THE WORLD WHO'S WHO
OF WOMEN

THE WORLD WHO'S WHO OF WOMEN

Published by the International Biographical Centre,
Cambridge, England

Hon. General Editor
ERNEST KAY
Author of Biographical and Other Works
Editor and Publisher (London)

Publisher
Nicholas S. Law

Editorial Production Manager
Diane Butcher

Sales and Promotion Manager
Dorothy M. Todd

Editorial Assistants
Lisa Mann
Gloria Walker

All communications to: The World Who's Who of Women
International Biographical Centre
Cambridge CB2 3QP, England.

THE WORLD WHO'S WHO OF WOMEN

TENTH EDITION

Hon. General Editor
ERNEST KAY

First Published 1973
Second Edition 1975
Third Edition 1976
Fourth Edition 1978

Sixth Edition 1982
Eighth Edition 1986
Tenth Edition 1990

First Published 1973
Second Edition 1975
Third Edition 1976
Fourth Edition 1978
Fifth Edition 1980
Sixth Edition 1982
Seventh Edition 1984
Eighth Edition 1985
Ninth Edition 1988
Tenth Edition 1990

ISBN 0 948875 10 0

Printed and bound in the UK by Bath Press, Lower Bristol Road, Bath, Avon.

FOREWORD BY THE HON GENERAL EDITOR

This completely new Tenth Edition of *The World Who's Who of Women* contains nearly 7,000 biographies from all parts of the world, bringing the total of those honoured in the series so far to more than 72,000.

Although *The World Who's Who of Women* was first published in 1974 its roots go back even further - to 1969 when the first of four editions of *Two Thousand Women of Achievement* was issued. In one form or another, therefore, this is the fourteenth edition of a work which has become highly respected by librarians, journalists, researchers and others in most countries of the world.

My thanks and those of my associates are offered to the many learned societies and other organizations for recommending selected members for biographical inclusion in *The World Who's Who of Women*. All recommendations are carefully researched and invitations are sent to the vast majority of them. It is largely because of personal and organizational recommendations that we have been able to highlight an important cross-section of the world's women achievers.

We always respect the privacy of those few who ask not to be listed: their wishes are strictly observed and no pressure is brought to bear upon them.

Only a few entries are repeated from edition to edition and then only because of *additional* achievements.

Once again I must emphasize that there is no charge or fee for entry in *The World Who's Who of Women* nor is there any obligation to purchase. Inclusion is solely by invitation and cannot be bought.

All entries have been checked meticulously by our own editors, then submitted in proof form to the entrants themselves for correction and amendment. But in spite of this rigorous double-checking it is still possible that an occasional error might have occured. In this event I offer my apologies in advance.

This edition of *The World Who's Who of Women* is specially dedicated to 46 women from all parts of the world. They were selected for this honour by my senior colleagues and myself. A special feature on each of them appears in the Dedications Section of this volume. They are, in alphabetical order:

Anneli Arms	Katarina-Zlata Defilipis
Jill Hart Barnes	Corinne Devlin
Ingrid Anne Berg	Estelle Cecilia Diggs Dunlap
Patricia Helen Breen	Lee Ellen Ford
Judith Lynne Cameron	Jeanne Elizabeth Harris
Mrs Gertrude Esther Carper	Gloria Hodgson-Brooks
Carmen Josefina Cividanes-Lago	Bettye D Kimble
Karen Sue Clippinger-Robertson	Gloria Dolores Knight
Joy Violetta Collins	Glorija Lawrence
Jean Elizabeth Comeforo	Josephine Gorliss Liebhaber
Arlene Dahl	Anneliese List

Chiyoe Matsumoto
Johanna Mitchell
Lourdes Gagui Mon
Peggy Sue Moore
Jean Mueller
Carole Ann Myers
Mary A Myers
Joyce Ann Wynn Oberhausen
The Hon Mrs Patricia E O'Neill
Carol Tommie Parker
Nanci Glick Reid
Belle Sara Rosenbaum
Lili Sarnoff

Geraldine Savary-Ogden
Anna Pearl Sherrick
Gail Penniman Turner Slover
Helen Chien-fan Su
June Conran Sutherland
Neva Bennett Talley-Morris
Naomi Cocke Turner
Amanda L Walton
Jan White
Zena Winifred Wickstein
Melva Jean Williams
Charin Yuthasastrkosol

More of our biographees have been added to the *The World Who's Who of Women* Honours List all of whom are named in the Honours List Section which follows the biographical listings.

Work has already begun on the Eleventh Edition and we would be glad to hear from any reader who feels that a particular individual should be included. Recommendations should be sent to the Research Department, International Biographical Centre, Cambridge CB2 3QP, England.

ERNEST KAY
Director General

International Biographical Centre
Cambridge CB2 3QP
England

April 1990

CONTENTS

INTERNATIONAL BIOGRAPHICAL CENTRE
RANGE OF REFERENCE TITLES

From one of the widest ranges of contemporary biographical reference works published under any one imprint, some IBC titles date back to the 1930's. Each edition is compiled from information supplied by those listed, who include leading personalities of particular countries or profession. Information offered usually includes date and place of birth; family details; qualifications; career histories; awards and honours received; books published or other creative work; other relevant information including postal address. Naturally there is no charge or fee for inclusion.

New editions are freshly compiled and contain on average 80-90% new information. New titles are regularly added to the IBC reference libary.

Titles include:

Dictionary of International Biography

Who's Who in Australasia and the Far East

Who's Who in Western Europe

Dictionary of Scandinavian Biography

Dictionary of Latin American and Caribbean Biography

International Who's Who in Art and Antiques

International Authors and Writers Who's Who

International Businessmen's Who's Who

International Leaders in Achievement

International Who's Who in Community Service

International Who's Who in Education

International Who's Who in Engineering

International Who's Who in Medicine

International Who's Who in Music and Musicians' Directory

International Who's Who in Poetry

International Who's Who of Professional and Business Women

Men of Achievement

The World Who's Who of Women

The World Who's Who of Women in Education

International Youth in Achievement

Foremost Women of the Twentieth Century

Enquiries to:
International Biographical Centre
Cambridge, CB2 3QP
England

Dedications

Anneli Arms

"For an Outstanding Contribution as an Artist, Sculptor, Painter and Printmaker".

ANNELI ARMS

Artist Anneli Arms works as a freelance sculptor, painter and etcher/monotypist. Her works of sculpture include "Gypsy Moth Caterpillar", "Spider", "Architect of his Dreams", "The Board of Education", "Jellyfish" etc. She is also responsible for the prints "Beetle", "Floral Jellyfish" and "Golden Sunfish" and for the paintings "Land Escape (I and II)".

Born in New York City, USA on 23rd May 1935, Anneli (or Anna Elizabeth) attended the School of Art of the University of Michigan and on an Art Students League of New York scholarship gained her BA in 1958. Subsequently, she studied at the Pratt Graphics Centre in Manhattan between 1982 and 1985. In September 1956, Anneli married John Arms and they have one son.

A member of the Federation of Modern Painters and Sculptors, Mrs Arms also belongs to the Manhattan Graphics Center, the Jimmy Ernst Artists' Alliance and the National Museum of Women in the Arts. She served as Chairman of exhibitions held at the Phoenix Gallery between 1977 and 1983.

Over the years, Anneli Arms has received a number of awards for her work, including the Jane Higby Award from the University of Michigan in 1956, and, more recently, the Nora Mirmont Award in 1984 and the Best Sculpture Award from the Guild Hall Museum in 1987.

Biographies of Mrs Arms also appear in "Contemporary American Women Sculptors" published by Oryx Press in 1986 and the Directors' Guild publication "Encyclopaedia of Living Artists in America" 2nd edition published in 1987, and "The New York Art Review" published in 1988 by American References Publishing Corporation. In addition to her love of nature, Anneli enjoys swimming, dance, literature, philosophy and attending movies, the opera and the theatre in her leisure time.

A biography of Anneli Arms appears in the main section of this Edition.

Jill Hart Barnes

"For an Outstanding Contribution in the Field of Education".

JILL HART BARNES

Educational Consultant, Jill Hart Barnes is the author of the publications "Reading is a Family Affair" 1981; "What Is It?", "I Can", "Help Me" and "I Want to Play" pre-primers and primer written for Tempe Elementary S D Chapter I Project, 1984.

Having attended the University of Arizona at Tucson from 1963 to 1966, Jill continued her education with Arizona State University in Tempe gaining a BA in Education in 1970, a Reading Endorsement in 1974 and her MA, also in Education in 1976. She served as a Teacher of Grade I with Carrollton-Farmers Branch ISD, Texas between 1970 and 1971, and then joined the Tempe Elementary School District in Arizona as a Teacher of Grades 2 and 3 and a Reading Specialist for Grades 2 - 6, serving from 1971 to 1986. Between 1975 and 1977 and again in 1980, Mrs Barnes was a Faculty Associate of Arizona State University. In 1986, she took up her present appointment as an Educational Consultant with D C Heath and Company.

A member of the International Reading Association, she also belongs to Arizona State Reading Council, chaired the Parents and Reading Committee from 1983 to 1986 and served on the ASRC State Board. After serving as Vice President in 1984, Mrs Barnes served as President of Ocotillo East Reading Council in 1985.

In addition, she belongs to Montana State Reading Council, California Reading Association and the Colorado and Utah Councils of the International Reading Association.

Mrs Barnes' publications have brought her awards. She won the 1st place Golden Bell Award from Arizona School Boards Association for "Reading is a Family Affair" in 1982 and again in 1983 for "Summer Correspondence for Elementary Students". She was semi-finalist for Arizona Teacher of the Year in 1984, and a member of the Arizona Governor's Committee to establish a state-wide parent involvement reading programme in 1985.

Born in Huron, South Dakota, USA on 2nd July 1945, Jill Barnes is divorced with a son John and a daughter Paige. In her spare time, Mrs Barnes enjoys reading, gardening, handicrafts, needlepoint, sewing, music and writing song parodies. She is also listed in Who's Who in American Education.

A biography of Jill Hart Barnes appears in the main section of this Edition.

Ingrid Anne Berg

"For an Outstanding Contribution to Showbusiness in Australia".

INGRID ANNE BERG

Australian Publicist, Ingrid Anne Berg, began her career as a Nurse. After undertaking General Nursing training between 1960 and 1963, she nursed at South Perth Hospital and Sir Charles Gairdner Hospital, Western Australia. In 1965, she was appointed Night Charge Sister in Yooralla, Victoria.

Deciding on a career change, Ingrid formed the Ingrid Berg Academy (Model and Deportment) School in Perth in 1966. After running the school for three years, Ms Berg joined Mullins Clarke and Ralph Advertising in 1969, and also had a spell of service for Murray Evans Advertising. In 1971, Ingrid set up her own publicity agency, Ingrid Berg and Associates.

Miss Berg serves as Chairman of the Australian Variety Artistes MO Awards Association. She is Convenor of the Paraquad 101 Club, and also a member of the Australian Ladies Variety Association and the Variety Club of Australia. The recipient of an MO award, in 1986 she received a Special Achievement Award for her services to Entertainment in Australia.

The contributor of numerous articles to journals and magazines, Ingrid Berg was born in Melbourne on 24th October, 1942. Her varied hobbies include music, walking, travel, knitting, cricket, Australian Rules Football and skiing.

A biography of Ingrid Anne Berg appears in the main section of this Edition.

Patricia Helen Hall Breen

"For an Outstanding Contribution to Finance and Nutritional Counseling".

PATRICIA HELEN BREEN

After studying Business Administration at Wayne State University for the year 1944 to 1945, Patricia Helen Breen attended the University of Michigan, where she obtained a BBA degree in 1949. She spent a short period during 1949 as a Trust Investment Analyst with the National Bank of Detroit and then joined the General Motors Corporation, serving as an Administrative Assistant from 1949 to 1951. Mrs Breen served on Policy Procedures and Bonus Committees with Union Securities, Cleveland in 1951 and as a Financial Organiser with Baxter and Co., also of Cleveland in 1952, before returning to the University of Michigan to undertake postgraduate study for the year 1953 to 1954. Since 1957 she has held the appointment of Senior Financial Consultant with Merrill Lynch Pierce Fenner and Smith, Inc., and is also currently owner, Chairman, President and Chief Executive Officer of the Good Food Company.

Born in Detroit, Michigan on 15th September, 1926, Patricia married Morton Breen in May 1951, and the marriage ended in divorce ten years later. In her leisure time, she enjoys a wide variety of hobbies, including silver and gold smithing, oil painting, writing, lecturing, snow and water skiing, swimming, sailing, golf, tennis and exhibition ballroom dancing.

In her early years, Patricia received the American Legion Award in 1939, an Allied Youth City Speech Writer award in 1940, followed by a Delivery Award in 1944. She has also been the recipient of academic scholarships from Wayne State University, University of Michigan and Vassar in 1945, of a Regents, Alumni Scholarship from the University of Michigan in 1947, plus a further two honorary scholarships. More recently, she received a Cranbrook Academy Award for Oil Painting in 1975.

Director of the University of Michigan Alumnae Association, Mrs Breen also belongs to Investment Analysts, Detroit and is President of NAFE Oakland. She serves as Organiser and President of Independent Women on Campus of the University of Michigan and is a Member, Organiser and Constitution Writer of the Business Administration Council. Reflecting her many hobbies, her club memberships include Otsego Ski Club, Bloomfield Surf Club, Kansas City Country Club, Detroit Boat Club and the 300 Oakland County Club.

A biography of Patricia Helen Breen appears in the main section of this Edition.

Dr Judith Lynne Cameron

"For an Outstanding Contribution as an Educator and Hypnotherapist".

JUDITH LYNNE CAMERON

After obtaining an AA in 1965 and BA in 1967, both in Psychology and German, and a California teaching credential in 1969, Judith Lynne Cameron taught at St Vincent's Elementary School in the San Francisco Archdiocese from 1969 to 1970 and then transferred to the Fremont Unified School District where she served as an elementary teacher from 1970 to 1972. In 1972 she was awarded her MA with specialisation in Reading Disorders. During the period 1972 to 1984, she was employed as an elementary special education teacher with the Bonita Unified School District, receiving a credential for teaching the learning-handicapped in 1978 and a California resource specialist certificate in 1980. Since 1984, Judith Cameron has served as a High School teacher within the Bonita Unified School District and since 1986 has also been a teacher-in-space consultant. In 1987 she was awarded her PhD in Hypnotherapy and Psychic Hypnotherapy and the following year received a junior college teaching credential and also her Doctorate in Clinical Hypnotherapy and Hypnotic Anaesthesiology. In addition to her teaching responsibilities, Dr Cameron has, since 1988 been owner and therapist of Southern California Clinical Hypnotherapy.

A member of the Association of Californian Resource Specialists and the Council for Exceptional Children, Dr Cameron also belongs to CTA/NEA; the National Space Society, the Planetary Society; Challenger Society for Space Education; the Association for Past-Life Therapists; the National Association of Hypnotherapists and the Association for Hypnotic Anaesthesiologists. An article by Judith Cameron was published in the National Board of Hypnotherapy Journal of March 1988.

In recognition of her services to education, Dr Cameron has received a number of honours and commendations. In 1984 she was the recipient of the California Teachers Honorary Service Award and the following year was honoured for her participation in the California teacher-in-space programme. Named California Teacher of the Month by Bonita High School in January 1988, she was appointed California mentor teacher-space education for 1988 to 1990 and Department Chairperson for Special Education at Bonita High School for two terms from 1985 through to 1991. For the 1988-89 school year, she was selected as Teacher of the Year at Bonita High School. She served as Advisor for both the Peer Counseling Programme at Bonita High School 1987-88 and the Children's Home Society of Santa Ana 1980-81. Since 1986 she has been advisor to the Students for the Exploration and Development of Space Chapter at Bonita High School.

Born in Oakland, California, USA on 29th April 1945, Judith married Richard I Cameron in December 1967 and they have one son, Kevin.

A First Lieutenant and aerospace officer with the Civil Air Patrol, Mrs Cameron has a great interest in astronomy and strophotography. She also enjoys playing the guitar and banjo and doing crewel embroidery and crochet. She is also currently writing a book.

In addition to this publication, Judith Cameron is listed in Who's Who in American Women, 16th edition, Who's Who in the West, and Who's Who in the World, 10th Edition.

A biography of Judith Lynne Cameron appears in the main section of this Edition.

Gertrude Esther Carper

"For an Outstanding Contribution to Humanity".

GERTRUDE ESTHER CARPER

Since 1955 the Owner and Developer of Essex Yacht Harbour, Baltimore, Maryland in the United States of America, Gertrude Esther Carper has several other interests, the main one being art. Born in Jamestown, New York in the United States on 13 April 1921, she showed an early aptitude for music, her other talent, and from 1931 until 1941 received violin tuition at the National Academy of Music. After two years at Business School in Covington, Virginia, she acted as Secretary to the Reverend Joseph Smith of Covington (1940-41). In 1942 Mrs Carper became a volunteer teacher of retarded people, as well as a portrait artist, continuing with these activities up to the present day. In addition, she was employed as an interior decorator at O'Neills (Importers), Baltimore from 1942-44 and as an Auditor for Citizen's National Bank in Covington (1945-56). Her next step was to pursue her interest in art, taking up studies at Maryland Institute of Art, and obtaining a Fine Arts Diploma in 1950. Between 1952 and 1955 she attended the Peabody Institute where she studied voice with Frazier Gange.

Mrs Carper has recently completed fifty paintings of North American ducks and geese, a choice of subject which reflects her love of wildlife. She has held various one-woman shows, as well as participating in group exhibitions, including one at Le Salon des Nations in Paris in 1985, where she received a citation. Among her other activities is her involvement in restoration of Lytton Hall in Baltimore, and she also works for Women's Rights. A fine Presbyterian, she has been a leader of the women's circle at the local church for twenty-six years and has sung in various choirs for forty years. She and her husband, J Dennis Carper were married on 5 April 1942 and they have two sons and one grand-daughter.

Mrs Carper believed that on the day man planted a flag on the moon all nations became one again, as was first intended. We should continue to believe in miracles. She enjoys seeing her ducks return in the spring and rear their young ones. She maintains that it is best to enjoy the small things of life then the miracles are tremendous.

It is her belief that success in life begins at an early age and that when challenges appear we should work through them and the answers will come. Through her caring, she tries to make life special for others. Her listings appear in numerous biographical works such as "Who's Who of American Women", "Who's Who in the World", "International Leaders in Achievement" and "Community Leaders of America". She is included in a special Art Book by Les Editions Arts et Images du Monde, Paris. A new Deputy Director General of International Biographical Centre.

A biography of Gertrude Esther Carper appears in the main section of this Edition.

Carmen Josefina Cividanes-Lago

"For an Outstanding Contribution as a Young Leader".

CARMEN JOSEFINA CIVIDANES-LAGO

After obtaining a high school honours diploma from St John's School, Puerto Rico in 1979, Carmen Josefina Cividanes-Lago attended Mount Holyoke College, USA where she did a triple major in Psychology, Education, and French and received a BA cum laude degree in Psychology in 1983. She also gained a Massachusetts State Teacher's Certificate enabling her to teach French to Grades 7 to 12. During the Spring of 1982, Carmen-Jo took part in the Wesleyan Program in Paris and also attended Lycée Chaptal. Returning to the US, she spent the year 1983-84 at Harvard University, gaining her EdM specializing in Human Development and also obtained a Licence for Administering Psychological Tests. She has been involved since in research for her D Phil with concentration in Developmental Psychology from the University of Oxford, England. Upon entering the University of Oxford, she was awarded the "Overseas Research Students' Award for outstanding merit and research potential administered by the Committee of Vice-Chancellors and Principals of the Universities of the United Kingdom", as well as the "Janet Watson Bursary Award from Somerville College, University of Oxford, for good academic ability and potential".

During June and July 1981, Carmen-Jo Cividanes-Lago served as an English Elementary Teacher at the Colegio Aurora, Puerto Rico, and from October 1982 to May 1983 was employed as a French Tutor at Mount Holyoke College, USA. She served as Secretary to the Admissions Officer at the John F Kennedy School of Government at Harvard University between September 1983 and May 1984. In addition, between 1980 and 1982, Ms Cividanes-Lago was Director of "Unidos", Holyoke Bilingual Learning Centre Programme, tutoring Hispanic children, ranging from 5 to 8 years old, in basic subjects.

With Columbia University psychologist Virginia V Valian, Carmen-Jo was co-author of "Memory for French Negation by Students of French" published in "Language Learning" volume 35 no 2, June 1985. With University of Oxford psychologist Peter E Bryant, Carmen-Jo has presented several papers at conferences, seminars, and discussion groups on children's understanding and perception of mathematical problems.

Elected an Associate Member of the Honorary Scientific Society of Sigma Xi in May 1983, Carmen Cividanes-Lago was also elected to the Professional Fraternity in Education, Phi Delta Kappa in May 1984, and in January 1987 she became a member of the British Society for Learning Mathematics. She received a French Government Book Prize for merit in May 1981. Whilst at Oxford University, Ms Cividanes-Lago was elected President of the Graduate Students of Somerville College in March 1985, in October 1984 was elected Social Secretary of the Graduate Students of Somerville College, and in March 1986 was elected House Chairperson of the Graduate Students of Somerville College living on campus. She was also the recipient of a Certificate of Appreciation for rendering invaluable services to improve the quality of life for individuals at Belchertown State School, USA.

The daughter of Mr Adolfo Cividanes-Freiría and Dr Carmencita Lago-Riera de Cividanes, Carmen was born in Puerto Rico on 6th May 1961.

A biography of Carmen Josefina Cividanes-Lago appears in the main section of this Edition.

Karen S Clippinger-Robertson
"For an Outstanding Contribution to Kinesiology".

KAREN SUE CLIPPINGER-ROBERTSON

Karen Sue Clippinger-Robertson, who is a clinical kinesiologist and lecturer, is the author of the books "Aerobic Dance Instructor's Manual" and "Flexibility", and is also responsible for book chapters on Principles of dance training; Patellofemoral pain in dancers; Turnout; Prevention of low back injuries in athletes; Components of an aerobic dance-exercise class.

Born in Santa Monica, California, USA on 8th October, 1951, Karen married John Wilbur Robertson in November 1981 and they have one son. She obtained a BA honours degree in Psychology, with dance therapy emphasis, from Sonoma State College in 1975 and in 1984 was awarded an MSPE in Exercise Science from the University of Washington.

Between 1980 and 1984, Mrs Robertson was employed at the Ballard Sports Medicine Clinic and since 1985 she has served as a kinesiologist with Seattle Sports Medicine. She has worked in a consultancy capacity for Pacific Northwest Ballet since 1981, for the US Weightlifting Federation since 1985 and for the US Men's Race Walking Team since 1986, and has also lectured throughout the United States and in Canada and Japan.

A Member of the American College of Sports Medicine, Karen Clippinger-Robertson also belongs to the International Society of Biomechanics in Sports and is Chairman of the Practical Committee of the International Dance-Exercise Association Foundation.

In addition to her interest in dance and human movement, Karen likes to travel.

A biography of Karen Sue Clippinger-Robertson appears in the main section of this Edition.

Joy V. Collins AM

"For an Outstanding Contribution to Community Service".

JOY VIOLETTA COLLINS

Although retired from the fields of journalism and television, Joy Violetta Collins is still an active Civil Marriage Celebrant.

Born in Launceston, Tasmania, Australia on 20th April 1917, she attended Launceston High School and Business College. After spending the War years in the WAAAF, Joy Collins did commercial work from 1946 to 1954. She then joined the Red Cross Society, Northern Territory serving as Administration/Field Officer and State Secretary from 1954 to 1956. She set up her own secretarial business and then spent twenty-five years in the media as a journalist and social/feature/travel writer with her own television show. Retiring in 1981, she serves as a Civil Marriage Celebrant.

Mrs Collins was Founder/President of the NT Order of Australia Association and the Royal Darwin Hospital Auxiliary. President/Governor of the Northern Territory Anti-Cancer Foundation, she was the inaugural Chairman of the first Board of Management of the Royal Darwin Hospital.

Joy Collins has held numerous voluntary appointments. Since coming to Western Australia in 1982, she has held executive positions in the Western Australia Arthritis and Rheumatism Foundation, the Better Hearing Association, RSL Women's Auxiliary, Bedingfeld Park Hostel for the Aged and the Western Australia Association of Civil Marriage Celebrants.

Appointed a Member of the Order of Australia in 1979, Mrs Collins was named Darwin Woman of the Year, also in 1979, and has been nominated for inclusion in the Register of Women Achievers of the Northern Territory, 1948-88 and 1988.

In October 1963, Joy married Ronald Kenneth Collins, now sadly deceased. She passes her leisure time in writing, tapestry and gardening.

A biography of Joy Violetta Collins appears in the main section of this Edition.

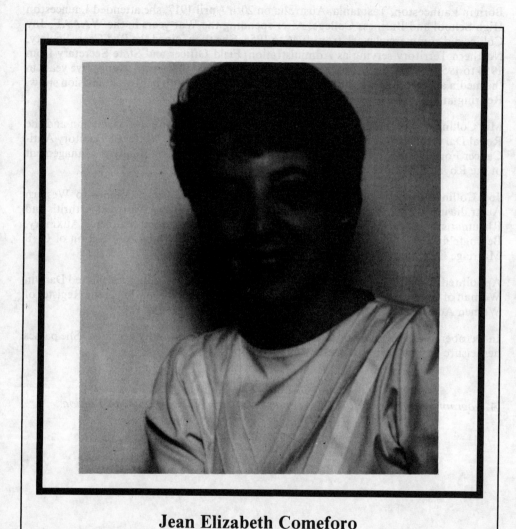

Jean Elizabeth Comeforo
"For an Outstanding Contribution to the Field of Education of the deaf".

JEAN ELIZABETH COMEFORO

Itinerant hearing therapist, Jean Elizabeth Comeforo obtained a BS degree in Biology from the College of St Elizabeth, New Jersey in 1969. She then served as a Houseparent at the Marie H Katzenbach School for the Deaf from 1969 to 1970. She was an Upper School Mathematics and Science Teacher at the Western Pennsylvania School for the Deaf between 1971 and 1976 and during this period was awarded her MED (Masters in Education of the Deaf) from Smith College, Massachusetts in 1972. Since 1976 Ms Comeforo has served as a Teacher of the Deaf and Oral Interpreter with the Delaware County Intermediate Unit, receiving, in 1982, her MEd degree from Cheney State College in Pennsylvania.

The presenter of a number of papers to professional conferences, she delivered "Comparison of Skills in Oral and Manual Interpreters" to the New York State Registry of Interpreters for the Deaf in 1986 and has given the following presentations to Alexander G Bell International Conventions: "You Should See What We Can Hear!" and "What's Happening! Come See" 1984; "Graduate Survey"; "Quota Job Bank for Hearing Impaired Youth" 1986.

A member of the international speech and hearing committee of Quota International Inc between 1974 and 1982, Jean Comeforo served as Chairman in 1979 and as interpreter for the deaf at international conventions from 1975 to 1979. She was Governor of District 2 from 1983 to 1985 and President for Philadelphia during the years 1977 to 1979. She also belongs to the International Organization for Educators of the Hearing Impaired.

An elected member of the Tri Beta National Biological Honour Society, Jean Comeforo won a scholarship to attend the Smith College/Clarke School for the Deaf Teacher Training Programme. In 1974 and 1975 she received Citations for Inspirational Teaching of Science Subjects from Buhl Planetarium, Pittsburgh, and, more recently, in 1983 and 1984 received an Award for Excellence in Community Service Programming from American Cablevision of Pennsylvania. The Program was also recognised by the President's Council for Private Sector Initiatives in 1984. Named as one of the first 75 people in the USA to be certified as an Oral Interpreter for the Deaf in 1979, Jean Comeforo was named Delaware County Intermediate Unit's First Anne Sullivan Award winner, for her extensive work with and for deaf people. She is also listed in Who's Who in American Education.

Born in Urbana, Illinois, USA on 2nd June 1947, Jean enjoys travel, bowling and swimming in her leisure time.

A biography of Jean Elizabeth Comeforo appears in the main section of this Edition.

Arlene Dahl

"For an Outstanding Contribution to Theater, Motionpictures and Television".

ARLENE DAHL

The successful acting, beauty and fashion career of Arlene Dahl began at the age of eight when she starred on a children's radio series in her hometown of Minneapolis and danced and sang at weekends with a group called the "Hollywood Review". She left Minnesota for New York to become a top photographer's model and cover girl. Her first singing and dancing appearance on Broadway in the musical "Mr Strauss Goes to Boston" was greeted with critical acclaim, and, at the request of Jack Warner she went to Hollywood, where she made her film debut as Rose in Warner Brothers' "My Wild Irish Rose". Miss Dahl has starred in 28 motion pictures and 18 stage plays, 7 of them musicals, including the Tony Award winning "Applause" at the famed Palace Theatre on Broadway. Her films include: "3 Little Words" with Fred Astaire and Red Skelton; "Desert Legion" with Alan Ladd; "Here Come the Girls" with Bob Hope; "Sangaree" with Fernando Lamas; "Woman's World" with Clifton Webb, Van Heflin and Fred McMurray; "Journey to the Center of the Earth" with James Mason and Pat Boone and "Kisses for my President" with Fred McMurray, all of which won the Box Office Magazine "Laurel Award". Among her stage credits are: "Cyrano de Bergerac" on Broadway; "The King and I" in Boston; "Blithe Spirit" Chicago and San Francisco; "Bell, Book and Candle" New York, Maine and Chicago; "Pal Joey" Ohio; "A Little Night Music" Chicago; "Life With Father" Chicago and "Murder Among Friends" in Phoenix.

The author of 16 best-selling books on Beauty, Health and Astrology, for twenty years Miss Dahl wrote an internationally syndicated beauty column, which was translated into five languages. Her books include: "Always Ask a Man" first published by Prentice Hall in 1965 and which ran into 7 reprints; 12 "Beautyscope" books, 1968 and 1978; "Arlene Dahl's Secrets of Hair Care" 1969; "Arlene Dahl's Secrets of Skin Care" 1972; "Beyond Beauty" 1980; "Arlene Dahl's Lovescopes" 1983. She is currently working on a novel to be entitled "The Corporate Body". Also successful in the world of business, she became an advertising executive at Kenyon and Eckhardt, a health and beauty director of Sears Roebuck and Company, and a health and beauty consultant to various cruise lines, inaugurating her now famous "floating beauty spa" and incorporating her innovative "beauty happenings" in 1980 aboard the QE II.

On the fashion scene, Arlene Dahl designed a successful line of sleepwear and started the 'baby doll' pyjama rage in the 50s. She has designed a complete fashion line for Vogue patterns called "In Vogue with Arlene Dahl", and is currently designing a jewelry line under her name.

Since 1981, Miss Dahl has had a recurring guest star role in ABC's popular day-time series "One Life to Live", appearing as the exciting Lucinda King and in 1982 began "Arlene Dahl's Lovescopes" in which she starred as well as co-produced. She continues to make television guest appearances and took part in the TV special "The Night of a Hundred Stars" and most recently, the salute to Hollywoods 100th anniversary "Happy Birthday Hollywood", a TV special in which she was honoured as one of Hollywood's legendary leading ladies.

Arlene Dahl is happily married to Cosmetic Executive, More Rasen, and is the mother of three children, Lorenzo Lamas, who has had a successful television acting career, Carole Christine Holmes, a recent honours graduate from Georgetown University, who is now one of the youngest editors at Vogue Magazine and Stephen Schaum, who, while still a student, has formed his own rock group "Aviation".

A biography of Arlene Dahl appears in the main section of this Edition.

Katarina-Zlata Defilipis

"For an Outstanding Contribution to Psychology".

KATARINA-ZLATA DEFILIPIS

Clinical Psychologist and Psychotherapist, Katarina-Zlata Defilipis was born in Zagreb, Yugoslavia on 1st April 1925. In April 1952, she married Berislav Defilipis, now sadly deceased. Katarina graduated from the Department of Psychology of the University of Zagreb in 1967 and then undertook postgraduate studies in Dynamic Psychotherapy at the Centre for Mental Health of the University between 1969 and 1979. For the year 1968 to 1969, she worked as an Assistant at the Clinic for Neurology, Psychiatry, Alcoholism and other addictions in Zagreb and then joined the staff of Zagreb University as an Assistant in the Centre for Mental Health. Currently she is a Lecturer in Clinical Psychology conducting undergraduate and postgraduate courses for medical students and doctors.

Between 1969 and 1981, Mrs Defilipis served as President of the Croatian Association of Clinical Psychologists. She developed the activities of the Section for Clinical Psychology of the Croatian Psychological Association, laid the foundation for modern developments in clinical psychology in Croatia and made a valuable contribution to the development of clinical psychology in Yugoslavia. She was the initiator, founder and first President (from 1972-75) of the Board of Clinical Psychologists at the Association of Health Organisations of Croatia set up to study various professional issues in the field of psychology in medicine. She was responsible for the introduction of psychotherapy into clinical psychology in Croatia in 1973. In addition, Mrs Defilipis founded the Board of Clinical Psychologists at the City of Zagreb Institute for the Protection of Health, the purpose of which was the planning and co-ordination of the work of the psychological services and health institutions in practice and research projects. She was initiator, organiser and President of the first Meeting of Clinical Psychologists of Yugoslavia in 1975 and in the same year authored the first Roster of Clinical Psychologists of Yugoslavia.

Founder and member of the Co-ordination Board of Clinical Psychologists of Yugoslavia from 1975 to 1988, she served on the Executive Committee of the Croatian Psychological Association between 1970 and 1981 and was a member of the Commission for Awards in 1984. Mrs Defilipis also belongs to the Yugoslav Psychological Association and the Yugoslav Psychotherapeutic Association. She initiated, organised and presided over the 3rd Meeting of Clinical Psychologists of Yugoslavia held in 1986.

Her successful career has brought her a number of honours and awards. She received a Diploma from the Health Organizations of SR Croatia in 1975, a Diploma from the Psychological Association of Yugoslavia in 1978 and a further Diploma from the Psychological Association of SR Croatia in 1983.

The author of numerous professional and scientific papers and articles on the problems of clinical psychology and psychotherapy, Katarina-Zlata Defilipis was also editor of "Selected Lectures of Clinical Psychology" published in 1979.

A biography of Katarina-Zlata Defilipis appears in the main section of this Edition.

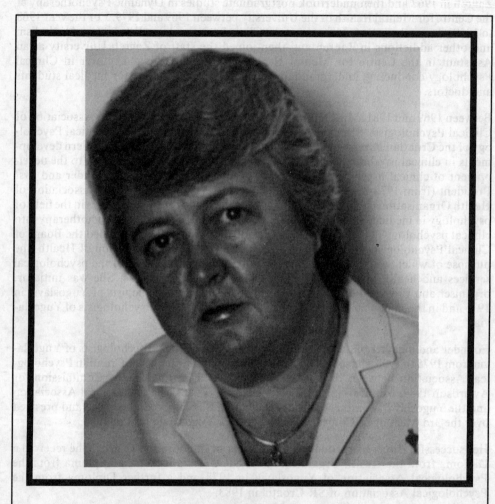

Dr Margaret Corinne Devlin

"For an Outstanding Contribution to the Sex-related Health Care of Women".

CORINNE DEVLIN

Corinne Devlin is a Professor of Obstetrics and Gynaecology in the Faculty of Health Sciences at McMaster University, Hamilton, Ontario, Canada. She is a founding member of the Canadian Menopause Foundation, a group committed to advancing the image and interests of women in the middle years from a consumer, provider and social perspective. Deciding on Nursing as a career, Corinne Devlin graduated from the Mack School of Nursing in St Catharines, Ontario, receiving the Birk's Medal for Theory in Nursing as an undergraduate and the Prize for Obstetrical Nursing upon graduation.

Her interest in health care issues led her into a second career in Medicine. She studied at the University of Western Ontario and entered the Faculty of Medicine at the University, graduating in 1967. She was elected to the Alpha Omega Alpha Honour Medical Society while at Western. After completing her internship in Detroit, Michigan, USA, Dr Devlin was accepted into the McGill University programme in Obstetrics and Gynaecology and was able to combine her interests in health care and women with particular reference to behavioural science, whilst also maintaining an enduring interest in surgical specialization.

Completing her residency training in Obstetrics and Gynaecology at the newly developed Faculty of Health Sciences at McMaster University, Hamilton, Ontario, Dr Devlin was, in 1972, certified as a specialist in that field by the Royal College of Physicians and Surgeons of Canada. After a further year of training, which included a direct emphasis in reproductive regulation and critical appraisal of medical evidence, Dr Devlin was invited to join the Faculty of Health Sciences at McMaster University in 1973. Her clinical activities embrace a range of Obstetrical and Gynaecological services, with special emphasis on fertility control, colposcopy and sexually transmitted diseases, from both a psychosocial and biomedical aspect. Through the use of academic forums, print and electronic media, Dr Devlin has spoken prolifically on sex-related health care issues, including fertility control and the Menopause. Although she has never sought administrative appointments, several such positions have provided a sense of pride and feeling of achievement. Two such appointments are President of the Medical Staff of Chedoke-McMaster Hospitals in the year of amalgamation and Chairman of the Graduate Committee of APOG. Also involved in research activities, Dr Devlin is currently investigating the psychosocial determinants of birth control failure, development and evaluation of an educational programme to decrease the incidence of adolescent pregnancy, evaluation of menstrual cycle impact of various contraceptives and an assessment of hormonal management of the menopause. A Licentiate of the Medical Council of Canada and a Member of the College of Physicians and Surgeons of Ontario, Dr Devlin also belongs to the Hamilton Academy of Medicine, the Niagara Society of Obstetricians and Gynaecologists, the Ontario Medical Association, the Canadian Medical Association and the Federation of Medical Women of Canada. She is a Fellow of the Royal College of Surgeons of Canada, of the American College of Obstetricians and Gynaecologists and the Society of Obstetricians and Gynaecologists of Canada.

Combining a busy career with her love for the Niagara District of Ontario, Dr Devlin enjoys the love and support of family and friends and is able to indulge her many interests such as hiking, camping, dogs and horses.

A biography of Corinne Devlin appears in the main section of this Edition.

Dr Estelle D C Dunlap

"For an Outstanding Contribution as an Educator and Mathematician".

ESTELLE CECILIA DIGGS DUNLAP

Although now retired from her teaching career, Dr Estelle Cecilia Diggs Dunlap continues to serve her community as an active member of the National Parks and Conservation Association, the National Trust for Historic Preservation, the United States Olympic Society, the Museum of African Art, the American Museum of Natural History and the Smithsonian Residents Association.

The daughter of John and Mary Diggs, Estelle was born in Washington, District of Columbia, USA on 26th September 1912. Having studied Mathematics, Science and the art of teaching at DC Teachers' College, she undertook graduate study and research in Pure Mathematics at Howard University between 1938 and 1940, gaining an MS degree. After postgraduate studies at the Catholic University of America, she obtained a teaching appointment at Garnet-Patterson Junior High School, where she was Head of the Mathematics Department from 1950 to 1956. She was Mathematics and Science Instructor at Macfarland Junior High School between 1954 and 1972 and Visiting Lecturer at the District of Columbia Teachers College from 1963 to 1964.

Awarded a National Science Foundation Fellowship to continue her studies, Mrs Dunlap gained a Cultural Doctorate in Philosophy of Education from the World University in 1982 and in 1984 was awarded a World Culture Prize from Accademia Italia. In 1985 she received an honorary doctorate from the International University Foundation. In addition, she has been awarded certificates from the US School of Music, Library of Human Resources, American Bicentennial Research Institute, Superior Court of the District of Columbia, United States District Court and other organisations.

A member of the American Mathematical Society, the American Association for the Advancement of Science, the National Council of Teachers of Mathematics and the Society for Industrial and Applied Mathematics, Estelle Dunlap has also been an active member in such social and civic organisations as the Northwest Boundary Civic Association, of which she was Recording Secretary, Petworth Block Club, and Vice President of the Benjamin Benneker Mathematics Club. She is a Charter Member of the Washington Performing Arts Society and a Founder Member of the National Historical Society.

In 1941, Estelle married Lee A Dunlap, a research scientist at the National Bureau of Standard, who served as a Staff Sergeant during World War II. Their daughters are Gladys and Dolly. An extensive world traveller, Mrs Dunlap also enjoys reading, playing musical instruments and bowling.

A biography of Estelle Cecilia Diggs Dunlap appears in the main section of this Edition.

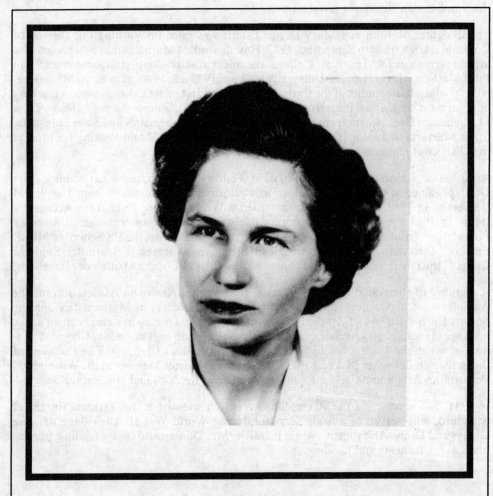

Dr Lee Ellen Ford

"For an Outstanding Contribution as a Researcher, Writer, Editor, Innovator, Pioneer, Feminist and Humanitarian".

LEE ELLEN FORD

Lee Ford was born on 16th June 1917 at Auburn, DeKalb County, Indiana, USA. Able to read at three years old, her earliest ambition was to go to college. However, when Lee graduated from High School at the age of 16, her parents were barely able to feed the family and pay the bills and taxes, so Lee took various unskilled low income jobs for the next ten years or so. However, during this period, Lee continued study in business and accounting and undertook 5 years of Accounting towards a CPA degree by correspondence. In the summer of 1944, Lee had an operation on her leg and lived at home with her parents. She wrote letters to colleges and was offered a very small grant to attend Wittenberg, Springfield, Ohio, her Lutheran Church college. She went for an interview and in the Autumn entered the College to study Science. In addition to full days of study, Lee worked nights in a manufacturing plant to pay for room and board, books and tuition. She graduated after two and a half years and then did nine months of teaching and graduate study at O S U followed by several years at the University of Minnesota in Minneapolis to gain a Master's degree. Miss Ford submitted her thesis for publication to an agronomy journal in her baptised name of Leola Ford but, perhaps because all the writers and editors were men, it was promptly rejected and returned to her. She changed the author to Lee Ford and sent it to another desk and it was published. After that for years Lee used the name "Lee Ford" on her research publications.

On completion of her Master's degree, Lee took a job teaching Science at Gustavus Adolphus College in St Peter, Minnesota, where she continued to carry on her hybrid corn research programme at her home. She also made contact with the scientists working on the Iowa State College corn programme and exchanged ideas on corn hybrid programmes and monoploids. At this stage monoploids could only be identified by the pollen of fully grown plants, and much time and money was spent in growing thousands of plants to obtain monoploids for use in the hybrid programme. Lee's research was to germinate the seeds in a few days, check out the roots by cytology and at that time pick out the monoploids by checking the number of chromosomes in the cells, and then to prove it by growing them. In twelve months she had proved it, published and saved the hybrid seed corn companies thousands or millions of dollars and years and years of time and labour. Refusing a job with the corn company as a laboratory worker, Lee went on to finish her thesis and was awarded her PhD from ISC in 1952. Lee did research at the Institute for Mental Retardation on Staten Island, New York into exercise therapy and work therapy for the retarded. Today her ideas are accepted as routine procedure.

In 1969, she returned to Indiana to care for her mother. Having no employment, Lee decided to retrain in some professional field. She was, at the age of 52, lucky enough to be accepted on a scholarship to the University of Notre Dame Law School. In 1969 this University Law School was not co-educational. That year the Dean decided to give a full 3 years tuition to women, older persons and minority persons to "see if they could do it?" Lee was accepted and in 1972, she graduated and in the same year the University Notre Dame Law School became co-educational, Lee was one of the few who helped make this happen. On graduation from Law School, Lee worked on the campaign of the prospective Governor of Indiana and on his election became the first woman aide to a Governor of Indiana, serving for three years. She also began her own private law practice. After leaving the Governor's office, Lee moved home and built her law practice whilst continuing to publish and care for her mother. Her clients are both male and female, the poor, handicapped, youth and aged and others of little social standing.

A biography of Lee Ellen Ford appears in the main section of this Edition.

Jeanne E Harris

"For an Outstanding Contribution to the Geosciences".

JEANNE ELIZABETH HARRIS

Geologist, Jeanne Elizabeth Harris attended the University of Michigan, where she obtained a BS in 1968 and an MS degree in 1975 in Geology. Between 1971 and 1975 she undertook graduate work in Computer Science. Further graduate studies in an MBA program were undertaken from the University of Denver between 1975 and 1978.

During the period 1970 to 1975, Jeanne Harris worked as a Researcher and geoscience computer programmer in the University of Michigan's Seismological Observatory and the Environmental Research Institute of Michigan. She then joined the Mobil Oil Corporation as an Exploration Geophysicist and Geologist, serving from 1975 to 1980. Between 1980 and 1985 she was a Project Manager and Team Leader with the Natural Gas Corporation of California engaged in oil and gas exploration and production. President and Consultant of the oil and gas exploration and production company, G & H Production Company from 1986 to 1987, Jeanne Harris has since 1988 held the appointment of Assistant Exploration Manager with the Equity Oil Company.

Named among the Outstanding Young Women of America in 1983, Ms Harris was awarded the title of Denver Woman of the Year by the Association for Women Geoscientists in 1984. The following year, she received a Community Service Award from Pacific Gas and Electric and in 1988 she was again honoured by the Association for Women Geoscientists, this time with a Distinguished Service Award.

A member of the American Association of Petroleum Geologists, Ms Harris served as Alternate Delegate from 1983 to 1986 and as Delegate between 1986 and 1989, as well as serving on several of the Association committees. She served as President of the Denver section of the Association for Women Geoscientists in 1981, was a Delegate between 1982 and 1985, Vice President 1985-86 and between 1987 and 1989 was President of the Association for Women Geoscientists Foundation. She has chaired several committees of the Rocky Mountain Association of Geologists and served as Colorado State Treasurer from 1984 to 1985 of the National Organization for Women. President of the Lake Village Homeowners' Association from 1984 to 1987, she is an Advisor for the University of Colorado at Denver Geology Department and also belongs to Wyoming Geological Society, Denver Geophysical Society, the American Geophysical Union, National Organization for Women, the Geological Society of America, the YMCA and the University of Michigan Alumni Association.

Married to Robert John Groth in October 1982, Jeanne has one son. In her leisure time she enjoys reading, travel, swimming, bicycling, riding, skiing, motorcycling, gardening, sketching and most team sports.

Jeanne was born in Detroit, Michigan on 4th July, 1947.

A biography of Jeanne Elizabeth Harris appears in the main section of this Edition.

Gloria Hodgson-Brooks

"For an Outstanding Contribution as a Psychotherapist and Artist".

GLORIA HODGSON-BROOKS

Gloria Hodgson-Brooks obtained a BA degree in Sociology and Art from Bennett College in 1965. Between 1976 and 1983 she studied Gestalt Body Centered Psychotherapy at the Hartford Family Institute and in 1979 was awarded her Master's degree in Social Work from Smith College School of Social Work. NASW qualification from the Academy of Certified Social Work in 1983 was followed by Certification in Independent Social Work from the State of Connecticut in 1986. In 1988 she received Board Certification as a Diplomate in Clinical Social Work.

A social worker with Child and Family Services Inc/Inter Agency Services between 1974 and 1977, Ms Hodgson-Brooks served as an intern private practice psychotherapist at the Hartford Family Institute from 1976 to 1978. She was a clinical social worker with Child and Family Services for the year 1979 to 1980, and between 1980 and 1981 held the appointment of Director of the Dr Issiah Clark Family and Youth Clinic. Returning to the Hartford Family Institute, Gloria served as an Associate private practice psychotherapist from 1978 to 1985 and also conducted staff training for Directions Unlimited between 1982 and 1985. During 1985 and 1986, she was a workshop leader and goal setter for PRO Disabled Entrepreneurs. In 1985 Brooks and Brooks Ltd was established and since then Gloria has served as President of psychotherapy and art, also engaged during the first year (1985-86) in staff training. She has also served as a psychotherapist and partner of Psychotherapy and Counseling Associates since 1985. In 1986, she undertook staff training and communication for the Sandler Sales Institute and the same year served as an Administrative Consultant for the Connecticut Centre for Human Growth and Development.

Ms Hodgson-Brooks is the author of "An Exploratory Study of the Diagnostic Process in Gestalt Therapy" published by Smith College Library in 1979. A keen sculptress, she has produced the following works: "Unfolding" in plaster 1987-88; "Awakening" soapstone 1987-88 and "Untitled" in wire 1987-88. During the same period, she was also responsible for paper collages, bearing the titles "Windows", "Lift Off", "Garden Life", "Illusion", "Shells by the Sea", "December in New England", "Winter '87", "Tin Cat", "Gay Head", "The Black Dog" and "Siesta". Her plaster sculpture "Unfolding" was at the ECKANKAR Creative Arts Festival in Chicago in 1987, and the same Festival held in New York City the following year for her sculpture "Awakening" in soapstone and her paper collage "Lift Off" were shown. The shows were juried and awards were given for exhibiting. Handweaving is another craft enjoyed by Gloria Hodgson-Brooks. She was a member of Connecticut Handweavers Guild from 1973 to 1976 and of New England Handweavers between 1974 and 1976.

Currently a member of the National Association of Black Social Workers, the National Association of Social Workers and the Smithsonian Association, Gloria was appointed a Charter Member of the National Museum of Women in the Arts in 1988 and a Professional Level Member of the International Sculpture Center in the same year. In 1974, she served as a Program Function Member on the Commission to Study the Consolidation of Children's Services Mandate of the 1974 Session of the Connecticut General Assembly and in 1988 was a member of the American Craft Council. Past memberships have included Connecticut Caucus of Black Women for Political Action 1984-86; PRO Disabled Entrepreneur Association 1985-86; and Farmington Valley Arts Center 1986-88.

A biography of Gloria Hodgson-Brooks appears in the main section of this Edition.

Bettye Dorris Kimble

"For an Outstanding Contribution to Music and Education".

BETTYE D KIMBLE

Born in Tulsa, Oklahoma, USA, Bettye D Kimble began playing and singing at her local Church, Vernon AME at the age of six. During her early teens, she sang, played and directed choirs at her church and other church, civic and school activities in Tulsa. Her late mother, the Evangelist, Ethel Kimble Weston was a continuous encouragement and inspiration to her, and together they toured the United States conducting revivals and concerts.

On graduation from college, Bettye Kimble taught for several years in the Sapulpa, Oklahoma School District. She served as Conference Musical Director for the 12th Episcopal District, where she was appointed Evangelist Gospel Singer. Moving to Kansas City, Missouri, she served as Co-ordinator of Vocal and Instrumental Music and was the first Black person to teach in the Hamlin Kansas School District. Whilst in Kansas City, she taught at Lincoln and Central High Schools, directed the choirs at Jamison Temple Church, performed with the Kansas City Philharmonic Orchestra and was the first Black person to conduct the All-City Band and Orchestra Festival in Topeka, Kansas. Coming to the Los Angeles area in 1967, she became pianist, organist and Minister of Music for Ward AME Church. She recorded her first album with the Chancel Choir of Ward AME Church and directed them in concert with the Watts Symphony Orchestra. She transferred to Bryant Temple AME Church as Director of the Chancel and Children's Choirs, and here had the opportunity to record her second album with the Chancel Choir and the Kimble Choral Ensemble in 1977.

She assisted in the auditioning of voices for the album "Roots" by Quincy Jones in 1977 and the following year was commissioned by the Rod McGrew Scholarship Fund to write a choral arrangement of "Inner City Blues" in honour of Marvin Gaye. She also directed the Interdenominational Community Choir at the McGrew Affair, appearing with Neil Diamond, Bob Dylan, Barry White, Stevie Wonder, Lou Rawls, Marvin Gaye and many others. Recently, Mrs Kimble performed with the Young Saints in a celebration to welcome President and Mrs Ronald Reagan back to California at the end of his presidential term.

The Kimble Community Choir, an interdenominational group of singers and instrumentalists was formed by Mrs Kimble in 1985, as an extension of the Kimble Choral Ensemble, and they have taken part in numerous church, community and civic performances.

Among the first Blacks to attend and graduate from Tulsa University, Bettye Kimble received a Bachelor of Music degree. She also holds Master of Arts and Master of Science degrees from Pepperdine University. For her dedicated service to church, school and community, Mrs Kimble has received numerous awards including honours from the County of Los Angeles, the City of Los Angeles, the City of Inglewood and a special tribute, which appeared in Jet Magazine, for 30 years service to the world of music. The composer of many songs, Mrs Kimble has published an outstanding book of songs entitled "Songs of Inspiration" and has also written a religious musical drama called "The Revelation".

Bettye Kimble is the mother of two children, Jay Charles and Cheleste Denine and grandmother of Saleeha.

A biography of Bettye D Kimble appears in the main section of this Edition.

Gloria Dolores Knight

"For an Outstanding Contribution to Urban Development".

GLORIA DOLORES KNIGHT

Gloria Dolores Knight is currently President of Mutual Life in Kingston, Jamaica. The recipient of a Jamaica Government Exhibition Scholarship, she attended the University of the West Indies/London gaining a BA in 1953, and then spent a year in England (1955-56) on a special course in Public Administration at Oxford University on a Commonwealth Development and Welfare Scholarship. Subsequently she undertook a two-year postgraduate course in Sociology at McGill University, Montreal on a Commonwealth Scholarship from 1962 to 1964 and in 1984 was awarded her MSc in Applied Behavioural Science from Johns Hopkins University, USA.

Mrs Knight began her career in the Jamaica Civil Service, serving in a range of posts from Administrative Cadet to Principal Assistant Secretary in the Ministries of Labour, Housing and Social Welfare, Development and Finance and Planning, between 1953 and 1966. She then joined the Kingston Waterfront Redevelopment Co, a fore-runner of the Urban Development Corporation, as Administrative Secretary. In 1968, she was appointed General Manager of the Urban Development Corporation. The U D C is responsible for urban expansion, renewal and development in designated areas. The Corporation has a total investment in land and development works of more than 109 million operating in six project areas of Kingston Waterfront, Hellshire, Ocho Rios, Oracabessa, Montego Bay and Negril. The U D C carries out developments which are too large or complex for the private sector to handle or which do not meet the profit requirement of private enterprise but which are necessary for development of the country. The Corporation has a number of subsidiaries, the major one being National Hotels and Properties Ltd, which owns eleven of the island's hotels, with a total of 3,750 rooms. Ten of these are leased to private operators. The U D C is currently engaged in designing and implementing employment creation projects aimed at the very poorest in its project areas and two of these projects are aimed at bringing women into productive employment.

As General Manager of the U D C, Gloria Knight is responsible for a staff of over 243 people, half of whom have professional training in such areas as architecture, planning, engineering, financial administration, estate and project management.

After the disastrous flooding in the West of the island in 1979, Mrs Knight was named co-ordinator of the Reconstruction Task Force. She has been selected as a member of Jamaica's delegations to meetings of the United Nations Environmental Programme and the United Nations Centre for Human Settlements (HABITAT), and has led these delegations on some occasions.

In 1975 Mrs Knight was selected as one of five distinguished women by the University Guild of Graduates, Mona Campus in celebration of International Women's Year. She received the Order of Distinction for her work in urban development in 1977 and in 1980 was awarded a Certificate of Honour for Distinguished Service for her work in connection with the flooding of June 1979.

Mrs Knight and her husband have four daughters and one son.

A biography of Gloria Dolores Knight appears in the main section of this Edition.

Glorija Lawrence

"For an Outstanding Contribution to Astrological Research and as a Writer".

GLORIJA LAWRENCE

Writer, lecturer, teacher and researcher, Glorija Lawrence is Proprietoress of Shiloko Astrological Services. Born in Auckland, New Zealand on 20th April 1945, she has been married to Lionel since 1964 and has two children.

In the Autumn of 1983, she undertook a six week beginners course in Astrology with top astrologer, Doris Greaves. She feels it was significant that this was the first beginners' course Doris had conducted for thirty years. Even though she had no astrological background, Glorija soon realised how much the subject had to offer, particularly for the contemporary person with modern thoughts and an inquiring mind. She finds it a unique way to try and understand people, their personality and their individuality, and also enjoys the challenge of modern methods of predicting, having had much success in this area.

The holder of a Diploma in Cosmobiology affiliated with the Cosmobiology Academy of West Germany, Mrs Lawrence is a member of the Federation of Australian Astrologers and of the Regulus Ebertin Study Group. A contributor to several magazines, she writes a star column for 'Tempo' Australia and articles of general interest for many astrological journals. Specializing in horse racing personalities, she also contributes a racing column for the 'National Trotting Weekly'.

Mrs Lawrence has taught a series of classes for the Council of Adult Education in Melbourne. She also teaches Astrology on the Mornington Peninsula and lectures for charitable groups such as the Yoralla Society and school clubs etc.

Having worked for eighteen months in the area of death and bereavement, Glorija gained access to many interesting dates of birth for study and research in all area of astrology.

A member and Accomplished Toastmaster of Toastmasters International, Mrs Lawrence is a Past President, Secretary and Educational Officer of her local branch. In 1984 she served as Area Governor and Convention Chairman for the district of Victoria, South Australia, Western Australia and Tasmania.

A biography of Glorija Lawrence appears in the main section of this Edition.

Dr Josephine Gorliss Liebhaber

"For an Outstanding Contribution to Education".

JOSEPHINE GORLISS LIEBHABER

Lecturer, Workshop Director, Poet, Literary Critic and Freelance Writer, Josephine Gorliss Liebhaber is the author of the play "Touches of Heritage" and the poetry books "The Song Alone" and "Lite News". She has also contributed to the "American Poetry Anthology" 1983; "Our World's Best Loved Poems" 1984, "A Treasure of Lyric Poetry", "Spotlight Review" and others.

Born in Thelan, North Dakota, USA on 2nd February, 1917, she obtained a BS degree from Winona State University in 1953 and an MS from Mankato State University in 1956. Her EdD was received from Teachers University in 1974. She also studied at the University of Minnesota, Duluth, Northwestern University, University of Hawaii, Colorado State University, and University of Minnesota.

On 19th June 1950, Josephine married Louis J Liebhaber.

Beginning her career as a saleslady in Dayton's Minneapolis, she then worked as a receptionist for David Shearer, Attorney, Minneapolis. She was appointed a Teacher of High School English, College Bound, Wells Minnesota in 1945 and served in this capacity until 1982.

Co-founder, Secretary and Vice-President of Wells Education Association, Josephine Liebhaber was also one of the founders of the Southern Minnesota Poetry Society, Mankato and founder of the Home and School Association, Wells. She served as PTA President and Secretary and was founder of the Wells Hospital Student Loan Fund and Wells Blue Birds Campfire Groups. Secretary of Graduate Women, Mrs Liebhaber is a member of Auxiliary of the American Legion, founded Local Girls State, American Association of University Women and is a member of the Minnesota Council of Teachers of English, legislative committee, AAUW Scholarship Committee.

Awarded an Honorary Doctorate of Divinity for her outstanding contribution to world peace by the Church Council, Josephine received an invitational audience with Pope Pius at Castle Gondolfo, Rome, Italy on 7th August, 1957.

She was the recipient of a Golden Poetry Award in 1985 and a Silver Poet Award in 1986 and received a Publication Evaluation from CTE Legislative Committee and an Award of Merit from the NCTE Speaker Committee. Other honours and awards include an MFT Citation and Life Membership in 1982, private reception and White House Tea, 1988, Governor's Reception at dedication of A L Vocational Technical College, 1989, School Board Award, President of Wells PTA.

Her hobbies include creative and freelance writing, fishing, reading, sports and music.

A biography of Josephine Gorliss Liebhaber appears in the main section of this Edition.

Anneliese List

"For an Outstanding Contribution as Author and Writer".

ANNELIESE LIST

Writer and Dancer, Anneliese (Pfenninger) List, who uses the pseudonym of Alice Pervin, was born in 1922 in Heroldsberg in the Federal Republic of Germany. After graduating from secondary school, she passed the government examination as a dancer in 1939. She performed as a dancer at the City Theatre in Guben between 1939-40 and 1940-41 and was a dance soubrette at the City Theatre in Landsberg/Warthe between 1941 and 1942. She performed at the City Theatre in Thorn, East Prussia 1942-44 and as an Operetten-Soubrette at the City Theatre, Elbing, East Prussia between 1944-45. Anneliese married Huldreich List in February 1947, deceased 1982. After serving as Secretary of the United States Embassy's Escapee Programme from 1956-60, she was Clerk in Charge of the Foreigners Office of the City of Nuremberg between 1960-82. Anneliese List holds membership in The World Literary Academy, England and the International Biographical Association, England. She won second prize in a story contest in the magazine "True Stories" in 1975, and among many other honors was awarded the Certificate of Merit by International Authors and Writers Who's Who in 1986. Stories she has contributed to books and magazines include: "The Tree", 1973; "The Work Was in Vain", 1974; "Miracles Happen Always Again", 1974; "Over and Over Again I Saw the Cross", 1975; "What I'll Never Be Able to Forget in All My Life", 1975; "My Long Way From the War until Today", 1976; "How I Earned My First Money", 1977; "The First Dance", 1977; "The Little Witch", 1977; "The Luck Behind the Mountains" (booklet with four stories), 1978; "The Gingerbread Heart", 1985; "Merry Christmas Everywhere", 1985; "A Fairy Tale", 1986; "Ten Promises", 1987; "First Love", 1987; "Realization", 1988; "Our Lumpi", 1989; "Prayer in the Sunshine", 1989.

In her leisure time Anneliese enjoys reading, the theatre, cinema, television and travelling.

A biography of Anneliese List appears in the main section of this Edition.

Professor Chiyoe Matsumoto

"For an Outstanding Contribution to Dance Aesthetics and Dance Education".

CHIYOE MATSUMOTO

Now a Professor Emeritus of Ochanomizu University, Japan, Chiyoe Matsumoto also spends her time as an author, lecturer and leader of professional and social organisations.

Born in Nara, Japan on 1st January, 1920, Chiyoe attended Tokyo Women's Higher Normal School (now Ochanomizu University) graduating in 1941, and was also awarded a Teacher's Certificate. She then undertook a period of postgraduate study at the same University.

She joined the staff of Tokyo University of Education as a Lecturer in 1952 and then served as a Professor of the University from 1963 to 1970. Transferring to Ochanomizu University, she held the appointment of Professor from 1971 to 1985, and during the same period (1977-85) undertook a Doctoral research course in Human Culture. Since 1985 she has been a Professor Emeritus of the University.

In addition to her teaching career, Professor Matsumoto is a distinguished author in her field. Her titles include "The Search for Beauty of Dance", "A Complete Guidebook to Dance Learning" and "Dance Expression". She is also responsible for three films on "Dance Research - Problem Situation and Problem Solving".

President of the Japan Association of Physical Education for Women, Chiyoe Matsumoto also serves as Vice President of the International Association of Physical Education and Sports for Girls and Women and of the Japanese Society for Dance Research. In January 1980, she received a letter of thanks from the Japanese Minister of Education for her long years of distinguished service to the promotion of physical education and sports.

On 4th April 1970, Chiyoe married Masakatsu Gunji. In her leisure time, Professor Matsumoto enjoys travelling, theatregoing, studying paintings and composing "Waka", 31 syllable Japanese poems. She also likes discussions with young people on such subjects as the aesthetics of dance and dance education.

A biography of Chiyoe Matsumoto appears in the main section of this Edition.

Johanna Mitchell

"For an Outstanding Contribution to Equality for Women in the work place".

JOHANNA MITCHELL

Business Executive and Company Owner, Johanna Mitchell was born in Germany on 14th June, 1917 and is now resident in Saskatoon, Saskatchewan, Canada. Educated at Max Reinhardt Seminar, Vienna, Austria from 1936 to 1938, she travelled to Canada to start a new life and in 1941 became a Director of Intercontinental Packers Ltd in Saskatoon, Saskatchewan. She served as Overseer for Vancouver, British Columbia, Canada Operations from 1963 to 1970, when she was appointed President of the company and since 1976 has held the titles of Chairman and Chief Executive Officer.

Whilst living in Europe Ms Mitchell was actively involved in horseracing. She was the registered owner of "Fuersten Brauch" winner of the Hungarian Derby in 1937, of "Credo" winner of the Hungarian Derby in 1939 and of the unbeaten mare "Melvynm" which won the Hungarian Oaks in the same year.

With hobbies such as Art collecting, writing, travel, cattle breeding and golf, Johanna Mitchell belongs to various social and professional organisations, including the Riviera Country Club, Riverside Golf and Country Club, Saskatoon Board of Trade and the Mendel Art Gallery.

A lady of varied creative talents, Johanna starred in the film "3 Stripes in the Sun" with Aldo Ray, Chuck Connors and Richard York in 1954. She is currently working on her autobiography.

Johanna Mitchell is the mother of two sons and one daughter.

A biography of Johanna Mitchell appears in the main section of this Edition.

Lourdes Gagui Mon
"For an Outstanding Contribution as a Humanitarian Asian Leader".

LOURDES GAGUI MON

Having served as a faculty member of San Sebastian College, St Joseph's College, Beloit Schools, Philippine Public Schools and Immaculate Conception School between 1963 and 1983, Lourdes Gagui Mon is currently Principal of St Josaphat School, Chicago, USA. In addition, she is a senior editor and columnist for VIA TIMES Newsmagazine, and was a contributing editor for TM Herald Newspaper and a columnist on MAYNILA Magazine.

Born in the Philippines on 6th March 1944, Lourdes obtained a BSc in Education from the University of the East, Manila, Philippines in 1963. Subsequently, she was awarded an MEd from Loyola University in Chicago, Illinois, USA in 1976. Lourdes married Francis Mon on 17th July 1968.

The first Filipino President of Asian Human Services, Mrs Mon is Charter President of the Illinois Chapter of Filipino American Women's Network and Charter Vice-President of Maharlika Lioness Club. She also belongs to the Association of Supervision and Curriculum Development and was a co-founder of Sining Kayumanggi Theatre Group.

In 1985, Lourdes Mon received the Outstanding Asians Award from the Asian American Coalition, Asian Human Services and has also been honoured by La Union Club and the Philippine Children's Museum and Library. She was awarded outstanding Filipino of the Midwest in 1988, by the Cavite Association of America. Her Biography also appears in Who's Who in American Education and Who's Who in the Midwest.

An amateur stage actress, Mrs Mon has appeared in "The Time Has Come" and also in the Philippine productions "Bayan-Bayanan" and "Secreto Ni Donya Rosario". In her spare time, she also serves as a volunteer with the United States Immigration Service. Mrs Mon was appointed Commissioner of the Skokie Fine Arts Commission recently and a member of the Advisory Board on Asian Affairs for the Governor of the State of Illinois.

A biography of Lourdes Gagui Mon appears in the main section of this Edition.

Peggy Sue Moore
"For an Outstanding Contribution as a Lady Entrepreneur".

PEGGY SUE MOORE

Entrepreneur, Peggy Sue Moore, is grateful for the many honours bestowed upon her during the past few years. She says "All that I have, all that I am, and all that I hope to be does not come from my ability, but comes from God and I am a steward of the blessings He gives me; therefore I give thanks to him." She maintains that success is only a word. Friends are the true measure of success, and she wishes to thank all the friends who have considered her a worthwhile investment all these years.

Peggy is the daughter of George Moore, who was an honours graduate of CIT in Los Angeles and holds US and Canadian patents for equipment for the food industry, and her loving mother, Marie. She is one of a family of six with children and grandchildren numbering fourteen.

Until 1969, Peggy was engaged in education and in accounting positions in Wichita, Kansas, but in 1969 she joined a very small company and in 1972 they merged with another small company to form CPI Corporation. They are a dry blend food processing company specializing in contract blending, research and development, private label packaging and sales to food franchises, distributors and institutional facilities.

In 1970, Peggy Moore purchased stock along with Ms Jo Herdt, a fellow co-founder. The other stockholders included her father (who had started the company in 1967) and four local oil men. Ms Herdt and Ms Moore were given $5,000 from the Corporation to develop the company. Over the next 18 years, the company grew from three full-time employees to 127 and their sales have developed from $50,000 annually to a twenty-million-dollar-a-year business with sales in the United States and Canada.

Peggy Moore served as a Director of the Wichita Bowling Association for ten years and as a Council Member and Treasurer of Good Shepherd Lutheran Church for five years. Recently she became a member of the International Platform Association in Winnetka, Illinois, and in 1989 was elected as a Director for the Kansas Restaurant Purveyors Association.

Believing that success is attainable through hard work, long hours, goals within reach and faith in God and yourself, Peggy is dedicated to the proposition that all women are created equal; therefore, the opportunities for success exist equally. It is her sincere hope that more women will venture into the corporate market, as there are a multitude of opportunities for women entrepreneurs.

A biography of Peggy Sue Moore appears in the main section of this Edition.

Jean Mueller

"For an Outstanding Contribution to Dancing, Ranching and Trail Riding".

JEAN MUELLER

Jean Mueller has spent eighteen years teaching dance including ballet, tap, jazz, gymnastics, twirling, ballroom, disco, and country western to all ages from three year olds, through college and adults. She is Instructor in Tap, Jazz, Country Western, Ballroom and Jitterbug at the University of Texas at Austin (since 1980).

Jean was born on 14 June 1952 in Austin, Texas in the United States of America and earned a B.Sc Degree in Home Economics and Child Development from the University of Texas at Austin in 1974. Her dance and musical theatre training has included: Dancing since the age of 3; Years of lessons and performing experience in ballet, tap, jazz, gymnastics, twirling, ballroom, disco, country western, voice, piano and drums. She is currently studying jazz with Rick Milland Dance Academy (former director-teacher of Dupree Dance Academy in Los Angeles) and Zachary Scott Theatre for drama and acting training. She was a Piano Teacher in Austin, Texas from 1973-75; Drummer, 1964-present; Dancer at famous pageants including the Tyler Rose Festival, Luckenbach World's Fair, Austin Aqua Festival and other special events in Texas from 1967-84; Dancer, chorus in "Kiss Me Kate", Oklahoma, 1969-70; Lead role of Sally Bowles in musical "Cabaret", 1976; Choreographer for musical "Cabaret" produced by Sul Ross State University, 1976; Head Cheerleader and Choreographer for Austin Texan Cheerleaders - Austin Texans Professional Football Team, 1981 (Awarded 1981 Outstanding Austin Texan Cheerleader and Miss Congeniality by Cheerleaders); Teacher at Shirley McPhail School of Dance, 1972-75; Instructor in country western, dance aerobics, Sul Ross State University, 1975-77; Instructor in ballet, tap, jazz, A & M Consolidated Community Education, 1977-78; Instructor in country western, jitterbug, Texas A & M University, 1977-80; Jean Mueller School of Dance: Alpine, Texas 1975-77 and College Station, Texas, 1977-80; From 1976-83 she produced and directed seven major shows and from 1981-84 was Director, Choreographer and Teacher at Jean Mueller School of Dance in Austin, Texas. She is a member of many professional, educational and civic organizations including Austin Chamber of Commerce, US Twirling and Gymnastics Associations, International Arabian Horse Association and Women's Symphony League of Austin. Jean has received many awards and honours for both dance and sports. In 1981 she received Austin Texan Professional Cheerleader Awards; Arabian Horse Show Awards and numerous awards and trophies for winning tennis and racquetball tournaments, best sportsmanship awards; Bryan College Station champion - represented city at State Regionals.

Jean Mueller has been making history on horseback since 1986 as Texas' First Lady Trail Boss of the Austin Founders Trail Ride which travels with horses and covered wagons through the Texas Hill Country over a week's time each year to officially start the Austin-Travis County Livestock Show & Rodeo. She has also been Trail Ride Chairman of the Austin-Travis County Livestock Show & Rodeo since 1986 and on the Equestrian Committee.

Jean has many interests including: dancing, theatre, piano, drums, singing, horseback riding, training and showing Arabian and quarter horses, trail riding, tennis, racquetball, golf, softball, volleyball, water skiing, swimming, canoeing, snow skiing, sailing, travel and photography.

A biography of Jean Mueller appears in the main section of this Edition.

Carole Anne Myers
"For an Outstanding Contribution to the Medical field of pre-hospital Emergency Medical Service".

CAROLE ANN MYERS

A certified paramedic, Carole Ann Myers has operated an ambulance service for the past 21 years. She and her late husband, Larry, founded Myers Ambulance Service in Greenwood, Indiana in 1967. On Larry's appointment as Mayor of Greenwood in 1976, Carole took over the family business as Chief Executive Officer. After her husband's death in an aeroplane accident in 1980, Carole decided to continue the family-operated service, the only private ambulance service in Johnson and Southern Marion Counties.

Nationally registered as an EMT in 1970, Carole was awarded state registration in 1975, following the formation of the Indiana EMS Commission. When she was registered as a Paramedic in 1979, she and her daughter Patti became the first mother-daughter paramedic team in the United States.

A member of the American Ambulance Association, Mrs Myers served as Secretary for the year 1983 to 1984 and as Treasurer between 1985 and 1986. She was Vice President of the Association for 1987 to 1988 and President 1989-90. President of the Indiana Ambulance Association from 1983 to 1985, she also served as Secretary between 1981 and 1983 and as Treasurer from 1987 to 1990.

Carole was appointed by Indiana's Governor, Robert Orr, to the Advanced Life Support Operations Committee, an advisory committee to the Indiana EMS Commission in 1984, and in September 1986 Governor Orr appointed her to the Indiana EMS Commission as a representative of commercial and private ambulance services.

A former Chairman of the Membership Services Subcommittee and former Chairman of the Finance Committee of the American Ambulance Association, Mrs Myers is the former Chairman of the Membership Development Committee. She also serves on the Industry Image, Accreditation, Education and Training and Privatization Task Force Committees.

A faculty member for workshops for the AAA, the IAA, other state conferences and for other state associations, Carole has instructed at local EMT classes and has been a CPR instructor for the American Heart Association since 1975.

In 1983, Carole was awarded the AAA's "Woman of the Year" award for her contributions and support of the American Ambulance Association and her tireless efforts to improve emergency medical services since 1970. She was also the recipient of the Distinguished Hoosier Award from the Governor of Indiana in 1984.

Active in community and civic organisations, Carole serves on the Board of Directors for both the Greenwood Chamber of Commerce (secretary) and the Greenwood Senior Citizens Center and is active in her local church. She is a Lifetime member of the Republican Senatorial Inner Circle in Washington and has been recognised at local, state and national levels for her contributions to pre-hospital emergency care and transportation of the sick and injured.

In addition to this publication, Mrs Myers is listed in the Marquis Who's Who of the Midwest and Who's Who of the World, 1988 edition, as well as The World Who's Who of Women. The mother of one son and three daughters, Carole enjoys reading and travelling in her leisure time.

A biography of Carole Ann Myers appears in the main section of this Edition.

Mary A Myers

"For an Outstanding Contribution to Foster Spiritual Unity Among Nations".

MARY A MYERS

Mary Myers, who was born in 1914, has spent her whole life in the search for spiritual knowledge and truth. As a young woman she taught the Sunday schools of churches of many denominations. She studied at various colleges and Universities in the United States for six years and was an accomplished athlete, receiving gold medals for swimming and diving and winning the City championship in Akron, Ohio, where she attended Akron University. She was a student at the University of California, Los Angeles from 1932 to 1935, majoring in Physical Education and Home Economics.

Mary then turned her attention to the study of journalism and writing and also undertook further religious study, exploring the inner-mystical teachings at the University of Cincinnati; she continued to study this field for twenty years. Her husband was a postgraduate student at the same University. When her husband was offered a position in Europe with the United States Army Recreational Programme, Mary followed with their three children shortly afterwards.

Called into service by the Chief of Chaplains, Mary assisted in the first Religious Conferences overseas, to train women to assist the chaplains overseas within the churches and was appointed an International Prayer Leader. Recognizing her abilities as a teacher, the National Organization of the American Business Women's Clubs (AWAG) in Germany called on her services to assist in their first training Conference to help women to become more effective in their business endeavours. During this period, she established "My Lady's News" a newspaper designed to assist in training potential women leaders, moving her into National circles.

Called to higher service in the religious field, Mary was invited to visit international spiritual organisations in Singapore, Malaysia, India, Africa, Italy, Germany and England where she lectured and taught.

When her husband was sent to Bangkok, Thailand, Mary had the opportunity to study the Buddhist Religion with the monks.

Returning to the United States, she was called to establish a spiritual study centre. Hundreds of booklets were printed monthly and distributed throughout the world. She then published four books "My Truth", "My Peace", "The Path of Light" and "The Parable of the Rose".

Receiving her Doctorate of Divinity from the State of Florida, she was ordained to work with spiritual leaders everywhere and she established a spiritual University. The leaders whom she had trained now began to assist her as leaders in the branch centres which sprang up in many areas and countries.

Mary has received numerous honours for her many years of service and many international organisations have sought her guidance and help. As her four children are now grown and raising families of their own, Mary devotes all her time in service to beneficent beings who are working to raise the spiritual level of mankind in the New Age.

A biography of Mary A Myers appears in the main section of this Edition.

Joyce Ann Wynn Oberhausen

"For an Outstanding Contribution to Excellence in Business and Art".

JOYCE ANN WYNN OBERHAUSEN

Aircraft Executive, Artist, Joyce Ann Wynn Oberhausen was born in Plain Dealing, Louisiana, USA on 12 November 1941. Joyce attended Ayers Business School, Shreveport, Louisiana, 1962-63; Seminars worldwide; Various art courses, University of Alabama, 1974-75.

Joyce began her business career as a Stenographer, secretary, Lincoln National Life, Shreveport, LA 1959; Secretary at Baifield Industries, Shreveport, LA 1963-66: International Art Teacher, Artist, Huntsville, Alabama, 1974-; Vice-President, co-owner Precision Specialty Corp., Huntsville, AL 1966-present; Vice-President, co-owner, Military Aircraft Sales, Inc., Huntsville, AL 1979-present; President, owner Wynnson Enterprises, Inc., Huntsville, AL 1984-present; owner Wynnson Galleries Collection (Limited Edition Prints) Florist, Meridianville, AL 1987-present. Owner Wynnson Enterprises Military Packaging Company 1988-present.

Joyce paints in oils, water colors and on porcelain. She is a member of International Porcelain Art Teachers, Porcelain Portrait Society, Co-founder of the National Museum Women in Arts, United Artist Association, American Society of Professional & Executive Women; Historial Society-Smithsonian, National Association of Female Executive, Huntsville Chamber of Commerce, Huntsville Better Business Bureau, Alabama Sheriffs Association, Metropolitan Museum of Art, National Member Smithsonian Association, Huntsville Art League and Museum Association, Association of Community Artist, People to People International, National Trust of Historic Preservation, International Platform Association, International China Painting School England, Lifetime Member International Biographical Association, Republican Senatorial Inner Circle, President Bush's Task Force Charter Member. Joyce has travelled to Communist China, the Democratic Republic of Germany, Europe, Mexico, the USSR and throughout the USA representing International Porcelain Art Cultures.

October 15, 1966 Joyce married James Joseph Oberhausen, she has one son Dale Henry Estein Oberhausen, two daughters Darla Renee Estein Oberhausen, Georgann Oberhausen, two grandchildren Audry Joanna Minor and Joyce Ann Summerhill Minor. In her leisure time, she enjoys gardening, rug hooking, skiing, tennis, travel, needlework, jewelry design and sewing. Joyce designed and built her home, swimming pool and tennis court and also two business buildings.

A biography of Joyce Ann Wynn Oberhausen appears in the main section of this Edition.

The Hon Mrs Patricia E O'Neill

"For an Outstanding Contribution to Wildlife and Animals".

PATRICIA E. O'NEILL

Patricia O'Neill was raised with animals and could ride before she could walk. The daughter of Brigadier General Cavendish, Colonel in Chief of the 9th Lancers, she was trained in horsemanship by Sergeant Higgens, a retired Cavalry Sergeant Major. After her father's death, Patricia's mother married the shipping magnate, Viscount Furness and Sergeant Higgens stayed with the family. Patricia was educated at home by a French governess, an English governess, a retired Oxford Don and a German teacher. Her step-father owned two famous thoroughbred studs and also kept 60 hunters and hacks and with Sergeant Higgens it was her job to exercise and school them. Her mother and Duke Furness spent half the year in Kenya and her mother returned with exotic animals to add to her collection. For years she had a cheetah which accompanied her everywhere and she also kept two silver foxes, a mongoose, a hyrax, parrots, budgies and numerous dogs.

When Patricia was ten they rented a large house in Muthaiga, Kenya and from then on she was determined to live in Africa. She finally went to live in Kenya in 1953. Her mother bought her a small farm overlooking the Ngong Hills at Karen and it was here that she started her collection of wild animals. Her first baby was a lion cub only a few weeks old, which she brought up on a bottle. It slept on her bed with all the dogs. She later acquired a cheetah, a baby chimp, various buck, 23 monkeys and, in fact, any suffering animal. Believing that animals should have their freedom, they were given the run of the house and even the deadliest enemies learned to live together. When the lion cub, called Tana, grew into a mature lioness she used to call in the males and Patricia would return home to find them sitting on her doorstep. Although Tana was no threat to the neighbouring farmers' herds or goats and cattle, wild lions were a different story and they threatened to shoot Tana. Therefore Ms O'Neill and her animals were forced to move and eventually settled in the Northern frontier of Kenya, where she, her animals and loyal Wakamba helpers and the local tribesmen were the only inhabitants for over 80 miles. She built a lodge on the banks of the Rojewire River with the help of the Meru tribesmen. After the death of Lord Furness, her mother married the Earl of Kenmare and Patricia named the lodge "Kenmare" after her. The Meru Game Park was the first to be established. With no roads, it was desert country - it was Africa at its magnificent best. She would watch herds of up to three hundred elephant watering in the river and would drive slowly through vast herds of buffalo. She lived there for years until the outbreak of the Shifta war when her greatest friend Beryl Markham persuaded her and her mother to move to South Africa as Beryl wished to race her horses.

On Beryl's persuasion, Patricia's mother bought Broadlands and they all moved to South Africa. After a few years Beryl returned to Kenya and Patricia would have loved to go too, but by now her mother was very ill and she remained at Broadlands until she died. Patricia then remarried her first husband Frank O'Neill, the ex-Australian Olympic swimmer, and they began a new collection of animals, which today consists of parrots, dogs, cats, donkeys, goats, sheep, ferrets and, of course, monkeys. In addition they own a stud consisting of 295 horses. Patricia firstly with her mother and then with her husband began training horses at Broadlands and managed to produce some of the greatest racing fillies in the country. Winning all the classics, they had champion after champion and these horses eventually became the basis of the stud. Gradually the racing gave place to breeding, and when they brought the stallion "Royal Prerogative" over from England, a new era started at Broadlands. He was to become the greatest sire South Africa had ever had and through him Broadlands became famous in the racing world.

A biography of Patricia E. O'Neill appears in the main section of this Edition.

Carol Tommie Parker
"For an Outstanding Contribution to the Field of Mental Health".

CAROL TOMMIE PARKER

Psychotherapist, Carol Tommie Parker is the author or co-author of a number of papers, mainly in the field of family therapy, which include 'A comparative study of family and professional views of the factors affecting positive adaptation to a disabled child' 1981; 'Utilizing a mental health-education outreach training model to prevent special education teacher career attrition' 1985; 'Multiple family therapy: evaluating a group experience for mentally retarded adolescents and their families' 1987; 'Dilemmas resulting from the application of extemporaneous ethics in interdisciplinary team decision-making' 1987; 'Family therapy case management' 1988 and 'The impact of special needs children on their parents' perceptions of family structural interaction patterns' 1989.

Born in Birmingham, Alabama, USA in 1928, Ms Parker studied at the University of Nebraska at Omaha, gaining a Bachelor of Social Work degree in 1977, followed by a Master of Social Work degree the next year. Between 1978 and 1979, she undertook postgraduate studies in Community Psychiatry at the Nebraska Psychiatric Institute of the University's Medical Centre. The recipient of a grant for a Traineeship in Alcoholism Studies in 1977, the following year she was awarded a Health Education and Welfare Grant for specialization in Child Welfare.

In addition to the practice of psychotherapy with families, groups and individuals, Carol has undertaken an active teaching career at the University of Nebraska. In 1987 she was appointed an Instructor in the Department of Special Education and the following year became a Graduate Lecturer at the Graduate College and an Assistant Professor at the School of Social Work. She has also served as an Instructor in the Departments of Psychiatry and Family Practice, College of Medicine and University of Nebraska Medical Centre.

A Fellow and Diplomate of the American Board of Medical Psychotherapists and a Diplomate of the International Academy of Behavioural Medicine, Counseling and Psychotherapy, Ms Parker is a Registered, Certified Family Mediator of the American Association of Family Counselors and Mediators and a Registered Clinician of the National Register of Clinical Social Workers. In addition, she serves as a Clinical Member of the American Association for Marriage and Family Therapy and the Academy of Certified Social Workers.

A biography of Carol Tommie Parker appears in the main section of this Edition.

Nanci Glick Reid

"For an Outstanding Contribution as a Health Care Professional".

NANCI GLICK REID

Nanci Glick Reid began her career as a Research Technician at the Children's Hospital in Boston, Massachusetts between 1961 and 1963 and then transferred to the New England Medical Center, Boston as a Senior Research Technician and Medical Technician, serving for two periods 1963 to 1965 and 1967 to 1969. In 1965 she was awarded a BA in Liberal Arts from Harvard University Extension College in Cambridge, Massachusetts. Between 1969 and 1984, she served as a Cytogeneticist Supervisor at Carney Hospital, Boston, and during the same period (1969-86) was an Instructor in Medicine at Tufts University Medical School. Other appointments held by Mrs Reid are Systems Analyst, Cognos/Coulter Corporation, Waltham, Massachusetts 1976-77; Medical Technologist, Milton (Mass) Hospital 1978-83 and Massachusetts Eye and Ear, Boston 1983 to 1984; Laboratory Manager, Harvard Community Health Plan, Braintree, Massachusetts, 1985 to 1988 and Quality Control Manager, Oncolab, Inc, Boston 1988-89. In 1983, Nanci Reid was awarded a BS degree in Health Science from Northeastern University, Boston where she is currently studying for her MBA.

The presenter of abstracts to the 12th and 13th International Haematology Society Conferences, Nanci Reid has also contributed articles to professional journals. She is a member of the Association of Cytogenetic Technologists, having served as Association President from 1976 to 1978, and is Lecturer of the American Society of Medical Technologists. A former Treasurer of Sigma Epsilon Rho she served as Vice President for the year 1987 to 1988. Mrs Reid, who is Jewish, is a Republican and a member of the Pythian Sisters.

Also listed in the 16th edition of "Who's Who in American Women", Nanci Reid has received a number of honours and prizes, including a Key Achievement award for outstanding management and a First Prize/Monetary Award for research presentation. Inducted into Sigma Epsilon Rho Honour Society, she appeared on the Dean's List at Northeastern University.

Born in Brookline, Massachusetts on 22nd September, 1941, Nanci married Raymond Augustus Reid in February 1985 and they have two daughters, Lori Sue and Staci Allison. Mrs Reid, whose hobbies include sailing, lobstering, game fishing, cranberry growing, photography, travel and skiing, belongs to the Plymouth Yacht Club and the Massachusetts Ski Club.

A biography of Nanci Glick Reid appears in the main section of this Edition.

Belle Sara Rosenbaum

"For an Outstanding Contribution to Promoting Judaic Art".

BELLE SARA ROSENBAUM

Belle Sara Rosenbaum is an interior designer and personal property appraiser, who was born in New York City, USA on 1st April 1922. In March 1939 she married Jack Rosenbaum and has one son and three daughters, eighteen grandchildren and thirteen great grandchildren.

Having gained a Certificate from the New York School of Interior Design in 1945, Belle Rosenbaum worked as a Design Consultant with the Marc Daniels company. She joined Jarvis Designs Inc in 1955 and was President of the company from 1959 to 1970. In addition she has served as Vice President of Lord and Lady Originals, Inc from 1955 to 1970, as Vice President of Cardio-Bionic Scanning Inc between 1975 and 1978 and as Vice President-Treasurer of Rapitech Systems Inc in 1985. From 1970 to 1978 she served as President of Design Associates BLS. In 1979, Mrs Rosenbaum was certified a Senior Member of the American Society of Appraisers.

A teacher of Judaica at Yeshiva University, Mrs Rosenbaum is completing a book on the subject entitled "Upon Thy Doorposts". She is also Director of the Rosenbaum Museum of Contemporary Judaica. One time author of short stories, she has contributed many articles on Interior Design to various professional journals.

A member of the Board of Governors of Yeshiva University Museum since 1987, Belle Rosenbaum also serves on the Board of New York State Council of Arts and is Honorary President of Yeshiva of Hudson County. She was Treasurer between 1948 and 1978 and President from 1955 to 1957 of AMIT Women and has been Treasurer of Brit AVROM since 1980. A member of the Board of Directors of American Friends of Migdal Ohr, she also serves on the editorial board of "Light Foundation".

The recipient of a Herald Tribune short story prize in 1939, Mrs Rosenbaum was more recently honoured by the State of Israel with a Woman of Valour Award in 1960 and in 1988 received a Founders Award from Migdal Ohr Schools of Israel.

A collector of art, antiques and people, Belle works as an artist in her leisure time and also enjoys gardening and communal and charity work.

A biography of Belle Sara Rosenbaum appears in the main section of this Edition.

Lili Sarnoff

"For an Outstanding Contribution to the Arts".

LILI SARNOFF

A Swiss citizen, Sculptor, Lili Charlotte Sarnoff was born in Frankfurt, Germany on 9th January, 1916. Having graduated from Reimann Art School in Berlin in 1934, she studied History of Art at the University of Berlin from 1934 to 1936. She then spent two years in Italy as a student at the University of Florence. Coming to the USA, Ms Sarnoff served as a Research Assistant at Harvard School of Public Health in Boston, Massachusetts between 1948 and 1954, and then moved to Maryland to take up the appointment of Research Associate at the National Heart Institute in Bethesda, a position she held until 1959. She then became President of Rodana Research Corporation in Washington DC, serving until 1961. Since 1968, Lili Sarnoff has worked as a freelance sculptor.

Her work has been the subject of numerous one-man shows, the most recent being at Gallery von Barhta, Basel, Switzerland, 1982; at the Alwin Gallery, London, 1982, at the Franz Bader Gallery, Washington DC, 1976; at Galerie de l'Hotel de Ville, Geneva, Switzerland in 1983; Pfalzgalerie, Kaiserslautern, West Germany, 1985; Gallery K, Washington DC 1987, and she has also taken part in group shows and juried shows, including Rockville Civic Center, Rockville, Maryland, 1988; Galerie Les Hirondelles, Geneva, Switzerland, 1988 and Washington Sculpture Group, Juried Show, 1989.

Museums in the USA and Israel, namely the National Museum for Women in the Arts, Washington DC; The Israel Museum, Jerusalem; The Corning Museum of Glass, Corning, New York and the National Academy of Sciences, Washington DC display the works of MS Sarnoff, and her pieces are also contained in private collections, which include those of King Birenda of Nepal, Katmandu; Mr James R Houghton of Corning, New York; Mr Vane Ivanovic, London, England; The Honorable and Mrs Randolph Kidder, Washington DC, His Excellency Anton Hegner, Berne, Switzerland. In addition her sculpture is in demand for inclusion in corporate exhibitions staged by such companies as Chase Manhattan Bank, New York, Federal National Mortgage Association, Washington DC and Survival Technology, Bethesda, Maryland.

She was commissioned by the National Institute for Music Theatre to create the sculpture entitled "Soaring Beyond" which is awarded annually to the First Prize winner of the George London and Mary Martin competition. Other commissions are a work called "The Flame" for the John F Kennedy Center for the Performing Arts in Washington DC and "Spiral Galaxy" for the National Air and Space Museum in Washington.

A Trustee of the Corcoran Gallery of Art, Ms Sarnoff is also Founder and President of Arts for the Aging, Washington DC. The recipient of the Sculpture Prize awarded by American Pen Women, she is listed in a number of other biographical registers, including Who's Who of American Women, American Artists, Who's Who of American Art and Dictionary of American Sculptures.

During her years as a scientific researcher, Lili Sarnoff authored or co-authored numerous scientific papers and was co-inventor of the Phrenic Respirator.

A biography of Lili Sarnoff appears in the main section of this Edition.

Geraldine Savary-Ogden

"For an Outstanding Contribution to Designer-White Dove Symbol for International Women's Liberation Movement 1970, as Pres, Sign of the Time, Selden, NY 1970-74".

GERALDINE SAVARY-OGDEN

Business entrepreneur, researcher, inventor, symbolist and author, Geraldine Savary Ogden is the owner of Ogden Research and Mail Order Business, Scottsdale, Arizona, Dove Medical Systems, USA, LAW Insurance Co, Scottsdale, Dove Landscaping and Citrus Nursery, Floral City, Florida and President of B G Micro-Purchasing, Inc, Scottsdale.

The daughter of Norman Pinkney and Maude (Bullard) Savary, Geraldine was born in Brooksville, Florida on 22nd September 1929. She received professional training in horticulture, research and writing and nursing.

Between 1961 and 1963, Ms Savary was owner and builder of the Ogden Trailer Court in Nenana, Alaska and at the same time (1962-63) was a stockholder and part-time worker for the Ogden Gold Mining Corporation at Candle Alaska on the Arctic Ocean. She was President of Sign of the Time in Selden, New York from 1970 to 1974, and then, returning to Florida owned and managed Ogden Nursery Products in Inverness, from 1974 to 1979. During the same period, from 1975 to 1978, she was owner, author and publisher of Ogden Advertising and Research, Floral City, Florida. Vice-President of Sales with the Computer Clinic in Mesa, Arizona from 1982 to 1984, she then served as a researcher with Geri-Health of Florida for the year 1984 to 1985.

An established author, Geraldine Savary's publications include: "Inverness and Citrus County Mapping Guide"; "What Florida Residents Should Know About Taxes"; "A Touch of Soul" 1983; "From A Liberated Mind" poetry 1972; "Favorite Recipes of 40 US Presidents" 1985 and children's books "Myrtle the Turtle"; "The Things I Like" and "The Death of a Bird". She has also contributed numerous articles to professional journals and popular magazines. In 1970, Ms Savary designed the white dove symbol for the Women's International Liberation Movement and in 1990 she designed the Women's Nouveau Movement symbol, The Grace of our International Dove symbol.

Over the years Ms Savary has had considerable success as an inventor. Her inventions have included a citrus tree freeze protection device in 1974, a hi-tech electronic time whistle, 1980, a work plan for a spring water bottling plant, 1987, a hi-tech protection devise against Radon gas in buildings, 1988, and a marketing plan for the national marketing of medical alarm systems for Lifecall USA, 1987. Ms Savary is the Founder of Dove Systems International Inc. 1990, a business and land development company (women owned and managed).

In 1950, Geraldine married Robert Thomas Ogden; they have two children, Robert Thomas Jr and Donna Lee, now Mrs Bonomi.

A biography of Geraldine Savary Ogden appears in the main section of this Edition.

Dr Anna Pearl Sherrick

"For an Outstanding Contribution as a Founder and Director of Montana State College of Nursing 1937-1965, Instructor 1965-1970".

ANNA PEARL SHERRICK

Anna Pearl Sherrick, RN, EdD, PhD, spent a total of thirty-three years in higher education at Montana State College and University (1937-70), serving twenty-eight years in Administration and Instruction on the Nursing program and the final five years until her retirement in 1970 on the University's Television Project. Dr Sherrick is now a Professor Emeritus of Montana State University.

The Nursing faculty, by use of the television method, sharpened their teaching skills by using visual aids and well-prepared teaching outlines, as well as other techniques that improved learning. Demonstrations, procedures, team conferences and lectures by general college and university faculty were put on video tapes for Nursing students at the associated hospitals. The purchase of television equipment for the University Television Department, the School of Nursing and the associated hospitals are assets that continue to assist faculty and Nursing students.

Between 1937 and 1965, the confederation of the three Deaconess hospitals, the Montana State Hospital, the Montana Tuberculosis Hospital, and a one-woman department of Nursing, with the co-operation and guidance from the Montana State College administrators, hammered out an accredited curriculum so that high school graduates in Montana might receive the baccalaureate degree. This was based on what the Roman Catholic Sisters, since 1864, and the Methodist Deaconesses since 1900 had promoted. Professor Sherrick feels privileged to have taken part in this exciting venture.

Through better funding for Schools of Nursing, the need for better prepared nurses in the military, public health, schools and hospitals, the establishment of the US Cadet Nursing Corps in World War II, and many other improvements, Dr Sherrick has, with satisfaction, seen the status of nurses rise dramatically in the United States.

Since her retirement, Professor Sherrick has become involved with the issues and problems of Senior Citizens, locally, statewide and nationally. In Gallatin County, she has been involved with the American Association of Retired Persons, the Gallatin County Council on Aging, the Bozeman Senior Social Center and the Retired Teachers Association. She was elected to the Area IV Board of Directors, of which Gallatin County is one of the seven counties. She attended the State of Montana annual Governor's Conferences on Aging and local forums to determine the needs of elders in Montana. She was a delegate to the White House Conference on Aging in both 1971 and 1981. Anna Sherrick chaired the committee that initiated and organised the building of the Bozeman Senior Centre, where meals are provided five days a week, meals are delivered to senior citizens confined to their homes, exercise classes are run for Seniors including swimming at Montana State University physical education buildings. She has been heavily involved with Gallatin County Council on Aging since its inception in the early 1970's. The Council works to provide funds for services to enhance the quality of living for the elderly. In addition, Dr Sherrick is a volunteer on the Retired Senior Volunteer Program.

Keeping as active as her arthritis and growing older permits, Anna Sherrick enjoys her home and garden, and her four poodles over the years have provided companionship. Her first poodle, Blackie, was a gift from a student, who, rightly, thought a dog would be good for her. She appreciates the concern shown by her nephew and his family for her welfare.

A biography of Anna Pearl Sherrick appears in the main section of this Edition.

Gail Penniman (Turner) Slover
"For an Outstanding Contribution as a Chronobiologist".

GAIL PENNIMAN TURNER SLOVER

Chronobiologist, teacher, researcher and lecturer, Gail Penniman Turner Slover is the author or co-author of a number of publications in her field, including '24-hour Synchronized Circadian Rhythm Before and After a Manic Episode Following a Norepinephrine Rhythm Alteration' in "Chronobiologia" 10 (2) 1983, co-author; author of 'Bringing Biological Rhythms into the Classroom' in "Connecticut Journal of Science Education" 1985 Fall-Winter; 'Urinary and Self-Measured Circadian and Circatrigintan Rhythms Before and After a Human Manic Episode', "Proceedings of II International Symposium on Chronobiologic Approach to Social Medicine" 1986 co-author and 'A Case Study of Psychophysiological Diary: Infradian Rhythms' co-author, in "Advances in Chronobiology, Part B", J E Pauly and L E Scheving eds, 1987. She also contributed to 'Jet Lag and Other Baggage' in "Off Camera" WFSB Channel 3, Fall-Winter, 1988.

After graduating from the Abbot Academy, Andover, Massachusetts in 1956, Gail Turner Slover attended Connecticut College, New London, Connecticut, gaining a BA degree in Zoology in 1960. Subsequently she was awarded her Masters in Education from the University of Hartford, West Hartford, Connecticut in 1978 and during the year 1979 to 1980 attended a Chautaqua Course in Chronobiology sponsored by the National Science Foundation. On gaining her BA in 1960, Gail spent a year as a Medical Technologist Trainee at the Harbor General Hospital, Torrance, California and then transferred to the Institute of Living, Hartford, Connecticut where she served as a Biochemistry Research Assistant from 1961 to 1964. She was an independent instructor of Parent Effectiveness Training and Teacher Effectiveness Training between 1978 and 1980. She joined the Talcott Mountain Science Center for Student Involvement in Avon, Connecticut as a chronobiologist, teacher and researcher for the period 1983 to 1987 and was also a substitute teacher of grades 6-12 within the Glastonbury and Manchester Public School System from 1984 to 1987. Since 1986, Ms Turner Slover has been an independent consultant and lecturer in Chronobiology and since 1988 has served as a Welcome Wagon representative.

Over the years, Ms Turner Slover has undertaken an extensive research programme. Since 1979 she has engaged in independent research in chronobiology in collaboration with the Institute of Living, University of Illinois and Talcott Mountain Science Center. In 1983 she presented a paper at the International Society of Chronobiology in Dublin, Ireland and in 1985 presented a further paper to the Society in Little Rock, Arkansas. Since 1986 she has lectured widely to corporations and organizations in the field of chronobiology (the study of timing within living things in the universe) emphasizing how to decrease jet lag and improve shift work rotation and maximize performance, and has also taken part in television programmes. A member of the Board of Directors of the Manchester Area Conference of Churches since 1988, Ms Turner Slover initiated two Christian Singles Ministries between 1984 and 1988. She is a member of the Orford Parish Chapter of Daughters of the American Revolution and is Chapter Chairwoman of the National Committee on American Indians.

On April 18th 1982 she took a personal step of faith and invited Jesus Christ into her life.

A biography of Gail Penniman Turner Slover appears in the main section of this Edition.

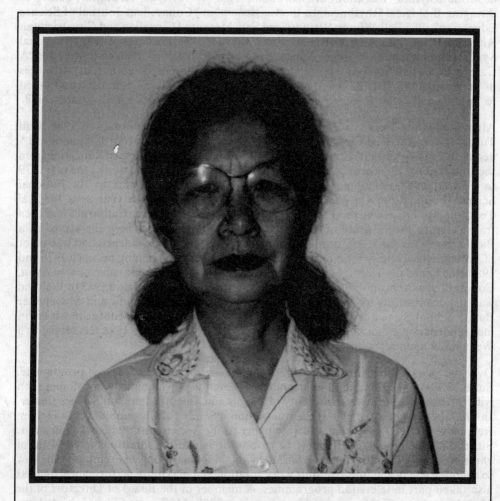

Dr Helen Chien-fan Su

"For an Outstanding Contribution to Chemistry".

HELEN CHIEN-FAN SU

Helen Chien-fan Su is a research chemist who has specialised in the field of natural product chemistry. After first researching into cancer chemotherapeutic chemicals and polymeric hydrophobic coatings she turned her attention to insecticides that occur naturally in edible foodstuffs. She synthesised insect pheromones in verification of chemical structure of the insect secretions, and is an advocate in the use of naturally occurring agents for insect control. Her research emphasises edible foodstuffs by utilising the secondary components of the foodstuffs that have adverse biological effects on stored-product insects. She is the author or co-author of 45 publications in scientific journals and the author of a book chapter entitled 'Isobutylamides' in "Comprehensive Insect Physiology, Biochemistry and Pharmacology" Volume 12 published by Pergamon Press (London) in 1985.

The daughter of Reverend Ru-chen Su and Sieu-Hsien Wang, Helen was born in Nanping, Fujian, China on 26th December 1922. After attending elementary and middle schools in Nanping, she studied at Hwa Nan College, Fuzhou, Fujian, China gaining a BA degree in 1944, with a major in Chemistry and minors in Biology and Mathematics.

She taught Chemistry at Hwa Nan College for five years and in 1949 came to the USA to undertake postgraduate studies at the University of Nebraska in Lincoln, Nebraska. Awarded her MS in Chemistry in 1951, she undertook research in organic chemistry and received her PhD in Chemistry (with minors in Physiology and Pharmacology) in July 1953.

Dr Su served on the faculty of Lambuth College, Jackson, Tennessee as Professor of Chemistry for two years, and then entered the Auburn Research Foundation, Auburn University (formerly Alabama Polytechnical Institute), Auburn, Alabama, where she conducted research on the synthesis of plant growth hormones for two years. She was then appointed a Senior Chemist and a Project Leader at the Central Research Laboratory, Borden Chemical Company, Philadelphia, Pennsylvania. Her research from 1957 to 1963 involved the synthesis of new chemotherapeutic compounds for cancer research and new enzymatic substrates for histochemistry. Transferring to the Lockheed-Georgia Research Laboratory, Lockheed Georgia Company, Marietta, Georgia, she conducted research into the development of water repellent coatings for aircraft windshields and submarine periscopes. She was a co-inventor of polymeric hydrophobic coatings which resulted in three patents granted from France, Italy and New Zealand, and she became one of the recipients of the Industrial Research Magazine IR-100 Award in 1966. In 1968 she took up her present appointment with the Agricultural Research Service of the US Department of Agriculture at the Stored-Product Insects Research and Development Laboratory at Savannah, Georgia.

A Certified Professional Chemist since 1968, Helen Chien-fan Su is a Fellow of both the American and Georgia Institutes of Chemists and also holds membership in the American Chemical Society, the American Association for the Advancement of Science, New York Academy of Science, Georgia Entomological Society, Sigma Xi and Sigma Delta Epsilon.
Her biography also appears in a large number of other biographical registers.

A biography of Helen Chien-fan Su appears in the main section of this Edition.

June Conran Sutherland

"For an Outstanding Contribution to Midwifery".

JUNE CONRAN SUTHERLAND

After graduating from Fintona Girls' School, June Conran Sutherland trained as a State Registered Nurse at the Royal Children's Hospital and Royal Melbourne Hospital between 1953 and 1955. The following year, she trained in Midwifery at the Queen Victoria Hospital and then undertook a further year's training, during 1957 at Berry Street Foundling Home. Now a qualified midwife, June joined the Victorian Health Department Maternal and Child Welfare Branch, serving from 1957 to 1959.

Married to Bruce Sutherland in March 1958, June raised a family of four sons. In 1980, she returned to nursing assuming the appointment of Sister-in-Charge of a Hospital Consultant's rooms and since 1984 she has been Director of Nursing at the Hawthorn Birth and Development Centre in Hawthorn, Victoria, Australia.

Born in Melbourne, Australia on 23rd June 1934, June Sutherland spends her leisure time doing tapestry, painting china, reading and travelling.

A biography of June Conran Sutherland appears in the main section of this Edition.

Neva Bennett Talley-Morris

"For an Outstanding Contribution to the World Association of Lawyers, Founder and Biennial Member of Planning and Goals Committee, World Peace through Law Centre".

NEVA BENNETT TALLEY-MORRIS

Lawyer, author and lecturer, Neva Bennett Talley-Morris was born in Judsonia, Arkansas, USA on 12th August, 1909. She obtained a BA degree, magna cum laude, from Ouachita Baptist University in 1930 and then served as a Classroom Teacher in Arkansas until 1937. Between 1937 and 1942 she was a High School Principal in McRae, Arizona, and during this period was awarded her MEd from the University of Texas in Austin in 1938. During World War II, Mrs Talley-Morris served as an Ordnance Inspector with the US Civil Service. In 1946, she entered the legal profession, serving as a Law Office Assistant in Little Rock for the year 1946 to 1947 and then becoming a lawyer, engaged in a general civil law practice until 1980. Her PhD in Law was awarded from the World University in 1984 and in 1987 Neva received an Honorary DDL from the International University.

Since 1974, Dr Talley-Morris has been the author of legal publications. Her titles include: "Family Law Practice and Procedure" 1974; "Civil Appealate Practice and Procedure" 1976; World Peace through Law pamphlets: 'Family Lawyer ; Problem Solver and Peace Maker' 1985, 'Alternate Dispute Resolutions' 1986 and 'Elevating Image of Family Lawyers' 1987.

During her successful career, Mrs Talley-Morris has achieved a number of notable "firsts". She was the First Woman Chairman of an American Bar Section in 1970, was the first woman elected member of Phi Alpha Delta, the International Legal Fraternity and was the first woman to serve on the Board of Governors of the American Academy of Matrimonial Law, between 1974 and 1980.

In addition, she has served on the Goals Committee of the World Peace Through Law Center, was Founder of the World Association of Lawyers in 1975 and held the Family Law Chair of the American Bar Association in 1970. President of the National Association of Women Lawyers in 1956 and of the Arkansas Association of Women Lawyers in 1950, Dr Talley-Morris was Chairman of the Arkansas Council for Children and Youth from 1952 to 1954 and has been a Life Member of the American Association of University Women since 1948.

She was honoured with appointment to the Board of Governors of the American Biographical Institute in 1984 and the same year was appointed an Executive Life President of the World Institute of Achievement.

Neva Talley-Morris has been married three times. In 1931, she married James L Woodfin and the marriage ended in divorce in 1945. She married Cecil C Talley in January 1946, but sadly Mr Talley died two years later. Her third marriage to Joseph Morris in March 1952 lasted until his death in 1974.

The interests of Mrs Talley-Morris include world travel for peace, the national preservation of historical buildings, writing and sewing.

A biography of Neva Bennett Talley-Morris appears in the main section of this Edition.

Naomi Cocke Turner

"For an Outstanding Contribution to Dental Health and Research".

NAOMI COCKE TURNER

Retired researcher, Naomi Cocke Turner is the author of over thirty research papers published in professional dental journals. A Fellow of the American Association for the Advancement of Science, her other memberships include the Radcliffe Chapter of Sigma Xi, the International Association for Dental Research, the American Public Health Association and the Royal Society of Health.

Born in Austin, Texas, USA on 19th December 1903, Naomi married Professor Clair Elsmere Turner on 24th December 1924 and is the mother of a son and a daughter. After obtaining her BA from the University of Texas in Austin in 1926, Naomi studied at Harvard University, gaining an EdM in 1930. During the years 1944 to 1957, she served as a Research Associate at Forsyth Dental Infirmary for Children in Boston, Massachusetts and between 1954 and 1960 held the same appointment with Harvard School of Public Health.

In retirement, Mrs Turner particularly enjoys gardening and doing needlepoint.

A biography of Naomi Cocke Turner appears in the main section of this Edition.

Amanda Loretta Walton

"For an Outstanding Contribution to Education".

AMANDA L WALTON

Amanda L Walton has served as a Teacher with the New York City Board of Education, Brooklyn, New York since 1981 and since 1987 has also been engaged as an Educational Consultant in private practice.

Having obtained an AA in Liberal Arts from BMCC in 1975, she attended York College from where she received an BA in Political Science in 1980. An MS in Special Education in 1983 and a Postgraduate degree and Advance Certificate in Supervision and Administration in 1985 were awarded by CCNY. She has also undertaken many courses and attended workshops on many health and education related topics.

Ms Walton began her career as an Auxiliary Trainer at the Public School on 7th Avenue and 149th Street, New York, where she introduced and trained para-professionals in the Creative Learning Reading Programme during 1970. Between September 1970 and September 1973, she worked as an Auxiliary Trainer at the Public School on Broadway and 168th Street, New York, engaged on the Intensive Reading Programme, planning and training educational assistants and working with groups of children in the area of language tests and reading skills. As an Auxiliary Trainer and Corrective Reading Teacher's Assistant from 1974 to 1981 she spent her time planning and working with small groups of children and testing reading.

Amanda Walton's studies have been assisted by various grants and awards. She received a Merit Award from ESEA District 6 in June 1971, a CSIP Grant in May 1989 and an Impact II Developer Grant for 1989-90. She was awarded a Recognition of accomplishment by Millen News, Miller, Georgia in 1988.

A member of the International Reading Association, Legislative Advisory Committee and the National Association for Female Executives, Ms Walton also belongs to the National Notary Association and the International Platform Association. A former Chairperson of Manpower Outreach Centre No 2, she is a member of the Manhattan Reading Council and is a Programme Developer for Impact II New York City Board of Education. She developed the Read to Reading Club 101A at the Public School 274K Brooklyn, New York and also established the John Paul Rutgers Memorial Award at the school.

Amanda Walton is also listed in many other biographical registers including Who's Who in American Education; Who's Who of American Women; Who's Who of Women Executives; International Leaders of Achievement; 2,000 Notable American Women and 5,000 Personalities of the World.

A biography of Amanda L Walton appears in the main section of this Edition.

Jan White

"For an Outstanding Contribution to the Global Society".

JAN WHITE

After obtaining a BS degree in Mathematics from Bates College, Lewiston, Maine, USA, Jan White attended Columbia University Graduate School of Business and was awarded her MBA in Marketing in 1967. She joined the corporate staff of the IBM Corporation in 1966 and served as Systems Engineer, Marketing Representative and Manager of the Harvard University Account. Between 1972 and 1975 she was Assistant to the Director of Information Processing Services at Massachusetts Institute of Technology (MIT) and from 1975 to 1981 was Managing Director of the Tuttle Family Trust. Since 1981 she has worked for the Digital Equipment Corporation holding the appointments of VAX Product Marketing Manager, Senior Product Management Manager, VAX Systems Marketing Programs Manager, Artificial Intelligence Market Conditioning Manager and Financial Systems Market Conditioning Manager.

Jan currently pursues many interests such as skiing, tennis, golf, riding, hiking, biking, music and horticulture. She is a sailing and swimming instructor and is also interested in the preservation of natural spaces and species worldwide.

A member of the American Association for Artificial Intelligence and the Columbia Club of New York, Jan White was a founding Director of the Columbia Club of New England and the Columbia Business Club of Boston. She was also the first woman Board member of the Columbia University Graduate School of Business Alumni Association.

Chairman of the Concord Council of Boston Symphony Orchestra, she also serves as Captain of the Centennial Major Gifts Campaign and is a supporter of ongoing Tanglewood Scholarship programs. As a member of the Guild Board of the Opera Company of Boston she helped establish the Boston Opera House and was a patron of the Fledermaus Ball in honour of Beverly Sills' retirement.

She served on the Board of Advisors, for the Museum of Science, Boston and Science Museum Exhibit Collaborative (SMEC), on the "Robots and Beyond: The Age of Intelligent Machines" exhibition which undertook a three-year national tour.

Chairman and Life Member of Emerson Hospital Auxiliary, she is also involved with Harwich Historical Association, Hannah Duston Garrison House Association, Garden Club of Concord, Trinitarian Congregational Church.

The recipient of several honours and awards, Ms White was nominated to the White House Fellows Program, received a VAX Tenth Anniversary Celebration Certificate of Appreciation in recognition of her outstanding support and contributions to the DECUS US Chapter VAX Systems Special Interest Group in January 1988 and in 1987 appeared in the Disney Channel documentary film "Silver Men" discussing the subject "The Future of Artificial Intelligence".

A frequent guest speaker, Jan White has recently addressed the Massachusetts Institute of Technology Sloan School Marketing Club.

She is listed in a number of other biographical registers.

A biography of Jan White appears in the main section of this Edition.

Zena Wickstein
"For an Outstanding Contribution to Education and the Community".

ZENA WINIFRED WICKSTEIN

The daughter of Winifred Ada (Wingrove) and Walter Thomas Barry Ricketts, Zena was born on December 9th 1940, one of four children. They lived on the family farm in the Cleve/Mangalo hills of South Australia until their mother Winifred died in July 1947 and Maureen and Zena went to live with their paternal grandparents and their uncle Hedley Gordon Ricketts. After taking lessons by correspondence, the girls went to Cleve School and on completion of her Intermediate Certificate, Zena went to Port Lincoln High School. When she obtained her Leaving Certificate, she was not old enough for college so she spent a year at Cleve Area School as a Junior Teacher before going to Adelaide Teachers' College to commence a two year Junior Primary training course. Having successfully completed the course, Zena was appointed to Cleve Area School and was thus able to spend some time with her father, prior to her marriage.

On 10th January, 1962 Zena married Richard Neil Wickstein, at St Michael's and All Angels Anglican Church in Cleve. After a year of sharefarming, Neil and Zena moved to the Ricketts family farm at Crossville, ten kilometres east of Cleve to sharefarm for a number of years before farming as RN and ZW Wickstein. Over the years they added to the original land until in 1980 they purchased the Benboy farm and the total area was 1691 hectares. Their crops are wheat, barley, lupins and oats and their stock are merino sheep and poll Dorset rams. In June 1965, their son Richard Grant was born, followed by Louise Ann in January 1968. Richard enjoys farm life and Louise is working in Real Estate in Melbourne. Richard married Angela Faye Story in March 1989 and commenced farming at Esperance, Western Australia.

A member of Cleve Country Women's Association in the early sixties, Zena had a term as secretary. She served as secretary of the Cleve Area School Council from 1977 to 1988 and continues as a committee member, while a member of the State committee of South Australian Association of State Schools Organisation Inc. In addition she serves as secretary of Sims Farm Operations Association Inc and is a member of local and regional committees of the Country Areas Programme for the Western Area of South Australia. Zena is also a member of the recently established Eyre Peninsula School Councils Network. Organist at the Cleve Anglican Church of St Michael and All Angels, where she was baptised, confirmed and married, Zena is treasurer of the Church Council and editor/producer of the church paper 'Manna'.

She first became involved with the Eyre Peninsula Field Days in 1973 when her husband Neil was inaugural President and again in 1976. Zena was President of the 1988 Bicentennial Eyre Peninsula Fields Days General Interest Section, a biennial event which attracts 20,000 to 30,000 visitors. Zena served four years as President of Cleve Netball Club and has held two year terms as Vice-President, President and Records Officer, Treasurer of the County Jervois Netball Association. She spent two years as President of Central Eyre Peninsula Netball Association and proxy delegate to South Australian Netball Association.

A committed Christian, Zena believes that life should be lived to the full, with joy, under the direction of God, taking every opportunity to serve others and giving God the glory for any good achieved.

A biography of Zena Winifred Wickstein appears in the main section of this Edition.

Melva Jean Williams

"For an Outstanding Contribution to Advancement of Women in Business".

MELVA JEAN WILLIAMS

The daughter of Wayne and Mildred Eva (Graham) Mulholland, Melva Jean Williams was born in Burke, South Dakota, USA on 11th June 1935. She married J B Williams on 29th April 1977 and has four children Mark, Doris, Robin and Jeannie.

After graduating from Roberta's Finishing School in Miami, Florida in 1950, Melva Jean attended the Charron-Williams Communal College, graduating in 1954. Now an oil and gas company executive, Mrs Williams has served with the Southeastern Resources Corporation, Fort Worth and Rising Star, Texas since 1968. She served as President of the company from 1979 to 1983 and since 1983 has been Vice-Chairman of the Board. She was a Director of the Delta Gas Co Inc, Tchula, Mississippi between 1973 and 1981 and also served as Secretary Treasurer from 1974 to 1981. Since 1977, Mrs Williams has been a Director of SERPCO Inc of Fort Worth and having served as Vice-President between 1980 and 1984, has been President of the company since 1984. A director of J J and L Drilling Co Inc of Fort Worth and Cisco, Texas, she served as Secretary Treasurer from 1979 to 1982. Her other directorships include: Rising Star Processing Corporation, Fort Worth (Secretary Treasurer 1981-); Brownwood Pipeline Corporation, Fort Worth (Secretary Treasurer 1981-) and Aero Modifications International Inc, Fort Worth and Waco, Texas. Also involved with the Real Estate business, Melva Jean Williams has been a general partner of B & W Real Estate Investments, Nashville since 1980, of F & W Real Estate Investments, Fort Worth since 1981 and is owner of Westward Properties, Fort Worth.

Mrs Williams was elected in 1989 as a member of the Advisory Board for the Center for the Study of Addiction, Texas Tech University, Lubbock, Texas.

Mrs Williams, who is a Republican, is also listed in the Marquis Who's Who of American Women 1987-88.

A biography of Melva Jean Williams appears in the main section of this Edition.

Charin Yuthasastrkosol

"For an Outstanding Contribution to endeavour to promote and support the Performing Arts, also many timeless hours spent in the organisation and donations to the many charitable organisations in the USA and abroad".

CHARIN YUTHASASTRKOSOL

"One of the most exceptional women of her times" are words that could best be used to describe Charin Yuthasastrkosol. A native of Thailand, Charin is internationally known for her love affair with "dance". A well-known pianist and sought-after teacher, she and her family moved to the United States in 1969. She and her husband, Senior Lieutenant (Retired) Prapakorn Yuthasastrkosol of the Royal Thai Navy, opened The Thai Royal Barge in Philadelphia, now one of the leading Thai restaurants in the United States. Successful in every endeavour, Charin's primary concern at that time was to provide the best education possible for her talented daughter, Anita.

While helping to foster her daughter's career in music and dance, she found a talent in herself that had gone undiscovered until the age of 47. She found she had exceptional talent for many forms of dance including Thai and classical ballet. The discovery of her ability in ballroom dance was proven at the Virginia Championship Competition in Washington, D.C. when she won first prize in four categories: tango, rumba, waltz and bolero. In 1983 and 1984 she was a finalist in the United States Ballroom Competitions. In 1988 she won first, second and third prizes in the Canadian Ballroom Competition. Also in 1988 she won a silver medal for the U.S. Ballroom Championships. Since that time she continues to be a top competitor in dance competitions around the world and to date has won over 200 awards and medals. She is listed in "2,000 Notable American Women", "World Who's Who of Women", 1990 and in "Marquis' Who's Who in the East of America".

Charin is often sought after by Thai as well as American media. Her picture has graced the cover of a major Thai magazine and she appears often in television and news articles. Performing for Their Majesties, the King and Queen of Thailand, Charin has won international acclaim for her beautiful dancing styles. She has performed for numerous charities in the United States and Thailand and continues to use this vehicle to promote a wonderful sense of pride and tradition among the Thai communities around the world. An inspiration to the young dancers in many countries, she recently performed a "one-woman show" in Washington, D.C. in which she demonstrated her love of dance. She will again be appearing in a one-woman show in June 1990 in Albuquerque, New Mexico raising funds for American organizations.

Charin is Vice President of Twining Land Corporation, whose goals are to economically revitalize land use in the Albuquerque area by providing new opportunities for investors and create new jobs for local residents. Charin is a master at the art of promotion, has introduced hundreds of friends and financial entrepreneurs to one of the most sensational developments in the Southwestern United States. Performing with magnificent style and grace, Charin continues to share her undying love of the "art of dance" with the world.

Charin is the Mother of three children and lives with her husband in Baltimore.

A biography of Charin Yuthasastrkosol appears in the main section of this Edition.

A

AALTONEN Ilta Annikki Tyyne, b. 21 May 1911, Pori, Finland. Author, pen name: Annikki Maruna. m. Erkki Aaltonen, 1 Sept. 1934. 2 sons, 1 daughter. *Education:* Studied at University of Hamburg, 1932; University in Helsinki, 1932-35 and 1946-47; Examination in Swedish Language, 1955. *Appointments:* Employed in editorial staff in order to get practical experience, 1931-32; Private lessons, 1932-72; Teacher, Workers' evening schools, 1967-73; Translations and writings in newspapers and journals, 1932-. *Publications:* Two novels, short stories, plays and Finnish translations. *Memberships:* Union of Finnish Authors; Union of Finnish Dramatists; Union of Defenders of Peace; Society Finland-Soviet Union; Pand, Artists for Peace. *Honours:* The Artist Pension of the State since 1975; 3rd Place, Historical Drama Competition, 1963. *Hobbies:* Reading; Study; The observation of life. *Address:* Ohjaajantie 3A3, 00400 Helsinki 40, Finland.

AARONSON Brenda Caryl, b. 13 Nov. 1938, Pittsfield, USA. Educator; Conductor; Author. *Education:* BMus., 1960; MA, 1967; SAS, SDA Certificate, 1979; PhD, New York University, 1979. *Appointments:* Assistant to Co-ordinator & Film Production Manager, Mills Music Inc., 1962-63; Music Librarian, New York University, 1963-65; Music Educator, Union Free School District, 1965-66, Acting Chairman, Music Dept., George Washington High School, 1966-71; Assistant Chairman, Music Department, Adlai E. Stevenson High School, 1971-78; Music Educator, Dean of Students, Martin L. King Jr., High School, 1978-; Examining Assistant Board Exams Board of Education, New York City, 1986-. *Publications:* Composer, Musical Comedy, Extension H., 1959; Secular & Sacred Works, 1962-; Author, childrens texts & musicology articles, 1964-. *Memberships:* Jurer, American Film Festival, 1961-63; Vice-President, executive offices, Gotham Unit, B'nai B'rith, 1979-82; Lecturer, State of Israel Bonds, 1980-; Vice-President, Golden Mier Group, Hadassah, 1980-82; Board of Directors, New Leadership Division, United Jewish Appeal 1980-82; President, Aviv Chapter B'nai B'rith Women, 1983-85; International Affairs Committee, Anti-Defamation League, B'nai B'rith, 1983-85. *Honours:* Orchestral Conducting Scholarship, Tanglewood Music Festival, 1959-60; Outstanding Service & Bulletin Awards, B'nai B'rith Women, 1979-86; Outstanding Service Awards, Hadassah, 1980-82; Israel Leadership Award, State of Israel Bonds, 1982. *Hobbies:* Jewish History; Painting; Sculpture. *Address:* 170 West End Avenue, New York, NY 10023, USA.

ABARBANELL Gayola Havens, b. 21 Oct. 1939, Chicago, Illinois, USA. Registered Financial Advisor. 1 son, 1 daughter. *Education:* University of California at Los Angeles, 1975; San Joaquin College of Law, 1976-77. *Appointments:* Regional Manager, Niagara Cyclo-Massage, 1969-72; Owner, Ad Enterprises, 1970-72; Field Supervisor, Equitable of Iowa, 1972-73; Pharmaceutical Rep, CIBA, 1973-75; Owner, Creativity Unlimited, 1975-76; Financial Advisor, Financial Network Investment Corp, 1976-. *Publication:* Co-author, Guidelines to Feminist Consciousness Raising, 1983. *Memberships:* Advisory Board, Financial Network, 1985-88; Business Advisory Board, Second Careers, 1986-; National Coordinator, NOW's Cr Task Force, 1975-76; ACLU, International Association of Financial Planners; Founding Member, S. Calif. Socially Responsible Investment Professionals, Whitman Brooks, NGRTF, GAU. *Honours:* Woman of the Year, Women in Insurance, 1972; Top producer and university club, University Securities, 1980, 1981, 1982, 1983; Top Producer, Financial Network, 1983, 1984, 1985, 1986, 1987, 1988; Golden Scales Award, Putnam Funds, 1985, 1986, 1987, 1988; All American Club, American Funds, 1987, 1988; Volunteer of the Year, Volunteer Association of Los Angeles, 1987. *Hobbies:* Art; Reading; Theatre; Plants; Outdoor Activities;

Photography; Travel. *Address:* 9724 Washington Blvd No 203, Culver City, CA 90232, USA.

ABBOTT Linda Mae Conger, b. 30 July 1942, Schenectady, New York, USA. Management Consultant; Author; Lecturer. m. John Standen Abbott, 28 Aug. 1980. 2 sons, 2 daughters. *Education:* BA, University of Colorado, 1964; MS, University of Wisconsin, La Crosse, 1976; PhD, Iowa State University, 1980. *Appointments:* Graduate Student, Research Assistant, Iowa State University, 1978-80; Dean, Minneapolis College of Art & Design, 1980-81; Dean, Assoc Professor, California School of Professional Psychology, 1981-86; Owner, President, Management Consulting Firm, Abbott & Associates, 1986-. *Publications:* Fresno, Valley of Abundance, 1988; Articles: Women work & self-esteem, 1987; Women's ambivalent affair with power, 1986, numerous other articles and reviews in field. *Memberships include:* Board, Fresno Chamber of Commerce; Fresno Community Council; Fresno Women's Network; Exec Council, National Association for Ethnic Studies. *Honours:* Invited Speaker, Governor's Conference on Women in Business, 1987; Phi Kappa Phi, Phi Kappa Delta; Leadership Fresno recognition, 1986-87; Invited Judge, Passport Fresno, 1986; Valedictorian, Schalmont High School, 1959. *Hobbies:* Travel; Photography; Pottery; Weaving; Folk arts and artifacts; Sailing; Flying. *Address:* 1455 W Menlo, Fresno, California 93711, USA.

ABBOTT Shelley, b. 10 Aug. 1954, Glens Falls, New York, USA. Paranormal Researcher; Entertainer. m. 1 son, 1 daughter. *Education:* New York State Regents Diploma 1972; College studies in Psychology, Sociology and Journalism, 1973-. *Appointments:* Editor/Manager, TV Data Incorporated, 1973-74; Computer Data, Off-Track Betting, 1974-75; President, The Enterprise, 1974-; Psychic Library Consultant, 1985-86. *Publications:* Cartoons and Columns to over 160 internationally distributed newspapers and magazines; Radio programme (astrology show) distributed nationally. *Memberships:* National Association of Female Executives; Smithsonian Associate; Association for Retarded Citizens; Cornell Feline Health center; Anti-vivisection groups. *Hobbies:* Breeding Siamese cats; Consumer advocate; World travel; Thrill seeker. *Address:* Glens Falls, NY 12801, USA.

ABDELA Lesley Julia, b. 17 Nov. 1943, London, England. Journalist; Broadcaster. Divorced, 1 son. *Education:* Hammersmith College of Art & Building; London College of Printing. *Appointments:* Advertising Executive, Royds Advertising, London; Derek Forsyth Design Partnership, Researcher, Liberal Whip's Office, House of Commons; Freelance Journalist/Broadcaster, 1980-; Senior Partner, Eyecatcher Journalism. *Publications:* Book on Women in Politics, due in 1989; Painting (Acrylics) of The Gambia. *Memberships:* Institute of Journalists Travel Specialists Group; Fellow, Royal Geographical Society; Founder, All Party Group for Women in Politics; Women in Management; Fawcett Society; Network; Friends of the Earth; Greenpeace; Amnesty International; etc. *Honours:* Stood for Parliament (Liberal), East Herts, 1979; Leadership Grant, US Government, 1983. *Hobbies:* Travel; Politics; Painting; Desert Agriculture; Third World Development. *Address:* Harper's Marsh, King's Saltern Road, Lymington, Hampshire, England.

ABE Graciela, b. 4 Dec. 1942, Mexico City, Mexico. Dentist; Professor. m. Alfonso Muray, 8 Oct. 1966, 3 sons. *Education:* Diploma, 1964 Odontology, Diploma, Dental Operatory, 1976, University of Mexico. *Appointments:* Assistant Professor, 1966-72, Professor, 1976, Odontology, University of Mexico. *Publications:* Radiotherapy in Estomatology; Director, 16 Professional Thesis of Odontology. *Memberships:* American Dental Association; Colegio Nacional de Cirujanos Dentistas; Academia de Operatoria Dental; Asoc. De Professores y Personal academico de la Universidad Nacional Autonoma de Mexico; Asoc. nisei de Estudios Estomatologicos; Federacion de Odontologas de Mexico. *Honours:* Diario De Mexico Award, 1964, Mexico-Japan

Society Award, 1965, Honorific Award, 1965, Silver Medal, 1987, University of Mexico. *Hobbies:* Reading; Music; Painting; Mexican Anthropology; Travel. *Address:* Prol. Rio San Angel 382, 01760 Mexico DF, Mexico.

ABELES, Kim Victoria, b. 28 Aug. 1952, Richmond Heights, Missouri, USA. Artist; Lecturer. m. Russell Parks Moore, 25 Oct. 1987, 1 daughter. *Education:* BFA, Painting, Ohio University, 1974; MFA, Studio Art, University of California, Irvine, 1980. *Appointments:* California State University, Fullerton, 1985-87; Claremont Graduate School, 1987; Lecturer, University of California, Irvine, 1987-. *Publications:* The Image of St Bernadette, 1987; Calamity Jane and Questions of Truth, 1986; Rara Aris, 1986; Solo Exhibitions: Bridge Gallery, Los Angeles City Hall, 1982; Phyllis Kind Gallery, Chicago, 1983; A I R Gallery, New York City, 1986; Karl Bornstein Gallery, Santa Monica, 1987; Institute for Design and Experimental Art, 1988; Anuska Gallery, San Diego, 1989; Numerous group exhibitions throughout USA. *Memberships:* Woman's Building; Los Angeles Contemporary Exhibitions; Sculpture International. *Honours:* Recipient, various honours and awards. *Hobby:* Reading. *Address:* 2401 Santa Fe, No 100, Los Angeles, CA 90058, USA.

ABELLAN Carmen Conde, b. 1907. Author. m. Antonio Oliver Belmas, 1931. *Publications Include:* Las Amistad en La Literatura Espanola, 1944; Juan Ramon Jimenez; Empezando La Vida, 1955; Cobe, 1953; La Rambla, 1977; Crecio Espesa La Yerba, 1979; Soy La Madre, 1980; por El Camino Viendo Sus Orilla, 1986, 3 volumes; Dilema, 1985; Memoria Puesta en Olvido, 1987; Children's Books: Don Juan De Austria, 1943; Don Alvaro de Luna, 1945; Aladino, 1945; El Caballito y La Luna, 1979; Aoquetin Y Martina, 1979; Belen, 1979; El Monje y El Pajarillo, 1980; Cuentos Del Romancero, 1987; Cantando Al Amanecer, 1988. *Address:* Calle Ferraj 67 5 Dereha, 28008 Madrid, Spain.

ABIDI Taquayya Sultana, b. 3 Sept. 1936, Jubbulpore, British India. Professor. m. 1965, 2 sons, 1 daughter. *Education:* FSc., Gordon College, Rawalpindi, 1953; MBBS, Fatima Jinneh Medical College, Lahore, 1958; M.Phil., Basic Medical Sciences Institute, Karachi, 1962. *Appointments:* House Surgeon, Lady Reading Hospital, 1958-59; Radiologist, TB Control Project, Sargodha, 1959-60; Lecturer, Anatomy, 1962-65, Assistant Professor, 1965-70, Professor, Head of Anatomy, 1970-74, Nishtan Medical College; Professor, Anatomy, Quaide Azza Medical College, 1974-75; Professor, Head, Anatomy, King Edward Medical College, Laahore, 1975-. *Publications:* Articles in professional journals including: Pakistan Biomedical Research Society; Pakistan Journal of Medical Research, etc. *Memberships:* President Anatomical Society of Pakistan; Finance Secretary, Medical Legal Association of Pakistan; Vice President, Medical Teachers Association of Pakistan; American Association of Anatomists. *Honours:* Recipient, various honours and awards including Research Fellowships, Scholarships, etc. *Hobbies:* Lecturing; Talking & Making Friends; Photography; Travel. *Address:* Anatomy Dept., King Edward Medical College, Lahore, Pakistan.

ABRAMS Edith Lillian, b. New York, New York, USA. Sculptor. 1 son, 1 daughter. *Education:* BA, Brooklyn College, 1974; MFA Sculpture, Pratt Institute, 1978. *Creative Works:* Nelita II, Acrylic, Evensville Mus Arts & Sic Ind; Grandmother & Child, Bronze, Brookdale Hospital, Brooklyn. Exhibited: National Academy of Design, 1986, 1988; Brooklyn Museum, 1979, 1980, 1981, 9184 and many other Museums and Universities. *Memberships:* American Soc of Contemporary Artists, ASCA; President of ASCA, 1983-85; National Association of Women Artists, NAWA; Catharine Lorillard Wolfe Art Club, CLWAC; Metropolitan Painters & Sculptors MPS; New York Artists Equity Association; Formally Salmagundi Club. *Honours:* Purchase Award, 1st Prize, Schulman Rehab Inst, Brookdale Hospital, 1976; Margaret Hirsh Levine Award, Audubon Artists 38th Ann, 1980; Ann Hyatt Huntington Bronze Medal,

CLWAC 84th Ann, 1980; CLWAC Award, 89th Ann, 1985; Harriet Frishmuth Memorial Award, CLWAC, 90th Ann, 1986; Charles D Murphy Award, NAWA, 93rd Ann, 1982; ASCA Sculpture Awards, 1980, 1981, 1983. *Address:* 2820 Ave J, Brooklyn, NY 11210, USA.

ABRAMS Nancy Beth, b. 14 Dec. 1954, Indiana, Pennsylvania, USA. Attorney. m. Frederick Segal, 12 Apr. 1987. *Education:* AB cum laude, Harvard University, 1976; JD, University of Pittsburgh Law School, 1979. *Appointments:* Associate, Rosenberg & Ufberg, Scranton, Pennsylvania, 1979-84; Associate, Pechner, Dorfman, Wolffe, Rounick & Cabot, Philadelphia, 1984-87; Associate, Myersin & Kuha, Phildelphia, 1988; Associate, Blank, Rome, Cormisky & McCauley, Philadelphia, 1988-. *Publications:* Articles: Unions on the DP Workforce, 1987; Labor Relations without Interferance, 1987; Countering New Union Organizing Techniques, 1987; Union Organizing - New Tactics for New Times, 1987. *Memberships:* Scranton Red Cross Center City Blood Council, Vice Chairman, 1982-83, Chairman, 1983-84; Lackawanna County Bar Association; Pennsylvania Bar Association (Labor & Employment Law Section); Philadelphia Bar Association (Theatre Wing member); American Bar Association (Labor & Employment Law Section); The Florida Bar (Labor & Employment Law Section). *Hobbies:* Theatre; Music; Dance; College football. *Address:* Blank, Rome, Cormisky & McCauley, 1200 Four Penn Center Plaza, Philadelphia, PA 19103, USA.

ABSHER Janet, b. 17 July 1955, Fairfield, Alabama, USA. Manager of Electronic Payments. *Education:* BS, Accounting, University of Alabama, Birmingham, 1976. *Appointments:* Auditor, American South Bank, 1975-78; Audit Supervisor, 1978-81, Manager, Auditing, 1981-83, Manager, Accounting, 1983-85, Manager, Electronic Payments, 1985-, Federal Reserve Bank. *Memberships:* Institute of Internal Auditors (Secretary 1983-84, Governor 1978-83); Friends of the Zoo, Atlanta; High Museum of Art; Young Careers; Atlanta Landmarks; Instructor, American Institute of Banks; Instructor, Federal Reserve Audit Training; Smithsonian Institution; Society for Historic Preservation. *Honours:* Certified Internal Auditor, 1984. *Hobbies:* Tennis; Softball; Colonial American history; Archaeology. *Address:* 1130 Willivee Drive, Dectur, GA 30033, USA.

ABT Sylvia Hedy, b. 10 October 1957, Chicago, Illinois, USA. General Dentist. *Education:* Registered Dental Hygienist 1977-79, Doctor of Dental Surgery, 1979-83, Loyola University School of Dentistry. *Appointments:* Dental Assistant General Dentistry, Chicago, Illinois, 1977-78; Dental Hygienist, Illinois, 1979-83; Dental Hygienist Periodontist, Illinois, 1980-83; Dentist General Dentistry, private Practice, Chicago, 1983- *Memberships:* American Dental Association, 1979-; Illinois State Dental Society, 1979-; Chicago Dental Society, 1979-; Psi Omega Fraternity Kappa Chapter, 1981-; Historian, Editor Psi Omega Fraternity Kappa Chapter, 1982-83; Vice Chairman for registration, 1986, Chairman for registration, 1987, Loyola Alumni Golf Tournament. *Honours:* 1st Oil Painting Award, St Apollonia Art Show, Loyola University of Dentistry, 1987; 2nd longest drive in golf tournament award, Loyola Dental Alumni, 1987; 1st Women's Tennis Tournament, Loyola Dental Alumni, 1987. *Hobbies:* Art; Singing; Dancing; Bicycling; Jogging; Tennis; Travelling; Reading; Golfing; Interior Decorating and design. *Address:* 6509 W Higgins, Chicago, IL 60656, USA.

ABU-LUGHOD Janet Lippman, b. 3 Aug. 1928, Newark, New Jersey, USA. Professor. m. Ibrahim Abu-Lughod, 8 Dec. 1951, 1 son, 3 daughters. *Education:* BA honours, 1947, MA honours, 1950, University of Chicago; PhD high distinction, University of Massachusetts, 1966. *Appointments:* Director of Research, American Society of Planning Officials, 1950-52; Instructor, University of Illinois, 1953-54; Research Associate, University of Pennsylvania, 1954-55; Consultant, American Council to Improve Our Neighborhoods, 1954-57; Assistant Professor,

Sociology, American University, Cairo, Egypt, 1958-60; Lecturer, Smith College, USA, 1963-67; Associate Professor, Sociology, 1967-71, Professor, Sociology, 1971-87, Northwestern University; Professor, Sociology, History, 1986-, Director, REALM Urban Research Center, 1988-, New School for Social Research, New York. *Publications:* Housing Choices and Constraints (with Nelson Foote), 1960; Cairo Fact Book (with Ezzedin Attiya), 1963; Cairo: 1001 Years of the City Victorious, 1971; Third World Urbanization (with Richard Hay Jr), 1979; Rabat: Urban Apartheid in Morocco, 1980; Changing Cities, 1990; Before European Hegemony: The World System A.D. 1250-1350, 1989; Numerous articles, book contributions, monographs, mainly on Cities. *Memberships include:* Council, Community Section and section of Political Economy, committees, American Sociological Association; Editorial Boards: Third World Review, Arab Studies Quarterly; Contemporary Sociology, International Journal of Middle East Studies, Comparative Urban & Community Research, Habitat; Associate Editor: American Sociological Review, American Journal of Sociology; Urban Affairs Quarterly. *Honours include:* Phi Beta Kappa, 1949; Ford Faculty Fellow, 1971; Guggenheim Fellow, 1976; National Endowment for the Humanities Senior Scholar, 1977; Fulbright Scholar, 1979. *Hobby:* Music. *Address:* Graduate Faculty, Department of Sociology, New School for Social Research, 64 University Place, New York, NY 10003, USA.

ABUL-HAJ Elizabeth, b. 15 Jan. 1924, Erie, Pennsylvania, USA. Senior Fine Arts & Antiques Appraiser. m. Suleiman K Abul-Haj, MD, 11 May 1948. 3 sons. *Education:* John Huntington Polytech Inst, 1942-46; Cleveland Art School, 1946; California Art School (now San Francisco Art Institute), 1946-48. *Appointments:* Office Supervisor & Sec, Federal Public Housing Auth, 1942-48; Medical Sec & Tech, Nursing, 1948-51; Senior Appraiser in Fine Arts & Antiques, American Society of Appraisers, 1971-89, President for 6 years. *Creative works:* Oil paintings and watercolours; Article on Charles Andre Boulle, French Cabinetmaker for ASA. *Memberships:* President, Board Director, Visiting Nurses Assoc; Dir, Forum of Arts Director, YWCA; Dir, American Cancer Soc; President, Ventura Co Medical Auxil; Dir, Heart Assoc; Dir, Forum of Arts; Dir, YMCA; Assistance League, Children's Home Soc. *Honours:* Recognition, American Cancer Society, 1967-68; Recognition and Honours, Visiting Nurses Association, 1973. *Hobbies:* Collection of Antiques; Paintings; Ivories; Coins; Snuff bottles; Bronzers; Oriental Carpets; Netsukes; Georgian silver; Tennis; Swimming; Hiking. *Address:* 105 Encinal Way, Ventura, CA 93001, USA.

ACCAD Evelyne, b. 6 Oct. 1943, Beirut, Lebanon. Professor; Author; Composer. *Appointments:* Professor French, Comparative Literature, Women's Studies, African Studies, South-west Asian Studies, University of Illinois, 1974-. *Publications:* Novels: Coquelicot du massacre (with Cassette of song), 1988; L'Excisee, 1982; Studies Sexuality War and Literature in the Middle East, 1989; Contemporary Arab Women and Poets, 1985. *Honours:* Social Science Research Award, 1987-88; Fulbright Award, 1983-85; Delta Kappa Gamma Society International Educator's Award, 1979. *Address:* 2090 FLB 707 S Mathews, University of Illinois, Urbana, Illinois 61801, USA.

ACHESON Alice B, b. 26 July 1936, Indiana, USA. Publicist. m. Donald H. Acheson, 12 Dec. 1970, deceased. *Education:* AB, English, Bucknell University, 1958; National Defence Education Act Scholarship to attend 1st Level Institute, University of Maine, 1960; NDEA Scholarship, 2nd Level, Quito, Ecuador, 1962; MA, Spanish French, CUNY, 1963. *Appointments:* Spanish Teacher, Mount Vernon, New York, 1958-69; Executive Assistant, Media Medica Inc., 1969-71; Associate Editor 1971-77, Publicity Associate, 1977-78, McGraw Hill Book Co.; Associate Publicity Director, Simon & Schuster Book Co., 1979-80; Associate Publicity Director, Crown Publishers Inc., 1980-81;

Founder, Alice B. Acheson Co., 1981-. *Memberships:* various professional organisations. *Honours:* Marquis Who's Who of American Women 1986-; Marquis Who's Who in the East, 1986-; Partner in Education awards, New York City Board of Education, 1977, 1978; Face to Face Publishing Conference & Exposition, 1977, 1979, 1981; Wilamette Oregon Writers Conference, 1981; Folio Publishing Week, 1983, 1984; New York University Publishing Institute, 1985; Panellist, National Writers Union 1985; Small Press Expo, 1987, 1988. *Address:* 2962 Fillmore Street, San Francisco, California 94123, USA.

ACKERLY Wendy S, b. 23 July 1960, Chicago, USA. Senior Engineer; Software Specialist. *Education:* BS, Atmospheric Science, University of California, Davis, 1982; Graduate Study, Computer Science, University of Nevada, 1985. *Appointments:* Programmer, University of California, 1982-83; Software Consultant, Tesco, Sacramento, 1983; Software Engineer, Bently Nevada Corp., 1984-85; Manager, Computer Sciences, 1985-86, Software Specialist, 1986-89, Jensen Elecric Co.; Senior Engineer, Aerojet Tech Systems, 1989-. *Membership:* American Meteorological Society. *Hobbies:* Tennis; Hiking; Travel; Piano; Camping; Fishing; Coin & Stamp Collecting. *Address:* 3280 Woodleigh Lane, Cameron Park, CA 95682, USA.

ACKERMAN Freda S, b. 17 Mar. 1947, New York, USA. Executive. *Education:* BA, Queens College, 1968; AMP, Harvard University Graduate School of Business, 1986. *Appointments:* Analyst, 1968-71, Senior Analyst, 1971-73, Vice President, Associate Director, 1973-75, Vice President, Associate Director, 1975-79, Senior Vice President, Director, 1979-81, Executive Vice President, Director, Public Finance, Dun & Bradstreet Inc., 1981-. *Memberships:* Past President, Board of Governors, The Municipal Forum of New York; Financial Women's Association & Bond Club. *Hobbies:* Travel; Film; Music; Art. *Address:* 99 Church Street, New York, NY 10007, USA.

ACOSTA Adolovni P, b. 3 Feb. 1946, Manila, Philippines. Concert Pianist; Art Administrator; Concert Manager; Piano Teacher. *Education:* Teacher's Diploma, Music, 1965, BMus., 1966, MMus., 1968, University of Philippines; MS. The Jiilliard School, 1971; PhD studies, Music Performance, New York Univesity. *Appointments:* Reseach Aide, Asian Music, University of the Philippines, 1966-68; Piano Faculty, Usdan Centre for Creative & Performing Arts, summers 1971-85; Piano Faculty 92nd Street Y School of Music, New York City, 1973-86; Piano Faculty, New York I Inivesity, 1976 77; Piano Faculty Brooklyn College Preparatory Centre for The Performing Arts, CUNY, 1981-85; Current positions: Founder, Executive Director, East & West Artists; Concert Manager, East West Directions. *Creative Works:* Recordings: Piano works of Carl Nielsen, Musical Heritage Society; Ernesto Lecuona's Danzas Afro-Cubanas and Andalucia for Orion Master Recordings. Solo Recitals include: Salle Cortot Ecole Normale de Musique, Paris, 1982; Merkin Concert Hall, New York City, 1982; Hallwyska Museet, Stockholm, 1982; Alice Tully Hall, 1975, 1982. *Memberships:* Pi Kappa Lambda; Phi Kappa Phi; Piano Teachers Congress of New York; mu Phi Epsilon. *Honours:* Recipient, numerous academic and musical awards & scholarships; one of ten Outstanding Young Women of America for 1982. *Hobbies:* Cooking; Walking. *Address:* East and West Artists, 310 Riverside Drive 313, New York, NY 10025, USA.

ACRIVOS Juana Luisa Adolfina (Vivo y Azpeitia), b. 24 June 1928, Habana, Cuba. Professor of Chemistry. m. Andreas Acrivas, 1 Sept. 1956. *Education:* BSc, 1951, DSc, 1956, Physical Chemistry, Mathematics, University of Habana; PhD, University of Minnesota, USA, 1956; Postdoctoral studies: Stanford University, 1956-59; University of California, Berkeley, 1959-61. *Appointments:* Assistant Professor of Chemistry, 1962-67, Associate Professor of Chemistry, 1967-71, Professor of Chemistry, 1971-, San Jose State University, San Jose, California, USA. *Publications:*

Book: Physics and Chemistry of Electrons and Ions in Condensed Matter (with N F Mott, A D Yoffe, D Reidel), 1984; Over 85 articles in refereed journals. *Memberships:* American Chemical Society; American Physical Society; Iota Sigma Pi. *Honours:* Fellow, Institute of International Education, 1951; Research Fellow, 1967, President's Scholar, 1982, San Jose State University; Elected Visiting Fellow Commoner, Trinity College, 1983; FACE Awardee, 1987; NSF Visiting Woman Professor, University of California, Berkeley, 1987. *Hobbies:* Sewing; Knitting; Painting. *Address:* San Jose State University, Department of Chemistry, One Washington Square, San Jose, CA 95192, USA.

ADAMS Beverly Jean Shackelford, b. 11 Nov. 1945, Middletown, Ohio, USA. Facial Plastic Surgeon. m. 24 Aug. 1969, divorced 1988. *Education:* BS, 1967; MD, 1977; Internships & Residencies, various Hospitals. *Appointments:* Clinical Assistant Professor, Otolaryngology, Duke University Medical Centre; McPherson Hospital, 1983-; Duke University Medical Centre, 1983-; Durham County General Hospital, 1986-. *Publications:* Articles in: Transplantation; Immunology; Ear Nose Throat Journal. *Memberships:* Fellow, American College of Surgeons, American Academy of Otolaryngology; American Academy of Facial Plastic & Reconstructive Surgery; American Medical Women's Association; American Medical Association; North Carolina, Durham-Orange County Medical Societies. *Address:* 1110 West Main St., Durham, NC 27707, USA.

ADAMS Catherine Marie, b. 29 June 1959, San Francisco, USA. Executive Officer; Planning Commissioner. m. Wayne P Adams, 9 Sept. 1983. *Education:* BSc., California Polytechnic State University, 1982. *Appointments:* Personnel Administration, Stanford School of Medicine, 1982-83; Executive Vice President, Antelope Valley Board of Realtors, 1984-86; Planning Commissioner, City of Lancaster, 1987-; Executive Officer, Palmdale Board of Realtors, 1987-. *Memberships:* American Society of Association Executives; Business and Professional Women, President, 1 Vice President; Society for Advancement of Management, Executive Board, Membership Chair; Lancaster Chamber of Commerce, Public Affairs Committee; etc. *Honours:* Recipient, various honours & awards including: Young Careerist Award, Antelope Valley Business & Professional Women, 1985; Appointment to Planning Commission, 1987. *Hobbies:* Waterskiing; Golf. *Address:* 526 E. Ave. J4, Lancaster, CA 93535, USA.

ADAMS Cindy, b. 24 Apr. New York, USA. Journalist, newspapers and television. m. Joey Adams, 14 Feb. *Appointments:* Commentator, WABC-TV, 1967-70; Journalist, NBC Monitor, 1970-73; Director, Miss Universe Pageant, 1970-77; Celebrity Interview, Fox-TV's A Current Affair, 1986-; Columnist, NY Post, 1981-. *Publications:* Author: Sukarno: An Autobiography, 1965; Lee Strasberg: The Imprefect Genius of the Actors Studio, 1980; My Friend the Dictator, 1967. *Honours:* Recipient of numerous honours. *Hobbies:* Travelling the world. *Address:* New York Post, 210 South Street, New York, NY 10002, USA.

ADAMS Iola N Hoag, b. 31 July 1909, Hudson, Iowa, USA. Teacher. m. Charles H Adams, 24 Nov. 1932. 1 son, 3 daughters. *Education:* Teachers Certificate, Iowa State Teachers College, 1929. *Appointments:* Teacher, 1929-33. *Creative Works:* Oil Paintings. *Memberships:* Iowa State Central Committee, 1974-76; Black Hawk Demo Committee, 1960-87; Chair of Third District, 1976; Founder of Democrat United Chair, Chair of Legion Aux, 1946-48; Sortoma Int, 1986-88; Common Cause, 1975-88; Gray Panthers Citizens for Community Improvement, 1978-88. *Honours:* Gem Award 1985, Centurian Award, 1986, Sortoma International; President's Award, American Legion Auxillary, 1948. *Hobbies:* Oil painting; Knitting; Sewing; Social concerns; Charities; Reading; Geneology. *Address:* 3720 Village Place, 5509, Waterloo, Iowa 50702, USA.

ADAMS Julia Davis, b. 23 July 1900, Clarksburg, West Virginia, USA. Writer. m. William McMillan Adams, 30 Mar. 1974. *Education:* Wellesley College, 1918-21; BA, Barnard College, 1922. *Appointments:* Reporter, Associated Press, New York, 1925; Children's Agent, State Charities Aid Association, New York, 1933-38. *Publications:* Swords of the Vikings, 1928; Vaino, 1929; Mountains Are Free, 1930; Stonewall Jackson, 1932; Remember and Forget, 1932; No Other White Men, 1937; Peter Hale, 1939; The Sun Climbs Slow, 1942; 10 others including Never Say Die, 1980; The Anvil (play), 1980. *Memberships:* The Children's Aid Society (Chairman of Child Adoption Service 1962-65). *Address:* 624 S. Mildred Street, Charles Town, WV 25414, USA.

ADBURGHAM Marjorie Vere Alison, b. 28 Jan. 1912, Yeovil, Somerset, England. Author. m. Myles Ambrose Adburgham, 22 Aug. 1936, 2 sons, 2 daughters. *Education:* Roedean School, 1925-29; Switzerland, 1930-31; Secretarial College, London, 1931-32. *Appointments:* London Press Exchange, 1933-36; Columnist, Night and Day, 1937; Feature Writer, Punch, 1953-67; Fashion Editor, Guardian, 1954-73. *Publications:* View of Fashion 1966; Punch History of Manners and Modes, 1841-1940; Shops and Shopping, 1800-1914; Women in Print - Restoration to Victoria; Liberty's - Biography of a Shop, 1875-1975; Shopping in Style - Restoration to Edwardian; Silver Fork Society, 1814 to 1840. *Memberships:* The Costume Society; The Queen's English Society; Society of Authors; University Women's Club. *Hobby:* Gardening. *Address:* Tredore Cottage, Little Petherick, Wadebridge, Cornwall PL27 7QT, England.

ADDIS Sara Cordelia Allen, b. 15 May 1930, El Paso, Texas, USA. Company President. m. Bobby Joe Addis, 5 June 1949, 3 sons, 1 daughter. *Appointments:* Executive Secretary: SW General Hospital, UTEP (Director of Personnel); Secretary, Reclamation Bureau, ADDCO Millworks; President, Founder, Sara Care Franchise Corporation. *Memberships:* International Franchise Association; National Association for Home Care; American Management Association; Presidents Association; National Association of Female Executives; Business & Professional Women; Association of Pioneer Women. *Honours:* Entrepreneur of the Year, 1982. *Hobbies:* Travel; Oil Painting; Music. *Address:* 8417 Parkland, El Paso, TX 79925, USA.

ADELMAN Deborah Susan (Proesel), b. 30 Nov. 1953, Chicago, Illinois, USA. Registered Nurse. m. Russell J. Proesel, 6 Apr. 1982, 1 son. *Education:* BSN, University of Illinois, 1980. *Appointments:* Instructor, Decatur Area Vocational Centre, 1982-83; Occupational Health Nurse, A. E. Staley Comp, 1983-85; Nurse Consultant, Russ Proesel DDS, 1982-; Allied Health Coordinator, Richland Community College, 1987-; Vice President, Nursing Administration, Heckman Educare, 1989-. *Memberships:* American & Illinois Nurses Associations; District 9 Nurses Association; Beta Beta Beta, biological honour society. *Honours:* Ward Duel Award, public health writing, 1980; Certified Occupational Health Nurse, 1983; Certified Nurse Administrator, 1989. *Hobbies:* Needlepoint; Reading; Foreign languages. *Address:* 713 Antler Drive, Mount Zion, Illinois 62549, USA.

ADELMAN Irma Glicman, b. 14 Mar. 1930, Rumania. Professor. m. Frank L Adelman, 1950, divorced 1979, 1 son. *Education:* BS, 1950, MA, 1951, PhD, 1955, University of California, Berkeley, USA. *Appointments:* Nontenure Ranks, 1955-57, Stanford University, 1958-62; Associate Professor, Johns Hopkins University, 1962-66; Professor, Economics, Northwestern University, 1966-72; Maryland University, 1972-79; Professor, Agricultural & Resource Economics, 1979-, University of California, Berkeley. *Publications:* Theories of Economic Growth & Development, 1958; Society, Politics & Economic Development: A Quantitative Approach, 1967; Economic Growth and Social Equity in Developing

Countries, 1973; Practical Approaches to Development Planning - Korea's Second Five Year Plan, 1969; Income Distribution Policy in Developing Countries: A Case Study of Korea, 1978; Comparative Patterns of Economic Development: 1850-1914, 1988. *Memberships:* American Economics Association, Vice President, 1979-80; American Academy of Arts & Sciences Fellow; Econometric Society, Fellow; Phi Beta Kappa. *Honours:* Recipient, various honours & awards. *Hobbies:* Art; Theatre; Music. *Address:* Dept. of Agricultural and Resource Economics, 207 Giannini Hall, University of California, Berkeley, CA 94720, USA.

ADES Dawn, b. 6 May 1943, Ripley, Surrey, England. Art Historian; Educator. m. Timothy Raymond Ades, 9 July 1966, 3 sons. *Education:* BA, Oxford University, 1965; MA, London University, 1968. *Appointments:* Research Fellow, Institute of Latin American Studies, 1975; Lecturer 1979-86, Senior Lecturer 1986, Professor 1990, University of Essex. *Publications:* Books: Photomontage, 1976; Dali, 1982; 20th Century Poster: Design of Avant-Garde, 1984. Also: Dada & Surrealism Reviewed, exhibition catalogue, Arts Council, 1978; Art in Latin America, Yale University Press, 1989. *Membership:* Cimam (ICOM), 1988. *Address:* Department of Art History & Theory, University of Essex, Wivenhoe Park, Colchester, Essex, England.

ADILETTA Debra Jean Olson, b. 1 Oct. 1959, Gloucester, Massachusetts, USA. Business Analyst/ Executive Systems Management. m. Mark Anthony Adiletta, 25 Aug. 1984. *Education:* BA, Mathematics, Economics, College of the Holy Cross, 1981; MBA, University of Rochester, 1986. *Appointments:* Computer Systems Analyst, 1981-85, Personal Computer Specialist, 1985-87, Business Analyst/Executive Information Systems, 1987-, Eastman Kodak Co. *Memberships:* Vice-President, Past Secretary, Past Treasurer, College of the Holy Cross Alumni Club; Association of Systems Management; College of the Holy Cross Class Agent. *Honour:* Outstanding Adult Student Award, 1986. *Hobbies:* Skiing; Boating. *Address:* Rochester, New York, USA.

ADKINS Marilyn Biggs, b. 3 July 1945, E Greenwich, Rhode Island, USA. Lawyer, Legislative Consultant. m. (1) John C Adkins, divorced 1978. 1 son, 1 daughter; (2) Charles T. Wood, April 16, 1989. *Education:* BA 1967, JD 1982, University of Denver; Called to Bar, Colorado 1982, US District Court Colorado, 1982; US Court of Appeals (10th cir), 1982. *Appointments:* Owner Texaco Service Stations, Denver, 1971-78; Legal Assistant, Paralegal, Hubert M Safran, Denver, 1974-82; Private Practice Bookkeeping, Denver, 1978-81; Legislative Director, Colorado Trial Lawyers Association, 1981-87; Partner, Safran & Adkins, Denver, 1982-. *Creative works:* Chairperson, Colorado Sup Ct Pub Ed Comm, Constitutional Bi-Centennial video and teaching manual; chapter on torts in Colorado Street Law. *Memberships:* ABA 1982-; Colorado Bar Association, 1982-; Denver Bar Association, 1982-; Association of Trial Lawyers America, 1981-; Colorado Trial Lawyers Association, 1982-; Board of Directors, CTLA, 1983-; Trial Lawyers for Public Justice, 1984-; University of Denver Alumni Association; Trustee Temple Sinai, 1986-88. *Hobbies:* Music; Gardening. *Address:* Safran and Adkins, 1832 Clarkson Street, Denver, CO 80218, USA.

ADLER Carole Schwerdtfeger, b. 23 Feb. 1932, Rockaway Beach, Long Island, New York, USA. Author of children's books. m. Arnold R Adler, 22 June 1952. 3 sons. *Education:* BA, Hunter College, 1952; Master of Science, Russell Sage College, 1967. *Appointments:* Advertising Dept, Worthington Pump Corp, 1952-54; Middle School English Teacher, Niskayuna Schools, 1968-77. *Publications include:* In Our House Scott Is My Brother, 1980; The Cat That Was Left Behind, 1981; The Evidence That Wasn't There, 1982; Get Lost Little Brother, 1983; Roadside Valentine, 1983; Fly Free, 1984; With Westie and the Tin Man, 1985; Good-bye, Pink Pig, 1985; Split Sisters, 1986; Kiss the Clown, 1986; Carly's Buck, 1987; Always and Forever Friends,

1988; If You Need Me, 1988; Eddie's Blue Winged Dragon, 1988; One Sister Too Many, 1989, etc. *Memberships:* Author's Guild; Society of Children's Book Writers. *Honours:* Child Study Book Award, 1984 for With Westie and the Tin Man; Golden Kite Award, 1979 for Magic of the Glits; William Allen White Award, 1979 for Magic of the Glits. *Hobbies:* Reading; Tennis; Snorkeling; Swimming; Biking; Travelling. *Address:* 1350 Ruffner Road, Schenectady, New York 12309, USA.

ADLER Naomi, b. 30 Sep. 1931, New York City, New York, USA. Realtor (Sales and Management). m. Gerson Adler, 1 Aug. 1950, 7 sons, 1 daughter. *Education:* Graduate, Beth Jacob Teachers Seminary, 1949; John Carroll University, 1979; Cuyahoga Community College, 1986; VIP, Century- 21, 1987. *Appointments:* Bod Milliken Realty, 1979; Fialkoff Bungalow Colony, Monticello, New York, 1980-89; Kenny Co, 1981-85; Century-21 Crysler-Kenny, South Euclid, Ohio, 1985-89. *Memberships:* Legislation Committee, Cleveland Area Board of Realtors; Heights Round Table; Former Member, National Association of Parliamentarians; Past President, Hebrew Academy of Cleveland Parent-Teachers Association; Past President, Union of Orthodox Jewish Congregations of Northern Ohio; Past President, Shomre Shabbos Sisterhood; Community Services Planning Committee, Jewish Community Federation, Cleveland; Treasurer, Hebrew Free Loan Association; President, N'Shei Agudah Women; Board of Directors, Heights Area Project; Jewish Vocational Service; President, Bais Yaakov, Cleveland; Mosdos Ohr Hatorah; Bikur Cholim, Cleveland. *Honours:* Award Certificate for Outstanding Volunteer to Project Head Start, 2 & 1 VIP Certificate of Achievement, Sar Haelef, Telshe Yeshiva, Chicago; Woman of Valor Award, Hebrew Academy, 1969; Award, Community Leaders of America. *Address:* 3595 Severn Road, Cleveland Heights, OH 44118, USA.

AFFLECK Julie Karleen Hall, b. 23 Dec. 1944, Upland, California, USA. Certified Public Accountant. m. William Affleck, 29 Aug. 1964. 1 son, 1 daughter. *Education:* BS, Bus, University of Colorado, Boulder, 1967; MSBA, University of Denver, Colorado, 1972. *Appointments:* IBM Corp, Boulder, 1967-71; Ernst and Whinney, CPA's, Denver, 1972-79; R Weiss, CPA, Denver, 1979-80; Partner in Affleck Melaragno & Co, Denver, 1980-. *Memberships:* American Institute of CPA's; Colorado Society of CPA's; American Society of Women Accountants, Past President, Denver Chapter; Women Business Owners Association, President, Colorado Chapter; Denver Chamber of Commerce; Bal Swan Children's Centre for Handicapped, Treasurer; Betterway Electric Inc, Director. *Honours:* CPA Certificate, Colorado, 1973; CPA Certioficate, Nebraska, 1981. *Hobbies:* Golf; Reading; Swimming; Skiing; Handiwork. *Address:* 3193 W 12th Avenue Ct, Broomfield, CO 80020, USA.

AGUTTER Jennifer Ann, b. 20 Dec. 1952, Taunton, England. Actress. *Education:* Elmhurst Ballet School, Camberley. *Creative Works:* Films; East of Sudan, 1964; Ballerina, 1964; Gates of Paradies, 1967; Star, 1968; Walkabout; I Start Counting; The Railway Children, 1969; Logan's Run, 1975; The Eagle Has Landed; Equus, 1976; Dominique; Clayton and Catherine, 1977; The Riddle of the Sands; Sweet William, 1978; The Survivor, 1980; An American Werewolf in London, 1981; Secret Places, 1983. Stage: School for Scandal, 1972; Rooted; Arms and the Man; The Ride Across Lake Constance, 1973. National Theatre: The Tempest; Spring Awakening, 1974; Hedda; Betrayal, 1980; Breaking the Silence, 1985. Royal Shakespeare Co: Arden of Faversham; King Lear; The Body, 1982-83. Television includes: Long After Summer, 1967; The Wild Duck; The Cherry Orchard; The Snow Goose, 1971; A War of Children, 1972; The Man In The Iron Mask, 1976; School Play, 1979; Amy, 1980; Love's Labours Lost; This Office Life, 1984; Silas Marner, 1985. *Publication:* Snap, 1983. *Honours:* Royal Variety Club Most Promising Artists, 1971; BAFTA Best Supporting Actress, 1977; Emmy Best Supporting Actress, 1971.

Address: c/o William Morris Agency, 31/32 Soho Square, London W1V 5DG, England.

AHMED-HUSSEIN Deborah Elizabeth, b. 15 July, 1950, Wailuku, Maui, Hawaii, USA. Freelance Editor; Photographer. m. Dr Mohsen Ahmed-Kamal Ahmed-Hussein, 11 Nov. 1984. 1 daughter. *Education:* BA, Classical Humanities, 1974; Postgraduate work in Ancient Greek and Ancient History, 1974-75, The George Washington University. *Appointments:* Freelance Editor/Photographer, 1974-; Copy Editor, The American Physiological Society, 1985-87; Press Photographer, The Gazette Newspapers, 1986-87. *Creative Works:* Photographs in The Gazette Newspapers, The Tampa Tribune, Mould Allergy. *Memberships:* Past Member of Washington DC, Area Board of Directors, The American-Arab Anti-Discrimination Committee; Past President, Epsilon Beta Chapter, Eta Sigma Phi Honor Fraternity; People for the Ethical Treatment of Animals; Association of Veterinarians for Animal Rights; Council of Biology Editors; American Medical Writers Association. *Hobbies:* Animal rights; Arab-American Civil Rights; Palestinian Civil Rights; Ancient Greek Epigraphy; Ecology; Pantheism; Holistic medicine; The legal issue of whether only humans have standing in the court system. *Address:* PO Box 785, Sebring, FL 33871, USA.

AHNEMAN Patricia Mae Eleanor, Jr., b. 29 Oct. 1951, Parkersburg, West Virginia, USA. Pilot. *Education:* Wagner College, 1969-73; Embry Riddle University, 1988-; Certified Airline Pilot (CW 46); Certified Flight Instructor, Ground Instructor & Aircraft Dispatcher. *Appointments:* Standardbred trainer, Saddle Rock Stables, 1975-78; Flight Instructor, Flight School Manager, DR Aviation Inc, 1978-80; Co-pilot CW 46, DC 3, 4, 6, CV 440, American Flyers Company Inc, 1978-85; Captain CW 46, Office Manager, Miami Air Lease Inc, 1985-86; FAA Liaison, Millon Air Inc, 1986-87; Captain CW 46, American Flyers Company Inc, 1987; Co-pilot ATR 42, Pan Am Express, Berlin, Germany, 1987-88; Captain CW 46, Evans Aviation Inc, Kodiak, Alaska & Miami Florida, 1988-. *Creative works:* Series, violin & cello duets, composed & performed, 1967-73. *Memberships:* Aircraft Owners & Pilots Association; Ninety-Nines; National Association of Female Executives; Alpha Eta Phi; National Trust for Historic Preservation. *Honours:* Voluntary service awards; American Cancer Society, St Brigid's Church, Southside Hospital, March of Dimes, various dates; Outstanding music awards, violin, 1963-73; 1st female airline pilot, Berlin, 1987; Only female flying Curtiss CW 46, 1978-. *Hobbies:* Art collecting; Music; Horse riding; Travel. *Address:* PO Box 330089, Coconut Grove, Florida 33233, USA.

AHOOJA-PATEL Krishna, Barrister. *Education:* PhD, International Relations, University of Geneva; Barrister at Law, Inner Temple, London. *Appointments:* UN Economic Commission for Africa in Addis Ababa, Ethiopia, Haile Selassie I University; Foreign Correspondent, Political & Economic Weekly, Bombay, and India Press Agency, New Delhi; International Labour Office, Geneva, 1969; Editor, Women at Work, 1977-86; Deputy Director, UN International Research & Training Institute for the Advancement of Women, Santo Domingo, 1986-. *Address:* Calle Nicolas Cesar Penson No 102A, Santo Domingo, Dominican Republic.

AHRLAND Karin Margareta, b. 20 July 1931, Torshalla, Sweden. Member of Parliament. m. Nils Ahrland, 29 Mar. 1964, 1 son. *Education:* LLB, University of Lund, 1958. *Appointments:* Assistant Judge, Judge, 1958-; Chief Lawyer, Regional government of Malmohus, 1971-; MP (Liberal), 1976-; Chairman, Standing Committee for Justice, 1985-. *Publications:* Contributor to various books and political debates; columnist, Svenska Dagbladet. *Memberships:* President, Fredrika Bremer Forbunder, 1970-76; President, Swedish Committee for Afghanistan, 1986-; Board, International Alliance of Women, 1973-86. *Honours:* Honourary Member, Varmlands nation,

University of Lund. *Hobbies:* Art; Gardening. *Address:* Faeoriksbergsgatan 2, 21211 Malmo, Sweden.

AINLEY Marianne Gosztonyi, b. 4 Dec. 1937, Budapest, Hungary. Author; Lecturer; Science Historian. m. David Ainley, 23 July 1966, 1 son, 1 daughter. *Education:* Diploma, Industrial Chemistry, Budapest Technical College, 1956; BA, Sir George Williams University, Canada; MSc, Universite de Montreal, 1980; PhD, McGill University, 1985. *Appointments:* Research Assistant, Immunology, Queen Mary Veterans Hospital, Montreal, Canada, 1964-66; Research Assistant, Chemistry, Loyola College, Montreal, 1966-69, 1973-74; Instructor in Chemistry, 1974-78, Lecturer, 1987-, Concordia University, Montreal. *Publications:* Despite the Odds, Essays on Canadian Women and Science, 1990. *Memberships:* American Ornithologists Union (Centennial Historian 1982-83); Canadian Representative, Commission on the History of Women in Science, Technology and Medicine, International Union of the History and Philosophy of Science. *Honours:* Research grant, American Ornithologists Union, 1981-82; Research grant, Frank M.Chapman Fund, American Museum of Natural History, 1983-84; Research grant, Canadian Research Institute for the Advancement of Women, 1984-85; 4 research grants, Social Science and Humanities Research Council of Canada, 1985-91. *Hobbies:* Nature study; Birdwatching; Pottery; Hiking; Travel; Reading; Classical music; Jazz. *Address:* 4828 Wilson Avenue, Montreal, Quebec, Canada H3X 3P2.

AISENSTEIN Clara, b. 15 Nov. 1939, Argentine. Psychiatrist. m. (2) Ronald Blanken, 5 May 1981. *Appointments:* MD, University of Buenos Aires, 1964; Internship, Residency, various Hospitals; Board Certification, Psychiatry, American Board of Psychiatry & Neurology, 1975, Child Psychiatry Board, 1978. *Appointments* Private practice, 1975-; Clinical Director, Research Project on Infants of Schizophrenic Mothers, 1979-85; Medical Director, Mothers/Infant Programme, 1985-; Faculty, Washington School of Psychiatry, 1985-. *Publications:* Articles in professional journals. *Memberships:* American Academy of child Psychiatry; American Psychiatric Association; American Association of Psychiatric Services for Children; American Medical Association; International Association for Child and Adolescent Psychiatry. *Honours:* Fellowship, James D. Putnam Children's Centre, Boston, 1970-72. *Hobbies:* Jewellery; Horticulture. *Address:* 5035 Rockwood Parkway NW, Washington, DC 20016, USA.

AIZEN Rachel K, b. Israel, Clinical Psychologist. m. June 1966, 3 sons. *Education:* BA, Hebrew University, Jerusaem, 1966; PhD, University of Illinois, 1970; Post Doctorate, University of Massachusetts, 1980-82; Fellow, Neuropsychological Assessment, Massachusetts Mental Health Hospital, 1988-89. *Appointments:* Psychologist, Northampton State Hospital, 1971-72; Assistant Professor, Counselling, Tel Aviv University, 1972-73; Psychologist, Amherst Schools, 1974-86; Private Practice, Psychology, 1975-; Sabbatical Visiting Psychologist, American School in Israel, 1976-77; Sabbatical Visitor, Child Psychiatry Unit, Sheba Hospital, Israel, 1985-86; Clinical Psychology Internship, VA Medical Centre, Northampton, 1982-83. *Publications:* Princples and Methods of Counselling, with A Klingman, 1978, second edition, 1989; articles in professional journals. *Memberships:* American Psychological Association, Division of Clinical Psychology; Western Massachusetts Association of Psychoanalytic Psychotherapy. *Honours:* Monitary Award for Scholastic Achievement, Hebrew University, 1967. *Address:* Amherst, MA 01002, USA.

AKAMATSU Ryoko, b. 24 Aug. 1929, Osaka, Japan. International Civil Servant. m. Tadashi Hanami, 15 Jan. 1954, 1 son. *Education:* Department of English, Tsuda College, 1947-50; Department of Law, Tokyo University, 1950-53. *Appointments include:* Counsellor, Prime Minister's Office, 1978-79; Minister, Japanese Permanent Mission, United Nations, 1979-82; Director-

General, Women's Bureau, Ministry of Labour, 1982-86; Japanese Ambassador, Uruguay, 1986-89; President, Institute of Women's Employment, 1989-. *Publications include:* Complete Comment on the Act for Equal Employment Opportunity for Men & Women & Revision of Labour Standards Law (in Japanese) 1985. *Memberships:* President, Japanese Association of International Women's Rights; Director, Japan Committee, UNICEF; Committee, Elimination of Discrimination Against Women, UN. *Hobbies:* Classical music; Golf. *Address:* 5-11-22-309 Roppongi, Minato-ku, Tokyo, Japan.

AKERS Cathay Ann Marie, b. 13 Aug. 1952, San Jose, California, USA. Company President. m. James Floyd Dorris, 1969, died 1974, 1 daughter. *Education:* Diploma, General Education, 1975. *Appointments:* Clerk-Receptionist, Hood River Abundant Food Stores, 1970; Guard, Lawrence Security, 1971-72; Store Detective, Lipman & Wolfe, 1972-74; Experimental Technician I, Weyerhaeuser Paper Co., Longview, 1977-79; Water Shed Technician, Washington State Dept. of Agriculture, 1979; Chemist, American Cyanamid Co., 1979-82; Lab. Technician, City of Monroe Wastewater Treatment Plant, 1984-85; Chief Executive Officer, GAP Plumbing Inc., 1987-. *Publications:* articles in various journals. *Memberships:* Society of Women Engineers; Veterans of Foreign Wars; Laidies Auxiliary; *Honours:* Pell Grantee, University of Toledo. *Hobbies:* Writing Poetry; Painting; Skiing; Tennis; Golf. *Address:* 237 White Oak Ct., Monroe, MI 48161, USA.

AKIN-BOWERS Gwynn Collins, b. 24 Mar. 1939, Florida, USA. Pharmaceutical Company Executive. m. Dr Albert Bowers, 23 Dec. 1985, 2 daughters, 3 stepdaughters. *Education:* BS, Florida State University, 1961; PhD, Tulane University, 1965. *Appointments include:* Executive Assistant to the President and Chief Executive Officer, 1981; Executive Assistant to the Chairman, President and Chief Executive Officer, 1982; Assistant to the Chairman and Chief Executive Officer, 1982-85; Director, Syntex Scholars Program, 1983-; Director of Health Policy, 1986-, Syntex Corporation, Palo Alto; Associate Adjunct Professor of Anatomy, Department of Anatomy, School of Medicine, University of California, San Francisco, 1972-, *Publications:* Author of numerous articles to professional journals and magazines. *Memberships include:* Consultant, National Science Board, 1978-; Pharmaceutical Manufacturers Association; Foundation for Advanced Education in the Sciences, Inc, 1984-; The Hastings Center: Western Advisory Council, 1986-; Board of Directors, National Association for Biomedical Research, 1987-; Board of Directors, National Leadership Coalition for AIDS, 1988-; Board of Directors, The Varsity Group, Inc., 1988-; Board of Overseers, University of California, San Francisco, 1989-. *Honours:* Mortar Board Scholarship Trophies, Florida State University; Certificate, National Academy of Sciences and American Radio Relay League; Scholarships: National Alpha Delta Pi; Florida State University's Alpha Lambda Delta Women; City of Tallahassee's Panhellenic. *Address:* Syntex Corporation, 3401 Hillview Avenue, A1-215, Palo Alto, CA 94304, USA.

AKINGBADE Oluyinka, b. 2 Apr. 1955, Nigeria. Lecturer; Author. m. Israel O Akingbade, 25 Aug. 1979. 2 sons, 2 daughters. *Education:* BSc Medical Physiology, 1978; MSc Medical Physiology, 1983; PhD Medical Physiology, 1986. *Appointments:* Lecturer at: School of Nursing, Lagos University Teaching Hospital, 1979-80; Department of Physiology, University of Ibadan, 1981-86; Department of Physiology, Ogun State University, 1987-88. *Publications:* Books: Effect of Stimulatory and Inhibitory Drugs on Gastric Acid Secretion; Hormonal Dynamics During Menopause in Nigerians; Some Aspects of Immunological and Physiological Changes induced by Plasmodium in Mice. *Memberships:* President; The Women; The Physiological Society of Nigeria. *Honours:* 1st senior prefect, Idia College, Benin City, Nigeria, 1972-73; Numerous prizes for first position throughout Secondary school education, 1968-72; Federal Government Scholarship for undergraduate and

postgraduate studies. *Address:* Department of Physiology, College of Medicine, University of Ibadan, Ibadan, Nigeria, West Africa.

AKINOSHO Babafunke Olayide Olubowale, b. 3 July 1935, Lagos, Nigeria. Chief Consultant, Community Physician. divorced. 1 son, 3 daughters, m.(2) Justice Ligali Akanni Ayorinde, 18 Jan. 1990. *Education:* Royal College of Physicians in Ireland, Dublin, Ireland, LRCP & SI,LM, 1956-62; DPH, University of Liverpool, England, 1968; Postgraduate, Colelge of Nigeria, FMCPH (Nig), 1976; West Africa College of Physician, FWACP, 1976. *Appointment:* Hospital Management Board, Lagos State Government, Nigeria, 1965-. *Memberships:* International Union Against Tuberculosis, President of the African region, 1972-74; International Association of Medical Women, Assistant Secretary Nigeria medical Women Association, 1976-80; International Epidemiological Association. *Hobbies and interests:* Chairperson of Management Home Committee of Caring for Motherless and abandoned babies; Keep fit exercises; Gardening. *Address:* 27A Jones Street, Ebute Metta, Lagos, Nigeria.

ALADJEM Sonia, b. 11 Oct. 1928, Montevideo, Uruguay. Sociologist; Researcher; Educator; Linguist; Lecturer. divorced. 1 daughter, 1 son. *Education:* MA French Literature 1977, PhD Sociology 1988, Loyola University of Chicago. *Appointments:* Sociologist/Researcher/Educator/Linguist/Lecturer, Loyola University of Chicago, 1979-. *Publication:* Dissertation: Structures of the Self: A Study of the Female Life-cycle through Autobiographies of Representative French Women Authors. *Memberships:* Sociologist for Women in Sociology; Modern Language Association; Assoc. for Humanistic Sociology; New York Academy of Sciences; Society for the Study of Symbolic Interaction; American Sociological Association; International Women Associates of the International Visitors Center, Chicago, Illinois. *Honours:* Research Assistantship, Modern Language Department, Loyola University of Chicago, 1974-76; Appointed to Alpha Sigma Nu (National Jesuit Honor Society), 1980; Research Assistantship, Sociology Department, Loyola University of Chicago, 1980-82. *Hobbies:* Art in general; Stress on painting and sculpture; Classical music; Cinematography. *Address:* 175 E Delaware Pl, No 5511, Chicago, Illinois 60611, USA.

ALAIN Marie-Claire, b. 10 Aug. 1926, Saint-Germain-en-Laye, France. Organist. m. Jacques Gommier, 1950, 1 son, 1 daughter. *Education:* Institut Notre-Dame, Saint-Germain-en-Laye: Conservatoire National Superieui de Musique, Paris. *Appointments include:* Organ teacher, Conservatoire National de Region, Rueil-Malmaison; Lecturer, Summer Academy for Organists, Haarlem, Netherlands, 1956-72; Lecturer, numerous universities, worldwide; Numerous concerts, worldwide, 1955-; Expert, organology, Ministry of Culture. Over 220 recordings including: Complete works of J. Alain, C. P. Bach, J. S. Bach, C. Balbastre, G. Bohm, N. Bruhns, D. Buxtehude, L. N. Clerambault, F. Couperin, L. C. Daquin, C. Franck, N. de Grigny, Guilain, Handel, Haydn, Mendelssohn, Vivaldi. *Honours:* Honorary Doctorates: Colorado State University Humane Letters, Southern Methodist University Music, USA; Officer: Legion of Honour, & Order of Merit, France; Officer, Arts & Letters, Chevalier du Danebrog, Denmark; Buxtehude Prize, Lubeck, Germany; Leonie Sonning Prize, Denmark; Franz Liszt Prize, Hungary; Numerous other awards, recordings & performances. *Address:* 1 avenue Jean-Jaures, 78580 Maule, France.

AL-ALOUSI Manal Younis Abdul Razzaq, b. 1 July 1949, Iraq. Secretary General of General Arab Women's Federation. m. Adnan Abdul Jalil Al-Hadithi, 17 July 1972, 3 sons, 1 daughter. *Education:* MA, Law. *Appointments:* Political Career, 1974-; MP, Iraqi National Assembly, 1980-84, 1985-88. *Publications:* Women and political Evolution in the Developing Countries, 1985; Women at War Time, 1985; Women and Political Evolution in the Arab World; articles in professional journals. *Honours:* First Order

Independence Medal, Jordan, 1982; First Order Distinguished Medal, Sudan, 1984; Peace Medal, Hungary, 1985; The Struggler's Medal for Freedom, Zambia, 1986. *Hobbies:* Political & Social Work. *Address:* Mahalla 304, Zuqaq 5, No. 33, Al-Yarmouk, Baghdad, Iraq.

ALBARELLA Joan Katherine, b. 22 Sept. 1944, Buffalo, New York, USA. Lecturer in Writing; Author. *Education:* BS, 1966, MSEd, 1971, State University of New York at Buffalo. *Appointments:* Publisher, Owner, Alpha Press, 1973-85; Actress, Director, Indigo Productions, 1975-88; Journalist, Western New York Catholic, 1986-; Lecturer in Writing, Educational Opportunity Center, State University of New York, 1986-. *Publications:* Poetry books: Mirror Me, 1973; Poems For the Asking, 1975; Women, Flowers, Fantasy, 1987; Over 40 freelance poems, articles, short stories in magazines and journals. *Memberships:* Poets and Writers Inc; Niagara Erie Writers. *Honours:* Poet of the Year, National Poetry Publications, 1974, 1975, 1976; 2nd Place, Romance Writing Competition, Buffalo, New York, 1983. *Hobbies:* Writing; Theatre. *Address:* 3705 Seneca Street, West Seneca, NY 14224, USA.

ALBERT Linda Isobel, b. 15 Nov. 1939, New York City, USA. Writer; Consultant. m. Byron C Eakin, 24 Sept. 1988, 2 sons, 1 daughter by former marriage. *Education:* BA, 1968, MSc., 1972, University of the State of New York; PhD, Psychology, William Lyon University, 1984. *Appointments Include:* Teacher, 1968-72; Teacher Specialist, 1972-81; Adjunct Professor, Education, Elmira College, 1978-86; Syndicated Columnist, 1979-; Author; TV Host, Family Focus, 1988-. *Publications:* Coping with Kids, 1982; Coping with Kids and School, 1984; Coping with Kids and Vacation, 1986; Strengthening Stepfamilies, 1986; Quality Parenting, 1987; Cooperative Discipline, 1989. *Memberships:* American Society of Journalists & Authors; National Family Resource Coalition; Stepfamily Association of America; Florida Network for Parent Education; North American Society of Adlerian Psychology; American Mensa. *Hobbies:* Folk Dancing; Scuba; Sailing; Opera. *Address:* 5238 Bon Vivant Dr. No 74, Tampa, FL33603, USA.

ALBET VILA Montserrat, b. 22 May 1927, Barcelona, Spain. Musicologist. m. J Gomis Sanahuja, 28 Sept. 1964. *Education:* Studied piano with B Selva, M Carbonell, J Llongueras and J Tomas; Chamber Music with J Massia and Chant with G Markova and C Badia in the Music Academy of Barcelona; Studied Musicology and musical Paleography with H Angles and J M Llorens in Barcelona and with B Rowenstrunck in Germany. *Appointments:* Director, Centre of Musical Documentation in Barcelona, 1983-; Librarian, Spanish Institute of Musicology, 1963-66; Adviser of music programmes, public television of Catalonia (TV3); Technical director of Ferrer Salat Foundation which awards the Queen Sofia Prize of Composition, 1983-85. *Publications:* Contemporanean Music, 1974; Critical bibliography of the Festa o Misteri d'Elx (a liturgic medieval celebration), Co-author with R Alier, 1975; Catalogue, One thousand years of music in Catalonia, 1976; Pau Casals, a lifetime of music, 1985; History of Catalan Music, 1986. *Contributions to:* Numerous magazines and encyclopedias. *Memberships:* International Society of Musicology, 1961-; Catalan Society of Musicology; Management Board, Orfeo Catala, 1975-; Vice President, 1978-, Representative, Generalitat de Catalunya (autonomous government) in the management of the Liceo-s Opera Theatre, 1980-. *Address:* Centre de Documentacio Musical, C/Rabida, s/n, 08034 Barcelona, Spain.

ALBRECHT Ruth E, b. 27 Oct. 1910, Perry County, Missouri, USA. Professor Emeritus, Sociology. *Education:* BSc, Washington University, 1934; MA 1946, PhD 1951, University of Chicago. *Appointments:* Research Associate, University of Chicago, 1948-50; Research Professor, Auburn University, Alabama, 1951-57; Head, Dept of Family Life, 1957-60, Professor of Sociology, 1960-75, University of Florida. *Publications:*

Books: Older People, with R J Havighurst; Aging in a Changing Society; Encounter: Love, Marriage & Family. Chapters in 6 other books; Articles in professional journals. *Memberships:* Secretary Family Section, 1970-73, American Sociological Society; Board of Directors 1971-74, Vice President 1974-75, Committee Chairmanships, Southern Sociological Society; Board of Directors 1967-70, National Council on Family Relation. *Hobbies:* Travel; Bridge; Opera. *Address:* 4078 Louisiana Street, Apt 8, San Diego, CA 92104, USA.

ALBRIGHT Ann Louise, b. 30 Oct. 1958, Chicago Heights, Illinois, USA. Doctoral Student in Exercise Science. *Education:* BA, U C Davis, 1980; MSc, California State University, 1987; Doctoral degree in progress, Ohio State University. *Appointments:* Physical test & Eval spec for State of California, 1983-85; Graduate Assistant, CSUS, part-time faculty at CSUS in Exercise Physiology, 1985-87; Research Assistant, Ohio State, Work in cardiac rehabilitation, cardiac testing, 1987-. *Publications:* Master's Thesis: Validation of Bioelectrical Impedance in Obese, Lean, Adolsecent, & Aging Populations, abstract published, 1987. *Memberships:* American College of Sports Medicine (ACSM); American Diabetes Association; ACSM, Midwest Chapter; Certified Exercise Test Technologist, ACSM; CPR and first aid instructor. *Honours:* Van Hagen/Cassidy Scholarship, California Association for Health, Phys Ed, Rec and Dance, 1987; Master's Thesis research presented at the Southwest Chapter of American College of Sports Medicine, 1986; Master's Thesis was selected for presentation at the California State University Research Competition; Dean's Honor Role, UC Davis, 1978-80. *Hobbies:* Exercise; Travelling; Movies. *Address:* 4848A Hollingbourne Ct, Columbus, OH 43214, USA.

ALBRIGHT Jodi Lee, b. 8 Sept. 1957, Cherry Point, North Carolina, USA. Teacher, Special Education Resource. *Education:* BS, Education, Mansfield University, 1979; Course work, Coppin State College, 1980; MA Psychology 1984, graduate courses 1985, Washington College. *Appointments:* Ethel Terrell Group Home, 1979-80; North East High School, 1980-85; Calvert Elementary School, 1985-; Swimming Coach, Glasgow High School, 1986 . Also: Co-operating teacher, research project, Johns Hopkins University. *Memberships:* Council for Exceptional Children, & its Learning Disabilities Division; Board, American Red Cross; National Education Association. *Honour:* Outstanding Senior, Special Education, 1979. *Hobbies:* Swimming including coaching, teaching, competing (Coach, Special Olympics); Sewing & needlework; Reading. *Address:* 25 Loran Court, Elkton, Missouri 21921, USA.

ALBRIGHT Lovelia Fried, b. 13 Dec. 1934, New York City, USA. Importer; Designer; Company President. m. Lee Albright, 30 Nov. 1958, 3 sons. *Appointments:* Acress, 1949-; Assistant Reporter, Bedford Villager, 1953; Publicist, Doubleday & Co., 1960-63; President, Owner, Design Consultants for Industry, 1964-72, Lovelia Enterprises Inc., 1972-, Foley & Robinson Inc., 1988-. *Memberships:* ASID/IF; MIAA; NAME; Jewellers Board of Trade. *Honours:* Recipient, many honours & awards. *Hobbies:* Swimming; Antique Shows; Designing Items for Miniature Dollshouses; Travel. *Address:* Viewpoint, Rte 100, RD 2, Katonah, NY 10536, USA.

ALCANTARA Rebecca D., b. 30 Sept. 1923, Philippines. Educator. m. Ernesto C. Alcantara, 2 Oct. 1949, 4 sons, 1 daughter. *Education:* Elementary Teacher's Certificate, 1942; Graduate Certificates, 1969, 1973; BSc, Education, 1947; MA Education 1952, English 1968; PhD, 1969. *Appointments:* Elementary school teacher, 1943-47; High school teacher, English, 1947-60; College teacher, 1960-70; Director of Publications, 1967-78; Professorial lecturer, English, Education, Drama Education Theatre Arts, Guidance, 1969-; Graduate Professor, Philosophy of Education, Values, Education, Research and Thesis Writing, 1969-; Head, English Department, 1978-80; Dean of

Instruction, 1980-87; Vice President, Academic Affairs & Research, 1987-88. *Publications:* Co-author, books for teachers &/or pupils including: Teaching Strategies I, 1987; Effective Writing; English Literature & Art; Strategies in Values Education; Educative Personnel Profiles & Training. *Memberships include:* President: Philippine Association of University Women; Teacher, Community Theatre; Philosophy of Education Society of the Philippines; Curia Maria Coronata, Legion of Mary; office and life member of various other professional groups and honour societies; Professor Emeritus, Philippine Normal College. *Honours:* Educational Leadership Award, 1967; National Award, Research & Writing, 1977; Kaunlaran Award, outstanding educator, 1982; Pontifical Award, 1983; Golden Harvest Award, 1983; Media Practitioners Award, 1984. *Hobbies:* Acting, directing & producing plays; Writing & editing; Advising Basic and Functional Literary Projects, Family visitation & catechetical instruction as apostolate, Legion of Mary; Planting flowering plants & fruit trees. *Address:* 555 Tolentino Street, Pasay City, Metro-Manila, Philippines.

ALCOCK (Garfield) Vivien, b. 23 Sept. 1924, Worthing, England. Author. m. Leon Garfield, 23 Oct. 1948, 1 daughter. *Education:* Oxford School of Art. *Publications:* The Haunting of Cassie Palmer, 1980; The Sonewalkers, 1981; The Sylvia Game, 1982; Travellers by Night, 1983; Ghostly Companions, 1984; The Cuckoo Sister, 1985; The Mysterious Mr Ross, 1987; The Monster Garden, 1988. *Membership:* Authors Society. *Address:* 59 Wood Lane, London, N6, England.

ALCOSSER Sandra Beth, b. 3 Feb. 1944, Washington, USA. Writer; Professor. m. Philip Maechling, 24 June 1978. *Education:* BA, Purdue University, 1972; MFA, University of Montana, 1982. *Appointments:* Director, Poets in the Park, Central Park, Glacier Park, 1975-77; Poet in the Schools, NEA 1977-85; Assistant Professor, Louisiana State University, 1982-85; Associate Professor, 1986-88, Director, Creative Writing, 1988-, San Diego State University. *Publications:* A Fish to Feed All Hunger, 1986; Chapbook: Each Bone & Prayer, 1982; Articles in: New Yorker; The Paris Review; Poetry; American Scholar; Yale Review; North American Review, etc. *Memberships:* Associate Writing Programmes; Poet & Writers Inc. *Honours Include:* Pushcart Prize for Poetry, 1988; Grant for Professional Performance SDSU, 1988; San Diego Combo Fellowship, Poetry, 1988; etc. *Hobbies Include:* Environmental Issues; Womens Issues. *Address:* NW 5791 West County Line Road, Florence, MT 59833, USA.

ALDAN Daisy, Writer. *Education:* BA, Hunter College; MA, Brooklyn College, PhD equivalent, NYU; Graduate Courses at City University; Studies in Philosophy, Eurythmy, Speech, Goetheanum, Switzerland. *Publications:* Poetry: Poems by Daisy Aldan, 1953; The Destruction of Cathedrals and Other Poems, 1963; The Masks Are Becoming Faces, 1964; Seven: Seven: Poems with Photographs by Stella Snead, 1965; Journey, 1970; 1 plus 1 equals 1 (with Elaine Mendlowitz), 1970; Or Learn to Walk on Water, 1970; Breakthrough, 1971; Love Poems of Daisy Aldan, 1972; Stones (Illustrated by B Krigstein), 1974; Verses for the Zodiac (Illustrated by Angiola Churchill), 1975; Between High Tides, 1978; In Passage, 1988. Prose: A Golden Story, a novella, 1979; Contemporary Poetry and the Evolution of Consciousness, 1980; Poetry and Consciousness, 1980; The Art and Craft of Poetry, 1981; Shakespeare and Spectator Consciousness, 1987. Translations: Stephane Mallarme, A Throw of the Dice, 1956; Albert Steffen, Selected Poems, 1968, The Death Experience of Manes, 1970, On the Mysteries of Eleusis, 1987; Rudolf Steiner, The Calendar of the Soul 1974, The Foundation Stone Meditation, The Twelve Harmonies, 1987; Herbert Witzenmann, The Virtues, 1974; Numerous articles to periodicals and anthologies; Editor: Folder Magazine of the Arts, 1953-60; Two Cities: Paris-New York, 1960-64. *Memberships:* PEN; Poetry Solciety of America; World Congress of Poets; Ecole Libre Des Hautes Etudes; Poets and Writers; National Book Critics Circle; Advisory Board, New York Quarterly; Advisory Board, American Biographical Association; English Teachers Association; Poets in the Public Service; Film Cooperative; Small Press Center, New York City; Small Press Centre, NY City 1987-. *Honours:* National Endowment Poetry Award; DeWitt American Lyric Poetry Award; Rochester Festival of the Arts, first prize for poetry; World Congress of Poets Bicenntenial Award; International Woman Artist, Radio Station WBAI for National Woman's Day; Honorary Doctor of Letters, Free University of Pakistan; Elected, Hunter College Hall of Fame; National Endowment for the Arts Award; 1 of 50 Outstanding Poets writing in America Today, EPOCH magazine, Cornell University; Included in Doubleday ballot of 500 greatest living writers in America; ALTA Award, University of Texas; Twice first runner-up, Columbia University Translation Award for Spanish Poetry Today; Runner-up for PEN translation award for The Death Experience of Manes by Albert Steffen. *Address:* 260 West 52 Street, Apartment 5-L, New York, NY 10019, USA.

ALDEA Patricia, b. 18 Mar. 1947, Bucharest, Romania. Architect. m. Val Alda, 17 Feb. 1971, 1 daughter. *Education:* MArch, 'Ion Mincu' School of Architecture, Bucharest, 1970. *Appointments:* Project architect, Historical Landmarks Preservation Institute, Bucharest, 1971-76; Architect, Edward Durell Stone Associates, New York, USA, 1977-79; Senior Associate, Alan Lapidus PC, NY, 1980-. *Creative works include:* Project architect for: Hilton Hotel, Lake Buenavista, Florida; Holiday Inn Crowne Plaza Hotel, Broadway, New York; World Disney Swan Hotel, Epcot Center, Florida. *Membership:* Registered Architect, New York. *Honour:* Citation, progressive architecture, World Disney Swan Hotel, 1989. *Hobbies:* Antiques; Arts; Reading. *Address:* c/o Alan Lapidus PC, 2112 Broadway, New York, NY 10023, USA.

ALDERMAN Minnis Amelia, b. 14 Oct. 1928, Douglas, Georgia, USA. Counselor; Educator; Psychologist; Business Woman; Executive. *Education:* AB, Music and speech-dramatics, Georgia State College, Milledgeville, Georgia, 1949; MA, Guidance, Counseling, Supervision, Murray State University, Murray, Kentucky, 1960; PhD, Psychology, Fine Arts and Performing Arts in process. *Appointments include:* Psychologist, Nevada Personnel, Ely Mental Health Center, 1969-75; Director, Retired Senior Volunteer Program, 1972-74; Originator, White Pine Senior Citizens Nutrition Program; White Pine Senior Citizens Center, 1974; Originator, White Pine Rehabilitation Center, 1974; Nevada Job Service, 1975-80; Originator, Creative Crafters Associates, 1976; Owner, Gift Gamut, 1977-; Private Instructor, Piano, Violin, Voice, 1981-; Band Director, Sacred Heart School, 1982-; Wassuk College; Organist, Sacred Heart Church, 1985-; Associate Dean, Professor and Head of Fine Arts Department, 1986-87, Academic Dean, 1987-; Ely Colony Child & Family Center, 1988-; etc. *Publications:* Numerous articles to newspapers, magazines and professional journals. *Memberships include:* Governor's Commission on Highway Safety, 1979-82; National Board of Advisors, American Biographical Institute, 1982-; Fellow, American College of Musicians and National Guild of Piano Teachers, 1986-; Society of Descendants of Knights of the Most Noble Order of the Garter, 1987; National Society Magna Charta Dames, 1987, etc. *Honours include:* Woman of the Year, 1964, Ely Business & Professional Women's Club; Scholarships, 1974 and 1975, University of Utah; Wisdom Award of Honor, 1979; Selected as 1 of 100 national participants in Leadership America, Foundation for Women's Resources, Washington, 1988. *Address:* Box 457, East Ely, Nevada 89315, USA.

ALDERSON Cheri Barnard, b. 20 Mar. 1946, Washington, Pennsylvania, USA. Family Psychotherapist. m. James Alderson, Nov. 1972, divorced 1981. 1 daughter. *Education:* BS Education, University of Nevada, 1972; Certified Hypnotherapist, 1980; MS Counseling, California State University, 1984; PhD Psychology, United States International University,

1988. *Appointments:* Vice President, Manager, 5A Ranches, Inc, 1972-80; Hypnotherapist terminally ill, 1980-; Psychological and Family Consultant, , 1983- ; USA Graduate Lecturer, 1984-; Seminar Presenter, Intervault, Inc, 1983- ; Marriage, Family & Child Therapist, 1986-. *Publications:* Articles: Psychological; Horse & Rider, 1977; Psychological Hypnotist Examiner, 1982; American Association of Marriage Therapist, 1988; Psychological AARP Resource Guide, 1988; Book in progress, Sexual Assault in United States, 1988. *Memberships:* PEO, International, Membership Chair, 1963-; Orange Co Sexual Assault Network, Board of Directors, Director of Programs, Shelter, 1986-; Soroptimist International, Health Chair, 1987-; American Psychological Association, 1986-; American Association of Marriage & Family Therapist; American Council of Hypnotist Examiner, Board of Directors, 1985-. *Honours:* Human Service Award, Delta Zeta, University of Nevada, 1972; Human Service Award, Christian Cowboys Association, 1982; Human Service Award, Batter Women's Shelter, 1983; Outstanding Contribution, American Council of Hypnotist Examiners, 1985; 4-H Leadership, Horses and Dogs, 1986-87; Psi Chi, National Honor Society in Psychology, 1988. *Hobby:* Breeding and showing (AKC) Fox Terriers. *Address:* 18336 Tamarind Street, Fountain Valley, California 92708, USA.

ALDRICH Joyce Bartolotta, b. 29 Sept. 1943, Lawrence, Massachusetts, USA. President, American Visages Inc. *Education:* BA, English, Regis College, Weston, MA, 1964; MEd, Administration, Lowell University, Lowell, MA, 1971. *Appointments:* Teacher of English, Town of Wilmington, Massachusetts, 1964-89; President, American Visages Inc, Lynn, Massachusetts, 1983-89. *Memberships:* Class President, Regis College Class of 1964; Lynn Area Chamber of Commerce; New England Coin Laundry Association; National Coin Laundry Assoc; Mass Teachers' Assoc; Republican Party. *Hobby:* Stock Market. *Address:* 3 Seal Harbor No 336, Winthrop, MA 02152, USA.

ALDRIDGE Nancy Louise Copelan, b. 24 Feb. 1946, Madison, Georgia, USA. Psychotherapist. m. Dale W Aldridge, 28 Oct. 1978. *Education:* Diploma in Nursing, Piedmont Hospital, 1967; Georgia Institute of Technology, 1971; Cardiovascular Nursing, University of Alabama, 1974; BS, Georgia State University, 1975; MSW, Atlanta University, 1982; Postgraduate training. *Appointments:* Psychiatric Nurse and Team Leader, Adult Psychiatric Unit, Peachford Hospital, Atlanta, 1974-76; Psychiatric Nurse, Inpatient Mental Health Unit 1976-77, Coordinator, Partial Hospitalization Treatment program 1977-80, Northside Hospital; Student Intern 1981-82, Marital and Family Therapist 1982-85, The Bridge Family Center; Private Practice, 1985-88; Executive Director, The Georgia Center for Children Inc, Decatur, 1988-. *Publications:* Prosecution of Child Sexual Abuse Cases (co-author), 1985; Presenter of numerous lectures in area of child sexual abuse. *Memberships:* American Professional Society on the Abuse of Children; American Association for Marriage and Family Therapy; National Association of Social Workers; Academy of Certified Social Workers. *Honour:* Diploma, Clinical Social Work. *Hobbies:* Equestrian events, ride and show horses, compete on national level; Tennis. *Address:* 290 Rucker Road, Alpharetta, GA 30201, USA.

ALENIER Karren LaLonde, b. 7 May 1947, Cheverly, Maryland, USA. Poet; Writer; Management Analyst. m. Howard Scott Alenier, 22 June 1969, divorced 1979. 1 son. *Education:* BA with honours, French, University of Maryland, College Park, 1969. *Appointments:* Computer Programmer, US Federal Power Commission, 1969-71; Computer Systems Analyst, US Department of Labor, 1972-77; Computer Specialist, US Department of Energy, 1977-82; Management Analyst, US Department of Justice, 1983-. *Publications:* Editor: Whose Woods These Are, 1983; The Dancer's Muse, 1981; Wandering on the Outside, 1975, 1978. *Memberships:* President and Chairperson of the Board,

1985-, Poetry Committee, Greater Washington DC Area, Folger Shakespeare Library; President & Chairperson of the Board, 1986-, The Word Works; Poetry Society of America, 1979. *Honours:* Finalist, Word Beat Press Fiction Competition (Arizona), 1988; 1st Prize, Billee Murray Denny Poetry Award, Lincoln College, Illinois, 1981; Finalist, Dellwood Award, Shenandoah College, Virginia, 1978 and 1979. *Hobbies:* Book collecting; Cross country skiing; Photography; Gourmet cooking; Foreign travel; Dancing; Bicycling. *Address:* 4601 North Park Avenue No 1212, Chevy Chase, MD 20815, USA.

ALEXANDER Cornelia, b. 30 Nov. 1924, Winona, USA. m. John W. Alexander, deceased, 4 sons, 2 daughters. *Education:* Youngstown State University. *Appointments:* Office Manager, Alexander's Garage, 1959-77; Supervisor, Salem Community Hospital Laundry, 1965-80; Beauty Consultant, Mary Kay Cosmetics, 1979-; Senior Aide NCSC, 1982-83; Deputy Recorder, Columbiana County, 1982, Salem County Council, 1984-, 1st Black. *Publications:* Lectures, Writing & composing, speaking amterial for groups of all ages. *Memberships:* Believers Christian FEllowship; YWCA; Board, Ladies Democrat Club; Board, Women's Aglow Fellowship; Volunteer, American Cancer Society. *Honours:* Recipient, many honours & awards. *Address:* 189 West Wilson Street, Salem, OH 44460, USA.

ALEXANDER Diane Marie, b. 31 Aug. 1945, Clinton, Oklahoma, USA. Telemarketing Consultant; Trainer; Author. m. (1) Larry Allen, divorced, 1972, 2 sons, (2) Nicol Alexander, divorced 1988, 1 son, 1 daughter. *Education:* Diploma, Lindenwood College for Women, 1963-65. *Appointments:* GTE Directories, District Telephone Sales Manager, 1974-78; Vice President, Marketing & Sales, Barakel Corp, 1981-82; Vice President, President, Telemarketing Enterprises, 1988-. *Publications:* Articles in professional journals. *Memberships:* National Associaiton of Female Executives; International Customer Service Association; American Society for Training & Development. *Honours:* Recipient, various honours and awards. *Hobbies:* Travel; Bridge; Reading. *Address:* 2307 Oak Lane Suite 115, Grand Prairie, TX 75051, USA.

ALEXANDER Geraldine Jane, b. 15 Nov. 1960, Leamington Spa, England. Actress. m. Michael Crompton. *Education:* Royal Academy of Dramatic Art, 1981. *Appointments:* Pitlochy Festival Theatre, 1982; Alison Teggert in Killer, STV, 1983; The Gay Lord Quex, BBC, 1983; Dr Who, BBC, 1984; You Can't Live on Cake, BBC, 1983; Ophelia, in Hamlet, The Royal Exchange, 1983, 1984; Taggart, STV, 1984; Marianne Nicholson, in The Nightingale Saga, CBS Film; Wendy, in Peter Pan, Bristol Old Vic, 1984-85; Sheila Birling in, An Inspector Calls, The Royal Exchange; Gwenda Reed in Sleeping Murder (Miss Marple) BBC; Jeannie McAllister, A Very Peculiar Practice, BBC; Helga, The Wall of Tyrany, HTV; Bust, LWT; Lady Anne in Richard III; Fidelia in The Plain Dealer, Royal Shakepeare Company. *Hobbies:* Art; Tennis; Swimming. *Address:* c/o Kate Feast Management, 43a Princess Road, London NW1, England.

ALEXANDER Jane Murray, b. 22 Jan. 1945, Lima, Ohio, USA. Teacher. m. Said Atamna, 14 June 1970, divorced 1983, 1 son. *Education:* BA from Ohio University, 1966; MA from the University of Illinois, 1969. *Appointments:* Taught English at Birzeit University, West Bank of Israel, 1977-79; Eckerd College, 1980-84. *Publications:* Articles in journals & magazines including: Listen; Kiwanis International; Obelisk. *Membeships:* International Association of Business Communications; Florida Freelances Association; Amnesty International; etc. *Hobbies:* Camping; Boating; Swimming; etc. *Address:* 5925 Shore Blvd. So., Lancaster No 215, Gulfport, FL 33707, USA.

ALEXANDER Jane, b. 28 Oct. 1939, Boston, Massachusetts, USA. Actress. m. Edwin Sherrin, 29 May 1975. 1 son. *Education:* Sarah Lawrence College; University of Edinburgh, Scotland. *Appointments:* Has appeared in numerous theatre roles on Broadway including: A thousand Clowns, 1963; The Great White Hope, 1968-69; Find Your Way Home, 1974; Hamlet, 1975; The Heiress, 1976; First Monday in October, 1978; Night of the Iguana, 1988. Off-Broadway: Losing Time, 1980; Misalliance, 1962; Old Times, 1983-84. Films Include: Kramer vs. Kramer, 1979; Brubaker, 1980; City heat, 1984; Sweet Country, 1985; Square Dance, 1986. Television films include: Welcome Back Johnny Bristol, 1970; Miracle of 34th Street, 1973; Eleanor and Franklin, 1976; Circle of Children, 1976; The White House Year, 1977; Lovey, 1977; A Question of Love, 1978; Calamity Jane, 1981; Dear Liar, 1981; Kennedy's Children, 1981; In The Custody of Strangers, 1983; Malice in Wonderland, 1985; Blood and Orchids, 1986; Open Admisions, 1988; A Friendship in Vienna, 1988. Has played in regional theatre, 1964-. *Honours:* Helen Caldericott Leadership Award, 1984; Academy Award Nominations for The Great White Hope; All the President's Men; Kramer vs Kramer; Testament. Emmy Award for Playing for Time. Emmy Nominations for Eleanor and Franklin; The White House Years; Malice in Wonderland. TV Critics Circle Award for The White House Years. Tony Award for The Great White Hope. Tony Nominations for 6 Roms Riv Vu; Find Your Way Home; First Monday in October. Drama Desk Award for The Great White Hope; Theatre World Award for The Great White Hope. St Botolph Club Award for Achievement in Dramatic Arts, 1979; Israel Cultural Award, 1982; Western Heritage Award, 1984. *Address:* c/o William Morris Agency, 1350 Avenue of the Americas, New York City, NY 10019, USA.

ALEXANDER Kathleen Ann, b. 4 Sept. 1955, Gary, USA. Exercise Physiologist. *Education:* BS, MS, University of Tenneree, 1978; PhD, Vanderbilt Univeristy, 1989. *Appointments:* Co-owner, STEPs. *Publications:* Contributing Editor, Cooking Light Magazine. *Membership:* American College of Sports Medicine. *Honours:* Outstanding Young Woman of America, 1985, 1986. *Hobbies:* Cycling; Nautiling; Rollerblading; Volleyball; Scuba Diving; Music; Reading. *Address:* 2108 Hayes St., No 312, Nashville, TN 37203, USA.

ALEXANDER Linda Dianne, b. 2 Apr. 1942, Atlanta, USA. Associate Broker/Real Estate. m. John Alan Alexander, 30 July 1965, 2 sons, 1 daughter. *Education:* GED, 1980; Real Estate License, 1981; Broker's License, 1986. *Appointments:* Waitress, Admiral Benbow Inn, 1958-65; Data Entry, Auto Dealer, 1965-66; Real Estate Investor, 1967-77; National Speaker, 1977- 84; Associate Broker, Metro Brokers, 1981-. *Memberships:* Women Council of Realtors; Board of Realtors. *Hobbies:* Interior Design; Boating; Dancing; Travel; People. *Address:* 6455 Windoor Trace Drive, Norcross, GA 30092, USA.

ALEXANDER HOLLAND Christina Ann, b. New Zealand. Author; Publisher; Educational Consultant. m. David Murray Alexander, 1 son, 1 daughter. *Education:* Teaching Certificate, New Zealand, 1955; Certificate of Diagnostic Testing and Remedial Teaching, Schonell Research Centre, 1971; BA, 1975, Queensland University, Australia, 1971; Diploma in Teaching, New Zealand, 1974. *Career:* Infant Teacher, New Zealand, 1955; Lecturer, Kindergarten Training College, 1956; Private Ceramics Teacher, Queensland, Australia, 1957-70, 1971-76; High School Teacher, Art, English, Queensland, 1977-85; Founder, Producer, Playwright, Brisbane Puppet and Marionette Theatre (charity fundraising), 1957-59; Established Liscanner Arabian Horse Stud, 1974; Founder, Turkey Tracks Press, 1981; Retrained 12 secondary teachers, Participation and Equity Programme (Australian Federal Government funded for projects to aid disadvantaged), 1985. *Publications:* Researcher, author, publisher, Banana Books all-ages remedial works, Turkey Tracks Press; Help for Dyslectics pocketbook; Paper presented at National Gifted and Talented Conference, 1985; Remedial Teaching Skills for Numeracy and Literacy, teacher's handbook, 1986. *Memberships:* Remedial Teachers Association, Queensland; Co-Founder,

Brisbane Dyslexia Association; Rural Environmental Planning Association; Australian Endurance Riders Association; Arabian Horse Society of Australia. *Honours:* Ceramics awards, Brisbane Fine Arts Exhibition, 1958; Christopher in Cowl sculpture, Brisbane Technical College Exhibition, 1959; Numerous halter awards for Liscanner-bred Arabian horses. *Hobbies:* Endurance riding; Bushwalking; Writing including numerous bush ballads; breeding Arabian horses; Reading omnivorously; Ceramics. *Address:* PO Box 134, Kenmore, Brisbane, Queensland 4069, Australia.

ALEXIOU Marina S, b. 12 Feb. 1940, New York City, USA. Business Executive. *Education:* Business Certification, Business Administration, University of North Carolina, 1959; Student Center for Degree Study Business Management, Scranton, Pennsylvania. *Appointments include:* Translator/Representative for Greek Orthodox Church, Greensboro, 1956-59; Legal Secretary, Jordan Wright, Henson and Nichols, Attorneys at Law, Greensboro, 1959-60; Executive Secretary to Manager, Licensing, 1961-65; Programme Coordinator for Management and Technical Staff, Netherlands and USA, North American Philips Company Incorporated, 1961-65; North American Philips Corporation: Executive Secretary to President, 1965-69, Administrative Assistant to Chairman, Chief Executive Officer, President and Director, 1969-77, Administrative Assistant to Chairman of the Board & Chief Executive Officer, 1978-80; Administrative Assistant to Chairman of the Board, Director and Chairman of the Governing Committee of the US Philips Trust, 1980-84; Manager, Corporate Purchasing, 1985-; Administrative Assistant to Director, North American Philips Corporation and Chairman of Governing Committee of the US Philips Trust, 1985-; Director/Secretary, 1973-75, Director Vice President, 1975-77, and 1986-, Northgate Cooperatives Inc. *Publications:* Public Speaking: I Speak for Democracy, 1958; Historical Essay on Thomas Jefferson, 1959. *Memberships:* National Association of Female Executives; American Society of Professional and Executive Women; Smithsonian National Associates; Womens Republican Club of Bronxville; Actively involved in fund raising for American Cancer Society and Century Club of United Way, 1976-79; US Senatorial Business Advisory Board; American Security Council, Republican Inner Circle; Republican Presidential Task Force Washington DC. *Honour:* Recipient, American Legion Award for Essay. *Hobbies:* Photography; Tennis; Golf. *Address:* Northgate, Alger Court, Bronxville, NY 10708, USA.

ALFORD Joan Franz, b. 16 Sept. 1940, St Louis, USA. Entrepreneur. m. Charles H. Alford, 28 Dec. 1978, 3 step-sons. *Education:* BS, St Louis University, 1962; Course work completed towards MPA, Consortium of California State Universities, 1975; Presidential/Key Executive MBA, Pepperdine University, 1987. *Appointments:* Deputy Head, Computer Centre, Lawrence Berkeley Laboratory, Dept. of Energy Lab., 1980-81; Regional Site Analyst Manager, Cray Research Inc., Supercomputer Company, 1981-83; President, Innovative Leadership Management Consulting Firm, 1983-. *Publications:* Numerous professional papers. *Memberships:* Past Chairman, Association for Computing Machinery's Special Interest Group on Computer Personnel Research; Board, Volunteer Centres of Alameda County; Lakeview Club. *Honours:* President's Club Award, Leadership Management Inc. *Hobbies:* Skiing; Swimming; Opera; Gardening; Reading; Physical Fitness. *Address:* Innovative Leadership, 1900 Embarcadero Suite 200, Oakland, CA 94606, USA.

ALGAZI Linda Pearlman, b. 24 Sept. 1941, New York, USA. Psychotherapist; Syndicated Columnist; Lecturer. m. Herman E. Algazi, 21 Oct. 1962, 1 son, 1 daughter. *Education:* BA, Queens College, 1963; MA, Chapman College, 1975; PhD, International College, 1983. *Appointments:* Psychotherapist, Private practice, 1975- ; National Syndicated Columnist; Co-Founder, Woman's Opportunity Centre. *Publications:* Helping Women,

1980. *Memberships:* AAMFCC; CAMFCC. *Honours:* Presswomen of California, 1st Place, 1985, 1986, 1987. *Hobbies:* Art; Travel; Humour. *Address:* No 8 Point Loma Drive, Corona del Mar, CA 92625, USA.

AL HUSSEIN Her Majesty Queen Noor, b. 23 Aug. 1951, Washington DC, USA. m. King Hussein of Jordan, 15 June 1978, 2 sons, 2 daughters. *Education:* BA, Architecture & Urban Planning, Princeton University, 1974. *Appointments:* Director of Planning & Design Projects, Royal Jordanian Airline; Noor Al Hussein Foundation, 1985. *Memberships:* Patron: General Federation of Jordanian Women; National Federation of Business and Professional Womens Clubs; National Committee for Public Building and Architectural Heritage; The Queen Noor Technical College for Civil Aviation; Naitornal Committee for the Protection of the Environment; Jordanian Welfare Society for the Care of the Deaf; Friends of St John's Ophthalmic Hospital in Jerusalem; Haya Arts Center Society; Jordanian Physiotherapy Association. *Honours:* Order of Al Hussein Bin Ali; Grand Cordon of the Jewelled Al Nahda; numerous decorations from other countries. *Hobbies:* Skiing; Water Skiing; Swimming; Tennis; Sailing; Horseriding; Photography. *Address:* Royal Palace, Amman, Jordan.

ALIE-DARAM Simone Julie, b. 12 May 1939, Toulouse, France. Lecturer; Assistant Professor. m. Leonce Daram, 29 Nov. 1983, 1 son, 1 daughter. *Education:* MD, Univerity of Toulouse Medical School, 1967; Diplomas of Haematology, 1964, Bacteriology, 1968, Immunology, 1968; MSc.,1971. *Appointments:* Touslouse Hospital, 1960-64; Teaching Assistant, 1964-69, Associate Professor, 1970-84, Assistant Professor, 1984-, University of Toulouse; Medical Practice, CRTS Toulouse, Lecturer, Head Researcher, FMI & Blood Products, 1976-. *Publications:* Articles in professional journals. *Memberships:* French Society of Immunology; Harvard Medical School. *Honours:* Specia Prize, Toulouse Hospital Non Resident Assistant Concourse, 1960; Gold Medal, Medical School Laureate 1967; French National Academy of Medicine, 1968. *Address:* Centre Hospitalier Universitaire Purpan, Centre Regional de Transfusion Sanquine Toulouse Purpan, 31052 Toulouse, France.

ALIESAN Jody, b. 22 Apr. 1943, Kansas City, Missouri, USA. Poet. *Education:* BA magna cum laude, English/American Literature, Occidental College, 1965; MA, 1966, ABD, 1968, English/American Literature, Brandeis University. *Career:* Performances, readings, workshops and courses at universities, colleges, high schools, conferences and other venues; Radio, TV and theatre appearances; Approximately 150 engagements in 6 states and District of Columbia, including joint performances with American Sign Language interpreters. *Publications:* Books: as if it will matter, 1978, 1985; Desire, 1985, Braille Edition, 1985; Soul Claiming, 1985; Chapbooks: Thunder in the Sun, 1971; To Set Free, 1972; Doing Least Harm, 1985; Poems in national and regional periodicals, also in books and anthologies including: Literature: A Contemporary Introduction; Leaving the Bough: 50 American Poets of the 80's; Crossing the River: Poets of the American West; Rain in the Forest, Light in the Trees: Contemporary Poetry from the Northwest; Iron Country: Contemporary Writing in Washington State; Anthology of Magazine and Yearbook of American Poetry; The Butterfly and Wuthering Heights: A Mystic's Eschatology (article), 1968. *Memberships:* Phi Beta Kappa. *Honours:* National Merit Scholarship, 1965; International Fellowship to Friesian Islands, 1965; Woodrow Wilson Fellowship, 1966; Performance Grant, Seattle Arts Commission, 1973; Snohomish County Arts Commission Poetry in the Cities Project, 6 Washington Poets, 1977; Literary Fellowship, National Endowment for the Arts, 1978; King County Arts Commission, Work-in-Progress, 1979, 1988; Seattle Arts Commission, Original Works, 1983; Thompson Visiting Poet, Babson College, Wellesley, 1988. *Address:* 5043 22nd NE, Seattle, WA 38105, USA.

ALISON Dorothy, b. 4 Mar. 1925, Broken Hill, New South Wales, Australia. Actress. m. 6 Dec. 1952. 1 son, 2 daughters. *Education:* Sydney Girls High School, 1939-42. *Appointments:* Films: Mandy; Reach for the Sky; The Long Arm; The Nun's Story; Georgie Girl; Blind Terror; Amazing Mr Blunden; Rikki and Pete; Evil Angels; Two Brothers Running. Television: Eustace and Hilda (BBC); Forgive Our Foolish Ways (BBC); A Town Like Alice (BBC/Channel 7, Australia); A Fortunate life (Channel 9 Australia); Tusitala (ABC Australia/Portnam Pro, UK); A Fortunate Life. Theatre: The Affair (CP Snow) Strand Theatre, London; Have You Any Dirty Washing Mother Dear, Hampstead Theatre Club; Beaux Stratagem, Royal Exchange, Mancester. *Honours:* Two nominations, British Film Academy Awards; Mandy best supporting actress; Reach for the Sky best actress; Logie Award for best supporting actress in TV mini-series A Town Like Alice; Television Society of Australia Commendation for TV series A Fortunate Life. *Hobbies:* Day-dreaming and plotting. *Address:* c/o International Casting Service, 147A King Street, Sydney, New South Wales 2000, Australia.

ALKALAY-GUT Karen Hillary, b. 29 Mar. 1945, London, England. Lecturer. m. 26 July 1980, 1 son, 1 daughter. *Education:* BA, 1966, MA 1967, PhD, 1975, University of Rochester. *Appointments:* State University of New York, Geneseo, 1967-70; Ben Gurion University of the Negev, 1972-76; Tel Aviv University, 1977-. *Publications:* Making Love, poetry, 1980; Butter Sculptures, poetry, 1983; Mechitza, poetry, 986; Alone in the Dawn: The Life of Adelaide Crapsey, biography, 1988. *Memberships:* PEN; Poetry Society of America; Israel Association of Writers in English, Founder, Chair 1982-84; Federation of Writers in Israel; Poets & Writers; MLA; American Studies Association, Central Board. *Honours:* Tel Aviv Fund Prize, 1980; Dulchin Prize, Israel, 1984. *Hobbies:* Poetry; Politics; Animals; Swimming. *Address:* Dept. of English, Tel Aviv University, Ramat Aviv 69978, Israel.

AL-KHALILI Farida Jafar, b. 25 Mar. 1938, Najaf-Irak. *Education:* BA (Hons) Sociology, University of Baghdad, 1961; Postgraduate Diploma, Anthropology, London School of Economics, University of London, 1965. *Appointments:* Research Assistant, Department of Sociology, College of Arts, Baghdad University, 1966-80; Lecturer, Community College of Social Work, Amman, Jordan, 1980-. *Publications:* Articles on women; Articles on modern poems. *Honours:* 2 Prizes from College of Arts, University of Baghdad-Irak. *Hobbies:* Travelling; Reading; Writing articles and Modern Arabic poems. *Address:* P O Box 17042, Amman, Jordan.

ALKON Ellen Skillen Bogen, b. 10 Apr. 1936, Los Angeles, California, USA. Physician; Paediatrician. m. Paul Kent Alkon, 30 Aug. 1957, 3 daughters. *Education:* BA, Stanford University, 1955; MD, University of Chicago, 1961; MPH, Certificate, Handicapped Children, University of California, Berkeley, 1968. *Appointments include:* Hospitals, Chicago & California, 1961-70; Chief, School Health, Anne Arunde County Health Department, Annapolis, Maryland, 1970-71; Paediatrician 1971-73, Director, Maternal & Child Health 1973-75, Commissioner of Health 1975-80, Minneapolis Health Department, Minnesota; Public Health Chief, Coastal Region 1980-81, West Area 1981-85, Acting Medical Director for Public Health 1986, Medical Director 1987-, Los Angeles County Department of Health Services. *Memberships:* Past President, Minnesota & Southern California Health Associations; Fellow, American College of Preventive Medicine, American College of Paediatrics; Secretary, California Conference of Local Health Officers, Health Officers Association of California. *Honour:* Elected, Delta Omega, 1967. *Address:* 313 North Figueroa, Los Angeles, California 90012, USA.

ALLAIN-NGUYEN Anmaise Charlotte, b. 15 June 1942, Coray, France. Educator; School director. m. (2) Georges Nguyen Xuan Hop, 10 Nov. 1988. 1 son, 1 daughter. *Education:* Diploma, Latin-American Institute,

NYC Bi-lingual translator, 1962; BA, City University of New York, 1975; MA, TESOL Teachers College, Columbia University, 1976. *Appointments:* ESL Teacher, various colleges of the University of the City of New York, 1972-79; Supervisor of the Writing Center, Hunter College, CUNY, 1976-78; Founder and director, Riverside Adult Learning Center, New York City, 1978- . *Memberships:* Executive Board 1983-85, President, 1984-85, Language Innovations, Inc; Chair of Applied Linguistics Special Interest Group, Creator and Chair of the Applied Linguistics Annual Winter Conference in NYC; ALSIG Newsletter editor, Executive Board member, 1979-81, New York State TESOL; Adult Education; Refugee Concerns Special Interest Groups, International TESOL. *Honours:* BA Summa Cum Laude, 1976; The Riverside Adult Learning Center received numerous Awards and Recognition for their work including: 1 of 12 programs chosen nationwide to be part of the President's Adult Literacy Innitiative; Nominated, New York State Education Department for the Secretary's Award, Outstanding Adult Basic Education Program, New York State; Chosen by the Ford Foundation as a site for their trustees' visit to view the plight of immigrants and refugees in the inner city; Chosen by the School for International Studies as a model to present to their visiting scholars from all over the world; Visitations: Puerto Rico Department of Education; Department of Education of Quebec, Canada; People's Republic of China's Peace Delegation; National Coordinator, Newsettlers Education of New Zealand; Minister of Foreign Affairs of Sweden and the Swedish Ambassador to the United Nations; Chosen by International TESOL and NYS TESOL as a site for teachers of adults from all over the world to observe the various methodologies and approaches at the Center; Recipient of a special grant to train teachers in the New York City area in the classroom application of suggestology and suggestopedic methodologies as applied to the teaching of languages, particularly English as a second language. *Hobbies:* Travelling; Reading, especially historical novels and biographies. *Address:* The Riverside Adult Learning Center, 490 Riverside Drive, New York, NY 10027, USA.

ALLAN Mabel Esther, b. 11 Feb. 1915, Wallasey, Cheshire, England. Author. *Publications include:* Author of over 160 books for young people, published in UK, USA, France, Germany, Iceland, Holland, Denmark, Japan etc, including: Pine Street Goes Camping, 1980; The Mills Down Below, 1980; Strangers in Wood Street, 1981; The Horns of Danger, 1981; The Pine Street Problem, 1981; A Strange Enchantment, 1981; Goodbye to Pine Street, 1982; Growing Up in Wood Street, 1982; Alone at Pine Street, 1983; The Crumble Lane Adventure, 1983; A Dream of Hunger Moss, 1983; A Secret in Spindle Bottom, 1984; Friends at Pine Street, 1984; Trouble in Crumble Lane, 1984; The Flash Children in Winter, 1984; The Pride of Pine Street, 1985; The Crumble Lane Captives, 1986; A Mystery in Spindle Bottom, 1986; The Road to Huntingland, 1986; The Crumble Lane Mystery, 1987; Up the Victorian Staircase, 1987; First Term at Ash Grove, 1988. Has also written under the pseudonym of Jean Estoril, Anne Pilgrim and Priscilla Hagon. *Memberships:* Crime Writers Association. *Honours:* Best Children's Book of Year, France for Lise en Italie, 1960; Mystery in Wales, Mystery Writers of American Award, 1971; Boston Globe Horn Book, An Island in a Green Sea, Hon. Book, 1973. *Hobbies:* Travel; Theatre; Photography. *Address:* Glengarth, 11 Oldfield Way, Heswall, Wirral, L60 6RQ, England.

ALLAN Sarah Katherine Meyers, b. 20 Feb. 1945, USA. University Lecturer. m. Nicol Allan, 28 Sept. 1963. *Education:* BA, UCLA, 1966; MA 1969, PhD 1974, University of California, Berkeley. *Appointments:* Lecturer in Chinese, School of Oriental and African Studies, University of London, 1972-. *Publications:* The heir and the sage: Dynastic legend in early China; Oracle bone collections in Great Britain (with Li Xueqin & Qi Wenxin); China (with C Barnett); Legend, lore and religion in China (ed with Alvin P Cohen); Articles on early Chinese myth, religion and art. *Memberships:* Founder and chairman, Early China Seminar, London;

Council of the British Association for Chinese Studies. *Address:* Far East Dept, SOAS, Malet Street, London WC1E 7HP, England.

ALLEN Belle, b. Chicago, Illinois, USA. Business Executive. Widowed. *Education:* Humanities, University of Chicago. *Appointments include:* President, Belle Allen Communications, 1961-; Consultant, Board member, American Diversified Research Corporation, 1967-70; Vice President, Treasurer, Board, Cultural Arts Surveys Inc, 1965-79; Vice President, Secretary, Board, Management Performance Systems Inc, 1961-66; Vice President, Treasurer, Board 1966-79, Chairman & President 1979-, William Karp Consulting Company Inc. Various consultancies, advisory boards, panels. (private, federal & state). *Publications:* Editor, contributor: Book, Operations Research & Management of Mental Health Systems, 1968; Numerous professional & business journals. Also reports, manuals. *Memberships include:* Offices, past/present: Affirmative Action Association, Industrial Relations Research Association, Chicago Press Club, Chicago Publicity Club, National Association of Inter-Group Relations Officials, Fashion Group. Member: American Association for Advancement of Science, Women's Equity Action League, National Organisation for Women. Also active, various community & civic associations. *Honours include:* Various awards from: Chicago Lighthouse for Blind, 1986; International Association of Official Human Rights Agencies, 1985; White House, 1961; Chicago Publicity Club, 1968; Chicago Cerebral Palsy Association 1954, 1955. Honorary citizen, Alexandria (Virginia), 1985; Numerous biographical listings. *Address:* 111 East Chestnut Street, Chicago, Illinois 60611, USA.

ALLEN Bessie, b. 10 Aug. 1942, Sumter, South Carolina, USA. Educator; Supervisor Curriculum & Instruction; Home Economist. m. Frederick D Allen, 28 June 1980. 2 sons, 5 daughters. *Education:* BS, Home Economics Education, 1964; MS, Education, 1974; MA, Admin & Supervision Education, 1984. *Appointments:* Home Economist, Teacher, Wagner, South Carolina, 1964-65; Extension Home Economist, Clemson University, Clemson, South Carolina, 1965-68; Home Economist Teacher Tackawama, New York, 1968-75; Home Economist Teacher, 1975-80, Supervisor 1980-89, Neptune, New Jersey. *Publications:* Contributing editor, Illinois Teacher Magazine, articles on Teaching, Nutrition Education, Grades K-12. *Memberships:* bb3Kappa Delta Pi, Education Honor Society; American Home Economist Association; Principal & Supervisors Association; Association for Supervision & Curriculum Dev. *Honours:* NY State Outstanding Young Educator, 1970-71; Lackawana, NY, Outstanding Young Educator by Jaycees, 1971; New Jersey Home Ec Teacher of the Year, 1987; Top Ten Home Ec Teacher of the Year, USA for Outstanding contributions to Home Ec Education in Grades K-12, 1987; Ocean Drifters Now Black Woman Achievement Award. *Hobbies:* Reading; Creating new recipies for good nutrition; Consulting and workshops on human relations and family management; Federal grant writing. *Address:* 19 Hartshorne Road, Wayside, New Jersey 07712, USA.

ALLEN Constance Olleen, 10 June 1923, Camphill, Alabama, USA. Artist; Designer. m. Walton S. Allen, 11 Mar. 1976. *Education:* George Washington University, Washington DC; Instituto Allende, San Miguel de Allende, Mexico, 1971; Diamond Certificate, Gemological Institute of America, Santa Monica, California, 1987. *Appointments:* Private art classes, 1969-74; Instructor, University of Science and Arts of Oklahoma, Chickasha, Oklahoma, 1974-75; Owner, Director, The Studio Gallery, Chickasha, Oklahoma and Green Valley, Arizona, 1979-. *Creative works include:* Numerous paintings in oil, pastel and watercolours exhibited in jurored shows. *Memberships:* Santa Rita Art League, Green Valley, Arizona (President 1983-84, Board of Directors 1984-88); Arts and Crafts Association, Green Valley (Vice-President 1986-87); President, National League of American Pen Women, Sonora Desert Branch, Arizona. *Honours:* 26th, 28th, 29th Festival of the Arts Jurored Show, Tubac, Arizona,

1985,-88; Honourable Mention, 27th Festival of the Arts, Tubac, 1986; 2 1st Places, Santa Rita Art League Show, Nogales, Arizona, 1986; 3rd Place, Sonora Desert Branch Juried Show, National League of American Pen Women, 1988. *Hobbies:* Gemology; Jewellery design and construction; Travel; Writing. *Address:* 2791 S. Calle Morena, Green Valley, AZ 85614, USA.

ALLEN Elaine Irene, b. 10 Dec. 1944, Lockport, USA. Minister. m. Gary Irving Allen, 13 June 1964, 1 son, 2 daughters. *Education:* State University of New York, College at Geneseo; International Christian Graduate University, School of Theology. *Appointments:* Bacteriology Laboratory, Buffalo General Hospital, 1965-66; Histologist, School of Medicine, SUNY, at Buffalo, 1967-68; International Student Ministry Development Base, University of California, Berkeley, 1976-79; UN Ministry, Christian Embassy, 1979-83; Vice President, Co-Founder, Christian Mission for the United Nations Community, 1983-. *Memberships:* America-Nepal Society; UN Delegates' Wives Club. *Hobbies:* Crafts; Flower Arranging; Reading. *Address:* 965 Knollwood Road, White Plains, NY 10603, USA.

ALLEN Elizabeth Colclough, b. 11 Aug. 1955, Reading, England. Trade Union Official. *Education:* BA Hons English & Related Literature, University of York, 1974-77; MA US Studies, Institute of US Studies, London University, 1977-78; DPhil English & American Literature, University of Sussex, 1978-80. *Appointments:* Women's Officer and National Organiser, Electrical, Electronic, Telecommunication & Plumbing Union, 1982-86; Private Sector Offical, National Association of Teachers in Further and Higher Education, 1986-. *Publication:* A Woman's Place in the Novels of Henry James, 1984. *Memberships:* Labour Party; Manufacturing, Science, Finance Union. *Address:* c/o NATFHE, 15-27 Britannia Street, London WC1, England.

ALLEN Jane, b. 15 June 1928, Dallas, Texas, USA. Concert Pianist; Teacher. m. Melvin Ritter, 26 July 1958, 1 son. *Education:* Private study with Paul van Katwijk, 1941-47; Southern Methodist University School of Music, 1944-46. *Appointments:* Private teaching, St Louis, 1952-; Member, Ritter-Allen Duo (violin & piano), 1959-; Official pianist, St Louis Symphony Orchestra, 1961-64; Artist-in-residence, Stephens College, 1966-75; Piano faculty 1976-, chairman, Piano Department 1985-, St Louis Conservatory. Master classes, Oberlin Conservatory, Spokane Music Festival, 1986; Frequent adjudicator, national & international competitions. Also: Soloist, St Louis & Baltimore Symphony Orchestras; Annual concert tours, USA & Canada; 10 recitals, New York Town Hall, 1959-; 3 European tours, 1962-; Concerts, UK, Holland, France, Norway, Sweden, Germany, Belgium, Spain, Italy, Yugoslavia, Switzerland, Austria. *Memberships:* Honorary member, Sigma Alpha Iota; Lifetime Master Teacher's Certification, member, Music Teachers National Association; Advisory board, Young Keyboard Artists Association; Past Arts Music Panel, National Foundation for Advancement in Arts. *Honours:* Award, St Louis Artist Presentation Society, 1958; Teaching awards, Mason & Hamlin 1970, 1980, Baldwin 1975, 1977, 1982, 1983; Certificates of excellence, Presidential Scholars Commission, US Department of Education, 1983, 1987. *Hobbies:* Cooking, Needlework. *Address:* 7471 Kingsbury Boulevard, St Louis, Missouri 63130, USA.

ALLEN Janet Marjorie, b. 22 Mar. 1953, Southport, Lancashire, England. Physician. *Education:* BSc(Hons), 1974; MB BS, 1977; MRCP (UK), 1980; MD, 1986. *Appointments:* Pre-registration house posts; Various junior hospital staff positions; Wellcome Trust Fellow, Royal Postgraduate Medical School, London, 1982-85. *Publications:* Various scientific publications. *Memberships:* Collegiate Member, Royal College of Physicians; Society for Endocrinology; American Society of Neuroscience; American Association for the Advancement of Science. *Honours:* Florence Hughes Scholarship for preclinical subjects, 1974; Lord Rank

Prize in Biochemistry, 1974. *Hobbies:* Sailing; Gardening. *Address:* Physiological Laboratory, University of Cambridge, Downing Street, Cambridge CB2 3EG, England.

ALLEN Judith Shatin, b. 21 Nov 1949, Boston, Massachusetts, USA. Composer; Professor. *Education:* AB, Douglass College, 1971; MM, The Juilliard School, 1974; PhD, Princeton University, 1979. *Appointments:* Assistant Professor, 1979-85, Associate Professor, 1985-, University of Virginia. *Creative works:* The Passion of St Cecilia, Piano and Orchestra; Ruah for Flute and Chamber Orchestra; Meridians for Solo clarinet; Fasting Heart for solo flute; Glyph for Viola, St Qt, and Piano; Ignoto Numine for Piano Trio. *Memberships:* National Officer, American Women Composers, 1981-85, 1988-; Member, Board of Directors, League of Composers, ISCM, 1975-78. *Honours:* NEA Composer Fellowships 1981, 1985; Sesquicentennial Award, University of Virginia, 1983, 1989; Meet the Composer Grants, 1979, 81, 85, 87, 88; New Jersey Arts Council Award, 1977-78. *Hobbies:* Swimming; Literature. *Address:* 113 Old Cabell Hall, University of Virginia, Charlottesville, VA 22903, USA.

ALLEN Learice Delorice, b. 15 July 1948, Chicago, USA. Manager. 1 son, 2 daughters. *Education:* AA, Business Education, 1975; BA, psychology, 1977; MA, Clinical Psychology, 1980. *Appointments:* Therapist, Bobby Wright Mental Health Centre, 1979-80; Therapist, Child and Adolescent Unit Community Mental Health Council, 1980-83; Associate Director, Community Mental Health Council, 1983-86; Victim Service Co- ordination, 1986-87; Manager, Mile Square Health Centre, 1987-88; Co-ordinator, Evangelical Health Systems, Inc, 1988-. *Memberships:* Illinois Coalition Against Sexual Assault, Board Member, Public Affairs Committee Member; Society for the Study of Traumatic Distress Disorder; Chicago Sexual Assault Network. *Honours:* Chicago Teacher Union Scholarship, 1975; Chicago State University Presidents List, 1977; Roosevelt University Scholar, 1978; Phi Beta Kappa. *Hobbies:* Reading; Dining; Aerobics. *Address:* 16603 S. Paulina, Markham, IL 60426, USA.

ALLEN Martha Leslie, b. 19 Feb. 1948, Chicago, Illinois, USA. Editor/Director. *Education:* BA, Oakland University, Rochester, 1969; MA 1978, PhD 1988, Howard University, Washington. *Appointments:* Staff, Southern Conference Educational Fund, Louisville, 1969-70; Organizer for the South, Operation Freedom, Memphis, 1971-75; Associate Director 1978-85, Director 1985-, Women's Institute for Freedom of the Press, Washington. *Publications:* Editor, Directory of Womens Media, 1975-; Editor, Celibate Woman Journal, 1982-88; Assoc Editor, Media Report to Women, 1976-83. *Memberships:* Board Member & Secretary, Women's Institute for Freedom of The Press, 1975-; Organization of American Historians; Coordinating committee on Women in the Historical Profession and Conference Group on Women's History. *Honours:* Black Belt, Tae Kwon Do, 1982; Black Belt, Ja Shin Do, 1983; Scholarship, Marion Davis Fund, Students for Social Justice and Peace, 1984-85; First degree Reiki Certification, 1987; Second degree Reiki Certification, 1987. *Hobbies:* Martial Arts; Reiki Healing Art; Political Activity (Peace & Justice Issues). *Address:* Women's Institute for Freedom of The Press, 3306 Ross Place, NW, Washington, DC 20008, USA.

ALLEN Randy Lee, b. 24 June 1946, Ithaca, New York, USA. Partner, Consulting Firm. 1 son. *Education:* BA, Physics, Cornell University, 1968; MBA Coursework, Seattle University. *Appointments:* Programmer, IBM, Endicott, 1968-69; Product & Industry Manager, Boeing Computer Services, Seattle, 1969-73; Director, Marketing, Androcor, 1973-76; Touche Ross, 1976-, Partner, 1981-. *Publications:* Point of Sales : Current Trends & Beyond, 1987; Bottom Line Issues in Retailing, 1984; POS Trends in the 80's, 1982; Management Development Series. *Memberships:* National Retail Merchants Association; American Management Association; Institute of Management

Consultants; Cornell University Alumni Association; etc. *Honour:* Academy of Women Achievers Award, YWCA of NY, 1984. *Hobbies:* Symphony; Art; Skiing; Stamp Collecting; Tennis; Travel. *Address:* Touche Ross & Co., 1633 Broadway, New York, NY 10019, USA.

ALLEN Susan Jean, b. 19 Jan. 1953 Pittsburgh, Pennsylvania, USA. Business Executive. *Education:* BA cum laude, Pennsylvania State University, 1974. *Appointments:* Production manager, account service, Korshak, Chinchar & Strickler Inc (now Korshak Hensley Associates), commercial art studio, 1974-78; President, Chinchar Visual Communication, illustration & design, advertising & marketing, 1978-81; Account Director, Baxter & Korge Inc, corporate image & advertising consulting, 1981-82; Manager, Corporate & Marketing Communications, Seiscom Delta Inc, 1982-85; Vice President, Account Executive, Wright Marketing Communications, 1985-. *Memberships include:* Officer of Chapter, District and International Boards, Numerous offices, International Association of Business Communicators (IABC); Committees, Space Business Roundtable; American Marketing Association. *Honours:* Awards, IABC Chapter Management, 1984; Excellence in Communiation Protrams, 1982, IABC; Silver Medal, Art Director' Club, Houston, 1982. *Hobbies:* Performing arts (dance, music, drama); Visual Arts; Travel. *Address:* 1338 Banks, Houston, Texas 77006, USA.

ALLEN Yvonne Griggs, b. 14 July 1951, Bolivar, Tennessee, USA. Career Level III Principal (K-8). 1 daughter. *Education:* BS, Lane College, 1973; MED 1975, MED45 1977, 21 Graduate Hours (Administration & Supervision), 1983, Memphis State University. *Appointments:* Jr Bookkeeper, Bendix After-Market Corp, 1973; Classroom Teacher 1973-79, Principal 1979-, Hardeman Co; Instructor (part-time) State Vocational school, 1977-. *Publication:* Non Financial Incentives to improve performance of Employees, research. *Memberships:* President, TN Assoc of Elem School Principals; National Assoc of Elem School Principals; President, West TN Assoc of Elem School Principals; Phi Delta Kappa Fraternity, Inc; Lane College National Alumni Assoc (Southern Regional Vice President). *Honours:* Principal of Leaders (one of ten in the Nation selected), 1988; Meritorious Service Award (Principal K-8), 1988; National Distinguished Principal, 1987; West Tennessee Black Heritage Award in Education, 1988; National Sorority of Phi Delta Kappa Inc, Achievement Award, 1986; Lane College Meritorious Award for Outstanding Achievement, 1980; Lane College United Negro College Fund Distinguished Leadership Award, 1987. *Hobbies:* Typing; Writing; Jogging. *Address:* Route 3, Box 565, Bolivar, TN 38008, USA.

ALLENDORFF S.b. 1 Oct. 1949, Federal Republic of Germany. Sociologist. m. Kurtis F. Johnson, 21 Dec. 1981, 1 son, 1 daughter. *Education:* BA, psychology, 1978; MA, 1981, PhD, 1988, Sociology. *Appointments:* Research Assistant, University of Illinois, 1980-82; Evaluation Assistant, Project Evaluator, Chicago Heart, 1983-84; Research Assistant, 1986-87. *Publications:* Articles in: Journal of School Health; The Chicago Fact Book. *Memberships:* Midwest Sociological Association; American Sociology Association. *Honours:* Foreign Student Tuition Waiver Award. *Hobbies:* Tennis; Politics; Women in Politics, at Work. *Address:* 112 E. Sinclair Dr., Tallahassee, FL 32312, USA.

ALLIES Victoria (Rossini), b. 27 May 1950, Southington, Connecticut, USA. Electronics Factory/ Process Design and Implementation Consultant. m. James M McCarron, 18 June 1980, 1 stepson, 2 stepdaughters. *Education:* Middlebury College, 1968-70; BA (Hons) 1972, MS 1979, University of Connecticut; MBA candidate, University of Phoenix, AZ 1980. *Appointments:* Adhesives Chemist 1972-76, Adhesives Technical Service Engineer 1976-78, Loctite Cpn, CT; Manager, Market Development, General Electric Co (Laminated Materials Department) 1978-79; Chemical Process Enginer, ITT Courier Terminal Systems Inc, Tempe AZ, 1980; Senior Chemical process

Engineer, Printed Circuit Board Start-up Team, Project Engineer, Environmental Enginering Supervisor, Digital Equipment Cpn, 1980-82; President and Founder, Training 'N' Technology Inc, Tempe, AZ, 1982-; has been named Technical Consultants to a 15 year Joint Venture Agreement among: SWC International, Vancouver, British Columbia; Zhuhai SEZ, People's Republic of China and Chinese Academy of Electronics Technology, Beijing; First Project is declared National Project Status. *Creative work:* Dry Film Photoresist Imaging, 1986. *Memberships include:* American Chemical Society, 1975-; American Electroplaters Society; Society for Women Engineers, Programmes Chairperson, 1980-82; American Soceity for Training and Development, 1982-; Technical Programmes Chairperson, Society for Manufacturing Engineers. *Honours:* Patentee, Temporary Bonding Adhesives; Life Instructor Certification, Arizona State Community Colleges; Named Industry Advisor to International Trade Committee of Arizona Chamber of Commerce. *Hobbies:* Photography; World-wide Travel. *Address:* Training 'N' Technology, Inc, 2121 W University Drive, Suite 123, Tempe, AZ 85281, USA

ALLINGTON Gloria Jean Ham, b. 21 May 1945, Northwood, North Dakota, USA. Educational Administrator. m. Gary F. Allington, 6 June 1966, divorced 1986. *Education:* BCS, 1976, MS, Ed., 1987, University of Miami, School of Medicine. *Appointments:* Staff Nurse, 1969-71, Associate Head Nurse, 1971-73, Jackson Memorial Hospital; Nurse Educator, 1973-75, Administrative Assistant, 1975-81, Assistant Director, Continuing Medical Education, 1981, Director, 1981-, University of Miami. *Memberships:* Society of Medical College Directors of Continuing Medical Education; Meeting Planners International. *Honours:* James W. Colbert Junior Award, 1977. *Hobbies:* Photography; Gourmet Cooking. *Address:* bb3University of Miami School of Medicine, PO Box 016960, D23-3, Miami, FL 33101, USA.

ALLISON Tomilea, b. 28 Mar. 1934, Madera, California, USA. Mayor of Bloomington, Indiana. m. James Allison, 1958. 2 daughters. *Education:* BA Sociology, Occidental College, Los Angeles, 1955; Postgraduate Sociology, Fresno State University, Fresno, California, 1956. *Appointment:* Mayor of Bloomington, Indiana, 1983-87. *Memberships:* League of Women Voters; Citizens for Good Government; Community Progress Council; Chamber of Commerce; Community Action Program Board. *Address:* 1127 East First Street, Bloomington, IN 47401, USA.

ALLNUTT Wendy, b. 1 May 1946, Lincoln, England. Actress. m. Colin McCormack, 16 Apr. 1968, 1 son, 1 daughter. *Education:* Elmhurst Ballet School, 1959-62; Central School of Speech & Drama, 1963-66. *Appointments:* Nottingham Playhouse, 1967; Film: Oh What a Lovely War, 1968; When Eight Bells Toll, 1971; All Coppers Are, 1972; Royal Shakespeare Company, 1973; The Regiment, BBC TV, Rough Justice, BBC TV, Son of Man, BBC TV, Waters of the Moon, BBC TV; Appearances In: Man About the House, Doctor in Charge, Robin's Nest, The Citadel; Toured UK in Good Morning Bill, 1984; Tour with Old Vic to USA as Lady McDuff in Macbeth, 1984; Andy in Stepping Out; Jennifer in Sorry; Wendy in Dear John, 1987-88. *Address:* c/o Roger Carey, 64 Thornton Ave., London W4 1QQ, England.

ALMAGUER Regina Zappala, b. 5 Nov. 1952, Berkeley, California, USA. Arts Administrator/Curator. m. Michael Rene Almaguer, 15 Aug. 1981. *Education:* BA, Anthropology, San Francisco State University, California, 1975; Certificate of Specialization, L'Universita dell'Arte, Florence, Italy, 1977; MA, Art History, University of California at Davis, 1981. *Appointments:* Administrative Assistant, Triton Museum of Art, Santa Clara, California, 1981-83; Curator, Art in Public Places, San Francisco Arts Commission, 1983-; Curator, Art in Public Places Programme, San Francisco International Airport; Freelance Curator and Public Art Consultant.

Publication: Art in Public Places, San Francisco International Airport, 1989. *Memberships:* Board of Directors, Berkeley Art Center, Vice-President 1988-89; Art Table; National Association of Museum Exhibitors; Alfa Romeo Association, Northern California Chapter. *Hobbies:* Art; Gardening; Gourmet cooking; Boxing; Historical automobiles. *Address:* 2415 Seventh Street, Berkeley, CA 94710, USA.

ALMOND Joan, b. 19 May 1934, Brooklyn, New York, USA. Associate Chemistry Instructor. m.(1)Randall Field, 15 Nov. 1952, divorced 1972, 5 sons, 1 daughter. (2)Bransford Wayne Almond, 9 Dec. 1986. *Education:* Erasmus Hall High School, Brooklyn, 1952. *Appointments:* Secretary, Fulton Savings Bank, Brooklyn, 1952-53; Manager, Reproduction Dept., Air Pre-heater Corp, Wellsville, 1958; Chemistry technician, Fibers Div, Allied Chem, Hopewell, 1963-76; Chemistry Technician, Virginia Power Co, North Anna Power Station, Mineral, 1976-86; Associate Chemistry Instructor, Nuclear Power Plant, 1987-. *Membership:* Women of the Moose, Chair-Mooseheart Hopewell Chapter, 1971. *Honours:* Basic Instructor Training/ Certification program, 1987; 3 year Advanced Instructor Training/Certification Program in 17 months, 1988; Certificate of Achievement, National Academy for Nuclear Training, 1988. *Hobbies:* Gardening, flowers in particular; Swimming; Fishing. *Address:* Route 1, Box 2160, Bumpass, VA 23024, USA.

ALTA b. 22 May 1942, Reno, Nevada, USA. Poet; Publisher. m. (1)Dan Bosserman, 26 May 1962, div. 1967, 2 daughters. (2)John Oliver Simon, 1 Oct. 1967, div. 1970. *Education:* Lastro Valley High School, California. *Appointments:* Founder and Publisher, Shameless Hussy Press, 1969-; Poetry Teacher, University of California Extension; Magazine Journalism, Maybeck High School. *Publications:* 12 books including: Momma: A start on all the Untold Stories; True Story; I am not a practicing Angel; The Shameless Hussy, etc. *Membership:* Before Columbus Foundation. *Honour:* American Book Award, 1981. *Hobbies:* Swimming; Hiking; Playing video games; Travel. *Address:* Box 5540, Berkeley, CA 94705, USA.

ALTER Joanne Hammerman, b. 3 July 1927, Chicago, USA. Commissioner, Water Reclamation District of Greater Chicago. m. James M. Alter, 17 May 1952, 2 sons, 2 daughters. *Education:* BA, cum Laude, Mount Holyoke College, 1949. *Appointments:* Commissioner, Metropolitan Water Reclamation District, elected 1972, re-elected 1978, 1984-. *Publications:* Articles in magazines; etc. *Memberships:* Board Member, Woman's Board, Art Institute of Chicago; Friends of Chicago River; Bright New City; Contemporary Art Workshop; etc. *Honours:* Audubon Service Award, 1979; Operation Lakewatch Award, 1982; Chicago Women's Hall of Fame, 1988. *Hobbies:* Skiing; Hiking; Sailing. *Address:* Metropolitan Sanitary District, 100 East Erie Street, Chicago, IL 60611, USA.

ALVAREZ Helen Holguin, b. 9 Jan. 1927, El Paso, Texas, USA. Teacher; Educator; Consultant. m. Edward Alvarez, Sr, 14 Nov. 1948. 3 sons, 1 daughter. *Education:* AA, Rio Hondo College, Whittier, 1975; BA 1979, MA 1981, Pacific Oaks College, Pasadena; UCLA and Cal State, Los Angeles, 1983; Adult Education Credential, 1987; Child Development Programs Teaching Credential. *Appointments:* Home Care for Children with Special Needs, 1952-72; Teacher, Mt View School District, El Monte, 1972-; Teacher, ESL and Amnesty Classes, El Monte High School (Evenings), 1983-87; Instructor and Consultant, Pacific Oaks College, Pasadena; Guided Study, Statewide, 1988-. *Memberships:* California Teachers Association; National Education Association, 1972-; Latin Americans Teacher's Organization. *Honours:* Mable Wilson grant to attend Pacific Oaks College; Certificate of Achievement in Early Childhood Education, Rio Hondo College; Building Rep for Teacher's District Bargaining Unit. *Hobbies:* Music; Dancing; Attending good plays; Reading. *Address:* 12636 Bonwood Road, El Monte, California 91732, USA.

AMADIO Bari Ann, b. 26 Mar. 1949, Philadelphia, Pennsylvania, USA. President & CEO, Food equipment fabricator. m. Peter Colby Amadio, MD, 24 June 1973. 1 son, 1 daughter. *Education:* BA, Psychology, University of Miami, 1970; Diploma in Nursing, Johnston-Willis School of Nursing, 1974; BSN (Nursing), Northeastern University, Boston, 1977; MS Nursing, Boston University, 1978; JD (Law), University of Bridgeport, 1983. *Appointments:* Nursing Faculty, Johnston-Willis School of Nursing, Virginia, 1974; Staff/Charge Nurse, Massachusetts General Hospital, Boston, 1975; Nursing Faculty, New England Deaconess School of Nursing, Boston, 1978-80; Nursing Faculty, Lankenau School of Nursing, Philadelphia, 1980-81; Legal Researcher, O'Brien Law Firm, Rochester, 1984; President & CEO, Original Metals, Inc, Philadelphia, 1985-. *Memberships:* Women's Association of the Minnesota Orchestra, newsnotes editor, 1984-86, Treasurer 1986, President 1987-; Rochester Friends of the Minneapolis Institute of Arts, vice president of arrangements, 1988-; Zumbro Valley Medical Society Association, Chairman of Finance, 1986, treasurer 1988-; American Society of Law & Medicine; Sigma Theta Tau; Phi Alpha Delta Law Fraternity; National Association of Food Equipment Manufacturers; National Association of Female Executives. *Hobbies:* Fencing; Equestrian sports; Painting; Writing; Playing piano and autoharp; Dance. *Address:* 816 9th Avenue SW, Rochester, Minnesota 55902, USA.

AMATEA Ellen Sherlock, b. 22 Apr. 1944, Apalachicola, Florida, USA. Family Therapist. m. Frank Charles Amatea. 2 sons. *Education:* BS, Psychology, Colorado State University, 1964; MS 1966, PhD 1972, Florida State University. *Appointments:* Counselor 1968-70, Research Assoc 1972-74, Florida State University; Assistant Professor 1974-84, Associate Professor Department of Counselor Education 1984-, University of Florida. *Publications:* Books: Brief Strategic Intervention for School Behavior Problems, 1989; Numerous research articles and monographs. *Memberships:* American Assoc for Counseling & Development; Amer Assoc for Marriage and Family Therapy; National Council for Family Relations. *Hobbies:* Reading; Quilting; Boy scouting. *Address:* Dept of Counselor Education, University of Florida, Gainesville, FL 32671, USA.

AMATO Carol Joy, b. 9 Apr. 1944, Portland, Oregon, USA. Writer; Environmental Anthropologist. m. Neville S Motts, 26 Aug. 1967, divorced. 1 son, 1 daughter. *Education:* BA, Spanish & French, University of Portland, Oregon, 1966; MA, Anthropology, California State University, Fullerton, 1986. *Appointments:* President, Systems Research Analysis, Inc, 1980-; Freelance Writer, 1973-. *Publications:* Short Stories: You're Only Old Once, 1975; The Secret of Wentworth House, 1975. Book Review: Colonies in Space, 1977. *Contributions to:* Over 50 articles in professional journals including: Menagerie; Speculative Anthropology; Anthro Perspectives; Cultural Futuristics; Oasis News; Space Shuttle External Tank Habitability Study; Communique; Mac D Vision. *Memberships:* American Institute of Aeronautics and Astronautics; Charter 100; Human Factor Society; Independent Writers of Southern California; Society for Technical Communication; Writer's Club of Whittier, Inc; Coalition Concerned with Adolescent Pregnancy, Board Member; Orange County Academic Decathlon, Board Member; Orange County Chamber of Commerce. *Honours:* Distinguished Leadership Award, 1988. *Hobbies:* Photography; Horses; Tap Dancing; Racquetball; Collecting Books; Interior Design. *Address:* 10151 Heather Court, Westminster, CA 92683, USA.

AMATOS Barbara Hansen, b. 30 Aug. 1944, Toledo, Ohio, USA. Fiscal Officer. m. (1)James D Mokren, 12 Sept. 1964. (2)David M Amatos, 27 Dec. 1974. 1 son, 1 daughter. *Education:* BSc, Business Admin, Franklin University, Columbus, Ohio. *Appointments:* Payroll Manager, City of Columbus, 1983-86; Auditor of State of Ohio, Management Advisory Services, 1986-87; Fiscal Officer, Amatos & Amatos, CPA's, McGuiness

Amatos Properties (Partnership), 1987-. *Memberships:* American Institute CPA's, AICPA; Association of Government Accountants, AGA. *Honour:* Certified Public Accountant, State of Ohio, 1984. *Address:* Auditor of State of Ohio, 88E Broad Street, Columbus, Ohio 43212, USA.

AMBROSE Alice, b. 25 Nov. 1906, Lexington, Illinois, USA. Professor retired. m. Morris Lazerowitz, 15 June 1938. *Education:* AB, Millikin University, 1928; MA 1929, PhD 1932, University of Wisconsin; PhD, Cambridge University, 1938. *Appointments:* University of Michigan, 1935-37; On Faculty of Smith College, 1937-72; Sophia and Austin Smith Professor of Philosophy, 1964-72; Visiting Professor of Philosophy, Hampshire College, 1977, 1979, 1981; Distinguished Visiting Professor of Philosophy, University of Delaware, 1975; Cowling Professor of Philosophy, Carleton College, 1979. *Publications:* Essays in Analysis, 1966; With M Lazerowitz: Fundamentals of Symbolic Logic, revised edition, 1962; Logic: The Theory of Formal Inference, revised edition, 1972; Philosophical Theories, 1976; Necesidad y Filosofia, 1985; Essays in the Unknown Wittgenstein, 1984; Necessity and Language, 1985. Co-editor and contributor (with M Lazerowitz), G E Moore. Essays in Retrospect, 1970; Ludwig Wittgentsein. Philosophy and Language, 1972; Editor, Wittgentstein's Lectures, Cambridge, 1932-35, 1979. *Memberships:* American Philosophical Association; Vice President, 1968, President 1974-75, American Philosophical Association (Eastern Division); Association for Symbolic Logic, 1953-68. *Honours:* LLD, Millikin University, 1958; Merit Award, 1986. *Address:* 126 Vernon Street, Northampton, MA 01060, USA.

AMES, Ruth Margaret, b. 8 Dec. 1918, New York City, USA. Professor. m. Anthony Gelber, 8 Apr. 1938, 3 sons, 2 daughters. *Education:* BA, Hunter College, 1940; MA, 1942, PhD, 1950, Columbia University. *Appointments:* Fellow, Tutor, Instructor, Hunter College, 1940-52; Professor, Queensborough Community College, City University, 1968-. *Publications:* Books: The Fulfillment of the Scriptures, Abraham, Moses and Piers Plowman, 1970; God's Plenty : Chaucer's Christian Humanism, 1984; articles on Chaucer & Langland. *Memberships:* MLA; New Chaucer Society; Newman Centre. *Honours:* Lisette Fisher Fellowship, Columbia University, 1949; Mellon Fellowship, City University of New York, 1980. *Hobbies:* Art History; Swimming; Grandchildren. *Address:* Queensborough Community College, City University of New YOrk, Bayside, NY 11364, USA.

AMONSON Johanne Leslie, b. 28 Mar, 1949, Edmonton, Alberta, Canada. Barrister; Solicitor. m., 6 Mar. 1981, 1 son. *Education:* BA, 1970, Teaching Certificate, 1971, University of Oregon, Eugene, Oregon, USA, 1970; LLB, University of Alberta, Edmonton, Canada, 1977; Called to Bar, 1977. *Appointments:* Teacher, Staatliche Realschule Nurnberg, Federal Republic of Germany, 1972-73; Exhibitions Registrar, Glenbow Museum, Calgary, Alberta, Canada, 1973-74; Partner, Peterson Ross, Edmonton, Alberta, currently; Sessional Instructor, Wills, Faculty of Law, University University of Alberta, 1987-88; Retirement and wills seminars. *Publications:* Administration of Estates for Legal Secretaries I, 1981, Updated, 1986; Administration of Estates II for Secretaries and Paralegals, 1982; Administration of Estates for Paralegals and Senior Secretaries, 1983; Papers: Proof in Solemn Form, 1984; Guarantees and Estates, 1984; Problems in Proof in Solemn Form, 1987. *Memberships:* Law Society of Alberta (Mentor, Wills & Estates); Canadian Bar Association, Alberta Branch (Chairman, Wills/Estates Section, 1987-88, former Vice-Chairman and Secretary/Treasurer, Wills & Trusts Section, Northern Alberta, Council and Executive Member, 1986-88, Coordinator, Northern Sections, 1986, 1987, 1988; International Commission of Jurists; International Bar Association; Edmonton Bar Association. *Honours:* Queen Elizabeth Scholarship, 1966; Dean's List and Foreign Student Scholarship, University of Oregon, 1967-68, 1969-70; Law Review, University of Alberts,

1975-77. *Hobbies:* Reading; Camping; Hiking; Travel; Figure- skating; Downhill skiing; Gardening; Sailing. *Address:* Peterson Ross, Barristers and Solicitors, 2700 CN Tower, 10004 104 Avenue, Edmonton, Alberta, Canada T5J OK1.

AMOR Anne Clark, b. 4 Feb. 1933, London, England. Author. m. Abdallah Amor, 23 Feb. 1982, 1 son, 1 daughter. *Education:* Honours Degree, English, London University. *Publications:* Beasts & Bawdy, 1975; Lewis Carroll: A Biography, 1979; The Real Alice, 1981; Mrs Oscar Wilde : A Woman of Some Importance, 1983; Madame Oscar Wilde: Une Femme Face au Scandale, 1984; contributor to: The New Book of Knowledge, 1988. *Memberships:* Lewis Carroll Society; Beatrix Potter Society. *Honours:* FWLA. *Hobbies:* Literature; Book Collecting; Antiques; Travel; Foreign Languages. *Address:* 16 Parkfields Avenue, London NW9 7PE, England.

AMORETTI Maria, b. 16 Nov. 1948, Costa Rica. University Professor; Lecturer; Author; Critic. m. Carlos Salazar, 26 June 1971, 2 sons. *Education:* Degree, Spanish Philology, University of Costa Rica, 1973; Doctorate, Hispanic-American Studies, University of Montpellier, France, 1982. *Appointments:* Assistant Director, Director, Philology School, 1978-79; Director, Journal of Arts & Letters, 1983-85; Member, University Council, 1985-80. *Publications:* Under the Singing, an Analysis of the National Anthem; Introduction to Sociotext; several articles in professional journals. *Memberships:* Costa Rican Association of Philology; Instituto Literario y Cultural Hispanico. *Honours:* Carlos Gagini Prize, Research, 1984. *Hobbies:* Cooking; Travel. *Address:* 738 Moravia, San Jose, Cosa Rica, Central America.

AMUNSON Patricia Ann, b. 26 May 1955, Iaeger, West Virginia, USA. Learning Disabilities Teacher. m. Dale Gene Amunson, 8 July 1978. 1 daughter. *Education:* AS Elementary Education, Cumberland Co College, 1976; BA, Special Education, Glassboro State College, 1978; MS, Special Education, Eastern Montana College, 1987. *Appointments:* Teacher, Orthopaedically Handicapped Children, 1978-80; Teacher, Learning Disabled Children, 1980-; Instructor, University of Wyoming, 1981-. *Publications:* Chapter One Handbooks for Parents and Teachers in State of Wyoming; Parents Guide to Learning Disabilities; Effective Schools and Effective Teaching. *Memberships:* Council for Exceptional children; Association for Supervision and Curriculum Development; Board of Directors for Epilepsy Foundation of America; Director of Very Special Arts Festival in State of Wyoming. *Honours:* Certified Trainer of TESA (Teacher Expectations for Student Achievement), USA, 1988; Summa cum laude, 1987; Teacher of Year Finalist, Wyoming, 1986; Outstanding Young Woman of America, 1985; Danced with Hearing Impaired children at White House for Mrs Reagan, Washington DC, 1984. *Hobbies:* Stamp and coin collecting; Photography; Crewel embroidery and cross-stitching; Candlewicking and quilting; Camping; Fishing; Reading. *Address:* 415 N Miller, Gillette, WY 82716, USA.

ANAND-SRIVASTAVA Madhu B., b. India. Research Scientist; Assistant Professor. m. Ashok K. Srivastva, 17 Feb. 1978, 2 daughters. *Education:* MSc, Delhi University, 1972; PhD, University of Manitoba, Canada, 1978. *Appointments:* Postdoctoral Fellow, Department of Physiology, Valderbilt University, Tennessee, USA, 1978-80; Senior Investigator, Clinical Research Institute, Montreal, Canada, 1982-. *Publications:* Various scientific articles & chapters, cellular regulation in cardiovascular system. *Memberships:* International Society for Heart Research; Canadian Biochemical Society; American Society for Pharmacology & Experimental Therapeutics; American Society for Biochemistry & Molecular Biology; Canadian Hypertension Society; Indian Academy of Neurosciences. *Honours:* Scholar, Canadian Heart Foundation, 1982-88; Member, Editorial Board: Molecular and Cellular Bichemistry, 1989; External reviewer, several professional journals; External member, grants review committee Canadian Heart Foundation, Grants, Scholarships Review committee Medical Research Council of Canada. *Hobby:* Reading. *Address:* Clinical Research Institute, 110 Pine Avenue West, Montreal, Quebec, Canada H2W 1R7.

ANDERS Barbara Lynne, b. 4 Sept. 1938, Jackson, Mississippi, USA. Professional Singer. m. The Hon Dan R Anders, 9 Mar. 1957. 2 daughters. *Education:* Voice Scholarship to Belhaven College, 1956. *Appointments:* Leading roles with American Light Opera, 1965 and 1967; Washington Civic Opera Assoc, 1968; The Friends of Opera, 1970-73; The Washington Opera, 1971-78; New York City Opera, 1972; The Wolf Trap Opera Co, 1972-79; Orchestra appearances from 1973-81; Recitals, 1981-87, including Lincoln Center, New York. *Memberships:* Pres, DC Fed of Music Clubs, 1978-80; America Opera Scholarship Society, 1980-81; The Friday Morning Music Club, DC, 1983-; Opera Chairman, Nat Fed of Music Clubs, 1983-87; Fairfax Co Alliance of Professional & Executive Women's Network; Scholarship Advisory Committee, National Federation of Music Clubs. *Honours:* Certificate of Appreciation, Goodwill Industries; Representative, Nat Music Council as part of a People-to-People Goodwill Tour to the Scandinavian Countries and Russia. *Hobbies:* Collecting dolls and costumes. *Address:* 3216 Prince William Drive, Fairfax, VA 22031, USA.

ANDERSEN Alice Evelyn Klopstad, b. 12 Apr. 1912, Union County, South Dakota, USA. Administrative Assistant, Congressman Carlos J Moorhead, California. m. Daniel J Andersen, 28 June 1937. 1 daughter. *Education:* University of South Dakota, 1929-30; AB, George Washington University, Washington, 1941. *Appointments:* Secretary, Prudential Life Insurance Company, South Falls, South Dakota, 1931; Secretary, Home Owners Loan Corporation, Sioux Falls, 1932-33; Secretary, US Senator William J Bulow, 1934-43; Clerk, US Senate Civil Service Committee; Executive Secretary, Religious Heritage of America, Washington, 1961-64; Administrative Assistant, Congressman H Allen Smith, 20th District of California, 1966-72; Administrative Assistant, Congressman Carlos J Moorhead, 22nd District of California, 1973-. *Memberships:* American News Womens' Club; Governing Board, General Alumni Association of George Washington University; Vice President, Columbia Women of George Washington University; US House of Representatives Administrative Assistants Association; Vice President, Dr O E Howe Foundation for Unfortunate Girls, Inc; President, Board of Managers, Florence Crittenton Home and Hospital; Vice President, George Washington University Women's Hospital Board; Co-chairman, American Cancer Crusade; Executive Women in Government; Republican Women's Federal Forum. *Honour:* Special Service Award, George Washington University General Alumni Association, 1967. *Hobbies:* Grandchildren; Music. *Address:* 4441 Lowell Street, NW, Washington, DC 20016, USA.

ANDERSEN Betty Margaret, b. 9 Aug. 1930, Sydney, Australia. Academic Dean. *Education:* RN, 1949-52; RM, 1953; Diploma, Nursing Education, 1967; BA, 1974; MA, Honours, Ed., 1978. *Appointments:* Clinical Nurse, Senior Tutor, Bangladesh, 1958-66; Nurse Educator, Curriculum Office, 1968-77; Researcher, Foundation, Head, Dept. of Health Studies, Newcastle C.A.E., 1977-84; Foundation Dean, School of Nursing & Health Studies, 1984-; foundation Professor of Nursing, University of Western Sydney, Macarthur 1989. *Publications:* Basic Nurse Ed. Curriculum Report incorporating Research in Judgment Making, 1976; Problem Based Curriculum for Diploma at Applied Sc. (Nursing), 1984. *Memberships:* Australian Baptist Missionary Scociety, Board; Newcastle Regional Nurse Training Council; South Western Sydney Regional Area Health Board. *Honours:* Member, Order of Australia, 1986. *Hobbies:* Photography; Stamp & Coin Collecting; Poetry; Gardening; Swimming; Golf. *Address:* 58 Springfield Road, Catherine Field, NSW 2171, Australia.

ANDERSEN Susan M, b. 6 June 1955, Santa Monica, California, USA. Professor of Psychology. *Education:* BA Psychology, University of California, Santa Cruz; PhD, Psychology, Stanford University, California. *Appointments:* Graduate Researcher, Stanford University, 1977-81; Professor of Psychology, University of California, Santa Barbara, 1981-87; Professor of Psychology, New York University, 1987-. Reviewer for various professional journals. *Publications:* Numerous published articles and book chapters on the nature of self-knowledge, Socialcognition, sex-role stereotypes and psychopathology, including Sex typing and androgyny in dyadic interaction: Individual differences in responsiveness to physical attractiveness, 1981, with S L Bem; Induced hearing deficit generates experimental paranoia, with P G Zimbardo and L G Kabat, 1981; Self-knowledge and social inference: The diagnosticity of cognitive/affective and behavioural data, 1984; Cognitive/affective reactions in the improvement of self-esteem: When thoughts and feelings make a difference with M Williams, 1985; The role of cultural assumptions in self-concept development, 1986; Traits and social stereotypes: Levels of categorization in person perception, with R L Klatzky; Anticipating undesired outcomes: The role of outcome certainty in the onset of depressive affect. *Memberships:* American Psychological Association; American Association for the Advancement of Science. *Honours:* National Danforth Finalist, 1977; Finalist, Annual Dissertation Award, Society for Experimental Social Psychology, 1982; Grant, National Institute of Mental Health, 1984-87; Harold J Plous Award, University of California, Santa Barbara, 1986. *Hobbies:* Playing flute and guitar; Singing; Listening to jazz; Sculpturing; Cross-country skiing. *Address:* Department of Psychology, New York University, 6 Washington Place 4th Floor, New York, NY 10003, USA.

ANDERSON Adele Konkel, b. 25 Jan. 1949, Winona, Minnesota, USA. Attorney. m. David S, 26 May 1984. *Education:* BA, English, St Mary College, 1971; JD, Washington University School of Law, 1981. *Appointments:* High School English Teacher, Salina, Kansas, 1971-73; Goodland, Kansas, 1974-75; District Magistrate Judge, Goodland, 1975-78; Attorney at Law, Pueblo, 1981-; Judicial Performance Commission, 1989-. *Memberships:* Pueblo County Bar Association, various offices; Pueblo Chamber of Commerce; Bar of Colorado Supreme Court; US District Court. *Honours:* Olin Fellowship, Monticello Foundation, 1978-81; Outstanding Young Lawyer, Pueblo County Bar Association, 1985. *Hobbies:* Gardening; Reading; Music. *Address:* Preston, Altman, et al., 501 Thatcher Building, Pueblo, CO 81003, USA.

ANDERSON Dame Judith, b. 10 Feb. 1898, Adelaide, Australia. Actress. m. (1) Professor B H Lehmann, 1937 divorced 1939. (2) Luther Greene, 1946 divorced 1950. *Education:* Norwood High School. *Career:* Stage debut in A Royal Divorce, Theatre Royal, Sydney, 1951; Went to New York, 1918. *Creative Works:* Stage appearances include: the Dove; Behold the Bridegroom; Strange Interlude; Mourning becomes Electra; Come of Age; The Old Maid; Hamlet; Macbeth; Family Portrait; Tower Beyond; Three Sisters; Medea; The Seagull; The Oresteia. Films: Rebecca; Edge of Darkness; Laura; King's Row; Spectre of the Rose; The Red House; Pursued; Tycoon; Cat on a Hot Tin Roof; Macbeth; Don't Bother to Knock; A Man Called Horse; Star Trek III. Television: The Chinese Prime Minister, 1974. *Address:* 808 San Ysidro Lane, Santa Barbara, CA 93103, USA.

ANDERSON Daphne, b. 27 Apr. 1922, London, England. Actress. *Education:* Kensington High School. *Career:* Stage debut in pantomime chorus, 1937; Screen debut in Trottle True, 1948. *Creative works:* Films include: Cloudburst; Beggar's Opera; Hobson's Choice; A Kid for Two Farthings; The Prince and the Showgirl; No Time for Tears; Snowball; Stork Talk; Captain Clegg; The Launching; I Want What I Want. Television: Silas Marner (serial); Gideon's Way (serial); Dr Finlay's

Casebook; Happy Family; The Imposter; The Harry Worth Show; The Whitehall Worrier; The Suede Jacket; Casanove; Haunted Series; Thirty Minute Theatre; Justice is a Woman; Paul Temple; Today; Z Cars.

ANDERSON Derrir Norah, Lady, b. 5 Aug. 1916, Derby, England. Housewife. m. Lt.Col. Richard Meville Anderson, 23 Dec. 1942, 2 sons. *Memberships:* Area President, BSPS; MPS; President, WJRC. *Hobbies:* Breeding Horses & Dogs; Hunting; Coursing. *Address:* Tarrale Keynston House, Blandford, Dorset, England.

ANDERSON Doris Elaine, b. 6 Nov. 1934, Elkhart, Indiana, USA. Attorney. *Education:* B.Mus., University of Michigan, 1956; JD, University of California, 1964. *Appointments:* Attorney, Fireboard Corporation, 1965-79; General Counsel: International Diamond Corporation, 1980-83, Kaiser-Crebs Mgt. Corp., 1983-85; Assistant Secretary & Counsel, AMFAC Inc., 1985-. *Memberships:* State Bar of California; American Society of Corporate Secretaries. *Hobbies:* Music; Tennis; Golf. *Address:* AMFAC Inc, 44 Montgomery St, San Francisco, CA 94104, USA.

ANDERSON Doris H., b. 10 Nov. 1925, Calgarry, Alberta, Canada. Journalist; Novelist. m. 24 May 1957, 3 sons. *Education:* BA, 1945. *Appointments:* Toronto Star Weekly, 1945; Eaton's, 1946-50; Various positions, 1951-57, Editor, 1957-77, Chatelaine Magazine; Canadian Advisory Council, 1978-80; Toronto Star, 1984-. *Publications:* Two Women (novel), 1978; Rough Layout (novel), 1982; Affairs of State, 1988. *Memberships:* President, National Action Committee, 1982-84; Board Member, York University, 1971-79; Institute on Research on Public Policy; Director, Maclean-Hunter Publishers and Macmillans Publishers, 1972-77; Board of Canadian Film Development Corporation, 1974-79; Board of Ontario Press Council, 1977-85. *Honours:* B'nai Brith Scholarship, 1942; History Prize, University of Alberta, 1942; Officer, Order of Canada, 1974; Hall of Fame, Canadian Press Council, 1981; Constance C. Hamilton Award, City of Toronto, 1981; YWCA Award, 1981. *Hobbies:* Antiques; Theatre. *Address:* Toronto Star, 1 Yonge Street, Toronto, Ontario, Canada.

ANDERSON Flavia (Lady), b. 20 Sept. 1910, Chorley Wood, England. m. Alasdair Anderson of Tullichewan, Nov. 1933. 1 son, 1 daughter. *Publications:* Keep Thy Wife; Jezebel and the Dayspring; The Ancient Secret; How to be a Deb's Mum; The Rebel Emperor; The Ancient Secret, Fire from the Sun. *Honour:* Medaille de Vermeil de la Reconnaissance Française, 1945. *Interests:* Portraits & wild life paintings by my son, Douglas Anderson; Crarae Garden in Argyll. *Address:* 13 Carlton Terrace, Edinburgh EH7, Scotland.

ANDERSON Gwendolynn Easson, b. 9 Apr. 1935, Montreal, Canada. Elementary School Teacher. m. Quentin Duane Anderson, 18 June 1960, 2 sons, 1 daughter. *Education:* BEd, National College of Education, 1957; MA, Education, University of North Alabama, USA, 1987. *Appointments:* Elementary teacher, 2nd Grade: Long Beach Public Schools, California, USA, 1957-59; Kenilworth Public Schools, Illinois, 1959-60; Fayetteville, Arkansas, 1960-61; Los Angeles, California, 1960-63; Shawnee Mission, Kansas, 1972-78; Athens, Alabama, 1979-. *Memberships:* National, & Alabama, Education Associations; Parliamentarian, Athens Education Association. *Honours:* Phi Delta Kappa, 1986-; Biographical recognition. *Hobbies:* Travel; Reading. *Address:* 104 Ridgelawn Drive, Athens, Alabama 35611, USA.

ANDERSON Janice Linn, b. 2 Sept. 1943, Henry County, Tennessee, USA. Real Estate Brokerage Assistant; Management Secretary; Executive Administration Coordinator; Property Researcher. *Education:* Graduate, E W Grove High School, Paris, Tennessee, 1961. *Appointments:* Real Estate Brokerage Assistant, Management Secretary, Executive Administration Coordinator; Property Researcher, J G Martin, Jr/Caudill Properties Inc., 1978-; Director of Leasing & Management, Fortune-Nashville Company, 1976-78; Property Management Assistant, Dobson & Johnson, Inc., 1974-76; Computer Operator/Assistant to Vice President, Medicare Administration/Equitable, 1973-74; Medical Transcriptionist/Insurance Processor, The Paris Clinic, 1965-73; Entertainer/Recording Artist, 4 Sons Recording Company, 1958-73. *Memberships:* Organizational: International Platform Association; National Association of Female Executives; Business and Professional Women's Club, President, 1968; Professional Musician Union; REALTORS Secretaries Association; Community: Citizen's Advisory Council - American Institute for Cancer Research; American Red Cross; M.A.D.D.; Causa U.S.A. Association; Christian Appalachian Project; Cancer Association of Tennessee. *Honours:* Honorary Appointment, Research Board of Advisors, American Biographical Institute, Inc. *Hobbies:* Camping; Guitar; Do It Yourself Projects. *Address:* 812 Elissa Drive, Nashville, TN 37217, USA.

ANDERSON Lois M., b. 1 Jan. 1927, Milwaukee, Wisconsin, USA. Artist; Librarian. *Education:* Wisconsin State College, Milwaukee, 1949; MLS, University of California, Berkeley, 1960. *Appointments include:* Director of Libraries: Larkspur School District 1962-69, Lagunitas School District 1970-75, California; Reference Librarian, Sausalito Public Library, 1983-. *Creative work includes:* Assemblage sculpture artist, 1970-; Works included, permanent collection, Oakland Museum; Exhibited widely, San Francisco Bay area. *Honours:* Visual fellowship grant, National Endowment for Arts, 1978; Grant, Art Matters Inc, New York, 1989. *Hobbies:* Art; Reading; Gardening. *Address:* 50 Catalpa, Mill Valley, California 94941, USA.

ANDERSON Lorna Kathryn Honley, b. 9 May 1942, Harrisonville, Missouri, USA. Supervisor. m. Thomas J. Anderson, 5 Mar. 1962, 2 sons. *Education:* BA, University of Northern Colorado, 1972; MPA, (Master of Public Administration), University of Missouri, Kansas City, 1989. *Appointments:* Deputy Recorder of Deeds, Cass County, 1966-68; Social Security Administration, Mid-America Programme Service Centre & Benefit Authoriser, 1973-77; Recovery Reviewer, 1977-80; Claims Authorizer, 1980-88; Assistant Module Manager, 1988-. *Memberships:* American Association of University Women, Past President, Independence MO Branch; Sigma Sigma Sigma; Citizens for Effective Leadership, Missouri Federation of Women's Clubs. *Honours:* Listed in Central Missouri State University Hall of Recognition, 1961; 500 Named Gift by Independence MO Branch American Association of University Women; Recipient, various other honours & awards. *Hobbies:* Writing; Walking; Reading. *Address:* 3924 Crackerneck Road, Independence, MO 64055, USA.

ANDERSON Lucinda K, b. 25 Mar. 1941, Dell Rapids, USA. Country Club Manager. m. Lauren Anderon, 18 June 1965, divorced 1975, 1 daughter. *Education:* BS, University of South Dakota, 1963; MEd.,1969, Certification in Special Education, 1971; M.Ed., 1978, South Dakota State University. *Appointments:* PE Teacher, Des Moines, 1963-65; PE, History Teacher, Dell rapids Public School,1965-68; Augustana College Sioux Falls, 1968-71; Manager, Alamo Country Club. *Membership:* PEO; American Personnel and Guidance Association; AAUW; Kappa Delta Phi; International Platform Association. *Honours:* Oustanding Young Homemaker of the Year, 1959; Outstanding Senior PE Major, 1963; Who's Who in America; Who's Who Among American Women; Outstanding Physical Education Major, University of South Dakota. *Hobbies:* Golf; Cooking; Travel; People; Reading. *Address:* 5005 N. 4th Street, McAlln, TX 78504, USA.

ANDERSON Madelyn Klein, b. 9 May 1926, New York City, USA. Author, Young People's Books. m. Douglas Ray Anderson, 2 Jan. 1960 (dec. 1970), 1 son. *Education:* BA, Hunter College, 1951; Certificate,

Occupational Therapy, New York University, 1958; MLS, Pratt Institute Graduate School of Library & Information Science, 1974. *Appointments:* Chief Occupational Therapist, Beth Israel Hospital, NY, 1959-63; Director, Occupational Therapy, New York Infirmary, 1968-72; Editor, Simon & Schuster, 1974-83; Freelance Editor, Writer, 1984-. *Publications:* 10 books including: Iceberg Alley; Sea Raids & Rescues, US Coast Guard; Counting on You, US Census; Oil on Troubled Waters; Greenland, Island at Top of the World; New Zoos; Soviet Life: A View of the Peoples of USSR; Arthritis. *Membership:* Beta Phi Mu, honorary library society. *Hobbies:* Collecting, Rare Books, Antiques; Travel. *Address:* 80 North Moore Street, New York City, NY 10013, USA.

ANDERSON Marilyn Nelle, b. 5 May 1942, Las Animas, Colorado, USA. Educator. m. George Anderson, 3 Sept. 1974. 2 sons, 1 daughter. *Education:* BEd, Adams State College, 1962; MEd, Arizona State University, 1967; Postgraduate, Idaho State University, 1971, 1986, 1987; University of Idaho, 1986. *Appointments:* Teacher, Wendell, Idaho, School District No 232, 1962-66; Teacher, Union-Endicott, New York School District, 1967-68; School Counselor and Librarian, Yuma Colo. School District, R-S-1, 1968-69; Elementary School Counselor, American Falls, Idaho School District No 381, 1969-73; Project Director, Gooding Co., Idaho, Senior Citizens Organization, 1974-75; Teacher, Castleford, Idaho School District No 411, 1982-. *Memberships:* PTA, 1962-66 and 1967-68; NEA, 1962-73 and 1986-; Idaho Education Association, 1962-66, 1969-73 and 1986-; Public Relations Chairman, Secretary and Treasurer, Wendell Hub City Ed. Association, 1962-66; Union-Endicott Teachers Association, 1967-68; GSA Brownie Leader, 1967-68; Yuma Public Library Board, 1968-69; High Plains Reading Council, 1968-69; American Personnel & Guidance Association, 1969-73; American Falls Ed. Association, 1969-73; Memberships Chairman, Secretary, Treasurer, Idaho Personnel & Guidance Association, 1969-73; Secretary, Treasurer, Idaho School Counselors Association, 1971-73; Secretary, Treasurer, 1984-87, Castleford Teachers Association; Castleford Parent Teacher Youth Org. 1986-; Gooding County 4-H Leader, 1983-; Idaho Council International Reading Association; Magic Valley Reading Association, 1988-; International Platform Association. *Honours:* AAUP Scholastic Award, 1962; AWS Service Award, 1962; NDEA Institute, Elementary School Guidance and Counseling, 1966-67. *Hobbies:* Reading; Writing poems and short stories; Painting; Photography; Camping; Sewing; Geology. *Address:* Route 1, Box 293, Wendell, Idaho 83355, USA.

ANDERSON Marjorie Elizabeth, b. 13 May 1941, USA. Professor, Physiology. *Education:* BS, Michigan State University, 1963; PhD, University of Washington, 1969. *Appointments:* Senior Fellow, The Rockefeller University, 1969-71; Assistant Professor, Associate Professor, Professor, Rehabilitation Medicine and Physiology & Biophysics, University of Washington, 1971-. *Memberships:* American Physiological Society; Society for Neuroscience; American Congress of Rehab Medicine; New York Academy of Sciences; American Assoc for the Advancement of Science; American Head of Clinical Neurophysiology. *Address:* Department of Rehabilitation Medicine, University of Washington RJ-30, Seattle, WA 98195, USA.

ANDERSON Pamela Ann, b. 9 Feb. 1941, Grantham, Lincolnshire, England. Head Mistress. m. Colin Peter Odell Anderson, 30 July 1966. 1 son, 1 daughter. *Education:* Teaching Diploma, 1963; Advanced Diploma in Education, 1971; BEd (Hons), 1974. *Appointments:* Assistant Teacher, Sarson School for Girls, 1963-64; Head of Geography Department, St Hugh's Grantham, 1964-73; 2nd Deputy Head, William Robertson School, Welbourn, Lincolnshire, 1973-80; Founder, Owner and Head Mistress, Heathlands Preparatory School, Grantham, 1981-. *Membership:* United Kingdom Federation of Business & Professional Women. *Hobbies:* Porcelain painting; Dress design; Drawing; Painting.

Address: Endahna House, Somerby Hill, Grantham, Lincolnshire, England.

ANDERSON Pamela Reakoff, b. 30 Dec. 1951, Detroit, Michigan, USA. Nurse; Educator; Consultant. m. Edward Lee Anderson, 8 Apr. 1978. *Education:* BS Nursing, Ohio State University, 1974; MS Nursing Administration, George Mason University, 1983; Cert. Med College, Virginia, 1975; Certificate in Nursing Education, George Mason University, 1988. *Appointments:* Staff nurse in Psychiatry, Med Coll. Virginia, 1974; CCU, 1975-76; Staff Nurse, CCU, Washington Hosp. Ctr, 1976; Asst Head Nurse, 1976-77, Cardiovascular instr., 1977-81, Cons. GAO, Washington, 1983; Research Asst. George Mason University, Fairfax, 1983; Cons. clin. Nurse C & P Telephone Co, Silver Spring, 1984; Instructor, Mary Washington Hospital, Fredericksburg, 1984-85; Instructor, profl devel and research, Washington Hosp Ctr, 1985-87; Dir. educational services, cons. Health M Connection, Falls Church, Virginia, 1987-. *Memberships:* Choir Member, St Andrews Episcopal Church, Arlington, 1977-84; Altar guild, 1980-; Women's Club Scholar, 1970; American Heart Association (trainer Basic Cardiac Life Support Inst, 1977-; affiliate faculty member, 1979-; instructor, Adv. Cardiac Life Support 1979-.); American Nurses Association; American Soc Health, Education and Training; American Association Critical Care Nurses; American Nurses Found Century Club (charter); Ohio State University Alumni Association; The Nightengale Society (Board of Regents); American Biographical Institute (life); Sigma Theta Tau. *Honours:* Certificate of Appreciation, American Heart Association, 1981; Distinguished member award, Education and Training 1987, Outstanding member award, President, (1988) Education and Training 1988 American Soc Health. *Hobbies:* Skiing; Sailing. *Address:* 2048 Hopewood Dr, Falls Church, VA 22043, USA.

ANDERSON Shirley Smith, b. 5 Jan. 1927, Detroit, Michigan, USA. Consultant. m. Edward L Anderson, Jr, 11 Dec. 1965, divorced 1974. 2 sons. *Education:* BS, George Washington University, 1948; Georgetown School of Languages and Linguistics, 1950; University of London School of Oriental & African Studies, 1951; MA, Political Science, Boston University, 1958. *Appointments:* Department of State Cultural Officer in Tangier, Nairobi & Leopoldville, 1952-56; African-American Institute, 1959-63; National Women's Committee for Civil Rights, 1963-64; Franklin Book Programs, 1964-65; President, Princeton Features, 1973-83; Executive Director, Buffett Foundation, 1983-84; Vice President, The Population Institute, 1986-87; Fund Raising Consultant and Exhibitor of Zimbabwe stone sculpture, 1987-. *Publications:* Search for Security: A Guide to Grantmaking in International Security & the Prevention of Nuclear War. *Memberships:* Co-Chairwoman, Center for the American Woman & Politics, Rutgers University, 1971-72; Board Member, Operation Crossroads Africa, 1968-. *Honours:* Kappa Kappa Gamma Foreign Fellowship Award, School of Oriental & African Studies, University of London, 1951; Distinguished Service Award, Department of State, 1954; Ford Foundation African Study Fellowship to Boston University, 1956. *Interests:* Advancement of the concept of partnership as a model for our global society in exhcnage for the continuing pattern of a dominator model. *Address:* 646 E Street SE, Washington, DC 20003, USA.

ANDERSON (Margaret)Anne (Brineman), b. 5 Oct. 1942, Caracas, Venezuela. Mental Health Counsellor. m. Richard Dean Anderson, 6 June 1964, divorced 1984. 1 son, 2 daughters. *Education:* BA, History, Grinnell College, Iowa, USA, 1964; Counsellor training with Patricia Webbink, PhD, 1972-74; Non-degree programme, Washington Community Therapy Guild, 1974-77; Supervision, Sheldon Kopp, PhD and Lora Price, LCSW, 1979-87. *Appointments:* Founder and Coordinator, Brookland Free Community Pre- School, 1971-72; Office Manager, Centre for Science in Public Interest, 1971- 73; Director, Clearing House for Options

in Children's Education, 1973-74; Self-employed
Mental Health Counsellor, Washington Community
Therapy Guild Associate, 1975-; Coordinator, national
office of Psychologists for Social Responsibility, 1983-
; Conference Director for 1983 and 1984 Annual
Conference and Newsletter Editor, 1984 for Common
Boundary, Division of Family Therapy Network.
Memberships: American Association of Counselling and
Development; American Mental Health Counsellors
Association; Chair, Board of Trustees, Somerset School;
American Association of University Women. *Hobbies:*
ALTERNATIVE education; Archaeology; Birding;
Camping; Spirituality; Reading; Kids. *Address:*
Washington Community Therapy Guild, 1841 Columbia
Road NW 209, Washington, DC 20009, USA.

ANDRADA Lucia Maria Lima Caldeira de, b. 20
June 1948, Rio de Janeiro, Brazil. Psychologist. m.
Ernan Mafia Caldeira de Andrada, 20 Dec. 1969, 1 son,
1 daughter. *Education:* Graduated as Primary Teacher,
1966; Graduated as Psychologist, National University,
Rio de Janeiro, 1981; Graduated as Junguian Analyst,
Sociedade Brasileira de Analise Arquetipeca, 1987.
Appointments: Psychologist, Founder of Psychology
Department, Pestalozzi Society of Rio de Janeiro, 1968;
Experimental Researcher, Flummense Federal
University, 1969; Psychologist for State Schools, 1969;
Clinical Psychologist in private practice, 1971-.
Publication: The position of the psychologist towards
the problems of the mentally deficient, article for
magazine on the mentally-retarded child. *Memberships:*
Sociedade Brasileira de Analise Arquetipeca; Approved
Supervisor, Regional Psychology Council, Rio de
Janeiro; Certificated Member, 3rd Brazilian Infantile
Neuropsychiatry Congress and 3rd Congress for Latin
American Neuropediatrics. *Hobbies:* Reading; Cinema;
Theatre; Sailing. *Address:* Rua Miguel de Frias 51, 8o
andar, Icarai Niteroi, Rio de Janeiro, Brazil CEP 24230.

ANDREAS Dorothy Inez, b. 9 July 1917, Earlham,
Iowa, USA. Patron of the arts and education. m. Dwayne
O Andreas, 21 Dec. 1947. 1 son, 2 daughters. *Education:*
BA, University of Minnesota, 1952; MS, Barry University
of Miami Shores, Florida, 1975. *Memberships:* Chair,
Barry University Board of Trustees; National City
BankHolding Board, Minn; Center for the Study of the
Presidency, NY; Millikin University, Decatur, IL; Director
of WPBT Public Television; Board of Founders, Dade
County Institute of Art. *Honours:* Honorary Doctor of
Laws, Hamline University, 1975; Honorary Doctorate
of Humanities, Barry University, 1983; Terrence
Cardinal Cooke Award for Distinguished Service in
Health Care at New York Medical College, Honorary
Doctorate, 1988; Citizen of the Day for service to the
community of South Florida, 1979; Women in
Communication, Community Headliner Award, 1982;
Association of Governing Boards of Universities &
Colleges AGB Distinguished Service in Trusteeship,
1983; Barry University Cornerston Award, 1983; Award
from Anti-Defamation League of B'nai B'rith, ADL
Florida Thousand, 1984, 1985, 1986; Charter Member,
Barry University Inter-American Council, 1985; Barry
College Corporate Leadership Award, Director of The
Andreas Foundation. *Address:* Sea View, 9909 Collins
Avenue, Bal Harbour, FL 33154, USA.

ANDRENCHUK Cori Gaye, b. 27 July 1953,
Lethbridge, Alberta, Canada. Lawyer. *Education:*
BA(Hons), Economics, University of Lethbridge, 1977;
LLB, University of Alberta, 1977. *Appointments:*
Barrister, Solicitor, Paterson North Law Office,
Lethbridge, 1978. *Memberships:* Executive, Lethbridge
Bar Association; Canadian Bar Association; Alberta Bar
Association; Alberta Advisory Council for Women's
Issues; Alberta Family Mediation Society; Canadian
Family Mediation Society; Alberta Arbitration Society;
Board of Referees, Unemployment Insurance
Commission. *Honours:* Numerous scholarships and
awards. *Hobbies:* Cooking; Golf; Reading. *Address:* 6th
floor Chancery Court, 220 4th Street South, Lethbridge,
Alberta, Canada.

ANDRESS Ursula, b. 1936, Berne, Switzerland.

Actress. *Career:* Motion picture debut, Hollywood, 1955.
Creative Works: Films include: Dr No; Fourt For Texas;
Fun in Acapulco; Toys For Christmas; She; Tenth Victim;
What's New Pussycat? Chinese Adventures in China;
Casino Royale; The Southern Star; Perfect Friday; The
Red Sun; Scaramouche; Clash of the Titans. Television:
Peter the Great. *Address:* c/o Danikhofenweg 9, 3072
Ostermundingen, Switzerland.

ANDREWS Grace Malekin, b. 14 June 1926,
Inverness, Scotland. College Principal. *Education:* BA,
Oxford University. *Appointments:* Personal Assistant,
Chairman, BMC, 1953-66; Director, M. Follett Ltd.,
1959-64; Director, Budapest HF Ltd., 1967-72;
Managing Director, Grace Andrews College Ltd., 1980-
. *Creative Works:* Articles in Health & Beauty Magazines;
Lecture Tours: US, 1980, Australia 1987, Singapore,
1988. *Memberships:* Chairman, International
Estheticiennes Phyto-therapists Association; Fellow,
Society Health & Beauty Therapists. *Hobbies:* Work;
Travel; Dry Fly Fishing; Golf. *Address:* Follett House,
Monument Lane, Lickey Rednal, Birmingham B45 9QJ,
England.

ANDREWS Julie, b. 1 Oct. 1935, Walton-on-
Thames, Surrey, England. Actress; Singer. m. (1) Tony
Walton, 1959, dissolved 1968, 1 daughter. (2) Blake
Edwards, 1969. *Career:* First stage appearance at the
age of 12 as singer, London Hippodrome; played in
reviews and concert tours; appeared in Pantomime
Cinderella, London Palladium. *Creative Works:* Plays:
The Boy Friend, 1954; My Fair Lady, 1959-60; Camelot,
1960-62; Television: High Tor; several television shows
including The Julie Andrews Hour, 1972-73. Films:
Mary Poppins, 1963; The Americanization of Emily,
1964; The Sound of Music, 1964; Hawaii, 1965; Torn
Curtain, 1966; Thoroughly Modern Millie, 1966; Star!
1967; Darling Lili, 1980; Victor/Victoria, 1981; That's
Life, 1986; Duet For One, 1986. *Publication:* Mandy,
Last of the Really Great Whangdoogles, 1973. *Honours:*
Academy Award (Oscar) Best Actress, 1964; Three
Golden Globe Awards. *Address:* c/o Suite 1616, Blake
Edwards Inc, 1888 Century Park East, Los Angeles, CA
90067, USA.

ANDREWS Lucy Harrison Gordon, b. 27 Mar. 1941,
Washington, USA. Assistant Professor. m. Charles
Lawrence Andrews, 28 Aug. 1965, 2 sons. *Education:*
AB, Agnes Scott College, 1963; PhD, University of
Georgia. *Appointments:* Professor, Chair, Natural
Science, Brenan College, 1967- 80; Director, Genetic
Services, North Health District, Gainesville, 1974-76;
Assistant Professor, Human Genetics, Mercer
University School of Medicine, 1981-. *Publications:*
Scientific Creativity, 1968; articles in journals &
magazines. *Memberships:* American Society Human
Genetics; AAAS; National Society of Genetic
Counsellors; Genetics Society of Georgia, Trustee &
Host of 1988 Annual Meeting; New York Academy of
Sciences. *Honours:* Recipient, honours & awards.
*Hobbies: (1)Research on Molecularbasis of Disease and
Aging; Horseriding; Gardening. Address:* Mercer
University School of Medicine, Macon, GA 31207, USA.

ANDREWS Mary Maria (Deaconess), b. 20 Mar.
1915, Cooma, New South Wales, Australia. Deaconess/
Chaplain. *Education:* Nursing Training, Sydney, 1933-
34; Diploma, Croydon Mission & Bible College, 1935-
36; Deaconess Diploma, 1st class honours, Deaconess
Institution, 1937-38. *Appointments:* Teacher, Pastoral
Worker, Church Missionary Society, China, 1938-45;
Children's Home & Home for Destitute Women, Lahore,
India, 1945-46; Teacher, Pastoral Worker, CMS,
Shaoxing, China, 1947-51; Head Deaconess, Diocese
of Sydney, NSW, Australia, 1951-82; Principal, Anglican
Deaconess Training College, 1952-75; Chaplain,
Goodwin Village, Elizabeth Lodge, St John's Lodge,
1976-. *Publications:* Articles in missionary and church
magazines; Book reviews; Newspaper and magazine
articles; Oral History, National Library Canberra.
Memberships: President, Sydney Deaconess
Fellowship, 1951- 82; Vice President, World Federation
of Deaconesses, 1972-75; Chairman, Asia Pacific

Regional Deaconess Association, 1972-75; Member of Council, Anglican Deaconess Institute, 1951-88; Vice President, NSW Women's World Day of Prayer, 1986-. *Honours:* Member of Order of Australia, 1980; Life Member, Australian Church Women, 1973; Life Member, NSW Unit of Australian Church Women, 1981; Fellow 1985, Life Member 1987, IBA. *Hobbies:* Gardening; Travel; Photography; Collecting miniatures; Welfare of Overseas students. *Address:* L8/250 Jersey Road, Woollahra, NSW 2025, Australia.

ANDREYEVA Victoria, b. 21 Jan. 1942, Omsk, USSR (emigrated to USA, 1974). Writer; Editor; Journalist; Teacher. m. Arkady Rovner, 5 Aug. 1969, 1 son. *Education:* MA, Russian Philology, 1965; Moscow Polygraphic Institute, 1966-67; PhD studies, Comparative Literature, New York University, USA, 1981-. *Appointments:* Editorial staff, Centrosoyuz Publishing House, 1965-68; Freelance journalist, journals including Junost, Outchitelskaya Gazeta, Detskaya Literatura, Sovietskaya Cultura, 1968-74; Editorial staff: Gnosis magazine (English & Russian) 1978-, This & That (bilingual children's magazine) 1980-81, Gnosis Anthology of Contemporary American & Russian Literature & Art 1981-83. *Publications include:* Poems, articles, prose in: Appollo-77, Paris; La Pensee Russe (Paris); Crossroads (USA); Echo (Paris); Gnosis (USA); RLT (USA). Book of poems, Dream of the Firmament, 1987. *Memberships:* Poets & Writers Inc; L'Egerete International; Writers' Union. *Honours:* Award, National Endowment for Arts, USA, 1980; Poet & critic in residence, Cummington Community for Arts, 1983. *Hobby:* Music. *Address:* PO Box 42, Prince Street Station, New York, NY 10012, USA.

ANDRIESKY Wilda Helen, b. 28 Nov. 1925, Rosseau, Ontario, Canada. Child Psychologist. m. Mitchell John Andriesky, 18 June 1961. *Education:* BA, Honours, Queen's University, 1959; MA, Psychology, 1961. *Appointments:* Elementary School Teacher, Ontario, 1944-55; Clinical Child Psychologist, Kingston Psychiatric Hospital, 1960-78; School Psychologist, Frontenac County Board of Education, 1978-86; Assistant Professor, Queen's University, Kingston, 1975-. *Memberships:* Ontario Psychological Association; Canadian Psychological Association; Nu Chapter, Delta Kappa Gamma. *Honours:* Susan Near Scholarship, Psychology, 1956; University Scholarship, 1957; Sir Wilfred Laurier Scholarship, Oral French, 1956; Eliza Fitzgerald Scholarship, 1957; Reuben Wells Leonard Scholarship, 1958; Prince of Wales Prize, Medal in Psychology, RS McLaughlin Fellowship, 1959. *Hobbies:* Gardening; Cooking; Preserving; Sewing; Reading. *Address:* RR No 8, Kingston, Ontario, Canada K7L 4V4.

ANFIELD Elizabeth Margaret, b. 20 Mar. 1949, London, England. Chartered Accountant. m. Alan Anfield, 19 July 1969, div. Dec. 1989. *Education:* BSc Hons, 1971; FCA, 1974; ATII, 1975. *Appointments:* Articled, Clark Whitehill, Reading, 1971-74; Casson Beckmann Rutley, London, 1974-75; Ernst & Whinney, Dusseldorf, Federal Republic of Germany, 1975-78; Finnie & Company, Newbury and Reading, England, 1980-83; Own Accountancy practice, 1983-; Managing Director, Thames Valley Residential Properties PLC, 1988-. *Memberships:* Executive Council, Newbury and West Berkshire Chamber of Commerce; Institute of Taxation, Thames Valley Branch; Chairman, Newbury Twin Town Association. *Hobbies:* Theatre; Skiing; Foreign travel. *Address:* 6 Tudor Road, Newbury, Berks RG14 7PU, England.

ANGEL Heather Hazel, b. 21 July 1941, Buckinghamshire, England. Wildlife Photographer; Author; Lecturer. m. Martin A. Angel, 3 Oct. 1964, 1 son. *Education:* BSc(Hons), 1962, MSc, 1965, Bristol University. *Career:* Self-employed; Kodak travelling exhibitions: The Natural World of Britain & Ireland, 1981-84; A Camera in the Garden, 1984; Other exhibitions: British Photography, Beijing, China, 1985; Nature in Focus, Aberystwyth Arts Centre, 1986; Gardens in Focus, Royal Botanic Garden, Edinburgh, 1986; Nature in Focus, Natural History Museum, London, 1987; Various photographic technique demonstrations on TV, 1981-84, 1988; Featured in Japanese TV documentary, 1983; Appeared on radio, 1984, 1988; Featured in magazines; Worked in numerous locations including tropical oceanic islands (Galapagos, Seychelles, Mauritius, Madagascar, Reunion, Hawaii), Sri Lanka, Japan, China, Uganda, Kenya, USA, Portugal, Mexico, Canaries, Alaska, Greenland. *Publications include:* Nature Photography: Its Art & Techniques, 1972; The Natural History of Britain & Ireland (co-author), 1981; The Book of Nature Photography, 1982; The Book of Close-Up Photography, 1983; Heather Angel's Countryside, 1983; A Camera in the Garden, 1984; A View from a Window, 1988; Nature in Focus, 1988; Landscape Photography, 1989; nature column for Camera Weekly, 1987-88; Heather Angel on Location, feature in What Camera?. 1988-. *Memberships:* The Royal Photographic Society (President 1984-86); Vice-President, Society for Wildlife Art for the Nation; Patron: Avon Wildlife Trust; Fellow: British Institute of Professional Photography; Linnean Society; Royal Photographic Society. *Honours:* Hood Medal, Royal Photographic Society, 1975; Medaille de Salverte, Societe Francaise de Photographie, 1984; Hon DSc, University of Bath, 1986. *Address:* Highways, Vicarage Hill, Farnham, Surrey GU9 8HJ, England.

ANGELL Bettie Ellen, b. 16 Mar. 1927, Centralia, Missouri, USA. Interior Designer. *Education:* Certificate, New York School of Interior Design, 1946. *Appointments:* Interior designer, Denver Dry Goods, Denver, Colorado, 1946-49; Home furnishings consultant, Barker Bros, Los Angeles, 1950-52; Interior Designer, Joske's Houston, Texas, 1952-55; Showroom of finer furniture, Corpus Christi, Texas, 1955-56; Braslau's, Corpus Christi, 1966-70; Browning Brothers, Corpus Christ, 1970-. *Publication:* The Layman's Handbook of Interior Design, 1972. *Memberships:* American Institute of Interior Design (AID), 1959-75, vice president, secretary, membership chairman, newsletter originator and editor, Texas Chapter board member 10 years, etc. American Society of Interior Designers, 1975-; Texas Chapter board member 6 years, national board member, 1984-86, Regional vice-president nationally, 1985-86; Long Range Planning Committee nationally, 1987- 89; Texas Association of Interior Designers, Board Member, 1984-88. *Honours:* Medalist Award (Highest award ASID gives at state level), 1984; Commendation for Outstanmding Service, ASID, 1986; Award for Special Service (one of five given in Texas), AID, 1974. *Hobbies:* Meditation and Meta-physics; Writing; Lecturing both on Interior Design and Meta-physics. *Address:* 346 Southern, Corpus Christi, TX 78404, USA.

ANGELO Eda Joanne, b. 11 Feb. 1936, Boston, Massachusetts, USA. Psychiatrist (Child, Adolescent, Adult, Hospice). *Education:* AB, Mount Holyoke College, 1957; MD, Tufts University Medical School, 1961; Diplomate, American Board of Psychiatry & Neurology (Psychiatry), 1972. *Appointments:* Internship, Pediatric Service, Boston City Hospital, 1961-62; Residency, General Psychiatry, Boston State Hospital, 1963-65; Fellowship, Child Psychiatry, James Jackson Putnam Chikldren's Center and Douglas Thom Clinic for Children, 1965-66; Fellowship, Child Psychiatry, Children's Hospital of DC and The Child Center of Catholic University, 1966-67; Medical Director, Canarsie Mental Health Center, Brooklyn, 1967-69; Staff Psychiatrist, Community Mental Health Service, Massachusetts Mental Health Center, Boston, 1969-73; Consultant in Psychiatry, Chandler School for Women, Boston, 1971-72; Consultant in Psychiatry, St Margaret's Hospital, Boston, 1976-83; Consultant in Child Psychiatry, Kennedy Memorial Hospital, Boston, 1971-74; Consultant in Child Psychiatry, North Suffolk Health Center, Boston, 1978-79 and 1980-81; Private Practice, Child and Adult Psychiatry, 1967-; Psychiatric Director, Laboure Center, South Boston, 1974-78. *Publication:* Communications Processes in School Consultation, 1973. *Memberships include:* American Academy of Child Psychiatry and Adolescent, (Chairperson Public Information Committee, 1985- 87);

American Psychiatric Association; New England Council of Child Psychiatry; Massachusetts Psychiatric Society; Massachusetts Medical Society, Suffolk County Branch (Co-chairperson, Comm on Religion & Med, 1985-87); American Orthopsychiatric Association; Seminar in the development of Infants and Parents (Steering Committee, 1976-79); Founding Member, New England Medical Ethics Forum; Regional Director for New England, National Federation of Catholic Physicians' Guilds, 1988-; Board of Trustees, St John of God Hospital, 1987-; Board of Trustees, Montrose School for Girls, Westwood, 1986- , etc. *Hobbies:* Horticulture; Outdoor activities; Sponsoring youth group; Music; Crafts. *Address:* 403 Commonwealth Ave, Boston, MA 02215, USA.

ANGLEMYER Roma Kathleen, b. 17 Sept. 1932, Wakarusa, Indiana, USA. Educator. m. Keith Alois Anglemyer, 10 June 1956, 2 daughters. *Education:* BS, Education, Goshen, 1955; MA, Education, St Mary's College, Notre Dame, 1966; Certified Endorsement in Special Education, 1966. *Appointments:* Public School Teacher: Bremen, Indiana, 1955-59, Wa-Nee Schools, 1960-; Enrichment Classes, 1984-86; Instructor, Assistant, College of Gifted & Talented, Indiana University, 1984. *Publications:* Wa-Nee Curriculum Writer, 3rd Grade. *Memberships:* National Education Association; Indiana State, & Wa-Nee Teachers Associations; Pi Lambda Theta; *Honours:* Certificate of Merit, Indiana Dept. of Education, 1985. *Hobbies:* Antique Cars; Travel; Collecting Candlewick Crystal. *Address:* 28584, County Road 38 R. 1, Wakarusa, IN 46573, USA.

ANNAND Louise Gibson, b. 27 may 1915, Uddington, Scotland. Artist. m. (1) Alistair Matheson, 1956, (2) Roderik MacFarquhar, 1989. *Education:* MA, Honours, English, Glasgow University, 1937. *Appointments:* Teacher, Glasgow 1939-49; Assistant Schools Museum Service, Glasgow, 1949-70; Museums Education Officer, Glasgow, Strathclyde, 1970-80. *Publications:* A Glasgow Sketchbook, 1988; illustrations for other authors; pictures in many private & public collections; educational & art films. *Memberships:* President, Scottish Women Artists, 1963-66, 1980-85; President, Society of Glasgow Women Artists, 1977-79 and 1988-91; Royal Fine Art Commission for Scotland. *Honours:* MBE, 1980. *Hobbies:* 16mm Film & Video; Mountaineering. *Address:* 22 Kingsborough Gardens, Glasgow, G12 9NJ Scotland.

ANSEVICS Nancy L, Psychologist. *Education:* BA, 1972; MA, Central Michigan University, 1977; Ed.D., University of South Dakota, 1986. *Appointments:* Clinical Supervisor, Adapt Inc., 1075-77, Instructor, Psychology, Grandview College, Des Moines, 1976-79; Associate Psychologist, Herbert S. Roth, 1977-79; Doctoral Internship, 1980-83; Psychologist, State of Kansas Psychology Dept., 1980-83; Clinical Psychologist, Human Development Center, Duluth, 1984; Psychologist, State of Missouri, 1985-88; Program Planning Director, State of Missouri, 1989-. *Publications:* Articles in professional journals. *Honours:* Psi Chi; Phi Delta Kappa; Outstanding Scientific Achievement, 1982; Certificate of Appreciation, School of Law, University of South Dakota, 1985. *Address:* 1102 Carol Drive, St Joseph, MO 64506, USA.

ANSON Elva Margaret, b. 9 Jan. 1932, Klamath Falls, Oregon, USA. Author; Psychotherapist. m. Everett F Anson. 1 son, 2 daughters. *Education:* BA, Education, Fresno State College, 1954; Gen Elem Credential; MA Counseling Psychology, University of San Francisco, 1979. *Appointments:* Teacher, San Diego Elementary Schools, 1953-54; Teacher, Sanger Elementary Schools, 1954-60; Counselor, Fair Oaks Presbyterian Counseling Center, 1978-86; Private practice, 1986-. *Publications:* Books: How to Keep The Family That Prays Together From Falling Apart; The Complete Book of Home Management; How To Get Kids To Help At Home. *Memberships:* California Association Marriage Family Therapists; California Writers Club; Christian Association for Psychological Studies; American Society

of Journalists and Authors. *Honour:* Valedictorian, Reedley High School, 1949. *Hobbies:* Reading; Photography; Tennis; The ocean; Sports; Food; Speaking; Teaching; Travel. *Address:* 10418 Fair Oaks Blvd, Fair Oaks, CA 95628, USA.

ANTHONY Betty Arlene, b. 14 July 1926, Jacksonville, Florida, USA. Corporate Secretary. m. Yancey Lamar Anthony, 13 Sept. 1983. *Education:* Jones Business College, Jacksonville, 1944; New Orleans Baptist Theological Seminary, 1952; University of Florida, Gainesville, 1953-54; University of Tampa, 1956. *Appointments:* Promotion Secretary, Florida Baptist State Convention, 1945-53; Pastor's Secretary, First Baptist Church, Tampa, 1955-59; Secretary, Assistant Administrator, 1960-65, Secretary to Executive Director, 1966-80, Corporate Secretary, 1980-, Baptist Health Inc; Secretary, Healthcare Management Services Inc., 1981-; Asst. Secretary-Treasurer, Southern Baptist Hospital of Florida, Inc., 1982-; Secretary Baptist Medical Center Foundation, Inc., 1983-; Secretary, Baptist Health Properties, Inc., 1983-; Asst. Secretary, Northeast Florida Breast Center, Inc.,1984-; Secretary-Treasurer, Southbank Advertising, Inc., 1987-; Asst. Secretary, The Pavilion Developer, Inc., 1987-. *Memberships:* Florida Hospitals, Executive Secretaries Association, Director 1973-76, President 1975-76; American Society of Corporate Secretaries Inc; National Association for Female Executives. *Honours:* Honorary Member, Florida Hospitals Executive Secretaries Association, 1983. *Hobbies:* Painting; Gardening; Reading; Jogging; Creative Writing; Church Activities. *Address:* Baptist Health Inc., 1300 Gulf Life Drive, Ste 303, Jacksonville, FL 32207, USA.

ANTHONY Geraldine Cecilia, b. 5 Oct. 1919, Brooklyn, New York, USA. English Professor Emeritus. *Education:* BA, 1951; MA, 1956; PhD, 1963. *Appointments:* Junior High School Teacher: St Margaret's School, 1942-48, St Peter's School, Lowell, 1948-51, St Barnabas School, Bellmore, 1951-62, Mount St Vincent Academy, Halifax, Nova Scotia, 1963-65; Professor, English, Mount St Vincent University, Halifax, 1965-. *Publications:* John Coulter, 1976; Profiles in Canadian Drama, 1977; Stage Voices, 1978; Gwen Pharis Ringwood, 1981; numerous articles in Canadian Literature, Canadian Theatre Review, Canadian Drama. *Memberships:* Founding Member, President, Association for Canadian Theatre History; Founding Member, Delta Kappa Gamma, Theta Province, Nova Scotia; Founder-Director, Orford University/MSVU; Canadian Association of University Teachers; Canadian Association of Chairmen of English. *Honours:* Fellowship, Journalism, University of Minnesota, 1965; Advisory Board, Canadian Drama, 1978-. *Hobbies:* Theatre; Travel. *Address:* 51 Marlewood Drive, Wedgewood Park, Halifax, Nova Scotia Canada B3M 3H4.

ANTHONY Julie Kathleen, b. 13 Jan. 1948, Los Angeles, California, USA. m. T Richard Butera, 28 Dec. 1976. *Education:* AB Psychology, Stanford University, 1969; MA Clinical Psychology 1971, PhD Clinical Psychology 1979, UCLA. *Appointments:* Professional Tennis Player, Virginia Slims Tour, Avon Tour, International Tour, 1968-79; Sport Psychologist for Philadelphia Flyers NHL Hockey Team, 1980-82; Owner/Operator, Aspen Club, Fitness and Sports Medicine Institute, 1982-. *Publications:* A Winning Combination, Scribner's, (Guide for parents with children who play or would like to play competitive tennis), 1981; Numerous articles for Tennis Magazine; Vogue, etc. *Membership:* American College of Sports Medicine. *Honour:* Stanford Athletic Hall of Fame, 1980. *Hobbies:* Skiing; Cycling. *Address:* 1450 Crystal Lake Road, Aspen, CO 81611, USA.

ANTIGNANI Gloria Riseley, b. 29 July 1935, Kingston, New York, USA. Teacher. m. Serafin Ralph Antignani, 30 June 1957, 3 sons, 2 daughters. *Education:* BS, New Haven State Teachers' College, 1956; MA, Fairfield University, 1960; 30 credits, St

Joseph's College, 1987. *Appointments:* Teacher: 2nd Grade, Jane Ryan School, Trumbull, Connectitut, 1956-60; 5th Grade, Wilcoxson School, Stratford, CT, 1977-. *Memberships:* National, Connecticut, & Stratford Education Associations; Teacher representative, Wilcoxson School Parent Teacher Association; Council, Sterling House Community Centre. *Honour:* Biographical recognition. *Hobbies:* Music; Crafts; Cooking; Travel. *Address:* 1037 North Avenue, Stratford, Connecticut 06497, USA.

ANTONE Linda A, b. 31 Aug. 1947, Minneapolis, USA. Programme Developer. *Education:* BA, University of Minnesota, 1969; Studies in Advertising, TV Production, Management, 1972-80; Seminars, Project Management Programme Design, 1979-82; Wilson Learning Courses in Management, Sales Customer Relations, Interpersonal Skills, Team Management, 1977-84. *Appointments:* Advertising Production Manager, Hoffman press, 1972-73; Advertising Director, Medallion Publishing, 1974-75; Associate Producer, Wilson Learning Corp, 1976-79, Producer-Director 1979-82, Director of Video Dept., 1982-83, Vice President, production, 1983-85, Vice President, Programme Developer, 1985-88. *Memberships:* Video Festival Judge, International TV Association; Women in Communications inc; American Film Institute; American Red Cross; Womens League for Peace & Freedom. *Honours:* Executive Producer, MIR Sightline Video, received JVC Video Award 1984. *Address:* 4700 Ewing Avenue South, Minneapolis, MN 55410, USA.

ANTONELLI Amy Solit, b. 23 Apr. 1941, New York City, USA. Assistant Dean, The Catholic Univers, School of Music. m. 29 July 1961. 1 son, 1 daughter. *Education:* BA, piano performance, Mary Hardin Baylor College, Belton, Texas; MM, University of Texas, Austin; PhD, Catholic University of America, Washington DC. *Appointments:* Accompanist, Oratorio Society, Washington under direction of Robert Shafer and guest conductors including Rafael Frubeck de Burgos, Mstislav Rostropovich, Charles Dutoit, 1971-88; Accompanist to Jessye Norman and Barbara Hendricks in rehearsal with Leonard Bernstein, 1982; Member of choir of Mass by Leonard Bernstein, 1971; Lecturer, Music Theory, Trinity College, 1976-88; Lecturer, Music theory 1971-88, Assistant Dean, School of Music 1988-, Catholic University of America. *Creative work:* Participated in original cast recording of Mass by Leonard Bernstein. *Memberships:* President, Oratorio Society, Washington, 1971- 88; Vice President, America-Israel Cultural Association, 1981-82; College Music Society, 1986-88; American Musicological Society. *Hobbies:* Travel; Sailing; Reading; Theatre; Concerts. *Address:* Catholic University of America, Washington, DC 20064, USA.

ANTOUN M. Lawreace, Sister, b. 30 Dec. 1927, Meadville, Pennsylvania, USA. College President Emerita. *Education:* BS, Chemistry, Villa Maria College, 1954; MS 1959, PhD (ABD), Chemistry, University of Notre Dame. *Appointments:* Chemistry instructor 1955-61, Assistant Professor of Chemistry 1965-66, President 1966-88, President Emerita 1988-, Villa Maria College, Erie, Pennsylvania. *Memberships:* Executive, Commission of Independent Colleges & Universities; Evaluator & Trustee, Middle States Association, Commission of Higher Educatin; Chair, Council of Higher Education, Erie Confercnce on Community Development, & Advisory Council, McMannis Educational Trust Fund; Boards of Incorporators, St Vincent Health Centre, & Hamot Medical Centre; Chair, State Board of Education, Commonwealth of Pennsylvania. *Honours:* Chemistry Research Grant, Atomic Energy Commission; Honorary Doctorates, Gannon University, Marymount Manhattan College; Award, distinguished service, Pennsylvania Association of Adult Education; Various biographical recognitions. *Address:* Villa Maria College, 2551 West 8th Street, Erie, Pennsylvania 16505, USA.

ANVARIPOUR Patricia Lynch, b. 12 Apr. 1935, Brooklyn, USA. Planning Associate in Nursing. Divorced, 1 daughter. *Education:* Diploma, Lutheran Medical Centre, 1955; BA, State University of New Jersey, 1973; MPA, New York University, 1977; CNAA. *Appointments:* Faculty, City College School of Nursing, 1980-; Faculty, New School for Social Research Management & Urban Professions, 1980-; Planning Associate in Nursing, Mount Sinai Medical Centre, 1987-; Faculty, Wagner College of Nursing, Staten Island, 1988-. *Publications:* Articles in: JONA; Nursing Management. *Memberships:* World Futures Studies Federation; American Nurses Association; Nurses House Inc. *Honours:* Sigma Theta Tau; various other honours & awards. *Hobbies:* Antiques; Bird Watching; Yoga. *Address:* 425 Riverside Drive, 9F, New York, NY 10025, USA.

APAGYI Maria, b. 11 Oct. 1941, Kosice, Czechoslovakia. Music Teacher. m. Ferenc Lantos, 28 July 1986. *Education:* Diploma in Piano and Solfeggio Teaching, 1964; Diploma in Oboe, 1969; Graduate, Ferenc Liszt Academy of Music, Teachers Training Insitute, Pecs, Hungary. *Appointments:* Music Teacher, Ferenc Erkel School of Music, Komlo, 1965-85; Music Teacher, Assistant Manager, Apaczai Csere Janos Education Centre Art School, Pecs, Hungary, 1985-. *Publications:* Construction and Improvisation series, 1980-81; Construction and Improvisation, 1984; Collection of exercises for teaching of musical improvisation, 1985. *Memberships:* International Society of Music Educators; Association of Hungarian Musicians. *Honours:* Audio-visual Studio Award, Institute of Popular Culture, 1976; Certificate of Merit, Ministry of Culture, 1976; Social Culture Medal, 1979; Distinguished Teacher Medal, 1981; Pro Urbe Komlo, 1984. *Hobbies:* Collecting gramophone records; Reading; Hiking. *Address:* Mogyoros-koz 5, 7624 Pecs, Hungary.

APHEK Edna, b. 16 Apr. 1943, Israel. Writer; Lecturer. *Education:* BA, Hebrew University, Jerusalem, 1966; MA, Hunter College, New York, USA, 1972; DHL, Jewish Theological Seminary, New York, 1976. *Appointments:* Hebrew Instructor, 1964-67, Assistant Director in Charge of Hebrew Studies, 1976-77, Jacob Hiatt Institute, Brandeis University, Jerusalem; Hebrew Instructor, Overseas Students Center, Haifa University, 1967-68; Hebrew Language and Literature, Teacher Training, Ramaz School, New York, USA, 1969-72; TESOL Instructor in Social Work, MA Program Hunter College, 1972; Hebrew Language and Literature lecturer, Jewish Theological Seminary, New York, 1973-76; Linguistic Coordinator of Mexico Project, Center for Jewish Education in the Diaspora, Hebrew University, Jerusalem, 1977-80; Senior Lecturer, Director Translation Institute, 1978-84, Senior Lecturer, 1984-. Jewish Theological Seminary; Senior Researcher, Head of Hebrew as a Second Language, South-Africa Project, 1982-86, Head of Project for the Development of Language and Thinking Skills, 1984-87, School of Education, Tel Aviv University. Consultant, 1977-86. *Creative works:* Art exhibit (painting) George Marcus Galleries, New York, 1976; Art exhibit (Painting), Shatz Gallery, Jerusalem, 1980. Poems: Eked, 1981. Short Stories: Hagar A Hated Woman; The Burial Customs of the Drus; To Sleep; The Song of the Great Waters; Where Do the Dreams Meet?; Where Shall I Go Tonight?; over 50 stories and over 30 poems for children. *Memberships:* Lyons, Israel, 1987; Board of Louis Waterman Youth Hostel, 1986; Secretary of the Israel Association of Applied Linguistics, 1977-79. *Honours:* Easifying second Language learning, Brandeis University, 1977-79; A Linguistic Analysis of Fortune Telling, Ben Gurion University of the Negev, 1979; Israel Academy of Science, 1981-82; Maxwell Abbell Research Grant, 1983. *Hobbies:* Painting; Writing. *Address:* 42 Hatayassim Street, Jerusalem 22509, Israel.

APOSTOL Antoaneta, b. 8 May 1945, Falticeni, Romania. Writer. m. 18 May 1936. *Education:* Painting school, Fine Arts, 1965. *Appointments:* Literary Critic; Secretary Literary Home U Eminescu; Contributor to Romania Literare Ramuri, Neue Banater Zeitug; Volk und Kultur, Convorkiri Literare; Cromice; Saptomana; Orizont; Informatia. *Publications:* Books: Scrisori ducteun concert de ieska, 1978, Fintim de Aer, 1980; Ceasul de Frunze, 1982; Mutrare Frevertibila, 1983; Lintec bentru Arleckin, 1989; Personel expositions, 1981. *Memberships:* Writers' Association; Fine Arts Association. *Honours:* Prizes, Song of Rumania, 1974-75; Diplome of Honour, 120 years Literary conversations. *Hobby:* Classical music. *Address:* Bd Dimitrie Cantemir Nr 17 BL.10 Sc.A Ap.2, Cod 75122 Bucharest Sect 4, Romania.

APPLE Jacqueline (Jacki), b. 11 Dec. 1941, New York City, USA. Intermedia; Performance artist; Writer; Producer. *Education:* Syracuse University, 1959-60; Graduate, Parsons School of Design, New York City, 1963. *Appointments:* Instructor, Art Center College of Design, Pasadena, 1983-; Producer/host, KPFK-FM Pacifica Radio, 1982-; Contributing writer, High Performance magazine, Artweek, Los Angeles Weekly, Media Arts. *Creative Works:* Performances/audiotapes: Palisade; The Amazon, The Mekong, The Missouri, The Nile; The Garden Planet Revisted. Film/video/audio: Free Fire Zone; The Mexican Tapes; Palisade. Radio: Last Rites after Angkor Wat; Swan Lake. Books: Truk Pieces; Partitions. Dance score: Urban Suite, etc. *Memberships:* The Cactus Foundation; Board of Directors, Los Angeles Contemporary Exhibitions, 1981-86; Arts Advisory Council, California State Universirty, Long Beach, 1988-. *Honours:* National Endowment for the Arts, Visual Artists Fellowship, 1979, 1981; NEA Inter-Arts Grant, 1984; New York State Council on the Arts, CAPS Program Multi-media grant, 1981; National/State County Partnership Grant, 1987. Commissions: Santa Monica Arts Commission, 1987; New American Radio, 1988. *Address:* 3827 Mentone Avenue, Culver City, CA 90232, USA.

APPLE Rima D, b. 6 Mar. 1944, New York City, USA. Historian. m. 20 June 1965. 2 sons. *Education:* BA, New York University, 1965; MA 1974, PhD 1981, University of Wisconsin-Madison. *Appointments:* Project Coordinator, Center for Photographic Images of Medicine and Health Care, 1981- 83; Visiting Assistant Professor, Univ Wisconsin-Madison, 1984; Adjunct Assistant Professor, University Wisconsin-Milwaukee, 1986-89; Assistant Editor, ISIS, 1989-90; Associate Editor, ISIS, 1990-. *Publications:* Illustrated Catalogue of Slide Archive of Historical Medical Photographs, 1984; Mothers and Medicine: A Social History of Infant Feeding 1890-1950, 1987; Women, Health and Medicine in America: A Historical Handbook, ed., 1990. *Memberships:* American Association for the History of Medicine (Program Committee, 1984-85); Berkshire Conference of Women Historians (Program Committee 1986-87, Prize Committee 1987-90); History of Science Society (Co-chair, Women's Committee 1987-89). *Honours:* Woodrow Wilson Research Grant in Women's Studies, 1978; Maurice L Richardson Research Grant, 1978-80; Women's Studies Research Center Honorary Fellowship, 1981-82, 1983-85; Honorary Fellow, Dept Hist Med, Univ Wisconsin, 1985-; History of Science Society Independent Scholars Travel Grant, 1987; National Science Foundation Grant, 1988-89. *Address:* University of Wisconsin-Madison, Department of the History of Medicine, Madison, WI 53706, USA.

AQUINO Corazon, nee Cojuangco, b. 25 Jan. 1933, Manila, Philippines. President of the Philippines. m. Benigno S Aquino Jr, 11 Oct. 1954, deceased 21 Aug. 1983. 1 son, 4 daughters. *Education:* BA French, Mathematics, College of Mt Saint Vincent, New York, USA, 1953. *Appointments include:* President of the Republic of the Philippines, 1986-. *Memberships:* Founder, Chairperson, Benigno S Aquino Jr Foundation; Kappa Gamma Pi. *Honours:* Woman of the Year, Catholic Educational Association of the Philippines, 1984; Woman of Distinction, Soroptimist International Award, 1986; Woman of the Year Award, Association of Outstanding Women in the Nation's Service, 1986; Collar Orden Del Libertador San Martin, conferred by President Raul Ricardo Alfonsin of Argentina, July 1986; 7 honorary degrees: Doctor of Humane Letters, College of Mt Saint Vincent, 1984, Doctor of Humanities, Stonehill College, Massachusetts, 1984, Doctor of Humane Letters, Ateneo de Manila University, 1985, LLD (hon causa) University of the Philippines, 1986, Doctor of Humane Letters, Xavier University, Cagayan de Oro, Philippines, 1986. *Address:* Malacanang, Metro Manila, Philippines.

ARAI Mary Needler, b. 18 Sept. 1932, Summerside, Prince Edward Island, Canada. Professor. m. Hisao Philip Arai, 23 Aug. 1958, 3 sons. *Education:* BSc, University of New Brunswick, 1952; MA, University of Toronto, 1956; PhD, University of California, Los Angeles, USA, 1962. *Appointments:* Instructor, Mount Holyoke College, 1956-57; Lecturer, University of British Columbia, 1960-61; Assistant Professor, Illinois State University, USA, 1961-62; Instructor, Research Associate, University of Illinois, 1962-63; Assistant Professor, Rice University, 1968-69; Instructor to Professor, University of Calgary, Calgary, Alberta, Canada, 1963-. *Publications:* 31 scientific papers. *Memberships:* Executive Council, Canadian Society of Zoologists; The Society of the Sigma Xi; American Society of Zoologists; American Society of Limnology and Oceanography. *Hobby:* Watercolour painting. *Address:* Department of Biological Sciences, University of Calgary, Calgary, Alberta, Canada T2N 1N4.

ARANGNO Deborah Catherine, b. 27 Nov. 1956, Rockville Centre, Long Island, NY, USA. Mathematician. *Education:* BS, Mercer University, 1977; MSc., Emory University, 1980. *Appointments:* Mathematician, Norad/Spacecom, 1981-83; Professor, Mathematics, University of Colorado, 1982- ; Project Specialist, United Airlines Services Corp, 1987-. *Publications:* Water Comets, 1980; Lunar/Solar Perturbations, NORAD, 1983; Collected Illustration, Childrens Books; Arangno/Calculus, 1985; The Ethics of Modern Science, AES, 1988; Music: Journey of the Fireflies, 1973; Water Comets, 1985; Fashion Design: Arangno Couture. *Memberships:* AIAA; ASG. *Honours:* Fellowship, Emory University, 1978; Recipient, various other honours & awards. *Hobbies Include:* Running; Modelling; Dance. *Address:* PO Box 25298, Colorado Springs, CO 80936, USA.

ARCHER Nuala Miriam, b. 21 June 1955, Rochester, USA. Professor. Poet. *Education:* BA, Wheaton College, 1976; Diploma, Trinity College, University of Dublin, Ireland, 1977; MA, 1978, PhD, 1983, University of Wisconsin, Milwaukee. *Appointments:* Lecturer, Marketing & Design, Parnell Square, Dublin, 1981-83; Lecturer, Dun Laoghaire College of Art & Design, Dublin, 1981-83; Assistant Professor, Editor, Midland Review; Co-Editor, Cimarron Review, Dept. of English, Oklahoma State University, 1984-. *Publications:* Whale on the Line, 1981; Contributor to: Unlacing: Ten Irish American Women Poets, 1987; many journals & magazines. *Memberships:* National Womens Studies Association; MLA. *Honours:* 1st Prize, Open Poetry Competition, 10th Annual Listowel Writers Week; Patrick Kavanagh National Poetry Competition, Ireland, 1980. *Hobbies:* Poetry; Photography; Travel; Women's Studies. *Address:* PO Box 754, Stillwater, OK 74076, USA.

ARCHER Violet Balestreri, b. 24 Apr. 1913, Montreal, Canada. Retired Composer; Educator; Pianist; Organist; Adjudicator. *Education:* B.Mus., McGill University, 1936; M.Mus., Yale University, 1949; Hon. D.Mus., McGill University, 1971. *Appointments:* Music Instructor, McGill University, 1943-47; Visiting Instructor, University of Alberta, summers, 1948, 1949; Resident Composer, North Texas State University, 1950-53; Visiting Professor, Cornell University, 1952; Assistant Professor, University of Oklahoma, 1953-61; Professor, Chairman, Theory & Composition, University of Alberta, 1962-78; Resident Composer, Banff School of Fine Arts, 1978-79; Professor, Music, University of Alberta, 1978-. *Publications:* Numerous compositions most recent being: Improvisatioins on Veni Creator, solo organ, 1987; Variations on Aberystwyth, solo organ, 1987; Six Miniatures for String Bass & Piano, 1987. *Memberships:* various professional organisations. *Hobbies:* Reading; Hiking; Theatre; Films. *Address:*

10805 85th Avenue, Edmonton, Alberta, Canada T6E 2L2.

ARD Saradell, b. 22 Mar. 1920, Macon, Georgia, USA. Art Professor; Paintr; Author. m. Robert A Frederick, 9 Sept. 1969, divorced, 1983. *Education:* BA, Asbury College, 1942; MA, University of Michigan, 1943; D.Ed., Columbia University, Teachers College, 1970. *Appointments:* Art Instructor, Asbury College, 1942-47; Assistant Professor Wheaton College, 1947-52; Educational Supervisor, US Army, Whittier, 1952-53; Arts & Crafts Supervisor, US Army, 1954, 1956, Europe 1956-62; Associate Professor, Alaska Methodist University, 1962-70, Professor 1970-73; Professor, University of Alaska, 1973-85, Dean, 1976-77, Emerita, 1985-. *Publications:* 7 One Woman Shows of Paintings, 35 group shows, 1965-84; Contributing Author, various journals. *Memberships:* Founding Board, Visual Arts Centre of Alaska; Founding Board, Anchorage Fine Arts Museum Association; Co-Director, All Alaska Juried Exhibition, 1969-73; Alaska Artists Guild; etc. *Honours:* Juror's Choice Award, All Alaska Juried Art Show, 1966; First Award, Drawing, 1967; Governor's Award in Art, 1980; Artist of the Year, Anchorage Fine Arts Museum Association, 1984. *Hobbies:* Reading; Painting; Research; Writing. *Address:* 12400 Toilsome Hill Road, Anchorage, AK 99516, USA.

ARDREY Saundra Curry, b. 26 Aug. 1953, Louisville, Georgia, USA. Assistant Professor, Political Science. m. William Ardrey, 5 Aug. 1977. 1 daughter. *Education:* BA, Winston-Salem State University, 1975; MA 1976, PhD 1983, Ohio State University. *Appointments:* Visiting Lecturer, University of North Carolina, Chapel Hill, 1979-80; Instructor, University of Kentucky, Louisville, 1981-82; Graduate Assistant, Ohio State, Columbus, 1982-83; Assistant Professor, Furman University, South Carolina, 1983-88; Assistant Professor, Western Kentucky University, Bowling Green, 1988-. *Memberships:* National Organization of Black Political Scientists; Bowling Green National Organization for Women, president; Kentucky NOW Executive Council; Board Member Child Advocacy; Board Member, Bowling Green Girls' Club; Board Member, Washington Center Internship Institute; Speaker, Kentucky Humanities Council. *Honours:* Women's Studies Grant, 1982; Furman Research Award, 1984; Outstanding Speaker Award, 1989. *Hobbies:* Playing the flute; Reading mystery books and feminist literature; Playing computer games. *Address:* Government Department, Grice Hall, Western Kentucky University, Bowling Green, KY 42101, USA.

ARENDELL Frances Louise Hussey, b. 19 Mar. 1918, New York, USA. Chemist. m. William Henry Arendell, 17 Oct. 1954. *Education:* BA/BS, Barnard College, Columbia University, 1943. *Appointments:* Chemist, General Electric Co., 1943-44; Research Engineer, Johns Manville Research Centre, 1944-53; Supervisor, Central Files, Squibb Institute for Medical Research, 1954-57; Supervisor, Information Services, Warner Lambert Research Institute, 1958-69; Resident Consultant, Mead-Johnson Research Institute; Demographic Data Analyst, Librarian, Amerco International; Process Engineer, Dickson Electronics; Process Engineer, Rogers Corp, 1977-85; Resident Consultant, Consolidated Technologies; Chemist, Tritech Manufacturing Inc. *Publications:* Articles in professional journals. *Memberships:* American Chemical Society; American Electroplaters & Surface Finishers Society; American Institute for Information Science; Arizona Printed Circuit Association. *Honours:* Recipient, various honour and awards. *Hobbies:* Hiking; Camping; Cooking; Rock Hounding; Carpentry. *Address:* Rt2 Box 594, Maricopa, AZ 85239, USA.

ARENSMAN Dorothy Marie, b. 9 Nov. 1942, Texarkana, USA. Educational Administrator. m. Benjamin Henry Arensman, 21 Nov. 1961, 3 sons, 1 daughter. *Education:* BS., Education, St Maary Plains, 1970. *Appointments:* Elementary Teacher, Dodge City, 1970-72; Camp for Blind & Visually Handicapped, 1973-83; Field Rep., Emporia State University, 1982- 84;

Special Education Director, Learned St Hospital, 1983-85; Elementary Principal, Kansas, 1985-89. *Publications:* Research & publications in visually impaired & blind; Family Structure, School Success, Quality Family Life; Educational Administrative Staffing Patterns. *Memberships:* Council for Exceptional Children, President; Southwest Kansas Association; *Honours:* Thomas Award, Outstanding Service to the Blind, 1978; Angel of Light, 1979; Elanor A. Wilson Outstanding Service Award, 1982; Kansas Master Teacher, 1982. *Hobbies Include:* Farming & Ranching. *Address:* River Road, Kinsley, KS 67547, USA.

ARIZAGA Lavora Spradlin, b. 29 Apr. 1927, Garvin County, Oklahoma, USA. Attorney; Counselor at Law. m. Francisco Depaula, 10 Aug. 1946. 2 sons, 2 daughters. *Education:* BA, University of Oklahoma, 1952; JD, University of Houston, 1979. *Appointments:* Private practice of law, 1979-87; US Government, 1987-. *Publications:* Women Under Texas Law, 1982; Exercising your Legal Rights, 1983. *Memberships:* State Bar of Texas; Houston Bar Association; American Bar Association; President, League of Women Voters of Houston; Vice President, League of Women Voters, Texas; President, Gethsemane United Methodist Women; President, Sharpstown High School; College of the State Bar of Texas, 1986, 1987, 1988; Board of Directors, Wesley Community Center, 1983-87; Chair, Affirmative Action Advisory Commission for the City of Houston, 1984-86; Board of Directors, Gethsemane School for Little Childern, 1985, 1986, 1987; United Nations Association, USA, 1958-88; Women in Action. *Hobbies:* Reading; Walking; Dancing, square-dancing; Travelling; The political process. *Address:* 8911 Sandstone Road, Houston, Texas 77036, USA.

ARMOUR Margaret-Ann, b. 6 Sept. 1939, Newton Mearns, Scotland. Chemist. *Education:* BSc Honours 1961, MSc 1966, Postdoctoral Fellow 1970-71, University of Edinburgh; PhD 1970, Postdoctoral Fellow 1971-73, University of Alberta, Canada. *Appointments:* Research Chemist, Alex Cowan & Sons Ltd, papermakers, 1961-66; Laboratory Supervisor 1973-77, Research Associate 1977-79, Supervisor, Undergraduate Organic Chemistry Laboratories 1979-, University of Alberta. *Publications:* Potentially Carcinogenic Chemicals Information & Disposal Guide, 1986; Organic Chemistry Experiments, 1987; Experiments in Organic Chemistry, 1987; Hazardous Chemicals Information & Disposal Guide, 3rd edition 1987. *Memberships:* Offices, Chemical Institute of Canada, Women in Scholarship Education, Science & Technology; American Chemical Society; New York Academy of Sciences; Canadian Association for Women in Science. *Honours:* Scholarship, National Research Council, Canada, 1968-70; Fellowships, National Research Council (UK) 1970-71, Medical Research Council (Canada) 1971-72. *Hobbies:* Encouraging young women to pursue careers in science & engineering; Theatre; Classical music; Gardening; Teaching adult Bible study. *Address:* Department of Chemistry, University of Alberta, Edmonton, Alberta, Canada T6G 2G2.

ARMS Anneli (Anna Elizabeth), b. 23 May 1935, New York City, USA. Artist. m. John Arms, 1 Sept. 1956, 1 son. *Education:* BA, School of Art, University of Michigan, 1958; Art Students League of New York (Scholarship; 1956-58) Pratt Graphics Centre, 1982-85. *Appointments:* Self-employed Artist. *Creative Works:* Sculpture: Gypsy Moth Caterpillar; Spider; Architect of His Dreams; The Board of Education; Jellyfish; Prints: Beetle; Floral Jellyfish; Golden Sunfish; Paintings: LandEscape, I & II. *Memberships:* Chairman, Exhibitions, Camino Gallery, 1960-63, Phoenix Gallery, 1977-83; Manhattan Graphics Centre; Federation of Modern Painters & Sculptors; Jimmy Ernst Artists Alliance, 1987; National Museum of Women in the Arts. *Honours:* Jane Highby Award, 1956; Tau Sigma Delta, 1956; Nora Mirmont Award, 1984; Best Sculpture, Guild Hall Museum, 1987. *Hobbies:* Landscape; Swimming; Films;

Theatre; Opera; Dance; Literature. *Address:* Box 498 Bridgehampton, NY 11932, USA.

ARMSTRONG Anne Legendre, b. 27 Dec. 1927, New Orleans, USA. Company Director; Educator. m. Tobin Armstrong, 12 Apr. 1950, 3 sons, 2 daughters. *Appointments:* Co-Chairman, Republican National Committee, 1971-73; Counsellor to Presidents Nixon and Ford, 1973-74; US Ambassador to Gt. Britain & Northern Ireland, 1976-77; Board of Regents, Smithsonian Institution, 1978-; Chairman, President's Foreign Intelligence Advisory Board, 1981-; Director, General Motors Corp., Halliburton Co., Boise Cascade Corp, American Express Co; Chairman, Board of Trustees, Center for Strategic and International Studies, 1987-. *Honours Include:* Texan of the Year Award, 1981; Presidential Medal of Freedom, 1987. *Address:* Armstrong Ranch, Armstrong, TX 78338, USA.

ARMSTRONG Ardell, b. 1 Oct. 1918, Hobart, Tasmania. Artist; Screen Printer. m. John Conacher Armstrong, 4 July 1940, 3 sons, 1 daughter. *Education:* Studied, Art Classes, Hobart Technical College. *Appointments:* Commercial Artist, The Mercury Newspaper, Hobart, 1938- 40; Teacher, Fahan School, 1938-41. *Publications:* Ardell Armstrong Serigraphy Ex. Art Poster, Hobart, 1982, 1983, 1984; Jointed Exhibition, 1984; Exhition at Zeehan, Tasmania, Burnie Rialto Gallery, Tasmania, 1986. *Memberships:* Art Society of Tasmania. *Honours:* Recipient, various honours & awards. *Hobbies:* Gardening; Travel. *Address:* 26 Derwentlaken Road, Otago Bay, Tasmania 7017, Australia.

ARMSTRONG Coralie Elizabeth, b. 20 Mar. 1945, Warren, New South Wales, Australia. Artist (Painter); Sheep Farmer. m. Francis Leslie Peddie, 25 Mar. 1975, 1 son, 1 daughter. *Education:* BSc Honours, Biochemistry, Sydney University 1965; PhD, Microbiology, New South Wales University, 1976. *Appointments:* Research assistant: Sydney Hospital 1966-67, Hammersmith Hospital, London, UK 1969, Royal North Shore Hospital, Sydney 1970, Biotechnology, NSW University, 1974-75. *Creative works include:* Portraits, oils; Landscapes, oils & watercolurs. *Memberships:* Associate, Royal Art Society of New South Wales; Associate, Royal South Australian Society of Arts; Member, Australian Watercolour Institute. *Honours:* Painting Open award, Condobolin, NSW, 1972, 1973, 1975; Oil painting, Wellington, NSW, 1976; Watercolour, Dubbo, NSW, 1983; Local & Jubilee Awards, Tea Tree Gully, South Australia, 1986; Oil painting, Campbelltown, SA, 1988. Commended, Doug Moran Portrait Prize, 1987. *Hobbies:* Painting; Growing trees & gardening; Riding for the Disabled; Family history & genealogy. *Address:* Lot 607, Richardson Road, Inglewood, New South Wales 5133, Australia.

ARMSTRONG Darlene Lillian, b. 20 June 1949, Skowhegan, Maine, USA. Elementary Schoolteacher. m. Rev. Robert W Armstrong, 5 June 1971. 1 daughter. *Education:* BSc, cum laude, Eastern Nazarene College, Quincy, Mass, 1971. *Appointments:* Teacher Grades 2 & 3, St Paul's Episcopal Parish Day School, Kansas City, 1971-73; Teacher Grade 2, Ridgedale Local School District, Maruion, 19730-76; Teacher Grade 6, School Administrative District No 54, Skowhegan, 1984; Teacher Grade 1, School Administrative District No 49, Fairfield, 1985-. *Memberships:* National Educational Association; Maine Teacher's Association; School Administrative District No 49 Staff Development Team; International Reading Association. *Honours:* Graduated from Eastern Nazarene College cum laude, 1971; Elected to Phi Delta Lambda honor society, 1971; Selected as an Outstanding Elementary Teacher of America, 1975; Elected Worker of the year in local church, 1988. *Hobbies:* Reading; Music; Travelling; Drama; Poetry; Crafts; Collecting antiques. *Address:* 29 North Ave, P O Box 187, Skowhegan, Maine 04976, USA.

ARMSTRONG Jennifer Taylor, b. 19 Jan. 1954,

Perth, Amboy, USA. Freelance Journalist; Editor; Publications Consultant. *Education:* BA, journalism, Marquette University, 1975. *Appointments:* Private Public Relations Practice, with National, Regional & Local Client Roster, 1978-85; Publisher, Footprints Publications, Phoenix, 1985-88; Freelance Journalist, Editor, Publications Consultant, 1988-. *Publications:* Contributor of articles to popular magazines & trade publications, 1978-. *Memberships:* Precinct Committeeman, Republican Party, 1986-. *Hobbies:* Reading; Writing; TV; Films. *Address:* Post Office Box 41921, Phoenix, AZ 85080, USA.

ARMSTRONG Judith Mary, b. 18 May 1935, Melbourne, Australia. University Lecturer. m. 22 May 1957, 2 sons. *Education:* MA, 1968, PhD, 1974, University of Melbourne. *Appointments:* Lecturer, 1974-82, Senior Lecturer, 1982-, University of Melbourne. *Publications:* The Novel of Adultery, 1976; In the Land of Kangaroos and Goldmines, translated from the French, 1981; Editor, Essays to Honour Nina Christesen, 1981; The Unsaid Anna Karenina, 1988. *Hobby:* Reviewing. *Address:* Queen's College, Parkville, Victoria 3052, Australia.

ARMSTRONG Mary Helen Hurlimann, b. 2 Jan. 1927, New York City, New York, USA. Artist. m. 4 Mar. 1977. 3 daughters, 3 stepdaughters. *Education:* Graduate, Chapin school, 1945; Graduate, Parsons School of Design, 1948; Courses at National Academy of Design; Studied with Edgar Whitney, Jack Pallew, Charles Reid, etc. *Appointments:* All covers for National Association for Fire Protection, Fire Journal magazine for 1984; Cover of Garden Club of America Bulletin, 1985. *Creative Works:* Prints of my paintings have been made by various printers; Many one-man shows in Maine, Connecticut, San Francisco, etc; Written up in Drawing with Pastels by Ron Lister-Prentice Hall. *Memberships:* American Society of Marine Artists; Pastel Society of America; National Arts Club, Painting Member; American Artists Professional League; Greenwich Art Society, Vice President in charge of fund raising. *Honours:* One Man Show, Bruce Museum, Greenwich, Connecticut, 1988; Monets Garden in Giverny, a continuing series of paintings, still ongoing. *Hobbies:* Gardening; Politics. *Address:* 8 Grahampton Lane, Greenwich, CT 06830, USA.

ARMSTRONG Nancy Jean, b. 7 Nov. 1924, Poona, India. Writer; Lecturer. m. John Frederick Armstrong, 18 Oct. 1946, deceased 1986. 3 sons, 1 daughter. *Education:* Cheltenham Ladies College; London University. *Appointments:* External Panel of Lecturers for: University of London; Victoria and Albert Museum; Hampton Court Palace; The National Trust; Design Centre; Society of Designer-Craftsmen; Associated Speakers; Foyles; National Association of Decorative and Fine Art Societies (NADFAS). *Publications:* Jewellery: An Historical Survey of British Styles & Jewels, 1973; A Collector's History of Fans, 1975; Victorian Jewellery, 1976; The Book of Fans, 1978; Fans, 1984; Fans from the Fitzwilliam, 1985. Numerous articles in magazines and professional journals. *Memberships:* Institute of Advanced Motorists, 1968; Fellow, Royal Society of Arts, 1975; Kentucky Colonel, 1977; Freeman of the City of Louisville, 1977; Captain of the Belle of Louisville, 1977; Patron of the Fan Circle International, 1985. *Honours:* First woman to give the annual Herbert Smith Memorial Lecture for the Gemmological Society at Goldsmiths' Hall; 3 times gave the Annual Lecture to all the NADFAS Societies, etc. *Hobbies:* Music; Travel; Gardening; Photography; People. *Address:* Priory Cottage, Prospect Place, Porthleven, Cornwall TR13 9DS, England.

ARMSTRONG Pamela, b. 25 Aug. 1951, Borneo. Journalist. *Appointments:* Capital Radio; Medical Journalist, Channel Four; Newscaster, Independent Television News; Broadcaster, Presenter, Daytime Live, BBC. *Hobbies:* Friends & Family. *Address:* c/o John Willcocks, 103 Charing Cross Road, London W1, England.

ARNAS-ISIK Ferial Servet, b. 14 Jan. 1946, Ann Arbor, Michigan, USA. Manager; Engineer. m. Sezai Isik, 5 Dec. 1974. *Education:* BS, Mechanical Engineering, 1965; MS, Mechanical Engineering (Design), 1966; MSE, Mechanical Engineering (Materials), 1968; MSE, Naval Architecture, Marine Engineering, 1972; MS, Public Systems Engineering, 1974. *Appointments:* Research Assistant, Teaching Fellow, 1966-68, 1972-74; Staff Engineer, Aerospace Co, 1969-70; Project Engineer, 1976-77, Superintendent, Plant Engineering Tech, 1977-82, Superintendent, Management Services, 1982-83, Manager, Plan Coordination, 1983-84, Tire Plant; Secretary-General, Tire Research and Development, 1984-87; Manager, Administration, Industrial Yarn Plant, 1987-. *Publications:* Termessos - City of Antiquity, 1986; Several professional papers and publications. *Memberships:* Holcuk Officers' Wives Association for Relief; Environmental and Green Association of Turkey; Treasurer, President, University of Michigan Turkish Students Association; Senior Member, Industrial Engineering Institute; Information Processing Association, Turkey; Mechanican Design and Manufacturing Association, Turkey; Founder, Eymir Foundation (educational); American Society of Plant Engineers; American Society of Mechanical Engineers; Alumnae Association of American Colleges; Alumni Association of Mid-East Technical University; Coordinator, University of Michigan Turkish Alumnae Group. *Honours:* Barbour Scholar, University of Michigan, 1967-68, 1972-73; Sloan Fellow, University of Michigan, 1973-74. *Hobbies:* Philately; Travel; Reading; Translations; Tutoring underprivileged children; Swimming; Hiking. *Address:* Yuzbasilar Cad Sanane Apt 23/4, Degirmendere-Golcuk, Kocaeli 41950, Turkey.

ARNDT Joan Marie, b. 9 July 1945, Stillwater, USA. Librarian. *Education:* BA, 1967; MA, University of Minnesota, 1970. *Appointments:* Elementary Teacher, Roseville Area Schools, 1967-69; Librarian Roseville Area Schools, 1969-; Continuing Studies Instructor, Hamiline University, 1984-. *Publication:* Book Reviews, University of Minnesota, 1988. *Memberships:* American Library Association; Minnesota Reading Association; Minnesota Education Association; Minnesota Education Media Organization. *Honours:* Guest Lecturer, various Universities, Schools & Colleges, 1985-89. *Hobbies:* Reading; Walking; Touring. *Address:* 5730 Donegal Drive, Shoreview, MN 55126, USA.

ARNDT Mary Jo Larsen, b. Chicago, USA. Entrepreneur; Educator; Freelance Writer. m. Paul W Arndt, 17 June 1956, 3 daughters. *Education:* BS, Education, Northern Illinois University, 1955. *Appointments:* Villa Park School District 45, 1955-56, 1957-59, 1962; Urbana School District, 1956-57; Entrepreneur, Managing Family Owned Enerprises, 1959-; Third Vice President, National Federation of Republican Women; President's Commission on White House Fellowships. *Publications:* Newspaper Columnist. *Memberships Include:* Republican National Committeewoman for Illinois; Illinois Republican State Committee; Board of Overseers, Illinois Institute of Technology; Family Shelter Dupage County, Advisory Board; American Association of University Women. *Honours:* Outstanding Woman Leader in Government and Politics, 1988; Delta Psi Kappa; Kappa Delta Pi; etc. *Hobbies:* Politics; Whale Watching in Maui; Wildlife Conservation. *Address:* 35 South Stewart, Lombard, IL 60148, USA.

ARNOLD Constance Ann Gidecumb, b. 12 Dec. 1948, Harrisburg, USA. Plastic Surgeon. m. Daniel Arnold, 21 June 1970, 1 son, 1 daughter. *Education:* BS, Medicine, 1969, MD, 1972, Northwestern University. *Appointments:* Plastic Surgeon, 1979-; Associate Clinical Professor, Surgery, Michigan State University. *Appointments:* Michigan Cleft Palate Association, Treasurer, 1986; Michigan Academy of Plastic Surgeons; American Society of Plastic & Reconstructive Surgeons; American Medical Association; American College of Surgeons. *Hobbies:* Sculpture; Painting; Cooking; Japanese Flower

Arranging. *Address:* 1414 W. Fair, Marquette, MI 49855, USA.

ARNOLD Janet, b. 6 Oct. 1932, Bristol, England. Writer; Lecturer. *Education:* NDD 1953, ATD 1954, West of England College of Art, Bristol. *Appointments:* Jubilee Research Fellowship, 1978-81; Leverhulme Research Fellowship, 1982-87. *Major Publications:* Patterns of Fashion 1660-1860, 1964, 1972; Patterns of Fashion 1860-1940, 1965, 1972; Perukes & Periwigs, 1970; A Handbook of Costume, 1973; Lost from Her Majesties Back, 1980; Patterns of Fashion 1560-1620, 1985; Queen Elizabeth's Wardrobe Unlock'd, 1988. Contributions to: Apollo, Waffen und Kostumkunde; The Times Educational Supplement; Costume; Burlington Magazine; Sweet England's Jewels and catalogue entries for portraits in Princely Magnificence (catalogue of the exhibition of European Court Jewels of the Renaissance 1500-1630 Victoria & Albert Museum, 1980); Contributor to series of six 15-minute programmes for BBC2 Television and others. *Memberships:* Society of Authors; Costume Society; Fellow, Society of Antiquaries, 1984; Honorary Advisor, International Association of Costume, 1983-. *Honour:* Recipient, Winston Churchill Travelling Fellowship, 1973. *Address:* Department of Drama, Royal Holloway College and Bedford New, University of London, Egham Hill, Egham, Surrey, TW20 0EX, England.

ARNOLD Marilyn, b. 26 Nov. 1935. Dean of Graduate Studies; Professor. *Education:* BS, 1955, MS, 1958, Brigham Young University; PhD, 1968, University of Wisconsin. *Appointments:* Assistant Professor, English, Weber St. College, 1968-69; Professor, English, 1969; Director, Center for the Study of Christian Values in Literature, Brigham Young University, Dean of Graduate Studies, 1985-, Brigham Young University. *Publications:* Willa Cather's Short Fiction, 1984; Willa Cather: A Reference Guide, 1986; Editor, Journal Literature & Belief, 1980-83; articles in professional journals. *Memberships:* MLA; Utah Academy of Sciences, Arts & Letters; Philological Association of the Pacific Coast; RMMLA. *Honours:* Karl G. Maeser Research Award, 1985; English Professor of the Year, 1983. *Hobbies:* Tennis; Skiing; Hiking. *Address:* D-341 ASB, Brigham Young University, Provo, UT 84602, USA.

ARNOLD Sheila, b. 15 Jan. 1929, New York City, USA. State Legislator. m. George Longan Arnold, 12 Nov. 1960. 2 sons. *Education:* College Courses. *Appointments:* Member, Wyoming State Legislature, 1978-; Legislative Committees-Appropriations, 1985-; Select Water Development, 1983-86; Agriculture, Public Lands & Water, 1983-84; Mines, Minerals & Industrial Development, 1978-84; Rules, 1985-; National Conference of St Legislators: Fiscal Affairs & Oversight Committee, 1987-; Special Task Force on Long Term Health Care, 1986; Member of the Board, First Interstate Bank of Laramie, 1983-. *Memberships:* Past president, University of Wyoming Faculty Women's Club; Past state land use chair, League of Women Voters; Zonta International; Past vice-chair, Albany County Democratic Central Committee; Secretary, Wyoming State Land Use Advisory Committee, 1975-79; Wyoming Democratic Committeewoman, 1977-79; Past president, Laramie Chamber of Commerce. *Honours:* Top Hand Award, Laramie Chamber of Commerce, 1977; Award for outstanding legislative efforts on behalf of the developmentally disabled citizens of Wyoming, 1985. *Hobbies:* Travel; Reading. *Address:* 1058 Alta Vista Drive, Laramie, Wyoming 82070, USA.

ARNSTEIN Sherry R., b. 11 Jan. 1930, New York City, USA. Executive Director. m. George E. Arnstein, 26 June 1951. *Education:* BS, University of California, Los Angeles; MS, Communications, American University; Graduate study, Systems Dynamics, Massachusetts Institute of Technology. *Appointments include:* Washington Editor, Current Magazine, 1961-63; Staff Consultant, President's Committee on Juvenile Delinquency, 1963-65; Special Assistant to Assistant Secretary, Department of Health & Human Services (HEW), 1965-67; Chief Citizen Participation Adviser,

Model Cities Administration, HUD, 1967-68; Public Policy Consultant, self-employed, 1968-75; Senior Research Fellow, HHS, 1975-78; Vice President (Government Relations), National Health Council, 1978-85; Executive Director, American Association of Colleges of Osteopathic Medicine, 1985-. *Publications include:* Co-author, Perspectives on Technology Assessment, 1975; Principal investigator, Health Technology Management at DHEW, 1977; Editor, Government Relations Handbook Series 1979-84, Washington Report Series 1984-85; Numerous contributions, professional reviews & journals; Editorial boards, various professional journals. *Memberships include:* Boards, Youth Policy Institute, Federation of Schools of Health Professions; Steering Committee, Health on Wednesday Network; Government Relations Committee, Independent Sector; Advisory Group, American Association for Advancement of Science. *Address:* American Association of Colleges of Osteopathic Medicine, 6110 Executive Boulevard, Suite 405, Rockville, Maryland 20852, USA.

AROGYASAMI Josephine Mary Stella, b. 3 Feb. 1951, India. Post Doctoral Research Fellow. m. M. Arogyasami, 26 Jan. 1978, 1 son, 1 daughter. *Education:* BSc., 1970, MSc., 1972, M.Phil., 1983, Zoology, Madras University; PhD, Zoology, Brigham Young University, USA, 1988. *Appointments:* Assistant Professor, Zoology, Holycross College, Tiruchirappalli, India 1972-75, Stanley Medical College, Madras, 1975-83, Tamilnadu Educational Service, 1983-84; Postdoctoral Research Fellow, Brigham Young University, USA, 1988-. *Publications:* Scientific articles in: American Journal of Physiology, Journal of Applied Physiology, Medicine & Science in Sports and Exercise. *Membership:* American College of Sports Medicine. *Honours:* Julia Greenwell Award, College of Biology & Agriculture, 1985, 1987. *Hobbies:* Reading; Travel; Classical Indian Music. *Address:* Wymount Terrace, 2A 63, Provo, UT 84604, USA.

AROIAN Lois Armine, b. 5 Nov. 1946, New York, USA. Diplomat; Historian. *Education:* AB, Occidental College, 1967; AM, 1969, PhD, 1978, University of Michigan. *Appointments:* Instructor, Occidental College, 1974; Lecturer, University of Ilorin, Nigeria, 1980-82; Adjunct Instructor, University of Michigan Extension Service, 1980-; Foreign Service Officer, US Dept. of State, 1984-. *Publications:* Co-author: The Modern Middle East & Norh Africa, 1984; The Nationalization of Arabic and Islamic Education in Egypt, 1983; Africa: A Dissertation Bibliography, editor, 1979. *Memberships:* Middle East Studies Association of North America; Middle East Institute; American Historical Association; Sudan Studies Association; AMerican Institute of Maghribi Studies; American Foreign Service Association; Sigma Alpha Iota. *Honours Include:* Rockefeller Congressional fellowship, American Historical Association, 1983-84; Postdoctoral Fellow: American Research Centre, Egypt, 1981, 1982, 1971-73; Fulbright-Hays Fellow, 1973. *Address:* American Embassy - Casa, APO New York, NY 09284, USA.

ARONSON Eva Beer, b. 6 July 1929, Vienna, Austria. College Professor. m. 6 June 1954. 1 son, 1 daughter. *Education:* BA Economics, Brooklyn College, 1951; MA Economics, New York University, 1954. *Appointments:* Marketing Research Manager, Family Circle Magazine, 1952-58; Principal, Continental Antiques Gallery, 1957-69; Administrator, Advertising Women of New York, 1971-72; Asst VP Thypin Steel Co, Inc, 1981-82; Professor of Economics and Business Management, Interboro Institute, 1982-. *Publications:* Textbook reviewer for Prentice Hall, Inc; Producer of Show-offs, a children's theatre. *Memberships:* New York State Association of Two-Year Colleges; Am Economic Association; Committee on the Status of Women in Economics; New York Women Economists. *Hobbies:* Travel; Alpine Skiing; Bridge; Rehabilitation and conversion of old houses. *Address:* 101-06 67 Drive, Forest Hills, NY 11375, USA.

ARONSON Hazel Josephine, b. 12 Jan. 1946,

Glasgow, Scotland. Sheriff of Lothian and Borders at Edinburgh. m. John Allan Cosgrove, 17 Dec. 1967. 1 son, 1 daughter. *Education:* LLB, Glasgow University. *Appointments:* Advocate Scottish Bar, 1968-79; Sheriff of Glasgow and Strathkelvin, 1979-83; Sheriff of Lothian and Borders at Edinburgh, 1983-. *Membership:* Parole Board for Scotland. *Hobbies:* Walking; Langlauf; Reading; Opera. *Address:* The Sheriff Court, Lawnmarket, Edinburgh, Scotland.

ARRINGTON Doris Ann Banowsky, b. 20 Mar. 1933, Nacoodoches, Texas, USA. Educator; Art Therapist. m. Robert Newton Arrington, 2 Feb. 1953, 3 sons. *Education:* BS cum laude, University of Houston 1965; MAT, College of Notre Dame, 1975; EdD, University of San Francisco, 1986. *Appointments:* Educational Curator, Contemporary Art Museum, Houston, 1966-69; Teacher, Burlingame, California, 1969-79; Associate Professor 1983-, Director, Master in Art Therapy programme 1979-, College of Notre Dame. *Creative work includes:* 12 publications & individual/group exhibitions, including co-creator, 1st major art therapy show in USA. *Memberships:* Standards Chair, American Art Therapy Association; Clinical member, American Psychological Association; American Association of Marriage & Family Therapists; President, Northern California Art Therapy Association. *Honours:* Faculty grant, College of Notre Dame; Research grant, American Art Therapy Association; HLM, Northern California Art Therapy Association. *Hobbies:* Skiing; Travel. *Address:* 30 Knoll Crest, Hillsborough, California 94002, USA.

ARROWSMITH Judith Mary (Pen Name: Judy Goldthorpe), b. 15 June 1944, York, England. College Lecturer. m. John Stanley Arrowsmith, 1 May 1976. *Education:* MA, Edinburgh University, 1965; Teaching Certificate, Distinction, Moray House College of Education, 1966; Advanced Diploma, Religious Education, 1966; MSc., Bradford University, 1974. *Appointments:* VSO Teacher, English, Simanggang, Sarawak, 1966-67; Teacher, English, Annan Academy, Dumfriesshire, 1967; Teacher English, Boroughmuir High School, 1968-71; Lecturer, Education (Psychology), Dunfermline College of Physical Education, Edinburgh, 1972-; Lecturer in Applied Social Science, Moray House College, Edinburgh, 1987-. *Memberships:* Founder Member, Yorkshire Poets Associatiron; Founder Fellow, International Academy of Poets, 1977; Fellow, WLA; Founder Member, Scottish Theatre Group; British Psychological Association. *Honours:* Edinburgh University Class Medal, 1963; Edinburgh University Blue, 1963, 1964; James Robertson Bursary, 1966. *Address:* 3 Strathalmond Park, Edinburgh, EH4 8AJ, Scotland.

ARTHUR Brenda Kay, b. 28 May 1951, Charleston, West Virginia, USA. Financial Planner; Consultant. *Education:* BA Sociology, West Virginia University, 1972; MSEd, Social Agencies Counselling, University of Dayton, 1975. *Appointments:* Field Representative, New York Life Insurance Co, 1981-85; Registered Representative New York Life Securities Corp, 1983-85; Financial Planner; Consultant CIGNA Securities, CIGNA Individual Financial Services Corp, Irvine, California, 1985-87; Financial Consultant; Planner, Financial Services Unlimited, Inc, Newport Beach, California, 1987-; Registered Representative, Southmark Securities Corp, 1987- *Memberships:* National Association of Life Underwriters, 1981-; Charter Member, Charitable Giving Council of Orange County; Planned Giving Roundtable of LA; International Association for Financial Planning; Planned Giving Committee, Adam Walsh Child Resource Centyer, Orange County; Board Member, 1987 & 1988, Vice President, 1986, Zonta International; Irvine Saddlebach Valley Chapter (International Association of Professional & Businesswomen. *Honours:* Distinguished West Virginian, 1986; Outstanding Young Woman of America, 1984; 2000 Notable American Women, 1987; Hall of Fame, 2000 Notable American Women, 1988; International Hall of Leaders, 1988; New Organization Leader, CIGNA Individual Financial Services Corp,

Newport Agency, 1986; Award of Merit, President's Conference, CIGNA Individual Financial Services Corp, 1986. *Hobbies:* Member various Animal Rights Organizations; Music; Working on possible Trademark; CLV/ChFC studies in progress; Travel. *Address:* 1737 N Oak Knoll Drive, Anaheim, CA 92807, USA.

ARTHUR Elizabeth Ann, b. 15 Nov. 1953, New York, USA. Assistant Professor; Writer. m. Steven Bauer, 19 June 1982. *Education:* BA, Distinction, University of Victoria, 1978. *Appointments:* Visiting Instructor, Creative Writing, University of Cincinnati, 1983-84; Assistant Professor, English, Miami Univerity, 1984-85; Assistant Professor, English, Indianapolis, 1985-. *Publications:* Island Sojurn, 1980; Beyond the Mountain, 1983; Bad Guys, 1986; Binding Spell, 1988. *Membership:* Poets & Writers. *Honours:* William Sloane Fellow, Prose, Bread Loaf Writers Conference, 1980; Vermont Council on the Arts Fellowship, 1980; NEA Fellow, 1982-83; Indiana Arts Commission Fellowship, 1988; NEA Fellow, 1989. *Hobbies:* Wildlife. *Address:* c/o Jean Neggar Literary Agency, 336 East 73rd St., New York, NY 10021, USA.

ARTHUR Margaret, Lady, b. 21 Dec. 1924, Manchester, England. Retired. m. Sir Geoffrey George Arthur, 31 July 1946, dec. *Education:* Cheltenham Ladies College, 1941-43; Scholar, Somerville College, Oxford, 1943-47; BA Hons; MA(Oxon). *Career:* Wife of Member of HM Foreign Service, 1948-75; Wife of Master of Pembroke College, Oxford, 1975-84. *Membership:* University Women's Club, South Audley Street, London. *Hobby:* Music. *Address:* 26 Cunliffe Close, Oxford OX2 7BL, England.

ARTHUR Toni, b. 27 Dec. 1946, Oxford, England. Media Presenter; Actress; Author; Playwright. m. D Arthur, 8 June 1970. 2 sons. *Education:* LRAM, Royal Academy of Music, 1964; Stanislavsky Institute of Drama; SRN, BA, University College. *Appointments:* State Registered Nurse, 1966-69; Musician, World Tours, 1969-74; TV and Radio Presenter, BBC and ITV, 1974-; Actress, various theatres. *Publications:* All the Year Round, children's book; Every day Singaway; 100 Ways to Amuse Your Kinds. 2 plays: Robin Hood; Jack the Lad. *Memberships:* Patron, Special Olympics UK; President, Spastics Society (Kent), Tonbridge Duke of Edinburgh's Award; Vice President, National Playbus, Mountbatten Adventure Centre. *Hobbies:* Music; Folklore; Reading; Theatre; Driving. *Address:* 3 Forge Cottages, Boards Head, Croborough, East Sussex TN6 3HD, England.

ARTYKIEWICZ-ZBOROWSKA Maria, b. 20 Feb. 1921, Ostrowiec Swietokrzyski, Poland. Actress; Singer. m. Tadeusz Zborowski, 15 Aug. 1960. *Education:* High State Theatrical School, & vocal studies, Professor Erazma Kopaczynska, Cracow, 1945-49. *Appointments:* Academic Theatre (during studies), 1946-47; Debut, operetta, Cracow Musical Theatre, 1948; State Theatre & State Philharmony, Cracow, 1949-52; State Silesian Operette, Gliwice, 1952-81. *Creative work includes:* Approx. 20 roles, dramatic theatre; Approx. 50 roles as primadonna, classic & contemporary operettas & musicals; Concerts, operatic & classical music. *Membership:* Union of Polish Stage Actors (ZASP). *Honours:* Gold Cross of Merit, 1960; Prize of the Wojewoda (District Chairman), Katowice, 1963; Award, merit in cultural activity, Ministry of Culture, 1973; Knight Cross of Poland, Order Polonia Restituta, 1975. *Hobbies:* Breeding cocker spaniels; Gardening. *Address:* ul Uzdrowiskowa 12, 43 450 Ustron, Poland.

ARTZT Alice Josephine, b. 16 Mar. 1943, Philadelphia, Pennsylvania, USA. Classical Guitarist. *Education:* BA 1965, Graduate Studies in Composition & Musicology, Columbia University; Studied Composition under Darius Milhald, and guitar under Julian Bream, Ida Prestl, and Alexander Lagoya. *Appointments:* Teacher, Mannes College of Music, 1966-69; Concert Guitarist, 1969-; Teacher, Trenton State University, 1977-80; Currently private tutor of Guitar. *Publications:* The Art of Practising, 1978; Editor, The GFA International Guitarists' Cookbook, 1986; numerous articles in guitar & music periodicals; 12 LP Records. *Memberships:* guitar Foundation of America; Board of Directors 1977-80, 1982-, current Chairman of Board of Guitar Foundation of America. *Honours:* several awards for LP recordings. *Hobbies:* Travel; Hi-Fi; Chaplin Films. *Address:* 180 Claremont Avenue, Apt 31, New York City, NY 10027, USA.

ARUM Barbara, b. 10 Oct. 1937, Des Moines, Iowa, USA. Sculptor. *Creative work includes:* Solo exhibitions New York City and environs 1979-. Group exhibitions, numerous venues throughout USA. Publications: New York Times, 1979-85; Reporters Dispatch, 1982; Art World, 1983. *Honours include:* 1st prize, sculpture, Beaux Arts Finale, Westchester, NY, 1981; Members Award, National Association of Women Artists, 1983; Purdue Frederick Award, New England Exhibition, Silvermine, Connecticut, 1984; Dan Rennick Award, Audubon Artists, New York, 1984; Dorothy Lubell Feigin Memorial Award, American Society of Contemporary Artists, 1984; Finalist, Certificate of Excellence, International Art Competition, Los Angeles, 1984; Business Community Award, North American Sculpture Exhibition, Golden, Colorado, 1987. *Address:* 138 West 17th, New York, NY 10011, USA.

ARVANITES Margherita Jessie, b. 29 Apr. 1955, Ipswich, Massachusetts, USA. Engineer. *Education:* BA, Pfeiffer College, 1978. *Appointments:* Evaluation engineer 1979-82, technical forecaster 1983- 84, Manager, Engine Testing 1985-86; Manager, Engine Test & Powerplant Engineering 1987, Quality Manager 1988, QEC Programme Manager 1988-, General Electric Company. *Memberships:* Senior member, American Institute of Aeronautics & Astronautics; Great Outdoors. *Honours:* Outstanding Business Woman 1977, Outstanding Professional Woman, 1986, YWCA. *Hobbies:* Skiing; Golf; Hiking. *Address:* 1741 Simmons Court, Claremont, California 91711, USA.

ASARO Catherine Ann, b. 6 Nov. 1955, Oakland, USA. Assistant Professor of Physics. m. John Kendall Cannizzo, 9 Aug. 1986. *Education:* BS, University of California at Los Angeles, 1978; AM 1983, PhD 1985, Harvard. *Appointments:* Research Physicist, Chemical Physics Theory Group, University of Toronto, Canada, 1985-87; Assistant Professor of Physics, Kenyon College, Ohio, USA, 1987-. *Publications:* Numerous articles in professional journals; PhD thesis: Multichannel Theory of Molecular Photodissociation. Poem: For John. *Memberships:* Association of Harvard Chemists; Tau Beta Pi; Sigma Xi; American Physical Society; Past President, Women in Science, Harvard and Radcliffe; Former Student Member, Royal Academy of Dancing, London England. *Honours:* Merck Index Award, 1978; Predoctoral Fellowship, Honourable Mention, National Science Foundation, 1978; NSF-URP participant, 1977; Highest Honours in Chemistry, University of California, 1978; Graduate, Magna cum laude, 1978. *Hobbies:* Classical piano; Ballet; Writer. *Address:* Dept of Physics, Kenyon College, Gambier, Ohio 43022, USA.

ASH Fayola Foltz, b. 24 Feb. 1926, Lansing, Michigan, USA. Musician. m. Major McKinley Ash, 2 Sept. 1947, 3 sons, 1 daughter. *Education:* BMus., Michigan State University, 1948; MA, Eastern Michigan University, 1985. *Appointments:* Private Piano Teacher, 1938-; Keyboard Soloist & Accompanist, 1938-; Church Organist, 1945-; Public School Teacher, 1949-51; Junior Choir Director, 1964-72; Private Organ Teacher, 1983-. *Memberships:* Ann Arbor Area Piano Teachers Guild, President, Vice President, Treasurer; American Guild of Organists; Michigan Music Teachers Association; Music Teachers National Association; Mu Phi Epsilon; etc. *Honours:* Tau Sigma, 1946; Phi Kappa Phi, 1948; Magna cum Laude, 1948; Grace Sponberg Scholar, 1985. *Hobbies:* Bird Watching; Gardening; Travel. *Address:* 1206 Snyder, Ann Arbor, MI 48103, USA.

ASHBY Anne, b. 2 May 1938, Shropshire, England. Fieldworker with Homeless Families. m. husband deceased 1981, 2 sons, 1 daughter. *Appointments:* Director, Co-Founder, First Refuge for Battered Women & Children, Chiswick, 1971-83; Fieldworker, Homeless Families in the London Boroughs, 1983-. *Publications:* Articles in: Woman; Womans Own; TV appearances; Lecturer, Holland, Italy, Spain, Belgium & UK on Family Violence. *Memberships:* Woman of the Year Association; Network; Chairwoman, Westminster Womens Aid. *Hobbies:* Anthropology; Swimming; Gardening; Reading; Social Science. *Address:* 12 Reynolds Place, Queens Road, Richmond, Surey TW10 6JZ, England.

ASHBY Wendy Coral, b. 27 Jan. 1953, Twickenham, Middlesex, England. Author; Glosa International Language Networker. *Career:* Shop Assistant, 1968; Manager of Newsagents and Confectioners, 1969-78; Started compiling Glosa dictionaries, 1978; Co-Founder, Glosa International Language Network, 1981-; Joint Editor, Plu Glosa Nota periodical, 1981-. *Publications:* Several dictionaries (with Ron Clark) including: Glosa 1000, Glosa 6000, Basic Dictionary of Glosa, Advanced Dictionary; 18 Steps to Fluency in Glosa; Editor, Dorset Wise, environmental Directory for the county of Dorset. *Memberships:* Tranet, USA; Green Party; CND; Peace Education Network; Christchurch Twinning Committee, 1981-83; Co-Founder, Trustee, Glosa Education Organisation education charity, 1987-. *Hobbies:* Swimming; Sewing; Nature study; Holistic health; Green movement; Travel; Networking. *Address:* Coraldene, 17 Wellington Avenue, Highcliffe, Christchurch, Dorset BH23 4HJ, England.

ASHDOWN Dulcie Margaret, b. 24 Feb. 1946, London, UK. Writer; Editor. *Education:* BA (Hons), History, Bristol University, 1967. *Publications:* 10 books, mainly historical biographies including: Royal Weddings, 1981; Victoria & The Coburgs, 1981; Contributor to many magazines including: Heritage; Majesty; Writer's Monthly. *Hobbies:* Gardening; Interior decorating; Dressmaking; Lay Preacher, Methodist Church since 1966. *Address:* c/o National Westminster Bank, 1302 High Road, Whetstone, London N20, UK.

ASHE Barbara Rose, b. 18 May 1928, Miami, USA. Retired. *Education:* Traphagen School of Art, 1947-49; University of Miami, 1947-53. *Appointments:* Head, Volunteers, Patient Counsellor and Assistant Director, Patient Relations, 1965-74; Group Employees Insurance Agent, 1975-82. As a volunteer, 1963-67: Chairman of Public Relations, The Junior League of Miami, Florida (1 year); Desk Chairman, American Red Cross, Day Grey Ladies -Veterans Hospital, Coral Gables, Florida (5 years); Lowe Art Gallery - University of Miami, Coral Gables, Florida - Workd with Children's Art Programs (Approx. 2 years). *Memberships:* English Speaking Union; Navy League. *Honours:* Recipient, awards with horses. *Hobbies:* Animals; Books; Art; Music. *Address:* 10852 North Kendall Drive, Bldg. No 2, Apt. 220, Miami, FL 33176, USA.

ASHER Jane, b. 5 Apr. 1946, London, England. Actress; Writer. m. Gerald Scarfe, 2 sons, 1 daughter. *Appointments:* Stage Appearances include: Will You Walk A Little Faster; Peter Pan; Bristol Old Vic, 1965; Strawberry Fields; To Those Born Whose Life is It Anyway? Blithe Spirit; Alan Ayckbourn's Henceforward, 1988-89; Films Include: Greengage Summer; Alfie, with Michael Caine; Deep End; Henry VII and His Six Wives; Runners, with James Fox; Dream Child; Numerous TV appearances including: The Mill on the Floss; Brideshead Revisited; Love is Old, Love is New; Voyage Round My Father; East Lynne; Bright Smiler; the series, The Mistress; Wish Me Luck. *Publications:* Jane Asher's Party Cakes, 1982; Jane Asher's Fancy Dress, 1983; Silent Nights for You and Your Baby, 1984; Jane Asher's Quick Party Cakes, 1986; The Moppy Stories, 1987; Easy Entertaining, 1987; Jane Asher's Childrens Parties; Articles in: Sunday Times; Daily Mail; London Standard; Taste Magazine; Family Circle; Country Homes and Interiors; Family Holiday; monthly Column, The Daily Telegraph; Weekly Column, The Independent. *Memberships:* Trustee, World Wildlife Fund; Trustee Child Accident Prevention Trust; FABTA; RADA; Governor, Molecule Theatre; Patron, numerous charities. *Honours Include:* Radio Actress of the Year, 1986. *Address:* Chatto & Linnit Ltd., Prince of Wales Theatre, Coventry Street, London W1V 7FE, England.

ASHER Lila Oliver, b. 15 Nov. 1921, Philadelphia, Pennsylvania, USA. Artist; Educator. m. Sydney S. Asher, 5 May 1946 dec. 1 son, 1 daughter. *Education:* Graduate, Philadelphia College of Art, 1943; Pupil, Frank B. A. Linton, Graphic Sketch Club, Philadelphia & Professor G. Raggi, New Jersey & Italy. *Appointments:* Instructor, Howard University, Washington DC 1947-51, Wilson Teachers College 1953-54, Howard University 1961-64; Assistant Professor 1964-66, Associate 1966-71, Professor 1971-, Howard University. *Creative work includes:* Group exhibitions throughout USA; Over 50 solo exhibitions, USA & abroad. *Memberships:* Past President, Society of Washington Artists; Treasurer, Society of Washington Print Makers; Washington Watercolour Association; Washington, & Philadelphia Print Clubs; Artists Equity. *Honours:* Works in permanent collections: National Museum of American Art; Corcoran Gallery of Art; Howard University; University of Virginia; Sweetbriar College; B'nai B'rith, Washington DC; University of Texas; Fisk University; National Museum of History, Taiwan; Kastrupgardsamlingen Kunst Museum, Denmark; Centre for Research in Education of Disadvantged, Israel; Numerous private collections. *Address:* 4100 Thornapple Street, Chevy Chase, Maryland 20815, USA.

ASHMEAD Allez Morrill, b. 18 Dec. 1916, Provo, Utah, USA. Private practice in Speech Pathology & Orofacial Myology. m. Harvey H Ashmead, 24 Sept. 1940. 1 son, 3 daughters. *Education:* BSc, Utah State University, 1938; MSc 1952, PhD 1970, University of Utah, Salt Lake City; ACE Continuing Education Award in Speech-Language-Hearing Pathology, American Speech-Language Hearing Association, 1985; Numerous post graduate courses in Speech-Language-Hearing Pathology and Orofacial Myology. *Appointments include:* Teacher various schools, 1938-51; Speech and Hearing Pathologist/Librarian, Bushnell General Hospital, 1942-44; Senior Speech Correctionist, Utah State Department of Health, 1952-55; Director, Speech and Hearing Department, Davis County School District, 1955-66; Assoicate Professor, University of Utah, 1965, 1966-70 and 1975-78; Teaching Specialist, Brigham Young University, 1970-72; Speech and Hearing Pathologist, Bux Elder County School District, 1970-74 and 1979- 84; Speech-Language Pathologist, Primary Children's Medical Center, 1974-75; Director, Speech-Language-Hearing Pathology, Head Start Programs of Ogden and Bear River, 1978-79, 1979-83; Speech Pathologist and Orofacial Myologist, Private Practice, 1970-88; Supervisor, Speech-Language Pathology, part-time, 1988-. *Publications:* Author of numerous articles, books and audio-visual slide films. *Memberships include:* Life Member, American Speech-Language and Hearing Association; Life Member, Utah Speech and Hearing Association; Western Speech Association; National Educational Association; Utah Educational Association; Davis County Educational Association; United States Council for Exceptional Children; Utah Council for Exceptional Children; Charter Member, Delta Kappa Gamma, Epsilon Chapter; American Association of University Women. *Honours:* Recipient of numerous honours including: Award for Scientific Contribution, International Assoication of Orofacial Myology, 1982; Delegate to Speech Pathology Professional Exchange Programme to the Soviet Union, 1984 and 1986; Delegate to Women's State Legislative Council for the State of Utah, 1958-70. *Hobbies:* International travel; Fine arts; Performing arts; Music; Drama; Reading; Handicrafts. *Address:* 719 East Center Street, Kaysville, Utah 84037, USA.

ASMUSSEN Inger Marie, b. 5 May 1945,

Frederikssund, Denmark. Senior Registrar; Assistant Professor. *Education:* MD, University of Copenhagen, 1971; Specialist: Internal Medicine, 1987, Cardiology 1987. *Appointments:* University Clinics in Cardiology & Internal Medicine, 1971-77, 1980-; Assistant Professor, University of Copenhagen, 1972-; Research Position, Copenhagen University, 1977-80. *Publications:* Articles in professional journals. *Memberships:* Danish Society of Cardiology; Danish Society of Internal Medicine; Danish Medical Association; European and Scandinavian Atherosclerosis Research Association; Danish Heart Association; European Vascular Biology Group. *Hobbies:* Painting; Drawing. *Address:* Dept. of Cardiology M, University Clinic Copenhagen, Frederiksberg Hospital, DK 2000 Copenhagen, Denmark.

ASSEL Barbara Gail, b. 18 Dec. 1951, North Dakota, USA. Physician. m. 27 May 1972, 2 sons. *Education:* BS, 1973; BS, 1977; MD, University of Nebraska, 1979; Resident Physician, University of Minnesota, 1979-83. *Appointment:* Obstetrician, Gynaecologist, Dakota Medical Centre, 1983-. *Memberships:* AMA; American Society of Colposcopy and Cervical Pathology; Amerikcan College of Obstetricians & Gynaecologists. *Hobbies:* Racquetball; Skiing. *Address:* 1702 S. University Drive, Fargo, ND 58103, USA.

ASSINK Anne Hoekstra, b. 3 July 1948, Groningen, Netherlands. Attorney. m. Roger A Assink, 22 Sept. 1967. 1 son, 1 daughter. *Education:* BA 1970, JD 1973, University of Illinois. *Appointments:* Full-time: Robinson Stevens & Wainwright, Albuquerque, 1973-75; Self-employed, Anne H Assink, 1975-. Part-time: Subst. Munic. Ct Judge, 1977-78; Municipal Court Judge, 1978-79 and 1985-. *Memberships:* New Mexico State Bar (Member Family Law Section); Albuquerque Bar Association; American Bar Association (Member Family Law Section); Hogares, Inc (Chair Personnel Committee); Governor's adoption Task Force; Mayor's Task Force on Homeless and Halfway Houses, 1986; Treasurer 1979-81, President 1981-83, El Cabellero Norte Property Owners; City of Albuquerque Task Force on Rescue Missions and Halfway Houses, 1986 (drafting zoning ordinances); New Mexico Department of Human Services Task Force, 1987-88 (drafting regulations). *Hobbies:* Racquetball; Softball; Hiking; Walking; Reading; Children. *Address:* Attorney at Law, 715 Tijeras NW, Albuquerque, NM 87102, USA.

ASTMAN Barbara, b. 12 July 1950, Rochester, New York, USA. Artist; Educator. m. Joseph Anthony Baker, 26 Aug. 1984, 1 daughter. *Education:* AA, Rochester Institute of Technology, 1970; Graduate, Ontario College of Art, Toronto, Canada, 1973. *Career:* Technician, Photographic Department, 1973-75; Faculty, 1975-, Ontario College of Art, Toronto, Canada; Coordinator, Colour Xerox Artists Programme, Visual Arts Ontario, Toronto, 1977-83; Faculty, York University, 1978-80; Board of Directors, Art Gallery at Harbourfront, 1983-85; Curatorial Team, WaterWorks Exhibition, Toronto, 1988; Numerous solo exhibitions, Ontario, Quebec, Saskatchewan, Alberta, also Annapolis, Maryland, Canton, New York, Newark, Delaware, USA, and Centre Culturel Canadien, Paris, France; Participant, numerous group exhibitions, Canada, USA, Milan, Italy, Paris, France, Hong Kong, Sheffield, England, Canada-Mexico Photography Exchange, Mexico; Many lectures and workshops; Commissions; Presenter, Polaroid Corporation's Crafty Camera taped radio shows, 1980. *Creative works include:* Cover art for Loverboy Album, CBS Records, 1980; Photographic mural for CIL Corporation, Toronto, 1981; Inlaid floor design for Speedskating Oval, Calgary Winter Olympics, 1987; Works in public collections, Canada, Bibiotheque Nationale, Paris, and Victoria & Albert Museum, London. *Memberships:* Public Art Commission, City of Toronto; Chairperson, Toronto Arts Awards, Visual Jury. *Honours:* Ontario Arts Council Grants, 1974-82; Canada Council Arts Grants B, 1976, 1977, 1980, 1981, 1983, 1984, 1986, 1988; Project Assistance Grant, OAC. *Address:* c/o The Sable-Castelli Gallery Ltd, 33 Hazelton Avenue, Toronto, Ontario, Canada M5R 2E3.

ASTOR Janet Elizabeth, b. 1 Dec. 1961, Taplow, England. Student. *Education:* Charterhouse, 1978-80; New College, Oxford, 1981-84; BA(Oxon), 1984. *Appointments:* Chanel, Paris, 1985-86. *Hobbies:* Ecology; Comparative religion; Psychology. *Address:* 7 Charles Street, London W1, England.

ATHERTON Arlene R. (Gilmore), b. 3 May 1956, Redlands, California. Financial Adviser. *Education:* Licensed Registered Representative & Life & Disability Agent, 1976; Graduate College of Financial Planners, 1981; Licensed Tax Preparer & Real Estate Agent, California, 1986. *Appointments:* Barclays Bank, 1974-76; Registered Representative 1976- 81, District Manager 1980-82, Waddell Reed; Registered Representative, FSC 1982-87, PSG 1987-; President, Atherton Advisory, 1982-. *Creative work includes:* Course, Unlocking the Golden Handcuffs, Employee Stock Options. *Memberships include:* Offices, various professional organisations. *Honour:* One of Top 20 Outstanding Brokers, Registered Representative Magazine, 1980. *Hobbies:* Skiing; Ballet; Symphony. *Address:* 1333 Lawrence Expressway, Suite 125, Santa Clara, California 95051, USA.

ATKIN Flora, b. 15 May 1919, Baltimore, Maryland, USA. Playwright; Writer; Educator; Lecturer. m. Maurice D. Atkin, 25 Dec. 1941, 2 sons, 1 daughter. *Education:* AB, Education, Syracuse University, 1940; Catholic University of America, 1959-61. *Appointments:* Director, Recreational Arts, Jewish Community Centre, Washington DC, 1941-44; Instructor, Dance Education, Howard University, 1942-43; Founding Director, Playwright, In-School Players of Adventure Theatre, Montgomery City, 1969-80; Freelance Director, Childrens Theatre Consultant, 1953-. *Publications:* Plays for Youth: Tarradiddle Tales, Tarradiddle Travels, Golliwhoppers, Skupper Duppers, Dig 'n Tel, Grampo/Scampo, Hold That Tiger; contributor to professional periodicals. *Honours:* Recipient, Charlotte Chorpenning Cup for Playwriting from Children's Theatre Assn of America, 1978, and other various honours & awards. *Hobbies:* Dance; Writing; Swimming; Theatre; Fishing; etc. *Address:* 5507 Uppingham Street, Chevy Chase, MD 20815, USA.

ATKINSON Janet, b. 9 Dec. 1947, Manchester, England. Director. Divorced, 1 daughter. *Education:* MBA, 1982; P.Adm., 1985. *Appointments:* Public Accounting, 1973-82; Director, Finance, Shuewap Lake General Hospital, 1982-85; Director, Finance & Administration, Vancouver Public Aquarium, 1985-. *Publications:* Articles in professional journals. *Memberships:* Canadian Association of Zoological Parks & Aquariums, Fellow; American Association of Zoological Parks and Aquariums, Fellow; Certified General Accountants Association of BC; General Accountants Association of Canada; Institute of Chartered Secretaries & Administrators. *Hobbies:* Natural History; Travel; Opera; Chess; Writing. *Address:* PO Box 3232, Vancouver BC, Canada V6B 3X8.

ATKINSON Natalie, b. 27 Aug. 1920, Plainfield, Indiana, USA. Instructor, English as a Second Language. *Education:* BA, University of California at Santa Barbara, 1947; MA, Stanford University, 1952; University of Vienna, 1962; San Francisco State University, 1962-67. *Appointments:* Vienna Dependents School, Vienna, Austria, 1948-50; Principal, Trieste Dependents School, Trieste, Italy, 1950-51; American School, Sao Paulo, Brazil, 1953-55; Consultant in Education, Indonesian Government, American School, Djakarta, Indonesia, 1956-58; Coordinator of Program for Mentally Gifted Minors, Millbrae, California, USA, 1959-60; Fulbright Exchange Teacher, Vienna, Austria, 1962-63; Instructor, San Bruno School District, 1960-85; Visiting Instructor, Chengdu College of Geology, Chengdu, Mainland China, 1980; Bilingual Teacher/Trainer, English as a Second Language Seminar (ESL). *Publication:* Marine Science Resource Handbook, 1978. *Memberships:* Academy of Science; Museum Society; Chinese Culture Foundation. *Honours:* Fulbright Exchange Teacher, Vienna, Austria. *Hobbies:* Classical

Music; Photography; Travel. *Address:* 3374 La Mesa Drive, San Carlos, CA 94070, USA.

ATKINSON Sallyanne, b. 23 July 1942, Sydney, Australia. Lord Mayor of Brisbane. m. Rupert Leigh Atkinson, 1 May 1964, 1 son, 4 daughters. *Education:* BA, History & Political Science, University of Queensland. *Appointments:* Cadet with Brisbane Telegraph, then Journalist on Sydney Telegraph & Brisbane Courier Mail, 1960-74; Freelance JOurnalist, UK & Australia, 1975-78; Research Assistant Hon. D.J. Killen, 1975-78; Elected to Council, Ward of Indooroopilly, 1979-82; Leader, Counil Opposition, 1983- 85; Elected Lord Mayor of Brisbane, 1985-. *Publications:* Around Brisbane, 1978. *Memberships Include:* Councillor, Australian Institue of Urban Studies; Vice President, Australian Commonwealth Games Association; Australian Elizabethan Trust Board. *Honours:* Recipient, International Visitor's Award; Honoray Fellow, Australian Marketing Institute; Honorary Life Member, Public Relations Institute of Australia; Fellow, Australian Institute of Management. *Hobbies:* Tennis; Theatre. *Address:* Lord Mayor's Office, City Hall, Brisbane, Queensland 4000, Australia.

ATTHOWE Jean Fausett, b. 26 Feb. 1931, Brooklyn, New York, USA. Writer. m. John M Atthowe, Jr, 17 Dec. 1954. 1 son, 1 daughter. *Education:* BA Humanities, University of Utah; MFA Creative Writing, University of Montana. *Appointments:* Instructor, Rutgers University College, 1975- 85; Adjunct Instructor, Fairleigh-Dickinson University, 1978-74; Instructor, Middlesex County College, 1978; Visiting Assistant Professor, University of Montana, 1975; Teacher, Gill, St Bernard's Upper School, 1974; Office manager/Production assistant, Anastation Advertising; Writing/editing etc, KSL (CBS) Radio; Writing/editing promotional material, Sunset Magazine. *Publications:* The Last Frontier, 1984; The Green Marble Pedestal, 1983; A Moon Over the Cherry Tree, 1983; Guardians, 1982; Old Houses, 1982; My Friend Murray, 1982; You Never Mention New York Anymore, 1982; A Measure of Sundrift, 1980. *Membership:* AWP. *Honours:* Best American Short Stories, 1981 and 1983; New Jersey State Council on the Arts Fellowship Grant, 1983; Nominated for Pushcart Prize, Writers Forum, 1982; Best Fiction Award, San Jose Studies, 1980; Nominated for inclusion in Dance with the West, proposed anthology, Colorado State Council on the Arts; Phelan Award in Creative Writing, San Jose State University, 1968. *Hobbies:* Gardening; Skiing; Hiking; Camping; Preserving plants, animals, people, the earth. *Address:* Box 163, R D 1, Far Hills, New Jersey 07931, USA.

ATWOOD, Margaret, b. 18 Nov. 1939, Ottawa, Ontario, Canada. Writer. *Education:* BA, 1961, University of Toronto; AM, Radcliffe College, 1962; Harvard University, USA, 1962-63, 1965-67. *Appointments:* Lecturer, English, University of British Columbia, 1964-65; Instructor, English, Sir George Williams University, Montreal, 1967-68; University of Alberta, 1969-70; Assistant Professor, English, York Town University, 1971-72; Writer in Residence, University of Toronto, 1972-73; Writer in Residence, University of Alabama, 1985. *Publications:* Poetry, including: The Animals in That Country, 1969; You are Happy, 1974; Two-Headed Poems, 1978; Selected Poems II: Poems Selected and New, 1976-1986, 1986. Fiction: The Edible Woman, 1969; Surfacing, 1972; Lady Oracle, 1976; Dancing Girls, 1977; Life Before Man, 1979; Bodily Harm, 1981; Encounters with the Element Man, 1982; Murder in the Dark, 1983; Bluebeard's Egg, 1983; Unearthing Suite, 1983; The Handmaid's Tale, 1985; Cat's Eye, 1988. Children's Books: Up in the Tree, 1978; Anna's Pet, 1980; Non-Fiction: Survival: A Thematic Guide to Canadian Literature, 1972; Days of the Rebels 1815-1840, 1977; Second Words, 1982; TV Scripts: Snowbird, 1981; etc. *Honours:* Numerous honours and awards including: Humanist of the Year Award, 1987; Fellow, Royal Society of Canada, 1987; YWCA Women of Distnction Award, 1988; American Academy of Arts and Sciences, Foreign Honorary Member, Literature, 1988; etc. *Address:* c/o Oxford University Press, 70 Wynford Dr., Don Mills, Ontario, Canada.

ATWOOD-PINARDI Brenda, b. 14 Mar. 1941, Hyannis, USA. Professor. m. 6 Aug. 1966. *Education:* BSE, Massachusetts College of Art, Boston, 1963; MFA, Painting, Rhode Island School of Design, 1967. *Appointments:* Professor, Art, 1967-, Chairperson, 1976-80, University of Lowell. *Creative Works:* Represented by Clark Gallery, Lincoln, Vorpal Gallery, New York City; Exhibitions include: Brockton Art Museum, Newport Art Museum, De-Cordova Art Museum, Laguna Gloria Art Museum; One person shows at: Clark, 1986, 1988; Germanou Gallery, Rochester, 1987; Winfisky Gallery, Salem, 1984; Kingston Gallery, Boston, 1983, 1985. *Memberships:* Boston Visual Artists Union; Artists for Survival. *Honours Include:* Several Best of Shows, various Festivals; Purchase Prize, Appalacian Nation Drawing, 1982. *Hobby:* Creative Writing. *Address:* 87 Child St., Hyde Park, MA 02136, USA.

AUBREY Rachel Lowe Rustow, b. Berlin, Germany. Psychotherapist; Author; Lecturer. m. Henry G Aubrey, 1963, deceased 1970. 1 son, 1 daughter. *Education:* AB, Smith College, Massachusetts, 1944; MSW, Smith School for Social Work, 1946; Certificate in Psychoanalysis, Alfred Adler Institute, New York, 1973; Diplomate in Clinical Social Work Board Certified, 1987. *Appointments:* Private practice of Psychotherapy, 1960- ; Adjunct Associate Professor of Sociology, City College, New York, 1968-85; Chief Psychiatric Social Worker, Teachers College, Psych. Cons. Center, 1963-67; Senior Consulting Clinical Social Worker, Columbia University, Mental Health Sve, 1973-; Mental Health Consultant, Columbia University, International Student Office, 1985-. *Publications:* Family Living in Modern Turkey, 1955; Family Living & Child Rearing in Modern Turkey, 1962; Death & Adolescents, 1977; The Courage to Mourn, 1987; Separation and Loss in University Mental Health Work, 1988. *Memberships:* President, Metropolitan College Mental Health Association; American Orthopsychiatric Association; American Group Psychotherapy Association; International Council on Social Welfare; Columbia University Seminar on Modern Society; Study Group on Transcultural Psychiatry, New York; Association for Humanist Psychology; Ethical Culture Society, New York. *Honours:* Commonwealth Fellow in social work, 1944; National Institute of Mental Health Fellow, 1958-60; PhD equivalency, voted by NY Board of Higher Education, 1974. *Hobbies:* Languages; Travel and study abroad; Music; Life-long amateur choral singer. *Address:* 560 Riverside Drive, Apt. 14J, New York, NY 10027, USA.

AUBREY-JONES Joan Marie, b. 18 Mar. 1919, London, England. Director. m. Rt. Hon. Aubrey Jones, 7 Sept. 1947, 2 sons. *Education:* MA, Oxford University, 1942. *Appointments:* Ministry of Agriculture & Fisheries, 1942-47; Young Conservatives, 1947-49; Organised Office Designs, 1966-. *Memberships:* Companion, British Institute of Management; Fellow, Institute of Management Consultants. *Hobbies:* Sailing; Travel; Music. *Address:* 89 North End House, Fitzjames Avenue, London W14 0RX, England.

AUCHINCLOSS, Eva Seed, b. 21 July 1933, New York City, USA. Consultant. m. James Stuart Auchincloss, 10 Dec. 1955, 1 son, 2 daughters. *Education:* BA, Vassar College, 1955. *Appointments:* Elementary School Teacher, 1955-57; President, Publisher, Schnell Publishing Co., New York City, 1971-72; Associate Publisher, Women's Sports Publishing C., California, 1974-76; Executive Director, Women's Sports Foundation, Caifornia, 1976-86; Consultant on Marketing to Women 1986-. *Publication:* The Women's sports Foundation Fitness & Sports Resource Guide. *Membership:* Womens Forum West, Director. *Honours:* Recipient, various honours & awards. *Hobbies:* Adventure Travel & Photography; Recreational Sports; Reading *Address:* 195 Moulton St., San Francisco, CA 94123, USA.

AUEL Jean M, b. 18 Feb. 1936, Chicago, Illinois, USA. Writer; Novelist. m. Ray B Auel, 19 Mar. 1954. 2 sons, 3 daughters. *Education:* MBA, University of Portland, Oregon, 1976. *Appointments:* Intermittant Clerical, 1954-64; Clerical, Ckt Brd, Designer, Technical Writer, Manager, Tektronix, Inc, 1964-76; Novelist, 1976-. *Publications:* The Clan of the Cave Bear, 1980; The Valley of Horses, 1982; The Mammoth Hunters, 1985. *Memberships:* MENSA; Authors Guild; PEN; American Center; International Women's Forum. *Honours:* Golden Plate Award, American Academy of Achievement, 1986; Honorary Doctorates: University of Maine, 1985; Mt Vernon College, 1985; University of Portland, 1983; Vicki Penziner Matsen Award, Chicago Friends of Literature, 1980; NW Booksellers Award, Excellence in Writing, nominated, Best First Novel, The American Book Awards. *Address:* c/o Jean V Naggar Literary Agency, 336 E 73rd Street, New York, NY 10021, USA.

AUER Barbara, b. 10 Aug. 1945, Pittsburgh, Pennsylvania, USA Educator. 1 son, 1 daughter. *Education:* BA, Millersville State University of Pennsylvania, 1969; MEd, Bowling Green State University, 1975; PhD, Ohio State University, 1984. *Appointments:* Administrator, School Liaison, Annie E Casey Foundation's New Futures Initiative, Dayton Public Schools, Ohio, 1987-; Director, Federal Dropout Prevention Programme, 1987-; Coordinator, Entry Year Teacher Programme, 1987-. *Publications:* Professional Preparation and Development (North Central Regional Educational Laboratory publication). *Memberships:* Human Development Council, Coshocton, Ohio (President); International Reading Association, Coshocton, Ohio, (President); Association for Supervision and Curriculum Development; Phi Delta Kappa. *Honours:* Jennings Scholar; Scholarship, Ohio International Reading Association. *Hobbies:* Presenter of effective teaching, creative visualisation, motivation; Art; Music; Film; Photography. *Address:* 100 Monteray, Dayton, OH 45419, USA.

AUGSTEIN Renate, b. 4 Dec. 1950, Cologne, Germany. Lawyer; Author. 1 daughter. *Education:* Examination for judicial officer, 1972; State examination lawyer, 1976; Assistant judge, Final State Examination, 1979. *Appointments:* Legal adviser, 1972-76; Referee for social policy, Friedrich-Naumann-Foundation, 1979-81; Head of Division on Women's affairs in the Federal Ministry for Youth, Family Affairs, Women and Health, Bonn, 1981-. *Publications:* Books about abortion; unmarried couples; sexuality; violence against women; witch-hunt; right of asylum, etc. (legal advice and women's policy). *Memberships:* Pro Familia; Female Lawyers Association; Union; Liberal Club (Chair). *Honour:* Roses of the Year by the Homosexuals Association, 1981 (for political engagement towards cancellation of 175). *Hobbies:* Reading; Writing; Travelling; History; Politics. *Address:* Seligenthaler Str 4, 5200 Siegburg, Federal Republic of Germany.

AUGUSTINE Jane, b. 6 Apr. 1931, Berkeley, California, USA. Professor; Writer. m. (1) 3 sons, 1 daughter, (2) Michael D. Heller, 5 Mar. 1979. *Education:* AB cum laude, Bryn Mawr College, 1952; MA, Washington University, St Louis, 1965; PhD, City University of New York, 1988. *Appointments:* New York University, 1975-77, 1986-88; Pratt Institute, 1977-; The New School (part-time), 1977-84; Parsons School of Design, 1985-87. *Publications:* Lit By The Earth's Dark Blood, poems, 1977; Journeys, chapbook, 1985. *Memberships:* Modern Language Association; Poetry Society of America; International Association for Philosophy and Literature; North-East Modern Language Association. *Honours:* Fellowships in Poetry, New York State Council on the Arts, 1976, 1979. *Address:* PO Box 981, Stuyvesant Station, New York, NY 10009, USA.

AULD Nancy Slomer, b. Cincinnati, Ohio, USA. Counsellor. m. John J. Auld, Jr, 20 Nov. 1962, 2 sons, 1 daughter. *Education:* BA, Maryville College, St Louis, 1960; MA 1975, EdS 1982, Seton Hall University, New Jersey; Licensed Professional Counsellor, Missouri. *Appointments:* Counsellor, Westfield, NJ, 1975-80; Catholic Family Services, St Charles, Missouri, 1982; Private practice, St Louis Family Institute, 1982-. *Memberships:* Clinical Member of American Association of Marriage & Family Therapy; National Board of Certified Counsellors; American Association for Counselling & Development. *Hobbies:* Fishing; Swimming; Travel; Art; Plays; Reading; TV; Animals; Nature. *Address:* 14487 Marmont Drive, Chesterfield, Missouri 63017, USA.

AUSBROOKS Carrie Yvonne, b. 26 Jan. 1954, Fort Worth, Texas, USA. Teacher. m. Kevin Ausbrooks, 27 May 1976. *Education:* AAS, Tarrant County Junior College, 1974; Texas Christian University, 1983; BBA, MEd, North Texas State University, 1981-84; Certified Office Automatin Professiona, 1986. *Appointments:* Vocational-academic Instructional Coordinator, Fort Worth ISD, 1983-; Teacher, business & computer use, 1983-87; Adjunct Professor, North Texas State University, 1985. *Creative work includes:* Author: OE/Computer Literacy Competency Profile, 1985; OE/Computer Applications Curriculum Guide, 1986. Developed & implemented computer applications & data processing programmes, & management system for teaching typewriting on computers; Keynote speaker/presenter, various professional organisations. Research: Business Education in Year 2000; Women in Business. *Memberships include:* Executive, Delta Pi Epsilon; Past President, Association for Supervision & Curriculum Development; Office Automation Society International; American Management Association; Various local & national education associations. *Honours:* Outstanding Teacher, Eastern Hills High School, 1986-87; National Dean's List, 1983; Phi Theta Kappa, 1974; Certificate, Forensic Merit, 1974. *Hobbies:* Photography; Calligraphy; Computer programming; Swimming; Fashion sketching & design; Cooking. *Address:* Route 26, Box 12, Fort Worth, Texas 76123, USA.

AUTRY Carolyn, b. 12 Dec. 1940, Dubuque, Iowa, USA. Artist (Printmaker); Teacher. m. Peter Elloian, 27 May 1966, 1 daughter. *Education:* Yale-Norfolk Summer School of Art & Music, 1962; BA 1963, MFA 1965, University of Iowa. *Appointments:* Instructor, Art & Art History, Baldwin-Wallace College, Berea, Ohio, 1965-66; Associate Professor, Art History, The Department of Art of the University of Toledo Museum of Art 1966-, Printmaking (Adjunct), School of Arts in France, Lacoste, France 1987. *Creative work includes:* Numerous exhibitions, USA, Italy, West & East Germany, Yugoslavia, Taiwan, Spain, Korea, Great Britain etc. *Memberships:* Boston Printmakers; Society of American Graphic Artists; Philedlphia Print Club; California Society of Printmakers; Los Angeles Printmkes Society; Women's Caucus for National Organisation; International Graphic Arts Foundation. *Honours:* Grants: Ford Foundation 1961-64, Ohio Arts Council 1979 & 1990; Awards: Boston Printmakers 1971, 1981, 1987, Library of Congress 1971, 1975, Philadelphia Print Club 1972, 75, 77, 79, Bradley University 1975, 1981; Society of American Graphic Artists 1985, 86; International Award of Merit, Wesleyn College, 1980. Works in public collections throughout USA, also Italy, *Hobbies:* Gardening (roses); Reading; past & contemporary fiction of merit; World travel. *Address:* 3348 Indian Road, Toledo, Ohio 43606, USA.

AVIEL JoAnn B. Fagot, b. 15 May 1942, Minneapolis, Minnesota, USA. Professor. m. Aug. 1970, 2 daughters. *Education:* BA, Lone Mountain College, 1964; MA, 1965, MALD, 1966, PhD, 1971, Fletcher School of Law and Diplomacy, Tufts University. *Appointments:* Assistant Supervisor of Social Studies, Ministry of Education, Costa Rica, 1966-68; Assistant Professor of Political Science, Humboldt State College, 1968-70; Professor of International Relations, San Francisco State University, California, 1970-. *Publications:* Resource Shortages and World Politics, 1977; Numerous articles including: Strategies to Influence US Commercial Policy, 1985; Nicaragua and the UN, 1988. *Memberships:* Board of Directors,

Northern California Political Science Association; Women's Caucus for Political Science (President 1973-74); American Political Science Association; Latin American Studies Association; Past Board of Governors, Pacific Coast Council for Latin American Studies; United Nations Association; Board of Directors, World Affairs Council of Northern California. *Honours:* Recipient of grants, Carnegie Foundation, 1972-73, US Office of Education, 1972-74, National Science Foundation, 1975; Fulbright Fellowship, Diplomatic Academy of Peru and University of Lima, 1984; Merit and Professional Achievement Award, San Francisco State, 1988. *Hobbies:* Travel; Skiing; Theatre. *Address:* Department of International Relations, San Francisco State University, 1600 Holloway, San Francisco, CA 94132, USA.

AVILA Kay Molly, b. 5 Feb. 1946, Whitstable, Kent, England. Television Journalist. m. Adam Hogg, 24 June 1978, 1 son, 1 daughter. *Education:* BSc., Honours, Human Relations, University of Surrey, 1968; London College of Secretaries, 1969-70. *Appointments:* Smith Hospital for Autistic Children, Save the Children Fund, 1969-70; Researcher, Daily Express 1969-70; Reader's Digest, 1971; House of Commons, 1972-73; BBC Jimmy Young Show, 1973; Thames TV, 1973-76; TV Reporter, Westward TV, 1977-79; Presenter, Thames TV, 1979-88. *Publications:* Take Six Cooks, 1984; Take Twelve Cooks, 1986; Take Six More Cooks, 1988; Documentaries and series. *Memberships:* ACTT; National Union of Journalists. *Honours:* Take Twelve Cooks topped the best seller list of hard-back books, Feb. 1986. *Hobbies:* Walking; Gardening. *Address:* 46 Wood Lane, London N6 5UB, England.

AVINA-RHODES Nina Alvarado, b. 29 Nov. 1944, Alamo, Texas, USA. Health Facility Director. m. James Lamar Rhodes, 14 Feb. 1977, 3 sons. *Education:* BS, California State University, 1973; MA, La Salle University, 1988; PhD Candidate, 1988-. *Appointments:* Instructor, Centre for Employment & Training, 1976-80; President, Avian Bros Trucking Co., 1982-84; Grants Writer, Quechan Nation Indian Tribe of Yuma, 1984-86; Executive Director, Western AZ Health & Education Centre, 1986-. *Publications:* Co-Host, Post Traumatic Stress Disorder, TV, 1983; Co- facilitator, Counselling Programme, Wives of Vietnam Veterans, 1983. *Memberships:* various professional organisations. *Honours:* Humanitarian Award, VA Administration, 1983; Humanitarian Award, Vietnamese of Santa Clara County, 1983; Citizen of Honour, Vietnam Combat Veterans Ltd., 1983; Woman of Achievement, Santa Clara Board of Supervisors, 1983. *Hobbies:* International Travel; Reading; Research; Baha' Faith. *Address:* 1740 West 24th Lane, Yuma, AZ 85364, USA.

AXINN June Morris, b. 30 Dec. 1923, New York City, USA. Professor; Lecturer; Editor. m. Sidney Axinn, 21 June 1947, 1 son, 1 daughter. *Education:* BA, Queen's College, New York City, 1945; New School for Social Research, 1946-47; PhD, Economics, University of Pennsylvania, 1964. *Appointments:* Research assistant to Financial Editor, Philadelphia Evening Bulletin, 1948-50; Economics Department, Wharton School, University of Pennsylvania, 1964-65; Faculty 1965-, Professor of Social Welfare current, University of Pennsylvania. Also: US Information Service 1986-87, Temple University 1987-88, Japan. *Publications:* Editor, Century of the Child, 1973; Co-author with H. Levin, Social Welfare: History of American Response to Need, 1975, 1982; Co-author with M. Stern, Dependence & Poverty, 1988; Numerous articles. *Memberships:* Past Chair, Faculty Senate, University of Pennsylvania; Past Treasurer, Association of Women in Social Work; American Economics Association; National Association of Social Work; Council for Social Education; Social Welfare History Group; Association for Philosophy of Law & Social Philosophy; International Council for Social Welfare. *Honours:* Kenneth L. A. Pray Professor, 1980-81; 1st annual teaching award (School of Social Work) 1985-86, Research Fund award 1985-86, University of Pennsylvania; Awards, Mellon Foundation 1986-87, Geriatric Centre 1984-85; Consultant, Ontario Council

for Graduate Studies, 1986; Reviewer, numerous journals & presses; Book Review Editor, Administration in Social Work. *Hobbies:* Tennis; Sailing; Travel; Member, programme committees, numerous conferences. *Address:* University of Pennsylvania, 3701 Locust Walk, Philadelphia, Pennsylvania 19104, USA.

AYERS Alice Lowndes, b. 29 May 1930, Atlanta, Georgia, USA. Executive Director. m. Glenn Shattuck, 30 Nov. 1985, 2 sons, 1 daughter. *Education:* BA, Honours, History, University of Bridgeport, 1965; Education Directors Certificate, 1984. *Appointments:* Director, New Careers for Women, 1977-79; Executive Director, Connecticut Trial Lawyers Association, 1979- . *Memberships:* National Association of Trial Lawyer Executives, President; Connecticut Society of Association Executives, immediate Past President; National Association of Bar Executives; Association of Continuing Legal Education Directors; Pro Arte Chamber Chorale of Connecticut, Board Member. *Hobbies:* Town Government; Music. *Address:* 229 Olmstead Hill, Wilton, CT 06897, USA.

AYERS Anne Louise, b. 22 Oct. 1948, Albuquerque, New Mexico, USA. Education Services Specialist. *Education:* BA, Univ Kans, 1970; MEd, Seattle Pacific University, 1971. *Appointments:* Staff cons in student devel, Cen Wash State U, Ellensburg, 19710-72; Dir, Chapman College for ND and Mont Chapman Coll Orange, California, 1972-74; Instr Psychology, Hampton (VA) Inst, 1973-78; Edn Service Specialist, Gen Ednl Devel Ctr, Fort Monroe, VA, 1975-77; Edn Specialist, US Army Transp Sch, Ft Eustis, VA, 1977-79; Nat Mine Health and Safety Acad, Beckley, W Va, 1979-89; Edn Services Specialist, NASA HQ, Washington DC, 1989- ; Appalachian Love Arts, Daniels, WVa, 1983-; Manufacture and market 2 U.S., 41 Canadian Patent. *Creative works:* 29 criterion referenced on-the-job training books for Federal Min Inspectors; 1 joint MSHA/NIOSH book; 1973 Gansfeld Research Psychology Publication; 1 international paper, Developing Criterion Referenced Instruction Based on Valid Performance Analysis. *Memberships:* Women in Aerospace; Nat Soc for Performance and Instrn; Am Ednl Research assn; Nat Assn Women Deans of Adminstrn and Counselors; Internat Platform Assn. *Honours include:* 3 Excellent oboe solo awards, 1963-66; Toastmaster Trophy for best speech, 1979; 2 scholarships to University of Kansas; Leadership Scholarship 1971; Elected 3 times as representative to the national Mine Health and Safety Academy-wide participating management group, 1985-89. *Hobbies:* Collecting gems, shells, coins, rocks and fossils; Oboe and clarinet. *Address:* NASA HQ, Code XEE, Washington, DC 20546, USA.

AYORINDE Julie Joke, b. 15 Dec. 1943. Ambassador. 1 daughter. *Education:* Teachers Training College, 1961-63; MA Philology, Patrice Lumumba University, Mosco, 1963-68; Diploma, Simultaneous Translation/Interpretation, Russian/English, 1973. *Appointments:* Federal Ministry of Finance, 1969-71; Federal Ministry of Establishments, 1971, Civil Service of Nigeria; Diplomatic Service, 1974-; Served as 1st Secretary, Switzerland, 1977-79; Counsellor, Gabon, 1979-82; Minister Counsellor, United Nations, New York, 1984-87; Ambassador, 1987-. *Memberships:* Young Women's Christian Association; Ikoyi Club. *Hobbies:* Travelling; Nature in it's crude form; Listening to music; Reading historical books; Cooking. *Address:* c/o Embassy of Nigeria, PO Box 2019, Cotonou, Benin Republic.

AYRES Gillian, b. 3 Feb. 1930. Painter; Artist. divorced. 2 sons. *Education:* Camberwell School of Art, 1946-50. *Appointments:* Art teacher, 1959-81, including senior lecturer, St Martin's School of Art, Head of painting, Winchester School of Art, 1978-81. *Creative Works:* One Woman Exhibitions include: Gallery One, 1956; Redfern Gallery, 1958; Moulton Gallery, 1960, 1962; Kasmin Gallery, 1965, 1966, 1969; William Darby Gallery, 1976; Women's International Centre, new York, 1976; Knoedler Gallery, 1979, 1982; Museum of Modern Art, Oxford, 1981; Retrospective Exhibition,

Serpentine Gallery, 1983; Also Exhibited: Redfern Gallery, 1957; 1st Paris Biennale, 1959; Hayward Gallery, 1971; Hayward Annual Exhibition, 1974, 1980; Silver Jubilee Exhibition, Royal Academy, 1977; Knoedler Gallery, New York, 1985. Works in Public Collections: Tate Gallery; Museum of Modern Art, New York; Olinda Museum, Brazil; Gulbenkian Foundation, Lisbon; Victoria & Albert Museum; British Council. *Honours:* Prize, Tokyo Biennale, 1963; 2nd Prize, John Moores, 1982; Major Arts Council Bursary, 1979; Order of British Empire (OBE), 1980. *Hobby:* Gardening. *Address:* The Old Rectory, Llaniestyn, Pwllheli, Gwynedd, North Wales.

AZCUENAGA Mary Laurie, b. 25 July 1945, Council, Idaho, USA. Commissioner. m. Ronald G. Carr, 24 Aug. 1968. *Education:* AB, Stanford University, 1967; JD, University of Chicago Law School, 1973. *Appointments:* Office, General Counsel-Attorney, 1973-74, Assistant to General Counsel, 1975-76, San Francisco Regional Office Attorney, 1977-79, Assistant Regional Director, SFRO, 1980-81, Assistant to Executive Director, 1981-82, Office of General Counsel Attorney, 1982-83, Assistant General Counsel, 1983-84, Commissioner, 1984-, Federal Trade Commission. *Memberships:* District of Columbia Bar, California Bar, Supreme Court Bar, American, and Federal Bar Associations. *Honour:* Chairman's Award, Federal Trade Commission 1982. *Address:* 5100 Manning Place NW, Washington, DC 20016, USA.

AZKALAY-GUT Karen, b. 29 Mar. 1945, London, England. Lecturer. m. 26 July 1980. 1 son, 1 daughter. *Education:* BA (Honours) 1966, MA 1967, PhD 1975, University of Rochester. *Appointments:* Teaching Assistant, University of Rochester, 1971; State University of New York at Genesco, 1967-70; University of Negev, 1972-76; Lecturer, Tel Aviv University, Israel, 1977-. *Publications:* Books: Alone in the Dawn: The Life of Adelaide Crapsey, 1988; Making Love: Poems, 1980; Butter Sculptures, 1983; Mechitza, 1986. *Memberships:* Poetry Society of America; Poets and Writers; Federation of Writers in Israel; PEN; Israel Association of Writers in English (Chair 1982-84, Secretary 1987); American Studies Association; Modern Language Association. *Honours:* Tel Aviv Fund, 1980; Arie Dulchin prize for Literature, Jewish Agency, 1985. *Address:* Department of English, Tel Aviv University, Ramat Aviv 69978, Israel.

B

BABB Sanora, b. 21 Apr. 1907, Oklahoma Indian Territory, USA. Writer. m. James Wong Howe, 16 Sept. 1948, deceased. *Appointments:* Reporter, Garden City Herald, 1926; Teacher, Country School, Kansas, USA; Associate Editor, Opportunity Magazine, 1927; AP Reporter, Midwest, 1928; Ghost Writer, Hollywood, California, 1929; Freelance Writer, Hollywood, 1930-; Editor, The Clipper Magazine, 1940-41; Editor, California Quarterly, 1951-52; Teacher, Short Story, UCLA Extension. *Publications:* The Lost Traveller, Novel, 1959; An Owl on Every Post, novel, 1970; Short Stories and Poems, US Magazines; The Dark Earth, Book of Short Stories, 1987. *Memberships:* Authors Guild. *Honours:* Best American Short Stories, 1950, 1960; National Five Arts Award (Story) Early 50's; Borestone Mountain Poetry Awards, 1966-67. *Hobbies:* Gardening; Wild Horses; Wildlife; Dogs; Conservation. *Address:* McIntosh and Otis Inc., 310 Madison Avenue, New York, NY 10017, USA.

BABCOCK Elaine Louise, b. 3 Dec. 1925, Hartford, Connecticut, USA. Public Relations Counsel Editor. div. 1974, 1 son, 1 daughter. *Education:* AB, Wellesley College, Wellesley, Massachusetts; MS, Boston University College of Public Communication, Boston, Massachusetts. *Appointments:* Teaching Fellow, Boston University, 1967-70; Technical Writer, Radio Corporation of America, 1960-61; Technical Editor, Technical Operations Incorporated, 1961-63; Partner, Dean Ross and Whitcomb Communications, 1963-66; Assistant Director, Dartmouth College News Service, 1965-66; Assistant Editor, Journal of Neurosurgery, 1966-74; Director, Publishing Division, Dartmouth Printing Company, 1974-80; President, Babcock Communications, 1980-. *Publications:* Contributor of numerous articles in books, journals and newspapers. *Memberships:* Trustee, Montshire Museum of Science; Society for Technical Communications, Director, Elected Associate Fellow; Society for Scholarly Publishing; Council of Biology Editors; American Medical Writers Association; Women in Communications Incorporated; Public Relations Society of America; The Counselors Academy; Wellesley; President, New Hampshire Wellesley Club; American Association of University Women, President, New Hampshire Division; National Programme Committee. *Honours:* Associate Fellow, Society for Technical Communication, 1982. *Hobbies:* Writing; Reading; Painting; Skiing; Tennis; Golf; Travel; Gardening; Women's issues; Community development projects. *Address:* PO Box A17, Hanover, NH 03755, USA.

BABCOCK Harriet L, b. 25 Aug. 1932, Blissfield, Michigan, USA. Educator. 2 sons, 2 daughters. *Education:* BS, 1962, MA 1972, Eastern Michigan University; EdD, Nova University, 1987. *Appointments:* Kindergarten Teacher, Wayne-Westland Community School, 1968-71; Kindergarten, First, Third Grade Teacher, Manattee County Schools, 1971-. *Memberships:* National Association Education of Young Children; Manatee Education Association. *Honours:* Outstanding Effort for Good Government, 1975; American Childhood International Mini-Grant, 1986; Teacher of the Year, Ballard Elementary School, 1988-89. *Hobbies:* Sailing; Astronomy; Quilting; Research in Education. *Address:* 411 Poinsettia Rd, Box 22, Anna Maria, FL 34216, USA.

BABENKO-WOODBURY Victoria A, b. 19 Mar. 1924, Odessa, USSR. Lecturer; Poet; Translator. m. James E A Woodbury, 25 May 1979. *Education:* PhD, University of Hamburg, Germany, 1959. *Appointments:* Technical University, Hanover, Germany, 1959-60; News magazine Der Spiegel, Germany, 1961-62; American Institute for Russian and East European Studies, Gamisch-Patenkirchen, Germany, 1964-68; Ohio State University, 1968-73; College of William and Mary, 1974-89. *Publications:* 2 books of original poems: Grust (Sadness); Struny serdtsa (Heartstrings), 1972. Contributor of articles and reviews to scholarly journals. *Memberships:* AATSEEL (American Association of Teachers of Slavic and East European Languages); SCSS (Southern Conference of Slavic Studies. *Hobbies:* Poetry; Painting; Parapsychology; Health and nutrition. *Address:* Route 2, Box 7T, Waynesville, MO 65583, USA.

BABER Harriet Erica, b. 6 Jan. 1950, Paterson, New Jersey, USA. Philosophy Professor. m. Roger S M Baber, 10 June 1972. 2 sons, 1 daughter. *Education:* BA, Lake Forest College, 1971; MA, PhD, The Johns Hopkins University, 1980. *Appointments:* Instructor, Northern Illinois University, 1980-81; Assistant Professor, Western Washington University, 1981-82; Assistant Professor, University of San Diego, 1982-; Associate Professor, University of San Diego, 1988-. *Publications:* Author of numerous articles, papers and abstracts to professional journals, magazines and to conferences. *Honours:* Phi Beta Kappa (Junior year), 1970; Scott Prize in Religion, 1971; MacPherson Award in Philosophy, 1971; Gilman Fellowship (Johns Hopkins), 1971. *Hobbies:* Computers; Bicycling; Running. *Address:* Department of Philosophy, University of San Diego, Alcala Park, San Diego, CA 92110, USA.

BACALL Lauren (Betty Joan Perske), b. 16 Sept. 1924, New York, USA. Actress; m. (1) Humphrey Bogart, 1945 died 1957. (2) Jason Robards 1961, divorced. 2 sons, 1 daughter. *Education:* American Academy of Dramatic Arts. *Creative Works:* Films include: To Have and Have Not; The Big Sleep; Confidential Agent; Dark Passage; Key Largo; Young Man with a Horn; Bright Leaf; How to Marry a Millionaire; Woman's World; The Cobweb; Blood Alley; Written on the Wind; Designing Woman; The Gift of Love; Flame over India; Sex and the Single Girl; Harper; Murder on the Orient Express, 1974; The Shootist, 1976; Health 1980; The Fan, 1981. Plays: Goodbye Charlie, 1960; Cactus Flower, 1966; Applause, 1970; Woman of the Year, 1981; Sweet Bird of Youth, 1985. *Publication:* Lauren Bacall By Myself, 1978. *Honours:* Tony Award, Best Actress in a Musical, 1970; Tony Award, 1981. *Address:* Dakota, Central Park West, New York, USA.

BACCUS Janet Glee, b. 27 Mar 1933, Roy, Pierce County, Washington, USA. Genealogist/Columnist. m. Dwaine C Baccus, 9 June 1951, 3 sons. *Education:* High school education. *Appointments:* Writing genealogy column, Routes to Roots, appearing in Pierce County Herald 1983-88, Column now appears in Nisqually Valley News, Yelm, Washington and Senior Scene, Tacoma, Washington. 1981 began teaching genealogy and researching for clients. Teaches at Tacoma Community College and Pacific Lutheran University and others. *Publications:* In preparation: Roy, Washington Voting Registers 1908-1910 and The Piano Tuner's Ledger 1924-1940; Helped Tacoma-Pierce County Genealogy Society compile several books. *Memberships:* Tacoma-Pierce County Genealogical Society, President, Secretary, Projects Chairman; Charter Member, Washington State Genealogical Society, Secretary; Pierce County Extension Homemakers, President, Secretary, Treasurer; Seattle Genealogical Society; National Genealogical Society; Council of Genealogy Columnists, Charter Member; Federation of Genealogical Societies, Regional Editor; Association of Professional Genealogists. *Honours:* Honorable Mention Award from Council of Genealogy Columnists for one Routes to Roots column written in 1988 published in Pierce County Herald. *Hobbies:* Genealogy; Grandchildren; Crocheting; Walking; Camping; Gardening. *Address:* 5817 144th Street East, Puyallup, WA 98373, USA.

BACHER Rosalie W., b. 25 May 1925, Los Angeles, California, USA. High School Counsellor & Administrator (Retired). m. Archie O. Bacher Jr, 30 Mar. 1963. *Education:* AB 1947, MA 1949, Occidental College; Graduate work, counselling & administration, University of Southern California. *Appointments:* Teacher, English, History, Latin, Jordan High School, 1949-55; Counsellor, Jordan, Lakewood & Polytechnic

High Schools, 1955-68; Vice Principal, Washington Jr. High School; Assistant Principal, Lakewood High School; Vice Principal, Jefferson Junior High School, Marshall Junior HS, until 1986; Counsellor, Millikan High School, Hill Junior HS, 1987-89. *Creative works include:* History of Long Beach Oil Fields & Their Influence on City of Long Beach, MA thesis, 1949. *Memberships:* Chapter President, Pi Lambda Theta; Chapter President, Area Director, State Officer, Delta Kappa Gamma; Past & current Chapter President, Phi Delta Gamma; Secretary, Phi Delta Kappa; Member, American Association of University Women. *Honour:* Phi Beta Kappa, 1947. *Hobbies:* Home; Gardening; Reading; Pets; Animal welfare. *Address:* 265 Rocky Point Road, Palos Verdes Estates, California 90274, USA.

BACHMAN Lois J, b. 23 Jan. 1930, Philadelphia, USA. Professor. m. William P. Bachman, 7 Aug. 1969, 1 son, 2 daughters. *Education:* BSc., Temple University; MEd., 1959; EDD, 1980. *Appointments:* Professor, Office Administration, 1969-, Head, Office Administration, 1982-, Community College of Philadelphia. *Publications:* Successful Business English, 1982, 2nd edition 1987. *Memberships:* International President of Association for Business Communications, 1986; various professional organisations. *Honours:* Recipient, Fellow & Distinguished Member Award (ABC). *Hobbies:* Travel; Needlecraft; Classical Music; Opera; Ballet. *Address:* 3032 David Drive, Abington, PA 19001, USA.

BACHRACH Eve Elizabeth, b. 3 July 1951, California, USA. Lawyer. *Education:* AB, cum laude, Boston University, 1972; JD, honours, George Washington University. *Appointments:* Associate, Stein Mitchell & Mezines, 1976-79; Associate General Counsel, 1980-83; Assistant General Council, 1985-87; Acting General Counsel, 1986-87; Associate General Counsel, Corporate Secretary, The Proprietary Association, 1987-. *Publications:* several articles on food & drug law; Editor, Small Business Resource Manual, 1984. *Memberships:* Food Drug Cosmetic Law Journal; Food & Drug Law Institute; Federal Bar Association; Food & Drug Law Committee. *Address:* The Proprietary Association, 1150 Connecticut Ave. NW, Washington, DC 20036, USA.

BACHUS Susan Etta, b. 24 May 1953, Flint, Michigan, USA. Psychobiologist. m. Robert E Sheridan, 25 July 1985. 1 son. *Education:* BA 1977, PhD, Psychobiology, 1987, University of Michigan. *Appointment:* Research Associate, Department of Psychiatry, University of Maryland, School of Medicine, 1988-. *Memberships:* Society for Neuroscience; American Psychological Association; Sigma Xi; New York Academy of Sciences; American Association for Advancement of Science; Association for Women in Science; International Organization of Psychophysiology. *Address:* Maryland Psychiatric Research Center, Catonsville, MD 21228, USA.

BACKE Pamela Renee, b. 25 Dec. 1955, Marinette, Wisconsin, USA. Internal Audit Manager. m. Steve Backe, 15 June 1984. *Education:* AA, 1981; AAS, Data Processing 1982, Truckee Meadows Community College; BBA, University of Nevada, Reno, 1987. *Appointments:* Information Systems Manager, Sierra Office Concepts, 1982-84; EDP Auditor 1984-86, Senior EDP Auditor 1986-87, Northern Nevada Internal Audit Manager 1987-, Harrah's. *Memberships:* Association of Information Systems Professionals, Board of Directors; Institute of Internal Auditors, Board of Directors; Data Processing Management Association; Silver State Striders. *Honours:* Dean's List, University of Nevada, Reno, 1986-87; Dean's List, Truckee Meadows Community College, 1979-82. *Hobbies:* Running; Skiing. *Address:* 12980 Broili Drive, Reno, Nevada 89511, USA.

BACKHAUS Patricia, b. 16 July 1959, Milwaukee, USA. *Education:* BA, Carroll College, 1981; MMus., 1983, DMA, 1986, University of Minnesota.

Appointments: 2nd Trumpet Milwaukee Ballet Orchestra; 2nd Trumpet Waukesha Symphony; Trumpet Instructor, University of Wisconsin, Waukesha & West Bend. *Publications:* Compositions Include: Brass Trio; Trumpet Ensemble. *Memberships:* International Trumpet Guild; Pi Kappa Lambda; Association of Concert Bands; International Congress on Women in Music; Windjammers Inc. *Address:* PO Box 2092, Waukesha, WI 53187, USA.

BACKSBACKA Mary-Ann Regina, b. 27 Feb. 1944, Pargas. Author; Journalist. m. Henrik, 17 Dec. 1967. 1 son, 1 daughter. *Education:* Student, 1962; Dispensing Chemist's Assistant, 1965; Master of Political Sciences, 1978. *Appointments:* Several appointments as Dispensing Chemist's Assistant, 1965-71; Sekr for the Summer University of Hanko, 1974-78; Reporter, Hufvudstadsbladet, 1980-82; Reviewer, Vastra Nyland, newspaper, 1982-. *Publications:* Langt till himlens bord, novel, 1982; I morgon blir det ljusare, novel, 1985; Minns du Shuangxi? poems, 1986; Dramas for radio in Finland and Sweden. *Memberships:* Member of Board, The Association of Finnish Authors; The Association of Finnish Journalists. *Honours:* 2nd prize, novel concurrence, Finland, 1982; Prize of the Foundation of Langman, Sweden, 1986. *Hobbies:* Books; Films; Art; Theatre; Politics. *Address:* Karrgatan 4, SF-10600 Ekenas, Finland.

BACON Margaret Keller, b. 20 Nov. 1909, Bourbon, Indiana, USA. Professor Emeritus. m. Solden D. Bacon, 25 May 1945, 2 sons. *Education:* BS, Purdue University, 1931; MA, 1933, PhD, 1940, Brown University. *Appointments:* Assistant, Brown University, 1931-33; Psychologist, Butler Hospital, 1933-39; Fellowship, Yale, 1939-40; Butler Hospital, 1943; Assistant Professor, Yale University, 1944-46; Part-time, Academy for Research, 1946-65; Associate Professor, 1968, Professor, 1973, Professor Emeritus, 1978-, Rutgers University. *Memberships:* Fellow: American, Eastern Psychological Associations; Fellow, American Antrhopological Association; Fellow, Psychological Anthropologist Society for Cross Control Research, Charter Member. *Honours:* Recipient, many honours & awards. *Hobbies:* Oil Painting; Gardening; Bridge. *Address:* 16 Renoar St , RFD 2 41B, Vineyard Haven, MA 02568, USA.

BADEN-POWELL Patience Helene Mary (Lady), b. 27 Oct. 1936, Zimbabwe (Rhodesia). Commonwealth Chief Commissioner. m. Robert Crause Baden-Powell (3rd Baron), 1 Aug. 1963. *Education:* Bulawayo. *Appointments:* Commonwealth Chief Commissioner, The Girl Guides Association, 1980-85; Patron, The National Playbus Association, 1980-; President, The Commonwealth Youth Exchange Council, 1982-86. *Membership:* Patron, Woodlands Camp Site Trust, 1978-. *Honour:* CBE, 1986. *Hobbies:* Gardening; Antique Furniture; Reading; Embroidery. *Address:* Grove Heath Farm, Ripley, Woking, Surrey GU23 6ES, England.

BADENI June, b. 13 June 1925, Leigh Delamere, Wiltshire, England. Writer. m. Count Jan Badeni, 7 July 1956, 1 son, 1 daughter. *Education:* Private. *Publications:* As June Wilson: Green Shadows: Life of John Clare; As June Badeni: Wiltshire Forefathers; The Slender Tree: A Life of Alice Meynell; Countributor to Country Life. *Membership:* Fellow, Society of Antiquaries. *Hobbies:* Reading; Local History. *Address:* Norton Manor, Malmesbury, Wiltshire SN16 0JN, England.

BADER-MOLNAR Katarina Elisabeth, b. 22 Jan. Berlin, Germany. Writer; Novelist; Poet. m. Dr Imre Molnar, deceased 1985. *Education:* MA, University of Nicolaus Copernicus, 1956. *Appointments:* Librarian in Gdansk, Poland, 1939; Professor and Librarian, Torun, Poland, 1945-57; Private teacher and Translator, 1957-64; Freelance Writer, novelist and poet, 1960-88. *Publications:* 15 books published including: Floeten im Rochricht (poems) 1934, 2nd edition 1979; Lyriden (poems) 1976; Romantisches Gefuege (stories & poems), 1978; Teufelskreis und Lethequelle, 1979 (novel); Neun Puppen (stories for the young), 1980; L'idee d'humanite dans l'oeuvre de Voltaire, 1980; Karola contra Isegrim und Reineke, 1981; Mira im Walfisch (poems) 1981; Konrad Adenauer, Essay, 1984, French edition, 1985; Rosen auf Baustellen (stories & Poems), 1985; Da waren Traeume noch suess, (novel), 1988. Contributions to numerous journals and 8 anthologies. *Memberships:* Swiss Writers Association; Zurich Authors Association; Anthropos. Society of Switzerland: Goetheanum; Dante Society; PEN Centre; Fr. Schiller Society; Marbach/N; Mozart Society; Rilke Society, Basel; Pro Litteris, Zurich, etc. *Honours:* Academie Internationale de Lutèce Diploma & gold medal, Paris 1985; Academie Internationale de Lutèce, Diploma & gold medal, Paris 1986; Academie Universelle de Lausanne, Diploma & silver medal. *Address:* Tobelhofstr 6, CH-8044 Zurich, Switzerland.

BADILLO-MARTINEZ Diana, b, 14 May 1946, Aguadilla, Puerto Rico, USA. Psychologist. m. Jose Martinez, 28 Sep. 1968, 1 son, 2 daughters. *Education:* BA, Psychology, Economy, 1967; MA, General Psychology, 1971; MA, Neurospsychology, 1982; PhD, Neuropsychology, 1984. *Appointments:* Bronx Psychiatric Center, 1976-85; Pain and Analgesia Research Laboratory, 1980-84; DATAHR Inc, 1985-; Neuropsychologist in Private Practice, 1986-; Adjunct Professor, Western Connecticut University, 1987-. *Memberships:* American Psychological Association; Society for Neuroscience; American Pain Society; Hispanic Psychological Association. *Honours:* Freshman Scholarship, 1963; Scholarship, Department of Labor, Puerto Rico, 1968; Member, Sigma Xi Research Society, 1984. *Hobbies:* Gardening; Music; Reading. *Address:* 27 Hospital Avenue, Suite 303, Danbury, CT 06810, USA.

BAENDER Margaret Woodruff, b. 1 Apr. 1921, Salt Lake City, Utah, USA. Author; Journalist; Novelist. m. Phillip Albers Baender, 17 Aug. 1946, deceased, 15 June 1980. 2 sons, 2 daughters. *Education:* BA, University of Utah, 1944; The Children's Institute of Literature, 1972 and 1975; American Society of Writers, 1976; National Writers Club Practical Magazine Writing, 1978. *Appointments:* Journalist, The Valley Pioneer, Danville, California, 1976-78; Editor, Diablo Inferno (Club magazine) 1972-77; Journalist, Author, 1976-88. *Publications:* Shifting Sands, YA Novel 1981; Tail Waggings of Maggie, Juvenile Novel, 1982; Newspaper and magazine articles, 1976-88. *Memberships:* AAUW, 1976-88; Alpha Delta Pi National Sorority, Life Member, 1939; The National Writers Club, 1978-88; Society of Childrens' Book Writers, 1985-88; International Women's Writing Guild, 1983-88; California Fed. Women's Garden Clubs, 1983-88; Contra Costa Music Theatre, 1986-88; Diablo Valley Panhellenic, 1965-77. *Honorus:* The American Society of Writers for the Bicentennial, 1976; The Directory of Distinguished Americans 5th Edition, Distinguished Leader Award for Extraordinary Achievement; Life Member, World Institute of Achievement. *Hobbies:* World Travel; Collector, artifacts, silver spoons, fans, etc; Photography; Music appreciation; Animals: Horses, dogs and cats; Pen pal writing to foreign children, currently to Nyzaura, Zimbabwe, Africa. *Address:* 1675 El Nido "B" Diablo, California 94528, USA.

BAER Frances Dorothea, b. Belserra, California, USA. Real Estate Broker. m. Benjamin Franklin Baer, 20 Mar. 1942. 2 sons, 1 daughter. *Education:* BA 1937-41, Certified Social Worker 1942, University of Southern California; Hastings College of Law, San Francisco, 1957-58. *Appointments:* Social Worker, Los Angeles County, 1942-44; American Red Cross, Los Angeles County, 1944-46; Probation Officer, Los Angeles County, 1946-47; Real Estate Broker, Iowa, California and Minnesota, 1968-; Community Organization, 1942-; Publisher Brooke Press, 1987; International Board of Realtors, Farm & Land Brokers, Minnesota, 1968-75. *Publications:* Study of the Habits of the Preschool Child, 1947; Contributor to National Mental Health & Social

Work publications; Hitting the Sale Trail (in process). *Memberships:* Publisher Brooke Press, 1987; President, National Institute for Crime Control, 1971-; National Council of Social Work; Farm & Land Brokers Association; Aux of National Council of Crime & Deliquency; National Association of Real Estate Brokers; Past President, PTA; Board, Boy Scouts & Campfire Girls; Past President, AAUW; Vice President, League of Women Voters; Past President, Coun of Coop Nursery Schools, California; Organizer, Sacramento Valley Nursery School Association; various other committees. *Hobbies:* Community activites; Publishing; Rancher Garden Valley California; Antiques; Silversmithing; American Silver Guild; Writing; Politics. *Address:* Box 465, Garret Park, MD 20896, USA.

BAEZ Joan Chandos, b. 9 Jan. 1941, Staten Island, New York, USA. Singer. m. David Harris, 1968, divorced 1973, 1 son. *Education:* School of Fine & Applied Arts, Boston University. *Appointments:* Began career as singer in coffee houses; appeared at Ballad Room, Club 47, 1958, Gate of Horn, Chicago, 1958, Newport RI Folk Festival, 1959, Town Hall and Carnegie Hall, 1962, 1967, 1968; gave concerts in black colleges in southern USA 1963; toured Europe, 1960s-, USA, 1960s-; Democratic Republic of Vietnam, 1972, Australia, 1985; numerous recordings. *Publications:* Joan Baez Songbook, 1964; Daybreak, 1968; Coming Out (with David Harris), 1971; And then I Wrote......(songbook), 1979; And a Voice to Sing With, 1987. *Memberships:* Founder, Vice President, Institute for Study of Non-Violence, 1965; National Advisory Council, Amnesty International, 1974-; Founder and President, Humanitas Int. Human Rights Comm. 1979-. *Honours:* Chevalier, Legion d'Honneur. *Address:* Diamonds and Rust Productions, PO Box 1026, Menlo Park, CA 94026, USA.

BAGBY Mary Jean, b. 27 Apr. 1938, Quincy, Illinois, USA. Social Worker; Hypnotist. m. Marvin O. Bagby, 31 Aug. 1957, 2 sons. *Education:* BS, Education, Illinois State University, 1973; MSW, University of Illinoiis, 1988. Certificates: Scientific Hypnosis 1977, Advanced Hypnosis 1978. *Appointments:* Teacher, Elementary Education, 1973-83; President & Director, Calla Hypnosis Centre Inc, 1978-; Case Manager, Zeller Mental Health Centre, State of Illinois, 1988-. *Publications:* 2 anecdotes, Kappa Delta Epsilon Journal; Poems, various occasions; Article, Tae Kwon Do Times, 1983. *Memberships:* Offices, Kappa Delta Epsilon; Universal Tae Kwon Do Association; National Association of Social Workers; Association to Advance Ethical Happiness; American Association of Professional Hypnotists. *Honours:* Kappa Delta Epsilon, national honourary education sorority, 1972; Adult Education Scholarship. *Hobbies:* 2nd Dan Black Belt, Tae Kwon Do; Reading; Writing; Travel. *Address:* Morton, Illinois, USA.

BAGLEY Constance Elizabeth, b. 18 Dec. 1952, Tucson, Arizona, USA. Attorney. *Education:* AB with distinction and honours, Political Science, Stanford University, 1974; JD magna cum laude, Harvard Law School, 1977. *Appointments:* Associate, Webster & Sheffield, 1977-78; Associate, Heller, Ehrman, White & McAuliffe, 1978-79; Associate, 1979-84, Partner, 1984-, McCutcheon, Doyle, Brown & Enersen, San Francisco, California; Lecturer in Business Law, Stanford University Graduate School of Business, California, 1988-. *Publications:* Mergers, Acquisitions and Tender Offers, 1983; Proxy Contests, 1983, Supplement, 1987; Contributing Editor, California Business Law Reporter, 1983-. *Memberships:* American Bar Association; San Francisco Bar Association; Commonwealth Club; Bureau of National Affairs; Corporate Practice Series Advisory Board. *Honours:* Phi Beta Kappa, 1973; Invited to join Harvard Law Review, 1976. *Hobby:* Tennis. *Address:* McCutchen, Doyle, Brown & Enersen, Three Embarcadero Center, Suite 2800, San Francisco, CA 94111, USA.

BAHR Lauren S, b. 3 July 1944, New Brunswick, New Jersey, USA. Marketing Executive. *Education:* Student, University of Grenoble, France, 1964; BA, MA,

University of Michigan, 1966. *Appointments:* Assistant Editor, New Horizons Publishers, Inc, Chicago, 1967; Scholastic Magazines, Inc, New York City, 1968-71; Supervising editor, Houghton Mifflin Co, Boston, 1971; Product development editor, Appleton-Century-Crofts, New York City, 1972-74; Sponsoring editor, McGraw-Hill, Inc, New York City, 1974-75; Editor, Today's Sec, magazine, 1975-77; Senior Editor, Media Systems, Corp, New York City, 1978; Senior Editor, 1978-82, Marketing Manager, 1982-83, CBS Coll. Pub, New York City; Director Development, 1983-86, Director Marketing, 1986-88, Harper & Row, New York City; Vice President Marketing, Willette Corp, New Jersey 1989- . *Address:* 444 East 82nd Street, New York, NY 100278, USA.

BAILEY Audrey Joyce, b. 4 Feb. 1935, Toronto, Canada. Hospital President. *Education:* Nurse Diploma 1956; BScN, 1964; MScN, 1968; FCCHSE, 1987. *Appointments:* Head Nurse, 1960-64; Director of Nursing, 1966-76; Assistant Administrator, 1976-81; Associate Executive Director, 1981-82; President, The Wellesley Hospital, 1982-. *Memberships:* Reg. Nurses Association of Ontario; Canadian Nurses Association; Canadian College of Health Service Executives; Canadian Association of Quality Assurance Professionals. *Honour:* Fellowship in Can. College of Health Service Executives. *Hobbies:* Reading; Music; Theatre; Travel. *Address:* 23 Wycliffe Crescent, Willowdale, Ontario, Canada M2K 1V5.

BAILEY Caroline, b. 13 Jan. 1943, London, England. Counsellor; Trainer; Lecturer; Writer; Agony Aunt; Director. m. Joseph Peter Ward-Bailey, 6 July 1968, 1 son, 1 daughter. *Education:* BA Honours, English & American Literature; Diploma, Health Education; Certificate, Life Management Skills; Diploma, Counseling Skills, 1989. *Appointments include:* (Current) Senior Counsellor, London Brook Advisory Centres; Director, Skills & People Ltd; Lecturer, City Lit, University of London Extramural Department; Agony Aunt, New Woman magazine; Administrator, Scats; Freelance trainer. *Publications:* Beginning in the Middle, 1983; A Loving Conspiracy, 1984; Developing Skills with People, training manual, with Sheila Dainow, 1988. *Memberships:* Committees, British Association for Counselling; Fawcett Society; National Union of Public Employees. *Hobbies:* Family, domesticity & friends; Entertaining; Theatre, Film, Concerts & Opera; Reading; Gardening; Sewing, knitting & crochet. *Address:* 15 Liberia Road, London N5 1JP, England.

BAILEY Daphne Magdalene, b. 23 Oct. 1938, Lillingston, Hampshire, England. Housewife; Business Proprietor. m. David Bailey, 19 Dec. 1961, 2 sons, 1 daughter. *Education:* Heathfield School, Ascot; Switzerland; Paris. *Appointments:* Self-employed in own businesss. *Creative works:* Manor House decorative woodwork; Colour artist. *Hobbies:* Gardening; Music. *Address:* The Manor House, Dry Sandford, Abingdon, Oxon OX13 6JP, England.

BAILEY Elizabeth Ellery Raymond, b. 26 Nov. 1938, New York City, New York, USA. University Dean. div., 2 sons. *Education:* BA magna cum laude, Economics, Radcliffe College, 1960; MS, Mathematics, Computer Science, Stevens Institute of Technology, 1966; PhD, Economics, Princeton University, 1972. *Appointments:* Several technical positions, 1960-73, Supervisor, Economics Analysis Group, 1973-75, Research Head, Economics Research Department, 1975-77, Bell Laboratories; Adjunct Assistant Professor, 1973-75, Adjunct Associate Professor, 1973-77, New York University; Commissioner, 1977-83, Vice-Chairman, 1981-82, Civil Aeronautics Board; Dean, Graduate School of Industrial Administration, Carnegie Mellon University, Pittsburgh, Pennsylvania, 1983-. *Publications:* Economic Theory of Regulatory Constraint, 1974; Selected Economics Papers of William J. Baumol (editor), 1976; Deregulating the Airlines (with David R Graham and Daniel P Kaplan), 1985; Public Regulation: Perspectives on Institutions and Politics (editor), 1987; Contributor to books, journals, newspapers.

Memberships: Past Vice-President, American Economic Association, Executive Committee 1981-83, Head, Committee on the Status of Women in the Economics Profession 1980-82; Past Vice-President, Harbor School for Children with Learning Disabilities; Beta Gamma Sigma; Board: Catalyst Inc; Presbyterian University Hospital, Pittsburgh; Brookings Institution; American Assembly of Collegiate Schools of Business; Philip Morris Companies Inc; Honeywell Inc; College Retirement Equity Fund; Former Board Member: Standard Oil; Kraft Inc; Pennsylvania Power & Light; Editor, several journals; Many governmental and academic advisory committees. *Honours:* Recognition Award, Radcliffe College Alumnae, 1985; Honorary LLD, DePaul University, 1988. *Hobbies:* Woodcarving; Travel; Reading. *Address:* Graduate School of Industrial Administration, Carnegie Mellon University, Pittsburgh, PA 15213, USA.

BAILEY Kathy Marie Clark, b. 21 Aug. 1956, Winston-Salem, North Carolina, USA. Nursing Administrator. m. (James) Donald Bailey, 14 Mar. 1987. *Education:* BSN (Greensboro) 1978, MPH (Chapel Hill) in progress, University of North Carolina. *Appointments:* Staff Nurse, Duke University Medical Centre 1978-81, Veteran's Administration 1981-82, Forsyth Memorial Hospital 1982-83; Director, ICU & Emergency Department, Lexington Memorial Hospital, North Carolina, 1983-. *Membership:* Nominated, National Office, American Association of Critical Care Nursing (AACN). *Honour:* Certified Critical Care Registered Nurse (CCRN), by AACN, 1982. *Address:* PO Box 1817, Lexington Memorial Hospital, Lexington, North Carolina 27293, USA.

BAILEY Louise S., b. 26 June 1930, Gainesville, Florida, USA. Emeritus Professor of English. m. Grayson A. Bailey Jr, 10 June 161 (div. 1983), 1 daughter. *Education:* BS Honours, University of Florida, 1951; MA 1953, postgraduate 1955-59, University of Tennessee. *Appointments:* Instructor, English, University of Tennessee, 1959-61; Instructor 1961-63, Assistant Professor 1963-87, Emeritus Professor 1987-, English, Marshall University. *Publications:* Critiques in: Masterplots II, short story series. Poetry in: Lucidity; North American Poetry Review; Earth Scenes; Moods & Mysteries; Summerfield Journal; Ashes to Ashes; Z Miscellaneous. Essays, various newspapers & journals. *Memberships:* Modern Language Association (MLA); South Atlantic MLA; Society for Study of Southern Literature; West Virginia Writers; Literary Landmarks Association; American Studies Association; Marjorie Kinnan Rawlings Society. Offices, active, American Association of University Women, Huntington Panhellenic Association, Delta Delta Delta, United Methodist Women. *Honours:* Phi Beta Kappa, 1951; Phi Kappa Phi, 1951; Sigma Tau Delta, 1950; Prizes, poetry & essay contests. *Hobbies:* Philately; Antiques; Huntington Museum of Art; Various Club & Association Memberships as above. *Address:* 1204 9th Avenue, Huntington, West Virginia 25701, USA.

BAILEY Margaret Anne, b. 10 July 1939, Birmingham, England. Education Consultant. m. Michael Bailey, 4 Sept. 1963. 3 sons. *Education:* BA (Hons), Durham, 1960; DipEd, Oxford, 1961; MLitt, Bristol, 1973; PhD, Macquarie, 1983. *Appointments:* Teacher, Dartington Hall School, 1961-64; Teacher, Bislington School, 1964-67; Lecturer, Redland College of Advanced Education, 1968-69; Teacher, Bristol Grammar School, 1972; Tutor 1974-75, Commonwealth Scholar 1976-80, Macquarie University; Lecturer, Sydney Teachers' College, 1976, 1979; Joint Principal, The Friends' School, Hobart, 1980-87; Assistant Director Education & Promotion, The Human Rights & Equal Opportunity Commission, Sydney, 1987-88. *Memberships:* Australian College of Education; Womens International League for Peace and Freedom; United Nations Association of Australia; Committee Member, UNESCO International Consultative Committee on Steps to promote the full and comprehensive implementation of the 1974 recommendation on International Education-

Rapporteur. *Interests:* Women's issues; Environmental issues; Education issues; Peace issues; China. *Address:* G P O Box 712, G P O Sydney, New South Wales 2001, Australia.

BAILEY R.A., b. 7 June 1947, Watford, England. Research Statistician. m. C.A. Rowley, 16 July 1971. *Education:* BA, Honours, 1968; MA, 1974; D.Phil, 1974. *Appointments:* Lecturer, Mathematics, Open University, 1972-75, 1978-81; SRC Research Fellow, Edinburgh University, 1976-78; Research Statistician, Rothamsted Experimental Station, 1981-. *Publications:* Contributor To: Proceedings of the Royal Society; Proceedings of the London Mathematical Society; Biometrika; Journal of Royal Statistical Society. *Memberships:* London Mathematical Society; Royal Statistical Society; International Statistical Institute; American Mathematical Society; Biometrics Society. *Hobbies:* Walking; Travel; Music; Drama; Good Food. *Address:* Statistics Dept., Rothamsted Experimental Station, Institute of Arable Crops Research, Harpenden, Herts AL5 2JQ, England.

BAILEY Susan McGee, b. 10 June 1941, Boston, USA. Director. Divorced, 1 daughter. *Education:* BA, Wellesley College, 1963; MA, 1970, PhD, 1971, University of Michigan. *Appointments:* Director, Policy Research Office, Harvard/Radcliffe, 1978-80; Director, Resource Centre on Education Equity, CCSSO, Washington, 1980-85; Director, Centre for Research on Women, Wellesley College, 1985-. *Memberships:* American Educational Research Associaiton; Founding Member, New England Coalition for Educational Leaders; Board of Directors, Connecticut Public TV, 1977; Board of Directors, National Council for Research on Women. *Honours:* Phi Lamba Theta, 1970; Phi Delta Kappa, 1975; State Policy Fellow,, 1978-80. *Address:* Wellesley College Centre for Research on Women, Wellesley College, Wellesley, MA 02181, USA.

BAILLIE Ramona V Balena. b. 2 June 1953, Quebec, Canada. Vice President. m. Ian Baillie, 3 Mar. 1986. *Education:* Courses towards BA, Ryerson Polytechnic, Ontario College of Arts. *Appointments:* Vice president, Tosi/Personnel World, 1974-. *Memberships:* Personnel Association of Ontario, Director of Annual Conference; Canadian Association of Women Executives; Commerce Court Merchants Association, Director. *Hobbies:* Skiing; Crosswords; Reading; Oil painting. *Address:* 58 Belcourt Road, Toronto, Ontario M4S 2T9, Canada.

BAILYN Lotte, b. 17 July 1930, Vienna, Austria. Professor. m. Bernard Bailyn, 18 June 1952, 2 sons. *Education:* BA, 1951, Swarthmore College: MA, 1953, PhD, 1956, Harvard (Radcliffe), USA. *Appointments:* Various Research positions, 1956-58; Research Associate, 1958-64, Lecturer, 1963-67, Harvard University; Research Associate, 1969-70, Lecturer, 1970-71, Senior Lecturer, 1971-72, Associate Professor, 1972-80, Professor, 1980-, Sloan School of Management, MIT. *Memberships:* Academy of Management; American Psychological Association; American Sociological Association. *Honours:* Sigma Xi; Phi Beta Kappa. *Address:* Sloan School of Management, E52-585, MIT, Cambridge, MA 02139, USA.

BAINES Patricia Margaret, b. 17 Mar. 1930, London, England. Author; Craftswoman; Musician. m. Anthony Cuthbert Baines, 16 June 1960. *Education:* Royal College of Music, 1947-50; Associate Certificate, RCM, 1948. *Appointments:* Principal Oboe, International Ballet, Ballet Rambert, Martha Graham Dance Company (1st European tour), 1950-54; Music Organiser, Royal Overseas League, London, 1957-61; Woodwind teacher, Bedales School, 1957-60; Full time music staff, Uppingham School, 1961-65; Solo Oboe, Cheltenham Chamber Orchestra, 1966-67; Woodwind teacher, boys' schools, Cheltenham & Gloucester, 1966-70. *Publications:* Spinning Wheels, Spinners & Spinning (award), 1977, 1982; Spinning Wheels at Snowshill Manor, 1978; Spindle Spinning, 1984; Spindle Spinning Cotton, 1985; Flax & Linen, 1985; Linen: Hand Spinning & Weaving, 1989; Linen Legacy, monograph & catalogue of Rita Beales weaving, 1989, Holborne Museum Crafts Study Centre, Bath. *Memberships:* Offices (past/present): Oxford & London Guilds of Weavers, Spinners & Dyers; Association of Guilds of Weavers, Spinners & Dyers; Oxfordshire Guild of Craftsmen. *Honours:* Exhibitioner, Royal College of Music, 1949-50; Dawson Prize, oboe playing, 1949; Prize, best craft book of year, Crafts Council, 1978. *Hobbies:* Textile history; Modern paintings; Artist's etchings; Decorative arts; Volunteer guide, Victoria & Albert Museum, London; Horse Racing. *Address:* 8 Lynette Avenue, Clapham, London SW4 9HD, England.

BAIRD Catherine Merena, b. 22 Jan. 1944, Detroit, Michigan, USA. Concert Pianist; Artist; Teacher. m. John Baird, 4 Sept. 1970. *Education:* BMus 1966, MMus 1968, University of Michigan. *Appointments:* University of Wisconsin, 1968-71; St Michael's College, 1976-; Faculty, American College of Musicians, 1982-. *Creative works include:* Recordings: Pianist, albums, Elsa Hilger: 1st Lady of the Cello, Volumes I, II & III, 1985-88. *Memberships:* Music Teachers National Association; National Guild of Piano Teachers. *Honours:* Sigma Alpha Iota, 1965; Phi Kappa Phi, 1965; Honours scholar, University of Michigan, Ann Arbor, 1965; Joseph Brinkman piano prize, 1966; Pi Kappa Lambda, 1966; Master Teacher's certificate, 1983; Hall of Fame, National Piano Guild, 1984. *Hobbies:* Persian cats; Spencerian script; Animal rights & welfare. *Address:* 35 Proctor Avenue, South Burlington, Vermont 05403, USA.

BAIRD Patricia A, b. 11 Oct. 1939, England. Professor of Medical Genetics. m. Robert M Baird, 22 Feb. 1964. 2 sons, 1 daughter. *Education:* BSc 1959, MD, CM, 1963, McGill University; FRCP (Canada), 1968; FCCMG, 1976. *Appointments:* Intern, Royal Victoria Hospital, 1963-64; Pediatric Resident, Vancouver General Hospital, 1964-68; Assistant Professor of Medicine, 1972; Associate Professor, 1977; Professor and Head, Department of Medical Genetics, University of British Columbia, 1979-. *Publications:* Over 200 scientific articles and abstracts related to medical genetics and birth defects. *Memberships:* Can College of Medical Geneticists, Medical Research Council of Canada; Board of Governors, UBC; Health Surveillance Registry of BC, Medical Consultant; Nat Advisory Board on Science & Technology to federal government; Science Council of Canada, Study committee on genetic predisposition; Chairman, MRC working group on guidelines for gene therapy;m Canadian Institute for Advanced Research, Research Council; American Society of Human Genetics; Nominating Committee American Society for Human Genetics; MRC Priorities and Planning Committee. *Honours:* Service on several research funding bodies and medical advisory boards. *Hobbies:* Skiing; Gardening; Music. *Address:* Department of Medical Genetics, University of British Columbia, 226-6174 University Blvd, Vancouver, BC, Canada, V6T 1W5.

BAIRSTOW Frances, b. 19 Feb. 1920, Racine, Wisconsin, USA. Arbitrator-Mediator, Labor. m. David Steel Bairstow, 17 Dec. 1954. 2 sons. *Education:* BS, University Louisville, 1949; Oxford University, England, 1953-54; Postgraduate, McGill University, Montreal, Canada, 1958-59. *Appointments include:* Research economist, US Senate Labor-Management Subcommittee, Washington, USA, 1950-51; Labor education specialist, University PR, San Juan, 1951-52; Chief Wage Data Unit, WSB, Washington, 1952-53; Labour Research Economist, Canadian Pacific Railway, Montreal, Canada, 1956-58; Asst Director, 1960-66, Associate Director, 1966-71, Director, 1971-; Lecturer, Industrial Relations Department, 1960-72, Assistant Professor Faculty Management, 1972-74, Associate Professor, 1974-83, Professor, 1983-, Industrial Relations Center, McGill University, Montreal; Deputy Commissioner, Essential Services, Province of Quebec, 1976-; Mediator So Bell Telephone, 1985; Consultant on collective bargaining to OECD, Paris, France, 1979; Consultant, National Film Board of

Canada, 1965-69; Arbitrator, Quebec Consultative Council Panel of Arbitrators, 1968-; Ministry Labour and Manpower, 1971; Mediator, Canadian Public Service Staff Relations Board 1973-. *Publication:* Contributing columnist to Montreal Star, 1971-. *Memberships include:* Board of Governors, National Academy Arbitrators; Nominating Committee Chairman, Industrial Relations Research Association; Canadian Industrial Relations Research Institute; National Coordinator of Regional Activities. *Honour:* Fulbright Scholarship, Oxford University, 1953-54. *Hobbies include:* Travel; Films. *b3Address:* 1430 Gulf Blvd Suite 507, Clearwater, FL 34630, USA.

BAJAS Maria Theresa, b. 7 Sept. 1968, Manila, Philippines. Student. *Education:* Albany Medical College Programme, 1986-. *Appointments:* Volunteer, Richmond Memorial Hospital, 1984; Volunteer, Institute for Basic Research, Department of Cytogenetics, 1986-87; Volunteer, Albany Medical Centre, 1986-87; Teacher, Religion, Sacred Heart Church, 1988. *Memberships:* Pingry Womens Glee Club, President; Pingry Balladeeers; Fisher Music Hall; American Field Service Club. *Honours:* Recipient, many honours & awards. *Hobbies:* Classical Ballet; Piano; Acting; Singing. *Address:* 1 Wilson Terrace, Staten Island, NY 10304, USA.

BAKANIC Eunice Yvonne, b. 26 Sept. 1954, Wilkinsburg, Pennsylvania, USA. Professor of Sociology. m. Floyd A Roberts, 30 Aug. 1974. 1 daughter. *Education:* BA 1977, MA 1980, University of South Carolina; PhD, University of Illinois, 1986. *Appointments:* Computer Consultant, 1980-81; Research Assistant, 1981-83; Visiting Instructor, University of Illinois, 1983-86; Assistant Professor, University of Southern Mississippi, 1986-. *Publications:* Who Complains to Journal Editors and What Happens, 1986; The Manuscript Review, decision making process, 1987; Mixed Messages, 1989. *Memberships:* American Sociological Association; Southern Sociological Soceity; Society for Social Study of Science; League of Women Voters (Chapter President). *Honours:* Giesert Fellow, 1983; Volunteer of the Year for State of South Carolina, 1977. *Hobbies:* Sailing; Horseback riding; Feminism; Bread Basket Community Hunger Project. *Address:* Rt 17, Box 1408, Hattiesburg, MS 39401, USA.

BAKER Alison Ruth, b. 30 Nov. 1962, Colchester, England. Concert Pianist. *Education:* Royal Academy of Music, 1972-78 with Professor Joan Last; ARCM (Hons), LRAM; Studied with Peter Katin and Imogen Cooper. *Career:* London debut, Queen Elizabeth Hall, 1977; Performed at Wigmore Hall; Fairfield Hall; Purcell Room etc. TV Appearances include: Mastermind; BBC People Documentary; Man Alive 1974. *Memberships:* Steinway Artist; European Piano Teachers Association; MENSA. *Honours:* 1st prize, Croydon Symphony Orchestra Soloist Award, 1984; 1st prize, Essex Young Musician of the Year, John Lill Award, 1985; Prizewinner, International Young Concert Artists Competition, Royal Tunbridge Wells, 1985; 1st Prize, Dudley National Piano Competition, 1987; Essex Symphony Orchestra Soloist Award, 1989. *Hobbies:* Languages; Old Testament studies; Architecture; World literature; Travel. *Address:* 26 Vicarage Gardens, Clacton-On-Sea, Essec CO15 1BU, England.

BAKER Bonni Winnifred Clark Perrott (Mrs Eugene R Baker), b. 4 Nov. 1938, Westfield, Massachusetts, USA. Assistant Professor; Human Resource; Workplace Health Education Consultant. m. Eugene R Baker, 19 June 1976. 1 son, 1 daughter, 2 step-daughters. *Education:* Associate of Arts, Berkshire Community College, Pittsfield, Massachusetts, 1976; Bachelor of Business Administration, University of Massachusetts, Amherst, 1982; MA, The Ohio State University, Columbus, 1986. *Appointments:* Assistant to Personnel Director, Berkshire Bank and Trust Co, Pittsfield, Massachusetts, 1971-74; Note Department Supervisor, First Agricultural Bank, Pittsfield, 1975-76; Personnel Director, United Presbyterian Board of Pensions, Philadelphia, 1977-79; Vice-President of Personnel,

Franklin Federal Savings and Loan Association, Columbus, Ohio, 1979-81; Employment Manager, Buckeye Federal Savings and Loan Association, Columbus, 1983-84; Owner/President, Humarn Resource and Workplace Health Consulting Firm, YWEM Enterprises, Inc, 1984-; Assistant Professor, Siena College, Loudonville, New York, 1987-. *Memberships:* Business: American Society for Personnel Administration; Association for Business Communications; Capital District Personnel Association; Association of Fitness in Business; American Alliance for Health, Physical Education, Recreation and Dance. Public Service/Community: Life Member, Advocacy Network for Retarded Citizens; Hampden County Association for The Retarded; Saratoga Performing Arts Centre; Friend of The University of Massachusetts Fine Arts Centre; Saratoga Springs Golf and Polo Club. *Honours:* Signifanct Contribution To Higher Education Award, Capital University, 1980; Academic Excellence Award, University of Massachusetts, 1982. *Hobbies:* Golf; Cooking; Reading; Travel; Theatre; The Arts. *Address:* 24 Collins Terrace, Saratoga Springs, NY 12866, USA.

BAKER Carroll, b.28 May 1931, Johnstown, Pennsylvania, USA. Actress. m. (1) Jack Garfein, 5 Apr. 1955, div. 1 son, 1 daughter, (2) Donald Burton, 1982. *Education:* St Petersburg Junior College, Florida, 1953. *Appointments include:* Broadway appearances: All Summer Long, 1954; Come On Strong, 1962. Motion pictures: Giant, 1956; Baby Doll, 1957; Big Country, 1958; Miracle, 1959; Something Wild, 1961; Carpetbaggers, 1963; Cheyenne Autumn, 1963; Harlow, 1965; Quiet Place to Kill, 1970; Captain Apache, 1971; Watcher in the Woods, 1980; Red Monarch, 1982; Native Son, 1986; Ironweed, 1988. Vietnam tour with Bob Hope, televised NBC, 1966; Various other TV appearances. *Publications:* Baby Doll, autobiography, 1983; To Africa with Love, autobiographical, 1985; Roman Tale, novel, 1989. *Memberships:* Academy of Motion Picture Arts & Sciences; British Academy of Film & Television; Authors Guild; Actors Studio; Cheyenne Tribe, honorary. *Honours:* Best Supporting Actress, National League of Women's Press Clubs, 1956; Nominated, Best Actress Academy of Motion Picture Arts & Sciences, 1957; Woman of Year, Hasty Pudding Club, Harvard, 1957; Film Achivement Award, Look magazine, 1957; Best Actress, San Francisco Critics, 1957; Best Dramatic Actress, Foreign Press Club, 1957; Kentucky Colonel, 1962. *Address:* c/o International Creative Management, 8899 Beverley Boulevard, Los Angeles, California 90048, USA.

BAKER Dorothy, b. 9 Sept. 1914, Mundoona, Australia. Artist. m. John V Baker. 2 sons. *Education:* National Gallery Art School, Melbourne, Australia. Geo Bell Art School; University Art Classes. *Appointments:* Dorothy Baker Art School, 1954-77; Tutor, Malvern Artists Soc School, 1957-71; Brighton Art Group, 1959-66; Victorian Artists Society, 1974-75; Writer, Articles for a Weekly Newspaper. *Creative works:* Major works: National Gallery of Victoria; Architecture School, Melbourne University; St Helen's College; City of Heidelberg Town Hall, Australia; Victorian Artists Society permanent collection; Historical Museum, Shepparton; Shire Officer Keilor; Shire Office Numuskah; Wakefield Collection; Collection of Reinhold Zunder, Oberburgermaster, City of Heidelberg, Germany; Collection of Professor Tein-Man-Str, Director of Taiwan University; Pan Asian Seoul, South Korea; Guangdong Academy of Fine Art, China; Yunnan Academy, Fine Art, Yunnan Province China; Collection of Huang Dok Wei, China; City of Albury Art Gallery, New South Wales. *Memberships:* President, 1980-83, Deputy President, 1979, Victorian Artists Society; Treasurer, 1957-63, Melbourne Society of Women Painters and Sculpters; Honorary Life Member, Victorian Artists Society, 1981; Honorary Life Member, Malvern Artists Society, 1973; Sesame Artists Society, 1967. *Honours:* Awarded, Victorian Artists Society Fellowship. *Hobbies:* Gardening; Travel. *Address:* 90 Pakington Street, Kew, Victoria 3101, Australia.

BAKER Therese Louise, b. 20 June 1939, Minneapolis, Minnesota, USA. Professor of Sociology; University Administrator. m. Keith Michael Baker, 25 Oct. 1961, 2 sons. *Education:* BA, Cornell University, 1961; PhD, University of Chicago, 1973. *Appointments:* Instructor to Full Professor, De Paul University, 1971-88; Assistant to Vice Provost, Stanford University, 1989-. *Publication:* Doing Social Research, 1988. *Memberships:* American & Midwest Sociological Associations; Sociologists for Women in Society; National Organisation for Women. *Honours:* Traineeship 1966-69, grant 1976-77, National Institute of Mental Health; Grants, National Institute of Child Health & Development 1979-81, Illinois Humanities Council/Arts Council, 1986. *Hobbies:* Jogging; Aerobics; Collecting plates, early 20th century dishes. *Address:* 914 Mears Court, Stanford, California 94305, USA.

BAKER Wendy Gertrude, b. 15 Mar. 1953, Kerrobert, Saskatchewan, Canada. Lawyer. *Education:* BComm with great distinction, 1976, LLB, 1978, University of Saskatchewan. *Appointments:* Articled student, 1977-78, Associate Lawyer, 1978-84, Partner, 1984-, Davis and Company, Vancouver, British Columbia. *Memberships:* Vice-President, British Columbians for Mentally Handicapped People; Governor, Law Foundation of British Columbia; Provincial Council and Executive, Canadian Bar Association, British Columbia Branch; Communications Committee, Canadian Bar Association. *Honours:* Governor General's Medal, 1971; University of Saskatchewan Continuing Scholarship, 1971-75; Citation for Citizenship, Secretary of State Department for Canada, 1988. *Hobbies:* Community development; Public speaking; Riding; Cross-stitch needlework; Politics. *Address:* 2800-666 Burrard Street, Vancouver, British Columbia, Canada V6C 2Z7.

BAKIARES Gina Marie Anne Santori, b. 27 Sept. 1956, Chicago, Illinois, USA. Podiatric Physician and Surgeon. m. Richard Santori, 5 Dec. 1987. *Education:* BS, Roosevelt University, Chicago, 1980; BA, Northeastern University, Chicago, 1981; Associate in Applied Sciences and Registered Nurse, Truman City College of Chicago, 1976; BS & DPM, College of Podiatric Medicine, 1981. *Appointments:* Director, Ability Podiatry and Happy Foot Centers located at: W Belmont Avenue, Chicago, 1981-83; W Lawrence Avenue, Chicago, 1981-; N Sheridan Road, Chicago, 1983-88; Glenview, Illinois, 1984-; Lisle/Naperville, Illinois area, 1989; Associate to Dr John Thomas, Barrington, Illinois, 1984-86. *Publications:* Advertising in different journals, etc. *Memberships:* American Podiatric Medical Association; Illinois Podiatric Medical Association; American Diabetes Association; Five Hospital Homebound Elderly Program; St Joseph Hospital Diabetic Center Consultant; Academy of Foot Surgeons; National Fraternal Society of the Deaf; Chicago Hearing Society; Variety Club of Illinois, President 1986-87. *Hobbies:* Flying (Private pilot's license); Boating; Piano; Singing; Swimming; Skiing; Snorkling. *Address:* 2324 West Lawrence Avenue, Chicago, Illinois 60625, USA.

BAKIN Gloria, b. 21 Nov. 1928, Braddock, Pennsylvania, (SA. Clinical Psychologist. m. 1948, divorced 1970. 4 sons, 1 daughter. *Education:* BA Psychology, Seton Hill College, 1962; MEd Counselling, Indiana University of Pennsylvania, 1966; CAGS Psychology, Duquesne University, 1970; Doctoral work, University of Pittsburgh, 1979. *Appointments:* Teacher Remedial Reading, Turtle Creek, 1962-63; Teacher/Dept Chair, Social Studies Department, Penn Trafford, 1963-66; Counselor/Dept Chair, Greensburg Salem Schools, 1966-70; Psychologist, Allegheny Intermediate Unit, Pittsburgh, 1970-84; Psychologist, Private Practice, 1973-. *Publication:* Diagnosis/Treatment of Sexual Abuse, 1982. *Memberships:* National Association of School Psychologists; American Psychological Associates; Office Secretary, 1978-82, Editor, Bulletin, 1978-79, Pennsylvania Psychological Association; Secretary, Pennsylvania Psychological Political Action Committee, 1982-; First Vice President, YWCA, 1987-89. *Hobbies:* Reading; Puzzles; Dancing;

Long Stitch; Volunteer activities including lectures for non-profit agencies as fund raiser. *Address:* 421 North Maple Avenue, Greensburg, PA 15601, USA.

BAKSH-SOODEEN Rawwida, b. 24 Dec. 1957, Trinidad & Tobago. Co- ordinator. m. Frank Soodeen, Jr, 13 Feb. 1979, 1 son, 1 daughter. *Education:* BA (Hons.-Literature & Linguistics), University of the West Indies, St Augustine, Trinidad & Tobago, 1982. *Appointments:* Teacher, Naparima Girls' High, 1977-79; Teaching Assistant, University of the West Indies, St Augustine, Trinidad & Tobago, 1982-87; Nuffield Visiting Fellow in Linguistics, University of York, England, 1987; Co-ordinator, Caribbean Association for Feminist Research & Action, 1988-. *Publications:* Articles in professional journals. *Memberships:* Founding Member, Women Working for Social Progress, (WWSP), Trinidad & Tobago; Society for Caribbean Linguists. *Honours:* Nuffield Visiting Fellowship, 1987. *Hobbies:* Writing; Yoga. *Address:* PO Bag 442, Tunapuna Post Office, Trinidad & Tobago, West Indies.

BALAZS Eva, b. 16 Nov. 1928, Nograd, Hungary. Author; Educator; Psychologist. m. Endre A. Balazs MD, 1945, divorced, 1 son, 1 daughter. *Education:* University of Budapest, 1944; MS, 1970, DEd, 1974, Boston University, USA; Postdoctoral training in Family System Theories, 1980-83. *Appointments:* Sargent College, USA, 1969-70; Boston State College, Massachusetts, 1970- 74; McLean Hospital, 1974-84; Metropolitan State Hospital, 1984-88; Psychologist in private practice, Arlington, Massachusetts, 1988-. *Books:* In Quest of Excellence, 1975; Dance Therapy in the Classroom, 1978; In Their Own Words, 1982; Spy Pond Stories, 1986. *Membership:* Clinical Member, American Association of Marriage and Family Therapy. *Hobby:* Playing jazz piano with a Dixieland band in Boston area. *Address:* 240 Pleasant Street, Arlington, MA 02174, USA.

BALAZS Mary Webber, b. 2 Aug. 1939, Cleveland, Ohio, USA. Poet; Professor of College. m. Gabriel George Balazs, 18 June 1960. 2 sons. *Education:* BA, University of Akron, 1960; MA, English, 1962, PhD, English, 1965, Pennsylvania State University. *Appointments:* Insructor, Pennsylvania State, 1962-65; Associate Professor of English, Virginia Military Institute, 1967-; Visiting Professor, Washington and Lee University; Randolph Macon's Woman's College; Poet in 40 schools, National Endowment for the Arts' Poets-in-the-Schools Programme, 1974-. *Publications:* The Voice of Thy Brother's Blood; The Stones Refuse Their Peace; Numerous poems in magazines. *Memberships:* Parent/Teachers Association; Academy of American Poets; National Council of Teachers of English; Poetry Society of Virginia; Alpha Lambda Delta. *Honours:* Sam Ragan Poetry Prize, 1987; 1st Hon Mention/Free Verse Irene Leache Literary Contest, 1985; 1st Hon Mention, Piedmont Literary Society Poetry Contest, 1983; 2nd Prize, Free Verse, Irene Leache Literary Contest, 1980; Best Poem of Issue, Baby John Literary Magazine, 1972; Best Poem of Issue, Patterns Literary Magazine, 1971. *Hobbies:* Travelling; Hiking; Jogging; Writing; Gardening; Swimming. *Address:* 503 Brooke Lane, Lexington, Virginia 24450, USA.

BALBOA Fernanda S., b. 8 Oct. 1904, Dagupan City, Pangasinan, Philippines. Lawyer; Civic Leader. m. Natalio Balboa, 26 Sept. 1926, (dec.), 4 boys, 3 girls. *Education:* BA 1925, LLB 1926, University of Philippines; Admitted, Philippines Bar, 1930; School for Social Work, Columbia University, 1955-56. *Appointments include:* Instructor, Spanish, College of Arts & Sciences, Far Eastern University, 1945-72; Founder, President 1964-65, 1973-75, 1980-, Women's Rights Movement of Philippines; Founder, Executive Vice President, Foundation for Gifted Children, 1986-; Honorary President, President International, Pan Pacific Southeast Asia Women's Association; Founder, President, Friendship Inc (rehabilitation, ex-convicts), 1950-; President, Moral Re-Armament Foundation of Philippines, 1960-; Founder, President, Children's Museum & Library Inc; President, Philippines League of Women Voters; Founder, Women's & Minors' Bureau; Numerous other involvements, community work of many kinds, including during the second world war, the setting up of a Home for disabled soldiers, work with teenage drug addicts and the establishment of a community kitchen and medical centre; International conferences & seminars attended, worldwide, 1957-84. *Honours include:* Scholarships, American Association of University Women 1950, Smithmund & Fulbright 1951. *Address:* c/o Women's Rights Movement of the Philippines, 90 M. Hemady, Quezon City, Philippines.

BALDASSANO Corinne, b. 16 May 1950, New York, USA. Radio Executive. *Education:* Ba cum laude in Communication Arts, Queens College, New York; MA Theatre, Hunter College, New York, 1975; MBA New York University, 1986. *Appointments:* Music Director/ Editorial Researcher, WHN-AM New York, 1970-73; Music Director, WPLJ-FM, New York, 1973-77; Programme Director/Operations Manager, KAUM-FM, Houston, Texas, 1977-79; Programme Director, WASI-FM, Cincinnati, Ohio, 1979-81; Director of Programming, ABC-FM and Contemporary Radio Networks, NY, 1981-84; Regional Manager, Affiliate Relations, United Stations Radio Networks, NY, 1985-. *Memberships:* International Radio and TV Society (On Planning Committee, 1986 and 1987, for Annual Faculty/Industry Seminar); American Women in Radio and TV; Women in Communications; New York Unviersity Business Forum; City Club of New York. *Hobbies:* Running (Ran 1986 NY Marathon); Theatre and Film; World Travel; Dancing; Art History. *Address:* c/o United Station Radio Networks, Affiliate Relations Department, 1440 Broadway, 5th Floor, New York, NY 10022, USA.

BALDWIN Kathleen Anne, b. 18 Jan. 1954, Elmira, New York, USA. Forensic Toxicology. *Education:* BS, Elmira, 1978; MS, University of Maryland, 1980; PhD, Medical College of Ohio, 1985. *Appointments:* Avian viral research, USDA, E Lansing, 1977; Agricultural research, Beltsville, 1977-80; American Red Cross Toledo, 1981-83; Senior Criminalist, Ventura Crime Laboratory, 1985-. *Publications:* Master's thesis: The Effect of Alkyl Amines on Volatile Fatty Acid Production and Cellulose Digestion by Rumen Microorganisms, 1980; Doctoral dissertation: Succinylcholine: Canine Pharmacokinetics, Pharmacodynamics and In Vitro Stability in Tissue, 1985; Correlation of Plasma Concentration and Effects of Succinylcholine in Dogs, 1988. *Memberships:* American Institute of Chemists, 1987; Society of Forensic Toxicologists, 1986; California Association of Toxicologists; American Academy of Forensic Sciences; American Association for Clinical Chemistry; Sigma Xi; Santa Paula Ninety Nines-scrapbook chairman; BBB; BSP; GBP. *Honours:* Outstanding Young Woman of America, California, 1986; Outstanding Young Woman of America, Ohio, 1984; Certificate of Recognition Sigma Xi, 1981 and 1982; Magna Cum Laude, Elmira College, 1978; Emerson Liscum Diven Award, Elmira College, 1978; Certificate of Academic Excellence, Louisiana State University, 1973; New York State Regents Scholarship, 1972; Good Sportsmanship Award, Watkins Glen, 1972; National Honor Society, 1970. *Hobbies:* Running; Aviation; Writing; Photography; Stained glass. *Address:* 702 Jasper Avenue, Ventura, California 93004, USA.

BALICE-GORDON Rita Juliana, b. 5 Sept. 1960, Chicago, Illinois, USA. Neurobiologist. m. Bruce Alan Gordon, 18 Aug. 1984. *Education:* BA Biological Sciences, Northwestern University, Evanston, 1982; Committee on Neurobiology, Department of Pharmacology and Physiology, University of Chicago, 1982-84; PhD Neurobiology, University of Texas at Austin, 1986. *Appointments:* Research Fellow, Washington University School of Medicine, St Louis, Missouri, 1987-. *Publications:* Numerous articles published in professional journals. *Memberships:* Society for Neuroscience; New York Academy of Sciences; American Association for Advancement of Science; Sigma Delta Tau, Sigma Chapter President, 1981 (fraternal organization). *Honours:* Muscular

Dystrophy Association Harry Zimmerman Postdoctoral Research Fellowship; National Institutes of Health Postdoctoral Research Fellowship; Visiting Lecturer, University of Texas at Austin; National Institutes of Health pre-doctoral traineeship; Student Marine Biological Laboratory Neurobiology, summer course, 1985; Phi Kappa Phi honorary society, University of Texas at Austin, 1986; University Fellowship, University of Texas at Austin, 1984-86; Summer Honors Research Fellowship, Northwestern University Medical School, 1981. *Hobbies:* Watercolour painter; History; Philosophy of science; Reading; Cooking; Wines; Travel; Music. *Address:* Washington University School of Medicine, Department of Anatomy and Neurobiology, 660 South Euclid, Box 8108, St Louis, MO 63110, USA.

BALL Jo-Anne Moreland, b. 22 Feb. 1930, Columbus, Ohio, USA. Freelance Public Relations; Singer. m. Donald E Ball, Snr, 22 July 1946, deceased. 1 son, 1 daughter. *Education:* BA, Music, Voice Performance, Otterbeing College, Westerville, Ohio. *Appointments:* Director of Development, Central Ohio Association of Builders and Contractors Inc, 1984-85. *Publications:* Feature story writer, Otterbein Tan and Cardinal student newspaper; Feature story writer, Otterbein Continuing Education newsletter. *Memberships:* Development Fund Steering Committee of Doctors Hospital; Public Relations Society of America; Women in Communications Inc; Columbus Area Leadership program; Columbus Chamber of Commerce, Public Relations Committee; Project Passage, Sustaining Board; Co-founder, Worthington Civic Arts Association (now Worthington Arts Council); Publicity Chairman: Orange PTA; Worthington United Methodist Church; Worthington Women's Club; Worthington Music Club; Columbus Women;s Music Club Inc; Olentangy Athletic Boosters; Orange Township Garden Club; Orange Township Volunteer Fireman's Association. *Honours:* Graduated cum laude and with departmental honours, Otterbein College, 1984; Arbegast Award in Music, 1984; Outstanding Woman in Associated Builders and Contractors Inc, Ohio, 1979. *Hobbies:* Golf; Gourmet cooking; Travel; Gardening; Bridge; Writing. *Address:* 715 Gatehouse Lane, Worthington, OH 43085, USA.

BALL Lucille, b. 6 Aug. 1911, Jamestown, New York, USA. Actress; m.(1) Desi Arnaz 1940, divorced 1960, 1 son, 1 daughter. (2) Gary Morton, 1961. *Career:* Film Actress, 1934-; Television Actress; President, Desilu Productions Inc, 1962-67; Lucille Ball Productions, 1967-. *Creative Works:* Films include: Roberta; Chatterbox; Follow the Fleet; Stage Door; Having a Wonderful Time; Affairs of Annabell; Room Service; Valley of the Sun; Seven Days Leave; DuBarry was a Lady; Best Foot Forward; Meet the People; Thousands Cheer; Without Love; Love from a Stranger; Her Husband's Affairs; Forever Darling; Facts of Life; Mame, 1974. Television: I Love Lucy, 1951-60; The Lucy Show, 1962-68; Here's Lucy, 1968-74. *Honours:* Kennedy Center Honor, 1986; Emmy Award, 1952, 1955, 1967, 1968. *Address:* 1041 North Formosa Avenue, Los Angeles, CA 90046, USA.

BALLANTYNE Edith, b. 10 Dec. 1922, Krnov, CSSR. Secretary-General, WILPF. m. Campbell Ballantyne, 28 July 1948. 2 sons, 2 daughters. *Appointments:* Editor, World Health Organisation; Editorial Assistant, Montreal Standard; German Section of the overseas service of the Canadian Broadcasting Corporation; Assistant, Provincial office of Co-operative Commonwealth Federation, Ontario, Canada; Farm Worker. *Publications:* Contributor of numerous articles on peace and disarmament and women's peace activities. *Membership:* Women's International League for Peace and Freedom. *Hobbies:* Music; Sports. *Address:* 7 ave de Secheron, 1202 Geneva 20, Switzerland.

BALLANTYNE Fiona Catherine, b. 9 July 1950, Bristol, England. Regional Director of the Scottish Development Agency. m. A Neil Ballantyne, 9 Aug. 1973. *Education:* MA, Edinburgh University, 1971. *Appointments:* Proctor & Gamble Ltd, Newcastle upon

Tyne, 1971-72; Market Research Manager, Nairn Floors Ltd, 1972-75; Research & Planning Manager, Thistle Hotels Ltd, Edinburgh, 1975-77; Assistant Marketing Manager, Lloyds & Scottish Finance Group, 1977-79; Scottish Development Agency, 1979-, Marketing Manager, 1979-84, Head, Small Business Division, 1984-87, Regional Director, Tayside & Fife, 1987-. *Memberships:* Institute Marketing; British Institute of Management; MENSA; BBC General Advisory Council; Board of Governors, Duncan of Jordanstone College of Art. *Honour:* Head Girl, Marr College, Troon, 1967-68. *Hobbies:* Arts; Gardening; Aerobics; Walking. *Address:* Scottish Development Agency, Nethergate Centre, Dundee DD1 4BU, Scotland.

BALLANTYNE Sheila, b. 26 July 1936, Seattle, Washington, USA. Writer; Professor. m. Philip M. Spielman, 22 Dec. 1963, 1 son, 1 daughter. *Education:* BA, Psychology, Mills College, 1958; English, University of California, Berkeley, 1980-81. *Appointments:* Professor, Department of English, Mills College, Oakland, California, 1984-. *Publications:* Novels: Norma Jean the Termite Queen, 1975; Imaginary Crimes, 1982; Story collection: Life on Earth, 1988. *Memberships:* The Writers Union; Authors Guild; PEN. *Honours:* O.Henry Award, 1977; Washington State Governor's Award for Fiction, 1982; John Simon Guggenheim Memorial Fellowship, 1983. *Hobbies:* Music; Dancing; Skiing; Jazz; Peace and environmental activism. *Address:* 2 Encina Place, Berkeley, CA 94705, USA.

BALLNER-BEAR Lisabeth G., b. 17 Aug. 1950, New York City, New York, USA. Business Executive; Writer. m. Paul Charles Ballner, 10 Aug. 1980, 1 son, 1 daughter. *Education:* BA, Goucher College, 1972; BM, Michigan State University, 1973; MA, Hunter College, 1978. *Appointments:* Media Planner, Ketchum, New York, 1980-81; Senior Media Planner, Bristol-Myers Company, 1981-87; Advertising Director, Sanofi Beauty Products/Parfums Nina Ricci USA, 1987-. *Publications:* Writer for Glamour, OMNI, Parents, Venture, New York Habitat, others. *Memberships:* New York Women in Communications; New York Representative, Religious Freedom Crusade; Elected Representative, New York County Democratic Committee; Life Member, International Association of Scientologists; Associate Research Director, Citizens Commission on Human Rights. *Honours:* Outstanding Young Women of America, 1984; Distinguished Leadership Award, 1987. *Hobbies:* Deep-sea fishing; Opera singing; Foreign languages. *Address:* 39 East 60th Street, New York, NY 10022, USA.

BALLWEG Mary Lou, b. 8 Feb. 1948, Madison, Wisconsin, USA. Writer; Executive Director; Founder *Education:* BA (Hons) Comparative Literature, University of Wisconsin-Madison. *Appointments:* Managing Editor, Investor, Wisconsin's Business Magazine, 1973-74; Scriptwriter/Director, Moynihan Associates, 1975; Mary Lou Ballweg writer, print/film (consulting business), 1976-81; President/Co-Founder, US-Canadian Endometriosis Association, 1980-. *Publications:* Writer/Editor, numerous articles. Scriptwriter/Director 19 films, videotapes, audiovisuals, 1975-81; Writer/Editor, numerous articles, kits and other materials on endometriosis, psychological issues, educational, scientific, 1980-; Writer/Editor, book, Overcoming Endometriosis, 1987; Consultant/on camera expert, videotape, You're Not Alone: Understanding Endometriosis, 1988. *Memberships:* Co-founder, Marg Sanger Community Health Clinic, Milwaukee, 1971-72; Board of Directors, Women in Communications, Southeastern Wisconsin, 1976-77; Board of Directors/President, US-Canadian Endometriosis Association. *Honours:* Recipient of numerous honours. *Interests:* Women's issues; Feminism; Health; Human Rights; Writing. *Address:* c/o US-Canadian Endometriosis Association, 8585 N. 76th Place, WI 53223, USA.

BALOROO Christina Kuuri Kanari, b. 1934, Dowine-Lawra. m. 20 Dec. 1955, 3 sons, 2 daughters. *Education:* Womens Training College, 1965-69. *Appointments:* Senior Superintendent of Education; Established Day Nursery School, 1984-. *Memberships:* Ghana National Association of Teachers; Co-operative Union Leader, Lambussie; Bakers Co-operative Leader, Lambussie. *Honours:* Recipient, various honours and awards. *Hobbies:* Netball; Rounders; Farming; Baking; Teaching. *Address:* PO Box 4, Lambussie Day Nursery, Lambussie, Jirapa-Lambussie District, Upper West Region, Ghana.

BALRAJ Elizabeth K, b. 11 Feb. 1939, Salem, India. Corner. m. Winfred Balraj, 20 May 1965, 1 son. *Education:* MBBS, Christian Medical College, Vellore, India, 1957-62; various Internships & Residencies at Hospitals in India & USA. *Appointments:* Staff Physician, Creighton-Freeman Christian Hospital, Vrindaban, 1964-65; Instructor, Pathology, 1973-78, Assistant Professor, Pathology, 1978-, University Hospitals, Cleveland; Forensic Pathologist, Deputy Coroner, 1973-87, Coroner, 1987-, Cuyahoga County. *Publications:* Articles in various journals including: Journal of Forensic Science. *Memberships:* American, Ohio, Cleveland Medical Associations; American Medical Womens Association; American Academy of Forensic Sciences; Cleveland Society of Pathologists; Ohio State Coroners Association; International Association of Coroners & Medical Examiners. *Hobbies:* Cooking; Reading; Tavel; Social Work. *Address:* 32795 Ledgehill Drive, Solon, OH 44139, USA.

BAMELA ENGO TJEGA Ruth, b. 8 Feb. 1943, Sakbayeme, Cameroon. m. Paul Bamela Engo, 21 Dec. 1974. 1 son, 1 daughter. *Education:* Doctorate, 3 cycle, Social Sciences, Paris, France, 1970; Diploma, Institute of Social Sciences, Paris; Diploma, Center for Social Security Studies, Paris, France. *Appointments:* Head, Trade Union Office 1971-73, Head, Social Problems in Labor Ministry 1973-76, Head, Research Division, Labor Ministry 1976-78, Technical Advisor, Minister of Labor, 1978-81, Director of Labor, 1981-84; Cameroon Head Delegate, International Labor Conference in Geneva, 1975-84; Cameroon Delegate, United Nations General Assembly, 1984; Conference Coordinator. *Publications:* Founder and editor, Le Monde du Travail, 1976-84; Numerous articles and book chapters to professional journals and magazines. *Memberships include:* President, Cameroonian Students' Association, Paris, France, 1965-66; Secretary General, Cameroonian Students' Association International, 1966-67; Founding Member, President, United Nations African Mothers Association, 1985-; Founder Member/Task force Member, Advocates for African Food Security-Lessening the Burden for Women, 1986-; Society of International Development, 1986-; Association of Women in Development, 1986-. *Hobbies:* Collect everything related with life and work of traditional African woman. *Address:* BP 4129, Yaounde, Cameroon.

BANCROFT Anne, b. 17 Sept. 1931, New York, USA. Actress. m. (2) Mel Brooks 1964, 1 son. *Education:* Christopher Colombus High School, New York. *Creative Works:* Plays: Two for the Seesaw, 1958; The Miracle Worker, 1959-60; The Devils, 1965; The Little Foxes, 1967; A Cry of Players, 1968; Golda, 1977. Films: The Miracle Worker; Don't Bother to Knock; Tonight We Sing; Demetrius and the Gladiators; The Pumpkin Eater; Seven Women; The Graduate, 1968; Young Winston, 1971; The Prisoner of Second Avenue, 1974; The Hindenberg, 1975; Lipstick, 1976; Silent Movie, 1976; The Turning Point, 1977; Golda, 1977; The Elephant Man, 1980; To Be or Not to Be, 1984. Wrote, directed and acted in Fatso; Agnes of God, 1985; 84 Charing Cross Road, 1986; 'night Mother, 1986. Television: Mother Courage and her Children; Annie, the Woman in the Life of a Man; Jesus of Nazareth, 1977; Marco Polo, 1981. *Honours:* Academy Award for The Miracle Worker, 1962; Golden Globe Award, 1968; Emmy Award for Annie, the Woman in the Life of a Man, 1970. *Address:* c/o 20th Century Fox Studios, PO Box 900, Beverly Hills, CA 90213, USA.

BANCROFT Margaret Anne Hart, b. 17 Apr. 1923, London, England. Writer. m. (1) K England, 19 May 1940, divorced 1948. (2) H Lobstein, 20 Mar. 1949, divorced 1960. (3) R Bancroft, 28 Apr. 1977, 2 sons, 2 daughters. *Education:* School Certificate, 1939; Certificate of Teaching, 1965. *Appointments:* Lecturer in English and Liberal Studies, Hammersmith College for Further Education, 1966-69; City Literary Institute, London, 1970-72. *Publications:* Religions of The East, 1974; Twentieth Century Mystics and Sages, 1976; ZEN: Direct Pointing to Reality, 1980; The Luminous Vision, 1981; Origins of the Sacred, 1987. *Memberships:* Vice-president, World Congress of Faiths; Buddhist Peace Fellowship; British Association for the History of Religions; United Nations Association, Religious Advisory Committee. *Interests:* Mysticism; Buddhism; Ecology; Peace. *Address:* 7A Dagmar Road, Exmouth, Devon EX8 2AN, England.

BANDARANAIKE Sirimavo, b. 17 Apr. 1916, Ratnapura. President, Sri Lanka Freedom Party. m. S W R D Bandaranaike, Prime Minister of Ceylon, 1956-59, 3 Oct. 1940. 1 son, 2 daughters. *Education:* St Bridget's Convent, Colombo. *Appointments:* Member of Parliament, Sri Lanka, 1960-80; Prime Minister of Sri Lanka (Ceylon until 1972), 1960-65, 1970-77; Minister of Defence and Foreign Affairs, Planning and Economic Affairs and Plan Implementation; President, Sri Lanka Freedom Party, 1960-; Leader of the Opposition, 1965-70; Minister of Information and Broadcasting, 1964-65; Chairman, non-Aligned Movement, 1976-77. *Membership:* Formerly President and Treasurer, Lanak Mahila Samita. *Honour:* Ceres Medal, FAO, 1977. *Hobbies:* Reading; Music; Gardening. *Address:* 65 Rosmead Place, Colombo 7, Sri Lanka.

BANDER Kay (Katherine) Walker, b. 24 Sep. 1936, St Louis, Missouri, USA. Executive. m. Martin S. Bander, 18 Aug. 1969. *Education:* BS magna cum laude, Miami University, Oxford, Ohio, 1958; Graduate study, Yale University School of Public Health, 1966-67; MS, Health Services Administration, Harvard School of Public Health, 1976. *Appointments:* Administrative Assistant to General Director, 1969-72, Assistant to General Director, 1973-80, Director of Staff Services, 1980-82, Massachusetts General Hospital, Boston; Visiting Lecturer, Health Services Administration, 1976-, Clinical Faculty Advisor, 1980-, Harvard School of Public Health; Management Consultant, consulting firm, Chicago, Illinois, 1980-83; Assistant to Executive Vice-President, Science & Administration, 1982-83, Director of Management Strategy, Science & Administration, 1983-86, Vice-President, Science & Technology, 1986-, E.R.Squibb & Sons, Princeton, New Jersey; Advisor to Administrative Fellowships, Massachusetts General Hospital. *Publications:* Hospital structures guidelines for coping with snowstorms, 1978; Strategic planning: reality versus literature, 1980; Multi-institutional arrangements in a teaching hospital setting (with C.A.Sanders), 1980; Third Parties in the Midst of Everyone's Expectations (with C.A.Sanders), 1986. *Memberships:* American College of Healthcare Executives; American Management Association; Massachusetts General Hospital Service League. *Honours:* USPHS Fellowship, 1966-67; Harvard University Scholarship, 1975-76; Management Innovation Award, Squibb/AHA Joint Venture Programme, American Collegge of Healthcare Executives, 1986; Tribute to Women and Industry, Princeton, 1987. *Hobbies:* Vounteerism and corporate relations work with not-for-profit bodies; Project BEST, Princeton University; Tennis; Travel. *Address:* 182 Beacon Street, Boston, MA 02116, USA.

BANFF Helen Thorburn, b. 20 Feb. 1927, Ipswich, Australia. Nursing. *Education:* General Nursing Certificate, 1952; Midwifery Certificate, 1953; Maternal and Child Welfare Certificate, 1956; Diploma in Nursing Administration, 1964. *Appointments:* Maternal and Child Welfare Service, Queensland, 1956-57; Repatriation Hospital, Perth, Western Australia, 1957-58; Maternal and Child Welfare Service, Papua, New Guinea, 1958-61; Registered Nurse 1961-68, Matron 1968-71, Royal Children's Hospital, Brisbane; Vietnam Service with the Australian Surgical Team (Senior Nurse, Jan-July 1971); Nursing Superintendent, The Wesley Hospital, Auchenflower, Brisbane, (1971-88). *Memberships:* Royal Australian Nursing Federation; College of Nursing, (National President, 1975-76); Queensland State Committee of College of Nursing (Chairman 1976); Blue Nursing Service Executive Council; Fellow of College of Nursing, Australia; Churchill Fellowship; Member of the Most Excellent Order of the British Empire (MBE), 1988. *Hobbies:* Arts and Crafts; Cooking. *Address:* 17 Hoskin Street, Sandgate, Queensland 4017, Australia.

BANFIELD Joanne, b. 21 Feb. 1954, Bronxville, USA. Benefits & Compensation Manager. m. Thomas A. Hanlon, 6 August 1978, divorced 1985. *Education:* BA, Iona College, 1976. *Appointments:* Outpatient Registrar, United Hospital, Port Chester, NY, 1976-78; Disability Benefits Specialist, UnionmMutal Insurance Co., Elmsford, NY, 1978-82; Staff Assistant to Executive Administrator, American Association of Advertising Agencies, New York, NY, 1982-83; Senior Claims Analyst, General Reassurance Corp, Stamford, CT, 1984-88; Benefits & Compensation Manager, Life Reassurance Corp of America, Stamford, CT, 1988-. *Membership:* NAFE. *Hobbies:* Music; Sign Language; Aerobic Exercise. *Address:* 7 Harris Lane, Harrison, NY 10528, USA.

BANIAK Sheila Mary, b. 26 Feb. 1953, Chicago, Illinois, USA. Accountant; Professional Speaker. m. Mark A Baniak, 7 Oct. 1972. 1 daughter. *Education:* Assocs in Accounting, Oakton Community College, 1986; Student, Roosevelt University, 1986-. *Appointments:* Owner Manager, Baniak and Associates, Park Ridge, 1984-; Accountant, Otto & Snyder, Park Ridge, 1984-87; Special projects coordinator, supplemental instructor, 1986-; Accounting computer instructor, 1987-, Advisory member accounting, 1986-, Cons mem Edn Found, 1986-, Oakton Community College, Des Plaines; Instructor, Ray Coll Design, 1987-, teaching financial mamagement, retail mathematics, business computers; Professional Speaker, 1988-; Director of Communiations, 1989-, National Association of Accountants. *Publication:* Author: A Small Business Collection Cycle Primer For Accountants, 1985. *Memberships:* National Association of Accountants; National Association of Tax Practitioners; Director of Community Responsibility, National Association of Accountants, Northwest Suburban Chicago Chapter, 1987-88. *Honours:* Illinois CPA Society Scholar, 1984; Roosevelt University Scholar, 1986; National Association of Accountants Scholar, 1985. *Address:* 1704 S Clifton Ave, Park Ridge, IL 60068, USA.

BANKS Iola Kelley, b. 10 Aug. 1935, Arcadia, Louisiana, USA. Teacher. m. Lovell Banks, 8 Oct. 1954. 1 son, 3 daughters. *Education:* BS 1967, MS 1975, University of Alaska; Licensed Practical Nurse, Denver General Hospital, Denver, Colorado, 1960; Professional Nursing School, Bear County Hospital, San Antonio, Texas, 1963-64. *Appointments:* Teacher, Eiclson Airforce Base, Fairbanks, Alaska, 1967; Teacher, Brookings Elementary School, Springfield Massachusetts, 1967-70; Mathematics Teacher, Kenai Junior High School, 1970; Teacher, Soldofnio Elementary School, 1970; Teacher, Searst Kenai Elementary School, 1975-86; Teacher, Mountain View Elementary, Kenai, 1986-. *Publications:* Children's class books, 1974-75, 1976-77, 1978-79, 1979-80, 1980-81, 1981-82, 1982-83, 1983-84, 1984-85, 1985-86, 1986-87. *Memberships:* KPEA; AEA; NEA/Building Representatives, 1974, Member of Minority Committee, 1982; Secretary, Treasurer, Membership Chairman, Vice-Chair, Alpha Delta Kappa, 1972-86; Delta Kappa Gamma, 1972-86; Chairman, Professional Affairs Committee, Phi Delta Kappa, 1982-86; Chairperson, House District 5 Democrats; Chairperson, Martin Luther King Scholarship Fund; Life Member NAACP. *Honours:* Delegate to Democratic national Convention, 1976, 1980; Honours Award, Grambling College, 1952; Offered membership, Phi Delta Kappa, 1982; Plaque for Service to Democratic Party, 1982. *Hobbies:* Tennis,

Dancing, Walking, Hiking, Reading, Writing. *Address:* 1202 3rd Avenue, Kenia, AK 99611, USA.

BANKS Rebecca Louise, b. 27 Feb. 1949, Ohio, USA. University Professor. *Education:* BS.Ed., University of Akron, 1971; MA, Kent State University, 1972; PhD Ohio State University, 1979; MS, Mankato State University, 1987. *Appointments:* Teacher, Perry Local Schools, 1972-76; Professor, Northern Kentucky Univesity, 1972-76; Assistant Professor, University of Minnesota, 1979-82; Associate Professor, Mankato State University, 1982-. *Publications:* 20 publications and 60 presentations in professional journals. *Memberships:* various professional organisations. *Honours Include:* Various Teaching Fellowships; Eta Sigma Gamma. *Hobbies:* Travel; Photography; Crafts; Gourmet Cooking. *Address:* Health Science Dept. Box 50, Mankato State University, Mankato, MN 56002, USA.

BANNISTER Jo, b. 31 July 1951, Rochdale, England. Author. *Appointments:* Newspaper Journalist, Editor, County Down Spectator, Bangor, Northern Ireland, 1968-87. *Publications:* The Matrix, 1981; The Winter Plain, 1982; A Cactus Garden, 1983; Striving with Gods, 1984; Mosaic, 1986; The Mason Codex, 1988; Gilga MEsh 1989; The Going Down of the Sun 1989. *Membership:* Society of Authors. *Honours:* Royal Society of Arts, Bronze Medal, 1968; Runner Up: Catherine Pakenham Award, 1974, British Press Awards, 1978; Provincial Journalist of the Year, Northern Ireland Press Awards, 1982. *Hobbies:* Horse Riding; Sailing; Archaeology; Astronomy; Archery. *Address:* 5 Hillfoot, Groomsport, County Down, Northern Ireland.

BANNON Kathleen Angela, b. 19 Jan. 1947, Washington, USA. Administrative Director. *Education:* College Conservatory of Music, Cincinnati, 1955-63; Washington School of Ballet, 1963-64; BA, American University, 1970. *Appointments:* Harkness Ballet of New York, Soloist 1964-67; Fellowship Programme Officer, NEA, 1972-77; International Programme Office, NEA, Washington, 1977-86; Executive Director, International Arts Enterprises, Washington, 1986-; Administrative Director, The Harid Conservatory, 1987-. *Honours:* Order of Leopold II, Government of Belgium, 1981; Order of Danneborg, Chevalier, Government of Denmark, 1983; Bicentennial Grant, Government of Sweden, 1986. *Hobbies:* Egyptology; Music; Dance; International Travel. *Address:* The Harid Conservatory, PO Box 1754, Boca Raton, FL 33429, USA.

BANUS Maria, b. 10 Apr. 1914, Bucharest, Romania. Writer. m. Sorin Banus, 19 Feb. 1936, 2 sons. *Education:* University of Bucharest. *Publications:* Poetry Girls Land, 1937; Joy, 1040, I Was Just Leaving the Arena, 1967; The Portrait of Fayvm, 1970; November the Innocent, 1981; Milano Nuovi Spazi, 1964; etc. *Memberships:* Writers Union of Romania; International Writers Association. *Honours:* Recipient, various honours and awards. *Address:* Str. Fundatiei 6, Bucharest 71116, Romania.

BANZER Cynthia Deane, b. 24 Jan. 1947, Portland, Oregon, USA. State Representative. m. (1) 2 sons, (2) V. Keith Martin, 9 Apr. 1988. *Education:* BS, Political Science, Oregon State University, 1969; Teacher Corps Intern, Ohio University Teacher Corps Programme, Parkersburg, West Virginia, 1969-70; MEd, Ohio University, 1973. *Appointments:* Research Associate, President's Commission on School Finance, 1971-; Legislative Assistant, Committee on Education & Labor, US House of Representatives, 1972-; Administrative Assistant, Senate Education Committee, State of Oregon, 1973-; Citizen Participation Coordinator, Oregon Land Conservation & Development Commission, 1974-; Community Services Director, City of Beaverton, Oregon, 1975-77; Presiding Officer, Metropolitan Service District, Portland, Oregon, 1978-85; Member, Oregon House of Representatives, Salem, 1985-; Development Director, Burnside Community Council, Portland, 1987-. *Publications:* Articles in professional journals; Education Policy Research at the Harvard Graduate School of Education, 1973; Equal Opportunity in Oregon Schools: A Proposal to the Ford Foundation to Study Basic School Finance in Oregon, 1973; Citizen Involvement Goal, 1974; Budget in Brief, City of Beaverton, 1975-76. *Memberships:* Board of Directors: United Way, Columbia-Wallamette; Junior League of Portland; Loaves and Fishes; President, Board of Directors, Metropolitan Family Services; Executive Board of Directors, Multnomah County Democratic Central Committee; Past Alternate Delegate, Democratic State Central Committee; Associates of Good Samaritan Hospital; Other past political activities; Past Member, Chairman, numerous civic and cultural bodies. *Honours:* Inspiration Award, Alpha Phi, 1969; Associated Women Students Scholarship Award; Panhellenic Senator; Outstanding Senior, Oregon State University; Ford Foundation Grant, 1973. *Address:* 7017 SE Pine Street, Portland, OR 97215, USA.

BAR Sylvia Sarah, b. 28 Nov. 1926, Java, Indonesia. Health Professional; Retired Teacher; Author. m. (1) Richard J. DuBois, 5 Feb. 1951, divorced, 1 daughter, (2) Rickey R. De Montrond, 4 July 1965, divorced, 1 son. *Education:* BA, University of California at Los Angeles, 1951; MA, California State University, Los Angeles, 1985. *Appointments:* Paramount Unified Schools, 1954-57; Los Angeles Unified Schools, 1957-85; Rosemead Adult, 1986-88; Newport Mesa Adult, 1988-; Santiago Community College, 1989-; Coastlines Community Colleges, 1989. *Publications:* Pasadena Tournament of Roses; Indonesia; Focusing on Awareness; numerous, columns articles. *Honours Include:* numerous organisations including: Pi Lambda Theta; AARP. *Honours:* 2 Awards for Articles in Educ-Teaching Music, 1955, Teaching Math., 1956; 3 Ceasar's Awards, 1974, 1975, 1977; Rollex Award Nominee, 1983-84. *Hobbies:* Lecturer; Author; Children's Books; Phtography; Singing; Designing Clothes. *Address:* 628 Joann Street, Costa Mesa, CA 92627, USA.

BARAN Dana, b. 17 June 1956, Montreal, Canada. Medical Doctor; Researcher. m. Benoit Vendeville, 8 Nov. 1986, 1 son. *Education:* MD, Clinical Medicine, McGill University Faculty of Medicine, 1979. *Appointments:* Intern, Queen Elizabeth Hospital, Montreal, 1979-80; Resident, internal medicine, Royal Victoria Hospital, 1980-83; Research, nephrology & immunology, Unite INSERM U28, Paris, France 1983-85, Institut Pasteur, 1985-. *Publications include:* Various scientific contributions to books & journals. *Memberships:* Professional Corporation of Physicians, Quebec; Fellow, Royal College of Physicians & Surgeons, Canada (FRCP); Diplomate, American College of Physicians. *Honours:* University Scholarship, J. W. McConnell Scholarship 1972-79, Campbell Howard Prize, clinical medicine & psychiatry, (Faculty of Medicine) 1979, McGill University; Bursaries, Kidney Foundation of Canada 1983-85, Medical Research Council 1985-. *Hobbies:* Literature & creative writing; Photography; Piano. *Address:* Unite d'Immunogenetique Cellulaire, Institut Pasteur, 25 rue Dr Roux, 75015 Paris, France.

BARAS Carol Formost, b. 1 Oct. 1930, Chicago, USA. Chief Executive Officer. m. Vascilios (Bill) Theophanis Baras, 15 Feb. 1969, 2 sons, 1 daughter. *Education:* San Diego State University, 1947-49; University of California, 1970-71; University of London Extension, 1971. *Appoinments Include:* Baras Foundation (educational and research foundation); Executive, Vice President, Originator, 291-KIDS; Owner, Executive Director, Hypnos Morpheus, 1968-; Owner, Formost Adv. & Promotions, 1969-; Universal Jet Inc., 1971-76. *Memberships Include:* National Academy of TV Arts & Science; Media Club of San Diego; etc. *Honours:* Recipient, numerous honours and awards. *Hobbies:* Reading; Travel. *Address:* PO Box 3189, San Diego, CA 92103, USA.

BARBANO Frances Elizabeth Dufresne, b. 28 May 1944, Corry, Pennsylvania, USA. Writer; Photographer; Editor. m. (1) John William Moyle, 1962 (div. 1967),

1 son, (2) Robert Lee Harkins, 1967 (div. 1974), 2 daughters (1 dec.), (3) Duane Louis Barbarno, 1974, 1 step-son, 1 step-daughter. *Education:* Licensed Cosmetologist, Phoenix Area Vocational College, Arizona, 1977; Certified Reflexologist, 1977. *Appointments:* Cosmetologist & owner, Carefree Hair Designs, Carefree, Arizona, 1978-84; Freelance writer, photographer, 1983-; Owner, Professional Images, providing services, graphic arts, editing, stock photos, 1983-; Supervisor, Boulders Club Restaurant, Carefree, 1986-87. *Publications:* Over 100 feature articles, national & regional magazines including: Field & Stream; Decision; Bassmasters; Women's Sports & Fitness; Bestways Health, 1984-; Numerous photographs, with/without articles. *Memberships:* Outdoor Writers Association; Southwest Outdoor Writers' Association; National Writers Club. *Hobbies:* Outdoor activities including camping, hiking, cycling, fishing, backpacking, travel; Photographing wildlife; Painting; Solitude by the pines, by the seashore; Writing poetry; Life in general. *Address:* 40240 North 69th Place, Cave Creek, Arizona 85331, USA.

BARBARA Agatha, b. 11 Mar. 1923, Malta. President, Republic of Malta. *Appointments:* School Teacher; Contested First General Elections, 1947, First Woman Elected to Maltese Parliament in 1947 and held her seat in House of Representatives until elected President, Republic of Malta, 1982-. *Memberships:* Numerous professional organisations including: Chairperson, Maltese National Committee, Community Chest Fund; Chairperson Welfare Committee, The Samaritans; Founder and Chairperson, Womens Political Movement in Malta. *Honours:* Stara Planina 1st Class with Ribbon, Republic of Bulgaria; Order of the National Flag, 1st Class, Democratic Peoples Republic of Korea; Hishan E Pakistan, Islamic Republic of Pakistan; Recipient, many honorary degrees; Given the Freedom of the Cities and presented with the keys of Lahore, Montivideo, Lima, Buenos Aires, San Jose, Bogatoa, Aiden. *Address:* Kenn Taghna, Triq Wied Il-Ghajn, Zabbar, Malta.

BARBER Judith Ann, b. 19 Sept. 1935, Bay City, Michigan, USA. Social Worker/Counselor. *FducAtlon:* BA, Aquinas College, 1959; MA, University of Michigan, 1968; MA, West Michigan University, 1983. *Appointments:* Junior High Teacher, 1960-62; College Registrar/Admin Officer, 1968-71; Residential Administrator, 1972-77; Youth Care Worker/Supervisor, 1980-82; Preg/Parent Teen Program Coordinator, 1983-87; Counselor-Social Worker, 1988-. *Memberships:* National Association of Social Workers; American Psych Association; Michigan Association of Inf Mental Health; Women's Therapist Network; Michigan Cert Social Worker. *Honours:* Achievement Award, National Association of County Commissioners, 1985; Achievement Award, American Pub Welfare Association, 1985. *Hobbies:* Outdoor activites; Arts and crafts; Gardening, Yard Work; Reading. *Address:* 2025 E Fulton, Grant Rapids, MI 49503, USA.

BARBER Sandra Powell, b. 15 Dec. 1941, Baltimore, Maryland, USA. m. Billy Owen Pickerill, 7 Nov. 1987. 3 sons, 4 daughters. *Education:* BA History, Mt St Agnes, 1963; MA, History, New Mexico State University, 1970; MA Political Science, Purdue University, 1975; EdD, Vanderbilt University. *Appointments:* 9th Grade Teacher, Baltimore County Schools, 1963-64; Research Assistant, History, New Mexico State University, 1967-69; Academic Adviser and Instructor, Political Science, Purdue University, 1973- 78; Lecturer, Political Science 1979-80, Academic Systems Analyst 1980-81, Instructor 1981-82, Indiana State University Evansville; Program Coordinator, Henderson Community College, 1983-88; Division Chair, Computer Technologies, Anne Arundel Community College, 1988-. *Publications:* It Was a Miracle, 1983; Light On Life, 1987; My Bear, Derek, 1986; Learning By Doing BASIC, 1983; Computer Learning By Doing, 1984; 10 published articles in field of Poltiical Science, Computer Science and Education. *Memberships:* Association for Computing Machiner, Vice President; Data processing Management

Association; Tecumseh Homemakers Club, President 1972-73; Kentucky Academic Computer User's Group, President, UMAP Consortium (department representative); American Political Science Association; International Studies Association, Midwest Board Member. *Honours:* Summer Teaching Fellowship, Univ of Kentucky, 1987; MD State Teachers' Scholarship, 1960-63; Pi Gamma Mu, social science honorary, 1966; Sloan Foundation Research Assistantship, 1973. *Hobbies:* Swimming; Gourmet cooking; Singing; Reading; Sewing. *Address:* 718 Broadmoor Drive, Annapolis, MD 21401, USA.

BARBER Shelley Inez, b. 27 Dec. 1949, Searcy, Arkansas, USA. Tax Service Executive. m. Ziba James Barber, 23 Aug. 1968. *Education:* BSE, University of Central Arkansas, 1971; Postgraduate study, Mississippi State University, 1976. *Appointments:* Paragould Public Schools, Arkansas, 1972; US Army Ludwigsburg, Federal Republic of Germany, 1973; Elaine Public Schools, Arkansas, 1973-76; Sewing Instructor, Singer Corporation, Pine Bluff, Arkansas, 1977-78; Star City Public Schools, Arkansas, 1978-80; Customer Relations, Sears Roebuck & Co, Pine Bluff, 1980-81; Franchise Owner, H & R Block Inc, Stuttgart, Arkansas, 1982-. *Memberships:* Stuttgart Chamber of Commerce; Board, First Christian Church (Disciples of Christ) of Stuttgart, Treasurer 1989; American Business Women's Association, Treasurer, Port O'Cotton Chapter, Pine Bluff, 1981-82. *Hobbies:* Her Cairn terrier Barber's Risky Business; Needlework; Reading science fiction; Youth work at First Christian Church LOGOS programme (Bible Studies Coordinator). *Address:* H & R Block, 208 East Third, Stuttgart, AR 72160, USA.

BARCA Kathleen, b. 26 July 1946, Burbank, California, USA. Regional Manager, A L Williams. m. Gerald A Barca, 8 Dec. 1967. 1 son, 1 daughter. *Education:* Pierce College, 1964; Business, Hancock College, 1984. *Appointments:* Teller, Security Pacific Bank, Pasadena, California, 1968-69; Teller, Bank of America, Santa Maria, California, 1972-74; Operator, 1974-83, Supervisor 1983-84, General Telephone Co, Santa Maria; Account Executive, KRQK/KLLB Radio, 1984-85; Owner, Advertising Unlimited, 1985-87; Regional Manager, A L Williams, 1987-. *Publications:* Author, Producer and Editor of TV Commercials, Family Portraits, Spas, Boudoir Portraits. Author and Editor of Promotional Sales Kits for Radio Stations; Author and Editor of Hot Tracks for Radio Stations; Author and Editor of Radio Commercials, Where Do You Go, Spas and Logo designs for businesses. *Memberships:* Chairperson, Casmalia Advisory Committee, includes Department of Health Services, California; Environmental Protection Agency and Regional Water Quality, 1987-; Activist Against Toxic Waste and Pollution with CADRE and PAC, 1984-; National Association of Female Executives, 1986-; Vice President, Tough Love, 1988-; Steering Committee of ASAP & Friends, Drug Rehabilitation for Adolescents, 1988-; Parents of Children recovering from Drug Addiction. *Honours:* Award of Excellence, TV Commercial Boudoir Portraits 1986, Radio Commercial, Where Do You Go 1984, Central Coast Ad Club, 1986; Award of Merit, TV Commercial, Spas 1986, TV Logo Central RV 1986, Radio Commercial, Spas 1986, Central Coast Ad Club. *Hobbies:* Raising Exotic Birds; Writing childrens books. *Address:* 509 Shaw Street, Los Alamos, CA 93440, USA.

BARCLAY Paula Jane, b. 6 Feb. 1952, Kansas City, Missouri, USA. Physician. *Education:* BS Biology, C W Post College, 1974; MDU of Kansas, 1978; Speciality Boards: Internal Medicine, 1983; Allergy and Immunology, 1985. *Appointments:* Research Collaborator for Brookhaven National Laboratory, 1982-; Emergency Room, Central General Hospital, Plainview, New York, 1986-; Internist, Kwajalein Missile Range Hospital, 1984-86. *Memberships:* American College of Physicians; American College of Allergists. *Hobbies:* Scuba Diving; Bicycling; Needlework; Reading; Piano. *Address:* 39 Jay Court, Northport, NY 11768, USA.

BARDERIS Dorothy Ellen Watkeys, b. 20 Sept. 1918, Newport News, Virginia, USA. Painter, watercolour, acrylic. m. Cesides V Barberis 17 June 1939, divorced 1956. *Education:* Syracuse University, College of Fine Arts, 1973-77; Studied with Milford Zornes, John Pike, Ed Whitney, Zigmund Jankowski; Paul Wood for 11 years in Studio. *Appointments:* Designer, Sherwin Bros Linens, 1938-39; Buyer of all material, Corning Glass, 1943; Designed fabrics & wallpaper, James Wynborough, 1943-44; Drafting-Triametric Projection of Motors, Johnson Cushing and Neville, 1944-45; Painter, 1973-. *Creative works:* Numerous paintings including Landscape, Still life, Flowers. *Memberships:* National Arts Club; Nat Assoc of Women Artists; Catharine Lorillard Wolfe Art Club; AAPL; Knickerbocker Artists; No Shore Art Assn; NJ Watercolor; Essex Wclr; Garden State Wclr; Southwest Wclr Society; Midwest Wclr; Artists Fellowship. *Honours:* Over 150 awards for paintings; 12 Best in Show; Recipient Creative Hands Award. *Hobbies:* Dressmaking; Collect stamps, antique silver and china. *Address:* 217 Lincoln Ave, Elmwood Park, NJ 07407, USA.

BARDOT Brigitte, b. 28 Sept. 1934, Paris, France. Actress. m. (1) Roger Vadim. (2) Jacques Charrier. (3) Gunther Sachs, 1966 dissolved, 1969. *Education:* Paris Conservatoire. *Creative Works:* Films include: Manina: la fille sans voile; Le fils de Caroline cherie; Futures vedettes; Les grandes manoeuvres; La lumiere d'en face; Cette sacree gamine; La mariee est trop belle; Et Dieu crea la femme; En effeuillant la marguerite; Une parisienne; Les bijoutiers du clair de lune; En cas de malheur; La femme et le pantin; Babette s'en va-t-en guerre; Voulez-vous danser avec moi?; La verite; Please not now?; Le mepris; Le repos du guerrier; Une ravissante idiote; Viva Maria; A coeur joie, 1967; Two weeks in September, 1967; Shalako, 1968; Les femmes, 1969; Les novices, 1970; Boulevard du rhum, 1971; Les petroleuses, 1971; Don Juan, 1973; L'Histoire tres bonne et tres joyeuse de Colinot trousse-chemise, 1973; Noonah, le petit phoque blanc. *Honours:* Etoile de Cristal from Academy of Cinema, 1966; Chevalier,Legion d'honneur, 1985. *Hobby:* Swimming. *Address:* La Madrague, 83990 Saint Tropez (Var), France.

BARDWICK Judith Marcia, b. 16 Jan. 1933, New York City, USA. Psychologist; Management Consultant. m. (2) Allen E. Armstrong, 10 Feb. 1984. 1 son, 2 daughters, previous marriage. *Education:* BS, Purdue University, 1954; MS, Cornell University, 1955; PhD, University of Michigan, 1964. *Appointments:* Teaching Fellow 1963-64, Lecturer 1964-66, Assistant Professor 1966-69, Associate Professor 1969-73, Professor 1973-83, Associate Dean, College of Literature, Science & Arts 1977-80, University of Michigan; President, In Transition, management consultants, 1983-; Clinical Professor of Psychiatry, University of California, San Diego, 1984-. *Publications:* Books: Author, In Transition 1981, Plateauing Trap 1986; Editor, Psychology of Women 1971, Readings in Psychology of Women 1972; 60 papers & book chapters. *Memberships include:* American Psychological Association. *Honours:* Fellow, APA; Senior Fellow, University of Michigan Society of Fellows, 1975-80; Phi Beta Kappa, Purdue & University of Michigan. *Hobbies:* Sailing; Cooking; Travel; Hatha Yoga. *Address:* 2285 Via Tabara, La Jolla, California 92037, USA.

BARKER A L, b. 13 Apr. 1918, Kent, England. Author. *Appointments:* Staff, Amalgamated Press, 1936; Reader, Cresset Press, 1947; Secretary, Sub-Editor, BBC, London, 1949-78. *Publications:* Apology for a Hero, 1950; A Case Examined, 1965; The Middling, 1967; John Brown's Body, 1969; A Source of Embarrassment, 1974; A Heavy Feather, 1978; Relative Successes, 1984; The Goose Boy, 1987; Short Story Collections: Innocents, 1947; Novelette, 1951; The Joy-Ride, 1963; Femina Real, 1971; Lost Upon the Roundabouts, 1964; Life Stories, 1981; No Word of Love, 1985. *Honours:* Atlantic Award in Literature, 1946; Somerset Maugham Award, 1947; Cheltenham Festival Award, 1963; SE Arts Creative Book Award, 1981; MacMillan Silver Pen Award, 1987; Society of Authors Travelling Scholarship, 1987; Fellow Royal Society of Literature. *Address:* 103 Harrow Road, Carshalton, Surrey SM5 3QF, England.

BARKER Bridget Caroline, b. 7 Mar. 1958, Kent, England. Solicitor. *Education:* 1st class Law Degree, Southampton University, 1979. *Appointment:* Partner, MacFarlanes Solicitors, 1988-. *Memberships:* International Bar Association; Association of Women Solicitors. *Honour:* Winston Churchill Memorial prize, Southampton University, 1979. *Hobbies:* Tennis; Travel. *Address:* 10 Norwich Street, London EC4A 1BD, England.

BARKER Michelle Diana King (Mikki), b. 15 Aug. 1956, New York City, USA. Psychiatrist. m. 29 July 1978, 2 sons, 1 daughter. *Education:* BA, Biology, California State University, Hayward, 1981; DO, Medicine, Comp, 1987. *Appointments:* Assistant Director, Public Affairs, KIQQ-FM, 1978; American Airlines, 1979; Mathematics Instructor, Laney College, 1979-83; King-Drew Medical Centre, 1987-. *Creative works:* Dance Theatre, Harlem. *Memberships include:* Various professional bodies including American Medical Association; China branch, National Association for Advancement of Coloured Peoples; Hawaii Jazz Preservation Society. *Honours:* Robert Wood Johnson Fellowships, 1983, 1984; BPW, Young Careerist Branch, 1988. *Hobbies:* Dance; Theatre; Collecting native American art. *Address:* 56 Brownfield Lane, Pomona, California 91766, USA.

BARLOW Laurie Patricia Hildebrand, b. 9 Sep. 1952, Pasadena, California, USA. Architect. m. James Paul Bochon, 29 Mar. 1980. *Education:* BA, Environmental Design, University of Washington, 1974; March, California Polytechnic University, San Luis Obispo, 1979; Registered Architect, California. *Appointments:* Lighting Designer, Sparling & Associates, Seattle, Washington, 1976; Draughtsperson, Ralph D Anderson, Seattle, 1977; Project Manager, Smith & Williams, South Pasadena, California, 1979-82; Project Manager, Whit Smith FAIA, South Pasadena, 1982-85; Architect, Neptune & Thomas, Pasadena, 1985-86; Project Architect, Administrator, Cashon, Horie, Cocke, Gonzalez, Los Angeles, California, 1986-. *Memberships:* Board of Directors, Chairman of Professional and Development Committee, Chairman of Bulletin, Pasadena Chapter, American Institute of Architects; Association of Women in Architecture (Committee for AIA exhibit Women in American Architecture, 1888-1988); Illuminating Engineering Society; Daughters of the American Revolution. *Hobbies:* Cycling; Art illustration; Design. *Address:* 623 Prospect Ave 3, South Pasadena, California 91030, USA.

BARNARD Kathleen (Katerina) Mae, b. 8 Aug. 1948, Joliet, Illinois, USA. Professor. m. Allen L Barnard, 19 June 1972, 1 daughter. *Education:* AA, Joliet College, 1968; BA, California State University, Long Beach, 1971; MA, Art History, Northern Illinois University, 1982; Foreign Studies in Greece, Turkey, Yugoslavia, Bulgaria, 1982-84. *Appointments:* Art Instructor, Joliet Twp. High Dist. 204, 1975-80; Art History, NIU, Dekalb, 1980-85; Instructor, Art History, Kishwaukee Community College, 1981-88. *Publications:* Numerous articles in Sacred Art Journal; Daphni: An Overview, 1989; The Anastasis..., Masters Thesis; Kastoria & Greece: Jewel of Middle Byzantine, in press. *Memberships:* St John of Damascus Association of Iconographers Iconologists & Architects, Vice Chaorman, Board of Directors; Greek Orthodox Philoptochos Society, President; Alpha Friends of Antiquity; Archaeological Institute of America; Chicago Art Institute; National Trust for Historic Preservation; etc. *Honours:* Outstanding Woman Student Leadership Award, NIU, 1982; MA, Art History Degree, 1982; etc. *Hobbies Include:* Writing Art Historical Articles; Music; Horticulture. *Address:* 2207 Arden Place, Joliet, IL 60435, USA.

BARNARD Rene, b. 8 June 1956, Upington, South Africa. Editor-in-Chief. m. 6 Oct. 1984. 1 son. *Education:*

Bachelor Home Economics. *Appointments:* Home Economist, Natal Dried Fruit Board, 1980; Cookery Editor 1980-84, Executive Editor 1985, Editor-in-Chief, 1985-, Rooi Rose. *Hobbies:* Interior Decorating; Entertaining. *Address:* P O Box 2595, Johannesburg 2000, Republic of South Africa.

BARNARD Susan M., b. 7 Mar. 1935, New York City, USA. Zoo Keeper. 1 son, 1 daughter. *Education:* AA, Santa Fe Community College, 1974; BSc, University of The State of New York, 1983. *Appointments include:* Lead Reptile Keeper, Zoo Atlanta, Georgia, 1979-. *Creative works include:* Lectures; Television appearances; Over 70 research publications; Manuscript reviewer. *Memberships include:* Water safety instructor, National American Red Cross, 1959-69; Board, American Association of Zoo Keepers, 1986-90. *Honours:* Sigma Tau Sigma, University of Florida honorary tutoring society, 1975-77; Excellence in Journalism award, Animal Keepers' Forum, 1985, 1986; Research grants. *Hobbies include:* Bat conservation & research; Technical & creative writing; Public speaking; Graphics & exhibition design; Carpentry; Gourmet cooking. *Address:* Department of Herpetology, Zoo Atlanta, 800 Cherokee Avenue SE, Atlanta, Georgia 30315, USA.

BARNES Jean, b. 7 Aug. 1923, Beaver Falls, USA. Retail Sales Executive; Retail Sales Writer; Speaker. m. Bruce Barnes, 11 Mar. 1947, deceased 1971, 4 daughters. *Appointments:* National Sales Manager, Empire Crafts Corporation, 1961-85; Founder, President, Tammey Jewels Inc., (35 stores in major shopping areas), 1986-; Founder, President, Hotel Gift Shops of America (Gina's Gifts); Founder, President, The Jean Barnes Collection. *Publications:* The Jean Barnes Newsletter; The Glamourlog. *Memberships:* Republication National Committee; President Reagan's Task Force; US Senatorial Committee; Honourable Order of Kentucky Colonels; etc. *Honours:* Recipient, many honours and awards. *Hobbies:* Non-Fiction Writing; Gourmet Cooking; Baseball games. *Address:* 725 Beach Street, Satellite Beach, FL 32937, USA.

BARNES Jill Hart, b. 2 July 1945, Huron, South Dakota, USA. Educational Consultant. m. John Paul Barnes, 11 Feb. 1966, div. 1972, 1 son, 1 daughter. *Education:* University of Arizona, 1963-66; BA Education 1970, Reading Endorsement 1974, MA 1976, Arizona State University. *Appointments:* Teacher, Grade 1, Carrollton-Farmers Branch Independent Schools District, Texas, 1970-71; Grades 2 & 3, & Chapter I Reading Specialist Grades 2-6, Tempe Elementary Schools District, Arizona, 1971-86; Faculty Associate, Arizona State University, 1975-77, 1980; Educational Consultant, D. C. Heath & Company, 1986-. *Publications:* Reading Is A Family Affair, 1981; What Is It?, I Can, Help Me, & I Want To Play, 4 pre-primers written for Tempe Elementary SD, Chapter I Project, 1984. *Memberships include:* International & California Reading Associations; Arizona & Montana State Reading Councils; Past President, Ocotillo East Reading Council; Past Chair, Parents & Reading Committee, ASRC State Board; *Honours:* 1st Place, Golden Bell Award, Arizona School Board Association, 1982, 1983; Semi-finalist, Arizona Teacher of Year; Member, Arizona Governor's Committee, to establish state-wide parent-involvement reading programme. *Hobbies:* Reading; Literacy; Gardening; Handcrafts, Needlepoint, Sewing; Music; Writing Song Parodies. *Address:* 6807 East Latham, Scottsdale, Arizona 85257, USA.

BARNES Julia Cobb, b. 27 Aug. 1935, Jacksonville, Florida, USA. Educational Administration and Supervision (Principal) AIDS Counselor and Consultant. m. Horace Barnes Snr, 14 Feb. 1981. 2 sons. *Education:* AA, St Petersburg Jr College, St Petersburg, Florida, 1961; BS, Florida A & M University, Tallahassee, 1964; MA, New York University, New York, 1970; PhD, Florida State University, Tallahassee, 1982. *Appointments:* Science Phys Ed Coach, First Street Jr High School, Bradenton, Florida, 1964-65; Phys Ed, Health, Coach, North Florida Jr College (Suwannee River Campus),

Madison, 1965-66; Phys Ed, Health Coach, Cook County Training School - Adel Elementary, Adel, 1966-68; Phys Ed, Coach, Franklin Jr High School, Yonkers, 1968-71; Assistant Prof, Phys Ed, Health Ed, Bethune Cookman College, Daytona Beach, 1971-79; District Intake Counselor and Social Rehabilitation Counselor, State of Florida, Health & Rehabilitative Services, 1979-81; Gen Sci, Health Ed, Polk Correctional Institution, 1981-85; Chapter I Teacher/Coordinator, Lincoln Avenue Elementary School, 1985-86; Principal, Academic and Vocation, Zephyrhills Correctional Institution, 1986-. *Publications:* The Perceived In-Service Training Needs of Florida Public School Teachers for Teaching Handicapped Students in Physical Education (PhD Dissertation), 1982; Suggested Guidelines for Teaching Black Disadvantaged Students in Physical Education (Master's Thesis), 1970; 2 AIDS pamphlets: Facts About AIDS; Do You Know? 1983, 1985, 1988; Contributions to magazines. *Memberships:* Correctional Education Association; National Education; The Charmettes, Inc of Hillsbourgh County - Chaplain/Public Relations; Kappa Delta Pi National Honor Society; Progressive United Order of Eastern Star No 12 - Chaplain; College Student Advisor NAACP - Bethune Cookman College; Florida Education Association; Polk Education Association; Special Olympics - Professional Consultant; Phi Epsilon Kappa Fraternity. *Honours:* Outstanding and Deducated Services Award, Zephyrhills Correctional Institution, 1987-88; Florida Department of Corrections Teacher of the Year 1982-83; Tampa Urban League Service Award, 1979; Rockefeller Foundation Grant, Columbia University Teachers' College, 1976; Denforth Award, Martha Graham School of Dance, 1975. *Hobbies:* Reading; Music; Sports; Geriatric Centres; Coaching; Modern Dance; Youth groups; Gymnastics; The handicapped; Community affairs. *Address:* 3212 Darlington Drive, Tampa, FL 33619, USA.

BARNES Karen Kay, b. 22 June 1950, Independence, Iowa, USA. Attorney. m. James Alan Barnes, 2 Dec. 1972. 2 sons. *Education:* BA, Valparaiso University, 1972; JD 1978, LLM, Taxation 1980, DePaul University College of Law, Chicago. *Appointments:* Staff Assistant, Sears, Roebuck and Co, Chicago, 1972-78; Attorney 1978-, Partner 1984-, McDermott, Will & Emery, Chicago. *Publications:* Editor, Taxation for Lawyers, 1986-; Author, Note, 25 DePaul L Rev 734, 1976. *Memberships:* Midwest Pension Conference; Assoc Member, Esop Association; WEB (Network of professionals working in employee benefits); Chicago Bar Association. *Honours:* Admitted to: Illinois Bar 1978, Federal District Court, Northern District of Illinois, 1978. *Address:* 3 S 102 Blackcherry Lane, GLen Ellyn, Illinois 60137, USA.

BARNES-SVARNEY Patricia Lou, b. 10 May 1953, Binghamton, New York, USA. Geologist; Author; Photographer; Lecturer. m. Thomas Eugene Svarney, 8 Jan. 1977. *Education:* BA, Geology, Catawba College, 1975; MA, Analytical Geography & Geology, State University of New York (SUNY), Binghamton, 1983. *Appointments:* Research specialist, Virginia Institute of Marine Science, 1977-78; Geochemical analyst, SUNY Binghamton, 1978-80; Freelance writer, photographer, lecturer, editorial consultant, 1985-. *Publications:* Books: National Science Foundation; Zimbabwe; Clocks in the Rocks. Articles, various journals including: Odyssey; Astronomy; Final Frontier; Earth Science; Cobblestone; Sports Afield; Women's Sports & Fitness; Sea Frontiers. *Memberships:* American Geophysical Union; Association of American Geographers; National Association of Science Writers. *Honour:* Elected, Gamma Theta Upsilon. *Hobbies:* Astronomy; Landscape & still-life photography; Bird watching; Cycle touring; Weight training; Cross-country skiing. *Address:* 2603 Smith Drive, Endwell, New York 13760, USA.

BARNETT Caroline Anne, b. 1 Mar. 1948, Decatur, Illinois, USA. Company Executive. *Education:* BS, Communications, University of Illinois, 70; Postgraduate study, Yale University, 1970-72. *Appointments:* Buyer, Yale Cooperative Corporation, 1970-72; Account Executive, 1972-75, Vice-President, 1975-84, Executive

Vice-President, 1985-, Denhard & Stewart, New York City. *Memberships:* President, Publishers Ad Club; University of Illinois Alumni Association; University of Illinois Foundation; Executive Committee: Publishers Hall of Fame; New York Is Book Country; Coordinating Committee: World Hunger Crisis; Friends of the Library. *Address:* c/o Denhard & Stewart, 240 Madison Avenue, New York, NY 10016, USA.

BARNETT Marilyn, b. 10 June 1934, Detroit, Michigan, USA. Advertising Executive. 1 son, 1 daughter. *Education:* BA, Wayne State University. *Appointments:* Professional Model, 1955-56; Hostess, Creator and Producer of Radio and TV Shows, 1956-58; National Spokesperson, TV, 1960-70; Vice-President 1973-74, Executive Vice-President 1974, Northgate Advertising; Co-founder, Executive Vice-President, Mars Advertising, 1974-80; President, Mars Advertising, 1981-. *Memberships:* Adcraft; AWRT; Economic Club; American Federation of Radio and TV Artists; Screen Actors Guild, Director. *Honours:* Outstanding Woman in Broadcast, AWRT, 1980; Advertising Woman of the Year, Women's Club of Detroit, 1986; Outstanding Woman in Agency Management, American Women in Radio & Television, Inc, 1987. *Hobbies:* Reading; Sailing. *Address:* 24209 Northwestern Highway, Southfield, MI 48075, USA.

BARNHILL-BROWN Donna Marie, b. 15 Sept. 1951, Waltham, Massachusetts, USA. Owner, President, Marketing Enterprises; Consultant, Lecturer. m. Stehen Frank Barnhill, 10 May 1987. *Appointments:* Personnel Director, City of Biloxi, 1972-73; Hotel Manager: Lodging Unlimited Hotels, 1973-79, Dunfrey Hotels, 1979-81, AIRCOA 1981-84; General Manager, Residence Inn, Denver, 1984-86; Regional Director, Operations, Residence Inn, 1985-86; Owner President, Marketing Enterprises, 1986-. *Memberships:* President, Colorado Wyoming HSMA, 1981-84; Chairman, Colorado Heart Association, 1984-87; Chairman RMBTA Hospitality; President, Baton Rouge/LA HSMA, 1977-79; Gulf Coas Carnival Association; etc. *Honours:* Outstanding Citizen Award, Denver Law Enforcement Association, 1985; Outstanding Person of the Week, NBC Affiliate, Denver, 1985; others. *Hobbies:* Big Game Bow Hunting; Camping; Hot Air Balloons. *Address:* 2283 S. Yosemite Circle, Denver, CO 80231, USA.

BARNWELL Adrienne Knox, b. 31 Jan. 1938, Indiana, USA. Clinical Child Psychologist. m. Franklin H. Barnwell, 13 June 1959, 1 daughter. *Education:* BS 1959, MA 1962, PhD 1965, Northwestern University. *Appointments:* Visiting Professor: Northwestern University 1966-69, Hamline University 1971-74; Director, Paediatric Psychology, Ramsey Hospital, 1974-88; Director, Child & Family Services, Gillette Hospital, 1987-. *Memberships:* American Psychological Association; American Women of Science; New York Academy of Sciences; Society of Paediatric Psychology. *Honour:* Carnegie Foundation Fellow, 1961-63. *Address:* Department of Child & Family Services, Gillette Children's Hospital, 200 University Avenue East, St Paul, Minnesota 55101, USA.

BAROLINI Teodolinda, b. 19 Dec. 1951, Syracuse, USA. Professor. m. Douglas G. Caverly, 21 June 1980. *Education:* BA, Sarah Lawrence College, 1972; MA 1973, PhD 1978, Columbia University. *Appointments:* Assistant Professor, Italian, University of California, Berkeley, 1978-83; Associate Professor, Italian, New York University, 1983-89; Professor, Italian, New York University, 1989-. *Publications:* Dante's Poets, 1984; essays on Dante, Petrarch, Boccaccio. *Memberships:* Vice President, Dante Society of America, 1983-86; Medieval Academy of America; Renaissance Society of America; Association of Teachers of Italian; MLA. *Honours Include:* John Nicholas Brown Prize, Medieval Academy, 1988. *Address:* Dept. of French & Italian, New York University, 19 University Place, Room 629, New York, NY 10003, USA.

BARR Elinor, b. 2 Apr. 1933, Fort William, Canada.

Author; Lecturer; Archivist. m. Peter S. Barr, 30 July 1954, 2 sons. *Education:* BA, 1974, BA, honours, History, 1989, Lakehead University. *Publications:* Silver Islet, 1988; Ignace: A Saga of the Shield; Filmstrip: Lady Lumberjack, 1988; Filmscript: The Castle of White Otter Lake, 1983; Booklet: White Otter Castle, 1984. *Memberships:* Writers Union of Canada; Writers Northward, Chairperson. *Honour:* Cultural Achievement Award, City of Thunder Bay, 1980; *Hobbies:* Tour Guide, White Otter Castle. *Address:* 104 Ray Blvd., Thunder Bay, Ontario, Canada P7B 4C4.

BARR Judith Harriett, b. 7 Sept. 1947, Hemel Hempstead, England. Radio Announcer. m. David Malcolm, 15 Jan. 1968. divorced. 2 sons, 1 daughter. *Education:* Otago University, New Zealand, 1964, 1965; Flinders University, 1974. *Appointments:* Announcer, Radio ADN TV, New Zealand Broadcasting Corporation; Television Newsreader, Australian Broadcasting Corporation. *Hobbies:* Passionate interest in World Peace; Family and their future. *Address:* 201 Tynte Street, North Adelaide, South Australia 5006 Australia.

BARR Patricia Miriam, b. 25 Apr. 1934, Norwich, Norfolk, England. Author. *Education:* BA, English Literature, Birmingham University, 1953-56; MA, English, University College, London University, 1964. *Appointment:* Freelance Journalist and Writer, 1966-. *Publications:* 13 books including: The Coming of the Barbarians, 1967; A Curious Life for a Lady, 1970; The Memsahibs, 1976; Taming the Jungle, 1977; Jade, 1984; Kenjiro, 1985; Coromandel, 1988. *Memberships:* Society of Authors; The Japan Society; PEN International. *Honour:* Churchill Fellowship for Historical Biography, 1971-72. *Hobbies:* Travel to the East; Eastern culture generally; Cats; Living on the Hebridean Island of Coll every summer. *Address:* 6 Mount Pleasant, Norwich, Norfolk, NR2 2DG, England.

BARR Susan Irene, b. 29 Nov. 1954, Vancouver, Canada. Nutritionist. *Education:* BHE, University of British Columbia, 1976, PhD, University of Minnesota, 1982. *Appointments:* Assistant Professor, Director, Continuing Education in Nutrition & Dietetics, University of British Columbia, 1981-. *Publications:* Numerous publications in scientific journals. *Memberships:* Canadian Dietetic Association, Vice President 1985-86; Society for Nutrition Education, Board of Editors, 1988-90; Canadian Society for Nutritional Sciences; American College of Sports Medicine; Sigma Xi. *Honours:* Recipient, various scholarships; Award, Best Published Paper in the Journal, Nutrition Research, 1985. *Hobbies:* Running; Cycling. *Address:* School of Family & Nutritional Sciences, University of British Columbia, 2205 East Mall, Vancouver, BC, Canada V6T 1W5.

BARR Tina (Elizabeth), b. 13 Apr. 1955, New York City, New York, USA. Teacher. *Education:* BA, Sarah Lawrence College, 1977; MFA, Columbia University, 1982; MA, Temple University, 1987. *Publication:* At Dusk on Naskeag Point, book, 1984. *Memberships:* Poets and Writers; Modern Language Association. *Honours:* Fellowship in Literature, Pennsylvania Council on the Arts, 1984; Temple University Fellowship, 1985; National Endowment for the Arts Fellowship, 1989. *Address:* English Department, Temple University, Philadelphia, PA 19122, USA.

BARRANGER Milly Slater, b. 12 Feb. 1937, Birmingham, Alabama, USA. Administrator; Theatre Producer; University Professor. m. Garic K. Barranger, 1961 (div. 1984), 1 daughter. *Education:* BA, University of Montevallo, 1958; MA 1959, PhD 1964, Tulane University, Louisiana. *Appointments:* Lecturer, New Orleans University, 1964-69; Assistant Professor 1969-73, Department Chair 1971-82, Associate Professor 1973-82, Tulane University; Visiting Professor, Humanities, University of Tennessee, 1981-82; Professor, Department Chair, University of North Carolina, Chapel Hill, 1982-; Producer, PlayMakers Repertory Company, 1982-. *Publications:* Author: Generations, 1971; Theatre: Past & Present, 1984;

Theatre: A Way of Seeing, 1980, 198, 1990; Understanding Plays, 1990. Co-Editor, Notable Women in the American Theatre, 1989. *Memberships:* Past President, offices, National Theatre Conference, & American Theatre Association. *Honours:* Achievement awards, New Orleans 1976, Southwest Theatre Conference 1978, University of Montevallo 1979; College of Fellows of the American Theatre, 1984. *Hobbies:* Films; Travel. *Address:* Department of Dramatic Art/PlayMakers Repertory Company, CB 3230, Graham Memorial, University of North Carolina, Chapel Hill, NC 27599, USA.

BARRELL Patricia Dawn, b. 7 Dec. 1940, Chattanooga, Tennessee, USA. Secretary, Delta Air Lines Inc. m. John MacMillin Barrell, 7 Oct. 1972. *Education:* School of Business Administration, Marketing Major, University of Georgia, 1958-62. *Appointments:* Secretary, Dr Wm Beaton, University of Georgia, 1960-62; Secretary to Superintendent of Operations, Delta Air Lines, 1963-; Director/Treasurer, Barrell Investments Inc, 1986-. *Creative work:* Poem, Windsong. *Memberships:* Daughters of the American Revolution; American Business Women's Association; Life Member, Republican Task Force. *Honours:* Dame of Justice, Sovereign Order of the Oak; Dame of Merit, Order of St John of Jerusalem; Holder of The Cross of the Holy Land; Holder of The cross Pro Ecclesia Et Pontifice; Elected Delegate to County and State Repbulican Convention, 1984, 1985, 1986; Honorary Lieutenant Colonel Aide-de-Camp Alabama State Milita, 1977; Lieutenant Colonel, Aide-de-Camp, Governor's Staff State of Greogia, 1979. *Hobbies:* Water skiing; Travelling; World wide stamp collecting; Antiques. *Address:* 101 Parkway Drive, Peachtree City, Georgia 30269, USA.

BARRERA Elvira Puig, b. 11 Dec. 1943, Alice, Texas, USA. Educator; Counsellor; Therapist. 1 son. *Education:* BA, 1971; MA, 1978; Specialist, Marriage & Family Therapy, 1989. *Appointments:* Teacher, Edgewood, 1965-74; Educational Consultant, 1974-79; Career Education Co-ordinator, 1979-84; Counsellor, SAISD, 1984-. *Publications:* Educational Guides, articles in professional journals. *Memberships:* Kappa Beta Chapter, Delta KappaGamma; San Antonio Area Women Deans Administrators & Counselors Association, Treasurer, 1984-86; South Texas Personnel & Guidance Association. *Honours:* Recipient, various honours and awards. *Hobbies:* Running; Reading; Interior Design. *Address:* 5015 Fairford Drive, San Antonio, TX 78228, USA.

BARRES Carmen I., b. 3 Dec. 1961, Puerto Rico. Physician. *Education:* University of Miami, USA, 1979-83; MD, Temple University School of Medicine, 1987; Internship, Residency, Internal Medicine, Cooper Hospital Medical Center, 1987-90. *Appointments:* Cashier Trainer, Grand Union and Research Assistant to Dr Jeffrey Seibert, 1979-83; Volunteer, Jackson Memorial Hospital, 6 years; RGIS Inventory Services, Public School Teacher, Dade County, and various voluntary positions in health field, 1983- 87. *Memberships:* Alpha Epsilon Delta (President 1982-83, Convention Delegate); Alpha Lambda Delta; Beta Beta Beta; Golden Key National Honor Society; Sigma Delta Pi; Phi Kappa Phi; American Medical Women's Association; Physicians for Social Responsibility; American Medical Student Association; Student National Medical Association. *Honours:* Undergraduate Honour Scholarship; Dean's List; Outstanding Member, 1981-82, 1982-83; Outstanding Services as President, 1982-83, Alpha Epsilon Delta; Distinguished Academic Achievement Award, University of Miami, 1982; 5-Year Pin for Volunteer Work, Jackson Memorial Hospital, 1977-82; Award for Maintaining Grade Point Average, Alpha Lambda Delta, 1983; Board of Trustees Award, Jackson Memorial Hospital, 1983; National Minority Fellowship Scholarship, 1983-84, 1984-85; Outstanding Alumni, Alpha Epsilon Delta, 1984-85; Service Award, Bascom Palmer Eye Institute, 1984; Thomas Brown McClelland Trust Scholarship, Rotary Club of Miami, 1985-86, 1986-87; Dean's Award, 1987;

Recipient, AMA/Burroughs Wellcome Co Leadership Programme for Resident Physicians. *Hobbies:* Writing poetry; Dance; Creating community programmes. *Address:* 2013 Arborwood II, Lindenwold, NJ 08021, USA.

BARRET Gisele, b. 13 May 1933, Oran, Algeria. Professor; Writer; Critic. m. Pierre Barret, 20 oct. 1956, 1 son. *Education:* Doctorat d'Universite, Sorbonne, 1967; Doctorat d'Etat, Paris France 1987. *Appointments:* Professor, Universite de Montreal, Quebec, 1967-88; Visiting Professor, McGill University, Quebec, 1970-74; Visiting Professor, Paris III, France, 1982-83. *Publications:* Books on Drama in Education; Videos on Drama in Education; Producer, Radio & TV (RTS Paris 1964-67). *Memberships:* President Founder, 1973-86, APEDQ; Union des ecrivains quebecois; Association quebecoise des critiques de theatre; Association canadienne des critiques de theatre. *Honours:* International Award, CTA, 1972. *Hobbies:* Arts; Music; Theatre; Dance. *Address:* Faculty of Education, University of Montreal, CP 6128 Suc.A, Montreal, Quebec, Canada H3C 3J7.

BARRETT Helen Hunt, b. 2 Nov. 1943, Paris, Texas. Account Executive. m. (1) Lawrence B. Hunt, 1961, divorced 1979, 1 daughter, (2) N. Lee Barrett, 11 Sept. 1982, 3 sons. *Education:* Midwestern State Univesity, 1970-74; Aladdin Beauty College, 1985. *Appointments:* Executive Secretary, Department of Defence, 1969-82; Consultant, 1977-79, Sales Director, 1979-85, Mary Kay Cosmetics; Manager, Director of Admissions, Vogue Beauty College, Austin, 1985-86; Field Manager, Welcome Wagon Intl., 1986-88; Account Executive, Master Check Corp, 1988-. *Memberships:* Various professional organisations. *Honours:* Queen of Sales, Campbell Unit, 1978, 1979. *Hobbies:* Gardening; Gourmet Cooking; Golf; Water Sports; Make up Artistry. *Address:* 4018 Outpost Trace, Lago Vista, TX 78645, USA.

BARRETT Kim Bernadette, b. 10 Oct. 1950, San Jose, California, USA. Communication Skills Consultant; Lecturer; Author; Teacher. *Education:* MBA, Human Relations Emphasis 1986, BBA, cum laude, General Business Administration, 1984, National University, San Diego; AS, Engineering Model Technology, 1981, AA Design, 1970, West Valley College, Saratoga. *Appointments:* Owner, K B Barrett & Associates; Communication Skills Consultant; Instructor Communication Skills, Calligraphy, San Diego Golf Academy; Special Programs Co-ordinator; Editor, Rub of the Green Newsletter; Special Communication Seminars, Male/Female Communication, 1982-. *Publications:* 1977 technical paper, Education's Role in the Model Industry, Anthology, Great Communicators II, Communicating with Women communicating with Men, 1987; Co-author, Calligraphy and the Golf Pro, 1988. *Memberships:* National Speakers Association, 1987 Showcase Committee; American Society for Training asnd Development, Chair Membership Committee; Carlsbad Chamber of Commerce, Education Committee, Vocational Education Committee; American Engineering Model Society, Member Board of Directors, Chair; Marketing, Seminar Moderator, 1987. *Honours:* National University Leadership Scholarship, 1985; Outstanding Supporter Award, Giving and Receiving Organization for Women, North County Chapter, 1984; Outstanding Achievement Award, Divisional Honours, Model Building, West Valley College, 1975. *Hobbies:* Woodworking; Metal Machining; Pencil Drawings; Scuba Diving; Tennis. *Address:* 6992 El Camino Real, Suite 104-450, Carlsbad, CA 92009, USA.

BARRETT Nancy Smith, b. 12 Sep. 1942, Baltimore, Maryland, USA. Economist; University Dean. m., 2 sons. *Education:* BA summa cum laude, 1965, Economics, Goucher College, 1963; MA, Economics, 1965, PhD, Economics, 1968, Harvard University. *Appointments:* Various positions, 1966-89, Chair, Department of Economics, American University, Washington DC; Congressional Budget Office, 1975-76; Carter-Mondale Transition, 1976-77; Council of Economic Advisers, 1977; The

Urban Institute, 1977-79; Department of Labor, 1979-81; Civil Aeronautics, 1981; currently Dean, College of Business Administration, Fairleigh Dickinson University. *Publications:* The Theory of Macroeconomic Policy; The Theory of Microeconomic Policy; Prices and Wages in W.S. Manufacturing; Numerous articles. *Memberships:* American Economic Association. *Honours:* Max Hoschild Award in Ecnomics, 1963; Phi Beta Kappa, Goucher College, 1963; Woodrow Wilson Fellowship and National Science Foundation Fellowship, Harvard University, 1963-64; Outstanding Woman Faculty Member, American University, 1971; Fulbright Scholar to University of Gothenburg, Sweden and Institute of Economic Studies, Belgrade, Yugoslavia, 1973; Outstanding Scholarship and Professional Achievement, College of Arts and Sciences, American University, 1984. *Address:* College of Business Administration, Fairleigh Dickinson University, Teaneck, NJ 07666, USA.

BARRETT Winnie W., b. 8 Dec. 1942, Durham, North Carolina, USA. Clinical Social Worker. m. Joseph Robert Barrett Jr, Oct. 1963, div. Aug. 1968. *Education:* BA, 1969, MSW, 1976, Denver. *Appointments:* Clinical Social Worker: The National Jewish Hospital, Denver, Colorado, 1976-79; Mt St Vincent Home, RCCF, Denver, 1979-81; The Children's Hospital, Denver, 1981-86; The Midtown Group, Associates in Psychotherapy, Denver, 1986-88; Private Practice, Denver, 1988-. *Publications:* Co-founder, Editor, Journal for Psychological and Spiritual Integration; Regular contributions to journal and newsletter. *Memberships:* Co-founder, Founding Board Member, Professional School for Clinical Social Work, Denver, 1984; Colorado Society for Clinical Social Work (Board Member, 1982, 1983); Colorado Chapter, National Association of Social Workers; Board Certified Diplomate, National Board of Examiners in Clinical Social Work. *Honours:* Special Recognition Plaque for contributions to development of the Professional School for Clinical Social Work, Denver, 1987. *Hobbies:* Classical music; Indian cuisine; Creative writing; World travel; Disciple of Avatar Meher Baba. *Address:* 360 South Monroe Street, Suite 250, Denver, CO 80209, USA.

BARRETT-CONNOR Elizabeth Louise, b. 8 Apr. 1935, Evanston, Illinois, USA. Professor of Community and Family Medicine. m. James D Connor, MD, 17 July 1965. 2 sons, 1 daughter. *Education:* BSc Zoology, Mount Holyoke College, 1952-56; MD, Cornell University Medical College, 1956-60; Post-Doctoral Diploma, Clinical Medicine of the Tropics, London School of Hygiene and Tropical Medicine, London, England, 1964-65. *Appointments:* Instructor of Medicine 1965-68, Assistant Professor of Medicine 1968-70, University of Miami, School of Medicine; Assistant Professor of Community Medicine & Medicine 1970-74, Associate Professor, 1974-81, Professor, 1981-, Acting Chair, Department of Community and Family Medicine, 1981-82, Chair, 1982-, University of California, San Diego School of Medicine. *Publications:* Author of numerous books and articles to professional journals. *Memberships include:* Fellow, American College of Physicians; Fellow, Council on Cardiovascular Epidemology, America Heart Association; Fellow, Royal Society of Health; Fellow, American College of Preventive Medicine; American Federation for Clinical Research; Association of Teachers of Preventive Medicine; Infectious Disease Society of America; International Epidemiological Association; Royal Society of Tropical Medicine and Hygiene; Society for Epidemiological Research; Association for Practitioners in Infection Control and many others. *Honours include:* Frederick Murgatroyd Prize, 1965; Kaiser Award for Excellence in Teaching, University of California San Diego, 1982; Living Legacy Award, Women's International Center, 1984; Merit Award, National Institute of Aging, 1987; Kelly West Memorial Lecture, American Diabetes Association, 1987; Recipient of many awards, grants and fellowships. *Hobbies:* Reading; Skiing. *Address:* Department of Community and Family Medicine, Division of Epidemiology M-007, University of California, San Diego, La Jolla, CA 92093, USA.

BARRIE Jane Elizabeth, b. 11 Sept. 1946, Brimingham, England. Stockbroker. m. William Robert Ian Barrie, 12 Dec. 1970. *Education:* Bishop Fox's Grammar School, Taunton, 1959-64; BSc(Hons), Imperial College of Science and Technology, London University, 1969; ARCS in Chemistry. *Appointments:* Investment Analyst, Fielding Newson-Smith & Co, 1969-73; Partner, Belisha & Co, 1973-76; Manager, Taunton Office, CL-Alexanders Laing & Cruickshank, 1976-. *Memberships:* International Stock Exchange (1 of 1st lady members, 1973); Vice-President, Soroptimist International of Great Britain and Ireland; Chairman, Taunton and West Somerset Crime Prevention Panel; Chairman of Governors, Bishop Fox School, Taunton; Royal Dart Yacht Club. *Hobbies:* Soroptimism; Education; Sailing; Bridge; Local politics, Conservative Party. *Address:* Hollydene, Kingston St Mary, Taunton, Somerset TA2 8HW, England.

BARRIS Bernice Margaret, b. Cleveland, USA. Drilling Company Executive. m. Robert Lee Barris, 22 Feb. 1941, 2 sons, 1 daughter. *Education:* AS, Real Estate, 1976; AA Arts, 1977; AS, Aviation, 1978; AS, Nursing, 1979; Registered Nurse, Cleveland; Licenced Commercial Pilot. *Appointments:* Real Estate Agent; Private Practice Nurse, Cleveland; Secretary, Hupp Well & Pump, Cleveland, 1968-82; President ABC Drilling, Willoughby, Ohio, 1982-; Major, Civil Air Patrol, Aux. United States Airforce. *Memberships:* Flying Nurses Association; President, Child Care Association, Cleveland, 1966-86. *Address:* 5480 Highland Rd., Highland Heights, OH 44143, USA.

BARRON Barbara A, b. 26 July 1953, Omaha, Nebraska, USA. Assistant Professor, Physiology. m. Mark C. Calidonna, 15 May 1988. *Education:* BS, Pharmacy, Creighton University, 1977; PhD, Pharmacology, University of Nebraska Medical Centre, 1985; Registered Pharmacist, California, Nebraska, 1977, Iowa & Kentucky 1986. *Appointments:* Postdoctoral Fellow, Northwestern University, 1985-86; University of Kentucky, 1986-88; Assistant Professor, Texas College Osteopathic Medicine, 1988-. *Publications:* Articles in: Biochemica Biophy Acta, Eur. Journal of Pharmacology, Journal of Neurochemistry, and British Journal Pharmacology. *Memberships:* Society for Neuroscience; American Association Advancement of Science; Sigma Xi. *Honours:* Health Professions Scholarship, 1975; Regents Tuition Fellowship, 1982-83; Herbert L. Davis Scholarship, 1982; Student Research Forum, Best Presentation, 1984. *Hobbies:* Softball; Gardening; Bicycling; Sewing; Crochet; Yoga; Dance. *Address:* Dept. of Physiology, Texas College of Osteopathic Medicine, 3500 Camp Bowie Blvd., Ft. Worth, TX 76107, USA.

BARROW (B.) Rosemary, b. 12 Jan. 1942, Davenport, Iowa, USA. Administrator; Counsellor. m. Lloyd H. Barrow, 5 June 1965, 1 son, 1 daughter. *Education:* BS, Mathematics, Iowa State University, 1964; MA, Counselling, University of Northern Iowa, 1968; EdD, Counsellor Education, University of Maine, 1982. *Appointments:* Various schools, Iowa, 1964-70; Catawba Valley Technical Institute, North Carolina, 1978-79; Lincoln University, Missouri, 1985-87; Moberly Area Junior College, Missouri, 1987-. *Publications:* Hands-On Computer Anxiety Reduction Workshop; Math Journals Used to Reduce Math Anxiety; Computer Software for a Computerised Math Testing Programme for David Novat Math Series. *Memberships:* American & Missouri Associations for Counselling & Development; American College Personnel Association; Association for Counsellor Education & Supervision; National & Missouri Associations of Developmental Educators; Treasurer, Maine Trio. *Honours:* Scholarship, University of Missouri, 1981; Various honour societies, 1961-78. *Hobbies:* Psychology; Music; Talking; Food. *Address:* 3011 Alsup, Columbia, Missouri 65203, USA.

BARTEL Pauline Christine, b. 7 May 1952, Poughkeepsie, New York, USA. Writer; Educator. *Education:* AA, Occupational Studies, Albany Business College, Albany, New York, 1972; BA magna cum laude,

English, The College of Saint Rose, Albany, 1983. *Appointments:* Freelance Writer and Editor, 1976-; Adjunct Instructor, State University of New York, Albany, 1985-present; Adjunct Instructor, Hudson Valley Community College, New York, 1981- 85. *Publications:* Biorhythm: Discovering Your Natural Ups and Downs, 1978; The Complete Gone With The Wind Trivia Book, 1989; Nonfiction in over 40 periodicals for children, teenagers and adults including: Jack and Jill, Ebony Jr, Christian Science Monitor, Seventeen, Boys' Life, True Romance, Mademoiselle, San Francisco Chronicle, Boston Herald, New York Daily News, Chicago Sun-Times. *Memberships:* Albany Women's Press Club; Delta Epsilon Sigma; Kappa Gamma Pi; Secretary, Writers Group. *Honours:* Winner, Patricia Nosher Memorial Writing Award, College of St Rose, 1983; Certificate of Achievement for ranking in top 100 winners, nonfiction category, Writer's Digest Annual Writing Competition, 40th, 1986, 25th, 1987, 15th, 1988. *Hobbies:* Reading; Cooking and baking; Needlework; Pace walking; Gone With The Wind memorabilia. *Address:* 12 1/2 Division Street, Waterford, NY 12188, USA.

BARTH Melissa Ellen, b. 24 Nov. 1948, Chewelah, Washington, USA. Associate Professor. *Education:* BA, English, 1971, MA, English, 1974, Washington State University; PhD, English, Purdue University, 1981. *Appointments:* Advisor, Foreign Study, Office of International Programmes, Washington State University, 1972-76; Assistant Professor, English, DePauw University, 1981-82; Associate Professor, English, Appalachian State University, 1982-; Visiting Associate Professor, English, Duke University, 1988. *Publications:* Strategies for Writing with the Computer, 1988; Hands On the Business Writer's Workbook, forthcoming; A Reader's Guide to Stephen R Donaldson, 1988; The Harbrace College Workbook: Writing for the World of Work, 1986; A Reader's Guide to Orson Scott Card, forthcoming. *Memberships:* Phi Kappa Phi; MLA; National Womens Studies Association; American Business Communications Association; Popular Culture Association; National Council of Teachers of English. *Honours:* David Ross Dissertation Fellow, Purdue University, 1979-81; Recipient, various other honours and awards. *Hobbies:* Bird Watching; Natural History; Computer Science; Feminist Issues. *Address:* Dept. of English, Appalachian State University, Boone, NC 28608, USA.

BARTH Patricia Esther, b. 10 Aug. 1949, Launceston, Tasmania, Australia. Freelance Calligrapher and Calligraphy Teacher. *Education:* Launceston Teachers College, 1969-71; CertT; DipT; Institute de Cursos Espanoles, Malaga, Spain, 1981; Donald Jackson Historical Scripts Workshop, Adelaide University, 1984; Calligraphy Summer School, Roehampton Institute of Advanced Education, London, England, 1986-87; Dave Wood Colour and Design Workshop, Calligraphy Society of Victoria, 1988; Charles Pearce Advanced Calligraphy Workshop, Melbourne, 1988. *Appointments:* Teacher, Montello Primary School, Burnie, 1972-73; English Teacher, School of Business Studies, Zurich, Switzerland, 1974-76; Sales Assistant, Bucherer Jewellery Store, Lucerne, 1977-78; Management Secretary, Foreign Department, Swiss Banking Corporation, Zurich, 1979; English Teacher, Oekreal Management School, Zurich, 1979; Secretary, Credit Department, Manufacturers Hanover Trust, Zurich, 1980; Management Secretary, Foreign Exchange Department, Citibank, Zurich, 1981, 1983; Full-time Freelance, Brighton, Victoria, 1984-: Calligraphy Teacher, CAE, Melbourne, 1984, School of Printing and Graphic Arts, Melbourne, 1985; Freelance Calligrapher, The Scriptorium, Melbourne, 1985-; Calligraphy Lecturer, P & O Sitmar Cruises, 1988-, Western Australian Genealogical Society, Genealogical Societies Victoria and of Tasmania, 1989; Calligrapher, Exhibitor, 1st International Congress on Family History, Sydney, New South Wales, Oct. 1988. *Memberships:* Victorian Society of Calligraphers, Committee Member and Editor of Post Script newsletter 1983-84; Australian Society of Calligraphers. *Hobbies:* Creative calligraphy; Genealogy; Gardening; Reading. *Address:* The Scriptorium, 25 Mills Street, Middle Park, Victoria 3206, Australia.

BARTLETT Elizabeth R., b. New York City, USA. Writer; Educator. m. 19 Apr. 1943, 1 son. *Education:* BS, Teachers' College; Postgraduate, Columbia University. *Appointments:* Instructor, Southern Methodist University, 1947-50; Director, Creative Writers Association, New School, New York, 1955; Assistant Professor of English, San Jose State University, 1960-61; Associate Professor, University of California Santa Barbara, 1962-64; Lecturer, Creative Writing, San Diego State University, 1978-79; Professor of English, University of San Diego, 1981-82; Poetry Editor, Crosscurrents, 1983-88 *Publications:* Poems of Yes & No, 1952; Behold This Dreamer, 1959; Poetry Concerto, 1961; It Takes Practice Not To Die, 1964; Threads, 1968; Selected Poems, 1970; House of Sleep, 1975; In Search of Identity, 1977; Dialogue of Dust, 1977; Address in Time, 1979; Zodiac of Poems, 1979; Memory Is No Stranger, 1981; Gemini Poems, 1984; Candles, 1987; Around the Clock, 1989. Also: Editor, Literary Olympians II, anthology, 1988. *Memberships:* Poetry Society of America; Authors League; PEN American Centre; International Women Writers Guild; International Society of General Semantics. *Honours:* Poetry award 1970, Combo creative writing 1988, National Endowment for Arts; Writing fellowships: Huntington Hartford Foundation 1959, 1960, Montalvo Association 1960, 1961, Yaddo 1970, MacDowell 1970, Dorland Mt Colony, fiction awards 1983, 1985; Ragdale 1983; PEN syndicated fiction awards, 1981, 1985. *Hobby:* Exhibiting own artwork. *Address:* 2875 Cowley Way- 1302, San Diego, CA 92110, USA.

BARTON Gladys, b. 9 Dec. 1940, New York City, USA. Advertising Art Director; Designer. m. Lawrence A Barton, 16 Dec. 1960. 1 son, 3 daughters. *Education:* BFA, Pratt Institute, 1960. *Appointments:* Art Director, Clairol Inc, 1960; Gladys Barton Design, 1962; Salisburg & Salisburg Studio, 1972; Wunderman Worldwide, 1974; Benton & Bowles Adv, 1981; Rosenfeld, Sirowitz, Humphrey & Strauss, 1984; McCaffrey & McCall, 1986-; Barry Blau & Partners, 1989. *Publications:* Numerous articles to professional magazines. *Memberships:* Art Directors Club of NY; Type Directors Club of NY; National Association of Female Executives; National Association of Interior Designers. *Honours:* 1st prize, Franklin Mint Bicentennial Medal Design, 1975; Echo Award, Desi Award, Creativity Awards, 1980, 1982, 1984, 1986; Art Directors Club Award, 1985; Type Directors Club TDC'32 Award, 1985; 45th Graphic Arts Exhibition/Certificate of Achievement, 1987. *Hobbies:* Skiing; Antiques; Interior Design; Gardening; Gourmet Cooking. *Address:* 245 Everit Ave, Hewlett Harbor, New York 11557, USA.

BARTON Phyllis Joan Loseke, b. 18 Apr. 1936, Gem, Kansas, USA. Owner, Mechatronics Office Machines. m. Benny Eugene Barton, 6 June 1960. 1 stepson, 1 stepdaughter. *Education:* BS 1957, Home Economics, Kansas State University, Manhattan, Kansas; MEd 1974, Certificate, Guidance and Counseling 1975, Certificate, Industrial Coop, Training 1977, Vocational Technical Education, Virginia Polytechnic Institute & State University, Blacksburg, Virginia. *Appointments:* Home Economics Teacher and Department Chairman: Trego Community High School, Wakeeney, KS, 1957-58; Russell City Schools, KS, 1958-60; Robert E Lee High School, Springfield, VA, 1960-63; Fort Hunt High School, Alexandria, 1963-69; Hayfield Secondary School, Alexandria, 1970-75; Child Care Services/Industrial Cooperative Teacher/Coordinator, Hayfield Secondary School, Alexandria, 1975-84, retired. *Publications:* Author of numerous articles in professional publications; Cookbook: Hush Puppies and Other Stories, 1975. *Memberships include:* National President, National Association of Vocational Home Economics Teachers; American Vocational Association, Home Economics Division; Virginia Vocational Association; National Education Association; National Board of Directors, Future Homemakers of America, Washington DC, 1981-84. *Honours include:* Honorary Member, Virginia Association, FHA, 1985; Special

Achievement Award for Women, Honorable Mention, Fairfax County Commission for Women, 1984; National Capitol Area, March of Dimes, Washington DC, Outstanding Service Award, 1979-84. *Hobbies:* Needlework; Genealogy; Gardening. *Address:* Lake Havasu City, Arizona 86403, USA.

BARTUSKA Doris Gorka, b. 18 Apr. 1929, Nanticoke, Pennsylvania, USA. Physician. m. Anthony John Bartuska, 23 June 1951, 6 daughters. *Education:* BS, Bucknell University, 1949; MD, Women's Medical College, Pennsylvania, 1954. *Appointments include:* Associate Professor of Clinical Pathology 1971-, Director, Division of Endocrinology & Metabolism 1973-, Professor of Medicine 1977-, Medical College of Pennsylvania. *Publications include:* Various research articles, medical journals; Abstracts, book reviews. Numerous presentations to professional bodies. *Memberships include:* President 1987-88, American Medical Women's Association; President elect, Philadelphia County Medical Society; Fellow, American College of Physicians. *Honours include:* Distinguished Daughter of Pennsylvania, 1988; Father Clarence E. Shaffrey SJ Award, St Joseph's University, 1982; Commonwealth Board Award, Medical College of Pennsylvania, 1981; Christian R. & Mary F. Lindback Distinguished Teaching Award, 1974; Biographical honours. *Hobbies:* Piano; Gardening; Taxonomy. *Address:* Medical College of Pennsylvania, 3300 Henry Avenue, Philadelphia, Pennsylvania 19129, USA

BARVICH Beverly Joyce, b. 26 Sept. 1940, St Paul, Minnesota, USA. Graphologist. m. Larry L Barvich, 28 Oct. 1960. 1 son, 1 daughter. *Education:* Certified Graphologist, American Handwriting Analysis Foundation, 1984. *Appointments:* Handwriting analyst working with personnel selection, personal analysis, lectures, classes in graphology. *Publication:* Course in Handwriting Analysis and your personal self-worth called, Write On. *Memberships:* American Handwriting Analysis Foundation, Historian, Hospitality Chairman; Erika Karoh's Inner Circle. *Hobbies:* Needlepoint; Target shooting; Fly fishing. Interest: Study of psychology by applying various graphological theories to determine why a person behaves in a particular manner; The Study of left-handedness and the implications of left slant writing. *Address:* BJB Handwriting Analysis, 3400 Sullivan Court No 269, Modesto, CA 95356, USA.

BASCH Norma, b. 4 July 1934, Norwich, Connecticut, USA. Professor of US History. m. Sheldon Basch, 10 June 1956, 1 son, 1 daughter. *Education:* AB, Barnard College; PhD, New York University. *Appointments:* Rutgers University, 1070-. *Publications:* In the Eyes of the Law: Women, Marriage & Property in 19th-Century New York; Contributor: Feminist Studies, Signs, Journal of Early Republic, Law & History Review. *Memberships:* Director, American Society for Legal History; Society for History of Early Republic; Organisation of American Historians; American Historical Association; New York Historical Society. *Honours:* Bayrd Still Dissertation Prize, 1979; Fellowships: Woodrow Wilson 1978, National Endowment for Humanities 1985-86, American Council of Learned Societies 1988-89; Best Article, Society for Historians of Early Republic, 1983. *Hobby:* Skiing. *Address:* Department of History, 312 Conklin Hall, Rutgers University, Newark, NJ 07102, USA.

BASIC Karmen, b. 25 June 1943, Zagreb, Yugoslavia. Councillor, Cooperation Yugoslavia, UN, EEC, OECD. div., 1 son. *Education:* MA, German and English Language and Literature, 1966; MA, Indian History and Literature, 1969. *Appointments:* Researcher, historical connections Yugoslavia/India (missionaries, merchants, soldiers, sailors), 1969-71; Lecturer in Serbo-Croatian, Delhi University, India, 1971-74; Rep. Administrator for International Cooperation, 1979-. *Publications:* Articles; Papers; Lectures. *Memberships:* Croatian Philological Society, Orientalists' Section (President 1984-87). *Address:* Marticeva 14 E, 41000 Zagreb, Yugoslavia.

BASKETT Belma Otus, b. 18 Jan. 1931, Istanbul, Turkey. Professor. *Education:* BS, Robert College, Istanbul, 1950; Honours Diploma, Faculty of Letters, Ankara University, 1958; MA, University of California, Berkeley, USA, 1965; Fulbright Scholarship for Study in USA, 1964-65; PhD, Faculty of Letters, Ankara University, 1969. *Appointments:* Middle East Technical University, 1960-83; Michigan State University, 1979-81, 1983-86; University of Pittsburgh, 1987; Kobe College & Kansai Gakuin University, Japan, 1988-89. *Publications:* Handbook for Composition and Term Papers for Freshmen, 1964; English Studies, 1969; The Concept of Death in Ernest Hemingway, 1969; Kurt Vonnegut : Connoisseur of Chaos, 1983; numerous articles in literary journals. *Memberships:* Hemingway Society; American and Popular Culture Associations; British Comparative Literature Association; International Comparative Literature Association; International Society for Contemporary Literature & Theatre, Chair 1977, 1987, Executive Committee 1977-79, 1987-89. *Honours Include:* Olmsted Scholarship, Istanbul, 1949-50; US State Department Grant to Salzburg, Austria, 1973; Italian Government Scholarship, University of Milano, 1975; British Council Grant, 1976; etc. *Address:* 201 Morrill Hall, Michigan State University, East Lansing, MI 48823, USA.

BASKIN Barbara Holland, b. 27 Aug. 1929, Detroit, Michigan, USA. Associate Professor. divorced. 2 daughters. *Education:* BA Special Education 1951, EdD Special Education & Vocational Rehabilitation 1968, Wayne State University; MA Administration & Supervision, University of Michigan, 1957. *Appointments:* Teacher, Special Education, Detroit Public Schools, 1951-54, 1955-56 and 1957-59; Lecturer, US Army Ft Knox, 1954-55; Assistant Professor 1971-76, Lecturer 1976-81, Associate professor, 1983-, State University of New York; Educational Consultant, Krell Software, 1982-83. *Publications:* The Special Child in the Library; Notes from a Different Drummer; More Notes from a Different Drummer; Books for the Gifted Child; How's Business?; The Mainstreamed Library; Numerous articles to professional journals. *Memberships:* Council for Exceptional Children; Assn for Supervision & Curriculum Development; VP & Treas, Verbal Intervention Project; National Assn for Gifted Children. *Honours:* President's Committee, Employment of the Handicapped Literary Presentation Award, 1980; American Library Association Citation, Outstanding Reference Book of 1980 for Books for the Gifted Child; ALA, 1978 for Notes for a Different Drummer. *Hobbies:* Travel; Computers; Reading; Puzzles; Bridge; Films; Theatre. *Address:* State University of New York, Social Sciences Interdisciplinary Program 239 S Social & Behavioral Sciences Bldg, Stony Brook, NY 11794, USA.

BASKOW Jacqueline Iris, b. 2 Aug. 1951, Camden, New Jersey, USA. *Education:* AA Degree. *Appointment:* Jaki Baskow Talent Agency. *Publications:* Author, TV Series on Wedding Chapels in Las Vegas. *Memberships:* Women In Film; Film Institute; AFM; SAG; ASAE. *Honours:* 1st Runner Up, Woman of the Year in Business in Las Vegas; Citation, etc. *Hobbies:* Helping Charities; Dancing; Good Music; Travel. *Address:* 4503 Paradise Rd No 1, Las Vegas, NV 89109, USA.

BASSET Elizabeth, (Lady) b. 5 Mar. 1908, London, England. Lady-in-Waiting to Queen Elizabeth the Queen Mother. m. 31 Oct. 1931, 2 sons. *Publications:* 3 Anthologies: Love is my Meaning; Each in His Prison; The Bridge of Love. *Honour:* CVO. *Hobbies:* Reading; Writing; Farming; Riding; Gardening. *Address:* 67 Cottesore Court, Stanford Road, London W8 5QW, England.

BASSI Karen (Kaki), b. 6 Apr. 1945, Pasadena, USA. Artist; Printmaker. m. 19 Dec. 1984. *Education:* BA, 1968, MFA, 1970, West Texas State University. *Appointments:* Houston Independent School District, 1970-76; North Harris County College, 1977-80; Homerton University, Cambridge, 1980; PPT Milan Italy, 1981-82; Rabfetti Spa Italy, 1983-85; Kaki Inc., 1986-

. *Creative Works:* One Man Shows: West Texas State University; Houston Baptist University; Sam Houston State University; Homerton University, Cambridge, England; Le Firma Gallery, Milan, Italy; La Parallele, Paris, France; Group Shows; Works in various collections including: Gulf Oil Corp, Houston; Ramondi Spa, Milan; Homerton University, Cambridge; Fulbrigh & Jaworski, Houston. *Memberships:* Texas, Houston Watercolour Societies; Cultural Art Council of Houston; Musem of Fine Art; Contemporary Art Museum; Centro Camuno Di Studi; Capo Di Ponte. *Hobby:* Reading. *Address:* 3217 Iola, Houston, TX 77017, USA.

BASSO Karen Margaret Nelson, b. 9 Apr. 1952, Wellsville, New York, USA. Reinsurance Intermediary. m. Derek Franklin Basso, 24 Nov. 1982. *Education:* BA, Colgate University, 1974; College of Insurance, New York City, 1978-79. *Appointments:* Brokers assistant, Towers, Perrin, Forster & Crosby, NYC, 1974-75; Underwriting Assistant, US Liability Insurance Company, NYC, 1975-77; Underwriter, Property Facultative, Reinsurance Department, Home Insurance Company, NYC, 1977-79; Assistant Manager, Property Facultative, Allstate Insurance Company, NYC, 1979-85; Senior Vice President, Treaty Marketing, Preferred Reinsurance Intermediaries Inc/Associated Intermediaries, South Carolina, 1985-. *Memberships:* Member 1979-81, Past Vice President, Wall Street Business & Professional Women's Club; Columbia Association of Insurance Women 1988-. *Hobbies:* Volunteer, Sistercare Inc, services for abused women & their children; Gourmet cooking; Reading; Hiking. *Address:* c/o Associated Intermediaries Inc, 1634 Main Street, Suite 100, Columbia, South Carolina 29201, USA.

BATES Dianne Nancy, b. 20 Mar. 1948, Sydney, Australia. Children's Author. m. David Bates, 1969. 1 daughter. *Education:* Diploma of Teaching, 1974; BA 1988. *Appointments:* Teacher; Newspaper editor/Manager; Youth worker; Assistant to editor, New South Wales Dept Education School Magazine; Co-editor, Puffinalia children's magazine. *Publications:* Books: Terri, 1981; Piggy Moss, 1982; The Belligrumble Bigfoot, 1984; Thirteen Going on Forty, 1986; Madcap Cafe and Other Humorous Plays (co-written with Bill Condon), 1986; Grandma Cadbury's Trucking Tales, 1987; The Worst Cook in the World, 1987; The Magician, 1988; The Slacky Flat Gang (co-written with Bill Condon), 1988; The New Writer's Survival Guide, 1989; When Melissa Ann Came to Dinner, 1989. Included in a number of anthologies. *Membership:* Children's Book Council of Australia. *Honours:* Writing Grants, Literature Board, Australia Council, 1982 and 1983; Writing Fellowships, Literary Arts Board, 1987 and 1988; Winner, West Australia Young Reader's Book Award, 1988. *Hobbies:* Ceramics; Painting; Reading; Gardening. *Address:* Lot 908, Ninth Avenue, Austral.2171, New South Wales 2500, Australia.

BATES Donnette Marie, b. 27 Nov. 1949, Sleepy Eye, Minnesota, USA. Rehabilitation Placement Spec/Career Con. m. 19 Sept. 1970. 2 daughters. *Education:* AB, Kellogg High, 1964-67; St Cloud State College, 1967-68. *Appointments:* A & B Personnel, 1978-79; West Cap, 1979-81; Metro Rehab Services, 1981-83; Bates Placement Services, 1983-. *Memberships:* American Society of Professional Women; Minnesota Rehabilitation Association; Vice President Board, Pre School Playhouse. *Honours:* Employer Trainer Office Education programme of Mahtomedi School District, 1983-84; Counselor of the Year 1976. *Hobbies:* Travelling; Cross Country Skiing; Crafts; Antique Collecting. *Address:* 80 W Co Rd C No 804, St Paul, MN 55117, USA.

BATES Eve Mary Widzenas, b. 18 Sept. 1918, Camden, New Jersey, USA. Retired Housewife; Author. m. 15 Mar. 1940. 2 daughters. *Education:* 12 years public school and various college courses. *Appointments:* Teller, Camden, New Jersey, Savings Bank, 1940-50; Correspondent, Wheaton, Illinois Daily Journal; Editor, Warrenville Illinois Naperville Clarion;

Real Estate Broker, New York State, 1970's. *Publications:* Sudiev (Goodbye) True Story, 1978; Ancestral Biography about Turn-of-the Century Lithuanian Immigrants. *Memberships:* Florida Freelance Writers Association; President's Council, Rutgers University; The State University of New Jersey. *Honours:* Scholastic endowments to Rutgers University and Burlington County College, New Jersey for the annual Bruns John and Antonina Widzenas Memorial Awards. *Hobbies:* Gardening; Fishing; Golf; Writing; Story telling; Touring and World Travel. *Address:* 180 Calle Madrid, St Augustine, FL 32086, USA.

BATES Margaret Jane, b. 27 Jan. 1918, New York, USA. University Professor. *Education:* MLA, Columbia University, 1940; PhD, Catholic University, Washington, 1945. *Appointments:* Library of Congress, Washington DC, 1940-45; and Office of Inter American Affairs, State Dept: Stationed at Rio de Janeiro, DASP, and Lima, Peru, National Library; Professor, Spanish & Portuguese, Catholic University of America, 1945-. *Publications:* Discrecion in the work of Cervantes; Editor, Gabriela Mistral, Poesias completas, 4th edition 1974; Editor, Gabriela Mistral, Desolacion, Tala, Lagar, 1973. *Memberships:* MLA; American Historical Association; Director, Institute of Ibero American Studies. *Honours:* Ford Faculty Fellowship, 1954-55. *Hobbies:* Tennis; Gardening; Fencing; Painting. *Address:* 5914 Carlton Lane Bethesda, MD 20816, USA.

BATHURST Joan Caroline (Lady), nee Petrie, b. 2 Nov. 1920, London, England. Member of H M Diplomatic Service (Retired). m. Sir Maurice (Edward) Bathurst, CMG, CBE, QC, 8 Aug. 1968. 1 step-son. *Education:* Wycombe Abbey School (Scholar); 1st Class Mediaeval and Modern Languages Tripos, Newnham College, Cambridge, 1942; MA (Cantab), 1964. *Appointments:* Entered HM Foreign Service, 1947; Foreign Office, 1947-48; 2nd Secretary, The Hague, 1948-50; Foreign Office, 1950-54; 1st Secretary, 1953; Bonn, 1954- 58; Foreign Office (later FCO), 1958-71; Counsellor, 1969. *Membership:* United Oxford and Cambridge University Club. *Honours:* Mary Ewart Scholarship, Newnham College, Cambridge, 1938; Officer, Order of Leopold (Belgium), 1966. *Hobbies:* Music; Genealogy. *Address:* Airlie, The Highlands, East Horsley, Surrey KT24 5BG, England.

BATTCHER-GARBE Jyce Karen, b. 24 Jan. 1945, t Paul, USA. Home Economist; Columnist; Writer. m. LeRoy Battcher, 20 Aug. 1966, 2 daughters. *Education:* BS, University of Minnesota, 1966. *Appointments:* Home Economist, Volunteer, Laos,, with International Voluntary Services, 1969-71; Foods Consultant, Writer, Cookbook Author, Syndicated Columnist, 1978-. *Publications:* Microwave Family Favorites; Microwave Candies; Microwaving with a Gourmet Flair; A Batch of Ideas Newsletter; Microwave Minues, syndicated column. *Memberships:* Minnesota and American Home Economics Associaitron; Minnesota & National Home Economists in business Associations; International Microwave Power Institute; Cooking Appliance Section; Electric Womens Round Table. *Hobbies:* Cooking; Food Facts; Nutrition; Travel; Reading; Collecting Cookbooks. *Address:* RR2 Box 162, Gaylord, MN 55334, USA.

BATTIN R. Ray, b. 29 May 1925, Rock Creek, Ohio, USA. Clinical Neuropsychologist-Audiologist. m. Tom C. Battin, 27 Aug. 1949. *Education:* BA, University of Denver, 1948; MS, University of Michigan, 1950; Clinical Fellow, 1952-54, PhD, University of Florida, 1959. *Appointments:* Instructor, Speech Pathology, University of Denver, 1949-50; Audiologist, Speech Pathologist, Ann Arbor School, 1950-51; Audiologist, Houston Speech & Hearing Center, Texas, 1954-56; Director, Speech Pathology-Psychology, Hedgecroft Hospital and Rehabilitation Center, Houston, 1956-59; Audiologist, Drs Guilford, Wright & Draper, Houston, 1959-63; Private Practice, Neuropsychology, Psycholinguistics, Audiology, Speech Pathology, Houston, 1959-; Director, Audiology, Vestibulography & Speech Pathology Lab, Houston Ear, Nose & Throat Hospital Clinic, 1963-73; Clinical Instructor, Department of Otolaryngology, University of Texas School of Medicine, Galveston, 1964-; Clinical Instructor, Psychology, Psychology Department, 1974-75, Adjunctor Instructor, Communication Disorders, 1981, University of Houston. *Publications:* Speech & Language Delay - A Home Training Program (with C.Olaf Haug), 1964, Revised, 1968; Private Practice: Guidelines for Speech Pathology & Audiology, 1971; Vestibulography, 1974; Pediatric Screening Tests, 1975; Hyperactivity, 1977; Private Practice, Audiology & Speech Pathology (editor with D.R. Fox), 1978; Psychoeducational Assessment of Children with Auditory Language/Learning Disorders in Schoool Children, 1981, Revised, 1987; Voice Therapy for Transexuals: Current Therapy, 1983. *Honours:* Awards, scientific exhibits: 2nd place, American Speech & Hearing Association Convention, 1961, 1971; 1st place, Texas Medical Association, 1964; Gold Award, Educational Exhibit, American Academy of Pediatrics, 1969; Sigma Alpha Eta; Fellow: American Speech & Hearing Association and World Academy Inc; Honours, American Academy of Private Practice in Audiology & Speech Pathology. *Hobbies:* Theatre; Art; Ballet. *Address:* 3931 Essex Lane, Suite F, Houston, TX 77027, USA.

BATTISCOMBE Georgina, b. 21 Nov. 1905, London, England. m. Lieutenant Colonel C F Battiscombe, OBE, FSA, 1 Oct. 1932. 1 daughter. *Education:* St Michaels School, Oxford; BA Honours History, Lady Margaret Hall, Oxford, 1924-27. *Appointments:* Reviewer and writer of articles etc, for The Times; Times Literary Supplement; Country Life and various other journals and papers, 1929-88. *Publications:* Charlotte M Yonge; Mrs Gladstone; John Keble; Queen Alexandra; Lord Shaftesbury; Christina Rossetti: Reluctant Pioneer; The Spencers of Althorp; Two on Safari; English Pictures. *Membership:* Fellow, Royal Society of Literature. *Honour:* James Tait Black Prize for best Biography (John Keble) of the Year, 1963. *Hobbies:* Church Art and Architecture; Bird watching. *Address:* 40 Phyllis Court Drive, Henley-on-thames, Oxon, RG9 2HU, England.

BATTISTA Sharon Lynn Diener, b. 13 July 1950, Cleveland, Ohio, USA. Paintings Conservator. m. Thomas Battista, 22 Aug. 1977, 1 son, 1 daughter. *Education:* BA, Indiana University, 1972; Apprenticeship, Conservation Laboratory, Indianapolis Museum of Art, 1979-85; IUPUI, Herron School of Art. *Appointments:* Conservation Laboratory, IMA, 1977-87; Own business, S. D. Battista Paintings Conservation Inc, 1987-. *Memberships:* Charter member, Midwest Regional Conservation Guild, & Conservators in Private Practice; American Institute of Conservation. *Hobby:* KyoKushin Karati. *Address:* 5430 North New Jersey Street, Indianapolis, Indiana 46220, USA.

BATTY SHAW Patricia Dorothy Mary, b. 18 Nov. 1928, England. m. Anthony Batty Shaw, 7 May 1954, 1 daughter. *Education:* University of Southampton. *Memberships:* Chairman, National Federation of Womens Institutes, 1977-81; Rural Development Commission, 1981-; Governor, Norwich High School for Girls, 1981-; Agriculture Board for England & Wales, 1984-; Charities Aid Foundation; English Advisory Committee on Telecommunications, 1985-. *Honours:* JP, Norfolk, 1968-; CBE, 1982. *Hobbies:* Life Member, Associated Countrywomen of the World; Walking; Caravanning; Gardening. *Address:* Appleacre, Barford, Norwich, Norfolk NR9 L1BD, England.

BAUDUIN Laura, b. 28 Apr. 1931, Djakarta, Indonesia. Psychologist; Psychotherapist. m. A. M. van Asch van Wyck, 19 Sept. 1962 (div. 1972), 2 daughters. *Education:* Registered Nurse, 1954; BA, Psychology, University of Amsterdam, Netherlands, 1974. *Appointments include:* Private Practice, Psychotherapy, especially for Homosexuals & Bisexuals, Men & Women. *Creative works:* Short stories, Lesbian Science Fiction, 1985, 1986; Various Speeches. *Memberships:* Het Nederlands Instituut van Psychologen; Vereniging van Rogeriaanse Psychotherapie; Board, Stichting Groep 7152 (group, lesbian & bisexual women). *Honour:* Harriet Freezer Ring Award, work for lesbian women,

given by OPZY feminist monthly, 1982. *Hobbies:* Animals & Animal Welfare; Playing Piano & Clarinet; Listening to Classical Music & Songs (Elisabeth Schwarzkopf); Alpine Skiing; White Water Canoeing. *Address:* Groote Peel 11, 1112 KC Diemen, Netherlands.

BAUER Nancy E, b. 4 Sept. 1953, Alexandria, Virginia, USA. Business Executive. *Education:* BA 1976, Graduate work, 1977-80, Glassboro State College. *Appointments:* Educator, Gloucester Township School District, 1976-80; Manager Group Services, Harrahs Holiday Inn, 1980- 83; Director Group Services: Resorts International, 1983-84; VP Business Development, Resorts International Hotel/Casino, 1984-85; Vice Preisdent, Trump Castle, 1985-89; Senior Vice President, Trump Castle/Trump Organization, 1989-. *Publications:* Industry periodicals, 1980-; Curriculum East Africa, 1979. *Memberships:* American Management Association, American Marketing Association; Promotion Marketing Assoc of America; National Assoc of Professional & Executive Women; AC Chamber of Commerce. *Honours:* Graduate summa cum laude, Glassboro State College; Project Kenya State department/Fulbright Foundation award Recipient; Served as NJ Dept of Education Representative to Kenya, Africa to research Global Education, 1979; NJCLD Award. *Hobbies:* Skydiving; Spelunking; Mountain climbing; Skiing; Reading; Riding; Ballooning. *Address:* 591 Fourth Street, Absecon, NJ 08201, USA.

BAUER Sheri (Cheryl F. Schuller), b. 4 Nov. 1945, Milwaukee, Wisconsin, USA. Public Relations Director. divorced, 1 son, 2 daughters. *Education:* BA, Business, 1964; Postgraduate courses, Communication, 1969-87. *Appointments:* Froedtert Mayfair Corporation, 1976-85; Milwaukee Board of Realtors, 1985-. *Publications:* Publisher, Editor, Realtor Esprit magazine; Special Section Editor, Milwaukee Magazine. *Honours:* Publication Excellence Awards, National Association of Realtors, 1986, 1987; Gold Circle Awards, Internal Communications 1986, Internal & External 1987, American Society of Association Executives. *Hobbies:* Ballet; Art; Metaphysics; Literature. *Address:* 12300 W. Center Street, Wauwatosa, Wisconsin 53222, USA.

BAUER Stefanie Gilmore, b. 29 June 1957, Detroit, Michigan, USA. National Sales Manager, Hotels. *Education:* Coral Shores High School, 1974; University of Montana, 1977. *Appointments:* Hotel Sales and marketing, 1975-88; Director of Sales, Howard Johnsons, 1975-76; Director of Catering, Hilton, 1976-77; Director of Sales, Regional Director of Sales, Ramada Hotel International, 1977-83; Director of Special Projects, Ramada Hotel Group International; National Sales Manasger, Peabody Hotels, 1983-85; National Sales Manager, Westin Hotle, 1985-86; National Sales Manager, Servico Hotels, West Palm Beach, Florida, 1986-. *Publication:* Article on Hotel Sales Career movement, 1979. *Memberships:* American Society Association; Hotel Sales Management Association; Board, National Association Exposition Managers; Board Member, Planned Parenthood; Board Member, Sales and Marketing Executives, ABWA. *Honours:* Edison Award, 1977; Distinguished Sales Award, Sales and Marketing Executives, 1984. *Hobbies:* Studying Management Philosophy; Reading; Skiing; Swimming; Art collecting; World travel. *Address:* 14706 Beech Daly, Redford, Michigan 48239, USA.

BAUGH Linda Sue, b. 27 May 1945, Kansas City, USA. Writer; Editor; Indexer. *Education:* BA, English, University of Iowa, 1967; MFA, Creative Writing, University of North Carolina, 1969. *Appointments:* Proof Reader, Commerce Clearing House Inc., Chicago, 1970-71; Senior Editor, Boox Allen & Hamilton, Chicago, 1971-78; Owner, Kairos Communications, Evanston, 1978-. *Publications:* Contributing Author (books): Good's World Atlas, 1982; Atlas of the United States, 1983; Rand McNally's Historical World Atlas, 1984; Rand McNally's World Facts in Brief, 1986, 1988; Rand McNally's Cosmopolitan World Atlas, 1987; Compton's Encyclopedia, 1988; Rebirth of Power: An Anthology, 1988; Poetry: For the Man Who Went North, World of

Poetry Anthology, 1976; Splitting and Seal Rock, Black Maria, 1980. *Memberships:* Chicago Women in Publishing, freelance Chair; American Medical Writers Association; American Society of Indexers. *Honours:* Recipient, various honours and awards. *Hobbies:* Music; Astronomy; Mythology; Fiction; Poetry. *Address:* Evanston, IL 60202, USA.

BAUMANN Carol Edler, University Professor and Administrator. *Education:* BA, University of Wisconsin, Madison, 1954; PhD, London School of Economics, England, 1957. *Appointments:* Chairman, International Relations Major, 1962-79, Director, International Studies and Programme, 1982-88, Professor, Department of Political Science, Director, Institute of World Affairs, University of Wisconsin, Milwaukee. *Publications:* Western Europe: What Path to Integration? (editor), 1967; The Diplomatic Kidnappings, 1973; Europe in NATO: Deterrence, Defense, and Arms Control (editor), 1987. *Memberships:* The China Council of the Asia Society Inc; Committee on Atlantic Studies; Council on Foreign Relations, New York; International Studies Association; National Committee on US-China Relations; National Council of World Affairs Organisations, President 1977-79. *Honours:* Phi Beta Kappa, Junior Year; Phi Kappa Phi; Phi Eta Sigma; Marshall Scholar, 1954-57; Honorary Woodrow Wilson Fellow, 1954-55; Fulbright Fellowship (declined), 1954-55. *Address:* 10810 Hidden Valley Drive, Cedarburg, WI 53012, USA.

BAUMANN Isabel Rotraud, b. 15 July 1942, Stuttgart, (Swiss). Pharmaceutical Management; Medical Consultant. *Education:* Dipl.med.cosmetol. 1966; Dipl.pharm, 1967, PhD, 1972, ETH Zurich; IFB Management Cadre, 1981; Swiss Federal Dipl.pharm, 1984. *Appointments:* Management of Screening Division, Pharmacy Dept., University Zurich, Lecturing and Research, 1967-72, Research and Lecturing, Department of Physiology, 1976-80, University of Zurich, Switzerland; Research and Lecturing, Consultant, University of San Marcos, Lima, Peru, 1972-73; Research and Lecturing, Department of Behaviour Biology, ETH Zurich, Switzerland, 1975; Management of Pharmacies, Medical Consultant to Pharmaceutical Industry, 1980-. *Publications:* The differential effects of the Amphetamine isomers on temperature regulationbehavioural effects; Contributions to various pharmacological and physiological journals. *Memberships:* International Brain Research Association; Swiss Society of Natural Sciences; Swiss Physiological Society; Swiss Pharmaceutical Society; President, Zurich Section, Swiss Academic Women's Association; Executive Committee, KVHO; Swiss Association of Business Women. *Silver Medal for doctoral thesis, ETH Zurich. Hobbies:* Skiing; Mountain climbing; Sailing; Tennis. *Address:* Buchholzstrasse 15, CH 8053 Zurich, Switzerland.

BAUMEL Joan Patricia French, b. Winona, Minnesota, USA. Teacher; Lecturer; Author. m. Herbert Baumel, 11 July 1971. *Education:* BA magna cum laude, Douglass College, 1952, (junior year, Sweet Briar Unit in Paris, including Institut de Phonetique, Ssorbonne); Post-graduate studies: University of Detroit, 1952-55; Case Western Reserve University, 1960, University of Akron, 1962, University of Notre Dame, 1963, Manhattanville College, 1971; Pre-doctoral work, MA in French, Rutgers University, 9 June 1965; PhD, Modern Languages (French), Fordham University, 25 May 1985. *Appointments:* Teaching French Language and Culture, Elementary, Secondary and College levels, Ohio, Michigan and New York including Mother House of the Religious of the Sacred Heart, Kenwood, Albany, New York, and University of Akron, 1955-66; French Teacher, White Plains (NY) High School, 1966-86; Curricula Creator, Akron Public Schools; Currently Director, Baumel Associates, Yonkers, New York; Lecturer, City University of New York Graduate Center, B'nai B'rith International Museum, Washington DC; The First Unitarian Society of Westchester, New York; Rocklany (NY) Center for Holocaust Studies; The Unitarian Church of All Souls, New York City; Barry University, Miami, Florida; and Temple Beth Israel, Port Washington, New York. *Publications:* Paul Claudel and the Jews: A Study in Ambivalence; Lecture topics include: French Anti-Semitism: The Gallic Road to the Concentration Camp; Klaus Barbie and The Children of Izieu; Jewish-Christian Dialogue; Cousin Daniel Chester French: From The Minute Man to the Lincoln Memorial; Americans in Paris: An Explosion of Genius in the 20's; Jewish Musician and Catholic Poet: Colleagues Darius Milhaud and Paul Claudel. *Memberships:* Phi Beta Kappa, Mark Brent Dolinsky Memorial Foundation (Advisory Board); American Association of Teachers of French; American Council on the Teaching of Foreign Languages; French Institute/Alliance Française, New York City; Alliance Française of Westchester, New York. *Honours:* High Honours in French (Douglass College), 1952; Woodrow Wilson Fellow, 1958-59; Yearbook Dedication by the White Plains High School Senior Class, 1980. *Address:* 86 Rosedale Road, Yonkers, NY 10710, USA.

BAUSCH-GALL Ingrid Mariluise, b. 13 Oct. 1950, Sindelfingen, Federal Republic of Germany. Mathematician; Independent Consultant. m. Hans Gall, 22 Oct. 1982. 1 son. *Education:* Diploma in Mathematics, 1974; PhD, 1979. *Appointments:* Assistant Professor, RWTH Aachen, 1975-79; Consultant, Mathematics and Simulation, Control Data, 1979-82; Independent Consultant, Simulation and mathematics and scientific programming, 1983-87; President with Hans Gall of Bausch-Gall GmbH, 1987- . *Memberships:* Gesellschaft fur Informatik; Vice Speaker, ASIMGI; Society for Computer Simulation; International Association for Computers and Mathematics in Simulation; Gesellschaft fur Angewandte Mathematik und Mechanik. *Honours:* Invited Speaker, 3rd Seminar on Advanced Vehicle Dynamics, International Center for Transporation, Amalfi, 1986; Member of Programme Committee: 1st European Simulation Congress, Aachen, 1983; 2nd to 5th Symposium Simulationstechnik, 1984, 1987, 1988, at Vienna, Ebernburg, Zurich, Aachen. *Hobbies:* Sports; Politics. *Address:* Wohlfartstrasse 21b, D- 8000 Munchen 45, Federal Republic of Germany.

BAWDEN Nina Mary, b. 19 Jan. 1925, London, England. Novelist. m. (1)H W Bawden, 1946, (2)Austen Steven Kark, 1954, 2 sons (1 deceased), 2 stepdaughters. *Education:* MA, Modern Greats, Somerville College, Oxford. *Publications:* Novels include: Tortoise by Candelight; A Woman of My Age; Afternoon of a Good Woman; Anna Apparent; George Beneath a Paper Moon; Familiar Passions; Walking Naked; The Ice House; Circles of Deceit; For Children: Carrie's War; The Peppermint Pig; The Finding; Keeping Henry; Squib; The Witch's Daughter and others. *Memberships:* Internaitonal Pen; Authors Lending & Copywright Society; Society of Women Writers & Journalists, President; Royal Society of Literature, Council Member; JP. *Honours:* Edwardian Award for Children's Literature; Yorkshire Post Novel of the Year Award, 1976; Short Listed for the Booker Prize, 1987. *Hobbies:* Reading Fiction; Travel; Friends; Garden Croquet. *Address:* 22 Noel Road, London N1 8HA, England.

BAXTER Betty Carpenter, b. 10 Oct. 1937, Sherman, Texas, USA. Educator; Administrator. m. Cash Baxter, 30 July 1959. 1 son, 1 daughter. *Education:* AA, Christian College, 1957; BM, SMU, Dallas, 1959; MA 1972, EdM 1979, EdD 1988, Teachers College, Columbia University, New York City. *Appointments:* Copy Writer, WLOF Radio, Orlando, Florida, 1959-60; Copy Chief, WDBO-CBS Radio, Orlando, 1960-61; Teacher Nursery 4's & 5's, Riverside Church Day School, New York City, 1966-71; Assistant Director of School & Director of Admissions, 1972-73; Head of School, Episcopal School, New York City, 1973-87; Founding Head of Presbyterian School, Houston, Texas, 1988-. *Creative Works:* Photo illustrations: Infant Caregiving. Articles: Death, Divorce & Separation, The Open Home Magazine; Morals, Values & Ethics in Early Childhood Education, Parents League Bulletin. *Memberships:* National Association Episcopal Schools, Gov. Board

Secretary; Independent Schools Admissions Association of Greater New York; NAEYC; ATIS; Kappa Delta Pi. *Hobbies:* Music; Theatre; Cooking. *Address:* 2205 Maroneal Blvd, Houston, Texas 77030, USA.

BAXTER Elaine Bland, b. 16 Jan. 1933, Chicago, USA. Secretary of State, Iowa. m. Harry Baxter, 2 Oct. 1954, 2 sons, 1 daughter. *Education:* BA, University of Illinois, 1954; Teaching Certificate, Iowa Wesleyan College, 1970; MA, Urban Planning, University of Iowa, 1978. *Appointments:* History Teacher, Burlington, Iowa High School, 1972; Council Member, Burlington, Iowa, City Council, 1973-75; Senior Liaison Office, Housing & Urban Development, Washington DC, 1979-81; Member, Iowa House of Representatives, 1982-86; Secretary of State, Iowa, 1987-. *Memberships Include:* Board of Directors, Womens Equity Action League, American Society for Public Administration; Advisory Board, 1988 Coalition for Womens Appointments. *Honours Include:* various awards & prizes. *Hobby:* Historic Preservation. *Address:* The Statehouse, Des MOines, IA 50319, USA.

BAXTER Violet, b. New York City, USA. Artist. m. Martin J. Leff, 25 May 1971, 1 daughter. *Education:* Diploma, Cooper Union, 1960; Columbia University, 1960-61; Pratt Graphic Art Centre, 1980-81. *Creative Works:* Solo Shows: Pleiades Gallery, New York City, 1985, 1987; Suffolk County College, New York, 1986; Washington Irving Gallery, New York, 1988; Group Shows include: Exhibitions in Monaco, New York City, Florida, Washington DC, Connecticutt, New Jersey, and Pennsylvania. *Memberships:* Pastel Society of America; American Society of Contemporary Artists; Artists Equity of New York, Board of Directors. *Hobbies:* Calligraphy. *Address:* 41 Union Square W (402), New York, NY 10003, USA.

BAYEFSKY Anne Fruma, b. 8 Nov. 1953, Toronto, Canada. Associate Professor. m. Raj K. Anand, 6 July 1986, 1 daughter. *Education:* BA, Honours, Philosopy, 1975, MA, Philosophy, 1976, LL.B., 1979, University of Toronto; M.Litt., Oxford University, 1981. *Appointments:* Legal Researcher, Ontario Human Rights Code Review, 1979; Special Adviser to Canadian Delegation to 39th Regular Session of the UN General Assembly, 1984; Chair, Boards of Inquiry under Ontario Human Rights Code, 1986-; Professor, University of Ottawa, 1986-. *Publications:* Canada's Constitution act 1982 and Amendments, forthcoming; Editor, Legal Theory Meets Legal Practice, 1988; Co-Editor, Equality Rights and the Canadian Charter of Rights & Freedoms, 1985; Associate Editor, Canadian Yearbook of Human Rights, Volumes 1,2,3,4, 1983, 1985, 1986, 1987; articles in professional journals. *Memberships:* various professional organisaitons. *Honours:* Recipient, various honours, scholarships & grants. *Address:* Common Law Section, University of Ottawa, Ottawa, Ontario, Canada K1N 6N5.

BAYLEY-JONES Coral Rita, b. 11 Aug. 1939, Sale, Cheshire, England. University Researcher; Consultant; Company Director. *Education:* BA, Geography (Hons.), University of Leeds, 1961; Dip.Ed., University of Cambridge, 1962; Dip.App.Sc., Recreation, Western Australia, 1976; M.Phil., Murdoch University, 1977; MSc., University of Salford, 1980; PhD, University of Newcastle, Australia, 1986. *Appointments:* Lecturer, Redland College of Advanced Education, 1966-70; First Residential Warden, St John Reade Residential Hall, Bristol, Senior Tutor, Research Staff, Geography, University of Western Australia, 1970-74; Part-time Teaching and Research Staff, Murdoch University, 1975-78, University of Salford, 1978-80; Research Consultant, University of Newcastle, 1980-; Director, Australian Centre for Tourism, Travel, Recreation & Leisure. *Publications:* articles in professional journals. *Memberships Include:* Fellow: Royal Geographical Society, Tourism Society, Royal Statistical Society; International Biographical Association; many other professional journals. *Honours Include:* Recipient, many honours and awards. *Hobbies:* Choral Singing - Soloist; Swimming; Water Skiing; Travel. *Address:* Australian Centre for Tourism, Travel, Recreation & Leisure, Ashdown 11, 32 Tyrrell Street, Newcastle, NSW 2300, Australia.

BAYOL Irene Sledge, b. 11 Oct. 1933, Franklin Co, North Carolina, USA. Program Manager, Information Resources Management. m. (1) Charlie Morton Hamlet, 23 Aug. 1950 div. Mar. 1956, 1 daughter. (2) Jerome Stollenwerch Bayol, 9 Aug. 1958, div. 1972, 2 sons, 1 daughter. *Education:* Business Certificate, Louisburg Jr College, Louisburg, North Carolina, 1952-53; Department of Agriculture, Grad School, 1957-75; University of Virginia, 1969-70; Nova Community College, 1980-84; American University, Washington, 1986-. *Appointments:* Computer Equipment Analyst, USAF, Washington, 1970-73; Supervisory Computer Equipment Analyst, 1973-84, Computer Equipment Analyst for Information Technology, 1984-85, Policy Officer, 1985-87, Program Manager, 1987-, General Services Administration, Washington. *Memberships:* Professional Women's Club; President, Vice President, Treasurer and Secretary, Toastmistress Club; Social Director, Travel Club; League of Women Voters; Realtor, Virginia Board of Realtors; Adv Committee, Federal ADP Council. *Honours:* Numerous Awards for superior and outstanding performance. *Hobbies:* Dancing; Gardening; Travel; Education/Studying. *Address:* 9012 Vernon Viuew Drive, Alexandria, VA 22308, USA.

BEACH-COURCHESNE Barbara Patricia Mary, b. 2 Mar. 1940, USA. Director; Psychologist. m. Norman George Courchesne, 6 Aug. 1983. *Education:* BA, 1969; MS, 1974. *Appointments:* Teacher, 1961-- 71; Vice Principal, School, 1972; Psychologist, 1974-87; Education Consultant, 1978-79; Director, Pupil Personnel Services, 1987-. *Memberships:* Southern California Women in Education Management; Association for Supervision & Curriculum Development; National Association for Female Executives. *Honours:* Pi Lambda Theta Honour Society; Delta Kappa; Catholic Authors Award, 1988. *Hobbies:* Swimming; Hiking; Classical Music. *Address:* 2021, Peaceful Hills Road, Walnut, CA 91789, USA.

BEACHCROFT Elinor Nina, b. 10 Nov. 1931, Kensington, London, England. Childrens Author. m. Dr Richard Gardner, 7 Aug. 1954, 2 daughters. *Education:* BA, St Hilda's College, Oxford. *Appointments:* Sub-Editor, Argosy Magazine, 1953-55, Radio Times 1955-57. *Publications:* Well Met by Witchlight; Under the Enchanter; Cold Christmas; A Spell of Sleep; A Visit to Folly Castle; others. *Memberships:* Society of Authors; Childrens Writers Group, Committee Member (twice); Writor with Eastern Arts Writers in Schools List. *Hobbies:* Walking; The Countryside; The Paranormal. *Address:* 12 Datchworth Green, Knebworth, Herts, England.

BEAL Janice Marie, b. 14 Apr. 1960, Houston, Texas, USA. Psychotherapist. *Education:* BA Psychology, University of St Thomas, 1983; MA Clinical Psychology, 1985, Doctoral student, Counselling & Guidance, Texas Southern University. *Appointments:* Urban Affairs Adolescent Clinic, 1986-87; Psychotherapist, Mental Health Mental Retardation, Northside Child & Adolescent Clinic, 1987-. *Memberships:* Alpha Kappa Alpha Sorority Inc; Houston Chapter of Black Psychologists; Urban League. *Hobbies:* Bicycling; Skating; Boating; Co-owner of J & K Resale Boutique. *Address:* 5518 Margarita St, Houston, Texas 77020, USA.

BEAMAN Margarine Gaynell, Scrap Metal Buyer/ Broker. m. Robert W. Beaman, 3 sons, 2 daughters. *Appointments:* Scrap Metal Buyer/Broker. *Memberships:* Texas Federation of Business & Professional Womens Clubs Inc; Executive Women International; Zonta International; numerous community organisations, including: CEACO; ARCIL; Private Industry Council, City of Austin - Travis County. *Honours:* Presidential Citation, Private Sector Initiatives Award, 1978; Recipient, many honours & Awards including: Governor's Volunteer of the Year Award, 1982; Mayor's Meritorious Award, 1982; Outstanding Volunteer Blind Workers of Texas, 1982; New York American Council of the Blind Award, 1986; Freedom Ft at Valley Forge - Citizen Leadership, 1986; Sertoma, Service to Manking Award, 1987; Austin's Most Worth Citizen, 1988. *Hobbies:* Quilting; Volunteering; Youth; Gardening. *Address:* 1406 Wilshire Blvd., Austin, TX 78722, USA.

BEANEY Jan, b. 31 July 1938, Worcester Park, England. Lecturer; Author; Occasional TV Presenter. m. Steve Udall, 14 July 1967. 1 son, 1 daughter. *Edcuation:* NDD Painting/Lithography, 1958; ATC, 1959; CGLI (Advanced) Embroidery, 1963. *Appointments:* Teaching Art and Embroidery, Grammar School, 1959-64; Lecturer, Whitelands College of Education, 1964-68; Part-time Teaching Courses for Junior/Secondary Teachers/Embroiderers Guild, 1968-76; Lecturer, C&G Embroidery, Windsor and Maidenhead College of Further Education, 1976-. *Publications:* The Young Embroiderer, 1966; Fun with Collage, 1970, 1979; Fun with Embroidery, 1975; Buildings in Picture, Collage and Design, 1976; Landscapes in Picture, Collage and Design, 1976; Textures and Surface Patterns, 1978; Embroidery: New Approaches, 1978; Stitches: New Approaches, 1985; The Art of the Needle, 1988; Exhibitions: As member of 62 Group has shown in numerous exhibitions including: Congress House, Festival Hall, Victoria and Albert Museum, National Museum of Wales, The Commonwealth Institute; Presenter of television series. *Memberships:* 62 Group, 1963-; The Embroiderers' Guild, 1963-. *Honours:* Joint designer (with Jean Littlejohn), Maidenhead Hanging to commemorate 400th anniversary of Charter given by Elizabeth I. *Hobbies:* Painting; Gardening; Reading. *Address:* c/o Windsor & Maidenhead College of Further Education, Clewer Hill Adult Centre, Clewer Hill, Windsor, Berkshire, England.

BEAR Isabel Joy, b. 4 Jan. 1927, Australia. Research Scientist. *Education:* AMTC, 1950; FRMIT, 1972; Doctor of Applied Science, 1978. *Appointments:* AERE Harwell UK, Experimental Scientist, 1950-51; Research Assistant, University of Birmingham, UK, 1951-53; Experimental Officer, CSIRO, Australia, 1953-67; Senior Research Scientist, 1967-72, Principal Research Scientist, 1972-79, Senior Principal Research Scientist, 1979-. *Publications:* Numerous scientific papers; several patents. *Memberships:* Royal Australian Chemical Institute, Fellow; Australasian Institute of Mining and Metallurgy, Fellow; Foundation Member, Women in Chemistry Network. *Honours:* Order of Australia, 1986; RACI Leighton Medallist, 1988. *Address:* 2/750 Waverley Road, Glen Waverley, Victoria, Australia 3150.

BEARDSLEY Alice McCarthy, b. 28 Mar. 1925, Richmond, Virginia, USA. Actress. m. James W. Carroll, 8 June 1968, 1 son. *Education:* BA, Agnes Scott College, Decatur, Georgia, 1947; Graduate work, School of Fine Arts, University of Iowa, 1949. *Appointments:* Appeared in Woody Allen Films, Fall Project, 1985, Purple Rose of Cairo, Zelig; other film appearances include: Honky Tonk Freeway; Where the Lilies Bloom, 1973; TV Appearances: American Playhouse, 1983; Too Far to Go, 1980; CBS Workshop, Sid Caesar Show; Soap Opera, Search for Tomorrow; Theatre: Broadway, The Wall; Off-Broadway, The Kid; A Man's A Man; Camino Real; In Good King Charles Golden Days. *Memberships:* Head, Board of Deacons, Presbyterian Church; Screen Actors Guild; American Federation of TV and Radio Artists; Actors Equity Association, Deputy. *Hobbies:* Bicycling; Quilting; Braiding Rugs; Bridge. *Address:* Abrams Artists, 420 Madison Avenue, New York, NY 10017, USA.

BEASLEY Norma Lea, b. 6 Sept. 1931, Springdale, Arkansas, USA. Attorney-at-Law; Title Company Director. *Education:* LLB, BSL, University of Arkansas, School of Law, 1953; Graduate Studies in Oil and Gas and Taxation, Southern Methodist University, 1957-60. *Appointments include:* Partner, Beasley and Pulliam, Approved Examining Counsel for numerous title insurance underwriters; Licensed Attorney of State of Arkansas, 1953; Licensed Attorney of State of Texas, 1958-; Licensed Attorney before all Federal Courts and Supreme Court of the USA; Chairman of the Board and Chief Executive Officer, Safeco Land Title of Dallas; Safeco Land Title of Tarrant County; Safeco Land Title of Collin County; Safeco Land Title of Denton County; Safeco Land Title of Rockwall County; Safeco Land Title of Kaufman County; North Texas Title of Hunt County; Trinity Abstract & Title Company of Ellis County. Past President, Dallas County Land Title Association; Past President, Index Corporation; Joint Platn Take-Off, Dallas; Past Executive Vice-President and General Counsell, Fidelity Title Company, Dallas; Past Attorney Closer, Owner and Manager, Hillcrest Office, Hexter-Fair Title Company, Dallas; Vice Chairman, Board of Texas American Bank, Prestonwood; Advisory Board, Texas National Bank Dallas; Organiser, New Charter National Bank, Plano, Texas; Past Member of Board of Directors, First Security Bank and Trust, Coppell, Texas; Past Vice-Chairman, Board of Brookhollow National Bank; Co-Partner, B and W Investments; Co-Partner, BPW Investments; Co-Partner BPWD Investments. *Contributions to:* Organizational Behaviour; Understanding and Managing People At Work; America's New Women Entrepreneurs. *Memberships include:* Bar Associations of Arkansas, Texas and Dallas; Bent Tree Country Club, Dallas; Caruth Institute of Southern Methodist University; Charter Member, Charter "100" Club, Dallas; Charter Member, Commercial Real Estate Women and Member, Advisory Board; Board of Governor's National Women's Economic Alliance; National Women's Coalition; Committee of 200 International Women; Director, Dallas Chapter Juvenile Diabetes Foundation International; Financial Advisory Board, Junior League of Dallas, Inc; Women's Advisory Board, Dallas Baptist University; Advisory Board, Dallas Chapter American Red Cross; Director, Girls Club of Dallas; Rotarian Club of Dallas, 1988; Dallas Women's Lawyers Association, 1988; Director of Coming Attractions, Inc; Director of MD Labs; Director of Verarex Med. Corp.; Chief Executive Officer of Flame/Pruf, Inc.; Member 200 Club of USA. *Honours include:* Recipient, Citation of Distinguished Alumni Award, University of Arkansas, 1986; Recipient Alumni of the Month Award, University of Arkansas School of Law, 1987; Recipient of Affiliate of the Year Award, 1987, Greater Dallas Board of Realtors; Founder, Southern Methodist University's Marie Mivelaz Scholarship Fund; Founder, University of Arkansas Norma Lea Beasley Endowed Scholarship; Founder, University of Arkansas School of Law Norma Lea Beasley Endowed Scholarship. *Address:* Safeco Land Title of Dallas, 8080 North Central Expressway No 120, Dallas, TX 75206, USA.

BEASLEY Rita Mae, b. 28 Jan. 1942, Cleveland, Ohio, USA. Vice President, Headquarters & Information Services. m. Jerry C Beasley, 6 Apr. 1966. 2 daughters. *Education:* BA, College of Wooster, 1963; MA, University of Kansas, 1966. *Appointments:* University of Delaware, 1976-82; Assistant Editor, Bureau of Economic & Business Research Produce Marketing Association, 1983-; Computer Systems Manager, Information & Memberships Services. *Memberships:* American Society of Association Executives; International Association of Hewlett-Packard Computer Users (INTEREX). *Hobbies:* Gardening; Reading; Piano; Aerobics. *Address:* Produce Marketing Association, 1500 Casho Mill Road, Newark, DE 19711, USA.

BEATH Betty, b. 19 Nov. 1932, Bundaberg, Queensland, Australia. Composer; Pianist; Educator. m. David Cox, 21 Feb. 1976. 1 son, 1 daughter. *Education:* Dip Mus, Queensland Conservatorium of Music, 1969; TMusA, Australian Music Examinations Board, 1969; AMusA (AMEB), 1969; LTCL, Trinity College of Music, London, England, 1948; Registered Teacher with Board of Teacher Education, Queensland. *Appointments:* Head, Music Department, St Margaret's Anglican Girls' School, 1967-; Lecturer, Queensland Conservatorium of Music, 1969-. *Publications:* With words by David Cox: Seawatcher, 1974; Abigail and the Bushranger, 1976; Abigail and the Rainmaker, 1986; Abigail and the Mythical Beast, 1985; The Strange Adventures of Marco

Polo, 1973; Francis, 1978; Reflections from Bali, 1981. *Memberships:* Executive Board, International League of Women Composers, 1984-; Musicological Society of Australia; Fellowship of Australian Composers; Australasian Performing Rights Association Ltd; Australian Society of Music Education; Full representation as an Australian Composer with the Australian Music Centre Ltd, Sydney. *Honours:* South East Asian Fellowship, awarded jointly with husband, David Cox, Australia Council, 1974; Schools' Commission Grant, School Opera, 1975; Australian Delegate, 3rd International Conference on Women in Music, Mexico City, 1984; Residency, North Adams State College, Massachusetts, USA, 1987; First Performance of commissioned work, Points in a Journey, Smith House, North Adams, 1987. *Hobbies:* Indonesian/Asian culture; Nature; Walking; Gardening; Animals; World music; Languages. *Address:* 8 St James Street, Highgate Hill, Queensland 4101, Australia.

BEATTY Martha Nell, b. 29 Oct. 1933, San Francisco, California, USA. Travel Agency Owner. m. Denis Beatty, 19 Sep. 1986, 1 daughter. *Education:* BA, Stanford University, 1955. *Appointments:* Gourdels Travel, 1964-66; World Wide Travel, 1966-69; President, Owner, Unravel Travel, 1969-; Project Chairman. *Publications:* Here Today, book on San Francisco architectural heritage (chairman of project), 1968; San Francisco At A Glance, 1970. *Memberships:* Institute of Certified Travel Consultants; Hamlin School Alumni Board; Board Member, Pacific Musical Society; Board Member, Episcopal Chaplaincy of San Francisco General Hospital. *Hobbies:* Cooking; Writing. *Address:* 2998 Jackson Street 3, San Francisco, CA 94115, USA.

BEAUCHAMP Else, b. 19 Sept. 1895, Copenhagen, Denmark. m. William, Viscount Elmley, later 8th Earl Beauchamp, 16 June 1936. *Memberships:* Dame Grand Cross, Order of St John; Dame of Dannebrog, Denmark. *Honour:* MBE, 1944. *Hobbies:* Travel; Music; Porcelain; Life in General. *Address:* Madresfield Court, Malvern, Worcestershire WR13 5AU, England.

BEAUDRY Mary Carolyn, b. 25 Nov. 1950, Great Lakes, Illinois, USA. Assistant Professor of Archaeology and Anthropology. *Education:* BA, College of William and Mary, 1973; MA 1975, PhD 1980, Brown University. *Appointment:* Assistant Professor, Boston University, 1980- *Publication:* Editor, Documentary Archaeology in the New World, 1988. *Memberships:* Society for Historical Archaeology; Council for Northeast Historical Archaeology; Editor of journal, Northeast Historical Archaeology; Editorial Board, Journal of Field Archaeology; American Archaeology. *Honours:* Brown University Fellow, 1973-75; Recipient of grants from National Endowment for the Humanities, 1981, 1985. *Hobbies:* Gardening; Basketball; Baseball. *Address:* Department of Archaeology, Boston University, 675 Commonwealth Avenue, Boston, MA 02215, USA.

BEAUFORT-SICKINGHE Cornelie Jeanne Louise Mathilde de, b. 3 Feb. 1923, The Hague, The Netherlands. Retired. m. A.J. de Beaufort, 30 May 1953, died 1966, 2 sons, 2 daughters. *Education:* MA, Romance Languages, Leiden University, 1950. *Appointments:* Teacher, French, Baarnsch Lyceum, 1951-53; Staff, Inter-faculty Institute, University of Utrecht, 1965- 85. *Publications:* Various articles in professional journals. *Memberships:* President, Association of Women Students; President, Association of University Women of the Netherlands; Board, National Refugee Council, 1977-82; Board, International Federation of University Women, 1986-89. *Hobbies:* Music - Flute; International Affairs. *Address:* 4-205 Julianlaan, 3743 JG Baarn, The Netherlands.

BEAUMAN Katharine Burgoyne Bentley, b. 30 Sept. 1903, Leeds, England. Writer. m. Wing Commander E. Bentley Beauman, 22 June 1940, 1 son. *Education:* MA, Lady Margaret Hall, History Scholar, Oxford, 1925. *Appointments:* Speaker, Organiser, Conservation Party in London & N.E. England, 1927-29; Women's Editor,

The Yorkshire Post, 1929-31; Public Relations Officer, Womens Auxiliary Air Force, 1939-41. *Publications:* Wings on her Shoulders, 1943; Partners in Blue: Story of the WRAF, 1971; Green Sleeves: Story of the WRVS, 1977; Viola player with Royal Amateur Orchestral Society. *Memberships:* Chairman, Patron, Lady Margaret Hall Settlement in Lambeth; Chairman, Crosby Hale Library; British Federation of University Women; Governor, Grey Coat Hospital, Westminster; HQ Staff, WRVS, University Women's Club; etc. *Honours:* British Ambassador Book Award, English Speaking Union, 1977. *Hobbies:* Music; Painting; Reading; Education; Social Work. *Address:* 59 Chester Row, London SW1, England.

BEAVEN Freda Margaret, b. 30 July 1923, Croydon, Surrey, England. Specialist Singing Teacher; Performer; Choralist; Theory Specialist; Adjudicator; Publisher. m. 18 Aug. 1945, 1 son. *Education:* LRAM Diplomas, Teacher and Performer, 1967-68. *Career includes:* BBC Choral Work, Recitals, London, 1968-; Director, The Lindsey Singers (madrigals), 1970-74; Private Teacher, 1967-; Ambrosian Singers, 1970-74; Choral Teacher, Accompanist, Voice and Language Tutor, Oldham, Lancs, 1980-1988; Adjudicator; Holiday Music Course Tuition. *Publications:* Music Theory Makes Sense, Ist Edition, 1985, 3-part Edition (includes Harmony), 1988. *Memberships:* Incorporated Society of Musicians; Royal Society of Musicians; Association of Teachers of Singing; Music Teachers Association; Adjudicator-Member, British Federation of Music Festivals; Institute of Advanced Motorists. *Hobbies:* Motoring; Antique glass and china collection; World travel. *Address:* Flat 4, 11A Alighton Road, Birkdale, Southport, Merseyside, England.

BEAVER Bonnie Veryle Gustafson, b. 26 Oct. 1944, Minneapolis, Minnesota, USA. Veterinarian; Educator. m. Larry J Beaver, 25 Nov. 1972. *Education:* BS 1966, DVM 1968, University of Minnesota; MS, Texas A&M University, 1972. *Appointments:* Instructor, Department of Veterinary Surgery and Radiology, University of Minnesota, 1968-69; Instructor, Department of Veterinary Anatomy, 1969-72, Assistant Professor, 1972-76, Associate Professor, 1976-82, Professor, 1982-86, Professor, Department of Small Animal Medicine and Surgery, 1986-, Texas A&M University. *Publications:* Your Horse's Health; Veterinary Aspects of Feline Behavior; Horse Color; Disection Guide for the Dog and Cat; Comparative Anatomy of Domestic Animals: A guide; Over 100 scientific articles. *Memberships include:* American Veterinary Medical Association; Brazos Valley Veterinary Medical Association; Texas Veterinary Medical Association; American Animal Hospital Association; American Veterinary Neurology Association; Animal Behavior Society; American Society of Veterinary Animal Behavior; American Association of Equine Practitioners; American Association of Veterinary Clinicians; American Veterinary Computer Society; Delta Society; Committee on Animal Models and Genetic Stocks; American Association for the Advancement of Science; Advisory Committee Member, Pew National Veterinary Education Program; Palomino Horse Breeders of America; Life member, University of Minnesota Alumni Association; Texas Palomino Exhibitors Association; Alamo Palomino Exhibitors Association, etc. *Honours:* Honored for contributions of women veterinarians to the profession, California Veterinary Medical Association, San Francisco, 1973; Citizen of the Week, The Press, 1981; Outstanding Woman Veterinarian of 1982, Association for Women Veterinarians, Salt Lake City, 1982; Phi Sigma; Sigma Epsilon Sigma; Phi Zeta; Phi Delta Gamma. *Hobbies:* Riding and showing Palomino Quarter Horses. *Address:* Department of Small Animal Medicine and Surgery, College of Veterinary Medicine, Texas A&M University, College Station, Texas 77843, USA.

BECHERER Deborah Zorn, b. 9 Feb. 1958, Youngstown, Ohio, USA. Bank Official. m. William B. Becherer Jr, 22 May 1983. *Education:* BS magna cum laude, Business Education, Youngstown State

University, 1980; MBA, College of William & Mary, Virginia, 1983; Graduate School of Banking, Madison, Wisconsin. *Appointments:* Loan Administrator 1983-85, Assistant Vice President 1986-, Commercial Loans, Bank One, Youngstown. *Memberships:* President, Lake to River Girl Scout Council; Past office, United Way; American Institute of Banking; National Association of Bank Women; Alumnae associations. *Hobbies:* Ballroom dancing; Travel; Aerobics; Swimming. *Address:* 7099 Oak Drive, Poland, Ohio 44514, USA.

BECK Donna Marie, b. 30 Apr. 1932, USA. Professor. *Education:* BSc., Music Education, 1962, MSc., 1966, Duquesne University. *Appointments:* Teacher, Music Education, 1952-76; Clinic Taining Supervisor, Polk State Center, 1976-79; Director, Music Therapy, Mary Wood College, 1979-82; Director, Music Therapy, Duquesne University, 1982-89. *Publications:* Varius articles in professional journals. *Memberships:* Sisters of St Joseph; National Association for Music Therapy; Mid-Atlantic Region Association of Music Therapy. *Honours:* Deans List; Pi Kappa Lambda. *Hobbies:* Liturgical Music; Dancing; Psychology; Reading; Working with Handicapped. *Address:* Sisters of St Joseph, St Joseph Convent, Baden, PA 15005, USA.

BECK Doreen, b. 12 Mar. 1935, Medomsley, County Durham, England. Writer; Producer; Fabric Artist. m. Leo Dink Siegel, 25 July 1974. *Education:* BA Honours, French (Upper II), London University External, 1957. *Appointments include:* Photo research, editing, Hulton Press, BBC Publishing, Observer newspaper, Thames & Hudson publishers (London), freelance magazine writing & translation (London), 1958-65; Staff & freelance writing, editing, producing, mainly with MD medical newspaper, Ved Mehta (New Yorker), United Nations Secretariat Department of Public Information, (New York), 1965-. *Creative work includes:* Book of American Furniture, Book of Bottle Collecting, Book of Country & Western Americana, published UK; History of British Isles, 3-part film strip, publishd USA; Numerous UN credits including initiation of printed Exhibit Series (Disarmament, Crisis in Africa, Soldiers of Peace); Apartheid South Africa. Quilted applique fabric hangings, including commissioned work, from husband's drawings of New York, 1979-. *Hobbies:* Amateur chamber music (cello); Tennis. *Address:* 100 West 57th Street, New York, NY 10019, USA.

BECK Francine, b. Pennsylvania, USA. Psychologist; Lecturer; Author. Widow, 1 son, 1 daughter (deceased). *Education:* Postgraduate Courses, Columbia University, 1959; PhD, The Union, 11961; Honorary Doctorate, World University, 1986; Research, Sexual Dysfunction Programming Clinic, 1984. *Appointments:* Educational Director, Academy of Creative Arts, 1970; Educational Administrator, Inner London School, 1973; School Psychologist, Hoffman School, 1975; City Mayor's Advisory Board, 1977; National Organisation for Women, Speech Writer, 1982. *Publications:* Gene or Jean, 1962; Choose Your Baby's Sex, 1962; Go Ahead and Cry; Sex Until You're 90!; Author, Producer, Director, Hostess, TV Talk Show, Medical News, 1976-85. *Memberships:* Director: Masters & Johnson Sexual Dysfunction Society; Keats-Shelley Association; American Psychological Association; Society for Women in Philosophy; Americna Guidance Association; Fellow, Centre for Advanced Studies in Behavioral Studies; Advisory Panel, Social Welfare Commonwealth Administration. *Honours:* George Foster Peabody Award, 1968; International Golden Eagle Award, 1966; National Teacher of the Year, 1967; Sylvania Award, 1971; Nobel Prize Candidate, Humanitarian Achievements, 1984. *Hobbies:* Painting; Sculpture; Travel; Signing; Dancing. *Address;* New York, NY 10010, USA.

BECK Helen (Lieland), b. 14 Oct. 1933, Indianapolis, Indiana, USA. Registered Social Worker. m. George J Beck, 13 May 1961. 4 daughters. *Education:* BA, Marian College, Indianapolis, 1955; Graduate work, part-time, Indiana University, 1956-58; Graduate student, social work, University of Illinois, currently. *Appointments:* Caseworker, Catholic Charities, Indianapolis, 1955-60; Probation Officer, Marion County, Juvenile Court, 1960-62; Omaha Girl Scout Council, 1973-74; Field Aide, Lakeview Girl Scout Council, Libertyville, 1979-82; Caseworker, Catholic Charities of Lake Co, Waukegan, 1982-87; Counsellor, Community Youth Network, Lake Villa, 1987-. *Membership:* National Association of Social Workers. *Hobbies:* Tennis; Soccer; Bridge; Theatre; Gardening; Reading. *Address:* 820 Crestfield Ave, Libertyville, IL 60048, USA.

BECK Kirsten, b. 23 Oct. 1942, Washington, District of Columbia, USA. Writer. *Education:* BA (Hons) Philosophy, Bucknell University, 1964. *Appointments:* Instructor, Dept of Philosophy, Duke University, 1968-70; Asst to Chairman, National Endowment for the Arts, 1970-73; Director Special Projects, Hospital Audiences Inc, 1974-75; Dir Public affairs, American Shakespeare Theatre, 1975; Managing Director, Women's Interart Center, 1978; Managing Director, Guest Relations, Radio City Music Hall, 1980; President, Beck Videotech, 1981-87; Senior Editor, Channels (Magazine), 1988; Senior Editor, Television Business International (Magazine), 1988; Director, Irondale Ensemble Project, 1988. *Publications:* How to Run a Small Box Office; Cultivating the Wasteland; Can Cable put the Vision back in TV?; Author of many articles on television and the arts; Editor: Artists in Schools; New Dimensions of the Arts; Our Programs. *Memberships:* Women in Cable; American Women in Economic Development. *Address:* 172 West 79th Street, New York, NY 10024, USA.

BECKER Mary Louise, b. St Louis, Missouri, USA. Political Scientist. m. 1966. 2 sons. *Education:* BS 1949, MA 1951, Washington University at St Louis; PhD, Radcliffe/Harvard University, 1957. *Appointments:* Research Analyst, Department of State, 1957-59; International Relations Officer, Agency for International Development, 1959- 64; Community Relations Officer, 1964-66, Research Officer, 1966-71; United Nations Relations Officer, 1971-. *Memberships:* American Political Science Association; Association of Asian Studies; Asia Society; Middle East Institute; Society of International Development; American Association of University Women. *Honours:* Blewett Fellow, Washington University, 1951; Resident Fellow, Radcliffe College, 1952-56; Fulbright Scholar, Pakistan, 1953-54. *Address:* Agency for International Development, Washington, DC 20523, USA.

BECKETT Margaret, b. 15 Jan. 1943, Ashton-under-Lyne, Lancashire, England. Member of Parliament. m. Leo Beckett, 7 July 1979. *Education:* Engineering Apprentice, Metallurgy, AEI Manchester. *Appointments:* Experimental Officer, University of Manchester; Researcher, Labour Party Headquarters, 1970-74; MP, Lincoln, 1974-79; Parliamentary Private Secretary, Minister of Overseas Development, 1974-75; Assistant Government Whip, 1975-76; Minister, Dept. of Education, 1976-79; Principal Researcher, Granada TV, 1979-83; MP, Derby South, 1983-; Front Bench, 1984-; Member, NEC, 1988-. *Memberships:* Transport & General Workers Union; National Union of Journalists; Association of Cinematograph Television & Allied Technicians; Fabian Society; Tribune Group; Anti-Apartheid Movement; Amnesty International, etc. *Address:* House of Commons, London SW1A 0AA, England.

BECKLES WILLSON Robina Elizabeth, b. 26 Sept. 1930, London, England. Author, Children's Books. m. 24 July 1952, 1 son, 1 daughter. *Education:* BA Honours, MA, Diploma of Education with Music, Liverpool University. *Appointments:* Teacher: Theresby High School, Leeds, 1952-54; Liverpool School of Art, 1954-56; Ballet Rambert Educational School, 1956-58. *Publications:* Children's books: Voice of Music, 1976; Musical Merry-Go-Round, 1977; Beaver Book of Ballet, 1979; Anna Pavlova, 1981; Eyes Wide Open, 1981; Secret Witch, 1982; Square Bear, 1983; Merry Christmas, 1983; Hungry Witch, 1984, Music Maker, 1986; Haunting Music, 1987. *Hobbies:* Music;

Gardening. *Address:* 44 Pope's Avenue, Twickenham, London TW2 5TL, England.

BECKWITH-COMBER Lillian, b. 25 Apr. 1916, Ellesmere Port, England. Author. *Major Publications:* The Hills is Lonely, 1959; The Sea for Breakfast, 1961; The Loud Halo, 1964; Green Hand, 1967; A Rope in Case, 1968; About My Father's Business, 1971; Lightly Poached, 1973; The Spuddy, 1974; Beautiful Just, 1975; Hebridean Cookbook, 1976; Bruach Blend, 1978; A Shine of Rainbows, 1984; A Proper Woman, 1986; A Proper Woman, 1986; The Bay of Strangers, 1988; The Small Party, 1989; contributor to various womens magazines (short stories). *Memberships:* Society of Authors; Mark Twain Society (USA); Women of the Year Association. *Address:* c/o Curtis Brown Ltd., 162-168 Regent Street, London W1R 5TA, England.

BEDFORD Frances Murray, b. Oregon, Missouri, USA. Professor of Music. 2 sons, 1 daughter. *Education:* MM, Southern Illinois University, 1969. *Appointments:* Professor of Music, 1970-, Chair, Music Department, currently, University of Wisconsin-Parkside, Kenosha, Wisconsin. *Publications:* Music for Movement; Music for Rest, 1973; Twentieth-Century Harpsichord Music: A Classified Catalog, 1974; Articles in the American Music Teacher, Woodwind World-Brass and Percussion, Instructor; Pleiades recordings. *Memberships:* Executive Board, Midwestern Historical Keyboard Society; Sigma Alpha Iota; Mortar Board; Phi Kappa Phi; Pi Kappa Lambda. *Honours:* Distinguished Service Award, Wisconsin Federation of Music Clubs, 1979; Touring grants, Wisconsin Arts Board. *Address:* 1654 College Avenue, Racine, WI 53403, USA.

BEDFORD Sybille, b. 16 Mar. 1911, Charlottenburg, Germany. Author. m. 1935, Walter Bedford. *Publications:* The Sudden View, A Visit to Don Otavio, 1953, revised 1982; A Legacy, 1956, 6th edition 1984, televised 1975; The Best We Can Do (The Trial of Dr Adams), 1958; The Faces of Justice, 1961; A Favourite of the Gods, 1962, revised 1984; A Compass Error, 1968, revised 1984; Aldous Huxley, a Biography, Vol I, 1973, Vol II 1974, revised 1987. *Memberships:* Vice President, PEN 1979; FRSL; Society of Authors. *Hobbies:* Wine; Reading; Travel. *Address:* c/o Coutts & Co, 1 Old Park Lane, London W1Y 4BS, England.

BEDIKIAN Mary Aslanian, b. 22 Jan. 1950, Detroit, Michigan, USA. Regional Vice-President, American Arbitration Association. m. 18 June 1972, 1 son, 1 daughter. *Education:* BA, European History, 1971, MA, Political Science, 1975, Wayne State University, JD, Detroit College of Law, 1980. *Appointments:* Labour Tribunal Administrator and Supervisor, 1975-78, Regional Director, 1978-87, Regional Vice-President, 1987-, American Arbitration Association. *Publications:* Contributor to Detroit Lawyer, Detroit College of Law Review, Michigan State Bar Journal, Wayne State Law Review, American Journal of Law and Medicine. *Memberships:* State Bar of Michigan, Labour Law Section, Committee on Arbitration and Alternate Methods of Dispute Resolution; American Bar Association; Michigan Trial Lawyers Association; American Trial Lawyers Association; Industrial Relations Research Association; Society of Professionals in Dispute Resolution; National Association of Women Lawyers; Women Lawyers Association of Michigan, Oakland County Branch; Economic Club of Detroit. *Honours:* Best Oralist Commendation, Spring 1978; Member, Moot Court Board; Nomination for Danforth and Woodrow Fellowship; Four-Year Board of Governors Academic Scholarship. *Address:* 15715 South Midway Avenue, Allan Park, MI 48101, USA.

BEE Adeline Mary, b. 6 Oct. 1954, Fort Belvoir, Virginia, USA. Tutor. m. Joseph D Galluzzo, 14 Apr. 1984. 1 son, 1 daughter. *Education:* BS Ed, University of Georgia, 1974; Harvard University, 1980; MBA Candidate, Suffolk University. *Appointments:* Teacher, English, Georgia, 1974-75; English and Social Studies,

Georgia, 1975-76; Kentucky, 1977; Active political worker and volunteer, Democratic Party, 1975-; Instructor, Chatahoochee Valley Community College, Alabama, 1976; Tax specialist, H & R Block, Massachusetts, 1979; Teacher, Massachusetts, 1980; Director, Purchasing Department, New England Paper Products, 1981; English teacher, Massachusetts, 1982-85; President, Consulting Unparalleled, 1982-. *Publication:* Reaching Out, poetry in Great Poems of the Western World, 1980; Microwave II, 1988. *Memberships include:* National Education Association; MTA; Association of MBA Executives Incorporated; Town Meeting Representative; Trustee, Leukemia Society of America; League of Women Voters; National Womens Political Caucus; National Association of Female Executives; Common Cause; Chair, Women's Caucus, Young Democrats of America, 1985-87; Region 1 Director, Young Democrats of America, 1983-85; Women in Politics and Government; Norfolk School Committee, 1988-; Chair, Norfolk Democratic Town Committee, 1988; Vice President, 1986-87 and Trustee, 1982-87, Leukemia Society, Greater Boston Chapter. *Honours:* Outstanding Young Woman of America, 1979; Lt Colonel, Alabama State Militia, Governor's Office, 1981; Certificate of Appreciation, Democratic National Committee, 1982; Ernie Boch's WJCC Community Salute Award, 1983. *Hobbies:* Reading; Politics; Golf; Racquetball; Bridge. *Address:* Consulting Unparalleled, 3 Day Street, Norfolk, MA 02056, USA.

BEEBE, Burdetta Faye, b. 4 Feb. 1920, Marshall, USA. Retired. m. James Ralph Johnson, 11 Oct. 1961. *Appointments:* Secretary, Love & Law Food Brokers, 1952-55; Secretary, Caston Lumber Co., 1955-57; Convention Manager, National Food Brokers Association, Washington, 1957-64; Writer, Santa Fe, 1962-72. *Publications:* Run, Light Buck, Run, 1962; Appalachian Elk, 1962; Coyote, Come Home, 1963; Chestnut Cub, 1963; American Lions & Cats, 1963; Assateague Deer, 1965; American Desert Animals, 1966; Ocelot, 1966; Little Red, 1966; Yucatan Monkey, 1967; Animals South of the Border, 1968; African Elephants, 1968; African Lions & Cats, 1969; African Apes, 1969; Little Dickens, Jaguar Cub, 1970; etc. *Honours:* Junior Literary Guild Selection, 1962, 1966. *Hobbies:* Travel. *Address:* Box 5295, Sante Fe, NM 87502, USA.

BEENSTOCK Vivian, b. 23 Oct. 1940, Brooklyn, New York, USA. Clinical Social Worker; Psychotherapist. m. Edward Beenstock Jr, 19 July 1964, 2 sons. *Appointments:* (Current) Clinical Director (outpatient mental health), Catholic Charities Mental Health Clinic, East Brunswick, New Jersey; Private practice, psychotherapy; Field instructor, Rutgers University. *Memberships:* National Association of Social Workers; American Association of Orthopsychiatry; American Association of Group Psychotherapy. *Honour:* Diplomate, Clinical Social Work, Academy of Certified Social Workers. *Hobbies:* Theatre; Tennis; Travel; Friends; Safe environment; World peace, Relationships; Child & Maternal Health. *Address:* 35 Independence Drive, East Brunswick, New Jersey 08816, USA.

BEERMANN Judith Countesa Ana, b. 19 May 1945, USA. Company President/Owner. m. Otto Von Bismarch, 22 June 1984, 2 daughter. *Education:* Kansas State University and Moana College. *Appointments:* President, Kappala-Donna Enterprises Systems Inc., 1967-. *Hobbies:* Travel; Church Activities; Family. *Address:* c/o 7316 Maple, Omaha, NE 68134, USA.

BEERY Mary, b. 16 Jan. 1907, Philadelphia, USA. Teacher; Writer; Researcher. *Education:* BA, College of Wooster, 1928; Studies, various Universities. *Appointments:* South High School, Lima, 1929-53; Director, Social Conduct, St Rita's School of Nursing, 1954-67; Programme Counsellor, 1967-68; Continuing Education Division, 1973-. *Publications:* Manners Made Easy, 1949; Guide to Good Manners, 1952; Young Teens Talk it Over, 1957; Young Teens Plan Dates and Proms, 1962; Young Teens Away from Home, 1966; Young Teens and Money, 1971; Newpaper Column, magazine articles. *Memberships:* Allen County Historical Society, Life Member; Smithsonian Associate. *Honours:* Recipient, many honours and awards. *Hobbies:* Gardening; Chess; Latchet Rugs. *Address:* Galvin Hall 420D, Ohio State University, Lima Campus, 4230 Campus Drive, Lima, OH 45804, USA.

BEESON Dorothy Patton, b. 10 Jan 1921, Kansas City, Missouri, USA. Artist. m. Donald Russell Beeson, 4 Dec. 1943. 1 son, 1 daughter. *Education:* School of Business Evanston Campus, Northwestern University. *Appointments:* Reinsurance, Home Insurance Co, San Francisco, 1945-46; Teacher, Boulder Public Schools, 1953-60; Treasurer, Mustard Seed Gallery, Boulder, 1968-72; Self employed since 1974-. *Creative works:* Paintings juried into shows in Rocky Mountain Region. *Memberships:* Juried membership, Southern Arizona Watercolour Guild; Arizona Watercolor Association; Tubac Art Center, Arizona. *Honours include:* Signature Member, Southern Ariz Watercolor Guild, 1987; First Prize, 7 state Arizona Aqueous, Tubac AZ, 1988; Honorary Mention, Arizona Aqueous, Tubac, 1986; Third Price, Natol Asson of American Pen Women of Arizona, 1988; Strickler Award, Award of Merit, Southern Arizona Watercolor Guild, 1984. *Hobbies:* Music; Reading; Travelling. *Address:* 1615 South La Canada, Green Valley, AZ 85614, USA.

BEGUM Syeda Firoza, b. 1 Apr. 1930, Comilla, Bangladesh. Physician, Gynaecology & Obstetrics. m. Prof M A Jalil. 1 son, 1 daughter. *Education:* MBBS, University of Dhaka, Bangladesh, 1953; MRCOG, 1964, FRCOG, 1977, University of London, England. *Appointments:* House Surgeon, Obstetrics and Gynaecology, Dhaka Medical College & Hospital, 1954; Civil Medical Practitioner, Pakistan Army Medical Hospital, Dhaka, 1954-55; House Surgeon, Dept of Medicine, 1955-56, House Surgeon, Dept of Surgery, 1956, Clinical Attachment, Dept of Obstetrics & Gynaecology, 1956-58, Registrar, Dept of Obstetrics & Gynaecology, 1958-59, Resident Surgeon, Dept of Obstetrics & Gynaecology, 1959-61, Dhaka Medical College & Hospital; Senior House Officer, Hammersmith Post Graduate Medical Institute, 1962; Welsh National School of Medicine, Cardiff, 1962; Associate Professor, Obstetrics & Gynaecology, 1964-67, Professor of obstetrics & Gynaecology, 1967-71, Professor and Head of the Department of Obstetrics & Gynaecology, 1971-86, Dhaka Medical College & Hospital. *Memberships:* President, Obstetrics & Gynaecological Society of Bangladesh, 1972-82; President, Bangladesh Association for Maternal & Neo-natal Health, 1979-; President, Bangladesh Association of Prevention of Septic Abortion, 1979-; President, Bangladesh Medical Association; Chairman, Board of Directors, Uttara Bank Ltd. *Honour:* Anniversary Medal, Path Finder Fund, Boston as a Leader in Maternal & child health, Physician, Teacher and Public Servant. *Address:* 19/E Green Road, Doad No 6, Dhanmondi R/A, Dhaka -1205, Bangladesh.

BEJI Blanka Jana, b. 7 June 1947, CSSR. Sociologist; Lecturer; Translator. m. (1)Toni Frisch, 1947, divorced 1975, (2)Fathi Beji, 1950, 1 daughter. *Educations:* MA, 1974. *Appointments:* Professor, German, University of Monastir, Tunisia, 1978-79; Institute of Social Research, Munich, 1980; Institute of Law, 1981-86. *Publications:* Encyclopedy of Visual Handicapped, co-author, 1989; Translations. *Memberships:* PEN; Institute of High Studies in Human Relations; Society of Sciences & Arts; Romain Rolland Society; Union of Interpretors & Translators. *Address:* E. Preetorius-Weg 6, 8000 Munich 83, Federal Republic of Germany.

BEKEY Michelle Elaine, b. 10 Oct. 1957, Los Angeles, USA. Writer. *Education:* BA, University of Southern California, 1978. *Appointments:* Los Angeles Herald Examiner, 1978; Stringer, Time Magazine, 1978-79; Self-employed 1979-. *Publications:* over 400 non-fiction magazine articles; contributor of book and home study course chapters. *Memberships:* President, Independent Writers of So. California, 1984; Regional Vice President, National Council of Writers Organizations, 1986; President, Council of Writers Organizations, 1987; American Society of Journalists & Authors. *Honours:* Phi Beta Kappa, Phi Kappa Phi Honorary Societies, 1978. *Hobbies:* Skiing; Back packing; Running.

BEL GEDDES Barbara, (Barbara Geddes Lewis) b. 31 Oct. 1922, New York, USA. Actress. *Career:* Stage debut in Out of the Frying Pan; toured USO camps in Junior Miss, 1941. Screen debut in the Long Night, 1946; Star of Tomorrow, 1949. New York Stage: the Moon Is Blue; Cat on a Hot Tin Roof; Mary, Mary; Everything in the Garden. *Creative Works:* Films include: I Remember Mama; Blood on the Moon; Caught; Panic in Streets; Fourteen Hours; The Five Pennies; Five Branded Women; By Love Possessed; Summertree; The Todd Killings. Television: Dallas, series. *Address:* c/o 15 Mill Street, Putnam Valley, NY 10579, USA.

BELCHER Phyllis Tenney, b. 10 Mar. 1927. Educator. m. 25 July 1975. *Education:* BA, 1949, BEd, 1950, Seattle Pacific College; MA, University of Washington, 1966. *Appointments:* Secondary School Teacher, 1950-53; Elementary School Teacher, 1954-57; Instructor Acting Director & Secondary Student Teacher Supervisor, Seattle Pacific College, 1957-63; Supervisor, Assistant Professor, director, 1965-68, Teaching Fellow with the Experimental School for the Neurologically Impaired, University of Washington, 1962-64; Curriculum Director, Bothell Regional Reading Centre, Programmer in Special Education, Federal Way Public Schools, 1969-70; Educational Specialist, 1970-73, Diagnostic Consultant/Teacher, 1973-, Tacoma Public Schools. *Memberships:* National Educational Association; Washington Educational Association; President, Federal Way Chapter, Internaional Reading Association, 1972-73; Council for Exceptional Children; Teacher Association of the Gifted; Association of Learning Disorders; Association of Behavioural Disorders; Council for Educational Diagnostic Services; Orton Society; Phi Lambda Theta; International Reading Association; Delta Kappa Gamma. *Address:* 1102 East Guiberson, Kent, WA 98031, USA.

BELCHER Vivian Carol Bray, b. 5 July 1932, Rush Run, USA. Elementary Supervisor. m. Robet Estel Belcher, 4 Jan. 1954, 1 son, 1 daughter. *Education:* BS, Elementary Education, Concord College, 1955; MA, Guidance & Counselling, Wayne State University, 1971; PhD, Curriculum & Supervision, University of Maryland, 1984. *Appointments:* Teacher, various schools, 1952-69; High School Biology, Physical Science & Art Teacher, 1967-71; Guidance Counsellor, Dr. Mudd School & Arthur Middleton School, 1971-73; Diagnostic Perscriptive Teacher, Dr Mudd School, 1973-74; Principal, Mt. Hope Elementary School, Nanjemoy, 1974-77; Principal, Eva Turner Elementary School, Waldorf, 1977-84; Principal, Dr James Craik Elementary School, 1984-; Elementary Supervisor, Elementary Education, 1989. *Publications:* Articles in various journals including: School Counselor; Reading; West Virginia Journal of Education; Journal of English Teachers. *Memberships:* International Reading Association; State of Maryland International Reading Association; Southern Maryland Reading Association; American Educational Research Association. *Honours:* Recipient, various prizes & awards. *Hobbies:* Gardening; Flower Arranging; Poetry; Square Dancing. *Address:* 820 Copley Avenue, Waldorf, MD 20602, USA.

BELINA Maria, b. 23 Jan. 1936, Mexico City (USA Citizen). Import & Government Contracts Manager. m. Abraham Munoz, 28 July 1979, 1 son. *Education:* BA, Teachers College, Mexico City, 1965; MA, Manhattan College, USA, 1974; Institute of Japanese Language & Culture, Tokyo, Japan, 1968. *Appointments:* Professor, Aoyama Gakuin University, Tokyo, Japan, 1967-69; Bilingual Teacher, St Catherine of Genoa, New York City, 1970-80; Professor, University of Technology, Monterrey, Mexico City, 1980-81; Manager, Administration, Sodick Inc., & Secretary of Corp., 1982-85; Import & Government Contracts Manager, Eiseman Ludmar Co. Inc., 1982-85, 1985-. *Publications:* Spanish Language & Culture for Japanese Speaking Students,

1969; The Nobody Bird, childrens story, 1980; Co-translator, Psychology of Personnel; Articles in professional journals. *Memberships:* National Association of Female Executives; Multiple Handicpped Association of New Jersey. *Honours:* Summa Cum Laude on BA Presentation Exam, 1965; St Catherine of Genoa Community Service Award, 1979. *Hobbies:* Reading; Ice Skating; Classical Music; Travel; Meeting People. *Address:* Teaneck, NJ 07666, USA.

BELINKI Karmela, b. 19 May, 1947, Helsinki, Finland. Journalist; Writer. *Education:* Trinity College, Cambridge, England; University College, London; Abo Academy, Finland; Helsinki University, Finland; Stockholm University, Sweden; Salzburg University, Austria; BA; MA; PhD. *Appointments:* Journalist; Writer; Lecturer in women's studies, journalism and international relations; Senior Programme Producer, Finnish Broadcasting Company. *Publications:* 3 books of essays; Text books on women's rights and history; Numerous papers, articles, television and radio programmes. *Honours:* Honorary positions in national and international women's organisations. *Address:* Stahlbergintie 6 B 13, 00570 Helsinki 57, Finland.

BELL Elizabeth, b. 1 Dec. 1928, Cincinnati, Ohio, USA. Composer. m. (1) Frank D. Drake, 7 Mar. 1953, 3 sons, (2) Robert E. Friou, 16 Apr. 1983. *Education:* BA, Music, Wellesley College, 1950; BS, Composition, Juilliard School of Music, 1953. *Appointment:* Music critic, Ithaca Journal, New York 1971-75. *Creative work includes:* Symphony No. 1; 1st String Quartet; Variations & Interludes (piano); Areciba Sonata (piano); 2nd Sonata (piano); Soliloquy for Solo Cello; Perne in a Gyre; Fantasy-Sonata; Songs of Here & Forever; Loss-Songs; Millenium; Kaleidoscope; Duovarios; Spectra. *Memberships:* Founder, Treasurer, New York Women Composers; Broadcast Music Inc; American Composers Alliance; American Music Centre; Composers Forum; International League of Women Composers; Cincinnati Composers Guild; American Women Composers; International Congress of Women in Music. *Address:* 114 Kelbourne Avenue, North Tarrytown, New York 10591, USA.

BELL Joanne M, b. 12 Sept. 1954, New Jersey, USA. Project Leader/Adjunct Assistant Professor of Pharmacology. m. Dr L Eric Hallman, 3 Sept. 1983. *Education:* BA, Franklin & Marshall College, 1976; MA, University of Hartford, 1978; PhD, Washington University, 1983; Postgraduate Fellow, Duke University Medical Centre, 1985. *Appointments:* Research Association, 1986, Assistant Medical Research Professor/Clinical Research Scientistll, 1988-, Department of Pharmacology, Duke University Medical Centre; Glaxo Inc. *Publications:* Contributing Author 2 books; Author of 17 Scienfic publications; 20 Scientific presentations; 4 Invited addresses. *Memberships:* Sigma Xi Research Society; American Association Adv of Science; NY Academy of Sciences; Society for Neuroscience; Int. Soc for Developmental Psychobiology; Assoc. Clinical Pharmacology; NC Society for Neurosciences; International Brain Research Organisations. *Honours:* Recipient of 2 Federally funded Research Grants. *Interests:* Consultant, Neurotoxicology; Volunteer, American Heart Association; Fitness Enthusiast; Dance/Choreography; Foreign Travel; Interior decorating; Collection of modern artwork. *Address:* Clinical Neuropharmacology, Medical Affairs, Glaxo Inc, Research Tringle Park, NC 27709, USA.

BELL Judith Carole Ransom, b. 4 Nov. 1938, Scranton, Pennsylvania, USA. Family Therapist. m. (1) Edward Landon Dovel, 17 Aug. 1956, div. 1975, 1 son, 2 daughters, (2) Jonathan Paul Bell, 17 Oct. 1981. *Education:* MA, Counselling, Psychology, 1978. *Appointments:* Part-time Counsellor, 1979, Full-time Counsellor, 1979, Director, 1983-, Bowie Youth Services. *Memberships:* Clinical Member, American Association for Marriage and Family Therapy, Approved Supervisor pending. *Hobbies:* Reading; Walking; Jazz;

Antiques. *Address:* 3028 Lake Avenue, Cheverly, MD 20785, USA.

BELL Nora Kizer, b. 25 July 1941, Charleston, West Virginia, USA. Professor/Department Chair/Medical Ethicist. m. David A Bell, 12 June 1976. 1 son, 2 daughters. *Education:* BA, Randolph-Macon Woman's College, 1962; MA, University of South Carolina, 1969; PhD, University of North Carolina, 1978; Graduate, MDP, Harvard University, 1987. *Appointments:* Instructor, Assistant and Associate Professor of Philosophy 1977-, Department Chair, Philosophy Department 1987-, Medical Ethicist, School of Medicine 1985-, University of South Carolina. *Publications:* Book: Who Decides? Conflicts of Rights in Health Care. Articles: Women and AIDS: Too Little, Too Late?; What Setting Limits May Mean; AIDS and Women: Remaining Ethical Issues; What is Wrong with Wrongful Life?; Ethical Dilemmans in Trauma Nursing and many others. *Memberships:* Advisory Boards: San Francisco AIDS Foundation; Coalition for Choice; Organ Procurement Agency; Commision on Aging; International Journal of AIDS Education; Leadership South Carolina; Department of Mental Health Advisory Board; Alzheimer's Day Care. *Honours:* Phi Beta Kappa, 1962; University Fellow, UNC, 1975; EXXON Fellow in Ethics and Medicine, 1984; Omicron Delta Kappa, 1986; Goldon Key National Honorary, 1987; Mortar Board Woman of the Year, 1988; J Marion Sims Award, SC Public Health Association, 1988; Mortar Board Excellence in teaching Award, 1989; Gubernatorial Appointee to SC Commission on Aging. *Hobbies:* Competitive tennis; Camping; Pianist. *Address:* 408 Park Lake Road, Columbia, SC 29223, USA.

BELL Sheila Leigh Cornish, b. 4 Oct. 1947, Great Falls, Montana, USA. School Administrator; Staff Development Coordinator. m. Bruce Arthur Bell, 27 June 1970. 1 daughter. *Education:* BA, Elementary Education, BS History 1969, University of Idaho; MEd, Spec Ed 1979, MA Admin & Curr 1984, Gonzaga University. *Appointments:* Chicago Home Base Field Secretary-Gamma Phi Beta Sorority- Public Relations , 1969-70; Teacher, Pocatello, Idaho School District, 1970-71; Writing Advertisements, Radio Station KPBX, Pocatello, 1971; Radio Programming, KHQ Radio, TV Station, 1971-73; Sepc Ed Teacher 1973-78, Learning Specialist 1979-81, Sp Ed Teacher 1981-83, Central Valley School District; Coordinator of Spec Ed Programm (4 Districts) 1983-84; Staff Development Coordinator, 1984-; Adjunct Professor, Eastern Washington University, 1980-; Adjunct Professor, Gonzaga University, 1979- . *Publications:* Articles in professional journals in USA, Canada, England. *Memberships:* Spokane Panhellenic, President; American Association of University Women; Delta Kappa Gamma; Phi Delta Kappa, Newsletter Editor; National State Teachers of the Year, Secretary; Central Valley Education Association, President. *Honours:* Teacher of the Year, Central Valley School District, 1978; Teacher of the Year, State of Washington, 1979; Kodak Grant Award, 1982; Dodge Grant Award. *Hobbies:* Skiing, downhill and cross country; Reading; Sewing; Bicycling. *Address:* East 12722 Guthrie, Spokane, WA 99216, USA.

BELLER Andrea H., b. 13 Sept. 1945, New York City, USA. Professor of Economics. m. Kenneth B. Stolarsky, 13 Dec. 1981, 1 son. *Education:* BA, Economics, Case-Western Reserve University, 1966; MA 1969, PhD 1974, Columbia University. *Appointments:* Institute for Research on Poverty, University of Wisconsin, 1975-77; Mary Ingraham Bunting Institute, Radcliffe College, Harvard University, 1977-79; University of Illinois, Urbana- Champaign, 1979-. *Publications:* Changes in Sex Composition of US Occupations 1960-81, Journal of Human Resources, 1985; Child Support Payments: Evidence from Repeated Cross-Sections (co-author), American Economic Review, 1988. *Memberships:* American Economic Association; Population Association of America; American Home Economics Association; Midwest Economic Association. *Honours:* Research grants, National Institute of Child Health & Human Development, 1984-87, 1987-90. *Hobbies:*

Tennis; Theatre; Gourmet Dining; Travel. *Address:* Division of Family & Consumer Economics, School of Human Resources & Family Studies, University of Illinois at Urbana-Champaign, 274 Berier Hall, 905 South Goodwin Avenue, Urbana, Illinois 61801, USA.

BELLINGHAM Lynda, b. 31 May 1948, Montreal, Canada. Actress. m. 22 July, 1981. 2 sons. *Education:* Central School of Speech and Drama, London, England, 1966-69. *Appointments include:* Repertory at Crewe, Coventry and Oxford; Various tours around England. West End appearances: Bordello, Queen's Theatre; Norman is That You? and Strippers, Phoenix Theatre; Look No Hans, Strand Theatre; Various television appearances including: Funny Man; Mackenzie, Oxo commercials; All Creatures Great and Small. *Hobbies:* Music; Films; Reading; Science Fiction. *Address:* c/o Saraband Associates, 265 Liverpool Road, London N1 1LX, England.

BELLO Shere Capparella, b. 4 Sept. 1956, Pennsylvania, USA. Sales Consultant; Freelance Model; Language translator. *Education:* BA, French/Spanish, 1978; Advanced Language Studios, ongoing; Postgraduate studies, Marketing, ongoing. *Appointments:* Sales, Spectrum Communications, 1977-79; Vice President/Choreographer/Dance Teacher, La Bella School of Performance/Modelling Agency, 1979-82; Salesperson, Administration Assistant, Tettex Instruments, 1979-83; Owner/ Director, Shere's World of Dance & Fine Arts, 1982-87; Bilingual Executive Secretary, Certain Teed Corp, 1983-84; Bilingual Executive Secretary, Syntex Dental Products, 1984-86; Manager, Sales/Marketing, Spectrum Communications, 1986-87; Vice President, Captrium Development, 1987- 88. *Publications:* Poetry, over 30 pieces; Dance Choreography, over 50 pieces. *Memberships:* Pageant Judge, Miss America Scholarship Program; America's Junior Miss; National Teen; National Pre-teen; All American Talent Awards; Official Little Miss America; Talent Unlimited; Talent Olympics; Producer/Choreographer, Miss Montgomery County Pageant, 1985 and Miss Delaware Valley Pageant, 1983-84; Kindergarten Teacher, Confraternity of Christian Doctrine, 1987-88; National Association Female Executives, 1986-89; Foster Parent, Christian Children's Fund, 1986-89; US Humane Society, 1987-89. *Honours:* Diamond Star Consultant, Mary Kay Cosmetics, 1989; Recognized Judge, Miss America Pageants, Inc, 1982-present. *Hobbies:* Travel; Dance; Fashion; Health and fitness; Astrology; Animals. *Address:* 1637 Sheridan Lane, Jeffersonville, PA 19403, USA.

BELLWARD Gail Dianne, b. 27 May 1939, Brock, Canada. University Professor. *Education:* BSc., 1960, MSc., 1963, PhD, 1966, University of British Columbia; Fellow, Clinical Pharmacology, Emory University, Atlanta, USA, 1968-69. *Appointments:* Assistant Professor, 1967-73, Associate Professor 1973-79, Professor, 1979-, Pharmacology, Associate Dean, Research and Graduate Studies, Faculty of Pharmaceutical Science, University of British Columbia. *Publications:* Articles in professional journals including: Journal of Neurochemistry; Molecular Pharmacology; BC Teacher; Clinical Pharacology and Therapeutics; Biochemical Pharmacology. *Memberships:* Pharmacological Society of Canada; Society of Toxicology (USA); Society of Toxicology of Canada; American Society for Pharmacology and Experimental Therapeutics; Federation of American Societies of Experimental Biolgoy; Lambda Kappa Sigma. *Honours:* MRC Visiting Professor, University of Toronto, 1971-72, University of Saskatchewan, 1975-76, Dalhousie University, 1975-76; Award of Merit, Labmda Kappa Sigma, 1980. *Hobbies:* Music; Gardening; Bicycling; Cross Country Skiing. *Address:* Faculty of Pharmaceutical Sciences, University of British Columbia, 2146 East Mall, Vancouver, BC. Canada V6T 1W5.

BELOFF Nora, b. 24 Jan. 1919. Author; Journalist. *Education:* BA Honours, History, Lady Margaret Hall,

Oxford University, 1940. *Appointments:* Political Intelligence Department, Foreign Office, 1941- 44; British Embassy, Paris, 1944-45; Reporter, Reuters News Agency, 1945-46; Paris Correspondent, The Economist, 1946-48; Observer correspondent, Parish, Washington, Moscow, Brussels, 1948-58; Political correspondent, 1964-76; Roving correspondent, 1976-78. *Publications:* The General Says No, 1963; The Transit of Britain, 1973; Freedom under Foot, 1976; No Travel Like Russian Travel, 1979 (US Inside the Soviety Empire: Myth & Reality, 1980); Tito's Flawed Legacy, London 1985, Boulder, the USA, 1986, Italian translation, 1987. *Address:* 11 Belsize Road, London NW6 4RX, England.

BELTZNER Gail Ann, b. 20 July 1950, Palmerton, Pennsylvania, USA. Teacher. *Education:* BS summa cum laude, Mus.Ed., West Chester University, 1972; Postgraduate Studies: Kean State College, Temple University, Westminster Choir College, Lehigh University. *Appointments:* Teacher of Music, Drexel Hill Junior High School, 1972-73; Music Specialist, Allentown School District, 1973-; participation in Teacher Corps Project Ecesis Programme, 1978-81; Teacher: Corps School and Community Developmental Laboratory Task Force 1978-80; Corps Community Resource Festival, 1979-81, Corps Cultural Fair, 1980-81. *Creative Works:* Musical compositions and articles, none published. *Memberships:* Women's Committee, Allentown Symphony Association; Allentown Area Ecumenical Food Bank, Board of Directors; Association for Supervision & Curriculum Development; American Associaton of University Women; National School Orchestra Association; Kappa Delta Pi; Phi Delta Kappa; Alpha Lambda; Music Educators National Conference; Pennyslvania Music Educators Association; American Orff-Schulwerk Association; Society for General Music; Choristers Guild; American Association for Music Therapy; International Society for Music Education; Allentown Art Museum; Life Member of Merit, Confederation of Chivalry, 1988; Ordre Souverain et Militaire de la Milice du Saint Sepulcre, 1988.etc. *Honours:* Swope Memorial Scholarship, 1971; Presse Foundation Scholarship, 1972. *Hobbies:* Painting; Composing Music; Travel. *Address:* PO Box 4427, Allentown, PA 18105, USA.

BEMENDERFER Shirley Ann, b. 10 July 1936, Fort Pierce, Florida, USA. Company President. m. Robert Leonard Bemenderfer, 3 June 1954, 2 sons, 1 daughter. *Education:* Indian River Community College. *Appointments:* Avon Saleslady, 1960-62; Cosmetologist, 1969-76; President Florida Properties of Fort Pierce, 1969-; School Teacher, 1975-78; President, Fort Pierce-Port Saint Lucio Board of Realtors, 1988. *Publication:* Theatre Work, Aunt Ethel in Harvey. *Memberships:* Florida Assocation of Realtors; Business & Professional Womens Club. *Honours Include:* Realtor Associate of the Year, 1976; Member, First Woman's Trade Mission to China, 1987. *Hobbies:* Tennis; Horse Riding; Fishing; Travel. *Address:* 1801 D Okeechobee Road, Fort Pierce, FL 34950, USA.

BENDOR Susan Julia, b. 5 Feb. 1937, Budapest, Hungary. Social Work Administrator; Professor. m. Edgar Bendor, 29 Nov. 1959, 2 daughters. *Educaiton:* World University Service Fellow, Heidelberg University, 1957-58; MSS, Adelphi University, USA, 1962; DSW, CUNY, 1986. *Appointments:* Associate Professor, Social Work, Molloy College, 1977- 81; Associate Director, Social Service Dept., Montefiore Medical Centre, 1981-86; Associate Director, Social Service, Beth Abraham Hospital, Bronx, 1986-. *Publications:* Articles in professional journals. *Memberships:* Community Advocates Inc; Treasurer, National Council of Community Mental Health Centres; Regional National Association of Social Workers; American Orthopychiatric Association. *Honours:* Social Worker of the Year, 1975; *Hobbies:* Folk Dancing; Skiing; Travel. *Address:* 38 Allenwood Road, Great Neck, NY 11023, USA.

BENENSON Esther Siev, b. 16 Aug. 1925,

Jerusalem, Israel. Gerontologist. m. William Benenson, 15 Sept. 1957, 1 son, 3 daughters. *Education:* AAS, Queen's College, 1957; B, Nursing 1972, MS, Community Health Education, Hunter College; EdD, Gerontology, 1981, Teachers College. *Appointments:* Assistant Administrator, Flushing Manor Nursing Home, 1953-56; Administrator, 1960-, Executive Director, 1970--, Executive Director, 1974-, Flushing Manor Care Center. *Publications:* Family Decision Making Styles and Their Relationship Towards Institutionalizing the Aged, in Long Term Care and Health Services Administration Quarterly, 1977; articles in various journals. *Memberships:* New York State Board of Examiners for Licensing Nursing Home Administrators, 1970-74; New York State Health Planning Commission Advisory Council; Fellow, Royal Society of Health; American College of Health Care Administrators; Gerontological Society; New York State Association of Gerontological Educators. *Address:* 36-21 Parsons Blvd., Flushing, NY 11354, USA.

BENESH Joan Dorothy Rothwell, b. 26 Mar. 1920, Liverpool, England. Retired Principal; Teacher. m. Rudolf Benesh, 12 Mar. 1949, 1 son. *Education:* Studio School of Dance & Drama; Lydia Sokolova School of Ballet. *Appointments:* Commercial Theatre, 1939-50; Royal Opera Company, 1950-51; Royal Ballet Company, 1951-57; Co-Founder, The Benesh Institute of Choreolgoy, 1956-76. *Publication:* Co-author, An Introduction to Benesh Dance Notation, 1956; An Introduction to Benesh Movement Notation, 1969; Reading Dance, 1977. *Memberships:* Benesh Institute, Consultant. *Honours:* All England Dance Competition Ballet Section, 1937; Parker Trophy for Dance, 1938; Queen Elizabeth II Coronation Award, 1987. *Hobbies:* Gardening; Sewing; Philosophy. *Address:* Flat 4, 15 The Grange, Wimbledon Common, London SW19 4PS, England.

BENEVIDES ROGERS Philomena Angela, b. 8 Mar. 1958, Fall River, USA. Research Associate. m. John L. Rogers, 6 Sept. 1986. *Education:* AB, Ripon College, 1980; MA, International Affairs, George Washington University. *Appointments:* Staff Assistant, 1980-81; Research Assistant, Analytical Assessments Corp., 1982; Research Consultant, George Washington University, 1983; Director of Research, The McLaughlin Group, 1983-84; Assistant to Senior Advisor, Ministry of Finance, Government of Japan, 1984-. *Memberships:* American Political Science Association; Women in International Trade; Japan-America Society of Washington DC; Asia Society; John Carrol Society. *Honours:* Recipient, various honours & awards. *Address:* 1760 North Rhodes Street No 346, Arlington, VA 22201, USA.

BENJAMINS Joyce Ann, b. 1 June 1941, Bay City, Michigan, USA. Neurochemist; Professor. m. David Benjamins, 23 Dec. 1964. 2 daughters. *Education:* BA, Albion College, 1963; PhD, University of Michigan, Ann Arbor, 1967. *Appointments:* Postdoctoral Fellow, Stanford University, Palo Alto, 1967-68; Instructor, Asst Prof Neurology, Johns Hopkins Sch Med, Baltimore, MD, 1968-73; Asst Prof, Biochemistry, U North Carolina School of Medicine, 1973-75; Asst Prof 1975-78, Assoc Prof 1978-85, Professor 1985-, Neurology, Way State University, School of Medicine. *Publications:* Over 50 scientific publications, reviews and chapters. *Memberships:* American Society for Neurochemistry, Councilor, 1988-; Society for Neuroscience. *Honour:* Javitz Neuroscience Inverstigator Award, 1987- *Address:* Department of Neurology, Wayne State University School of Medicine, 540 E Canfield Road, Detroit, MI 48201, USA.

BENNETT Barbara, b. 14 Aug. 1945, Pontiac, Illinois, USA. Consumer Relations Director/Hospital Marketing. m. (1) Kenneth Blumenthal, 2 May 1964, div., 1 daughter, (2) Charles W. Stuart II, 20 Dec. 1969, div., (3) David L. Eason, 23 Nov. 1975, div. *Education:* BS, Radio and TV, Southern Illinois University, Carbondale, 1976; MS, Urban Affairs, University of Wisconsin, Milwaukee, 1979. *Appointments:* Instructor, University of Wisconsin, Milwaukee, 1979-81; Assistant Programme Director, Community Access Director, Viacom Cablevision, Greenfield, Wisconsin, 1981-83; Member Services Director, FHP-Utah, Salt Lake City, Utah, 1984-86; Consumer Relations Director, Women's Services Director, LAS Hospital, Salt Lake City, 1986-. *Memberships:* Vice-Chair, Salt Lake City Community Development Advisory Committee; Vice-Chair, Salt Lake City Mayor's Budget Advisory Committee; Utah Issues Fund Raising Committee; Public Relations Society of America; Women in Business, Salt Lake City; Chamber of Commerce. *Hobbies:* Civil War History; Archaeology; Reading; Travel; Cooking. *Address:* 1164 Herbert, Salt Lake City, UT 84105, USA.

BENNETT Bernice Spitz, b. 4 Sept. 1923, Boston, Massachusetts, USA. Freelance Professional Writer. m. Jack Bennett, 5 June 1942. 1 son, 1 daughter. *Education:* Copley Secretarial Institute; Attended: Brandeis University, Waltham; Boston University, Boston; Simmons College, Boston. *Appointment:* President, Traveling Meals of Newton (Gratis). *Publications:* Columnist, Newton Graphic; Contributor to: Confidential Chat; Boston Globe; DCAA Government Bulletin; Senior Citizen News; Story to be published in December Rose, 1989. *Memberships:* Teacher of Creative Writing, Newton; Inter/Agency Council Member, Newton; Retired Executives Volunteers, Newton; Public Relations Consultant; Professional Member, National Writers Club, Aurora, Colorado; Member of the Association for Research and Enlightenment - Cayce Foundation, Virginia; Massachusetts Cultural Alliance - located in Boston, Massachusetts. *Honours:* Award for poem given by the National Professional Writers Union. *Hobbies:* Walking; Philanthropic and related volunteer works; Reading; Nature Study; Decorating; Drawing. *Address:* 9 Ithaca Circle, Newton Lower Falls, Massachusetts 02162, USA.

BENNETT Betsy Dianne, b. 28 Sept. 1948, Charlotte, Tennessee, USA. Pathologist; Professor. *Education:* BA summa cum laude, General Biology, Vanderbilt University, 1970; PhD, Pathology, 1975, MD, 1976, Vanderbilt University School of Medicine; Resident, Pathology, 1976-78, Fellow, American Cancer Society, 1978-79, Chief Resident, Instructor, 1979-80, Vanderbilt University Hospital; Certified, American Board of Pathology, 1980. *Appointments:* Acting Assistant Chief, Laboratory Service, Director of Clinical Chemistry Laboratory and Autopsy Service, VA Medical Center, Assistant Professor, Vanderbilt University School of Medicine, Nashville, Tennessee, 1980-81; Assistant Professor, 1981-85, Medical Director, Clinical Chemistry, Associate Director, Clinical Laboratories, 1981-, Minority Affairs Officer, 1983-85, Assistant Dean, Student Affairs, 1983-87, Women's Liaison Officer, 1983-, Associate Professor, 1985-, Associate Dean, Academic Affairs, 1987-89, University of South Alabama College of Medicine, Mobile; Director, Health Services Foundation Laboratory, 1987-. *Publications:* Articles and book-chapters including: Preneoplastic Lesions of the Breast (with W H Hartmann), 1980; Network Television News: A Resource in Medical Education (with W A Gardner), 1982; Pathology of the Prostate, A Review (with W A Gardner Jr), 1985; Histochemistry and Quantitative Microscopy of Prostate Cancer, 1987; Abstracts. *Memberships:* Academy of Clinical Laboratory Physicians & Scientists; American Society of Clinical Pathology; US-Canadian Academy of Pathology; Association of Clinical Scientists; American Medical Association, Section Committee; American Medical Women's Association; Group for Research in Pathology Education; Gulf Coast Pathology Society; Sigma Xi; Southeastern Region Chair, Women's Liaison Officers, AAMC, 1985-87; Phi Beta Kappa; Alpha Omega Alpha. *Honours:* Founder's Medal, Vanderbilt University College of Arts & Sciences; Several others. *Address:* 201 Grand Boulevard, Mobile, AL 36607, USA.

BENNETT Donna Jean (Walker), b. 10 Oct. 1956, Warwick, Rhode Island, USA. Film Producer; Accountant. *Education:* School for Performing Arts, 1976; Radcliffe College, 1977; University of Houston,

1978. *Appointments:* Concert Promoter, Concert West Cobblestone Productions, Dallas and Houston, Texas, 1974-77; Programme Director, Bellaire Cable TV, CBS, Houston, 1974-75; Assistant Manager, Dow Jones & Co Inc, 1977-78; President, Chief Executive Officer, Controller, VIP Toy Store, Los Angeles, California, 1978-81; President, VIP Productions, Beverly Hills, 1981-84; President, Chief Executive Officer, Jordan, Bennett, Walker & Associates, Los Angeles, 1984-; Executive Administrator, Corporate Secretary, Ford & Daze, Los Angeles, 1986-; Director, Finance Committee, Victims for Victims, 1987-; President, Don Hill Productions. *Creative works:* Producer, Widow Chiche (play); Executive Producer (films): Mama's a Little Weird; Not 'till the Wedding; Dominick & Carmelia; Others; Co-author, children's musicals; Poetry; Analytical Analysis Explained, textbook, 1975. *Memberships:* Institute of Political Science; SAG; AFTRA; Writers Guild; Association of Female Executives. *Honours:* Daughters of the American Revolution, 1966; Miss Missouri, Miss Universe Pageant, 1977. *Hobbies:* Polo; Reading; Victims rights activist; Volunteer work; Drug prevention work; Women's rights work; Her sweetheart. *Address:* PO Box 10786, Beverly Hills, CA 90213, USA.

BENNETT Jalynn Hamilton, b. 12 Mar. 1943, Toronto, Canada. Company Vice President. 2 sons. 1 daughter. *Publications:* Assistant Investment Office, 1965-70; Part-time Consultant, Alfred Bunting & Co., 1971- 72; Assistant Investment Officer, 1972-76, Investment Manager, 1976-79, Assistant Vice President, Investments, 1979-82, Investment Vice President, 1982-85, Corporate Develoment Vice President, 1985-88, Vice President, 1988-, Manufacturers Life Insurance Company. *Publications:* Co-Editor, Background Papers: Pensions Reform, 1984; articles in various journals & magazines. *Memberships:* Toronto Society of Financial Analysts; Toronto Association of Business Economists. *Honours:* Woman of Distinction, YWCA of Metro Toronto, 1988. *Address:* c/o The Manufacturers Life Insurance Company, 200 Bloor Street East NT-11, Toronto, Ontario M4W 1E5, Canada.

BENNETT Jill, b. 24 Dec. 1929, Penang, Federated Malay States. Actress. m. (1) Willis Hall, 1962, dissolved 1965, (2) John Osborne, 1968, dissolved 1977. *Education:* Tortington Park and Priors Field, Stratford-upon-Avon. *Career:* First London appearance in Captain Carvallo, St James's Theatre, 1950; appeared in productions of classical and contemporary plays in London (Royal Court Theatre), Chichester, Nottingham, etc. *Creative Works:* Films include: Lust for Life; The Nanny; The Criminal; The Charge of the Light Brigade; Inadmissible Evidence; Julius Caeser; I Want What I Want; Quilp; Full Circle; For Your Eyes Only; Britannia Hospital; Lady Jane. Numerous television appearances. Film script: Paradise Postponed. *Publication:* Godfrey: A Special Time Remebered, 1983. *Honours:* Evening Standard Award and Variety Club's Best Actress for Pamela in Osborne's Time Present, 1968. *Hobbies:* Riding; Water Skiing; Art. *Address:* James Sharkey Associates, 15 Golden Square, London W1, England.

BENNETT Jo Anne Williams, b. 16 Apr. 1915, Brooklyn, New York, USA. Writer; Anthropologist. m. David Bennett, 19 July 1969, 2 sons, 1 daughter. *Education:* BA, 1966; MA, New York University, 1971; PhD, University of Cambridge, 1980. *Appointments:* Adjunct Associate Professor, Queen's University. *Publication:* Downfall People, novel. *Memberships:* Canadian Ethnology Association; Writers Union of Canada. *Honour:* Winner, Seal Books First Novel Award, 1986. *Hobbies:* Riding; Canoeing. *Address:* 664 MacLaren St., Ottawa, Ontario, Canada K1R 5L2.

BENNETT Lilian Margery, b. 22 Aug. 1922, London, England. Director. m. Ronald Bennett, 1 son. *Appointments:* Director, Thermo Plastics Ltd., 1957-68; Director, Manpower Plc, Girlpower Ltd., Overdrive Plc, 1968-. *Memberships:* Member, Parole Board, 1983-87; Community Service Volunteers Employment Panel; Fellow, Royal Society of Arts. *Hobbies:* Reading; Music;

Community work. *Address:* c/o Manpower Plc., Manpower House, 272 High Street, Slouth, Berkshire SL1 1LJ, England.

BENNETT-KASTOR Tina Lynne, b. 8 Feb. 1954, La Mesa, California, USA. Linguist; Professor. m. Frank Sullivan Kastor, 28 Oct. 1979. 2 sons, 1 daughter. *Education:* BFA, California Institute of the Arts, 1973; AM 1976, PhD 1978, University of Southern California. *Appointments:* Research and Teaching Assistant, University of Southern California, 1975- 78; Research Consultant, Los Angeles, California, 1977-; Research Associate, John Tracy Clinic, Los Angeles, 1977-; Assistant Professor 1978-, Associate Professor 1987-, Wichita State University, Kansas. *Publications:* Book: Analyzing Children's Language. Articles: Cohesion and Predication in Child Narratives; The Two Fields of Child Language Research; Noun Phrases and Coherence in Child Narrative, and numerous other articles. *Memberships:* American Speech-Language-Hearing Association; American Association of University Professors; Linguistic Society of America; Modern Language Association; New York Academy of Sciences. *Honours:* Wichita State University Research Award, 1979, 1981, 1983; Hall Fellowship, University of Kansas, 1987. *Hobbies:* Photography; Film; Traditional music; Child development. *Address:* 115 N Fountain, Wichita, KS 67208, USA.

BENNINGHOFF Anne Stevenson, b. 3 Aug. 1942, Shelby, Ohio, USA. Research Investigator. m. William Shiffer Benninghoff, 14 June 1969. *Education:* BS, Wittenberg University, 1964; MS 1967, PhD candidate 1969, University of Michigan. *Appointments:* Influenza vaccine development, Parke-Davis & Co, 1964-65; Teaching Fellow, Dept of Bot; Rsch Asst in pollen analysis, University of Michigan, 1965-69; Sec to Dir, Int Biol Prog, Aerobiology, 1969-74; Research Investigator, Dept of Biology, University of Michigan, 1977-. *Publications:* Various contributions to professional journals and books. *Memberships:* Ecological Society of America; Botanical Society of America; Ohio Academy of Sciences; International Association for Great Lakes Research; Sigma Xi; Science Research Club (Univ of Mich); Women of the University Faculty (Univ of Mich). *Hobbies:* Music, flute and piano; Sports, badminton, swimming, biking, skiing. *Address:* Department of Biology (Botany), University of Michigan, Ann Arbor, Michigan 48109, USA.

BENNION (Barbara) Elisabeth, b. 27 Sept. 1930, London, England. m. Francis Alan Roscoe Bennion, 1951, diss. 1975. 3 daughters. *Publications:* Antique Medical Instruments, Sotheby, 1978; Antique Dental Instruments, Sotheby, 1986. *Address:* 96 Pelham Road, London SW19, England.

BENO Candice Lynn, b. 25 Mar. 1951, New Brunswick, New Jersey, USA. Biochemist; Administrator. *Education:* BA Honours magna cum laude 1973, MS 1974, postgraduate 1974-75, University of Connecticut. *Appointments:* Laboratory Technician 1976-78, Senior Laboratory Technician 1978-79, Regional Technical Supervisor 1979, Assistant Staff Engineer 1979-82, Staff Engineer 1982-84, 1985-87, Teachnical Business Consultant, 1984-85, Manager 1987, Linde Division, Union Carbide Corporation (UCC). *Memberships include:* Chairman, Compressed Gas Association, & Semi-Conductor Equipment & Materials International (SEMI); American Society for Quality Control; Offices, Werner Erhard Associations. *Honours:* Outstanding Service Award 1984-88, Standards Leadership Award 1988, SEMI; Special Recognitions, Linde Division, UCC, 1984, 1988; Various honour societies. *Hobbies & interests:* Nutrition; Swimming; Reading. *Address:* 405 Newark Avenue, Point Pleasant Beach, New Jersey 08742, USA.

BENSON Chief Opral Mason, b. 7 Feb. 1935, Arthington, Liberia. Business Entrepreneur. m. Otunba T S Benson, 1962, 1 daughter. *Education:* BSc., Education, 1958; MA, Education, 1959; Dip.Admin,

1961. *Appointments:* Teacher, School Princpal, Liberia; Chief Administrative Officer, Ministry of Agriculture, Commerce & Labour, Liberia; Secretary General, Oau Conference; Assistant Principal Registrar, University of Lagos; Chairman, Chic Afrique Ltd., & Johnson Products Ltd. *Publication:* Otunba T O S Benson, His Life & Views. *Memberships:* Zonta Internaitonal; International Womens Society; National Association of University Women; Ex President, Junior Organisation, National Council of Womens Societies. *Honour:* CSA, Liberia. *Hobbies:* Reading; Music; Designing. *Address:* No. 8 Thorburn Avenue, Yaba-Lagos, Nigeria.

BENSON Harriet, b. 17 May 1941, Kansas City, USA. Principal Scientist. *Education:* BA, Chemistry, Wellesley College, 1963; PhD, Organic Chemistry, University of Kansas, 1967; Postdoctoral Fellow, The University, Groningen, Netherlands, 1968. *Appointments:* Info. Chemist, Shell Develop. Co., Emeryville, 1963-64; Head, Literature, Alza Corp, Palo Alto, 1969-74; Area Director, Alza Corp, Palo Alto, 1974-87, Vice President, Regulatory Affairs, 1987-, Alza Corp. *Publications:* Articles in various journals including: American Pharmacist; American Journal Public Health; Journal Pharmaceutical Science; Drug Info. Journal. *Memberships:* American Association for the Advancement of Science; American Chemical Society; American Medical Writers Association; Drug Information Association; National Association of Female Executives. *Honours:* Wellesley College Scholar, 1962-63; NIH Predoctoral Fellow, 1965-67; Sigma Xi, 1967; Fellow, American Medical Writers Association, 1978. *Hobby:* Gardening. *Address:* 2825 Ramona, Palo Alto, CA 94306, USA.

BENSON Janet Elizabeth, b. 1 Apr. 1954, Ewell, Surrey, England. Airline Director. *Education:* BA (Hons), University of London, England, 1976; MBA, University of Pennsylvania, Philadelphia, USA, 1983. *Appointments:* Transport Economist, Rendel, Palmer & Tritton, London, England, 1976-81; Financial Analyst, Morgan Guaranty Trust of New York, London, 1982; Financial Analyst, 1983-85, Controller 1985, Vice President Finance, AADNC, 1986-87, American Airlines, Inc, Dallas, Texas, USA; Director, Reservations Operations, Eastern Airlines Inc, Miami, 1987-. *Publications:* Why Knock the New Towns?, 1978; Syrians Improve Roads to Encourage Transit Traffic, 1980; The Value of Passenger Time in Project Evaluation, 1981. *Honours:* ESU Scholar, English Speaking Union, London, England, 1981; Two Undergraduate Awards, University of London, 1976; Teagle Scholar, Exxon Corp, New York, USA, 1982. *Hobbies:* Rowing; Classical Music; Middle Eastern History; Flying; Sailing; Railroad travel. *Address:* Eastern Airlines, Inc, Miami International Airport, Miami, FL 33148, USA.

BENSON Susan, b. 22 Apr. 1942, Bexley Heath, Kent, England. Theatre Designer. m. Michael Whitfield, 5 June 1971. *Education:* National Diploma of Design, 1962; ATD, West of England College of Art, Bristol, 1963. *Appointments:* Freelance Designer in Canada, USA and England, 1966-; Designer for Stratford Shakespearean Festival, 1974-; other companies include: National Ballet of Canada, Citadel Theatre Edmonton, National Arts Centre, Ottawa, Canadian Opera Company, New York City Opera, Denver Centre Theatre Company, Birmingham Repertory Theatre, Canadian Broadcasting Corporation, Opera Theatre of St Louis, Mirvish Productions, Toronto, The Australian Opera Company. *Memberships:* Royal Canadian Academy; United Scenic Artists; Associated Designers of Canada. *Honours:* Represented Canada at 1979 and 1983 Prague Quadrennial; Dora Mavor Moore Award for Theatre Design, 1980, 1981, 1986, 1987; Winner, American Cable TV Awards (Arts and Entertainment Channel), 1986. *Address:* 236 William Street, no 3, Stratford, Ontario, Canada N5A 4Y3.

BENTLEY Helen Delich, b. 28 Nov. 1923, Ruth, Nevada, USA. US Government Official. m. William Roy Bentley, 1959. *Education:* BA Journalist (honours),

University of Missouri, Columbia, 1944; University of Nevada; George Washington University. *Appointments:* Reporter, Ely Record, 1940-42; Political Campaign Manager for Senator James G Scrugham, White Pine County, Nevada, 1942; Bureau Manager, United Press, Fort Wayne, Indiana, 1944-45; Reporter, Baltimore Sun, 1945-53; Maritime Editor 1953-69, Television Producer 1950-64, Public Relations Advisor 1958-67, American Association Port Authories; Chairwoman, Federal Maritime Commission, 1969-75; Chairwoman, American Bicentennial Fleet Inc, 1973-76; President, International Resources & Development Corporation, 1976-77; President, HDP International, 1977-84; Elected to United States Congress, 1984-. *Memberships:* Women's National Republican Club Inc; Valley Forge Freedoms Foundation; North Atlantic Ports Association. *Honours:* George Washington Honour Medal, Valley Forge Freedoms Foundation, 1976; Silver Citizenship Award, Maryland State Society, Sons of American Revolution, 1975; Distinguished Republican Service Medal, 1972; Faculty Alumni Gold Medal, University of Missouri, 1971; Honorary degrees: LLD, University of Michigan, University of Maryland, University of Alaska, Long Island University, Goucher College Baltimore; Honorary DHL, University of Portland Oregon, Bryant College of Business Administration, Providence, Rhode Island, numerous other awards and honours. *Address:* PO Box 10619 Towson, MD 21204, USA.

BENTLEY Lisa Jane Ricker, b. 20 Mar. 1936, Lansdale, USA. Minister; Lecturer; Company President. m. John Lee Bentley, 30 July 1972, 1 son. *Education:* Ordained Minister, Living Bible Centre, 1987. *Appointments:* Owner, Manager, Arthur Murray, New York, Philadelphia, Key West, 1956-65; Interior Designer, Lisa's Interiors, Philadelphia, 1965-75; Executive Consultant, Snelling & Snelling, 1975-78; President, Bentley Glass & Mirror Inc., 1979-89; President, Treasurer, Bentley Interiors Worldwide, 1982-89; Minister, Lecturer, Founder Minister, Nevada Institute of Applied Metaphysics, Las Vegas. *Memberships:* Legalisative Chairman, Glazing Contractors Association; Finance Chairman, Membership Chairman, Glazing Contractors Association. *Hobbies:* Writing; Designing; Skiing; Dancing; Cooking; Reading; Hiking. *Address:* 4351 Flandes Street, Las Vegas, NV 89121, USA.

BENTON Suzanne, b. 21 Jan. 1936, New York City, New York, USA. Sculptor; Mask Ritualist. 1 son, 1 daughter. *Education:* BA, Fine Arts, Queens College, 1956. *Career:* Creator, Mask Ritual Theatre; Over 130 performances throughout US and abroad including: Woudschoten, Ziest, Netherlands, and Geilsdorfer, Cologne, Federal Republic of Germany, 1982; Maskmaking/storytelling workshop, London, England, 1982; Winter-Term, Artist-in-Residence, Oberlin College, Ohio, USA, 1983; Affiliate, Image Theatre, New York City; Led Art/Mythology tour, Greece, 1985; 1-woman shows, sculpture, include: Hartford, Connecticut, 1975, Tokyo, Japan, 1976, Bombay, India, 1977, Athens, Greece, 1977, New Orleans, 1978, Belgrade, Yugoslavia, 1978, New York City, 1981, -82, 1986-89, Dusseldorf and Cologne, Federal Republic of Germany, 1983, Connecticut, 1983-1987, Stuttgart, Federal Republic of Germany, 1986; Ossining, New York, 1987, London, England; Group shows include: USIS, Eastern Europe, 1971-75, Expo '74, Seattle, Washington, 1974, National Sculpture Conference, Kansas University, 1974, Stamford Museum, Connecticut, 1976, Athens, Greece, 1985 Joods Historical Museum, Amsterdam, Netherlands, 1986. *Publications:* The Art of Welded Sculpture, 1975. *Memberships:* Convenor, Connecticut Feminists in the Arts, 1970-72; National Coordinator, NOW Women in the Arts, 1973-76; Grants: United Methodist World and Women's Division, 1976; United Presbyterian Program Agency, 1976; United Church Board Homeland Ministries, 1976; Artists Equity, New York City; Honorary Member, National Association of Women Artists; National Korean Women's Sculpture Association; National Association of Women Artists; Silvermine Guild of Artists. *Honours:* Grantee, Connecticut Commission on Arts, 1973, 1974; Amelia

Peabody Award, National Association of Women Artists, 1979; USIS Grantee, Tunisia, 1983, Istanbul, Turkey, 1986. *Address:* 22 Donnelly Drive, Ridgefield, CT 06877, USA.

BENTZEN Lynda Lea Crocker, b. 27 Sept. 1959, Oklahoma City, Oklahoma, USA. Literary Agent and Translator. m. Kjetil Bentzen, 4 June 1982. *Appointments:* Literary Agent and Translator, 1985-, freelance since 1988-; Secretary, Orthopaedic High School, 1986 and 1987-88; Sales Consultant with Publisher, 1987. *Publications:* Translations: 1 non-fiction (medicine); 1 anthology, fiction, several short stories; 1 novel fiction; currently working on a series, fiction. *Memberships:* Co-worker with the Second International Feminist Book Fair, 1986. *Hobbies:* Singing; Cats; Painting; Flower-binding; Linguistic; Morphology; Renaissance culture; Mythology and folklore; Alternative Philosophy; Ecology. *Address:* Walckendorfsgt 5, 5012 Bergen, Norway.

BERAN Barbara Nancy Black, b. 9 Feb. 1934, Newburyport, Massachusetts, USA. Writer; Editor. m.Dr Mark J Beran, 29 Dec. 1953. 1 son, 2 daughters. *Education:* BA, Sociology and Anthropology, Wellesley College, 1955; MA, Sociology, University of Pennsylvania, 1967. *Appointments:* Director of Research and Evaluation, CMHC of Yaffo, Israel, 1975-87; Self-employed Professional Writer and Editor, 1985-; Director of Communications, Statcon Inc, Washington DC, USA, 1984-. *Publications:* Numerous professional articles in Geriatrics and Psychohypnosis; Edited Psychogeriatrics by P Ernst; Developed Computer Software. *Memberships:* American Sociology Association; Sociology Society of Israel; Society for Technical Communication; Gerontological Association of Israel. *Honours:* Wellesley College Scholar, 1954, 1955; Roy M Dorcas Award, Society for Clinical and Experimental Hypnosis for the best clinical paper on hypnosis during 1979. *Hobby:* Computing. *Address:* 20 Ben Yehuda, Herzlia, Israel.

BEREDIK Hilda, b. 19 Oct. 1906, Vienna, Austria. Retired Special Inspector. *Appointments:* Inspector in Public Service; Author; Poet. *Publications:* Ein paar Kleinigkeiten, 1948; Aus dem Bilderbuch der Natur, 1966; vom Morgen zur Nacht, 1967; So?...oder So!, 1970; Fabeln and Parabeln, 1975; Frohe Fahrt, 1976; Balladen, 1984; Die Kinder aus dem Kuckuckshaus; Aus jenen Tagen, 1985; Zugvögel, 1986. *Memberships:* Member, European-American Eurafok, 1973; Geistig Schafende Osterreichs; Osterreichs Autorenverband; Schiftstellerinnen und Künstlerinnen; Der Kreis; honorary member of Winifried. *Honors:* Silbernes Verdienstzeichen der Republik Osterrich, 1960; Silbernes Ehrenzeichen der Republik Osterrich, 1982, both medals awarded by the Federal President of Austria, Albert Rotter-Lyrikpreis. *Hobbies:* Literature; Art; Music. *Address:* Veitingergasse 147, A-1130 Vienna, Austria.

BERENDES M. Benedicta (Sister), b. 28 Nov. 1927, New York City, USA. Musicologist; College Professor; Member, Congregation of the Sisters, Servants of the Immaculate Heart of Mary. *Education:* BMus, Marywood College, 1955; Choir Master's Certificate, American Guild of Organists, 1962; MMus, University of Notre Dame, 1962; PhD Musicology 1973, MS Religious Studies 1979, Marywood College. *Appointments:* Elementary & Secondary School Music Specialist, 1948-70; Doctoral study, 1970-72; Professor, Musicology, Marywood College, 1973-. *Publications:* Transcription & Analysis, Works of Cadeac; Versus & Its Use in Medieval Roman Liturgy. *Memberships:* American Musicological Society; American Association of University Professors; National Pastoral Musicians. *Honours:* 1st prize, musicology, National Catholic Music Educators Association, 1962; National Endowment for Humanities' Summer Seminar, 1982. *Address:* Marywood College, Box 864, Scranton, Pennsylvania 18509, USA.

BERG Ingrid Anne, b. 24 Oct. 1942, Melbourne, Australia. Publicist. *Education:* Matriculation; General Nursing Certificate, Alfred Hospital, England. *Appointments:* General Nursing, 1960-63; Sir Charles Gairdners Hospital, 1963-65; South Perth Hospital, Yooralla, Victoria, 1965-66; Ingrid Berg Academy, 1966-69; Mullins Clarke Ralph, 1969-71; Murray Evans Advertising, 1971; Ingrid Berg & Associates, 1971-89. *Publications:* Various articles in Australia. *Memberships:* Australian Variety Artistes MO Awards Association, Chairman, 1988; Convenor, Para Quad 101 Club; Committee Member, Publicist, Variety Club of Australia, Tent 56; Australian Ladies Variety Association. *Honours:* Special Achievement Award, MO Awards, 1986. *Hobbies:* Music, Classical to Rock; Walking; Travel; Art; Cricket; Australian Rules Football; Skiing. *Address:* 85E Wigram Road, Glebe, NSW 2037, Australia.

BERG Jean Horton, b. 30 May 1913, Clairton, Pennsylvania, USA. Writer. m. John Joseph Berg, 2 July 1938, 1 son, 2 daughters. *Education:* BS, Education, 1935, MA, Latin, 1937, University of Pennsylvania. *Appointments:* Teacher, Latin, English, Delaware Public Schools, 1936-38; Teacher, Creative Writing, Main Line School Night, 1960-; Workshops, College of General Studies, University of Pennsylvania, 1979-. *Publications:* 50 books for young people; many articles in magazines and newspapers. *Memberships Include:* School Parent Associations; National Association American Pen Women; Authors League; Authors Guild; ASCAP; Children's Reading Round Table; Board Member, St Davids Christian Writers Association; Board Member, Philadelphia Writers Association. *Honours:* Follet Award, 1961; City of Philadelphia Medallion, 1963; Alumni Award of Merit, University of Pennsylvania, 1969; Distinguished Alumna, Friends Central School, 1979. *Hobbies:* Tennis; Sewing; Gardening. *Address:* 207 Walnut Avenue, Wayne, PA 19087, USA.

BERG M Carin, b. 12 Dec. 1937, Oestersund, Sweden. Director, Unesco European Center for higher education. Divorced, 1 daughter, 2 sons. *Education:* Cand phil, Linguistics, 1970; Dipl information techniques, 1971. *Appointments:* University of Lund, Sweden, 1971-75; Council for research in Social Sciences, Stockholm, Sweden, 1975-76; Liber Publishing House, Stockholm, 1976-78; Nat. Board of Universities, Stockholm, 1978-88; Director, Unesco European Center for higher education, Bucharest, Roumania, 1988-. *Memberships:* Advisory Committee, Swedish Educational Broadcasting Company, 1980-88; Planning Council, National Board of Education, Sweden, 1984-88; International Round Table for the Advancement of Counselling; President, Regional Committee for the Application of the Diploma Convention for the Europe Region (Unesco), 1986-88. *Address:* 39 Str. Stribei Voda, Bucharest, Roumania.

BERG Siri, b. 14 Sept. 1921, Stockholm, Sweden. Artist; Instructor. m. Robert Berg, 28 June 1954, 2 sons, 2 daughter. *Education:* BA, University of Brussels, 1940. *Appointments:* Instructor, Colour Theory Workshops, New School Parsons School of Design, New York, 1977-. *Creative Works:* Solo Exhibitions include: Paula Allen Gallery; American Swedish Museum; Bjorn Lingrew Gallery, New York; American Scandinanvian Foundation; Galerie d'Art, Sweden; One man Shows; Permanent Collection of the Solomon R. Guggenheim Museum. *Memberships:* American-Scandinavian Society; Swedish Womens Educational Alliance. *Honours:* Recipient, various honours & awards. *Address:* 93 Mercer Street 6E, New York, NY 10012, USA.

BERGEN Candice, Actress. m. Louis Malle. 1 daughter. *Education:* Westlake School for Girls, Los Angeles; Cathedral School, Washington DC; Attended School in Switzerland; Studied Art History and Creative Writing, University of Pennsylvania. *Appointments:* Role of Lakey in the film, The Group. Starred in The Sand Pebbles. Co-star, Rich and Famous. Appeared in the role of Margaret Bourke-White in Ghandi. Appearances in: The Day the Fish Came Out; Vivre Pour Vivre; Starred in T R Baskin; The Adventurers; Soldier Blue; The Magus; The Hunting Party; 11 Harrow Houre: The Wind and the Lion; Bite the Bullet; The Domino Principal; Night Full of Rain; Oliver's Story. Starred on Broadway as Darlene in Hurleyburly; Starring role in Hollywood Wives on television. *Publications:* Articles for magazines including: New York Magazine; Life; Playboy; Esquire; Vogue; Cosmopolitan and Ladies Home Journal. Feature articles on the Masai Tribe in Kenya; Emperor Haile Selassie of Ethiopia, both written for Playboy. An account of her 4 week trip to Red China, Can A Cultural Worker from Beverly Hills find Happiness in The People's Republic of China? Photographed and wrote cover story on Charles Chaplin's return to United States for Life magazine. *Hobbies:* Writing; Photography; Travelling. *Address:* One Lincoln Plaza, 2nd floor, New York, NY 10023, USA.

BERGEN Marcelene Betsy, b. 12 May. 1928, Carbondale, Kansas, USA. Professor. m. Gerald R Bergen, 30 June 1967. 3 sons, 2 daughters. *Education:* BA, Ottawa University, 1949; MS 1964, PhD 1972, Kansas State University. *Appointments:* Highland Park Schools, Topeka, 1949-52; Kanopolis High School, 1952-56; St John High School, 1958-64; Dept of Human Devel & Family Studies, Kansas State University, 1965-. *Publications:* Book: Century of Family Living in Flinthills; Videos: From the Heartland: AIDS; From the Heartland: STDs. *Memberships:* Delta Kappa Gamma; National Council Family Relations; American Home Economics Association; Society for Scientific Study of Sex; Amer Assoc Sex Educators, Counselors & Therapists; Phi Kappa Phi; Omicron Nu; Kansas Council Family Relation. *Honours:* Outstanding Instructor, Kansas State University, 1969; International Fellowship, Delta Kappa Gamma, 1970; Certified AASECT, Sex Education and Sex Therapist, 1982; Certified NCFR, Family Life Educator, 1987; Certified AHEA, Home Economist; Postdoctoral Research Award, Delta Kappa Gamma, 1987; Omicron Nu, Outstanding Alumni Award, 1989. *Hobbies:* Quilting; Dressmaking. *Address:* 5732 S W 33, Topeka, KS 66614, USA.

BERGER Eugenia Hepworth, b. 30 Jan. 1925, Lawrence, Kansas, USA. College Professor. m. Glen Berger, 18 June 1946, 2 sons, 1 daughter. *Education:* BME, University of Kansas, 1946; MA 1964, MA 1966, PhD 1968, University of Denver. *Appointments:* Teacher, Ppublic Schools, 1946-50; Director, Parent Education/Pre-School, 1960-64; Instructor, University of Denver, 1966-68; Professor, Metropolitan State College, Denver, 1968-. *Publications:* Books: Parents as Partners in Education, 1981, 1987; Beyond the Classroom, 1983. *Memberships:* Past President, Rocky Mountain Council of Family Relations; Culurado Board, Association on Childhood Education International; Life Member, National Association for Education of Young Children; American Sociological Association; National Council for Social Studies; National Council on Family Relations; Building Family Strengths. *Honours:* Distinguished Service Award, Metropolitan State College, 1986; Pi Kappa Lambda, 1946; Mu Phi Epsilon, Pi Lambda Theta, 1945; Foremost Mother, Littleton, 1969; Mortar Board, University of Kansas, 1946. *Hobbies* Music; Family Therapy; Building Family Strengths; Hiking; Camping. *Address:* Box 21, Metropolitan State College, 1006 11th Street, Denver, Colorado 80204, USA.

BERGER Francine Ellis, b. 27 July 1949, Albany, New York, USA. Radio Executive; Educator. m. Jerome M. Berger, 9 Oct. 1977. *Education:* BS, Broadcasting & Film, Boston University, 1971; EdM, Administration, Planning & Social Policy, Harvard University, 1981. *Appointments:* Traffic Manager, WCAS-AM/WJIB-FM (Kaiser Globe Broadcasting), 1971; Continuity Supervisor, WBZ AM (Westinghouse Broadcasting), 1971-75; Traffic Director, Producer, WMEX-AM/ WITS-AM, 1975-78; News Writer, WEEI-AM (CBS Radio), 1980; General Manager, WERS-FM, Emerson College, 1980-; Assistant Professor, Emerson College, 1981-; Head, Radio Department, Emerson College, 1983-;

Member Brookline, Massachusetts Cable Television Monitoring Board, 1988-. *Memberships:* National Academy Television Arts & Sciences; Alpha Epsilon Rho; Kappa Gamma Chi. *Hobbies:* Music; Cooking. *Address:* WERS-FM, 126 Beacon Street, Boston, MA 02116, USA.

BERGER Judith Ellen, b. 17 Mar. 1948, Brooklyn, New York, USA. Businesswoman. m. Stephen G. Schoen, 1 son. *Education:* Psychology, Franklin Pierce College, Rindge, New Hampshire, 1966-67; Sociology, New School of Social Research, New York City, 1977-78; Professional Pilot, Miami-Dade Community College, Florida. *Appointments:* Vice President, Senior Search Consultant, Corson Group (NYC) 1977-79, Vice President, Training, Education & Consulting Services Division (Florida) 1985-; President, MD Resources Inc, Miami, Florida (executive & physician recruiting firm), 1979-. *Publications:* Author, co-author, articles in Group Practice Journal, Healthcare Marketing Quarterly. *Memberships:* Medical Group Management Association; Board, National Association of Physician Recruiters; American Group Practice Association; Society of Hospital Planners & Marketing; American College of Healthcare Executives; American Marketing Association. *Honours:* Recognitions, various journals including Glamour magazine 1984-85, Insight 1987; Distinguished Entrepreneur lecture series, Shearson Lehman Brothers at Marquette University, 1987-88; Biographical listings. *Hobbies:* Flying; Cycling; Skiing; Tunning. *Address:* MD Resources Inc, 7385 Galloway Road no. 200, Miami, Florida 33173, USA.

BERGER Julie Ann (Monestersky), b. 18 Sept. 1950, Newark, New Jersey, USA. Social Work Consultant. *Education:* Honours programme, University of Wisconsin; BA, Jackson College, Tufts Universty, 1972; MSW, Rutgers University Graduate School of Social Work, 1974. *Appointments include:* Medical social worker, Haemodialysis Unit 1974-76, Outpatient Clinic & Hospital-Based Home Care Unit 1976-77, VA Hospital, East Orange, NJ; Medical social worker, Haemodialysis Unit, Morristown Memorial Hospital, 1977- 81; Social worker, private practice, 1981-84; Freelance market researcher, health care, telecommunications, office automation, 1984-85; Associate editor, research assistant, Probe Research Inc, 1985-88. Also: Field instructor, Rutgers University Graduate School of Social Work. *Publication:* New Product Study on a Disposable Health Care Item. *Memberships include:* Past president, NJ Dialysis & Transplant Association; Past council secretary, various offices, NJ Renal Network Council; National Association of Social Workers; Academy, & Register, of Clinical Social Workers, American Association of Kidney Patients; National Association of Female Executives. *Honours:* Dean's List, Jackson College, 1971-72; Guest speaker, Critical Care Nursing course 1978, Chronic Renal Failure workshop 1979, Chronic Renal Failure, prospects for vocational rehabilitation 1980, National Association of Patients on Haemodialysis & Transplant; In-service presentation, Social Work Department, 1980. *Hobbies:* Community Corrections Council; Microcomputers; Psychopharmacology. *Address:* Morristown, New Jersey, USA.

BERGER-HAZZARD Carolyn E., b. 26 Dec. 1944, Springfield, Massachusetts, USA. Clinical Psychologist. m. Gary C. Hazzard, 17 Sep. 1983. *Education:* BA, Psychology, University of Massachusetts, Amherst, 1966; MA, Marriage, Family and Child Clinical Services, 1979, PhD, Psychology, 1984, US International University, San Diego, California. *Appointments:* Computer Consultant/Instructor, 1966-84; Substance Abuse Counsellor, 1984- 87; Private Practitioner in Psychology, 1986-; Clinical Psychologist, University of California Medical Center/Owen Clinic, San Diego, 1987-. *Memberships:* American Psychological Association; National Association of Female Executives; Society of Psychologists in Addictive Behaviors; New York Academy of Sciences; Academy of San Diego Psychologists; National Association of Adult Children of Alcoholics; California Women's Commission on

Alcoholism and Drug Dependencies; California Association of Adult Children of Alcoholics. *Honours:* Outstanding Young Women of America, 1978; Appointed to San Diego County Regional Task Force on AIDS, Subcommittee on IV Drug Abuse, 1988. *Interests:* Space exploration; Spiritual development; World hunger; 12-step programmes; *Hobbies:* Growing roses; Vegtable gardening; Country and Western dancing; Regular exercise; Reading; Ceramics. *Address:* 911 Third Street, Suite C, Encinitas, CA 92024, USA.

BERGHEL Victoria Smouse, b. 20 Nov. 1952, Oakland, Maryland, USA. Attorney. m. Robert J. Berghel, Jr., 1 Feb. 1981, 1 son, 2 daughters. *Education:* BA 1974, JD 1977, University of Maryland. *Appointments:* Associate 1977-84, partner 1985-, Weinberg & Green, Baltimore. Also: Lecturer, legal writing 1977-78, real estate drafting & negotiation 1986-, University of Maryland; Lecturer, Maryland commercial transfer taxes, Maryland Institute for Continuing Professional Education for Lawyers, 1985. *Publications:* Various articles. *Memberships:* Vice chair, Committee on Condos, Coops & HOAs, American Bar Association; Maryland, & Baltimore City Bar Associations. *Honours:* bb3Phi Beta Kappa, 1974; Editorial board, Maryland Law Review, 1976-77. *Address:* 100 South Charles Street, Baltimore, Maryland 21201, USA.

BERKETT Marian Mayer, b. 29 Mar. 1913, Baton Rouge, Louisiana, USA. Lawyer. m. Dr George D B Berkett, 26 Jan. 1943. *Education:* BA 1933, MA 1935, Louisiana State University; LLB, Tulane University, 1937; Geneval School of International Studies, Geneva, Switzerland, 1933. *Appointments:* Associate 1937-61, Partner 1961-, Deutsch, Kerrigan & Stiles, New Orleans, LA. *Publications:* Author: Workmen's Compensation Law in Louisiana, 1937; Articles in Tulane Law Review. *Memberships include:* Honorary Chairman, Louisiana Civil Service League; Member, Board of Directors, New Orleans Chapter National Conference of Christians and Jews; Officer and Member of Board of Directors, Family Service Society; Council of Social Agencies; American Law Institute; American Bar Association; New Orleans Bar Association; Louisiana Bar Association. *Honours include:* Valedictorian, Tulane Law School Class 1937; Salutatorian Louisiana State University graduation class 1933; Scholarship 1933 Geneval School of International Studies; Pi Sigma Alpha Award; Honorary Members Order of Coif. *Hobbies:* Tennis; Travel. *Address:* 755 Magazine Street, New Orleans, Louisiana 70130, USA.

BERLIOUX Monique, b. 22 Dec. 1925, Metz, France. Technical Advisor to the Mayor of Paris. m. Serge Groussard, 29 Feb. 1956. *Education:* BA, MA, Fenelon Lycee, Paris Faculty of Letters, Sorbonne. *Appointments:* Journalist, special reporter and columnist of the written press; Correspondent for provincial and foreign newspapers (English, Belgian, Spanish, North African), etc; Director for French Television; (Women's magazines, short stories and features); Head of the Press Department, 1960-66; In charge, General Inspection, 1966-67 Ministry of Youth and Sport; Director, Press & Public Relations, 1967-69, Director of Information responsible for administration, 1969-71, Executive Director, 1971-85, International Olympic Committee; Technical Advisor to Mayor of Paris, 1985-. *Publications:* La Natation; Mon sejour chez Mao Tse Toung; Les Jeux Olympiques; Olympica; Femmes; D'Olympie a Mexico; Jacques Chirac - La Victoire du Sport; Participant in a great many works. *Memberships:* Literary Society of France; Board, Sports Writers Association; Board, Academie des Sports (1st woman to be elected); Board, Racing Club de France; Cercle de l'Union Interalliee. *Honours:* Officer of the Legion of Honour; Officer of National Merit; Knight of Arts and Letters; Gold Medal of Youth and Sport; Great Medal of the City of Paris; Foreign decorations. *Hobbies:* Swimming, Cycling, Philately, Needlework. *Address:* 16, avenue de Valmont, 1010 Lausanne, Switzerland.

BERMAN Karen Faith, b. 25 June 1951, Detroit, Michigan, USA. Physician; Neuroscientist; Clinical Neuropsychiatry Researcher. m. 18 Dec. 1985.

Education: BA, University of Rochester, 1973; MD, St Louis University Medical School, 1977; Intern, Washington University 1977-78; Resident, Psychiatry, University of California, San Diego, 1978-80, National Institute of Mental Health, 1980-81; Board Certified, American College of Neurology & Psychiatry, 1983. *Appointments:* Research Ward Director, Saint Elizabeths Hospital, Washington DC, 1980-81; Clinical Associate, Staff Psychiatrist, 1980-, Associate Director, Regional Cerebral Blood Flow Laboratory, 1982-87, Director, Regional Cerebral Blood Flow Laboratory, 1987-, Clinical Brain Disorders Branch, National Institute of Mental Health, Saint Elizabeths Hospital; Lieutenant, 1980-81, Lt Commander, 1981-85, Commander, 1985, Commissioned Corps, USPHS. *Publications:* Articles & book chapters including: Blink rates, neuropharmacological & clinical evidence of dopaminergic control (with C.N.Carson, P.A.LeWitt, S.Burns, R.Newman, R.J.Wyatt), 1983; Neuroradiology in psychiatry (with D.R.Weinberger), 1984; Schizophrenia dementia (with D.R.Weinberger), 1986; Cortical stress tests in schizophrenia: Regional cerebral blood flow studies, 1987; Prefrontal cortical blood flow & cognitive function in Huntington's disease (with D.R.Weinberger, M.Iadarola, N.Driesen, R.F.Zec), 1988; Abstracts. *Memberships:* Society for Neuroscience; Reviewer, Science Magazine; American Association for the Advancement of Science; American Medical Women's Association; American Medical Association; International Brain Research Organization; Occupational Safety & Health Association, Adult Psychiatry Branch. *Honours:* Administrator's Award for Meritorious Achievement, Department of Health & Human Services, Public Health Service, 1984; A.E.Bennett Foundation Award for Neuropsychiatric Research, Society of Biological Psychiatry, 1986. *Address:* Clinical Brain Disorders Branch, National Institute of Mental Health, NIMH Neuroscience Center at St Elizabeths, Washington DC 20032, USA.

BERNARD Desiree Patricia, b. 2 Mar. 1939, Georgetown, Guyana. High Court Judge. *Education:* LLB, Honours, London, UK, 1963. *Appointments:* Solicitor, admitted to practice, Guyana, Dec. 1964-; Established own law practice, 1967-80; Appointed to High Court Bench, Guyana, Oct. 1980-; Chair, United Nations Committee on Elimination of Discrimination Against Women, 1982-89. *Publications:* Several paper & articles, on legal status of women. *Memberships include:* President, Guyana Association of Women Lawyers; Past President; Georgetown Toastmistress Club, Law Society of Guyana, Commonwealth Caribbean Bar Associations; Past Treasurer, Business & Professional Womens Club, Guyana. *Honours:* Cacique Crown of Honour (3rd highest national award), Guyana, 1985; Award, Outstanding Guyanese Woman, University of Guyana, 1989; Honorary member, Canadian Bar Association, 1978. *Hobbies:* Reading extensively; Travel; Women's issues. *Address:* 79 Ixora Avenue, Bel Air Park, Georgetown, Guyana.

BERNARD Linda Diane, b. 1 Nov. 1950, Detroit, Michigan, USA. Attorney; Executive Director. *Education:* BA, Wayne State University 1970; JD, WSU Law School, 1973; LLM, University of Pennsylvania, 1975. *Appointments:* Ford Motor Company, 1974-76; City of Detroit Law Department, 1976-81; Management-Port Authority, 1981; L. D. Bernard & Associates, 1982-. *Memberships:* American, National, Detroit & Wolverine Bar Associations; National Urban League; Board, Parents Anonymous, Michigan. *Honours:* Appreciation: Friends of Street Law 1987, Wolverine Bar Association 1988; Outstanding Young Woman of America, 1987; Fellow, Michigan State Bar Foundation, 1988. *Address:* 3500 Cadillac Tower, Detroit, Michigan 48226, USA.

BERNARDEZ Teresa, b. 11 June 1931, Buenos Aires, Argentina. Professor. m. Jorge Bonesatti, 26 Dec. 1956, 1 son. *Education:* MD, University of Buenos Aires. *Appointments:* Psychiatry Residency, Menninger, 1957-60; Staff Psychiatry, 1960-65, Psychotherapy Dept., 1965-71, Menninger Memorial Hospital; Professor, 1971-87, Dean's Office, 1987-89, Michigan State

University. *Publications:* Book Chapter in Handbook of Short Term Therapy Groups, 1983; Articles in various journals. *Memberships:* American Psychiatric Association; American Medical Womens Association; American Orthopsychiatric Association; Michigan Psychiatric Society; Michigan Society for Psychoanalytic Psychology. *Honours:* Physician's Recognition Award, American Medical Association, 1970; Teacher's Recognition Award, Menninger School of Psychiatry, 1971; Peace Award, Pawlowski Foundation, 1974; Distinguished Faculty Award, Michigan State University, 1982. *Hobbies:* Sailing; Skiing; Peace Work. *Address:* 118 W Fee Hall, College of Human Medicine, Michigan State University, E. Lansing, MI 48823, USA.

BERNDT Karen Ann, b. 12 Jan. 1947. Lawyer. *Education:* BB, Journalism in Advertising, University of Texas, 1968; JD, 1970. *Appointments:* Trial Attorney, US Dept. Justice, Washington, 1971-74; Attorney, Corp. & Securities, Childs Fortenback Beck and Guyton, Houston, 1974-76; Partner, Woodward, Berndt & Teeter, Houston, 1976-78; Senior Attorney, Texaco Inc., Houston, 1978-87; Assistant to President, Texaco USA., 1987-. *Memberships:* various professional organisations. *Address:* Texaco Inc., PO Box 52332, Houston, TX 77052, USA.

BERNI Frances M, b. 6 Apr. 1954, Long Island, New York, USA. Assistant Vice President, Citicorp. m. Joseph T Krysztoforski, 31 Dec. 1986. 1 son. *Education:* Suffolk College, 1974; State University of New York, 1976; BA, MA, New York Institute of Technology, 1978-79. *Appointments:* Programmer Analyst Data Compass, 1977; Vice President/Co-owner, SCDPI, 1978-80; Sr Analyst 1979-81, Manager, Investment Savings 1982-84, Assistant Vice president 1984-, Citicorp. *Creative works:* Developed computer software system for small business management, 1977-78; Applied Digital Data Systems, operating system development 4 user application system, 1979. *Memberships:* American Management Association; Data Processing Management Association. *Honour:* Citicorp Service Excellence Award, 1984. *Hobbies:* Gardening; Photography; Private Adoption Associations. *Address:* Phoenix, Maryland 21131, USA.

BERON Gail L, b. 13 Nov. 1943, Detroit, Michigan, USA. Real Estate Valuation, Consultation and Market Analyses. 2 sons. *Education:* Professional training: Society of Real Estate Appraisers, Course 101, 1972; Course 201, 1974; Course 301, 1983; Designation: Senior Real Estate Analyst (SREA), 1984; American Institute of R E Appraisers, Course 1, 1975; Course VI, 1980; Designation: Member, Appraisal Institute (MAI), 1979. *Appointments:* Plant and Office Manager, 1968-71; Loan Underwriter, American Federal Savings, 1971-73; Staff Appraiser, 1973-75, Chief Appraiser, 1975, Fort Wayne Mortgage Company; Fee Appraiser, private practice, South Carolina, Iowa and Michigan, 1976-80; Principal, The Real Estate Counseling Group of America, Inc; Consulting Partner, Real Estate Counseling Group of Connecticut; President, The Beron Company, 1980-. *Publications include:* Co Author of: An Introduction to Real Property Valuation, revised 6th Edition, 1984; Applied Residential Appraising, revised 5th edition, 1984; Summary of Accrued Depreciation Procedures (with Special Emphasis on Residential Properties), 1984; What Value? Of What? To Whom?, 1985; The Challenge of Measuring Economic Obsolescence, 1985; R-41c and the Appraiser, 1986. *Memberships:* Society of Real Estate Appraisers; Society of Real Estate Appraisers, SE Michigan Chapter No 13; American Institute of Real Estate Appraisers; American Institute of Real Estate Appraisers, MI Chapter 10; American Real Estate Society; Institute of Property Taxation; National Association of Realtors; South Oakland County Board of Realtors; Detroit Board of Realtors; Women's Commercial/Industrial Brokerage Association; Young Mortgage Bankers' Association. *Honour:* Recipient M William Donnally award, Mortgage Bankers Association of America, 1975. *Hobbies:* Art; Music; Piano; Dancing. *Address:* 17228 West Hampton, Southfield, Michigan 48075, USA.

BERRIAN VIOLA Diane Marie, b. 1 May 1956, New York City, New York, USA. Owner, Architectural lighting design company. m. Denis Francis Viola, 6 June, 1981. *Education:* BFA, Environmental Design, Parson School of Design, 1981. *Appointments:* Project Manager, Jules G Horton Lighting Design, Inc, New York, 1980-81; Lighting Specialist, Kallen and Lemelson Cons. Engrs. New York, 1981-83; President, Owner, Berrian Viola Associates Inc, New York, 1983-. *Publications:* Articles: A New Site for Site, 1984; Designing Lighting Systems for Health Care Facilities, 1985. *Memberships:* Guest Lecturer Cooper Union School, Architecture; International Association Lighting Designers Senior Association, 1983; Illuminating Engineering Society, Architectural League, New York. *Honour:* IALD Award of Excellence, 1986. *Address:* Berrian Viola Associates Inc, 153 Conant Valley Road, Pound Ridge, NY 10576, USA.

BERRY Cornelia (Connie), b. 28 Mar. 1944, Rock Hill, South Carolina, USA. Pharmacist. m. Paul Douglas Berry Jr, 9 June 1962 (div. 1982), 1 son, 2 daughters. *Education:* Martinsville Community College, 1972- 73; Virginia Commonwealth University, 1973-75; BS, Pharmacy, Medical College of Virginia, 1978. *Appointments:* Pharmacist, Drug Fair, 1978-81; Staff Pharmacist, Laurens District Hospital, 1981-84; Director of Pharmacy, Laurens County Health Care System, 1984-; Consultant Pharmacist, Bailey Nursing Home, 1984-. *Creative work:* Oil painting. *Memberships:* Panel, Delta Marketing Dynamics; Instructor, Laurens County Arts Council; American Society of Hospital Pharmacists; South Carolina Pharmaceutical Association; Past President, Student Pharmaceutical Association. *Hobbies:* Painting; Calligraphy. *Address:* Route 1, Box 166, Pineland Shores, Cross Hill, South Carolina 29332, USA.

BERRY Edna Helen, b. 24 Oct. 1953, Bellefontaine, Ohio, USA. Assistant Professor of Sociology. m. George Stanley Laughlin, 9 Sept. 1986. 1 daughter. *Education:* BA, Sociology, Westminster College, 1975; MA, Sociology, Ohio State, 1979; PhD, Sociology, Ohio State University, 1983; NICHD Post-doctoral Scholar, University of Michigan, 1983-84. *Appointments:* Adjunct Professor of Sociology, Population Studies Center, University of Michigan, 1983-84; Assistant Professor of Sociology, Utah State University, 1984-. *Publications:* Articles: Fear of Crime in Rapidly Changing Rural Communities: A Longitudinal Analysis, with R S Krannich and T Greider; Perceptions of Distrust and Social Isolation, with R S Krannich and T Greider; A Longitudinal Analysis of Neighboring, with R S Krannich and T Greider; Structural Influences on Migrant Selectivity: A Panel Study of Three Rural Colombian Communities, with D W Wimberley and W L Flinn; 3 other articles in preparation. *Memberships:* Secretary, American Association of University Professors, USU Chapter, 1988-90; Co-Director, Women and Gender Research Institute, USU, 1986-88; American Sociological Association; Population Association of America; Rural Sociological Society. *Honours:* Mortar Board, 1974; Phi Alpha Theta, 1974; Phi Kappa Phi, 1980; University Research Faculty Grants, 1985; Election to state board of Planned Parenthood Association. *Hobbies:* Cross-country skiing; Hiking; Birding; ACLU. *Address:* Department of Sociology, Social Work and Anthropology, Utah State University, Logan, Utah 84335, USA.

BERRY Jacqueline Carol Peltz, b. 7 May 1946, Bronx, New York, USA. Individual & Family Therapist; Social Worker; Sociologist. m. Ralph L. Berry, 24 July 1976, 2 daughters. *Education:* BA, Queens College, 1968; MA, 1972, PhD, 1977, Sociology, MSW, 1982, Family Mental Health Social Work, Syracuse University. *Appointments:* Instructor, Sociology, State University College, Brockport, 1972; Psychiatric Nurse, 1972; Instructor, Psychiatric Nursing, Eastern Maine Medical Centre, 1976-77; Private Practice, Family, Individual and Couples Therapy, 1983-. *Publications:* Black Jews: A Study of Status Malintegration and (Multi) Marginality, 1977; articles in various professional journals, papers.

Memberships: National Association of Social Workers; American Sociological Association. *Honours:* Diplomate in Clinical Social Work, 1987. *Hobbies:* Downhill Skiing; Tennis. *Address:* Suite 107, 713 East Genesee St., Syracuse, NY 13210, USA.

BERRY Kristin Elizabeth Highberg, b. 23 Feb. 1943, Walla Walla, Washington, USA. Arid Lands Ecologist. m. Raymond W. Butler, 17 Dec. 1983. *Education:* Occidental College, 1960-63; BA, Stanford University, 1964; MA, University of California, Los Angeles, 1968; PhD, UC Berkeley, 1972. *Appointments:* Biologist & information specialist, Naval Weapons Centre, China Lake, California, 1965-68; Biological consultant, 1972-74; Zoologist, US Bureau of Land Management, Riverside, California, 1974-; Staff leader, wildlife, 1974-80. *Publications:* Book 1987, various papers, desert tortoise. *Memberships:* Past trustee, Maturango Museum, China Lake; Founder, trustee, Desert Tortoise Preservation Committee; Founder, co- chairman, various offices, Desert Tortoise Council, 1976; Past elected director, Southern California Academy of Sciences; Past director, Southern California chapter, Nature Conservancy; Tortoise Species Group, International Union for Conservation of Nature. *Honours:* Best scientific paper, Sigma Xi, 1975; 4 awards, US Bureau of Land Management, 1974-79; Annual conservation award, Desert Tortoise Council, 1977; National conservation award, American Motors, 1979. *Hobbies:* Photography of rare & endangered plants; International travel & study. *Address:* US Bureau of Land Management, 1695 Spruce Street, Riverside, California 92507, USA.

BERRY Nira Etons, b. 15 Nov. 1958, Israel. Business Owner. m. Philip Berry, 7 Sept. 1987. *Education:* BSc., Journalism, Univeirty of Maryland, USA, 1980. *Appointments:* Public Affairs, Giant Food Inc., 1979-80; President, Maryland Opticians. *Memberships:* National Association of Women Business Owners; Business & Professional Womens Club, Silver Spring. *Honours:* US Small Business Administration's Young Entrepreneur of the Year, 1984; Young Careerist of the Year, Business & Professional Women, Silver Spring, 1985; White House Ceremony Witness to Signing of Women's Commission on Business to the President, 1985. *Hobbies:* Travel; Photography; Collecting Antique Eyewear; Painting. *Address:* Potomac, Maryland, USA.

BERTRAM Cicely Kate, J.P., b . 8 July 1912, London, England. Retired Academic. m. Colin Bertram, 4 sons. *Education:* Brighton Technical College, 1929-30; Newnham College, Cambridge, 1931-34; Part I National Science Tripos, 1934; Girton College, Yarrow Research Student 1937-40. PhD degree 1941. *Appointments:* Field Work in Central Africa, 1935-36; Member, Colonial Office Nutrition Survey in Nyasaland, 1937; Adviser, Freshwater Fishes to Palesine Government, 1941; Tutor, then President, Lucy Cavendish College, Cambridge, 1965-79. *Publications:* various papers on Fish, Fisheries and on Sea Cows in biological journals. *Memberships:* Fellow, Linnean Society of London; British Federation of University Women, Chairman, Cambridge Branch, 1978-79; Trustee, 300 Group, until 1988; Member, Fawcett Society. *Hobbies:* Travel; Gardening. *Address:* Ricardo's, Graffham, nr. Petworth, West Sussex GU28 0PU, England.

BESCH Bibi, b. 1 Feb. 1942, Vienna, Austria. Actress/Seminar Leader/Producer/Writer. 1 daughter. *Education:* Connecticut College for Women, 1963; American Academy of Dramatic Art; HB Studio; Specialized Training with Milton Katselas, Amri Galli Campi. *Appointments:* Played, Eliza in Pygmalion; Starred in a daytime serial, The Secret Storm, Love is a Many Splendoured Thing, and The Edge of Night; Has worked on Broadway, off Broadway and in regional theatres; Played in classics such as: Macbeth as the Lady; The Cherry Orchard; Private Lives; Medea; Starred in Feature Film Productions: Slammer; Star Trek II; Distance; The Best Within; The Promise; Meteor; The Lonely Lady, and Paul Schrader's Hardcore. Television appearances in specials, movies-of-the-week, and pilots

total 26 and include: Mrs Delafield Wants to Marry, 1986, 2 Emmy winning After School Specials, Dead Wrong and Hear Me Cry; The Day After; Backstairs at the White House; Victory at Entebbe; Centrefold: The Dorothy Stratton Story. Regularly guest-starred in Dallas; Who's the Boss; Falcon Crest; Dynasty; Helltown and Highway to Heaven; Founded, with Rae Allen, Besch-Allen International, 1985; In 1984, organised readings of the Anti-Nuclear Play, Handy Dandy at 16 theatres throughout Los Angeles; With Paul Lance, has several film and television projects iun development. *Membership:* Academy of Motion Picture Arts and Sciences; Academy of Television Arts and Sciences; Actors Equity Association; Screen Actors Guild; American Federation of Television & Radio Artists. *Hobbies:* Gardening; Tennis; Sailing; Hot-air ballooning; Billiards. *Address:* c/o Harris & Goldberg, The Fox Plaza, Century City, CA 90067, USA.

BESSANT-BYRD Helen Pearl, b. 27 Feb. 1943, Waynesboro, Burke County, Georgia, USA. Professor. m. 16 June 1979. 1 son. *Education:* AA, Warren Wilson Junior College, 1961; BA, Berea College, 1963; MEd, Temple University, 1965; PhD, University of Connecticut, 1972; Postdoctoral study: Columbia University, 1973 and 1978, University of California-Riverside, 1978, Long Island University, 1986. *Appointments:* Teacher of Retarded Educables, School District of Philadelphia, 1963-65; Teacher of Educable Mental Retardates, Atlanta Public Schools, 1966-67, Summer 1967; Teacher of Children with Learning Problems, Atlanta Public Schools, 1967, 1968; Visiting Professor, Special Education Department, Atlanta University, Summer 1968; Assistant Professor, Special Education Department, Norfolk State College, 1968-72; Visiting Professor, Special Education Program, Savannah State College, Summer 1971; Graduate Assistant, University of Connecticut, Storrs, 1971-72; Associate Professor 1972-74, Professor 1974-, Department Chair 1978- 81, Special Education Department, Norfolk (VA) State College (renamed Norfolk State University 1979). *Publications:* Author of numerous articles to professional journals and magazines. *Memberships include:* International Council for Exceptional Children; American Association on Mental Deficiency; Association of Retarded Citizens National, Virginia and Tidewater. *Honours include:* Special Olympics Award, 1986; Certificate of Appreciation, 1987; Distinguished Scholar, Fayetteville (NC) State University, 1988. *Hobbies:* Reading; Volunteer service; Spectator sports. *Address:* 7112 Hunters Chase, Norfolk, Virginia 23518, USA.

BESSETTE Denise Rae, b. 25 Aug. 1954, Midland, Michigan, USA. Actress. m. Paul Schneeberger, 4 Sept. 1982. *Education:* BA, Marymount Manhattan College, 1976. *Appointments:* Theatrical Performances at: Cohoes Music Hall, New York, 1978; New Jersey Shakespeare Festival, 1979, 1981; Meadowbrook Theatre, Michigan, 1979; Asolo Theatre, Florida, 1982; Kennedy Centre & American Shakespeare Theatre, Connecticut, 1980; Huntington Theatre, Boston, 1982; Geva Theatre, 1983, 1986; Cincinnati Playhouse, 1984; Peoples Light & Theatre Company, 1984, 1985; Manhattan Punchline, New York City, 1984; TV: Kate & Allie, Kay O'Brien, 1986; Film: Agent on Ice, 1986. *Memberships:* AEA; SAG; AFTRA; Writers Theatre, New York City; Peoples Light & Theatre Company, Pennsylvania. *Honours:* Drama Critics Award, 1980. *Hobbies:* Piano; French Culture & Language. *Address:* 302 West 79th St. 8C, New York, NY 10024, USA.

BETTINSON Brenda, b. 17 Aug. 1929, King's Lynn, Norfolk, England. US citizen, 1966-. Artist; Teacher. *Education:* St Martin's School of Art, London, 1946-48; National Diploma in Design, Central School of Arts & Crafts, 1948-50; Academie de la Grande Chaumiere, Paris, France, 1951; Ecole des Hautes Etudes, Sorbonne, University of Paris, 1951-53. *Appointments:* Caligraving Ltd, 1954-59; Art Editor, WRVR-FM Radio, New York, USA, 1961- 65; Faculty, Department of Art 1963-, currently Professor of Art, Pace University, New York; Lecturer, Katonah Museum, NY, 1988. *Creative work* *includes:* Numerous solo & group exhibitions, USA; Paintings in numerous public & private collections, USA, Canada, Europe, Israel. *Honour:* Gold Medal, International Exhibition, National Arts Club, NY, 1966. *Address:* West Side Road, Barter's Island, Maine 04571, USA.

BETTS Katheleen, b. 2 Nov. 1953, Wilmington, Delaware, USA. Textile Conservator; Lecturer; Design Consultant. *Education:* Liberal Arts Degree, Hartford College for Women, 1973; BA, Wheaton College, Norton, 1975. *Appointments:* Staff Conservator, The Society of The Cincinnati, Washington DC, 1976-; Private Textile Conservator/Lecturer and Design Consultant; Acting Museum Director, The Society of the Cincinnati, Washington, DC, 1990-. *Memberships:* American Institute for Conservation of Historic & Artistic Works, National Newsletter Editor; Board of Directors, Washington Conservation Guild; Co-founder and Co-chairman, The Harpers Ferry Regional Textile Group; Conservation Advisor, American Standard Testing Methods; Advisory Council, Textile Arts Foundation; Textile Conservation Group (New York); Textile Society of America; National Volunteers Association. *Honours:* Delegate, Citizen Ambassador Program, People to People International, Preservation Consultant in China, 1989; Royal Oak Foundation, British National Trust, 1979. *Hobbies:* Multiple Sclerosis Society, Movers and Shakers Committee; Potomac Polo Club; Bravo, Washington Opera Society. *Address:* The Society of The Cincinnati, Anderson House - Headquarters and Museum, 2118 Massachusetts Avenue NW, Washington, DC 20008, USA.

BETTS, Dianne Connally, b. 23 Sept. 1948, Tyler, Texas, USA. Economist; Instructor. m. Floyd G. Betts, 14 Feb. 1973. *Education:* BA, 1976, MA, 1980, Southern Methodist University; MA, University of Chicago, 1986; PhD, University of Texas, 1988. *Appointment:* Instructor, Southern Methodist University, 1985-. *Memberships:* American Economic Association; Economic History Association; Cliometric Society; American Association of Univeriy Professors; North American Conference on British Studies; American History Association. *Address:* 6267 Revere Place, Dallas, TX 75214, USA.

BEVERLEY-BURTON Mary, b. 10 June 1930, Abergavenny, Wales. University Professor. m. John Bull, 27 Dec. 1968. 1 son, 2 daughters. *Education:* BSc, University of Wales, 1953; PhD 1958, DIC 1958, University of London (Imperial College). *Appointments:* Department of Agriculture, Scotland, 1953-55; Imperial College of Science & Technology, 1955-58; Post Doctoral (Nuffield Fellow), University College, Rhodesia & Jyasaland, 1958-61; Lecturer, University of West Indies, 1961-66; CAB, Inst Parasit, St Albans, 1966-68; Assistant Professor, Department of Zoology 1968-73, Associate Professor, 1973-85, Professor 1985-, University of Guelph, Canada. *Memberships:* American Soc of Parasitology; British Society for Parasitology; Canadian Society of Zoologists; Helmingthological Society of Washington. *Hobby:* Horses. *Address:* Department of Zoology, College of Biological Science, University of Guelph, Guelph, Ontario, Canada, N1G 2W1.

BEVERLY Virginia Q, b. 20 Oct. 1926, Wilmington, North Carolina, USA. Circuit Judge. m. Phillip C Beverly, 24 Apr. 1954. 3 sons, 1 daughters. *Education:* Graduate work Child Welfare, 1948-49; LLB, University of North Carolina, Chapel Hill, 1953. *Appointments:* General Practice of Law, Wilmington, North Carolina, 1953-60; Assistant United States Attorney, Middle District of Florida, 1965-68; Milam, Martin & Ade, 1968-74; Circuit Judge, 1977-. *Memberships:* Florida Bar; Georgia Bar; Jacksonville Bar Association; Jacksonville Women's Network; First President, Uptown Civitan; Supreme Court Committee, Standard Jury Instructions. *Hobbies:* Reading; Museums; Travelling. *Address:* 10157 Lake Lamar Court, Jacksonville, Florida 32216, USA.

BEVILACQUA WEISS JoAnn, b. 17 Aug. 1931, Pittsburgh, Pennsylvania, USA. Podiatrist. m. Oliver F. Weiss, 11 June 1955, 4 sons, 1 daughter. *Education:* Duquesne University; DPM, Ohio College of Podiatric Medicine. *Appointment:* Staff, St Francis Medical Centre, Pittsburgh. *Memberships:* American Podiatric Medical Association; Western Division, Pennsylvania Podiatry Association; American Association of Women Podiatrists; Council, International Poetry Forum; Pittsburgh Symphony Society; Carnegie Business & Professional Women; Carnegie Chamber of Commerce. *Hobbies include:* Children: Christopher, Drew, Bennett, Oliver II, Jennifer. *Address:* 411 East Main Street, Carnegie, Pennsylvania 15106, USA.

BEWLEY Beulah R., b. 2 Sep. 1929, Londonderry, Northern Ireland. Physician. m. Thomas Bewley, 20 Apr. 1955, 1 son, 4 daughters. *Education:* BA, 1951, MBBCh, 1953, MA, 1963, MD, 1974, Trinity College, Dublin University; House training, 1953-56; Paediatric Resident, Children's Hospital, Cincinnati, Ohio, USA, 1957-58; MSc, Social Medicine, University of London, 1971; MFCM, 1972, FFCM, 1980, Faculty of Community Medicine, Royal College of Physicians. *Appointments:* Assistant Medical Officer, London Boroughs of Southwark, Lambeth, Lewisham, and Medical Officer, Family Planning Association, South London Hospital for Women, Clapham, St James' Hospital, Balham, 1958-68; Medical Officer, Marks & Spencer Ltd, 1966-68; Lecturer, 1971-74, Senior Research Fellow, Senior Lecturer, Consultant, 1974-79, Department of Public Health Medicine, St Thomas' Hospital Medical School, London; Senior Lecturer, Consultant, Community Medicine: King's College Hospital Medical School, London, 1979-83; London School of Hygiene & Tropical Medicine, 1979-86; Currently Regional Postgraduate Tutor, Community Medicine, St George's Hospital Medical School, and Regional Consultant, South West Thames Regional Health Authority. *Publications:* Choice not Chance: A Handbook of Fertility Behaviour (with J.Cook and P.Kane), 1977; Book chapters (with T.H.Bewley): Don't get addicted, 1979; Dependence as a Public Health Problem (Alcohol, Tobacco and Other Drugs), 1979; Over 50 articles in professional journals on aspects of smoking especially in children, and other topics. *Memberships:* Life Member, Medical Defence Society; General Medical Council (several committees); Executive Council, Past President, Medical Women's Federation; Past Member Council, Central Committee for the Education and Training of Social Workers. *Hobby:* Music. *Address:* Department of Clinical Epidemiology and Social Medicine, St George's Hospital Medical School, Cranmer Terrace, London SW17 0RE, England.

BEYER Barbara Lynn, b. 16 Feb. 1947, Miami, Florida, USA. Aviation Consultant. *Education:* BA Business Administration, George Washington University, 1978. *Appointments:* Saudi Arabian Airlines, 1966-67; Modern Air Transport, 1968-72; Johnson International Airlines, 1974- 75; Avmark Inc, 1975; Avmark International UK, 1985; Avmark Asia Ltd, Hong Kong, 1988. *Publication:* Employee Productivity - The Key to Airline Profits. *Memberships:* Aviation/Space Writers Association, International Director, 1986-88; International Aviation Club; Aero Club; Regional Airline Association; American Chamber of Commerce Hong Kong; Foreign Correspondents Club Hong Kong; National Business Aircraft Association. *Honour:* Writing Award, Aviation/Space Writers Association, 1978. *Hobbies:* Horseback riding; Reading; Home repair. *Address:* 1911 North Fort Myer Drive, Suite 1000, Arlington, Virginia 22209, USA.

BEYER-MEARS Annette, b. 26 May 1941, Madison,. Wisconsin, USA. Associate Professor of Physiology & Ophthalmology. *Education:* BA, Vassar College, 1963; MS, Farleigh Dickinson University, 1973; PhD, UMD-N J Medical School, 1977; NIH Postdoctoral Fellow, 1978-80. *Appointments:* Assistant Professor, 1979-85, Associate Professor, 1986-, Department of Ophthalmology; Assistant Professor, 1980-85, Associate Professor, 1986-, Department of Physiology. *Publications:* Contributor of articles in field of diabetic lens and kidney therapy to professional journals.

Memberships: American Associate for Advamancement of Science; American Diabetes Association; American Physiological Society; American Society of Pharmacology & Experimental Therapeutics; Assoc. Research in Vision & Ophthalmology; International Soc. for Eye Research; International Diabetes Federation; NY Academy of Sciences; The Royal Society of Medicine; Sigma Xi; Society For Neuroscience. *Honours:* NIH Nat. Research Service award, 1978-80; NIH Research awardee, 1980-; Found. UMDNJ Research award, 1980; Grantee Juvenile Diabetes Found, 1985-87; Pfizer Inc, 1985-88, Sigma Xi. *Address:* Department of Physiology-H649, UMD-New Jersey Medical School, 185 South Orange Avenue, Newark, NJ 07103, USA.

BHARADWAJ Krishna, b. 21 Aug. 1935, Karwar, India. Professor. m. 30 Sept. 1960, divorced, 1 daughter. *Education:* BA, 1955; MA, 1957; PhD, 1960. *Appointments:* Lecturer, 1963-64, Senior Research Officer, Economics, University of Bombay; Fellow, Clare Hall, Cambridge, England, 1967- 71; Senior Research Officer, Applied Economics, Cambridge, 1969-70; Visiting Professor, Delhi School of Economics, Delhi University, 1971-72; Professor, Centre for Economic Studies & Planning, Jawaharlal Nehru Univerisy, 1972- . *Publications:* Production Conditions in Indian Agriculture, 1974; Classical Political Economy and Rise to Dominance of Supply and Demand Theories, 1976; On Some Issues of Method in Analysis of Social Chane, 1980; Thmes on Value and Distribution : Classical Theory Reappraised, 1988; articles in numerous journals. *Memberships:* Council Member, Indian Council for Social Science Research. *Hobbies:* Indian Classical Music; Writing. *Address:* 4 New Campus, Jawaharlal Nehru University, New Delhi 67, India 110067.

BHARDWAJ Neelam, b. 12 Jan. 1951, India. Obstetrician & Gynaecologist. m. Vijay Bhardwaj, 1 Oct. 1973. 2 sons. *Education:* MB BS, Maulana Azad Medical College, New Delhi, India, 1972; MRCOG, London, England, 1980; FRACOG, Melbourne, Australia, 1983. *Appointments:* Private medical practice, Melbourne, 1983; Consultant, Family planning clinic, Western General Hospital, 1985; Director, Family planning clinic, Maribyrnong Medical Centre, 1987-; Sessional specialist, obstetrics, Royal Women's Hospital, 1985- . *Memberships include:* Fellow, Royal Australian College of Obstetricians & Gynaecologists. *Hobby:* Painting, French Impressionists. *Address:* 7 Eldale Avenue, Greensborough 3088, Victoria, Australia.

BHUIYAN Syeda Nurjahan, b. 21 Dec. 1939, Dhaka, Bangladesh. Professor of Obstetrics and Gynaecology. m. Aminuz Zaman Bhuiyan, 20 Oct. 1967, 1 son. *Education:* MBBS, Dhaka Medical College, 1961; MRCOG, 1967, FRCOG, 1982, Royal College of Obstetrics and Gynaecology. *Appointments:* House Officer, Senior House Officer, Registrar, various hospitals, UK, 1963-68; Assistant Professor, 1969-72, Associate Professor, 1972-77, Professor, 1977-, Obstetrics and Gynaecology, Dhaka Medical College and Hospital, Bangladesh; World tour, lecturing Los Anfgeles, Masuri and Boston, USA on training midwives for menstrual regulation, 1982; Conferences: Geneva, 1972, Manila and Bombay 1974, Seoul, 1976, Baltimore, 1977, Netherlands and Singapore, 1986; Delhi, 1988. *Publications:* A Comparative Study of Multiload M-250Vs CU-T200 from June 1980 to 1982; Characteristics of Tubectomy Clients; Female Sterilization; Male Sterilization; Hospital Abortion; Experience with Menstrual Regulation and Family Planning Service; Training of Midwives for Menstrual Regulation; Acceptance of Voluntary Surgical Contraception, Bangladesh, 1986; Social Responsibility of Medical Practitioners in Maternity Care, presentation, 1989. *Memberships:* Royal College of Obstetrics and Gynaecology; Vice- President, Bangladesh Association for Prevention of Septic Abortion; Project Director, Bangladesh Association for Voluntary Sterilization; Bangladesh Fertility Programme; Project Director, Menstrual Regulation Programme, Bangladesh. *Hobbies:* Reading; Music; Games; Friendship. *Address:* K. B. Fazlul Kader Road, Chittagong, Bangladesh.

BIAFORA Rosanne, b. 2 Apr. 1962, Morgantown, West Virginia, USA. Marketing Executive. *Education:* BSc, Public Relations, University of Florida, 1984; MBA, Nova University, 1988. *Appointments:* Public relations specialist, 1985-87; Marketing & communications coordinator, Shands Hospital, 1987-88; Director of Marketing, Winter Park Pavilion, 1988-. *Memberships:* Society for Marketing & Public Relations (American Hospital Association); Society for Healthcare Public Relations & Marketing (Florida Hospital Association); Florida Alcohol & Drug Abuse Association; Seminole Chemical Awareness Network; United Way. *Honours:* Awards: Virginia Society for Hospital Marketing & Public Relations, Florida Public Relations Association, Gainesville Advertising Association, Florida Hospital Association's Society for Healthcare Public Relations & Marketing, 1986. *Hobbies:* Physical fitness; Reading; Swimming; Tennis. *Address:* 3733 Goldenrod Road, Apt. 1012, Winter Park, Florida 32792, USA.

BIAGI Shirley Anne, b. 21 June 1944, San Francisco, California, USA. Professor; Writer. m. 1964, 3 sons. *Education:* MA, English Literature, 1975. *Appointments:* Assistant Editor, California Journal, 1969-72; Lecturer, Assistant Professor, Associate Professor, Professor, 1972-. *Publications:* How to Write & Sell Magazine Articles, 1981; Interviews That Work, 1985; News Talk, I & II, 1987; Media/Impact: Introduction to Mass Media, 1988; Media/Reader, 1989. *Memberships:* Association for Education in Journalism & Mass Communication; Western Communications Educators Association. *Honours:* Award, California State University, 1985; Several University Grants & Awards; Teaching Award, Poynter Institute for Media Studies, 1983; Distinguished Teaching Award, American Society of Newspaper Editors, 1983. *Hobbies:* Swimming; Tennis. *Address:* 6000 J Street, Sacramento State University Journalism Department, CTR 308, Sacramento, California 95819, USA.

BIAGIOTTI Laura, b. 4 Aug. 1943, Rome, Italy. Fashion Designer. divorced. 1 daughter. *Appointments:* Foundation, Biagioti Export srl, for distribution & diffusion of pret-a-porter lines, 1965; 1st Laura Biagiotti collection presented, Florence, 1973. *Membership:* Amici del Teatro dell'Opera di Roma (Friends of Rome Opera). *Honours:* Leone d'oro di Venezia, fashion, July 1985; Fil d'or Internationa Linen Association, Jan. 1985. *Hobbies:* Antiques; Collecting scent bottles. *Address:* Via Palombarese Km 17, 300, 00012 Guidonia, Rome, Italy.

BIBEL Debra Jan, b. 6 Apr. 1945, San Francisco, California, USA. Medical Microbiologist. *Education:* AB, Bacteriology 1967, PhD Immunology 1972, University of California, Berkeley. *Appointments include:* Captain US Army/Microbiologist, LAIR, 1972-78; Tech Writer, Hoefer Scientific Instruments, 1979; Res Assoc, Dermatology, UC San Francisco, 1961- 83; Prod Mgr, Tago Inc, 1983-85; Res Assoc, Kaiser Foundation Res Inst, 1987-; Director, Elie Metchnikof Mem Library, 1977-. *Publications:* Book: Milestones in Immunology; Column: Rummagings Along the Dusty Shelf; 38 articles in research and history of science. *Memberships:* Amer Soc Microbiol; Amer Assoc Advancement Sci; Fed Amer Sci; Assoc Women in Science; Inst of Noetic Sciences; N Calif. Branch of Amer Soc Microbiol. *Honours:* US Public Health Service Traineeship, 1967-72; US Army Commendation Medal, 1976. *Hobbies:* History of Microbiology & Immunology; Buddhist Philosophy and Zen; Music; Painting and Photography; Hiking. *Address:* 230 Orange Street 6, Oakland, California 94610, USA.

BICKER Edwina Carole, b. 20 Sept. 1943, Sheffield, England. Solicitor. m. David Charles Bicker, 11 Nov. 1972. *Education:* Ilkley College of Housecraft, 1962-64; LLB, London University, 1972. *Appointments:* Teacher, Sheppey Technical High School, 1965-67; Articled Clerk, 1967-72; Solicitor (practising as Edwina Millward), Gill Turner & Tucker, Maidstone, Kent; Deputy Registrar, County Court; District Registry of the High Court. *Memberships:* Law Society; Kent Law Society; National President, UK Federation of Business and Professional Women; Company Secretary,

Maidstone Hospice Appeal; Chairman, Construction Advisory Committee of the International Federation of Business and Professional Women; Member, South Eastern Region Electricity Consumers Committee (a new committee operating under the office of Electricity Regulation). *Honours:* Appeal Patron for Lucy Cavendish College, Cambridge; Trustee, The International Federation of Business and Professional Women. *Hobbies:* Swimming; Reading; Needlework. *Address:* Loan Head, Simmonds Lane, Otham, Maidstone, Kent ME15 8RH, England.

BICKLEY Gillian Barbara, b. 3 Aug. 1943, Aberdare, South Wales. Wife; College Professor; Writer; Scholar; Consultant. m. Dr Verner Courtenay Bickley, MBE, 7 May 1986. *Education:* BA (Hons) 1965, Cert. Ed 1966, MLitt 1969, Bristol; PhD, Leeds, 1973. *Appointments:* University of Lagos, Nigeria, 1968-70; University of Hong Kong, 1971-74; University of Auckland, New Zealand, 1974-77; Longman (Far East), 1978-79; Hong Kong Examinations Authority, 1979-82; Hong Kong Baptist College, 1982-. *Publications:* Articles on: George Orwell; Leonard Woolf; Swinburne; Carlyle; African and Asian writing in English; The Governor Eyre Controversy; Hong Kong Education; Hong Kong Educational History. *Memberships:* Committee for the Award of International Fellowships, 1980-86, Chairman, 1986-89, International Federation of University Women; Committee Member 1977-, President 1985-87, Hong Kong Association of University Women; Society of Authors; Royal Commonwealth Society; Royal Asiatic Society, Hong Kong Branch; Hong Kong Association of Applied Linguistics; Hong Kong Journalists' Association; Spaclals; Aulla; Council Member, 1987-, Asian Federation of University Women. *Honours:* State Studentship, 1966-68; British Academy Overseas Visiting Fellowship, 1974; Research Awards: University of Lagos, 1969; University of Hong Kong, 1971, 1972, 1973; University of Auckland, 1974; Hong Kong Baptist College, 1985, 1987/88; Winifred Cullis Grant, 1972; Kathleen Elliott Scholarship, 1972; Theodora Bosanquet Bursary, 1974. *Hobbies:* The history of Hong Kong education; Interior design; Travel; Giving parties; Theatre; Walking. *Address:* c/o Invico S-O-S, Roc Escolls 3-4D, Avenida Meritxell 20, Andorra La Vella, Principat D'Andorra, Spain.

BIDDULPH Elizabeth Mary, b. 17 June 1927, Port Elizabeth, South Africa. Painter. m. 15 July 1961. 1 son. *Education:* Honours Certificate, Royal Drawing Society, 1942; National Diploma, Design, Drawing & Painting, Wimbledon School of Art, 1947; Slade School of Fine Art, 1949-51; Self-employed painter, portraits, landscapes, flowers, still-life; Demonstrations, amateur art clubs. *Creative works.* Ceiling panels for writer Ralph Dutton (originals destroyed by fire), 1961-62; Illustrated articles, Leisure Painter, magazine, 1980-81; Solo exhibitions, Hornsey 1971, Egham 1977, 1985; Pastoral Murals in Shop in Virginia Water, Surrey, 1984. *Membership:* Past committee member, Egham & District Music Club. *Honours:* Elected member, Royal Institute of Oil Painters, 1952; Elected honorary Senior Member, ibid, 1982. *Hobbies:* Piano playing; Gardening; Cooking. *Address:* 74 Clarence Street, Egham, Surrey TW20 9QY, England.

BIEHL Kathy Anne, b. 27 Jan. 1956, Pittsburgh, Pennsylvania, USA. Attorney; Writer. *Education:* BA German, Southern Methodist University, 1973-76; JD, University of Texcas School of Law, 1976-79. *Appointments:* Associate, Schlanger, Cook, Cohn, Mills & Grossberg, Houston, 1979-82; Lecturer in Political Science, Rice University, 1982; Sole Law Practice, 1982- ; Adjunct Professor, University of Houston, 1988; Cofounder, Metaphysiques Fitness Studio, 1988. *Publications:* Contributing writer, Our Kids Magazine; numerous articles to professional journals and local newspapers. *Memberships:* University of Texas Law Review; American Bar Association; State Bar of Texas; Houston Bar Association; Houston Folklore Society; Texas Accountants & Lawyers for the Arts; Phi Beta Kappa; Friends of Goethe, founding director and president, 1983-86. *Hobbies:* Choral singing; Writing

and performing acoustic music; Rubber stamp art; Folk art (environmental). *Address:* 909 Kipling, Houston, Texas 77006, USA.

BIELKE Patricia Anne, b. 11 May 1949, Bay Shore, New York, USA. Psychologist. m. Stephen Roy Bielke, 10 July 1971. 1 son, 1 daughter. *Education:* BA, Carleton College, 1971; PhD, University of Minnesota, 1979. *Appointments:* Research Assistant, National Institute of Mental Health, 1972-74; Psychologist, Southeastern Wisc Medical & Social Services, 1979-; Brief Family Therapy Center, Psychologist, 1981-; Psychologist, Elmbrook Memorial Hospital, 1986-; Supervisor, Consultant, Catalyst Counseling Center, 1981-86; Consulting Psychologist, Family Health Plan, 1985-. *Memberships:* American Association of Marriage & Family Therapists; Board of Directors, League of Women Voters. *Honour:* Graduated cum laude, Carleton College, 1971. *Hobbies:* Skiing; Camping; Tennis; Hiking; Travelling. *Address:* 17455 Bedford Dr, Brookfield, WI 53005, USA.

BIELSKI Alison Joy Prosser, b. 24 Nov. 1926, Newport, Gwent, Wales. Writer. m. (1)Dennis Treverton Jones, 19 June 1948, deceased 1950, 1 son. (2)Anthony Edward Bielski, 30 Nov. 1973, 1 daughter. *Education:* Newport High School, Gwent; Kerr Sander Secretarial College. *Appointments:* Personal Assistant, Bristol Aircraft, 1944-46; Secretarial posts, Morris Prosser Engineering, 1946-48; Offa's Mead Primary School, 1976-78; Tenby Bookshop, Dyfed, 1978-83; Lectured, Welsh Arts Council Writers on tour for over 20 years. *Publications:* The Story of the Welsh Dragon, 1969; Across the Burning Sand, 1970; The Love Tree, Poems, 1974; Tales & Traditions of Tenby, 1982; Eagles, Poems, 1983; The Story of St Mellons, 1985. *Memberships:* Association of Little Presses; Society of Women Writers & Journalists; Past Honorary Secretary, Welsh Academy (English Language Section); Folklore Society; Writers Union of Wales; Traditional Cosmology Society; Vegetarian Society UK Ltd. *Honours:* 2nd prize Julia Cairns Trophy, Society of Women Writers & Journalists, 1984; Orbis, Poems for Peace, 1984; Alice Gregory Memorial Competition, 1972; Anglo-Welsh Review Summer Prize, 1970; Arnold Vincent Bowen Poetry Prize, 1971; 2nd Prize Festival Spoken Poetry, 1967; Premium Prize, Poetry Review, 1964. *Hobbies:* Music, play 3 keyboard instruments and Bardic harp; Chess; Gardening. *Address:* 24 Kingfisher Close, St Mellons, Cardiff CF3 0DD, Wales.

BIGGS Elise Delano, b. 10 Sept. 1936, Baltimore, USA. Certified Public Accountant *Education:* DA, University of Delaware, 1957; MA, 1964; BA, Accounting, University of West Florida, 1979. *Appointments:* Assistant to Dean of Graduate School, University of Delaware, 1961-71; CPA, Self-employed, 1980-; Trustee, Okaloosa Walton Junior College, 1987-. *Memberships:* Treasurer, Republican Party of Florida, 1984-; Florida Institute of CPA's. *Honours:* Phi Beta Kappa; Phi Kappa Phi; Mortar Board. *Address:* PO Box 1009, Santa Rosa Beach, FL 32459, USA.

BIGGS Margaret Annette Key, b. 26 Oct. 1933, Needmore, Pike County, Alabama, USA. Author. m. Wayne Saunders Biggs, 1 Apr. 1956. *Education:* BS, English, Troy State University, Troy, Alamaba, 1954; MS, Humanities, California State University, Dominguez Hills, 1979. *Appointments:* Instructor, Port Saint Joseph Junior-Senior High School, Florida, 1954-86; Adjunct Professor, Gulf Coast Community College, 1984-85. *Publications:* Books of poetry: Swampfire, 1980; Sister to the Sun, 1981; Magnolias and Such, 1982; Petals from the Womanflower, 1983; Plumage of the Sun, 1986. *Memberships:* Life Member, Panhandle Writers Guild; Alabama State Poetry Society; National League of American Pen Women. *Honours:* Recipient of numerous national and international awards for poetry and prose; Pulitzer Prize Nominee, 1982, 1986. *Hobbies:* Post Office Box 551, Port Saint Joseph, FL 32456, USA.

BIGLAND-RITCHIE Brenda R., b. 23 Sep. 1927,

Jordans, England. Physiologist; Professor. m. J. Murdoch Ritchie, 28 July 1951, 1 son, 1 daughter. *Education:* BSc, 1949, PhD, 1968, University College, London; DSc, University of London, 1987. *Appointments:* Assistant Professor, University College, London, 1949-53; Research Associate, Albert Einstein College of Medicine, New York City, USA, 1963-66; Assistant Professor, Marymount College, Tarrytown, New York, 1967-70; Associate Professor, Quinnipiac College, Hamden, Connecticut, 1970-73, Professor, 1973-; Fellow, John B. Pierce Foundation, New Haven, Connecticut, 1985-. *Publications:* About 50 scientific publications in refereed journals and books. *Memberships:* American Physiological Society; British Physiological Society; Society for Neuroscience; Fellow, American College of Sports Medicine. *Address:* John B. Pierce Foundation, 290 Congress Avenue, New Haven, CT 06519, USA.

BILLINGS Carolyn Veronica, b. 10 Dec. 1938, Montpelier, Vermont, USA. Nurse. m. W. Curtis Fitzgerald, 1 son, 1 daughter. *Education:* Diploma, Nursing, 1959; BA, Psychology, North Carolina State University, 1973; MSN, Nursing, University of North Carolina, Chapel Hill, 1980; Certification as a Clinical Specialist, Psychiatric-Mental Health Nursing, American Nurses' Association, 1983. *Appointments:* Various positions, Nursing Service & Education, 1959-; Graduate Faculty, School of Nursing, East Carolina University, 1982-84; Nurse Therapist, Private Practice, 1983-. *Publications:* Contributor to: American Journal of Nursing; Nursing Management; Supervisor Nurse; Nursing; RN. *Memberships:* Board of Directors, North Carolina Nurses Association, Chair of Commission on Member Services, Officer of Conference Group of Clinical Specialists in Psychiatric- Mental Health Nursing; Board of Directors, Wake County Mental Health Association; Alpha Alpha Chapter, Sigma Theta Tau; ANA Council of Psychiatric and Mental Health Nursing. *Honours:* Volunteer of the Year, Wake County Mental Health Association, 1985; Writing Award, American Nurses Association, 1985; North Carolina Governor's Award. *Hobbies:* Family; Tennis. *Address:* 3410 Hillsborough Street, Raleigh, NC 27607, USA.

BINDMAN Lynn Janice, b. 14 July 1938, London, England. Senior Lecturer. m. Geoffrey Bindman, 9 Apr. 1961, 2 sons, 1 daughter. *Education:* BSc., 1960, PhD, 1964, University College, London. *Appointments:* Assistant Lecturer, 1965-69, Research Associate, 1969- 72, Lecturer, 1972-82, Senior Lecturer, 1982-, Physiology, University College, London. *Publications:* The Neurophysiology of the Cerebral Cortex, with Olof Lippold; MCQS in Physiology, with B R Jewell & L H Smaje; MCQS in Neurophysiology, with P. Ellaway; numerous scientific papers in professional journals; invited chapters on research. *Memberships:* Physiological Society, Committee Member, 1987-; The Brain Research Association, Committee Member, 1988-; Society for Neurosciences, USA; International Brain Research Organization. *Hobbies:* ILEA School Governor. *Address:* Dept. of Physiology, University College London, Gower St., London WC1E 6BT, England.

BINNEY Caroline Thorn, b. Newport, Rhode Island, USA. Ballet Dancer. *Education:* Mary C. Wheeler School. *Appointments include:* American Festival Ballet; New York Dancing Ensemble; New York City Opera; New York Folk Ballet; Metropolitan Opera Company; Stuttgart Ballet, Germany; Royal Ballet, UK; Paris Opera Ballet, France; La Scale Opera Ballet, Italy; *Creative work includes:* Choreography: Italian tarantellas & waltzes; Carmen, gypsy dance; La Traviata, gypsy dance. *Membership:* American Guild of Musical Artists. *Hobbies:* Photography; Sewing costumes; Swimming; Cycling; Running; Horseback riding; Music; Singing; Films. *Address:* 314 West 58th Street, Apt. 3B, New York City, NY 10019, USA.

BINNIE Jean Catherine, Writer. 3 daughters, 1 son. *Creative Work:* Joss the Boss, Children's Book, 1984; Chota, Radio 4 play; Just a Tick, 1 act stage play, 1985; Stories on Radio & TV; Co-Writer, Sticks & Stones, and

The Backway, BBC London & Germany, etc; Boudicca's Victory, Radio 4, BBC; Lady Macbeth, Edinburgh Fringe, 1985; Premiere of play, Colours, at the Abbey Theatre, Dublin, 1988, British premiere at the Leeds Playhouse, 1988 . *Membership:* Writers Guild. *Hobbies:* Oil Painting; Films; Jumble Sales; Photography; Travel; etc. *Address:* c/o Cecily Ware's Agency, 19c John Spencer Square, Canonbury, London N1 2LZ, England.

BINSFELD Connie, m. John E. Binsfeld, 947, 4 sons, 1 daughter. *Education:* BS, Secondary Education, Siena Heights College. *Appointments:* Michigan State Senator, 1982-. *Memberships:* North Country Scenic Trail Council; National State Legislative Council; Zonta International; Girl Scouts Council; League of Women Voters. *Honours Include:* Northwestern Michigan College Fellow; Honorary DHL, Siena Heights College; Michigan Mother of the Year, 1977. *Address:* 36th District Rt- 2, Maple City, MI 49664, USA.

BIRAULT Mary Alice Collier, Dr., b. Denver, Colorado, USA. Educational Communications, Human Relations & Business Consultant. 1 daughter. *Education:* BA, Elementary Education Early Childhood, California State University, Los Angeles, 1966; MEd, Inner City Education Administration, Loyola Marymount University, Los Angeles, 1974; PhD, Multicultural Education Administration, Claremont Graduate School, Claremont, California, 1985. *Appointments:* Supervisor, Coordinator, Teacher, Multicultural, Multimedia Education & Communication Center, 1966-85; Compensatory-Urban Classroom Teacher; Reading Specialist; Bilingual Coordinator, Community & Public Relations, Cortez School, Magnolia Avenue School, Loren Miller School, Los Angeles, California, 1970-80; Organizer, political campaigns, charity activities, Hollywood & Los Angeles, 1970-81; President, Partner, Mon-Mar Enterprises consultancy, 1973-; Consultant, Lecturer, Instructor, California State University, Los Angeles, Pepperdine University, Los Angeles City College, Immaculate Heart College, Los Angeles, 1975-81; Public Relations Coordinator, National Rehabilitation Annual Conference, 1981-82; Owner, Coordinator, Teaching-Training & Research Services, 1984-; Coordinator, Leader, TV & Children (seminar/ workshop), International Association for Mass Communication Research, Prague, Czechoslovakia, Aug. 1984; President, Co- Owner, 4-E-Z Communications Inc multi-media educational cultural publishing company, 1986-. *Publications:* Many news media articles in English and Spanish newspapers, 1970-80; Multicultural Multimedia Systematized Resource Catalogue, 1977; Children's TV Viewing Experiences vs Academic, Cultural and Social Activities, 1985. *Memberships:* National Association for the Advancement of Colored People; National Education Association; International of Mass Communication Researchers; National Association of Women Business Owners; Association of Black Women Entrepreneurs; Public Interest Radio & Television Education Society; Many others. *Honours:* Various awards for services to minority education. *Address:* 1313 Edgecliffe Drive, Los Angeles, CA 90026, USA.

BIRD Agnes Thornton, b. 15 Sept. 1921, Wichita Falls, Texas, USA. Attorney at Law. m. Frank B Bird, 10 Mar. 1946. 1 daughter. *Education:* BS, Texas Women's University, 1943; MA 1959, PhD 1967, JD 1974, University of Tennessee. *Appointments:* Instructor of Political Science, University of Tennessee, 1966-68; Assistant Professor of Political Science, Maryville College, 1968-70; Partner in Law Firm, Bird, Navratil, Bird & Kull, 1975-. *Publications:* Articles in professional journals. *Memberships:* American Bar Association, Committee on Immigration Law, 1987-; National Federation of Democratic Women, Parliamentarian, 1974-; President, Tennessee Division, American Association of University Women, 1985- 87; Chair, Tennessee Commission on the Status of Women, 1977-78; Tennessee Human Relations Commission, 1965-68; Tennessee Democratic Executive Committee, member 23 years, Vice Chair, 1975-82; Democratic National Committee, 1976-82. *Honours:* Delegate,

Prominent American Women's Tour of People's Republic of China, 1979; Distinguished Alumna Award, Texas Women's University, 1980; Annie Selwin Award, 1988; Grant for Monograph, Citizens Research Foundation, 1964. *Hobbies:* Promoting Women's Rights; Politics; Reading. *Address:* Cold Springs Road, Walland, Tennessee, USA.

BIRD Florence Bayard, The Honourable, C.C. b. 15 Jan. 1908. Retired Senate of Canada Member. m. John Bird, 1928, deceased 1978. *Appointments:* Commentator on National and International News, CBC, 1941-67; Chairman, royal Commission on the States of Women, 1967-70; Consultant to Task Force, Status of Women in the CBC, 1974; Special CIDA Consultant: Government of Jamaica 1975, Barbados 1976; The Senate of Canada, 1978-83; Status of Refugees Advisory Committee, 1983-85. *Publications:* Anne Francis - An Autobiography, 1974; Holiday in the Woods, 1976; articles in journals & magazines. *Memberships:* National Liberal Party of Canada; UN Association; Institute of Cultural Affairs; Hon. Life Member, Canadian Research Institute for the Advancement of Women; Patron, MATCH; etc. *Honours:* 2 Wommen's National Press Club Prizes; Companion of the Order of Canada, 1971; LL.D, Hon: York University, 1972, Carleton University, Queen's University, 1975; Persons Award, 1983. *Address:* Apt. 201 -333 Chapel Street, Ottawa, Ontario K1N 8YS.

BIRMINGHAM Maisie Poynter, b. 28 Sep. 1914, Darjeeling, India. Housewife. m. Walter Birmingham, 17 Dec. 1948, 2 sons, 1 daughter. *Education:* St Hilda's College, Oxford University, 1932-35; 2nd Class Honours Degree, Philosophy, Politics and Economics. *Appointments:* Staff Manager, John Lewis's, London, England, 1936-38; Personnel Manager, Rowntree's, 1938-41; HM Inspector of Factories, 1941-43; Personnel Manager, D'Arcy Exploration Co, 1943-45; Tutor in Social Studies, University College of South Wales and Monmouthshire, 1945-49; Lecturer in Social Administration, University of Ghana, 1958-60. *Publications:* Crime novels: You Can Help Me, 1974; The Heat of the Sun, 1976; Sleep in a Ditch, 1978. *Memberships:* Cwmbran New Town Corporation, 1950-52; Toynbee Housing Association Committee, 1967-90; Shaftesbury Christian Council (Secretary 1979, Chairman 1983); Crime Writers Association. *Hobbies:* Reading; Corresponding; Walking; Doing what she can to help meet needs especially in the Third World. *Address:* 7 Gold Hill, Shaftesbury, Dorset SP7 8JW, England.

BIRNEY Alice Lotvin, b. 6 Mar. 1938, New York City, USA. Literature & Theatre Specialist. m. G. Adrian Birney, 4 June 1964, 1 daughter. *Education:* AB, Barnard College, Columbia University, 1959; MA, Ohio State University, 1962; PhD, University of California, San Diego (UCSD), 1968. *Appointments:* Editorial assistant, Billboard, 1959-61; English Professor, Ohio State University, University of California (Los Angeles & San Diego), 1961-72, Mansfield State College, 1968-69; Specialist in English and American Literature, Library of Congress, 1973-. *Publications:* Books: Satiric Catharsis in Shakespeare, 1973; Literary Lives of Jesus, 1989. Also: Journalism, reviews, poetry, various publications; Director, 2 short films; Staff contributor, World Shakespeare Bibliography. *Memberships:* Modern Language Association; Treasurer, Library of Congress Employee Film Society; MENSA. *Honours:* Scholarship, Barnard College, 1959; Dissertation fellowship, UCSD, 1967; Summer fellowship, Folger Shakespeare Library, 1974; Awards, Library of Congress, 1975, 1983, 1984; Film showings, American University 1980, Hirschorn Museum 1982. *Hobbies:* Film maker (Hannah Sennesh, Photograph); Dramatist (Retakes, Daughters of Zion, Rappaccini's Daughter, Capitol Combat, Cold War in the Catskills). *Address:* 112 5th Street, NE, Washington DC 20002, USA.

BIRNKRANT Jeanne-Ann, b. 17 July 1951, New York City, USA. Artist; Actress; Social Worker; Politician. *Education:* BA, 1971; MSW, 1973. *Appointments:* New

School for Social Research, 1968-70; Art Students League, 1970-75; Chief Psychiatric Social Worker, New York City. *Publications:* Bronze Sculpture. *Memberships:* Academy of Certified Social Workers; Diplomate, Clinical Social Work; Screen Actors Guild. *Honours:* Recipient, many honours & awards. *Hobbies:* Jazz Dancing; Painting. *Address:* 240 Central Park South, New York City, NY 10019, USA.

BIRSAY Robina Margaret (Lady), b. 2 Aug. 1914, Stromness, Orkney. Retired. m. Sir Harald Leslie, Hon. Lord Birsay, KT, CBE, TD, QC, DL, 27 Dec. 1945. 1 son, 1 daughter. *Education:* Stromness Academy, Orkney, 1919- 32; MB ChB, University of Edinburgh, 1937. *Appointments:* Elsie Inglis Memorial Maternity Hospital, 1938-39; Sunderland Children's Hospital, 1939; Medical Officer, Sanday, Orkney, 1939-42; Captain, RAMC, 1943-46. *Memberships:* President, Edinburgh Ladies Lifeboat Guild, 1967-; President, Edinburgh Association of University Women, 1987-88. *Honour:* Mentioned in Despatches, 1945. *Address:* 27 Queensferry Road, Edinburgh, EH4 3HB, Scotland.

BISHOP Beverley, b. 19 Oct. 1922, Corning, New York, USA. Professor of Physiology. m. Charles William Bishop, 2 May 1944, 1 son. *Education:* BA, Syracuse University, 1944; MA, University of Rochester, 1946; PhD, University of Buffalo, 1958. *Appointments:* Assistant, physiology, University of Glasgow, Scotland, UK, 1956-57; Assistant Professor of Physiology, University of Buffalo, USA, 1958-67; Associate Professor 1975, Professor of Physiology 1975-, State University of New York (SUNY), Buffalo. *Publications:* Over 100 papers, refereed scientific journals including Basic Neurophysiology. Also: Illustrated lectures, neurophysiology, Audio- Visual Medical Marketing Inc, NYC, 1976-80. *Memberships:* American Physiological Society; Society for Neurosciences; American Thoracic Society; American Congress of Rehabilitation Medicine; American Physical Therapy Association; International Society of Electromyography & Kinesiology; American Association for Advanced Sciences. *Honours:* Golden Pen Award, APTA, 1976; Faculty recognition award, HRP, 1981; Chancellor's Award, teaching, 1975; Innovative teaching awards, SUNY, 1973, 1974; Dean's Award, academic contribution, 1969; Outstanding contribution, Alumni Association, 1969; Elected, Council, American Physiological Society, 1988-. *Hobbies:* Flying; Snorkeling; Travel; Swimming; Reading. *Address:* Department of Physiology, Sherman Annexe, School of Medicine, State University of New York, Buffalo, New York 14214, USA.

BISHOP Helen Louise, b. 8 Sept. 1941, Des Moines, Iowa, USA. Administration/Microbiologist. *Education:* BA, Grinnell College, 1963; MS, Syracuse University, 1965; PhD, University of California, 1968. *Appointments:* Predoctoral fellow, University of California, Davis, 1966-68; Postdoctoral Research Associate, University of California, Davis, Purdue University, & University of Michigan, 1968-72; American Society for Microbiology, 1972-. *Publications:* Articles in professional journals. *Memberships:* American Society for Microbiology; Sigma Xi; Delta Sigma Epsilon. *Honours:* Danforth Fellowship, 1982; NIH Predoctoral Fellowship, 1966-68; Fellow, American Academy of Microbiology. *Hobbies:* Travel; Bridge; Reading. *Address:* American Society for Microbiology, 1913 I St., NW, Washington, DC 20006, USA.

BISHOP Mary Chambers, b. 30 Nov. 1955, Pittsburgh, Pennsylvania, USA. Analyst. m. David Bishop, 30 Jan. 1981. 1 daughter. *Education:* BS Health & Phys Ed, West Chester State College, 1978; MA, Sport Science, 1979, University of Denver; MS, Administration, Health Care Services, West Chester, 1987. *Appointments:* Chief Cardiology Tech, Paoli Memorial Hospital, 1981-86; Analyst, Shared Medical Systems, Malvern, 1986-. *Publications:* Adult Echocardiography, A Handbook for Tech, 1985; An In-House Cardiology Technician Training Program, 1983. *Memberships:* American College of Sports Med, 1979-; American Cardiology Tecyhnologists Association,

1982-87. *Honours:* 3rd place, American Cardiology Technologists Association National Conference; PA State Champion, Womens C Division Racketball Championships, 1988; Regional 2nd place, Racketball, 1988. *Hobbies:* Sports especially Racketball; Renovating our home, a barn; Personal computer. *Address:* 9 Tiburon Lane, Malvern, PA 19355, USA.

BISHOP Susan Katharine, b. 3 Apr. 1946, Palm Beach, Florida, USA. Executive Search Consultant. m. Robert Uchitel, 27 Dec. 1973, divorced 1979, 1 daughter. *Education:* BA, Briarecliff College, 1968; MBA, Fordham University. *Appointments:* Actress, 1968-72; Producer, Hostess, KIMO TV, Anchorage, 1972-75; Programme Director, Visions TV, Anchorage, 1976-79; Partner, Johnson Smith & Knisely Inc., 1982-88; Director, Schmitt Bishop Inc., 1989-. *Memberships:* National Board, Women in Cable; Chair, Human Resource Committee, Cable TV Administration & Marketing Society. *Honours:* TAMI Award, 1987. *Hobbies:* Piano; Music; Theatre; Sports. *Address:* 400 Central Park West, New York, NY 10025, USA.

BISS Christine Helen, b. 31 May 1940, New Jersey, USA. Management Professional. m. Ronald M. Biss, 2 June 1962, divorced 1984. *Education:* BS, 1986. *Appointments:* Secretarial positions, 1958-74; Executive Secretary, 1974-81, Engineering Administrator, 1981-85, Singer Kearfott Division, Wayne; Senior Engineering Administrator, Singer Electronic Systems Division, 1985-88; Senior Engineering Administrator, Plessey Electronics System Corp., 1988-. *Memberships:* NAFE; Oak Ridge Civic Association. *Honours:* Cum Laude, Montclair State College, 1986. *Hobbies:* Travel; Theatre; Ballet; Concerts. *Address:* Plessey Electronic Systems Corp., 164 Totowa Road, Wayne, NJ 07474, USA.

BISSELL LeClair, b. 18 May, 1928, Virginia, USA. Physician. *Education:* BA, University of Colorado, Boulder, 1950; MS 1952, MD 1963, Columbia University, New York City. *Appointments:* Librarian, later Supervising Librarian, New York Public Library, 1952-59; Founder, Chief, Smithers Alcoholism Treatment and Training Centre, 1960-79; President and Chief Executive Officer 1979-81, Consultant/Researcher 1981-82, Edgehill- Newport, Inc; Writer, Lecturer, Consultant, 1982-. *Publications:* Books: The Cat Who Drank Too Much, with R Watherwax, 1982; Alcoholism in the Professions, with P W Haberman, 1984; Ethics for Addiction Professionals, with J E Royce, 1987; Chemical Dependency in Nursing, The Deadly Diversion, with E J Sullivan and E Williams, 1988; numerous articles in professional journals. *Memberships include:* American Assn of Physicians for Human Rights; American Civil Liberties Union and NYCLU; American Medical Society on Alcoholism, past president, Membership Chairperson; Chairperson, Impaired Physician Committee, American Medical Womens Assn; American Medical Writers Assn; Amnesty Internation, Urgent Action Network; ALMACA; Advisory Board Member, Intercongregational Alcoholism Program (for women religious); Board of Trustees, JACS Foundation (for Jewish Alcoholics). *Honours:* Mel Schulsted Award, National Assn of Alcoholism Counselors, 1981; Merit Award, Public Health Assn of New York City, 1976; Named one of the Top 25 Americans by 50 Plus Magazine, 1979; Women of the Year, Rhode Island Business and Professional Women's Club, 1981 also SECAD Award, 1988. *Hobby:* Textile arts. *Address:* 130 West 16th Street No 63, New York, NY 10011, USA.

BITTMANN Susan Wilkins, b. 10 Nov. 1946, Lumberton, North Carolina, USA. Professional Educator of Social Sciences. m. Christopher Jacob Bittmann, Jr, 20 Apr. 1973. *Education:* BA, Education, 1968; MA, History, 1971; Additional postgraduate work in Humanities and Political Science, 1980. *Appointments:* Great Bridge High School, Chesapeake, Virginia, 1968-69; Joe P Moore Junior High School, Lumberton, North Carolina, 1971-72; Chamberlain High School, Tampa, Florida, 1972-. *Publications:* Co-author, Instructional Manual for Limited English Proficient students, 1986;

World History Curriculum development for Hillsborough County, Florida; Humanities and World History test development for state of Florida-continuing development. *Memberships:* National Education Association; Florida Teaching Profession; Hillsborough Classroom Teachers Assoc; National Council for the Social Studies; Florida Council for the Social Studies; Phi Delta Kappa; Alpha Delta Kappa, educational fraternities; Pi Sigma Alpha, Political Science honorary; Member, Association for Supervision and Curriculum Development. *Honours:* Selected, AP European Reader and test developer for Educational Testing Service, Princeton, 1986-; Secretary, Carrollwood Service League 1974-76, Ways and Means Chairperson, 1978-79; Hillsborough County Social Studies Teacher of the Year, 1986; Teacher of the Year, Chamberlain High School, 1987 & 1989; Florida Humanities grantee, 1985-86; Hillsborough CTA grantee, 1988-89; Elected Democratic Party Precinct Chairperson, Hillsborough County, 1988; Recipient, Master Teacher Award, 1986; Phi Mu alumna secretary, 1975-77; Chairperson of textbook selection committee, Hillsborough County, 1985-86. *Hobbies:* Raquetball; Swimming; Basketball; Reading. *Address:* Chamberlain High School, 9401 North Blvd, Tampa, FL 33612, USA.

BIVENS Ernestine, b. Jacksonville, USA. Teacher. m. Woodrow B. Bivens, 17 Oc.t 1942, 1 sons. *Education:* AA, 1941; BS, 1969. *Appointments:* Light House Nursery School, 1953-54; Division of Day- Care, New York City, 1961-64; Rochdale Village Nursery School, Jamaica, 1964- 60; Lawrence Public School District, 1969-. *Publications:* Early Childhood Study Composition District 15 (School)Theme, A Birthday of Hope - What is a Friend; All Children Join Hands; Dr Martin Luther King, Jr. *Memberships:* NAEYC; Alpha Kappa Alpha; Life Member, National Association for the Advancement of Coloured People. *Honours:* Leadeship Award, Bethune Cookman College, 1970; Outstanding Service Award, Epsilon Pi Omega Chapter, AKA, 1983. *Hobbies:* Crafts Reading; Music; Travel. *Address:* 129-17, 158th Street, Jamaica, NY 11434, USA.

BIZIERE Kathleen Emilie Paula, b. 17 June 1946, Poona, India. Neuropsychiatric Researcher. m. Jean-Maurice Biziere, 11 Aug. 1966, 2 sons, 1 daughter. *Education:* Chemistry degree, 1969; Medical Doctorate, 1975; PhD, Neuroscience, & Board Certified, Neurology, 1980. *Appointments:* Intern 1975-76, Neurology Resident 1980-87, University Hospital, Tours, France; Postdoctoral Fellow, Johns Hopkins School of Medicine, Baltimore, USA, 1976-78; Head, Neurophysiology Research, Sanofi, France, 1980-87; Senior Clinical Research Physician, Hoffman-LaRoche, Basle, Switzerland, 1987-. *Creative work includes:* Research, neuroexcitatory amino-acids, depression, epilepsy, anxiety; 1st description, link between cerebral cortex & immune system; Over 90 research articles published, various international journals. *Memberships:* Society for Neuroscience; British Pharmacological Society; British Association for Psychopharmacology; New York Academy of Sciences. *Honours:* 1st prizes, These de Tours, & These des Facultes de l'Ouest, 1978. *Address:* 60, rue de la Couronne, 68400 Riedisheim, France.

BIZORIK Susan Hamilton, b. 25 Mar. 1951, Kansas City, Missouri, USA. Mathematics Resource Teacher. m. James Bizorik, 1 Oct. 1983, 1 daughter. *Education:* AA, Penn Valley College, 1971; BA 1973, MA 1979, Education Specialist 1982, University of Missouri. *Appointments:* Specialist, Remedial Mathematics, 1974-83; Instructional Assistant to Principal, 1983-85; Adjunct Mathematics Instructor, Donnelly, St Mary, Avila, University of Missouri Kansas City, Area Colleges, 1981-88; Resource Teacher, Elementary Mathematics, 1985-. *Publications:* Teacher consultant, Mathemtics Unlimited, 1987; Research articles. *Memberships:* Offices: National, Missouri, Kansas City Councils, Teachers of Mathematics; Phi Delta Kappa; Junior League. *Honours:* Biographical recognition. *Hobbies:* Volunteer work, Junior League; Kansas City History; Antiques. *Address:* 11704 East 41st Street, Independence, Missouri 64052, USA.

BJORKLUND Janet Vinsen, b. 31 July 1947, Seattle, Washington, USA. Speech Pathologist. m. Dan Robert Young, 4 Dec. 1971. 1 son, 2 daughters. *Education:* Student, University of Vienna, Austria, 1966-67; BA, Pacific University, 1969; Student, University of Washington, 1970-71; MA, San Francisco State University, 1977; Cert. Clinical Speech Pathologist, Audiologist. *Appointments:* Speech pathologist, audiological cons. USN Hospital, Rota Spain, 1972-75; Traineeship in Audiology, VA Hospital, San Francisco, 1976; Speech Pathologist San Lorenzo, California Unified Schools, 1975-77 and 1978-81; Dir. speech pathology, St Lukes Speech & Hearing Center, San Francisco, 1977-78; Audiologist, XO Barrios, MD, San Francisco, 1977-81; Cons. Visually Impaired Infant Program, Seattle, 1981-82; Speech Pathologist, Everett Washington Schools, 1982-; Cons. Madison House, Kirkland, Washington, 1983-87; NW Devel. Therapists, Everett, 1985-87; Pediatric Diagnostic and Treatment Ctr., Everett, 1985-; Pacific Hearers and Speech Centre, 1988-. *Publications:* Author (with others) Screening for Bilingual Preschoolers, 1977, (TV Script); Clinical Services in San Francisco, 1978; Developing Better Communication Skills, 1982. *Memberships:* Co-ordinator pre-school Christian edn. Kirkland Congregational Church, Washington, 1983-85; Organizer, Residents Against Speeding Drivers, Madison Park, Seattle, 1985-87; American Speech and Hearing Association; American Speech and Hearing Foundation, Washington; Speech and Hearing Association, Regional Rep 1985-86, Chair licensure task force, 1986-88; President Pacific U Chpt 1968, Phi Lambda Omicron. *Hobbies:* Numismatics; Travelling; Needlwork; Cooking. *Address:* 2015 41st Avenue E, Seattle, WA 98112, USA.

BLACK Barbara Aronstein, b. 6 May 1933, Brooklyn, New York, USA. Dean, Faculty of Law. m. Charles L. Black, 11 Apr. 1954, 2 sons, 1 daughter. *Education:* BA, Brooklyn College, 1953; LL.B., Columbia 1955; M.Phil., 1970, PhD, 1975, Yale Univesity; LL.D., New York Law School, 1986; LLD, Vermont Law School, 1987; LLD, College of New Rocchelle, 1987. *Appointments:* Associate in Law, Columbia, 1955-56; Acting Instructor, History, 1971-72, 1973-74, Lecturer, History, 1974-76, Assistant Professor, History, 1976-79, Associate Professor, 1979-84, Yale University; Visiting Lecturer, Harvard University, 1978-79; George Welwood Murray Professor of Legal History, 1984, Dean, Faculty of Law, 1986-, Columbia University. *Publications:* Articles in: Pennsylvania Law Review; Law and History Review. *Memberships:* New York, Connecticut Bar Associations; Bar of the US Court of Appeals; American Society of Legal History, President; Selden Society. *Honours:* Recipient, many honours and awards. *Address:* Columbia University School of Law, 435 West 116th Street, New York, NY 10027, USA.

BLACK Barbara Ellen, b. 22 June 1938, Brooklyn, New York, USA. University Treasurer. *Education:* BA 1960, MA 1962, History; DPS, Management, 1982. *Appointments include:* Vice president, Business Affairs & Administration, Molloy College, New York City, 1973-83; Director of Finance, Hunter Colege, NYC, 1984-85; Financial Vice President & Treasurer, Fordham University, Bronx, NY, 1985-. *Publications:* Papers on: Commuter Education, 1973; Indicators of Financial Health (unpublished doctoral dissertation), 1982; Woman Business Officer, 1983. *Memberships:* President, Eastern Association of College & University Business Officers; College Board; Treasurer, Middle States Association; Trustees Board Chair, Consolation Residence; Trustee, National Association of College & University Business Officers. *Honours:* Veritas Alumni Award 1978, Distinguished Service Medal 1975, President's Medal 1983, Molloy College; Citation, volunteer work, Diocese of Rockville Centre, 1982; Outstanding Young Woman, NYS Representative, 1972. *Address:* 1285 Lake Shore Drive, Massapequa Park, New York 11762, USA.

BLACK Claire Alexander, b. 11 May 1953, Fayette, USA. Attorney. m. Duane Albert Wilson, 1 Apr. 1988. *Education:* BA, 1974-, JD, 1978, University of Alabama. *Appointments:* Attorney, Lee, Barrett & Mullins, Tuscaloosa, 1978-80; Self-employed, Prince & Black, Tuscaloosa, 1980-82; Attorney, Crownover & Black, Tuscaloosa, 1982-87; Attorney, Dishuck, LaCoste & Black, Tuscaloosa, 1987-. *Memberships Include:* Alabama, American, Tuscaloosa County Bar Associations, many offices; Alabama Trial Lawyers; American Association of Trial Lawyers. *Honours Include:* Recipient, many honours, awards & scholarships. *Hobbies:* Music; Ballet; Horse Riding. *Address:* 2125 Glendale Gardens, Tuscaloosa, AL 35401, USA.

BLACK Joan, b. 21 Nov. 1917, Birkenhead, England. Tutor of modern languages. m. Misha Black, 15 July 1955. 1 son. *Education:* BA, Hons, St Anne's College, Oxford University. *Appointments:* Served in WRNS, 1943-46; UNESCO, Paris, France, 1946-55; Social Care Worker (voluntary) 1955, Part-time Remedial Teacher, 1970-83, St George's School Battersea; French Tutor, Hugh-Jones Tutors, Hammersmith, 1983-86; French tutor various London tutorial colleges; French Tutor, Milestone Tutorial College, South Kensington; Teacher, Hornsby House School, Wandsworth. *Membership:* Trustee, St Mungo Community Trust. *Address:* 78 Primrose Mansions, Prince of Wales Drive, London SW11, England.

BLACK Linda Cabot, b. 17 Dec. 1928, Boston, USA. Opera Presentor & Producer. m. (1)David Goldmark Black, 21 Dec. 1951, divorced, 1978, 2 sons, 1 daughter, (2)Roger E. Clapp, 1989. *Education:* AB, Music, Radcliffe College, 1951. *Memberships:* President 1958-60, Board 1964-86, Board of Overseers, 1986-88, Opera Co. of Boston; Opera New England, Vice President, 1975-88; Fairfield Co. Association for Opera New England, President 1974-88. *Honours:* Governor Ella Grasse Distinguished Award in the Arts, 1982; United Nations Association Outstanding Connecticut Women Award, 1987. *Hobbies:* Opera; Nature. *Address:* 3 Hilliard Place Cambridge, MA 02138, USA.

BLACK Lisa Y., b. 15 Apr. 1963, St Louis, Missouri, USA. Legislative Author. *Education:* BBA magna cum laude, Electrical Engineering, Columbia University, 1981-84; Accounting, University of the District of Columbia, 1988. *Appointments:* Bookkeeper, T.Head & Company, Washington DC, 1986-87; Accounting Intern, Coopers & Lybrand, Washington DC, 1987-88; Legislative Author, Division of Audits, Baltimore, Maryland, 1988-. *Memberships:* Secretary, University of the District of Columbia Accounting Club, 1986; Phi Sigma Pi, 1987 *Honours:* Dean's List Award, University of the District of Columbia, 1985-88; Outstanding Junior Award, 1986; National Dean's List, 1986-87; Top Graduating Senior Award, Wall Street Journal, 1988. *Hobbies:* Reading; Playing tennis; Films; Dancing. *Address:* 6435 13th Street NW, Washington, DC 20012, USA.

BLACK-WILSON Ann Elizabeth, b. 9 June 1943, Logansport, Indiana, USA. Scientist. m. Robert C Black, 22 May 1976. 1 son. *Education:* BS 1965, MS Pharm 1972, University of Michigan; Wayne State Med School, 1967. *Appointments:* University of Michigan, 1966-73 and 1974-77; Lafayette Clinic of Detroit, 1973-74; Warner-Lambert/Parke-Davis, 1977-. *Publications:* 26 publications in major scientific journals and books. *Memberships:* Society for Neuroscience; New York Academy of Sciences. *Honours:* International Society for the Study of Xenofiotus; University of Michigan Scholarship, 1961-65. *Hobbies:* Gardening; Reading; Conservation. *Address:* 2800 Plymouth Road, Ann Arbor, MI 48106, USA.

BLACKBURN Christine Louise, b. 29 Nov 1948. Chicago, Illinois, USA. Campus Minister. *Education:* BA cum laude, Religion, Hamline University, St Paul, Minnesota, 1970; MDiv, with honours, Andover Newton Theological School, Newton Centre, Massachusetts, 1974. *Appointments:* Prudence Crandel Centre for

Women, summer 1974; United Ministries in Higher Education, University of Wisconsin, River Falls, 1974-77; Director, University Christian Movement in New England, Cambridge, Massachusetts, USA, 1978 - . *Publications:* Published in Images: Women in Transition. *Memberships:* National Campus Ministry Association; Campus Ministry Women; International Association of Women Ministers; National Organization for Women; World Student Christian Federation; Methodist Federation for Social Action. *Honours:* Ordained in United Methodist Church, 1973; Travels to People's Republic of China; Led tour to the USSR. *Hobbies:* International issues; Women's issues; Travel; Reading; Peace and justice work. *Address:* 9A Direnzo Terrace, Vernon Street, Somerville, MA 02145, USA.

BLACKLEY Rebecca Mae (Becky), b. 11 June 1947, Bay Shore, New York, USA. Publisher; Editor; Author; Musician; Teacher. m. Gordon Blackley, 4 July 1974. *Education:* BA, summa cum laude, University of California, Santa Barbara, 1969; Teaching credential, University of British Columbia, Canada, 1971. *Appointments:* Editor, publisher, founder, Autoharpoholic magazine, 1980-; Performed with Bluegrass Band, Woodshed, 1983; Performed as duo with Jim Stevens, 1984; Currently solo, autoharp & guitar with vocals, major music events throughout USA; Teacher, autoharp, festivals & workshops, Davis & Elkins College, West Virginia, 1985-. *Publications:* Author, Harp! The Herald Angels Sing! 1981, Autoharp Book 1983; Editor, Care & Feeding of the Autoharp, 6 volumes 1980-86; Winning Ways on the Autharp, 2 volumes 1985. Record Album, Flower of Loudoun County. *Memberships:* Committee of Small Magazine Editors & Publishers; Sonneck Society; California Traditional Music Society; Phi Beta Kappa. *Hobbies:* Music; Handicrafts; Painting; Screen printing. *Address:* PO Box 504, Brisbane, California 94005, USA.

BLACKMAN Honor, b. London England. Actress. *Creative Works:* Film debut in Fame is the Spur, 1947. Films include: Quartet, 1948; So Long at the Fair, 1948; Conspirator, 1959; Green Grow the Rushes, 1951; Come Die My Love, 1952; The Rainbow Jacket, 1953; The Glass Cage, 1954; Dead Man's Evidence, 1955; A Matter of Who, 1961; Goldfinger, 1964; Life at the Top, 1965; Twist of Sand, 1967; The Virgin and the Gipsy, 1970; To the Devil a Daughter, 1975; Summer Rain, 1976; The Cat and the Canary, 1977. Television appearances include: Four Just Men, 1959; Man of Honour, 1960; Ghost Squad, 1961; Top Secret, 1962; The Avengers, 1962-64; The Explorer, 1968; Visit from a Stranger, 1970; Out Damned Spot, 1972; Wind of Change, 1977; Robin's Nest, 1982; Never the Twain, 1982; The Secret Adversary, 1983; Dr Who, 1986; Voice of the Heart, 1987. *Address:* c/o Michael Lactkin, 2a Warwick Pl. Nth, London, SW1V 1QW, England.

BLACKMORE Susan Jane, b. 29 July 1951, London, England. Parapsychologist; Broadcaster; Writer. m. Tomasz S. Troscianko, 16 Sept. 1977, 1 son, 1 daughter. *Education:* BA, Psychology & Physiology, Oxford University, 1973; MSc Environmental Psychology 1974, PhD Parapsychology 1980, Surrey University. *Appointments:* Part-time Lecturer, London Polytechnic, 1974-79; Lecturer, Surrey University, 1975-80; Research Fellow, Brain & Perception Laboratory, University of Bristol, 1980-. Also: Freelance journalist, TV presenter. *Publications:* Books: Beyond the Body, London, 1982; Adventures of a Parapsychologist, New York, 1986. *Memberships:* Council, Society for Psychical Research; Parapsychological Association. *Hobbies:* Skiing; Gardening; Do-it- Yourself; Painting. *Address:* Brain & Perception Laboratory, University of Bristol, Bristol BS8 1TD, England.

BLACKSTOCK Charity (Pseudonym for Ursula Torday), b. 19 Feb. 1912, London, England. Writer. *Publications:* 60 novels including: (As Ursula Torday) The Ballad Maker of Paris, 1935; No Peace for the Wicked, 1937; The Mirror of the Sun, 1938. (As Paula Allardyce) After the Lady, 1954; The Doctor's Daughter, 1955; A Game of Hazard, 1955; Adam and Evelina, 1956; The Man of Wrath, 1956; Dewey Death, 1956; The Lady and the Pirate, 1957; Southern Folly, 1957; The Foggy, Foggy Dew, 19578; All Men are Murderers, 1958; Beloved Enemy, 1958; My Dear Miss Emma, 1958; The Bitter Conquest, 1959; Death My Lover, 1959; A Marriage Has Been Arranged, 1959; The Briar Patch, 1960; Johnny Danger, 1960; The Exorcism, 1961; Witches' Sabbath, 1961; The Gentle Highwayman, 1961; The Gallant, 1962; Mr Christopoulos, 1963; Adam's Rib, 1963; The Factor's Wife, 1964; The Respectable Miss Parkington-Smith, 1964; When the Sun Goes Down, 1964; Octavia or The Trials of a Romantic Novelist, 1965; The Children, 1966; The Knock at Midnight, 1966; The Moonlighters, 1966; Party in Dolly Creek, 1967; Six Passengers for the Sweet Bird, 1967; Waiting at the Church, 1968; The Melon in the Cornfield, 1969; The Ghost of Archie Gilroy, 1970; The Daughter, 1970; The Encounter, 1971; The Jungle, 1972; The Lonely Strangers, 1972; Miss Jonas's Boy, 1972; The Gentle Sex, 1974; Miss Philadelphia Smith, 1977; Haunting Me, 1978; Miss Charley, 1979; The Rogue's Lady, 1979; With Fondest Thoughts, 1980; The Vixen's Revenge, 1980. (As Charlotte Keppel) Madam You Must Die, 1974; People in Glass Houses, 1975; Ghost Town, 1976; My Name Is Clary Brown, 1976; I Met Murder on the Way, 1977; I Could Be Good to You, 1980; The Villains, 1980; Dream Towers, 1981; The Ghosts of Fontenoy, 1981. *Honour:* Romantic Novelist of the Year. *Address:* 23 Montagu Mansions, London W1H 1LD, England.

BLACKSTOCK Heather Winifred, b. 4 June 1933, Dorrigo, New South Wales, Australia. Artist; Art Teacher. m. Matthew Blackstock, 10 Nov. 1964, 1 son. *Education:* Various art courses, including Mitchell College of Advanced Education, winters 1976-79; Associate Diploma, Creative Arts (distinction), 1982; TAFE Certificate, Sculptural Mechanics, 1985. *Career:* Participant, many exhibitions including: Canberra Agricultural Show, 1979; Royal Easter Show, Sydney, 5 years, In Search of Gold Centennial, Gold Coast, Queensland, 1988; Group exhibitions: Goulburn, New South Wales, 1976, 1979, Canberra, 1978, Ashmore, Queensland, 1982, Nerang Art Festival, Queensland, 1982; 1-man exhibitions: Laggan Community Hall, New South Wales, 1978; St Mary's Community Centre, Crookwell, New South Wales, 1979; Teaching: Art group, Crookwell, 1980; Workshops, Bega and Pambula Art Society, 1980-81; Art, Goulborn College of Advanced Education, 6 weeks 1981-82; Art Teacher (part- time), TAFE College, Benowa Gold Coast, Queensland, currently; Judge, art competitions. *Creative works include:* Works in major collections: Griffith City Collection; Goulborn City Council (2); Albury City Collection: Stonequarry, Blue Circle Collection; Commissioned drawings: Bishopthorpe, Goulborn, 1978; Goulborn Building Society, 1979; Radio 2GN, 1981; Oil painting of Goulborn Building Society building (commission), 1981; Articles for Hinterlander local art paper, 1980-81. *Memberships:* Foundation Member, Australian Society of Miniature Art, Queensland; Exhibiting Member, Royal Art Society, New South Wales; Royal Art Society, Queensland; Foundation Member, Watercolour Society, Brisbane; Foundation Member, Creative Arts Group; Former Publicity Officer, Secretary and Vice-President, Goulborn Art Club; Foundation Committee member (Treasurer), Miniature Art Society. *Honours include:* Over 100 art prizes; Guest Artist, Nerang Art Festival; Commended, Doug Moran National Portrait Prize, 1988; First Prize and overall Trophy Award (Sects. 1-11), R.M. Galley (Sydney), 1989; Bronze Medallion, Bond University Open Award, Save our Sands, 1989. *Hobbies:* Tap dancing; TAFE; Tennis; *Address:* 4 Kurnell Court, Pindari Hills, Worongary, Queensland 4211, Australia.

BLACKSTONE Tessa Ann Vosper, b. 27 Sept. 1942, London, England. College Principal. divorced, 1 son, 1 daughter. *Education:* BSc., 1964; PhD, 1969. *Appointments:* Associate Lecturer, Enfield College, 1965-66; Assistant Lecturer, then Lecturer, Social Administration, LSE, 1966-75; Adviser, Central Policy Review Staff, Cabinet Office, 1975-78; Professor, Educational Administration, University of London

Institute of Education, 1978-83; Deputy Education Officer, then Clerk and Director of Education, ILEA, 1983-87; Special Rowntree Visiting Fellow, Policy Studies Institute, 1987; Master, Birkbeck College, 1988-. *Publications:* Students in Conflict, co-author, 1970; A Fair Start, 1971; Education & Day Care for Young Children in Need, 1973; The Academic Labour Market, jointly, 1974; Social Policy and Administration in Britain, 1975; Disadvantage and Education, jointly, 1982; Educational Policy & Testing Children, jointly, 1983; Politics and Consensus in Modern Britain, jointly, 1988. *Memberships:* Fabian Society, Executive, 1979-, Chairman 1984-85; Arts Council Planning Board, 1986-; Director, Project Fullemploy, 1984-; Director, Royal Opera House, 1987-; Chairman, General Advisory Council, BBC, 1988-. *Honours:* Barroness, Life Peerage, Stoke Newington, Greater London. *Hobbies:* Opera; Ballet; Tennis. *Address:* Birkbeck College, Malet Street, London WC1E 7HX, England.

BLADES Ann, b. 16 Nov. 1947, Vancouver, British Columbia, Canada. Artist; Illustrator of Children's Books. m. David Morrison, 19 Oct. 1984, 2 sons. *Education:* Standard Teaching Certificate, University of British Columbia, 1967; Registered Nurse, BCIT, 1974. *Appointments:* Elementary School Teacher, 1967-71; Registered Nurse, part-time, 1974-80. *Creative works:* Writer, Illustrator, books: Mary of Mile 18; A Boy of Tache; The Cottage at Cresart Beach; By the Sea: An Alphabet Book; Illustrator, books: Jacques the Woodcutter (Michael Macklem); A Salmon for Simon (Betty Waterton); Six Darn Cows (Margaret Laurence); Anna's Pets (Margaret Attwood and Joyce Barkhouse); Pettranella (Betty Waterton); A Candle for Christmas (Jean Speare); Ida and the Wool Smugglers (Sue Ann Alderson); Paintings on sale, Bau Xi Gallery, Vancouver and Toronto. *Memberships:* CANSCAIP. *Honours:* CACL Book of the Year Award for Mary of Mile 18, 1973; Canada Council Children's Literature Award for Illustrations for A Salmon for Simon, 1979; CACL Amelia Frances Howard-Gibbon Award for A Salmon for Simon, 1979; Elizabeth Mrazik-Cleaver Canadian Picture Award for By the Sea: An Alphabet Book, 1986; Canadian Nominee for Hans Christian Andersen Award for Illustration, 1987. *Hobbies:* Gardening; Garage sales. *Address:* 2701 Crescent Drive, Surrey, British Columbia, Canada V4A 3J9.

BLAGBROUGH Elizabeth M., b. 8 Sep. 1926, Orlando, Florida, USA. Fine Arts Appraiser. m. Harry Putnam Blagbrough, 30 June 1951, 1 son, 2 daughters. *Education:* BA, Washington University, St Louis, Missouri, 1949. *Appointments:* Gallery Affiliation, 1948-68; Fine Arts Appraiser, 1970-; Lecturer. *Publications:* Articles in professional journals, USA and Great Britain. *Memberships:* Fellow, American Society of Appraisers, various offices, St Louis Chapter, 1973-77, President, St Louis Chapter, 1977-78, Chairman, ASA APPRAISAL Foundation Advisory Committee, 1989-90, Member, The Appraisal Foundation Advisory Council, Washington, DC, 1990, Advisor, Board of Governors, American Society of Appraisers, 1989-1991; international offices: State Director, Missouri, 1983-84, International Secretary, 1984-86, International Vice-President, 1986-87, International Senior Vice-President, 1987-88, International President, 1988-89, Past Co-Chairman, Fine Arts Recertification Board, Past Chairman, International Board of Publications, Past Co-Chairman, International Board of Examiners, Fine Arts, Chairman, Omniconx, 1990, Chairman, Fine/Decorative Arts Symposia (Cornucopia I-V), 1981-85; Appraisers Association of America Inc; Fellow, Incorporated Society of Valuers and Auctioneers, London, England. *Honours:* Appraiser of the Year, St Louis Chapter, American Society of Appraisers, 1978. *Hobbies:* Music; Sports. *Address:* 340 South Elm, St Louis, MO 63119, USA.

BLAINEY Ann Warriner, b. 22 June 1935, Australia. Author. m. Geoffrey Norman Blainey, 15 Feb. 1957, 1 daughter. *Education:* BA, Honours, University of Melbourne, 1956. *Appointments:* President, Lyceum Club, 1980-82; Council Member, University of Melbourne, 1986-; Board Member, Melbourne University Press, 1986-. *Publications:* The Farthing Poet: A life of Richard Hengist Horne, 1968; Immortal Boy: A Portrait of Leigh Hunt, 1985; Life of Fred Cato, 1990; contributor to journals, magazines. *Memberships:* Board, Percy Grainger Museum; Committee Member, Victoria State Opera Society; Vice President, Australian Bicentenniel Beacons, 1987-88. *Hobbies:* Opera; Cattle Farming; Travel. *Address:* PO Box 257, East Melbourne, VIC 3002, Australia.

BLAIR Margaret Elaine, b. 28 July 1932, Kansas City, Kansas, USA. High School Reading Teacher. m. Carl Raymond Blair, 14 June 1957. 1 daughter. *Education:* BS Education, Central Missouri State University, 1955; MA Education, University of Missouri at Kansas City, 1966. *Appointments:* Kansas City Public School System, 1955-57; Bob Jones University, 1957-88. *Memberships:* President, 1970 & 1985-87, Greenville Club, Business & Professional Women's Club; Public Relations Chairman, South Carolina Business & Professional Women's Club, 1972. Recording Secretary, 1986-88, Alpha Pi Chapter, Delta Kappa Gamma; Recording Secretary, 1975, Chaplain 1984-88, Greenville County Republican Women's Club; International Reading Association. *Honours:* Career Woman of the Year, 1971, Downtown Greenville Business & Professional Women's Club; Boethia Award, 1984, in appreciation for assistance in publication of The Challenger. *Hobbies:* Interest in Fine Arts; Reading; Travel; Golf. *Address:* Greenville, South Carolina, USA.

BLAIR Patricia Jean, b. 17 Mar. 1939, Fairhaven, USA. Director- Corporate Personnel. *Education:* BS, Management, 1978, MBA, 1982, University of San Francisco. *Appointments:* Junior Escrow Officer, Transamerica Title Corp, 1966-68; Administrator, Transamerica Information Services, 1968-72; Manager, Syner Graphics Inc., 1972-80; Director, Adminstrative Services, 1980-85, Director, Corporate Personnel, 1985-, Transamerica Corp. *Publications:* Author-Editor, handbook of Secretaries, 1970. *Memberships:* League of Women Voters; American Compensation Association; American Society Personnel Administrators. *Honours:* Historical Costumes; Early Music; Mystery Buff; Knitting. *Address:* 1619-5th Street, Alameda, California 94111, USA.

BLAIR Ruth Virginia, b. 9 June 1912, St Michael, Alaska, USA. Freelance writer. m. 27 June 1934. 1 son, 1 daughter. *Education:* Graduate, Elementary Education, Seattle Pacific University, 1932; Studied voice privately, NYC, 1937-38; Studied Voice, Seattle, 1929-37; Vocal Soloist, Everett. WN, Urbana & Champaign, Illinois Churches. *Appointments:* Teacher, Everitt, WN, Public Schools, 1932-34; Kindergarten Teacher, 1952- 61; Played piano for fitness classes, Urbana, Illinois; High School, Champaign, Illinois YMCA, 1961-74. *Publications:* Children's Books: Puddle Duck; A Bear Can Hibernate-Why Can't I?; Willa-Willa, the Wishful Witch; Mary's Monster; Numerous articles, stories and poetry published in magazines and journals. *Memberships:* Clearwater Branch, National League of American Pen Women, President 1980-82; Soceity of Children's Book Writers; FL State Poetry Association; Chicago Childrens Reading Roundtable; Friends of the Library. *Honours:* Winner of more than 100 awards for single poems; 3 Writers Digest Awards, 1964, 1965; 1st prize, Children's Story, Florida Free Lance Writers, 1987; Numerous awards in State Contests of National League of American Pen Women, 1980-88. *Hobbies:* Travel; Music; Art; Archaeology. *Address:* 51 Island Way Apt 510, Clearwater, FL 34630, USA.

BLAKE Esther Jean Morrone, b. 8 June 1939, Pueblo, USA. Educator. m. Ronald Edward Blake, 22 Oct. 1961, 1 son, 1 daughter. *Education:* BS, Bethany College, 1961; Diploma, Penrose School of Medical Technology, 1961. *Appointments:* Teacher, St Mary Corwin Hospital, 1956-65; Teacher, Immanuel Lutheran School, 1977-78; Teacher, Rockrimmon Elementary Academy School District, 1978-. *Publications:* It's in the Bag; Maximizing the Mini Page. *Memberships:* NEA;

CEA; PPEA; Council for Elementary Science International; International Reading Association; American Society of Clinical Pathology. *Honour:* Presenter, Colorado Council of International Reading Association; Presenter, Newspaper in Education. *Hobbies:* Teaching Sunday School Classes; Gardening; Bowling; Fishing; Poetry. *Address:* 1405 Yuma St., Colorado Springs, CO 80909, USA.

BLAKE Jane Salley, b. 3 Sep. 1937, Tallahassee, Florida, USA. Small Business Owner; Publisher. m. Arthur C. Blake Jr, 5 Sep. 1959, 1 son, 1 daughter. *Education:* BA, Art, Florida State University. *Appointments:* Executive Secretary, Historic Homes Foundation, 1975-76; Chair, Kentucky Heritage Bicentennial Celebration, 1976; Founder, President, Chairman, Arts Forum Inc, 1978-84; President, Blake Publications Inc, Louisville, Kentucky, 1983-86; President, Owner, The Center Magazine Inc, Louisville, 1986-; President, Owner, J.S.Blake Publications Group, Louisville, 1986-. *Publications:* The Farmington Cookbook (publisher), 2nd Edition, 1974; Public Relations for Volunteers & Entry Level Practitioners (publisher, editor), 1985; Kentucky Heritage Recipes (publisher), 1986; Publisher and executive editor: The Center Magazine, 1983-89; Kentucky Magazine, 1986-89. *Memberships:* Public Relations Society of America; Women in Communications; Executive Committee, The Entrepreneur Society; Business Advocates; Women's Alliance; YWCA; Professional Women's Society; Society of Professional Journalists; Louisville Chamber of Commerce; Sales and Marketing Executives; Advertising Club of Louisville; Vice-President, Art Center Association, 1967-72; Board of Directors, Publicity Chair, Children's Theatre, 1968; Vice-President, Board of Directors, Crusade vs Crime, 1972-74; Board of Directors, Farmington Historic Home, 1973-75, 1977-80; Public Relations Committee, Jefferson County Police Department, 1987-88. *Honours:* 13 Louie Awards, Advertising Club of Louisville, 1981-84; 2 Landmarks of Excellence Awards, Public Relations Society of American and IABC, 1988. *Hobbies:* Reading; Nutrition; Playwriting; Entrepreneurism/Business; Music; Art; Creative problem-solving. *Address:* The Center Magazine Inc, 118 Bauer Avenue, Louisville, KY 40207, USA.

BLAKE Jane, b. London, England. Editor. *Appointments:* Researcher, Field Publications, 1969-71; Sub-Editor, Diary Column, 1971- 76, Editor, 1976-, Anglian Magazine. *Creative Works:* Contributor of Articles to: All magazines published by Field Publications; Hare and Hounds; Country; Times; Daily Telegraph. *Hobby:* Walking. *Address:* Flat 1, 3 Regal Lane, Soham, Cambs CB7 5BA, England.

BLAKESLEE Joan Helen, b. 14 Nov. 1930, New Haven, Connecticut, USA. Physician. *Education:* RN, 1951; BS, Nursing, 1955; MS, Biology, 1960; MD, 1967; Internship, 1967-68; Residency, Internal Medicine, 1968-71. *Appointments:* Solo Practice, Internal Medicine, 1971-81; Associate Medical Director, 1981-86, Medical Director, 1986-, Medical Department, Travelers Insurance Co, Hartford, Connecticut. *Memberships:* Admissions Committee, Hartford County Medical Association; Secretary, Board of Directors, Hartford Medical Society; Connecticut State Medical Society; Connecticut State Medical Examining Board; Parish Council, Sacred Heart Church, Vernon. *Hobbies:* Photography; Travel. *Address:* 15 Lake Street, Vernon, CT 06066, USA.

BLANCH Emma Jeanne, b. 30 Mar. 1920, Brussels, Belgium. Writer. m. William S Blanch, 14 June 1945. *Education:* BSc Education 1959, MSc French in Secondary Education 1961, University of Bridgeport. *Appointments:* French teacher, The Gateway Private School, New Haven, CT, 1955-57; French teacher, Amity Regional Senior High School, Woodbridge, CT, 1959-65; French teacher, West Haven High School, West Haven, CT, 1965-80. *Publications:* 2 collections of French poems: Poemes D'Outre-Mer, 1959; Tourments, 1974; 3 collections of English poems: Golden Glow,

1982; Blossoms, Birds and Berries, 1986; Symphony of Tides, 1988. *Memberships:* Connecticut Poetry Society, 1974-78; The Milford Fine Arts Council, 1975- (Board member 1981-85); The West Haven Council of the Arts, 1979-; Editor in Chief, High Tide, 1981-85 and co-editor, 1976-87; Co-editor, Sound and Waves of West Haven, 1979-; Chairman, national Poetry Contest, 1984, 1985 (Judge, 1986); Conservatory of American Letters, 1988-. *Honours:* Award, Board of Education, City of West Haven, 1981; Award of Distinction from President and Board, Milford Fine Arts Concil, 1982; 1st prize, National Short Story Contest, VEGA Press, 1981; Honorable Mention (7th prize), Florida State Poetry Association, 1983; Cash Award (4th place), International Contest by AHNENE PUBLICATIONS, Maxville, Ontario, Canada; Poetry Contest, 1983; 1st prize, Annual Poetry Contest, 1986; 1st prize in Poetry Contest by Creative With Words Publications, Carmel, California, and numerous other honours and awards. *Hobbies:* Fine lines drawing and illustrations of books; Poetry; Fiction; Lecturing on famous painters of France, England and USA; Editor-Publisher, Laurels, 1985-. *Address:* 21 Ludlow Drive, Milford, CT 06460, USA.

BLANCHARD Helen Mae, b. 17 May 1926, Pender, Nebraska, USA. Federal Manager. m. John Blanchard, 26 June 1946, 1 son, Bruce Blanchard, 1 daughter, Cheryl Sonnenwald. *Appointments:* Physical Science Technician, 1960-75, Head, Navy Sensor Data Bank, 1975-83, Communications Specialist, 1983-84, Head, Visitor Information & Pres. Branch, 1984-85, Head, Technical Information Division, 1985-, all at NEL or NOSC, San Diego. *Publications:* Author, numerous reports on Fleet Testing for US Navy Department; UK Report on Navy Sensor Test Results, 1974. *Memberships:* Toastmasters International: District Governor, San Diego, 1976-77, International Director, 1978-80, 3rd VP, 1982-83, 2nd VP, 1983-84, Senior Vice President, 1984-85, President, 1985-86. *Honours:* Woman of the Year, Navy Electronics Lab, 1971; Award for Conducting Special Study for UK Navy, 1974; Candidate for Federal Woman of the Year, 1977; Award for Instructing NATO Engineers in Norway, 1978; Developing & Conducting Workshops on Better Technical Briefing, 1980. *Hobbies:* Public Speaking; Conducting Technical Briefing Workshops. *Address:* 430 San Antonio Avenue, No 2, San Diego, CA 92106, USA.

BLANCHET Jeanne Ellene Maxant, b. 25 Sept. 1944, Chicago, Illinois, USA. Educator; Lecturer; Ethnic Music Performer. m. William B. Blanchet, 21 Aug. 1981. *Education:* BA, Northwestern University, 1966; MFA, Tokyo, 1970; MA, Arizona State University, 1978; EdD (pending), Illinois State University. *Appointments:* Freelance Artist, 1973-; Ethnic Musical Performer, 1973-; Freelance Writer, 1985-; Arizona State University, 1985-. *Publications:* Original Songs and Verse of the Old (and New) West; Pistol Packin' Mama; Pencil Sketching for the 'Doubting Thomas'; A Song in My Heart (in press). *Memberships:* National League of American pen Women, Local Secretary 1987-88, Vice President, 1988; national press Women; National Rifle Association, Distinguished Expert; Sun Health Foundation; etc. *Honours:* Phi Beta Kappa; Woodrow Wilson Fellowship, 1966; Ada B C Welsh Fellowship, 1979; etc. *Hobbies:* Hiking; Riding; Pistol Marksmanship; Travel; Languages; Miniatures. *Address:* Rio Salado College, West, 10451 Palmeras Dr., Sun City, AZ 85373, USA.

BLANCHFIELD Jonee Catherine (Sierra), b. 26 Aug. 1942, Cape Town, South Africa. Managing Director. m. Patrick Blanchfield, 26 May 1962, 1 son, 1 daughter. *Education:* Diploma, Marketing Management; Retail Marketing Certificate, Johannesburg. *Appointments:* Private Secretary, Rhodesian Printing & Publishing Co., 1959-63; Owner, Director, Employment Consultants, 1965-68; Self employed stage & TV Singer, Fashion Model & Property Marketer, 1969-74; Personnel Manager, Operations Manager, Truworths, 1975-78; Retail Manager, Merchandise Manager, Edgars, 1979-81; Retail Director, Managing Director, Truworths,

1981-. *Memberships:* Fellow, Institute of Directors, UK; Zimbabwe Institute of Management; Director, Zimbabwe National Property Association. *Honours:* Cambrian Cup for Singing, 1958; Miss Rhodesia, entrant in Miss Universe Beauty Pageant, 1961; Businesswoman of the Year, Zimbabwe, 1983; IMM Student of the Year, Zimbabwe, 1983; IMM Student of the Year, Merchandising & Distribution, South Africa, 1983. *Hobbies:* Theatre; Bridge; Tennis; Philosophy; Cooking. *Address:* PO Box 2898, Harare, Zimbabwe.

BLANCO Amanda, b. 23 Oct. 1933, El Salvador. Photographer. m. Mario Escobar, divorced, 15 Sept. 1954, 2 sons, 2 daughters. *Education:* BFA, Brooks Institute, 1970; MFA, Cal Arts-Valencia, California, 1980. *Appointments:* Photographer, Aduio Visual Dept., 1973-78, Photographic Teacher, 1976-78, Calstate Northride; Advanced Photography Teacher, Isomata-USC, Idyllwild, 1980-82. *Publications:* Type-Faces: A Photographic Study of Ward Ritchie, 1988; Richard Hoffman at Seventy, 1985; ISOMATA: The Place and Its People, 1983; About Norman Corwin, 1979; The Many Faces of Jake Zeitlin, 1978. *Memberships:* California Women in Higher Education, Executive Board; American Association of University Women; Chicano News Media Association. *Honours:* Fellowship, Brook Institute of Photography; Ahmanson Foundaitron Grant; etc. *Hobbies:* Painting; Travel. *Address:* 10551 Yarmouth Avenue, Granada Hills, CA 91344, USA.

BLANDING Sandra Ann, b. 16 June 1951, Providence, Rhode Island, USA. Attorney-At-Law. 1 son. *Education:* BS, summa cum laude, Jackson College of Tufts University, 1973; JD, cum laude, National Law Center, George Washington University, Washington DC, 1978. *Appointments:* RI Protection and Advocacy Services, Providence, 1978; Children's Code Commission, Legal Counsel, 1980-; Counsel, Partner 1983-, Revens Blanding, Revens & St. Pierre, Warwick. *Memberships:* RI Bar Association; Delegates, Executive Committee, Kent County Representative, 1981-; RI Bar Association Civil Liberties, 1981-82, 1990; RI Bar Association Federal Bench Bar Committee, 1982-89, Chairperson, 1986-89; Federal Bar Association, 1979-; Assistant Secretary RI Chapter, 1982-83; Secretary, RI Chapter 1983-85, President-Elect 1985-86, President 1986-87; National Delegate 1987-; RI Trial Lawyers; Association, 1978-, Board of Governors, 1987-; RI Women's Bar Association, 1978-, Secretary 1978-80, President 1980-81; National Association of Women Lawyers, 1980-; American Civil Liberties Union, Member of Board of Directors, RI Affiliate, 1981-87; RI Legal Services, Member of Board of Directors, 1987, Chairperson, 1988-90; Industrial Research and Relations Association, 1983-89; National Organization of Social Security Claims Representativo, 1001-, RI Women's Network. *Honours:* Phi Beta Kappa, Tufts University, 1973; Psi Chi, Tufts University, 1972. *Hobbies:* Gardening; Boating; Horseback riding. *Address:* c/o Revens, Blanding, Revens & St. Pierre, 946 Centerville Road, Warwick, RI 02886, USA.

BLANKHART Susan, b. 31 Dec. 1951, Bandoeng, Indonesia. Coordinator, International Women's Affairs. *Education:* Candidate in Geography, 1974; Doctorate in Geography (Non-Western countries), 1978. *Appointments:* Royal Tropical Institute, Amsterdam, 1978; Department of Town and Country Planning, Government of Zambia, 1979-82; Coordinator for International Women's Affairs, Directorate General for International Cooperation, Netherlands Ministry of Foreign Affairs, The Hague, 1983-. *Memberships:* Board Member, Netherlands Council, Women Working in Development Cooperation; Consultative Committee, UNIFEM. *Address:* Ministry of Foreign Affairs DGIS/SA, PO Box 20061, 2500 EB The Hague, The Netherlands.

BLANPAIN Monique Francoise, b. 29 November 1928, Brussels, Belgium. Professor. m. Jean Temmerman, 26 April 1952. *Education:* Licence in Political Science and Diplomacy, 1951; Studies in Psychology. *Appointments:* Various positions, Institut Superieur des Carrieres Auxiliaires de la Medicine, Divisions of Kinesitherapy, Ergotherapy and Podotherapy, 1959-. *Publications:* Introduction a la psychologie; Bases en psychologie, 2nd and 3rd Editions; Visite au Parlement (with J.Temmerman); Various oral presentations. *Memberships:* Federation Belge des Femmes Diplomees des Universites; International Federation of University Women; Society of the Order of Leopold. *Honours:* Chevalier, Order of Leopold. *Hobbies:* Music; Dance (ballet). *Address:* Place du Roi Vainqueur 10/6, 1040 Brussels, Belgium.

BLASER Cathy Barbara, b. 31 Oct. 1950, Cleveland, Ohio, USA. Editor; Theatrical Stage Manager. *Education:* BFA, University of Detroit, 1973; MA, William Paterson College, 1975. *Appointments:* Broadway Shows: Whose Life Is It Anyway; Ain't Misbehavin'; Duet For One; Children of a Lesser God; Penn & Teller; Founder of Broadway Press. *Publications:* Publisher: The New York Theatrical Sourcebook, 1984, 1985-86, 1987 editions; Editor: The Stage Managers Directory, 1984, 1985, 1986, 1987 editions. *Memberships:* United States Institution of Theatre Technology; Actors Equity Association; Stage Managers Association. *Honours:* The Heart of the Center Award, L & G Community Services Center, New York; Dean's Key, University of Detroit; Gamma Pi Epsilon, National Honors Society, University of Detroit; Nomination Theatre Library Association Award. *Hobbies:* Scuba diving; Computer consultant. *Address:* 350 West 85th St No 67, New York, NY 10024, USA.

BLASS Elizabeth Victoria, b. 30 Aug. 1949, Little Rock, Arkansas, USA. Writer; Creative Consultant. *Education:* Graduated, Cranbrook Kingswood, Bloomfield Hills, Michigan, 1967; attended, Florida Presbyterian College, St Petersburg, Florida. *Appointments:* Columnist and Editor, Arkansas Gazette, Little Rock, Arkansas, 1969-77; Marsteller Inc, New York, New York, 1980-82; Copywriter, Robert Landau Associates, New York, 1982-83; Senior Copywriter, The Hanley Partnership, New York, 1982-84; Senior Copywriter, Muir Cornelius Moore, New York, 1988-. *Memberships:* Society of Professional Journalists Sigma Delta Chi; Junior League of Little Rock. *Honours:* Award for Excellence, Society of Technical Communications; Little Rock Metropolitan Drug Abuse Committee, 1972-73; Board Directors, Newburgh, New York, Community Photo-Film Workshop, 1980-83. *Address:* 78 Pomona Road, Suffern, NY 10901, USA.

BLAU Francine Dee, b. New York City, USA. College Professor; Economist. m. Lawrence Max Kahn, 1 Jan. 1979, 1 son, 1 daughter. *Education:* BS, Cornell University, 1966; AM 1969, PhD 1975, Harvard University. *Appointments:* Instructor, Economics, Trinity College Hartford, Connecticut, 1971-74; Research Associate, Ohio State University, 1974-75; Assistant, Associate, Full Professor, Economics & Industrial Relations, University of Illinois Urbana-Champaign, 1975-; Research Associate, National Bureau of Economic Research, Cambridge, Massachusetts, 1988-. *Publications:* Equal Pay in the Office, 1977; Economics of Women, Men & Work, 1986; Contributor, articles to scholarly journals. *Memberships:* American Economic Association; Executive Committee, 1987-89, Industrial Relations Research Association; Past Vice President, Midwest Economics Association. *Honours:* Grants, US Department of Labour, 1971-74, 1977-78, 1979-80. *Hobbies:* Swimming; Aerobics; Crossword puzzles; Reading mystery stories. *Address:* Institute of Labour & Industrial Relations, University of Illinois, 504 East Armory Avenue, Champaign, Illinois 61820, USA.

BLAU Judith R, b. 27 Apr. 1942, Lansing, Michigan, USA. Professor of Sociology. m. Peter M Blau, 31 July 1968. 1 daughter. *Education:* BA 1964, MA 1967, University of Chicago; PhD, Northwestern University, 1972. *Appointments:* Assistant Professor to Associate Professor, State University of New York at Albany, 1978-88; Visiting Associate Professor, New York University, 1986-87; Professor of Sociology, University of North Carolina, Chapel Hill, 1988-. *Publications:* Architects and Firms, 1984; The Shape of Culture, 1989; Cultural Life - Region and Place, with Gail Quets, 1988. *Memberships:* Executive Council, 1987-89, American Sociological Association; Co-Chair, Committee on Professions, Eastern Sociological Society; International Sociological Association; Sociologists for Women in Society. *Honours:* American Council of Learned Societies Award, 1988; Rockefeller Foundation Bellagio Residency, 1988; National Endowment for the Arts research award, 1986; National Science Foundation research grant, 1984-86; National Institutes of Mental Health Postdoctoral Fellowship, 1976-78; US Department of Labor Research grant, 1970-72. *Hobbies:* Travel; Gardening. *Address:* Hamilton Hall, Sociology Department, University of North Carolina, Chapel Hill, North Carolina 27514, USA.

BLAU Zena Smith, b. 4 Aug. 1922, New York, USA. Professor. m. Peter M. Blau, 7 Aug. 1948, divorced 1968, 1 daughter. *Education:* AB, 1943, MSW, 1946, Wayne State University; PhD, Columbia University, 1957. *Appointments:* Assistant Professor, University of Illinois, 1957-65; Senior Research Scientist, Institute for Juvenile Research, Chicago; Associate Professor, Northwestern University, 1969-74; Professor, Richmond College, CUNY, 1975-76; Professor, Sociology, University of Houston, 1976-, Chairman, Sociology Dept., 1976-79. *Publications:* Old Age in a Changing Society, 1973; Aging in a Changing Society, 1981; Black Children/White Children: Competence, Socialization & Social Structure, 1981; Work Retirement & Social Policy, 1985; numerous articles in professional journals. *Memberships:* American Sociological Association; Gerontological Society of America; Society for Sociological Study of Jewry; Sociologists for Women in Society; Society for Study of Social Problems. *Honours:* HEW Social and Rehabilitation Administration Grantee, 1967-72; Texas Dept. Human Resources Grantee, 1977-79. *Address:* Dept. of Sociology, University of Houston-UP, Houston, TX 77204, USA.

BLAXALL Martha, b. 2 Feb. 1942, Haverhill, Massachusetts, USA. Economist. m. 15 May 1970, 2 daughters. *Education:* BA, Economics, Wellesley College, 1963; PhD, International Economics, Fletcher School of Law and Diplomacy, Tufts University, 1971. *Appointments:* Director of Research, Health Care Financing Administration, Washington DC, 1976-79; Director, Office of Utilization and Development, National Marine Fisheries Service, Department of Commerce, 1979-82; President, BBH Corporation, Washington DC, 1982-87; Vice-President, ICF Inc, Fairfax, Virginia, 1987-1989; Senior Consultant, DPAC Inc., Washington, DC, 1990-. *Publications:* Women in the Workplace: The Implications and Occupational Segregation (co-editor). *Memberships:* American Economic Association; Washington Women Economists. *Hobbies:* Tennis; Member, Board of Directors, Washington-Moscow Exchange (people to people association for contacts with Soviet Union). *Address:* 3516 Winfield Lane NW, Washington, DC 20007, USA.

BLEDSOE Janeva Leigh Woods, b. 1 July 1949, Caney, Kansas, USA. Interior Designer. m. Newton Dale Bledsoe, 8 Nov. 1987, 2 sons. *Appointments:* Real Estate Sales, 1973-77; Gesnariade Dept., Alex R. Masson Greenhouse, 1977-80; Cost Estimator, Decker Construction, 1980-82; Interior Designer, Architecture Unlimited, 1982-. *Publications:* Articles in various journals. *Memberships:* Epsilon Sigma Alpha, Delta Rho Chapter, Vice President; Coffeyville Jaycees Jaynes, Secretary Treasurer, 1971; Montgomery Co. March of Dimes Chairman, 1974. *Honours:* Outstanding Sister of Chapter, City & Zone, Epsilon Sigma Alpha, 1974. *Hobbies:* Aerobics; Weight-Lifting; Walking; Camping. *Address:* 1226 W. 2nd Street, Coffeyville, KS 67337, USA.

BLISS Anna Campbell, b. 10 July 1925, Morristown, USA. Artist; Architect. m. Robert Lewis Bliss, 2 Apr. 1949. *Education:* BA,. 1942; M.Arch., Harvard University, 1950. *Appointments:* Partner, Bliss & Campbell, Architects & Consultants, Salt Lake City,

1956-; Lecturer, Color to Professional Groups, 1970-; Consultant. *Creative Works:* Paintings & Prints in Collections of Metropolitan Museum, New York City, Art Institute of Chicago. *Memberships:* American Society of Interior Designers, Chairman, 1976-86; Inter Society Color Council, Board. *Honours:* Graham Foundation Fellowship, 1980; ASID Presidential Citation for Colour, 1981; American Academy in Rome, Mid-Career Fellowship, 1984. *Hobbies:* Travel; Reading; Theatre; Modern Dance; Tennis; Gourmet Cooking. *Address:* 27 University Street, Salt Lake City, UT 84102, USA.

BLISS Lee, b. 9 Aug. 1943, Buffalo, USA. Professor. *Education:* BA, Stanford University, 1965; MA, 1967, PhD, 1972, University of California, Berkeley. *Appointments:* Visiting Assistant Professor, Scripps College, 1972-73; Lecturer, English & Humanities, 1974-75, Assistant Professor, 1975-82, Associae Professor, 1982-88, Professor, 1988-, University of California, Santa Barbara; Visiting Associate Professor, Claremont Graduate School, 1986. *Publications:* The World's Perspective: John Webster and the Jacobean Drama, 1983; Francis Beaumont, 1987. *Memberships:* MLA; Shakespeare Association of America; Renaissance Society of America; Malone Society. *Honours:* Recipient, various honours & awards. *Address:* Dept. of English, University of California, Santa Barbara, CA 93106, USA.

BLISSITT Patricia Ann, b. 23 Sept. 1953, Knoxville, Tennessee, USA. Neuroscience Clinical Nurse Specialist. *Education:* BSc Nursing, High Honours 1976, MSc 1985, University of Tennessee, Memphis; RN, 1976; MSN, CCRN, CNRN. *Appointments:* Medical-Surgical-Trauma ICU Staff Nurse, University of Tennessee Memorial Hospital, Knoxville, 1982-83; Neurosurgical ICU Staff Nurse 1985-86, Neuroscience Clinical Nurse Specialist 1986-, Baptist Memorial Hospital, Memphis. *Publications:* Article, Nursing Management of Diabetic Peripheral Neuropathies; Neuroscience Nursing Speciality Modules & Patient Teaching Sheets. *Memberships:* Offices: Greater Memphis Chapter, American Association of Critical Care Nurses; Mid-South Chapter, American Association of Neuroscience Nurses; American Nurses' Association. *Honours:* Sigma Theta Tau, 1985; Certificates, Critical Care Nursing 1986, Neuroscience Nursing 1987; Biographical recognition. *Hobby:* Music. *Address:* Blair Tower Apartments no. 315, 810 Washington Avenue, Memphis, Tennessee 38105, USA.

BLIX Susanne, b. 29 Oct. 1949, Crawfordsville, Indiana, USA. Physician; Psychiatrist; Child and Adolescent Psychiatrist. m. William Charles McGraw, 20 June 1971. 2 daughters. *Education:* BA, DePauw University, 1971; MD, Indiana University, 1975; Internship, Internal Medicine, 1976; Residency, Psychiatry, 1979; Fellowship, Child Psychiatry, 1981. *Appointments:* Assistant Professor of Psychiatry, Indiana University School of Medicine, 1981-; Assistant Director, Psychiatric Services 1981-85, Director of Psychiatric Services, 1985-, Riley Hospital for Children; Acting Director, Section of Child Psychiatry, 1988; Consultant, Cummins MHC, 1981-84; Consultant, Midtown, MHC, 1984-85. *Publications:* Numerous articles in professional journals. *Memberships:* American Academy of Child and Adolescent Psychiatry; American Medical Association; American Psychiatric Association; Association for Academic Psychiatry; Indiana Council of Child & Adolsecent Psychiatry; Indiana Psychiatric Society; Indiana State Medical Association; Marion Co Medical Society. *Honours:* Alpha Lambda Delta, 1968; Phi Beta Kappa, 1971; Mortar Board, Pres De Pauw U Chapter, 1970-71; Outstanding Sr Woman in Chemistry & Zoology, 1971; Student Chemistry Grant, De Pauw, 1969. *Hobbies:* Children; Church activites; Counted cross stitch. *Address:* Indiana University School of Medicine, Riley Hospital, 3rd Fl North, 702 Barnhill Dr, Indianapolis, IN 46202-5200, USA.

BLOCH Chana (Florence), b. 15 Mar. 1940, New

York City, USA. m. Ariel Bloch, 26 Oct. 1969, 2 sons. *Education:* BA, Cornell University, 1961; MA, Near Eastern & Judaic Studies, 1963, MA, English Literature, 1965, Brandeis University; PhD, English Literature, University of California, Berkeley. *Appointments:* English Dept., Hebrew University, Jerusalem, 1964-67; Dept. Near Eastern Studies, University of California, 1967-69; English, Mills College, 1973-, Chair, English Dept., 1986-89, Lynn T White Junior Professor of English, 1987-. *Publications:* The Window: New & Selected Poems of Dahlia Ravikovitch, editor, translator, 1989; Selected Poems of Yehuda Amichai, editor, translator, 1986; Spelling the Word: George Herbert and the Bible, 1985; The Secrets of the Tribe, poetry, 1981; A Dress of Fire: Poems of Dahlia Ravikovitch, editor, translator, 1978. *Honours:* Discovery Award, 92nd Street Y Poetry Center, 1974; Translation Award, Columbia University Translation Centre, 1978; NEH Fellowship, 1980; Book of the Year Award, Conference on Christianity & Literature, 1986; Translation Award, Bay Area Book Reviewers Association, 1987; Poets and Writers Exchange Writers Award, 1988; NEA Fellowship in Poetry, 1989. *Address:* 12 Menlo Place, Berkeley, CA 94707, USA.

BLOCK Carolyn Rebecca, b. 8 July 1943, Columbus, Ohio, USA. Senior Research Analyst. m. Richard L Block, 30 June 1966. 1 son, 1 daughter. *Education:* BA Social Science, Ohio State University, 1965; MA Sociology 1968, PhD Sociology 1975, University of Chicago. *Appointments:* Lecturer, Loyola University of Chicago, 1968-77; Statistical Analysis Center, Illinois Criminal Justice Information Authority, 1976-; Research consultant, WODC, Ministry of Justice, The Netherlands, 1985-86. *Publications:* Homicide in Chicago, 1986; Numerous articles in professional journals. *Memberships:* American Society of Criminology; American Sociological Association; Criminal Justice Statistics Association; Am. Statistical Association; Research Committee for the Soc of Deviance & Social Control, International Sociological Association. *Honours:* Excellence in Analysis Award, Criminal Justice Statistical Association, 1986; Research grants: Application of Spatial and Temporal Analysis to Law Enforcement, 1987-88; Time Series Pattern Description for Criminal Justice Decision Makers, 1982-83. *Hobby:* Gardening. *Address:* Illinois Criminal Justice Information Authority, 120 South Riverside Plaza, Chicago, Illinois 60606, USA.

BLOCK Ruth S, Director and Consultant. Married. *Education:* BA, Adelphi University. *Appointments:* Executive Vice-President, and Chief Insurance Officer, Equitable Life Assurance Society of the United States, 1080 87; Chairman and CEO Equitable Variable Life Insurance Company, 1981-85; Board Member: Informatics, 1973-76; Equitable General Life Insurance Company, 1977-80; Equitable Casualty Insurance Company, 1983-85; Equitable General of Oklahoma, 1983-85; Medical Information Bureau 1981-82; Equitable Money Market Account, 1981-86; Equitable Tax Free Account, 1981-86; Equitable Investment Management Company 1983-86; Equitable Real Estate Group 1984-86; National Association of Security Dealers 1983-85; Life Underwriter Training Council, 1984-87; YWCA, Stamford, CT., 1982-85; Donaldson, Lukfin and Jenrette, 1984-88; Integrity Life Companies, 1985-86; Monumental National Life 1985-86; Avon Products, Inc, 1985-; Ecolab, Inc, 1985-; Amoco Corporation, 1986-; Tandem Financial Group, 1985-89; Alliance Capital Management, Thirteen Mutual Funds, 1986-. *Memberships:* Emeritus Member, The Research Board; Member: Business Executives for National Security; Women's Forum; Committee of 200; Women's Economic Roundtable; WEAL; YWCA, New York. *Address:* Box 4653, Stamford, CT 06905, USA.

BLOCKSOM Rita Verlene Haynes, b. 13 Sept. 1952, Decatur, Illinois, USA. Educational Consultant; Author. m. (1) Richard Brian Day, 21 June 1970, divorced 1 Apr. 1976. 1 son, 1 daughter. (2) Bruce Willard Blocksom, 22 Nov. 1978. *Education:* BS, Education, Eastern Illinois University, 1984; MA, Education, Wright

State University, 1989. *Appointments:* Director, Private School for Gifted Children, 1980-84; Consulting Editor, 1986-; Educational Consultant, 1984-. *Publications:* Create-A-Kid Workbook series, 1984-86; Preprimary and Primary Gifted, 1988; Gifted Education, 1989. *Memberships:* National Association for Gifted Children; National Association for Education of Young Children; Council for Exceptional Children. *Honours:* Certificate of Merit for Excellence in Publishing from Ohio Association for Gifted Children, 1986, 1987 and 1988; Phi Delta Kappa. *Hobbies:* Reading; Writing; Researching about creativity. *Address:* 7622 Woodland Drive, Newburgh, Indiana 47630, USA.

BLOEDEL Joan Stuart Ross, b. 21 Sept. 1942, Boston, Massachusetts, USA. Artist. m. David S. Bloedel, 25 Aug. 1969. *Education:* BA, Connecticut College, 1964; Yale University, 1964-65; MA 1967, MFA 1968, University of Iowa. *Appointments:* Art instructor: St Nicholas School, Seattle 1969-70, Seattle Pacific University 1970-73, 1988, Green River Community College 1978, City of Seattle 1978-80, University of Washington 1988-. *Creative work includes:* Numerous paintings, prints, assemblages, exhibited Seattle Art Museum 1981, 82, 88, Foster White Gallery 1979-present, Whatcom Museum 1988. Also Book, 50 Northwest Artists, 1983. *Membership:* Charter member, Northwest Print Council. *Honours:* New Proposals, King County Arts Commission, 1976, 1980; Seattle Arts Commission & National Endowment for Arts, 1976; Artist-in-the-City, Seattle, 1978-80; Betty Bowen Memorial Award, Seattle Art Museum, 1981; Artist-in-Residence, Centrum Foundation, & Pilchuck School, 1986. *Hobbies:* Film; Poetry. *Address:* c/o Foster White Gallery, 311 1/2 Occidental Street S, Seattle, Washington 98104, USA.

BLOMDAHL Carolyn Anne, b. 4 Sept. 1959, Houston, Texas, USA. Manager of Member Services, National Glass Association. *Education:* Public Policy Certificate, American Studies Programme, 1981; BS Business Admin & Economics, 1982; MA Biblical Studies, 1986; Masters in Association Management, 1988. *Appointments:* Office of Senator John Tower, US Senate, 1982; US Senate Judiciary Subcommittee on Separation of Powers, 1983; The National Automotive Technicians Education Foundation, 1983-86; National Glass Association, 1986-. *Publication:* Article: Earning Your Masters Makes Sense..in Association Management. *Memberships:* American Society of Association Executives; Associated Institute of Marketing; Director Marketing Association. *Honours:* National Dean's List, 1982; May Queen, The King's College, 1982; Outstanding Young Women of America, 1983, 1086; Summa Cum Laude, The King's College and George Washington University, 1982 and 1988. *Hobbies:* Tennis; Biking; Reading; Travelling; Music; Languages. *Address:* 2349 N Quebec Street, Arlington, VA 22207, USA.

BLOOM Jane Ira, b. 12 Jan. 1955, Boston, Massachusetts, USA. Saxophonist; Composer; Record Producer. m. 10 Sep. 1984. *Education:* Private instrumental study with Joe Viola, Boston, Massachusetts, 1969-77; BA magna cum laude, Music major, Yale University, 1976; MM, Saxophone Performance, Yale School of Music, 1977. *Appointments:* Soprano/Alto Saxophonist, Composer, Leader, Record Producer, 1976-89; Saxophonist, Composer, 1977-78. *Recordings:* We Are, Outline Records, 1978; Second Wind, Outline Records, 1980; Mighty Lights, Enja Records, 1982; As One, JMT Records, 1984; Modern Drama, CBS Records, 1987; Slalom, CBS Records, 1988. *Memberships:* National Space Society. *Honours:* National Endowment for the Arts Grants, 1977, 1985; Downbeat International Critics Poll, for soprano saxophone, 1979-88; 1st Musician commissioned by NASA Documentary Art Program, 1988-89. *Hobby:* Manned and planetary space programme. *Address:* c/o Agency for the Performing Arts, 888 7th Avenue, New York, NY 10106, USA.

BLOOM Pauline, Writer; Teacher; Lecturer; Critic;

Consultant. *Appointments:* Teacher, Writing Courses, Brooklyn College, 1948-69; Conduct own mail course in fiction writing, 1950-. *Publications:* Toby, Law Stenographer, 1959; Analysis of Vanity Fair, 1957; Chapter in Mystery Writer's Handbook, 1956 and 1977; Chapter in Short Story Writing Handbook, 1970; Short story in Killers of The Mind, 1975; Numerous articles and stories in national magazines. *Address:* 20 Plaza Street, Booklyn, NY 11238, USA.

BLOOMQUIST Lorraine E. Colson, b. 28 Ma. 1932, Boston, USA. Professor. m. Carl W. Bloomquist, 6 Aug. 950, 3 sons. *Education:* BS, 1966, MS, 1968, University of Rhode Island; Ed.D., Boston University, 1974. *Appointments:* Physical Education Dept., University of Rhode Island, 1967-. *Publications:* Adapted Aquatics Program Manual, 2nd edition 1987; Curriculum Guide, Weight Control Programmes & nutrition Education, 1976; 19 journal articles. *Memberships:* American College of Sports Medicine; New England Chapter, Past President, Trustee, American College of Sports Medicine; American Alliance of physical Education Health Recreation & Dance. *bb3Honours:* Recipient various honours including: Fellow, American College of Sports Medicine; Phi Kappa Phi. *Hobbies:* International Travel; Swimming; Music. *Address:* Dept. of Physical Education & Health, University of Rhode Island, Kingston, RI 02881, USA.

BLOUCH Susan Elizabeth, b. 23 Aug. 1947, Cleveland, Ohio, USA. Training Specialist. *Education:* BS Education, Miami University, Oxford, 1969; MHRD in progress, University Associates, San Diego. *Appointments:* Program Director, YWCA, 1971-73; Asst Dir, Family Resource Center, 1974-75; Social worker, Supervisor, Program Developer Adult Services, 1976-82; Consultant, Change HRD, 1981-85; Seminar Leader, Learning Centers, Intl, 1984-86; Training Specialist, The Taubman Company, 1985-. *Publications:* It'll Do Model, 1985; Stress Management, 1984; Self Image, 1983; Customer Service. *Memberships:* Lippitt Cluster; ASTD; OD Network. *Honour:* Mortarboard, 1969. *Hobbies:* Marathon swimmer; Reading; Travel; Scrabble. *Address:* The Taubman Company, 200 East Long Lake Road, Bloomfield Hills, Michigan 48303, USA.

BLOUNT Marie-Louise, b. 15 Mar. 1935, Hackensack, New Jersey, USA. Educator; Occupational Therapist. m. Arthur W Blount, 7 Nov. 1964. 1 son, 1 daughter. *Education:* BS, Education, Tufts University, Boston School of Occupational Therapy, 1957; AM, Sociology, Boston University, 1964. *Appointments:* Tufts University, 1967-72; Howard University, 1974-75; Chair, Prog Dir & Associate Professor, Occupational Therapy Department, Towson State University, Maryland, 1976-88; Clin Associate Professor & Dir Basic Progs, Department of Occupational Therapy, New York University, 1988-. *Publications:* Papers: Factors Affecting Faculty Recruitment in Two American Universities, with Gail Maguire; The Contemporary Meaning of Work, 1967 with Louis Orzack; Proceedings of the 1982 Congress of the World Federation of Occupational Therapists, Hamburg, Germany. *Memberships:* Maryland Occupational Therapy Association; American Occupational Therapy Association; World Federation of Occupational Therapists; Sociologists for Women in Society; American Association of University Professors; American Sociological Association. *Honours:* Prize Essay Contest, Tufts University, 1953; Honours, AOTA Registration Examination, 1957; OVR grant, 1956; OVR-AOTA Traineeship, 1962-63; Three AOTA-VRA Traineeships, 1965-68; Maryland Occupational Therapy Associations Recognition of Excellence, 1979; University Merit Award, Towson State University, 1986; Roster of Fellows, American Occupational Therapy Association, 1987. *Hobbies:* Running and Walking; Reading; Films. *Address:* 2 Washington Square Village, Apt 4J, New York, New York 10012, USA.

BLOXHAM Christine Gillian, b. 10 Mar. 1948, Bogner Regis, England. Lecturer; Writer; Broadcaster. m. Norman Richard Blanks, 15 May 1982, 2 sons. *Education:* BA, Honours, History, Leeds University, 1969; AMA, Human History, 1974. *Appointments:* Museum Secretary, Scunthorpe Museum & Art Gallery, 1969-71; Museum Assistant, Banbury Museum, 1971-74; Assistant Keeper, Antiquities, Oxfordshire County Museum, 1974-83; Editor, Embroidery Magazine, 1984-88. *Publications:* The Book of Banbury, 1975; Portrait of Oxfordshire, 1982. *Memberships:* Folk Life Society; Folklore Society. *Hobbies:* Embroidery; Archaeology; Local History. *Address:* 146 Leiden Road, Headington, Oxford OX3 8QU, England.

BLUMBERG Grace Ganz, b. 16 Feb. 1940, New York City, New York, USA. Professor of Law. m. Donald R. Blumberg, 9 Sep. 1959, 1 daughter. *Education:* BA, University of Colorado, 1960; JD, State University of New York, Buffalo, 1971; LLM, Harvard Law School, 1974. *Appointments:* Professor, Law School, State University of New York, Buffalo, 1974-80; Professor, Law School, University of California, Los Angeles, 1980-. *Publications:* Community Property in California, 1987. *Address:* UCLA Law School, 405 Hilgard Avenue, Los Angeles, CA 90024, USA.

BLUMBERG Julia Baum, b. Hazelton, Pennsylvania, USA. Community Leader; Educator. m. Dr Leo Blumberg, 9 Aug. 1938. *Education:* PhB, summa cum laude, Muhlenberg College; Graduate Study, Columbia University, New York University. *Appointments:* Faculty Member, Bethlehem, Pennsylvania Senior High School, Chairman, Survey Committee for Evaluation of Bethlehem Senior High School so that school could become accredited by Middle Atlantic States Association of Colleges & Secondary Schools. *Creative Works:* The Philosophy of Secondary Education; Aims and Objectives; wrote directives on Career Counselling & Group Guidance and Individual Counselling; Adult Jewish Education. *Memberships Include:* Life Member: Betty Emith Sisterhood; B'nai B'rth Women; Hadassah; National Council of Jewish Women; Auxiliary of the Kutz Home for the Aged; Served on Boards of National Federation of Temple Sisterhoods; B'nai B'rth; President, Greater Wilmington Federation of Womens Organization; 56 of the leading womens organizations: AAUW; Business & Professional Women; Church Womens, et al; Active Member of the Wilmington New Century Club; President, Hillel Counsellorship, University of Delaware; Committee Member: Art, Music, International Affairs. *Honours Include:* Recipient, many honours and awards. *Hobbies:* Music; Art; Helping People. *Address:* 1401 Apartments, No 406, 1401 Pennsylvania Avenue, Wilmington, DE 19806, USA.

BLUMBERG Leda, b. 19 July 1956, Mt Kisco, New York, USA. Author; Photographer; Horseback Riding Instructor. m. 4 Sept. 1983, 2 daughters. *Education:* Franconia College, 1974-76. *Appointments:* Teacher, Creator of Nature Exhibits, Teatown Lake Nature Reservation, 1974; Horseback Riding Instructor, Horse Trainer, 1974-; Veterinarian's Assistant, 1980; Author, children's books, Freelance Writer and Photographer, 1980-; Manuscript Editor, Junior Riders, 1985. *Publications:* Books: Pets, 1983; The Simon and Schuster Book of Facts and Fallacies (with Rhoda Blumberg), 1983; The Horselover's Handbook, 1984; Lovebirds, Lizards, and Llamas: Strange and Exotic Pets (with R. Blumberg), 1986; Breezy, 1988; Articles and photographs in numerous periodicals such as The Chronicle of the Horse, Cobblestone, Horse and Rider, Suburban Horseman, Pet Lovers' Gazette, Junior Riders. *Memberships:* Authors Guild; Society of Children's Bookwriters; United States Dressage Federation; American Horse Shows Association; 4-H Club Leader. *Honours:* Winner, numerous horse show championships. *Hobbies:* Outdoor activities (hiking, camping, gardening, cross-country skiing, riding). *Address:* Baptist Church Road, Yorktown Heights, NY 10598, USA.

BLUME Judy, b. 12 Feb. 1938, Elizabeth, New Jersey, USA. Author. m. George Cooper. 1 son, 1 daughter and 1 stepdaughter. *Education:* BS, Education, New York University, 1961. *Publications:* Books: Younger children:

The Pain and the Great One; The One in the Middle Is the Green Kangaroo; Freckle Juice; Tales of a Fourth Grade Nothing; Otherwise Known as Sheila the Great; Superfudge. Older children: Starring Sally J Freedman as Herself; Blubber; Iggie's House; Are You There God? It's Me, Margaret; Then Again, Maybe I Won't; It's Not the End of the World; Deenie; Just As Long As We're Together. Young Adult: Tiger Eyes; Forever. Adults: Wifey; Smart Woman. For parents and kids to share: Letters to Judy: What Kids Wish They Could Tell You. *Memberships:* Founder and Trustee, Kids Fund; Authors Guild Council; PEN; American Center; Board member, Society of Children's Book Writers; Board member, SIECUS (Sex Information and Education Council of the US); Planned Parenthood Advocates; Council, Advisors on the National Coalition Against Censorship. *Honours:* Carl Sandburg Freedom to Read Award, Chicago Public Library, 1984; Civil Liberties Award, American Civil Liberties Union, Atlanta, 1986; John Rock Award, Center for Population Options, Los Angeles, 1986; Honorary doctorate, Humane Letters, Kean College, 1987. *Address:* c/o Harold Ober Associates, 40 East 49th Street, New York, NY 10017, USA.

BLUMENTHAL Eileen Flinder, b. 1 Dec. 1948, New York City, USA. Essayist; Theatre Critic; Professor of Theatre. *Education:* BA, Eng & Am Lit 1968, MA, English & Amer Lit 1968, Brown University; PhD, History of Theater, Yale University, 1977. *Appointments:* Chaminade Coll, Honolulu, 1968-69; Chapman Coll, World Campus Afloat, 1969; Queensborough Community College, NY, 1970-71; Wesleyan University, 1976-77; Rutgers University, 1977-. *Publications:* Joseph Charkin, 1984; Dance of Death: Preserving Cambodian Culture, 1988; Stranger in Paradise: Trance & Transience in Bali, 1984; Reviews and articles in numerous magazines and newspapers. *Memberships:* PEN; Am Theater Critics Assoc. *Honours:* Guggenheim Fellowship, 1988; Woodrow Wilson Fellowship, 1968. *Address:* Theater Arts Dept, Rutgers University, New Brunswick, NJ 08903, USA.

BLYTHE Marguerite Maryanna Elizabeth, b. 17 Feb. 1947, Manhattan, USA. Psychiatrist. *Education:* AB, Barnard College, 1971; MA, Teachers College, 1973; BSN, Cornell University, 1978; MD, University of Cincinnati, 1985. *Appointments:* St Hilda's School, 1971-74; Trees Group, New York, 1974-76; Psychiatric Nurse: Bellevue Hospital, 1978-79, VA 1979-82; University of Cincinnati, 1985-; Psychiatrist, PW Lewis Centre, 1986-. *Publication:* The Christ Tree, musical album, 1975. *Memberships:* American Medical Association; Fellow, American Orthopsychiatric Association; American Psychiatric Association, 1984-; American Psychiatric Association. *Honours:* Recipient, several honours and awards including: Burrows Welcom Fellowship, 1987-89. *Hobbies:* Gardening; Oboe; Calligraphy. *Address:* Dept. of Psychiatry, University of Cincinnati, 231 Bethesda Ave., Cincinnati, OH 45267, USA.

BOADLE-BIBER Margaret Clare, b. 18 Jan. 1943, Australia. Professor of Physiology. m. Thomas Ulrich Leonard Biber, 1 son. *Education:* BSc Special, Physiology, London University, UK, 1964; DPhil, Oxford University, 1967. *Appointments:* USA Instructor 1969-71, Assistant Professor 1971-75, Department of Pharmacology, Yale University School of Medicine; Associate Professor 1975-87, Professor 1987-, Department of Physiology, Medical College of Virginia, Virginia Commonwealth University. *Publications:* Scientific articles, neurotransmitter synthesis & metabolism (specifically catecholamines & 5-hydroxytryptamine), journals including Biochemical Pharmacology, British Journal of Pharmacology, Neurochemisty International. *Memberships:* Society for Neuroscience; American Society for Neurochemistry; American Society of Pharmacology & Experimental Therapeutics; International Society of Neurochemistry. *Honours:* Postgraduate scholarship, biochemical pharmacology, Linacre College, 1964-67; A. B. Coke Memorial Fellow, Yale University School of Medicine, 1967-68; Established Investigator, American Heart Association, 1975- 80. *Hobbies:* Hiking; Skiing; Wildflower Photography. *Address:* Department of Physiology, Box 551 MCV Station, Medical College of Virginia, Virginia Commonwealth University, Richmond, VA 23298, USA.

BOATRIGHT Ann Morgan Long, b. 11 Jan. 1947, Louisville, Kentucky, USA. Dancer; Musician; Choreographer; Pianist; Educator. m. Ned Collins Boatright, Jr, 15 June 1968. 1 daughter. *Education:* Student, Jordan Coll Music, 1960-65; Butler University, 1965-68; BA, SUNY, Plattsburgh, 1970; MM, Ithaca College, 1974, Cert Teacher, NY, Ohio. *Appointments:* Music Teacher, public schools Plattsburgh, Ithaca and Rochester, New York, 1970-76; Head Dance Program Columbus (Ohio) School for Girls, 1977-82; Instructor, Suzuki piano, Capital University, 1982-85; Instructor, Eurythmics, 1982-; Clincian for Ohio Music Teachers Association, 1986-87; Developed Teacher training/Music & Movement, Capital University, 1985-88; past teacher, eurythmics, music, movement, Lake Forest College; Wittenberg University; Ohio State University; Eastern Michigan University; Denison University; Utah State University; Teacher Suzuki and traditional piano, Columbus, 1985-; Ballet soloist with Jordan Coll Music Co, Butler University, Ithaca Ballet Co; Dancer with Indianapolis Civic Ballet Co; Columbus Theatre Ballet Co. Pianist with Butler University String Trio. *Creative works:* Choreography: ballet, musicals & modern dance: Little Match Girl, 1979; Odds 'n Ends, 1980; Crusades, 1982; Ballet of Unhatched Chicks, 1982; Wheels, 1979; Marathon, 1981. *Memberships:* Arts for Peace-Unify Ohio, 1986; Women's service board, Grant Med Ctr; Franklin Park Conservatory; St Mark's Episcopal Church; Jr Council, Columbus Mus Art, Zephyrus League; Music Teachers Nat Assn; Ohio Music Teachers Assn; Nat Guild Piano Teachers; Am Coll Musicians (faculty); Suzuki Assn; Ams Suzuki Assn Ohio. *Hobbies:* Skiing; Bicycling; Travel; Gardening. *Address:* 4000 Newhall Road, Columbus, Ohio 43220, USA.

BOAZ Donalee, b. 8 Apr. 1934, Grand Junction, Colorado, USA. Management Consultant; Psychotherapist. 3 daughters. *Education:* Certificates: Pastoral Ministry, Seattle University, 1978, Clinical Pastoral Education, Virginia Mason Hospital, 1979; BA, Antioch West, 1980; Certificate, Neuro Linguistic Programming, 1983; Cross cultural Study, Lanting Institute, Wu Yi Mnt, Fujian Province, Peoples Republic of China and C G Jung Institute, 1986, 1987. *Appointments:* Owner, Donalee's Studio of Dance, Kirkland, 1952-63; Administrative Assistant, Church of the Redeemer, Kenmore, 1974-76; Counsellor, Eastside Mental Health, Bethell, 1976-79; Psychotherapist, Private Practice, 1979-; Owner, Management Consultant, Optimum Options, 1979-; Member, Adjunct Faculty, Seattle University, 1979-84; Northwest College, Holistic Studies, 1982-84; Huston School of Theology, 1980- 85; Consultant: Government, Business & Non-profit Boards of Management. *Memberships:* Seattle Association of Counseling & Development; National Speaker's Association, Vice President; Episcopal Church Standing Committee on Stewardship, 1980-82; Active, local politics, 1968-80; Associate Member, Clinical Pastoral Education; Northwest Speakers Association. *Hobbies:* Philosophy; Travel; Laughter; Carpentry; Friends; Spirituality. *Address:* Grosvenor House, 500 Wall Street Suite 322, Seattle, WA 98121, USA.

BOBACK Karen Passerella, b. 24 May 1951, Scranton, USA. m. 7 Sept. 1974, 1 son, 1 daughter. *Education:* BS, College Misericordia, 1973; MS, Marywood College, 1977; PhD, University of Pennsylvania, 1985. *Appointments:* Elementary School Teacher, Tunkhannock Area School District, 1973-75; Middle School Guidance Counsellor, Tunkhannock Area School District, 1975-85; Adjunct Professor, Wilkes College, 1985-; Elementary School Teacher, Tunkhannock area School District, 1989-. *Memberships:* PA State Education Association; Delta Kappa Gamma; Alpha Alpha; Alpha Rho; Phi Delta Kappa; Dallas Women of Rotary; Past President, National Federation of Women's Service Clubs. *Honours Include:*

Miss America Preliminary Winner, 1973; Miss Wyoming Valley United Way, 1974; Mrs Pennsylvania, 1979; Mrs America, semi-finalist, 1979; many other honours and awards. *Hobbies:* Reading; Writing; Knitting; Crochet; Travel. *Address:* RD No 3, Box 201, Lakeside Drive, Harvey's Lake, PA 18618, USA.

BODENHEIMER Henriette Hannah, b. 21 July 1898, Cologne, Federal Republic of Germany. *Education:* Certificate, Municipal Lyceum II, Cologne, 1915; Matriculated, Friedrich-Wilhelm University, Bonn, 1921; went on to the College of Agricultural Sciences, Teacher of Agriculture and Domestic Science Certificate, Prussian Ministry of Agriculture, Domains and Forests, Berlin, 1931; Certificate, Vocational Teacher in technical Schools, Prussian Provincial School Board, Berlin. *Career:* Founded and managed, The Wirtschaftliche Frauenschule auf dem Lande, Wolfratshausen, near Munich, 1926-32; Actively involved in pioneer work, Palestine, Israel, 1933; Writing. *Publications:* Published Father's memoirs and works of her own; Written in Hebrew, English and German. English works: The Memoirs (Prelude to Israel, edited her father's work), 1963; The Statutes of the Keren Kayemeth, 1964-65; The Three Delegates Conferences of German Zionists (1897), 1971. German: Max Bodenheimer: So Wurde Israel, 1958, 2nd edition, 1986; Im Anfang der Zionistischen Bewegung, documentation from 1896 to 1905, 1965; Vom Judischen Koln und seinem Anteil an der Entwicklungsgeschichte Israels, 1959; Die Zionisten und das kauserliche Deutschland, 1972; Der Durchbruch des politischen Zionismus in Koln 1890-1900, Dokumentation 321S, 1978; Von den Geburtswehen der Zionistischen Organisation, pamphlet, 1983; Max Bodenheimer: Ein zionistisches Lebensbild, 1986. Hebrew: Wohin mit den russischen Juden?; Jehudea Russia lean?, 1972; Hazionim Wegermaniah Hakaiserit, 1980; Toldoth Tochnith Basel, 1947; Max Bodenheimer: Lebensbeschreibung in Hamesilat Harishonim, 1950; M I Bodenheimer, Darki Lezian Sichronoth, 1952; Bereshit Hatnuah, 1965. *Hobbies:* Travelling; Gardening; Studying the history of art and literature. *Address:* Sadja Gaon Street 8, Jerusalem, Israel.

BODKIN Ruby Emma Pate, b. 11 Mar. 1926, Frostproof, Florida, USA. Vice President, Marketing, The Bodkin Corporation. m. Lawrence Edward Bodkin, 15 Jan. 1949. 1 son, 2 daughters. *Education:* BA, Education, Florida State University, 1948; Florida Banking Institute, 1949; Florida Insurance School, 1950; Jacksonville University, 1968; University of North Florida; Masters Education, University of Florida, 1972; Florida Real Estate Institute, 1975. *Appointments:* Barnett Bank, Avon Park, Florida, 1943; Lewis State Bank, Tallahassee, Florida, 1944-49; John Hunt Insurance Agency, Tallahassee, Florida, 1950-52; Duval County School Board, Jacksonville, Florida, 1952-76; SWD, Real Estate, 1977; Bodkin Corporation, 1985-; Florida Real Estate Broker, 1985-. *Creative Works:* Publications: Karen, 1952; Sketches: An Orange Tree for Me, 1958; Genius Inventor Relaxes, 1958; 100 Teacher Chosen Recipes, 1975; Why I Love Where I Live, 1982; Conception, Birth, Life and Death, 1982; My Mother Lucy Latham Pate, 1982 and numerous other books and articles; You Can Be A Teacher, 1987. *Memberships:* National Association of Realtors; Florida Association of Realtors; Jacksonville Board of Realtors; Florida Education Association; Duval County Classroom Teachers Association, Vice President; NEA Insurance Women of Jacksonville; Florida Association of Insurance Agents; Florida State Board of Education, Licensee; San Jose Country Club and Ponte Vedra; Woman's Club. *Honours include:* American Legion School Award, 1941; Florida House of Rep. Scholarship, 1944; Personnel Problems Committee, State of Florida, 1957; Eligibility List for Principal (Duval County), 1972; EVE Award in Education, 1974; 25 year Service Award, DSCB, 1976, etc; Teacher of the Year, 1981. *Hobbies include:* Genealogy; Writing; Typing; Reading; Walking etc. *Address:* 1149 Molokai Road, Jacksonville, Florida 32216, USA.

BOECKMAN Patricia Ellen (Patti) Kennelly, b. 23 June, Chicago, Illinois, USA. Professional Writer. m. Charles Boeckman, 25 July 1965, 1 daughter. *Education:* BA, North Texas State University, 1962; MA, Texas A&I University, 1972. *Appointments include:* Teacher, English, Spanish, Creative Writing, public schools, 1962-70, 1972-74; Professional writer, 1973-; Consultant & workshop leader, annual Southwest Writers Conference, University of Houston 1974-80, Tri-State Writers Guild seminar 1984; Guest speaker, Byliners writers organisation, 1987. *Publications include:* 24 novels (including one for teenagers, Please Let Me In (bestseller), one inspirational, With the Dawn), over a dozen foreign language editions. Titles include: Captive Heart, Louisiana Lady, Forbidden Affair, Danger in His Arms. Columnist, feature articles, Corpus Christi Voice Chronicle newspaper, 1973; Numerous articles for national publications, 1973-; Children's short story. *Memberships:* Texas Press Women; National Federation of Press Women; Romance Writers of America; Eastern Star. *Honours:* Nominated, one of best children's writers, national Literary Peer Awards, 1985; Biographical listings. *Hobbies:* Painting; Crafts; Reading; Travel; Music, plays electric bass in husband's Dixieland jazz band; Flew in Powder Puff Derby, 1964, as co-pilot. *Address:* 322 Del Mar Boulevard, Corpus Christi, Texas 78404, USA.

BOGAT Marie, b. 29 Dec. 1932, Glen Cove, USA. School Director. m. Lesly L, 16 Aug. 1960, 1 son (deceased), 1 daughter. *Education:* BA, Oberlin College, 1953; MA, Hofstra College, 1955; PhD, University of Alabama, 1975. *Appointments:* Teacher, Malverne Junior High School, New York, 1954-58; Teacher, 1958-, Director 1969-, Union School Port-au-Prince, Haiti. *Publications:* Contributor to: Teaching Overseas, 1984, 1988. *Memberships:* Association of Colombian-Caribbean American Schools, President; Phi Delta Kappa; Kappa Delta Pi; Association for the Advancement of International Education. *Honours:* Ordre National du Travail, Grade de Officier, 1978, Grade de Chevaillier, 1976. ssa 20Hobbies: Theatre; Amateur Acting; Bridge. *Address:* PO Box 515, Port-au-Prince, Haiti.

BOGDANOWICZ Marta, b. 23 Nov. 1943, Cracow, Poland. Psychologist. m. 5 Aug. 1966, 1 son, 1 daughter. *Education:* Master's degree, Psychology, Jagiellonian University, Cracow, 1966; Doctor's degree 1976, Doktor habilitowany & Assistant Professor 1987, University of Gdansk. *Appointments:* (Specialities include: Clinical child psychology, specific difficulties in reading & writing, psychotherapy of children & parents.) Psychologist, Outpatient Clinic for Neurotic Children, Gdansk, 1966; Academic teacher, clinical child psychology, University of Gdansk, 1972. *Publications:* Books: From New-Born to Pre-School Age, 1979; Children's Writing Difficulties, 1983; Materials for Teaching the Diagnostic Methods in Psychology, 1984; Method of the Good Start, 1985; Clinical Child Psychology of Pre-School Children, 1985; Perceptive Motor Integration & Special Difficulties in Reading of Children, 1987; Left- Handedness of Children, 1989; Practical Child Psychology, 1989; Try to be a child, 1990 (translator and wrote preface). *Memberships:* Vice President, International Study Group on Special Educational Needs; Orton Dyslexia Society; Neuropsychology Committee, Polish Academy of Science; Board, Polish Psychologic Society. *Honours:* Silver Cross of Merit, 1972; S. Blachowski All-Poland Award, doctoral thesis, 1979; Award, Ministry of Education, 1987. *Address:* Pomorska 18 B/21, 80-333 Gdansk, Poland.

BOGGS Joan Marie, b. 18 Aug. 1946, Endicott, New York, USA. Scientist; Professor. m. Steven Allan Boggs, 24 May 1968. *Education:* BA, Reed College, 1968; MSc, 1970, PhD, 1975, University of Toronto, Canada. *Appointments:* Senior Research Associate, 1978, Assistant Professor, 1980, Associate Professor, 1985-, Hospital for Sick Children, Toronto, Ontario, Canada; Assistant Professor, 1980, Associate Professor, Department of Clinical Biochemistry, 1985-, University of Toronto. *Publications:* Membrane Fluidity in Biology,

Vols III and IV (edited with R C Aloia), 1985; Over 60 papers in scientific peer-reviewed journals. *Memberships:* Canadian Biochemical Society, Secretary 1983-86; American Society for Neurochemistry; Biophysical Society; New York Academy of Sciences; American Oil Chemists Society; Canadian Association of Women in Science. *Honours:* Postdoctoral Fellowship, 1977-78, Scientist Award, 1983-88, Medical Research Council of Canada, 1975-77; Postdoctoral Fellowship, 1977-78, Career Development Award, 1978-82, Multiple Sclerosis Society of Canada. *Hobbies:* Gardening; Hiking; Canoeing. *Address:* Biochemistry Department, Hospital for Sick Children, 555 University Avenue, Toronto, Ontario M5G 1X8, Canada.

BOGUS SDiane Adams, b. 22 Jan. 1946, Chicago, Illinois, USA. Professor of Literature; Publisher; Editor. *Education:* BA, Stillman College, 1968; MA, Syracuse University, 1969; PhD, Miami University, 1988. *Appointments:* Professor, Freshman Studies, Miles College, 1970-71; English Teacher, Chicago Public Schools, Illinois, 1971-73; English Teacher, Los Angeles Unified Schools, California, 1973-74; Teacher, Compton Unified Schools, 1975-81; Professor of English, Southwest College, 1975-81; Professor of English, Miami University, 1981-84; Professor of American Literature, California State University, 1987-88; Publisher/Editor, WIM Publications. *Publications:* Books: I'm Off to See the Czerbama Wizard, 1970; Women in the Moon, 1979; Sapphire's Sampler, 1982; The Chant of the Women of Magdalena, 1990; Essays, 1989; Contributions to various journals. *Memberships:* National Women's Studies Association; San Francisco Museum; Modern Art; San Francisco Zoological Society; National Organization for Women in the Arts; Committee of Small Press and Magazine Publishers. *Honours:* Syracuse University Fellowship, 1969; Walser Award, Miami University, 1984. *Hobbies:* Music; Walking; Chinese lays and culture; African-American women writers; Poetry reading, performance and writing; Myths; 19th century literature and history; Politics. *Address:* 3601 Crowell Road 100, Turlock, CA 95380, USA.

BOHANNON-KAPLAN Margaret Anne, b. 6 July 1937, Oakland, California, USA. Publisher; Speaker; Author; Attorney. m. Melvin Jordan Kaplan, 2 Feb. 1961, 5 sons. *Education:* BA, Philosophy, University of California, 1960; LLB Law, La Salle Chicago, 1981. *Appointments:* Property Management and Investments, Kaplan Real Estate, 1961-77; Consultant Financial Planning Law, Wellington Financial, San Francisco, 1977-, and Carmel Branch, 1982-; Publishing & Advertising Carmel, 1983-. *Publications:* Everyone's Guide to Financial Planning, 1984; The Election Process, 1988; The Deficit, 1988; American Deficit, 1988; Social Security, 1986; Writes and lectures under pseudonym, Helen P. Rogers. *Memberhips:* CA Real Estate Association; CA and American Bar Associations; International Association for Financial Planning; Institute of Certified Financial Planners; International Platform Association; Federalist Society; Estate Planning Council; National Center for Financial Education. *Hobbies:* Figure Skating; Hiking. *Address:* PO Box 223159, Carmel, CA 93923, USA.

BOHNEN Mollyn V, b. 1 Nov. 1941, Aklan, Philippines. Professor, Nursing. m. Dr Robert F Bohnen, 20 June 1965. 2 sons; 1 daughter. *Education:* BS, Nursing, University of The Philippines, 1962; MS, Nursing, University of Utah, 1971; Doctor of Education, University of San Francisco, 1984. *Appointments:* Lecturer 1979-82, Assistant Professor 1982-84, Associate Professor 1984-87, Professor 1987-, California State University, Sacramento. *Creative Work:* Bohnen Maternal Receptivity to Instruction Clinical Nursing Model. *Memberships:* American Nurses Association; Sigma Theta Tau, International Honor Society of Nursing; University of the Philippines Alumni Association. *Honours:* Certificate of Appreciation, Filipino Association of Nurses in Sacramento (FANS); Doctoral Dissertation presented at Doctoral Saturday, University of San Francisco; Philippine Delegate to World Girl Scout Jamboree in Du Valais, Switzerland, Baden Powell Centenial. *Hobbies:* Travel; Classical music; Match book collection; Sports. *Address:* 5670 Rolling Oak Drive, Sacramento, CA 95841, USA.

BOHNING, Elizabeth, b. 26 June 1915, Brooklyn, USA. Professor Emeritus. m. William H. Bohning, 18 Aug. 1943, 2 daughters. *Education:* BA, Wellesley College, 1936; MA, 1938, PhD, 1943, Bryn Mawr. *Appointments:* Faculty Member, Language & Literature, University of Delaware, 1947-85, Department Chairman, 1971-78. *Publications:* The Concept 'Sage' in Nibelungen Criticism; 40 articles in professional journals. *Memberships:* American Association of Teachers of German; Delta Phi Alpha; Phi Beta Kappa; Phi Kappa Phi; Board of Directors, Delaware Library Association. *Honours:* Lindbeck Award, 1962; Goethe Hanus Award, 1982; Delaware Council for the Teaching of Foreign Languages, Teacher of the Year, 1984. *Address:* Box 574, Newark, DE 19715, USA.

BOHRK Gisela, b. 8 June 1945, Leipzig, German Democratic Republic. Minister for Women. 1 daughter. *Appointments:* Technical Assistant, Mathematics; Teacher; Member, Parliament of Schleswig-Holstein, FRG, 1975; Minister for Women, FRG, 1988-. *Memberships:* Social Democratic Party of Germany, 1970; Numerous responsible positions in different Committees of Social Democratic Party of West Germany. *Hobby:* Cooking. *Address:* Minister for Women of Schleswig-Holstein, Beseler Allee 41, 2300 Kiel, Fedaral Rupublic of Germany.

BOIMAN Donna Rae, b. 13 Jan. 1946, Columbus, Ohio, USA. President, Central Ohio Art Academy; Educator; Professional Artist, Corporate. m. David Charles Boiman, 8 Dec. 1973. *Education:* Ohio State University, 1964-66 and 1966-69; BSc Pharmacy, College of Pharmacy, 1969; Columbus College of Art and Design, 1979-83. *Appointments:* Registered Pharmacist-Manager Retail, Cleveland, Ohio, 1970-73; Pharmacist-Manager Retail, Columbus, Ohio, 1973-77; Owner, L'Artiste, Reynoldsburg, Ohio, 1977-81; President, Central Ohio Art Academy, Reynoldsburg, Ohio, 1981-. *Creative Works include:* Painting: Free Flow Series, opened 1984 Zanesville Art Center; Split Field Series, opened 1985 Capital University Law Library; Photographs: Human nature, opened 1985 Columbus Art Museum; New Surfaces-New Lights, opened 1986 in Franklin University Gallery; Book: Anatomy and Structure: A Guide for Young Artists, 1988. *Memberships:* National Society of Layerists in Multimedia; Allied Artists of America; Central Ohio Watercolour Society, President, 1983-84; Pennsylvania Society of Watercolour Painters; Columbus Art League; Ohio State University Alumni Association; Ohio State University Pharmacy Alumni Association, Charter Member; American Quarterhorse Association. *Honours:* Numerous awards, 1977-1987 in painting and photography; Artworks 1983, 1985, celebrating Women in the Arts, invitational; Mayoral Appointment to Municipal Gallery Consultant, 1986-87, City of Reynoldsburg; John Lennon Memorial Award for Arts, 1987, International Art Challenge, Los Angeles; Infinite Diversity-Infinite Combination, Massillon Museum, 1987 invitational; Nominated, YWCA Women of Achievement, 1988. *Hobbies:* Show horses & Showhorse jumping; Dressage; Skiing; White water river running. *Address:* c/o Central Ohio Art Academy, 7297 E Main Street, Reynoldsburg, Ohio 43068, USA.

BOIVIN Carole Anne, b. 5 Mar. 1957, Quebec City, Canada. Sports Marketing Manager. *Education:* BSc, Occupational Therapy, McGill University, 1978; MBA, University of Western Ontario, 1983. *Appointments:* Occupational Therapist, Montreal Children's Hospital, 1979-81; General Foods, 1982, Bank of Nova Scotia, 1983-84; Holiday Inn - Canada, 1984-88; Director Trans World International - Canada, International Management Group, 1988-. *Memberships:* Travel Tourism Research Association; American Marketing Institute; Toronto Women's MBA Association; Multiple Sclerosis Association. *Honours:* Honours, Canadian

Securities Institute. *Hobbies:* Skiing; Tennis; Golf; Aerobics; Knitting; Drawing. *Address:* 150 Bloor Street W, Suite 630, Toronto, Canada M5S 2X9.

BOJARSKA Anna, b. 1 Oct. 1948, Warsaw, Poland. Writer. 1 son. *Education:* MA, Philosophy, University of Warsaw. *Publications:* Author of books including novels: Varnish, 1979; Me, 1984; Aqitka, 1987; Glory of the Lunapart, 1988; also 2 volumes of essays. Play, A Lesson of Polish, first staged by A. Wajda, Warsaw, 1988. Screenplays for television. Some underground publications under a pen-name. *Honours:* The Maximilian Kolbe-Reinhold Schneider Peace Award,Hamburg, 1976; The Pol-Cul Foundation Prize, Sydney, 1986; Prize of the Committee of the Independent Culture for the best polish essayist, Warsaw, 1988. *Hobbies:* Astrology; Tarot; Occult sciences. *Address:* Targowa 84/14, 03-448 Warsaw, Poland.

BOJAXHIU Mother Tereza, b. 27 Aug. 1910, Skopje, Yugoslavia. Roman Catholic Nun. *Appointments:* Joined Loreto Sisters, Rathfarnam, Republic of Ireland, 1929; Moved to Calcutta, India, January 1929; Founded, Missionaries of Charity (Sisters), 1950; Missionary Brothers of Charity, 1963; International Co-Workers of Mother Tereza which includes Active and Sick and Suffering Coi-Workers, Youth Co-Workers, officially established, 1969; Her works of love include: Silum Schools; Nirmal Friday Homes for Sick and Dying Street Cases; Shishu Bhavan Homes for Unwanted, Crippled and Mentally-retarded Children; Mobile centres and General Clinics for the Malnourished; Mobile Clinics and Rehabilitation Centres for the malnourished; Homes for Drug Addicts and Alcoholics; Night Shelters for the Homedless; natural Family Planning and Visiting of Families in Need; Relief Work, in cash and kind. *Awards:* Padma Shri, 1962; Roman Magsaysay Internnational Award, 1971; Pope John XXIII Peace Prize, 1971; Kennedy International Award, 1971; Jwaharlal Nehru International Award, 1972; The Templeton Foundation Prize, 1973; The First Albert Schweitzer International Prize, 19785; Order of the British Empire, 1978; Nobel Peace Prize, 1979; BharAT Ratna, 1980. *Address:* 116 54A Acharya Jagadish Chandra Bose Road, Calcutta 700016, India.

BOLAND Hon. Janet Lang, b. 6 Dec. 1928, Kitchener, Canada. Judge. m. 1 Oct. 1949, 2 sons. *Education:* BA, University of Western Ontario; DCL (Hon.), Wilfrid Laurier University, 1974; LLD, Hon, 1976. *Appointments:* Called to Bar of Ontario, 1950; QC, 1966; Private Law Practice, 1950; Joined White, Bristol, Beck & Phipps, Toronto, 1958; Partner, Lang, Mitchener, Farquharson, Cranston & Wright, Toronto, 1968; Appointed Judge, County of York, 1972; Judge, Trial Division, Supremem Court of Ontario, 1976-. *Hobbies:* Skiing; Tennis; Travel. *Address:* 164 Inglewood Dr., Toronto, Ontario, M4T 1H8, Canada.

BOLES Shari Lynne Reynolds, b. 20 Nov. 1949, Clinton, Iowa, USA. Owner, Typing and Word Processing Service. m. Glen Ernest Boles, 24 May 1985, 1 son, 3 stepsons, 1 stepdaughter. *Education:* Date Entry Operator Studies, Kees Business College, 1975; Degree in Psychology/Humanities, Sauk Valley College, Association of Liberal Studies, 1985. *Appointments:* General Electric, 1968-70; Precision Service Electronics Inc, 1970-72; Systems Management Associates Inc, 1978-80; Western Temporaries Inc, 1985-88; Owner, Scotties Typing and Word Processing Service, Morrison, Illinois, 1988-; Legally deaf individual. *Publications:* The Doll's Corner, newspaper column in Whiteside Sentinel, Morrison, 1988-89. *Memberships:* Clinton Area Association of Hearing Impaired, Secretary and Board Member 1988-89; Northwestern Illinois Center for Independent Living, Board Member 1988-89. *Hobbies:* Working with deaf adults teaching Bible studies in Sunday School; ASL and SEE languages for the deaf; Hand quilting; Making porcelain dolls and miniature dolls-houses; Volunteer, United Way Drive and local youth clubs, 1986-87; Coaching Little League, 1984. *Address:* 802 Keith Drive, Morrison, IL 61270, USA.

BOLEY Jacqueline, b. 14 Apr. 1951, Columbus, Ohio, USA. Professor. *Education:* Columbia University, 1966-68; Licenza Ginnasiale, Liceo G Parini, Milan, Italy, 1967; BA, Cornell University, 1970; VBA 1973, MA 1978, Cambridge University, England; University of London, 1973- 80; Trinity College of Music, London, England, 1975-80 (harpsichord). *Appointments:* Lecturer in Classics, Trinity College, Hartford, Connecticut, 1983-85; Lecturer in Italian, Central Connecticut State University, 1985-. *Publications:* The Hittite hark - Construction, 1984; The Sentence Particles in Old and Middle Hittite, 1989; Articles on Hittite and Indo-European, 1985-90; Latin poetry, 1985-87. *Membership:* American Oriental Society. *Honours:* National Endowment for the Humanities grants, 1986 Munich, Germany; 1988 Berkeley, California, USA; Women's Studies grant, Trinity College, 1984. *Hobbies:* Harpsichord building; Skiing; Gardening. *Address:* Old Saybrook, Connecticut, USA.

BOLEY BOLAFFIO Rita, b. 7 June 1898, Trieste, Italy. Artist. m. Orville F. Boley, 22 Dec. 1918, 2 sons. *Education:* Faculty of Architecture (Josef Hoffmann), Kunstgewerbeschule, Vienna, Austria; Violin Diploma, Music Conservatory, Vienna. *Creative work includes:* Murals, display work, for private commissions & leading department stores, USA. *Memberships:* American Red Cross Arts & Crafts Unit, World War II; Artists of America. *Honours:* Exhibits, various museums & galleries; Publications, USA, Europe, including encyclopaedias on contemporary art; Critical reviews, New York Times & other newspapers. *Hobbies:* Horseback riding; Skiing; Swimming. *Address:* 310 West 106th Street, New York, NY 10025, USA.

BOLI Sarah Helen Collins, b. 18 July 1958, Warren, Pennsylvania, USA. Property Manager. m. Robert McPherson Boli, 22 Dec. 1982. 1 son. *Education:* AA Liberal Arts (Honours), Jamestown Community College, 1978; BA, Environmental Studies, Alfred University, 1980; Presently studying, Landscape Architecture, University of Washington. *Appointments:* Director, Commercial Operations, Tech-Turf Inc, 1980-81; Image Analyst and Intelligence Analyst, US Army, 1981-84; Property Manager, Pacific Land Assoc, 1984-; Owner, Plandscape, 1987-. *Publication:* Field Guide Jamestown Community College Preserve, 1978. *Memberships:* City of Enumclaw Design Review Board, 1987-; District IV Washington State Business and Professional Women Young Career Woman Chair, 1987-88; City of Enumclaw Tourism Committee, 1985-87; American Society for Photogrammetry and Remote Sensing; American Society of Landscape Architects. *Honours:* Washington State Chapter American Society of Landscape Architects Student Merit Award, 1988; District IV Washington State Business and Professional Women Young Career Woman, 1986; United States Army Achievement Medal, 1984; Jamestown Community College Phalynx Society, 1978; National Honor Society, New York State Music Association Award, I Dare You Award, Panama Central School Drama Award, John Phillip Sousa Award, 1976. *Hobbies:* Skiing; Golf; Painting; Landscape design. *Address:* 1334 Roosevelt Way East, Enumclaw, WA 98022, USA.

BOLLINGER Taree (Teresa Vir), b. 21 Dec. 1949, Forks, Washington, USA. Editor; Writer. m. Robert Patrick Bollinger, 5 May 1979, 1 son, 1 daughter. *Education:* Washington State University, 1967-71. *Appointments:* Advertising copy writer, Sears, Seattle, Washington, 1973-79; Manager, forms & procedures, Airborne Freight Corporation, Seattle, 1973-79; Office manager, Stan Wiley Real Estate, Portland, Oregon, 1979-81; Chief executive officer, Word Marketing, editorial & writing services, 1981-. *Publications include:* Author, Baby Gear Guide, 1985; Contributor, Baby!, Expecting, Family Circle, Glamour, Baby Talk magazines; Editor, Journal of Forms Management 1981-88, Today's Home: Investment 1985-86, Inside Pocatello 1985, In Focus 1988-, Templates for Information Resources Management 1988-. *Memberships:* Authors Guild; Authors League of America; Society of Childrens Book Writers. *Hobbies:* Golf; Quilting; Computers; Gardening.

Address: 6431 Linville Court, Moorpark, California 93021, USA.

BOLT Christine Anne, b. 10 Aug. 1940, Nelson, Lancashire, England. Professor of American History; University Pro-Vice-Chancellor. m. 18 Aug. 1962. *Education:* Westfield College, University of London, 1958-61; BA Hons, History, 1961; University College, London, 1963-65; PhD, London, 1966. *Appointments:* Assistant Lecturer, 1966-67; Lecturer, 1967-73; Senior Lecturer, 1973-77, Reader, 1978-84, Professor of American History, 1984-, History Board of Studies, University of Kent, Canterbury; Visiting Assistant Professor of History, Wayne State University, Detroit, USA, 1969-70; Visiting Associate Professor, Northern Illinois University, USA, 1970-71. *Publications:* Books: The Anti-Slavery Movement and Reconstruction, 1969; Victorian Attitudes to Race, 1971; A History of the U.S.A., 1974; Power and Protest in American Life (with A.Barbrook), 1980; Anti-Slavery, Religion and Reform (with S.Drescher), 1980; American Indian Policy and American Reform, 1987, paperback edition 1989. *Memberships:* British Association for American Studies; Historical Association; American Historical Association. *Honours:* For research in USA: British Academy/Newberry Library Fellowshsip, 1975; Huntington Library Fellowship, 1975; Leverhulme Trust Fund Fellowship, 1978; Wolfson Foundation Fellowship, 1978; Leverhulme Trust Fund Grant, 1987; Appointed Pro-Vice-Chancellor, University of Kent, 1988-91. *Address:* Eliot College, University of Kent, Canterbury, Kent CT2 7NS, England.

BOMBECK Erma Louise, b. 21 Feb. 1927, Dayton, Ohio, USA. Author; Syndicated Columnist. m. William L. Bombeck, 13 Aug. 1949, 2 sons, 1 daughter. *Education:* BA, University of Dayton, 1949. *Publications:* Books: At Wit's End, 1967; Just Wait Till You Have Children Of Your Own!, 1971; I Lost Everything In The Post-Natal Depression, 1974; The Grass Is Always Greener Over The Septic Tank, 1976; If Life Is A Bowl Of Cherries - What Am I Doing In The Pits?, 1978; Aunt Erma's Cope Book, 1979; Motherhood: The Second Oldest Profession, 1983; Family - The Ties That Bind...And Gag!, 1987; I Want To Grow Hair, I Want To Grow Up, I Want To Go To Boise, 1990. *Honours:* Theta Sigma Phi Headliner Award, 1969; Mark Twain Award, 1973; 14 honorary doctorates, 1974-88; Golden Plate Award, American Academy of Achievement, 1978; Grand Marshal, Tournament of Roses Parade, 1986. *Address:* Universal Press Syndicate, 4900 Main Street, Kansas City, MO 64112, USA.

BOMIA Goldie Rose, b. 7 June 1949, Monroe, Michigan, USA. Lyricist; Song Writer; Freelance Writer; Barber Stylist. m. 23 Nov. 1968, 1 son, 1 daughter. *Education:* Stautzenberger Business College, 1967-68; Certificate, Licence, Ohio State Barber Styling College, 1977-78. *Appointments:* Owner, President; Williams Hair Care Centre, Indianapolis, 1979-; Bomia & Carman Enterprises Inc publishing company, 1984-. *Creative work includes:* Numerous song lyrics and/or music; 13 poetry anthologies, 1982-; 2 songs recorded on album; Music contract pending. *Memberships:* Association of Songwriters, Composers & Performers; Arizona, & Indianapolis Songwriters Associations; American Astrology Association. *Honours:* Golden Poet Awards 1985, 86, 88, 13 merit awards 1982-, World of Poetry Press. *Hobbies:* Music; Travel; Astrology; Numerology; Cycling; Bowling. *Address:* Bomia & Carman Enterprises Inc, 11322 Allens Cove Beach, Luwa Pier, MI 48157, USA.

BOND Alma Halbert, b. Philadelphia, Pennsylvania, USA. Psychoanalyst; Author; Lecturer; Teacher. m. Rudy Bond, 1 Feb. 1948, 2 sons, 1 daughter. *Education:* BA Honours, Temple University, 1944; MA, New York University, 1951; PhD, Developmental Psychology, Columbia University, 1961. *Appointments:* Private Pactice, Psychoanalysis, 1953-; Fellow, Faculty Member, Training Analyst, Institute of Psychoanalytic Training & Research (IPTR), 1963-; Author, Lecturer. *Publications:* Co-editor with Dr Gladys Natchez, Guru

Therapist's Notebook, 1976; Author: Aspects of Psychoanalysis, 1983; Who Killed Virginia Woolf: Psychobiography, 1989; On Becoming a Grandparent, in preparation; Numerous professional articles. *Memberships:* IPTAR; American Psychological Association; Modern Language Association. *Honours include:* Diplomate, American Board of Psychotherapy, 1987; Fellow, IPTAR, 1863; Research Grant, Similac, 1960; Various Academic Honours, School & College. *Hobbies:* Reading; Poetry; Running; Swimming; Sculpting. *Address:* 11 East 87th Street, New York, NY 10128, USA.

BOND Sharon Anne, b. 1 July 1947, Belleville, Illinois, USA. Banker. m. 18 Mar. 1972. *Education:* BSc., Cornell University, 1969; MA, Urban Planning, Michigan State University, 1972. *Appointments:* Administrative Assistant, Urban Extension, University of Missouri, 1969- 70; Urban Planner, City of East Lansing, 1970-72; Assistant Director, Michigan State Housing Development Authority, 1972-75; General Manager, Real Estate Operations, 1975-79; Vice President, Properties, Continental Illinois Corp, 1979-. *Memberships:* National Trust for Historic Preservation; Landmarks Preservation Council of Illinois; Chicago Historical Society. *Hobbies:* Historical Architecture; Antique Furniture; Porcelain; Textiles; Fine Arts; Classical Music; Needlework. *Address:* 9437 Hamlin Avenue, Evanston, IL 60203, USA.

BONDAR Roberta Lynn, b. 4 Dec. 1945, Sault Ste Marie, Ontario, Canada. Neurologist; Researcher; Payload Specialist. *Education:* BS, Zoology, Agriculture, University of Guelph, 1968; MSc, Experimental Pathology, University of Western Ontario, 1971; Doctorate, Neurobiology, University of Toronto, 1974; MD, McMaster University, 1977; Fellow, Neurology, Royal College of Physican and Surgeons of Canada, 1981; Intern, Toronto General Hospital; Postgraduate training: Neurology, University of Western Ontario; Neuro- Ophthalmology, Tuft's New England Medical Center, Boston, USA and Playfair Neuroscience Unit, Toronto Western Hospital. *Appointments include:* Assistant Professor, Medicine (Neurology), McMaster University, Director, Multiple Sclerosis Clinic, Hamilton-Wentworth Region, 1982-; Payload Specialist, Canadian Astronaut Program, Space Division, National Research Council, Ottawa, 1984-; Civil Aviation Medical Examiner. *Memberships:* American Academy of Neurology; Canadian Neurological Society; Canadian Aeronautics and Space Institute; Canadian Society of Aerospace Medicine; College of Physicians and Surgeons of Ontario; Flying Ninety-Nines; Aerospace Medical Association; International Women Pilots Association; Canadian Stroke Society; Royal Astronomical Society of Canada. *Honours:* National Research Council of Canada Scholarship, 1971-4; Fellowships: Ontario Graduate and National Research Council of Canada Postdoctorate, 1971; Ontario Ministry of Health, and Medical Research Council, 1981; Career Scientist Award, Ontario Ministry of Health, 1982; Honorary Member: Zonta International, 1984; Canadian Federation of University Women, 1985; Girl Guides of Canada (Life), 1986; Vanier Award, Jaycees of Canada, 1985; Co-recipient, F.W.(Casey) Baldwin Award for Best Paper, Canadian Aeronautics and Space Journal, 1985. *Hobbies:* Flying; Hot air ballooning; Canoeing; Biking; Target Shooting; Fishing; Cross-country skiing; Squash. *Address:* Canadian Astronaut Program, Space Division, National Research Council, Ottawa, Ontario, Canada K1A 0R6.

BONETTI Ruth Helen, b. 4 Sept. 1951, Hughenden, Queensland, Australia. Musician; Teacher; Writer. m. Antoni Bonetti, 16 Mar. 1974. 2 sons. *Education:* AMusA, 1972; BMus (Performing) University of Queensland, 1973; Associate, Royal College of Music, London, England, 1976. *Appointments:* Principal Clarinettist and soloist, Queensland Youth Orchestra tour of Switzerland and Italy, 1972; Freelance with Queensland Symphony Orchestra, 1969-72; Principal clarinettist, Norrlands Opera and Regionmusiken, Sweden, 1976-77; Masterclasses, concerts in Australia,

1987; Teacher, Queensland Conservatorium of Music, Australia, 1983-; Performed at numerous festivals in Australia and Europe. *Publications:* Enjoy Playing the Clarinet, 1985; Numerous articles for professional journals. *Membership:* Secretary/Editor, Queensland Clarinet Society. *Honours:* Winner, ABC Instrumental Concerto Complettion, Queensland, 1971; Participated in Hoguakt Ceremony, Stockholm Palace (first foreigner to be included); Numerous recordings. *Hobbies:* Sculpture; Sketching; Bushwalking; Travelling; Reading. *Address:* 17 Allambic St, The Gap, Queensland 4061, Australia.

BONHAM Barbara Lee, b. 27 Sept. 1926, Franklin, Nebraska, USA. Novelist. m. 24 Dec. 1950. *Education:* University of Nebraska. *Publications:* Juvenile books: Challenge of the Prairie, 1965; Crisis at Fort Laramie, 1967; To Secure the Blessings of Liberty, 1970; Willa Cather, 1970; Heroes of the Wild West, 1970. Adult Novels: Diagnosis: Love, 1964; Army Nurse, 1965; Nina Stewart, RN, 1966; Sweet and Bitter Fancy, 1976; Jasmine for My Grave (pseudonym Sara North), 1978; Proud Passion, 1976; Passion's Prize, 1977; Dance of Desire, 1978; The Dark Side of Passion, 1980; Green Willow, 1982; Bittersweet, 1984. *Memberships:* Nebraska Writers Guild; Authors Guild. *Honour:* New York Times Paperback Best Seller List with Passion's Price. *Hobbies:* Travel; Gourmet dining. *Address:* Route 2 Box 123, Franklin, Nebraska 68939, USA.

BONNER Ruth Johanna Margarethe, b. 6 Aug. 1917, Zurich, Switzerland. Retired. m. Charles Edmond Bradlaugh Bonner, 1937, 1 son, 2 daughters. *Education:* Diploma, Languags, University of Lausanne. *Appointments:* London Institute of Child Psychology; Language Teacher; Language Examiner, Cambridge Examination Board; Executive Secretary, International Schools Association (DSA); International Baccalaureate Organization, 1964-80; ISA Consultant: Health & Social Education. *Publications:* Articles on Education, Peace & Disarmament; Status of Women; WHO; MWIA International Representative UN, WHO, UNICEF etc., Geneva; Member Editorial Boards, JUNIC - Educational Kits for the Advancement of Women (to date). *Memberships:* International Association Bryologists, Botanic Society, Geneva. *Honour:* Founding Member, International Baccalaureate Organization; Member of Honour, Medical Womens International Association (MWIA) 1989. *Hobbies Include:* Research; Music; Family Life; Education. *Address:* 34 chemin Pont Ceard, 1290 Versoix Switzerland.

BOOBBYER Juliet Honor (The Honourable Mrs), b. 28 Oct. 1930, London, England. m. Brian Boobbyer, 5 July 1957, 2 sons. *Education:* Westonbirt School, Tetbury, Gloucestershire, 1944- 49. *Appointments:* Worked with Moral Rearmanent on 5 continents, over 35 years. *Creative works:* Cross Road, multi-media production (co-author with Ailsa Hamilton and Ronald Mann); Columba, play with music (co-author with Joanna Sciortino and Elaine Gordon). *Memberships:* Society of Antiquaries of Scotland. *Hobbies:* Painting; Gardening; Local history of Welsh Borders. *Address:* 4 Victoria Road, Oxford OX2 7QD, England.

BOON Beverly Eizabeth, b. 4 May 1951, Paterson, New Jersey, USA. Chiropractor. 1 daughter. *Education:* AA Business, Katherine Gibbs School, Montclair, NJ, 1974; AA, Applied Arts, Somerset County College, NJ, 1980; Dr of Chiropractic, Life Chiropractic College, Marietta, Georgia, 1984; Licensed, Virginia & Georgia. *Appointments:* Chiropractic associate, general practice, Kennesaw, Georgia 1984-85, Denbigh Chiropractic Clinic, Newport News, Virginia 1985-86; Self-employed, Boon Chiropractic, Newport News, 1986-. *Memberships:* International, American, Virginia, Tidewater Chiropractic Associations. *Honours:* Dean's List, Life Chiropractic College, 1982-84; National Dean's List, 1980-84; Pi Tau Delta, national chiropractic honour society, 1984. *Address:* Boon Chiropractic pc, 12458 Warwick Boulevard, Newport News, Virginia 23606, USA.

BOOTE Barbara Mary, b. 8 June 1954, Petts Wood, Kent, England. Editorial Director, Paperback publishing. *Appointments:* Teach Yourself Books, 1973-74; Coronet Books, 1974-77; Magnum, 1978-80; Sphere Books Ltd, 1981-. *Hobbies:* Walking; Reading. *Address:* c/o Sphere Books Ltd, 27 Wrights Lane, London W8 5TZ, England.

BOOTH Jody, b. 4 Aug. 1944, Norton, Kansas, USA. Assistant Personnel Director; Educator. m. Michael Gerard Booth, 11 Feb. 1984. *Education:* BA, Ottawa University, 1967; MS, Emporia State University, 1977; EdD student, Kansas University, current. *Appointments:* Teacher: Belvoir, Topeka 1967-68, Central, Olathe 1968-77; Principal: Westview, Olathe 1977-80, Tomahawk, Olathe 1980-88; Assistant Personnel Directr, Olathe, 1988-. *Creative work includes:* Presentations: Leadership Plus Goal Setting; Techniques to Develop Teacher Ownership; Effective Discipline; Interviewing Strategies; Communication Techniques; Bridge the Channel; Professionalism; Motivation; Iron Bars or Goal Posts. *Memberships:* President, Kansas Association of Elementary School Principals; United School Administrators; National Association of Elementary School Principals; Association for Supervision & Curriculum Development. *Honours:* Outstanding Jayne Award, 1972; Outstanding Young Woman, 1979-80; Outstanding Young Woman of Kansas, 1980; Excellence in Education, Tomahawk Elementary, 1985-88; Kansas Outstanding Principal of Year, 1987-88; National Distinguished Principal Award, 1987-88. *Hobbies:* Travel; Writing; Aerobics; Reading; Bridge; Jogging; Films. *Address:* 1005 Pitt Street, Olathe, Kansas 66061, USA.

BOOTH Kathleen Hylda Valerie, b. 9 July 1922, Stourbridge, England. Managing Director. m. Andrew D. Booth, 30 Aug. 1950, 1 son, 1 daughter. *Education:* BSc., Honours, Mathematics, London, 1944; PhD, Applied Mathematics, London, 1950. *Appointments:* Junior Scientific Officer, Royal Aircraft Establishment, 1944-46; Research Scholarship, King's College, 1946-50; Research Fellow, Lecturer, Birkbeck College, 1950-62; Lecturer, Professor, University of Saskatchewan, 1963-72; Hon. Full Professor, Mathematics, Lakehead University, 1972-78; Director, Autonetics Research Associates, 1978-. *Publications:* 2 books; over 30 papers on machine translation etc; many reviews. *Hobbies:* Gardening; Sewing. *Address:* 5317 Sooke Road, RR 1, Sooke, BC VOS 1NO, Canada.

BOOTH Margaret, b. 1898, Los Angeles, California, USA. Film Editor. *Creative Works:* Films include: Why Men Leave Home; Husbands and Lovers; Bridge of San Luis Rey; New Moon; Susan Lenox; Strange Interlude; Smilin' Through; Romeo and Juliet; Barretts of Wimpole Street; Mutiny on the Bounty; Camille, etc. Supervising editor on Owl and the Pussycat; The Way We Were; Funny Lady; Murder by Death; The Goodbye Girl; California Suite; The Cheap Detective (also associate producer); Chapter Two. Editor: Annie. Executive Producer: The Slugger's Wife. *Honour:* Honorary Oscar 1977.

BOOZ Gretchen Arlene, b. 24 Nov. 1933, Boone, Iowa, USA. Marketing Services Manager. m. Donald R Boox, 3 Sept. 1960. 1 son, 2 daughters, 1 deceased. *Education:* AA, Graceland College. *Appointments:* Medical Assistant, Des Moines, Iowa, 1955-61; Herald Publishing House, 1975-. *Publication:* Book: Kendra, 1979. *Memberships:* Board of Trustees, Graceland College; Board of Directors, Comprehensive Mental Health, 1981-83; Board of Directors, Hope House; Board of Directors, Child Placement; General Council of Women (RLDS Church), 1970-74; Citizens Advisory Committee, Blue Springs R-IV School District; Personal Diplomat, Independence Chamber of Commerce. *Honour:* Outstanding Chamber of Commerce Member Award (Independence Chamber of Commerce), 1981. *Hobbies:* Writing and performing monologues of biblical and historical women. *Address:* Herald Publishing House, 3225 So Noland Road, Independence, Missouri 64055, USA.

BORACCHIA Beatrice Mabel, b. 25 Aug. 1935, Bergen, Norway. Medical Doctor; Psychiatrist. m. Dr Carlos Alberto Boracchia, 21 Sept. 1957. *Education:* Medical School, University of Buenos Aires, 1956; Resident, Anaesthesia, University of Toronto, Canada, 1960; University of Washington, Seattle, USA; Fellow, Cardiovascular Research, University of Alberta, Edmonton; Postgraduate Training, Psychiatry, University of Toronto, 1971. *Appointments:* Intern, Hospital Juan A Fernandez, Buenos Aires, 1956- 58; Chief Resident, Surgery, 1957-58, Staff, Anaesthesia, Hospital Fernandez Rivadavia and Clinic Buenos Aires, 1958-60; Resident, Anaesthesia, University of Washington, USA, 1961-62; Internship, Holy Cross Hospital, Calgary, Canada, 1965-66; Resident, ST Michaels Hospital, Toronto, 1970-71; Psychiatrist Consultant, Private Practice, 1971-. *Publications:* Articles in professional journals, presentations etc; Use of Dogs in Psychotherapy. *Memberships:* Royal College of Physicians and Surgeons, Ontario; Canadian Medical Association; Ontario Medical Association; Canadian and Ontario Psychiatric Associations; Canadian Group Psychotherapy Association (Toronto Section); American Orthopsychiatry Association; Canadian Group and American Group Psychotherapy Associations; Canadian Opera Company; Canadian Childrens Dance Theatre; Ontario Tennis Association, etc. *Honours:* CMA Research Award for original work on Artificial Placenta, 1962-63. *Hobbies:* Opera; Dancing; Dog Training; Oil Painting; Wood working; Tennis; Jogging. *Address:* 94 Cumberland St No 512, Toronto, Ontario M5R 1A3, Canada.

BORDELON Kathleen Frances Weiss, b. 17 Oct. 1947, New Orleans, Louisiana, USA. Teacher. m. Ronald Joseph Bordelon, 27 Oct. 1973. 2 sons. *Education:* BA, Sociology 1981, MEd 1988, University of New Orleans; Elementary Education Certification; Reading Specialist Certification. *Appointments:* Tutorial program Coordinator, Lafayette Area Community Development Program, Lafayette, 1973-74; Statistical Assistant, Veterans Administration Medical Center, New Orleans, 1976-80; Elementary Teacher, St Cecilia School, New Orleans, 1981-87; Reading and Language Arts Teacher, 4th Grade, J F Gauthier School, St Bernard, 1987-. *Publications:* Sexism in Reading Materials, Reading Teacher, 1985; Bridges: A Tool to Interethnic Communication, LACDP, 1974. *Memberships:* International Reading Association; Louisiana Reading Association/St Bernard Council, Vice President Elect, 1988-89; St Bernard Association of Educators; St Bernard Council International Reading Association, Vice-President, 1989-90. *Honours and Awards:* Mini-Grant Recipient, Louisiana Reading Association, 1989-90; Mini-Grant Recipient, South Central Bell, 1989-90 *Hobbies:* Reading; Writing; Louisiana-style cooking (Cajun). *Address:* 2401 Margaret Lane, Meraux, Louisiana 70075, USA.

BORENSTEIN Audrey, b. 7 Oct. 1930, Chicago, USA. Freelance Writer. m. Walter Borenstein, 5 Sept. 1953, 1 son, 1 daughter. *Education:* BA, 1953, MA 1954, University of Illinois; PhD, Louisiana State University, 1958. *Appointments:* Assistant Professor, Louisiana State University, 1958-60; Assistant Professor, Cornell College, 1965-69; Adjunct Professor, SUNY, New Paltz, 1970-86. *Publications:* Chimes of Change and Hours, 1983; Redeeming the Sin, 1978; Fiction in: Oxalis; North Dakota Quarterly; Northwest Review. *Memberships:* National League of American Pen Women; Poets & Writers; Hudson Valley Writers Guild; Ulster County Historical Society. *Honours:* Fellow, NEA, 1976-77; Humanities Fellow, Rockefeller Foundation, 1978-79; Award for Excellence, 1986. *Hobbies:* Journal Keeping; The Letter as Literature; Creativity & Aging. *Address:* 4 Henry Court, New Paltz, NY 12561, USA.

BORER Mary Irene Cathcart, b. 3 Feb. 1906, London, England. Writer. m. 7 June 1935, divorced 1939. *Education:* BSc., University College, London, 1928. *Appointments:* Research Assistant, Ethnographical Dept., Wellcome Historical Medical Museum, 1928-35; Excavation, Egypt Exploration Society, 1935-38; Script Writer, Rank Organisation, and Editor, Rank Childrens Film Dept., 1941-50. *Publications:* Childrens Books Include: Kilango, 1935; Taha the Egyptian, 1937; The House with the Blue Door, 1938; The Highcroft Mystery, 1939; Distant Hills, 1951; The Baobab Tree, 1955; Sophie and the Countess, 1960; The Dragons Remembered, 1956; Books of Childrn's Films: Two Thousand Years Ago, 1948; The Little Ballerina, 1949; Bush Christmas, 1950; The Secret Tunnel, 1950; The Mystery of the Snakeskin Belt, 1951; Trapped by the Terror, 1952; The Dog and the Diamonds, 1956; The Quest of the Golden Eagle; Educational: People Like Us, 1960; Mankind in the Making, 1962; Women Who Made History, 1963; Famous Rogues, 1966; Agincourt, 1970; Liverpool, 1970; The Boer War, 1971; Two Villages, 1973; The Years of Grandeur, 1975; The City of London, 1977; London Walks and Legends, 1981; The Story of Covent Garden, 1984; An Illustrated Guide to London in 1800, 1988. *Address:* 4 Station Road, Tring, Hertfordshire HP23 5NG, England.

BORGERDING Shirley Ruth, b. 19 Dec. 1929. Civic Worker. m. George Norman Borgerding, 3 sons, 4 daughters. *Education:* BS, Temple University, 1951. *Appointments:* Former Business Office Supervisor, Bell Telephone Company of Pennsylvania. *Memberships Include:* Belgrade (Minnesota) Precinct Chairwoman, 1958-; District Convention Delegate, 1960-; State Convention Delgate, 1960-; National Convention Delegate, 1980-; Belgrade Bicentennial Festival, CMTE, 1976; Belgrade Art Festival, Chairwoman; Belgrade Readers Club, Past President; Christian Mothers Society, Past President. *Address:* 1060 Washburn, Belgrade, MN 56312, USA.

BORGESE Elisabeth Mann, b. 24 Apr. 1918, Munich, Germany. Professor. m. G A Borgese, 23 Nov. 1939. 2 daughters. *Education:* BA Classical Studies, Freies Gymnasium, 1935; Diploma, Zurich Conservatory of Music, 1936. *Appointments:* Research Associate, University of Chicago, 1946-52; Editor, Inter-cultural Publications Inc, 1952-63; Senior Fellow, Center for the Study of Democratic Institutions, California, 1964-78; Professor, Political Science, Dalhousie University, 1979-. *Publications:* To Whom It May Concern, short stories; Ascent of Woman; The Language Barrier; The Ocean Regime; The Drama of the Oceans; Seafarm; The Mines of Neptune; The Future of the Oceans. Plays: Only the Pyre; Eat Your Fish Balls, Tarquin. *Memberships:* World Academy of Arts and Science; Third World Academy of Science. *Honours:* Cross for High Merit, Government of Austria, 1982; Honorary Doctorate, Mount Vincent University, 1986; United Nations Environment Prize, 1986; Gold Medal International Studies, Malta, 1987; Ordor of Canada, 1988. *Hobbies:* Music; Animal intelligence; Skiing; Swimming; Hiking. *Address:* Sambro Head, Halifax, Nova Scotia, Canada.

BORLAND Lorelei Joy, b. 16 Sept. 1941, USA. Attorney. m. Arthur Gundersheim, 19 July 1970. *Education:* BSc., University of Illinois, 1963; JD, De Paul College of Law, 1969. *Appointments:* Legal Assistance, Found of Chicago, 1969-75; Food Research & Action Centre, 1975-78; US Dept. of Labour, 1978-80; New York Attorney General's Office, 1980-82; Morgan Melhuish (Partner), 1982-87; Partner, Edwards & Angell, 1988-. *Membership:* American Bar Association, Natural Resources Section, Litigation Committee. *Hobbies:* Cooking; Sailing; Scuba. *Address:* 145 Nassau Street, New York, NY 10038, USA.

BOROWSKI Jennifer Lucile, b. 23 Oct. 1934, Jersey City, New Jersey, USA. Payroll & Payroll Tax Manager. *Education:* BS, St Peter's College, 1968; Postgraduate, Pace College, 1976-77. *Appointments:* Manager, benefits, Amerada Petroleum Corp, New York City, 1951-66; Benefits Manager, Mt Sinai Hospital, New York City, 1966-67; Manager Payroll, Haskins & Sells, New York City, 1967-74; Manager Payroll and Payroll Tax, Cushman & Wakefield, Inc, New York City, 1975-. *Memberships:* Am Payroll Assn (bd dirs 1979-81, cert); Am Mgmt Assn; American Society of Payroll

Management. *Hobbies:* Golf; Opera; Boating. *Address:* 36 Front Street, North Arlington, NJ 07032, USA.

BOSC Joyce L, b. 26 Oct. 1952, Washington, District of Columbia, USA. Advertising Agency President. *Education:* AA, Prince George's College, Largo, Maryland; BA, University of Maryland, College Park, Maryland. *Appointments:* Promotion Manager and Product Manager, Arbitron Co, Laurel, Maryland; Assisted in new product development and client service 1974- 80; President and Owner, Boscobel Advertising Inc, Kensington, Maryland; Developed a high-tech, bio-tech, commercial and residential real estate client base, 1980-. *Memberships:* Direct Marketing Association; Advertising Club of Washington; American Marketing Association; American Association of Advertising Agencies; American Advertising Federation; National Association of Women Business Owners. *Hobbies:* Weight-lifting; Dancing; Reading; Family and friends. *Address:* 7711 Erica Lane, Laurel, MD 20707, USA.

BOSKEY Adele Ludin, b. 30 Aug. 1943, USA. Professor of Biochemistry; Researcher. m. James Bernard Boskey, 30 June 1970, 1 daughter. *Education:* BA, Barnard College, 1964; PhD, Boston University, 1970; Postdoctoral Fellow, Hospital for Special Surgery. New York City, 1970-73. *Appointments:* Instructor, Department of Chemistry, Boston University, Boston, Massachusetts, 1969-70; Assistant Professor, 1973-78, Associate Professor, 1978-83, Professor of Biochemistry, 1983-, Columbia University Medical College, New York City; Senior Scientist, Hospital for Special Surgery, New York City, currently. *Publications:* Over 90 contributions to refereed journals. *Memberships:* Orthopedic Research Society (Member at Large 1981, Nominations Committee 1987); International Association for Dental Research (President, Mineralised Tissues Group, 1985-86, Chair, Constitution Committee, 1985-88); American Crystallographic Association; Fellow, American Institute of Chemists; American Chemical Society; American Society for Bone Mineral Research. *Honours:* Kappa Delat Award for Distinguished Research in Orthopaedics, 1979; NIH Grants from NIDR, NIAMKDD, NICa; NIH Merit Award, 1987. *Hobbies:* Music; Theatre. *Address:* The Hospital for Special Surgery, 535 E 70th Street, New York, NY 10021, USA.

BOSS Evelyn Maurine, b. 15 June 1929, Quinter, Kansas, USA. Elementary Teacher. m. Marion L Boss, 18 June 1950. 2 daughters. *Education:* BA, Elem Ed, University of No Colorado, 1963; MA, Elem Ed, Adams St, Col, 1977; Utah State University; University of Connecticut; Ft Hayes State University (Kansas); Emporia (Kan) State University. *Appointemtns:* Teacher, Quinter, Kansas, 1949-50; Teacher, Beuhler, Kansas, 1958-60; Teacher, LaJunta, Colorado, 1960-64; Teacher, School District 60, Pueblo, Colorado, 1964-. *Memberships:* 2nd VP, Delta Kappa Gamma; President, Beta Chapter, 1982-84; State Recording Secretary, 1987-89; American Assn University Women, Pres Elect, 1987-88, President 1988-90 (Pueblo Branch); Vice Pres 1972-74, President 1974-76, Assn Childhood Ed Intl. *Honours:* Delta Kappa Gamma Scholarship, 1964; Participant, Delta Kappa Gamma Leadership/Management Seminar, Austin, Texas, 1989. *Hobbies:* Reading; Sewing; Playing bridge; Working with children. *Address:* 114 Cornell Circle, Pueblo, CO 81005, USA.

BOSS Nancy M, b. 21 Apr. 1933, Washington, USA. School Director. m. Richard Boss, 3 June 1954, 2 sons, 2 daughters. *Education:* BA, Barrington College; MA, TESL, Fairleigh Dickinson University. *Appointments:* Teacher, Latin America Mission, 1955-69; Teacher, Colegio Jorge Washington, 1969-70; Department Head, Miami Dade Community College, Florida, 1977-81; Director, International School of Panama, 1982-84; Director, Caribbean International School, Colon, 1986-. *Memberships:* Phi Delta Kappa; TESOL. *Hobbies:* Music; Needlework; Church Activities. *Address:* Box 2401, Cristobal, Colon, R. Panama.

BOSSOM Barbara Joan, Lady, b. 28 Sept. 1929, London, England. m. The Hon. Sir Clive Bossom, 28 Sept. 1951, 3 sons, 1 daughter. *Appointments:* Personal Secretary to Sir Miles Thomas, 1947-51; Director, (Exports) Coats Viyella, 1976-87. *Memberships:* Management Committee, Habinteg Housing Association. *Honour:* Order of St John. *Hobbies:* Travel; Snorkeling; Reading; Music; Art; China Mending. *Address:* 97 Cadogan Lane, London SW1X 9DU, England.

BOSTICK Ruby Nan Roach, b. 26 Oct. 1954, Brookhaven, Mississippi, USA. Educator; Administrator. 1 son. *Education:* BE 1975, MEd 1980, EdD 1984, University of Mississippi. *Appointments:* Teacher, 5th Grade Remedial Mathematics, Brookhaven, 1978-80; Graduate Instructor, School of Education, University of Mississippi, 1980-84; Director, Instructional Resource Centre, University of Arkansas, Monticelo. *Publications:* Co- author, book, Math Instruction Using Media & Modality Strengths, 1988; Various eductional articles. *Memberships:* Vice President 1988-89, Monticello Chapter, Phi Delta Kappa; Board, Arkansas Association of Instructional Media; Office, Association for Educational Communications & Technology; Association for Supervision & Curriculum Development. *Honours:* Research Grant, Mississippi Educational Television, 1984; Biographical recognition. *Hobbies:* Working with teachers concerning learning styles & modality based instruction; Reading; Good films; Dancing. *Address:* 122 Mark Circle, Monticello, Arknsas 71655, USA.

BOSWELL Nathalie Anne (Spence), b. 9 May 1924, Cleveland, Ohio, USA. Speech Pathologist, retired. m. 11 June 1946, divorced 1953. 1 son, 2 daughters. *Education:* Bachelor of Music Education, Northwestern University, 1945; MA, Western Reserve University, 1961. *Appointments:* Speech Clinician, Highland View Hospital, 1961-64; Speech Pathologist, Cleveland Veterans' Administration Medical Center, 1964-86. *Publications:* Booklets: Guidelines for EEO Counselors, 1973; Laryngectomy-orientation for Patient & families, 1985; Noninvasive Electrical Stimulation for the Treatment of Radiotherapy Side-effects, 1983; Elimination of Xerostomia During Radiotherapy of the Pharynx: A Case History, 1985. *Memberships:* American Speech & Hearing Association; Ohio Speech & Hearing Association; Adjunct Clinical Instructor, Case-Western Reserve University, 1982-86; Advisory Boards: National Institute Electromedical Information; School of Electromedical Sciences; City University of Los Angeles, 1985-; Associate Editor, American Journal of Electromedicine. *Honours:* Performance Award, VA for establishing EEO program, 1974; Superior Performance Award, VA Hospital, 1978; Federal Woman of Achievement, 1982; Commendation from Regional Director, Great Lakes Area, VA; Award for Laryngectomy-Orientation for Patient & family, 1983. *Hobbies:* Volunteer for: Cleveland Seamens' Service, Asst. Treasurer; Cleveland Orchestra Chorus, 1968-81; Music Director, Highland Heights RLDS Church; Mineralogy Dept, Cleveland Museum of Natural History; Endowed Tuba Chair, Cleveland Orchestra, 1983; Sailing; Gardening; Music; Mineralogy. *Address:* 2946 Berkshire Road, Cleveland Heights, Ohio 44118, USA.

BOULDING Elise Marie, b. 6 July 1920, Oslo, Norway. Professor Emeritus of Sociology. 4 sons, 1 daughter. *Education:* BA, English, Douglass College, USA, 1940; MS, Sociology, Iowa State University, 1949; PhD, Sociology, University of Michigan, 1969. *Appointments:* Research Associate, 1967-78, Professor, 1967-78, University of Colorado; Chair, Department of Sociology, Dartmouth College, 1978-85. *Publications:* Translation of Dutch Polak's Image of the Future, 1961; Underside of History, 1976; Handbook of International Data on Women, 1977; Women in 20th Century World, 1977; Children's Rights and Wheel of Life, 1979; Bibliography on World Conflict and Peace (with Passmore and Gassler), 1979; Building Global Civic Culture, 1988; One Small Plot of Heaven, 1989. *Memberships:* International Peace Research

Association, Secretary-General 1989; Fellow, Dickey Endowment, Dartmouth; UN University Governing Council, 1980-85; UNESCO Peace Prize Jury, 1981-86; US Commission for Peace Academy, 1979-82; American Sociological Association; International Sociological Association; International Peace Research Association; COPRED; World Futures Federation. *Honours:* Lentz International Peace Research Award, 1986; Woman of Conscience Award, National Council of Women, 1980; Jessie Bernard Award, American Sociological Association, 1981; Athena Award, University of Michigan Alumnae Council, 1983; The Women Who Made a Difference Award, National Women's Forum, 1985; Adin Ballou Peace Award, Unitarian Universalist Peace Fellowship, 1986; Celebration of Practise Award, Sociological Practise Association, 1986. *Hobbies:* Her 15 grandchildren; Solitude; Imaging A World without War workshops; Local and global networking; Voluteering at local parenting center. *Address:* 624 Pearl Street 206, Boulder, CO 80302, USA.

BOULET Tami, b. 12 Sept. 1958, Lawton, Oklahoma, USA. Social Worker. *Education:* BA, Social work, BA Religion, Azusa Pacific University, 1980; MSW, University of California in Los Angeles, 1984. *Appointments:* Social Worker, United Cerebral Palsy, 1980-82; Social Worker 1984-87, Director of Clinical Services 1987-, Hollygrove Children's Home. *Memberships:* Vestry member, St Augustine's Episcopal Church, 1986-; Amnesty International; National Association of Social Workers; UCLA Social Welfare Alumni. *Hobbies:* Reading; Art; Theatre; Film; Travel; Yoga; Skiing; Human rights; Women's issues. *Address:* 1626 Armacost No 5, Los Angeles, CA 90025, USA.

BOUNDS Nancy, b. Rodney, Arkansas, USA. Modelling and Talent Company Executive. m. Mark C Sconce, 28 Oct. 1972. 1 daughter. *Education:* Student, Northwestern University, 1950. *Appointment:* President, Nancy Bounds International, 1959-. *Publications:* Fashion Show choreography, music and production; Contributing author to various professional journals. *Memberships:* Executive Director, International Fashion/Modelling Association, New York City, 1978; Founding President, International Talent and Model Schools Association, New York, 1979-80; Chairperson, Douglas/Sarpy County Heart Association, Omaha, 1973-74; Producer, TV Heart Fund Auction, 1965. *Honours:* Recipient, National Teachers Award, Milady Publications Co, 1965; Commendation from President Lyndon B Johnson's Council on Youth Opportunity, 1968; Heart Fund Citation, 19672; Omaha Mayor's Award for Outstanding Service, 1984; Uta Halle Girls Village Service Award, 1983-87. *Hobbies:* Reading; Painting; Travel; Golf; Tournament bridge. *Address:* 4803 Davenport, Omaha, NE 68132, USA.

BOURNE Judith Louise, b. 2 July 1945, New York City, New York, USA. Attorney-at-Law. *Education:* BA, Cornell University, 1966; JD, 1972, LLM, International Law, 1974, New York University Law School; Junior Fellow, New York University Center for International Studies, 1972-73; Bar admissions: New York State; US Courts of Appeals; South Carolina; US District Courts; US Supreme Court; US Virgin Islands. *Appointments include:* Legal Intern, National Council on Crime & Delinquency, New York City, 1970-71; Graduate Intern, Staten Island Community College, 1971; Various short-term positions in research and community work; Instructor, Political Science, School of Continuing Education, New York University, 1973; Associate, Bernard R Fielding, Attorney at Law, Charleston, South Carolina, 1973-74; South Carolina State Coordinator, Emergency Land Fund, 1974; Assistant Federal Public Defender, Office of the Federal Public Defender, St Croix and St Thomas, US Virgin Islands, 1977-81; Private Law Practice, St Thomas, 1982-. *Memberships:* National Conference of Black Lawyers, National Co-Chair, 1976-79, South Carolina State Director 1973-76, Political Affairs Task Force Chair 1979-80, International Affairs Task Force; American Trial Lawyers Association; Past Secretary, Treasurer and member Board of Governors,

Virgin Islands Bar Association, 1987; District Court Lawyers Advisory Committee; Founder, Chair, Virgin Islands Anti-Apartheid Committee; Past Treasurer, Anguilla Virgin Islands Society; Almeric L Christian Lawyers Association; Former Member and Chair, Division of Mental Health Community Support Programme Advisory Board; Caribbean Development Coalition; CDC Community Cooperative, Chair 1983-84. *Honour:* 1st Black Female Attorney to practice in Charleston, South Carolina. *Address:* PO Box 6458, St Thomas, VI 00801, USA.

BOURQUE Linda Anne, b. 25 Aug. 1941, Indianapolis, Indiana, USA. Professor. m. Don Philippe Bourque, 3 June 1966, div. Nov. 1974. *Education:* BA, History, Indiana University, 1963; MA, Sociology, 1964, PhD, Sociology, 1968, Post Doctoral Trainee, 1968-69, Duke University. *Appointments:* Assistant Professor, Department of Sociology, California State University, Los Angeles, 1969-72; Assistant Professor, then Associate Professor, 1972-86, Professor, 1986, School of Public Health, University of California, Los Angeles. *Publications:* Defining Rape, 1989 and Author or co-author, 33 articles in professional journals. *Memberships:* American Sociological Association (Co-Chair, Committee on Freedom of Research and Teaching, 1978-80); Pacific Sociological Association (Vice-President 1983); American Public Health Association; Sociologists for Women in Society; American Association for the Advancement of Science; American Association for Public Opinion Research; The Association for Research in Vision and Ophthalmology. *Honours:* Phi Alpha Theta, 1963; Delta Omega Society, 1976; Award for Distinguished Service in Teaching, UCLA School of Public Health Alumni Association, 1976-77; Certificate of Recognition for Outstanding Service to the Association, American Sociological Association, 1980. *Hobbies:* Violoncello player, Los Angeles Doctors Symphony Orchestra and Santa Monica Symphony orchestra; Librarian, Santa Monica Symphony Orchestra. *Address:* School of Public Health, University of California, Los Angeles, CA 90024-1772, USA.

BOURQUE Susan Carolyn, b. 9 Oct. 1943, Detroit, Michigan, USA. Professor of Government; Project Director. *Education:* BA, 1965, PhD, 1971, Cornell University. *Appointments:* Assistant Professor of Government, 1970-75, Associate Professor of Government, 1975-81, Director, Project on Women and Social Change, 1978-, Professor of Government, 1981-, Smith College, Northampton, Massachusetts; Reader in Politics, School of Social Science, University of Sussex, Brighton, England, 1981. *Publications:* Learning About Women (co-editor and contributor with Jill Conway and Joan Scott); Women Living Change (co-editor and contributor with Donna Robinson Divine); Women of the Andes (with Kay Warren); Articles. *Memberships:* Discipline Screening Committee for Fulbright Scholars Awards in Political Science for Council for International Exchange of Scholars, 1987-90; Past President, Member, Executive Council of Latin American Studies; Board of Directors, Association for Women and Development. *Honours:* Hamilton Prize for Women of the Andes, 1979; Rockefeller Foundation Grant for International Conference on Gender, Technology and Education, 1985; Prize for Best Article, New England Council on Latin American Studies, 1987; National Endowment for the Humanities Grant for development of international material in the Sophia Smith Collection, 1987; Research Grant on Current Latin American Issues, Howard Heinz Endowment, 1989. *Hobbies:* Gardening; Swimming. *Address:* Department of Government, Smith College, 138 Elm Street, Northampton, MA 01063, USA.

BOUTON Lalea Mardiana Ika, b. 22 Jan. 1952, P. Siantar, Sumatra, Indonesia. Fashion Designer; Administrator. m. Jay H. Bouton, 1 Sept. 1979. *Education:* Literature, University of Indonesia, 1970; Far East Dressmaking & Design School, Hong Kong, 1972; London College of Fashion, UK, 1977-79. *Appointments:* Flight purser, Cathay Pacific Airways, 1972-77;

Freelance designer, London, UK, 1977-79; In-house designer, L'Estelle, West Berlin, Germany, 1979-83; Managing Director, own firm, 1983-. *Creative work includes:* Designing evening dresses, Miss Hong Kong pageants, & presentation at Miss Universe, 1983-86; Panel of judges, designers' competition, Indonesia & Hong Kong Polytechnic. *Memberships:* Committee, Hong Kong Fashion Designers Association; Hong Kong Designers Association (HKDA). *Honours:* Excellence Award, HKDA competition, 1984; Outstanding Designer in Indonesia (among 5), Iwan Tirta, Peter Sie, 1988. *Hobbies:* Reading; Buying books & magazines; Accessories; Mountain & Seas; Swimming, jogging, walking, cycling. *Address:* 4 FL, Humphrey's Building, 11 Humphrey's Avenue, Kowloon, Hong Kong.

BOUVARD Marguerite, b. 10 Jan. 1937, Trieste, Italy. Professor; Writer. m. 25 Nov. 1959, 1 son, 1 daughter. *Education:* BA, Northwestern College, USA, 1958; MA, Radcliffe College, 1960; PhD, Harvard University, 1965; MA, Boston University, 1977. *Appointments:* Professor, Regis College, USA, 1966-. *Publications:* Labor Movement & Common Market, 1972; The Intentional Community Movement, 1975; Journeys Over Water, 1982; Landscape and Exile, 1985; Voices from an Island, 1985; The Path Through Grief, 1988. *Memberships:* Board, Women West of Boston; American Poetry Society. *Honours:* Bunting Institute Fellow, 1971-72; Outstanding Educators of America; Scholarship in Poetry, Breadloaf Writers Conference, 1978; Fellow: Ossabaw Island Project, Virginian Center for the Creative Arts, Ragdale Foundation, MacDowell Colony, Yaddo Foundation, Djerassi Foundations, 1978-88; Visiting Research Scholar, Wellesley College Center for Research on Women, 1990-92. *Hobbies:* Quilting; Hiking. *Address:* 6 Brookfield Circle, Wellesley, MA 02181, USA.

BOWDEN Ruth Elizabeth Mary, b. 21 Feb. 1915, Madras, India. Sir William Collins Professor of Anatomy, Royal College of Surgeons of England. *Education:* MB BS, London (Royal Free Hospital) School of Medicine for Women, 1934-40; Rockefeller Travelling Fellowship, 1949-50; DSc London; FRCS England. *Appointments:* House Surgeon and later House Physician, Elizabeth Garrett Anderson Hospital, 1940-42; House Surgeon, Royal Cancer Hospital, 1942; Graduate Assistant, Nuffield Department of Orthopaedic Surgery, 1942-45; Assistant Lecturer, 1945, Lecturer, Reader & Professor, 1951-80, Royal Free Hospital School of Medicine; Hunterian Prof., RCS, 1950; Part-time Lecturer, Department of Anatomy, St Thomas's Hospital Medical School, 1980-83; WHO Consultant in Anatomy, Khartoum University, 1972, 1974, 1977. *Publications:* Peripheral Nerve Injuries, 1958; Contributions to Peripheral Nerve Injuries Report of Medical Research Council; Oxford Companion to Medicine; and to medical and scientific journals. *Memberships:* President: Anat Sco of Great Britain and Ireland, 1970; Medical Women's Federation, 1981; Member Executive Committee, Women's Nat. Commn, 1984-; FRSM; Fellow, British Orthopaedic Association; Linnean Society Vice President; Chartered Society of Physiotherapy (Chairman 1960-70); Institute of Science Technology (President, 1960-65) Riding for the Disabled Association. *Honours:* Jubilee Medal, 1977; DLJ, 1978; OBE, 1980; DCLJ, 1988. *Hobbies:* Reading; Music; Painting; Walking; Gardening; Carpentry. *Address:* 6 Hartham Close, Hartham Road, London N7 9JH, England.

BOWEN Barbara C, b. 4 May 1937, Newcastle, England. Professor of French and Comparative Literature. m. 12 Jan, 1963. 2 daughters. *Education:* BA 1958, MA 1952, Oxford University; Doctorat de l'Université de Paris, France, 1962. *Appointments:* Instructor, 1962- 63, Assistant Professor, 1963-66, Associate Professor, 1966-73, Professor, 1973-87, University of Illinois; Professor, Vanderbilt University, 1987-. *Publications:* Les caractéristiques essentielles de la farce française, 1964; The Age of Bluff, 1972; Words and the Man in French Renaissance Literature, 1983; One Hundred Renaissance Jokes, 1988. *Memberships:*

Organising Committee, Central Ren Conference, 1973-87; Modern Language Association; Executive Committee, Medieval Association of the Midwest, 1982-85. *Honours:* Basil Zaharoff Travelling Scholarship, 1958-59; ACLS Travel Grants, 1973 and 1984; John Simon Guggenheim Memorial Fellowship, 1974-75; NEH Summer Seminar for College Teachers, 1980; NEH Senior Fellowship, 1981-82 and 1988-89. Non-stipendiary Fellow, Villa I Tatti, Florence, 1981-82. *Hobbies:* Art History; Hiking. *Address:* P O Box 1647-B Vanderbilt Univeristy, Nashville, TN 37235, USA.

BOWEN Gwen Lorrayne, b. Denver, Colorado, USA. Dance Educator; Choreographer. *Education:* BA, University of Denver, 1951. *Appointments:* Teacher: Lillian Cushing Dance School, 1945-48, Denver Public Schools 1951-53, Metro State College, 1973; Teacher, Owner, Gwen Bowen School of Dance Arts, 1953-; Artistic Director, Premiere Dance Arts Company, 1959-. *Publications:* Author, Graded System for Ballet & Tap Dance; Choreographer, numerous ballets, operas, musicals. *Memberships:* Colorado dance Teachers, Vice President 1963-64; Dance Educators of America, Life Member; Professional Dance Teachers Association; Dance Masters of America, Life Member; Metro Denver Arts Alliance; South Central Improvement Association; etc. *Honours:* University of Denver Mathematics Honorary, 1950. *Hobbies:* Knitting; Gardening. *Address:* 714 So. Pearl St., Denver, CO 80209, USA.

BOWERS Beverly Mary, b. 6 Nov. 1954, Ogden, Utah, USA. Doctoral Candidate, Exercise Physiology. *Education:* BA, Biological Sciences 1979, MA, Exercise Physiology 1988, Doctor of Philosophy, in process, Kent State University. *Appointments:* Neurobiology Research Technician, Northeastern Ohio University, College of Medicine, 1981-83; Graduate Assistant, Kent State University, 1983-. *Memberships:* American College of Sports Medicine; Canadian Association of Sport Sciences. *Honours:* Graduated with honors, Biological Sciences, 1979; Graduate Assistantships, Exercise Physiology, 1983-87, Kent State University. *Hobbies:* bb3Travelling; Recreational tennis; Cycling; Softball; Soccer; Camping; Backpacking. *Address:* Applied Physiology Research Lab, 163 Memorial Gym Annex, Kent State University, Kent, Ohio 44242, USA.

BOWERS Janette Lawhon, b. 13 Nov. 1933, Conroe, Texas, USA. Retired Educator; Direct Sales. m. Richard E. Bowers, 4 sons, 2 daughters. *Education:* BSc., Sam Houston State University, 1954; MA, Sul Ross State University, 1970. *Appointments:* Elementary PE Teacher, Pasadena ISD; Junior High School PE Teacher, Cypress Fairbanks ISD; Health & PE Instructor, Sul Ross State University, 1968-75, Director, Division for Adult & Continuing Education, 1975-83. *Memberships Include:* American Cancer Society; Governor, Texas District of Pilot International, 1981-82; Pilot Club of Alpine; American Association of Retired Persons. *Honours:* Outstanding Volunteer in Texas, 1977; Finalist, National Volunteer Activist Award, 1977; Outstanding Woman of Alpine, 1981. *Address:* Drawer 1440, Alpine, TX 79831, USA.

BOWERS Mary, b. 16 July 1923, Oklahoma, USA. Schoolteacher. m. William Russell Bowers, 25 Sept. 1953, 1 son, 1 daughter. *Education:* BS, Elementary Education, Oklahoma Baptist University, 1961; MS, Educational Psychology, Oklahoma University, 1965; further studies: Central State University, Edmond, University of Oklahoma, Neuropsychology Workshops under Ralph Reitan. *Appointments:* Elementary School Teacher, 1st Grade Remedial Reading, Educator of Mentally Handicapped and Learning Disabled, Elementary School Counsellor, Shawnee, 1961-68; Child Psychologist, Oklahoma State Health Dept., 1968-81; Middle School Counsellor, 1981-82; 4th Grade Classroom Teacher, 1981-. *Memberships:* Southwestern Psychological Association; Association for Counselling Development; NEA; Oklahoma Education Association. *Hobbies:* Oil Painting; Stained Glass; Ceramics; Gardening. *Address:* Rt 2, Box 86, Shawnee, OK 74801, USA.

BOWMAN Marilyn Laura, b. 30 July 1940, McLennan, Alberta Canada. Associate Professor. *Education:* BA, University of Alberta, 1961; MSc., 1965, PhD, 1972, McGill University. *Appointments:* Director, Psychology Services, Lethbridge Rehab Centre, 1965-70; Assistant Professor, Queens University, Kingston, 1972-76; Associate Professor, Simon Fraser University, 1976-. *Memberships:* Fellow, Canadian Psychological Association; American & BC Psychological Associations. *Hobbies:* Symphonic & Choral Music; Literature of Ancient Japan & Ancient China; Travel. *Address:* Dept. of Psychology, Simon Fraser University, Burnaby, BC, V5A 1S6, Canada.

BOX Betty, b. 1920, Beckenham, Kent, England. Producer. m. Peter Rogers. *Career:* Assistant to Sydney Box, Riverside Studios; In charge of Production, Islington Studios, 1946-47; High Commissioner, USA, 1969; Director, Ulster Television. *Creative Works:* Productions include: The Seventh Veil; The years Between; A Girl In a Million; Daybreak; The Upturned Glass; Dear Murderer; When The Bough Breaks; Miranda; The Blind Goddess; It's Not Cricket; Here Come The Huggetts; Vote For Huggett; The Huggetts Abroad, 1949-52; Marry Me; So Long At The Fair; The Clouded Yellow; Appointment With Venus; The Venetian Bird; A Day To Remember; Doctor In The House; Mad About Men; Doctor At Sea, 1956; The Iron Petticoat; Checkpoint, 1957; Doctor At Large; Campbell's Kingdom; A Tale of Two Cities; The Wind Cannot Read; The Thirty-Nine Steps, 1959-60; Upstairs and Downstairs; Conspiracy Of Hearts; Doctor In Love, 1960; No Love For Johnnie, 1961-62; No, My Darling Daughter; A Pair of Briefs, 1962; The Wild And The Willing, 1963; Doctor In Distress; Hot Enough For June, 1964; The High Bright Sun; Doctor in Clover, 1965; Deadlier Than The Male, 1967; Nobody Runs Forever; Some Girls Do, 1970; Doctor In Trouble, 1971; Percy, 1972; It's A 2 Feet 6 Inch Above The Ground World, 1974; Percy's Progress. *Honour:* OBE, 1958. *Address:* c/o Pinewood Studios, Iver, Bucks, England.

BOXALL Linda Louellen, b. 6 Apr. 1945, Regina, Saskatchewan, Canada. Farmer; Businesswoman. m. John A Boxall, 11 July 1967. 3 daughters. *Education:* Diploma in Business Administration & Accounting, Saskatchewan Technical Institute, 1965. *Memberships:* Saskatchewan Egg Producers Board; Grand Coulee School Division; Canadian Egg Producers Council; Canadian Egg Marketing Agency; Saskatchewan School Trustees Association; Canadian Club; Business & Professional Womens Club. *Hobbies:* Raised and showed registered American Saddlebred Horses; Past Ladies Foil Fencing Champion for Saskatchewan. *Address:* PO Box 491, Regina, Saskatchewan, Canada, S4P 3A2.

BOXER Arabella, b. 11 July 1934, Edinburgh, Scotland. Food Writer. m. Mark Boxer, 10 Dec. 1956, divorced 1982, 1 son, 1 daughter. *Appointments:* Food Writer, Vogue Magazine, 1966-68, Food Editor 1975-. *Publications:* First Slice Your Cookbook; A Second Slice; Arabella Boxer's Gaden Cookbook; Medditerranean Cookbook; The Sunday Times Complete Cookbook; etc. *Memberships:* Founder Member, Guild of Food Writers. *Honours:* Glenfiddich Food Writer of the Year Award, 1975, 1978. *Hobbies:* Cooking; Travel; Sight Seeing. *Address:* 44 Elm Park Road, London SW3 6AX, England.

BOYAN Mariana, b. 16 June 1947, Cimpia-Turzii, Romania. Writer; Painter; Painting Restorer. m. Vasile Gheorghita, 4 Aug. 1972. 1 daughter. *Education:* Ion Andreescu, Institute of Fine Arts in Cluj-Napoca, 1967-73; Specilization in painting restoring, Bucharest 1973-77 and Brussels, 1978. *Appointments:* Museum of Fine Arts, Cluj-Napoca, 1973-85. *Creative works:* Elegy for the Last Meadow (volume of verse), 1976; Poetry: The Judge of Puppets, 1980; The Linen Coat, 1984; Phantasticon, 1987; 10 personal exhibitions of painting. *Memberships:* Union of Writers in SR of Romania, 1980-; Union of Painters, Cluj-Napoca, 1975-. *Honours:* Debut Prize, awarded by Dacia Publishing House, Cluj-Napoca, 1976; Prize, Union of Writers awarded by Cluj-Napoca Branch, 1980; Prize awarded by Tribuna review for

painting, 1987. *Hobbies:* Russian and South American literature; Italian poetry; Culinary art; Collecting aquecheeks. *Address:* Cluj- Napoca 3400, 12 Paring str Blk 4, Sc II apts, S R of Romania.

BOYD Beverly M, b. Brooklyn, New York, USA. Professor. *Education:* BA, Brooklyn College, 1946; MA, 1948, PhD, 1955, Columbia University. *Appointments:* Instructor, English, University of Texas, 1955-58; Professor, English, Radford College, Virginia, 1958-62; Assistant Professor to Professor, English, University of Kansas, 1962-. *Publications:* Philippine's Windows and Other Poems, 1987; 5 books on medieval literature. *Memberships:* American Association of University Professors; MLA; Medieval Academy of America. *Honours:* Lizette A. Fisher Fellowship, Columbia University, 1954-55; Guggenheim Fellow, 1969-70; Huntington Library Fellowship, 1975. *Address:* Dept. of English, University of Kansas, Wescoe Hall, Lawrence, KS 66045, USA.

BOYD Liona Maria, b. London, England. Musician; Guitarist. *Education:* BMus, University of Toronto, 1972; Private student with Alexandre Lagoya, Paris, France; Master classes with Julian Bream. *Appointments:* International performer; Royal Command Performance for Queen Elizabeth II, England; Played for world leaders Economic Summit in Canada, Fidel Castro, Schmitt, Thatcher, Manley, Mitterand. Television artist. *Creative works:* Composer for guitar; 13 LP's, CBS Recording artist: The Guitar; Artistry of Liona Boyd; Miniatures for Guitar; Guitar for Xmas; Liona Boyd and English Chamber Orchestra; Liona in Tokyo; Spanish Fantasy; Persona; Music books: Miniatures; Folk Songs; Liona's Favourites; Xmas songs. ssa 20Memberships: AFTRA; AF of M; President, Liona Boyd Prod, Inc. *Honours:* Honorary Doctorate, University of Lethbridge; Honorary Mayor of San Antonio; Vanier Award, 1979; 4 time winner of readers poll of Guitar Player for best classical guitarist; 4 time Juno Award winner for best instrumentional of year; Order of Canada, CM; 2 gold records; 1 platinum record. *Hobbies:* Song writing; Travel. *Address:* 3 Canterbury Road, Islington, Ontario, Canada, M5A 5B2.

BOYD Sue Abbott, b. 31 Aug. 1921, Cedar Rapids, Iowa, USA. Poet; Lecturer; Critic; Executive Editor; Publisher. m. Arnold Boyd, 28 Aug. 1943. *Education:* Adjatant General School, 1943; New School for Social Research, 1949-50; Draughn's business College, 1950-51. *Appointments:* Womens Army Corp, 1943-45; Poet, Writer, 1949-; President, South and West Inc., 1962-. *Memberships:* Life Fellow, International Institute of Arts & Letters; Poetry Society of Amerioa; etc. *Hobbies:* Recipient, various honours and awards. *Hobbies:* Politics; Poetry; Family. *Address:* 2406 South S Street, Fort Smith, AR 72901, USA.

BOYD Virginia Ann Lewis, b. 15 Nov. 1944, Shreveport, Louisiana, USA. Professor; Research Scientist. m. James Pierce Boyd, 4 June 1964, 1 son, 1 daughter. *Education:* BS, Chemistry, 1965, MS, Microbiology, 1968, Northwestern State University; PhD, Microbiology, Louisiana State University, 1971; Postdoctoral Fellow, Baylor College of Medicine, 1971-73. *Appointments:* Instructor: Jacksonville State University, 1968-69; Baylor College of Medicine, Houston, Texas, 1972-73; Senior Scientist, 1973-75, Scientist II, 1975-76, Principal Scientist, 1976-82, Principal Scientist, Section Head, 1982-88, NCI-Frederick Cancer Research Facility, Frederick, Maryland; Adjunct Associate Professor, 1981-82, Associate Professor, Biology, Director, Biomedical Sciences MS programme, 1982-88, Professor and Chairman of Biology, 1989-, Hood College, Frederick. *Publications:* Symposia chapters: The DNA-transfer technique: Relevance to virus-cell relationship (with J.L.Melnick and J.S.Butel), 1973; Demonstration of infectious deoxyribonucleic acid in transformed cells: I. Recovery of simian virus 40 from yielder and non-yielder transformed cells (with J.S.Butel), 1974; Review of interaction of onconaviruses and herpes- viruses: A hypothesis proposing a co-carcinogenic role for herpesviruses in transformation (with B.Hampar), 1978; 24 scientific publications in journals. *Memberships:* American Society for Virology; American Society for Microbiology; Tissue Culture Association; New York Academy of Sciences; American Association for the Advancement of Science; American Association of University Professors; American Association of University Women; American Institute of Biological Sciences; International Association for Antiviral Agents; Professional Ethics Forum; Associate Member, Park Ridge and Hastings Centers; National Association of Advisors for the Health Professions; International Association for Research on Epstein-Barr Virus and Associated Diseases. *Honours:* Phi Kappa Phi, 1971; Sigma Xi, 1971; Penn Laurel Pin for Volunteer Service, 1982; Teaching Excellence Award, Hood College, 1983-84. *Hobbies:* Reading; Travel; Fishing; Tennis. *Address:* 8821 Indian Springs Road, Frederick, MD 21701, USA.

BOYD-FOY Mary Louise, b. 30 June 1936, Memphis, USA. Corporate Manager. m. James Arthur Foy, 16 Mar. 1975, 1 stepson, 1 stepdaughter. *Education:* BA, Sociology, Columbia University, 1977. *Appointments:* Assistant to Director, United Negro College Fund Inc., 1958-60; Administrative Assistant, Foreign Policy Association, 1960-70; Executive Assistant, School of Engineering and Applied Science, Columbia University, In the City of New York, 1970-78; Sales Manager, 1978-80, Corporate Manager, 1980, Ebasco Services Inc. *Memberships Include:* Board, YWCA of New York, 1989-; American Association of Blacks in Energy; United Negro College Fund. *Honours:* Woman of the Year, National Association of University Women, 1984; Recognition award, 1984; many other honours and awards. *Hobbies:* Tennis; Theatre; Opera; Travel. *Address:* 117-20 232 Street, Cambria Heights, Queens, NY 11411, USA.

BOYD-LEOPARD Norree, b. 10 June 1951, Beckley, USA. Fine Arts Administrator; Musician. m. Lewis Boyd-Leopard, 15 Dec. 1979, 1 son. *Education:* BS, Music, East Tennessee State University, 1974; MM, Voice, College Conservatory of Music, University of Cincinnati, 1976. *Appointments:* Administration Services Co-ordinator, National Association of Campus Activities, 1979-82; Property Management State of South Carolina, 1982-83; Research Parks Manager, South Carolina Research Authority, 1983-89; Executive Director, Fine Arts Center of Kershaw County, 1989-. *Memberships:* Delta Omicron; Columbia Music Festival Association, Board Member; Columbia Choral Society, President. *Honours:* Orion Award, 1969; Jane Hobson Haward, Metropolitan Opera Auditions, 1974; Outstanding Young Artist, Women's Voice, National Federation of Music Clubs, 1985-87; Outstanding Young Women in America, 1986. *Hobbies:* Opera; Choral Music; Children's Choirs; Reading; Travel. *Address:* 201 Greengate Drive, Columbia, SC 29223, USA.

BOYER Alta E., b. 18 Oct. 1914, Lodi, New York, USA, Medical Librarian; Preservationist. m. (1) Charles H. Boyer, 8 May 1940, 1 son, 1 daughter, (2) Charles A. Blohm, 9 July 1980. *Education:* BA, William Smith College, 1936; MLS, Stte University of New York, Genesco, 1963; Certification, Medical Library Association 1975, New England Centre for Document Preservation 1976. *Appointments include:* WPC, retired 1978; Chief, Library Services, Willard Psychiatric Centre, NY, 1957-78. *Publications:* Siltstone Houses of Seneca County; Regional Study of Early Dutch Style Barns; ABC for John; Houses of Lodi, New York; Brochures, bibliographies, NY State Department of Mental Hygiene. *Memberships include:* Offices, past/present: Regional Council of Historic Agencies, Syracuse, NY; Mental Health Committee, Seneca County Community Counselling Services; Finger Lakes Library System; Lodi Historical Society; American Legion Auxiliary. Member, various other professional & community organisations. *Honour:* Alumnae Citation, professional & community services, Hobart-William Smith Colleges, 1986. *Hobbies:* Playing piano & organ; Gardening; Travel; Braided Rugs; Paper Restoration.

Address: 8678 Watkins Glen Road, Lodi, New York 14860, USA.

BOYER Ruth Eleanor Gasink, b. 18 May 1913, Minneapolis, Minnesota, USA. Researcher; Writer. m. 20 Dec. 1943, divorced 1951. 2 sons, 1 daughter. *Education:* BA, University of Minnesota, 1934; MSS, Smith College for Social Work, Psychiatric Social Work, 1936; Workshops related to human behaviour, psychotherapy and social work education, 1936-76; DSW, Catholic University of America, National Catholic School of Social Service, 1966. *Appointments:* Investigator, Federal Emergency Relief Administration, 1934-35; Caseworker, Milwaukee Family Welfare Association, 1936-39; Senior Caseworker, Children's Protective Society, Minneapolis, 1939- 40; Assistant Professor, Florida State College for Women (now Florida State University), 1940-43; Assistant Field Director, American Red Cross, Hospital Service, 1943-45; School Social Worker and Chairman of Special Education, School District No 124, Robbinsdale, 1951-58; Associate Professor, Graduate School of Social Work, Richmond Professional Institute (now Virginia Commonwealth University); Associate Professor, Graduate School of Social Service Administration, Arizona State University, 1963-66; Associate Professor, Graduate School of Social Work, University of Georgia, 1966-67; Professor, Department of Social Work, Florida State University, 1967-68; Professor, Graduate School of Social Work, University of Arkansas at Little Rock, 1968-76. *Publications:* Books: Be Gentle With Yourself:You have a right to be Happy, 1982; Be Gentle With Yourself: Your Feelings and The Bad Guys, 1982; The Happy Adolescent, 1981; An Approach to Human Services, 1975; Tomorrow is Living, 1968; Numerous articles, monographs, chapters and speeches to professional journals, magazines and conferences. *Memberships:* Order of the Eastern Star; Alpha Omicron Pi; President Milwaukee Alumnae Chapter, 1937-39. *Honours:* Personal Representative, Governor of Arkansas, White House Conference on Aging, 1971; Dr Ruth G Boyer Day, City of North Little Rock, Arkansas, 11 Feb. 1975; Professor Emeritus, University of Arkansas, 1977. *Hobbies:* Bridge; Gardening; Singing; Acting. *Address:* 1091 Cheltenham Court, Longwood, Florida 32750, USA.

BOYES Megan, b. 7 July 1923, Cardiff, Wales. Author. m. Ivor Jardine Johnstone Boyes, 31 Dec. 1949. 1 daughter. *Education:* Matriculation, London University, 1939. *Appointment:* Civil Servant, War Office, Whitehall, London, 1940-49. *Publications:* Books: Auntie Blodwen & The Pageant, 1967; Allestree Hall, 1983; Queen of A Fantastic Realm, 1986; Love Without Wings, 1988. Radio Serial: Bess of Holmepierrepont; Mary of Annesley; Margaret of Welbeck; Mary of Thoresby. Short stories, articles. *Memberships:* Society of Authors; Royal Overseas League; British Byron Society; Newstead Abbey Byron Society, Committee; Thoroton Society; Friends of Derby & Nottingham; National Trust; English Heritage; Derbyshire Archaeological Society; Nottingham Mechanics Institute; Kirkby & Ashfield Conservation Society. *Hobbies:* Reading; Gardening; Local history research. *Address:* The Glade, 49 Evans Avenue, Allestree, Derby DE3 2EP, England.

BOYLAN Clare Catherine, b. 1948, Dublin, Ireland. Novelist. m. A Wilkes, 1970. *Education:* NUJ Journalists School. *Appointments:* Journalist, newspapers, magazines, TV and Radio, Ireland, 1968-78; Edited, Image magazine, Ireland, 1981-84; Novelist. *Publications:* Novels: Holy Pictures, 1983-84; Last Resorts, 1984, 1986; Black Baby, 1988; Doubleday, 1989. Short stories: A Nail on The Head, 1983, 1985; Concerning Virgins, 1990; Included in magazines and anthologies. *Honours:* Benson and Hedges Prize for Outstanding work in Irish Journalism, 1974; Film version of short story Some Retired Ladies on a Tour, filmed by All female crew as Making Waves, nominated for Hollywood Oscar, 1988. *Interests:* Lit criticism: book reviews for numerous papers and magazines; Introduction to Molly Keane's Taking Chances;

Interviews and essays; Conducted Writers' Workshops; Booker Prize Judge, 1978. *Address:* c/o Rogers, Coleridge & White Ltd, Literary Agency, 20 Powis Mews, London W11 1JN, England.

BOYLE Barbara Dorman, b. 11 Aug. 1935, New York City, USA. President, Sovereign Pictures Inc. m. Kevin Boyle, 26 Nov. 1960. 2 sons. *Education:* BA, University of California, Berkeley, 1957; JD, University of California, Los Angeles, 1960. *Appointments:* Corporate Counsel, Business Affairs, American International Pictures, 1960-65; Partner, Cohen and Boyle, 1967-74; Entertainment Law Firm, Executive Vice President, General Counsel and COO, New World Pictures, 1974-82; Senior Vice President Production, ORION Pictures Corporation, 1982-85; Executive Vice President Production, RKO Pictures, 1986-88; President, Sovereign Pictures Inc., 1988-. *Memberships:* California Bar, 1961; New York Bar, 1964; US Supreme Court Bar, 1964; Academy of Motion Picture Arts and Sciences; Women in Film (President, 1977-78); Women Entertainment Lawyers Association; UCLA Law School Entertainment Symposium Advisory Board. *Address:* 557 Spoleto Drive, Pacific Palisades, CA 90272, USA.

BOYLE Kammer, b. 17 June 1946, New Orleans, USA. Organisational Psychologist; Consultant. m. Edward Turner Barfield, 23 July 1966, divorced 1975, 1 son, 1 daughter. *Education:* BS, magna cum laude, Univeity of West Florida, 1976; PhD, University of Tennessee, 1982. *Appointments:* Private Consultant, University of Tennessee, Graduate Research & Teaching Assistant, 1976-81; US State Dept., Washington DC, 1978; Management Consultant, PRADCO, Cleveland, 1982-83; Principal, Organisational Psychologist, Management and Assessment Systems Inc., 1984-. *Publications:* Author-Presenter, Annual Conference of American Psychological Association, 1980; Task Characteristics and Pay Expectations : The Mediating Effects of Perceived Equity Under conditions of Job Enrichment and Job De-Enrichment, 1982; Annual Conference for Society of Industrial/Organisational Psychology, 1987; Trends in Worker Values and Changing Organisation Cultures; Annual Conference of American Society for Training and Development, 1988; New Directions in Management Development for Meeeting New Corporate Challenges. *Memberships:* American Psychological Association; Cleveland Psychological Association; Ameriaca Society for Training and Development; Member of Editorial Review Board for Journal of Managerial Issues. *Honours:* Phi Kappa Phi; Mensa; Walter Bonham Fellow, 1980-81; Recipient, various other honours and awards. *Hobbies:* Bowling; Swimming; Public Speaking. *Address:* Management & Assessment Systems Inc., 24200 Chagrin Boulevard, Cleveland, OH 44122-5509, USA.

BOYLE Lilian Garner, b. 14 Feb. 1947, Scotland. General Manager. m. Patrick J M Boyle, 16 Feb. 1973, 2 sons. *Education:* MA, University of Glasgow, 1968; MBA, University of Witwatersrand, South Africa, 1985. *Appointments:* ManagEmEnt Services Adviser, Rolls Royce, Scotland, 1968-70; Market Research Analyst, Cape Asbestos, 1970-73; Economist, SA Breweries, 1973-79; Corporate Planning Manager, Rennies Group, 1979-86; General Manager, Thomas Cook Rennies Travel, 1986-. *Publications:* An Examination of Strategy Formulation for Competitive Advantage, 1985. *Memberships:* Institute of Directors; Soroptimist International; Institute of International Affairs. *Hobbies:* b3Ballet; Music; Wild Life; Tennis; Running. *Address:* 16 Uranus Street, Atlasville, Boksburg, South Africa 1459.

BOYSEN Melicent Pearl, b. 1 Dec. 1943, Houston, Texas, USA. Finance & Business Consultant. m. Stephen Boysen, 10 Sept. 1961, 1 son, 2 daughters. *Education:* Central Missouri State University, 1973-75. *Appointments:* Owner & President, Boysen Enterprises, Kansas City, Missouri, 1973-; Underwriter, financial consultant, New England Life Insurance Company, Kansas City, 1978-81; President, Boysen Agri-Services, 1984-. Companies provide financial, business management & agri-business consulting to American Indian Tribes including: San Luis Rey Tribal Water Authority, California; Wind River Reservation, Wyoming; Cheyenne River Sioux & Iroquois Nations, South Dakota. *Memberships:* Founding Director: Rose Brooks Centre (for battered women) 1979-, Visible Horizons (American Indian youth organisation) 1978-. Member: International Financial Planners Association; International Agri-Business Association; Kansas City Chamber of Commerce & Industry; KC Chamber of Commerce; Daughters of American Revolution; International Platform Association. *Hobby:* Stamp collecting. *Address:* Boysen Enterprises, PO Box 9104, Shawnee Mission, Kansas 66201, USA.

BOZSA Deborah Ann, b. 8 Aug. 1953, Belleville, Illinois. Vice- President, Advertising Agency; Associate Media Director. m. 18 Jan. 1975. *Education:* BA, 1974, MS, 1978, Southern Illinois University, Edwardsville. *Appointments:* Production Assistant, Jonah video, 1974; Assistant Producer, No Single Thing Abides, video art for Bicentennial Celebration, St Louis, Missouri, 1976; MIS Specialist, OFC Manpower Development, Edwardsville, Illinois, 1976-78; College Instructor, BAC, Belleville, Illinois, 1978-81; Territorial Advertising Manager, CPI Corporation, St Louis, 1979-81; Associate Media Director, 1987-88, Media Manager 1985-87, Media Supervisor, 1983-85, Media Planner 1983, Broadcast Buyer, 1981-83, Vice-President, Associate Media Director, D'Arcy, Masius, Benton & Bowles, St Louis, 1988. *Publications:* Research article (co-author) in APA Journal, 1974; Book chapter on student financial aid options (co-author), 1976. *Memberships:* St Louis Chapter, Business and Professional Advertising Association, 1986-88; Board of Directors, Director of Project Review Committee, St Louis Health Systems Agency, 1978-82; Vice- President, Board of Directors, Madison County Information Line, Edwardsville, 1975-76. *Honours:* Dean's College, 1972-74, Outstanding College Student Award, 1973-74, Activities Honor Society, 1973-74, Graduate Fellowship, 1975- 76, Southern Illinois University. *Hobbies:* Trout fishing; Canoeing; Reading. *Address:* c/o D'Arcy, Masius, Benton & Bowles, 1 Memorial Drive, St Louis, MO 63102, USA.

BPANDT Yanna Kroyt, b. 6 Sept. 1933, Berling, Germany. Television Producer, Writer & Director. m. 5 Apr. 1955. 1 son, 1 daughter. *Education:* AB, Vassar College, 1953; MS, Columbia Graduate School of Journalism, 1954. *Appointments:* CBS 1954-55; Scholastic magazines, 1955-57; Eductional broadcasting, 1957-59; CBS 1959-60; NBC, 1961-69; PBS, 1969-71; Freelance, 1971-; Own production company, Kroyt Bpandt Productions, 1977-. *Produced:* The Nutcracker with Baryshnikov; Vegetable Soup (NBC, PBS); High Feather (NBC, PBS); Denmark Vesey's Rebellion (PBS); Solomon Northup's Odyssey (PBS); Charlott Forten Mission (PBS); Concerto at Work (Bravo). *Memberships:* 10 National Academy of TV Arts & Sciences; Writers Guild of America, Awards Committee; Executive Committee, Columbia Graduate School Alumnae Council. *Honours:* 7 EMMY Awards, 1980-83; Award, Wrtiers Guild of America, 1975; Cine Golden Eagle, 1981; ACT Award, 1981; American Women in Radio & TV 1982; International TV & Film, 1982; American Academy of Paediatrics, 1982; Informational Producers of America, 1981; Ohio State Awards, IFPA 1976; CINE 1976. *Hobbies:* Tennis; Theatre; Music; Swimming. *Address:* 1349 Lexington Avenue, New York City, NY 10128, USA.

BRAATVEDT Susan Pamela, b. 21 Oct. 1952, Eshowe, Zululand, South Africa. Opera Singer. m. Frederick Snyders, 30 Mar. 1986. *Education:* BA, University of Natal, 1973. *Appointments:* Operatic roles include: Zerlina in Don Giovanni, 1980; Emilia in Otello, 1981; Maddalena in Rigoletto, 1982, 1986; Amneris in Aida, 1982; Cherubino in Nozze di Figaro, 1983; Bersi in Andrea Chenier, 1984; Page in Salome, 1984; Marzellina in Il Barbiere di Siviglia, 1984; Alicia in Lucia di Lammermoor, 1985; Czipra in Der Zigeunerbaron, 1985; Anita in La Navarraise, 1986; Un Musico in

Manon Lescaut, 1986; Auntie in Peter Grimes; Carmen, title role, 1988, 1989. Musical: Julie in Showboat, 1984; Appeared on radio and television. Oratorios and concerts include: Stabat Mater, 1984; Magnificat, 1985; Salve Regina, 1985; Messe Solennelle, 1986; Verdi Requiem, 1985. *Honours:* Nederburg prize for Opera, 1983; Vita Award from AA Mutal Insurance Company, Most Outstanding Female Singer in Transvaal, South Africa, 1985. *Hobbies:* Theatre; Painting stones; Making tapestries; Reading biographies. *Address:* 39 Rockynook, Malden, MA 02148, USA.

BRACHMANN Claire Ruth, b. 14 Oct. 1955, Windsor Locks, Connecticut, USA. Computer Specialist. *Education:* University of Connecticut, 1973-75; Asnuntuck Community College, 1988-. *Appointments:* Machinist, Stanadyne Diesel Systems, 1976-83; Machinist, Kennametal Inc, Windsor Locks, 1983-85; Customer Service Representative, Bausch & Lomb Telescope Division, 1983-85; Computer Specialist, Great American Ins Co, 1985- *Honour:* Creativity Award, Bausch & Lomb, 1985. *Hobbies:* Poetry; Public speaking; Astronomy; Reading; Education; Swimming. *Address:* P O Box 604, Windsor Locks, CT 06096, USA.

BRACIALE Vivian Lam, b. 5 June 1948, New York City, New York, USA. Assistant Professor. m. Thomas Joseph Braciale Jr, 5 Aug. 1972, 1 son, 2 daughters. *Education:* AB, Mathematics, 1969; PhD, Microbiology, 1973. *Appointments:* Visiting Fellow, Australian National University, 1976-78; Research Instructor, Pathology, 1978-83, Research Assistant Professor, Pathology, 1983-89, Assistant Professor, Pathology, 1989-, Washington University School of Medicine, St Louis, Missouri. *Publications:* Contributions to professional journals. *Memberships:* American Association of Immunologists. *Honours:* New York State Regents Scholarship, 1965-69; Service Award, National Institute of Health and National Research, 1976-78. *Address:* Department of Pathology, Washington University School of Medicine, 660 South Euclid, Box 8118, St Louis, MO 63110, USA.

BRADBURY Barbara Laura, b. 28 Apr. 1940, New South Wales, Australia. Psychotherapist; Clinical Psychologist. m. (1) 29 Dec. 1962; (2) Professor Max Wilcox, 1988. *Education:* Teachers' Certificate, NSW Education Department, 1962; AMusA (Performing Piano), AMEB, 1966; BA Hons, 1970, Dip Psychol, 1980, Sydney University. *Appointments:* Secondary School Teacher of English, History and Music, 1959-66; Music Teacher, 1967-71; Educational/Clinical Psychologist, 1971-77; Clinical Psychologist, 1978-83; Psychoanalytic Psychotherapist, 1984-88. *Publications:* Numerous papers in professional journals; Assessment of the Disturbed Child, 1980; Wholistic Assessment of the Disturbed Child, 1983; The Effect of the News of Mother's Imprisonment on the Child, Implications for Treatment, 1984; We Die Not for Ourselves but for One Another, 1985; Coping with Scleroderma: The Role of a Self-Help Organisation, 1985; Survey of People's Experience with Sclerodema, 1985. *Memberships:* Australian Psychological Society, Clinical and Counselling Boards; International Association of Applied Psychology. *Honours:* Mathematics Prize and Bursary, 1950; Teachers College Scholarship, 1957-58; Commonwealth Mature Age Scholarship, 1968-78; Walter Reid Memorial Fund Award, 1967, 1968. *Hobbies:* Music; Creative Writing; Travel; Book collecting; Theatre; The Arts; Bush camping; Photography; Square-rig sailing; Bird watching. *Address:* PO Box 156, Cammeray, NSW 2062, Australia.

BRADBURY Elizabeth Joyce, b. 12 Dec. 1918, Newcastle-upon-Tyne, England. Retired. *Education:* BA, Honours, History, 1940, Diploma, Education, 1941, University of Leeds. *Appointments:* Various Teaching Appointments, 1941-57; Deputy Headmistress, Stand Grammar School for Girls, Whitefield, 1957-59; Headmistress, Bele Grammar School for Girls, 1959-67; Headmistress, Pennywell School, Sunderland, 1967-72; Headmistress, Thornhill School, 1972-78. *Publications:* Contributor, Chapter on Management, in Headship in Secondary Schools, 1977. *Memberships:* Fellow, Royal Society of Arts; Soroptimist International, Sunderland President, 1966-67; Association of Headmistresses, National President 1974-76; Honorary Member, Secondary Heads Association. *Honours:* CBE, 1970; Moir Cullis Fellowship, British American Association, 1979. *Hobbies Include:* Travel; Photography; Literature. *Address:* 6 Cliffe Court, Roker, Sunderland SR6 9NT, England.

BRADFISCH Jean Tilden, b. 5 Feb. 1926, St Louis, USA. Editor. m. (1)Robert Dale Hall, 31 Aug. 1946, 2 daughters, (2)Robert K. Bradfisch, 30 Dec. 1959. *Education:* BA, University of Miami, 1975. *Appointments:* Copywriter, 1947-50; Graphic Designer, Univesity of Miami, 1955-59; Staff Writer, Village Post, 1960-68; Executive Editor, Sea Frontiers Magazine, 1965- *Publications:* Articles in National, regional and local periodicals. *Memberships:* Women in Communication Inc; Society of Professional Journalists; National Federation of Press Women; Florida Magazine Association. *Honours:* Recipient, various honours and awards. *Hobbies:* Photography; Crafts; Arts; Travel. *Address:* Sea Frontiers, International Oceanographic Fdn, 3979 Rickenbacker Cwy, Miami, FL 33149, USA.

BRADFORD Barbara Taylor, b. Leeds, England. Writer. m. Robert Bradford, 1963. *Appointments* include: Cub reporter, Women's Page Editor, Yorkshire Evening Post; Fashion Editor, Woman's Own, London; Feature writer & columnist, Evening News, Today magazine; Executive Editor, London American weekly newspaper; Column, Designing Woman, for Newsday Syndicate, later syndicated by New York Daily News Syndicate, Los Angeles Times Syndicate, ran in 185 US newspapers, 12 years. *Publications:* Complete Encyclopaedia of Homemaking Ideas; Woman of Substance, novel (sold 7 million copies, worldwide); Voice of the Heart, novel; Hold the Dream, novel. *Honours include:* Award, 1st Women's Bank, New York City, 1983. *Address:* c/o Grafton Books, 8 Grafton Street, London W1X 3LA, England.

BRADFORD Louise Mathilde, b. 3 Aug. 1925, Alexandria, Louisiana, USA. Social Worker. *Education:* BSc, Business Administration, Louisiana Technical University, 1945; Social Work Certificate, LA State University, 1949; MSc, Columbia University School of Social Work, 1953; Graduate study, various establishments. Certified, State & National Boards; Diplomate in Clinical Social Work. *Appointments:* Stenographer, 1945-48; Welfare visitor 1948-50, case worker 1950-53; Children's case worker 1953-57, Supervisor 1957-59; Child Welfare Consultant, Tallulah Region, 1959-63; State Consultant on Day Care, 1963-66; Social Services Consultant, Alexandria Region, 1966-78; Adjunct Assistant Professor of Sociology, Louisiana College, Pineville, 1970-86; Director of Social Services, St Mary's Training School, Alexandria, 1978-; Private Consultant, Louisiana Special Education Centre, Alexandria, 1980-86. Numerous national & state committees & conferences; Delegate, International Conferences on Social Welfare, Kenya 1974, Israel 1978, Hong Kong 1980, England 1982, Canada 1984. *Memberships:* International Council on Social Welfare; National Association of Social Workers; Central Louisiana Professional Advisory Committee, Parents Without Partners; Louisiana Conference on Social Welfare; American Association on Mental Deficiency; Various community & leisure organisations. *Honours:* Social Worker of Year, local chapter, National Association of Social Workers, 1974; 2 awards, Louisiana Conference of Social Welfare, 1987. *Hobby:* Travel. *Address:* 5807 Joyce Street, Alexandria, Louisiana 71302, USA.

BRADLEY Betty Hunt, b. 17 Dec. 1932, Oelwein, Iowa, USA. Psychologist. m. Ray P. Bradley, 21 Apr. 1962, 1 daughter. *Education:* BA, Coe College; MA, Ohio State University; Psychology License, State of Ohio. *Appointments:* Psychologist, State of Ohio, Dept. of Mental Retardation, 1955-. *Publications:* Co-Author: Teaching Moderately & Severely Retarded Children -

a Diagnostic Approach, 1971; Book Chapters: The Slow Learner, In The Difficult Child, 1964; The Use of Teaching Machines with the Mentally Retarded, 1965; articles in journals. *Honours:* Phi Kappa Phi; Crescent Mortar Board *Hobby:* Detiology. *Address:* 1601 West Broad Street, Columbus Developmental Center, Columbus, OH 43223, USA.

BRADLEY Connie D, b. 1 Oct. 1945, Shelbyville, Tennessee, USA. Southern Regional Executive Director. m. Jerry Bradley, 12 June 1976. *Appointments:* Receptionist, WLAC-TV Station; Executive Secretary, Dot Records; Assistant, Bill Hudson & Associates Advertising Agency; Executive Secretary, RCA Records; Southern Regional Executive Director, American Society of Composers, Authors and Publishers. *Memberships:* President, Country Music Association; Past Chairman, Nashville Area Chamber of Commerce; Board of Directors: Country Music Foundation; Nashville Songwriters International Assoc; Gospel Music Association; National Academy of Recording Arts and Sciences; Copyright Society of the South; Alabama Hall of Fame. *Honours:* Named Lady Executive of the Year, National Womens Executives, 1985; Featured in Nashville! magazine, one of seven leading ladies of Nashville, 1988; Featured on cover and article of Advantage magazine, 1989. *Hobbies:* Travelling; Reading; Community activities. *Address:* American Society of Composers, Authors and Publishers, 2 Music Square West, Nashville, TN 37203, USA.

BRADLEY Myra James (Sister), b. 1 Feb. 1924, Cincinnati, Ohio, USA. Hospital and Healthcare President. *Education:* BS, Education, Athenaeum of Ohio, 1950; RN Nursing, Good Samaritan Hospital, Dayton, Ohio, 1954; BS, Nursing, Mt St Joseph, Ohio, 1954; MS, Hospital Administration, St Louis University, 1959. *Appointments:* Assistant Administrator, St Mary Corwin Hospital, Pueblo, Colorado, 1960; Administrator, St Joseph Hospital, Mt Clemens, Michigan, 1960-65; President, Penrose Hospitals, Colorado Springs, Colorado, 1965-; President, Penrose-St Francis Catholic Healthcare, 1987-. *Memberships:* Colorado Hospital Association Board, 1982-88; National Council of Community Hospitals Board, 1974-88; American College of Hospital Administrators; Association of Western Hospitals Board, 1986-88. *Honours:* Distinguished Service Award, University of Colorado, Colorado Springs, 1983; Civis Princeps, Regis College of Colorado Springs, 1984; Sword of Hope, American Cancer Society, 1988. *Hobbies:* Painting; Cross-country skiing. *Address:* Penrose Hospitals, 2215 North Cascade, Colorado Springs, CO 80907, USA.

BRADNA Joanne Justice, b. 1 May 1952, Evergreen Park, Illinois, USA. Assistant Professor. m. William Charles, 20 Aug. 1972. 2 sons. *Education:* BS, Northwestern University, Illinois, 1974; MS, University of Illinois at Chicago, 1981. *Appointments:* Med Tech, Northwestern University Medical School, Chicago, 1974-76; Med Tech, Good Samaritan Hospital, Illinois, 1977-78; Instructor, Dept of Med Lab Sciences, University of Illinois at Chicago, 1976-81; Technical Sales Representative, Analytab Products, New York, 1981-84; Assistant Professor and Clinical Coordinator, Dept of Med Lab Sciences, University of Illinois at Chicago, 1987-. *Publications:* Contributor of articles and abstracts to professional journals. *Memberships:* American Society of Clinical Pathologists; American Society for Medical Technology; Chicago Society for Med Tech; Illinois Med Tech Association; American Soc Micro; Illinois Soc Micro; South Central Assoc Clin Micro; Hinsdale Jr Woman's Club, Treasurer, President; Illinois Fed Women's Club, 3rd Vice president of 5th District, Treasurer 5th District. *Honours:* Outstanding Member, Hinsdale Jr Woman's Club, 1981, 1982; Certificate of Recognition, American Society Med Tech, 1977; Certificate of Recognition, Chicago Society Med Tech, 1978, 1979, 1980; Who's Who in the Midwest. *Hobbies & Interests:* Golf; Football Fan; Children; Family. *Address:* Dept of Medical Laboratory Sciences, 808 South Wood Street, Room 690 CME, Chicago, IL 60612, USA.

BRADSHAW Alice Linda, b. 11 June 1957, Indiana, USA. Attorney-at-Law. *Education:* BA, Georgetown College, 1979; JD, University of Kentucky College of Law, 1982. *Appointment:* Attorney, sole practitioner, 1982-. *Creative work:* Original lost wax jewellery design & casting; Gemstone cutting. *Memberships:* Committee member, American Bar Association; Secretary & Treasurer, Kentucky & Clark County Bar Associations; Kentucky Academy of Trial Attorneys; Past and present president, Historic Thomson subdivision, American Trial Lawyers Association; Past president, Rockhounds of Central Kentucky; Journal editor, League of Women Voters. *Honours:* Biology award, Georgetown University, 1974; Moot Court Oral Advocacy Award, 1980; Continuing legal education award, Kentucky Bar Association, 1987. *Hobbies:* Jewellery design; Lapidiary; Horticulture; Stained glass. *Address:* 31 North Main Street, Winchester, Kentucky 40391, USA.

BRADSHAW Dove, b. 24 Sep. 1949, New York City, New York, USA. Artist. *Education:* BFA, The Boston Museum School of Fine Arts, 1973. *Appointments:* The School of Visual Arts, 1976-81; Artistic Advisor, The Merce Cunningham Dance Company, 1984-. *Creative works:* Paintings; Sculptures, videos, performance, photographs, thearte designs; nothing (artist book); Works in permanent collections at: Museum of Modern Art, New York; Metropolitan Museum of Art, New York; Brooklyn Museum, New York; Philadelphia Museum of Art; Whitney Museum of American Art, New York; Kunst Museum, Dusseldorf, Federal Republic of Germany; Getty Museum, Santa Monica, California; The Art Institute of Chicago. *Honours:* National Endowment for the Arts, 1975-76; Pollock Krasner Award, 1985-86. *Hobbies:* Reading; Running. *Address:* 640 Riverside Drive, New York, NY 10031, USA.

BRADSHAW Renee Sara, b. 13 Apr. 1965, Washington, District of Columbia, USA. Paralegal Student. *Education:* Paralegal Certificate 1988, BA Psychology 1986, George Washington University; Diploma, Immaculate Conception Academy, 1982. *Appointments:* Reasoner, Davis & Fox, paralegal, 1988-; Legal assistant, Clone, Adams & Dean. *Memberships:* Treasurer, Glee Club; Treasurer, Youth Council; Troop Leader, Girl Scouts of America. *Honours:* National Honor Society of secondary Schools, 1982; Future Business Leaders of America, 1982; Mount Vernon HI/Ship Program, 1982; Organizer, Thurgood Marshall Law Society, GWU, 1984; PTA Volunteer Pan-5years, 1988; Outstanding Service to Goding Elem, 1987; Academic Scholarship, Shiloh Baptist Church, 1982; American Legion Auxilary Cherry Blossom Girls State Award, 1982; Youth Speaker & Director, Shiloh Baptist Church. *Hobbies:* Teaching sign language; Swimming; Reading; Writing; Poetry; Speaking in public; Track and volleyball. *Address:* 7517-16th Street NW, Washington, DC 20012, USA.

BRADY Darlene Ann, b. 4 Aug. 1951, Fort Hood, Texas, USA. Artist; Designer; Professor. m. Mark M. English, 26 Dec. 1984. *Education:* BFA, Ohio University, 1976; MA, University of Pittsburgh, 1980; MS Arch, University of Cincinnatti, 1986. *Appointments include:* Teaching: Assistant, University of Pittsburgh, 1978-80; Various capacities, Departments of Design, Architecture, Interior Design (currently Adjunct Assistant Professor, Architecture), University of Cincinnati. Design: Co-Partner, Archi-Textures, Cincinnati, 1984-. Various administrative positions (arts): Frick Fine Arts Gallery, University of Pittsburgh, 1979-80; Stained Glass Association of America, 1980-81; Tulane University, 1981-83. *Creative work includes:* Various commissions, stained glass, 1977-. Participant, group exhibitions including: 6 National Exhibitions of Stained Glass, 1980; Vitraux des USA (juried), Chartres, France, 1985; Stained Glass in Architecture (juried), Corning Museum of Glass, New York, 1987. Various monographs & articles, Le Corbusier, stained glass. *Honours:* Dean's Scholarship 1977, Provost Scholarship 1978, University of Pittsburgh; J. Wayland Morgan & Phi Kappa Phi scholarships, 1977; Best use of hand-blown glass, National Exhibition of Stained Glass,

Toronto, Canada, 1985; Biographical listings. *Hobby:* Landscaping. *Address:* 1665 Pullan Avenue, Cincinnati, Ohio 45223, USA.

BRAHAM Delphine Doris, b. 16 Mar. 1946, L'Anse, Michigan, USA. Government Accountant. m. John Emerson Braham, 23 Sept. 1967. 1 son, 2 daughters. *Education:* BS, summa cum laude, Drury College, Springfield, Missouri, 1983; MA, Webster University, St Louis, 1986. *Appointments:* Bookkeeper, Community Mental Health Center, Marquette, Michigan, 1966-68; Accounting Technician, St Joseph's Hospital, Parkersburg, 1972-74; Material Manager, 1982-86, Accountant, 1986-, US Dept of Army, Ft Leonard Wood, Missouri; Instructor, Adjunct Faculty, Columbia College, 1987-; Instructor, Adjunct Faculty, Park College, 1987-. *Memberships:* American Society of Military Comptrollers, 1986-; Association of Government Accountants, 1987-; Alpha Sigma Lambda, 1983; National Association of Female Executives, 1983-; Federal Women's Program Executive Committee Secretary, 1986-88; American Association of University Women, Treasurer-Waynesville, Missouri Branch, 1986- 88; Girl Scout Leader 1972-74 and 1977-79. *Honours:* National Dean's List, 1982 & 1983 editions; National Merit Scholar Finalist, 1963; Valedictorian, Class of 63, Champion High School, 1963. *Hobbies:* Volksmarching; Reading. *Address:* Rt 2, Box 248L No 28, Waynesville, Missouri 65583, USA.

BRAMAN Heather Ruth (Hansford), b. 27 Apr. 1934, Wilmington, Ohio, USA. Technical Writer; Consultant. m. Barr Oliver Braman, 29 June 1957 div. 1974, 1 son, 1 daughter. *Education:* BA, Hiram College, 1956; Additional courses, Sinclair Community College, Wright State University. *Appointments:* Personnel clerk, Wright-Patterson Air Force Base, Ohio, 1956; Specifications editor 1956-57, Publications editor, writer 1957-63; Homemaker, & volunteer, Children's Medical Center, Dayton Public Schools, 1963-86; Teacher, Gloria Dei Montessori School, Dayton, 1973-77; Assistant Manager, Acting Manager, Manager, tennis club, 1977-81; Technical Writer, Miclin Inc., Alpha, Ohio 1982, Industrial Design Concepts, Dayton, 1982-83; Technical Writer & Consultant, Belcan Corporation, Cincinnati, 1984-. *Memberships include:* Founder, Past Board Member, Trotwood (Ohio) Women's Open Tennis Tournament; Past President, Dayton Tennis Commission; Harrison Township Parks Board; Parents' Executive Committee, Hiram College; Court-appointed Special Advocate & Guardian Ad Litem, 1988-; Various other community associations. *Honours:* Sustained Superior Performance Awards, 1962, 1963. *Hobbies:* Antiques & collectables; Tennis; Reading; Real estate investment. *Address:* 320 Elm Hill Drive, Dayton, Ohio 45415, USA.

BRAMWELL Elinda Lois, b. 8 Jan. 1923, South Africa. m. John Edgar Dale Bramwell, 5 July 1947. 1 son, 3 daughters. *Education:* BA, Social Studies (Rand), 1947. *Appointments:* Probation officer, Dept of Social Welfare, 1947-49; Voluntary Capacity in many allied fields. *Publications:* Booklet on Day Care Facilities for the Pre school Child; Booklet on After School Care on the Witwatersrand. *Memberships:* National Executive Member, South African Association for Early Childhood Education; Chairman, Committee of Concern for Children; President, national Council of Women of South Africa. *Honour:* Appointed one of the Women of our Time 1986 in South Africa. *Hobbies:* Reading; Needlework. *Address:* P O Box 87, Himeville, Natal 4585, South Africa.

BRAMWELL Marvel Lynnette, b. 13 Aug. 1947, Durango, Colorado, USA. Registered Nurse. *Education:* BS, South Oregon State College; Graduate Programme, University of Utah, ongoing. *Appointments:* Staff Nurse, Monument Valley Seventh-day Adventist Mission Hospital, 1973-74; Staff Nurse, LaPlata Community Hospital, Durango, Colorado, 1974-75; Health Coordinator, Tri-County Head Start Program, Durango, 1974-75; Nurse Therapist/Team Leader, Portland Adventist Medical Center, Portland, 1975-78; Staff Nurse, Indian Health Service Hospital, Barrow, Alaska, 1980-81; Village Health Services Coordinator, North Slop Borough Health and Social Service Agency, Barrow, 1981-83; Home Care Nurse, QA Nurse, Supervisor for Home Health Aides and Homemaker/Companions, Bonneville Health Care Agency, Salt Lake City, 1984-85; Adolescent Psychiatric Unit, Staff Nurse, LDS Hospital, Salt Lake City, 1985-86; Adolescent Nursing Coordinator, CPC Olympus View, Salt Lake City, 1986-87; Adult Psychiatric Unit, Staff Nurse, Part-time Charge Nurse, University of Utah Medical Center, Salt Lake City, 1987-88. *Publications:* Articles: North Slope Borough Telehealth, 1982; Nursing in the Alaskan Arctic, in press. *Memberships:* National League of Nurses; Association for Women in Science; National Organization of Women. *Honours:* Voted Most Supportive NSB Health Department Staff by the Community Health Aides, 1983; Certificate of Appreciation, Barrow Lions Club, 1983. *Address:* P O Box 511282, Salt Lake City, Utah 84151, USA.

BRANCHAW Bernadine P, b. 23 Jan. 1933, Joliet, Illinois, USA. Professor. *Education:* BA, College of St Francis, 1964; MS, Education 1970, EdD 1972, Northern Illinois University. *Appointment:* Western Michigan University, 1971-. *Publications:* Author: English Made Easy; Co-author, Business Communication From Process to Product; Business Report Writing; SRA Reference Manual for Office Personnel; several other textbooks; Successful Communication in Business; Effective Business Correspondence. *Memberships:* Association for Business Communication, Board Member and Vice President of Midwest Region; National Business Education Association; Michigan Business Education Association; Zonta Club of Kalamazoo, Past President. *Honours:* Francis W Weeks Award of Merit, Association for Bus Com, 1982; Professional Achievement Award, College of St Francis, 1986; Distinguished Faculty Award, Michigan Assn of Governing Boards, 1987; Distinguished Member Award, Association of Bus Com, 1987. *Hobbies:* Writing; Consulting; Travelling. *Address:* 809 Weaver Avenue, Kalamazoo, MI 49007, USA.

BRAND Mona Alexis, b. 22 Oct. 1915, Sydney, Australia. Freelance Writer. m. Len Fox, 26 Sept. 1955. *Appointments:* Advertising Copywriter, 1935-41; Industrial Welfare & Personnel Management, 1942-48. *Publications:* Poems, Short Stories, Plays, etc; Here Under Heaven; Strangers in the Land; Better a Millstone; No Strings Attached; Barbara; Our Dear Relations; And a Happy New Year; Here Comes Kisch. *Memberships:* Australian Society of Authors; Australian Writers Guild; Fellowship of Australian Writers; Society of Women Writers; etc. *Honours:* James Picot Memorial Poetry Prize, 1945; Moomba Festival Prize, 1972; Noosa Arts Theatre Prize, 1985. *Hobbies:* Reading; Theatre; Cryptic Crosswords. *Address:* 10 Little Surrey St., Potts Point, NSW 2011, Australia.

BRANDT Kathleen Weil-Garris, b. 7 Apr. 1934, Surrey, England. Art Historian. m. Werner Brandt, 1982, deceased 1983. *Education:* BA Honors, Vassar College, 1956; MA 1958, PhD 1965, Harvard University. *Appointments:* Asst Prof 1963-67, Assoc Prof 1967-72, Professor 1973-, New York University College of Arts & Science; Assoc Prof, 1967-72, Professor 1973-, New York University Institute of Fine Arts; Visiting Professor, Harvard, 1980; Editor, Art Bulletin, 1977-81; Consultant, Vatican Museums, 1987-. *Publications:* Leonardo & Central Italian Art, 1974; Problems in Cinquecento Sculpture, 1977; The renaissance Cardinal's..Palace (with J d'Amico), 1981; numerous articles on Renaissance art, architecture; Films on art; with J Ackerman, Looking for Renaissance Rome, 1974. *Memberships:* College Art Assn, board, 1973-74, 1977-81; Renaissance Soc of America; Soc of Architectural Historians; Phi Beta Kappa, NYU Chapt VP, 1972-76; NY Academy of Sciences; Metropolitan Soc for Hist of Sciences; Friends Vassar Coll Art Gall, VP, 1979-81. *Honours:* American Academy of Poets, 1955; Phi Beta Kappa, 1955; Lindback Award for Distinguished Teaching, 1967; Alexander von Humboldt Research

Prize, 1985; Fellowships include: Fulbright 1956, National Endowment for the Humanities, 1975, 1981-84; Guggenheim, 1976; elected NY Academy of Science, 1988. *Hobbies:* Film; Music; Collecting; Dance. *Address:* Institute of Fine Arts, One East 78th Street, New York, NY 10021, USA.

BRASHEAR Rama Maxine, b. 12 Mar. 1925, Apperson, Oklahoma, USA. Apartment Manager, 176 Unit complex. m. T C Brashear, 8 Mar. 1946. deceased. 2 sons, 1 daughter. *Education:* High School Graduate, Joplin, Missouri, 1943; Tulsa Business College, 1954. *Appointments:* Secretary to President, Century Geophysical Corp, 1962; Executive Secretary to Vice President, ENGR of Seismograph Service, 1976-82; Secretary to General Director of Metropolitan YMCA, 1974-76. *Memberships:* National Association of Female Executives; American Society of Professional and Executive Women. *Honour:* Certificate of Merit, Thomas Gilcrease Institute of American History & Art, 1955. *Address:* 1937 South 68th East Avenue, No 124A, Tulsa, Oklahoma 74112, USA.

BRATTON Ida Frank Button, b. 31 Aug. 1933, Glasgow, Kentucky, USA. Teacher. m. Robert Franklin Bratton, 20 June 1954. 1 son. *Education:* BA Major Mathematics and English, 1959; MA, Leadership, 1962, Western Kentucky University; Standard Teaching Certificate, Standard Leadership Certificate, Kentucky. *Appointments:* Teacher of Mathematics and Science, Gottschalk Junior High School, Louisville, 1959-65; Teacher of Mathematics, Iroquois High School, Louisville, 1965-79; Teacher, Mathematics and English, Waggener High School, Louisville, 1979-. *Memberships:* National Education Association; Kentucky Education Association; Jefferson County Teacher's Association; American Association of University Women. *Hobbies:* Travel; Needlecrafts. *Address:* 304 Paddington Court, Louisville, KY 40222, USA.

BRAUN Barbara Ann, b. 13 Nov. 1923, Whitewater Twp, Michigan, USA. Homemaker. m. Gilbert L Braun, 1 Sept. 1947. 3 sons, 2 daughters. *Education:* High School, 1940; Secretarial School, 1941. *Appointments:* Michigan Public Service, 1941-44; Great Lakes Naval Base, 1944-47; RR Donnelly & Sons, Chicao, 1947-49. *Memberships:* Numerous Offices including: President, Women Diocese of Eau Claire, 1977- 79; Delegate, National Women's Triennial, 1973, 1976, 1979, 1982, 1985; Director, Teen's Encounter Christ, 1975-79, 1985-86, Episcopal Church; Leader 1954-79, National Council Member 1969-75, President Board of Directors, Eau Claire Council, 1974-76, 1978-81, Treaasurer 1986-, Campfire; State Discussion Leador 1983, State Convention Chairman, 1977, Secretary Board of Directors, Eau Claire, 1975-77, Leage of Women Voters; Co-Director, 1st Handicapped Swim Class, Wisconsin, 1965-72, Red Cross Handicapped Swim Programme; Board of Directors, Indianhead AAU Swim Club, 1969-75; Episcopal Church; Chairman National Books Fund Committee; National Board of Church, Periodical Club; Chairman, PEWSACTION, 22 organizations of the Episcopal Church, 1986-. *Honours:* Luther Halsey Gulick Medalion, Camp Fire, 1980; Distinguished Service Award, Jaycees, 1981. *Hobbies:* Bridge; Golf; Games. *Address:* 9 Dolphin Lane, Bella Vista, AR 72714, USA.

BRAUN-MOSER Ursula, b. 25 May 1937, Frankfurt-am-Main, Germany. Economist; Member, European Parliament. m. Dr Bernd Braun, 20 Oct. 1960, 2 sons. *Education:* Dip.rer.pol., Goethe University, Frankfurt, 1963. *Appointments:* Scientific Assistant, Institute for Monetary & Currency Theory, Frankfurt University; member, Town & District councils, Bad Vilbel, 1968-79; Deputy Mayor, Wetterau District, 1979-86; Member, European Parliament, 1984-. *Publications:* various journalisticc writings. *Memberships:* Board Member, Women of the Christian Democratic Union, Hessen; President, Christian Democratic Women, Wetterau; Various women's Associations, Hessen; Speaker, Association of Small shareholders in Germany; President, European Union of Small and Medium Sized Enterprises, Section Germany. *Address:* Erzweg 55, 6368 Bad Vilbel, Federal Republic of Germany.

BRAVERMAN Louise Marcia, b. 23 Nov. 1948, New York, USA. Architect. m. Steven Z. Glickel, 1 July 1984, 1 daughter. *Education:* BA, University of Michigan, 1970; M.Arch, Yale University, 1977. *Appointments:* Partner, Austin Braverman Patterson Architects, 1982-. *Memberships:* American Institute of Architects; Association of Real Estate Women; Yale Club; Charter Member, National Women's Museum. *Honours:* Guest Architectural Design Critic, 1978-88: Yale, Pennsylvania, Syracuse Ohio State & Columbia Universities. *Hobbies:* Aesthetic Interests; Ahletics. *Address:* Austin Braverman Patterson Architects, 39 East 31 Street, New York, NY 10016, USA.

BREAKEY Gail Farrington, b. 5 June 1934, Rochester, New York, USA. Health Director. *Education:* Nursing Diploma, Rochester, 1958; BA Political Science 1967, MPH International Health 1968, University of Hawaii. *Appointments include:* Director, child abuse prevention programme for infants (model for statewide programme), Kapiolani Medical Centre, Hawaii; Planning & implementation, child abuse & drug abuse treatment programmes in Hawaii, 15 years; Child Health Care Plan; Conducted health survey, Laos; Director, Hawaii Family Stress Centre, current. *Publications:* Nutritional Status of Villages in Laos, HSMHA Reports, 1972; Mekong Valley Health Survey, University of Hawaii Press, 1975; Prevention of Child Abuse & the Medical Home, HMA Journal, 1986. *Memberships:* President, Big Sisters of Hawaii; Director, Hawaii Bound; Secretary, Wainae Kai Development Inc; Vice President, Hawaii Flight for Life; Hawaii Public Health Association; University of Hawaii School of Public Health Alumni Association. *Honours:* 2 scholarships, 1966; Yachtsman of Year, Hawaii Yacht Club, 1973; Honoree, Children & Youth Conference on Prevention of Child Abuse, Honolulu, 1988. *Hobbies:* Yacht racing; Scuba diving; Soaring; Hiking; Reading; Music apreciation. *Address:* Hawaii Family Stress Centre, 2919 Kapiolani Blvd no. 30, Honolulu, Hawaii 96826, USA.

BREAKWELL Glynis Marie, b. 26 July 1952, Tipton, West Midlands, England. Senior Lecturer. *Education:* BA, honours, Psychology, Leicester University, 1973; MSc., Research Methods, University of Strathclyde, 1975; PhD, University of Bristol, 1976. *Appointments:* Lecturer, Bradford University, 1976-78; Prize Fellow, Tutor, Nuffield College, Oxford, 1978-82; Lecturer, 1981-87, Senior Lecturer, 1987-88, Reader, 1988-, Psychology, University of Surrey. *Publications:* The Quiet Robot, 1000, Coping with Threatened Identities, 1986; Facing Physical Violence, 1989. *Memberships:* Fellow, British Psychological Society; European Association of Experimental Social Psychologists. *Honours:* MA, by Special Resolution, University of Oxford, 1978; British Psychological Society's Young Social Psychologist Award, 1978; Associate, 1984, Fellow, 1987, British Psychological Society. *Hobbies:* Racquet Sports; Painting. *Address:* Dept. of Psychology, University of Surrey, Guildford, Surrey GU2 5XH, England.

BREDIMA-SAVOPOULOU Anna, b. 3 June 1949, Athens, Greece. Lawyer. Married with one daughter. *Education:* LLB, Law Degree, University of Athens Law School, 1971; LLM, Master of Laws in Shipping Law, 1972; PhD, Doctor of Philosophy in EEC Law, 1976, University College, London; Certificate in EEC Law, University of Paris Centre for European Studies, 1973. *Appointments:* Legal Assistant on EEC, Ministry of Economic Coordination, Greece, 1977-81; Special Advisor on EEC, Union of Greek Shipowners, 1977-81; Special Advisor on International/EEC Affairs, Union of Greek Shipowners, 1981-; Member, Economic and Social Committee of the European Communities, 1981-. *Creative Works:* Methods of Interpretation and Community Law, 1978. *Membership:* Pierce College Alumnae Association. *Hobbies:* Swimming; Sailing; Gardening; Reading. *Address:* 13 Papadiamantopoulou Street, Athens 11528, Greece.

BREEN Katherine Anne, b. 31 Oct. 1948, Chicago, USA. Speech Language Pathologist. *Education:* BS, Northwestern University, 1970; MA, University of Missouri, 1971. *Appointments:* Fulton Missouri Public Schools, 1971-73; Easter Seal Society, summers 1972-73; Shawnee MIssion, Kansas Public Schools, 1973-; St Joseph's Hospital, Kansas City, 1978-81; Midwest Rehabilitatiron Centre, 1985. *Memberships:* American, Kansas Speech Language Hearing Association; National Education Association; Missouri State Teachers Association; Zeta Phi Eta. *Honours:* US Rehabilitation Services Trainee, 1971; Certificate, Clinical Competence, American Speech Language Hearing Association, 1973; Outstanding Leadership Award, Northwestern University Alumni Admissions Council. *Hobbies:* Reading; Historic Preservation; Art; Architecture; Travel; Needlecraft; History; Psychology. *Address:* 6865 W. 51st Terr. No 1C, Shawnee Mission, KS 66202, USA.

BREEN Patricia Helen, b. 15 Sept. 1926, Detroit, Michigan, USA. Senior Financial Consultant; Chairman, President and Chief Executive Officer. m. Morton I Breen, 26 May 1951, divorced 1961. *Education:* BBA 1945-49, Post Graduate 1953-54, University of Michigan; Bus Ad, Wayne State University, 1944-45. *Appointments:* Trust Investment Analyst, National Bank of Detroit, 1949; Administrative Assistant, General Motors Corp, 1949-51; Policy Procedures & Bonus Committees, Union Securities, Cleveland, 1951; Financial Organisation, Baxter & Co, Cleveland, 1952; Senior Financial Consultant, Merrill Lynch Pierce Fenner & Smith, Inc, 1957-; Owner, Chairman, President and Chief Executive Officer, Good Food Co. *Creative Works:* Air Cargo Research, International Reciprocal Trade Book Credits. *Memberships:* Otsego Ski Club; Bloomfield Surf Club; Kansas City Country Club; Detroit Boat Club; 300 Oakland County Club; Republican Committee; Organizer, President, Independent Women on Campus, University of Michigan; Organizer and Writer Constitution, and Member, Bus Ad Council; Tuesday Musical; Director, University of Michigan, Alumnae Association; Investment Analysts, Detroit; President, NAFE Oakland. *Honours:* Am Legion Award, 1939; Allied Youth City Speech Writer, 1940, Delivery Award, 1944; Scholarships: Wayne S U, University of Michigan, Vassar, 1945; Regents, Alumni Scholarship, University of Michigan, 1947, plus 2 more honorary scholarships; Oil Painting, Cranbrook Academy Award, 1975. *Hobbies:* Silver & Gold Smithing; Oil Painting; Writing; Lecturing; Radio; Television; Snow and Water Skiing; Swimming; Sailing; Golf; Tennis; Exhibition ballroom dancing; Consul Natural Nutrition USA and Internationally. *Address:* 17959 University Park Drive, Livonia, Michigan 48152, USA.

BREGGIN Janis Ann, b. 5 Mar. 1955, Rochester, New York, USA. Attorney at Law. m. Bruce A Jomez, 14 May 1983, 2 sons, 2 daughters. *Education:* BA, 1976, JD, 1980, University of Denver. *Appointments:* Sherman & Howard, Denver, 1980-82; Nobel & Associates, Denver, 1982-84; Deutsch & Sheldon, Englewood, 1985-87; Breggin & Associates PC, 1987-. *Publications:* Co-author, Annexation: Today's Gamble for Tomorrow's Gain, The Colorado Lawyer, 1988. *Memberships:* Colorado Women's Bar Association; Denver, Colorado & American Bar Associations; Commercial Real Estate Women; Alliance of Professional Women; Mothers Against Drunk Drivers. *Honours:* Martin Marietta Scholar, 1973-76; National Merit Scholar, 1973-76; Phi Beta Kappa, 1975; American Jurisprudence Awards, many other awards. *Address:* 2028 Glencoe Street, Denver, CO 80207, USA.

BREGOLI-RUSSO Mauda Rita, b. 30 Mar. 1938, Italy. Assistant Professor. m. Franco Russo, 27 June 1964, 1 daughter. *Education:* PhD, Romance Languages, 1978. *Appointments:* University of Illinois, Chicago, 1976-80, 1983-; Northwestern University, 1981-82. *Publications:* Boiardo Lirico, 1979; Edition and Commentary of Galeotto Del Carretto Li Sei Contenti and Sofonisba, 1982; Renaissance Italian Theatre,

1984. *Memberships:* MLA; MMLA; RMMLA; SAMLA; Newberry Library Associates; AATI; AAIS; Renaissance Society of America. *Honours:* NEH, 1981, 1983. *Hobbies:* Theatre; Films; Opera. *Address:* University of Illinois, Dept. of Spanish, Italian & Portuguese, Box 4348 M/C 315, Chicago, IL 60680, USA.

BREINES Estelle B, b. 7 Mar. 1936, Brooklyn, New York, USA. Occupational Therapist. m. Ira S. Breines, 30 May 1956, 1 son, 2 daughters. *Education:* BA, New York University, 1957; MA, Kean College, 1977; PhD, Occupational Therapy, New York University, 1986. *Appointments:* Staff OT, Director, OT, Coney Island Hospital, Brooklyn, 1965-67; Staff OT, Senior OT, Meadowbrook Hospital, 1967-69; Director, OT, Brunswick Hospital Centre, 1975-78; Private Practice, 1978-; Teaching Fellow, New York University, 1983-85; Clinical Assistant Professor, New York University, 1987-; President, Geri-Rehab, Inc., 1978-; Executive Director, Developmental Rehabilitation Services, 1987-. *Publications:* Perception: Its Development and Recapitulation, 1981; Functional Assessment Scale, 1983; Origins and Adaptations: A Philosophy of Practice, 1986; Pragmatism: A Philosophical Foundation of Occupational Therapy 1900-1922, and 1965-1985, 1986. *Memberships:* various professional organisations. *Honours:* Recipient, various honours & awards. *Hobbies:* Belgian Sheepdogs; Painting; Needlecrafts. *Address:* Groenendahl Farm, 170 Hibbler Road, Lebanon, NJ 08833, USA.

BRENDEL Bettina, b. Lueneburg, Germany. Artist; Lecturer. m. Arthur Spitzer, 1949, divorced 1965, 1 daughter. *Education:* University of South California, 1955-58; New School of Social Research, New York, 1968- 69. *Appointments:* Art Teacher, Landhochschule, Marienau, Germany, 1947; Faculty, University of California Extension, 1958-61, 1976; Lecturer, Institute of Optics, Rochester University, 1971, University of South California, 1980, Gulbenkian Foundation, Paris and Lisbon, 1987. *Creative Works:* Included in major international group exhibitions in USA and Europe; 15 One man shows; Author, articles in art journals; etc. *Memberships:* UCLA Art Council; Los Angeles County Museum of Art; Museum of Contemporary Art. *Honours:* various honours and awards including Purchase Prizes in Competetive Exhibitions. *Hobbies:* Swimming; Classical Music; Computer Art. *Address:* 1061 N Kenter Ave, Los Angeles, CA 90049, USA.

BRENER Rochelle Diane, b. 27 Feb. 1945, Syracuse, New York, USA. Freelance Writer; Photographer. m. Donald Arthur Squire, 1965. 1 son, 1 daughter. *Education:* BA English, BA Philosophy, Russell Sage College, 1974; MFA, Vermont College, of Norwich University, 1989. *Appointments:* Features Writer, Capitol News Group/Albany Times-Union, 1973-75; Contributing Editor, Poetry Forum, 1973-76; Drama Critic, Feature Stories, Photographs, KITE, 1974-76; Editor, Woman Locally Magazine, 1977; Associate Editor, Albany Magazine, 1986; Poetry Editor, The Albany Review, 1987-. *Creative Works:* Chapbook: The Bottom Line; Packrat The Poet; Poetry Forum; The Albany Review; The Answer. Pen and ink sketches and poems in Poetry Forum; Short Story, Of the Coin, in Between the Sheets; Poems, Book reviews, Albany Magazine and The Albany Review; Several photo exhibits; Judge, Utah State Writing Contest. *Memberships:* Costume Society of London; Costume Society of America; Professional Photographers of America; Associated Photographers International; Freelance Photographers International; National Writers Club; Hudson Valley Writer's Guild; Writers Union of America; Poets and Writers Inc; International Women Writers Guild; American Diabetes Association; Alliance for the Mentally Ill. *Hobbies:* Photography; Swimming; Reading; Needlework. *Address:* 69 Huntersfield Road, Delmar, NY 12054, USA.

BRENNAN Frances Margaret Myers, b. 13 Feb. 1921, Paris France. Artist. m. Francis E. Brennan, 1946, 2 sons. *Education:* France & Switzerland until 1934; Graduate, Spence School New York, USA, 1938; Studied

Drawing, Atelier Art et Jeunesse, Paris, France, 1938-39. *Appointments:* Assisted Alexie Brodovitch, Art Director, Harpers Bazaar, New York City, 1940-41; Education Dept., Exhibition Dept., Metropolitan Museum, 1941-44; Office of War Information, London & Paris, 1944-45; 2 group exhibitions of paintings, Wakefield Bookshop Gallery, New York City. *Creative Works:* Group Exhibitions at Betty Parsons Gallery, New York City, 1973, 1975, 1977, 1978; Solo Exhibitions, Betty Parsons Gallery, 1977, 1979, 1981; Solo Exhibitions, Coe Kerr Gallery, new York City, 1984, 1986, 1988; Chicago Art Fair, 1987-88. *Address:* 123-35 82nd Road, Kew Gardens, NY 11414, USA.

BRENNEMAN Mary, b. 14 Oct 1923, USA. Divorced. *Education:* MD, 1947; MA, Public Health, Univeristy of Pittsburgh, 1948; Various positions as Intern and Resident, 1947-50. *Appointments Include:* Pediatrician, various hospitals 1950-62; Psychiatrist, Camarillo State Hospital, 1971-73; Private Psychiatric Practice, 1973-; Psychiatric Consultant, St JOhn of God Nursing Hospital, Los Angeles, 1975-; Psychiatric Consultant, Beverlywood Mental Health Centre, Los Angeles, 1985-87; Psychiatric Director, El Portal Guest Home, Los Angeles, 1987-88; Staff Psychiatrist, Robert F Kennedy Hospital, Hawthorn, 1987-; Staff Psychiatrist, Metropolitan State Hospital, Norwalk, CA. *Memberships:* many professional organisations. *Address:* 10477 Santa Monica Blvd., Westwood, CA 90025, USA.

BRENNER Anita Susan, b. 18 Aug. 1949, Hollywood, USA. Attorney. m. 19 Aug. 1973, 1 son, 1 daughter. *Education:* BA, History, 1970, JD, 1973, University of California, Los Angeles. *Appointments:* Law Clerk: Richard Levin, Esq., Los Angeles, 1971-72; Robert N. Harris, Esq., Beverly Hills, 1972-73; Attorney, Greater Watts Justice Center, Los Angeles, 1974-75; Private Practice, Los Angeles, 1975-. *Publications:* Co-Editor, Jury Selection Handbook, 1981; articles in professional journals. *Memberships:* Los Angeles County Bar Association; Criminal Courts Bar Association; Los Angeles County Medical Association. *Hobbies:* Mountaineering; Classical Music; California Cooking. *Address:* 301 East Colorado Blvd., Suite 614, Pasadena, CA 91101, USA.

BRENT Nancy Jean Weiss, b. 28 June 1947, Erie, PA, USA. Nurse-Attorney. m. George W. Brent, June 1979. *Education:* BS, Villa Maria College, 1969; MS, University of Connecticut, 1975; JD, Loyola University, 1981. *Appointments:* Assistant Professor, University of Illinois, 1975-77; Staff Attorney, Law Office of T J Keevers, 1981-82; Principal, Nye Brent & Shoenberger, 1982-85; Associate Professor, St Xavier College, 1984-; Law Office of Nancy J. Brent, 1985-. *Publications:* Articles in various journals. *Memberships:* American and Illinois Nurses Association; Chicago, Illinois; American Bar Association; American Association of Nurse Attorneys; Sigma Theta Tau. *Honours:* Recipient, various honours & awards. *Address:* 5445 N. Sheridan, Suite 1906, Chicago, IL 60640, USA.

BRERETON Bridget Mary, b. 13 May 1946, India. Reader. m. Ashton Brereton, 23 Sept. 1966, 3 sons. *Education:* BA, University of West Indies, Jamaica, 1966; MA, University of Toronto, 1968; PhD, University of the West Indies, Trinidad, 1973. *Appointments:* Reader, Caribbean Social History, University West Indies. *Publications:* Race Relations in Colonial Trinidad, 1979; A History of Modern Trinidad 1783-1962, 1981; Social Life in the Caribbean 1838-1938, 1985. *Memberships:* Secretary/Treasurer, Association of Caribbean Historians, 1977-83; Head, History, University of West Indies, 1985-87, 1988-91. *Address:* Dept. of History, University of the West Indies, St Augustine, Trinidad & Tobago, West Indies.

BRESKIN ZALBEN Jane, b. 21 Apr. 1950, New York City, USA. Author; Artist; College Teacher. m. Steven, 25 Dec. 1969, 2 sons. *Education:* BA, Art, Queens College, 1971; pratt Graphics Centre, 1972.

Appointments: Assistant to Art Director, Dial Press, 1972; Designer, T Y Crowell, 1974; School of Visual Arts, 1976-; Art Director, Charles Sribners, 1976. *Publications:* Published 20 books. *Memberships:* Society of Childrens Book Writers. *Honours:* International Reading Association, Children's Choice; American Institute of Graphic Arts; Art Directors Club. *Hobbies:* Cooking; Gardening; Renovating/Constructing Old House; Lecturing. *Address:* Curtis Brown Ltd., 10 Astor Place, New York, NY 10003, USA.

BRETT Tybe Ann, b. 6 May 1954, Johnstown, Pennsylvania, USA. Lawyer; Law Professor. m. Mervin Hayman, 22 Aug. 1979. 1 son; 1 daughter. *Education:* BA, magna cum laude, History, Barnard College, 1977; JD, Columbia University School of Law, 1979. *Appointments:* Associate, Drinker Biddle & Reath, Philadelphia, Pennsylvania, 1979-82; Associate Professor, University of Maine School of Law, Portland, 1983-. *Publications:* Insuring against the innovative liabilities and remedies of superfund, Journal of Environmental Law & Policy, 1986; General Discretion under Maine's Site Location of Development Law, Maine Law Review, 1989. *Memberships:* Admitted to practice before: US Supreme Court; Pennsylvania Supreme Court; Maine Courts; Third Circuit Court of Appeals; US District Court for the Eastern District of Pennsylvania and the District of Maine; American Bar Association; Founder, Director, Cape Elizabeth Land Trust. *Hobbies:* Hiking; Cross-country skiing; Biking; Swimming; Gardening. *Address:* University of Maine School of Law, 246 Deering Ave, Portland, ME 04102, USA.

BREWER Annie M, b. 31 Mar. 1925, Rahway, New Jersey, USA. Vice President/research. m. Donald Edward Brewer, 12 Aug. 1943. 3 sons. *Education:* Purdue University, 1942-43; Henry Ford Community College, 1960-64; BA, University of Michigan, Dearborn, 1966; AMLS, University of Michigan, Ann Arbor, 1968. *Appointments:* Senior editor/research and librarian, Gale Research Company, 1969-87; Vice President/research, Omnigraphics, Inc, 1987-. *Publications:* Dictionaries, Encyclopedias and Other Word Related Books, 1975, 1975, 1982, 4th edition, 1987; (with Elizabeth Geiser) Book Publishers Directory, 1977, 1979, 1980; Youth-Serving Organizations Directory, 1978, 1980; Abbreviations, Acronyms, Ciphers and Signs, 1981; Biography Almanac, 1981, 1983; Indexes, Abstracts and Digests, 1982; Library of Congress Subject Headings: A Cumulation, 1985, 1986, 1987. *Memberships:* American Libraries Association; American Society of Indexers; Past chairperson, Detroit Metropolitan Book & Author Society; Past chairperson, Book Club of Detroit; Charter member and past chairperson, Friends of the Dearborn Library; Association of American Publishers as liaison from Special Libraries Association, 1988. *Honour:* Special Libraries Association, Publishing Division 1988 Roll of Honor Award. *Address:* Omnigraphics, Inc, Penobscot Building, Detroit, Michigan 48226, USA.

BREWER Joan, b. 29 July 1923, Adelaide, South Australia. Librarian. m. John Thomas Brewer, 8 June 1965. *Education:* BA 1944, DipEd 1948, University of Adelaide; MLib, Monash University, 1982; ALAA (Assoc of Library Assoc of Australia), 1951. *Appointments:* Teacher, Naracoorte High School, 1944-47; Library Assistant, University of Adelaide, 1947-49; Librarian, Defence Centre, Salisbury, South Australia, 1949-57; 1952- 53 overseas; Lecturer, Principal Lecturer in Librarianship 1957-84, South Australia College of Advanced Education. *Publications:* A History of the Catholic Parish of St Peters, 1984; Loreto Convent, Marryatville 1905-1975, 1975; Also chapters in several books. *Memberships:* Library Assoc of Australia (State President/Member of the General Council at various times/Member Board of Education/Examiner, 1973-80); Aust College of Education (Sth Aust Chapter Committee); Alumni Assoc of University of Adelaide (Membership Officer 1985-). *Honours:* AM, Member of the Order of Australia, 1985; FACE, Fellow of the Australian College of Education, 1976; FLAA, Fellow of the Library Association of Australia, 1979. *Hobbies:* Travel; Theatre; Gardening. *Address:* 13 Thornton Street, Dulwich (Adelaide), South Australia 5065, Australia.

BRIANS Suzanne Gary, b. 21 Aug. 1949, New Iberia, Louisiana, USA. University Instructor; Counselor. m. Robin, 30 Apr. 1977. 1 son, 1 daughter. *Education:* BA, elem educ, 1971; MEd, education, 1974; EdS, 1976; MS, 1988. *Appointments:* Elementary Teacher, St Martinville Primary, Louisiana, 1971-76; Supervisor of Student Teachers, Instructor, Curriculum & Instruction, Special Education, Reading, University of Texas, Tyler, 1977-; Counselor, Counseling & Testing, 1989-. *Memberships:* International Reading Assn; Phi Psi Psychology Honor Fraternity; Phi Delta Kappa, past vice president, past foundations representative; Faculty sponsor to the student chapter, IRA. *Honours:* Honor Graduate, USL, 1971; Phi Kappa Phi Honor Fraternity, 1976; Outstanding Young Educator, St Martinville, 1976. *Hobbies:* Reading; Walking; Cooking, French gourmet; Travels; Music. *Address:* 512 Oxford Dr, Tyler, TX 75703, USA.

BRIDGES Mary Patricia (Dame), b. 6 June 1930, Chesterfield, England. m. Betram Marsdin Brudges, 28 Mar. 1951, deceased. *Memberships:* Member of Executive, St Loys' College, Exeter; Devon FFPC; President, South Western Area Conservative Association; Chairman, Devon County Royal British Legion Women's Section; National Vice Chairman, Royal Bitish Legion Women's Section; Member of Political Committee T.S.W.; Founder President Exmouth Branch, British Heart Foundation; National Central Committee, Royal British Legion Women's Section; Dering Court House Committee, RBL; Founder Trustee, Exmouth Lympstone Hospiscare; Trustee, Resthaven; Director, The Home Care Trust Ltd; Trustee, Exmouth Welfare Trust; Life Member, Retford Cricket Club; Hon Vice President, Exmouth Cricket Club; Founder Trustee, Girls Adventure Trust, Exmouth. *Honour:* DBE, 1980. *Hobbies:* Cricket; Reading. *Address:* Walton House, 3 Fairfield Close, Exmouth, Devon EX8 2BN, England.

BRIDGES P. Elaine, b. 11 Nov. 1932, Antigua, West Indies. High School Teacher. div, 1 son. *Education:* BA, College of New Rochelle, New York, USA, 1980; MS, Fordham University School of Education, 1982. *Appointments:* Paraprofessional Counsellor & Financial Aide 1973-83, High School Teacher 1983-, Board of Education, New York City. *Creative work includes:* Associate Producer, various high school plays. *Membership:* Network Organisation of Bronx Women. *Hobbies:* Reading; Sewing; Caribbean cooking. *Address:* 630 Pugsley Avenue, Bronx, New York 10473, USA.

BRIDGEWATER Geraldine Diana Noelle, b. 26 Dec. 1952, Sutton, Surrey, England. Futures Broker and Dealer; Association Administrator. *Education:* London College of Fashion and Clothing Technology. *Appointments:* S & W Berisford PLC, 169-71; J H Rayner, Mincing Lane, London, 1971-86; 1st Woman Dealer, 1976, 1st Woman Individual Subscriber, 1986, London Metal Exchange; Currently Head of Public Affairs and Training, Association of Futures Brokers and Dealers, London. *Publications:* All That Glitters Is Not Gold; Futures and How to Invest. *Memberships:* Freeman of City of London; Rosicrucian; Institute of Complementary Medicine; Network; Greenpeace; CND; UNICEF; Action Aid. *Hobbies:* Metaphysics; Alchemy; Philosophy; Holistic healing; Religious history; Global economics; Mythology; Astronomy; Tennis; Painting; Reading; Riding; Walking. *Address:* Association of Futures Brokers and Dealers, B Section, 5th Floor, Plantation House, 5-8 Mincing Lane, London EC3, England.

BRIDWELL Charmaine Claudette, b. 25 June 1953, Chula Vista, California, USA. Financial Executive. m. 1971 (div. 1976), 1 son. *Education:* Southwestern College, 1971; Contractor's License, Class A, 1988. *Appointments:* Summer work 1969, 1970, Bookkeeper

1973, Chief Financial Officer & part-owner (purchased 12.5% of stock) 1981-, Erreca's Inc (general engineering contractor, $20-25 million volume pa). *Memberships:* National Association of General Contractors; National Association of Women in Construction; International Platform Association; Zoological Society; National Rifle Association; World Wildlife Foundation; Ducks Unlimited. *Hobbies:* Softball; All spectator sports; Collecting Antiques. *Address:* 1507 Sunrise Shadow Court, El Cajon, California 92019, USA.

BRIEGHEL-MULLER Gunna, b. 11 Dec. 1925, Copenhagen, Denmark. Teacher of Eutony; Director of School of Eutony. *Education:* Diploma in Eutony, Gerda Alexander School, Copenhagen, 1948; BA, Music, French, University of Copenhagen, 1956; Diploma in Eurythmics, Jaques Dalcroze Institute, Geneva, Switzerland, 1956. *Appointments:* Teaching Eutony, 1948-, including Jaques Dalcroze Institute, Geneva, Switzerland, 1954-, University of Geneva, 1974-; Director, Swiss School of Gerda Alexander Eutony, Geneva, 1974-. *Publications:* Eutonie et relaxation, book, translated into Spanish, Dutch, Swedish. *Memberships:* International Association of Gerda Alexander Eutony; Dalcroze Teachers Association. *Hobbies:* All methods of keeping healthy especially alternative methods; Painting; Literature; Music. *Address:* 2 pl. Eaux-Vives, CH-1207 Geneva, Switzerland.

BRIERLEY Caroline, b. 22 Dec. 1937, Oxford, England. m. David Brierley, 23 Apr. 1960, 1 daughter. *Education:* BA, Honours, Philosophy, Politics & Economics, Lady Margaret Hall, Oxford, 1959. *Appointments:* Economist, International Sugar Council, 1959-61; Political & Economic Planning, 1961-63, Head of Food & Services Unit, 1963-, National Economic Development Office. *Publications:* Food Prices & the Common Market, 1961; The Making of European Policy, 1963; Textiles - Industrial Review, 1974; Lifting the Barriers to Trade, 1986. *Memberships:* Romney Street Group; Centre for Service Management Studies. *Hobbies:* Gardening; Travel; Making Exotic Jams & Pickles. *Address:* Old Farm, Harthall Lane, Kings Langley, Herts WD4 8JW, England.

BRIGGS Eva Lucille Clark, b. 6 Apr. 1907, Luther, Michigan, USA. Portrait Photographer; Artist (Painter). 1 daughter. *Education:* Cadillac High School plus special studies for 60 years; Meinzinger Art School; Greason Art School; Wayne State University; Oakland University; Winona School of Photography and over 25 private teachers in photography, art, business, advertising, merchandising, public relations, publicity and public speaking. *Appointments:* Baby Photographer with Hinkston Studio, Detroit, 1931-43; Owner, Eva Briggs Galleries, Detroit, 1943-55, Pleasant Ridge, Michigan, 1955-73; Art Teacher, Lecturer, Juror, Photography and Art, Painter, Freelance, 1973-; Photographic clientele was international including stage, screen, music, government and financial greats. *Creative works:* Photographic Paintings (Portrait) in Junior Achievement Headquarters, New York City; Business and Professional Women Headquarters, Washington, DC; Oakland University; Michigan State University and many Corporate and Private Collections in USA; Over 100 magazine articles. *Life Memberships include:* Life Member: Detroit Professional Photographers Association (Past President), Professional Photographers of Michigan, Professional Photographers of America, Pleasant Ridge Foundation, (Founding President), Photographic Society of America and American Society of Photographers, Honorary Life Member, Palette and Brush Club, Member National League of American Pen Women, etc. *Honours include:* National Award, Professional Photographers of America, 1970; Several Honorary and Earned Degrees; First Eva Briggs Annual Good Citizens Award Pleasant Ridge Foundation, 1985; The Burton Historical Collection, Detroit, Michigan Public Library, Main Branch has set aside one room to house the "Eva Briggs Photographic Collection" containing over 93,000 negatives and hundreds of images by Eva Briggs from

1931-73. *Hobbies:* Duplicate Bridge; Clothes Designing; Gardening; Painting; Public Speaking; Writing; Cooking; Entertaining; Walking; Genealogy, etc. *Address:* 334 Paseo Azul, Country Club North, Green Valley, AZ 85614, USA.

BRIGHT Betty Suida, b. Harbor Beach, Michigan, USA. *Education:* European Study, Comparable Government, Bachelor Degree, Political Science, Wayne State University; Certificate, Dartmouth Alumni College; Congressional Candidate School, Washington DC; Master Business Administration, Central Michigan University. *Appointments:* State Air Pollution Commissioner, State of Michigan; Congressional Candidate, 18th Congressional District, 1980; State Central Committee: Executive Budget Committee; Officer, 17th Congressional District; National Delegate-Alternate, Republican National Convention, Kansas City; Precinct Delegate; Oakland County Executive Committee; Board Member, Lincoln Republican Club; Oakland County Campaign Committee; Honorary Sergeant of Arms, Republican National Committee, Miami Beach. *Memberships:* Past Vice President, Royal Oak Area Republican Club; Republican Business and Professional Women's Forum; Gold Key; Beta Sigma Phi; Pi Sigma Alpha; Sigma Iota Epsilon; PR Committee, Women's Economic Club of Detroit; Chrysler Management Club, Photographic Committee; Executive Board, March of Dines PROs; Executive Board, American Lung Association. *Honour:* Recipient Women to Watch award, Cobo Hall. *Address:* 32608 Inkster Road, Franklin, MI 48025, USA.

BRIGHT-WHITE June Louise, b. 17 June 1956, Dover, New Jersey, USA. Satellite Programme Control. m. Timothy H. White, 30 May 1987. *Education:* BSCE, Bucknell University, 1978; MBA, Florida Institute of Technology, 1986. *Appointments:* Civil Engineer, Interpace Corporation, 1978-79; Mechanical Engineer, Systems Engineer, Department of Defense, 1979-84; Systems Engineer, Programme Manager, Space and Strategic Division, Hughes Aircraft Co, 1984-87; Programme Control, Advance Communications Technical Satellite (ACTS), GE Astro Space, Princeton, New Jersey, 1987-. *Memberships:* American Preparedness Association; Technical Marketing Society of America. *Honours:* Outstanding Federal Employee. *Hobbies:* Golf; skiing; Water-skiing; Tennis; Cycling; Volleyball; Making beaded jewellery; Cooking. *Address:* 4 Colebrook Court, Princeton, NJ 08540, USA.

BRIGHTLEAF Ana (Dr), b. 21 Mar. 1946, Alexandria, Virginia, USA. Dentist. 1 daughter. m. John David, 9 Apr. 1989. *Education:* BS, University of North Carolina, 1968; DMD, University of Florida, 1982. *Appointments:* Private practice, 1982-. *Publications:* Co-Creator, video tape programme. *Memberships:* ADA; AGD; Pinellas County Dental Association; American Association of Women Dentists. *Honours:* Fellowship, Academy of General Dentistry, 1989. *Hobbies:* English Saddle Horse Riding; Sailing; Kayaking; Reading; Yoga. *Address:* 744, 32 Avenue N., St Petersburg, FL 33704, USA.

BRINKER Connie Juge, b. 15 July 1928, New Orleans, Louisiana, USA. Graphoanalyst; Document Examiner. m. Robert William Brinker, 4 Jan. 1948. 4 sons, 1 daughter. *Education:* Graduate, New Orleans Beauty College, 1964; International Graphoanalysis Society, 1972; Masters, IGAS, 1978. *Appointments:* Cosmetologist, 1967-; Graphoanalyst, 1972-; Instructor, NOCCD, 1974-85; Question Document Examiner, 1974-. *Publications:* Author of articles published on handwriting and documents; Book: Reflections: History of the Writing Instrument. *Memberships:* Life Member, International Graphoanalysis Society; World Association of Document Examiners; Southern Cal Chp IGAS, President Emeritus. *Honours:* Sharron Topper Humanitarian Award, Fullerton College, 1976; Graphoanalyst of the Year, Sou Cal Chp, 1977; Cooperator of the Year, 1977; Excellence of Performance, 1980; President Emeritus Honour, Sou Cal Chp, 1980; Graduation Speaker, IGAS, 1982; Proficiency Recognition Award, 1984; Honorary

Appointment, Research Board of Advisors, National Division, ABI. *Hobbies:* Jewellery designing; Antique clock repair; Nutrition; Herbal study. *Address:* Brinker and Associate, 107 North Woods Ave, Fullerton, CA 92632, USA.

BRINKLEY Christie, b. 2 Feb. 1954, Los Angeles, California. Model; Photographer. m. Billy Joel, 23 Mar. 1985, 1 daughter. *Education:* Studied art, Paris, France. *Career:* As model has appeared in numerous magazines including: Life; Us; People; Time; Vogue; Cosmopolitan; Paris Match; Harper's Bazaar. Television appearances include: Johnny Carson's Tonight Show; The David Letterman Show; The Dinah Shore Show; Good Morning America; You Magazine; Guest on Bobe Hope's Birthday Special 1982 and 1983 shows; Co-hosted with Lee Majors, The Face of the Eighties, 1982. Acting debuty with Chevy Chase, National Lampoon's Vacation. *Creative works:* Numerous documentaries; Calendars; Videos: Cover Girl's Guide to Basic Make-Up with Christie Brinkley; Uptown Girl; Keeping the Faith; Book: Christie Brinkley's Outdoor Beauty and Fitness Book, 1983; Photographs appeared in: Ring Magazine; Photo; Autosprint; Kodak's Ampersand; American Photographer. *Memberships:* Greenpeace; The Cousteau Society; SANE. *Honours:* Humane Society Award; Sexiest Mom. *Hobbies:* Photography; Reading; Art & design; English horseback riding. *Address:* c/o Frank Management, 1775 Broadway, Suite 401, New York, NY 10019, USA.

BRINTON Margo A., b. 6 Feb. 1945, Hanover, Pennsylvania, USA. Virologist; Artist. m. G. Stephen Bowen, 31 Mar. 1979, 1 stepson, 1 stepdaughter. *Education:* BS, Duke University, 1966; PhD, University of Pennsylvania, 1972; Postdoctoral Fellow, University of Minnesota, Minneapolis, 1971-73. *Appointments:* Instructor, Microbiology, University of Minnesota, Minneapolis, 1973-74; Senior Microbiologist, Riker Research Laboratories, St. Paul, 1974-77; Assistant Professor, 1977-83, Associate Professor, 1983-, Wistar Institute, Philadelphia, Pennsylvania; Wistar Associate Professor, Department of Microbiology, University of Pennsylvania, Philadelphia, 1983-; Co-Organizer, UCLA Molecular Biology Symposium, Keyston, Colorado, 1986; Paintings exhibited: 7 1-woman shows, 5 juried shows. *Publications:* 12 book chapters; Articles in professional journals. *Memberships:* Microbiology and Infectious Diseases Committee, NIH; Pennsylvania Watercolor Society; Philadelphia Watercolor Club; American Society for Microbiology; American Society for Virology; Reticulo-endothelial Society; Sigma Xi;, Board of Directors, Brinton Family Association; Board of Directors, South Eastern Pennsylvania Orchid Society. *Address:* 61 A Line Road, Malvern, PA 19355, USA.

BRISSON Marcelle Liliane, b. 18 Dec. 1931, Canada. Secretary General. 4 sons, 1 daughter. *Education:* BA, Ottawa University; MSW, University of California, 1967. *Appointments:* Child Psychiatry, UCLA, 1968-70; Regional Centre for Mentally Retarded, Orange, 1971-75; Clinical Social Worker, American Airforce Base, Athens, 1975-80; Clinical Social Worker, Ottawa General Hospital, 1980-83; Director, Social Work Services, St Paul's Hospital, Vancouver, 1983-84; Clinical Social Worker, Regional Palliative Care Services, Ottawa, 1984-86; Secretary General, International Social Services, Geneva, 1986-89; Immigration and Refugee Board of Canada, Montreal, 1989-. *Memberships:* NASW; CASW; Professional Advisory Board, Palliatiro Care Foundation. *c/o International Social Service, 32 Quai du Senjit, 1201 Geneva, Switzerland.*

BROADBENT Amalia Sayo Castillo, b. 28 May 1956, Manila, Philippines. Graphic Artist/Designer. m. 14 Mar. 1981, 1 son, 1 daughter. *Education:* Charm and Modelling courses, Karilagan Finishing School, 1972; BFA, Advertising, 1976; Production Art, Academy of Art College, San Francisco, USA, 1980-81; French, Alliance Francaise de San Francisco, 1981-82. *Appointments:* Designer, import company, 1976-77;

Assistant Advertising Manager, Dale Corporation, 1977-78; Art Director, Resort Hotels Corporation, 1978-80; Production Artist, Cato Yasumura Behaeghel, 1981-83; Graphic Artist/Deisgner, Owner, A.C.Broadbent Graphics, San Francisco, California, 1983-; Freelance Art Director, Ogilvy & Mather Direct, 1986. *Creative works include:* Work for Pepsi Colouring Contest - Christmas; Daing Na Isda charcoal painting, 1st runner up; 1988 book cover design and art direction, Better Business Bureau, Marin-Sonoma; 1988 book cover design and art direction, Better Business Bureau, San Francisco; Several logos and collateral materials. *Memberships:* YWCA; National Association of Female Executives; President, Pax Romana, College of Architecture and Fine Arts; Vice-President, Atelier Cultural Society; San Francisco Prayer Group. *Honours:* Certificate of Merit, Pepsi-Cola Christmas Colouring Contest, 1964; Dean's List, Outstanding Leader, 1975-76; Certificate of Merit, UNESCO, 1976; Pax Romana Award for Leadership, 1976; Silver Medal for Freehand Drawing, University of Santo Tomas, Philippines, 1976. *Hobbies:* Gardening; Painting and sketching; Classical music; Designing clothes; Interior decorating. *Address:* 1265 Princeton Court, Pittsburg, CA 94565, USA.

BROCCHINI Myra Mossman, b. 26 July 1932, Palo Alto, USA. Architect. m. Ronald G. Brocchini, 3 Feb. 1957, 1 son. *Education:* BA, 1955, MA, 1956, Architecture, University of California. *Appointments:* Howard Moise, 1954; Kitchen Hunt, 1955; Campbell Wong Associates, 1956-63; R.G. Brocchini Arch., 1964-67; Myra M. Brocchini, 1967-80; Wong, Brocchini Assoc., 1980-87; Brocchini Architects Inc., 1987-. *Publications:* Co-Author, Head Royce Centennial History. *Memberships:* American Institute of Architects; Head Royce School Board of Trustees; Board, Cal Arks UCB; BAE Board of Architectural Examiners; NCARB National Council of Architectural Registration Board Examination Committee. *Honours:* Design Medal, 1955, Chi Alpha Kappa Award, 1955, School of Architecture; AIA Sunset Architecture Honour Award, 1968; University of California Alumni Citation, 1988; University of California Bear of the Year, 1989. *Hobbies:* Travel; Architecture; Education; Art. *Address:* 2836 Garber Street, Berkeley, CA 94705, USA.

BROCK Karena Diane, b. 21 Sept. 1942, Los Angeles, California, USA. Artistic Director; Principal Dancer; Choreographer; Teacher. *Education:* Graduate of Barstow School, Kansas City, Missouri, 1960. *Appointments include:* National Ballet of the Netherlands, Amsterdam, 1962; Corps-Soloist-Principal, American Ballet Theater, New York City, USA, 1963-78; Teacher-Faculty member, State University of New York at Purchase, brooklyn College New York, 1978-79; Artistic Director, Prima Ballerina, Choreographer, Savannah Ballet Company, Savannah, Georgia, 1978-. *Creative Works:* Choreographed ballets include: Vignettes by Robert Schumann; Tribute to Sousa by John Phillip Sousa; Celebration by Glazounov; Midsummer Night's Dream by Mendelsohn; Suite en Sept by Satie; Movements by Poulenc; Baiser de Lafee by Stravinsky; Gotcha by Gottschalk; Nutcracker by Tschaikovsky; Rhythm in Blues by Gershwin. *Address:* 20 Hanging Moss Road, Savannah, GA 31410, USA.

BRODIE Elizabeth, b. 4 Sept. 1923, Budapest, Hungary. Psychiatrist. m. Tom Philbrook, 1 son. *Education:* MD, University of Vienna, Austria, 1957; Intern, McKellar General Hospital, Thunder Bay, Ontario, Canada, 1958; Resident: Internal Medicine, Women's College Hospital, Toronto, 1959, Psychiatry, Ontario Hospital, Hamilton, 1960, Clarke Institute, University of Toronto, 1961-63; LMCC, Medical Council of Canada, 1959; DPsych, University of Toronto, 1963; Fellow, Psychiatry, Addiction Research Foundation, Toronto, 1964; CRCP(C), 1963, FRCP(C), 1973, Royal College of Physicians and Surgeons of Canada. *Appointments:* Director, Day Hospital for Alcoholics, Addiction Research Foundation, Toronto, 1966-69; Adjunct Associate Professor, Faculty of Environmental Studies, York University, Toronto, 1973-76; Private Practice in Psychiatry, Toronto, Ontario, 1968-78;

Private Practice in Psychiatry, Houston, Texas, USA, 1978-. *Publications:* Contributions to McLeans, Chatelaine, Association for Planned Parenthood; Exerpta Medica, IV World Congress of Psychiatry, Madrid, 1966. *Memberships:* American Psychiatric Association; Texas Medical Association; Houston Psychiatric Society; American Medical Association. *Honours:* Rockefeller Fellowship, Vienna, 1956. *Hobbies:* Piano; Gourmet cooking; Tennis; Travel. *Address:* 1700 West Loop South, Suite 1155, Houston, TX 77027, USA.

BROEDER Nancy Hunzinger, b. 8 Dec. 1932, Davenport, Iowa, USA. Archaeologist. m. (1)William Herbert Giragosian, 25 Aug. 1956, 1 son, 2 daughters. (2)Robert Edmund Broeder, 30 Aug. 1966, 1 son. *Education:* BA, State University of New York, 1980; MA, Religion 1985, Research Fellow, 1985-88, Yale University. *Appointments:* Editorial Assistant, Columbia University, New York, 1966-68; Financial Secretary, 1st Presbyterian Church, Greenwich, 1974-79; National Leadership Team, Prisoner Visitation and Support, Philadelphia, 1986-; Archaeologist, Dead Sea Plain Expedition, Pittsburgh, 1983-. *Publications:* Author: Gemological reports: Excavations of Dead Sea Plain, 1985; Early Bronze Age Beads from Maadi, Egypt, 1987; Photographer: Photo essays: Dead Sea Plain Tombs, 1981; Vernacular Architecture of Chinese Turkestan, 1982; Journeys of St Paul, 1983. *Memberships:* American Schools of Oriental Researchl; Archaeological Institute of America; Connecticut Academy of Arts and Sciences; Sierra Club. *Honour:* Honours Thesis, State University of New York, 1980. *Hobbies:* Tennis; Golf; Amateur Radio Operator, WA1NDS. *Address:* 11 Linwood Avenue, Riverside, CT 06878, USA.

BROER Eileen Dennery, b. 7 Sept. 1946, Philadelphia, USA. Management Consultant. m. (1) Paul Alan Broer, 26 Nov. 1970 (div. 1980), (2) Charles Kenneth Recorr, 10 Sept. 1981. 1 son, 2 stepsons. *Education:* BA, Mount St Vincent College, 1969. *Appointments:* Media Director, Control Manager, Merrill Anderson Company, New York City, 1970-72; Administrative assistant, finance, McCall Pattern Company, NYC, 1972-74; Personnel Specialist 1974-77, Employee Relations Manager 1978, Personnel Director 1978-79, Notions Marketing Inc, NYC; Lecturer, Business Writing, New York University, 1975-78; 2nd Vice President (Personnel) 1979, Vice President (Human Resources) 1980-82, Manhattan Life Insurance Company, NYC; VP (Human Resources), McM Corporation, Raleigh, North Carolina, 1982-85; President, Human Dimension, 1985-; Board, Centre for Health Education Inc, NC, National Association of Women Business Owners (NAWBO). *Memberships:* Human Resources Planning Society; Organisation Development Network; Gestalt Institute, Cleveland; NAWBO; Raleigh-Wake Personnel Association; American Society for Training & Development. *Address:* Suite 354, 975 Walnut Street, Cary, North Carolina 27511, USA.

BROINOWSKI Alison Elizabeth, b. 25 Oct. 1941, Adelaide, South Australia, Australia. Writer; Diplomat. m. Richard Philip Broinowski, 14 Dec. 1963, 1 son, 1 daughter. *Education:* BA, University of Adelaide. *Appointments:* Department of Foreign Affairs and Trade, 1963-88; Journalist, The Canberra Times, 1968-69; Consultant, IDP, 1988; Visiting Fellow, Australian National University, 1987; Research Associate, Yonsei University, Korea, 1988-89. *Publications:* Take One Ambassador, 1973; Understanding ASEAN (editor), 1982; Australia, Asia and the Media (editor), 1982. *Memberships:* Past Vice-President, Australian Institute of International Affairs; Past Vice-President, Australian National Word Festival; American Association of Australian Studies. *Honours:* Hubbard-Cooke Prize for French, 1960, Archibald Strong Essay Prize and James Gartrell Prize for English, 1961, Adelaide University; Special Purpose Grants, Literature Board, Australia Council, 1981, 1986; Research Grant, Australia-China Council, 1987; Research Grant, Australia-Japan Foundation, 1987; Research Fellowship, Korea

Research Foundation, 1988. *Hobbies:* Skiing (snow and water); Running; Swimming; Tennis; Chamber music (piano). *Address:* c/o Department of Foreign Affairs and Trade, Canberra, ACT 2600, Australia.

BROMKA Elaine, b. 1 June 1950, Rochester, New York, USA. Actress. m. Peter Phillips, 27 Nov. 1976. 1 son. *Education:* AB, magna cum laude, Smith College, 1972; MAT, Smith College, 1973. *Appointments:* Appearances on Broadway, Off-Broadway and television; Films include: Without a Trace. Appeared in Macbeth on Broadway; Over 12 leading roles in regional theatre. *Honour:* New England Emmy for Catch a Rainbow, 1978. *Address:* 214 Lincoln Road, Brooklyn, NY 11225, USA.

BROMLEY (Amey) Ida, b. 18 July 1929, Lancashire, England. Physiotherapist. *Education:* Member, Chartered Society of Physiotherapy (MCSP), Liverpool School of Physiotherapy, 1949-52. *Appointments:* Various hospitals, UK & Australia, 1952-66; Senior Physiotherapist 1966- 77, Superintendent Physiotherapist 1966-77, Stoke Mandeville Hospital (UK national spinal injuries centre); Superintendent, King's College Hospital, London, 1977-79; District Physiotherapist, i/c all physiotherapy services, Hampstead Health District, based Royal Free Hospital, London, 1979-86; Member, Health Advisory Service teams, national basis, 1984-; Freelance consultant, Lectures & workshops worldwide, 1986-. Work has covered: Treatment, spinal cord injuries; Sport for disabled; Rehabilitation; Problem-orientated medical recording; Peer review audit. *Publications:* Author: Tetraplegia & Paraplegia, A Guide for Physiotherapists; Series Editor, International Perspectives in Physical Therapy, 8 volumes; Numerous journal articles. *Memberships:* Fellow, Chartered Society of Physiotherapy (FCSP), 1982-; Past President, Society for Research in Rehabilitation; Past Council Chair, Chartered Society of Physiotherapy. *Honour:* Member, Order of British Empire, 1981. *Hobbies:* Bridge; Walking; Country pursuits; Bird Watching; Music; Theatre. *Address:* 6 Belsize Grove, London NW3 4UN, England.

BRON Eleanor, Actress; Writer. *Education:* North London Collegiate School, Cannons, Edgware; BA Hons, Modern Languages, Newnham College, Cambridge. *Career:* De La Rue Co., 1961. *Creative works:* Appearances include: Revue, Establishment Nightclub, Soho, 1962, New York, 1963; Not so much a Programme, More a Way of Life, BBC TV, 1964; several TV series written with John Fortune and TV series: Making Faces, written by Michael Frayn, 1976; Pinkerton's Progress, 1983. TV Plays include: Nina, 1978; My Dear Palestrina, 1980; A Month in the Country, 1985; Quartermaine's Terms, 1987; The Attic, 1988. Stage Roles include: Jennifer Dubedat, The Doctor's Dilemma, 1966; Jean Brodie, The Prime of Miss Jean Brodie, 1967, 1984; title role, Hedda Gabler, 1969; Portia, The Merchant of Venice, 1975; Amanda, Private Lives, 1976; Elena, Uncle Vanya, 1977; Charlotte, The Cherry Orchard, 1978; Margaret, A Family, 1978; One Woman Show: On Her Own, 1980; Goody Biddy Bean; The Amusing Spectacle of Cinderella and her Naughty, Naughty Sisters, 1980; Betrayal, 1981; Heartbreak House, 1981; Duet for One, 1982; Title role, The Duchess of Malfi, 1985; The Real Inspector Hound and The Critic (double bill), 1985, Vanya, The Cherry Orchard; Jocasta and Ismene, Oedipus, and Oedipus at Colonus, 1987; Flaminia, Infidelities, 1987; Tittle role, The Mad Woman of Chaillot, 1988. Films include: Help!; Alfie; Two for the Road; Bedazzled; Women in Love; The National Health; The Day that Christ Died, 1980; Turtle Diary, 1985; Little Dorrit. Author: song-cycle with John Dankworth, 1973; verses for Saint-Saens' Carnival of the Animals, 1975 (recorded). *Publications:* Is Your Marriage Really Necessary (with John Fortune), 1972; Contributed: My Cambridge, 1976; More Words, 1977. Written: Life and Other Punctures, 1978; The Pillow Book of Eleanor Bron, 1985. *Address:* c/o Jeremy Conway Ltd, 109 Jermyn Street, London SW1.

BRONER Esther M., b. 7 Aug. 1930, USA. Writer.

m. Robert Broner, 2 sons, 2 daughters. *Education:* BA, MA, Wayne State University; PhD, Union Graduate School, 1978. *Appointments:* Professor, Department of English, Wayne State University, 1963-87; Visiting Writer, Sarah Lawrence College, 1983-88; Guest Professor, University of California Los Angeles, Oberlin College, Haifa University (Israel). *Publications include:* Co- Editor, with Cathy N. Davidson, Lost Tradition: Mothers & Daughters in Literature, 1980. Author: A Weave of Women, novel; Her Mothers, novel; Journal-Noctural. *Memberships:* Women's Committee, PEN; Modern Language Association. *Honours:* National Endowment for Arts (Literature), 1980, 1987; Wonder Woman Award, 1984; Distinguished Alumna, Distinguished Faculty, Wayne State University; Michigan Council for Arts (2); Michigan Foundation for Arts. *Hobbies:* Feminist actions, pro choice; Peace actions, East-West & Mideast. *Address:* 40 West 22nd Street, 7A, New York, NY 10010, USA.

BRONSTEIN-GREENWALD Eva Mindy, b. 18 May 1954, USA. Market/Media Research Executive. m. Mark Barry Greenwald, 18 Nov. 1984. *Education:* BA, Brooklyn College, 1975; MA, University of Maryland, 1976; PhD, CUNY, 1983. *Appointments:* Assistant Manager, Literary Rights, ABC TV Network, 1979; Producer, Production Managr, WPIX TV (NY), 1979-81; Assistant Professor, Communications, University of New Haven, Instructor, Radio TV, Brooklyn College, 1981-85; Manager, Market Research CBS College Publishing, 1985-. *Publications:* Sex in Public Places: The Discussion of Sex on Call-in Radio, Aberrant Sexuality; You're on the Air!, Dissertation; Entertaining the Troops: MASH and War Personality Adaptations; Sociological Abstracts. *Memberships:* American Marketing Association; Popular Culture Association; Eastern Communication Society; American Association of Public Opinion Research. *Honours:* Recipient, many honours & awards. *Hobbies Include:* Qualitative Research for Small business; Theatre; Photography; Art. *Address:* 12 Westchester Avenue, White Plains, NY 10601, USA.

BRONSTHER Ellyn Kaiser, b. 12 Jan. 1929, New York, USA. Executive Vice President. m. 17 June 1951, 1 son, 2 daughters. *Education:* BA, Psychology, Adelphi University, 1949; BS, Education, Brooklyn College, 1950. *Appointments:* Teacher, New York Public Schools, 1951-65; Originator, Planner, Schneider Childrens Hospital, New Hyde Park, 1962-82; Resident, PTA Central Council, Hewlett, 1967-69; Chairperson, Mental Health Nassau County, 1969-71; Trustee, Schneider Childrens Hospital, 1970-; Vice President, Money Talks, 1978-81; Vice President, Rika Art & Design Ltd., 1978-, Board Member, NY Statewide Health Co-ordinating Council, Albany, 1980-; Mayor, Incorporated Village of Hewlett Bay Park, 1980-86; Executive Vice President, Co-Founder, Surgical Aid to Children of the World, 1980-. *Publication:* Introducti on to, The Surgeon and the Child, 1988. *Memberships:* Numerous professional organisations. *Honours:* Recipient, many honours and awards. *Hobbies:* Travel; Collecting Antiques; Collecting Paperweights; Gardening. *Address:* 114 Cedar Avenue, Hewlett Bay Park, NY 11557, USA.

BRONZAFT Arline Lillian, b. 26 Mar. 1936, New York, USA. Professor of Psychology. m. Bertram Bronzaft, 7 Oct. 1956. 2 daughters. *Education:* BA, Hunter College, 1956; MA 1958, PhD 1966, Columbia University. *Appointments:* Lecturer, Hunter College, 1958-65; Instructor, Finch College, 1965-67; Associate Prof 1967-75, Associate Professor 1975-81, Professor 1981-, Director of Women's Studies 1985-89, Chair, Psych Department 1988-, Lehman College, Bronx, New York; Consultant, NYC Transit Authority, 1977-85. *Publications:* Over 35 publications in professional journals, 2 chapters in books, articles in magazines. *Memberships:* Secretary, NY Phi Beta Kappa Assoc, 1977-86; Chair, Phi Beta Kappa Assoc (Nationally), 1985-; Sigma Xi, Pres Lehman College Chapter, 1980-81; Chair, Noise Comm, Council on the Environment of NYC, 1985-; NYS Pres of Women's Equity Action League, 1974-76; Board member, Hebrew Immigrant

Aid Society 1985-, President Women's Division, 1988-. *Honours:* Phi Beta Kappa; Sigma Xi; Kappa Delta Pi; Pi Lambda Theta; Psi Chi; Fellowship, Hunter College, 1956-58; Research Awards, City Univ of NY, 1971, 1977; Regional Certificate of Appreciation, US Environmental Protection Agency, 1976; Hall of Fame, Hunter College, 1987; Honoured by Brooklyn Chapter of National Organization of Women (NOW) 1974 and Bronx Chapter, 1988. *Hobbies:* Peace issues; Current events; Environmental issues. *Address:* c/o Lehman College, Bronx, NY 10468, USA.

BROOK Meriel Monica, b. 30 Oct. 1932, Malaysia. Actress. m. (1) 1 son, 1 daughter. (2) Roger Spencer Withnell, 25 Mar. 1982. *Education:* State Registered Nurse, St Bartholomew's Hospital, London, England, 1950-54; Drama Course, British Council, 1963; LLAM (Teaching), 1988. *Appointments:* State Registered Nurse, St Bartholomew's Hospital, London, 1954; Plastic Surgical Assistant to Patrick Clarkson, 1954-63; Royal Court Studio; Royal Shakespeare Company, 1974-75; National Theatre, 1979-80; New York Shakespeare Festival, USA, 1982. *Memberships:* British Actors Equity; Royal College of Nursing. *Honours:* Dean Robinson Best Actress Award. *Hobbies:* Theatre; Reading; Writing; Tennis; Skiing; Animals. *Address:* Kingswood, 10 Gipsy Lane, London SW15 5RG, England.

BROOK Susan G, b. 7 Dec. 1949, New York, USA. State Agency Administrator; Michigan Department of Transportation. *Education:* BA, Northwestern University, 1971; MA, Michigan State University, 1975. *Appointments:* Community Representative, Region V Office, Child Development, Department of Health, Education & Welfare, 1971-72; Program Assistant, Region V Office of Economic Opportunity, 1972-73; Executive Coordinator, Michigan Community Coordinated Child Care Council, Governors Office and Michigan Department of Management & Budget, 1973-80; Administrator, Office of Interagency Transportation Coordination 1980-83, Administrator, Freight Division 1983-, Bureau of Urban & Public Transportation, Michigan Department of Transportation. *Memberships include:* National Association for the Education of Young Children; Michigan Association for the Education of Young Children; National Association of State Directors for Child Development; Society for Women in Transportation; Women in State Government; National Association of Female Executives; National Conference of State Railway Officials; Michigan League of Human Services; Animal Protection Institute. *Hobbies:* Horseback Riding; Cross Country Skiing; Jogging; Walking; Needlework. *Address:* Michigan Department of Transportation, 425 West Ottawa Street, P O Box 30050, Lansing, MI 48909, USA.

BROOKS Hindi, b. 31 Jan. 1926, Detroit, Michigan, USA. Playwright; Television Writer. m. Manny Kleinmuntz, 6 Oct. 1951, 1 son, 1 daughter. *Education:* Wayne University, Detroit, Michigan, 1944-46; University of Judaism, Los Angeles, Los Angeles City College, University of California, Los Angeles, 1946-55. *Career:* Freelance Playwright, 1946-; Freelance TV Writer, 1951-; Artistic Director, Academy Writers Repertory Group; President, New Wrinkles Productions, Inc.; Drama and Film Critic, Columnist, various magazines and newspapers; Lecturer, various universities, writers seminars and organisations. *Publications:* Plays: That's No Lady; What's His Name Gets All The Good Musicians; A Minor Incident; Getting There; Wising Up; Exeunt O'Brien and Krasnov; Captain Noah; TV films: Before and After; Reversals; Fear of Climbing; Long Days of Summer. *Memberships:* Writers Guild of America, Board of Directors 1977-81; Board of Governors, Academy of TV Arts and Sciences; Dramatists Guild; Women in Film, Vice-President 1977-78; Advisory Board, Los Angeles Arts Council; Resident Playwright, Nomads Theatre; Theatre 40; Actors Studio; First Stage; Ensemble Studio Theatre; Playwrights Coordinator, Theatre Western Century City Playhouse. *Honours:* 1st Prize for 1-act plays, Jewish Centers Association, 1950; Back Stage Magazine, Full Length

Play, 1952; Grant, Office for Advanced Drama Research, 1962; Humanitas Award, 1974; Writers Guild Award, 1974. *Hobbies:* Support groups for peace and ecology; Swimming; Yoga; Knitting. *Address:* 2343 Hill Street, Santa Monica, CA 90405, USA.

BROOKS Patricia K, Author; Journalist. m. Lester Brooks, 10 Sept. 1950, 3 sons. *Education:* BA, Vassar College, 1947; University of Minnesota, 1948; University of London,1949. *Appointments:* Copywriter, W Lee Radio Station, Richmond, 1949-50; Radio Script Writer, WMBS, New York, 1950-51; Freelance Writer, 1951-. *Publications:* Crown Insider's Guide to Britain; Crown Insider's Guide to New York; Fisher Guide to Spain & Portugal; The Presidents' Cookbook; Meals that Can Wait; Christmastime Cook Book; Best Restaurants of New England; Country Inns of New England. *Memberships:* New York Travel Writers, Treasurer; Society of American Travel Writers; American Society of Journalists & Authors; Travel Journalists Guild. *Hobbies:* Art; Architecture; Food; Folk Art; History; Music; *Address:* 43 Marshall Ridge Road, New Canaan, CT 06840, USA.

BROOKS Suzanne May, b. 11 Feb. 1945, Australia. Public Official. *Education:* B Econ, Latrobe University, 1977; Accounting major. *Appointments include:* Administrator, State Bank of Victoria, 1961-75; Researcher 1978-79, Manager, Research Unit 1979-80, Accounting Manager 1980- 81, Money Market Manager 1981-83, ibid; Ministerial Adviser (seconded) 1983-85, Senior Ministerial Adviser, 1985-86, Treasurer of Victoria; 1st Assistant Secretary, Office of the Status of Women, Department of the Prime Minister & Cabinet, 1986-1988; Member, Australian Broadcasting Tribunal 1988-. *Work undertaken includes:* Head of Australian Delegation, CSW, UN 1987-88, Local government councillor, City of Doncastor & Templestowe, 1979-82; Prison Industries Commissioner, 1984-86; Member, Technical & Further Education Finance Committee, 1984-85; Member, Steering Committee, Financial Institutions Review, 1984; Task Force member, Worker's Compensation Reform, 1985. *Honours:* 1st woman in State Bank awarded a full-time university bursary, 1975-78. *Address:* 1/10 Ross Street, Waverton, 2060, NSW, Australia.

BROSMAN Catharine Hill (Pen Name Catharine Savage Brosman), b. 7 June 1934. Professor, French. m. (2) 1970, 1 daughter. *Education:* BA 1955, MA 1957, PhD 1960, Rice University, Houston; Postgraduate Study, University of Grenoble, France, 1957-58. *Appointments:* Instructor, French, Rice University, 1960-62; Assistant Professor, French, Sweet Briar College, 1962-63; Assistant Professor, French, University of Florida, 1963-66; Associate Professor, French, Mary Baldwin College, 1966-68; Associate Professor, French, Tulane University, 1968-72; Professor, French, Tulane University, 1972-. *Publications:* Poems: Watering, 1972; Abiding Winter, 1983; Critical Works: Andre Gide: l'evolution de sa pensee religieuse, 1962; Malraux Sartre and Aragon as Political Novelists, 1964; Roger Martin du Gard, 1968; Jean Paul Sartre, 1983; Jules Roy, 1988; Art as Testimony: The Work of Jules Roy, 1989; Dictionary of Literary Biography: Twentieth Century French Novelists, 3 volumes, 1988-89, Editor. *Address:* 7834 Willow Street, New Orleans, LA 70118, USA.

BROUSSARD Elsie Rita, b. 30 Jan 1924, Baton Rouge, USA. Professor. m. (1) F.P. Cassidy, 30 Jan. 1945, (2) Lloyd H. Cooper, 1 Jan. 1972, 1 son, 1 daughter. *Education:* MD, Louisiana State University, 1944; MPH, 1962, Dr.PH, 1964, University of Pittsburgh. *Appointments:* Private Practice, 1949-51; Assistant County Health Officer, Escambia County Health dept., 1952-61; Associate Professor, 1966-61, Assistant Professor, 1967-73, Professor, 1972-, Child Psychiatry, University of Pittsburgh. *Publications:* Measurement Instrument: Broussard's Neonatal Perception Inventories, 1964; Editor, Prevention of Psychosocial Disorders in Infancy: Emerging Perspectives for the 80's,

1981. *Memberships Include:* American Public Health Association, Fellow; American Medical Association; American & Pennsylvania Psychiatric Associations; Pennsylvannia State Medical Society. *Honours:* Recipient, many honours & awards. *Hobbies:* Golf; Gardening. *Address:* University of Pittsburgh, Graduate School of Public Health, 209 Parran Hall, 130 DeSoto Street, Pittsburgh, PA 15261, USA.

BROUSSARD Margaret Faye, b. 26 Nov. 1952, Lafayette, USA. Office Manager. *Education:* BSc., Texas Southern University, 1978. *Appointments:* CRT Operator, First City National Bank, Houston, 1974-75; Secretary, Librarian, Southern University Banking Centre, Houston, 1975-78; Secretary, Accounts Payable Analyst, Temporaries Inc., Houston, 1978-79; Secretary, Temporaries Inc., 1979-80; Office Assistant, 1981-82; Word Processing Specialist, Tenneco Oil Co., 1982-83; Administrative Assistant, Hoover Keith & Bruce Inc., 1983-87; Office Manager, Collaboration in Science & Technology Inc., 1987-. *Memberships:* National Association of Female Executives; March of Dimes. *Honours:* Recipient, various honours and awards. *Address:* Collaboration in Science & Technology Inc., 15835, Park Ten Place, Suite 105, Houston, TX 77084, USA.

BROWDE Selma, b. 21 July 1926, Cape Town, South Africa. Therapeutic Radiologist, retired; Honorary Consultant in Pain Management. m. Julian Browde, 21 Dec. 1947. 3 sons. *Education:* MB BCh, 1959; MMedRadT, 1967. *Appointments:* Consultant Radiotherapist, 1967-82, Acting Head of Department, 1982-84, Professor and Head of Department of Radiation Therapy and Oncology, 1984-86, University of Witwatersrand and Johannesburg Hospital. *Publications:* Articles in medical and non- medical journals and magazines. *Memberships:* City Councillor, Johannesburg, 1972-82; Provincial Councillor, TVL Province, 1974-77; NMDA (regional council); MASA; Soweto Electricity Advice Centre (Founder and Director); Trustee, TVL Black Blind Association; Founder, Hunger Concern Programme forerunner of Operation Hunger; American Association of Clinical Oncology. *Honours:* Awarded grant to USA to study new techniques in Hodgkins Disease, 1971; Grant to Breast Cancer Conference, 1980; Invited Guest Speaker, World Health Day in Lesotho, 1974. *Hobbies:* Tennis; Community work; Art; Game and bird watching; Travel. *Address:* 23 Third Avenue, Lower Houghton, Johannesburg 2198, South Africa.

BROWES Pauline, b. 7 May 1938, Harwood, Ontario, Canada. Member of Parliament; Educator. m. George Browes. 1 son, 2 daughters. *Education:* Coburg District Collegiate Institute, Cobourg; R H King Collegiate Institute, Scarborough; Toronto Teachers' College; BA Political Science, York University, McLaughlin College Faculty of Arts. *Appointments:* Teacher, Scarborough Board of Education, prior to 1975; Member, Practitioner Review Committee, Ministry of Health, Ontario, 1975-80; Member, Scarborough Board of Health, 1979-84; Chairman, 1982-84; Member, Metropolitan Toronto Housing Authority, 1980-81; Appeal Commissioner, Residential Tenancy Commission, Government of Ontario, 1981-84; Elected to House of Commons of Canada, September 1984; Appointed Parliamentary Secretary to the Minister of the Environment, October 1986; Between 1984-86 served as Chairman, Secretary of State; Member of Health Welfare and Social Affairs; Labour, Employment and Immigration; Justice and Legal Affairs; Vice-Chairman, Sub-Committee on Equality Rights, all Standing Committees of the House of Commons; Also between 1984-86 served on Caucus Committees as Chairman, Health and Welfare; Employment and Immigration, Labour and Youth; Served as Chairman of a Committee to commission a statue of the late Rt Hon John G Diefenbaker, former Prime Minister of Canada. The statue was placed on Parliament Hill on 18 Sept. 1986. *Memberships:* Member, Executive of the Canada-Europe Parliamentary Association; Canada-Greece Parliamentary Friendship Association; Royal Canadian Legion; Canadian Institute

of International Affairs; Scarborough Historical Society; Arts Scarborough; Scarborough Centenary Hospital Association; Friends of Scarborough Philharmonic Orchestra; Dental Auxiliary, Academy of Dentistry, Toronto; President 1969-70; Canadian Cancer Society and Red Shield Appeal; Scarborough Women's Centre; Member of Board of Directors, 1983. *Address:* 251 Confederation Building, House of Commons, Ottawa, Canada K1A 0A6

BROWN Adele Margaret Ashmore, b. 26 Aug. 1945, London, England. Caterer. m. (1)David Hamilton Parker, 6 May 1968, divorced 1972, 1 son, 1 daughter, (2) Neil Anthony Brown, 5 July 1984. *Appointments:* Secretary, 1971-73; Catering Business, 1975-. *Memberships:* Liberal Party of Australia; Red Cross; Lauriston Music Society; President, Local Association for Girl Guides, 1982-83; Riley Car Club of Australia. *Hobbies:* Music; Walking; Cycling; Reading; Gardening. *Address:* Cherry Trees, 32 Kent Hughes Road, Eltham 3905, Victoria, Australia.

BROWN Angela Royster, b. 21 Apr. 1948, Baltimore, Maryland. Educator, School Principal. m. James Elton Brown, 4 Oct. 1975, 1 daughter. *Education:* BS, Health Education, Psychology, Morgan State University, 1971; MS, Adult Education, Health Education, Guidance Counselling, 1977; Computer and Data Processing courses, Charles County Community College, LaPlata, Maryland, 1983; Administrative/Supervisory Endorsement Programme, Utah State University, Logan, 1987-89. *Appointments:* Counselor, 7th grade, Dededo Junior High School, Dededo, Guam, 1977-78; Teacher, Physical Science, Chemistry, Walker Mill Junior High School, Capital Heights, Maryland, 1979-82; Assistant Director, Instructor, Pre-Employment Training Programme, Charles County Community College, LaPlata, Maryland, 1982-84; Counsellor, Vocation and Drug Counseling, Crisis Intervention, Clearfield Job Corp, Clearfield, and Educational Director, Teacher, Odyssey Alternative School, Salt Lake City, Utah State employment, 1984-85; Teacher, Physical Science, Chemistry, Earth Science, Astronomy, North Davis Junior High School, 1985-89; Principal, Island Paradise School (private elementary school), Hawaii, 1989-. *Publications:* The Ins and Outs of ABE, in Phi Delta Gamma Journal. *Memberships:* Alpha Kappa Alpha Sorority Inc; Phi Delta Gamma Fraternity of Graduate Women; Association for Supervision and Curriculum Development; National Association for Female Executives. *Honours:* Martin Luther King Fellowship. *Hobbies:* Foster parenting; Juvenile Court volunteering; Tutoring; Travel; Reading science fiction; Writing. *Address:* 107 A 20th Street, Honolulu, HI 96818, USA.

BROWN Beatrice, b. 17 May 1917, Leeds, England. Conductor; Violist; Music Teacher. m. Morris Rothenberg, 1 Jan. 1981. *Education:* BA, Hunter College, USA, 1937; MA, New York University, 1939, Scholar, Berkshire Music Center, 1948-49. *Career:* Instructor of Music, Hunter College, 1937-43; Music Teacher, Public Schools, New York City, 1944-61; Bronx High School of Science, New York City, 1970-79; Violist: symphony orchestras, 1944-, Chamber Music Group, Musique Vivante, American Symphony Orchestra, Latvian Choir Orchestra, 1979-; Conductor, Chamber Music Associates, New York City, 1950-53; Music Director, Conductor: Scranton (Pennsylvania) Philharmonic Orchestra, 1963-72, Ridgefield (Connecticut) Orchestra, 1969-, Western Connecticut Symphony Orchestra, Danbury, 1981-, Housatonic Chamber Orchestra, 1982-; Conductor, New York, New Jersey and Connecticut companies; TV appearances; Adjunct Assistant Professor, Lehman College, 1972-74; Lecturer. *Memberships:* American Symphony Orchestra League; Conductors Guild; Phi Beta Kappa. *Honours:* Fulbright Grant in Conducting, 1953-55; Martha Baird Rockefeller Grant in Conducting, 1957-59; Named to Hunter College Hall of Fame, 1972; 1 of 100 Distinguished Women in Connecticut, 1976; 1 of 5 Outstanding Women in Ridgefield, Connecticut, 1979; UN Peace Award, 1980; Wellington Award, 1981.

Address: 3 Seir Hill Road, Apt C-2, Norwalk, CT 06850, USA,

BROWN Billie Augustine, b. 1 Aug. 1924, Pangburn, Arkansas, USA. Educator. m. James A Brown, 26 Nov. 1969, 2 sons, 2 daughters by previous marriage. *Education:* BS, Harding University, 1962; MSEd, 1966; MA, University of Central Arkansas; University of Arkansas Graduate Centre, 1980-84. *Appointments:* Librarian, White County, 1947-52; US Postal Clerk, 1954; Public School Teacher, 1959-78; Art Specialist, Palaski County, 1979-80; Instructional Co-ordinator, Art, Pulaski County School District, 1980-87; UALR Lecturer, 1987-. *Creative Works:* Editor, Committee Chair, art L. Curriculum Guide-Exploratory Art 6 and 7, Level 8 Art Curriculum Guide; Commercial Art Guide 10-12; Contributor to Arkansas Educator, 1957; numerous paintings. *Memberships:* various professional organisations. *Honours:* Co-Founder, Board of Advisors, Arkansas Young Artists Association (Art Patron of the Year, 1985); Democratic Committeewomen, 1978-86; 1st Place Award, Pastels, White County, 1957; Fair Housing Special award, 1985; League of Artists Award, 1986. *Hobbies:* Reading; Walking; Caring for Animals. *Address:* 5302 Dreher Lane, Windemere, Little Rock, AR 72209, USA.

BROWN Blanche R, b. 12 Apr. 1915, Boston, USA. Professor Emeritus. m. Milton W. Brown, 15 July 1938. *Education:* BFA, 1936, MA, 1938, PhD, 1967, New York University. *Appointments:* Staff Lecturer, Metropolitan Museum of Art, 1942-66; Associate Professor, 1967-73, Professor 1973-85, Emeritus 1985-, New York University. *Publications:* Ptolemaic Paintings & Mosaics, 1957; Five Cities: An Art Guide to Athens, Rome, Florence, Paris, London, 1964; Anticlassicism in Greek Sculpture of the 4th Century BC, 1973. *Memberships Include:* Archaeological Institute of America, Board of Directors of New York Society; Alumni Association, Institute of Fine Arts, President 1985-. *Honours:* Carnegie Foundation, 1973; American Council of Learned Societies, 1959-60; American Association of University Women, 1971; NEH, 1976-77; Guggenheim Memorial Foundation, 1978-79. *Hobbies:* Sailing. *Address:* 15 West 70 Street, New York, NY 10023, USA.

BROWN Carolyn, b. 23 Jan. 1944, Bridgeport, Connecticut, USA. Microbiologist; Ecologist. m. Frank D. Davis, Sr, 25 Jan. 1985. *Education:* BA, Biology, University of Bridgeport, 1968; MS, Southern Connecticut State University, 1971; PhD, Zoology, University of Connecticut, 1980. *Appointments:* Research microbiologist (diseases of bivalve larvae), Milford Laboratory 1967-85, Ecologist, advising/ assisting Director of Research & Environmental Information (disease & ecological problems), National Marine Fisheries Service. *Publications include:* Numerous scientific articles, book chapter, diseases of bivalve larvae. *Memberships:* American Association for Advancement of Science; American Society for Microbiology; Society for Invertebrate Pathology. *Honour:* Professional Award, Greater Bridgeport Negro Business & Professional Women's Club, 1982. *Hobbies:* Cooking & baking; Working with adolescents. *Address:* 2013 Alabaster Drive, Silver Spring, Maryland 20904, USA.

BROWN Deborah Sharon Miller, b. 6 Feb. 1955, Danville, Pennsylvania, USA. Oil Company Official. *Education:* AA, Business Administration, Brandywine College, 1975; BS, Business Management, University of Maryland, 1978; MS, Business Communication, American University, 1979. *Appointments:* Administrator, Pentagon, Washington DC, 1975-77; Press Officer, Food & Drug Administration, 1977-79; Official, Shell Oil Company, Houston, Texas, 1979-. *Memberships:* Offices: National Association of Female Executives; Association of Information Processors. *Honour:* Award, outstanding achievement, Shell Oil Company, 1984. *Hobbies:* Painting; Cycling; Skiing; Tennis. *Address:* Shell Oil Company, 777 Walker, Houston, Texas 77002, USA.

BROWN Delores Elaine Robinson, b. 10 Dec. 1945, Wildwood, Florida, USA. Retired Engineer; Minister; Hospital Volunteer. m. Marshall L. Brown, 21 Dec. 1966, 1 daughter. *Education:* Pre-Engineering, Fla., A & M University, 1962-64; BSEE, Tuskegee University, 1967. *Appointments:* Electrical Engineering positions: General Electric Corp, 1967-68; Florida Power Corporation, 1968-70; Honeywell Aero, 1971-76; Sperry Univac, 1975; ECI Div., E-Systems, 1976-79. *Publication:* The Way to Salvation, 1985 *Memberships:* Tuskegee Alumni Association; IEEE; St Anthony's Hospital Foundation; Computer Programmers Association; Society of Women Engineers. *Honours:* Recipient, several awards. *Hobbies:* Studying the Bible; Coin Collecting; Collecting Miniature Antiques & Magnets; Writing Poetry. *Address:* 2630 Queen Street South, St Petersburg, FL 33712, USA.

BROWN Dorothy Ann, b. 9 Apr. 1953, Minden Louisiana, USA. Certified Public Accountant. m. Frankie C Brown, 20 July 1984. 1 daughter. *Education:* BS Accounting, Southern University, Baton Rouge, 1975; MVA Finance, Depaul University, 1981. *Appointments:* Staff Accountant, Commonwealth Edison, 1975-77; Auditort, Arthur Anderson & Co, 1977-80; Senior Auditor, First National Bank of Chicago, 1981-84; Audit Manager, Odell Hicks & Company, 1984-. *Memberships:* American Institute of CPA's; Illinois Society of CPA's; National Society of CPA's; National Association of Black Accountants. *Honours:* Certified Public Accountant Certificate, 1977; Notary Public, 1976; National Editorial Award, National Association of Black Accountants, 1985; Nominated, Board of Trustees, Chicago City Colleges, 1984. *Interest:* Coordinating activities for youth of the Church. *Address:* 8816 South Constance, Chicago, Illinois 60617, USA.

BROWN Faith, b. 28 May 1943, Liverpool, England. Impressionist; Actress; Singer. m. 8 Sept. 1968, 1 daughter. *Education:* St Francis De'Sales, Liverpool. *Memberships:* Full Equity. *Honours:* The TV Times Award, Funniest Lady, 1979-80; The Club Mirror Award, 1981; LA Award for Outstanding Services, USA, 1981. *Hobbies:* Music; Fishing; Cooking; Reading. *Address:* c/o Tony Lewis, 233 Regent St., London W1, England.

BROWN Frances Anne, b. 13 Feb. 1946, Newport News, USA. Psychotherapist. *Education:* AA, Nursing, 1968; BS, St Joseph's College, 1980. *Appointments:* Staff Nurse, Psychiatry, Duke University Medical Centre, 1968-71; Head Nurse, Psychiatry, DUMC, 1971-76; Private Practice, Counselling, 1976-; Distributor Success Motivation Institute, 1988-. *Publications:* Photographer, art display in several galleries. *Memberships:* various professional organisations including: Rape Crisis Centre; Hillsborough Historical Society; NOW; National Association Women Business Owners. *Honours:* Recipient of the World Decoration of Excellence; Member, International Platform Association; Member, Associated Photographers International; Member, National Trust for Historic Preservation; Invited to become Member of ABI Research Board of Advisors. *Hobbies:* Photogrpahy; Walking; Music. *Address:* 29 Bluff Trail, Chapel Hill, NC 27516, USA.

BROWN Freda, b. 9 June 1919, Sydney, Australia. Journalist. *Appointments:* Journalist, 1945-. *Membership;* Australian Women's Movement; President, Union of Australian Women, 1962, Honorary Vice President, 1964; Vice President, 1964-75, President, 1975-, WIDF; President, International Preparatory Committee, World Congress in International Women's Year, 1974; Vice President, World Peace Council, 1977-. *Honours:* International Lenin Prize. *Address:* Women's International Democratic Federation, Unter den Linden 13, Berlin 1080, German Democratic Republic.

BROWN Helen Gurley, b. 18 Feb. 1922, Green Forest, Arkansas, USA. Editor-in-Chief, Cosmopolitan Magazine. m. David Brown, 25 Sept. 1959. *Education:*

Texas State College for Women, 1941; Woodbury College, 1942. *Appointments:* Executive Secretary, Music Corp. 1942-45; Executive Secretary, Wm Morris Agency, 1945-57; Copywriter, Foote Cone & Belding, 1948-58; Advertising Account Executive, Kenyon & Eckhardt, 1958-62; Editor-in-Chief, Cosmopolitan Magazine, 1965-. *Publications:* Sex and the Single Girl, 1962; Sex and the Office, 1965; The Outrageous Opinions of Helen Gurley Brown, 1967; Helen Gurley Brown's Single Girl's Cookbook, 1969; Sex and the New Single Girl, 1970; Having It All, 1982. *Memberships:* Authors League of America; American Society of Magazine Editors; The Establishment of the Helen Gurley Brown Research Professorship at Northwestern University's Medill School of Journalism. *Honours:* Francis Holmes Achievement Award for Outstanding Work in Advertising, 1956-59; Dist. Achievement Award, University of Southern California, School of Journalism, 1971; American newspaperwomans Association Annual Award, 1972; American Soc. Journalism School Administrators, 1972; Distinguished Achievement Award in Journalism Hon Alumnus Stanford University, 1977; New York Women in Communications annual Matrix Award in Magazine Category, 1985; Doctor of Laws, Woodbury University, 1987; Publishing Hall of Fame, 1988. *Interests:* Health fanatic; Feminist; Workaholic; Relationships between men and women. *Address:* 1 West 18st Street, New York, NY 10024, USA.

BROWN Jacqueline Calder, b. 19 July 1947, Corbin, USA. Teacher. Divorced, 2 sons. *Education:* BS, Mobile College, 970; MEd., Science Education, University of Southern Alabama, 1982. *Appointments:* Teacher, Adams Middle School, 1974-89; Geology Consultant, Mobile College, 1983-89; Aerospace Education Consultant, 1985-89. *Publications:* Author, Field Guide to Alber S. Dix Rock & Mineral Museum. *Memberships:* Phi Delta Kappa; National Association of Geology Teachers; Alabama Science Teachers Association, Treasurer; NEA; National Association of Marine Science Educators; Earth Science Teachers. *Honours:* Recipient, many honours & awards including: Woman of Year, 1985; NASA Teacher in Space Finalist, 1985; Heart of Gold Winner, 1989. *Hobbies:* Rock & Mineral Collecting; Reading; Gardening; Cycling; Horse Riding. *Address:* 824 Norma Circle, PO Box 625, Saraland, AL 36571, USA.

BROWN Jean B., b. 22 Jan. 1947, Springfield, Missouri, USA. Speech and Communication Counsellor. div., 1 son. *Education:* BA, 1973, MA, 1974, PhD, 1981, Memphis State University. *Appointments:* Several positions associated with graduate assistantships, 1973-79; Instructor, Diroctor of Audiology Programmes, 1979-81, Assistant Professor, Director of Audiology Programmes, Department of Communicative Disorders, 1981-82, University of Minnesota, Duluth; Private Practitioner, Albuquerque Aphasia and Speech Consultants, Albuquerque, New Mexico, 1982-86; Private Practitioner, Director, Owner, Vocal Point Therapies, Inc., Communication and Cognitive Treatment Center Inc, Albuquerque, 1986-. *Publications include:* Examination of the Grammatical Morphemes in the Language of Hard-of-Hearing Children, 1984; Review of Can't Your Child Hear, Journal of the American Speech-Language- Hearing Association, 1983-86. *Memberships include:* American Speech-Language-Hearing Association; National Head Injury Foundation; New Mexico Speech-Language-Hearing Association; New Mexico Head Injury Foundation; National Board of Certified Counselors; New Mexico Counseling Association. *Honours include:* Named Most Valuable Professor, College of Education, University of Minnesota-Duluth, 1982; Cooperative Training Programme between Twin Cities and Duluth Campuses, University of Minnesota, 1981-84. *Address:* 11901 El Dorado Place NE, Albuquerque, NM 87111, USA.

BROWN Jennifer Mary, b. 26 Aug. 1930, London, England. Housewife. m. Edward Peter Moncriefe Brown, 14 Oct. 1954, 4 sons. *Appointments:* Voluntary Helper, MacMillan Unit, Midhurst. *Hobbies:* Interior Decorating;

Tennis; Sailing; Bridge. *Address:* Wotton, Grove Lane, Petworth, West Sussex GU28 0BT, England.

BROWN Joan Abena, b. 8 May, Chicago, Illinois, USA. Manager Arts Organization. divorced. *Education:* BA, Roosevelt University; MA, University of Chicago. *Appointments:* Director of Program Services, YWCA of Metropolitan Chicago, 1963-82; President, ETA Creative Arts Foundation, 1982-. *Publications:* Monography, Politics of/and Black Theatre, 1979; The Challenge of the 21st Century, article, 1988. *Memberships:* Womans Board Chicago Urban League; President, Midwest African American Theatre Alliance, Chair; Personnel Committee, African American Arts Alliance. *Honours:* Hull House Fellowship, 1962; Kool Achiever Award, finalist, 1988; Top 100 Black Business and Professional Women, Dollars & Sense Magazine, 1988; Black Rose Award, League of Black Women, 1987; 100 women influencing Chicago's Future, Today's Chicago Woman, 1988; Builder Award, Institute of Positive Education, 1987; Paul Robeson Award, African American Arts Alliance, 1978; Hazel Joan Bryant Award, Midwest African American Theatre Alliance, 1988; Governor's Award In the Arts (Illinois), 1981; Harriet Tubman Award Black Woman Hall of Fame, 1985; Fine Arts Award, national Association of Negro Business & Professional Women, 1986. *Hobbies:* Theatre; Reading; Dance; Travel. *Address:* 7637 So Bennett Street, Chicago, IL 60649, USA.

BROWN June Gottlieb, b. 21 June 1932, Dunn, North Carolina, USA. Artist; Teacher; Gallery Owner. m. 16 Apr. 1976. 1 son, 5 daughters. *Education:* Queens College; 6 years study under William Leon Stacks. *Appointments:* Owner, Art Gallery; Art Instructor Brunswick Community College. *Creative Works:* Exhibitions: One Person Shows at: Robinette Gallery, Charlotte, North Carolina, 1975; Brunswick Southport Public Library, 1975; Riverbend Gallery, Wilmington, North Carolina, 1975. Group Shows: Hanes Community Centre, 1975; Temple Beth El, Charlotte, 1975; Salem College, 1981; Many in private collections in United States and Israel. *Memberships:* American Artists Professional League; Salmagundi Club; Artists Fellowship Incorporated; Catharine Lorillard Wolfe Arts Club; International Society of Women Marine Artists and COGAP (Coast Guard Artists); Guild of Charlotte Artists, Charlotte, North Carolina; Associated Artists of Winston-Salem, North Carolina; Associated Artists of Southport, North Carolina; The Painters Group, Southport. *Honours:* Mae Berlind Bach Award 1982; Oil: Catharine Lorillard Wolfe Arts Club; Henley's Southeastern Specturm Annual Open Juried Show, 1983; Butler Institute of American Art, 1982/83; Hoyt Institute of American Art, 1982; Allied Artists of America, 1982, 1986; 112th International Dogwood Festival Art Show, Honourable Mention, 1984; 15th Annual River Road Art Competition, 1984; Woodstock School of Art 2nd Annual, 1984; Leslie Levy Gallery 2nd Annual Contemporary Realism Show, 1984; Dorothy Watkey Barberies, Oil Award 1986, Merit Award 1987, Catharine Lorillard Wolfe Art Club; Emily Morse Memorial Award, Salmagundi Club, 1983; Southdown Fine Arts Biennial, 1988. Gallery Affiliation: Riverfront Gallery, Wilmington; The Treasure Room, Oak Island; Colorworks Club, Hilton Head Island; City Art Works, New Bern. *Hobbies:* Cross Country Skiing; Swimming. *Address:* 230 River Drive, Southport, NC 28461, USA.

BROWN Kay, Artist. *Education:* Vassar College, USA; MS, Columbia University; Study sculpture, Corcoran Gallery, Washington DC. *Recent painting exhibitions:* American Stage Festival, New Hampshire, 1986; Obsidian Gallery, Tucson, Arizona, 1986; Collage, Simmons College, Boston, 1986; Collage, Paper & Steel, Cambridge Art Association, 1985. Dance & Multimedia: Martin Street Collage Group, Sharon, New Hampshire, 1986; Dance & Life Music, Cambridge Art Association/ Martin Street College Dance Company, 1985; Dance Improvisation with Music & Painting, Greensboro, Vermont, 1984, 1985. One-man exhibitions: Radcliffe College, Massachusetts, 1975, 1982, 1985; Wordsmith

Gallery, Cambridge, 1983, 1984; Marion Art Centre, Massachusetts, 1983; World Affairs Council, Boston, 1981. Corporate collections: Boston Globe; Bank of America, Boston; Dean, Witter; First National Bank, Boston; Hearthstone Insurance Company, Massachusetts; Mitchell & Company, Cambirdge, Massachusetts. *Memberships include:* Founder/Director, Martin Street Dance Company (mixed media improvisational dance group); Boston Visual Artists Union; Cambridge Art Association; Copley Society, Boston; Concord Art Association; Sharon Art Centre; Massachusetts Craftsmens Council. *Honours include:* 2nd Prize, Regional Juried Show, Cambridge Art Association, 1983; Honorable Mention, Cambridge Art Association, 1984; 1988, Grumbacher Gold Medal, painting, Concord, Massachusetts. *Address:* 16 Avon Street, Cambridge, MA 02138, USA.

BROWN Leanna Young, b. 11 May 1935, Providence, Rhode Island, USA. State Senator. m. W Stanley, 16 June 1956. 2 sons. *Education:* BA Honours, Smith College, 1956. *Appointments:* Chatham Borough Council, 1969-72; Morris County Freeholder, 1972-80; Freeholder Director, 1976; New Jersey General Assembly, 1980-83; New Jersey Senate, 1984-. *Memberships:* Governor's Commission on International Trade, 1986-; New Jersey Historical Commission, 1986-; Vice-Chair, Gateway National Recreation Area Advisory Commission, 1983-86; President, New Jersey Association for Elected Women, 1982-84; chair, Northeast New Jersey Transportation Co-ordinating Committee, 1979-80; President, New Jersey Association of Counties, 1978. *Hobbies:* Reading; Yoga. *Address:* 123 Columbia Turnpike, Florham Park, NJ 07932, USA.

BROWN Margaret J, b. 7 Sept. 1941, Rhineland, Texas, USA. Managing Editor, Tutorials and Monographs. *Education:* BSE Education with English & Social Sciences, 1970; MPA Public Administration with HUD Fellowship, 1973. *Appointments:* Secretary, Congressman John Paul Hammerschmidt, 1973-75; Production Editor, Journals & Books, American Geophysical Union, 1976-79; Managing Editor of Tutorials and Monographs, Computer Society of the IEEE, 1980-. *Membership:* ASAE. *Honours:* Meritorious Service Award, 1987; Dinner for two Award, 1986. *Hobbies:* Stamp collecting; Antiques; Books; Music; Politics, assisted many people running for office (federal, state and local candidates). *Address:* 8802 Plymouth St, No 3, Silver Spring, MD 20901, USA.

BROWN Michelle Ann Roose, b. 25 Dec. 1953, Detroit, Michigan, USA. Executive Vice President. m. Scott Brown, 18 Dec. 1976, divorced, 1985, 1 son, 1 daughter. *Education:* AA, Business Administration. *Appointments:* Escrow Secretary, Burton Abstract & Title Co., 1971-73; Closing Director, Ed McNulty Realty, 1973-77; Administrative Assistant, Family Service Agency, 977-79; Closing Director, Real Estate Counselors Inc., 1981- 82; Co-Owner, Decorator, Port Huron Decorating Studio, 1982-85; Executive Officer, St Clair County Board of Realtors, 1984-85; Executive Vice President, Ann Arbour Area Board of Realtors, 1985-. *Publications:* Writer, Personnel Policies & Procedures Manual, Ann Arbor Area Board of Realtors; Articles in various journals. *Memberships:* American and Michigan, Societies of Association Executives; Michigan Executive Officers Council; Ann Arbor Area Chamber of Commerce; etc. *Honours:* Recipient, various honours and awards including: 1st Place, Entrepreneurship, Michigan Career Development Conference, 1984; Salute to Women in Business, Ann Arbor Area Chamber of Commerce, 1987. *Hobbies:* Music; Dance; Live Theatre; Running; Skiing. *Address:* 502 Rosemont, Saline, MI 48176, USA.

BROWN Mona Wright, b. 18 Feb. 1958, Washington, DC, USA. Administrative Coordinator. *Education:* University of Nevada, Las Vegas, 1977-; Clark County Community College, 1987-. *Appointments:* Radiology Department Secretary, Valley Hospital, Las Vegas, 1979-80; Receptionist/Branch Manager's Secretary,

Wells Fargo Mortgage Company, Las Vegas, 1980-81; Residential Installation Control Clerk, 1981-82, Secretary, Customer Services Assistant Manager, 1982-84, Central Telephone Company, Las Vegas; Administrative Coordinator, Science Applications International Corporation, Las Vegas, 1984-. *Memberships:* CITY, 1987-; American Diabetes Association, Nevada Affiliate, Inc, 1985-; American Business Women's Association, Gambleier's Chapter, 1983-86; Toastmasters International, I'll Drink to That Club, 1983-85; Las Vegas Chamber of Commerce, Membership Committee, 1982. *Honours:* President's Volunteer Action Award, Nominee, 1987; Most Outstanding Member, American Diabetes Association, Nevada Affiliate, 1986; For leadership that earned the Chapter top awards from the National Organization, American Business Women's Association, Gambleier's Chapter, 1985; For work with the Membership Committee, Greater Las Vegas Chamber of Commerce, 1982; Assistant to the Company Campaign Coordinator, Centel United Way Campaign, 1982. *Hobbies:* Writing poetry and short stories; Ceramics; Swimming; Animals; Community service. *Address:* SAIC, 3349 S Highland Dr., Suite 403, Las Vegas, NV 89109, USA.

BROWN Monica Julienne, b. 3 July 1938, Colon, Republic of Panama. Assistant Professor of Medicine. *Education:* BSc, National Institute, 1964; MD, University of Panama, 1966-68; Residency in Internal Medicine, Hospital Santo Tomas, Panama; Training in Endocrinology and Nuclear Medicine, Royal Postgraduate Medical School, London, England, 1968-70; Study tour on Radiation Dosimetry in Medicine and Biology in Europe, 1973. *Appointments:* Assistant Professor of Pro-pedeutics and Physiopathology, 1966-68, Assistant Professor of Medicine, 1977-, Clinical Professor of Biochemistry, 1986, University of Panama; Head, Endocrine Unit and Diabetic Clinic, Hospital Santo Tomas, Panama, 1977-. *Publications:* Contributor of numerous articles to medical and scientific journals; The Problems of Type 1 diabetes in Latin America. *Memberships:* Founder Panamanian Diabetic Association; Panamian Academy of Medicine and Surgery, Board of Directors, 1986-92; Honorary President, Panamanian Diabetic Association; Human Rights Committee, Gorghas Memorial Laboratory; International Vice-President for Panama of Pan-American Women's Alliance; Past President, Central American and Caribbean Association of Endocrinology and Metabolism; American Diabetes Association; President, Female Doctors Society of Panama; Panama's Delegate, Latin America Diabetes Association. *Honours:* 1st place Honours, National Institute, 1957; 1st place Honours, Sigma Lambda Chapter, University of Panama, 1964; Achievement Award, Panamanian Academy of Medicine and Surgery, 1964; Distinguished Citizen of Colon Award, 1976; Plaque of Honour, Panama's Professional and Business women. *Hobbies:* Classical and jazz Music; Reading; Travel. *Address:* PO Box 4968, Panama 5, Republic of Panama.

BROWN Ollie Dawkins, b. 30 May 1941, Stanton, Texas, USA. Scientific Researcher; Author; Psychotherapist; Educator. m. Robert Jerry Brown, 28 Sept. 1958, div. 2 sons. *Education:* BS, Texas Tech University, 1965; MEd, University of North Texas, 1973; MS, East Texas State University, 1983. *Appointments:* Schoolteacher, 1965-73; Diagnostician, with Dr Lillian Solomon, 1973-82; Medical Researcher, Environmental Health Centre, Dallas, Texas, 1982-87; Medical Researcher, Psychotherapist (Pastoral Counselling Centre), Instructor, University of Texas Dallas, 1987-. *Publications include:* Contributions, professional journals & medical textbooks, areas of: Medical Imaging of the Brain; Death & Dying; Relationship Between Length of Birth Labour & Learning Problems; Environmental Aspects of Health & Disease; Food & Chemical Sensitivities with Emphasis on Cardiovascular Effects. Editor, co-author, various popular manuals including: Tips for Non-Toxic Household Maintenance. *Memberships include:* Current American & Texas Psychological Associations; Texas Association of Marriage & Family Therapists; New York Academy of Sciences; Dallas Museum of Art. *Hobbies:* Birding;

Gardening; Family & friends; Dance; Theatre; Art; Gourmet food; Travel. *Address:* 634 Williams Way, Richardson, Texas 75080, USA.

BROWN Pamela, b. 31 Dec. 1924, Colchester, Essex, England. Writer. m. Donald Masters, 24 June 1949, 2 daughters. *Education:* Royal Academy of Dramatic Art. *Appointments include:* Director, BBC Children's Programmes, 1950-55; Freelance, Granada & Scottish TV, 1955-60. *Publications include:* Over 20 books, children & teenagers, including The Swish of the Curtain. *Address:* Casa Moreno, Cuxach, Pollerusa, Mallorca, Spain.

BROWN Ritamary, Sister, b. 15 Sept. 1939, Illinois, USA. Assistant Administrator. *Education:* BA, Fontbonne College, 1964; MS, Purdue University, 1972; MA, Xavier University, 1986. *Appointments:* Dietitian, St Mary's, Decatur, 1965-66; Director, Food Services, St Francis Hospital, Washington, Missouri, 1966-68; Director, Food & Nutrition Services, St John's Hospital, Springfield, 1969-84; Assistant Administrator, St Elizabeth's Hospital, Belleville, 1986-. *Publications:* Articles in journals including: Diabetes Forecast. *Memberships:* Board, American Cancer Society; American Dietetic Association; Illinois Dietetic Association, President 1978-79; American Diabetes Association. *Honours:* Recipient, various honours and awards including: Editorial Board, Diabetes Forecast, 1983-85; Governor's Appointee, Illinois State Council on Nutrition. *Hobbies:* Classical Music; Reading. *Address:* St Elizabeth's Hospital, 211 S. Third Street, Belleville, IL 62222, USA.

BROWN Ruby Joyce, b. 30 June, 1931, Claremont, St Ann, Jamaica, West Indies. Attorney-at-Law (Legal Draftsman). m. Glester Samuel Brown, 25 May 1959. 1 daughter. *Education:* Commonwealth Drafting Course (Advanced), 1984; Inns of Court School of Law, London, England, 1968-72; Called to Bar, Lincoln's Inn, 1972. *Appointments:* Criminal Clerk, Falmouth Courts Office, 1949; Trust Officer, Administrator General's Office, 1953-68; Legal Officer, Ministry of Social Security, 1973-74; Legal Draftsman, Parliamentary Counsel's Office, 1974-. *Publications:* Poems: BBC Caribbean Voices; Welfare Reporter Magazine; Poetry International. *Memberships:* Commonwealth Lawyers Association; Civil Service Association; President, St Hilda's Alumnae, 1980-83; Commissioner, Girl Guide Association. *Honour:* Civil Service Long Service Medal, 1988. *Hobbies:* Reading; Poetry writing; Guiding. *Address:* 15 Begonia Drive, Kingston 6, Jamaica, West Indies.

BROWN Sandra Dernstein, b. 18 Oct. 1940, Brooklyn, New York, USA. Customs Broker; International Freight Forwarder. m. Herbert H. Burstein, 22 Mar. 1980. 1 son, 2 daughters. *Education:* BA, Newcome College, Tulane University, 1962. *Appointments:* Teacher, New Orleans Public Schools, 1962-64; Comptroller 1968-74, President 1974-, Irwin Brown Company. *Memberships:* Past Boards, Jewish Welfare Federation, & Junior Achievement, New Orleans; Past President, Offices, Jewish Family Service; Past Council President, United Way; Past Offices (New Orleans), Women's Business Enterprise Commission, & International Freight Forwarders & Customs Brokers Association; National Customs Brokers & Forwarders of America (NCBFA). *Honours:* Merit Award, NCBFA, 1975; One of 10 Businesswomen of Year, Mayor of New Orleans, 1985. *Hobbies:* Music; Reading; Interior design. *Address:* Irwin Brown Company, 212 Chartres Street, New Orleans, Louisiana 70130, USA.

BROWN Sandra Marie Hale, b. 10 July 1957, La Follette, USA. Professional Dog Breeder; Clothes Designer. m. Thomas Barrett Brown, 12 Dec. 1981. *Education:* BS, Home Economics, Lincoln Memorial Univerity, 1976. *Appointments:* Assistant Restaurant Manager, Senior Service Co- ordinator, Holiday Inns Co., 1973-80; President, Co-Owner, Sandy's Kennels, Co-Owner, Vice President, Paw Pals Mail Order Catalog,

1981-. *Publications:* Life Applachia, 1973. *Memberships:* Girls Auxiliary; Greenpeace; Tennessee Republican Party; Smithsonian Institute. *Honours:* Breeder of the Year, Knox County, 1986. *Hobbies:* Horseriding; Shell Collecting; Painting; Crafts; Singing. *Address:* 308 Bridgewater Road, Knoxville, TN 37923, USA.

BROWN Verlia Monica, b. 16 July 1947, Jamaica, West Indies. Registered Professional Nurse. *Education:* Diploma, Nursing, 1974; BSc., 1977, MA, 1982, Brooklyn College. *Appointments:* Staff Nurse, Surgical Intensive Care Units, Kings County Hospital Center, 1974-77; Assistant Head Nurse, SICU, Kings County Hospital, 1977-82; Head Nurse, Surgical Intensive Care Unit, Kings County Hospital Center, 1982-; Per-Diem-Registered Nurse, Surgical Intensive Care Unit, Beth Israel Medical Center, 1983-. *Publications:* Letters in: RN Nursing Journal; American Journal of Nursing. *Memberships:* American Nurses Association; New York State Nurses Association. *Honours:* Marion Doyle Nursing Scholarship, 1976- 77; Brooklyn College Graduate Student Association Awards, 1981, 1982. *Hobbies:* Travel; Photography; Animal Lover. *Address:* 1462 Crown Street, Wantagh, Long Island, NY 11793, USA.

BROWN, (Mary) Charline Hayes, b. 13 Dec. 1919, Cotton Valley, Louisiana, USA. Manager, Hayes Co. m. Joseph Cecil Brown, Jr, 30 Sept. 1945. 1 son, 2 daughters. *Education:* BS Business Administration, Louisiana State University, 1941. *Appointments:* Accountant Secretary, H R Hayes Lbr Co, 1941-45; Personnel Clerk and Insurance Examiner, Veterans Adm. 1945- 46; Secretary/Treasurer, Lumbermen's Supply Co, Inc, 1953-85; Estate Administrator, 1977- 78 and 1983-84, Manager, 1978-, Hayes Company. *Publications:* Poems: Brief Lightning, 1979; Contributed to: Vignettes of LA History; Louisiana Leaders; Lyric LA, etc. *Memberships:* President North LA Branch, National League of American Pen Women; Secretary, President of Northeast Branch twice, Louisiana State Poetry Society; Miss. State Poetry Society; Junior Charity League; Daughters of the American Revolution. *Honours:* 4 first prizes, Louisiana State Poetry Society, 1955. *Hobbies:* Poetry; Gardening; Cooking; Travel. *Address:* Monroe, LA 71203, USA.

BROWN-MINER Kathleen Marie, b. 8 Sept. 1959, Dearborn, Michigan, USA. Registered Dietitian; Exercise Physiologist. m. Mark Miner, 13 Aug. 1983. *Education:* BS, University of Wisconsin-Stout, 1981; MS, University of Wisconsin-LaCrosse, 1988. *Appointments:* Assist. Chief Clinical Dietitian; Health Promo/Cardiac Dietitian; Chief Dietitian, Food Service Manager, 1982; Health Promotion & Cardiac Rehabilitation Dietitian, 1985; Nutrition Coordinator/Exercise Leader, 1987; Nutrition and Fitness Consulting, KBM Consulting, 1988. *Publications:* Author, HELP (Healthy Eating & Lifestyle Program); Contributing author to Clinical Exercise; Evaluation to Application. *Memberships:* American Dietetic Association; American College of Sports Medicine; Association for Fitness in Business, Sports & Cardiovascular Nutrition Practice Group; American Running & Fitness Association. *Honours:* Preston Clayton Memorial Scholarship, 1988; Phillip Morris Scholarship for academic achievement, 1977-81; University of Wisconsin-Stout Foundation Scholarship, 1979, 1980. *Hobbies:* Volleyball; Softball; Bike touring; Cross country skiing; Fitness walking; Crafts and sewing; Being with my family. *Address:* Route 1, Box 50, Avoca, Wisconsin 53506, USA.

BROWN-STANDRIDGE Marcia Dorothy, b. 5 June 1955, St Louis, USA. Assistant Professor. m. Charles Robert Standridge, 13 July 1985. *Education:* BSW, Valpariso University, 1977; MSW, Tulane University, 1978; PhD, Purdue University, 1986. *Appointments:* Clinical Social Worker, Luheran Medical Centre, 1979-82; Research/Teaching Assistant, Purdue University, 1982-85; Consultant, Lutheran Child & Family Sevices, Texas Tech University, 1984-85. *Publications:* Articles in: Family Process; American Journal of Family Therapy;

Journal of Psychotherapy and the Family; Family Therapy; Journal of Early Adolescence; Family Therapy News. *Memberships:* National Association of Social Work; American Association of Marriage & Family Therapy; American Home Economics Association. *Honours:* Outstanding Student - Proposed and Completed Research Awards, 1984, 1986. *Hobbies:* Piano; Voice Choir; Bell Choir. *Address:* Texas Tech University, Dept. of Human Development & Family Studies, Box 4170, Lubbock, TX 79409, USA.

BROWNE Coral (Edith), b. 23 July 1913, Melbourne, Australia. Actress. m.(1) Philip Westrope Pearman, 1950. (2) Vincent Price, 1974. *Education:* Claremont Ladies; College, Melbourne; Studied painting in Melbourne. *Career:* First stage appearance in Loyalties, Comedy Theatre, Melbourne, 1931; Acted in 28 plays in Australia, 1931-34. First London appearance in Lover's Leap, Vaudeville, 1934. *Creative Works:* Theatre since 1940 includes: The Man Who Came to Dinner, 1941; My Sister Eileen, 1943; The Last of Mrs Cheyney, 1944; Lady Frederick, 1946; Canaries Sometimes Sing, 1947; Jonathan, 1948; Castle in the Air, 1949; Othello, 1951; King Lear, 1952; Affairs of State, 1952; Simon and Laura, 1954; Nina, 1955; Macbeth, 1956; Troilus and Cressida, 1956; (Old Vic Season) Hamlet, A Midsummer Night's Dream and King Lear, 1957-58; The Pleasure of His Company, 1959; Toys in the Attic, 1960; Bonne Soupe, 1961-62; The Rehearsal, 1963; The Right Honourable Gentleman, 1964-66; Lady Windermere's Fan, 1966; What the Butler Saw, 1969; My Darling Daisy, 1970; Mrs Warren's Profession, 1970; The Sea, 1973; The Waltz of the Toreadors, 1974; Ardele, 1975; Charley's Aunt, 1976; The Importance of Being Ernest, 1977; Travesties, 1977. Has also appeared in USA and Moscow. Films: Auntie Mame; The Roman Spring of Mrs Stone; Dr Crippen; The Night of the Generals; The Legend of Lylah Clare; The Killing of Sister George, 1969; The Ruling Class, 1972; Theatre of Blood, 1973; The Drowning Pool, 1975; Dreamchild, 1985. Television series: Time Express, 1979. TV Films: Eleanor, First Lady of the World, 1982; An Englishman Abroad, 1983. *Hobby:* Needlepoint.

BROWNE Kathleen, b. June 1905, Christchurch, New Zealand. Artist; Painter. m. Polish Artist, Marian Kratochwil, Mar. 1961. *Education:* Canterbury School of Art, New Zealand, 1920; Chelsea School of Art, 1932-34. *Appointments:* Taught at Art School, 1925; Art Mistress at Marsden Girls Collegiate and Diorcrsan High School, Auckland New Zealand; Art and History of Art teacher in Schools from 1935-49; Art Advisor to George Rowney, Colour Manufacturer; Started own School, 1949-79. *Creative works:* Numerous Articles in The Artist; Exhibited regularly at Leicester Galleries, London, 1943-62. *Memberships:* Membver of a number of societies including the Senefelder Club, Lithographic Society, all of which now retired from. *Honours:* Bursary, Royal Academy, 1934; Paintings in several private collections in England and abroad; Women of the Year luncheons; Early portrait of Marian Kratochwil in Crocow Museum, Poland; Portrait of Arnold Dolmetsch, Instrument Maker hanging in the National Gallery,London; Three drawings and lithographs in the British Museum, London. *Hobbies:* Writing; Music. *Address:* 56 Compayne Gardens, London NW6 3RY, England.

BROWNE Moyra Blanche Madeleine, b. 2 Mar. 1918, London, England. Honorary National Chairman, Support Groups Research into Ageing. m. Sir Denis John Browne, 10 dec. 1945, died 1967, 1 son, 1 daughter. *Education:* Privately Educated, SEN, 1945. *Appointments:* Research into Ageing; Deputy Superintendent in Chief, 1964-70, Superintendent in Chief, 1970-83, St John Ambulance Brigade; Vice President, Royal College of Nursing, 1970-85; Honorary National Chairman, Support Groups, 1987-, Governor, 1988-. *Honours:* OBE, 1962; DStJ, 1970; DBE, 1977; DGC St J, 1984. *Hobbies:* Travel; Music; Fishing. *Address:* 16 Wilton Street, London SW1X 7AX, England.

BROWNE Sally Elizabeth, b. 24 May 1947,

Melbourne, Victoria, Australia. Company Director; Fashion Designer. m. (2) Graeme Williams, 27 May 1983. 3 sons, 1 daughter. *Education:* Matriculation, St Leonards PGC, Victoria. *Appointments:* Trainee, Lucas, 1964-65; Buyer, Controller, Sportsgirl, 1965-69; Founded Sally Browne pty Limited, 1970-. *Memberships:* Fashion Industries Association of Australia; Australia Council, Member of Design Forum Committee; Fellow, Institute of Directors; Regional Director, Fashion Group Inc; Les Femmes Chef D'Enterprises; Society of Senior Executives. *Honours:* Fashion Industry Awards: Lifestyle Fashion, 1979; Fantasy Fashion, 1982; Daywear Fashion, 1984 and 1985; Casual Weekend Wear, 1987; Hall of Fame, 1987. Rotary Club Prahran Employer of the Year, 1985; Concord D'Elegance Award, Grand Prix, 1986. *Hobbies:* Bridge; Community Work; Tennis; Cooking; Reading; Public Speaking. *Address:* Sally Browne Pty Limited, 229 Lennox Street, Richmond, Victoria 3121, Australia.

BROWNELL Kelly D., b. 31 Oct. 1951, Evansville, Indiana, USA. Professor of Psychiatry. m. M. J. Gabriele, 20 Aug. 1977, 2 sons, 1 daughter. *Education:* BS, Psychology, Purdue University, 1973; MS 1975, PhD 1977, Clinical Psychology, Rutgers University. Postgraduate, Brown University School of Medicine, 1975-77. *Appointments include:* Assistant Professor 1977- 82, Associate Professor 1982-87, Professor 1987-, Department of Psychiatry, University of Pennsylvania School of Medicine; Visiting Scientist, National Cancer Institute, 1983-84; Adjunct Professor, Psychology, Temple University, 1984-. *Publications:* Author, co-author, co-editor, 8 books including: Behaviour Therapy for Obesity: Treatment Manual, 1979; Annual Review of Behaviour Therapy, Vols. 8, 9, 10, 1982-85; Handbook of Behavioural Medicine for Women, 1988. Numerous articles, professional journals. *Memberships include:* President, Society of Behavioural Medicine; President elect, Association for Advancement of Behaviour Therapy, & Division of Health Psychology, American Psychological Association; Programme Chair, World Congress on Behaviour Therapy. *Honours:* Numerous Awards, Fellowships, Honour Societies including: Phi Beta Kappa, 1973; James McKeen Award, Psychology Dissertation, New York Academy of Sciences, 1978; Fellow, Society of Behavioural Medicine 1985, American Psychological Association (Division 25) 1986, Academy of Behavioural Medicine Research 1988; Chair, Small grants review committee, National Institute of Mental Health, 1986-87; Consultant, President's Council on Physical Fitness & Sports, 1988-; NCAA Committee, Eating Disorders in Athletes, 1988-. *Address:* Department of Psychiatry, University of Pennsylvania, 133 South 36th Street, Philadelphia, Pennsylvania 19104, USA.

BROWNELL Mary Barbara, b. 6 Jan. 1954, Seattle, Washington, USA. Writer; Editor. *Education:* BS, University of Virginia, 1976; MFA, American University, 1986. *Appointments:* Researcher, writer, Time-Life Books, Alexandria, Virginia, 1976-84; Researcher, writer, Children's Division (books & magazines), Managing Editor, Geo-Whiz! & Amazing Things Animals Do, & Managing Editor, World magazine, National Geographic Society, 1984-; Continuity editor, Faculty, American University, 1985. *Publications include:* Author: Busy Beavers & Amazing Otters; Collette & Nature: Circular Love (microfilm). Contributor: 16 Time-Life Books, various NGS publications. *Memberships:* Volunteer, American Red Cross; Phi Kappa Phi. *Honours:* Lawn Residency, University of Virginia, 1975-76; Graduate scholarships, American University, 1982, 1985; Citations, Editor's letters, Time-Life Books, 1980-82; Breadloaf Writers' Conference, Vermont, 1983; Phi Kappa Phi honour society, 1986. *Hobbies:* Tennis; Golf; Photography; Travel; Poetry. *Address:* 6772 Perry Penney Drive, Annandale, Virginia 22003, USA.

BROWNING Cassandra Nell, b. 4 Aug. 1957, Houston, USA. Technical Information Manager. *Education:* BA, Southwest Texas State University, 1980. *Appointments:* Manager, Technical Information

Systems, Continental Airlines, 1988-. *Publicatirons:* Contributor to Public Broadcasting Service & Veterans of Foreign Wars. *Memberships:* International Alliance; Associatoin of professional & Executive Women; Notary Public; Phi Beta Lambda; Phi Theta Kappa. *Honours Include:* Certificate, National Honour Fraternity, 1977; Nominated for Executive Council, Continental Airlines, 1987-88; etc. *Hobbies:* Piano; Guitar; Ballet; Squash; Golf. *Address:* 15615 Blue Ash Dr. No 3204, Houston, TX 77090, USA.

BROWNING Vivienne (Elaine Baly), b. 1 Dec. 1922, Sydney, New South Wales, Australia. Author; Broadcaster. m. Wilfred Frank Baly. 1 son, 3 daughters. *Education:* Clothworkers Exhibition Tenable at Westfields College, London, 1942. *Appointments:* Intelligence Corps, ATS, repatriation of prisoners of war, 1942-46; CID, Metropolitan Police; Leach Pottery Cornwall; Department of Health and Social Security, London. *Creative Works:* BBC Radio and Television: Living in Addis Ababa; From Stores Detective to Private Eye; Going on Fungus Expedition; My Father was a Medium, etc. Kansas and Texas Articles on Browning Books; My Browning Family Album, 1979; Brownings and Spiritualism; The Uncommon Medium, to be published 1989. *Memberships:* Former President, Chairman, Browning Society; Former President, Honorary Life Vice President, New Barnet Literary & Debating Society; Society of Authors; International PEN; Friend of Royal Academy; Sadlers Wells; Boston Browning Society, Browning Institute, New York, USA; International Browning Society; Armstrong Browning Library, Baylor University Texas. *Hobbies:* Music; Sculpture; Theatre; Ballet; Ballroom Dancing; Debating; Swimming; Opera; Tapestry; Travel; Cooking. *Address:* Oakleigh Park, Hertfordshire, England.

BROWSE Lillian Gertrude, b. London, England. Private archivist. m. (1) Ivan Joseph, 3 Sept. 1934. (2) Sidney Lines, 17 June 1964. *Education:* Johannesburg, South Africa. *Appointments:* Leger Galleries, Old Bond Street, London, England, 1930-39; Founder Director, Roland, Browse & Delbanco Gallery, Cork Street, London, 1940-77; Founder Director, Browse & Darby, London, 1977-81. *Publications:* Augustus John Drawings, 1941; Sickert, 1943; Degas Dancers, 1949; Wm Nicholson, Catalogue Raisonné, 1955; Sickert, 1960; Forain, 1978; numerous articles in magazines. *Membership:* Honorary Fellow, Courtauld Art Institute, University of London. *Hobby:* Gardening. *Address:* Little Wassell, Ebernoe, Nr Petworth, West Sussex, England.

BRUBECK Anne Elizabeth Denton, b. 5 Mar. 1918, USA. Artist. m. William E Brubeck, 14 Dec. 1940, 1 son, 1 daughter. *Education:* B.Des., Newcomb College Tulane University, 1939; AA, Honorary, Wabash Valley College, 1981. *Appointments:* Instructor, Painting, Wabash Valley College, 1962-67; Painter. *Creative Works:* 1 Man Shows include: New York City, 1961, 1963-67; Evansville, Indiana, 1963-69; Juried Exhibitions include: Evansville Museum, 1963, 1964, 1965; Swopes Gallery, Terre Haute, 1964, 1968; Nashville, 1967. *Memberships:* Illinois Library Assocation; National League of American Penwomen. *Honours:* Brubeck Art Center named in her and her husband's honour, 1976; Named to Mt. Carmel High School Centennial Hall of Fame, 1982. *Address:* 729 Cherry St., Mount Carmel, IL 62863, USA.

BRUCE Debra M. b. 4 Apr. 1951, Bristol, Connecticut, USA. Poet; English Professor. m. 21 Aug. 1981. *Education:* BA, English, Univerity of Massachusetts, 1974; MA, English, Brown University, 1976; MFA, University of Iowa Writers Workshop, 1978. *Appointments:* Instructor, English, Old Dominian University, 1978; Assistant Professor English, Northeastern Illinois University, 1984-. *Publications:* Sudden Hunger, 1987; Pure Daughter, 1983; Dissolves, 1977. *Memberships:* Academy of American Poets; Poets and Writers; Poetry Society of America; PEN Midwest; Midland Society of Authors. *Honours:* NEA Writing Grant, 1982; NEH Scriptwriting Grant, 1983; Poetry Prize, Academy of American Poets, 1985; Illinois Arts Council Grant, 1986. *Address:* Dept. of English, Northeastern Illinois University, 5500 North St Louis Avenue, Chicago, IL 60625, USA.

BRUCKNER Christine, b. 10 Dec. 1921, Schmillinghausen, Waldeck, Germany. Author. m. Otto Heinrich Kuhner, 1967. *Education:* Librarian's Diploma, Stuttgart; Assistant, Kunstinstitut, University of Marberg, 1947-51. *Appointments:* Editor, Frauenwelt Nurnberg, 1951-; Freelance Author. *Publications:* Ehe die Spuren verwehen, 1954; Die Zeit danach, 1961; Der Kokon, 1966; Das gluckliche Buch der a.p., 1970; Uberlebensgeschichten, 1971; Jauche und Levkojen, 1975; Nirgendwo ist Poenichen, 1977; Erfahren und erwandert, 1979; Das eine sein, das andere lieben, 1981; Mein schwarzes Sofa, 1981; Wenn du geredet hattest, Desdemona, 1983; Die Quints, 1985; Deine Bilder, meine Worte, 1987; Hat der Mensch Wurseln?, 1988; Die Letzte Strophe, 1989. Novels, short stories, radio plays, dramas. *Memberships:* Vice-President, German PEN, 1980-84. *Honours:* Prize for Novel, Bertelsmann Verlag, 1954; Goetheplakette, State of Hessen, 1982; Honorary Citizen, City of Kassel, 1987. *Hobbies:* Modern art; Travel especially on foot. *Address:* Ullstein Verlag, Lindenstrasse 76, 1000 Berlin 61, Federal Republic of Germany.

BRUENING Deborah S., b. 12 Apr. 1954, Kansas City, Missouri, USA. Health & Welfare Executive. *Education:* Surgical Technician, Davenport Community College, Iowa, 1976; Certified Welder, Welding & Drafting School, 1980. *Appointments:* Assistant to veterinary surgeon, 1973-74; assistant to plastic surgeon, 1978-81; Oil rig welder, Gonzales Inc, Pascagoula, Mississippi, 1981; Quality Control Inspector, Gonzales Marine Enterprises, Waveland, Mississippi, 1981-83; Director of Activities & Administrative Assistant, Immacolata Manor (residential care for developmentally disabled), 1984- . Also: Missionary, Micronesia, 1986-87, 1987- 88. *Memberships:* Association of Licensed Surgical Technicians; Development Board, Our Lady of Mercy Country Home; Immacolata Manor Auxiliary; Internatinal Biographical Association. *Honours:* Awards: Caring for Disabled Persons, 1985; Caring Service to People, 1987. *Hobbies:* Photography; Music; Painting; Reading; Lawn beautification & landscaping; Boating; Foreign cars; Real estate development. *Address:* PO Box 194, Liberty, Missouri 64068, USA.

BRUES Alice Mossie, b. 9 Oct. 1913, Boston, USA. Professor Emerita. *Education:* AB, Bryn Mawr College; PhD, Radcliffe College. *Appointments:* Assistant Professor, 1946-53, Associate Professor, 1953- 60, Professor, 1960-65, Anatomy, Univesity of Oklahoma; Professor, 1965-84, Emerita, 1984-, University of Colorado. *Publications:* People and Races, 1977. *Memberships:* American Association of Physical Anthropologists, President, 1971-73; Human Biology Council; American Society of Naturalists. *Honours:* American Academy of Forensic Sciences, Physical Anthropology Award, 1986. *Address:* 4325 Prado Drive, Boulder, CO 80303, USA.

BRUNDAGE Marjorie Underwood, b. 5 Feb. 1940, Bellefontaine, Ohio, USA. Director of Computing Services. m. Richard Keith Brundage, 20 Dec. 1967. 2 daughters. *Education:* BS, Bowling Green University, 1962; IBM School, 1962; NCR School, 1964; EDP at OSU, 1984. *Appointments:* Systems Trainee, IBM Corp, 1962-63; Systems Analyst, Kaiser, 1963-64; Systems Analyst, Lazarus, 1964-66; Director of Computing Services, Ohio State University College of Business, 1966-. *Publication:* Simulation on Computer Utility, 1969. *Memberships:* Central Ohio Chapter Association of Computer Machinery; Executives Club of Columbus; Columbus Landmarks; National Historic Preservation; National Assoc of Female Executives. *Honour:* Most Valuable Staff, 1986. *Hobbies:* Violinist Metropolitan Chamber Orchestra; Ordained Elder, Presbyterian Church; Swimming; Reading; Boating. *Address:* 328 Glenmont Avenue, Columbus, Ohio 43214, USA.

BRUNSON Dorothy Edwards, b. USA. Broadcasting Executive. 2 sons. *Education:* BS, State University of New York. *Appointments Include:* Assistant General Manager, Radio Station WWRL, 1964-68; Vice President, Marketing & Media Director, Stockholder, Howard Sanders Advertising, 1968-70; Vice President, Marketing/Media Director, Eden Advertising & Communications Inc., 1970; General Manager, Inner City Broadcasting Corporation; Owner, Radio Stations: WLIB/AM, WBLS/FM, 1973-79; President, Brunson Communications Inc, Owner, various Radio Stations, Georgia, North Caorlina, Consultant banks, Radio Station Owners, etc, 1979-. *Publications:* Black Woman's Career Guide, 1983; Outstanding Women, booklet, 1985. *Memberships Include:* Park Heights Advisory Board, Baltimore; Baltimore Economic Development Corporation; United Way, Central Maryland; Harlem Commonwealth Council, New York City; Johns Hopkins Matro Centre; etc. *Honours Include:* Numerous citations & recognitions as 1st Black Woman Radio General Manager, Station Owner, from businesses & civic organisations throughout USA. *Address:* c/o Brunson Communications Inc., Baltimore, MD, USA.

BRUSH Karen Alexandra, b. 5 Oct. 1960, New York City. Author; Student. *Education:* BS, Yale University, 1982; MA, Anthropology, Columbia University, 1986; M.Phil., Archaeology, 1987, PhD Candidate, 1987-, Cambridge University, England. *Publications:* The Pig, The Prince & The Unicorn, 1987; The Demon Pig, in press. *Memberships:* Yale Science & Engineering Association; Society for American Archaeology; Science Fiction Writers of America; New York Junior League. *Honours:* Graduated, Yale University, cum laude, 1982; Honorary Fellowship, Columbia University, 1985- 87; Overseas Research Students Award, Cambridge, 1988-89. *Hobbies:* Scuba; Painting; Drawing; Sailing; Hiking. *Address:* Queens' College, Cambridge, CB3 9ET, England.

BRYAN Dora (Mrs William Lawton), b. 7 Feb. 1924, Southport, Lancashire, England. Actress. m. William Lawton, 1954. 1 son (1 son and 1 daughter adopted). *Education:* Hathershaw Council School, Lancashire. *Creative works:* Pantomimes: London Hippodrome, 1936; Manchester Place, 1937; Alhambra, Glasgow, 1938; Oldham Repertory, 1939-44; Peterborough, Colchester, Westcliff-on-Sea. ENSA, Italy during War of 1939-45; London, 1945 appeared in West End Theatres: Peace in our Time; Travellers' Joy; Accolade; Lyric Revue; Globe Revue; Simon and Laura; The Water Gypsies; Gentlemen Prefer Blondes; Six of One; Too True to be Good; Hello, Dolly!; They Don't Grow on Trees; Rookery Nook, Her Majesty's, 1979; The Merry Wives of Windsor, Regent's Park, 1984; She Stoops to Conquer, National Theatre, 1985; The Apple Cart, Haymarket; Charlie Girl, Victoria Palace, 1986; Pygmalion, Plymouth, New York, 1987; Chichester Festival Seasons, 1971-74; London Palladium season, 1971; London Palladium Pantomime season, 1973-74; Farces televised from Whitehall Theatre. Films include: The Fallen Idol, 1949; A Taste of Honey, 1961; Two a Penny, 1968. Television series: Appearances on A to Z; Sunday Night at the London Palladium; According to Dora, 1968; Both Ends Meet, 1972. Cabaret in Canada, Hong Kong and Britain. Has made recordings. *Honours:* British Academy Award. *Hobbies:* Reading; Patchwork quilts. *Address:* 118 Marine Parade, Brighton, East Sussex, England.

BRYANT Sandra Renee, b. 29 July 1959, Norfolk, Virginia, USA. Assistant City Manager; Municipal Executive. *Education:* BA Political Science, 1981; MA Urban Studies, 1988, Old Dominion University. *Appointments:* Municipal Executive, 1984-; Assistant City Manager, City of Emporia; Senior Analyst, City of Suffolk; Executive experience in administration and management. *Publications:* Master's Thesis: Impact of Real Estate Property Tax Relief on City of Suffolk, Va's Tax Base, 1985. *Memberships:* Delegate, National Parks & Recreation Society; Secretary- Treasurer, Emporia-Greensville Affiliate American Heart Association; Vice-

Chairman Chesterfield Community Diversion Advisory Board. *Honour:* Delegate, Omicron Delta Kappa, 1980. *Hobbies:* Reading, Recreation and leisure services. *Address:* 3845 North Ingleside Drive, Norfolk, VA 23502, USA.

BRYANT-REID Johanne, b. 11 Mar. 1949, Farmington, West Virginia, USA. Vice President, Human Resources Manager. *Education:* BS Psychology, West Virginia University, 1971. *Appointments:* Senior Recruiter; Vice President Employment Manager; Vice President Corporate Human Resources, Merrill Lynch. *Memberships:* Employment Comm Manager, Edges; Council of Concerned Black Executives; ASPA; Employment Managers Association; Executive Board, Women's Center; Advisory Board for BMCC; Black World Championship Rodeo. *Honour:* Black Achiever in Industry, 1981. *Hobbies:* Art collecting; Book reading; Painting. *Address:* Merrill Lynch, WFC South Tower, New York City, NY 10080-6111, USA.

BRYON Dilys Muriel, b. 27 Sept. 1930, Nottingham, England. Artist; Printmaker; Potter. m. D Banham, 31 July 1954. 3 daughters. *Education:* National Diploma in Design, Painting, Wimbledon School of Art, 1951; Art Teacher's Diploma, London University, 1952. *Appointments:* Crohamhurst School, Croydon, 1952-54; Thornhill Senior School, Dewsbury, 1957-59; Stanley Park Institute of Adult Education, Wallington, 1967-70; Supply Teaching in Adult Education, 1970-83; Brooklands College of Further Education, Weybridge, Surrey, 1983-. *Creative works:* Paintings; Drawings; Prints (etchings, mezzotints); Pottery and Ceramic sculpture including terracotta figures, 1967-; Exhibitions: Solo: Connaught Gallery, Surrey, 1973; Gallery 20, Brighton, 1978; Embankment Gallery, London, 1979; Bishop Grosseteste College, Lincoln, 1983; Wandle Gallery, Surrey, 1986; Pots an Prints Gallery, Northants, 1988. 2 persons, 39 Steps Gallery, Whitechapel, London, 1987. Mixed include: National Theatre, London, 1984; Royal Society of Painter-Etchers, London, 1985; Cabo Firio International Print Biennale, Brazil, 1985; US/UK Touring Exhibition PMC, 1987; US/UK Print Connection Touring Exhibition, 1989. *Membership:* Printmakers' Council of Great Britain (Chairperson 1988-89). *Honours:* Collections: Embragel University, Cabo Frio, Brazil. Private Collection: Gilly Fraser; Agent, Anthony Hopkinson, Art for Today Ltd., Melbourn Bury, Herts SG8 6DE. *Hobbies:* Studying French literature; Music listening; Playing tennis; Swimming; Yoga; Visiting places of historic interest; Theatre. *Address:* Monksgreen Farm, Cobham Road, Fetcham, Surrey KT22 9RU, England.

BUCHANAN Enid Jane, b. 20 June 1950, Winnipeg, Canada. Civil Servant. m. 15 Nov. 1986, 1 son. *Education:* BA Honours, Queen's University, 1973; MA, Urban & Regional Planning, University of British Columbia, 1978. *Appointments:* General Manager, Inuit Non-Profit Housing Corporation, 1975-78; Senior Policy Analyst, Housing Department, Government of Alberta, 1978-80; Senior Inter-Government Officer, Alberta, 1980-81; Director of Policy Planning & Research 1981-83, Director of Policy & Programmes 1983-85, Director of Social Housing 1985-, Government of British Columbia. *Memberships:* Member 1984-86, Board 1985-86, Pacific Region Chair 1985-86, Canadian Housing Design Council; Urban Development Institute. *Honours:* Scholarships, British Columbia Telephones 1973-74, Canadian Mortgage & Housing Corporation, 1974-75. *Hobbies:* Skiing; Art; Reading; Playing with children. *Address:* c/o British Columbia Housing Management Commission, Suite 1701, 4330 Kingsway, Burnaby BC, Canada V5H 4G7.

BUCHANAN, Brenda J, b. San Diego, California, USA. Computer Manufacturing Manager. *Education:* BS, Math, Physics & Chemistry, University of Denver; MA, Math, Washington University, 1973; Postgraduate Studies, 1973-75. *Appointments:* Maths Instructor, Washington Univerity, 1969-71; Programmer/Analyst, United Aircraft of Canada, 1971-73; Operations Research Analyst, Consolidated Bathurst Ltd., Montreal,

1973-75; Corp New Products Planning Manager, Digital Equipment Corp., 1976-80, New Products Programme Manager, Digital, Springfield, 1980-84, Tapes Business Manager, Springfield, 1984-86, Corp Purchasing Programme Office Manager, Digital, Northboro, 1986-88, District Manufacturing Manager, 1988-. *Memberships Include:* League of Women Voters, Board of Directors; Strathmore Shire Association, Board of Trustees, 1987-; The Professional Council, Boston Chapter. *Honours:* Fulbright Fellow, Federal Republic of Germany; Experiment in International Living, Germany; Ivy of the Year, Alpha Kappa Alpha, Denver; Centennial Scholar, University of Denver. *Hobbies:* Leader, Canadian Girl Guides; Participant, Core Groups (networking); Cross Country Skiing; Travel. *Address:* 4E Strathmore Shire, PO Box 49, N. Uxbridge, MA 01538, USA.

BUCHEISTER Patricia Louise (Patt), b. 27 Mar. 1942, Waterloo, Iowa, USA. Artist; Author. m. Raymond Cecil Bucheister, 14 Jan. 1961, 2 sons. *Publications:* Novels: Make the Angel Weep, 1979; Summer of Silence, 1980; Feather in the Wind, 1981; The Sheltered Haven, 1981; The Amberley Affair, 1983; Escape the Past, 1985; Lifetime Affair, 1985; Night and Day, 1986; The Dragon Slayer, 1987; Touch the Stars, 1987; Two Roads, 1987; The Luck of The Irish, 1988; Flynn's Fate, 1988; Time Out, 1988; Near the Edge, 1989; Short Stories include: Echo of the Past, 1982, On the Stormy Side, 1982, both in Romance Readers Guide; Articles in numerous journals and magazines. *Memberships:* Romance Writers of America; Virginia Romance Writers; National Society of Tole and Decorative Painter; Tidewater Decorative Painters. *Honours:* Silver Palette Award, 1986. *Address:* 901 Shady Hollow Lane, Virginia Beach, VA 23452, USA.

BUCHWALD Jennifer Sullivan, b. 20 Oct. 1930, Okmulgee, Oklahoma, USA. Professor of Physiology, UCLA School of Medicine; Associate Director, Brain Research Institute. 1 son, 2 daughters. *Education:* AB magna cum laude, Lindenwood College, 1951; PhD, Tulane University, 1959; Honorary LLD, Lindenwood College, St Charles, 1970. *Appointments:* Assistant Professor, Department of Pediatrics 1963-66, Associate Professor, Department of Physiology 1967-73, Professor, Department of Physiology 1973-, UCLA School of Medicine; Member, Mental Retard Res Center, 1972-; Brain Research Institute, 1963-. *Publications:* Author of 200 original research papers, review articles, abstracts on research in human brain function, normal, Alzheimer, autistic groups and in animal functional models. *Memberships:* Neuroscience Society, Treasurer 1975-77; Association of Academic Women, UCLA, President 1982-83; American Physiology Soc; American Assoc of Anatomists; American Women in Science; Intern Brain Res Organization. *Honours:* Senior Fellowship Award, Parkinson Foundation, 1963-66; Career Development Award, USPHS, 1965-69; Woman of Science Award, UCLA, 1969; Merit of Achievement Award and Honorary LLD, Lindenwood College, 1970; USPHS-NIH, Research Grant Awards, 1966-90; Advisory Com to the Director, NIH-NINCDS, 1982-86. *Hobbies:* Reading; Tennis; Skiing; Hiking. *Address:* Dept of Physiology, UCLA School of Medicine, Los Angeles, CA 90024, USA.

BUCK Carolyn Elizabeth Burrell, b. 10 Dec. 1948, Benham, USA. Co-ordinator; Learning Skills Counsellor. 1 son, 1 daughter. *Education:* BA, Psychology, 1971; MSc., 1977. *Appointments:* Co-ordinator, Academic Studies, 1980-83; Co-ordinator, Summer Bridge and Academic Success Programme, 1983-84; Intern Student Financial Services, UCSD, 1986-87; Co-ordinator, Tutorial Programme, University of California, San Diego, 1987-. *Publications:* Articles in journals & magazines. *Memberships:* Association for Study of Higher Education. *Honours:* Fellowship, SOSU Work in Graduate Dean;s Office; Management Skills Assessment Programme, 1987. *Hobbies:* Sewing; Aerobic; Weight Lifting; Poetry. *Address:* 10405 Caminito Mayten, San Diego, CA 92131, USA.

BUCK Joan, b. 1 Oct. 1930, East Orange, New Jersey, USA. Course Coordinator, University of Connecticut. m. Raymond J Buck, Jr, 14 Mar. 1953. 3 daughters. *Education:* BA, Sociology, Wellesley College, 1952; MA, Political Science, University of Connecticut, 1977. *Appointments:* Tutorial Instruction, Remedial Reading, Elementary grades, Town of Stafford, Connecticut, 1970-72; Research Intern, State Department of Banking, Hartford, 1975; Educational Assistant III, Urban management Curriculum Development Project, Institute of Public Service, 1976-77; University Lecturer (now Course Coordinator), Survival of Humanity and Violence in the Global Village, 1986-, University of Connecticut. *Publications:* Long River Region Simulation, 1977; Women and Credit in Connecticut, 1978; Report of the Mansfield Ad Hoc Housing Committee, 1983; Report of the Mansfield Study Committee on Community Sewerage Systems, 1984. *Memberships:* League of Women Voters of Mansfield; Programme Vice President, 1978-80, Chair, Alternative Living Study, 1978-80, Chair, Guidance Services Study, 1978-79, Board Member, League of Women Voters of Connecticut, 1980-82; World Federalists of Mansfield; Vice President, 1980-81, Public Relations Chair, 1980-81; Membership Chair, 1981-83; Nominating Committee, 1982-84; Recording Secretary, 1984-, Mansfield Democratic Town Committee and Executive Committee; Town Council, Town of Mansfield; Housing Study Committee, 1983; Personnel Committee Chair, 1983-85; Chair, Study Committee on Community Sewerage Systems, 1984-85; Chair, Finance Committee, 1985-. *Honours:* Fellow, New England Rural Leadership Program; Recipient of $4,000 in-kind training, 1982-84. *Hobbies:* Public policy-making; Reading; Research; Gardening; Hiking; Swimming; Gourmet cooking; Travel. *Address:* 6 Sumner Drive, Storrs, CT 06268, USA.

BUCKAWAY Catherine Margaret, b. 7 July 1919, North Battleford, Saskatchewan, Canada. Poet. m. Edward James Buckaway, 1 Apr. 1941. 1 daughters. *Education:* Grade Twelve, Dale Carnegie Course. *Appointments:* Lifeguard & Swimming Teacher, 1940-41; Post Office Assistant, 1941-42; Municipal Office, School Unit, Village and set up books for Jansen-Esk Credit Union, 1942-76. *Publications:* Author of 8 books including, Blue Windows, 1988; Stardust Chapbook, 1989; Riding Into Morning, 1989. 2,975 poems published; 7 plays published; 5 plays produced. *Memberships:* League of Canadian Poets; Sask Writer's Guild; CANSCAP; Saskatoon Writers Club. *Honours:* Canada Council Grant, 1971; Carlings Community Arts Foundation Grant, 1972; Saskatchewan Arts Board Grant, 1973 and 1975; First place, Canada, USA & Japan Yukuharu and First California Bank Award; Don MacIntosh Award, 1985; Private Grant, 1087-00, Intermediate Certificate, Bronze Medal and Bar, Silver Medal and Bar, First Class Instructor, Royal Life Saving Society. *Hobbies:* Haiku; Contemporary poetry; Plays; Children's literature. *Address:* Porteous Lodge, 833 Avenue P North, Saskatoon, Saskatchewan, Canada S7L 2W5.

BUCKHAM Jeanette Mary Landell, b. 29 May 1926, Melbourne, Victoria, Australia. Educational Administrator. *Education:* BA, DipEd, University of Melbourne. *Appointments:* Teacher, Geography & Social Studies, Presbyterian Ladies' College, Melbourne, 1948-55; Lecturer, Mercer House Teacher Training Institute, Melbourne, 1953-55; Principal, Presbyterian Ladies' College, Goulburn, New South Wales 1956-67, Pymble Ladies' College (formerly Presbyterian Ladies' College, Pymble), NSW 1968-89. *Memberships:* Fellow, Australian College of Education; Geography Teachers Association, Great Britain & New South Wales; Association for Classical Archaeology; Council for Educational Administration; Past office (NSW), Association of Heads of Independent Schools; NSW State Development Committee for Inservice Education; Past President, Council, NSW Teachers Guild; Vice President, Association of Heads of Independent Girls Schools, NSW; Commission, National Mission of Uniting Church, 1980-85; Royal Life Saving Society, Australia; Justice of the Peace, 1957-. *Honours:* Recognition Badge 1975, Distinguished Service Membership 1982,

Badge 1975, Distinguished Service Membership 1982, Royal Life Saving Society; Citizenship Award, Municipality of Ku-ring-gai, Sydney, 1978. *Hobbies:* Surfing; Music; Collecting antiques, paintings, books; Travel. *Address:* The Lodge, Pymble Ladies' College, Avon Road, Pymble, New South Wales 2073, Australia.

BUCKINGHAM Karen Webster, b. 10 Nov. 1956, Baltimore, Maryland, USA. Financial Planner. m. William A. Buckingham Jr, 26 June 1981. *Education:* Certificate, College for Financial Planning, Denver, Colorado, 1984; BS, Marketing, University of Baltimore, 1985. *Appointments:* Assistant to board chairman, Maryland National Bank, 1979-85; Vice president & sales director, Plan First Company, 1985-88; Director of Financial Planning, PSA Financial Centre, 1988-. *Creative works:* Numerous contributions, professional journals & publications; Speaker to civic groups & professional organisations, personal financial planning & similar topics. *Memberships include:* Board, offices, Baltimore Association for Financial Planning; International Association for Financial Planning; Institute for Certified Financial Planners; Planned Giving Committee, American Heart Association. *Honours:* Biographical listings. *Hobbies:* Reading, Gardening, Tennis. *Address:* 6421 Murray Hill Road, Baltimore, Maryland 21212, USA. 2, 5, 6, 132.

BUCKMAN Maire Tults, b. 25 Sept. 1939, Tartu, Estonia. Medical Educator; Physician; Researcher. m. (1)James F. Buckman, 1 Jan. 1966, divorced 1980, 1 son, 1 daughter, (2)Walter L Brink, 29 Mar. 1987. *Education:* MD, University of Washington, 1966. *Appointments:* Captain, MCUS Army, 1966-68; Instructor, Medicine, University of New Mexico School of Medicine, 1973-74; Assistant Professor, medicine, Chief Endo/Metab and Director IRA Lab, VA Medical Centre, Albuquerque, 1980-86; Associate Professor, Medicine, University of New Mexico School of Medicine, 1980-. *Publications:* Over 100 including 9 book chapters; over 50 presentations at local, regional, national and international scientific meetings. *Memberships:* American College of Physicians; American Federation Clinical Rsearch, Counsellor, 1977-80; Endocrine Society; Western Society Clinical Research; Pacific Coast Fertility Society; West Coast Endocrine Club, Chairman, 1978. *Honours:* Recipient, various honours and awards. *Hobbies Include:* Reading; Hiking; Cross Country Skiing; Art Collecting; Writing Poetry. *Address:* 2900 El Tesoro Escondido NW, Albuquerque, NM 87120, USA.

BUCKNER Rose Laminack, b. 4 Feb. 1945, Dallas, Texas, USA. Missouri Licensed Clinical Psychologist. m. 1 son, 1 daughter. *Education:* BS 1967, MS 1972, North Texas State University; PhD, University of Arkansas, 1985. *Appointments:* Director of Occupational, Recreational and Group Therapy, Ft Worth Neuropsychiatric Hospital, 1968-70; Diagnostic Consultant, New Learning Opportunities Program, Willard Public Schools, 1979-80; Family and individual therapy, Missouri Division of Family Services, Federal Veterans Administration Grant for Veterans of Viet Nam and their families, Green County Juvenile Court for status offenders and their families, 1980-85; Clinical Psychologist, Private Practice, Springfield, Missouri, 1972-; Instructor in Psychology 1970-78, Instructor in Abnormal Psychology 1984, Southwest Missouri State University. *Publications:* The Effects of Hypnosis on the Overhand Vollyball Serve, 1974; Presented papers to conferences; Seminars. *Memberships:* American Association of Counseling & Development; Missouri Psychological Association; Ozark Area Psychological Association; Missour Association of Social Welfare. *Address:* 1111 South Glenstone Suite 2-101, Springfield, Missouri 65804, USA.

BUDD Ruth, b. 20 June 1924, Winnipeg, Manitoba, Canada. Musician. m. Philip, divorced, 1 son, 1 daughter. *Education:* British Columbia School of Pharmacy & Science, University of Toronto, Faculty of Music. *Appointments:* Vancouver Symphony, 1942-45; Toronto Symphony, 1947-51; CBC Stymphony; Stratford Festival

Orchestra; Hart House Orchestra, Boyd Neel; Toronto Symphony, 1964-. *Memberships:* Founding Chairman, organization of Canada Symphony Musicians; Chairman and Secretary, T S Players Committee. *Honour:* Woman of Distinction, 1983. *Hobbies:* Folk Music; Pottery; Music Education for Children; etc. *Address:* Toronto Symphony, c/o Roy Thomson Hall, 60 Simcoe St., Toronto, Ontario M51 2H5, Canada.

BUGBEE Victoria Jean, b. 1 Sept. 1951, Northampton, Pennsylvania, USA. Playwright; Film Director/Producer. m. (1) Santo M. Bruno, 29 Dec. 1973, div. 1982, 1 daughter, (2) George A. Warren III, 27 July 1985, 1 son. *Education:* Universidad Nacional de Argentina, 1970; Kutztown State University, USA, 1970-73; Moravian College, 1971. *Appointments:* Head of Sales, Digital Effects Inc, 1982-84; Executive Producer, George Parker Productions, Doros Animation, 1984-85; President, Director, Writer for Victory Press International, Backstage, American Cinematographer, Computer Pictures, Millimeter, Sequence, 1985-88; Founder, Victory Productions Ltd, New York City, 1987-. *Creative works:* Plays: Life and Death with Business in Between; Boxer Shorts; The Vacation: Worlds of Desperation; Murder (adapted from short story by David Lee; Drawings: Music Series, 1973-77; Le Pavilion Hotel Series, 1977-80; Fireworks Series, 1981-85. *Membership:* Founding Member, Secretary, Atlanta Art Workers Coalition Ltd. *Honours:* Rotary Exchange Student, Argentina, 1969-70; Individual Artist Grants, Bureau of Cultural Affairs, City of Atlanta, 1978, 1979, 1981; Fellowship for Playwriting, New York State Council for the Arts, 1988. *Hobbies:* Gardening; Movies; Swimming. *Address:* Victory Productions Ltd, 308 Mott Street, Suite EE, New York, NY 10012, USA.

BUGBEE-JACKSON Joan, b. 17 Dec. 1941, Oakland, California, USA. Sculptor. m. John Michael Jackson, 21 June 1973, 1 daughter. *Education:* BA Art 1964, MA 1966, San Jose State College; National Academy School of Fine Arts, New York City, 1968-72; Art Students League, NYC, 1968-70; Apprentice, Joseph Kiselewski, 1970-72. *Appointments:* Instructor: Art, Foothill Junior College, California, 1966-67; Design, De Anza Junior College, CA, 1967-68; Pottery, Greenwich House Pottery (NYC) 1969-71, Craft House Institute (NYC) 1970-72, Cordova Extension Centre, University of Alaska 1972- 79, Prince William Sound Community College 1979-. *Creative work:* Solo exhibitions, Maine, NYC, Alaska, California; Group exhibitions including Allied Artists of America 1970-72, National Academy of Design 1971, President, Cordova Arts & Pageants 1975-76. Commissions include: Commemorative plaques, Merlek Smith 1973, Bob Korn Pool 1975; Eyak Native Monument, 1978; Ceramic mural, Anchorage Pioneer's Home, 1979; Bronze Medal, Alaska Wildlife Series, 1980; Sculpture murals & portraits, Alaska State Capitol, 1981; Numerous other portraits, plaques, memorial sculpture. *Honours:* Scholarship, National Academy School of Fine Arts, 1969-72; J. A. Suydam Bronze Medal, 1969; Dr Ralph Weiler Prize, 1971; Helen Foster Barnet Award, 1971; Daniel Chester French Award, 1972; Frishmuth Award, 1971; Allied Artists of America Award, 1972; C. Percival Dietsch Prize, 1973; Citations, Alaska Legislature, 1981, 1982. *Address:* Box 374, Cordova, Alaska 99574, USA.

BULL Angela Mary, b. 28 Sept. 1936, Halifax, Yorkshire, England. Writer. m. Rev. Martin Wells Bull, 15 Sept. 1962, 1 sons, 1 daughter. *Education:* Edinburgh University MA, Honours; and St Hugh's College, Oxford, 1961. *Appointments:* Teacher, English, Casterton School, Cumbria, 1961-62; Assistant, Medieval Mss Dept., Bodleian Library, Oxford, 1962-63. *Publications:* The Friend with a Secret, 1965; Wayland's Keep, 1966; Child of Ebenezer, 1974; Treasure in the Fog, 1976; Griselda, 1977; The Doll in the Wall, 1978; The Bicycle Parcel, 1980; The Machine Breakers, 1980; The Accidental Twins, 1982; Noel Streatfield, 1984; Anne Frank, 1984; Florence Nightingale, 1985; A Hat for Emily, 1986; Marie Curie, 1986; The Visitors, 1986; Green Gloves, 1987; Elizabeth Fry, 1987; A Wish at the Baby's Grave, 1988. *Honours:* Runner Up, Guardian Award for Children's Books, 1974; Children's Rights Workshop Other Award, 1980. *Hobbies:* Reading; Church Activities; Contemplative Prayer & Meditation; Historical Research; Theatre; Country Walking. *Address:* The Vicarage, Hall Bank Drive, Bingley, W. Yorkshire BD16 4B2, England.

BULLARD Judith E, b. 10 May, 1945, Oneonta, New York, USA. Human Factors Engineer; Systems Engineer. divorced. 1 son, 1 daughter. *Education:* BA, Political Sci/ SP 1964, MA, Political Science 1969, MA, Experimental Psychology 1973, University of Oregon. *Appointments:* Manager, Lane Co Mental Health Prog for Criminal Offenders, 1977-80; Small Business Consultant, System Develop, 1980-83; Social Psychology Research, Oregon Research Institute, 1983-85; Researcher, Product design and test, Bell Laboratories, 1985-. *Publications:* Affirmative action newsletter articles; Contributor AT&T Technical Journal; Technical Memoranda; Human Factors Eval of Key Systems; Comparative Analysis of Two Sys 75 Switch releases. *Memberships:* Bell Laboratory Women's Network, Program Coordinator; Board of Directors, Women's Resource and Survival Center; Secretary, Short Athletic Club; Human Factors Society. *Honours:* New Jersey Division, Bell Laboratories Affirmative Action Recognition Award, 1988; Shore Athletic Club President's Award, most improved Athlete, 1987; 1st place age award, E Murray Todd half Marathon, 1985, 1986, 1987, 1988. *Hobbies:* Running, marathons; Biking; Swimming; Reading; Cooking. *Address:* Bell Laboratories, 1E521 Crawfords Corner Road, Holmdel, NJ 07733, USA.

BULLOWA Catherine E., b. 21 July 1919, Larchmont, New York, USA. Professional Numismatist. m. (1)David M. Bullowa (dec. 1953), (2)Earl E. Moore, 27 June 1959, 2 stepsons. *Education:* BA, Connecticut College for Women, 1941; Pre-medical studies, New York University, Columbia School of Pharmacy. *Appointments:* Assistant, Physiology Department, Long Island College of Medicine, 1943-46; Research Assistant, Physics Department, Cornell Medical School, 1946-49; Research Assistant, Sloan/Kettering Institute, 1949- 52; Owner, Coinhunter (business specialising in rare coins), 1953-. *Publications:* Numismatic articles for trade publications. *Memberships:* Board of Directors, Professional Numismatists Guild; Board of Directors, Vice-President, International Association of Professional Numismatists; Fellow, American Numismatic Society (Benefactor 1957); Life Member, American Numismatic Association; Senior Member, American Society of Appraisers; Several other related organisations and associations. *Honours:* Leonard Forer Bronze Medal, International Association of Professional Numismatists. *Hobbies:* Horses; Art; Early European and American Antiques. *Address:* 1616 Walnut Street, Suite 2112, Philadelphia, Pennsylvania, USA.

BULMAN Susan Lesley, b. 31 Dec. 1948, Glasgow, Scotland. Head of Education, The Industrial Society. divorced. *Education:* BSc Biochemistry Hons, London Hospital Medical College, 1967-71; PGCE, London Institute of Education, 1971-72. *Appointments:* Head of Chemistry, Archbishop Michael Ramsey, 1972-76; Head of Science, Hydeburn, 1976-80; Head of Science, N Westminster Community, 1980-82; Deputy Head, Abbey Wood, 1982-85; Head, Kingsdale, 1985-89. *Publications:* Teaching Language & Study Skills in Secondary Science, 1985; The Pastoral Curriculum, 1988; Many articles in professional journals and magaziners; Television and radio appearances. *Memberships:* Secondary Heads Association; Conference of Comprehensive Heads (London) Chair, 1988-89. *Honour:* Judge on Times Educational Supplement Senior Information Book Award, 1986-88. *Hobbies:* Japanese and French novels; Classical music especially opera; Watercolours. *Address:* 19 Walcot Sq, London SE11 4UB, England.

BUMAGIN Victoria Edith, b. 20 June 1923, Free City of Danzig. Director. m. Victor I Bumagin, 16 Mar. 1946. 5 daughters. *Education:* BA, 1945; MSSW 1969; Doctoral Study, 1973-74. *Appointments:* Caseworker, Supervisor, New Jersey, 1946-48 and 1968-69; Senior Social Worker, Dept Social Services, Berkshire County Council, England, 1970-73; Director, Social Services, Council for Jewish Elderly, Chicago, USA, 1974-84; Director, Center for Applied Gerontology, 1984-; Associate Professor, Layola University School of Social Work. *Publications:* The Appliance Cookbook, 1971; Aging Is a Family Affair, 1979; Helping the Aging Family, 1989; Challenge of Working With Old People, 1972; Growing Old Female, 1982; Observations on Changing Relationships for Older Women, 1982; Book reviews and monographs. *Memberships:* American Society on Aging; National Council on the Aging; Gerontological Society of America; National Association of Social Workers; Academy of Certified Social Workers; Editorial Board, Gerontological Society of America; Commission, Senior Resources Commission, Wilmette, 1988-91. *Honours:* Distinguished Chicago Gerontologist, Association of Gerontology in Higher Education, 1988; Chicago Senior Citizens Hall of Fame, 1986; Fellow, Gerontological Society of America, 1984. *Hobbies:* Miniaturist; Needlework; Gardening. *Address:* 1224 North Branch, Wilmette, Illinois 60091, USA.

BUNKER Mary Louise Condie, b. 11 Aug. 1923, Utah, USA. Chairman, Redevelopment Agency; Mayor; Councilwoman, City of Alhambra. m. Earle Robert Bunker, Jr, 22 May 1944. 2 sons, 1 daughter. *Education:* BA, Magna cum laude, 1971, MA 1977, California State University; Registered Dietitian. *Appointments:* Director, Progressive Savings Bank, 1977-87; Controller, 1955-65; President, 1965-68, James I Condie & Associates Inc; President, ELF Investments, 1969-; Councilwoman, Alhambra, 1982-. *Publications:* Federation Proceedings, 1972, 1973, 1974; American Journal of Clinical Nutrition, 1975; Journal of American Dietetic Association, 1979. *Memberships:* American Dietetics Association; Soroptomist, International; Director, LA Co, Sanitation Distr. *Honours:* Phi kappa Phi; Pi Lambda theta; Alumni Honor Award, 1973; Graduate Award, 1975. *Hobbies:* Nutritionist, Instructor at Community College & University. *Address:* 132 So El Molino, Alhambra, California 91801, USA.

BUNKER-FULLER Paula Barie, b. 27 May 1949, Cincinnati, Ohio, USA. Nurse Anaesthetist. m. Bryant Fuller, 30 May 1987, 1 son. *Education:* BS, Nursing, Florida State University, 1971; BA, Zoology, University of South Florida, 1977; Certificate, Nurse Anaesthesia, North Carolina Baptist Hospital & Bowman Gray School of Medicine, 1979; MS, Nursing Administration, University of Florida, in process. *Appointments:* Nurse Anaesthetist: North Trident Regional Hospital, Charleston, South Carolina, 1979-80; Humana Hospital, Greensboro, North Carolina, 1980-82; Moses Cone Memorial Hospital, Greensboro, 1982-83; University Hospital, Jacksonville, Florida, 1983-. *Publications:* Articles, professional journals: Critical Care for the Newborn, 1976; Multiple Trauma: Problematic Issues for the Anesthetist, 1980. *Memberships:* American, & Florida Associations of Nurse Anaesthetists; Sigma Theta Tau; Northeast Florida Marlin Association; Ancient City Gamefish Association. *Honours:* Scholarships, Florida State Department of Education 1967, North Carolina Baptist Hospital & Bowman Gray School of Medicine, 1977-79. *Hobbies:* Fishing; Golf; Skiing; Scuba Diving. *Address:* 620 20th Street, North Beach, St Augustine, Florida 32084, USA.

BURA Corina, b. 15 Feb. 1948, Cluj, Rumania. Violinist; Professor. *Education:* Bachelorship, Emil Racovitza Lyceum, Cluj, 1967; Bachelorship, Lyceum of Music Profile, Cluj, 1967; Diploma, Conservatoire of Music, Bucharest, 1972. *Career:* Debut as Soloist with Philharmony of Cluj, 1967; Recitals, radio and TV appearances, recordings; Professor, Conservatoire of Music, Bucharest, 1972-. *Publications:* Studies concerning modern music and aesthetics in Conservatory publications. *Membership:* Professional Association of the Conservatory. *Honours:* Diplomas of chief promotion: Lyceum, 1965, 1966, 1967;

Conservatoire of Bucharest, 1972. *Hobbies:* Literature; Theatre; Plastic arts; Dogs; Cats. *Address:* Str Ecaterina Teodoroiu No 17, 78108 Bucharest I, Rumania.

BURACK Sylvia E Kamerman, b. 16 Dec. 1916, Hartford, USA. Editor; Publisher. m. Abraham S. Burack, 28 Nov. 1948, 3 daughters. *Education:* BA, Smith College, 1938; Honorary Degree, Doctor of Letters, Boston University, 1985. *Appointments:* Editor, Publisher, The Writer Magazine, and The Writer Inc., 1978-. *Publications:* Editor, numerous collections of plays for Young People: Little Plays for Little Players, 1952; Blue Ribbon Plays for Girls, 1955; Blue Ribbon Plays for Graduation, 1957; A Treasury of Christmas Plays, 1958; Children's Plays from Favorite Stories, 1957; 50 Plays for Junior Actors, 1966; 50 Plays for Holidays, 1969; Dramatized Folk Tales of the World, 1971; On Stage for Christmas, 1978; Christmas Play Favorites for Young People, 1982; Holiday Plays Round the Year, 1983; Plays of Black Americans, 1987; Patriotic and Historical Plays for Young People, 1987; Plays from Favorite Folk Tales 1987; The Big Book of Christmas Plays, 1988; The Big Book of Comedies, 1989. Editor: Writing the Short Story, 1942; Book Reviewing, 1978; Writing and Selling Fillers, Light Verse and Short Humor, 1982; Writing & Selling the Romance Novel, 1983; Writing Mystery and Crime Fiction, 1985; The Writer's Handbook, 1989. *Memberships:* Numerous professional organisation. *Address:* 72 Penniman Rd, Brookline, MA 02146, USA.

BURCH Linda Jane Cash, b. 17 Feb. 1950, Portsmouth, Ohio, USA. Transportation Company Executive. m. (1)George M. Crickard, divorced 1976, 1 daughter, (2)Nick Burch, 12 Oct. 1989. *Appointments:* Import Specialist, Rogers & Brown, 1976-77; Import Specialist, John S. James, 1977- 78; Sales Coordinator, Transworld Shipping, Toledo, 1982; Associate Executive, Pilot Air F, 1985; McClean Trucking, Dayton, 1985-86; Duff Truck Lines, 1986; Emery Air Frt., 1986-87; Air Express International, 1987-89; Air Express International, 1989-. *Memberships:* Miami Valley International Trade Association; National Association Female Executives. *Honours:* Recipient, various honours and awards. *Hobbies:* Ceramics; Sewing; Reading; Gardening; Photography. *Address:* 116 SW 144th Street, Oklahoma City, OK 73170, USA.

BURCH Margaret Smith, b.19 Juy 1935, Waco, USA. Teacher. m. Jack Charles Burch, 28 Dec. 1962. *Education:* BA, Baylor University, 1957. *Appointments:* Teacher, Sonora, 1958-61, 1968-present. *Memberships:* TSTA; Delta Kappa Gamma; Tau Beta Sigma. *Hobbies:* Stamp Collecting; Travel; Genealogy. *Address:* 612 Allen Dr., Sonora, TX 76950, USA.

BURFORD Anne McGill, b. 21 Apr. 1942, Casper, Wyoming, USA. Attorney. m. Robert Fitzpatrick Burford, 20 Feb. 1983. 2 sons, 1 daughter. *Education:* BA 1961, LLB 1964, University of Colorado. *Appointments:* Assistant Trust Adm, 1st National Bank Denver, 1966-67; Assistant District Attorney, Denver, 1968-71; Deputy District Attorney, Denver, 1971-73; Hearing Officer, Adm Law Judge, Colorado State, 1971-74; Corp Counsel, Mtn Bell Tel, Denver, 1975-81; Administrator, EPA, Washington DC, 1981-85. *Publication:* Are You Tough Enough?, 1985. *Memberships:* Colorado House of Representatives, 1976-78, 1978-80; American, Colorado and Denver Bar Associations; Mortar Board; Phi Alpha Delta; Board Member, YMCA, Denver; Board of Advisors, Mercy Hospital, Denver; National Conference on Uniform St Law, 1979. *Honours:* Fulbright Scholarship to Jaipur, India, 1964-65; Outstanding Freshman Legislator, Colorado, 1976. *Hobbies:* Reading; Swimming; Travel. *Address:* 5505 Seminary Road No 105N, Falls Church, VA 22041, USA.

BURGANGER Judith, b. Buffalo, New York, USA. Concert Pianist; Professor of Music. m. Leonid Treer, 3 July 1985. 3 daughters. *Education:* Studies with Laura Kelsey, Rudolf Serkin; Hubert Giesen and Wladimir Horbowski; Matriculated, State Conservatory of Music,

Stuttgart, 1961; Graduate work, Stuttgart Conservatory. *Appointments:* Orchestral engagements throughout Europe, North America and Japan including: The Chicago Symphony; The Cleveland Orchestra; The Pittsburgh Symphony; The Baltimore Symphony; The American Symphony in Carnegie Hall; The Minnesota Orchestra; The Vancouver Symphony; The National Symphony; Buffalo Philharmonic; Syracuse Symphony; New Orleans Philharmonic Symphony Orchestra; Rochester Philharmonic; Winnpeg Symphony; The Bayerischer Rundfunk orchestra, Munich, Germany; The Hessischer Rundfunk Orchester, Frankfurt; The Symphony Orchestra of Berlin; The Zurich Radio Orchestra; Innsbruck Symphony orchestra; Hetgelders Orchestra; The Philharmonica Hungarica; Tokyo Symphony; Philharmonic Orchestra of Florida. Teacher at Cleveland Institute of Music, Artist in residence at Texas Tech and Carnegie-Mellon University; Full professor/Artist-in-resident, Florida Atlantic University. *Creative works:* Chamber music performances included: Cleveland Quartet; Emerson Quartet; Dorian Wind Quintet and Ridge Quintet. Created the Brahms Festival at Florida Atlantic University and founded Fall Chamber Soloists. *Memberships:* Florida State Music Teachers Association; National Music Teachers Association; Broward County Music Teachers Association; National Federation of Musicians; Boca Raton Music Guild, Adviser; National Society of Arts and Letters, Hibel Museum, Palm Beach & Florida Singing Sons. *Honours:* 1st Prize, Merriweather Post Competition; Principals' Medals for excellence in languages and music; Special Diploma for high Scholastic Achievement, Cleveland Hill High School; 1st Prize, International Piano Competition, Munich becoming first American to obtain this honour; Laureate in International Piano Competition, Geneva, Switzerland; grant from Kulturkreis der Deutsche Industrie, Köln, (Cologne) Germany. *Hobbies:* Chamber music; Gardening; Interior Decorating; Pottery; Bicycling; Hiking. *Address:* Music Department, Florida Atlantic University, 500 NW 20th Street, Boca Raton, FL 33431, USA.

BURGE Harriet A., b. 19 June 1938. Associate Research Scientist. m. Walter G. Burge, 15 June 1963, 1 son, 2 daughters. *Education:* BA, MA, San Francisco State University, 1956-62; PhD, University of Michigan, 1966. *Appointments:* Assistant Research Scientist, 1977-88, Associate Research Scientist, Department of Internal Medicine, 1988-, University of Michigan, Ann Arbor. *Memberships:* Chair, Committee on Bioaerosols, American Conference of Governmental Industrial Hygienists; Fellow, American Academy of Allergy and Immunology; Chair, Pollen and Mold Committee. *Honours:* Horace H.Rackham Predoctoral Fellowship, 1965-66; NSF Summer Fellowship, 1965; Sigma Xi, 1966; Phi Beta Kappa, 1966; Distinguished Service Award, American Academy of Allergy and Immunology, 1988. *Hobbies:* Piano; Birdwatching; Spinning. *Address:* Allergy Research Laboratory, University of Michigan Medical Center, R6621 Kresge I, Box 0529, Ann Arbor, MI 48109, USA.

BURGER Mary Jane, b. 2 July 1920, Chicago, Illinois, USA. Homemaker; Artist; Wife of State Legislator. m. John Burger, 17 Aug. 1940, 2 sons, 2 daughters. *Education:* Certificate, National College of Education, Evanston, Illinois, 1940; Courses, Art Center of Minnesota, 30 years; Certificates: American Floral Art School, Chicago; Dale Carnegie courses; Many watercolour workshops. *Career:* Nursery School Teacher, Wayzata Community Church, 2 years, 50s; Bachmans Floral Department, Daytons, 60s; Many art shows and sales, Crosscreek Gallery, Art Center of Minnesota, Participant, flower shows, Ikebana International; Leader, Painting and Ikebana workshops; Assistant to State Legislator husband; Responsible for 11-acre estate, Lake Minnetonka; Entertaining groups. *Creative works include:* Floral arrangements for Ikebana shows, University of Minnesota Landscape Arboretum and church; Many watercolours including: Sea Gull River, First Snow in the North Woods, Arboretum Dancing Nymphs, Superior Seascape, Cascade River, The Wine Table, On the Scene at the Metrodome, Blue Abstracts 1, 2, Color Shimmers. *Memberships:*

Legislative and Life Member, Dome Club of Minnesota; Volunteer, University of Minnesota Landscape Arboretum; Artist Volunteer, Art Center of Minnesota; Wayzata Community Church; Twin City Watercolor Society; Midwest Watercolor Society; Ikebana International; Republican Women's Association; Minneapolis Institute of Arts; Charter Member, National Museum of Women in the Arts. *Honours:* 1st Premium, flower show, Wayzata Bay Shopping Center, 1975; Best of Show, 1976, Honourable Mention, 1979, 2nd Prize, Watercolour, 1988, Art Center of Minnesota; Life story included in Dale Carnegie's book How to Win Friends, How to Stop Worrying and Start Living. *Hobbies:* Art work of all kinds; Sewing; Flower arranging; Home and family. *Address:* 3750 Bayside Road, Long Lake, MN 55356, USA.

BURGER Ronna, b. 5 Dec. 1947, Cleveland, Ohio, USA. Professor. m. Robert Berman, 16 Mar. 1979, 1 son. *Education:* BA, Philosophy, University of Rochester; MA, 1972, PhD, 1975, New School for Social Research, New York. *Appointments:* Professor, Philosophy, Tulane University, 1980-. *Publications:* Plato's Phaedrus: A Defense of a Philosophic Art of Writing, 1980; The Phaedo: A Platonic Labyrinth, 1985. *Memberships:* American Philosophical Association; Society for Ancient Greek Philosophy. *Address:* Dept. of Philosophy, Tulane University, New Orleans, LA 70118, USA.

BURGESS Rachel L, b. 9 Nov. 1935, Grand Falls, Canada. Counsellor; Consultant. m. Lee Burgess, 4 Sept. 1956, 2 sons, 3 daughters. *Education:* Nursing School, Montreal, 1951-52; BPsy, 1975; Teachers Licence, 1976; MA, Counselling, 1979; Honorary PhD, University of St Thomas, 1980; CAS, University of Maine, 1986. *Appointments:* Past Principal and Director, Burgess Centre for Handicapped; Founder, School & Sheltered Workshop, Teacher; Counsellor; Private Practice, 1987-; Hypnotist. *Memberships:* Literacy Association; Mental Association; Psychological Associaiton; Mentally Retarded Association; Teachers' Association, Director; Counsellors Association. *Hobbies:* Guitar; Skiing; Reading; Thinking; Meditation; Philosophy. *Address:* SS No 1, Site No 306, Box 40, Grand Falls, NB, Canada, EOJ 1MD.

BURK Jennie Marie, b. 14 Aug. 932, Peoria, USA. Teacher; Librarian; Literary Coach. m. Clarence M. Burk, 1 Nov. 1963, 1 son, 1 daughter. *Education:* BS, Business Administration, 1954; BA, Elementary Education, 1956; MA, School Administration, 1960; Reading Specialist Certification, 1983. *Appointments:* Teacher, 1952-53; Teaching Principal, 1953-55; Teacher, 1955-58; Superintendent, 1958-60; Teacher, 1960- 03; Superintendent 1963-64; Chapter I Teacher, 1967-89. *Memberships Include:* Illinois Valley Reading Council, Treasurer; Illinois Reading Council; International Reading Council; American Legion Auxilary. *Honours Include:* Presidential Citation, US Civil Defense, 1976; Distinguished Service Award, Illinois Civil Defense, 1976. *Hobbies:* Sewing; Cooking; Working with Youth. *Address:* 106 South Pine Street, Tremont, IL 61568, USA.

BURKE Earla Blanche, b. 12 Aug. 1935, Kirkland Lake, Canada. Company President. m. (1)Charles Robb, 23 June 1951, divorced, 2 sons, 2 daughters, (2)Harold Taylor, 3 Apr. 1965, divorced 1970, 1 son. *Education:* BA, Psychology, York University, 1975; BJ, Carleton University, 1978; CFP, College for Financial Planning, 1988. *Appointments:* Personnel Manager, 1963-67; Owner, Association Management Firm, 1967-70; College Teacher, 1969-81; Financial Planner, 1981-Present; Owner, Financial Planning Firm, 1983-. *Publications:* Freelance Writer. *Memberships:* Investment Funds Institute of Canada, Governor, 1986-; Canadian Institute of Management, Director, Education 1984-86; Seneca College, Advisory Committee, 1987-. *Hobbies:* Private Pilot; Skiing; Diving; Tennis. *Address:* Suite 214, 1177 Yonge St., Toronto, Ontario, Canada.

BURKE Elizabeth H. Ferguson, b. 19 Mar. 1950,

Denver, Colorado, USA. Speech/Language Pathologist. m. James D. Burke, 20 Oct. 1973, 2 sons. *Education:* BS, 1972, MS, 1973, University of Wisconsin. *Appointments:* Speech/Language Pathologist, Easter Seal Society of Metro Chicago, 1973-77; Speech Language Pathologist, East Dubuque Public Schools, 1979-86; Speech Language Pathologist, Mercy Hospital, 1986-; Speech Pathologist, Medical Associate Clinic, 1988. *Memberships:* Neurodevelopmental Treatment Association; Iowa Speech Hearing Association; American Speech Language Hearing Association. *Hobbies:* Needlepoint; Drawing; Wood Carving; Books; Children. *Address:* 410 N. Booth St., Dubuque, IA 52001, USA.

BURKE Jacqueline Yvonne, b. 10 Apr. 1949, Newark, New Jersey, USA. Telecommunications Executive. m. Harry C. Burke, 20 Aug. 1967 div. 1977, 1 son. *Education:* Howard University, Washington DC. *Appointments:* Self-employed, developed & conducted management workshops, 1974-77; Manager, developed training courses, AT&T, 1977-83; Rating & routing data, supporting telephone industry, Bell Communications Research, 1984-. *Publications:* Author, book, Career Assessment, Development & Planning; Co-author, article, One Stop for Routing & Rating Information. *Memberships:* Career Option Committee, Tribute to Women in Industry; American Society for Training & Development; Union County President, Board Chair, National Association of Negro Business & Professional Women; Adviser, Archway Pregnancy Centre; Brothers & Sisters Inc. *Honours:* Awards & Rcognitions from: Tribute to Women in Industry; YMCA; Outstanding Young Women of America; Bellcore; International Roll of Honour; NANB & PWC. *Hobbies:* Reading; Voluntary Youth Work; Rug Latching; Needlepoint. *Address:* 229 West Avenue, South Plainfield, New Jersey 07080, USA.

BURKE Janet Chorkey, b. 2 Mar. 1950, Detroit, Michigan, USA. Publications Editor, Design & Production; Advertising. *Education:* BA, Honours, Wayne State University. *Appointments:* Director, Public Relations, Cranbrook Bloomfield Hills, 1976-84; President, Chief Executive Officer, JB Communications Inc., 1984-. *Publications:* Editor, Publisher, The Cranbrook Quarterly, 1978-84; Editor, Publisher, Cranbrook Journal, 1984-87. *Memberships:* Women in Communications Inc, Chairman 1983-84; Michigan Advertising Agency Council; International Association of Business Communicators; Council for Advancement & Support of Education; etc. *Honours Include:* Best Magazine, IABC, 1983, 1984; Award of Excellence, NSPRA, 1983, 1984, 1086; Gold Medal, CASE, 1986; Grand Gold Medal, CASE, 1984, 1985. *Address:* JB Communications Inc., 30800 Telegraph Road, Suite 2820, Birmingham, MI 48010, USA.

BURKE Mary Thomas, b. West Port, Ireland. Professor; Chairperson. *Education:* BA, Social Science & Mathematics, 1958; MA, Modern European & Renaissance History, 1965; PhD, Counselling, 1968. *Appointments:* (USA) Academic Dean 1967-69, Chair, Education Department 1969-70, Sacred Heart College; Associate Professor of HDL 1970-76, Professor & Chair, Department of Human Services 1976-, University of North Carolina, Charlotte. *Publications:* Professional papers: Religious & Spiritual Dimensions of Counselling; Being & Becoming a Woman of Integrity; Becoming a Woman of Excellence: An Ethical Challenge for Today's Woman. *Memberships:* American Association for Counselling & Development; Association for Counsellor Educators & Supervisors; Board, Association for Religious Values in Counselling; Honour societies. *Honours:* Awards: B'nai B'rith Anti- Defamation, Ray Thompson Human Relations, 1978; WBT Woman of Year, 1979; Delta Kappa Gamma honour society, 1981; Ellen Stephens Barratt Leadership Award, 1983; Crusade, American Cencer Society, 1986. *Hobbies:* Classical Music; Golf; Reading; Travel. Ministering to depressed, deprived & marginal peoples; American Cancer Society; Needs of women & elderly. *Address:* College of Education & Allied Professions, Department of Human Services, University of North Carolina, Charlotte, NC 28223, USA.

BURKE Sheila Mary, b. 26 May 1956, London, England. Company Director. *Appointments:* Director of Studies, KMG Thomson McLintock, 1980-86; Graduate Recruitment Manager, Binder Hamlyn, 1987-88; Managing Director, SB Business Support, 1989-. *Memberships:* Country Gentlemans Association; International Teddy Bear Club; Club Cognac. *Hobbies:* Art; Music; Antiques; Photography; Theatre; Tennis; Badminton. *Address:* Ridley Hall, Honington, Suffolk, England.

BURKHART Deborah A., b. 9 Dec. 1956, San Diego, California, USA. Architect. *Education:* BS, Environmental Design, BArch, Ball State University, 1980; MBA, MArch, University of Illinois, 1987. *Appointments:* Architect, Woollen Molzean and Partners, Indianapolis, Indiana, 1980-85; Teacher, University of Illinois School of Architecture, Champaign, Illinois, 1985-87; Management Consultant, Shepley Bulfinch Richardson and Abbott, Boston, Massachusetts, 1986; Architect, Decker and Kemp Architecture and Urban Design, Chicago, Illinois, 1987-. *Memberships:* National Women's Task Force Regional Director, Indiana Society of Architects Board of Directors, Indianapolis Chapter Board of Directors, Chicago Chapter Professional Practice Committee, American Institute of Architects; Alpha Omicron Pi; Gargoyle Society; Mortar Board. *Honours:* Indiana Concrete and Masonry Design Award, 1977; Most Valuable Player Award, Indianapolis Chapter, American Institute of Architects, 1984; Creative and Performing Arts Fellowship, University of Illinois, 1986-87. *Hobbies:* Travel; Theatre; Softball; Quilting. *Address:* 930 West Dakin, Chicago, IL 60613, USA.

BURLESON Helen Louise, b. 8 Dec. 1929, Chicago, Illinois, USA. Realtor; Writer; Lecturer; Consultant. m. 24 June 1956, divorced, 1987. 1 son, 1 daughter. *Education:* BS, Central State University, Wilberforce, 1950; MA, Northwestern University, Evanston, 1954; DPA, Nova University, Ft Lauderdale, 1983. *Appointments:* Coowner, Operator Sweet Shop, 1947-56; Teacher, High School English, 1951-61; Radio Commentator, WBBM (CBS); Writer, Poetry Reader, Lecturer and Consultant, 1974-; Real Estate Multi-million Sales, 1988-. *Publications:* No Place Is Big Enough To House My Soul (Poetry), 1974; Where Did You Last Find Me?, Anthology, Prose, Poetry and Songs, 1975. *Memberships:* Illinois Humanities Council, 1971-76; Elected 3 terms Flossmoor Board of Ed, Vice President Flossmoor Board of Education, 1972-81; Appointed Illinois State Board of Education, 1981-83; 1958-87, President 1960-62, Auxiliary Cook County Physicians' Association; Alpa Kappa Alpha Sorority, 1950; Appointed: Governor's Task Force for Medical Malpractice, 1985. *Honours:* 1 of 100 Women Worldwide Honored for Freedom of the Arts, 1975; Humanitarian Award, St Matthews AME Church, 1974; Humanitarian Award, Gavin Foundation, 1977; Humanitarian Award, Links, Inc, 1978; Outstanding Contribution Award, United Negro College Fund, 1980; Literary Award, Central State University, 1981; Plaque (recognition service) Illinois State Board of Education, 1983. *Hobbies:* Study of World culture with emphasis on African and African American; History and culture; Writing poetry; Reading; Gourmet cooking; Motivating youth. *Address:* 56 Graymoor Lane, Olympia Fields, IL 60461, USA.

BURMAN Marsha, b. 9 Jan. 1949, Baltimore, Maryland, USA. Director, Marketing Training & Development. m. John R Burman, 6 June 1986. 2 sons, 2 daughters. *Education:* BS, cum laude, 1970, MA, magna cum laude, 1971, Kent State University, Kent, Ohio. *Appointments:* Teacher, Garfield Heights, OH, 1972-73; Education Director, Atlanta Humane Society, 1976-78; Director, Special Projects, Planned Parenthood Chicago, IL, 1978; Program, Admin, Gould Mgmt Education Ctr, Chicago, 1979-80; Manager, Training & Education, 1981-85, Director, Marketing

Training & Development, 1986-present, Lithonia Lighting, Atlanta, GA. *Publications:* Putting Your Best Foot Forward, Booklet, 1982; Editor, Dictionary of Lighting Industry Terminology & Jargon, 1988, second edition 1989. *Memberships:* Board of Directors 1983, American Society of Training & Development; Toastmasters International. *Honours:* Georgia Athlete of Year, 1967; National History Honorary 1969-70, National Education Honorary 1969-70, Honors College Member 1967-70, Kent State University; ASTD Volunteer of Year, 1982; Vice President, Lithonia Lighting Management Club, 1982-83. *Address:* Lithonia Lighting, P O Box A-1400 Lester Road, Conyers, GA 30207, USA.

BURMEISTER Kristen Schnelle, b. 25 Aug 1960, USA. Trade Association Executive. m. David J. Burmeister, 30 June 1984. *Education:* BS, Southwest Missori State University, 1981; MA, Webster University, 1986. *Appointments:* Managing Editor, Southwest Standard; Facility Management Internship, Hammons Student Centre; Sales Manager, Tulsa Excelsior Hotel; Assistant Vice President, Farm Equipment Manufacturers Association. *Memberships:* Phi Kappa Phi; American Society of Association Executives; St Louis Society of Association Executives, Programme Committee; Naitonal Agri-Marketing Association Program Committee. *Honours:* Missouri 4-H Key award, 1977; 4-H I Dare You Award, 1978; Class Citizenship Award, 1978; Miss Missouri candidate, 1980. *Hobbies:* Volunteer Work; Running; Sailing; Tennis. *Address:* 12551 Round Robin Ct., Creve Coeur, MO 63146, USA.

BURN Mary Wynn, b. 2 July 1910, London, England. Retired Archaeologist; Lecturer in Art History. m. Andrew Robert Burn, 31 Dec. 1938. *Education:* BA, 1932; MA, Oxon, 1936. *Appointments:* Assistant Keeper, Victoria & Albert Museum, 1935-38; Signals & Intelligence, RAF, Navy, Army, Athens, Crete, 1940-41, Cairo GHQ Middle East, 1941-43; British Embassy to Gk Govt. in Exile, 1943-44, Third Secretary British Embassy, Athens, 1944-46; Excavations at Old Paphos, Cyprus, 1950-53; Lecturer, Greek Art, Extra Mural Dept, Glasgow University, 1956-66; Lecturer, Greek & Byzantine Art, Athens, 1969-72. *Publications:* Guide to the Byzantine Monastery of Daphni; Guide to the Byzantine Monastery of Holy Luke of Stiris; The Living Past of Greece, with A. R. Burn, 1980; Contributor to: The Glory that is Greece, H. Hughes, 1944. *Memberships:* British School of Archaeology at Athens; Friends of the Ashmolean Museum; Friends of Christ Church Cathedral, Oxford. *Hobby:* Photography. *Address:* Flat 23, 380 Banbury Road, Oxford OX2 7PW, England.

BURNET Jean Robertson, b. 10 June 1920, Toronto, Canada. Sociologist. *Education:* BA, 1942, MA, 1943, University of Toronto; PhD, University of Chicago. *Appointments:* Instructor to Associate Professor, University of Toronto, 1945-67; Visiting Lecturer, University of New Brunswick, 1948-49; Professor, York University, 1967-85. *Publications:* Next Year Country, 1951; Ethnic Groups in Upper Canada, 1972; Editor, Looking into My Sister's Eyes, 1986; Coming Canadians, 1988. *Memberships:* American Sociological Association; Canadian Sociology and Anthropology Association; Canadian Ethnic Studies Association; Multicultural History Society of Ontario, Board Chairman. *Honours:* Guggenheim Fellowship, 1955-56; Life Membership, Canadian Sociology and Anthropology Association, 1969; D.Litt, hc, York University, 1985. *Hobbies:* Reading; Canoeing; Bird Watching. *Address:* 494 St Clements Avenue, Toronto, Ontario, Canada M5N 1M4.

BURNETT Carol, b. 26 Apr. 1936, San Antonio, Texas, USA. Actress; Comedienne; Singer. m. Joseph Hamilton, 1963. 3 daughters. *Education:* Hollywood High School; University of California at Los Angeles. *Creative works:* Introduced comedy song: I Made a Fool of Myself Over John Foster Dulles, 1957; Broadway debut in Once Upon a Mattress, 1959; regular performer Garry Moore TV show, 1959-62; appeared several CBS-

TV specials, 1962-63. Broadway play Fade Out-Fade In, 1964; Plaza Suite, 1970. Musical play: I Do, I Do, 1973; Same Time Next Year, 1977. Club engagements: Harrah's Club; The Sands; Caesar's Palace. Star, Carol Burnett Show, CBS-TV, CBS-TV Spec. 6 Rooms Riv Vu, 1974; Twigs, The Grass Is Always Greener; Friendly Fire; The Tenth Month; Fresno; Plaza Suite. Films: Pete 'n Tillie, 1972; Front Page; A Wedding; Health; The Four Seasons; Chu Chu and the Philly Flash; Annie; Between Friends. *Honours:* Outstanding commedienne award, American Guild Variety Artists, 5 times; 5 Emmy Awards for Outstanding Variety Performance, Academy of TV Arts and Sciences; TV Guide Award for Outstanding Female Performer, 1962, 1962, 1963; Peabody Award, 1963; Golden Globe Award for Outstanding Comedienne of Year, Foreign Press Association; Woman of Year Award, Academy of TV Arts and Sciences; One of the World's 20 most admired women, voted in poll conducted by George Gallup, 1977; First Annual National Television Critics Award for Outstanding Performance, 1977; Best Actress, San Sebastian Film Festival.

BURNETT Janet Flora Wiedenbein, b. 26 Mar. 1936, Cincinnati, Ohio, USA. Educator; Writer. m. Lonnie Avril Burnett, 15 June 1957, 1 son, 1 daughter. *Education:* BSc., 1957, MA, Special Education, 1975, University of Cincinnati; PhD, Miami University, 1987. *Appointments:* Teacher, various schools, 1957-74; Special Education Consultant, Supervisor, Teen Challenge, 1975-76; Graduate Assistant, Special Education Consultant, Cincinnati Centre for Developmental Disorders, 1977-78; Education Consultant, 1979; Assistant to Director, Miami University, 1980-82, 1982-83; Educational Co-ordinator, Care Unit Hospital, Cincinnati, 1985-. *Publications:* Articles in journals & magazines. *Memberships:* Council for Exceptional Children; National Middle School Association; Ohio Middle School Association, Board, Editor, Newsletter. *Honours:* Outstanding Student Teacher, 1957. *Hobbies:* Gardening; Needlepoint. *Address:*7216 Quail Hollow, Cincinnati, OH 45243, USA.

BURNETTE Ada Puryear, b. Darlington, South Carolina, USA. College Professor; Programme Director. m. (2) Thomas C. Burnette, 25 Aug. 1984. 2 sons, 3 daughters. *Education:* BA, Talladega College, 1953; MA, University of Chicago, 1958; Early childhood certificate, Texas Southern University, 1980; PhD, Florida State University, 1986; Certified Public Supervisor, 1987. *Appointments:* High school teacher, mathematics, North Carolina, 1953; Elementary teacher, Chicago Public Schools, 1954; Reading clinic director, Norfolk State College 1958, Tuskegee University 1961; Mathematics Professor, director freshman mathematics, Fisk University, 1966; Administrator, Florida Department of Education, 1973; Professor & programme Director, Bethune-Cookman College, Florida, 1988-. *Publications include:* Various reports, book chapters, reading & phonetics; Regular columns, Children Our Concern, Florida Journal. Also: Radio talk show hostess. *Memberships include:* Offices, Florida Elementary School Principals Association; Florida Council on Elementary Education; Florida Reading Association; Secretary, Societas Docta Inc; Numerous other professional bodies. *Honours:* Numerous plaques, certificates, awards including: Head Start Awards, 1985, 1987; Phi Kappa Phi, Phi Delta Kappa, Pi Lambda Theta Honour Societies. *Hobbies:* Reading; Helping others; Speaking; Cooking; Bridge. *Address:* PO Box 15154, Daytona Beach, Florida 32015, USA.

BURNHAM Sophy, b. 12 Dec. 1936, Baltimore, USA. Writer. m. 12 Mar. 1960, 2 daughters. *Education:* BA, Smith College. *Appointments:* Contributing Editor, Town & Country, 1975-80; Staff Writer, New Woman, 1984-; Staff Writer, Columnist, Museum & Arts/Washington, 1987-. *Publications:* The Art Crowd, 1973; The Landed Gentry, 1978; The Threat to Licensed Nuclear Facilities, 1975; Buccaneer, 1977; The Dogwalker, 1979; A Book of Angels, 1990; numerous essays & magazine articles; Plays: Penelope, 1976; The Study, 1979; The Witch's Tale, 1979; The Nightingale, 1980. *Honours:* Recipient, many honours & awards. *Hobbies and interests:* Pottery; Beekeeping; Arts; Travel; Metaphysics; The Spiritual. *Address:* 1405 31st St. NW, Washington, DC 20007, USA.

BURNISTON Karen Sue, b. 20 May 1939, Hammond, Indiana. Vice President Nursing. *Education:* Diploma, Parkview Methodist School of Nursing, 1961; BS in Nursing, Purdue University, 1974; MS in Nursing, Northern Illinois University, 1976. *Appointments:* Staff Nurse, Parkview Memorial Hospital, Ft Wayne, 1961-63 and 1971-73; Physician Off Nurse & Operating Rm Nurse, 1963-67; Served, US Air Force Nurse Corps, 1967-71; NW Ind. VNA 1974; Faculty Michael Reese School of Nursing, Chicago, 1977-79; Asst Director of Nursing, mt Sinai Hospital & Medical Center, Chicago, 1977-79; Asst Adm PT Care Services, St Margaret Hospital, Hammond, Indiana, 1980-85; Asst Adm PT Care Services, 1985-86; Chief Operating Officer, 1986-1988, St Catherine Hospital; Regional Director Patient Care Services, Lake Shore Health System, 1986-1988. *Memberships:* Board of Directors, South Lake Center Mental Health; Board of Directors, Hospice of NW Indiana; Board of Directors, E Chicago Chamber of Commerce; ANA; Indiana State Nurses' Association; Indiana Organization Nurse Executives, Board Member 1981- 85, President 1984; American Organization Nurse Exec.; Visiting Associate Professor, Purdue University, Department of Nursing; Adjunct Faculty Indiana University School of Nursing; Sigma Theta Tau; Christian Church (Disciples of Christ). *Hobbies:* Reading; Fishing; Travel. *Address:* St Joseph Hospital and Health Center, 1907 W. Sycamore St., Kokomo, Indiana 46904, USA.

BURNS Carol, b. 27 Oct. 1934, London, England. Writer; Painter; Lecturer in Creative Writing. m. 5 Jan. 1954, dov., 1 son, 1 daughter. *Education:* Courtauld Institute, 1953; Chelsea School of Art, 1954-55; Diploma in Fine Art, Slade School of Fine Art, London University, 1959. *Career:* Lecturer in Creative Writing, City Lit, London, 1973-88; Lecturer in Creative Writing, Morley College, London, 1974-86; Lay-out Designer, Christian Action Journal, 1979-88; Editor, Matrix and More magazines; Held 1-woman show of paintings and drawings, New Art Centre, 1961; Exhibited with Young Contemporaries and London Group. *Publications:* Novels: Infatuation, 1967; The Narcissist, 1967; Articles and reviews in Books and Bookman, Times Higher Literary Supplement. *Memberships:* City Literary Association. *Honours:* Slade Postgraduate Scholarship, 1958; French Government Travelling Scholarship, 1959; Arts Council Award, 1959; C.D.Lewis Fellowship 1075, Boise Scholarship in Stage Design, 1978; Winner, Sunday Telegraph Mini-Saga Competition, 1982. *Hobbies & Interests:* Art; Literature; Music; Psychology; Politics. *Address:* 26a Ladbroke Gardens, London W11 2PY, England.

BURNS Maretta Jo, b. 7 Nov. 1941, San Antonio, Texas, USA. Accountant. *Education:* BBA, Accounting. *Appointments:* Supervisory Accountant Assistant, Pueblo Army Depot, US Federal Government, 1962; Assistant to Administrative Officer, Labour, Denver, 1965, Budget Analyst, Budget Accounting Officer, 1976. *Memberships:* Beta Alpha Psi; Phi Gamma Nu; Beta Gamma Sigma; National Association Female Executives; American Management Associatirn; Digital Equipment Company Users Association. *Honours:* Cash awards, 1978, 1986; Letters of Commendation, 1978-80. *Hobbies:* Swimming; Crochet; Knitting; Sewing; Piano; Youth Work. *Address:* 3784 South Quince Street, Denver, CO 80237, USA.

BURNS Mary Elizabeth Crew, b. 30 July 1946, Vermillion, South Dakota, USA. Lawyer; Real Property Manager. m. (1) Damon Russell Jorgenson, 21 Sept. 1968, divorced 30 Jan. 1976, 1 daughter. (2) William Mason Burns, 12 May 1978, divorced 8 Nov. 1986. *Education:* BA English, Mills College, Oakland, 1968; MA History 1977, JD (Law) 1980, University of South Dakota, Vermillion. *Appointments:* Law Clerk, South

Dakota Supreme Court Justice Jon Fosheim, 1980; Associate Attorney, Dial, Looze & May, Pocatello, 1981-83; Law Clerk, Niels Pearson, PC, Las Vegas, 1984-85; Partner, Crew Law Offices, Vermillion, 1985-. *Memberships:* American Bar Association; Phi Delta Kappa; State Bar of South Dakota; Council Board of Directors, Silver Sage Council, ID, 1983, Girl Scouts of America; Personnel Committee Chair, Frontier Council, NV, 1984-85. *Honour:* Sterling Honor Graduate, University of South Dakota, School of Law, 1980. *Hobbies:* Writing, fiction; Weaving; Needlework; Travel; Reading. *Address:* 508 Poplar Street, Vermillion, South Dakota 57069, USA.

BURNS Norma DeCamp, b. 14 Dec. 1940, Flushing, Long Island, New York, USA. Architect. m. Robert Paschal Burns, 4 Dec. 1973. 1 daughter. *Education:* BS, Florida State University, 1962; University of Florida, 1967-68; University of Maryland, 1972; MArch, North Carolina State University, 1976; Department of Cultural Resources Historic Preservation Workshop, North Carolina State University, 1977; Loeb Fellowship, Harvard University, 1986-87. *Appointments:* High School Teacher, FL and MD, 1962-73; Graduate Teaching Assistantship, North Carolina State University, 1973-75; Principal, Burnstudio Architects, PA, 1977-; Visiting Lecturer 1978, Visiting Assistant Professor 1979, North Carolina State University; Research Consultant, NC Courthouse Study, 1976-79; Graphic and Editorial Consultant, 1978; President and Director of Design, Workspace Inc, 1981-. *Publications:* Numerous articles in professional journals and magazines. *Memberships:* American Institute of Architects; AIA National Interiors Design Committee, Appointed Member 1985-87; NC AIA Historic Resources Committee, Current Member, Past Chairman; NC AIA Awards Committee, 1981-84; The National Trust for Historic Preservation; The Preservation Foundation of NC Board of Advisors, 1985-; Business Advisory Committee, Peace College, 1983-; Councillor at Large, Raleigh City Council, 1985-. *Honours:* Graduate Fellowship, NC State University, 1973; Loeb Fellowship, 1986-87; AIA School Medal, NC State University School of Design, 1977; Owens-Corning Energy Conservation Award, 1984; Triangle J Development Award, 1984; Spectator Architecture Award, 1984, 1985; NC AIA Award for Excellence in Architecture, 1984; Sir Walter Raleigh Appearance Award, 1985; Ten Best Designs of 1984, TIME Magazine, 1985; American Planning Association of NC, Outstanding Appointed Official, 1984; Top 50 Triangle Leaders, National Business Yearly Mag, 1988; Invited Lecturer, Linc School of Business, 1988. *Address:* Burnstudio Architects PA, PO Box 25688, Raleigh, NC 27611, USA.

BURNS KIBENS Betty X., b.16 Sept. 1926, St Louis, Missouri, USA. Director of Music Academy. m. (1) Douglas Corzine Burns, 8 Sept. 1945, 3 sons, 1 daughter, (2) Valdis Kibens, 27 Nov. 1988, 1 stepson, 1 stepdaughter. *Education:* High School Diploma; College, 2 years. *Appointments:* Selp-employed Piano Teacher; Clinician, National Piano Foundation, 1961-73; Faculty Member, Webster College, 1962-73; Jazz Singer, 1968-74; Director, New Music Academy, 1968-. *Publications:* You Do It books (7 books on jazz and blues improvisation), 1973-75. *Memberships:* National Music Teachers Association; Past President, Piano Teachers Forum; Former Guild Chairman. *Hobbies:* Psychic healing; Stock market. *Address:* St Louis, Missouri, USA.

BURNSTEIN Frances, b. 18 Oct. 1935, New York City, USA. President, Greater Cherry Hill Chamber of Commerce. m. 16 Oct. 1955. 1 son, 2 daughters. *Education:* City College, City of New York, 1953-55; Institute for Organizational Management, University of Delaware, 1983. *Appointments:* Elected Deputy Mayor, Cherry Hill Township, 1975-77; Executive Director 1977-88 title changed to President 1988-, Greater Cherry Hill Chamber of Commerce; Commissioner, Camden Co Parks, 1986-88. *Memberships:* Board of Trustees, Cooper Foundation, Cooper Hospital/University Medical Center, 1982-; Marketing Committee, Cooper Hospital/University Medical Center, 1983-; Vice President, New Jersey Association of Chamber Executives, 1987-; Board of Trustees, United Way, Camden County, 1982-, Vice President, Communications, 1986; Executive Advisory Council, Rutgers University School of Business, 1985-; Board of Directors, American Red Cross, Camden County Champter, Disaster Appeal Committee, 1981-; Board of Trustees, Police Athletic League, 1976-; Member, World Affairs Council. *Honours:* Humanitarian Award, National Conference of Christians and Jews, South Jersey Chapter, 1987 and 1988; Featured on the cover of New Jersey Woman Magazine, Feb 1986; Newsmaker of the Year, Cherry Hill Chamber of Commerce, 1984; Person of the Year Award, Garden State Rotary, 1980; Recognized by Joint Republican Leadership of the US Congress, 1980. *Address:* 1060 Kings Highway North, Cherry Hill, New Jersey 08034, USA.

BURRILL Melinda Jane, b. 31 Mar. 1947, Washington, District of Columbia, USA. Professor; Geneticist. *Education:* BS, University of Arizona, 1969; PhD, Oregon State University, 1979. *Appointments:* Research Fellow, University of Minnesota, 1975-76; Professor Animal Science, California State Polytechnic University, 1976-. *Publications:* Numerous articles in professional journals and magazines. *Memberships:* Am Soc Anim Sci; Can Soc Anim Sci; Brit Soc Anim Prod; Am Genetics Assn; Sigma Xi, the Scientific Research Soc. *Honours:* Phi Beta Kappa 1969; Phi Kappa Phi 1969; Sigma Xi, the Scientific Research Society, 1974; Women in Development Fellow, 1984; Faculty Exchange Fellow to France, CIES, 1980; NDEA Fellow, 1970-71; Beta Beta Beta; Gamma Sigma Delta; Sigma Delta Epsilon; Phi Beta Delta. *Hobbies:* Medieval architecture, especially British; Medieval British History; Science fiction. *Address:* Department of Animal Science, California State Polytechnic University, Pomona, CA 91768, USA.

BURROWS Elizabeth MacDonald Lafeyette, b. 30 Jan. 1930, Portland, Oregon, USA. International Lecturer; Author; Emissary for World Peace. *Education:* Research, Ancient Christian Manuscripts; Studies of Comparative Religions; self-educated. *Appointments:* President, Founder, Christian Church of Universal Philosophy; President, Archives International; Vice President, James Tyler Kent Institute of Homeopathy. *Publications:* Pathway of the Immortal; Jesus - the True Story; Odyssey of the Apocalpse; Maya Sangh; Chrystal Planet; Commentary for Gospel of Peace of Jesus the Christ according to John; Moses of Sinai (in preparation). *Memberships:* Board of Directors, International Institute of Complimentary Psychology, International Speakers Platform, Assn., International New Thought Alliance, The Cousteau Society, Inc. *Honours:* Recipient, numerous honours and awards. *Address:* 10529 Ashworth Ave. N, Seattle, WA 98133, USA.

BURROWS Eva Evelyn, (General), b. 15 Sept. 1929, Newcastle, Australia. General of the Salvation Army. *Education:* BA, Queensland University, 1950; Postgraduate Certificate of Education, London University, England, 1952; M.Ed., Sydney University, 1959. *Appointments:* Various Teaching Positions in Zimbabwe, 1952-67; Principal, Usher Institute, Zimbabwe, 1967-69; Vice Principal, 1970-73, Principal, 1974-75, International College for Officers, London, England; Leader, Women's Social Services in Great Britain and Ireland, 1975-77; National Leader, (Territorial Commander): Salvation Army: Sri Lanka 1977-79, Scotland 1979-82, Australia, 1982-86; General, World Leader of the Salvation Army, 1986-. *Honours:* Officer, Order of Australia, 1986; Honorary DLA, EWHA Womans University, Seoul, Korea, 1988; Honorary Doctor of Laws, Ashbury College, USA, 1988. *Hobbies:* Classical Music; Reading; Travel. *Address:* The Salvation Army, 101 Queen Victoria Street, PO Box 249, London EC4P 4EP, England.

BURSON Lorraine E., b. 20 Dec. 1925, Omaha, Nebraska, USA. Librarian. m. Francis Mark Burson, 25

Apr. 1948 (dec. 1986), 2 sons, 1 daughter. *Education:* BA, Portland State University, 1975. *Appointments:* Congregational Librarian, 1961-88; Congregational Library Consultant, 1975-; Executive Director, Church & Synagogue Library Association (CSLA), 1987-. *Publications:* Book, Recruiting & Training Volunteers for Church-Synagogue Libraries, 1986; Over 50 articles, numerous religious periodicals, 1983-; Editor, CSLA bi-monthly, Church & Synagogue Libraries, 1988-. *Memberships include:* Church & Synagogue Library Association; Pacific Northwest Association of Church Libraries; Association of Christian Librarians; Evangelical Church Library Association; Lutheran Church Library Association. *Honours:* Outstanding Scholar 1974, Baccalaureate candidate with honours 1975, Portland State University. *Hobbies:* Writing; Editing; Vocal & instrumental music; Organist; Reading. *Address:* 1312 SW Texas Street, Portland, Oregon 97219, USA.

BURSON Michele Aleta, b. 28 Mar. 1947, Los Angeles, USA. Airline Coupon Broker. 2 sons, 1 daughter. *Education:* AA, Delta College, 1979. *Appointments:* Caddilac Sales, 1984-85; BMW Sales Executive, 1985-87; F & I Manager Sales, 1987-88; Discount Travel Network Supervisor, 1988-. *Publications:* Poetry to American Journals; Editor, Writer, Middle Eastern World. *Memberships:* SPCA; Archaeological Institute of America; Greenpeace; World Wildlife; National Association of Female Executives. *Hobbies:* Egyptology; Photography; Middle Eastern Studies; Travel. *Address:* 4201 Spring St., No. 17, La Mesa, CA 92041, USA.

BURTON June Rosalie Kehr, b. 19 June 1941, New Jersey, USA. Professor. *Education:* AB, 1965, MA, 1967, Stetson University; PhD, University of Georgia, 1971. *Appointments:* new Smyra Beach Senior High School, Florida, 1966-67; University of Georgia, 1968-71; University of Akron, 1971-. *Publications:* Napoleon and Clid, 1979; Historical Dictionary of Napoleonic France, 1985, co-editor; Human Rights: A Historical Bibliography, 1987; Essays in European History, 1989, Editor. *Memberships:* Southern Historical Association; European History Section, editor; American Historical Association; CCWWP; SAWH; American Association of University Professors, Chapter President 1979-80, 1987-88. *Honours:* Ford M-A 3 Fellowship, 1966-67; Phi Alpha Theta, 1965; Rockefeller Foundation, 1976-78; Dorothy Danforth Compton Fellowship, 1977-78. *Hobbies:* Painting. *Address:* 64 Waldorf Drive, Akron, OH 44313, USA.

BURTON Karen Poliner, b. 18 Feb. 1952, Albuquerque, New Mexico, USA. Assistant Professor. m. 30 June 1974, 1 son. *Education:* BS, Southern Methodist University, Dallas, 1974; PhD, University of Texas, Health and Science Center, Dallas, 1978. *Appointments:* Graduate Assistant, 1975-78, Postdoctoral Fellow, 1978- 79, Faculty Associate, Dept. Pathology, 1979, Instructor 1979-81, Assistant Professor, 1983-, Physiology, University of Texas, Southwestern Medical Center; Assistant Professor, Pharmacology & Physiology, University of South Alabama, 1981-82. *Publications:* Contributor of numerous articles in professional journals. *Memberships:* American Physiological Society; American Heart Association; American Heart Association Basic Science Council; American Association for Advancement of Science; American Section, International Society for Heart Research; Electron Microscopy Society of America; The Oxygen Society; Sigma Xi. *Honours:* NIH New Investigator Research Award, 1982-85; NIH Research Grant, 1985-88; NIH Research Career Development Award, 1986-. *Hobbies:* Skiing; Heart Research. *Address:* Dept. of Physiology (9040), University of Texas Southwestern Medical Centre, 5323 Harry Hines Boulevard, Dallas, TX 75235, USA.

BURTON Lynn Elen, b. 6 Oct. 1946, Nova Scotia, Canada. Educator; Senior Policy Advisor. m. Mario Piamonte, 1 Oct. 1988, 2 daughters. *Education:*

Teaching Certificates, Ottawa University; BA, Towson State University, 1976, USA; MSc, Johns Hopkins University, 1978; MA, 1986, DEd pending, Columbia University. *Appointments:* Senior Programme Officer, Canadian Labour Market and Productivity Centre, 1985-87; Senior Advisor, Prime Minister's National Advisory Board on Science and Technology, 1987-; Director, National Skill Development Leave Task Force. *Publications:* Learning a Living in Canada; Adult Learning and Human Resource Development in a Knowledge-Based Economy; The People Prescription - Adult Learning in a Knowledge-Based Economy. *Memberships:* Director, Canadian Association for Adult Education; Director, Canadian Association for the Study of Adult Education; Education Sub-committee, Canadian Commission for UNESCO; Advisory Board, Countdown 2001; Advisory Board, Human Resource Development and Assessment Centre, Shanghai, China; TV Ontario, Distance Education Advisory Committee; Interdepartmental Committee on Futures Forecasting; World Future Society; Canadian Association for the Club of Rome. *Honours:* Head, Canadian Delegation on Adult Education to UK, 1984; Canadian Voting Delegation to World Congress on Adult Education, Buenos Aires, 1986; UN Senior Advisor to 1st International Human Resource and Assessment Centre Conference, Shanghai, 1988; Phi Delta Kappa. *Hobbies:* Skiing; Gardening; Futures studies; Writing for discussions and publications. *Address:* 364 Thomas Dolan Parkway, Dunrobin, Ontario, Canada K0A 1T0.

BURTON Truly (Aka Demetra), b. 5 Mar. 1951, Miami, Florida, USA. Associate Director for Government Affairs. m. Richard Jay Burton, 10 June 1972. 1 son. *Education:* BA cum laude, University of Miami, 1973; Coursework toward MBA, 1978 did not complete degree. *Appointments:* Legislative Assistant, House Com. on Pub. Works and Transport, US Congress, Washington, 1976-78; Lobbyist, Fed. Nat. Mortgage Assiciation, Washington, 1978-80; Creative Services Manager, Prose Management Co, Miami, 1980; Public Relations Coordinator, Arvida So, Miami, 1980-81; Associate Director for Government Affairs, Builders Association of South Florida, 1981-. *Publications:* Contributed to professional journals, 1978-80. *bb3Memberships:* League of Women Voters, 1981-; Chairman, Construction Industry Advisory Council, 1986; Treasurer, Taxpayers for Fire Board Repeal, 1988; Events Chair, Greater Miami Jewish Federation, 1984-85. *Honours:* President's Award for Outstanding Service given by the Builders Association of South Florida, 1986; Recipient, Women In Business & Industry Award, YWCA, 1986. *Hobbies:* Snow skiing; Art collecting; Watersports; Reading. *Address:* 15225 NW 77th Avenue, Miami Lakes, FL 33014, USA.

BURTON Verona Devine, b. 23 Nov. 1922, Reading, Pennsylvania, USA. Professor of Biology (retired). m. Daniel F. Burton, 22 July 1950, 1 son. *Education:* AB, Hunter College, City of New York, 1944; MA, 1946, PhD, 1948, State University of Iowa. *Appointments:* Instructor, 1948, Assistant Professor, 1948-67, Associate Professor, 1967-70, Professor of Biology, 1970-86, Compliance Officer, 1973-75, Mankato State University, Minnesota. *Publications:* Floral abscission of Lychnis alba, 1946; Note on the culture of Lychni embryos, 1948; Embryogeny of Lychnis alba, 1950. *Memberships:* American Assocaition of University Women (President Mankato branch, 1970-72, 1988-90, Education Representative, Minnesota Division, 1980-82); Fellow, Iowa Academy of Science; Charter Member, International Society of Plant Morphologists; Business and Professional Women (President Mankato Club, 1972-73); Chairperson, Minnesota Legislative Task Force. *Honours:* Sigma Xi (member, 1946-, President Mankato State University Chapter 1985-86); Sigma Zeta, 1948; Sigma Delta Epsilon; Delta Kappa Gamma (President Mankato Chapter, 1988-90); Hubert H. Humphrey Award, Minnesota Democratic-Farmer-Labor Party, 1986. *Hobbies:* Gardening; Canning; Politics; Travel. *Address:* 512 Hickory Street, Mankato, MN 56001, USA.

BURY Mairi Elizabeth, Lady, b. 25 Mar. 1921, Mount Stewart, New Townards, Co. Down, N. Ireland. Estate Owner; Farmer. m. 10 Dec. 1940, 2 daughters. *Appointments:* JP, Co. Down; Past President and Chairman, Ards Womens Unionist Association, 1945-72; Liveryman, Guild of Air Pilots & Air Navigators; Fellow, Royal Philatelic Society, London; President, County Down Branch, British Red Cross Society. *Honours:* Twice Winner, Royal Ascot Gold Cup; 5 Philatelic Medals; 6 Photographic Awards. *Hobbies:* Philately; Ornithology; Reading; Politics. *Address:* Mount Stewart, Newtownards, Co. Down, Northern Ireland, BT22 2AD.

BUSBY Shannon G Nixon, b. 30 Nov. 1955, Gainesville, Texas, USA. Educational Diagnostician. m. Larry W Busby, 3 Apr. 1982. 1 son. *Education:* BS, Home Economics Education, Texas Technical University, Lubbock, 1977; MEd, Sul Ross State University, Alpine, 1982; Texas Teaching Certificate; Professional Educational Diagnostician, teacher of language and/or learning disabilities; teacher of vocational homemaking. *Appointments:* Home Economics Teacher, Pecos, Barstow, Toyah, ISD, 1978-82; Educational Diagnostician, Special Education Department, Pecos, Barstow, Toyah ISD, 1985-. *Memberships:* Board of Directors, Department of Mental Health and Mental Retardation, 1980-85; Chairperson, Texas War on Drugs, 1980-83; American Association of University Women (Local president 1982-86, local vice president 1978-81); Texas State Board of Directors, 1982- 83; Texas Educational Diagnosticians' Association; Texas Society for Autistic Citizens; International Platform Association. *Address:* 1519 Mary Street, Pecos, TX 79772, USA.

BUSCH Marianna Anderson, b. 28 Oct. 1943, Pittsburgh, Pennsylvania, USA. University Professor; Educator. m. Kenneth Walter Busch, 15 Dec. 1968. *Education:* BA, Randolph Macon Woman's College, 1965; Certificate, University of Heidelberg, Germany, 1965; PhD, Florida State University, 1972. *Appointments:* Postdoctoral Assoc, Cornell University, Ithaca, New York, 1972-74; Robert A Welch Fellow 1974-75, NSF Fellow 1976, Assistant Professor 1977-84, Associate Professor Chemistry 1984-, Baylor University, Waco, Texas; Visiting Scientist, Caltech, Pasadena, 1983 and E I Dupont & Nemours, Wilmington, 1986. *Publications:* Contributor of numerous articles to scientific journals. *Memberships:* Fellow Amer Inst Chemists; AAUW; Am Chem Soc; Amer Water Works Assoc; Sigma Xi; Phi Lambda Upsilon; Consultant, National Bureau of Standards, 1984-; American Association of University Professors, 1986-; Water & Waste Water Analysts Association. *Honours:* AAUW Woman of the Year, Waco Branch, 1986; Waco-McLennan County Pathfinder Award (Science), 1987; Recipient of numerous grants and awards. *Hobbies:* Early American antiques; Art. *Address:* Department of Chemistry, Baylor University, Waco, TX 76798, USA.

BUSCH Nancy Elizabeth, b. 7 Sept. 1944, Manitowac, Wisconsin, USA. Marketing Communications Consultant. m. Charles Nels, 21 Aug. 1965, 1 son. *Education:* BA, Journalism, 1966, Postgraduate study, Center for Creative Studies, 1984-, University of Michigan. *Appointments:* Account Executive, Grosse Pointe News, Grosse Pointe, Michigan, 1966-68; President, Nels Associates Inc, Birmingham, Michigan, 1968-75; President, The Woman's Market Group, Birmingham, 1973-75; President, Busch & Associates, Birmingham, 1975-. *Memberships:* Health Care Division, American Marketing Association; American Society for Hospital Public Relations; Michigan Hospital Public Relations Association; Southeastern Michigan Hospital Public Relations Association; Economics Club of Detroit; Adcraft Club of Detroit. *Honours:* Publication Awards for Excellence, 1975-85. *Hobbies:* Writing; Painting; Travel; Trekking; Aerobics; Skiing. *Address:* Busch & Associates, PO Box 1024, Birmingham, MI 48012, USA.

BUSH Barbara, Wife, President Elect of the USA.

m. George Bush, 6 Jan. 1945, 4 sons, 1 daughter. *Appointments Include:* Volunteer Work, various organisations. *Publications:* C. Fred's Story, 1984. *Memberships:* Board Member, Reading is Fundamental; Sponsor, Laubach Literacy International; Honorary Member, Board, Kingsbury Center, Washington; Honorary Chairperson, National Advisory Council of Literacy Volunteers of America Inc. *Honours Include:* Dameshek Award, Leukemia Society of America, 1982; Woman of the Year Award, National Republican Club, 1983; Woman of Achievement Award, Girls Club of New York, 1983; National Outstanding Mother of the Year, 1984; many other honours and awards including honorary degrees. *Hobbies:* Needlepoint; Reading; Being with her Family.

BUSH Helen Virginia (Ginger), b. 15 Mar. 1940, Jacksonville, Florida, USA. Psychotherapist; Marital Sex Therapist. m. 25 Jan. 1963, 2 sons, 1 daughter. *Education:* BA, University of Miami, 1962; MSW, University of Pittsburgh, 1974. *Appointments:* University of West Indies, Jamaica, 1968-69; Various hospitals, Pittsburgh, Pennsylvania, 1973-74; Mental health centre, Florida, 1974-77; Private practice, 1977-. *Publications:* Articles: Sex Therapist as Advocate for Treatment in Sex Offender Case; Sexual Discomfort & Dysfunction Within the Incestuous Family; Incest, Interrelationship Between Legal System & Treatment. *Memberships:* American Association of Sex Educators, Counsellors & Therapists; Society for Scientific Study of Sex; American Association of Marriage & Family Therapists; American Association for Advancement of Science. *Honours:* Scholarships, music 1959-62, social work 1973; Professional of Year, Palm Beach County Mental Health, 1979; Women of Stress Award, 1980. *Hobbies* Research; Writing, professional & fiction; International Travel; Reading; Sewing & Designing Clothes; Soccer; Theatre; Art. *Address:* 2828 Seacrest Boulevard, Suite 212, Boynton Beach, Florida 33435, USA.

BUSWELL Debra Sue, b. 8 Apr. 1957, Salt Lake City, USA. Business Owner; Programmer; Analyst. m. Randy James Buswell, 17 Aug. 1985. *Education:* BA, University of Colorado, 1978. *Appointments:* Programmer, Analyst, Trail Blazer Systems, Palo Alto, 1980-83; Data Processing Manager, Innovative Concepts, San Jose, 1983-86; Owner, Egret Software, San Jose, 1986-. *Memberships:* Commonwealth Club of California; Northern California Pick Users; Institute of Electrical & Electronics Engineers Inc; National Audubon Society. *Hobbies:* Art Collecting; Stamp Collecting; Reading; Gardening; Computers. *Address:* 883 Del Vaile Ct., Milpitas, CA 95035, USA.

BUTCHER Elizabeth Ann, b. 19 May 1938, Gundagai, Australia. Administrator. *Education:* Leaving Certificate, SCEGGS, Darlinghurst. *Appointments:* Secretary, Butcher & Heaton, 1959; Administrative Secretary, International Convention of Architects, 1962; Secretary to Director, Institute of Dental Research & Clinical Research Supervisor to Dean, University of Sydney, 1963-67; Research Co-ordinator, Proctor & Gamble, Ohio, USA, 1968-69; Administrator, National Institute of Dramatic Art, Kensington, New South Wales, 1969-; Seconded, Assistant Director, Cultural Activities, 1978; Interim Administrator, Inaugural Season, Sydney Theatre Company, 1979. *Memberships:* Australia Council, 1982-84; Chairman, Theatre Board of Australia Council, 1982-85; Council Member, University of New South Wales, 1982-84; Seymour Centre Management Board, 1984-; Sydney Opera House Trust, 1986. *Honour:* Order of Australia, 1984. *Hobbies Include:* Theatre; Opera; Ballet; Lace-making; Gardening. *Address:* c/o NIDA, PO Box 1, Kensington, NSW 2033, Australia.

BUTIN Judie T. (Judith LaVonne Tomlonovic), b. 15 July 1941, Iowa, USA. Probation & Parole Officer. m. 14 Jan. 1972, 2 sons, 2 daughters. *Appointments:* Administrative Assistant, School Without Walls, Newton School System, 1970-76; Probation & parole officer, Department of Correctional Services, 5th

Judicial District, 1976-. *Memberships include:* President, Iowa Corrections Association; Affiliate Board Representative, American Probation & Parole Association; Boards, Iowa Children & Family Services, Central Iowa Foundation for Alcoholism & Drug Abuse; Substance Abuse Committee, Newton Chamber of Commerce; Vice President, Newton Community School Board. *Honours:* Selected Co-Chair, Spring Symposium, American Probation & Parole Association/Iowa Corrections Association, 1986; Certificate of Appreciation, American Correctional Association, 1987. *Hobbies:* Gardening; Entertaining; Decorating. *Address:* PO Box 761, Newton, Iowa 50208, USA.

BUTLER (Muriel) Dorothy, b. 24 Apr. 1925, Auckland, New Zealand. Author; Bookseller; Lecturer. m. Roy Edward Butler, 11 Jan. 1947, 2 sons, 6 daughters. *Education:* BA, University of New Zealand, 1946; Diploma in Education, 1976. *Publications:* Author: Cushla & Her Books, 1979; Babies Need Books, 1981; Five to Eight, 1986; Come Back, Ginger, 1987; A Bundle of Birds, 1987; My Brown Bear Barney, 1989; Bears, Bears, Bears, 1989; Lulu, 1990; A Happy Tale, 1990; Higgledy Piggledy Hobbledy Hoy, 1990. Co-author, with Marie Clay: Reading Begins at Home, 1979. Editor: The Magpies Said; For Me, Me, Me; I Will Build You A House. *Memberships:* PEN; New Zealand Children's Literature Association; NZ Reading Association. *Honours:* Eleanor Farjeon Award, UK, 1979; May Hill Arbuthnot Lectureship, USA, 1982; American Library Citation, 1983. *Hobbies:* Reading; Gardening; Walking; Children & their books; Music. *Address:* The Old House, Kare Kare, R. D. Piha, Auckland, New Zealand.

BUTLER Elizabeth (Liz), b. New Zealand. Editor. m., 3 sons. *Education:* BA, University of Victoria. *Appointments:* Freelance, 1970-79, Chief Associate Editor, 1979-82, Editor, 1987-, Fair Lady, National Magazines, South Africa; Editor, Cosmo Man, Jane Raphaely & Associates, 1982-85. *Memberships:* Arag; 100 Club. *Hobby:* Keen interest in historic houses. *Address:* Fair Lady, PO Box 1802, Cape Town 8000, Republic of South Africa.

BUTLER Gwendoline, b. London, England. Author. m. Lionel Butler, 15 Oct. 1949, 1 daughter. *Education:* Lady Margaret Hall, Oxford; BA, 1947. *Appointments:* Temporary teaching, Westfield College, London, 1944; Lecturing in Medieval History; Tutorial work, Somerville College and St Anne's, Oxford, 1949-54. *Publications:* Various books under own name including Receipt for Murder, 1955; Others under pseudonym Jennie Melville. *Memberships:* Crime Writers Association; Detective Club; Royal Society of the Arts. *Honours:* Silver Dagger for Coffin for Pandora, Crime Writers Association, 1974; Prize for Best Romantic Novel of the Year for The Red Staircase, Romantic Novelists Association, 1980. *Hobbies:* Reading; Travel; Writing. *Address:* 32 Harvest Road, Englefield Green, Egham, Surrey, England.

BUTLER Lucilla, b. 16 Nov. 1955, Oxford, England. Ophthalmology. *Education:* Lady Margaret Hall, Oxford University, 1974-77; MBBS, University College Hospital, London, 1980; FRCS ED, 1986; FC Opth, 1988. *Appointments:* Royal United Hospital, Bath, 1980; University College Hospital, London, 1981-82; Department Anatomy, St Andrews, 1982-; Birmingham and Midland Eye Hospital, Birmingham, currently senior Register. *Memberships:* British Medical Association; Fellow, Royal College Surgeons, Edinburgh; Fellow, College of Opthalmologists; Midland Ophthalmological Society. *Honours:* Serving Sister, Order of St John of Jerusalem. *Hobbies:* St John Ambulance. *Address:* The Birmingham and Midland Eye Hospital, Church St., Birmingham, England.

BUTLER Margaret Kampschaefer, b. 7 Mar. 1924, Evansville, USA. Senior Computer Scientist. m. James W. Butler, 30 Sept. 1951, 1 son. *Education:* AB, Mathematics, Indiana University, 1944. *Appointments:* Statistician, US Bureau of Labour Statistics, 1945-46,

1949-51, US Air Force in Europe, 1946-48; Mathematician, Argonne National Lab, 1948-49, 1951-80; Senior Computer Scientist, 1980-. *Publications:* Chapter in Application of Digital Computers to Problems in Reactor Physics, 1968; Chapter in, Advances in Nuclear Science & Technology, 1976; articles & reports in professional publications. *Memberships:* American Nuclear Society, variuos offices; Association for Computing Machinery, Executive Committee Chicago Chapter; Association for Women in Science. *Honours:* Fellow, American Nuclear Society, 1980; Elected Illinois Delegate Republican National Convention, 1980. *Hobbies:* Working to Assist Women in Developing Their Full Potential. *Address:* 17 W 139 Hillside Lane, Hinsdale, IL 60521, USA.

BUTLER-SKURATOWICZ Charlotte Gabrielle, b. 27 May 1951, Valetta, Malta. Ballet Dancer. m. Marek Skuratowicz, 7 Aug. 1982, 1 daughter. *Education:* Arts Educational Trust Schools, Tring, 1961-67, London Branch, 1967-70. *Career:* Performed with: Ballet de la Jeunesse Romande, Lausanne, Switzerland, 1970-71; Ballett der Stadtische Bühmen, Freiburg, 1971-73 Demi-Soloist, Wuppertaler Ballet, Federal Republic of Germany, 1973-74; Ballet of the Berlin Opera, 1974-, Principal, 1980-; Danced Queen of the Willis in Giselle, Big Swans and Spanish Solo in Swan Lake, Van Manen's Pas De Deux Twilight and Sarcasm, Solos in Balanchine's, Apollon, Agon, Symphony in C, 4 Temperaments, Solos in Coppelia, La Fill Malgardee, Les Sylphides, *Memberships:* Union of German Theatre Members (Examiner, Dance Examinations). *Hobbies:* Theatre; Concerts; Opera; Knitting and sewing children's clothes; Travel. *Address:* Laubenheimerstrasse 19, 1000 Berlin 33, Federal Republic of Germany.

BUTNER Mary Boemker, b. Kentucky, USA. Counsellor. m. William Francis Butner, 14 Aug. 1976, divorced, 1 daughter, Victoria Leigh Butner. *Education:* BS, Nursing, 1976; BS Education, 1983; MS, Education & Counselling, 1980; PsyS, Counseling Psychology, 1986. *Appointments:* Psy. Nurse, Kentucky Baptist Hospital, 1976-77; Counsellor, South Louisville Substance Abuse Centre, 1977-79; Consultant, Treasurer, Changing Patterns Inc., 1981-84; Counsellor, Lecturer, Indiana University School of Nursing, 1984-88. *Publications:* articles in Kentucky Nurse; Imprint. *Memberships:* Sigma Theta Tau; Pi Lambda Theta; Kappa Delta Phi; Fellow, World Association Social Psychiatry; Kentucky Nurses Association; American Nurses Association; Chair, KNR Committee on Ethics. *Honours:* Academic Achievement Awards, Indiana University, 1978, 1979, 1981; Charter member Wilson Center; Member, Gatorade Sports Science Institute. *Hobbies Include:* Girl Scout Programme Co-ordinator; Breeding Boston Terriers; Reading; Hiking; Swimming. *Address:* 1209 Curlew Ave., Louisville, KY 40213, USA.

BUTNER Victoria Leigh, b. 19 Nov. Louisville, Kentucky, USA. Student. *Memberships:* Lakeside Swim Team; Audubon Park Dogwood Princess; Server, St Stephen Martyr; Nominee for Student Council Developer of operation, Adopt-a-Ship; Military Mailcall. *Honours:* Academic Merit Award, 1985-89 annually; Certificate of Merit for Community Service, 1989; Louisville Young Authors Award, 1989; Certificate for Achievement in Swimming Skills, Level 3; G.I. Joe Great American Hero Award; Naval Appreciation Award. *Hobbies:* Swimming; Penpals from around the world; Reading; Collecting postcards; Cycling; Travel; Tennis; Hiking. *Address:* 1209 Curlew Avenue, Louisville, KY 40213, USA.

BUZZI Ruth Ann, b. 24 July 1946, Westerly, Rhode Island, USA. Actress. m. Kent Perkins, 10 Dec. 1978. *Education:* West Broad street Grammar School in Pawcatuck, Connecticut; Stonington High School, Pawcatuck, Connecticut; Pasadena Playhouse Graduate. *Creative works:* 18 musical revues in New York City including: Julius Monk's Plaza Nine and Upstairs at the Downstairs; Off Broadway shows: Mis-Guided Tour, revue and Babes in the Woods by Rick Besoyan, musical, also a Brecht play; Broadway show

Gwen Verdon's Sweet Charity; 5 year contract for voice over in Linus the Lionhearted; 150 on-camera TV Commercials in New York City; Television appearances include: Rowan and Martin's Laugh In, Carol Burnett's The Entertainers; The Steve Allen Comedy Hour; The Days of Our Lives; The Lost Saucer; Betsy Lee's Ghost Town Jamboree; Whatever Turns You On. Films include: Freaky Friday; Record City; The Trouble with Hello; The Villian; The Bad Guys; Indian Summer. *Honours:* Golden Globe Award, 1972; Nominated for 4 Emmy Awards; IMAGE Award presented by NAACP; Rhode Island Hall of Fame; Achievement Award from Pasadena Playhouse, 1979. *Hobbies:* Book-binding; Crewel work; Watercolour painting; Pencil sketching; House cleaning; Cooking for large dinner parties. *Address:* c/o The Artists' Group, 1930 Century Park West, Los Angeles CA 90068, USA.

BYAM M Elizabeth, b. 31 Oct. 1949, Cooperstown, New York, USA. Data Processing Management Consultant. *Education:* BA, Georgia State University, Atlanta, 1972; Post Graduate, Columbia Southern School of Law, Atlanta, 1976-88; Certified Systems Professional, 1988. *Appointments:* Programmer, Coastal States Life Insurance, Atlanta, 1973-75; Analyst, Southern Airways, Atlanta, 1975-76; Independent Contractor, Atlanta and Scotts Valley, 1978-82; Senior Consultant, Field Manager, Computer Dynamics, Woodland Hills, California, 1983-84; Principal Consultant & Owner, MEB Associates, Canoga Park, 1984-. *Memberships:* Data Processing Management Association; Association for Women in Computing; Opera Guild of Southern California; Los Angeles Science Fantasy Society; Sierra Club. *Honour:* 1st Prize, National Newsletter Contest, Data Processing Management Association, 1988. *Address:* MEB Associates, 6846-D Hatillo, Canoga Park, CA 91306, USA.

BYE Beryl Joyce Rayment, b. 7 Aug. 1926, Maida Vale, London, England. Freelance Writer. m. Dennis Robert Bye, 9 Aug. 1945, 2 sons, 2 daughters. *Education:* Adult Correspondence, Wolsey Hall, Oxford. *Career:* Author; Speaker; Broadcaster. *Publications:* Books: Three's Company; Wharf Street; Nobody's Pony; Pony for Sale; Belle's Bridle; Looking into Life; Learning from Life; Prayers at Breakfast; Start the Day Well; Please God; About God; Jesus Said; Jesus at Work; People Like Us; More People Like Us; To Be Continued; Teaching Children the Christian Faith; Following Jesus; Prayers for All Seasons; What about Lifestyle?; Time for Jesus; Hear a Minute, 1990. *Hobbies:* Walking; Reading; Swimming; Folk dancing. *Address:* The Old Coach House, Lye Lane, Cleeve Hill, Cheltenham, Glos, England.

BYERS Amy Irene, b. 30 Dec. 1906, London, England. Writing; Painting in oils. m. 4 June 1932. 1 son, 1 daughter. *Creative Works:* One woman Art Exhibition. Books: Mystery of Midway Mill; Verses for Children, 1946; Mystery at Barber's Mill, 1950; Jim of Tamberly Forest, 1954; Adventure of Floating Flat; Catherine of Corners; Stage Under the Cedars; Tim Returns to Tamberly, 1962; The Merediths of Marpins, 1964; Flowers for Melissa, 1958; Sign of Dolphin, 1968; Missing Masterpiece, 1957; Timothy and Tiptoes, 1974; Tiptoes Wins Through, 1987; Tiptoes and the Big Race-Fox on Pavement, 1988; Tiptoes and the Big Race, 1987; War Memoirs, Me and Mine accepted for the Archives of the Imperial War Museum Publications Department. *Membership:* Croydon and District Writers Association. *Honours:* Second Prize for poem, Women Writers. *Address:* 69 Baldry Gardens, London SW16 3DR, England.

BYRD Sandra Judith, b. 14 July 1960, Detroit, Michigan, USA. Circulation Director. m. Michael Keith Byrd, 23 Nov. 1984. 1 daughter. *Education:* Southern Illinois University, Carbondale, Illinois, 1978- 84. *Appointments:* Manager, Colony West Swim Club, Springfield, Illinois, 1979-84; Assistant Manager, Body Shop, Vero Beach, Florida, 1984; Office Manager, Insta-Med Clinics, Inc, Vero Beach, 1984-86; Business Manager, Treasure Coast Diagnostics, Inc, Sebastian, Florida, 1987-88; Circulation Manager, Redgate Communications Corporation, Vero Beach, 1986-88; Circulation Director, T T Publications, Inc, Longwood, Florida, 1988-. *Membership:* National Association of Female Executives. *Honours:* National Honor Society, Springfield Illinois, 1978; Illinois State Scholarship, 1979-82. *Hobbies:* Swimming; Scuba diving; Drawing; Running. *Address:* 1013 Pond Apple Court, Oviedo, Florida 32765, USA.

BYRNE Julie Ann Marlane, b. 28 Apr. 1951, Pembroke, Ontario, Canada. Deputy Director of Nursing. m. Michael Thomas Alexander Byrne, 3 Sept. 1970. 2 sons. *Education:* Diploma in Nursing, Ottawa Civic Hospital, Ottawa, Canada, 1972; Diploma, Applied Science (Nursing and Unit Management), Queensland Institute of Technology, Australia, 1979; Bachelor of Health Administration, University of New South Wales, 1987. *Appointments:* Staff Nurse, Medical Unit, 1972-73, Staff Nurse, Renal Unit, 1973-74, Ottawa Civic Hospital; Staff Nurse, Haemodialysis Unit, 1974-79, Charge Nurse, Renal Transplant Unit and Acute Dialysis Ward, 1979-84, Acting Nursing Supervisor, Night Duty 1984, Nursing Supervisor, Day Duty, 1985-86, Acting Senior Nursing Staff Officer/Acting Staff Allocation Nursing Supervisor/Acting Deputy Nursing Superintendent/Deputy Director of Nursing, 1986; Acting Director of Nursing, 1987-, Princess Alexandra Hospital, Brisbane, Australia. *Memberships:* Fellow, College of Nursing Australia (FCNA); Associate, Australian College of Health Service Administrators (ASCHA) (AHA); Queensland Branch Education and Training Committee; Royal Australian Nursing Federation (RANF); Queensland Nurses Union. *Honours:* Anthony Suleau Prize for the best performance in Behavioural Science I at the University of New South Wales, 1983. *Hobbies:* Politics; Counselling (Career); Feminist Literature; Travelling; Environmental issues. *Address:* Deputy Director of Nursing, Princess Alexandra Hospital, Ipwsich Road, Woollorgabba, Queensland 4102, Australia.

BYRNE Tamara Ebert, b. 23 Mar. 1960, Mobile, Alabama, USA. Accountant; Business Administrator. m. Thomas Robertson Byrne, 14 Feb. 1985. *Education:* BSc, Commerce, University of Virginia, 1982. *Appointments:* Auditor, Charles E. Smith Management Inc, 1982-83; Certified Public Accountant, S. F. Parker & Company, 1983-86; Internal Auditor 1986-87, Assistant Director Business Services, Medical Centre 1987-, University of South Alabama. *Memberships:* Offices, Past/Present: Business & Professional Women's Club; South Baldwin Jaycees; Foley Civic League. Member: Alabama Sheriff's Ranch; American Institute of Certified Public Accountants; Healthcare Financial Management Association. *Honours:* Young Career Woman, District 1, Alabama Federation of Business & Professional Women's Clubs, 1987; Intermediate Honours, University of Virginia, 1980. *Hobbies:* Reading; Cooking; Camping & canoeing; Astronomy; Environmental Issues. *Address:* 10231 Bayou Circle, Fairhope, Alabama 36532, USA.

BYRON Kathleen, b. 11 Jan. 1922, London, England. Actress. *Education:* London University; Old Vic Co., student, 1942. *Appointments:* Screen debut in Young Mr Pitt, 1943. *Creative Works:* Films include: Silver Fleet; Black Narcissus; Matter of Life and Death; Small Back Room; Madness of the Heart; Reluctant Widow; Prelude to Fame; Scarlet Thread; Tom Brown's Schooldays; Four Days; Hell is Sold Out; I'll Never Forget You; Gambler and the Lady; Young Bess; Night of the Silvery Moon; Profile; Secret Venture; Hand in Hand; Night of the Eagle; Hammerhead; Wolfshead; Private Road; Twins of Evil; Craze; Abdication; One of Our Dinosaurs is Missing; The Elephant Man; From a Far Country. Television: The Lonely World of Harry Braintree; All My Own Work; Emergency Ward 10; Probation Officer; Design for Murder; Sergeant Cork; Oxbridge 2000; The Navigators; The Worker; Hereward the Wake; Breaking Point; Vendetta; Play to Win; Who Is Sylvia; Portrait of a Lady; Callan; You're Wrecking

My Marriage; Take Three Girls; The Confession of
Mariona Evans; Paul Temple; The Worker; The
Moonstone; The Challengers; The Golden Bowl; The
Edwardians; The New Life; Menace; The Rivals of
Sherlock Holmes; The Brontes; On Call; Edward VII;
Sutherland's Law; Crown Court; Anne of Avonlea; Heidi;
Notorious Woman; General Hospital; North & South;
Angelo; Within these Walls; Jubilee; Z Cars; Tales from
the Supernatural; Secret Army; An Englishman's Castle;
The Professionals; Forty Weeks; Emmerdale Farm; Blake
Seven; The Minders; Together; Hedda Gabler; Nancy
Astor; God Speed Co-operation; Take Three Women;
Reilly. *Address:* c/o Rolf Kruger Management Ltd,
Morley House, 314-322 Regent Street, London W1,
England.

C

CABRAL Olga Marie, b. 14 Sept. 1909, Trinidad, West Indies. Poet; Writer. m. Aaron Samuel Kurtz, 27 June 1951, deceased. *Education:* Art courses, New School for Social Research. *Appointments:* Director of Children's Art Workshop, 1951-57; Owner and Manager, Art Gallery, 1958-66. *Publications:* Poetry: Cities and Deserts, 1959; The Evaporated Man, 1968; Tape Found in a Bottle, 1971; Occupied Country, 1976; The Darkness in My Pockets, 1976; In the Empire of Ice, 1980. Books (Juvenile): The Seven Sneezes, 1948; The Four-in-One Book, 1948; Tony the Tow Car, 1949; So Proudly She Sailed, 1981. Contributor to 31 poetry anthologies in the USA and Europe and 32 literary journals. *Memberships:* The Poetry Society of America; Authors Guild; National Writers Union. *Honours:* Poetry Society of America: Emily Dickinson Award, 1971; Lucille Medwick Memorial Award, 1976. *Hobby:* Painting. *Address:* 463 West St Apt H-523, New York, NY 10014, USA.

CACCAMISE Genevra Louise Ball, b. 22 July 1934, Mayville, New York, USA. Media Specialist, retired. m. Alfred Edward Caccamise, 7 July 1974. *Education:* BA, Stetson University, DeLand; MSLS, Syracuse University. *Appointments:* 5th Grade Teacher, Sanford, Florida, 1956-57; 2nd Grade Teacher, Longwood, Florida, 1957-58; 4th Grade Teacher, Enterprise, Florida, 1958-73; School Librarian, Boston Avenue School, DeLand, 1963-82; Head Media Specialist, Blue Lake Elementary School, DeLand, 1982-86. *Memberships:* President, 1980-82, American Association of University Women; President, 1982-84, Board of Trustees, DeLand Public Library; Director, Alhambra Villas Home Owners' Association; Treasurer, Volusia County Association for Media in Education; Lt Governor, Frances Cooke Colony, General Society of Mayflower Descendants; President, Retired Teachers Volusia County. *Honours:* Delta Kappa Gamma Society, Beta Psi Chapter, Mu State, Women's Educational Honorary President, 1982-84; National Scholastic Press Association Journeyman Award, 1952. *Hobbies:* Genealogy; Reading; Travelling; Photography; Sewing. *Address:* PO Box 241, DeLand, Florida 32721, USA.

CACCIATORE Vera, b. 9 Nov. 1911, Rome, Italy. Writer. m. Edoardo Cacciatore, 24 Feb. 1941. *Education:* Doctor of Literature, University of Rome, Italy, 1934. *Appointment:* Curator, Keats-Shelley Memorial House, Rome, 1933-75. *Publications:* Novels: La Vendita all'Asta, 1953; The Swing, 1959, New York, 1961; Shelley and Byron in Pisa, 1961; La Palestra, 1961; La Forza Motrice, 1968; A Room in Rome, 1970; La Scalinata, 1984. *Honours:* MBE, UK, 1958; Honorary Member, Poetry Society of America; Honorary Member, Keats-Shelley Association of America. *Hobbies:* Travel; Mountains; Art. *Address:* Largo Cristina di Svezia 12, 00165 Rome, Italy.

CAHAN Judith Eleanor, b. 3 May 1951, New York City, New York, USA. Attorney (Partner). m. Ronald Jacobs, 1 Aug. 1987. *Education:* BS, Cornell University, 1972; JD, cum laude, Yeshiva University, Benjamin N Cardozo School of Law, 1979. *Appointments:* Richard T Gallen & Co, 1979-80; Judicial clerkships, 1980-82; Associate, Brownstein Hyatt Farber & Maddey, 1982-84; Associate and Partner, Sherman & Howard, 1984-. *Publication:* The Unmarried Couple's Legal Handbook, with Richard T Cullen and Joseph Brianco, 1981. *Memberships:* Colorado Bar Association; Denver Bar Association; American Bar Association; Colorado Women's Bar Association; New York State Bar; Alliance of Professional Women. *Honour:* Samuel Belkin Scholar, 1978-79. *Hobbies:* Jazz dance; Skiing; Bicycling; Reading; Car rallying. *Address:* 315 Vine Street, Denver, Colorado 80206, USA.

CAHILL Teresa Mary, b. 30 July 1944. Opera & Concert Singer. *Education:* Guildhall School of Music & Drama, AGSM Piano, LRAM Singing; London Opera Centre. *Appointments:* Opera & Concert Singer, Glyndebourne debut 1969; Covent Garden Debut, 1970; La Scala Milan, 1976; Philadelphia Opera, 1981; specialising in Mozart & Strauss; Concerts: all the London Orchestras, Boston Symphony Orchestra, Chicago Symphony Orchestra, Berlin Festival, 1987, Vienna Festival, 1983, Rotterdam Philharmonic, 1984, Hamburg Philharmonic, 1985; West Deutscher Rundfun Cologne, 1985; Promenade Concerts, BBC Radio & TV; Recordings including Elgar, Strauss and Mahler for all major companies; recitals, concerts throughout Europe, USA & Far East; Silver Medal Worshipful Company of Musicians; John Christie Award, 1970. *Hobbies:* Cinema; Theatre; Travel; Reading; Collecting Antique Furniture. *Address:* 65 Leyland Road, London SE12 8DW, England.

CAHN Susan, b. 18 Dec. 1952, Los Angeles, California, USA. Historian; Teacher; Writer; Reviewer. m. Stephen Allen Downs, 4 May 1985. *Education:* BA, cum laude, Cornell University, 1974; AM 1976, PhD 1981, University of Michigan. *Appointments:* University of Michigan, 1977; Visiting Lecturer, Rutgers University, 1982-83; Coordinator, National Association to Stop the Family Protection Act, 1983; Staff, Columbia University Senate, 1984-87; Teacher, Horace Mann School, 1987-. *Publications:* Book: Industry of Devotion: The Transformation of Women's Work in England 1500-1660, 1987; Article: Women's Self-Organization, 1981; Escape to New York, 1989. *Membership:* AHA, District 65-UAW (Local Officer 1985-87). *Hobbies:* Films; Books; Dogs; Bicycling.

CAIN Linda C., b. 5 Oct. 1941, USA. Communications Executive; Writer; Educator. *Education:* BA, History, Government, Boston University, 1963; MEd, Northeastern University, 1967; Journalism Techniques, Boston Globe, Boston, 1982. *Appointments:* Admissions Officer, Children's Hospital Medical Group, Boston, Massachusetts, 1964-65; Executive Assistant, Massachusetts Republican State Committee, 1965-67; Teacher, Dover Public Schools, Dover, Massachusetts, 1967-81; President, Dover-Sherborn Education Association, 1976-77, 1979-81; President, Beehive Communications Inc, Medfield, Massachusetts, 1982-; Adminstered fundraising programmes on public TV, 1973-76. *Publications:* Blast-Off, children's book; Fifty Top-Notch Tips to Help You Travel Smarter; Smart Shopping Tips....for the Traveller; Smart Dining Tips....for the Traveller; Fifty Savvy Security Tips....for the Traveller; How to Survive a Hotel Fire: Over Twenty-Five Timesaving, Lifesaving tips; How to Share the Christmas Spirit: Twenty-Five Clever Ways....; How to Survive Holiday Shopping: Thirty Sure-Fire Shopping Shortcuts; How to Hide Your Valuables: Fifty Easy Ways to Fool Burglars; How to Keep Burglars out of Your House: Fifty Easy Ways to Help Burglarproof Your House; How to Protect Your Vacation House: Fifty Easy Ways to Keep Your Property Safe.... *Address:* Beehive Communications Inc, 11 Pleasant Street, Medfield, MA 02052, USA.

CAIRD Janet Hinshaw, b. 24 Apr. 1913, Livingstonia, Malawi. Writer. m. 19 July 1938, 2 daughters. *Education:* Dollar Academy; MA Honours, University of Edinburgh, 1935; Sorbonne, Paris, 1935-36. *Appointments:* Teacher of English, Park School, Glasgow, Scotland, 1937-38; Teacher of English, Dollar Academy, 1942-43, 1957-62. *Publications:* Angus The Tartan Partan (children's book); Novels: Murder Reflected; Perturbing Spirit; Murder Scholastic; The Loch; Murder Remote; The Umbrella-Maker's Daughter; Poems: Some Walk A Narrow Path; A Distant Urn; John Donne You Were Wrong; Various short stories. *Honours:* Scottish Arts Council Bursary, 1981. *Hobbies:* Art; Archaeology; Travel. *Address:* 1 Drummond Crescent, Inverness, Scotland.

CAIRNS Lorraine Joyce, b. 14 Jan. 1939, Winnipeg, Manitoba, Canada. Training & Development Officer. m. Gerald Stuart Cairns, 12 Oct. 1957. *Education:*

University of Winnipeg, 1982-84; Fellow, Life Management Institute. *Appointments:* Administrator, Winnipeg Free Press, 1955-64; Executive assistant 1964-71, Training Assistant 1971-76, Assistant Training & Development Manager 1976-, Great-West Life Assurance Company. *Memberships include:* Past President, Manitoba Society for Training & Development; Past President, Human Resources Canada; Chairman, United Way Loaned Rep Training Programme; Chair, YWCA Women of Year Awards; Life Office Management Training & Development Management Committee; International Toastmasters. *Hobbies:* Cottage at lake; Reading; Cooking; Volunteer work. *Address:* Great-West Life Assurance Company, 100 Osborne Street North, Winnipeg, Manitoba, Canda R3C 3A5.

CAIRNS Marion G, b. 8 June 1928, USA. State Representative, Missouri. m. Donald F. Cairns, 2 Sept. 1950, 1 son. *Education:* BA, 1950. *Appointments:* Principal, Ellis Groves Elementary School, 1951-52; Teacher, Nebraska High School, 1952-54; Layout Designer, Hallmark Co., 1954-55; Instructor, Evening College, Washington University, 1959; Instructor, Hickey Business School, 1966-70; State Legislator, Missouri, 1977-; Adjunct Professor, Webster University, 1978-. *Memberships:* American Association of University Women; National Federation of Republican Women; National Order of Women Legislators. *Hobbies:* Golf; Gardening; Antiques; Reading. *Address:* 17 East Swon Ave., Webster Groves, MO 63119, USA.

CAIRNS-REINA Susan Glenda, b. 10 May 1947, Huntington Park, California, USA. Administrative Assistant; Office Manager; Freelance photographer. *Education:* 3 years, California State Polytechnic University; New York Institute of Photography. *Appointment:* Administrative Assistant-Office Manager, Risley & Associates, 1974-. *Memberships:* Order of St Stanislas of Poland; Sovereign Order of the Oak; Job's Daughters; Order of the Eastern Star. *Honours:* Grand Cross, Order of St Stanislas of Poland; Grand Cross, Sovereign Order of the Oak; Grand Bethel Officer, representing the State of Montana, 1965; Grand Bailiff, Sovereign Order of the Oak; Award winning photojournalist; Recipient of First Bronze Medal of Merit, Sovereign Order of the Oak. *Hobbies:* Photography; Travelling; Snow skiing; Handicrafts. *Address:* 2518 Back Bay Loop, Cost Mesa, CA 92626, USA.

CALANCHINI Elizabeth Ellen, b. 6 Oct. 1925, Melbourne, Australia. Investor. m. Dr William Calanchini, 3 Jan. 1949, 3 sons, 2 daughters. *Education:* BA, Melbourne, Australia, 1945. *Appointments:* Translator of French for International Red Cross; Investor; Running an estate of over 10 million dollars. *Memberships:* Lyceum Club, Melbourne; Chairman, Toorek Womens Branch of Liberal Party; Chairman, Penguin Club, Toorek; Executive Australian Britain Society; Patron, Australia & New Zealand Scientific Exploration Society. *Hobbies:* Swimming; Bridge; Business activites; Travel. *Address:* 2 St Georges Road, Toorek 3142, Victoria, Australia.

CALDERINI Gabriella, b. 29 June 1949, Udine, Italy. Head, FIDIA Bioskin Division. *Education:* BA, Biological Science, 1973; PhD, Neuropharmacology, 1976; Certificate, Business Administration, 1987. *Appointments:* Researcher, Farmintalia Laboratories, 1977-78; Group Leader, Fidia Research Laboratories, 1979-85; Scientific Assistant, 1985-86, Assistant, Commercial Committee, 1987, Head, FIDIA Bioskin Division, 1988-. *Publications:* 84 scientific publications; 2 editorials. *Memberships:* American, European Societies for Neuroscience; European Society for Neurochemistry; Italian Study Group on Brain Aging; Italian Society for Biochemistry; Italian Society for Pharmacology. *Hobbies:* Literature; Music. *Address:* FIDIA Bioskin Division, via Ponte Della Fabbrica 3/A, 35031 Abano Terme, Italy.

CALDWELL Brenda Joyce Matson, b. 10 Jan. 1944, Fayetteville, North Carolina, USA. Gemmologist. m. Dallas Caldwell, 18 May 1963, div. 1981, 1 son. *Education:* Guild Gemmologist, 1970, Certified Diamontologist, 1971, DCA; Graduate Gemmologist, GIA, 1980; Master Gemmologist Appraiser, American Society of Appraisers, 1983. *Appointments:* Crescent Jewellers, Tucson, Arizona, 1962-80; Founder, President, Caldwell Jewellery Corporation, 1980-. *Creative works:* Jewellery for fundraising campaigns; Articles on gemmology and gemstones in local newspapers and magazines; Article on insuring fine jewellery in Good Housekeeping, 1986. *Memberships:* Association of Women Gemologists; Tucson Chapter, American Society of Appraisers, Secretary 1986, Treasurer 1987, Vice-President 1989, President 1990; Accredited Gemologists Association, Vice-President 1985-86, 1987-88, Public Relations Director; Board Member, Arizona Jewellers Association. *Honours:* Ribbons and trophies for riding, 1975-80; Awards for local lectures to high school groups etc, 1983-; Chairman, Jewellers Promoting Professionalism, 1986; Woman Gemmologist of the Year, 1987. *Hobbies:* Snow and water skiing; Camping; Hiking; Target shooting; Riding including gymkhanas; Swimming; Running; Jazzercise; Collecting coloured diamonds; Opera, symphony and theatre; Learning including college classes in psychology, foreign languages, computers. *Address:* 7225 North Oracle Road, Tucson, AZ 85704, USA.

CALDWELL Judy Carol, b. 28 Dec. 1946, Nashville, USA. Advertising; Public Relations; Business Owner. m. John Caldwell, 24 June 1984, 1 daughter. *Education:* BS, Wayne State University, 1969. *Appointments:* Teacher, Bailey Mid. School, West Haven, 1969-72; Editorial Assistant, Vanderbilt University, 1973-74; Editor, Graphics Designer, Field Researcher, Urban Observatory of Met. Nashville, 1974-77; Account Executive, Holden & Co., Nashville, 1977-79; Business Teacher, Federated States of Micronesia, 1979-80; Director, Advertising, American Association for State & Local History, Nashville, 1980-81; Director Production, Marketing Communications Co., Nashville, 1981-83; Owner, President, Ridge Hill Corp, 1983-. *Hobbies:* World Conservation; Photography. *Address:* 4004 Hillsboro Road, A-201, Nashville, TN 37215, USA.

CALDWELL Nancy Louise, b. 16 Dec. 1939, Monroe, Wisconsin, USA. Registered Nurse/Military Officer. m. Douglas Lorimer, 31 July 1965. *Education:* RN, Sparks School of Nursing, Ft Smith, Arkansas, 1960; BSN, Texas Christian University, 1976; MA, University of Oklahoma, 1985; Certiified Practitioner in Infection Control. *Appointments:* Colonel in USAF; Chief Nurse, Reg Hospital, MacDill AFB, Florida, 1983-85; Chairperson, Dept of Nursing, USAF Medical Center, Scott AFB, Illinois, 1985-87; Command Nurse, Tactical Air Command, USAF, Langley AFB, Virginia, 1987-; Consultant to the Air Force Surgeon General in Infection Control. *Memberships:* American Nurses Association; Association of Operating Room Nurses; Association of Practitioners in Infection Control; Sigma Theta Tau; Aerospace Medical Association; Air Force Association; Past President, Misawa Chapter, Air Force Association. *Honours:* 5 Meritorious Service Medals, USAF, 1979, 1981, 1983, 1985, 1987; Sikorsky Winged-S Award, 1973; Commissioned 1Lt, USAF, 1963. *Hobbies:* Camping; Black labrador retrievers. *Address:* 33A Eagan Avenue, Langley AFB, VA 23665, USA.

CALHOUN Monica Dodd, b. 3 June 1953, New York City, USA. Attorney. m. Charles Hallett Calhoun, 4 Feb. 1983. *Education:* BA, State University of New York at Albany, 1975; JD, State University of New York at Buffalo, 1978; LLM, Taxation, New York University. *Appointments:* Attorney, Windsor Life Ins Co, New York City, 1978-79; Assoc General Counsel, Manhattan Life Ins Co, New York City, 1979-84; Associate Counsel, Teachers Ins & Annuity Association, College Retirement Equities Fund, New York City, 1984-. *Memberships:* American Life Insurance Counsel; NYS Bar Association.

Address: TIAA-CREF, 730 Third Avenue, New York, NY 10017, USA.

CALLAHAN Cheryl Elizabeth Mann, b. 9 Mar. 1949, Greenville, USA. University Administrator. m. Thomas Michael Callahan, 15 July 1972, 2 daughters. *Education:* BA, Sociology, honours, 1971, PhD, Child Development & Family Relations, 1987, University of North Carolina, Greensboro; MEd., Counselling, University of North Carolina, Chapel Hill, 1972. *Appointments:* Director, Orientation, Delaware State College, 1972-76; Counsellor, Guilford County Schools, 1977-79; Assistant to the Vice Chancellor for Student Affairs, 1979-83, Assistant Vice Chancellor, 1984-87, Associate Vice Chancellor, 1987-, University of North Carolina, Greensboro. *Publications:* Article in: Sociology of Education, 1974. *Memberships:* Junior League, Greensboro, Community Vice President, Board of Directors 1986-; National Association of Student Personnel Administrators. *Honours:* Outstanding Young Woman of the Year, State of Delaware, 1975; Distinguished Service Award, National Association of Student Personnel Administrators, Region III, 1986, 1987; Omicron Nu. *Hobbies:* Volunteer Work in Community; Reading; Needlework. *Address:* University of North Carolina, 147 Mossman Building, Greensboro, NC 27412, USA.

CALLAHAN Pia Iris Laaster, b. 21 Sept. 1955, Belgium. Research Virologist. m. Lynn T. Callahan, 26 June 1981. *Education:* BS, Cornell University, USA, 1977; MCM, Hannemann University, 1979. *Appointments:* Research Assistant, Temple University, 1979-80; Clinical Microbiologist, Thomas Jefferson University Hospital, 1980-81; Staff Virologist, Merck Sharp & Dohme Research Labs, 1981-84; Research Virologist, Merck Sharp & Dohme Research Labs, 1984-. *Publications:* Contributor to professional journals & books. *Memberships:* American Society for Microbiology; National Registry of Microbiologists; National Association for Female Executives. *Hobbies:* Golf; Gardening. *Address:* 907A, Stockton Court, Lansdale, PA 19446, USA.

CALLAN Clair Marie, b. 18 May 1940, Lincolnshire, England. Physician. m. John P Callan, 4 Apr. 1964. 2 sons, 2 daughters. *Education:* MB BCh BA, University College, Dublin, Ireland, 1963. *Appointments:* Intern/Resident, Mater Hospital, Dublin, Ireland, 1963-65; Medical Director, State of Connecticut, Department of Income Maintenance, 1978-84; Senior Staff Physician 1984-, Director Medical Affairs, 1985-, Abbot Laboratories. *Publications:* Several articles, Women in Leadership; Guest editor, Connecticut Medicine, 1980 Issue devoted to Women Physicians. *Memberships:* President, 1985, Finance Chair, 1986-, American Medical Women's Association; Member Ad Hoc Committee, Women in Medical Project, American Medical Association; Delegate to ISMS and Board Member, Lake County Medical Society, 1988. *Honours:* Woman in Management, Charlotte Denstrom Award, 1987; Women of Achievement, Corporate Category, Winner of both Lake Surban and National Awards; Leader, Women Physician Delegation to China, Topic Nutrition, 1986. *Hobbies:* Tennis; Golf; Needlecraft; Bridge. *Address:* Abbott Laboratories D970, Abbott Park, Illinois 60064, USA.

CALLANDER Kay Eileen Paisley, b. 15 Oct. 1938, Coshocton, Ohio, USA. Teacher, Columbus Public Schools. m. Don Larry, 18 Nov. 1977. *Education:* BSc, Education, Muskingum College, New Concord, 1956-60; MA, Speech Education, 1961-64, Postgraduate work, 1964-84, The Ohio State University. *Appointments:* Classroom teacher, various grades, 1960-70; Drama Specialist, Arts Impact Program, 1970-80; Drama Specialist, Classroom teacher, Gifted and Talented Educator, 1980-88, All at Columbus Public Schools, Columbus, Ohio. *Creative Works:* Teacher & Director The Trial of Gold E Locks, a video tape designed to teach about the law, nationally distributed. *Memberships:* Vice President, Executive Board of Directors, Neoteric Dance Theater Company, 1987,

Board of Directors, 1985-87; Central Ohio Teachers Association; Columbus Education Association; Ohio Education Association; National Education Association; Benefactor of the Columbus Jazz Arts Group; Liturgical Art Guild of Ohio; Columbus Museum of Art; The Ohio State Alumni Association; National Organization of Women; National Trust for Historic Preservation; The Navy League; The Humane Society of the United States. *Honours:* Excellence in Schools Grant, 1987-88; Commendation, Ohio House of Representatives, 1986-87; Good Apple Award, Columbus Public Schools, 1983; Educator of the Year Award, Local Parent-Teacher Association, 1982; Nominated, Ohio Teacher of the Year Award, 1981. *Hobbies:* Painting; Photography; Sculpting; Cartooning; Swimming; Walking; Reading; Music, play both piano and organ; Artistic director, Shady Lane Music Festival, Columbus; Church. *Address:* 570 Conestoga Drive, Columbus, Ohio 43213, USA.

CALLINICOS Aedgyth Berth Milburg Mary Antonia Frances (The Honorable Mrs), b. 15 Dec. 1920, Bridgnorth, England. Hotelier. m. John Alex Callinicos, 7 July 1949. 2 sons. *Appointments:* Temp Assistant Principal, POW Dept, later Consular, Foreign Office, 1941-49; Ambassador Hotel, 1961-68; Park Lane Hotel, 1968-86; Holiday Inn, 1986-. *Memberships:* Hon Secretary, Zimbabwe Britain Society; Past Vice President, National Unifying Force; Chairperson, Prankard-Jones Trustee's; Soroptimists. *Honours:* Greek Order of Merit, 1962; Order of the British Empire, 1987. *Hobbies:* Reading; Politics; History; Languages; Travel. *Address:* P O Box 7, Harare, Zimbabwe.

CALLWOOD June, b. 2 June 1924, Chatham, Canada. Journalist. m. Trent Frayne, 13 May 1944, 2 sons (1 deceased), 2 daughters. *Education:* Honorary Degrees: LLD, University of Toronto, Osgoode Hall, York University, Memorial University, Newfoundland; Doctor of Sacred Letters, Trinity College; Doctor of Letters, University of Alberta; Doctor of Literature, Carleton University. *Appointments:* Reporter, Brantford Expositor, 1941; Globe & Mail, 1942; Freelance Journalist, 1942-; Column, Globe & Mail, 1983-. *Publications:* 25 books most recent: Emma, 1984; Emotions, 1986; Twelve Weeks in Spring, 1986; Jim: A Life with Aids, 1988; 500 magazine articles; CBC TV Host, In Touch, 1976-79. *Memberships:* Canadian Civil Liberties Association, Founding Member, 1964, Vice President 1964-88; Nellie's Hostel for Women, Founder, 1974, President, 1974-79; Jessie's Centre for Teenagers, Founder 1982, President 1982-83, 1987-89; Casey House Hospice, Founder, 1987, President 1987-88. *Honours:* Order of Canada, Member 1978, Officer 1986; City of Toronto Award of Merit; Canadian News Hall of Fame, 1984; Windsor Press Club Quill, 1987; Order of Ontario, 1988; Gardiner Award for Citizenshiip, 1988; etc. *Hobbies:* Reading; Swimming. *Address:* 21 Hillcroft Drive, Islington, Ontario, Canada M9B 4X4.

CALMESE Linda, b. 3 June 1947, East St Louis, Illinois, USA. Owner; Director. *Education:* BSc 1969, MSc Business Education 1972, Specialist Degree Counselor Education 1978, Southern Illinois University. *Appointments:* Teacher Business Education, St Teresa Academy, East St Louis, 1969-73; DODDS, Madrid, Spain, 1973-84; Computer Consultant: Scott AFB, Illinois, 1984-87; Norton AFB, California, 1986; Owner/Director, Bits and Bytes Computer Training Centre, Belleville, Illinois, 1985-; Instructor, State Community College, East St Louis, 1986-87; Computer Consultant: Army Aviation Systems Command, St Louis, 1986-87; Ohio Army NG, Worthington, Ohio, 1986; Military Personnel Records Center, St Louis, 1986; Navy Finance Center, Cleveland, 1987; Billy Mitchell Air Field, Milwaukee, 1987; NASA, Cleveland, 1988; Army Corp of Engineers, St Louis, 1988; National University, San Diego, 1988. *Publication:* Co-author Chapter, Business Education for the Seventies, 1969. *Memberships:* National Association of Female Executives; Pi Omega Pi (Honorary Undergraduate Business Education); Delta Pi Epsilon (Honorary Graduate Business Education). *Hobbies:* Travelling; Computer Operating; Reading;

Learning; Teaching; Aerobics. *Address:* 3124 Trendley Avenue, East St Louis, Illinois 62207, USA.

CALMORIN Laurentina P, b. 3 Feb. 1946, Olingan, Dipolog City, Philippines. Dean, Higher and Technical Education. m. Melchor A Calmorin, 30 Dec. 1971. 1 daughter. *Education:* BSE, 1966; BSF, 1971; MA, 1977; PhD, 1980. *Appointments:* Elementary grades Teacher, 1966-69; Secondary School Teacher, 1973-74; Jr College Instructor, 1974-78; Instructor, 1978-82; Voc Inst Supervisor, 1982-84; Assistant Professor, 1984, Associate Professor 1984-87, Dean, Higher & Tech Education, 1987-. *Publications:* Books: Educational Measurement and Evaluation, 1984; Introduction to Fishery Technology, 1989; Numerous articles to professional journals. *Memberships:* Life Member, Philippine Phycological Society, Inc; Treasurer, Junior Fishery Educators of the Philippines; Fishery Research Society of the Philippines; President, Philippine Association for Vocational Education (Local Chapter); Philippine Association for Teachers Education; Treasurer, Council of Department Chairmen for English; Associate Member, National Research Council of the Philippines, *Honours:* Golden Scroll of Honor, Outstanding Educator of the Year, 1985; Graduated with high distinctions, 1966; Kagitingan Award, Outstanding Educator of the Year, 1983; Bantayog Award, Outstanding Educator, 1985; Highest Achievement Award, 1985. *Hobbies & Interests:* Conducting researches; Writing books; Reading; Crocheting. *Address:* Northern Iloilo Polytechnic State College, Estancia, Iloilo, Philippines.

CALVERT Barbara Adamson, b. 30 Apr. 1926, Leeds, England. Chairman; Recorder. m. John Thornton Calvert, 3 Apr. 1948, died 1987, 1 son, 1 daughter. *Education:* London University, 1943-46. *Appointments:* Trainee Personnel Manager, 1946-48; Statistician, City & Guilds, 1960-61; Practising Barrister, 1961-86; Chairman, Industrial Tribunal, Recorder, South Eastern Circuit, 1986-. *Memberships:* Honourable Society of the Middle Temple; Institute of Arbitrators. *Honour:* QC, 1975. *Hobbies:* Music; Poetry; Gardening. *Address:* 158 Ashley Gardens, London SW1P 1NW, England.

CALVERT Laura Merle, b. 29 June 1922, Ohio, USA. Writer. m. Edward H Calvert, 12 Feb. 1942, 1 daughter. *Edcuation:* BA 1956, MA 1957, University of New Mexico; PhD, Ohio State University, 1966. *Appointments:* University of Maryland, Baltimore, 1968-75; University of Massachusetts, 1967-68; University of New Mexico, 1962-67 and 1956-57; Ohio State University 1957-58 and 1961-62; Queens College, 1960. *Publications:* Book: Francisco de Osuna and the Spirit of the Letter. Articles: The Exercise of Recollection According to Osuna; Osuna's Meditations: Between Preaching and Poetry; Images of Darkness and Light in Osuna's Spiritual Alphabet Books; Meditation of the Creatures; The Mode of Incongruity: Notes on Three Hymns in the Nahuatl Style; The Widowed Turtledove and Amorous Dove of Spanish Lyric Poetry; An Etymological Basis for the Pastor-Amador Equation; The Role of Written Exercises in an Audio-Lingual Program; Notes on the Peace Corps Language Training Program. *Memberships:* Modern Language Association; American Association of Teachers of Spanish and Portuguese; American Literary Translators Association. *Honour:* Roberts Memorial Poetry Prize, 1979. *Hobbies:* Linguistics; Gardening. *Address:* 1029 Guadalupe del Prado NW, Albuquerque, New Mexico 87107, USA.

CALVERT Phyllis, b. 8 Feb. 1915, London, England. Actress. m. Peter Murray Hill, 14 June 1941. 1 son, 1 daughter. *Education:* French Lycee & Margaret Morris School of Dancing, Acting & Painting. *Creative Works:* Films include: Kipps; The Young Mr Pitt; Man in Grey; Fanny by Gaslight; Madonna of the Seven Moons; They Were Sisters; Time out of Mind; Broken Journey; My Own True Love; The Golden Madonna; A Woman with No Name; Mr Denning Drives North; Mandy; The Net; It's Never Too Late; Child in the House; Indiscreet; The Young and The Guilty; Oscar Wilde; Twisted Nerve; Oh! What a Lovely War; The Walking Stick; TV Series, Kate,

1970: Death of the Heart; All Passions Spent; Boon; The Woman He Loved; Sophia and Constance; Across the Lake; Capsticks Law; Recent Plays, The Cherry Orchard, Oxford Playhouse; All Over, York Theatre Royal; Clown Matrimonial, Haymarket Theatre London; Dean Daddy, The Ambassadors Theatre; Before The Party, Apollo Theatre. *Hobbies:* Swimming; Gardening; Collecting costume books. *Address:* Hill House, Waddesdon, Buckinghamshire, England.

CALVERT Sarah Jane, b. 27 Aug. 1953, England. Consultant Psychologist. *Education:* BSc., Social Science, 1973; Master, Social Science (honours), 1974; PhD, 1982. *Appointments:* Tutor, University of Waikato, 1973-78; Tutor, Waikato Technical Institute, 1978-79; Tauranga Hospital, 1980; Private Practice, Psychologist, Willow Street Medical Centre, 1980-; Researcher, Womens Mental Health Project, 1981-84; Consultant Psychologist, Social Welfar Dept; Member, Tauranga Hospital Board. *Publications:* Healthy Women, as a Women's Health Book, 1982. *Memberships:* New Zealand Psychological Society; Broadstreet Managazine; Amnesty International; Federation of University Women; Tauranga Womens Centre. *Honours:* Winter Lecturer, Massey University Winter Lecture Series, 1984. *Hobbies:* Writing; Gardening; Sailing; Skiing. *Address:* 205 Fraser Street, Tauranga, New Zealand.

CAMACHO Leonarda, b. 6 Nov. 1923, Manila, Philippines. Writer; Lecturer; Journalist. m. Teodoro Camacho, 28 Nov. 1950, deceased, 1975, 4 sons, 2 daughters. *Education:* BA, Journalism. *Appointments:* Public Information Office, Rizal province, 1961-76; Member of Board, National Cottage Industries Development Authority, 1966-70. *Publications:* Editor, Ang Pilipina; Contributor to National & International newspapers. *Memberships:* National Committee Against Apartheid; Metro Manila Council of Women World Ecologists Foundation. *Honours:* Awards for Volunteer Service. *Hobbies:* Reading; Writing. *Address:* 82A Midland 11, Washington Street Greenhills West, San Juan, Metro Manila, Philippines.

CAMENZIND-WUEST Margrit Mathilde, b. 13 Nov. 1939, Lucerne, Switzerland. Politician. m. Hans Camenzind, 14 May 1962. 1 son, 1 daughter. *Education:* Commercial diploma of Switzerland; Political courses. *Appointments:* Business in international commerce; President general of the Ligue of Catholic Women organisations of Switzerland, 1982-88; Member of the Swiss National Parliament, 1987; Member of the Parliament of Thurgan, 1988-. *Memberships:* Ligue of Catholic Women Organisations; Swiss Christ-democratic Party; President of the family-political commission of the Swiss Christ-democratic party; Member of several social organisations. *Hobbies:* Skiing; Swimming. Interest: Politics; History; Art. *Address:* Wellhauserweg 50, CH-8500 Frauenfeld, Switzerland.

CAMERER Sheila Margaret, b. 15 Dec. 1941, Cape Town, South Africa. Member of Parliament. m. Alexander Camerer, 29 May 1965, 1 son, 2 daughters. *Education:* BA, 1961; LLB, 1964. *Appointments:* State Prosecutor, 1964-65; Reporter, Feature Writer, Financial Mail, 1966-75; Practising Attorney, 1976-87; City Councillor, 1982-87; Provincial Councillor, 1984-86; Member of Parliament for Roschenville, Johannesburg, 1987-. *Memberships:* Chairman, Johannesburg Publicity Association, 1982-87; Member, Womens Legal Status Committee. *Hobbies:* Portrait Painting; Reading; Bridge; Tennis. *Address:* c/o House of Assembly, PO Box 15, Cape Town 8000, South Africa.

CAMERON Judith Lynne, b. 29 Apr. 1945, Oakland, California, USA. Resource Specialist; Teacher-in-Space Consultant; Clinical Hypnotherapist. m. Richard I Cameron, 17 Dec. 1967. 1 son. *Education:* AA 1965, BA 1967, Califronia Teaching Credential, 1969; MA 1972; Credential for teaching learning handicapped, 1978; Calif resource specialist certificate, 1980; PhD, Hypnotherapy/Psychic hypnotherapy, 1987; Jr College teaching Credential, 1988; Doctorate, Clinical Hypnotherapy & Hypnotic Anaesthesiology, 1988. *Appointments:* SF Archdiocese, St Vincent's Elem, 1969-70; Elem Teacher, Fremont Unified S Dist, 1970-72; Elem Spec ed teacher 1972-84, High School Teacher 1984-, Bonita Unified; Teacher-in-space Consultant, 1986-; Owner/Therapist, Southern Calif Clinical Hypnotherapy, 1988-. *Publication:* Article in professional journal, 1988. *Memberships:* CTA/NEA; Assoc Calif Resource Specialist; National Space Society; Planetary Society; Council for Exceptional Children; Challenger Center for Space Education; Association of Past-life Therapists; National Association Hypnotherapists; Association for Hypnotic Anaesthesiologists. *Honours:* California Teachers Honorary Service Award, 1984; California Participant Teacher-in-space Program, 1985; California Teacher of the Month, Bonita High School, January 1988; California Mentor Teacher, Space Education, 1988-; Dept Chairperson, Spec Educ Bonita High School, 1985-; Advisor-Peer counseling program, Bonita High, 1987-88; Advisor, Students for the exploration & development of space chapter, Bonita High School, 1986-. *Hobbies:* First lieutenant, Aerospace Officer, Civil Air Patrol; Astronomy/astrophotography; Guitar & banjo; Crewel embroidery; Crochet; Writing. *Address:* 3257 La Travesia Drive, Fullerton, CA 92635, USA.

CAMMARATA Joan Frances, b. 22 Dec. 1950, New York, USA. College Professor of Spanish. m. Richard M. Montemarano, 9 Aug. 1975. *Education:* BA summa cum laude, Fordham University, 1972; MA, 1974, MPhil, 1977, PhD, 1982, Columbia University. *Appointments:* Taught Spanish Language and Literature: Columbia College, New York, 1974-82; Fordham University, New York, 1982-84; Iona College, New York, 1982-84; Associate Professor of Spanish, Manhattan College, New York, 1982-. *Publications:* Mythological Themes in the Works of Garcilaso de la Vega, 1983; Several articles on literary criticism in professional journals. *Memberships:* Asociacion Internacional de Hispanistas; Modern Language Association; Cervantes Society of America; Renaissance Society of America; NEMLA; American Association of Teachers of Spanish and Portuguese; ACTFL; NYSAFLT; Instituto Internacional de Literatura Iberoamericana; Hispanic Institute. *Honours:* Spanish Medal, Fordham University, 1972; University Fellowship, 1972-73, President's Fellowship, 1973-75, Columbia University; Computer Literacy Project Grant, Manhattan College, 1985; University Associate, Faculty Resources Network Program, New York University, 1985-; Grant for summer institute, National Endowment for the Humanities, 1987, 1988; Andrew W Mellon Foundation Grant, 1990. *Hobbies:* Needlework; Crafts; Plants; Piano; Cooking. *Address:* Modern Foreign Languages, Manhattan College, Riverdale, NY 10471, USA.

CAMP Katherine Merrill Lindsley, b. 10 July 1918, Mount Kisco, New York, USA. Public Policy Advocate; Disarmament Consultant. m. William P. Camp, 11 June 1941, 3 sons. *Education:* BA, Swarthmore College. *Appointments:* Teacher, 1940-42; Founder, Director, Fairmont Kindergarten, Havertown, Pennsylvania; National President 1968-71, International Vice President 1971-74, International President 1974-80, Womens International League for Peace & Freedom (WILPF); Representative, United Nations ECOSOC, 1977-. *Creative work includes:* Listen to the Women for a Change, 1975; Columnist, Peace & Freedom, Pax et Libertas; Lecturer, disarmament, United Nations, foreign policy, women. *Memberships include:* Boards: Institute for Defence & Disarmament Studies 1979-89, In the Public Interest 1980-83; Special adviser, US delegation, UN Special Session on Disarmament, 1978; National Commission, UNESCO, 1980-85; Board of Managers, Swarthmore College, 1975-79; Women's Foreign Policy Council, 1986-; Leader, WILPF Missions, Vietnam, Chile, Israel, USSR, Central America, Iran; Elected Democratic Nominee for US Congress. *Honours:* Bersh Brotherhood Award, 1965; Gimbel Philadelphia Award, 1983; Pomerance Award for Disarmament, 1983; Gandhi Peace Award, 1984; Honorary LLD degreees, Haverford College, Swarthmore College.

Hobbies: Camping; Sailing; Reading; Growing things; Theatre; Music; Travel; Crossword puzzles. *Address:* 3300 Darby Road, no. 7212, Haverford, Pennsylvania 19041, USA.

CAMPANIZZI-MOOK Jane, b. 27 Nov. 1947, USA. Business Executive. m. William H. Mook, 31 Dec. 1978. *Education:* PhD, Ohio State University, 1978. *Appointments:* Consultant, State of Ohio, 1978-81; Analyst, OCLC Inc, 1981-85; President, JCM Enterprises, 1985-. *Publications:* Contributor, Quality Progress journal; Editor, Quali-News newsletter. *Memberships:* Board, Rapi-Serv Cash Systems Inc; Trustee, Treasurer, Artreach; Member: American Society for Quality Control, Institute of Electrical & Electronics Engineers; Midwest Committee, National Quality Month. *Honours:* Leadership programme award, Columbus Area, 1985; Certified Quality Analyst, 1986. *Hobbies:* Astronomy; Visual & performing arts; Electronics. *Address:* 4453 Masters Drive, Columbus, Ohio 43220, USA.

CAMPBELL Bonnie Jean, b. 9 Apr. 1948, Norwich, New York, USA. Attorney. m. Edward L. Campbell, 24 Dec. 1974. *Education:* BA, 1982, JD, 1984, Drake University. *Appointments:* Clerk, Dept. of Housing & Urban Development, 1965-67; Subcommittee, Inter-Governmental Relations, US Senate, 1967-69; Caseworker, Hon. Harold E. Hughes, 1969-74; Field Director, US Senator, John C Culver, 1974-80; Attorney, Wimer Hudson Flynn & Neugent, 1983-. *Memberships:* State Chair, Iowa Democratic Party; Democratic National Committee; Iowa Bar Association. *Hobbies:* Reading; Hiking; Political Activites. *Address:* 300 Walnut No. 187, Des Moines, IA 50309, USA.

CAMPBELL Carol Nowell, b. 16 Dec. 1944, Phoenix, Arizona, USA. Lawyer. m. Harding B Cuve, 28 June 1984. 1 daughter. *Education:* BA 1972, JD 1978, Arizona State University. *Appointments:* Partner, O'Connor, Cavanagh, Anderson, Westover, Killingsworth & Beshears, 1978-. *Memberships:* American Trial Lawyers Association; American Bar Association; State Bar of Arizona; State Bar of California; Maricopa County Bar Association; Phoenix Association of Defense Counsel; Arizona Women Lawyers Association. *Honours:* E Blois du Bois Scholarship, 1976; Kappa Delta Pi, Education Honorary, Reporter and Board Member, 1972; Graduated with Distinction, 1972; Dean's List, 1970-72; Arizona State University Academic Scholarship, 1970-72; American Association of University Professors' Scholarship, 1969-70. *Hobbies:* Hiking; Cross country and downhill skiing; Travel; Reading. *Address:* 1E Camelback Road, Phoenix, AZ 85018, USA.

CAMPBELL Connie Lynn, b. 11 July 1954, Liberty, Liberty County, Texas, USA. Vice President, Virgin Islands Power (VIP) Yachts. m. Omer H Campbell, Jr, 21 Nov. 1974. 1 son. *Education:* Robert E Lee College, Baytown, Texas; Liberty High School, Liberty, Texas. *Appointments:* Manager, Red Carpet Real Estate; President, Brownstone Consolidated; Secretary Treasurer, Financial Land Concepts; Vice President, VIP Yachts. *Memberships:* Democratic Party; Virgin Islands Yacht League; Heart Association; American Cancer Society. *Hobbies:* Reading; Crafts; Swimming; Tennis; Animals; Gardening; Travel. *Address:* 1312 Maple Street, PO Box 6088, Liberty, TX 77575, USA.

CAMPBELL Diane Davis Hoye, b. 2 Sept. 1942, Waltham, USA. Psychiatrist; Lecturer; Consultant. m. Gordon, 23 Apr. 1983, 1 daughter. *Education:* BA, Wellesley College, 1964; MD, Tufts University School of Medicine, 1975; Resident, University of California, San Diego, Psychiatry, 1975-77; Fellow, Child Psychiatry, 1977-79. *Appointments:* Private practice, 1979-; Consultant, Child Guidance Clinics of San Diego, 1979-80; Child Psychiatrist, Childrens Division, San Diego County Mental Health, 1980-82. *Publications:* Chapter, The Pregnant Therapist: Countertransference & Transference Issues, in press. *Memberships:*

American Academy of Child Psychiatry; American Psychiatric Association; American Psychoanalytic Association; San Diego Society of Psychiatric Physicians; etc. *Honours:* Diplomate: National Board of Medical Examiners, American Board of Psychiatry & Neurology, Pscychiatry and Child Psychiatry. *Hobbies:* Lecturing. *Address:* 1011 Camino del Mar, No 270, Del Mar, CA 92014, USA.

CAMPBELL Dianne Olive, b. 5 Nov. 1944, Melbourne, Australia. Director of Nursing. m. David Campbell, 20 Apr. 1968, divorced. *Education:* General Nurse Training, Royal Melbourne Hospital School of Nursing, 1965; Diploma, Nursing Administration, Lincoln Institute of Health, 1977. *Appointments:* Staff Sister, 1965-66, 1967-68, Acting Charge Sister, 1968, Deputy Charge Sister, 1968-69, Charge Sister, 1969-75, Assistant Director, Nursing, 1975-81, Deputy Director of Nursing (Admin), 1981-86, Royal Melbourne Hospital; Theatre Sister, Entabeni Hospital, Durban, South Africa, 1966-67; Acting Director, Nursing, 1986-86, Director, Nursing, 1987-, Amalgamated Melbourne & Essendon Hospitals. *Memberships:* FCNA; AIMM; Australian Management College; Association of Directors of Nursing. *Hobbies:* Tennis; Reading; Travel; Gardening. *Address:* The Amalgamated Melbourne & Essendon Hospitals, C/-Post Office, Royal Melbourne Hospital, Victoria, 3050, Australia.

CAMPBELL Kathryn Dee, b. 21 Apr. 1949, USA. University Professor. m. Dean Campbell, 1970, divorced 1972, 1 son. *Education:* BS, New Mexico State University, 1972; MS, 1977, Ed.D., 1987, Oklahoma State University. *Appointments:* Teacher, Junior High School, 1975-77; Research Assistant, 1975-77, Graduate Assistant, 1984-87, Oklahoma State University; Basketball, Volleyball Coach, W New Mexico University, 1983-84; Exercise Physiologist, Wichita State University, 1987-. *Publications:* various research papers, presentations, and book chapters. *Memberships:* American Alliance of Health Physical Education Research & Dance; American College of Sports Medicine; Oklahoma and Kansas AHPERD. *Honours:* Recipient, various scholarships and awards including: A B Harrison Scholarship, 1984; OAHPERD Graduate Scholarship, 1984; Exercise Test Technologist, American College of Sports Medicine, 1988. *Hobbies Include:* Professionnal Jockey 1979-84; Racquetball; Jogging; Golf; Tennis. *Address:* Dept. of HPER, Box 16, Wichita State University, Wichita, KS 67208, USA.

CAMPBELL Mona Louise, b. 3 Feb. 1919, Toronto, Canada. Company President; Director. m. Kenneth Laidlaw Campbell, 1 son, 2 daughters. *Appointments Include:* President, Director, Dover Industries Limited; Director: Canada Development Investment Corp; Rothmans Inc, Toronto; The Toronto-Dominion Bank, Toronto; Churad Properties Limited, Toronto; The Capstone Investments Trust, Toronto; National Sea Products Limited, Halifax. *Memberships Include:* Life Member, Toronto General Hospital Auxilliary; Metropolitan Toronto Zoo; Founder, Royal Ontario Museum. *Address:* 30 Glen Edyth Place, Toronto, Ontario M4V 2W2, Canada.

CAMPBELL Olga Margaret, b. 20 June 1943, Altrincham, England. Psychologist. *Education:* BS, Marywood College, Scranton, USA, 1972; MA, Clinical/Counselling Psychology, Abilene Christian University, Texas, 1975; PhD, Educational Psychology, University of Texas, Austin, 1983. *Appointments:* Psychologist, 1973-74, Clinical Psychologist, 1980-84, Big Spring State Hospital, Big Spring, Texas; Psychologist, Vernon Centre, 1974-76; Psychologist, Rusk State Hospital, Texas, 1976-77; private practice, Psychology, Midland, Texas 1984-. *Memberships:* American, Texas Psychological Associations; Society for Personality Assessment; Licensed Psychologist, Texas State Board of Examiners of Psychologists. *Hobbies:* Swimming; Knitting; Parapsychology; Mysticism; High IQ Organizations. *Address:* 3325 W Wadley Ste 231, Midland, TX 79707, USA.

CAMPBELL Virginia Anne, b. 12 Aug. 1930, St John, New Brunswick, Canada. University Professor. *Education:* BSc, Acadia University, 1951; MSc Public Health Nutrition 1959, PhD Foods & Nutrition 1963, Pennsylvania State University, USA. Dietetic intern, Harper Hospital, Detroit, Michigan, USA, 1951-52. *Appointments:* Therapeutic Dietitian, Hartford Hospital, Connecticut, USA, 1952-58; Instructor, Pennsylvania State University, 1963-64; Assistant Professor, Department of Paediatrics, University of Washington School of Medicine, Seattle, 1964-71; Dean, School of Home Economics 1971-83, Professor, School of Nutrition & Home Economics 1983-, Acadia University, Nova Scotia, Canada. *Publications:* Various articles, periodic journals. *Memberships:* Canadian, & Nova Scotia Dietetic Associations; Canadian, & Kings County Diabetes Associations. *Honours:* Good Host Award, Canadian Dietetic Assocition, 1982; Award, Nova Scotia Dietetic Association, 1986. *Hobbies:* Golf; Fishing; Oil painting; Curling; Carpentry. *Address:* 1033 Old Farm Lane, New Minas, Nova Scotia, Canada B4N 4L5.

CAMPOS Anisia, Concert Pianist and Pedagogue. *Education:* Graduate, Ecole Normale de Musique de Paris; Mozarteum Academy of Music, Salzburg; Studied with Reine Gianoli and K Leimer; Received advice from Alfred Cortot and Claudio Arrau. *Appointments:* Full Professor, State Conservatory of Music, Montreal, Canada; Master Classes and Lectures, Ecole Superieure de Musique Vincent-D'Indy of Montreal; International Summer Courses, Orford Arts Center (Jeunesses Musicales du Canada) and University of Ottawa. *Creative works:* Recitals and soloist with Orchestra in Europe, Canada and South America. Radio and TV Broadcasts in Brazil, Portugal, Canada, Romania. *Memberships:* President, Co-Founder, Enesco Foundation, Canada; Member of the Jury, Ecole Normale de Musique de Paris. *Honours:* French Government Grant; Austrian Government Grant. *Hobbies:* Gardening; Photography; Backgammon. *Address:* 632 Avenue Herve-Beaudry, Laval, Quebec, H7E 2X6, Canada.

CANDRIS Laura A., b. 5 Apr. 1955, Frankfort, Kentucky, USA. Attorney. m. Aris S. Candris, 22 Dec. 1974. *Education:* BA, Distinction & Departmental Honours, Transylvania University, Kentucky, 1975; JD, University of Pittsburgh School of Law, 1978; Holland Law Centre, University of Florida, Gainesville, 1977-78. *Appointments:* Associate: Coffman, Coleman, Andrews & Grogan PA, Jacksonville, Florida 1978-80; Alder, Cohen & Griesby, Pittsburgh 1981-85; Associate 1985-86, Partner 1987-, Eckert, Seamans, Cherin & Mellott, Pittsburgh. *Publications:* Law articles, Hocpital Law Newsletter. *Memberships:* Labour & Litigation Sections, Member of the Equal Employment Opportunity Law Committee of the Labor Law Section, American Bar Association; Labour & Litigation Sections, Pennsylvania Bar Association; Member, Continuing Legal Education Committee; Labour and Litigation Sections and Civil Rights and Continuing Legal Education Committees, Allegheny County Bar Association; Florida Bar; National Health Lawyers Association; Society of Hospital Attorneys, Western PA; Pittsburgh Personnel Association. *Honours:* Outstanding Young Woman of America, 1984; Certificate of Merit, Labour Section, Florida Bar, 1980; Kentucky Colonel, 1974; National Merit Foundation Scholar, 1973. *Hobbies:* Council Member, O'Hara Township, Pennsylvania, 1986-89; Member, O'Hara Township Planning Commission, 1990-; Cycling; Alpine Skiing; Travel. *Address:* c/o Eckert, Seamans, Cherin & Mellott, 600 Grant Street, 42nd Floor, Pittsburgh, Pennsylvania 15219, USA.

CANNAVA Lucille Casey, b. 30 Dec. 1929, Brooklyn, New York, USA. Alcoholism Specialist. m. Robert E Cannava, 11 Nov. 1950. 2 sons, 2 daughters. *Education:* A, Burlington College, 1948; AB College of Notre Dame, 1950; Rutgers Centre of Alcohol Studies, 1972. *Appointments:* Medical Assistant, 1963-70; Alcoholism Counsellor, New Jersey Community Action, 1970-72; Supervising Counsellor, US Department of Army, Ft Dix,

New Jersey, 1972-74; Administrator, Burlington County Alcoholism Programme, 1974-84; Programme Specialist, New Jersey Department of Health, Division of Alcoholism, 1985-. *Memberships:* South New Jersey Health Systems Agency, Board Directors, 1977-79; Comprehensive Alcohol Recovery Programme, President, 1980-84; New Jersey Task Force, Women and Alcohol, 1978; New Jersey Association of Alcoholism Counsellors, President, 1985-. *Honours:* Outstanding Achievement Award, US Department of Army, 1974; YWCA Leadership Award, 1980; Woman of the Year, New Jersey Women and Alcohol Association, 1981; Chairperson Emeritus, NJ Alcoholism Counsellor Certification Board, 1977-. *Hobbies:* Horticulture; Aerobics. *Address:* 8 Pinecrest Court, Deptford, NJ 08096, USA.

CANNON Barbara, b. 10 July 1946, Wallasey, England. Professor. m. Jan Nedergaard, 10 Mar. 1979. 2 sons. *Education:* BSc, biochemistry, London University, 1967; PhD, physiology 1971, Docent (DSc) physiology 1974, Stockholm University, Sweden. *Appointments:* Research Assistant 1967-73, Research Associate 1974-80, Reader in Physiology 1980-83, Professor in Physiology 1983-; Director, Wenner-Gren Institute 1985-92, Chairman and Dean, Faculty of Biological and Earth Sciences 1984-90, Stockholm University; Post-doctoral fellow, National Research Council of Canada, Ottawa, Canada, 1974. *Publications:* Some 100 research papers and review articles on mammalian heat production, energy turnover and brown adipose tissue. *Memberships:* British, Swedish Biochemical Societies; Scandinavian Physiological Society. *Honour:* Elected to, Royal Swedish Academy of Sciences, 1989. *Address:* The Wenner-Gren Institute, The Arrhenius Laboratories F3, University of Stockholm, S-10691 Stockholm, Sweden.

CANNON Davita Louise, b. 17 Mar. 1949, Jersey City, New Jersey, USA. Owner, Cannon Clues; Word Processing Specialist/Trainer. *Education:* BS, Marketing Management, St Peter's College, 1973; Advanced Diploma, Advanced Management Programme, NYU Graduate School of Business, UBAC Division, 1983. *Appointments:* Executive Secretary/ Admin. Assistant, Office Force, 1978-84; Dicta. Secretary, J M Fields, 1978; Word Processing Specialist/Trainer, 1985-; Principal Owner, Cannon Clues, 1981-. *Publication:* Unpublished song: Paradise is Where You Are, 1968. *Memberships:* Concerned Community Women of Jersey City, Inc; Board of Directors, Bayonne Youth Center; National Board of Advisors, American Biographical Institute; Board of Directors, New Jersey Development Authority; Council Member, Governor's Advisory Council on Minority Business Development; National Policital Congress of Black Women. *Honours:* Woman of Achievement, Jersey Journal, 1985; Mary McLeod Bethune Achievement Award, 1984; The Com-Bi-Na-tions; VIP Award, Concerned Community Women of Jersey City, Inc, 1984; Salute to Black Businesses, Roselle Branch, NAACP, 1984; Outstanding Young Women of America, 1982. *Hobbies:* Photography; Songwriting; Lecturing; Collecting Keychains; Reading. *Address:* 528 Avenue A-5, Bayonne, NJ 07002, USA.

CANOVA-DAVIS Eleanor, b. 18 Jan. 1938, San Francisco, California, USA. Protein Biochemist; Scientist. m. Kenneth Roy Davis, 10 Feb. 1957, 2 sons. *Education:* BA 1968, MS 1971, Chemistry, San Francisco State University; PhD, Biochemistry, University of California, San Francisco, (UCSF) 1977. *Appointments:* Laboratory assistant, San Francisco State University, 1969-71; Research assistant (UCSF) 1972-77, NIH postdoctoral fellow 1977-80, University of California, Berkeley (UCSF); Assistant research biochemist, Anaesthesiology, Veterans Administration Medical Centre, UCB, 1980-84; Senior Scientist, Liposome Technology Inc, 1984-85; Scientist, Genentech Inc, 1985-. *Publications:* Author, co-author, numerous research papers & abstracts, professional journals. *Memberships:* American Chemical Society; Past President, California Scholarship Federation.

Honours: Awards & grants: National Institute of Arthritis, Metabolism & Digestive Diseases, 1977-80; Technischen Hochschule, Aachen, West Germany, 1979; Chancellor's Patent Fund 1976, Earl C. Anthony Trust 1975, Graduate Division Fellowship 1972-73, University of California, San Francisco, Honours Convocation, Department of Chemistry 1966, San Francisco State University. *Hobbies:* Reading fiction, historical novels, scientific articles; Collecting stamps & coins; Sewing & knitting; Playing bridge, Trivial Pursuit. *Address:* c/o Genentech Inc, 460 Point San Bruno Boulevard, South San Francisco, CA 94080, USA.

CANTIN HOOPER Carol, b. 5 Nov. 1959, Sanford, Maine, USA. Exercise Physiologist/Fitness Trainer. m. James William Hooper, 3 Oct. 1987. *Education:* BSc, Physical Education, University of Maine, 1982; MSc, Cardiovascular Health/Exercise, Northeastern University, Boston, 1986. *Appointments:* Research Assistant, Human Performance Center, University of Maine, 1979-82; Cardiac Rehabilitation Internship, The Health Institute, Methodist Hospital, 1982; Assistant Director, YMCA, Physical, Health and Wellness Center, 1982-83; Coordinator, Health/Fitness Corporate Program, Polaroid Corporation, 1984-85; Graduate Teaching Assistantship, Northeastern University, 1983-85; Exercise Physiologist, Cardiac Rehabilitation, New England Rehabilitation Hospital, 1986; Exercise Physiologist, Le Pli Health and Spa Club, 1986-88; Fitness Consultant, 1987-. *Publication:* Thesis: The Prediction of body density of middle-age male marathoners, 1986. *Memberships:* American College of Sports Medicine; International Dance and Exercise Association. *Honours:* Invitation for presentation of Aerobic Games, American College of Sports Medicine; Exercise Specialist Certification, Northeastern University, 1987 and 1988. *Hobbies:* Running; Skiing; Tennis; Golf; Racquetball; Swimming; Dance. *Address:* 1055 Southern Artery No 707, Quincy, MA 02169, USA.

CAPLAN Paula Joan, b. 7 July 1947. Psychologist. *Education:* AB, Radcliffe College, 1969; MA, 1971, PhD, 1973, Duke University. *Appointments:* Various hospitals & institutes, 1974-80; Assistant Professor, 1980-81, Associate Professor, 1982-87, Professor, 1987-, Ontario Institute for Studies in Education. *Publications:* Don't Blame Mother: Mending the Mother-Daughter Relationship, 1989; The Myth of Women's Masochism, 1985; Between Women: Lowering the Barriers, 1981; Children's Learning and Attention Problems, 1979; numerous articles in professional journals. *Memberships Include:* Feminist Therapy Institute; Canadian Mental Health Association's Women and Mental Health Committee, 1986; Fellow, American Orthopsychiatric Association; Fellow, Canadian Psychological Association; many other professional organisations. *Address:* Dept. of Applied Psychology, Ontario Institute for Studies in Education, 252 Bloor Street West, Toronto, Ontario M5S 1V6, Canada.

CAPLIN Barbara Ellen, b. 1 May 1954, Framingham, Massachusetts. USA. Bookkeeper; Accountant; Dancer. *Education:* AS, Early Childhood Assistant, Massachusetts Bay Community College, BS, Early Childhood Education, Boston State College, 1977. *Appointments:* Student teaching, Jonathan Maynard School, Framingham, Massachusetts, 1977; Keypunch Operator, Assessor's Officer, Framingham, 1979; Enumerator-Clerk, US Census, 1980; Bookkeeper, Sam & Frances Caplin, 1980-; Dancer, 1982-. *Memberships:* National Association of Female Executives; International Tap Association; American Film Institute; National Association of Unknown Players; Humane Society; World Wildlife Federation; Doris Day Animal League. *Honour:* Dean's List, Boston State College, 1974. *Hobbies:* Entering contests and sweepstakes. *Address:* 26 McAdams Road, Framingham, MA 01701, USA.

CAPODILUPO Elizabeth Jeanne Hatton, b. 3 May 1940, McRae, Georgia, USA. Public Relations Executive. m. Raphael S. Capodilupo, 21 Jan. 1967. *Appointments Include:* Secretary, 1958-59; Receptionist, 1960-69; Clerk, Woodlawn Cemetery, Bronx, 1969-71, Historian,

Community Affairs Co-ordinator, 1971-, Editor, Woodlawn Cemetery News, 1979-, Assistant to President, 1984. *Memberships:* Various professional organisations including: President, Bronx Council on the Arts, 1987-89; Secretary, Bronx Chamber of Commerce, 1989. *Honours Include:* Outstanding Cemeterian award, 1987-88; Honorary Grand Marshall Columbus Day Parade, 1987-88; Grand Marshall Memorial Day Parade, 1989; Community Service Award Italian Heritage and Culture Committee. *Address:* 371 Scarsdale Road, Crestwood, New York 10707. USA.

CAPPELLO Eve, b. 4 Dec. 1922, Sydney, Australia. International Business Consultant; Employee Training Specialist. 1 son, 1 daughter. *Education:* AA French, Santa Monica CC, 1972; BA Art History, CSU, Dominguez Hills, 1974; MA Psychology 1977, PhD Psychology 1978, Pacific Western University. *Appointments:* Singer/pianist, Los Angeles Hotels, Clubs and Cruise ships, 1958-76; International Keynote Speaker; Private Practice Director/Founder ACT Institute; Instructor, Loyola Marymount University; Instructor, West Los Angeles CC, 1976-. *Publications:* Act Don't React (3rd edition), 1988; The New Professional Touch (2nd edition), 1988; Let's Get Growing, 1979; Game of The Name; Newspaper column, Behavior & You, 1977-81; Articles to magazines and newspapers. *Memberships:* Century City Chamber of Commerce; 1st President, Founder & Chairman of the Board, Women's International Network; Past 1st Vice President, Business & Professional Women; Past President, Leads Professional Business Women; Associate for Advancement of Behavior Therapy; International Platform Association. *Honours:* Lifetime membership, Alpha Gamma Honor Society; Century City Woman of Achievement, 1988; Lawrence Welk Scholarship for proficiency in French, SMCC, 1972; Coordinator of 1st Women's Entrepreneurial conference, Australia, 1986; Invited to address World Congress of Behavior Therapy, Israel, 1980; University of Melbourne, Australia, 1985. *Hobbies:* Travel; Art; Reading; Writing; Music. *Address:* 10600 Eastborne Avenue, No 16 Los Angeles, CA 90024, USA.

CAPRA Louise Antoinette, b. 4 July 1948, Paterson, New Jersey, USA. Teacher. *Education:* BA, General Elementary, Paterson State College, 1969; Sp Ed 1976, MA Ed Admin, 1979, William Paterson College; NJ Permanent Teaching Certificate 1969; Learning Disabilities Teacher Consultant, 1976; Supervisor, Principal, Supervisor, 1979. *Appointments:* Teacher, Grades 6-8, Maths Science, Social Studies, Language Arts, Health, Reading, Learning Disabilities, Paterson Board of Education, 1969-. *Publications:* Research: The Effects of Programmed Instructional Materials on Reading and Mathematics Achievement Test Scores; The Research and Administration of a Complete Reading Program from Pre-school to Adult Education; Bilingual Education. *Memberships:* New Jersey Education Association; WPC Alumni Association; WPC Club; Beta Chi Chapter of Pi Lambda Theta, Kappa Delta Pi. *Honours:* Perfect Attendance Awards, 1969-89; Undergraduate Four Year State Scholarship, 1965-69; Graduated cum laude, 1969. *Hobbies:* Dancing; Reading; Crossword puzzle enthusiast; Learning to bowl; Shopping. *Address:* 477 Totowa Road, Totowa Boro, New Jersey 07512, USA.

CARAPICO Sheila, b. 24 July 1951, Bridgeport, Connecticut, USA. College Professor, Political Science. *Education:* BA, 1973; MA 1976; PhD, 1984. *Appointments:* Social Sciences Tutor, Empire State College, 1976-77; Instructor, Wilkes College, 1981-84; Faculty, School for Int Training, 1984-85; Assistant Professor, University of Richmond, Virginia, 1985-. *Publications:* Autonomy & Secondhand Oil Dependency of the Yemen Arab Republic; Yemeni Agriculture in Transition; Self-Help and development Planning in the Yemen Arab Republic; Yemeni Agriculture and Economic Change: Case Studies of two Highland Regions, co-author R Tutwiler. *Memberships:* American Institute for Yemeni Studies, President; Middle East Studies Association of North America; American

Professors for Peace in the Middle East; Board of Directors, Richmond Peace Education Center. *Honours:* Research Award, Center for Study of Philanthropy, City University of NY, 1989; Faculty Summer Fellowship 1987, Faculty Field Research Grant 1986, University of Richmond; NEH Summer Seminar Participant, 1985; Field Research Grant, Cornell University, 1982; Co-Principal researcher, American Institute for Yemeni Studies, 1980-; Dissertation grant, Department of Political Science, SUNY, 1977. *Hobbies:* Homemaking; Gardening; Water sports. *Address:* Department of Political Science, University of Richmond, VA 23173, USA.

CARBONNEL Katrina Vanderlip de, b. 9 May, 1952, Los Angeles, USA. Art Conservator. m. Charles Eric de Carbonnel, 4 Aug. 1979. 1 son, 1 daughter. *Education:* BFA, Cornell University, USA, 1974; Certificate in Art Conservation, Harvard University Fogg Art Museum, 1977. *Appointments:* Painting & Textile Conservation at: Los Angeles County Museum of Art, 1977; Boston Museum of Fine Arts, 1978; Service de la Restauration des Peintures des Musees Nationeaux, Musee du Louvre, Paris, France, 1977-79; Corcoran Gallery of Art, 1979-83; Textile Museum, Washington DC, USA, 1980-81; Director, Carbonnel Faience, Desures, France. *Memberships:* American Institute for Conservation; International Institute for Conservation; Friends of French Arts, Vice President. *Address:* 79 Chemin des Princes, 1244 Coulex, Switzerland.

CARD Claudia Falconer, b. 30 Sept. 1940, Madison, Wisconsin, USA. Professor; Author; Lecturer. *Education:* BA, Philosophy, University of Wisconsin, 1962; AM, 1964, PhD, 1969, Philosophy, Harvard University. *Appointments:* Instructor, 1966-69, Assistant Professor, 1969-72, Associate Professor, 1972-84, Professor, 1984-, University of Wisconsin, Madison; Visiting Associate Professor, Dartmouth College, 1978-79, University of Pittsburgh, 1980. *Publications:* Editor, with R. Ammerman, Religious Commitment & Salvation: Essays in Secular and Theistic Religion, 1974; articles in: The Philosophical Review, American Philosophical Quarterly, Ethics, Journal of Social Philosophy, Canadian Journal of Philosophy, etc. *Memberships:* American Philosophical Association; Society of Women in Philosophy; Hastings Centre; National Women's Studies Association. *Honours:* NEH Fellowship, 1974-75; Woodrow Wilson Fellowships, 1962-63, 1965-66; Harvard University Fellowships, 1963-64, 1964-65; Phi Beta Kappa; Phi Kappa Phi; etc. *Hobbies:* Classical Piano; T'ai Chi; Feminist Politics. *Address:* Department of Philosophy, 600 N. Park St., Madison, WI 53706, USA.

CARDEA Jane Mannweiler, b. 8 Nov. 1943, Williamsport, Pennsylvania, USA. Nurse Educator. m. George Cardea, 27 Dec. 1965, 1 son, 1 daughter. *Education:* BSN, University of Colorado, 1965; MA, Chapman College, 1978; PhD, Texas Tech University, 1983; MSU, University of Arizona, 1985. *Appointments:* Antelope Valley Medical Centre, 1979-80; Methodist Hospital School of Nursing, 1980-82; Texas Tech University, 1981-82; University of Arizona, 1984-87; Director of Graduate Nursing, Azusa Pacific University, 1988-. *Creative work includes:* Various articles, research interest re: community maintenance of chronically mentally ill; Dissertation, friendship & social network characteristics of young adults. *Memberships:* American Nurses Association; Board, Arizona Nurses Association; American Association of Marital & Family Therapists; World Federation of Mental Health; National Council on Family Relations; Groves Conference on Marriage & Family. *Honours:* Elected, Sigma Theta Tau, & Sigma Xi, 1986; Outstanding contribution award, Arizona Nurses' Association, 1987; Biographical recognition. *Hobbies:* Crewel Embroidery; Skiing; Gardening. *Address:* School of Nursing, Azusa Pacific University, 921 E Alosta, Azusa, California 91702, USA.

CARDWELL (Margaret) Thelma, b. 19 July 1920, Toronto, Canada. Occupational Therapist. *Education:* Diploma, Occupational Therapy, University of Toronto. *Appointments:* Staff Occupational Therapist, Ontario

Hospital, 1943-44; Lieutenant (OT), Royal Canadian Army Medical Corps, UK, 1944-45; Instructor 1945-47, lecturer 1951-72, Assistant Professor 1972-74, Associate Professor & Assistant Director 1974-80, Associate Professor & Acting Director 1980-83, Occupational Therapy Department, University of Toronto; Sole Occupational Therapist, St John's Convalescent Hospital, Toronto, 1947-48; Charge Occupational Therapist, Dalmeny Hospital, Toronto, 1948-51. *Memberships:* Past president, various offices, Canadian Association of Occupational Therapists (CAOT), & World Federation of Occupational Therapists (WFOT); Founder 1983-, past Vice President, Canadian Occupational Therapy Foundation (COTF). *Honours:* Honorary Doctor of Laws, Dalhousie University, 1985; Founding membership, COTF, 1983; Life membership, Ontario Society of Occupational Therapists, 1983; Queen's Silver Jubilee Medal, 1977; Honorary fellowship, WFOT 1972, life membership, CAOT 1969. *Hobbies:* Travel; Art. *Address:* 12 Sheppard Square, Willowdale, Ontario, Canada M2K 1A1.

CAREY Cynthia, b. 17 July 1947, Denver, Colorado, USA. Professor. *Education:* AB, 1969, MA, 1970, Occidental College; PhD, University of Michigan, 1976. *Appointments:* Department of EPO Biology, University of Colorado, Boulder, 1976-. *Publications:* 35 contributions to physiological, ornithological and herpetological journals. *Memberships:* American Association for the Advancement of Science; American Society of Zoologists; American Physiological Society; American Ornithologists Union; Board of Directors, Cooper Ornithological Society; American Society of Ichthyologists and Herpetologists; Sigma Xi. *Honours:* American Association for the Advancement of Science Fellow, 1981; Elective Member, American Ornithologists Union, 1981; Teaching Recognition Award, University of Colorado, 1983. *Hobbies:* Mountain and rock climbing; Bicycle touring; Skiing. *Address:* Department of EPO Biology, University of Colorado, Boulder, CO 80309, USA.

CAREY Ernestine Gilbreth, b. 5 Apr. 1908, New York City, USA. Author; Lecturer. m. Charles Everett Carey, 13 Sept. 1930, 1 son, 1 daughter. *Education:* BA, Smith College, 1929. *Appointments:* Buyer, R. H. Macy & Company Inc, NYC 1930-44, James McCreery 1947-49. *Publications include:* Books: Cheaper by the Dozen, with Frank B Gilbreth Jr, 1949; Belles on Their Toes with Frank B Gilbreth Jr, 1951; Jumping Jupiter, 1952; Rings Around Us, 1956; Giddy Moment, 1958; Also; Magazine articles, lectures, book reviews, syndicated newspaper articles. *Memberships:* PEN; Past Council, Life Member, Authors Guild of America; Board, Right to Read Inc; Lay Adviser, Manhasset Board of Education, NY; Past Trustee, Manhasset Public Library, Smith College; Various college associations. *Honours:* Co-recipient, Prix Scarron, French International Award (humour) 1951, McElligott Medallion, Association of Marquette University Women 1966; Recipient, Montgomery Award, Friends of Phoenix Public Library, 1981. *Address:* 6148 East Lincoln Drive, Pardise Valley, Arizona 85253, USA.

CAREY Kathryn Myatt, b. 16 Mar. 1946, Alameda, California, USA. Conservator of works of Art on Paper; Teacher. *Education:* BAT, Seattle University, 1969; Harvard University, 1977; Studies, various Universities including University of London, England, 1987-89. *Appointments:* Director of Art, John Howell Books, 1970-73; Intern, Boston Museum of Fine Arts, 1974-76; Conservator, Isabella Stewart Gardner Museum, 1976-78; Director of Records Preservation, Supreme Judicial Court, 1979-84; Conservator, Society for the Preservation of New England Antiquaties, 1984-88; Paper Conservator, Boston College, 1988. *Memberships:* International Institute for Conservation; American Institution for Conservation of Historic & Artistic Works; American Association of Museums; Board of Directors, New England Conservation Association, Founding Member; American Chemical Society. *Honour:* Samuel H. Kress Foundation Fellowship, 1988, 1989, 1990. *Hobbies:* Performer of 19th Century Historic Dance. *Address:* 24 Emery Street, Medford, MA 02155, USA.

CAREY Margaret J. Standish, b. 28 Nov. 1926, Albany, USA. Writer; Publisher. m. Robert E. Carey, 3 Sept. 1949, 1 son, 1 daughter. *Appointments:* Advertising Dept., Albany, Oregon Democrat-Herald, 1947-48, Corvallis, Oregon Gazette-Times, 1949-50; News Correspondent, Brownsville, Oregon Times, 1958-82; Historical Past Times Column, 1976-87; Partner, Calapoola Publications, Brownsville, 1976-. *Publications:* Brownsville: Linn County's Oldest Town, 1976; Halsey: Linn County's Centennial City, 1977; Shedd: Linn County's Early Dairy Center, 1978; Sweet Home in the Oregon Cascades, 1979; Indian Lize: Last of the Calapooias, in Anthology, Daughters of the Land, 1988. *Memberships:* President, Linn County Historical Society; Oregon Historical Society; Chair Person, Linn County Historical Museum Advisor Commission; Western Writers of America; etc. *Hobbies:* Music; History. *Address:* 32865 Lake Creek Drive, Halsey, OR 97348, USA.

CARIC Helen Lora, b. 1 Jan. 1939, Yugoslavia. m. (1) Ernest, 14 Dec. 1959, divorced 1971, 1 son, 1 daughter, (2) Caric, 3 Nov 1973, divorced 1981, 1 son. *Appointmens:* various Positions 1956-66; Showroom Sales Manager, Import-Export Co., 1968-72; Travel Representative, 1972; Owner, Walter's Bake Shop, 1973-79; Sales Lady, Bond's Clothing, 1979; Nurse's Aide, Hillside Manor, 1980; Clerical Worker, 1979-81, Molloy College, 1980-81, Long Island University, 1981-82; Chiropractor Assistant, 1982; Bakery-Restaurant Owner, Linden Motel, 1983-; Vice President, Universal Centre of New Age Consciousness Inc., 1985-89; Sales, Abatelli Realty, 1988; Chairperson, Republican National Hispanic Assembly for Orange County, New York. *Memberships:* International Consultants Exchange; Universal Spiritualist Association; Warwick Art League. *Hobbies:* Oil Painting; Piano; Guitar; Dancing. *Address:* PO Box 954 Linden Motel, Linden Court, Greenwood Lake, NY 10925, USA.

CARICO Margie Helton, b. 18 June 1938, Benham, USA. Principal. m. Billy Stevenson Carico, 17 Dec. 1960, divorced 1981, 1 son, 2 daughters. *Education:* BS, 1960, MS, 1964, MS45, 1976, Ed.D., 1985, University of Tennessee, Knoxville. *Appointments:* Speech Therapist, Oak Ridge, 1960-61; Teacher, Tennessee School for the Deaf, 1961-67; Special Education Teacher, 1973-83, Vision Consultant, 1983-86, Principal, 1986-, Maryville. *Publications:* Articles in journals & magazines. *Memberships Include:* Local, State, National Professional Education organizations; National Association for Elementary School Principals; Phi Delta Kappa; Delta Kappa Gamma. *Honours:* Delta Kappa Gamma Scholarship, 1980; Graduated, summa cum laude, University of Tennessee, 1985. *Hobbies:* Stained Glass; Knitting; Harpist; Skiing; Aerobics. *Address:* 2802 Wildwood Rd, Maryville, TN 37801, USA.

CARLISLE Patricia Ann Howes-Davis, b. 20 Jan. 1943, Flint, Michigan, USA Educational Administrator. m. John C. Carlisle, 8 Apr. 1967, 2 daughters. *Education:* BS, Central Michigan University, 1965; MA, Michigan State Universiy, 1969. *Appointments:* Research Assistant, 1964-65; Assistant Instructor, 1963-66, Counsellor, 1966-72, Oakland Community College; Purdue University Calumet, 1973-82; Acting Director, Non-Credit Continuing Education, Purdue University, 1982-84; Director, Student Support Services, Purdue University, Indiana, 1984-. *Memberships:* American Association for Affirmative Action; American Association for Counselling & Development; American College Personnel Association; Indiana & Mid-American Associations of Educational Opportunity Programme Personnel. *Honours:* Phi Kappa Phi, 1965; Kappa Delta Pi, 1965; Award, Creative Programming for Women, 1988. *Hobbies Include:* Reading; Family; Gardening. *Address:* Purdue University North Central, 1401 S U.S 421, Westville, IN 46410, USA.

CARLL Elizabeth K, b. 4 May 1950, Budapest, Hungary. Psychologist. m. Alan A Carll, 17 June 1972. *Education:* BA Psychology, 1972; MA Psychology, 1976; PhD Psychology, 1978; Fellow and Diplomate, American Board of Medical Psychotherapy, 1988. *Appointments:* Psychologist, Private Practice, Huntington & Centerport, New York, 1979-; Kings Park School District, 1979-, Adjunct Faculty, Hofstra University, N.Y.; District Psychologist, 1981-86, Chief Psychologist, 1986-. *Memberships:* American Psychological Association; New York State Psychological Association; Suffolk County Psychological Association, Executive Board Member; Eastern Psychological Association; National Register of Health Service Providers in Psychology; Nassan County Psychological Association; American Association for Advancement of Psychology. *Address:* 4 Bittersweet Ct, Centerport, New York 11721, USA.

CARLSEN Laurie Beth, b. 10 Feb. 1961, Milton, Massachusetts, USA. Administrator. *Education:* BSc, University of Rhode Island, 1982. *Appointments:* Regional Office Administrator 1982-85, National Conference Coordinator 1985-87, Manager, Trade Shows & Conferences 1987-88, Director, Trade Shows & Conferences 1988, Director, Associate Market Manager 1989-, Fidelity Investments, Boston. *Memberships:* International Exhibition Association; Meeting Planners International. *Hobbies:* Golf; Skiing; Travel. *Address:* 12 Greenough Lane, Boston, Massachusetts 02113, USA.

CARLSON Cynthia Joanne, b. 15 Apr. 1942, Chicago, Illinois, USA. Artist; Professor. m. Mitchell Rosen, 6 June 1979. *Education:* BFA, 1965; MFA, Pratt Institute, 1967. *Appointments:* Philadelphia Colleges of the Arts, 1967-87; Queens College, CUNY, Flushing, 1987-. *Creative Works:* Solo Exhibitions: Milwaukee Art Museum, 1982; Pam Adler Gallery, New York, 1983; Albright Knox Art Gallery, Buffalo, 1985; School 33 Art Center, Baltimore, 1987. *Membership:* College Art Association, Board, 1984-88. *Honours:* NEA, 1975, 1978, 1980, 1987; Creative Artist Public Service Grant, 1978; Faculty, Venture Fund Grants, 1983, 1986; MacDowell Colony Resident. *Address:* 139 West 19th Street 4NE, New York, NY 10011, USA.

CARLSON Jane Elizabeth, b. 19 Nov. 1918, Hartford, USA. Concert Pianist; Teacher. *Education:* BMus., Shenandoah Conservatory of Music, 1940; Professional Diploma, Juilliard Graduate School, 1946. *Appointments:* As Pianist: Assistant to Carl Friedberg, Juilliard Summer School, 1947-52; Faculty, Juilliard Preparatory Division, 1946-, College Division, 2 Piano Ens. 1962-, Piano Ped. 1965-; many summer schools. *Publications:* Recordings with MGM, Odeon & Musical Heritage of Paul Hindemith's Ludus Tonalis. *Membership:* Treasurer, Carl Friedberg Alumni Association, 1951-52. *Honours:* Naumburg Foundation Award, 1947; Honorary PhD, Shenandoah Conservatory of Music, 1982. *Hobbies:* Photography; Crossword Puzzles. *Address:* 257 West 86th St., New York, NY 10024, USA.

CARLSON Loraine Belle, b. 6 May 1923, Los Angeles, California, USA. Writer. m. Neil Walter Carlson, 31 Dec. 1958. *Education:* BA, History and Education, University of Redlands, California, 1944; Study in Physics, University of Southern California, 1950-53. *Appointments:* Technical Writer for Hughes Aircraft Company, Space Technology Laboratories (TRW) and as independent contractor. *Publications:* Mexico: An Extraordinary Guide, 1971; The TraveLeer Guide to Mexico City, 1978, 1981; The TraveLeer Guide to Yucatan and Guatemala, 1980; The TraveLeer Guide to Yucatan, 1982. *Address:* 2021 West Homer Street, Chicago, IL 60647, USA.

CARLSON M Susan, b. 2 Nov. 1949, Lincoln, Nebraska, USA. Law Professor. m. Gerald Phillip Greiman, 2 May 1982. 1 son, 1 daughter. *Education:* AA, Cottey College, Nevada, 1970; BFA, University of Nebraska, Lincoln, 1972; Notre Dame in Japan, Tokyo, Japan, 1974; JD, University of Nebraska College of Law, Lincoln, 1976. *Appointments:* Staff Law Clerk, US Court of Appeals for the Eighth Circuit, 1976-78; Associate, Kilcullen, Smith & Heenan, Washington, 1978-79; Trial Attorney, Civil Div, US Dept of Justice, Washington, 1980-86; Trial Attorney, Lands Div, US Dept of Justice, Guam, 1981; Visiting Assistant Professor, Washington University School of Law, St Louis, 1987-. *Memberships:* NOW, NARAL, ABA, Nebraska, DC and Missouri Bar Associations. *Hobbies:* Scuba Diving; Painting. *Address:* Washington University School of Law, Box 1120 One Brookings Drive, St Louis, MO 63130, USA.

CARLSON Margaret, b. 7 Feb. 1951, Salt Lake City, Utah, USA. Dancer; Arts Administrator; Choreographer. m. John Joseph Braham IV, 21 Aug. 1983. *Education:* BA Social Services 1974, MEd, Curriculum and Instruction 1985, Cleveland State University; Schools of Cleveland Ballet, San Francisco Ballet and Harkness House. *Appointments:* Two episodes, Jackie Gleason's for the Stars, 1968; Teacher and Dancer, Karamu Dancers, 1969-74; Teacher, principal dancer, regisseur, Cleveland Ballet, 1972-; The American Ballet Company, 1979; Second City TV, 2 episodes, 1979; Head, Dance Department, University of Akron, 1985-. *Creative works:* Musical Theatre with Kenley Players and the Muny Light Opera, Circuits; The Merry Widow; Sweet Charity; Mame; Hello Dolly; Ballroom; Brigadoon; How to Succeed in Business Without Really Trying, 1974-79; Choreographed following operas for The Cleveland Opera: Daughter of the Regiment; Die Fleidermaus; Carmen; The Masked Ball; Faust; Rigoletto; The Marriage of Figaro; The Merry Widow; Hansel and Gretel; Falstaff, 1976-88; Choreographed following musicals for Kids on Broadway: HMS Pinafore; Pirates of Penzance; Oklahoma; Joseph and the Amazing Technicolor Dreamcoat, 1982-86; Video: Ballet's Beginning, produced and wrote script, 1988. *Memberships:* Secretary, Council of Dance Administrators (CODA); Nominating Committee, National Association of Schools of Dance (NASD); Actors Equity; Founding President, National Association of Female Executives (NAFE); The American College of Sports Medicine; American Alliance of Dance Artists (AADA); Board of Trustees, Dance Cleveland; Tom Evert Dance Company; Ohio Ballet; Cleveland Ballet Council; Shore Cultural Centre of Euclid. *Honours:* Mayor's appointment to Board, Shore Cultural Arts Centre of Euclid, 1988; Employee Recognition Award, University of Akron, 1987/88; Nominated, Euclid Senior High School Hall of Fame, 1986-87; Nominated, Outstanding Teacher of the Year, University of Akron, 1985-86. *Hobbies:* Scuba diving, Swimming. *Address:* 34 Church Street, Hudson, Ohio 44236, USA.

CARLTON Claudia Dowdy, b. 20 May 1955, Richmond, Virginia, USA. Independent Library Automation Consultant. m. James John Carlton, 28 June 1983. 1 stepdaughter. *Education:* BS, Art Education and Library Science, Longwood College, Virginia, 1976. *Appointments:* Librarian, Cumberland Co Schools, Virginia, 1976-79; Librarian, Goochland Co Schools, 1979-80; Media Specialist, Seminole Co Schools, Florida, 1980-81; Software Consultant, Follett Library Book Co, Crystal Lake, Illinois, 1981-83; Private Practice Library Automation Consultant, 1983-. *Memberships:* National Education Association; Virginia Education Association; Georgia Library/Media Directors; American Library Association; Florida Association of Instructional Materials. *Address:* P O Box 426, Howey-in-the-Hills, FL 32737, USA.

CARLTON Diane Michele, b. 26 Sept. 1950, Los Angeles, California, USA. Attorney; Judge. m. Greg Carlton, 12 Sept. 1969. 2 sons. *Education:* BA Spanish, 1972; BA Crim. Justice, 1972; JD, University of Denver, 1976. *Appointments:* Partner, Carlton & Jacobi, 1983-; Municipal Judge, Aurora, 1984-. *Memberships:* Colorado Bar Association; American Bar Association; Municipal Judges Association; Colorado Trial Lawyers Association; Criminal Defense Bar Association. *Honour:*

Valedictorian University of California, Irvine, 1972. *Hobbies:* Reading; Gardening; Hiking; Skiing. *Address:* 300 So Jackson, No 320, Denver, Colorado 80209, USA.

CARLTON Yvonne Annette, b. 23 May 1949, Minneapolis, Minnesota, USA. Contingency Planning Specialist. m. Donald D Carlton, 4 Mar. 1972. 1 daughter. *Education:* BS, St Cloud State University, 1971; MBA, College of St Thomas, 1987. *Appointments:* FBS Mortgage, 1978-81; Norwest Bank Mpls, 1981-84; Red Owl Foods, 1984-86; Norwest Technical Services, 1986-. *Memberships:* Minnesota Association of Contingency Planners (Secretary, 1987-); National Association Female Executives, 1985-. *Honour:* National Honor Society (1965-67). *Hobbies:* Needlework; Reading. *Address:* 4750 Oakview Ln, Plymouth, MN 55442, USA.

CARMEN Marilyn Elain (Aisha Eshe), b. 23 Nov. 1941, Harrisburg, Pennsylvania, USA. Writer; Administrator. divorced. 2 sons, 2 daughters. *Education:* AA, Harisburg Area Comm College, 1977; BS, Penn State, 1979; MA, Iowa State University, 1987I. *Appointments:* Teachers and Writers, New York, 1983-85; Iowa State Council of Arts, 1986-87; Research Assistant, Iowa State University, 1985-87; Administrator, La Salle University, 1988-. *Publications:* Blood at the Root, a novella; I Usta Be Afraid of the Night, poems; Images of What's Goin' On, poetry book; Poems published in numerous magazines. *Honours:* Hob-Nob, Honourable mention, Best in book, 1987; White Rock Poetry Journal, best in book, 1984; Focus poetry contest, Honourable mention, 1986. *Hobbies:* Horticulture; Reading. *Address:* 11803A Academy Road, Philadelphia, PA 19154, USA.

CARNEGY Elizabeth Patricia, Baroness Carnegy of Lour, b. 28 Apr. 1925, London, England. Working Peer. *Appointments include:* Cavendish Laboratory, Cambridge, 1943-46. Girl Guides Association, 1947-, including: County Commissioner, Angus, 1956-63; Training Adviser, Scotland 1958-62, Commonwealth HQ 1963-65; President for Scotland, 1979-89. Co-opted to Education Committee, Angus County Council, 1967-75. Councillor, Tayside Regional Council, 1974-82 including: Chairman, Recreation & Tourism Committee, 1974-76; Chairman, Education Committee, 1977-81. Chairman, Working Party on Professional Training for Community Education in Scotland, 1975-77; Commissioner, Manpower Services Commission, 1979-82; Chairman, MSC Committee for Scotland, 1981-83; Chairman, Scottish Community Education Council, 1981-88; Council, Open University, 1984-; Administrative Council, Royal Jubilee Trusts, 1985-88; Trustee, National Museum of Scotland, 1987-; Honorary President, Scottish Libraries Association, 1989-; Honorary Sheriff, 1969-84; Farmer. *Membership:* Fellow, Royal Society of Arts. *Honours:* Life Peer, 1982; Deputy Lieutenant, Angus, 1988. *Address:* Lour, Forfar, Angus DD8 2LR, Scotland.

CARNEY Deborah Leah Turner, b. 19 Aug. 1952, Great Bend, Kansas, USA. Attorney. m. Thomas J. Carney, 20 Mar. 1976, 1 son, 2 daughters. *Education:* BA, Human Biology, Stanford University, 1974; JD, Denver College of Law, 1976. *Appointments:* Shareholder, Employee, 1976-84, Of Counsel, 1984-, Turner & Boisseau, Chartered; Associate, Lutz & Oliver, 1984-85; Attorney, Deborah Turner Carney PC, Lakewood, Colorado, 1985-. *Publications:* Numerous articles for use of computers in trial; Past publisher, Apple Law Newsletter. *Memberships:* American Bar Association (Past Vice-President, Trial Tactics Committee); American Trial Lawyer Association; Kansas Bar Association; Colorado Bar Association; Phi Delta Phi; Denver Kiwanis Club. *Honours:* Recipient of Plaque of Appreciation for Seminar Presentation on Litigation in High Technology. *Hobbies:* Horses; Computers; Hiking; Science; Cooking. *Address:* Deborah Turner Carney PC, 12600 W Colfax Avenue, Suite C-400, Lakewood, CO 80215, USA.

CARON Leslie Clair Margaret, b. 1 July 1931, Boulogne-Billancourt, Paris, France. Dancer; Actress. m. (1) George Hormel. (2) Peter Reginald Frederick Hall, 1956, dissolved 1965, 1 son, 1 daughter. (3) Michael Laughlin, 1969. *Education:* Convent of the Assumption, Paris, France; Conservatoire de Danse; Ballet des Champs Elysees, 1947-50; Ballet de Paris, 1954. *Creative works:* Films include: An American in Paris; Man with a Cloak; Glory Alley; Story of Three Loves; Lili; Glass Slipper; Daddy Long Legs; Gaby; Gigi; The Doctor's Dilemma; The Man Who Understood Women; The Subterranean; Fanny; Guns of Darkness; The L-Shaped Room; Father Goose; A Very Special Favor; Promise Her Anything; Is Paris Burning?; Head of the Family; Madron; The Contract; The Unapproachable, 1982; Deathly Moves, 1983; Genie du Faux, 1984. Stage appearances: Paris; London; USA; Australia. *Publication:* Vengeance, 1983. *Address:* c/o James Fraser, Fraser & Dunlop, 91 Regent Street, London W1R 8RU, England.

CARPENTER Adelaide Trowbridge Clark, b. 24 June 1944, Athens, Georgia, USA. Professor of Biology. *Education:* BS Biology, NC State University, 1966; MS Genetics 1969, PhD Genetics 1972, University of Washington; Postdoctoral Cytogenetics, University of Wisconsin, 1972-74. *Appointments:* NIH Postdoctoral Fellow, University of Wisconsin, 1972-74; Adjunct Assistant Professor/Research Associate, Duke University, 1974-76; Assistant Professor 1976-79, Associate Professor 1979-85, Professor 1985-, University of California, San Diego. *Publications:* Author of numerous articles to professional journals, magazines and to conferences. *Memberships:* Associate Editor, Genetics; Board of Directors, Executive Committee, Genetics Society of America; Genetics Society of Canada; American Association for the Advancement of Science; American Society of Naturalists; Society of the Sigma Xi; American Society for Cell Biology; Gemetical Society (UK); Society for Developmental Biology; International Platform Association. *Honours:* Recipient of numerous grants. *Hobbies:* Backpacking; Skiing; Squash; Weaving; Music. *Address:* Department of Biology, B-022, University of CA, San Diego, La Jolla, CA 92093, USA.

CARPENTER Anna-Mary P, b. 14 Jan. 1916, Ambridge, Pennsylvania, USA. Professor of Pathology. *Education:* BA, Geneva College, 1936; MS 1937, PhD 1940, University of Pittsburgh; MD 1958, University of Minnesota; DSc, Geneva College, 1968. *Appointments:* Research Assistant, University of Pittsburgh, 1938-40; Instructor, Moravian College for Women, 1941-42; Chair Biology, Keystone College, 1942-44; Research Associate Pathology, University of Pittsburgh School of Medicine, 1945-53; Instructor to Professor, University of Minnesota School of Medicine, 1954-80; Professor Pathology, Indiana University, 1980-87. *Publication:* Color Atlas of Human Histology, 1958. *Memberships:* Sigma xi; Phi Sigma; Am Diabetes Association; International Society for Sterology, 1971-89; Histochemical Society, 1974-88; Society for Quantitative Morphology, Founder and President; AAAS; American Association Anatomists. *Honours:* Teaching Award, Indiana University School of Medicine, 1986; International Federation of Societies for Histochemistry and Cytology, Provers Award, 1988. *Hobbies:* Piano and organ; Porcelain painting; Needlework. *Address:* 6424 Hayes, Merrillville, IN 46410, USA.

CARPENTER Barbara, b. 17 Mar. 1943, New Orleans, Louisiana, USA. Assistant Director, Mississippi Humanities Council. m. Charles Harrell Weathersby, 18 Mar. 1972. *Education:* BA, Southeastern LA University, 1965; MA, University of Georgia, 1966; PhD, Tulane University, 1982. *Appointments:* Instructor in English, Southeaster LA University, 1966-69; Teaching Assistant, Tulane University, 1970-72; Assistant Professor, St Joseph Seminary College, 1972-76; Assistant Professor, University of Southern Mississippi, 1980-86; Assistant Director, Mississippi Humanities Council, 1986-; Partner, WordWorks Consultants.

Memberships: Mississippi Folklife Council, Co-chair; Modern Language Association; South Atlantic Modern Language Association; Mississippi Philological Society; Phi Delta Kappa, 1990; Mississippi Historical Society. *Honours:* Woodrow Wilson Fellow, 1965; Phi Kappa Phi, 1965; University Fellow, Tulane, 1969. *Address:* P O Box 16651, Jackson, MS 39236, USA.

CARPENTER Vicki J, b. 8 Mar. 1957, Evanston, Illinois, USA. Journalist; Writer. m. 27 Aug. 1983. *Education:* BA French Literature, University of Illinois, 1979; MA Coursework, University of Missouri, 1980-83. *Appointments:* Correspondent, Croin Publications, Chicago, South-North News Service, 1983-; Stringer Washington Post, London Guardian, 1988-. *Publications:* Series of published articles in various magazines, newspapers, trade and company publications. *Memberships:* Life Member, Pi Delta Phi, French Honorary and University of Illinois Alumni Association; Society of Professional Journalists (SPJ); Sigma Delta Chi, 1983-86; American Association of Chile, 1983-. *Honours:* Illinois State Scholar, 1975; Dean's List, American College of Switzerland, 1977; Dean's List, University of Illinois, 1979; Inter American Press Association Scholarship, 1983. *Hobbies:* Reading; Writing; Painting; Photography; Tennis; Skiing; Swimming; Horseback Riding; Films; Travel. *Address:* Tobago 1355, Las Condes, Santiago, Chile.

CARPENTER-MASON Beverly Nadine, b. 23 May 1933, Pittsburgh, Pennsylvania, USA. Executive Health Care Quality Assurance Professional. m. Sherman Robert Robinson Jr, 26 Dec. 1953, divorced Jan 1959, 1 son. (2) David Solomon Mason, Jr, 10 Sept. 1960, 1 daughter. *Education:* RN, Shadyside Hospital School of Nursing, Pittsburgh, 1954; BS, St Josephs' College, North Windham, 1979; MS, So Illinois University, 1981. *Appointments:* Clinic Manager, clinician dermatol. services, Malcolm Grow Medical Centre, Camp Spring, Maryland, 1968-71; Pediatric Nurse Practitioner, Department Human Resources, Washington, 1971-73; Assistant Director Nursing, Glenn Dale Hospital, Maryland, 1973-81; Nursing Coordinator medicaid division, Forest Haven, Laurel, 1981-83; Special Assistant to supervisor for medical services, 1983-84; Special assistant to Supt for quality assurance, Bur. Habilitation Services, Laurel, 1984-; Board of Directors, ABQAURP, Inc, Sarasota, Florida; Consultant and Lecturer. *Publications:* Contributor of articles to professional journals. *Memberships:* Star Donor, ARC Blood Drive, Washington, Maryland, 1975-; Chairman nominations committee, Prince Georges National Council Negro Women, 1984-85; American Coll. Utilization Rev, Physicians, 1983-; Assistant Treasurer, 1988- (Member editorial board and case study Ed. journal, 1985-); American Board Quality Assurance and Utilization Rev. National Association of Female Executives; Chi Eta Phi. *Honours:* Recipient awards, Dept Air Force and DC Government, 1966-; Della Robbia Gold Medallion, American Academmy Pediatrics, 1972; John P Lamb Jr Memorial Lectureship Award, East Tennessee State University, 1988. *Hobbies:* Language study; Travel; Reading; Writing; Collecting antiques. *Address:* 11109 Winsford Avenue, Upper Marlboro, MD 20772, USA.

CARPER Gertrude Esther, b. 13 Apr. 1921, Jamestown, NY., USA. Artist; Marina Owner. m. 5 Apr. 1942, 2 sons. *Appointments:* Secretary, 1940-41; Interior Decorator, O'Neills Importers, 1943-44; Auditor, Citizen's National Bank, Covington, 1945-46. *Publications:* Expressions for Children 1986; articles in numerous journals, newspapers & magazines. *Memberships:* Essex Chamber of Commerce; Guilford Association; Alumni Association of Maryland; Institute of Art. *Honours:* Life Member, Alumni Association of Maryland Institute of Art, 1955; Citation, Le Salon des Nations a Paris 1985. *Hobbies:* Growing Orchids; Making Tiny Books; Writing Poetry; Spending Time with her Granddaughter. *Address:* c/o Essex Yacht Harbour Marina, 500 Sandalwood Road, Baltimore, MD 21221, USA.

CARR Jayge (Margery Morgenstern), b. 28 July 1940, Houston, Texas, USA. Writer; Physicist. m. Roger Carr Krueger, 8 Sept. 1961, 2 daughters. *Education:* BA, Physics, Wayne State University, 1962. *Appointments:* Nuclear Physicist, NASA Lewis Research Centre, Cleveland, 1962-65. *Publications:* Novels: Leviathan's Deep, 1979; Navigator's Sindrome, 1983; The Treasure in the Heart of the Maze, 1985; Rabelaisian Reprise, 1988; Knight of a Thousand Eyes, in press; many short stories in magazines & journals. *Memberships:* Science Fiction Writers of America; Futurism; World Future Society; etc. *Address:* 310 Country Club Blvd, Slidell, LA 70458, USA.

CARR Mary Lois, b. 13 May 1948, Quincy, Florida, USA. Mental Health Professional. m. Edward J. Scholl, 24 Oct. 1988, 1 son, 1 step-daughter. *Education:* AA, pensacola Junior College, 1969; BS, University of South Florida, 1981; MS, Nova University, 1988. *Appointments:* Resource Centre Director, 1981-83, Associate Director, 1983, Executive Director, 1983-86, Girls Club of Sarasota. *Publications:* Quarterly Article for Tomorrow's Woman, 1984-86; Author, local TV Announcement Coast Update, 1985; Designer/Devloper: Latchkey Programme, Ater School Hotline for Latchkey Children, Pediatric Visitation to Hospital. *Memberships:* various professional & civic organisations. *Honours:* Presidents Award, University of South Florida, 1980; Phi Kappa Phi, 1981. *Hobbies:* Volunteer Work; Travel. *Address:* 1729 Lakeside Drive, Venice, FL 34293, USA.

CARR Patricia Warren, b. 24 Mar. 1947, Mobile, USA. Adult Education Resource Teacher/Consultant. m. Joyn Lyle Carr, 26 Sept. 1970, 1 son, 1 daughter. *Education:* BS, 1968, MEd., 1970, Auburn University. *Appointments:* Teacher, DeKalb County Schools, Atlanta, 1969-70; Counsellor, Dept. of Defence Schools, Okinawa, Japan, 1972-75; Teacher, Jefferson County Schools, 1975-76; Counsellor, Clark County Schools, 1976-78; Adult Education Teacher, Fairfax County Schools, 1980-; Consultant, State VA Dept. of Education, 1984-; Consultant, VA Association of Adult & Continuing Education, 1987; Consultant, Commission of Adult Basic Education 1988. *Publications:* No Easy Answers, Newsletter, 1983. *Memberships:* American Association of Adult & Community Education; Fairfax County Association of Volunteer Administrators; Virginia Association of Adult & Community Education; Smithsonian National Associates. *Hobbies:* Tennis; Horseriding; Interior Decorating. *Address:* Fairfax Co. Adult & Community Education, 7510 Lisle Ave., Falls Church, VA 22043, USA.

CARR Vikki (born Florencia Bisenta de Casillas Martinez Cardona), b. El Paso, Texas, USA. Singer. *Appointments include:* Singer with touring band; Solo engagements, various clubs; Contracts, Liberty Records, Columbia CBS-Mexico. Tours worldwide; Numerous performances, live & TV, including Royal Command Performance, London, UK 1967, Vietnam military bases, 1967, US White House, President Nixon's inaugural celebration; Performed for US Presidents Ford, Regan and Bush; 1st major success in Australia with song, He's A Rebel, then UK with It Must Be Him. Host, own TV shows, frequent guest star, major network variety shows; Stage performances worldwide; Own TV & film production company, current. *Honours include:* Record sales almost 20 million, including 30 best-selling records, 14 gold albums; Visiting Entertainer of Year, Mexico, 1972; Grammy award, 1985; Hispanic Woman of Year, 1984; Entertainer of Year, American Guild of Variety Artists, 1972; Woman of Year, Los Angeles Times, 1970. *Hobbies include:* Vikki Carr Scholarship Foundation, providing higher education scholarships for Mexican-American youth, founded 1971-. *Address:* PO Box 5126, Beverley Hills, California 90210, USA.

CARRICK Diana Margaret (Angela), Lady b. 14 Oct. 1927, Papua New Guinea. m. John Leslie Carrick, 2 June 1951. 3 daughters. *Education:* St Vincent's College, Sydney, New South Wales, Australia. *Memberships:* Deputy State Commissioner, Girl Guides

(NSW), 1974-78; Assistant Chief Commissioner, Girl Guides Association of Australia, 1979-83; Chief Commissioner, Girl Guides Association of Australia, 1983-88; NSW Government Womens Advisory council, 1988-. *Honours:* Red Kangaroo, Highest Award of Girl Guides Association of Australia, 1984; Officer of the Order of Australia (A6) 1988. *Hobbies:* Reading; Swimming; Music. *Address:* 8 Montah Avenue, Killara, New South Wales 2071, Australia.

CARRINGTON Connie Kay, b. 23 Apr. 1952, San Antonio, Texas, USA. Professor. m. Samuel Stephen Rusell, 22 Dec. 1983. *Education:* BA, Mathematics, University of Rochester, 1974; MA, University of Virginia, 1979; PhD, Virginia Tech, 1983. *Appointments:* Engineering & Programmer, Research Labs Engineering Sciences, UVA, 1975-77, 1979; Engineer, Sperry Marine Systems, 1977-79; Assistant Professor, GMI Engineering & Management Institute, 1983-84; Assistant Professor, University of South Carolina, 1984-. *Publications:* Technical papers in professional journals. *Memberships:* Managing Editor, AAS Journal of the Astronautical Sciences; Guidance & Control Technical Committee, AIAA; Sigma Xi. *Honours:* VPI & SU Cunningham Fellow, 1982-83; USAF/UES Summer Faculty Research Fellow, 1985; NASA/ASEE Summer Faculty Research Fellow, 1988. *Hobbies:* Sailing; Sailboat Racing; Aerobics. *Address:* 330 Grantham Road, Irmo, SC 29063, USA.

CARROLL Barbara Anne, b. 20 Oct. 1945, Beaumont, Texas, USA. Professor; Physician. m. Olaf T. von Ramm, 5 Apr. 1986. *Education:* BA magna cum laude, Liberal Arts, University of Texas, Austin, 1967; MD, 1972, Internal Medicine Internship, 1972-73, Radiology Residency and Fellowship, 1973-76, Stanford University Medical School. *Appointments:* Research Assistant, 1963-67, Genetics Foundation, National Science Foundation Teaching Assistant, 1967, University of Texas, Austin; Research Assistant, Department of Hematology, 1968-69, Assistant Professor, Radiology, 1977-84, Associate Professor, Radiology, 1984-85, Stanford University; Clinical Instructor in Medicine, University of California, Santa Cruz, 1972-76; Clinician, Planned Parenthood, Santa Clara, California, 1973-76; Associate Professor, Radiology, Duke University Medical School, Durham, North Carolina, 1985-. *Publications:* Over 60 original scientific manuscripts; 18 book chapters; Numerous invited articles and reviews; 10 instructional video tapes for medical education purposes. *Memberships:* Medical Advisory Committee, Planned Parenthood, Santa Clara; Board of Governors, American Institute of Ultrasound in Medicine; Education Committee, American College of Radiology; Associate Editor, Radiology; Faculty Advisor, North Carolina Ultrasound Society; Association of University Radiologists. *Honours:* Phi Beta Kappa, 1963; Agnes Axtell Moule Faculty Scholar, Stanford University, 1980; Elected to Society of Radiologists in Ultrasound, 1980; National Cancer Institute Research Contract, Ultrasound Contrast Agents, 1980-84; Fellow, American Institute of Ultrasound in Medicine, 1986; Honorary Member, Venezuelan Ultrasound Society, 1986. *Hobbies:* Gardening; Raising Abyssinian cats; Gourmet cooking; Phiotography; Writing poetry; Riding; Hiking. *Address:* Department of Radiology, Box 3808, Duke University Medical School, Durham, NC 27710, USA.

CARROLL Barbara Wake, b. 28 July 1947, Winnipeg, Canada. Assistant Professor of Political Science. m. Dr Terrance G Carroll, 22 Aug. 1969. *Education:* BA, University of Manitoba, 1967; MA, Carleton University, 1969; PhD, American University, 1985. *Appointments:* Managerial and policy advisory positions, Canadian Government and Alberta Government, 1969-82; Assistant Professor of Consumer Studies, University of Guelph, 1983-85; Assistant Professor of Political Science, McMaster University, 1985-. *Publications:* Articles on housing policy, construction industry and administration in a number of professional journals. *Memberships:* Canadian Institute of Public Administration (Member of Executive Committee 1986-

87, Member of Regional Executives 1978-85); Canadian Political Science Assoc; American Society of Public Administration; Phi Alpha Alpha (Public Administration Honour Society). *Honours:* Recipient of several research grants, Social Science and Humanities Research Council, 1982-. *Hobbies:* Wilderness camping; Volunteer work on non-profit Boards of Director, primarily in the housing field (Jubilee Management Services 1980-83, Victoria Park Community Homes 1984-, Canadian Mental Health Association 1987-). *Address:* 16 Robinson St South, Grimsby, Ontario, Canada.

CARROLL Elisabeth, b. 19 Jan. 1937, Paris, France. Associate Professor in Ballet/Educator. m. Felix Smith, 18 July 1957. 1 daughter. *Education:* College de Jeunes Filles, Cannes, France, 1948-51. *Appointments:* Soloist, Monte-Carlo Opera Ballet, 1952-54; First Soloist, American Ballet Theatre, 1954-61; Principal Dancer, Robert Joffrey Company, 1961-63; Ballerina, Harkness Ballet, 1963-70; Faculty, Harkness School for Ballet Arts, New York City, 1970-76; Assistant Professor, Associate Professor, 1976-, Skidmore College. *Honours:* Master Teacher, Dance Masters of America; Chicago National Dance Masters of America (Honorary Award, 1969). *Hobbies:* Outdoor work and activites; Animal supporter. *Address:* Skidmore College, Saratoga Springs, NY 12866, USA.

CARROLL Gladys Hasty, b. 26 June 1904, Rochester, New Hampshire, USA. Writer. m. Herbert A. Carroll, 23 June 1925, 1 son, 1 daughter. *Education:* AB, Bates College, 1925; Graduate courses, literature, fine arts, University of Chicago, Harvard & Columbia Universities. *Publications include:* Over 20 books, fiction & non-fiction. *Memberships:* Phi Beta Kappa; Board, Dunnybrook Historical Foundation. *Honours:* Several titles, Book Club choices; Honorary degrees, University of New Hampshire, Bates College, University of Maine, Nasson College; Deborah Morton Award, Westbrook College, 1986. *Hobbies:* Everything historical, especially local records & all objects associated with daily life of earlier generations; Education, all family members teachers, past/present. *Address:* 8 Earls Road, South Berwick, Maine 03908, USA.

CARROLL Linda Louise, b. 10 June 1949, Seattle, USA. Professor; Author. m. Edward W. Muir Jr, 8 June 1986. *Education:* AB, Princeton University, 1971; MA 1972, PhD 1977, Harvard University. *Appointments include:* Assistant Professor 1977-81, Chair, Department of Modern Languages 1978-81, Gonzaga University; Assistant Professor 1981-87, Associate Professor 1987-, Tulane University. *Publications:* Language & Dialect in Ruzante & Goldoni, 1981; Angelo Beolco (Il Ruzante), forthcoming; Contributions, 16th Century Journal. *Memberships:* Past Trustee, Washington Association of Foreign Language Teachers; Renaissance Society of America; 16th Century Society; Linguistic Association of Canada & US. *Honours:* McConnell Fellow, 1970; Fulbright Fellow, 1984; Grant, National Endowment for Humanities, 1985; Delmas Fellow, 1985; Newberry Library Fellow, 1986. *Address:* Department of French & Italian, Tulane University, New Orleans, Louisiana 70118, USA.

CARROLL Mary Ann, b. 31 May 1947, Baton Rouge, Los Angeles, USA. Professor of Philosophy. m. Bruce N Richter, 1 Sept, 1967, divorced Dec. 1978. *Appointments:* BA, University of New Orleans, 1969; MA 1971, PhD 1973, University of North Carolina at Chapel Hill. *Appointments:* Lecturer, University of North Carolina, Chapel Hill, 1973; Assistant Professor 1973-77, Associate Professor 1977-83, Professor 1983-, Appalachian St University; Visiting Professor, University of Richmond, 1986-87. *Publications:* Co-Author: Moral Problems in Nursing; Ethics in the Practice of Psychology; Author: The Right to Treatment and Involuntary Commitment; Book reviews. *Memberships:* Am Philosophical Association; American Association of Philosophy Teachers; Southern Society of Philosophy and Psychology. *Honours:* NDEA Fellowship, 1972-73; Exxon Fellowship in Medicine & Ethics (Baylor College of Medicine), 1985. *Hobbies:* Photography; Borzoi Dogs; Weightlifting. *Address:* c/o Department of Philosophy & Religion, Appalachian State University, Boone, NC 28608, USA.

CARROLL Mary Beth, b. 17 Apr. 1944, Hartford, Connecticut, USA. Theatrical General Manager. *Education:* MFA, Stage Management, Catholic University of America, 1972; Film Administration, New School, New York City, 1983-86. *Appointments:* General Manager: Roundabout Theatre 1975-77, Light Opera of Manhattan 1977-80, Acting Company 1980-. *Memberships:* Independent Feature Project; Association of Theatrical Press Agents & Managers; National Association of Female Executives. *Hobbies:* Fishing; Horseback Riding; Dogs; Travel. *Address:* Acting Company, 420 West 42nd Street, Times Square Station, Box 898, New York, NY 10108, USA.

CARROLL Paula Marie, b. 17 July 1933, Fresno, USA. Company President. m. Herman S. Carroll, 25 Apr. 1954. *Appointments:* Co-owner, 1963, Vice President, 1977, Pesident, Manager, 1988, Central Valley Alarm Co. Inc.; President, founder, Consumers for Medical Quality Inc., 1981-. *Publication:* Book, Life Wish, 1986. *Memberships:* Republic Womens Club; Beta Sigma Phi; Ombudsman; Order of Eastern Star; Society of Law & Medicine. *Honours:* Woman of Distinction, Soroptimist International, 1986; Merced County Celebrating Women Award, 1987; President's Award, California Trial Lawyers Association, 1987; Consumers for Medical Quality Inc., Grantee, California Trial Lawyers Association, 1987. *Hobbies:* Oil Painting; Writing. *Address:* 3271 Alder Avenue, Merced, CA 95340, USA.

CARSON Gayle, b. 19 Feb. 1938, Albany, New York, USA. Professional Speaker; Author; Consultant. m. Norman De Vecht, 27 Nov. 1963. 2 sons, 1 daughter. *Education:* BA Communication Art, Emerson College, Boston; Music Degree, Octavo School of Musical Art, Albany; EdD, Nova University, Fort Lauderdale. *Appointments:* Director, Florida Casting Agency, Miami, 1959-80; Gayle Carson's Florida School of Real Estate, Maimi, 1975-80; Founded, Gayle Carson Career Schools, Inc, Miami, 1959-80; Self-employed Lecturer and Writer, Miami, 1959-; Founder and President, Gayle Carson Presents, Miami Beach, 1973-. *Publication:* Winning Ways: How to Get to the Top and Stay There, 1988. *Memberships:* National Speakers Association; Florida Society Association of Executives; Florida Speakers Association; South Florida Meeting Planners International; Chairman of the Board, Better Business Bureau of South Florida, 1987 and 1988; National Alumni Board, Emerson College, 1986-89; Board of Directors, Hotel Sales Management Association, Gold Coast, 1978-, etc. *Honours:* Florida's Outstanding Young Woman of the Year, 1970; Dade County's Oustanding Business Woman, 1980; School of the Year Award, 1974-75; National Alumni Achievement Award for Excellence in Education, Emerson College, 1987; National Award, ASTD, 1985, 1986. *Hobbies:* Reading; Aerobics; Waterskiing; Swimming; Animals. *Address:* 2957 Flamingo Drive, Miami Beach, Florida 33140, USA.

CARSON Margaret Marie, b. 30 Dec. 1944, Windber, Pennsylvania, USA. Director of Competitor Anal. m. Brian Charles Scruby, 6 July 1975. 3 stepsons, 1 daughter. *Education:* BA, University of Pgh, Pennsylvania, 1971; M Science, Houston Baptist University, 1985. *Appointments:* Manager & Anal. Gulf Oil Corporation, Pgh, Pennsylvania and Houston, Texas, 1971-84; Director, Cabot Energy Consulting, Marketing, 1985-86; Director Natural Gas Competitor Anal, Enron Corp, Houston, 1986-. *Publications:* Cathedral Poets, 1980; University of Pgh, Poetry Workshop, 1979; Columnist, The Collegian HBU University in Houston on Careers and Business Issues, 1983-85. *Memberships:* International Association Energy Economists, 1980-; University Club of Houston; Gas Proc Association, 1985-. *Honours:* Forecasting NGL Plant Profit & Performance, Technical Speaker, Gas Processors Association, Houston and New Orleans,

1985-86; American Petrol Institute Commendation, Oil and Water Pollution Control, 1973; United Way Award, Koppers Corp, Pgh, 1981. *Interests:* Piano Music; Board of Directors, Houston Classical Guitar Society; Board of Directors, Indiana University of Pennsylvania Business Advisory Board, 1981. *Address:* Enron Corp, 1400 Smith Street, Enron Building, Houston, TX 77002, USA.

CARSTAIRS Sharon, b. 26 Apr. 1942, Nova Scotia, Canada. Leader of the Opposition; Leader of the Liberal Party in Manitoba; Member of Legislative Assembly. m. John, 1966. 2 daughters. *Education:* BA Political Science and History, Dalhousie University, 1962; MA, Teaching of History, Smith College, Massachusetts, 1963. *Appointments:* Teacher, Dana Hall for Girls, Wellesley, Massachusetts, 1963-65; Teacher, Calgary Separate School Board, 1965-71; Scriptwriter and Narrator (TV), Calgary and Region Educational TV, 1967-69; Chairman, Board of Referees, Unemployment Insurance Commission, 1973-77; Teacher, St John's Ravenscourt School, 1978-80; St Norbert Collegiate, St Norbert, Manitoba, 1981-84. *Hobbies:* Reading; Swimming. *Address:* Room 172, Legislative Building, 450 Broadway, Winnipeg, Manitoba, R3C 0V8, Canada.

CARTER Betsy, b. 9 June 1945, New York City, USA. Editor. *Education:* BA English, University of Michigan, Ann Arbor, 1967. *Appointments:* Editorial Assistant, McGraw Hill, 1967-68; Editor, American Security and Trust, 1968-69; Editorial Assistant, Atlantic Monthly, 1969-70; Associate Editor, Newsweek, 1970-79; Senior Editor, Executive Editor, 1981, Senior Executive Editor, 1982, Editorial Director, 1983-85, Esquire; Creator and Editor in Chief, New York Woman, 1986-. *Memberships:* American Society of Magazine Editors; Executive Committee, American Society of Magazine Editors, 1988-; Women in Communications. *Address:* 339 East 18th Street, New York, NY 10003, USA.

CARTER Daisy, b. 17 Oct. 1931, Stuart, Florida, USA. Therapeutic Recreation Specialist. 1 daughter. *Education:* BSc., Temple University. *Appointments:* District Coordinator, Philadelphia Dept. of Recreation, 1968-71; Centre Supervisor, 1969-70; Senior Citizens Community Worker, Zion Church, 1971-72; Day Camp Director, East Germantown Recreation Centre, 1972-78; Senior Citizens Programme Supervisor, Crafts Instructor, 1971-82; Centre Supervisor, Penrose Playground, 1981-88; Thereapeutic Recreation, Northeast Older Adult Centre, 1988-. *Publication:* On Common Ground, 1987. *Memberships:* Pennsylvania Park and Recreation Society; Temple University Alumni Association; Black Social Workers Association; National Park and Recreation Association; etc. *Honours:* Recipient, numerous honours and awards. *Hobbies:* Walking; Dancing; Writing. *Address:* The Fairmount Apartments W104, 357 W. Johnson Street, Philadelphia, PA 19144, USA.

CARTER Frances Tunnell, b. Mississippi, USA. Educator; Executive Director, Kappa Delta Epsilon. m. John T. Carter, 16 Mar. 1946, 1 son, 1 daughter. *Education:* AA: Wood Junior College, Mathison, Mississippi, 1940, Elementary Education, Blue Mountain College, 1942; BS, Home Economics, Science, University of Southern Mississippi, 1946; MS, General Home Economics, University of Tennessee, 1948; EdD, Education, Home Economics Education, University of Illinois, 1954; Post-doctoral study, Elementary and Early Childhood Education, Psychology. *Appointments include:* Teacher, Home Economics, Art, Wood Junior College, 1947-48; Department Head, Home Economics: East Central Junior College, 1948-49; Clarke College, 1950-56; Assistant Professor, Associate Professor, Professor, Education, Home Economics, Samford University, 1956-84; Visiting Professor, Hong Kong Baptist College, 1965-66; Editor, Woman's Missionary Union, 1983-85; National Executive Director, Kappa Delta Epsilon, currently. *Creative works:* Children's books: Sammy in the Country, 1960; 'Tween-age Ambassador, 1970; Sharing Times Seven, 1971; Ching Fu and Jim, 1978; Curriculum units, Aware & Start magazines; Programmes on missions; Study guides; Articles; Poems; Children's song; 3 underprivileged children's study units; 2 brochures; Principles of Early Childhood Education (draft textbook); charcoal/acrylic artwork. *Memberships:* Kappa Delta Epsilon; Kappa Delta Pi; Kappa Omicron Phi; Pi Gamma Mu; Alpha Delta Kappa; Delta Kappa Gamma; Phi Delta Kappa; Director of Public Affairs, SE Region, Civil Air Patrol; State/local bodies including: Alabama League of American Pen Women; Association for Childhood Education; Alabama Federation of Women's Clubs; Advisory Panel, State Council on Arts and Sciences; Many more; Held office in most. *Honours:* Art, poetry, writing awards; Frances Tunnell Carter Day, National Kappa Delta Epsilon, 1983; Outstanding Clubwoman of Alabama, 1988; Various other honours. *Hobbies:* Reading; Writing; Club and church work; Spectator sports. *Address:* 2561 Rocky Ridge Road, Birmingham, AL 35243, USA.

CARTER Gwendolyn Marie Burns, b. 21 Nov. 1932, Lufkin, Texas, USA. Resource Teacher. m. Purvis Melvin Carter, 2 June 1956. 2 sons, 1 daughter. *Education:* BS, Huston Tillotson College, Austin, Texas, 1954; MEd, Prairie View A & M University, 1960; Attended: Universities of Denver, Southern Illinois, Colorado, and Texas. *Appointments:* Brandon Elementary School, Lufkin, Texas, 1954-56; A W Jackson Elementary School, Rosenberg, 1959-61; Lincoln Elementary School, College Station, 1962-64; San Schwarz Elementary School, Hempstead, 1964-70; Hempstead Elementary School, Hempstead, 1970-. *Memberships:* President 1970-72, Vice President 1988-90, Prairie View Chapter, Delta Sigma Theta Sorority; President, Prairie View Chapter, Jack & Jill of America, 1980-82; President, Waller County Teachers Association, 1983-84; President, Top Ladies of Distinction, Prairie View Chapter, 1987-. National Education Association. *Honours:* Excellent Service to the Prairie View Chapter & Community, Delta Sigma Theta Sorority, 1972; Outstanding Leadership, Girl Scout Award, 1984; San Jacinto Council Appreciation Girl Scout Award, 1984; Distinguished Service, Prairie View Local Alumni Association, 1984; Certificate of Recognition Mount Corinth Baptist Church, 1985; Human Relations Award, Waller County Teachers Association, 1986; Outstanding Service Award, Top Teens of America, Inc, 1986; Recognition of Outstanding Service in the Area/Areas of Public Service and Community Relations, Jack and Jill of America, Inc. 1978. *Hobbies:* Working with children; Writing; Helping others; Travelling. *Address:* 319 Pine Street, Post Office Box 2243, Prairie View, Texas 77446, USA.

CARTER Jaine Marie, b. 29 Oct. 1946, Chicago, USA. Human Resources Development Company Executive. m. James Dudley Carter, 8 Apr. 1970, 2 sons. *Education:* BS, Northwestern University, 1968; PhD, Walden University, 1978. *Appointments:* President, Baherlorette Association, Los Angeles, 1962-64; Management Consultant to Business, 1964-69; Chairman of Board, Personnel Development Inc., Palatine, 1969-; Director, Womens Division, Lake Forest College, Advanced Management Institute, 1970-75; Writer, Lecturer, Teacher, Consultant. *Publications:* How to Train for Supervisors, 1969; Career Planning Workshop for Women, 1975; Training Techniques that Bring About Positive Behavioural Change, 1976; Assertive Management Role Plays, 1976; Understanding the Female Employee, 1976; Rx for Women in Business, 1976; New Directions Needed in Management Training Programmes, 1980; The Burnout of Retirement, 1983; Successfully Working with People, 1984; Assertiveness Training for Supervisors, 1985; Successfully Managing People, 1986; Satellite Television series, Seminars by Satellite, 1987-88; National Viseo Confereces Successfully Working with people, 1989; Cable Television show, Lifeskills, 1989-90. *Memberships:* International Transactional Analysis Association; National Speakers Association; Screen Actors Guild; AFTRA; AGVA; Executive Club of America; American Management Association. *Address:* 4401 Gulfshore Blvd N, Naples, FL 33940, USA.

CARTER Jessie Anita, b. 3 June 1948, Ft. Worth, Texas, USA. Mathematics Teacher. *Education:* BA, Mathematics, 1970; MEd., 1976. *Appointments:* Sales Clerk to Personnel Dept., 1970-72, Leonards Department Store; FWISD Instructional Aide, 1972; Teacher, Dept. Chairman, Gifted Teacher. *Publications:* Co-author, Hexiamonds, Computing Teacher, 1986. *Memberships:* NEA; TSTA; FWCTA; NCTM; FWCTM; ICCE. *Honours:* Recipient, various honours and awards. *Hobbies Include:* Painting; Stained Glass; Needlework; Computers; Reading. *Address:* Box 9471 Arl Hts Sta., Ft. Worth, TX 76147, USA.

CARTER Margaret L, State Representative. *Education:* BA, Portland State University; MEd., Oregon State University. *Appointments:* Counselor, POrtland Community College; Instructor, Albina Youth Opportuniy School; Assistant Director, Community Action Agency; State Representative, Salem, Oregon. *Memberships:* Founder, Oregon Black Leadership Conference, 1986-; Oregon Alliance for Black School Educators; Alpha Kappa Alpha. *Honours:* Jeanette Rankin Award, Oregon Womens Politicla Caucus, 1985; Elliott Award, Human Rights, Oregon Education Association, 1987; March of Dimes, White Rose Award, 1987; Woman of Achievement Award, 1987; National Fellow, American Leadership Forum, 1987. *Address:* House of Representatives, Salem, OR 97310, USA.

CARTER Margaret Louise, b. 29 Apr. 1948, Norfolk, Virginia, USA. m. Leslie R Carter, CDR, USN, 21 Sept. 1966. 4 sons. *Education:* BA, College of William & Mary, 1972; MA, University of Hawaii, 1974; PhD, University of California, Irvine, 1986. *Appointments:* Teaching Assistant English, University of Hawaii, 1972-74; Instructor, English, Chaminade College, 1974-75; Instructor, Business Admin, Hawaii Pacific College, 1974-75; Teaching Assistant, English, University of California, 1981-82; Instructor, English, Trident Technical College, Charleston, SC, 1985-86. *Publications:* The Vampire in Literature: A Critical Bibliography, 1989; Specter or Delusion? The Supernatural in Gothic Fiction, 1987; Shadow of a Shade: A Survey of Vampirism in Literature, 1975. ED: Dracula: The Vampire and the Critics, 1988; Demon Lovers and Strange Seductions, 1972; Curse of the Undead, 1970; Contributions of fiction and poetry in various periodicals. *Memberships:* Phi Beta Kappa; Modern Language Assn; Mythopoeic Society; Society for the Study of Narrative Literature; International Association of Fantasy in the Arts. *Hobby:* Dungeons and Dragons game. *Address:* 105 Phipps Lane, Annapolis, MD 21403, USA.

CARTER Rosalynn, b. 18 Aug. 1927, Plains, Georgia, USA. Author; Lecturer. m. James Earl Carter Jr, 7 July 1946. 3 sons, 1 daughter. *Education:* Georgia Southwestern College, 1946; Honorary Doctor of Humanities, Tift College, Georgia, 1979; Honorary Doctor of Humane Letters, Morehouse College, Altanta, Georgia, 1980. *Career:* As First Lady of Georgia appointed to Governor's Commission to Improve Services for the Mentally and Emotionally Handicapped; Volunteer at the Georgia Regional Hospital in Atlanta for 5 years; Honorary Chairperson for the Georgia Special Olympics for Retarded Children; First Lady, 1977. *Creative Works:* Autobiography First Lady From Plains, 1984. *Memberships include:* Honorary Chair, President's Commission on Mental Health whilst First Lady; Board of Advisors of Habitat for Humanity Inc; Honorary Fellow, American Psychiatric Association; Numerous other memberships. *Honours include:* Numerous honous and awards during years at the White House including: Volunteer of the Decade by the National Mental Health Association; Presidential Citation from the American Psychological Association; The Distinguished Service Award for Leadership in Christian Social Ethics from the Christian Life Commission of The Southern Baptist Convention; Elected to Board of Directors, Gannett Company Inc. *Address:* Plains, GA 31780, USA.

CARTERET Anna, b. 11 Dec. 1942, Bangalore, India.

Actress. m. Christopher Thomas Morahan, 12 Oct. 1974, 2 daughters. *Education:* Advanced RAD Ballet; Advanced Ceccetti Ballet. *Appointments:* Repertory, Lincoln, Windsor, Bristol, 1958-67; Lead Parts, National Theatre, 1967-75; Portia, The Merchant of Venice; Isabella in Measure for Measure and Mistress Page in Merry Wives, St Georges Theatre; As You Like It; Sisterly Feelings; Man and Superman; She Stoops to Conquer; The Reluctant Debutante; The Pallisers; The Man Who Liked Elephants; Send in the Girls; Little Mrs Perkins; A Piece of My Mind; Currently playing lead in BBC Serial: Juliet Bravo; most recent film, Gipsy House. *Publications:* Helped to compile, Raving Beauties in the Pink, 1983, and No Holds Barred, 1985, both poetry. *Memberships:* Equity; International Committee for Artists Freedom. *Honours:* Clarence Derwent Award for Most Promising New-Comer for The Maid in Saturday, Sunday, Monday, National Theatre, 1973. *Hobbies:* Running; Gardening; Walking; Music. *Address:* 55 Winterbrook Road, Herne Hill, London SE24 9HZ, England.

CARTIER Celine R, b. 10 May 1930, Lacolle, Canada. Consultant; Text Reviser. m. Georges Cartier, 29 Nov. 1952, 1 son, 1 daughter. *Education:* MLS, Univeristy of Montreal; MAP, Ecole nationale d'administration publique. *Appointments:* Director, Central Library, Montreal Cath. Sc., Commission, 1964-73; Director, Sector Libraries & Special Collections, University of Quebec, 1973-77; Director, Social Sciences Library, 1977-78, Director General, Library Services, 1978-88, Laval University; Text Reviser, 1989-. *Publications:* Le Plan Directeur Pluri-Annuel; Cours de Francais; Rencontre surla Bibliotheconomie Quebecoise; articles in journals. *Memberships:* Corporation of Professional Librarians of Quebec; Association pour l'avancement des sciences et des techniques de la documentation; IFLA; CLA, etc. *Hobbies:* Piano; Cello; Reading; Writing; Sailing; Skiing. *Address:* 750 Place Fortier No 701, Ville St Laurent, Quebec, Canada H4L 5C1.

CARTLAND Barbara Hamilton, Author; Playwright. m. (1) Alexander George McCorquodale, 1927, divorced 1933, 1 daughter, (2) Hugh McCorquodale, 2 sons. *Publications:* Published 1st novel aged 21; numerous novels most recent being: Kiss the Moonlight; Love Locked In; The Marquess who hated Women; Rhapsody of Love; Look Listen & Love; The Wild Unwilling Wife; Punishment of a Vixen; The Curse of the Clan; A Touch of Love; The Naked Battle; The Hell Cat and the King; No Escape from Love; A Sign of Love; The Castle Made for Love; The Saint and the Sinner; A Fugitive from Love; Love Leaves at Midnight; The Problems of Love; Love is a Maze; A Circus for Love; The Temple of Love; A Necklace of Love; The Marquis Wins; Love is the Key: Free as theWind; Desiro in the Desert; A Heart in the Highlands; The Music of Love; The Wrong Duchess; The Magic of Paris; Love at First Sight; The Scent of Roses; The Secret Princess; Heaven in Hong Kong; Paradise in Penang; A Game of Love; Cookery Books Include: Barbara Cartland's Health Food Cookery Book; Food for Love: Magic of Honey Cookbook; Recipies for Lovers; The Romance of Food; Radio Operetta: The Rose and the Violet, 1942; Radio Plays; Autobiography: The Ishmus Years 1919-939, The Years of Opportunity 1939-45; I Search for Rainbows 1946-66; We Danced All Night 1919-1929; I Seek the Miraculous; Childrens Books; Historical Books; Books on Sociology. *Memberships:* Member, numerous professional organisation including: Founder, Barbara Cartland-Onslow Romany Gypsy Fund; President, National Association of Health, 1966. *Address:* Camfield Place, Hatfield, Herts, England.

CARTMER Deborah Joan, b. 20 Jan. 1961, New Brunswick, Canada. Film Producer; Director; Writer. *Education:* Niagara College of Applied Arts & Technology, 1978-81. *Appointments:* Broadcaster, Chow Radio, 1979-84; CJOR, 1984-86; President, Esprit Films Limited, 1983-; Instructor, Film Programme, Niagara College of Applied Arts, 1985-86. *Publications:* Films: Being There, 1983; Video: Child Abuse: Definition & Causes, 1984; Growing Together, 1986; Break the

Cycle, 1987. *Memberships:* various professional organisations. *Honours:* Recipient, honours & awards. *Hobbies:* Cross Country Skiing; Handweaving. *Address:* PO Box 2215 Stn.B, St. Catharines, Ontario, Canada L2M 6P6.

CARTWRIGHT Inez P. Gesell, b. 25 Feb. 1917, Fosston, USA. Retired. m. (1) William J. Gessel, 31 Dec. 1938, deceased 1975, 2 sons, 1 daughter, (2) Myron R. Cartwright, 30 Jan. 1982. *Education:* Bagley High School, 1936. *Appointments:* Office Manager, Owner, President 1975-81, Gesell Concrete Products Inc. *Memberships:* St Joseph Roman Catholic Church, Bagley; Treasurer, Ladies Auxiliary, St Ann Roman Catholic Church; North Country Unit, Marine Corps League Auxiliary, Bagley, Treasurer. *Hobbies:* World Travel. *Address:* 110 Lakeview Drive, Bagley, MN 56621, USA.

CARTWRIGHT Mary Lucy (Dame), b. 17 Dec. 1900, Aynho, Northants, England. Mathematician; Head of Girton College; Emeritus Reader in the Theory of Functions, University of Cambridge; Life Fellow of Girton College. *Education:* DPhil, Oxon, 1930. *Appointments include:* Staff, Fellow, Lecturer, Girton College, 1934-49; University Lecturer, University of Cambridge, 1935-59; Mistress, Girton College, 1949-68; Reader, Theory of Functions, Cambridge University, 1949-68. *Publications include:* Integral Functions, 1956, reprinted 1962; Religion & the Scientist. Contributions to numerous professional journals and magazines. *Memberships include:* Fellow, Royal Society; President and Vice President, London Mathematical Society; American Mathematical Society; Honorary Fellow, Institute of Mathematics & its Applications. *Honours include:* Commander, Order of Dannebrog, 1964; DBE 1969. *Hobby:* Travel. *Address:* 38 Sherlock Close, Cambridge CB3 0HP, England.

CARY Arlene D, b. 19 Dec. 1930, Chicago, Illinois, USA. Hotel Company Sales Executive. m. Elliot D Hagle, 30 Dec. 1972, divorced. *Education:* BA, University of Miami, 1953. *Appointments:* Public Relations Account Executive, Robert Howe & Co, 1953-55; Sales Manager, Martin B Iger & Co, 1955-57; Sales Manager/General Manager, Sorrento Hotel, Miami Beach, Florida, 1957-59; General Manager, Mayflower Hotel, Manomet, Massachusetts, 1959-60; Numerous positions with Aristocrat Inns of America, 1960-71; VP Sales, McCormick Center Hotel, Chicago, 1972-. *Memberships:* Active Nat Women's Polit Caucus; International Organisation Women Executives, membership promotion chairman, 1979-80; Board of Directors, 1980-81; Profl Conv Mgmt Association, National Association Exposition Managers; Hotel Sales Management Association; Meeting Planners Internat; American Society Assn Executives; NY Society Assn Executives; Chicago Society Assn Executives; Ind Hotel Alliance (Sec, 1986-). *Honours:* Distinguished Salesman Award, Sales and Marketing Execs International, 1977. *Address:* 1130 S Michigan Ave, Apt 3203, Chicago, IL 60605, USA.

CASE Karen A, b. 7 Apr. 1944, Milwaukee, Wisconsin, USA. Secretary of Revenue. *Education:* BS, 1960-63, JD 1963-66, Marquett University; LLM, New York University, School of Law, 1972-73. *Appointments:* Mat Teacher, Milwaukee Pub Schools, 1968-72; Guest Lecturer, Marquette Law School, 1976-80; UW Milwaukee School of Business Tax Instructor, 1975-80; Private Law Practice, Mulcahy & Wherry, 1973-87; Secretary of Revenue, State of Wisconsin, 1987-. *Memberships:* State Bar of Wisconsin; ATS-CLE Comm; Interest on Lawyers' Trust Accountants Comm; Prepaid Legal Service Comm; Milwaukee Bar Association; Association of Women Lawyers, Milwaukee County; Professional Dimensions; TEMPO; Wisconsin Bar Foundation; Friends of the Boerner Botanical Gardens; Park People of Milwaukee County. *Honour:* Madison Rose Show, Queen of Show, 1979. *Hobbies:* Cross country skiing; Gardening; Swimming; American Rose Society, judge and qualified rosarian. *Address:* P O Box 8933, Madison, WI 53708, USA.

CASE Sue-Ellen, b. 22 June 1942, Ventura, California, USA. Associate Professor. *Education:* BA, Humanities 1964, MA 1966, California State University, San Francisco; PhD, Dramatic Arts, University of California, Berkeley, 1980. *Appointments:* Instructor, CSUSF, 1966-68; Instructor, Calif Institute of Arts, 1968-72; Professor, University of Washington, 1981- . *Publications:* Book: Feminism & Theatre, 1988; Editor, Theatre Journal, 1986-89; Articles on German Theatre, Feminist & Lesbian Theory in professional journals and magazines. *Memberships:* ATHE; International Brecht Society; MLA. *Honours:* Director's Fellowship, Intl Theatre Institute, Berlin; Mark Goodson Scholarship for Outstanding Theatrical Takut, 1978, 1979; American Council Literary Scholarship, summer grant, 1984; Inter Nations Cultural tour of Germany, 1984; Goethe Institute Language Grant, Berlin, 1988. *Hobbies:* T'ai Chi; Film noir. *Address:* School of Drama, University of Washington, Seattle, Washington 98195, USA.

CASEY Helen Angell, b. 7 July 1940, Pierre, South Dakota, USA. Marketing & Sales Consultant; Businesswoman. m. (2) Samuel Brown Casey Jr, 8 Nov. 1980. 2 sons, 2 daughters. *Education:* Related arts, University of Minnesota. *Appointments include:* Senior director, Mary Kay Cosmetics, Dallas, Texas, 1974-78; Chairman & founder, Angell-Brown Inc (marketing & sales consultants, outplacement careers, multinational & self-help seminars), 1980-. *Creative works:* Cassette tapes: 10 Ways To Get Ahead; Marketing Yourself; Meeting & Greeting: Developing Your Lifelist. *Memberships:* Regional Director, President Elect, Director, Fashion Group Inc; Director, Minnesota Goldstein Gallery; Womens Advertising Club, Chicago; President's Council, various offices, Museum of Science & Industry; Creator, Fashion Group Designers Gift, Children's Memorial Adviser, Minneapolis Symphony; National Advisory Committee, St Louis Symphony Roto Magazine; Various offices, community & charitable organisations. *Honour:* One of Top Saleswoman Recruiters, Mary Kay Cosmetics. *Hobbies:* Orchid growing; World travel; Collecting folk art; Promoting Caribbean artists; Creating & marketing table settings for hotels & inns. *Address:* 1420 North Lake Shore Drive, Chicago, Illinois 60610, USA.

CASH Grace (Savannah), b. 13 Apr. 1915, Hall County, Georgia, USA. Freelance Short Story Writer. *Education:* BA, Brenau College, 1974. *Appointments:* Silk Mill, 1937-41; Textile-Pacolet, 1942-44; Steno-Typist, Leprosy Mission Office, 1945-46, National Red Cross, 1946-49, Georgia State Department, 1950-68. *Publications:* Promise unto Death, 1966; Highway's Edge, 1965; 600 Fiction stories in literary and religious magazines; 1000 poems. *Memberships:* Honorary Member, Mark Twain International Society, 1950. *Hobbies:* Reading; Writing; Music. *Address:* Route 2, 4466 Strickland Road, Flowery Branch, GA 30542, USA.

CASH Rosalind, b. New Jersey, USA. Actress. *Appointments:* Motion Pictures include: Melinda with Calvin Lockhart; Hickey and Boggs with Bill Cosby and Robert Culp; The New Centurians with George C Scott and Stacey Keach; The Omega Man with Charlton Heston; The All American Boy with John Voight. Television appearances include: Barney Miller; Starsky and Hutch; Police Woman; Kojak; The Mary Tyler Moore Show; Ceremonies in Dark Old Men (Mobile Theatre of the Air-ABC); King Lear (PBS). Roles in theatre productions including: The Negro Ensemble Company; The World Theatre Festival (Aldwych Theatre, London, England); Rosalind Cash in Concert (Paoli Theatre, Rome, Italy); The Arena Stage (Washington DC, USA); The Harlem Y Little Theatre Group (Harlem, USA). *Hobbies:* Guitar; Painting. *Address:* c/o John Sekura, 7469 Melrose Avenue, Suite 30, Hollywood, CA 90046, USA.

CASPER Ellen, b. 16 Feb. 1951, Camden, New Jersey, USA. Clinical Psychologist. *Education:* BA, University of Rochester, 1973; MA, Psychology, Columbia University, 1974; PhD, Clinical Psychology, University of Virginia, 1981. *Appointments:* Ursuline College, 1979-; Cleveland Heights-University Heights Board of Education, 1981-85; Centre for Effective Living, 1981-85; Behaviour Management Association, 1985-87; Ellen F. Casper PhD & Associates, 1987-. Also: Consultant, local radio & TV talk shows, psychology-related topics. *Memberships include:* American, Ohio, & Cleveland Psychological Associations; Cleveland Chapter, Adam Walsh Foundation; Executive, Goodwill Industries of Cleveland. *Honour:* Proclamation (practice of psychology), State of Ohio. *Hobbies:* Tennis; Scuba diving; Jogging; Cinema; Travel. *Address:* 24075 Commerce Park Road, Suite 210, Beachwood, Ohio 44122, USA.

CASPER Regina Claire, b. 13 Aug. 1938, Berlin, Germany. Physician, Professor of Psychiatry. m. Gerhard Casper. 1 daughter. *Education:* The Free University of Berlin, 1957-59; University Geneve, Switzerland, 1960; Albert-Ludwig University, Freiburg, Germany, 1960-62; MD degree, Freiburg, 1964; Med Lic 1966, Germany, 1972, Illinois, Psychiatry, 1974. *Appointments:* Associate Professor, Abraham Lincoln School Med, University of Illinois, 1973-84; Associate Dir. Dept Research, Illinois State Psych. Inst, 1974-83; Director, Eating Disorders Research & Treatment Program, Michael Reese Hospital & Medical Center, Chicago, 1984-; Associate Professor, The University of Chicago, 1984-89; Professor, The University of Chicago, 1989. *Publications:* About 70 scientific articles and chapters on depression, eating disorders and neuroendocrinology in professional journals. *Memberships:* American Psychiatric Association; American College of Neuropsychopharmacology; International Society of Psychoneuroendorcinology; International College for Psychosomatic Med; International Society for Adolescent Psychiatry. *Address:* Department of Psychiatry, Michael Reese Hospital and Medical Center, Lake Shore Drive at 31st Street, Chicago, IL 60615, USA.

CASPERS Mary Lou, b. 9 Apr. 1950, Wyandotte, Michigan, USA. Biochemist; Professor. *Education:* BS, University of Detroit, 1972; PhD, Biochemistry, Wayne State University, 1977. *Appointments:* Assistant Professor, 1972-81, Associate Professor, 1981-, University of Detroit. *Publications:* 13 articles in scientific journals; 19 presentations. *Memberships:* American Society of Biological Chemists & Molecular Biologists; Society for Neuroscience; American Chemical Society; Sigma Xi; AAAS. *Honours:* Visiting Researcher, University of Michigan, 1978; Travel Award to 12th International Congress, 1982; Guest Research, NIMH, 1984-85. *Hobbies:* Cross Country Skiing; Backpacking; Gardening; Knitting. *Address:* Dept. of Chemistry, University of Detroit, 4001 W. McNichols Road, Detroit, MI 48221, USA.

CASSAB Judy, b. 15 Aug. 1920, Wein, Austria. Artist; Painter. m. John Kampfner, 30 Apr. 1939. 2 sons. *Education:* Art School, Budapest, 1942-44, 1946-49. *Appointments:* Represented at numerous Art Galleries in England, Australia, USA. Has held numerous exhibitions including: Macquarie Galleries, Sydney, Australia, 1953, 1955, 1961; Crane Kalman Gallery, London, England, 1959, 1961; Newcastle City Art Gallery, 1959; Argus Gallery, Melbourne, Australia, 1962; Skinner Galleries, Perth, 1967, 1969, 1973; White Studio Gallery, Adelaide, 1969; Reid Gallery, Brisbane, 1973; South Yarra Gallery, Melbourne, 1976; New Art Centre, London, England, 1978, 1981; Greenhill Galleries, Perth, Australia, 1982 and Adelaide, 1982; Solander Gallery, Canberra, 1983; Twon Gallery, Brisbane, 1984; Holdsworth Gallery, Sydney, 1985; Benalla Regional Gallery; Hamilton Regional Gallery, Caulfield Arts Centre and David Ellis Fine Art, Ballarat, 1985; Holdsworth Gallery, Sydeny, 1986; David Ellis Fine Art, Melbourne, 1987; S.H. Ervin Gallery, Sydney, 1988; Brisbane City Hall, 1988; National Library, Canberra, 1988-89. *Publications:* Places, Faces and Fantasies, Co-author, 1984; Porfolio of Lithographs published in Australian Portraits, 1984; Artists and Friends, 1988. *Memberships:* Council of the Order of Australia, 1975-79; Trustee, The Art Gallery of New

South Wales, 1980-87. *Honours:* The Perth Prize, 1955; Australian Women's Weekly Prize, 1955, 1956; The Archibald Prize, 1961; Helena Rubenstein Portrait Prize, 1964, 1965; Sir Charles Lloyd Memorial Prize, 1965, 1971, 1972, 1973; The Archibald Prize, 1968; Awarded CBE, 1969; Awarded A.O., 1988. *Hobbies:* Writing; Music. *Address:* 16C Ocean Avenue, Double Bay, Sydney, New South Wales 2028, Australia.

CASSADY Ann Belden Rentschler, b. 22 Oct. 1927, New York, USA. Politician. m. William Francis Cassady. 2 sons, 6 daughters. *Education:* Diploma, Ethel Walker School, 1940-45; AA, Bennett College, 1974. *Appointments:* Medical Secretary, Hartford Hospital, 1947-49; Florida Republican State Committee, Executive Board, 1966-84; Boca Raton City Council, 1975-80; Tourist Development Commission, 1981-88; Vice President, Program Chairman, Loggerhead Club 1987-; Republican County Committee executive Board, 1988-. *Memberships:* Consultant, Presidents Commission on Mental Retardation; Life Member, Capitol Hill Club, Washington DC; International Oceanographic Foundation; American Horse Show Association; National Steeple Chase Hunt Association; Daughters of the American Revolution, PB Chapter; JR League of Boca Raton; International Platform Association; Programme Co-Chairman, The Loggerhead Club, 1985-. *Honours:* Certificate of Appreciation, Republican Party, 1970-84. *Hobbies:* Horses; Riding; Fishing; Water skiing; Flowers; Gardening; Children's Rights. *Address:* Boca Raton, FL 33429, USA.

CASSAN Dagmar A, b. 7 Oct. 1941, Munster, West Germany. Finance Officer. m. Vito J Cassan, 9 Nov. 1972. *Education:* BA, Economics, Fordham University, New York City, 1977; MBA, Finance, Graduate School of Business, New York University, 1980. *Appointments:* Financial Analyst/Specialist, General Foods Corp, White Plains, New York, 1980-83; Financial Manager, Asia/Pacific, Nabisco International Corp, New York, 1984; President, DAC Associates, International Capital Advisors, New York, 1985-. *Memberships:* Financial Womens Association, New York City; New York University Finance Club. *Honour:* Magna Cum Laude, Economics, Fordham University, New York. *Hobbies:* Classical music; Painting; Antique furniture; Swimming; Tennis. *Address:* 301 East 66th Street, Suite 12E, New York, NY 10021, USA.

CASSELLE Dawne Astride, b. 16 Apr. 1943, Philadelphia, Pennsylvania, USA. Advertising Specialties Media Consultant, Businesswoman/owner. m. (1) Frank Poindexter, 5 Feb. 1961, divorced 6 Jan. 1968, 1 son. (2) Raymond Spurlock, 6 Oct. 1968, divorced 12 Jan. 1980. *Education:* AA, LA Pierce College, 1973; BA 1975, JD 1980, University of California at Los Angeles (UCLA). *Appointments:* Administrative Specialist, IBM Corp. 1968-73; Independent Contractor Paralegal, 1975-88; Advertising Specialties Media Consultant, 1982-; Real Estate Salesperson. *Creative work:* Yarn Art Creations, Wall Tapestries. *Memberships:* California Women Business Owners (CWBO); Wilshire Chamber of Commerce, 1984-88, Board of Directors, 1987-88; National Association of Female Executives (NAFE); UCLA Law Alumni Association; National Organisation of Women (NOW); International Platform Association; National Museum of Women in the Arts, Charter Member; NAACP; Crystal Cathedral Church of the Air; 2nd Baptist Church; Founders Church of Religious Science. *Honours:* UCLA Letters & Science Honors Program, 1974-75; Staff Writer, UCLA Black Law Journal, 1979, 1980; UCLA Law Moot Court Honors Program, Invitee, 1976-79; Newton Manufacturing Company, National Sales Topper Award, 1984,1985 and 1987; Who's Who in California, 1987-89. *Hobbies:* Swimming; Theatre; Concerts; Opera; Plays; Photography; Downhill snow skiing; Gourmet cooking; Travelling; People. *Address:* 3333 W 2nd Street, Suite No 53-204, Los Angeles, CA 90004, USA.

CASTANIS Muriel Julia Brunner, b. 27 Sept. 1926, New York City, USA. Sculptor. m. 23 Nov. 1955, 3 sons,

1 daughter. *Education:* Self-taught artist. *Creative work includes:* 21 solo exhibitions, New York, Massachusetts, Pennsylvania, Florida, Colorado, 1974-; Numerous group exhibitions, New York, Maine, Virginia, Ohio, Connecticut, New Jersey, 1968-; Work reviewed, numerous books & journals including New York Times, Village Voice, American Craft Magagazine, Art News; Listed, various biographical directories. *Honours:* Sculpture grant, Tiffany Foundation, New York, & Stage Set Award, Show Business, 1977; Award of Distinction, Virginia Museum of Fine Art (Biennal), 1979. *Hobbies:* Roller skating; Cycling; Swimming; Thinking. *Address:* 444 6th Avenue, New York, NY 10011, USA.

CASTELL Claire Louise, b. 29 June 1960, Woking, England. Personnel Executive. *Education:* HNC, Distinction, Business Studies, 1983. *Appointments:* Personnel Officer, Rank Xerox HQ, London, 1979-84; Managing Director & major shareholder, Hughes-Castell (Hong Kong) Ltd, recruitment consultants to legal profession, 1986-. *Hobbies:* Sports; Theatre; Travel; Antiques; Restaurants. *Address:* Room 602, East Town Building, 41 Lockhart Road, Wanchai, Hong Kong.

CASTELO-SOTTO Herminia, b. 1 July 1910, Philippines. Physician. m. Marcelino O. Sotto, 7 June 1944, 4 sons. *Education:* MD, University of the Philippines, 1935; various courses & studies. *Appointments:* Private Practice, 1936-52; Medical Officer, Workmen's Compensation Commission, 1952-63; Chief Compensation Rating Medical Officer, WCC, 1963-68; Medical Commissioner, WCC, 1968-76. *Publications:* over 30 articles in professional journals. *Memberships:* 1st Chairman, Board, Araullo University, 1950-54; 1st Lady President: Philappine Association of Occupational Health, Philippine Association of Compensation Medicine, Philippine Specialty Board of Compensation Medicine. *Honours:* Recipient, numerous honours including: Dona Aurora Aragon Quezon Medal, 1959; Emeritus Professor, 1980; Rizal's Women of Malalos Award, 1988. *Hobbies:* Reading; Knitting; Singing; TV & Films. *Address:* No 20 Asparagus, Valle Verde V, Pasig, Metro Manila, Philippines.

CASTEN JoAnn Daly, b. 30 Sept. 1941, Peekskill, New York, USA. Antiquarian Book Dealer. m. 6 June 1964. *Education:* BA, St Joseph's College, West Hartford, Connecticut, 1963; MS, Southern Connecticut State College, 1965; Student, financial planning, Adelphi University, current. *Appointment:* Vice President, JoAnn & Richard Casten Ltd, 1975-. *Publications:* Numerous catalogues, antiquarian books. *Memberships:* Antiquarian Booksellers Association of America; American Association of University Women. *Hobbies:* Skiing; Tennis; Backpacking. *Address:* 4 Dodge Lane, Old Field, New York 11733, USA.

CASTLE Barbara Anne, b. 6 Oct. 1910, Chesterfield, England. Member, European Parliament. m. 29 July 1944. *Education:* BA Honours Degree, St Hugh's College, Oxford, 1932. *Appointments:* Member, House of Commons, 1945-79; Member, British Cabinet, 1964-70; 1974-76; Member, European Parliament, 1979-; Minister, Overseas Development, 1964; Minister, Transport, 1964; Secretary of State for Employment, 1968; Secretary of State for Social Services, 1974-76. *Publications:* The Castle Diaries 1974-76, 1980; The Castle Diaries 1964-70, 1984; Sylvia and Christabel Pankhurst, 1987. *Memberships:* President, Anti-Apartheid Movement, Great Britain, 1962-64. *Honour:* Honorary Fellow, St Hugh's College, Oxford. *Hobbies:* Gardening; Walking with the dogs. *Address:* 2 Queen Anne's Gate, London SW1, England.

CASTON Anne Louise, b. 24 Oct. 1956, Los Angeles, California, USA. Doctoral candidate. *Education:* BA, UCLA, 1978; MA, California State University, Northridge, 1987; Doctoral candidate at Pennsylvania State University. *Appointments:* Employee Relations Assistant, Vivitar Corporation, California, 1978-79; Employee Relations Representative, Delphi Communications Corporation, San Francisco, CA, 1979-

80; Assistant Dept Manager, Bullock's Department Stores, 1980-83; Exercise Physiologist, Los Angeles Athletic Club, 1984-85; Exercise Physiologist, Pritikin Programs Inc, 1985-87. *Creative works:* Presentations: American College of Sports Medicine, 1987; California State University Student Research Competition, 1987; American Alliance of Health, Physical Education, Recreation and Dance, 1986. *Memberships:* American College of Sports Medicine; American Alliance of Health, Physical Education, Recreation and Dance; Phi Beta Kappa Honor Society; Phi Kappa Phi Honor Society; California Association for Health, Physical Education, Recreation and Dance. *Honours:* Phi Beta Kappa, Summa Cum Laude, UCLA, 1978; Dean's List, 1978; Dean's Award, Outstanding Graduate Student, California State University, 1985; Robert Schiffman Memorial Scholarship; Mable W Richards Scholarship, 1986. *Hobbies:* Track clubs; Running clubs; Volunteer time with Vetrans Administration Track club and rehabilitation organizations; Volunteer for Big Brothers/ Sisters. *Address:* 245 So Almont Drive, Beverly Hills, CA 90211, USA.

CASTON Christine Marie Lowman, b. 13 Jan. 1951, Laporte, Indiana, USA. Commercial Real Estate Broker. m. Robert W Caston, 25 July 1980. 1 daughter. *Education:* Bert Rogers School of Real Estate, 1975; Mid Cities Commercial College, 1986. *Appointments:* Real Estate Broker, Deltona Corporation, Miami, Florida, 1976-80; Assistant to President, Worth Enterprises, Ft Worth, Texas, 1982-85; Morrow Investment Co, Ft Worth, Texas, 1985-87; Caston Commercial Interests, 1987-. *Memberships:* The International Platform Association; Commercial Real Estate Women; National Association of Realtors; Texas Association of Realtors; Florida Association of Realtors; Texas State Bar Association Auxiliary. *Honours:* Quill and Scroll Award, 1969. *Hobby:* Writing. *Address:* 1201 Medford Drive, Bedford, Texas 76021, USA.

CASTRO Jan Garden, b. 8 June 1945, St Louis, USA. Author; Arts Consulant; Educator. 1 child. *Education Includes:* BA, English, University of Wisconsin, 1967; Publishing Certificate, Radcliffe College, 1967; MAT, Washington University, St Louis, 1974. *Appointments:* Teacher, Writer, St Louis, 1970-; Executive Director, Big River Association, St Louis, 1975-85; Lecturer, Lindenwood College, 1980-; Co-Founder, Director, Duff's Poetry Series, St Louis; Founder, Director, River Styx PM Series, 1981-83; Arts Consultant, Harris-Stowe State College, 1986-87. *Publications:* Contributing Author: San Francisco Review of Books, 1982-85; Author books including: Mandala of the Five Senses, 1975; The Art & Life of Georgia O'Keeffe, 1985; Editor, River Styx Magazine, 1975-86; Co-Editor: Margaret Atwood: Vision and Forms, 1988; TV Host & Co-Producer, The Writers Circle, Double Helix, St Louis, 1987-88. *Memberships:* MLA; Founder, Margaret Atwood Society. *Honours:* Editors Award, River Styx Magazine from Co-ordinating Council for Literary Magazines, 1986; NEH (National Endowment for Humanities) Summer Fellow; UCLA, 1988; YWCA Leadership Award in Arts, 1988. *Address:* 7420 Cornell Ave., Saint Louis, MO 63130, USA.

CASWELL Paulette Reva, b. 8 June 1951, Chicago, Illinois, USA. Attorney-at-Law. m. 7 Jan. 1981, 1 son. *Education:* AA cum laude, West Los Angeles Community College, 1971; BA, California State University, 1975; JD, Whittier College School of Law, Los Angeles, 1982. *Appointments include:* Freelance Consultant, efficiency in workplace, 1975-; Clinical experience, labour law, Lionel Richman, 1980, 1982; Notary Public, State of California, 1980-; Attorney, sole practice, specialising representation of disabled persons, 1982-; Founder & president, Amicus, non-profit corporation for legal services and information to persons with disabilities; Lecturer, legal issues, various groups. *Publications:* Numerous articles, papers. *Memberships include:* State Bar of California; US District Court (Central California); LA Trial Lawyers Association; Past Board, Greater Los Angeles, Mensa; Magician member, Academy of Magical Arts & Sciences, LA; Board, Legal Adviser,

World Recreation Association for the Deaf; Various other organisations concerning disabled people. *Honours include:* Award of Excellence, Administrative Law, Whittier College School of Law, 1979-82; 2 scholarships; Honour societies. *Hobbies include:* Helping people make dreams come true; Flying. *Address:* Amicus, 645 N Gardner Street, Los Angeles, CA 90036, USA.

CATALFO Betty, 1 son, 1 daughter. *Appointments:* Secretary, ABCTV, New York City; Lecturer, Weight Watchers, Manhasset, New York; Founder President, Everybodys' Diet Inc; Get Slim & Stay Slim Diet Centers; Director, In-Home Program NYS Dept of Health; Director, Senior Citizen Diet & Nutrition Centyers, Queens & Bronx, New York. *Publications:* 101 Stay Slim Recipes; Isometrics for Spot Reducing; Never Say Dietl; Videos: Dancercize for the Overweight; Eating Right for Life; Get Slim and Stay Slim Diet Class in Action!; Hello Its Me & I'm Thin!; Dance Your Calories Away!; Isometric Techniques for Weight Reduction, 1986; Revised Get Slim & Stay Slim Diet Cookbook, 1987; Video: Positive & Negative diet Forces, 1987. *Memberships:* Business & Professional Womens Club; Association for fitness in Business Inc; National Chamber of Commerce; Presidents Council for Physical Fitness; National Association Female Business Owners; Roundtable for Women in Food Service; American Red Cross; League of Women Voters; American Italian Association; Council of Churchs & Synagogues; United Way of Greenwich; Sponsor, St Pauls Center, Brooklyn; Throggs Neck Retarded Children Association 1985-; etc. *Honours:* Woman of Year, 1986-87; Richmond Boys Club; Women of Year 1987, National Chamber of Commerce; Mother of Year, 1987, Bronx Press Association; Woman of Year, 1987, Senior Citizens of Sacred Heart League 1987 Merit award for Community Service, Brooklyn Queens Archdiocese. *Address:* 208-05 15 Road Bayside, New York 11360, USA.

CATCHINGS Yvonne Parks, b. 17 Aug. Atlanta, Georgia, USA. m. 30 May, 1960. 1 son, 2 daughters. *Education:* AB, Spelman, 1955; MA, Columbia, 1959; MA 1970, PhD 1981, University of Michigan; Art Therapy Certificate, Wayne, 1985. *Appointments:* Valdosta State College; Detroit Board of Education; Marygrove College; Spelman College; Atlanta Board of Education. *Creative Works:* Book: You Ain't Free Yet, Notes From a Black Woman; Collage: The Detroit Riot; Watercolour: Backyard Wash; Pen & Ink: Country Madonna. *Memberships:* American Association of University Professors; American Association of University Women; National Art Educ. Association; National Conference of Art; American Art Therapy Assoc, Archivist, Michigan Association; Phi Delta Kappa Fraternity; Delta Sigma Theta Sorority, Nat Board Member, Chair, Heritage & Archives; Detroit Genealogy Society, Program Chairman. *Honours:* James D Parks Special Award, National Conference of Artists; First Award Print; President's Special Award, National Dental Association, 1973; Mayor's Award of Merit, 1978; Spirit of Detroit Award, 1978; Special Award, Afro American Museum, 1983. *Hobbies:* Painting; Tracing Ancestors; Writing. *Address:* 1306 Joliet Place, Detroit, Michigan 48207, USA.

CATCHPOLE Nancy Mona, b. 6 Aug. 1929, Hampstead, London, England. Part-time Consultant to Royal Society of Arts. m. 19 Aug. 1959. 1 son, 1 daughter. *Education:* BA Hons, History, Bedford College, PGCE, Maria Grey College, London University. *Appointments:* History Teacher, Gravesend G S, 1952-56; Head of History, Ipswich HS, 1956-62; Part-time Teacher of History, 1965-68; Part-time Lecturer in History, 1977-89; Joint Secretary, Women's National Commission, 1985-88; Consultant to Industry Matters, 1989-. *Memberships:* British Federation of University Women, National President 1981-84; Historical Association, Bath Branch Secretary, 1975-79; Fellow, Royal Society of Arts, 1986-; Member, Wessex Regional Health Authority, 1986-. *Honours:* OBE, 1986; FRSA, 1986; John Stowe Memorial Prize, 1946-47. *Hobbies:* Promotion of women's non-traditional employment;

Social education; Theatre; Knitting. *Address:* 66 Leighton Road, Weston, Bath, Avon BA1 4NG, England.

CATHCART Helen, Author; Biographer, British Royal Family, 1958-. *Publications:* The Queen and the Turf, 1959; Prince Philip, Sportsman, 1961; Her Majesty, 1962; Sandringham, 1964; The Queen Mother, 1965; Royal Lodge, Windsor, 1966; Princess Alexandra, 1967; Lord Snowdon, 1968; The Royal Bedside Book, 1969; The Married Life of the Queen, 1970; The Duchess of Kent, 1971; Princess Margaret, 1974; The Queen in her Circle, 1977; The Queen Mother Herself, 1979; The Queen Herself, 1982; The Queen Mother, 50 Years a Queen, 1986; The Queen and Prince Philip, 1987; Anne, the Princess Royal, 1988; Charles, Man of Destiny, 1988; etc. *Memberships:* Society of Authors. *Address:* c/o Rupert Xrew Ltd, Kings Mews, London WC1N 2JA, England.

CATHOU Renata Egone, b. 21 June 1935, Milan, Italy. Scientist; Consultant to industry in biotechnology. m. Pierre-Yves Francois Cathou, 21 June 1959, divorced. *Education:* BS 1957, PhD 1963, Massachusetts Institute of Technology. *Appointments:* Research Associate, Chemistry, MIT, 1962-65; Research Associate, Massachusetts General Hospital, 1965-69; Instructor, Harvard Medical School and MGH, 1970; Professor, Tufts Medical School, 1970-81; Independent consultant, 1981-82; President, Technical Evaluations, 1983-. *Publications:* 60 research articles in professional journals and contributed chapters to books. *Memberships:* Amer Soc of Biol Chemists; American Association Immunologists; NY Academy of Sciences; Clinical Ligand Assay Soc; American Chemical Society; Amer Assoc for Clinical Chemistry; American Association for the Advancement of Science; US Power Squadrons; Museum of Fine Arts (Boston) Council; American Institute of Chemists. *Honours:* Senior Investigator, Arthritis Foundation, 1970-75; Grantee, American Heart Association, 1969-81; Grantee, US Public Health Service, 1970-81; Member, Board of Scientific Counselors, National Cancer Institute, 1979-83; Member Editorial Board, Immunochemsitry, 1972-75. *Hobbies:* Photography: Fine arts; Sailing. *Address:* Technical Evaluations, 430 Marrett Road, Lexington, MA 02173, USA.

CATLETT Mary Jo, b. 2 Sept. 1938, Denver, Colorado, USA. Actress. *Education:* BA Drama, Loretto Heights College, 1960. *Creative Works:* Performances in: Broadway Shoes: Hello Dolly (Ernestina), 1964-67; Canterbury Tales (Nun, Miller's Wife), 1967-68; Lysistrata, with Melina Mercouri (Beta), 1968; Different Times (Characters ranging from 16 to 67), 1970; Fashion (Mrs Tiffany), 1960; Promenade (Mother), 1971; Pajama Game (Mabel), 1974; Play Me A Country Song (Penny), 1982. Films include: Some Tough; The C Lamp. Off Broadway: Commercials, television. *Memberships:* Various professional associations. *Honours:* Drama Critics Award, Washington DC, 1976; Los Angeles Dramalogue Award, 1977, 1980; Louisiana Drama Critics Award for Come Back Little Shiba, 1977 and for Philadelphia Here I Come, 1982, etc. *Hobbies:* Bowling; Bingo; Swimming; Collecting Hummel figurines; Auction sales. *Address:* California, USA.

CAUWELS Janice Marie, b. 8 Dec. 1949, New Jersey, USA. Writer; Consultant. *Education:* MA, 1973, PhD, 1976, University of Virginia. *Appointments:* Visiting Assistant Professor, Emory University, 1977-78; University of Minnesota, 1978-79; Writing Consultant, J.A. Johnson Co., 1980-83; Copy Editor, Minnesota Educational Computing Consortium, 1982; Woman's World, 1983; Physicians Weekly, 1985; United Research Co. 1988-; Biotechnology consultant, RLS International, 1987-. *Publications:* Bulimia: The Binge-Purge Compulsion, 1983; The Body Shop: Bionic Revolutions in Medicine, 1986; 16 articles. *Memberships:* MLA; American Society of Journalists & Authors; Authors Guild. *Honours:* Recipient, various awards including: Lychnos Honour Society, 1973. *Hobbies:* Professional Acting; Furniture Refinishing;

Lecturing; Exercising. *Address:* 515 Mount Prospect Avenue, Apt 17-F, Newark, NJ 07104, USA.

CAVANAUGH Margaret Anne, b. 17 July 1947, Dayton, Ohio, USA. Professor of Chemistry. m. Joseph C. Cavanaugh, 6 Jan. 1968. *Education:* BS, Chemistry, University of Pittsburgh, Pennsylvania, 1968; PhD, Physical Inorganic Chemistry, Catholic University of America, Washington DC, 1973. *Appointments:* Visiting Assistant Professor, Postdoctoral Research Associate, Department of Chemistry, University of New Orleans, 1973-75; Assistant Professor, Chemistry, 1975-79, Associate Professor, 1979-86, Professor and Chair, Department of Chemistry, 1986-, Saint Mary's College, Notre Dame, Indiana; Visiting Scientist, Chemistry Division, National Science Foundation. *Publications:* 12 publications in inorganic chemistry, chemical education, women in chemistry. *Memberships:* American Chemical Society: Chair, 1981, Councilor, 1984-, St Joseph Valley Section; Chair, Women Chemists Committee, 1986-88; Nominations and Elections Committee, 1988-; Iota Sigma Pi: President, 1978-81, Treasurer, 1981-, Samarium Chapter; National Editor, 1981-87; National Vice-President, 1987-; Fellow, American Institute of Chemists; Sigma Xi: Chair, 1985-87, Secretary, 1982-84, Notre Dame Chapter; Regional Nominating Committee, 1987; Midwestern Association of Chemistry Teachers at Liberal Arts Colleges; Indiana Academy of Science (Chair, Chemistry Division, 1982 and 1989); Member, Women Chemists Committee, 1983-88. *Honours:* Spes Unica Award for Outstanding Teaching and Service to the College, Saint Mary's College, 1983; Local Section Service Award, St Joseph Valley Section, American Chemical Society, 1983. *Hobbies:* Theology; Philosophy of science. *Address:* Chemistry Division, National Science Foundation, Washington, DC 20550, USA.

CAVENS Sharon Sue, b. 15 Feb. 1942, Manhattan, USA. Director. 5 sons. *Education:* Trained Crisis Counsellor for battered women, youth and alcohol/drugs. *Appointments:* Field Co-ordinator, Friendly Neighbors Aging Nutritional Programme, 1972-76; Outreach Co-ordinator, Supervisor, Shawnee County Community Assistance & Action, 1976-79; Executive Director, East Topeka Senior Centre, 1979-. *Memberships:* Exodusters Awareness Inc; Topeka Black Womens Network. *Honours:* Recipient, various honours and awards. *Hobbies:* Fishing; Reading; Poetry; People. *Address:* 2323 SE Ohio, Topeka, KS 66605, USA.

CAWS Mary Ann, b. 20 Sept. 1933. Distinguished Professor of English, French and Comparative Literature. *Education:* BA, Bryn Mawr College, 1954; MA, Yale, 1956; PhD, Kansas, 1962; Doctor Humane Letters, Union College, 1982. *Appointments:* Assistant Professor, University of Kansas; Sarah Lawrence Faculty; Hunter College; Associate, Full, Distinguished Professor, Graduate Center, City University of New York. *Publications:* The Eye in The Text; Reading Frames in Modern Fiction; The Art of Interference; Textual Analysis. *Memberships:* President, Modern Language Association; President, Academy of Literary Studies; President Elect, American Comparative Literature Association. *Honours:* Fellowships: Guggenheim; Fulbright, NEH. *Address:* 140 E 81st, New York, NY 10028, USA.

CAZALET Camilla Jane, b. 12 July 1937, London, England. Art Gallery Director. m. Edward Stephen Cazalet, 24 Apr. 1965, 2 sons, 1 daughter. *Education:* Benenden School, 1950-54. *Appointments:* Foreign Office, 1955-57; Various art galleries, UK and USA, 1957-63; Assistant Foreign Manager, Financial Times, London, 1964-65; Founder, Lumley Cazalet Ltd, 1967-. *Memberships:* Trustee, Glyndebourne Festival Opera; Council Member, Friends of Covent Garden. *Hobbies:* Music; Tennis; Art; Theatre. *Address:* 58 Seymour Walk, London SW10 9NF, England.

CAZALET-KEIR Thelma, m. David Keir, 1939 (died 1969). *Appointments:* Member, London County Council,

East Islington, 1925-31; Alderman, City of London, 1931; Contested by-election, East Islington, 1931; MP (Nat.C) East Islington, 1931-45; Parliamentary Private Secretary to Parliamentary Secretary to Board of Education, 1937-40; Parliamentary Secretary to Ministry of Education, May 1945; Member, Committee of Enquiry into conditions in Women's Services, 1942; member, Committee on Equal Compensation (Civil Injuries), 1943; Chairman, London Area Women's Advisory Committee, Conservative & Unionist Associations, 1943-46, Chairman, Equal Pay Campaign Committee; Member, Cost of Living Committee; Member, Arts Council of Great Britain, 1940-49; Member, Executive Committee of Contemporary Art Society; Member, Transport Users Conultative Comittee for London, 1950-52; A Governor for the BBC, 1956-61; Member,Transport Users Consultative Committee for London, 1950-52; Governor of the BBC, 1956-61; Member, Committee, Royal UK Beneficial Association, 1962; President, Fawcett Society, 1964. *Publications:* From the Wings, Editor, 1967; Homage to P G Wodehouse, 1973. *Honour:* CBE, 1952. *Hobbies:* Music; Lawn Tennis. *Address:* Flat J, 90 Eaton Square, London SW1W 9AG, England.

CECIL Dorcas Ann, b. 31 Mar. 1945, Greensboro, North Carolina, USA. Property Manager; Real Estate Broker. m. Richard L. Cecil, 8 June 1968, 1 daughter. *Education:* BA, University of Arkansas, 1967. *Appointments:* President, Property Manager, Owner, B & C Enterprises Property Management Ltd., 1977-. *Memberships:* Vice President, St Louis Chapter, Institute of Real Estate Management, 1987-; President-Elect, 1989-; Managing Committee, St Louis Multi-Housing Council, 1986-; Professional Housing Management Association; O'Fallon Library Board of Trustees, President; O'Fallon Chamber of Commerce Board of Directors, Vice President; Belleville Board of Realtors; National Association of Realtors. *Honours:* Certified Property Manager; Accredited Resident Manager; Registered Apartment Manager. *Hobbies:* Reading; Walking; Boating. *Address:* 15 Brandonwood, O'Fallon, IL 62269, USA.

CEDEL Melinda Irene, b. 31 July 1957, Fort Worth, Texas, USA. Musician. *Education:* North Carolina School of Arts, 1974-77; BMusEd, University of South Carolina, 1979. *Appointments:* Teacher, Charleston County Public Schools, 1979-; Violinist, Charleston Symphony Orchestra, 1979-; Conductor, Charleston County Prep Orchestra, 1983-84; Private String Teacher, 1983-; Violinist, Manager, Charleston String Quartet, 1983-. *Creative work includes:* Violin performances: Florence Symphony Orchestra, Columbia Philharmonic Orchestra, SC Chamber Orchestra, Augusta (Georgia) Symphony Orchestra, Long Bay (SC) Symphony Orchestra, Charleston Opera Company; Regular Performances: Piccolo Spoleto Festival, Charleston Symphony Orchestra, Charleston Symphony Chamber Orchestra. *Memberships:* Music Educators National Conference; American Federation of Musicians; American String Teachers Association; Kappa Phi Kappa. *Honour:* Member, Mensa. *Hobbies:* Travel; Water Sports; Reading; Sailing. *Address:* 302 Grimball Avenue, Charleston, South Carolina 29412, USA.

CENTENO-BELTRAN Violeta, b. 18 Oct. 1930, Manila, Philippines. MD. Widow, 3 sons, 1 daughter. *Education:* MD, 1954; Diplomate, 1973, Fellow, 1974, American Academy of Obstetrics & Gynaecology. *Appointments:* Attending Obstetrican, Salvation Army Booth Hospital, 1972-83; Attending Obstetrician, Ravenswood Hospital, 1972-, Chairman of Department, 1986-. *Publications:* Look I'm Flat Again, 1985. *Memberships:* Chicago Medical Society; Illinois Medical Society; American Medical Association. *Honours:* Golden Apple, 1976. *Hobbies:* Travel; Collecting Porcelain. *Address:* 2256 W. Lawrence, Chicago, IL 60625, USA.

CENTERS Louise Claudena, b. 21 Jan. 1931, Hunt Park, California, USA. Psychologist; Attorney. *Education:* BA 1953, PhD 1958, University of Southern California;

JD, Detroit College of Law, 1979. *Appointments:* Chief of Psycholgical Services and Director of Psychology Training, Sinai Hospital, Detroit, Michigan, 1970-88; Associate Clinical Professor of Psychology, University of Windsor, Ontario, Canada; Full-time private clinical psychology practice, 1988-. *Publications:* 9 publications in psychological journals. *Memberships:* Michigan Psychological Association, President, 1981; Michigan Society of Clinical Psychologists, President, 1975; American Psychological Association, Committee on Legal Issues, 1979-89; American Orthopsychiatric Association, Fellow; State Bars of Michigan and Florida. *Honour:* Distinguished Psychologist, Michigan Psychological Association, 1984. *Hobbies:* Harpsichord and classical music; Travel; Theatre. *Address:* 25052 Sherwood Circle, Southfiled, MI 48075, USA.

CERASANO Susan, b. 17 June 1953, Cleveland, Ohio, USA. Professor of English. *Education:* AB, West Chester State College, 1975; MA, 1976, PhD, 1981, University of Michigan. *Appointments:* Department of English, Colgate University, Hamilton, New York, 1981-. *Publications:* Articles and review essays in Shakespeare Quarterly, Medieval and Renaissance Drama in England, Biography, Shakespeare Bulletin, and other professional journals. *Memberships:* International Shakespeare Association; Shakespeare Association of America; British Theatre Association; London Topographical Society; Modern Language Association of America. *Honours:* Rackham Fellowships, 1979-81; Rackham Travel Grants, 1979-81; Rackham Doctoral Fellow, University of Michigan, 1980-81; National Endowment for the Humanities Fellowship, 1982, 1988-89. *Hobbies:* Gardening; Photography; Equestrian sports; Music. *Address:* Department of English, Colgate University, Hamilton, NY 13346, USA.

CHADWELL Susie, b. 26 Aug. 1940, Jellico, Tennessee, USA. Real Estate & Mortgage Broker; Lecturer; Teacher; Practitioner, Mantic Arts. m. Richard Rodriguez, 30 May 1957, 1 son, 1 daughter. *Education:* Business University of Tampa, Florida, 1965-67; Midland Technical College, Columbia SC, 1972-73; University of South Carolina, 1972-73; Hillsborough Community College, Tampa, 1975-78; Tampa College, 1982-83; University of South Florida, 1988-89. *Appointments:* Assistant, Chad Supply, Tampa, 1977-79; Real Estate Sales, Chadwell Homes, Tampa, 1979-; Owner, Susie's Creations, 1975-82; Sales Manager, Eastfield Slopes Condominiums, 1982-84; Owner/Operator, Susie Chadwell, Real Estate Broker, 1985-; Lecturer, Universal Centre, Cassadaga, 1987-88; Affiliate, Ruth Rogers Centre, Tampa, 1988-; Owner, Susie Chadwell Association, 1989-. *Creative works:* Numerous lectures & workshops, real estate, self-improvement, parapsychology, relationships. *Memberships include:* Past/present Tampa Lyric Society; YWCA Educational Group; Association for Research & Enlightenment; National Association for Female Executives; Networking; Tampa Board of Realtors; Lobbyist, Florida Association of Mortgage Brokers; Friends; Charter Member, Tampa Bay Performing Arts Centre; International Platform Association. *Hobbies:* Art; Handicrafts; Photography. *Address:* 9540 Field View Circle, Thonotosassa, Florida 33592, USA.

CHADWICK Fiona Jane, b. 13 May 1960, Morecambe, England. Ballet Dancer. *Education:* Trained Junior and Senior Royal Ballet Schools, 1971-78. *Appointments:* Joined Royal Ballet Company, 1978 as Corps de Ballet; Promoted to Soloist 1983; Principal, 1985. *Appearances:* Danced all major classical roles including: Swan Lake; Sleeping Beauty; Giselle; Nutcracker; Romeo & Juliet; Other main roles included: Mayerling; Rite of Spring; Firebird; Symphonic Variations; Scenes of Ballet; Serenade, etc. *Hobbies:* Theatre; Cinema; Cooking; Gardening; Football. *Address:* The Royal Opera House, Covent Garden, London WC2, England.

CHADWICK Virginia Anne, b. 19 Dec. 1944, Newcastle, Australia. Parliamentarian. m. Bruce

Sheldon Chadwick, 4 Jan. 1965. 1 son, 1 daughter. *Education:* BA; Diploma in Education. *Appointments:* Teacher, Lecturer, Australia and United Kingdom, 1965-71; Family business, 1971-78; Elected to New South Wales Parliament, 1978. *Address:* Parliament House, Sydney, New South Wales, Australia.

CHAFFIN Lillie D (Mrs Kash), b. 2 Jan. 1925, Varney, Kentucky, USA. Writer. m. (1) Thomas Chaffin, 6 Aug. 1942, 1 son. (2) Dr Vernon O Kash, 6 Apr. 1983. *Education:* Akron University; MA, Doctor of Letters, Eastern Kentucky State Universtiy; Morehead State University; BSc, Doctor of Letters, Pikeville College. *Appointments:* Lecturer, Teacher and/or Librarian: Alice Lloyd College; Berea College; Bevins School; Eastern Kentucky State University; Hindman Settlement School; Johns Creek School; Johns Creek High School; Kimper School; Morehead State University; Morris Harvey College; Pikeville College; University of Kentucky. *Publications include:* Included in over 33 Anthologies and Textbooks. Books: Poetry: Appalachian History and Other Poems, 1980; A Stone for Sisyphus, 1967; Eighth Day Thirteenth Moon, 1975; First Notes, 1969; In My Backyard, 1969; Lines and Points, 1966; Star Following, 1976; Waiting for Love, 1982. Picture books: A Garden is Good, 1963; Bear Weather, 1969; I Have a Tree, 1969; Tommy's Big Problem, 1967; We Be Warm till Springtime Comes, 1980. Non-Fiction: America's First Ladies (2 volumes with Miriam Butwin), 1969; A World of Books, 1969; Coal: Energy and Crisis, 1974. Fiction: John Henry McCoy, 1971; Freeman, 1972. Contributions to numerous magazines, journals and newspapers. *Memberships:* Academy of American Poets; Florida State Poetry Association; Kentucky State Poetry Society; National League of American Pen Women; National Poetry Association; Poetry Society of America; Society of Children's Book Writers. *Honours:* Alice Lloyd College Poetry Award; Anita Boggs Award for Poetry; Child Study Association Book Award; Distinguished Alumna Eastern Kentucky State University; Distinguished Alumna Pikeville College; Fiction Award, Kentucky Literary Guild; International Poetry Prize; Jane Tinkham Broughton Award; Kentucky Colonel (Governor's Award); Marion Doyle Memorial Award for Poetry; Outstanding Teacher, Eastern Kentucky State University. *Address:* 2284 Spanish Drive, Clearwater, FL33575, USA.

CHAFIN Sara Susan, b. 24 Mar. 1952, Huntington, USA. Teacher; Administrator. *Education:* BA, 1977. *Appointments:* Teacher, Woods Academy, 1982-83; Head Teacher, Children's House of Washington, 1983; Headteacher, Vera Camder Montessori School, 1984-85; Administrator, President, Manhattan Montessori School, 1985-. *Publications:* Articles in: East West Journal. *Memberships:* North American Montessoi Teachers Association; Association Montessori Internationale. *Honours:* Recipient, various honours and awards. *Hobbies:* Acting; Painting; Environmental Concerns; Animal Rights; Swimming. *Address:* 255 West 92nd Street, Apt. 3C, New York, NY 10025, USA.

CHALFIN Alycia Robin Shapiro, b. 20 Jan. 1952, Long Beach, New York, USA. President Sales/Merchandiser. m. Seth David Chalfin, 30 Aug. 1987, 1 son. *Education:* BS, Education, New York University, 1973. *Appointments:* Buyer, Alexanders Dept Stores, 1974-78; Buyer, Paul Harris Stores, 1978-81; Buyer, Limited Express Stores, 1981-83; President, Evie B, 1983-. *Hobbies:* Collect Italian/French art deco objects and furniture. *Address:* 22 West 38 Street 9th Floor, New York City, NY 10018, USA.

CHALOVICH Pamela Sue, b. 7 July 1954, Gary, Indiana, USA. Vocational Rehabilitation Counsellor/General Partner. *Education:* BA, Psychology, St Mary's College, Notre Dame, Ind; Master of Arts, Loyola Marymount University, Los Angeles. *Appointments:* New Opportunities: Evaluation and assessment of aptitudes, skills & interests, job placements, vocational counsellor, vocational intervention. *Memberships:* HARPPS; CARP; CAL-NARPPS; SCRE; APA; CSPA; RNS; Academy of Science; National Rehabilitation Assoc.

Honour: CAL-NARPPS Program Chair Honour. *Hobbies:* Art; Music; Theatre; Reading; Writing; Cooking; Collectibles. *Address:* 12304 Santa Monica Bl Ste 300, Los Angeles, CA 90025, USA.

CHAMBERS Joan Louise, b. 22 Mar. 1937, Denver, Colorado, USA. University Library Director. m. Donald R. Chambers, 17 Aug. 1958. *Education:* BA, University of North Colorado, 1958; MS, Library Science, 1970, University of California, Berkeley, MS Systems Management, University of Southern California, 1985. *Appointments:* Librarian, University of Nevada, Reno, 1970-79; Assistant University Librarian, University of California, San Diego, 1979-81; University Librarian, University of California, Riverside, 1981-85; Director of Libraries, Colorado State University, 1985-. *Publications:* Articles in: DLA Bulletin; Microform Review; Energy and Nevada. *Memberships:* Research Libraries Group, Board of Governors; Association of Research Libraries; American Library Association. *Honours:* Beta Phi Mu; Senior Fellow, UCLA. *Hobbies:* Local History; Sierra Club; Audubon Society; Biking; Skiing; Jogging. *Address:* Fort Collins, Colorado, USA.

CHAMBERS Margaret Horsell, b. 19 Jan. 1916, Waynsboro, Pennsylvania, USA. Retired Musician; Poet; Writer; Explorer; Traveller for Peace and Rights of Handicapped. *Education:* Honour High School Graduate; Special Student Eg. Columbia University, NYC; Alvin College, Eng., Math; Honour Graduate Phi Theta Kappa, Fine Arts, College of the Mainland. *Appointments:* Draftsman Engrs Asst, Scomet Engr. 1935-41; Draftsman, M W Kellog, 1942; Draftsman, Special engrs. Panama Canal Zone, 1942-45; Pioneer Woman Engineering 1934-81. Illustrator, Cartog., Corps of Engrs. 1963-72; Bluebonnet Art & Sculpture Studio, 1971; Bluebonnet Lapidary/Art studio 1974-. *Publications and Creative Works:* Poetry; Illuminated relig./ publ; Illustrations AIChE, ACS chem. journals; Children's Stories; Reports & Illustrations, Congressional record; Articles, The Courier, Year book illustrations; Ed & Illustrator, The Flair; Paintings: Psalm 121, Sumi-E Paintings (Dan Fong Liang Method). Sculpture: Eye of the Needle; Madonna; Nativity; Custom designed jewellery; Gemstone sculpture. *Memberships:* VP, Treas. Sec., Desk & Derrick, Founder & Charter Member, 1954-62; VP, Prog Chmn, TC, Phi Sigma Alpha; Charter Memb, all offices, PSALM; VP, GC Area Asssembly; VP, Galv Coast Gem & Min Assn, 1988; VP, Prog Ch. AARP LM Chapter; Fndr Dir., Choir Mother, Jr & Youth Choirs; St Michael's Snr Choir; COM Singers; Women of St Michael's Lay Minister Order of St Luke; Order of the Holy Cross; Minister Order of St Luke; Graduate, School of Theology, Swanee University; Episcopal Ministry, Priest; AARP; Galveston Alliance Snr Citizens; Grad. Asst., Dale Carnegie Assn, 1966-79; Composer Religious/secular music. *Honours:* Woman of the Year; Phi Sigma Alpha Sweetheart, also yr award; Cert of Appreciation St Michael's Ch. *Hobbies:* Writing Poetry, children's stories; Ikibana Flower Arrangement; 3 dimensional needlepoint; Working with handicapped children & the elderly. *Address:* Box 1263, La Marque, TX 77568, USA.

CHAMBLEE-SWAIN Anna, b. Manhattan, USA. Marketing Consultant; Writer; Lecturer. *Education:* International Marketing, Baruch College. *Appointments:* Secretary to President, Bleuette Inc, 1970-73; Assistant to Director of Classified Advertising, Fairchild Publications, 1974-75; Assistant to Publication Director and National Sales Manager, Lebhar-Friedman Publishing, 1975; Assistant Account Executive, Gaynor & Lucas Advertising, 1976; Assistant Manager, Real Estate Advertising, Fairchild Publications (Women's Wear Daily), 1976-77; Research Analyst and Client Service Representative, Time Incorporated (Selling Area Marketing Incorporated), 1977-80; Marketing Consultant, 1980; Marketing Coordinator, Metropolitan Opera, 1982-. *Creative Works:* Articles: A Night of Super Stars, 1980; The Music of George Gershwin, 1981; Minority Business Calls for Increased Support, 1981; Freedom: Most Profitable Bank in new York City, 1981; Analysis of Minority Business Ownership in the US,

1981; Boom Year at Freedom, 1981. *Memberships:* Public Relation Liaison, Black Liberation Thru Action Collectiveness & Knowledge, Baruch College, 1979-80; President, American Society for Personnel Administration, Baruch College Chapter, 1980-81; Volunteer, United Negro College Fund, 1982; National Business League, 1981-; Founder, Baruch Arts & Letters Society, 1981; Volunteer, United Jewish Appeal Federation of Jewish Philanthropies, 1982; Women for Racial & Economic Equality, 1982-; Founder, International Arts Forum, 1982. *Honours:* Harry M Sherman Award, ASPA, Metropolitan New York, 1981; Designated International Muse of Art by Tenth World Congress of Poets, 1987. *Hobby:* Horticulture. *Address:* PO Box 1142, Ansonia Station, New York, NY 10023, USA.

CHAMLIN Suzanne, b. 18 Feb. 1963, West Long Branch, New Jersey, USA. Artist/Painter. *Education:* BA, Barnard College, 1985; MFA, Yale University, 1989. *Career:* The Spence School, 1985-87; Teachers Assistant, Yale University, summer 1988; Solo exhibitions: Fine Arts Museum of Long Island, 1987; Group exhibitions: Wolden International, New York City, 1986; 5th Annual Juried Show, Fine Arts Museum of Long Island, 1987; Living in New York, Aubes 3935, Montreal, Canada, 1988. *Honours:* Virginia Center for the Creative Arts, Sweet Briar, Virginia, 1986; The Millay Colony Residency, Austerlitz, New York, 1987. *Hobbies:* Music; Running; Dancing. *Address:* 123 York Street, Apt 20K, New Haven, CT 06511, USA.

CHAN Lau C, b. Hong Kong. Actuary. m. Kam F Chan, MD. 2 sons. *Education:* AA, Packer Collegiate Institute, 1948; BS 1950, MS 1952, Fordham University. *Appointments:* Buck Consultants, Inc, 1968-. *Memberships:* Conference of Actuaries in Public Practice, Editor; Society of Actuaries; American Academy of Actuaries; International Actuarial Association; American Pension Conference; Actuarial Society of Greater New York. *Honours:* Graduated with highest honour, Packer Collegiate Institute, 1948; Magna cum laude, Fordham University, 1950. *Hobbies:* Horticulture; Travelling; Opera and music; Tennis. *Address:* Buck Consultants, 500 Plaza Drive, Harmon Meadow, NJ 07094, USA.

CHAN Lois Mai, b. 30 July 1934, Nanking, China. Teacher. m. Shung-Kai Chan, 22 June 1963, 1 son, 1 daughter. *Education:* AB, National Taiwan University, 1956; MA English, 1958, MS Library Science, 1960, Florida State University, USA; PhD, Comparative Literature, University of Kentucky, 1970. *Appointments Include:* Various positions in University Libraries, 1960-67; Assistant Professor, 1970-74, Associate Professor, 1974-80, Professor, 1980-, University of Kentucky; Visiting Professor, Graduate School of Library Studies, Univerity of Hawaii, 1982; Project Consultant, OCLC (DDC Online Project), 1983-86. *Publications:* Library of Congress Subject Headings : Principles and Application, 1978; Marlowe Criticism: A Bibliography, 1978; Immroth's Guide to the Library of Congress Classification, 1980; Cataloging & Classification: An Introduction, 1981; Theory of Subject Analysis: A Source Book, 1985; Library of Congress Subject Headings: Principles and Application, 1986; numerous articles in journals & magazines. *Memberships:* Decimal Classification Editorial Policy Committee, Chairman, 1986-; American Library Association. *Hobbies:* Travel. *Address:* University of Kentucky, Lexington, KY 40506, USA.

CHAN Sucheng, b. 16 Apr. 1941, Shanghai, China. Professor of History. m. Mark Juergensmeyer, 21 Sept. 1969. *Education:* BA, Economics, Swarthmore College, 1963; MA, Asian Studies, University of Hawaii, 1965; PhD, Political Science, University of California, Berkeley, 1973. *Appointments:* California State University, Sonoma, 1971-73; University of California, Berkeley, 1974-84; University of California, Santa Cruz, 1984-88; University of California, Santa Barbara, 1988-. *Publications:* This Bittersweet Soil: The Chinese in California Agriculture, 1860-1910, 1986; Asian

Californians, 1989; Quiet Odyssey: A Pioneer Korean Woman in America, 1989. *Memberships:* Association for Asian American Studies (President, 1980-83); Organization of American Historians; American Historical Society; Immigration History Society; Agricultural History Society; California History Society. *Honours:* Distinguished Teaching Award, 1978; Louis Knott Koontz Prize, 1985; Theodore Saloutos Memorial Book Award for Agricultural History, 1986; American Historical Association Pacific Coast Branch Book Award, 1987; Association for Asian American Studies Outstaanding Book Award, 1988; National Endowment for the Humanities Post-doctoral Fellowship, 1973; University of California Los Angeles Institute of American Cultures Post-doctoral Fellowship, 1980; John Simon Guggenheim Fellowship, 1988. *Hobbies:* Reading; Raising dogs.

CHANCE-PETERS Mary Ann, b. 6 Oct. 1937, Muscatine, Iowa, USA. Chiropractic Physician. m. Rolf E. Peters, 23 Apr. 1983, 3 sons, 1 daughter. *Education:* Doctor in Chiropractic, Palmer College of Chiropractic, 1959. *Appointments:* Private Practice, Mount Gambier, 1959-60; Clinician, McLeod Chiropractic Clinic, Melbourne, 1961-63; Director, Clinician, McLeod Chiropractic Clinics Pty Ltd., 1963-75; Part-time Private Practice, Melbourne, 1975-82; Part-time Lecturer, 1977-82; Executive Secretary, Australian Chiropractors Association, 1975-82; Publications Consultant, Australian Chiropractors Association, 1982-83; Editor, Journal of the Australian Chiropractors Association, 1983-; Director, Research Officer and part time chiropractor, Peters Chiropractc Center, Wagga Wagga. *Publications:* Articles in professional journals. *Memberships:* Various professional organisations. *Honours:* Chiropractor of the Year, 1980, Meritorious Service Award, 1982, 1988, Australian Chiropractors Association. *Hobbies:* Travel; Languages; Music; Horticulture. *Address:* 84 Peter Street, PO Box 748, Wagga Wagga 2650, Australia.

CHANDLER Viney Polite, b. Wichita, Kansas, USA. Community Worker. 1 daughter. *Education:* Graduate, Wichita Business College; BA, Psychology & Sociology, Wichita State University; MSSW, University of Missouri School of Social Work. *Appointments:* Campaign planner, Cleveland United Way, Ohio, 1978-85; Vice President, United Way of Toledo, Ohio, 1985-88; President, United Way of Central Iowa, 1988-. *Publications:* Whom Does United Way Serve; Setting Funding Priorities for United Way. *Memberships:* Rotary Club, Des Moines; Board, Junior Achievement; Appeals Review Board, Des Moines Chamber of Commerce; National Association of Social Workers; Junior League, Des Moines; Board, Executive, National Association for Advancement of Coloured People; Treasurer, Roosevelt High School PFC. *Honours:* 50th anniversary award, American Marketing Association, 1987; Certificate, completion of management skills programme, United Way of America National Academy of Volunteerism, 1978-84. *Hobbies:* Running; Tennis; Collecting antiques. *Address:* United Way of Central Iowa, 1111 9th Street, Suite 300, Des Moines, Iowa 50314, USA.

CHANDLER-MANNING Ellen, b. New York City, USA. m. Alexander Manning, 20 Nov. 1979, 1 son. *Education:* BSc., Long Island University, 1966; MA, English, Brooklyn College, 1969; Litt. D., University of South Africa, 1972. *Appointments:* Administrative Assistant, 1970-71; Instructor, 1971-72, 1972-73, University of Miami; Instructor, Broward Community College, 1973-74; Director, Cultural Affairs & Special Programmes, Broward Community College, 1974-88. *Memberships:* Alpha Epsilon Delta; Phi Sigma, President, 1965; Psi Chi; Sigma Tau Delta; AAUW; ACUCAA; Florida League for the Arts, etc. *Address:* PO Box 22-3854, Hollywood, FL 33022, USA.

CHANDNI Joshi, b. 30 Oct. 1946, Nepal. Under-Secretary. m. Mohan Raj Joshi. *Education:* MA, English Literature, 1965; Diploma Linguistics, SIL/Tribhuvan University; Numerous certificates and diplomas. *Appointments:* Lecturer, English Literaure 1965-70,

Head of Department, English Faculty 1970-75, Padma Kanya College, Nepal; Chief, Training Material Production Center, Ministry of Panchayat and Local Development, 1975-84; Coordinator, Audiovisual Seminar Workshop, 1976; Project Coordinator, Country Review on Role and Participation of Women in Rural/Agriculture Development, Nepal, 1979-80; Project Coordinator, International Year of the Disabled programmes, 1982; Executive Member, Community Services Coordination Committee, 1982-86; Taksforce Member, VII National Development Plan of Nepal, 1984-85; Consultant, UNICEF; Chief, Women Development Section, Ministry of Panchayat and Local Development, 1981-; Consultant, CIRDAP, 1988. *Publications:* Country Review Analysis opf the Role and Participation of Women in Rural/Agricultural Development in Nepal, 1980; Training Material Production Centre, 1980; How to Prepare and Use Audio Visual Aids, 1981; Successful Income Generating Projects for Women in Nepal, 1984; Co-author, Manual for Field Workers on Income Generation Programmes for Women, 1984; Some Successful Technology to Redcuce the Drudgery of Women's Work in Nepal, 1984; Off-Farm Employment for Women in Nepal, 1985; Planning for Women's programme, 1985; Institutions for Women in Nepal, 1985; Role of Women in Forestry Conservation and Utilization in Nepal, 1986; The Role of Women in Resource Conservation and Development, 1986; Credit for Women in South Asia, 1987; Model to Apply Guidelines and Checklists for Integration of Women Farmers Into Development Planning and Implementation at District Level in Nepal, 1987; Co-author, Regional Study on the Role of Women in Rural Industries in Nepal, 1988; Empowering and Releasing the Creativity of Rural Women for Participatory Development, 1987. *Memberships:* Member of numerous committees. *Honours:* Awarded Gorkha Dakshin Bahu, His Majesty the King of Nepal, 1982; Awarded SAARC Award, Her Majesty the Queen of Nepal, 1988; Coronation Award. *Address:* Cha 1-42 Maligaon, Kathmandu 2, Nepal.

CHANEY Jill, b. 5 June 1932, Hertfordshire, England. Author; Gardener. m. Walter Francis Leeming, 26 Aug. 1960. 1 son, 2 daughters. *Education:* Royal Horticultural Society Diploma. *Appointments:* Jewish Board of Guardians, 1954-59; Partner, Chorleywood Bookshop, 1973-88. *Publications:* For Children: On Primrose Hill; Taking the Woffle to Pebblecombe on Sea; Woffle RA; A Penny for the Guy; Christopher's Dig; Christopher's Find. For Young adults: Mottram Park; Return to Mottram Park; Leaving Mottram Park; Angel Face; Half a Candle; Canary Yellow; Vectis Diary; The Buttercup Field. *Hobbies:* Gardening; Natural History; Birdwatching; Travelling; Reading. *Address:* Glen Rosa, Colleyland, Chorleywood, Hertfordshire, England.

CHANG Isabelle, b. 20 Feb. 1925, Boston, USA. Library Media Co-ordinator. m. Dr Min Chueh Chang, 28 May 1948, 1 son, 2 daughters. *Education:* BSLS, Simmons College, 1946; AM, Clark University, 1967; MA, Anna Maria College, 1982. *Appointments:* Library Cataloguer, Yale Sterling Library, 1946-48; Library Director, Shrewbury Public Library, 1959-64; Media Co-ordinator, Shrewsbury School System Library, 1964-. *Publications:* What's Cooking at Changs; Chinese Fairy Tales, 1965; Tales from Old China, 1969; Gourmet on the Go, 1971; The Magic Pole, 1978. *Memberships:* Massachusetts Library Round Table, Secretary-Treasurer, 1962; NE Library Association; American Library Association; National Education Association; MEAM; NEMA. *Honours:* John Chandler Award, 1966. *Hobbies:* Bridge; Gardening; Photography; Stamp & Coin Collecting. *Address:* Shrewsbury High Media Center, 45 Oak St., Shrewsbury, MA 01545, USA.

CHANG Patricia L, b. 9 Dec. 1943, Hong Kong. Professor. *Education:* BSc 1967, PhD Biochemistry, 1971. *Appointments:* Assistant Professor, 1979-84, Associate Professor, 1984-, McMaster University, Canada. *Publications:* Numerous scientific publications in professional journals. *Memberships:* American Soc Human Genetics; Canadian Society Biochemistry;

American Society Biological Chemistry. *Address:* Department of Pediatrics, McMaster University, Hamilton, Ontario, Canada.

CHANG Pauline Wuai Kimm, b. 19 Jan. 1926, Shanghai, China. Chemist. m. Sung-Un Chang, 27 Dec. 1952. 1 son, 1 daughter. *Education:* National Central Unviersity, Chongqing, China, 1944-46; BA, Wellesley College, USA, 1949; MS 1950, PhD 1955, University of Michigan, Ann Arbor. *Appointments:* Research Assistant 1955-58, Research Associate 1958-66, Senior Research Associate 1966-83, Research Scientist 1983-88, Department of Pharmacology, Yale University School of Medicine, retired June 1988. *Publications:* Organic Synthesis; Synthesis of Anti-cancer, Anti-viral agents and isotope-labelled compounds. *Memberships:* Former Member, American Chemical Society; Royal Society of Chemistry. *Honours:* Wellesley College Scholar, 1948-49; Barbour scholarship for Oriental Women, 1949-52; University of Michigan; Sigma Xi (Associate), 1949. *Hobbies:* Reading; Gardening; Swimming; Travel; Watching good television programmes; Cinema-going. *Address:* 50 Allendale Drive, North Haven, CT 06473, USA.

CHAPEY Roberta, b. 9 Dec. 1942, Brooklyn, USA. Professor. *Education:* BA, Marymount Manhatten College, 1964; MA, New York University, 1965; EdD, Columbia University, 1975. *Appointments:* Professor, Speech, Brooklyn College, 1974-. *Publications:* Language Intervention Strategies in Adult Aphasi, 1984, 2nd edition 1986; 25 articles in professional journals; book chapters. *Memberships:* American Speech Hearing Association; New York State Speech Hearing Language Association; Academy of Aphasia. *Honours:* Recipient, various honours, grants. *Hobbies:* Golf; Reading; Writing; Travel. *Address:* 225 East 66 St., New York, NY 10021, USA.

CHAPIN Mary Della Real, b. 5 Sept. 1953, East St Louis, Illinois, USA. Attorney. m. Mark Chapin, 26 June 1981, 1 daughter. *Education:* BA magna cum laude, Art & English, St Mary's Dominican College, 1975; JD, University of Georgia, 1983; Admitted, Georgia Court of Appeals, Supreme Court of Georgia, 1984. Also: Interior design studies, Art Institute, Atlanta, Georgia, 1976, Augusta College 1977. *Appointments:* Teacher, St Thomas Aquinas High School, Augusta, Georgia, 1975-77, 1979-80; Manager, retail sales, Sound Probe Inc, 1977-78; Book store manager, St Mary's Dominican College, 1978-79; Law clerk 1981-82, Associate Attorney 1983-84, John L. Thompson PC, Augusta; Law clerk 1981, Attorney & Partner 1984-, Vice President 1986, Richard L. Powell PC; Secretary, Real & Real Dental Associates Inc 1983-87, Wermic Enterprises Inc 1987-; Admitted State Bar of Georgia, 1983; Secretary, director, advisory board, Safe Homes of Augusta Inc, 1988-; Assistant Attorney, Columbia County, Georgia, 1989-. *Memberships:* American & Augusta Bar Associations; Young Lawyers Association (Augusta Bar); Lay minister, St Mary-on-the-Hill Catholic Church, Augusta. *Honours include:* Outstanding Young Women of America, 1984; Delta Epsilon Sigma, 1974; Cardinal Key National Honour Sorority, 1974; Biographical recognition. *Hobbies:* Reading; Art; Sewing. *Address:* 254 Silver Maple Road, Martinez, Georgia 30907, USA.

CHAPLIN Geraldine, b. 3 July 1944, Santa Monica, California, USA. Actress. 1 son. *Education:* Royal Ballet School, London, 1961. *Appointments:* Starred in over 20 European productions including 7 with Spain's leading film-maker, Carlos Saura; Pictures include: Doctor Zhivago; Stranger in the House; I Killed Rasputin; The Hawaiians; Zero Population Growth; Innocent Bystanders; The Three Musketeers; Nashville; Buffalo Bill and the Indians; Welcome to LA; Roseland; Remember My Name; The Mirror Crack'd; L'Amour Par Terre; The Moderns; TV: The Corsican Brothers; My Cousin Rachel; etc. *Address:* c/o William Morris Agency, 1350 Ave. of the Americas, New York, NY 10019, USA.

CHAPMAN Constance Elizabeth, b. 5 Jan. 1919,

Barnsley, Yorkshire, England. Writer. m. Frank Chapman, 22 Nov. 1941. 3 sons. *Education:* Technical College, Barnsley. *Publications:* Childrens books: Marmaduke the Lorry; Marmaduke and Joe; Marmaduke and His Friends; Riding with Marmaduke; Merry Marmaduke; Marmaduke and the Lambs; Marmaduke and the Elephant; Marmaduke goes to France; Marmaduke goes to Italy; Marmaduke goes to Holland; Marmaduke goes to America; Marmaduke goes to Morocco; Marmaduke goes to Spain; Marmaduke goes to Switzerland; Marmaduke goes to Scotland; Marmaduke goes to Wales; Marmaduke goes to Ireland. Stories broadcast on Listen with Mother BBC Radio and Rainbow Thames Television. Frequent contributer to Sunny Stories edited by Malcolm Saville. *Memberships:* Pinner Sketch Club; Friend of the Royal Academy; National Trust; RSPB. *Hobbies:* Painting in oils and water-colours; Gardening. *Address:* 88 Grange Gardens, Pinner, Middlesex, HA5 5QF, England.

CHAPMAN Debra Ann Bouchard, b. 22 July 1957, New Haven, Connecticut, USA. Optician. 1 daughter. *Education:* Pearle Eyecare University, Dallas, Texas, 1988. *Appointments:* Bradlees Optical, 1976-79; Midwest Vision Centre, 1979-80; Stigers Optical, Santa Maria, California, 1980-82; Own business, Opticaly A-Wear, 1983-85; Manager, Pearle Vision Centre, Norwalk, Connecticut, 1985-. *Membership:* Connecticut chapter, Opticians Association of America, 1987-88. *Honours:* Opticians licenses, Massachusetts 1979, California 1982, Connecticut 1987. *Hobbies:* Sailing; Cooking; Gardening. *Address:* 35 Coram Street, Hamden, Connecticut 06517, USA.

CHAPMAN Janet Goodrich, b. 26 May 1922, Brooklyn, New York, USA. Professor of Economics. m. John Chapman, 10 Feb, 1943, 1 daughter. *Education:* BA, Economics, Swarthmore College, 1943; MA, Economics, 1951, Certificate of Russian Institute, 1951, PhD, Economics, 1963, Columbia University. *Appointments:* Analyst, National War Labor Board, Philadelphia, Pennsylvania, 1943; Economist, Board of Governors, Federal Reserve System, 1945-46; Consultant, The Rand Corporation, 1949-69; Associate Professor, then Professor of Economics, University of Pittsburgh, Pennsylvania, 1964-. *Publications:* Real Wages in Soviet Russia Since 1928, 1963; Wage Variation in Soviet Industry, 1970; Equal Pay for Equal Work, Women in Russia, 1977; Articles in books and journals. *Memberships:* American Association for Advancement of Slavic Studies (Board of Directors 1974-79); American Economic Association; Association for Comparative Economic Studies (President 1983); Editorial Boards: Comparative Economic Studies, and Economic Books: Current Selections; Journal of Comparative. *Honours:* Garth Fellow, Columbia University, 1946-47; New York State Fellow, American Association of University Women, 1948-49; American Council of Learned Societies Grant, 1973; National Science Foundation Grant, 1973-74; National Council for Soviet and East European Research Grant, 1982; IREX Travel Grant, 1985. *Address:* Economics Department, Room 4A34 Forbes Quadrangle, University of Pittsburgh, Pittsburgh, PA 15260.

CHAPPELL Joan, b. 4 Sept. 1921, Birkenhead, England. m. (1) Ted Chappell, deceased, (2) Norman Mathias, deceased. *Education:* Universities of St Andrews & Liverpool; MBChB; FRANZCP; MRCPsych; DPM; MRNZCGP; MRCGP. *Appointments:* General Practice, London, 1953-; Psychiatrist, Sunnyside Christchurch, New Zealand, Retired 1986; Visiting Psychiatrist, Womens Prison. *Publications:* The Black Void. *Memberships:* Hon. Life Member, Past President, New Zealand Association of Psychotherapists; Director, Christchurch Institute for Training in Psychotherapy; Hon. Life Member, New Zealand Medical Womens Association; Zonta. *Hobbies:* Native Flora of New Zealand & Pacific; Gardening; Music; Tennis. *Address:* 195 Hackthorne Road, Christchurch 2, New Zealand.

CHAPUT WILLIAMS Marie-Therese, b. 13 Nov. 1949, Montreal, Quebec, Canada. Executive Director.

m. Leo Williams, 4 May 1973. 3 daughters. *Education:* BA, Anthropology, 1980; MLS, Library Science, 1984, McGill University. *Appointments:* Singer and Composer under the stage name, Marie Merlin, 1968-76; Director, chess magazine, Echect, 1984-87; Director General, Quebec Chess Federation, 1984-87; Organizer, Quebec International Chess Tournament, 1986; Executive Director, Quebec Special Olympics, 1988-. *Contributions to:* A chess bibliography: Des livres d'eches pour tous. *Honours:* (Women) Quebec Chess Champion 1972, 1973, 1974; Participant in the 22nd Chess Olympiad in Israel, 1976. *Address:* 142 Cameron Crescent, Point Claire, Quebec, Canada, H9R YE1.

CHARNAS Suzy McKee, b. 22 Oct. 1939, New York City, New York, USA. Author. m. Stephen Charnas, 1968, 1 stepson, 1 stepdaughter. *Education:* Art major, High School of Music and Art, 1957; BA, Economic History, Barnard College, 1961; MAT, Social Studies (high school level), School of Education, New York University, 1965. *Appointments:* Peace Corps Teacher, History, English, Drawing, Girls' High School, Ogbomosho, W.R., Nigeria, and Introductory Economic History, University of Ife, Ibadan, 1961-63; Teacher, Ancient History, African History, New Lincoln School, New York City, USA, 1965-67; DCMH, Department of Psychiatry, Flower Fifth Avenue Hospital, New York City, 1967-69; Instructor, Clarion West Writers Workshop, Seattle, Washington, 1984, 1986; Instructor, Clarion Writers Workshop, Michigan, 1987. *Publications:* Walk to the End of the World, 1974, 1979; Motherlines, 1978, 1979; Scorched Supper on New Niger, in New Voices III, 1980; The Ancient Mind at Work, 1980; Unicorn Tapestry, in New Dimensions II, 1980; The Vampire Tapestry, 1980, 1981, 1986; The Bronze King, 1985, 1987; Dorothea Dreams, 1986, 1987; Listening to Brahms, 1986; The Silver Glove, 1988; The Golden Thread, 1989; Evil Thoughts, in Seaharp Hotel, 1989; Vampire Dreams (unpublished play from Unicorn Tapestry), premiere performance, Magic Theatre, San Francisco, 1990. *Memberships:* Science Fiction Writers of America; Authors Guild; Horror Writers of America; Chair, Archive Project Committee, National Council of Returned Peace Corps Volunteers. *Honours:* Nominee, John W.Campbell Award, for Walk to the End of the World, 1975; Winner, Nebula Award for Best Novella, Unicorn Tapestry, 1980. *Hobbies:* Needlepoint; Flea markets; Oriental rugs. *Address:* 520 Cedar N E, Albuquerque, NM 87106, USA.

CHARPENTIER-SIMON Manon, b. 6 Aug. 1957, Madrid, Spain. Financial Consultant. m. Colin Leslie Simon, 28 June 1985, 1 son. *Education:* BA, Honours, Hispanic Studies, University of Ottawa, Canada, 1980; MBA, Finance, McGill University, 1982. *Appointments:* Journalist, Radio Canada International, 1977-80; Banker, The Bank Of Nova Scotia, Management Trainee, 1982-83, Assistant Supervisor, International Corporat Credit, Toronto, 1983-84, Account Manager, Dublin, Ireland, 1984-87, Assistant Supervisor, Corporate Credit, UK, Toronto, 1987-88 ; Financial Consultant, Simon & Associates, 1988-. *Memberships:* Fellow, Institute of Canadian Bankers; MBA Women's Association, Toronto. *Hobbies:* Travel; Micro-computers; Tennis. *Address:* 240 Broadway Ave., TH 22, Toronto, Ontario M4P 1V9, Canada.

CHARTERS Ann, b. 10 Nov. 1936, Bridgeport, Connecticut, USA. University Professor and Administrator. Writer. m. 14 Mar. 1959, 2 daughters. *Education:* BA, University of California, Berkeley, 1957; MA, 1960, PhD, 1965, Columbia University. *Appointments:* Professor of English, University of Connecticut, Storrs, Connecticut, 1974-89; Associate Dean of the College, Brown University, Providence, Rhode Island, 1989-. *Publications:* Olson/Melville, 1968; Nobody, 1970, Reprinted, 1984; Kerouac: Straight Arrow, 1973, Paperback, 1974, Reprinted, 1987; Bibliography of Works by Jack Kerouac, 1975; I Love: The Story of Vladimir Mayakovsky and Lili Brik (with S Charters), 1979, Reprinted, 1988; Beats and Company, 1986; Editor: Special View of History, by C. Olson, 1969; Scattered Poems, by J. Kerouac, 1970; Scenes Along the Road, by J. Kerouac and A. Ginsberg, 1970; The Story and Its Writer, 1983, 2nd Edition, 1986; The Beats: Literary Bohemians in Post-War America, 1983; Three Lives and QED, by G Stein, 1990. *Honour:* Fulbright Professor, Uppsala University, 1980. *Address:* Brown University, Box 1939, Providence, RI 02912, USA.

CHARTOFF Melanie, b. 15 Dec. 1950, New Haven, Connecticut, USA. Actress; Singer; Comedienne; Writer; Host; Producer. *Education:* BA Adelphi University, 1970. *Appointments:* Host, Indian Child Conference for Save the Children, Spokane, Washington, 1982; Co-starred in Having It All, ABC-TV Movies, 1982; Starred in March of the Falsettoes, 1982; Co-starred and wrote for Fridays late night comedy series, ABC, 1980-82; Co-starred and produced, What's Hot, What's Not, syndicated national magazine format Entertainment, 1985-86; Co-produced and hosted, We Belong to the City, Concert Fundraiser for Los Angeles homeless; Co-starred in Fresno Comedy on CBS; Starred in Sunday in the Park with George, American Conservatory Theater in San Francisco, 1986. *Memberships:* SAG; AFTRA; AGVA; AEA; Alpha Psi Omega; Women in Film. *Honours:* Dramalog Critics Award for musical performance March of the Falsettoes, 1982; Mayor's Certificate of Appreciation, Concert for the Homeless, 1986; United Jewish Appeal of Hawaii Award of Appreciation, 1985. *Hobbies:* Philosophy; Holistic Cuisine; Dance. *Address:* c/o William Morris Agency, 151 El Camino Drive, Beverly Hills, CA 90212, USA.

CHASEN Heather Jean, b. 20 July 1927, Singapore. Actress. *Education:* Notre Dame, Dahung, Malaya; Princess Helena College, United Kingdom. *Appointments include:* 1st Professional appearance, the Castle Farnham, 1945; 1st London appearance at the Arts, 154; Repertory, Oxford and Salisbury; Numerous parts including: Mercelle, Hotel Paradiso, 1957; Mollie Ralston, The Mousetrap, 1958; Helena, Midsummer Night's Dream, open-air in Regents Park, 1962; Martha, Who's Afraid of Virginia Woolf, 1962; Matron in 40 Years On, Apollo, 1969; Marchioness of Mwereston in Lady Frederick, Vaudeville and Duke of Yorks, 1970; Contesse de Saint Ford in Madame de Sade, King's Head, Islington, 1975; Toured Canada with Pleasure of His Company, 1974 and Rebecca, 1977. Television appearances since 1957 include: The Newcomers; The Navy Lark; Isabel in Marked Personal, 1973-74; BBC Play of the Month, Waste, 1977; Mary Queen of Scots in A Traveller in Time, a serial, 1978; A Picture of Innocence with Robert Morley, 1978; Valerie Pollard in Central Television's Crossroads; Appeared for 2 years at the Garrick Theatre in No Sex Please We're British, 1984-86. *Memberships:* British actors Equity. *Honour:* Tony Nomination for Best Actress for Antonia Lynch Gibbon in A Severed Head, 1964. *Hobby:* Rescuing and Collecting old teddy bears.

CHATER Shirley Sears, b. 30 July 1932, Shamokin, Pennsylvania, USA. Vice President, Texas Woman's University. m. Dr Norman Chater, 5 Dec. 1959. 1 son, 1 daughter. *Education:* BS, University of Pennsylvania, 1956; MS, UC, San Francisco, 1960; PhD, UC-Berkeley, 1964; MIT Sloan School of Management Program for Senior Executives, Certificate, 1982. *Appointments:* Vice Chancellor, Academic Affairs, Unviersity of California at San Francisco, 1977-82; Council Associate, American Council on Education, 1982-84; Senior Associate, Presidential Search Consultation Service, Association of Governing Boards of Colleges & Universities, 1984-86; President, Texas Woman's University, 1986-. *Memberships:* National Advisory Committee, Leadership America; Women's Forum West; Council of Presidents, Association of Governing Boards of Colleges and Universities. *Honours:* Member, Institute of Medicine, National Academy of Science; Distinguished Alumnae Award, University of Pennsylvania. *Hobby:* Antique collecting. *Address:* P O Box 23925, Texas Woman's University, Denton, TX 76204, USA.

CHAUVENET Beatrice Champion, b. 22 July 1902, Iola, USA. Writer; Lecturer; Retired Public Health Administrator. m. William Chauvenet, 8 Sept. 1924, divorced 1934, 1 daughter. *Education:* BA, 1923, MA, 1939, University of Michigan. *Appointment:* Executive, Santa Fe New Mexico, American Red Cross, 1942-49; Director, Hospital Facilities, New Mexico Department Public Health, 1950-52; Hospital Analyst, US Public Service, Washington, 1952-53; Executive, New Mexico Heart Association, 1954-60; Teacher, Navajo Resevation, Arizona, 1964-65. *Publications:* The Buffalo Head, 1972; Holy Faith in Santa Fe, 1977; Hewett & Friends, 1983; John Gaw Meem, Pioneer, 1985; short stories, articles, radio drama. *Memberships:* Phi Beta Kappa; Mortarboad; American Association University Women, President. *Honours:* Recipient, various honours & awards. *Hobbies:* Travel; Painting; Oils; Acrylics. *Address:* 10501 Lagrima de Oro NE, Apt. 373, Albuuerque, NM 87111, USA.

CHAVERS Blanche M., b. 2 Aug. 1949, Clarksdale, Mississippi, USA. Physician. m. Gubare R. Mpambara, 21 Apr. 1982, 1 son. *Education:* BS 1971, MD 1975, University of Washington, Seattle; Diploma, American Board of Paediatrics, 1981. *Appointments:* Paediatric Resident, University of Washington Hospitals, 1975-78; Paediatric Nephrology Fellow, University of Minnesota Hospitals, 1978-81; Instructor 1981-83, Assistant Professor 1983-, Department of Paediatrics, University of Minnesota. *Publications:* Co-author, papers in professional journals, various abstracts; Reviewer, Diabetes Care, 1985-86. *Memberships:* American Societies of Nephrology & Paediatric Nephrology; International Society of Nephrology; National Association for Advancement of Coloured People; Alpha Kappa Alpha. *Honours:* Awards, grants, fellowships including: National Research Service, 1978-80, 1981-83; Vikings Children's Fund, 1980-81, 1980-82, 1986-88; Minnesota Medical Foundation, 1980-81; American Diabetes Association, 1981-82; etc. Also: Clinical Investigator Award, National Institutes of Health, 1982-87; Biomedical Research Support Grant & Reference Lab Contract, 1983. *Hobbies:* Afro-aerobics; Collecting African artifacts; Black literature. *Address:* 5425 Grand Avenue South, Minneapolis, Minnesota 55419, USA.

CHAWLA Vera Vaswani, b. 4 Dec. 1950, Bombay, India. Executive Vice President, Information Systems & Networks Corporation. m. Inder Chawla, 5 Mar. 1978. 2 daughters. *Education:* BS Applied Math 1972, MS Computer Science/Electrical Engineer 1973, University of Virginia. *Appointments:* NASA (Goddard Space Flight Center), 1973-74; Boeing Corp, 1974-76; General Electric, 1976-81; Executive Vice President, Information Systems & Networks Corporation, 1981-. *Memberships:* Air Force Comm Electronics Association; American Management Association; IEEE; Assoc of the US Army; US Navy League, US Air Force Assoc; American Defense Preparedness Assoc; Greater Washington Board of Trade; President's High Technology Task Force. *Honours:* Dean's List for BS and MS, 1972 and 1973. *Hobbies:* Real Estate; Dancing; Tennis. *Address:* Information Systems & Networks Corporation, 10411 Motor City Drive, Bethesda, Maryland 20817, USA.

CHEE Gracia Tay, b. 2 June 1923, Singapore. Actress; Author; Director; Lecturer. m. Keng Long Chee, 23 July 1955, 2 sons. *Education:* LRAM (London); IPA (London). *Appointments:* Lecturer, Speech & Drama (Singapore): Teachers' Training College 1959-74, Institute of Education 1974-75, Nanyang University 1965, Singapore University 1965, Polytechnic 1966. Acted in Teahouse of August Moon, London Haymarket Thetre, UK, 1953-56. *Memberships:* Founder, President 1960-81, Theatre World Association; Founder, President 1975-, National Council of Women; President, Pan-Pacific Women's Association; Director, Asia Arts Association. *Hobbies:* Reading; Writing; Attending Plays & Concerts; Chinese Brush Painting; Watching TV. *Address:* Balmoral Road, Singapore 1025.

CHELIUS Anne Virginia Kirby, b. 22 July 1944, New York City, USA. Stockbroker; Computer Consultant. m. 25 Nov. 1965, 3 sons, 2 daughters. *Education:* BS, St Joseph's College for Women. *Appointments:* Teacher:

NYC Board of Education, Poughkeepsie School System, & Half Hollow Hills; Vice President, Software Enterprises Inc; President, Seven C's Charter Corporation; Asset Management Consultant, FASCO. *Memberships include:* Past President, Data Processing Management Association; Boards, Long Island Forum for Technology, & Cold Spring Harbor Soccer; Secretary, Fiddlers Green Association; LI Business & Professional Women. *Honours:* Certified Systems Professional; Certificate, Data Processing. *Hobbies:* Writing; Reading; Sailing; Windsurfing; Swimming. *Address:* 1 Dolphin's Rise, Lloyd Harbor, New York 11743, USA.

CHELLIS Elizabeth Jean Colp, b. 9 Apr. 1903, Robbinsdale, Minnesota, USA. Author; Lecturer; Collector. m. Robert Dunning Chellis, 14 June 1929. 1 son. *Education:* BA, Carleton College, 1925; Postgraduate work in English Literature, Wellesley College, 1925-27. *Appointments:* English Instructor and Assistant Dean of Women, Carleton College, 1927-29. *Publications:* Author of articles in Antiques including: Sources of Child Motifs, From the Nile to the Trent. in Hobbies Magazine, Kate Greenaway and Wedgwood; Artiles on Lessore's Aesop's Fables plates and on Wedgwood majolica salts for the American Wegwoodian. *Memberships:* Founding member, President, Wedgwood International Seminar; Founder, President, Wedgwood Society of Boston, 1969; Boston Browning Society; President, Warren and Prescott Chapter, DAR; Museum of Fine Arts, Boston, Visiting Committee, European Decorative Arts Dept; Boston Public Library, Library Committee; American Ceramic Circle; Life Member, Wedgwood Society of New York, London and Australia; Fellow, Royal Society of Arts, London; English Ceranmic Circle. *Honour:* Distinguished Achievement Award, Carleton College, 1985. *Hobby:* Collections of bookplates, fine bookbinding, decorated papers, rare bells. *Address:* 17 Windemere Lane, Wellesley Hills, MA 02181, USA.

CHEMPIN Beryl Margaret, b. Edgbaston, Birmingham, England. Piano Teacher; Pianist; Lecturer; Adjudicator. m. (1) Arnold Chempin (dec.), 2 daughters, (2) Bernard While (dec.), (3) Denis Matthews. *Education:* Birmingham School of Music; FTCL; LRAM; ARCM; LTCL; ABSM. *Appointments:* Private Music Teacher; Piano Teacher, Birmingham Conservatoire, Birmingham University and Birmingham Junior School of Music; Solo Performer; Freelance Lecturer and Adjudicator, internationally. *Publications:* Various articles in musical journals including Music Teacher, Musical Times, Music Journal. *Memberships:* Birmingham Conservatoire Association; National Council, Chairman of Birmingham Centre, Incorporated Society of Musicians; International Society for Music Education; Royal Society of Musicians; European Piano Teachers Association; International Piano Teachers Consultants; City of Birmingham Symphony Orchestra Society; British Federation of Music Festivals; King Edward's High School Old Edwardians. *Honours:* Midland Woman of the Year, 1977; National Award for Piano Teaching, 1983. *Hobbies:* Music; Reading; Languages; Art; Cooking. *Address:* 10 Russell Road, Moseley, Birmingham B13 8RD, England.

CHEN Kok-choo, b. 24 Oct. 1947, Hong Kong. Attorney-at-Law. 1 son, 1 daughter. *Education:* Barrister-at-Law, England, 1968; Advocate and Solicitor, Singapore, 1970; Attorneyat-Law, California, USA, 1974; Admitted to US District Court, Northern District of California, 1974. *Appointments:* Associate, Law Officers of Tan, Rajah and Cheah, Singapore, 1969-70; Lecturer in Commercial Law, Nanyang University, Singapore, 1970-71; Law Clerk, Sullivan and Cromwell Law Offices, New York, USA, 1971-74; Attorney-at-Law, Heller, Ehrman, White and McAuliffe, San Francisco, California, 1974-75; Partner, Ding & Ding Law Offices, Taipei, Taiwan, Republic of China, 1975-87; Founding Partner, Ding, Ding & Chan Law Offices, San Francisco, California, USA, 1983-; Founding Partner, Chen & Associates Law Offices, 1988-; Associate Professor, Graduate School of Law, Soochow University, Taipei, Taiwan, Republic of China, 1981-. *Publications:*

Licensing Technology to Chinese Enterprises, 1986; Mergers and Acquisitions (co-author). *Memberships:* Honourable Society of Inner Temple, England; California Bar Association, USA; Zonta International, Taipei III Club; Young Women's Christian Association, Republic of China. *Honours:* Elected as one of Most Outstanding Women of the Year, Taiwan, 1982. *Hobby:* Music. *Address:* 824, No 602 Min Chuan E Road, Taipei, Taiwan, China.

CHEN Linda, b. 1 Nov. 1951, Somerville, New Jersey, USA. Medical Doctor. *Education:* SCB, Brown University, 1973; MS, University of Rhode Island, 1979; MD, Brown University Programme in Medicine, 1979; Intern in Medicine, PUPMC, Philadelphia, 1979-80; Resident in Anesthesia, 1980-82, Cardiac Anesthesia Fellow, 1982-83, HUP, Philadelphia; Postdoctoral Research, 1983-84. *Appointments:* Assistant Professor of Anesthesia, University of Pennsylvania School of Medicine, Philadelphia, 1983-. *Appointments:* 4 contributions to Anesthesiology, 1985, 1987, 1988 (2). *Memberships:* American Society for Anesthesiology; IARS; ATS. *Honours:* Tuition Scholarship, University of Rhode Island, 1974-75; Sigma Xi, 1979; Physicians Recognition Award, 1982, 1985, 1988; NIH Post Doctorate Research Training Grant, 1983-84. *Hobbies:* Movies; Travel; Boating; Skiing. *Address:* Department of Anesthesia, HUP, Dulles 7788, 3400 Spruce Street, Philadelphia, PA 19104, USA.

CHEN May Jane, b. 3 Jan. 1940, Taipei, Taiwan. m. John Jawyaw Chen, 20 Dec. 1962, 1 son, 1 daughter. *Education:* BSc., 1962; MSc., 1964; PhD, 1973. *Appointments:* Lecturer, National Taiwan University, 1964-68; Lecturer, Senior Lecturer, Australian National University, 1971-86; Senior Lecturer, Chinese University of Hong Kong, 1987-. *Publications:* Articles in: British Journal of Developmental Psychology; Australian Journal of Psychology; etc. *Memberships:* International Society for the Study of Behavioral Development; International Association of Cross-Cultural Psychology. *Honours:* Asian Foundation, UN, 1967-68; National Science Council, Taiwan, 1978-79; Australian Research Grants Scheme, 1983-85; Centre for Hong Kong Studies, 1987-89. *Hobbies:* Music; Reading. *Address:* Dept. of Psychology, Chung Chi College, Chinese University of Hong Kong, Shatin, New Territories, Hong Kong.

CHENAULT Sheryl Ann Catt, b. 16 May 1953, Springfield, Missouri, USA. Elementary Teacher. m. Daniel Alden Chenault, 7 June 1975. *Education:* BS, East Texas State University, 1975; MEd, University of North Texas, 1987. *Appointments:* Brentfield Elementary, 1975-82; Liberty Jr High, 1982-85; Jess Harben Elementary, 1985-88; Rise Academy, 1988- (all Richardson Independent School District). *Memberships:* Richardson Education Association; Richardson Association of Children with Learning Disabilities; Association of Tx Professional Educators; International Reading Association; Association for Supervision and Curriculum Development. *Honours:* Honour Stipend for Outstanding Special Education Student Teacher, 1975; Scholarship (Richardson Association of Retarded Children), 1973; Scholarship (Richardson Council of PTAs), 1986; Certificate of Honour for Outstanding Service (Alpha Delta Pi), 1983; Dean's List, 1974. *Hobbies:* Reading; Teaching. *Address:* Garland, Texas, USA.

CHEONG Doreen, b. 23 Jan. 1941, Sydney, Australia. Management Consultant; Industrial Psychologist. m. Lanman Cheong, 25 Feb. 1961, divorced 1978. 2 sons. *Education:* BA, Economics and Psychology, Sydney University, 1979. *Appointments:* Chequers Theatre Restaurant, 1960-62; Lanman Cheong Jewellery, 1963-77; Coopers & Lybrand Consultants, 1980-. *Memberships:* Institute of Management Consultants; Victorian Psychological Council; Affiliate, Australian Psychological Society. *Hobbies:* Opera; Theatre; Ballet; Keeping fit (aerobics); Reading. *Address:* 71 Hargrave Street, Paddington, NSW 2021, Australia.

CHERMAK Gail D., b. 30 Sept. 1950, New York City, USA. Professor of Speech & Hearing Sciences. *Education:* BA, State University of New York, Buffalo, 1972; MA 1973, PhD 1975, Ohio State University. *Appointments:* Southern Illinois University, 1975-77; Washington State University, 1977-. *Publication:* Handbook of Audiological Rehabilittion, 1981. *Memberships:* American Speech-Language-Hearing Association; American Audiology Society; International Society of Audiology; American Association for Advancement of Science; American Association for Higher Education. *Honours:* Fulbright Scholar, 1989-1990; Kellogg National Fellow, 1986-89; Phi Beta Kappa, 1972. *Hobbies:* Ornithology; Opera. *Address:* Department of Speech & Hearing Sciences; Washington State University, Pullman, WA 99164, USA.

CHERNOFF Maxine Hahn, b. 24 Feb. 1952, Chicago, Illinois, USA. Writer; English Professor. m. 5 Oct. 1975, 2 sons, 1 daughter. *Education:* BA, English, 1972; MA, English, 1974. *Appointments:* University of Illinois, 1977-80; Columbia College, 1979-85; City Colleges of Chicago, 1980-; School of the Art Institute of Chicago, 1988. *Publications:* Stories: Bop, 1987; Books of Poems: Japan, 1988, New Faces of 1952, 1985, Utopia TV Store, 1979. *Memberships:* President, Poetry Centre, School of the Art Institute, Chicago, 1982-85; Co-ordinating Council of Literary Magazines; Associated Writing Programmes; etc. *Honours:* Recipient, various honours & awads. *Hobbies:* Writing Childrens Stories; Reading; Co-Editor of New American Writing. *Address:* 2920 W. Pratt, Chicago, IL 60645, USA.

CHERRY Rose Ellen Reed-Loomis, b. 13 Sept. 1929, Hundred, West Virginia, USA. Teacher, 6th Grade. m. (1) Raymond A. Loomis, 26 June 1948, dec. 1 son, 3 daughters, (2) Hilliard C. Cherry, 15 Apr. 1973. *Education:* BSc Education 1970, MEd 1985, Lake Erie College, Painesville, Ohio. *Appointments:* Teacher: 3rd & 4th Grades, St Mary's, Chardon, Ohio, 1961-66; 6th Grade & Libraries 1967-70, 6th Grade 1970-89, Burton Elementry School, Berkshire School District, Ohio. *Creative work:* Social Studies, study with Project TEACHER, 1970. *Memberships:* Offices including past Matron, twice, Lily Chapter, Order of Eastern Star; President, Geauga County Business & Professional Women's Club; Treasurer, American Association of University Women; Librarian, Moderator, Burton Congregational Church. *Honours:* Member, North Central Evaluation Team elementary schools, 1988; Numerous awards, ceramics, 1976-86. *Hobbies:* Many committees, church work; Teacher, school workshops, computers, creative writing; Teacher, ceramics, many students win top prizes; Former school coordinator, Red Cross; Chairperson 1987-88, 1000-89, Young Author Programme. *Address:* PO Box 147, Burton, Ohio 44021, USA.

CHERTOW Doris S., b. 23 Apr. 1925, New York City, USA. County Legislator. m. Bernard Chertow, 2 Feb. 1947, 4 sons, 1 daughter. *Education:* BA, Political Science, Hunter College, 1945; MA, Radcliffe College, 1947; PhD, Social Science, Syracuse University, 1968. *Appointments:* Instructor, Douglass College, New Jersey, 1948-49; Assistant to Director, Inter-University Case Programme 1963-64; graduate teacher 1964-66, Editor, continuing education publications 1968-75, Syracuse University; Onondago County Legislator, 1975-89. *Publications:* Co-editor, University & Community Service & Challenge of Modern Church-Public Relations, 1970; Author, Participation of Poor in War on Poverty, in Adult Education, 1974; Last Disgrace, in Central New Yorker, 1972. *Memberships:* Board, United National Association, 1984; Discovery Centre, 1980-; Resolve Dispute Settlement Centre, 1982-85; CHIPS Sub-Area Council, Health Systems Agency, 1977-84. *Honours:* Phi Beta Kappa; Magna cum laude; Head Start grant, Office of Economic Opportunity, 1967; Woman of Achievement (politics), Post-Standard, 1976. *Hobbies:* Swimming; Reading; Playing piano. *Address:* 139 Sunnyside Park Road, Syracuse, New York 13214, USA.

CHESSON Catherine Leona, b. 29 May 1928, Monrovia, Liberia. Lawyer. m. Joseph J F Chesson, 21 Apr. 1951, divorced 1970, 2 sons, 2 daughters. *Education:* BSc., Mathematics, Education, Howard University, USA, 1953; LLB, University of Liberia, Monrovia, 1956. *Appointments:* Secretary, to US Police Advisor to Liberia, 1947; Mathematics Instructor, University of Liberia, 1953-54; Legal Advisor, Liberia American Swedish Minerals Company, 1957-69; Liberian Government Labour Office, 1969-72; Assistant Minister of Justice for Taxation, 1972-76; Assistant Minister of Foreign Affairs, 1976-79; Member, House of Representatives, National Legislature of Liberia, 1979-80. *Publications:* Songs: A Nation's Prayer; Song of Praise; Just for Thee; I'm Graeful to the Lord; Christmas Poems for Children. *Memberships Include:* President, Liberia Federation of Women Organizations; International Federation of Women Lawyers. *Honours:* Meritorious Services Award, Bible Society of Liberia, 1985; 10 Year Service Award, Opportunities Industrialisation Centre, International 1986; Liberia OIC Inc. Service Award, 1988. *Hobbies:* Piano; Writing; Reading; Sewing. *Address:* PO Box 198, Monrovia, Liberia.

CHESTER Stephanie Ann, b. 8 Oct. 1951, Minneapolis, USA. Lawyer. *Education:* JD, University of South Dakota School of Law, 1977; National Graduate Trust School, 1984. *Appointments:* Law Clerk, South Dakota Supreme Court, 1977-78; Originations Representative, Dain Bosworth Inc., 1978-79; Vice President, Trust Officer, First Bank of South Dakota, 1979-86; Vice President, Team Manager, First Trust NA, 1986-. *Publications:* articles in professional journals. *Memberships:* South Dakota State, Minnesota State & American Bar Associations. *Honours:* Recipient, various honours including: Augustana Scholar, 1973; University of South Dakota Law Review Projects & Research Editor, 1977. *Hobbies:* Skiing; Golf; Jogging; Sailing; Dancing; Reading. *Address:* First Trust National Association, First Trust Centre, PO Box 64488, St Paul, MN 55164, USA.

CHEUNG Gretchen Hughes, b. 6 Feb. 1945, Cinderford, England. Librarian. m. Cheuk Yin Cheung, 8 Oct, 1966. 3 sons. *Education:* BA, University of British Columbia, Canada; MLS, McGill University, British Columbia. *Appointments:* Librarian, Pacific Press, 1972-73; Librarian, St Jean Public Library, 1973-75; Teacher of English as a Second Language, 1975-82; Acquisitions Librarian 1982-85, Chief Librarian 1986-, College Militaire Royal de Saint Jean. *Memberships:* Canadian Library Association; Quebec Library Association; Special Library Association; Editor, ABQLA Bulletin, 1985-88. *Address:* Library, College Militaire Royal de Saint Jean, Saint-Jean- Sur-Richilieu, Quebec, Canada J03 1R0.

CHEUNG Man Yee, b. 25 Dec. 1946, Hong Kong. Director of Broadcasting. *Education:* BA, Chinese University of Hong Kong, 1968. *Appointments:* Part-time Script Translator rising to TV Producer, Rediffusion (HK) Ltd, 1965-70; Account Executive, Young Nichol & Co Ltd, 1971; Programme Officer rising to Controller, Radio 1972-82; Assistant Director of Broadcasting 1983-84, Deputy Director 1984-86, Director 1986-, Radio Television Hong Kong, 1972-82; Assistant Director of Information Services 1983-84, Deputy Director 1984-85, Director 1985, Government Information Services. *Memberships:* President, Commonwealth Broadcasting Association, 1988-92; Hong Kong Red Cross Advisory Council; Henley Association; Outstanding Young Persons Association; Hong Kong Community Chest PR Committee; Council Member, Hong Kong Family Planning Association; Patron, The Social Sciences Society, Hong Kong University Student's Union. *Hobbies:* Music; Bridge; Reading. *Address:* No 4 Gough Hill Path, The Peak, Hong Kong.

CHEVIS Felicia K, b. 3 Nov. 1961, Houston, Texas, USA. Mechanical Engineer-Project Manager. *Education:* BSc, Mechanical Engineering, 1985. *Appointments:* Naval Technical Intelligence Center, 1985-. *Memberships:* National Association for Female Executives; Junior Advisory Board, Chairperson; Federal

Women's Program, Co-leader; Senior Class, President; NIC, New Building Committee, Design Team Leader. *Honours:* Pi Mu Epsilon (Mathematics Honor Society), 1982; Beta Kappa Chi (Science Honor Society), 1982; President's Honor Roll, 1980-82; Academic Scholar Award, 1981; National Dean's List, 1981; 4-Year Engineering scholarship. *Interests:* Networking; Managing people; Conducting professional seminars. *Address:* 6200 Westchester Park Dr No 1110, College Park, Maryland 20740, USA.

CHEW Nancy Jane, b. 19 Jan. 1942, Lakewood, Ohio, USA. Consulting Regulatory Pharmacologist. *Education:* BA, Biology, Woman's College, University of North Carolina, 1963; MS, Physiology, Florida State University, 1968. *Appoinments Include:* various positions as Technician, Senior Research Technician, 1964-71; Assistant Biochemist, Hoffman LaRoche Inc., 1971-74; Professional Consultant, Appleton Century Crofts, 1971; Freelance Copywriter, Jarman and Spitzer Advertising Agency, 1973-74; Freelance Copywriter, Klemtner Advertising Inc, 1974; Freelance Medical Writer, 1974-76; Biomedical & Regulatory Affairs Consultant, 1976-. *Publications:* Articles in: Endcrinology; Medical World News; Contemporary Surgery, BioPharm. *Honours:* Beta Beta Beta, 1962; NDEA Title IV predoctoral Fellowship, 1963-64; Florida State University Teaching Fellowship, 1965-66; Special Recognition Award for Education Programmes, RAPS, 1986; Regulatory Affairs Professional of the Year, 1986; Elected Board of Directors, RAPS, 1987-88; Appointed Chair Regulatory Affairs Board, 1988-. *Address:* NJC Enterprises Ltd., 700 Washington St., New York, NY 10014, USA.

CHIARAMIDA Angeljean, b. 12 Apr. 1949, Lawrence, Massachusetts, USA. Executive Director; Professional Administrator. *Education:* BA, History, Merrimack College, 1970; Graduate Work, Merrimack College, Fitchburg State College and Tufts University, 1971-75. *Appointments:* History Teacher, Reading & No Andover High School, 1974-76; Admin. Asst. VP Devel. & Res. Staff Dir. Merrimack College, 1977-79; Director of Public Relations, Notre Dame College, 1979-80; Director of Community Relations, NH Lung Association, 1980-83; Executive Vice President, NH Hospitality Assoc. Inc, 1983-84; Director of Resturants, Dunfey Management Co., 1984-85; Executive Director, Martha's Vineyard Chamber of Commerce, Inc, 1985- *Publications:* Various photographic works & Editor, Martha's Vineyard Visitor's Guide. *Memberships:* Mass. Advisory Committee on Vacation Travel; American Society of Association Executives; Mass. Association of Chamber of Commerce Executives; Chairman of Martha's Vineyard Airport Advisory Committee; Martha's Vineyard Community Services Program Advisory Committee; Zonta International. *Honours:* Elected Outstanding Young Woman of America, 1981; Elected Alumna of the Year, Merrimack College, 1981. *Hobbies:* Photography; Creative Writing; White Water Rafting and Canoeing; Travelling. *Address:* PO Box 1698, Vineyard Haven, MA 02568, USA.

CHICK Victoria, b. 8 Apr. 1936, Berkeley, California, USA. Reader in Economics. *Education:* BS (BSc) 1958, MA 1960, University of California, Berkeley. *Appointments:* Assistant Lecturer, 1963-64, Lecturer, 1964-84, Reader, Department of Economics, 1984-, University College London; Research Economist, Federal Reserve Bank of New York, 1963; Visiting Assistant Professor, University of California, Berkeley, 1964; Visiting Economist, Reserve Bank of Australia, Sydney, 1975-76; Visiting Lecturer, University of Southampton, 1977; Visiting (Full) Professor, University of California at Santa Cruz; Visiting Professor, University of Aarhus, Denmark, 1980; Visiting (Full) Professor, McGill University, Montreal, Canada, 1981; Research Fellow, Universite Catholique de Louvain, Louvain La Neuve, Belgium, 1986. *Publications:* The Theory of Monetary Policy, 1973, revised, 1977; Macroeconomics After Keynes: A Reconsideration of the General Theory, 1983. *Contributions to:* Numerous articles in professional journals. *Memberships:* Royal Economic Society;

American Economic Association; Editorial Board, European Journal of Political Economy, Review of Political Economy; Executive Committee Member, ESRC Money Study Group. *Hobbies:* Singing; Travelling; Art Galleries; Theatre. *Address:* Department of Economics, University College London, Gower Street, London WC1E 6BT, England.

CHILDERS Elsie Trusty, b. 26 Sept. 1924, Henderson, Kentucky, USA. Businesswoman; Music Publisher; Song Writer. m. James Madison Childers, 1 Dec. 1943, 2 sons. *Education:* Business College, 1942. *Appoinments:* Hospital Secretary, 1953-56; Clerk, US Department of Agriculture, 1956-80; Executive Director, 5 Days for Famous Kentucky Country Music Artists, 1968-72; Recording studio owner & engineer, music publisher, 1980-. *Creative works include:* Over 450 songs, words & music (best known, award-winner, 3 national record releases, There's A Boat Leaving Ev'ryday), approx. 55 on commercial records or cassettes; Writing copy for own music publication, Trusty International Newsletter, 1974-; Booklet, Instant Know How: Money At Your Finger Tips, 1978. *Memberships:* National Academy of Songwriters; Nashville Songwriters Association International; Country Music Association; Business & Professional Women's Association. *Honours:* Kentucky Colonel, 1971; 3 Citations, US Department of Agriculture; Winner, Nashville Music Survey Contest, 1968. *Hobbies:* Church pianist & soloist, Johnson Island Baptist Church, 37 years; Live concerts, country music & gospel; Playing Yamaha synthesiser; Fishing; Meeting creative people. *Address:* 8781 Rose Creek Road, Nebo, Kentucky 42441, USA.

CHILDS Beryl Ann, b. 17 Sept. 1943, Surrey, England. Director; Principal. m. John C Childs, 23 Apr. 1966. *Education:* Tante Marie Cordon Bleu Diploma; City & Guilds 730 Teacher Training Certificate. *Appointments:* Legal Executive, London, 1962-72; Brussels, 1972-75; Director, Principal, Tante Marie School of Cookery Limited, 1982-. *Publications:* Food Garnishes and Decorations, 1984; Tante Marie Book of French Cooking, 1985; Economic Entertaining, 1986. *Memberships:* Cookery and Food Association; Certified Member, International Association of Cooking Professionals. *Hobbies:* Wine and Food appreciation; Entertaining. *Address:* Woodham House, Carlton Road, Woking, Surrey GU21 4HF, England.

CHILDS Francine C., b. 8 Feb. 1940, Wellington, Texas, USA. Professor & Chair, Afro-American Studies. 1 son (adopted). *Education:* BS, Paul Quinn College, Waco, Texas; MEd, EdD, East Texas State University. *Appointments:* Assistant Resident Director, McKinney Job Corps, Texas, 1969-70; Dean of Women 1971, Dean of Students 1972, Wiley College, Marshall, TX; Project Director, Special Services, East Texas University, 1973; Associate Professor 1974-76, Professor 1977-85, Professor & Chair 1985-, Afro-American Studies, Ohio University; Peace Corps Southeastern Ohio; University Professor, 1989-90. *Creative work includes:* Coordinator, Afro-Arts Symposium 1985, Black Music Seminar 1988; Author, script, Sweet Land of Liberty, Musical, 1984. *Memberships:* National Alliance of Black School Educators; Offices, National Council for Black Studies (NCBS); Offices, Ohio Chapter, National Association for Advancement of Coloured Peoples; National Council of Black Family. *Honours include:* 1st Black Full Professor, Ohio University, 1977; Fulbright-Hayes Scholar, India, 1986; One of 10 participants, Ohio University Management Development Programme, 1986; At-Large Board Member, NCBS, 1988; Dr Francine C. Childs Award established, Black Student Cultural Programming Board; Peace & Justice Award, United Campus Ministry; Black Educator of the Year; Award Received; Can design and teach two special courses of choice. *Hobbies:* Jogging; Walking; Reading; Cooking; Meeting New People. *Address:* 25 Elliott, Athens, Ohio 45701, USA.

CHILDS Julie, b. 5 Oct. 1950, Atlanta, USA. Attorney. *Education:* AB, 1971, JD, 1978, University of Georgia.

Appointments: Cofer Beauchamp & Hawes, 1978-85; Private practice, 1985-86; Attorney, McLain & Merritt, 1986-. *Memberships:* Atlanta Bar Association; State Bar of Georgia; Atlanta Lawyers Club. *Honours:* Order of the Coif, 1978; State Chairman, Junior Leagues of Georgia, 1986- 87; Leadership DeKalb, Dekalb County, 1987-88. *Hobbies:* Golf; Volunteer Work; Local Politics. *Address:* 1250 Tower Place, Atlanta, GA 30326, USA.

CHILLDERS Mary Wynelle Henry, b. 13 Mar. 1919, Wood Co, Winnsboro, Texas, USA. Instructor (Medical), Amarillo College. m. Luel V Chillders, 30 Oct. 1933. 1 son, 3 daughters. *Education:* Graduated, Amarillo College School of Vocational Nurisng, 1963; Graduated, Amarillo College School of Associate Degree Nursing, 1973. *Appointments:* Co- owner & Secretary, Chillders Plumbing & Heating Co, Amarillo, 1946-68; Owner and Administrator, Twilight Nursing Home, 1957-65; Private Duty Nurse, 1967-69; Supervisor and Director of Nursing Service, Medical Drive Convalescent Center in Amarillo, 1969-70; Director of Nursing, 1974-77, Board of Directors, 1974-77, Medi Park Care Center; Instructor, Medication Administration and Medical Terminology, Amarillo College, 1975-. *Publications:* Handbook: Drew Star Unit Dose System Services, 1968; Maxor Drug Procedure Manual, 1968; Patient Care Policy, 1975; Orientation Handbook for Registered Nurse, Licenses Vocational Nurse, Orderly, Nurse Aid, Medication Aide, 1975; Job Description Handbook, 1975; Personnel Policy Handbook, 1975; Policy Handbook for Medipark Care Center, 1975; Medication Terminology Handbook, 1977; Infection Control Procedure & Guideline Manual, 1975; Nursing Care Procedure Manual, 1975; Drug Procedure Manual, 1975, etc. *Memberships include:* PTA, Amarillo School District, 1940-63; Troup Leader in Brownie & Girl Scouts, 1942-54; Charter Member, South Amarillo Garden Club, 1944-60; American Rose Society, 1945-65; Palo Dura Chapter of International Toastmistress, 1968-79; Organizing President, Alpha Delta Rho Chapter of Beta Sigman Phi, 1974; Amarillo Genealogical Society, 1977. *Honours:* Accredited Jr Flower Show Judge, 1962; Appointed to the Texas State Board of Vocational Nurse Examinations, 1975-81. Hobbies: Civic Affairs; Antique Collecting; Travel; Genealogical Research. *Address:* 4000 Julie Drive, Amarillo, TX 79109, USA.

CHIN Janet Sau-Ying, b. 27 July 1949, Hong Kong. Computer Scientist. *Education:* BSc Honours, Mathematics, 1970; MSc, Computer Science, 1972. *Appointments:* Systems programmer, research, secured operating systems, Lawrence Livermore National Laboratory (LLNL), USA, 1972-75; Application programmer, laser research 1975-77, systems programmer, graphics group 1977-79, LLNL; Project leader, decision support 1979-80, manager, graphics unit 1980-82, manager systems products section 1982-83, Tymshare; Manager, software, Fortune Systems, 1983-85; President, Chin Associates, 1985-. *Creative works:* Author, published reports; Invited speaker, international conferences. *Memberships:* Vice chairman, technical committee on computer graphics (X3H3), American National Standards Institute, 1979-82; International representative, X3H3, 1982-88; International Standards Committee on Computer Graphics, 1980-88. *Hobbies:* Science fiction books; Piano; Racquetball; Tennis; Karate; Iaido. *Address:* 5837 Snake Road, Oakland, California 94611, USA.

CHIN Penny Chu, b. 29 Feb. 1948, New York City, New York, USA. Interior Spatial Planner. m. Chester Chin, div. 1983, 1 son, 4 daughters. *Education:* Gibbs Secretarial School, 1968; AS, Interior Design, Redwood City, California, 1984. *Appointments:* New Account Teller, Lincoln Savings Bank, Brooklyn, New York, 1965-66; Executive Secretary, Stauffer Chemical Co, New York City, 1966-69; Domestic Engineer, 1969-82; Sales Designer, Kitchen and Bath Association, Palo Alto, California, 1982-84; Spatial Interior Intraplan Design (Formerly Designer, P.C.Design), 1984-. *Publications:* Bath by Professionals, 1989; Kitchen by Professionals, 1989 & 1990; California Edition, Designers, 1989;

Kitchen and Bath Business, 1990. *Memberships:* American Society of Interior Designers Program 1990; (Secretary, Student Chapter, 1982); International Society of Interior Designers, 1984-85; National Kitchen and Bath Association; San Francisco Medical Society (Director of Health Education 1980-81); Coordinator, Health Lectures, American Cancer Society, San Mateo, 1981; Student Liasion, College of San Mateo, 1989 & 1990; Special Event Chair, Designers Showcase, 1990; Education Advisory Committee to College of San Matoe, 1988, 1989, 1990. *Honours:* Miss New York Chinatown, 1965; Miss Congeniality, Miss USA Chinatown, 1966; Miss Chinatown, Miss New York, 1966; National Recognition in Health Education, American Medical Society, 1981. *Hobbies:* Tennis; Home. *Address:* 1060 Crystal Springs Road, Hillsborough, CA 94010, USA.

CHIN Sue S (Suchin), b. San Francisco, USA. Artist; Photographer; Community Affairs Activist. *Education:* California College Art; Minneapolis Art Institute; Schaeffer Design Centre; Student, Yasuo Kuniyoshi, Louis Hamon, Rico LeBrun. *Appointments:* Photojournalist, All Together Now Show, 1973, East-West News, Third World Newscasting, 1975-78, KNBC Sunday Show, Los Angeles, 1975, 1976, Live on 4, 1981, Bay Area Scene, 1981; Graphics Printer. *Creative Works:* Exhibitions Include: Kaiser Center, Zellerbach Plaza, Chinese Culture Center Galleries, Capricorn Asunder Art Commission Gallery, San Francisco; Newspace Galleries, New College of California, Los Angeles County Museum of Art. *Memberships:* Delegate National State Conventions, National Women's Political Caucus, 1977-83, San Francisco Chapter, Affirmative Action Chairperson, 1978-82; San Francisco Women Artists; California Chinese Artists; Japanese American Art Council. *Honours:* Recipient, many honours & awards. *Address:* PO Box 1415 San Francisco, CA 94101, USA.

CHINN Phyllis Zweig, b. 26 Sept. 1941, Rochester, New York, USA. Mathematician. m. Daryl Ngee Chinn, 31 Dec. 1968, 1 son, 1 daughter. *Education:* BA, Brandeis University, 1962; MAT, Harvard Graduate School of Education, 1963; MA (San Diego) 1966, PhD (Santa Barbara) 1969, University of California. *Appointments:* Instructor, State College, Salem, Massachusetts, 1964; Assistant Professor, Towson State College, Baltimore, Maryland, 1969-75; Assistant, Associate, now full Professor, Humboldt State University, California, 1975-; Visiting Professor, University of Central Florida, 1983-84. *Publications:* Women in Science & Mathematics, bibliography, 1983; Editor, 3 volumes Congressus Numerantium; Over 30 articles, various professional journals. *Memberships:* Mathematical Association of America; National Council of Teachers of Mathematics; Association for Women in Science; Association for Promotion of Methematical Education of Girls & Women; Math/Science Network. *Honours:* Phi Beta Kappa, 1962; Award, innovation in instruction, Chancellor's Office, California State Colleges & Universities, 1976-77; Outstanding Professor, Humboldt State University, 1989-90. *Hobbies:* Juggling; Work for male/female equity in science & mathematics. *Address:* Department of Mathematics, Humboldt State University, Arcata, California 95521, USA.

CHISSELL Joan Olive, b. Cromer, Norfolk, England. Musicologist. *Education:* Royal College of Music, London; ARCM: GRSM. *Appointments:* Lecturer in Music for Extra-Mural Departments of Oxford and London Universities, 1943-48; Piano teacher, Junior Department, Royal College of Music, 1943-53; Assistant Music Critic, The Times, 1948-79; Regular broadcaster for BBC and reviewer for The Gramophone; Jury Member for International Piano Competitions in Milan, Leeds, Zwickau, Budapest and Sydney. *Publications:* Schumann, 1948; Chopin, 1965; Schumann's Piano Music, 1972; Brahms, 1977; Clara Schumann, 1983; Contributor to various symposia, professional periodicals. *Memberships:* Critics Circle; Royal College of Music Union; Royal Lifeboat Society. *Hobbies:* Boating on the Thames; Swimming in the Aegean sea. *Address:*

Flat D, 7 Abbey Road, St Johns Wood, London NW8 9AA, England.

CHITI Patricia Adkins, b. 17 Nov. 1946, Oxford, England. Mezzo-soprano; Opera Singer; Musicologist. m. Gian Paolo Chiti, 22 Dec. 1967. *Education:* Guildhall School of Music & Drama; Teatro dell'Opera, Rome. *Appointments:* Debut as Azucena in Il Trovatore, with Teatro Comunale Bologna; Guest Artist with orchestras & theatres in Europe, Americas, USA and Asia. *Memberships:* Lansdown Club; Artistic Director, Festivals in Italy. *Hobbies:* Reading; Cooking; Knitting; Musical Research. *Address:* Via Proba Petronia 82, 00136 Rome, Italy.

CHITTISTER Joan D, b. 26 Apr. 1936, Dubois, Pennsylvania, USA. Religious Superior; Social Psychologist; Author; Lecturer. *Education:* Saint Benedict Academy, Erie, PA, 1956; BA, Mercyhurst College, Erie, 1962; MA, University of Notre Dame, Notre Dame, IN, 1968; PhD, Pennsylvania State University, 1971. *Appointments:* Elementary Teacher 1955-59, Secondary Teacher 1959-74, parochial schools, diocese of Erie; Taught, Pennsylvania State University, 1969-71; Executive Secretary, Inter Monastic Aid, 1990-; American Benedictine Academy; Executive Board, Ecumenical and Cultural Institute, St John's University, Collegeville, 1976-; Prioress, Benedictine Sisters of Erie, 1978-90. *Publications:* Climb Along the Cutting Edge: An Analysis of Change in Religious Life, 1977; Living the Rule Today, 1982; Faith and Ferment: An Interdisciplinary Study of Christian Beliefs and Practices, with Martin Marty, 1983; Women, Church and Ministry, 1983; A Psalm Journal, Books I and II, 1985; Winds of Change: Women Challenge the Church, 1986; Wisdom Distilled from the Daily, 1990; Numerous articles, tapes, video cassettes, workshops and lectures on religious life and peacemaking. *Memberships include:* Council Member, Federation of St Scholastica, 1969-; President, Conference of American Benedictine Prioresses, 1974-90; Board of Directors, National Catholic Reporter, 1983-; Board of Directors, Hamot Health Systems Inc, 1984-88; Board of Corporators, St Vincent Foundation, 1986-. *Honours:* Promotion of Religious Life Award, Serra Club International, 1976; Distinguished Pennsylvanian Award, Gannon University, 1984; Honorary LLD, Chestnut Hill College, 1986, Villa Maria College, 1987, St Mary's College, 1989, Loyola University of Chicago, 1989; Aquinas College, 1990, Loyola University of New Orleans, 1990; Distinguished Alumna Award, Mercyhurst College, 1986. *Hobbies:* Fishing; Music; Reading. *Address:* Mount Saint Benedict, Erie, PA, USA.

CHITWOOD Phyllis Ann Adams, b. 28 June 1959, Rocky Mount, Virginia, USA. Certified Public Accountant (CPA). m. Walter Michael Chitwood, 12 Dec. 1981. *Education:* ASc magna cum laude, Applied Science, Patrick Henry Community College, 1982. *Appointments:* Bookkeeper, Secretary, James K. Sells CPA, Martinsville, Virginia, 1977-82; Senior Staff Accountant, Hertz Herson & Company, CPA's, Charlotte, North Carolina, 1982-. *Memberships:* National Association of Accountants; American Institute, & North Carolina Association of CPA's; Offices including past Area Council Chairman, American Business Woman's Association. *Honour:* CPA licence, Mar. 1985. *Hobbies:* Reading; Travel; Golf; Crafts; Bowling. *Address:* 6333 Lake Forest Drive, Charlotte, North Carolina 28227, USA.

CHIU Sharon Cho, b. 29 May 1942, Canton, China. Musician. m. 5 Dec. 1969, 2 sons. *Education:* BA, Chinese Culture University, 1967; MA course, Elizabeth Music College, Japan, 1973-75. *Appointments:* Instructor of Piano, 1967-72, Associate Professor, Department of Music, 1973-80, Chinese Culture University; Professor, Kuang-Jen Music School, 1973-80; Music Director, Chiu's Art Institute, 1981-; Director of Music, Chinese Festival, Asian Expo, 1970. *Publications:* A Study of Cha-Cho Folk Music, 1971; A Theoretical and Practical Study of Piano Petal, 1978. *Memberships:* Chinese Music and Dance Association;

American Music Teachers Association, Pasadena, Director 1981-82, Chairperson; The Southwestern Youth Music Festival; National Guild of Piano Teachers. *Honours:* Honorary Certificate for Asian Expo, Ministry of Education, Republic of China; Honorary Certificate for Active Membership of MTAC; Honorary Certificate for Outstanding Teacher in California, Committee of The Confucius Commemorative Day Ceremony, USA. *Hobbies:* Music especially piano and singing; Art appreciation; Touring; Dancing. *Address:* 1937 San Gabriel Boulevard, San Marino, CA 91108, USA.

CHMIELEWSKI Margaret Ann Kakaley, b. 13 Dec. 1946, Detroit, Michigan, USA. Adjunct Assistant Professor. m. James Chmielewski, 19 May 1973, 1 son, 1 daughter. *Education:* BA, 1969, MA, 1972, Wayne State University. *Appointments:* English Teacher: Our Lady Star of the Sea High, 1969-70, Bishop Borgess High, 1972-73, Wayne County Community College Speech Instructor 1972-74; Assistant Professor, Madonna College, 1977-. *Memberships:* Delta Zeta; Michigan Harness Horsemen and US Trotting Association. *Honours:* Miss Wheelchair America, 1978-79; Miss Wheelchair Michigan, 1976. *Hobbies:* Harness Horse Racing; Bridge. *Address:* 36600 Schoolcraft, Livonia, MI 48150, USA.

CHODOROW Nancy Julia, b. 20 Jan. 1944, New York City, New York, USA. Professor of Sociology. m. 2 children. *Education:* AB summa cum laude, Social Relation, Radcliffe College, 1966; Graduate work, Social Anthropology: London School of Economics & Political Science, England, 1966- 67, Harvard University, 1967-68; MA, PhD, Sociology, Brandeis University, 1975; Postdoctoral Intern, Pyschology Clinic, University of California, Berkeley, 1984-86; Marriage, Family and Child Counselling Intern, 1986. *Appointments:* Instructor, Women's Studies, Wellesley College, 1973-74; Lecturer, Stevenson College and Board of Studies in Sociology, 1974-76, Assistant Professor, Kresge College and Board of Studies in Sociology, 1976- 79, Associate Professor, Board of Studies in Sociology, 1979-86, University of California, Santa Cruz; Associate Research Sociologist, Institute of Personality Assessment & Research, 1981-, Associate Professor, Department of Sociology, 1986-, University of California, Berkeley. *Publications:* The Reproduction of Mothering: Psychoanalysis and the Sociology of Gender, 1978; Feminism and Psychoanalytic Theory, 1989; Articles and book-chapters including: Family Structure and Feminine Personality, 1974; Gender, Relation and Difference in Psychoanalytic Perspective, 1980; Oedipal Asymmetries and the Marital Age Gap, 1986; Reviews, commentaries. *Memberships:* American Sociological Association; National Women's Studies Association; Sociologists for Women in Society; Affiliate: San Francisco Psychoanalytic Institute; American Psychoanalytic Association; Advisory Editor, Editorial Board Member, several journals. *Honours:* Phi Beta Kappa, 1965; Jessie Bernard Award, American Sociological Association, 1979; Fellow, Center for Advanced Study in the Behavioral Sciences, 1980-81; Elected to Sociological Research Association, 1988; Many research grants and fellowships. *Address:* Department of Sociology, University of California, Berkeley, CA 94720, USA.

CHOURA LOUGHRAN Bana, b. 21 May 1956, Damascus, Syria. Architect. m. Edward Loughran, 14 Apr. 1987, 1 son. *Education:* BA, Architectural Design, Damascus University, 1979; MA, Pratt Institute, New York, USA, 1984. *Appointments:* (USA) Architect, Project Manager, Easton & Larocca Inc 1982-83; Michael R. Larocca Ltd 1983-84, 1985-87, New York City; Freelance architect, Westchester & New York City, 1987-. *Creative work includes:* Renovation, several residential projects, NYC & Westchester, including: Palmieri Loft, Soho, NYC; Palace, for member of Royal Family, Riyadh, Saudi Arabia; Office building, Tunis, Tunisia. *Memberships:* American Institute of Architects; Syrian Society of Engineers & Architects. *Hobbies:* Photography; Tennis; Crafts. *Address:* 137 Bayberry Close, Chappaqua, New York 10514, USA.

CHOYKE Phyllis May Ford, b. 25 Oct. 1921, Buffalo, USA. Business Executive; Editor; Poet. m. Arthur Davis Choyke, 18 Aug. 1945, 2 sons. *Appointments:* Reporter, City News Bureau, Chicago, 1942-43, Met. Section, Chicago Tribune, 1943-44; Feature Writer, OWI, New York City, 1944-45; Secretary Corp. Artcrest Products Co. Inc., Chicago, 1958-, Vice President 1964-; Founder Director, Harper Square Press Division, 1966-; President, Partford Corporation, 1988-. *Publications:* Author as Phyllis Ford: Apertures to Anywhere, 1979; Editor, Gallery Series One, Poets, 1967; Gallery Series Two, Poets, 1968; Gallery Series 3, 1970; Gallery Series Four, Poets, 1973; Gallery Series Five, 1977. *Memberships:* Mystery Writers of America; Chicago Press Veterans Association; Historical Alliance of Chicago Historical Society; DAR. *Address:* 29 East Division St., Chicago, IL 60610, USA.

CHRISTENSEN Carol Lynette, b. 10 Aug. 1941, Long Beach, California, USA. Professor of Human Performance. *Education:* BA, San Jose State University, 1963; MA, University of California, Santa Barbara, 1976; PhD, University of Utah, 1980. *Appointments:* High school teacher, physical education, 1963-74; Graduate assistant, University of Utah, 1976-80; Assistant, Associate, full Professor of Human Performance, San Jose State University, 1980-. *Creative work:* Author or co-author: 20 research articles & abstracts; 24 scholarly, 17 professional presentations at local, regional, national & international professional meetings. *Memberships:* Fellow, American College of Sports Medicine, American Alliance of Health, Physical Education, Recreation & Dance (AAHPERD); Various offices, California AHPERD. *Honours:* 4 graduate fellowships; Grant, National Collegiate Athletics Association; 7 grants, faculty development, California State University & Colleges Affirmative Action; 2 awards, meritorious performance, professional promise. *Hobbies:* Tennis; Jogging; Hiking; Photography; Gardening. *Address:* Department of Human Performance, San Jose State University, San Jose, California 95192, USA.

CHRISTIE Clare Willis, b. 10 Sept. 1946, Amherst, Canada. Barrister; Solicitor; Notary Public. *Education:* BA, Honours, 1967, LLB, 1984, Dalhousie University; B.Ed., Mount Alison University, 1969. *Appointments:* Teacher, English, New Brunswick & Nova Scotia, 1969-71, 1976-78; New Options School for Dropouts, Halifax, 1974-76; Resource Centre Co-ordinator, Stikine School District, BC, 1978-81; Articled Clerk, Stewart MacKeen & Covert, Halifax, 1984-85; Associate Lawyer, Kenneth A MacInnis Associates, Halifax, 1986-. *Memberships:* Canadian Bar Association; Nova Scotia Barristers' Society; Family Mediation Canada; many other professional organisations. *Hobbies Include:* L'Arche & Other Organizations for the Mentally Handicapped; Outdoor Activities; Travel. *Address:* Kenneth A MacInnis Associates, Suite M 101, 1809 Barrington Street, Halifax, Nova Scotia B3J 3K8, Canada.

CHRISTIE Gerri, b. 17 June 1945, Kapunda, South Australia. Marketing Manager. m. Bruce Alexander Christie, 30 Oct. 1982, 1 son, 1 daughter. *Education:* Teachers' Diploma, 1965; APMA Diploma, 1981. *Appointments:* Teacher, 1965-70; Medical representative, 1979-83; Marketing director, 1983-85; Recruitment consultant, 1985-88; Marketing manager, 1988-. *Memberships:* Company Directors Association; Australian Marketing Institute; Australian Institute of Management. *Hobbies:* Bridge; Classical music; Gardening; Ballet; Tennis; Golf. *Address:* Myrtle Bank, 78 Cross Road, Adelaide, South Australia 5064, Australia.

CHRISTIE Julie Frances, b. 14 Apr. 1940, Assam, India. Actress. *Education:* Brighton Technical College; Central School of Speech and Drama. *Creative Works:* Films: Crooks Anonymous, 1962; The Fast Lady, 1962; Billy Liar, 1963; Young Cassidy, 1964; Darling, 1964; Doctor Zhivago, 1965; Fahrenheit 451, 1966; Far From the Madding Crowd, 1966; Petulia, 1967; In Search of Gregory, 1969; The Go-Between, 1971; McCabe & Mrs Miller, 1972; Don't Look Now, 1973; Shampoo, 1974;

Demon Seed; Heaven Can Wait, 1978; Memoirs of a Survivor, 1980; Gold, 1980; The Return of the Soldier, 1981; Les Quarantiemes rugissants, 1981; Heat and Dust, 1982; The Gold Diggers, 1984; Miss Mary, 1986. *Honours:* Motion Picture Laurel Award, Best Dramatic Actress, 1967; Motion Picture Herald Award, 1967; Academy Award for Darling, 1966; Donatello Award for Doctor Zhivago, 1965. *Address:* c/o International Creative Management, 22 Grafton Street, London W1, England.

CHRISTINE Virginia, b. Stanton, Iowa, USA. Actress. *Education:* University of California at Los Angeles. *Creative Works:* Has appeared in more than 400 motion pictures and television productions including: Films: Mission to Moscow; Counter Attack; The Killers; Cover Up; The Men; Cyrano De Bergerac; Cobweb; High Noon; Not as a Stranger; Spirit of St Louis; Three Brave Men; Judgment in Nuremberg; The Prize; Four for Texas; A Rage to Live; Guess Who's Coming to Dinner; Hail Hero; Daughter of the Mind. Television: Dragnet; Abbot & Costello; Dangerous Assignment; Racket Squad; Superman; Schiltz Playhouse; Four Star Playhouse; The Whistler; Code 3; Ford Theatre; You Are There; Stage 7; Passport to Danger; Soldier of Fortune; Heinz Show; Anthology; Cavalcade of America; Alfred Hitchcock Presents; Father Knows Best; Crusader; Kellogg; Front Row Center; The Twisted Road; Matinee; Private Secretary; Fort Laramie; Big Town; Science Fiction; Frontier Detective; Lone Ranger; Jim Bowie; Wire Service; Whirlybirds; Gunsmoke; Las Vegas Story; Trackdown; The Thin Man; San Francisco Beat; Stranger in Town; T Men; Casey Jones; Climax; Mickey Spillane; The Millionaire; Behind Closed Doors; Target; Peter Bunn; Zane Grey Theatre; Wyatt Earp; Secret Mission; The Donna Reed Show; Wanted Dead or Alive; Buckskin; Loretta Young Show; Starperformance; Rescue 8; Steve Canyon; State Trooper; Twilight Zone; General Electric Theatre; How to Marry A Millionaire; Rifle Man; June Allyson Show; Rawhide; M Squad; Coronado 9; Man From Black Hawk; Grand Jury; Riverboat; 77 Sunset Strip; Happy; The Thriller; Lawless Years; The Untouchables; Death Valley Days; Verdict Is Yours; Deputy; Perry Mason; Wagon Train; Mr Ed; Maverick; The Shirley Temple Show; Asphalt Jungle; Harrigan and Son; Tales of Wells Fargo; Bronco; Line of Duty; The New Breed; Going my Way; Stoney Burke; Bonanza; The Eleventh Hour; Ben Casey; The Virginian; The Fugitive; Day in Court; Hazel; Singing Nun; Billy The Kid; The Big Valley; The FBI; Laredo; A Man Called Shenandoah; Jericho; Judd for the Defense; The Invaders; Lancer; Nanny and the Professor. Stage: Hedda Gabler; Mary, Queen of Scots; Miss Julie; Desdemona.

CHRISTO-JAVACHEFF Jeanne-Claude de Guillebon, b. 13 June 1935, Casablanca, Morocco. Art Dealer; Company President. m. Christo Javacheff, 1 son. *Education:* Baccalaureat, Latin and Philosophy, University of Tunis, 1952. *Appointments:* Art Dealer for artist Christo, 1958-; President, CVJ Corporation (formerly Valley Curtain Corporation and Running Fence Corporation), 1970-; Faculty Member, Colorado State Univesity, Fort Collins, Colorado, USA. *Creative works:* Collaborates with artist Christo on all projects. *Memberships:* Museum of Modern Art, New York; International Center of Photography; Architectural League of New York. *Honour:* LLD (honoris causa), The College of Saint Rose, Albany, New York. *Address:* 48 Howard Street, New York City, NY 10013, USA.

CHRISTOPHER Alexandrina Kimi, b. 26 Aug. 1926, Port of Spain, Trinidad. Travel & Marketing-Conference/Incentive Specialist. m. Alyt Bain Christopher, 10 May 1958. 2 daughters. *Education:* Primary/Secondary/Commercial Trinidad, London Business School, Executive Marketing Programme, Strategy Planning, 1979. *Appointments:* BWIA International, 37 years; Manager, New York Office, 1979-84, Manager, UK/Europe Office, 1984-87, Trinidad and Tobago Tourist Board; Chairman, Mystique Isles International Ltd, 1988. *Memberships include:* BWIA/Tourist Board Appointed Member at various overseas exhibitions etc, 1975-79; Trinidad & Tobago Representative Member, Association of National Tourist Offices (ANTOR), New York, 1980-84; Government Member, appointed on Caribbean Tourism Association Board, New York, 1980-84; Trinidad & Tobago Representative Member, ANTOR, London; Association for Female Executives, USA, 1984; Association of Women Travel Executives, 1985; Committee Member, South Save The Children Appeal Fund, London, 1986. *Honours:* International Women's Year Award, 1975; Gold Medal of Merit Award and Charter Member, Republican Presidential Task Force, 1984. *Hobbies:* Reading; Theatre; Interior Decorating; Horse & Dog Racing; Dancing; Concerts. *Address:* 3 Abbotsbury House, Abbotsbury Road, Holland Park, London W14 8EN, England.

CHRISTOPHER Ursula, b. 25 Feb. 1940, Australia. Doctor of Medicine; General Practitioner. m. Semisi David, 15 Mar. 1985, 2 daughters. *Education:* Sydney Technical College, 1959; Sydney University, 1960-70, 1971, 1972, 1973, 1974. *Appointments:* Royal North Shore Hospital, 1975, 1976; Royal Alexandra Hospital for Children, 1977; Monar Vale Hospital, 1978; Lewisham Hospital, 1979. *Memberships:* Australian Medical Association; Est Subs Medical Association. *Hobbies:* Her home on Rotuma Island (600 km north of Fiji), attending twice yearly; Fundraising for Rotuma Island Hospital. *Address:* 76 Hall Street, Bondi, New South Wales 2026, Australia.

CHRZAN-SEELIG Patti, b. 3 Mar. 1954, Springfield, Massachusetts, USA. Systems Integrator. m. Harold C Seelig, 5 Nov. 1977. 1 son, 1 daughter. *Education:* BS, Human Development, University of Massachusetts, Amherst, 1974. *Appointments:* Director, Tri-City Information & Referral, 1975-76; Planner, Secty of Human Resources, 1976-77; Data Analyst, Department Mental Health & Retardation, 1977-78; Vice President, Preferred Custom Software, 1979-88; President, Focused Systems, Inc, 1988-. *Memberships:* National Association for Female Executives; Blackstone Town & Hobby Garden Club, President 1987-88, Programme Chairman 1986-87; Blackstone Women's Club, Vice President, 1985-86; President, Hopewell Jaycettes, 1975-76. *Honour:* Graduate cum laude, 1974. *Hobbies:* Gardening; Photography; Painting. *Address:* Rt 1, Box 26A, Wilsons, VA 23894, USA.

CHUBB Virginia, b. 3 NOv. 1942, Roanoke, USA. Educator. m. 24 Oct. 1980, 1 son. *Education:* BS, Bluefield State College, 1966; MEd., University of Virginia, 1972. *Appointments:* Teacher, Amherst, 1966-67; Roanoke City, 967-85; Elementary Studies Co-ordinator, 1985-87; First Summer Gifted Programme, 1985; Roanoke City Teacher, 1987-. *Publication:* Outstanding Blacks Past & Present of Roanoke. *Memberships;* American Associatiron of Univerity Women; Founder, Northwest Investors; Virginia Education Association; Roanoke Education Association; National Education Association. *Honours:* Outstanding Social Studies Teacher of the Year Award, 1980; Outstanding Women of Southwest Virginia, 1983. *Hobbies:* Travel; Cooking; Reading; Music. *Address:* 2721 Cove Rd, NW, Roanoke, VA 24017, UsA.

CHUHRAN Linda Jo, b. 28 Aug. 1949, Ypsilanti, USA. Elected Official. m. Terry Edward Chuhran, 14 Feb. 1970, 1 son, 1 daughter. *Education:* AAS, various subjects including: Small & General Business Management; BS, Social Science. *Appointments:* Senior Clerk General Motors, 1969-; Elected Official, 1984-. *Publications:* Handbook for election workers rules, guidelines and legal information. *Memberships:* American Management Association; Southeastern Michigan Councils of Michigan; NAFE; Business & Professiona Womens Organization. *Honours:* Recipient, various honours and awards. *Hobbies:* Photography; Painting; Writing; Boating; Ceramics. *Address:* 44184 Wiclif Court, Canton, MI 48187, USA.

CHURCH Irene Zaboly, b. 18 Feb. 1947, Cleveland,

Ohio, USA. Personnel Services Executive. 1 son, 3 daughters. *Education:* Certified Personnel Consultant, National Association of Personnel Consultants, 1975. *Appointments:* Consultant, recruiter, 1965, 1968-70; Chief Executive Officer & President, Oxford Personnel 1973-, Oxford Temporaries 1979-. Professional & civic activities include: Guest lecturer, community, business, educational & civic sectors, 1974-; Generated, implemented, consumer/industry self-regulation & self-improvement programme (local, state & national use), 1975-80; Expert witness, court testimonies, 1982-. *Publication:* Chapter, Employment Practices, in book, How to Start a Business, 1981. *Memberships include:* Offices: National, Ohio & Greater Cleveland Associations of Personnel Consultants; Rotary International; Euclid & Chagrin Valley Chambers of Commerce. Member: Council of Small Enterprises, Greater Cleveland Growth Association; Cooperative Office Education. *Honours:* Service awards, Greater Cleveland Association of Personnel Consultants 1977, Ohio Association 1987. *Hobbies include:* Various activities, Federated Church (United Church of Christ), Chagrin Falls, Ohio; Girl Scout Leader, 1980-81; Chapter Leader, National Coalition on Television Violence. *Address:* Oxford Personnel, Executive Commons, Suite 300, 29425 Chagrin Boulevard, Pepper Pike, Ohio 44122, USA.

CHURCH Nancy Jeanne Suway, b. 16 Aug. 1950, Middletown, New York, USA. Marketing Professor; Consultant. m. Walter H. Church III, 9 July 1977, 1 daughter. *Education:* BS, Business Administration, State University of New York, Albany; MBA, Marist College, Poughkeepsie, New York; PhD, Administration, Concordia University, Montreal, Canada. *Appointments:* Business Teacher, Krissler Business Institute, 1974-76; Business Teacher, Dover Plains High School, 1976-77; Marketing Professor, State University of New York, Plattsburgh, New York, 1977-. *Publications:* Future Opportunities in Franchising: A Realistic Appraisal, 1979; Tips for Waiters and Waitresses, 1981; Marketing for Nonprofit Cultural Organizations, 1986. *Memberships:* American Marketing Association; Academy of Marketing Science; Administrative Sciences Association of Canada; Division 23, American Psychological Association; Kiwanis Club, Plattsburgh; Champlain Valley Business and Professional Women's Organization. *Honours:* District Young Careerist, Business and Professional Women's Club, 1981; Woman of the Year Award, Business and Professional Women's Club. *Hobbies:* Travel; Public Speaking; Antique dishes; Entertaining. *Address:* Department of Management and Marketing, School of Business and Economics, Redcay Building Room 102, State University of New York at Plattsburgh, Plattsburgh, NY 12901, USA.

CHURCH Virginia Anne, b. 21 Dec. 1929, Sarasota, Florida, USA. Psychologist; Lawyer. m. Gaylord Church, MD, divorced 1975. 4 sons, 1 daughter. *Education:* BA 1949, MA Program, JD (Law) 1953, University of Miami; MA Program (Psychology, University of South Florida, 1969-71; PhD (Psychology), Union Graduate School; Union of Experimenting Colleges & Universities Ohio, 1972; 2 year postdoctoral fellowship, Institute for Emotive Therapy, NYC. *Appointments:* Practice of law, Tampa Bay Area, 1956-72; Executive Director, Interprofessional Family Council, Tampa, Florida, 1959-72; Executive Director, Institute for Rational Living, Florida Branch 1974; San Francisco Branch 1975-81; Dean, College of Law, Lewis University, Chicago, 1974-76; Management Consultant, Church & Association, San Francisco, 1982-87; Principal Psychologist, Mid Staffordshire Health Authority, District Psychological Services, England, 1987-; Steering Committee, European Conferences on Post Traumatic Stress, 1989-90. *Publications:* Behaviour Law & Remedies, 1975; Rational Approach to Legal Counseling, 1976-78; Help for Lawyers Who Want to Help People; Numerous articles and columns in journals. *Memberships:* American Bar Association, Family Law Section; AAMFT; AASECT. *Honours:* ABA Award of Merit for founding Legal Aid Society in Tampa, 1957; National Legal Aid Assn, 1959; Grumacher Award of Merit for Sculpture at Florida International Show, 1956. *Hobbies:* Writing novels; Tree (exotic); Farming (trees from seed); Medieval history; Travel. *Address:* 101 Stone Road, Stafford, ST16 2RB, England.

CHURCHLAND Patricia Smith, b. 16 July 1943, Oliver, British Columbia, Canada. Professor. m. 9 Aug. 1969. 1 son, 1 daughter. *Education:* BA, University of British Columbia, 1965; MA, University of Pittsburgh, USA, 1966; BPhil, Oxford, 1969. *Appointments:* University of Manitoba, Canada, 1969-84; Professor, University of California, San Diego, USA, 1984-. *Publication:* Neurophilosophy, 1986. *Memberships:* American Philosophical Association; Society for Neuroscience; Society for Philosophy and Psychology, President 1984-85; Philosophy of Science Association, Governing Board, 1987-89. *Address:* Philosophy Dept B-002, University of California, San Diego, La Jolla, CA 92093, USA.

CHWATSKY Ann R., b. 11 Jan. 1942, Philadelphia, Pennsylvania, USA. Photographer; Teacher. m. Howard Chwatsky, 2 Nov. 1965, 1 son, 1 daughter. *Education:* BS 1963, MS 1965, Art Education, Hofstra University; Postgraduate, C. W. Post, Long Island University. *Appointments:* Freelance photographer, Photography Editor 1980-82, Long Island Magazine; Adjunct Professor 1982-, Director, Master Workshop in Art (Southampton Campus) 1986-, Long Island University. *Publications:* Photos for book, 4 Seasons of Shaker Life, 1986; Author, interviews & photographs, book, Man in the Street, 1989. *Memberships:* Professional Women Photographers; Association of American Magazine Photographers; University Women's Club. *Honours:* Kodak Professional Photographers Award, 1984; Hofstra Distinguished Alumni Award, 1985; Leica Award for Excellence, 1987. *Hobbies:* Gardening; Tennis. *Address:* 85 Andover Road, Rockville Centre, New York 11570, USA.

CIACCIO Karin McLaughlin, b. 9 Feb. 1947, Galesburg, Illinois, USA. Attorney at Law. m. Frederick Steven Ciaccio, 4 May 1968, 1 son, 1 daughter. *Education:* BS, Southern Illinois University, Carbondale, 1969; Temple University School of Law, Philadelphia, 1971-72; JD, DePaul University School of Law, Chicago, 1975. *Appointments:* French Teacher, Sherrard High School, Sherrard, Illinois, 1969-70; Law Professor: University of Wisconsin, Racine, 1975; College of DuPage, Glen Ellyn, Illinois, 1976; Attorney-at-Law: Lombard/Chicago, Illinois, 1975-80; Woodhull/Galesburg, Illinois, 1980-. *Publication:* Lawyers Forum, newspaper article (real estate), 1979. *Memberships:* Zoning Official, Lombard Zoning Board, Lombard, Illinois, 1978-80; Alpha Cemetery Board, Alpha, Illinois; Officer, St John's Cemetery Board, Woodhull, Illinois; Director, AlWood Business Association, Woodhull, 1984-86; Vice-President, AlWood Music Boosters, 1987. American Bar Association; Illinois Bar Association; Henry County Bar Association; 9th Judicial Circuit Women's Bar Association; Republican Women, Henry County, Legislative Chairman 1981-83; Phi Alpha Delta, Secretary 1971-72; Altrusa. *Honours:* President's Scholar, 1965-66, Honors Day Recipient, 1969, Southern Illinois University, Carbondale. *Hobbies:* Photography; Knitting; Sewing. *Address:* 545 Lake Drive, Woodhull, IL 61490, USA.

CICHANOWICZ Edana Regina McCaffery, b. 26 Jan. 1952, Greenport, New York, USA. Librarian. m. William David Cichanowicz, 20 Feb. 1988. *Education:* University of Nottingham, England, 1972; Autonomous University of Mexico, 1973; BA (English/Spanish), State University of New York, Genesco, 1974; MLS, St John's University, 1978. *Appointments:* Assistant Archivist, New York Hospital, Cornell Medical Center, New York, 1975-78; Assistant Reference Librarian, Television Information Office, National Association Broadcasters, New York, 1978-84; Head, Reference Services, Riverhead Free Library, Riverhead, New York, 1984-. *Memberships:* American Library Association; Beta Phi Mu; Association of Professional Genealogists; Suffolk County Historical Society. *Hobbies:* Family history/genealogy; Ballet; Modern dance; Ballroom dancing;

Tartan, Clan history; Gaelic; Knitting. *Address:* c/o Riverhead Free Library, 330 Court Street, Riverhead, NY 11901, USA.

CICHOSZ Joan Mary, b. 12 Sept. 1939, Winona, Minnesota, USA. Probation & Parole Officer. *Education:* BA 1962, graduate work, University of Minnesota; Numerous seminars, continuing education credits, various educational sources. *Appointments:* Probation Officer 1963-67, Community Corrections worker Grades II & III 1967-, Ramsey County Community Corrections, St Paul. *Publications:* Author, presenter, Human Side of the Addict, numerous professional & government publications; Various other articles, professional publications. *Memberships:* American Correctional Association; Minnesota Community Corrections Association; Minnesota Association of Women in Criminal Justice; Mensa; ReEntry Metro Advisory Board. *Honours:* Appreciation Award, Youth Service, Catholic Boys Sub, 1962; Appreciation Award 1974, Robert H. Robinson Service Award 1986, Minnesota Corrections Association. *Hobbies:* Travel; Reading; Cake Decorating; Losing at the race track. *Address:* Ramsey County Community Corrections, Adult Division, 965 Payne Avenue, St Paul, Minnesota 55101, USA.

CIERACH Lindka Rosalind Wanda, b. 8 June 1952, Basutoland, Africa. Fashion Designer. *Education:* Diploma, City & Guild, London College of Fashion. *Appointments:* Vogue Magazine, 1 year; London College of Fashion, 2 years; Designer, Yuki, 6 months; Started own business couture for private clients, now expanded to ready to wear day and evening. *Creative work:* Couture designer, Duchess of York's Wedding Dress, 1986. *Honours:* Honour of designing the Royal Wedding Dress for Sarah Ferguson, 1986; Women of Achievement Award, for Top British Designer, 1988. *Hobbies:* Travelling; Photography; Swimming; Cooking; Opera and classical music; My aquarium. *Address:* 54 Hartismere Road, London SW6 7UD, England.

CIGARROA Sunny Savoy, b. 29 June 1958, Mamou, Louisiana, USA. Dancer; Choreographer; Professor. m. Leonides G Cigarroa, 24 Aug. 1979. *Education:* BFA with honours in Dance, University of Texas, 1982; MFA in Dance, University of Illinois, 1984. *Appointments:* Founder/Director, Sunny & Company, 1984; Professor, Instituto Tecnologico de Estudios Superiores (ITESM), 1984-; Founder/Director, Ballet IMPULSO de Monterrey, 1985-. *Creative works:* Choreography: Dialogue, 1987; Intersect, 1987; Form in Motion, 1987; Support System, 1986; Psychic Injury, 1986; Solo Con Jose, 1986; Preliminaries, 1986; Dealing with It, 1984; Molluscan Myriad, 1984; Redbono'o Dones, 1986; Only 24 hours, 1983; Back to Bach, 1986. *Membership:* Vice president, IMPULSO Arte Danza, AC. *Honours:* Finalist, 1 of 4, Premio Nacional de Danza, 1987 with Dialogue; Finalist, 1 of 5, Premio Nacional de Danza, 1986 with Psychic Injury; Selected to participate in International Competition for Choreographers in Paris, France with Molluscan Myriad, 1986; Creative and Performing Arts Fellowship, University of Illinois, 1982-83; Brown Award, University of Texas, 1981. *Hobbies:* Drawing; Reading; Music; Swimming; Visual Arts. *Address:* Camino de Los Colibries 543, Col San Jemo, 64640 Monterrey, NL, Mexico.

CILENTO Diane, b. 1934, Queensland, Australia. Actress. *Education:* Toowoomba, Australia; American Academy of Dramatic Art, USA; Royal Academy of Dramatic Art, London, England. *Creative Works:* Toured USA with Barter Co; Repertory, Manchester Library Theatre, England. Films include: Angel Who Pawned Her Harp; Passing Stranger; Passage Home; Woman for Joe; Admirable Crichton; Truth About Women; Jet Storm; The Full Treatment; The Naked Edge; The Breaking Point; Once Upon A Tractor for UN; Hombre. Stage: New York: Tiger at the Gates; I Thank a Fool; The Third Secret; Tom Jones; The Rattle of a Simple Man; The Agony and the Ecstacy; Hombre; Once Upon a Tractor; Negatives; The Four Seasons; The Bonne Soup; Heartbreak House; The Big Knife; Orpheus;

Altona; Castle in Sweden; Naked Marys; I've Seen You Cut Lemons. Television: La Bell France (series); Court Martial; Blackmail; Dial M for Murder; Rogues Gallery; Rain; Lysistrata. *Address:*

CINCIOTTA Linda Ann, b. 18 May 1943, Washington Dc, USA. Lawyer; Administrator. m. John P. Olguin, 4 Aug. 1979. *Education:* BS, Georgetown University, 1965; JD, George Washington University, 1970. *Appointments:* Associate 1970-77, Partner 1978-83, Arent, Fox, Plotkin & Kahn, Washington DC; Director, Office of Attorney Personnel Management, US Department of Justice, 1983-. *Memberships:* Past President, Past Delegate, Federal Communications Bar Association; Past President, Washington DC chapter, American Women in Radio & TV; Federal & DC Bar Associations. *Honours:* US Law Week Award, George Washington University National Law Centre, 1970; Order of Coif.

CIOCHETTI Virginia Marie, b. 11 May 1956, Waterbury, Connecticut, USA. Physical Therapist; Athletic Trainer. *Education:* BSc, Physical Therapy, Quinnipiac College, Hamden, Connecticut, 1979, Registered, 1979; Internship for Athletic Training, 1979-81, Certified, 1981, Yale University, New Haven, Connecticut; Dale Carnee Course Graduate, 1987. *Appointments:* Staff Physical Therapist, Grove Hill Clinic, New Britain, Connecticut, 1979; Athletic Trainer, Yale University, 1979-81; Physical Therapist and Athletic Trainer, Phoenix Physical Therapy, 1980-82; Athletic Trainer and Massage Therapist, United States Women's Tennis Association, Volvo Tournament and US Open, 1982; Managing Director, Physical Therapist/ Athletic Trainer, Physical Therapy & Sports Medicine Center of Waterbury, 1983-88; Owner/Director, Physical Therapy & Sports Medicine Center of Southbury, 1986-; Center Coordinator of Clinical Education, Clinical Associate, Quinnipiac College and the University of Connecticut, 1981-; Athletic Trainer, Women's Professional Softball Association, 1980; Athletic Trainer, Greater Waterbury Soccer Camp, 1980 and 1981; Athletic Trainer/Consultant to 6 local high schools, 2 colleges and 1 prep school, 1981-; Physical Therapist, Waterbury Double A Professional Baseball Teams, 1983-86; Athletic Trainer for Nutmeg Games, 1986. *Creative Works:* Annual article contributor to Waterbury Republican and American; Established and Director of Athletic Training Programme for local cities, 1988. *Memberships:* American Physical Therapy Association; National Athletic Trainers Association; American College of Sports Medicine; Connecticut Physical Therapy Association; Eastern Athletic Trainers Association; Connecticut Athletic Trainers Association. *Honours:* Dale Carnegie Award, 1987; Completed 20 hour tennis marathon for the Multiple Sclerosis Society of Connecticut, 1979. *Hobbies:* Tennis; Running; Bicycling; Coin Collecting; Music; Fitness. *Address:* 42 Bradley Avenue, Waterbury, CT 06708, USA.

CIPKUS Loretta Ann, b. 27 Apr. 1957, Cleveland, Ohio, USA. Biochemist. m. Raymond T Dubray, 4 June 1988. *Education:* BS 1979, MS 1988, John Carroll University; Ohio Teaching Certificate, 1980; Real Estate License, 1981. *Appointments:* Environmental Resource Assoc, Cleveland Mus Nat History, 1977-80; Junior Res Assistant, Research Assistant I, Research Assistant II, Case Western Reserve University, 1982-85; Biochemist, Cardiovascular Diseases Research, The Upjohn Company, 1985-. *Publications:* Newsletter Editor, The Upjohn Company-Greater opportunities for women, 1985-; numerous scientific journal publications. *Memberships:* American Association for the Advancement of Science; American Association for Women in Science; Kalamazoo Network, Programme Committee; Steering Committee, Greater Opportunities for Women; Corporate Info Liaison, Catalyst; Smithsonian; Michigan Society for Med Research, Chair Ed Committee; Women's Leadership Roundtable, Coordinator; Willowick Clown Company, Pres; Leader, Programme Coordinator, Lithuanian Scouting. *Honours:* National Dean's List, 1979; Outstanding Secondary Teacher, 1980-81; Lily Award, Lithuanian Scouting

Award, 1983. *Interests:* Women's issues; Environmental issues; Humanitarian concerns; Religious education; Political issues; Bicycling; Aerobics. *Address:* 118 East Candlewyck Apt 1001, Kalamazoo, MI 49001, USA.

CIVIDANES-LAGO Carmen Josefina, b. 6 May 1961, Puerto Rico. Student. *Education:* BA cum laude, Mount Holyoke College, USA, 1983; Ed.M, Harvard University, 1984; PhD, University of Oxford, England, 1989. *Appointments Include:* English Elementary Teacher, Colegio Aurora, Puerto Rico, 1981; French Tutor, Mount Holyoke College, USA, 1982-83; Secretary to Admissions Officer, John F. Kennedy School of Government, Harvard University, 1983-84. *Publications:* Articles in various journals and magazines; Co-author, Memory for French Negation, in Language Learning, volume 35 No. 2, 1985. *Memberships:* Phi Delta Kappa; President, Graduate Students, Somerville College, Oxford, England, 1985; Sigma Xi. *Honours:* French Government Book Prize for Merit, 1981. *Hobbies:* Tennis; Writing Poetry. *Address:* PO Box 24, Dorado Beach, Dorado, Puerto Rico 00646.

CIZEWSKI Jolie Antonia, b. 24 Aug. 1951, Frankfurt, Federal Republic of Germany. Professor of Physics. *Education:* BA, University of Pennsylvania, USA, 1973; MA, 1975, PhD, 1978, State University of New York, Stony Brook. *Appointments:* Postdoctoral Staff, Los Alamos National Laboratory, New Mexico, 1978-80; Assistant Professor, 1980-85, Associate Professor, 1986, Yale University, New Haven, Connecticut; Associate Professor, Rutgers University, New Brunswick, New Jersey, 1986-. *Publications:* 60 professional articles; 10 contributions to books. *Memberships:* American Physical Society; Association for Women in Science; Sigma Xi. *Honour:* A.P.Sloan Foundation Fellow, 1983-87. *Hobbies:* Gourmet cooking; Travel. *Address:* Department of Physics and Astronomy, Rutgers University, New Brunswick, NJ 08903, USA.

CLAASSEN Sharon Elaine, b. 23 Jan. 1953, Beatrice, USA. Attorney. m. Robert M. Still, 10 Sept. 1983, 1 daughter. *Education:* BA, University of Nebraska, 1975; JD, University of Oklahoma, 1980. *Appointments:* Paralegal, Legal Services, Ft. Wayne, 1976-77; Legal Intern, Legal Services, Western Oklahoma, 1979-80; Nevada Indian Rural Legal Services, Carson City, Staff Attorney 1980-84, Directing Attorney, 1984-86; Partner, Claassen & Olson, 1986-. *Publications:* Articles in professional journals. *Memberships:* American Bar Association; ABA Young Lawyers Division; Nevada, Oklahoma, Washoe First Judicial District County Bar Associations. *Honours:* John B Cheadle Memorial Award, University of Oklahoma, 1979; Silver Key Award, ABA Law Student Division, 1979; Certificate of Appreciation: Nevada Indian Rural Legal Services, 1986, Nevada Network Against Domestic Violence, 1987. *Address:* PO Box 209, Carson City, NV 89702, USA.

CLAMPITT Amy Kathleen, b. 15 June 1920, New Providence, USA. Writer. *Education:* BA, Honours, English, Grinnell College, 1941. *Appointments:* Editor, E.P. Dutton, 1977-82; Writr in Residence, College of William & Mary, 1984-85; Visiting Writer, Amherst College, 1986-87. *Publications:* The Kingfisher, 1983; What the Light Was Like, 1985; Archaic Figure, 1987; Editor, The Essential Donne, 1988; poetry in numerous journals. *Memberships:* Editorial Freelancers Association; PEN American Centre; Authors Guild; Fellow, Academy of American Poets; National Institute of Arts & Letters. *Honours:* Phi Beta Kappa, 1941; Guggenheim Fellowship, 1982; DHL, hc, Grinnell College, 1984; Award, Institute of Arts & Letters, 1984; Fellowship Award, Academy of American Poets, 1984; Harvard University Literary Exercises, 1987. *Address:* c/o Alfred A Knopf Inc., 201 East 50th Street, New York, NY 10022, USA.

CLANCY Antoinette Mary, b. 13 June 1938, Dublin,

Ireland. Writer & President of the Women's Political Party. m. Dr Martin O'Boyle, 15 Oct. 1960. 2 sons, 2 daughters. *Education:* Children's Hospital, Dublin, SRSCN, 1955-58; German Hospital, London, 1958-60; University of Manitoba, Canada, 1972-73. *Appointments:* Nurse, Secretary, Sierra Leone, West Africa, 1966-68; Newspaper Columnist, Canada, 1971-74; Managing Director, The Pas Day Care Centre, Inc, Canada, 1970-74; Writer, 1976-. *Publications:* Budgies, 1984; Articles in: World Medicine; Daily Mail; Irish Independent; Women's magazines, etc. *Memberships:* Founder, The Women's Political Party (Ireland), President, 1981-; Women's Political Association, 1979-85; Pro WPA Waterford, 1980-81; Founder Member Dolphin (Youth) Club, 1981-83; Founder, WIGS Drama Group, 1987-. *Hobbies:* Debating; Walking; Member of Toast Masters International; Art; Drama; Bird breeding; Play writing. *Address:* The Cove, Tramore, Co Waterford, Ireland.

CLAPHAM Elisabeth Russell (Hon. Lady), b. 2 May 1911, London, England. Retired. m. Sir Michael Clapham, 18 May 1935. 3 sons, 1 daughter. *Education:* Newnham College, Cambridge, 1931-34. *Appointments:* Welfare Officer, Ministry of Labour, 1940-42; Justice of the Peace, Birmingham, 1955-61; Justice of the Peace, SW London, 1963-81; Chairman, 1972-75. *Membership:* Chairman, Birmingham Settlement, 1953-61. *Hobbies:* Painting; Looking at pictures; Reading; History. *Address:* 26 Hill Street, London W1X 7FU, England.

CLAPP, Patricia, b. 9 June 1912, Boston, Massachusetts, USA. Writer. m. 3 Mar. 1933, 1 son, 2 daughters. *Education:* Columbia University School of Journalism. *Publications:* Constance; Jane Emily; Witches' Children; Dr Elizabeth; I'm Deborah Sampson; King of the Dollhouse; The Tamarack Tree; etc. *Honours:* Runner-up, National Book Award. *Hobbies:* Theatre. *Address:* 83 Beverley Road, Upper Montclair, NJ 07043, USA.

CLARK Beatrice, b. 28 Aug. 1922, Lancaster, England. Political Writer. m. Morris Clark, 16 Apr. 1945, 2 sons, 1 daughter. *Education:* BA, University of Lancaster, 1948; Honorary Degree, Political Science, London University, 1972. *Appointments:* Librarian, City Bank, 1957-59; Chief Researcher, Government Departments, 1959-63; Freelance Writer, Political & Recent Historical Affairs, particularly in Middle East, 1963-. *Publications:* The Princes of the Middle East, 1964; The Cradle of Modern History, 1965; Article, The Sands of Time Run Out, 1979. *Memberships:* National Trust; British Historical Society; British Universities Club. *Honours:* Hon. Fellow, Islamic Research Institute. *Hobbies:* Reading; Writing; Travel. *Address:* 418 Milton Road, Cambridge CB4 1ST, England.

CLARK Carol Lois, b. USA. Administrator; Educator. *Education:* BA cum laude, English, 1970, MEd, 1972, PhD, 1979, University of Utah; Postdoctoral study, Teachers College, Columbia University, 1980. *Appointments:* Teacher, Curriculum Developer, Jordan School District, 1972-78, 1981-82; Instructor, Lecturer, Curriculum Consultant, Brigham Young University, 1978-; Programme Specialist, Utah System Approach to Individualised Learning, 1980-81; Editor, Dian Thomas Enterprises, 1981; Freelance Editor, Curriculum Developer, Utah State Office of Education, 1981-82; Consumer Education Specialist, Utah Attorney General's Office, 1982-85; Special Assistant, Education and Communications, Utah Governor's Office, 1985-87; Consultant, Instructor: Educators Mutual Communication Programme, 1985, Intermountain Health Care, 1985-, Shipley Associates, 1987-; Director of Communications and Research, Department of Community and Economic Development, Salt Lake City, Utah, 1987-; Columnist. *Publications:* A Singular Life, 1974; Principles of Learning (with Evelyn Murdock), 1980; The Relief Society Magazine: A Legacy Remembered, 1914-1970, 1982; How to Avoid Getting Ripped Off, 1985; A Singular Life: Perspectives From Sixteen Single LDS Women, 1987; Contributor,

Consumer's Resource Handbook, 1986. *Memberships:* Home Economics Association, Board 1985-87; National Futures Association Consumer Education, Advisory Council 1984-87; National Association of Consumer Agency Administrators, Board of Directors 1984-86; Board of Directors, Better Business Bureau; Society of Consumer Agency Professionals, 1983-85; Chair, Governor's Advisory Council on Drugs; Project 2000 Kid Speak Steering Committee Council; National Advisory Board, Fund for the Improvement of Postsecondary Education; US Department of Education Elementary School Recognition Programme; Former member, other boards, committees, commissions. *Honours:* Phi Kappa Phi, 1979; 2 Annual Achievement Awards, National Association of Consumer Agency Administrators; Several other honours. *Address:* 2147 Broadmoor Street, Salt Lake City, UT 84109, USA.

CLARK Carol Morrow, b. 12 Feb. 1962, Minneapolis, Minnesota, USA. Investment Research Analyst. m. 20 Dec. 1986. *Education:* Business Administration, William Woods College, Salutatorian, 1983; Chartered Financial Analyst, 1986. *Appointments:* Market Strategist, Piper, Jaffray & Hopwood, 1983-87; Investment Research Officer, First Trust, 1987-. *Publications:* Managing Editor, Informed Investor, Bi-weekly Newsletter (Investments); Numerous Quotes in professional journals and newspapers. *Memberships:* Alpha Chi National Honour Society; Financial Analysts Federation; Twin Cities Society of Securities Analysts. *Honours:* William Woods College Distinguished Scholar Award, 1983; Alpha Chi National Honour Society, 1982-83; Salutatorian, William Woods College, 1983. *Hobbies:* Horse training; Black laboradors; Aerobics; Camping; Teaching; Swimming lessons; Volunteering; Music; Art. *Address:* First Trust, S4E540, First National Bank Building, St Paul, MN 55101, USA.

CLARK Carolyn Faye Archer, b. 16 Feb. 1944, Texas, USA. Scientist. m. Frank Ray Clark, 20 Nov. 1960, divorced 1979, 2 sons, 1 daughter. *Education:* BA, Sam Houston State University, 1961; MS 1973, PhD, 1977, Texas A & M University. *Appointments:* Lecturer 1977, Research Associate 1977-79, Texas A&M University, College Station; Scientist Senior 1979-82, Scientist Principal, 1982-85, Lockheed; Scientist, Staff, 1986-, Lockheed EMSCO, 1986-. *Publications:* Articles in professional journals. *Memberships:* American Society of Plant Taxonomists; Botanic Society of America; America Society of Photogrammetry; Sigma Xi. *Hobbies:* Sailing; Scuba Diving; Tennis; Piano; Travel. *Address:* PO Box 580221, Houston, TX 77258, USA.

CLARK Charlene Elizabeth Miller, b. 8 Jan. 1941, Spokane, Washington, USA. Associate Professor; Director, Learning Resources Unit. m. Robert Stephen Clark, 14 Apr. 1962, 2 sons. *Education:* Diploma, 1962, Sacred Heart School of Nursing; BS, 1965, M.Ed., 1974, Whitworth College. *Appointments:* Office Nurse, 1962; Instructor, Sacred Heart Medical Centre, 1962-66; Instructor, Spokane Community College, 1968; Associate Professor, Director, Learning Resources, Intercollegiate Centre for Nursing Education, 1969-. *Publications:* Numerous articles in professional journals. *Memberships:* WSNA; NLN; Sigma Theta Tau; Sacred Heart School of Nursing Alumni, President; AECT. *Honours:* 4 Academic Scholarships for Nursing Education, 1959-62; number of Grant Awards, 1980-87; etc. *Hobbies:* Skiing; Knitting; Piano; Bridge; Lake Activities. *Address:* Learning Resources Unit, Intercollegiate Center for Nursing Education, W. 2917 Ft. George Wright Drive, Spokane, WA 99204, USA.

CLARK Daphne M, b. 2 May 1923, London, England. College Director. m. (1) Max Richardson, 1943, (2) Terence Clark, 1963, 1 son, 2 daughters. *Education:* Dip.Ed, 1951; BA, 1974; MA 1976; Australian College of Education, 1976. *Appointments:* Teacher, UK & Australia, 1951-73; Senior Librarian, Barker College, Sydney, 1974-80; Executive Officer, NSW State Development Committee, 1980-87; Director, International College of Languages, 1987-. *Publications:* Editor, Teacher Librarian, 1970-75; articles in professional journals. *Memberships:* Australian School Library Association, National Council 1970-72; President, NSW School Library Association, 1971; Member, NSW Committee Australian College of Educaiton, 1976-; Historian, Archivist, ACE, 1978-. *Honours:* British Council Scholarship, 1973; JP, 1980; Overseas Study Award, 1986. *Hobbies:* Guild of Craft Bookbinders; Paintings; Spinning; History. *Address:* 641 41-49 Roslyn Gardens, Elizabeth Bay, NSW 2011, Australia.

CLARK Denise Lynn, b. 14 Oct. 1954, Norristown, Pennsylvania, USA. Accounts Receivable Regional Manager. *Education:* BBA, Ursinus College, Collegeville, Pennsylvania, 1985; MBA candidate, St Joseph University, Philadelphia. *Appointments:* Customer Service Supervisor, Upjohn Co, King of Prussia, Pennsylvania, 1976-80; Manager, Credit and Collection, Smith Kline Clinical Laboratory, King of Prussia, 1980-85; Manager, National Credit and Collection, Smith Kline Bio-Science Laboratories, King of Prussia, 1986-87; Accounts Receivable Regional Manager, International Clinical Laboratories, Nashville, Tennessee, 1987-; Manager, Accounts Receivable, Smith Kline Bioscience Lab, 1989-. *Memberships:* National Association of Female Executives; New Jersey Association of Credit Executives. ssa 20Hobby: Travel. *Address:* 2753 Apple Valley Lane, Audubon, PA 19403, USA.

CLARK Eleanor, b. Los Angeles, California, USA. Author. m. Robert Penn Warren, 7 Dec. 1952, 1 son, 1 daughter. *Education:* BA, Vassar College, 1934. *Appointments:* Editorial Work, W W Norton, 1936-39, OSS, Washington, 1943-45; Ghost Writer, Translator, Editor, Freelance. *Publications:* The Bitter Box, novel, 1946; Rome and A Villa, 1952, expanded edition, 1975; The Oysters of Lochmariaquer, 1964; Baldur's Gate, novel, 1971; Dr Heart, A Novella, and Other Stories, 1974; Eyes Etc., a Memoir, 1977; Gloria Mundi, novel, 1979; Tamrart: 13 days inthe Sahara, 1982, Camping Out, novel, 1986; translation, Dark Wedding by Ramon Sender, 1945; Four Children, The Song Roland. Contributor to various journals and magazines. *Honours:* Guggenheim Fellowship, 1946, 1949; National Institute of Arts & Letters Award, 1946; National Book Award Arts & Letter, 1965. *Address:* 2495 Kedding Road, Fairfield, CT 06430, USA.

CLARK Emma Jean, b. 27 Aug. 1931, Yuma, Arizona, USA. Substitute Teacher; Author. m. Harold Henry Clark, 11 Aug. 1951. *Education:* Diploma, Arizona Bible Institute, 1954; BSEd, Grand Canyon College, 1958; MEd, Sul Ross State College, 1968; Graduate work, Arizona State University; Graduate Work, Northern Arizona University; Graduate work, University of Arizona. *Appointments:* First Grade 1958-73, Kindergarten 1973-75, Third Grade 1975-76, Fourth Grade 1976-79, Third Grade 1979-80, Second Grade 1980-84, Kindergarten 1984-88, Cartwright Elementary School. *Publications:* Bible vol 401; It's In The Book, in process. *Memberships:* National Education Association; Arizona Education Association; Cartwright Education Association; Past Secretary, Maricopa County Chapter, National Association of Christian Educators; Past Chaplain, Ponderosa Republican Women's Club. *Honours:* Education Scholarship for Highest Grade in Education Dept, Grand Canyon College, 1957-58; Kappa Delta Pi, Honor Society in Education, Sul Ross State College, 1967. *Hobbies:* Bible study; Teaching; Reading; Writing; Cooking; Children; Knitting; Embroidery; Computers; Travel; Homemaking; Letter writing; Pen pals; People; Biographies; Pets. *Address:* 4248 N 31st Avenue, Phoenix, AZ 85017, USA.

CLARK Helen Elizabeth, b. 26 Feb. 1950, New Zealand. Cabinet Minister. *Education:* BA, 1971, MA Honours, 1974, Auckland University. *Appointments:* Junior Lecturer, 1973-75, University Postgraduate Scholar, 1976, Lecturer, 1977-81, Political Studies, Auckland University; Member of Parliament, 1981-, Cabinet Minister 1987-. *Publications:* numerous articles on New Zealand Foreign Policy. *Hobbies:* Classical Music; Opera; Drama; Reading; Racquet Sports. *Address:* Parliament House, Wellington, New Zealand.

CLARK Jane Colby, b. 22 July 1928, Smith County, Kansas, USA. Instructor. M. William K. Clark, 27 May 1951, divorced, 2 daughters. *Education:* BS, Kansas State University, 1951. *Appointments:* Teacher, Rural School, Smith County, Kansas, 1946-47; Secretary, Home Service Worker, American Red Cross, 1952-55; Instructor, English, Kansas State University, 1968-, Director, Writing Lab, 1985-. *Publications:* Book Reviews, Manhattan Mercury. *Memberships:* National Council of Teachers of English; Midwest Writing Centers Association, Executive Board; National Writing Centers Association, Executive Board. *Honours:* Mortar Board; Phi Kappa Phi. *Hobbies:* Animal Welfare; Travel; Reading; Swimming. *Address:* 2105 McDowell Avenue, Manhattan, KS 66502, USA.

CLARK Joyce Naomi Johnson, b. 4 Oct. 1936, Corpus Christi, Texas, USA. Registered Professional Nurse; Certified Instrument Flight Instructor. m. William Boyd Clark, 4 Jan. 1960, 1 daughter. *Education:* RN, Trinity University, 1958; Certified Instrument Flight Instructor, FAA, 1986; Currently studying for Airline Dispatcher. *Appointments:* Registered Nurse; Ft. Sill, Oklahoma, Labour & Delivery, USPH Indian Hospital, 1960; Surgical Staff Nurse, Van Nuys Community Hospital; Memorial Medical Centre, Obstetrics, 1964; US Naval Hospital, 1965-68; Assistant Clinical Manager, Operating Suite, Memorial Medical Centre; Flight Instructor, 1983-. *Memberships:* Association of Operating Room Nurses, Vice President, 1969 Aircraft Owners & Pilots Association; Civil Air Patrol, USAF Search & Rescue, Texas Wing; Air Force Association; Smithsonian Institute. *Honours:* Charles A Mella Award, Corpus Christi Surgical Society, 1981; Grover Loening Aerospace Award, 1986; Paul E. Garber Award, National HQ Cap, 1986; Charles E (Chuck) Yeager Aerospace Education Achievement Award, 1985; Gill Rubb Wilson Award Exceptionally Distinguished Service Cap 1988; Award of Merit for a Drug Free America National Association Chiefs of Police, 1988; Community Leaders of America, 1988. *Hobbies:* Pilot; Flight Instruction; Volunteer Air Search & Rescue. *Address:* 1001 Carmel Parkway No. 15, Corpus Christi, TX 78411, USA.

CLARK Julie Elizabeth, b. 27 June 1948, USA. Airline Pilot. m. Mark Cacioppo, 3 Aug. 1988, 1 stepson, 1 stepdaughter. *Education:* University of California, 1968. *Appointments:* Hostess, TransWorld Airlines, 1968-71; SFO Helicopter Airlines, 1971; World Airways, 1972-75; Western Sierra Aviation/US Navy, 1975-76; First Female Airline Pilot, Golden West Airlines, 1976-77; Captain, Northwest Airlines, 1977-; American Aerobatics, 1981-. *Publications:* Valley Flying, 1975; Par Avion Catalogue, 1988; Serenade in Smoke, Airshow Performance 10 years; Sponsorship with Chupler Corp.-MOPART-34. *Memberships:* 99's International Organisation of Licensed Woman Pilots; Confederate Air Force; Experimental Aircraft Association; Warbirds of America; T34 Association; T34 Association Incorporate Membership Chairman World Wide; ISA21 Charter member of First 21 Women pilots in USA for a major US Airline. *Honours:* Certificate of Appreciation presented by FAA for contributions as Outstanding Woman in Aviation, 1989; Recipient, many honours & awards. *Hobbies:* Aircraft Restoration; Antiques; Water Skiing; Skiing; Co-founder/Director, Aerobics. *Address:* 3114 Boeing Road, Cameron Park, CA 95682, USA.

CLARK LaVerne Harrell, b. 6 June 1929, Smithville, Texas, USA. Writer. m. L D Clark, 15 Sept. 1951. *Education:* BA, Texas Women's University, 1950; MA, University of Arizona, 1962. *Appointments Include:* Reporter, Librarian, Fort Worth Press, 1950-51; Columbia university Press, 1951-53; Assistant, Promotions Dept., Episcopal diocese of New York, 1958-59; Director, Poetry Centre, University of Arizona, 1962-66; Writer, Photographer, Lecturer, 1966-. *Publications:* They Sang for Horse: The Impact of the Horse on Navajo and Apache Folklore, 1966, 1971, 1984; The Deadly of Chicago, 1967; Editor, The Face of Poetry: 101 Poets in Two Significant Decades, 1976, 1979; Revisiting the Plains Indian Country of Mari Sandoz, 1977; Focus 101, 1979; Swarm & Other Stories, 1985, 1986. *Honours:* University of Chicago Folklore Award (1st Prize), 1967; Creative Writer of the Year, National League of American Pen Women, Tucson, 1977; etc. *Hobbies:* Cycling; Travel in Indian Country. *Address:* 4690 North Campbell Ave., Tucson, AZ 85718, USA.

CLARK Margaret Goff, b. 7 Mar. 1913, Oklahoma City, Oklahoma, USA. Freelance Writer; Lecturer. m. Charles R. Clark, 2 Sept. 1937, 1 son, 1 daughter. *Education:* BS, Education, State University College of New York, Buffalo, 1936. *Appointments:* Elementary teacher, Niagara & Buffalo, NY, 1933-34, 1934-39. *Publications:* Over 50 poems; Over 200 short stories, adults & children; 21 books for young readers, 1961-, including: Danger at Niagara 1968, Freedom Crossing 1969, Benjamin Banneker (biography) 1971, Mystery Horse 1972, Barney & the UFO 1979, Who Stole Kathy Young? 1980, Latchkey Mystery 1985; The Vanishing Manatee, 1990. *Memberships:* Judge (3 times), Juvenile Edgar Award, Mystery Writers of America; 2nd Vice President, National League of American Pen Women; Honorary member, Delta Kappa Gamma; Authors Guild; President, Association of Professional Women Writers. *Honours:* Honorary adoption by Seneca Indian Tribe, 1962; 4th place, Texas Bluebonnet Award, 1986; Short list, Georgia Children's Book Award, 1981; Children's Choice, 1981, for Who Stole Kathy Young; Distinguished Alumni, Buffalo State University, 1979. *Hobbies:* Swimming; Travel; Bridge; Local history; Preservation of endangered wildlife, especially Florida manatee. *Address:* 5749 Palm Beach Boulevard, Lot 334, Fort Myers, Florida 33905, USA.

CLARK Mary Romayne Schroeder, b. Fergus Falls, Minnesota, USA. Communications Consultant; Civic Worker. m. Donald Arthur Clark, 24 Aug. 1946 (dec. 1975), 2 sons, 1 daughter. *Education:* BA, College of St Teresa, 1944; Diploma, Fine Arts, Conservatory of St Cecelia, 1944; MA, Marquette University, 1978; Postgraduate, University of Salzburg, Austria. *Appointments include:* Instructor: Ottumwa Heights College, Iowa 1944-46, University of North Dakota 1946-48, Marquette University 1948-52, Milwaukee Area Technical College 1962-66, Mount Mary College, Milwaukee 1976-81; Communications Consultant, 1978-80; Coordinator, Community Relations, 1980-; Director, Training & Development, First Bank, Milwaukee, 1981-84; Instructor, Seminar Leader, Division of Continuing Education, Marquette University & University of Wisconsin Extension, 1984-. *Memberships include:* Committee on Education, US Catholic Conference, Washington, 1971-75; State voluntary adviser, National Foundation, 1971-; Advisory Board, Sickle Cell Disease Centre, Deaconess Hospital, Milwaukee, 1970-73; Board of Education 1965-71, President 1967-71, Archdiocese of Milwaukee; Board, Woman to Woman Inc. *Honours include:* Wisconsin Woman of Year, Catholic War Veterans, 1963; Alumna of Year, St Teresa Colege, 1969; Numerous other awards, voluntary work, teaching. *Address:* 317 North Story Parkway, Milwaukee, Wisconsin 53208, USA.

CLARK Mary Twibill, b. 23 Oct. Philadelphia, Pennsylvania, USA. Professor of Philosophy; Author. *Education:* BA, Manhattanville College, 1939; MA 1952, PhD 1955, Fordham University. *Appointments:* Instructor, Assistant Professor, Associate Professor, Professor, 1951-84, Manhattanville College; Visiting Professor, Villanova University, 1980; Visiting Professor, Fordham University, 1981; Visiting Professor, Santa Clara University, 1983; Visiting Professor, University of San Francisco, for 6 summers. *Publications:* Augustine, Philosopher of Freedom, 1959; Logic, A Practical Approach, 1963; Discrimination Today, 1966; Augustinian Personalism, 1970; An Aquinas Reader, 1972; Problem of Freedom, 1973; Marius Victorinus: Theological Treatises on the Trinity, 1981; Augustine of Hippo (Classics of Western Spirituality), 1984. 30 Articles in Journals. *Memberships:* Vice President, 1975-76; President 1976-77; Executive Council 1961-

64, 1971-74, American Catholic Philosophical Association; Executive Council, 1988-91; Chair, Conference of Chairmen, 1974-76; American Philosophical Association; Executive Committee 1985-88, Metaphysical Society; Secretary/Treasurer, 1979-, Society for Medieval & Renaissance Philosophy; Executive Committee 1974-86, Conference of American Philosophical Societies; Executive Committee, 1981-84, Society of Christian Philosophers; Sophia, 1988-; Executive Committee, 1988-, Catholic Commission on Intellectual and Cultural Affairs. *Honours:* Kappa Gamma Pi, 1939; Postdoctoral Fellowship, Yale University, 1968-69; Inter-racial Justice Award, 1967; Outstanding Educator of America Award, 1971; Honorary LHD: Villanova University 1977, Manhattanville College 1984. NEH Fellowship for College Teachers, 1984-85; Honorary Membership in Augustinian Order, 1987; Charter Day Outstanding Alumna Award, Manhattanville, 1988; Aquinas Medal for Eminence in Philosophy, American Catholic Philosophical Association, 1988. *Interests:* Politics and Social Justice. *Address:* Manhattanville College, Purchase, NY 10577, USA.

CLARK Ouida Ouijella, b. 7 Dec. 1949, Birmingham, Alabama, USA. Public Relations. *Education:* BA, Spanish Education, Dillard University, New Orleans, 1971; Graduate Cert. Pub. relations, American University, 1973, University of Valencia, Spain, 1974; Cert. Journalism, NYU, 1972; Postgraduate, University of Chicago, 1980. *Appointments:* Foreign Service Intern, USIA, 1971; Freelance public relations consultant, 1972-76; Teacher, English as a Second Language, Arlington, Public Schools, 1976-78; Founder, President, Clark Prodns, Ltd, Inc, Little Rock, 1981; President Founder, Global Public Relations, Inc, Washington, 1976 and Little Rock, 1981-. *Publications:* Contributor of articles to professional journals. *Memberships:* Public Relations Society of America; America Film Institute; National Press Club; Capital Press Club. *Honours:* Recipient Public Relations award, National Powderly Alumni Association, 1977; Ark. Endowment Humanities grantee, 1982. *Address:* Global Public Relations Inc, PO Box 583, Little Rock, AR 72203, USA.

CLARK Patricia Chamberlin, b. 18 Mar. 1933, Seattle, Washington, USA. Writer; Editor; Education Consultant. m. Arthur W. Clark, 19 Sept. 1951, 4 daughters. *Education:* BA, English 1963, MA 1968, University of Alaska; EdD, University of Southern California, 1986. *Appointments:* Lecturer, English, University of Alaska, 1967-68; Teacher, Fairbanks North Star Borough School District, Alaska, 1968-87; Reporter, Jessens Daily, 1968-; Editor, Arctic Oil Journal, 1969-71. *Publications:* Classroom Reality & Creative Non-Use; Cooperative Learning for Student Success; Martin Luther King, Study Skills Unit for Middle Grades. *Memberships:* National Education Association, retired; American Society for Curriculum & Development; American Educational Research Association; National Middle Schools Association; Phi Delta Kappa. *Hobbies:* Politics; Crisis intervention; Writing poetry; Freelance public relations. *Address:* 612 Sprucewood, Fairbanks, Alaska 99709, USA.

CLARK Petula (Sally Olwen), b. 15 Nov. 1934, Epsom, England. Singer; Actress. m. Claude Wolff, 1961. 1 son, 2 daughters. *Career:* Started career as child singer entertaining troops during Second World War; Early appearances in films under contract to Rank Organization; Numerous recordings and television appearances in England and France; success of record Downtown started career in the USA. *Creative Works:* Films: Medal for the General, 1944; Murder in Reverse, 1945; London Town, 1946; Strawberry Roan, 1947; Here Come the Huggets; Vice Versa; Easy Money, 1948; Don't Ever Leave Me, 1949; Vote for Huggett, 1949; The Huggetts Abroad; Dance Hall; The Romantic Age, 1950; White Corridors; Madame Louise, 1951; Made in Heaven, 1952; The Card, 1952; The Runaway Bus, 1954; My Gay Dog, 1954; The Happiness of Three Women, 1955; Track the Man Down, 1956; That Woman Opposite, 1957; Daggers Drawn, 1964; Finian's

Rainbow, 1968; Goodbye Mr Chips, 1969; Second Star to the Right, 1980. Stage appearance: Sound of Music, 1981. *Honours:* Two Grammy Awards; Ten Gold Discs. *Address:* c/o PROGENAR, 82 rue de Lausanne, Fribourg 1701, Switzerland.

CLARK Sandra L, b. 17 Dec. 1949, Adrian, Michigan, USA. Medical Administrator; Author. m. Frank L. Clark, 1 Sept. 1974, 1 son, 2 daughters. *Education:* BA, Wayne State University, 1978. *Appointments:* Hospital Social Worker, 1976-78; Writer, 1978-83, 1988-; Medical Clinic Administration Aurdra Corporation: Secretary and one-third owner, 1988; Corporate Vice President, Americare, 1983-; Corporate President, Datasolutions Inc., 1983-88. *Publications:* Inspection; The Brave Brothers; minor works of poetry, radio & TV marketing. *Memberships:* National and Michigan Associations of Ambulatory Care; American Public Health Association; Chamber of Commerce. *Hobbies:* Raising & Showing Great Danes; Horse Breeding; Showing & Eventing & Dressage; Music; Reading; Art; Literature. *Address:* 544 Onondaga, Benton Harbor, MI 49022, USA.

CLARK Sandra Marie, b. 17 Feb. 1942, Hanover, Pennsylvania, USA. School Principal. *Education:* BS, Elementary Education, Chestnut Hill College, 1980; MS, Child Care Administration, Nova University, Florida, 1985. *Appointments:* Elementary school teacher, private schools, 1962-75, 1976-77; Assistant Vocation Directress, 1975-76; Assistant Manager, truck stop, 1977-81; Administrator, Regional Resource Coordinator, Day Care, 1981-88; Principal, Elementary School, 1988-. *Publication:* Introducing an Individualised Primary Education Programme at Kindergarten Level, practicum abstract, 1986. *Memberships:* Offices, past/present: St Vincent's School Board, Little People of Hanover, Hanover Area Council of Churches, Hanover Chapter American Red Cross. *Honours:* Federal training grant, Selection Research Inc, Pennsylvania Department of Public Welfare, 1986; Diploma, Institute of Children's Literature, 1981. *Hobbies:* Fine arts, working in pastels, oils, watercolours; Walking; Swimming; Playing piano & organ, singing. *Address:* 348 Barberry Drive, Hanover, Pennsylvania 17331, USA.

CLARK Sheree L., b. 10 Oct. 1956, Saratoga Springs, New York, USA. Co-Owner, Graphic Design Company. *Education:* BS, Retailing, Rochester Institute of Technology, New York, 1978; MEd, Higher Education, University of Vermont, 1980. *Appointments:* Coordinator of Greek Life, Drake University, Des Moines, Iowa, 1980-85; Co—Owner, Sayles Graphic Design Inc, Des Moines, 1985-. *Publication:* ETSIS: A History of the Fraternities and Sororities of Drake University, book, 1984. *Memberships:* Alpha Phi Fraternity; PEO Sisterhood, President of Chapter HX 1985-87; National Association of Women Business Owners; Advertising Professionals of Des Moines, President 1988-89; Public Relations Society of America. *Honours:* Inducted into Alpha Sigma Lambda, RIT Leadership Society, 1978; Named Advertising Professional of the Year, Des Moines, 1986, 1987. *Address:* c/o Sayles Graphic Design Inc, 308 Eighth Street, Des Moines, IA 50309, USA.

CLARK Susan (Nora Goulding), b. 8 Mar. 1944, Sarnia, Ontario, Canada. Actress. *Education:* Student, Toronto Children's Players, 1956-59; Academy Scholar, Royal Academy of Dramatic Art, London, UK. *Appointments include:* Partner, Georgian Bay Productions, California, USA, current. Producer: Jimmy B. & Andre, 1979; Word of Honour, 1980; Maid in America, 1982. Star, Webster, ABC Television. Member: London Shakespeare Festival Company, British Repertory Company; Appearances, US, British & Canadian TV productions; Co-star, British premiere, play, Poor Bitos. Films include: Apple Dumpling Gang; Night Moves; North Avenue Irregulars; Airport '75; Midnight Man; Porky's; Murder by Decree; Tell Them Willie Boy Is Here; Skin Game; City On Fire; Madigan; Promises in the Dark; Double Negative. *Memberships:* ACLU; American Film Institute. *Honours:* Emmy award

1975. *Address:* c/o Georgian Bay Productions, 3815 West Olive Avenue, Suite 101, Burbank, California 91505, USA.

CLARK Sylvia Dolores, b. 5 June 1959, New York City, USA. Instructor. m. Allen Lewis Spiegel, 19 Aug. 1984. *Education:* BBA, Baruch/CUNY, 1979; MBA, New York University, 1982. *Appointments:* Media Research Analyst, 1979-80; Assistant Project Co-ordinator, General Foods, 1980-82; Research Associate, Lord Geller, 1982-83; Instructor, Business, College of Staten Island, 1984-. *Memberships:* American Marketing Association; American Stat. Association; American Association of Public Opinion Research. *Honours:* Recipient, various honours and awards. *Hobbies:* Fitness & Aerobics Instructor; Scholarship - PhD Candidate; Reading. *Address:* 62 Renwick Ave, Staten Island, NY 10301, USA.

CLARKE Anna, b. 28 Apr. 1919, Cape Town, South Africa. Author. Divorced. *Education:* BSc., London University, 1945; BA, Open University, 1974; MA, University of Sussex, 1975. *Appointments:* Private Secretary to Victor Gollancz, Publisher, 1947-50; Eyre & Spottiswoode, Publishers, 1951-53; Administrative Secretary, British Association for American Studies, London, 1956-63. *Publications:* Novels: The Darkened Room, 1968; A Mind to Murder, 1971; The End of a Shadow, 1972; Plot Counter-Plot, 1974; My Search for Ruth, 1975; Legacy of Evil, 1976; The Deathless and the Dead, 1976; The Lady in Black, 1977; Letter from the Dead, 1977; One of Us Must Die, 1978; The Poisoned Web, 1979; Poison Parsley, 1979; Last Voyage, 1980; Game Set and Danger, 1981; Desire to Kill, 1982; We the Bereaved, 1982; Soon She Must Die, 1983; Last Judgement, 1985; Cabin 3033, 1985; The Mystery Lady, 1986; Last Seen in London, 1987; Murder in Writing, 1988. *Address:* c/o Wendy Lipkind Agency, 165 East 66 Street, New York, NY 10021, USA.

CLARKE Joan Lorraine, b. 23 Aug. 1920, Sydney, Australia. Author; Freelance Editor. m. R. G. Clarke, 1946 (div. 1958), 1 son. *Education:* Secretarial Diploma, 1938. *Appointments:* Private secretary, radio, 1939-46; Publisher's copy writer, 1947; Editor, 1948; Manager, secretarial offices, until 1975. *Publications include:* Books: Author, Max Herz Surgeon Extraordinary 1976, Dr Who Dared 1982, Just Us 1988; Co-author, Girl Fridays in Revolt 1969, Gold 1981; Contributing author, Australian Political Milestones. Also: Author, 2 plays, various radio scripts, stories, poems; Editor, Australian Author, 1977-81. *Memberships:* Past offices, Australian Society of Authors, Fellowship of Australian Writers, International PEN (Sydney); Member, Editors' Society, New South Wales. *Honours:* Co-recipient, Woman of Year Award, 1969; Commonwealth Literary Fellowship, 1978. *Hobbies:* Music; Films; Drama; History. *Address:* 42/114 Spit Road, Mosman, New South Wales, Australia.

CLARKE Lorna Jane, b. 13 Jan. 1944, Oban, Scotland. Farmer; Housewife; Horse rider. m. Richard Clarke, 12 Dec. 1977. 1 son. *Membership:* British Horse Society. *Honours:* Winner, Burghley, 1967, 1978; Winner, Munich pre-olympics, 1971; Boekelo, Holland, 1972; Reserve, Olympics, 1972; Team Silver, European Championships, 1983; Winner, Luhmuhlen, Germany, 1984; 2nd Burghley, 1984, 1985; Team Gold, Individual Silver, European Championships, Burghley, 1985; Team Gold and individual Bronze, World Championships, Gawler Australia, 1986; Reserve, Olympics, Korea, 1988. *Hobbies:* Almost all sports; Farming; Gardening. *Address:* The Old Manse, Keir Mill, Thornhill, Dumrfriesshire, DG3 4DF, Scotland.

CLARKE Mary b. 23 Aug. 1923, London, England. Writer; Editor. *Education:* Mary Datchelor Girls' School, London. *Appointments:* Correspondent, Dance magazine, New York, 1943-55; London Editor, Dance News, New York, 1955-70; Assistant Editor and Contributor, Ballet Annual, 1952-63; Editor, The Dancing Times, 1963-. *Publications:* The Sadler's Wells

Ballet: a history and an appreciation, 1955; Six Great Dancers, 1957; Dancers of Mercury: the story of Ballet Rambert, 1962; Ballet, an Illustrated History, with Clement Crisp, 1973; Making a Ballet, with Clement Crisp, 1974; Introducing Ballet, with Clement Crisp, 1976; Editor, Encyclopedia of Dance and Ballet, with David Vaughan, 1977; Design for Ballet, with Clement Crisp, 1978/Ballet in Art, with Clement Crisp, 1978; The History of Dance, with Clement Crisp, 1981; Dancer, Men in Dance, with Clement Crisp, 1984; Ballerina, with Clement Crisp, 1987; contributor to Encyclopedia Britannica. *Address:* 11 Danbury Street, London N1 8LD, England.

CLARKE Nina Honemond, b. 13 Nov. 1917, Dickerson, Maryland, USA. Retired Teacher. m. Samuel Ellis Clarke, 21 Apr. 1941, 1 daughter. *Education:* Bowie State University, 1937; BS, Hampton Institute, Virginia, 1942; MEd, Boston University, 1952; Postgraduate, American & George Washington Universities, 1967-73. *Appointments:* Classroom teacher, 1937-66; Assistant Principal, 1967-68; Principal, 1968-73. *Publications:* Co-author, History of Black Public Schools, Montgomery County, Maryland 1972-1961; Author, History of 19th Century Black Churches, Maryland & DC; Contributions, Flower of Forest Journal, Montgomery County Journal, Afro-American Newspaper. *Memberships include:* Association of Black Women Historians; Maryland, & Montgomery County Historical Societies; Bethune Museum Archives; Banneker-Douglass Museum Inc; National Trust for Historic Preservation; Maryland Retired Teachers Association. *Honours include:* Academic honours & awards; Various recognitions, National Academy of School Executives 1972, Bannneker-Douglass Museum 1980, Kiwanis Club 1986, Government of Montgomery County 1987, Senator Sidney Kramer 1984, National Association for Advancement of Coloured Peoples 1984. *Hobbies & interests include:* Local black history, & general history; World travel; Flower gardening; Lecturing, consulting, voluntary teaching, black history, high schools & colleges. *Address:* 600 Great Falls Road, Rockville, Maryland 20850, USA.

CLARKE Rosemary, b. 23 June 1921, Daytona Beach, Florida, USA. Semi-retired musician; Composer; Accompanist; Concert Artist; Church Musician. *Education:* BMus, Stetson University, 1940; MM 1941, 3 year Organ Diploma 1942, Philadelphia Music Academy; AAGO, 1943; PhD, Eastman University of Rochester, 1950; FAGO, 1953. *Appointments:* Associate Professor, Stetson University, 1942-57; Head of Organ Department, Organist, Director, Community Methodist Church, Daytona Beach, 1943; Organist-Director, St Barnabas Church, Deland, Florida 1951-57; Associate Professor, Music, Artist-in-Residence, University of Dubuque, Iowa, 1957-61; Organist, Director, 1st Congregational Church, Dubuque, 1960-62; Professor of Music, University of Wi at Platteville, 1962-84; Organist, Westminster Presbyterian Church, Dubuque, 1962-65; Organist, Director, St John's Church, Dubuque, 1977-82; Organist, Director, St Thomas Church, Dubuque, 1983-87; Trinity Church, Platteville, 1987-90. *Creative works:* Composer: Symphony in E flat, 1946; 2nd pf concerto, 1947; Pf Trio, 1947; Passion for soloist, chorus & orchestra, 1950; A Canticle of Praise for chorus, organ & Pf, 1984; Wrath for soprano & Orchestra, 1971; Skyrocket No 101 for symphony band, 1966; Fantasy for piano solo & band, 1964; Sound Structures for orchestra, 1979; 11 commissioned works for chorus, symphony band, chamber and solo instruments. *Memberships include:* FL Composers League (Past Pres); Southeastern Composers League; T.U.B.A.; M.T.N.A; Iowa Composers League; American Women Composers Inc; American Music Center; Organ Historical Society; New Music Chicago; The Hymn Society. *Honours include:* At age 9 won for entire state in composition (piano solo) and age 11 (two-piano piece), Nat Fed Mus Clubs, FL. *Hobbies:* Conchology and malachogy; Stamps. *Address:* P O Box 615, Dubuque, IA 52001, USA.

CLARKSON E Margaret, b. 8 June 1915, Melville,

Saskatchewan, Canada. Freelance writer; Retired teacher. *Education:* Toronto Teacher's College, 1935; 2 years at University of Toronto. *Appointments:* Teacher, Barwick, Ontario, 1935-37; Supervisor of Music for the schools of Kirkland Lake, Ontario, 1937-42; Teacher in the Public School System of Ontario, 1942-70. *Publications:* Let's Listen to Music, 1947; The Creative Classroom, 1958; Susie's Babies, 1960; Our Father, 1961; Clear Shining After Rain, 1962; Growing Up, 1962; The Wondrous Cross, 1966; Rivers Among The Rocks, 1967; God's Hedge, 1967; Grace Grows Best in Winter, 1972; Conversations With a Barred Owl, 1975; Booklets of Bible Studies from 1976-79; So You're Single, 1978; Destined for Glory: The Meaning of Suffering, 1983; All Nature Sings, 1986; A Singing Heart, 1987; Theme Hymns for Conventions etc. *Membership:* Audubon Society. *Honours:* Winner of numerous international competitions for hymns, 1948-. *Hobbies:* Serious music; Hymnology; Writing; Natural science; Homemaking; Dressmaking; Gardening; Reading; Christian studies and activities. *Address:* 72 Gwendolen Crescent, Willowdale, Ontario M2N 2L7, Canada.

CLARY Sydney Ann, b. 13 Feb. 1948, Auburn, Alabama, USA. Writer. m. Bishop David Clary, 26 Sept. 1967. 2 daughters. *Education:* 2 years at College. *Appointments:* Professional dressmaker, 1967-84 retired; Writer, 1983-. *Publications:* Her Golden Eyes; Let Passion Soar; Home at Last; The Wildfire Magic; A Touch of Passion; Look Beyond Tomorrow; Undercover Affair; When the Wandering Ends; Double Solitaire; Shadow Watch; Devil and The Duchess; To Tame the Wind; Southern Comfort. *Memberships:* National Writers Club; Romance Writers of America; Florida Romance Writers; East Orange Romance Writers Association. *Honours:* Her Golden Eyes nominated best Desire of 1983; A Touch of Passion nominated best Desire of 1985; Double Solitaire, finalist in Gold Medallion Award. *Hobbies:* Sewing; Swimming; Tai Chi; Horses; Computers; Antique salt cellar collecting (currently has 175); Reading. *Address:* 104 Eganfusku Street, Jupiter, Florida 33477, USA.

CLASON Patricia Ann Turzinski, b. 11 Nov. 1950, Milwaukee, Wisconsin, USA. Consultant; Author; Entrepreneur. m. Steven W Clason, 6 Jan. 1986. 1 daughter. *Education:* University of Wisconsin, Milwaukee, 1969- 70. *Appointments:* Supr Mortgage Servicing, A L Grootemaat & Sons, Milwaukee, 1969-72; Legal Secretary, 1973; Executive Secretary, Plastronics Inc, Milwaukee, 1974; Manager, Mortgage Servicing, University Mortgage Co, Milwaukee, 1975; Manager, Outpost Natural Foods, Milwaukee, 1975-76; Owner, Genesis, 1976-79; Owner, Manifestation Management Inc, 1978-; Owner, Great Ideas! Speakers Bureau and Meeting Planning Consultants, 1983-; Owner, Center for Creative Learning, 1983-; Professional Speaker and Business Consultant, 1975-. *Creative works:* Life Organization Game, time management system and seminar; Claim Your Unlimited Potential, book; Guide to Growth, cassette album; Numerous audio cassettes, seminars and training programs. *Memberships:* WI Professional Speakers Association, Secretary-Treasurer, 1984-85, Vice President, 1986; Association Advancement of Human Animal Bond, Co-Founder, President, 1984-; Co-Founder, Women's Resource Network; Woman to Woman Inc, President, 1985-87; Meeting Planners International; National Speakers Assn. *Honours:* Commendation for Community Service, 1984; Chapter Member of the Year, WI Professional Speakers Assn, 1986; Special Friend of Woman to Woman Conference, 1980. *Hobbies:* Reading; Metaphysics. *Address:* Center for Creative Learning, 6040 W Lisbon Avenue, 200, Milwaukee, WI 53210, USA.

CLAY Jennifer Mary Ellen, b. 27 Sept. 1941, Aberdeenshire, Scotland. Airline Executive. m. John Peter Clay, 1972. *Education:* BA Honours, MA, University College Cardiff, University of Wales; Cornell University, New York, USA; LTCL, MCIT. *Appointments:* Sales Training Manager 1974-79, Manager Western

USA 1979-82, Manager Scotland 1982-84, Controller Corporate Identity 1984-86, British Airways; General Manager, Product Design & Development, Pan American World Airways, USA, 1986-. *Memberships:* Various clubs, London & New York. *Hobbies:* Music; Travel; Royal tennis; Squash; Dressmaking. *Address:* 123 East 30th Street, New York, NY 10016, USA.

CLAY Lori Lee, b. 19 Mar. 1957, Gary, Indiana, USA. Retail Manager, m. Terry D Clay, 2 Jan. 1982. *Education:* BBA, Honours, New Mexico State University, 1980; MBA, Columbus College, Georgia, 1985. *Appointments:* Retail Manager, Fort Bragg, North Carolina, 1980-81, Elgin AFB, Florida, 1981-82, Pope AFB, North Carolina, 1982-83, Army and Air Force Exchange Service; Operations Manager, Ft Benning, Georgia, 1983-84; Sales and Merchandise Manager, 1985-87; Army and Air Force Exchange Service - Europe, Store Manager, Munich, Germany, 1988-. *Membership:* National Association Female Executives. *Honours:* Suggestion Award, Army and Air Force Exchange Service, 1985; Excellence Award, 1986. *Hobbies:* Water skiing; Aerobic dancing; Poetry; Reading. *Address:* 30 Leifstrasse 306 A-4, 8000 Muenchen 90, Federal Republic of Germany.

CLAYTON Gloria Florence, b. 2 July 1935, Thames, New Zealand. State Manager, HST Western Australia. divorced, 3 sons. *Education:* Diploma Anatomy & Physiology, 1965, 1980; Diploma, Advanced Beauty Tutor, 1965, 1983; Diploma, Auricular Therapy, 1981; Diploma, Therapeutic Massage, 1965, 1982; Diploma in Modelling; ADMA Australian Certificate in Direct Marketing, 1986. *Appointments:* Marjory McGann, 1969-88; Director, own business, Public Relations International, 1975-88. *Publication:* Bi-monthly column in Western Australia Health and Beauty Magazine. *Memberships:* World President, Salesman with a Purpose (SWAP); Council Member, Public Relations Institute of Australia (PRIA); Society of Senior Executives; L'Entrepreneuse Inaugural member SBDC for Women. *Honours:* Manager of the Year Swan Swap WA 1985-86; National Manager of the Year, 1985-86; President Swan Swap WA 1985-86; National Presidents Special Recognition Award for outstanding service to SWAP, 1986; Responsible for launching youth SWAP WA, 1986; International Liaison Officer, SWAP Club Australia, 1986-88; Marketing Officer for SWAP WA 1986-87. *Hobbies:* Writing; Music; Singing; Compering organising events on a voluntary basis; Modelling, TV Commercials, Catwalk; Community work; International Compere; Organiser of Community events on a Voluntary Basis. *Address:* PO Box 164, Applecross 6153, Western Australia, Australia.

CLAYTON Margaret Ann, b. 7 May 1941, Cheltenham, England. Assistant Under Secretary of State; Director of Services, Prison Dept., Home Office. *Education:* BA, Honours, English, 1964, MSc., Organisational Behaviour, 1988, Birkbeck College, London. *Appointments:* Civil Servant, Home Office, 1960-, Civil Service Commission, 1983, Head, Personnel, Home Office, 1983-86, Chairman, Prison Service Industries & Farms Board, 1986-; Chairman, Prisons Building Board, 1987-. *Memberships:* Liveryman, Farriers Company; Freeman, City of London; Fellow, Royal Society of Arts. *Hobbies:* Riding & Training Horses & Riders; Theatre; Gardening. *Address:* c/o Reform Club, Pall Mall, London SW1, England.

CLAYTON Xernona, b. 30 Aug. 1930, Muskogee, Oklahoma, USA. Broadcasting System Executive, m. Paul L. Brady, 22 June 1974. *Education:* BS with honours, Tennessee State University; Graduate study, University of Chicago. *Appointments:* Teacher, Public Schools, Chicago and Los Angeles; Southern Christian Leadership Conference (working with Martin Luther King Jr), Atlanta, Georgia; Entered broadcasting, 1967; Host, The Xernona Clayton show, WAGA-TV, Atlanta; Various positions, Turner Broadcasting Inc, Atlanta, 1979-, including; Host, Producer, Open Up, 1981, Coordinator of Minority Affairs, 1982, currently Assistant Corporate Vice-President, Urban Affairs; Guest Lecturer, Institute of Politics, Kennedy School of

Government, Harvard University. *Publications:* The Peaceful Warrior (with Ed Clayton), editions in several languages. *Memberships include:* Board of Trustees, Martin Luther King Jr Center; Board of Directors, Multiple Sclerosis Society; Board of Directors, Science and Technical Museum, Atlanta; Board, National Association of Sickle Cell Disease; National Issues Forum, Jimmy Carter Presidential Library; Motion Picture and Television Commission, Georgia; Commissioner, Board of Review, Appellate Board of Unemployment Compensation, Georgia; Alpha Kappa Alpha; National President, National Association of Media Women. *Honours:* Bronze Woman of the Year, 1969; Superior Television Programming Award, 1971; Kizzy Award, 1979; Black Georgian of the Year, 1984; Inducted into the Academy of Women Achievers, YWCA, 1986; Communications Award, OICs of American, 1986; American Spirit Award, US Air Force Recruiting Service, 1987; 1st recipient, Trailblazer Award, Greater Atlanta Club of Business and Professional Women; Many other awards and honours for her achievements. *Hobbies:* Painting; Photography; Browsing in art galleries and decorators' shops. *Address:* Turner Broadcasting System Inc, Urban Affairs, One CNN Center, Atlanta, GA 30348, USA.

CLELAND Rachel (Dame), b. 19 Jan. 1906, Perth, Western Australia. Retired. m. Donald Mackinnon Cleland, 18 Dec. 1928. 2 sons. *Education:* Methodist Ladies College; Kindergarten Training College. *Appointment:* Teacher, Guildford Grammar Prep School. *Publication:* Pathways to Independence, 1984, 2nd edition 1985. *Memberships:* Honorary Secretary, Sydney Torchbearers for Legacy, 1948-51; President, Girl Guides Association PNG, 1952-66; President, Red Cross Association, 1952-66; President, Pre School Association, PNG, 1952-66; Patron, Sporting Bodies, PNG; Patron WA Branch, Women Writers Association. *Honours:* MBE, 1960; Girl Guide Beaver Award, 1962; CBE, 1966; Red Cross Gold Life Hon Member, 1966; Queen Elizabeth Silver Jubilee Medal; PNG Independence Medal, 1975; DBE, 1980. *Hobbies:* Gardening; The Arts; Music; Welfare of children and youth. *Address:* 2/24 Richardson Ave, Claremont 6010, Western Australia, Australia.

CLEMENT Kathleen Ruth, b. 28 May 1928, Ord, Nebraska, USA. Artist (Painter-graphics). m. Richard Sibley, 28 Aug. 1955. divorced 1972. 1 son, 2 daughters. *Education:* Milton College, 1946-48; BA, University of Nebraska, 1950; Frank Gonzalez painting classes, 1967-69; Art Critic seminars, Toby Joysmith, 1977-79; Museum Studies, Paris, France, 1980; Hand Made Course, 1984. *Appointments:* Professional painter, self employed. *Creative works:* Individual exhibitions: Margolis Galeries, 1985; Rossi Gallery; Kin Gallery; San Angel Gallery; Stuhr Museum; Walker Art Gallery. Group Exhibitions: VI Bienial Iberoamericana, Palacio bellas Artes; National Museum of History, Mexico; Banamex, Mexico; Sheldon Memorial Art Gallery, USA. *Memberships:* Delta Phi Delta, art honorary; SOMART; Foro de Arte Contemporaneo; Churubusco Book Club, Pres, 1985; Panhellenic (Mexico City Chapter); Pro-Salud Maternal (Treasurer & Founding member); Conservation International; St Ceclia Choir; Director children's choir. *Honours:* Prize graphics, 1949; Honorary Commercial Attache, State of Nebraska to Mexico 1985-88; World Culture Prize, Parma, Italy. *Hobbies:* Reading; Piano; Swimming. Address: Tulipan 359B, Mexico 10610 DF, Mexico.

CLEMENTE Lilia, b. 21 Feb. 1941, Manila, Philippines. Financier. m. Leopoldo M. Clemente Jr, 24 June 1964. *Education:* BSc, Business Administration, University of Philippines, 1960; MA, Economics, University of Chicago, 1962. *Appointments:* Investment Analyst, CNA Financial Corporation, 1967-69; Director of Research & Assistant Treasurer, Ford Foundation, New York City, 1969-76; 1st Vice President & Chief Executive Officer, International Investment, Paine Webber, NYC, 1983-86; Chairman & CEO, Clemente Capital Inc, NYC, 1986-; Consultant, various organisations, national & international. *Publications:*

Publisher, Clemente Asian-Pacific Report. *Memberships:* Offices, past/present: NY Association for International Investment; NY Society of Security Analysts; Financial Analysts Foundation; Women's World Banking; Philippine American Foundation. Also: Trustee, Manhattan College. *Honour:* 1st woman & youngest officer appointed in foundation's history, Ford Foundation, 1976. *Address:* 767 Third Avenue, 33rd Floor, New York, NY 10017, USA.

CLEMENTS (Lady Eyre) Anne, b. 19 Mar. 1953, London, England. Actress; Writer. m. Sir Reginald Eyre, 6 Apr. 1978, 1 daughter. *Education:* LGSM, GSMD, Guildhall School of Music & Drama. *Appointments:* Appearances in Repertory Companies: Cheltenham, 1970; Sheffield, 1971; Chichester, 1972; Glyndbourne Festival Opera Company; Chesterfield, 1977; West End Performance, Susan in No Sex Please - We're British, Strand Theatre, 1971; Stand and Deliver, Round House, 1972; Original Production, Godspell, Wyndhams Theatre, 1974; TV Appearances include: YTV Stars on Sunday; ATV's Songs That Matter; BBC Ragtime Girls; Basil Brush Show; Grange Hill; Dr Who; Oxford Road Show; Sorry; Fresh Fields; Film: Ike; over 300 appearances on Radio. *Publications:* Contributor to BBC, Week Ending, Oxford Road Show, The Jason Explanation, Newsreview, Gate Theatre, etc. *Memberships:* Fellow, Royal Society of Arts; Committee Member, Population Concern; Patron, Womens Advisory Committee, Hall Green Conservative Association. *Honours:* Freeman, City of London; Raymond Rayner Memorial Prize; Poetry Society Silver Medal. *Hobbies:* Travel; Sculpture; Literature; Art; Music. *Address:* c/o June Epstein Associates, 16 Golden House, 29 Great Pultney Street, London W1R 3ND, England.

CLEMINSHAW Helen Marie, b. 16 May 1938, New Jersey, USA. Director, Center for Family Studies; Professor, Child & Family Development; Psychologist. m. John Greenwood Cleminshaw, 24 June 1960. 1 son, 1 daughter. *Education:* BS, Rutgers University, 1960; MA 1972, PhD 1977, Kent State University. *Appointments:* Director, Centre for Family Studies and Professor, Child & Family Development, University of Akron, 1977-; Psychologist, private practice, Hudson Psychological Associates, 1980-. *Publications:* Alcoholism: new perspectives, 1983; Book chapters on family issues in 6 books; Articles on family issueds in 9 professional journals. *Memberships:* American Psychological Assoc; American Orthopsychiatric Assoc; National Council on Family Relations; Association for Care of Children's Health; Child Life Council; Council on Advancement & Support of Education; Society for Family & Divorce Mediators; Chair, Family Center Directors. *Honours:* Outstanding Faculty Achivement Award 1987-88, Outstanding Faculty (College of Fine & Applied Arts) 1987, University of Akron; Akron Woman of the Year, 1987; Ohio Professor of the Year (CASE), 1987; Professor of the Year (Bronze medalist, CASE), 1987; Recipient of numerous grants. *Hobbies:* Tennis; Hiking; Travelling; Painting (art). *Address:* University of Akron, Schrant Hall South 215, Akron, Ohio 44325, USA.

CLEMMONS Frances Anne (Polly), b. 21 Dec. 1915, Camden, USA. Medicare Hearing Officer. m. Slaton Clemmons, 21 NOv. 1965, 3 sons, 2 daughter. *Education:* BS, BMus., Belhaven College, Jackson, 1937. *Appointments:* Owner, Operator, Crowder Art Gallery, Jackson, 1946-50; Department Store Manager/Buyer, 1953-56; Social Security Administrator, 1956-83, Assistant District Manager, 1962-83. *Memberships:* Toastmasters; Quota International Inc. *Honours:* Polly Clemmons Art Award to Senior Georgia State School for the Deaf (annually). *Hobbies:* Gardening; Music; Art. *Address:* 412 East Third Ave., Rome, GA 30161, USA.

CLIFTON Judy Raelene Johnson, b. 8 Nov. 1946, Safford, Arizona, USA. Executive Secretary. m. Richard Clifton, 5 Mar. 1982, 2 sons. *Education:* BA, Christian Education, Southwestern College, 1970. *Appointments:*

Editorial Assistant, Accent Publications, Denver, Colorado, 1970-73; Expediter, Phelps Dodge Corporation, Douglas, Arizona, 1974-78; Administrative assistant, Southern Arizona International Livestock Association, Tucson, 1978-81; Executive Secretary, Phelps Dodge Corporation, Playas, New Mexico, 1981-. *Creative work:* Publications: Watch it Grow; Good Humour Man; Openers for Elementary. Also oil & finger paintings. *Memberships:* Past Advisory Board, Arizona Lung Association; Past Leader, 4-H; Republican National Committee; Republican Senatorial Committee; Conservative Caucus; Secretary, Executive Board, Phelps Dodge Employees Committee for Responsible Government; Numerous other memberships, community, voluntary, political. *Honours:* Good Citizen award, American Legion, 1964; Award, Daughters of American Revolution, 1964; Chair, annual event Navidad en November, Arizona Lung Association, 1980. *Hobbies:* Reading; Tennis; Collecting glass, Western art, old books. *Address:* PO Drawer M, Playas, NM 88009, USA.

CLINE Catherine Ann, b. 27 July 1927, West Springfield, Massachusetts, USA. Professor of History. *Education:* AB, Smith College, 1948; MA, Columbia University, 1950; PhD, Bryn Mawr College, 1958. *Appointments:* St Mary's College, 1953-54; Notre Dame College, Staten Island, New York, 1954-68; Catholic University of American, Washington, District of Columbia, 1968-. *Publications:* Recruits to Labour, 1963; E.D.Morel: The Strategies of Protest, 1981. *Memberships:* American Historical Association; American Catholic Historical Association; Conference on British Studies. *Address:* History Department, Catholic University, Washington, DC 20064, USA.

CLINE Eileen Tate, b. 25 June 1935, Chicago, Illinois, USA. Music Educator; Conservatory Dean. m. William P. Cline, 15 Feb. 1958, dec., 1 son, 1 daughter. *Education:* BMus, BMusEd, Oberlin Conservatory of Music, 1956; MMus, University of Colorado, 1960; DME, Indiana University, 1985. *Appointments:* Music Teacher, public schools, Gary, Indiana, 1956-58; Piano Instructor, 1960-75, Coordinator, Continuing Education Piano, 1965-75, University of Colorado; Independent Piano Studio, Boulder, Colorado, 1960-75; Executive Director, Neighborhood Music, New Haven, Connecticut, 1980-82; Associate Dean, 1982-83, Dean, 1983-, Peabody Conservatory of Music, Johns Hopkins University, Baltimore, Maryland. *Publications:* Piano Competitions: An Analysis of their Structure, Value & Educational Implications (book); The Competition Explosion: Impact on Education Parts I-III (article), 1982. *Memberships:* Trustee, Oberlin College, 1002-87, Director, National Guild of Community Schools of the Arts, Board, 1982; College Board Test Development Committee, 1982-86; Panelist, National Endowment for the Arts, 1980-83; Music Educators National Conference; College Music Society. *Honours:* Pi Kappa Lambda, Oberlin Conservatory, 1956; Danforth Foundation Fellowship, 1975; Outstanding Woman Award, National Executive Club, 1984; Distinguished Alumna Award, University of Colorado College of Music, 1985. *Hobbies:* Mountaineering; Skiing; Cycling; International folkdance. *Address:* Peabody Conservatory of Music, One East Mt Vernon Place, Baltimore, MD 21202, USA.

CLINE Robbie G, b. 29 May 1952, Garden City, Kansas, USA. Insurance Sales Agent; Commercial Account Executive. *Education:* BA, English/Foreign Languages, Friends World College, 1974; Diploma, Insurance Risk Management & Suretyship, School of Insurance for USF&G, 1981; Certificate, General Insurance, 1982, Insurance Institute of America; Chartered Property Casualty Underwirter, 1984; Certified Insurance Counselor, 1986. *Appointments:* Rutter/Cline/Association, 1978-86, Sales Executive 1986-; Taught Insurance Course, St Mary of Plains College, 1987. *Publications:* Articles in professional journals, magazines and newspapers. *Memberships:* National Association of Insurance Women, state legislative Chairman; Insurance Women of Western KS, Leg & PR Chair; Past Board member, Crossroads;

Western KS Foundation; Finney County Women's Chamber of Commerce, past secretary, Vice Pres currently; Society of CPCU; Society of CIC; Local IIA affiliate past president, VP & Sec; Toastmaster's Intl. *Honours:* Outstanding Performance Award, Dale Carnegi, 1986; Region VII Rookie of the Year, NAIW, 1984; Rooking of the Year, Insurance Women of Western KS, 1983. *Hobbies:* Physical Fitness; Aviation (private pilots license); Home Technologies; Music; Gardening; Foreign languages, cultures and cuisines. *Address:* P O Box 1121, Garden City, KS 67846, USA.

CLINE Sarah (Sue) Louise, b. 21 Nov. 1948, New Haven, Connecticut, USA. Professor; Historian. m. Marvin Shinbrot, 21 Dec. 1976, dec. 18 Sept. 1987, 1 daughter. *Education:* BA, Northwestern University, 1970; MA, 1976, PhD, 1981, University of California, Los Angeles. *Appointments:* Assistant Professor, Harvard University, 1981-84; Assistant Professor, 1985-86, Associate Professor, 1986-, University of California, Santa Barbara. *Publications:* The Testaments of Culhuacan (with Miguel Leon-Portilla), 1984; Colonial Culhuacan, 1580-1600: A Social History of an Aztec Town, 1986; The Conquest of New Spain (editor), 1989. *Memberships:* American Historical Association; Conference on Latin American History; Trustee, Santa Barbara Mission Archives; Bishop's Committee, St Michael's University Episcopal Church. *Honour:* Harold J Plous Award for Outstanding Assistant Professor, University of California, Santa Barbara. *Hobbies and Interests:* Latin American Social History; History of Religion; History of Indians; Linguistics. *Address:* History Department, University of California, Santa Barbara, CA 93106, USA.

CLINGAN Judith Ann, b. 19 Jan. 1945, Sydney, New South Wales, Australia. Composer; Conductor; Music Educator. m. David Huntly Dixon, 12 Feb. 1974, separated. 1 daughter. *Education:* BA, ANU, 1966; DipMusEd, Kecskemet, Hungary, 1982. *Appointments:* Founder, Canberra Children's Choir, 1967; Founder Summer Music Schools for Children, Canberra, 1969; Founder Young Music Society, Canberra, 1975; Co-Founder Canberra Recorder and Early Music Society, 1975; Founder, current director, Gaudeamus Community music, Canberra, 1983. *Creative works:* The Compleat Chorister, (compilation), 1971; So Good a Thing (5 volumes) (Compilation), 1981; Modal Magic,(Song cycle), 1984; Lux Mundi (Cantata), 1985; Francis (an opera), 1986; Nganbra (music theatre), 1988. *Memberships:* Australia Choral Conductors' Association; Australia Music Centre; Kodaly Music Education Institute (Australia and International); Australia Society for Music Education; Life member, Young Music Society; Life member, ANU Choral Society. *Honours:* Composition prize, Hobart Festival, 1972; Numerous conducting prizes in Eisteddfods (Australia National Eisteddfod, Sydney, Hobart), 1967-85; Hungarian Government Scholarship, 1981; ACT Capital Territories grant, 1981; Many commissions from Music Board, Australia Council; AM (Member of the Order of Australia), 1986. *Hobbies:* Visual arts: portraiture (drawing, painting), leatherwork, book illustration; Writing, children's books, poems; Bushwalking; Member of Christian House Church. *Address:* 3 Cornelian Place, Lyons, ACT 2606, Australia.

CLINTON Dorothy Louise Randle, b. 6 Apr. 1925, Des Moines, Iowa, USA. Writer. m. 17 June 1950. 1 son. *Education:* BFA, Drake University, 1949. *Appointments:* Bookkeeper, 1949; Recreation Leader, 1949; Teacher, 1950-61; Government Worker, 1961-85. *Publications:* The Look and the See; Ascending Line; poetry included in numerous books, magazines and journals. *Honours:* Clover Award for Clouds, 1975; Clover Award for A Cruise, 1974. *Hobbies:* Coin collector; Flowers; Rocks. *Address:* 1530 Maple, Des Moines, Iowa 50316, USA.

CLINTON Hillary Rodham, b. 26 Oct. 1947, Chicago, USA. Attorney. m. William Jefferson Clinton, 11 Oct. 1975, 1 daughter. *Education:* BA, Wellesley College, 1969; JD, Yale University, 1973. *Appointments:* Impeachment Inquiry Staff, Judiciary Committee, US House of Representatives, 1974; Professor, Law, University of Arkansas School of Law, 1974-77; Partner, Rose Law Firm, 1977-. *Publications:* Articles in professional journals. *Memberships:* Chairman, Board, Children's Defense Fund, 1986-; Chairman, Board, New World Foundation, 1987-; Board, Wal-Mart Stores Inc., 1986-; Chairman, American Bar Association Commission on Women in the Profession, 1987-. *Honours:* Arkansas Woman of the Year, 1983; Honorary LLD, University of Arkansas, 1985; The Best Lawyers in America, 1987. *Address:* Arkansas Governor's Mansion, 1800 Center St., Little Rock, AR 72206, USA.

CLIPPINGER-ROBERTSON Karen Sue, b. 8 Oct. 1951, Santa Monica, USA. Clinical Kinesiologist; Lecturer. m. John Wilbur Robertson, 1981, 1 son. *Education:* BA, Psychology, Sonoma State College, 1975; MSPE, Exercise Science, University of Washington, 1984. *Appointments:* Ballard Sports Medicine Clinic, 1980-84; Consultant, Pacific Northwest Ballet, 1981-, US Weightlifting Federation, 1985-, US Mens Race Walking Team, 1986-; Kinesiologist, Seattle Sports Medicine, 1985-. *Publications:* Aerobic Dance & Japan Instructor's Manual; Flexibility; Chapters in various books; Lectures throughout USA & Canada. *Memberships:* American College of Sports Medicine; International Society of Biomechanics in Sports; International Dance-Exercise Association, committee Chair. *Hobbies:* Dance; Human Movement; Travel. *Address:* Seattle Sports Medicine, 501 First Avenue South, Seattle, WA 98104, USA.

CLOCKER Camilla Ann, b. 28 May 1940, Saratoga, USA. Rare Book Conservator. *Education:* BA, French, College of William & mary, 1965. *Appointments:* Assistant Division Secretary, Welfare, Library of Congress, 1961-64; National Gallery of Art, summer 1965; Cataloguer, Library of Congress, 1966-87; Rare Book Conservator, private practice, 1987-. *Memberships:* American Institute for Conservation; Guild of Book Workers; Womens National Book Association; American Horticultural Society; Potomac Branch, American Begonia Society. *Honours:* National HOnour Society. *Hobbies Include:* Restoration & Repair of Books; Nature Photography; Ice Dancing; Folk Dancing. *Address:* 7108 Marine Drive, Alexandria, VA 22307, USA.

CLOUD Mary Elaine, b. 27 May 1951, Denver, Colorado, USA. Corporation Executive Officer. *Education:* High School Diploma, 1969; Bar Management Certificate, National Beverage Institute, 1982; Minority Business Development Certification Program, 1988. *Appointments:* Personal Bartender, Governor Richard Lamm, State of Colorado; Owner, Feminine Elegance Bartending Service; Corporate Executive Officer, Feminine Elegance Bartending and catering, Inc. *Creative works:* Presented Entrepreneurial Strategies at the 10th Annual Women and Business Conference, 1988. *Memberships:* Business Women Owners Association; The Women's Foundation of Colorado; Colorado Black Chamber of Commerce; Denver Chamber of Commerce; Minority Business Enterprise; Colorado Black Women for Political Action; National Association of Female Executives. *Honours:* Recipient of Women at Work Award, The Council of Working Women, 1986; Clairol Take Charge Award, National Women's Economic Foundation, 1986; Profiled in Sunday Edition of the Rocky Mountain News People to Watch segment, 1986; Feature in segment of Channel 4 TV Evenings News on Executive Women, 1986; Feature in Rocky Mountain Business Journal, 1986; Profiled in the October/November 1985 Edition of Odessey West Magazine of Black Business Women. *Hobbies:* Art; Dance; Physical fitness. *Interests:* Business networking; Working with the poor and homeless. *Address:* Feminine Elegance Bartending & Catering Inc, 8965 East Florida Avenue, Bldg No 6, Apt No 205, Denver, Colorado 80231, USA.

CLOUTIER Patricia Ayotte, b. 9 Mar. 1938, Franklin, NH, USA. Human Resource Administrator. m. (1) Edward

Roby, 1956, divorced 1962, 3 sons, (2) Donald Cloutier, 1962, divorced 1978, 1 son. *Education:* Hesser Business College, 1956; Johnson & Wales College, 1975; New Hampshire College, 1989. *Memberships:* Founder, 1st Presidnet, Local Chapter, National Organisation of TOPS-North Stonington, 1966; National Association of Female Executives. *Honours:* Betty Crocker Homemaker of Tomorrow, 1955. *Hobbies:* Plate Collecting; Reading; Travel. *Address:* RR9, Box 602-2, Laconia, NH 03246, USA.

CLUTTER Mary Elizabeth, b. 29 Mar. 1930, USA. Science Administrator. *Education:* BS, Allegheny College, 1953; MS 1957, PhD 1960, University of Pittsburgh. *Appointments:* Yale University, 1960-78; Programme Director, Developmental Biology, National Science Foundation, 1976-81; Section Head, Cellular & Physical Biosciences, 1981-84; Director, Cellular Biosciences, 1984-88, Senior Science Advisor, Office of the Director, 1985-87, Assistant Director for Biological and Social Sciences, 1988-; National Science Foundation. *Memberships:* American Association for the Advahcement of Science, Board, 1986-90; American Society for Cell Biology; American Society of Plant Physiology; Association for Women in Scince; Sigma Xi. *Honours:* Fellow, AAAS, 1981; Presidential Rank Award, 1985; DSc., HC, Allegheny College, 1986; Bicentennial Medallion of Distinction, University of Pittsburgh, 1987. *Hobbies:* Bird Watching; Hiking; Opera; Ballet; Reading; Sports. *Address:* 940 25th St., NW, Washington, DC 20037, USA.

CLWYD Ann Clwyd Roberts, b. 21 Mar. 1937, Denbigh, Wales. Member of Parliament; Former Journalist, Broadcaster. m. May 1963. *Education:* University College, Bangor. *Appointments:* Student-Teacher, Hope School, Flintshire; BBC Studio Manager; Freelance Reporter Producer, Welsh Correspondent, Guardian & The Observer, 1964-69; Member, European Parliament, Mid & West Wales, 1979-84; Chairperson, Parliamentary Labour Party Health and Social Services Backbench Committee; Vice Chair, POL Defence Backbench Committee; MP, 1984-. *Memberships:* Vice Chair, Welsh Arts Council, 1975-79; Welsh Hospital Board, 1970-74; Cardiff CHC, 1975; Royal Commission on HHS, 1976-79; Working Party Report, Organisation of Out-Patient Care for Welsh Hospital Board; Working Party, Bilingualism in Hospital Service, etc. *Hobbies:* Swimming; Walking; Sailing. *Address:* House of Commons, Westminster, London SW1A 0AA, England.

CLYMER Eleanor, b. 7 Jan. 1906, New York City, USA. Writer. m. Kinsey Clymer, 7 Mar. 1933, 1 son. *Education:* Barnard College, 1925; BA, University of Wisconsin, 1927; Postgraduate. Rank Street College, New York University, Columbia. *Publications include:* 58 juvenile books including: Trolley Car Family, 1947; Search for a Living Fossil, 1963; My Brother Stevie, 1968; Spider, Cave & Pottery Bowl, 1971; We Lived in the Almont, 1972; Luke Was There, 1974; Get-Away Car, 1978; My Mother is the Smartest Woman in the World, 1982; Horse in the Attic, 1983. *Memberships:* Past Council Member, Chairman Children's Book Committee, Authors' Guild. *Honours:* Woodward School Award, 1968; Border Regional Library Association Award, 1971; Children's Book Award, Child Study Association, 1974; Film of book, Luke Was There, Learning Corporation of America, 1975; Sequoyah Book Award, 1980. *Hobbies include:* Natural history & conservation; Native American history & culture. *Address:* 11 Nightingale Road, Katonah, New York 10536, USA.

COAKLEY Mary Lewis, b. 8 Dec. 1907, Baltimore, USA. Writer. Widow, 1 son. *Publications:* Mister Music Maker, 1958; For the Know Your Bible Paperback Series: Women of the New Testament, Children of the Old Testament; Children of the New Testament, Temptations of the Bible; Fitting God into the Picture; Our Child-God's Child; Never Date Women; Rated X: The Moral Case Against TV; Not Alone; How To Live Life to the Fullest; Long Liberated Ladies, 1989; numerous articles in magazines & newspapers; Contributing Editor, Life

& Family News, 1982-. *Address:* 110 Hewett Road, Wyncote, PA 19095, USA.

COALE Genevieve Marie, b. 4 June 1946, Philadelphia, USA. Director; Educational Consultant. m. James S. Coale, 1 Dec. 1972. *Education:* BS, West Chester University, 1968; MEd., 1972, PhD, 1981, Temple University. *Appointments:* Teacher, Penn-Delco School District, 1968-78; Lecturer, Community College of Delaware County, 1971-74; Assistantship, Temple University, 1978-79; Director, Special Services, Spring-Ford Area School District, 1979-. *Publications:* Articles in professional journals; presentations. *Memberships:* Treasurer, Montgomery County Council for Gifted Education; American Educational Research Association; American Association of School Administrators; Association for Supervision & Curriculum Development; International Reading Association, many others. *Honours Include:* Distinguished & Dedicated Service Award, Reading is Fundamental, 1986; Van Essen Award, 1987. *Hobbies:* Writing Poetry; Hiking; Skiing. *Address:* 510 William Salesbury Drive, Downingtown, PA 19335, USA.

COATES Carolyn Noble, b. Oklahoma City, Oklahoma, USA. Actress. m. 19 May 1956. 1 daughter. *Education:* University of California at Los Angeles, 3 years. *Appointments:* Leading roles on Broadway, off Broadway and in regional theatre. *Creative works:* Films: Buddy System; Mommie Dearest; The Effect of Gamma Rays on Man in the Moon Marigolds. Television: This Child is Mine; Blood Feud; Starflight One; Female Sheriff; Powder Puff Platoon; Sacred Straight-Another Story; Murder in Texas; Glitter; St Elsewhere; Ryan's Four; Cutter to Houston; Remington Steele; Benson; Waltons, Lou Grant; The Doctors, Search for Tomorrow, Where the Heart is All my Children, Poets on Russian Street Corners, Barn Burning-Great American Short Stories. Broadway: The Death of Bessie Smith; The American Dream; The Condemned of Altona; The Country Wife. Off Broadway: In the Summerhouse; Courtship; The Effect of Gamma Rays on Man in the Moon Marigolds; The Trojan Woman; The Balcony; The Whitman Portrait; The Party of Greenwich. Commissioned to do stained glass ceiling panel for Lucille Fairbanks Crump, 1981. *Memberships:* Church of St Mary the Virgin, New York City; National Museum of Women in the Arts. *Honours:* Theatre world Award for The Trojan Women; Golden Straw Award, Chicago Daily News. *Hobbies:* Painting; Volunteer work for AIDS project, Los Angeles. *Address:* 4249 Danes Ave, Studio City, CA 916011, USA.

COBB Vicki, b. 19 Aug. 1938, Brooklyn, New York, USA. Writer. m. 31 Jan. 1960 (div. 1975), 2 sons. *Education:* Ford Foundation Early Admission Scholarship, University of Wisconsin, 1954; BA, Barnard College, 1958; MA, Science Education, Teachers' College, Columbia University. *Publications:* Numerous non-fiction books for young people, including: Logic, 1969, 1971; Cells: Basic Structure of Life, 1970; Making Sense of Money, 1971; Science Experiments You Can Eat, 1972, 1974; Heat, 1973; Long & Short of Measurement, 1973; Truth on Trial: Story of Galileo Galilei, 1979; Secret Life of School Supplies, 1981; Monsters Who Died: Mystery About Dinosaurs, 1983; Secret Life of Cosmetics: Science Experiment Book, 1985; More Power To You!, 1986; Getting Dressed, 1988; Why Doesn't the Earth Fall Up? And Other Such Not So Dumb Questions About Motion, 1989; Why Doesn't the Sun Burn Out? 1989. *Memberships:* Authors Guild; American Society of Journalists & Authors. *Honours:* Book awards: New York Academy of Sciences; Eva L. Gordon Award, children's science literature; Washington Irving Award, Children's Book Choice; American Library Association. *Hobbies:* Tennis; Skiing; Music; Early American crewel. *Address:* 910 Stuart Avenue, Mamanneck, New York 10543, USA.

COBBS Dorothy Lee, b. 6 Dec. 1946, Olive Branch, USA. Healthcare Professional. *Education:* BA, 1971; MPS, AAA, Cornell University. *Appointments:* American Hospital Association, 1976-. *Publications:* Financial

Growth and Diversification of Hospitals and Multihospital Systems; articles in journals. *Memberships:* Board, American Association of Preferred Provider Organizations; National Association of Health Services Executives. *Honours:* Service Leader Award, AHA, 1985. *Hobbies:* China & Porcelain Collection; Weightlifting; Reading; Creative Writing. *Address:* 421 E. 45th Place, Chicago, IL 60653, USA.

COCHRAN Carolyn Collette, b. 4 Mar. 1951, Dallas, Texas, USA. Renal Dietitian. m. R. Keith Cochran, 26 Apr. 1980. *Education:* BS 1973, MS 1978, Texas Tech University; RD after dietetic internship, P. B. Brigham Hospital, Boston, Massachusetts, 1974. *Appointments:* Memorial Hospital, Garland, Texas, 1974-76; Part-time positions, nutrition consultant, 1976-78; Parkland Memorial Hospital, Dallas, 1978-80; Southwestern Dialysis Centre, Dallas, 1980-. *Creative works:* Taking the First Bite: Basics of Renal Nutrition, slide/tape 1981, VHS 1987; Magic Menus, cookbook for renal patients, 1985; Studies, clinical nutrition research; Professional writing, several articles published; Numerous engagements, public speaking. *Memberships:* Offices, American Dietetic Association, ADA Renal Practice Group; President, Dallas Dietetic Association; 1st vice president 1985-86, Texas Dietetic Association, President, 1989-90; Offices, National Kidney Foundation, Dallas Fort Worth Council on Renal Nutrition. *Honours:* Traineeship, US Department of Health, Education & Welfare, 1977; Scholarship, Texas Tech, 1977-78; Service award, Dallas Dietetic Association, 1987; Outstanding CRN Council, 1987; Distinguished service award, National Kidney Foundation, 1988; Dallas Hephrology Associates Special Recognition Award. *Hobbies:* Arts & crafts; Entertaining; Reading. *Address:* Southwestern Dialysis, 6010 Forest Park Road, Dallas, Texas 75235, USA.

COCHRAN Patricia Luella, b. 13 Nov. 1944, Modesto, California, USA. Small Business Owner. m. (1) Ronald Lee Campbell, 13 May 1961, divorced 1984. 2 sons, 2 daughters. (2) Adrian Lester Cochran, 20 June 1984. *Education:* Diploma, CLS Design Academy, 1983; Student, University of California, Berkeley, 1983-; Certificate, Keye Productivity Centre, 1984. *Appointments:* Foreclosure officer Cen State Title Ins Co, Modesto, 1974-79; Bookkeeper, North Adrians, Modesto, 1979-82; Instructor Adrians Beauty College, Modesto, 1982-84, also board directors. *Publication:* Author, Adrians Beauty College Student Handbook, 1985. *Memberships:* National Association Cosmetology Schools (diploma 1985); California Cosmetology Association; CARODC, 1987. *Honours:* National and International Olympic Judge, WINBA, 1987. *Address:* 2209 Cedarwood Circle, Riverbank, CA 95367, USA.

CODD Ellen Elizabeth, b. 28 July 1943, Staten Island, New York, USA. Scientist. m. Vincent J. Aloyo, 18 Oct. 1976, 1 son. *Education:* BA, Chemistry, Alverno College, 1966; MS, Biochemistry, Center for Health Science, University of Tennessee, 1976. *Appointments:* University of Tennessee, 1972-79; State University of Utrecht, Netherlands, 1980-82; University of Kentucky, Kentucky, USA, 1983-85; Research and Development Division, Smith Kline and French Labs, King of Prussia, Pennsylvania, 1985-90; Department of Biological Research, RW Johnson Pharmaceutical Research Institute of McNeil Pharmaceutical Spring House Pennsylvania. *Publications:* Contributions to scientific journals including Neuropharmacology, Psychopharmacology, Regulatory Peptides, Journal of Neurochemistry, Life Sciences, Biological Psychiatry, Psychiatry Research. *Memberships:* International Society for Neurochemistry; Society for Neuroscience; International Brain Research Organization; International Narcotics Research Conference. *Address:* RW Johnson Pharmaceutical Research Institute at McNeil Pharmaceuticals, Department of Biological Research, McKean and Welsh Rds, Spring House, PA 19477-0776, USA.

CODDING Peggy Ann, b. 11 Mar. 1933, Denver, USA. University Assistant Professor. *Education:* BM

1975, MM 1982, PhD Music Education/Therapy, 1985, Florida State University, Tallahassee; Therapist Registered, Nat Assoc Music Therapy, Phillips University, Enid. *Appointments:* Therapist, Music Faculty, University Wisconsin Eau Claire, Training school for the Blind, 1977-79; School of Music, 1982-85; Research Association, Center for Music Research, 1985; Director of Music Therapy, Ohio University School of Music, 1986-. *Publications:* Numerous articles in professional journals and magazines. *Memberships:* National Association for Music Therapy; Music Educator's National Conference; National Symposium for Research in Music Behaviour. *Honours:* Phi Kappa Lambda National Music Honor Society, 1976; Cardinal Key National Honor Society, 1974. *Hobbies:* Music; Art; Photography; Travel. *Address:* School of Music; Ohio University, Athens, Ohio 45701, USA.

CODELL Julie Francia, b. 19 Sept. 1945, Chicago, USA. Associate Professor; Art Department Chairman. 1 son. *Education:* AB, Vassar College, 1967; MA, University of Michigan, 1968; MA, 1975, PhD, 1978, Indiana University. *Appointments:* English Instructor, Western Illinois University, 1968-71; Teaching Assistant, 1973-75, Editor, Continuing Education, 1975-79, Indiana University; Associate Professor, Art History & Criticism, University of Montana, 1979-. *Publications:* 25 Essays, and articles in journals & magazines. *Memberships:* Executive Board, Midwest Victorian Studies Association; Executive Committee, Montana Committee for the Humanities; College Art Association; Popular Culture Association. *Honours:* NEH Grant, 1986; William Nelson Award, 1987; NEH Summer Stipend, 1988. *Hobbies:* Music; Dance; Films; Gardening; Art; Travel. *Address:* c/o Art Dept., University of Montana, Missoula, MT 59812, USA.

COE Elisabeth Ann, b. 12 Nov. 1946, El Paso, USA. Educator. m. Raymond H. Coe, 6 July 1968, 2 daughters. *Education:* BS, 1968; MEd.; PhD, 1988. *Appointments:* Educator: Mad River Township Schools, Honeysuckle Montessori School; Adjunct, University of Houston; Teacher, Houston Montessori Centre; Educator, School of the Woods. *Publications:* Articles in various journals & magazines. *Memberships:* American Montessori Society, Board; Montessori Education Association; National Association for Education of Young Children. *Honours:* Outstanding Leadership, 1982; Super Leader, 1980. *Hobbies:* Arts; Crafts; Reading; Gardening. *Address:* 1002 Glacier Hill, Houston, TX 77077, USA.

COE Elizabeth Beaubien, b. 16 Dec. 1919, Topeka, Kansas, USA. English Language Teacher. m. W R Deitz, 17 Apr. 1942, divorced 1963. 1 son, 1 daughter. *Education:* AB English, 1967, MA 1969, University of Illinois; EdD Linguistics, University of Houston, 1984; Undergraduate attendance at: University of Pittsburgh; Washburn College and University of Kansas. *Appointments:* College Santiago Apostol, Puerto Rico, 1970-71; University of Costa Rica, 1972; National University, 1973-76; Houston Community College, 1977-78; University of Houston, 1981-85; Fulbright Fellow, Rwanda, Africa, 1985-87; University of Houston, 1987-89. *Publications:* Rwanda, Africa: 5 tapes on grammar, pronunciation, story: 4 books; Costa Rica: 9 tapes on stories; 2 books; Puerto Rico: More than 10 tapes on publicity stories for Puerto Rico; Doctoral dissertation on Afro-American English. *Membership:* TEX-TESOL. *Honours:* Puerto Rican Fellowship, 1968-69; Fulbright Fellowship, Resource specialist, 1985-87. *Hobbies:* Repairing Furniture, particularly old clocks; Skiing; Clothing design; Reading of history and social aspects of all countries. *Address:* English Language Institute, University of Houston DT, Suite 369-Number One Main Street, Houston, TX 77002, USA.

COE Mirian (Myrilla), b. 1 July 1902, Liverpool, England. Author/Illustrator, State Representative for American Society of Artists Inc. (Volunteer Repsentation). *Education:* Skerry's Civil Service College; Oulton College (Union of Lancashire and Cheshire Inst); Liverpool City School of Art; Liverpool University; Columbia University, NY, USA; Long Island University;

CW Post College; University of Rochester, NYS; NY School of The Theatre; School of Chinese Brush Work; Geo. Peabody College for Teachers, Vanderbilt University; Florida State University; Utah State University; Louisiana State University; Honours Diploma from Union of Lancashire and Cheshire Institutes; BFA, Louisiana State University; PhD (Honours), Colorado State Christian College; Valid Teachers Certificate, Florida State University. *Appointments:* Secretary, John Ogden and Co; Teacher, Violin Playing; Inventor of Spectra Colour System, correlating colour in art with colour in musical sounds; Invented colour system codifying touch in developing skill in typewriting; Article Writer, Liverpool Express; Lecturer, Psychology of Creating Musical Themes, Rochester, NY, USA; Delivered Series of Lectures over Station WHAM; Solicited for orders for: Periodical: Childhood Interest; Dickens Stories for Children sponsored by the British Royal Society for Lighthouse Work; Consignment Writer, Platt and Munk; Self-employed Writer and Illustrator of Books; Invented original typeface The Enolidean; currently Louisiana Representative for The American Society of Artists, Inc., Palatine, Illinois, staging shows of Art and Literature. *Creative works:* Author: Anthology of World Literature; A Sociological Cyclopedia; Dictionary and Handbook of Photogrammetry and Related Terms; Poems of Louisiana; Poems for the Young; Poets, Poems, Portraits and Pictures, Selected Collection International; Pitimm Sorakin: His Life and His Work; Haiku East/West: Review of New Book for Hildref Publishers, Washington DC Summer Learning and The Effects of School by Barbara Heynes; Russian Intelligensia, by Vladimir Naherny. *Memberships include:* Liverpool Psychological Society; Liverpool Little Theatre Group; American Library Association; Louisiana Library Association; Parish Library Association; Academy of American Poets; Haiku Society of America; American Society of Political and Social Sciences. *Honours:* Recipient of various Honours and Diplomas in recognition of contribution to creative works. *Hobbies:* Psychology; Sociology; Progressive Methods in Education; Anthropology and Preanthropology; Semantics. *Address:* PO Box 18184, Louisiana State University, Baton Rouge, LA 70893, USA.

COGAN Elaine, b. 24 Sept. 1932, Brooklyn, New York, USA. Writer; Consultant in Communications. m. Arnold Cogan, 21 Dec. 1952, 2 sons, 1 daughter. *Education:* BS with high honours, Oregon State University, 1954. *Appointments:* Weekly Editorial Columnist, Oregon Journal and Oregonian newspapers, 1970-85; Partner, Cogan Sharpe Cogan, Planning and Communications Consultants, 1975-; President, Elaine's Tea Co, 1984; Editor, Oregon Jewish Review, 1985-87. *Publications:* You Can Talk to (Almost) Anyone About (Almost) Anything, public speaking for professional people; Book on effective public meetings, in progress. *Memberships:* Chair, Providence Medical Center, 1985; Chair, Governor's Special Commission on Liquor Control, 1979; Chair, Task Force on Emergency Preparedness, Portland, 1982; Chair, Portland Development Commission, 1973-74; 1st Women President, Congregation Neveh Shalom. *Honours:* Phi Kappa Phi and Omicron Nu, 1954. *Hobbies:* Baking bread; Sailing; Reading; Political campaigns. *Address:* The Penthouse, 10 NW Tenth Avenue, Portland, OR 97209, USA.

COGER Greta Margaret Kay McCormick, b. 13 June 1934, Cardale, Manitoba, Canada. College Educator. m. (1) William Leslie Avery, 3 Sept. 1960, (2) Dalvan M. Coger, Oct. 1979, 3 stepsons. *Education:* BA, Manitoba, 1959; BRE, Toronto, 1962; MLitt, Strathclyde, Scotland, 1969; PhD, University of Colorado, USA, 1980; Certificates: Elementary Education (McMaster), 1959; Secondary Education, Toronto, 1962; Piano, Toronto Conservatory of Music. *Appointments:* Cartwright High School, Manitoba, 1953-54; Dundee, Scotland, 1960-61; Sydenham High School, Ontario, Canada, 1962-67; Fourah Bay College, University of Sierra Leone, Freetown, West Africa, 1969-73; Albert Academy, Freetown, 1973-74; University of Colorado, USA, 1974-76; Christian Brothers College, Memphis, Tennessee, 1979; Instructor in English and World Literature,

Northwest Mississippi Community College, Senatobia, Mississippi, 1980-. *Publications:* Index of Subjects, Proverbs, and Themes in the Writings of Wole Soyinka, 1988; Margaret Laurence Essays on Her Works, 1990; Margaret Laurence's Manawaka: A Canadian Yoknapatawpha, article, 1986. *Memberships:* Founder, President, Editor, Margaret Lawrence Society; Modern Languages Association; South Atlantic Modern Languages Association; African Literature Association; Association of Canadian Studies in the United States; African Studies Association; American Association of Australian Literary Studies; Mississippi Philological Association; President, Memphis State University Wives Club, 1987-88. *Honour:* Manitoba Scholar. *Hobbies:* Piano; Violin; Reading; African art; Swimming. *Address:* 1433 West Crestwood Drive, Memphis, TN 38119, USA.

COGGINS Cynthia Anne, b. 29 Apr. 1954, Greenville, South Carolina, USA. Assistant Principal. *Education:* BA, 1976, MA, 980, Furman University. *Appointments:* Athens Elementary-Travelers Rest, 1976-77; Arrington Elementary, Greenville, 1977-80; Elementary Learning Disabilities Resource, 1980-88; Brushy Creek Elementary, Assistant Principal, 1988-. *Memberships:* Council for Exceptional Children; South Carolina Association of School Administrators; Delta Kappa Gamma; Kappa Delta Pi; Division for Learning Disabilities; Council for Children with Behavior Disorders. *Hours:* Arrington Elementary Teacher of Year, 1987; Greenville Council for Exceptional Children Teacher of Year, 1987; South Caorlina Council for Exceptional Children State Special Education Teacher of the Year, 1987; Outstanding Young Woman of South Carolina, 1987. *Hobbies:* Music; Racquetball. *Address:* 14 Batesview Drive, Greenville, SC 29607, USA.

COHEN Anne Silberstein, b. 12 Aug. 1928, Baltimore, Maryland, USA. Psychotherapist; Marriage/Family Counsellor. m. Robert J. Cohen, 7 Sept. 1952, 1 son, 1 daughter. *Education:* Goucher College, 1949; MA, Montclair State College, 1974; MSW, Rutgers University, 1975; Certificate, New Jersey Academy Group Psychotherapy, 1976-78; Postgraduate study including Certificate, Psychoanalytic Psychotherapy, New York Center for Psychoanalytic Training, 1979-; Licensed Marriage Counsellor, New Jersey. *Appointments:* Social Worker: Children's Division, Department of Public Welfare, Baltimore, Maryland, 1950-53; Children's Protective Services, Pennsylvania Society to Protect Children from Cruelty, Philadelphia, 1953-56; Staff, Social Work, Family Life Improvement Project, Rutgers University Graduate School, New Brunswick, New Jersey, 1964-68; Social Worker, Catholic Family & Community Services, Paterson, New Jersey, 1974-75; Psychotherapist, Clinical Social Worker, Essex County Guidance Center, East Orange, New Jersey, 1975-83; Private Practice in Psychotherapy, Marriage & Family Counselling, Livingston, New Jersey, 1980-. *Memberships:* Planning Committee, Mental Health Association, New Jersey, 1980; Board of Directors, Community Psychiatric Institute, East Orange, New Jersey; Trustee, Community Mental Health Center of Oranges, Maplewood & Millburn, New Jersey; Fellow, American Orthopsychiatric Association; Academy of Certified Social Workers; New Jersey Academy of Group Psychotherapy; Fellow, Director, Membership Chair, New Jersey Society for Clinical Social Work; National Association of Social Workers; American Association of Marriage & Family Therapists; New Jersey Association of Women Therapists; New Jersey Psychological Association; Society for Advancement of Self-Psychology; National Registry of Health Care Providers; LWV; National Council of Jewish Women. *Hobbies:* Travel; Reading; Theatre; Swimming; Tennis; Gourmet cooking. *Address:* Roosevelt Plaza, Suite 305, Two West Northfield Road, Livingston, NJ 07039, USA.

COHEN Gloria Carol, b. 3 Mar. 1953, Montreal, Quebec, Canada. Physician (Sports Medicine and Family Practice). m. David S Cohen, 1 June 1975. 1 daughter. *Education:* Diploma of Collegial Studies, Science (CEGEP) McGill, 1972; BSc, Physical Therapy, McGill

University, 1975; Years I-III, MD 1980, Faculty of Medicine, University of Ottawa; Year IV, Faculty of Medicine, University of British Columbia, 1979-80. *Appointments:* Locum tenens, 1981-87; The Fitness Institute, Toronto, 1985-86; Director, Sports Medicine Unit, Women's College Hospital, Family Practice Toronto, 1985-86; Private Practice, Vancouver, 1987-; Medical Director, Y Sports Medicine Clinic, Vancouver, 1987-. *Publications:* Video: The Female Athlete, 1986; TV Ontario, Ontario's Best: Injury Forum with Dr Gloria Cohen, 1986; Intense Exercise During the First Two Trimesters of Unapparent Pregnancy, The Physician and Sports medicine, January, 1988. *Memberships:* College of Family Physicians of Canada; Canadian Academy of Sport Medicine, Women's Committee; Canadian Summer Olympic Medical Team, Seoul, Korea, 1988; Coordinating Physician Canadian Cycling Association; Board of Governors, YMCA of Vancouver. *Honours:* Pfizer Clinical Prize for Highest Standing in Psychiatry, 1979; Steinberg's University Scholarship, 1970-75; McGill University Scholarship, 1971. *Hobbies:* Long distance running; Cycling; Aerobics instructor; Reading. *Address:* Suite 705-750 West Broadway, Vancouver, British Columbia, V5Z 1H6, Canada.

COHEN Judith Jacqueline, b. 7 Feb. 1926, Coogee, New South Wales, Australia. Judge. m. Senator S H Cohen, 3 May 1953, deceased. 2 daughters. *Education:* BA, LLB, University of Sydney; Dip of Education, University of Melbourne. *Appointments:* Admitted as a Solicitor, Supreme Court of New South Wales, 1950; Practised in Sydney until 1953; Admitted as a Barrister and Solicitor, Supreme Court of Victoria, 1953; Practised as a Solicitor in Melbourne, 1953-55, 1962-66 and 1970-75; Teacher, Banyule High School, 1966-69; Commissioner 1975, Deputy President 1980, Australian Conciliation and Arbitration Commission; Deputy President, Australian Industrial Relations Commission, 1989-. *Memberships:* Council, National Library, Canberra, 1984-; Women Lawyers Assoc of Victoria; Industrial Relations Society, Victoria; Lyceum Club, Melbourne. *Address:* c/o Australian Industrial Relations Commission, Nauru House, 80 Collins Street, Melbourne, Vic 3000, Australia.

COHEN Mollie Louise, b. 6 Oct. 1941, Hartford, Connecticut, USA. Writer and Editor. m. Daniel Seth Harrison, 28 Aug. 1987. *Education:* BA, History, Smith College, 1963; MA, Teaching of Social Studies, Columbia Teachers College, 1964. *Appointments:* American History Teacher, New Rochelle High School, 1964-65; Reading Skills Teacher, Baldridge Reading and Study Skills, Greenwich, 1965-66; Training Assistant, Macy's New York, 1966-68; Copy Editor, Matthew Bender & Co, 1968-69; Copy Editor, 1969-70, Assistant Editor, 1970-73, Associate Editor, 1973-75, Random House School Division; Associate Editor, 1976-80, Editor, 1980-, Scholastic Inc. *Publications:* Articles in professional journals: The Computing Teacher, 1982; Social Education, 1983-84; The Social Studies, 1987; Software Review: The Computing Teacher, 1982. Filmstrips: Labor Unions: What You Should Know, 1977; Career Choice: A Lifelong Process, 1976. Presentations to Conferences. *Membership:* National Council for the Social Studies. *Address:* 8 Gramercy Park South, New York, NY 10003, USA.

COHEN-ADDAD Nicole, b. 24 Jan. 1949, Algiers, Algeria. Physician. *Education:* BS, Lycee de Chantilly, Chantilly, France, 196; MD, CHU Pitie-Salpetriere, Paris, 1972. *Appointments:* Instructor 1981-83, Assistant Professor of Paediatrics 1983-89, University of Medicine & Dentistry, New Jersey, USA, State University of new York, 1989-. *Publications:* Author, co-author, 3 book chapters, numerous contributions to professional journals, various abstracts. *Memberships:* American Academy of Paediatrics; American Society for Photobiology; American College of Nutrition; American Medical Womens Association; President, New Jersey Medical Women's Association. *Hobbies:* Skiing; Philosophy. *Address:* 5 Charles Street Apt 2F, New York, NY 10014, USA.

COHN Anne Harris, b. 16 Jan. 1945, Evanston, Illinois, USA. Health Planner. *Education:* BA, Sociology, University of Michigan, 1967; MA, Medical Sociology, Tufts University, 1970; MPH 1972, DPH 1975, Health Administration, University of California, Berkeley. *Appointments:* Associate & member, Board of Directors, Berkeley Planning Associates (designer & director, 1st national study, child abuse & neglect treatment programmes), 1973-78; Congressional Science Fellow, office of Honourable Albert Gore Jr, 1978-79; White House Fellow, & Special Assistant to Secretary, Department of Health & Human Services, 1979-80; Executive Diretor, National Committee for Prevention of Child Abuse, 1980-. *Publications:* Various articles, professional journals. *Memberships:* Maternal & Child Health Council, American Public Health Association; Executive, International Society for Prevention & Treatment of Chid Abuse; Board, National Congress of Parents & Teachers; Board, The Independent Sector; Fellow, American Association for Advancement of Science. *Hobbies:* Photography; Triathlons. *Address:* National Committee for Prevention of Child Abuse, 332 South Michigan, Suite 950, Chicago, Illinois 60604, USA.

COHN Lucile M, b. 17 Apr. 1924, Kokomo, Indiana, USA. Professor; Nurse/Psychotherapist; Consultant. m. Norman, 20 Apr. 1947. 2 sons. *Education:* Diploma, School of Nursing, 1944; BS 1964, MS 1966, University of Wisconsin; PhD, Marquette University, Milwaukee, 1972. *Appointments:* Army Nurse Corps, 1st Lt, 1947-49; Employee Counselor 1964-72; Vice President, 1972-73, Mt Sinai Medical Center; Chair Dept of Psychiatric Services, Milwaukee Regional medical Center, 1973-82; Professor, Columbian Carroll College of Nursing, 1965-89; Private Practice, 1972-89. *Publications:* Author of numerous articles to professional journals. *Memberships:* American Nurses' Association; Wisconsin Nurses Association; Milwaukee Mental Health Association; Myasthenia Gravis Association; American Association for Counseling & Development; American Medical Psychotherapists; American Orthopsychiatric Association; Council of Psychiatric Mental Health Nursing; American Mental Health Counselors Association; Wisconsin Counselors Association. *Honours:* 1 of 9 Outstanding Counselors in US, American Personnel & Guidance Assor, 1980; Milwaukee Nurses Association Award of the Year, 1977; Phi Lambda Theta, 1972; Sigma Theta Tau, 1970; Phi Kappa Phi, 1964; Yearly graduate (commencmenet) addresses for schools of Nursing, 1976-; Fellow & Diplomate, American Medical Psychotherapists, 1986-. *Hobbies:* Gardening; Reading; The arts; Swimming. *Address:* 136 East Mall Road, Milwaukee, Wisconsin 53217, USA.

COLBURN Janet, b. 6 Nov. 1942, Rahway, New Jersey, USA. Data Processing Manager. m. Alan S. Newman, 3 June 1963, divorced 1968, 2 sons. *Education:* BA, Classical Languages, Muhlenberg College, 1964. *Appointments:* Manager, Data Processing Operations, National Tool & Mfg. Co., kenilworth, 1972-75; Supervisor, Data Processing, Mailing Services, hillside, 1975-79; Manager, data Processing: Whitestone Products, Piscataway, 1979-86, Lladro USA Inc., Carlstadt, 1986-; Microcomputer Consultant, Ad-A- System, Gaarwood, 1979-. *Memberships:* NAFE; Data Processing Management Association; American Management Association; Founder & Chairperson of Garwood Teenage Recreation Committee, 1979-81. *Hobbies:* Camping, Writing, Language Study, Woodcarving, Rug Hooking. *Address:* PO Box 9434, Elizabeth, NJ 07202, USA.

COLBY Jean, b. 26 July 1907, Pine Orchard, Connecticut, USA. Writer. m. Dr Fletcher H Colby, 1932. 1 son, 2 daughters. *Education:* Graduate, Noah Webster School, 1920; Graduate, Oxford School, 1924; Graduate, Wellesley College, 1928; PhD, University of Colorado. *Appointments:* Actress: Copley Players, Boston, 2 years; Tamworth Players, New Hampshire, 2 years; Blanche Yurka Co, London, England as Electra in Euripides, 2 seasons. Editor: Houghton Mifflin, 1945-

50; Farrar, Straus, 1950-54; Hastings House, 1954-60. *Publications:* Childrens Books: The Elegant Eleanor Jennie; Jim the Cat; Peter Paints USA; Jesus and The World. Adult books: The Children's Book Field Writing; Illustrating and Editing Plimouth Plantation; Lexington and Concord What Really Happened; Mystic Seaport, The Age of Sail; The Greatest Golf Tournament of All - The 1913 USGA Golf Open, 1988. *Memberships:* Actors Equity; Children's Book Association; Writers Guild. *Honours:* One of the Ten Best Bicentennial books, Lexington and Concord, What Really Happened, 1976; Ladies Golf Champion, Duxbury, 1956, 58, 60; Ladies Golf Champion, The Country Club, Brookline, 1970. *Hobbies:* Music; Gardening; Golf. *Address:* 73 Eagles Nest Road, Duxbury, MA 02332, USA.

COLCORD Linda Miller, b. 7 Sept. 1953, Washington DC, USA. Ballet Dancer; Director. m. 23 Aug. 1985, 1 son. *Education:* High School Diploma, North Carolina School of Arts, 1970. *Appointments include:* Principle ballet dancer: North Carolina Dance Theatre 1970-74, Feld Ballet 1974-80; Instructor, Washington University, 1980-81; Gino Thompson Revue, 1981-84; Director, Ballet 106, 1984-. *Creative works include:* Choreographer: Tricia's Dances 1985, Progressions 1986, Walk Like An Egyptian 1986, Cameos 1987, Handle with Care 1988, Ancient Airs 1989. *Membership:* Former member, AGMA. *Honour:* Scholarship student, Ford Foundation, 1965-70. *Hobbies:* Flute; Needlework; Reading; *Address:* 106 South Frederick Avenue, Gaithersburg, Maryland 20877, USA.

COLDREY Jennifer Morton May, b. 13 Aug. 1940, Perth, Scotland. Writer; Editor. m. Nigel William May, 29 Aug. 1986. *Education:* BSc., Honours, Botany, University of London, 1962; Postgraduate Certificate, Education, St Hllds College, Durham, 1975. *Appointments:* Oxford University, 1964-66; Librarian, Edward Grey Institute, 1966-72; Primary School Teacher, Oxford, 1975-77; Teacher, Field Studies Centre, Oxford, 1977-79; Manager, Slide Library, Writer of Texts, Oxford Scientific Films, 1979-86; Freelance Writer, 1986-. *Publications:* 6 Titles in Nature's Way Series, 1981-83: Harvest Mouse; Jellyfish and other Sea Jellies; Grey Squirrel; Mosquito; Penguins; The Silkworm Story; 4 Titles in, Discovering Nature Series: Discovering Worms, 1985; Flowering Plants, 1986; Slugs and Snails, 1987; Fungi, 1987; 8 Titles in Animal Habitats Series: The Crab on the Seashore, 1986; The Squirrel in the Trees, 1986; The Rabbit in the Fields, 1986; The Swan on the Lake, 1987; The Chicken on the Farm, 1987; The Owl in the Tree, 1988; Co-author, The Man-of-War at Sea, 1987; Co-Author: The Pond, 1984, How Life Begins - a Look at Birth in the Animal Kingdom, 1004. *Memberships:* numerous professional organisations including: World Wildlife Fund; National Trust. *Hobbies:* Natural History; Classical Music; Walking. *Address:* Rose Cottage, Cutmere, Tideford, Saltash, Cornwall PL12 5JU, England.

COLDWELL Joan, b. 3 Nov. 1936, Huddersfield, England. Professor. *Education:* BA, Honours, 1958, MA, Distinction, 1960, Bedford College, University of London; PhD, Harvard University, USA, 1967. *Appointments:* Assistant Professor, English, University of Victoria, Canada, 1960-72; Associate Professor, Professor, English, Mcmaster University, 1972-. *Publication:* Charles Lamb on Shakespeare, Editor, 1978. *Memberships:* Canadian Research Institute for the Advancement of Women; International Shakespeare Association; Canadian Association for Irish Studies. *Honours:* Social Sciences & Humanities Research Council of Canada, Leave Fellowship, 1977-78, 1984-85; McMaster University Students Union Teaching Award, 1982. *Hobbies:* Women's Issues; Swimming; Theatre; Travel. *Address:* Dept. of English, McMaster University, Hamilton, Ontario, Canada L8S 4L9.

COLE Josephine Elizabeth, b. 18 Jan. 1913, San Francisco, California, USA. Educator; Dramatic Lecturer. m. Audley L Cole, 18 June 1941. *Education:* BA 1932, MA (Educ) 1958, Univ of California, Berkeley; Genl Administrative Credential, San Francisco State University, 1968. *Appointments:* Teacher, St Vincent's Parochial High, 1936-42; Raphael Weill (Public), 1943-46; Balboa High School, 1948-64; Director, District Youth Guidance Centers, 1966-67; Supervisor AA, 1968-74, retired; Consultant to Superintendent of SF Schools, 1988-. *Creative works:* Liaison and curriculum writer for US Dept of State Reception Center, 1974-76; Leader of student mission to Osaka, Japan; Author: Have you Met your Inner Self?, 1986. *Memberships:* Delta Kappa Gamma; Nobirukai, Japanese Newcomers; Act-So, Chairman of Judges for scholastic awards (Youth programme of NAACP); Intl Training in Communication; National Parliamentarians. *Honours:* International Awareness Award, Delta Kappa Gamma, 1985; Distinguished Service Award, 6th Army of US, 1988; Speaker of the Year, Kiwanis (SF), 1984 and 1985; Woman of the West, Iota Phi Lambda, 1984; 2nd place, International Woman of the Year, Iota Phi Lambda, 1985. *Hobbies:* The art and use of beautiful English; Study of French, Spanish, Japanese; Study of religions-comparative. *Address:* 1598-36th Avenue, San Francisco, CA 94122, USA.

COLE Leona Lewis, b. 16 Mar. 1916, Roberts County, Texas, USA. Elementary Gifted, Talented Teacher. m. 22 Dec. 1943. 4 daughters. *Education:* BS, Huntington College, Montgomery, 1960; MEd 1977. Master's Plus 30 and Gifted Certification 1979, University of New Orleans. *Appointments:* Teacher, Dependent Schools, Misawa Air Base, Japan, 1960-63; Teacher Public Schools, Fairfax County, Virginia, 1964-67; Teacher, Dependent Schools, Ankara, Turkey, 1967-70; Teacher, Public Schools, Austin, Texas, 1970-71; Teacher, Public Schools, Jefferson Parish, Louisiana, 1972-. *Memberships:* American Association of University Women; Delta Kappa Gamma; Business and Professional Women; World Aerospace Education Organization; Honorary Alpha Theta Epsilon; Phi Delta Kappa; Past President, Louisiana Alpha Rho Chapter, Alpha Delta Kappa; Lieutenant Colonel, Civil Air Patrol. *Honour:* Participant in People to People Aerospace Education Delegation to Peoples Republic of China, Summer 1986. *Hobbies:* Travel; Photography; Aerospace education; Civil air patrol. *Address:* 4500 Leo Street, Marrero, Louisiana 70072, USA.

COLE Susie Cleora, b. 21 Feb. 1939, Bloomsburg, Pennsylvania, USA. Employee Relations Officer. m. (1)Richard E Miller, 31 July 1959, divorced 1977, 1 daughter, (2)Gerald E Nelson, 18 Feb. 1978, divorced 1982. *Education:* Northern Virginia Communicty College, History Courses, 1982; Numerous Federal Government Courses including Managing the Training Function, 1985. *Appointments:* Washington DC: Navy Dept. Clerk Typist Secretary, 1957-60, Military Pay Regulations Specialist, 1962-67, Head Performance Review & Analysis Section, Manager, Navy Error Detection & Reduction Programme for Military Pay, Allowances & Travel, 1967-71, Fiscal Accounting Specialist, Military Pay Regulations Specialist, 1971-74; US Dept. of State Fiscal Clerk, 1975-77, Senior Retirement Claims Examiner, 1977-83, Employee Relations Officer, Manager, Federal Health Benefits & Life Insurance Programme, 1983-. *Publications:* Navy Department Semi Annual Error Detection & Reduction Programme for Military Pay, Allowances & Travel Report, 1967-71; Navy Department Disbursing Officer's Digest on Military Pay Allowances & Travel articles. *Memberships:* Citizens Band Radio Club, Fairfax, 1974-82; Volunteer Worker, Retarded Childrens Centre, Fairfax, 1981- 82; National Association of Female Executives. *Honours:* Recipient, various honours & awards. *Hobbies:* Reading; Travel; History; Music; Art. *Address:* US Dept. of State, Office of Employee Relations, 2201 C Street NW, Washington, DC 20520, USA.

COLEMAN Alice Mary, b. 8 June 1923, London, England. University Professor. *Education:* Teachers' Certificate, 1943; BA, Honours, 1st Class, Birkbeck College, 1947; MA, Distinction, 1951, London University. *Appointments:* Teacher, in Charge of

Geography, Northfleet Central School for Girls, 1943-48; Assistant Lecturer through to Professor, Geography, King's College, London, 1948-. *Publications:* approximately 200 geographical papers; Utopia on Trial, 1985; The Planning Challenge of the Ottawa Area, 1969. *Memberships:* Royal Geographical Society, Council Member; Geographical Association; Institute of British Geographers. *Honours:* Gill Memorial Award, Royal Geographical Society, 1963; Times/Veuve Clicquet Award, 1974; First Holder, Visiting Professorship for Distinguished Women Social Scientists, University of Western Ontario, 1976; Busk Gold Medal, Royal Geographical Society, 1987. *Hobbies:* Problems of Crime and Social Breakdown; Geographical Study Tours; Analysis of Character through Handwriting. *Address:* King's College, Strand, London WC2R 2LS, England.

COLEMAN Jane Candia, b. 9 Jan. 1939, Pittsburgh, Pennsylvania, USA. Writer. m. Bernard Coleman, 27 Mar. 1965 (div. 1989), 2 sons. *Education:* BA, University of Pittsburgh, 1960. *Appointments:* Director, Women's Creative Writing Centre, Carlow College, Pittsburgh, 1984-86; Teacher, Creative Writing, Cochise College, Douglas, Arizona, 1988- 89. *Publications include:* Books: Voices of Doves, fiction, 1988; No Roof But Sky, poetry, 1999; Shadows in my Hands, non-fiction. *Memberships:* Western Writers of America; Associated Writing Programmes; Poets & Writers; International Poetry Forum. *Honours:* Plainswoman Fiction Award, 1983; Pennsylvania Historical & Museum Award, 1985; Writing grant, Pennsylvania Arts Council, 1986; Blue Moon fiction award, 1987; Amelia fiction award, 1988; Gila review fiction chapbook award, 1986; Poetry included, Anthology of American Poetry, 1988, 1989. *Hobbies:* Training horses; Playing harpsichord. *Address:* PO Box 40, Rodeo, NM 88056, USA.

COLEMAN Jane Dexter, b. 24 Aug. 1942, Boston, Massachusetts, USA. Communications Executive. m. Peter S Coleman, 18 Aug. 1969. 1 son. *Education:* AB, Barnard College, 1965; MPhil, PhD, 1976, Columbia University. *Appointments:* Manager, Program Analysis, CBS Broadcast Group, 1976-77; Director, Program Analysis, East, 1977-80; Station Manager, WINS Radio, New York City, 1980-81; Vice President & General Manager, WIND, Chicago, 1981; President, Oberland Productions, New York City, 1982-84; Associate Director/Administration, Gannett Center for Media Studies, New York City, 1985-. *Creative Works:* Various photographs and films. *Memberships:* National Academy Television Arts & Sciences; International Radio & Television Society; National Academy of Cable Programming. *Honours:* Red Ribbon Award, American Film Festival, 1985; Montreal World Film Festival Selection, 1983; Tyneside Film Festival Selection, 1983; Columbia University International Fellows Program, 1971-72; United Nations Summer Internship, 1974. *Hobbies:* International cultural exchange; The Arts, especially Film and Theatre; Sports, Tennis, Badminton, Football; Politics, encouraging women to run for public office. *Address:* 110 Bleecker Street, New York, NY 10012, USA.

COLLART, Marie E, b. 23 Nov. 1945. *Education:* BS, Nursing, 1967, MS, Nursing Education, 1970, PhD, 1979, Ohio State University, Columbus. *Appointments Include:* Perceptor to Medical Communications, School of Allied Medical Professions, 1973-; Advisory Committee, Respiratory Therapy, 1975-; Ohio State University; Co-Founder, Partner, Grey Squirrel Antiques Inc., 1983-. *Publications:* Articles in: American Journal of Nursing; Modern Hospital; Nursing Outlook; Audiovisual Instruction; and many other professional journals. *Memberships:* Sigma Theta Tau; President, Executive Director, Central Ohio Lung Association, 1981-; Secretary, Assistant Treasurer, The Lung Foundation; Ohio Thoracic Society, Director, 1973-81; Ohio Lung Association; many other professional organisations. *Honours:* American Lung Association Allied Health Professional Educator Award, 1976- 77; Chris Bronze Plaque Award, Columbus International Film Festival, 1977; Hattie Lazarus Health Award, 1987;

Woman of Distinction Award, Soroptimist International, Columbus, 1988. *Address:* 4063 Fairfax Drive, Columbus,OH 43220, USA.

COLLETTE Carolyn, b. 2 Aug. 1945, Boston, Massachusetts, USA. Professor of English. m. David Raymond Collette, 9 July 1967, 2 sons. *Education:* AB, Mount Holyoke College, 1967; MA 1968, PhD 1971, University of Massachusetts. *Appointments:* Faculty, Mount Holyoke College, 1970-. *Publications:* Articles in: Chaucer Review, English Literary Renaissance, Journal of William Morris Society. *Memberships:* William Morris Society; Modern Language Association; New Chaucer Society; Medieval Academy of America. *Honours:* Phi Beta Kappa, 1967; Woodrow Wilson fellowship, 1967-68; NDEA fellowship, 1969-70; Summer stipend, National Endowment for Humanities, 1976. *Address:* Department of English, Mount Holyoke College, South Hadley, Massachusetts 01075, USA.

COLLIER Alice Louise (Tschanen), b. 18 Sep. 1931(larion, Ohio, USA. Speech/Language/Hearing Pathologist. m. Charles Theodore Collier Jr, 18 Sep. 1954, 3 sons, 1 daughter. *Education:* BS, Education, Bowling Green State University, Ohio, 1953; MS, Education, Western New Mexico University, 1955; Postgraduate study, Portland State University, Oregon, 1963. *Appointments:* Speech Therapist, Huron County Schools, Norwalk, Ohio, 1953-54; Teacher, Bagdad (Arizona) Public School, 1961-62; Speech Pathologist, Beaverton (Oregon) School District 48, 1962-66, 1970-88. *Publications:* Editor, Speech and Language Development, Beaverton Schools, 1985-. *Memberships:* President, Bagdad Parent-Teacher Association, 1961-62; Vice-President, Whitford Parent Teachers Club, 1967-68; President, Whitford Parent Teachers Club, 1968-69; Council Member, Band Parents Association, Beaverton, 1971-76; Former Member, Mary Lee Singers, Beaverton; American Speech-Language-Hearing Association; Oregon Speech-Language Association (State Council 1965-68); Delta Zeta; Beaver School District Professional Enhancement Committee, 1986-88; National Education Association; Oregon Education Association; Beaverton Education Association. *Honours:* Employee Service Recognition Award, 1986, Employee Recognition Award, 1987, Beaverton School District. *Hobbies:* Tennis; Cycling; Sewing; Singing. *Address:* PO Box 546, Beaverton, OR 97075, USA.

COLLIER Ellen Clodfelter, b.19 Oct. 1927, Lawrence, Kansas, USA. Specialist, US Foreign Policy. m. Edwin Collier, 25 May 1951, 2 sons, 3 daughters. *Education:* BA, Ohio State University, 1949; MA, American University, 1951; Diploma, National War College, 1978. *Appointments:* Analyst, 1949-69, Specialist, US Foreign Policy, Congressional Research Service, Library of Congress, Washington, 1969-. *Publications:* Editor, Congress and Foreign Policy, annual volume published by Foreign Affairs Committee; Author, Co-Author: The Congressional Role in Nuclear Arms Control; Treaties and Other International Agreements; The Role of the United States Senate; other congressional publications. *Memberships:* International Studies Association, President, Washington Chapter, 1983-84; American Society of International Law; Executive Women in Government. *Honours:* Phi Beta Kappa; Pi Sigma Alpha; Mortar Board. *Hobbies:* Bicycling; Quilting. *Address:* Foreign Affairs & National Defense Division, Congressional Research Service, Library of Congress, Washington, DC 20540, USA.

COLLIER Zena, b. 21 Jan. 1926, London, England. Writer. m. (2) Thomas M. Hampson, 30 Dec. 1969. 2 sons previous marriage, 1 dec. *Education:* Henrietta Barnett School for Girls, London. *Appointment:* Teacher, Writers' Workshop, Nazareth College, Rochester, New York, USA, 1984-. *Publications include:* 1 Novel, A Cooler Climate, 1990; 5 novels, young adults: Year of the Dream, 1962; First Flight, 1962; Shutterbug, 1963; Tangled Web, 1967; Next Time I'll Know, 1981. Non-fiction book for teens: Seven for the People: Public Interest Groups at Work, 1979. Also: Short stories, articles, national magazines & literary journals. *Memberships:* Poets & Writers; Mystery Writers of America; Associated Writing Programmes; Writers & Books. *Honours include:* Fellow, Yaddo, Virginia Centre for Creative Arts, Alfred University Summer Place; Stories on Honour Roll Best American Short Stories, Nominated, Pushcart Prize, Winner, Winner, Hoepfner Award, best story in Southern Humanities Review 1985. *Hobbies:* Reading; Films; Theatre. *Address:* 83 Berkeley Street, Rochester, New York 14607, USA.

COLLIN Clarissa (Lady), b. 11 Oct. 1938, London, England. Farmer; Landowner. m. 14 Dec. 1963. 1 son, 1 daughter. *Appointments:* Charity Work, The Rainer Foundation, 1959; Sec Embassy, Washington, DC, USA, 1963; Correspondent, Queen Magazine, 1964. *Memberships:* Constituency Officer, Treasurer, Deputy Chairman, Conservative Party, 1957-89; President, York Area Appeals Committee for Mental Health; Chairman various fund raising committees. *Honour:* Justice of the Peace for Ryedale. *Hobbies:* Gardening; Photography; Dried flower arrangements; Walking. *Address:* Pockly, York YO6 5TE, England.

COLLINGS Patricia Gay, b. 29 July 1941, Shifnal, Shropshire, England. Head Teacher. m. 1963, 1 son, 1 daughter. *Education:* BA Honours, University of Hull, 1963. *Appointments:* Part-time teacher (French), Hull, Wallasey, Nottingham, 1963-72; Head of House, Head of Modern Languages, Chilwell Comprehensive School, 1972-79; Deputy head, Rushcliffe School, 1980-84; Head, Sinfin Community School, Derby, 1984-. *Memberships:* Founder Member, Secretary, NE Midlands branch, National Association PCE; Past Vice-Chair, Derbyshire, SHA; Board of Trustees, Central Bureau. *Hobbies:* People; Appreciation of the Arts, Concerts, Galleries, Literature; Music, Choral Singing; Gastronomy; Sport, Skiing, Tennis, Jogging; Homecrafts. *Address:* Glebe Villa, 4 Glebe Street, Beeston, Nottingham NG9 1BZ, England.

COLLINS Barbara-Rose, b. 13 Apr. 1939, Detroit, USA. Councilwoman. m. 19 Jan. 1958, deceased, 1 son, 1 daughter. *Appointments:* Elected to Detroit School Board, Region 1, 1970; Elected to Michigan State House of Representatives, 1974-82; Elected to Detroit City Council, 1981-. *Memberships:* National Political Congress of Black Women; National Council Negro Women; Detroit Symphony; Association of Municipal Professional Women. *Hobbies:* Piano; Harp; Reading; Travel; Oriental & African Art; Opera; Symphony. *Address:* PO Box 07167, Detroit, MI 48207, USA.

COLLINS Bernice Elaine, b. 24 Oct. 1957, Kansas City, Kansas, USA. Circus Dancer; Showgirl. *Education:* Diploma, RBBB Clown College, 1977; Diploma, Transworld Travel College, 1985; Studied dance in New York and Kansas City. *Appointments:* Clown 1978-79, Dancer 1980-84, Tiger Trainer 1983, Dancer 1988-, Ringling Bros, Barnum & Bailey Circus; Int Flight Attendant, TWA, 1985-86; Singer, Kansas City Riverboat, 1986-87. *Honours:* First Black Female Clown, 1978; First Black Female Tiger Trainer, 1983. *Hobbies:* Art; Music; Animal training. *Address:* 3507 Oak Ave, Kansas City, Kansas 66104, USA.

COLLINS Imogene M, b. 5 Feb. 1939, Liberia. Administrator. m. Benjamin T. Collins, 24 May 1957, 2 sons, 2 daughters. *Appointments:* Chief Dietician, Maternity Hospital, 1960-65; Librarian, Cultural Assistant, 1965-75; Director, Publications, Government of Liberia, 1975-81; Programme Representative, African-American Institute, 1981-; Executive Secretary, Liberian Council of Churches, 1982-. *Memberships:* Liberia Baptist Missionary & Educaiton Convention; Baptist Sunday School Convention; etc. *Hobbies:* Working with People. *Address:* Logan Town, Bushrod Island PO Box 2432, Monrovia, Liberia, West Africa.

COLLINS Joan, b. 23 May 1933, London, England. Actress. m (2) Anthony Newley, divorced, 1 son, 1 daughter. (3) Ronald S Kass, 1972, divorced, 1 daughter. (4) Peter Holm, divorced. *Creative Works:* Films include: I Believe in You, 1952; Our Girl Friday, 1953; The Good Die Young, 1954; Land of the Pharaohs, 1955; The Virgin Queen, 1955; The Girl in the Red Velvet Swing, 1955; The Opposite Sex, 1956; Island in the Sun, 1957; Sea Wife, 1957; The Bravados, 1958; Seven Thieves, 1960; Road to Hong Kong, 1962; Warning Shot, 1966; The Executioner, 1969; Quest for Love, 1971; Revenge, 1971; Alfie Darling, 1974; The Stud, 1979; The Bitch, 1980; The Big Sleep; Tales of the Unexpected; Neck, 1983; Georgy Porgy, 1983; The Nutcracker, 1984. Numerous Television appearances including: Dynasty (serial); Cartier Affair, 1985; Sins, 1986; Monte Carlo, 1986. *Publications:* Past Imperfect, 1978; The Joan Collins Beauty Book, 1980; Katy, A Fight for Life, 1982. *Address:* c/o Judy Bryer, 15363 Mulholland Drive, Los Angeles, CA 90077, USA.

COLLINS Joy Violetta, b. 20 Apr. 1917, Launceston, Tasmania. Retired; Active Marriage Celebrant. m. Ronald Kenneth Collins, 26 Oct. 1963, died 1981. *Appointments:* Member WAAAF, 1942-46; Commercial Work, 1946-54; Administration, Field Officer, State Secretary, Red Cross Society, 1954-56; Own Secretarial Business, then 25 years as Journalist, Social/Feature/Travel Writer, TV Show, Civil Marriage Celebrant, 1981. *Publications:* Tapestries, given to charitable organisations; 50 years History of Red Cross Society and the 1st World War of the Northern Territory, 1914-19, 1937-87. *Memberships:* Red Cross Society; Girl Guides, District Commissioner; Royal Commonwealth Society; Pensioners Association; Quota International; Founder, President, Royal Darwin Hospital Auxiliary; etc. *Honours:* Member, Order of Australia, General Division, 1979; Darwin Woman of the Year, 1979; Nominated to Appear in Register of Women Achievers of the Northern Territory, 1948-88, 1988. *Hobbies:* Reading; Writing; Tapestry; Gardening. *Address:* Unit 2, No 15 Rockford Street, Mandurah, Western Australia 6210, Australia.

COLLINS Kathleen Elizabeth, b. 14 Jan. 1951, Rock Island, Illinois, USA. Sales Representative. *Education:* Foreign student, University of Grenoble, France, 1970; BA, French & English, St Ambrose College, 1972; Secondary Education 1975, Pre-Med 1980-83, Augustana College. *Appointments:* Salesperson: Burroughs Wellcome Company, 1976-80; Phil Collins Company, 1980-85; Lederle Laboratories, 1985-88; Summit Pharmaceuticals, 1988-. *Memberships:* Various offices, Quint Cities Pharmaceutical Association; Self Realisation Fellowship. *Honours:* Valedictorian & Staffers Award, 1968; Bausch & Lomb Science Award, 1968; No. 1 Sales, Lederle Laboratories, 1987; American Legion, 1965. *Hobbies:* Fashion modelling, Rosen Agency; Scuba diving; Holistic medicine; Health & beauty spas & resorts; Teaching French to gifted children; Hospice work. *Address:* 3649 Cedarview Court, Bettendorf, Iowa 52722, USA.

COLLINS Mary, b. 26 Sept. 1940, Vancouver, Canada. Member, Canadian House of Commons. 2 sons, 1 daughter. *Education:* BA, Political Science, Queens University. *Appointments:* President, Mary Collins Consultants Ltd., 1973-81; Consultant in Communications; Director, Public Affairs, Brinco Ltd., 1981-83; Re-elected to the House of Commons November 21st 1988 - Member of Parliament for Capilano-Howe Sound. *Memberships:* Chairman, British Columbia PC Caucus; Standing Committee on Finance & Economic Affairs; Chairman, Standing Committee on Consumer & Corporate Affairs; Executive Member, Canada Japan Parliamentary Association; Founding Member, Canada China Parliamentary Association. *Honours:* Woman of the Year, Public Affairs, Calgary YWCA, 1982. *Hobbies:* International Trade; Human Rights. *Address:* House of Commons, Ottawa, Ontario, Canada K1A 0A6.

COLLIS Louise Edith, b. 1 Jan. 1925, Burma. Writer. *Education:* BA, Modern History, Reading University, 1945. *Publications:* Novels: Without a Voice, 1951; A

Year Passed, 1952; After the Holiday, 1954; The Angle's Name, 1955; The Great Flood, 1966; Biographies: Seven in the Tower, 1958; The Apprentice Saint (Margery Kemp), 1964; Soldier in Paradise (John Steadman), 1965; A Private View of Stanley Spencer, 1972; Maurice Collis Diaries, Editor, 1977; Impetuous Heart, Ethel Smyth, 1984; contributor to numerous magazines on art & literature. *Memberships:* Society of Authors; International Association of Art Critics. *Address:* 65 Cornwall Gardens, London SW7, England.

COLLISON Diane Marie, b. 11 May 1939, Carroll, Iowa, USA. Public Speaker, Consultant, Collison & Associates; 5 sons, 1 daughter. *Education:* BA, Iowa State University, 1979; Post-Graduate Studies, Iowa State University, 1980. *Appointments:* Organization & Communications Director, Republican Party of Iowa, Presidnetial, US Senate and Gubeunatorial Campaigns, 1979-85; Arts Management, Denver Symphony Orchestra, Boulder, 1985-87; Business Communications Consultant, US West, Denver, 1987-; Coordinator, Regis College Career Program; Public Relations Director, International Couide Academy; Consultant, Collison and Associates, Career and Organisational Development; Project Management, Denver, Colorado. *Publication:* Transitions, 1983-. *Memberships:* Centennial Philharmonic Orchestra, Board Member; Served on Dole Presidential State Steering Committee, Colorado, 1987; National Speakers Association; Colorado Federation of the Arts; NAFE. *Honours:* International Platform Association, Certified Team Management Systems, National Consulting and Training Institute; Arion Foundation Music Award. *Hobbies:* Semi-professional Musician, Violinist and Pianist; Art; Politics. *Address:* 801 Pennsylvania, Apt. 207, Denver, CO 80203, USA.

COLLYER Janet Louise, b. 30 Mar. 1942, Melbourne, Australia. Certified Practising Accountant. m. Hugh Richard Collyer, 3 Dec. 1966. 1 son, 2 daughters. *Education:* Diploma, Royal Melbourne Institute of Technology, 1963; Associate 1963, Fellow 1985, Australian Society of Accountants; Registered Tax Agent, 1972; Registered Company Auditor, 1984. *Appointments:* E V Nixon & partners, 1960-63; McGills, 1964-66; Arthur Young & Co, 1967-69; Partner, Bede Collyer Alderton & Co, 1975-. *Memberships:* Australian Society of Accountants; Australian Taxation Institute. *Honours:* Award of Distinction, 1986, Confederation of Australian Sport. *Hobbies:* Family; Athletics (Administration); Music; Reading. *Address:* 14 High Street, Mont Albert 3127, Victoria, Australia.

COLVIN Iris, b. 15 Apr. 1914, Ashlond, USA. Businesswoman. m. Lloyd Dayton Colvin, 11 Mar. 1938. *Education:* BA, University of California, 1937. *Appointments:* Staff, W.A. Bechtel Corp; GSA, General Accounting Office, Tokyo, 1945-47; General Contractor, Vice Presidnet, Drake Builders, 1947-. *Publications:* Co-author, How We Built Our Own Home and Went on to Make a Million Dollars in the Construction Business; many articles. *Memberships:* RCA; ARRL. *Honours:* Delta Epsilon; various other honours. *Hobbies:* Artist; Writer; Amateur Radio Operator. *Address:* 5200 Panama Avenue, Richmond, CA 94804, USA.

COLWILL Nina Lee, b. 9 Feb. 1944, Gaspe, Canada. Professor. m. C Dennis Anderson, 7 Nov. 1964. 1 son, 1 daughter. *Education:* BA, University of Western Ontario, 1974; MA 1976, PhD 1981, University of Manitoba. *Appointments:* University of Manitoba, Faculty of Management, 1978-, Adjunct Professor, Department of Psychology, 1984-. *Publications:* The Psychology of Sex Differences with Hilary Lips; The New Partnership: Women and Men in Organizations; Numerous journal articles and conference presentations. *Memberships:* Nominating Committee, Canadian Psychological Association; President, 1982-83; Manitoba Psychological Society; Academy of Management; International Association for Research on Economic Psychology; Administrative Sciences Association of Canada. *Honours:* Touche Ross Consultants' Award for Outstanding Contribution to

Business Quarterly, 1988; Canada Council Masters Scholarship, 1974-75; Canada Council Doctoral Fellowship, 1978-79, 1979-80; Vineberg Prize in Psychology for Excellence in Research by a Graduate Student, 1977-78; Manitoba Fellowship, 1975-76, 1977-78. *Hobby:* Writing poetry. *Address:* 100 Cornell Drive, Winnipeg, Manitoba, Canada, R3T 3C3.

COMBIER Elizabeth Irene, b. 11 July 1949, New York City, USA. Journalist; Development Communication Consultant. m. David Kapel, 5 May 1984. 2 daughters. *Education:* BA, Northwestern University, 1971; Certificate, Harvard, 1970, Columbia 1973; Johns Hopkins School for Advanced International Studies, 1975; MPS, New York University, 1984. *Appointments:* Sales, Memorex, 1971-72; Mergers & Acquisitions, 1972-73; Producer, Cue TV Magazine, 1975-77; Producer, Egypt, Israel, Jordan, TV News & Documentaries, 1978-83; President, Ecomedia, 1978-; Director, The Business Circle, 1986-. *Publications:* PCBS & Breastfeeding; Gifts for Health, American Health Magazine; Nutritional Anti-Cancer Diet Therapies; Video: Cultural Awareness: An Egyptian Experience, Cultural Survival Quarterly. *Memberships:* Membership Committee, International Radio & TV Society; National Academy of TV Arts & Sciences; Society for International Education, Training and research; International Institute of Communications; Sierra Club. *Honours:* Nominated for Fellowship Award, Marconi International, 1981; Winner, AECT Memorial Scholarship Award, 1984; Fellow, Salsburg Seminars 1980, 1981, 1982, 1984; Mentioned in Rolex Awards book, Spirit of Enterprise, 1984; Winner, Washington Square Outdoor Art Exhibit, 1975, 1976. *Hobbies:* Nutrition; Drawing children; Miniatures; Travel. *Address:* 315 E 65 Street, New York, NY 10021, USA.

COMEFORO Jean Elizabeth, b. 2 June 1947, Urbanna, USA. Teacher of the Deaf. *Education:* BS, Biology, 1969; MED, Smith College, 1972; MEd., Cheyney State College, 1982. *Appointments:* Houseparent, Marie H. Katzenbach School for the Deaf, 1969-70; Math & Science Teacher, Western Pennsylvania School for the Deaf, 1971-76; Teacher of Deaf, Interpreter, Delaware County Intermediate Unit, 1976-. *Publications:* Presentations; articles in professional journals. *Memberships:* Quota International Inc; Alexander G. Bell Association for the Deaf; International Organization for Educators of the Hearing Impaired. *Honours:* Tri Beta National Biological Honour Society; Scholarship to Smith College; many other honours & awards. *Hobbies:* Travel; Bowling; Swimming. *Address:* 616 North Lemon Street, Media, PA 19063, USA.

COMER Marian Wilson, b. 26 Nov. 1938, Gary, Indiana, USA. Scientist; Teacher. m. (1) Samuel Wilson, 1956, 1 son, 1 daughter (div. 1974), (2) Richard Comer, 1979, 1 son, 1 daughter. *Education:* BS, Roosevelt University, Chicago, 1966; MAT, Indiana University, 1969; PhD, University of Illinois, 1975; Postdoctoral, National Institutes of Health, 1978-79. *Appointments:* Assistant to Vice President Research & Development 1978-79, Acting Dean Student Development 1979-81, Associate Vice President Academic Affairs 1981-84, Professor of Biology 1984-, Chicago State University; Chief Executive Officer, Institute of Transition, Gary, Indiana, 1984-. *Publications:* (Research) High Tech for the Population at Greatest Risk; Plant Biochemistry; Biosystematics; Paleobotany; Ethics of Research on Recombinant DNA. *Memberships:* Extramural Associate, NIH; American Institute of Biological Sciences; Botanical Society of America; Council, ACE Fellows in Academic Administration; American Association for Higher Education. *Honours:* NIH, 1983; Fellow, American Council of Education, 1977-78; Rockefeller Fellow, 1977-78; Distinguished Minority Speaker, 1976; Dr Marian Wilson Scholarship, Chicago State University, 1976; Award, Indiana University, 1968. *Address:* 7612 Forest Avenue, Gary, Indiana 46403, USA.

COMINI Alessandra, b. 24 Nov. 1934, Winona,

Minnesota, USA. University Professor; Author; Lecturer. *Education:* BA, Barnard College, 1956; MA, University of California at Berkeley, 1964; PhD with distinction, Columbia University, 1969. *Appointments:* Teaching Assistant, University of California, Berkeley, 1964; Visiting Inst 1967, Preceptor 1965-66, Columbia University; Inst 1968-69, Assistant Professor 1969-74, Visiting Assistant Professor 1973, Yale University; Visiting Assistant Professor, Summers 1970, 1972, Associate Professor Art History 1974-75, Professor 1975-, Southern Methodist University; University Distinguished Professor of Art History, 1983-. *Publications:* Author of: Schiele in Prison, 1973; Egon Schiele's Portraits, 1974; Gustav Klint, 1975, 1986; Egon Schiele, 1976, 1986; The Fantastic Art of Vienna, 1978; The Changing Image of Beethove, 1986; Numerous articles in magazines and various catalogue essays. *Memberships:* American Society of Composers, Authors & Publishers; College Art Ass of America, Board of Directors, 1980-84; Women's Caucus for Art, director 1974-78; Texas Institute of Letters. *Honours:* Alfred Hodder resident, Princeton University, 1972-73; Recipient, Charles Rufus Book Award, College Art Association of America, 1976; Laurel Award, Association of University Women, 1979; Named Outstanding Professor, SMU Rotunda, 1977, 1979, 1983, 1985-88; Named Meadows Distinguished Teaching Professor, 1986-87. *Hobby:* Flute and Piano duets. *Address:* 2900 McFarlin, Dallas, Texas 75205, USA.

COMISEL Emilia, b. 28 Feb. 1913, Romania. Professor. m. 10 Feb. 1941, 1 son, 1 daughter. *Education:* Music Academy, Bucharest, 1933-37; Sociology Faculty, 1941-42. *Appointments:* Music Teacher, 1941-43; Ethnomusicologist, Folklore Archives, C. Brailoiu, 1943-49; Ethnomusicologist, Folklore Instutute, Bucharest, 1949-64; Professor, Music Conservatory, Bucharest, 1949-74; Research, South-East Institute, 1968-72. *Publications:* Romanian Ballard, 1955; The Doina, 1964; Children's Folklore and Lullaby, 1959; C. Brailoiu, Little Monography, 1965; Melody Structure of Dances, 1965; Architectonic Form of Folk Music, 1967; Romanian Folklore, 1968. *Memberships:* Many professional organisations including: Ethnomusicology Studies. *Honours:* Recipient, various honours and awards. *Hobbies:* Painting; Literature. *Address:* Str. Popa Petre, 26 A 70249, Bucharest Romania.

COMISKEY Donna Jean, b. 26 Aug. 1949, Hazleton, Pennsylvania, USA. Board Certified Diplomate in Clinical Social Work; Human Development Specialist. m. Walter Phillip Comiskey, 8 Apr. 1973. 1 son, 2 daughters. *Education:* BA, Saint Francis College, Loretto, 1971; Master of Social Work, Marywood College, Scraton, 1975. *Appointments:* Casework Trainee, Children and Youth, Department of Social Service, Harford County, 1970; Casework Interne, Cresson State School and Hospital, Cresson, 1970-71; Social Worker, White Haven Center, White Haven, 1971-73; Corrections Counselor, Chase State Prison, Dallas, 1973-74; Psychiatric Social Worker, Veterans Administration Hospital, Wilkes Barre, 1974-75; College Misericordia Field Instructor, Social Work, Dallas, 1977-; Specialist, Hazleton-Nanticoke, MH/MR Center, 1975-78; Director for Mental Retardation/Developmental Disabilities Services, Hazleton-Nanticoke Mental Health/Mental Retardation Center, 1978-. *Memberships:* National Association of Social Workers; Secretary and first Vice President, Association for Retarded Citizens; National Association for the Dually Diagnosed; American Association on Mental Retardation; Alpha Delta Mu, National Social Work Honor Society; Academy of Certified Social Worker; Horizon House Documentary Film Panelist; Scranton Diocese, Marriage Preparation class Facilitator. *Honours:* Clifford Bigalow Advocate of the Year Award, Association for Retarded Citizens, 1987; Juliette Low International World Friendship, Girl Scout Award, 1967. *Address:* 445 Carver Street, Larksville, Plymouth, PA 18651, USA.

COMMENS Muriel Jasper, b. 22 May 1922, Sydney,

Australia. m. 6 Oct. 1945, 2 sons, 1 daughter. *Education:* Teachers Certificate, Sydney Teachers College, 1942. *Appointments:* Teacher, Maimuru Public School, 1942-45; Partner, wih husband, in the Farm. *Memberships:* Country Womens Association of NSW, State Treasurer, 1978-82, State President 1983-86; CWA Club Management Committee Chairman, 1983-87; CWA of Australia, National Treasurer, 1979-81; National Women's Consultative Council, 1986-88. *Honours:* Order of Australia Medal, 1988. *Hobbies:* Reading; Gardening; Sewing. *Address:* Glenfield, Junee NSW 2663, Australia.

CONANT Jan Royce, b. 14 Sept. 1930, Boston, USA. Artist; Pro-Horsewoman. m. Richard W. Conant, 22 Mar. 1952, divorced 1978, 2 sons. *Education:* Boston Museum School of Fine Arts, 1948-51; Cincinnati Arts Academy, 1951-53. *Appointments:* Owner, Manager, Tinker Hill Farm, 1965-73; Stonefield Farm, 1974-; Managing Director, Chukka Cove Farm, Jamaica, West Indies, 1982-84. *Publications:* Half Pint and Others; The Winning Streak, illustrator; Horsemanship, illustrator; Judge and Jr. Exhibitor, illustrator; 7 limited edition Lithographs; over 300 paintings in private & corporate collections. *Memberships:* US Pony Clubs Inc., Life Member, Ex Vice President, Governor, Regional Supervisor, National Examiner; New England Dressage Association; US Dressage Federation; US Horse Show Association; International Judge; FEI Judge. *Hobbies:* Photography; Classical Guitar. *Address:* 23 Three Bridges Road, East Haddam, CT 06423, USA.

CONARD Brenda Ruth Dorn, b. 1 Aug. 1940, Madison, Ohio, USA. Multicultural Education Consultant. m. Dennis Conrad, 14 Aug. 1971, 1 son, 1 daughter. *Education:* BS, 1961, MA, 1964, Ohio State University. *Appointments:* Teacher, 1962-69; TV Teacher, 1969-70; Elementary Teacher, 1970-78; Multicultural Education Consultant, Columbus, 1978-. *Publications:* Cooperative Learning and Prejudice Reduction, (April/May 1988 issue of Social Education). *Memberships:* Phi Delta Kappa; National Education Association; Ohio, Columbus Education Associations; Central Ohio Council for Social Studies; Ohio Folklore Society. *Honours:* Recipient, various honours and awards. *Hobbies:* Singing; Tennis; Oil Painting. *Address:* Alum Crest Centre, Columbus Public Schools, 2200 Winslow Drive, Columbus, OH 43207, USA.

CONAWAY Carol Beth, b. 20 Feb. 1948, Philadelphia, Pennsylvania, USA. Political Scientist. *Education:* AB, Bryn Mawr College, 1970; SM, 1981, PhD, 1990, Massachusetts Institute of Technology. *Appointments:* Policy Adviser to Mayor of Philadelphia, 1971-73; Policy Analyst, Abt Associates Inc, 1973-75; Programme Coordinator, The Boston Sickle Cell Center, 1975-76; Private consulting, non-profit organisations, 1976-77; Researcher on politics and economics of Middle East, 1977-89. *Creative works:* Arab and American Banks and the New International Economic Order, Master's thesis, 1981. *Memberships:* Joint Seminar on Political Development; American Political Science Association. *Honour:* Goodwin Medal for Outstanding Teaching by a Graduate Student, Massachusetts Institute of Technology, 1988. *Hobbies:* Violinist (plays chamber music); Gardening. *Address:* 153 West Brookline Street, Boston, MA 02118, USA.

CONDIE Carol Joy, b. 28 Dec. 1931, Provo, Utah, USA. Consulting Anthropologist. m. M. Kent Stout, 18 June 1954, 1 son, 2 daughters. *Education:* BA, Anthropology, University of Utah, 1953; MEd, Elementary Education, Cornell University, 1954; PhD, Anthropology, University of New Mexico, 1973. *Appointments:* Education Coordinator 1973, Director of Interpretation 1974-77, Maxwell Museum of Anthropology, University of New Mexico; Assistant Professor of Anthropology 1975-77, UNM, President, Quivira Research Centre 1978-. *Publications:* Article, Weavers of the Jade Needle, in Fiberarts, 1976; Senior Editor, Anthropology in the Desert West, 1986. *Memberships:* Past Chair, Native American Relations Committee, Society for American Archaeology; Past

President, New Mexico Archeological Council; Past Chair, Albuquerque-Bernalillo County Archaeological Resources Planning Advisory Committee. *Honours:* Albuquerque Conservation Award, 1986; Award, American Planning Association, 1985-86; Governor's Award 1986, New Mexico Archeological Council award 1988, historic preservation. *Hobbies:* Spinning; Weaving; Dyeing. *Address:* Quivira Research Centre, 1809 Notre Dame NE, Albuquerque, New Mexico 87106, USA.

CONE Martha Caroline, b. 11 Apr. 1933, Columbus, Ohio, USA. TV Production Manager. m. E. David DeVoe, 30 Jan. 1953, divorced 1965, 1 son, 1 daughter. *Education:* Ohio State University, Columbus, 1951-53. *Appointments:* Director, Women's Programming, WPTA-TV, Fort Wayne, Indiana, 1963-65; Assistant Director, Press & Publicity, KNBC TV Burbank, 1965-70; Syndicatoe, Don Fedderson Productions, The Lawrence Welk Show, 1971-77; Production Manager, 1984-, Manager, Syndication Operations, 1977-, Mark Goodson Productions. *Publications:* Consultant, The Silent Witness, 1980. *Memberships:* Foothill Civitan Club, California District Civitan International, Board Member, President-Elect, President, Delegate, International Convention, Oslo, 1986; Burbank Communty Hospital Health Care Foundation, Board; GLAZA; Burbank Community Hospital Volunteer. *Hobbies:* Cooking; Interior Decorating; International Special Olympic; Working with Mentally & Physically Handicapped; Horses; Gardening; Reading. *Address:* 6614 Clybourn, Unit 3, North Hollywood, CA 91606, USA.

CONEY Elaine Marie, b. 9 Aug. 1952, Magnolia, Mississippi, USA. Foreign Language Teacher, Secondary School. *Education:* BA, Millsaps College, Jackson, Mississippi, 1974; MEd, University of Southern Mississippi, Hattiesburg, 1979; PhD, Universidad Interamericana, Saltillo, Mexico, 1977. *Appointments:* Teacher, South Pike High School, Magnolia, 1977-; Teacher, Liberty Attendance Center, Liberty, Mississippi, 1976-77; Instructor, Jackson State University, Jackson, 1982. *Memberships:* National Education Association; Mississippi Association of Educators; South Pike Association of Educators; Mississippi Foreign Language Association, 2nd Vice President; Chairperson, Mississippi Association of Educators, Instructional and Professional Development Committee, 1985-90. *Honour:* Teacher of the Year, South Pike High School, 1988. *Hobbies:* Travelling to foreign countries; Playing the piano and flute. *Address:* P O Box 208, Magnolia, Mississippi 39652, USA.

CONGER Martha (Marti), b. 10 Feb. 1950, Tillamook, Oregon, USA. Consultant. Divorced, 1 son. *Education:* BA, Western Washington University, 1972; M.Ed., Technology, 1977. *Appointment:* Owner/Manager, Yours Mine & Ours, Mt. Vernon, WA, 1980-83; Manager of Training, F W Woolworth Co., Milwaukee, WI, 1983-85, Director of Training, F W Woolworth Co., 1985-88; Corporate Resouice Associates, INc., 1988-. *Memberships:* American Society of Training & Development; Boy Scouts of America; Girl Scouts of America. *Honours:* Speaker, American Society for Training & Development, National Convention, 1987; Director-Elect, Retail Industry Group, American Society for Training & Development, 1987/88; Director, Retail Industry Group, American Society for Training & Development, 1988/89. *Hobbies:* Needlework; Travel. *Address:* 815-102 sea Spray Lane, Foster City, California 94404, USA.

CONLIN Roxanne Barton, b. 30 June 1944, Huron, South Dakota, USA. Attorney. m. James Clyde Conlin, 21 Mar. 1964. 2 sons, 2 daughters. *Education:* BA 9164, JD 1966, MPA 1979, Drake University. *Appointments:* Private Practice, 1966-67; Deputy Industrial Commissioner, 1967-68; Assistant Attorney General, State of Iowa, 1969-76; Consultant, United States Commission on the Observance of International Women's Year, US Department of State, 1976-77; Adjunct Professor of Law, University of Iowa Law School, 1977-79; US Attorney, Southern District of Iowa, 1977-81; Democratic nominee for Governor, State of Iowa, 1982; James, Galligan and Conlin, PC, 1983-. *Creative works:* Numerous articles to professional journals and to conferences. *Memberships include:* Chair, Education Department, Association of Trial Lawyers of America; ATLA-PAC Board of Directors; President, Civil Justice Foundation; Council on Judicial Selection; Board of Directors, YWCA; Steering Committee, Key Person Committee of Association of Trial Lawyers of America; Board of Governors, Association of Trial Lawyers of Iowa; Board of Directors, NOW Legal Defense and Education Fund; Board of Directors, Dowling High School; Des Moines Chamber of Commerce, *Honours:* Iowa Women's Hall of Fame, 1981; Omicron Delta Kappa, Alumni Member, 1981; Outstanding Assistance, US Secret Service, 1981; Special Commendation, Director of FBU, 1979; Special Commendation, US Postal Inspection Service, 1978, etc. *Hobbies:* Reading; Raising African Violets and other Gesneriads; Knitting. *Address:* The Plaza Suite 5, 300 Walnut Street, Des Moines, Iowa 50309, USA.

CONLON Karen D, b. 9 Nov. 1951, Amarillo, Texas, USA. Director of Community Associations and Development Services. *Education:* BS, Economics, 1975; Guidance Counseling, Para Professional Program-AS, 1973. *Appointments:* Regional VP, Mercury Property Management, Irvine, CA, 1982-83; Director, Property Management, George Elkins Co, Palm Desert, 1983-85; Shappell Industries Inc, 1985-. *Creative Works:* Publication: The Invisible Sales Force: Your Community Association, 1989; Speaker at numerous national conferences for the Building Industry; Several papers presented at conferences. *Memberships:* Community Associations Institute, National Trustee, 1986-; Past President, Business & Professional Women, Coachella Valley Chapter. *Honour:* Community Association Institute, National Volunteer of the Year, 1989. *Hobbies:* Horseback riding; Reading; Travelling; Theatre going; Dancing. *Address:* 3805 E 2nd St No B, Long Beach, CA 90803, USA.

CONLON Pepita Helen Marilla, b. Sydney, Australia. Radio Producer. *Education:* BA Honours, Sydney University, 1965; Simultaneous Interpreter's Certificate, Macquarie University, Sydney, 1975. *Appointments:* Program Officer, Radio 2 EA, Special Broadcasting Service; Radio Producer, Current Affairs, Australian Broadcasting Corporation, The World Today and PM programmes, Sydney. *Publications:* Monthly column on language, Pepita's Pick. *Memberships:* Australian Broadcasting Corporation, Standing Committee on Spoken English. *Honours:* Gold Citation, Media Peace Prize, 1979. *Hobbies:* Tennis; Skiing; Travel; Reading; Languages. *Address:* c/o Australian Broadcasting Corporation, Radio Current Affairs, GPO Box 9994, Sydney 2001, Australia.

CONN Eunice M. Janicki, b. 2 Jan. 1938, Chicago, USA. Entrepreneur. m. Donald F. Conn, 10 May 1958, 2 sons, 2 daughters. *Education:* University of Illinois, 1957. *Appointments:* Secretary, Bookkeeper, Strom Construction Co., 1954-58; Part-time Bookkeeeper, ARC Steak House, Glenview, Illinois, 1959-63; Salesgirl, Studio Girl Cosmetics, 1963-65; Regional Manager, Studio Girl, Hollywood, 1965-68; Regional Manager, Fashion Frocks, Ohio, 1968-70; E.B. Conn Vending Inc., 1972- ; Formed Playhouse Productions, Inc., Niles, 1983. *Creative Works:* Writer, Producer, many plays & original music; Write, Editor, 8 page newsletter, 1980-, National Association of Postal Stamp Vendors, 1986-. *Memberships:* Numerous professional organisations including: President, Independent Business Association of Illinois, 1985-86; Chicago Association of Commerce and Industry. *Honours Include:* Certificate of Recognition, National & Local Government Liaison for Small Businesses from Senator John Nimrod, 1981; President's Award, National Association of Stamp Vendors, 1982. *Hobbies:* Creating & Performing & Directing Music & Theatre; Computers; Gardening; Small Business; Politics. *Address:* 9245 Maple Court, Morton Grove, IL 60053, USA.

CONNELL Linda, b. 30 Jan. 1957, Williamsport, Pennsylvania, USA. Registered Dietician. *Education:* BS 1980, MS 1982, University of Arizona; Work experience, Tucson Medical Centre, 1982. *Appointments:* Dietician, Tucson Medical Centre 1982-83, Canyon Ranch Resort, Tucson 1983-85; President, Connell & Associates, Consultants, 1982-; Director, Nutrition Services, Canyon Ranch Resort, 1985-. *Publications:* Articles, diet, nutrition, fitness, journals including Tucson Business Journal, Tucson Magazine, Fitness Plus, New Woman. *Memberships:* American & Arizona Dietetics Associations; National Council Against Health Fraud; Centre for Science in the Public Interest; American Running & Fitness Association; National Association for Female Executives. *Honour:* National Honour Society, 1975. *Hobbies:* Triathlons; Hiking; Travel. *Address:* 2016 East Water Street, Tucson, Arizona 85719, USA.

CONNOR Marie Stella, b. 7 Mar. 1918, Chicago, Illinois, USA. Psychotherapist; Consultant; Medical/ Psychiatric Social Worker. *Education:* University of Chicago High School, 1935; AM, University of Chicago School of Social Service Administration, 1943; BS, Northwestern University, Evanston, Illinois, 1940; *Appointments:* Michael Reese Hospital, 1943-47; St Louis University Hospitals, 1948-50; Child Welfare Worker and Supervisor, State of Illinois, department of Public Welfare, Division of Child Welfare, 1950-61; Medical Social Consultant, University of Illinois, Division of Services for Crippled Children, 1961-66, 1969; Director of Social Work, Angel Guardian Home for Children, Chicago; Psychiatric Social Worker and Field Work Preceptor, Veterans Administration Medical Centre, North Chicago, Illinois, 1971-. *Memberships:* National Association of Social Workers; Lake Shore Animal Foundation; Academy of Certified Social Workers; Pullman Civic Organisation; Register of Clinical Social Workers; Therapy Dogs International; Save A Pet; Delta Society; South Shore Country Club Alumni; Historic Pullman Foundation; Yorkshire Terrier Club of America; Red Carpet Room of United Airlines; Goldcoast Kennel Club; Admirals Club of American Airlines. *Honours:* VA Letter of Appreciation, 1975; VA Commendations, 1976, 1977; Superior Performance Award, 1986. *Hobbies:* Raising and showing Yorkshire Terriers; Horseback riding; Tennis; Golf; Ballet; Interior Decorating; Restoration of old houses of Historic Landmark status. *Address:* 11222 Champlain Avenue, Chicago, Illinois 60628, USA.

CONRAN Shirley Ida, b. Sept. 1932, London, England. Designer; Writer. m. Sir Terence Conran, 24 June, 1955. dissolved 1962. 2 sons. *Education:* St Paul's Girls' School, London; la Chatelainie, Switzerland, Portsmouth College of Art. *Appointments:* Fabric Designer and Director of Conran Fabrics, 1956-62; Member, Selection Committee, Design Centre, 1961-69; Journalist; (first) Woman's Editor, Observer Colour Magazine, 1964; Woman's Editor, Daily Mail, 1969; Life and Style Editor, Over 21, 1972-74. *Publications:* Superwoman, 1975; Superwoman Year Book, 1976; Superwoman in Action, 1977 (with E Sidney); Action Woman, 1979; Lace (novel), 1982; The Magic Garden, 1983. *Hobbies:* Skiing; Swimming; Reading; Yoga. *Address:* c/o Birkett Wesson, 20 Princes Street, London W1, England.

CONSTANT Patricia Reed, b. 14 Mar. 1949, Chandler, Arizona, USA. Attorney. m. Anthony Field Constant, 12 Oct. 1976, 2 daughters. *Education:* BA, Texas A & I University at Corpus Christi, 1976 (Summa cum Laude); JD, University of Texas Law School, 1979. *Appointments:* Law Clerk, Texas Trial Lawyers Association, 1978- 79; Associate, 1979-85, Partner, 1985-, Wood & Burney, now known as Wood, Burney, Cohn and Bradley, a Professional Corporation. *Memberships:* President, Nueces County Young Lawyers, 1984-85 Board Member, Nueces County Bar Association, 1980-82. *Honours:* Boss of the Year, Nueces County Legal Secretaries Association, 1985-86. *Hobbies:* Reading; Singing; Horses. *Address:* Wood & Burney, PO Box 2487, Corpus Christi, TX 78403, USA.

CONTRERAS Margarita Luisa, b. 25 Nov. 1956, Denver, Colorado, USA. Scientist; Assistant Professor. *Education:* BS, Biological Sciences, Colorado State University, 1978; PhD, Pharmacology, University of Colorado, 1985. *Appointments:* Postdoctoral Fellow, National Institute of General Medical Sciences, National Institutes of Health, Bethesda, 1985-87; National Institute of Child Health & Human Development, NIH, 1987-88; Assistant Professor, Michigan State University, 1988-. *Memberships:* Society of Neuroscience; Michigan State University Faculty, Professional Womens Association. *Honours:* Honorary Scholarship, 1974, President's Scholarship, 1975-78, Colorado State University; Phi Kappa Phi; Phi Beta Kappa; NICHD Intramural Research Training Award, 1987-88. *Hobbies:* Swimming; Reading; Cooking; Knitting. *Address:* Michigan State University, Dept. of Pharmacology and Toxicology, B403 Life Science Bldg., East Lansing, MI 48824, USA.

CONWAY Jennifer, b. 7 Aug. 1943, Kodaikanal, South India. Engraver on Glass. *Education:* Colchester School of Art. *Appointments:* Self employed. *Creative Works:* Large memorial screens in Barcombe Parish Church, Lewes, Sussex and in Little Waltham Parish Church, Essex; Windows in Weston Favell Parish Church, Northampton and in Sandhurst Parish Church, Kent; Doors in Bramford Parish Church, Suffolk; Screen in Irthingborough Parish Church, Northants.; Wainfleet Parish Church, Lincolnshire; Numerous engravings on private collections. Exhibitions: Invitations into group exhibitions: British Craft Centre, 1975; Victoria and Albert Museum, 1977; Portsmouth City Art Gallery, 1979; Ashmoleon Museum, 1979; Rochester Cathedral, 1979; The Bowes Museum, 1980; St Lawrence Jewry, 1980 and 1986; Prophesy and Vision, Bristol, Durham, London, 1982-83. *Membership:* Fellow, Guild of Glass Engravers. *Hobbies:* Playing violin; Growing and drawing plants; Intricate knitting. *Address:* 31 Oxford Road, Mistley, Manningtree, Essex, CO11 1BW, England.

CONWAY Jill Kathryn, b. 9 Oct. 1934, Hillston, Australia. Historian. m. 22 Dec. 1962. *Education:* BA, University of Sydney, Australia, 1958; PhD, Harvard, USA, 1969. *Appointments:* Lecturer, University of Sydney, Australia, 1958-60; Teaching Fellow, Harvard University, USA, 1961-63; Lecturer, 1964-68, Assistant Professor 1968-70, Associate Professor 1970-75, Graduate Faculty 1971-75, University of Toronto, Canada; Sophia Smith Professor, Smith College, 1975-85; Vice President, Internal Affairs, University of Toronto, 1973-75; President, Smith College, 1975-85; Visiting Scholar, Program in Science, Technology and Society, Massachusetts Institute of Technology, USA, 1985-. *Publications:* The Female Experience in 18th and 19th Century America, 1982; Women Reformers & American Culture, 1987; The Road from Coorain, 1989. *Memberships:* American Historical Association; Canadian Historical Association, Conference Board; Council on Foreign Relations. *Honours:* Honorary Doctorates from: St Thomas University, New Brunswick, Canada, 1974; Mount Holyoke College, South Hadley, Massachusetts, 1975; Amherst College, Massachusetts, 1976; York University, Toronto, Ontario, Canada, 1977; University of New Hampshire, 1977; Westfield State College, Massachusetts, 1979; Mount St Vincent University, Halifax, Nova Scotia, 1980; Wesleyan University, Middletown, Connecticut, 1980; University of Massachusetts, Amherst, 1981; University of Toronto, 1984; Queen's University, Kingston, Canada, 1984; Trinity College, Hartford, Connecticut, 1985; McGill University, Montreal, 1985; Potsdam College, SUNY, New York, 1986; Providence College, 1987; Smith College, 1988. *Hobbies:* Gardening; Music. *Address:* E-51, 209, MIT, Cambridge, MA 02139, USA.

CONWAY Pamela Ruth, b. 27 Sept. 1942, Keighley, Yorkshire, England. Company President. *Education:* Degree in Hotel and Catering Management, 1963. *Appointments:* Sales & Marketing Executive, Thomson Newspapers, 1963-67; Business Development Manager, Trident TV, 1967-78; Marketing Director,

1978-81, Managing Director, 1985-87, Michael Peters & Partners Ltd; Managing Director, Brand New Ltd., 1981-85; President, International Division, Michael Peters Group PLC, 1987-. *Memberships:* Institute of Directors; Marketing Society. *Honour:* Sir William Teeling Cup (Top Graduate), 1963. *Hobbies:* Tennis; Badminton; Theatre; Music; Ballet; Travel. *Address:* Putney, London SW 15, England.

COOK Alicia Skinner, b. 20 Jan. 1951, Greenville, Alabama, USA. University Professor; Psychologist, Private Practice. *Education:* BS 1971, MS 1972, University of Alabama; PhD, Arizona State University, 1975; Licensed Psychologist. *Appointments:* Psychologist, Private Practice, 1975-; Technical Specialist, United States Agency for International Development, 1988-89; Professor, Colorado State University, 1976-. *Publications:* Adult development and aging: Contemporary Perspectives, 1983; Dying and grieving: Lifespan and family perspectives, 1989; Over 30 research articles in professional journals. *Memberships:* American Psychological Association; Clinical Mwember, American Association for Marriage and Family Therapy; National Council on Family Relations. *Honours:* Fulbright Fellowship, 1979; Radcliffe Research Scholar, 1984; Women in Development Fellowship, 1988; Selected, one of top 50 family scholars in United States, 1989. *Address:* Department of Human Development and Family Studies, Colorado State University, Fort Collins, CO 80523, USA.

COOK Ann Jennalie, b. 19 Oct. 1934, Wewoka, Oklahoma, USA. Professor of English. m. (1) Howard L. Harrod, 31 Mar. 1956, 2 daughters, (2) John D. Whalley, 10 Sept. 1975. *Education:* BA 1956, MA 1959, University of Oklahoma; PhD, Vanderbilt University, 1972. *Appointments:* Instructor, English, University of Oklahoma, 1956-57; Secondary school teacher, North Carolina & Connecticut, 1958-61, 1964; Instructor, Southern Connecticut State College, 1962-63; Assistant Professor, University of South Carolina, 1972-74; Executive Secretary, Shakespeare Association of America, 1975-87; Professor of English, Vanderbilt University, 1977-. *Publications:* Books: Privileged Playgoers of Shakespeare's London 1576-1642, 1981; Making a Match: Courtship in Shakespeare & his Society, forthcoming. Associate Editor, Shakespeare Studies, 1973-80; Numerous articles & editorial boards. *Memberships include:* Offices: International Shakespeare Association; Folger Shakespeare Library; Renaissance Society of America. Member: Modern Language Association; American Association of University Professors; Malone Society; American Society for Theatre Research. *Honours include:* Phi Beta Kappa, 1955; Research Grant, Vanderbilt University, 1980; Study centre residence, Rockefeller Foundation, 1984; Guggenheim Foundation Fellow; Numerous fellowships, 1967-85. *Hobbies:* Theatre; Travel; Cooking; Art; Reading. *Address:* Department of English, Vanderbilt University, Nashville TN 37205, USA.

COOK Evelyn Margaret (Lyn) Waddell, b. 4 May 1918, Weston, Canada. Author. m. Robb John Waddell, 19 Sept. 1949, 1 son, 1 daughter. *Education:* BA, 1940, B.LSC, 1941, University of Toronto. *Appointments:* Librarian, Toronto Public Libraries, 1941-42; RCAF, 1942-46; Children's Librarian, 1946-47; Script Writer, Director, Narrator, A Doorway in Fairyland, CBC 1947-52; Creative Drama Teacher, New Play Society, 1956-65; Creator, Story Hour, Drama Festivals, Scarborugh Public Library, 1962-76. *Publications:* The Bells on Finland Street; The Little Magic Fiddler, 1951; Rebel on the Trail, 1953; Jady and the General, 1955; Pegeen and the Pilgrim, 1961; The Road to Kip's Cove, 1961; Samantha's Secret Room, 1963; The Brownie Handbook for Canada, 1965; The Secret of Willow Castle, 1966; The Magical Miss Mittens, 1970; A Treasure for Tony, 1981; Picture Story Books include: Toys from the Sky; Jolly Jean Pierre; If I Were All These; The Magic Pony; Sea Dreams. *Honours:* Recipient, many honours & awards. *Address:* 72 Cedarbrae Blvd., Scarborough, Ontario, Canada M1J 2K5.

COOK Janice Eleanor Nolan, b. 22 Nov. 1936, Middletown, Ohio, USA. Teacher. m. Kenneth John Cook, 16 May 1980. 1 son, 2 daughters, previous marriage. *Education:* BS, Miami University, 1971; MEd 1982, Kentucky Rank I 1987, Reading Specialist 1982, Special Education 1988, Xavier University. *Appointments:* Grades 1-2 1957-58, Pre-School-3, 1971-80, Middletown Public Schools, Ohio; Grades 1-2, Boone County Schools, Kentucky, 1980-, including Resource Teacher, Kentucky Intership Programme, 1985-89. *Memberships:* National & Kentucky Education Associations; Offices, Boone County Education Association; Association for Supervision & Curriculum Development; International Reading Association. Also: Offices, Boone County Republican Party. *Honours:* Kentucky Incentive Grant, 1986-87; Kentucky Colonel. *Hobbies & interests:* Computers; Reading; Children; Politics. *Address:* 2028 West Horizon Drive, Hebron, Kentucky 41048, USA.

COOK Lyn (Evelyn Margaret Waddell), b. 4 May 1918, Weston, Ontario, Canada. Author; Lecturer. m. Robb John Waddell, 19 Sept. 1949, 1 son, 1 daughter. *Education:* BA 1940, BLS 1941, University of Toronto. *Appointments:* Librarian, Toronto Public Libraries, 1941-42; Meterological observer, Royal Canadian Air Force, WD, 1942-46; Children's Librarian, Sudbury Public Library, 1946-47; Script Writer, Director, Narrator, CBC Radio, 1947-52; Creative Drama Teacher, New Play Society, 1956-65. *Publications include:* Children's Literature: Bells on Finland Street, 1950, German translation; Little Magic Fiddler, 1951, 1981; Jady & the General, 1955; Samantha's Secret Room, 1963, 1973; Secret of Willow Castle, 1966, 1984; Treasure for Tony, 1981. Picture-Story Books: Toys from the Sky, 1972; If I Were All These, 1973; Sea Dreams, 1981. *Memberships:* Writer's Union of Canada; Canadian Society of Authors, Illustrators & Performers. *Honour:* Vicky Metcalf Award, 1978. *Hobbies:* Music; Reading; Walking; Landscape Painting. *Address:* 72 Cedarbrae Boulevard, Scarborough, Ontario, Canada M1J 2K5.

COOK Mary Lynn Bostick, b. 3 June 1934, Portales, New Mexico, USA. President, nonprofit organization; Instructor/Facilitator. m. Curtis Clifton Cook, 27 Feb. 1954. 1 son, 1 daughter. *Education:* Studied numerous courses, 1975-88. *Appointments:* Director, Driver Improvement, 1973-80; President, Oklahoma Training Systems Institute, nonprofit organization offering alternative programs such as driver improvement and alcohol/drug abuse, 1980-; Red Cross volunteer worker and telerecruiter, 1988; Instructor, three phases of CPR (Cardiopulmonary Resuscitation) adult, child and infant, 1989. *Publications:* Books: Driver Improvement, 1980; Alcohol/Drug Abuse Programs, 1980; revised annually. *Memberships:* National Association of Female Executives; Oklahoma DUI School Administrators; American Red Cross Volunteers; Cage Bird Society; American Budgerigar Society. *Honours:* National Honour Society; Three Linz Scholastic Awards; Picture in local newspaper when working with Cub Scouts; Instructor Achievement Award, National Safety Council, 3 times; Special article, local newspaper for ability as an instructor and outstanding rapport with teenagers. *Hobbies:* Aviculture; Horticulture. *Address:* Oklahoma Training Systems Institute, 9999 N 112th E Avenue (Rear), Owasso, Oklahoma 74055, USA.

COOK Nancy Ellen, b. 9 Sept. 1945, San Diego, California, USA. Educator, University Professor. m. Jerry E Cook, 30 Jan. 1965. 1 son, 1 daughter. *Education:* Graduate in Japanese with honors, Army Language School, 1966; BS, University of California, San Diego, 1967; MBA, Harvard, 1972; PhD, University of California, Los Angeles, 1978. *Appointments:* Consultant, Pierl Imports, Fort Worth, Texas, 1971-72; Japan Manager, Trammell Crow Company, Tokyo, Japan, 1972-74; Associate Professor of International Business & Accounting, University of San Diego, San Diego, USA, 1977-. *Publications:* Control of Foreign Subsidiaries: The Electronics Industry Case, with Greg Gaerther; Auditor Stress and Time Budgets: A Replication, with Tim Kelley; Working Women: A US and Japanese Comparison. *Memberships:* American Association of Accountants, President of Behavioral Section, 1984-85; Academy of International Business, Annual Meeting Local Chair, 1988; National Association of Accountants, Student Chapter Advisor, 1988. *Honours:* Beta Gamma Sigma, 1976; Beta Alpha Psi, 1977. *Hobbies:* Music (vocal, piano, organ). *Address:* University of San Diego, Alcala Park, San Diego, CA 92110, USA.

COOK Rebecca Johnson, b. 2 Dec. 1946, Bennington, Vermont, USA. Law Teacher. m. 26 Apr. 1987. *Education:* AB, Columbia University, 1970; MA, Tufts University, 1972; MPA, Harvard University, 1973; JD, Georgetown University Law Centre, 1982; Attorney, Washington DC Bar, 1983; LLM, Columbia University School of Law, 1988. *Appointments include:* Director, Law Programme, International Planned Parenthood Federation, London, UK, 1973-78; Associate, Beveridge, Fairbanks & Diamond, Washington DC, USA, 1980; Various offices including Assistant Professor of Clinical Public Health, Division of Population & Family Health, School of Public Health, Columbia University, 1983-87; Assistant Professor, Faculties of Law & Medicine & Member, Law & Health Administration, School of Graduate Studies, University of Toronto, Canada, 1987-. Adjunct Faculties, Columbia University & University of Minnesota; Legal consultancies & appointments, World Health Organisation (Geneva), International Federation of Gynaecology & Obstetrics (London), Commonwealth Secretariat (London); Various editorial advisory boards, board of directors. *Publications include:* Author, co-author, editor, numerous books, chapters, monographs, articles in fields of law, health, population. *Address:* Faculty of Law, University of Toronto, Toronto, Canada M5S 2C5.

COOK Sue, b. 30 Mar. 1949, Ruislip, Middlesex, England. Broadcaster. m. 20 May 1981, 1 son, 1 daughter. *Education:* BA, honours, Leicester University, 1971. *Appointments:* Broadcaster/Producer, Capital Radio 1972-74; Presenter, You and Yours, Radio 4 programme, and BBC World Service, 1974-78; Presenter, Nationwide, 1978-83; Out of Court, Crimewatch UK, Daytime Live, Children in Need, BBC TV; Various TV & Radio Quiz programmes including: Call My Bluff; Face the Music. *Hobbies:* Singing; Travelling Abroad; Crosswords; Learning Piano & Saxophone; Listening to People Talking. *Address:* c/o Michael Ladkin, 2a Warwick Place North, London SW1, England.

COOK-LYNN Elizabeth, b. 17 Nov. 1930, Fort Thompson, South Dakota, USA. Associate Professor of Native American Studies. m. (1) Melvin Traversie Cook, 1953, (2) C. J. Lynn, 1973, 1 son, 3 daughters. *Education:* BS, Journalism, English, South Dakota State University, Brookings, 1952; MA, Psychology, Education, South Dakota University, Vermillin, 1971; Further graduate work: UNL, Lincoln, Nebraska and New Mexico State University, Las Cruces. *Appointments:* Secondary teaching; Newspaper work; Associate Professor, Eastern Washington University, Cheney, Washington, 1972-. *Publications:* The Badger Said Thus, poetry chapbook, 1981; Seek the House of Relatives, 1984; Novel in progress; The Power of Horse, collection of short stories, 1990; Founding Editor, The Wicazo SA Review, Journal of Native American Studies, 1985. *Honours:* NEH Fellowship, Historical Sociological Perspectives on Literary Criticis, Stanford University, 1978; Ford Foundation Fellowship Panelist for Minority Scholars, 1989; Writer-in-Resident, Summer, Evergreen College, Olympia, Washington, 1989. *Address:* MS 25-188 Indian Studies, Eastern Washington University, Cheney, WA 99004, USA.

COOKE Cynthia Hughes, b. 18 Oct. 1959, Farmville, North Carolina, USA. Commercial Real Estate Broker & Financier. 1 son. *Education:* Pitt Commercial College, 1980; Memphis College, Tennessee, 1981; Cecil Lawter School of Real Estate, 1981; Arizona School of Real Estate, 1983. *Appointments:* Dan Stewart Company, 1981; Cottonwood Real Estate & Investment, 1982; DDI Properties, 1983; Owner/broker, Paragon Financial, & C&H Realty Resources, 1983-; Developer, Blue Ridge Park. *Memberships:* Arizona Association of Realtors; Executive Females National Association; Women's Council of Realtors. *Honours:* 3 Outstnding Young Women of Phoenix, 1985; President's Round Table Award, 1982; Recognition, Governor Moffard, 1985; Baseball coaching awards, 1987, 1988; Soccer coaching award, 1984. *Hobbies:* Tennis; Baseball; Soccer; Skiing; Horseback riding. *Address:* 109 West Honeysuckle, Litchfield Park, Arizona 85340, USA.

COOKE Marcia, b. 16 Oct. 1954, Sumter, South Carolina, USA. US District Court Magistrate. m. Marc R. Shelton, 15 June 1985. *Education:* BS, Foreign Service, Georgetown University, Washington DC, 1975; JD, Wayne State University Law School, 1977. *Appointments:* Staff Attorney, Wayne County Neighborhood Legal Services, Michigan, 1978-79; Deputy Defender, Deputy Defenders Office, Michigan, 1979-80; Assistant US Attorney, Criminal Division, US Attorneys Office, Eastern District of Michigan, 1980-83; Associate, Litigation Department, Miro, Miro and Weiner, 1983-84; US District Court Magistrate, Eastern District of Michigan, 1984-; Adjunct Professor, Wayne State University Law School, 1986-. *Publications:* TWM Mfg Co., Inc. v. Dura Dorp, Report of Special Master, 1984; Sixth Annual Survey of Sixth Circuit Law - Criminal Procedure (with Amy R.Snell), 1985. *Memberships:* American Bar Association; Federal Bar Association; Michigan Black Judges Association; National Institute for Trial Advocacy. *Hobbies:* Movies; Travel. *Address:* 238 US Courthouse, Detroit, MI 48226, USA.

COOKE Sara Mullin Graff, b. 29 Dec. 1935, Philadelphia, Pennsylvania, USA. Kindergarten Teacher; Child Care, Fundraising, Daisy Day, the Childrens Hospital of Philadelphia. m. Peter Fischer Cooke, 29 June 1963, divorced 1984. 1 son, 4 daughters (two sets of twins). *Education:* BA, The Madeira School, Virginia, 1953; AA, The Bennett College, New York, 1955; Child Education Foundation, New York City; West Chester State College, Pennsylvania. *Appointments:* The Woodlynde School, 1956-58; Sara Bircher's Kindergarten, 1958-62; The Tarleton School, 1962-63; Marketing Executive, FCI Marking Coordinators, New York City, 1982-86; Child Care Fundraising, Childrens Hospital of Philadelphia, 1969-90. *Memberships:* GOP Victory Fund Sponsor, 1983-; The Philadelphia Cricket Club; The Acorn Club; National Society of Colonial Dames; The St Martin-in-the-Fields Episcopal Church; PA Association of Hospital Auxiliaries, Health Chairman, 1980-; Women's Committee, Children's Hospital of Philadelphia, President, 1987-88; Sustainers Garden Club, Jr League of Philadelphia, on Board, 1987-; Commonwealth Board of Women's Medical College, 1984-. *Honours:* Mentioned in A Tricentennial History of The William Penn Charter School for originating and leading their school fund raising. *Hobbies:* Started Mothers of Twins Club; Tennis; Antiques; collecting dolls; Photography; Entertaining. *Address:* Oak Hall, 529 East Gravers Lane, Philadelphia, Pennsylvania, USA.

COOL Kim Patmore, b. 1 Feb. 1940, Cleveland, Ohio, USA. Retail Store Owner; Artist; Author. m. Kenneth A Cool, Jr, 11 Mar. 1963. 1 daughter. *Education:* BA, Sweet Briar College, 1962. *Appointments:* Psychometrist, Pradco, Cleveland, Ohio, 1962-63; Self employed Artist, 1963-72; Owner, Vice President, And Sew On, Inc, Ohio, 1974-. *Publications:* How to Market Needlepoint - The Definitive Manual, Co-author with Iona Dettelbach, 1988. *Memberships:* Regional Director/Exec. Board/Class Secretary/Club President, Sweet Briar College Alumnae Association; Gold Test Judge/Senior Competition and Sectional Precision Judge/Member Judges Education & Training Committee/Singles and Pairs Committees, United States Figure Skating Association; Associate Retail Member, The National Needlework Association; Southeastern Yarncrafters Association; National Standards Council of American Embroiderers. *Honours:* Regional Champion, Ladies Curling, United States

Curling Association, ranked 7th in US, 1986 and 1987; Invited and attended first US Olympic training Camp for Women Curlers, 1986; Numerous awards for needlework. *Hobbies:* Figure skating; Curling; Tennis; Photography; Writing; Needlework. *Address:* 14500 Washington Blvd, University Heights, Ohio 44118, USA.

COOLEY Loralee Coleman, b. 17 Jan. 1943, Charleston, Illinois, USA. Storyteller. m. Edwin Mark Cooley, 1 July 1967, 4 foster-daughters. *Education:* BA, Music, Eastern Illinois University, 1965; Graduate work, Southern Baptist Theological Seminary 1965-67, Arizona State University 1972-74. *Appointments:* Piano, music teacher, various schools, 1967-69; Women's Programme Director, WDXB-Radio, Chattanooga, Tennessee, 1969-70; Assistant Editor, New Age magazine, Washington DC, 1970-72; Publicity Coordinator, Firebird Lake, Phoenix, Arizona, 1975; Assistant Librarian, Casa Grande Public Library, Arizona, 1975-76; Professional storyteller, 1977-. *Creative works include:* Wedding Cantata, 1967; Various choral compositions; Current project: Stories of the 2 Georgias, Soviet & US (book & theatre piece). *Memberships:* Founder, President (Chairman of Bards, Chief Bard), Southern Order of Storytellers, professional guild, Southeastern USA; National Association for Preservation & Perpetuation of Storytelling; American Guild of Organists; International Reading Asociation; Co-Chair, Casa Grande Bicentennial Committee, 1976. *Honours:* Miss Louisville, Kentucky, 1966; Seanachie Award, Southern Order of Storytellers, 1986; Invited Member, Conference on Communications, Kansas City, Missouri, 1984. *Hobbies:* Travel; Reading; Thinking of new ideas for storytelling, workshops, theatre; Playing with dogs. *Address:* Storyspinning, 2600 South Highway 187, Anderson, South Carolina 29624, USA.

COOLIDGE Martha Patterson, b. 17 Aug. 1946, New Haven, Connecticut, USA. Motion Picture Director. m. Michael Backes, 22 Mar. 1984. *Education:* BFA, Rhode Island School of Design, 1968; MFA, Institute of Film and Television, New York University School of the Arts, 1971. *Appointments:* Produced films independently, 1972-79; Directed films for cinema and TV, 1973, 1978-. Participated in various film festivals. *Creative works:* David: Off and On, 1972; More than a School, 1973; Old-fashioned Woman, 1974; Not a Pretty Picture, 1975; Trouble Shooters, Phoenix Films, 1978; Bimbo, 1978-79; The Winners, CBC, 1980; The City Girl, Moon Pictures, 1981-84; Valley Girl, Atlantic Releasing, 1983; Joy of Sex, Paramount, 1984; Real Genius, Tri-Star, 1985; Twilight Zone, Night of the Meek, Quarentine, CBS, 1985, 1986; Sledge Hammer (pilot), ABC, 1986. *Memberships:* Director's Guild of America; Director;s Guild of Canada; Screen Actor's Guild; The Association of Independent Film and Videomakers Inc, Founder, Past Chairman of Board, Past Vice-President. *Honours:* John Grierson Award, American Film Festival, 1973; 3 Blue Ribbons, American Film Festival, 1974, 1975, 1976; 1st prize, Melbourne Film Festival, 1979; 1st Prize, Thessaloniki Film Festival, 1979; prix de Publique, Chamrousse Comedy Film Festival, 1986. *Hobbies:* Theatre; Singing; Skiing; Oz; Painting and drawing. *Address:* 2040 Avenue of the Stars, Suite 400, Century City, CA 90067, USA.

COOMBS Elizabeth F, b. 2 July 1910, Wildwood, New Jersey, USA. Retired. *Education:* BS, Ursinus College, 1931; MA, Columbia University, 1939; Boston University; Rutgers University; Glassboro State; Trenton State. *Appointments:* Teacher, Mathematics, Millville Bd of Education, Millville, New Jersey, 1931-64. *Memberships:* PTA, Millville High School, Secretary 2 terms; First Advisor of Nat Honor Society; Chr Senior Class Trip; Speaker on New Math, Millville Educ Assoc; Truancy Assistant; Juvenile Conference Committee of City of Millville; Red Cross; Leadership in Professional and Community activities. *Honours:* Chairman, Mathematics Dept, Millville High School; Delta Kappa Gamma International; Beta Chapter; Teacher of the Year (twice), Millville High School. *Hobbies:* Tutoring; Knitting; Gardening; Clerking; Assisting with bazaar

work. *Address:* 320 E 22nd Ave P O B 28, North Wildwood, NJ 08260, USA.

COOPER Artemis Clare, b. 22 Apr. 1953, London, England. Writer. m. Antony Beevor, 1 Feb. 1986. *Education:* BA (2nd class) English, St Hugh's College, Oxford, 1972-75. *Appointments:* Assistant English Teacher, Alexandria University, Egypt, 1975-76; Odd jobs in USA, 1976-80; Assistant Historic Buildings Representative, The National Trust, 1981-82. *Publications:* A Durable Fire, 1983; The Diana Cooper Scrapbook, 1987; Cairo in The War, 1989. *Memberships:* The National Trust; Amnesty International; The Royal Geographical Society. *Hobbies:* Travelling; Cooking; Peering through other people's windows. *Address:* 54 St Maur Road, London SW6 4DP, England.

COOPER Dona Hanks, b. 5 Nov. 1950, Oklahoma City, USA. Story Analyst. *Education:* BA, Theatre, American University, 1972; Postgraduate Work, Theatre, University of Minnesota, 1972-73. *Appointments:* Caseworker, US Senator Marlow Cook, Washington DC, 1973- 74, US Representative B. A. Gilman, 1974-75; Artistic Director, American Society of Theatre Arts, 1975-79; Producer, Mr Henry's Dinner Theatre, 1979- 80; Managing Director, Ensemble Studio Theatre, Los Angeles, 1979-81; Freelance Story Analyst, HBO, NBC and Metro Media, 1982-87; Director, Story Dept., NB TV Network, 1987. *Publications:* (Plays) The Works of Lizzie Bordon, 1981; California Calico, 1982; The Lone Star State, 1983; Rules of the House, 1984. *Memberships:* National Organization of Women; National Organization of Female Executives; Dramatist Guild. *Honours:* Phi Beta Phi, 1972. *Hobbies:* Quilting; Researching Womens Roles in American History. *Address:* Star Rute Box 8068 Frazier Park, CA 93225, USA.

COOPER Joan Davies, b. 12 Aug. 1914, Droylsden, Lancashire, England. Researcher. *Education:* BA 1935, Teacher's Diploma and Social Work Training, 1936-38, University of Manchester; Social Work Studies, London, 1976-77. *Appointments:* Teaching Posts, 1938-41; Assistant Director of Education, Derbyshire, 1941-48; Children's Officer, East Sussex, 1948-65; Chief Inspector, Children's Department Home Office, 1965-71; Director, Social Work Service, Department of Health and Social Security, 1971-76. *Publications:* Patterns of Family Placement, 1978; Group work with Elderly People in Hospital, 1980; Creation of the British Personal Social Services, 1983. *Memberships:* Vice President National Children's Bureau, 1965-; Social Science Research Council, 1972-76; Chairman Parents for Children, 1979-87; Chairman Council for Education & Training in Social Work, 1984-87; Chairman, International Expert Conference on Access to Personal Records, 1987. *Memberships:* CB, 1972; Fellow Royal Anthropological Institute since 1972; Social Science Research Council Award, 1980-81; Leverhulme Fellowship, 1984-85; Honorary Visiting Research Fellow, University of Sussex, 1979. *Hobbies:* Walking; Travel; Opera. *Address:* 2A Gallows Bank, Abinger Place, Lewes, Sussex BN7 2QA, England.

COOPER Marilyn Mace, b. 9 Aug. 1950, Los Angeles, California, USA. Bank Card Executive. 3 sons. *Education:* BA Mathematics 1971, MA Education 1975, California State University, Los Angeles; MBA, Finance, University of Southern California, 1985; Bank Card Management School, 1987; MISR Certificate, Harvard Business School, 1988. *Appointments:* Trust Systems Development 1980-82, Elec Systems Development 1982-85, SPNB; Global Openings Development 1985, Executive Information Systems 1985-86, Bank Card Services 1986-89, Security Pacific Automation Company; Bank Card Executive, Security Pacific Bank, 1989-. *Memberships:* Past President, member, San Gabriel Board of Education; Various professional organisations. *Hobbies:* Golf; Tennis; Sewing; Reading. *Address:* 1032 West Roses Road, San Gabriel, California 91775, USA.

COOPER Sandra Lenore Aka Sonni, b. 9 July 1934, Brooklyn, New York, USA. Writer. m. 23 Jan. 1955, 1 son, 1 daughter. *Education:* BFA, University of Colorado, 1955; Cooper Union Art School. *Education:* Assistant Director, Council, 8 Northern Indian Pueblos, 1971-75; President, Creative Enterprises, 1976-; Vice President, Board Chair, Apogee Research Corporation, 1986-. *Creative works include:* Books: Black Fire; Forbidden Passion; Love Trap. Paintings in private collections & museums. *Memberships:* Past Vice President, New Mexico branch, Screen Actors Guild; Science Fiction Writers of America. *Hobbies:* American Indians; Space sciences. *Address:* 76 Santa Ana Avenue, Long Beach, California 90803, USA.

COOPER Virginia Leah Adkins, b. 15 Sept. 1940, Clintwood, Virginia, USA. President, Cooper & Associates. m. Lieutenant General Kenneth Banks Cooper, 29 Dec. 1979. *Education:* BA Communications, University of Alabama, 1977. *Appointments:* US Army Medical Command, Europe (Heidelberg), 1973-76; Jacksonville Florida Chamber of Commerce, 1978-79; Alexandria Economic Development Authority, 1982-84; Vice President Corporate Affairs, Mount Vernon Realty, Inc, 1984-88. *Memberships:* Kiwanis Club of Washington DC; Greater Washington Board of Trade; Founder and Honorary Lifetime Member, Greater Washington Employee Relocation Council; Public Relations Society of America; Alexandria Volunteer Bureau. *Honours:* Joseph P Kennedy Jr, Foundation Award, 1969; Outstanding State Chairman, Alabama Jayceettes, 1969; Outstanding Young Women of America, 1969. *Hobbies:* Writing cookbook; International travel. *Address:* 6101 Edsall Road No 1801, Alexandria, VA 22304, USA.

COPELAND Ann (Virginia W. Furtwangler), b. 16 Dec. 1932, Hartford, USA. Author; Teacher. m. 17 Aug. 1968, 2 sons. *Education:* BA, College of New Rochelle, 1954; MA, Catholic University of America, 1959; PhD, English, Cornell University. *Appointments:* Instructor, English, College of New Rochelle, 1963-66, Indiana University, 1970-71; Assistant Professor, English, Mt. Allison University, 1976-77; Visiting Fiction Writer, College of Idaho, 1980; Professor, English, Linfield College, 1980-81; Visiting Fiction Writer, University of Idaho, 1986. *Publications:* At Peace, 1978; The Back Room, 1979; Earhen Vessels, 1984; The Golden Thread, 1989; many stories in American & Canadian journals. *Memberships:* Writers Union of Canada; International Womens Writing Guild; Associated Writing Programmes. *Honours:* Contributors Prize, Canadian Fiction Managazine, 1975; Canada Council Short Term Arts Grant, 1977; NEA Creative Writing Fellowship, 1978; Canada Council Arts Grant, 1980, 1988. *Hobbies:* Music; Piano, Organ. *Address:* P.O. 1450, Sackville, N.B. Canada EOA 3C0.

COPELAND Ida Elaine, b. 3 Nov. 1943, Catawba, South Carolina, USA. Associate Dean, Graduate College. m. Robert McDaniel Copeland, 26 Sept. 1964. 1 son. *Education:* BS, 1964; MAT, 1971; PhD, 1974, MBA, 1987. *Appointments:* High School Science Teacher, 1964-70; Psychological Counsellor, 1970-74; Assistant Dean Graduate College 1976-83, Associate Dean 1983-, Associate Professor 1988-, University of Illinois, Champaign. *Publications:* Trends in Participation in Graduate Education; Cross- Cultural Counselling and Psychotherapy: An Historical Perspective; A Minority Graduate Student Orientation Program; Minority Populations and Traditional Counselling Programs: Some Alternatives; Oppressed Conditions and the Mental Health Needs of Low-Income Black Women. *Memberships:* American Psychological Association; American Association of Counselling and Development; American Educational Research Assoc; National Association for Women Deans, Administrators and Counsellors Vice President, 1983-85, President Elect 1987-88, President 1988-89. *Honours:* President, National Association for Women Deans, Administrators and Counsellors, 1988-89; Outstanding Faculty Award, Black Student Association, 1987; Distinguished Alumni Award, National Equal Opportunity Education

Association, 1986; Alpha Kappa Mu, National Honour Society. *Interests:* Cross-Cultural Counselling; Minorities in Higher Education. *Address:* 34 Ashley Lane, Champaign, Illinois 61820, USA.

COPPS Sheila Maureen, b. 27 Nov. 1952, Hamilton, Ontario, Canada. Member of Parliament. m. Ric Marrero, 6 July 1985, 1 daughter. *Education:* Hon. BA, University of Western Ontario, 1974. *Appointments:* Journalist: Ottawa Citizen, 1974-76, Hamilton Spectator, 1977; Constituency Assistant, 1977-81; Member of Ontario Legislation, 1981-84; Member, Federal Parliament, 1984-. *Publication:* Nobody's Baby, 1986. *Memberships:* Standing Committee on National Health & Welfare. *Address:* 440 C, House of Commons, Ottawa, Ontario, Canada K1A 0A6.

CORBIT Irene Elizabeth, b. 18 July 1930, Detroit, Michigan, USA. Art Psychotherapist. m. Bernard Gerald Corbit, 7 Jan. 1949. 2 sons, 1 daughter. *Education:* BA, Houston International University, 1976; MA, University of Houston, Clear Lake, 1978; Certificate in Group and Family Psychotherapy, HGPS, 1981; PhD, Union Graduate School, 1985. *Appointments:* Private practice, Houston, 1979-; Adjunct Faculty, University of Houston, Clear Lake, 1982-; Faculty, Houston International University, 1988-; Faculty the C G Jung Educational Center, Houston, 1973-. *Publications:* Chapter in book Advances in Art Therapy, Visual Transitions: Metaphor for Change, with Jerry L Fryrear, 1989; Reflections on Integrative Art Therapy, 1987. *Memberships:* Speaker, Executive Board Member, The American Art Therapy Association; President, South Texas Art Therapy Association; Advisory Board, Institute Chair, Houston Group Psychotherapy Society; American Group Psychotherapy Association. *Hobbies:* Art and sculpting; Photography; Hiking; Presenting growth workshops in art therapy and photo therapy. *Address:* 7722 Braesview Lane, Houston, Texas 77071, USA.

CORBITT Gretchen Johnson, b. 20 Dec. 1920, Delway, North Carolina, USA. Retired General Music Teacher. m. John C. Corbitt, 22 Dec. 1949, 1 son, 3 daughters. *Education:* Mars Hill Junior College, 1938-40; AB, Meredith College, 1943; Southwestern Theological Seminary, 1948-50; Graduate studies, Appalachian State University, 1975. *Appointments:* Teacher, General Music, Marion, North Carolina, 1969-78; Private Teacher, Organ and Piano, 1969-78; Director, Children's Theatre, 1971-72; Director, Marion Boys Choir, 1974-75; Columnist, local newspaper, 1979-82. *Publications:* Staff Notes, article, 1976; Gone, non-fiction, 1976. *Memberships:* North Carolina Music Association; National Music Association; PEN Women; North Carolina Chapter, North Carolina Symphony; Daughters of the American Revolution. *Honours:* Trustee, Meredith College, 1984-88; 1st Place Award for paper on Associational Missions: Mountain Style, sponsored North Carolina Baptist Historical Society. *Hobbies:* Reading; Hiking; Cooking. *Address:* PO Box 303, Ridgecrest, NC 28770, USA.

CORCORAN Mary (Elizabeth), b. 15 Aug. 1921, Providence, Rhode Island, USA. Professor Emeritus of Educational Psychology. *Education:* BA, cum laude, Hunter College, 1947; MA, Stanford University, 1948; PhD, University of Minnesota, 1957; Lic Consulting Psychologist, State of Minnesota, 1976. *Appointments:* Instructor, Psychology, University of Vermont, Burlington, 1948-50; Assoc Ed, Education Testing Service, Princeton, New Jersey, 1950-53; Assistant then Associate Professor 1957-67, Professor Educactional Psychology & Higher Education 1967-86, Professor Emeritus, 1987-, University of Minneapolis. *Publications:* Contributor of articles in professional journals. *Memberships:* Association for Institutional Research, Bd of Directors, Forum Publications Ed; Assoc for Studies in Higher Education, Chair of Governing Board; American Educational Research Association; American Psychological Association. *Honours:* Merit Award, Association for Studies in Higher Education, 1980; Distinguished Member, Association for Institutional Research, 1981; Best Paper Award,

Association for Institutional Research, ·1984. *Hobby:* Nature study. *Address:* 400 Groveland Ave So No 209, Minneapolis, MN 55403, USA.

CORDES Loverne Christian, b. 13 Feb. 1927, Cleveland, Ohio, USA. Interior Designer. m. William Peter Cordes, 14 Nov. 1959, 1 son, 1 daughter. *Education:* BS, Purdue University, 1949. *Appointments:* Interior Designer, Buyer, Fred Epple Co, 1949-67; Owner, Loverne Christian Cordes FASID interior design firm, 1967-. *Memberships:* Fellow, Member, National Committee of Fellows and National Awards Committee, former Vice-President, East Central Region, former National Board Member, former Ohio North Chapter President, American Society of Interior Designers; Professional Affiliate, American Institute of Architects; Past President, Ohio Chapter, National Home Fashion League; Past President, Kappa Kappa Gamma Cleveland Alumnae Association; Board, Dunham Tavern Museum; Past President, Dunham Dames; Steering Committee, American Furniture Collectors; National Trust for Historic Preservation; Western Reserve Historical Society; Women's Advisory Council; Cleveland Museum of Art; Chagrin Falls Historical Society; International Platformm Association; Nature Conservancy; Audubon Society; Plymouth Church, United Church of Christ; Cleveland Garden Center; Past President, Arcadian Garden Club; Dogwood Valley Garden Club; Architectural Historians; Chagrin Valley Country Club; The Cotillion Society of Cleveland. *Honours:* 1st National Presidential Citation, 1973, Presidential Citations, 1974, 1975, 1978, American Society of Interior Designers; Represented USA at 1st International Design Federation Conference, Stockholm, Sweden; Represented USA at 1st design seminar, USSR. *Address:* 60 S Franklin Street, Chagrin Falls, OH 44022, USA.

CORDNER Jacqueline Telfer Willingham, b. 28 Feb. 1922, Sparkill, New York, New York, USA. Registered Nurse; Author. m. Harold J. Cordner Jr., 24 Nov. 1969. *Education:* RN, 1942; BA, 1970. *Appointments:* Assistant Supervisor, Operating Room, Roosevelt Hospital, 1951-54; Director, Operating Room, Hackenseck Medical Centre, 1955-74; Director, Operating Room, Riverside General Hospital, Secaucus, N.J., 1975-81. *Publications:* Logic of Operating Room Nursing, 3rd edition 1984; Operating Room Management, 1982; Teaching Film for Aorn. *Membership:* Association of Operating Room Nurses. *Honours:* Writing Award. *Address:* 9 Lynn Court, Woodcliff Lake, NJ 07675, USA.

COREA Genoveffa (Gena), b. 18 July 1946, Weymouth, Massachusetts, USA. Writer; Feminist Activist. m. Thomas E. Marlin, 22 May 1971. *Education:* BA, University of Massachusetts, 1971. *Appointments include:* Journalist, including Amherst Record 1969-70, Berkshire Eagle 1967-68, Holyoke Transcript 1971-73; Syndicated columnist, New Republic Features Syndicate, 1973-75; Latin & North American co-editor, co-founder, journal Reproductive & Genetic Engineering: International Feminist Analysis; Lecturer, USA & abroad; Associate director, Institute on Women and Technology. *Publications include:* Books: Hidden Malpractice: How American Medicine Mistreats Women, 1977, 1985; Mother Machine: Reproductive Technologies from Artificial Insemination to Artificial Wombs, 1985 (German & Japanese translations). Numerous book chapters, obstetrics & reproduction, USA, UK, France, Germany, Austria, Canada; Articles on Northern Ireland, South Africa, Israel, obstetrics reform, various journals; Research, 1st world survey revealing success rate deception, in-vitro fertilisation (test-tube baby) clinics. *Honours include:* Grants, Fund for Investigative Reporting 1984 and 1989; European Parliament & Skaggs Foundation 1985, Skaggs Foundation 1987 and 1990; Book selected, Editor's Choice, New York Times Review of Books, 1977. *Address:* 34 Lloyd Street, Winchester, Massachusetts 01890, USA.

CORLEY Diana, b. 4 Dec. 1946, Russelleville, Arkansas, USA. College Professor. *Education:* Diploma,

United Township High School; BS, 1968, MS, 1970, Illinois State University; PhD, University of Maryland, 1986. *Appointments:* Cooperative Extension Service, summers 1967; Teacher, Davenport Public Schools, 1969-70; Teaching Assistant, Illinois State University, 1969-70; Faculty, Black Hawk College, 1970-; University of Maryland, 1981-83. *Publications:* Poetry in National Anthology of College Poetry, 1967, 1968; Articles in professional journals, 1971-86; Articles in religious magazines, 1978, 1986. *Memberships:* Convention Delegate, Speech Communication Association; Friends of Art; US-China People's Friendship Association, 1984-85; Central States Speech Association, 1971-75, Convention Delegate, 1983; Convention Delegate, Chairperson of Publication Committee, Chairpersons of Awards Committee, Treasurer, International Listening Association; Board of Directors, Towne Crest Home Owners, 1983-87; Cooperative Extension Foundation Board of Directors, 1985; National Geographic Society. *Honours:* 4-H awards, 1958-67; Academic awards, Illinois State University, 1965-68; Outstanding Leader, Cooperative Extension, 1967; President and Vice-President, Sigma Tau Delta, 1967-68; Nominated Outstanding Young Educator, 1974; Co-recipient, University of Maryland Research Grant. *Hobbies:* Walking; Reading; Theatre; Collecting photography, art and trinket boxes; Photography. *Address:* 1315C Ninth Street, Moline, IL 61265, USA.

CORNE Sharron Zenith, b. Winnipeg, Canada. Artist; Activist. *Education:* Bachelor of Pedagogy, Faculty of Education; BFA (Hons), School of Art, University of Manitoba, Canada; Feminist Art Program, Los Angeles, California, USA. Prominent feminist activist in Canada during the 1970s, campaigning for equal rights for female artists. *Creative works:* Numerous One-person, Group and Co-ordinated Art Exhibitions including: Powerhouse Gallery, Montreal, 1981; Gallery III, University of Manitoba, Winnipeg, 1985; Augsburg College, Minneapolis, 1986; Ace Art, 1988; Articule, Montreal; Plug In, Winnipeg; Main Access Gallery, Arstpace, Winnipeg, Thomas Gallery Winnipeg, Plains Museum, Moorhead, Minnesota, Katherine Nash Gallery, University of Minnesota, Saskatchewan Cultural Exchange Society, Winnipeg Art Gallery, 1987; Del Bello Gallery Toronto; Woman As Viewer exhibition, Winnipeg Art Gallery, First national juried exhibition of Canadian women artists, 1975. *Publications:* Author of numerous articles and reports to professional journals and lectures to associations. *Memberships include:* International Women's Art Conference 1987, Visual Arts Commission; Manitoba representative, Planning Committee, National Women Art Conference, London; Chairperson, Women in the Arts, Manitoba; Board Member, Manitoba Arts Council; National Capital Commission, Ottawa, Advisory Committee on the Arts, Government of Canada; Manitoba Department of Education, consultant. *Honours:* Canada Council, Secretary of State, Dept of Cultural Affairs, Manitoba Government and City of Winnipeg grants to organize exhibition at Winnipeg Art Gallery, 1975; Woman of the Year Award, Arts, YWCA, 1980; Secretary of State research grant, 1981; Manitoba Department of Cultural Affairs and Secretary of State Department, Canada grants, 1984. *Hobbies:* Collecting collectables and junk; Walking; Travel; Films; Reading. *Address:* 207 Park Blvd North, Winnipeg, Manitoba, R3P 0G6, Canada.

CORNER Beryl Dorothy, b. 9 Dec. 1910, Bristol, England. Consultant Paediatrician. *Education:* MBBS, 1934; MRCS, LRCP, 1934; MD, London,1936; MRCP, London 1936; FRCP, London, 1953. *Appointments:* Consultant Paediatrician, Bristol Royal Hospital for Sick Children, 1937-76, and United Bristol Hospitals, 1948-76, and Southead Hospital Group, 1942-76; Clinical Lecturer, University of Bristol, 1942-76; Hon. paediatrician, Bristol Zoo, 1972-83. *Publications:* Prematurity, 1960; Textbook for Health Visitors, jointly 1951, 1963; many articles in professional journals. *Memberships:* Medical Womens International Association, President 1978-80; Royal Society of Medicine, President, Paediatric Section; Medical Womens Federation, President; Bristol Medico Chirurgical Society. *Honours:* Margaret Todd

Scholarship, 1929; Beaverbook Fellowship, 1939-42; Markham Skerritt Prize, 1956. *Hobbies:* Violin; Photography; Foreign Travel. *Address:* Flat 4, Chartley, The Avenue, Sneyd Park, Bristol BS9 1PE, England.

CORREA PEREZ Alicia, b. 7 Jan. 1944, H. Zitacuaro, Michoacan, Mexico. Professor; Author. m. Julian V. Tarasuk, 17 Dec. 1975 (div. 1986), 2 sons. *Education:* BA, Spanish Language & Literature, National Autonomus University of Mexico, 1968; Teaching degree, Hispanic Culture Institute, Madrid, Spain, 1972; Master's degree (Letters) 1974, PhD 1976, UNAM; Extensive postgraduate studies. *Appointments:* Librarian, National Library, UNAM, 1965; Professor, Spanish & Literature, Secretariat of Public Education 1965-70, Mexican & World Literature, National Preparatory School (ENP), UNAM 1966-75; Coordinator, College of Letters, ENP/UNAM, 1968-70; Full Professor, Department of Mexican & Iberoamerican Literature, University of Veracruz 1969-70, Spanish & Mexican Literature, College of Philosophy & Letters (FyL), UNAM 1970-; Various other scholarly positions, UNAM & other universities. *Publications include:* Spanish Literature of Middle Age, 1976; Golden Age: Baroque, 1976; Culture, Education & Literature, 1982; Numerous articles, university journals. Co-author: Hispanic Language & Literatures, 1978; Spanish textbooks for junior high school, 1985-88. Also numerous conferences, public lectures. *Memberships:* Academy of Professors & Investigators of Letters; Academic Council, Cristobal Colon University, Veracruz; Association of Academic Personnel, UNAM. *Honours include:* Numerous academic successes; Recognitions, university & government bodies. *Hobbies:* Literature; Films; Travel; Academic personnel improvement; Cultural diffusion. *Address:* Edificio 25, Suite 803, Villa Olimpica, Tlalpan, DF Mexico, CP 14020, Meixco.

CORSAR Mary Drumond, b. 8 July 1927, Edinburgh, Scotland. m. Charles Herbert Kenneth Corsar, 25 Apr. 1953. 2 sons, 2 daughters. *Education:* MA Honours History, Edinburgh University. *Memberships:* Deputy Chief Commissioner, Girl Guides Association, Scotland, 1972-77; Visiting Committee, Glenochil Young Offenders Institution and Detention Centre, 1976-; Parole Board for Scotland, 1982-; Governor, Fettes College, 1982-; Convocation, Heriot-Watt University, 1986-; Chairman Women's Royal Voluntary Service, 1988-; Honorary President, Scottish Women's Amateur Athletic Association; Executive Committee, Trefoil Centre for the Handicapped. *Hobbies:* Hill Walking; Needlework. *Address:* 11 Ainslie Place, Edinburgh, EH3 6AS, Scotland.

CORSELLE Lily Joann, b. 30 Mar. 1953, Newark, New Jersey, USA. Minister; Counsellor; Educator. m. George M. Neel. *Education:* BA, Florida State University, 1974; MEd, Florida Atlantic University, 1977; MA, Southwestern Baptist Theological Seminary, 1987. *Appointments:* Educator, Broward County School System, Florida, 1974-84; Minister, Park Place Baptist Church, Houston, Texas, 1985-87; Counsellor, Executive Director, Single Plus Inc, 1989-. *Publications:* Articles: What Is Faith?; Loneliness: The Hidden Horror; The Liberty of Surrender; Needs and Identities of Today's Single Adults; The Close of the Age, poem. *Memberships:* American Personnel and Guidance Association; International Platform Association; Women in Ministry. *Honours:* Medal, Daughters of the American Revolution, 1968; Life Member, Lambda Iota Tau. *Hobbies:* Reading; Writing; Crafts; Aerobics; Computers (using a microcomputer). *Address:* 2801 Hamlett Lane, Flower Mound, TX 75028, USA.

CORTI KOSTIC Ivanka, b. 3 May 1926, Leskovac, Yugoslavia. Politician; Lecturer; Journalist. m. Bruno Corti, 10 June 1961, 1 son. *Education:* 2 years courses and examinations, Faculty of Law, Paris, France, 1950-51; 1st degree, Ecole du Louvre, Paris, 1950; Degree in French and English Literature and Language, Belgrade University, Yugoslavia, 1956. *Appointments:* International Secretary, Member of Executive, Social Democratic Party, Italy, 1979-; Vice-President, Socialist International Women, 1980-86; Italian Government's Committee for Equality of Men and Woman, 1984-; UN Expert Member, CEDAW, 1987-90. *Publications:* Book: Time of Crisis (introduction by Mario Soares), 1983; Several articles on equality issues and international policy in various newspapers and reviews; Declaration Principles of Socialist International Women. *Memberships:* Executive Member, AIDOS-Italian NGO for Development Aid for Women; Institute of International Affairs; Founder Member, Woman and Health Association. *Hobbies:* Study of equality problems; Study of demographic issues; Archaeology. *Address:* Via Cardinal de Luca 10, 00196 Rome, Italy.

COSKY Judith Ann, b. 20 Jan. 1953, Farmington, Michigan, USA. Referral Coordinator. m. M. Williams, 12 Dec. 1986, 1 son. *Education:* BSN, Oakland University, Rochester, Michigan, 1978; MSN, Wayne State University, Detroit, Michigan, 1982. *Appointments:* Nursing Instructor, Mercy College of Detroit, 1981-82; Clinical Nurse Specialist, University of Michigan Hospital, 1982-83; Coordinator of Infant Programme, Fairlawn Center, 1983-85; Referral Coordinator, Havenwyk Hospital, 1985-. *Publications:* Co-author, chapter on assessment in child and adolescent psychiatry in textbook Psychiatric-Mental Health Assessment, 1984. *Honour:* Clawson Jaycees Scholarship, 1970. *Hobbies:* Theo-philosophy; Tennis; Needlework. *Address:* 600 East 14 Mile, Clawson, MI 48017, USA.

COSTA Patricia Ann, b. 10 Jan. 1953, Cambridge, USA. Media Technician. *Education:* University of Massachusetts, 1974-79, 1987-88. *Appointments:* Musician, Audio Engineer, AAA Recording Studios Inc., 1970-; Media Technician, Harvard University, 1975-80; Media Technician, Computer Lab Co-ordinator, Lesley College, 1986-. *Publications:* Composer, Five Boston Composers, 1976; Slide Tape, Keeping Harvard's Books, 1981; Videotape, Welcome to HGSE, 1985; Peter Rabbit Instructional Interactive Video Disc, 1986; Neon Tetra, guitarist, 1988-. *Memberships:* International Interactive Communications Society; American Film Institute; John F. Kennedy Library Associate Fellow. *Hobbies:* Music; Golf; Skiing. *Address:* RFD Route 2, Lincoln, MA 01773, USA.

COSTELLO Dawn E, b. 12 July 1940, Allentown, Pennsylvania, USA. Nurse Administrator. m. Robert G Costello, 5 Dec. 1962, 1 son, 1 daughter. *Education:* BS, Nursing, University of Pennsylvania, 1962; MS, Education, Temple University, 1967; EdD, Administration, Lehigh University, 1973; Enrolled MS Nursing, Allentown College St Francis des Salles. *Appointments:* Nurse, Allentown School Dist, 1963-67; Director Research & Records, Lehigh County Community College, 1972-74; Associate Director Nursing, Lehigh Valley Hospital Center, 1974-78; Associate Director Personal Health Service, Allentown, 1979-81; Consultant, NCHE, 1978-; Director of Nursing, Coaldale State General Hospital, 1981-. *Memberships:* Secretary, Advisory Board Volunteers of America, 1974-78; Board Lehigh Valley Area Health Education Center; President, Lehigh Valley Association for Children with Learning Disabilities, 1981-83; President, Pa Eastern Region Organisation of Nurse Executives 1988; Secretary, Advisory Board Association Degree Nursing, Lehigh County Community College, 1989; PADONA; LV Council on Nursing Educ and Nursing Service. *Honours:* Certified by American Nurses Assoc in Nursing Administration, Advanced 1983; Instructor-Management Development for Department of Welfare, 1983-; 1st Director Public Health Nursing, B City Health Bureau, 1979. *Hobbies:* Computers; Gardening; Fishing; Hunting. *Address:* RD No 1 Box 240A, Schnecksville, PA 18078, USA.

COSTIGAN Constance Frances, b. 3 July 1935, New Jersey, USA. Artist; Teacher. m. Michael Krausz, 14 May 1976. *Education:* BS, Simmons College & Boston Museum School of Fine Arts, 1957; MA, American University, 1965; Postgraduate, University of California, Berkeley, University of Virginia, District of Columbia

University. *Appointments include:* Exhibits designer 1957-59, design & public education services, museum shops & services 1963-67, Smithsonian Institution, Washington DC; Freelance illustrator, graphic designer, & private tutor, studio art, art history, textile design, 1959-70; Instructor: Sidwell Friends School, Sulgrave Club, Arlington County Public Schools, Smithsonian Institution, Artists' Cooperative (all Washington DC), 1968-83; Associate Professor, Fine Arts, Smith Hall of Art, George Washington University, 1976-; Various lectures, juries. *Creative work includes:* 9 solo shows, USA, England, Scotland, 1973-, including 10-year retrospective, Northern Virginia Community College, 1983; Exhibitor, numerous juried or invited group shows, USA; Works in public collections, Washington DC, Iowa City, George Washington University; Private collections USA, Canada, UK, Europe, Egypt. *Memberships:* College Art Association; American Crafts Council; Coalition for Washington Artists. *Honours:* Distinguished Visiting Professor, American University, Cairo, Egypt, Dec-Jan 1980-81; Fellow, Ossabaw Island Project 1980, MacDowell Colony 1977; Fellow, Royal Society of Arts, UK, 1974-; Grant, Lester Hereward Cook Foundation, 1978-79. *Hobbies:* Music; Hiking; Sailing; Cooking; Gardening. *Address:* Art Department, Smith Hall of Art, George Washington University, Washington DC 20052, USA.

COTE Sally S (Stevie), b. 16 Nov. 1946, Huntington, USA. Manager. m. 14 Mar. 1980, 5 stepsons, 2 stepdaughters. *Education:* BS, Mathematics, Univerity of Kentucky, 1968; MBA, University of Detroit, 1983. *Appointments:* Ford Motor Company Finance & Insurance Operator, 1968-86; Ford Finance Staff, 1986-87; Systems Dept. Manager, Ford Office of the General Counsel, 1987-. *Memberships:* Society for Information Management; Association for Systems Management; US Olympics Society; University of Detroit, President's Cabinet; University of Michigan, Henry Ford's Fairlane Friend; Michigan Humane Society. *Honours:* First Woman Systems Manager, Ford Motor Company, 1987; Guest Lecturer, University of Michiggan; Hole-in-One. *Hobbies:* Environmental & Wildlife Protection; Animal Rights & Assistance; Golf. *Address:* One Parklane Blvd., PO Box 65, Dearborn, MI 48126, USA.

COTHORN Marguerite Esters, b. 23 Dec. 1909, Albia, Iowa, USA. Social Worker (retired). m. John L. Cothorn, 4 Nov. 1934 (div. 1945), 1 son. *Education:* BA, 1930, Masters, 1932, Drake University, Des Moines, Iowa; MSW, University of Iowa, 1954. *Appointments:* Probation Officer, 1930-33; Social Welfare Department, Balto, Maryland, 1934-40; Director, Willkie House, 1940-45; Director, Booker Washington Center, Rockford, Illinois, 1945-52; Psychiatric Social Worker, Veterans Administration Hospital, Knoxville, Iowa, 1952-56; Council of Social Agencies, 1956-65. *Publications:* Booth Case, 1954; Adaptation of Role Playing as a Basic Method of Inter-disciplinary Reaching, 1956. *Memberships:* League of Women Voters of M; Des Moines Playground Association; Recreation Workshop; Drake University Alumni; Formerly: National Association for the Advancement of Coloured People; National Association of Social Workers; Delta Sigma Theta. *Honours:* National Honor Society, 1926; Drake University Women's Athletic Association, 1926; Music Society, 1926; Alice Whipple Award from Labor, 1973; Plaque for Outstanding Leadership in Black Community, 1973; Key to City for organising and promotion of Volunteerism, Des Moines, 1973; Drake University Distinguished Alumnae Award, 1973; Community Service Award, 1973; Service Award, Polk County Republic Central Committee, 1984; Inducted into Iowa State Women's Hall of Fame, 1984. *Hobbies:* Crafts; Bridge; Music; Political activity - civil rights. *Address:* 1249 43rd Street, Des Moines, IA 50311, USA.

COTTON Eileen Giuffre' b. 23 Apr. 1947, Oakland, California, USA. University Administrator and Professor. m. 3 Apr. 1971. *Education:* BA, Social Science, CSU, Hayward, 1968; MA, Elementary Education, California State University, Sacramento, 1976; PhD, Administration, Supervision & Curriculum, University of Maryland, 1979. *Appointments:* Teacher, 1969-76; Program Director, Crownsville Hospital Center, 1976-77; Associate Professor of Education, 1984-85 and 1986-, Coordinator, Multiple Subjects Program 1986-, Director of Credential Services 1988-, California State University. *Publications:* Author of numerous articles in professional journals. *Memberships include:* American Educational Research Assoc; American Psychological Assoc; Assoc for Supervision and Curriculum Development; International Reading Association; National Council of Teachers of English; Phi Delta Kappa; Kappa Delta Pi. *Honours:* Grant, California State University, 1987; Phi Delta Kappa Leadership Grant, 1983. *Hobbies:* Reading; Computers; Camping/motorhoming; Travelling. *Address:* Department of Education, California State University, Chio, California 95929, USA.

COUCHMAN Mary Catherine, b. 24 Aug. 1945, Centerville, Iowa, USA. Administrative Assistant; Support Staff Coordinator; Bookkeeper. m. Gary Joe Couchman, 7 Nov. 1965. 2 sons. *Education:* NE Mo State, 1963-65; Indian Hills CC, 1965; Parsons College, Mt Pleasant, Iowa, 1971. *Appointments:* Secretary Dean of Women, NE Mo State, 1964-65; Secretary, DVM Wm Cooper, 1963-65; Recp Milani & Milani, Law Firm, 1965-67; Sub Teacher, R3 Unionville, Missouri and Wayne School, 1974-77; Secretary, Rathbun Area Mental Health, 1977-89; Admin Assistant, 1982-; Support Staff Coordinator, 1983-89. *Memberships:* Community Betterment Com, Seymour, Iowa; Extension Council Wayne Co, Corydon, 1984-86; President, United Methodist Women, 1983-85; Finance Chairman, United Methodist Church Seymour, 1985-87; National Association for Female Executives, 1988. *Honours:* Worthy Advisor, Rainbow, 1962-63; Grand Cross of Colors Member, 1967; Beta Tau Delta. *Hobbies:* Sewing; Horseback riding; Craft items; Reading. *Address:* Rural Route No 1, Box 77, Seymour, Iowa 52590, USA.

COUCOULIOS Connie, b. 29 June 1944, Torrance, California, USA. Accountant. m. Nat Coucoulios, 1 Aug. 1984, 1 son, 3 daughters. *Education:* BA, University of California, Santa Barbara, 1966. *Appointments:* Sperry Univac, 1966-69; Denny's Restaurants, 1969-74; City of Albuquerque, New Mexico, 1974-79; Mitchell Energy and Development, 1979-84; Kauai Data Processing, Hawaii, 1984-. *Memberships:* Treasurer, Quota Club of Kauai; Hawaii Association of Public Accountants; American Institute of Professional Bookkeepers; American Society of Professional and Executive Women. *Hobbies:* Computers; Medicine; Fitness walking; Classical music. *Address:* PO Box 627, Lawai, HI 96765, USA.

COULSON Juanita Ruth, b. 12 Feb. 1933, Anderson, Indiana, USA. Freelance Writer. m. Robert Stratton Coulson, 21 Aug. 1954, 1 son. *Education:* BA, 1954, MA 1961, Ball State University. *Publications:* Novels: Crisis on Cheiron, 1967; The Singing Stones, 1968; The Secret of Seven Oaks, 1972; Door into Terror, 1972; Unto the Last Generation, 1975; Stone of Blood, 1975; Space Trap, 1976; Fear Stalks the Bayou, 1976; Dark Priestess, 1976; The Web of Wizardry, 1978; Fire of the Andes, 1979; The Death Go's Citadel, 1980; Tomorrow's Heritage: Book One, Children of the Stars, 1981; Outward Bound: Book Two, Children of the Stars, 1982; Legacy of Earth: Book Three, Children of the Stars, forthcoming; The Past of Forever: Book Four, Children of the Stars, forthcoming; short stories in: Magazine of Fantasy & Science Fiction; Worlds of If Science Fiction; Fantastic Science Fiction & Fantasy; etc. *Memberships:* Science Fiction Writers of America. *Honours Include:* Recipient, various honours and awards. *Hobbies:* Music; Reading; Natural Science; Amateur Astronomy; Gardening; Travel; etc. *Address:* 2677W - 500N, Hartford City, IN47384, USA.

COULSON Zoe Elizabeth, b. 22 Sept. 1932, Sullivan, Indiana, USA. Food Processing Executive. *Education:* BS, Purdue University, 1954; AMP, Harvard Business School, 1983. *Appointments:* Assistant Director, Home Economics Public Relations, American Meat Institute,

Chicago, Illinois, 1954-57; Account Executive, J Walter Thompson, Chicago, 1957-60; Consumer Services Director, Creative Department, Leo Burnett Co, Chicago, 1960-64; Editorial Director, What's New, Donnelley/ Dun and Bradstreet, New York City, 1964-68; Food Editor, 1968-75, Director, 1975-81, Good Housekeeping Institute, New York City; Vice-President, Campbell Soup Co, Camden, New Jersey, 1981-. *Publications:* Good Housekeeping Cookbook, 1973; Good Housekeeping Illustrated Cookbook, 1980; Case history in Harvard Business Review, 1987. *Memberships:* Board of Governors, National Women's Economic Alliance; Comsumer Affairs Committee, National Food Processors Association; Sponsor, Women Executives in State Government; American Home Economics Association; Kappa Alpha Theta Alumnae Association. *Honours:* Distinguished Alumna, School of Home Economics, Purdue University, 1970; Old Master, Purdue University, 1972; Academy of Women Achievers, Young Women's Christian Association, New York City, 1976. *Hobbies:* Meso-American archaeology; International travel. *Address:* 220 Locust Street, Philadelphia, PA 19106, USA.

COULTER Deborah Ann, b. 11 Oct. 1952, Seattle, Washington, USA. Building Official; Code enforcement. *Education:* Applied science degree, Building Construction Technology, 1986-. *Appointments:* Supply Specialist, US Dewline, Operations Maintenance Service, Barter Island, Alaska, 1973-74; Division Manager, A & P Griswold Expeditors, Inc, Fairbanks, Alaska, 1974-76; Construction Coordinator, Saudi Development & Commercial Co, Jeddah, Saudi Arabia, 1977-78; Installation Coordinator, Star Machinery Cio, Seattle, Washington, 1979-80; Construction Inspector/ Field Rep/Contract Administrator, Seattle Housing Authority, Seattle, 1980-83; Building Official/Fire Marshal, City of Fife, Washington, 1983-85; Building Official/Code Administrator, City of Issaquah, Washsington, 1985-87; Building Official, Yakima County Washington, 1987; Code Enforcement Official/ Contract Consultant, City of Mercer Island, Washington, 1987; Deputy State Fire Marshal, Department of Community Development Fire Protection Servicision Division, Seattle, Washington, 1988-. *Publication:* Women in Construction, in progress. *Memberships:* Chairman - Legislative/State Liaison Committee, 1986-87, Washington Association of Building Officials; International Conference of Building Officials; National Association of Women in Construction. *Honour:* Certificate of Achievement & Participation, International Conference of Building Officials, Western Washington Chapter, 1985. *Hobbies:* Skiing; Bicycling; Painting; Boating; Fishing; Swimming; Games; Sewing; Reading; Snow Machining. *Address:* PO Box 891, Mercer Island, Washington 98040, USA

COURTEMARCHE Paula Jean, b. 22 June 1948, Quincy, USA. Wang Word Processing Specialist. m. Charles T. Courtemarche, 19 Sept. 1969, 1 son. *Education:* Evening Student, Classical Piano, New England Conservatory of Music, 1967-69. *Appointments:* Boston Financial Technology Group, 1978-82; Goldstein & Manello, Boston,1984-86; Boston Edison Company, 1984-86; Nutter, McClennen & Fish Boston, 1986-88. *Publications:* For Survivors Only-the Journey of Unbeaten Woman, poetry, 1986; Poetry includes: The Wedding; My Friend; The Rescuer has a Fortress; Two Lovers Parting; Sisters; Timeless Word. *Memberships:* American Society of Notaries; Religious Charities. *Honours:* Poetry Published in American Poetry Anthology, Quill Books and World of Poetry Press. *Hobbies:* Writing; Classical Pianist; Crochet; Volunteer Work. *Address:* PO Box 2241, Quincy, MA 02269, USA.

COURTER Gay, b. 1 Oct. 1944, Pittsburgh, Pennsylvania, USA. Writer; Filmmaker. m. Philip Courter, 18 Aug. 1968, 2 sons. *Education:* BA, Drama/ Film, Antioch College, Yellow Springs, Ohio. *Appointments:* Various film production companies, 1966-70; Own film production company with husband, 1970-. *Creative works:* The Beansprout Book (non-fiction), 1973; Novels: The Midwife, 1981; River of Dreams, 1984; Code Ezra, 1986; Flowers in One Blood, 1990; More than 100 educational/documentary films. *Memberships:* Writers Guild of America; Authors Guild. *Honours:* Several film awards including Cine Gold Eagles and EFLA American Film Festival awards. *Hobbies:* Scuba diving; Flying; Growing orchids; Family; Waterfront pursuits; Cooking; Travel. *Address:* 121 N W Crystal Street, Crystal River, FL 32629, USA.

COURTNEY Angela Maria, b. 11 Aug. 1943, Gateshead, Co. Durham, England. Worker, Belfast Womens Aid. m. Adan Dewton Courtney, 12 Sept. 1964, 2 sons, 1 daughter. *Appointments:* University Library, Newcastle upon Tyne, 1959-64; University Library, Queens University of Belfast, 1967-69, 1974-85. *Publications:* Some magazine articles & poetry. *Memberships:* Northern Ireland Womens Aid Federation, Secretary; Benburb Centre Co. Tyrone. *Hobbies Include:* Community Activities; Workshops; Writing Poetry. *Address:* 129 University St., Belfast, Ireland.

COVEY Ellen, b. 26 Sept. 1947, Elmhurst, USA. Scientist. m. J.H. Casseday, 1981, 1 son. *Education:* BS, 1974, MS, 1976, Biology, University of Houston; PhD, Psychology, Duke University, 1980. *Appointments:* Research Associate, Princeton University, 1980-81; Research Associate, Duke University, 1981-. *Publications:* Articles in professional journals. *Memberships:* Society for Neuroscience; Sigma Xi. *Honour:* Visiting Scientist, Zoologisches Institut, Munich, Germany, 1985, 1986, 1987. *Hobbies:* Painting; Running. *Address:* PO Box 3943, Duke University Medical Centre, Durham, NC 27710, USA.

COVINGTON Patricia Ann, b. 21 June 1946, Mt Vernon, Illinois, USA. Professor; Administrator; Artist. m. Burl Vance Beene, 10 Aug. 1964. divorced 1981. *Education:* BA, University of New Mexico, 1968; MS in Education, 1974, PhD 1981, So Illinois University. *Appointments:* Lab Director, Anasazi Origins Project, 1968; Teacher, Public Schools, Albuquerque, 1969-70; Teaching Assistant 1971-74, Professor of Art 1974-88, Administrator 1988-, So Illinois University College, Carbondale, Illinois. *Publications:* Diary of a Workshop, 1979; History of the School of Art at SIUC, 1981; Paper castings shown nationally and internationally. *Memberships:* Board of Directors, 1973-86, Fellow, Illinois Ozarks Craft Guild; Chairman and Board of Directors, 1978-88, Illinois Higher Education Association; Sphinx Club; Phi Kappa Phi; National Organization of Women; National Association of Female Executives; Panel Member, Illinois Arts Council, 1982; Board of Directors, Humanities Council, John A Logan College, 1982-88. *Honours:* Grantee Kresge Foundation, 1978; Grantee National Endowment for the Arts, 1977 and 1981; Named Oustanding Young Woman of the Year for Illinois, 1981; Scholarship Phi Kappa Phi. *Interests:* Director, Artist of the Month for US Rep. Paul Simon, Washington, 1974-81; Visiting Curator, Mitchell Museum, Mt Vernon, 1977-83; Faculty Advisory, European Business Seminar, London, England, 1983; Education Consultant, Illinois Department of Aging, Springfield, 1978-81; Judge, University of Illinois, 1978-87; Judge, Dept of Conservation, Springfield, 1984-86; Judge, Mitchell Museum, 1985. *Address:* Rt 6 352 Lake Drive, Murphysboro, IL 62966, USA.

COWAN Larine Y, b. 25 Mar. 1949, Kensett, Arkansas, USA. Human & Civil Rights administrator; Director of Affirmative Action Support Staff. *Education:* BA Sociology 1968-71, Master of Social Work 1971-73, University of Arkansas; Continuing Education at Texas Southern University 1987; National Coalition Building Inst, Prej Reduction & Conflict Resolution, 1987. *Appointments:* Director, Com Relations Dept, City of Champaign, 1974-79; Equal Opportunity Officer, 1982-85; State Coordinator, Industrialization Ctrs of America, 1983-87; Director, Affirmative Action Nonacademic Office, 1985-. *Publications:* Co-author: Police Community Relations, A Process Not a Product, 1st edition 1976, 2nd edition 1977; Human Rights

Ordinance for City of Champaign; Editor, Status of Affirmative Action, 1986. *Memberships:* American Association for Affirmative Action; American Association for Higher Education; American Association of University Women; College & University Personnel Association; Industrial Relations Research Association; Illinois Aff Act Officers Association; NAACP; National Association for Female Executives; Illinois Concerns for Blacks in Higher Education; Executive Women's Club. *Honours:* Boss of the Year Award, 1978; Proclamation for Outstanding Contributions in the Field of Human Rights, 1979; Outstanding Services in Human & Civil Rights, 1979; Proclamation, Special Achievements in Human Rights, 1979; Outstanding Achievement in Volunteerism, 1985; Special Services Award, Chanute Air Force Base, 1988; Chancellors Award of Appreciation for Outstanding Service as Chair of the Campus Charitable Fund Drive, 1988; Outstanding Achievement for Running the Best Charitable Campaign at any State University, United Way of Campaign Country 1988. *Hobbies:* Cooking; Walking; Reading; Movies; Painting. *Address:* 349 W Paddock Drive, Savoy, IL 61874, USA.

COWGILL Ursula M., b. 9 Nov. 1927, Bern, Switzerland. Biochemist. *Education:* AB, Hunter College, USA, 1948; MS, Kansas State University, 1952; PhD, Iowa State University, 1956. *Appointments include:* Massachusetts Institute of Technology, 1957-58; Doherty Foundation, Guatemala, 1958-60; Biology Department, Yale University, 1960-68; Professor, Biology 1968-81, Joint Professor, Anthropology 1971-81, University of Pittsburgh; Environmental sciences research 1981-83, research associatie; Manager, environmental regulatory activities 1983-84, Associate Environmental Consultant, Environmental Quality 1984-87, Mammalian & Environmental Toxicology 1987-, Dow Chemical Company. Numerous committees, US Federal Government, National Bureau of Standards, professional bodies. *Publications:* Numerous research Papers, Physics, Chemistry, Anthropology, Professional Journals, 1953-; Editorial Boards, Reviews. *Memberships include:* American Society for Limnology & Oceanography; Analytical Chemistry Division, American Chemical Society; Society of Bio-Inorganic Chemists; International Society for Theoretical & Applied Limnology; Iota Sigma Pi; Sigma Xi. *Honours include:* Grants: National Science Foundation, 1961-80; Sigma Xi, 1965-66; Wenner Gren Foundation, 1965-66; American Philosophical Society, 1978-81. *Address:* Dow Chemical Company, 1702 Building, Midland, Michigan 48674, USA.

COWLES Fleur, Author; Painter. m. Tom Montague Meyer, 18 Nov. 1955. *Education:* LLD; SF, RCA. *Appointments:* Associate Editor, 1946-55, Foreign Correspondent, 1955-60, Look Magazine. *Creative Works:* 40 One Man Painting Exhibitions, worldwide, 1959-88; Books: If I Were an Animal, 1987; To Be a Unicorn, 1986; People as Animals, 1986; Flower Decorations, 1985; The Flower Game, 1983; All Too True, 1981; Friends and Memories, 1975; The Case of Salvador Dali, 1959; Bloody Precedent, 1951; contributor to books. *Memberships:* various professional organisations. *Honours:* Legion of Honour, 1951, France; Chevalier Cuziero de Sud, 1950; Queen's Coronation Medal, 1953; Commander Cuziero de Sud, 1970; Ribbon of La Dama of The Order of Isabel La Catolica, Spain, 1977; Senior Fellow, Royal College of Art, 1988. *Address:* A5 Albany, Piccadilly, London W1V 9RD, England.

COX Frances, b. 15 Oct. 1919, Goodyear, Arizona, USA. Teacher; Resource Specialist, Retired. m. N James Cox, 24 Nov. 1948. 2 sons. *Education:* BA, Arizona State University, 1941; CSU San Francisco, Santa Clara University, Notre Dame Coll, UC Santa Cruz, UC Berkeley, CSU San Jose; Tchg cred, Elementary (Life Cert), Arizona 1941, Oregon 1950, California 1954, Resource Specialist, Learning Handicapped, California 1972. *Appointments:* Classroom teacher, Phoenix City Schools, 1941-49; Fresno (CA) City Schools, 1949-50; Fresno County Schools, 1953-56; Portland (Ore) City Schools, 1960-63; Teacher/Resource Specialist, Palo Alto Unified Schools, 1964-86; Devel curriculum in Kdg literature and elementary science, Phoenix, 1941-43; Lead panel Association for Childhood Education Convention, Arizona State University, 1946; Lead demonstrator for 2d gr games for Fresno Co Schools, Fresno St Coll, 1954; Lead demonstrator for social studies for Portland City schools, Portland Teachers Institute, 1962; Master teacher Fresno St College, 1953; Oregon St University. *Memberships:* Palo Alto Tchrs Assn; Remedial Reading Teachers, 1961-73; Resource Specialist Organisation; National Teachers Association; California Teachers Association (Political action rep); NEA; Tchr orgns in Phoenix, Fresno and Portland, PTA, 1941-; Nat Profl Sigma Phi Gamma Treasurer 1945-47; Bus Sor, 1941-47; Valley of The ? Mortar Board Alumni; CA Retired Teachers Association. *Honours:* Recipient WHO Award for outstanding service, 1986. *Hobbies:* Travel; Politics; Environment; Art. *Address:* 911 La Mesa Drive, Portola Valley, CA 94028, USA.

COX Geraldine Anne Vang, b. 10 Jan. 1944, Philadelphia, USA. Technical Director. m. Walter G. Cox, 10 Sept. 1965. *Education:* BS, 1966, MS, 1967, PhD, 1970, Environmental Science, Drexel University. *Appointments:* Environmental Co-ordinator, Raytheon Oceanographic & Environment Services, 1970-76; White House Fellow, 1976-77; Environmental Scientist, American Petroleum Institute, 1977-79; Vice President, Technical Director, Chemical Manufacturers Association, 1979-. *Publications:* Oil Spill Studies: Strategies & Techniques, 1977; Marine Bioassays, 1975; How Serious is the Toxics Problem, 1983; Soul Searching in the Chemical Industry, 1985; Industry Initiatives Now Under Way, 1985; A Trade Association's Role in Crisis Management, 1987. *Memberships Include:* US Coast Guard Chemical Transport Advisory Committee; Health & Safety. *Honours Include:* Outstanding Young Woman in America, 1975; Harriet E. Wornell Medal, 1977; Rhode Island Governor's Citation, 1975; Panhellenic Woman of the Year, 1966, Drexel University. *Hobbies:* Photography; Breeding & Showing Cats; Gemology & Jewel Design. *Address:* Chemical Manufacturers Association, 2501 M St., NW, Washington, DC 20037, USA.

COX Marjorie Herrmann, b. 10 July 1918, New York, USA. Retired. m. William Gould Cox, 23 Jan. 1943, 3 sons, 3 daughters. *Education:* AA, Catley College; BS, University of Minnesota. *Appointments:* Teacher, 1941-42; Teacher, St Lukes Parochial School, 1942-43, Lincoln Unified School, Stockton, California, 1955-57, Randolph School, Minnesota, 1966-78; Council Member, Northfield Assesment Tester for Minnesota Department of Education. *Publications:* Poetry & articles in journals & magazines. *Memberships:* Delta Kappa Gamma; National Collegiate Players; Zeta Phi Eta; Northfield Arts Guild, Board Member. *Hobbies:* Writing; Theatre; Knitting; Sewing; Volunteer, many Organisations. *Address:* 610E. 6th St., Northfield, MN 55057, USA.

COX Wendy Bertha (Kerlin), b. 15 July 1934, Aliquippa, Pennsylvania, USA. Executive Director. m. Thomas M S Cox, 21 Aug, 1954. 1 son, 1 daughter. *Education:* Hopewell High School, Aliquippa, Pennsylvania, 1953. *Appointments:* Store Manager, 1965-68; Director, Headquarters Bedford County Bicentennial, 1968-71; Executive Secretary, Bedford County Heritage Commission, 1972-78; Executive Director, Bedford County Travel Promotion Agency Inc, 1978-. *Publications:* Co-author of three cookery books. *Memberships:* National Association Female Executives; National Federation Business & Professional Women, Pennsylvania Chapter; Administrative Board, Girl Scouts of America; Bedford United Methodist Church. *Honours:* District Award, Girl Scouts of America, 1972; Trophy Award, Torch Relay, Statue of Liberty, 1985; Hand Across America Award, 1986; Manager of the Year Award, Silco Dept Stores, 1967; Traveller Award, 1986, S Alleghenies Travel Council. *Hobbies:* People; Travel; Special projects or challenges; Good music;

Attending musicals; My grandchildren. *Address:* 798 Echo Vale Drive, Bedford, Pennsylvania 15522, USA.

COYE Molly Joel, b. 11 May 1947, Bennington, Vermont, USA. Medical Doctor; Administrator. m. Mark D. Smith, 22 Feb. 1986, 1 son. *Education:* BA, 1968; MA, 1972; MPH, 1977; MD, 1977. *Appointments include:* Chief, Occupational Health Clinic, University of San Francisco School of Medicine, 1979-84; Medical Officer, National Institute for Occupational Safety & Health, 1980-85; Special Adviser, Health & Environment, Governor's Office of Policy & Planning, New Jersey, 1985-86; Deputy Commissioner of Health 1986, State Commissioner of Health 1986-, New Jersey. *Publications:* Cancer Prevention, Strategies in Workplace; China, Inside People's Republic; China Yesterday & Today. *Memberships:* Offices, past/present, American Public Health Association, Association of State & Territorial Health Officials; American Medical Association; American College of Preventive Medicine; Society for Occupational & Environmental Health. *Honours:* Award, Central New Jersey chapter, March of Dimes, 1988; Woman of Year, Jersey Woman magazine, 1989. *Hobbies:* Cinema; Travel. *Address:* New Jersey State Department of Health, CN 360, Trenton, New Jersey 08625, USA.

COYNE Ruth Lillian, b. 6 May 1925, Pittsburgh, USA. Psychiatrist; Psychoanalyst. m. Thomas J. Coyne, 23 Nov. 1968, 1 daughter. *Education:* BS, 1946, MLitt, 1949, MD, 1953, University of Pittsburgh; Board Certification, American Board of Psychiatry (Adult) 1960, (Child), 1966. *Appointments:* University of Pittsburgh, 1958-60; Consultant Psychiatrist, Pittsburgh Public Schools, 1965; Director, Child & Adolescent Mental Health Services, 1965-; Private Practice, 1965-. *Publications:* Articles in professional journals including: American Journal of Psychiatry. *Memberships:* Fellow, American Psychiatric Association; American Orthopsychiatric Association; Pennsylvania, Pittsburgh Psychiatric Societies; President, Regional Council, Child Psychiatry; etc. *Honours:* Phi Tau Pi; United Mental Health Pittsburgh Award, 1988. *Hobbies:* Music; Eating Disorders; Bowling; Opera. *Address:* St Francis Medical Center, 45th St Off Penn Avenue, Pittsburgh, PA 15201, USA.

CRAIG Gail Heidbreder, b. 20 Jan. 1941, Baltimore, USA. Architect; Educator. m. 9 Jan. 1984, 2 sons, 2 daughters. *Education:* BA, Stanford University 1966. *Appointments:* Registered Architect, State of California with various firms, 1969-85; Owner, Gail Craig AIA, Poterville, California, 1985-; Instructor, California Community Colleges, Kern Community College District, 1985-. *Creative Works:* Structures have been constructed throughout USA, Asia & Middle East. *Memberships:* American Institute of Architects; International Conference of Building Officials; Poterville Chamber of Commerce, Board of Directors, 1985-87; Main Street Inc., President 1989-; Back Country Horsemen of California. *Hobbies:* Horse Training; Back Country Stock Packer. *Address:* 639 A North Main, Porterville, CA 93257, USA.

CRAIG Wendy, b. County Durham, England. Actress. m. Jack Bentley. 2 sons. *Education:* Central School of Dramatic Art, London. *Appointments:* Played Monica Twigg for J B Priestley; Has appeared in numerous stage roles in the West End including: George Dillon in London and on Broadway; The Wrong Side of the Park; Three; A Resounding Tinkle; Sport of My Mad Mother, Royal Court Theatre; The Ginger Man; Ride A Cock Horse; I Love You Mrs Patterson; Finishing Touches; Breezeblock Park; Beyond Reasonable Doubt, by Jefferey Archer, 1988. Played the last Peter Pan in the redeveloped Scala Theatre. Film roles include: Room at the Top; The Mindbenders; I'll Never Forget What's-his-Name; Joseph Andrews; The Servant; Just Like a Woman. Has starred in many leading roles in television dramas including: Candida; Wings of a Dove; Nanny, BBC Television, 1981-83; Not in Front of the Children for 12 years; Mother Makes Three; Mother Makes Five; Butterflies; Laura and Disorder, 1989. Has appeared in many stage revivals of The Taming of the Shrew; A Doll's House; Hobson's Choice; A Bed Before Yesterday and the 1985 version of The Constant Wife; Mary, Mary, 1986. Has made many recordings especially for children. *Publications:* Busy Mum's Cookbook; Busy Mum's Baking Book. *Honours:* Nominee, British Film Academy Award for The Servant; Edinburgh Festival Award for Just Like a Woman; TV Drama Actress of the Year, The Guild of Television Producers and Directors (now BAFTA), 1968; BBC Personality, The Variety Club, 1969; ITV Personality of the Year, 1973; Voted by Readers of the TV Times as The Funniest Woman on Television, 1972, 1973, 1974; Variety Club's Choice as BBC Television's Woman of the Year, 1983. *Address:* c/o Wentley Productions Limited, Bowdens, Winter Hill, Cookham, Berkshire, England.

CRAMER Marjorie, b. 26 Apr. 1941, London, England. Plastic Surgeon. m. Philip Cramer, 1964. 2 daughters. *Education:* BA, Barnard College, 1964; MD, Downstate College of Medicine, 1968. *Appointments:* Surgical Intern, 1968-69, Surgical Resident, 1969-72, Plastic Surgical Resident, 1972-74, Kings County Hospital, Downstate Medical Center; Private Practice, 1974-. *Memberships:* Fellow, American College of Surgeons, 1977-; Diplomate, American Board of Plastic Surgery, 1976-. *Hobby:* Sculpting. *Address:* One Fifth Avenue, New York, NY 10003, USA.

CRANDALL Jane Leigh Ford, b. 11 Dec. 1933, Fort Wayne, Indiana, USA. Businesswoman. m. Dr Ira Carlton Crandall II, 29 Jan. 1954. 1 son, 2 daughters. *Education:* AA, Summa Cum Laude, 1975, BBA, Summa Cum Laude, 1986, LaSalle University. *Appointments:* Sales Clerk, Mary Leigh Variety Store, 1949-50; Sales Clerk, G C Murphy Co., 1950-51; Actuarial Clerk, Lincoln National Life Insurance Co., 1952-53; Billing Clerk, General Telephone Co., 1953-54; Salesperson, Snellenberg's Department Store, 1957-58; Sales Representative, Bestline Products, 1969-70; Sales Representative, Avon Products, 1970-73; Sales Representative, Sara Coventry Products, 1970-73; Vice President, IC Crandaqll and Associates, 1972-82; Vice President, 7C's Enterprises, 1972-; Clerical Temporary, Kelley Services, Inc., 1978; Machinist, 1978-80, Customer Service Representative, 1980-82, Micropump, Inc; Administrative Assistant, Diablo Realty, 1982-85; Administrative Temporary, Kelley Services Inc., 1986-; Board of Directors, Fly-in Fish, Inc., 1987-. *Memberships include:* American Business Women's Association (Treasurer, Board of Directors, Past President, Past Recording Secretary, Bay Winds Charter Chapter); Bay Area Council, ABWA, Associate Member; Women's Network of Contra Cocta County, Past Secretary; National Association of Female Executives, Associate Member, Concord Chamber of Commerce; Alpha Alpha Pi; Beta Sigma Phi; National Travel Club; National Wildlife Federation; Smithsonian Institution; National Historical Society; Neptune Society; American Association of Retired Persons; Concord Stitch and Chatter Society; Dana Farms Homeowner's Association; Concord Child Care Task Force, etc. *Honours:* Woman of the Year, American Business Women's Association, 1987; Lee Award for Historical Presentation, Concord Women's Club, 1976; Band Parent of the Year, Clayton Valley High School, 1974, 1976, 1977. *Hobbies:* Music; Sewing; Crafts; Reading; Camping; Travel; Gourmet Cooking. *Address:* 5754 Pepperridge Place, Concord, California 95421, USA.

CRANDALL Norma Rand, b. New York, USA. Biographer; Book Review Editor. m. Wilson C McCarty, deceased. *Education:* Passy Lycee, Paris, France, 1924-25; Barnard College, USA, 1926-27. *Appointments:* Editorial Consultant, Harcourt Brace Co., New York City, 1939-40. *Publications:* Book Reviews, essays in: The New Republic, New York Times, New Leader, North American Review, Humanist, Chicago Review, the 19th Century, American Book Collector, etc. *Creative Works:* An Evening With The Brontes - A Dramatic Reading, presented by the Library Players; Various Lectures on Charlotte and Emily Bronte in the 1970s and 80s. *Hobbies:* Swimming; Bridge; Art Galleries; Theatre.

Address: Apt 1B - 44 East 63rd Street, New York, NY 10021, USA.

CRANE Barbara, b. 19 Mar. 1928, Chicago, Illinois, USA. Photographer; Educator. 1 son, 2 daughters. *Education:* Mills College Oakland, California, 1945-48; BA, Art History, New York University, 1950; MS, Photography, Illinois Institute of Technology, Institute of Design, 1966. *Appointments:* Professor, School of Art, Institute of Chicago, 1967-; Visiting Professor, Philadelphia College of Art, Pennsylvania, spring 1977; Visiting Lecturer, Tufts University, Boston, Massachusetts, spring 1979; Visiting Professor, Cornell University, Ithaca, New York, autumn 1983; Visiting Professor, Bezalel Academy of Art and Design, Jerusalem, Israel, spring 1987. *Publications:* Barbara Crane: 1948-1980 (monograph), 1981; Barbara Crane: the Evolution of a Vision (exhibition catalogue), 1983. *Memberships:* Trustee, Friends of Photography, 1975-80; Society for Photographic Education (Board of Directors 1972-76); Chicago Network; Advisory Board to Polaroid Corporation Education Programme. *Honours:* Grant for Photography, National Endowment for the Arts, 1975, 1988; John Simon Guggenheim Memorial Fellowship in Photography, 1979; Polaroid Corporation Materials Grant, 1979-; Illinois Arts Council Completion Grant, 1985; Honoured Educator and Artist, Society for Photographic Education, Midwest Regional Conference, 1987; Outstanding Achievement Award, YWCA, 1987. *Address:* 3164 North Hudson, Chicago, IL 60657, USA.

CRANE Charlotte, b. 30 Aug. 1951, Hanover, New Hampshire, USA. Law School Professor. m. 5 July 1975, 2 daughters. *Education:* AB magna cum laude, Radcliffe College, Harvard University, 1973; JD magna cum laude, University of Michigan Law School, 1976. *Appointments:* Law Clerk to Hon W.McCree, US Court of Appeals 6th Circuit, 1976-77; Law Clerk to Hon H.Blackmun, US Supreme Court, 1977-78; Associate, Hopkins & Sutter, 1978-82; Northwestern University School of Law, Chicago, Illinois, 1982-. *Publications:* Ex Post Facto Limitations on Legislative Power, 1975; Constitutional Limits on Retroactive Tax Laws, 1987; Matching and the Income Tax Base. *Memberships:* American Bar Association; National Tax Association, Tax Institute of America. *Honours:* Permanent Class Marshall, Radcliffe Class of 1973; Member, United States Women's Rowing Team, 1973. *Hobbies:* Crewing; Windsurfing; Gardening. *Address:* Northwestern University School of Law, 357 East Chicago Avenue, Chicago, IL 60611, USA.

CRANE Laura Jane, b. 2 Nov. 1941, Middletown, Ohio, USA. Biochemist. m. Robert K. Crane, 13 Apr. 1972. *Education:* BS, Carnegie-Mellon University, 1963; MA, Harvard University, 1964; PhD, Rutgers University, 1972; Postdoctoral research, Roche Institute of Molecular Biology, 1972-75. *Appointments:* Assistant Scientist 1966-68, Group Leader 1976-79, Warner-Lambert; High School Teacher, English, Manila, Philippines, 1969; Manager 1979-80, Assistant Director 1980-85, Director of Research 1985-, J. T. Baker Inc. *Publications:* Numerous scientific journal reports, original research; Chapters, various books, biochemical research; Editor, reference book, Chiral Chromatographic Separations. Also: Invited lecturer, scientific symposia; Numerous patents. *Memberships:* American Chemical Society; American Society for Biological Chemistry; President, Al Khamsa, national society, Arabian horse breeders. *Honours:* Full scholarship, Armco Corporation, 1955-59; Nationl Merit Scholar, 1955; Fellowship, National Science Foundation, 1963-64; Du pont fellowship, 1965; Fellowship, National Department for Education & Arts, 1969-72; President's Scholar, 1956-59; Warner Prize, Chemistry, 1963; Hamilton Watch Award, 1963. *Hobbies include:* Breeding, training (classical dressage), showing Arabian horses. *Address:* J. T. Baker Inc, 222 Red School Lane, Phillipsburg, New Jersey 08865, USA.

CRANE Maida R. b. 14 Mar. 1955, Pittsburgh, Pennsylvania, USA. Lawyer. *Education:* Chatham College, 1972-75; BA 1976 summa cum laude, JD cum laude 1982, University of Pennsylvania. *Appointments:* Summer associate 1981, associate 1984-87, Schnader, Harrison, Segal & Lewis; Law clerk, US District Court, New Jersey, 1982-84; Assistant general counsel, Rorer Group Inc, 1988-. *Memberships:* American, Pennsylvania, Philadelphia, Montgomery County Bar Associations; Office, Delaware Valley chapter, American Corporate Counsel Association; Office, Pharmaceutical Manufacturers Association; Volunteer, Support Centre for Child Advocates. *Honours:* Phi Beta Kappa, Mortar Board, 1975. *Hobbies:* Horseback riding; Sculpting; Reading contemporary fiction; Home design. *Address:* c/o Rorer Group Inc, 500 Virginia Drive, Fort Washington, Pennsylvania 19034, USA.

CRANE Teresa Yancey, b. 18 Mar. 1957, Durham, North Carolina, USA. Publisher & Editor. m. W Carey Crane III, 27 Sept. 1980. 2 children. *Education:* BA, Economics, Randolph Macon Woman's College; Additional studies in business, Washsington & Lee University, The University of Richmond. *Appointments:* Public Relations, Reynolds Metals, 1979; Business Manager, Howard Chase Enterprises, 1980-81; Founder and President, Issue Action Publications Inc, 1982-; Founder, The Issue Exchange (TIE), 1988. *Publications:* Editor and Publisher, Books and periodicals on issue management including: Corporate Public Issues & Their Management; LINC Linking Issue Networks for Coopration. *Memberships:* The Issue Exchange, Board member; Newsletter Association of America; World Future Society. *Honour:* Poffenberger Award for Service, The Collegiate Schools, 1975. *Hobbies:* Writing; Reading; Music; Art; Swimming. *Address:* 219 South Street SE, Leesburg, Virginia 22075, USA.

CRANFORD Eula Forrest, b. 24 Sept. 1923, North Carolina, USA. Executive Director. m. John Henry Cranford, 4 July 1942, 2 daughters. *Appointments:* Acting Director, Stanly Co. Vocational Workshop, 1966-67; Executive Director, Stanly Co. Vocation Workshop Inc., 1967-85; Director, Adult Day Program for Association for Retarded Citizens, 1985-87. *Publications:* TV appearances. *Memberships:* President, North Carolina Rehabilities Facilities Inc, 1977; NC Rehabilitation Association Facility; President, Stanly Actioneers Civitation Club, 1986-87. *Honours:* Citizen of the Year, Albemarle Civitan Club, 1970-71; Citation of Merit, 1973; Citation of Merit, 1977; Community Service Award, 1978; Coordinator Christian Social Involvement, Albemarle District, 1988-89. *Hobbies:* Travel; Flower Gardening; Reading; Walking; Sports. *Address:* 1623 West Park Avenue, Albemarle, NC 28001, USA.

CRAVEN Gemma, b. 1 June 1950, Dublin, Republic of Ireland. Actress; Singer. *Education:* Loretto College, Dublin; St Bernard's Convent, Westcliff-on-Sea, England Bush Davies School, England. *Appointments:* Appeared in numerous stage shows including: South Pacific; They're Playing Our Song; Loot; Song and Dance; Songbook; Dandy Dick; Trelawny; Black Comedy; Polly in the Threepenny Opera; Cats; A Chorus of Disapproval; Jacobowsky and The Colonel; The Magistrate; Three Men on A Horse. Films: Cinderella in The Slipper and the Rose, 1976; Why Not Stay for Breakfast; Minna in Wagner. Television roles: Joan in Pennies from Heaven; Title role in Emily; Barbara Hare in East Lynne; Amalia in She Loves Me; Lilith in Robin of Sherwood. Has appeared in several musical specials including: Gemma, Girls and Gershwin; Must Wear Tights; Song by Song by Alan Jay Lerner; Song by Song by Noel Coward. Appearances in Call My Bluff; Child's Play; Give Us a Clue; This is Your Life; The Morecambe and Wise Show; 2 Royal Variety Performances; Treasure Hunt; Dangerous Days. Has appeared numerous times on the concert platform singing with the City of London Orchestra at the Barbican; BBC Concert Orchestra for several major broadcasts on radio; Star singer in Filmharmonic 85 concert, Royal Albert Hall with the London Symphony Orchestra. *Honours:* Best Actress in a musical for They're playing our song, societey of West End Theatre; Best Comedy Actress of the Year for Loot; Film Actress of the Year for The Slipper and the Rose, the Variety Club; The Most Promising New Actress for The Slipper and the Rose, The Evening News Awards. *Address:* c/o Stella Richards Management, 42 Hazlebury Road, London SW6 2ND, England.

CRAWFORD Amanda Clements, b. 15 June 1960, Gastonia, North Carolina, USA. Technical Sales Representative. *Education:* BSc, Biology, Belmont Abbey College 1982. *Appointments:* Gaston Memorial Hospital, 1980-81; Dixie Yeast Corporation, 1981-83; ICI Americas, 1984-85; Frito-Lay, Inc, 1985-87; Remel, Inc, 1987-. *Memberships:* National Association for Female Executives; South Eastern Association of Clinical Microbiologists; American Society of Microbiologists. *Honour:* Tau Upsilon Chapter Beta Beta Beta, National Biological Honor Society. *Hobbies:* Calligraphy; Drawing. *Address:* 8300-D Runaway Bay Drive, Charlotte, North Carolina 28212, USA.

CRAWFORD Linda Sibery, b. 27 Apr. 1947, Ann Arbor, USA. Assistant Attorney General. m. Lelouc A. Crawford, 4 Apr. 1970, 1 son, 2 daughter. *Education:* BA, University of Michigan, 1969; J.D., University of Maine, 1977. *Appointments:* Teacher, 1969-72; Assistant District Attorney, Trial Lawyer, 1977-79; Assistant Attorney General, Trial Lawyer, State of Maine 1979-. *Publications:* Articles in professional journals. *Memberships:* National Association of State Mental Health Attorneys, Vice Chair, 1987-89; American, Man & Kansas Bar Associations; American & Maine Trial Lawyers Associations; Trustee, Arthritis Foundation. *Honour:* National Book Award, 1976. *Hobbies:* Running; Music; Cooking; Needlework; Mountain Climbing. *Address:* 25 Winthrop St., Hallowell, ME 04347, USA.

CRAWFORD Mary Virginia Greer, b. 28 May 1919, Marshall, Texas, USA. College Professor. m. Cranford L. Crawford, 11 Nov. 1937, div., 1 son, 1 daughter. *Education:* BA, Wiley College, 1947; MA, New Mexico Highlands University, 1953; East Texas State University, 1972, 1983; East Texas Baptist College, 1985. *Appointments:* Wiley College, Marshall, Texas, 1947-. *Creative works:* Thesis; Research papers. *Memberships include:* Texas Business Educators Association; American Association of University Professors; National Business Education Association; Texas Business Education Council; Various honour societies. *Honours:* Numerous awards including: Woman of Year; Alumnus of Year; Outstanding Citizen of Year; Piper Scholar; Outstanding Educator; Texas Black Women's Hall of Fame; Teacher of Excellence; Commission on Status & Role of Women, Texas annual conference. *Hobbies:* Creative writing; Reading; Dramatic & public speaking; Community volunteer, worthwhile causes; Worker with children & young people. *Address:* 808 Atkins Boulevard, Marshall, Texas 75670, USA.

CRAWFORD Patricia A Farren, b. 6 Sept. 1928, Middleton, USA. Member, Crime Victims Compensation Board. m. Robert J. Crawford, 14 June 1947, divorced, 1 son, 1 daughter. *Appointments:* State Representative, 1968-76; Deputy Secretary, Commonwealth of Pennsylvania, 1979-84; Member, Crime Victims compensation Board, 1985-. *Publications:* Producer, 2 One Act Musicals, Turning Points, 1987, Out of This World, 1988. *Memberships:* various professional organisations. *Honours Include:* Woman of the Year, 1974; Honorary member: Junior Women's Club of Malvern, Para Medical Society, West Chester State College. *Hobbies:* Travel; Composing Music. *Address:* Crime Victims Compensation Bd., Room 307, Finiance Building, P.O. Box 1323, Harrisburg, Pas. 17120, USA.

CRAWFORD Priscilla R, b. 13 Oct. 1941, Ferndale, Michigan, USA. Social Psychologist. *Education:* BA, Butler University, 1962; Fulbright Scholar, Goethe University, Frankfurt, Germany, 1963; MA 1965, PhD 1970, The Ohio State University, Columbus, Ohio, USA. *Appointments:* Research Associate, Gary Income Maintenance Experimenta, 1970-73; Independent consulting, 1973-77; Director of Manpower, Development for the Indiana Department of Mental

Health, 1978-86; Director of Operations Research and Policy Analysis, 1986-. *Publications:* Numerous articles and papers to professional journals and conferences. *Memberships:* American Sociological Association; Eastern, Midwest and North Central Sociological Societies; Ohio Academy of Science; American Association of University Professors; American Management Association; Various Training Societies; Board, Indiana Academy of the Social Sciences; Board, Indiana Conference on Social Concers. *Honours include:* President, Mortar Board; Outstanding Freshman Woman; Outstanding Woman Student Alumni Association Award; Phi Kappa Phi; Phi Kappa Phi Alumni Award; Alpha Lambda Delta Scholarship Award; Special University Fellow, Ohio State University; Fellow, National Institute of Mental Health; Nominated for national award, American Society of Training and Development, 1980-81; Committee to Select Recipients, Governor's Showcase, Mental Health Awards, 1983. *Address:* 1653 E Kessler Blvd, Indianapolis, IN 46220, USA.

CREASON Mary Helen (Rawlinson), b. 20 Nov. 1924, Greenwood, Delaware, USA. Assistant Director, Michigan Aeronautics Commission. m. William Creason, 21 Oct. 1944, 3 sons, 1 daughter. *Education:* BS, Western Michigan University, 1944; Licensed, private pilot 1943, commercial pilot 1946, airline transport 1966. *Appointments include:* Self-employed, fixed base operation, Ottawa Air Training & Transport, owner & chief pilot, Grand Haven Memorial & Muskegon County Airports, 1964-77; Manager, Grand Haven Memorial Airport, 1974-75; Assistant Administrator 1983-84, Administrator 1984-86, Safety & Services Division, Bureau of Aeronautics, Michigan Department of Transportation; Assistant Deputy Director, Michigan Aeronautics Commission, 1987-. *Creative works:* Articles, flying, flight safety; Editor, Michigan Aviation, 1977-83; Various film programmes, aviation subjects. *Memberships include:* Chapter Chair, Ninety-Nines (women pilots international); President, Grand Haven Area League of Women Voters, Grand Haven Pilots & Owners Association; Women's, & Citizen's Advisory Committees on Aviation (to Federal Aviation Administration) 1969-74; Civil Air Patrol; Aerospace Education Council, Michigan. *Honours:* Amelia Earhart Scholarship, Ninety-Nines, 1964; Frank C. Brewer Memorial Aerospace Award, Great Lakes Region Civil Air Patrol, 1979. *Hobbies:* Writing; Photography; Skiing; Travel. *Address:* 824 Lake Avenue, Grand Haven, Michigan 49417, USA.

CREMER Lyall Millicent, b. 13 Jan. 1923, Kokstad, South Africa. m. Jack Stewart Cremer 16 June 1945, 1 son. *Education:* Diplomas: General Nursing, 1945; Midwifery, 1966, Psychiatric Nursing, 1976; University Diplomas: Nursing Education, 1970, Nursing Administration, 1981. *Appointments:* Ward Sister, 1947-49; Clinical Instructor, 1950-65, Tutor Sister, 1970-72, Nursing College; Senior Matron, 1972-75, Principal Matron, 1975-78, Chief Matron, 1978-87 (retired), Hospital. *Memberships:* South African Nursing Association; Board Member, TAFTA; Executive Member, Natal Coast Council for The Aged; Founder, Chairman, Durban & District Geriatric Discussion Group; Founder, Vice Chairman, Hospice Association of Natal; National Vice President, Chairman, SAVES. *Honours Include:* Honorary Life Membership, South African Nursing Association, 1985; Upjohn Achievement Award for Community Nursing, 1987. *Hobbies:* Reading; Gardening. *Address:* 10 Park Lane Mews, 9 Park Lane, Kloof, 3610 Natal, South Africa.

CREWE Candida Annabel, b. 6 June 1964, London, England. Novelist; Journalist. *Education:* Headington School, Oxford, 1978-82. *Appointments:* Quartet Books Ltd, 1983-86; Weekly Column, The Evening Standard, 1986-87; Freelance Journalist for The Telegraph, The Spectator, Tatler, Independent, The Standard, The Sunday Times, The Observer, Harpers & Queen, 1987-. *Publications:* Books: Focus, 1985; Romantic Hero, 1986; Accommodating Molly, 1989. *Honour:* Runner-up in Catherine Pakenham Memorial Award for

Journalism, 1987. *Address:* 1 Arundel Gardens, London W11 2LN, England.

CRICHTON-STUART Anna Rose, b. 30 May 1940, Cork, Ireland. Mother. m. 11 Feb. 1970, deceased 1982, 3 sons. *Education:* New Hall School Chelmsford, 1951-57. *Memberships:* President, Basingstoke Branch, Multiple Sclerosis Society; Part-time Welfare Officer, Multiple Sclerosis Society; First Lady Govenor, Farleigh School, Andover; Vice President, Deaf Club Association, London. *Hobbies:* Riding; Drawing; Gardening; Fund-Raising; Racing - Horses Owned: Spanish Line & Dry Gin; Music. *Address:* Upton Grey House, Upton Grey, Basingstoke, Hampshire, England.

CRIST Judith (Klein), b. 22 May 1922, New York City, USA. Journalist; Film and drama critic. m. William B Crist, 3 July 1947. 1 son. *Education:* AB Hunter College, 1941; Teaching Fellow, State College, Washington, 1942-43; MSc Journalism, Columbia University, 1945. *Appointments:* Civilian instructor, 3091st AAFBU, 1943-44; Reporter, 1945-60; Editor Arts, 1960-63, Associate Theater Critic, 1957-63, Film critic, 1963-66, New York Herald Tribune; Film, theater critic, NBC-TV Today Show, 1963-73; Film critic, World Jour, Tribune, 1966-67; Critic at large, Ladies Home Journal, 1966-67; Contributing editor, film critic, TV Guide, 1966-87; New York magazine, 1968-75; The Washingtonian, 1970-72; Palm Springs Life, 1971-75; Contributing editor, film critic Saturday Review, 1975-77, 1980-84; New York Post, 1977-78; MD/Mrs, 1977-; 50 Plus, 1978-83; L'Officiel/USA, 1979-80; arts critic Channel 9 News Station, WWOR-TV, 1981-87; Goodlife, 1985-86; Coming Attractions, 1985-; Instructor journalism, Hunter College, 1947; Sarah Lawrence College, 1958-59; Associate Journalism, 1959-62, Lecturer journalism, 1962-71, Adjunct professor, 1971-, Columbia Graduate School of Journalism. *Publications:* The Private Eye; The Cowboy and the Very Naked Girl, 1968; Judith Crist's TV Guide to the Movies, 1974; Take 22; Moviemakers on Moviemaking, 1984; Contributor of articles to magazines. *Memberships:* Columbia Journalism Alumni (President 1967-70); New York Film Critics; National Society of Film Critic; Sigma Tau Delta. *Honours:* Trustee Anne O'Hare McCormick Scholarship Fund; Recipient Page One award, New York Newspaper Guild, 1955; George Polk award, 1961; New York Newspaper Women Club awards, 1955, 1959, 1963, 1965, 1967; Edn. Writers Association award, 1952; Columbia Graduate School of Journalism Alumni award, 1961; Named to 50th Anniversary Honors List, 1963; Centennial President's medal, Hunter College, 1970; Named to Hunter Alumni Hall of Fame, 1973. *Address:* 180 Riverside Drive, New York, NY 10024, USA.

CRISWELL Eleanor Camp, b. 12 May 1938, Norfolk, Virginia, USA. Psychologist; Professor. m. Thomas L. Hanna, 24 June 1974. *Education:* BA 1961, MA 1962, University of Kentucky; EdD, University of Florida, 1969. *Appointments:* Jacksonville University, Florida, 1966; University of Florida, 1968; California State College, Fullerton 1967, Hayward 1969; College of Holy Names, 1969-75; Founding director, Humanistic Psychology Institute (now Saybrook Institute), 1970-77; Professor of Psychology, Sonoma State University, California, 1969-; Clinical director, biotherapeutics, Kentfield Medical Hospital, 1984-. *Publications:* Co-editor, Biofeedback & Family Practice Medicine, 1983; Author, research section, Somatics magazine (journal of bodily arts & sciences), 1982-; Managing editor, ibid, 1976-; Articles, various magazines, journals & books. Also US patent, optokinetic perceptual learning device. *Memberships:* Past president, Association for Humanistic Psychology; Aerospace Medical Association; American Psychological Association; Association for Transpersonal Psychology; American Association for Advancement of Science; Biofeedback Society of America; Past executive director, Biofeedback Society, California; California State Psychological Association. *Hobbies:* Guitar; Gardening; Writing; Travel; Computers; Horses. *Address:* Psychology Department, Sonoma State University, Rohnert Park, California 94928, USA.

CROCKER Olga Lillian, b. 9 Mar. 1930, High Prairie, Alberta, Canada. University Professor. m. Leo B. Crocker, 12 Apr. 1952, 3 sons. *Education:* BEd, MBA, University of Alberta, Canada; PhD, University of Washington, Seattle, USA. *Appointments include:* High School Teacher, 1956-74, Adjunct Professor, Central Michigan University, USA, 1970-89; Professor, Business Administration, University of Windsor, Canada, 1976-89; President, An. Advantage 1987-89, Educational Skills Process 1986-89, Centre for Workplace Dynamics 1986-89. *Publications include:* Incidents & Cases in Canadian Personnel Administration, 1986; Experimental Exercises in Canadian Personnel Administration, 1986; Quality Circles: Guide to Participation & Productivity, 1984, 1986; MSA Integrative Paper, 1988; Various other articles & documents. Editorial board, Canadian Public Policy. *Memberships include:* Offices: University of Windsor Faculty Association, Ontario & Windsor Personnel Associations, Chamber of Commerce. *Honours:* Senior Faculty Award, S. Bronfman Foundation, 1978; E. J. Benson Award, 1977; Scholarships: Government of Alberta, & Imperial Order of Daughters of Empire 1948, Edmonton Women Teachers 1972. *Hobbies:* Writing; Stamp Collecting. *Address:* Faculty of Business Administrtion, University of Windsor, Ontario, Canada.

CROMAN Dorothy Young, b. 25 Dec. 1906, Waverly, Washington, USA. Author. m. (1) Harrison Croman, 1 Aug. 1943, divorced 1952, 1 son, 2 daughters. (2) George Rosenberg, 21 Aug. 1970, deceased 23 Nov. 1970. *Education:* Reed College, Portland, Oregon, 1937-39; University of Seattle, Washington, 1956, 1957, 1962. *Appointments:* Secretary and Writer, Seattle Public Schools, 1954-64; Night Supervisor, University of Washington, Seattle, 1965-69. *Creative works:* Novels for children: Mystery of Steamboat Rock, 1956, 1984; Danger in Sagebrush Country, 1984; Trouble on the Blue Fox Islands, 1985; Secret of the Poison Ring, 1986; 6 Readers for Slow Learners, 1962-74; Sprinter in Life - Charles Richard Drew, 1988. *Memberships:* Smithsonian Associates; American Association of Retired Persons; Pioneer Assocition of State of Washington; Seattle Historical Society; Reed College Alumni Association; National Urban League; NAACP; Authors Guild Inc; National League of American PEN Women, 1960-, Secretary Seattle Branch, 1968-70, Editor Whistling Swan, NLAPW Seattle Branch Newsletter, President, 1984-86. *Honours:* Two NLAPW Gold Biennial Awards in Writing, 1972; NLAPW Owl Award for outstanding achievement in writing, 1984. *Hobbies:* Folk dancing; Swimming (volunteer teacher of senior citizens to pattern dance and to swim); Volunteer work at Orthopedic Hospital in Seattle, 1979; Travelling. *Address:* Kamlu-Apt 20, 1000 NE 82nd Avenue, Vancouver, WA 98664, USA.

CRONIN Audrey Kurth, b. 14 Jan. 1958, Jacksonville, Florida, USA. Assistant Professor. m. Patrick Maurice Cronin, 8 June 1985. 1 son. *Education:* AB, Public and International Affairs, summa cum laude, Princeton University, 1981; MPhil, International Relations 1983, DPhil, International Relations 1985, St Anthony's College, Oxford University, England. *Appointments:* Assistant Professor, Government and Foreign Affairs, University of Virginia, 1985-88; Assistant Director, Center for International Security Studies at Maryland, 1988-89; Assistant Professor, Security Studies, School of Public Affairs, University of Maryland, 1988-. *Publications:* Great Power Politics and The Struggle Over Austria 1945- 55, 1986; Numerous articles in edited volumes and journals. *Memberships:* President, Oxford University Strategic Studies Group, 1983-84; Council on Foreign Relations; American Political Science Association; International Studies Association; Women in International Security; Committee on Atlantic Studies; International Institute for Strategic Studies; American Association for the Advancement of Slavic Studies. *Honours:* Phi Beta

Kappa, 1981; Marshall scholar, 1981-84; Post-doctoral Fellow, European Society and Western Security, Center for International Affairs, Harvard University, 1984-85; Herman Kahn Visiting Fellow, Hudson Institute, 1987-88. *Hobbies:* Jogging; Aerobics and other sports; Ballet; Music; Needlework. *Address:* School of Public Affairs, Morrill Hall, University of Maryland, College Park, MD 20742, USA.

CRONIN-GOLOMB Alice Mary, b. 27 Mar. 1957, New Haven, Connecticut, USA. Research Scientist. m. Mark Cronin-Golomb, 17 May 1981. *Education:* BA, Wesleyan University, 1979; PhD, California Institute of Technology, 1984. *Appointments:* Assistant Professor, Department of Psychology, Barton University, 1989-; Research Fellow, Department of Brain and Cognitive Sciences, Massachusetts Institute of Technology, 1985-89; Graduate Research 1979-84, Research Fellow and Visiting Associate 1985-86, Division of Biology, California Institute of Technology; Lecturer in Psychology, Harvard University, 1989. *Publications:* Articles published in scientific journals; Author: The Concept Comprehension Test; Translation from German of play by G E Lessing, Emilia Galotti; Stage adaptations of children's classics: The Wind in the Willows, Puss-in-Boots; Direction and production of German radio play, Draussen vor der Tur, by W Borchert, 1979; Directed US premier of German/English production of L Tieck's Der gestiefelte Kater (Puss in Boots), 1984; Directed plays including Emilia Galotti (using the above-mentioned translation); Mark Twain's Bizarre Shorts. *Memberships:* Society for Neuroscience; American Psychological Association; Eastern Psychological Association; American Association for the Advancement of Science; Women in Neuroscience; National Organization for Women; National Museum of Women in the Arts; National Archery Association. *Honours:* Alzheimers Association, Pilot Research Grant, 1989; Biomedical Research Support Grants, National Institutes of Health, 1985 and 1987; National Research Service Award, National Institute on Aging, NIH, 1985-88; Phi Beta Kappa, Wesleyan University, 1979; Scott Prize for Excellence in Modern Languages (German), Wesleyan University, 1979. *Hobbies:* Gardening; Beer-brewing; Theatre Arts; Archery; Travelling; Translation of written works (from German); Hiking; Skiing; Skating; Baseball, specifically following the Boston Red Sox. *Address:* 669 Pearl Street, Reading, MA 01867, USA.

CROPPER Anna, b. 13 May 1938, Brierfield, England. Actress. *Education:* Sorbonne, Paris; Central School of Speech and Drama, London. *Memberships:* Transpersonal Pyschology Centre, London. *Hobbies:* Philosophy; Cooking; Swimming; Travel. *Address:* c/o Kate Feast Management, 43A Princess Road, Regents Park, London, England.

CROPPER Hilary, b. 9 Jan. 1941, Bollington, Cheshire, England. Chief Executive. m. Peter Cropper, 16 Sept. 1963, 1 son, 2 daughters. *Education:* BSc., 1964. *Appointments:* ICL, Bridge House, Putney, 1970-85; Chief Executive, F.I. Group Plc, 1985-; Director, TSB Bank Plc, 1987-. *Honours:* Freedom of the City of London, 1987. *Address:* F.I. Group Plc., Chesham House, Church Lane, Berkhamsted HP4 2HA, England.

CROSHAW Susan, b. 17 Mar. 1959, Northamptonshire, England. Public Speaker & Voluntary Worker, Aspects of Disability (has suffered fom Chronic Juvenile Arthritis since age 2). m. Robert Thomas Croshaw. *Publications:* Essay, Physical Perfection, 1987; Contributions, disability magazines & periodicals, animal rights magazines, national & international educational pamphlets & booklets. Also: TV appearances, including Jimmy Young TV programme, 1985; Video, Health with Humanity, 1988. *Memberships:* Treasurer, telephone operator, Disabled Information & Advice Line, 1980-84; Founder & Coordinator, international animal rights group, Disabled Against Animal Research & Exploitation, 1986. *Honours:* Achievement award, East Anglia & Midlands DISTA, 1986; Finalist, Midlands Women of Year, 1987; Gold award (video), 31st International Film & Television Festival, New York, 1988. *Hobbies:* Public speaking; Lectures to medical profession on problems of disability; Attending animal rights exhibitions; Reading; Theatre. *Address:* 22 The Severn, Grange Estate, Daventry, Northants NN11 4QR, England.

CROSS Janis Alexander, b. 8 Sept. 1954, Plainview, Hale County, Texas, USA. Corporate Counsel/Attorney. m. Stephen Douglas Cross. 19 Aug. 1978. 1 son, 1 daughter. *Education:* BA, History, 1976, JD, Law 1979, Texas Tech University School of Law, Lubbock. *Appointments:* Private Practice of Law, Amarillo, Texas, 1979-81; Corporate Attorney, Pioneer Corporation, 1981-84; Corporate Attorney, Cabot Corporation, 1984-87; Corporate Counsel, Mason & Hanger-Silas Mason Co, Inc, Amarillo, 1987-. *Memberships:* American Bar Assoc; Texas Bar Assoc; Amarillo Bar Assoc; Delta Theta Phi Legal Fraternity; Gamma Phi Beta, Sorority; Board of Directors: Plemmons-Echols Neighborhood Association; March of Dimes; Campfire Inc. President 1988-89, Amarillo Women's Network; American Association of University Women. *Hobbies:* Reading; Snow skiing; Bicycling. *Address:* P O Box 30020, Amarillo, Texas 79177, USA.

CROSS K Patricia, b. 17 Mar. 1926, Normal, Illinois, USA. University Professor. *Education:* BS, Illinois State University, 1948; AM 1951, PhD 1958, University of Illinois. *Appointments:* Dean of Students, Cornell University, 1959-64; Sr Program Director 1964-67, Distinguished Research Scientist 1967-80, Educational Testing Service; Professor, Harvard University, 1980-88; Conner Professor, University of California, 1988-. *Publications:* Adults as Learners, 1981; Accent on Learning, 1976; Beyond The Open Door, 1971; Classroom Assessment, 1988. *Memberships:* Academy of Education, Vice Chair, 1981-85; American Association of Higher Education, President 1975; President Elect 1988 Board of Trustees, Bradford College 1984-88, Antioch College 1976-78; NCHEMS; ASHE. *Honours:* Borden Medal for Accent on Learning, 1976; E F Lindquist Award, American Association for Educational Research, 1986; National Person of The Year, National Council on Community Service & Cont Education, 1988; Outstanding Service Award, Coalition of Adult Education, 1987; Medal of Honor, New York Regents, 1985; Honorary Doctoral Degrees: Northeastern University, Illinois State University, Hood College, Loyola University of Chicago and others. *Address:* Graduate School of Education, University of California, Berkeley, CA 94720, USA.

CROSS Shelley Ann, b. 2 Dec. 1948, Beacon, New York, USA. Physician: Neurologist, Neuro-ophthalmologist. *Education:* AB, Wellesley College, 1970; MD, Med Coll Pennsylvania, 1975. *Appointments:* Intern, Montreal General Hospital, Canada, 1975-76; Resident in Medicine, Royal Victoria Hospital, Montreal, 1976-78; Resident in Neurtology, Massachusetts General Hospital, Boston, USA, 1978-81; Fellow in Neuro-ophthalmology, Bascom Palmer Eye Inst, Miami, Florida, 1981-82; Consultant in Neurology, Mayo Clinic, Rochester, 1982-. *Publications:* Numerous articles to professional journals. *Memberships:* Fellow, Royal College Physicians & Suregons (Canada), FRCP(C); Fellow, American College of Physicians; American Academy of Neurology; Frank Walsh Society; North American Neuro-ophthalmology Society. *Hobbies:* Classical music; Travel; Literature; Languags. *Address:* Department of Neurology; Mayo Clinic, 200 SW 1st Street, Rochester, MN 55905, USA. ·

CROUCH Dora Polk, b. 15 Feb. 1931, Ann Arbor, Michigan, USA. Professor of Architectural History. m. Ralph G Crouch, 12 June 1953, divorced 1976. 4 sons, 3 daughters. *Education:* BA 1965, MA 1967, PhD with distinction, 1969, UCLA. *Appointments:* California State University, San Francisco, 1969-70; University of California, Berkeley, 1970-71; University of California at Los Angeles, 1971-72; California State University, Dominguez Hills, 1972-75; Rensselaer Polytechnic Institute, 1975-. *Publications:* Co-author, Spanish City Planning in North America, 1982; Co-author,

Architecture Thesaurus, Volume 1 of Art & Architecture Thesaurus, 1983-84; Author, History of Architecture-Stonehenge to Skyscrapers, 1984; Numerous articles. *Memberships:* Society of Architectural Historians, 1972-; College Art Association; American Institute of Archaeology. *Honours:* AAUW Fellowship, 1984-85; National Gallery of Art Fellowship, 1980-81; University Research Grant, Berkeley, 1970-71; NDEA Fellowship, UCLA, 1967-69; Kress Fellowship, 1967. *Hobbies:* Needlework; Photography; Gardening. *Address:* 37 Pinewoods Avenue, Troy, NY 12180, USA.

CROUCH-RUIZ, Evelyn, b. 18 May 1945, Ponce, Puerto Rico. Professor of Nursing. m. Julio Rivera, 8 Aug. 1970, divorced, 1978, 2 sons, 1 daughter. *Education:* BSN, Catholic University of Puerto Rico, 1972; MSN, 1978, PhD, 1987, University of Texas, Austin, USA. *Appointments:* Staff Nurse, St Lukes Episcopal Hospital, Puerto Rico, 1966-67; Staff Nurse, Columbia Presbyterian Medical Center, New York, 1967-69; Instructor, 1972-80, Professor, 1983-, Catholic University, Puerto Rico; Clinical Nurse, US Public Health, Houston, Texas, 1980-81. *Publications:* Perceptions of and Emotional Cognitive and Behavioral Responses to Premature & Fulltime Birth. *Memberships:* Puerto Rico College of Professional Nurses, President, Research Commission, 1988-. *Honours:* Cum Laude, 1972. *Hobbies:* Needlepoint; Swimming; Cooking. *Address:* BE 33, 4th Street, Las Delicias, Ponce, Puerto Rico 00731, USA.

CROUTHER Betty Jean, b. 2 Mar. 1950, Carthage, Mississippi, USA. Assistant Professor. m. Eddie Pate, 1970 divorced 1978. 1 daughter. *Education:* BSc, Jackson State University, Mississippi, 1972; Master of Fine Arts, University of Mississippi, 1975; Doctor of Philosophy, University of Missouri, 1985. *Appointments:* Assistant Professor of Art and Art History, Lincoln University, Jefferson City, 1978-80; Assistant Professor of Art and Art History, Jackson State University, Mississippi, 1980-83; Assistant Professor of Art and Art History, University of Mississippi, 1983-. *Publications:* Deciphering the Mississippi River Iconography of Frederick Oakes Sylvester, 1986; Black American Art in the South Before 1900, to be published. *Memberships:* Southeastern College Art Conference; National Art Education Association; Mississippi Art Education Association; Phi Kappa Phi; Kappa Pi International Honorary Art Fraternity. *Honours:* J Paul Getty Postdoctoral Fellowship, Stanford University, 1986-87; Ford Foundation Fellowship for Black Americans, 1974-78. *Hobbies:* Gardening; Comic Books; Needlework; Photography. *Address:* Department of Art, University of Mississippi, University, Mississippi 38677, USA.

CROW Lynne Smith, b. 13 Oct. 1942, Buffalo, New York, USA. Insurance Saleswoman; Life Underwriter. m. William D. Crow II, 16 Apr. 1966, 2 sons, 1 daughter. divorced. *Education:* BA, Sweet Briar College, Virginia, 1964; CLU, ChFC, American College, Pennsylvania, 1986. *Appointments:* Claims representative, Brooklyn & NYC 1964-66, East Orange NJ 1967-68, Liberty Mutual Insurance Company; McGraw Hill Book Company, 1966-67; Sales Associate, Realty World, Allsopp Realtors, 1981-82; Field representative, Guardian Life, Millburn NJ, 1982-. *Memberships include:* Offices, Newark Association of Life Underwriters, United Way, Junior League; Association of Chartered Life Underwriters; Chartered Financial Association; Women's Life Underwriters Association; Qualifying Member, Million Dollars Round Table. *Honours:* Sales Associate of Year, 1984; National Sales Award, 1988; National Quality Achievement Award, 1988; Health Achievement Award, 1988. *Hobbies:* Travel; Reading; Tennis; Paddle Tennis; Skiing; Sailing. *Address:* 22 The Crescent, Short Hills, New Jersey 07078, USA.

CROWDER Barbara Lynn, b. 3 Feb. 1956, Mattoon, Illinois, USA. Attorney. m. Lawrence O. Taliana, 17 Apr. 1982, 2 sons. *Education:* BA with distinction, Speech Communication, 1978; HD, University of Illinois, 1981.

Appointments: Associate, Louis Olivero, Peru, Illinois, 1981-82; Assistant State's Attorney, Madison County, Illinois, 1982-85; Partner, Robbins, Crowder & Bader, Attorneys, Edwardsville, Illinois, 1985-. *Memberships:* Women's Lawyers Association of Metro East, President 1985, Vice-President 1984; Edwardsville Zoning Board of Appeals, Chairman 1986-87, Vice-Chairman 1985-86; Edwardsville Plan Commission, 1985-87; American Trial Lawyers Association; Illinois State Bar Association; Madison County Bar Association. *Honours:* Parliamentary Debate Award, University of Illinois, Champaign, 1978; Best Oral Advocate, Moot Court, University of Illinois Law School, 1979; Distinguished Senior, Phi Alpha Delta, 1981; Woman of Achievement, Edwardsville Business and Professional Women, 1985; District XIV Young Career Woman Award, Business and Professional Women, 1986; Junior Service Award, Edwardsville Business and Professional Women, 1987; Alice Paul Award, Alton/Edwardsville NOW, 1987. *Hobbies:* Reading; Politics. *Address:* 1538d Troy Road, Edwardsville, IL 62025, USA.

CROWE Sylvia, b. 15 Sept. 1901, Banbury, Oxon, England. Landscape Architect. *Education:* Swanley Horticultural College, 1920-23. *Appointments:* Designing Gardens, 1926-39; Military Service, 1939-45; Private Practice, Landscape Architect, 1945-. *Publications:* Garden Design; Tomorrows Landscape; The Landscape of Roads; The Landscape of Power; Forestry in the Landscape; The Patterns of Landscape. *Memberships:* Landscape Institute, Past President; IUCN; Australian Institute; Landscape Architecture; American Society Landscape Architecture; Hon. Fellow, Royal Institute of British Architects; Hon. Fellow, Royal Institute Town Planning. *Honours:* DBE; Landscape Institute Medal, 1985; John D. Bracken Fellow in Landscape Architecture Award, USA, 1988. *Hobbies:* Gardens; Country Walks; Writing; Sketching. *Address:* 59 Ladbroke Grove, London W11 3AT, England.

CROWLEY Rosemary Anne, b. 30 July 1938, Melbourne, Australia. Senator, Parliament of Australia. m. James Raymond Crowley, 5 Feb. 1964. 3 sons. *Education:* Kilmaire Brigidine Convent, Hawthorn, Victoria, 1943-55; MBBS, Melbourne University, 1960. *Appointments:* RMO, St Vincent's Hospital, Melbourne; Pathology Registrar, Royal Childrens Hospital, Melbourne, 1964; Part-time Pathology appointments, 1970-74; Part-time General Practitioner, Southern Clinicl, 1974-75; Parent Education Counsellor, Clovelly Park Community Health Centre, 1975-83; Elected to Senate, 1983 (1st ALP Woman elected to Federal Parliament from South Australia); Convenor, Federal Government Working Group on Women in Sport. *Memberships:* Director, Australian People for Health Education and Development Abroad, 1984-; Foundation Member, Mental Health Preview Tribunal, 1979-83; Member, ANZSERCH/APHA; Doctors Reform Soceity; Holds numerous positions within Australian Labour Party. *Hobbies:* Jogging; Gardening; Reading; Theatre; Music. *Address:* 354 King William Street, Adelaide, South Australia 5000, Australia.

CROWLEY Suzan Elizabeth, b. 10 Sept. 1954, Lincolnshire, England. Actress. *Education:* Bristol Old Vic Theatre School; London Academy of Film and Television. *Career:* Repertory Theatre includes: Salisbury Playhouse; Glasgow Citizens, 1977; Liverpool Playhouse, 1978; Liverpool Everyman, 1981. West End: Under the Greenwood Tree, Vaudeville Theatre, 1980. Films include: Draughtsmans Contract; Success is the Best Revenge; Giro City; Inside Out; Year of the Bodyguard; Ullysees; Dantes Inferno. Television includes: Plays for Today, Treatment, BBC; Byron, BBC. *Membership:* Director, Actorum Actors Co-op; Boundary Road Co-operative. *Hobbies:* Horse Riding; Sub Aqua Diving; Skiing; Alto Saxaphone. *Address:* c/o Libby Glenn Associates, 1-3 Charlotte Street, London W1, England.

CROWTHER Connie Justice, b. 16 June 1944, Ohio, USA. Journalist; Editor; News Bureau Director. m. Michael Timothy Crowther, 20 Mar. 1971. *Education:*

BSc, Journalism, Ohio University, 1966. *Appointments:* Correspondent, Time Magazine & UPI, 1970-72; Lecturer, Journalism, College of the Bahamas, 1972-74; Reporter: Miami Herald, Nassau Guardian, Huntington Herald-Dispatch, 1965-75; Florida Legislature, 1975-76; Chamber of Commerce, Coral Gables, 1976-80; News Bureau Director, Florida International University, Miami, 1980-. *Publications:* Presentation, Suppose They Gave a News Conference and Nobody Came, to professional groups, students, peers; Freelance writing for many magazines and newspapers including South Florida Magazine, Americas. *Memberships include:* Women in Communications Inc, President, Miami Chapter, 1985-86, (Outstanding WICI Chapter, National Award 1985-86) National WICI Committee Member, 1983-84, 1985-86, 1987-88, National WICI Committee Chair, 1984-85, 1986-87; Miami Chapter, Headliner, 1989; Zeta Tau Alpha; Society of Professional Journalists; International Association of Business Communicators; Founding Chair, Education Network (EdNet). *Honours include:* National Honour Society, Latin & English scholarship Teams, High School; Pershing Rifles Princess & Homecoming Queen Candidate, Ohio University, 1964; Best of Category and Grand Award, 1989; Awards of Excellence 1988 and 1987 (District III) and National Gold Medal, Council for the Advancement and Support of Education (CASE); National Award of Excellence Winner, Chamber of Commerce of the US, 1979 and 1980; Award Winner (Public Relations Projects), elected member, CASE District III Board of Directors; Several Journalism awards. *Hobbies:* Scuba Diving; Hiking; Travel; Reading; Boating; Writing; Photography. *Address:* 3612 Palmarito St, Coral Gables, FL 33134, USA.

CRUICKSHANK Maureen Doris, b. 20 Oct. 1941, Hereford, England. College Principal. m. Brian Cruickshank, 14 Aug. 1964, 2 sons, 1 daughter. *Education:* BA, 2nd Class Honours, Philosophy, Politics & Economics, Lady Margaret Hall, University of Oxford, 1963; MED, University of Warwick, 1975. *Appointments:* St Felix School, Southwold, Suffolk, 1963-64; Pool Hayes Comprehensive School, Willenhall, 1964; Southfields Junior School, 1970-71; Sidney Stringer School, Coventry, 1972-74; Binley Park Comprehensive School, 1975; Hind Leys College, Shepshed, 1976-81; Principal, Beauchamp College, Leicestershire, 1981-. *Publications:* Co-Editor (1 of 4), book, Girl Friendly Schooling, 1985; Various professional articles. *Memberships:* Council 1986-89, Secondary Heads Association; Committee, Lady Margaret Hall Association; Governor, Leicestershire Dance & Drama Workshop; Fawcett Society; Invited member, Windsor Meeting 7, St George's House, Windsor Castle, 1983, 1988. *Hobbies:* Gender issues; Skiing; Swimming; Art; Theatre; Travel. *Address:* 15 Stoneygate Road, Leicester, LE2 2AB, England.

CRUM Helen Louise, b. 18 July 1920, Kempton, Illinois. Teacher, Learning disabled and emotionally disturbed adolescents. m. Albert Carl Sundberg Jr, 26 Dec. 1943, divorced 1982. 2 daughters. *Education:* AA, Los Angeles Pacific College, 1940; BA 1972, MA 1975, Northeastern Illinois University, 1980; PhD, Northwestern University, 1980; Attended: Heidelberg University, Germany 1958-59, St George's College, Jerusalem, 1967, Cambridge University, England, 1973-74. *Appointments:* Teacher, Grades 1-8, Georgetown School, Pontiac, Illinois, 1941-43; Teacher, Grades 5 & 6, Special Education, Winnetka Public Schools, 1972-73; Teacher, Grades 7 & 8, Iroquois Junior High School, Des Plaines, 1975-85; Extension Course Teacher, National College of Education, Evanston, 1982-83. *Publications:* Dissertation: Values clarification: An intervention strategy for use with adolescent drug abusers. MA Thesis: An appraisal of Frank Hewett's Strategies for working with emotionally distrubed children in the classroom. *Memberships:* National Educ Association; Illinois Educ Association; Des Plaines Educ Association; American Psychological Association; Special Educator, Learning Disabled, Emotionally disturbed and Educable Mentally retarded; Episcopal Church of America. *Honours:* Scholarship, Seattle

Pacific College, 1940; Foremost Women of the Twentieth Centure, Northwestern University; Honours graduate, Northeastern Illinois University, 1972. *Hobbies:* Travel; Sewing; Gardening. *Address:* 36 Willowbrook Ct, Kingsport, TN 37660, USA.

CRUM DE GROOT Susan, b. 16 Mar. 1953, Queens, New York, USA. Licensed Psychologist. m. Bruce Anthony De Groot, 12 Aug. 1973, 1 son. *Education:* BS, Evangel College, 1975; MA, Montclair State College, 1978; PhD, Cognitive Psychology, Rutgers University, 1986. *Appointments:* School Neuropsychologist, Nyack Public Schools, 1986-88; Director, Clinical Services, Neuro Rehab Center, Warwick, NY, 1988-. *Publications:* Articles in various journals including: Psychology of Women Quarterly. *Memberships:* American Psychological Association; National Academy of Neuropsychology; American Orthopsychiatric Association. *Honours:* Recipient, various honours & awards. *Address:* 8 Mountainside Road Extension, Warwick, NY 10990, USA.

CRUMRINE June, b. 1 Jan. 1957, Canada. Nurse. m. Paul Richard Crumrine, 10 July 1976, 1 son. *Education:* RN; BSN. *Appointments:* Staff Nurse, Intensive Care, Coronary Care, 1977-81; Medical/ Surgical Staff Development Instructor, 1981-82; Adjunct Professor, Nursing, 1982-86; Manager, Cardiac Rehabilitation & Physical Fitness Dept., 1986-. *Publications:* articles in journals. *Memberships:* American College of Sports Medicine; American Running and Fitness Association; Purdue University Alumni Association. *Honours:* Member, Chancillors Forum for Academic Honoress, Purdue University, 1980-81; Outstanding Graduating Senior, School of Science & Nursing, Purdue University. *Hobbies:* Physical Fitness; Oil Painting; Sports Medicines. *Address:* 3101 Candlewood Court, Flossmoor, IL 60422, USA.

CRUTCHER Betty Joy, b. 21 Nov. 1949, Tuskegee, USA. Administrator. m. Ronald Andrew Crutcher, 24 Nov. 1979, 1 daughter. *Education:* BS, Sociology, Tuskegee Institute, 1971; MPH, University of Michigan, 1973. *Appointments:* Co-Director, Ann Arbor Community Coalition, Black Caucus Against Drugs, 1972-74; Institute for the Study of Mental Retardation & Related Disabilities, University of Michigan, 1974-75; Office of Substance Abuse Services, Michigan Dept. of Public Health, 1975-80; Assistant to the Chancellor, University of North Carolina, Greensboro, 1980-85; Assistant to the President: Guilford College, Greensboro, 1972-1985. *Memberships:* Delta Sigma Theta Sonority, 1988 - 100 Black women Coalition, Greensboro; American Association for Affirmative Action Leadership; Alumni Association, 1972-85; American Public Health Organization. *Honours:* Recipient, various honours & awards. *Hobbies Include:* Classical Music; Ballet; Walking; Travel. *Address:* 1402 McDowell Drive, Greensboro, NC 27408, USA.

CULBERTSON Frances Mitchell, b. 31 Jan. 1921, Boston, Massachusetts, USA. Professor of Psychology; Licensed Clinical Psychologist. m. John M Culbertson, 27 Aug. 1949. 1 son, 3 daughters. *Education:* BS Psychology, 1944-47, MS Psychology, 1947-49, PhD Psychology, 1949-55, University of Michigan; Postdoctoral Retraining, Clinical Psychology, University of Wisconsin, 1959-61. *Appointments:* Clinical Child Psychologist, Wisc Diag Centre, 1961-65; Chair, Psychology Dept, Child Psychiatry, University of Wisconsin, 1965-66; Res Psychol, NIMH, Berkeley, 1966-67; School Psychologist, Madison, 1967-68; Private Psychology Practice, Clinical Psychologist, 1984-; Professor of Psychology, University of Wisconsin, 1968-88. *Publications:* Book: Voices in International Psychology; articles and book chapters to professional journals. *Memberships:* International Council of Psychol; Wisconsin School Psychol Association; Honorary President, Brazilian Clinical Psychol Association; Madison Society of Clinical Hypnosis; Committee on International Rel APA; Director, School Psychology Program, University of Wisconsin. *Honours:* Pi Lambda Theta, 1949; Sigma Xi, 1950; Fellow, APA,

1979; Pacific Cultural Foundation Grant for Study on Gifted Children, 1981; Elected Vice President Midwest, Psi Chi, 1981; Honorary Lecturer, University of Paris, Sorbonne, 1983. *Hobbies:* Hiking; Cross-country skiing; Reading, book group; Dancing; Travelling. *Address:* 5305 Burnett Drive, Madison, WI 53705, USA.

CULBERTSON Janet Lynn, b. 15 Mar. 1932, Greensburg, Pennsylvania, USA. Artist. m. Douglas Kaften, Sept. 1964. *Education:* BFA, Carnegie Institute of Technology, 1949-53; MA, New York University, 1963. *Appointments:* Art Instructor, Pace College, New York City, 1964-68, 1971; Drawing Instructor, Pratt Art Institute, Brooklyn, 1973-74; Southampton College, NY, 1976; Parrish Museum, Southampton, NY, 1979. *Creative works:* One Woman Exhibitions include: Lerner-Heller Gallery, NYC, 1971, 1973, 1975, 1977; Heckscher Museum, Huntington, NY, 1980; Elaine Benson Gallery, Bridgehampton, 1978, 1981; Nardin Gallery, NYC, 1981; Aronson Gallery, Atlanta, 1982; William Penn Museum, Harrisburg, 1988. Group Exhibitions include: Bronx Museum, 1976; Carnegie Mellon Univ Alumni Exhibit, West B'way Gallery, 1976; Guild Hall, East Hampton, NY Invitational, 1976, 1989; Organization Ind Artists, 1978; Heckscher Museum, Huntington, 1978; Parrish Museum, Southampton, 1978; Guild Hall, NY, 1979; CAPS Graphics Recipients Exhibit, 1979; Western Carolina University, Cullowhee, 1979; Memorial Art Gallery, Rochester, 1979; Phoenix Museum and Tucson Museum of Art, 1980; Department of Parks, NYC, 1981; Edison Community College Art Gallery, Fort Myers, 1982; Silverpoint-Norton Gallery of Art, West Palm Beach, Florida, 1985-86. *Membership:* Womens Caucus for Art. *Honours:* Creative Artists Public Service Grant, 1979; Ossabaw Art Fellow, 1983; Numerous awards and honours. *Interests:* Ecology; Music; Hiking in wilderness; Tennis; Reading. *Address:* P O Box 455 Heights, Shelter Island, NY 11965, USA.

CULBRETH Luann Janine, b. 26 Sept. 1961, Chattanooga, USA. Educational Consultant/Instructor. m. Stephen A. Culbreth, 20 Mar. 1982. *Education:* AS, 1981; BMSc., 1984; M.Ed., 1986; MRI Intern, 1987. *Appointments:* Staff Radiologic Technologist, Emory University Hospital, 1981-84; Clinical Instructor, Radiology, Grady Memorial Hospital, Atlanta, 1984-87; MRI Instructor, Emory University, Atlanta, 1987-. *Memberships:* Society for Magnetic Resonance Imaging; Atlanta, Georgia, American Societies of Radiologic Technologists; Association of Educators in Radiological Sciences; Omicron Gamma; NAFE. *Honours:* Kappa Delta Pi. *Hobbies:* Outdoor Activities. *Address:* 1376 Oakengate Drive, Stone Mountain, GA 30083, USA.

CULJIS Jane A., b. USA. Executive; Yacht Broker. *Education:* AA, Stephens College, Columbia, Missouri, 1961; University of Vienna, Austria, 1962; BA, California State University, San Francisco, 1963; Graduate studies, University of Los Angeles. *Appointments:* Western States Director, Leader of student tours to Europe, US National Student Association, Educational Travel Inc; Editor, California Girl Magazine, Los Angeles, California; Assistant to Creative Director, Lennen & Newell Advertising Agency, Beverly Hills, California; Executive Vice-President, Robert Howell Associates Advertising Agency, Beverly Hills; Advertising/Public Relations Director, Weight Watchers International; Marketing Director, Lion Country Safari, Laguna Hills, California; Account Executive, Cochrane, Chase, Livingston & Co Advertising and Public Relations Agency, Newport Beach, California; Founder, President, International Charter Association Yacht Charter Brokers, Laguna Beach, California, currently. *Memberships:* Aegean Turkish Coast Yacht Charter Brokers; Orange County Performing Arts Center; Women in Business; Virgin Island Charteryacht League; Caribbean Tourist Association; Business and Professional Women; Society of Executive and Professional Women of America; Newport Harbor Chamber of Commerce; Laguna Beach Chamber of Commerce; Dana Point Chamber of Commerce; Stephens College Alumnae Association; Laguna Beach Greenbelt; Laguna Beach Neighborhood Watch; MENSA; Australian Wine Society. *Honours:*

Writer of the Year Award, Atlantic Monthly Magazine; Winner, Short Story Competition, Mademoiselle magazine; Runnerup, National Creative Writing Contest, Saturday Review. *Hobbies:* Sailing; Writing; Painting; Photography; Chess. *Address:* 31548 Bluff Drive, Laguna Beach, CA 92677, USA.

CULLEN Barbara Jocelyn, b. 9 July 1908, Sydney, Australia. Retired. m. William Hartland Cullen, 17 Feb. 1930, 2 daughters. *Memberships Include:* State President 1953-56, National President 1955- 57, Country Women's Association of NSW; Vice President, 1959-62, Deputy President 1962-68, Associated Country Women of the World; Immigration Advisory Council, 1957-71; Board, Rachel Forster Hospital, 1957-78; Vice President, Council of Social Service NSW, 1955-73; Chairman, Executive, 1957-59; Committee Member, Home Help Service, 1964-80; Executive Member, Anglican Retirement Villages Foundation for Aged Care, 1987-. *Honours:* OBE, 1961. *Hobbies:* Reading; Sewing; Knitting; Travel. *Address:* 180 Hopetoun Village Castle Hill, NSW 2154, Australia.

CULVERHOUSE Barbara Mary, b. 16 Apr. 1921, Slough, England. Chartered Accountant. m. Patrick Emerson Culverhouse, 8 Feb. 1947, 2 sons, 1 daughter. *Appointments:* Articled to Hemsley Miller, 1939-44; Various appointments 1945-65; Group Accountant, 1965-66; Sole Practitioner, Chartered Accountant, 1966-. *Memberships:* Council of Institute of Chartered Accountants in England and Wales, 1981-87; Court of the Worshipful Company of Chartered Accountants, 1981-; City Livery Club; Trustee, Old Roedeanian Association. *Hobbies:* Travel; Music; Walking. *Address:* Wayside, Penn, High Wycombe, Bucks HP10 8LY, England.

CULVERHOUSE Renee Daniel, b. 10 Nov. 1950, Tuskegee, Alabama, USA. Assistant Vice-Chancellor for Academic Affairs. m. Charles E Culverhouse III, 27 May 1978. 1 daughter. *Education:* BA Foreign Languages 1973, MA Spanish 1973, Auburn University; JD Law, Cumberland School of Law of Samford University, 1978. *Appointments:* Associate, Dinsmore, Waites and Stovall, Attorneys at Law, Birmingham, 1978-81; Associate Professor, Department of Management 1986-, Assistant Professor, Department of Management 1981-86, Acting Head, Management Department, 1983-84 and 1988-89, Undergraduate Coordinator, School of Business 1985-88, Assistant Vice-Chancellor for Academic Affairs, 1989-, Auburn University at Montgomery. *Publications:* Author of numerous articles, papers and chapters to professional journals and magazines including: Aids and the (Un)Availability of Health Insurance: Ethical Considerations, Volume 15 Selected Papers of the American Business Law Association Regional Proceedings, 1988; Presenter of papers to conferences nationally. *Memberships:* Secretary-Treasurer, Southeastern Regional Business Law Association, 1988-89; Southern Regional Business Law Association; American Business Law Association; Atlantic Marketing Association; Alabama Academy of Science; Society for the Advancement of Management; Southwest Social Sciences Association; Women's Caucus. *Honour:* Dean's Award for Excellence in Teaching, School of Business, Auburn University at Montgomery, 1988. *Hobbies:* Distance running; Racquetball. *Address:* Office of Academic Affairs, Library Tower, Auburn University at Montgomery, Montgomery, AL 31693, USA.

CUMBER Carol Jane, b. 24 Nov. 1956, Jamestown, USA. Instructor. m. Craig Fairbanks, 29 May 1982, 1 son. *Education:* BA, 1979; MBA, North Dakota State University, 1984. *Appointments:* Job Site Office Manager, 1980-82; Instructor of Business Economics, University of Minnesota, 1984-; Adjunct Professor, Business, Southwest State University, 1987-. Consultant on Labor and personal issues. *Memberships:* Industrial Relations Research Association; Business & Professional Women; Midwest Economics Association; University Association; Countryside Council, Board. *Honours:* Dakota Paper Scholarship for Outstanding

MBA Student; University of Minnesota Presidents Distinguished Faculty Mentor; Graduate Student Representative to Graduate Council. *Hobbies:* Music; Travel. *Address:* 630 County Road 9, Watson, MN 56295, USA.

CUMMINGS Caroline, b. 13 Apr. 1946, Los Angeles, California, USA. President, Cummings Communications. *Education:* Orange Coast College, Newport Beach, California; Burklyn Business School, San Diego, California. *Appointments:* Over 20 years in hotel industry. Director of Sales, Meridien Hotels, Beverly Hills, 1984-85; Sales & Marketing posts included: Hilton, Hyatt & Sheraton Hotel Corporations; The Anchorage Convention and Visitors Bureau; 4 years as President, Caroline Cummings & Associates, La Jolla; Director of Sales, Preferred Hotels Worldwide, 1985-86; President, Cummings Communications, International sales and marketing firm for independent, luxury hotels and resorts, 1987-. *Memberships:* American Society of Asson. Executives; American Society of Travel Agents; Chicago Convention & Visitors Bureau; Hotel Sales and Marketing International; Meeting Planners International; Pacific Area Travel Association. *Hobbies:* Skiing; Tennis; Jogging; Spiritual Development. *Address:* Cummings Communications, 2021 Midwest Road, Suite 300, Oakbrook, Illinois 60521, USA.

CUNLIFFE Corinna, b. 18 Apr. 1929, Leatherhead, England. Novelist. m. Frederick Starr Wildman, 18 May 1957, divorced 1962, 1 son. *Education:* Chelsea School of Art, 1946-50. *Appointments:* Pritchard Wood & Partner,s 1952-53; Ladies Home Journal, USA, 1953-59; Homes & Gardens, 1963-80; Good Housekeeping, 1980-81. *Publications:* How Fear Left the Forest, illustrated only, 1950; Hand of Fortune, 1985; Play of Hearts, 1986; The Unsuitable Chaperone, 1988. *Memberships:* South Vermont Art Centre, Trustee; Merck Forest; Dorset Village Library, Trustee; Hildene, Advisor, 1985-88. *Hobbies:* Gardening; Breeding Horses; Needlework; Painting; Travel. *Address:* C/o J. C. A. Agency, 242 W. 27th St., New York City, NY 10001, USA.

CUNNINGHAM Cherry Larson, b. 21 Aug. 1944, Austin, Texas, USA. Nursing Executive; Consultant. m. Ronald W Cunningham, 14 Jan. 1967, 1 son. *Education:* BSN, 1966, MSN, 1985, University of Texas; MS, 1972, Currently Doctoral Student, East Texas State University. *Appointments:* Huntsville Memorial Hospital, 1967; Memorial Hospital of Garland, 1968; Paris Junior College, 1969-71; Grayson County College, 1972-75; East Texas State University, 1976-77; Texoma Medical Centre, 1978-. *Publications:* Song: In the Autumn of My Days; Presenter, Many papers, seminars & workshops. *Memberships:* Altrusa Inernational; Phi Delta Kappa; Sigma Theta Tau; American Association of Marriage & Family Therapists. *Honours:* Nominated, Piper Professor, 1972; Nursing Excellence Award, 1988. *Hobbies Include:* Designing & Creating Stained Glass Windows; Needlepoint; Cooking; Reading; Walking. *Address:* Route One, Box 801, Denison, TX 75020, USA.

CUNNINGHAM Jeannette R., b. 26 Oct. 1941, Cameron, Texas, USA. Doctor of Dental Surgery. m. Thomas C. Cunningham, 18 Aug. 1962, 3 sons. *Education:* University of St Thomas, Houston, Texas, 1960-63; Graduate, University of Texas Health Science Dental Branch, 1977. *Appointments:* Self-employed, private dental practice, Moody (Texas) 1977-80, Waco 1980-. *Memberships:* American Dental Association; Texas, & Central Texas Dental Societies; Waco Dental Study Club; Academy of General Dentistry; American Orthodontic Society; American Association of Functional Orthodontists; International Association for Orthodontists; Past President, St Mary's Parish Board. *Hobbies:* Reading; Hiking; Cycling; Skiing. *Address:* 421 North Robinson, Waco, Texas 76706, USA.

CURLE Robin Lea, b. 23 Feb. 1950, Denver, USA. Company President. m. Lucien Ray Reed, 23 Feb. 1981, divorced 1983. *Education:* BSc., Business Communications, Kentucky University, 1972. *Appointments:* Systems Analyst, SW Bancshares, 1972-77; Sales Person, Software International, 1977-80; District Manager, UCC, 1980-81; Vice President, Sales, Tesseract, 1983-85, 1987; Vice President, Sales, Foothill Research, 1985-86; President, Curle Consulting Group, 1987-. *Memberships:* University of Kentucky Alumni; Delta Gamma Alumni. *Hobbies:* Skiing; Scuba Diving; Cooking; Entertaining; Exercise. *Address:* Curle Consulting Group, 140 Arguello Blvd., San Francisco, CA 94118, USA.

CURNS Eileen Bohan, b. 22 May 1927, Chicago, Illinois, USA. Stress Counsellor; Consultant; Author. m. John R. Curns, 1 July 1950, div. 1 son, 1 daughter. *Education:* BA, DePaul University, 1949; MEd, Loyola University, 1975; Certificate, Gestalt Institute, Chicago, 1975; Graduate Credits, health education, University of Wisconsin, 1985, 1987. *Appointments:* Lecturer, Author, Consultant on Stress & Health, self-employed, 1973-; Co-founder, Stress-Wellness Team, & Stress Counsellor, Doctors of Northbrook Court, Northbrook, Illinois, 1982-86; Co-founder, Wellness Expo Council, 1985-. *Creative work:* Chart, 1st Aid for Stress; Workbooks: From Stress to Balance, Negatives to Positives, Pathways to People; Discovered & named stress emergency, & stress flu; Advanced theory of stress process. *Memberships:* Co-Chair, Chicago Wellness Expo Council; International Human Learning Resource Network; Vice President, Midwest Society for Professional Consultants. *Honours:* Golden Deeds Award helping poor in Salvador, Bahia, Brazil, Exchange Club, Waukegan, Illinois, 1965; Various art fair awards. *Hobbies:* Sculptress, wood & welded steel; Choir Member; Golf; Various other sports. *Address:* PO Box 393, Deerfield, Illinois 60015, USA.

CURRIE Barbara Flynn, b. 3 May 1940, LaCrosse, Wisconsin, USA. Member, Illinois House of Representatives. m. David Park Currie, 29 Dec. 1959. 1 son, 1 daughter. *Education:* AM, cum laude, 1968; AM 1973, University of Chicago. *Appointments:* Instructor, Political Science, DePaul University, 1973-74; Assistant Study Director, National Opinion Research Centre, Chicago, 1973-77; Member, Illinois House of Representatives, 1979-. *Publications:* Political Attidues Among American Ethnics: A Study of Perceptual Distortion in Andrew Greeley Ethnicity in the United States, New York, 1974. *Memberships:* Advisory Board, Harriet M Harris Centre, YWCA; Past Vice-President, Chicago League of Women Voters; Member, Midwest Women's Centre, Hyde Park-Kenwood Community Conference, South Shore Commission, Hyde Park Neighbourhood Club, South Shore and Hyde Park Historical Societies, Illinois Task Force on Child Support. *Honours:* IVI-IPO Best Legislator, National Association of Social Workers; Best Legislator-84, Illinois Women's Political Caucus Award, Illinois Environmental Council, Illinois Public Action Council, Illinois Nurses' Association-Best Legislator-84, Illinois Women's Substance Abuse Coalition, Legislator of the Year-84, Welfare Rights Coalition of Organizations; Distinguished Service Award. *Address:* Rm 2107, Sratton Building, Springfield, IL 62706, USA.

CURRIE Edwina, b. 13 Oct. 1946, Liverpool, England. Member of Parliament. m. Raymond Frank Currie, 1 July 1972. 2 daughters. *Education:* BA, Oxford University, 1969 (MA 1972); MSc, London School of Economics, London University, 1972. *Appointments:* Arthur Andersen & Company, Chartered Accountants, 1969-70; Department of Trade and Industry, 1970-71; Teaching posts in Economics, Economic History and Business Studies, 1972-81; Birmingham City Councillor, 1975-86; Parliamentary Private Secretary, Depaartment of Education and Science, 1985-86; Parliamentary Under secretary, Department of Health and Social Security, 1986-88. *Publications:* Various articles and pamphlets on Health, Housing, Welfare, etc. *Address:* House of Commons, London SW1A 0AA, England.

CURRIER Una King Conway, b. Birmingham, Alabama, USA. Supervisor. m. 9 Jan. 1960, 2 sons. *Appointments:* BS, Secondary Education, 1962, BS, Elementary Education, 1974, Samford University; MEd., Early Childhood Education, 1979, MEd., Administration & Supervision, 1984, University of Alabama at Birmingham; EdS, Early Childhood Education, 1987, University of Alabama at Birmingham. *Appointments:* Teacher: Shelby County Board of Education, 1964, Birmingham City Schools, 1964-71, Calhoun County, 1971-74, Jefferson County, 1974-79; Resource Consultant and Supervisor, 1974-. *Memberships:* President, Vice President, Kappa Delta Epsilon, Beta Omega; Kappa Delta Phi; Phi Delta Kappa; Women Educators Network; International Reading Association; Alabama Reading Association. *Honours:* Recipient, many honours & awards. *Hobbies:* Travel; Interior Decorating; Arts; Crafts; Reading. *Address:* 3713 Fitzgerald Mountain Drive, Pinson, AL 35126, USA.

CURRY Ginger Simpson, b. 5 Feb. 1939, Middletown, Ohio, USA. Freelance Writer. m. (1) Bob Thacker 1956, divorced 1962, 1 son; (2) James I Curry, 11 July 1964. 1 son. *Education:* AA English, 1973; BA Psychology, 1977. *Appointments:* Book Review Editor, 1980-81, Fiction Editor, 1981-82, Florida Arts Gazette; Fiction Chairman, Florida State Writing Competition, 1983-; Freelance Writer. *Publications:* Short Stories: Rendezvous with Death, 1981; Love's Ebbing Tide, 1981; Never Obsolete, 1981; Iron Shadows Wave, 1986; Guardians of the Secret, 1986; Sea-Serpents of Domnudale, 1988; Survivors: At Face Value, 1988. *Memberships:* Adult Fiction Contest Chairman, Florida Freelance Writers; National Writers Club; Science Fiction Writers of America; Founder & Market Analyst, ANRALD; Phi Kappa Phi; Palm Beach County Council of Arts; Florida Audubon Society. *Honours:* Fiction Contests: Writer's Digest, 1977; National Writers Club, 1981-84 and 1986, 2nd, 3rd, 6th, 7th, 8th; Inkling Literary Journal, 1985, 2nd; Bylines Magazine, 1982, 2nd; Chronoscope Literary Magazine, 1988, 1st, etc; Artist in Literature Fellow, Florida Arts Council, 1982-83; Broward Cultural Arts Award Finalist, 1983; National Audubon Society Ecology Camp Scholarship, 1984. *Hobbies:* Slogging through Florida scrubs; Snorkeling the Atlantic Ocean reefs; Nature photography; The environment. *Address:* 722 West Ocean Drive, Boynton Beach, FL 33426, USA.

CURRY Mary Earle Lowry, b. 13 May 1917, Seneca, South Carolina, USA. m. Reverend Peden Gene Curry, 25 Dec. 1941. 1 son, 1 daughter, deceased. *Education:* Furman University, 1944-45. *Publications:* Poetry books: Looking Up, 1949; Looking Within, 1961, reprinted 1980. Hymn: Church in The Heart of the City, 1973. Contributions to numerous magazines, journals and papers. Personal Poetry Broadcasts (Virginia). *Memberships:* Aux Rotary, Charleston, South Carolina, 1972-74; Centro Studi Scambi International Roma; United Methodist Women's Organizations; United Methodist Ministers' Wives Club, President, Charleston, 1973-74. *Honours:* World Award for Culture represented by the Statue of Victory, 1985 (Centro Studi E Riccerche Delle Nazioni, Italy). *Hobbies:* Photography; Music. *Addres:* R-5, Box 371, Seneca, South Carolina 29678, USA.

CURTIN Phyllis, b. 3 Dec. 1921, Clarksburg, West Virginia, USA. Professor of Music (Voice); Dean, School for the Arts Boston University, Boston, Massachusets. m. Eugene Cook, 6 May 1956, deceased. 1 daughter. *Education:* BA, Wellesley College, 1943; Private Musical Education; Opera Study, Tanglewood Music Center, 1946, 1948, 1951. *Appointments:* Leading Soprano, NY City Opera, 1953-64; Leading Soprano, Metropolitan Opera, 1961-74; Vienna Staatsoper, 1959-62; Recitalist around USA, Europe, Australia, New Zealand, Israel, 1951-84; Guest Artist, La Scala, Teatro Colon, Italy; Artist in Residence, Tanglewood Music Center (Boston Symphony Orchestra), 1963-; Master Classes in many schools, Conservatories in USA, Canada, China, Soviet Union. *Address:* 24 Cottage Farm Road, Brookline, MA 02146, USA.

CURTIS Jean Marie, b. 8 July 1931, Lewisburg, Ohio, USA. Political Director Ohio Republican Party. m. 12 May 1984, 2 sons, 1 stepdaughter. *Education:* BS, Education, University of Dayton, 1967. *Appointments:* Substitute Teacher, 1959-60; Elementary Teacher, Lincoln School, Middletown, 1960-68; Butler County Recorder, 1969-81; District Service Director, Congressman Thomas N. Kindness; Campaign Manager, Kindness for US Senate; Ohio Scheduler George Bush for President; Alternate Delegate, 1988 Republican National Convention; Political Consultant; Political Director, Ohio Republican Party. *Memberships:* Ohio and National Federations of Republican Women; Business & Professional Women; Delta Zeta; State Central Committee, Ohio Republican Party; Butler County Republican Womens Club. *Hobbies:* Travel; Fishing; Needlework; Antique Jewelry. *Address:* 80 Carlton Drive, Hamilton, OH 45015, usA.

CURTIS Linda Lee, b. 18 Apr. 1950, Stafford, Kansas, USA. m. Ronald Benson Curtis, 8 June 1979. *Education:* AA, Barton Country, 1978. *Appointments:* Editor, Publisher, Winter Wheat Newsletter, 1985-. *Publications:* Over 400 poems published in various magazines including; Bronte Sreet; Soundboard; Arizona Womens Voice; Poetry Books incude: Intermission; Smoke Rings; Midnight Echoes; More than My Share; others. *Honours:* Arizona Womens Partnership Songwriting Award 1985; Soundboard Poet of the Year Award, 1984. *Hobbies:* Writing Poetry; Contest Judge. *Address:* 1919 West Adams, Phoenix, AZ 85009, USA.

CURTIS Lisa, b. Munich. President, International Sophrology Institute. m. 1 son, 1 daughter. *Education:* New York University; New School of Social Research. *Appoinments:* Publicity, Advertising Promotion, Mr. Fred, Fur and Sport, Inc., 1964-71; Zuzu Angel Rio de Janiero, 1969-73; Ben Thylan Furs Inc., 1972-83; Communications Director, 1979-82, President 1983-, International Sophrology Institute; Lecturer/Speaker Turning Stress in to Energy and The Chief Executives Survival Programme presented to Conventions, Corporations and Organizations *Creative Works:* Articles in professional journals and Newspapers. *Memberships:* Walters International Speakers' Bureau; Women in Communication; Zen Studies Society Inc; Advertising Women of New York; World Future Society. *Hobbies:* Photography; Languages; Music; Skiing; Hiking. *Address:* International Sophrology Institute, 381 Park Avenue South, New York, NY 10016, USA.

CURTIS Winifred Mary, b. 15 June 1905, Charlton, London, England. Botanist. *Education:* University College, London, 1924-30; BSc 1927, MSc 1939, PhD 1950, DSc 1968, University of London; Cambridge Training College for Women, 1930-31; Cambridge Teachers' Certificate, 1931. *Appointments:* Senior Science Mistress, Levenshulme Girls High School, Manchester, England, 1931-32; Biology Specialist, S Hampstead High School, London, 1933- 39; Science Mistress, Fahan Girls School, Hobart, Tasmania, Australia, 1939-43; Demonstrator in Botany & Zoology 1939-43, Assistant Lecturer in Biology 1943, Lecturer in Botany 1945, Senior Lecturer 1951, Reader 1956-66, retired, Hon Research Associate currently, University of Tasmania. *Publications:* Books: Biology for Australian Students, 4 eds, 1948-62; The Student's Flora of Tasmania, Parts 1-4a, 1956-80; Text for The Endemic Flora of Tasmania with paintings by Margaret Stones, 6 vols 1967-78; 25 papers in scientific journals. *Memberships:* Fellow, Linnean Society of London; International Association of Plant Taxonomists; Honorary Member, British Ecological Society; Honorary Member, ANZAAS; Patron, Launceston (Tasmania) Field Naturalists Club; Honorary Member, Society for Growing Australian Plants, Tasmanian Section. *Honours:* London University Scholarship in Botany, 1926; Carnegie Corporation, New York, Travel Grant 1959; Clive Lord Memorial Medal, Royal Society of Tasmania, 1966; Australian natural History Medallion, 1967; Order of Australia (AM), 1977; Honorary DSc degree, University of Tasmania, 1987. *Hobbies:* Field work in botany;

Reading history. *Address:* Tasmanian Museum Herbarium, Unviersity of Tasmania, Box 252C, GPO Hobart, Tasmania 7001, Australia.

CURTIS-VERNA Mary V., b. 9 May 1921, Salem, Massachusetts, USA. Professor of Voice. *Education:* Abbot Academy; AB, Hollins College. *Career:* Sang, All Italian Opera House, La Scala, Rome, Vienna; Leading Soprano, Metropolitan Opera, New York, 10 years; 45 operas in repertoire performed worldwide; Extensive recital tours; Professor and Chair of Voice Division, University of Washington. *Memberships:* President, Friends of Opera, University of Washington; AGMA; Senate and Executive Council, University of Washington. *Honours:* Gold Medal, Hollins College; Outstanding Teacher, Past Pres Association, Seattle. *Hobbies:* Gardening; Needlepoint; Reading. *Address:* 1600 East Boston Terrace, Seattle, WA 98112, USA.

CURTISS Vienna Ione, b. 1909, Eau Claire, Wisconsin, USA. Author-Designer-Illustrator. *Education:* Interior Design Graduate, Parsons School of Design, New York City, succeeded by professional practice in Hollywood; AFD, Columbia University, 1960. *Appointments:* Professor of Design in Art, Colleges of Liberal Arts, Human Ecology and Education at the University of Maryland and Arizona State University, 1935-75. *Publications:* Adult books: Pageant of Art: A Visual History of Western Culture; I Should be Glad to Help You Madame: Europe Minus One's Wardrobe!, 1979; Cappy-Rollicking Rancher Atop Arizona's Mighty Rim. Children's Books: Life's Great Show!, Poems for Tomorrow's Men and Women; Zip, Zing, Ping, Pop!, Poems and pictures for the very young, companion volumes, 1966. *Honours:* International Award, Printing Industries of America Graphic Arts Competition, 1977; National Award, 1st prize for Nonfiction Books, National League of American Pen Women, 1980. *Address:* 1727 Massachusetts NW, Washington, DC 20036, USA

CURZON Elizabeth Mae (Liz), b. 29 Nov. 1947, Edinburgh, Scotland. Homemaker Supervisor. m. Anthony Paul Curzon, 29 Aug. 1978, 3 sons, 1 daughter. *Appointments:* License Issuing Clerk, Department of Transport, 1964-67; Pioneer Pool Co., Sales, 1972-78; Scarborough Red Cross, 1978-; Supervisor, Homemaking/Outreach Scarborough Red Cross, 1986-87. *Memberships:* George Brown College, Advisory Board. *Honours:* Communication Excellence Award, United Way of America, 1986; Certificate of Achievement, Scarborough Board of Education, 1987; Certificate of Recognition, Canadian Red Cross Society, Ontario Division, 1988. *Hobbies:* Wildlife; Reading; Music; Plants; Parasailing. *Address:* Scarborough Red Cross Society, 1095 Bellamy Road North, Scarborough, Ontario, Canada M1H 3B8.

CUSACK Mary Jo, b. USA. Attorney. *Education:* AB, Marquette University, 1957; JD, Ohio State University, 1959; Admitted: Ohio Supreme Court 1959, US Supreme Court 1962, US District Court 1965. *Appointments:* Attorney, Industrial Commission of Ohio 1960-61, Ohio Department of Taxation 1961-65; Private practice, Cotruvo & Cusack, 1961-; Special Counsel, Attorney General William J. Brown, 1971-82; Adjunct Professor, Family & Probate Law, Capital University Law School; Lecturer, various organisations. *Memberships* include: Fellow: American, Ohio State & Columbus Bar Foundations; Past President: National Association of Women Lawyers, Franklin County Trial Lawyers, & Democratic Attorneys Associations, Women Lawyers of Columbus; National Panel of Arbitrators, American Arbitration Association; Offices: American, Ohio State & Columbus Bar Associations, Ohio Academy of Trial Lawyers, Kappa Beta Pi International Legal Association, National Board of Trial Advocacy; Member, Thomas More Society; *Address:* Cotruvo & Cusack, 50 West Broad Street, Columbus, Ohio 43215, USA.

CUTHBERT Amanda Cherry, b. 8 Sept. 1946, Lythan St Annes, England. Actress; Broadcaster. m. Ashton Chadwick, 6 Mar. 1982. 1 son. *Education:* LUDDA, New College of Speech and Drama, London, 1968-71. *Appointments:* Freelance Actress radio, television, theatre, 1971-81; West End work includes: Crown Matrimonial; Dirty Linen. Radio work includes: Waggoners Walk. Television work includes: Tinker Tailor Soldier Spy. Founder Member, Director on Board, 1982-83, Head, Presentation, 1984-, Satellite Television. *Memberships:* National Union of Journalists; British Actors Equity Association. *Honours:* American Field Service Scholarship, 1964- 65. *Hobbies:* Travel; Writing; Gardening; Playing Piano and Guitar. *Address:* 27 Farrer Road, London N8, England.

CUTLER Ethel Rose, b. USA. Artist; Painter. *Education:* BA, Fine Arts and Education, Hunter College; MA, Fine Arts and Fine Arts Education, Teachers College, Columbia University; New York University; University of Missouri; Illinois Institute of Technology; Teachers College, Columbia University; New School for Social Research; American Artist School; PhD, Walden University, Institute for Advanced Studies; Fashion Institute of Technology; Metropolitan Museum of Art. *Appointments:* Instructor and Head of Arts Program, Highland Manor School and Junior College, New Jersey, 1942-43; Instructor, Women's College of the University of North Carolina, Greensboro, 1943-47; Instructor, Adelphi College, Long Island, 1947-50; Assistant Professor, University of Missouri, 1950-55; Assistant Professor, Rhode Island School of Design, 1955-59; Artist/Designer/Consultant/Educator, 1959-. *Creative Works:* Exhibitions: Young American Artist Group, New York; Macy's Gallery; University of Missouri; Institute of Design Illinois Institute of Technology; Rhode Island School of Design; Design Derby, Hialeah, Florida; Lynn Kottler Galleries, New York; World's Fair '65, New York; Artist Equity Exhibits, 1973 & 1974; South Street Museum Gallery, 1973; 80 Washington Square East Galleries, 1977; Palazzo Vagnotti, Cortona, italy, 1982; New York City center Gallery; National Academy of Design, 1986, 1987; Ayos Constantinas Samos, Greece, 1987. *Memberships:* Art Directors Club; Allied Board of Trades; Artist Equity; College Arts Association; National Society of Interior Designers. *Honours:* Scholarships: American Artists School, 1939-40; Metropolitan Museum of Art, 1968-69; Grant, Walden University, 1980. *Address:* 230 East 88th Street, New York, NY 10128, USA.

CUTNER Helen Hull, b. 26 Sept. 1933, Pittsburgh, Pennsylvania, USA. Attorney; Freelance writer; Editor; Word-processor. divorced. *Education:* AB 1963, JD with honours 1967, Temple University. *Appointments:* Trial Attorney, Harold E Kohn, PA, 1967-70; Trial Attorney, Wolf, Block, Schorr & Solis-Cohen, 1970-72; Trial Attorney, Atlantic Richfield Co, 1972-75; Sole practitioner, 1975-79; Civil rights consultant, Freelance writer, Editor and word-processor, 1981-. *Publications:* Discovery-Civil Litgation's Fading Light: A Lawyer Looks at the Federal Discory Rules after Forty Years of Use, 1979. *Memberships:* National Writers Club; Anti-Vivisection Society; Defenders of Wildlife; In Defense of Animals; Nature Conservancy; Sierra Club; World Wildlife Fund; Democratic National Committee; The Smithsonian Associates; Past Chairman, Committee on Law and Mental Retardation, Philadelphia Bar Association. *Honours:* Article Editor, Temple Law Q., 1966-67; Lectured on women's legal rights and other civil rights subjects at Rutgers University, Drexel University and CCNY, to women's groups and other associations, 1970-78. *Hobbies:* Animal rights activist; Concerned with the rights of the elderly; Gardening; Listening to music. *Address:* 1346 Chestnut Street, No 620, Philadelphia, Pennsylvania 19107, USA.

CUTRUBUS Christina Nina, b. USA. *Education:* University of Utah; Further study, Europe including Gtreece. *Appointments include:* Publicist, Metro-Goldwyn-Meyer, Paramount Pictures, Walt Disney Productions, United Artists, Cinerama Productions, 7 years; Founder, owner Phonic Arts Agency, full-service advertising firm, special emphasis electronic media production; Founder, University Services Corporation, publishing firm serving all 4 universities in Utah, 1971-

; Personal representative & press agent, Archbishop Iakovos, Primate, Greek Orthodox Archdiocese of North & South America. *Publications include:* Editor, publisher, Utah Ballet West magazine; Originator, owner, publisher, editor, Utah Preservation & Restoration magazine; Publisher, book, Consecration of Transfiguration Greek Orthodox Church; Compiler, editor, designer, publisher, book, Salt Lake Temple: Monument to a People; Compiler, author, designer, publisher, book, D. Alt: Impressions of an Impressionist. *Memberships:* Zeta Phi Eta; Salt Lake Advertising Club; Salt Lake Chamber of Commerce. *Honours include:* Power of the Pen award, National Trust, Washington DC; Recognition, ecclesiastical-related work, Greek Orthodox Church; World award, collector's edition Salt Lake Temple; Biographical listings. *Hobbies:* Fine arts, especially sculpture; Classical philosophy. *Address:* University Services Corporation, 1159 Second Avenue, Salt Lake City, UT 84103, USA.

CUTTER MODLIN Beverly, b. 31 Dec. 1947, New York City, USA. Vice Chancellor. Married, 2 sons, 2 daughters. *Education:* BS, Family Services, University of New Hampshire, 1978. *Appointments:* Co-ordinator, Special Programs, Duke University, 1978-80; Consultant, Ross Johnston & Kersting Inc., 1980-84; Director, Development, National Child Welfare Leadership Center, 1984-85; Assistant Dean, Development, School of Law, 1985-89, Vice Chancellor, University Relations, 1989-, University of North Carolina-Asheville. *Publications:* Articles in professional journals. *Membership:* Council for Advancement & Support of Education. *Address:* University of North Carolina, One University Heights, Asheville, NC 28802, USA.

CZAJKOWSKI Eva Anna, b. 4 Sept. 1961, New Britain, USA. Research Assistant; Aerospace Engineer. *Education:* BSc., 1983, M.Eng., 1983, Rensselaer Polytechnic Institute; MSc., Massachusetts Institute of Technology, 1985; PhD, Virginia Polytechnic Institute & State University, 1988. *Appointments:* Teaching Assistant, 1983,Rensselaer Polytechnic Institute; Engineering Analyst, Pratt & Whitney Aircraft, 1984; Research Assistant, MIT, 1984-85; Teaching Assistant, 1985-, Research Assistant, 1985-, Virginia Polytechnic Institute & State University. *Memberships:* New York Academy of Sciences; American Helicopter Society, Director at Large, 1983-84, President, RPI Chapter, 1983; Sigma Gamma Tau. *Honours Include:* Recipient, various scholarships; Bausch & Lomb Medal, 1978; Rensselaer Medal for Excellence in Science and Mathematics, 1978; Sikorsky Scholarship, 1983; Amelia Earhart Fellowship Award, Zonta International, 1983-84, 1984-85; etc. *Hobbies:* Horse Riding; Art; Music; Flying; Swimming; Skiing; Tennis. *Address:* 170 Carlton Street, New Britain, CT 06053, USA.

CZALCZYNSKA Barbara, b. 21 Aprl. 1929, Lwow, Poland. Writer; Translator. *Education:* Graduate in Philosophy, University of Jagiellonski, Krakow. *Publications:* Pierwszy zakret, short stories; Proba zycia; Magdalena; Wielka cisza, short stories; Rozmowy z babka, short stories. *Memberships:* PEN club; Catholic Inteligentsia Club. *Hobbies:* Music; Art. *Address:* ul Karlowicza 5 m 5, 30-047 Krakow, Poland.

CZARNECKI Mary, b. 20 Jan. 1957, California, USA. Professional Artist. *Education:* Indian Valley Colleges, 1985; College of Marin, 1988. *Appointments:* Fine Art Oil Painter & Creator of Sculptural Masks & Ceramic Tiles. *Publications:* Series of Paintings: Joy, Abstractions from the Earth, Portraits of the Self, The Stone People, and The Big Women. *Memberships:* Artists Equity; Allied Women Artiss of America; Creative Growth; National Museum of Women in the Arts; Lillian Paley Centre for the Visual Arts. *Honours:* Recipient, various honours & awards including: Grant, Barbara Deming Memorial Fund, New York, 1987. *Hobbies:* Study of Art History; Use of Colour. *Address:* 193 Mill Street, San Rafael, CA 94901, USA.

D

DACE Tish, b. 13 Sept. 1941, Washington, District of Columbia, USA. Professor. 2 sons. *Education:* AB, Drama, magna cum laude, Sweet Briar College, Virginia, 1963; MA, Drama 1967, PhD English, 1971, Kansas State University. *Appointments:* Graduate Teaching Assistant, Speech & English, 1963-67, Instructor, Speech and Associate Director of Theatre 1967-71, Kansas State University; Assistant Professor of Speech, Drama and English, 1971-74, Associate Professor, 1975-80, Deputy Chair or Chair, 1974-80 at John Jay College of Criminal Justice, City University of New York; Professor of English 1980-, Dean, College of Arts and Sciences 1980-86, Southeastern Massachusetts University. *Publications include:* Books: LeRoi Jones (Imamu Amiri Baraka): A Checklist of Works by and about Him, 1971; (the first five of 8 chapters in:) The Theatre Student: Modern Theatre and Drama, 1973; The Osborne Generation: A Bibliography of Works by and about and a List of Production Data on Twenty Contemporary English and Irish Dramatists, in progress; Langston Hughes: American Critical Archives, in progress; Contributor to books, author of articles and papers to professional journals, magazines, newspapers and to conferences. *Memberships include:* American Theatre Critics Association; American Society for Theatre Research; Women & Theatre Program (ATHE); Outer Critics Circle. *Honour:* NEH Summer Research Stipend, 1987. *Address:* English Department, Southeastern Massachusetts University, No Dartmouth, MA 02747, USA.

DACHS Erika, b. 22 July 1932, Berlin. Lawyer. *Appointments:* Evangelische Framenarbeis in Germany; Verbond der Wuttembergiulem Modzindustrue und Kinrroffverberlung e.v. *Memberships:* Evangelische Kirche, Germany; Evangelisch Akademi Kerscheff; Sorialchemokirchsche Parti; Deutscher funstin em bund e.v.; Deutscher fortemry ev; Deutscher fapamische geschelleshaft Baden-Wurtemburg. *Hobbies:* English; French; Russian Japanese. *Address:* Mahdachstr. 20, D-7000 Stuttgart 31, Federal Republic of Germany.

DACKOW Sandra Katherine, b. 19 May 1951, Paterson, New Jersey, USA. Orchestra Conductor. *Education:* Bachelor of Music, 1973, Master of Music, 1976, PhD 1987, Eastman School of Music. *Appointments:* Faculty, Slippery Rock University, Slippery Rock, Pennsylvania, 1981-86; Supervisor of Music, Ridgewood New Jersey Public Schools, 1986-88; Conductor, Ridgewood Symphony, Ridgewood, 1986-; Conductor, Brandeis University Orchestra, Waltham, 1988-. *Creative works:* Arranger of over 30 musical compositions for student orchestra; Co-author, The Complete String Guide. *Memberships:* Music Educators national Conference; New Jersey Music Educators Association; American String Teachers Association; National School Orchestra Association; College Music Society; American Federation of Musicians. *Honours:* Slippery Rock University Town/ Gown Award, 1984; Mu Kappa Gamma Outstanding Professor, Slippery Rock University, 1985. *Hobbies:* Chamber music; Travel; Books. *Address:* 1220-B Shetland Drive, Lakewood, NJ 08701, USA.

DACRE OF GLANTON Alexandra Henrietta Louisa, (Lady), b. 9 Mar. 1917, London, England. Painter. m. 4 Oct. 1954, 2 sons, 1 daughter. *Education:* N. Foreland Lodge, Art Course, Brussels; Pupil of Pierre Bernac, 1948-50. *Appointments:* Journalist, Daily Mail; Interior Decorator; Founder, Music Therapy Charity; Patron, Cambridge University Opera. *Publications:* Oil & Watercolour Paintings. *Memberships:* Life Member, Victorian Society; National Art Collections Fund; Friend, ENO; Friend, Fitzwilliam Museum; Friend, Northern Sinfonia Orchestra; Chairman, Edinburgh Festival Guild, 1960-75; Chairman, Blenheim Concerts, 1969-80. *Hobbies:* Music; Collecting Pictures; Garden Design;

Organizing Concerts. *Address:* The Old Rectory, Didcot, Oxon, OX11 7EB, England.

DAGG Anne Innis, b. 25 Jan. 1933, Toronto, Canada. Professor. m. Ian Ralph Dagg, 22 Aug. 1957, 2 sons, 1 daughter. *Education:* BA, 1955, MA, 1956, University of Toronto; PhD, 1967, University of Waterloo. *Appointments:* Part-time Lecturer, Waterloo Lutheran University, 1962-65; Assistant Professor, University of Guelph, 1967-72; Resource Person, Academic Director, Independent Studies Program, University of Waterloo, 1978-. *Publications:* Canadian Wildlife and Man, 1974; Mammals of Ontario,1974; The Giraffe, with J.B. Foster, 1976; Running, Walking & Jumping, 1977; The Camel, with Hilde Gauthier-Pilters, 1981; Harems and Other Horrors, 1983; The 50% Solution, 1986; MisEducation, with Patricia J. Thompson, 1988. *Memberships:* Canadian Society of Environmental Biologists, National Director, 1977-80; Writers' Union of Canada, National Council, 1981-82; Harold Innis Foundation, Director, 1983-. *Honours:* Gold Medal, Biology, University of Toronto, 1955; Chosen as One of Top 8 Living Women Biologists in Canada, 1975; Kitchener-Waterloo Status of Women Group Human Rights Award, 1984. *Hobbies:* Wildlife; Mammals; Feminism; Tennis; Badminton. *Address:* Box 747, Waterloo, Ontario, Canada N2J 4C2.

DAHBANY Avivah, b. 3 Jan. 1951, Brooklyn, New York, USA. Psychologist. *Education:* BA 1974, MS 1978, City College, New York (CCNY). *Appointments:* Fellow, clinical psychology, Albert Einstein College of Medicine, 1976-77; Psychologist, Adams School, NYC, 1977-78; Director Special Education, Psychologist, Dov Revel Yeshiva, Forest Hills, NY, 1978-79; Psychologist, Franklin Twp Public Schools, Somerset, New Jersey, 1979-; Adjunct lecturer, CCNY, 1977-78; Adjunct instructor, Monmouth College, 1981, 1988; Psychology consultant, Robert Wood Johnson Memorial Hospital, Laurie Development Institute, Child Evaluation Centre, 1985-; Instructor, Raritan Valley College, 1986-. *Memberships:* National Association of School Psychologists; Past office, NY Association of School Psychologists; American Psychological Association; National Education Association. *Address:* 101 Aspen Drive, North Brunswick, New Jersey 08902, USA.

DAHL Arlene, b. 11 Aug. 1928, Minneapolis, Minnesota, USA. Actress; Author; Designer. m. Marc A Rosen, 30 July 1984. 2 sons, 1 daughter. *Education:* Minneapolis College of Music, Opera; Minneapolis Business College; University of Minnesota, Drama; Student, Walker Art Gallery; Zell McConnell's School of Modelling. *Appointments include:* Model and Assistant Buyer Lounging Apparel, Marshall Field & Co, 1945; President Arlene Dahl Enterprises, 1950-75; National Beauty Director, Sears, 1970-75; President, Dahlia Parfums, 1975-80; President Woman's World, 1967-72; Vice President, Kenyon & Eckhart, 1967-72. *Stage Appearances include:* Broadway: Mr Strauss Goes to Boston, 1945; Questionable Ladies, 1946; Cyrano Bergerac, 1952; Applause, 1972. On Tour: I Married an Angel; Lilliom; Roman Candle; The King & I; One Touch of Venus; The Camel Bell; Blithe Spirit; Bell Book & Candle; Pal Joey; Marriage Go Round; Life with Father; 40 Carats; Murder Among Friends; A Little Night Music. 29 Starring Films; Slightly Scarlet; Watch the Birdie; Wicked as They Come; Journey to the Center of the Earth; Who Killed Maxwell Thorne? Nightclub Appearances; Flamingo Hotel, 1962; The Latin Quarter, 1962. Records: Three little Words (soundtrack-MGM); Costar Records: Casablanca. Numerous television appearances. *Publications:* Always Ask a Man, 1965; 12 Beautyscope Books, 1969, revised 1979; Arlene Dahl's Secrets of Haircare, 1969; Arlene Dahl's Secrets of Skin Care, 1971; Beyond Beauty, 1980; Arlene Dahl's Lovescopes, 1983. *Memberships:* Academy of Motion Picture Arts & Sciences; Academy of TV Arts & Sciences; Le Comanderie du Bontemps de Medog; Ambassador at Large, City of Hope; International Platform Association; American Film Institute; Sierra Club; Smithsonian Institute. *Honours:* 1st, 2nd & 3rd Scholastic Fashion Awards for Designs 1943; Hollywood Walk of Fame Bronze Star, 1953; 8 Box office Laurel

Awards for Films 1948-63; Best Coiffed 1970-71-72; Heads of Fame Award, 1971, 1983. *Hobbies:* Painting; Sculpting; Interior & Fashion design; Dancing; Collecting Tanagra Figurines, Roman Glass, Fans, Lions and Clocks. *Address:* c/o Dahlmark Productions, POBox 116, Sparkill, New York 10976, USA.

DAHL Carol Ann, b. 2 June 1947, Grantsburg, USA. Associate Professor. *Education:* BA, University of Wisconsin, 1969; PhD, Economics, University of Minnesota, 1977. *Appointments:* Assistant Professor, Illinois State University, Normal, 1976-77; Wayne State University, 1977-79; University of Wisconsin, 1980-83; Associate Professor, Economics, Louisiana State University, 1983-. *Publications:* Articles in journals and magazines. *Memberships:* American Economic Association; International Associate for Energy Economics; Volunteers for Technical Assistance; Association for Environmental & Resource Economics. *Awards:* NSF Science, 1963; Scholarships, 1965-66, 1968-69; Thesis Fellowship, 1975-76; various other Grants. *Hobbies:* Travel; Writing. *Address:* Dept. of Economics, Louisiana State University, Baton Rouge, LA 70803, USA.

DAHLIN Elizabeth Carlson, b. USA. University Administrator. m. Douglas G. Dahlin, 1963 (dec. 1988), 3 daughters. *Education:* BA, Wellesley College, 1953; Graduate study, Harvard University 1953, 1964, George Washington University 1971. *Appointments include:* Neurology research assistant, 1956-58; Substitute teacher, Fairfax County, Virginia, 1958-75; Chief Election Judge, Fairfax County Electoral Board, 1967-75; Administrative assistant 1978-79, assistant to Executive Director 1979-80, National School Volunteer Programme, Alexandria, Virginia; Assistant to Vice President for Development 1980-83, Acting Director of Development 1983, Director of Development 1984-87, Vice President for University Development 1987-, George Mason University, Fairfax, Virginia. *Creative work includes:* Talks, professional fund-raising groups, 1979-. *Memberships:* Numerous community organisations including: Assistant Treasurer, Treasurer, Girl Scout Council, Washington DC, 1972-78; Assistant Folklife Specialist 1977, Concessions Manager 1976, Coordinator of Participants (4th of July Celebration) 1981, Smithsonian Institution, Washington DC; Education Council, Public Relations Committee, George Washington University; National Women's Political Caucus. *Honours include:* Graduate fellowship, psychology, Brown University, 1953; Award, Girl Scout Council, 1978; Biographical recognitions. *Hobbies:* Travel; Grandchildren; Swimming; Folk & ethnic festivals; Cooking; Reading; Visiting museums. *Address:* 6041 Edgewood Terrace, Alexandria, Virginia 22307, USA.

DAHN Daniela, b. 9 Oct. 1949, Berlin, Germany. Author. 1 daughter. *Education:* Diploma, Journalist, 1972. *Appointments:* TV Journalist, 1972-82; Writer, 1982-. *Publications:* Spitzenzeit, 1980; Prenzlauer Berg-Tour, 1987; Radio Plays: Auf dass wir klug werden, 1983; Warum ausgerechnet ich?, 1985, Mitgerissen 1989. *Membership:* Writers Association, GDR. *Honours:* Fontane Prize, 1988; Berlin Prize, 1988. *Address:* Husstrasse 126, Berlin 1199, German Democratic Republic.

DAI Ailian (Tai Ai-lien: Ai-lien Tai), b. 1916, Trinidad, West Indies (Cantonese parents). Dancer; Dance Adviser. *Education:* Studies, classical ballet, modern dance, various teachers including Anton Dolin, Margaret Craske, Marie Rambert, Leslie Borrowes-Goosen, Ernest Berk, London, & Joose-Leeder School of Dance, Dartington Hall, Devon, UK, 1930's. *Appointments include:* Residence in China, 1940-; Research, Chinese dance, continuing; Principal, Beijing Dance School (classical ballet), 1954; Founding member, Labanotation Society of China (recording Chinese dances); Research & popularisation, Chinese ethnic folklore dance; Teacher & coach, classical ballet; Frequent juror, national & international ballet, dance & choreography competitions; Lecture-demonstrations, Chinese Dance & Its History; Artistic Adviser, Central Ballet of China, current. *Creative work includes:* International Prize Choreography works: Tibetan Spring, Berlin, 1951; Lotus Dance, Bucharest, 1953; Flying Apsaras, Warsaw, 1955. *Memberships:* Vice President, Chinese Dancers Association; Chair, China Ballet Society; Chair, China Labanotation Society; Vice President, Conseil International de la Danse (CIDD-UNESCO); President, China National Committee, CIDD; International Council Kinetography Laban/Labanotation; Chair, Dance for All (Chinese Ethnic) Club, Beijing. *Honours:* As Creative works. *Address:* Central Ballet of China, 3 Taiping Street, Shuen Wu Section, Beijing 100050, China.

DALE Lorraine Annie Henderson, b. 30 Aug. 1942, Philadelphia, Pennsylvania, USA. Vice Principal, High School. 2 sons. *Education:* BA, Elementary Education 1975, MEd, Reading 1977, University of Guam; University of Hawaii, 24 graduate credits, 1977-85; EdD Programme currently, University of Southern California. *Appointments:* Administrator at elementary, intermediate and secondary levels (Public Schools), 1985-; District Resource Teacher, 1983-85; Classroom teacher, elementary-secondary, 1975-83; Instructor, University of Hawaii, College of Continuing Education, 1986; San Jose State University, 1981; Department of Education, Repbulic of Palau, 1980. *Publication:* Co-author, Instructional Basic Skills Manual, 1985. *Memberships:* Hawaii Association of Secondary School Administrators, Secretary 1988-89, Executive Board Member 1987-88; National Staff Development Council; Assoc for Supervision & Curriculum Development; Hawaii Education Association; Hawaii Community Education Association; Hawaii State Teachers Association (associate member); Hawaii Government Employees Association; Alpha Delta Kappa; International Honorary Sorority for Women Educators. *Honours:* Chi Omicron Gamma, Honorary Scholastic Society, University of Guam, 1977. *Hobbies:* Running, completed the 1983 & 1984 Honolulu Marathon; Scholarly research. *Address:* 290 C Kawaihae Street, Honolulu, Hawaii 96825, USA.

DALE Margaret Neil, b. 10 Aug. 1950, Bangor, North Wales. Director of Communications. m. Ian Monro Cartwright Dale, 23 May 1980. *Education:* BA Hons History, 1971; DEd History/Theatre Arts, 1973; MA History, 1976; MA Journalism, 1979. *Appointments:* Lecturer, University of Western Ontario, 1976-77; Editor of Publications, Norcen Energy Resources, 1979-85; Assistant Director, 1985-87, Director, 1987-, National Communications Price Waterhouse, Canada. *Publication:* Articles in Canadian Banker Magazine, 1987. *Memberships:* American Marketing Association, 1986-87; International Association of Business Communicators, 1979-; Board of Directors, Adelaide Court Theatre, Toronto. *Honour:* Lynne Bailey Cup for Service to the Community, 1965. *Hobbies:* Photography; Tennis; Bicycling; Movies. *Address:* 207 Queen's Quay West, Suite 500 Box 134, Toronto, Ontario, Canada, M5J 1A7.

DALE Patricia, b. 12 Jan. 1942, Sunderland, England. Software Technical Author. m. (1) Francis Rowland Dale, 16 Aug. 1969, divorced 1986, 2 sons, 1 daughter. (2) Michael William Gerwat, 23 July 1988. *Education:* BA Hons 2.1 English, Sheffield University, 1965; Diploma in Education, 1966. *Appointments:* English teacher, Sheffield High School, 1966-69; 2nd in Department of English, Pudsey Grammar School, 1969-71; Administrative/Secretarial Assistant, North Friends Peace Board (Quakers), 1977-83; Part-time Lecturer of English, Joseph Priestley Institute of Education, Morley, 1977-82; First National Coordinator, Mothers for Peace, 1982-87; Literacy tutor/adviser, Leeds Education Committee, 1983-86. *Memberships:* N E Leeds UNA, 1969-77; CND, Oxfam, War on Want at various times; Society of Friends (Quakers), 1977; Committee Member, Mothers for Peace. *Honours:* Renee Fisher Prize for English, Sheffield University, 1965; One of four mothers visiting the USA on the first Mothers for Peace initiative, 1981; Delegate from Mothers for Peace to World Congress of Women in Moscow, 1987. *Hobbies:*

Creative writing; Dressmaking; Music; Theatre; Walking; Gardening; Current affairs. *Address:* c/o Mothers for Peace, 70 Station Road, Burley-in-Wharfedale, Leeds, LS29 7NG, England.

DALE Theresa, b. 16 Mar. 1947, Flushing, USA. Bio-energetic Medical Consultant; Nutritionist; Researcher. *Education:* MS, 1981, PhD, 1982, Donsbach University; PhD, 1988, FACACN, Clayton University. *Appointments:* Xerox Corp, 1971; Sales professional Health practitioner, 1981-. *Publications:* Beyond M.D's, in progress; Custom Jewelry Design. *Memberships:* National Trainingo-ordinator, Hans Brugemann Institute, Germany; American Naturopathic; Medical Association; American Holistic Health Sciences Association; National Institute of Electro-Medical Information Inc. *Hobbies:* Designing Jewelry; Walking; Racquetball; Classical Music; Reading. *Address:* 1801 N. Beverly Drive, Beverly Hills, CA 90210, USA.

DALEY Therese Fay, b. 15 Jan. 1968, Provo, Utah, USA. Student. *Education:* Communications & Public Relations, Brigham Young University, graduation expected 1990. *Appointments:* Office Manager, Oakwood Chiropractic Clinic, 1986-87; Assignment Desk Editor, KBYU-TV/FM, 1987. *Creative works:* Musical compositions (piano); Radio writer, Times & Seasons, Religion in our Lives; Producer, anchor, announcer, writer, editor, reporter, KBYU television; Public speaker. *Memberships:* Society of Professional Journalists; Numerous honour societies. *Honours:* Communications Talent Scholarship 1986, Festival of Arts Gala Award 1987, BYU; 3rd runner-up, Illinois Modern Miss (scholarship received), 1987; Illinois State Scholar, Phi Eta Sigma, 1987; Scholarships, Waukegan Altrusa Club, Lake County Homemaker's Extension Association, 1986; Miss Teen of Illinois, 1986; Presidential Award, Academic Fitness, 1986; Young Womanhood Recognition Award, 1986; Forensics Awrd, 1986. *Hobbies:* Modern language club, Spanish language (study abroad, Mexico, 1988); Public relations; Piano; Public speaking, community, school, church; Church involvement; Community service, mentally handicapped, fund-raising, organisation; Reporter, Commwrold magazine (BYU alumni). *Address:* 21545 West Brentwood Lane, Lake Villa, Illinois 60046, USA.

DALKEITH Elizabeth Marian Frances, Countess, b. 8 June 1954, Derbyshire, England. Freelance Journalist. m. Earl of Dalkeith, 31 Oct. 1981, 2 sons, 1 daughter. *Education:* BSc., Sociology, London School of Economics, 1975. *Appointments:* Research Assistant, House of Commons, 1976-77; Producer, Talks & Documentaries, BBC Radio 4, 1977-80; Researcher, Readers Digest Magazine, 1980-81. *Memberships:* Deputy Chairman, Scottish Ballet Co.; Scottish President, JMB Development Training; National Union of Journalists. *Hobbies:* Freelance Radio Production; Music; Ballet; Literature; Politics; Gardening. *Address:* Dabton, Thornhill, Dumfriesshire, Scotland DG3 5AR.

DALL'AVA-SANTUCCI Josette, b. 7 June 1942, Corsica, France. Professor; Biologist. m. Jean Marie Targowia, 1966, divorced 1970, 1 son, (2) Remi Dall'Ava, 1977, divorced 1985. *Education:* MD, 1967, University of Paris. *Appointments:* Instructor, Physiology, 1967; Assistant Professor, 1973; Professor, Medicine, Cochin University Hospital, Paris, 1978; Visiting Professor, University of Lisbonne, Portugal, 1981; Director, Laboratory of Pathophysiology of Noise, 1984-. *Publications:* Articles in professional journals. *Membership:* President, French Medical Womens Association; Medical Womens International Association; President, Association for Research on Biological Effects of Noise; American Thoracic Society; European Society for Clinical Respiratory Physiology. *Address:* 69 Rue de la Tombe Issoire, 75014 Paris, France.

DALLMAN Elaine G., b. 8 Mar. 1934, Sacramento, California, USA. Poet; Author; Editor; Publisher; Academic Tour Developer. m. Willard Ross, 18 Dec.

1954, 1 son, 1 daughter. *Education:* BA, Stanford University; MA, Creative Writing, San Francisco State University; PhD, Cretive Writing & English Literature, Southern Illinois University, 1975. *Appointments:* English Teacher: Southern Illinois University, Carbondale 1970-74, University of Nevada, Reno 1975-76; Founder & President: ARRA International Inc 1981-, Women-in-Literature Inc 1977-, Reno, Nevada. *Publications:* Editor, publisher, Woman Poet series regional anthologies, Women-in-Literature Inc, 4 volumes, 1980-89; Author, Parallel Cut of Air, book of poems, 1990. *Memberships:* PEN; Authors Guild; Poetry Society of America; Poets & Writers Inc; Modern Language Association; American Association of University Professors; Academic Board, Board of Directors, Consortium for International Education. *Honours:* Grants: National Endowment for Arts (via Nevada State Council on Arts), 1979, 1981-82; American Association of University Women, 1980, 1983-84; Illinois Arts Council, 1977. *Hobbies:* Travel; Jewellery. *Address:* PO Box 60550, Reno, Nevada 89506, USA.

DALLY Rebecca Leigh Polston, b. 4 Dec. 1955, Columbus, Georgia, USA. Attorney at Law. m. Hal W. Dally, 28 June 1980, 1 son, 1 daughter. *Education:* Mercer University, Atlanta, 1973-75; BA cum laude, Georgia State University, 1976; JD, University of Georgia School of Law, 1979. *Appointments:* Attorney, private practice, 1980-; Assistant District Attorney, Alcovy Judicial Circuit, 1982-84; Special Assistant, Attorney General, 1984-. *Memberships include:* Professional: Past President, Alcovy Judicial Circuit Bar Association, Walton County Bar Association; Member: American Bar Association, Georgia Trial Lawyers Association, State Bar of Georgia, Phi Alpha Delta international law fraternity. Community: Boards, Social Circle Historic Preservation Society, Chairperson-Legislative Committee 1988, 1st Vice President 1989, President 1990, Walton County Chamber of Commerce; Trustee, Walton County Arts Council; Social Circle Merchant & Trade Association; Affiliate, Walton County Board of Realtors; The Alcove (Youth Shelter); Social Circle Family Education Committee 1989; Charter Member, Social Circle Rotary Club 1989-; Georgia Civil Justice Foundation, Inc., Instructor, People's Law School, 1989. *Hobby:* Antiques. *Address:* 317 North Cherokee Road, Social Circle, Georgia 30279, USA.

DALTON Katharina Dorothea, b. 12 Nov. 1916, London, England. Consultant Gynaecological Endocrinologist. m. (1) Wilfred Thomson, Killed in Action 1942, 1 son. (2) Thomas Ernest Dalton, 7 July 1944, 1 son, 2 daughters. *Education:* Registered Chiropodist, Royal Masonic School and London Foot Hospital; MRCS; LRCP, 1948; FRCGP, Royal Free Hospital Medical School. *Publications:* Once a Month, 4th edition 1987; Depression After Childbirth, 3rd edition, 1988; Premenstrual Syndrome & Progesterone Therapy, 2nd edition, 1984; Over 80 papers in Medical Journals on Premenstrual Syndrome *Memberships:* Royal Society of Medicine, Past President, Section of General Practice; Founder Member, Royal College of General Practitioners. *Honours:* British Medical Association prize, three times; British Migraine Association prize; Royal Free Hospital prize, twice; Royal College of General Practitioners prize, twice. *Hobbies:* Cooking; Dressmaking; Painting. *Address:* 100 Harley Street, London W1N 1AF, England.

DALY M. Virginia, b. 10 Sept. 1945, Washington, USA. President, Ginny Daly & Friends. m. Garrett Sanderson, 1 Nov. 1982. *Education:* AB, English, College of Saint Elizabeth, New Jersey, 1967. *Appointments:* Doubleday, 1968-70; Princess Hotels International, 1970-75; Bureau of National Affairs, 1975-76. *Publications:* Expect the Unexpected!, 1987. *Memberships:* Board of Directors, Direct Marketing Association, 1987-90; American News Women's Club, President, 1986-88; Co-Founder, The Creative Group. *Honours:* Professional of the Year, 1985, Gold Maxi Winner, 1986, Echo Winner, 1986, Direct Marketing Association of Washington. *Hobbies:* Flying; Sailing;

Gardening; Breeding Dogs; Travel. *Address:* 918-16th Street NW, Suite 702, Washington, DC 20006, USA.

DALY Margaret Elizabeth, b. 26 Jan. 1938, Belfast, Northern Ireland. Member of European Parliament. m. Kenneth Anthony Edward Daly, 1964. 1 daughter. *Appointments:* Department Head, International Insurance Group, 1956-59; Trade Union Official, 1959-70; Consultant, Conservative Party Central office, 1976-79; Director, Conservative Trade Unionists Organisation, 1979-74; Member for Somerset and Dorset West, European Parliament, 1984-. *Hobbies:* Travel; Reading; Opera; Cooking. *Address:* The Old School House, Aisholt, Bridgwater, Somerset, TA5 1AR, England.

DALYELL Kathleen Mary Agnes, b. 17 Nov. 1937, Edinburgh, Scotland. Lecturer. m. Tam Dalyell, 26 Dec. 1963, 1 son, 1 daughter. *Education:* MA, Edinburgh University, 1960; Teaching Diploma, Craiglockhart College of Education, 1961. *Appointments:* Teacher of History, St Augustine's High School, Glasgow, 1961-62; James Gillespies High School for Girls, Edinburgh, 1962-63. *Publications:* The House of the Binns, Booklet for National Trust, Scotland. *Memberships:* Historic Buildings Council for Scotland, 1975-87; Vice Chairman, Architectural Heritage Society of Scotland, 1988; Chairman, Bo'Ness Industrial Heritage Trust, 1987-; Heritage Education Trust, 1988; Trustee, Paxton Trust, 1988-; Member Ancient Monuments Board, Scotland, 1989-. *Hobbies:* Reading; Travel; Hill Walking. *Address:* The Binns, Linlithgow, West Lothian. Scotland EH49 7NA.

DAMONE Debbie (Debra Joyce), b. 3 May 1953, Lenox Hill, Manhatten, USA. Director of Heritage Outreach. m. Dennis J Damone, 11 June 1972. 1 son, 1 daughter. *Education:* Attended Cosmotlogy School; Lic Inst of NY, 1982. *Appointments:* Substitute Teachers Aid, 1980-83; Haridresser, 1983-85; Director of Heritage Outreach, 1987-89. *Publications:* America the Blest, 1979, Song; Collection of Christian Songs, 1978; Orchestra of Love, 1978; Gave a singing concert, 1978; Sang for Walk-A-Thon for Life, 1988; Wrote, directed and sang in Majesty, 1987; Made a record, 1980. *Memberships:* People Active for Virtuous Education (PAVE) Preisdent; Concerned Women for America (CWA) Prayer Chapter Leader; Coalition for Better Ed, President. *Honour:* Award from Southside Hospital, Caring Award. *Hobbies:* Singing at Weddings, Churches, choir and parties; Reading; Sew clothes and curtains; Crochet. *Address:* 1380 5th Ave, P O Box 692M, Bay Shore, New York 11706, USA.

DANDOY Maxima Antonio, b. Philippines. Educator. *Education:* Philippine Normal College, 1938; AB, National Teachers College, Manila, 1947; MA, Arellano University, 1949; EdD, Stanford University, USA, 1952. *Appointments:* Elementary School Teacher, 1927-37; Laboratory School Teacher, Philippine Normal College, 1938-49; Curriculum Writer & General Office Supervisor, Department of Education, Manila (jurisdiction, schools countrywide), 1944-45; Instructor, Arellano University, 1947-49; Associate Professor of Education 1952-55, Laboratory School Principal 1953-54, University of East, Manila; Visiting Professor, University of California, Los Angeles, USA, 1956; Professor of Education, California State University Fresno, 1956-82. *Publications:* Various articles, teachers' journals, Philippines, 1945-47; Teaching Competencies, Workbook & Log, 1985. *Memberships include:* Offices, past/present: California Federation of Business & Professional Women's Clubs; American Association of University Women; National Council for Social Studies; Filipino-American Women's Club; State Filipino-American Coordinating Council; Honour societies. *Honours:* California Governor's Committees, Juvenile Delinquency 1958, Traffic Safety 1959; Scholarship Award Panel, Bank of America, 1968; Committee for Selection of Social Studies Textbooks, California, 1970. Numerous scholarships, service recognitions, most recent: Special Award, higher education & international understanding, Philippine Normal College Alumni Association, 1986. *Address:*

1419 West Bullard Avenue, Fresno, California 93711, USA.

DANDRIDGE Rita B. College Professor. *Education:* BA, Virginia Union University, 1961; MA, 1963, Phd, 1970, Howard University. *Appointments:* Instructor, Morgan State College, 1964-70; Assistant Professor, University of Toledo, 1971-74; Associate to Full Professor, 1974-, Norfolk State University. *Publications:* American and Ethnic Studies Associations; College Language Association. *Honour:* Virginia Foundation & Public Policy Grant. *Hobbies:* Quilting; Photography; Real Estate Management. *Address:* 1905 Popes Head Arch, Virginia Beach, VA 23464, USA.

DANGAR, Elizabeth, b. 18 Nov. 1944, Australia. Chief Executive Officer, Fortune Communication Holdings. 1 daughter. *Education:* BA, Sydney University. *Appointments:* Founder and MD, The Dangar Research Group. *Memberships:* The Australian Caption Centre, Director; The Geraldine Pascall Foundation, Trustee; The Salvation Army Red Shield Appeal; The Stewart Foundation; The Australian Market Research Society; IAA. *Honour:* First woman appointed as Chief Executive Officer in top ten Agencies in Australia. *Hobbies:* Film; Theatre; Literature; Antiques; Horse Riding. *Address:* Fortune Communication Holdings, 11th Floor, 100 William Street, East Sydney, NSW 2011, Australia.

DANIEL Yvette Felice, b. 18 Nov. 1959, Hammond, Indiana, USA. Sales Representative. *Education:* BA, University of Denver, 1978-83. *Appointments:* Lab Aide, Kaiser Permanenet, 1983; Marketing Rep, National Home Health Care, 1984; Representative, Bristol Laboratories, 1983- 84; Environmental Tech, City of Houston, 1984-87; American Standard Inc, 1987- *Creative works:* Oil on canvas, Mother's portrait; Pencil, self portrait. *Memberships:* University of Denver Alumni Association, 1983-; National Association of Female Executives, 1984-; United Negro College Fund Raiser Associations Links, Houston Chapter; Dorothy Smith Educational Foundation, Board Member, Secretary & Officer; Associate Member, AIA, 1984-. *Honours:* Junior & Senior High school Honor Roll; Houston Independent School District Volunteer Certificate of Appreciation, 1976; Governor of Texas Volunteer Certificate of Appreciation, 1978; Miss National Teenager State Preliminaries, Miss Essay, 1978; Kartrina McCormick Barnes Scholarship, 1978- 83. *Hobbies:* Arts and crafts; Drawing; Painting; Physical fitness; Interior design; Medically related issues pertaining to psychiatry, in particular cat scans and metabolic disorders. *Address:* 6000 North Brookline, Unit 74, Oklahoma City, Oklahoma 73112, USA.

DANIELS Doria Lynn, b. 22 Apr. 1951, Ohio, USA. Production Planner. *Education:* BBA, Kent State Universiy, 1974. *Appointments:* Quality Assurance Supervisor, Little Tikes Co., 1979-83; Production Planner, Little Tikes Co., 1983-. *Memberships:* Founer, Thames-Anderson Development Corporation, 1986; National Association of Female Executives; National Council Negro Women; NAACP; Kent Board of Education; Kent City Council. *Honours:* Kent CitizonScholarship Award, 1969; Governor's Recognition Award, 1986; Ohio House of Representation Commendation, 1987. *Hobbies:* Church Organist; Pianist; Reading; Composing Gospel Music. *Address:* 234 Dodge St., Kent, OH 44240, USA.

DANIELS Dorothy, b. 1 July 1915, Waterbury, Connecticut, USA. Writer. m. Norman Daniels, 7 Oct. 1937. *Education:* Central Connecticut State College, 1932-36. *Appointments:* Training Teacher, 1937-39; Actress, 1939-49. *Publications:* Over 132 books published including: No Tears Tomorrow, 1962; Cruise Ship Nurse, 1963; The Tower Room, 1964; The Unguarded, 1965; The Lily Pond, 1966; Screen Test for Laurel, 1967; The Sevier Secrets, 1968; Affair in Hong Kong, 1969; Web of Peril, 1970; Man from Yesterday, 1971; Dark Island, 1972; The Stone House, 1973; Island of Bitter Memories, 1974; Tidemill, 1975;

Nightshade, 1976; Juniper Hill, 1977; In the Shadows, 1978; Cormac Legend, 1979; Purple and the Gold, 1980; Monte Carlo, 1981; For Love and Valcour, 1983; Crisis at Valcour, 1985. Also published under the pseudonyms: Suzanne Somers, Cynthia Cavanaugh and Angela Gray. *Address:* 6107 Village 6, Camarillo, CA 93010, USA.

DANIELS Elizabeth, b. 23 Sept. 1938, Florida, USA. Dentistry. Divorced, 1 daughter. *Education:* BS, Biochemistry, Tennessee State University, 1958; MS, Howard University, 1963; PhD, Organic Chemistry, University of California, 1968; DMD, Dentistry, University of Connectuct, 1977. *Appointments:* Assistant Dean, Academic Affairs, 1985-87, Associate Dean, Academic Affairs, 1987-88, Faculty Member, Periodontics,1988-, Meharry Medical College. *Publications:* Article in professional journal. *Memberships:* American Association of Dental Schools; National Dental Association; National Association for the Advancement of Coloured People; National Urban League; etc. *Honours:* Alpha Kappa Mu; Beta Kappa Chi; National Aeronautics & Space Agency Fellowship, 1964-68. *Hobbies:* Reading; Films. *Address:* 2933 Stanwyck Drive, Nashville, TN 37207, USA.

DANIELS Elizabeth Adams, b. 5 Aug. 1920, Westport, Connecticut, USA. Educator. m. John Lothrop Daniels, 21 Mar. 1942, 1 son, 3 daughters. *Education:* BA, Vassar College, 1941; MA, University of Michigan, 1942; PhD, New York University, 1954. *Appointments:* Instructor to Professor of English 1948-85, Dean of Freshmen 1954-57, Dean of Studies 1965-73, Acting Dean of College 1976-78, Emeritus Professor of English & College Historian current, Vassar College. *Publications:* Jessie White Mario: Risorgimento Revolutionary, 1972; Main to Mudd, 1987; Editor, Vassar: Remarkable Growth of a Man & his College (Edward Linner); Numerous articles, Victorian literature. *Memberships:* American Association of University Professors; Modern Language Association; Various boards. *Honours:* Phi Beta Kappa; Graduate Alumnaeli Award, New York University, 1954; Summer Grant, National Endowment for Humanities 1980. *Hobbies:* Tennis: Oral history. *Address:* Box 74, Vassar College, Poughkeepsie, New York 12601, USA.

DANIELS Madeline Marie, b. 14 Oct. 1948, Newark, New Jersey, USA. Psychotherapist; Author. m. Peter Walden Daniels, 18 Oct. 1976. 3 sons. *Education:* BA, City College of New York, 1971; PhD, Union Graduate School, Ohio, 1975; PhD, Union Graduate School, Ohio, 1988. *Appointments:* Executive Director, Cross Roads Center, 1979-87; Administrator, Spectrum Cross-Cultural Institute for Youth, East Kingston, 1988-. *Publications:* Books: Living Your Religion In the Real World, 1985; Realistic Leadership, 1983; A Culturally-Different Perspective on Psychology, 1988. *Memberships:* State Chair, International Council of Psychologists; American Psychological Association; Biofeedback Society of America; American Anthropological Association; Biofeedback Society of New England, Secretary-Treasurer, 1982. *Honours:* Certified as Biofeedback Practitioner, Biofeedback Certification Institute of America, 1982; Visiting Consultant, Gopakrishna Piramel Memorial Hospital, Bombay, India, 1987. *Hobbies:* Costumes; Drama and performance; Story telling and expressive arts. *Address:* SCIY Inc, 5 Pow Wow River Road, East Kingston, NH 03827, USA.

DANIELS Molly Anne, b. 2 July 1932, India. Writer; Teacher; Editor. 1 son, 1 daughter. *Education include:* PhD, University of Chicago Committee on Social Thought. *Appointments:* Founder, Director, The Clothesline School of Writing, Chicago, Illinois, USA; Organiser, numerous public performance readings of original poems and fiction. *Publications:* Fiction: The Yellow Fish, 1966; The Salt Doll, 1978; A City of Children, 1986; G.V.Desani: Writer and Worldview, literary criticism, 1984; The Clothesline Review Manual for Writers, with 400 Writing Exercises and Lessons, textbook, 1987: Editor of The Clothesline Review (1986-90); Prophecy in A Passage to India, forthcoming.

Honours: Fulbright Award; Award for Best Fiction and Literary Criticism, Illinois Arts Council; PEN Syndicated Fiction Award. *Hobbies:* Interests focused on creative arts (poetry, fiction, playwriting). *Address:* The Clothesline School of Writing, 5629 Dorchester, Chicago, IL 60637, USA.

DANILOVA Alexandra, b. 20 Nov. 1906, Pskoff, Russia. Lecturer; Teacher; Choreographer; Actress; Former Ballerina. m. (1) Giuseppe Massera (dec. 1936), (2) Kazimir Kokie (div. 1949). *Education:* Theatrical School, Petrograd. *Appointments include:* Maryinski Theatre, Leningrad, 1923-24; Diaghileff Company, 1925-29; Waltzes from Vienna, 1931; Colonel de Basil Company, 1933-37; Prima Ballerina, Ballet Russe de Monte Carlo, 1938-58; Guest artist, Royal Festival Hall, London 1955, Oh Captain musical, New York 1958; Faculty, School of American Ballet. With own company toured West Indies, Japan, Philippines, USA, Canada, South Africa. Guest choreographer, Metropolitan Opera House, New York; Guest teacher & choreographer, Krefeld Festival of Dance (Germany) & Amsterdam (Holland), 1959-60; Choreographed Coppelia, La Scala, Milan 1961, New York City Ballet (with G. Balanchine) 1975; Guest choreographer, Washington Ballet, USA, 1962-64; Screen acting debut, The Turning Point, 1977. Lecture performances throughout USA. *Honours include:* Capezio Award, services to dance, 1958; Kennedy Center Award, 1989; Handel Medal, 1989. *Hobbies: include:* Needlework; Ping-pong; Gardening. *Address:* Carnegie House, 100 West 57th Street, New York, NY 10019, USA.

DANNA Jo Josephine, b. New York City, USA. Author; Publisher. m. David Pender, 9 July 1960. *Education:* BA, Hunter College; MA, 1964, PhD, 1974, Columbia University. *Appointments:* Co-Director, Villaggio del Superdotato, Sicily, 1967-70; Director, Ethnic Studies, New York State Education Dept., 1975-76; Assistant Professor, LaTrobe University, Melbourne, Australia, 1976-79; Author, Publisher, 1982-. *Publications:* It's never Too Late to Start Over; Living in a New Lind: Guide for Immigrants; Starting Over in a Changing Economy; Anthropological Study: Influence of a Sicilian Peasant Culture on Cognitive Development. *Memberships:* Founder, Network of Independent Publishers of Greater New York; Institute for Immigration & Ethnic Studies, Melbourne. *Honours Include:* New York Mensa Fellowship, 1968; Kappa Delta Pi; National Science Foundation Graduate Fellowship, Honourable Mention, 1968; National Institute of General Medical Sciences Fellowship, 1968; Gold Medal, Community Service, Petralia Soprana, Sicily, 1970. *Hobbies:* Museums; Science & Technology. *Address:* 86-07 144 St , Briarwood, NY 11435, USA.

D'ANNIBALLE Priscilla L., b. 28 Oct. 1950, Martins-Ferry, Ohio, USA. Businesswoman. *Education:* BBEd, University of Toledo, 1973. *Appointments:* Credit Manager, Kabat Distributing Company, 1973-80; Commercial Operations Officer, Credit Analyst Officer, Marketing Officer, Martgge Banking Officer, Ohio Citizens Bank, 1980-85; President, D'Ann Enterprises Inc, 1985-. *Memberships:* Past President, various offices, National Association of Credit Management, NACM Educational Forum; Various offices (past/present), National Credit Congress, Midwest-Eastern Credit Women's Conference, Floor Covering Industry Group, Executive Network. Also: Board 1981, 1982, Voluntary Action Centre. *Honours:* Credit Person of Year, 1982; Credit Executive of Year, 1987. *Hobbies:* Golf; Swimming; Gardening; Antiques; Travel. *Address:* 1050 Valley Grove, Maumee, Ohio 43537, USA.

DAOUK Hassana Fathallah, b. 6 June 1922, Beirut, Lebanon. President, Child and Mother Welfare Society; Member, Lebanese Red Cross Central Committee. m. Hassan Omar Daouk, 30 Apr. 1944. 3 sons, 1 daughter. *Education:* Baccalaureat, High school, 1942; Licence, School of French Literature, 1952; History of Arts, American University, 3 years; Public Relation, Beirut, AUB, 1970-74. *Appointments:* Voluntary Occupations: Lebanese Red Cross, 1965-; Youth Committee, Civil

Defense, International and Public Relations until 1988; Member and Vice President, 1955-69, President 1970-, Child and Mother Welfare Society. *Creative works:* Cooperating in many Lebanese Welfare, Cultural, Artistic, Social and Political (for women) activities; Delegate for many conferences and congresses, regional and international. *Memberships:* Friends of American University Museum; YWCA, Beirut; YWMuslima; Lebanese Council for Women; Alumni of American University of Beirut; Founder member and active for 12 years, Baalbek Artistic Festival and Anjar Festival, Lebanon. *Honours:* Merite Libanais (Golden), 1972 and Merite Libanais Chevalier (Golden Knight) 1983, Lebanese Republicane Honnours. *Hobbies:* Sports; Golf; Swimming; Exercise; Art exhibits; Books; Travelling. *Address:* Villa Hassana F Daouk, Rue Mme Curie, Beirut, Lebanon.

D'ARCY Margaretta Ruth, b. 14 June 1934. Playwright; Video & Radio Maker; Cultural Worker. 4 sons. *Appointments include:* Ronald Ibbs Players, Ireland, 1950; 37 Theatre Club, Dublin, 1951-53; Hornchurch Repertory Company, Essex, UK, 1953-55; Royal Court Theatre, London, 1958; New York University, USA, 1967; University of California, Davis, 1973. *Creative works include:* Books: Tell Them Everything, 1982; Awkward Corners, 1988. Film: Circus Expose of New Cultural Church, 1987. Plays: Non-Stop Connolly Show, 1975; Whose is the Kingdom? 1988. *Memberships:* Aosdana (Ireland); Founder Member: Corrandulla Arts & Entertainment, Galway Theatre Workshop, Galway Women's Entertainment, Women's Sceal Radio (Galway), & Ducas na Saoirse; Society of Irish Playwrights; Writers Guild, Great Britain. *Honours:* Membership, Aosdana, 1981; Award, for Island of the Mighty, & Little Gray Home in the West, Arts Council, Great Britain, 1973. *Address:* 10 St Bridget's Place (Lower), Galway, Ireland.

D'ARCY-MACULAITIS Jean, b. 26 Oct. 1949, New York City, USA. Business Owner; Author; Professor; Lecturer. m. Joseph P Maculaitis, 10 Dec. 1966, 2 sons, 4 daughters. *Education:* BA, Jersey City State College, 1968; MA, 1973, PhD, 1978, New York University. *Appointments:* ESL & English Teacher, West New York Public Schools, 1968-72; Programme Administrator, Teacher, Dover (NJ) Public Schools, 1972-74; Lecturer, ESL & Bilingual Vocational Education, New York University, 1978-; Freelance Consultant, Career Counsellor, Business, Academic & Personal Issues, 1978-; CEO, President, Career Wise Inc., & MAC Testing & Consulting Inc., 1987-. *Publications:* Viva El Espanol: Assesment Component, 1988; Hello, English: Assessment Component, 1988; The Complete ESL/EFL Resource Book, 1988; Odyssey: Assessment Component, 1986; Centennial Celebration of the Death of Venerable Father Lodovico, 1985; Maculaitis Assessment Program: A Coordinated Series of Test Batteries for ESL Students in Grades K-12, 1983; Standards for the Preparation and Certification of International Studies Teachers in the USA, 1982; several other books. *Memberships Include:* International TESOL Association; American Booksellers Association; National and New Jersey Associations of Women Business Owners; etc. *Honours:* Recipient, many honours & awards. *Address:* 103 South Ward Avenue, Rumson, NJ 07760, USA.

DARDEN Betty Everett Worrell, b. 28 Jan. 1930, Franklin, Virginia, USA. Assistant Professor; Office Technology Teacher. m. W Thomas Darden, 27 Dec. 1953. 2 sons, 2 daughters. *Education:* AA, Louisburg Jr College; BS, East Carolina University; MED, Virginia State University. *Appointments:* Business Ed Teacher, Newsoms High School, 1952-53; 6th Grade Teacher, Newsoms Elementary School, 1960-61; Business Education Teacher, Franklin High School, 1961-69; Office Technology Teacher, Paul D Camp Com College, 1971-. *Publication:* History of Barnes United Methodist Church, 1st and 2nd Edition. *Membership:* Vice President, Delta Kappa Gamma. *Honours:* FBLA Sponsor of Year, PBL National Award, 1969; 1st Woman Lay Leader, Barnes Methodist Church, 1989-. *Hobbies:* Raising four children; Fishing. *Addres:* Route 1 Box 90, Newsoms, VA 23874, USA.

DARKE Edith Olstad, b. 6 Feb. 1923, Staten Island, NY, USA. Poet. m. (1) Vincent Sapone, 1942, divorced 1970, 1 son, 4 daughters, (2) George Olstad, 1972, widowed 1986, (3) Frederick E Darke, 1987-. *Appointments:* Secretary, City University, retired 1978. *Publications:* Award winning Poems, essays, articles, songs, chldrens story; contributor to magazines. *Memberships:* Space Coast Writers; Florida Federation Womens Clubs; ASCAP; Song Writers Guild; Womens Club of Cocoa; etc. *Honours:* various honours & awards, estate and national levels. *Hobbies:* Reading; Swimming; Cooking. *Address:* 791 Apollo Circle NE, Palm Bay, FL 32905, USA.

DARKE Marjorie, b. 29 Jan. 1929, Birmingham, England. Writer. m. 1952. 2 sons, 1 daughter. *Education:* Leicester College of Art, 1947-50; Central School of Art, London, 1950-51. *Appointments:* Textile Designer, 1951-54; Writer, 1962-. *Publications:* Young Adult Novels: Ride the Iron Horse, 1973; The Star Trap, 1974; A Question of Courage, 1975; The First of Midnight, 1977; A Long Way to Go, 1978; Comeback, 1981; Tom Post's Private Eye, 1982. For younger readers: Mike's Bike, 1974; What Can I Do? 1975; The Big Brass Band, 1976; Kippers Turn, 1976; My Uncle Charlie, 1977; Carnival Day, 1979; Kipper Skips, 1979; Imp 1985; The Rainbow Sandwich, 1989. Short Story Collection: Messages, 1984. Numerous other short stories in anthologies and for television. *Memberships:* The Society of Authors; Committee Member, Children's Writers Group, 1979-85; International PEN. *Honour:* Runner up, Guardian Award for The First of Midnight, 1978. *Hobbies:* Reading; Music; Sewing; Gardening; Walking; Cycling. *Address:* c/o Rogers, Coleridge and White Ltd, Literary Agency, 20 Powis Mews, London W11 1JN

DARLING Alberta, b. 28 Apr. 1944, Hammond, Indiana, USA. Company Director. m. William A Darling, 12 Aug. 1967, 1 son, 1 daughter. *Education:* BS, University of Wisconsin, 1967. *Appointments:* English Educator: Nathan Hale High School, 1967-69; Castle Kock High School, Colorado, 1969-71; Director, Marketing & Communications, Milwaukee Art Museum, 1982-88; Director, Marketing, Beckley Myers, 1988-. *Publications:* Project '85, Plan for United Way; Long Range Plan 80-82 Junior League; 5 Year Plan, Milwaukee Art Museum. *Memberships:* Founder, Goals for Greater Milwaukee 2000, 1980-84; Co-Chair, Action 2000, 1980-84; Board of Directors, Executive Committee, United Way; etc. *Honours Include:* Marketer of the Year, American Marketing Association, 1985; Milwaukee Leader of the Future Award, 1985; Today's Girls/Tomorrow's Women Leadership Award, 1987. *Hobbies:* Reading; Travel; Art; Art History. *Address:* 1325 West Dean Road, Milwaukee, WI 53217, USA.

DARLING Marsha Jean, b. 1 Feb. 1947, New York City, USA. Professor. *Education:* AA, 1971; BA, Vassar College, 1973; MA, 1975, PhD, 1982, History, Duke University. *Appointments:* Fellow, Harvard Univesity, 1978-79; Professor, Wellesley College, 1979-88; Professor, Women's Studies, Hunter College, 1987; Research Consultant, National Committee for Responsible Philanthrophy, Washington, 1988-89. *Publications:* Articles in professional journals. *Memberships:* Board of Directors, National Black Womens Health Project; Board of Directors, Massachusetts Foundation for Humanities & Public Policy; American Association of University Women; Black Achievers Linkage Programme. *Honours:* Greater Boston Black Achievers Award, 1983; Anna and Samuel Pinanski Endowed Award for Distinguished Teaching, 1984; NEH Fellowship, 1984; Rockefeller Foundation Post-doctoral Research Scholar, Spelman College, 1984-85; Research Scholar, Spelman College, 1984-85; Associate, WEB Dubois Institute, 1985-87; Associate, Centre for Research on Women, Wellesley College, 1987-88; Fulbright Senior Scholar's Award, India, 1988. *Hobbies:* International Travel; Tao; Hatha

Yoga; Aerobics. *Address:* 1540 44th Street NW, Washington, DC 20007, USA.

DARLING Vera Hannah, b. 18 July 1929, Walthamstow, London, England. Director. *Education:* Registered General Nurse, 1951; Registered Nurse Tutor, 1959. *Appointments:* Inspector, Training Schools/Examinations Officer, General Nursing Council, 1968-78; Principal Officer, JBCNS, 1978-83; Professional Officer, ENB, 1983-84; Associate Lecturer, University of Surrey, 1984-86; Director, Lisa Sainsbury Foundation, 1985-. *Publications:* Co-author, Ophthalmic Nursing, 1981; Research for Practising Nurses, 1986; Series Editor, The Lisa Sainsbury Foundation Book Series, 1987-; contributor to: Nursing, Midwifery & Health Visiting since 1900. *Memberships:* Eastbourne Health Authority, 1983-88; East Sussex Family Practitioner Committee, 1985-87; Council Member, Cancer Relief Macmillan Fund, 1987. *Honour:* OBE, 1985. *Hobbies:* Classical Music; Gardening. *Address:* Lisa Sainsbury Foundation, 8-10 Crown Hill, Croydon, Surrey CRO 1RY, England.

DASHER Cornelia Watson, b. 9 Nov. 1943, Sheffield, Alabama, USA. Occupational Therapy Director. *Education:* BA, Biology, Converse College, 1965; BS, Occupational Therapy, University of Florida, 1967; MA, Education, University of Alabama at Birmingham, 1972. *Appointments:* Easter Seal Rehabilitation Centre, Aiken, 1967-69; University Hospital, Birmingham, Alabama, 1969-, Director, Occupational Therapy, 1974-. *Publications:* Discharge Planning, 1976; Joint Protection/Energy Conservation, 1977; Low Back Pain - Self Inst. Unit, 1978; Film, Architectual Barriers, 1979. *Memberships:* American Occupational Therapy Association, 1967-; Alabama Occupational Therapy Association. *Honours:* Mortar Board, 1965; Outstanding Young Woman in America Nominee, 1979; Award of Excellence, Alabama OT Association, 1982, Roster of Fellows, 1983, American Occupational Therapy Association. *Hobbies:* Organ Playing; Tennis; Tap Dancing; Deacon, Presbyterian Church. *Address:* 101 Virginia Drive, Birmingham, AL 35209, USA.

DATÉ Barbara, b. 22 Aug. 1946, Chicago, USA. Counselor and Education Consultant. *Education:* BA, Manchester College, 1969; MA, 1978, PhD, Counseling Psychology, 1987, University of Oregon. *Appointments:* Private Practice, 1979-. *Publications:* Articles in professional journals. *Memberships:* American Association for Counselling & Development. *Honours:* American Psychological Association Minority Fellowship Program, 1980-83; Outstanding Young Woman of America, 1981; Outstanding Young Woman of Orogon, 1001. *Address:* Oregon Caring Skills Project, 1475 Ferry Street, Eugene, OR 97401, USA.

DAUBENAS Jean Dorothy, b. New York, USA. Librarian. m. Joseph A. Daubenas, 29 May 1965. *Education:* AB, Barnard College, Columbia University; MA, New York University; MLS, University of Arizona; PhD, University of Utah. *Appointments:* Actress, Boothbay (Maine) Playhouses & others, 1967-70; Reference Librarian, Arizona State Univerity, Tempe, 1972-75; Assistant Librarian, Avila College, Kansas City, 1979-83; Associate Professor, Librarian, St John's University, 1983-. *Publication:* Book reviews in Catholic Library World; Modern Drama. *Memberships:* American Library Association; Actors Equity Association; AAUP; Beta Phi Mu; Phi Kappa Phi. *Honours:* New York State Regents Scholarship; University of Arizona Graduate Assistantship & Tuition Waiver Scholarship, 1971-72; University of Utah Graduate Assistantship, 1976, 1977. *Hobbies:* Classical Music; Theatre; Art. *Address:* Library, St John's University, Jamaica, NY 11439, USA.

DAUNTER Maria Teresa, b. 26 Oct. 1946, Malta, Europe. Clinical Psychologist. m. 1 Mar. 1968, 1 son, 1 daughter. *Education:* AS, 1978; BA, 1980; MA, 1982; PhD, 1985. *Appointments:* Co-Owner, Family Medical & Mental Health Clinic, 1982-84; Clinical Director, Owner, Family Psychological Services, 1984-.

Publications: Audio Tape on mediation; Frequent speaker to professional groups. *Memberships:* American, Michigan Psychological Associations; American Association of Marriage & Family Therapy; World Mental Health Organisation. *Hobbies:* Meditation; Reading; Walking; Swimming. *Address:* Family Psychological Services, 3491 Harman Road, SuiteB, Traverse City, MI 49684, USA.

DAVENPORT Evi, b. 18 Feb. 1940, St Peter, Minnesota, USA. Coordinator of Learning Resourses. m. (1) Craig Lawson, 27 Aug. 1960, divorced 1975, 2 sons, 1 daughters. (2) Manuel Davenport, 8 Nov. 1978. *Education:* BA, Kansas State University; Graduate student, Texas A&M University. *Appointments:* Campus Ministry Associate, University of Houston, 1973- 75; Research Associate 1975-77, Instructional Mat Specialist 1977-85, Coordinator, Learning Resources 1985-, Texas A&M College of Medicine. *Memberships:* Health Sciences Communications Association, Secretary, Board of Directors, 1985-, Coordinator, Learning Resources Center, 1984-; Board of Directors, Health Sciences Consortium, 1982-; Secretary, Phi Delta Gamma, 1982-84. *Honours:* Student Friend Award, Texas A&M University College of Medicine, 1985; Nominee for President of Health Sciences Communications Association, 1988. *Hobbies:* Reading; Gourmet cooking; Sewing. *Address:* Learning Resources, 109 Medical Sciences Library Building, Texas A&M University, College Station, TX 77843-4462, USA.

DAVID Evelyn R, b. 2 Feb. 1929, Chicago, USA. Flight Purser. *Education:* AA, North Park Junior College, 1947; Studies at various colleges & universities. *Appointments:* Assistant to Mrs Ambrose Diehl, Director of Recreation for the San Francisco State Department, 1954-69; Flight Purser, Pan American Airlines. *Memberships:* ACIC. *Hobbies:* Travel; Tennis; Skiing; Hiking; Arts. *Address:* 800 Bush St., No 505, San Francisco, CA 94108, USA.

DAVID Janet, b. 13 May 1936, Brooklyn, New York, USA. Psychologist. m. Stephen Mark David, 23 Aug. 1962. *Education:* BA, Brandeis University, 1957; MA, New School for Social Research, 1967; PhD, Fordham University, 1982. *Appointments:* The Childrens' Village, 1976-78; The Clearview School, 1978-81; Metropolitan Institute for Training in Psychoanalytic Psychotherapy, 1980-82; Center for the Study of Anorexia & Bulimia, 1981-; Institute for Contemporary Psychotherapy, 1982. *Publications:* Articles in professional journals. *Memberships:* American Psychological Association; NY State Psychological Assn; American Orthopsychiatric Association; Association for Professionals Treating Eating Disorders; NY Society of Clinical Psychologists; Council for the National Register of Health Service Providers in Psychology. *Hobby:* Travelling. *Address:* 303 W 66th St 6BW, New York, NY 10023, USA.

DAVID Joanna, b. 17 Jan. 1947, Lancaster, England. Actress. m. Edward Fox. 1 daughter. *Education:* Elmhurst Ballet School; Webber Douglas Academy of Dramatic Art. *Career includes:* Theatre: The Importance of Being Earnest; The Cherry Orchard; Breaking the Code. Television: When Johnny Comes Marching Home; The Last of the Mohicans; Colditz; Jenni; Ballet Shoes; The Duchess of Duke Street; Within These Walls; Just William; The Dancing Princess; Lillie; Rebecca; Lady Killers; Dear Brutus; The South Bank Show; Charlotte and Jane; Fame is the Spur; Alexa; The Red Signal; Lady Maid's Bell; Rumpole; Brass; Time for Murder; Tender is the Night; Paying Guests; First Among Equals. Film: Comrades. *Address:* c/o Peter Browne Management, 13 St Martins Road, London SW9, England.

DAVIDOVICH Bella, b. 16 July 1928, Baku, USSR. Concert Pianist. m. Julian Sitkovetsky, violinst, deceased. 1 son. *Education:* Moscow Conservatory. *Appointments:* Engagements in recitals as soloist with orchestras and in chamber music in all major music centers internationally; Duo rectials with son, violinist Dmitry Sitkovetsky; Professor of Piano, The Juilliard School of Music, 1983-; Professor of Piano, Moscow Conservatory, 16 years. *Honours:* First Prize, Chopin International Piano Competition, Warsaw, Poland, 1949. *Hobbies:* Opera; Literature; Films. *Address:* c/o Agnes Bruneau, 155 West 68 Street No 1010, New Mexico, NM 10023, USA.

DAVIDSON Sylvia A, b. 14 Apr. 1922, Porland, Oregon, USA. Civic Health Worker. m. (1) Norman Nemer, 21 Dec. 1947, deceased, 2 sons, (2) C. Girard Davidson, 4 Oct. 1967. *Education:* Stanford University, 1942; BA, Reed College, 1947. *Publications:* Editor, Conning Tower, US Navy WWII; Editor, Metropolitan Arts Committee News Letter, 1976; Alternatives to Nursing Home Care, 1976. *Memberships Include:* Multnomah County Planning Commission; Home Rule Charter Commission; Portland State University Goals Committee, 1965-66; Portland Multnomah County Consolidation Committee, 1970-72; Metropolitan Arts Commission; Oregon Health Commission (Chairman), 1972-80; Northwest Oregon Health Systems (President); National Council Health Planning (Federal Advisroty Commision), 1980-86; Oregon Health Council, 1982. *Honours:* Outstanding Effort Award, Oregon Jewish Welfare Fund, 1951; Harry Truman Freedom Bell Award, 1960; Forrest E. Rieke, MD Achievement Award in Community Health Planning, 1980; White Rose Award Community Service (March of Dimes), 1988. *Address:* 1054 S.W. Douglas Place, Portland, OR 97205, USA.

DAVIES Angela Leicester, b. 22 Apr. 1957, West Kirby, Wirral, Merseyside, England. University Lecturer in Restorative Dentistry; Warden of Hall of University Residence. *Education:* Bachelor of Dental Surgery, Liverpool University, 1980. *Appointments:* Junior Hospital post, Liverpool Dental Hospital, 1981-82; Sheffield Dental Hospital, 1983-; Subwarden & Tutor, Sorby Hall of Residence, Sheffield, 1983-87; Warden, Halifax Hall of Residence, Sheffield University, 1987- . *Creative works:* Presented papers at International conferences, e.g. The Hague, Netherlands at at many national conferences, London, Glasgow, Newcastle, etc. *Memberships:* Elected Council Member, Liverpool Odontological Society, 1982; British Dental Association; International Association of Dental Research and British section; School Governor, 1985-88; Member of many University committees. *Hobbies:* Sport; Squash; Badminton; Skiing; Postcard collecting; Water-colour painting; Collecting reverse-glass paintings; Travel. *Address:* Warden, Halifax Hall of Residence, Endcliffe Vale Road, Sheffield S10 3ER, England.

DAVIES Bronwyn, b. 10 Jan. 1945, Armidale, New South Wales, Australia. Academic; Senior Lecturer. m. (widowed 1970), 3 sons. *Education:* BA 1965, DipEd 1972, BEd 1974, PhD 1980, University of New England (UNE), Armidale. *Appointments:* School teacher, English, science, drama, 1967-72; Tutor 1973, 1974, Lecturer, Behavioural Studies 1975-81, Social & Cultural Studies 1982-84, UNE; Senior Lecturer, Centre for Social & Cultural Studies, UNE, 1985-; Remedial Reading Tutor, aboriginal children & adults, 1974. *Publications include:* Books, sole author: Life in the Classroom & Playground: Accounts of Primary School Children, 1982; Frogs and Snails and Feminist Tales. Preschool Children and Gender, 1989. Co-author: Women's Studies Research Directory, 1985, 1988. Also: Monograph, Gender, Equity & Early Childhood; Numerous book chapters, articles in refereed & professional journals, book reviews. *Address:* Social & Cultural Studies, University of New England, Armidale, New South Wales 2351, Australia.

DAVIES Lucy Myfanwy, b. 8 Apr. 1913, Plymouth, England. Retired. m. Jaor D W Davies TD, RAMC, 23 Apr. 1955, deceased 1959. *Education:* Sorbonne, 1930-31. *Appointments:* Joined ATS 1938; Served Egypt, 1945-48; Assistant Director, Cyprus, 1957-59; Comdt WRAC Depot, 1961-64; Deputy Director, WRAC, 1964-68; Deputy Controller Comdt 1967-77. *Memberships:*

Life President, WRAC Association; Underwriting Member, Lloyds. *Honours:* Order of St John, 1938; OBE, 1961; CBE, 1968. *Hobbies:* Horse racing; Travel. *Address:* 6 Elm Place, London SW7, England.

DAVIES Margaret Constance, b. 4 May 1923, Manchester, England. Professor of French. m. (1) 1 son, 1 daughter, (2) E. W. J. Mitchell, 25 Jan. 1984. *Education:* Somerville College, 1941-44; MA(Oxon); La Sorbonne, Paris, France, 1946-49; Doctorat, University of Paris, 1949. *Appointments:* Lecturer, Westfield College, University of London, 1963-65; Lecturer, 1965-72, Reader, 1972-76, Professor of French, 1976-88, University of Reading, Reading, Berkshire; Special Professor, University of Nottingham, 1989-. *Publications:* Two Gold Rings, novel, 1954; Colette, critical biography, 1961; Apollinaire, critical biography, 1962; Une Saison en Enfer de Rimbaud, 1975; Numerous learned articles. *Honours:* Sarah Smithson Modern Languages Prize, Somerville College, Oxford; Emeritus Professor, University of Reading, 1988-. *Hobbies:* Music, particularly opera; Writing; Art; Theatre; Cooking. *Address:* Department of French Studies, University of Reading, Reading, Berkshire, England.

DAVIES Margaret, b. 8 Nov. 1944, Hobart, Tasmania. Zoologist. *Education:* BSc (Tas), 1966; BSc., Honours, 1967; MSc., ANU, 1970; PhD, Adelaide, 1987. *Appointments:* Tutor, Zoology, ANU, 1967-70; Research Assistant, University of British Columbia, Canada, 1970-71; Tutor, 1972-73, Senior Tutor, 1974-81, Principal Tutor, 1982-, Zoology, University of Adelaide. *Publications:* Co-editor, 3 books; Co-author, 1 book; Author, Co-author, 52 scientific papers; Editor, Transactions of the Royal Society of South Australia, 1982-. *Memberships:* Royal Society of South Australia, Secretary, 1978-82; Australian Society of Herpetologists, Secretary/Treasurer, 1978-83; Australian Institute of Biology; Society for the Study of Amphibians & Reptiles. *Hobbies:* Scientific Illustration; Photography; Old Books; Cooking. *Address:* c/o Dept. of Zoology, University of Adelaide, GPO Box 498, Adelaide, South Australia 5001, Australia.

DAVIES Nicola Elizabeth, b. 6 July 1949, London, England. Actress; Writer; Producer. *Education:* Haberdashers' Aske's Public School, 1954-64. *Career:* Acting Debut: Jenny, juvenile lead in the original West End Production of The Prime of Miss Jean Brodie at Wyndham's Theatre, 1967; Stage work includes: Peer Gynt at the 1970 Chichester Festival, musicals, pantomime and repertory. Recent Roles: Annie in The Norman Conquests; Karen in Plaza Suite; Doris in Same Time Next Year and Rita in the Scandinavian premiere of Educating Rita in Stockholm. TV Debut: Esther Hargreave in the BBC Classic Series of Bronte's The Tenant of Wildfell Hall. TV Appearances include: Saturday Theatre, The Open University; Z Cars; Crossroads; The Regiment; Pathfinders; That's My Boy; The Gaffer; Help; Casualty, etc. Film debut: Kathleen in Walt Disney's Guns in the Heather. Films include: The Chairman; All Coppers Are...; Duet for One. Voice Producer for EMI Broadcast Programmes Ltd, 1974-76; Administrative Director, London Centre for Psychotherapy, 1976-79; Company Director, Medical and Electyrical Instrumentation Co Ltd. *Creative Works:* Pop record: Infatuation on the SNB label, distrubted by CBS. Full-length stage play: Sex and the Single Man; Screenplay: Sleep to Wake. Novel: Baize. *Memberships:* British Actors; Equity Association; Association of Cinematograph and Television Technicians; British Mensa Limited, 1975; Executive Member, The Young Variety Club of Great Britain, 1974-77. *Honours:* Kilburn Polytechnic Chess Champion, 1966; Certificate of the Faculty of Astrological Studies, 1981. *Hobby:* Snooker, has own full-size snooker table. *Address:* 632 Kingsbury Road, London NW9 9HN, England.

DAVION Ethel Pauline Johnson, b. 21 July 1948, North Carolina, USA. Educator. m. Joel Davion, 6 Aug. 1988, 1 daughter. *Education:* BA, 1971; MA, 1983. *Appointments:* Teacher, various high schools & colleges, 1971-87; Supervisor, Language Arts (K-12) &

Facilitator, Curriculum Workshops,, Irvington Board of Education, New Jersey, 1987-. *Publications:* Teachers' Resource Manual, 1988; Tutorial English Program at Westfield; Reading Approach to Basic Skills; Strategies for Passing Mandated Testing. *Memberships:* Secretary, Linden Scholarship Guild; Historian, Obsidian Club; Principals' & Supervisors' Association; Association for Supervision & Curriculum Development; Irvington Administrators' Association; Jolly Samaritans Civic Club. *Honours:* Woman of Year, 1968; Urban Initiative Award, District Writing Programme, 1988; Supervisor, programme with highest writing test scores, 1988; Presidential Scholarship, 1966. *Hobbies:* Writing poetry & short stories; Golf; Reading; Public speaking; Aerobics; Curriculum workshops. *Address:* 610 East Blancke Street, Linden, New Jersey 07036, USA.

DAVIS Abigail F., b. 13 Aug. 1950, Margaretville, New York, USA. Airline Pilot. *Education:* BA, English & Philosophy, Ithaca College, New York, 1972; University of Minnesota Graduate School, 1983, 1988. *Appointments:* New Haven Airways Inc, Connecticut, 1974-76; Stauffer Chemical Company, Westport, CT, 1976-77; IBM Corporation, New York, 1977-79; Northwest Airlines, Minneapolis, 1979-. *Memberships:* President 1984-86, Vice President 1982-84, Board of Directors 1986, International Society of Women Airline Pilots; Daughters of American Revolution. *Hobbies:* Skiing; Tennis; Whitewater rafting; Running; Theatre; Literature. *Address:* 11149 Drew Avenue South, Bloomington, Minnesota 55431, USA.

DAVIS Ann Elizabeth, b. 17 Sept. 1932, Cleveland, Ohio, USA. professor of Sociology. divorced. 2 sons. *Education:* BA 1954, PhD 1971, Ohio State University; MS SW, University of Louisville, 1960. *Appointments:* Insurance Sales, Washington National Insurance Company, 1954-56; Social Worker, Kentucky Department of Mental Health, 1956-63; Counselor, West Covina Mental Health Center, 1963-65; Professor of Sociology, Miami Unviersity, 1970-. *Publications:* Schizophrenics In the New Custodial Community; Chapters in books; The Insurmountability of Alienation (in German); The Professional Woman. *Memberships:* The Association for Humanist Sociology, Vice-President, 1985-86; Co-Founder 1975, Regional Representative 1979, 1980; North Central Sociological Association, Secretary 1977-80; Kent School Alumni Association, President, 1961; Editor, Central Issues Newsletter, North Central Sociological Association, 1977-80. *Honours:* Research Award, New York Department of Mental Hygiene, 1968; NIGMS Fellowship, University of California, Los Angeles, 1965; NIMH Grant Recipient, 1968. *Hobbies:* Writing; Swimming; Counseling; Analytic Therapy; Certified Hypnotist; Fourwheeling a Jeep; Painting on Silk, Golf; Raquetball; Dancing. *Address:* 788 W Sharon Road, Cincinnati, OH 45240, USA.

DAVIS Carolyne Kahle, b. 31 Jan. 1932, Penn Yan, New York, USA. Health Care Consultant. m. Howard Davis, 28 June 1953. 1 son, *Education:* BS Nursing, Johns Hopkins University, Baltimore, 1954; MS Nursing Education 1965, PhD Higher Education Administration 1972, Syracuse University. *Appointments:* Various full and part-time staff nurse and supervisory positions at: Lankenau Hospital, Philadelphia, Garfield Memorial Hospital, Washington and Syracuse Memorial Hospital; Assistant to Chairperson 1966-67, Assistant Chairperson 1967-68, Acting Chairperson 1968-69, Chairperson 1969-73, Baccalaureate Nursing Program, Syracuse University; Dean School of Nursing 1973-75, Professor of Nursing, School of Nursing 1973-81, Professor of Education, School of Education 1973-81, Associate Vice President for Academic Affairs 1975-81, University of Michigan; Administrator, Health Care Financing Administration, Dept of Health and Human Services, 1981-85; Board of Directors: Beverly Enterprises; Smith Kline Corporation; American Red Cross; Beckman Instruments; The Prudential Insurance Company of America Inc; National and International Health Care Advisor, Ernst & Whinney. *Memberships include:* Board of Governors, American Red Cross, 1988-; Community Health Accreditation Program, Chairperson 1987-. *Honours include:* Recipient of numerous honorary degrees and awards including: Cullen prize Administration, Johns Hopkins Hospital, 1954; Distinguished Leadership Award, Dept Health & Human Services, 1985; Special Recognition Award, American Association of Medical Colleges, 1986. *Hobby:* Gardening. *Address:* c/o Ernst & Whinney, 1200 19th Street, Washington, DC 20036, USA.

DAVIS Coleen Cockerill, b. 20 Sep. 1930, Pampa, Texas, USA. Educator; Author. m. Richard Harding Davis, 22 June 1952, 2 sons. *Education:* BS, University of Oklahoma, 1951; MS, University of California, Los Angeles, 1952; Graduate work, University of Southern California, Whittier College and University of California, Los Angeles; International Tour Management Institute. *Appointments:* Teaching, Whittier Union High School District, Whittier, California, 1952-85; Founder, President, Executive Director, Co-Host, America's Bed & Breakfast, Whittier, 1983-; Substitute Teacher, 1985-; Consultant, 1986-; Tour Guide. *Publications:* Contributor of articles to newspapers including the Register, The Leader, The Daily Trojan. *Memberships:* Founder, President, Children of Murdered Parents, Whittier, 1984; Founder, President, Coalition of Organizations and People, Whittier, 1984; Founder, President, Whistle Ltd, Whittier; Southeast/Long Beach Chapter Leader, Parents of Murdered Children, 1984. *Hobbies:* Volunteer work; Writing. *Address:* PO Box 9302, Whittier, CA 90608, USA.

DAVIS Faith Margaret, b. 16 Aug. 1939, Detroit, Michigan, USA. Psychiatric Social Worker. div., 2 sons, 1 daughter. *Education:* BA, Marygrove College, 1959; MSW, San Francisco State University, 1972; Licensed Clinical Social Worker, 1981. *Appointments:* Social Worker, San Diego Welfare Department, San Diego, California, 1962-64; Social Work Supervisor, Alameda County Welfare Department, Oakland, California, 1964-72; Psychiatric Social Worker, West Oakland Health Center, 1971-72; Child Welfare Worker, Alameda County Human Resources, Oakland, 1972-73; Psychiatric Social Worker, 1973-77, Director, 1977-78, Alameda County Substance Abuse; Clinical Director, East Oakland Drug Abuse, 1977-78; Consultant: Verbal Exchange Programme, 1968-70; Public Health Nurses, 1973-77; Oakland Public Schools, 1973-83. *Memberships:* National Association of Social Workers; Counselors West; Marygrove College Alumni Association; San Francisco State University Alumni Association; Alpha Kappa Alpha; Various Parent-Teacher Associations; Toler Heights Citizens Council; World Peace Organisation, Nichiren Shoshu Soka Gakkai of American Buddhism. *Honours:* Numerous appreciation awards, Oakland Schools and various organisations; The well-being and growth of the people she has tried to help. *Hobbies:* Attending human service and world peace conferences in other countries; Travel; Dancing; Photography; Cultural exchanges. *Address:* Oakland, California, USA.

DAVIS Grania Eve, b. 17 July 1943, Milwaukee, USA. Author; Teacher. m. Stephen L. Davis, 2 June 1968, 2 sons. *Education:* BA, University of Hawaii, 1977; BA, Sonoma State University, 1977. *Appointments:* Teacher, various schools, 1968-; Author, 1972-. *Publications Include:* Doctor Grass, 1978; The Great Perpendicular Path, 1980; The Rainbow Annals, 1980; Moonbird, 1986; Marco Polo and The Sleeping Beauty, co-author, 1988; Short Fiction Includes: Young Love, Orbit 13, 1974; To Whom it May Concern, 1975; David's Friend The Hole; What Happened on Cranberry Road, 1985; Word Woman of Dza, 1986; Fantastic Magazine. *Membership:* Science Fiction Writers of America. *Hobby:* World Travel. *Address:* 557 Whitewood Drive, San Rafael, CA 94903, USA.

DAVIS (A) Jann, b. 1 Sept. 1941, Shattuck, Oklahoma, USA. Author; Lecturer; Nursing Consultant. m. 27 Dec. 1962, 1 son, 1 daughter. *Education:* Registered Nurse, Wesley Medical Centre, Wichita,

Kansas, 1962; BA, Nursing & Communications, Metropolitan State University, Minnesota, 1976; MA, Counselling, University of Northern Iowa, 1979. *Appointments:* Staff Nurse, Charge Nurse, Missouri & Iowa, 1962-74; Director, Nursing Education, Floyd County Memorial Hospital, Iowa, 1974-77; Author, Lecturer, Consultant, 1977-; Owner & Director, Jann Davis & Associates Inc, 1979-. *Publications:* Books: Please See my Need, 1981; Listening & Responding, 1984. Monthly Column, American Journal of Nursing, 1983-84; Numerous Articles, Nursing Journals. *Honours include:* Outstanding Book of Year, 1984; 1st Place Writing Award, American Journal of Nursing, 1979; 2nd Place, National Creative Nursing Award, 1978; Outstanding Young Woman of Iowa, 1978; One of Ten Outstanding Young Women of America, 1978. *Hobbies:* Collecting Antique Quilts; Flying (pilot). *Address:* 706 2nd Avenue, Charles City, Iowa 50616, USA.

DAVIS Jean Reynolds, b. 1 Nov. 1927, Cumberland, Maryland, USA. Composer; Author; Poet; Teacher; Arranger; Lecturer. m. The Rev Warren H Davis, Jr, 9 Dec. 1949, divorced. 2 sons. *Education:* BM, University of Pennsylvania, School of Fine Arts, 1949. *Appointments:* Teacher (piano, theory, composition), 44 years; Composer/arranger, 50 years; Author (books, articles, poetry), 40 years. *Publications:* Books: A Hat On The Hall Table; To God with Love; Parish Picnic; Music; Sacred & secular; Doors Into Music (a 10-volume teaching method); Shenandoah Holiday (a ballet story); Symphonies; Choral works; Teaching materials. *Memberships:* American Society of Composers, Authors & Publishers; American College of Music; National Guild of Piano Teachers; AARP; Mature outlook. *Honours:* Thornton Oakley Medal; Benjamin Franklin Medal; Grant from ASCAP for performance of Ballet. *Hobbies:* Oil painting; Gourmet cooking; Sewing. *Address:* The Mermont Plaza Apt 104, Merion & Montgomery Avenues, Bryn Mawr, PA 19010, USA.

DAVIS Judy, b. Australia. Actress. *Education:* Studied at West Australia Institute of Technology; National Institute of Dramatic Art. *Appointments:* Theatre companies in Adelaide and Sydney. Theatrical film debut in My Brilliant Career, 1979. *Creative Works:* Films: Hoodwink; Heatwave; Winter of Our Dreams; The Final Option; A Passage to India; Kangaroo; High Tide. Television: A Woman Called Golda. *Address:* c/o Chatto & Linnit Ltd, Prince of Wales Theatre, Coventry Street, London W1, England.

DAVIS Lauren, b. 1 Apr. 1959, Cleveland, Ohio, USA. Neuroscientist. *Education:* BA, New York University, 1981; Doctor of Philosophy, Neuroscience, University of Virginia, 1988. *Publications:* Selective Dendritic Transport of RNA in Hippocampal Neurons in Culture (with G.A.Banker and O.Steward), 1987; Ultrastructural characterization of the Synapses of the Crossed Temporo-dentate Pathway in the Rat (with S.L.Vinsant and O.Steward), 1988. *Memberships:* Society for Neuroscience; International Brain Research Organization. *Address:* Department of Neuroscience, Medical Center, Box 230, University of Virginia, Charlottesville, VA 22908, USA.

DAVIS Linda Macrae, b. 7 Dec. 1942, Batavia, New York, USA. Musician; Pianist Teacher and Performer. m. 6 June 1968. divorced. 3 sons, 2 daughters. *Education:* BS, Fredonia State University, Fredonia, USA, 1964; Conservatory of Music, Antwerp, Belgium, 1964; MM, Manhattan School of Music, USA, 1972; Doctoral Study, Columbia University and Juilliard School of Music, New York City, 1970-72. *Appointments:* Director of Music, Bronx Music Association, 1967-68; Taught piano, theory and chorus at NYC Community College, 1971; Teacher of piano, Brooklyn Conservatory of Music, 1972-75; Solo pianist with Orechestras in new York and New Jersey; Solo concert tours in Boston and New York, 1970- and 1972; Recital, Gardner Museum, Boston, 1971; Solo Piano recitals, Europe and England, 1963; Pianist with Antwerp Philharmonic Orchestra Quartet, 1963-65; Pianist with New Art Trio,

1971-74; Accompanist and Chamber artist with hundreds of vocalists and instrumentalists including Placido Domingo, John McCormack and Robert Guerra; Concerts on WNYC NYC and WLAD; Past Director of Music, United Jewish Center, Danbury, 1976-86; Church of Jesus Chirst of Latter Day Saints, Newton, 1976-86; Director of Piano Studio, Newtown, 1976-81; Director and teacher of music school, Pittsford, 1986-. *Memberships:* Past President Danbury Conn, Chapter of the CSMTA, 1980-82. *Honours:* 1st prize concerto contest at Fredonia State University; Fellowship, Antwerp Conservatory of Music, Antwerp, Belgium; Full scholarships of study of trio chamber music with William Kroll, Kroll String Quartet and Loren Munro, principal cellist of the NY Philharmonic orchestra; Winner, Visiting Artists series, Gardner Museum, Boston. *Address:* Pittsford, New York, USA.

DAVIS Lydia Joanna, b. 4 May 1958, Indiana, USA. Vice President. *Education:* BA, Howard University, 1980. *Appointments:* News Reporter Trainee, 1980-81; Writer, Researcher, 1981-83, Associate Producer, 1983, Assistant Director, Public Relations, 1983, Director, Promotion, 1983-85, Vice President, 1985-, Johnson Publishing Co. *Publication:* Naked Thoughts: The Fire's Inside. *Memberships:* Executives Club of Chicago; Womens Advertising Club of Chicago; Chicago Association of Direct Marketing; Cosmpolitan Chamber of Commerce; Howard University Alumni Association; League of Black Women. *Honours:* CEBA Communications Excellence to Black Audiences, 1986. *Hobbies:* Creative Writing; Painting; Singing; Biking; Cooking. *Address:* Johnson Publishing Co. Inc., 820 S. Michigan Ave., Chicago, IL 60605, USA.

DAVIS Mary Helen, b. 2 Dec. 1949, Kingsville, Texas, USA. Child Psychiatrist; Psychoanalyst; Medical Educator. *Education:* BA, University of Texas, 1970; MD, University of Texas Medical Branch, Galveston, 1975; Psychiatric Residency, State University of New York, Buffalo, 1975-78; Fellowship in Child Psychiatry, University of Cincinnati, 1978-80; Psychoanalytic training, Institute for Psychoanalysis, Chicago, Illinois, 1982-. *Appointments:* Assistant Professor, Child Psychiatry, Medical College of Wisconsin, 1980-89; Clinical Association Professor, 1989-; Clinical Director, Adolescent Treatment Center, 1981-86, Medical Director, Schroeder Child Center, 1986-, Milwaukee Psychiatric Hospital. *Memberships:* American Psychiatric Association; American Academy of Child and Adolescent Psychiatry. *Honours:* KASS Award for Excellence in Research, University of Texas Medical Branch, 1975; APA Falk Fellowship, 1977-79; Outstanding Young Women, 1985. *Hobbies:* Crochet; Computers; Science Fiction. *Address:* 1220 Dewey Avenue, Wauwatosa, WI 53213, USA.

DAVIS Myrtle Hilliard, b. 13 June 1926, Texarkana, Arkansas, USA. President, Chief Executive Officer. 1 son. *Education:* RN 1943; MS, Health Planning/Administration, University of Cincinnati, 1977. *Appointments:* Admin, St Louis Comp Health Center, 1969-82; President, Harvard St Health Centers, Boston, 1982-83; President, Chief Executive Officer, St Louis Comp Health Center, 1983-. *Memberships:* Board of Directors, Urban League E, Chairman Med Committee; President Board of Directors, Tower Village Nursing Home; Co Chairman, NAACP Freedom Fund Dinner; President, Board of Directors, Primary Care Covnor; Missouri Minority Health Task Force; Task Force, Operation Child Save; Board of Directors, Maternal-Child Health Council. *Honours:* Role Model Program, St Louis Public Schools; Certificate of Appreciation, Missouri Senate; Outstanding Achievement, Homer Phillips Nurses Alumni; Masonic Award for Community Service; Community Health Sv Award Northside Preservation Corp; Woman of Year, St Louis Argus Newspaper, Greyhound Bus Corp; Distinguished Service Award, Sigma Gamma Rho Sorority, et al. *Hobbies:* Photography; Travel. *Address:* 5471 Dr M L King Drive, St Louis, MO 63112, USA.

DAVIS Shirley E, b. 23 Feb. 1935, New Haven,

Connecticut, USA. National Secretary of trade Union. m. Eldridge E Davis, 26 May 1956. 1 daughter. *Education:* Certificate course, New Haven College, 1969; Certificate course, Southern Connecticut State College, 1971; Cornell School of Labor Management. *Appointments:* Sub-clerk, 1958-62, Clerk, 1962-74, PSDS Technician, 1974-, United States Postal Service; National Secretary, NAPFE, 1980-; District Eight Vice President, 1970-72, District Eight President, 1972-80, NAPFE; President Local 811 New Haven, Connecticut, 1969-72. *Memberships:* Board of Directors, Urban League of Greater New Haven, 1974-80; Commissioner of Equal Opportunity, 1974-80, Vice Chairwoman, 1977-80; President, Board of Directors, Newhallville Day Care Center, 1973-78. *Honours:* First Black Female career Postal Employee in New Haven Connecticut Post Office, 1958; First female president Local 811 New Haven NAPFE, 1969; First female president of District Eight NAPFE, 1972; First National Secretary NAPFE, 1980; Second full time National Secretary in history of NAPFE. *Hobbies:* Sports; Reading. *Address:* 317 Clifton Street, New Haven, Connecticut 06513, USA.

DAVIS Susan Ann, b. 18 Nov. 1946, Wausau, Wisconsin, USA. Public Relations Executive. m. Robert S Wilkerson, 11 May, 1985. *Education:* BA, University of Wisconsin, 1968. *Appointments:* Press Staff, Office of Governor Warren Knowles, Wisconsin, 1968-69; Volunteer Advanceperson, Committee to Reelect the President, 1976; Volunteer Advanceperson, President Ford Committee, 1976; Inaugural, Director, Hospitality Committee, 1973; Chairman, National Self-Help Resource Center, Inc, 1974-81; President, The Davis Company, Executive Search, 1981-82; Office of the President, Elect Neighborhood Policy Advisory Group, 1982; Inaugural, Deputy Director, First Family Office, 1982; President, Susan Davis and Associates, 1975-83; Chairman, The Susan Davis Companies, 1983-. *Publications:* Uplift - What People Themselves Can Do, 1974; Community Resource Centers: The Notebook, 1976; Various handbooks, articles etc. *Memberships:* Immediate Past President, International Women's Forum; Economic Club of Washington, DC; Women in Advertising, Marketing, Board of Advisors; World Affairs Council; Greater Washington Board of Trade; National Museum of Women in the Arts; Board Member, The Center for Democracy; Children's Hospice International; Techmatics, Inc; Overseas Education Fund; KIDS. *Honours:* Women Business Advocate of the United States, US Small Business Administration, 1984; Outstanding Achievement in National and International Public Affairs, National Association of Women Business Owners; Personalities of America, 1981-82; Community Leaders of America, 1981-82; Outstanding Young Women of America, 1979-80. *Hobbies:* Travel; Tennis; Skiing. *Address:* 1146 19th Street, NW, Washington, DC 20036, USA.

DAVITT Christine Mary, b. 15 May 1950, New York City, USA. Research Associate; Electron Microscopist. m. Bruce B Davitt, 3 Apr. 1971. *Education:* BS, Natural Sci, Niagara University; BS Microbiology, PhD Zoology, Washington State University. *Appointments:* Teaching Assistant 1977-84, Electron Microscopist 1984-, Research Associate/Instructor, Dept of Zoology, 1988-, Washington State University. *Publications:* Scientific articles to professional journals. *Memberships:* American Society Zoologists; Association for Women Faculty, Washington State University; Society for the Study of Amphibians & Reptiles (SSAR). *Honour:* Graduated cum laude, 1977. *Hobbies:* Scientific illustration; Photography; Drawing, pen and ink. *Address:* Dept of Zoology, Washington State University, Pullman, WA 99164, USA.

DAVY Patricia Mary, b. 29 Apr. 1920, Edinburgh, Scotland. Retired. m. I. A. G. Davy, 11 June 1941, 1 son, 4 daughters. *Education:* Oxenfoord Castle; Abbot's Hill; Brillantmont, Lausanne, Switzerland. *Appointments:* F.A.N.Y., 1939-41; Executive, J. Walter Thompson, Lexington, 1968-81. *Memberships:* Local Representative, Suffolk Preservation Society. *Hobbies:*

Fishing; Embroidery; Gardening. *Address:* Clare, Suffolk, England.

DAWSON Carol Gene, b. 8 Sept. 1937, Indiana, USA. Commissioner. m. Franklin Dean Smith, 2 Aug. 1986, 2 sons, 2 daughters from previous marriage. *Education:* BA, Dunbarton College, 1959. *Appointments:* White House Staff, News Analyst, 1969, Deputy Press Secretary, US Dept. of Energy, Washington, 1981-82; Deputy Special Assistant to Secretary, US Dept. of Energy, Washington, 1982-84; Commissioner, US Consumer Product Safety Commission, 1984-. *Memberships:* National College Young Republicans, co-chairman, 1959-61; Board of Directors, Young Americans for Freedom, 1960-64; Board of Visitors, Institute for Political Journalism, Georgetown University, 1985. *Honour:* Award of Merit, Young Americans for Freedom. *Hobby:* Foxhunting. *Address:* 320 Canterwood Lane, Great Falls, VA 22066, USA.

DAWSON Judith Montague Sheehan, b. 3 Nov. 1939, Honolulu, Hawaii, USA. Director of Development, Punahou School. m. Donald D. Dawson, 4 Apr. 1964, div. 1979, 1 son, 1 daughter. *Education:* Wellesley College, 1957-59; BA, University of California, Berkeley, 1962; MA, University of Hawaii, 1977. *Appointments:* Executive Secretary, Halekulani Hotel, Hawaii, 1962-64; Community Relations Officer, East-West Center, Honolulu, Hawaii, 1964-66; Director of Development, Punahou School, Honolulu, 1978-. *Memberships:* Vice-President, Atherton Family Foundation; President, Board of Trustees, Hawaiian Mission Children's Society; Docent, Chairman of annual fund-raising dinner, Honolulu Academy of Arts; Board Member, Daughters of Hawaii; Board Member, Boys and Girls Club of Hawaii; Board Member, Oriental Art Society, Hawaii. *Hobbies:* Chinese and Japanese art; Travel; Marathon runner. *Address:* 3155 Kaohinani Drive, Honolulu, HI 96817, USA.

DAWSON Nancy B, b. Jan. 1952, Cincinnati, Ohio, USA. Director. m. Terry Wells, 14 June 1986, 1 stepson. *Education:* MEd., Business, Xavier University, 1985. *Appointments:* Clinic Supervisor, Planned Parenthood, 1974-75; Clinic Supervisor, City of Cincinnati Health Dept., 1975- 76; Assistant Director, Health Services, 1976-78, Director, Nursing & Health Service, 1978-85, Director, Workplace Health Service, 1985-87, American Red Cross, Cincinnati Area Chapter; Director, Deaconess Womens Care, Centre for Womens Health & Medicine, Deaconess Hospital, 1987-88; Adjunct Professor, Northern Kentucky University, 1988-. *Memberships Include:* American Marketing Association; American Public Health Association, Association of Fitness in Business. *Honours:* President's Academic Award, Alpha Lambda Delta Academic Award, Purdue University. *Hobbies Include:* Wine; Cooking; Skiing; Swimming; Singing. *Address:* 3428 Ferncroft Dr., Cincinnati, OH 45211, USA.

DAYHOFF Ruth Elizabeth, b. 16 May 1952, New York, USA. Physician. m. Vincent M. Brannigan, 26 May 1975, 2 daughters. *Education:* BS summa cum laude, University of Maryland, 1973; MD, Georgetown University, 1977; Residencies, clinical pathology, George Washington University 1977-79, Johns Hopkins University 1979-80. *Appointments:* Research associate, Veterans Administration, Washington DC, 1980-82; Research associate, research assistant professor, Georgetown Medical School, 1982-88; Instructor, Johns Hopkins University, 1980-; President, Ruth Dayhoff Research Associates, Maryland, 1988-. *Publications include:* Editor, Proceedings, 7th annual symposium, Comparative Applications of Medical Care, 1983; Editor, MUMPS Users Group Quarterly, 1980-; Co-author, Computer-Based Information Systems, 1981; Co-author, various articles, Journal of Law & Medicine, Journal of Legal Medicine. *Memberships:* Board, offices, Symposium on Computer Applications in Medical Care; Past Executive, Past Chair, Board, MUMPS Users Grup; Fellow, American College of Informatics. *Honours:* Phi Beta Kappa, 1972; General honours certificate, 1973; Career development award,

Veterans Administration, 1980-82. *Address:* 4309 Rosedale Avenue, Bethesda, Maryland 20814, USA.

DAYTON Donna Irene Fisher, b. 26 Sept. 1914, Flushing, Ohio, USA. Teacher; Librarian. m. Wilber T. Dayton, 24 Dec. 1938, 2 sons, 2 daughters. *Education:* BA, Religious Education, Northern Baptist Theological Seminary, 1945; MA, University of Kentucky, 1963. *Appointments:* various Teaching positions, 1935-73; Assistant to the Librarian, Houghton College, New York, 1973-76; Librarian, Assistant Professor, Christian Education, 1976-83, Professor Emeritus, 1983-, Wesley Biblical Seminary, Jackson MS; Summer Librarian, Kingsley College, Melbourne, Australia, 1985. *Memberships Include:* National Education Association; Retired Teachers Association; Kentucky Retired Teachers Association; etc. *Honours:* Recipient, various honours and awards. *Hobbies:* Reading; Swimming; Travel; Church; Library Work. *Address:* 2655 Cherokee Ave., Macon, GA 31204, USA.

DAYTON Irene Catherine G, b. 6 Aug. 1922, Lake Ariel, Pennsylvania, USA. Poet; Novelist. m. Benjamin B. Dayton, 16 Oct. 1943, 2 sons. *Publications:* Poetry Books: In Oxbow of Time's River, 1978; Seven Times the Wind, 1977; The Panther's Eye, 1974; The Sixth Sense Quivers, 1970; Novels: Tale of the Vercors, completed, 1984; The House of Zorayan, in progress; Represented in numerous anthologies, journals & magazines. *Memberships:* Poetry Society of America; North Carolina Poetry Society; Fellow, International Academy of Poets. *Honours:* Distinguished Submissions Award, Dellbrook Writer's Conference, 1979. *Hobbies:* Reading; Map Research; Mountain Trail Hiking; Travel. *Address:* Pine Stone, 209 S. Hillandale Drive, E. Flat Rock, NC 28726, USA.

DEAN Alberta LaVaun, b. 12 Apr. 1925, Lafayette, USA. Registered Nurse. m. Guy, 16 Oct. 1948, 1 son, 5 daughters. *Education:* Diploma, Hurley Hospital School of Nursing, 1948. *Appointments:* Hurley Hospital, 1948-53; McLaren General Hospital, Flint, 1953-54; Home Hospital, Lafayette, 1954-. *Memberships:* Hurley Hospital Alumni; Nurses Association American College Obstetrics Gynecology; Smithsonian Institution. *Honour:* Outstanding Nurse of the Year, 1982. *Hobbies:* Knitting; Crocheting; Needlepoint; Baking & Decorating Cakes. *Address:* 276 Dayton Road, Dayton, IN 47941, USA.

DEAN Carol Carlson, b. 1 Aug. 1944, Fort Worth, Texas, USA. Accountant. m. William Franklin Dean, 17 June 1966. 1 son, 1 daughter. *Education:* BBA 1966, MBA 1987, Midwestern State University; PhD student programme, University of North Texas, currently. *Appointments:* Accountant, Parkland Memorial Hospital, Dallas, 1966-67; Accountant, Federal National Mortgage Association, Dallas, 1967-69; Instructor of Management, Midwestern State University, 1987-88. *Publications:* Contributor to Texas Business magazine, 1988. *Memberships:* Wichita County Medical Auxiliary, former President, 1983-84; Board of Directors, YMCA, Wichita Falls; Archer County Republican Party (Chairman, 1984-87); Texas Commission for Health Care Reimbursement Alternatives. *Hobbies:* Snow skiing; Scuba diving; Running. *Address:* Wichita Falls, Texas, USA.

DEAN Elizabeth M, b. 2 Dec. 1948, Birmingham, England. Rehabilitation Medicine Educator, Physical Therapist, Cardioresp Physiologist. m. Daniel Perlman, 22 Aug, 1975. *Education:* BA 1972, PhD 1987, University of Manitoba; Diploma in phys therapy 1975; MS, University of So California, USA, 1978. *Appointments:* Research Assistant, Can Agr Winnipeg, Man, Canada, 1966-71; Phys therapist, St Boniface Gen Hosp, Winnipeg, 1975-78; Research Assoc 1978-79, part-time Teacher 1978-81, University Man, Winnipeg; Instructor, U of BC, School of Rehab Med, Vancouver, 1983-87; Research Fellow 1985-87, Physical Therapist Dir Ergometric Performance lab, Sch Rehab Med, 1985-, Assistant Profesor, Sch Rehab Med, 1987-.

Publications: Contributor of articles to professional journals and chapters to books on cardioresp phys therapy. *Memberships:* American Physical Society; Can Physical Therapy Association; American Physical Therapy Association. *Hobbies:* Walking; Cycling; Plays; Reading; Hiking. *Address:* 3493 W 23rd Ave, Vancouver, BC, Canada V6S 1K2.

DEAN Lydia Margaret Carter, b. 11 July 1919, Bedford, Virginia, USA. Author; Food and Nutrition Consultant, Coordinator. m. Halsey Albert Dean, 24 Dec. 1941, 2 sons, 1 daughter. *Education:* BS, Madison College, 1941; MS, Virginia Polytechnic Institute & State University, 1951; Micjigan State University and UCLA; DSc.; PhD. *Appointments:* Various Dietition positions, 1942-53; Community Nutritionist, Roanoke, 1953-60; Director, Nutritions & Dietetics, Southwestern Virginia Medical Center, 1960-67; Food & Nutrition Consultant, National Headquarters ARC, Washington, 1967-; Staff, and Volunteer, 1973-, Nutrition Scientist, Army, Washington, 1973-, Department of Agriculture, 1973-; 1973-, Nutrition Coordinator, Public Health, US Government. *Publications:* Co-Author, Community Emergency Feeding, 1972; Help My Child How to Eat Right, 1973; The Complete Gourmet Nutrition Cookbook: The Joy of Eating Well and Right, 1978; The Stress Foodbook, 1980; contributor of articles to professional journals. *Memberships Include:* Trustee, International World University, Member Nutrition Policy Committee; Fellow, American Public Health Association; American Dietetic Association; American Association University Women; etc. *Address:* 7816 Birnam Wood Dr., McLean, VA 22102, USA.

DEAN Monica Alexis, b. 24 July 1972, USA. Student. *Appointments:* Clerk, The Voter Education Project, Inc, May 1987; Librarian's Assistant, John F Kennedy Summer Camp Library, June 1987; Chief Babysitter and Founder, Dean Infant and Children's Sitting Service, 1988-. *Memberships:* Arrive Alive; Student Government Association; Center for Applied Technology, Megnet Program, Morris Brown Pre-Freshman Engineering Program, Mass Communications Club, NAACP, Youth Council; Friendship Baptist Church League of Youth, Youth Handbell Choir; Science & Technology Awareness Program. *Honours:* 1988 Georgia Governor's Honor Program-Science; National Honor Society; Smith College Book Award; Georgia Certificate of Merit Winner. *Address:* 87 Burbank Drive NW, Atlanta, Georgia 30314, USA.

DEARAGON RaGena Cheri, b. 29 May 1952, Boulder, Colorado, USA. College Professor. *Education:* BA, 1974, MA, 1977, PhD, 1982, History. *Appointments:* Visiting Assistant Professor, History, Wichita State University, Kansas, 1981-83; Assistant Professor, History, Gonzaga University, 1983-. *Publications:* Articles in: Journal of Medieval History; Albion. *Memberships:* North American Conference on British Studies; Haskins Society; American Historical Association. *Honours:* NEH Summer Seminar, 1978, 1985; Visiting Scholar, Summer, Fitzwilliam College, Cambridge, 1987. *Hobbies:* Photography; Wine Tasting. *Address:* Dept. of History, Box 35, Gonzaga University, Spokane, WA 99258, USA.

DEBLASIS Celeste Ninette, b. 8 May 1946, California, USA. Writer. *Education:* BA, English, Pomona College, 1968. *Publications:* Novels: The Night Child, 1975; Suffer a Sea Change, 1976; The Proud Breed, 1978; The Tiger's Woman, 1981; Wild Swan, 1984; Swan's Chance, 1985; A Season of Swans, 1989; translations into Danish, Dutch, French, German, Hebrew, Italian, Swedish. *Memberships:* Authors Guild; ACLU; California Historical Society; California State Library Foundation; National Museum of Women in the Arts; etc. *Hobbies:* Birdwatching; Walking; Travel; Gardening; Reading. *Address:* c/o Jane Rotiosen Agency, 318 E 51st St, New York, NY 10022, USA.

DECAMPO Rossana, b. 24 Feb. 1963, Toronto, Canada. Scenic Painter. m. Paul DeCampo, 15 Apr.

1983, 1 daughter. *Education:* Ryerson Polytechnical Institute, 1981-83; Ontario College of Art, 1984-85. *Appointments:* Various positions including: Box Office, Reception, Costume Mistress, Fund Raiser, Stage Manager, Window Dresser. *Creative Works:* Leather Wreaths; Floor Cloths with painted Marble, Granite, Textures; Scenic Painter. *Memberships:* Association of Canadian Film and Crafts People. *Honour:* High School Drama Festival Stage Management Award. *Hobbies:* Leather Wreaths; Floor Cloths; Own Paintings. *Address:* 9 Winnett Ave., Toronto, Ontario M6C 3L2, Canada.

DE CHANT-MORRIS Betsy A., b. 21 Oct. 1943, Youngstown, Ohio, USA. Psychotherapist; Clinical Social Worker. m. Roger Jay Morris, 31 Mar. 1979, 2 daughters. *Education:* BS cum laude, Youngstown University, 1965; MSW, University of Pittsburgh, 1969. *Appointments:* Warren City Schools, Ohio, 1965-67; St Francis Hospital & Community Mental Health Centre, Pittsburgh, 1969-73; Allegheny East Mental Health Centre, Pittsburgh, 1974-83; Private practice, Monroeville, Pennsylvania, 1979-. *Creative work includes:* Contributor, National Banner Exhibition (nationwide tour), Christian Art Guild, 1968; Editorial Board, Proceedings, American Association of Partial Hospitals, 1980-86. *Memberships:* Various offices, American Group Psychotherapy Association; National Registry of Clinical Social Workers. *Honours:* Fellow: American Group Psychotherapy Association 1989, Pennsylvania Society for Clinical Social Workers 1985; Diplomate, American Board of Examiners, Clinical Social Work; Teacher of Year, LAS Warren City Schools, 1966-67; Academy of Certified Social Workers, 1971; Awards, Federal MR Grants, 1968, 1969; Honour societies. *Hobbies:* Jewellery, silversmithing & design; Sculpture; Pastel drawing; Editorial work including Chief Editor, text, Women, Gender & Group Psychotherapy. *Address:* 100 James Place, Monroeville, Pennsylvania 15146, USA.

DE CRISTOFORO Mary Agnes, b. 5 Dec. 1918, New York City, New York, USA. Freelance Writer; Columnist. m. Romeo John De Cristoforo, 7 June 1941, 3 sons. *Education:* High School Diploma, 1936; Invitational courses in Journalism, Literature, Radio, Drama, Art; Editing and Creative Writing. *Career:* Under pen-name Mary A. Cristy: Freelance contributor to national newspapers, periodical and magazines; Weekly newspaper column; Regular contributor to daily newspapers (columns, poems, inspirational articles, fiction). *Creative works:* Horses In The Living Room Let Me Love Again; Professional paintings, Huguette's Gallery. *Memberships:* Professional Member, National Writers Club; Society of Western Artists; Pacific Art League; San Francisco Museum Society; Sunnyvalo Art Club; Los Altos Historical Society. *Honours:* Best Radio Show, Stanford University, 1959; Award for Best Painting in Oils, Sunnyvale Art Club, 1976. *Hobbies:* Hiking; Literature; Art; Gardening; Decorating; History; Music; Travel; Ecology. *Address:* 27861 Natoma Road, Los Altos Hills, CA 94022, USA.

DECKER-REESE Deborah, b. 12 Aug 1950, Milwaukee, USA. Freelance Writer/Photographer. m. Clyde W Reese, 22 Oct. 1983, 1 son. *Education:* University of Wisconsin, 3 years. *Appointments:* Freelance Writer/Photographer, 1982-. *Publications:* Johnny Rutherford, Biography; numerous magazine articles and author of greetings cards. *Memberships:* National Writers Club; International Freelance Photographers Organisation. *Honours:* Beta Phi Gamma. *Hobbies:* Photography; Motor Racing; Travel. *Address:*4858 South Hoyt St., Littleton, CO 80123, USA.

DEE Helen, b. 18 May 1944, Manila, Philippines. Business Executive. m. Peter S. Dee, 18 July 1964, 1 son, 2 daughters. *Education:* BSc, Commerce, Assumption College, Manila, 1963; MBA, De la Salle University, 1987. *Appointments include:* Board Chairman: Z Fishing Corporation, 1st Nationwide Assurance Corporation, Manila Memorial Park Cemetery Inc, American Bristol Insurance Company, Malayan Zurich Insurance (Guam)(also President), Malayan Zurich Insurance Company Inc, Hi Rubber Products; Director, Vice Chairman, President, Executive, Trustee, numerous other companies. *Memberships include:* Past President, Philippine Insurers Club; Philippine Insurance Institute; Past President & Chairman, Insurance & Surety Association, Philippines; Past Chairman, Past Advisory Board, Asean Insurance Council; Electoral College, Insurance Hall of Fame; Charter Member, International Insurance Society Inc. *Hobby:* Tennis. *Address:* 1150 Tamarind Road, Dasmarinas Village, Makati, Metro Manila, Philippines.

DE FERREIRE Mary Elizabeth, b. 13 Sept. 1949, Rio Grande City, USA. Clinical Psychologist. m. Peter Joseph Rowen, 24 Jan. 1970, 1 daughter. *Education:* BA, University of Texas at Austin, 1970; MSc., Wright University, 1973; PhD, University of Texas at Austin, 1984. *Appointments:* Various positions, 1970-78; Psychology Intern, Audie L. Murphy Memorial VA Hospital, San Antonio, 1980-81; Psychotherapist, Robert E. Buxbaum & Associates, San Antonio, 1981-82; General Land Office, Austin, 1983-86; Texas Department of Mental Health, 1986-. *Publications:* Articles in: Journal of Genetic Psychology; various other journals. *Memberships:* National Partners of the Americas; Texas Partners of the Americas; Capital Area Psychological Association; Institute of the Humanities; American Civil Liberties Union; National Hispanic Womens Network; American Cancer Society; American GI Forum; American Heart Association; Hispanic Women's Network of Texas; Mexican American Democrats of Texas. *Honours Include:* Phi Kappa Phi; Kappa Delta Pi; National Institute of Child & Health Department Research Fellow, Washington, 1977-78; National Partners of the Americas Kellogg Fellow in International Development, 1988-. *Hobbies:* Photography; Classical Music; Arts. *Address:* 2506 Cascade Drive, Austin, TX 78757, USA.

DEFILIPIS Katarina-Zlata, b. 1 Apr. 1925, Zagreb, Yugoslavia. Clinical Psychologist and Psychotherapist. m. Berislav Defilipis, 6 Apr. 1952 (deceased). *Education:* Graduated 1967, Studies in dynamic psychotherapy, Centre for Mental Health, 1969-79, Zagreb University. *Appointments:* Assistant, Clinic for Neurology, Psychiatry, Alcoholism and other addictions, Zagreb, 1968-69; Assistant, Centre for Mental Health, Zagreb University, 1969-. *Publications:* Numerous professional and scientific papers and articles on the problems of clinical Psychology and psychotherapy; Selected Lectures of Clinical Psychology (editor), 1979. *Memberships:* Member Croatian Association of Clinical Psychologists, President, 1969-81; Croation Psyhchological Association. Member; Board of Executives, 1970-81, Initiator, Organizer, President, 1st Meeting of Clinical Psychologist of Yugoslavia, 1975; Croatian Psychological Association, Member, Commission for Awards, 1984-; Yugoslav Psychological Association; Yugoslav Psychotherpeutic Association. *Awards:* Diploma of Association of Health Organisations of S R Croatia, 1975; Diploma of Psychological Association of Yugoslavia, 1978; Diploma of Psychological Association of SR Croatia, 1983. *Hobbies:* Classical music; Painting; Poetry. *Address:* 95 Mosa Pijade, 41000 Zagreb, Yugoslavia.

DEFLEUR Lois B, b. 25 June 1936, Aurora, Illinois, USA. Provost and Professor of Sociology. *Education:* AB, Blackburn College, 1958; MA, Indiana University, 1961; PhD Sociology, University of Illinois, 1965. *Appointments:* Assistant Professor, Sociology, Transylvania College, Lexington, 1963-67; Associate Professor 1967-74, Professor 1975-86, Dean College of Arts & Science 1981-86, Washington State University; Provost, University of Missouri-Columbia, 1986-; Distinguished Visiting Professor, US Air Force Academy, 1976-77; Visiting Professor, University of Chicago, 1980-81. *Publications:* Author: Deliquency in Argentina, 1965; Sociology: Human Society, 3rd edition 1981 (with others), 4th edition 1984; The Edward R Murrow Heritage: A Challenge for the Future, co-author, 1986; Numerous articles to professional journals. *Memberships:* Board of Curators, Stepehs College;

American Sociological Association; Pacific Sociological Association; Sociol for Women in Society, Law & Society Association; Sociol Study Social Problems; Inter-University Seminar on Armed Forces & Society; Council of Coll of Arts & Sciences; American Society Criminology. *Honours:* Washington State University Invited Address for Distinguished Scholars, 1973; Alumni Achievement Award, Blackburn College, 1985; Grantee: NIMH 1969-79, NSF 1972-75, Air Force Office 1978-81. *Hobbies:* Flying, licensed pilot since 1966; Horseback riding. *Address:* University of Missouri-Columbia, Columbia, Missouri 65211, USA.

DEGKWITZ Eva Gertrud, b. 31 July 1926, Greifswald, Democratic Republic of Germany. University Professor. *Education:* Diploma in Biology, 1953; Promotion, Zoology, 1955; Habilitation, Biochemistry, 1970. *Appointments:* Professor of Biochemistry, University of Giessen, 1970-. *Creative works:* Research on biochemistry of vitamin C. *Memberships:* German Society for Biological Chemistry; German Society for Nutrition; German Society for Laboratory Animal Science (GV-SOLAS). *Hobby:* Riding. *Address:* Biochemisches Institut, Friedrichstrasse 24, D-6300 Giessen, Federal Republic of Germany.

DEHART Panzy Lavonne, b. 18 May 1934, North Carolina, USA. Social Worker. m. Henry Oss De Hart, 18 June 1966, 1 son, 1 daughter. *Education:* BA, 1956, MSW, 1958, Howard University. *Appointments:* Social Worker: Washington DC, 1958-61, VA Hospital, Buffalo, 1961-63, Bronx, 1963-65; District Social Work Consultant, New York City, 1968-70; Supervisor, Inwood House, New York City, 1970-72; Social Worker, Rusk Institute of Rehabilitation Medicine, New Yorkk University Medical Centre, 1976-. *Memberships:* New York City Howard Univeristy Alumni Club, President 1970-74; Director, Queens Chapter, Jack & Jill, 1986-87. *Honours:* Lambda Kappa Mu National Achievement Award, 1974; Howard Alumni Service Award, 1974; Jack & Jill Service Award, 1987. *Hobbies:* Cooking; Bible Study; Interior Decorating. *Address:* 110-06 214th Street, Queens Village, NY 11429, USA.

DE HAVILLAND Olivia Mary, b. 1 July 1916, Tokyo, Japan. Actress; Author; Lecturer. m. (1) Marcus Aurelius Goodrich, 1946, div. 1952. 1 son. (2) Pierre Paul Galante, 1955, div. 1979. 1 daughter. *Creative Works:* Films: A Midsummer Night's Dream; Captain Blood; Anthony Adverse; Call it a Day; Charge of the Light Brigade; The Great Garrick; Robin Hood; Gold is Where You Find It; Dodge City; Gone With the Wind; Sante Fe Trail; Strawberry Blond; Hold Back the Dawn; They Died with Their Boots On; Princess O'Rourke; To Each His Own; Dark Mirror; The Snake Pit; The Heiress; My Cousin Rachel; Not As A Stranger; Proud Rebel; Libel; Light in the Piazza; Lady in a Cage; Hush, Hush, Sweet Charlott; The Adventurers; Airport 77; The Swarm. Plays: Midsummer Night's Dream; What Every Woman Knows; Candida; Romeo and Juliet; The Dazzling Hour; Gift of Time. Television Appearances: Noon Wine; The Screaming Woman; Roots II, The Next Generations; Murder is Easy; Charles and Diana: A Royal Romance; North and South II; Anastasia. *Publications:* Every Frenchman Has One, 1962; Mother and Child, (Essay), 1975. Contributor to Look Magazine. *Memberships:* 1st Woman President, Jury of International Cannes Film Festival, 1965; Screen Actors Guild; Academy of Motion Picture Arts and Sciences. *Address:* Postal Box BP 156-16, Paris Cedex 16, 75764 France.

DEIBLER Barbara Ellen, b. 11 Aug. 1943, Pottsville, Pennsylvania, USA. Librarian. *Education:* BA, Pennsylvania State University, 1965; MSLS, Drexel University, 1966. *Appointments:* Cataloguer, State Library of Pennsylvania, 1966-82, Head Cataloguer, 1972- 82, Rare Book Librarian, 1980-; Assistant Co-ordinator, Collection Management, 1982-. *Publications:* Articles include: Pennsylvania German Barn Signs, 1978; Books of State: A Peripatetic Collection, 1983; A Treasure Trove of Books, 1986; Anne Royall's Visit to Carlisle in 1828, 1987; Indomitable Eccentric, 1987. *Memberships:* Pilot club of Harrisburg, President 1979-

81, 1987-88, Vice President 1985-87, Secretary 1985, Treasurer 1978-79, Director, 1981-83, 1988-89; Society for Political Enquiries, Secretary, 1987-; Historical Society of Pennsylvania. *Address:* 301 Chestnut St No 906, Harrisburg, PA 17101, USA.

DEITZ Susan Rose, b. 21 Mar. 1934, Long Island, New York, USA. Columnist; Author. m. (1) Richard Alan Deitz, deceased, 1 son, (2) Morris J. Mandelker, 3 step-daughters. *Education:* Smith College; Barnard College; Stella Adler Theatre Studio; Art Students League; St John's University, New York. *Appointments:* National syndicated: Advice Columnist, LA Times syndicate, 1975-; Radio Talk Show Host; Part-time Professor, New School, New York City, 1979. *Publications:* Valency Girls, co-author, 1976; Joint Custody, 1977; Single in New York, week long series, New York Post, 1977; Conceived, developed thrice weekly advice column, Single File, 1975-; Conceived Developed, hosted 2 hour weekly radio programme, WMCA, 1977; speaking engagements include: Purdue Univesity, 1983, Smith College, 1985; numerous Womens Singles Groups; TV appearances. *Memberships:* Authors Guild; Women in Communications Inc; Newspaper Features Council. *Honours:* Interviewed on Today Show; Elected Outstanding Member, Women in Communications Inc., 1984. *Hobbies:* Reading; Gardening; Designing Clothes & Jewelry. *Address:* New York.

DEIZ Mercedes Frances, b. 13 Dec. 1917, New York City, USA. Circuit Court Judge. m. Carl H Deiz, 5 Oct. 1949. 2 sons, 1 daughter. *Education:* Undergraduate study, Hunter College, New York City; Juris Doctor, Northwestern College of Law, Portland, 1959. *Appointments:* Law Library Assistant, Bonneville Power Administration, Portland, 1949-53; Legal Secretary, Portland, 1954-59; Trial Lawyer, general practice of law, Portland, 1960-68; Administrative Law Judge with Oregon Workmen's Compensation Board, 1968-70; Judge of the District Court of the State of Oregon, 1970-72; Judge of the Circuit Court of the State of Oregon, 1973-. *Memberships include:* Woodrow Wilson Visiting Fellow; Lecturer, Harvard Law School on Trial Techniques; Director of National Center for State Courts and Chairman, Committee on Research; Education and Central; Member of several Bar Associations and American Judicature Society, etc. *Honours:* Urban League Award, Devotion to League's Concept of Equality, 1977; Honorary Member, Oregon United Nations Association; Woman of Accomplishment, 1969; First Black elected to remunerative office in the State of Oregon; Selected by the Willamette week (local newspaper), one of 10 Most Influential Blacks in this area, 1978; One of 10 Outstanding Women in Oregon, 1983; Distinguished Service Award, Citizens for Children, 1983; Woman of Excellence Award, Delta Sigma Theta Sorority, Inc, 1984. *Hobbies:* Travel to different countries and learning about their cultures; Reading everything and anything; My grandchildren. *Address:* Multnomah County Courthouse, 1021 SW 4th Avenue, Room 308, Portland, Oregon 97204, USA.

DEJONGH Donna Geal Criner, b. 18 Sept. 1944, Beaumont, Texas, USA. Architect. m. Robert Charles deJongh, 22 Apr. 1967, 1 son, 1 daughter. *Education:* BA, Howard University School of Architecture, 1971. *Appointments:* Draftsman: Marcou O'Leary & Associates, Washington, 1965; US Government, Arlington, 1966; Hudgins Thompson & Ball Inc., Washington, 1968; Stuart L Werner & Associates, 1968-72; Freelance Architectural Illustrator & Designer, Washington, 1972-73; Architectural Designer, Perkins & Will Architects, Washington, 1973; Architectural Designer, Robert de Jongh & Associates, 1973-74; Partner, deJongh Associates, St Thomas, 1974-. *Memberships Include:* Tau Beta Pi; American Institute of Architects, Chapter President, 1981-82; Virgin Islands Board of Zoning & Land Use Appeals; Virgin Islands Board of Architects Engineers & Land Surveyors; National Council of Architectural Registration Boards/Southern Conference. *Honours Include:* Jesse H Jones Fellowship, 1962-66; Bronze Medal, Excellence in Design, Howard University, 1967; Tau BEta Pi, 1970;

Gold Medal, Excellence in Design, Howard University, 1971; First Annual Howard University Young Firm Award, 1989. *Hobbies:* Art; Literature; Music; Languages; Tennis; Swimming. *Address:* 26/27 Dronningens Gade, Kings Quarter, Charlotte Amalie, St Thomas, US Virgin Islands 00802, USA.

DEKANIC Darinka Ozegovic, b. 31 Oct. 1943, Samobor, Yugoslavia. Consultant in Rheumatology; Head of Laboratory of Human Metabolism. m. Slavko Ozegovic, Nov. 1973. 1 son, 1 daughter. *Education:* MD 1968, MSc, Faculty Natural Sciences, 1971, DSc, Medical Faculty, 1975, University of Zagreb; Subspeciality training, MRC Miner Metab Unit, General Infirmary, Leeds, England, 1977 and 1979. *Appointments:* University Hosp Clinic, University of Zagreb, 1968-69; Institute for Medical Research and Occupational Health, Zagreb, 1969-; Consultant in Rheumatology, 1981-. *Publications:* Author of 20 scientific papers and contributions to 3 books. *Memberships:* Croatian Society of Physicians, 1970; Croatian Society of Physiologists, 1970; Board member, Rheumatological Association, 1972-75; Croatian Society of Physicians, 1978; Physical Medicine and Rehabilitation Association, Croatian Society of Physicians, 1978. *Honour:* The Republican Scientific Award Rodjer Boskovic for 1980. *Hobbies and Interests:* Gardening; Reading: Metabolic bone and stone diseases, calcium metabolism, osteoporosis. *Address:* Institute for Medical Research and Occupational Health, Mose Pijade 158, 41000 Zagreb, Yugoslavia.

DE LA TORRE Lillian (pen name Lillian Bueno McCue), b. 15 Mar. 1902, New York City, USA. Writer. m. Professor George S McCue, 2 July 1932. *Education:* BA, College of New Rochelle, 1921; MA, Columbia University, 1927; MA, Harvard/Radcliffe, 1933; Colorado University, 1934-35. *Appointments:* Teacher, New York High Schools, 1923-34; University of Colorado Extension, 1937-41; Technical adviser, Twentieth Century Fox, 1945; Freelance writer, 1946-. *Publications:* Dr Sam Johnson, mystery short stories, collected in 4 volumes, 1946, 1960, 1985, 1987; True crime books; juveniles; poetry; plays etc. *Memberships:* President, Mystery Writers of America, 1979; Johnson-Boswell Society; Star Bar Players; President, Colorado Springs Chorale, 1957. *Honours:* Awards: Ellery Queen's Mystery Magazine; Colorado Authors League; Mystery Writers of America, 1947-57; Medal of Distinction in the Fine Arts, Colorado Springs Chamber of Commerce, 1980; Honorary Doctorate of Humane Letters, Colorado College, 1987. *Hobbies:* Amateur theatre; Choral singing; Cookery. *Address:* 16 Valley Place No 302, Colorado Springs, CO 80903, USA.

DE LA VINA Lynda Yvonne, b. 29 July 1950, Edinburg, Texas, USA. Professor; Institute Director. *Education:* BA, Pan American University, 1972; MA, 1977, PhD, 1982, Rice University. *Appointments:* Assistant Director, Human Resources Management and Development Programme, 1979-82, Assistant Professor, 1982-85, Associate Professor of Economics, 1985-, Director, Institute for Studies in Business, 1985-, University of Texas, San Antonio. *Memberships:* American Economic Association; Southwestern Economic Association; Vice-President, Southwestern Society of Economists. *Honours:* Rice Young Alumni Achievement Award, 1985; Faculty of the Year Award, 1986; San Antonio Women's Hall of Fame, 1987. *Hobby:* Tennis. *Address:* Institute for Studies in Business, University of Texas at San Antonio, San Antonio, TX 78285, USA.

DELANEY Mary Murray, (Mary D. Lane), b. 1 Jan. 1913, New Richmond, USA. Author; Travel Agent. m. Thomas J. Delaney, 1 June 1932, 2 sons, 1 daughter. *Education:* Twin Cities Business College, 1930. *Appointments:* Secretary, Montgomery Ward & Co., 1930-32; Auditor, E.I. Dupon de Nemours, Rosemount, 1942; Vice President Tour Escort for Delaney, Joyce & O'Dell, Travel Agency, 1963-. *Publications:* Author, short stories in various magazines & journals including: The Writer; The Pen Woman; Redbook; Wrote and published Family Album, a history of their Irish ancestors. *Memberships:* National League American Pen Woman. *Hobbies:* Psychic Phenomenon; Reading; History. *Address:* 1606 Highland Parkway, St. Paul, Minnesota 55116, USA.

del CASTILLO Jeanne L Taillac, b. 15 May 1933, New Orleans, Louisiana, USA. Energy Source Executive. m. Roberto del Castillo, 19 Dec. 1951, divorced 12 Feb. 1969. 2 sons, 3 daughters. *Education:* Charity Hospital Nursing School, 1951-52; Various Business/Computer Courses, 1962-. *Appointments:* Manager, Louise's Gift Shop, Bay St Louis, 1947-51; Assistant Manager, Ray Mercantile Co, New Orleans, 1958-64; Consul & Maritime Commercial Officer, Consulate General of Panama, New Orleans, 1964-72; Administrator, McDermott International Inc, New Orleans, 1972-86; Manager, McDermott International Inc, Domiciliary Office in Panama/New Orleans, 1986-; Owner, Kiddie Kare Train'n Station, Waveland, Mississippi, 1985-89. *Memberships:* Consul, New Orleans Consular Corps, 1964-72; Director, New Orleans & Louisiana Soccer Associations, 1968-77; Executive Director, Spanish Programming WNNR, 1969-73; Public Relations Director, International Club, 1970-72; Co-Chairman, The Jerry Lewis Telethon, 1977; Co-Chairman, New Orleans Handicapped Children Easter Parade, 1982-83; Fund Raising, Bayside Volunteer Fire Department, 1985-89; Coordinator, Panamanian Maritime Exam Board, 1985-86; Panama Chamber for Industry & Commerce, 1986-89; Panama/American Chamber of Commerce, 1986-89; Co-Chairman Handicapped Children Sex Education (State) Committee, 1986-88; Panama Industry Advisory Committee for Offshore Industry, 1987-89; Founder, Handicapped Children Xmas Program, 1987-89. *Honours:* Merit Award, Bayside Fire Department; Promotion Soccer, New Orleans Soccer Association; *Hobbies:* Floral arrangements; Camping; Recreations with handicapped children. *Address:* 4413 Senac Drive, Metairie, Louisiana 70003, USA.

DELIMAR Natasa, b. 16 Sep. 1940, Rijeka, Yugoslavia. Mathematician. m. Vjekoslav Delimar, 31 Aug. 1963, 2 sons. *Education:* BSc, 1963; MSc, 1973; PhD, 1985. *Appointments:* Assistant, Republic Institute for Statistics, 1964-66; Institute of Immunology, Zagreb, 1966-, Head, Department of Biometry, currently. *Memberships:* Yugoslavian Society for Microbiology; Yugoslavian Society for Statistics; International Society for Mathematical Biology. *Hobbies:* Music; Reading novels; Skiing. *Address:* Institute of Immunology, Rockefellerstr 2-10, 41000 Zagreb, Yugoslavia.

DELL Miriam Patricia, b. 14 June 1924, Hamilton, New Zealand. Honorary President, International Council of Women. m. Richard K Dell, 3 Aug. 1946. 4 daughters. *Education:* BA, Aukland University, 1940-45; Secondary School Teachers Certificate, Auckland Teachers' Training College, 1944. *Appointments:* Teaching Full/Part-time, 1945-47, 1957-58 and 1961-71. Public Appointments: National Development Council, 1969-74; Committee of Inquiry into Equal Pay, 1971-72; National Commission for UNESCO and sub-Committee on Social Science, 1974-85; Social Security Appeal Authority, 1974-; Convener, Sub-Committee, National Development Council on the Role of Women in National Development, 1969-74; Chairwoman, Committee on Women, 1974-81; National Convener International Women's Year, 1975; Justice of the Peace, 1975-; National Advisory Committee on Women and Education, 1979-82; Appointed to numerous working groups, steering committees etc., including: Burns (Royal Society) Task Force on Nuclear Energy; Ross Committee on Human Development and Relationships in Schools; Review of the Education and Initial Employment of Nurses, 1986-; Council, Conference of ANZAAS, Palmerston North, 1986- 87;Honorary President,International Council of Women, 1986-. *Creative Works:* Chair and Convener of numerous Conferences in New Zealand; New Zealand Government Delegate to Conferences in Mexico, Vancouver, Canada, Paris; International Council of Women Representative to Conferences in Copenhagen, Paris, New York, Nairobi. Numerous magazine articles and papers. *Memberships include:* President, National Council of Women of New Zealand, 1970-74; Provincial Public and Social Affairs Committee of the Anglican Church, 1981-; Co-Chair, Environment and Conservation Organisation, (N.Z.) 1988-; Foundation Member, Hutt Valley Branch and Convener Public Affairs Committee, Federation of University Women; Joint Committee on Women and Employment, etc. *Honours:* CBE 1975; Adele Ristori Prize, 1976; Queen's Jubilee Medal, 1977; DBE 1980. *Hobbies:* Gardening; Reading; Handcrafts; Family and Friends. *Address:* 98 Waerenga Road, Otaki, New Zealand.

DE LONG Erika V., b. 14 Oct. 1925, Riga, Latvia. Medical Doctor. m. Mark E. De Long, 12 Apr. 1952, 1 daughter. *Education:* Cand.med, University of Goettingen, Federal Republic of Germany; MD, University of Vienna, Austria, 1957; Cleveland Psychology Institute, USA, 1959-63; Diplomate, American Board of Psychology and Neurology, 1968. *Appointments:* Cardiovascular Research, Harold Brunn Institute, Mt Zion Hospital, USA, 1957-58; Private Practice, 1963-; Director, Psychology Department, Fairview General Hospital, Ohio, 1981-. *Publications:* Cardiovascular research published in journals, 1958, 1959. *Memberships:* American Medical Association; Ohio State Medical Association; Cleveland Psychological Society; Cleveland Academy of Medicine; New York Academy of Sciences; Smithsonian Institute; Animal Protection League of Cleveland. *Hobbies:* Skiing; Horsebreeding and Racing. *Address:* 4495 Valley Forge Drive, Fairview Park, OH 44126, USA.

DELONG Nancy Glyn, b. 2 Oct. 1946, Columbus, Ohio, USA. Journalist; Public Relations and Communications Consultant. *Education:* BA, Journalism and English, Ohio State University, 1969. *Appointments:* Exec dir, Tri-County Dental Health Council, Detroit, 1971-76; Reporter, The Detroit News, 1970-71; The Columbus (Ohio) Dispatch, 1965-68; Editorial photographer, contributing editor, Amusement Bus, 1968-73; Producer, The Oz of Prevention, Detroit, 1971-74; Partner, Real to Reel, 1973-77; President project promotion, Glyn Prodn Ltd, 1977-79; President N Glynn & Assocs, Inc, Southfield, Michigan, 1979-82; Business Consultant, 1976-; Interior designer, 1976-; Associate, Walt Peabody Advt Service Inc, Ft Lauderdale, Florida; Beauty consultant, Mary Kay Cosmetics, Inc, Dallas, 1982-85; Dir employee assistance programs and public relations, Shepherd Hill, Newark, Ohio, 1985-86; Dir communication, liaison, CompCare Corp, Irvine, California and Columbus, Ohio, 1987-; President Recovery Assistance and Director Communications, liason, Snow Babies Inc, Orlando, FL, 1989-; Professional boxing judge, State of Michigan. *Publications:* Contributor of articles to various magazines; Contributing editor, Downbeat, 1966-68, Billboard 1968-73; Producer educational films on health and rehabilitation; Producer, director, Super Party '82. *Address:* 1040 Waverly Drive,Longwood, FL 32750, USA.

DELOUGHERY Grace Leone, b. 17 Jan. 1933, Iowa, USA. Nurse-Educator. m. Henry Otis Deloughery, 30 Nov. 1964, 1 son. *Education:* BS, Nursing, 1955, MPH, 1960, University of Minnesota; PhD, Political Science & Education, Claremont Graduate School & University, 1968. *Appointments Include:* Various nursing positions, 1955-66; Associate Professor, Nursing, University of North Dakota, 1967-68; Assistant Professor in Residence, Universiy of California Los Angeles School of Nursing, 1968-72; Associate Professor, Dean, Centre for Nursing Education, Spokane, 1972-74; Associate Professor, Nursing, Winona Stat University, 1975-77; Associate Professor, Indiana University, 1985-87; Associate Professor, Bellarmine College, Louisville, 1987-. *Publications:* Contributor to numerous journals and magazines including: Journal of Psychiatric Nursing; Journal of Nursing Education; Nursing; Educational Horizons; Journal of School Health; Scholar & Educator, Managing Editor, 1988; Editor, Lansing

Journal; etc. *Memberships Include:* Fellow, American Association for Social Psychiatry; Fellow, American Public Health Association; Indiana Public Health Association; Society of Midwest Researchers; etc. *Honours:* Recipient, various scholarships; Recognition of Achievement, educational Innovation, Research & Evaluation Techniques, Southwest Regional Lab, Inglewood, 1967. *Address:* Rte 2, Circle Drive, Georgetown, IN 47122, USA.

DEL RIO-DIAZ Estyne, b. 30 July 1945, Chicago, USA. Behavioral Psychologist. m. Raul Diaz, 21 Nov. 1987. *Education:* PhD, Jackson State University, 1974. *Appointments:* President, Psycheologistics Inc., New York, 1960-80; Principal Psychologist, Ghana, 1975; Practicing Psychologist, Parapsychologist, New York, 1975-89; Host, Encounters TV, New York, 1986-89. *Publications:* Columnist, The Health & Diet Times, 1980. *Memberships:* National Academy for Cable Programming; American Board of Christian Psychology; American Society for Psychical Research; Association for Research & Enlightenment; International Spiritual Associates of America; Association of National Christian Counselors. *Honours:* Recipient, many honours & awards. *Hobbies:* Collector of Art, Gold Coins, Dolls, Rare Books; Horse Riding; Metaphysical Investigations; Parapsychological Research. *Address:* 30 East End Avenue, Suite 6B, New York, NY 10028, USA.

DE MAERTELAER Viviane, b. 11 Nov. 1946, Brussels, Belgium. Professor in Statistics. 1 son. *Education:* Bachelor's degree in Physics, 1968; Bachelor's degree in Radiobiology, 1973; PhD, Physics, 1978. *Appointments:* Euratom, Ispra, Italy, 1968; Professor, CERIA, Belgium, 1969; Researcher, 1969, Assistant Professor, 1973, Professor in Statistics, 1981-, University of Brussels. *Memberships:* European Study Group for Cell Proliferation; International Society for Clinical Biostatistics. *Address:* IRIBHN - CP 602, 808 rue de Lennick, B-1070 Brussels, Belgium.

DEMAS Jean V, b. 30 Dec. 1940, Oak Park, Illinois, USA. Lawyer. m. (1) Harry T Dallianis, 8 Dec. 1962, div. July 1979. 1 son, 1 daughter. (2) Emil Athineos, 24 Apr. 1983. *Education:* BA, Northwestern University, 1962; JD, DePaul University, 1982. *Appointments:* Teacher, Von Steuben High School, Chicago, 1962-65; Secretary, Treasurer 1965-72, Vice President, exec director 1972-79, Director Corp Relocation 1975-81, Ideal Real Estate and Ins Brokerage Inc, Chicago; Associate, Kois & McLaughlin PC, Chicago, 1982-84; Sole practice, Lincolnwood, Illinois, 1984-85; Staff counsel, The Options Clearing Corp, Chicago, 1985-; Board of Directors, Ideal Real Co. *Publications:* Contributor of articles to professional journals. *Memberships:* Lincolnwood Community Council, Illinois, 1972-75; Lincolnwood Friends of Library, Lincolnwood Steering Com, 1978-; Lincolnwood Bicentennial Com; Lincolnwood PTA; Treasurer, Lincolnwood Homeowners Association, 1974-75; Den leader, Cub Scouts America, 1978-79; Precinct worker, Lincolnwood Citizens Action Party, 1975; Coordinator 15th dist Illinois ERA, 1977-78; Board of Directors, Sts Peter and Paul Greek Orthodox Church School, 1977-79; ABA (banking and bus law com young lawyers division); Illinois Bar Association; Chicago Bar Association (real property com, corp law depts com); Women's Bar Association, Illinois; Chicago Real Estate Board (chairman sales council 1980-81); North Suburban Real Estate Bd (President 1976-77, Board of Directors 1978-80); RELO/Inter-City Relocation Service (Chairperson Chicago met area 1975-76); LWC; Zeta Tau Alpha. *Address:* 6842 N Kostner, Lincolnwood, IL 60646, USA.

DEMASSA Jessie G, b. Aliquippa, USA. Freelance Writer. m. Frank R. DeMassa, divorced, 3 sons. *Education:* BS, Temple University; MLS, San Jose State University, 1967. *Appointments:* Teacher, Palo Alto School District, 1966; Librarian, Antelope Valley Joint Union High School District, 1966-68; ABC Unified School District, 1968-72; Media Specialist, District Librarian, Tehachapi Unified School District, 1972-81.

Publications: Articles in: Collier's; The Woman; Read; Today's Woman; short stories: Decade of Short Stories; Family Weekly. *Memberships:* American Association of University Women, Bulletin Editor; California Association of School Librarians; National Museum of Women in the Arts, Charter, 1988; Hon. Fellow, John F. Kennedy Library Founding Member; National Writers' Club. *Hobbies:* Reading; Writing; Travel; Art; Music. *Address:* 9951 Garrett Circle, Huntington Beach, CA 92646, USA.

DE MENESES Mary Louise Roades, b. 16 Apr. 1939, Alton, Illinois, USA. Associate Professor; Coordinator of Graduate Programme in Nursing. m. William C Meneses, 31 May. 1973. 2 sons, 1 daughter deceased. *Education:* RN diploma, ST Luke's Hopsital, 1960; BS Nursing, 1970, MA Education 1973, MS Nursing, 1975, De Paul University, Chicago; EdD Education, Northern Illinois University, 1982. *Appointments:* Staff Nurse, ER, St Luke's Hospital, 1960-61; Staff Nurse, ICU, Our Lady of Lourdes, 1961-64; Head Nurse, Supervisor, St Joseph's Alton, 1964-66; Head Nurse, St Joseph's Chicago, 1966-69; Instructor, Michael Reese Hospital School of Nursing, 1969-74; Associate Professor, De Paul University, 1974-82; Associate Professor, Southern Illinois University, 1982-. *Publications:* Book: Nursing Process: Theory, application and related processes, with N Pinnel, 1986. numerous articles in professional journals and magazines. *Memberships:* American Nurses Association, Vice President, 10th District (Illinois) Association; American Association of Critical Care Nurses; ANA Council of Nurse Researchers; Illinois Legislative Research Network. *Honours:* Danforth Scholar, 1957-60; USPHS Nurse Trainee, 1969-70; Kappa Delta Pi, 1975; Sigma Theta Tau, 1974; Phi Delta Kappa, 1980; Phi Kappa Phi, 1983; Graduate Status I 1982; Graduate Status II, 1985; Sabbatical Leave, 1988. *Hobbies:* Reading; Walking; Sewing; Arts and crafts; Writing and Research; Swimming; Travelling. *Address:* School of Nursing, Box 1066, Southern Illinois University, Edwardsville, Illinois 62026, USA.

DEMLER Linda Kass, b. 17 Feb. 1954, Pocatello, Idaho, USA. Corporate Manager. m. Frederick Russel Demler, 26 Aug. 1976, 1 son. *Education:* BS, cum laude, Psychology, Mathematics, Pennsylvania State University, 1976. *Appointments:* Dining Manager, Holiday Inn, State College, 1976-77; Restaurant Manager, Corner Room, State College, 1977-78; Accounting Manager, Heim, Heckendorn & Bruce, State College, 1978-80; Divisional Manager, New York Life Insurance Co., New York City, 1980-. *Memberships:* National Association Female Executives; American Management Association; Chi Omega. *Address:* 4 Effingham Road, Yardley, PA 19067, USA.

DE MONTE Claudia A., b. 25 Aug. 1947, Astoria, New York, USA. Artist; University Professor. m. William Edward McGowin, 28 May 1978. *Education:* BA, College of Notre Dame of Maryland, 1969; MFA, Catholic University, 1971. *Career:* Professor, Art Department, University of Maryland, College Park, 1972-; Director, Art Workshop, New School for Social Research, New York City, 1980-; Many 1 person shows, projects, performances including: Corcoran Gallery of Art, Washington DC, 1976; Contemporary Arts Center, New Orleans, Baltimore Museum of Art, 1978, Marianne Deson Gallery, Chicago, 1979; Fort Worth Art Museum, Washington Project for the Arts, Mississippi Museum of Art, Jackson, 1980; Marion Locks Gallery, Philadelphia, Miami-Dade Community College, Xochipilli Gallery, Birmingham, Michigan, 1981; Shipka Gallery, Sofia, Bulgaria, 1982; Gracie Mansion Gallery, New York City, 1984; Galerie Joyce Goldman, Montreal, 121 Gallery, Antwerp, Belgium, Stamford Museum and Nature Center, Gracie Mansion Gallery, Jones Troyer Gallery, Washington DC, New School for Social Research, Queens Museum, New York, 234 Gallery, University of Wyoming, 1985; Harris Samuels Gallery, Conconut Grove, Xochipilli Gallery, 1986; Gracie Mansion Gallery, Brentwood College, St Louis, 1987. *Creative works include:* Works in public collections, Museum of Modern Art, Indianapolis Museum of Art,

Mississippi Museum of Art, Bellevue Hospital, Chemical Bank, Prudential Life Insurance, Best Products, University of Maryland, Alternative Museum, New Orleans Museum, Miami-Dade Community College, Hyatt Regency Hotels, Stamford Museum and Nature Center, Exxon Corporation, Delaware Museum. *Honours:* American Italian Award in the Arts, 1972; Head Award, Baltimore Museum of Art, 1972; Creative Award Summer Grant, University of Maryland, 1972, 1983, 1987; Ariana Foundation Award, 1983; Special Research Award, University of Maryland, 1984. *Hobbies:* Travel; Reading. *Address:* 96 Grand Street, New York, NY 10013, USA.

DE MUNNIK Mary Baptista, b. 23 Feb. 1941, Slagharen, Netherlands. Barrister; Solicitor. *Education:* BA honours, Psychology, York University, Toronto, Canada, 1973; LLB, University of Toronto, 1977; Called to the Bar, 1979. *Appointments:* Self-employed Lawyer, Toronto, 1979-, Specialist in family law, residential real estate, and wills and estates; Lecturer in family law, 1980-. *Publications:* Essay on differences in male/female socialization, in Chatelaine, 1973; Editor, Fernways Flyer newsletter, 1985, 1986. *Memberships:* Director, Canadian Netherlands Business and Professional Association; Treasurer, Toronto Adoption Group; Founding Member, Toronto Women Lawyers Support Group; Women's Law Association of Ontario; Don Valley Chorus of Sweet Adelines, Public Relations Committee; Past Vice-President, Toronto Women's Breakfast Club; Past President, Uptown Network; Past Committee Member, Scarborough Family Services Association; Student Representative to Canadian Bar Association, 1977; Chairman, Aid Committee, Stong College, 1971; Student Representative to Status of Women Council, 1970; Steering Committee on Programmes for Immigrant Women, Toronto YWCA, 1980; Atkinson College Committee for Student Housing, 1968. *Honours:* IODE Book Prize, 1953; IODE Bursary, 1970-73; Scholarship to Ontario Institute of Education, 1973; Scholarship to University of Waterloo, 1973. *Hobbies:* Singing; Travel; Writing; Music. *Address:* 183 Donlea Drive, Toronto, Ontario, Canada M4G 2M9.

DENCH Judith Olivia (professionally known as Judi Dench), b. 8 Dec. 1934, York, England. Actress. m. Michael Williams, 1 daughter. *Appointments Include:* Debut as Virgin Mary in York Cycle of Mystery Plays, 1957; 1st appeared with Old Vic Company in 1957 as Ophelia in Hamlet, other roles including, Maria, Twelfth Night on tour of USA & Canada, 1958-59, Juliet, in Romeo and Juliet, directed by Franco Zeffirelli; joined RSC, Stratford upon Avon, 1961, returning to tour with them, West Africa, 1960, Japan and Australia, 1970, Japan, 1972, and seasons at Stratford, 1971, 1976-77, 1979, London, 1970, 1977-78, 1980-81, 1984-85; other stage appearances include: Lady Bracknell in The Importance of Being Ernest, National Theatre, 1982-83; Barbara in Pack of Lies, Carrie in Mr and Mrs Pooter, Cleopatra in Antony and Cleopatra, 1984-87; Films include: He who Rides a Tiger; A Study in Terror; Four in the Morning; A Midsummer Night's Dream; The Third Secret; Dead Cert; Wetherby; A Room with a View, 1986; TV appearances include: TV series with husband, A Fine Romance; Make and Break; Ghosts; Mr and Mrs Edgehill. *Honours Include:* Most Promising Newcomer, 1965; OBE, 1970; Best TV Actress, 1981; Best Actress Award, Plays and Players Award, 1984; BAFTA Best Supporting Actress, for A Room with a View, 1987. *Hobbies:* Sewing; Drawing; Catching up with Letters. *Address:* leading Artists Ltd., 60 St James's Street, London SW1, England.

DENES Magda, b. Budapest, Hungary. Psychologist. m. Michel Radomisli, May 1963, divorced Jan. 1976. 2 sons. *Education:* BA, CCNY, 1956; MA, Boston University, 1958; PhD, Yeshiva University, 1961; Cert Psychoanalysis & Psychotherapy, 1967; Lic Psychologist, New York. *Appointments:* Clinical Prof & Supervisor, Derner Institute of Advanced Psychological Studies, Adelphi University, 1970-; Assoc Clinical Professor & Supervisor Post Doctoral Program in Psychotherapy & Psychoanalysis, NYU, 1970-; Faculty

& Supervisor, Department of Psychiatry, Mt Sinai School of Medicine, New York, 1980-; Private Practice, 1962- . *Publications:* Author: In Necessity & Sorrow: Life & Death in an Abortion Hospital, 1976; Articles in professional journals, newspapers and magazines. *Memberships:* Fellow, American Psychological Association; New York Society Clinical Psychologists, President 1978-79; NYS Psychol Assn, President 1986-87; Eastern Psychological Association; Psychoanalytic Society of NYU; Adelphi Society of Psychoanalysis & Psychotherapy. *Honours:* Teacher of the Year, Doctoral Programm on Psychology, Adelphi University, 1972; Psi Chi, Honorary Society (Psychological), 1977. *Hobbies:* Reading; Horseback riding. *Address:* 40 East 84th Street, New York, NY 10028, USA.

DENHOLM Diana B, b. 29 Dec. 1944, Milwaukee, Wisconsin, USA. Psychotherapist. *Education:* BSEd, University of Wisconsin, 1967; MEd, University of Hartford, Connecticut, 1971; PhD, Philosophy, Columbia Pacific University, Mill Valley, Pennsylvania, 1982. *Appointments:* Guidance Counselor, Middle & High School, Avon, CT, 1971-75; Testing Supervisor & Guidance Counselor, 1975-79; School Psychologist, Naragansett, Rhode Island, 1979-83; Hypnosis Consultant, Private practice, 1981-83; Staff Member, Humana Hospital and Psychotherapist and Pres, Association in Behavioural Change, 1983-. *Publications:* Numerous. *Memberships:* Kappa Kappa Gamma Fraternity; Executive Women of the Palm Beaches; National Mental Health Counselors Association; American Association for Counseling & Development; Association to Advance Ethical Hypnosis; U Wisconsin Alumni Association; International Society for Professional Hypnosis. *Honours:* National Honor Society; University Wisconsin Tuition Scholarship, Cum Laude graduate, Teaching Internship; Kappa Kappa Gamma Alumnae Scholarship; University of Hartford, Graduate Assistantship; University of Connecticut, Honors Student. *Hobbies:* Warm weather sports; Macro nature photography; Landscaping; Knitting. *Address:* Gould Professional Center, 2151 45th Street Suite 304, West Palm Beach, FL 33407, USA.

DENIZ Clare Frances, b. 7 Apr. 1945, Highgate, London, England. Solo Concert Cellist; Teacher. *Education:* Junior Exhibition, 1956-66, LRAM, 1966, Royal Academy of Music; International Master Classes, 1976-80. *Appointments:* Royal Ballet, 1967, Principal Solo Cellist, 1968; Welsh National Opera, 1970; English National Opera, 1971-77; Sub Principal, English National Opera, 1973-77; numerous recitals; Debut as Soloist, Purcell Room, South Bank, London, 1983; Concertgebouw, Amsterdam, 1987. *Memberships:* Correspondance Secretary, Childrens Variety Appeals; The Church of England Childrens' Society Appeals Committee; Musicians Union; Amateur Fencing Association; C.S. Lewis Society, Oxford University; Incorporated Society of Musicians & Solo Performers Section. *Hobbies:* Researching Music; Gardening; Literature; Fencing; Badminton; Art Theology. *Address:* 31 Friday Street, Henley-on-Thames, Oxfordshire RG9 1AN, England.

DENNIS Patricia Diaz, b. 2 Oct. 1946, Santa Rita, New Mexico, USA. Commissioner; Lawyer. m. Michael J. Dennis, 3 Aug. 1968, 1 son, 2 daughters. *Education:* AB, English, University of California, Los Angeles, 1970; JD, Loyola University, 1973. *Appointments:* Associate Attorney, Paul Hastings, Janofsky, Walker, 1973-76; Attorney, Pacific Lighting Corp, 1976-78; Attorney, 1978-79, Assistant General Attorney, 1979-83, American Broadcasting Co; Member, National Labor Relations Board, 1983-86; Commissioner, Federal Communications Commission, 1986-. *Publications:* Articles in: Stetson Law Review; The Labour Lawyer. *Memberships:* Womens Forum of Washington; National Advisory Board, Leadership America; National Network Hispanic Women; Mexican American Bar Association of Los Angeles, Secretary 1980-81; Columbia Bar Association. *Honours:* honours and awards including: Member, US Delegation, World Conference, Nairobi, Kenya, 1985. *Hobbies:* Skiing; White Water Rafting;

Aerobics; Travel; Camping and Hiking; Reading. *Address:* Federal Communications Commission, 1919 M. Street, NW, Rm 832, Washington DC, 20554, USA.

DENNY Judith A, b. 18 Sept. 1946, Lamar, Missouri, USA. Attorney. m. Thomas M. Lenard, 29 May 1976, 1 son, 1 daughter. *Education:* BA, Louisiana Tech University, 1968; JD, George Washington University, 1972. *Appointments:* Various positions, 1968-72; Assistant Special Prosecutor, Watergate Special Prosecution Force, 1973-75; Trial Attorney, US Dept. of Justice, 1975-78; Director, Division of Compliance, BSFA, Office of Education, 1978-80; Acting Assistant, Inspector General, US Dept. of Education, 1980; Deputy Director, Office of Revenue Sharing, 1980-83; Counselor to the General Counsel, 1984-87; Deputy Assistant General Counsel, US Dept. of the Treasury, 1987-. *Hobbies:* Church and School Activities. *Address:* 3214 Porter Street NW, Washington, DC 20008, USA.

DENSEN-GERBER Judianne, b. 13 Nov. 1934, New York City, USA. Psychiatrist; Lawyer; Educator. m. Michael M Baden, 14 June 1958, 2 sons, 2 daughters. *Education:* AB, Bryn Mawr College, 1956; LLB, Columbia University, 1959, JD, 1969; MD, New York University, 1963; various hospital residencies, 1963-67. *Appointments Include:* Founder, Odyssey House, New York City, Michigan, Maine, New Hampshire, Utah, Lousiana, Australia New Zealand, 1967, Clinical Director 1967-69; Executive Director, 1967-74, President, 1974-82; President, Founder, Chief Executive, Odyssey Institute of America, 1974-82; President, Odyssey Institute, Australia, 1977-86; Odyssey Institute International Inc., 1978-; Attending Physician, Gracie Square Hospital, New York City, 1982- , Park Hospital, Bridgeport, 1985-, Bridgeport Hospital, 1985-; Coutesy Staff, St Vincents Hospital, Connecticut, 1986-88. *Publications Include:* Co-author, Drugs, Sex, Parents and You, 1972; We Mainline Dreams, The Odyssey House Story, 1973; Walk in My Shoes, 1976; Co-author, The Role of Child Abuse in Delinquency and Juvenile Court Decision-Making, 1984; Chronic Acting-Out Students and Child Abuse: A Handbook for Intervention, 1986; paper: Co-author, The United States Age of Consent Laws Governing the Sexual Conduct of Minors - A Proposal for Reform; articles in professional journals & magazines. *Memberships:* Member, numerous professional organisations including: American Academy of Forensic Sciences; Institute of Womens Wrongs, etc. *Honours:* Recipient, various honours & awards. *Address:* 817 Fairfield Avenue, Bridgeport, CT 06604 USA.

DENT Rosamond Mary, The Hon. (Sister Ancilla), b. 3 June 1933, Canton, China. Nun. *Appointments:* Entered Religion, Order of St Benedict, 1956. *Publications:* Lettering - Illuminating; various articles. *Memberships:* Committee Member, Benedictine Association; Committee Member, Commission on Contemplative Life in Britain. *Hobbies:* Farming (Livestock); Writing Poetry; Music; Reading; Spinning; Calligraphy. *Address:* Minster Abbey, Minster, Nr. Ramsgate, Kent CT12 4HF, England.

DENTON Jean, b. Wakefield, England. Director. Divorced. *Education:* BSc., Economics, London School of Economics, 1958. *Appointments:* Managing Direbtnr, Herondrive, 1981-85; Director, External Affairs, Austin Rover, 1985-86; Non-Executive Director, Ordnance Survey, 1986; Director, Burson-Marsteller, 1987; Vice Chairman, Black Country Development Corporation, 1987; Non-Executive Director, British Nuclear Fuels, 1987; Director Wolverhampton Grand Theatre, 1988- . *Publications:* Frequent contributor to radio programmes, and articles in professional journals. *Memberships:* Chairman, Women on the Move against Cancer; Chairman, Marketing Group of Great Britain; Fellow, Institute of Marketing; Fellow, Institute of Motor Industry; Fellow, Royal Society of Arts; Vice President, National Organisation for Womens Management Education; Governor London School of Economics; Trustee of Brooklands Museum; Hansard Society

Commission on Women into Power; Interim Advisory Committee on Teachers Pay and Conditions, 1988; B.I.C. Womens' Institute; Director, Think Green; Vice President, British Womens' Racing Drivers Club. *Honours:* Adwoman of the Year, 1980; Female Executive of the Year, 1983. *Address:* 32 Gilbert Road, Kennington, London SE11 4NL, England.

DE OLARTE Gloria Acosta, b. 28 July 1948, Colombia, South America. M.D.; Plastic Surgeon. m. 26 May 1973, 1 son, 1 daughter. *Education:* University of Antioquia, Colombia, 1971; Intern, Baptist Memorial Hospital, Houston, Texas, USA, 1973-74; Resident in General Surgery, 1974-77, Resident in Plastic Surgery, 1977-79, Albany Medical College; Fellow in Microsurgery, Ralph Davis Medical College, San Francisco, California, 1979; Fellow in Craniofacial Surgery, Hopital des Enfants Malades, Paris, France, 1979-80; Diplomate, American Board of Plastic Surgeons. *Appointments:* Private Practitioner, Pasadena and Downey, California, USA, 1981-. *Publications:* Reduction Mammoplasty and Correction of Ptosis with a Short Inframmary Scar, article, 1982. *Memberships:* American Medical Association; California Medical Association; American Medical Women's Association; American Society for Plastic and Reconstructive Surgery. *Hobbies:* Scuba diving; Snorkelling; Water skiing. *Address:* 65 North Madison Avenue, Suite 606, Pasadena, CA 91101, USA.

DERHAM Rosemary Joan Brudenell, Lady, b. 29 Jan. 1921. m. Prof Sir David Plumley Derham, KBE CMG MBE (Mil), 1944. 1 son, 2 daughters. *Education:* Toorak College (Frankston); BA, University College, University of Melbourne. *Career:* President, Committee of Management, Royal Children's Hospital, 1979-83 (member 1964-83, honorary secretary 1970-72, honorary treasurer 1972-77, vice president 1977-79); Director, Research Foundation, Royal Children's Hospital, 1978-83; Member, Vic Council of Australian Hospitals Association, 1981-83; Vice President, Volunteer Service Royal Children's Hospital, 1966-79; President, Women of the University Fund, 1968-82; President, University of Melbourne Auxiliaries, 1977-82; Honorary Vice President, University of Melbourne Staff and Distaff Association. *Publication:* Author: A Changing View of Childhood, 1979. *Clubs: Alexandra; Lyceum; Graduate House Melbourne; Barwon Heads Golf Club. Hobbies:* Tennis; Gardening; Writing; The Arts; Birdwatching. *Address:* 13 Selborne Road, Toorak, Victoria 3142, Australia.

DERION Toniann, b. 11 Dec. 1954, Buffalo, New York, USA. National Institutes of Health Postdoctoral Fellow Research Physiologist. *Education:* BS, SUNY College at Brockport, 1976; MEd, University of Texas at Austin, 1982; PhD Exercise Physiology, University of Wisconsin, Madison, 1988. *Appointments:* Phys Ed Specialist, Austin, 1978-83; Research Assistant, University of Wisconsin, Madison, 1983-88; NIH Postdoctoral Fellow, School of Medicine, University of California, San Diego, 1988-. *Publications:* Contributions to: FASEB Journal; Fed Proc; Undersea Biomedical Research. Designed, built model to scale, helped construct safe playground at Allan Elem School, Austin, 1982. *Memberships:* Aerospace Medical Association; American College of Sports Medicine. *Honour:* Kappa Delta Pi, national education honor society, 1981. *Hobbies:* Masters swimmer (Nationally ranked in age group in 50 metre butterfly, 1986); Scuba diver. *Address:* Physiology/NASA Lab, M-023A, Department of Medicine, School of Medicine, University of California, San Diego, La Jolla, CA 92093, USA.

DERISE Nellie L, b. 9 Aug. 1937, Jeanerette, Louisiana, USA. Nutrition Education; Researcher. *Education:* BS, University Southwestern Louisiana, 1962; MS, University of Alabama, 1964; PhD, Virginia Polytechnic Institute & State UNiversity, 1973. *Appointments:* Graduate Assistant, University of Alabama, Tuscaloosa, 1962-64; Assistant Professor Home Economics 1964-68; Associate Professor 1973-81, Professor, 1981-, University SW Louisiana,

Lafayette; Assistant Professor Home Economics, Iowa State University, Ames, 1968-70; Graduate Assistant, Virginia Polytechnic, 1970-73. *Publications:* Contributed numerous articles to professional journals. *Memberships:* Chairman Louisiana State Nutrition Council, 1978-80; American Home Economics Association; Louisiana Home Economics Association (Board director, 1973-75); American Dietetic Association; Louisiana Dietetic Association (Board director, 1982-86, Secretary 1984-86); Soc Nutr Education; Sigma Xi Research Society (President local chapter, 1980-81). *Honours:* Sigma Xi Research Society Regional Lecture Poster, 1982-84; Phi Kappa Phi; Phi Sigma; Phi Tau Sigma; Phi Epsilon; Omicron; Kappa Omicron Phi; Louisiana Education Quality Support Fund Research Grant, 1987-88 and 1988-89. *Hobbies:* Music; Designing and making clothes; Hand sewing; Reading; Physical fitness. *Address:* 142-1/2 Clark Court, Lafayette, Louisiana 70503, USA.

DE ROO Anne Louise, b. 23 Sep. 1931, Gore, New Zealand. Writer. *Education:* BA, 1952, LTH Honours, 1985, Canterbury University. *Appointments:* Assistant, 1955, Assistant Librarian, 1956-58, Dunedin Public Library. *Publications:* Children's books: The Gold Dog; Moa Valley; Boy and the Sea Beast; Cinnamon and Nutmeg; Mick's Country Cousins; Scrub Fire; Traveller; Because of Rosie; Jacky Nobody; The Bat's Nest; Friend Troll Friend Taniwha. *Honours:* ICI Writer's Bursary, 1981; Choysa Bursary, 1983; Children's Book of the Year, 1984. *Hobbies:* Gardening; Reading; Various community and church activities including lay reader. *Address:* 38 Joseph Street, Palmerston North, New Zealand.

DE RUBERTIS Patricia Sandra Uhl, b. 10 July 1950, Bayonne, New Jersey, USA. Vice-President, Computer Services. m. Michael De Rubertis, 1 Mar. 1986. *Education:* BS, Business Administration, University of Maryland, 1972. *Appointments:* Account Representative, General Electric co., San Francisco, 1975-77; Technical Representative, Computer Sciences Corporation, Sna Francisco, 1977-78; Consultant/ President, UHL Associates, Tiburon, California, 1978-81; Consulting Manager, Ross Systems, Palo Alto, California, 1981-83; Vice President, Distributed Planning Systems, Calabasas, 1983-. *Memberships:* National Association Female Executives; University of Maryland Alumni Association; Delta Delta Delta. *Hobbies:* Gardening; Sailing; Skiing. *Address:* Distributed Planning Systems, 23632 Calabasas Road No. 107, Calabasas, CA 91302, USA.

DESFOSSES Helen Roberta, b 24 April 1945, Dover, New Hampshire, USA. University Administrator and Official. 1 son. *Education:* BA, Mount Holyoke College, 1965; MA, Harvard University, 1967; PhD, Boston University, 1971. *Appointments:* Associate Dean, University of Michigan, Dearborn, 1976-78; Assistant VP for Academic Affairs 1978-82, Associate VP for Academic Affairs 1982-83, Director Public Policy Program 1983-, SUNY, Albany. *Publications:* Soviet Policy Toward Black Africa; Socialism in the Third World; Soviet Population Policy. *Memberships:* American Society of Public Administration; African Studies Association. *Honours:* Hoover Institution Fellowship; NDEA Fellowship; Coretta Scott King Fellowship, American Assoc of University Women; Research Fellowship, Harvard Russian Research Center; Mellon Foundation; Aspen Institute Fellowship. *Hobbies:* Public speaking; Hiking. *Address:* State University of New York at Albany, 135 Western Avenue, Albany, NY 12222, USA.

DESJARDINS Alice, Honourable Madame, b. 11 Aug. 1934, Montreal, Quebec. *Education:* University of Montreal; Harvard Law School; Called to the Quebec Bar in 1958. *Appointments:* Appointed QC, 1974; Assistant Professor 1961-68, Associate Professor 1968-69, Faculty of Law, University of Montreal; Legal Couns, Privy Council Office, Ottawa, 1969-74; Director, Adv & Admin. Law, Department of Justice, Ottawa, 1974-81. *Memberships:* Board of Governors, Donner

Canadian Found, 1974-81; Board, Foundation Internationale Roncalli, 1982; Association of Quebec Law Teachers, 1968-69; President of Local Chapter, Ottawa, Canadian Branch Internat, Law Association, 1977-79; Vice President, Candian Branch International Law Association 1984; Institute of Pub Admin 1975 (National Board 1975-78, President, Local Chapter Ottawa 1975); Committee Member, American Society of International Law, 1971-72; National Board Candian Association of University Professors (Ottawa) 1968-69; Executive Committee Mount Royal Tennis Club. *Honours:* MacKenzie King Travelling Scholarship, 1958-59; Ford Foundation Scholarship, 1966; Appointed Judge of the Superior Court of Quebec, 1981; Judge of the Federal Court of Canada, Appeal Div and ex officio member of the Federal Court of Canada Trial Div, 1987; Judge of the Court Martial Appeal Court of Canada, 1988. *Address:* The Federal Court of Canada, Ottawa, Ontario, K1A 0H9, Canada.

DESMOND Patricia Ann, b. 13 May 1956, Boston, USA. Educational Supervision. *Education:* BS, Boston University, 1978; MEd., Reading Seton Hall University, 1981; Ed.D. Candidate, 1981-. *Appointments:* English Teacher, 1978-80; Graduate Assistant, Seton Hall University, 1980-81; English Teacher, Rahway High School, 1981-82, Rutherford High School, 1982-83; Instructor, Middlesex County College, 1984, Valley County College, 1984-85; Co-ordinator, Learning, Instruction & Assessment, Seton Hall University, 1987-88; Supervisor, Instruction-Secondary Reading, Orange Board of Education, 1988-; School Administrator, Assistant Superintendent of Schools, 1988-. *Memberships:* NABSE; NAFE; COMP; American Federation of Teachers; National Society for the Study of Education. *Honours:* Kappa Delta Pi; Teaching Asssistantship, Teachers College, Columbia University, 1981-86. *Hobbies:* Writing; Research; Reading; Sewing; Roller & Ice Skating; Skiing. *Address:* 10 Alden Place, Maplewood, NJ 07040, USA.

DEUCHLER Suzanne Louise, b. 21 July 1929, Chicago, USA. State Legislator. m. Walter E. Deuchler, 1 son, 1 daughter. *Education:* BA, University of Illinois. *Appointments:* Elected to Illinois General Assembly, 1980. *Memberships:* American Association of University Women; League of Women Voters, President, 1973-75; Business & Professional Womens Club. *Honours:* Beta Sigma Phi Woman of the Year, 1978; YWCA Woman of the Year, 1979; Women in Management, Charlotte Dansford National Award, 1982; Woman of the Year, Aurora Business & Professional Womens Club, 1984. *Hobbies:* Reading; Travel; Painting. *Address:* 1128 A Prairie Street, Aurora, IL 60506, USA.

DEVAPRIAM Emma, b. 5 Aug. 1933, Kodaikanal, Indian. Senior Curator. *Education:* BA, 1955, MA, 1964, Stella Maris College, Madras; PhD, Case Western University, USA, 1972. *Appointments:* Tutor, Fine Arts, 1955-62, Lecturer, 1962, Stell Maris College, Madras; Assistant Curator, Cleveland Museum of Art, Ohio, 1974-75; Student Advisor, USEFI, 1975-76; Assistant Curator, 1975-76, Senior Curator, 1975-76, Senior Curator, European Paintings, 1976-, National Gallery of Victoria, Australia. *Publications:* Articles in Profesisonal Journals. *Memberships:* Various organisations including: Art History Association, USA; Australian Art Galleries Associations. *Honours:* Fulbright Scholarship, USEFI, USA, 1967-68; Graduate Assistantship, Cleveland Museum of Art, USA, 1968-70; Research & Travel Grant, JDR 3rd Fund, USA, 1970-71; etc. *Hobbies:* Painting; Reading. *Address:* 9-1st Main Road, Seethamma Colony, Alwarpet, Madras 600018, South India.

DEVAUGHN-TIDLINE Donna Michelle, b. 20 Sept. 1954, Houston, Texas, USA. Director, Health Care Management; Plan Administrator. m. Eric Tidline, 27 Aug. 1988. *Education:* BBA, Southern Methodist University in Dallas, Texas, 1977. *Appointments:* Associate Manager of Financial Services, Prudential Insurance Company, 1977-83; Director of Administration, Prulare (subsidiary of Prudential), 1983-85; Director, Health Care Management/Plan Administrator, Prudential, 1986-. *Memberships:* National Association of Female Executives; Volunteer for the Big Sisters Program; Delta Sigma Theta Sorority; Friends of Lemoyne Owens College. *Honour:* Outstanding Young Women in America, 1984. *Hobbies:* Reading; Crafts. *Address:* 845 Crossover Lane, Suite 220, Memphis, TN 38117, USA.

DEVERE Julia Anne Bonjour, b. 2 Nov. 1925, Onaga, Kansas, USA. Retired Elementary Teacher. m. Robert E DeVere, 18 Aug. 1964. 1 son. *Education:* BA 1957, MD 1961, University of Denver. *Appointments:* Teacher: Buckeye School, Jackson Co, 1943-45; Bancroft Elementary, Kansas, 1945-46; Belvue Grade, 1946-53; Westmoreland Grade School, 1953-56; Stockton Unified School; 1957-64; Cupertino Union School, 1964-88. *Publications:* Articles in magazines and journals. *Memberships:* California Teachers Association, NEA and Cupertino Education Association; Council for Exceptional Children; Academy of Political & Social Science; Delta Kappa Gamma Society; Chi State, Delta Rho Chapter. *Honour:* Scholarship, Delta Kappa Gamma, 1955. *Hobbies:* Reading; Socialising with friends; Dancing. *Address:* 950 Chehalis Drive, Sunnyvale, California 94087, USA.

DEVILLE Sue Caroline Burden, b. 2 June 1940, Cleveland, Ohio, USA. Lecturer; Corporate Executive Director. m. S. Bruce Deville, 9 June 1962, 1 son, 1 daughter. *Education:* RN, 1961; BA, 1980; MA Economics, 1983; PhD, 1988. *Appointments:* Corporate Executive, Sun Shore Services; Lecturer, Baldwin-Wallace College. *Memberships:* American Economic Association; Ohio Association Political Scientists & Economists; American Horse Council; American Quarter Horse Association; Cleveland Museum of Art; National Wildlife Association. *Honours:* Estelle Koch Award, 1961; Amling Investment Award, 1979; OAPS & E Student Paper, 1980; Hudson Fellowship, 1981-84. *Hobbies:* Entrepreneurial Endeavors; Physical Fitness; Horse Riding; Hiking; Nature; Interior Design; Drag Racing; etc. *Address:* 1985 Salem Parkway, Westlake, OH 44145, USA.

DEVLIN Margaret Corinne, b. 12 Nov. 1937, St Catherines, Ontario, Canada. Professor. *Education:* Registered Nurse, 1958; MD, University of Western Ontario, 1967; FRCS (C), 1972; FACOG, 1978; FSOGC, 1984. *Appointments:* Faculty Member, Health Sciences, 1973-, Professor, Obstetrics & Gynaecology, Health Sciences, McMaster University. *Publications:* Numerous scientific presentations & papers in professional journals concerning sex related health care. *Memberships:* NSOGC; OMA; CMA; CPSO: SSSS; CSRF; New York Academy of Science. *Honours:* Alpha Omega Alpha, 1967. *Hobbies:* Naturalist Activities. *Address:* Health Science Center 471, 1200 Main Street West, Hamilton, Ontario, Canada L8N 3Z5.

DEWAR Marion, b. 17 Feb. 1928, Montreal, Quebec, Canada. Federal President, New Democratic Party. m. Kenneth J Dewar, 15 Sept. 1951. 2 sons, 3 daughters. *Education:* RN, ST Joseph's School of Nursing, 1949; BScN, Public Health Diploma, University of Ottawa, 1969. *Appointments:* Registered Nurse, 1949-52; Public Health Nurse, 1969-72; Alderman, then Controller, then Deputy Mayor, 1972-78; Mayor, City of Ottawa, 1978-85; Federal President, New Democratic Party of Canada, 1985-. *Memberships:* Canadian Women for Political Representation; World Federationalists of Canada; Ottawa Women's Network; National Action Committee of Status of Women; Group of 78; Board, Canadian Centre for Arms Control and Disarmament; Canadian centre for Policy Alternatives; Canadian Institute of Child Health; International Institute of Concern for Public Health; Council of Canadians. *Hobbies:* Reading; Swimming; Bridge; Curling; Theatre. *Address:* 869 Rex Avenue, Ottawa, Ontario, Canada K2A 2P6.

DEWINE Sue, b. 27 June 1944, Xenia, Ohio, USA.

Professor and Director. m. James Michael DeWine, 20 Aug. 1966. 1 son, 1 daughter. *Education:* BA Education 1966, MA 1967, Miami University; PhD, Indiana University, 1977. *Appointments:* Graduate Assistant, 1966-67, Instructor 1967-75, Senior Instructor 1973-75, Miami University; Associate Instructor, Indiana University, 1975-77; Assistant Professor 1977-81, Assistant Department Chair 1981-82, Associate Professor 1981-85, Faculty Planning Administrator, Provost's Office 1981-83, Professor 1985-, Ohio University. *Publications include:* Women in organizations, 1983; Communication in the organization: An applied approach, 1978; Instructor's Manual for Communication in the organization: An applied approach, 1978; Interpersonal Communication Journal, 1976; Instructor's manual for Interpersonal Communication Journal, 1976; Ten designs for integration in experienced based learning environments, 1976. Numerous articles and papers to professional magazines and conferences. Editor: Speech Communication Association of Ohio Journal, 1982-84; Communication Monographs; Communicaton Education; World Communication Association; Central States Speech Journal; Southern Speech Communication Journal; Progress in Communication Sciences; Communication Management Journal; Journal of Applied Communication Research, 1982-. *Memberships include:* International Communication Association; Speech Communication Association; Central States Speech Association; Ohio Speech Communication Association; American Society for Training and Development; Program Associate, Organization Renewal, Inc; American Psychology Association; Academy of Management, etc. *Honours:* Commencement Speaker for Graduate Students, Ohio University, 1987; Student Affairs Faculty Contribution Award, Ohio University, 1987; Outstanding University Graduate Faculty Award, Ohio University, 1986; Elected Member-at-large by members of ICA; Elected Chair of Organizational Communication Division of ICA; Distinguished Teaching Award, Indiana University, 1977. *Address:* 8 York Drive, Athens, Ohio 45701, USA.

DEWITT Bonnie St Clair, b. 13 Jan. 1954, Bethesda, Maryland, USA. Senate Liaison Officer. m. Charles Barbour DeWitt, 25 Mar. 1989. *Education:* BS 1976, MA (Government & Politics) 1984, University of Maryland; Diploma, Senior Managers of Government, Kennedy School of Management, Harvard University, 1982. *Appointments:* Staff director & administrator, US Senate Select Committee on Ethics, 1978-88; Senate liaison, Federal Relations, Tobacco Institute, 1988-. *Hobbies:* Skiing; Hiking. *Address:* 3344 'P' Street, N.W., Washington, DC 20007, USA.

DEXTER Dallas-Lee, b. 30 Nov. 1950, Rockville Centre, New York, USA. Businesswoman. *Education:* Bachelor of Science Degree, Mills College, 1972; MA, Columbia University 1973; Special Education Roundtable, Georgetown University, 1987. *Appointments:* Consultant, Administrator, Teacher, Kingdom of Saudi Arabia, Islamic Saudi Academy, 1986-87; Manager, telesales Division, Best Programs Inc., Arlington, 1987-. *Memberships:* Society for International Development; World Affairs Council & Foreign Policy Association; National Academy of Television Arts & Sciences; American Defense Preparedness Association, Life Member. *Honours:* Phi Delta Kappa; Columbus Mutual Golden Key Club Award for Personal Sales Achievement, 1985. *Address:* 1280 21st Street NW, Washington, DC 20036, USA.

DEYOUNG Yvonne Marie, b. 9 Dec. 1951, Milwaukee, Wisconsin, USA. Senior Computer Programmer Analyst. *Education:* BBA, Accounting and Data Processing, University of Wisconsin-Eau Claire, 1970-75. *Appointments:* General Accountant, Laboratory Computing Inc, Madison, 1975-78; Systems Analyst, State of Wisconsin Department of Industry, Labor and Human Relations, Madison, 1978; Tax Pension Accountant, Telephone and Data Systems, Madison, 1978-79; Computer Programmer, Wisconsin Dairy Herd Improvement Cooperative, Madison, 1979-80; Computer Programmer/Analyst, Professional Insurance Management Company, Jacksonville, 1980-81; Senior Computer Programmer/Analyst, Rayovac Corporation, Madison, 1981-; Independent Sales Representative, Avon Products Inc, New York, 1986-. *Memberships:* Data Processing Management Association, 1984-, (Southern Wisconsin Chapter); Secretary 1985-87, Chairman, 1987-89, Rayovac Credit Union, Board of Directors. *Honours:* Avon President's Club, 1986, 1987, 1988, 1989; Numerous Avon Selling awards, 1986, 1987, 1988, 1989. *Hobbies:* Performing Arts; Sports; Cars; Domestic Arts; Physical Fitness. *Address:* 5216 Piccadilly Drive, Madison, WI 53714, USA.

DIAMOND Adele Dorothy, b. 14 June 1952, New York City, USA. Professor in the fields of Child Development and Neuroscience. *Education:* BA, Swarthmore College, 1975; PhD, Harvard University, 1983. *Appointments:* Postdoctoral Fellow in Neuroanatomy, Yale University School of Medicine, 1982-85; Research collaboration, University of California, San Diego, 1986; Assistant Professor of Psychology, Washington University, 1986-88; Assistant Professor of Psychology, University of Pennsylvania, 1988-; Associate in Child Neurology, St Christopher's Hospital, Philadelphia, 1988-; Member, Institute of Neurological Sciences, University of Pennsylvania School of Medicine, 1988-. *Publications:* Author of numerous articles to professional scientific journals; Convener, Conference on Development and Neural Bases of Higher Cognitive Functions, Philadelphia, 1989. *Memberships:* American Association of the advancement of Science; American Association of University Professors; American Psychological Association; Association for the Advancement of Psychology; International Brain Research Organization; International Society for the Study of Behavioural Development; Piaget Society; Sigma Xi; Society for Neuroscience; Society for Research in Child Development; American Psychological Society. *Honours:* Recipient of numerous Grants and Fellowships, most recently: NSF Doctoral Dissertation Grant, 1980; Radcliffe Grant for Graduate Women, 1981; Sloan Foundation postdoctoral fellowship award, 1982. *Hobbies:* Dancing (especially contra dance and swing); Sports; Outdoor (hiking, camping, canoeing). *Address:* University of Pennsylvania, Department of Psychology, 3815 Walnut Street, Philadelphia, PA 19104, USA.

DIAMOND Linda Ann, b. Panama. Choreographer; Modern Dancer; Teacher. Divorced, 1 son. *Education:* BA, USC. *Appointments:* Artistic Director, Linda Diamond & Co; Performing Arts Teacher, NYC Board of Education; New York Foundation for the Arts, Artist in Residence, 1988. *Publications:* Dance Visions of Picasso; Homage to Chagall; A Dancer's View of Calder's Universe; Shadoflash; Inti Raymi; Secret Annexe; Portrait of Beck Danzon Cubano. *Memberships:* Fulbright Scholarship Committee-Dance Panellist; New York Foundation for the Arts-Artist in Residence. *Honours:* Recipient, various honours and awards. *Hobbies:* Writing; Swimming. *Address:* 418 W. 51 St., New York City, NY 10019, USA.

DIAMONSTEIN-SPIELVOGEL Barbaralee, b. New York City, USA. Writer; TV Interviewer/Producer. m. Carl Spielvogel, 27 Oct. 1981. *Education:* BA, BC, MA, New York University, 1954; Doctorate, 1963. *Appointments:* Staff Assistant, White House 1963-66; Director, Cultural Affairs, City of New York, 1966-67; Director, Forums, McCall Corp, 1967-69; Editor, Columnist, Harper's Bazaar, 1969-71; Special Projects Director, Guest Editor, Art News, 1973-; Columnist, Ladies Home Journal, 1979-84; TV Interviewer, Producer, 1980-86. *Publications:* Open Secrets: 94 Women in Touch with Our Time, 1972; The World of Art 1902-77, 75 Years of Art News, 1977; Buildings Reborn: new Uses, Old Places, 1978; Inside New York's Art World, 1979; American Architecture Now, 1980; Interior Design: The New Freedom, 1982; Handmade in America, 1983; Fashion: The Inside Story, 1985; American Architecture

Now, 1985; Visions and Images: American Photographers on Photography, 1986; Remaking America, 1986; The Landmarks of New York, 1988; Editor, Our 200 Years: Tradition and Renewal, 1975; Moma at 50, 1980; contributor to numerous journals & magazines. *Memberships:* Board of Directors, Landmarks Conservatory; The Big Apple Circus; Chairperson, New York Landmarks Preservation Foundation, 1985-; Numerous other professional organisations. *Address:* 720 Park Ave., New York, NY 10021, USA.

DIBLEY Nancy Priscilla, b. 27 Apr. 1931, Portsmouth Dockyard, England, Writer; Musician; Composer; Artist. *Appointments:* Royal Academy of Music, 1948-81; Private study with Max Rostal, 1952; RAM (2), Guildhall School of Music and Drama, 1954; Children's Authorship Writing Diploma, Arthur Waite School of Writing, 1978; *Career:* Part-time Teacher, Violin, Viola, beginners Cello, 1952-56; Conducted Grammar School Orchestras; Taught at Westminster Abbey Choir School; Freelance recitals include 2nd Viola, BBC Light Orchestras, Variety, Revue and New Radio Orchestra, 1956-67; Second Viola, 1956-67; Recitals, Public House, Prison, Asylum; Recitals, Wigmore Hall, 1963, St Martins-in-the-Fields Lunch Hour, London; Studied poetry/poems in anthologies, also 2 on Radio for Children: How to make and Bread and Butter in Verse, How to Make a Sandwich; Wrote poetry and stories for Marylebone Brownies, 1975-77; Talks, including Victoria League; Read poem at Speakers Corner, Hyde Park; Recorded 30 light poems for 4 hospital radios including Middlesex and St Thomas's Hospital; Played piano, recited her poems in Nursery School, 1988; *Creative works:* Religious poetry in Springs of Joy; Book accepted by Lee-on-the-Solent Library; Author, several plays performed at Player Playwrights Club; Plays for Age Concern and playreading groups; Portrait painting. *Memberships:* Associate Red Cross Visitor; Women's Royal Voluntary Society; Age Concern; Foundation Member, The Woman of the Year Luncheon party, 1955-. *Honours:* Numerous honours and awards including Cheltenham Viola Cup; Bolton Viola Prize, Guildhall School of Music, 1954; Bronze, Silver and Gold Medals, Royal Academy of Music. *Hobbies:* Walking; Cinema; Photography; Travel. *Address:* 23 Upper Berkeley Street, London W1H 7PE, England.

DICK Susan Marie, b. 6 Nov. 1940, Battle Creeek, Michigan, USA. University Professor. *Education:* BA, Western Michigan University, 1963; MA, 1964, PhD, 1967, Northwestern University. *Appointments:* Queen's University, Kingston, Ontario, 1967-. *Publications:* Critical Edition of George Moore's Confessions of a Young Man; Edition of the Original Holograph Draft of Virginia Woolf's To the Lighthouse; Editor, The Complete Shorter Fiction of Virginia Woolf; articles in professional journals. *Memberships:* Canadian Association of University Teachers; Association of Canadian University Teachers of English; Humanities Association; Association of Women Teaching at Queen's; Virginia Woolf Society. *Honours:* Woodrow Wilson Fellowship, 1963; Woodrow Wilson Dissertation Year Fellowship, 1966. *Hobbies:* Gardening; Music. *Address:* 177 Churchill Crescent, Kingston, Ontario K7L 4N3, Canada.

DICKENS Patricia Allen, b. 16 Jan. 1938, Richmond, Virginia, USA. College Professor. m. Charles E. Dickens, 27 Aug. 1960, 3 sons. *Education:* BA, History, William and Mary University, Norfolk, Virginia, 1959; MEd, Elementary Education, Lynchburg College, Virginia, 1984; EdD, University of Virginia, Charlottesville, 1987. *Appointments:* Adjunct Assistant Professor, Lynchburg College, Virginia, 1988-89; Visiting Instructor, Sweet Briar College, Virginia, 1989. *Memberships:* Delta Kappa Gamma International; ASCD; AECT. *Honours:* National Science Foundation Fellowship at Boston University, 1976; Delta Kappa Gamma International Scholarship, 1986. *Hobbies:* Reading; Travel; Photography; Painting. *Address:* 102 Millbrook Terrace, Forest, VA 24551, USA.

DICKENSON Donna Lee, b. 15 Nov. 1946, New Haven, Connecticut, USA. Writer; University tutor.

Christopher Britton. 1 son, 1 daughter. *Education:* BA, 1st class, Wellesley College, Massachusetts, 1967; MSc, London School of Economics and Political Science, 1968; PhD candidate, The Open University. *Appointments:* Journalist, The Associated Press, New York City, USA, 1966-67; Associate in Research, Yale University, 1968-73; Lecturer, Albertus Magnus College, 1971-73; Tutor and Consultant, The Open University, England, 1974-. *Publications:* Feminist critical biographies: Emily Dickinson, 1985; George Sand, 1988; Flora Tristan (forthcoming); Margaret Fuller (forthcoming); Poetry: In Four Minds, 1976; Peterloo Preview 1, 1988. BBC Radio Drama, The Archers, 1985; Translations from the French: Louis Aragon, Prospice and The Malahat Review. Frequent contributor to London Magazine. Poetry Readings at Edinburgh Festival and other venues. *Memberships:* Religious Society of Friends (Quakers); CND; Amnesty International. *Honours:* Prize-winning poems at Oxford Poetry Festival, 1982 and 1984. *Hobbies:* Gardening; Classical piano. *Address:* 39 Lonsdale Road, Summertown, Oxford, OX2 7ES, England.

DICKINSON Dana Lynne, b. 6 Oct. 1951, Dayton, Ohio, USA. Engineer; Computer Consultant. *Education:* SB, SM, Chemical Engineering, Massachusetts Institute of Technology, Cambridge, 1974. *Appointments:* Consulting Engineer, Arthur D Little Co, Cambridge, Massachusetts, 1975-76; Principal Engineer, General Electric Knolls Atomic Power Laboratory, Schenectady, New York, 1976-; Computer Consultant, Dickinson Computer Services, Saratoga Springs, New York, 1984-. *Honour:* GE Outstanding Young Engineer Award, Power Systems Sector, 1982. *Hobbies:* Cycling; Piano; Volleyball; Skiing; Aerobics; Cooking. *Address:* PO Box 1198, Saratoga Springs, NY 12866, USA.

DICKINSON Margaret Maria (AKA Muggy Do), b. 11 Aug. 1949, Washington, District of Columbia, USA. Special Assistant to the Administrator, Mental Retardation/Developmental Disabilities Administration. *Education:* BA, Wilbeforce University, Wilbeforce, Ohio, 1972; MA, The University of the District of Columbia, Washington, DC, 1979; PhD, The Union Graduate School, Cincinnati, Ohio, 1987. *Appointments:* Co-founded an experimental Family Group Home for people with Mental Retardation, Telataipale, Finland, 1975-76; Mental Health Officer (Unit Chief), DC Children's Center, Laurel, Maryland, 1977-84; Acting Chief of Program Monitoring, Bureau of Community Services, Washington, DC, 1985-86. *Creative works:* In-service workshops (Finland & USA); paper presentations (Common Boundary Conferences); Plays: Jesse, 1975 and Herkko Wants To Go Home, 1977 (co-author), broadcast by the Finnish Broadcasting Company. *Honours:* Social Services Certificate of England, 1970; President of the Class, Wilbeforce University, 1972; Most Oustanding Psychology Student Award, Wilbeforce University, 1972; Award for Outstanding Service to individuals with Mental Retardation, Department of Human Services, Washington, 1984; Served a Student Internship with the President's Committee on Mental Retardation, Washington, 1985-88. *Hobbies:* Hunting antiques; Collecting art; Blowing bubbles; Reading spiritual books; Tae Kwan Do Karate; Meditating; Travelling; The Finnish Language. *Address:* 429 O Street NW, Room 200, Washington, DC 20001, USA.

DICKSON Doris Rose, b. 7 Dec. 1922, Cleveland. Psychologist. divorced, 1 son, 1 daughter. *Education:* BS, 1958, MEd, 1963, University of Toledo; PhD, Walden University, 1978; Licensed Psychologist, Ohio. *Appointments:* Psychologist, Columbus (Ohio) Public Schools, 1957-; Private practice, Columbus, 1980-. *Memberships:* International Transactional Anaylsis Association; Ohio Psychological Association; National Schools Psychological Association; Ohio Consultant Psychologists; Ohio Psychological Association; AAUW. *Hobbies:* Gardening; Sewing; Cooking; Pets. *Address:* 5623 Chowning Way, Columbus, OH 43213, USA.

DICKSON Katharine Joan Balfour, b. 21 Dec. 1921,

Edinburgh, Scotland. Musician; Cello performer; Teacher. *Education:* LRAM 1939; ARCM 1943; Royal College of Music, London, England, 1945-46. *Career:* Performer, London Promenade Concerts (many); Edinburgh Festival; Broadcasts on Television; Concert tours in Europe; Professor of Cello, Royal Scottish Academy of Music, 1953-79; Professor of Cello, Royal College of Music, London, 1968-. *Creative works:* Radio talks; Numerous articles to professional magazines; Film: Bowing Principles for string players. *Memberships:* European String Teachers Association, British Branch (ESTA), Member of Executive Committee. *Honours:* FRSAMD; FRCM; Honorary MMus (Dunelm); Gold Medal of Worshipful Company of Musicians for services to Chamber music. *Hobbies:* Golf; Stamp collecting. *Address:* Garden Flat, 5 Leamington Road Villas, London W11 1HS, England.

DICKSON Kristina Anne (Krista), b. 16 Mar. 1961, London, England. Writer; Artist; Performance Poet. m. Andre Dickson, 23 July 1977, 1 son. *Career:* Worked in parents' jewellery firm, several years; Freelance Writer, Performer and Community Artist; Numerous stage performances of own poetry and prose for juveniles and adults, Kent and surrounding localities; Workshops, Kent Schools; Performed poetry personally in Britain, and by other poets in USA and Greece; Aims to achieve publication on equal terms with men and to foster peace, wellbeing and happiness through her work. *Creative works include:* Various reviews and articles; Commissioned paintings including Coco; Poetry and illustrations in small press issues; Children's work; Adult work, unpublished: The Pussywillow Thrillers; Chasing Rainbows; Morbida; Mystika; The Little Velvet Baby Bag; Included in the forthcoming Womens' Press anthology, In The Gold of The Press . *Memberships:* President, Founder, Ashford Poeteers. *Honours:* Poetry read at International Poetry Congress, Florida, USA, mid-1980s; Award of Merit, The Yeats Club Poetry Competition on Theme of Ecstasy, 1988. *Hobbies:* Gardens; Children; Sixties music; Fabric design; Exterior and interior design; Painting (portraits and murals); Good friends. *Address:* Kingsnorth, Ashford, Kent, England.

DICKSTEIN Leah Joan, b. 17 Aug. 1934, Brooklyn, USA. Professor; Psychiatrist. m. Herbert Dickstein, 23 Aug. 1955, 3 sons. *Education:* BA, 1955, MS 1961, Brooklyn College; MD, University of Louisville School of Medicine, 1970. *Appointments:* Professor, Psychiatry & Behavioral Sciences, Associate Dean, Student Affairs, University of Louisville School of Medicine. *Publications:* Editor: Women Physicians in Leadership Roles, 1986, Family Violence, 1988. *Memberships:* American Psychiatric Association; American Medical Women's Association; President, Association of Women Psychiatrists. *Honours:* Golden Apple Award, Teacher of the Year, 1982; Kentuckiana Metroversity Grawemeyer Award for Instructional Development, 1987. *Hobby:* Photography. *Address:* University of Louisville, Health Sciences Centre, Louisville, KY 40292, USA.

DIDIER Francette Keilocker, b. 18 Dec. 1936, Pittsburgh, USA. Curriculum Consultant. m. Paul J. Didier, 12 Apr. 1982, 1 son, 2 daughters. *Education:* BA, Seton Hill College, 1965; MEd., Duquesne University, 1970; DEd, University of Florida, 1973. *Appointments:* Director, Guidance, 1973-75, Assistant Professor, 1975-77, Seton HIII College; Assistant Professor, Univesity of San Francisco, 1977-80; Regional Administrator, Chase Econometrics, 1980-82; Fulfillment Specialist, A T & T, Bell Laboratories, 1983; Curriculum Consultant, 1984-. *Publications:* Model Kindergarten Programme, 1988; Helped Design: First Doctoral Programme, Private School Leadership, 1977-80, Florida Middle School Competency Programme, 1972-73. *Memberships:* Board, Morris Habitat for Humanity; National Audubon Society; World Future Society; National Catholic Education Society. *Honours:* Pi Lambda Theta, 1973; Trainer, Northwest Regional Laboratory, 1973. *Hobbies Include:* Bird-watching; Future's Study; Tennis; Square Dancing; Opera. *Address:* 13 Girard Avenue, Chatham, NJ 07928, USA.

DIDRICKSON Loleta Anderson, b. 22 May 1941, Chicago, Illinois, USA. State Legislator. m. Charles A Didrickson, 17 June 1961. 2 sons, 1 daughter. *Education:* Student, University of Illinois, 1958-61; BA, Governors State University, 1974. *Appointments:* Former Senatorial aide; General Manager, Manufacturing Company; Junior League of America; Past President, Homewood Flosswood High School Parents Board; Vice-President, Board of Directors, Prairie State College; Illinois Dangerous Drugs Advisory Council; Taylor Institute; Y-Me Board Directors; Director, Women's Republican National Club of Chicago; Alternate Delegate-at-Large, National Convention, 1984; South Suburban Association of Commerce and Industry, LVW. *Address:* 1111 Brassie Avenue, Flossmoor, IL 60422, USA.

DIEMER Emma Lou, b. 24 Nov. 1927, Kansas City, Missouri, USA. Composer; University Professor. *Education:* BMus 1949, MMus 1950, Yale School of Music; PhD, Eastman School of Music, 1960. *Appointments:* Ford Foundation Composer-in-residence, Arlington, Virginia Schools, 1959-61; Professor of Theory & Composition, University of Maryland, 1965-70; Professor of Theory & Composition, University of California, Santa Barbara, 1971-. *Publications:* Over 100 choral and instrumental works published (Carl Fischer, Boosey & Hawkes, Oxford University Press, Plymouth Music Co, Seesaw Music Corp). *Memberships:* ASCAP; American Guild of Organists; American Music Center; American Women Composers, Inc; Mu Phi Epsilon. *Honours:* Fulbright Scholarship, 1952-53; Louisville Orch Student Award, 1955; Ford Foundation Young Composers Grant, 1959-61; National Endowment for the Arts Fellowship, 1980. *Hobbies:* Walking; Reading; Computers. *Address:* Department of Music; University of California, Santa Barbara, CA 93106, USA.

DIENSTAG Eleanor Foa, b. 13 Apr. 1938, Naples, Italy. Writer; Consultant. m. Jerome Dienstag, 29 June 1958, divorced, 2 sons. *Education:* BA, Smith College, 1959. *Appointments:* Assistant Editor, Harpers/Random House, 1959-61; Editor, Writer, Monocle Magazine, 1961-65; Columnist, Reviewer, Feature Writer, 1965-78; Senior Writer, American Express, 1978-83; President, Eleanor Foa Associates, 1983-. *Publications:* Whither Thou Goest, 1976; articles in: New York Times; McCalls; Savvy; Travel & Leisure and other national publications. *Memberships:* American Society of Journalists & Authors; National Writers Union. *Honours:* Speechwriting Awards, New York Association of Business Communicators, 1981, 1982; Outstanding Member Award, New York Women on Communication, 1984; Community Relations Rupert Bellinger Awards, 1988. *Hobbies:* Reading; Writing; Travel; Photography; Tennis. *Address:* 435 East 79th Street, New York, NY 10021, USA.

DIERS-TAYLOR Carol Jean, b. 16 July 1933, Bellingham, USA. University Professor. m. Herbert C. Taylor, 17 Aug 1973. *Education:* BA, 1956; BA, Ed., 1956; MA, 1958; PhD, 1961. *Appointments:* Public School Teacher, 1956-57, 1958-59; Community College Instructor, 1961-63; Assistant Professor, Associate Professor, Professor, Western Washington University, 1963-. *Publications:* Articles in research journals. *Memberships:* Sigma Xi; Animal Behavior Society; Delta Society; American Association Advancement of Science; American Psychological Society. *Honours:* USPHS pre-Doctoral Rsearch Fellowship, 1960-61; Director, Honours Programme, 1970-74. *Hobbies:* Golf; Hiking; Photography. *Address:* Dept. of Psychology, Western Washington University, Bellingham, WA 98225, USA.

DIETZ Dorothy Brill, Artist-Designer. *Education:* Student, Mills College, University of Southern California, Oregon State University; Sorbonne, L'Ecole de Cordon Bleu; Academie Julien, Washington School of Art; Japanese Art Center. *Appointments:* Court Reporter, American Superior Courts; Interior Designer and Artist; Teacher, Counsellor, Unity School of Christianity.

Memberships: Alpha Chi Omega; Republican party; Honlulu Academy of Arts. *Honours:* Recipient, 3 1st prizes, National Art Contests. *Hobbies:* Golf; Tennis; Bridge; Swimming; Chess. *Address:* Royal Iolani, 581 Kamoku Street, No. 408, Honolulu, HI 96826, USA.

DIGERONIMO Suzanne Kay, b. 27 Mar. 1947, Berwick, Pennsylvania, USA. Architect. m. Louis Anthony DiGeronimo, 19 Sept. 1969, 2 sons. *Education:* Associate of Applied Science (highest honours), Interior Design, Fashion Institute of Technology, New York, 1967; School of Architecture, Pratt, 1968; School of Architecture, Columbia, New York, 1970; Bachelor of Architecture, Cooper University, New York, 1973. *Appointments:* Port Authority of New York and New Jersey Aviation Planning Division, 1968-69; Greydanus DiGeronimo, 1970-73; Architect/Engineers Division, Prudential Insurance Company, 1974; DiGeronimo, A Hillier Group Company, 1975; Architects DiGeronimo PA, currently. *Creative works:* United Methodist Church, Morristown, New Jersey, 1973; Locker/Laundry Facility, US Coast Guard, Governors Island, New York, 1982; Lincoln Tunnel Emergency Garage Extension, Weehawkin, New Jersey, 1986. *Memberships:* Society of American Military Engineers, New Jersey Post, Secretary; American Institute of Architects; New Jersey Society of Architects, Legislative Committee; Architects League of Northern New Jersey; Chamber of Commerce and Industry, Legislation Committee. *Honours:* Design Excellence, Mantolokin Residence, 1983. *Address:* Fair Lawn, NJ 07410, USA.

DIGGINS Lauraine Beth, b. 7 Mar. 1946, Melbourne, Australia. Fine Art Dealer. m. Michael Manning Blanche, 19 Dec. 1975, 1 daughter. *Education:* Diploma, OT Lincoln House. *Appointments:* Occupational Therapist, Alfred Hospital, Melbourne, 1968, 1969; Travel Researcher, Australian Tourist Commisison, Melbourne, 1971-75; Director, Bartoni Art Gallery, 1975-78; Director, Lauraine Diggins Gallery, 1978-85, Lauraine Diggins Fine Art P/L, 1985-. *Publications:* Fine Art Books including: Haughton Forrest, 1826-1925; Art Catalogues on Sidney Nolan; articles in professional journals. *Hobbies:* Collector of Paintings, Sculpture, Ceramics & Primitive Artefacts; Travel; Theatre; Tennis; Wine; Music. *Address:* 9 Malakoff Street, North Caulfield, Victoria 3161, Australia.

DILKE Caroline Sophia, b. 28 May 1940, London, England. Journalist. m. Timothy Fisher Wentworth Dilke, 4 Sept. 1965, divorced 1988. 1 son, 1 daughter. *Education:* 1st Class degree in Biology, Open University, 1982. *Appointments:* School Teacher, 1978-84; Journalist, 1984-. *Publications:* The Sly Servant, 1975; Contributions to: Woman magazine; The Sunday Times; Woman's Journal, etc. *Address:* HB Viva, 106 Cheyne Walk, London SW10 0DG, England.

DILLARD J.M. (Jeanne), b. 17 Dec. 1954, Winter Haven, Florida, USA. Science Fiction Novelist; Instructor. m. Georg C. Kalogridis, 11 Nov. 1978. *Education:* AA, 1974; BA, Russian, 1976, MA, Linguistics, 1980, University of South Florida. *Appointments:* Student Teacher, University of South Florida, 1979-80; Language Specialist, American University of Washington, 1981-88; Writer, 1988-. *Publications:* Mindshadow, 1986; Demons, 1986; Bloodthirst, 1987; War of the Worlds: The Resurrection, 1988; The Lost Years, 1989; Star Trek V: The Final Frontier, 1989; short stories. *Membership:* Science Fiction Writers of America. *Honours:* Citation, Lutheran Council, USA, 1975; Polk Community College Distinguished Alumni Awad, 1986; New York Times Bestseller, 1986, 1987. *Address:* PO Box 290665, Temple Terrace, FI 33687, USA.

DILLINGHAM Marjorie Carter, b. 20 Aug. 1915, Bicknell, Indiana, USA. m. William Pyrle Dillingham, deceased, 2 sons (1 deceased), 1 daughter. *Education:* PhD, Spanish, Florida State University, 1970. *Appointments:* Teacher, Duke University, University of Georgia, Florida State University, Panama Canal Zone College, etc. *Memberships:* National President, La Sociedad Honoraria Hispanica; President, Foreign Language Division, Florida Education Association; President, Florida Chapter, American Association of Teachers of Spanish and Portuguese; President, Alpha Lambda Chapter, Delta Kappa Gamma; President, Delta Kappa Gamma; President, Foreign Language Teachers of Leon County, Florida, etc. *Honours:* Putnam County Educational Archives Hall of Fame, 1986. *Address:* 2109 Trescott Drive, Tallahassee, FL 32312, USA.

DILLON Janet Jordan, b. 2 Feb. 1947, Denver, USA. Attorney. m. 17 Sept. 1983, 1 daughter. *Education:* BA, Columbia University, 1969; PhD, University of Connecticut, 1974; JD, University of California, Berkeley, 1981. *Appointments:* Assistant Professor, Colorado State University, 1974-78; Director, Mondocino County Family Violence Division Programme, 1980; Associate, Vlassiso Ott, 1982-83; Associate, de Mers & Thomson, 1983; Sole Practice, Tacoma, 1983-. *Publications:* Articles in professional journals. *Memberships:* American Bar Association; American Anthropological Association; American Ethnohistorical Society; Washington Women Laywers. *Honours:* Phi Beta Kappa; Phi Kappa Phi; National Institute of Mental Health Fellowship, 1971; Faculty Grant, Florida University, 1976. *Hobbies:* Sailing; Swimming. *Address:* 802 South Oakes Street, Tacoma, WA 98405, USA.

DILWORTH Mary Elizabeth, b. 7 February 1950, New York, New York, USA. Director, Educational Research. *Education:* BA, Elementary Education, 1972; MA, Student Personnel Adm in Higher Education, 1974, Howard University; EdD, Higher Education Administration, Catholic University of America, 1981. *Appointments:* Research Fellow, Institute for the Study of Educational Policy, 1983-85; Coordinator, Education and Training, Howard University Hospital, 1985-87; Director, ERIC Clearinghouse on Teacher Education, 1987-; Director, Research, American Association of Colleges for teacher Education, 1987-. *Publication:* Book: Teacher's Totter: A Report on Teacher Certification Issues, 1984. *Memberships:* National Association Advancement Colored People (NAACP); Education Advisory Board Member; Section President, 1976-78, National Cnc of Negro Women (NCNW); Board Member, National Center Research Teacher Education (NCRTE); American Ed Research Association; Phi Delta Kappa; Washington Urban League. *Honours:* Frito Lay, National Council of Negro Women, Black Women Who Make it Happen, Honoree; Bethune Recognition Award, National Council of Negro Women. *Address:* AACTE, 1 Dupont Circle, NW, Suite 610, Washington, DC 20036, USA.

DIMEDIO Angela, b. 2 July 1955, Bryn Mawr, Pennsylvania, USA. Company Vice President. *Education:* BS, Cabrini College, 1977; American Banker Associaiton National School, 1985; Graduate School, 1986. *Appointments:* Elementary School Teacher, Archdiocese of Philadelphia, St Callistus, 1973-83; Personnel Assistant, 1983-84, Personnel Manager, 1984-85, Personnel Officer, 1985-86, Vice President, Personnel, 1987, Vice President, Training & Development, 1988-, Bryn Mawr Trust Co. *Memberships Include:* International Association of Personnel Women, President Elect, 1985-86, Membership Chair, 1985-86, President, 1986-87; Wellness Council of Delaware Valley, Board of Directors, 1985-; American Society of Personnel Administrators; National Association of Banking Women; American Bankers Association; National Employees Service & Recruitment Association; American Institute of Banking; etc. *Hobbies:* Reading; Assembling Mini Dolls' Houses; Writing; Antiques; etc. *Address:* 3036 Darby Road, Ardmore, PA 19003, USA.

DINESCU Violeta, b. 13 July 1953, Bucharest, Rumania. Composer. *Education:* Bachelor's degree, Lazar College, Bucharest, 1972; Master's degree, C.Porumbescu Conservatory, Bucharest, 1978. *Appointments:* Teaching Harmony, Counterpoint, Theory, Aesthetics, Piano, G.Enescu Music School,

Bucharest, 1978-82; Teaching Harmony, Counterpoint, Theory Hochschule für Kirchenmusik, Heidelberg, Federal Republic of GErmany, 1986-. *Creative works:* Chamber music, orchestral compositions: Memories; Akrostichon; Anna Perenna; Concerto; Opera: Hunger and Thirst; 35 Mai; Film music for Murnau's 1930 film Tabu. *Memberships:* Union of Composers, Rumania; Union of Composers, West Germany; Executive Board, ILWC, New York. *Honours:* Awards, Union of Composers, Rumania, 1975, 1976, 1980, 1982; Prize, County of Stuttgart, West Germany, 1983; Grand Prize for Composition, Composers Guild, USA, 1983; IAM Prize, Kassel, West Germany, 1985; Carl Maria von Weber Prize, Dresden Festspiele, 1986; Prizewinner, New York, Poland and Austria, 1987. *Hobbies:* Literature; Travel; Sport; Mathematics. *Address:* c/o von Knorr, Jahnstrasse 3, 6907 Nussloch-Heidelbert, Federal Republic of Germany.

DINKINS Carol E, b. 9 Nov. 1945, Mathis, Texas, USA. Attorney. m. O Theodore Dinkins, Jr. 2 daughters. *Education:* BSc, University of Texas at Austin, 1964-68; University of Texas School of Law, 1968-69; JD, University of Houston, 1971. *Appointments:* Principal Associate, Texas Law Institute of Coastal & Marine Resources and Adjunct Assistant Professor of Law, University of Houston College of Law, 1971-73; Associate 1973-80, Partner, 1980-81 and 1983-84, Vinson & Elkins; Assistant Attorney General, Land and Natural Resources Division, US Department of Justice, Washington, 1981-83; Deputy Attorney General of the United States, 1984-85. *Memberships include:* Director, Environmental and Energy Study Institute, 1986-89; Director, Environmental Law Institute, 1986-88, (elected for a second term); Director, National Ocean Industries Association, 1986-89; Board Member, Houston Law Center Foundation, 1986-89; Board Member, Houston Law Review, 1986-89; American Bar Association; State Bar of Texas; Texas Bar Foundation Fellow; Federal Bar Association; Houston Bar Association; Board of Advisors, Environmental Liability Law Program, University of Houston Chamber of Commerce; Texas Water Conservation Association. *Honours:* Delegate, British program, Anglo-American Successor Generation, School of Advanced International Studies, The Johns Hopkins University, 1985; Delegate, Japanese-American Environmental Conference, Osaka, Japan, 1982. *Address:* Vinson & Elkins, First City Tower, Houston, Texas 77002, USA.

DINTELMAN Sharon Faye Clemons, b. 28 Feb. 1949, DeWitt, Arkansas, USA. Educator. m. George Edward Dintelman, 10 June 1966 div. 1984, 1 son, 1 daughter. *Education:* BSE 1969, MEd 1982, University of Arkansas; EdSc, University of Central Arkansas, in progress. *Appointments:* Elementary teacher, various schools, Arkansas, 1969-80; Elementary Principal, Stuttgart Public Schools, 1981-86; Director of Curriculum, Searcy Public Schools, 1986-. *Creative work includes:* Editor & publisher, Singles Newsletter, Searcy & district; Development & presention, workshops for churches, teachers & parents, topics including self-esteem, stress management, parenting, drug prevention, effective teaching. *Memberships:* National & Arkansas Associations, Supervision & Curriculum Development; Arkansas Association of Education Administrators; National Association of Female Executives; National & Arkansas Associations, Federal Coordinators; Arkansas County Child Abuse Task Force; Phi Delta Kappa; Daughters of American Revolution. *Honours include:* Alpha Chi, 1968; Outstanding Elementary Teacher of America, 1972; Stuttgart Teacher of Year, 1980; Audio-Visual Screening & Selection Committee, Arkansas State Department of Education, 1985; Elementary Council, 1986; Governor's School Screening Committee, 1987; Winthrop Rockefeller Foundation At-Risk Youth Grant Planning Committee, 1988. *Hobbies:* Genealogy; Travel; Music; Drug education & prevention. *Address:* 200 Western Hills Drive, Searcy, Arkanss 72143, USA.

DIOMATARI Ourana, b. 28 Mar. 1920, Chios Island, Greece. Author. *Education:* Graduated Civil Sciences, Pandios, 1952; Graduated Law, University of Athens, 1955. *Appointments:* Ministry of the Interior Affairs, 1948-72. *Publications:* Happiness is not a Dream, Essay; Homer's Echo, Essay; People who conquer, People who are conquered (Historical essay); Theatrical plays in many pictures; The woman's position in Platon's philosophy (essay); Platon in the reality and the legend (essay); Lily's Book (critical study of the poetic work of Lily Lakovidou; The poet writes the world's history (essay); Greek poetresses (critical study). *Memberships:* Council Member, National Society of Greek Authors, 1970-. *Honours:* Prize of the Greek Academy for the essay, The Woman's position in Platon's philosophy, 1976. *Hobby:* Study of the Ancient and Classic works. *Address:* Michala Kopoulou Str, No 38, Athens 115 28, Greece.

DI PALMA Vera June, b. 14 July 1931, London, England. Chairman, Mobile Training Ltd. m. Ernest Jones, 4 July 1973. *Appointments:* Accountant, Public Practice, 1947-64; Taxation Accountant, Dunlop Co., 1964-67; Senior Lecturer, City of London Polytechnic, 1967-71; Taxation Consultant, 1971-80; Chairman, Mobile Training Ltd., 1978-. *Publications:* Capital Gains Tax, 1972; Your Fringe Benefits, 1978. *Memberships:* Fellow, Chartered Association of Certified Accountants, President 1980-81; Fellow, Institute of Taxation; Public Works Loan Commissioner; Deputy Chairman, Air Travel Trust Committee; VAT Tribunal; Finance Member, Think British Campaign. *Membership:* OBE, 1986. *Hobbies:* Tennis; Dog-Walking; Gardening. *Address:* Temple Close, Sibford Gower, Banbury, Oxon OX15 5RX, England.

DITCHBURN (Elizabeth) Ann, b. 4 Oct. 1949, Sudbury, Ontario, Canada. Choreographer; Film maker; Performer. *Education:* National Ballet School Graduate, 1967. *Appointments:* Dancer Choreographer, National Ballet of Canada, 1968-80; Founder Ann Ditchburn Enterprises, 1988; Independent Choreographer/Film maker. *Creative Works:* Created over 30 ballets including: Kisses featuring Lynn Seymour of the Royal Ballet; Mad Shadows, National Ballet of Canada, 1977, Toronto, London and New York. Choreographed and performed in films: Slow Dancing in the Big City, 1978; Curtains, 1982; Six Weeks, 1982; Elusive Prayers, 1984; The Bathers, 1985; Ann Ditchburn: A Moving Picture, 1987. *Memberships:* Screen Actors Guild, USA; ACTRA, Canada; The Academy of Motion Pictures; Toronto Women in Film; Dancer's Transition Center. *Honours:* Ford Foundation Scholarship, 1965; Jean A Chalmers Award for Choreography, 1975; Film Awards: Nominated for Golden Globe Award for Best Performance by a new actress for Slow Dancing in the Big City, 1978; I am a Hotel, Anik Award, Best Choreography and Best Performance; Golden Rose of Montreux and 7 other awards; Gold Medal, New York International Festival of Film and Video and a Gemeni award for Best Arts Program, 1987 for A Moving Picture. *Hobbies:* Acting classes; Film editing; Writing technique; North American Indian Rights; Vegetarian; House builder. *Address:* 1061 Craven Road, Toronto, Ontario M4J 4V7, Canada.

DIX Barbara Mary, b. 23 Oct. 1944, Southport, England. Singer; Teacher. m. Alexander Abercrombie, 21 Dec. 1973. *Education:* Royal Manchester College of Music, 1964-71. *Appointments include:* Glyndebourne Festival Opera, 1971-75; BBC Northern Singers, 1970's; London recital debut, Purcell Room, 1973; Opera, television appearances, UK & France; Founder, secretary, inaugural year, National Mozart Competition, 1987. Currently Head of Singing, Independent Academy of Music & Drama, Southport. *Hobbies:* Embroidery; Detective stories. *Address:* Independent Academy of Music & Drama, Talbot Street, Southport, Merseyside PR8 1LU, England.

DIXON Jill Ann, b. 19 July 1939, Galion, Ohio, USA. Registered Nurse; Instructor. m. Howard E Dixon, 24 June 1966. 3 daughters. *Education:* BS, Nursing 1961, MS 1988, Ohio State University. *Appointments:* Assistant Instructor Medical-Surgical Nursing,

Samaritan Hospital School of Nursing, Ashland, Ohio, 1961-63; Staff Nurse 1964-65 and 1969-82, Galion Community Hospital, Galion, Ohio; Instructor in Medical-Surgical Nursing 1965-66, Coordinator and Instructor 1966-68 and 1982-, Mansfield General Hospital, Mansfield, Ohio. *Memberships:* Sigma Theta Tau, Nursing Honorary, 1987; First United Church of Christ; Order of the Eastern Star; Galion Past Matrons Club; Galion Rainbow Girls Advisory Board; Girl Scouts; Galion Shrine Ladies; School Parent's Organizations; Ohio State University Alumni Association, Life Member; Ohio State University Nursing Alumni Association, Life Member. *Hobbies:* Sewing; Knitting; Handwork; Cooking; Baking; Reading; Refinishing furniture; Designing houses; Spectator sports. *Address:* 310 E Brandt Rd, Galion, Ohio 44833, USA.

DIXON Katie Loosle, b. 10 Oct. 1925, Clarkston, Utah, USA. Salt Lake County Recorder. m. Rodney Paul Dixon, 23 Nov. 1946, divorced 1972, 3 sons, 1 daughter. *Education:* BSc., Utah State University, 1945. *Appointments:* Teacher, various schools, Idaho, Utah, 1945-59; Public Relations Director, Salt Lake County Recreation Dept., 1956-64; Teacher, Murray High School, 1962-64; Instructor, English, University of Utah, 1965-68; Executive Director, Utah Association for Retarded Citizens, 1972-74; Development Director, Pine Canyon Ranch for Boys, Salt Lake City, 1974-75; Salt Lake County Recorder, 1975-. *Publications:* Articles in: Life; Time; Newsweek; Sports Illustrated. *Memberships:* National Association of Counties, Board of Directors; National Association of County Recorders & Clerks, President, 1983-84; Women Official in the National Association of Counties, Chairman, 1980-81; Institute for Land Information, President, 1988-89; National Womens Education Fund; many other organisations. *Honours:* Susa Young Gates Award, 1980; Clerk/Recorder of the Year, NACRC, 1980; Scholarship Recipient, 1986; Pi Alpha Alpha, 1987; Commencement Speaker, Westminster College, 1988; others. *Address:* 3781 Lois Lane, Salt Lake City, UT 84124, USA.

DIXON Ora L. Wright, b. 27 July 1950, Monroe, Louisiana, USA. Research Microbiologist. m. Clark A. Dixon Jr, 4 June 1977, 2 sons, 1 daughter. *Education:* BSc, 1972; Certification, Fisheries Academy, 1977. *Appointments:* Instructor, counsellor, Alabama Lutheran Academy & College, Selma, 1973; Biological technician, Eastern Fish Disease Laboratory, Kearneysville, West Virginia, 1973-77; Research microbiologist, National Fisheries Centre, 1977-; Host, international symposium, Fish Biologics, 1981; Assistant organiser, North American Foundation, Marcel Merieux Talloires, France, 1982. *Publications:* Author, co-author, various scientific publications, fish diseases, 1977-. *Memberships:* Potomac Chapter, American Fisheries Society; Almech Chapter, Federally Employed Women; National Association of Female Executives; Blue Ridge Chapter, Toastmasters International; National Association for Advancement of Coloured Peoples. *Honours:* Special Achievement Award, US Fish & Wildlife Service, 1981; Featured, Black Collegian Magazine, 1980; Plaques, Boy Scouts 1986, Girl Scouts 1987-88. *Hobbies:* Camping; Reading; Sewing; Voluntary work, Scouting. *Address:* 416 North Samuel Street, Charles Town, West Virginia 25414, USA.

DIXON Shirley Juanita Clark, b. 29 June 1930, Haywood. Business Owner. m. Clinton M Dixon, 1 Sept. 1953. 1 son, 3 daughters. *Education:* Accounting, Wayne State University; Institute of Government, UNC Chapel Hill; Meredith College, NC State University; Haywood Tech College. *Appointments:* Standard Oil Co, Detroit Mich; Statler-Hilton Hotel, Detroit; Osborne Lumber Co, Canton; Business Owner, Dixon's Restaurant, 1961-. *Memberships:* National Association of Female Executives; NC Women's Forum; Canton Business and Professional Assoc; Chamber of Commerce; DAV Commanders Club; Governor's Advisory Council on Aging for the State of North Carolina; Vice-Chair, State Crime Prevention-Community Watch Board of Directors; International Platform Association, 1987; Chairperson, Haywood County, North Carolina Museum of History Associates, 1987; Board of Directors, North Carolina Conference of Social Services, 1987-. *Honours:* Outstanding Service to Crime Prevention in North Carolina, 1982 and 1986; Governor's Special Volunteer Award, 1983; Outstanding Service in Community Watch for State of North Carolina, 1984; Community Service Award to Handicapped, 1983-84; Employer of the Year for Hiring Handicapped, North Carolina Association for Retarded Citizens, 1985; Woman of the Year, Canton Business and Professional Women, 1984; Outstanding Service Award, Community Watch, 1986. *Address:* 104 Skyland Terrace, Canton, NC 26716, USA.

DOAN Rebecca Miles, b. 8 Dec. 1955, Pennsylvania, USA. Sociologist. m. Peter L Doan, 8 Aug. 1981. 1 daughter. *Education:* BA, Harvard University, 1977; MRP 1983, PhD 1988, Cornell University. *Appointments:* Project Administrator, Gaza Strip, 1978-80; Project Administrator, Washsington DC, 1980-81; Community Development Adviser, Amman, Jordan, 1984-86; Research Fellow, UNC, Chapel Hill, 1988-89. *Memberships:* Population Assoc of America; American Sociological Association; Middle East Studies Association; Rural Sociological Association. *Honours:* Outstanding Teaching Assistant Award, 1987; Mary G Williams Teaching and Travel Award, 1977. *Hobbies:* Middle East politics and development; Camping; Hiking; Swimming; Music, singing, guitar and piano. *Address:* Center for the Study of Population, College of Social Sciences, Florida State University, Tallahassee, FL 32306, USA.

DOBRYSZYCKA Wanda Maria, b. 26 Feb. 1921, Dabrowa Gornicza, Poland. Professor. Married, 2 sons. *Education:* Magister Pharm, 1952; Doctor, Pharm. Sci, 1960; Dozent Dr.habil. Bioch., 1965. *Appointments:* Medical School, Poznan, 1952-53; Faculty of Pharacy, Medical Academy, 1953-. *Publications:* Articles and papers in international journals. *Memberships:* Vice President, Clinical Analysis, FIP, 1976-79; National Representative, IFCC, 1970-79; Polish Biochemical Society; Polish Pharmaceutical Society; Polish Society of Laboratory Diagnostics. *Honours:* Recipient, various honours & awards. *Hobbies:* Travel; Bridge. *Address:* Swierczewskiego 1/9, 50-048 Wroclaw, Poland.

DOBSON Susan Angela, b. 31 Jan. 1946, Maidstone, Kent, England. Magazine Editor. m. Michael Dobson, 28 July 1966, divorced 1974. *Education:* Dip.HE, BA Honours (CNAA), 1974-77. *Appointments:* Editor, City Magazines, 1963; Argus Newspapers, 1965; Feature Writer, Fair Lady Magazine, National Newspapers, 1969; Editor, S.A. Institute of Race Relations, 1972; Editor, Wedding Day & First Home, Socio Communications, 1978; Editor, IPC Magazines, 1981-. *Publication:* The Wedding Day Book, 1981, 1989. *Hobbies:* Travel; Travel Writing; Photography; Books; Theatre; Music; Opera; Food. *Address:* IPC Magazines, Kings Reach Tower, Stamford Street, London SE1 9LS, England.

DOCKRY Nancy, b. Niagara Falls, New York, USA. Feature Movie and TV Producer; Consultant. m. John Dockry, 19 Aug. 1961, div. 1968. *Education:* BS, Syracuse University; PhD, Mathematics, Columbia University; Corporate Training Programme, ABC. *Appointments:* Freelance Writer, 1956-60; Director, Programming Department, 1962-64; Media Director, 1964-67, Account Executive, 1967-69, Account Supervisor, 1969-70, Dancer, Fitzgerald, Sample Inc; Vice-President, Advertising, American Home Products, 1970-75; Senior Agent, Vice-President: New York City Office, 1975-76, Los Angeles Office, 1976-78, William Morris Agency; Vice-President, Nephi Productions, 1978-79; Vice-President, Television, MCA-Universal, 1979-80; Vice-President, Time-Life Television Inc, 1980-81; Vice-President, Television, Columbia Pictures, 1981-82; Producer, Consultant, Dockry Productions, 1983-; Consultant for investment firms, advertisers and foreign film companies. *Creative works include:* Numerous short stories and TV serial scripts; Produced numerous TV movies and series and feature films, music videos. *Memberships:* ATAS; MPAA; Board of Directors, Entertainment Industries Council; Republican Party. *Hobbies include:* Tennis; Swimming; Skiing; Travel. *Address:* 2528 Hutton Drive, Beverly Hills, CA 90210, USA.

DODOHARA Jean Noton, b. 21 Feb. 1934, Monroe, USA. Music Educator. m. (1) Rev. Laurence G. Landers, 7 June 1955, (2) Edward R. Harris, 27 Nov. 1981, 3 sons, 2 stepdaughters. *Education:* BA, Monmouth College, Illinois, 1955; MS, 1975, EdD, 1985, University of Illinois. *Appointments:* Music Teacher, Matteson, Illinois, Schools, 1955-56, Choral and Band, Grafton, Ohio Schools, 1958-60; Church Music for Children, Churches in Illinois, Ohio and Missouri, 1957-72; Music Teacher, Glenwood, Illinois Schools, 1970-75, Choral, Miami, Florida Schools, 1975-76; Music Teacher, Choral, Schaumburg, Illinois Schools, 1976-79; Teaching Assistantship, University of Illinois, 1979-. *Publications:* Historical booklets & articles for schools & churches in Illinois, Ohio & Missouri; The Instructional Philosophies Reflected in the Elementary Music Series, published by Silver Burdett Company, 1885-1975. *Memberships:* Music Educators National Conference, Life Member; National Education Association, Life Member; American Choral Directors Association; etc. *Honours:* Outstanding Young Woman of the Year, St Charles (Missouri) Jaycee Wives, 1968. *Hobbies:* Research on 18th & 19th Century Music Instructional Methods; Family Genealogy; Church Leadership; Music; Travel; Reading. *Address:* 914 Roxbury Lane, Schaumburg, IL 60194, USA.

DODSON Jill Marietta, b. 10 Oct. 1955, Baltimore, Maryland, USA. Equine Artist; Social Worker/Addictions Counselor. *Education:* BS Fine Art, Towson State University, 1977; Certified Family Therapist, 1985; Licensed Graduate Social Worker; Master of Social Work, University of Maryland, School of Social Work and Community Planning, 1987. *Appointments:* Equine Artist/Photographer/Instructor, Jill Dodson's Studio of Equestrian Artwork, 1976-; Woman's Program Coordinator, Francis Scott Key Addictions Unit, Baltimore, Maryland, 1987-; Consultant for Adult Children of Alcoholics, Pathfinders Addiction Services, 1988-. *Creative works:* Paintings of: Horse Racing, Stable, Pastoral and Fox Hunting scenes in Watercolours and Oils exhibited nationally; Equine portraits commissioned by: T Mellon Evans; Jack Klugman; Jim McKay etc. Cover Illustrations: Preakness Guides 1980-85; Thoroughbred Record, Horseman's Journal. Magazine articles: Equine Images; The Blood Horse. *Memberships:* Full Membership of The American Academy of Equine Art; The National Association of Social Workers; National and Maryland Associations of Adult Children of Alcoholics (Baltimore Representative in 1985); Junior Advisory Board, Baltimore Museum of Art, 1973. *Honours:* 2nd place award, Popular Vote, Invitational Exhibition of the American Academy of Equine Art, 1982; Accepted and exhibited in all annual Juried Exhibitions of the Academy, 1981-88; Preakness Press Guide featuring cover illustration Spectacular Bird voted Best Media Guide in Racing by New York Racing Association, 1980; Artwork used for Racing Trophies: Maryland Million, Laurel Race Course, 1986; Maryland Sales Agency Stakes, Bowie Racecourse, 1983, Delaware Park Race Course. *Hobbies:* Horseback riding; Visiting museums; Horse races and steeplechases; Playing guitar and harmonica; Ballet; Swimming. *Address:* Jill Dodson's Studio of Equestrian Artwork, 717 Old Belfast Road, Sparks, MD 21152, USA.

DOHERTY Evelyn Marie, b. 26 Sept. 1941, Philadelphia, Pennsylvania, USA. Owner, Computer Consulting Firm. *Education:* IBM Misc Data Processing Courses; RCA Tech Inst DP Courses. *Appointments:* Freelance Programmer, 1968-81; Consulting Firm, serving banking, brokers, transportation, manufacturing, medical, publishing, food wholesaling and contracts, 1981-. *Publications:* Articles relating to data processing. *Memberships:* Founder, Babe Didikson Collingswood Girls' Softball Team; DPMA; DPMA, Educational Chairwomen; DPMA Board Member; Democratic committee Woman, Collingswood, NJ. *Hobbies:* Chess; Tennis; Fishing. *Address:* P O Box 3780, Cherry Hill, NJ 08034, USA.

DOLL CAMPISI Kristine Ann, b. 27 Mar. 1955, Boston, USA. Professor; Speechwriter; Translator. m. Joseph Paul Campisi, 9 July 1983. *Education:* BA, University of Massachusetts, 1976; MA, Distinction, Boston College, 1979; PhD, Brown University, 1984. *Appointments:* Instructor, College of William & Mary, 1982-83; Corporate Speechwriter, Michelin Tire Corporation, 1983-85; Professor, Modern Languages, State University of New York, Old Westbury, 1985-. *Publications:* Towards a Revaluation of Joan Alcover's Elegies, in The Catalan Review, Volume II, 1987; The Expression of Death in Catalonia, 1987; The Elegiac Verse of Rosalia de Castro, 1982; The Theme of Death in the Family in Rosalia de Castro and Joan Alcover, 1982. *Memberships:* Asociacion Internacional de Hispanistas; Modern Langage Association of America; North American Catalan Society; Northeast Modern Language Association. *Honours:* SUNY/Old Westbury Faculty Development Awards, Spring, 1987, Autumn, 1987; United States Department of Education grant in Critical Foreign Languages, 1988; New York State Department of Education Title II grant in Foreign Languages, 1988. *Hobbies:* Travel; Literature; Skiing; Gardening; Music. *Address:* SUNY, College at Old Westbury, Modern Languages, Old Westbury, NY 11568, USA.

DOLMETSCH Mary Douglas, b. 16 Feb. 1916, Glasgow, Scotland. Retired. m. Carl Frederick Dolmetsch, 24 Feb. 1937, 2 sons, 2 daughters. *Education:* Glasgow College of Domestic Science; Diploma, Domestic Sciences, 1934; Studing, Making & Playing Early Instruments with Arnold Dolmetsch, 1935. *Appointments:* Director, Arnold Dolmetsch Ltd., 1938-81; Life Member, Dolmetsch Foundation, Organising Secretary 1947-58. *Memberships:* British Red Cross; National Arts Collection Fund; Royal Horticultural Society; Secretary, The Record in Education Summer Schools, 1947-63. *Hobbies:* Gardening; Reading; Travel; Music. *Address:* Greybield, Peebles, Scotland EH45 9JB.

DONAHUE Mary Rosenberg, b. 20 Dec. 1932, New York, USA. Psychologist. m. George T Donahue, 27 Dec. 1967. 2 daughters. *Education:* BA, Adelphi University, 1954; MA, New York University, 1957; Graduate courses in Psychology, Yeshiva University, 1958; PhD, St Johns University, 1968. *Appointments:* Classroom Teacher, 1954-57; School Psychologist, Union Free School, Elmont, NY, 1957-62, 1965-66 and 1966-67; Consultant Psychologist, NIMH, 1964-65; Associate in Private clinical practice, 1969-71; Private Clinical Practice, Rockville, 1971-. *Publications:* Community Educational program for the Emotionally Disturbed Child, 1961; Project for some Exceptional Children, 1961; American Bar Association, invited speaker, Family Law Division, 1986; TV/Issues surrounding joint custody, 1986. *Memberships:* Maryland Psychology Association; American Psychology Association; Association Practicing Psychologists; Orthopsychiatric Association. *Hobbies:* Theatre; Travel. *Address:* 12017 Edgepark Ct, Potomac, MD 20854, USA.

DONALD Christine Mary, b. 21 Dec. 1950, Chesterfield, Derbyshire, England. Freelance Editor. *Education:* MA, Cambridge University, 1977. *Publications:* The Fat Woman Measures Up, book & audio cassette, 1986 and 1987; The Breaking Up Poems, tape & audio cassette, 1987 and 1988. *Memberships:* Coalition for Lesbian & Gay Rights in Ontario (CLGRO), Spokesperson; League of Canadian Poets. *Interest:* Feminism. *Address:* c/o Box 822, Sta 1, Toronto, Ontario, Canada, M5W 1G3.

DONALDSON Dorothea E., b. 1 Mar. 1911, New Rochelle, New York, USA. Arbitrator/Mediator; Retired Judge; Lawyer. *Education:* BA, Hunter College, New York City, 1931; MA, Teachers College, Columbia

University, 1932; LLB, JD (retroactive), St John's University School of Law, 1935; Honorary LLD, St Johns University, 1977. *Appointments:* Teacher, New Rochelle New York School System, 1934-43; Private Practice of Law, 1943-50; Referee, Supervising Referee, Board Member, Workmen's Compensation Board, New York State, 1944-60; Chairman, Unemployment Insurance Appeal Board, New York State, 1960-63; Judge, Court of Claims, New York State, 1963-77; Arbitrator/ Mediator, American Arbitration Association, 1977-. *Memberships:* American Bar Association; New York State Bar Association; Westchester Bar Association; New Rochelle Bar Association (Treasurer 1941-48); Business and Professional Women's Clubs, New York State, New Rochelle, Orlando, Florida (President, New Rochelle, 1942-44, state-wide chairmanships). *Honours:* Golden Eaglet, Girl Scouts, 1928; Achievement Award, 1949, Woman of the Year, 1963, New Rochelle Business and Professional Women's Club; Benjamin Potoker Brotherhood Award, 1961; Trustee, St John's University, 1969-87; President's Medal, 1971; Pietas Medal, 1976; Medal of Honor, 1981; Hall of Fame Hunter College, 1972; Westchester Community College Foundation Medallion, 1974; 1st woman appointed Supervising Referee, as Chairman of Appeals Panel, Workman's Compensation Board, as Chairman of Unemployment Insurance Appeal Board, as Court of Claims Judge. *Hobbies:* Swimming; Walking; Cycling; Dance; Jewellery making; Gardening. *Address:* 915 Euclid Avenue, Orlando, FL 32806, USA.

DONALDSON Loraine, b. Clearwater, Florida, USA. Professor of Economics. *Education:* BSBA 1960, MA 1961, University of Florida; DBA, Indiana University, 1965. *Appointments:* Research Assistant, Brookings Institute, 1962; International Development and Research Center, Indiana University, 1963-64; Faculty member, Georgia State University, Atlanta, 1964-. *Publications:* Development Planning in Ireland, 1966; Economic Development, Analysis and Policy, 1984; Journal articles. *Memberships:* Scottish Rite Auxiliary; Shepherd Spinal Center Auxiliary; American Economic Association; American Association of University Professors. *Honours:* State of Florida Teacher Scholarship, 1958; JH Miller Scholarship, 1960; Beta Gamma Sigma Achievement Award, 1960; Phi Kappa Phi, 1960. *Hobbies:* Art; Painting; Tennis. *Address:* Department of Economics, Georgia State University, University Plaza, Atlanta, Georgia 30303, USA.

DONOHO Betty B, b. 12 Oct. 1934, Henderson County, USA. Corporate Secretary. m. 6 Apr. 1959, 1 son, 1 daughter. *Appointments:* Corporate Officer, Contrc. Company, 27 years. *Memberships:* Sub Contractors Association; National Association Female Executives; National Geographic Society; NC Electric Association. *Honours:* Advisory Board, Local School Board; Jerry Silverman Scholarship Board Member. *Hobbies:* Boating; Travel.

DONOVAN Mary Patricia, b. 25 Mar. 1943, Jersey City, New Jersey, USA. Teacher. 1 son, 1 daughter. *Education:* BA, State University of New York SUNY Albany, 1964; MLS, SUNY Stony Brook, 1972; Ed.D, Columbia University Teachers' College, 1986. *Appointments:* Teacher 1967-. *Creative work includes:* Research, Study, 8 Young Children's Uses of Language with a Partner, 1986; Research measurement, purity of babies' milk & fruit; Guest teacher, International Dispatch Programme, Tokyo Metropolis High School, 1985; Videotaped lesson, World Peace. *Memberships:* World Wildlife Federation; Planetary Society; Union of Concerned Scientists; Smithsonian Associates. *Honours:* National Museum of Women in Arts, Washington DC, 1988; Kappa Delta Pi, Teachers' College, 1985. *Address:* 8 Woodcutter's Path, St James, New York 11780, USA.

DORIAN Nancy Marilyn, b. 27 May 1933, Shaker Heights, Ohio, USA. Clinical Psychologist. m. Alex Dorian, 1960, divorced 1961, 1 daughter. *Education:* BA, University of Chicago; MA, Case-Western Reserve University, 1966. *Appointments:* Psychologist,

Cleveland State Hospital, 1956-60; Psychologist, Fallsview Psychiatric Hospital, 1962-64; Psychologist, Euclid Public Schools, 1965-74; Office Manager, Realtek Industries, 1975-77; Psychologist, Vocational Guidance & Rehabilitation Services, 1977-79; Coordinator, Psychological Services, Townhall II, 1979-81; Chief Psychologist, Trumbull County Children Services, 1982-. *Memberships:* American Psychological Association; Sugarbush Kennel Club, Secretary, 1981, 1982; Board of Trustees, Ohio District XI Forensic Board. *Honours:* Recipient, various honours. *Hobbies:* Breeding & Showing Dogs; Music; Gardening. *Address:* Trumbull County Children Services Board, 2282 Reeves Road NE, Warren, OH 44483, USA.

DORION Dorothy Mae, b. 19 Feb. 1934, Floral Park, New York, USA. RN Consultant - Health & Wellness; Special Education. m. George H Dorion, 7 Sept. 1957. 3 sons, 1 daughter. *Education:* BS, RN, Columbia University, 1957; MS Special Education, Southern Connecticut State College, 1969. *Appointments:* Staff Nurse, Instructor, Yale-New Haven Med Center, Stamford Hospital, Norwalk Hospital, Connecticut, 1957-69; Instructor, Special Education, California, Puerto Rico, 1969-72; Special Education, Director, Kadis Learning Center, Jacksonville, 1972-74; Director, Learning Disabilities Summer Day Camp, Jacksonville, 1975-78; Hospice NE Florida, 1978-82, Director 1980-82, Jacksonville; Coordinator, Sports Medicine Clinic, Nemours Childrens Hospital, Jacksonville, 1983-86. *Publications:* Birth of a Learning Disabilities Day Camp, 1976; Guidelines for Learning Disabilities Day Camp, 1977; Jacksonville Community Council, Inc, Studies: Handicapped, Youth & Family, Civil Service, Disaster Preparedness, Financial Health Care Medically Indigent, 1977; Junior Olympics Study on Injuries & Dehydration, 1984. *Memberships include:* Sigma Theta Tau, Nursing Honor Society, 1957-; Florida State Hospice, National Hospice Organization, Delegate, 1982; First Woman President, Osprey Club, University of North Florida, 1985; Trustee, Aloha Foundation; Florida Athletics Congress Registered Nurse, Florida, etc. *Honours include:* Outstanding Achievement Award (FACLD), Learning Disabilities Day Camp, 1985; Certificate of Outstanding Achievement, Florida Governor's Council on Fitness & Sports, 1984; Proclamation by President, University of North Florida, Dorothy S Dorion Day, 1986; Dorothy S Dorion Endowed Scholarship for Women Athletes, University of North Florida, 1986-; Organizer, Founder, Director, Jacksonville's First Women's Race, North Florida Triathletes, Greater Jax Masters Swim Team, Jacksonville Track Club, River Run, etc. *Hobbies:* Competed in World Masters Track & Field Championships; Completed two Ironman World Triathlon Championships, Hawaii, 1985, 1987; Competed in World Masters Swim Championships, Holmes Lumbar Jax, Brisbane, Australia, 1988; Brass/ Stone rubbings; Gourmet cooking; Hostess/sponsor for World Class Athletes. *Address:* 7922 Hunters Grove Road, Jacksonville, Florida 32256, USA.

DORN Dolores, b. 3 Mar. Chicago, Illinois, USA. Actress; Teacher. m. Franchot Tone (deceased), 14 May 1966. *Education:* BFA, Art Institute of Chicago. *Appointments:* Has appeared in numerous television roles including: Simon and Simon; Charlies Angels; Tenafly; Girls of Huntington House; Run for Your Life; Strawberry Blonde; Studio 5B; Superior Court; Capitol. Films include: Tell Me a Riddle; The Stronger; Thirteen West Street; The Bounty Hunter; Uncle Vanya; Murders of the Rue Morgue; The Stronger. Theatre includes: Broadway: The Midnight Sun; Starward Ark; Hide and Seek. Off-Broadway: The Pinter Plays; Plays for Bleeker Street; Between Two Thieves; A Mighty Man is He. Acting Coach, KTTV Starsearch 1982. *Publications:* Contributor of articles in professional magazines. *Memberships:* Women in Film; Actor's Studio; Senior Faculty Member, American Film Institute, 1977-; The Lee Strasberg Theatre Institute, 1982-85. *Honours:* Best Actress Award for Uncle Vanya, San Francisco Film Festival. *Hobbies:* Dogs; Working out. *Address:* c/o American Film Institute, 2021 N Western Avenue, Los Angeles, CA 90027, USA.

DORN Georgette Magassy, b. Budapest, Hungary. Historian. m. Paul Austin Dorn, 9 June 1961, 1 son, 3 daughters. *Education:* BA. Creighton University; MA, Boston College; PhD, Georgetown University. *Appointments:* Descriptive Cataloging, Library of Congress, 1963-64; Specialist, Hispanic Culture, Library of Congress, 1964-; Adjunct Lecturer, History, Georgetown University, 1982-. *Publications:* The Indian Tribes of Texas by Jose F., 1972; Archive of Hispanic Literature on Tape, 1974. *Memberships:* Latin American Studies Association, Executive Council; American Catholic Historical Association; Inter American Council, President. *Honours:* Phi Alpha Theta; Alpha Sigma Nu. *Hobbies:* Painting; Skiing. *Address:* 4702 Essex Avenue, Chevy Chase, MD 20815, USA.

DORNIN Catharine Quillen, b. 19 Apr. 1946, Louisville, USA. Concert Pianist; Teacher. m. Christopher Laird Dornin, 24 Nov. 1967, 2 sons, 3 daughters. *Education:* Bachelor, Piano performance, Oberlin Conservatory, 1968. *Appointments:* Pittsfield Community School, 1968-69; Hochstein Community School, 1969-71; St Paul's School, Concord, 1981; Concord Community Music School, 1984; Notre Dame College Community Music School, 1986. *Memberships:* Vice President, New Hampshire Music Teachers Association, 1983-87; Piano Guild; New England Piano Teachers Association. *Honours:* Recipient, various honours and awards. *Address:* 52 Whipple Ave., Lacomia, NH 03246, USA.

DOST Jeanne Ebbert, b. 12 Aug. 1929, Walla Walla, USA. Economist. m. Frank N Dost, 3 Sept. 1950, 1 son, 1 daughter. *Education:* BA 1951, Washington State University; MA, 1953, PhD, 1959, Harvard University. *Appointments:* Instructor, Economics, Washington State University, 1959-61; Economic Consultant, Oregon State Department of Education, 1962-67; Assistant Professor, 1967-73, Director, Associate Professor, 1973-87, Womens Studies, Professor 1987-, Oregon State Univesity. *Publications:* Introduction to Women Studies, 1989; Guide to Eliminating Sexism in Classroom, 1986. *Memberships:* Royal Economic Society; American Economic Association; National Women's Studies Association; President Oregon Women's Political Caucus, 1973-74. *Honours:* Susan B Anthony Womens Rights Award, Oregon Public Employees Union, 1986; Woman of the Year Oregon State University Womens Centre, 1985. *Address:* Dept. of Women Studies, Oregon State University, Corvallis, OR 97331, USA.

DOTSON Nancy Jean Davis, b. 5 Feb. 1941, Houston, Texas, USA. Teacher Adviser. m. Earl Leslie Dotson Jr, 2 Oct. 1964, 2 sons, 1 daughter. *Education:* BS, Southern University, Louisiana, 1962; University of Southern California, 1964-66; MS, Pepperdine University, California, 1974. *Appointments:* Teacher, various subjects, Houston, Texas, 1962-64; Mathematics Teacher 1964-72, Mathematics Adviser 1972-76, Teacher/Adviser, Drew Junior High School, 1976-, Los Angeles Unified School District. *Publications:* Helpful Hints for Teaching & Learning; E's of Learning; Teacher's Pledge; What Parents Can Do To Help Their Child(ren). *Memberships:* Various professional bodies; Secondary Coordinators Association; Wheatley West Alumni; California Mathematics Council; Los Angeles City Teachers Mathematics Association; Council of Mathematics; Association of Curriculum and Supervision (ASCD); National Staff Development Council; Basic Council of Education. Also various community organisations. *Honours include:* Honorary Life Member, California Congress of Parents & Teachers, 1969; Outstanding Teacher, LA Unified School District, 1969; University Grants, 1973, 1974; Biographical recognition. *Hobbies:* Collecting quotations; Developing library, human relations, school management, time management, supervision, curriculum development, communication; Meeting people; Collecting butterflies; Travel; Own business, Agape Resource Centre. *Address:* 19420 South Fariman Drive, Carson, California 90746, USA.

D'OTTAVIANO Itala Maria Loffredo, b. 18 July 1944, Campinas, Brazil. Mathematician; Logician. m. Carlos Roberto d'Ottaviano, 29 Apr. 1968, 1 son, 2 daughters. *Education:* BA 1960, graduate course 1962, Music, BSc Mathematics 1966, MSc 1974, DSc 1982, Livre Docente Logic & Foundations of Mathematics 1987, State University of Campinas (UNICAMP). *Appointments:* Concert pianist, pre-1966; High School Mathematics Teacher, 1967-68; Professor, Catholic University of Campinas (PUCC), 1967-68; Assistant Professor 1969-86, Professor 1986-, (Department of Mathematics), Director, Centre of Logic, Epistemology & History of Science (CLE) 1986-, Founder, Centre of Documentation on History of Science 1987, UNICAMP; Director, Education Department, City of Campinas, 1978; Visiting Scholar, University of California, Berkeley, & Stanford University, USA 1984-85, Wolfson College, Oxford University, UK 1988. *Publications:* Various papers, Brazilian & International Scientific Meetings, Scientific Journals; Didactical Works; Book chapters. *Memberships:* Founding Member, Brazilian Logic Society, CLE; Offices, Brazilian Logic Society; Brazilian Society for History of Science; Association for Symbolic Logic. *Honours include:* Elected trustee, UNICAMP, 1983-84, 1985-86; Editor-at-large, Marcel Dekker, 1985-; Editorial Board, Journal of Non-Classical Logic, 1986-; President, CLE, UNICAMP, 1986-; Reviewer, various prestigious journals; Editor, Colecao CLE, book collection, 1987-; National Scholar, Brazilian National Research Council, 1987-; Invited Speaker, Brazil, USA, Europe; Organising Committess, Scientific Meetings. *Hobbies:* Music; Dance; Opera; Reading; History, Politics; Animals; Riding. *Address:* CLE UNICAMP, Caixa Postal 6133, 13-081 Campinas, SP, Brazil.

DOTTO Lydia Carol, b. 29 May 1949, Cadomin, Alberta, Canada. Executive Editor; Freelance Science Writer. *Education:* Honours degree (Class Medal), Journalism, Carleton University, 1971. *Appointments:* Reporter, Toronto Star, 1970-71; Science writer, Toronto Globe & Mail 1972-78, freelance 1978-; Executive Editor, Canadian Science News Service, 1982-. *Publications include:* Books: Ozone War, 1978; Planet Earth in Jeopardy: Environmental Consequences of Nuclear War, 1986; Canada in Space, 1987; Thinking the Unthinkable: Social Consequences of Rapid Climate Change, 1988; Asleep in the Fast Lane, 1990. Also: Numerous magazine articles; Film, radio & TV scripts. *Memberships:* Past President, Canadian Science Writers Association; Advisory Board, Marc Garneau Collegiate Institute. *Honours:* Sandford Fleming Medal, 1983; Awards, magazine/newspaper articles, Canadian Science Writers Association, 1974, 1981, 1984; 2 US best book lists, 1986; One of 3 finalists, Gemini Awards, 1988; Award, Canadian Meteorology Society, 1975. *Hobbies:* Computers; Flying; Diving; Skiing; Swimming; Theatre & dance; Reading. *Address:* Canadian Science News Service, Room 45, University College, University of Toronto, Ontario, Canada M5S 1A1.

DOTY Carolyn Ruth House, b. 28 July 1941, Tooele, Utah, USA. University Teacher; Author. m. (1) William Doty, 2 Feb. 1963 (div. 1983), 1 son, 1 daughter, (2), Gardner H. Mein, 16 June 1986. *Education:* BFA Painting, University of Utah, 1963; MFA, Creative Writing, University of California-Irvine, 1979. *Appointments:* Teacher, University of California, Irvine, 1977-79, 1984-86; Teacher, San Francisco State University, 1980; Assistant Professor, University of Kansas, 1986-. *Publications:* A Day Late, novel, 1980 (UK 1981); Fly Away Home, novel, 1982; What She Told Him, novel, 1982; Bonniers in Sweden, 1986. *Memberships:* Authors Guild; Poets & Writers Inc; Modern Language Association; Board, Squaw Valley Community of Arts. *Honours:* Scholarships, Squaw Valley Community of Writers, 1975, 1976; Teaching fellowships, University of California, Irvine, 1977, 78, 79; New Faculty grant 1986, General Research Fund grant 1987, Kansas University; Santa Barbara Award, excellence in writing. *Hobby:* Painting. *Address:* 1630 Barker Avenue, Lawrence, Kansas 66044, USA.

DOUGLAS Carole Nelson, b. 5 Nov. 1944, Everett, Washington, USA. Novelist. m. Sam Scott Douglas, 25 Nov. 1967. *Education:* BA, College of St Catherine, St Paul, Minnesota, 1966. *Appointments:* Journalist, 1967-84, copy & layout Editor, 1981-84, Editorial Page Copy & Layout Editor, Occasional Editorialist 1983-84, St Paul Pioneer Press & Dispatch. *Publications include:* Novels: Amberleigh, 1980; Fair Wind, Fiery Star, 1981; Six of Swords, 1982; In Her Prime, 1982; Her Own Person, 1982; The Best Man, 1983; Lady Rogue, 1983; Exiles of the Rynth, 1984; Azure Days, Quicksilver Nights, 1985; Probe, 1986; Keepers of Edanvant, 1987; Counterprobe, 1988; Heir of Rengarth, 1988; Seven of Swords, 1989. *Memberships:* Authors Guild; Science Fiction Writers of America; Romance Writers of America; Sisters In Crime. *Honours:* Finalist, single title release 1987, Historical Romance 1984, Contemporary Mainstream 1983, Historical Mainstream 1982, Romance Writers of America; Silver Medal, Historical Romance, West Coast Review of Books 6th annual Porgie Awards, 1982; SF/Fantasy Award 1984, Science Fiction Award 1986, Romantic Times. *Hobbies:* Vintage Clothes & Jewellery; Art & Illustration. *Address:* 3920 Singleleaf Lane, Fort Worth, Texas 76133, USA.

DOUGLAS Cynthia, b. 7 Oct. 1952, Appleton, Wisconsin, USA. Physician. *Education:* BA, summa cum laude, Central Washington State University, 1975; MD 1978; Pathology Residency, 1979-82, Affiliated Residency Programme, University of Washington, Seattle. *Appointments:* Lecturer, Medical Technologist and Medex Physician Assistant Programs, University of Washington, 1979-82; Locum Tenens, Chelan County Coroner, Wenatche, 1982-83; Locum Tenens, Laboratory Director, Northwest Medical Labs, Seattle, 1982-83; Inspector for Laboratory Accreditation, College of American Pathologists, 1983; Co-director of Laboratories 1983-85, Director of Laboratory 1985-, Twin Cities Community Hospital, Templeton. *Publications:* Letter to the Editor, Chest, 1987; Goin' Home, Patterns of Stardust, 1970. *Memberships include:* College of American Pathologists, 1981-; American Society of Clinical Pathologists, 1982-; San Luis Obispo County Medical Society, 1983-; American Medical Association, 1983-; California Medical Association, 1983-; Tissue and Transfusion Committee, Twin Cities Community Hospital, 1983-; Infection Control Committee, Twin Cities Community Hospital, 1984-; Quality Assurance Committee, 1989; Twin Cities Hospital Executive Committee, 1989; Women's Medical Society, 1985-; San Luis Obispo Pathology Society, 1986- (President 1986, 1987, 1988, 1989); Central Coast Chapter of Hypnosis Society, 1987-; Flying Samaritans, 1988-. *Honours:* Physicians Recognition Award, AMA, 1984-; 4th place Afghan Award, SLO Co Fair, 1986. *Hobies:* Playing piano; Knitting; Crocheting. *Address:* P O Box 959, Templeton, CA 93465, USA.

DOUGLAS Esther, b. 6 Aug. 1927, Cordoba, Argentina. Research Scientist; Engineer. m. (1) Juan R Pene, 28 Dec. 1948, divorced 1969, 2 daughters, (2) W J M Douglas, 30 Oct. 1970, divorced 1983. *Education:* Eng., Chemical Engineering, University of the Litoral, Santa Fe, Argentina, 1957; PhD, Soil Physics, McGill University, Canada, 1978. *Appointments:* Research Engineer, 1976-78, Research Associate, 1978-82, McGill University; Research Scientist, CANMET, 1982-. *Publications:* Articles in: Canadian Agricultural Engineer; Soil Scientist; Cement & Concrete Research, American Ceramic Faculty Bulletin, Cement, Concrete and Aggregate. *Memberships:* Canadian Engineering Manpower Council, Director, 1981-84, Member 1982-; Canadian Society for Chemical Engineering, Director, 1981-84; Chemical Institute of Canada; Argentine Association of Chemical Engineers. *Hobbies:* Music; Literature; Tennis; Swimming. *Address:* Canmet, Energy Mines & Resources Canada, 405 Rochester St., Ottawa, Ontario, Canada K1A 0G1.

DOUGLAS Susan Margaret, b. 29 Jan. 1957, London, England. Journalist. *Education:* BSc, 1st Class Honours Physiology & Biochemistry, Southampton University. *Appointments:* Writer, Medical

Correspondent 1983-85, Features Editor 1985, Assistant Editor 1986, Associate Editor 1987, Mail on Sunday; Assistant Editor, Daily Mail newspaper, 1988. *Hobby:* Horses. *Address:* c/o Daily Mail, Tudor Street, London EC4, England.

DOUGLASS Sue Nan, b. 7 Nov. 1938, Los Angeles, California, USA. Artist; Registered Nurse. m. John M. Douglass, 14 May 1962, 2 daughters. *Education:* RN, Hollywood Presbyterian Hospital, Los Angeles, 1960; BSN, Pacific Western University, 1987. *Appointments:* Nurse, Hollywood Presbyterian Hospital, 1960-62; Vice President, Douglass Enterprises, 1962-; Art Instructor, Conejo Valley Unified School District, 1981-84; Nurse, Health Improvement Service, Kaiser Permanente, Los Angeles, 1980-; Designer, A Stamp in the Hand, 1982-; Instructor, 5th International Calligraphy Symposium, Scripps College, Claremont, 1985. *Publications:* Health Improvement Service Handbook, 1983; Regional Handbook, Society for Calligraphy, LA, 1985; Eraserstamp: Alphabet & Image, 1986; Tapiglyphics, 1980; Effects of Raw Food Diet on Hypertension & Obesity, Southern Medical Journal, 1985; Mona: Variations on a Theme, video, 1985. *Memberships:* Past Regional Coordinator, Society for Calligraphy, Los Angeles; LA County Art Museum; International Hajji Baba; Women in Arts; Friends of Calligraphy. *Honours:* 2 1st places, calligraphy, Ventura County Fair, 1982; Outstanding service, Ventura County, Society for Calligraphy. *Hobbies:* Antique oriental rugs; Calligraphy; Stamp designing, carving, printing; Real estate; Health improvement; Studies, chemical dependency; Creativity; World peace. *Address:* Bell Canyon, California 91307, USA.

DOUTHITT Vicki Lynne, b. 20 Aug. 1960, Dallas, Texas, USA. Physical Education Professor. m. Cameron Bennett Douthitt, 22 Dec. 1984. *Education:* BSc., 1986; MSc., 1988; PhD Candidate. *Appointments:* Fitness Consultant, Gold's Gym, 1983-84; Personal Fitness Trainer, 1983-; Fitness Consultant, Instructor, University College Health Centre, 1988-. *Publications:* Body Building; Weight Training: Getting Started; The Dynamics of Fitness & Conditioning. *Memberships:* American College of Sports Medicine; National Strength & Conditioning Association; Colorado Association of Health, Physical Education Recreation and Dance. *Honours:* Phi Theta Kappa; Graduate cum laude, BS and MS Degrees; Ms North Texas, 1982; Ms East Texas, 1983; Ms Texas, 1983; National Deans List, 1985-86. *Hobbies:* Bodybuilding; Skiing; Acrylic Painting; Aerobics. *23515 Currant Drive, Golden, CO 80401, USA.*

DOW Marguerite Ruth, b. 13 June 1926, Ottawa, Ontario, Canada. Professor Emerita. *Education:* BA Honours, English, 1949, MA 1970, BEd 1971, University of Toronto; High School Specialist's Certificate, Ontario, 1952; Drama Certificates, Queen's University 1955, Banff School of Fine Arts, University of Alberta 1956. *Appointments:* Laboratory assistant 1944-46, librarian, Aeronautical Library 1947-48, National Research Council; Librarian, Joint Intelligence Bureau, Defence Research Board, 1949-50; English Teacher, Ontario high schools, 1950-65; Associate Professor 1965-72, Professor 1972-85, Professor Emerita 1985-, Faculty of Education, University of Western Ontario. Also: 7 consultative & research committees, Ontario Ministry of Education, 1958-64; Creative Arts & Theatre Arts Committees, Ontario Institute for Studies in Education, 1966-69. *Publications:* Magic Mask, theatre arts textbook, 1966; Numerous articles, professional journals. Co-author: Courses of Study in Theatre Arts, grades 7-12, 1969; Loyalist Vignettes & Sketches, 1984. Editor, co-editor, various other books. *Memberships include:* Past offices: Ontario Secondary School Teachers Federation; Ottawa Theatre Foundation; United Empire Loyalists Association of Association; Monarchist League of Canada; Canadian College of Teachers; Heraldry Society of Canada, librarian, 1988-89. *Honours include:* Armorial bearings, Kings of Arms, England, 1972; Various recognitions, International Institute of Community Service, World Academy of

Scholars, World University, Monarchist League, World Literary Academy, MacDonald Stewart Art Centre. *Hobbies:* Travel; Drama; Early Canadian history; Chinese culture & art. *Address:* 52 First Avenue, Apt. 2, Ottawa, Ontario, Canada K1S 2G2.

DOWELL Flonnie, b. 7 Feb. 1947, Marietta, GA, USA. Research Physical Scientist (Theoretical). *Education:* BA, University of South Florida, 1969; MS, Texas Woman's University, 1974; PhD, Georgetown University, 1977. *Appointments:* Teacher, Florida and Texas, 1970-71; Research, Teaching Assistant, 1971-73, 1973-77; National Bureau of Standards, Washington, 1977-79; Research Scientist, Oak Ridge National Laboratory, 1979-81; Los Alamos National Laboratory, 1981-, Project Leader 1984-. *Publications:* Articles in professional journals. *Memberships:* American Physical Society; Royal Society of Chemistry, London; New York Academy of Sciences; American Association for the Advancement of Science; Sigma Xi. *Honours:* National Science Foundation NATO Travel Award, 1977; National Research Council Postdoctoral Research Associate, 1977-79. *Address:* Theoretical Division, MS-B221, Los Alamos National Laboratory, University of California, Los Alamos, NM 87545, USA.

DOWN Lesley-Ann, b. 17 Mar. 1954, London, England. Actress. *Career:* At age of 10 modelled for TV and film commercials, leading to roles in features. At 14 appeared in All the Right Noises (debut). *Creative Works:* Films include: Pope Joan; Scalawag; Brannigan; The Pink Panther Strikes Again; The Betsy; A Little Night Music; The Great Train Robbery; Hanover Street; Sphinx; Rough Cut; Nomads. Television: Series: Upstairs, Downstairs; Heartbreak House; North & South II. Movies: The One and Only Phyllis Dixey; The Last Days of Pompeii; Arch of Triumph. Stage: Great Expectations; Hamlet, etc. *Address:* c/o William Morris Agency, 147-149 Wardour Street, London W1, England.

DOWNING Elizabeth Ann, b. 15 Aug. 1946, Iowa City, USA. Health Educator. m. David G. Everett, 26 Apr. 1986. *Education:* BS, Miami University, 1968; MAT, Simmons College, 1972; PhD, University of Virginia. *Appointments:* Wellness Co-ordinator, Federal Executive Institute, Charlottesville, 1984-89; President, The Health Advantage, 1988-. *Publications:* Cassettes: Stretching & Relaxation, 1983; Hatha Yoga Practice Tape, 1978. *Memberships:* National Wellness Association; American College of Sports Medicine; Physicians for Social Responsibility; Associaiton for Applied Sport Psychology; Association for the Advancement of Health Education; Adjunct Faculty Member, Federal Exoeutive Institute, 1983-. *Honours:* Recipient, various honours including: Panel Member for Patnership '87. *Address:* 11917 Moss Point Lane, Reston, VA 22094, USA.

DOYLE Judith Warner, b. 18 Aug. 1943, Los Angeles, California, USA. Psychotherapist. 1 son. *Education:* BA, Theatre Arts, 1975; MS, Counselling Psychology, 1977. *Appointments Include:* Owner, Psychotherapist, private practice, 1977-; Director, Counselling, Gay/Lesbian Community Service Centre, 1985-88; Executive Director, One in Long Beach Inc., 1988-. *Memberships:* Co-Chair, Aidswalk, Long Beach, 1988-; Co-Chair, Southland Political Action Committee; Long Beach Lesbian & Gay Pride Inc., President, 1983-87; President, California Association Marriage & Family Therapists, 1981-87. *Honours:* Woman of the Year, 1981, Lambda Democratic Club; Woman of the Year, 1986, Christopher Street West; Who's Who of California; Who's Who of America; Distinguished Clinical Member, Califoria Association of Marriage & Family Therapists; Special Recognition, Long Beach Lambda Democratic Club, Human Rights Award. *Address:* 4041 E 4th St., Long Beach, CA 90814, USA.

DRACHNIK Catherine Meldyn, b. 7 June 1924, Kansas City, Missouri, USA. Clinical Psychiatric Counselor; President, American Art Therapy Association; Art Therapist. m. Joseph Brennan Drachnik, 6 Oct. 1946. 1 son, 1 daughter. *Education:* BA Home Education, University of Maryland, 1945; MA Art Education, California State University, Sacramento, 1975. *Appointments:* Art Therapist: Arlington Mental Health Day Treatment Center, Fairfax Mental Health Day Treatment Center, Vincent Hall Retirement Home, 1971-72; Art Therapist, Sequoia Hospital, Redwood City, 1972-73; Supervising Teacher, Adult Education, Sacramento Society for the Blind, 1975-77; Partner, Sacramento Divorce Mediation Services, 1981-82; Instructor, California State University, Sacramento, 1975-82; Instructor, College of Notre Dame, Belmont, 1975-88; Art Therapist, Mental Health Counselor, Eskaton American River Mental Health Clinic, 1974-88; Instructor, University of Utah, 1988-. *Publications:* Article: A Historical Relationship Between Art Therapy and Art Education, 1976; Art Therapy with a Girl Who Lived in Two Worlds, 1978. *Memberships:* American Art Therapy Association; Northern California Art Therapy Association; California Coalition of Rehabilitation Therapists; National Art Education Association; American Association of Marriage and Family Therapists. *Honours:* Omicron Nu, Home Economics, Alpha Psi Omega, Drama, University of Maryland; Honorary Life Member, Northern California Art Therapy Association; Citation Award, California Parks and Recreation Society, Therapeutic Section; Certificate of Recognition, Alumnae Association of California State University, 1984. *Hobbies:* Painting; Visiting art galleries; Walking the dog; Golf; Swimming; Travelling. *Address:* 4124 American River Drive, Sacramento, CA 95864, USA.

DRAGNEA Emilia Irina Victoria, b. 29 Dec. 1941, Izvoarele-Prahova, Romania. Music Teacher. *Education:* Ciprian Porumbescu Music Academy, Bucharest, 1960-65; Shorthand Section 1971-73, English Language Section 1973-76, University Extension Scheme. *Appointments:* Teacher, vocal music, No. 21 School 1965-70, No. 70 School 1970-, Bucharest; Teacher, instrumental music (violin), No. 1 School, Bucharest, 1965-67. *Creative work:* Preparation, numerous children's musical formations, including large & chamber choirs, vocal-instrumental folk music groups 1976-83, vocal-instrumental group of French & English songs, vocal & instrumental soloists. *Memberships:* Romanian Music & Drawing Teachers Society; International Union of Anthropological and Ethnological Sciences (ICAES); National Jury, Children's Artistic Competition. *Honours:* 1st prize 1979 (children's folksong group), Honourable Mention 1983 (vocal-instrumental group, folk customs), 2nd prize 1985, 1987 (large chorus), numerous prizes Folkloric Flute Group, Children's National Artistic Competition (Republican Degree); Honour Diploma, National Pioneers Council. *Hobbies:* Literature; Tourism; Motoring. *Address:* Str. Popa Petre nr. 26A, Sector 2, Bucharest, Romania 70 249.

DRAGOESCU Serbana, b. 1 July 1943, Craiova, Romania. Fine Artist. *Education:* Fine Arts Institute Nicolae Grigorescu, Bucharest. *Appointment:* Freelance Artist. *Creative Works:* Tapestries; Graphical Works; Fashion Design; Art Deco. *Membership:* Union of Plastic Artists of Romania. *Honours:* Diploma, Quadrennial of Decorative Arts, 1978; 1st Prize, Decorative Arts Competition, 1979. *Hobbies:* Music; Literature; Sports. *Address:* 24 Turbinei Str., 71431 Bucharest 2, OP 30, Romania.

DRAHOS Leslie Ann, b. 12 Nov. 1942, USA. Business Press Editor. m. Dean F. Drahos, 8 June 1965. *Education:* BS, Case Western Reserve University. *Career:* Writer, assistant/associate Managing Editor, Printing Production & Newspaper Production magazines, 1971-74; Managing Editor, Veterinary Economics 1974-77, Handling & Shipping 1977-81; Editor, Government Prouct News, 1981-. *Memberships:* American Society of Business Press Editors; American Business Press; Cleveland Press Club; Sigma Delta Chi; American Public Works Association; National Park & Recreation Association; National Institute of Government Purchasing; American Correctional

Association; Women in Communications. *Honours:* 28 direct citations, writing/graphic excellence (current position). *Hobbies:* Contemporary art & architecture; Antiques; Travel; Films; Persian cats; Wild flowers; Bird watching; House plants. *Address:* 24000 Rainbow Drive, Olmsted Turnpike, Ohio 44138, USA.

DRAKE Joan Howard, b. Wallasey, Cheshire, England. Children's Author; Housewife. m. John Emyr Davies, 2 Jan. 1954. *Publications:* 20 books for young children; contributor to children's papers and to BBC. *Membership:* JP, 1970-85. *Hobbies:* Ballet; Dogs; Music; Cooking; Entertaining. *Address:* Castle Rock, 46 Marine Drive, Barry, South Glamorgan CF6 8QP, Wales.

DRAKE Mimi Kuo Cary, b. 15 Dec. 1947, Hong Kong. Real Estate Investment Banking. m. William Moffat Drake, 8 Aug. 1988. *Education:* AB, Radcliffe College, 1970. *Appointments:* Vice President, Grubb & Ellis, 1982-85; Senior Vice President, Bear, Stearns, 1985-87; Chief Executive Officer, The Amerin Group. *Publications:* Author of numerous articles in professional journals. *Memberships:* Urban Land Institute; Asian Business League; Commonwealth Club. *Hobbies:* Raise Arabian Horses; Abyssinian Cats; Harpsichord; Hunt upland game and waterfowl. *Address:* 41 Sutter Street Suite 1563, San Francisco, CA 94104, USA.

DRAPER Ellinor Elizabeth Nancy, b. 17 Feb. 1915, Oundle, Northants, England. Retired. m. (1) G A I D Draper, 5 Jan. 1940. divorced. (2) J D W Pearce, 20 Mar. 1964. 1 daughter, deceased. *Education:* Edgbaston Church of England College, Birmingham, England; Jena, Munich, Hamburg Universities. *Appointments:* Assistant Secretary, ASLIB (Information Management); Secretary to Managing Director, F C Pritchard, Wood & Partners (Advertising); Secretary to Managing Director, A C Neilson (Market research); Supervisor, Kent Education Committee; Head of Casework, Assistant General Secretary, National Association for Mental Health (MIND); General Secretary, ISTD (Institute for Scientific Treatment of Delinquency); General Secretary, British Italian Society; Secretary and Researcher, Lafitte Committee Family Planning Association; Consumers Association and Federation of Consumer Groups; Secretary & Investigator, Aves Committee on Volunteers in Social & Medical Services. *Publications:* Birth Control in the Modern World, 1965 and 1972; Conscience et Contrôle, 1971; Contributions to books and journals. *Memberships:* Howard League for Penal Reform; Int. Planned Parenthood Association; Researcher & Committee, Hampstead Consumers Group; Committee Member, CPRE, Hatfield Broad Oak; Chairman, Christchurch Area Neighbourhood Committee; Committee Member, Hampstead Conservation Area Advisory Committee. *Address:* Flat 28, 2 Barnton Avenue West, Edinburgh EH4 6EB, Scotland.

DRAPER Line Bloom (born Leopoldine Anne-Marie Voisin), b. Verviers, Belgium. Artist. m. (1) Nelson H. Bloom (deceased), (2) Glen C. Draper (dececeased), (3) Anthony Rubba, 25 Nov 1987. 1 son, 1st marriage. *Education:* Belgium: Ecole des Arts Decortifs, Verviers; Academie Royale, Tournai. USA: Bowling Green State University; Skowegan School of Art, Maine. *Creative work includes:* Painter, printmaker, engrosser-illuminator, enamallist. Over 50 solo exhibitions, Ohio & Florida, USA, 1952-; Numerous group touring exhibitions. Work in private collections throughout USA, also Boca Raton College & Community Hospitals, Florida; Cannon County Museum, North Carolina; Defiance College, Ohio; Eldercare, Delray Beach, Florida; International Institute, Toledo, Ohio; Miami Children Centre, Ohio; Stuart Historical Museum, Florida; Sylvania Country Club, Ohio. *Memberships include:* American Watercolour Society; Past President, Athena Art Society; English Speaking Union; Past local President, National League of American Pen Women; Navy League. *Honours:* Numerous awards & recognitions, various art exhibitions, 1955-. Most recent include: Honour award, Athena Art Society, Toledo, Ohio, 1978; 2nd award, Broward Art Guild, Florida,

1979; Honourable Mention, American Artists National Show, 1985; Florida State Distinguished Service Award, Boca Raton branch, National League of American Pen Women, 1986; 2nd award, College of Boca Raton, 1988. *Address:* 401 East Linton Boulevard 668, Delray Beach, FL 33483, USA.

DREIER Wanda Kay, b. 2 May 1949, Waterloo, Iowa, USA. Education- Elementary Counsellor. *Education:* BA, Junior High Education with Secondary Mathematics emphasis, University of Northern Iowa, 1971; MAT, Special education, Western New Mexico University, 1987. *Appointments:* Maths Teacher, Gregory, South Dakota, 1971-75; Maths Teacher, Wakpala, South Dakota, 1976-77; Teacher, Gallup-McKinley County Schools, Gallup, New Mexico, 1977-88; Counsellor, Lincoln Elementary School, Gallup, 1988-89. *Creative works:* Designed inservice Teaching Special needs Students in Regular Education Classrooms, 1988; Designed inservice Stress Reduction Techniques, 1982. *Memberships:* Association for Supervision and Curriculum Development; American Association for Counselling and Development; American School Counsellors Association; New Mexico School Counsellors Association; Council for Exceptional Children; Council for Children with Behavioural Disorders. *Hobbies:* Reading; Sewing; Hiking. *Address:* 310 Bortot No 6, Gallup, New Mexico 87301, USA.

DRELICH Iris M., b. 20 Feb. 1951, Israel. Pharmacist. m. Lee Drelich, 21 Aug. 1972, 2 sons. *Education:* BSc, Chemistry 1972, MEd 1974, University of Tel Aviv; BS, Pharmacy, Brooklyn College of Pharmacy, New York City, USA, 1978; Doctor of Pharmacy studies, South Eastern College of Pharmacy, Miami, Florida, current. *Appointments:* 2nd lieutenant, Israeli Army, 1969-73; Staff Pharmacist 1979-85, Director of Pharmacy 1985-, Plantation General Hospital, Florida, USA; Faculties, Broward Community College, South Eastern College of Pharmacy. *Memberships:* American, Florida, & East Central Societies of Hospital Pharmacists; Florida Pharmacists Association; Mortar & Pestle Society. *Hobby:* Painting. *Address:* Plantation General Hospital, 401 NW 42nd Avenue, Plantation, Florida 33317, USA.

DRESSEL Irene Emma Ringwald, b. 26 Oct. 1926, Enderlin, USA. Alcoholism and Family Therapist. m. Clarence Irvin Dressel, 13 Mar. 1946, divorced 1972, 1 son. *Education:* Certificate, Master Addiction Counsellor, North Dakota; Certificate, Chemical Dependency Counsellor. *Appointments:* Alcoholism Counselling Trainee, Heartview Foundation, 1974-75; Family Therapy Intern, 1975-76; Family Counsellor, 1976-77; Sup. Family Mems. Programme, 1978; Director, Consultation Dept., Johnson Institute, 1979-81; Associate Director, Chemical Dependency Unit, Presbyterian Hospital, Oklahoma City, 1981-83; Supervisor, Adolescent Counselling Staff, United Recovery Centre, Grand Forks, 1983-85; Director, Irene Dressel Counselling, 1985-. *Memberships:* Oklahoma and Kansas Alcoholism Counsellors Association; Oklahoma Association Alcoholism and Drug Abuse. *Address:* 1951 28th Ave. S, Apt. 303, Grand Forks, ND 58201, USA.

DRINKWATER Carol, b. 22 Apr. 1948, London, England. Actress; Author. *Education:* Holy Trinity Convent, Bromley, 1952-66; Diploma Drama, Drama Centre London Limited, 1967-70. *Appointments:* Performances include: Glasgow Citizens Theatre, 1971-72; National Theatre, 1973-74; Bristol Old Vic, 1975; Edinburgh Theatre, 1976; Lyric Theatre, London, 1984. Television and Film: A Clock-work Orange, Stanley Kubrick, 1971; The Shout, Jerzi Skolomowski, 1977; All Creatures Great and Small, BBC Television (3 series and 2 films), 1978-85; Sam, 1974; The Lady Killers, 1982; Tales of the Unexpected, 1983; Bouquet of Barbed Wire (2 series); Chicky (2 series), 1983 and 1984; Golden Pennies, 1984; The Haunted School (based on her first novel), 1986; Overseas Theatre: Tour of South East Asia for British Council. *Publication:* The Haunted School. *Memberships:* Greenpeace; World Wildlife Fund. *Honours:* Festival Fringe Award, 1976; Variety Club TV

Personality of Year, 1978. *Hobbies:* Travelling; Reading; Gardening; Scuba Diving.

DRINKWATER Penelope Ann, b. 26 July 1929, London, England. Wine Speaker; Writer. m. Hugh Michael Self, 24 June 1950, 2 daughters. *Education:* Rollins College, Winter Park, Florida, USA. *Appointments:* Tutored Tastings; Talks on Wine; Speaker, Luncheon Clubs, etc. *Publications:* To Set Before a King; Time for a Party; A Passion for Garlic, with Elaine Self. *Memberships:* Compagnons du Beaujolais; Trade Judge, International Wine Competitions; Circle of Wine Writers, Past Programme Secretary. *Hobbies:* Table Tennis; Reading; Theatre, Concert & Opera Going. *Address:* 59 Maresfield Garden, Hampstead, London NW3 5TE, England.

DRISKILL Mary Elizabeth, b. 28 May 957, Portsmouth, USA. Architect. *Education:* BSc., Architecture, University of Virginia, 1979; MArch., Columbia University, 1981. *Appointments:* Todd Williams & Assoc., New York City, 1979; hartman Cox Architects, washington, 1981; Visiting Lecturer, University of Virginia, 1982; Charles Scott Hughes & Associates, Washington, 1983; Microtecture Corp., Charlottesville, 1985; VMDO Architects, Charlesville, 1985; M.E. Driskill & Associates, Charlottesville, 1986-. *Memberships:* American Institute of Architects. *Honours:* Recipient, many honours & awards. *Hobbies:* Sports; Trail Riding; Fox Hunting; Show Jumping; Racing; Polo. *Address:* PO Box 381, Ivy, VA 22945, USA.

DRIVER Glenda Jewel, b. 28 Oct. 1951, Texas, USA. Social Worker. 1 daughter. *Education:* AA, Sacramento City College, 1980; BA, California State University, 1984; MSW, California State University, 1988. *Appointments:* Co-ordinator, Econ. Ops. programme, Albuquerque, 1965-66; Head Start Programme, Famrington, 1967-69; Office Supervisor, Sunrise Realty Mix, Sacramento, 1972-75; Assistant to Co-ordinator, Womens Research Centre, Sacramento, 1983-84; Adoptive Social Worker, Childrens Home Society, Sacramento, 1983-84; President, Chairman, Chief Executive Officer, Insight Communications Systems, 1986-. *Memberships:* Fellow, California State University; National Association for Female Executives; American Management Association; Centre for Entrepreneurial Management. *Hobbies:* Table Games; Bicycling; Reading; Art; Theatre. *Address:* Insight Communication Systems, 3000 Sunrise Blvd Suite 3, Rancho Cordova, CA 95670, USA.

DRUM Joan Marie, b. 31 Mar. 1932, Waseca, USA. Government Official. m. William Merritt Drum, 13 June 1954, I son, 1 daughter. *Education:* BA, University of Minnesota, 1962; MEd, College of William and Mary, 1975. *Appointments:* Government Official, Foreign Claims Branch, 1962-64; Freelance Writer, 1967-73; Educator, Newport News, 1975-79; Writer, Consultant, Drum Enterprises, 1980-82; Developer, trainee, US Army, 1982-86; Government Official, Army Training Support Centre, 1986-. *Publications:* Author, Ghosts of Fort Monroe, 1972; Travel for Children in Tidewater, 1974; Editor, Army newsletter for Families, 1968-73; contributor of articles to professional journals. *Memberships:* National Society for Performance Instruction; The Virginia Writers Club; National Association Government Communicators; Tidewater Writers Association; Kappa Delta Pi. *Honours:* Numerous awards including: North Shore Community Service Award, Hialeah, Hawaii, 1966; Home Bur Service Award, 1975; Service Award, Girl Scouts, US, Tokyo Japan. *Hobbies:* Writing; Volunteer Civic Service. *Address:* 9 Bray Wood, Williamsburg, VA 23185, USA.

DRUMMOND Alice, b. 21 May 1928, Providence, Rhode Island, USA. Actress. *Education:* BA English Literature, Brown University, 1950. *Appointments:* Appeared in numerous Broadway Plays including: The Ballad of the Sad Cafe, 1963; Malcolm; The Chinese; Thieves; Summer Brave; Some of my Best Friends; You Can't Take It With You; A Memory of Two Mondays;

Secret Service; Boy Meets Girl. Off Broadway productions include: Royal Gambit, 1959; The American Dream; The Carpenters; Wonderland; Sweet Bird of Youth, The Haymarket Theatre, London, England, 1985. Film appearances: Hide in Plain Sight; Ghostbusters; King of the Gypsies. *Honours:* Entrance Premium in Mathematics, Phi Beta Kappa in junior year, Elisha Benjamin Andrews Scholar, 1947, 1948, 1949, Brown University; Antoinette Perry Nomination for performance in The Chinese. *Address:* New York, NY 10022, USA.

DRUMMOND Willa Hendricks, b. 5 Dec. 1943, Harrisburg, Pennsylvania, USA. Neonatologist. *Education:* AB, Brown University, 1966; MD, University of Pennsylvania School of Medicine, 1970; Intern (Pediatrics), 1970-71, Resident (Pediatrics) 1971-72, Fellow (Pediatric Cardiology) 1972-74, Children's Hospital of Philadelphia. *Appointments:* Instructor in Pediatrics, University of Pennsylvania, 1973-74; Staff Pediatrician, Philadelphia General Hospital, 1973-74; Research Fellow (Perinatology), University of Oregon, 1974-75; Staff Pediatrician and Nursery Consultant, Kaiser-Permanente Clinics, 1975-76; Instructor in Residence and Fellow, Cardiovascular Research Institute, 1976-78, Fellow (Neonatology), 1977-78, University of California; Assistant Professor 1978-81, Affiliate Assistant Professor 1981, Associate Professor, Department of Pediatrics 1981-88, Associate Professor, Department of Physiology 1981-88, Associate Professor, College of Veterinary Medicine 1984-88, Professor, Departments of Pediatrics (Neonatology), Physiology and Veterinary Medical Sciences, 1988-, University of Florida. *Publications:* Several published poems; Numerous articles and abstracts published in professional journals; Chapters in Books; Over 60 lectures to conferences, in USA and England. *Memberships include:* Society for Pediatric Research; Southern Society for Pediatric Research; American Physiological Society; New York Academy of Sciences; American Association for the Advancement of Science; American Academy of Pediatrics, Section of Cardiology; American Health Association, Section of Pediatric Cardiology; Founder, International Society for Veterinary Perinatology; Southern Perinatal Association; Florida Society of Neonatal-Perinatologists; Alachua County (Florida) Medical Society. *Honours include:* Recipient of numerous scholarships and fellowships; Sigma Xi Election, 1965. *Hobbies:* Mountain climbing; Backpacking; Farming; Gardening; Scuba diving. *Address:* Box J 296, JHMHC, Department of Pediatrics, University of Florida College of Medicine, Gainesville, FL 32610, USA.

DRURY-GANE Margaret, b. 18 Nov. 1926, Toronto, Canada. Novelist. m. James Thomas Gane, 4 Oct. 1951. 3 sons, 1 daughter. *Education:* MA equivalent, English; Studied Politics and Music. *Appointments:* Senior Copywriter, T Eaton Co, 1948-55; Freelance Journalist, 1965-80; Contributing Editor, Weekend magazine, 2 years; Novelist. *Publications:* 9 Short stories including: A Few Words Before Dinner, Saturday Night magazine; Child's Book; Novels: Parade On An Empty Street, Blissland; Novel in progress. *Memberships:* The Writers' Union of Canada; Arts for Peace; Special interest in organizations dealing with feminist issues. *Hobbies:* Music, piano; Opera; Gardening; Good rock; Jazz; Interest in furthering and upgrading the status of women. *Address:* c/o The Writers' Union of Canada, 24 Ryerson Avenue, Toronto, Ontario, Canada, M5T 2P3.

DRYDEN Judy Canaday, b. 14 Dec. 1930, Elkhart, Kansas, USA. Supervisory Information System Management Specialist. m. Donald W Dryden, 6 May 1949. 2 sons, 1 daughter. *Education:* Iola Junior College, 1947-49; Northwestern State University, 1975. *Appointments:* Computer Systems Analyst, Management Information Systems Office, Fort Polk, 1970-74; Computer Specialist, Management Information Systems Office, Fort Dix, NJ, 1974-76; Computer Specialist, HQ US Army Training & Doctrine Command, Fort Monroe, Va., 1976-82; Chief, Customer

Services Branch, Data Processing Field Office, 1982; Chief, Customer Spt Div, 1982-83; Chief, Office Automation & Management Branch, 1983-85; Chief ADPE Accountability, Acquisition and Contracting, 1985-87; Chief, Logistics Spt Br, 1987-88. *Memberships:* International Platform Association; National Association of Female Executives; Association of the US Army; National Trust for Historic Preservation. *Honours:* Sustained Superior Performance Award, 1979; Outstanding Performance Award, 1981. *Hobbies:* Travel; Reading. *Address:* USAISC-DOIM, Attn: Atid Tol (Mrs Dryden), Fort Monroe, VA 23651, USA.

DUBERSTEIN Helen, b. 3 June 1926, New York City, USA. Writer. m. 10 Apr. 1949, 2 daughters. *Education:* BS, College of the City of New York, 1946. *Appointments:* Guest Lcturer: Manhatten Community College, 1987; Editorial Collective, Heresies, 1987-88; Liaison, PEN Outreach Committee, 1987. *Publications:* Eidos, 1985; Latucca, 1986; Audio-Visual, poetry, 1986; Earth's Daughters, 1986; & Then, 1987; Heresies, 1988;The Human Dimension; Arrived Safely; The Voyage Out; etc. *Memberships:* PEN; Poetry Socity of America; Dramatists Guild. *Address:* PO Box 134 Prince St. Station, New York City, NY 10012, USA.

DUBIE Maria Rudman, b. 1 Jan. 1938, Gary, Indiana, USA. Assistant Principal. m. Kenneth M Dubie, 18 June 1960. 1 daughter. *Education:* BA, Baldwin-Wallace College, 1961; MA, Ball State University, 1964; Prof Diploma, C W Post College. *Appointments:* English/Sp Teacher, N Olmsted, (Ohio) High School, 1961-; English/Sp Teacher, Perrysburg (Ohio) High School; English Teacher, Adams TWP (Ohio) Jr High School; English Reading Teacher 1968-80, Assistant Principal, 1988-, Weber Jr High School, Port Washington, New York; English Dept Chairperson, Sousa Jr High School, Port Washington, 1980-85; English Teacher, Pt Washington, 1985-87. *Memberships:* Association for Supervision & Curriculum Development (ASCD); National Association of Secondary School principals (NASSP); National Staff Development Council (NSDC); NASSP, Long Island; National Council of Teachers of English (NCTE). *Honours:* Presenter at local and state conferences on Team Teaching, Teaching Thinking in The Reading Program, Teaching Writing Through Social Studies, Credibility as a substitute, Assertive Discipline for Paraprofessionals; Awarded summer sabbatical from District. *Hobbies:* Jogging; Reading; Professional development. *Address:* Cedar Lane, Sands Point, NY 11050, USA.

DUBS Rosalind Vivienne, b. 6 July 1952, Newport, Gwent, Wales. Registrar, Australia National University. m. Andreas Dubs, 5 July 1978, 1 son, 1 daughter. *Education:* SCEGGS, Wollongong, 1969; BSc., Honours, Australian National University, 1973; Dr ès Sc., Université de Lausanne, Switzerland, 1977. *Appointments:* Secretary, CSIRO Institute of Physical Sciences, 1983-85; Registrar, Australian National University, 1985-. *Membership:* ACT Schools Authority Council, 1985-87. *Hobbies:* Music; Windsurfing. *Address:* 5 Galbu Place, Aranda, ACT 2614, Australia.

DUCKWORTH Carol Kay, b. 21 Apr. 1941, Wichita, Kansas, USA. University Administrator; Teacher. *Education:* BA, Oklahoma Baptist University, 1965; MSE, Education, Arkansas State University, 1975; Graduate Study, University of Arkansas, 1984-; Oklahoma State University, 1988-. *Appointments:* Midway High School Denton, 1965-69; Potosi High School, Potsoi, Missouri, 1969-72; Counselor, Green Forest High School, Harrison, Arkansas, 1972-74; Professor, Business Administration, Weatherford College, Weatherford, Texas, 1974-77; Director, Co-operative Education, North Arkansas Community College, Harrison, Arkansas, 1976-81; Assistant University Registrar, Kansas State University, 1981-83; Secondary Counsellor, Rogers High School, 1983-87; Business Professor, North Arkansas Community College, 1987; University Registrar, University of the Ozarks, 1987-88; Teacher Educator, Oklahoma State University, Stillwater, 1988-. Author, Business

Education Textbooks on individualised instruction & programmed instruction. *Memberships:* Phi Delta Kappa, Past President; Phi Beta Kappa, Past President; many other professional organisations. *Honours:* Recipient, many honours & awards. *Hobbies:* Oil Painting; Porcelain Dolls; Writing. *Address:* 350 North Giles, PO Box 434, Gentry, AR 72734, USA.

DUCORNET Rikki, b. 19 Apr. Canton, New York, USA. Writer; Illustrator. m. 24 June 1962, 1 daughter. *Education:* BA, Bard College, 1964. *Appointments:* Teaches Creative Writing, University of Denver, Autumn 1988-. *Publications:* Novels: The Stain, 1984; Entering Fire, 1987; The Fountains of Neptune, 1989; Short fiction: The Butcher's Tales, 1980; Haddock's Eyes, 1988; Poetry: From the Star Chamber, 1974; Wild Geraniums, 1975; Weird Sisters, 1976; Knife Notebook, 1977; The Illustrated Universe, 1979; The Cult of Seizure, 1989; Illustrations for Tlon, Ugubar, Orbis tertius (Jorge Luis Borges); Spanking The Maid (Robert Coover); others. *Honours:* Travel Grant, 1976, Publishing Grants, 1977, 1987, Ontario Arts Council; The Mary Ingram Bunting Institute, 1988; The Ingram Merrill Foundation, 1988; The Eben Demarest Trust, 1990. *Hobbies:* Ceramic sculpture; Lithography. *Address:* Atelier de la Jaleterie, 49260 Le Puy Notre Dame, France.

DUCOTE Marjorie Ellen Tate, b. 28 Oct. 1938, Chattanooga, Tennessee, USA. Research Chemist. m. (1) Calvin Cucksee, Jan. 1962, divorced 1978, 2 sons, 1 daughter, (2) Jere D. Ducote, 9 Aug. 1980, deceased 1986. *Education:* AB, University of Chattanooga, 1959; University of Tennessee, 1960; Doctoral candidate, Southeastern Institute of Technology. *Appointments:* Research & development chemist, Tennessee Eastman, 1961; Analytical Chemist, NNS & DD Company, 1962-64; Research chemist, solid rocket propellants, Army Missile Command, MICOM, Redstone Arsenal, Alabama, 1964-. *Creative work:* 36 scientific publications; 19 patents. *Memberships:* President, Federally Employed Women; President, Toastmistress, ADPA. *Honours:* Awards, science & engineering, US Army MICOM, 1970, 1979; Chemistry Awards, 1956, 1959; Mary Jane Hearn Award, 1984; Commanders Award, Civil Service, 1985. *Hobbies:* Ballroom dancing; Ju-jitsu & karate, 2nd degree black belt; Gardening; Parapsychology. *Address:* 2037 Bankhead Parkway, Huntsville, Alabama 35801, USA.

DU CROS Rosemary Theresa, Lady, b. 23 Sept. 1901, London, England. m. Sir Philip Du Cros, Nov. 1950. *Education:* Attended dancing classes of S Astafieva, Nicolas Legat and Ninette de Valois. *Appointments:* Dancing, 1924-33; Paris Life, Catlins Pierrots, Lavender; Army Co-operation (Flying), 1938-39; Ferry Pilot for RAF, 1939-46; Running own Air Taxi service Skytaxi, 1946-50. *Publications:* ATA girl, Memoirs of a Wartime Ferry Pilot; Contributions to The Aeroplane; Flight and other magazines. *Memberships:* Air Transport Auxiliary, 1939-46; Captain, Deputy CO, Hamble Ferry Pilots Pool; Dame President, Torrington Conservative Association, Vice Chairman 1959-71; Patron, Turridge & West Devon Conservative Assn, 1987-. *Honour:* MBE, 1946. *Hobbies:* Reading; Garden; Animal welfare societies. *Address:* Bocombe, Parkham, Bideford, Devon EX39 5PH, England.

DUCZMAL Agnieszka Elzbieta, b. 7 Jan. 1946, Krotoszyn, Poland. Conductor; Artistic Director. m. Jozef Jaroszewski, 6 May 1972, 1 son, 2 daughters. *Education:* Diplomas: Piano 1966, Flute 1968, Poznan Conservatory; Diploma, Conducting, Akademy of Music, 1971. *Appointments:* Founder, Chamber Orchestra, 1968-; Conductor, Poznan Opera House, 1972-81; Artistic Director, conductor, Chamber Orchestra of Polish Radio, 1977-; Assistant Conductor, State Philharmonic Society, Poznan, 1979-82. *Membership:* Society of Polish Musicians. *Honours:* Recipient, many honours & awards. *Hobby:* Gardening - Tropical Plants. *Address:* Chamber Orchestra of Polish Radio, ul. Strusia 10, 60-711 Poznan, Poland.

DUDEK Stephanie Z, b. 18 Dec. 1921, Lithuania. Professor. m. Louis Dudek, 16 Sept. 1944, 1 son. *Education:* BA, McGill University, 1943; MA, Columbia University, 1948; PhD, New York University, 1960. *Appointments:* New York Psychiatric Institute Research, 1947-49; Columbia Medical Centre, Staff Psychologist, 1950-58; Bellevue Medical Centre, Staff Psychologist, 1950-53; New York University, Instructor, 1956-58; Allan Memorial Institute, Montreal, Head, Clinical Psychology, 1960-69; Professor, University of Montreal, 1969-. *Publications:* numerous articles in professional journals & books. *Memberships:* American Psychological Association; Canadian Psychological Association. *Honours Include:* Founders Day Award, NYU, 1960; Canada Council Award, 1964; Award, Distinguished Contributions to the Profession of Psychology, Canadian Psychological Association, 1988. *Hobbies:* Swimming; Painting. *Address:* 3476 Vendome Ave., Montreal, Quebec, H4A 3M7, Canada.

DUDER Tessa, b. 13 Nov. 1940, Auckland, New Zealand. Writer. m. John Nelson Duder, 23 Apr. 1964, 4 daughters. *Appointments:* Auckland Star, 1959-64; Daily Express, London, 1964-66; Freelance Journalist, editor, 1979-. *Publications:* Childrens Books: Night Race to Kawau; Jellybean; Alex; The Story of Auckland; Waitemata - Aukland's Harbour of Sails; Spirit of Adventure; 3 educational school readers, short stories, magazine articles, *Memberships:* PEN; New Zealand Writers Guild; Childrens Literature Association. *Honours:* Silver Medal, Womens Butterfly (Swimming), Empire Games, Cardiff, 1958; Choysa Bursary for Childrens Writer, 1985; Alex, New Zealand Childrens Book of the Year, 1988, Esther Glen Medal, 1988. *Hobbies:* Music; Theatre; Sailing; Reading. *Address:* 94a Shakespeare Rd, Milford, Auckland, New Zealand.

DUE Jean Margaret Lucinda, b. 19 Sept. 1921, Peterborough, Ontario, Canada. Agricultural Economist. m. John Fitzgerald Due, 18 Aug. 1950. 2 sons. *Education:* BCom, University of Toronto, 1946; MSc 1950, PhD 1953, University of Illinois. *Appointments:* Dept of Agric, Ottawa, Canada, 1946-49; Res Assistant 1949-50, Visiting Professor 1965-70, Professor 1970-, University of Illinois, UC. *Publications:* Book: Costs, Returns and Repayment Experience of Ujamaa Villages in Tanzania 1973-76, 1980; More than 40 articles in refereed journals. *Memberships:* American Women in International Development; American Economic Assoc; American Agri Econ Association; International Agric Econ Association; YWCA. *Honours:* College of Agriculture Extension Award for recruiting, assisting and advising foreign students, 1985, 1987; Sigma Xi, Gamma Sigma Delta. *Hobbies:* Travel especially in Africa; Golf; Persons adversely affected in life. *Address:* 808 Dodds Dr, Champaign, IL 61820, USA.

DUERR Dianne Marie, b. 14 July 1945, Buffalo, New York, USA. Educator. *Education:* BS, SUNY College at Brockport, 1967; Premedical, Canisius College, 1971; Permanent teaching certificate, SUNY College at Oswego, 1982. *Appointments:* Educator, North Syracuse Central School District, 1967-; Project Director in Sports Medicine, SUNY Health Science Center, Syracuse, 1987-. *Creative works:* Creator of SUNY Sports Medicine and Human Performance Study Center; Creator of Scholastic Sports Injury Reporting Systems (SSIRS); Creator of Scholastic Head and Spine Injury Reporting System (SHASIRS). *Memberships:* American College of Sports Medicine; American Alliance of Health, Physical Education, Recreation and Dance; American Federation of Teachers; New York United University Professions; New York United Teachers; North Syracuse Teachers Association. *Hobbies:* Recreational sports: swimming, cycling, ice-skating; Reading; Photography; Music; Computers. *Address:* 8810 Woodside Drive, Clarence, New York 14031, USA.

DUERR-LEVINE Diane, b. 8 Mar. 1938, Tulsa, Oklahoma, USA. Marketing & Management Consultant. m. Matthew A. Levine, 9 June 1963, 1 son, 1 daughter. *Education:* BA, Mathematics, University of Michigan, 1960; MBA, Graduate School of Business, Columbia University. *Appointments:* various administrative positions: Lever Brothers, New York City, 1963-68; American Home Products Corportion, NYC, 1968-71; Honig-Cooper Herrington (now Foote, Cone Honig), San Francisco, 1971-72; Continental Airlines, Los Angeles, 1973-76; San Francisco Bay Area Transit District, 1976-78. Current: President & Founder, Institute for Health Management, 1978-; Professor, School of Business, San Francisco State University; President & Founder, DD-L Inc, 1982- *Publications:* Executive Edge, 1981; Vital Living After 50, 1982. Also: Large-print books for partially sighted, developed for Xerox Corporation. *Memberships:* Board, Greybridge Pacific Select Corporation; Resource Centre for Women: Northern California American Friends Service Committee; Business Advisory Committee, SFSU School of Business. *Honours:* Fellowship & grant, Columbia University Business School, 1961-63; Honorary member, Beta Sigma Gamma, SFSU; Achievement award, Direct Marketing Association; One of Top 100 advertising campaigns, Advertising Age. *Hobbies:* Reading; Skiing; Parenting; Horseback riding. *Address:* 6509 California Street, San Francisco, California 94121, USA.

DUFF Ann MacIntosh, b. Toronto, Canada. Artist. *Education:* Central Technical School, Toronto, 1943-46; Queen's University Summer School, 1944 and 1945. *Creative works:* Watercolourist and Printmaker. Works in may public collections in Canada, USA and Great Britain; Also in many corporate collections. *Memberships:* Royal Canadian Academy of Arts; Canadian Society of Painters in Water Colour; Print and Drawing Council of Canada. *Honours:* Queen Elizabeth Silver Jubilee Medal, 1977; Canadian Society of Painters in Water Colour, Honour Award, 1984; Curry Award, 1980, 1981; London Art Gallery Award, 1975. *Address:* 133 Imperial Street, Toronto, Canada M5P 1C7.

DUFFY Carol Ann, b. 23 Dec. 1955, Glasgow, Scotland. Poet. *Education:* BA, Honours, Philosophy, University of Liverpool, 1977. *Appointments:* Full Time Writer, C. Day Lewis Fellowship, 1982-84. *Publications:* Standing Female Nude, 1985; Selling Manhattan, 1987. *Honours:* Eric Gregory Award, 1983; Scottish Arts Council Book Award of Merit, 1985; Somerset Maugham Awardd, 1988. *Address:* 4 Camp View, London SW19 4UL, England.

DUGGAN Jacqueline Dacus, b. 25 Oct. 1956, El Paso, Texas, USA. Registered Music Therapist. m. Mark Nicolas Duggan, 22 Aug. 1981. *Education:* BSc., Music Therapy, Texas Woman's University, 1980. *Appointments:* Denton State School, 1980; Fort Worth State School, 1981-83; Music/Art Teacher, St John the Apostle Catholic Day School, 1983-84; Music Therapist, Private Practice, Bedford 1985-88, San Antonio, 1988-; Preschool Music Teacher, Piano, Organ, Theory, Alamo Music, 1989-. *Publications:* Development of Music Theory Games, Puzzle Match; Music Moves, 1987-88. *Memberships:* NAMT; National Association for Music Therapy; Fort Worth Music Teachers Association, Historian, 1986; Mid Cities Music Teachers, Charter Member. *Honours:* Arion Foundation Award, 1976; Feature Speaker, Fort Worth Music Teachers Association, 1986; Guest Speaker, Arlington Music Teachers Association, 1986. *Hobbies Include:* Equine Geriatrics; Life Science; Wildlife Conservation; Child Development. *Address:* 501 Val Oak Court, Hurst, TX 76053, USA.

DUGGAN Julia Ann, b. 11 May 1960, Denver, Colorado, USA. Treasurer. *Education:* Certificate of Financial Management, Certificate, Oil and Gas, University of Denver, 1985. *Appointment:* Treasurer, Duggan Petroleum Co., 1980-. *Memberships:* Denver Chamber of Commerce; Republican Party, Precinct Chairman. *Hobbies:* Reading; Cooking; Stained Glass; World History; Animals. *Address:* 4495 So Santa Fe Drive, Englewood, CO 80110, USA.

DUGGIN Lorraine Jean, b. 21 Sept. 1941, Omaha, Nebraska, USA. Lecturer, Writer. m. (1) Jack Kiscoan, 19 Dec. 1964, divorced 1974, 1 son, 1 daughter. (2) Richard C Duggin, 16 July 1977, divorced 1983. *Education:* BA English, University of Omaha, 1965; MA English, University of Nebraska, Omaha, 1979; PhD English/Creative Writing, University of Nebraska, Lincoln, 1988. *Appointments:* Coordinator of Special Projects and Instructor, University of Nebraska, Omaha Writer's Workshop, 1974-82; Assistant to President, Bellevue College, 1983-85; Artist in Residence, Nebraska Arts Council, 1983-89; Lecturer, Creighton University English Department, Omaha. *Publications:* Numerous stories, poems, essays and articles including: Translations From the Mother Tongue; Wintering at Home; Thursday's Child. *Memberships:* Associated Writing Programs; Nebraska Writer's Guild; Nebraska Council of Teachers of English; Teachers and Writers Collaborative; Metropolitan Arts Council. *Honours:* John R Vreeland Graduate Award in Writing, University of Nebraska, 1981; First Prize, Academy of American Poets, 1982; Nominee, Pushcart Prize IX, 1984; First Prize, Mari Sandoz Prairie Schooner Fiction Award, University of Nebraska, 1984; Golden Poet, World of Poetry, 1987; Maude Hammond Fling Fellowship, University of Nebraska, 1986-87; Stanislav Serpan Scholarship for Czech Studies, 1987. *Hobbies:* Reading; Walking; Music; Travel. *Address:* 932 North 74th Avenue, Omaha, Nebraska 68114, USA.

DUKAKIS Olympia, b. 20 June 1931, Lowell, Massachusetts, USA. Actress. m. L Zorich, 28 Nov. 1961. 2 sons, 1 daughter. *Education:* BSc 1951, MFA 1957, Boston University. *Career:* Actor, Founder, Charles Playhouse, Boston, 1958; Actor, Founder, Buzzards Bay, Cape Cod, 1957; Actor, Founding Member, Eggertown Playhouse, Martha's Vineyard, 1959; Master Teacher New York Unviversity; Visiting Instructor, Yale University, Sarah Lawrence College; Director of numerous plays in New York City and regional theatre; Has appeared in over 120 plays on Broadway, Off-Broadway, national tours, regional theatres and summer stock; Has played at the American Place Theatre and Circle Repertory, Phoenix; Featured Co-star in over 50 films; Artistic Director of the Whole Theatre, Montclair, New Jersey for 7 years. *Memberships:* Actors Equity; Screen Actors Guild; AFTRA; New Jersey Humanities Coalition; Board Member, Women in Theatre. *Honours:* OBIE Award for Man is Man; OBIE Award for The Marriage of Bette and Boo; World Theatre Award for A View From a Bridge; CLIO Award for H and R Block Commercial with Henry Winkler; New England Fencing Champion. *Hobbies:* Ecology; History of Religion. *Address:* Montclair, New Jersey, USA.

DUKES Dorothy, b. 24 Jan. 1926, Birmingham, Alabama, USA. Law Church Worker. m. Leonard Dukes, 11 Mar. 1957. 2 daughters. *Education:* Graduate, Detroit Bible College, 1976. *Appointments:* Owner, Dorothy Dukes House of Coiffure, Detroit, 1957-; Evangelist 1965, State ean Sunday School Department 1969-71, Chairman of Lay Delegation to International Sunday School Convention 1971, International Coordinator of Sunday School Convention Pageant 1974, Chairman Education Committee of South West Michigan District 9, 1982-; Public Relations Director, Baileys Temple, 1976, Church of God in Christ. *Memberships:* Women's Conference of Concern, 1974; National Council of Negro Women, 1974; Board of Directors, Charles Harrison Mason Systems of Bible College, Detroit, 1972; Southwest Michigan State Director 1968, Business and Professional Womans Federation; International Platform Society; Democratic Association; President Scholarship program, 1984, Public Relations Committee 1986, Second Ecclesiastical Jurisdiction of Southwest Michigan, Editor COGIC Womens Magazine 1973, COGIC. *Honours:* Honorary DH, Trinity Hall College, 1981; Religious Workers Guild Honorium Award, Church of God in Christ, 1982. *Address:* 4181 Burns Drive, Detroit, MI 48214, USA.

DUKES Rebecca Weathers (Becky), b. 21 Nov. 1934, Durham, North Carolina, USA. Singer; Songwriter; Entertainer. m. Charles Aubrey Dukes Jr, 20 Dec. 1955, 2 sons, 1 daughter. *Education:* BA, Duke University, 1956; Licensed Elementary School Teacher; Vocal student of Todd Duncan. *Career:* Teacher: Durham City Schools, North Carolina, 1956-57, Arlington County Schools, Virginia, 1958-59; Secretary, USMC, Arlington, 1957-58; Office Manager, Dukes and Kooken, Landover, Maryland, 1976; Musical Performer, Washington DC, Virginia, Maryland, 1982-; Pianist, Vocalist, Back Alley Restaurant Lounge, 1982; Presented A Life Cycle in Song orginal programme, throughout mid-Atlantic states and Washington; Operatic solo recital, 1983; Frequent performer, private functions and public events, venues include Capitol Center, George Washington University, Chateau de La Gesse, France, Andrews Air Force Base, Sigma Alpha Iota; Operatic solo concert with pianist Glenn Sales, 1985; Benefit appearances for: National Symphony Orchestra, 1984, Prince George's Civic Opera, 1985, University of Maryland Concert Series, 1986, 1987; Currently singing at Four Ways Bermuda Lounge, Washington DC. *Creative works:* Over 70 copyright songs including: Between the Lovin' and the Leavin'; Covers of My Mind; Gentle Thoughts; Headin' Home Again; I Would Like To Be Reborn; Miss You; Tears; You Played a Part in My Life; Pottery, collection of 32 poems. *Memberships:* Past President, National Capitol Law League, Washington DC; Women's Committee, National Symphony; Executive Committee, Duke University Annual Fund; International Platform Association; Riversdale Presbyterian Church, Deacon, President, Women's Group, 1968-70; Songwriters Association, Washington DC; William Preston Few Association, Duke University. *Honours:* Honorary Trustee, Prince George's (MD) Arts Council, 1984; Winner, American Women Composers Song Contest, 1986; Many other song contest awards; Friend of Year Award, University of Maryland Summer Institute, 1986. *Address:* 7111 Pony Trail, Hyattsville, MD 20782, USA.

DU LAC Lois Arline, b. 17 July 1920, Ohio, USA. Professional Writer. m. Leo Joseph Du Lac, 20 Apr. 1941, 3 sons, 2 daughters. *Education:* BA cum laude 1942, MA 1962, University of California, Los Angeles; JD, Western State University, 1982. *Appointments:* Various schools, California, 1962-69. *Publications include:* Contribution, Professor Vincent Schmieder's Constitutional Law, 3rd edition; Short story, in Murder California Style (anthology); Various other works, prose & poetry. *Memberships include:* Mystery Writers of America. *Honours:* Phi Beta Kappa, also German & classics honorary societies, 1941; Dean's Honour Roll, Western State University College of Law, 1981. Poetry awards: Honourable Mention, The Writer, 1972; 5th California, American Association of University Women, 1959; 8th place, California Chaparrel Poets & City of Sierra Madre, 1969; 4th place, California Writers Guild, 1973. *Hobbies:* Reading; Cooking; Gardening; Singing. *Address:* PO Box 3301, Hesperia, California 92345, USA.

DULEBOHN Diana Gay, b. 2 Feb. 1950, Lima, Ohio, USA. Attorney. m. William Joe Dulebohn, 17 Oct. 1969. 2 sons, 1 daughter. *Education:* BS, cum laude, Ohio State University, 1977; JD, Ohio Northern University College of Law, 1980. *Appointments:* Instructor, Business Law & Real Estate Law, Lima Technical College, 1979-82; Assistant Domestic Relations Investigator, Auglaize County Common Pleas Court, 1984-86; Private Practice, Attorney, 1980-; Village Solicitor, Village of Waynesfield, Ohio, 1984-; Democratic Candidate, Court of Appeals Judge for the Third Judicial District of Ohio. *Honours:* Phi Kappa Phi National Honour Society, 1977; Ohio Northern University Scholarships; Ohio State University Scholarships. *Hobbies:* Painting; Writing; The Environment; The American justice system; The Church. *Address:* 215 West Mulberry St, Waynesfield, OH 45896, USA.

DUMAS Sandra Lee, b. 27 Mar. 1957, Malone, New York, USA. Personnel Manager. *Education:* Associates Degree, University of NY Canton ATC, Canton, NY, 1976;

Tunxis Community College, Farmington Ct, 1977-81. *Appointments:* Business Clerk, Alice Hyde Memorial Hospital, Malone, New York, Summer 1972; Receptionist, Northwest Enterprises, Malone, Fall 1972; Receptionist/Secretary, Summer 1973; Time Study Estimator, part-time 1974-76; Production Control Clerk, 1976-77; Personnel Assistant, 1977-79; Assistant Personnel Manager, 1979-82; Personnel Manager, 1982-, Wasley Products, Inc.; Consultant, Wasley Lighting, 1982-; Consultant, Precision Molding, 1985-; Consultant, Hi-Tech Precision Machining Inc, 1987-88; Consultant, Eastern Plastics, 1987-88. *Memberships:* National Association for Female Executives; American Society for Personnel Administration; International Foundation of Employee Benefit Plans; Manufactuers of Hartford County; National Safety Council; Connecticut Business and Industry Association; Board of Directors, 1985-, Campaign Chairperson, 1987-88, United Way of Plainville; Board of Directors, Wheeler Clinic, Inc, 1984-88; Trustee, United Auto Workers Local 376 Welfare Fund, 1984-; Crisis Intervention Counsellor, HELP LINE, 1983-84; Rape Crisis Counselor/Advocate, YWCA, 1984-85; Strike Back Against Crime Representative, 1984-; Consultant (Teaching Instructor) Junior Achievement, Project Business Plainville, 1986; Advisor, Cooperative Work Experience, Bristol Eastern High School, 1982-85. *Honors:* Student Advocate, Bristol Cooperative Work Experience Program, Bristol Eastern High School, 1984; Outstanding Young Woman Award, Jaycee Women Bristol, 1984; CT Outstanding Young Citizens Award, WFSB Channel 3/CT Jaycees, 1985; Proclamation Mayor, City of Bristol, 1985. *Hobbies:* Bowling; Ceramics. *Address:* Wasley Products, Inc., Plainville Industrial Park, Plainville, CT 06062, USA.

DUNAWAY Faye, b. 14 Jan. 1941, Bascom, Florida, USA. Actress. *Education:* US Army Schools in Texas, Arkansas, Utah and Mannheim, Germany; University of Florida; Boston University of Fine Applied Arts. *Appointments:* Appeared on New York Stage in: A Man for All Seasons, After the Fall (with Lincoln Center Repertory Co., 3 years), Hogan's Goat; Films Include: The Happening; Bonnie and Clyde; Hurry Sundown; The Thomas Crown Affair; The Extraordinary Seaman; A Place for Lovers; The Arrangement; Puzzle of a Downfall Child; Little Big Man; Doc; Oklahoma Crude; The Three Musketeers; Chinatown; The Towering Inferno; The Four Musketeers; Three Days of the Condor; Network; Voyage of the Damned; Eyes of Laura Mars; The Champ; The First Deadly Sin; Mommie Dearest; The Wickeder; Beverly Hills Madam; Casanova. *Honours:* Best Actress, Academy Nomination for Bonnie and Clyde, 1967; Most Promising Newcomer, British Academy, for Bonnie and Clyde, 1967; Best Actress Academy Nomination, for Chinatown, 1974; Best Actress Academy Award, for Network, 1976. *Address:* c/o William Morris Agency, 151 El Camino, Beverly Hills, CA 90212, USA.

DUNBAR Marilyn L Nurse, b. 12 Apr. 1939, Atlantic City, USA. Teacher. Divorced 4, sons, 1 daughter. *Education:* BA, Glassboro College, 1978; Teacher of the Handicapped, Rutgers Sate College, 1986-87. *Appointments:* Teacher of Handicapped: Merchantville, 1979, Atlantic County Board of Elections, 1975-78, Pine Hill Board of Education, 1980-; Tutor, Physically Sick Children, 1982-. *Publication:* Who Will Win? *Memberships:* NJEA; Red Cross Blood Bank; Heart Association. *Honours:* Outstanding Young Women of America, 1976; Deans list, 1976; Foster Parent Society Haitian Refugees Award, 1983. *Hobbies:* Reading; Dancing; Horticulture; Skiing. *Address:* 22 Villanova Court, Sicklerville, NJ 08081, USA.

DUNCAN Frances Mary (Sandy), b. 24 Jan. 1942, Vancouver, Canada. Authors. 2 daughter. *Education:* BA, 1962, MA 1963, University of British Columbia. *Publications:* Cariboo Runaway, 1976; Kap-Sung Ferris, 1977; The Toothpaste Genie, 1981; Dragonhunt, 1981; Finding Home, 1982; Amanda et le Genie, 1984; Pattern Makers, 1989; Contributor to professional journals & magazines. *Memberships:* Writers Union of Canada; Federation of British Columbia Writers; PEN International; Canadian Association of Childrens Authors, Illustrators Performers. *Address:* c/o Writers' Union of Canada, 24 Ryerson Ave., Toronto, Ontario Canada M5T 2P3.

DUNCAN Joan A., b. 8 Sept. 1939, Butte, Montana, USA. Businesswoman. *Education:* Syracuse University, New York, 1957-58; Carroll College, Helena, Montana, 1958-67; University of Montana, 1968; Montana Tech, Butte, 1960. *Appointments include:* Teacher, librarian, St Mary's of the Mount High School, 1962-67; Camp director, ibid, 1964-67; Assistant Dean of Women, Carroll College, 1961-69; Director, Foster Grandparent programme 1969-75; Chief, Womens Bureau, Montana Department of Labour & Industry, 1975-81; Owner, Topflight Executive Assistance; Sales Associate, Hennessys department store, 1981-; Administrative assistant, Office of Political Practices, State of Montana, 1986; Chief bills clerk, Senate, Montana State Legislature, 1985-88; Executive director, Helena Food Share Inc, 1987-. *Creative works:* Contributor, newsletters; Creator, producer, hostess, several local TV programmes, statewide radio programme. *Memberships include:* Local & State offices, American Women in Radio & TV; Board, Model City; Regional & State representative, NISC/National Council on Ageing; Board, United Way; Economic Development Blue Ribbon Study Commission, Campaign for Human Development; Advisory council, Region VIII, Small Business Administration; Numerous other civic & community organisations & offices. *Honour:* Elected City Commissioner, Helena, Montana, 1981-85. *Hobbies:* Collecting pottery; Attending antique & art auctions; Skiing. *Address:* 712 Harrison, Helena, Montana 59601, USA.

DUNDON Margo Elaine, b. 3 July 1950, Cleveland, Ohio, USA. Museum Director. *Education:* BS Communications, cum laude, Ohio University, 1972; Currently studying for MLS in Museology, University of Oklahoma. *Appointments:* General Staff 1974-75, Education Coordinator, 1976-78, Co-director, 1979-87, Director, 1988-, Grout Museum of History & Science. *Memberships:* President, 1984-86, Iowa Museum Assoc; President, 1988-, Midwest Museums Conference; Regional Councillor, 1988-, American Association of Museums, AAM Museum Assessment Program, site surveryor, 1982-; AAM Accreditation Examiner, 1987-; Chairperson, City of Waterloo Historic Preservation Commission, 1987-. *Honours:* Scholarship 1979 and 1986, American Law Institute; American Bar Assoc seminar, Legal Problems of Museum Administration; Mayor's Volunteer Performance Award for Outstanding Community Service, 1983; My Waterloo Days Leadership Award, 1982. *Hobbies:* Snorkling, Scuba Diving; Personal computers; Museum consultant. *Address:* Grout Museum of History & Science, 503 South Street, Waterloo, Iowa 50701, USA.

DUNDONALD Ann Margaret, (The Dowager Countess of) b. 3 Aug. 1924, Jerusalem, Palestine. m. C.F.E. Stalb, 21 Oct. 1949, divorced, (2) The Earl of Dundonald, 15 July 1978. *Education:* Diploma, Business Studies. *Appointments:* WVS, 1940-43; Womens Royal Naval Service, 1943-46. *Memberships:* Anglo Chilean Society, General Committee; Anglo Peruvian Society, Chairman, Ladies Committee. *Hobbies:* Painting; Travel; Archaeology. *Address:* Lochnell Castle, Ledaig, Argyll, Scotland.

DUNETZ Lora Elizabeth, b. New York, USA. Occupational Therapist, Registered. *Education:* MA, Education of the Exceptional, Teachers College, Columbia University, 1943; Certificate in Occupational Therapy, NYU, 1945; Diplome, Ecole de Hautes Etudes, PAU, France, 1962. *Appointments:* Occupational Therapist, University Hospital, Baltimore, Maryland, 1947-57; 10 years as Occupational Therapist, Special Schools, Maryland; Teacher of French, 4 years; Teacher of Retarded, 3 years. *Publications:* Poetry: Recent collections: To Guard Your Sleep and other poems, 1987; Editorial staff, poetry magazine, Without Halos; Contributor of articles to numerous publications.

Memberships: American Occupational Therapy Association; New Jersey Occupational Therapy Association; Poetry Society of America; New Jersey Poetry Society; American Legion. *Honours:* Lyric Memorial Award (Poetry), 1982; Kellogg Foundation Grants, 1945. *Interest:* Poetry. *Address:* Box 113, Whiting, NJ 08759, USA.

DUNHAM Patricia Ann Garvey, b. 13 May 1948, Jersey City, USA. Educator. m. David W. Dunham, 21 July 1973, 1 son, 1 daughter. *Education:* BA, 1976. *Appointments:* National Employment Exchange, 1967-71; Teacher, Jersey City Board of Education, 1971-. *Publications:* various journals. *Memberships:* Jersey City Education Association; Hudson County Education Association; National Education Association; Parents Council of Jersey City, Official President of Chapter 30, 1981-. *Honours:* Recipient, various honours and awards. *Hobbies:* Reading; Crochet; Embroidery; Music; Ceramics; Country Crafts. *Address:* 30 Linden Avenue, Jersey City, NJ 07305, USA.

DUNLAP Emma Magdalene, b. 14 Mar. 1933, Greenville, Ohio, USA. Registered Nurse. *Education:* Diploma, Miami Valley Hospital School of Nursing, 1954; BS Ed 1973, MEd 1978, University of Cincinnati; Psychology and Counseling, Graduate School, University of Dayton. *Appointments:* Staff Nurse, MVH, Dayton, 1954-55; Staff RN 1955, Supervisor & ICN, simultaneously, Instructor Pharm, LPN Dayton Night School & Greenville Schools, DON & In-Ser Education, 9 years, Coor Pt Comm Health Education & Emp Health, 1982-, Wayne Hospital, Greenville. *Memberships:* Delta Kappa Gamma; Kappa Delta Pi; AAUW; University Women-Darke Co; VFW 7262 Ladies Auxiliary; Sec, Western Ohio American Association; Diab Educators; Board, numerous community service organizations. *Honours:* Nurse of Hope, American Cancer Society, 1986 and 1987; Distinguished Voluntary Leadership, March of Dimes, 1985, 1987, 1988, 1989; Appreciation Plaque, Wayne Hospital Medical Staff, 1985. *Hobbies:* Collecting salt and pepper shakes; Travelling; Shopping; Watching football; Basketball; Horse racing (harness). *Address:* P O Box 406, Greenville, Ohio 45331, USA.

DUNLAP Estelle Cecilia Diggs, b. 26 Sept. 1912, Washington, DC, USA. Educator; Mathematician. m. Lee Alfred Dunlap, 16 May, 1941. 2 daughters. *Education:* Teachers College, District of Columbia, 1933-37; BS 1937, MS, Howard University, 1940; Postgraduate, Catholic University; Federal City College, 1954-62. *Appointments:* Instructor and Head of Mathematics Department, Garnet-Patterson Junior High School, 1941-56; Mathematics and Science Instructor, MacFarland Junior High School, 1956-72; Visiting lecturer of Mathematics, District of Columbia Teachers College, 1963. *Publications:* Contributor: Talent Magazine; Atoms for Peace Exhibit. *Memberships include:* National Council of Teachers of Mathematics; American Mathematical Society; Benjamin Banneker Mathematics Club (Vice president); American Association for the Advancement of Science; Society for Industrial and Applied Mathematics; National Defense Preparedness Association; National Educational Association; American Association of Retired Persons; Member of over 40 other associations and societies. *Honours include:* Mathematics Fellowship, Howard University, 1938-40; National Science Foundation Fellowship, 1959-62; Cultural Doctorate, World University, 1982; Certificates of Appreciation: Superior Court of District of Columbia, 1971, United States District Court, 1975, Institute for American Strategy, Young Americas Foundation; Honorary Doctorate, International University Foundation, 1985; Bronze Medal Award, Albert Einstein International Academy, 1985; Executive Life Representative, World Institute of Achievement, 1985; World Culture Prize, Italian Academia, 1984. *Hobbies:* Bowling; Reading; Playing musical instruments, especially piano. *Address:* 719 Shepherd Street, NW, Washington, DC 20011, USA.

DUNLOP Carol Elizabeth, b. 22 Apr. 1945, Andover,

Massachusetts, USA. Structural integration practitioner (Rolfer); Cranial/Sacral Therapist. *Education:* BS, Education 1967, BS, Specialized Education, 1967, Tufts University; Certified Rolf Practitioner, 1979; Cranial/Sacral Therapist, Upledger Institute, 1987. *Appointments:* Head of Department, Specialized Education, Katerine Burke School, 1967-70; Head of Department, Specialized Education, International School of Rome, 1970; Owner, Safari Co Kenya, East Africa, specializing in Educational Safaris; Advanced Rolf Practitioner, Kenya, East Africa, 1979-88. *Membership:* Rolf Institute, Boulder, Colorado. *Honour:* Member of group invited by Chinese Government to lecture/demdonstrate structural integration work in five major cities in China under auspices of Medical Services, 1983. *Hobbies:* Organized Film Society, Nairobi, Kenya; Run a small furniture factory making tables, etc from tree roots; Restore antique cars, especially upholstery; Osteopathic work on Racehorses; Horses; Tennis; Most general sports. *Address:* Box 30181 Muthaiga Club, Nairobi, Kenya, East Africa.

DUNLOP Eileen, b. 13 Oct. 1938, Alloa, Scotland. Teacher; Children's Writer. m. Antony Kamm, 27 Oct. 1979. *Education:* Diploma with distinction in Primary Education, Moray House College of Education, Edinburgh, 1959. *Appointments:* Teacher, Eastfield School, Penicuik, and Sunnyside School, Alloa, 1959-79; Headmistress, Preparatory School, Dollar Academy, Dollar, 1980-. *Publications:* Robinsheugh, 1975; A Flute in Mayferry Street, 1976; Fox Farm, 1978; The Maze Stone, 1982; Clementina, 1985; The House on the Hill, 1987; The Valley of Deer, 1989. *Memberships:* PEN Scottish Centre. *Honours:* Runner-up, Austrian State Book Prize, Fox Farm, 1978; Scottish Arts Council Book Awards for The Maze Stone, 1983, Clementina, 1986; Commended by the Library Association, Carnegie Medal, for The House on the Hill, 1987. *Hobbies:* Gardening; Theatre. *Address:* 46 Tarmangie Drive, Dollar, FK14 7BP, Scotland.

DUNLOP Joan Banks, b. 20 May 1934, London, England. Chief Executive Officer. m. Edwin A. Deagle, 27 Sept. 1980. *Appointments:* Secretary, Administrative Assistant, BBC, Associated Rediffusion TR, Ford Foundation, New York City Government, 1952-70; Associate of John D. Rockefeller 3rd, 1973-78; Assistant to President, New York Public Library, 1981-84; President, International Women's Health Coalition, 1984-. *Memberships:* Community Family Planning Council, Board Member; Hampshire College, National Advisory Council. *Hobbies:* Reading; Travel; Tennis; Gardening. *Address:* International Women's health Coalition, 24 East 21st Street, New York, NY 10010, USA.

DUNN Carol Fischer, b. 5 Nov. 1952, White Plains, New York, USA. Chiropractic Physician. m. Alan S. Dunn, 30 Aug. 1980. *Education:* BS Honours, Environmental Sciences, University of California, Berkeley, 1975; Doctor of Chiropractic, Logan College of Chiropractic, 1985. *Appointments:* Entrepreneur, 1976-80; Chiropractic assistant, 1981; Assistant Coordinator, Dellwood Health Centre, Logan College, 1985; Private practice, 1985-. *Memberships:* Amerian Chiropractic Association (& past offices, student body); Fellow, International Academy of Clinical Acupuncture; Omega Sigma Phi. *Honours:* Special recognition, Logan College, 1985; Honour Students Society, University of California, 1975; National Board of Chiropractic Examiners, 1984. *Hobbies:* Gardening; Skiing; Cycling; Swimming; Reading. *Address:* 3234 Candelaria NE, Albuquerque, New Mexico 87107, USA.

DUNN Jennifer Blackburn, b. 29 July 1941, Seattle, Washington, USA. Political Worker. 2 sons, *Education:* BA, Stanford University, 1959-60, 1962-63; University of Washington, 1960-62. *Appointments:* International Business Machines Corporation (IBM), 1964-65; Freelance systems analyst, 1965-70; Department of Assessments, King County, Washington, 1978-80; Chairman, Washington State Republican Party, 1980-89. *Memberships:* Sustaining member, Junior League,

Seattle; Metropolitan Opera National Council; Vice chairman, Western Region, & chairman of chairmen, Republican National Committee. *Honours:* Delegate, Republican National Conventions, 1980, 1984, 1988; Cathedral Fellow in World Affairs, 1983-84; Shavano Summit Award, national leadership, Hillsdale College, 1984; US delegate, 30th United Nations Commission on Status of Women, Vienna, Austria, 1984; Delegation member, Conservative Party conference, Blackpool, UK 1985, Kuomintang convention, Taipei, Taiwan 1988: Presidential appointee, President's Advisory Councils, Voluntary Service, & Historic Preservation. *Hobbies:* Reading political novels; Tennis. *Address:* Bellevue, Washington, USA.

DUNN Patrice Marie, b. 19 Aug. 1956, Scott, USA. Consultant; Writer. m. Dr S. Thomas Dunn. *Education:* BS, University of Wisconsin, 1978; MR, San Francisco State, 1983. *Education:* Production Editor, Medical Self Care Journal, 1978-82; Senior Editor, Computer Graphics World Magazine, 1982; Vice President, DTI, 1985-. *Publications:* Articles in: Digital Portfolio; etc; Collection of Digital Imagery; Tiger Eye, 1 Act Play. *Memberships:* Technical Association of the Graphic Arts; American Institute of the Graphic Arts; Art Directors Club; Charter Member, National Museum of Women in the Arts; Association of Computing Machinery. *Honours:* Wisconsin Academy of Arts Letters & Sciences Short Story Award, 1974; American Film Institute Award, 1981. *Hobbies:* Gardening; Photography; Hiking; Swimming. *Address:* 2090 Casa de Vereda, Vista, CA 92084, USA.

DUNN Sandra Puncsak, b. 28 May 1946, Melbourne, Australia. University Administrator. m. Roger A. Dunn, 24 Feb. 1983. *Education:* USA BA, Environmental Design, University of California, Berkeley, 1968; MA, Special Education, San Francisco State University, 1970; MA, Counselling & Guidance, Lewis & Clark College, 1974; Further studies, various institutions. *Appointments:* Various personnel offices, Oregon, Washington DC, California, 1973-85; Assistant Executive Director for Consumer Affairs, Dallas Area Rapid Transit, 1985-; Associate Vice President, University Relations, Southern Methodist University, 1987-. *Memberships include:* Past President, California State Council on Vocational Education; Past Chair, Governor's Task Force on Youth Employment; Board, American Diabetes Association; Board, US Film Festival, Dallas; Leadership Texas, 1987. *Honours:* Various awards, marketing & public relations, including: Presidential White House Award, & White House Fellows finalist, 1984; Community Relations Gold Award, 1984; Twin Award, Women in International Industry, YWCA, 1983; 3 Matrix Awards, 1987-89; Semi-finalist, Outstanding Young Working Woman, Glamour magazine; Grand Gold Award, Case, 1989; Biographical recognition. *Hobbies:* Tennis; Skiing; Travel; Reading. *Address:* 7702 Marquette Street, Dallas, Texas 75225, USA.

DUNNE Diane Cantine, b. Milwaukee, USA. Advertising Executive. 1 son. *Education:* BS, Marquette University, 1970; MBA, New York University, 1985. *Appointments:* Manager, Advertising, NBC, 1975-77; Director, Marketing Communication, CBS, 1977-81; Director, Bloomingdale's, 1981-. *Publications:* Guidelines to Advertising All News Radio; Guidelines for Catalogue Copywriters; Associate Editor, The Gourmet Guide for Busy People by Famous People. *Memberships:* Women's Economic Round Table, Board of Directors ; The Fashion Group, Co-Chair, Regional Director's Committee; Chairman, American Cancer Society, 1980-; Committee to Feed the homeless, Chairwoman; Board of Directors, 750 Park Avenue Corporation. *Hobbies:* Opera, Jogging, Theatre, Skiing. *Address:* 750 Park Avenue, New York, NY 10021, USA.

DUNNETT Dorothy, b. 25 Aug. 1923, Dunfermline, Scotland. Author. m. Alastair M. Dunnett, 17 Sept. 1946, 2 sons. *Appointments:* British Civil Service: Assistant Press Officer, Scottish Government Departments, Edinburgh, 1940-46; Scottish Economic Research

Department, Board of Trade, Glasgow, 1946-55; Director, Scottish Television plc, 1979-; Professional Portrait Painter. *Publications include:* Novels: Game of Kings, 1961, 8th edition 1986; Queens' Play, 1964, 8th edition 1986; Disorderly Knights, 1966, 8th edition 1987; Dolly & the Singing Bird, 1968, 4th edition 1984; Pawn in Frankincense, 1969, 8th edition 1987; Dolly & the Cookie Bird, 1970, 4th edition 1985; Ringed Castle, 1971, 8th edition 1987; Dolly & the Doctor Bird, 1971; Dolly & the Starry Bird, 1971, 4th edition 1985; Checkmate, 1975, 8th edition 1987; Dolly and the Nanny Bird, 1976; King Herefter, 1982, 3rd edition 1983; Dolly and the Bird of Paradise, 1983; Niccolò Rising, 1983, 4th edition 1985; Spring of the Ram, 1987, 4th edition 1989; Race of Scorpions, 1989; The Scottish Highlands (text jointly with Alastair M Dunnet) 1988; Untitled Johnson novel, 1990. *Memberships include:* Fellow, Royal Society of Arts; Other Trusteeships and Directorships include: Trustee, National Library of Scotland; Trustee for Secretary of State for Scotland, Scottish National War Memorial; Board Member, Edinburgh Book Festival. *Honour:* Award, Scottish Arts Council, 1976. *Interests include:* Medieval History; Travel; Sailing; Opera; Orchestral Music; Ballet. *Address:* 87 Colinton Road, Edinburgh EH10 5DF, Scotland.

DUNSHEATH Joy, Music Dealer; Teacher. m. David H J Dunsheath, 11 June 1973. 2 sons. *Education:* BA (Hons); Dip Tchg; ATCL; Auckland University; Conservatorio di Musica, Luigi Cherubini; Victoria University. *Appointments:* Various teaching posts, Seconday schools, United Kingdom and New Zealand; Music Dealer, specialist in Antiquarian and Oceanic Music. *Publications:* Occasional contributor of theatre criticism, programme notes and music articles. *Memberships:* Federation of University Women; Composers Association of New Zealand; Historic Places Trust. *Hobbies:* Tennis; Music. *Address:* 9 Easdale St, Wellington 1, New Zealand.

DUNSON Karyl Lea, b. 8 Feb. 1945, Wichita, Kansas, USA. Assistant Operator. divorced. 2 daughters. *Education:* Wichita St University, 1965; Lamar University, 1979. *Appointments:* Traffic Dir Public Relations, KFDI Radio, 1966-69; KS Production Mgr Traffic Manager, Media Director, McCormick-Armstreong Adv Agency, Wichita, 1969-77; Assistant Operator-Oil Movements, Mobil Oil Corp, 1977-. *Publications:* Contributing Author, Getting Job Hazards out of the Bedroom; Various poetry pieces published. *Memberships:* Oil Chemical & Atomic Workers Union, Trustee, Health & Safety Director, Local 4-243; OCAW-IU OSHEC HAZMAT Trainer on Hazardous Material Handling, Sabine Area Central Labor Council; COSH Director, First Collation on Safety & Health in Texas. *Honours:* Public Speaker for OCAW and AFL-CIO; Set up first divorce counselling centre in Kansas; Set up first Coalition on Occupational Safety & Health in state of Texas. *Hobbies:* Editor, OCAWA4-243 Newsletter; Co-editor, OCAW International Hazardous Material Handling newsletter; Educating Women on their rights under Union Contracts. *Address:* Oil Chemical & Atomic Workers Union, 2490 So 11th St, Beaumont, TX 77701, USA.

DUNZ Diane Dewar, b. 13 Sep. 1960, New York, USA. Health Researcher Analyst. m. Karl Heinz Dunz, 12 Oct. 1985. *Education:* Music Diploma, Catholic Central High School Troy, New York; BA, Economics, 1982, MA, Economics, 1985, PhD, Economics, in progress, State University of New York, Albany. *Appointments:* Market Research Statistician, New York State Division of the Lottery, 1982-84; Senior Biostatistician, New York State Department of Health, 1987; Health Researcher Analyst, Empire Blue Cross and Blue Shield, Albany, New York, 1987-. *Publications:* The Influence of Economic and Demographic Factors on Cause Specific Mortality in an Elderly Population Aged 65-74, 1987. *Memberships:* American Public Health Association; American Economic Association; American Economic Association Committee on the Status of Women in the Economics Profession; Vice-

President, Empire State Capital Volkssporters; Participant, Career Advisory Network, State University of New York, Albany. *Honours:* Graduate Fellowship, Economics Department, State University of New York, Albany, 1984-86. *Hobbies:* Activist, animal welfare groups (American Association for the Prevention of Cruelty to Animals, PETA, World Wildlife Fund); Playing the piano; Hiking. *Address:* Utilization Economics and Research, Division of Health Affairs, Empire Blue Cross and Blue Shield, 18 Corporate Woods Boulevard, Albany, NY 12208, USA.

DUPLANCIC-SIMUNJAK Ruzica, b. 3 July 1936, Jurjevcani, Zagreb, Croatia, Yugoslavia. Paediatrician. m. Dr Ivan-Vanja Duplancic, 6 Aug. 1960. 1 son. *Education:* Diploma, Medical School University of Zagreb, 1961; Diploma Specialist in Pediatrics, Zagreb, 1970; Master's degree, University Zagreb, 1979; Primarius, 1983; Subspecialist in Social Pediatrics, 1988. *Appointments:* Medical Practice, Gen Hospital, Split, 1961-63; General Practice, 1963-66; Pediatric Residency, Medical Center, Split, 1966-70; Pediatric Dep Clin Hospital, Split; Mother and Child Welfare Institute, Zagreb, 1970-89; Head of Pediatric Dep Gen Hosp, Misurata, Lybia, 1976-77. *Publications:* Morbidity of preschool children and mother's sick leave, Manual Zagreb, 1982; Co-author, The first year of Life, 1987. *Memberships:* Medical Association of Croatia; Pediatric Association of Yugoslavia. *Hobbies:* Literature, especially poetry in original language (English, French and Croatian); Classic literature; Theatre (drama); Cinema. *Address:* Srednjaci 24, 41000 Zagreb, Yugoslavia.

DUPLESSIS Yvonne, b. 26 Jan. 1912, Paris, France. m. Herbert Tuchmann, 22 Dec. 1936. 1 son, 1 daughter. *Education:* Diplome d'Etudes Superieures, Sorbonne, Paris, 1932; PhD, 1934; Doctor of the University, Montpellier, 1945. *Appointment:* Head of the study Committee on Dermo-optical Sensitivity of the Centre Information de la Couleur, Paris, 1970-. *Publications:* Le Surrealisme, 1987; The Paranormal Perception of Color, 1975; Les Couleurs Visibles et Non Visibles, 1984. *Memberships:* Parapsychological Association; Institut Metapsychique International Paris, Vice Presidente. *Honours:* 1st Prize, Schweizerische Vereiningug fur Parapsychology, 1976; Advisor of the Sittaram Bhartia Institute of Scientific Research, New Delhi, India, 1985; Ehre Member von Imago Mundi Innsbruck Austria, 1988. *Hobby:* Parapsychology. *Address:* 67 Avenue Raymond-Poincare, Paris 75116, France.

DUPONT Frances Marguerite, b. 23 May 1944, Duluth, USA. Scientist. m. Gene Frederick Dupont, 15 July 1969, divorced 1980. *Education:* BA, 1965, MA 1971, PhD, 1979, University of California. *Appointments:* Teacher: Peace Corps, Gulu, Uganda, 1965-68, Homer High School, Alaska, 1971-72; Research Assistant, UC Riverside, 1975-79; Research Associate: Cornell University, 1979-81, ARCO Plant Cell Research Institute, 1981-83; Plant Physiologist, USDA Agricultural Research Service, Albany, 1983-. *Memberships:* American Association for Advancement of Science; American Society of Plant Physiologists. *Honours:* USDA Competative Research Grant, 1986-88; US-Israel Bilateral Agricultural Research & Development Grant, 1987-89. *Hobbies:* Natural History; Sailing; Reading; Travel. *Address:* USDA Agricultural Research Service, Western Regional Research Centre, 800 Buchanan St., Albany, CA 94710, USA.

DUPREE Sherry, b. 25 Nov. 1946, Raleigh, North Carolina, USA. Researcher; Librarian. m. Herbert Clarence Dupree, 11 Jan. 1975, 3 sons. *Education:* BS 1968, MA 1969, North Carolina Central University; AMLS 1974, EdS 1978, University of Michigan; Graduate courses, University of Florida, 1980-81. *Appointments:* Media specialist, Ann Arbor Public Schools, 1970-77; Visiting Professor, Eastern Michigan University, 1975; Associate Reference Librarian 1977-83, Project Director, IBC 1985-, University of Florida; Reference Librarian, Santa Fe Community College, 1983-; Professor, Bethume Cookman College, 1986-88;

Afro-American Religious Researcher. *Publications:* Books: Displays for Schools, 1976; Busy Bookworm, Good Conduct Book, 1980; Card Catalog Book, 1989. Papers: Library Media Center & Classroom Displays, 1976; Black Pentecostal Resources, 1987. *Memberships:* American & Florida Library Associations; Society of American Archivists; Society for Pentecostal Studies; Alachua Library League; National Association for Advancement of Coloured Peoples. *Honours:* Grant, University of Michigan, 1976; Fellowship, Florida Board of Regents, 1981; Governor's Award, outstanding Florida Citizen, 1986; Travel Awards, National Endowment for Humanities 1986, Southern Regional Education Board 1988; Smithsonian Visiting Scholar, 1987; Gatorade Foundation Award, University of Florida, 1988. *Hobbies:* Reading; Playing Piano. *Address:* Santa Fe Community College; 3000 NW 83rd Street, PO Box 1530, Library P-105, Gainesville, Florida 32602, USA.

DUPUY-BOURY Marie Catherine, b. 12 May, 1950, Neuilly/Seine, France. Associate Manager and Creative Director, BDDP. m. Paul Boury, 12 Sept. 1987. 3 sons. *Education:* Baccalauréat Philosophie, Universite Paris, Dauphine, 1968-70. *Appointments:* Copy Writer, Dupuy Compton, 1970-81; Assistant Creative Director, 1981-83; Co-Founder, Member and Creative Director, BDDP Advertising Agency, 1984-. *Hobbies:* Reading; Swimming; Bicycling; Cinema; Theatre. *Address:* BDDP, 162.164 Rue de Billancourt, 92100 Boulogne, France.

DURACK Mary, b. 20 Feb. 1913, Adelaide, Australia. Author. m. Horace Clive Miller, 1938, died 1980, 3 sons, 3 daughters. *Publications:* All-about, 1935; Chunuma, 1936; Son of Djaro, 1938; The Way of the Whirlwind, 1941, 1979; Piccaninnies, 1943; The Magic Trumpet, 1944; Keep Him My Country, 1955; Kings in a Grass Castles, 1959; To Ride a Fine Horse, 1963; The Courteous Savage, 1964; Yagan of the Bibbulmun, 1976; Kookanoo & Kangaroo, 1963; An Australian Settler, 1964; A Pastoral Emigrant; The Rock and the Sand, 1969; To Be Heirs Forever, 1976; Tjakamarra - Boy between Two Worlds, 1977; Swan River Saga, 1975; Sons in theSaddle, 1983; Play: The Ship of Dreams, 1968; author numerous scripts for Australian Broadcasting Commission, Drama Department; etc. *Memberships:* Hon. Life Member, Fellowship of Australian Writers, President, WA Branch, 1958-63; Australian Society of Authors; National Trust; many other professional organisations. *Honours:* Commonwealth Literary Grant, 1973, 1977; DBE, 1978; Australian Research Grant, 1980, 1984-85; Emeritus Fellowship, Literature Board, Australia Council, 1983-86; Foundation Fellow, Curtin University of Technology, 1987. *Address:* 12 Bellevue Avenue, Nedlands, WA 6009, Australia.

DURAN June C., b. 10 June 1919, California, USA. Company President. widowed, 1 son, 1 daughter. *Education:* AB, Social Studies, University of Southern California; Graduate work, University of California; LLB, LaSalle University; Psychometrist Credential. *Appointments:* Director of Operations, 1955-59, Administrative Vice-President, 1959-65, California Test Bureau, Monterey, California; Assistant Vice-President, CTB/McGraw-Hill, Monterey, 1965-84; President, Legal Research and Services Center Inc, Monterey, 1984-. *Memberships:* Copyright Society of the USA, President, Willis W. & Ethel M.Clark Foundation; Director, First National Bank of Monterey County; Governing Board, Monterey Community College; Board of Trustees, Community Hospital of the Monterey Peninsula, 1978-84; Monterey County Agency on Aging Advisory Council, 1977-82; Board of Directors, Alliance on Aging, 1971-77; Board of Directors, Monterey Peninsula Chamber of Commerce, 1973-75; Board of Directors, American Cancer Society, 1972-75; Board of Directors, District 7 Agricultural Association, 1968-76; Board of Directors, Leadership Monterey Peninsula, 1983-86; Monterey County Republican Central Committee, 1963-78; California State Republican Central Committee. *Address:* PO Box 23, Pebble Beach, CA 93953, USA.

DURHAM Kathleen Erickson, b. 3 June 1944, Mojave, California, USA. Speech/Language Pathologist. divorced. 1 son. *Education:* BS 1968, MA, Speech Pathology, 1969, University of Utah. *Appointments:* CD Spec, 1969-70, 1971-72, Resource Teacher 1972-76, Communication Disorders Specialist, 1976-, Salt Lake City Schools, 1969-70, 1971-72; CD Spec, Orange Unified Schools, 1970-71; Clinical Instructor, Dept Communication Disorders, University of Utah, 1976-; Naval Reserve, SACLANT DET 120, Salt Lake City, 1968-. *Publication:* Masters Thesis, Subgroup study of the effectiveness of Public School Speech Therapy, 1969. *Memberships:* American Speech/Language/Hearing Association; Jr League of Salt Lake City, Recording Sect Project Chair; Board of Directors, Salt Lake Jr Achievement, Chair Committees, PR, Awards, Banquet; Board of Directors, Youth Services Advisory Board; Pi Beta Phi Alumnae, numerous offices. *Honours:* Golden Key Honour Society, 1987; Certificate Clinical Competence, American Spch/Hearing Assoc, 1971; Salt Lake County Commission, Vital Volunteer, 1986. *Hobbies:* Snow skiing; Bicycling; Golfing; Travel; Cooking; Decorating; Volunteerism. *Address:* 5219 So Gravenstein Park, Murray, Utah 84123, USA.

DURON Mary Salinas, b. 30 Apr. 1952, Los Angeles, California, USA. Vice President, Banking. m. Armando Duron, 16 Dec. 1978. 1 daughter. *Education:* BA, Loyola Marymount University, 1975; Master of Business Administration, Graduate School of Management, University of California at Los Angeles, 1978. *Appointments:* First Interstate Bank of California (formerly United California Bank) 1977-, currently Vice President & Manager, Urban and Community Affairs Unit. *Memberships:* Chairman of the Board, Bilingual Foundation of the Arts, 1987 and 1988, Board Member, 1983-88; Advisory Committee, 1987-88, Hispanic Women's Council; Program Council Chair, Member, 1983-88, National Network of Hispanic Women; President, 1985 and 1986, Hispanic Bankers Association. *Honours:* Caminos Magazine, Hispanic of the Year: Community Development, 1985; Richard M Dominquez Award for Excellence in Banking, Hispanic Bankers Association, 1986; Corporate Leader Award, National Network of Hispanic Women, 1985; Mexican American Alumni Association Award, Loyola Marymount University, 1985; YWCA Leader Luncheon VII Award, 1981; Hispanic Business Magazine, 100 Hispanic Influentials. *Hobbies:* Reading; Chicano art; Mexican artifacts. *Address:* Urban and Community Affairs, First Interstate Bank of California, 1055 Wilshire Boulevard, B9-75, Los Angeles, CA 90017, USA.

DUSCHEK Maria, b. 24 June 1929, Hungary. President 2 sons. *Education:* Political Academy, Hungarian Socialist Worker's Party, 1961. *Appointments:* Secretary, 1971-80, Vice President, 1980-86, National Council of Trade Unions; Vice President, 1971-80, President, 1980-, National Council of Women. *Memberships:* Foreign Affairs Committee of Parliament; National Council and Presidium of the Patriotic Peoples Front; Vice President, Soviet-Hungarian Friendship Society. *Honours:* Order of Labour in Silver, 1964, Gold 1973; Commemorative Medal for the Liberation, 1970; Order for Socialist Hungary, 1983. *Address:* National Council of Hungarian Women, Nepkoztarsasag u. 124, 1391 Budapest, Hungary.

DUSSERRE Liliane Denise France, b. 6 Mar. 1932, Dijon, France. Department head of medical informatics; Professor of Statistics and Medical Informatics. m. Dr Pierre Dusserre, 30 Sept. 1954. 2 sons, 1 daughter. *Education:* Medical Doctor, Paris, 1961; Master of Sciences, Dijon, 1961; Human Biology Doctor, Paris, 1975; Professor, University, 1976; Master of Social and Economic Health Science, Paris, 1985. *Appointments:* Interne des hoptiaux de Dijon, 1957-61; Assistant de Biologie, 1966-69; Chef de Travaux de Mathematiques, statistique, informatique medicale, Assistant de Biology, 1969-76; Maitre de Conferences, Biologiste des Hopitaux depuis, 1976; Chef de Service (Laboratoire Informatique Medicale de la Faculte de Medecine et du Chru de Dijon. *Publications:* Informatique Medicale,

1985; Informatique et soins infirmiers, 1986. *Memberships:* Biometrics; Past-president, AIM/IF (association for medical applications of informatics Paris, Ile de France); National Medical Order., *Honour:* Decorated by the Ministry of Education (Chevalier des Palmes Academiques). *Hobby:* Ski. *Address:* Laboratoire d'Informatique Medicala, Batiment administratif, Hopital du Bocage, BP 1542, 21034 Dijon Cedex, France.

DUTCHER Janice Jean Phillips, b. 10 Nov. 1950, Bend, Oregon, USA. Physician and Medical Scientist, area of Cancer Research. Divorced. *Education:* BA, Hons, magna cum laude, University of Utah, 1966-71; MD, University of California, 1971-75; Medical Internship and Residency, Rush Presbyterian St Lukes Medical Centre, Chicago, 1975-78. *Appointments:* Clinical Associate, Baltimore Cancer Research Programme, DCT National Cancer Institute, NIH 1978-81; Clinical Investigator, BCRC, DCT, NCI, NIH, 1981-82; Assistant Professor, University of Maryland School of Meedicine, University of Maryland Centre for Cancer, 1982; Assistant Professor of Medicine, 1983-86, Associate Professor of Medicine, 1986-, Division of Oncology, Albert Einstein College of Medicine, Montefiore Medical Center, New York. *Publications:* 72 scientific publications including 22 book chapters; 62 scientific abstracts at national and international meetings, 31 invited presentations in areas of leukemia, transfusion supportive care and biologic response modifiers, given in US, South America and Europe. *Memberships:* Fellow, American College of Physicians; American Society of Clinical Oncology; American Society of Haematology; International Society of Haematology; American Federation of Clinical Research; American Society of Cancer Research; American Association of Blood Banks; American Society for Clinical Pharmacology and Therapeutics; American Radium Society; Alpha Lambda Delta, Freshman Women Honor Society; Phi Kappa Phi; Phi Beta Kappa; Alpha Omega Alpha; NOW. *Honours:* National Merit Finalist and Scholar, 1968; Sterling scholar in general Scholarship, Utah, 1968; Presidential Scholar from State of Utah, 1968; Lange Medical Publishers Award, 1975; Beecham Award Finalist, South Blood Bank, 1983; First Distinguished Alumnus awardee, University of California, Davis School of Medicine. *Hobbies:* Swimming; Cycling; Skiing; Knitting; Sewing; Travel; Reading; Viola and Violin orchestral chamber music. *Address:* Albert Einstein College of Medicine, 1300 Morris Park Avenue, Bronx, NY 10461, USA.

DUTT Aroti, b. 23 Sept. 1924, India. Social Worker. m. 19 July 1942, 1 son. *Education:* BA, Calcutta University, 1942; diploma, Social Science, Institute of Social Studies, The Hague, Holland, 1958. *Appointment:* Social Worker, Rural Women, Children & Urban Poor. *Publications:* Unkown People and Strange World, in Bengali. *Memberships:* President, Saroj Nalini Association; Country Womens Association of India; Founder President, Soroptimist International, Calcutta; Founder President, Inner Wheel, S.W. Calcutta; Past Area Vice President, Asia, & Past World President, Associated Country Women of the World; etc. *Honours:* Member of Honour Associated Country Women of the World, 1983. *Hobbies:* Reading; Music. *Address:* 6/1 Gwrn Saday Dutt Road, Calcutta 700019, India.

DUTTON Diana C, b. 27 June 1944, Sherman, Texas, USA. Attorney. m. Anthony R Grindl, 8 July 1974. 1 son, 1 daughter. *Education:* BS, Georgetown University, Washington, DC, 1967; JD, University of Texas School of Law, 1971. *Appointments:* US Environmental Protection Agency, Region 6, 1971-81; Partner, Akin, Gump, Strauss, Hauer & Feld, 1981-. *Memberships:* State Bar of Texas, Environmental & Natural Resources Law Section, Chairman, 1984-85; Dallas Environmental Law Section, Chairman, 1985; American Bar Association. *Address:* 4150 First City Center, 1700 Pacific Avenue, Dallas, TX 75201, USA.

DUVA Donna Marie, b. 28 June 1956, Paterson, USA. Financial Executive. *Education:* AAS, Bergen Community College, 1976; BS, 1985. *Appointments:*

CFO/Controller, Al Duva Enterprises Inc., 1976-; Accountant, Beecham Inc., 1980-85; CFO/Accounting Manager, Power Battery Corp, 1986-. *Publications:* Newspaper Editorials, Paterson Evening News, 1976; Editor's Choice Editorial of the Year. *Memberships:* New Jersey Society of Notary Publics; National Association of Female Executives; Board, Bergen Community College. *Honours:* Berkeley School Award, 1974; Dean's List, 1974-76. *Hobbies:* Games of Chance; Bowling; Tennis; Travel. *Address:* bb3205 Vernon Avenue, Paterson, NJ 07503, USA.

DUVAL Jill, b. 23 Oct. 1940, Morristown, New Jersey, USA. Publisher; Insurance Agent. div., 1 son, 3 daughters. *Education:* Art study, University of New Mexico. *Appointments:* Insurance Agent, 1980-; Publisher, 1981-. *Publications:* Albuquerque Women in Business Directory, annually 1981-; Albuquerque Woman bi-monthly (publisher, editor), 1989-. *Memberships:* Incorporator, New Mexico Women's Foundation; Women Entrepreneurs. *Honours:* New Mexico Governor's Award for Outstanding Women, 1986. *Address:* PO Box 6133, Albuquerque, NM 87197, USA.

DWIGHT Margaret L, b. 12 Dec. 1947, Hattiesburg, Mississippi, USA. Assistant Professor Afro-American & African Studies. *Education:* Diploma 1966; BS, USM, 1970; MA, So Ill. University, 1973; PhD, University Missouri, Columbia, 1978. *Appointments:* Instructor, Lincoln University, 1973-74; Dir. Blk Cult. Ctr/Asst Professor University of Virginia, 1977-80; Assistant Professor History, Alcorn University, 1980-85; Fulbright Professor, University of Niamey, 1985-87; Visiting Lecturer, UTSA, 1988; Assistant Professor, History, UNCC. *Publications:* Miss Black History Makers, 1984; Changing Roles and Status of Cameroonian Women; Book reviews: Journal Sou. Hist; Journal Negro History. Poem: Africa's Rape. *Memberships:* Assoc. Study Afro-American Life and History; NAACP; Delta Sigma Theta Sorority; Phi Delta Kappa Honorary Frat; Phi Alpha Theta; Southern Rural Women Network; Southern Historical Association; National Council Black Studies. *Address:* 1044 Spencer Street, Hattiesburg, Mississippi USA.

DWYER Judith A, b. 29 Nov. 1948, Philadelphia, USA. Associate Professor; Member, Sisters of St Joseph (Roman Catholic Nun). *Education:* BA, English, Chestnut Hill College, 1972; MA, Theology, Duquesne University, 1975; PhD, Theology, Catholic University of America, 1983; STL, Weston School of Theology, 1987. *Appointments:* Assistant Professor, Religious Studies, Chestnut Hill College, 1980-85; Assistant Professor, Moral Theology, Western Schoola of Theology, Cambridge, Massachusetts, 1986-88; Associate Professor, 1988-. *Publications:* Edited, contributed to Questions of Special Urgency: The Church in the Modern World two decades after Vatican II, 1986; Edited, contributed to The Catholic Bishops and Nuclear War, 1983; Contributor of Harvard Educaitonal Review, Religious Studies Review. *Memberships:* The Catholic Theological Society of America, Steering Committee Moral Theology Section; The Society of Christian Ethics; American Academy of Religion. *Honours:* Fulbright Post-doctoral Fellowship, 1988-89; University of TüßingenPresidential Scholar, The Catholic University of America. *Hobbies:* Classical Music; Opera; Ballet. *Address:* Weston School of Theology, 3 Phillips Place, Cambridge, MA 02138, USA.

DYER Lois Edith, b. 18 Mar. 1925, Gosport, England. *Education:* MCSP, 1945; Fellow, 1986. *Appointments:* Physiotherapist, Middlesex Hospital, London, 1945-47; Senior Physiotherapist, Coronation Non-European Hospital, Johannesburg, South Africa, 1948-51; Superintendent Physiotherapist, Johannesburg Group of Hospitals, 1951-56; Superintendent Physiotherapist, Westminster Hospital, London, 1958-61; Superintendent Physiotherapist, Royal National Orthopaedic Hospital, Stanmore, 1965-70; Physiotherapy Officer, Department of Health & Social Security, London, 1976-86. *Publications:* Numerous articles in professional journals; Care of the Orthopaedic Patient, 1977; Co-editor, Physiotherapy practice, 1985. *Memberships:* Chartered Society of Physiotherapy, Honorary Life Vice President, South African Society of Physiotherapy; Founder Member of Society for Research in Rehabilitation. *Honours:* OBE, 1984. *Hobbies:* Music; Country Pursuits; Bridge; Food & Drink; Conservation. *Address:* Garden Flat, 6 Belsize Grove, London NW3 4UN, England.

DYKE Beverley Janis, b. 9 May 1951, Sydney, Australia. Managing Director of Public Affairs Consultancy. *Education:* BA, Political Science, 1980. *Appointments:* Tjuringa/Ipec Group & Australia Party (Investment Group and Political Party), 1969-76; Radio 2GB, 1976; Harris Robinson Courtenay, 1977-80; The Consultancy, 1980-82; Fox Communications, 1982-86; Mojo Corporate, 1986-; Federal Government Trade in Services Advisory Committee; Federal Governments Bicentennial Youth Foundation Committee. *Creative works:* Led team of 8 businesswomen to research, fund raise and produce video and book on careers for young women, Work it Out. *Memberships:* Australian Institute of Political Science; Australian Marketing Institute. *Honour:* First Life Member Women and Management, 1987. *Interests:* Women's issues; Trade. *Address:* 9 Collins Street, Annandale, NSW 2038, Australia.

DYTELL Rita Scher, b. 9 May 1943, New York, USA. Assistant Professor. m. Robert M. Dytell, 30 Jan. 1965, 1 daughter. *Education:* BA, City College, 1964, PhD, Social Psychology, 1970, City University of New York. *Appointments:* New York Institute of Technology, 1975-81; President, Analytical Research Consulting, 1981-; Assistant Professor, Psychology, College of Mount St Vincent, 1985-. *Publications:* 14 papers presented, American or Eastern Psychological Convention, 1980-; 9 papers published in scientific journals. *Memberships:* Society for the Psychological Study of Social Issues; Eastern Psychological Association; Greater New York Area Social Psychologists; American Association of University Professors. *Honours:* New York State Regents Scholarship, 1961-64; New York State Incentive Award, 1964-70; Research Grants, New York Institute of Technology, 1978-79, College of Mt. St. Vincent, 1988. *Hobbies:* Theatre; Cooking; Entertaining. *Address:* Dept. of Psychology, College of Mount St Vincent, Riverdale, NY 10471, USA.

DZELZKALNS LeeAnn, b. 5 Sept. 1956, Milwaukee, USA. Fitness Consultant; Entrepreneur. m. Raymond Robert Dzelzkalns, 5 June 1981, 2 sons. *Education:* BS, Social Work, 1981; MS, Physical Education, 1985; Certified Idea Foundation Fitness Instructor, 1986. *Appointments:* Director, Owner, Stretchercise, 1981-87; Fitness Consultant, Shape Magazine, 1985; Co-Director, Editor at Large Programme, Shape Magazine, 1986-; Lecturer, Instructor, University of Wisconsin, 1988-. *Publications:* Efficacy of Educational Awareness Programming on Self-directed Physical Activity of Older Female Adults; Stretchercise Instructor Training and Educational Manual; numerous articles in professional journals. *Memberships:* International Dance-Exercise Association; International Dance-Exercise Association Foundation; American College of Sports Medicine; International Exer-Safety Association; etc. *Hobbies Include:* Cross Country Skiing; Bicycling; Hiking; Crafts. *Address:* LA Fitness Design, 1715 E. Cumberland Blvd., Whitefish Bay, WI 53211, USA.

E

EAKIN Margaretta B Morgan, b. 27 Aug. 1941, Ft Smith, Arkansas, USA. Lawyer. m. Harry D Eakin, 7 June 1959. 1 daughter. *Education:* BA with honours, University of Oregon, 2969; JD 1971; Bar: Oregon 1971, US District Court Oregon, 1971; US Court of Appeals (9th circuit), 1977. *Appointments:* Law Clerk to Chief Justice Oregon Supreme Court, 1971- 72; Reginald Heber Smith Law Reform Fellow, 1972-73; House Counsel, Hyster Co., 1973-75; Associate, N Robert Stoll, 1975-77; Margaretta Eaking, PC, Portland, Oregon, 1977-; Teacher Business Law, Portland State University, 1979-80. *Memberships:* Speaker, Member State Board, professional responsibility, Oregon State Bar, 1979-82; Ann. fund com. Oregon Episcopal School, 1981; Chairman, Subcom. country fair, 1981; Paul Patterson fellow; ABA; Association of Trial Lawyers of America; Oregon Trial Lawyers Association; Oregon Bar Association; Multnomah County Bar Association; Board of Visitors, University of Oregon, School of Law, 1987-90. *Address:* 1000 Jackson Tower, Portland, OR 97205, USA.

EARLY-BOWLAND Jane, b. 22 Apr. 1936, Los Angeles, California, USA. Director. m. Donald Bowland, 21 Nov. 1981, 2 daughters. *Education:* BA, San Francisco State University, 1960; MEd 1969, EdD 1985, University of Nevada, Reno. *Appointments:* First and Third Grade Teacher, So Lake Tahoe, California, 1960-66; Third Grade Teacher, Carson City, Nevada, 1966-68; Special Education Teacher, Reno, Nevada, 1969-71; Consultant, 1971-85, Director 1985-, Special Education, Nevada Dept of Education. *Publications:* A Ten-Year Study of Programs for the Academically Talented in Nevada; A Ten-Year Study of Nevada Revised Statues, Chapter 395; Learning Disabilities Don't Show; Gains for the Gifted; Developing a State Plan for the Education of Gifted and Talented Students. *Memberships:* National Association of State Directors of Special Education; Council of State Directors of Programs for the Gifted; Chairperson, Regional State Directors Association; Phi Delta Kappa; Nevada Association of School Administrators. *Honours:* Certificate of Recognition, US Office of Education, 1976; Master's Fellowship, Nevada Dept of Education, 1968-69; Vocal Music Scholarship, 1953- 54; California Scholarship Federation, 1951-53; Phi Beta Kappa Award, 1952. *Hobbies:* Reading; Swimming; Gardening; Walking; Singing. *Address:* Nevada Department of Education, Capitol Complex, Carson City, Nevada 89710, USA.

EASTEP Lou Ann (Radford), b. 9 Sep. 1939, Martin, Tennessee, USA. Educator; Assistant Elementary School Principal. m. Buford Allen Eastep, 23 Aug. 1959, 1 son, 1 daughter. *Education:* BS, University of Tennessee, 1962; MS, Texas A&I University, 1989. *Appointments:* Henry County Education Department, Paris, Tennessee; Los Fresnes, CISD, Texas, 1974-80; Gifted and Talented Coordinator, Harlingen CISD, Texas, 1980-88; Assistant Principal, Lamar Elementary School, 1988-. *Publications:* Curriculum Handbook for Gifted and Talented - Teachers and Administrators. *Creative Works:* 2 musicals for elementary students, citywide featuring 600 students. *Memberships:* Association for Supervisors and Curriculum Directors; Delta Kappa Gamma; President, Alpha Delta Kappa; President, Association for Childhood Education International; State and National Associations for Gifted and Talented. *Honours:* State Officer, Future Homemakers of America, 1956-57; Danforth Foundation Award, 1962; Honoured by Harlingen CISD, 1985, 1986, 1987, 1988. *Hobbies:* Music; Reading; Collecting antiques. *Address:* 910 N 21st Street, Harlingen, TX 78550, USA.

EASTMAN Carolyn Ann, b. 8 Sept. 1946, Potsam, New York, USA. Scientist; Business Owner. *Education:* AAS, Professional Photography, Rochester Institute of Technology, NY, 1976; BS, Biology, Nazareth College,

Rochester, 1968. *Appointments:* Chemistry technician, University of Rochester, 1968-69; Chemist, Castle-Sybron, Rochester, 1969-79; Owner, Vice- President, Sterilization Technical Services, Rush, NY, 1979-; Partner, EFC Properties, 1983-; Owner, Fairfield Cosmetics, Rush, 1986-. *Creative work includes:* Several articles, various professional journals, 1969-83; Patentee, scientific field, 1976. *Memberships:* Association for Advancement of Medical Instrumentation; National Association of Female Executives; National Organisation of Women; Sierra Club; Amnesty International. *Honours:* 1st & 3rd places, art show, Greater Rochester, 1977. *Hobbies:* Racquet sports; Skiing; Restoring antiques, old houses; Stained glass; Oil & watercolour painting; Sculpture. *Address:* 6 Genesee Street, Scottsville, New York 14546, USA.

EASTON Margaret Mary, b. 14 Oct. 1935, Pittsburgh, Pennsylvania, USA. Psychotherapist. formerly m. David Ryan Schuchts, 24 June 1953, 4 sons, 3 daughters. *Education:* AA, University of Pittsbsurgh, 1972; BS, Psychology & Sociology, Barry University, School of Social Work, 1973; MSW, 1975; PhD, Psychotherapeutics, Cambridge University, University of London England, 1982. *Appointments:* City of North Miami Day Camp Director, 1970; Taughat at Universities including Nova 1975, Barry 1975-79 Pepperdine 1981; St Thomas 1989, Clinical practice with Dr Henry Merritt 1981, Dr Burton Cahn 1981-89. *Publications:* Works on: Leadership training, Stress reducation, Post-Traumatic Stress Disorders, Family relationships; Also art, poetry. *Memberships:* American Association of Marriage & Family Counsellors; Biofeedback Society of America; Council on Social Work Education; President, Christian Family Movement, Family Life Commission; International Society for Professional Hypnotherapists; National Association of Social Workers. *Honours:* Honour societies: Phi Beta, Delta Epsilon Sigma, Kappa Gamma Phi, Psi Chi. *Hobbies:* International Travel; Swimming; Hiking; Cycling; Gourmet Cooking; Flower arranging; Creative writing; Public speaking; Poetry. *Address:* 1201 South Ocean Drive, Hollywood, Florida 33019, USA.

EASTON-BERGER Miriam, b. 4 Apr. 1924, New York City, New York, USA. Psychotherapist; Relationship counselor. m. (1) 1950; (2) 1985. 2 daughters. *Education:* BA Psychology, Queens College, 1946; MSW, Columbia University, School of Social Work, 1950. *Appointments:* Pre- professional social worker, Bureau of Foster Care, 1946-49; Family Counselor, Family Service Bureau, 1950-55; Field Work Supervisor, NY University Graduate School of Social Work, 1953-55; Snr Social Worker and Psychotherapist, 1955- 56, Group I herapist, 1964-67, LI Consultant Center; Private practice in Psychotherapy, 1955-; Group discussion leader, League for Parent Education, 1960-67; Faculty member, Group Relations Ongoing Workshops, 1970-73; Adjunct Instructor, Lehman College, CUNY, 1973-74; Faculty, YWCA, 1974-81; Faculty, LI Institute for Mental Health, 1978-79; Option Center for Psychotherapy, New York, 1975-81; Private practice in San Diego, 1981-; Peer Reviewer for CHAMPUS, 1984-. *Publications:* Numerous articles to professional journals; Papers/Workshops presented to conferences. Casettes: Psychotherapy by the Option Method; Introduction to Option Therapy; Options for Harnessing the Placebo Effect; Options for Reducing Stress in Family Relationships. *Memberships:* National Association of Social Workers; Charter member, Academy of Certified Social Workers; Fellow, Society for Clinical Social Work; American Group Psychotherapy Association; American Association of Marriage & Family Therapists; American Association of Sex Educators, Counselors & Therapists; American Academy of Psychotherapists & San Diego Chapter Secretary; Association for Women in Psychology. *Hobby:* Creative writing. *Address:* PO Box 40073, San Diego, CA 92104, USA.

EAVES Virginia Lee, b. 31 Oct. 1928, Dustin, USA. Fiscal Operations Assistant. m. (1)Floyd P. Deegan, 15 Sept. 1950, divorced 1954, 1 son (deceased), 1 daughter, (2)Charles H. Eaves, 28 Dec. 1959, divorced 1975.

Education: BS, Public Affairs, 1983; MA, Business Management, 1984. *Appointments:* US Government Bureau of Indian Affairs, 1956-63; US Government, Dept. of Health & Human Services, Bureau of Indian Affairs, 1963- 88; Fiscal Operations Assistant, 1988- . *Memberships:* President, native American Indian Vision Quest; Vice President, Secretary, Newsletter Editor, Federally Employed Women, Heart of America; Chairperson, National Womens Conference Committee American Indian Women. *Honours:* Outstanding Achievement Award, 1981, 1980; Recipient, several other honours & awards. *Hobbies:* Travel. *Address:* 5404 Skyline Drive, Mission, KS 66205, USA.

EBBETT, Frances Eva (Eve), b. 6 June 1925, Wellingborough, England. Author. m. Trevor George Ebbett, 22 Oct. 1949, 1 daughter. *Appointments:* Freelance Writer. *Publications:* (As Eva Burfield): Yellow Kowhai; A Chair to Sit On; The Long Winter; Out of Yesterday; After Midnight; The White Prison; The New Mrs Rainier; The Last Day of Summer; (As Eve Ebbett): Give Them Swing Bands; To the Garden Alone; In True Colonial Fashion; Victoria's Daughters; When the Boys Were Away; short stories in magazines. *Memberships:* New Zealand Women Writers Society, Chairman, 8 years, Secretary 2 years Hawkes Bay Branch; New Zealand Centre. *Hobbies:* Reading; Television; Walking; Current Affairs; Genealogy. *Address:* 908 Sylvan Road, Hastings, Hawkes Bay, New Zealand.

EBERLEY Helen-Kay Marie, b. 3 Aug. 1947, Sterling, Illinois, USA. Opera Singer; Classical Record Company Executive; Company President/Chairman. m. Vincent P Skowronski, 15 July 1972. *Education:* BMus, 1970, MMus, 1971, Northwestern University. *Career includes:* Artistic Coordinator, President, Chairman, Eberley-Skowronski Inc, 1973-; Founder, Teacher, Coach, EB-SKO Production, 1976-; Executive Director, Performance Consultant, E-S Management, 1985-; Opera debut, Lyric Opera, Chicago, Illinois, 1974; Leading roles: Cosi Fan Tutte, Le Nozze di Figaro, Falstaff, Peter Grimes, La Boheme, Faust, Don Giovanni, Brigadoon, Dido & Aeneas, La Traviata, Old Maid & the Thief, many others; Performing Artist, A.M.America, ABC-TV, 1977-79; Numerous concert, orchestra, recital appearances, Europe, USA; Featured Artist, WFMT; Continental Bank Concerts, 1982-89, United Airlines, Schumann, 1986, Schubert, 1987, Brahms, 1988, Mendelssohn, 1989; Poet. *Recordings:* Artist, Executive Producer, EB-SKO: Separate but Equal, 1976; All Brahms, 1977; Skowronski: Opera Lady, 1978; Eberley Sings Strauss, 1980; Helen-Kay Eberley: American Girl, 1983; Helen-Kay Eberley: Opera Lady II, EB-SKO, 1984; Producer, Annotator, EB-SKO: Gentleman Gypsy, 1978; Strauss & Szymanowski, 1979; One Sonata Each: Franck & Szymanowski, 1982. *Memberships:* Finance Chair, Board of Directors, Chicago Youth Orchestra, 1973-77; Mayor's Founding Committee, Evanston Arts Council, 1974-75; American Guild of Musical Artists; Alumuni Association of St Mary's Academy; Public Relations, Delta Gamma, 1968- 69. *Honours:* Creative/ Performing Arts Award, Indiana Jr Miss, 1965; Sudler Award, Excellence in Oratorio, 1966; Chramer Award, Excellence in Opera, 1967; Weyerhauserm Award, Opera, 1967; Milton J.Gross Metropolitan Opera Award, 1968; Prizewinner, Metropolitan Opera National Auditions, 1968; Honoured Artist, Northwestern University Honours Concert, 1970; Listed Artist, Illinois Arts Council Artists Registry, 1986. *Hobbies:* Swimming; Figure-skating; White-water canoeing; Animal rights; Needlepoint; Poetry. *Address:* 1726 Sherman Avenue, Evanston, IL 60201, USA.

EBERT Darlene Marie, b. 29 Dec 1951, Milwaukee, Wisconsin, USA. Attorney. m. Lee A Ebert, 30 Dec 1972, 1 son, 1 daughter. *Education:* BA, International Economics, 1973; MS, Agricultural Economics, 1974; JD, Law, 1977. *Appointments:* Attorney, Lobato-Bleidt, Bleidt and Haight, 1977-78; Supervisor, Employment Law Section, Denver City Attorney's Office, 1979-. *Memberships:* City Club of Denver; Beta Sigma Phi; Colorado Women's Bar Association; Colorado Bar Association; National Institute of Municipal Law

Officers, Chair, Local Government Personnel Committee. *Address:* 4015 South Niagara Way, Denver, CO 80237, USA.

EBLE Janice Johanna Grotpeter, b. 30 Nov. 1942, St Louis, Missouri, USA. Educator. m. John Eble, 10 June 1967 dec. 1 daughter. *Education:* BA, Fontbonne College, 1964; MA, St Louis University, 1966. *Appointments:* Instructor, Webster College 1968-74, Maryville College 1974-78; Instructor in History, now Professor, St Louis College, 1978-. *Publications:* Co-author, History of Namibia, publication pending; Research Assistant, Historical Dictionaries, Swaziland & Zambia; Book reviews, African Book Publishing Record. *Memberships:* Past Board Vice President, Mid-City Community Congress; Past Board, University Chapter, Missouri Citizens for Life; African Studies Association. *Honours:* Outstanding service, Mid-City Community Congress Library, 1968; Educator of Year, Alpha Zeta Omega, 1982. *Hobbies:* Numerous theatre performances, college, community & professional including lead roles, The Lesson, Harvey. *Address:* Liberal Arts Division, St Louis College, 4588 Parkview, St Louis, Missouri 63110, USA.

ECKERT Arlene Gail Lough, b. 28 July 1956, Euclid, Ohio, USA. Child Protective Services Specialist. m. Theodore Eckert, 14 May 1983, divorced 1985. *Education:* BS, Law Enforcement, University of North Alabama, 1978. *Appointments:* Probation/Parole Counsellor, Dept. of Corrections, Columbia, Tennessee, 1978-83; Child Protective Services Specialist, Dept. of Human Services, Killeen, 1984-86; Business co-ordinator, Associated Counselling Services, Harker Heights, TX 1986-88; Child Protective Services Specialist, Gatesville, 1988-. *Memberships:* Certified Social Worker; American Correctional Association; Multidisciplinary Child Abuse Review Team; Tennessee Employees Association; NAFE. *Honour:* Deans List, University of North Alabama, 1977. *Hobbies:* Horse Riding; Country Western Dance; Hiking; Boating; Camping; Stamp Collecting. *Address:* 4310 A Shawn Drive, Killeen, TX 76542, USA.

EDDY Martha Hart, b. 16 July 1957, New York City, USA. Dance Teacher; Movement Therapist. *Education:* BA, Dance Education, Hampshire College, 1979; CMA, Certified Laban Movement Analyst, 1981; Certified Teacher of Body-Mind Centering, 1982; Certified, Holistic Health, 1984; MA, Exercise Physiology, Columbia University, 1985; Registered Movement Therapist, 1988. *Appointments:* Faculties: Department of Dance & Dance Education, New York University; Certificate programme, Laban Institute of Movement Studies, University of Washington; Rotterdam Dansacadamie; Movement specialists, New School for Social Research; Graduate dance, Connecticut College. *Publications:* Dance Teacher's Handbook, in press; Articles: Vision, Movement & Children 1984, Designing a Fitness programme 1986. *Memberships:* Past Vice President, Alumnae Association, Laban Movement Analysts; Founding Member, Body-Mind Centering Association; American College of Sports Medicine; International Movement Therapists Association. *Honours:* Featured, NY Woman magazine, 1987; Keynote speaker, International Wholistic Vision Conference, Frankfurt, Germany, 1988. *Hobbies:* Peace Education; Conga drumming; Watercolours; Aikido; Trapeze Arts; Women's Health. *Address:* c/o School for Body-Mind Centering, 189 Pondview Drive, Amherst, Massachusetts 01002, USA.

EDEN Lorraine Diane Lesniak, b. 8 Aug. 1942, Utica, USA. m. Ronal Dean Eden, 28 June 1969. *Education:* BS, 1964, MS, 1974, Syracuse University. *Appointments:* Account Executive, Software Corporation of America, 1985-86; Loan Officer, Great Western Mortgage Corp., 1987-88; Realtor Trainer, Better Homes Realty Inc., 1986-. *Memberships:* Lockmeade Home Owners Association, Board; Syracuse University Alumnae; Northern Virginia Board of Realtors; NAFE; Volunteer Fundraiser for Hospice of Northern Virginia, 1989. *Honours:* Sales & Management

Awards, 1982-85. *Hobbies:* Tennis; Art; Music; Travel; Photography. *Address:* 1156 Riva Ridge Drive, Great Falls, VA 22066, USA.

EDEN-FETZER Dianne Toni, b. 1 Mar. 1946, Washington, District of Columbia, USA. Registered Nurse; Project Coordinator, Stroke Data Bank. m. (1) William Earle Eden, 1967, divorced 1982, 1 son. (2) John Thompson Fetzer, 1987. *Education:* AA, Nursing, State University of New York and Farmingdale, 1978; University of Maryland, Balto County, 1987; BSN, Towson State University, 1987-. *Appointments:* Charge Nurse, Neurosurgery 1978-79, Nurse Clinician I Neurologic ICU 1979-84, Project Coordinator, Stroke Data Bank 1984-, University of Maryland Hospital. *Publications:* Reliability of the ADL scale and its use in telephone interview, 1987; The sensitivity & specificity of the CESD scale in screening for post-stroke depression, 1988. *Memberships:* Fellowship, Stroke Council of the American Heart Association; American Assoc of Neuroscience Nurses. *Hobbies:* Sailing; Tennis; Travel. *Address:* 1303 Maywood Avenue, Ruxton, Maryland 21204, USA.

EDMOND Lauris Dorothy, b. 2 Apr. 1924, Dannevirke, New Zealand. Freelance Writer; part-time University Tutor. m. Trevor Charles Edmond, 16 May 1945. 1 son, 5 daughters. *Education:* Teacher's Certificate, 1943; Speech Therapy Diploma, 1944; BA 1969; MA (1st class Honours), 1972; Hon DLitt, 1988. *Appointments:* High School Teaching, 1969-72; Editor, Post Primary Teachers Journal, 1973-81; Part-time University Tutor, 1980-. *Publications:* Poetry: In Middle Air, 1975; The Pear Tree and other poems, 1977; Wellington Letter A Sequence of Poems, 1980; Seven, 1980; Salt from the North, 1980; Catching it, 1983; Selected Poems, 1984; Seasons and Creatures, 1986; Summer near the Arctic Circle, 1988. Plays: The Mountain, 1981 and 1986; Between Night and Morning, 1981. Fiction: High Country Weather, 1984; Stories published in Women's Fiction, New Zealand Listener; Overland; More; Magazine; Metro. Editorial: Dancing to my Tune, 1973; Young Writing, 1979; Selected Letters of A R D Fairburn, 1981; Women in Wartime, 1986. *Honours:* Best First Book Award, PEN New Zealand, 1975; Katherine Mansfield Memorial Fellowship, 1981; Writer's Residency, Deakin University, Melbourne, 1985; Visiting Performer: Cambridge Poetry Festival, 1985; Commonwealth Poetry Prize, 1985; Laufen Conference in Commonwealth Literature, West Germany, 1986; Member of Writers' Group sent by Ministry of Foreign Affairs to tour in the USA, 1986; OBE 1986; Lilian Ida Smith Award for Poetry, PEN New Zealand, 1987; Perth Arts Festival, 1987; National Word Festival Canberra, 1987; Victoria University Writer's Fellowship, 1987; Adelaide Festival, 1988; New Zealand Festival of the Arts, 1988; Poetry reader and speaker for Academy of American Poets, New York, 1988. *Hobbies:* Piano music; 8 Grandchildren. *Address:* 22 Grass Street, Oriental Bay, Wellington, New Zealand.

EDWARDS Jane Elizabeth, b. 31 Mar. 1932, USA. Freelance Author. m. Richard Byron Edwards, 26 Sept. 1953, 3 sons, 2 daughters. *Education:* Catholic Schools, California. *Publications:* What Happened to Amy?, 1961; Carol Stevens, Newspaper Girl, (as Jane Campbell), 1964; The Houseboat Mystery, 1965; Lab Secretary, 1964; The Affair of the Albatross; Believe No Evil, 1969; Co-Author: Mexican American, His Life Across Four Centuries, 1973; Listen with Your Heart, 1986; The Ghost of Castle Kilgarrom, 1987; Susannah is Missing, 1988; The Hesitant Heart, 1988; novelettes; articles & short stories. *Hobbies:* Travel; Gardening; Seashells. *Address:* 2525 Rocky Point Road, Bremerton, WA 98312, USA.

EDWARDS Phyllis, b. 7 Nov. 1944, California, USA. Educational Consultant. m. Hugh A Patterson, 30 Aug. 1966, divorced Feb. 1979. 1 son. *Education:* BA, Wheaton College, 1966; MEd, Boston University, 1973. *Appointments:* Teacher, Boston Public Schools, 1967-72; Teacher, Department Head, Wayland Public Schools, 1972-76; Project Director, Oakland Public Schools,

1977-81; Principal, Greenfield USD, 1981-86; Curriculum Consultant, Monterey Peninsula, USD, 1986-. *Publication:* Reading in the Content Areas, 19072. *Memberships:* Association for California School Administrators; Association for Supervision and Curriculum Development; California Association for Supervision and Curriculum Development; International Reading Association; California Reading Association; National Council for Teachers of English; National Council for Social Studies; Sierra Club. *Hobbies:* Music; Little Theatre; Jogging; Skiing. *Address:* 46 Los Encinos Drive, Del Rey Oaks, CA 93940, USA.

EGELSTON Diane Carroll, b. 26 Mar. 1955, Shirley, Massachusetts, USA. Human Recources Manager; Writer. m. 27 Mar. 1981. *Education:* BA, Humanities, University of California, Berkeley, 1977. *Appointments:* Management Associate, 1980, Operations Supervisor, 1981-82, Senior Training Specialist, 1982-83, Security Pacific Bank; Training Officer, 1983-85, Assistant Vice-President, Training Manager, Consumer Credit Division, 1985-88, Vice President, Human Recources, Wells Fargo Bank, Business Banking group, Wells Fargo Bank, San Francisco, California. *Publications:* Numerous articles in magazines including Ms, Business Week's Careers, Collegiate Career Woman, Business Woman, Working Writer. *Memberships:* Board of Directors, Vice-President Public Relations/Communications, Former Editor, Golden Gate Chapter, American Society for Training and Development; Professional Member, National Writers Club; Professional Member, California Writers Club. *Honours:* Elizabeth Crothers Mills Prize for Literary Composition, University of California, 1977. *Hobbies:* Gardening; Cooking; Running; Hiking; Biking; Guitar; Travel. *Address:* Merchant Card Services HR, 1200 Montego, Walnut Creek, CA 94598, USA.

EGENDORF-POMERANTZ Norma Lucy, b. 7 Oct. 1928, Philadlephia, USA. President, Advertising Agency. m. Jerry Pomerantz, 27 Sept. 1986. *Educationn:* Diploma, Charles Morris Price School of Advertising & Journalism, 1948; Temple University, 1950-52. *Appointments:* Advertising Assistant 1952-54, Advertising Sales Pormotion Manager 1954- 61, International Resistance Company; Account Executive, 1961-68, Vice President, Account Supervisor, 1968-72, Mel Richman Inc.; President, The Advertising People Inc., 1972-84; President, de Marco Egendorf, 1984-; Lecturer, Communications Industry. *Publications:* Contributor to professional journals. *Memberships:* Numerous professional organisations. *Honours:* Gold Mail Boax Award, National Director Marketing Association, 1968; Silver Medal, American Advertising Federation, 1980; Award of Merit, Artists Guild of Delaware, 1981; Distinguished Alumna, Charles Morris Price School of Advertising & Journalism, 1982. *Hobbies:* Tennis; Art; Music; Sculpture. *Address:* 730 S. American Street, Philadelphia, PA 19147, USA.

EHMEN Betty Hersey, b. 29 Oct. 1927, Butler County, Iowa, USA. Manager. m. George Ehmen, 21 May 1946, died 1979, 1 son, 1 daughter. *Education:* Iowa State Teachers College, 1945. *Appointments:* Rural Schoolteacher, 1945-48; Farmwife, Homemaker, 1948-68; Grain Elevator Manager, 1968-79; Senior Services Manager, 1979-. *Publications:* Weekly column, Parkersburg Eclipse. *Memberships:* Federated Woman's Club, President, County Chairman; Republican Party; Goodwill Industries Volunteer Services, Membership Chairman; Parkersburg Chamber of Commerce. *Honours:* Recipient, various honours. *Hobbies:* Photography; Camping; Reading; Travel. *Address:* 301 First Street, Parkersburg, IA 50665, USA.

EHRMANN Susanna, b. 17 Oct. 1944, Detroit, Michigan, USA. Foreign Language Teacher. *Education:* French Summer School, Laval University, Canada, 1965; BA, Antioch College, 1966; MAT, University of Chicago, 1968. *Appointments:* Foreign languages teacher: Laboratory Schools, University of Chicago, 1967-74; Maimonides School, Brookline, Massachusetts, 1975-76; North Shore Country Day School, Winnetka, Illinois, 1977-78; Copenhagen International Junior School,

1978-79; Houston Community College, Texas, 1979-81, 1984; Kinkaid School, Houston, 1980-82; Alief Independent School District, Houston, 1982-85; Private instructor, freelance researcher/editor, 1986-. *Publications:* German Grammar Game, 1982; Erasing Mitt, 1987. *Memberships:* American Associations, Teachers of German, Teachers of French. *Honours:* National Defence Education Act Fellowships, US Government, 1966-68; Grant, Goethe Institute, 1983. *Hobbies:* Writing; Sewing; Needlework; Reading; Tennis; Horseback Riding; Art; Music. *Address:* 651 Bering Drive, No. 703, Houston, TX 77057, USA.

EICHELBERGER Alyce Faye, b. 28 Oct. 1944, Frederick, Oklahoma, USA. Child Psychotherapist; Clinical Psychologist. m. Martin Davis Eichelberger Jr, 22 Jan. 1966, 2 sons. *Education:* BS Honours, Oklahoma State University, 1965; MA 1974, MSc 1975, graduate certificates 1976, 1977, Baylor University; Graduate work, Tavistock Clinic & University of London Institute of Education, London, UK, 1979-87. *Appointments include:* Secondary school teacher, Texas, 1962-69; Teaching assistant, special education, Baylor University, 1974-75; Educational psychologist, Waco, Texas, 1975-78; Secondary teacher, emotionally disturbed children 1980-83, children with medical & emotional problems 1983-84, Inner London Education Authority UK; Trainee 1981-85, child psychotherapist 1985-, Tavistock Clinic; Child psychotherapist, emotionally disturbed children, ILEA, 1985-. *Publications include:* Various professional articles & case studies. *Memberships include:* Fellow, Diplomate, American Medical Psychotherapist Association; Association of Child Psychotherapy; American Psychological Association; Associate, Chartered Psychologist, British Psychological Society; Royal Society of Medicine. *Address:* 70 Scott Ellis Gardens, St John's Wood, London NW8 6PE, England.

EICHINGER Marilynne H, Executive Director. *Education:* BA, magna cum laude, Boston University, 1965; MA 1971, 1971, Michigan State University. *Appointments:* Ingham County Medical Health Center, 1972; Numerous workshops, 1973-89; Instructor, Lansing Community College, 1978; Partnership, Eyrie Studio, 1982-85; President/Executive Director, Impression 5 Museum, 1973-85; Executive Director, Oregon Museum of Science and Industry, 1985-. *Publications:* Lexington Montessori School Survey, with Jane Mack, 1969; Manual on the Five Senses, 1974; Publisher, Boing magazine, Michigan Edition; Presented numerous workshops to schools, organisations and professional societies. *Memberships:* Association of Science & Technology Centers (ASTC); American Association of Museums; Portland Rotary Club; Oregon Museum Association; City Club of Portland; Portland Chamber of Commerce. *Honours:* Recipient of numerous grants. *Hobby:* Travel; Painting. *Address:* Oregon Museum of Science and Industry, 4015 SW Canyon Road, Portland, Oregon 97221, USA.

EIFFLER-ORTON Carol A., b. 25 Dec. 1948, Chicago, Illinois, USA. Professional Writer. m. 18 June 1975. *Education:* BA, Elmhurst College, Elmhurst, Illinois, 1982; MBA, Rosary College, River Forest, Illinois, 1985. *Appointments:* Executive Secretary to Vice-President, Inryco Inc, 1974- 82; Professional Writer, Resumes and Promotional Materials, 1982-; Secretary to Chairman of Board, Warren Barr Supply Co, 1983-84. *Publications:* Senior's Pastime, in Elmhurst College Magazine; Numerous articles in local publications. *Memberships:* Association of MBA Executives; National Association for Female Executives; Women in Management; National Network of Women in Sales, National Recording Secretary 1987, NW Chapter President 1988-89, NW Chapter Career Opportunity Co-Chair 1987. *Honours:* National Chairman's Award for Outstanding Achievement, National Network of Women in Sales, 1987; Beverly Kievman Leadership Award, National Network of Women in Sales, NW Chapter, 1988. *Hobbies:* Needlepoint; Periodical reading; Cycling; Opera. *Address:* Words By CEO, 304 East Lyndale, Northlake, IL 60164, USA.

EILLAM Esther, b. 12 July 1939, Israel. *Education:* BA, Philosophy 1968, BA Psychology, 1973, Tel Aviv University. *Appointments:* Founder Member, Israel Feminist Movement, Oranizer, Lecturer, 1972-; Re-evaluation Co-Counselling Teacher, 1978-; Founder, Rape Crisis Centre, Tel Aviv, 1978-. *Publications:* Numerous Papers. *Memberships Include:* ICPR; Womens Personal Growth Centre; Womens Guard; Womens Forum; Women Against Violence; Secretariat Member, Citizens Rights & Peace Party. *Honours:* Grants include: ISIS International, Geneva, 1983; Skaggs Foundation, San Francisco, USA, 1985. *Address:* 5 Blum Street, Tel Aviv 69461, Israel.

EILOART Mildred Joy, b. 31 Oct. 1930, Iver, Buckinghamshire, England. Secretary/PA. *Education:* Claremont, Esher, Surrey; Diploma, Mayfair Secretarial College, 1948-49. *Appointments:* Secretary, Colefax & Fowler Ltd., 1954-58; Secretary, Federation of British Industries, 1959-63; Secretary, Chief of Navy Section, Operations Division, Supreme Headquarters Allied Powers in Europe, Paris, 1963-64; Temporary Secretary, Fleet Street Bureau, 1964-65; Secretary, Assistant Librarian to Economic Adviser, Rio Tinto-Zinc Corp., 1965-81; voluntary Prison Work. *Membership:* European Association of Professional Secretaries. *Hobbies:* Theatre; Ballet; Music; Horse-racing; Walking; Travel. *Address:* Flat 38, 7 Elm Park Gardens, London SW10 9QG,, England.

EISEMAN Leatrice, Education: BA, Psychology. *Appointments:* Counseling Specialist, Color Consultant; Executive Director, Pantone Color Institute; Radio & TV appearances. *Publications:* Alive with Color; Pantone Color News. *Memberships:* Womens International Network; Color Association of US; Color Marketing Group; Fashion Group; ASID, Organization. *Honours:* Occupational Training Award, 1975; Color Marketing Group Chairholder, 1987; Governor's Converence for Women in Business, 1988; Key Award: Notable Author. *Hobbies:* Reading; Music; Gardening; Antiques. *Address:* 1677 Elmsford Place, West Lake Village, CA 91361, USA.

EISLER Ann, b. 17 Jan. 1954, Whittier, California, USA. Clinical Director, Rape Crisis Center. m. Richard Eisler, 11 Sept. 1976, 1 son. *Education:* Valedictorian, Pacific High School, San Bernardino, California, 1972; BS, Iowa State University, 1976; MSW, University of Texas at Austin, 1985. *Appointments:* Copy Editor, Feature Writer, The Albuquerque Tribune, Albuquerque, New Mexico, 1976-79; Sexual Abuse Intake Worker, Department of Human Services, Austin, Texas, 1985-86; Therapist, 1986- 87, Clinical Director, 1987-, Albuquerque Rape Crisis Center. *Memberships:* Phi Beta Kappa; Mortar Board; Phi Kappa Phi; Kappa Alpha Theta, Treasurer, Vice-President; National Association of Social Workers; Temple Albert, Board of Trustees, Sisterhood President. *Honours:* Bank of America Award for Fine Arts, 1972; California Scholarship Federation State Champion, 1972; Elks Club Young Leaders State Champion, State of California, 1972; William Kershner Scholarship Award Winner for the Study of Journalism, 1974. *Hobbies:* Bridge; Drama. *Address:* Albuquerque Rape Crisis Center, 1025 Hermosa SE, Albuquerque, NM 87108, USA.

EISNER Susan Pamela, b. 19 Apr. 1950, New York, USA. Communications Executive and Management Consultant. *Education:* BA, Wellesley College, 1971; MPA Kennedy School of Government, Harvard University, 1974. *Appointments:* Staff Intern to Senator Javits, US Senate, Washington, 1970; Staff, Department of Health Education and Welfare, Washington, 1971; Assistant to Director of Communications, Democratic National Committee, Washington, 1972; National Coordinator, Press Operations, McGovern Presidential Campaign, Washington, 1972; Director of Communications, Democratic National Committee Telethons II and III, Washington and Los Angeles, 1973-74; Creative Director, Ways and Means, Inc, Louisville, 1974; Producer/Writer 1975-79, Assistant Director of Broadcasting 1979-81, Director of Acquisitions,

Scheduling and Specials 1981, Director of Broadcasting 1981-83, Special Adviser to Senior Vice President 1983, WNET/THIRTEEN Television; President, Susan Eisner Associates, New York, 1983-; Director of Communications, March of Dimes Birth Defects Foundation National, New York, 1985-86; Folk Singer, Boston, 1969-71; Special consultant to Whitney Young, Executive Director, National Urban League, New York, 1969-71; Tutor, MIT, 1972. *Creative works:* Director of Broadcasting for various television programmes and mini series; Executive producer and producer various television specials, spots, reports and segments; Author of speeches, presentations. *Memberships include:* American Ballet Theatre, 1980-; Manhattan Theatre Club, 1984-. *Honours include:* NAEB Graphics and Design Awards, 1978 and 1979. *Hobbies:* Travel; Film; Arts & Culture; Photography; Writing; Athletics/health and fitness. *Address:* One Lincoln Plaza, Suite 38-U, New York, NY 10023, USA.

EISNER Wendy Jane, b. 5 Apr. 1953, New York City, USA. Assistant Professor, Psychology. *Education:* BA, Philosophy, Wellesley College, 1971-75; MA, Anthropology, Columbia University, 1977-79; PhD, Psychology, CUNY, 1980-87. *Appointments:* Instructor, Nassau Community College (SUNY), Garden City, 1988-; Psychology Instructor/Assistant Professor, Hunter College, New York City, 1980-88; Adjunct Faculty, Neurophysiology, Rockefeller University, New York City, 1988-; Guest Investigator, Neurophysiology, Rockefeller University, New York City, 1987-88; Research Assistant, Anthropology, American Museum of Natural History, 1980. *Publications:* Doctoral dissertation: Cerebral asymmetry during visual pattern recognition: A dynamic view, 1987. *Memberships:* American Psychology Association (Psychology and Art Division); Eastern Psychology Association; International Association of Empirical Aesthetics; National Art Education Association; NY Academy of Sciences; New York Neuropsychology Group; Society for Philosophy and Psychology; Society for Neuropsychology Group; Society for Philosophy & Psychology; Society for Neuro-Science. *Honours:* Helena Rubenstein Foundation Tuition Grant, 1985; Biopsychology Distinguished Student Award, 1984, First recipient; Sigma Xi, 1984; Phi Beta Kappa, 1975; Wellesley College Freshman Honours, 1972, Scholar 1975; National Merit Scholar, 1971. *Address:* Nassau Community College, Psychology Department, Garden City, NY 11530, USA.

ELDEFRAWI Amira Toppozada, b. 10 Feb. 1937, Giza, Egypt. Professor of Pharmacology. m. Mohyee E. Eldefrawi, 18 July 1957, 2 sons, 1 daughter. *Education:* BSc, Agriculture, University of Alexandria, Egypt, 1957; PhD, Entomology (Toxicology), University of California, Berkeley, USA, 1960. *Appointments:* Assistant Professor, University of Alexandria, Egypt, 1960-68; Research Assistant, then Research Associate Professor, Section of Neurobiology and Behaviour, Cornell University, Ithaca, New York, USA, 1968-76; Research Associate Professor, then Professor, Department of Pharmacology and Experimental Therapeutics, School of Medicine, University of Maryland, Baltimore, 1976-. *Publications:* Book: Myasthenia Gravis; 190 scientific publications. *Memberships:* Society for Toxicology; Society for Neuroscience; Entomology Society of America; American Society for Pharmacology and Experimental Therapeutics. *Honours:* Exemption from out-of-state tuition, University of California; Scholar-in-Resident, Queen's University School of Medicine, Kingston, Canada. *Hobbies:* Travel; Gardening. *Address:* University of Maryland, School of Medicine, Department of Pharmacology & Experimental Therapeutics, 655 W Baltimore Street, Baltimore, MD 21201, USA.

ELKINS Margreta Anne, b. 16 Oct. 1930, Brisbane, Queensland, Australia. Opera Singer; Lecturer. m. Henry James Elkins, 30 Dec. 1950, 1 daughter. *Education:* Government Opera Scholarship, Education Department. *Appointments include:* Brisbane Opera Company; National Opera Company, Australia; Carl Rosa Opera Company; Dublin Opera Company; Royal Opera House, Covent Garden, London, Concerts & operas, Europe, USA, Canada, Australia, Australian Opera Company. Lyric Opera, Brisbane; Victorian Opera, Melbourne. *Memberships:* Life Member, Lyric Opera (Queensland), Joan Sutherland Society (Sydney). *Honours:* Australia Medal; Honorary Doctorate of Music, Queensland University; Honorary Ambassador, World Expo, 1988. *Hobbies:* Horse Riding; Painting; Gardening. *Address:* c/o Jenifer Eddy Artists Management, Suite 11, The Cliveden, 596 St Kilda Road, Melbourne 3004, Australia.

ELLARD Cynthia Orrick, b. 7 Oct. 1957, Fayette County, Kentucky, USA. Exercise Physiologist; Administrator. *Education:* BS, Lander College, 1979; MS, University of Southern Mississippi, 1986. *Appointments:* Director, women's programmes & phase III rehabilitation, Institute for Wellness & Sports Medicine, Hattiesburg, Mississippi, 1986-87; Director of Wellness, Oktibbeh County Hospital, Starkville, 1987-. *Memberships:* American College of Sports Medicine; Association for Fitness in Business; Worksite coordinator, American Heart Association. *Honours:* Thomas & Blanche Hope Memorial Scholarship, 1975-78; Alumni scholarship, Morehead State University, 1975; Scholarship, Atheneum Club, 1978. *Hobbies:* Music; Jogging; Travel. *Address:* Wellness Connection, Oktibbehy County Hospital, Hospital Road, Starkville, Mississippi 39759, USA.

ELLES Diana, (Baroness) b. 19 July 1921. Life Peer; Member, European Parliament. m. Neil Elles, 14 Aug. 1945, 1 son, 1 daughter. *Education:* BA, Honours, London University, 1941; Barrister at Law, Lincoln's Inn, 1956. *Appointments:* Voluntary Social Work, 1956-72; Chairman, Conservative Party International Office, 1973-79; UK Delegate to UN, 1973; Member, UN Sub-commission, 1974-75; Opposition Spokesman, House of Lords, 1975-79. *Publications:* numerous articles, studies on social subjects, European and foreign policy issues, human rights of non-citizens & UN publications *Memberships:* Institute of International Affairs, Council Member, 1977-85; Governor, British Institute, Florence, 1986-; Member, European Parliament, 1979-, Vice President, 1982-87; Chairman, Legal Affairs Committee, 1987-. *Hobbies:* Reading; Music; Swimming. *Address:* House of Lords, London SW1, England.

ELLIOT OF HARWOOD Katharine, (Baroness) b. 15 Jan. 1903. Peer of the Realm. m. Rt. Honourable Walter E Elliot, 2 Apr. 1934. *Education:* Hon. LLD, Glasgow University, 1959. *Memberships:* Roxburgshire County Council, 1946-75; Chairman, National Association Youth Clubs, 1930-49; Carnegie Unitted Kingdom Trust, 1940-86, Chairman 1965; King George's Jubilee Trust, 1936-68; Delegate, UN General Assembly, 1954-57. *Hobbies:* Farmer, President Royal Highland Agricultural Society, 1986-; Social Services; Youth Work; Fox Hunting; Golf. *Address:* Harwood, Bonchester Bridge, Hawick, Roxburghshire TD9 9TL, Scotland.

ELLIOTT Carol Harris, b. 26 Mar. 1950, Chicago, Illinois, USA. Registered Dietitian. m. Craig C Elliott, 12 Aug. 1973. 1 son, 1 daughter. *Education:* BS Dietetics, Michigan State University, 1972; Dietetic Internship, Henry Ford Hospital, Detroit, Michigan, 1973. *Appointments:* Chief Therapeutic Dietitian, Seiler's Corporation, 1973-75; Consultant Dietitian, Homestead Rest Nursing Home, 1973-77; Consultant Dietitian, Mountain View Nursing Home, 1973-74; Consultant Dietitian, Crescent Manor Nursing Home, 1974-77; Clinical Dietitian, Berkshire Medical Center, 1975-78; Clinical Dietitian, Humana Hospital of Daytona Beach, 1979-81; Faculty Therapeutic Dietitian, Family Practice Center, Halifax Medical Center, 1982-83; President, Carol H Elliott, RD, Inc, Nutritional Counseling Services, Daytona Beach, 1980-. *Publications:* Prenatal Nutrition Booklet/Classes; Nursing Care Nutrition Booklet/Classes; Policy & Procedure Manual, Corporate for Dietary Services. *Memberships include:* American Dietetic Association, 1973-; Florida Dietetic Association, 1978-; Florida East Central Dietetic Association, 1978-; Delta Delta Deltam, Michigan State University, 1969-

; American Business Women's Association, Ormond Beach Chapter, 1981-. *Hobbies:* Physical fitness; Walking; Swimming; Bicycling; Sewing; Tailoring. *Address:* 18 Lake Vista Way, Ormond Beach, Florida 32174, USA.

ELLIOTT Myra Ruth, b. 22 Nov. 1940, Atlanta, Georgia, USA. Writer; Photojournalist. m. 20 Nov. 1965. 3 sons, 2 daughters. *Education:* Attended University of Southern California. *Appointments:* Freelance writer and photographer, 1968-88; Editor, Writer and Photographer, Lanakila Rehabilitation Newsletter, 1968-70; Writer, Editor and Photographer, Property Management News, 1986-88. *Publications:* Books: Maui & the Sun, 1976; The Sixth Great Deed of Maui, 1976; Kimo and the Whale, 1977; Numerous articles to magazines and newspapers. *Memberships:* National Writers Club; Society of Children's Book Writers; Romance Writers Club; Board of Directors for LA Girl's Club. *Hobbies:* Professional quiltmaker; Needlepoint; Embroidery designer. *Address:* 1540 Silver Street, Hermosa Beach, CA 90254, USA.

ELLIOTT-WATSON Doris Jean (born Esther Grace Kriegh), b. 6 Dec. 1932, Caney, Kansas, USA. Educator; Certified Psychiatric/Gerontological Nurse. m. John Stanley Watson, 1 Aug. 1952, 1 son, 1 daughter. *Education:* BEd 1953, MEd 1954, University of Miami, Florida; EdD, Pacific Western University, 1982; BS, Nursing, University of Kansas, 1985; Associate of Science, Psychology, Kansas City, Kansas Community College, 1989. *Appointments:* Journalist, Editor, Park Stylus, 1950-52; Author & speaker, 1950-90; Librarian, University of Miami 1952, Kansas University 1978; Teacher, Shawnee Mission, Kansas, 1961-76; Certified Psychiatric/Gerontological Nurse & Educator, 1985-. *Publications:* Papers: Mainstreaming Special Children; Teaching Non-Readers; Kindergarten Teaching; Sexuality in Nursing Home Patients; Kansas City Rat Infestation & Control. *Memberships include:* Sustaining, Republican National Committee; President, Young Republicans, 1960; Red Cross Nurse, Gerontological Nursing Council, Psychiatric Nursing Council American Nurses Association; Various honour societies. *Honours include:* Featured, National Chamber of Commerce paper, 1960; Breakfast guest, Vice President & Mrs Nixon, 1960; Honourable Mention, Quill & Scroll, 1986; Guest (Republican leaders), President & Mrs Bush, White House, 1989. *Hobbies:* Holistic healing; Gardening; Talking to friends; Republican politics; Camping; Studying; Community involvement. *Address:* 231 Sheidley Avenue, Bonner Springs, Kansas 66012, USA.

ELLIS Ella Thorp, b. 14 July 1928, Los Angeles, California, USA. Novelist. m. 17 Dec. 1949, 3 sons. *Education:* BA, English, University of California, Los Angeles, 1966; MA, San Francisco State University, 1975; Junior College Credential, 1977. *Appointments:* Teacher: Acalanes Adult School, Argentina, 1970-75; San Francisco State University, 1975-80, University of California Extension, 1975-80, 1988: Buenos Aires Seminars, 1980-85. *Publications include:* Celebrate the Morning; Sleepwalker's Moon; Riptide; Where the Road Ends; Hugo & Princess Nena; Roam the Wild Country; Hallelujah. *Memberships:* Authors Guild; Sierra Club; Amnesty International; California Writers Club; Society of Childrens Book Writers. *Hobbies:* Reading; Visiting friends. *Address:* 1438 Grizzly Peak, Berkeley, California 94708, USA.

ELLIS Helen Elizabeth (Oickle), b. 16 Dec. 1926, Brighton, Massachusetts, USA. College Professor Emeritus. m. Frederick E. Ellis, 30 July 1949, 2 sons. *Education:* Diploma, Northampton Commercial College, 1946; BA cum laude, honours in English, 1963, PhD, 1973, University of Massachusetts; MAT, Smith College, 1964. *Appointments:* English Teacher, Mahar Regional School, 1964-65; Associate Professor of English, 1965-77, Chair, Humanities, 1977-86, Professor, 1986-88, Greenfield Community College, Greenfield, Massachusetts. *Publications:* Structures for Composition, 1974, 1978; Exploring Literature, 1983;

Archibald Macleish: Reflections (editor), 1986; Proceedings of the Macleish Symposium (editor), 1988; Many poems in literary journals. *Memberships:* Delta Kappa Gamma; College Media Associates; Pocumtuck Valley Association; Vice-President, Friends of the Macleish Collection; Smith College Alumnae. *Honours:* GCC Trustees Citation for Outstanding Performance, 1982; Walter H.Taylor Award for Leadership in Development of Co-Curricular Activities, 1984; Massachusetts Citation for Outstanding Performance, 1985; Honourable Mention, Billie Murray Denny Poetry Competition, 1986. *Hobbies:* Sewing; Crochet; Bowling; Reading; Writing; Lecturing; Swimming; Walking; Stamp collecting. *Address:* Greenfield Community College, Greenfield, MA 01301, USA.

ELLIS Janet Michell, b. 16 Sept. 1955, Kent, England. TV Presenter. m. Robin Ellis Bextor, 5 Sept. 1976, 1 daughter, divorced 1985. (2) John Leach, 30 July 1988, 1 son. *Education:* Central School of Speech and Drama, 1974-77. *Appointments:* Jackanory Playhouse, BBC; Sundry TV and Theatre including: The Misanthrope, Manchester Royal Exchange; Repertory in Harrogate, Leeds, Fringe Theatre; Jigsaw, TV Series and Blue Peter; Open Air, Motor Show TV Series. *Hobbies:* Walking; Shopping for Clothes; Changing my Mind. *Address:* c/o Arlington Enterprises, 1-3 Charlotte Street, London W1, England.

ELLIS Joyce Eileen, b. 31 Aug. 1950, St Louis, Missouri, USA. Freelance Writer; Editor. m. Steven Wayne Ellis, 29 Nov. 1969, 1 son, 2 daughters. *Appointments:* Food Preparer, Dairy Queen, 1966-68; Clerical Worker, Dayton's Department Store, 1968-70; Freelance Writer, Editor, 1972-; Craft Teacher/Sales, Artcraft Concepts, 1979. *Publications:* Wee Pause, 1977; The Big Split, 1979; Overnight Mountain, 1979; Tell Me a Story, Lord Jesus, 1981; Snowmobile Trap, 1981; The Big Split, reissued, 1983; Plug into God's Rainbow, 1984; Tiffany, 1986. *Memberships:* National League of American Penwomen; Minnesota Christian Writers Guild, past President, Seminar Director. *Honours:* Nominee, Gold Medallion Award, fiction, Evangelical Christian Publishers Association, 1980; Outstanding Young Woman of America, 1980; etc. *Hobbies:* Music; Needlework; Camping; Swimming; Reading; Travel. *Address:* 17372 Evener Way, Eden Prairie, MN 55346, USA.

ELLIS Melody Genneane, b. 25 Apr. 1952, Houston, Texas, USA. Investment Banker; Educator. m. McKen Vincent Carrington, 25 July 1987. *Education:* BS, Business, Texas Southern University, 1974; MEd 1976, EdD 1984, University of Houston. *Appointments:* Educator, 1974-83; Marketing Manager, IPI, 1983-85; Legislative Liaison, TSU, 1985-87; Consultant, Apex Securities, Inc, 1988-; Educator, University of Houston, 1988-. *Memberships:* American Management Society; Association of Information Processors; National Association of Notaries; Association for the Advancement of Black Americans in Vocational Education; National Association of School Board Members; Delta Pi Epsilon National Business Education Honor Society; Texas Association of School Boards; Houston Area Urban League; Leadership Houston; American Leadership Forum; Houston Chapter NAACP; Coalition of 100 Black Women; Task Force for the Recruitment and Retention of Foster Parents; Enron Scholarship Foundation Board; Houston Independent School Board of Education, 1988-92; Houston Community College, Board of Trustees, 1988-89. *Honours:* Texas State Board of Education Fellowship, 1979; Outstanding Young Woman of America, 1979, 1980, 1983; Human Enrichment for Life Young Black Achiever Award, 1985; Houston Area Urban League Whitney B Young Volunteer of the Year Award, 1985. *Hobbies:* Music; Crafts; Biking. *Address:* 3240 Holly Hall, Houston, Texas 77054, USA.

ELLSTROM CALDER Annette Elaine, b. 19 Dec. 1952, Duluth, Minnesota, USA. Clinical Social Worker; Lecturer; Researcher. m. Jeffrey Ellstrom Calder, 30 July 1982. *Education:* BA, Social Work, Psychology,

Sociology, Concordia College, Moorhead, Minnesota, 1974; MS, Social Work, University of Wisconsin, Madison, 1978. *Appointments:* Social Worker, Department of Social Services, Jackson County, 1975-77; Lecturer in Medicine, Medical School, 1979-82, Lecturer in Social Work, Graduate School of Social Work, 1979-, University of Wisconsin, Madison; Clinical Social Worker, 1979-, Principal Investigator in Research, 1985-86, University of Wisconsin Hospital, Madison. *Publications:* Reference Handbook: A Guide for Patients and Families (editor), 1984, 2nd Edition, 1986; Self Help Resource Guide, 1985; Developmemt of a Psychosocial Intervention Assessment Tool (principal investigator), 1985-86; Articles in Perspectives, American Journal of Kidney Diseases. *Memberships:* Council of Nephrology Social Workers (National Vice-President 1984-86); National Research Committee, American Association of Spinal Cord Psychologists & Social Workers; Wisconsin Chapter, Council of Nephrology Social Workers; National Association of Social Workers; National Delegate/Board of Directors, National Training & Education Committee, National Patient Services Committee, National Kidney Foundation; Former Chairman, Board of Directors, other former offices, National Kidney Foundation of Wisconsin. *Honours:* Pi Gamma Mu, 1974; Honorary adoption, Winnebago Indian tribe, 1978; Volunteer Service Award, 1983, Volunteer of the Year Award, 1984, Health Advancement Award, 1985, National Kidney Foundation of Wisconsin; National Nephrology Social Worker of the Year Award, Council of Nephrology Social Workers, 1987; Outstanding Young Wisconsinite, Wisconsin Jaycees, 1988. *Hobbies:* Community service; Hiking; Camping; Skiing; Gardening; Swimming; Travel. *Address:* 3538 Topping Road, Madison, WI 53705, USA.

ELLSWORTH Cynthia Ann, b. 19 Jan. 1950, Springfield, Ohio, USA. Teacher. *Education:* BS, El.Ed., Western Connecticut State University, 1972; MS, Sp.Ed., Ohio University, 1976; MS, Counselor Education, University of Dayton, 1986. *Appointments:* Teacher, Federal Hocking Schools, Stewart, 1972-76; Supervisor, EMR/LD Vinton County Schools, MacArthur, 1976-77; Teacher, Southwestern City Schools, 1977-. *Memberships:* Council for Exceptional Children; Phi Delta Kappa; National Education Association; Southwestern Education Association; Ohio School Counselor Association. *Honours:* Outstanding Young Woman of America, 1980; School Bell Award, 1984. *Hobbies:* Gardening; Reading; Bicycling. *Address:* 421 East Whittier Street, Columbus, OH 43206, USA.

ELLWOOD Edith Elizabeth Muesing, b. 18 Sept. 1947, New York City, New York, USA. Writer; Researcher; Editor. m. 15 Sept. 1980, 1 son, 2 daughters. *Education:* BA, Fordham University, Bronx, New York, 1969; MA, New York Univesity, New York City, 1971. *Appointments:* Freelance Writer, The Academic Research Group, 1975-78, 1980-82; Administrative Assistant, English-Speaking Union, 1979; Editor, Publisher, Colin-Press, 1984-88; Currently Ellwood Editing and Research Services. *Publications:* United States Democracy: Myth vs Reality, 1985; The Alternative to Technological Culture, 1986; Tips on Self-Publishing, 1988; The Individual in High Technological Society, 1989; The First Day of School, 1989; Haiku in small press magazines, 1979-89. *Memberships:* Professional Member, National Writers Club; International Women's Writing Guild; National Organization for Women; Women in Scholarly Publishing, Newsletter Column Writer and Editor; National Trust for Historic Preservation. *Honours:* Invited Paper on Technological Culture, Ethics and Religion, delivered at international seminar; Tied 1st Place, Readers Vote for Best of the Spring Issue, for Dragonfly, East/West Haiku Quarterly, 1985. *Hobbies:* Sketching; Music; Country Furniture. *Address:* 229B Pond Way, Staten Island, NY 10303, USA.

ELORANTA Nancy J, b. 16 Dec. 1955, Fort Wayne, Indiana, USA. Architect. *Education:* Bachelor of Architecture and Environmental Science, Ball State University, 1980. *Appointments:* Schenkel & Shultz, Inc, 1979-83; Cole, Matoit, Riley, 1983-84; LeRoy Troyer & Assoc, 1984-86; National Architectural Services, 1986-. *Creative works:* Buildings: Menno Hof, Shipshewana, Indiana (Museum); Carmelite Monastery, Maryland; Trinity Evangelical Free Church, Michigan. *Memberships:* American Institute of Architects; Indiana Society of Architects; Northern Indiana Chapter/AA Board of Directors, 1986-87; Habitat for Humanity of Lafayette (Vice Pres/Bd of Directors 1987-88); Habitat for Humanity of Elkhart County (Vice Pres/Bd of Directors 1986). *Hobbies:* Calligraphy; Music; Photography; Gardening; Volunteer work in local community. *Address:* 1719 Vermont Ave, Fort Wayne, Indiana 46805 USA.

EL-SAFFAR Ruth Anthony, b. 12 June 1941, New York City, New York, USA. Professor; Psychotherapist. m. Zuhair El-Saffar, 11 Apr. 1965, 2 sons, 1 daughter. *Education:* BA, Colorado College, 1962; PhD, Johns Hopkins University, 1966. *Appointments:* Assistant Professor, University of Maryland, 1967-68; Professor, 1968-88, Research Associate, Professor, 1989-, University of Illinois, Chicago; Professor, Northwestern University, Illinois, 1988-89. *Publications:* Novel to Romance, 1974; Distance and Control in Don Quixote, 1975; Beyond Fiction, 1984; Over 50 articles; Over 40 poems; Many book reviews. *Memberships:* Modern Language Association, Executive Council 1974-78, Committee on Future of Profession, 1980-81; Cervantes Society, Executive Committee 1979-88, Vice-President/President 1989-95. *Honours:* Woodrow Wilson Fellow, 1962; National Endowment for the Humanities Fellow, 1970, 1990, Guggenheim Fellow, 1975; Newberry Library Fellow, 1983; Senior University Scholar Award, University of Illinois, 1986- 89; Doctor of Humane Letters (honorary), Colorado College, 1987. *Hobbies:* Poetry; Philosophy; History of science; Recorder music. *Address:* 7811 Greenfield, River Forest, IL 60305, USA.

ELSHTAIN Jean Bethke, b. 6 Jan. 1941, Windsor, Colorado, USA. Professor; Writer; Lecturer. m. Errol L. Elshtain, 3 Sept. 1965, 1 son, 3 daughters. *Education:* AB, Highest Distinction, History, 1963; MA, 1965; PhD, Politics 1973. *Appointments:* Assistant to full Professor, University of Massachusetts, 1973-88; Centennial Professor of Political Science, Vanderbilt University, 1988-; Visiting Professor, Yale University, Oberlin College. *Publications:* Books: Public Man, Private Woman, 1981; The Family in Political Thought, 1982; Meditations on Modern Political Thought, 1986; Women & War, 1987; Women, Militarism & War (with Sheila Tobias), 1989. Also: Over 100 articles & essays. *Memberships include:* American Political Science Association; National Book Critics Circle; PEN International; International Political Science Association; Amnesty International. *Honours include:* Writer-in-Residence, MacDowell Colony, 1981; Fellow, Institute for Advanced Study, Princeton, New Jersey, 1981-82; Scholar-in-Residence, Bellagio Conference & Study Centre, 1983; President's Writing Award, University of Massachusetts, 1985; Numerous fellowships & grants. *Hobbies:* Animal welfare; Rock music; Films; Fiction; Travel; Pop culture. *Address:* Department of Political Science, Vanderbilt University, Nashville Tennessee 37235, USA.

ELSY Winifred Mary, Journalist; Travel Writer. *Education:* Diploma, Oakley Training College for Teachers. *Appointments:* Teaching, 3 schools; Realist Film Studio; Assoc Rediffusion TV; Children's Encyclopedia; BPC, Evans Bros; Children's Book Editor, Abelard-Schuman. *Publications:* Travels in Belgium & Luxemburg; Brittany and Normandy; Travels in Brittany; Travels in Normandy; Travels in Alsace and Lorraine; Travels in Burgundy. *Memberships:* Society of Authors; Institute of Journalists; British Guild of Travel Writers; PEN International; Camden History Society; Royal Overseas League. *Hobbies:* History; Travel; Art. *Address:* 519c Finchley Road, London NW3 7BB, England.

EMBLETON Sheila Margaret, b. 18 Nov. 1954, Ottawa, Canada. *Education:* BSc., 1975, MSc, 1976, PhD, 1981, University of Toronto. *Appointments:* Professor, York University, 1980-. *Publications:*

Statistics in Historical Linguistics, 1986; articles in: Diachronica, Language, Word, Canadian Journal of Linguistics. *Memberships:* Linguistic Society of America, Editorial Board; International Linguistic Association, Executive Board; Linguistic Association of Canada and US, Executive Board; Canadian Society for the Study of Names, President; Canadian Linguistic Association, Programme Committee. *Honours:* various Grants, Fellowships, prizes. *Hobbies:* Classical Music; Figure Skating; Languages; Travel. *Address:* Dept. of Languages Literatures & Linguistics, South 561 Ross Building, York University, North York, Ontario, Canada M3J 1P3.

EMEK Sharon Helene, b. 23 Oct. 1945, Brooklyn, New York, USA. Business Consultant. 1 son, 2 daughters. *Education:* BA, City College, New York, 1967; MA, Brooklyn College, 1970; EdD, Rutgers University, 1977. *Appointments:* Director, Preliminary English Skills, Small College Programme, Brooklyn College, 1968; Director, American Centre for Reading Skills, Tel Aviv, Israel, 1971; Assistant Professor of English, Brookdale Community College (New Jersey) 1973, Livingston College, Rutgers University 1977; Vice president, Radzik & Emek business consultants, 1980- . *Publications:* The Manager's Keys, 1987; Managing Employees the Easy Way, 1986; Dealing Successfully with Key Management Issues, 1986; Various articles, professional journals & business magazines. *Memberships:* American Management Association; American Society for PC. *Honour:* Award, promising research, National Council of Teachers of English, 1978. *Hobbies:* Writing; Music; Sports. *Address:* 547 North Main Street, Hightstown, New Jersey 08520, USA.

EMERSON Tamsen Leigh, b. 16 Dec. 1956, Denver, USA. Librarian; Historian. *Education:* BA, American History, Colorado State University, 1979; MLS, Emporia State University, 1984; MA, American History, Emporia State University, 1988. *Appointments:* Documents Dept., University of Wyoming Libraries, 1986-88; Reference/Collection Development Librarian, University of Wyoming Libraries, 1988-. *Publications:* Articles in various journals and magazines including: The Great Plains Newsletter. *Memberships:* American, Wyoming, Mountain Plains, Library Associations; American Association of State & Local History; Western History Association, Vice President; Pi Gamma Mu; Wyoming State Historical Society. *Honours:* Recipient, various honours and awards. *Hobbies:* Outdoor Sports; Watching Rodeos; Travel; Counted Cross Stitch. *Address:* Coe Library Reference Dept., University of Wyoming Libraries, PO Box 3334, University Station, Laramie, WY 82071, USA.

ENGEL Susan Charlotte, b. 25 Mar. 1935, Vienna, Austria. Actress. m. Sylvester Morand, 9 Feb. 1968. 1 daughter. *Education:* BA Bristol University; Sorbonne University, Paris, France; Bristol Old Vic Theatre School, England. *Appointments:* Bristol Old Vic Theatre, 1959; Royal Court Theatre, London, 1960; Mermaid Theatre, 1961; Member of Royal Shakespeare Company, Stratford and Aldwych Theatre, playing lead roles including: Queen Elizabeth in Wars of the Roses. Numerous leading roles in West End Theatre productions including: Olga in Three Sisters; Gertrude in Hamlet; Watch on the Rhine, National Theatre; A kind of Alaska, by Harold Pinter, Duchess Theatre; Brighton Beach Memoirs, Aldwych Theatre, 1986-87; Constance in King John, Royal Shakespeare Theatre, Stratford-upon-Avon and the Barbican, 1988-89. Numerous television and film roles including: Regan in King Lear; Grand Duchess Olga in Anastasia. *Address:* 15 Compayne Gardens, London NW6 3DG, England.

ENGEL Tala, (F) b. 29 Aug. 1933, New York City, USA. Attorney. m. James Colias, 22 Nov. 1981. *Education:* BA, 1954, JD, 1957, University of Miami. *Appointments:* Private Practice, Miami, 1957-61; Attorney, Immigration Service, Chicago, 1961-62; Parole Agent, Illinois Youth Comm., Chicago, 1963-66; Private Practice, Immigration Law: Chicago, 1966-86, Washington DC, 1987-. *Publications:* Miami Law Quarterly, articles on criminal & insurance law, 1955. *Memberships:* District of Columbia, American, Chicago, Illinois State, Florida and Federal Bar Associations; American Immigration Lawyers Association. *Honours:* Recipient, various honours and awards. *Hobbies:* Theatre; Singing; Travel; Mensa; Speaking Russian & Spanish; etc. *Address:* 1730 K St., NW, Suite 304, Washington, DC 20006, USA.

ENGELHARDT M Veronice (Sister, OSF), b. 29 Mar. 1912, Syracuse, New York, USA. Educational Psychologist; Guidance Counsellor. *Education:* BS Education 1937, MA Education, MA Psychology 1938, PhD Educational Psychology 1962, Catholic University, Washington DC; Graduate work, various universities. *Appointments:* Elementary & secondary school teaching & administration, college & university instructor, Associate Professor. Positions include: Head, Department of Education & Psychology, & Founder-Director, Reading & Speech Clinics, Maria Regina College, Syracuse, NY, 1962- 68; Founder, Director, Franciscan Learning Centre, Syracuse, 1968-83; Counsellor, Educational Psychologist, Remedial Instructor, Most Holy Redeemer School, Tampa, Florida, 1983-. Lecturer, speaker, various educational conventions, teachers' institutes, Diocesan meetings, 11 US States including Hawaii; Guest Lecturer, workshops. *Memberships include:* Various offices, Community of Sisters, Third Franciscan Order, Syracuse; Consultant- Evaluator, Catholic University; Reading Consultant (Central New York), Educational Development Laboratories, Huntingdon, NY; Member, various professional organisations. *Publications:* Author: 1st series science textbooks based on Catholic Philosophy of Education; 1st 3 books, & 1st 4 teachers manuals, God's World series; Various science articles; Poetry; High school plays. Editor, Creative Arts (newsletter, Central NY), National League of American Pen Women, 1981-82. *Honours:* Miriam Joseph Farrell Award, distinguished teaching, NCEA, 1988; Numerous biographical recognitions. *Address:* 304 East Linebaugh Avenue, Tampa, Florida 33612, USA.

ENGELHART Margaret Stevens, b. 19 June 1924, Flint, Michigan, USA. Teacher; Editor. m. Carl W.E. Engelhart, 11 June 1949, 3 sons, 1 daughter, adopted family 2 sons, 3 daughters. *Education:* BA, University of Michigan, 1945; MA, Columbia University, 1947. *Appointments:* Instructor, University of Minnesota, 1947-50; Instructor, State University College, Plattsburgh, 1960's; Editor, Tundra Books of Montreal & Northern New York, 1972-88; Foreign Expert, Nankai University, Tianjin, 1985-86. *Publications:* They Sought a New World, 1985; The Mother of Us All, 1979. *Memberships:* President, Clinton County Mental Health Association, 1971-74; Chairman, Unitarian Universalist Fellowship, Plattsburgh, 1977-. *Honours:* Recipient, various honours and awards. *Hobbies:* Reading; Writing; Family History; Gardening; Politics. *Address:* 72 Brinkerhoff Street, Plattsburgh, NY 12901, USA.

ENGELS Patricia Louise, b. 2 July 1926, Joliet, Illinois, USA. Attorney; Educator. m. Henry William Engels, 1 Feb. 1947, 3 sons. *Education:* BE, 1970, MEd, 1971, Olivet Nazarene College; Advanced Education study, University of Illinois, 1972; JD, John Marshall Law School, 1979; Admitted to practise Law: Illinois, 1979; Indiana, 1979; Certified to teach Elementary, High School, College, Education Administration, Illinois; Licensed Real Estate Broker, Illinois, 1979. *Appointments:* Teacher, Bourbonnais, Illinois; Teacher, Momence (Illinois) Unit Schools, 1970-76; Instructor, Kankakee Community College, Illinois, 1975; Sole Law Practice, Indiana and Illinois, 1979-. *Memberships:* Lake Village (Indiana) Civic Association, 1980-87; Lowell (Indiana) Chamber of Commerce; Educational Coordinator, St August Catholic Church, 1985-87; Lake County Bar Association; American Bar Association; Indiana Bar Association; Illinois Bar Association; Public Defender Bar Association; Theta Chi Sigma; Kappa Delta Pi; Former Member: Newton County Bar Association; Kankakee County Bar Association. *Hobbies:* Exercise;

Swimming; Sewing; Square dancing; Reading. *Address:* Route 1, Box 448, Momence, IL 60954, USA.

ENGERRAND Anne Sawyer, b. Atlanta, Georgia, USA. Executive. m. Kenneth Gabriel George Engerrand, 16 Mar. 1985, 1 daughter. *Education:* BA, Honours, Southwest Texas State University, 1977; JD, Honours, South Texas College of Law, 1984. *Appointments:* Paralegal Litigation, Exxon County, USA, 1978; Law Clerk, 1983; Law Clerk, Hon. John R. Brown, 1984-85; Attorney, Houston Lighting & Power Co., 1985-86; Vice President, Texas Institute for Arts in Education, 1987-. *Publications:* Articles in journals & magazines. *Memberships:* Order of the Lytae; Phi Delta Phi; Presidents Council, Houston Grand Opera. *Honours:* Recipient, various honours and awards. *Hobbies:* Volunteer, Houston Grand Opera. *Address:* 773 West Creekside Drive, Houston, TX 77024, USA.

ENGERRAND Doris Alma Dieskow, b. 7 ug. 1925, Chicago, USA. College Professor. m. Gabriel H. Engerrand, 26 Oct. 1946, (deceased), 2 sons, 1 daughter. *Education:* BS, Business Administration, 1958; BS, Elementary Education, 1959; MBE, 1966; PhD, 1970. *Appointments:* Teacher 1960-63, Teacher & Dept. Head, 1966-68, Lumpkin County High School, Dahlonega, Georgia; Assistant Professor, Troy State University, 1969-71; Assistant Professor, 1971-74; Associate Professor, 1974-78, Georgia College; Professor, Chairperson, Business Information Systems & Communications, Georgia College, 1978. *Publications:* Contributor of various professional articles. *Memberships:* Association for Business Communication; Georgia Business Educatiron Association; Southern Management Association; American, Georgia Vocational Associations; National Association of Business Teacher Educators; Office Systems Research Association. *Honours:* American Business Communication Association Fellow, 1983; Georgia Vocational Association Educator of the Year for Business Education, 1984. *Hobbies:* Swimming; Golf; Gardening. *Address:* 1674 Pine Valley Road, Milledgeville, GA 31061, USA.

ENGHOLM Mary Korstad, b. 7 May 1918, Seattle, Washington, USA. Art Consultant; Author. m. (1) Walter Weigel, 1949, 1 daughter; (2) Paul Mueller, 1968, deceased; (3) Glenn Stanley Engholm, 1982. *Education:* BA, University of California, Los Angeles, 1940; MA, St Lawrence University, New York, 1949; Postgraduate, Syracuse University; various other universities. *Appointments include:* Art Teacher, Supervisor, Canton Schools, New York. 1946-48; Assistant Professor, Art, State University of New York, Potsdam, 1948-58; Supervisor, Art, Watertown City Schools, New York, 1966-67; Art Education Consultant, Bakersfield City Schools, 1967-68; Freelance Art Consultant, 1978-; Adjunct Professor, California State College, Bakersfield, 1982, 1983. *Creative works include:* Art for Elementary Schools, co-author, 1967; Murals: Creating an Environment, 1979; Contributing author, various art education and professional magazines. *Memberships include:* National and Californian Art Education Associations; AAUW; Delta Kappa Gamma; President, Young Audiences of Kern County; President of the Board, Child Guidance Clinic; Community Advisor, Junior League; President, Monterey Chapter, American Scandinavians of California, Monterey Bay Chapter; Board of Directors, Monterey History and Art Association; Docent, Monterey Art Museum on Wheels. *Honours:* Chosen Bakersfield Chamber of Commerce, 1983 Woman of the Year Award. *Hobbies:* Writing; Photography; Travel. *Address:* 867 Grove Street, Monterey, CA 93940, USA.

ENGLE Mary Allen English, b. 26 Jan. 1922, Madill, Oklahoma, USA. Paediatric Cardiologist. m. Ralph Landis Engle Jr, 7 June 1945, 1 son, 1 daughter. *Education:* BA cum laude, Baylor University, Waco, Texas, 1942; MD, Johns Hopkins University School of Medicine, 1945; Internship, Residency, Paediatrics, Johns Hopkins Hospital, The New York Hospital; Fellowship, Paediatric Cardiology, Johns Hopkins Hospital, Cornell University Medical College; Board Certified, Paediatrics, Paediatric Cardiology. *Appointments include:* Director, Paediatric Cardiology Training Programme, 1956-, Attending Paediatrician, Director of Paediatric Cardiology, 1962-, Founder, Director, Greek Children's Cardiac Programme, 1973-, The New York Hospital, New York City; Professor of Paediatrics, 1969-; Stavros S Niarchos Professor of Paediatric Cardiology, 1979-; Visiting Professor, 45 medical schools, USA and abroad. *Publications include:* 184 scientific articles; 95 chapters; 10 editorials; 8 books; 7 symposia. *Memberships:* American Academy of Pediatrics; Board of Trustees, American College of Cardiology; Board of Directors, American and New York Heart Associations; American Pediatric Society; Association of European Paediatric Cardiologists; Board of Directors, Executive Board, New York Cardiological Society (President 1986-87); Pediatric Cardiological Society of Greater New York; Board of Directors, Royal Society of Medicine Foundation; Society of Pediatric Research; Medical Science Advisory Committee, US Information Agency; Editorial boards including: ACCEL, American College of Cardiology; American Heart Journal; Heart and Lung; Year Book of Cardiology; Cardiac Advisory Committee, State of New York, 1974-. *Honours:* Phi Beta Kappa; Alpha Omega Alpha; DSc(hon.causa), Iona College; Honorary Alumnus Award, Cornell University Medical College; Numerous others. *Hobbies:* Gardening; Antiques. *Address:* One Country Club Lane, Pelham Manor, NY 10803, USA.

ENGLISH Barbara Ann, b. 5 Sept. 1933, Dundee, Scotland. University Lecturer; Author. Widowed, 2 sons. *Education:* MA 1955, PhD 1969, St Andrews Univerity; Fellow, Society of Antiquaries; Fellow, Royal Historical Society. *Career:* Archivist, 1958-60; Publisher (assistant editor), 1960-62; Lecturer, Senior Lecturer, History, University of Hull. *Publications:* John Company's Last War; Lords of Holderness; Strict Settlement. *Hobbies:* Travel: Romanesque architecture; Yorkshire history. *Address:* The University, Hull, England.

ENGLISH Brenda Harks, b. 24 Jan. 1897, Sleights, North Yorkshire, England. Retired from Medical Practice. m. Dr Alec Warner Riddolls, MRCS, LRCP. June 1927. 1 son, 1 daughter. *Education:* MRCS, LRCP, Royal Free Hospital, London, 1926. *Appointment:* Medical Practice, Author. *Publications:* Into the North; The Gabriel Hounds; These Yellow Sands; The Goodly Heritage; The Proper Standard; This Freedom; Hob of High Farndale; Except Ye Repent; Sins of the Fathers; Crying in the Wilderness; Five Generations; Rhymes of a Yorkshire Village (3 Vols), with Irene Sutcliffe; Rhymes of a Yorkshire Hamlet (2 Vols); Rhymes of a Rural Railway. *Memberships:* Society of Authors. *Address:* Groves Bank, Sleights, Whitby, North Yorkshire YO21 1RY, England.

ENGLISH Hildegard Maria, b. 27 Feb. 1945, Chemnitz, Germany. Lawyer. m. John English, 5 May 1967, 1 son. *Education:* BA, University of Waterloo, Canada, 1967; Harvard University, USA, 1968-70; LLB, University of Western Ontario, 1974. *Appointments:* Lawyer, Haney, White, Ostner, English and Linton, Waterloo, Ontario, 1974-. *Memberships:* Director, Chairperson, Government Policies, Waterloo Chamber of Commerce; Canadian Bar Association; Advocate Society; Trial Lawyers Association of America; Board Member: Grand River Conservation Foundation; YWCA Kitchener; Waterloo Liberal Association; Canadian Institute of International Affairs; Waterloo Law Association. *Honours:* Dean's List, University of Western Ontario, 1974. *Address:* Haney, White, Ostner, English and Linton, 45 Erb Street East, Waterloo, Ontario, Canada N2J 4B5.

ENGLISH Marlanda, b. 14 Apr. 1962, Chicago, USA. Manufacturing Engineering. *Education:* BS, Industrial Engineering, 1983, MS, Manufacturing Engineering, 1986, Northwestern University. *Appointments:* Industrial Engineer, Erlicon, 1983-85; Manufacturing

Engineer, Borg Warner Automotive, 1985-. *Publications:* Numerous original musical compositions. *Memberships:* American Institute of Industrial Engineers; Women United for Professional Advancement. *Honours:* 1st Place, fine Arts Scholarship, C.H. Mason Foundation, 1979; First Female Graduate of Northwestern University's Manufacturing Engineering Programme, 1986. *Hobbies:* Music; Composition; Classicla Piano. *Address:* 9912 South Prairie Avenue, Chicago, IL 60628, USA.

ENGLISH Nichola, b. 28 Aug. 1922, Grantworth, North Carolina, USA. Writer; Researcher. m. Thomas Paters English, 16 Apr. 1945, 2 sons, 1 daughter. *Education:* BA, University of North Carolina, 1944; Doctorate Candidate, 1947. *Appointments:* Staff Writer, 1947-49, Sub-Editor, 1949-54, Editor, 1954-55, The Carolina Star; Publisher, Independent Observer Magazine, 1956-66; Publisher, Southern Literary Review, 1968-. *Publications:* Articles in: Independent Observer, 1956-66; Southern Literary Review; Poems for Summer, 1953; More Poems for life, 1954; As I Saw the Planet, 1957; The Winter of Our Life (poems), 1960; Anthology of a Woman, 1962; etc. *Memberships:* Literary Society of America; Southern Poets Inc; Poets and Writers of Modern America. *Honours:* Recipient, various honours and awards. *Hobbies:* Walking; American Literature. *Address:* 5126 Bur Oak Circle, Raleigh, NC 27622, USA.

ENTWISTLE Phillida Gail Sinclair, b. 7 Jan. 1944, Nagpur, India. m. John Nlcholas McAlpine Entwistle, 6 Sept. 1968, 1 son, 1 daughter. *Education:* BSc., Honours, London University, 1965; PhD, Liverpool University, 1971. *Appointment:* Inland Revenue, 1965-66; Director, J Davey & Sons, Liverpool Ltd., 1983-. *Memberships:* JP Liverpool, 1980-; General Commissioner for Income Tax, 1985-; Mersey Regional Health Authority, 1987-; Governor, Liverpool Polytechnic, 1988-; Fellow, RSA. *Address:* Gorstage Hall, Cuddington, Cheshire CW8 2SG, England.

EPP Margaret, b. 1 Aug. 1913, Waldheim, Saskatchewan, Canada. Writer. *Education:* 5 years Theological training, Bible Institute. *Publications:* Juvenile: Peppermint Sue; Jack Tandy of Baskatong; North to Sakitawa; Come Back; Jonah; Light on Twin Rocks; The Long Chase; the Sign of the Tumbling T; Thirty Days Hath September; Vicki Arthur; Sap's Running; Anita and the Driftwood House; No Hand Sam; Mystery at Pony Ranch; The Brannans of Bar Lazy B; The North Wind and the Caribou; Jungle Call; Trouble on the Flying M; Search down the Yukon; No help Wanted; The call of the Wahoa; The Great Frederick; Runnaway on the Running K; Prairie Princess; The Princess and the Pelican; The Princess Rides a Panther; Sarah and the Magic Twenty- fifth; Sarah and the Pelican; Sarah and the Lost Friendship; Sarah and the Mystery of the Hidden Boy; Sarah and the Darnley Boys; Sarah and the Persian Shepherd. Adult Non-Fiction: But God Hath Chosen (Biography); This mountain is Mine (Biography); Come to My Party; Walk in my Woods (Autobiography); Into all the World; Proclaim Jubilee; 8, Tulpengasse; Adult fiction: A Fountain Sealed; The Earth is Round. Chariots in the Smoke; All in the April Evening, short stories. *Hobbies:* Flower culture; Flower arranging; Embroidering; Cooking, baking. *Address:* Box 178, Wakldheim, Saskatchewan, S0K 4R0, Canada.

EPPS Constance Arnettres, b. 8 Feb. 1950, Portchester, New York, USA. Dentist. m. Charles Ray Epps, 24 June 1974. 1 son, 1 daughter. *Education:* BS, Bennett College, 1971; DDS, Howard University, College of Dentistry, 1979; Currently studying for MPH, University of North Carolina at Chapel Hill. *Appointments:* General Dentist Resident, St Elizabeth's Hospital, Washington, DC, 1979-80; Public Health Dentist, North Carolina Department of Human Resources, 1980-85; Public Health Dentist, Guilford County Health Department, 1985-. *Memberships:* North Carolina Public Health Association; American Dental Association; North Carolina Dental Society; Old North State Dental Society; National Dental Association; Guilford County Dental Society; Minority Women In Science; Delta Sigma Theat; Academy of General Dentistry. *Honours:* Outstanding Young Women of America, 1982; Achievement in Black Women's Health, Bennett College, 1987; Third District Nominee North Carolina Dental Society, Young Dentist of the Year, 1988; Outstanding College Student of America, 1988; Awarded $6,000 for purchase of portable dental equipment for Dental Treatment for the Homebound Patient (principal author of the grant application). *Hobbies:* Reading; Swimming. *Address:* 2024 Arden Place, High Point, NC 27260, USA.

EPSTEIN Cynthia F. b. 17 Oct. 1933, Brooklyn, New York, USA. Occupational Therapist. m. Alan J. Epstein, 16 Apr. 1961, 1 son. *Education:* BA, Brooklyn College, 1954; Certificate, Occupational Therapy, Tufts University, 1956; MA, Vocational Rehabilitation, New York University, 1961. *Appointments:* Consultant occupational therapist, self-employed, Flemington, New Jersey, 1964-; Executive director, Occupational Consultants, Bridgewater, NJ, 1979-. *Publications include:* Wheelchair Management Guides, 1979; Chapter, Consultation: Communicating & Facilitating, in Occupational Therapy Manager, ed. Bair & Gray, 1985; Chapter, Case Study: Alzheimer's Elderly Patient, in COTA: Roles & Relationships, ed. S. Ryan, 1986. *Memberships:* NJ Representative 1973-80, American Occupational Therapy Association (AOTA); World Federation of Occupational Therapists; Executive Board 1970-80, NJ Occupational Therapy Association; Gerontology Societies of America & New Jersey; National Council on Ageing; Sigma Phi Omega. *Honours:* Service Award, AOTA, 1986; Awards, Merit in Practice 1985, Administration 1980, Appreciation Certificate 1976, NJOTA; Certificate of Appreciation, Hunterdon County Mental Health Board, 1979; Roster of Fellows, AOTA, 1978. *Address:* Occupational Therapy Consultants Inc, 350 Grove Street, Bridgewater, New Jersey 08807, USA.

EPSTEIN Cynthia Fuchs, b. 9 Nov. 1933, New York City, New York, USA. Professor of Sociology; Sociology Educator. m. Howard M. Epstein, 3 July 1954, 1 son. *Education:* BA, Political Science, Antioch College, 1955; University of Chicago Law School, 1955-56; MA, Sociology, New School for Social Research, 1960; PhD, Sociology, Columbia University, 1968. *Appointments:* Instructor, Anthropology, Finch College, 1961-62; Associate, School of General Studies, 1964-65, Instructor, Barnard College, 1965, Senior Research Associate, Bureau of Applied Social Research, 1971-77, Senior Research Associate, Center for the Social Sciences, 1977-82, Columbia University, New York; Instructor, 1966-67, Assistant Professor, 1968-70, Associate Professor, 1971-74, Professor, 1975-84, Mellon Professor, 1983-84, Queens College, City of New York; Professor of Sociology, Graduate Center, City University of New York, 1975-; Visiting Scholar, Newnham College, Cambridge, England, 1975; Visiting Professor: State University of New York, Stony Brook, 1975, University of Oslo, 1986, University of Helsinki, 1986; Faculty, Salzburg Seminar, Austria, 1980; Resident Scholar, Russell Sage Foundation, 1982-88; Consultant. *Publications:* Books: Woman's Place: Options and Limits in Professional Careers, 1970; The Other Half: Roads to Women's Equality (edited with William J.Goode), 1971; Access to Power: Cross-National Studies of Women and Elites (edited with Rose Laub Coser), 1981; Women in Law, 1981, Paperback, 1983; Deceptive Distinctions: Sex, Gender and the Social Order, 1988; About 50 articles and book chapters on women's issues. *Memberships:* Past President, Committee Member, Eastern Sociological Society; American Sociological Association, committees; Sociological Research Association; American Association for the Advancement of Science; International Scientific Commission on the Family; Sociologists for Women in Society; Editorial and other boards. *Honours:* I.Peter Gellman Award, Eastern Sociological Society, 1966; Various fellowships. *Address:* 425 Riverside Drive, New York, NY 10025, USA.

EPSTEIN June Sadie, b. 29 June 1918, Perth, Western Australia, Australia. Musician; Author. m. Julius Guest, 7 Mar. 1949, 2 sons (1 dec.), 1 daughter. *Education:* Perth College, 1931-33; Lic.Music, Australian Universities, 1934; Lic.Royal Schools of Music, 1935; ATCL, Speech Training, 1937; Lic. Trinity College of Music, London (Teachers Training Diploma), 1938; Lic. Royal AC Music, 1938. *Appointments:* Scriptwriter, Broadcaster, ABC, 1930s-; On tour, Australian Broadcasting Commission, 1940; Director of Music, Melbourne Church of England Girls Grammar School, Melbourne, Victoria, 1946-49; Senior Lecturer in Music, Melbourne College of Advanced Education, Institute of Early Childhood Development. *Publications:* Some 60 books (biographies of people with disabilities, educationists, children's books) including: No Music by Request, a Portrait of the Gorman Family; June Epstein, Woman with Two Hats; Mermaid on Wheels, the Story of Margaret Lester; Tapes; Records; Musical compositions. *Memberships:* Foundation President, Kew Cottage Parents Association; Australian Society of Authors; Society of Women Writers; Fellowship of Australian Writers; Honorary Graduate, Institute of Early Childhood Education. *Honours:* Overseas Scholar, Trinity College of Music, London, 1936-39; Silver Medal, Worshipful Company of Musicians, 1938; Grantee, Australian Council for the Arts; Various awards for Best Children's Books; Order of Australia Medal, 1986. *Hobbies:* Family; Welfare of people with disabilities; embroidery. *Address:* 2 Alexander Street, Bentleigh East, Victoria 3165, Australia.

EPSTEIN Lee Joan Spole, b. 17 Mar. 1958, New York, USA. Professor, Political Science. m. Jay Epstein, 21 June 1980. *Education:* BA 1980, MA 1982, PhD 1983, Emory University. *Appointments:* Instructor/Assistant Professor, Emory University, 1983-85; Assistant Professor, Southern Methodist University, 1986-. *Publications:* Books: Conservatives in Court, 1985; Public Interest Law, forthcoming. Numerous articles in professional journals and magazines. *Memberships:* American Political Science Association; Midwest Political Science Association; Southern Political Science Association; Southwestern Social Science Association; Law and Society Association. *Honours:* Margareta Deschner Teaching Award, 1988; Earhart Research Fellowship, 1988-89; Magna Cum Laude, graduate 1980; SMU Research Council Grant, 1987-88. *Address:* Department of Political Science, Southern Methodist University, Dallas, Texas 75275, USA.

EPSTEIN Sarah Louise Gamble, b. 31 Oct. 1925, Philadelphia, Pennsylvania, USA. Population Consultant; Social Workor; Art collector and lecturer. *Education:* BA, Oberlin College, Oberlin, 1946-48; MSW, Simmons College, School of Social Work, Boston, 1949-51. *Appointments:* Junior Counselor, Counselor, Head Counselor, Green Mountain Camp, West Dummerston, 1949-50; Counselor, Half Moon Ranch, Jackson, 1943-44; Nurse's Aide, Boston City Hospital, 1943-44; Group Member, Austria, 1949, Leader, Holland, 1952, Council Member, 1952-, National Board Member, 1981-, Experiment in International Living. *Creative works:* Produced pots for over 30 years, some of which have been in juried exhibitions; Catalogue: The Prints of Edvard Munch: Mirror of his Life. *Memberships:* Board Member, Potomac School, 1967-73; Board Member, Planned Parenthood of Washington, 1974-; Board Member, The Pathfinder Fund, 1965-; Board Member, Center for Development and Population Activities, 1980-; Board of Policy Advisors, The Population Institute; Center for Defense Information; Board Member, Federation for American Immigration Reform; Board of Advisors, Washington-Moscow Capitals Citizens Exchange; Board member, Arena Stage, 1980-. *Honours:* Delegate to National Women's Conference for the Prevention of Nuclear War, Washington; Delegate to United Nations Conference on World Population in Mexico City; Delegate to NGO Forum, UN Women's Decade Conference, Nairobi; 50th Anniversary honoree, Planned Parenthood of Washington, 1986. *Hobbies:* Tennis; Horseback riding;

Jogging; Skiing; Skating; Hiking; Travel. *Address:* 5620 Oregon Avenue NW, Washington, DC 20015, USA.

EPSTEIN Selma, b. 14 Aug. 1927, Brooklyn, New York, USA. Musician. m. Joseph Epstein, 28 May 1950. 2 sons, 2 daughters. *Education:* Graduated, Juilliard School; Diploma in Piano, 1949. *Appointments:* Concerts, seminars, master classes, international tours, 1950-. *Publications:* 8 manuals on group teacher; Editor, music by Lily Boulanger, P Grainger and others; Numerous pastel paintings and sketches. *Memberships:* Founder & President, AM Graingher Society; Int League of Women Composers; Mid Atlantic Reg Director, Intl Congree on Women in Music; Founder, W Point Parents Club of MD, VA & Washington DC; Vice Pres, Thyroid Assoc of US, MD Chapter; Founder, MD Women's Symphony. *Hobbies:* Music & History medal, public school graduation; USIS grants, Europe, Asia, Australia & S America; Winner, D Hendrick Engleman Foundation school Competition, 1950; Juilliard scholarship grants, 1946-49. *Hobbies:* Gardening; Reading; Painting; Cooking. *Address:* 2443 Pickwick Road, Dickeyville, Maryland 21204, USA.

ERDONMEZ Denise Elizabeth, b. 24 July 1946, Victoria, Australia. Lecturer in Music Therapy. m. Hasan Erdonmez, 20 June 1970, 1 son, 1 daughter. *Education:* BMusic, 1967; BMusic Therapy, 1970; MMus, 1987. *Appointments:* Music Therapist, Larundel Psychiatric Hospital, 1970-80; Lecturer in Music Therapy, University of Melbourne, Victoria, 1980-. *Publications:* Many articles in professional journals. *Memberships:* National President, Australian Music Therapy Association; Consultant, New Zealand Society for Music Therapy. *Honour:* Honorary Life Membership, Australian Music Therapy Association. *Hobbies:* Dance; Ceramics; Poetry; Reading; Long walks. *Address:* Faculty of Music, University of Melbourne, Parkville, Victoria 3052, Australia.

ERICKSON Carol A, b. 26 Dec. 1933, Worcester, USA. Pychoherapist. m. Jean LaRue Barnes, 20 Mar. 1952, divorced 1962, 2 sons, 4 daughters. *Education:* BS, Arizona State University, 1964; MSW, California State University, 1977. *Appointments:* Social Worker, Los Angeles City, 1964-83; Private Psychotherapy Practice, Berkeley, 1977-; Director, Erickson Institute, Berkeley, 1981-; Adjunct Faculty, University of California, Berkeley, & Vermont College, San Francisco, 1986-. *Publications:* Co-Writer, Composer, Deep Self Appreciation, 1983; Self Hypnosis - A Relaxing Time Out, 1984; Natural Self Confidence, 1985. *Memberships:* Board of Directors, YWCA, Torrance, 1981-83; International Sooioty of Hypnosis; Northern & Southern California Societies of Clinical Hypnosis; California Association of Marriage & Family Therapists; Society of Clinical & Experimental Hypnosis; Society of Clinical Social Workers; etc. *Honour:* Phi Kappa Phi, 1964. *Hobbies:* Writing; Music; Reading; Camping. *Address:* PO Box 739, Berkeley, CA 94701, USA.

ERICKSON Charlotte Joanne, b. 22 Oct. 1923, Oak Park, Illinois, USA. University Professor. m. 19 July 1952, 2 sons. *Education:* BA, Augustana College, 1945; MA, 1947, PhD, 1951, Cornell University. *Appointments:* Instructor Vassar College, 1950-52; Research Fellow, National Institute of Economic & Social Research, 1952-55; Assistant Lecturer, Lecturer, Senior Lecturer, Reader, Professor, London School of Economics, 1955-83; Paul Mellon Professor, American History, Cambridge University, 1983-. *Publications:* American Industry & the European Immigrant, 1957; British Industrialists, 1959; Invisible Immigrants, 1974; Emigration from Europe, 1976. *Memberships:* British Association for American Studies, Chairman, 1983-86; American Historical Association; Organisation of American HIstorians; Economic History Society. *Honours:* AAUW, 1948-49; Fulbright Fellow, 1949-50; Guggenheim Fellow, 1966-67; LDH Augustana College, 1977; Sherman Fairchild Professor, California Institute of Technology, 1976-77. *Hobbies:* Music Gardening. *Address:* 8 High Street, Chesterton, Cambridge CB4 1NG, England.

ERIKSSON Anne-Marie, b. 30 Mar. 1932, Dunkirk, New York, USA. Educator. m. (2) Erik A. Eriksson, 1 Jan. 1984. 2 sons, 1 daughter, previous marriage. *Education:* BS, Early Childhood Education, State University of New York, Fredonia, 1955; Graduate studies, Hunter College School of Social Work, City University of New York, 1960. *Appointments:* Social worker, NY State Department of Social Welfare, 1960-64; Probation Officer, NY State Supreme Courts, Kings, NY & Queens Counties, 1972-84; Founder, Board Chair, Incest Survivors Resource Network International (Adjunct to Quaker Task Group on Family Trauma), 1983-. Specialises, education on inter-generational transmission of verbal & physical violence, especially concerning overt & emotional incest. *Memberships include:* Co-Clerk, Quaker Task Group on Family Trauma, NY Yearly Meeting, Religious Society of Friends; Quaker Studies on Human Betterment; Society for Traumatic Stress Studies; International Society for Prevention of Child Abuse & Neglect; National Council of Juvenile & Family Court Judges; World Federation for Mental Health; World Society of Victimology; Presenter, 1st and 3rd International Conferences on Incest & Related Problems, Switzerland, 1987 and London, 1989; Expert Consultant, World Federation for Mental Health's Consultation on Mental Health Needs of Victims, United Nations Headquarters, NY, 1987. *Address:* Incest Survivors Resource Network International, PO Box 911, Hicksville, New York 11802, USA.

ERLICHSON Miriam, b. 26 July 1948, Bronx, USA. Fundraiser. m. Victor Petrusewicz, 17 July 1980. *Education:* BA, 1969, MA, 1976, English, City College of New York. *Appointments:* Teacher, English, Intermediate School, Bronx, 1972-78; Senior Secretary to Director of Annual Giving, New York Hospital-Cornell Medical Center, 1979-80; Annual Giving Co-ordinator, New York-Cornell, 1980-. *Memberships:* Secretary, 77th Settler Corp; Gamma Chapter, Phi Beta Kappa; Direct Mail Fundraisers Association; National Association of Female Executives; Life Member, Jane Austen Society. *Honours:* Recipient, various honours & awards. *Hobbies:* Writing Poetry; Art; Classical Ballet. *Address:* Development Office, New York Hospital-Cornell Medical Center, 525 East 68th Street, Box 123, New York, NY 10021, USA.

ERTEL Grace Roscoe, b. 10 Oct. 1921, Santa Monica, California, USA. Teacher; Writer. m. Donald J. Ertel, 28 Sep. 1946, 2 daughters. *Education:* BA, University of California, Los Angeles; Graduate courses, Sacramento University and University of Southern California; Teaching Credential, Sacramento University. *Appointments:* Social Worker, 1944- 50; Teacher, English and English as a Second Language, chiefly adult education classes, 1963-; Freelance Writer, 1975-. *Publications:* Plant an Ecology Garden, 1975, 1976; Contributions to over 100 US and foreign publications, chiefly in field of travel, fitness and the environment, including: Travel/Holiday, Globehopper, Westways, Golf, Health, Friendly Exchange, Voyager, Los Angeles Times, New Zealand Times, London Free Press, Better Health & Living. *Memberships:* American Society of Journalists and Authors; National Writers Club; American Medical Writers Association; International Food, Wine and Travel Writers Association; California Writers; Secretary, American Association of University Women. *Hobbies:* Photography; Gourmet but heathful cuisine; Nature study and wildlife conservation. *Address:* 6350 Dorchester Court, Carmichael, CA 95608, USA.

ERVIN Betty J., b. 14 Oct. 1951, Savannah, Georgia, USA. Psychologist; Military Officer. *Education:* BA, Ohio State University, 1972; MA, Eastern New Mexico University, 1978; EdS, University of New Mexico, 1981. Diplomas, US Army Institute of Personnel & Resource Management, 1983, 1984. *Appointments:* Personnel Officer & Manager, US Army National Guard, 1975-; Counsellor, Job Corps Centre, Teledyne Corporation, Albuquerque, New Mexico, 1979-83; Assistant Professor, Military Science, Bishop College, US Army, 1984-87; Psychologist, State of New Mexico, 1988-.

Memberships: National Association for Female Executives; Amry & Navy Club; Reserve Officers Association; National Guard Association. *Honours include:* Promotion to Major 1988, Achievement Medal 1987, Commendation Medal 1984, Officer's Direct Commission 1975, US Army; National Guard Commander, New Mexico, 1978, 1983; Psi Chi honour society, 1977, 1978; American Spirit Honour Medal, 1973. *Hobbies:* Museums; Sculpture; Aquaria; Music; Travel; Boating; Trains; Cooking; Physical conditioning; Skiing; Spectator sports. *Address:* 2719 Golden Creek Lane, no. 406, Arlington, Texas 76006, USA.

ERVIN Hazel Arnett, b. 19 Dec. 1948, Washington, Georgia, USA. College Instructor. divorced. 1 son, 1 daughter. *Education:* AB, English, Guilford College, 1980; MA, English and Afro Am Literature, North Carolina A&T State University, 1985; PhD, English and Afro Am Literature, Howard University, expected 1991. *Appointments:* Eng Techer, Reidsville City Schools, North Carolina, 1980-81; Eng Teacher, Hancock County School, Sparta, Georgia, 1981-82; Eng Teacher, Montgomery County Schools, Troy, North Carolina, 1982-85; Instructor, Shaw University, Raleigh, North Carolina, 1985-. *Publications:* Reviews: Angelou's Is Story of Vision and Hope, 1986; Lyrical Novel Deines Woman's Struggle, 1984; A Vivid Look at the Haslem Renaissance, 1982; Classic Works by Langston Hughes, 1981; Over 20 articles published; Interview with Ann Petry, Black American Literature Forum, shared interview with Yvonne Carter, 1989. *Memberships:* Langston Hughes Society; Black Scholar; Callaloo; Zora neale Hurston Forum; Black american Literature Foruma; Smithsonian Institution (Associate Member); Absidian II. *Honours:* United Negro College Fund Grant, 1987-88; National Consortium for Educational Access, Fellow, 1988-; Internship with American Quarterly, Copy Editor, 1989. *Hobbies:* Writing; Photography; Hiking. *Address:* 1330-301 Park Glen Drive, Raleigh, NC 27610, USA.

ESBENSEN Barbara Juster, b. 28 Apr. 1925, Madison, Wisconsin, USA. Poet; Author. m. Thorwald S Esbensen, 24 June 1953. 4 sons, 2 daughters. *Education:* BS, University of Wisconsin, 1947. *Appointments:* Art Teacher, 1947-50 and 1953-56; Art/Creative Writing, 1957-58; Classroom Teacher, 1961-63; College Consultant for Creative Arts, 1970-73. *Publications:* Books: Swing Around the Sun, 1965; A Celebration of Bees, 1975; Cold Stars and Fireflies, 1984; Words with Wrinkled Knees, 1986; The Star Maiden, 1988; Ladder to the Sky, 1989; Great Northern Diver-the Loon, 1990; Who Shrank My Grandmother's House, 1991; Tiger with Wings-The Great Horned Owl, 1991; Dance With Me, forthcoming. *Memberships:* Society of Children's Book Writers; American Poetry Society. *Honours:* Minnesota Book Award for The Star Maiden, 1988; Teachers Choice Award for Words with Wrinkled Knees, 1987 and for The Star Maiden, 1989; Colorado Childrens Book Nomination, 1989. *Hobbies:* Gardening; Reading; Cooking; Natural world. *Address:* 5602 Dalrymple Road, Edina, MN 55424, USA.

ESBORG Patricia Keith, b. 19 Oct. 1938, Santa Monica, California, USA. Family Therapist; Psychiatric Nurse; Doctoral Candidate. m. Svend Esborg, 27 Jan. 1962. 1 son, 2 daughters. *Education:* Diploma, Bishop Johnson College of Nursing, 1959; BS, Bowie State University, 1982; MS 1985, Doctoral Candidate 1988, University of Masryland. *Appointments:* Nursing positions at hospitals in California, Maryland, Alaska and Belgium, 1959-85; Psychological Services Inc, Annapolis, MD, 1985-88; Private Practice, Bowie, MD, 1988-. *Memberships:* Sigma Theta Tau, Nursing Honor Society; American Nurses' Association; National Council for Family Relations. *Honours:* Certified Clinical Specialist in Psychiatric Nursing, 1986; Clinical Member, American Assn for Marriage and Family Therapy, 1986; MD State Scholarship for Graduate Students, 1983-84; Graduate Student Fellowship, University of MD, 1985 and 1987; Pre-Doctoral Fellowship, Natl Institute of Mental Health, 1989; Nurses' Educational Funds Grant, 1989. *Hobbies:*

Travel; Languages; Family systems especially family stories and myths; Women's roles especially dual-career mothers. *Address:* 12808 Buckingham Drive, Bowie, Maryland 20715, USA.

ESPAILLAT Rhina Polonia, b. 20 Jan. 1932, Dominican Republic. Poet; Lecturer; Workshop director. m. Alfred Moskowitz, 28 June 1952. 2 sons. *Education:* BA, Hunter College, 1953; MSE, Queens College, 1964. *Appointments:* English Teacher, NYC public school system, 1953-54; English Teacher, NYC high school system, 1965-80; Consultant for NYC Board of Education, 1986-. *Publications:* Over 200 poems published in numerous anthologies, newspapers and magazines. *Memberships:* Women Poets of NY; Poetry Society of America; Fresh Meadows Poets; Alliance of Queens Artists; Queens Council on the Arts, member of Board of Directors and editor of QCA Newsletter; United Federation of Teachers. *Honours:* Prizes from: Lyric magazine 1981, 1984-87; Amelia magazine, 1985-88; World order of Narrative Poets, 1981, 1984-86; First prize, Croton Review's Annual Competition, 1987; Gustav Davidson Memorial Award, Poetry Society of America, 1987. *Hobbies:* Gardening; Needlework; Volunteer teacher for the UFT Retired Teachers Chapter, community work to further the arts. *Address:* 72-04 162 Street, Flushing, NY 11365, USA.

ESPINET Ramabai, b. 25 May 1948, Trinidad, West Indies. Writer; Researcher; Lecturer. m. Peter Espinet, 31 Mar.1969, divorced, 1 son, 1 daughter (not of this marriage). *Education:* BA, Honours, 1977, MA, English, 1980, York University, Toronto. *Appointments:* Lecturer, York University, 1977, 1979, 1980, 1981; Lecturer, University of the West Indies, 1982, 1987-88; Management of Information Science, Trinidad, 1982-87. *Publications:* Creation Fire, anthology, 1989; numerous articles. *Memberships:* CAFRA; Centre for Caribbean Dialogue; ACURIC. *Address:* c/o Sister Vision Press, PO Box 217, Station E, Toronto, Ontario Canada M6H 4EZ.

ESSBERGER Karin Lise-Lotte Margaret, b. 30 Dec. 1962, Cape Town, South Africa. Publisher. *Education:* BA Legal, Witwatersrand University. *Appointments:* Brigadiers Film Company (Pty) Ltd; Lynton Stephenson Productions CC; Who's Who of Southern Africa. *Hobbies:* Aerobics; Horse riding; Art. *Address:* P O Box 81284, Parkhurst 2120, Johannesburg, South Africa.

ESSLINGER Nell Daniel, b. 13 June 1903, Huntsville, Alabama, USA. Writer. m. Raymond G Miller, 18 Aug. 1979. 1 stepdaughter. *Education:* Vocal Certificate, Agnes Scott College, 1922; BA, University of Alabama, 1954; MMus, University of Illinois, 1962; TV Directing, Boston University, summer 1953; Voice study with Cox, Rider-Kelsey. *Appointments:* Soloist in Church & Oratorio, 1919-40 and 1951-52; NY Japanese Garden and the Winter Garden, 1924; Adrienne & Roxy's Gang, 1925; Kenilworth Inn and Battery Park Hotels, Asheville, NC, 1926; Music Clubs Concerts in Alabama and FL, 1927; Christian Science Monitor, Boston, 1942-47; TV Traffic, J Walter Thompson, Chicago, 1956-60; Director, Koch School of Music, 1963-64; Voice Teacher, Baldwin Wallace College, Berea, 1964-65; Voice Teacher, Choral Director, Northeast State Junior College, Rainsville, 1965-68. *Creative works:* Revised Notation 1965 and 1987 (textbook); Poetry: Song Lyrics; Specifications. Choruses: Magnolia; Ode to Summertime; 3 Christmas Carols. Solos: Immortal; I Love You This Well. *Memberships:* Honorary Life Member, Hunstville Music Study Club; AE Rho Radio-TV Fraternity; Charter Member, Agnes Scott Poetry Club; Rainsville Bus & Prof Women's Club; Past member of other associations. *Honours:* Winner of numerous scholarships and prizes as Singer. *Hobbies:* Swimming; Cooking; Writing poetry. *Address:* Rt 1, Box 336-X, Auburn, AL 36830, USA.

ESTES Elaine Rose, b. 24 Nov. 1931, Springfield, Missouri, USA. Director. m. John Melvin Estes, 1953. *Education:* BS, Drake University; Teaching Certificate; MS, Library Science, University of Illinois. *Appointments:* Senior Librarian, 1962-65, 1965-70, Supervising Librarian, 1970-77, Co-ordinator, External Services, 1977-78, Director, 1978-, Des Moines Public Library. *Publications:* Articles in professional journals. *Memberships:* Iowa Library Association; American Library Association; Des Moines Art Centre. *Honours:* YWCA Recognition for Outstanding Working Women, 1975; Drake Univesity Distinguished Alumni Award, 1979; Des Moines Architects Council Community Reward, 1981. *Hobbies:* Studying & Collecting Antiques; Playing Bridge; Travel. *Address:* Public Library of Des Moines, 100 Locust, Des Moines, IA 50308, USA.

ESTRIN Thelma, b. 21 Feb. 1924, New York City, USA. Professor fo Computer Science; Assistant Dean. m. Gerald Estrin, 21 Dec. 1941, 3 daughters. *Education:* BSEE, 1948, MSEE, 1949, PhD, 1952, University of Wisconsin, Madison. *Appointments:* Division Director, National Science Foundation, 1982-84; Assistant Dean, University of California, Los Angeles, School of Engineering, Director, Engineering, UCLA Extension, 1984-88; Professor of Computer Science, 1988-. *Publications:* over 50 articles in journals of the field. *Memberships:* Board of Trustees, Aerospace Corporation; Board of Directors, Institute of Electrical & Electronics Engineers; Association for Advancement of Medical Instrumentation; *Honours:* Distinguished Service Citation, University of Wisconsin, 1976; Society of Women Engineers' Achievement Award, 1981; IEEE Centennial Medal, 1984; Distinguished Professional Engineering Contributions to Education Award, National Society of Professional Engineers. *Hobbies:* Cinema; Theatre; Folk Dancing. *Address:* 3732 Boelter Hall, School of Engineering & Applied Science, University of California, Los Angeles, CA 90024, USA.

ETZEL Theresa Marie Hill, b. 7 Aug. 1959, DeKalb, Illinois, USA. Lecturer; Writer. m. David Frederick Etzel, 20 June 1987. *Education:* BA, magna cum laude, Saint Marys College, Notre Dame, Indiana, 1981; MA 1982, PhD expected 1990, Miami University, Oxford, Ohio. *Appointments:* Graduate Assistant, Career Planning & Placement Office 1981-82, Teaching Assistant 1982-83, Teaching Fellow 1983-86, Instructor 1986-, Miami University; Editor-in-Chief, The Pluralist, Washington, DC, 1989; Visiting Lecturer, Eastern Michigan University, 1989; Lecturer, Lourdes College, 1990. *Publications:* Soviet Ethnic Policy in the 1980's, co-author Prager, 1985; Pre revolutionary & Post revolutionary Leadership in Soviet Russia, 1984; Dementia and Day Care: A perfect Union, 1987. *Memberships:* American Association for the Advancement of Slavic Studies; American Political Science Association; Academy of Political Science; International Studies Association; Alzheimer's Association; President, Class of 1981, Saint Marys; President, Graduate Students Association, 1986. *Honours:* High Scholastic Award, Department of Government, Saint Marys College, 1981; Dissertation Fellow, Miami University, 1987; Kappa Gamma Phi, 1981; Delta Phi Alpha, 1981; Member, Board of Directors, The Democracy International, Washington, DC, 1988-. *Hobbies:* Tennis; Board games; Volunteer work with The Alzheimer's Association; Gardening; Linguistics; Culinary arts; Photography; Skiing. *Address:* 4217 Lancelot, Toledo, Ohio 43623, USA.

EUBANKS Mary Wilkes, b. 21 May 1947, Hattiesburg, USA. Anthropologist; Biologist. *Education:* BA, 1970, MA 1973, PhD, 1977, University of North Carolina. *Appointments:* Harvard University Botanical Museum, 1972; Instructor, Univesity of North Carolina, Chapel Hill, 1975; Research Associate, Southern Methodist University, 1976; Research Associate, Tulane University, 1977-78; Vanderbilt University Research Associate, 1978-80; University of Cincinnati Visiting Scholar & Lecturer, 1981-84; Indiana University Postdoctoral Research Associate, 1984-85; Vanderbilt University Teaching Assistant, 1985-87; North Carolina State University Visiting Assistant Professor, 1988-; Biological and Environmental Sciences Writer. *Memberships:* Many professional organisations.

Honours: Recipient, various grants and awards; Vanderbilt University Research Award, 1985-86; Nashville Banner Certificate of Recognition, 1986; Inventor U.S. plant patent. *Address:* 312 Dixie Trail, Raleigh, NC 27695, USA.

EUBANKS Rachel, b. San Jose, USA. Executive Administrator; Teacher. *Education:* BA, University California, Berkeley, 1945; MA, Columbia University, 1947; DMA, Pacific Western, 1980. *Appointments:* President, Founder, Eubanks Conservatory of Music & Arts, 1951-. *Creative Works:* Cantata for Chorus & Orchesta; Symphonic Requiem; Trio for Violin, Clarinet & Piano; etc. *Memberships:* Society of Ethnomusicology; National Music Teachers Association; National Piano Guild; Inglewood Philharmonic Board of Directors, Vice President; Southeast Symphony Association. *Honours:* Alpha Mu. *Hobby:* Travel. *Address:* 4928 Crenshaw Blvd., Los Angeles, CA 90043, USA.

EVANS Cathryn Dwyer Campbell, b. 3 Dec. 1947, San Francisco, California, USA. Medical and Science Writer. m. John H Evans, 16 Feb. 1973. 1 daughter. *Education:* Attended for coursework: San Francisco State University, 1966-67, College of Marin 1968, Foothill College, Los Altos; Continuing education courses in Pharmacology, Medical Writing and Communications. *Appointments:* Technical Writer, Mellonics Division of Litton Industries, 1970-71; Medical Writer, Syntex Corporation, 1971-80; President, Chandos Communications, 1980-; Associate Editor, The Apothecary, 1981-. *Publications:* Numerous publications in healthcare field, many ghost-written, including: The Apothecary; You and Your Health and numerous other professional journals. Workshops taught: Business Aspects of Freelancing; Video Production for the Pharmaceutical Industry; The Scope of Medical Communications; Freelance Writing; Careers for Writers in the Pharmaceutical Industry. *Memberships:* American Medical Writers Association, Programme Chairman, 1981, Toronto, Pharmaceutical Section Chairman, 1978 and 1979, Executive Committee 1980-84, Local Arrangements Chairman 1978, San Francisco, Fellowships Chairman, 1986, National Vice President, 1981, President, 1983; Drug Information Association; Pharmaceutical Advertising Council; American Association for the Advancement of Science, Delegate to the Board, 1979-80; National Association of Executive Women. *Honour:* Fellow, American Medical Writers Association, 1978. *Hobbies:* Jungian psychology; Video production; Astrology; Bicycling; Classical music and opera; Instructor for American Medical Writers Association. *Address:* 200 Page Mill Road, Suite 150, Palo Alto, CA 94306, USA.

EVANS Cheryl Ruth, b. 6 Nov. 1944, Westerly, Rhode Island, USA. Businesswoman. m. Brooks Edward Evans, 15 Aug. 1987. *Education:* AA 1983, BA in progress (correspondence), Murray State University, Kentucky. *Appointments:* Executive Secretary, 1975-80; Sales Clerk, Secretary, 1980-81; Data Transcriber, 1981; Executive Secretary, Contracts Clerk, 1981- 85; Acquisition Manager, 1985-. *Memberships:* Past President, Business & Professional Womens Club; Naval Enlisted Reserve Association; National Association for Female Executives. *Honours:* 6 Recognition awards, superior accomplishment, 1973-; Sailor of Quarter, 1981; Employee of Quarter, 1983. *Hobbies:* Golf; Reading; Collecting antiques; Travel. *Address:* PO Box 356, LaCenter, Kentucky 42056, USA.

EVANS Evelyn Jane Alice, b. 22 Mar. 1910, Coventry, England. Retired Librarian. *Education:* ALA, 1931; FLA, 1933. *Appointments:* Junior Assistant to Branch Library Inspector, Coventry City Libraries, 1927-41; University of Michigan Library, 1935-36; Deputy City Librarian, York, 1941-45; British Council Librarian, Gold Coast, 1945-50; Director, Library Services, Ghana, 1950-65; UNESCO Library Consultant, Ceylon, 1966-70; Consultant, Ranfurly Library Service, 1970-. *Publications:* The Development of Public Library Services in the Gold Coast; A Tropical Library Service - the Story of Ghana's Libraries; Editor, Grafton Basic Texts. *Memberships:* Library Association; Commonwealth Institute, Governor, 1966; CPRE Area Chairman, 1987-. *Honours:* MBE, 1955; CBE, 1960; Honorary Fellow, Library Association, 1968. *Hobbies:* Reading; Gardening; Local Government. *Address:* 8 Park Close, Bladon, Oxford OX7 1RN, England.

EVANS Janet Ann, b. 26 Aug. 1936, Muskegon, USA. Music Educator. 1 son. *Education:* B.Mus., 1958, M.Mus., 1959, University of Michigan; Michigan Secondary Permanent Teacher Certificate. *Appointments:* Vocal Director, South Redford Schools, 1959-63; Orchestra, Band, Vocal Director, South Redford Schools, 1966-79; Band Director, Detroit Public Schools, 1979-. *Publications:* Build Leadership NOW, 1983; Michigan NOW Policies and Guidelines, 1986. *Memberships:* NOW, Michigan Conference, Vice President 1984-86, various other offices; Alpha Delta Kappa, District II President, 1980-82; Farmington Hills Business & Professional Womens Club, Recording Secretary, 1981; Women in the Arts, Washington DC Charter Member; Woman Band Directors National Association, Recording Secretary, 1988-; Older Womens League; Michigan Women Studies Association; Sigma Alpha Iota; Tau Beta Sigma; etc. *Honours Include:* Recipient various honours and awards including; Certificate of Achievement, Metro Detroit YWCA, 1985; Certificate of Appreciation, Michigan Democratic Party, 1986; Certificate of Leadership, Detroit Public Schools, 1988. *Hobbies Include:* Swimming; Camping; Reading; Music. *Address:* Clinton School, 8145 Chalfonte, Detroit, MI 48238, USA.

EVANS Judith Futral, b. 18 Feb. 1931, Fort Smith, Arkansas, USA. Fine Artist; Painter. m. Jeptha A Evans Jr, 16 June 1963, divorced 1976, 1 son, 1 daughter. *Education:* BA, University of Arkansas, 1961; MFA, University of Iowa, 1964. *Appointments:* United Scenic Artists, 1984. *Creative works include:* Paintings in public collections, E F Hutton, New York City, Dewey Ballantine Bushby Palmer Wood, New York City, Cedar Crest College, Allantown, Pennsylvania; Mural - After Diego Rivera, The Alameda, New York City. *Membership:* Founder, The Blue Mountain Gallery, New York City. *Honours:* Participating Member, The American/French Art Exchange, Auvers-sur Oise, France; Medal of Excellence, City of Auvers-sur-Oise. *Address:* 1801 Dorchester Road, Apt 4-L, Brooklyn, NY 11226, USA.

EVANS Louise, b. San Antonio, Texas, USA. Clinical Psychologist; Lecturer. m. Thomas Ross Gambrell, 23 Feb. 1960. *Education:* BS, Northwestern University, 1949; MS 1952, PhD (Clinical Psychology) 1955, Purdue University; Intern 1953, Postdoctoral Fellow 1956, (both, 1st woman) in training program Menninger Clinic; Diploma, American Board of Professional Psychology, 1966. *Appointments include:* Kankakee State Hospital, Illinois, 1954; US Public Health Service, Menninger Clinic, Topeka, Kansas, 1955-56; Head Staff Psychologist, Child Guidance Clinic, Kings County Hospital, Brooklyn, New York, 1957-58; Clinical Research Consultant, Episcopal City Diocese, St Louis, Missouri, Director, Psychology Clinic, Barnes-Renard Hospitals & Instructor, Medical Psychology, Washington University School of Medicine, St Louis, 1959; Private practice, clinical & consulting psychology, Fullerton, California, 1960-. Various hospital affiliations. *Publications include:* Various scientific papers & projects. *Memberships include:* Life Fellow, American Orthopsychiatric Association; Diplomate, American Board of Professional Psychology; American Board of Professional Psychology; Fellow: International Council of Psychologists, International Council on Sex Education & Parenthood, Royal Society of Health (UK), American Association for Advancement of Science, American Psychological Association, various biographical associations; Member, numerous professional bodies. *Honours include:* Numerous certificates, plaques, medals, commendations from biographical, educational & civic institutions. *Address:* 905-907 West Wilshire Avenue, Wilshire West Professional Centre, Fullerton, California 92632, USA.

EVANS Nancy Remage, b. 19 May 1944, Massachusetts, USA. Astronomer. m. Martin Griffith Evans, 13 Aug. 1968, 2 daughters. *Education:* BA, Wellesley College, 1966; MSc, 1969, PhD, 1969, Postdoctoral Fellow, 1975-82, University of Toronto, Canada. *Appointments:* Assistant Professor, Erindale College, University of Toronto, 1982-83; Resident Astronomer, IOE Satellite, 1983-86; Research Associate, University of Toronto, 1986-88; Associate Scientist, Institute of Space and Terrestial Sciences, York University, North York, Ontario, 1988-. *Publications:* Numerous articles in professional journals. *Memberships:* American Astronomical Society; Canadian Astronomical Society; International Astronomical Union. *Honours:* Duncan Prize in Astronomy, Wellesley College, 1966; Chant Fellowship, 1966-67; Ontario Graduate Fellowships, 1967- 68. *Address:* Space Astrophysics Laboratory, Institute for Space and Terrestial Sciences, York University, 4700 Keele Street, North York, Ontario, Canada M3J 1P3.

EVANS Pamela Roye, b. 25 Aug. 1957, Hoisington, Kansas, USA. Group Director, Marketing. *Education:* BSc., 1980. *Appointments:* Sales Representative, 1981, District Sales Manager, 1981-82, Syracuse, Marketing Associate, Simonize, 1982-84, Associate Product Manager, Simonize/Division Acquisitions, 1984, Union Carbide Corp.; Product Manager, 1984-85, Mainstay/Field Master, Churck Wagon 1985-86, Grocery Products Division; Product Manager, New Products Group, 1986, Classic, super Heavy Duty, 1986-88, Group Director, Marketing, 1988-, Eveready Battery Co. Inc.,; Ralston Purina Co., 1989-. *Hobbies:* Trumpet; Racquet Sports; Photography; Bicycling; Hiking. *Address:* Eveready Battery Company Inc., Chekerboard Square 3EBC, St Louis, MO 63164, USA.

EVANS Roxanne Elizabeth Romack, b. 14 Feb. 1952, Idaho Falls, USA. Military Officer; Registered Dietitian. m. Paul Evans, 12 Nov 1988, 1 son by previous marriage. *Education:* BS, University of Idaho, 1974; MHA, Baylor University, 1982. *Appointments:* Private First Class 1973, advanced through ranks to Major 1985; Dietetic Intern, Brooke Army Medical Centre, 1974-75; Staff Dietitian, Walker Reed Army Medical Centre, 1975-77; Chief Food Service, Ft. Meade, 1977-80; Administrative Resident Tripler, Army Medical Centre, Hawaii, 1981-82; Chief, Clinical Dietetics, Tripler Army Medical Centre, 1982-85; Chief, Nutrition Care, Moncrief Army Hospital, 1985- 87; Chief, Clinical Dietetics, Walter Reed Army Medical Centre, Washington, 1987-89; Chief, DC/SP/VC Program Activity, Health Professional Support Agency, Falls Church Virginia, 1989-. *Memberships:* American College of Health Care Executives; American Dietetic Association; American Running & Fitness Association; American Hospital Association. *Hobbies:* Running; Cycling; Sewing. *Address:* 11669 Newbridge Court, Reston, VA 22091, USA.

EVANS Suzanne Marie, b. 29 Oct. 1953, Hartford, Connecticut, USA. Medicinal and Computational Chemist. *Education:* BS, magna cum laude, Fairfield University, CT, 1975; MS, Purdue University, IN, 1977; Certificate in Management, Elmhurst College, IL, 1982; PhD Candidate, Rutgers University, NJ, 1988-; Postgraduate, University of Illinois at Chicago, 1985-88. *Appointments:* Teaching and Research Assistant, Purdue University, West Lafayette, IN, 1975-77; Research Chemist 1981-82, Data Base Co-ordinator 1982-83, Biomolecular Structure Analyst, Medicinal Chemistry Dept, G D Searle & Co, Research and Development, Skokie, IL, 1978-81, 1983-85, Senior Computational Chemist 1985-88, Chemlab Inc, Lake Forest; Computational Chemistry Educator, Consultant 1986-88, Senior Scientist, Technical Center 1988-, The BOC Group Inc, Murray Hill, New Providence, NJ; Teaching Assistant, University of Illinois at Chicago, IL, 1985-87; University Fellow, 1987-88; Consultant, Computational Chemist, Intersoft Inc, Lake Forest, IL, 1985-88; Speaker in Field, 18 invited lectures 1977-88. *Publications:* Author: Opiates, 1986; Proceedings of the First European Seminar on Computer-Aided

Molecular Design, London, England, 1984; Contributor to professional journals; Patentee in field (holds 5 patents as inventor). *Memberships:* American Chemical Society, Organic Division, 1971-78; Computers in Chemistry Division, 1982-; Medicinal Chemistry Division, 1978-; Lecturer, Milwaukee, WI Section, 1985; Volunteer work: Career educator, National Science Foundation, 1980; Area High schools, 1980-84; Tutor, Center for Continuing Education, Fairfield, CT, 1974-75. *Honours:* ACS National Analytical Chemistry Award, 1974; Outstanding Personal Achievement Award, Alumni Assoc Fairfield University, 1975; Special Incentive Award, G D Searle & Co, 1982; Patent Achievement Award, G D Searle & Co, 1983; University of Illinois at Chicago University Fellow, 1987-88. *Address:* The BOC Group Inc, Technical Center, 100 Mountain Avenue, Murray Hill, New Providence, NJ 07974, USA.

EVANS-MCNEILL Elona Anita, b. 22 Nov. 1945, Washington, USA. Ambulatory Services Ombudsperson. m. James McNeill, 7 Oct. 1967, divorced 1973. *Education:* Howard University, 1963-64; American University, 1968-71. *Appointments:* Independant Contractor, 1973-84; Ambulatory Services Ombudsperson, Patient Advocate, Washington Hospital Center, 1986-. *Memberships:* numerous professional organisations including: National Association of Real Estate License Law Officials; Womens Political Caucus; Calvary Shelter for Homeless Women, Board; RedCross Volunteer. *Honours:* Scholastic Excellence Awards, Americna University, 1970-71; Outstanding Community Volunteer Award, Black Policemen's Association, 1980. *Hobbies:* Reading; Travel; Backgammon & Dominoes; Politics. *Address:* 3055 16th Street Northwest, Washington, DC 20009, USA.

EVATT Elizabeth Andreas, b. 11 Nov. 1933, Sydney, Australia. President, Australian Law Reform Commission. *Education:* LLB, Sydney, Australia, 1955; LLM, Harvard, USA, 1956; Barrister, Inner Temple, London, England, 1958. *Appointments:* Deputy President, Australian Conciliation & Arbitration Commission, 1973-; Chair, Royal Commission on Human Relationships, 1974-77; Chief Judge, Family Court of Australia, 1976-88; President, Australian Law Reform Commission, 1988-. *Memberships:* Chancellor, University of Newcastle, 1988-; United Nations Committee on the Elimination of Discrimination against Women, 1984-. *Honours:* University Medal in Law, 1955; Order of Australia, Officer (AO), 1982; Honorary Doctor of Laws, Sydney University, 1985. *Hobbies:* Music; Italian. *Address:* Law Reform Commission, 99 Elizabeth Street, Sydney, NSW 2000, Australia.

EVDOKIMOVA Eva, b. 1 Dec. 1948, Geneva, Switzerland. Prima Ballerina Assoluta. m. Michael Gregori, 1982. *Education:* Student, Munich State Opera Ballet Sch; Royal Ballet Sch, London, England; studied privately with Maria Fay, London; Vera Volkova, Copenhagen; Natalia Dudinskaya, Leningrad. *Appointments:* Debut, Royal Danish Ballet, Copenhagen, 1966; Prima Ballerina Assoluta, Deutsche Oper Berlin, 1969-; Frequent guest artist with numerous major ballet companies worldwide including: London Festival Ballet; Am Ballet Theatre; Paris Opera Ballet; La Scala; Kirov Ballet; Tokyo Ballet; Teatro Colon; Nat Ballet of Can; Most frequent partner of Rudolf Nureyev, 1971-; Premiered roles in all Rudolf Nureyev's classical ballet prodns; Repertoire of more than 85 roles includes: Swan Lake; Giselle; La Sylphide; Sleeping Beauty; Romeo and Juliet; Don Quixote; La Bayadere; Onegin; Raymonda; Created roles in ballets including Aspects (by Frank Schaufuss); Cinderella; The Idot (both by Valery Panov); Sphinx (by Glen Tetley); Tristan and Isolde (by Loyce Houlton); Unicorn (by John Neumeier); Medea, A Family Portrait (both by Birgit Cullberg); Carmencita (by Patrice Montagnon); Transfigured Night, Child Harold (both by Hans Spoerli); Undine (By Tom Schilling); Film appearances include: The Nutcracker; La Sylphide; Cinderella; A Family Portrait; The Romantic Era; Invitation to the Dance; Portrait of Eva Evdokimova. *Honours:* Recipient Diploma, Internat Ballet

Competition, Moscow, 1969; Winner Gold Medal Varna Internat Ballet competition, 1970; Awarded title Prima Ballerina, Berlin Senate, 1973; First fgn mem, Royal Danish Ballet; First Am and Westerner to win any internat ballet competition; First Am to perform with Kirov Ballet, 1976; First Am to perform in Peking after the Cultural Revolution, 1978; First and only Am dancer with portrait in peramenent collection, Mus Drama and Dance, Leningrad; First Am ballerina to perform as Guest Artist, Great Theatre, Warsaw, 1988. *Address:* c/o Michael Gregori, 400 East 56th Street, New York, NY 10022, USA.

EVERETT Cherry Sarff, b. 14 Dec. 1938, Jacksonville, Illinois, USA. Agribusiness/Development Company Officer/Director. m. Woodrow W. Everett Jr, 23 Aug. 1958, 1 son, 1 daughter. *Education:* Mary Washington College, University of Virginia, 1957-58; The George Washington University, 1958-59. *Appointments:* Director, Corporate Secretary, Masonwood Incorporated, 1959-; Director, Secretary-Treasurer, Device Associates Corporation of New York, 1971-; Director, The Sunoric Corporation, 1980-; Panel Member, Rotary Student Exchange, Rotary International Convention, 1968; Workshop Participant, Scholarly Research Workshops, Syracuse University, 1978- 83; Conference Participant, The Social Impact of Technology, Beijing, People's Republic of China, 1983. *Memberships:* Groton Community Church; Leader, Executive, Girl Scouts of America; Leader, Executive, 4-H Clubs of America; Little League Board of Directors; Corporate Member, Illinois Farm Bureau Federation; Corporate Member, King George Chamber of Commerce. *Honours:* Student Exchange Award, Rotary International, 1968; Service Awards, New York 4-H Clubs, 1971, 1973, 1974. *Hobbies:* Creative crafts. *Address:* Cherwood Pond, Walsingham-at-Port-Conway, Locked Box 68, Port Royal, VA 22535, USA.

EVERNDEN Margery E, b. 6 June 1916, Okeechobee, Florida, USA. Freelance Writer; Professor Emerita. m. Earl A Gulbransen, 2 July 1938. 1 son, 2 daughters. *Education:* AB, Univesity of California at Berkeley, 1938; MA, University of Pittsburgh, 1967. *Appointments:* Professor of English, University of Pittsburgh, retired 1986; Currently teach part-time. *Publications:* Novels for young readers: Secret of the Porcelain Fish; The Sword with the Golden Hilt; The Runaway Apprentice; The Golden Nail; Knight of Florence; Wilderness Boy; Simon's Way; Lyncoya; The Kite Song; The Dream Keeper; Plays for young audiences; Short stories; Essays and Poetry. *Address:* 63 Hathaway Court, Pittsburgh, PA 15235, USA.

EVERT Chris, b. 21 Dec. 1954, Fort Lauderdale, Florida, USA. m. Andy Mill, 30 July 1988. *Career:* Professional Tennis Player; President, Women's International Tennis Association. *Publications:* Autobiography, Chrissie with Neuil Amdur, 1982; Lloyd on Lloyd, co-authored with John Lloyd, 1985; Regular contributor of articles to World Tennis Magazine and USA Today newspaper. *Honours include:* Won four Singles titles, 1988; Leads all professional players with 157 singles titles; Named Greatest Woman Athlete for last 25 years, Women's Sports Foundation, 1985; Winner WITA Player of the Year Award, 1981. *Address:* The Polo Club, 5400 Champion Blvd, Boca Raton, FL 33496, USA.

EVERTON Louise Mathews, b. 22 Oct. 1934, Providence, Utah, USA. Publisher. m. George Baugh Everton, 10 Sept. 1952, 4 sons, 3 daughters. *Education:* Logan Latter Day Saints Seminary, 1951; Bridgerland Area Vocational Centre & Utah State University, 1974. *Appointments:* Book Review Editor, Genealogical Helper Magazine, 1970; Lecturer, Genealogy, US & Abroad; Vice President, Everton Publishers. *Memberships:* President, Utah Federation of Republican Women; Board, Freedom Foundation, Valley Forge; Board, Cache County Child & Family Support Centre (child abuse); Past President, Junior Chamber of Commerce Womens Organisation. *Hobbies: include:* Chairman, Providence Beautification (Providence Pioneer Days); Gardening; Oil Painting; Genealogy. *Address:* 825 South 4th East, Providence, Utah 84332, USA.

EWART Betty Ruth, b. 4 Jan. 1931, Portsmouth, USA. Health Educator. m. John Edward Ewart, 28 Dec. 1968, 1 daughter. *Education:* B.Church Mus., Capital University, 1952; MA, Education, Columbia University, 1955. *Appointments:* Christian Education Director, 1955-61: Episcopal Church; Assistant Dean of Women, Boston University, 1961-64; Assistant Dean of Women, Oberlin College, 1964-65; Director, Student Activities, Kent State University, 1965-68; Health Educator, West Virginia School of Osteopathic Medicine, 1974-. *Memberships:* AAUW,Past President, Lewisburg, WV; Quota Club; Interagency Council; United Way; West Virginia, Affiliate American Heart Association, Chairman of Board. *Honours:* Volunteer of the Year, Programming for West Virginia Affiliate of the American Heart Association, 1986. *Hobby:* Music. *Address:* 326 Longview Avenue, WV 24901, USA.

EWING Margaret Anne, b. 1 Sept. 1945, Lanark, Scotland. Member of Parliament. m. Fergus Stewart Ewing, 30 Nov. 1983. *Education:* MA, University of Glasgow, 1967; Secondary Teacher's Certificate, Jordanhill College, 1968; BA, Honours, University of Strathclyde, 1974. *Appointments:* Schoolteacher: Our Lady's High School, Cumbernauld, 1968-70; St Modan's High School, Stirling, 1970-74; MP, East Dunbartonshire, 1974-79; Social Work Administrator, 1981-87; MP for Moray, 1987-. *Memberships:* SNP:NEC, 1974-79, Vice President 1980-84, Deputy Leader 1984-87, Parliamentary Leader 1987-, Vice President 1987-. *Hobbies:* Self Government for Scotland; Arts in General; Gardening. *Address:* Goodwill, 22 Kinneddar Street, Lossiemouth, Moray IV31, Scotland.

EWING Mary, b. 1948, USA. Attorney. m. R. Craig Ewing, 1 son. *Education:* BA, History, University of Colorado, 1972; JD, University of Denver College of Law, 1975. Admitted: Colorado State Bar, 1975; US District Court, Colorado, 1975; US Court of Appeals, 1977; US Supreme Court, 1979. Certified Trial Specialist, 1984. *Appointments include:* Law Clerk 1972-75, Attorney 1975-80, Johnson & Mahoney, PC; Partner, Branney, Hillyard, Ewing & Barnes 1980-86, Bucholtz, Bull & Ewing PC 1986-. Also: Assistant Professor of Law 1978, Adjunct Professor 1979-, University of Denver College of Law; Numerous speaking engagements, professional seminars & conventions. *Publications:* Contributions, various legal publications. *Memberships include:* Past President, Kappa Beta Pi; Offices, past/present: Colorado Trial Lawyers Association, Denver Bar Association; Member: Colorado Women's & American Bar Associations, various college (professional) & community associations. *Address:* Nonesuch Farm, 816 West Quarry Road, Littleton, Colorado 80214, USA.

EWING Winifred Margaret, b. 10 July 1929, Glasgow, Scotland. Member of European Parliament; Solicitor. m. 25 June 1956, 2 sons, 1 daughter. *Education:* MA, LL.B, Glasgow University. *Appointments:* Solicitor, 1952-; Paid President, Glasgow Bar Association. *Memberships:* Law Society; President, Solicitors National Party; Vice President, European Democratic Alliance. *Hobbies:* Art Collecting; Walking on Hills. *Address:* 52 Queens Drive, Glasgow, Scotland.

EYJOLFSDOTTIR Steinunn, b. 8 July 1936, Iceland. Hospital Worker. m. Hilmar Albertsson, 24 May 1968, 4 sons, 2 daughters. *Appointments:* Farmer; Fish Production Worker; Hospital Worker. *Publicatins:* The Old Acquaintance, short stories, 1969; Wildrhyme, poem, 1981; Life of a Cat, Children's Story, 1985; The Nursery Home, Childrens Story, 1986; The Book of the Road, poems, 1987. *Memberships:* Icelandic Writers Association; Anti-Militarybase Association of Iceland. *Hobbies:* Reading; Politics; Nature Conservancy; etc. *Address:* Einigrund 11, 300 Akranesi, Iceland.

F

FAATZ Jeanne, b. 30 June 1941, Cumberland, Missouri, USA. State Representative; College Instructor. 2 daughters. *Education:* Honour Graduate, University of Illinois; MA Communications, University of Colorado at Denver, 1985. *Appointments:* Colorado State Representative, 1978-; Instructor, Metro State College, Denver, Regis College, Denver; Substitute Teacher, Denver Public Schools. *Memberships:* South-West Denver Community Mental Health Administration Board; Southwest Mental Health Center Citizens Advisory Board; Past President, Harvey Park Improvement Association; Fort Logan Mental Health Center Citizens Advisory Board; SW YMCA Board of Managers; Past President, SW YMCA Adult Education Club; Represented GOP Women at National Conference for Women State Legislators. *Honours:* Named, Denver Post Gallery of Fame 1978 for work with charities, politics and communities; Named as YWCA outstanding Colorado Woman Leader; Recipient President's Award for exemplary service to Warren Village, 1982; Graduated University Illinois, Cum laude; Gates Fellowship, Harvard JFK School of Government, 1984. *Hobbies:* Reading; Music; Theatre; Aerobics. *Address:* 2903 So Quitman Street, Denver, CO 80236, USA.

FABACHER Diane Hains, b. 6 Sept. 1941, Baton Rouge, USA. Social Worker. m. Edward Boos Fabacher, 2 Sept. 1963, 3 sosn, 2 daughters. *Education:* BS, 1984; MSW, Tulane University, 1984. *Appointments:* Director, Parent Aide Programme, YWCA of New Orleans, 1985-86; Psychiatric Socialworker, Greenbrier Hospital, 1986-; Private Practice, 1987- *Publications:* Seminars; articles in journals. *Memberships:* National Association of Social Workers; Northshore Social Workers Association; Society of Clinical Social Workers; NAFE; National Organization of Women. *Honours:* Dean's List, Southwestern Louisiana University, 1982; President's List, Our Lady of Holy Cross Academy, 1983; National Dean's List, 1983. *Hobbies:* Painting; Sailing. *Address:* 516 Woodridge Blvd., Mandeville, LA 70448, USA.

FADER Ellen Strahs, b. 9 Dec. 1952, New York City, USA. Communications Company Executive. m. Robert Steven Fader, 30 July 1976. *Education:* BA, SUNY, 1974. *Appointments:* Managing Editor, Oracle Newspaper, 1974-78; Assistant Editor, Random House/ A A Knopf, 1979-81; Contracts Co-ordinator, Hammond Music, 1981; Executive Vice President, Republic Broadcasting Corp., New York, 1981-; Vice President, Corporate Secretary, Price Communication Corp, 1981-; Vice President, Secretary; Atlas Broadcasting Corp, 1983-, Federal Broadcasting Corp, 1984-, New York Law Publishing Co., 1985-, Telemation Inc.; Director, Vice President, Secretary, 1986-; Director, Fairmont Communications Corporation, 1987-. *Memberships:* Women in Communications; American Women in Radio & TV; American Society of Corporate Secretaries; Rockefeller Centre Club. *Honours:* Alexander Medal, Board of Education, New York City, 1969; Haney Award, Metropolitan Museum of Art, 1970. *Address:* Price Communications Corp, 45 Rockefeller Plaza, Suite 3201, New York, NY 10020, USA.

FAGG Jenny Martin, b. 26 July 1930, Oklahoma City, Oklahoma, USA. Genealogical Editor and Writer. m. 20 Nov. 1948, 1 son, 2 daughters. *Education:* Computer course, Business School, Houston Community College. *Appointments:* President, JMF Publication, 1975-89; Chair, Board, Arlington Century Printing, 1983-88; President, JMF Computer Service, 1985; Secretary/Treasurer, Managing Editor, Chief Executive Officer, Martin/Barnett Genealogical Co Inc. *Publications:* The Family History of Thomas Martin, Sr, a North Carolinian American Revolutionary Soldier, 1975; Index to Marriage License Carroll County, Georgia 1827-1980, Vol I Groom Index, Vol II Bride Index, 1984; Texas Genealogical Societies and Their Publications; The Birth of the Martin Family Association; The Rigney Family of Coryell County; Register of Medical Practitioners Carroll County Georgia, 1986; How to Start Tracing Your Family Tree (co-author), 1986; Co-editor, Genealogical Compendium of Books and Articles in Print, bi-annually, Vol I, 1987, Vol II, 1988, Vol III, 1989. *Memberships:* Texas State Genealogical Society, Recording Secretary 1978-79, 1st Vice-President 1980-81; 1st Vice-Regent, Alexander Love Chapter, Daughters of the American Revolution, Treasurer 1979-81, Registrar 1987-89; National Genealogical Society; Campbell Clan, USA; United Daughters of the Confederacy; HAL Personal Computer Users Inc. *Hobbies:* Genealogy; History; Computers; Needlepoint. *Address:* 4314 Nenana, Houston, TX 77035, USA.

FAHRENKAMP Bettye, b. Wilder, Tennessee, USA. Consultant; Retired Teacher. *Educaiton:* BS, University of Tennessee; MA, University of Alaska. *Appointments:* Director, Curriculum Service Center, Fairbanks School District; Chairman, Alaska Education Television Association; Commissioner, Fairbanks North Star Borough Planning/Zoning Commission. *Memberships:* National Retired Teachers Association; American Legion; Alaska State Senate Resources Committee; Alaska State Legislative Council, etc. *Hobbies:* Bridge; Golf. *Address:* 119 No. Cushman Street, Suite 201, Fairbanks, AK 99701, USA.

FAHS Marianne Cullen, b. 16 July 1949, Rio de Janeiro, Brazil. Professor. m. John Frederick Padgett, 1973, divorced 1978. *Education:* BA, Sweet Briar College, 1971; MPH 1973, PhD 1985, University of Michigan. *Appointments:* National Center for Health Services Research, 1979-83; Mount Sinai School of Medicine, 1983-. *Publications:* The Cost-Effectiveness of Cervical Cancer Screening Among Indigent Elderly Women; The Economic Cost of Occupational Disease; The Effect of Increased Cost Sharing on the Health Care of the United Mine Workers. *Memberships:* American Public Health Association; Committee on the Status of Women, American Economics Association; Association for Health Services Research; Association for the Social Sciences in Health. *Honour:* Member, Advisory Panel to Office of Technology Assessment, US Congress. *Hobbies:* Sailing; Classical violin and country fiddle; Camping and backpacking; Squash. *Address:* Box 1043, Division of Health Economics, Mount Sinai Medical Center, 1 Gustave Levy Place, New York, NY 10029, USA.

FAIRBAIRN Joyce, The Honourable, b. 6 Nov. 1939, Lethbridge, Alberta, Canada. Journalist. m. Michael Gillan, 28 Oct. 1967. *Education:* BA, English, University of Alberta, 1960; B.Journalism, Carleton University, 1961. *Appointments:* News Reporter, Ottawa Journal, 1961- 62; Political Reporter, Columnist, Parliamentary Press Gallery Bureau of the United Press International, 1962-64; Political Correspondent, Parliamentary Press Gallery Bureau of F.P. Publications serving The Winnipeg Free Press, The Calgary Albertan, The Lethbridge Herald, The Vancouver Sun, The Victoria Times and The Ottawa Journal, 1964-70; Legislative Assistant to The Prime Minister of Canada, Rt. Honourable Pierre Elliott Trudeau, 1970-84; Summoned to The Senate of Canada for the Province of Alberta, Lethbridge, 1984-. *Memberships:* Canada US Interparliamentary Group; Canada Japan Interparliamentary Group; Canadian Branch, Commonwealth Parliamentary Association; Canada-Europe Parliamentary Association; Canadian Group, Interparliamentary Union; Human Rights Institute of Canada; National Press Club of Canada; Liberal Party of Canada, Alberta. *Address:* 34 Harmer Avenue North, Ottawa, Ontario, Canada K1Y 0T4.

FAIRFAX Mary (Lady), m. Sir Warwick Fairfax, 4 July 1959, 3 sons, 1 daughter. *Education:* University of Sydney, Australia. *Appointments Include:* Life Governor & Founder, Opera Foundation, Australia; Founder, Australia Opera Auditions in co-operation with Metropolitan Opera, New York; Founder, Australia Opera Scholarships to Bayreuth, German, La Scala, Italy and London Opera Centre, England; Founder, President,

Friends of the Ballet; Past Member, Cultural Grants Committee, Ministry for Culture, Sport & Recreation, New South Wales; Founder, Juilliard Scholarship, Lincoln Centre, New York, USA, 1977; Director, Industrial Equity Ltd; Honorary Consul of Monaco, 1979; Founder, Lady James Fairfax Memorial Prize for Painting (Australian Birds and Flowers for the Royal Agricultural Society of New South Wales, 1980); Founder, Donor, Lady James Fairfax Memorial Prize for Photography, Art Gallery of New South Wales, 1981. *Publications:* Short stories, poetry in various journals and magazines. *Memberships:* Queen's Silver Jubilee Committee. *Hobbies:* Working; The Arts; Writing; Poetry; Sculpture; Fashion; Entertaining; Reading; Swimming; Walking; Travel. *Address:* Fairwater, 560 New South Head Road, Double Bay 2028, Australia.

FAIRLEIGH Marlane Paxson, b. 28 Feb. 1939, Three Rivers, Michigan, USA. Account Executive. m. James P. Fairleigh, 25 June 1960, 1 son, 1 daughter. *Education:* BM, University of Michigan, 1960; MBA, Jacksonville State University, 1986. *Appointments:* Adjunct Faculty, Providence College, 1976-80, Rhode Island College, 1978-80; Graduate Assistant, News Bureau, 1983-84, College of Commerce, 1984-85, Jacksonville State University; Account Executive, Small Business Development Centre, 1985-. *Publications:* Articles in: News and Views; Troy State University Business and Economic Review. *Membership:* International Management Council, Anniston, Secretary. *Honours:* Recipient, various Scholarships; Outstanding Chairperson Awards: International Management Council, 1984-85, 1985-86. *Hobbies:* Waterskiing; Swimming; Music; Reading. *Address:* 70 Fairway Drive, Jacksonville, AL 36265, USA.

FAITH Sheila, Dental Surgeon; Member European Parliament. m. Dennis Faith. *Education:* Durham University. *Appointments:* Member, Northumberland County Council, 1970-74; Contested Conservative, Newcastle Central, 1974; Member of Parliament for Belper, 1979-83; Member, European Parliament for Cumbria & Lancashire North, 1984-. *Memberships:* various professional organisations. Chairman, several school governing bodies; JP. *Address:* Flat Two, 39 Royal Avenue, London SW3 4QE, England.

FAITH-ELL Age (Anna Margareta), b. 9 July 1912, Vaxjo, Sweden. Textile Designer; Teacher. *Education:* Weaving teacher's degree, Johanna Brunsson's Weaving School, Stockholm, 1931-34; Academy for Applied Art, Vienna, Austria, 1935; National Teachers & Experimental Institute for Textile Industries, 1943. *Appointments:* Textile designer, Swedish Handicraft Society, 1936-42; Teacher, Academy for Applied Art, Vienna, Austria, 1942-45; Designer & Instructor, R. Atkinson, Irish Poplin House, Belfast, Northern Ireland, UK, 1946-49; Textile designer, AB Claes Hakansson (AB Kinnasand), Kinna, Sweden 1955-56, 1964-65, Eriksbergs Vaveri AB, Kinna (with department store, Nordiska Kompaniet, Stockholm) 1960-61, AB Marks Jacquerdvaveri, Bjorketorp 1961-63; Freelance designer, own studio. *Creative work includes:* Numerous decorative textiles for public buildings. Solo & group exhibits, Sweden & abroad, including: Vienna, 1944; Stockholm, 1945; Munich, 1959; Darmstadt, Germany, 1959; Stockholm, 1960; London, 1961; Milan, 1960; New York, 1962; Stuttgart, 1962, 1963; Stockholm, 1946, 1956, 1964, 1973, 1982, 1987; Malmö, 1987; Stockholm, 1988, 1989; Kalmar, 1988; Malmö, 1989. *Honours include:* Silver Medal, Stockholm Craft Association, 1934; Gold Medal, XII Triennal, Milan, 1960; Distinction, Swedish Design, 1961; AID Interior Design Award, USA, 1963; Excellent Swedish Design Award 1987; Excellent Swedish Design Award, 1989; Numerous biographical listings. *Hobby:* Classical music. *Address:* Kungsvagen 54, S-352 33 Vaxjo, Sweden.

FAITHFULL Lucy, (Baroness), b. 26 Dec. 1910, Boxburg, South Africa. Social Worker. *Education:* Social Science Diploma, Birmingham University, 1932; Family Casework Training, 1936; Certificate in Child Care, 1969. *Appointments:* Club Leader and Sub-Warden of the Birmingham Settlement, 1932-35; Assistant Organiser of Child Care, London County Council, 1936-40; Regional Welfare Officer for Evacuees, Ministry of Health, 1940-48; Inspector, Children's Branch, Home Office, 1948-58; Children's Officer, Oxford City, 1958-70; Director, Social Services, Oxford City, 1970-74. *Memberships:* Association of Directors of Social Services; British Association of Social Workers; British Association of Counselling; President, National Children's Bureau. *Honours:* Honorary MA, Oxford University, 1974; Honorary DLitt, Warwick University, 1978. *Hobbies:* Friends; Travel. *Address:* House of Lords, Westminster, London SE1, England.

FALK Candace Serena, b. 30 July 1947, New York, USA. Writer; Editor and Director, Emma Goldman Papers. m. Lowell Finley, 23 Oct. 1977. 1 son, 1 daughter. *Education:* BA, Humanities 1969, MA, Humanities 1971, University of Chicago; PhD, History, Political Theory, University of California, Santa Cruz, 1984. *Appointments:* Research Associate, Woodlawn Mental Health Center, 1970-71; Instructor, Stockton Staff College, Methods of Inquiry, 1971-72; Instructor, Teaching Assistant, University of California, Santa Cruz, 1972-76; Editor, Center for Research & Education, 1972-79; Editor & Research Associate, Southeast Asia Resource Ctr, 1976-79; Editor and Director, The Emma Goldman Papers, 1980-. *Publications:* Love, Anarchy and Emma Goldman (a biography), 1984, 1989, Berlin 1986; Comprehensive Papers of Emma Goldman, 1989-; Many articles and reviews. *Memberships:* Organization of American Historians; American Historical Association; Association of Documentary Editors; American Studies Association; Institute for the Study of Social Change (University of California); President of Board of Directors, Catticus Documentary Film Company; Society of American Archivists. *Honours include:* American Council of Learned Societies, 1988; Recipient of numerous grants. *Hobbies:* Writing; International and community politics; Art; Balancing children's development with work. *Address:* c/o Emma Goldman Papers, University of California, 2224 Piedmont, Berkeley, CA 94720, USA.

FALK Elizabeth Moxley, b. 21 Sept. 1942, Memphis, Tennessee, USA. Producer, Opera & Music. m. Lee Falk, 31 Dec. 1976. *Education:* Blytheville, Ark High School. *Appointments:* Promotional Manager, Chesebrough-Pond's International, 1961-65; Account Executive, Lintas Advertising, Durban, South Africa, 1965-67; Director of New Product Development, Chemway Corporation, New York, USA, 1967-69; Marketing Manager, Revlon, Inc, New York, 1969-70; Account Supervisor, BBDO Advertising, New York, 1971-72; New Product Director, Alexandra de Markoff, Division of Charles of the Ritz, New York, 1972-74; Director of Product Development, Almay Cosmetics, Inc, 1974-76; Producer, Vineyard Theatre, 1986; Company Manager, New Artists Coalition, 1986; Associate Producer 1987, Producer 1988, Project: Music Rediscovery; Stage Manager 1987, Producer 1988, Producer 1989, Vineyard Opera, New York City; Producer, Elizabeth Falk Presents, 1987; Project Chairman, American Landmark Festivals, 1988; Producer, Newport Music Festival, 1988; Associate Producer, Vineyard Opera at Berkshire Opera Festival, 1988. *Publications:* Novels: The Evil Within, 1980; Mirror Images, 1981; Plays: Goldsmith's Last Rites, 1983; White Tie and Veils, 1984. *Creative works:* Most recently, Producer: Il Viaggio a Reims, La Gazza Ladra. *Memberships:* Players Club, Admissions Committee, 1989-; Provincetown Academy for the Living Arts (PALA), Vice-President 1986-; American Guild of Musical Artists (AGMA); AGMA Relief Fund, National Advisory Board, 1988-; The Women's Project of American Place Theatre; Alliance of Resident Theatres (ART); Foundation for the Extension and Development of American Professional Theatres (FEDAPT); Central Opera Services; Development Professionals Roundtable; Mystery Writers of America; Castle Hill School for the Arts, Advisory Board, 1984-87; National Museum of Women in the Arts, Founding Member; Confrerie de La Chaine des Rotisseurs, Dame de la Chaine, 1977-; Patron, Metropolitan Opera Guild; MENSA; National Association of Underwater

Instructors. *Hobbies:* Scuba diving. *Address:* Seven West 81 Street, New York, NY 10024, USA.

FALKENDER Marcia Matilda, b. 10 Mar. 1932, England. Writer; Company Director. m. 1 Dec. 1955, 2 sons. *Education:* Queen Mary College, London University, 1951-54. *Appointments:* PA to General Secretary, British Labour Party, 1954-56; Private & Political Secretary to Rt. Harold Wilson, 1956-83. *Publications:* Inside No. 10, 1972; Perspective on Downing Street, 1983. *Memberships:* British Screen advisory Council; Governor, Queen Mary College, London University; Deputy Chairman, UK, Unifem. *Honours:* CBE, 1970; Life Peerage, 1974. *Hobbies:* Reading; Films; Parapsychology. *Address:* 3 Wyndham Mews, Upper Montagu St., London W1H 1RS, England.

FALKOWSKI Patricia Ann Crawford, b. 12 Apr. 1947, New Brunswick, New Jersey, USA. Investment Analyst. m. Walter S. Falkowski, 1 son, 1 daughter. *Education:* BS summa cum laude, Marketing Management, Rider College, Trenton, New Jersey, 1969; MBA, Finance, Accounting, University of Chicago, 1980. *Appointments:* Federal Loan Bank Board, Washington DC, 1970-72; SEC, Washington DC, 1972-73; Economic Development Administration, Philadelphia, Pennsylvania, 1975-76; FDIC, Chicago, Illinois, 1977-79; Kemper Financial Companies Inc, Chicago, 1980-81, 1983-; Harris Trust and Savings, Chicago, 1981-83. *Memberships:* President, Chicago Financial Stock Association; Committee Co-Chair, University of Chicago Women's Business Group; Chicago Investment Analysts Society (Committee Member, Public Relations); Placements Member, New York Bank and Financial Stock Analysts Association; St Francis Hospital Auxiliary, Evanston Inc. *Hobbies:* Travel; Jogging; Politics. *Address:* 505 Sunset Road, Winnetka, IL 60093, USA.

FANTHORPE U. A., b. 22 July 1929, Kent, England. Writer. *Education:* MA, St Anne's College, Oxford University, 1953; PGCE, London University, 1954; DipSc, University College of Swansea, 1971. *Appointments:* Assistant English teacher, then Head, English Department, Cheltenham Ladies' College, 1954-70; Receptionist, Burden Neurological Hospital, 1973-86; Arts Council Writer Fellow, St Martin's College, Lancaster, 1983-85; Northern Literary Arts Fellow, 1987. *Creative work includes:* Poetry. *Honours:* 3rd prize, Arvon-Observer South Bank Poetry Competition, 1980; Travelling scholarship, Society of Authors, 1983; Hawthornden Fellowship, 1987; Elected Fellow of the Royal Society of Literature, 1988. *Hobbies:* Reading; Birdwatching; Narrowboats; Walking. *Address:* Culverhay House, Wotton-under-Edge, Gloucestershire GL12 7LS, England.

FARBER Phyllis Gwendolyn Ingler, b. 21 Sept. 1942, Franklin, USA. Teacher. m. Frank Dale Farber, 2 Aug. 1961, 1 son, 1 daughter. *Education:* BA, Trenton State College, 1965; Certified in Elementary Education. *Appointments:* Kindergarten Teacher, 1965-80; Slow First Grade Teacher, 1980-85; First Grade Teacher, 1985-89. *Memberships:* Vernon Township, Sussex County, New Jersey, National Education Associations; Sussex County Association of Kindergarten Educators, Past President. *Honours:* Vernon Township Teacher of the Year, 1978-79; Sussex County Teacher of the Year, 1st Runner Up, 1978-70. *Hobbies:* Sponser, Save the Children's US programmes; Photography; Music; Crafts; Gardening. *Address:* 30 Mountain Road, RD1 Box 611, Hamburg, NJ 07419, USA.

FARIAN Babette Sommerich, b. 6 June 1916, New York City, USA. Artist. m. Robert Alan Farian, 27 Sept. 1942. 1 son. *Education:* Arts Student League; Parsons School of Design; Museum of Modern Art; Cooper Union. studied with Joseph Margulies, Morris Cantor and Donald Stacy. *Appointments:* Designed textiles and greeting cards; Assistant Studio Manager; Teacher, Cooper Union. *Creative works:* Works permanently on exhibit in: Tammassee DAR School Gallery; The

Women's Inter-art Gallery; The First Unitarian Church; Sloan-Kettering Memorial Center; Brooklyn Botanic Garden, also in many fine private collections. Most recent shows include, Audubon Artists; National Society of Painters in Casein & Acrylics; National Art Club; Queens Community College Works on Paper and Visual Individuals United; 1989: Discoveries II; Flushing Council on Culture and the Arts; The American Flag Museum, Virginia; The Paul VI Institute for the Arts, Washington DC; Passaic County Community College; Audubon Art Association, 1988. *Memberships include:* Burr Artists (Catalog Chairwoman); National League of American Pen Women (Corresponding Secretary); Composers, Authors and Artists of America; Eleanor Gay Lee Gallery Foundation; National Art Club. *Honours:* Winner of numerous prizes including: First prize, Jackson Heights Art Club, oils, 1989; First prize, National Art Club, oils, 1988; Sea Heritage Foundation Show, 1986; Exhibiting finalist, FACIT Gallery, Taos, 1984-85; 1st prize watercolour, Composers, Authors and Artists of America, 1983; Jackson Heights Art Club, 1988. *Hobbies:* Sketching; Reading; Theatyre; Music; Nature; Gardens. *Address:* 3448 81 Street, Jackson Hts, NY 11372, USA.

FARIAS Anna Maria, b. 15 Oct. 1952, San Antonio, Texas. Attorney; Deputy Director. *Education:* BA, cum laude, Boston University, 1976; Temple Law School, 1980. *Appointments:* Administrative Clerk, Massachusetts' Criminal Justice Department, 1976-77; Legal Clerk, United States Treasury Dept., 1978; Attorney, General Counsel's Merit Systems Protection Board, 1980-85; Special Assistant, Attorney Advisor, US Secretary of Education, 1985-; Deputy Director, Office of Bilingual Education & Minority Langues Affairs, 1985-; Attorney Advisor to Assistant Secretary in the office for Civil Rights, US Department of Education, Washington DC; Attorney Advisor to Commissioner of National Labor Relations Board. *Memberships:* Legal Bar of the Commonwealth of Pennsylvania; US Supreme Court; Federal and American Bar Associations; Federal Court of Appeals; Military Court of Appeals. *Honours:* Recipient numerous honours and awards including: Special Achievement Award, 1984; Meritorious Achievement Award, 1987; Houston, Texas Award of Excellence, 1987; Pennsylvania State Award, 1987; Las Vegas Nevada Award, 1988; Brownsville, Texas Award, 1988; Clark County, Nevada Award, 1988; etc. *Hobbies:* Photography; Baseball; Travel. *Address:* 6618 Boulevard View C-2, Alexandria, VA 22307, USA.

FARINA Rachele, b. 30 Jan. 1930, La Spezia, Italy. Editor, The Biographical Dictionary of Lombard Women. m. Luigi Gruppi, 27 Nov. 1954. 1 daughter. *Education:* Degree in Philosophy, University, Turin, 1954. *Appointments:* Telephone Operator, 1948-54; Teacher, 1955-83; Chief Organizer of the Exhibition Exist as a Woman, 1983. *Publications:* La Prestazione with M Novero, 1974; La Resistenza taciuta, with A M Bruzzone, 1976; Un nocciolo di Verita, with F Ferrero, 1978; Vita Sociale alla Scala in Bicentenario della Scala 1778/1978 Articoli storici sulle riviste Il Risorgimento e Ca' de Sass di Milano. *Memberships:* CGIL National Representative for Telephone workers, 1952-54; President, Unione Femminile Nazionale, 1985-88; Presidente dalla fondazione di Exist as a Woman, 1986-, research Association. *Honours:* Guzzo Award for best Philosophy Dissertation, 1954; Exploit Atkinsons Award, 1983; Europa Award, 1983; Cavaliere della Repubblica Italiana, 1986. *Hobbies:* Swimming; Historical research. *Address:* Via Stendhal 55, 20144 Milan, Italy.

FARLEY Carol, b. 20 Dec. 1936, Ludington, Michigan, USA. Writer; Editor; Lecturer. m. 21 June 1956, 1 son, 3 daughters. *Education:* Teaching Certificate 1956, MA (Children's Literature) 1983, Western Michigan State University; BA, Communication, Michigan State University, 1980. *Appointments:* Freelance writer, 1959-; English teacher, Seoul, Korea, 1978, 1979; ICL teacher, 1983-88. *Publications:* The Garden is Doing Fine; Mystery of the Fog Man; Mystery of the Melted Diamond; Case of the Vanishing Villain; Case of the Lost Look Alike.

Memberships: Society of Children's Book Writers; Mystery Writers of America; Washington DC Book Guild; Chicago Reading Round Table; Authors Guild. *Honours:* Best Book Award, Child Study Association, 1977; Golden Kite Award, childen's writing, 1987; Children's Choice Book, 1977. *Address:* 8574 West Higgins Lake Drive, Roscommon, Michigan 48653, USA.

FARLEY Carole, b. 29 Nov. 1946, Le Mars, Iowa, USA. Opera Singer. m. Jose Serebrier, 29 Mar. 1969. 1 daughter. *Education:* BM, Indiana University, 1968; Munich Hochschule, 1970. *Career:* American debut, Town Hall, New York City 1969; Paris debut, Nat Orch, 1975; London debut, Royal Philahrmonic Soc, 1975; South American debut, Teatro Colon, Philharmonic Orchestra, Buenos Aires, 1975. Soloist with major American and European Symphony orchestras, 1970; Soloist, Welsh National Opera, 1971, 1972; Cologne Opera, 1972-75; Phila Lyric Opera, 1974; Brussels Opera 1972; Lyon Opera, 1976, 1977; Strasbourg Opera, 1975; Linz Opera, 1969; NYC Opera 1976; New Orleans Opera, 1977; Cin Opera, 1977; Met Opera Co, NYC 1977-; Zurich Opera, 1979; Chicago Lyric Opera 1981; Can Opera Co, 1980; Dusseldorf Opera, 1980, 1981, 1984; Palm Beach Opera 1982; Theatre Chatelet, Paris, 1983; Theatre Royale de la Monnaie Brussels, 1983; Teatro Regio, Turin, Italy, 1983; Nice Opera, France, 1984-88; Cologne Opera, 1985; Teatro Comunale, Florence, Italy, 1985; Nice Opera, 1987; BBC Opera, 1987. *Publications:* About Salome, series of articles compiled in book form; TV film, ABC Australia La Voix Humaine, recorded for Deutsche Gramophone, Chandos, CBS, BBC records, ASV Records. *Memberships:* Am Guild Mus Artists (AGMA); Metropolitan Opera Guild. *Honours:* Alumni of Year, Indiana University 1976; Abiati prize, for Lulu, Italy, 1984; Musician of the Month, Musical America, February 1977. *Hobbies:* Reading; Swimming; Cooking; Gardening; Jogging. *Address:* Stafford Law Associates, 26 Mayfield Road, Weybridge, KT13 8XB, England.

FARLEY Irene Daly, b. 9 Feb. 1923, New York City, New York, USA. Civic Worker. m. Edward R. Farley Jr, 19 Feb. 1948, 2 sons, 2 daughters. *Education:* Hunter College, 1941-42. *Appointments:* Secretary, US Treasury Department, New York City, 1942-44; Smith Barney & Co, Investment Bankers, New York City, 1944-47; Public Relations Executive, Newell Emmett Advertising Agency, New York City, 1947-48. *Publications:* Contributor to Treasure Chest Magazine. *Memberships:* Chairman, Princeton, Hospital Fete, 1966; Chairman, Princeton Hospital Christmas Boutique, 1973; Chairman, Steering Committees, 1966, 1973; President of Board, New Jersey Neuro Psychiatric Association, 1969-71; Executive Officer, Board of Managers, 1969-71; President, Friends of Princeton Public Library, 1985; Executive Officer, Board of Directors, 1985, Council Member, 1980-89, Princeton Public Library; Vice-Chairman, 1989, Board of Directors, 1988-89, Eden Institute for Autistic; Present Day Club, Princeton; Pretty Brook Tennis Club, Princeton; Bedens Brook Country Club, Skillman, New Jersey. *Hobbies:* Civic works; Committee work; Organizing benefits; Reading; Travel. *Address:* 188 Parkside Drive, Princeton, NJ 08540, USA.

FARMER Carol Ann, b. 14 Aug. 1944, Columbus, Ohio, USA. President, Carol Farmer Associates. m. Alton Doody, 14 May 1976, divorced 1980. *Education:* BA, De Pauw University, Greencastle, Ind, 1964. *Appointments:* Senior Consulting Assoc, Management Horizons, Columbus, Ohio, 1971-74; Chief Operating Officer, Co-Founder, The Doody Company, 1974-80; President, Retail Design Research, 1980-83; Exec VP, Lerner Store, New York City, 1982-84; Vp Corp Development Specialty Retailing, American Can Co, 1984-85; Founded, Carol Farmer Associates, 1985-. *Membership:* The Fashion Group International. *Hobbies:* Tennis; Painting. *Address:* Carol Farmer Associates, P O Box 470, Boca Raton, Florida 33429, USA.

FARMER Cathy Lee, b. 18 Jan. 1957, Nashville, Tennessee, USA. Geologist; Petroleum Exploration Engineer. *Education:* BS Geological Engineering 1979, MS Geology 1981, Colorado School of Mines. *Appointments:* Geologic Associates, 1976-77; Amoco Production Company, summers 1978-79, 1981-87; Staff Geologist, Africa & Middle East Region, Amoco International, 1987-. *Publication:* Co-author, Tectonic Influence on Sedimentation, CSM Quarterly, 1982. Also: Numerous recommendations for drilling oil & gas wells, for company reports (unpublished). *Memberships include:* American Association of Petroleum Geologists; Rocky Mountain Association of Geologists; Houston Geologic Society; Sigma Xi; Various honour societies; Speaker 1981, International Association of Sedimentologiss; Past President, CSM Geology Club. *Honours:* High School Valedictorian, 1975; Awards, Tau Beta Pi 1976, Texas Oil & Gas 1978, Colorado Engineering Council 1979; Outstanding Geologist, CSM, 1979; Most Outstanding Woman Geoscientist, 1981; Geosciences Distinguished Leadership Award, 1988. *Hobbies include:* Private pilot; Horse riding; Scuba diving; Skiing; Backpacking & hiking; Mineralogy; Directors' Circle, Houston Grand Opera. *Address:* Amoco International, 501 Westlake Park Boulevard, Houston, Texas 77253, USA.

FARMER Mary Ann Bauder, b. 30 Nov. 1953, San Diego, California, USA. Consultant; Nurse Practitioner. *Education:* Ida V. Moffett School of Nursing, Samford University, 1975; Ob/Gyn Nurse Practitioner Programme, University of Alabama, 1978; BS, Auburn University, 1986. *Appointments:* Staff Registered Nurse, University of Alabama Hospital, 1973-75; Regional Director, Women's Medical Clinics, 1975-80; Owner, Beacon Clinic, 1980-83; Partner, Hill, Rose & Farmer, 1988; Affiliated Resources, Vice President. *Memberships:* Board Member, Planned Parenthood of Greater Atlanta; Business Committee for the Arts; Outstanding Young Women of America; Action Committee, League of Women Voters; National Museum of Women in the Arts; NOW; ODK. *Honours:* Outstanding Young Women of America, 1978; Women's Freedom Award, National Women's Political Caucus, 1980; Scholar's Colloquium, 1983-86. *Hobbies:* Sailing; Skiing; Reading; Theatre; Cooking; Historic Preservation; Political events, fundraising and campaigns; Collecting antique perfume bottles; Golf. *Address:* 1810 Rockridge Place NE, Atlanta, GA 30324, USA.

FARMER Susan L, b. 29 May 1942, Boston, USA. Broadcast Executive. m. Malcolm Farmer, 6 Apr. 1968, 2 daughters. *Appointments Include:* Court Appointed Special Advocate for Abused Children, 1978-83; Elected Providence Home Rule Commission, 1979-80; Elected RI Secretary of State, 1983-87; Chief Executive Officer, General Manager, WSBE TV Channel 36, 1987-. *Memberships:* various professional organisations including: National Fund for America's future; National Womens Campaign Advisory Committee. *Honours:* Woman of the Year: National Womens Political Caucus, RI Chapter, 1980, Business & Professional Women, 1984. *Address;* WSBE TV, 24 Mason Street, Providence, RI 02903, USA.

FARR Jennifer Margaret, b. 20 July 1933, London, England. m. Sydney Hordern Farr, 28 July 1956, died 1981, 2 sons, 1 daughter. *Education:* Middlesex Hospital & Royal Victoria Infirmary, Newcastle-upon-Tyne, 1951-54. *Appointment:* Chartered Physiotherapist (MCSP), 1954-56. *Memberships:* JP 1979-; Chairman, Nottingham & District NSPCC; President, Thurgarton Cricket Club. *Hobbies:* Music; Gardening; Golf; Tennis. *Address:* Lanesmeet, Epperstone, Nottingham NG14 6AU, England.

FARRAR Elaine Willardson, Painter; Sculptor; Graphic Artist; Art Educator. m. H Gordon Farrar, 1947, divorced 1964, 4 sons, 2 daughters. *Education:* BA, Arizona State University, 1955; BA, MA, 1968; Currently PhD Candidate in Art Education; private study with various experts in field. *Appointments:* Instructor, Art, Camelback desert School, Scotsdale, 1966-68; Instructor 1969-72, Chairperson & Instructor 1973-78, Instructor, Painting, Printmaking, 1973-, Yavapai

College, Prescott. *Creative Works include:* Exhibitions, 1967-; Solo Shows: Art Centre, Battlecreek, Michigan, Scottsdale, Arizona, Costa Mesa, California. *Memberships Include:* Registered Representative, State of Arizona, Arizona Art Education; Ex-President, Mountain Artists Guild Inc; Fine Arts Superintendent, County Fair, 8 years; Registered Board Scholastics Arts Exhibitions; International Society Artists; National League of American Pen Women; Kappa Delta Pi; Phi Delta Kappa. *Honours Include:* Numerous awards including 1st places national juried competitions and exhibitions, 1967-86. *Hobbies:* Flying; Golf. *Address:* Yavapai College, 1100 E Sheldon, Prescott, AZ 86301, USA.

FARRAR Pauline Elizabeth, b. 2 July 1928, Madison, USA. Broker; Business Owner. m. (1) James Walter Byers, 15 Aug. 1950, deceased 1972, 2 sons, 2 daughters, (2) Dr Robert B. Farrar, 14 Apr. 1974. *Education:* BBA, University of Wisconsin, 1949; University of Houston, 1956-57. *Appointments:* Accountant, Sterling Hogan Interest, 1951-54, Prokop Interests, 1954-57, Holland Mortgage & Investments, 1959-64; Administrative Assistant, Jetero Cor., 1968-71; Real Estate Sales, 1976-86; Mills Paulea Realtors, 1980-81; Era Nelson & Assoc., 1981-; Property-Wise Realty, Broker/Owner. *Memberships:* Ft. Bend County Board of Realtors; Houston Board of Realtors; Ft. Bend Chamber of Commerce; Houston Apartment Association. *Honours:* Top Listing Agent, 1978; Top Sales Leader, 1977; *Hobbies:* Travel; Camping; Grandchildren. *Address:* 6730 Highway 6, Sugar Land, TX 77478, USA.

FARREN Grainne Teresa, b. 15 Oct. 1936, Dublin, Republic of Ireland. Freelance Journalist/Editor/Translator. 1 son. *Education:* Secondary Education Leaving Certificate, 1954; Studied Music, French, Spanish; Correspondence course in Indexing. *Appointments:* Various secretarial positions, Dublin, London, England and Paris, France, 1955-67; Translator, Patent Agency, Paris, 1968-72; Translator, Selection du Reader's Digest, Paris, 1973-80; Proof Reader/Editor, Tycooly International Publishing, Dublin, 1984. *Publications include:* Short stories in magazines and on RTE Radio 1; Articles for Jazznews International; The Secretary Trap (book manuscript). *Memberships:* Chairwoman, Cherish (Association of Single Mothers); National Jazz Society; Irish Translators Association; Association of Freelance Editors and Indexers. *Hobbies:* Music; Photography; Cinema; Theatre; Reading. *Address:* c/o Cherish, 2 Lower Pembroke Street, Dublin 2, Republic of Ireland.

FARROW Maureen Anne, b. 20 July 1943, England. Economist. m. John E. L. Farrow, 1969, 1 son. *Education:* BSc., Honours, Hull University, England, 1966; Postgraduate Studies, London Business School. *Appointments:* Partner in Charge, Economics, Coopers & Lybrand (Canada); President, C. D. Howe Institute, 1987-. *Memberships:* Social Sciences and Humanities Research Council of Canada; Past President, Canadian Association for Business Economics; numerous other professional organisations. *Address:* The Cooper & Lybrand Consulting Group, 135 King Street East, Toronto, Ontario M5C 1G6, Canada.

FARROW Mia Villiers, b. 9 Feb. 1945, California, USA. Actress. m. (1) Frank Sinatra, 1966, divorced 1968. (2) Andre Previn, 1970, divorced 1979. 3 sons, 3 daughters. *Career:* Stage debut in The Importance of Being Earnest, New York, 1963. *Creative Works:* Stage appearances: In London: Mary Rose; The Three Sisters; House of Bernarda Alba, 172-73; The Zykova, 1976; The Marrying of Ann Leete, 1975; Ivanov, 1976 both Royal Shakespeare Company. Romantic Comedy (Broadway), 1979. Films include: Guns at Batasi, 1964; Rosemary's Baby, 1968; Secret Ceremony, 1969; John and Mary, 1969; See-No Evil, 1970; The Great Gatsby, 1973; Full Circle, 1978; A Wedding, 1978; Death on the Nile, 1978; The Hurrican, 1979; A Midsummer Night's Sex Comedy, 1982; Zelig, 1983; Broadway Danny Rose, 1984; Purple Rose of Cairo, 1985; Hannah

and her Sisters, 1986; Radio Days, 1987. Television appearances: Peyton Place, 1964-66; Johnny Belinda, 1965; Peter Pan, 1975. *Honours:* French Academy Award for best actress, 1969; David Conatello Award, (Italy), 1969; Rio de Janeiro Film Festival Award, 1969; San Sebastian Award. *Hobbies:* Reading; Mind wandering; Listening to music and certain people. *Address:* c/o Lionel Lamer Ltd, 850 7th Avenue, New York, NY 10019, USA.

FASEL Ida Drapkin, b. 9 May 1909, Portland, Maine, USA. Professor Emerita. m. Dr Oskar A Fasel, 24 Dec. 1946. *Education:* BA, 1931, MA, 1945, Boston University; PhD, University of Denver, 1963. *Appointments:* Teacher: various universities in USA; Professor, English, 1962-77, Professor Emerita, 1977-, University of Colorado, Denver. *Publications:* Poetry: On the Meanings of Cleave; Thanking the Flowers; West of Whitecaps; All of Us, Dancers; Amphora Full of Light; Available Light; Basics; contributor of Poetry, translations, book reviews, and professional articles to journals, magazines & anthologies. *Memberships:* Phi Beta Kappa; Poetry Society of America; Milton Society of America; Friends of Milton's Cottage; South Central & Midwest Modern Language Associations; Conference on Christianity and Literature. *Honours:* Elected to Collegium of Distinguished Alumni, Boston University, 1979; other honours and awards. *Hobbies:* Collecting Angels; Playing Piano; Cooking. *Address:* 165 Ivy Street, Denver, CO 80220, USA.

FAULL Lesley Alice Margaret, b. 11 Dec. 1922, Durban, Natal, South Africa. m. George Langdon Faull, 31 Oct. 1942. 4 sons, 1 daughter. *Appointments:* Lecturer, International School of Cookery, 1950-58; Public Relations Office, Royal Dairy South Africa, 1958-64; Founded Silwood Kitchen Cordon Bleu Cookery School, 1969-. *Publications:* Author of 30 cooking books latest: Good Morning - A Book of Breakfasts, 1988; Numerous articles to professional journals and magazines. *Memberships:* President, Southern Hemisphere Cordon Bleu de France; International Wine & Food Society; Professional Culinary Circle; Professional Member, International Association of Cooking Schools; Certified member, de l'Ecole de Cuisine La Varenne. *Honours:* Commandeur Associe de la Commanderie des Cordons Bleus de France; Chevalier de la Confrerie des Chevaliers du Tastavin; Confrerie de la Chaine des Rotisseurs; Fellow, South African Chef's Association; Tas de Vin du Cap. *Hobbies:* Wine; Food; 6 grandchildren. *Address:* Silwood House, 40 Silwood Road, Randebosch, Cape 7700, South Africa.

FAUMAN Beverly Joyce (Freedman), b. 18 Jan. 1943, Detroit, Michigan, USA. Psychiatrist; Educator. m. Michael A. Fauman, 27 Aug. 1972, 1 son, 3 daughters. *Education:* BA, Mathematics, Florida State University, 1962; MD, Tufts University School of Medicine, 1968. *Appointments:* Director, Psychiatric Emergency Services, University of Chicago 1973-78, Henry Ford Hospital, Detroit 1978-81; Director, Psychiatric Education, Sinai Hospital, Detroit, 1981-. *Publications:* Book, Emergency Psychiatry for the House Officer, 1981; Over 30 contributions, scientific journals & books. *Memberships:* Councillor, Michigan Psychiatric Society; American Psychiatric Association; American Association of Directors of Psychiatry Residency Training; Association of Women Psychiatrists. *Honours:* Fellowship, APA, 1984; President's Service Awards, American College of Emergency Physicians 1979, 1980, Michigan Psychiatric Society 1983, 1984. *Hobbies:* Needlework; Cooking; Music. *Address:* 6767 West Outer Drive, Detroit, Michigan 48235, USA.

FAURIOL Sandra Ann Ellis, b. 19 June 1949, Tokyo, Japan. Nonprofit organization executive. m. Georges A Fauriol, 16 Apr. 1977. *Education:* BA, Ohio University, 1971; Certificate in Management Skills, Georgetown University. *Appointments:* Campaign Director, Vietnam Veterans Memorial Fund, 1980-83; Fund Raising Consultant, 1983-; Executive Director, Center for the Study of the Vietnam Generation, 1985-87; Founder and President, Center for The New Leadership, 1987-

. *Publications:* Enduring Legacies: Expressions from the Hearts and Minds of the Vietnam Generation, 1987; various articles and book reviews. *Memberships:* President, Greater Washington DC Area Chapter of National Society of Fund Raising Executives, 1988-90; Vice President Programs and Vice President Education, NSFRE, 1984-87; President, National Council of Career Women, 1980. *Honours:* Outstanding Fund Raising Executive of the Year, NSFRE, 1983; Nominated for the Presidential Medal of Freedom. *Hobbies:* Travelling; Dancing; Jogging; Bicycling. *Address:* 2641 Mann Court, Falls Church, VA 22046, USA.

FAUST Naomi F, b. Salisbury, North Carolina, USA. Educator; Poet; Author. m. Roy M Faust. *Education:* AB, Bennett College, Greenboro; MA, University of Michigan, Ann Arbor; PhD, New York University, New York City. *Appointments:* Elementary Teacher, Granard School, Gaffney, USA; English Teacher, Atkins High School, Winston Salem; Instructor of English, Bennett College; Instructor, English, Southern University, Scotlandville, Louisiana; Professor, English, Morgan State College, Baltimore; Teacher in Public School, Greensboro; Teacher, Public Schools, New York City; Professor, English Education, Queens College, City University of New York, Flushing. *Publications:* Speaking in Verse (A Book of Poems); All Beautiful Things, poetry; Discipline and the Classroom Teacher. *Memberships:* World Poetry Society Intercontinental; New York Poetry Forum; Womens National Book Association; National Council of Teachers of English; American Association of University Professors, United Negro College Fund; NAACP; Alpha Kappa Alpha Sorority. *Honours:* Teacher, Author of the Year; Certificate of Merit for Poem, Cooper Hill Writers Conference; Alpha Epsilon Honour Society; Alpha Kappa Mu Honour Society. *Hobbies:* Reading; Dancing. *Address:* 112-01 175th Street, Jamaica, NY 11433, USA.

FAWCETT Farrah, b. 2 Feb. 1947, Corpus Christi, Texas, USA. Actress. *Education:* University of Texas. *Career:* Signed by Screen Gems, Hollywood. Made films, TV shows and over 100 Television commercials. *Creative Works:* Films include: Love is a Funny Thing; Myra Breckenridge; Logan's Run; Somebody Killed Her Husband; Sunburn; Saturn III; Cannonball Run; Extremities. Television: Owen Marshall; Counselor at Law; The Six Million Dollar Man; Charlie's Angels (regular). Movies: The Feminist and the Fuzz; The Burning Bed; Between Two Women; Nazi Hunter; Poor Little Rich Girl; The Barbara Hutton Story. *Address:* c/ o 3130 Antelo Road, Los Angeles, CA 90077, USA.

FAYE Sefi, b. 22 Nov. 1943, Dakar, Senegal. Ethnologist; Film-maker. 1 daughter. *Education:* Teacher's Certificate, 1962; Sorbonne, University of Paris and Louis Lumiere Film School, France, 1970-74; Diplomas in Ethnology Sorbone, 1975, 1977; PhD, Ethnology, University of Paris VII, 1979. *Appointments:* Teacher, Dakar School System, 1963-69; Commenced film-making career in 1972, becoming 1st woman film-maker in black Africa; Specialises in Documentaries of varying length concerning culture and problems of Black Africa; Guest Lecturer, Free University of Berlin, 1979-80. *Creative Works:* The Passer-by, 1972; Revenge (collective production), 1973; Kaddu Beykat, 1975; Fad, Jal, 1979; Goob na nu, 1979; Man sa yay, 1980; Souls under the Sun, 1981; Selbe one among others, 1982; 3 Years 5 Months, 1983; Embassys of Traditional Cuisine, 1984; Black Roots, 1985; Elsie Haas, Woman Painter and Film-maker from Haiti, 1985. *Memberships:* Societe Civile des Auteur Multimedia; Societe des Gens de Lettres. *Honours:* Georges Sadoul Award, 1975; International Critic Award, Forum, Berlin, 1976; FIFEF Award, Geneva 1975, for Kaddu Bykat; Official selection of Fad Jai, Un Certain Regard, Festival of Cannes, 1979; Award, Festival de Carthage, Tunisia, 1980; Special Award for Selbe one among others, Festival of Leipzig, 1983; Commissioned to produce a film for United Nations, 1980. *Address:* 12 Rue Morere, 75014 Paris, France.

FAYEMI Phebean Olusola, b. 15 Oct. 1929, Abeokuta

Ogun State, Nigeria. Provost, Adeyemi College of Education. m. 17 July 1952. 3 sons, 2 daughters. *Education:* Teachers' Certificate, 1948; Senior Teachers' Domestic Science, 1951; Diploma Domestic Science, 1958; BSc Home Economics, 1965; MSc Home Economics, 1966; PhD, Teacher Education, 1983. *Appointments:* Teaching in Elementary Schools, 1948-55; Teacher Training College, 1959-69; Comprehensive High School, 1969-74; Lecturer, Adeyemi College, Obafemi Awolowo University, Ondo, 1974-; Provost, Adeyemi College, 1985-. *Publications:* Home Economics books for Primary, Secondary and Tertiary institutions in Nigeria; Home Economics curriculum developer in collaboration with Comparative Education Study and Adaptation Centre (CESAC) and Nigerian Educational Research Council (NERC). *Memberships:* Formerly Secretary, President, now Executive Member, Home Economics Teachers' Association of Nigeria; American Home Economics Association; National Association of Teachers of Home Economics, England; International Federation of Home Economics; Association of Home Economists; Home Economics Society Illinois State University, Illinois, 1966; Home Economics Society of Nigeria. *Honours:* Dean's List, Illinois State University, Illinois, 1966; Oak Leaf, Girl Guides Association of Nigeria for Long Useful Service, 1983; Iyalode Trinity Methodist Church, Abeokuta, 1982; Iyalode Methods Church, Ondo, 1985; Certified Home Economist, 1987. *Hobbies:* Writing; Guiding; Music; Gardening. *Address:* Obafemi Awolowo University, Adeyemi College of Education, PMB 520, Ondo, Ondo State, Nigeria.

FEATHERBY Natalie Hope Newton Petrov (Countess), b. 31 Jan. 1958, New Bern, North Carolina, USA. Writer; Public relations. m. the Count Terry Alan Petrov Featherby, 14 Nov. 1987. *Education:* BA, Writing & Editing, North Carolina State University, 1976-80; MA, Professional and Creative Writing, Antioch University, 1985-88. *Appointments:* Freelance Writer, 1978-88; Editor, William Collins Publishers, Australia, 1988-; Editor in chief of West Australian Business World newspaper, 1988-; Media Liaison & Cyclist, Across Down Under, Inc (Fundraiser Cross country trek of Australia), 1986-87. *Publications:* Publish under the name of Natalie Newton: Across the Never Never; Island Man; Across Down Under, documentary; Ultrarunning, documentary; Poetry in 12 USA Anthologies. Television appearances: The Today Show, USA; Good Morning America, USA; Good Morning Australia, twice; The Today Show, Australia. *Memberships:* Florida Freelance Writers Association, USA; National Association of Female Executives, USA; NCSU Alumni Association, North Carolina, USA; Jaycees, North Carolina, USA; Small Businessmen's Association, USA; Florida Board of Television & Film (Mayor's Advisory Committee), USA. *Honours:* State Award for Short Story, North Carolina Writers Association, 1976; Homecoming Queen, North Carolina State University West Campus, 1980; Investigative Reporting Commendation, North Carolina Dept of Hew, 1980; State award for Essay, Florida Freelance Writers Association, 1983; National (USA) Poetry Award, New York Poetry Society, 1984; Finalist, Florida Woman of the Year, 1985; Mascot for the America's Cup in Australia, 1987. *Hobbies:* Cycling, 2 world records for endurance cycling; Equitation, Expert Advice columnist syndicated to the equine magazines. *Address:* 14 Doongall a Road, Attadale, Western Australia 6156, Australia.

FEDDEERSEN Jutta Ella Lore Erika, b. 5 Aug. 1931, Briesen Kreis Belgart, East Germany. Lecturer; Artist. m. Lorenze Heinrich Feddersen, 29 Dec. 1959. 2 daughters. *Education:* Degree in Textiles and Restoration, Facchochschule, Bremen, Germany, 1955; Master Degree, Visual Arts, Sculpture, 1985-88. *Appointments:* Teacher, Sturt Workshops, Frensham, Mittagong, Australia, 1957-59; Occupational Therapy Department, Concord Repatriation Hospital, 1959-63; Part-time Lecturer, National Art School, East Sydney, 1962-67; Fibre Art Teacher, Aboriginal Women, St Theresa Mission near Alice Springs, 1972; Teacher, Silverwater Women's Prison, Sydney, 1973; Part-time Lecturer, Alexander Mackie College, Sydney, 1977-80; Part-time Lecturer 1980, Full-time Lecturer, 1981-,

Newcastle College of Advanced Education. *Creative works:* Numerous Solo and Group Exhibitions; Commissions and Collections. *Honours:* Australia Council Grant to travel Africa, 1974; Warringah Shire Art Prize, 1978; Diamond Valley Art Prize, 1981; Australia Council Grant, 1982; Visual Arts Board Studio Paretaio, Italy, 1982. Represented: National Gallery, Victoria; Art Gallery of Western Australia; McClelland Art Gallery, Victoria; Ballarat Gallery, Victoria; Gold Museum Ballarat, Victoria; Carnation Mild Head office, Chicago, USA; Brisbane Art Gallery; Private Collections in Australia, Germany, USA and Austria. *Hobbies:* Sailing; Walking; Theatre. *Address:* 78 Elanora Road, Elanora Heights, NSW 2101, Australia.

FEE Susan Kay, b. 14 Mar. 1956, Sidney, New York, USA. Art Consultant. m. 12 Oct. 1980, divorced 1989. *Education:* BS, Environmental Sci 1974-78, Landscape Architecture 1975-79, SUNY College of Environmental Science & Forestry, Syracuse, NY. *Appointments:* Landscape Architect, Marmon Mok & Green, Houston, Texas, 1980-83; Landscape Architect, John Blevens Association, Fremont, CA, 1984-85; Gallery Director, Victor Fischer Gallery, Oakland, CA, 1985-87; Western Manager, California Fine Art Directory, San Francisco, CA, 1987; Art Consultant, Editions Limited, San Francisco, 1988-; Western Manager, Kraus Sikes Publishers, San Francisco, 1989-. *Creative works:* Editor/Rep Book, The Guild, 1989; Landscape architect designed, San Antonio Airport, 1983; Art Consultant, large public sculpture, various artists, 1986-89. *Memberships:* Board of Directors, Public art Works, 1989-92; Secretary, American Society Landscape Architects, 1975-89; Seminar leader, American Society Landscape Architects, 1978; Seminar Leader, Landscape Architect & Specifier News Magazine Conference, 1987. *Honours:* Honored Service, American Society Landscape Architects, 1988; Hi Sales Award, California Fine Arts Directory, 1987. *Hobbies:* The Arts; Environment; Flying; Tailoring; Travel. *Address:* 279 Mangels Avenue, San Francisco, CA 94131, USA.

FEIL Naomi Weil, b. 22 July 1932, Munich, Germany. Executive Director. m. 29 Dec. 1963, 2 sons, 2 daughters. *Education:* BS, cum laude, 1954, MSW, 1956, Columbia University. *Appointments:* Director, Group Work, W. Hodson Centre, 1960-62; BS Coler Hospital Welfare Island, 1960-62; Director, Group Work, Montefiore Home for the Aged, 1963-80; CWR, School of Applied Social Sciences, 1963-80; Executive Director, Valid. Institute, 1988. *Publications:* Films: Where Life Still Means Living, 1963; The Inner World of Pahasia, 1967; Looking for Yesterday, 1978; Validation: The Feil Method, book, 1982; articles in journals and magazines. *Memberships:* Association for Humanistic Psychology; Association for Transpersonal Psychology; Gerontological Association. *Honours Include:* Christ Award, various international awards, Intenational Film Festivals for documentary films on aging, 1965, 1968, 1982. *Hobbies:* Biking; Reading; Exercise. *Address:* 21987 Byron Road, Cleveland, Oh 44122, USA.

FEIN Helen, b. 17 Sept. 1934, New York City, USA. Sociologist; Administrator. m. Richard J. Fein, 10 Sept. 1955, 2 daughters. *Education:* BA 1955, MA 1958, Brooklyn College; PhD, Columbia University, 1971. *Appointments:* Research Fellow, City College, New York, 1973-75; Lecturer, Queens College, 1977-78; Director, Indochinese Refugee Sponsorship Development Project, Dutchess Interfaith Council, 1979-80; Senior Research Associate, Centre for Policy Research, 1980-87; Guest Professor, Technical University, West Berlin, Germany, 1983-84; Research Director 1987, Executive Director 1987-, Institute for Study of Genocide; Visiting Scholar, Center for International Affairs, Harvard University, 1989-. *Publications:* Imperial Crime & Punishment: Jallianwala Bagh Massacre & British Judgement 1919-20, 1977; Accounting for Genocide: National Responses & Jewish Victimization During the Holocaust (award), 1979, 1984; The Persisting Question: Social Contexts & Sociological Perspectives of Modern Anti-Semitism, 1987; Congregational Sponsors of Indochinese Refugees in the US 1979-81: Helping Beyond Borders, 1987; Also essays, various books & journals. *Memberships:* American Sociological Association; Board, Cambodia Documentation Commission, Institute of International Conference on Holocaust & Genocide. *Honour:* Sorokin Award, American Sociological Association, 1979. *Address:* 33 Elting Avenue, New Paltz, New York 12561, USA.

FEIN Leah Gold, b. 10 Dec. 1910, Minsk, Russia. Clinical Psychologist. m. Alfred Gustave, 10 June 1944, 1 son. *Education:* BS, 1939; MA, 1942, PhD, 1944, Yale University. *Appointments Include:* Health Educator, 1930-43; Assistant Professor, Carleton College, 1944-45; Research Associate, 1946; Chief Psychologist, Seattle, 1947-48; Professor, University of Bridgeport, 1946-47, 1952-58. *Publications:* The 3 Dimensional Personality Tests, 1960; The Changing School of Scene: Challenge to Psychology, 1974; articles in professional journals. *Memberships Include:* American Academy of Psychotherapists; International Council of Psychologists; Fellow, Society Personality Assessment. *Honours:* Many Honours and Awards. *Address:* 1450 Washington Blvd., N706, Stamford, CT 06902, USA.

FEIN Leona M, b. 6 Apr. 1930, New York, USA. Artist; Craftsman; Lecturer. m. Harris A Fein, 25 May 1952, 2 sons, 1 daughter. *Education:* BA, Studio Arts, Queens College, 1980. *Appointments:* Sculptor & Decoupeur, Owner, Leona M Fein Artist, Douglaston, 1974-; Lecturer, New York State Council of Arts, New York, 1978. *Creative Works:* Sculpture; Ceramic & Mixed Media: a) Pavlova; b) In Tribute to Fred; c) Amelia; d) Between the Cracks; e) Beverly; f) Roseland Ginger Also Known as Jenny; g) Rocky; h) Pooped; i) Boris; j) Poppa; k) Street Lady; l) Uncle Joe; etc. *Memberships:* National Association of Women Artists; Contemporary Sculptors Guild; National Guild of Decoupeurs; International Sculptors Association; American Craft Council. *Honours:* One Woman Sculpture Shows, Queens College Art Gallery, 1980; Gallery Shows, various locations. *Hobbies:* Travel; Archaeology. *Address:* 245-03 62nd Ave., Douglaston, NY 11362, USA.

FELD Karen Irma, b. 23 Aug. 1947, Washington, DC, USA. Syndicated Columnist. *Education:* BA, American University, 1969. *Appointments:* Columnist, Contributing Editor, Capitol Hill Magazine, 1980-; Broadcaster, Voice of America, 1984; Writer, Broadcaster, United States Informaion Agency, 1986-87; Celebrity Columnist, Washington Times, 1986-87; Syndicated Columnist, Universal Press Syndicate, 1988-. *Publications:* Contributor to numerous magazines & newspapers including: People; Time; Money; ParAde; Family Circle, Vogue; American Politics; New York Times syndicate; Los Angeles Times syndicate; Washingtonian; Detroit News; Dallas Morning News; Contributor of Chapter to Readings in Brain Injury, 1984. *Memberships:* Capital Press Women, Vice President; Sigma Delta Chi; American Association of Journalists and Authors; Women in Communications; National Press Club; Senate Pres Gallery; National Federation of Press Women. *Honours:* 1st Place, Magazine Interview & Personal Column, 1985, 1st Place, Radio Interview, Public Relations Brochure, 1987, National Federation of Press Women; 1st Place, Personal Column, Radio Interview, Public Relations Brochure, 1987, 1st Place, Personal Column, Radio Interview, Newspaper Feature, 1988, Capital Press Women. *Hobbies:* Politics. *Address:* 1698 32nd St. NW, Washington, DC 20007, USA.

FELDBAUM Eleanor G., b. 14 Aug. 1935, Philadelphia, Pennsylvania. Researcher; Professor. m. Ronald Feldbaum, 30 Sept. 1956, 4 daughters. *Education:* RN, Albert Einstein Medical Center, 1956; BA, 1969, MA, 1970, American University; PhD, University of Maryland, 1973. *Appointments:* University of Maryland, 1973-80, 1985-86; Consultant, 1980-85, 1986-89; Professor, Troy State University, Alabama, 1989-. *Publications:* 2 texts on state and local politics; 8 research publications; 14 articles on health manpower and political behaviour. *Memberships:* American Political Science Association; American Society of Public

Administrators; American Public Health Association. *Honours:* University Scholarships and Fellowships; Research Grants, US Department of Health and Human Services and Department of Defense; Elected to Pi Sigma Alpha and Phi Kappa Phi. *Hobbies:* Walking; Hiking; Cycling; Aerobic dance. *Address:* 9102 Jones Mill Road, Chevy Chase, MD 20815, USA.

FELDMAN Gwen Diane, b. 27 Apr. 1959, Manhasset, USA. Paleobotanist. *Education:* BSc., Honours, Marlboro College, 1981; Internship, New York Botanical Garden; Presently in Doctoral program, University of Conn, (degree to be awarded in 1989). *Appointments:* Herbarium Assistant, Muttontown Nature Preserve, New York, 1979; Research Assistant, Botany, New York Botanical Gardens, 1980-82; Research Technician, Paleobotany, 1984-85, Research Assistant, 1985-86, Research Associate, 1986-, Paleobotany, University of Connecticut. *Publications:* Articles in various journals including: American Journal of Botany. *Memberships:* American Association of University Professors; Botanical Society of America; International Organization of Paleobotany; American Society of Plant Taxonomists. *Hobbies:* Botanical Illustration; Photography; Stamp-Collecting; Backpacking; Canoeing. *Address:* Dept. of Ecology & Evolutionary Biology U-43, University of Connecticut, 75 N. Eagleville Road, Storrs, CT 06268, USA.

FELDMAN Lenore Helen Spiewak, b. 5 Sept. 1935, Brooklyn, NY, USA. Volunteer. m. George Feldman, 6 Apr. 1957, 3 sons, 1 daughter. *Education:* BS, Cornell University, 1956; MBA, Adelphi University, 1978. *Career:* Textile Advertising, Eastman Chemical Products, 1956-57; Lecturer, Consultant, Creative Resources Associates, 1978-84. *Memberships:* National Council of Jewish Women, President, 1987-90. *Honours:* Delta Mu Delta, 1978; Hannah G. Solomon Award, 1969. *Hobbies:* Tennis; Music. *Address:* 411 Mistletoe Way, Lawrence, NY 11516, USA.

FELDMAN Ruth Duskin, b. 13 June 1934, Chicago, USA. Writer; Editor; Photographer; Lecturer. m. Gilbert Feldman, 14 June 1953, 1 son, 2 daughters. *Education:* BS, Northwestern University, 1954. *Appointments:* Quiz Kid, Radio & TV, 1941-50; Quizmistress, Chicago Sun Times Quizdown, 1947-50; Teacher: Nichols School, 1954-55, Fort Sheridan, 1964; Correspondent, Staff Writer, Lerner Newspapers, 1973-81; Creative Editor, Humanistic Judaism, 1983-. *Publications:* Chemi the Magician, 1947; Whatever Happened to the Quiz Kids, 1982; Human Development, 4th edition, co-author, 1989; contributor to many journals and magazines. *Memberships:* Phi Beta Kappa; American Socity of Journalists & Authors; Society of Professional Journalists; Authors Guild. *Honours:* Mortar Board, 1951; James Alton James Scholar, 1953-54; Benjamin Fine Award, 1983. *Hobbies:* Tennis; Music; Theatre. *Address:* 935 Fairview Road, Highland Park, IL 60035, USA.

FELL Diana Dickson, b. 13 Dec. 1946, Glensfalls, New York, USA. Manager; Administrative Services. m. Kennedy Fell, 8 May 1965, 1 son, 1 daughter. *Education:* University of Delaware, 1970-72; Oakland University, 1972-73; Pontiac Business Institute, 1973; Thomas A. Edison State College, 1986-. *Appointments:* Membership & Communicatirons Co-ordinator, 1973-75; Staff Assistant, 1975-78; Office Administrator, 1978-84; President, Plato enterprises, 1984-86; Instructor Computers 1984-. *Publications:* Articles in professional journals. *Membership:* National Association of Female Executives. *Honour:* Honour Student. *Hobbies:* Writing; Studying; Research. *Address:* 3330 Warrensville Ctr., No 305, Shaker Heights, OH 44122, USA.

FELTON Marianne Victorius, b. 20 Aug. 1929, Berlin, Germany. Professor of Economics. m. Donald Charles Felton, 14 May 1958, 1 son and 1 daughter. *Education:* BA, French, Guilford College, 1950; BA, Music, 1968, MA Economics, 1971, PhD, Economics, 1979, Indiana University. *Appointments:* US State Department, Seoul, Korea, 1956-57; Indiana University, Southeast, 1976-. *Publications:* The Economics of the Creative Arts: The Case of the Composer, 1978; Policy Implications of a Composer Labor Supply Function, 1980; Is Baumol's Disease Alive and III in Louisville, Kentucky? 1987. *Memberships:* American & Midwest Economic Associations; Association for Cultural Economics. *Hobbies:* Singing Member of Louisville Bach Society. *Address:* Division of Business & Economics, Indiana University Southeast, New Albany, IN 47150, USA.

FENBY Barbara Lou, b.29 Apr. 1938, New York City, USA. Social Worker. m. George Fenby, 25 June 1960, divorced 1985, 1 son, 1 daughter. *Education:* AB, University of Rochester, 1960; MSW, UCLA, 1962. *Appointments:* Chief, Clinical Unit, 1976-80; Childrens Mental Health Co-ordinator, 1980-86; Associate Area Director, Concord, 1986-88; Director, Mental Health, 1988-. *Publications:* Articles in professional journals. *Memberships:* NASW; ACSW; AGPA; Association of Women in Social Work; National Register of Clinical Social Workers. *Honours:* Recipient, various honours and awards. *Hobbies:* Hiking; Travel. *Address:* 1 Cullinane Dr., Marlborough, MA 01752, USA.

FENN Margaret, b. 23 Mar. 1921, Ironwood, Michigan, USA. Professor Emeritus. m. 3 Aug. 1948. 2 sons. *Education:* BS, LaCrosse State University, Wisconsin, 1942; MBA 1950, PhD 1963, University of Washington. *Appointments:* Teaching contributions to: Institute of Financial Management; Pacific Coast Banking School; Women in Management Seminars; National Training Lab (2 years-intern in OD); University of Washington, School of Dentistry, School of Social Work, School of Nursing, School of Librarianship; Visiting Professor at: University of California, Tulane University, Victoria University, New Zealand, Graduate School of Library & Information Science, University of Washington. Consultant to: Industrial Health Tecna; Financial Pacific national Retailing; national Association of Bank Women; Government Post Office, FTC, GSA, FEW, ERDA, Personnel, HEPB, Law and Justice; Service Organizations; American Nursing Foundations. *Publications:* Books: Making It in Management: A Behavioral Approach for Women, 1978; In the Spotlight: Women Managers in a Changing Environment, 1980; Vrouwen in Management, 1981; Contributions to professional journals and a forthcoming Encyclopedia of Women. *Memberships:* Leadership for Tomorrow, 1982-85; Seattle Chamber of Commerce, 1980-81; Alumni Association, University of Washington, 1979-82; Retirement Association, University of Washington, 1979-82; Women and Business, Inc, 1978-81; Private Issues in Public Education, Sr Advisory Board, 1986-89; Unviersity Prepatory Academy, 1987-. *Honours:* Beta Gamma Sigma; Matrix Table, Woman Achievment Honoree, 1979; Women Business and Professional Network Honoree, 1980; AACSB Award for Women Training Innovations, 1981; Small Business Advocate of the Year Award, State of Washington, 1982; President Western Academy of Management, 1982; Fulbright Lecturer, New Zealand, 1983; Distinguished Alumnus, University of Wisconsin, LaCrosse, 1986. *Hobbies:* Hiking; Cross-country skiing; Swimming; Cooking; Embroidery; Golf. *Address:* Graduate School of Business Administration, University of Washington (DJ-10), Seattle, WA 98195, USA.

FERGUS Patricia Marguerita, b. 26 Oct. 1918, USA. Writer; Composer. *Education:* BS, 1939; MA 1941; PhD, 1960. *Appointments:* Administrative Positions, US Government, 1943-59; Faculty, University of Minnesota, 1964-79; Associate Dean, Professor, Writing, Mount St Mary's College, Maryland, 1979-81; Editorial Assistant to President, Metro, State University, 1984-85. *Publications:* Spelling Improvement, 4th edition, 1983; contributor of articles to: English Journal; ABI Digest; Downtown Catholic; Voice; Mountaineer Briefing; Poetry in: English Journal; Minneapolis Muse; Moccasin; Heartsong and Northstar Gold; The Poetry Letter. *Memberships Include:* IBC; AAUW; ABIRA; World Literary Academy; Minneapolis Poetry Society,

President; National League of American Pen Women, 1st vice-president, Minnesota Branch; Pi Lambda Theta; Midwest Federation of Chaparral Poets; League of Minnesota Poets. *Honours:* Outstanding Contributions Award, Twin Cities Student Assembly, University of Minnesota, 1975; Morse-Amoco Foundation Award, 1976; Mount St Mary's College Hearst Grant, 1980; Bronze Medalist, IBC, 1986; Poetry Prizes, 1984-89. *Hobbies:* Reading; Speaking; Travel; Choral Singing; Singing. *Address:* 111 Marguette Avenue, 712, Minneapolis, MN 55401, USA.

FERGUSON Anne, b. 9 Jan. 1951, Glasgow, Scotland. Hairdressing; Public Relations. m. Taylor Ferguson, 22 Mar. 1971. 1 son. Worked with own Company Taylor Ferguson, 1966-. *Creative works:* Avante Garde Hairstyling demonstrated and viewed throughout the World. *Honours:* National Hairdressing Federation, 1986; Numerous British Hairdressing Awards, 1987, awards were from Hairdressing Teachers. *Address:* 106 Bath Street, Glasgow, G2 2EN, Scotland.

FERGUSON Dee A Lucas, b. 13 July 1947, Columbus, Ohio, USA. Academic Director.m. David E. Ferguson, 11 Apr. 1968, deceased 1969, 1 son. *Education:* BA, Ohio State University, 1966; MBA, University of Exeter, England, 1975. *Appointments:* Managing Director, Law of London International, 1973-80; Administrator, Gucci Watches, Los Angeles, 1980-82; Director, Facilities, Marlborough School, Los Angeles, 1983-. *Publications:* Chemical Patent (Cosmetic); 2 Mechanical Patents: Roll 'r Shoe and Load Stabilizer. *Memberships:* American Institute of Plant Engineers; Association of Physical Plant Administrators of Universities & Colleges; American Institute of Plant Engineers, Treasure, 1988; American Management Association. *Hobbies:* Skiing; Reading; Music; Bicycling; Jogging. *Address:* 1147 North Wilcox Place, Los Angeles, CA 90038, USA.

FERGUSON Sybil, b. 7 Feb. 1934, Barnwell, Alberta, Canada. Franchise Business Executive; Founder, Diet Center Inc. m. Roger N Ferguson, 10 July 1952. 2 sons, 3 daughters. *Creative works:* The Diet Center Program: Lose Weight and Keep It Off Forever, 1983; The Diet Center Cookbook, 1986. *Memberships:* National Advisory Council, School of Management, Brigham Young University; Dept of Business, Advisory Board, Ricks College; Board of Directors, Boise State University, Community Health Sciences Division; Founding Member, Committee of 200; Rexburg Civic Club; Soroptomist Club; Chamber of Commerce; International Franchise Association; American Entrepreneur Association; Founding Sponsor, Children's Miracle Network Telethon; Board of Advisors, Working Mother's Network. *Honours:* Business Leader of the Year, 1980; Woman of the Year, Soroptomists, 1987; Great Figure of Franchising; Savvy magazine, Top 60 Women Entrepreneurs. *Hobbies:* Golf; Painting; Gardening. *Address:* 220 South Second West, Rexburg, ID 83440, USA.

FERNANDEZ Aurora Fernandez, b. 3 May 1920, Mexico D.F., Mexico. Sociologist; Politician. *Education:* BA, Political Science, 1960; BA, Social Sciences, 1965; BA, Latin American Studies, 1975. *Appointments:* Adviser, PRI (Institutional Revolutionary Party), 1950; Head, Women's Affairs, Department of DF, 1952; Acting Federal Deputy, 1967; Federal Deputy, 1970. *Publications:* Book: Adelante Campesinal; Mujeres que Honran a la Patria; Escritores America; Mini Semblanzas. *Memberships:* Federation of Mexican University Women; Council of Mexican Women; National Association of Sociologists; Mexican Ateneo of Women; Association of Mexican Women Civil Servants; Institutional Revolutionary Party. *Honours:* Medal, Academia de Estudies Militares; Pergamine de la Confederacion Nacional Campesina; Diploma, Derecho de Anahuac; Honorary President, Academia Interamericana de Letras Argentinas; Diploma of Honour, Association of Writers of America; Sor Juana Ines de la Cruz Medal, Ateneo Mexicano de Mujeres;

Medal as Exemplary Citizen of Mexico, Institutional Revolutionary Party. *Hobbies:* Reading; Listening to music; Working. *Address:* Peten Norte Street, 24 Dpto 3, Colonia Narrarte, Delegacion Benito Suarez, CP 03020, Mexico DF, Mexico.

FERNANDEZ Isabel Lidia, b. 23 Jan. 1964, Miami, USA. Programme Director. *Education:* BBA, 1984; MSc., Candidate. *Appointments:* Director, Personnel, Sheraton River House Hotel, 1987-88; Programme Director, Hospitality Management, Dade Community College, 1988-. *Publications:* Freelance Writer, Panther Gazette, City & Country Club Life; Editor: The Sunblazer, 1983-84; The New International, 1983. *Memberships:* Greater Miami Chapter, Educational Institute of American Hotel & Motel Association, President; AmericanSociety of Training & Development, Associate; Greater Miami Hotel & Motel Association. *Honours:* Employee of the Month, Coconut Grove Hotel, 1985; Finalist, Up and Comer's Award, Tourism, 1988. *Hobbies:* Singing; Writing; Sunday School Teacher. *Address:* 201 NW 60 Avenue, Miam, FL 33126, USA.

FERRARINI Elizabeth Mary, b. 8 Sept. 1948, Cambridge, USA. Journalist. *Education:* BSc., Journalism, Suffolk University, 1982; MSc., 1988. *Appointments:* Information Gatekeepers, 1980-84; Consulting Editor, Leading Edge, 1986-87; Proprietor, Infomania, 1987-. *Publications:* Confessions of an Infomaniac; Infomania: The Guide to Essential Online Services; numerous articles. *Membership:* International Association of Business Communicators. *Honours:* Recipient, various awards. *Hobbies:* Drama; Personal Computers; Antiques; Racquetball; Bowling. *Address:* 204 Mystic Street, Arlingotn, MA 02174, USA.

FERRARO Geraldine A., b. 26 Aug. 1935, Newburgh, New York, USA. Attorney; Author; Lecturer. m. John A. Zaccaro, 16 July 1960, 1 son, 2 daughters. *Education:* BA, Marymount Manhattan College, 1956; JD, Fordham University School of Law, 1960; Postgraduate, New York University Law School, 1978. *Appointments:* Private practice, New York City, 1961-74; 1974-78; Staff 1974-78, Chief, Special Victims' Bureau 1977-78, Queen's District Attorney's Office, NY; Member, US Congress, NY 9th District, 1979-84; Author, lecturer, 1985-; Fellow, JFK Institute of Politics, Harvard University, 1988. *Publication:* Ferraro My Story, 1985. *Memberships:* President, International Institute of Women Political Leaders; National Democratic Institute for International Affairs; Trustee, Marymount Manhattan College. *Honours:* Honorary degrees: Marymount Manhattan Collge 1982, New York Law School 1984, Hunter College 1985, College of Boca Raton 1988; Various Awards, Federal, State, City, Civic, Private Organisations. *Hobbies:* Swimming; Tennis; Golf. *Address:* 218 Lafayette Street, New York, NY 10012, USA.

FERRARS Elizabeth, b. 6 Sept. 1907, Rangoon, Burma. Writer. m. 5 Nov. 1945. *Education:* Diploma, Journalism, London University, 1927. *Appointments:* Writer, Detective Stories, 1940-. *Publications:* Author of 62 books the first Give a Corpse a Bad Name, 1940, the latest, A Murder Too Many, 1988. *Memberships:* Crime Writers Association Chairman, 1978; Detection Club. *Honours:* Silver Dagger, Crime Writers Association, 1980. *Address:* 5 Treble House Terrace, London Road, Blewbury, Didcot, Oxon, OX11 9NZ, England.

FERRERO DE ESTABLE PUIG Rosita Mercedes, b. 8 May 1930, Montevideo, Uruguay. Professor of Pathology. m. Dr Juan F Estable Puig, 17 July 1952, 4 sons, 4 daughters. *Education:* BA, 1949; PhD, 1964; Lic Es Biological Sciences, 1969; MD, 1978. *Appointment:* Associate Instructor, Physiology and Pathology, Montevideo, 1952-60; Associate Experimental pathology, Ames Research Centre, NASA, USA, 1962-65; MRC, Canada Associate, 1967, 1978; Professor, pathology, Laval Medical School, Canada, 1968-. *Publications:* Over 140 articles in professional journals. *Memberships:* Corporation Professionnelle des Medecins due Quebec; International Academy of athology; Microscopical Society of Canada; Electron Microscopy Society of America; Society for Neurosciences; etc. *Honours:* OAS Fellowship, 1961; American Cancer Society Fellow, 1965; Council Member, SMC, 1976-87; many other honours and awards. *Address:* Dept. de Pathologie, Faculte de Medecine, Universite Laval, Quebec G1K 7P4, Canada.

FERRI Fleur, b. 26 May 1929, Pretoria, South Africa. Artist. m. Count Ludovico Ferri, 1956, 1 son. *Education:* Natal Technical College; Johannesburg Technical College. *Appointments Include:* Own Business, 1950. *Creative Works:* Designed & executed stands for leading South African Industries, at Industrial Exhibitions in major centres; 18 One Man Art Exhibitions; 25 Group Exhibitions; Radio & TV interviews; Portrait Painter of Ministerial, Academic and Business Leaders; and of last five Presidents in Office; commissioned by Government to paint the full Cabinet of twenty-nine Ministers of the Houses of Parliament to commemorate the last sitting of the Cabinet of the Westminster System; Prose Poetry, Borne on the Breeze, 1983. *Address:* 24 Valley Road, Bordeaux, Randburg 2194, Republic of South Africa.

FERRY Joan Evans b. 20 Aug. 1941, Summit, New Jersey, USA. College Instructor; Elementary School Counsellor. *Education:* BS, University of Pennsylvania, 1964; Ed.M., Temple University, 1967; MSc., Villanova University, 1981. *Appointments Include:* Teacher, Elementary Schools, Pennridge, 1964-74, 1975-77; Riding, Sailing, Tennis, Swimming Instructor, self-employed, 1965-74; Ski Patroller, 1966-74; Ski Instructor, 1967-74; Elementary School Counsellor, Pennridge Schools, 1981; Private Counsellor, 1981-; Instructor, American Institute of Banking 1982-; Adjunct Faculty, Bucks County Community College, 1983-; Municipal Auditor, Hilltown Township, 1984-; Notary Public, 1986-. *Publications:* Co-author, Life-Time Sports for the College Student, 1971; Contributor to College Textbook, 1976. *Memberships Include:* Kappa Delta Pi; AIB; PEA PSEA; NEA; IFUW; AAUW; PSCA; National Association of Female Executives; PAN; ASN; BCATO; PEWA; NSPS; USPTR; PMSTA; Research Board of Advisor, American Biographical Institute, 1989-; Board of Governors, American Biographical Research Association, 1989-. *Honours:* Recipient, many honours and awards including: Athletics Awards for Basketball, Bowling, Field Hockey, Riding, Sailing, Softball, Surfing, Tennis and Track; Judith Netzky Memorial Fellowship award; Philanthropic Education Organization Grantee; American Management Associations Scholarship; American Red Cross 5 Year Service Pin; National Science Foundation Research Grant; Hall of Fame; World Decoration of Excellence Medallion; Statesman's Award; International Cultural Diploma of Honor; Numerous listings in biographical reference books. *Hobbies Include:* Archery; Coin & Stamp Collecting; Private Pilot; Music; Parasailing; Photography; Sailing; Scuba Diving. *Address:* 834 Rickert Road, Perkasie, PA 18944, USA.

FERSHTMAN Julie Ilene, b. 3 Apr. 1961, Detroit, Michigan, USA. Lawyer. *Education:* BA, 1983, JD, 1986, Emory University. *Appointments:* National Labor Relations Board, Law School Intern, 1985; Alumni Officer, Emory University, 1983-; Summer Associate, Kitch, Saurbier, Drutchas, Wagner & Kenney, Detroit, 1985; Associate, Miller, Canfield Paddock and Stone, Detroit, 1986-88; Associate, Miro, Miro and Weiner, P.C., Bloomfield Hills, Michigan, 1988-. *Memberships:* American Bar Association; American Trial Lawyers Association; Common Cause; National Organization for Women; Women Lawyers Association; National Museum of Women and the Arts; Michigan Women's Historical Centre & Hall of Fame; Phi Alpha Delta Law Fraternity. *Honours:* Omicron Delta Kappa; Phi Sigma Tau; Pi Sigma Alpha; Society for Collegiate Journalists; Jr. Phi Beta Kappa. *Hobbies:* Art Collecting; Theatre; Horse Riding; Reading. *Address:* 31700 Briarcliff, Franklin, MI 48025, USA.

FIELD Shirley Anne, b. London, England. Actress. *Appointments:* Entered films after repertory experience, 1955. Under contract to Ealing-MGM, 1958. *Creative Works:* Theatre: The Lily White Boys; Kennedy's Children; Fire; Wait Until Dark; The Life and Death of Marilyn Monroe; How the Other Half Loves. Films include: Saturday Night and Sunday Morning; The Man in the Moon; War Lover; Lunch Hour; Kings of the Sun; Doctor in Clover; Alfie; Hell is Empty; The Entertainer; The Damned; My Beautiful Laundrette. Television: Risking It; Buccaneer. *Address:* c/o Julian Belfrage Associates. 40 St James Street, London SW1, England.

FIELDER Mildred, b. 14 Jan. 1913, Quinn, South Dakota, USA. Freelance Author. m. Ronald Fielder, 17 Sept. 1932, 2 sons. *Education:* Huron College, 1929-31; University of Colorado, 1946. *Appointments:* Society Editor, Rapid City Daily Journal, 1930-31; Freelance Author, 1942-. *Publications:* Wandering Foot in the West, 1955; Railroads of the Black Hills, 1960, 7th Edition 1985; The Edzards Family and Related Lines, 1965; Wild Bill and Deadwood, 1965, 2nd edition 1969; The Treasure of Homestake Gold, 1970, 3rd edition 1984; A Guide to Black Hills Ghost Mines, 1972, 3rd edition 1983; The Chinese in the Black Hills, 1972; Potato Creek Johnny, 1973; Hiking Trails in the Black Hills, 1973, 3rd edition 1981; Wild Bill Hickock, Gun Man, 1974; Theodore Roosevelt in Dakota Territory, 1974; Deadwood Dick and the Dime Novels, 1974; Sioux Indian Leaders, 1975; 1982 Plant Medicine and Folklore, 1975; 1977 Poker Alice, 1978; Silver is the Fortune, 1978; Preacher Smith of Deadwood, 1981; Fielder's Herbal Helper for Hunters, Trappers and Fishermen, 1982; The Legend of Lame Johnny Creek, 1982; Wild Fruits, An Illustrated Field Guide & Cookbook, 1983; Captain Jack Crawford, Poet & Military Scout, 1983; Invitation to Fans, 1988; articles in numerous journals and magazines; poetry in many anthologies. *Memberships:* Many professional organizations. *Honours Include:* 424 Awards; Special Awards for Distinguished Achievement, South Dakota Historical Society, 1975, National League of American Pen Women, 1980. *Hobbies:* Travel; Music; Golf; Photography; Friendships. *Address:* 264 San Jacinto Dr., Los Osos, CA 93402, USA.

FIELDING Joy, b. 18 Mar. 1945, Toronto, Canada. Author. m. Warren Fielding, 11 Jan. 1974, 2 daughters. *Education:* BA, University of Toronto. *Appointments:* Book reviewer: Canadian Broadcasting Corporation, Radio approx 7 years, CBC TV Journal 1986-87; Book reviewer, contributor, Globe & Mail newspaper. *Publications:* The Best of Friends, 1972; The Transformation, 1976; Trance, 1978; Kiss Mommy Goodbye, 1980; The Other Woman, 1982; Life Penalty, 1984; The Deep End, 1986; Good Intentions, 1989. *Memberships:* Association of Canadian Television & Radio Artists; Authors Guild of America. *Honour:* Book of Year, Canadian Periodicals, 1981. *Hobbies:* Bridge; Reading; Tennis; Crossword puzzles; Piano; Swimming; Travel. *Address:* 15 Clarendon Avenue, Toronto, Ontario, Canada M4V 1H8.

FIELDS Bessie Marie Williams, b. 14 Sep. 1940, USA. Associate Professor. m. 16 Aug. 1958, divorced 1973, 1 son, 1 daughter. *Education:* BS, 1971, MS, 1981, Portland State University; EdD, Nova University, 1989. *Appointments:* Portland State University, 1971-83; Associate Professor, University of Alaska, Anchorage, 1983-. *Publications:* An evaluation of University of Alaska, Anchorage, orientation and advising programmes' impact on student retention. *Memberships:* National Association for the Advancement of Colored People; Alpha Kappa Alpha; Black Caucus; United Nations Association; Urban League; International Toastmasters. *Honours:* Virginia Salir Award; American Management Association Award; Managing Interpersonnel Conflicts Award; Emerging Women in Management Award; Award for Appreciation and Recognition of Dedication to Education, Anchorage School District. *Hobbies:* Reading; Tennis; Racketball; Jogging; Theatre; Music;

Cycling. *Address:* University of Alaska at Anchorage, 3211 Providence Drive, Anchorage, AK 99508, USA.

FIELDS Karla Jo, b. 27 Jan. 1959, Fayette, Alabama, USA. Senior Accountant & Auditor. *Education:* AS, Faulkner State Junior College, 1979; BS, Troy State University, 1981. *Appointments:* Staff accountant, Troy State University, 1980-82; Comptroller, Baldwin County Commission, 1982-86; Senior accountant & auditor, Wood Robertson & Associates, CPA's, 1986-. Also: Elected member, Robertsdale City Council, 1988-. *Memberships include:* Chair, Vocational Advisory Council; National Association of Female Executives; Laubach Literacy International; South Baldwin Literacy Council; Baldwin Library Library Board of Directors; Various other community associations; Alumni & honour societies. *Honours:* Senator James B. Allen Leadership Award, 1979; President's Award, academic excellence, 1979; George C. Wallace Scholarship, 1979-81. *Hobbies include:* Laubach reading tutor; Avid animal lover; Music; Sport. *Address:* 23175 Pecan Street, Robertsdale, Alabama 36567, USA.

FIFE Emma Hafen, b. 28 May 1940, Ivins, Washington County, Utah, USA. Teacher/Education. m. William S Fife, 30 Dec. 1964. 1 son, 4 daughters. *Education:* AA, Dixie Jr College, St George, Utah, 1960; BS Elem 1964, Special Education 1966, Brigham Young University, Provo, Utah; Resource Certificate, State of Utah, 1985. *Appointments:* Teacher, Grade 2, Clark County school District, Las Vegas, 1964; Teacher, Intellectually Handicapped, Jordan School District, Draper, 1965-67; Reading Aide 1982-85, Homebound Teacher 1982-87, Washington County School District; Resource Teacher, Santa Clara Elementary, Santa Clara, Utah; Washington County School District, St George, Utah, 1985-. *Publications:* The Postmistress of Ivins, Beehive Postmaster, 1975; Ode to the Town of Ivins, 1980; Ada Blake and Charles Hafen Family History; Weston and Fern Hafen Family Picture History; Emma Fife Family poetry and pictures, all private publications. *Memberships:* Council of Learning Disabilities; International Reading Association; Council of Exceptional Children; Utah Education Association; National Education Association; Heritage Writers Guild (League of Utah Writers); Daughters of Utah Pioneers; Ivins Camp Historia; Historian for Town of Ivins; LDS Relief Society Woman's Organization. *Honours:* LDS Golden Gleaner Award, 1961; High Honor Award, Dixie High School, 1958. *Hobbies:* Family; Writing poetry; Reading; Photography; Puppets; Nursery rhymes; Fund raiser for several charities. *Address:* Box 356 (200 East 235 South), Ivins, Utah 84738, USA.

FIFKOVA Eva, b. 21 May 1932, Czechoslovakia. Professor of Psychology. *Education:* MD, School of Medicine, Prague, 1957; PhD, Czechoslovak Academy of Science, 1963. *Appointments:* Lecturer, anatomy, Prague School of Medicine, 1954-60; Staff member, physiology, Czechoslovak Academy of Science, 1960-68; Research associate, biology, California Tech, USA, 1968-74; Professor, psychology, University of Colorado, 1974-. *Creative work:* Research, numerous publications, neurobiology on fine structure & plastic changes in nervous system. *Memberships:* American Association for Advancement of Science; American Physiological Society; Society for Neuroscience; American Association of Anatomists; Electron Microscopy Society of America; International Brain Research Organisation. *Honours:* Faculty fellowships, University of Colorado, 1979-80, 1984-85; Member, Cajal Club, 1980-; Delegate, Southeast Asia, American Association of Anatomists, 1985. *Address:* Department of Psychology, University of Colorado, Campus Box 345, Boulder, Colorado 80309, USA.

FIKE Theora Belle Hardy, b. 7 Nov. 1926, Haxton, USA. Retired Teacher. m. Harold Landis Fike, 22 Aug. 1948, 3 sons, 6 daughters. *Education:* BS, Chemistry, 1948; MS, Education, 1969. *Appointments:* Teacher, Durham, Kansas, 1951-52; Assistant Clinical Lab Assistant, 1952- 54; Teacher, Science, Richwood High School, 1969-82; Homebound Teacher, 1984- 87.

Memberships: Girl Scouts; Life Member, NSTA; LSTA; NEA. *Honours:* Recipient, various honours and awards. *Hobbies Include:* Teaching Sunday School; Piano. *Address:* 116 Hilbert, West Monroe, LA 71291, USA.

FILER Elizabeth A., b. 16 Oct. 1923, New York City, New York, USA. Psychotherapist. *Education:* Diploma, Early Childhood Education, Ann-Reno Institute, 1943; BS, 1944, MA, 1945, Teachers College, Columbia University; MS, Columbia University School of Social Work, 1954; Board Certified in Clinical Social Work (BCCSW). *Appointments:* Head Teacher, Assistant Director, Mallay Nursery School, 1943-52; Guidance Staff, New York School for Nursery Years, Columbia School of Social Work, 1954-60; Field Foundation Research Project, 1956-58. *Creative works:* Study of educational and therapeutic techniques with prelatency children in a nursery school setting. *Memberships:* National Association of Social Workers; New York State Society of Clinical Social Work Psychotherapists; National Institute for Clinical Social Work Advancement; World Federation for Mental Health. *Honours:* Columbia University Bicentennial Medal for role in establishing New York School for Nursery Years, 1954; Anonymous Foundation Grant for study with prelatency children. *Hobbies:* Travel; Art; Music; Sports; Swimming; Reading; Voluntary psychological rehabilitation work homebound persons in English-speaking families in Switzerland, summers 1981-86, 1988. *Address:* 240 East 79th Street, New York, NY 10021, USA.

FILIPPONE Ella Finger, b. 2 Feb. 1935, Kearny, New Jersey, USA. Administrator; Environmentalist. m. 3 Mar. 1962. 4 sons. *Education:* Katharine Gibbs School, 1954; BA University of Beverly Hills, 1980; PhD, University of Beverly Hills, 1982. *Appointments:* Vice President 1959-60, Board of Directors, 1960-64, Partner, 1961-64, Executive Vice President, Stricker Research Associates, Inc, New York; Executive Administrator, 1976-, Board of Trustees, 1971-, Chairman, 1971-76, Passaic River Coalition, New Jersey. *Publication:* Editor, Goals & Strategies, quarterly newsletter of the Passaic River Coalition, 1971-; Columnist, Along the Passaic, 1989-. *Memberships:* Member of numerous committees including: Secretary, Passaic Valley Ground Water Protection Committee, 1980-; Director, Passaic River Restoration Project Master Plan, 1981-; Advisory Committee, Great Swamp Point/Non Point Water Quality Study Task Force, 1983-; Ground Water Data Management Committee, 1987. *Honours:* Special Award of Merit, US Environmental Protection Agency, Region II, 1975; Community Achievement Award, City of East Orange, New Jersey, 1980; Achivement Award, US Department of the Interior, Heritage Conservation and Recreation Service, 1981; Recipient, German-Marshall Fund, 1982; Certificate of Appreciation, North Jersey Water Supply District, 1987; United States Japan Friendship Commisiion, 1988. *Hobbies:* International travel; Gourmet cooking; Needlepoint. *Address:* 246 Madisonville Road, Basking Ridge, NJ 07920, USA.

FINCH Sheila Rosemary, b. 29 Oct. 1935, London, England. Author; Professor of English. m. Clare Grill Rayner, 8 June 1957, divorced 1980. 3 daughters. *Education:* Diploma, Bishop Otter College, England, 1956; BA English 1959, MA English 1962, Indiana University, USA. *Appointments:* Cuesta College, California, 1965-67; California State University, Long Beach, 1967-70; El Camino College, California, 1974-. *Publications:* Novels: Infinity's Web, 1985; Triad, 1986; Garden of the Shaped, 1987; The Shadow of Shaping, 1989; Shaper's Legacy, 1989; Shaping the Dawn, 1989; Shaper's Child, 1989; Numerous short stories and scholarly articles about science fiction. *Memberships:* Science Fiction Writers of America; Asilomar Writers' Consortium; Science Fiction Research Associates. *Honours:* National Endowment for the Humanities Award, 1978; Compton-Crook Award for best 1st novel in the Science Fiction and Fantasy Field, 1986. *Hobbies:* Reading; Hiking; Sailing; Travelling. Interests: Alien contact; Xenolinguistics. *Address:* Humanities Division, El Camino College, Crenshaw Blvd, Torrance, CA 90506, USA.

FINE Anne, b. 7 Dec. 1947, England. Writer. m. Kit Fine, 3 Aug. 1968, 2 daughters. *Education:* University of Warwick. *Publications:* Children's Books: The Summer House Loon; The Other Darker Ned; The Stone Menagerie; Round Behind the Icehouse; The Granny Project; Madame Doubtfire; others for younger readers; Adult Novel: The Killjoy. *Honour:* Scottish Arts Council Book Award, 1986. *Hobbies:* Reading; Walking. *Address:* c/o Murray Pollinger, 4 Garrick Street, London WC2E 9BH, England.

FINGERMAN Sue Whitsell, b. 4 May 1932, Kentucky, USA. Environmental Toxicologist. m. Milton Fingerman, 31 Mar. 1958, 2 sons. *Education:* BA, 1955, Transylvania Collge; MS 1959, PhD, 1975, Tulane University. *Appointments:* Various positions as Teaching Assistant & Research Assistant, 1953-58; Assistant Editor, Copeia & Tulane Studies in Zoology, 1957-58; Instructor, Biology: Ursuline Academy, 1967-68, Dominican College, 1968-69, Xavier Univerity, 1969-71; Research Assistant, Biology, Marine Biological Laboratory, 1970-73 (summers); Research Assistant, 1972-75, Research Associate, 1975-77, Biology, Research Associate, Biology & Chemistry, 1977-78, Research Associate, Biology, 1978-80, Tulane University; Environmental Toxicologist, Oklahoma State University, 1980-81; Biological Consultant, 1980-; Visiting Assistant Professor, Tulane University, 1984. *Memberships Include:* American Society Zoology; Sigma Xi; *Honours:* Sigma Xi Award for Outstanding Graduate Research, 1975; Assistant Editor, Scientific Journals. *Hobbies:* Sewing; Pets; Knitting. *Address:* 1730 Broadway, New Orleans, LA 70118, USA.

FINIFTER Ada Weintraub, b. 6 June 1938, New York City, New York, USA. Professor of Political Science. *Education:* BA, Brooklyn College, 1959; MA, 1961, PhD, 167, University of Michigan. *Appointments:* Assistant Professor to Professor of Political Science, Michigan State University, East Lansing, 1967-. *Publications:* Many articles in political science journals; Alienation and the Social System (editor), 1972; Political Science: The State of the Discipline (editor), 1983; Using the IBM Personal Computer: EasyWriter, 1984. *Memberships:* American Political Science Association, Vice-President 1983-84; Programme Chairperson 1982, Committee on Professional Ethics Chair 1985-87; Midwest Political Science Association, President 1986-87; International Political Science Association, Programme Committee 1986-88. *Honours:* University Fellow, University of Michigan, 1959-60; Graduate Fellow, National Science Foundation, 1966-67; Congressional Fellow, 1973-74; Research Grant, National Science Foundation, 1977-78; Research Grant, Russell Sage Foundation, 1979-83; Visiting Scholar, University of California, Berkeley, 1988-89. *Hobbies:* Computing; Travel; Theatre. *Address:* Department of Political Science, Michigan State University, 303 South Kedzie Hall, East Lansing, MI 48824, USA.

FINK Janet Rose, b. 10 May 1950, New York, USA. Attorney. *Education:* AB, Bryn Mawr College, 1971; JD, Georgetown Law Centre, 1974. *Appointments:* Fellow, Metropolitan Applied Research Centre, 1970-71; Urban Institute, 1972-73; Russell Sage Foundation, 1974-75; Staff Attorney, 1974-79, Director, Special Litigation Unit, 1979-84, Assistant Attorney in Charge, 1984-, Juvenile Rights Division, Legal Aid Society. *Publications:* Articles in professional journals; book chapters. *Memberships:* Board, National Centre for Youth Law; Chairman, American Bar Association, Juvenile Justice Committee; Editorial Board, Criminal Justice Magazine. *Address:* Legal Aid Society Juvenile Rights Division, 15 Park Row, 21 Floor, New York, NY 10038, USA.

FINKE Blythe Foote, b. 24 Nov. 1922, Pasadena, California, USA. Freelance writer. m. 15 Nov. 1958. 1 stepson, 1 stepdaughter. *Education:* BA, International Affairs, University of California, Berkeley; BB, Woodbury Business College, Los Angeles. *Appointments:* United Nations and New York City Correspondent for US Information Agency; American Foreign Service Information Officer and Writer/Editor; Administrator in Austria, Germany, Turkey, Washington DC; Administrator, International Cultural Exchange Programme, New York; Radio News Commentary Writer, Japan; Director of Public Relations, Brooklyn Public Library System (52 libraries); Editor, Shell Oil Company house organ; Employee and Industrial Relations, Union Oil Company; Freelance assignments for organizations; Volunteer, Foreign Policy Association, United Nations Association; UN Delegate, National Council of Women of the US Inc; Vice Convenor, International Council of Women. *Publications:* Books: Aleksandr Solzhenitsyn: Beleaguered Literary Giant of the USSR; Assassination Case Studies: Bernard M Baruch, Speculator and Statesman; Berlin, Divided City; Charlie Chaplin, Famous Silent Movie Actor and Comic; China Joins The United Nations; General Patton, Fearless Military Leader; George Meany, Modern Leader of the AFL; Howard R Hughes, Twentieth Century Multi-Millionaire and Recluse; John Foster Dulles, Master of Brinkmanship & Diplomacy; Konrad Adenauer, Architect of the New Germany; Our Besieged Environment, The Pollution Problem; W C Fields, Renowned Comedian of the Early Picture Industry; Numerous articles to newspapers and magazines. *Memberships:* National Press Club; Overseas Press Club of America; American Society of Journalists; Authors Travel Journalist Guild; Women in Communications. *Address:* 45 Kylerwood Place, Inverness, Califonia 94937-1079, USA.

FINKE Leonda Froelich, b. 23 Jan. 1922, Brooklyn, New York, USA. Sculptor. m. Arnold I. Finke, 30 Mar. 1947, 1 son, 2 daughters. *Appointments:* Sculptor; Adjunct Professor, Sculpture & Drawing, Nassau Community College, 1969-. *Creative Works:* Women in the sun, at Galleria, Atlanta, Georgia; 3 figures; many sculptures in public spaces & museums; Collections in: National Portrait Gallery, Smithsonian Museum; British Museum, London; Museum of Foreign Art, Sofia, Bulgaria; Chrysler Museum, Norfolk, Virginia, etc; and many private collections. *Memberships:* National Sculpture Society; Sculptors Guild; National Association of Women Artists; New York Society of Women Artists; American Medallic Sculptors Association. *Honours:* National Sculpture Society, Bronze Medal, 1974; National Association Women Artists, Medal of Honour, 1980; Audubon Artists, Medal of Honour, 1984; National Accademy of Design Award, 1984; Yaddo Fellowships. *Address:* 10 The Locusts, Roslyn, NY 11576, USA.

FINLAY Audrey Joy, b. 18 Sept. 1932, Davidson, Saskatchewan, Canada. Consultant, Environment & Education. m. James Campbell Finlay, 18 June 1955. 2 sons, 1 daughter. *Education:* BA, University of Manitoba, 1954; Profl diploma in Education, 1974, MEd 1978, University of Alberta. *Appointments:* Social Worker, Children's Aid, Brandon, Manitoba, 1954-55; Foster Home worker, Social Services, Province of Saskatchewan, Regina, 1954-56; Social Service, City of Edmonton Alta, 1956-59; Naturalist City of Edmonton, 1965-74; Education Consultant, Coordinator, Edmonton Public School Board, 1974-85; Private Consultant Environment and Education, 1985-; Interpretation numerous projects, 1965-. *Publications:* Winter Here & Now, 1982; Co-author: Parks In Alberta, 1987; Nature Guide to BC, 1989. Contributions to numerous professional journals; Weekly columnist, Edmonton Journal & Calgary Herald. *Memberships:* Board Directors, North American Environmental Education ASS, 1983-; Board Directors, American Nature Study Soc, 1984-; Vice President, Canadian Nature Federation, 1984-; Board Directors, Federation Alberta Naturalists, 1970's; Chairman and Chief Executive Officer Wildlife '87 The Canadian; Centennial of Wildlife Conservation, 1985-88; Founding President Environmental Outdoor Council of Alberta Teachers Association. *Honours:* First life membership award, Environmental & Outdoor Education Council of Alberta Teachers Association; Ms Chatelaine, Chatelaine Magazine, International Year of Women, 1975; Order of the Bighorn, Alberta, 1987; Ralph D Bird distinguished Award, Manitoba, 1988; Loran Goulden Award, Alberta, 1979. *Hobbies:* Exploring nature; Photography; Pottery. *Address:* Box 8644, Station "L" Edmonton, Alberta, Canada T6C 4J4

FIORATTI COSTANTINO Helen, b. New York, USA. Interior Designer; Antiques Dealer. m. Nereo Fioratti, 21 Nov. 1963, 1 daughter. *Education:* BS, Parson's School of Design in conjunction with New York University, 1963, 1950. *Appointments:* President: The Connoisseur Inc., 1952, L'Antiquaire Inc., 1965-83. *Publications:* How to Know French Antiques. *Memberships:* NSID; Antique Dealers Association. *Hobbies:* Art Collector; Cooking. *Address:* 555 Park Ave., New York City, NY 10021, USA.

FIRTH Tazeena Mary, b. 1 Nov. 1935, Southampton, England. Theatre Designer. *Education:* St Mary's School, Wantage. *Appointments:* Theatre Royal, Windsor, 1954-57; English Stage Company, Royal Court, 1957-60; Partnership, stage design, with Timothy O'Brien, 1961-; Independent design work, 1969. *Creative Works:* Recent joint work includes: Tales from the Vienna Woods; Bedroom Farce, National Theatre; Falstaff, Berlin Opera; The Cunning Little Vixen, Goteborg; Evita, London, Later USA, Australia, Vienna; A Midsummer Night's Dream, Sydney Opera House; Peter Grimes, Royal Opera; Turendot, Vienna State Opera. Recent solo work includes: Rape of Lucretia, Karlstad, 1982; Katerina Ishmailova, Goteborg, 1984; Traviata, Umea, 1985; Bluebeard's Castle, Copenhagen, 1985; Trojan Women, Goteborg's Statstertern, 1985; Il Seraglio Goteborg, 1986; Costumes for Marilyn Monroe, the Musical, 1984. *Honour:* Gold Medal, Set Design, Prague Quadriennale, 1975. *Hobby:* Sailing. *Address:* London, England.

FISCHER Margaret Jane, b. 25 Apr. 1946, Chicago, Illinois, USA. Lecturer; Independent Artist/Craftsman. *Education:* Diploma, Silversmithing, 1968, BFA, Enamelling, 1969, Cleveland Institute of Art; MA, Art Education, Case Western Reserve University, 1977. *Appointments:* Sacristan, St Dominic Church, Shaker Heights, Ohio, 1965-71; Instructor, Enamelling, Silversmithing, Jewish Community Center, Cleveland Heights, Ohio, 1970-86; Lecturer, Enamelling, Jewellery, Art Studios, Case Western Reserve University, Cleveland, Ohio, 1971-; Instructor, Enamelling, Jewellery, Valley Art Center, Chagrin Falls, Ohio, 1972-74; Instructor, Ceramics, School of Fine Arts, Willoughby, Ohio, 1977; Instructor, Ceramics, Cuyahoga Community College, Warrensville, Ohio, 1987. *Creative works:* Tabernacle and sanctuary lamp, St Francis-St George Hospital Inc, Cincinnati; Communion Pateus, St Joseph Cathedral, Columbus; Eucharistic vessels: London Correctional Institute; Newman Center, Slippery Rock University; Christ Our King Church, Mt Pleasant. *Memberships:* American Crafts Council; Secretary, Northeast Regional Trustee, Ohio Designer Craftsmen; Chairman, Liturgical Arts Committee, Art and Architecture Commission, Diocese of Cleveland; Cleveland Representative, Liturgical Art Guild of Ohio; Executive Committee for Pastoral Liturgy, Diocese of Cleveland; Cleveland Institute of Art Alumni Association. *Honours:* Teaching Assistantship, Case Western Reserve University, 1975; Graduate Alumni Fund Scholarship, Case Western Reserve University, 1976; Honourable Mention, Annual Hallinan-Newman Religious Art Show, 1977, 1978; Juror's Mention, Liturgical Arts Exhibit, McFall Gallery, Bowling Green State University, 1981; Ohio Designer Craftsmen Purchase Award, Honourable Mention, Liturgical Arts VIII, 1981; Honourable Mention, Visual Arts Award, Modern Liturgy magazine, 1986. *Hobbies:* Choral singing; Kite flying; Photography; Reading; Cooking. *Address:* 3475 Avalon Road, Shaker Heights, OH 44120, USA.

FISCHER Sandra Kay Klein, b. 18 June 1950, Salem, Oregon, USA. Professor. m. Philip John Fischer, 20 June 1969, divorced 1987. 1 son. *Education:* BA, Calif State Univ, Dominguez Hills, 1972; MA, Univ Calif, Los Angeles, 1974; PhD, Univ of Oregon, 1980. *Appointments:* Instructor, West Los Angeles College, 1974; Graduate Teaching Fellow, University of Oregon, 1976-79; Lecturer 1980-81, Assistant Professor 1981-87, Associate Professor and Director of Undergraduate Studies in English 1987-, State University of New York

at Albany. *Publications:* Econolingua, 1985; Reviews and articles in Shakespeare Quarterly; Henry James Review; Theatre Survey and others. *Memberships:* Modern Language Association of America; Shakespeare Association of America; American Society for Theatre Research (Associate Editor, Theatre Survey). *Honours:* Kirby Award, 1976; Erns Fellowship, 1979-80, University of Oregon; State University of New York Faculty Research Grants, 1982, 1985; American Council of Learned Societies Grant, 1986; Research Fellow, Center for the Humanities, Oregon State University, 1989. *Hobbies:* Music; Sports; The Arts. *Address:* English Dept, University at Albany, 1400 Washington Ave, Albany, NY 12222, USA.

FISH Barbara, b. 31 July 1920, New York City, USA. Professor of Psychiatry. m. Max Saltzman, 12 Dec. 1953, 1 son, 1 daughter. *Education:* BA summa cum laude, Barnard College, Columbia University, 1942; New York University College of Medicine, 1945; Certificate, Psychoanalysis, William A. White Institute, 1956. *Appointments:* Faculty, Cornell University Medical College, 1955-60; Director, Child Psychiatry & Associate Professor to Professor 1960-72, Professor of Psychiatry 1972-, New York School of Medicine, 1960-72; Professor of Psychiatry, UCLA, 1972-; University of California, Los Angeles (UCLA). *Publications:* Numerous scientific articles including: Infant Predictors of the Longitudinal Course of Schizophrenic Development; Psychoses of Childhood; Neurobiologic Antecedents of Schizophrenia in Children. *Memberships:* Committee on Certification in Child Psychiatry, American Board of Psychiatry & Neurology, 1969-77; Clinical Programme Projects Research Review Committee, National Institute of Mental Health, 1976-79; American Psychiatric Association; American Academy of Child Psychiatry; American College of Neuropsychopharmacology; Society for Research in Child Development. *Honours:* Numerous academic awards, fellowships, honour societies, including: Woman of Science Award, UCLA, 1978; Agnes P. McGavin Award, American Psychiatric Association, 1987. *Hobbies:* Research, antecedents in infancy of schizophrenia & related disorders; Music; Painting; Gardening. *Address:* Neuropsychiatric Institute, UCLA, Los Angeles, California 90024, USA.

FISHER Ann, b. 5 Apr. 1939, Governor's Island, New York, USA. Attorney. m. William J Danaher, 22 Feb. 1958, divorced 1963. 2 daughters. *Education:* MBA 1976, JD 1981, University of Miami, Florida. *Appointments:* Sales Promotion Manager, Family Finance Management Corp, Miami, 1965-71; Director of Institutional Sales, Terner's of Miami Corp, 1971-80; Attorney, Associate with Helliwell, Melrose and DeWolf, 1981-83; Co-owner Vice President, Now Courier, Inc, Hialeah, Florida, 1983-84; Co-owner, President, Cannon & Fisher Corp, Coral Gables, Florida, 1984-86; Owner/President, Ann Fisher, PA, 1986-; Owner/President, Corporate Records Inc., 1986-. *Memberships:* President, South Miami Business Network; President, Entrepreneurial Club of South Florida; Vice President, National Association of Women Business Owners, Miami Chapter; Director, Coral Gables Bar Association; Director, University of Miami School of Business Alumni Association; Rotary Club of Coral Gables. *Honours:* Class Valedictorian, 1976; Beta Gamma Sigma, 1976; Cum Laude, 1981. *Hobbies:* Golf; Reading; Music. *Address:* 1514 Zuleta Avenue, Coral Gables, FL 33146, USA.

FISHER Beatrice Awura Oboshie Allua, b. 3 May 1933, Lagos, Nigeria. Barrister and Solicitor of Supreme Court of Nigeria. m. Babatunde Adekunle Olanrewaju Fisher, 28 Sept. 1957. 2 sons, 1 daughter. *Education:* Ophthalmic Nursing Diploma, London, England; SRN, Guys Hospital, London; Midwife Certificate, Glasgow, Scotland, 1953-58; LL.B. (Hons) BL, Nigeria, 1972. *Appointments:* Barrister and Solicitor of Supreme Court of Nigeria, Obafemi Awolowo & Co, 1972-75; Barrister and Solicitor of Supreme Court of Nigeria, Principal Partner, Beatrice Fisher & Co, 1975-; Appointed Notary Public, 1979. *Memberships:* Nigerian Bar Association; The Nigerian Association of University Women;

President, Corona Society, 1978; Treasurer, International Women's Society, 1982-84; Women's Auxilliary Guild (Cathedral Church); President Elect, Soroptimist International of Eko; UN Representative, International Federation of Women Laywers (FIDA), 1988-90. *Honours:* Scholarship, Annie Walsh Memorial Girls School, Freetown, Sierra Leone; Scholarship, Fourah Bay College, Freetown, Sierra Leone. *Hobbies:* General Reading; Gardening; Flower Arrangement; Gourmet Culinary Skills; Travel; Theatre; Opera; Classical music. *Address:* No 1 Taiwo Koya Street, Ilupeju Estate, PO Box 8032, Lagos, Nigeria.

FISHER Florence Rose, b. 20 June 1929, USA. Environmental Company Chairman. m. William Fisher, 30 Mar. 1952. 3 daughters. *Education:* BSc, Chemistry. *Appointments:* Founder and Chairman, Environmental Resources Ltd (ERL), London, 1971-; Director, ERL (Asia) Ltd, 1978-; Research Fellow and Assistant Director for Environment at John F Kennedy School of Government, Harvard University, Energy and Enviroment Policy Center. *Memberships:* Fellow, Royal Society of Arts; Trustee, Environment Foundation; Founding Member, International Association of Environemtnal Affairs. *Honours:* Queens Award for Export, ERL, 1984 and 1988; Roll of Honour for Achievements for the Environment. *Hobby:* Music, past concert pianist, command performance before a USA President. *Address:* RDI, Box 222, Chatham, NY 12037, USA.

FISHER Phyllis Kahn, b. 30 Mar. 1919, Oakland, California, USA. Licensed Clinical Social Worker. m. Leon H. Fisher, 2 Dec. 1941, 3 sons, 1 daughter. *Education:* BA, 1940, MSW, 1966, University of California, Berkeley. *Appointments:* Senior Social Worker, Children's Health Council, Palo Alto, California, 1966-79; Senior Social Worker, Supervisor, Tokyo Community Counselling Service and International School Sacred Heart, Tokyo, Japan, 1979-82; Private Clinical Practice, Atherton, California, USA, 1982-; Invited delegate to China with People to People by Chinese Medical Association to discuss one couple/ one child policy and problems. *Publications:* Los Alamos Experience, 1985, Japanese version From Los Alamos to Hiroshima; Professional articles in American and Japanese journals. *Memberships:* Beyond War; National Association of Social Workers; Jewish Community Relations Council. *Honours:* Pi Phi Delta; Womens Economics Society, University of California, 1939; Prytanean Women's Honor Society, University of California, Berkeley, 1940. *Hobbies:* Music; Hiking; Children and grandchildren. *Address:* 102 Encinal Avenue, Atherton, CA 94027, USA.

FISHER Robin Leeann, b. 12 Oct. 1955, Latrobe Pennsylvania, USA. Product Assurance Supervisor of Tubing Manufacturer. *Education:* BA, political science 1973-77, Post graduate courses, Indiana University of Pennsylvania. *Appointments:* Quality Control Inspector 1978-81, Production Coordinator 1983-84, Product Assurance Supervisor 1984-89, Maufacturing Supervisor, 1989-, Westinghouse Electric Corp Specialty Metals Plant. *Memberships:* National Association of Female Executives; Smithsonian Institute, National Member; Westinghouse Foreman's Association; Indiana University of Pennsylvania Alumni Assoc, Life Member; National Arbor Day Foundation. *Hobbies:* Snow skiing; Water skiing; Vollyball; Reading. *Address:* RD No 3 Box 437, Blairsville, PA 15717, USA.

FISHER Wendy Astley-Bell, b. 23 Jan. 1944, London, England. Company President. m. (1) 21 Mar. 1970, divorced 1980, (2) Lester E. Fisher, 23 Jan. 1981. *Education:* BA, Northwestern University, 1965. *Appointments:* Okamoto/London Studio, 1966-70; Communications International, 1970-71; Freelance Artist, 1971-76; The Lincoln Park Zoological Society, 1976-81; President, Direct Marketing Agency, Mailworks Inc., 1981-. *Publication:* The First Hundred Years, with Richard Van Mell, 1975. *Memberships:* The Economic Club of Chicago; National Society of Fund Raising Executives, Chicago Chapter, Board of Directors; Chicago Association of Direct Marketing, Board of Directors; American Association of Zoological Parks and Aquariums; Junior League of Chicago, Board of Directors. *Honours:* Recipient, various honours & awards including: Award of Merit, Golden Pyramid Competition, 1979; Graphics Design Selection, Print Magazine, 1981; Outstanding Woman Entrepreneur, Women in Communications, Chicago Chapter, 1983; President's Award, National Society of Fund Raising Executives, Chicago Chapter, 1987. *Hobbies Include:* Sailing; Hiking; Travel; Art. *Address:* 3180 North Lake Shore Drive, Chicago, IL 60657, USA.

FISK Caroline Susan, b. 7 May 1946, Simla, India. Scientist. *Education:* BSc., Honours, University of Alberta, Canada, 1968; PhD, University of Paris, 1972. *Appointments:* Research Associate: University of British Columbia, 1972-77, University of Montreal, 1977-80; Assistant Professor, University of Illinois, 1980-84; Research Scientist, University of Auckland, 1985-. *Publications:* Over 35 articles in professional journals. *Memberships:* Operations Research Society of America, Council Member; New Zealand Operations Research Society. *Hobbies:* Music; Sport. *Address:* 52 Rauhuia Crescent, Parau, Auckland 7, New Zealand.

FITCH-HAUSER Margaret Erin, b. 17 July 1953, Pusan, South Korea. Professor. m. Jerry Hauser, 19 June 1979. *Education:* BA, 1974, MA, Stephen F. Austin, State University, 1975; PhD, University of Oklahoma, 1982. *Appointments:* Assistant Professor, Universiy of Oklahoma, 1980-87; Associate Professor, Auburn University, 1987-; President, Windward Communication Associates, 1988-. *Publications:* Strategic Business Messages: Applied Theory & Practice, 1986; numerous journal articles. *Membership:* International Listening Association and the Speech Communication Association. *Honours:* Fantus Outstanding Teaching Award, 1986, 1987, 1988; Ralph Nichols Award, 1986, 1987. Trainer, Consultant to a number of organisations. *Address:* Dept. of Speech Communication, Auburn University, 6030 Haley Centre, Auburn, AL 36849, USA.

FITZALAN Marsha, b. 10 Mar. 1953, Bonn, Federal Republic of Germany. Actress. m. Patrick Ryecart, 4 July 1977. 2 daughters. *Education:* German Governess, West Berlin; The Beehive School, Nanyuki, Kenya, 1959-62; Convent of the Sacred Heart, Woldingham, Surrey, England; Webber Douglas Academy of Dramatic Art, 1971-74. *Appointments:* Television appearances include: Upstairs Downstairs; Duchess of Duke Street; Pride and Prejudice; The Professionals; Diamonds; Angels; Pygmalion; Nancy Astor; Shelley; Three Up Two Down; Paradise Postponed; Inside Story; Anna Karenina; The New Statesman; Hedgehog Wedding. Theatre appearances include: 84 Charing Cross Road, Ambassadors Theatre. Film: International Velvet; Handful of Dust. *Hobbies:* Riding; Foxhunting; Dressage; Show jumping; My children and husband. *Address:* Fraser & Dunlop Ltd., Chelsea Harbour, Lots Road, London SW10, England.

FITZGERALD Carrie Eugenia, b. 28 Mar. 1929, Atlantic City, New Jersey, USA. Professor; Gerontologist; Lecturer. 2 daughters. *Education:* AA, Atlantic Community College, Mayslanding, New Jersey, 1972; BA, Rutgers University, Camden, 1974; Master Social Work, 1976, EdD, 1985, Temple University, Philadelphia. *Appointments:* Temple University, 1976-84; Adjunct Faculty Professor, Glassboro State College, Glassboro, New Jersey, 1984-. *Publications:* The Perceptions of Black Nursing Home Aides and Supervisors Concerning Training Programs for Entry-level Employees, Doctoral Dissertation, 1984; Planning and Developing Inservice Training: A Needs Assessment for Nursing Home Employees who work in Urban Nursing Homes, Masters Project, 1976; Striving for Excellence, Past, Present and Future Goals, 1988. *Memberships:* Rutger's Alumni Association; Temple Alumni Association; Philadelphia Urban League; NAACP, National Member; National Black Women's Political Association; National Council on Aging; Juvenile Conference Committee Member. *Honours:*

Ford Foundation Scholarship, 1970, 1971, 1972, 1973, 1974; Mental Health Aging Grant, 1974, 1975, 1976; Proclamation, House of Representatives, Commonwealth of Pennsylvania, 1985; Television Broadcast: Black History Special, Camden, New Jersey, 1988. *Hobbies:* Reading; Teaching Sunday School; Counseling Juveniles; Working with the Elderly and Community Out-Reach. *Address:* Post Office Box 362, Camden, NJ 08101, USA.

FITZGERALD Julia, b. 18 Sept. 1943, Bangor, North Wales. Author; Astrologer; Nutritionist. m. 1981. 1 son, 1 daughter. *Career:* Author since 1961; Regular lecturer on Writing, Health and diet, Astrology; Reviewer. *Publications:* Royal Slave, 1978; Slave Lady, 1980; Scarlet Woman, 1979; Salamander, 1981; Fallen Woman, 1981; Venus Rising, 1982; The Princess and the Pagan, 1982; Firebird, 1983; The Jewelled Serpent, 1984; Taboo, 1986; Desert Queen, 1987; Beauty of the Devil, 1988; Earth Queen, Sky King, 1989; Non-fiction: Healthy Signs, 1989. Astromance Series: Daughter of the Gods; Pasodoble; Flame of the East; A Kiss from Aphrodite; Castle of the Enchantress; Glade of Jewels; Devil in my Arms; Jade Moon; Temple of Butterflies; Bridge of Rainbows. As Julia Watson: The Lovechild, 1968; Medici Mistress, 1969; A Mistress for the Valois, 1970; The King's Mistress, 1970; The Wolf and the Unicorn, 1971; Winter of the Witch, 1971; The Tudor Rose, 1972; Saffron, 1972; Love Song, 1981. As Jane de Vere: Scarlet Women, 1969. As Julia Hamilton: The Last of the Tudors, 1971; Katherine of Aragon, 1972; Anne of Cleves, 1972; Son of York, 1973; The Changeling Queen, 1977; The Emperor's Daughter, 1978; Pearl of the Habsburgs, 1978; The Snow Queen, 1978; The Habsburg Inheritance, 1980. *Memberships:* Society of Authors; Crime Writers Association; Romantic Novelists Association; British Fantasy Society; Romance Writers of America; Astrological Association; Astrological Lodge of London. *Honours:* Romanti Times (USA) Award for Historical Romance, 1984; Nominated for Romantic Times Award for Most Exotic Book, 1985; Winner of Romantic Times Reviewers' Choice Award for Most Exotic Book, 1988/89. *Hobbies include:* Reading; History; Costume; Ancient Religions; Astrology, etc. *Address:* c/o June Hall Agency, 5th Floor, The Chambers, Chelsea Harbour, Lots Rd., London SW10 OXF, England.

FITZMAURICE Kerry Clare, b. 7 Dec. 1951, Melbourne, Australia. Lecturer; Orthoptist. m. Alan Leslie Pearce, 25 Mar. 1984. *Education:* Higher Diploma, Secondary Teaching, 1973; Diplomas, Applied Science (Orthoptics), Orthoptic Board of Australia, 1982; Master's degree research (rehabilitation of visually impaired), in progress. *Appointments:* Secondary school teacher, biology, 1974-79, Lecturer, Orthoptics, Lincoln Institute of Health Science, & Orthoptist, Royal Victorian Institute for Blind, 1983-; Lecturer Coordinator, Visual Rehabilitation Research & Consultantcy Centre, La Trobe University, 1988-. *Publications:* Scientific papers, Australian Orthoptic Journal, various conference transactions. *Memberships:* Councillor, Publicity Officer, & representative on Australian Orthoptic Board, Orthoptic Association of Australia; Associate, Royal Australian College of Ophthalmologists; Australian Institute of Training & Development. *Honour:* Queen's Guide Award, 1968. *Hobbies:* Bush walking; Kayaking. *Address:* 27 Howell Road, Plenty, Victoria 3090, Australia.

FJELDSTAD Lise, b. 17 June 1939, Oslo, Norway. Actress. 1 son, 1 daughter. *Education:* Studied Psychology, Oslo University, 1958-61; Theatre School, Oslo, 1961-64. *Creative Works:* Performances at: The Norwegian Theatre, Oslo, 1964-71; TV Theatre, Oslo, 1971-74; National Theatre, Oslo, 1975-; Roles include: Soeveig, Peer Gynt; Nora, A Doll's House; Hedda, Hedda Gabler; Agnes, Brand; Asta, Little Eyolf; Maja, When We Dead Awaken; Elena, Uncle Vanja; Madame Ranevesky, The Cherry Orchard; Rosalinde, As You Like It; Desdemona, Othello; Yerma, Yerma; Blanche, Streetcar Named Desire; Elisabeth, Don Carlos; Mary, Mary Queen of Scots; Martha, Who's Afraid of Virginia

Woolf, etc and several leading parts in films. *Memberships:* Artistic Board, National Theatre, Oslo; Vice-member, Board, State Drama School, Norway. *Honour:* Best Swedish Film Actress, 1983. *Address:* Prof Dahlsgt, 27C, Oslo 2, Norway.

FLAGLER Christine Elizabeth Fleischer, b. 9 Dec. 1943, Madison, Wisconsin, USA. International Adoption Specialist. m. David Girard Flagler, 29 Aug. 1964, 2 sons, 2 daughters. *Education:* Beloit College, 1961-63; University of Wisconsin, 1963-64; BA, University of Houston, 1965; MSW, Western Michigan University, 1979. *Appointments:* Coordinator, respite care cooperative, Family & Children's Services, Kalamazoo, 1980-83; Director, Council of International Programs, Kalamazoo, 1980-84; Adoption Specialist, Bethany Christian Services, Grand Rapids, 1983-. *Memberships:* Board Chair, Council of International Programmes; Kalamazoo Oratorio Society; Founder, Heal the Children, Kalamazoo, 1986-88; Prince of Peace Lutheran Church; Academy Street Peace Society. *Hobbies:* Walking; Backpacking; Reading; Singing. *Address:* 1510 Academy Street, Kalamazoo, Michigan 49007, USA.

FLANAGAN Judith Ann, b. 28 Apr. 1950, Lubbuck, Texas, USA. Entertainment and Special Events Specialist. *Education:* BS., Memphis State University, 1972; Walt Disney World, 1972-81. *Appointments:* Entertainment Production Manager, 1982, 1984 World's Fairs: Director of Sales/Conventions, River Terrace, Gatlingsburg Tennesee; Gatlingburg C of C Christmas Parade Director, 1981-85; Universal Studios, Florida, 1988-; Parades, Special Events, Grand Openings & Closing Ceremonies. *Memberships:* NAFE; Tennessee Society of Association Executives; Hotel/Motel Association; Hospitality Industry Association. *Honours:* Best Actress, Wizard of Diz, Disney World Entertainment, 1974-75; America on Parade Flag, 1976. *Hobbies:* Photography; Filming; Bicycling. *Address:* 511 East Magnolia Street, Kissimmee, FL 34744, USA.

FLAUGHER Jeanine Karen Sue, b. Belleville, USA. Mathematics Educator. m. John Wesley Flaugher, 9 Aug. 1968, 1 step-daughter. *Education:* AA, Belleville Junior College, 1959; BS, Mathematics, 1961, MS, 1964, Southern Illinois University. *Appointments:* Mathematics Educator, Belleville Township High School, District 201 with BTHS West 1961-66, with BTHS East 1966-89; Owner Flowers Travel. *Honours:* Recipient, various honours including: American Federation Teachers Local 434 Scholar; Business & Professional Womens Org. Scholar; Delegate to Madeline Hunter Quincy Education Conference. *Hobbies:* Travel; Swimming; Boating; Bowling; Macrame. *Address:* Belleville Township High School East Dist 201, 2555 West Boulevard, Belleville, IL 62221, USA.

FLEEMAN Frances de Sales Stallkamp, b. 4 Apr. 1938, Lima, Ohio, USA. Behaviour Management Specialist; Early Childhood Special Educator. m. (1) David P. Gibson (deceased), 27 Aug. 1960, 3 sons, 3 daughters, (2) Frederick M. Fleeman, 1 Sep. 1971, 1 daughter. *Education:* BA cum laude, Siena Heights College, Adrian, Michigan, 1960; MEd, Bowling Green State University, Ohio, 1985; EdS, University of Toledo, Toledo, Ohio, 1989. *Appointments:* St Joseph School, Killeen, Texas, 1959-60; Wm County Board of MR/DD, Montpelier, Ohio, 1986-88. *Publications:* Night & Day, Employee Stress Retreat; Attention, Behavior Management Inservice; Fathers, Implications for Educators. *Memberships:* Board Member, Sandusky County United Way; Board Member, NORCA; Career Counselling Board Member, Terra Technical College; Board Member, Cedar Clinic; Board Member, Beginning Experience; Lakota Community Advisory Council. *Honours:* Siena Heights Student Teachers Award, 1960; Theology Award, Siena Heights College, 1960; Early Childhood Specialist Degree Grant, University of Toledo, 1988. *Hobbies:* Clown ministry; Creative writing; Drama productions; Theme designs for environments; Perinatal coaching; Parenting exceptional children. *Address:* 6681 County Road 21, Risingsun, OH 43457, USA.

FLEMING Alice Carew Mulcahey, b. 21 Dec. 1928, New Haven, Connecticut, USA. Writer. m. Thomas Fleming, 19 Jan. 1951, 3 sons, 1 daughter. *Education:* BS, Trinity College, Washington DC, 1950; MA. Columbia University, New York, 1951. *Publications:* Books for young people: The Key to New York, 1960; Wheels, 1960; A Son of Liberty, 1961; Doctors in Petticoats, 1965; Great Women Teachers, 1965; General's Lady, 1965; The Senator from Maine, 1969, Paperback, 1976; Alice Freeman Palmer, Pioneer College President, 1970; Reporters at War, 1970; Highways into History, 1971; Pioneers in Print, 1971; Ida Tarbell: First of the Muckrakers, 1971, Paperback, 1976; Psychiatry: What's It All About? 1972; The Moviemakers, 1973; Alcohol: The Delightful Poison, 1975, Paperback, 1979; Trials That Made Headlines, 1975; Contraception, Abortion, Pregnancy, 1975; Something for Nothing, 1978; The Mysteries of ESP, 1980; What To Say When You Don't Know What To Say, 1982; Welcome to Grossville, 1985; The King of Prussia and a Peanut Butter Sandwich, 1988; Editor, poetry anthologies: Hosannah The Home Run! 1972; American Is Not All Traffic Lights, 1976. *Memberships:* PEN American Center; Authors Guild. *Honours:* National Media Award, Family Service Society of America, 1973; Alumnae Achievement Award, Trinity College, 1979. *Hobbies:* Reading; Tennis; Volunteer work. *Address:* c/o Raines & Raines, 71 Park Avenue, New York, NY 10016, USA.

FLEMING Mary Crist, b. 10 Sept. 1910, Boston, USA. Educator; Director, Founder, TASIS Schools. m. William Thomas Fleming, 15 Sept. 1938, 1 son, 1 daughters. *Education:* BA, Radcliffe College, 1933. *Appointments Include:* Headmistress, Mary Lyon School, Swarthmore, 1933-41; Founder, Director, Frog Hollow Farm Children's Camp, 1942-48, Frog Hollow Country Day School, 1948-55, Swiss Holiday 1953-67, Summer School in France, 1964-70, Project Europe, 1968-70, Fleming College, 1968-70, American Repertory Theatre in Europe, 1969-73, Fleming College, Florence, 1972-77; Founder Director, American School in Switzerland (TASIS) 1955, TASIS Summer Language Programme, Switzerland, 1972; Le Château des Enfants, 1968; TASIS England, 1976, TASIS English Language Programme, England, 1977; TASIS Greece, 1979; TASIS France, 1985. *Memberships:* Founding Member, Executive Committee, European Council of International Schools. *Honours:* Commendation, US Dept. of Education and Radcliffe College for 50 years service to international education. *Address:* TASIS England, Coldharbour Lane, Thorpe, Surrey TW20 8TE, England.

FLORENCE Verena M, b. 4 Nov. 1946, Interlaken, Switzerland. Business Executive. m. Kenneth Florence, 10 Dec. 1967. *Education:* BA, University of California, Berkeley, 1974; MS, 1979, PhD, 1982, University of California, Los Angeles. *Appointments:* Research Scientist, Procter & Gamble, Cincinnati, 1983; Administrator, Swerdlow, Florence, Beverly Hills, 1984-89; President, Chief Executive Officer, Chairman of the Board, Böl Designs, Inc., Los Angeles, 1989-. *Publications:* Articles in scientific journals. *Membership:* Association of Legal Administrators. *Honours:* Numerous awards in Womens Road Running Events, 1978-83. *Hobbies:* Reading; Computers; Running; Skiing; Backpacking. *Address:* 1063 Stradella Road, Los Angeles, CA 90077, USA.

FLORES Joan Milke, b. 9 May 1936, Sheboygan Falls, Wisconsin, USA. City Councillor. (divorced), 1 daughter. *Appointments include:* Former aide, John S. Gibson Jr (LACC President Emeritus), 25 years, 13 as Chief Deputy; 1st woman to qualify (competitive Civil Service examination), No. 1 ranking, Assistant City Clerk, City of Los Angeles; Elected representative (1st woman), 15th District, Los Angeles City Council (LACC), 1981-; Elected President Pro Tempore, LACC, 1983-87; Chair, Industry & Economic Development Committee, & Vice Chair, Grants, Housing & Community Development Committee, LACC; Member, numerous other council committees. *Memberships include:* Vice President, Board of Trustees, World Opportunities International

(missionaries); California Elected Women's Association for Education & Research; San Pedro-Palos Verdes Assistance League; Business & Professional Women's Association; Board, Harbor View House (mentally disabled); Trustee, Verbum Dei High School; Governor, Los Angeles Actors' Theatre; Citizens for Law & Order; Civic Centre Speakers Club (1st woman); LA Junior Chamber of Commerce (one of 1st women). *Honours include:* City Employee of Month, All City Employees Association, LA; Woman of Achievement, Business & Professional Women's Association, San Pedro; Woman of Year, Harbor Area YWCA. *Hobbies:* Collecting Olympic pins; Computers; Reading. *Address:* Room 230, City Hall, 200 North Spring Street, Los Angeles, California 90012, USA.

FLORI Anna Di Blasi Le Poer, b. 29 Oct. 1940, Amsterdam, New York, USA. Director of School. m. Gilberto Flori, 24 May 1986, 3 daughters. *Education:* Graduated, Albany Medical Centre School of Nursing, 1962, Fairfax Hospital School for Nurses Anesthetics, 1972; PhD, Columbia Pacific University, San Rafael; MBA, MPA, Southeastern University, Washington; BSc., Anesthesia, George Washington University, 1979. *Appointments:* Paediatrics, West Seattle General Hospital, 1962-64; Office Nurse, Filmore Buckner MD, Seattle, 1964-66; Staff, CRNA, Fairfax Hospital, 1972-73, Staff CRNA (part-time), Woodbridge, 1973; Chief Nurse, Anesthetist, 1973-84; Director, Potomac Hospital School for Nurse Anesthetists, Faculty Member, Columbia Pacific University, 1973-. *Publications:* Faculty Manual; Administrative Manual; Outpatient Surgery Informatiron Booklet; A Student Manual and a Brochure, Potomac Hospital School of Anesthesia. *Memberships:* American Associatiron of Nurse Anesthetists; Virginia Nurse Anesthesia Association. *Honours:* 1st Place, Essay Contest 1959; Special Academic Diploma, State of New York; Graduation Award, Scholastic Scholarship, Academich Achievement Award, Southeastern University, 1982. *Address:* 6368 Brampton Ct., Alexandria, VA 22304, USA.

FLORIN Irmela Gertrud, b. 14 Apr. 1938, Dortmund, Germany. Professor of Psychology. *Education:* Diplompsychologin, 1964; Dr Rer Soc, 1972. *Appointments:* Director, Student Counseling Center, Augsburg University, 1973-76; Professor of Psychology, University of Tubingen, 1976-78; Professor of Psychology, University of Marburg, 1978-. *Publications:* Books: Behandlung kindlicher Verhaltensstorungen; Leistungs-storung und Prufungsangst; Therapie der Angst; Entspannung/Desensibilisierung; Neurobiology and Human Disease; Frontiers of Stress Research. *Memberships:* Deutsche Gesellschaft fur Psychologie; Deutsche Gesellschaft fur Verhaltens medizin und Verhaltensmodifikation; Deutsches Kollegium fur Psychosomatische Medizin; American Psychological Association. *Address:* Calvinstr 1a, D-3550 Marburg, Federal Republic of Germany.

FLOWERS Loma Kaye, b. 27 Feb. 1944, Chardon, Ohio, USA. Psychiatrist. m. Edgar Flowers Jr, 21 Aug. 1971, 2 sons. *Education:* BA Honours, Biology, 1965; MD, 1968; Internship, 1968-69; Psychiatry residency, 1969-72. *Appointments include:* Director of Mental Health, HEW Charles Drew Health Centre, California, 1971-73; Chief of Mental Hygiene, Veterans Administration Hospital, San Francisco, 1974-77; Private practice, 1977-. *Publications:* Various articles, professional journals. Also papers & lectures. *Memberships include:* Past offices, American Psychiatric Association, Black Psychiatrists of California; Past Board Chair, Association for Study of Dreams; Black Psychiatrists of America; Offices, Northern California Psychiatric Society; California & San Francisco Medical Societies; American Medical Association. *Honours:* QBK, 1964; Faculty research award, 1968; Fellow, APA, 1988. *Hobbies:* Cooking; Hiking; Music; Fiction. *Address:* c/o Delaney & Flowers, Dream Center, 337 Spruce Street, San Francisco, California 94118, USA.

FLOYD Mary Alice, b. 27 Feb. 1928, Fairhope,

Alabama, USA. Counselor; Educator. m. Gerald L Floyd, 22 Mar. 1952. 1 son. *Education:* San Francisco University, 1945-47; BA, Alabama University, 1949; Postgraduate, Tulane University, 1951-52; San Jose State University, 1958; University of California Santa Barbara, 1966-72; MA, University of So Ala, 1969. *Appointments:* Guidance Cons and Coordinator, Careers for Women project, Santa Barbara (Calif) Sch Dist, 1973-74; Counselor terminally ill, Luife Acceptance Unit, Pinecrest Hospital, Santa Barbara, 1975-77; Counselor-Director, Women's Center, Santa Barbara City College, 1977-78; Teacher, Adult Education, Santa Barbara, 1972-; Teacher, Golden Gate University, Santa Barbara, 1988-; Private Practice Cons, counseling; Cons Coordinator, Alienated Youth Program, 1971; Faculty, University California at Santa Barbara Extension, 1976; Board Directors, Californian Luth U Grad Studies, 1984-85. *Memberships:* American Personnel and Guidance Association; National Vocational Guidance Association; California Personnel and Guidance Association; Santa Barbara C of C; Council International Students (pres 1983-85); California Coll Personnel Association; South Coast Bus Network. *Address:* 3233 Lucinda Ln, Santa Barbara, CA 93105, USA.

FLOYD-TENIYA Kathleen, b. 23 June 1953, Berwyn, Illinois, USA. Executive President, Chief Executive Officer for Sales Consulting Corporation. m. Robert D. Teniya, 20 June 1982, 1 son. *Education:* Certificate for Credit & Financial Analysis, National Credit Office, New York, 1977; Realtor Licence, State of Illinois, 1979. *Appointments:* Industrial Specialist, Technicon Instruments Corporation, Elmhurst, Illinois, 1971-74; Contract Administrator, 1974-76; Assistant to the President, 1976-77; Elmed Addison Illinois, Credit Rep. Manager, Memorex Corportion 1977-79; National Sales Representative, Midcontinet Adjustment Co., Glenview, Illinois, 1979-83; Assistant Vice-president of Sales, 1983-86; President, Chief Executive Officer, 1986-, Innovative Telemarketing Techniques Inc., Itasca, Illinois. *Publications:* Creator of INTELETEK, Commercial Telemarketing Sales Training Programme, 1986. *Memberships:* Elected to a two year term on the Board of education/Trinity Lutheran School Lombard II; National Association of Female Executives; The Direct Marketing Association of Chicago; Citizens Utility Board; Women's Republican Club American Society of Professional and Executive Women; Citizen's for a Better Environment. *Hobbies:* Interests; Environmental Issues; Women's Rights in the Workplace; Writing; Painting; Camping; Fishing. *Address:* PO Box 0163, Itasca, IL 60143, USA.

FLUGSRUD Liv Birkeland, b. 5 May 1929, Oslo, Norway. Physician; Deputy Head. m. Sverre Flugsrud, 22 Dec. 1056. 2 sons, 1 daughter. *Education:* Cand med. University of Oslo, 1954. *Appointments:* Deputy Head, Department of Virology, National Institute of Public Health, Oslo, Norway, 1963-. *Publications:* Numerous publications in scientific journals. *Memberships:* Norwegian Association of Medical Women; Norwegian Medical Association; Norwegian Society for Medical Microbiology; Norwegian Society for Infectious Medicine. *Hobbies:* Music; Out-of-door life. *Address:* National Institute of Public Health, Geitmyrsveien 75, 0462 Oslo 4, Norway.

FLYNN Beverly C., b. New Jersey, USA. Professor; University Administrator. m. Patrick Flynn, 30 Aug. 1969, 1 son, 1 daughter. *Education:* BSPHN, University of Michigan, 1959; MS, Boston University, 1963; PhD, University of Wisconsin, 1972. *Appointments:* Public Health Nurse, Washtenaw County Health Department, Ann Arbor, Michigan, 1959-62; Instructor, Public Health Nursing, University of Wisconsin School of Nursing, Madison, 1963-67; Research Associate, Regenstrief Institute for Health Care Delivery, Indianapolis, Indiana, 1970-77; Associate Professor, School of Medicine/School of Nursing, 1970-77, Professor, 1977-, Department of Community Health Nursing Chairperson, 1975-89 and Director, International Programmes, 1975-, Indiana University, Indianapolis, USA. *Publications:* Current Perspectives in Nursing, Vol I, 1977, Vol II, 1980; Articles & chapters include: Demystifying Political Envolvements; Community Health Nursing Education, Research Trends and Recommendations; Research as a Guide to Commnuity Health Nursing Practice. *Memberships:* American Nurses Association; American Public Health Association, Public Health Nursing Section Council 1978-81, Governing Council 1986-88; Association of Graduate Faculty in Community Health, Vice-President 1980-81; Past Secretary, Vice-President, President Elect and President, Indiana Public Health Association, Affiliate Representative to Governing Council 1988-; National Council for International Health. *Honours:* Sigma Theta Tau, 1977; Fellow Commoner, Churchill College, University of Cambridge, England, 1981-82; American Journal of Nursing Company Scholar, 1981-82; Sigma Xi, 1982; Community Health Nurse of the Year, American Nurses Association, Council of Community Health Nurses, 1986; Distinguished Lecturer, Sigma Theta Tau International, 1988; President's Award, Indiana Public Health Association, 1988. *Hobbies:* Travel; Swimming; Waterskiing; Biking. *Address:* Indiana University School of Nursing, Department of Community Health Nursing, 610 Barnhill Drive, Indianapolis, IN 46223, USA.

FLYNN Mary Ellen (Sister), b. 4 Jan. 1899, Tenterfield, Black Swamp, Australia. *Education:* Leaving Certificate. *Appointments:* Social Worker; Organised homes for the elderly and sick. *Publications:* Visits to the Blessed Sacrament; Prayers of Dying. *Honours:* MBE; Justice of the Peace. *Hobby:* Visiting sick people. *Address:* St Basil's Nursing Home, 71 Wilson Street, Wentworth Falls, New South Wales 2782, Australia.

FLYNN Suzanne Kennedy, b. 9 Jan. 1937, New York City, USA. Writer-Producer; Beauty Health & Fashion Workshop Executive. m. Arthur E.P. Flynn, 25 Mar. 1961, divorced 1967, 2 daughters. *Appointments:* Senior Health & Beauty Editor, Seventeen Magazine, New YOrk City, 1966-69, 1973-76, Harper's Bazaar, 1971-73; Associate Editor, Town & Country Magazine, 1969-71; Founder, President, Chief Executive Officer, The Creative Eye, Nantucket, 1976-; Senior Consultant, Revlon Inc., 1976, Click Models, 1980-, Estee Lauder Inc., 1985-. *Publications:* Copy Voice for Princess Marcella Borghese, Revlon, Pierre Balmain Perfume; Columnist Trends, New York Post; Writer, Producer, The Contemporary Woman; Co-author, 17 Book of Beauty and Fashion, 1969; Author, Beauty Begins at Sixty; How to Save Your Hair....A man's Guide, 1985; contributor to numerous journals. *Memberships:* various professional organisations. *Honours:* Recipient, Execellence in Writing Award, Fragrance Foundation, 1967, 1969, 1971, 1978; Fashion Video Award, In Fashion, 1986, 1980. *Address:* The Creative Eye, 12 E 86 St., New York, NY 10028, USA.

FOBES Jacqueline Theresa Mitchell, b. 5 June 1946, Calgary, Albert, Canada. Educational Psychologist; Consultant. m. James Lewis Fobes, 28 Feb. 1970. *Education:* AA, Pasadena City College, California, USA, 1970; BA 1973, MEd 1974, University of Arizona; PhD, Educational Psychology, Claremont Graduate School, 1988. *Appointments:* Private practice as Educational Psychologist, Marriage & Family Therapist & Consultant, 1975; Contracts include: Monterey Peninsula Unified Schools, Pajaro Valley Unified Schools, Monterey County Office of Education, Monterey Rape Crisis Centre, etc, also private clients. *Publications:* Article, Neonatal Development, in journal, Developmental Psychobiology, 1974; Book, A Papago Boy & His Friends, Sahuaro Impressions in Tucson, Arizona, 1975; Honorary Editor, Ostomy Quarterly, 1985. *Memberships:* Past office, American Association of University Women; Past Board, Foundation to Support Monterey Peninsula Unified Schools. *Honours:* Various certificates of appreciation, Monterey Rape Crisis Centre, 1982-86. *Hobbies:* Reading; Gourmet cooking; Walking; Gardening; Restoring antique furniture, Needlepoint. *Address:* 3067 Larkin Road, Pebble Beach, California 93953, USA.

FODOR Mariana (Therese) Duarte, b. 8 Mar. 1938,

New York City, USA. US Army Officer; Educator; Nurse. m. Joseph E. Fodor, 1 Sept. 1972. *Education:* RN, Bellevue School of Nursing, 1958; Basic Officers Training, US Army, 1967; BA, Hunter College, 1972; MA, New York University, 1975; US Army Defense Information School, 1977; Strategic Defense Studies, 1985. *Appointments Include:* In-Service Training Director, Trafalgar Hospital, New York City, 1958-60; Teacher, French, Sciences, Sacred Heart Academy, Puerto Rico, 1961-63; Assistant Principal, Teacher French, St John's Cathedral High School, Puerto Ricco, 1963-64; Owner-Manager, Casa Medici, Arts & Antiques, Puerto Rico, 1964-65; Nursing Supervisor, Hospital for special Surery, New York City, 1966-67; US Army Japan, 1967-69 DOD Schools Japan, 1969-72; Nursing Educator, New Rochelle, 1972-74; Adjunct Lecturer, Spanish Language, Hunter College, 1972-74; Educator, then Bio-Med Co-ordinator, Lehman High School, Bronx, 1974-81; US Army, Active duty, Lieutenant Colonel, 1981-. *Publications:* DOD Health Curriulum; Comuter Technology and Health Careers, New York City Board of Education. *Memberships Include:* Life Member, Association of Military Surgeons; Presidential Task Force, Charter Member; National Security Council Foundation. *Honours Include:* Outstanding Service Award, 77th Army Reserve, 1985. *Address:* Riverside Drive, New York, NY 10025, USA.

FOGARTY Elizabeth Rummans, b. 1 Nov. 1916, Portsmouth, Ohio, USA. Librarian. m. Joseph C. Fogarty, 6 Oct. 1945, 3 daughters. *Education:* BA, Ohio Wesleyan University, 1938; MLib.Sc., University of Illinois, 1939. *Appointments:* Public Library Administrator, Miamisburg, 1940-42; Post Librarian, Camp Atterbury, US Army 1942-45; Organised, Legislative Auditors Library, Capital, Sacto, 1952-53; Organised Library, University of Kentucky, 1966-67; Organised Medical Research Library, US Army Medical Centre, Rxukyui, 1967-70; Medical Librarian, Fort Polk, US Army, 1970-72; Public Services Librarian, McAllen, Texas, 1974-76. *Publications:* Contributions to professional journals. *Memberships Include:* US Daughters of 1812; Daughters of American Colonists; Jamestowne Society; American Library Association; American Association of University Women. *Honours:* Certificates of Merit, US Army Medical Centre, 1970; Phi Beta Kappa; Mortar Board. *Hobbies:* Travel; Methodist Church. *Address:* 405 Vermont, McAllen, TX 78503, USA.

FOGEL Marguerite Martindale Stone, b. 12 Sept. 1912, Graysville, USA. Psychotherapist. m. 28 May 1952, 1 son, 1 daughter. *Education:* BA, Columbia Union College, 1937; MA, 1943, PhD, 1953, University of Maryland; MSSW, Catholic University of America, 1947. *Appointments:* Spanish Teacher, WCTS Canal Zone, Panama, 1929-30; Head, Commerce Dept., OMC, Oshawa, 1937-39; Teacher, 1939-40; Teacher, Arlington Institute, 1941-42, Marjorie Webster Schools Inc., DC, 1943-44; Caseworker, Social Service league, Rockville, 1944-48; Therapist, Arlington Guidance Centre, 1948-50; Administration Board of Education, Mont. County, 1950-52; Psychotherapist, Private Practice, 1950-; Supervisor, Fogel Foundation, 1980-. *Memberships Include:* AAMFT; ASSECT; Diplomate, Marital and Family Therapy; American Board of Family Psychotherapy. *Honours:* President, Middle Atlantic Division, AAMFT, 1970. *Hobbies:* Swimming; Planning Houses. *Address:* 2948 Brandywine St. NW, Washington, DC 20008, USA.

FOGLESONG Susan Lyn (Minges), b. 7 July 1948, Southwest City, Missouri, USA. Office Manager; RGO Group Specialist. m. Marion David Foglesang, 17 June 1972, divorced 1974, 1 son, 1 daughter. *Education:* Kansas City Metropolitan Junior College; Business Administration, Kansas City Business College; Medical Assistance. *Appointments:* Various positions: Simon Johnson, 1968-71; Internal Revenue, 1971; Midwest Orthopaedic Clinic, 1971-72; Kansas City General Hospital, 1973; Lakeside Osteopathic Hospital, 1974-76; Esco Life Consultants, 1977-82; Bankers Life and Casualty, 1982-84; Administrative Assistant, Sales Group Representative, Association Services International, 1985; US Life Insurance, 1985-87; Office Manager, Service Assistance, American United Life Insurance Co, 1987-. *Publications:* Clay, People Finders Magazine; His Happiness Is My Reward; Bimonthly column in People Searching News; Quarterly newsletter, KCAAO; Monthly legislative column, Cub Communicator. *Memberships:* National Association for Female Executives; Kansas City Underwriters; Regional Director, State Representative, Legislative Reporter, Concerned United Birthparents; Editor, Corresponding Secretary, Legislative Director, Liaison Coordinator, KCAAO; Regional Director, Legislative Reporter, AAC; 1st Vice-President, Parent-Teachers Association. *Hobbies:* Writing (non-fictional legislative and birthparent material, children's stories); Quilting; Gardening; Home improvement; Counted cross stitch; Reading; Poetry. *Address:* 7000 Jackson, Kansas City, MO 64132, USA.

FOLEY Alexandra Mary, The Hon. b. 3 Apr. 1960, London, England. Antique Weapons Cataloguer. m. Somerset Carlo De Chair, 25 July 1987, divorced March 1989. *Appointments:* Sotheby's, Los Angeles, California, 1979-81; First Female Arms & Armour Cataloguer at an Auction House, Sotheby's, London, 1981-. *Hobbies:* Shooting; Table Tennis; Cycling; Travel. *Address:* 36 Rosary Gardens, London SW7 4NT, England.

FOLEY Joan Eleanor, b. 31 May 1936, Sydney, Australia. University Professor and Administrator. m. 5 Oct. 1964. 2 sons. *Education:* BA Hons 1957, PhD 1960, University of Sydney. *Appointments:* Defence Research, Medical Laboratories, Downsview, Ontario, 1960-62; Jan. 1962-; Special Lecturer, Assistant Professor, Associate Professor, Professor, Department of Psychology, University of Toronto; Associate Dean, Faculty of Arts and Science, University of Toronto, 1971-74; Principal, Scarborough College, University of Toronto, 1977-84; Vice President and Provost, University of Toronto, 1985-. *Creative Works:* Articles in scientific journals on Learning, Perception and Spatial Cognition. *Memberships:* Fellow, Canadian Psychological Association; Member, Royal Society of Arts. *Honours:* University of Toronto Alumni Faculty Award; City of Scarborough Civic Award of Merit in Education, 1985. *Hobbies:* Printmaking; Tennis; Cross-country Skiing. *Address:* Office of the Vice President and Provost, Simcoe Hall, University of Toronto, Toronto, Ontario, Canada M5S 1A1.

FOLK Sharon Lynn, b. 13 June 1945, Bellefontaine, Ohio, USA. Business executive. *Education:* AA, Liberal Arts, Sacred Heart Junior College, 1965; AB, Business administration and Economics, Belmont Abbey College, 1968; Doctor of Humane Letters, Sacred Heart College, 1985. *Appointments:* Executive Vice-President, National Business Forms, Inc, Greeneville, 1968-73; Secretary and Treasurer 1969-73, Chairperson, Board of Directors and President 1973-79, National Forms Company Inc, Gastonia; Chairperson, Board of Directors and President, National Business Forms, Inc, Greeneville, 1973-; Chairperson, Board of Directors and President, SF Enterprises, Inc, Greeneville, 1987-; Chairperson, Board of Directors and President, Andrew Johnson Golf Club, Inc, Greeneville, 1987-. *Memberships include:* Board of Directors, Andrew Johnson Bank, 1981-; Founding Member, Committee 200, 1981-; International Business Forms Industries, Arlington, 1978-; Associate Member, National Business Forms Association, Alexandria, 1977-; Forms Manufacturers Credit Interchange, 1975-; Board of Directors, Takoma Adventist Hospital, 1987-; Takoma Foundation Board, 1987-; Honorary Business Advisory Committee, Business Partners Inc, 1987-; Major, Civilian Guard, Middlesboro, 1986-; Board of Trustees, Sacred Heart College, 1985-; First Lieutenant, Search & Rescue Pilot, Civil Air Patrol, 1984-; Life member, Republican National Committee, 1981-; Life member, United States Tennis Association, 1981-; The Ninety-Nines, Inc, 1980-; Airplane Owners and Pilots Association, 1977-; Oblate, Order of Saint Benedict, Our Lady Help of Christians Abbey, 1967-. *Hobbies:* Tennis; Private airplane pilot;

Photography; Golf; Reading; Music; Water skiing. *Address:* 1131 Hixon Avenue, Greeneville, TN 37743, USA.

FONDA Jane, b. 21 Dec. 1937, New York, USA. Actress. m. (1) Roger Vadim, 1967, dissolved 1973. (2) Tom Hayden, 1973. 2 children. *Education:* Vassar College. *Creative Works:* Films include: Tall Story, 1960; A Walk on the Wild Side, 1962; Period of Adjustment, 1962; Sunday in New York, 1963; The Love Cage, 1963; La Ronde, 1964; Histoires extraordinaires, 1967; Barbarella, 1968; They Shoot Horses Don't They? 1969; Klute, 1970; Steelyard Blues, 1972; Tout va bien, 1972; A Doll's House, 1973; The Blue Bird, 1975; Fun with Dick and Jane, 1976; Julia, 1977; Coming Home, 1978; California Suite, 1978; The Electric Horseman, 1979; The China Syndrome, 1979; Nine to Five, 1980; On Golden Pond, 1981; Roll-Over, 1981; Agnes of God, 1985; The Morning After, 1986. Television: The Dollmaker (ABC-TV), 1984. *Publications:* Jane Fonda's Workout Book, 1982; Women Coming of Age, 1984; Jane Fonda's New Workout and Weight Loss Program, 1986. *Honours:* Emmy Award; Academy Award for Best Actress, 1972, 1979; Golden Globe Award, 1978. *Address:* Fonda Films, P O Box 491355, Los Angeles, CA 90049, USA.

FONTAINE Joan, b. 22 Oct. 1917, Tokyo, Japan as Joan de Beauvoir de Havilland. Actress. m. (1) Brian Aherne, 1939, divorced 1944. (2) William Dozier, 1946, divorced 1951. (3) Collier Young, 1952, divorced 1961. (4) Alfred Wright, 1964, divorced 1965. *Education:* High School, Los Gatos, California; American School in Japan (Tokoyo); May Runthardt's Drama School. *Career:* Stage debut in Kind Lady with May Rubtson and Call It a Day, 1935; Film debut in No More Ladies. Used the names Joan St John and Joan Burfield. Leading role in Rebecca, 1940. Formed Rampart Productions with William Dozier, 1948. *Creative Works:* Roles include: No More Ladies, 1935; Quality Street, 1937; The Man Who Found Himself; You Can't Beat Love; Music for Madame; A Damsel in Distress; A Million to One, 1938; Maid's Night Out; Blond Cheat; Sky Giant; The Duke of West Point, 1939; Gunga Din; Man of Conquest; The Women; Rebecca, 1940; Suspicion, 1941p; This Above All, 1942; The Constant Nymph, 1943; Jane Eyre; Frenchman's Creek, 1945; The Affairs of Susan; From This Day Forward, 1946; Ivy, 1947; Letter From an Unknown Woman, 1948; The Emperor Waltz; Kiss the Blood Off My Hands; You Gotta Stay Happy; Born to be Bad, 1950; September Affair; Darling, How Could You, 1951; Something to Live For; Ivanhoe; Decameron Nights, 1953; Flight to Tangier; The Bigamist; Casanova's Big Night, 1954; Othello, 1955; Serenade, 1956; Beyond a Reasonable Doubt; Island in the Sun, 1957; Until They Sail; A Certain Smile, 1958; Voyage to the Bottom of the Sea, 1961; Tender is the Night; The Witches (The Devil's Own), 1973; The Users, 1978. Plays: Tonight at 8.30; Tea and Sympathy; Cactus Flower; Private Lives; Dial M for Murder. *Honours:* Best Actress Academy nomination for Rebecca, 1940; Best Actress Academy Award for Suspicion, 1941; Best Actress, New York Film Critics for Suspicion, 1941; Best Actress Academy nomination for The Constant Nymph, 1943; Lion in Winter; Spiders Web; Tonight at 8.30. *Address:* c/o P O Box 222600, Carmel, CA 93922, USA.

FONTAINE Nicole (nee Garnier), b. 16 Jan. 1942, Grinville- Ymauville (Seine-Maritime), France. Deputy to European Parliament. m. 1 daughter. *Education:* Law degree, Paris; State Doctorate in Law; University of Paris; Graduate, Institute of Political Studies, Paris. *Appointments:* Teacher, 1964; Director, Legal Service, 1965-84, Adviser 1970, General Secretariat of Catholic Education in France; Member of Permanent Committee, Member Higher Council of National Education, 1975-81; Member of Economic and Social Council, 1980; Elected Deputy to European Parliament, 1984. *Publications:* Guide juridique de l'enseignement prive associe a l'Etat par contract, 1970, 4th Edition 1986; L'Ecole libre et l'Etat, 1981. *Memberships:* Adviser, Parliamentary Association for Freedom of Education. In European Parliament: Member of Legal Commission,

Commission on Young People, Education, Culture, Sport, Information, Commission on Women's Rights, Europe-Latin American Delegation. *Hobby:* Tennis. *Address:* 13 rue Pierre Nicole, 75005 Paris, France.

FONTANIVE Lynn Marie, b. Detroit, Michigan, USA. Educator; Audiologist; Speech and Language Pathologist. m. Paul Adasek, 8 Nov. 1985. *Education:* BA, Marygrove College, Detroit; MA, Michigan State University, East Lansing; EdS, EdD, 1981, Wayne State University, Detroit, Michigan. *Appointments:* Department Director of Hearing Impaired, Visually Impaired Physically Impaired Department, 1985-; Department Head of Center Programs, 1981-85; Consultant for Hearing Impaired, 1978-81; Educational Audiologist, 1975-78, Oakland Schools, Pontiac, Michigan; Insturctor, Wayne State University, Detroit, Michigan, 1984; Associate Director, Detroit Hearing and Speech Centre, 1973-75; Audiologist, Plymouth Centre for Human Development, Plymouth, Michigan. *Publications:* The American Educational Audiologist: An Exploration of Role and Responsibilities, 1981; The Audiologist in the Educational Setting, (Project Director and Editor), 1977; The Public School Audiologist, with Kitchen D, and Bradshaw R, 1976; The Self Concept and Self Related Attitudes of Normal Hearing Adults Assuming the Role of Hearing Impaired Individuals, with Frankman, Schwimmer and Oyer; Application of the World Intelligibility by Picture Identification (WIPI) Test to a Mentally Retarded Sample, with K Wilson, R McLaughlin, D W Kitchen, C Tait. *Memberships:* President, Metropolitan Detroit Audiological Society, 1985-86; Advisory Board, Michigan School for the Deaf, Flint Michigan, 1984-89; Chairperson, Michigan Supervisors of Hearing Impaired Programmes; Board Member, Michigan Association for Better Hearing and Speech; Board Member, Cranbrook Institute of Science, Bloomfield Hills, Deaf/Blind Advisory Group, 1988; Associate Journal Editor, Michigan Speech and Hearing Association; Vice President, Hearing Impaired Programmes, Michigan Speech and Hearing Association; American Association of University Women. *Honours:* Certificate of Appreciation, American Speech and Hearing Association, 1980; Rehabilitation Services Administration Traineeship; United Foundation Volunteer Award, 1973; Lions Club Speaker, 1975, 1976; Rotary Club Speaker, 1977; Optimist Club Speaker and Volunteer, 1982-. *Hobbies:* Reading; Physical fitness; Skiing; Golf; Travel; Dance; Photography. *Address:* 32705 Chalfonte Drive, Warren, MI 48092, USA.

FOODEN Myra, b. 20 June 1926, New York City, USA. Psychologist. m. Richard Fooden, 16 Apr. 1950, 1 son, 2 daughters. *Education:* BA, Hunter College, 1946; MS, Adelphi University, 1967; PhD, Yeshiva University, 1974. *Appointments:* Associate Professor, St John's University, 1969-71; City University of New York, 1971-75; State University of New York, 1975-81; Long Island University, 1980-. *Publications:* Editor, The Second X and Womens Health; professional articles. *Memberships:* American, Eastern and Nassau City Psychology Associations; American Women in Science; New York Academy of Science. *Honour:* NDEA Fellowship. *Hobby:* Weaving. *Address:* 83 Nassau Road, Great Neck, NY 11021, USA.

FOOKES Janet Evelyn, b. 21 Feb. 1936, England. Member of Parliament. *Education:* BA Honours, Royal Holloway College, London University. *Appointments:* Teacher, 1958-70; Councillor, County Borough of Hastings, 1960-61, 1963-70 (Chairman of Education Committee, 1967-70); Member of Parliament, Conservative, Plymouth, Drake, 1974-, Merton and Morden, 1970-74; Secretary, Conservative Parliamentary Education Committee, 1971-75; Parliamentary Animal Welfare Group, 1974-82; Chairman, Education, Arts and Home Affairs Sub-Committee of the Expenditure Committee, 1975-79; Member, Speaker's Panel of Chairman, 1976-; Unopposed Bills Committee, 1973-75; Services Committee, 1974-76; Select Committee on Home Affairs, 1984-; Chairman, 1976-77, Conservative West

Country Members Committee. *Memberships:* Council Member and Past Chairman, Royal Society for the Prevention of Cruelty to Animals; National Art Collections Fund; Council, SSAFA; Council, Stonham Housing Association, 1980-; Member Commonwealth War Graves Commission, 1987-. *Hobbies:* Swimming; Gymnasium Exercises; Gardening. *Address:* House of Commons, Westminster, London SW1A 0AA, England.

FOOT Sarah Dingle, b. 24 Sept. 1931, Bath, England. Journalist; Author. m. Timothy Nicholas Percival Winter Burbury, 13 May 1961, 1 son, 1 daughter. *Education:* Senior Cambridge, History, Health Science, English Literature, English Language; Priory School, Jamaica, West Indies. *Appointments:* Journalist, London Evening News, 1959-61; Freelance Journalist, Chester, 1968-73; Executive Secretary, Africa Bureau, London, 1973-75; Freelance Journalist and Editor of Cornish Scene Magazine, 1986-88. *Publications:* 7 books relating to West Country subjects including: Rivers of Cornwall; My Grandfather Isaac Foot. *Memberships:* Committee Member: Broadreach House (treatment centre for drug addicts and alcoholics); Durnford Society for the Mentally Handicapped; The Rural Development Commission of Cornwall. *Hobbies include:* Interest in the arts and social problems. *Address:* Ince Barton, Elm Gate, Saltash, Cornwall PL12 4QZ, England.

FORAKER-THOMPSON Jane, b. 23 Oct. 1937, Alhambra, California, USA. Professor. m. (1) 2 sons, 2 daughters, (2) Edwin Watson Stockly, 22 July 1979. *Education:* AB, 1959, MA, 1965, Political Science, University of California, Berkeley; Government, University of New Mexico, 1955-56; Criminal Justice, University of Leiden, Netherlands, summer 1973; PhD, Political Science, Stanford University, 1985. *Appointments:* Criminal Justice Specialist, Bernalillo County Mental Health Center, Albuquerque, New Mexico, 1974-75; Chief Planner, New Mexico State Police, Santa Fe, 1975-78; Project Manager, New Mexico Restitution Project, Criminal Justice Department, State of New Mexico, Santa Fe, 1978-80; President, Analysis, Innovation, Development Inc, Santa Fe, 1980-81; Assistant Professor of Criminal Justice, 1981-86, Associate Professor of Criminal Justice, 1986-, Department of Sociology, Anthropology & Criminal Justice, Boise State University, Boise, Idaho. *Publications include:* Surveys, reports, New Mexico State Police; Alternatives to Prison - A More Rational Approach That Involves Accountability of the Offenders, essay, 1980; Victims and Offenders, Our Rights and Needs As Members of Society, Cause and Effect, essay, 1981; Teaching manuals on Social Justice and Criminal Justice Planning. *Memberships:* Past President, Western Association of Sociology & Anthropology; Academy of Criminal Justice Sciences; American Society of Criminology; American Bar Association, Criminal Justice Section; World Society of Victimology; National Organization of Victim Assistance; American Political Science Association; American Society for Public Administration; International Society of Law Enforcement & Criminal Justice Instructors; Idaho Law Foundation Inc; Foreign Relations Committee of Boise; Various community service bodies. *Honours include:* Woman of the Year, Santa Fe Business & Professional Women, 1981; Research Grant, Boise State University, 1983; Canadian Studies Grant, 1986; BSU Alumni Outstanding Faculty Award, 1987, 1988. *Address:* HC 33, Box 1690, Boise, ID 83706, USA.

FORD Lee Ellen, b. 16 June 1917, Auburn, USA. Attorney at Law. *Education:* Petersburg Junior College; Ohio State University; Ft Wayne Business College. *Publications:* Over 2000 publications. *Memberships:* Business & Professional Women; Sigma Beta; Lutheran Church; DeKalb County Humane Society; Indian Federation of Humane Society. *Honours:* Various awards for work & support of humane rights. *Hobbies:* Writing; Travel; etc. *Address:* 824 E. Seventh St., Auburn, IN 46706, USA.

FORD Linda (Hooton), b. 14 Aug. 1948, Tipton, Oklahoma, USA. Dietician. m. Gary L. Ford, 21 Dec. 1973, 2 daughters. *Education:* AA, 1968; BSc summa cum laude, Institutional Management & Dietetics, 1970; Dietetic internship, administrative & therapeutic, 1971. *Appointments:* Therapeutic, travelling, & managing dietician, ARA Ford Services, 1971-73; Assistant Food Service Director, Spring Branch Schools, 1974-75; Food Service & Nutrition Director, Jackson County Hospital, 1974-77; State Dietetic Assistant Training Programme Instructor, 1975, 1977-79; Food Service & Nutrition Consultant, 1975-87; Public Health Nutritionist, Oklahoma State Health Department, 1986-. *Publications:* Diabetes Mellitus: Proposed Mechanism, literature review, 1971; Dietary Policies & Procedures, manual, 1972; Microbiology in Food Service, employees' course, 1972; Psalm 23, exogetical study, 1986. *Memberships:* American & Oklahoma Dietetic Associations; Donor, American Red Cross; Volunteer, American Cancer Society, American Heart Association; Active member, teacher, Prague Church of Christ. *Honours:* PEO scholarship award, 1968; Alpha Chi national honour society, 1970; Various biographical listings. *Hobbies:* Bible study; Teaching Bible classes; Studying motivational materials. *Address:* PO Box 626, Prague, Oklahoma 74864, USA.

FORD Lisa, b. 12 Nov. 1956, Knoxville, Tennessee, USA. Professional Speaker; Consultant. m. John Emerson, 20 Feb. 1988. *Education:* Alliance, Francaise, Paris, France, 1976; BA, University of Tennessee, 1977. *Appointments:* Energy Education Specialist, Oak Ridge Associated Universities, 1977-78; Training Consultant, Vernine & Assoc, 1978- 83; Ford Associates, 1983-. *Creative works:* Audiotapes: How to Give Exceptional Customer Service; Personal Power. *Memberships:* National Speakers Association; American Society for Training & Development. *Honours:* Careertrack No 1 Speaker, 1986-87; Outstanding Alumni, University of Tennessee, 1987-88. *Hobbies:* Tennis; Travel; Reading. *Address:* 140 Seville Chase, Atlanta, GA 30328, USA.

FORDE Norma Monica, b. 9 Oct. 1927, Barbados, West Indies. Lawyer; University Lecturer. *Education:* Qualifications, Therapy & Radiography, Royal Northern Hospital School of Radiography, London, UK, 1953- 56; LLB 1973, LLM 1976, University of West Indies; Summer course, Academy of International Law, 1976. *Appointments:* Assistant Radiologist, General Hospital, Barbados, 1947-53; Radiographer General, Queen Elizabeth Hospital, 1956-67; Broadcaster, Caribbean Broadcasting Corporation, 1967-73; Lecturer 1973-79, Senior Lecturer 1979-, Head, Teaching Department 1984-86, Faculty of Law, University of West Indies. Also: Chair, National Commission on Status of Women, 1978; Deputy Chair, Public Service Commission, 1977-86; Board, Insurance Corporation of Barbados, until 1986; Member, National Advisory Commission on Education; Member, Commonwealth Caribbean Law Reform Task Force; Elected member, United Nations Committee on Elimination of Discrimination Against Women 1986, International Council of Environmental Law 1988; Numerous other positions, national & international. *Publications:* Articles, legal & social questions, various journals; Research papers, various government bodies. *Memberships:* Soroptimist International; Royal Commonwealth Society. *Honours include:* Educational travel grant, Directorate of Educational & Cultural Affairs, US Information Agency, 1984. *Hobbies:* Collecting antiques; Gardening; Music; Travel; Reading; Research. *Address:* Valley View, St George, Barbados, West Indies.

FOREMAN Arlene Raina, b. 19 Aug. 1945, Detroit, Michigan, USA. Insurance Marketing & Training Consultant. m. George Johnson Black, 23 Sept. 1980. *Education:* MSc., Financial Services, 1980; Chartered Financial Consultant, 1982; Chartered Life Underwriter, 1975. *Appointments:* Assistant to President, Gene Galasso Association, 1965-67; Co-Owner, Manager, Efficient Business Service, 1967-70; Consultant, Manufacturers Life Ins. Co. Toronto, Canada, 1978-80; Agent, Manufacturers Life Ins. Co., Washington, 1971-82; Vice President, Life Underwriter Training Council, 1982-85; Insurance Marketing & Training Consultant,

1985-. *Publications:* Editor: Financial Planning Skills; Multiline Skills; Co-author: Group Insurance; Life Insurance Concepts; Author: Sales Builder; Time Builder; AIDS and the Insurance Industry. *Memberships:* S.W. Florida Life Underwriters Association, President; DC Life Underwriters Association, Director; DC Estate Planning Council. *Honours:* Million Dollar Round Table, 1973-74; National Quality Award, 1973-79; National Sales Achievement Award, 1973-78; Associate of the Year, 1974. *Hobbies:* Golf; Plants. *Address:* 4841 Springline Drive, Fort Myers, FL 33919, USA.

FORER Lois G., b. 22 Mar. 1914, Chicago, Illinois, USA. Retired Judge. m. Morris L. Forer, 30 June 1940, 2 sons, 1 daughter. *Education:* AB with honours, Northwestern University, Evanston, Illinois, 1935; JD, Northwestern University Law School. *Appointments:* US Senate Committee on Education and Labor, 1938-40; US Rural Electrification Administration, 1940-41; Law Clerk, US Judge John Biggs Jr, 3rd Circuit, 1941-46; Deputy Attorney General, Commonwealth of Pennsylvania, 1952-58; Attorney in Charge, Community Legal Services Office for Children, 1966-68; Judge, Court of Common Pleas, Philadelphia, Pennsylvania, 1971-87. *Publications:* Books: No One Will Listen, 1970; Death of the Law, 1975; Criminals and Victims, 1980; Money and Justice, 1984; A Chilling Effect, 1987; Over 100 articles in scholarly journals and general periodicals. *Memberships:* National Board, American Civil Liberties Union; Philadelphia Bar Association; Pennsylvania Bar Association; American Bar Association; Board Member, Seybert Foundation; Board Member, Planned Parenthood of Philadelphia; Board Member, Settlement Music School, Germantown. *Honours:* Ross Essay Prize, American Bar Association, 1953; Hannah Solomon Award, National Council of Jewish Women, 1973; Special Citation for Non-Fiction, Athenaeum of Philadelphia, 1982; Gavel Award for Money and Justice, American Bar Association, 1985; Award of Merit, Northwestern University Alumni, 1986. *Hobbies:* Music; Travel; Archaeology and anthropology.

FOREVILLE Raymonde Germaine, b. 14 Feb. 1904, Montpellier, France. Emeritus Professor; Director of Research. *Education:* University of Montpellier; Practical School of High Studies, Paris-Sorbonne; School of Paleography (Vatican Archives); State Doctor of Letters & Religious Sciences, Paris, 1944. *Appointments:* Taught History, Lycees of Perigueux, 1926-27, Agen, 1927-28, Bordeaux, 1928-32, Montpellier, 1932-38, Paris, 1938-41; Professor, Mediaeval History, Universities of Lille, 1942-45, Rennes, 1945-64, Caen, 1964-74; Director of Research, CNRS, Paris. *Publications:* L'Eglise et la Royaute en Angleterre sous Henri II Plantagenet (1154-89), 1943; Un proces de canonisation a l'aube du XIIIe siecle (1201-1202), 1943; Histoire de Guillaume le Conquerant par Guillaume de Poitiers, 1952; Histoire de l'Eglise du premier concile du Latran a l'avenement d'Innocent III (1123-1198), 1953; Le Jubile de saint Thomas Becket du XIIIe au XVe siecle (1220-1270). Etude et Documents, 1958; Latran I, II, III et Latran IV, 1965; Vie montoise et Rayonnement du Mont Saint-Michel, 1967; Thomas Becket, 1979; Thomas Becket dans la tradition historique et hagiographique, 1979; Gouvernement et vie de l'Eglise au Moyen age, 1981; Les mutations socio-culturelles au tournant des XIe-XIIe siecles, 1984; St Gilbert of Semoringham (1083/89-1189). His Life and Achievement, 1986; The Book of St Gilbert, 1987; Over 100 articles in historical reviews. *Memberships:* Society of Ecclesiastical History of France; International Society of Law; International Society of Canon Law; Society of History and Institutions of Western Countries, France; Soroptimist International, France (Vice-President 1964-66, President, Union of French Clubs, 1966-68, Representative, UNESCO, 1972-78). *Honours:* Officer, Legion of Honour; Commander, Ordre des Palmes Academiques; Officer, National Order of Senegal; Etienne Tempie Prize, City of Montpellier; Bordin Prize, Academie des Inscriptions et Belles Lettres; Budget Prize, Fondation Pouchard. *Hobby:* Archaeology. *Address:* 7 Avenue de Lamballe, 7501 Paris, France.

FORGEY Donna Marie, b. 5 Feb. 1948, Marysville, Kansas, USA. Psychologist; Nurse. *Education:* BSN, Nursing, University of Kansas, 1970; MA, Counselling 1976, PhD, Counselling Psychology 1984, University of Missouri, Kansas City. *Appointments:* Registered Nurse, University of Kansas Medical Center, 1970-73; Psychiatric Nurse, Spofford Home, 1973-74; Nursing Instructor, Johnson County Community College, 1974-75; Nursing Instructor, St Luke's School of Nursing, 1975-80; Private practice, Psychologist, 1983-89; Psychologist, Midwest Diabetes Care Center, 1986; Psychologist, Community Mental Health Center, 1984-86; Faculty (Psychologist), Trinity Lutheran Family Medicine Residency Program, 1986-89. *Publication:* Dissertation: The Effects of Mood and Ability to Fantasize on the Auto-regulation of Skin Temperature, 1984. *Memberships:* American Psychological Association; Missouri Psychological Association; Greater Kansas City Psychological Associationn (Secretary, President); Sigma Theta Tau (Nursing Honorary); University of Kansas Nurses' Alumni; Society of Teachers of Family Medicine. *Honour:* Joslyn Award (Research Grant), University of Missouri, Kansas City Women's Council, 1983. *Hobbies:* Tennis; Skiing; Classical guitar; Art; Photography. *Address:* Trinity Lutheran Family Medicine Residency, 2900 Baltimore Suite 400, Kansas City, Missouri 64108, USA.

FORMAN Joan, b. Louth, Lincolnshire, England. Professional Author. *Appointments:* Educational administration; Training College Bursar; University Conference Organizer; Full-time Writer, 1960's-. *Publications:* Drama General: Portrait of the Late, 1961; Midwinter Journey, 1961; The Accusers, 1961; Ding-Dong-Belle, 1961; Night of the Fox, 1961; The Pilgrim Women, 1962; Maid in Arms, 1960; The Wise Ones, 1968; Three Plays for Girls; The Walled Garden, (prod. Salisbury Arts Company), 1961; A Search for Comets (prod. The Unnamed Society, Manchester), 1958; The King's Knight. Educational Books: See for Yourself (Books 1 and 2), 1967; Galaxy (books 1-4), 1967; Look Through a Diamond, 1971; The Romans (Poetry Anthology), 1975. Drama Educational: The Freedom of the House, 1971; The End of a Dream, 1969; Westward to Canaan, 1972; The Turning Tide, 1971. Juvenile Fiction: The Princess in the Tower, 1973. General Adut (Non-fiction): Haunted East Anglia, 1974; The Haunted South, 1978; The Mask of Time, 1978 (2 TV series by BBC in 1978 and 1980); Haunted Royal Homes, 1987; Royal Hauntings, 1987; The Golden Shore, 1988. *Memberships:* The Society of Authors; Educational Writers' Group; The League of Dramatists; Society for Psychical Research; Eastern Arts Association (as lecturer); East Anglian Writers' Association. *Honour:* Runner-up, Bridie Memorial Competition. *Hobbies:* Drama; Painting; Natural History; History; Country life; Good food and cooking. *Address:* Newton St Faith's, Norwich, Norfolk, NR10 3AD, England.

FORRAI Katalin, b. 25 Sept. 1926, Debrecen, Hungary. Music Teacher; Researcher. m. Laszlo Vikar. 2 sons, 1 daughter. *Education:* Training Diploma, Teachers College. *Career:* Music Teacher; Choir Conductor; 264 Kindergarten Broadcast Programmes, 26 TV appearances; 2 films (dealing with own activity); Elaboration of Music Teaching; Methodology for pre-school age based upon the Kodaly concept; Professor in the Kindergarten Teachers College, 1950-60; Supervisor of Music Education and Postgraduate Courses at the Hungarian Pedagogical Intitute, 1960-68; Research of Early Childhood, 1968-; Broadcast Programmes for Kindergarten regularly, 1952-; Clinician: 27 Universities and Music Schools in Australia, Europe, Canada, Japan, USA, 1966-; Music Director of the Videocasette Series Kodaly Pedagogical Legacy, 1984. *Creative Works:* Music Methodology and Song Material for Kindergarten, 1951-, 1957-, 1974-. European Childrens Songs I and II, 1966; Contributor to various journals: Music Pedagogy for Teacher Training Scholars, 1981; Music Education for Babies, 1986; Music in Preschool (in English), 1988. *Memberships:* Hungarian Union of Composers; Franz Liszt Society; Hungarian Pedagogical Research Society; International Society of Music Education, Board

Member, 1976-86, President, 1988, Founding Chairman of Early Childhood Commission; International Kodaly Society, Vice President, 1979-83. *Honours:* Prize of Master Teaching, 1963; Apaczai Price for Excellent Teaching, 1983; Award for the Radio Broadcast Programmes, 1982; Order of Labour, Golden Medal for Hungarian Music Education in 40 Years, 1986. *Address:* Budapest, Bajcsy 60., H-1054, Hungary.

FORRESTER Helen, b. 6 June 1919, Hoylake, Cheshire, England. Writer. *Publications:* Alien There is None, 1959; The Latchkey Kid, 1971; Twopence to Cross the Mersey, autobiography, 1974; Most Precious Employee, 1976; Minerva's Stepchild, autobiography, 1979; Liverpool Daisy, 1979; Fiction Editor, Anthology 80, 1979; By the Waters of Liverpool, autobiography, 1981; The Suicide Tower, short story, 1981; Three Women of Liverpool, 1984; Lime Street at Two, autobiography, 1985; The Moneylenders of Shahpur, 1987; Yes, Mama, 1988. *Memberships:* Writers' Union of Canada; Society of Authors, London; Canadian Association of Children's Authors, Illustrators and Performers; Authors' Lending & Copyright Society Ltd, London. *Honours:* Hudson's Bay Beaver Award, 1970, 1977; Edmonton Journal Literary Competition, Honourable Mention; City of Edmonton, Honoured for Distinguished Contribution to Literature & to Life of the City; Government of Alberta Achievement Award, 1979; YWCA Woman of the Arts, 1987; Doctor of Literature, University of Liverpool, England, 1988. *Hobbies:* Fan Collecting; Reading. *Address:* c/o The Writers' Union of Canada, 24 Ryerson, Toronto, Ontario, Canada.

FORSBERG, Randall, b. 23 July 1943, Huntsville, USA. Executive Director. 1 daughter. *Education:* BA, English, Barnard College, 1965; MIT, 1975-79. *Appointments:* English Teacher, Baldwin School, Bryn Mawr, 1965-67; Editor, 1968-69, Research Fellow, 1970-74, Stockholm International Peace Research Institute, Sweden; Teaching Assistant: Harvard University, 1978, MIT, 1979; Instructor, Political Science, Boston University, 1978-81; Executive Director, Institute for Defense & Disarmament Studies, 1979-. *Publications:* The Role of Arms Control in US Defense Policy, 1984; two Bulletin articles; Articles in various journals and magazines including: World Policy Journal; Congressional Record; SIPRI Yearbook. *Honours:* Board of Directors: Arms Control Association, Women for a Meaningful Summit, Nicaragua Network, Mershon Centre; Womens Action for Nuclear Disarmament, Advisory Board. *Address:* Institute for Defense and Disarmament Studies, 2001 Beacon St., Brookline, MA 02146, USA.

FORSYTHE Mary McCornack, b. May 1920, Whitehall, Wisconsin, USA. Member of Minnesota House of Representatives. m. Robert A Forsythe, July 1942. 1 son, 4 daughters. *Education:* BMus, St Olaf College, Minnesota. *Appointments:* Political Appointments: Precinct Chairwoman Republican Party; Republican Workshop State Board of Directors; Delegate to Village, County District and State Conventions; Delegate (1976) to the National Republican Convention and member of the National Platform Committee; Chairman of Arrangements Committee for the 1972 Republican 100 Dinner; Campaigner statewide for many candidates for public office; Chairman 1972 Republican Task Force on Health and Welfare; Hennepin-Anoka County Republican Legislative Campaign Committee; Conductor of workshops on the political and electroate process throughout the state of Minnesota. *Memberships include:* Former Public School Music Teacher and Homemaker; Former member: Board of Directors Guthrie Theatre Foundation; Legislative Review Commission, Minnesota Commission on the Economic Status of Women; Minnesota News Council; National Conference of State Legislatures (1973-86); Human Resources Committee Vice Chairman (1977-789); Board of Trustees of Fairview-Riverside Hospital (1980- 86); Member: Fairview Corporate Board, Board of Trustees of Fairview-Southdale Hospital, 1986-; Community Resources Pool of Edina Public Schools; Advisory Task Force on Women Offenders in Corrections; Advisory Board of Life-Planning Services for Older Children; Governor's Residence Council; Bethlehem Lutheran Church, Minneapolis. *Honours:* Distinguished Alumni Award, St Olaf College, 1974; Dr I Michael Kuhn Award, National Hemophilia Foundation, 1978; Outstanding Woman of Edina Rotary Bicentennial Award, 1978. *Address:* 5308 Brookview Avenue, Edina MN 55424, USA.

FORTSON Sanna Gail, b. 8 July 1944, Newton, Mississippi, USA. Freelance Writer. *Education:* University of Southern Mississippi. *Appointments:* Broadcast Journalist, 1973-84; WJDX-WZZQ FM, Jackson, Mississippi; WOKJ-WJMI FM, Jackson; Mississippi News Network, Jackson; WBKH, Hattiesburg, Mississippi; Freelance Writer, 1984-. *Publications:* Contributor of numerous articles in journals, magazines and newspapers. *Memberships:* Professional member, National Writer's Club. *Honours:* Certificate of Merit, National Poetry Society 1962; Poem published in Voice of America, Best Poems of the last 5 years, National Poetry Press, 1965. *Hobbies:* Photography; Conservation; Wildlife. *Address:* 213 Patton Avenue, Hattiesburg, MS 39401, USA.

FOSTER Joyce Geraldine, b. 10 Oct. 1951, Farmville, Virginia, USA. Research Plant Biochemist. *Education:* BS, Chemistry, Mathematics, Education, 1974; MS, Biochemistry & Nutrition, 1976; PhD 1979. *Appointments:* Research associate: Department of Horticulture, University of Wisconsin, Madison, 1979-80; Department of Botany, Washington State University, 1981; Research biochemist, US Department of Agriculture (USDA) Agricultural Research Service, 1982-. *Publications:* Articles & papers: Plant physiology, planta, plant & cell physiology, phytochemistry, applied environmental microbiology, Communications in Soil Science & Plant Analysis, & Journal of Experimental Botany. *Memberships:* American Society of Biological Chemists; American, Scandinavian & Japanese Societies of Plant Physiologists; American Chemical Society; American Society of Agronomy; Crop Science Society of America; Phytochemical Society of North America; Plant Growth Regulator Society of America; Sigma Xi. *Honours:* Numerous awards & recognitions including: USDA special achievement awards; Honour societies; Academic honours. *Hobbies:* Furniture refinishing; Sewing, needlework, handicrafts; Gardening; Sheep production. *Address:* USDA-ARS-ASWCRL, PO Box 867, Airport Road, Beckley, West Virginia 25802, USA.

FOSTER Judith Christine, b. 25 Nov. 1952,. Columbus, Ohio, USA. Attorney at Law. m. Dr Sabah Amin Wali, Dec. 1973. 2 sons. *Education:* BA Linguistics, BSc, Science Penn State University, 1973; JD, Marshall-Wythe School of Law, College of William and Mary, Williamsburg, Virginia, USA, 1979. *Appointments:* Private practice of immigration, nationality and private international law, 1979-. *Publications:* New Amerasian Legislation: Appearance or Substance? 1982; Sanctuary: A People's Primer, with Erich Pratt, 1986. *Memberships:* Fairfax County Bar Association; Virginia State Bar; American Immigration Lawyers Association; Republican Party, state delegate, 1981, 1985. *Honour:* Oustanding Young Women of America, 1984. *Address:* 4021 University Drive, Fairfax, VA 22030, USA.

FOSTER Julia, b. 1944, Lewes, Sussex, England. Actress. *Appointments:* Acted with the Brighton Repertory Company; 2 years with the Worthing, Harrogate and Richmond companies. TV debut as Ann Carson in Emergency Ward 10, 1956. *Creative works:* Films include: Term of Trial; the Loneliness of the Long Distance Runner; The Small World of Sammy Lee; The System; The Bargee; One Way Pendulum; Alfie; Half a Sixpence. Television: A Cosy Little Arrangement; The Planemakers; Love Story; Taxi; Consequences; They Throw It At You; Crime and Punishment; The Image. Stage: No 1 tour of The Country Wife; What the Butler Saw, 1969. *Address:* c/o I.C.M. 388-396 Oxford Street, London W1N 9HE, England.

FOSTER Sarah Rachel Jane, b. 18 July 1950, England. Designer. m. (1) Richard Francis Foster, 31 Oct. 1970, 1 son, 2 daughters, (2) Peter Robert Figgins, 2 stepchildren. *Education:* Studio Simi, Florence, Italy, 1966-67; City and Guilds Art School, London, 1967-68. *Appointments:* China Restorer, 1968-72, 1978-; Tapestry Designer, 1980-88; Freelance Designer, 1980-. *Creative Works:* Tapestry Commissions for private and commercial, National & International Clients. *Hobbies:* Reading; Needlework; Freelance Design. *Address:* Flat 15, 16 Pembridge Square, London W2 4EH, England.

FOSTER Susan K. b. 1 Jan. 1955, Owensboro, Kentucky, USA. Examination Network Co-ordinator. *Education:* BS, Educational Psychology, 1977; Post graduate studies, Experimental Psychology, University of Louisville. *Appointments:* Interpreter for Deaf, 1972-; Teacher (Pre-school), 1973-77; Women's Program Co-Ordinator, 1979-81; Training & Development Specialist, 1982-83; Exam Network Co-ordinator, 1984-; Technical Writer and Advisor for Visual Media Unit, 1984-. *Publications:* Annotated Bibliography, University Attrition Rates, 1977; Contributing Editor, Career Digest, 1985-86; Contributing Co-Editor, GMF Informer, 1983-84. *Memberships:* Kentucky Colonel, Junior Achievement Advisor, 1980; Organization of Business and Professional Women; We Speak your Language; Greenpeace; Amnesty International. *Honours:* Award for Patriotism; Dean's List. *Hobbies:* Photography (Freelance); International travel; Sponsoring International Families; Reading. *Address:* POBox 90031, Long Beach, CA 90809, USA.

FOSTER Wanell B, b. 7 May 1928, Hartford, Kentucky, USA. Oncology Social Worker. 2 sons, 1 daughter. *Education:* AA, University of Kentucky, 1975; MS Social Work, University of Louisville, 1977. *Appointments:* Teacher, Jefferson County Public Schools, Louisville, 1978-79; Social Worker, Department Human Services, Louisville, 1979-80; Social Worker, VA Med Center, Long Beach, 1980-; Adjunct Professor, California State University, Long Beach, 1986-; Consultant at Large, 1981-. *Publication:* Author of article in Health and Social Work Journal, 1981. *Memberships:* National Association Social Workers; National Association Oncology Workers. *Honour:* Named to Honorary Order of Kentucky Colonels. *Hobbies:* World travel; Music; Reading. *Address:* PO Box 90031, Long Beach, CA 90809, USA.

FOULDS Elfrida Vipont, b. 3 July 1902, Manchester, England. Writer. m. 21 Apr. 1926, 4 daughters. *Education:* Mount School, York, 1915-20; Further studies in History and Music. *Publications:* 44 books including Tho Lark on the Wing; Occasional writings. *Memberships:* PEN; Society of Authors; Various offices, Society of Friends (Quakers). *Honours:* Carnegie Medal for The Lark on the Wing, 1950; Honorary Doctorate in Humane Studies, Carlham College, USA. *Hobbies:* Formerly fell-walking and rock-climbing; Music; History; Rural studies. *Address:* Green Garth, Yeeland Conyers, Carnforth, Lancashire, England.

FOUNTAIN Linda Kathleen, b. 30 Apr. 1954, Fowler, Kansas, USA. Health Science Association Executive. m. Andre Fountain. *Education:* BS, Nursing, 1976. *Appointments:* Staff Nurse, Presbyterian Hospital, 1976-79; Manager, Hillcrest Osteopathic Hospital, 1979-80; Staff Nurse, Manager, Oklahoma University Teaching Hospital, 1980-82; New Life Programs, President, 1981-88; Co-ordinator, Lactation Consultant, Infant Car Seat Rental, Nursing Entrepreneurs Ltd., 1988-. *Memberships:* American Nurses Association; International Childbirth Education Association; International Lactation Consultants Association. *Honours:* Mentor of the Year, Oklahoma Metroplex Childbirth Network, 1984. *Hobbies:* Gemology; Travel. *Address:* PO Box 75393, Oklahoma City, OK 73107, USA.

FOURCARD-BULTRON Sharon Lynne Elizabeth, b. 8 Oct. 1953, Lake Charles, Louisiana, USA. Registered Nurse. m. Gilbert C Bultron, 18 June 1983. *Education:* Graduate, BS, 1978, McNeese State University, Lake Charles; Masters Candidate. *Appointments:* Charge Nurse, Medical & Surgical Unit, Lake Charles Memorial Hospital, 1978-80; Staff Nurse, 1980, Charge Nurse & Assistant Head Nurse, 1980-86, Oncological Unit, Methodist Hospital, Houston; Assistant Co-ordinator, Oncology Unit, Memorial City Medical Centre, Houston, 1986-. *Publications:* Research project, A Comparison of Nursing Degrees in Relationship to Performance; co-author, New Employee Orientation Package for the Medical Nursing Service-Hematology and Oncology; Conducted inservice workshops for continuing education for nurses; Video Tape of inservice on Cancer Screening & Early Detection, et. *Memberships:* American & Texas Nurses Association; Past Member, Louisiana Association for Sickle Cell Anaemia; Past Secretary, Board Member, South West Sickle Cell Anaemia Foundation Incorporated; Past Member, Oncology Task Force, Methodist Hospital. *Honours:* Recipient, numerous honours and awards. *Address:* 17530 Garnercrest Drive, Houston, TX 77095, USA.

FOUTZ Shirley Laudig, b. 8 Mar. 1934, Indianapolis, USA. Newspaper Executive. m. William C. Foutz, 17 Aug. 1956, 2 sons, 1 daughter. *Education:* BA, Religion/Education, 1956; MEd., Counsellor Education, 1974; PhD, Human Resource Development, 1987. *Appointments:* Teacher, 1956-58; Newspaper in Education Co-ordinator, Richmond Newspapers Inc., 1974- 80; Director, Educational Services, Richmond Newspapers Inc., 1980-. *Publications:* Contributing Author, Aliteracy: People Who Can Read But Won't, 1983; Conference Proceedings: Lifelong Learning Research Conference, 1988. *Memberships:* American Society for Training & Development; International Reading Association; Virginia State Reading Association; Association for Supervision & Curriculum Development; Adult Association of Adult & Continuing Education. *Honours:* Presenter: Lifelong Learning Research Conference, 1988, Adult Education Research Conference, 1988; many other honours & awards. *Address:* 6200 River Road West, Columbia, VA 23038, USA.

FOWKE Helen Shirley, b. 5 Mar. 1914, Oshawa, Canada. Author; Playwright; Novelist. *Education:* BA, Modern Languages, 1935, Governor-General's Medal, Italian Prize, University of Toronto. *Appointments:* Censorship Dept., World War II, Halifax, Nova Scotia; Teacher, French, Private Girls' School, Halifax; Supply Teacher, Ladies' College. *Publications:* Joe, or A Pair of Corduroy Breeches; Top of the Stove Cook and Bake Book; Radio & TV plays; Short Stories. *Membership:* Nova Scotia Writers' Association. *Honours:* Recipient, various honours & awards. *Hobbies:* Golf; Painting. *Address:* 105-323 Michigan St., Victoria, BC, Canada V8V 1R6.

FOWLER Austine Brown, b. 6 Apr. 1936, DC, USA. Education Supervisor. m. Milton Otis Fowler, 18 June 1959, 1 son. *Education:* BS, Elementary Education, 1960; MA, Education, Early Childhood Education, 1969; Ed.S, Administration & Supervision, 1972. *Appointments:* Teacher, 1960-70; Director, Head Start, 1970-77; Education Specialist, 1977-78; Director, Health Services, 1978-79; Education Specialist, National Head Start Office, 1979-80; Social Science Research Analyst, 1980-82; Management Analyst, 1983-85; Education Supervisor, 1985-. *Memberships:* National Association for the Education of Young Children; National Capital Area, March of Dimes Chairperson; Delta Sigma Theta. *Memberships:* National Science Foundation Fellow, 1967; Rockefeller Foundation Fellow, 1977-78; Pi Lambda Theta, 1971; Phi Delta Kappa, 1972; Distinguished Public Service Awards, 1972, 1973, 1974, 1982. *Hobbies:* Public Service; Reading; Spectator Sports; Crochet. *Address:* 4530 Fort Totten Drive NE, No 412, Washington, DC 20011, USA.

FOWLER Dona Jane Wilson, b. 8 May 1928, Muncie, Indiana, USA. Professor of Biology. m. Dale J. Fowler,

15 May 1948, divorced 15 May 1950, 1 son, 1 daughter. *Education:* BS, 1955, MS, 1962, PhD, 1965, Purdue University. *Appointments:* Registered Nurse, 1950-53; Research Associate, 1954-57, Teaching and Research Assistant, 1960-65, Purdue University; Analytical Chemist, Eli Lilly Co, 1957-60; Assistant Professor, 1965-70, Associate Professor, 1970-78, Professor, 1978-, Western Michigan University, Kalamazoo. *Publications:* Research publications in refereed scientific journals on neurosecretion, light cycles and seasonal physiology; Recent papers: Neurobehavioral Chronobiology; Effects of Monochromatic Lights on Drosophila Development. *Memberships:* American Association for the Advancement of Science; American Society of Zoologists; AIBS; Sigma Xi; American Association of University Professors; American Arachnologists; International Society of Chronobiology; Biometerological Section, Society of Meterology; American Society for Photobiology; American Physical Society; American Society of Chronobiology. *Honours:* Research Grant, Purdue University, 1962; Research Associate, NSF, 1962-65; Faculty Research Fellowships, Western Michigan University, 1967, 1974, 1981, 1985; Research Director, Serotonin Associated Regulative Functions, NSF, 1968-70; Guest Scientist, CNRS, Gif-sur-Yvette, France, 1973; Research Director, Pterins, Indole Amine Metabolism and Photoperiod, 1977-79; Distinguished Visiting Professor, University of Arizona, 1980-81, 1987-88; Visiting Scientist, Argonne National Labs, 1983-87. *Hobbies:* Gardening; Ranching; Development of arid land plants by biotechnology; Needlework; Writing; Master's swimming; Mountain hiking. *Address:* Biology Department, Western Michigan University, Kalamazoo, MI 49008, USA.

FOX Aileen Mary, (Lady), b. 29 July 1907, Kensington, London, England. Archaeologist. m. Sir Cyril Fox, 6 July 1933. 3 sons. *Education:* Downe House School, Newbury; MA, Newnham College, Cambridge, 1926-29. *Appointments:* Lecturer in Archaeology, University College, Cardiff, 1940-45; Senior Lecturer, Exeter University, 1947-72; Auckland University, New Zealand, 1973-74; Auckland Museum, 1974-76. *Publications:* Roman Exeter, 1952; Roman Britain, with Alan Sorrell, 1961; South West England, 1964, 2nd edition, 1973; Prehistoric Maori Fortifications, 1976; Carved Maori burial chests, 1983. *Memberships:* Fellow, Society of Antiquaries, 1947; Honorary Fellow, University College, Cardiff, 1981. *Honours:* Honorary DLitt, Exeter University, 1985. *Hobbies:* Walking; Gardening; Bird-watching. *Address:* 2 The Retreat, Topsham, Exeter, Devon, England.

FOX Eleanor M, b. 18 Jan. 1936, Trenton, New Jersey, USA. Lawyer; Professor of Law. m. Byron E. Fox, 2 sons, 1 daughter. *Education:* BA, Vassar College, 1956; LLB, New York University School of Law, 1961; Bar admissions: New York State Courts, 1961; Southern and Eastern Districts, New York, 1964; US Supreme Court, 1965. *Appointments:* Associate, 1962-70, Partner, 1970-76, Counsel, currently, Simpson Thacher & Bartlett, New York; Director, Root-Tilden Program, 1978-81, Professor of Law, Associate Dean of JD Division, New York University School of Law, currently; Lecturer, Federal Judicial Center; Appointed by President Carter to National Commision for the Review of Antitrust Law and Procedure, 1979. *Publications include:* Corporate Acquisitions and Mergers, 4 vols (with Byron E.Fox), 1968, revised half-yearly; W.L., Esquire 1977; Industrial Concentration and the Market System, 1979, Antitrust Policy in Transition: The Convergence of Law and Economics, (editor with James T.Halverson, contributing author), 1984; A Visit with Whitney North Seymour (editor, contributor), 1984; Antitrust: Cases and Materiels (with Lawrence A Sullivan) 1989; Reign of Reason, 1979; Various articles, especially relating to antitrust matters. *Memberships include:* Trustee, New York University Law Center Foundation; Trustee, Lawyers Committee for Civil Rights Under Law; Fellow, American and New York Bar Foundations; Advisory Board: Bureau of National Affairs Antitrust & Trade Regulation Report, Antitrust Law & Economics Review; Editorial Board: The Antitrust Bulletin, New York Law Journal; Board of Directors, New York University Law Alumni Association; American Law Institute; Various former offices, New York State Bar Association, American Bar Association, Association of the Bar of the City of New York. *Address:* 69 West 89th Street, New York, NY 10024, USA.

FOX Hazel Mary, (Lady), b. 22 Oct. 1928. Director, British Institute of International & Comparative Law. m. Sir Michael Fox, 3 sons. *Education:* MA, 1st Class, Jurisprudence, Somerville College, Oxford, 1949; Called to the Bar, Lincoln's Inn, 1950. *Appointments:* Practised at the Bar, 1950-54; Lecturer, Jurisprudence, Someville College, 1951-58; Lecturer, Council of Legal Education, 1962-76; Fellow, Somerville College, 1976-81; Chairman, London Rent Assessment Panel, 1977-; London Leasehold Valuation Tribunal, 1981-. *Publication:* International Arbitration, with J L Simpson, 1959. *Memberships:* Home Office Departmental Committee on Jury Service, 1963-65; JP London, 1959-77; Chairman, Tower Hamlets Juvenile Court, 1968-76; General Editor, Internaitonal and Comparative Law Quarterly, 1987-. *Address:* c/o British Institute of International & Comparative Law, 17 Russell Square, London WC1B 5DR, England.

FOX Lorraine E., b. 27 Aug. 1941, Staten Island, New York, USA. Consultant. *Education:* BA, 1973; MA, 1976; Certificate in Organisational Development; Doctoral Candidate in Clinical Psychology, currently. *Appointments:* Executive Director, Des Plaines, Illinois, 1975-81; Assistant Professor, Joliet, Illinois, 1981-84; Director of Clinical Services, San Luis Rey, California, 1984-86; Consultant, Professional Growth Facilitators, San Clemente, California, 1986-88. *Publications:* Who Put the Care in Child Care?, 1985; The Child and Youth Care Worker: Marginal Employee or Professional Team Member? (with T. Linton and M. Forster), 1986; Teachers or Taunters: The Dilemma of True Discipline for Direct Care Workers with Children, 1987; The Risks of Dealing with Assaultive Behavior (with P. Smith), 1987; Review of Jesse E Crone's Getting started as a Residential Child Care Worker?, 1985; The Effect of Incest/Rape on Adolescent Sexual Development (videotape); Tapes of lectures and presentations. *Memberships:* National Academy of Child and Youth Care Professionals; American Psychological Association; California Association of Child Care Workers; Past President, Illinois Association of Child Care Workers. *Hobbies:* Reading; Camping; Outdoor activities. *Address:* Post Office Box 5981, San Clemente, CA 92672, USA.

FRADKIN Mindy Sue, b. 3 June 1955, Baltimore, Maryland, USA. Fashion stylist; Costume designer. *Education:* Art Centre College of Design, 1979-80; AA Honours, Fashion Institute of Design and Merchandising, 1983. *Appointments:* Assistant Freelance Stylist, 1983-84; Production Coordinator & Stylist, Cailor-Resnick Studio, 1984; Freelance Fashion Stylist, 1985-. *Publications:* Barry Blackmans Special Effects Book; Television appearance, World of Photography. *Memberships:* National Association of Broadcast Employees & Technicians; Association of Stylist & Coordinators; Stylists & Allied Services Inc. *Honours:* Nominee, Outstanding Young Women of America, 1988; National Deans List, 1983. *Hobbies:* Writing; Reading; Movies; Travelling; Opera; Jazz and classical music; Theatre. *Address:* 313 West 75th St No 4B, New York City, NY 10023, USA.

FRAME Nancy Davis, b. 13 Dec. 1944, Brookings, South Dakota, USA. Lawyer; Government Executive. m. J. Davidson Frame, 28 Mar. 1970, 1 daughter. *Education:* BS, South Dakota State University, 1966; MA, 1968, JD, 1976, Georgetown University. *Appointments:* Research Assistant, The Brookings Institution, 1968-70; Foreign Language Teacher, 1970-73; Attorney, Agency for International Development, 1976-86; Deputy Director, Trade & Development Programme, 1986-. *Memberships:* American & Federal Bar Associations. *Honours:* Fulbright Fellowship, France, 1966-67; NDEA Fellow, 1967; Superior Honor Award, AID, 1984. *Hobbies:* Hiking; Bicycling; Skiing;

Gardening; Reading. *Address:* 5819 Magic Mountain Drive, Rockville, MD 20852, USA.

FRANCE Valerie Edith, b. 29 Oct. 1935, London, England. Headmistress. m. Christopher Walter France, 15 Apr. 1961. 1 son, 1 daughter. *Education:* BA 1958, MA 1978, St Hugh's College, Oxford; Cert Ed, Hughes Hall, Cambridge, 1958-59. *Appointments:* Assistant Teacher, North London Collegiate School, 1959-62; Teacher, Bromley High, 1970-86; Senior Mistress 1982-83, Deputy Headmistress 1983-86, Bromley School GPDST; Headmistress, City of London School for Girls, 1986-. *Memberships:* Fellow, Royal Geographical Society; Girls' Schools' Association. *Hobbies:* Family; Friends; Places; Reading; Walking. *Address:* City of London School for Girls, Barbican, London EC2Y 8BB, England.

FRANCIS Babette Avita, b. 3 Nov. 1930, Lucknow, India. Homemaker; Freelance writer. m. Charles Hugh Francis, 28 Oct. 1953. 4 sons, 4 daughters. *Education:* BSc (Hons) Microbiology & Chemistry, University of Bombay. *Appointments:* Chowgule & Co, Bombay, India, 1950; The Onlooker Magazine, Bombay, 1951; Burmah Shell Oil Co, Bombay, 1952; Imperial War Graves Commission, London, England, 1953; Commonwealth Fertilisers & Chemicals, Melbourne, Australia, 1954-55. *Publications:* Author of Minority Report, Victorian Committee on Equal Opportunity in Schools, 1977; South Africa, Namibia & Sanctions, 1988; Numerous short stories, articles, book reviews and newspaper columns. *Memberships:* Director, Asthma Foundation of Victoria, 1976-85; National & Overseas Coordinator, Endeavour Forum, 1979-88. *Honour:* Phyllis Schlafly Award for Homemaker of Australia, 1987. *Hobbies:* Badminton; Contract bridge; Reading. *Address:* 12 Denham Place, Toorak, Victoria 3142, Australia.

FRANCIS Lorna Owens-Bath, b 30 June 1931, McAllen, Texas, USA. Artist; Teacher. m. 28 Aug. 1952, 2 sons. *Education:* BFA, 1953, MFA 1965, University of Texas, Austin; Graduate Study, Ceramics, Texas Womans University, Denton, 1970-78. *Appointments:* Instructor, Art, University of Texas, Austin, 1965-66; Texas Womans University, Denton, 1966-68; North Texas State University, 1969-76; Our Lady of the Lake University, San Antonio, 1988-. *Publications:* 1 Woman Show, Sumatra, Indonesia, 1958; Group Shows, Texas, 1969-76; Book: Twirly Hurly, Helicopter Rabbit, Illustrated, 1962. *Memberships:* Texas Fine Arts Association; Texas Watercolour Society. *Honours:* Recipient, many honours & awards most recent: 2nd Place, Austin Watercolour Exhibition, 1987; Award, San Antonio Art League, 1987. *Address:* PO Box 530, Castroville, TX 78009, USA.

FRANCK Ardath Amond, b. 5 May 1925, USA. Director. m. Fred Franck, 15 Mar. 1945, 1 son, 1 daughter. *Education:* BS, 1945, MA, 1947, Education, Kent State University; PhD, Case Western Reserve University, 1956. *Appointments:* Speech Therapist, Coventry Schools, 1950-52, 1953-55; Instructor, University of Akron; Consultant, School Psychologist, Summit County Schools, 1955-60; Director, Special Title I, Elyria Schools, 1970-75; Instructor, Western Reserve University, 1958; Consultant, Psych. Wadsworth Schools, 1978-86; Director, Akron Speech & Reading Centre. *Memberships:* OSHA; ASHA; OPA; IRA. *Hobbies:* President, Twirling Unlimited. *Address:* 700 Ghent Road, Akron Oh 44313, USA.

FRANCK Martine, b. 2 Apr. 1938, Antwerp. Belgium. Photographer. *Education:* Madrid University, 1956-57; Ecole du Louvre, Paris, 1958-62. *Appointments:* Agency Vv, 1970; Co-Founder, Agency Viva, 1972; Associate Member, 1980, Member, 1983, Magnum Photos photographic cooperative, Paris, France. *Publications:* Les Luberons, photos (text Yves Berger), 1978; Le Temps de vieillir, 1980; I Grandi Fotografi (texts Vera Feyder and Attilio Colombo), 1982; Des Femmes et le Creation Le Havre, 1983; La B.P.I. en toute liberte, 1986; Portraits. Photographs by Martine Franck (text Yves Bonnefoy),

1988. *Hobbies:* Looking at paintings; Walking; Skiing. *Address:* Magnum Photos, 20 Rue des Grands Augustins, 75006 Paris, France.

FRANCY Faye Ilene, b. 13 Oct. 1956, Steubenville, Ohio, USA. Businesswoman. *Education:* BA, Towson State University; MS, University of Pittsburgh. *Appointments:* Forensic Chemist, Maryland State Police, 1979-81; Teaching Assistant, University of Pittsburgh, 1981-82; Adjunct Professor, Florida Keys Community College, 1984-85; Crime Laboratory Director, 1983-85, Criminalist, 1985-87, Monroe County Sheriff's Department; Associate Instructor, United States Department of State Antiterrorism Assistance Program, 1987-88; Senior Analyst and Program Manager, MiTech, Inc, Washington, 1988-; President, Intersec, Inc, 1988-. *Memberships:* American Academy of Forensic Scientists; American Chemical Society; Association of Analytical Chemists; Southern Association of Forensic Scientists; American Association of Crime Laboratory Directors. *Honours:* Junior Scientist Award, Southwestern High School, 1975; Optimist Scholarship, 1975-79; Maryland Senatorial Scholarship, 1975-79; Scientific Scholarship, Mid-Atlantic Association of Forensic Scientistis (MAAFS) 1982. *Address:* 412 S Beechfield Avenue, Baltimore, Maryland 21229, USA.

FRANK Charlotte K, b. 5 Apr. 1929, New York City, USA. Businesswoman; Teacher. m. Sidney, 3 June 1950, 2 sons, 1 daughter. *Education:* BBA, 1950; MSEd., 1963; Ed.D., 1989. *Appointments:* New York City Board of Education 1963-68, 1970-87; Educational Consultant, Olivetti Corp., of America, 1968-70; Vice President, Educational Publishing, McGraw-Hill Inc., 1988-. *Publications:* Supervised Development of: Minimum Teaching Essentials; Global History: Cultural Diffusion; I Can Learn Language Series; Liberty Enlightening the World. *Memberships:* American Association of School Administrators; Association for Supervision & Curriculum Development; American Educational Research Association. *Honours:* Kappa Delta Pi Distinguished Educational Leadership Award; Woman of the Year Award, National Council of Administrative Women in Education. *Hobbies:* Non-Fiction Reading; Golf; Swimming. *Address:* McGraw-Hill Inc., 1221 Ave. of Americas, New York City, NY 10020, USA.

FRANK Mari J., b. 9 Dec. 1947, Chicago, Illinois, USA. Attorney at Law. m. Joel J. Frank, 7 June 1970 (divorced 1989), 1 son, 1 daughter. *Education:* BS, University of Wisconsin, 1970; MA, Hofstra University, New York, 1973; JD, Honours, Western State University School of Law, California, 1985. *Appointments:* High school teacher, 1970-76; University Instructor, 1980-87; Educational Consultant, 1980-85; Associate Attorney, Harris D. Himes & Associates, 1985-88; Sole Proprietor, Mari J. Frank Esq, 1989-. *Publications:* Author: Cross Cultural Communications: Handbook for Teachers, 1976; Law review article. Editor: What To Do With An Educational Degree Upon Dissolution. *Memberships:* Saddleback Unified Board of Education; Vice President, Auxiliary, Orangewood Home for Abused Children; Orange County Bar Association; Speakers' Bureau; Office, Deva Point Chamber of Commerce. *Honours:* Best Editor, Law Review, 1985; Various American Jurisprudence Awards, 1984; Exchange Club Award, contributions to education, 1986. *Hobbies:* Skiing (water & snow); Gourmet cooking; Tennis; Writing; Aerobics. *Address:* Far West Bank Building, 24591 Del Prado, Suite 201, Dana Point, California 92629, USA.

FRANK Patricia Anne Collier, b. 12 Nov. 1929, Cleveland, Ohio, USA. Florida State Senator. m. Richard Frank, 21 Dec. 1951. 3 daughters. *Education:* BSBS, Hall of Fame and Mortar Board, University of Florida, 1947-51; Georgetown University School of Law, 1951-52. *Appointments:* Business Economist, Department of Justice, Anti-Trust Division, Washington, 1951-53; Member of Staff of Congressman John R Foley, US Capitol, 1959-60; School Board, Hillsborough County,

1972-76; Chairman, 1975-76; Florida House of Representatives, 1976-78; Elected, 1978, Re-elected, 1980-, 1982, 1984-, Florida State Senate. *Memberships include:* Chairman, Economic, Community and Consumer Affairs Committee, Senate Committee; Vice Chairman, Assessment Policy Committee, National Assessment of Educational Progress, 1982-86; Southern Regional Education Board, 1979-82, 1982-86; National Science Foundation Task Group on Governments, National Science Board Commission on Precollege Education in Mathematics, Science and Technology, 1982-84. *Honours Include:* Special Ambassador for the USA to Independence of St Vincent's Island, 1979; Distinguished Service Award, National Kidney Foundation, 1985; Honoured by and Speaker to National Task Force on Organ Transplantation, Dallas, Texas, 1985; Best Public Servant Award, national Association of Industrial and Office Parks, 1985; Florida Phosphate Council Award, 1985; Leadership and Support of Growth Management Legislation Award, Tampa Bay Regional Planning Council, 1985; 1 of 30 women Legislators chosen nationwide to participate in Roundtable discussion on Womens Rights, National Conference of State Legislators, 1985; numerous other state and national civic and professional honours, awards and certificates of merit and appreciation. *Hobbies:* Music; Needlepoint. *Address:* 401 South Albany Avenue, Tampa, FL 33609, USA.

FRANKE Kathi Jane Weber, b. 11 Nov. 1958, West Bend, Wisconsin, USA. Cytotechnologist. m. Mark A Franke, 24 Aug. 1985. *Education:* BSc, Marian College of Fonddulac, 1976-80; Certification, School of Cytotechnology, 1980-81. *Appointments:* Part-time, Columbia Hospital, 1982-84; Part-time, PCL Laboratory, 1983-84; Cytotechnologist, Gundersen Clinic, La Crosse, 1984-. *Memberships:* Marian College Alumni; Secretary, Wisconsin Society of Cytology, 1987-89. *Hobbies:* Travelling; Needlepoint; Music; Horseback riding; Reading; Furthering my education. *Address:* 3335 East Avenue South No 230, La Crosse, Wisconsin 54601, USA.

FRANKLIN Barbara Hackman, b. 19 Mar 1940, Lancaster, Pennsylvania, USA. President; CEO. m. Wallace Barnes. *Education:* BA, with distinction, Pennsylvania State University, 1962; MBA, Graduate School of Business Administration, Harvard University, 1964. *Appointments:* Manager, Office of Environmental Analysis, Singer Company, New York; Assistant Vice President, Corporate Planning Department, then Head, Government Relations Department, Citibank of New York, 1969-71; Established and directed first program to recruit women into senior policy and decision-making positions in Federal Government, based at White House, 1971; One of first Commissioners in newly-created US Consumer Product Safety Commission, 1973. Joined University of Pennsylvania's Wharton School as a Senior Fellow and director of its Public Policy Fellowship Programs, 1979; Appointed to the Advisory Committee for Trade Negotiations, chairing Task Force on Tax Reform, 1982; Current appointments: President and Chief Executive Officer, Franklin Associates, Washington, management consulting firm (founded by Barbara Franklin in 1984); Serves on Board of Directors of seven major American corporations. *Publications:* Frequent contributor to national publications on matters of corporate governance, business and public policy. *Memberships:* Women's Forum, Washington; National Women's Economic Alliance Foundation; National Women's Forum; F Street Club, Washington DC. *Honours:* Award for excellence in management, Simmons College, Boston, Massachusetts; Award for corporate Leadership from Catalyst, a national non-profit organization, New York City; Citation, National Women's Party; The Mother Gerard Phelan Award from Marymount University; 3 awards for her work in child safety while a Commissioner, including one from American Academy of Pediatrics; Penn State's Distinguished Alumni Award. 1972, youngest person to receive the award. *Address:* 2700 Virginia Avenue NW, Suite 506, Washington, DC 20037, USA.

FRANKLIN Ellen, b. 16 July 1952, New York City, USA. Television Network Executive. *Education:* BA, Conrell University, 1974; MA, Sociology, State University at Buffalo, 1976. *Appointments:* Department of Research (marketing, social research, audience analysis) ABC-TV, 1976-79; Programme executive, ABC Department of Current Comedy, 1979-81; Director, ABA Comedy series, responsible for production of all comedy series on prime time, 1981-. *Memberships:* Hollywood Radio & Television Association; International 15 Aerobics; es ing; Judaic uies. *Address:* 1600 Camden Avenue, Los Angeles, CA 90025, USA.

FRANKLIN Grace, b. 25 Oct. 1944, Glasgow, Scotland. Journalist. m. Kenneth Franklin, 6 Dec. 1969, 2 step-daughters. *Education:* National Council for the Training of Journalists, Proficiency Certificate. *Appointments:* Trainee Librarian, Ayr County Library, 1963-64; Junior Reporter, Troon, Prestwick Times, 1964-67; News Reporter, Scottish Daily Mail, 1967-68; News Reporter, Assistant Women's Editor, Glasgow Herald, 1968-73; Women's Writer, Features Writer, Scottish Daily Record, 1973-. *Publications:* Our Times, monthly bulletin for women; Co-Editor, Scottish Plan of Action Produced for United Nations Decade for Women; etc. *Memberships:* National Union of Journalists, Past Chair of Glasgow Branch; NUJ Provident Fund; Chairwoman, Scottish Joint Action Group. *Hobbies:* Womens Rights, Trade Union Rights; Travel; Food; Gardening. *Address:* Seacroft, 13 Titchfield Road, Troon KA10 6AN, Ayrshire, Scotland.

FRANKLIN Kelorah M. b. 15 Jan. 1941, Belize City, Central America. Educator. *Education:* AA, Chaffey College, 1961; BA, California State University, Fullerton, 1963; MEd 1976, MS Counseling, 1986, University of LaVerne. *Appointments:* Teacher, Assistant Principal, 1963-67; Teacher, Reading Coord, 1974; Instructional Advisor, Director, Region C Urban Ethnic Center, 1981; Chapter 1 Program Coordinator, 1983; Dean of Students, 1986; Coordinator/Counselor Gifted Students, 1988-. *Publications:* Thesis: Multi-cultural Education and Children's Learning, 1976; Thesis: The Effect of Group Counseling on Gifted Underachievers, 1986. Play: A Symphony of Brotherhood, 1983. *Memberships:* Phi Beta Kappa; California Teachers Association; National Education Association; CACED Counseling Association. *Honours:* International Relations Club Scholarship, Chaffey Wives School Speech Contest Awards, 1961; Commissioned by Governor, State of California, Member Special Task Force on Juvenile arson and firesetting, 1987; Commissioned by Governor, State of California as Member, Board of Directors, California Afro-American Museum, 1988. *Hobbies:* Public speaking; Creative writing, essays, poetry, plays; Music, instrumental, vocal; Travel; Multi-cultural activities; Art; Photography. *Address:* 5419 Victoria Avenue, Los Angeles, California 90043, USA.

FRANKLIN Linda Campbell, b. 4 Feb. 1941, Memphis, Tennessee, USA. Writer; Lecturer. *Education:* BA, English and Fine Arts, 1962. *Appointments:* Librarian, Brooks Art Museum, Memphis, Tennessee, 1963- 65; Numerous part-time posts and full-time writing, 1965-76; Editor, Writer, Creative Director, Tree Communications Inc, New York City, 1976-83; Full-time Writer, 1983-. *Publications include:* Books: Bibliography of Antiques and Collectibles, 16th Century to 1976, 1978; From Hearth to Cookstove, Encyclopedia of Kitchen Antiques, 1976, 1978; Library Display Ideas, 1980; Old-Fashioned Country Diary, Keepbook Series, annually 1980-; 300 Years of Kitchen Collectibles, 1982, 1984, 1990; Publicity and Display Ideas for Libraries, 1985. *Memberships:* Early American Industries Association; Ephemera Society of America, Editor of monthly newsletter. *Hobbies:* Collecting American folk art; Rock and roll; Animal welfare. *Address:* 2716 Northfield Road, Charlottesville, VA 22901, USA.

FRANKLIN Margaret Lavona Barnum, b. 19 June 1905, Caldwell, Kansas, USA. Former Teacher. m. C Benjamin Franklin, 20 Jan. 1940, deceased 1983. 1

son, 1 daughter. *Education:* University of Northern Iowa, 1923- 25; University of Iowa, 1937-38; BAA, Washburn University, 1952. *Appointments:* Advance Representative and Junior Supervisor, Redpath-Vawter Chautauqua, Summer 1926; Advance Representative, Associated Chautauquas, Summer 1927, 28, 29, 30; Teacher: Public Schools, Union, Iowa, 1925-27, Kearney, Nebraska, 1927-28, Marshalltown, Iowa, 1928-40. *Publications:* Contributor to magazines and newspapers. *Memberships:* 1st Vice President, Topeka Woman's Club, 1952-54; PEO Sisterhood, Chapter CS President, 1956-57; President, Cooperative Board, 1964-65; Chapter Honoree Centennial PEO, 1969; Western Sorosis, President, 1960-61; Minerva Club, 2nd Vice President, 1984-85; Topeka Stamp Club, Stamp Cover Cachet by Club in 1974; Shawnee County Historical Society, Secretary, 1964, 1966, Director, 1963, 1969-75; Topeka Public Library Board of Trustees, Chairman, 1965-67; Daughters of the American Revolution; American Association of University Women (50 years); Nonoso, Washburn University; Stevengraph Collectors Association; Doll Collectors of America; Civic Symphony Board of Directors, 1952-57; Topeka Genealogy Society. *Honours:* Service Citation, Topeka Civic Symphony, 1960; W B Haywood Award, Topeka Civic Theatre, 1967; Outstanding Alpha Delta Pi Mother of Kansas, 1971; Distinguished Service Award, Board of Directors, Topeka Public Library, 1977; Award for Distinguished Service, Board of Friends of the Library, 1980; Topeka Public Library Foundation Board, 1984- . *Address:* 4808 West Hills Drive, Topeka, KS 66606, USA.

FRANKLIN Margaret Ann, b. 5 July 1929, Melbourne, Australia. Sociologist. m. Richard Langdon Franklin, 20 Dec. 1952, 4 sons, 1 foster daughter. *Education:* LLB, Melbourne, 1953; BSocSci, University of New England, 1976. *Appointments:* Housing Officer, Melbourne University, 1951; Columnist, Perth Daily News, 1957-58; Honorary Welfare Officer 1960-65, Divinity Teacher 1965-68, Lucy Creeth Home for Crippled Children; Honorary Welfare Officer, Armidale Association for Aborigines, 1968-71; Representative, Aboriginal Legal Service, New South Wales, 1971; Tutor, casual lecturer 1976-83, honorary research associate 1985-, Departments of Sociology & Continuing Education, University of New England. *Publications:* Books: Black & White Australians, author, 1976; Force of the Feminine, editor, 1986; Opening the Cage, co-editor, 1987; New England Experience, editor, 1988; White Culture Black Health: Social Causes of Aboriginal Illness, co-author, in press. Also book chapters, articles in learned journals, papers, mostly relating to Australian Aboriginals. *Memberships include:* Vice President, past President: Australian Federation of University Women, Australia-China Friendship Society. Member: Black Women's Action; Management Committee, Armidale Women's Centre; Women in Science Network; Australian Medical Anthropologists Association. *Honours:* Awards: Armidale Zonta, & All China Women's Federation, 1986. *Hobbies:* Aboriginal Health; Women & Christianity; Status of Chinese women. Also: Meditation; Gardening; Entertaining; Listening to music. *Address:* 8 Burgess Street, Armidale, New South Wales 2350, Australia.

FRANKLIN Phyllis, b. USA. Executive Director, Modern Language Association. div., 1 son, 1 daughter. *Education:* AB, Vassar College, 1954; MA, 1965, PhD, 1969, University of Miami. *Appointments:* Assistant Professor, Associate Professor of English, University of Miami, 1969-80; Special Assistant (American Council on Education Fellow in Academic Administration) to Dean Ernestine Friedl, Duke University, 1980-81; Director, Association of Departments of English, 1981-85; Director, English Programmes, 1981-85, Executive Director, 1985-, Modern Language Association, New York City; Adjunct Professor of English, New York University, 1987. *Publications:* Show Thyself a Man: A Comparison of Benjamin Franklin and Cotton Mather, 1967; Traditional Literary Study-in the Subjunctive Mood, 1972; Sexual and Gender Harrassment in the Academy: A Guide for Students, Faculty, and Administrators (chief author), 1981; Various articles and

book- chapters; Several reviews. *Memberships:* Women's Caucus for the Modern Languages, 1st Vice-President 1976-78; Commission on Curriculum, National Council of Teachers of English, 1981-85; Modern Language Association, Commission on Status of Women 1980-83, Committee on the Centennial 1980-83; American Council of Learned Societies, Conference of Secretaries Chair 1987-89, Board of Directors 1987-89; Board of Directors, National Humanities Alliance, 1986-88; USSR Academy of Sciences ACLS Commission on the Humanities and Social Sciences, 1987-88. *Honours:* New York State Scholarship, 1950-54; Graduate Fellowship, Danforth Foundation, 1966-68; Summer Stipend, National Endowment for the Humanities, 1971; Florence Howe Award for Feminist Criticism, 1974; May A. Brunson Award for Outstanding Contributions to Women at University of Miami, 1978; Doctor of Humane Letters, George Washington University, 1986. *Address:* Modern Language Association of America, 10 Astor Place, New York, NY 10003, USA.

FRASER Anthea Mary, b. 18 Aug, Blundellsands, Lancashire, England. Author. m. 22 Mar. 1956. 2 daughters. *Education:* Cheltenham Ladies' College. *Publications:* 22 published novels including: Laura Possessed; Whistler's Lane; Breath of Brimstone; Presence of Mind; Island-in-Waiting; The Stone; A Shroud for Delilah; A Necessary End; Pretty Maids All in a Row; Death Speaks Softly; The Nine Bright Shiners; Six Proud Walkers, 1988. *Memberships:* Crime Writers' Association; Society of Women Writers and Journalists. *Hobbies:* Travelling; Reading; Cookery; Theatre; Conservation. *Address:* c/o Laurence Pollinger Ltd, 18 Maddox Street, Mayfair, London W1R 0EU, England.

FRASER Arvonne S, b. USA. Administrator. m. Donald M. Fraser, 6 children (2 deceased) *Education:* BA, Liberal Arts, University of Minnesota. *Appointments:* Staff Assistant, 1963-70, Administrative Assistant, 1970-76, Office of Congressman Donald M. Fraser; Regional Coordinator, Carter-Mondale Committee, 1976; Counsellor, Office of Presidential Personnel, The White House, 1977; Coordinator, Office of Women in Development, US Agency for International Development, Washington DC, 1977-81; Director, Minnesota/Chicago Committees, Peace Petition Drive, Albert Einstein Peace Prize Foundation, Chicago, Illinois, 1981-82; Senior Fellow, Humphrey Institute of Public Affairs, University of Minnesota, Minneapolis, 1982-; Project Director, Women, Public Policy & Development, Co-Director, International Women's Rights Action Watch, also Center on Women & Public Policy, Humphrey Institute. *Publications:* Insiders & Outsiders, in Women in Washington: Advocates for Public Policy, 1983; UN Decade for Women: Documents & Dialogue, 1987. *Memberships:* Women's Equity Action League (Legislative Chair, National President 1972-74, Board, 1970-77, 1981-83, Fund Treasurer 1974-77, Project Director); Board: National Democratic Institute for International Affairs; Women's Economic Development Corporation; National Women's Law Center; Trustee, Overseas Education Fund; Former Board Member, various organisations including: Nameless Sisterhood of Washington; National Leadership Conference on Civil Rights; Minneapolis Board of Public Welfare; Trustee, Macalester College, St Paul, 1982-84. *Honours:* Distinguished Service Award, 1977, Elizabeth Boyer Award, 1984, Women's Equity Action League; Minneapolis Woman of the Year, 1979, Outstanding Achievement Award as Leader of Leaders, 1986, Minneapolis YWCA; Honorary LLD, Macalester College, 1979; Superior Honour Award, US Agency for International Development, 1981. *Address:* 821-7th Street SE, Minneapolis, MN55414, USA.

FRASER Flora Elizabeth, b. 30 Oct. 1958, London, England. Writer. m. Robert Powell-Jones, 29 Mar. 1980. 1 daughter. *Education:* Honours Degree, Literae Humaniores, Wadham College, Oxford, 1977-81. *Publications:* Double Portrait, 1983; Maud: The Diaries of Maud Berkeley, 1985; Beloved Emma: The Life of Emma Lady Hamilton, 1986; The English Gentlewoman,

1987. *Hobbies:* Italy; Greece. *Address:* c/o Curtis Brown, 162-168 Regent Street, London W1, England.

FRASER Flora Marjory (The Lady Saltoun of Abernethy), b. 18 Oct. 1930. Peer of the Realm; Chief of the Name of Fraser. m. Captain Alexander Ramsay of Mar, 6 Oct. 1956. 3 daughters. *Education:* St Mary's, Wantage, 1944-48; Cordon Bleu Diploma, 1950. *Interests:* Music; Reading; Needlework; Gardening; Cooking; Geneology. *Address:* The House of Lords, London SW1, England.

FRASER Kathleen Joy, b. 22 Mar. 1937, Tulsa, Oklahoma, USA. Writer (Poet & Essayist); Professor of Creative Writing. m. (1) Jack Marshall, 1 son. (2) A K Bierman, 30 June 1984. *Education:* BA, English Lit, Occidental College, 1959; PhD, SF State University, 1976. *Appointments:* Editor, Fashion Writer, New York City, 1961-66; Writer/Lecturer, Iowa Writers' Workshop, University of Iowa, 1969-71; Writer-in-Residence, Reed College, 1971-72; Director, The Poetry Center 1972-75, Professor of Creative Writing 1972-, San Francisco State University. *Publications:* Collections of Poetry: Change of Address, 1967; What I Want, 1974; New Shoes, 1978; Something (even human voices), 1984; Notes Preceding Trust, 1988. *Membership:* Founder, American Poetry Archive, 1974. *Honours:* Dylan Thomas Poetry Prize, The New School, NYC, 1964; Young Writers Award, NEA, 1971; National Endowment for the Arts, Fellowship in Poetry, 1978; Guggenheim Fellowship in Poetry, 1981. *Address:* 1936 Leavenworth Street, San Francisco, CA 94133, USA.

FRASER Mary Charteris Love, b. 29 Nov. 1933, Kirkconnel, Scotland. Principal of International School. m. Dr William S Fraser, 28 Dec. 1957. 2 sons, 2 daughters. *Education:* MA 1954, MEd 1956, Edinburgh University, Scotland. *Appointments:* Child Psychologist in various Child Guidance Clinics, 1956-68; Various Teaching Posts, 1968-79; Director, International School, Sifundzani, Swaziland, 1981-. *Publication:* Thesis: Evaluation of an English Test, 1956. *Memberships:* British Psychological Society; President of Association of International Schools in Africa, 1986-87, 1987-88; Executive Board, Association of International Schools in Africa. *Honour:* Dux Laudorum, Sanquhar Academy, Scotland, 1948. *Hobbies:* Choral singing; Church work; Sewing; Tennis. *Address:* P O Box 1301, Mbabane, Swaziland.

FRASER Sheila Janet, b. 5 July 1947, Glasgow, Scotland. Freelance Television Producer. *Education:* Associate, Royal College of Music, 1968; Certificate of Education with Distinction, Gipsy Hill College, 1975. *Appointments include:* Studio Manager (radio), 1968-74; Producer (radio), 1981-85, Assistant Producer (television), 1985-88, British Broadcasting Corporation, London, England; Primary School Teacher, 1975-79; Freelance Stage Manager, Teacher, 1979-81. *Publications:* Numerous songs, stories and addaptations for children's radio and television. *Memberships:* ACTT; PRS. *Hobbies:* Music; Travel. *Address:* 22 Borneo Street, London SW15 1QQ, England.

FRASER Shelagh Mary, b. Purley, Surrey. Actress; Writer. m. Anthony Squire, 15 Dec. 1960. *Education:* Diplomas, Medals, Voice Production, London Royal Academy of Music; Scholarship, Dramatic School. *Creative Works include:* This was a Woman, Comedy Theatre, London, 1944; Numerous theatre work including: The Country Wife; The Menagerie; Peer Gynt; A Delicate Balance by Edward Albee; The Slight Ache, by Pinter; Knuckle, David Hare; Who's Afraid of Virginia Woolf; Sam Sam, Trevor Griffith. TV appearances include: many leading parts in Family at War series; Frankie & Johnny, Old Men at the Zoo, Angus Wilson; Woman of Substance; Over 500 radio plays; Film appearances include: Star Wars; Hope and Glory, etc. *Publications include:* Children's Books: Gypsy's Great Adventure; Princess Tai Lu; Tai Lu Flies Abroad; Tai Lu Talking; Clare Goes Cooking; Captain Johnnie; Come to Supper; Cheese of Old England; Theatre plays: Judith,

1950; Sundown, 1955; Fools of Fortune; Always Afternoon (Garrick Theatre); Time of Departure, (Theatre Royal, Windsor); Also radio and television plays including: Ernest; The Maid's Room; Salt of the Earth. *Memberships:* British Actors Equity; Welsh Corgi League; The Writers Guild; Authors Society. *Honours:* Silver & bronze Medals, Royal Academy of Music. *Hobbies:* Swimming; Sailing; Art; Music. *Address:* 12 Caroline Terrace, London SW1 W8JS, England.

FRASER Sylvia Lois, b. 8 Mar. 1935, Hamilton, Ontario, Canada. Writer; Lecturer; Journalist. Divorced. *Education:* BA, University of Western Ontario, 1957. *Appointments:* Feature Writer, Toronto Star Weekly, 1957-68; Freelance Writer, 1968-; Guest Lecturer, Banff Centre, 1973-79, 1987-89. *Publications:* Novels: Pandora, 1972; The Candy Factory, 1975; A Casual Affair, 1978; The Emperor's Virgin, 1980; Berlin Solstice, 1984; Memoir, 1987, Film Script, 1988, My Father's House. *Membership:* PEN International. *Honours:* Womens Press Club Awards, 1967, 1968; President's Medal, Magazine Journalism, 1968; Canadian Authors' Association Non-Fiction Book Award, My Father's House, 1987. *Address:* c/o Doubleday, (Canada) Ltd., 105 Bond St., Toronto M5B 1Y3, Canada.

FRAZIER Lois Elizabeth, b. 20 June 1920, Spray, North Carolina, USA. Professor of Business Administration. *Education:* BS, 1942, MS, 1948, University of North Carolina, Greensboro; EdD, Indiana University, 1961. *Appointments:* Leaksville High School, 1942-44; Chairman, Department of Business, Brevard College, 1944-46, 1947-52; University of North Carolina, Greensboro, 1946-47, 1952-53; Associate Professor of Business, Flora Macdonald College, 1953-54; Head, Department of Business and Economics, 1954-85, Director, MBA Programme, 1985-, Meredith College, Raleigh, North Carolina. *Publications:* Guide to Transcription (co-author); History of N. C. Business Education Association. *Memberships:* President: Southern Business Education Association; North Carolina Federation of Business & Professional Women's Clubs; Research Triangle Chapter, Administrative Management Society; Treasurer, National Federation of Business & Professional Women's Clubs; Board Member: National Business Education Association; North Carolina Council on Economic Education; President of Brevard College Alumni Association. *Honours:* Outstanding Leadership Award, Southern Business Education Association; Honorary Member and Member of the Year, North Carolina Business Education Association; Wake County Women of the Year; Wake County Academy of Women; Outstanding Alumni Award, Brevard College; Lois E Frazier Scholarship and Member of the Year, Raleigh Business and Professional Women's Club; Outstanding Teachers Award, Meredith College; Laura Harrill Presidential Award for Service to Meredith College; Administrative Management Society Diamond Merit Award for Service; Lois E Frazier Award to Outstanding Senior in Business at Meredith College. *Hobbies:* Travel; Reading; Participation in church and community organisations. *Address:* John E. Weems Graduate School, Meredith College, 3800 Hillsborough Street, Raleigh, NC 27607, USA.

FREDERICK Virginia Fiester, b. 24 Dec. 1916, Rock Island, Illinois, USA. State Legislator. m. (1) C Donnan Fiester, 1 Sept 1937, deceased 1975, 2 sons, 1 daughter. (2) Kenneth J Frederick, 9 Nov. 1978. *Education:* BA, University of Iowa, 1938; Post graduate, Lake Forest College, 1942-43. *Appointments:* Freelance Fashion Designer, Lake Forest, Illinois, 1952-78; President, Mid Am China Exchange, Kenilworth, Illinois, 1978-80; Illinois State Legislator, District 59, 1979-. *Memberships:* LWV (local president 1958-60, State director, 1969-75, Member National comm, 1975); AAUW (local president, 1968-70, State president, 1975-77; state director, 1963-69; member national commns 1967-69); UN Association; Director, Chicago Associaton Commerce and Industry. *Honours:* AAUW, Virginia Fiester Frederick Research Grant, 1988; Delta Kappa

Gamma Outstanding Legislator Award, 1985; Lake Co YWCA Award, Woman of Achievement, 1983; Jane Addams Award, Leadership on Women's Issues, 1981; Lottie Holman O'Neal Award, Outstanding Freshman Award, 1980; Chicago Area Woman of Achievement, 1979 and many others. *Hobbies:* Far East, especially China; Foreign travel; Creative design; Genealogy. *Address:* 1540 Greenleaf Avenue, Lake Forest, IL 60045, USA.

FREDERICKS Lillian Elizabeth, b.23 Jan. 1914, Vienna, Austria. Physician. m. Hans A. Abraham, 10 Mar. 1944, 1 son, 1 daughter. *Education:* MD, 1941; Diplomate, American Board of Anesthesiology, 1954; Diplomate, American Board of Medical Hypnosis, 1976. *Appointments:* Senior Attending Physician, Co-Chairman, Department of Anesthesiology, Albert Einstein Medical Center, Philadelphia, 1964-72; Assistant Professor, Department of Anesthesiology, University of Pennsylvania Hospital, 1972-85. *Publications:* Numerous medical publications. *Memberships:* American Medical Association; American Society of Anesthesiologists; AM; Medical Women's Association; Fellow, ASCH; Fellow, SCEH; American Board of Medical Hypnosis; American Board of Anesthesiology. *Hobby:* Sculpture. *Address:* 3360 South Ocean Boulevard, Apt 3H2, Palm Beach, FL 33480, USA.

FREDRICKSON Sharon Wong, b. 24 Nov. 1956, Cleveland, Ohio, USA. Accountant. m. Brant M. Fredrickson, 19 Mar. 1988, 1 son. *Education:* BS summa cum laude, Accounting, 1978, MBA, International Management, 1987, Case Western Reserve University, Cleveland; Certified Public Accountant, State of Ohio, 1980. *Appointments:* Staff Accountant, Audit Department, 1978-81, Senior Accountant, Special Services Audit, 1981-84, Price Waterhouse; Accounting Research and Planning Analyst, Corporate Control, Standard Oil Company (now part of BP America Inc), 1984-85; Senior Financial Analyst, Research and Development Accounting, 1985-88, Business Analyst, Corporate Control Reporting, 1989-, BP America Inc, Cleveland, Ohio. *Memberships:* Ohio Society of Certified Public Accountants, State Director 1985-86, 1988-89, Cleveland Chapter Secretary 1987-88, Chapter Director 1986-87; American Woman's Society of Certified Public Accountants, Affiliate President 1985-86, Vice-President 1984-85, Secretary 1983-84; American Institute of Certified Public Accountants; National Association of Accountants; Young Professionals of Cleveland, Trustee 1983-85; Inroads Cleveland Inc, Business Advisor to Student Intern at Price Waterhouse 1982-84. *Hobbies:* Travel; Physical fitness; Tai Chi; Reading. *Address:* BP America Inc, 200 Public Square, 37 5255-A, Cleveland, OH 44114, USA.

FREE Helen, b. 20 Feb. 1923, Pittsburgh, USa. Consultant. m. Alfred H. Free, 18 Oct. 1947, 3 sons, 3 daughters. *Education:* BS, College of Wooster, 1944; MA, Central Michigan University, 1978. *Appointments:* Chemist, Miles Laboratories Inc., 1944-78; Manager, Miles Research Products, 1978-82; Chemist Consultant, Miles Ames Division, 1982-; Adjunct Faculty Indiana University, 1977-. *Publications:* Co-author: Urodynamics and Urinalysis in Clinical Lab practice, 1972; Urinalysis in Clinical Lab, 1975; 176 articles in professional journals. *Memberships:* Numerous professional organisations. *Hobbies:* Travel; Tennis. *Address:* Miles Inc, PO Box 70, Elkhart, IN 46515, USA.

FREEDMAN Joyce B., b. 17 Jan. 1945, Brooklyn, New York, USA. University Administrator. m. Stuart J. Freedman, 16 Dec. 1968, 1 son. *Education:* University of Southern California, 1962-65; BA, Psychology, University of California, Los Angeles, 1967; Graduate courses in Education, 1968. *Appointments:* Staff, Youth Services, Area West, Los Angeles Board of Education, Los Angeles, California, 1962-68; Receptionist, 1969-71, Graduate Admissions Secretary, 1971-72, Department of History, University of California, Berkeley; Assistant to Director of Graduate Studies, Department of Statistics, 1972, Office Coordinator, Assistant to

Chairman, Department of Statistics, 1973-75, Director of Admissions, Graduate School, 1975-76, Princeton University, Princeton, New Jersey; Administrator for Contract Services, Maintenance Operations, 1977-78, Assistant to Director, Services and Facilities, 1978-79, Manager, Research Coordination, School of Engineering, 1979-82, Stanford University, Stanford, California; Associate Controller for Restricted Funds, Office of the Comptroller, 1982-86, Assistant Vice-President for Research, Director of Research Administration, Office of Vice-President for Research, 1986-, University of Chicago, Illinois. *Memberships:* Council on Government Relations; NUCRA; Quadrangle Club. *Hobbies:* Cross-country skiing; Tennis. *Address:* 5946 Greenview Road, Lisle, IL 60532, USA.

FREEDMAN Nancy, b. 4 July 1920, Chicago, Illinois, USA. Novelist. m. Benedict Freedman, 29 June 1941. 1 son, 2 daughters. *Education:* Art Institute of Chicago, 1939 and 1940. *Publications:* Novels: (in collaboration with Benedict Freedman), Mrs Mike, 1947; This and No More, 1950; The Spark and the Exodus, 1954; Lootville, 1957; Iresa, 1959; The Apprentice Bastard, 1966. (Under single authorship) Joshua Son of None, 1973; Cyclone of Silence, 1969; The Immortals, 1978; Prima Donna, 1981; Dear Murderess, in progress. *Membership:* Writers Guild of America. *Honours:* Collection of work in Mugar Memorial Library, Boston University; Mrs Mike: Main selection, Literary Guild 1947, Motion picture 1948; Joshua Son of None, Literary Guild selection, 1973; The Immortals, Main selection of Backen Club Success, 1978; Prima Donna Book of the Month selection. *Hobbies:* Theatre; Sung dynasty painting; Classical music; Climbing waterfalls; Snorkelling.

FREEDMAN Wendy Laurel, b. 17 July 1957, Toronto, Canada. Astronomer. m. Barry F. Madore, 23 June 1985, 1 son, 1 daughter. *Education:* BSc, 1979, MSc, 1980, PhD, 1984, University of Toronto. *Appointments:* Carnegie Fellow, 1984-87, Staff Member, 1987-, The Observatories of the Carnegie Institution of Washington, Pasadena, California, USA. *Publications:* Theses: Time Evolution of Disk Galaxies Undergoing Stochastic Self-Propagating Star Formation; The Young Stellar Content of Nearby Resolved Galaxies. *Memberships:* American Astronomical Society; Canadian Astronomical Society; Astronomical Society of the Pacific; Association for Women in Science; Canadian Association for Women in Science. *Honours:* Anelia Earhart Fellowship Award, Zonta International, 1980, 1981. *Hobbies:* Swimming; Playing the piano; Reading. *Address:* The Observatories of the Carnegie Institution of Washington, 813 Santa Barbara Street, Pasadena, CA 91101, USA.

FREEMAN Lelabelle Christine, b. 27 Oct. 1923, Chicago, USA. Physician. m. James Robinson, 22 Aug. 1958, divorced 1972, 1 son, 1 daughter. *Education:* BA, 1944, Spelman College; MD, Howard University, 1949. *Appointments:* Laboratory Technician, 1944-45; Various Paediatric positions, various hospitals, 1951-72; Health Resources, Cleveland, 1975-77; Consultant, Maternity & Infant Care Project, Cleveland, 1983-86; Paediatrician, Cuyahoga County Board of Health; Clinical Instructor, Paediatrics, Case Western Reserve School of Medicine, 1986-. *Publications:* Articles in professional journals including: Illinois Medical Journal; Pediatrics; AMA American Journal of Diseases of Children. *Memberships Include:* AMA Womens Medical Society; Illinois State, Chicago Medical Societies; American Medical Association; New York Academy of Science. *Honours Include:* C.V. Mosby Co. Scholarship Prize, 1949; Distinguished Women in Sciences, Shaw High School, 1985. *Address:* 16306 Aldersyde Drive, Shaker Heights, OH 44120, USA.

FREER Maureen, b. 2 Aug. 1931, Toowoomba, Queensland, Australia. Business Administrator; Author; Famer; Housewife; Mother. m. Gerard Freer, 23 Jan. 1954. 1 son, 5 daughters. *Education:* Arts Degree, University of Queensland, 1954. *Appointments:* Company Director: Superfoods Pty Ltd, 1959-87; Red

Seal Pty Ltd and Freers Pty Ltd, 1961-87; Freer Foods Pty Ltd, 1988-; Coottha Coottha Stud, 1968-; Costwold Station Condamine, 1981-. *Publications:* Author/editor of: Square Poets, 1971; Writers' Guide, 1973-74; The Day We Saw the Marigolds (Stage Play) 1977; A Common Wealth of Words, 1982; Tealeaf Oracles (Poetry), 1982. *Memberships:* First woman president, Fellowship of Australian Writers, 1970-74; First woman member, Warana Festival's Board of Directors, 1977-79; Founding member, Queensland Festival of Arts; Chairman, Warana Literary Arts Festival, 1968-82. *Honours:* Medal of the Order of Australia for services to Australian Literature, 1984; Warana Poetry Prixe, 12967; Poetry Society of Australia, New Poetry prize, 1968; Shell Poetry Prize, 1976; Jean Trundle prize for play, The Day We Saw the Marigolds, 1977; Minister for the Arts Poetry Award, 1987. *Hobbies:* Horseriding; Fishing. *Address:* St Joseph's Forest, 445 Simpsons Road, Bardon 4065, Australia.

FREERICKS Mary, b. 26 Mar. 1935, Tabriz. Writer; Teacher; Puppeteer. m. Charles Knox Freericks, 2 May 1959. 2 sons. *Education:* BA, Beaver College, 1959; Graduate work, Northwester University; MFA, Writing, Columbia University, 1989. *Appointments:* Poetry Teacher, Dodge Foundation, 1986-88; Poet-in-the-Classroom, NJ State Council on the Arts, 1988; Poet Instructor, Nyack Library; Poets and Writers of NY; NY State Council on the Arts, 1987-88. *Publications:* Creative Puppetry in The Classroom, New Plays, 1979; Articles in numerous magazines and journals. *Memberships:* Poets and Writers of NY; Bergen Poets, North Jersey; Children's Book Writers; Puppeteers of America; Story Tellers Guild. *Honours:* Eve of St Agnes Poetry Prize, Negative Capability, 1988; NJ State Council on the Arts, Fellowship in Poetry, 1985; Newark Library Poetry Contest, 1987; Distinguished Achievement Award, Educational Press Assoc of America, 1981; Alex Manoogian Literary Contest, 1979; Poem selected for Cantat 1978, set to music for performance of Ars Musica Chorale, performed and taped. *Hobbies:* Swimming; Dancing; Attending plays in NY; Reading. *Address:* 450 Vera Pl, Paramus, NJ 07652, USA.

FREIBERT Lucy Marie, b. 19 Oct. 1922, Louisville, Kentucky, USA. Professor of English. *Education:* AB, Spalding College, 1957; MA, St Louis University, 1962; PhD, University of Wisconsin, 1970. *Appointments:* Spalding College, 1960-71; Professor of English, University of Louisville, 1971-. *Publication:* Hidden Hands: An Anthology of American Women Writers 1790-1870 edited with Barbara A White. *Memberships:* Modern Language Association; National Women's Studies Association; Melville Society. *Honours:* Distinguished Teaching Award, University of Louisville, 1987; Susan Koppleman Award for Hidden Hands, 1986, from Popular Culture and American Culture Association. *Address:* Department of English, University of Louisville, 315. Bingham Building, Louisville, KY 40292, USA.

FRENCH Dorris Towers Bryan, b. 15 May 1926, Kississimmee, Florida, USA. m. 2 sons. *Education:* BFA, Sophie Newcomb College, 1946; Studied, Sculpture and Art, University of Mexico. *Appointments:* Head, Art, Private School. *Publications:* Editor, Publisher, Paw Prints; Columnist, From the Mayors Desk. *Memberships:* Vice President, Peoples Animal Welfare Society, 1977-; etc. *Address:* 3510 Aransas Street, Corpus Christi, TX 78411, USA.

FRESCH Marie Beth Spiegel, b. 16 Jan. 1957, Norwalk, Ohio, USA. Freelance Court Reporter; Firm owner-operator. m. James Richard Fresch, 5 Aug. 1978. *Education:* AB, Court Reporting, Tiffin University, 1977; Certificate of Completion, Cleveland Academy of Court Reporting, 1979. *Appointments:* Official Court Reporter for Seneca County Common Pleas Court, 1979-80; Freelance Court Reporter, 1980-; Owner/Operator of firm. *Memberships:* National Shorthand Reporters Association; Ohio Shorthand Reporters Association (student promotions & public relations committees, 1986-87); Baron Users Group (computer support);

National Organization for Women/Port Clinton Area NOW Chapter (various offices); American Legion Auxiliary; Kappa Delta Kappa Sorority; Democratic Party; First United Methodist Church; Order of the Eastern Star. *Honour:* Member of the Year, Port Clinton Area NOW Chapter, 1988. *Hobbies:* Reading; Walking; Swimming; Fishing; Target shooting; Women's rights; Gardening. *Address:* 47 Warren Drive, Norwalk, Ohio 44857, USA.

FREUD Jill, b. 22 Apr. 1927, London, England. Actress; Theatre Manager. m. Clement Freud, 4 Sept. 1950, 2 sons, 2 daughters. *Education:* Royal Academy of Dramatic Art, 1945-47; Diploma, Drama, London University, 1947. *Appointments:* Theatre & Radio, TV; Founder, Jill Freud & Company (touring company), 1980-; Southwold Summer Theatre, 1984-. *Memberships:* Executive, Welfare Committees, Actors Charitable Trust. *Hobby:* Riding; Vice President, RDA (Riding for the Disabled Association). *Address:* 22 Wimpole Street, London W1, England.

FREUND Miriam Kottler, b. 17 Feb. 1906, New York City, USA. Teacher. m. (1) Milton Freund, 3 July 1927, deceased 1968, 2 sons, (2) Harry Rosenthal, 1974. *Education:* BA, Hunter College, 1925; MA, New York University, 1927; PhD, 1936. *Appointments:* Teacher, Public High Schools, until 1944. *Publications:* Jewish Merchants in Colonial America, 1936; Jewels for a Crown, 1963; articles in various magazines. *Memberships:* National Board, Hadassah, 1940-; World Zionist Organisation; Co-Chairman, American Zionist Youth Commission, 1944-49; Founding Charter Member, Brandeis Youth Foundation, 1944; National Vice President, Jewish National Fund, 1960-; various other organisations. *Address:* 11 Island Ave., Belle Isle Apt., Miami Beach FL 33139, USA.

FREY Julia Bloch, b. 25 July 1943, Louisville, USA. University Professor of French/Art History. m. Roger G Frey, 27 Dec. 1968, divorced 1976. *Education:* BA, Antioch College, 1966; MA, University of Texas, 1968; MPhil 1970, PhD 1977, Yale University. *Appointments:* Instructor, Brown University, Providence, 1972-73; Chargé de cours, Université de Paris, 1974-75; Lecturer, Yale University, New Haven, 1975-76; Professor of French, Inst Internat. Comparative Law University of San Diego, Paris, 1979-; Associate Professor, University of Colorado, Boulder, 1976-; Guest Professor, Sarah Lawrence College, Bronxville, New York, 1983. *Creative works:* Editor, Gustave Flaubert's La Lutte du Sacerdoce et de L'Empire (1837), 1981; Contributor of articles and monographs to professional publications; chapters to books; Translator: René. *Memberships:* Modern Language Association; Unitarian Church. *Honours:* First Prize, University of Texas Graduate Poetry Award, 1967; Yale University Prize Teaching Fellowship, 1972; Rotary Club International Award, regional finalist, 1977; Faculty Mentor for Alice E Nichols, Jacob Van Ek Award Winner, University of Colorado, 1977; Nominated for CU Teaching Excellence Award, 1978; Faculty Mentor for Gwen Wells, Jacob Van Ek Award Winner, University of Colorado, 1979; Honorable Mention, Rocky Mountain Poetry Society, 1979; Associate, New York University Institute for the Humanities, 1983-84; Honored at dinner given by David Rockefeller for contributors to Museum of Modern Art Exhibition, 1985. *Address:* Department of French & Italian, Campus Box 238, University of Colorado, Boulder, CO 80309, USA.

FRICK Charlotte Ann, Higher Education Administration; Coordinator of Student Information Services. *Education:* BA English Language and Literature, 1975; MA Creative Writing, 1976; MA English Language and Literature, 1985, The City College of the City University of New York; Studying for Master and Doctor of Philosophy at The Graduate School and University Center of the City University of New York; Courses at Exeter College, Oxford University, 1986, 1987 and The University of London, England, 1985. *Appointments:* Promotion Editor, Acting Promotion Manager, Alan R Liss, Inc (Scientific and Scholarly Publications), 1970-73; Public Service and Self-generated Income Committee, Member; Educational Extension Program Planning Committee, Member; Contributing Writer and Assistant Managing Editor of MAI Newsletter; Coordinator of Volunteers; Membership Coordinator, The Museum of the American Indian, 1974-80; Research Assistant, 1980-82; Assistant to the Dean and Associate Dean of Graduate Studies, 1982-84; Assistant to the Associate Provost for Academic Affairs, 1984-85; Coordinator of Enrollment Services, 1985-87, Queens College Adjunct Lecturer, 1987-88; Coordinator of Student Information Services, 1987-; The Graduate School and University center of the City University of New York. *Publications:* Contributions to: The Crimson Crier; The Watchtower; The Graduate School and University Center Computer Center Newsletter; Newsreport. Delivered papers at Plymouth State College; The Graduate School and Center of the City University of New York. *Memberships:* The Frick Collection; The Museum of the American Indian; The Society for Textual Scholarship; The Modern Language Association; The Julliard Association; The National Museum of Women in the Arts, Charter Member; American Federation of Teachers; The One-Hundred Club of the Riverside Shakespeare Company; The GSUC Medieval Study; CUNY Academy for the Humanities and Sciences; Natural Resources Defense Council. *Honours:* Certificate of Achievement, Who's Who Among Professional and Executive Women, 1987; Queen's College Teaching Internship, Academic 1987-88; Fellow, International Biographical Association. *Hobbies:* Drawing; Oil on Canvas. *Address:* 910 Riverside Drive, 5B, New York, NY 10032, USA.

FRIED-CASSORLA Martha, b. 18 Jan. 1950, New York City, New York, USA. Clinical Psychologist. m. Albert Fried-Cassorla, 17 June 1973. 1 son, 1 daughter. *Education:* BA, Music, SUNY, Binghamton, New York, 1971; PhD, Clinical Psychology, Temple University, Philadelphia, 1981. *Appointments:* Private Practice, Philadelphia Medical Institute, 1985-; Chief Psychologist, Cooper Medical Center, Camden, New Jersey, 1981-85. *Memberships:* American Psychological Association; Philadelphia Society of Clinical Psychologists. *Interests:* Child-rearing; Books. *Address:* 21 South 5th St, Suite 640, The Bourse, Philadelphia, PA 19106, USA.

FRIEDLANDER Sherry, b. 16 Nov. 1938, New Orleans, Louisiana, USA. Publisher. m. 4 June 1983. *Education:* University of Cincinnati, 1958; University of Miami, Oyford, 1960. *Appointments:* CF Communication, 1969; Lauderdale Publishing, Fort Lauderdale, Florida, 1978-. *Publications:* Developed magazines: Business in Broward; Business in Palm Beach; Prism magazine; Storage magazine. *Memberships:* Sales and Marketing Executives International (Executive Vice-President, 1979); Women in Communication; National Association of Women Business Owners. *Hobbies:* Tennis; Books; Photography; Travel. *Address:* Lauderdale Publishing, PO Box 7375, Fort Lauderdale, FL 33338, USA.

FRIEDMAN Dorothy, b. 3 Oct. 1921, New York, USA. Freelance Writer. m. 23 Aug. 1938, 2 sons, 1 daughter. *Education:* Art Scholarship, 1956; AA, Van Nuys Junior College, 1968; Northridge State College, 1970. *Publications:* Several paintings exhibited in Brooklyn Museum, Museum in Vienna, others in New York; etc. *Honours:* Readings on Monitor Radio; Honoroulbe Mention, Writers Digest, 1986. *Hobbies:* Acting; Dancing; Hiking. *Address:* 1825 N. Edgemont St., No 1, Los Angeles, CA 90027, USA.

FRIEDMAN Janet T., b. 21 Aug. 1957, Houston, Texas, USA. Mortgage Company & Consulting Specialist. *Education:* BS magna cum laude, Elementary Education, University of Houston, 1978; Licences: Texas Real Estate Broker, Certified Teacher for Texas, Airline Sales Agent. *Appointments include:* Sales consultant, real estate, & sales representative, Continental Airlines, 1978; Real estate entrepreneur, 1982; Senior Residential Loan Originator, Richard Gill Company/Gill Savings & Loan, 1983; Production Manager,

Development Mortgage Group Inc, 1984; President, Friedman Financial Services Inc, 1985-. *Publications:* Book, Safecracking Mortgage Secrets; Nationally syndicated column, Dear Ms Mortgage; Contributing writer, various publications; Contributing Editor, Uptown Express. *Memberships include:* Offices, Houston Board of Realtors; Greater Home Builders Association, Houston; Houston Association of Professional Mortgage Women; Houston Area Business Women's Exchange Group; Forum Club of Houston; American Business Women. *Honours:* Founder, Chair, Houston Proud's CARE Seminars (Creating Alternatives in Real Estate); Houston Proud's Chair, Continuing Education Committee; Nominee, Houston Woman on the Move, 1986, 1987; Biographical listings; Honour societies. *Address:* 8300 Bissonnet, Houston, Texas 77074, USA.

FRIEDMAN Jo-Ann, b. 14 Mar. 1946, Brooklyn, New York, USA. President, J. Friedman Communications. m. Michael Friedman, 31 May 1970, divorced 1973. *Education:* BS, Brooklyn College, 1967; MS, University of Michigan, 1968; CCC, Speech Pathology. *Appointments:* Chief of Speech Pathology, Albert Einstein College Hospital, Bronx, New York, 1968-71; Account Supervisor, Medcom, New York City, 1972-75; President, Health Marketing Systems, New York City, 1975-86; President, J.Friedman Communications, New York City, 1986-. *Publications:* Home Health Care, 1986; Articles: The Omni-marketing Approach, 1980, Reprint, 1982; Home Care and Telephony, 1983; Getting Well at Home, 1986; Guiding Patients Through the Labyrinth of Home Health Care Services, 1986; Home Health Care News, Bottom Line Personal, 1986; Home Health Care; Choice, Not Chance, 1987. *Memberships:* National Spokesperson, Director, American Women's Economic Development Corporation; Advisor, Community Health Accreditation Programme; Clinical Associate, Columbia University; Chairman, Codanceco. *Honours:* Grant, NIH Neurological and Sensory Disease, Ann Arbor, Michigan, 1968. *Hobbies:* Dance; Swimming; Tennis. *Address:* PO Box 6729, Grand Central Station, New York, NY 10017, USA.

FRIEDMAN, Rosemary, b. 5 Feb. 1929, London, England. Writer; Reviewer. m. Dennis Friedman, 2 Feb. 1949, 4 daughters. *Education:* Queens College, Harley St., 1942-47; University College, London, 1947-48. *Publications:* Aristide, 1987; Aristide in Paris, 1987; To Live in Peace, 1987; A Second Wife, 1986; Rose of Jericho, 1984; A Loving Mistress, 1983; Proofs of Affection, 1982; The Long Hot Summer, 1980; The Life Situation, 1977; (As Robert Tibber) Practice Makes Perfect, 1969; The General Practice, 1967; The Commonplace Day, 1964; The Fraternity, 1963, Patients of a Saint, 1961; We All Fall Down, 1960; Love on My List, 1959; No White Coat, 1957. *Memberships:* Fellow, English PEN; Writers Guild; Society of Authors; Royal Society of Literature. *Hobbies:* Walking; Reading. *Address:* 2 St Katharine's Precinct, Regents Park, London NW1 4HH, England.

FRIERMOOD Elisabeth Hamilton, b. 30 Dec. 1903, Marion, Indiana, USA. Writer. m. H T Friermood, 26 June 1928. 1 daughter. *Education:* Northwestern University, 1923-25; University of Wisconsin (5 summers) 1934-39. *Appointments:* Children's Librarian, Marion, Indiana, 1921-28; Children's Librarian, Dayton, Ohio, 1930-42. *Publications:* The Wabash Knows the Secret, 1951; Geneva Summer, 1952; Hoosier Heritage, 1954; Candle in the Sun, 1955; That Jones Girl, 1956; Head High, Ellen Brody, 1958; Jo Allen's Predicament, 1979; Promises in the Attic, 1960; Luck of Daphne Tolliver, 1961; Ballad of Calamity Creek, 1962; The Wild Donahues, 1963; Whispering Willows, 1964; Doc Dudley's Daughter, 1965; Molly's Double Rainbow, 1966; Focus the Bright Land, 1967; Circus Sequins, 1968; Peppers' Paradise, 1969; One of Fred's Girls, 1970; (Autobiography) Frier and Elisabeth-Sportsman & Storyteller, 1979. *Honours:* Indiana University Writers' Award for distinguished work in Juvenile Literature, 1959; The Ohioana Award in Juvenile Literature, 1968; 6 books selected by Junior Literary Guild; 3 books translated and published in Italy, Sweden and Germany; 1 book published in England. *Hobby:* Rewriting 3-act plays to be performed by mature people in our retirement residence. *Address:* 3030 Park Avenue-2-W-16, Bridgeport, Connecticut 06604, USA.

FRIERSON Lorraine Hess McKnight, b. 4 Apr. 1928, Tulsa, Oklahoma, USA. Interior Designer. m. Roy Elwood Frierson, 20 Nov. 1953. 1 son, 3 daughters. *Education:* University of Tulsa, 1945; University of Oklahoma, 1945. *Appointments:* Interior Designer, Ethan Allen Furniture Store, Dallas Texas, 1975-84; Self employed Interior Designer, 1984-. *Memberships:* United Daughters of the Confederacy; Pres, Pro-Seeders Garden Club, Tulsa; President, Town North Antique Study Club, Dallas; Professional Interior Design Society; Pres, Friends of the Library, Kaufman; Kaufman County Library, Texas; Member of the First Families of the Twin Territories, Oklahoma. *Hobbies:* Antiques; Reading; Bridge; Sewing; Genealogy; History. *Address:* P O Box 636, Kaufman, Texas 75142, USA.

FRIMML Jaymee Jo, b. 18 Oct. 1949, Watertown, South Dakota, USA. Chiropractic Physician. m. Steven James Frimml, 1 July 1984, 1 son. *Education:* AA, Nursing, Southern College, 1970; Doctor of Chiropractic, Palmer College of Chiropractic, 1985. *Appointments:* Staff Nurse, Madison Hospital, 1970-71; House Supervisor, Wilson N Jones Hospital, Sherman, 1972-74; Obstetrics, Reynolds Army Hospital, Ft. Sill, 1974; Neonatel Nurse Specialist, Lansing General Hospital, 1974-78; Clinical Nurse Leader, Pulmonary Nurse, Tucson Medical Centre, 1978-82; Doctor of Chiropractic, Chiropractic Center, 1986-. *Publications:* Biweekly Health Articles, Idaho Press Tribune; Director, better Living Committee, Caldwell Seventh Day Adventist. *Memberships:* International, American & Idaho Chiropractic Physicians; Sigma Phi Chi; etc. *Honours:* Women Helping Women Award, Soroptomist International, 1988; etc. *Hobbies:* Backpacking; Music; Stamps; Physical Fitness. *Address:* Chiropractic Center, 228 Holly, Nampa, ID 83651, USA.

FRISCHAUF Elisabeth Claire, b. 2 Jan. 1947, New York City, USA. Doctor. m. Edward J. Bridge, 17 Feb. 1979, 1 son, 1 daughter. *Education:* BS, cum laude, City College of New York, 1967; MA, New York Univerity, 1970; MD, New York Medical College, 1975; Certified American Board Neurology & Psychiatry, 1980. *Appointments:* Head, Pedeatric Consultation-Liaison Service, Bronx Municipal Hospital, 1982-83; Director, Research, The Studio Elementary School, 1988; Consultant, King's Harbor Cure Center, 1988-. *Publication:* Poetry book in progress. *Memberships:* American Psychiatric Association; American Academy for Advancement of Science; American Academy of Child & Adolescent Psychiatry; New York Council for Children & Adolescents. *Honour:* Phi Beta Kappa, 1966. *Hobbies:* Citizen Street Tree Pruner; Gardening; Skiing. *Address:* 565 West End Avenue, No 20A, New York, NY 10024, USA.

FROST Arline Ross Moodie, b. 17 Apr. 1909, Superior, Wisconsin, USA. Retired Architect & Architectural Historian; Modèl Maker; Miniaturist. m. Hampson Lockwood Frost, 10 Feb. 1948, deceased 1978, 1 son, 1 daughter. *Education:* BA Architecture, magna cum laude, University of Minnesota, 1931; Extensive graduate study, various universities. Registered Architect: Illinois 1939, Hawaii, 1st woman 1945. *Appointments include:* Furniture designer, draughtsman, head draughtsman, various firms, 1930-40; Own practice, architecture, Winnetka, Illinois, 1940-42; Professional architect, various cities 1942-44, Honolulu, Hawaii 1944-46, National USO Building Staff; International YMCA Building Bureau, & self-employed, 1946-51; Owner-operator with husband, Ke Aka Studios, Honolulu, arts & crafts 1946-55, figurines 1962- ; Assistant to Building Superintendant, City & County of Honolulu, 1955; Partner, Frost & Frost Architects, 1956-78; Self-employed 1978-. *Creative works include:* Numerous & varied building projects; Reports, historical Hawaii; Restoration, conservation, historical buildings. *Memberships include:* Past/present

offices, memberships, local & national architectural & historical associations. *Honours:* Phi Beta Kappa, Mortar Board, Tau Sigma Delta, 1930; Honorary member, Hawaiian Mission Children's Association research & architectural work, Mission Houses Museum, 1970; Award historical report, local chapter, American Institute of Architects, 1982; Award from Historic Hawaii Foundation for the Historical Report, co-authored with husband, on the Ali'iolani Hale, Honolulu . *Hobbies:* Books; Historical architecture; Architectural models; Miniatures, including Hawaiian quilts, some exhibited locally & nationally; Cooking. *Address:* 3715 Crater Road, Honolulu, Hawaii 96816, USA.

FROST Elizabeth Ann McArthur, b. 29 Oct. 1938, Glasgow, Scotland. Physician. m. Wallace Capobianco, 4 Sept. 1965, 4 sons. *Education:* MB ChB, University of Glasgow, 1961; Diplomate, Royal College of Obstetricians and Gynecologists, 1963; Diplomate, American Board of Anesthetists, 1967; Licensed MD, New York State. *Appointments:* Assistant Professor, 1967, Associate Professor, 1974, Professor, 1980-, Albert Einstein College of Medicine, New York City, New York, USA. *Publications:* Textbooks: Recovery Room Care; Clinical Anesthesia in Neurosurgery; History of Anesthesia; Preanesthetic Assessment. *Memberships:* Association of University Anesthetists; American Society of Anesthetists; President, Anesthesia History Association; International Anesthesia Research Society; American Association of Neurological Surgeons. *Hobbies:* Tennis; Books; Antiques. *Address:* 9 Heathcote Road, Scarsdale, NY 10583, USA.

FROULA Barbara Sue, b. 30 Nov. 1955, Hot Spring, Arkansas, USA. Artist; Art Publisher. m. Timothy W. Adams, 3 Sept. 1983. *Education:* BArch, Auburn University, 1978; Certificate, Royal Danish Academy of Fine Arts, Copenhagen, 1977. *Appointments:* Architect, Baer & Hickman, Denver, Colorado, 1979-80; Administrator, State Buildings Division, 1980-81; Architect, SLP Inc, 1981-82; Instructor, Auburn University 1978-79, University of Colorado (Boulder) 1982. *Creative works include:* Book cover illustrations: Denver; City Beautiful; Visit to Capitol Hill; Afternoon in the City; Afternoon in Boulder; Landmarks in Boulder; The Mayan; San Francisco; Vail; Evolving Mountain Landscape; Visit to Victorian Highlands; Book illustrations, Undiscovered Denver Dining. *Memberships include:* American Institute of Architects; Colorado Lawyers for Arts; Foothills Art Centre; Denver Art Museum; Association for Preservation Technology; Friends of Mayan Temple. *Honours:* Award, Historic Denver Inc, 1985; Juror's Award, AIA Art by Architects, 1982; Student Medal, AIA, 1979; 1st place, Symphony of Art, 1983; Poster Composite Award, Colorado Lawyers for Arts, 1983; Scholar, Rotary International Foundation, 1976. *Hobbies:* Travel; Skiing; Hiking; Photography. *Address:* 108 West Byers Place no. 208, Denver, Colorado 80223, USA.

FROWEN Irina, b. 17 Aug. 1915, Moscow, USSR. Writer; Lecturer. m. Stephen Francis Frowen, 21 Mar. 1949, 1 son, 1 daughter. *Education:* BA, 1st Class Honours, University College, London, 1941. *Appointments:* Assistant Lecturer, University of Durham, 1941-43; Lecturer, University of Leeds, 1943-55; Lecturer, University College, London, 1960-80. *Publications:* Contributions to leading journals on Goethe & Aristotle, Nietzsche, Rilke and Lou Andreas-Salomé. *Memberships:* Association of University Teachers of German; Hölderlin Society; Rilke Society (committe member). *Honours:* Establishment of Irina Frowen Memorial Fund, at University College, London. *Hobbies:* Reading; Theatre; Cinema; Travel; Friendships & Human Communication. *Address:* 40 Gurney Drive, London N2 0DE, England.

FRY Dolores M, b. 6 Feb. 1934, Chicago, Illinois, USA. President, Dial-A-Grandparent Inc; Ultimate Home Care and Dial-A-Meal Inc. m. Robert B Fry, 4 July 1975. 3 sons, 2 daughters. *Education:* Business Degree, Elmhurst College, Elmhurst, Illinois, 1973. *Appointments:* Accountant, Illinois Bell, 1952-60;

Accountant, White Motors, 1973-76; Accountant, Central Dupage Hospital, 1976-80; Accountant, D & B Management Real Estate, 1980-84; Owner/President of: Dial-A-Grandparent, 1982-89; Ultimate Home Care, 1986-89; Dial-A-Meal, 1987-89. *Memberships:* Bay Area Continuity of Care Association; Pinellas County Better Living for Seniors, Co-Chairman; Member, Tampa Bay Regional Planning Council. *Hobbies:* Art; Fishing. *Address:* 240 Windward Passage No 1203, Clearwater, FL 34630, USA.

FRY Joanna B. Wiedeman, b. Junction City, USA. Educational Consultant; Clinical Hypnotherapist; Lecturer. m. S. Edwin Fry, 2 sons, 1 daughter. *Education:* BA, University of Laverne, 1979; MA, 1985; PhD, AIH, 1989. *Appointments:* Teacher, Fontana Unified School District, 1985-. *Publications:* Mythology: Paradigm for Creating a Writing Environment; Learning Achievement through NLP; An Electric Approach to the Teaching of Reading; Uses of Baroque Music to Stimulating Writing; Education & Hypnosis. *Memberships:* Pi Gamma Mu; California Teachers Association; National Council Teachers of English; International Reading Association; American Board of Hypnotherapy; NEA; Mensa. *Honours:* Fellowship, Inland Area Writing Project, University of California, 1987. *Hobbies:* World Travel; Writing; Seminars; Swimming; Reading. *Address:* 124 East F Street, Suite 1, Ontario, CA 91764, USA.

FRYE Della Mae, b. 16 Feb. 1926, Roanoke, Virginia, USA. Portrait Artist; Fine Arts Painter. m. James Frederick Frye, 1 Nov. 1944, 2 sons, 1 daughter. *Education:* Hope College, 1968; Grand Valley State University, 1969-71. *Appointments:* Assistant Medical Records Librarian, Baptist Hospital, Little Rock, 1944; Stenographer, University of Missouri, 1945; Receptionist-Secretary, Stephens College, Columbia, 1945-47; Art Teacher, Jenison Chrisian School, 1965-67; Portrait Artist, 1965-; Realtor, 1978-80; Diversified Financing, 1978-82. *Publications:* Paintings in collections throughout USA & Europe; Poetry, The Caterpillar in John Frost, 1982; Poetry in local newspapers etc. *Memberships:* President, Mother's Club; Treasure, Band Boosters; Song Authors Guild; Charter Member, NAUR; Kalamazoo Artists. *Honours:* Recipient, various honours and awards. *Hobbies:* Swimming; Walking; Reading; Composing Poems; Hymn Writing, etc. *Address:* 7677 Steele Avenue, Jenison, MI 49428, USA.

FRYM Janet Carolyn, b. 30 Oct. 1946, San Francisco, California, USA. Sole owner, H&I Water Systems; Distributor. *Education:* Sonoma State College, 1964-65; Healds Business College, 1965. *Appointments:* Entered retail travel field, 1964; Sole Owner, Small World Travel, Mill Valley, California, 1970-76; Commercial Manager, Traveltime Inc, Laguna Hills, California, 19780-83; General Manager, Bay Travel, Newport Beach, California, 1983-84; Southern Region Sales Manager, Automated Accounting, Travel Industry Systems, Woodland Hills, California, 1984-85; Finance Executive, Snider Organization, Sacramento; Sole Owner, H&I Water Systems, currently; Distributor, NSA (water filtration systems), Houston, Texas, currently. *Creative works:* Designed 4 restaurants; Writer of lyrics. *Memberships include:* International Platform Association; Life Fellow, International Biographical Research Association. *Honours:* Recipient of several honours and awards including: Nominated, Board of Governors, American Biographical Research Assoc. *Hobbies:* Music; Gourmet cooking; Travel; Investments. *Address:* c/o The Griffins, 250 Kachina Drive, Sedona, AZ 86336, USA.

FUENNING Esther Renate, b. 10 July 1912, Florence, Missouri, USA. Teacher. *Education:* BS, University of Nebraska; MA, Columbia University, 1952; Doctoral programme, University of Illinois. *Appointments include:* Dean of Women, Carthage College, Illinois 1949-50, Southern State Teachers College, Springfield, South Dakota 1961-63; Assistant Social Director, Illinois Union University, 1955-61; Assistant Director Student Activities, Illinois Teachers

College, 1963-64; Professor, Wilbur Wright College, Chicago, & Director, Public Relations, Wright City College, 1964-77; Substitute teacher, Chicago Public Schools, 1977-82; Teacher, Department of Ageing & Disability, Senior Citizens Centres, Chicago, 1980-. Also: Organiser, Art Fair, 1968-; Delegate, senior citizens conference, Wilbur Wright College, 1984; Tour guide, adults abroad, Wright City College, 1986-. *Publications:* Pamphlets in field. *Memberships include:* Delegate, International Leisure & Recreation Congress, Krefeld, Germany, World Leisure & Recreation Association, USSR. *Honours:* Governor Thompson's Award, Senior Leadership; Outstanding Service, Wilbur Wright College Alumni; Leadership Award, Physical Education Department, Wright City College, 1977; Chicago Senior Citizens' Hall of Fame. *Address:* 2936 North Kolmar, Chicago, Illinis 60641, USA.

FUENTES Martha Frances Ayers, b. 21 Dec. 1923, Ashland, Alabama, USA. Author. m. Manuel Solomon Fuentes, 11 Apr. 1943. *Education:* BA, English, University of South Florida, Tampa, 1969. *Appointments:* Jewellery Sales Clerk, Tampa, Florida, 1940-43; Clerk Typist, Bookkeeper, Western Union, 1943-48; Author, 1953-. *Creative works:* Publications, productions: Two Characters In Search Of An Agreement, 1-act play, published 1970; The Rebel, TV drama; Faith For Today; Mama Don't Make Me Go To College, My Head Hurts, produced University of South Florida, 1969; 30 unpublished plays (some with readings); Articles for young adults and adults in national and regional magazines; A Cherry Blossom For Miss Chrysanthemum, 1983. *Memberships:* United Daughters of the Confederacy; Florida Women in the Arts, Literary Representative 1983; Authors Guild; Authors League of America; Dramatists Guild; Society of Children's Book Writers; Southeastern Writers Union, Staff Instructor, Drama, TV; American Association of University Women; University of South Florida Alumni; The International Women's Writing Guild; Florida Theatre Association; Blue Army; The Association of the Miraculous Medal; The Society of the Little Flower; Others. *Honours:* Ione Lester Creative Writing Award, University of South Florida, 1965; George Sergel Drama Award for Go Stare At The Moon full-length play, University of Chicago, 1969. *Hobbies:* Gourmet cooking; Animal rights and protection; Theatre; Swimming; Gardening; Travel; Birdwatching. *Address:* 102 Third Street, Belleair Beach, FL 34635, USA.

FUGATE Virginia Kimbrough, b. 31 July 1940, Birmingham, Alabama, USA. Computer Sales Professional. m. Neil Peter Clarke, 21 May 1970 (div. 1973). *Education:* BMucEd, Florida State University, 1962. *Appointments include:* Trainee draughtsman, Broward County Tax Assessor's Office, Florida, 1963; Systems engineer to advertising marketing representative, IBM, 1963-70, 1978-82; Programmer, analyst, 1st National Bank, Atlanta, 1970-71; Program administrator, Insurance Systems America Inc, 1971-72; Senior systems analyst, Trusco Data Systems/Trust Company Bank, Georgia, 1972-73; Systems engineer to marketing representative, Data 100 Corporation, 1973-78; Senior sales representative, Datapoint Corporation, New York City, 1982-84, 1985-89; Account Manager, Systems Automation, Inc, 1989-90. *Memberships:* Sigma Kappa; Daughters of American Revolution; Metropolitan Opera Guild, 1982-88; Director of Volunteers, 1985-88. *Honours:* Various, within employment industry. *Hobbies:* Opera; Ballet; Ocean cruises; Golf. *Address:* 6271 Bay Club Drive, Ft Lauderdale, FL 33308, USA.

FUKUDA Haruko, b. 21 July 1946, Tokyo, Japan. Stockbroker. m. J. I. Dunnett, 28 Sept. 1973, divorced 1986. *Education:* BA Hons, 1968, MA Hons, 1971, Cambridge University, England. *Appointments:* Trade Policy Research Centre, London, England, 1968-70; ODI, London, 1970-71; IBRD, Washington, District of Columbia, USA, 1971-72; Vickers da Costa Ltd, 1972-74; James Capel & Co, London, 1974-. *Publications:* Britain in Europe: Impact on the Third World, 1973; Japan in World Trade, 1974; Contributions to books, journals. *Membership:* Trade Policy Research Centre, London. *Hobbies:* Art; Gardening; Reading. *Address:* Creems Wissington, Nayland, Suffolk, England.

FULBROOK Mary Jean Alexandra, b. 28 Nov. 1951, Cardiff, Wales. University Lecturer. m. Julian George Holder Fulbrook, 28 June 1973, 2 sons, 1 daughter. *Education:* MA, Cambridge University, 1973; AM, 1975, PhD, 1979, Harvard University, USA. *Appointments:* Lecturer, LSE, 1977-78; Lecturer, Brunei University, 1978-79; Research Fellow, New Hall, Cambridge University, 1979-82; Research Fellow, King's College, London University, 1982- 83; Lecturer, University College London, 1983-. *Publications:* Piety and Politics: Religion and the Rise of Absolutism in England, Württemberg and Prussia, 1983; In preparation: Germany 1918-1988: Tension, Trauma and Transformation; The Cambridge Concise History of Germany; Articles in journals including: European Studies Review; British Journal of Sociology; etc. *Memberships:* German History Society, Executive Committee, Journal Editor; Association for the Study of German Politics; Fellow, Royal Historical Society; Mayoress, London Borough of Camden, 1985-86. *Hobby:* Family Life. *Address:* Dept. of German, University College London, Gower St., London WC1E 6BT, England.

FULKES Jean Aston, b. Chatanooga, USA. Writer; Musician. m. James Sherman Fulkes, deceased, 2 sons, 1 daughter. *Education:* AB, University of Tennessee; Advanced French Institute, University of Missouri; Graduate, Programmes in French & Music, University of Missouri, 1970-82. *Appointments:* Chairman, Foreign Languages, Mexico, Missouri Schools, Teacher, English & Creative Writing, 1960-77; Director, Vocal Music, Chapel Activities, Missouri Military Academy, 1978-82; Freelance Writer. *Publications:* 8 books-Little Collectables, 1986; Composer, Words & Music, for piano & voice; Oil Paintings. *Memberships:* Quadrangle (later Mortar Board, Vice President); Presbyterian Women, various offices; Missouri State Teachers Association, Convention Speaker, 1982; PEO, Education Chairman; Delta Kappa Gamma. *Honours:* USA French Institute Fellowship; Shakespeare Fellow, Yale, 1961; Founder, President, Old Books and New Association, 1972. *Hobbies Include:* Speaking; Antiques; Music; Gardening; Gourmet Cooking; Travel; Creative Writing. *Address:* Old Books & New Association, 1605 Pallo Cte Road, Mexico, MO 65265, USA.

FULLER Ruth Louvenia, b. 26 Apr. 1937, Anderson, South Carolina, USA. Psychiatrist; Psychoanalyst. m. (1) Courtney Callender, 17 June 1961 (divorced 1981), 1 son, 1 daughter, (2) Rick Pope, 30 May 1981 (divorced 1986). *Education:* BS, magna cum laude, Howard University, 1957; MD, State University of New York (Downstate), 1961; Certificates, Psychiatry 1965, Psychoanalysis 1975. *Appointments include:* Psychiatric Director, James Weldon Johnson Family & Children's Counselling Centre, 1969-78; Assistant Professor 1978-87, Associate Professor 1987-, University of Colorado School of Medicine. *Publications:* Author or co-author, papers: Mental Health Educational Processes for Minority Populations, 1984; Significance of Skin Colour in a Newborn, 1985; Communicating with the Grieving Family, 1985. *Memberships:* Past President, New York Council on Child & Adolescent Psychiatry; Past Councillor, Colorado Child & Adolescent Psychiatric Society; American Psychoanalytic & Psychiatric Associations; Black Psychiatrists of America. *Honours:* Phi Beta Kappa, Beta Kappa Chi, Woman of Year, 1956; Phi Sigma Tau, 1957; Scholarship, Jessie Smith Noyes Foundation, 1957-61; Dicori Award, 1966; Certificate, NY Council on Child & Adolescent Psychiatry, 1979; Fellow, American Psychiatric Society, 1983; Examiner, American Board of Psychiatry & Neurology, 1988. *Hobbies:* Music, solo & ensemble singing; Swimming; Needlework; History. *Address:* University of Colorado Health Sciences Centre, Campus Box C-231, 4200 East 9th Avenue, Denver, Colorado 80262, USA.

FULLERTON Fiona Elizabeth, b. 10 Oct. 1956,

Kaduna, Nigeria. Actress. m. Simon Maccorkindale, 10 July 1976, divorced 1982. *Appointments:* Stage Includes: Guinevere in Camelot; Polly Brown in The Boyfriend; Gypsy Rose Lee, in Gypsy; Polly Peacham in The Beggar's Opera; Sally Bowles, I Am a Camera; Cinderalla; Ethel, The Royal Baccarat Scandal; TV appearances include: Clarice, The Charmer; Nurse Rutherford, Angels (series); Lev Tolstoy, A Question of Faith; Gaugin the Savage; Dick Barton Special Agent; A Friend Indeed; Shaka Zula; Hold the Dream; A Hazard of Hearts; A Taste for Death; The Life of Hemmingway; A Ghost in Monte Carlo; The Secret Life of Ian Fleming; Films include: Diana, Run Wild Run Free; Anastasia, Nicholas & Alexandra; Alice, Alice's Adventures in Wonderland; The Human Factor; Pola Ivanova, A View to a Kill. *Memberships:* Board, Savoy Theatre. *Address:* c/o Jean Diamond, London Management, 235 Regent Street, London W1, England.

FULLMER June Z, b. 16 Dec. 1920, Illinois, USA. Emeritus Professor of History; Writer. m. Paul Fullmer, 6 June 1953. *Education:* BS 1943, MS Chemistry 1945, Illinois Institute of Technology; PhD, Bryn Mawr College, 1948. *Appointments:* Associate Professor & Head, Department of Chemistry, Newcomb College, 1954-63; Associate Professor & Professor of History 1966-84, Emeritus Professor 1984-, Ohio State University. *Publications include:* Book, Sir Humphry Davy's Published Works, 1969; Numerous articles, scientific & historical journals. *Memberships:* Council 1970-73, History of Science Society; Chair, History of Chemistry Division 1971, American Chemical Society; Fellow, American Association for Advancement of Science. *Honours:* Guggenheim Fellow, 1963; Fellow: American Council of Learned Societies 1961, American Association of University Women 1948; Fellow, Coordinator of Sciences, Bryn Mawr College, 1946-48. *Hobbies include:* 19th century British physical science; Scientific biography; 19th century encyclopaedias. *Address:* 781 Latham Court, Columbus, Ohio 43214, USA.

FUNCK-BRENTANO Liselotte, b. 21 Aug. 1931, Saarebruck, Germany. Attorney at Law. m. 23 Sept. 1956, 1 son, 1 daughter. *Education:* Law degree, University of Strasbourg, 1952; PhD cum laude, German Law, Frankfurt/Main University, 1962. *Appointments include:* Attorney, Paris, France (Avocat a la Cour de Paris), current. *Publications:* French & German legal & financial journals, articles including: Compensatory Monetary Amounts; West Berlin Fiscal Paradise; European Fiscal Harmonization; Free Movement of Goods; Common Agricultural Policy & Law; Wine War. *Memberships:* President, European Law Association; German Bar Association; German-French Chamber of Commerce; Deutscher Juristinnenbund; Deutsche Vereinigung fur gewerblichen Rechtsschutz und Urheberrecht; Association Capitan; International Union of Lawyers; Ligue Internationale contre la Concurrence Deloyale. *Hobbies:* Art (painting, sculpture); Travel. *Address:* Funck-Brentano & Associes, 198 Avenue Victor Hugo, 75116 Paris, France.

FURR Ann Longwell, b. 25 May 1945, USA. Judge; Lawyer. divorced, 1 daughter. *Education:* BA 1967, JD 1976, University of South Carolina. *Appointments:* Partner, Furr & Delgado, 1976-; Assistant Municipal Judge, 1980-86; Chief Judge, 1986-. *Memberships:* South Carolina Bar Association; SC House of Delegates. *Honour:* Saigon Social Service Medal, 1970. *Hobbies:* Travel; Reading. *Address:* 515 Woodrow Street, Columbia, South Carolina 29205, USA.

FURUTO Sharlene Bernice Choy Lin, b. 29 Sept. 1947, Honolulu, Hawaii. Social Worker; Educator. m. David Masaru Furuto, 1 Apr. 1977, 3 sons, 1 daughter. *Education:* BS 1969, EdD 1981, Brigham Young University, Hawaii; MSW, University of Hawaii, 1972. *Appointments:* Department of Social Services, Hawaii, 1969-70; Maile Community Services Centre, 1972-73; Faculty 1975-, currently Associate Professor, social work, Brigham Young University, Hawaii. *Publications:* Article, Effects of Affective Treatment & Cognitive

Treatment on Attitude Change Toward Ethnic Minority Groups (International Journal of Intercultural Relations), 1983. Analyzing Intervention in Social Welfare, 1987. *Memberships:* Council on Social Work Education; President 1988-90, National Association of Social Workers; Secretary-treasurer, Asian-American Social Work Educators; American Business Womens Association; Chair, Koolauloa Community Council. *Honours:* Woman of Year, Koolauloa charter chapter, American Business Womens Association, 1982; Outstanding Young Woman of America, 1978-82. *Hobbies:* Parenting; Reading; Sewing. *Address:* Brigham Young University Hawaii, Box 1858, Laie, Hawaii 96762, USA.

FUSCO Jacqueline Teece, b. 23 Apr. 1956, New York City, USA. Systems/Management Consulting. m. 7 Apr. 1984. 1 daughter. *Education:* BA, Psychology 1978, AAS Business Administration, 1978, cum laude, St Francis College; Seminars attended, Dale Carnegie Institute; Associated Management Institute, working with the people; Association of Executive Search Consultants. *Appointments:* Assistant Director, Lease Administration, Retail Headquarters, 1979-81, Coordinator, Information Services, Richard Kove Associates Inc, Management Consultants, 1981-86; Vice President, Bilco Mechanical Corporation, 1985-; Owner and President, JTF Word Pros, legal systems processing, 1987-. *Memberships:* National Association Female Executives, 1984-; Anti Vivisection Society, 1978-; Save our Strays, 1978-. *Honours:* St Francis College Presidential Award, 1974; Phillip Morris Marketing Communications Award, 1975; Psi Chi and Chi Beta Phi, 1978. *Hobbies:* Photography; Dancing; Art; Volunteer work with handicapped children. *Address:* 8 Guilford Road, Port Washington, NY11050, USA.

FUTRELL Mary Alice Hatwood, b. 24 May 1940, Alta Vista, Virginia, USA. President, National Education Association; Educator. m. Donald Lee Futrell. *Education:* BA, Business Education, Virginia State College, Petersburg; MA, Business Education, George Washington Unviersity, Washington DC; Graduate studies: Universities of Virginia and Maryland, Virginia Polytechnic Institute, Virginia State University. *Appointments:* High School Teacher, Business Education, Alexandria, Virginia, 1963-; President, Education Association of Alexandria, Virginia, 1973-75; President, Virginia Education Association, 1976-78; Board of Directors, 1978-80, Secretary- Treasurer, 1980-83, President, 1983-89, National Education Association, Washington, DC. *Memberships:* American Association of Colleges of Teacher Education; American Association of State Colleges and Universities; National Chair, America; Board of Directors, National Foundation for the Improvement of Education; National Board for Professional Teaching Standards; National Council for the Accreditation of Teacher Education, Education Committee Chair; National Select Committee on Education of Black Youth; Democratic Labor Council, Democratic National Committee; Education Commission of the States; Trustee, Joint Council on Economic Education; Editorial Board, Pro-Education Magazine; WCOTP, several committees; International Committee of Educators to Combat Racism, Anti-Semitism and Apartheid; Board of Directors, US Committee for UNICEF; UN National Commission for UNESCO; National Democratic Institute for International Afairs; Study Commission on Global Perspectives in Education; Various others. *Honours:* 6 honorary doctorates; Medal of Distinguished Service, Teachers College, Columbia University; Fitz Turner Human Rights Award; Excellence in Education Award, Pi Lambda Theta; President's Award, National Association for the Advancement of Colored People; Many others. *Address:* National Education Association, 1201-16th Street NW, Washington, DC 20036, USA.

FYFE Maria, b. 25 Nov. 1938. m. James Fyfe, 4 Apr. 1964, deceased. 2 sons. Member of Parliament. *Education:* BA Honours 2.1, Economic History, 1975. *Appointment:* Senior Lecturer, Central College of Commerce, 7-87; Labour Front Bench Spokespersor ɔmen. *Memberships:* T&GWU; EIS. *Address:* Hoᴜ Commons, Westminster, London, England.

FYSON Jenny Grace, b. 3 Oct. 1904, Bromley, Kent, England. Writer. m. Christopher Fyson, 8 Mar. 1940, 1 son adopted from babyhood. *Publications:* Saul & David, Dramatic Interlude for BBC Schools, 1952; The Three Brothers of Ur; The Journey of the Eldest Son; Friend Fire and the Dark Wings; The Daughter of the Coppersmith; etc. *Membership:* Society of Authors. *Honours:* Honours: Runner Up for Carnegie Medal: 1964, 1965. *Hobbies:* Gardening; Wildlife; Preservation. *Address:* Oxford University Press, Walton Street, Oxford, England.

G

GAAL Magdolna, b. 9 Jan. 1928, Budapest, Hungary. Medical Doctor. m. John laszlo, 14 Apr. 1952, 2 daughters. *Education:* Medical Diploma, 1952; Diploma: PathologicalSciences, 1955, Genetic Sciences, 1979. *Appointments:* Pathology Anatomy & Experimental Cancer Research, Medical University, Budapest, 1950-53; Pathology Dept., Hungarian State Railways Hospital, Budapest, 1953-57; Head, Pathological & Genetic Dept., Institute for Medicine in Physical Education Sports, 1957-. *Publications:* Gynecologic Pathology Medicina Budapest, 1967, 1976. *Memberships:* Hungarian Society of Pathologists; Hungarian Society of Sports Medicine; Hungarian Society of Genetics. *Honours:* Honoured Doctor of the Hungarian Republic, 1976. *Address:* Dept. of Pathology, Institute for Medicine in Physical Education & Sports, Alkotas u. 48, Budapest XII, Hungary.

GABE Caryl Jacobs, b. 7 Dec. 1949, New York City, USA. Attorney. m. Allen S Gabe, 25 May 1980. *Education:* Brooklyn College, 1972; John Marshall Law School, 1976. *Appointments:* Special Assistant, Attorney General for the State of Illinois, 1976-77; Self-employed, 1977-80; Kaufman & Litwin, 1980-83; Senior Partner, Gabey Gabe & Associates, 1983-. *Memberships:* Illinois State Bar Association; Chicago Bar Association; American Bar Association; Illinois Trial Lawyers Association; North Suburban Association of Community & Industry. *Honour:* Order of John Marshall, 1976. *Hobbies:* Cellist; Jogging; Raquetball; Painting; Sculpting. *Address:* 180 North LaSalle Street, Suite 3110, Chicago, IL 60601, USA.

GABLE Martha Ann, b. 16 Sept. 1905, Philadelphia, USA. *Education:* BED, University of Indiana, 1927; MEd, Temple University, 1935. *Appointments:* Teacher, Philadelphia Public Schools, 1927-41; Assistant Director Health and Physical Education, 1942-48, Assistant Director, Communications 1948-55, Philadelphia Public Schools; Director, Radio & TV, 1955-68; Editor, American Association School Administrations 1965-74; Vice President, Communications, Women for Greater Philadelphia, 1976-. *Publications:* Editor, Museum Showcase, 1984. *Memberships:* Public Relations Society of America; American Women in Radio-TV; Women in Communications; TV Radio Advisory Club; National Press Club, Washington; American News Women's Club; Philadelphia Club Advertising Women; American Association University Women; Philadelphia Museum of Art; Pennsylvania Academy of Fine Arts; Franklin Institute. *Honours:* John B Kelly Award, 1962; Alumni Award, Temple University, 1964; Pioneer Award, Frankford High School, distinguished graduate 1974 (1st woman); Hall of Fame, Philadelphia Public Relations Association, 1979; Distinguished Daughter of Pennsylvania, 1980; President's Award, Philadelphia Chamber of Commerce, 1982; Pennsylvania Sports Hall of Fame, 1984; Museum Council of Philadelphia and Delaware Valley Annual Award, 1985; Silver Medal, Phila-Club Advertising Women, 1987. *Hobbies:* Promoting Museums; Sport. *Address:* 2601 Parkway, Philadelphia, PA 19130, USA.

GABLIK Suzi, b. New York City. Artist; Author; Critic. *Education:* BA, Hunter College, New York, 1955. *Creative Works:* Exhibitions: Alan Gallery, New York, 1963, 1966; Landau-Alan Gallery New York, 1967; Henri Gallery, Washington, 1971; Dintenfass Gallery, New York, 1972; Hester Van Royen Gallery, 1978; etc.; Books: Magritte, 1970; Progress in Art, 1977; Has Modernism Failed? 1984; The Re-enchantment of Art, in progress; Pop Art Redefined, with John Russell, 1969; Critic, Art News, 1962-66; London Correspondent, Art in America, 1975-; articles in: Artscribe; Art and Australia; Art New Zealand; Times Literary Supplement; New York Times Book Review; New Art Examiner.

Memberships: Numerous professional organisations. *Address:* 5 Westmoreland Street, London W1, England.

GABOR Georgia M, b. 30 Aug. 1930, Budapest, Hungary. Author; Educator; Lecturer. *Education:* AA, Los Angeles City College, LACC, 1965; BA, Mathematics, 1966, MA, Educational Psychology, 1968, University of California Los Angeles. *Appointments:* Dressmaker/Designer, 1956-60; Research and Development Computer Programmer and Systems Analyst, Todd Shipyards' Naval Research Division, 1962; Douglas Aircraft Company's space research division, 1963-64; General Precision, 1964-65; Mathematics Instructor, Los Angeles and San Marino School Systems, 1969-. *Publications:* Numerous articles in professional journals. *Memberships include:* HOX Philosophy Club, founder and past president; Jewish Society of Americanists; The Jewish Right, founder and past executive director; Jewish Identity Center; Brotherhood to Prevent Genocide; Philadelphia Holocaust Museum, Honorary Member; Southern California Motion Picture Council; National Association of Professional Educators; Internatiodnal Platform Association. *Honours include:* Outstanding Philosophy Student Honor Award, LACC, 1964; Outstanding Service Award, Tutorial project, LACC, 1965; Dedication to God and Country-Service on Behalf of Freedom, Jewish Society of Americanists, 1967; Outstanding Mathematics Teachers Award and Certificate of Honor for Service to School, Children and Community, San Marino Founders' Lodge, 1979; Honorary Cultural Doctorate, World University, 1986; Outstanding Teacher of the Year, Daughters of the American Revolution, 1987. *Address:* P O Box 3612, Arcadia, CA 91066, USA.

GABOR Zsa Zsa, (Sari Gabor), Princess Frederick von Aubalt, Duchesse de Laxon. b. 6 Feb. 1925, Hungary. Actress. *Education:* Budapest, Hungary; Lausanne, Switzerland. *Creative works:* Stage debut in Europe. Films include: Lovely to Look At; We're Not Married; The Story of Three Loves; Lili; Moulin Rouge; Three Ring Circus; Death of a Scoundrel; Girl in the Kremlin; For The First Time; Boys' Night Out; Picture Mommy Dead; Jack of Diamonds; 22 more films. 300 television appearances; Las Vegas 7 times. *Address:* c/o 1001 Bel Air Road, Los Angeles, CA 90077, USA.

GADDIS ROSE Marilyn, b. 2 Apr. 1930, Fayette, Missouri, USA. University Professor; Translator. m. Stephen David Rose, 6 Nov. 1968, 1 son. *Education:* BA 1952, DHumane Letters 1987, Central Methodist College; MA, University of South Carolina, 1955; PhD, University of Missouri, 1958. *Appointments:* Stephens College, 1958-68; Faculty 1968-, currently founding Director, translation programme, & Professor of Comparative Literature, State University of New York, Binghamton. *Publications:* Author: Axel, 1970, 1986; Eve of the Future Eden, 1982; Lui by Louise Colet, 1986. Editor: Translation Spectrum, 1981; Women Writers in Translation, 1987;. Managing Editor: ATA Series; Translation Perspectives. *Membership:* Board, American Translation Association. *Honours:* Senior Fellowship, Australian National Humanities Centre, 1977; Institutional Grants, US Department of Education, 1981-; ATA Gold Medal, 1988. *Address:* 4 Johnson Avenue, Binghamton, New York 13905, USA.

GAFNEY Louvenia Magee, b. 22 Mar. 1942, Garysburg, North Carolina, USA. Science Resource Teacher, Elementary Level. divorced. 1 son, 1 daughter. *Education:* BS, Elizabeth City State University, 1964; MA 1980, EdD 1985, George Washington University. *Appointments:* Biology Teacher, South Hill, Virginia, 1964-65; Maths Teacher, Gates Co, North Caroline, 1966-67; Science Resource Teacher, DC Public Schools, 1967-; Adult Education Teacher, Prince Georges Co, Maryland, 1977-88; Tutor for Foster Children, 1984-. *Publications:* Dissertation research: Incentive Pay Systems as viewed by selected DC Public school Teachers; Article: Towards Reduced Adult Illiteracy. *Memberships:* National Science Teachers Assoc; DC Science Educators Assoc; PDH-GWU Foundation Rep; Newsletter Staff, AAACE; AKA Sorority; MAACCE; GWU

Education Alumni. *Honours:* Honour Graduate, Elizabeth City State University, 1964; Award for Dedicated Services, Birney Elem School, 1988; Outstanding Teacher, 1980-88; Incentive Award, 1987-88. *Hobbies:* Reading; Theatre; Walking. *Address:* 13102 Keverton Drive, Upper Marlboro, MD 20772, USA.

GAILLARD Mary Katharine, b. 1 Apr. 1939, New Brunswick, USA. Professor. *Education:* BA, Hollins College, 1960; MA, Columbia University, 1961; Doctorat de Troisieme Cycle, 1964, Doctorat d'Etat, 1968, University of Paris, Orsay. *Appointments:* Attache de research, 1964- 68, Charge de research, 1968-73, Maitre de Research, 1973-80, Directeur de research, 1980-81, CNRS; Visiting Scientist, Fermilab, 1973-74; Theory Group Leader, LAPP, 1979-81; Professor, Physics, University of California, Berkeley, 1981-. *Publications:* 84 articles in scientific journals; 43 articles in conference proceedings; Editor: Gauge Theories in High Energy Physics, 1982; Weak Interactions, 1977. *Honours:* Woodrow Wilson Scholarship, 1960; Pri Thibaud, 1977; Loeb Lecturer, Physics, Harvard University, 1980; Regents Lecturer, 1981, Miller Research Professorship, 1987-88, University of California, Berkeley; Fellow, American Physical Society, 1985; E.O. Lawrence Memorial Award, 1988. *Address:* Dept. of Physics, University of California, Berkeley, CA 94720, USA.

GALANE Irma Adele Bereston, b. 23 Aug. 1921, Baltimore, USA. Electronics Engineer. 1 daughter. *Education:* BA, Goucher College, 1940; Postgraduate, Johns Hopkins University 1940-42, Massachusetts Institute of Technology 1943, George Washington University 1945, 65, 73, 77, 79, University of Maryland 1958, Army Management School 1964. Registered Professional Engineer, District of Columbia. *Appointments:* Physicist, Naval Ordnance Laboratory, 1942-43; Electronics engineer, Navy Bureau of Ships 1943-49, Army Office Chief Signal Officer 1949-51, Navy Aerospace Bureau 1951- 56, Air Research & Development Command, US Air Force 1956-57, FCC 1957-60, NASA 1960-62; Supervisory electronics engineer, US CG Headquarters, 1962-64; Scientific specialist, engineering sciences, Library of Congress, 1964-65; Project engineer, Advanced Aerial Fire Support Ssystem, Army Material Command, 1965-66; Engineer, Naval Air Systems Command, 1966-71; Electronics engineer, Spectrum Management Task Force 1971-76, senior research engineer 1976-, FCC. Also: Judge, National Capitol Awards (engineers & architects), 1975. *Memberships include:* Senior member, Institute of Electrical & Electronics Engineers; Past offices, National Society of Professional Engineers, Society of Women Engineers (senior member); Armed Forces Communications & Electronics Association; American Ordnance Association; US Naval Institute. *Address:* 4201 Cathedral Avenue NW, Washington DC 20016, USA.

GALAZKA Helen G. MacRobert, b. 8 June 1915, Paisley, Scotland, Thanatologist; Minister. m. Michal Galazka, 9 Sept. 1941, 1 son. *Education:* MA, Glasgow University, 1935; BD, Trinity College, Scotland, 1938; DMin, Psychology & Counselling, Andover Newton Theological School, USA, 1974. *Appointments:* Pastorates, Scotland, 1939-53; Executive, Minneapolis Council of Churches, USA, 1962-69; Pastor, 1st Church, Ludlow, Massachusetts, USA, 1969-81; Thanatalogist (specialist death & bereavement), Baystate Medical Centre, Springfield, Massachusetts, 1978-; Interim Minister, Thru Rivers, Massachusetts; Lecture tours, UK, 1989, 90. *Publications:* Articles, job-relatd magazines including Journal of Pastoral Care, My Church, Cystic Fibrosis Bulletin. Also poetry, plays. *Memberships:* Various committees, United Church of Christ; Clinical member, American Association of Marriage & Family Therapy; American Psychiatric Association; Adviser, Compassionate Friends. *Honours:* Woman of Year, Beta Sigma Phi, 1976; Outstanding Citizen, Channel 22 TV, 1982; Woman of Achievement, Business & Professional Women, 1980; Various college awards & scholarships; School gold medal. *Hobbies:*

Physical fitness; Oil painting; Photography; Travel. *Address:* 769 Allen Street, Springfield, Massachusetts 01118, USA.

GALE Cynthia Rose, b. 29 Sept. 1949, Buffalo, New York, USA. Graphic Designer. m. Paul Gale, Aug. 1971 (div. 1978). *Education:* Kent State University, 1967; Otis Reed Art Centre, 1967-69; Art Centre, Los Angeles, 1969-70; Parsons School of Design, New York City, 1979. *Appointments:* Art Director: Fashion Week, Los Angeles 1970-71, Daisy Publishing, LA 1971-73; Representative, R. Tyme Gallery, LA, 1973-78; Art Director, Interart Advertising, New York City, 1978-79; President, Gale Graphics Studio, NYC, 1979-. *Creative works:* Paintings in private collections, Los Angeles, New York City, London. *Memberships:* Offices, Graphic Artists Guild; NYC Chamber of Commerce; NYC 3-D Illustrators Group. *Honours:* Inclusion in: 2nd volume, North American Illustrators, 1983; 1st volume, NY York Gold, 1987. *Hobbies:* Politics (Democrat); Ice skating; Aerobics; Jazz; Theatre; Hiking & camping; Foreign travel (including 1 month in Australia, 1986); Lecturer, Motivation & Procrastination, School of Visual Arts, NYC. *Address:* Gale Graphics Studio, 229 East 88th Street, New York, NY 10028, USA.

GALIK Candace, b. 23 Apr. 1952, Brooklyn, New York, USA. Journalist. m. Richard Galik, 14 May 1978. *Education:* BA cum laude, History Honours, Brooklyn College, 1973; MA, Anthropology, State University of New York, Binghamton, 1979. *Appointments:* Archaeologist, 1977-83; Newspaper reporter, editor, 1983-86; Freelance journalist, 1986-. *Publications:* Feature articles in: USAIR; Harrowsmith; Women's Enterprise; New York Alive; Upstate; Country Woman. *Memberships:* National Writers Club; Vice President, Natural Organic Farmers Association, New York. *Honours:* Award, journalism, NY State Agricultural Society, 1988; Certificate of achievement, Natural Organic Farmers, New York. *Hobbies:* Gardening; Aerobics; Hiking; Organic food; Square dancing; Photography; Travel. *Address:* Box 237, Newfield, New York 14867, USA.

GALLAGHER Abisola Helen, b. 13 Oct. 1950, Chicago, Illinois, USA. Educator. *Education:* BA, Northeastern Illinois University, 1972; MS, University of Wisconsin, 1974; EdD, Rutgers University, 1983. *Appointments:* Educational Admin Intern, 1974-75, Counselor, Program Coordinator, 1975-78, University of Wisconsin; Residence Director, Rutgers College, 1978-81; Asst Dean of Student Life, Douglass College, 1981-85; Consultant, self-employed, 1985-87; Assistant Dean, Rutgers College, 1987-. *Publications:* Book chapter with F T Trotman, Group Therapy with Black Women, in Women in Therapy Groups: Paradigms of Feminist Treatment, 1987. *Memberships:* American Psychological Association; New Jersey Psychological Association; New Jersey Academy of Psychologists; New Jersey Chapter, Association of Black Psychologists, Vice President, 1983-87, Membership Chair, 1983-87, Fundraiser Committee, 1987-89; Eastern Deans Association. *Honours:* Paul Robeson Outstanding Service Award, 1985; Kappa Alpha Psi Fraternity-Eta Epsilon Chapter Distinguished Service Award, 1984; Douglass College Minority Advisory Board Service Recognition Award, 1985; Douglass College Black Student Congress Service Award, 1982; Martin L King Scholarship, Rutgers University Graduate School of Education, 1979, 1980; Zeta Phi Beta Scholarship, 1968. *Hobbies:* Travel; Jazz; Classical music; Art; Dancing. *Address:* 111 Livingston Avenue, New Brunswick, NJ 08901, USA.

GALLAGHER Jayne, b. 19 Nov. 1938, New York City, New York, USA. Federal Government Agency Administrator. m. Peter C. Gallagher, 10 Dec. 1957, dec. 1986, 2 sons, 1 daughter. *Education:* Neighborhood Playhouse School of Theatre. *Appointments:* Special Assistant, Office of US Senator James L. Buckley, 1970-74; Executive Director, Urban Priorities, New York City, 1974-79; Vice-President for Finance, Concrete Elements Corporation, New York City, 1979-81;

Director, Office of Public Affairs, Department of Housing and Urban Development, Washington, District of Columbia, 1984-. *Memberships:* Crusade for America; Executive Secretary, Home Rule Party of Rockville, New York; Executive Committee, American Conservative Union; Human Rights Commission, Rockville Center, New York. *Honours:* Gold Screen Award, National Association of Government Communicators, 1986; W.Bill Calloway Public Service Award, National Association of Real Estate Brokers, 1987; American Cancer Society Citation. *Hobbies:* Theatre; Arts. *Address:* 2301 Jefferson Davis Highway, Arlington, VA 22202, USA.

GALLAGHER Nancy Elizabeth, b. 6 June 1950, Ontario, Oregon, USA. Tax preparation, financial planning. 1 son, 1 daughter. *Education:* Student, University of Oregon, 1968-72; Certified as Tax preparer 1974; Licensed as Tax Consultant, 1976; Notary Public. *Appointments:* Tax Preparer, H&R Block. Eugene, Oregon, 1973-77; Tax Consultant, Partner, Gallagher, Gleason and Raven, Eugene, 1977-81; Tax Consultant, Partner, Gallagher, Raven & Ass, Eugene, 1981-87; Instructor, Amer Inst Taxation, Vancouver, 1984-85; Tax Consultqant, Financial planning, sole proprietor, Gallagher & Assoc, Eugene, 1987-. *Memberships:* Chairperson, Aslan House Counseling Center, 1976-; External Adv Bd, Lane Comm Coll Business Center; International Assn Fin Planners; Association Tax Consultants (Vice President 1981-82); Eugene Business Women (Vice President); Alliance for Career Advancement; International Association of Financial Planning, 1984-, Treasurer 1987. *Honours:* Distinguished Service Award, Association of Tax Consultants, 1979; Pan Hellenic Award, 1968. *Hobbies:* Reading; Gardening; Being involved in community affairs; Travelling. *Address:* 4560 Larkwood St, Eugene, OR 97405, USA.

GALLERY Leslie Mesnick, b. 21 Feb. 1943, Pennsylvania, USA. Urban Planner; Architect; Special Events Designer. m. John Andrew Gallery, 1972, divorced 1982. 2 sons. *Education:* BA Medieval Studies 1964, BArch, Architecture 1968, MArch 1970, MLandscape Arch 1971, University of Pennsylvania. *Appointments:* President, City Gardens, Philadelphia, 1970-72; Assistant Professor, University of Texas, School of Architecture, Austin, 1972-77; Executive Director, Philadelphia AIA, 19799-83; Founding Director, Foundation for Architecture, 1980-88.*Creative works:* Producer, Philadelphia Architecture-A guide to the City; Design competition, City Visions; Design competition, City Hall; Beaux Arts Ball; Sign Study and Design, Direction Philadelphia; City wide special events. *Memberships:* American Institute of Architects; Urban Land Institute; AIA Urban Design Com; Bermantown Historic Society; Citizens for Arts in Pennsylvania, Executive Board; Friends of Philadelphia Museum, Executive Board; Austin Heritage Society, Advisor; Womens Equity Action League, President; Business Volunteers for Arts, Advisor. *Honours:* Senatorial Fellowship, Dale Travelling Fellowship, 1967; Burlington Industries Design Award, 1972; National Ednowment for the Arts Design Fellow, 1979; Rolan P Gallimore Award for Design, 1987; Phoebe W Haas Trust Fellowship, 1988-90. *Interests:* American Indian Architecture; Southwestern American Landscape. *Address:* 2979 Schoolhouse Lane, Philadelphia, PA 19144, USA.

GALLEYMORE Frances, b. 21 May 1946, London, England. Novelist and Television Dramatist. m. Stephan Bird, divorced. 1 daughter. *Publications:* Novels: The Orange Tree; Ground Wave Sailing. Television Drama: A Divorce; Little Girls Don't; Ladykillers; A Mother Like Him; Time for Murder; Wish Me Luck. *Membership:* Writers Guild of Great Britain. *Honour:* Pye Colour Television Award, 1977. *Address:* c/o Peters, Fraser & Dunlop, The Chambers, Chelsea Harbour, London SW10 0XF, England.

GALLUP Lee, b. 27 Jan. St Louis, Missouri, USA. College Professor of Theatre; Theatrical Director;

Actress. m. Arthur Feldman, 20 Dec. 1 daughter. *Education:* BA, MA, University of Illinois; PhD, University of Denver. *Appointments:* University of Illinois; University of Denver; Theatre in the Square, Denver; Third Eye Theatre, Denver; Theatre Under Glass, Denver; Colorado Women's College, Denver, Arvada Center of the Arts & Humanities; Loretto Heights College. *Creative Works:* Plays: Lysistrata an adaptation; For Whom the Belle Told, with G Giem; The Green Witch; Rumpelstiltzkin. Roles (a selection): Mary Stuart; The Matchmaker; Time Remembered; The Hostage; The Birthday Party; 12th Night; Canterbury Tales; Macbeth; You Never Can Tell. Plays directed (selection): The Norman Conquests; Absent Friends; 12th Night; The Threepenny Opera; The House of Bernarda Alba; the Imaginary Invalid; Vanities; Kiss Me Kate; The Mikado; Yeomen of the Guard; The Music Man; Lysistrata; The Man in the Glass Booth. *Memberships:* American Federation of Television & Radio Artists (AFTRA); Zeta Phi Eta, American Theatre Association; Brecht Society of America; Greater Denver Council for the Arts & Humanities (Board member); Regis College Arts Advisory Council (Board Member). *Honours:* Outstanding Faculty Member, Loretto Heights College, 1987; One of Colorado's Outstanding Women in the Performing Arts, Network Magazine, 1986; Best Actress, Bonfils Theatre, Denver, 1978; Best Actress, University of Denver, 1962. *Hobbies:* Anglophile; Astronomy; Archaeology. *Address:* 2045 S Fillmore Street, Denver, Colorado 80210, USA.

GALLUPS Vivian Lylay Bess, b. 14 Jan. 1954, Vicksburg, Mississippi, USA. Contract Administrator. m. Ordice Alton Gallups, Jr, 12 July 1975. *Education:* BA, Psychology, 1975; MA Education, 1975; MA, Public and Private Management, 1985. *Appointments:* Counsellor, Columbia College, 1975-76; Case Manager, SC Dept of Social Services, 1976; Recovery Reviewer, USA Social Security Administration, 1977-85; Contract Administration, Defense Logistics Agency of the USA Department of Defense, 1985-. *Memberships:* National Contract Management Association (Chapter secretary, 1987); Cathedral Church of the Advent (Episcopal); National Cathedral Association; Alabama Zoological Association. *Hobbies:* Dance; Music. *Address:* 566 12th Court, P O Box 126, Pleasant Grove, Alabama 35127, USA.

GALVIN Martha Blackwell, b. 11 Nov. 1948, Biltmore, USA. Interior Designer. m. Lance Scott Galvin, 31 May 1970, divorced 1983. *Education:* BA, Norh Carolina State University, 1970; BFA, University of Georgia, 1976. *Appointments:* Design, Ivan Allen Co., 1976-79; Director of Design, Todd Commercial Interiors, 1979; Designer, The Coca Cola Co., 1979-80; Designer, Southern Bell, 1980-83; Director of Interiors, Turner Broadcasting System Inc., 1983-. *Memberships:* American Society of Interior Designers; Institute of Business Designers; Colour Marketing Group; National Trust for Historic preservation. *Hobbies:* Water Colour; Volunteer - CARE. *Address:* 55 Lafayette Drive NE, Atlanta, GA 30309, USA.

GAMBINO Elaine Helen, b. 9 May 1936, Milwaukee, Wisconsin, USA. Banker. m. Vito Gambino, 3 Mar. 1962. 2 sons. *Education:* BA Accounting, Northwestern University, Chicago, Illinois, USA. *Appointments:* Accounting Supervisor, Chicago Eye, Ear, Nose and Throat Hospital, 1975; Executive Vice-President, Capitol Federal Bank for Savings, 1975-; Director/Secretary, Capitol Federal Mortgage Corp, 1986-; President, Workshop Inc, 1983-. *Creative works:* Interior Design of Professional Offices, Beauty Salons, Private Homes. *Memberships:* National Association of Female Executives; Chicago Council on Foreign Relations. *Hobbies:* Art; Travel; Horses. *Address:* Capitol Federal Bank For Savings, 4011 North Milwaukee Avenue, Chicago, IL 60641, USA.

GAME Patricia Jean (Pat), b. 13 Nov. 1926, Jamestown, South Australia. Medical Practitioner. m. David Aylward Game, 8 Dec. 1949, 2 sons, 2 daughters. *Education:* MB,BS, Adelaide University, 1949; Specialist

Register, Anaesthesia, 1968. *Appointments:* Resident Medical Officer 1950, Honorary Anaesthetist (Orthopaedics) 1951-63, Royal Adelaide Hospital; Private practice, anaesthetics, various hospitals 1951-. *Publications:* Sliding Sheet (video, lectures, method of preventing back damage in nurses & orderlies); Pre-Operative Visiting; Doctor's Family (lectures, seminars); Pre-Operative Anaesthetic Assessment of the Patient; Anaesthetist's Family. *Memberships include:* Australian Medical Association; South Australian Division, National Safety Council; Australian Society of Anaesthetists; Association of Medical Specialists; Associate, College of General Practitioners; World Organisation of National Colleges & Academies of General Practice; Various community organisations. *Honours:* 4 well-educated children (surgeon, physiotherapist, lawyer, sociologist), 5 grandsons. *Hobbies include:* Talking to women's groups (anaesthesia), National Safety Council; Lecturing, professional meetings (Sliding Sheet method); Gardening; Bridge; Homemaking & family. *Address:* 50 Lambert Road, Royston Park, South Australia 5070, Australia.

GANLEY Gladys D, Writer. *Education:* BA in Government and Politics, University of Maryland; ALM, History, Harvard University. *Appointments:* Writer, Public Relations Officer, 1965-68, Information Officer, Computer Research, 1968-69, Writer, Public Relations Officer, 1975-76, Contract Research & Writer, 1977-78, National Institutes of Health, Bethesda, MD; Independent Writer & Researcher, 1979-. *Publications:* Political Significance of the Changing Media, in preparation; Global Political Fallout. The VCR's First Decade, 1987; Co-author, To Inform or To Control? The New Communications Networks, First Edition, 1982, Second Edition 1989; several monographs; contributor to various professional journals. *Address:* 1572 Massachusetts Avenue, Apartment 26, Cambridge, MA 02138, USA.

GANN Jo Rita, b. 2 June 1940, Talihina, Oklahoma, USA. YWCA Executive Director. *Education:* BS, Oklahoma Baptist University, 1962; Master of Theatre Arts, Portland State University, 1970; Advanced Management Qualifications 1975, 1977, 1978 and 1980; Professional Institute of American Management Association. *Appointments:* Teacher, Oklahoma City Schools, 1962-64; Teen Director, Oklahoma City YWCA, 1964-67; Camp and Teen Director, Portland, Oregon, 1967-72; Program Coordinator/Assistant Director, Flint, Michigan, YWCA, 1972-75; Executive Director Salem, Oregon YWCA, 1975-. *Publications:* Co-author manual A New Look at Supervision. *Memberships:* Chair, United Way Agency Executives, Salem, Oregon, 1980- 81; Board Member, Renewable Resources Corporation, Salem, Oregon, 1980-82; chair, YWCA NW Region Staff, Portland, 1983; Delegate, United Nations for Non- Governmental Organisations, New York, 1984; Exeutive Directors of YWCA of USA; National Organisation of Female Executives. *Honours:* Fellowship (Masters Degree), National YWCA, New York, 1970; International Study Program, National YWCA, Ghana, Africa. *Hobbies:* Public speaking on global concerns, Portland and Salem, Oregon, 1981-86; President's Council, Salem Summerfest, Salem, Oregon, 1985-86; Photography; Hiking; Swimming; Travel. *Address:* Salem YWCA, 768 State Street, Salem, OR 97301, USA.

GANTRESS Louise T., b. 17 June 1947, Buffalo, New York, USA. Financial Consultant. m. David Hiromura, 11 Sept. 1976, 1 son. *Education:* BA, History, State University of New York, Buffalo, 1969; MPA, New York Universty Graduate School of Public Administration, 1977. *Appointments:* Senior municipal analyst, Moody's Investors Service, 1977-81; Senior institutional analyst, Dean Witter Reynolds Inc, 1981; Director of Research, Lebenthal & Company Inc, 1982-84; Consultant, 1984-: Adviser, Japan Credit Rating Agency, Tokyo, (1986-88); Interviewed on NHK Radion (Tokyo) on credit ratings, July 1987; re-broadcast December 1987; Adviser, Yasuda Trust & Banking Company Ltd, Tokyo, 1988-90; Nth Degree, (1990).

Publications: Japanese-English Dictionary Fundamental 1200 Business and Banking Terms, 1990. Co-authored articles: Business Tokyo, 1988; Borrowing in Japan. Authored articles: review of Second to None, ACCJ Journal (Tokyo), 1987; review of Financial Innovation and Monetary Policy, Bank of Japan Conference Papers, ACCJ Journal (Tokyo), 1987; The Chronicle of the Horse (Middleburg, VA), 1987, Riding in Japan; Winds (Japan Airlines), 1986, Kendo in Paris; Institutional Investor, 1985, Survey of leading economists; Empire State Report (New York), 1985, The New York Convention Center; Regional Economic Digest (New York), 1985, The Changing World of Municipal Bonds; review of Trading Places, ACCJ Journal (Tokyo), 1988; *Hobbies:* Horse riding; Scuba diving; Cross-country skiing. *Address:* 35 West 93 Street, New York, NY 10025, USA.

GARCIA Eva, b. 12 Dec. 1950, McAllen, Texas, USA. Attorney at Law. m. John F. Mendoza, 17 Jan. 1987, 1 son, 2 daughters. *Education:* BA, University of Nevada, 1973; JD, University of San Diego, 1981. *Appointments:* Social Worker, Nevada State Welfare Agency, 1973; Interpreter, 8th Judicial District Court, 1975-78; US District Court, 1981. *Publications:* Handbook for Court Interpreters; Manual for Spanish Court Interpreters. *Memberships:* Association of Trial Lawyers; Latin American Bar Association, President 1983-85; Latin Chamber, Vice-President 1984-85, President 1987-88; Nevada Bar Association; Nevada Trial Lawyers Association; Nevada Association of Latin Americans, Vice-President 1981-84; Southern Nevada Association of Women Attorneys, Board of Directors 1982-83; Clark County Bar Association. *Honours:* Named Outstanding Young Women, 1980; Professional Award, Nevada Economic Development Co, Las Vegas, 1984-86; Named Ambassador for Nevada by Governor, 1987; Women Helping Women Award, Soroptimists of Las Vegas, 1988. *Hobbies:* Scuba diving; Classical music. *Address:* 501 South 7th Street, Las Vegas, NV 89101, USA.

GARCIA Mariella, b. 18 Aug. 1950, Guayaquil, Ecuador. Artist Painter; Teacher; Lecturer. m. E. Manrique T, 9 Aug. 1971, 3 daughters. *Education:* Art school, Incarnate Word College, San Antonio, Texas, USA, 1970-71; Licenciada en Arqueologia, Escuela Superior Politecnica, Guayaquil, 1980-85. *Career:* Plastic Arts Commissioner, Centro Municipal de Cultura, Guayaquil, 1975; Cultural Assistant, USIS, 1976-78; Ayudante de Catedra Antropologia ESPOL, 1987. *Creative work includes:* Numerous exhibitions, paintings, 1974-. Paintings in permanent collections: Casa de la Cultura Museum; Municipal Museum, Quito; Banco Central Museum; Banco Continental; COFIEC, Guayaquil. Also essay on Valdivia culture. *Memberships:* Plastic Arts Section, Casa de la Cultura Nucleo del Guayas; Agrupacion Cultura y Fraternidad, Hiliar; Agrupacion Cultural las Penas, Guayaquil; FIBA. *Honours:* Acquisition award, Salon Nacional de Artes Plasticas, Casa de la Cultura, Quito, 1976; 1st prize, acquisition, Salon Nacional de Pintura y Escultura Mariano Aguilera, Quito, 1977; 1st prize, Salon Fundacion de Guayaquil, 1978; Participant, Art Biennials, Valparaiso (Chile) 1979, 1981, La Habana (Cuba) 1985, Miami (USA) 1986, Cuenca (Ecuador) 1986, Sao Paulo (Brazil) 1987. *Hobbies:* Literature; Sports including tennis, swimming, water skiing. *Address:* PO Box 427, Guayaquil, Ecuador, South America.

GARCIA-SALAS ALVARADO Olga Marina, b. 10 Oct. 1938, Guatemala, Central America. Elementary School Principal; University Professor. *Education:* BS, George Peabody College for Teachers, USA, 1966; MS, University of Tennessee, 1967; Licenciatura en Educacion, Universidad de San Carlos de Borromeo, Guatemala, 1969; EdD, Michigan State University, USA, 1977. *Appointments:* Professor, School of Education, Universidad del Valle de Guatemala, 1968-; Assistant Principal, 1968-80, Elementary School Principal, 1981-, The American School of Guatemala. *Publications:* Word Frequency Count in Spontaneous Conversations of Five-year-old Guatemalan Spanish speaking Children. *Memberships:* Colegio de Humanidades, Universidad de

San Carlos de Borromeo; Delta Kappa Gamma Society International Alpha Chapter President, Guatemala State President, Latin American Representative in the Committee to consider the Regional Reorganization. *Honours:* Institute of International Education, Latin American Convention Scholarship, 1964-66; Institute of International Education, Academic Year Development Fellowship Award, 1967; Organization of American States, Cordell Hull Foundation Scholarship, 1966-67; Fundacion de la Universidad del Valle scholarship, 1972-75; Delta Kappa Gamma Society International Golden Fund Scholarship, 1981. *Hobbies:* Reading; Sewing; Knitting; Hiking. *Address:* 1 Calle C 1-29, zona 1 Guatemala, Guatemala, Central America.

GARCZYNSKI Carol Joan J., b. 7 Dec. 1945, Trenton, New Jersey, USA. Reading Diagnostician. *Education:* AA, Manor Junior College, Pennsylvania, 1965; BA, Holy Family College, Torresdale, PA 1967; MEd, Monmouth College, New Jersey, 1970; MA, Rider College, NJ 1975; Postgraduate studies, Nova University, Monmouth College; Various certifications, New Jersey. *Appointments include:* Classroom teacher, Ocean County 1968, Manchester Township 1969-70, Toms River School District 1970-83; Reading Specialist, 1984-85; Language Arts Specialist, 1984-86; Reading Diagnostician, 1986-. *Memberships include:* Professional; College, & NJ Reading Associations; Worldwide, & New Jersey branch, International Reading Association; National, & NJ Education Associations; Offices, local associations; Delegate, annual Teachers' Convention. Community: Active, numerous organisitions, church, educational. *Honours include:* Outstanding Teaching of a Science Unit, Grade 3, Manchester Township School District; Outstanding Young Woman of America, Holy Family College, 1971; Certification, Barbizon School of Modelling, 1971; Outstanding Service Award, Manor Junior College; Awards, environmental project, Dover Township, 6 years; Leadership awards, 4H Club, 4 years. *Hobbies include:* Writing children's stories; Attending lectures & conferences; Travel; Educational research; Theatre; Opera; Antiques; Horse riding; Sport; Conversation. *Address:* 525 Ship Avenue, Beachwood, New Jersey 08722, USA.

GARDE Karin, b. 24 Mar. 1938, Copenhagen, Denmark. Medical Doctor; Psychiatrist; Head of a Psychiatric Department. m. Kjeld Garde, MD, 31 May 1958. 3 sons. *Education:* Medical Doctor, 1965; Psychiatrist, 1975. *Appointments:* Trained at Copenhagen University Hospitals; Head of Psychiatric Department D, Sct Hans Hospital, Roskilde, 1983-. *Publications:* Author of: Voksne Kvinder (adult women, not translated), a description of female sexual behaviour, experience, knowledge and attitudes among women, born 1936; Co-author in several publications about women in psychiatry (in Danish). *Memberships:* Danish Psychiatry Association; Danish Women's Society. *Honour:* Danish Women's Societies Award "Mathilde" 1982. *Address:* Sct Hans Hospital, adfeling D, 4000 Roskilde, Denmark.

GARDEN Nancy, b. 15 May 1938, Boston, Massachusetts, USA. *Education:* BFA, School of Dramatic Arts, Columbia University, 1961, MA Teachers College, 1969. *Appointments:* Actress & Theatrical lighting designer, 1954-64; Teacher of speech and dramatics, 1961-64; Editor, 1964-76 (educational materials; text books); Teacher of writing (adult education; correspondence school), 1979-. *Publications:* What Happened in Marston, 1971; The Loners, 1972; Maria's Mountain, 1981; Fours Crossing, 1981; Annie On My Mind, 1982; Watersmeet, 1983; Prisoner of Vampires, 1984; Peace, O River, 1986; The Door Between, 1987; Mystery of the Night Raiders, 1987; Mystery of the Midnight Menace, 1988; Mystery of the Secret Marks, 1989; Favorite Tales from Grimm, 1982; Berlin: City Split in Two, 1971; Vampires, 1973; Werewolves, 1973; Witches, 1975; Devils and Demons, 1976; Fun with Forecasting Weather, 1977; The Kids' Code and Cipher Book, 1981. *Memberships:* Society of Childrens Book Writers; Authors Guild (past member).

Honours: Scholarship, Peterbrough Players, Peterbrough, New Hampshire, 1955; Professional Internship META-TV, 1961; Book, Annie on My Mind an ALA Best of the Best, 1970-83, and a Best Book for 1982. *Hobbies:* Running; Hiking; Cross-country skiing; Gardening; Weaving. *Address:* c/o McIntosh & Otis, Ins, 310 Madison Avenue, New York NY 10017, USA.

GARDETTO Sondra Lynn, b. 11 Nov. 1961, McKeesport, USA. Director. m. Gerry D. Gardetto, 11 Apr. 1987. *Education:* BMus., Michigan State University, 1983; MSc., University of NOtre Dame, 1989. *Appointments:* Intern, 1983-84; Co-Ordinator, 1984, Rehabilitation Therapist, 1984-86, New Castle State Developmental Centre, Indiana; Rehabilitation Therapist, 1986-88,, Director, Community/Volunteer Services, 1988-, Northern Indiana State Developmental Centre. *Memberships:* National Association for Music Therapy Inc; Indiana Music Therapist Association; Sigma Alpha Iota. *Address:* 2124 Spring Hill Drive, South Bend, IN 46628, USA.

GARDNER Ava, b. 24 Dec. 1922, Smithfield, North Carolina, USA. Actress. m. (1) Mickey Rooney, 1942. (2) Artie Shaw, 1945. (3) Frank Sinatra, 1951, divorced. *Education:* Atlantic Christian College. *Creative Works:* Films include: Lost Angel; Three Men in White; Singapore; One Touch of Venus; Great Sinner; East Side West Side; My Forbidden Past; Show Boat; Love Star; The Snows of Kilimanjaro; Ride Vaquero; Mogambo; The Barefoot Contessa; Bhowani Junction; The Little Hut; The Sun also Rises; Naked Maja; On the Beach; 55 Days to Peking; Night of the Iguana; The Bible; Mayerling; Tam-Lin; The Life and Times of Judge Roy Bean; Earthquake; The Bluebird; The Cassandra Crossing; City on Fire; The Kidnapping of the President; Priest of Love; Regina. *Address:* c/o Jess S Morgan & Co Inc, 6420 Wilshire Boulevard, Los Angeles, CA 90048, USA.

GARDNER Mary Adelaide, b. 19 July 1920, USA. Professor of Journalism. *Education:* AA, Stephens College, 1940; BA 1941, MA 1953, Ohio State University; PhD, University of Minnesota, 1960; Studied at Mexico City College and Universidad de San Marcos, Lima, Peru. *Appointments:* Bacteriologist, Mead Johnson & Co, 1942-43; US Marine Corps, 1943-46; Civilian with Special Services, US Army, Austria, 1948-51; Program Asst, World Affairs Program 1957-60, Copy Editor, 1960-61, Minneapolis Star; Assistant Professor, University of Texas, 1961-66; Professor, Michigan State University, 1966-; Consultante, El Norte, Monterrey, Mexico, 1970-. *Publications:* Latin America (Print), 1987; Colegiación: Another Way to Control the Press?; Mexico: Mass Communications, 1980; Inter American Press Association and It's Fight for Freedom of the Press, 1967; numerous articles and papers to professional journals and magazines. *Memberships:* Midwest Association on Latin America; Women in Communications, Inc; Association for Education in Journalism and Mass Communication (President, 1979); Inter American Press Association. *Honours include:* Woman Achiever, Michigan State University, 1986; Phi Kappa Phi, national honorary, 1983; Honorary Member and Board of Directors, El Renacimiento, 1983; Distinguished Faculty Award, Michigan State University, 1982; National Headliner Award, Women in Communications, Inc, 1978; Special Citation, Inter American Press Association, 1975, etc. *Hobbies:* Swimming; Reading; Travelling. *Address:* School of Journalism, Communications Arts Building No 305, Michigan State University, East Lansing, Michigan 45824, USA.

GARDNER Nancy Hazard, b. 17 Feb. 1949, Washington, District of Columbia, USA. President, Computer Sales and Consulting Firm. *Education:* BS, University of Maryland, 1972. *Appointments:* Trainer, Equitable Trust Bank, 1970-74; Program Analyst, University of Maryland, 1974-77; Comptroller, Carltech Assoc, 1981-83; Financial Director, Helschiem Health Center, 1983-84; President and Chair of Board,

Sensitive Systems Inc, 1983-. *Memberships:* National Assoc of Female Executives. *Hobbies:* Computers; Auto racing; Softball; Skiing. *Address:* 9567 Transfer Row, Columbia, MD 21045, USA.

GARDNER Shirley Mae, b. 7 Mar. 1932, Chicago, Illinois, USA. Company Director. m. William Rex Gardner, 9 June 1973. *Education:* AA, North Park College; BS, University of Illinois. *Appointments:* Director of Purchasing, Mindscape Inc.; Senior Purchasing Agent, Society for Visual Education, Chicago; Senior Production Operator, Regensteiner Corp, Chicago; Owner, Founder, Eagle Bindery Inc. *Memberships:* National Association of Female Executives; Purchasing Management Association of Chicago; Printing Industries of Illinois Association; VFW Auxilary. *Honours:* Recipient, various honours and awards. *Hobbies:* Gardening; Fishing; Reading; Humane Societies for Animals. *Address:* 8924 Robin Drive, Des Plaines, IL 60016, USA.

GARDNER Susan Beth Ross, b. 25 Oct. 1941, New York City, USA. Art Professor. m. Bruce Brook, 24 June. 1983. 2 sons, 1 daughter. *Education:* BA, Antioch College, 1963; MA, Ohio State University, 1966. *Appointments:* Assistant Professor of Art, Manhattan Community College, City of New York, 1966-70; Head, Art Department, Stern College/Yeshiva University, New York City, 1979-. *Creative works include:* Numerous One Person and Group Shows/Exhibitions including: Eve Whiles Away the Hours, 30ft installation Twining Gallery, 1983; Darwin Triptych, St Peters at Citicorp, 1983; Sacred Pig, Ruth Seigel. *Honour:* Awarded a large scale commission by NYC Department of Cultural Affairs through the Board of Education to create two entry way 24ft murals for a NYC Public School, completed 1987, dedicated by Mayor Koch & Department of Cultural Affairs Chair, 26 October, 1987. *Hobbies:* History; Nature studies. *Address:* 108 Wyokoff Street, Brooklyn, NY 11201, USA.

GARDNER OF PARKES Rachel Trixie, Baroness, b. 17 July 1927, Parkes, Australia. Dental Surgeon. m. Kevin Anthony Gardner, 7 July 1956. 3 daughters. *Education:* BDS, University of Sydney, 1954; Diplome de Cordon Bleu de Paris, France, 1956; Director, London Electricity Board, England, 1984-. *Appointments:* Dental Practitioner, 1955-; Member, Westminster City Council, 1968-78; Member, Greater London Council for Havering, 1970-73, for Enfield Southgate, 1977-86; Governor, national Heart Hospital, 1974-; Governor, Eastman Dental Hospital, 1971-80; Member, Industrial Tribunal Panel for London, 1974-; Department of Employment's Advisory Committee on women's Employment: .IP,North Wootminster, 1971-; North Thames Gas Consumer Council, 1980-82; United Kingdom Representative on the United Nations Status of Women Commission, 1982-; Fellow, Institute of Directors; President, UK Women in Dentistry, 1985-88; Director, Woolwich Building Society, 1988-. *Memberships:* Honorary President, War Widows Association of Great Britain, 1984-87; Chairman, British Section, European Union of Women, 1978-82; Member, Westminster Kensington and Chelsea Area Health Authority, 1974-81; Member, Inner London Executive Council, NHS, 1966-71. *Honour:* Life Peer, 1981. *Hobbies:* Family Life; Travel; Gardening; Reading. *Address:* House of Lords, Westminster, London SW1 0PW, England.

GARFIELD Nancy Jane, b. 24 Oct. 1947, New York City, USA. Psychologist. *Education:* BA, Pasons College, 1968; MA, Western Illinois University, 1971; PhD, University of Missouri, 1975. *Appointments:* Counselling/Career, Specialist, Oklahoma State University, Stillwater, 1975-77; Associate Dean of Student, Wichita State Univesty, 1977-80; Director of Training, Psychology, Topeka, 1980-. *Publications:* Contributor to: ACPA Developments; Journal of Counselling & Development; Journal of College Student Personnel. *Memberships Include:* Vice-Chair, Topeka AIDS Project; American Association of Counselling & Development; American College Personnel Association;

American Psychological Association. *Honours:* VA Superior Performance Award, 1983; American College Personnel Assocation Presidential Service Award, 1985. *Hobbies:* Reading; Gardening; Classical Music. *Address:* Psychology Service (116B), Colmery-O'Neil VA Medical Centre, Topeka, KS 66622, USA.

GARG Mridula, b. 25 Oct. 1938, Calcutta, India. Creative Writer; Columnist. m. A. P. Garg, 4 May 1963, 2 sons. *Education:* BA Hons, Economics, Delhi University, 1957; MA, Economics, Delhi School of Economics, 1960. *Appointments:* Lecturer in Economics, Indraprastha College, University of Delhi, 1960-61; Lecturer in Economics, Jankidevi Mahavidyalaya, Delhi, 1961-63. *Publications:* Novels in Hindi: Uske Hisse ki Dhoop; Vanshaj; Chittkobra (also in German translation); Anitya; Main aur Main; Collection of short stories in Hindi: Duniya ka Kayda; Tukra tukra Aadmi; Daffodil Jal Rahain Hain; Glacier Se; Urf Sam; Plays in Hindi: Ek Aur Ajnabi; Tum Laut Aao; Jadoo Ka Kaleen; In English: A Touch of Sun (novel); Daffodils on Fire (collection of short stories); Skyscraper transcreation of short stories of Yogesh Gupt). *Memberships:* Board of Directors, Centre for Science and Environment, Delhi; Life Member, India International Centre, Delhi; Authors Guild of India. *Honours:* Madhya Pradesh Sahitya Academy Award for novel Uske Hisse ki Dhoop, 1975; All India Radio Award for play Ek Aur Ajnabi, 1979. *Hobbies:* Reading; Flower arrangement; Acting. *Address:* E 118 Masjid Moth, N. Delhi - 110048, India.

GARMAN Teresa Agnes, b. 29 Aug. 1937, Fort Dodge, Iowa, USA. State Representative. m. Merle A. Garman, 5 Aug. 1961, 1 son, 3 daughters. *Education:* High school. *Appointments:* Breeding pure bred Landrace pigs; Employee relations, 3M Company, 11 years. *Memberships:* Advisory Council, Institute for Decision Making; State Republican Agricultural Council; Story County Porkettes; Veterans of Foreign Wars Auxiliary; Kate Shelley chapter, American Business Women's Association; Boone Women's Club; Farm Bureau; Story County Board of Adjustment, 7 years. *Hobbies include:* Homemaker; Grandmother; Horseback Riding. *Address:* Rural Route 2, Ames, Iowa 50010, USA.

GARMS-HOMOLOVA Vjenka, b. 8 Sept. 1944, Lulec, Czechoslovakia. Psychologist. m. Erik Notthoff, 1981, 1 daughter. *Education:* University degree, Psychology, University of Brno, 1966; PhD, Ludwig-Maximillian University, Munich, Federal Republic of Germany, 1973. *Appointments:* Research fellowship, Max-Planck Institute of Psyohiatry, Munich, 1969-72; German Centre for Youth, Munich, 1973-74; German Centre for Old Age, Berlin, 1974-78; Assistant Professor 1978-, Research Associate 1984-, Free University, Berlin. *Publications:* Over 250 scientific publications; Co-editor, Intergenerational Relationships, 1984. *Memberships include:* Past Chair, Section for Psychological & Social Sciences, German Gerontological Association; International Sociological Association. *Hobbies:* Music; Reading; Travel. *Address:* Freie Universitat Berlin, AG Gesundheistsanalysen und soziale Konzepte, Albrechtstrasse 36A, D-1000 Berlin 41, Federal Republic of Germany.

GARNETT Eve Cynthia Ruth, Author; Illustrator. *Education:* Royal Academy Schools, London. *Publications:* Books: The Family from One End Street; Further Adventures of the Family from One End Street; Holiday at The Dew Drop Inn, A One End Street Story; A Book of the Seasons: an Anthology; To Greenland's Icy Mountaints. The story of Hans Egede, Explorer, Coloniser, Missionary; Pencil illustrations to Stevenson's A Child's Garden of Verses; Is it well with the Child?; In and Out and Roundabout, Stories of a Little Town; Lost and Found, 4 stories; First Affections: some autobiographical chapters of Early Childhood. Paintings: Mural decorations at the Children's House; Exhibited Tate Gallery, 1939. *Memberships:* Society of Authors; PEN. *Honours:* Carnegie Gold Medal, 1937 for The Family from One End Street. *Hobbies:* Wild flowers;

Beach combing. *Address:* c/o Lloyds Bank Ltd, 29-31 Grosvenor Gardens, London SW1W 0BU, England.

GARRON OROZCO Victoria, b. 8 Oct. 1920, San Jose, Costa Rica. Vice President, Republic of Costa Rica. m. Edward Doryan, 1 Mar. 1951, 1 son. *Education:* Licenciatura in Arts & Philosophy, 1945. *Appointments:* Escuela Normal de Heredia, 1942; Professor, North American-Costa Rican Cultural Centre, 1946-48; Professor, Aliance Francaise, 1950; Professor, several high Schools, 1945-55; Professor, University of Costa Rica, 1946-55; Director, Liceo Anastasio Alfaro, 1972; Vice President, Costa Rica. *Publication:* 5 Biographies; 6 Essays; 2 Poetry Books; 1 Text book on Spanish Etymology; 1 novel. *Memberships:* various professional organisations. *Honours:* ⌐3Recipient, various honours and awards. *Address:* Avenida 11, Calle 5 y 3 Bis, Casa No 393, Barrio Amon, San Jose, Costa Rica, Central America.

GARSON Greer, b. 29 Sept. 1908, Northern Ireland. Actress. m. (1) Edward A Shelson, dissolved. (2) Richard Ney, 1943, dissolved. (3) Col. E E Fogelson, 1949. *Education:* BA Hons, London University; Grenoble University. *Creative works:* Birmingham Repertory Theatre, 1932, 1933; London Theatre debut, Whitehall, 1935; lead roles in 13 London plays; entered films in 1939. Films include: Goodbye Mr Chips; Pride and Prejudice; When Ladies Meet; Blossoms in the Dust; Mrs Miniver; Random Harvest; Madame Curie; Mrs Parkington; Valley of Decision; That Forsyte Woman; Julius Caesar; The Law and the Lady; her Twelve Men; Sunrise at Campobello; Strange Lady in Tow; the Singing Nun; The Happiest Millionaire. Stage appearances include: Auntie Mame; Tonight at 8.30; Captain Brassbound's Conversion. Appeared in pioneer British TV, on American TV. *Memberships:* Member of Board, Dallas Theater Centre; State Commn on the arts in Texas and New Mexico; National Committee, St John's College, Santa Fe. *Honours:* Academy Award; Golden Globe Award; Hon. DHum. Rollins College, Florida, 1950; Hon. Dr in Communication Arts, College of Santa Fe, 1970; Hon. DLitt Ulster, 1977; Winner of many awards and medals; Adjunct Professor in Drama, SMU University, Dallas. *Hobbies:* With husband operates Forked Lightning Ranch, Pecos, New Mexico; Breeding and racing thoroughbred horses (stable includes Ack Ack, horse of the year, 1971); Nature study; Music; Golf; Primitive art. *Address:* c/o Republic Bank Building, Dallas, Texas 75201, USA.

GARVEY Olive White, b. 15 July 1893, Arkansas City, Kansas, USA. Executive, retired. m. Ray Hugh Garvey, 8 July 1916, deceased 1959. 2 sons, 2 daughters, 18 grandchildren, 39 great grandchildren. *Education:* AB, Washburn University, 1914. *Appointments:* Chairman of the Board & Director, Garvey Inc, Garvey Center Inc, SRI, Inc; President and Trustee, Family Charities Foundation; Trustee, Olive White Garvey Trust, Garvey Charitable Trusts One-Eleven, inclusive; Eighteen R H Garvey Trusts; Three R L Cochener Trusts; Director and Honorary Trustee, Friends' University, Wichita, 1961-76; Herbert Hoover Presidential Library Association, 1974-; Kansas 4-H Foundation, Wichita, 1960-; Music Theatre of Wichita, Inc, 1973-; Wichita Festival Committee; Kansas Coliseum Board, 1976. *Publications:* Several published plays, poems and articles including: The Obstacle Race, Biography, 1970; Produce or Starve? Commentary, 1976; Once Upon a Family Tree, Autobiography, 1980. *Memberships:* National Board of Governors, Institute of Logopedics, 1970-; International Institute of Education, Honorary Member; Republican Women; Wichita Metropolitan Council. *Honours include:* Phi Kappa Phi, Honorary Scholastic Fraternity; Martin Palmer Humanitarian Award, Institute of Logopedics, 1970; HD Letters, Oklahoma Christian College, 1970; Distinguished Service Award in Agriculture, Kansas State University, 1971; Honorary Member, Clovia, Kansas State University; Over the Years Award, Wichita C/C, 1971; Uncommon Citizen Award, Wichita C/C, 1975; Rose Award, Delta Gamma Fraternity, 1976; 4-H Hall of Fame, 1977; Honor Roll, American Society

of Colonial Dames, 1979; Daughters of American Revolution Medal of Honour, 1983; Distinguished Service Citation, Kansas University, 1983; Kansan of the Year, 1984; Olive W Garvey, Uncommon Citizen, Dr Billy Jones Wichita State University Business Heritage Series, 1985. *Address:* Parklane Towers, 5051 E Lincoln, Wichita, KS 67218, USA.

GASKELL Jane b. 7 July 1941, Grange-over-Sands, Lancashire, England. Writer. 1 daughter. *Appointments:* USA Correspondent, Daily Mail, 1974-76. *Publications:* Strange Evil, 1957; King's Daughter, 1958; Attic Summer, 1960; The Serpent, 1961; Atlan, 1962; The Shiny Narrow Grin, 1963; The Fabulous Heroine, 1963; The City, 1964; All Neat in Black Stockings, 1965 A Sweet Sweet Summer, 1971; Summer Coming, 1973; Some Summer Lands, 1979; Contributor to: Astrological Column, Observer, 1977-79, Vogue Magazine 1986-87; SHE Magazine, 1987-. *Honour:* Somerset Maugham Award, 1971. *Address:* c/o MBA, 45 Fitzroy Street, London W1, England.

GASKIN Catherine Majella, b. 2 Apr. 1929, Co Louth, Republic of Ireland. Novelist. m. Sol Cornberg, 1 Dec. 1955. *Education:* Holy Cross College, Sydney, Australia. *Publications:* This other Eden, 1946; With Every Year, 1947; Dust in Sunlight, 1950; All Else is Folly, 1951; Daughter of the House, 1952; Sara Dane, 1955; Blake's Reach, 1958; Corporation Wife, 1960; I know my Love, 1962; The Tilsit Inheritance, 1963; The File on Devlin, 1965; Edge of Glass, 1967; Fiona, 1970; A Falcon for a Queen, 1972; The Property of a Gentleman, 1974; The Lynmara Legacy, 1975; The Summer of the Spanish Woman, 1977; Family Affairs, 1980; Promises, 1982; The Ambassador's Women, 1985; The Charmed Circle, 1988. Television: The File on Devlin was adapted as a 90 minute Hallmark Hall of Fame Production, USA; Sara Dane 8-part series. Many titles have been adapted for magazine, radio serials or readings. *Memberships:* Society of Authors; Authors Guild of America. *Hobbies:* Reading; Music. *Address:* White Rigg, East Ballerterson, Maughold, Isle of Man, England.

GASKIN Felicia, b. 17 Jan. 1943, Carlisle, USA. OMRF Professor. m. Shu Man Fu, 29 Nov. 1969, 1 son, 1 daughter. *Education:* AB, 1965; MA, Bryn Mawr College, 1967; PhD, University of California Medical School, 1969. *Appointments:* Reseach Associate, NINDS Special Fellow, Columbia University, 1972-74; Assistant & Associate Professor, Pathology, 1974-82, Albert Einstein College of Medicine; OMRF Professor, Biochemistry & Molecular Biology, Oklahoma Medical Research Foundation, 1982-88; Professor Behavioral Medicine and Psychiatry and Neuroscience, University of Virginia School of Medicine, 1988-. *Publications:* 36 publications in scientific journals and books. *Memberships:* American Association of Neuropathologists; American Chemical Society; Americna Society for Biological Chemists; American Society for Cell Biology; Biophysical Society; New York Academy of Science; Oklahoma Academy of Science; Sigma Xi; Society for Neuroscience. *Honours:* Ninds Special Fellowship, 1972-74; Research Career Development Awad, 1975-80. *Address:* University of Virginia School of Medicine, Department of Behavioral Medicine and Psychiatry, Charlottesville, VA 22901, USA.

GASPER Jo Ann, b. 25 Sept. 1946, Providence, Rhode Island, USA. m. Louis Clement Gasper, 21 Sept. 1974. 1 son, 4 daughters. *Education:* BA 1967, MBA 1969, University of Dallas. *Appointments:* Assistant Administrator, Britain Convalescent Center, Inc, Irving, 1964-68; President and Administrator, Turtle Creek Convalescent Center, Medicare Centers, Inc, Dallas, 1968-69; Business Manager/Treasurer, University of Plano, 1969-72; Sales Representative, John Hancock Insurance Co, Dallas, 1972-73; Systems Analyst, Texas Instruments, Richardson, 1973-75; Instructor, George Mason University, Fairfax, 1976; Editor and Publisher, The Right Woman, 1976-81; Deputy Assistant Secretary for Social Services Policy, Office of the Assistant Secretary for Planning and Evaluation, 1981-85, Deputy

Assistant Secretary for Population Affairs, Public Health Service, 1985-87, US Department of Health and Human Services, Washington; Policy Advisor to the Under Secretary of Education, US Department of Education, Washington, 1987-. *Memberships:* Reagan Deputy Assistant Secretaries Association; Executive Women in Government. *Honours:* US Department of Health and Human Services: Secretary Richard Schweiker, Bronze Medal, Secretary Margaret Heckler, Commendation; Wanderer Foundation; Eagle Forum; Outstanding Conservative Woman, Conservative Citizen, Christendom College; Defender of Liberty, Liberty Foundation; Recognition, National Right to Life; Reagan/Bush Family Policy Advisor. *Address:* 6253 Park Road, McLean, VA 22101, USA.

GASS Elizabeth Periam Acland-Hood (Lady), b. 2 Mar. 1940, London, England. Member of Somerset County Council. m. Sir Michael Gass, KCMG, 21 Aug. 1975. *Education:* BA 1961, MA, Girton College, Cambridge. *Appointment:* Member of Somerset County Council, 1985-. *Hobby:* Gardening. *Address:* Fairfield, Stogursey, Bridgwater, Somerset, TA5 1PU, England.

GATES Martina Marie, b. 19 Mar. 1957, Minneapolis, Minnesota, USA. Director of Franchise Development. *Education:* Music/Piano Performance study: College of St Scholastica, Duluth, Minnesota, 1975-76; College of St Catherine, St Paul, Minnesota, 1976-77; Certificates: Professional Tailor, 1979; Executive Secretary, 1979; BA cum laude, Business Administration, Marketing Management, 1984, MBA, Marketing, Finance, 1987, College of St Thomas, St Paul. *Appointments:* Teachers Assistant, Minneapolis Area Vocational/Technical Institute, Minneapolis, Minnesota, 1978-79; Secretary, 1979-80, Customer Service Representative, Regional Accounts, 1980-81, Customer Service Representative, National Accounts, 1981-82, Credit Coordinator, Industrial Foods Division, 1982-85, Assistant Credit Manager, Consumer Foods Division, 1985, Advertising/Sales Promotion Manager, Industrial Foods Division, 1985-86, Credit Manager, Fast Food and Restaurant Division, 1986-87, Director, Franchise Development, Fast Food and Restaurant Division, 1987-89, International Multifoods, Minneapolis; Director, Franchise Development, International Dairy Queen, Minneapolis, 1989-. *Memberships:* Association of MBA Executives; National Association for Female Executives; New College Student Advisory Council, College of St Thomas Alumni; Minneapolis Aquatennial, Committee Volunteer, 1988; St Thomas Alumni Association, College of St Thomas. *Honours:* Member, Omicron Delta Epsilon, 1987-. *Hobbies:* Travel; Numerous summer/winter outdoor sports; Needlework; Reading; Fine Arts. *Address:* 5000 Washburn North, Minneapolis, MN 55430, USA.

GAUCHER Ellen, b. 4 Apr. 1941, Worcester, Massachusetts, USA. Hospital Administrator. m. Stephen Arthur Gaucher, 28 Nov. 1981. 5 sons, 4 daughters. *Education:* RN, St Vincent's Hospital, 1960; ADS, Quinsigamond Comm, 1972; BSN, Worcester State University, 1975; MSPH, Clark University, 1979; MSN equivalent, Boston University, 1980; Postgraduate, University of Michigan, 1980-82. *Appointments include:* Clinical Director of Nursing 1980-81, Acting Administrator 1981-82, Administrator Ambulatory Care 1982-83, Associate Hospital Director Ambulatory Care 1983-87, Chief Operating Officer 1987-, University of Michigan Hospital; Senior consultant & partner, MacKenzie Associates Ltd, 1985-. *Publications:* Author: Article, Software in Healthcare, 1986; Book, Hospital Based Ambulatory Care, 1988. Co-author, articles: A University Helicopter Program, 1985; Entrepreneurship, 1988. Also: Editorial Board, Health Care Competition Week. *Memberships:* American College of Health Care Executives; Local chapter, Society for Ambulatory Care Professionals; Michigan Hospitals Association; Centre for Biomedical Ethics; 1st Vice President, Mid-Michigan, Planned Parenthood; Chair, Visiting Care. *Honours:* Grant, Hartford Foundation, 1988; Recognitions, Worcester Chapter, National Organisation of Women 1977, Worcester State College 1978. *Hobbies:* Cross-

country Skiing; Antiques; Hiking; Travel. *Address:* 9429 Huron Rapids, Whitmore Lake, Michigan 48189, USA.

GAUL Jennifer Daphne, b. 7 Oct. 1947, Durban, Natal, Republic of South Africa. Teacher. m. Patrick Anthony Gaul, 15 Apr. 1968, 1 son, 3 daughter. *Education:* ATCL, 1974; LTCL, 1978. *Appointments:* Teaching piano in private studio, 1978-; Lecturer in Piano, Durban Westville University, 1983, 1984. *Memberships:* Vice-Chairman, South African Society of Music Teachers. *Hobbies:* Gardening; Sewing; Writing music. *Address:* 6 Seaton Place, Durban North 4051, Natal, Republic of South Africa.

GAULKE Mary Florence, b. 24 Sept. 1923, Johnson City, Tennessee, USA. Library Administrator. m. (1)James Wymond crowley, 1 Dec. 1939, 1 son. (2)Bud Gaulke, 1 Sept. 1945, deceased Jan. 1978. (3)Richard Lewis McNaughton, 21 Mar. 1983. *Education:* BS Home Economics, Oregon State University, 1963; MS, Library Service, University of Oregon, 1968; PhDF in Special Education, 1970; Certificate standard personnel supr., standard handicapped learner, Oregon. *Appointments:* Head Department of Home Economics, Riddle School District, Oregon, 1963-66; Library Cons, Douglas County Intermediate Edn Dist, Roseburg, Oregon, 1966-67; Head resident, Head Counselor, Prometheus Project, So Oregon College, Ashland, summers 1966-68; Supr Librarians, Medford School District, Oregon, 1970-73; Instructor in Psychology, So Oregon College, Ashland, 1970-73; Library Supr, Roseburg School Dist, 1974-; Resident psychologist, Black Oaks Boys School, Medford, 1970-75. *Publications:* Vo-ED Course for Junior High, 1965; Library Handbook, 1967; Instructions for Preparation of Cards For All Materials Cataloged for Libraries, 1971; Handbook for Training Library Aides, 1972; Coordinator Laubach Lit Workshops for High School Tutors, 1972. *Memberships:* Oregon Governor's Council on Libraries, 1979; So Oregon Library Federation, secretary 1971-73; ALA, Oregon Library Association; Pacific NW Library Assocaition; Delta Kappa Gamma, president, 1980-82; Phi Delta Kappa, historian, research rep. *Address:* 1625 Days Creek Road, Days Creek, OR 97429, USA

GAULT Marian Holness, b. 1 Oct. 1934, Panama, Canal Zone. Consultant Health/Support Services. 1 son, 1 daughter. *Education:* BA Health Education, 1968-71, MA Education, 1976-78, Glassboro College; Management Certificate, Drexel University, Philadelphia, 1980; Computer Programming, Basic Language Level I and II, NJ State Department of Education, Trenton, 1983-84. *Appointments:* Administrative Supervisor, West Park Hospital, Philadelphia, 1963-64; Nurse Education, Roxborough School of Nursing, Philadelphia, 1965; Teaching/Research Nurse, SUNY Downstate Medical Center, Brooklyn, 1966-67; Director, Nursing, Washington Memorial Hospital, Turnersville, 1972-78; Assistant Director, Nursing Administrator, Einstein Medical Center, Daroff Division, Philadelphia, 1979-81; Consultant Health and Support Services, NJ State Department of Education, Trenton, 1981-87. *Publications:* Manuals for: Maternal Child Health Development Program; Guidelines for a Mixed Obstetrical-Gynecological-Clean Surgical Program; Medical-Surgical Nursing Policies and Procedures; Emergency Procedures; Operation of Central Supply Department; Criteria for Patient Classification System and Categorization System; Guidelines for Operation of a Nursing Personnel Pool-Budgeting and Staffing Procedures; Guidelines for the Statewide Delivery of Migrant Health and Support Services; Evaluation Report for the New Jersey Migrant Education Programe, Fiscal Year 1985 and 1986. *Memberships:* Consultant-Urban Education, NJ State Department of Education; Chairperson- Committee for Action, NJ Society Nursing Administrators; National Consultant (JONA listing), Palpack Enterprises; Chairperson, Sub-Committee for Action of Southern NJ Society for Nursing Service Administrators; New Jersey Migrant Health Task Force; Chairperson, Committee for Health Workshop, National Conference for Panamanians; Board Member, Utopia

Youth Mission; National Association Female Executives; American Nurses Association; National League Nursing. *Honours:* LaBoca High School, Honor Society (Top Ten Students), 1952; Special delegate to the National Student Nurses Panel, St Agnes Medical Center, 1954; Letter Commendation for Public Service, US Senator William Cahill, 1969; Distinguished Alumna, St Agnes Medical Center, Class of 1955, 1980. *Address:* 11 Yale Road, Atco, New Jersey 08004, USA.

GAUTHIER Paule, b. 3 Nov. 1943, Joliette, Quebec, Canada. Lawyer. m. Gilbert J. Cashman, 4 Apr. 1974. *Education:* BA, MBL, Laval University. *Appointment:* Partner, Stein Monast Pratte & Marseille. *Memberships:* Canadian Bar Association, President, Quebec Branch, 1984- 85. *Honour:* Member, Privy Council, Canada, 1984. *Hobbies:* Travel; Music. *Address:* Le St-Amable, 1150 Claire Fontaine, Bureau 300, Quebec G1R 5G4, Canada.

GAVIN, Catherine, b. Aberdeen, Scotland. Author. m. John Ashcraft, 6 July 1948. *Education:* MA, PhD, Aberdeen University, Sorbonne, Paris. *Appointments:* Lecturer, History, Aberdeen Uiversity, 1932-34, 1941-43, Glasgow University, 1934-36; Leader Writer, Kemsley Newspapers, London, 1943-44; War Correspondent, 1944-46, We. Europe, Middle East. *Publications:* 23 published works including: Madeleine; The Cactus and the Crown; The Fortress; The Moon into Blood; The Devil in Harbour; The House of War; Give Me the Daggers; The Snow Mountain; Traitors' Gate; None Dare Call it Treason; How Sleep the Brave; TheSunset Dream; A Light Woman; The Glory Road; A Dawn of Splendour. *Honours:* University Medal of Honour, Helsinki, Finland, 1970; Honorary D.Litt, Aberdeen University, 1986; Military Decoration, World War II, France & Germany Star. *Hobbies:* Travel; Lecturing. *Address:* Apartment 506, 120 California Street, San Francisco, CA 94109, USA.

GAY Alice Felts, b. 3 Oct. 1949, Atlanta, Georgia, USA. Law student. m. 12 June 1971, divorced 1978. 1 daughter. *Education:* AB Psychology 1971, ABJ Radio-TV-Film 1971, MEd Mental Retardation 1973, University of Georgia; Georgia State University, College of Law, 1988-. *Appointments:* Spec Ed Teacher, Commerce Junior High School, 1972-73; Community Relations Specialist, Georgia Retardation Center, Athens, 1978-80; Director of Public Relations, St Mary's Hospital, Athens, 1980-83; Advertising Account Executive, The Adsmith, Athens, 1983-86; Co-owner, And Associates, Athens, 1986-88. *Creative works:* Directed numerous videos and commercials. *Memberships:* President elect, Jr League of Athens, Georgia, 1988-89; President, Athens Jr Woman's Club, 1978-79; State Ed State Education Committee Chairman, Georgia Federation of Women's Clubs, 1980-82; Board Member, American Cancer Society, Clarke Co Unit, 1978-85; Delta Gamma Fraternity. *Honours:* Grand Award, Communications Council of the American Chamber of Commerce Executives; 1984 Gold Award of the Archie Awards; Award of Merit, Southern Industrial Development Council; 1984 Video Communications Award, Atlanta Chapter of the International Television Association for the video The Spirit of Athens. *Hobbies:* Needlework; Gourmet cooking; Rose gardening; Karate; Photography. *Address:* 260 Skyline Parkway, Athens, GA 30606, USA.

GAY Dawn Virginia, b. 9 Jan. 1951, New York City, New York, USA. Executive Recruiter; Health Care Consultant. 1 son. *Education:* Graduate, Hopkins Fellows Program Community & Organizational Systems, Johns Hopkins University, 1981; BA ABS, National College of Education, 1985. *Appointments:* Med Consultant, Prof Medical Services, 1980l; Physician Recruiter, Prof Search Int, 1983-84; Sales/Marketing Rep, Addison Medical Center, 1982-84; Gen Manager, Catalyst Health Care, Div Catalyst Search Ltd, 1984-86; President, Allister & Assoc, Inc, 1986-. *Publication:* Article: How to Find the Right Practice Opportunity?. *Memberships:* National Association of Physician Recruiters; American Hospital Association; MGMA, Illinois Group Mngmt Association; American Assoc

Medical Assistants; American Society Professional & Executive Women; Addison Indust Association; Addison Chamber of Commerce; Leader, Discovery Ministry to Unemployed Willow Creek Community Church. *Hobbies:* Reading; Dancing; Sewing; Crafts; Travelling. *Address:* P O Box 195, Bensenville, IL 60106, USA.

GAY Kathlyn R, b. 4 Mar. 1930, Zion, Illinois, USA. Author. m. Arthur L Gay, 28 Aug. 1948, 2 sons, 1 daughter. *Education:* Northern Illinois University. *Publications:* Childcraft Annual, 1969; Proud Heritage on Parade, 1972; Core English, 1972; Young America Basic Reading Series, 1972; Our Working World, 1973; Body Talk, 1974; Look Mom! No Words, 1977; Eating What Grows Naturally, 1980; Junkyards, 1982; Cities Under Stress, 1985; Civics, 1989; Family Living, 1982; Acid Rain, 1983; Crisis in Education, 1986; Science in Ancient Greece, 1988; Bigotry, 1989; Silent Killers, 1989; Ozone, in press numerous other books; contributor to professional journals, magazines & newspapers. *Honours Include:* Outstanding Book, 1984; Outstanding Book on Education, National Education Association, 1987. *Hobbies:* Reading; Bicycling; Knitting; Cooking. *Address:* 1711 East Beardsley Avenue, Elkhart, IN 46514, USA.

GAY Renate Erika, b. 11 Nov. 1949, Halle, Germany. Physician; Researcher. m. Steffen Gay, 6 Jan. 1973, 1 son, 2 daughters. *Education:* Allgemeinbildende Polytechnische obserschule Lutzen, 1956-64; Erweiterte Oberschule Lutzen, Abitur, Summa cum laude, 1964-68; Medical School, University of Leipzig, DDR, 1968-73; Medical School, University of Munich, FRG, 1973-74; MD Thesis, 1975; Postgraduate Medical Training, University of Munich, 1974-75. *Appointments:* Research Specialist, Biochemistry, Rutgers Medical School; Research Assistant, Institute Dent Research, 1976; Associate Scientist, Comprehensive Cancer Centre, 1981-; Research Assistant Professor, Dermatology, 1981-; Research Assistant Professor, Clinical Immunology & Rheumatology, 1982-84; Research Associate Professor, Medicine, 1984-, University of Alabama, Birmingham, USA. *Honours:* Carol Nachman Prize for Rheumatology, 1984. *Hobbies:* Music; Books; Swimming. *Address:* 1100 Beacon-Parkway, East Regency Villa V-102, Birmingham, AL 35209, USA.

GAYLORD Clarice Elaine, b. 14 Apr. 1943, Los Angeles, USA. Deputy Director. m. Thaddeus Johnson Gaylord, 26 Aug. 1970, 1 son, 1 daughter. *Education:* BA, Zoology, UCLA, 1965; MS, 1967, PhD, 1971, Zoology, Howard University. *Appointments:* Lab Instructor 1965-68, Zoology Instructor, 1968-69, Research Assistant, 1969-71, Howard University; Programme Administrator, Immuno-epidem, National Cancer Institute, 1972-76; Chief, Breast Cancer Programme, 1976-78, Executive Secretary, Tumor Imm. 1980-84, Executive Secretary, Pathology, 1984-80, NIH; Director, Research Grants Programme, EPA, 1984-89; Deputy Director, OHRM, EPA, 1989-. *Memberships:* Senior Executive Service; Minority Women in Science; Women in Science & Engineering; NAFE; Sigma Xi; Delta Sigma Theta; Beta Kappa Chi. *Honours:* Recipient, many honours & awards. *Hobbies:* Swimming; Skating; Bicycling; Painting. *Address:* 605 Camelot Way, Fort Washington, MD 20744, USA.

GAYLORD Karen Lynn Whitacre, b. 25 Dec. 1951, Stuttgart, Germany. Financial Executive; Certified Public Accountant. m. John William Gaylord, 7 May 1988. *Education:* BS cum laude, Accounting, Pennsylvania State University, USA, 1973; CLU, ChFC, American College, 1984. *Appointments:* Peat, Marwick, Mitchell & Company, CPA's, 1973-75; Chief Management Analyst, New Jersey Housing Finance Agency, 1975-81; President, P&R Financial Services & Tax Planning, 1984-87; Senior Sales Trainer, Merrill Lynch, Pierce, Fenner & Smith, 1987-. *Memberships:* American Institute, & New Jersey Society of Certified Public Accountants; American Women's Society of CPA's; National Association of Female Executives. *Honours:* Forum Award, & Top 50 Award, MONY, 1984. *Hobbies:*

Real estate; Physical fitness. *Address:* 1 Witherspoon Court, East Windsor, New Jersey 08520, USA.

GAYNOR Mitzi, b. 4 Sept. 1930, Chicago, Illinois, USA. Actress. *Education:* Powell Professional High School, Hollywood. Studied ballet since age four. Was in Los Angeles Light Opera production, Roberta. *Creative Works:* Opera: Fortune Teller; Song of Norway; Louisiana Purchase; Naughty Marietta; Great Waltz. Pictures include: My Blue Heaven; Take Care of My Little Girl; Golden Girl; The I Don't Care Girl; We're Not Married; Bloodhounds of Broadway; There's No Business Like Show Business; Anything Goes; Three Young Texans; Down Among the Sheltering Palms; Birds and the Bees; The Joker; Les Girls; South Pacific; Surprise Package; Happy Anniversary; For Love or Money.

GAYNOR Suzanne Marie, b. 10 Jan. 1941, Philadelphia, USA. Health Care Executive. m. John Michael Hayes, 26 May 1962, divorced 1982, 1 son, 2 daughters. *Education:* BS, Health Care Administration, Marymount College, 1977; MBA, Finance, Marymount College, 1981; Dr.Ph., University of Michigan, 1989. *Appointments:* Service Co-ordinator, 1972-74, Training Co-Ordinator, 1974-75, Upjohn Health Centre, Washington; Congressional Intern, US Senate, Washington, 1977; Health Analyst, American BloodComm. Arlington, 1977-79; Director, Regionalization Programme, American BloodComm, 1979-83; Director, Regional Services, Greater New York Blood Programme, 1983. *Publications:* Author, various papers, reports & articles. *Memberships:* State, Regional and National Blood Bank Mtgs; American Association of Blood Banks; National Association of Female Executives; Delta Sigma Epsilon. *Honours:* Delta Sigma Epsilon; Scholarships, Fitzgerald-Mercy School of Nursing, & Marymount College; PEW Fellowship, Health Policy, University of Michigan, 1986-89. *Address:* New York Blood Centre, 310 E. 67th Street, New York, NY 10021, USA.

GECKINLI Ayse Emel, b. 1 Feb. 1943, Istanbul, Turkey. University Professor. m. Melih Geckinli, 6 Sept. 1969, 2 daughters. *Education:* Dipl.Eng, Metallurgy, Istanbul Technical University, 1965; MS, Materials Science, 1969, PhD, Materials Science, 1973, Stanford University. *Appointments:* Research Associate, Research Assistant, Stanford University, California, USA, 1969-74; Assistant Professor, 1974-78, Associate Professor, 1978-88, Full Professor, 1988-, Istanbul Technical University, Turkey; Visiting Professor, Ecole Polytechnique, Montreal, Canada, 1981-82. *Publications:* Materials Science and Engineering Materials; Metallography; Phase Transformations; Advance Ceramics. *Hobbies:* Handcrafts; Archaeology; Travel. *Address:* I.T.U. Kimya-Metalurji Fak, Ayazaga, Istanbul, Turkey.

GEE Elaine, b. 14 Feb. 1949, Oakland, California, USA. Psychotherapist. *Education:* BA, University of California, 1969; MA, University of Chicago, 1971. *Appointments:* Supervisor, Social Worker, Governer Hospital, New York City, 1973-81; Psychotherapist, Private Practice, 1981-; Adult Educator, 1982-85; Manager, Employee Services, Mervyn's Corporate Office, 1985-86. *Publications:* 2 research articles, 1973, 1974. *Memberships:* Diplomate, American Board of Examiners in Clinical Social Work; Academy of Certified Social Workers; National Association of Social Workers; American Orthopsychiatric Association, Fellow; American Association for Marriage and Family Therapy. *Honours:* HEW Fellowship, 1969-71; Regents Scholar, 1969, University of California. *Hobbies:* Hiking; Biking; Piano; Choral Singing; Gardening; Writing. *Address:* 1315 Culver Place, San Lorenzo, CA 94580, USA.

GEE Shirley A. b. 25 Apr. 1932, London, England. Playwright. m. 30 Jan. 1965, 2 sons. *Education:* Webber Douglas Academy of Music and Drama. *Career:* Actress, stage, radio, TV, 1953-65; Playwright, 1974-. *Creative works:* Theatre, radio and TV plays: Stones; Moonshine;

Bedrock; Typhoid Mary; Never in My Lifetime; Long Live the Babe; Flights; Against the Wind; Ask for the Moon; Warrior. Adaptations, Children's programmes. *Memberships:* Society of Authors (Broadcasting Committee 1983-85); Theatre Committee, Women's Committee, Writers Guild of Great Britain. *Honours:* Radio Times Drama Bursary, 1974; Giles Cooper Award, 1979, 1983; Pye Award, 1979; Special Commendation, Prix Italia Jury, 1979; Sony Award, 1983; Samuel Beckett Award, 1984; Susan Smith Blackburn Prize, 1985. *Address:* c/o David Higham Associates Ltd, 5-8 Lower John Street, Golden Square, London W1R 4HA, England.

GEESON Judy, b. 10 Sept. 1948, Arundel, Sussex, England. Actress. *Education:* Corona Stage School. *Appointments:* Began professional career on British Television 1960. *Creative Works:* Films include: To Sir With Love; Circus of Blood; Here We Go Round the Mulberry Bush; Hammerhead; Three into Two Won't Go; Two Gentlemen Sharing; The Executioner; 10 Rillington Place; Brannigan; The Eagle Has Landed. Television: Dance of Death; Lady Windermere's Fan; Room with a View; The Skin Game; Sar Maidens; Poldark; She. Theatre: Othello; Titus Andronicus; Two Gentlemen of Verona; Section Nine; An Ideal Husband. *Address:* c/o Richard Stone Partnership, 18-20 York Buildings, London WC2N 6JU, England.

GEFFNER Donna Sue, b. New York City, USA. Speech Pathologist/Audiologist; Educator. *Education:* BA magna cum laude, Brooklyn College, 1967; MA, New York University, 1968; PhD, 1970. *Appointments:* Assistant Professor, Lehman College, 1971-76; Professor, 1976-, Director, Speech & Hearing Centre, 1976-, Dept. Chairperson, 1983-, Speech, Communication Sciences & Theatre, St John's University; Consultant to Corporations in Communications, TV Producer & Hostess, NBC, Emmy Nominee, 1977-78; appeared on ABC, CBS TV and Radio. *Publications:* Articles to professional journals & textbooks; Issue Editor, Journal Topics in Language Disorders, 1980; Editor, Contributor to Monograph, Speech, Language and Communication Skills of Deaf Children, 1987. *Memberships Include:* President 1978-80, New York State Speech Language & Hearing Association; Fellow, Legislative Councillor, 1978-87, 1990-92, American Speech Language Hearing Association. *Honours:* NDEA Fellow, 1970; CUNY Research Foundation Grantee, 1972; Faculty Achievement, Presidents Medal, St John's University; Distinguished Service, New York State Speech, Language Hearing Association. *Address:* St John's University, Jamaica, NY 11439, USA.

GELBART Nina, b. 24 Sept. 1946, New York City, USA. Associate Professor of History. m. William Gelbart, 23 June 1968, 1 son, 1 daughter. *Education:* BA, Harvard Univesity, 1968; MA, 1969, PhD, 1974, University of Chicago. *Appointments:* Lecturer, Mills College, 1972-73; Assistant Professor, Mt. St. Mary's, 1976; Assistant Professor, 1978-86, Associate Professor, 1986- , Occidental College. *Publications:* Feminine and Opposition Journalism in Old Regime France, Le Journal des Dames, 1987; many articles in professional journals. *Memberships:* AHA; SFHS; AAHM; WSFH; HSS; ASECS; WAWH. *Honours:* Recipient, Sierra Prize for Feminine and Opposition Journalism, awarded by Western Association of Women Historians; Fellowships from American Council of Learned Societies, National Endowment for the Humanities, National Institute of Health, etc.; many honours & awards. *Hobbies:* Playing Cello; European Travel. *Address:* 967 Bluegrass Lane, Los Angeles, CA 90049, USA.

GELBER Linda C, b. 30 Oct 1950, Hackensack, New Jersey, USA. *Education:* BA, 1972, MBA, 1974, JD, 1978, Indiana University; National Graduate Trust School, 1983; Indiana Bar 1978; US Supreme Court, 1983; New Jersey, 1988. *Appointments:* Legislative Analyst, Legislative Services Agency, Indianapolis, Indiana, 1978-80; Vice President, Trust Officer, First

National Bank, Kokomo, Indiana, 1980-85; Assistant Vice President and Assistant Trust Counsel, Merchants National Bank, Edison/Englewood, New Jersey, 1987-. *Memberships:* American, New Jersey State and Bergen County Bar Associations; Board of Directors, United Way of Howard County, Kokomo, Indiana 1984-85; North Central Indiana Chapter of American Institute of Banking, Vice President, 1984-85. *Honour:* Awarded the designation of Certified Financial Services Counsellor (through National Graduate Trust School) 1983. *Address:* Midlantic National Bank, One Engle Street, Englewood, NJ 07631, USA.

GELFMAN Mary Hughes Boyce, b. 3 Apr. 1935, Boston, Massachusetts, USA. Attorney at Law. m. Nelson A. Gelfman, 1 son, 2 daughters. *Education:* BA, Swarthmore College, 1957; MA, Columbia University, 1959; JD, University of Connecticut, 1978. *Appointments:* Teacher, New Rochelle, New York, 1957-58; Teacher, New Haven, Connecticut, 1958-60; Connecticut State Department of Education, 1979-84; Private Practice of Law, 1984-. *Memberships:* American Bar Association; Connecticut Bar Association; League of Women Voters; American Association of University Women; Connecticut School Attorneys' Council; Ridgefield Board of Education, 1969-80; State Advisory Council on Special Education, 1972-76; Board Member, Ridgefield Community Kindergarten, 1965-77. *Honours:* Appointed by the Governor to State Department of Education Panel of Arbitrators, 1987. *Address:* 374 North Salem Road, Ridgefield, CT 06877, USA.

GELLER Estelle Hecht, b. 1 Jan. 1927, New York City, USA. Researcher/Educator; Spec Laboratory Animal Medicine. m. Lester M Geller, 5 Sept. 1948. 2 sons, 1 daughter. *Education:* BS, DVM, Cornell University, 1942-47; MPH, Columbia University, 1970-71. *Appointments:* Director, Experimental Surgery Lab, New York Medical College, 1947-48; Research Vet, USVA Hospital, Bronx, NY, 1948-54; Small Animal Practice, New York, 1954-55; Director and Vet, Animal Institute; Asst Professor of Pathology, Albert Einstein College of Medicine, Bronx, NY, 1956-; Vice President and Treas, Consultant Laboratory Animals, New York State Society for Medical Research, 1972-74. *Publication:* Health Hazards for Man in text The Laboratory Rat and other publications. *Memberships:* Nature Conservancy of Long Island; AVMA, reviewer for Journal of AVMA, 1986-; Assn for Women Vets (founding and charter memb, vice-president for charter membs, editor of Bulletin 1950-55); Amer Assn for Laboratory Animal Science (orig member of Animal Care Panel, Book reviewer for Laboratory Animal Science 1986-); Conference of Public Health Vets; Vet Med Assn of New York City. *Honours:* Fellow, International Agency for Research on Cancer, World Health Organization, 1969; Diplomate, American College of Laboratory Animal Medicine. *Address:* 53-20 213 Street, Bayside, NY 11364, USA.

GELLIS Roberta Leah, b. 27 Sept. 1927, Brooklyn, New York, USA. Author. m. Charles Gellis, 14 Apr. 1947, 1 son. *Education:* BA, Hunter College, 1947; MS, Brooklyn Polytechnic Institute, 1952. *Appointments:* Chemist, Foster D. Snell Inc., 1947-53; Copy Editor, McGraw Hill Book Company, 1953-55; Freelance Editor, 1955-. *Publications:* Knight's Honor, 1964; Bond of Blood, 1965; The Dragon and the Rose, 1977; The Sword and the Swan, 1977; The Rope Dancer, 1986; Masques of Gold, 1988; Roselynde Chronicles: Roselynde, 1978, Alinor, 1978, Joanna, 1979, Gilliane, 1980, Rhiannon, 1982, Sybelle, 1983; The Royal Dynasty Series: Siren Song, 1981, Winter Song, 1982, Fire Song, 1984, A Silver Mirror, 1989; Tales of Jernaeve: Tapestry of Dreams, 1985, Fires of Winter, 1987, Napoleonic Era: The English Heiress, 1980, The Cornish Heiress, 1981, The Kent Heiress, 1982, Fortune's Bride, 1983, A Woman's Estate, 1984; other books. *Memberships:* Authors League; Pen and Brush; Romance Writers of America. *Honours Include:* Romantic Times Award, 1982; West Coast Review of Books, Silve Medal Porgy, 1983; West Coast Review of Books, Gold Medal Porgy, 1984; Romantic Times Reviewer's Award, 1988; etc.

Hobby: Reading. *Address:* Box 483, Roslyn Heights, NY 11577, USA.

GELSINGER-BROWN Linda M, b. 8 Jan. 1950, Robesonia, Pennsylvania, USA. Senior Clinical Scientist. m. Richard A Brown, 13 Aug. 1973. *Education:* BA, St Joseph's University, 1975; Diplomas: American Management Association, 1980-87. *Appointments:* Supervisor, Cardiovascular Research, Lankenau Hospital, 970-76; Sales Representative, Medical Monitors, 1976-77, Data Medical, 1977-81; Senior Research Specialist, Cardio Data Systems, Bloomfield, 1986-88; Senior Clinical Scientist, Wyeth- Ayerst Research, Radnor, 1988-. *Memberships:* National Association of Female Executives; Associates in Clinical Pharmacology; American Association of Professional & Executive Women; etc. *Honours:* Dale Carnegie Sales Course, Continuous Oustanding Performance Award. *Hobbies:* Foreign Travel; Classical Music; Volunteer Work. *Address:* Box 1036 RD No 2, Robesonia, PA 19551, USA.

GENSHEIMER Elizabeth Lucille, b. 25 Jan. 1955, Louisville, USA. Manager. *Education:* BS., Computer Science, 1976. *Appointments:* Weapons Analyst, CIA, 1975-76; Graduate Teaching Assistant, University of Louisville, 1977-78; Software Engineer, Texas Instruments, 1978-81; Software Engineer, Northern Telecom Inc., 1981-83; Bell Northern Research, 1983-; Bell Northern Research, 1983-89; Convex Computer Corporation, 1989-. *Memberships:* Association for Computing Machinery; German Choral Society; Nature Conservancy; National Audubon Society; Whale Adoption Project; *Honours Include:* Kentucky Girls State, 1972; National Merit Scholar, Getty Oil, 1973; National Merit Scholarship, University of Louisville, 1973; CWENS, 1973-74; Delta Phi Alpha, 1976; Bell Northern Research Achievement Award, 1988. *Hobbies Include:* Photography; Volleyball; Power Lifting; Reading. *Address:* PO Box 796005, Dallas, TX 75379, USA.

GENTRY Hilda Arleen, b. 4 Mar. 1963, Houston, USA. School Administrator. *Education:* BA, 1983; MEd., 1985; Currently pursuing Ed.D. degree. *Appointments:* Junior Newscaster/Editor, Channel 39 KHTV, 1975-80; Teacher, Hogg Middle School, 1984; Teacher, Bellaire High School, 1984-88; Dean of Instruction, High School for the Performing and Visual Arts, 1988-. *Publications:* Developer, Computer Software Programme, Keys to Sentence Structure. *Memberships:* National, Texas & Houston Junior Chambers of Commerce; Association for Curriculum & Development; National, Texas & Houston Council of Teachers of English; Phi Delta Kappa. *Honours:* Outstanding Young Educator, 1987; Semi-Finalist, Teacher of the Year, Houston Independent School District, 1987. *Hobbies Include:* Reading; Aerobics; Chess. *Address:* High School for the Performing & Visual Arts, 4001 Stanford, Houston, TX 77006, USA.

GENTZLER Yvonne Sharon, b. 14 June 1953, Norfolk, Virginia, USA. Assistant Professor. *Education:* BA, Biblical Studies, 1975; BS, Home Economics, 1977; MEd., 1982, PhD, 1986, Home Economics Education. *Appointments:* Home Arts Instructor, 1977-82; Graduate Assistant, 1982- 84, Instructor, 1984-86, Assistant Professor, 1986-, Home Economics Education, Pennsylvania State University. *Publications:* Profesional Competence for Home Economists; The Twelve Goals of Quality Education; Professional Commitment: An Analysis of Meaning; Toward Professional Competence: A Conceptualization of Self Directed Behaviour; Transforming the Home Economics Profession: A Role for Educators. *Memberships:* Omicron Nu; Pennsylvania Home Economics Association, Vice President, External Relations. *Honours:* Distinguished Leadership Award, 1986; Home Economics Division Fellowhship, 1987; Recipient, various other honours and awards. *Hobbies:* Reading; Needlework; Antique Collecting. *Address:* Home Economics Education, 212 Rackley Building, The Pennsylvania State Uiversity, University Park, PA 16802, USA.

GEORGE D. Kay, b. 21 Sept. 1953, Columbus, Ohio, USA. Senior Account Executive. m. Denis J. Doyle, 20 Sept. 1980, 2 stepsons. *Education:* BA, University of Maine, 1975. *Appointments:* Sales Representative, Dunfey Eastland Hotel, Portland, Maine, 1971-75; Sales Manager, Dunfey Sheraton Lamies and Meadowbrook Inns, Hampton, New Hampshire, 1976; Sales Manager, Dunfey Hyannis Hotel, Boston, Massachusetts, 1977-80; Senior Account Executive, Targeted Media in Time Inc. Magazines, Boston, 1980-90. *Honours:* Dunfey Sales Award, 1979; Fortune Sales Award, 1981; Targeted Media/Time Inc. Sales Award, 1984, 1987, 1988, 1989. *Hobbies:* Horseback riding and jumping; Cooking; Reading; Swimming; Entertaining. *Address:* Targeted Media/Time Inc., PO Box 297, Brookline, MA 02146, USA.

GEORGE Joyce J, b. 4 May 1936, Akron, Ohio, USA. Judge. 1 son, 1 daughter. *Education:* BA, 1962, JD, 1966, University of Akron; LL.M, 1986, SJD Candidate 1987-, University of Virginia. *Appointments:* Assistant Director of Law, Akron, 1966-70; Private Practice, Akron, 1970- 73; Referee, Akron Muni Court, 1975-76; Judge, Akron Muni. Court, 1976-83; Judge, 9th District Court of Appeals, 1983-. *Publications:* Articles in professional journals. *Memberships:* Akron Bar Association; American Bar, Ohio State Bar Associations; Ohio Judicial Conference. *Honours Include:* Alumni Honour Award, University of Akron, 1983; Woman of the Year, Government & Politics, Summit County, 1983; President, Class of 1986, Masters in Judicial Process, University of Virginia Law School. *Address:* Ninth District Court of Appeals, 161 South High Street, Akron, OH 44308, USA.

GEORGE Kathleen Elizabeth, b. 7 July 1943, Johnstown, Pennsylvania, USA. Associate Professor of Theatre. *Education:* BA English 1964, MA Theatre 1966, PhD Theatre 1975, MFA Fiction 1988, University of Pittsburgh. *Appointments:* Instructor, Carlow College, 1968-76; Assistant Professor 1976-81, Associate Professor 1981-, Academic Dean, Semester-at-Sea 1987, University of Pittsburgh. *Creative work includes:* Publications: Book, Rhythm in Drama, 1981; Article, Anagrams, Wind Literary Journal, 1981; 50 theatre productions, including Country Wife, Much Ado About Nothing, Hamlet, King Lear. *Memberships include:* Poets & Writers; Board, Institute of Shipboard Education. *Honours:* Phi Beta Kappa, summa cum laude, 1964; Graduate fellowships, 1964-68; Directing awards, 1977-79; Writing residencies, 1981-83; Grant, Bowman, travel to London, 1984; Grants, Pennsylvania Council of Arts, 1981, 1987. *Hobbies:* Cooking; Travel; Fiction. *Address:* 6605 Rosemoor Street, Pittsburgh, Pennsylvania 15217, USA.

GEORGE Patricia Ann, b. 17 Mar. 1950, Port Arthur, USA. Certified Public Accountant. m. Stephen Craig George, 28 Apr. 1972, 1 son, 1 daughter. *Education:* BS, Accounting & Management, Houston Baptist University, 1979. *Appointments:* Feasibility Analyst, United Investors Inc., Houston, 1970-74; Assistant Controller, Browne of Houston, 1974-75; Chief Accountant, Owen Company, Houston, 1975-77; Vice President, Eco Resources Inc., Houston, 1978-85; Private Practice, Consultant, Houston, 1985-. *Memberships:* American Institute of CPA's' Texas Society of CPA's; Houston & Tulsa Chapters of CPA's; Clear Lake Area Chamber of Commerce; Girl Scout Leader, San Jacinto Council. *Honours:* Recipient, Scholastic Achievement Award, Wall Street Journal, 1979; Distinguished Leadership Award for Accounting, 1986. *Address:* 15931 Parchester, Houston, TX 77062, USA.

GEORGE Susan Melody, b. 26 July 1950, Surbiton, Surrey, England. Actress; Producer, Amy International Productions Limited. m. Simon Charles Pendered MacCorkindale, 5 Oct. 1984. *Education:* Corona Academy of Dramatic Art, 1962-66. *Appointments:* Films: Billion Dollar Brain, 1965; The Sorcerers, 1966; Up the Junction, 1966; The Strange Affair, 1967; The Looking Glass War, 1967; All Neat in Black Stockings, 1968; Twinky (Lola), 1968; Spring and Port Wine, 1969; Eye Witness, 1969; Die Screaming Marianne, 1969; Fright, 1970; Straw Dogs, 1970; Sonny and Jed, 1971; Dirty Mary Crazy Larry, 1973; Mandingo, 1973; Out of Season, 1974; A Small Town in Texas, 1975; Tiger Shark, 1975; Tomorrow Never Comes, 1977; Venom, 1980; A Texas Legend, 1980; Enter the Ninja, 1981; The House Where Evil Dwells, 1981; The Jigsaw Man, 1982-83; The White Stallion, 1986; Stealing Heaven, (Executive Producer), 1987-88; White Roses, (Executive Producer), 1988-89. TV: Swallows and Amazons, BBC 1962; Adam's Apple, 1963; Weaver's Green, 1966; Compensation Alice, 1967; The Right Attitude, 1968; Dracula, 1968; Life Class, 1969; Dr Jekyll and Mr Hyde, 1972; The Final Eye, 1976; Lamb to the Slaughter, Anglia, 1979; Royal Jelly, 1979; The Bob Hope Special, NBC, 1979; US Against the World, NBC 1979; Pajama Tops, 1982; Czechmate, UK-TV, Movie, 1984; Jack The Ripper, Thames TV, 1988. Theatre: The Sound of Music, 1962; Pyjama Tops, 1982; The Country Girl, 1984; Producer, The Importance of Being Oscar, 1985; Rough Crossing, 1987. *Publications:* Song, Please Just Go; Song, Save Me for a Rainy Day; Song, Singing This One for Me; Songs to Bedroom Walls, 1987. *Memberships:* various professional organisations. *Honours:* Recipient, various honours and awards. *Hobbies:* Horse Riding; Singing/Song Writing; Skiing; Tennis; Travel. *Address:* Amy International Productions Ltd., Lee International Studios, Studios Road, Shepperton, Middlesex TW17 0QD, England.

GEORGE Sylvia James, b. 13 Oct. 1921, Syracuse, New York, USA. Professional Painter; Portraitist. m. Henry H, 5 Aug. 1946, 5 sons, 3 daughters. *Education:* Pratt Institute, 1944; American University, 1954. *Appointments:* Tobe Syndicates, 1942-44; Contemp Artists, New York City, 1943-44; Johnson Studio, Columbia, 1974-75; S & G Art Studio. *Publications:* Commissioned portraits in large number of private & public collections worldwide. *Memberships:* Maryland Society of Portrait Painters; Howard County Society of Portrait Painters; Artist Equity; new Art Centre; etc. *Honours:* Gold Seals, 1st Prize, Honorable Mentions, 1939-40, etc. *Hobbies:* Sailing; Photography. *Address:* 6510 Beeechwood Drive, Columbia, MD 21046, USA.

GEORGE, Wilma, b. 19 Dec. 1918, Manchester, England. Author; Lecturer. m. George Crowther, 20 July 1956. *Education:* BA, MA, Oxford University. *Appointments:* Fellow, St Anne's College, 1945-48, Lecturer, Somerville College, 1962-77, Fellow, Lady Margaret Hall, Lecturer, 1959-86, University of Oxford; Visiting Professor, University of Oregon, 1962-63. *Publications:* Elementary Genetics, 1951, 1965; Animal Geography, 1962; Biologist Philosopher, 1963; Eating in Eight Languages, 1968; Animals and Maps, 1969; Gregor Mendel & Heredity, 1975; Darwin, 1982; over 50 articles in professional journals. *Memberships:* Genetical Society; Society for Experimental Biology; British Society for History of Science; Zoological Society; Royal Geographical Society; Society for the History of Natural History; Exploration Club, Oxford University. *Hobbies:* Travel Photography; Walking Swimming; Skiing. *Address:* 7 Tackley Place, Oxford OX2 6RR, England.

GEORGESCU Bianca Camelia, b. 18 June 1938, Bucharest, Romania. Doctor. m. Georgescu Florin, 12 Apr. 1972. *Education:* Dentist Technician Diploma; Dentist Doctor (Medicine), Institute of Bucharest; X-ray course for Dentist Profession; Exam for specialist doctor, 1974. *Appointments:* High scholl nv 1 Hasdeu, 1964-72; Carol Davila Hospital, 1972-79; Grivita Hospital, 1973-88. *Membership:* Society for Medical Sciences. *Hobbies:* Literature; Poetry. *Address:* Radu voda nv 16, District 4, Bucharest, Romania.

GEORGOPOULOS Maria, b. 2 Apr. 1949, Moussata, Cefalonia, Greece. Architect. divorced. 1 son. *Education:* BArch, National Polytechnic School of Greece, 1972; MSc, Columbia University, New York, USA, 1976. *Appointments:* Project Manager, Architects Design Group, New York City, 1976-79; Project Manager,

Griswold, Heckel & Kelly, New York City, 1979-80; Project Director, Lehman Brothers, Kuhn Loeb Inc, New York City, 1980-85; Vice President, L F Rothschild Inc, New York City, 1985-. *Memberships:* AIA; American Women Entrepreneurs; Greek Institute of Architects. *Hobby:* Tennis. *Address:* 14 Melrose Lane Douglaston, New York, NY 11363, USA.

GERARD-SHARP Monica Fleur, b. 4 Oct. 1951, London, England. Publisher; Media Executive. m. Ali E Wambold, 21 Nov. 1981. 1 daughter. *Education:* BA (Hons), University of Warwick; MBA, Columbia University Graduate Business School, 1980. *Appointments:* Editorial assistant then Staff Editor, The Chemical Engineer, 1973-74; Features Sub-Editor, TV Times, 1974-75; Press Officer, Editor 1975-78, Organizer Conference on Science & Technology for Development 1977-78, United Nations; Manager, Time Life Video, 1980; Director, Time Life Films/Time Life Television, 1981; Vice President, TVIS, 1982; Director, Video Group, Time Inc, 1983-85; Board Member, USA Network, 1984-785; Assistant Treasurer, Corporate Officer, Time Inc, 1985-87; Fairchild Publications, Capital Citites/ABC Inc, 1987-; Associate Publisher, Travel Today, 1987-88; Director, Video, 1988-89; Publishing Director, Entree Magazine and Home Fashions Magazine, 1989. *Publications:* Editor, Everyone's United Nations, 1965-76; Contributing Editor, Asian Pacific Forum; Articles published; Produced Clara Hancox on Europe. *Memberships:* Distinguished Leaders Lecture Series, Chairman; Magalink Foundation; American Film Institute; National Academy of Cable Programming. *Honours:* Beta Gamma Sigma, 1980; Samuel Bronfman Fellow, Columbia University, 1978- 80. *Hobbies:* Antiques; Wildlife; Minority education; Gadgets. *Address:* 161 West 86th Street, New York, NY 10024, USA.

GERBER Jane, b. 17 June 1938, New York, USA. Professor. m. Roger A. Gerber, 24 Sept. 1964, 3 daughters. *Education:* BA, Wellesley College, 1959; MA, Harvard University, 1962; PhD, Columbia University, 1972. *Appointments:* Herbert Lehman College, 1972-77, Graduate School amd University Center, 1977-, City University of New York. *Publications:* Books: Jewish Society in Fez 1450-1750; Jews in Muslim Lands. *Memberships:* President, Association for Jewish Studies; Vice- President, American Society of Sephardic Studies; Executive Board, World Union of Jewish Studies; Academic Council, American Jewish Historical Society; Academic Council, American Friends of Hebrew University; American Jewish Committee, Westchester Board; Board, Institute of Contemporary Jewry, Jerusalem. *Honours:* Phi Beta Kappa, 1959; Durant Scholar, 1959; Wellesley Scholar, 1958, 1959; Radcliffe College Fellow, 1961; Columbia Faculty Scholar, 1962; NDFL Fellow in Arabic, 1961-65; NEH Junior Faculty Fellow, 1975; CUNY Faculty Research Grants, 1977, 1978, 1981. *Hobby:* Music. *Address:* 26 Sage Terrace, Scarsdale, NY 10583, USA.

GERMAN Joan Alice, b. 9 Feb. 1933, Philadelphia, Pennsylvania, USA. Writer. m. (1) Donald R. German (dec.), 1 son, (2) David R. Grapes, 1 Oct. 1988. *Education:* Temple University, Philadelphia, 1951-54. *Appointments:* Various secretarial positions, 1954-57; Administrative assistant, public relations department, Vertol Aircraft, Morton, PA, 1958; Freelance writer, editor, 1964-. *Publications:* Author: What Am I?, 1979; Guess What?, 1979; Money Book, 1981. Co-author with Donald R. German, numerous books including: Passkeys, 1967; Dividends, 1969; Bank Teller's Handbook, 1970, 1981; Successful Job Hunting for Executives, 1974; Make Your Own Convenience Foods, 1979; Checklists for Profitability, 1983; Money A to Z: A Consumer's Guide to Language of Personal Finance, 1984; 90 Days to Financial Fitness, 1986. Also: Numerous articles, various journals & magazines; Author/editor, Branch Banker's Report 1968-87, Bank Teller's Report 1969-, contributing editor, Bank Marketing Report 1967-86. *Memberships include:* Past State President, Past Branch President, National League of American Pen Women; Chair, Berkshire Hills Chapter,

American Society of Journalists & Authors; Board Chair, Learning Connection; Authors Guild; Boston Authors Club; Founder, Berkshire Poets Workshop. *Hobbies:* Writing poetry; art needlework. *Address:* 1008 West Mountain Road, Cheshire, Massachusetts 01225, USA.

GESCHKA Ottilia Maria, b. 27 Dec. 1939, Haintchen, Hesse, Federal Republic of Germany. Secretary of State, Government of Hesse. m. Dr Horst Geschka, 16 Aug. 1963. 1 son, 1 daughter. *Education:* Agricultural School, 1953-56; State Diploma, Nurse for Children, 1957-59. *Appointments:* Nurse for Children at: Stadtkrankenhaus Zell a.d. Mosel, 1959-61; Universitatskinderklinik Mainze, 1961-65; Member of Parliament of Hesse, 1978- 87; Secretary of State for Womens Affairs, Government of Hesse, 1987-. *Memberships:* Member of various committees on federal and national level, Christian Democratic Union; Member, Federal Executive and National Executive, Christian Democratic Union. *Honour:* Bundesverdienstkreuz, Federal Republic of Germany, 1987. *Hobbies:* Accommodation of guests; Art; Literature; Music. *Address:* Sifterstrasse 2, 6100 Dramstadt- Arheilgen, Federal Republic of Germany.

GHEZZI Grace Baranello, b. 26 May 1955, Syracuse, New York, USA. Certified Public Accountant. m. Reno Ghezzi, Jr, 7 Oct. 1978, 1 son, 1 daughter. *Education:* Powelson Business Institute, 1973-74; BS magna cum laude, Accounting, LeMoyne College, 1977; CPA, New York State, 1979. *Appointments:* Corporate Auditor, McGraw-Hill Inc, 1979-80; Staff Accountant, Deloitte Haskins & Sells, CPA's, 1977-79; Self-employed CPA, 1980- 87, 1989-; Partner, Peters, Ghezzi & Kawa, 1987-89. *Memberships:* American Institute, National & New York State Societies, of Certified Public Accountants; Past Chair, member, St Charles Borromeo Finance Committee. *Hobbies:* Piano; Cake decorating; Needlework. *Address:* 600 Bronson Road, Syracuse, New York 13219, USA.

GIANUTSOS Rosamond Ingalls Rockwell, b. 1 Apr. 1945, Lawrence, USA. Psychologist. m. John Gerasimos Gianutsos, 11 Sept. 1965, 2 sons. *Education:* BA, Barnard College, 1966; PhD, New York University, 1970. *Appointments:* Assistant, & Associate Professor, Adelphi University, 1970-83; Senior Psychologist, New York University Medical Centre, 1978-83; Consultant, Neuropsychology, 1983-. *Publications:* Computer Programmes for Cognitive Rehabilitation; over 25 articles. *Memberships:* National Co-ordinator, Psychologists for Social Action; Chair, Linguistics Section, New York Academy of Sciences; Editorial Board, Neuropsychology, Journal of Clinical & Experimental Nueropsychology. *Honours:* National Finalist, Johns Hopkins Personal Computing to Active Handicapped, 1981; Fellow, New York Acadmey of Sciences. *Hobbies:* Jogging; Cycling; Computer Software Design; Weight Management. *Address:* Cognitive Rehabilitation Services, 38-25 52nd St., Sunnyside, NY 11104, USA.

GIARDELLI Bim, b. 19 May 1917, Croydon, Surrey, England. Artist. m. (1) Kennedy Axten, 1938, divorced 1946. (2) Terence Brinsley John Danvers Butler, 1947, divorced 1969, 4 daughters. (3) Vincent Charles Arthur Giardelli, 1973. *Education:* Byham Shaw School of Art, London, 1934-36. *Appointments:* Lemay Studio London; Illustrations for Harpers Bazaar, The Queen, Vogue etc, 1936-38; WRNS MT Driver and Officer, 1942-47; Feature Writer, Times of Malta, 1949-53; Librarian Durham Cathedral, 1948. *Publications:* Interviews and Woman's Page in Dyfed and Milford Reporter, 1953-55; Reports and Critical Articles for Link Art Magazine. Illustrations for The Lord and Son by Madeleine Mayne, Edge Press 1980. Paintings in National Museum of Wales, Welsh Arts Council, University of Wales, Bankok Embassy etc. Exhibitions: Centaur Gallery London; Galerie Convergence Nantes; University College Wales; Glyn Vivian, Swansea; National Museum Wales; Arnolfini, Bristol, etc. *Memberships:* Secretary and Chairman West Wales, AADW; Member of Welsh Group: Vice Chairman, Dyfed KGV Fund for Sailors, RNLI Committee. *Honours:* Welsh Arts Council Awards, 1975 and 1977; British Council selection 1986. *Hobbies:*

Acting, producing and stage design for Malta Amateur Dramatic Club, 1949-53; Orchid growing; Sailing Ocean Racing with John Illingworth; Riding; Wild flowers; Seals; Music. *Address:* The Golden Plover, Warren, Pembroke, Dyfed, SA71 5HR, Wales.

GIBBS Barbara Francesca, b. 23 Sept 1912, Los Angeles, California, USA. Housewife. m. 1. James V Cunningham, June 1937, divorced 1942, 1 daughter; 2. Francis Golffing, 2 Feb 1942. *Education:* BA, Stanford University, 1934; MA, University of California, Los Angeles, 1935; Studies, University of California, Berkeley, 1936. *Appointments:* Assistant Editor and de facto business manager, production manager, design editor, The Journal of Pre-Raphaelite Studies (original title The Pre- Raphaelite Review). Teaching, Bennington College. *Publications:* Books of Poems: The Well, 1941; The Green Chapel 1958; Poems Written in Berlin, 1958; The Meeting Place of the Colors, 1972. Reviews of poetry published in The Western Review, Stand, Poetry and Accent. *Honours:* Oscar Blumenthal Prize for Poetry, 1949; James Phelan Fellowship, 1942; Guggenheim Fellowship in Creative Writing, 1955-56 (2 years). *Hobbies:* Gardening; Travel; Photography; Music; Animals. *Address:* 272 Middle Hancock Road, Peterborough, NH 03458, USA.

GIBBS Barbara Jill, b. 4 May 1955, Dayton, Ohio, USA. Art Therapist. m. Allen Doefel, 19 Aug. 1984. *Education:* BA, Education, 1979; MA, Therapy, 1985. *Appointments:* Art Therapist, Westview School for Mentally Retarded, 1981-82; Art Therapist, 1982-88, Consultant on Art Therapy with Severe behaviour handicaps, Samaritan Center for Youth Resources. *Memberships:* American Art Therapy Association; Buckeye Art Therapy Association (Membership chair, 1985-88); Sierra Club; Costeau Society. *Hobbies:* Art; Dance; Reading; Nature. *Address:* 4746 49th St, SW, Seattle, WA 98116, USA.

GIBBS Carol Ann (nee Carol Le Feuvre), b. 18 Oct. 1951, Jersey, Channel Islands. Housewife; Golfer. m. Roderick James Gibbs, 25 Jan. 1975. 1 son. *Honours:* LGU touring teams to Australia & Canada, 1973; Runner- up, English Ladies, 1973; South Eastern Ladies Champion 1974; Avia Foursomes, Champion, 1974; Jersey Ladies Champion, 1966, 1967, 1968; English International, 1971, 1972, 1973, 1974; Hampshire Ladies Champion, 1970. 71. 72. 73. 74. 76; Dutch Ladies Champion, 1972; English Girls, 1966-70; British Girls, 1970; Girl International, 1968, 69, 70; Curtis Cup, 1974. *Hobbies:* Swimming; Squash. *Address:* Les Arches, 14 Brackenborough, Brixworth, Northamptonshire NN6 9JW, England.

GIBBS Fannye Irving, b. 9 Mar. 1914, USA. Retired. m. (1)Charles U. Bouldes, 15 Sept. 1941 (div.), (2) Cecil Eric Gibbs, 8 Dec. 1966. 3 daughters. *Education:* AA, University of Albuquerque, 1982; BA, University of New Mexico, 1988. *Memberships:* Leader, offices, Girl Scouts; Club President, Secretary, Civitan International; Branch Secretary, Treasurer, National Association for Advancement of Coloured Peoples (NAACP); Secretary, Women United for Youth. *Honours:* Numerous awards, voluntary service, including: American Red Cross, 1950, 1965; Girl Scouts, 1951-83; New Mexico Secretary of State, 1979, 1981, 1982, 1988; NM Conference of Churches,1983; NM Department of Corrections, 1983; NAACP, 1936-; International Civitan Club, 1982-. *Hobbies:* Compiling Afro-American history library; Volunteer work, various community & church organisations. *Address:* PO Box 15752, Rio Rancho, New Mexico 87174, USA.

GIBBS Kaye Louise, b. 11 Sept. 1943, Moscow, Idaho, USA. Psychotherapist. div. *Education:* BS, Education, 1965; MEd, Northeastern University, 1969; Postgraduate courses, University of Miami, & Humanistic Psychology Institute. *Appointments:* Teacher, Georgia, California, Massachusetts, 1965-68; Editor, Houghton Mifflin Publishing Company, Boston, 1968-69; Career Counsellor, University of Miami, 1969-

72; Counsellor, vocational rehabilitation, mental health, 1973-74; Family Therapist, Village South Inc, Miami, Florida, 1974-76; Private practice, individual, marriage & family therapy, Miami 1973-79, Atlanta, Georgia 1981-; Social worker, Good Shephard Retirement Centre, Phoenix, Arizona, 1979-80. *Membership:* American Association of Marriage & Family Therapists. *Honour:* Kappa Delta Pi. *Address:* c/o Real Life Institute, 3960 Peachtree Road NE, Suite 427, Atlanta, Georgia 30319, USA.

GIBSON Dorothy E, b. 9 Feb. 1923, Colombus, Ohio, USA. Clinical Social Worker. *Education:* BA, 1940; Certificate Admin., NYU, 1944; MSS, Smith College, 1952. *Appointments:* Children's Home Society, 1952-56; California State Dept. Mental Hygiene, 1956-61; University of California, Social Work Dept., 1961-66; Yale University, Psychiatry Dept., 1968-70; Planned Parenthood, 1970-72; Private Practice, 1972-. *Publications:* Professional papers. *Memberships:* National Association Social Workers, State Board, Regional Board; Society Clinical Social Work, State Board; American Osteopsychiatric Association, Fellow. *Honour:* Scholarship, Smith College, 1951. *Hobbies:* Hiking; Camping; Cooking; Skiing; Bicycling; Travel. *Address:* 429 1/2 Johnson St., Sausalito, CA 94965, USA.

GIBSON Kathleen Rita, b. 9 Oct. 1942, Philadelphia, Pennsylvania, USA. Professor of Anatomical Sciences. *Education:* BA Anthropology, University of Michigan; MA Anthropology, University of California, 1969; PhD Anthropology, University of California, Berkeley, 1970. *Appointments:* Teaching Associate, University of California, 1965-70; Assistant Professor of Anatomical Sciences, 1970-73, Associate Professor, 1973-80, Professor, 1980-, University of Texas Dental Branch; Adjunct, Rice University, Department of Anthropology, 1980-. *Publications:* With A Petersen, Brain & Behavioural Maturation: Biosocial Dimensions, ed. book in press; Language & Intelligence in Animals, with S T Parker, ed book in progress. Numerous articles in Journal of Human Evolution; Primate biosocial Development; The Behavioral and Brain Sciences; Infancy and Epsistemology; Advanced Views in primate Biology; Glossogenetics; Primate Ontogeny, Cognitive and Social Behaviour; Evolution and Development; The Genesis of Language: a Difference Judgement of Evidence; Handbook of Symbolic Intelligence; American Journal of Physical Anthropology. *Memberships:* Social Science Research Council, Committee on Parenting and Child Development; American Association of Primatologists, Publications Committee; American Association of Dental Schools, Section on Anatomical Sciences, Secretary; American Anthropological Association; American Association of Physical Anthropologists; American Anatomical Association. *Hobbies:* Anthropology; Photography; Travel. *Address:* 4837 Waycross; Houston, Texas 77035, USA.

GIBSON Melverene Stevens, b. 27 Dec. 1937, Texas, USA. Insurance Broker; Business Administrator. m. Carroll Raymond Gibson, 12 Feb. 1962, 1 son, 1 daughter. *Education:* Accounting, Griffin Murphy Business College, Seattle, Washington, 1955-58; Accounting, LaSalle Extension University, 1968-69. *Appointments:* Typing Instructor, Seattle, 1960- 62; Co-owner, Vice President, Carmark Transp. Company, Chicago, 1966-69; Assistant Administrator, American Bar Endowment, Chicago, 1970-77; Deputy Administrator, 1977-82; Insurance Consultant, Yates Insurance Agency, Chicago, 1982-83; Administration, American Hospital Association, Chicago, 1985; Insurance Agent, Equiable Assurance Society US, also Mutual of Omaha Insurance Company, Pioneer Life Insurance Company of Illinois, 1983-88; Consultant, Professional Services Group, Chicago, 1984-. *Memberships:* Board of Directors, University Park Condominium Association, 1987-88; Director, 1979-80, Secretary, 1980, Marcy Newberry Agency, Chicago; Word Processing Association of Chicago; National Association of Female Executives. *Honours:* Kizzy Award for Outstanding Accomplishments Personifying Black

Women, 1980; Various Service Awards from American Bar Endowment, 1977- 82. *Hobbies:* Reading. *Address:* 1401 E. 55th Street, Chicago, IL 606715, USA.

GIDWITZ Betsy R, b. 13 Nov. 1940, Chicago, Illinois, USA. Lecturer; Consultant; Author. *Education:* BA, University of Iowa, 1962; EdM, Boston University, 1965; PhD, University of Washington, Seattle, 1976. *Appointments:* Teacher, Public Schools of Westford and Medford, Massachusetts, 1962-68; Consultant, 1972-74; Lecturer at MIT, Consultant, Author, 1974-. *Publications:* The Politics of International Air Transport, 1980; Numerous articles in professional journals, newspapers and magazines. *Memberships:* Executive Board, Council of Jewish Federations (New York), National Conference on Soviet Jewry (New York), Combined Jewish Philanthropies (Boston) and Jewish Community Relations Council (Boston); Board of Directors, Union of Councils for Soviet Jews, (Washington) and Action for Soviet Jewry, (Waltham, MA); Member, American Academy of Political and Social Sciences, American Association for the Advancement of Slavic Studies, American Political Science Association. *Address:* Cambridge, Massachusetts, USA.

GIFFIN Mary Elizabeth, b. 30 Mar. 1919, Rochester, USA. Medical Director. *Education:* BA, Smith College, 1939; MD, Johns Hopkins Medical School, 1943; MS, University of Minnesota, 1948. *Appointments:* Staff, Mayo Clinic, 1949-58; Josselyn Clinic, 1958-. *Publication:* Her Doctor Will Mayo; A Cry for Help, co-author. *Memberships:* American Psychiatric Association; American Acadmey of Child Psychiatry; American, Chicago Societies for Adolescent Psychiatry; Chicago, Illinois Psychiatric Societies. *Honours Include:* Illinois Association of School Social Workers, Citation, 1976; Smith College Medal, 1978. *Hobbies:* Creative Writing; Nature; Music. *Address:* 1190 Hamptondale Road, Winnetka, USA.

GIGLI Irma, b. 22 Dec. 1931, Cordoba, Argentina. Doctor; Professor of Medicine. m. Hans J. Muller-Eberhard, 29 June 1985. *Education:* MD, Universidad Nacional de Cordoba, 1957; Intern, Cook County Hospital, 1957-58; Dermatology Resident, Cook County Hospital, 1958-60; Fellow, New York University Skin & Cancer Unit, 1960-61; Immunology Fellow, Howard Hughes Medical Institute, 1961-64. *Appointments:* Professor, Dermatology & Experimental Medicine, New York University, 1976-82; Professor, Medicine & Head, Dermatology, University of San Diego, 1982-. *Publications:* Original publications in Immunology & Dermatology. *Memberships:* Association of American Physicians; Americna Federation for Clinical REsEarch; Western Association of Physicians; American Dermatological Association; American Acadmey of Dermatology; etc. *Honours:* Faculty Research award, American Cancer Society, 1970-72; Research Career Development Award, National Institutes of Health, 1972-76; Guggenheim Memorial Foundation Award, 1974-75. *Address:* Division of Dermatology/H-811J, University of California Medical Centre, 225 Dickinson Street, San Diego, CA 92103, USA.

GIL-DEL-REAL Maria Teresa, b. 5 Jan. 1941, Colombia. Epidemiologist. m. John R. Romano, 10 Oct. 1964, 1 son, 1 daughter. *Education:* AB, Colombia, 1959; BA, Rutgers University, USA, 1979; MPH, Columbia University, New York, 1986. *Appointments:* Bilingual Editor, Princeton International Translations, 1979-80; Research Assistant, Robert Wood Johnson Foundation, 1980-83; Researcher, University of Madrid, 1983-85; Analyst, NJ State Department of Health, Cancer Epidemiology Programme, 1985-. *Memberships:* Philadelphi Epidemiology Society; Epidemiologic research Association; American Biographical Institute Research Association; Alpha Sigma Lambda. *Hobbies:* Reading; Nature. *Address:* 76 Princeton Ave., Rocky Hill, NJ 08553, USA.

GILBERT Anna (Marguerite Lazarus), b. 1 May 1916, Durham, England. Writer. m. Jack Lazarus, 5 Apr. 1956.

Education: BA, Honours, 1937, MA, 1945, Durham University. *Appointments:* Teacher, English, various grammar schools, 1941-73. *Publications:* Novels: Images of Rose; the Look of Innocence; A Family Likeness; Remembering Louise; The Leavetaking; Flowers for Lilian; Miss Bede is Staying; The Long Shadow; A Walk in the Wood. *Membership:* Society of Authors. *Honour:* Romantic Novelists' Association Major Award, 1976. *Address:* Pickering, Yorkshire, England.

GILBERT Anne, b. 1 May 1927, Chicago, USA. Author; Fine Arts & Antiques Appraiser. m. 7 Apr. 1951, 2 sons. *Education:* BS, Northwestern University, Evanston, 1949. *Appointments:* Joined, Chicago Daily News, 1971, United Features Syndicate of Column, Antiques Staff, 1971-83; Self Syndicator of Column, Antique Detective, 1983-89. *Publications:* Antique Hunting - A Guide for Freaks & Fancies; Antique Hunting-Collecting the New Antiques; Antique Hunting - Antique Detective; Antique Hunting - Investing in Antiques Market; Chasing the Chocolate Chippendale; Collectors Guide to American Illustrator Art. *Memberships:* Alpha Gamma Delta; Social Register, Fort Lauderdale; Newspaper Features Council. *Hobbies:* Gourmet Cooking; Architecture; Decorating; Theatre. *Address:* 4794 NE 17 Ave., Fort Lauderdale, FL 33334, USA.

GILBERT Florence Ruth, b. 26 Mar. 1917, Greytown, New Zealand. Retired. m. John Bennett Mackay, 15 Aug. 1945, 2 sons, 2 daughters. *Education:* Diploma, Physiotherapy, Dunedin School of Physiotherapy, 1938. *Appointments:* various New Zealand Hospitals. *Publications:* Lazarus & Other Poems; The Sunlit Hour; The Luthier; Collected Poems. *Memberships:* New Zealand Women Writers' Society; Past President, Honorary Vice President, PEN (N.Z. Centre). *Honours:* Jessie Mackay Memorial Award for Poetry (three times). *Hobbies:* Reading; Dreaming. *Address:* 23 Teece Drive, Motueka, New Zealand.

GILBERT Harriett Sarah, b. 25 Aug. 1948, London, England. Writer. *Education:* Diploma, Rose Bruford College of Speech and Drama, 1966-69. *Appointments:* Co-Books Editor, City Limits Magazine, 1981-83; Deputy Literary Editor, 1983-86, Literary Editor, 1986-88, New Statesman Magazine. *Publications:* Novels: I Know Where I've Been, 1972; Hotels with Empty Rooms, 1973; An Offence Against the Persons, 1974; Tide Race, 1977; Running Away, 1979; The Riding Mistress, 1983. Non Fiction: A Women's History of Sex, 1987. *Memberships:* National Union of Journalists; Writers' Guild. *Address:* c/o Richard Scott Simon, 43 Doughty Street, London WC1N 2LF, England

GILBERT Joyce Ann, b. 9 June 1958, Washington DC, USA. Research Assistant; PhD Candidate. *Education:* BS, University of South California, 1980; MS, Univerity of Clemson, 1983; PhD Candidate, University of Florida, 1987-. *Appointments:* Instructor, University of Florida, 1986- 88. *Publications:* TV Series, Public TV, Current Nutrition Topics; Research papers, etc. *Memberships:* American College of Sports Medicine; Institute of Food Technologists; Americna Dietetic Association; Florida Dietectics Association; Sports and Cardiovascular Nutritional Group. *Honours:* Alpha Epsilon Delta, Recognized Young Dietitian. *Hobbies:* Athletics, Painting. *Address:* 211 NW 28th Street, Gainesville, FL 32607, USA.

GILBERT Linda Sue, b. 17 May 1948, Springfield, Illinois, USA. College Mathematics Professor; Textbook author. m. Dr Jimmie D Gilbert, 20 Dec. 1974. 1 son, 1 daughter. *Education:* BS, summa cum laude, Mathematics, 1970; MS, Mathematics, 1972; PhD, Mathematics, 1977, Louisiana Tech University. *Appointments:* Computer Programmer, Continental Can Co, Hodge, LA, 1973-75; Instructor of Math 1977-80, Assistant Professor of Math 1980-84, Associate Prof of Math 1984-86, Louisiana Tech University, Ruston, LA; Associate Professor of Math, University of South Carolina at Spartanburg, 1986-89, Professor of Math.,

1989-. *Publications:* College Algebra, 1981, 2nd edition 1986; Intermediate Algebra, 1983, 2nd edition 1987; Elements of Modern Algebra, 1984, 2nd edition, 1988; College Trigonometry, 1985; College Algebra and Trigonometry, 1986, Precalculus: Functions and Graphs, 1990. *Memberships:* American Mathematical Society; Mathematical Association of America; Textbook Author Association; Spartanburg County Council of Teachers of Mathematics; Phi Kappa Phi; Pi Mu Epsilon. *Honour:* Recipient Outstanding Achievement Award, Louisiana Tech University, 1984. *Hobbies:* Needlepoint; Flower and vegetable gardening; Salt-water fishing. *Address:* Division of Mathematics and Sciences, University of South Carolina at Spartanburg, Spartanburg, South Carolina 29303, USA.

GILBERT Lucia Albino, b. 27 July 1941, Brooklyn, New York, USA. Psychology Educator. m. John Carl Gilbert, 18 Dec. 1965, 1 daughter. *Education:* BA, Wells College, 1963; MS, Yale University, 1964; PhD, University of Texas, 1974; Licensed Psychologist, Texas. *Appointments:* Supervisor, Research Information, G.S.Gilmore Research Laboratory, New Haven, Connecticut, 1964-67; Teacher, St Stephen School, Austin, Texas, 1967- 69; Assistant Professor, Iowa State University, Ames, 1974-76; Assistant Professor, 1976-81, Associate Professor, 1981-86, Professor, 1986-, University of Texas, Austin. *Publications:* Men in Dual Career Families, 1985; Sharing It All: The Rewards and Struggles of Two-Career Families, 1989; Editor, special issue Parenting Dual Career Families. *Memberships:* Fellow, Council Representative, American Psychological Association; Association of Women in Psychology; Texas Psychological Association. *Honours:* Excellence in Teaching Award, University of Texas, 1981-86. *Hobbies:* Swimming; Progressive country music; Ecology. *Address:* 4402 Balcones Drive, Austin, TX 78731, USA.

GILBERT Sharon, b. 15 Feb. 1944, Brooklyn, New York, USA. Artist. m. Vyt Bakaitis, 23 Jan. 1970, 1 son, 1 daughter. *Education:* Skowhegan School, Maine, 1965; BFA, Cooper Union, 1966. *Creative works:* Books: Nuclear Atlas; Waste; 80 Faces, 3-Mile Island Reproductions (1-8). Sculpture: The Look; Commerce; Meat & Bones; Etymography; Country; Topography; Here/After; Poison America; Green the Fragile. *Memberships:* Advisory Board 1979-83, New York Chapter, Women's Caucus for Art; Artist Equity. *Honours:* Women's Studio Workshop, Rosendale, New York, 1982; Carl Schurz Haus, German-American Institute, Freiburg, Germany, 1980; New York Foundation for the Arts, 1988. *Address:* 323 Atlantic Avenue, Brooklyn, New York 11201, USA.

GILBOA Netta, b. 5 Jan 1958, Israel. Sales Manager. m. Alan Scheckter, 4 Jan. 1989. *Education:* BA, State University College, USA, 1979; MS, Advertising, 1980, MA, Sociology, 1985, Northwestern University. *Appointments:* Instructor, College of Lake County, 1984-85; Instructor, Northeastern University, 1984-85; Midwest Sales Representative, Wadsworth Inc., 1985-86; District Sales Manager, Avon Products Inc., 1987-88; East Coast Sales Representative, Harcourt Brace Jovanovich Inc., 1988-. *Publications:* Editor, Slideshow, I Know it When I See It: Pornography, Erotica & Sexual Deviance. *Memberships:* Popular Culture Association; Associate, Womens Institute for Freedom of the Press; American Sociological Association; Society for the Scientific Study of Sex. *Honours:* Recipient, various honours and awards. *Hobbies:* Astrology; Films. *Address:* 111 S. Olive St., No 532, Media, PA 19063, USA.

GILCHRIST Paula Lizak, b. 13 Jan. 1953, Pittsburgh, Pennsylvania, USA. Podiatric Physician & Surgeon; Physical Therapist. m. Joseph A. Gilchrist, 7 July 1979, 2 daughters. *Education:* BS, Physical Therapy, University of Pittsburgh, 1974; Ohio College of Podiatric Medicine, 1982; Surgical Residency, Podiatry Hospital, Pittsburgh, 1983. *Appointments:* Physical Therapist, VA Hospital, Staff Therapist, Director InServices, Director Student Education, Guest Lecturer University of Pittsburgh, speaker & Lecturer, Gait Analysis, Prosthetics, 1977-78; Private Practice, 1977; Staff Therapist, Montefiore Hospital, 1979-82; Home Health Cre, Physical Therapy, 1980-82; Surgical Podiatric Resident, 1982; Guest Lecturer, University of Pittsburgh, 1982-; Self-Employed Podiatric Physician, 1983-. *Creative work includes:* Lectures: Gait Analysis, 1982, 1983, 1984; Prosthetics & Orthotics, 1977, 1978; Adult Haemiplegia, 1983. *Memberships:* Numerous Professional Organisations including: American, & Pennsylvania Podiatric Medical Associations; American & Pennsylvania Physical Therapy Associations; *Honours:* Clinical Instructor 1976-78, Assistant Clinical Professor 1982-, University of Pittsburgh. *Hobbies:* Reading; Lecturing, lower extremity gait analysis. *Address:* St Francis Medical Office Building, Suite 501, 4221 Penn Avenue, Pittsburgh, Pennsylvania 15224, USA.

GILL Alice Janet Swaim, b. 1 July 1934, Brooklyn, New York, USA. Teacher, Editor. m. William Gill div. 1968, 2 sons, 3 daughters. *Education:* BFA, Ohio University, 1955; MA, John Carroll University, 1974. *Appointments:* Director, Continuity, Traffic, Public Relations, WDCN-TV educational television, 1963-65; Teacher, Toledo Public Schools 1967- 68, Cleveland Public Schools 1968-. *Publications:* Editor: Ohio Teacher; CTU Critique, 1977-88. Author: Pamphlet, Giving Your Child the Edge; Articles, American Teacher. *Memberships include:* American Federation of Teachers; Executive, Ohio Federation of Teachers; Past Chair, Ohio Inservice Advisory Committee; Past member, Ohio Teacher Education & Certification Advisory Commission; Offices, Cleveland Teachers' Union, Union Teacher Communication Association. *Honours:* Awards: Ohio Federation of Teachers 1984, Education Commission of States 1986; Grants 1983-84, 1985-86, scholarship 1984-85, Martha Holden Jennings; Grant, Cleveland Education Fund, 1987-88; Teacher of Year, 1984-85; Numerous awards, journalism, UTCA, 1977-; Member, evaluation teams for Colleges of Education, Ohio Department of Education. *Address:* 4073 Verona Road, South Euclid, Ohio 44121, USA.

GILL Becky Lorette, b. 16 Mar. 1947, Phoenix, Arizona, USA. Physician. m. 5 Aug. 1978. *Education:* BA, Biology, Stanford University, Stanford, California, 1964-68; Spanish Conversation, Summer Session in Guadalajara, Mexico, 1968; MD 1968-73, University of Arizona College of Medicine. *Appointments:* Surgical Extern, Tucson Medical Center, 1970; Medical Extern, COSTEP, Federal Reformatory for Women, Alderson, West Virginia, 1972-73; Straight Medidal Internship, United States Public Health Service Hospital, Baltimore, Maryland, 1973-74; Poychiatry Residency, National Naval Medical Center, Bethesda, Maryland, 1974-77; Head and Staff Psychiatrist, Alcohol Rehabilitation Service/Substance Abuse Department, Naval Hospital, Camp Lejeune, North Carolina, 1977-85; Head, Alcohol Rehabilitation Service/Substance Abuse Department and Chief of Psychiatry, Naval Hospital, Millington, Tennessee, 1985-. *Memberships include:* Stanford Cap and Gown, 1968-; Life Member, Stanford Alumni Association, 1968-; Life Member, University of Arizona Alumni Association, 1973-; Stanford Cardinal Club, 1977- ; American Medical Society on Alcoholism and Other Drug Dependencies, 1977-; Association of Military Surgeons of the United States. 1977-; Alcoholism Professionals of North Carolina, 1978-; American Psychiatry Association, 1978- ; National Association of Alcoholism and Drug Abuse Counselors, 1979-; Stanford Personal Solicitation Program, 1982-, Southern Regional Vice Chairman, 1984-; Founding Member, American Academy of Psychiatrists in Alcoholism and Addictions, 1985-. *Hobbies:* Tennis; Jogging. *Address:* P O Box 207, Naval Hospital, Millington, TN 38054, USA.

GILL Lunda Hoyle, b. Covina, California, USA. Artist. 1 son, 1 daughter. *Education:* BFA, Pomona College, Claremont; Art Students League, New York; Academia de Belli Arti, Florence, italy. *Exhibitions:* The Tribal People of Kenya, 1976; Alaska's Native People - Eskimos, Aleuts and Indians, 1979; People of China,

1986, held at the Smithsonian Institution's National Museum of Natural History; Exhibitions held at Hammer Galleries, New York City, 1978, 1980, 1982, 1987; Exhibitions held throught the USA including: National Academy of Design, Allied Artists of America, Mid-America Annual; work also appears in museums and private collections including: Metropolitan Museum of Art, New York City, and Hermitage Museum, Leningrad, USSR; *Publications:* numerous newspaper and magazine articles; featured on national radio & TV. *Honours:* David Prescott Barrows Award, 1987; Stacey Fellowship, 1st woman to win the top fellowship in the Stacy Awards; Rolex Awards for Enterprise; recipient, numerous awards for exhibitions. *Address:* 500 Via La Paloma, Riverside, CA 92507, USA.

GILL Rosemary Eva Gorell, b. 9 July 1925, London, England. Writer; Freelance Cook. m. Peter Douglas Gill, 16 July 1966, 1 son, 2 daughters. *Education:* B.Ed., London; BA, Honours, Bedford College, London University; Fellow, IHR. *Appointments:* Teacher, LCC, 1946; Teacher, Private School, 1949-52; Market Research, 1976-87. *Publication:* Wigley a Fairy Story, 1950; Silver Apples of Avalon, in press; The White Book of Canterbury, 1959. *Memberships:* Chairman, Yorks European Movement, 1972-77; Council, Order of St John; General Synod C of E, 1981-88; *Hobbies:* Reading; Gardening; Cooking. *Address:* The Thatched Cottage, Wormsley Park, Stokenchurch, Bucks HP14 3YG, England.

GILLAM Lynne Ormond, b. 10 Jan. 1948, Trussville, Alabama, USA. Realtor; Broker/Co-owner, Realty World, McCrimmon Realty. m. G Gillam, 19 Aug. 1967. 1 son, 1 daughter. *Education:* BS 1973, MS 1975, Jacksonville State University. *Appointments:* Teacher, Talladega Co, Alabama, 1974- 75; Teacher, Gadsden Co, Florida, 1975-77; Instructor, Jacksonville State University, 1977-84; Sales Manager, Locklear & Co, Alabama, 1984; Broker/Co- owner Realty Work McCrimmon Realy, Alabama, 1985-. *Memberships:* Calhoun Co Board of Realtors, Chair Education Committee, 1988; President, Million Dollar Club, 1989; ALA Assoc of Realtors, National Assoc of Realtors. *Honours:* Outstanding Young Women, 1981; Manager of the Year Realtyworld Sunbelt Region, 1986; Million Dollar Producers Club, 1986. *Address:* 115 E 18th Street, Anniston, AL 36201, USA.

GILLAN Maria Mazziotti, b. 3 Dec. 1940, Paterson, USA. Poet; Poetry Centre Director. m. Dennis Gillan, 30 Feb. 1964, 1 son, 1 daughter. *Education:* BA, 1961, MA, 1963, Literature, New York University. *Appointments:* Adjunct English Instructor, University of Missouri, 1969-72, Bloomfield College, 1974-80; Poetry Centre Director, Passaic County Community College, 1980-. *Publications:* Flowers from the Tree of Night, 1980; Winter Light, 1985; Luce D'Inverno, 1988; The Weather of Old Seasons, 1989; Editor, Fottwork Magazine, since 1980; New Jersey Poetry Resource Book, 1988. *Memberships:* Poetry Society of America; Poets & Writers Inc; MLA; Associate Writing Programmes. *Honours:* New Jersey State council on the Arts Fellowship in Poetry, 1980-81, 1985-86; American Literary Translator's Award, 1987. *Address:* 40 Post Avenue, Hawthorne, NJ 007506, USA.

GILLARD Julia, b. 29 Sept. 1969, United Kingdom. Lawyer. *Education:* Law degree, University of Melbourne. *Appointments:* Education Vice President 1982, President 1983-, Australian Union of Students; Organiser, Socialist Forum, 1984-85; Solicitor, Slater & Gordon, 1987-. *Memberships:* Australian Labour Party, Carlton Branch President, 1984-; Victorian State Conference Delegate, 1985-86; Member, Council of the University of Adelaide, 1981; First President, Union Council, Adelaide University Union; Australian Higher Education Round-Table, 1982; One of the Convenors, Commonwealth Students Conference, 1983; Socialist Forum Management Committee; Socialist Forum Public Issues Committee, 1984-89. *Honour:* Butterworth's Book prize, University of Melbourne, 1984. *Interests:* Politics, particularly political education; Women's art;

Literature. *Address:* 67 Rae St, North Fitzroy, Melbourne 3068, Australia.

GILLEO Sandra V, b. 8 May 1944, Somerville, N.J., USA. Educator. m. Robert James Gilleo, 26 Nov. 1967, divorced 1981, 1 son, 1 daughter. *Education:* BA, Trenton State College, 1967; MA, Newark State College, 1971. *Appointments:* Teacher, Franklin School District, 1966-67, Bricktown School District, 1967-69; Reading Specialist, Lawrence School District, 1969-72; Educator, New Hope-Solebury School District, 1972-. *Memberships:* Franklin, Bricktown, Lawrenceville, New-Hope Solebury Education Associations; Staff Development Committee, Second Monday-Women's Advisory Council. *Hobbies:* Volunteer Work; Tennis; Hiking; Computer Programming. *Address:* 2650 Windy Bush Road, Newtown, PA 18940, USA.

GILLESE Eileen Elizabeth, b. 8 July 1954, Edmonton, Alberta, Canada. Barrister; Solicitor; Professor. m. Robert Donald Badun, 14 Aug. 1982, 1 daughter, 1 son. *Education:* BCom., Honours, University of Alberta, 1977; BA, Honours, Jurisprudence, 1979, BCL, 1st class, 1980, Oxford University; Called to Alberta Bar, 1981; Called to Law Society of Upper Canada, 1988-. *Appointments:* Student at Law, Reynolds Mirth & Cote, Edmonton, 1980-81; Barrister, Solicitor, Reynolds, Mirth & Cote, 1981-83; Sessional Lecturer, Commerce, 1982, Sessional Lecturer, Law, 1983, University of Alberta; Assistant Professor, University of Western Ontario, 1983-87; Associate Professor, 1987-; Pension Commission of Ontario, 1988-; Associate Dean, 1988-89. *Publications:* Co-author: A.H. Oosterhoff, Text, Commentary and Materials on the Law of Trusts, 3rd edition, 1987; Introduction to the Law Governing Physicians, 1986, co-author; Legal Research, Writing and Moot Court Materials, 2nd edition, 1985; articles in professional journals. *Memberships:* various professional organisations. *Honours:* Various honours & awards. *Hobbies:* Public Speaking; Community Work; Travel; Sports. *Address:* Faculty of Law, University of Western Ontario, London, Ontario N6A 3K7, Canada.

GILLESPIE Dana, b. 30 Mar. 1949, London, England. Singer; Songwriter; Actress. *Career:* Films: The Lost Continent; Mahler; People That Time Forgot; Bad Timing; Scrubbers; The Hound of the Baskervilles; Parker; Strapless. LP's: Foolish Seasons; Box of Surprises; Weren't Born A Man; Ain't Gonna Play No Second Fiddle; The Boogie Woogie Flu; Blue Job; Below the Belt; Solid Romance; It Belongs To Me; Hot News; Amor; Jesus Christ Superstar, Live LP. Musicals: Catch my Soul; Jesus Christ Superstar; Mardi Gras; Tommy; Cora; Cinderella. Plays: The Tempest (National Theatre); Playthings. *Honour:* British Junior Water Ski Champion, 1963-66. *Hobbies:* Water skiing; Snow skiing; Indian and Morroccan music. *Address:* c/o Belinda Wright, Apartment 20, 47 Courtfield Road, London SW7, England.

GILLESPIE Rhondda Marie, b. 3 Aug. 1941, Sydney, Australia. Concert Pianist. m. 1976. *Education:* MusB, New South Wales Conservatorium. *Appointments:* Concert Pianist, soloist, recitalist Worldwide; recordings for EMI, Decca, Chandos. *Honours:* Harriet Cohen Commonwealth Medal. *Hobbies:* Exotic Cooking; Golf. *Address:* 2 Princes Road, St Leonards on Sea, East Sussex TN37 6EL, England.

GILLETT Margaret, b. 1 Feb. 1930, Wingham, Australia. Professor; Author. *Education:* BA, Sydney, 1950; Dip.Ed., Sydney, 1951; MA, Russell Sage, New York, 1958; Ed.D., Columbia, New York, 1961. *Appointments:* Registrar, Haile Sellassie I University, Ethiopia, 1962- 64; Associate Professor, 1964-67, Professor, 1967-82, Education, McDonald Professor of Education, 1982-, McGill University, Canada. *Publications:* Dear Grace: A Romance of History, 1986; A Fair Shake: Autobiographical Essays by McGill Women, 1984; We Walked Very Warily: A History of Women at McGill, 1981; Educational Technology: Toward Demystification, 1973; Foundation Studies in

Education: Justification and New Directions, 1973; Readings in the History of Education, 1969; The Laurel and the Poppy, 1968; A History of Education: Thought and Practice, 1966. *Memberships Include:* Sub-Commission, Status of Women; Canadian Commission, UNESCO, 1980-; Board of Directors, Womens Information & Referral Centre, 1980-83; Founder Member, Canadian History of Education Association; Canadian Research Institute for the Advancement of Women. *Honours:* Research Grants; Appointed MacDonald Professor of Education, 1982; Awarded LL.D, hc, University of Saskatchewan, 1988. *Hobbies:* Tennis; Gardening; Cross Country Skiing. *Address:* 220 Olivier Ave., Apt. 502, Westmount, Quebec, Canada H3A 1Y2.

GILLETTE Ethel Perry, b. Plainfield, New Jersey, USA. Registered Nurse. m. John H Gillette, 1943. 1 son, 1 daughter (deceased). *Education:* Scholarship Nursing, 1970; Assoc Degree, St Petersburg Jr College, 1975; BA, St Leo's College, 1977. *Appointments:* Inservice Instructor, Metropolitan General Hospital, Pinellas Park, Florida. *Creative Works:* Numerous articles in Point of View, Fitness Industry, Simply Living. Video: Let's live; Golden Years; Camp Orama. *Memberships:* American Nurses Foundation Century Club; Consumer Advocate Nursing Homes, 1978; Chairwoman Ombudsman Committee, 1979. *Honours:* Magna cum laude; Fellowship Fine Arts Committee, 1978; Writers Award for Book, 1987, Ashley Publishing Company; Contracts News America Syndication, 1987-88. *Address:* 4409 58th Avenue North, St Petersburg, FL 33714, USA.

GILLIN Loris Olwyn, b. 25 June 1935, Melbourne, Australia. Consulting Psychologist. m. Laurence Murray Gillin, 29 Nov. 1958, 1 son, 1 daughter. *Education:* BA, 1982; Dip.Ed.Psych, 1985. *Appointments:* Clinical Psychologist, El Kanah Counselling Service, 1983-. *Publications:* articles in journals etc. *Memberships:* Member, Australian Psychological Society; Christian Counsellors Association; Victorian Association of Family Therapists; Research into Adolescent Indentity Formation. *Address:* El Kanah, 934 Whitehorse Road, Box Hill 3128, VIC, Australia.

GILLIOM Bonnie Lee, b. 1 Mar. 1933, Mansfield, Ohio, USA. Consultant; Educator. m. M. Eugene Gilliom, 27 Dec. 1956, 1 son, 1 daughter. *Education:* BA, Heidelberg College, 1955; MA, 1960, PhD, 1971, Ohio State University; Other study: University of Wisconsin, 1954; Tucson Creative Dance Center, 1975; Chelsea School of Human Movement, England, 1978; 18 study tours, 30 countries, Ohio State University, 1969-87. *Appointments:* Television Teacher, WVIZ-TV, NIT and KPIX-TV, WOSU, 1959-68; Lecturer, Movement and Education, San Francisco State University, California, 1962-65; Assistant Professor, Creative Movement for Children, 1971-78, Director, 4M Programme, Associate Director, Institute for the Advancement of the Arts in Education, 1982-present, Ohio State University; Director, Developer, Meanings, Modes and Moods of Movement Programme, ESEA Title IV-C, 1979-82. *Publications:* Basic Movement Education for Children, 1970, Hebrew Edition, 1977; ITV: Promise into Practice (with Ann Zimmer), 1972; 4M: A Training Manual for Designing a K-6 Movement Curriculum, 3rd Edition, 1981; The 4M Program is..., 1981; Guest editor/author; Many other articles, booklets, chapters, newsletters. *Memberships:* Kappa Delta Pi; Pi Delta Epsilon; Pi Lambda Theta; National Academy of Television Arts & Sciences; Ohio Advisory Council to State Department of Education (Executive Committee 1980-85); American and Ohio Alliances of Health, Physical Education, Recreation & Dance (Ohio Editorial Board 1981-87); National Dance Association; Upper Arlington Cultural Arts Commission Associate. *Honours:* Best Education Series, Institute for Education by Radio & Television, 1962; Meritorious Award, Ohio Association for Health, Physical Recreation & Dance, 1984. *Hobbies:* Art; Music; Dance; Travel; Skiing; Snorkelling. *Address:* 2495 Haverford Road, Columbus, OH 43220, USA.

GILLISON Helen L Jackson, b. 9 July 1944, Colliers, West Virginia, USA. Attorney at Law. m. Edward Lee Gillison, 18 Nov. 1963, 1 son. *Education:* BA, cum laude, West Liberty State College, 1977; JD, West Virginia University, 1981. *Appointment:* Sole practitioner, Weirton, 1981-. *Memberships:* West Virginia State Bar Association, various offices including Board of Governors, 1986; West Virginia Trial Lawyers Association, Board of Governors, 1986; American, Mountain State, National and Hancock County Bar Associations; American Trial Lawyers Association; Mountatin State Bar, Board of Directors; West Virginia Community College, Board of Advisors; Weirton Police Civil Service Commission, Chairman of Board; American Bar Association; National Bar Association. *Honours:* Black Attorney of the Year Award, BALSA West Viginia College of Law, 1986; Member of Million Dollar Club. *Hobbies:* Reading; Writing. *Address:* 3139 West Street, Weirton, WV 26062, USA.

GILMORE Jane Murray, b. 27 Mar. 1952, Philadelphia, Pennsylvania, USA. Counselling Psychologist; Professional Musician. m. Michael David Gilmore, 5 Aug. 1972. 1 son, 2 daughters. *Education:* MusB, Boston University, 1972; MusM, Philadelphia College of Performing Arts, 1975; MEd, Antioch University, 1977; DMA, Cambs College, 1988. *Appointments:* School District of Philadelphia, 1974-; Music Teacher, 1974-85; Counselling Psychologist, 1985-; Director of Children's Junior and Young Adult Choirs, Tindley Temple UM Church; Organist-Director, local Churches, 1987-; Director of Choral Activities, Cambs College of Music; Understudy Aida Opera North. *Publication:* The Musical Elements of Mendelssohn's Elijah, as they relate to the drama of the oratorio. *Memberships include:* Fellowship, United Methodists in Worship, Music & Other Arts; Chairperson, Commission on Worship of the Eastern PA Conf of UM Church; Tindley Temple UM Church. *Honours include:* Honoured by UWCA (SW Belmont branch), 1988; Mele Foundation Fellowship, Nightingale Recital Series, 1987; Recipient of numerous Scholarships; Mother of Year Award; Teacher of Year Nominee; Conference Presenter, Girl Scouts of USA. *Hobbies:* Vocal and choral music, particularly Sacred Music; Vocal performance; Conducting choirs; Piano; Organ; Reading; Writing (literature). *Address:* 8409 Newbold Lane, Laverock, PA 19118, USA.

GILROY Beryl Agatha, b. 30 Aug. 1924, British Guiana. Author; Psychologist; Lecturer. m. 30 July 1954, 1 son, 1 daughter. *Education:* Teacher Training, 1943-45; London University, 1953-57; Sussex University, 1978-79; Century University, 1983-85. *Appointments:* Teacher, 1950-56; Deputy Head Teacher, 1967-68; Head Teacher, 1969-81; University London Multicultural Centre Researcher, 1981-89. *Publications:* Blue Water Readers, 1962; Green & Gold Readers, 1967-71; Nipper, 1969-75; Black Teacher, 1976; In for a Penny, 1982; Frangipani House, 1985; Boy Sandwich, 1989. *Memberships:* Network; Association of Head Teachers; Friend of Connonwealth; Camden Black Sisters. *Honours:* BSc., Psychology, 1954; MA, Education, 1979; PhD, 1984; GLC Caribbean Writers Award, 1985. *Hobbies:* Walking; Collecting Pictures; Reading; Museums; Music. *Address:* 86 Messina Ave., London NW6 4LE, England.

GINGOLD Hermione Ferdinanda, b. 12 Sept. 1907, London,. England. Actress. m. (1) Michael Joseph, (2) Eric Maschwitz. 2 sons. *Appointments:* Roles in Pinkie and the Fairies, 1908; Seasons at the Old Vic, Stratford on Avon; The Gate Review, 1938; Sweet and Low; John Murray Andersons Almanac (Broadway), 1954; From A to Z; Milk and Honey; Oh Dad, Poor Dad; First Impressions; A Little Night Music; Side by Side by Sondheim. Films include: Gigi; Bell, Book and Candle; Around the World in 80 days; The Music Man. Records: La Gingold; Babar; Chitty Chitty Bang Bang; Lysistrada; Peter and the Wolf. *Creative Works:* Author: The World is Square; Sirens Should be Seen and Not Heard; Hermoine Gingold Wrote These. *Honours:* Broadway: Donaldson Award, John Murray Anderson's Almanac;

Film: Golden Globe Award, Gigi. *Hobbies:* Writing; Needlepoint. *Address:* 405 East 54th Street, New York City, NY 10022, USA.

GINSBERG Elizabeth Gail, b. 15 Dec. 1942, New York City, USA. Artist. m. William R Davis. *Education:* BFA, Rhode Island School of Design, Providence; European Honours Program, Rhode Island School of Design, Rome, Italy. *Creative works:* Solo exhibitions: Chuo Gallery, Tokyo, Japan, 1965; Salt Lake Art Center, Utah, 1973; Atlantic Monthly Gallery, Boston, 1973; Susan Caldwell Gallery, New York, 1976; Hemisphere Club, New York, 1978; US Courthouse, Foley Square, New York, 1981; Marsha Mateyka Gallery, Washington DC, 1982 & 1988; Museum of the Huedson Highlands, Cornwall-on-Hudson, New York (2 person), 1985; John Nichols, New York, 1985; Kinokuniya Gallery, Tokyo, Japan, 1988; E. Montana College, Billings, Montana, 1988; Cultural Arts Center, Columbus, Ohio, 1990. Group exhibitions include: Museum of the Hudson Highlands, 1988; McNay Art Museum, San Antonio, Texas, 1986; Woods-Gerry Gallery, Rhode Island School of Design, 1986; Arts for Living Center, Henry Street Settlement, New York, 1986; Art in City Hall, Mayor's Office, Philadelphia, 1986; Moore College of Art, Philadelphia, 1986; Lubbock Arts Festival, Texas, 1986. Work in many collections. Numerous contributions to reviews and journals. *Honours:* Commission for Parsippany Place Corporate Center, New Jersey, 1985; Recipient of numerous grants. *Address:* 5 Great Jones Street, New York, NY 10012, USA.

GIPPS Ruth Dorothy Louisa, b. 20 Feb. 1921, Bexhill-on-Sea, East Sussex, England. Composer; Conductor; Organist. m. Robert Baker, 19 Mar. 1942, 1 son. *Education:* Bexhill School of Music, 1925-36; ARCM, Piano Performance, 1936; Scholar, Royal College of Music, London, 1937-42; BMus(Dunelm), 1941; DMus(Dunelm), 1948. *Career:* Freelance Pianist and Oboist, 1931-55; Chorus Master, City of Birmingham Choir, 1948-50; Conductor, London Repertoire Orchestra, 1955-86; Conductor, London Chanticleer Orchestra, 1961-; Professor, Royal College of Music, London, 1967-77. *Creative works:* 5 symphonies; 6 concertos; Choral works: The Cat; Goblin Market; Chamber music including wind octet etc; Radio feature Concert Pianist, BBC 3rd programme. *Memberships:* Composers Guild of Great Britain (Chairman 1967, opened Music Information Centre); President, Hastings Musical Festival, 1957-88; President, John Bate Choir; Chairman, Presentation of New Artists Society. *Honours:* Winner, all 5 composition prizes, Royal College of Music, 1940, 1941, 1942; Cobbett Prize, Society of Women Musicians; Honorary RAM; FRCM; MBE, for services to music, 1981. *Hobbies:* Organ playing (Organist, Parish Church, High Hurstwood, 1986-); Photography; Animals (cats, goats, ponies); Old houses particularly own 16th-century one. *Address:* Tickerage Castle, Pound Lane, Framfield, Uckfield, East Sussex TN22 5RT, England.

GIRE Sharon, b. 13 Jan. 1944, Ohio, USA. State of Michigan Representative. m. Dana L. Gire. *Education:* BS, Education, 1965; MSW, Wayne State University, 1975. *Appointments:* Programme Director, 1969-71, Central Region Teen Programme Consultant, National Board, 1971-73, YWCA; Macomb Area Supervisor, Big Brothers/Big Sisters, 1975-77; Director, Northeast Interfaith Centre, 1977-84; Mount Clemens City Commissioner, 1979-84, Major Pro-Term, Mount Clemens City Commission; State Representative, Michigan, 1987-. *Memberships Include:* Macomb County Commissioner; Chairperson: Budget Committee, Data Processing Subcommittee, Building & Grounds Subcommittee, Personnel Committee, 1985; Michigan Municipal League; Michigan Women in Municipal Government. *Address:* 37567 Radde, Mount Clemens, MI 48043, USA.

GISEL Erika G., b. 24 May 1942, Switzerland. Assistant Professor, Physical and Occupational Therapy. *Education:* BA, Education, 1963; BS, Occupational Therapy, 1972; MS, Physiology, Biophysics, 1976; PhD, Biology, 1979. *Appointments:* Teacher, Textile Arts, 1963-67; Occupational Therapist, 1972-79; Teaching Assistant, 1973-79; Assistant Professor, Occupational Therapy, 1979-83, School of Occupational Therapy, Washington University, St Louis, MO; Assistant Professor 1983-89, Associate Professor 1989-, Occupational Therapy, School of Physical and Occupational Therapy, McGill University, Montreal, Quebec, Canada. *Publications:* 23 contributions to American Journal of Physiology Brain Research, Journal of Developmental Physiology Physiology and Behavior, American Journal of Occupational Therapy, The Lancet, Physical and Occupational Therapy in Pediatrics. *Memberships:* American Occupational Therapy Association; Sigma Xi; International Society for Developmental Psychobiology; Society for Neuroscience. *Honours:* Simon Komarov Prize in Gastrointestinal Research, Philadelphia, 1976; Postdoctoral Fellow, American Occupational Therapy Foundation, 1986. *Hobbies:* Hiking; Cycling; Skiing; Swimming; Music (plays classical repertoire on violin); Arts and crafts; Cooking; Gardening. *Address:* McGill University, School of Physical and Occupational Therapy, 3654 Drummond Street, Montreal, Quebec, Canada H3G 1Y5.

GLACEL Barbara Pate, b. 15 Sept. 1948, Baltimore, Maryland, USA. Human Resource Consultant, Manager. m. Robert Allan Glacel, 21 Dec. 1969, 3 daughters. *Education:* AB, College of William & Mary, 1970; MA, Human Relations, 1973, PhD, Political Science, 1978, University of Oklahoma. *Appointments Include:* Academic Appointments, 1970-85, most recent being Suffolk University, Boston, 1975-77; John Jay College of Criminal Justice, 1979-80, St Thomas Aquinas College, 1981; Anchorage Community College, 1983, University of Alaska, 1983-85; Barbara Glacel & Associates, Human Resource Consultants, 1980-86; Vice President, Director, Chesapeake Broadcasting Corporation, 1982-; Senior Management Trainer, ARCO Alaska, 1984-85; General Manager, Hay Systems Inc., Washington, 1986-88; Owner, Pace Consulting Group, Virginia, 1988-. *Publications:* Family; Sourcebook on Municipal County & State Government, 1970; Regional Transit Authorities, 1983; numerous articles. *Memberships:* US Army Science Board; ASTD, Director, Anchorage Chapter; NMFA, Governor; APA, Division 14. *Honour:* US Army Commander's Award for Public Service. *Hobbies:* Travel; Writing. *Address:* 8996 Burke Lake Road, Suite 305, Burke, Virginia 22015, USA.

GLADNEY Heather Jeanne, b. 2 Feb. 1957, Hawthorne, USA. Writer. *Publications Include:* Teot's War, 1987; Teot's Warning, opera libretto, 1988; Teot's War II: Bloodstorm, 1989; A Devotee of Conscience, short story, 1988. *Memberships:* Science Fiction Writers of America; African Violet Society of America; Secretary, President, Yolo Violeteers. *Honours:* Nominated, John W. Campbell award, 1987; Certificate of Appreciation, Oustanding Contribution to AVSA Magazine, 1987. *Hobbies:* Native Plant & Japanese Style Gardening; Tropical Fishkeeping; Classical Music. *Address:* Ace/Berkeley, 200 Madison Ave., New York, NY 10017, USA.

GLANTZ Wendy Newman, b. 16 Dec. 1956, Brooklyn, New York, USA. Attorney; Lecturer. m. Ronald Paul Glantz, 29 Jan. 1984, 1 son, 1 daughter. *Education:* BA, State University of New York, Stony Brook, 1978; JD, Nova University, Florida, 1982. *Appointments:* Associate attorney, Glazer & Glazer, 1983-85; Partner, attorney, Glantz & Pasin 1985-86, Glantz & Glantz 1986-present. *Publications:* Florida Bar Journal, Extra-Ordinary Writs (Habeas Corpus & Ne-exeat) in Family Law; Valuation of Professional Goodwill; Legal series of articles including child support, temporary relief, shared parental responsibility, tax ramifications in divorce; Mystique magazine publication; extensive legal articles in civil newsletter publications. *Memberships:* President, Broward County Women Lawyers' Association; President, West Borward Bar Association; Board of Directors, Florida Association for Women Lawyers; Program Coordinator, Continuing Legal Education for Family Law Section of Broward County

Bar Association; Delegate to All Bar Conference; Project Chairperson of the Floriday Bar Family Law Section Law School, Liaison Committee; American Trial Lawyers Association; Family Law Section Florida Bar; American Bar Association, Family Law Section; Advisory Board of Parents Anonymous; President of National Association of Female Executives; Chairperson, National Association of Women Business Owners (Broward Chapter); Chairperson, Special Programs, Chairperson of Business and Professional Group; Sunrise Jewish Center; Plantation Chamber of Commerce; Fund Raising Committee, Jewish Community Center; South Florida Symphony; Women of Fine Arts.. *Hobbies:* Tennis; Writing; Ceramics; Gourmet cooking; Homemade Chocolates. *Address:* 150 South Pine Island Road, Suite 500, Plantation, Florida 33324, USA.

GLASS Julie Kay Ball, b. 27 Aug. 1960, Oklahoma City, Oklahoma, USA. Entertainment PR Advertising. m. John Edward Glass, 24 May 1986. *Education:* Magna cum laude, Casady High School, 1979; BA, Sociology, Pomona College, 1983; Graduate studies, PR, USC and UCLA Extension, 1983-86. *Appointments:* Exhibit Floor Manager, Omniplex Sci Centre, Oklahoma City, 1977-80; Intern, Michael Levine Pub Rels, Los Angeles, 1983; Acct Exec, New Image Pub Rels, Los Angeles, 1983-86; Acct Exec, Brocato & Kelman Inc, Los Angeles, 1986-. *Publications:* Columnist, Tower Records' Pulse!, 1984- 85; Columnist, Goldmine Magazine, 1984-85. *Membership:* Hollywood Women's Press Club. *Hobbies:* Making stained glass windows; Walking; Jazzexercise; Arabian horse shows; Music. *Address:* Apt 244, 8635 Southwestern Blvd, Dallas, TX 75206, USA.

GLASSMAN Lorna R, b. 16 Aug. 1935, Philadelphia, Pennsylvania, USA. Neuropsychologist; Music Therapist. m. Donald Glassman, 26 Dec. 1954. 1 son, 2 daughters. *Education:* AAS, Early Childhood Education, Montgomery County Community College, 1977; BS, Music Education, Chestnut Hill College, 1980; MCat, Music Therapy, Hahnemann University, 1982; MS, Neuropsychology, Drexel University, 1989. *Appointments:* Music Therapist, Moss Rehabilitation Hospital, 1981-86; Private Practice, Music Therapy, 1982-; Music Therapist, David Neuman Senior Center, 1981-85; Faculty Member, Hahnemann University, 1983-86; Research Assistant, Psychology Dept, Philadelphia Geriatric Center, 1988-89; Faculty Member, Chestnut Hill college, 1988. *Publications:* Production, Educational Videotape; Author, narrator and featured music therapist, Music Therapy in the Rehabilitation of Brain Injured Patients, 1985; Articles in professional journals; Presentations at professional conferences *Membership:* Board Member, Delaware Valley Chapter, Dystonia Medical Research Foundation, 1983-; Board Member, Center for Autistic Children, 1982-87. *Honour:* Delta Epsilon Sigma National Scholastic Honour Society, 1980. *Hobbies:* Music performance, therapeutic entertainment; Songwriting; Poetry writing; Physical fitness; Tennis. *Address:* 8 Latham Parkway, Melrose Park, Pennsylvania 19126, USA.

GLAZER Daphne Fae, b. 21 Apr. 1938, Sheffield, England. Lecturer. m. Peter Glazer, 14 July 1973. 1 son, 1 daughter. *Education:* BA, German/English 1959; Certificate in Education 1960; MEd 1971; Advanced Dip Psychol 1970, Hull University. *Appointments:* Head of German, Newland High School, Hull, 1960-63; Lecturer, Goethe-Institut, Lagos, Nigeria, 1963- 68; Lecturer, Hull Maximum Security Prison, England, 1971-72; Lecturer, Everthorpe Borstal, 1973-74; Lecturer, Hull College of Further Education, 1974-. *Publications:* Three Women, 1984; Short stories in Critical Quarterly, Bananas, Spare Rib, Everyday Matters, Vol II, Writing Women, broadcast on BBC Radio 4 and World Service. *Memberships:* PEN; The Society of Friends. *Honours:* Guardian Short Story Award, 1979; Runner- up, Constable Trophy competition for best unpublished novel in North of England, 1986. *Hobbies:* Yoga; Swimming; Theatre; Foreign travel; Speaking and reading German. *Address:* 198 Westbourne Avenue, Hull, HU5 3JB, England.

GLEASNER Diana, Writer. *Education:* BA (cum laude), Ohio Wesleyan University, 1958; MA, University of Buffalo (now State University of New York at Buffalo), 1964. *Appointments:* Secondary School Teacher, Kenmore Senior High School, Kenmore, New York, 1958-64; Part-time instructor, State University of New York at Buffalo, 1970-76; Freelance writer, 1966-; Co-founder with husband, Bill and Diana Gleasner Inc, photojournalism team. *Publications:* Books: Touring By Bus At Home and Abroad, 1989; RVing American's Backroads-Florida, 1989; Governor's Island- From the Beginning, 1988; Florida Off The Beaten Path, 1986; Lake Norman-Our Inland Sea, 1986; Windsurfing, 1985; Woodloch Pines-An American Dream, 1984; Charlotte: A Touch of Gold, 1983; Breakthrough: Women in Science, 1983; Inventions That Changed Our Lives: The Movies, 1983; Inventions That Changed Our Lives: Dynamite, 1982; Callaway Gardens, 1981; Rock Climbing, 1980; Sea Islands of the South, 1980; Illustrated Dictionary of Surfing, Swimming and Diving, 1980; Breakthrough: Women in Writing, 1980; Maui Traveler's Guide, 1978; Big Island Traveler's Guide, 1978; Oahu Traveler's Guide, 1978; Kauai Traveler's Guide, 1978; Hawaiian Gardens, 1978; Women in Track and Field, 1977; Women in Swimming, 1975; Pete Polar Bear's Trip Down the Erie Canal, 1970; The Plaid Mouse, 1966; Contributor of numerous articles. *Memberships:* American Society of Journalists and Authors; Society of American Travel Writers; Travel Journalists Guild. *Address:* 132 Holly Court, Denver, North Carolina 28037, USA.

GLEESON June, b. 11 June 1933, Melbourne, Australia. Deputy Director. m. Leo John Gleeson, 12 June 1957, deceased. 1 son, 2 daughters. *Education:* BEcon, Monash, 1972; MS, San Diego State, 1974; PhD, La Trobe, 1980. *Appointments:* Principle Lecturer, David Syme Business School, 1974-86; Deputy Director, Western Institute, 1987-. *Publications:* Australian Case Studies in Financial Management, 1972; Microcomputers & Financial Planning, 1987; Various journal articles. *Memberships:* Fellow, Australian Society of Accountants; Associate, Royal Institute of Public Administrators. *Honours:* Official Representative of Australian Society of Accountants; Commonwealth Conference of Accountants, New Delhi, 1975. *Hobbies:* Bushwalking; Swimming. *Address:* c/o Western Institute, McKechnie Street, St Albans, Victoria 3021, Australia.

GLEN Beverly Ruth, b. 20 Sept. 1940, Windsor, Canada. Executive Director, YWCA, North Orange County. m. Todd Veazie Glen, 14 Apr. 1963, divorced 1983, 1 son, 1 daughter. *Education:* BA, Middlebury College, 1962. *Appointments:* Career Councillor, Yale University, 1963-65; Publicist, Costume Design, Fullerton Collee, 1973-83; Administrative Assistant, 1983-85, Executive Director, 1985-, YMCA, North Orange County. *Memberships:* President, Fullerton College Faculty Wives, 1967-69; Board, Fullerton College Theatre Festival, 1981; Vice President, Resident Theatre Co., 1981; Treasurer, So. California Council YWCA, 1988-89; NAFE; Soroptomists International of Fullerton. *Hobbies:* Theatre; Reading; Writing; Yoga. *Address:* YWCA of North Orange County, 321 N. Pomona Ave., Fullerton, CA 92632, USA.

GLIBERT Patricia Marguerite, b. 2 Apr. 1952, Hackensack, New Jersey, USA. Biological Oceanographer. m. Todd Milan Kana, 10 June 1978, 1 son, 1 daughter. *Education:* BA, Skidmore College, 1974; MS, University of New Hampshire, 1976; PhD, Harvard University, 1982. *Appointments:* Postdoctoral Scholar, Woods Hole Oceanography Institute, 1981-82; Assistant Scientist, Woods Hole, 1982-86; Assistant Research Scientist, Horn Point Labs, University of Maryland, 1986-. *Publications:* Author, Co-Author, 29 scientific publications. *Memberships:* American Society of Limnology and Oceanography; American Society for the Advancement of Science; American Geophysical Union. *Address:* Horn Point Environmental Laboratories, PO Box 775, Cambridge, MD 21613, USA.

GLICK Deborah Kelly, b. 9 Sept. 1953, Waterbury, USA. CPA. m. William Glick, 30 June 1973, divorced 1978, 1 son, 1 daughter. *Education:* BS, Accounting, Post College, 1982; MA, Taxation, in progress. *Appointments:* Staff Accountant, De Angelis Lambardi & Kelly, 1981-82; Staff Accountant, John J. Baldelli, 1982-84; Partner, Baldelli Glick & Co., 1984-. *Memberships:* American Institute of Certified Public Accountants; Connecticut Society of CPA's; National Society of Public Accountants; National Society of Executive Females. *Honours:* Graduate Fellowship, University of New Haven, 1988-89. *Hobbies:* Drawing; Cake Decorating; Puzzles; Reading. *Address:* 357 Spring Street, Naugatuck, CT 06770, USA.

GLICKLICH Lucille Barash, b. 1 Oct. 1926, USA. Medical Director; Educator. m. John A Rosenberg, Snr. 3 sons, 2 daughters. *Education:* BA, University of Wisconsin, 1947; MD, University of Wisconsin Medical School, 1950; Internship, Youngstown Hospital Association, 1950-51; Residency, Pediatrics, Milwaukee Children's Hospital, 1951-53; Residency, General Psychiatry, Marquette Medical School Associated, 1967-69; Child Psychiatry Fellowship, Marquette/Milwaukee Children's Hospital, 1969-71. *Appointments:* Chief Resident, Department of Pediatrics Instructor 1953-54, Instructor 1956-57, Marquetee University; Assistant Professor 1965- 86, Assistant Professor, Department of Physicatry 1971-81; Associate Clinical Professor, 1981-, Associate Professor and Vice Chairperson 1986-, Medical College of Wisconsin; Child Psychiatrist 1971-86, Consultantion/Liaison Service 1978-86, Milwaukee Childrens Hospital; Medical Director, Child and Family Team, Sinai Samaritan Medical Center, 1986-. *Publications:* Numerous articles in professional journals; Presentations. *Memberships include:* Fellow, American Academy of Child and Adolescent Psychiatry; Fellow, American Psychiatric Association; American Society for Adolescent Psychiatry; Wisconsin Council for Adolescent and Child Psychiatry; American Orthopsychiatric Association; Fellow, American Academy of Pediatrics Wisconsin Branch; Milwaukee Pediatric Society. *Address:* 950 North 12th Street, Milwaukee, Wisconsin 53233, USA.

GLIMM Adele, b. 27 Aug. 1937, New York City, New York, USA. Writer. m. James Glimm, 30 June 1957, 1 daughter. *Education:* AB, Barnard College, 1958; AM, Columbia University, 1962. *Appointments:* Assistant Editor, Harvard University, 1961-63; Freelance Writer, 1963-; Lecturer, University of New York at Stony Brook, 1989-. *Publications:* 28 short stories in US magazines and literary quarterlies; Stories reprinted in 8 foreign countries; Novel in Redbook Magazine. *Hobby:* Travel. *Address:* 530 East 72nd Street, New York, NY 10021, USA.

GLOBERMAN Linda M, b. 15 May 1951, Los Angeles, California, USA. Physician; Dermatologist. m. 19 Aug. 1984. *Education:* BA, University at Los Angeles, 1972; MD, University of Southern California School of Medicine, 1976; Internship, Mercy Hospital, San Diego, 1976-77; Residency, University of California, Irvine, 1977-80; Fellowship, Interdisciplinary Program, Rancho, Los Amigos, 1973. *Appointments:* Valley Dermatologic Medical Group, 1980-84; Self employed, 1982-. *Publications:* Articles to professional journals. *Memberships:* Orange County Medical Assoc; American Academy of Dermatology; Society for Investigative Dermatology; Business & Professional Women; Salerni Collegium; Orange County Dermatologic Society, Treasurer, 1987-88; Irvine Medical Association, Treasurer, 1986-88; California Medical Assoc. *Honours:* Woman of the Year, Tarzana Chamber of Commerce, 1982; Phi Beta Kappa, 1972; Woman of Achievement, Irvine Business & Professional Women, 1984-85; Chief Resident, Dermatology Training Program, UCI Affiliated Hospitals, Irvine, 1980. *Hobbies:* Music; Theatre; Walking; Animals. *Address:* 4902 Irvine Center Drive Ste 105, Irvine, CA 92714, USA.

GLOGOWSKI Patricia Carol Duff, b. 22 Dec. 1942, Rahway, New Jersey, USA. Real Estate Broker. Divorced

2 sons. *Education:* Drakes Business College. *Appointments:* Real Estate Salesperson, 1971-77; Real Estate Broker/Owner, Happy Homes Realty, 1977-83; Real Estate Broker, Union County Director of Berg Realtors, 1983-85; Real Estate Broker, Commercial Investment Manager, 1985-86; Real Estate Broker, Glogowski Realty, 1986-. *Memberships:* President, 1986-87, GEUCBR, various other offices 1983-87; President, Multiple Listing Service, 1986-87. *Honours:* Recipient, many awards including: Make America Better, NJAR, 1980, 1983; President's Excellence, New Jersey Association of Realtors, 1987. *Hobbies:* Skiing; Golfing; Tennis; Swimming; Snorkeling; Boating; Fishing. *Address:* Glogowski Realty Inc., 342 E. Westfield Ave., Roselle Park, NJ 07204, USA.

GLOS Margaret Beach, b. 20 Jan. 1936, New York City, New York, USA. Management Company Executive. m. Stanley Glos, 1 June 1961, 2 sons, 1 daughter. *Education:* BA summa cum laude, Smith College, 1958; Postgraduate studies: Columbia University, 1959-61, Massachusetts Institute of Technology, 1978. *Appointments:* Editor, McGraw-Hill Book Co, New York City, 1958-61; Editor, Nucleonics magazine, 1961-68; Managing Editor, Science Research Magazine, 1966-68; Executive Director, Society for Nuclear Medicine, 1968-79; Administrator, American Board of Nuclear Medicine, 1968-79; Executive Secretary, Education and Research Foundation; President, G & T Management Inc, New York City, 1979-89; Senior Vice-President, Ecumed, New York City, 1984-85; Senior Vice-President, Tishman Speyer Medig, New York City, 1986-89; General Partner, Ami EXPO, 1987-; President, The Glos Group, Inc., New York City, 1989-. *Publications:* Numerous children's books; Professional articles. *Memberships:* Board of Directors, Vice- President, British American Educational Foundation; Director, American Society of Association Executives; Board of Directors, Professional Convention Management Association; Meeting Planners International; Vice-President, Institute of Association Management Companies; Society for Nuclear Medicine; Phi Beta Kappa; Sigma Xi. *Address:* 129 East 94th Street, New York, NY 10028, USA.

GLOVER Betty R, b. 27 Apr. 1916, Hamilton County, Tennessee, USA. Homemaker; Teacher; Author. m. William L Glover, 10 Aug. 1940. 2 sons. *Education:* Berry College Cadek Conservatory of Music; BS, Home Economics, University of Tennessee, 1940. *Appointments:* US Farm and Home Administration, Athens, Tennessee; Teacher, Home Economics, Tiptonville and Ridgely High Schools Lake County Board of Education, Tiptonville, Tennessee, 1945-51. *Publications:* The Lees and Kings of Virginia and North Carolina (co-author with sister, Reba Wilson), 1976. *Memberships:* Past President, Ridgely Womans Club; Ridgely Review Club; Magna Charta Dames; DAR; Treasurer, Henry Lee Society; Vice President, Henry Lee Society, UDC; Music Director, First Baptist Church, Ridgely, Tennessee, 1945-63. *Hobbies:* Travel; Genealogy; Music. *Address:* 571 Headden Drive, Ridgely, TN 38080, USA.

GLOVER Hilary Ethel Bartlett, b. 18 Nov. 1947, Liverpool, England. Research Scientist. Divorced. *Education:* HNC, Liverpool College of Technology, 1968; Bsc., Microbiology, 1st Class Honours, University of Sussex, 1971; PhD, University College, London. *Appointments:* Technician, J.H. Bibby & Sons, Liverpool, 1966-68; Post-graduate Fellow, NERC, 1971-74; Post-doctoral Travelling Fellow, NERC, 1974-76; Lecturer, University College, London, 1974-76; Research Scientist, Bigelow Lab., USA, 1976-. *Publications:* Articles in professional journals including: Marine Biology; Science; Nature; Deep Sea Research. *Membrships:* American Society for Limnology & Oceanography; American Association for the Advancement of Science; American Society of Microbiology. *Honours:* Recipient, various honours & awards. *Address:* Bigelow Laboratory for Ocean Sciences, McKown Point, W. Boothbay Harbor, ME 04575, USA.

GLOVER Janet Reaveley, b. 3 Dec. 1912, Cambridge, England. Retired. *Education:* First class degree, History, Somerville College, Oxford, 1931-34. *Appointments:* Teaching History, 1934-43; Head Mistress, 1946-59, Laurel Bank School, Glasgow, Scotland; Head of History, Selhurst Grammar School, Croydon, England, 1943-46; Head Mistress, Sutton High School, Surrey, 1959-73. *Publications:* Joint Editor, A Contribution to the History of Lanarkshire by J A Wilson, 1937; The Retreat at York, 1985; Epsom Common, 1981. Author: The Story of Scotland, 1960 republished 1977. *Memberships:* Association of Head Mistresses, President of the Scottish Branch for 2 years in the 1950's; President of the whole Association, 1970-72; Member of the Royal Society of Arts. *Honour:* CBE, 1973. *Hobbies:* Music; Gardening; Reading; Country pursuits. *Address:* 73 Christchurch Mount, Epsom, Surrey, KT19 8LP, England.

GLOVER Judith Mary, b. 31 Mar. 1943, Wolverhampton, Staffordshire, England. Author. m. (1) Anthony Rowley, 2 daughters, divorced 1970, (2) Stanley Martin, deceased 1987. *Education:* Aston Polytechnic, 1960. *Appointments:* Newspaper Reporter, 1960-62; Freelance Feature Writer, 1962-74; Author, 1974-. *Publications:* The Place Names of Sussex, 1975; The Place Names of Kent, 1976; Drink Your Own Garden, 1979; The Stallion Man, 1982; Sisters and Brothers, 1984; To Everything a Season, 1986; Birds in a Gilded Cage, 1987; The Imagination of the Heart, 1989. *Memberships:* Black Country Society; Catholic Social Service for Prisoners. *Hobbies:* Country Walking; Art; Historical Research. *Address:* Albrighton, Shropshire, England.

GLOVER Sarah Louise, b. 27 Apr. 1954, Detroit, Michigan, USA. Public Relations Officer. *Education:* Shaw University, North Carolina, 1972-76; Writers Workshops, NC State University 1981, NC University Chapel Hill 1984; Masters programme, media education, NCCU, Durham, 1985. *Appointments:* Store clerk, store manager, 1977-79; Activity assistant 1980, public relations director 1981, Bloodworth Street YMCA; Public Relations director, Garner Road Family YMCA, 1981-. *Memberships:* Former Debutante, Zeta phi Beta Sorority; Public Relations Society of America; YMCA Professional Directors Association. *Honours:* Scholarship, Zeta Phi Beta, 1975-76; Awards: Garner Road Family YMCA 1984, Triangle Area United Way 1987, WAUG 750 AM Radio Broadcast 1988; Public relations award, 7th Annual Back-a-Child Campaign, 1988; Professional Director's Grant, National YMCA, 1987. *Hobbies include:* Travel & business; Talk show host & producer (health & community issues) for Garner Road YMCA, Shaw University Radio, 1984-; Producer, bi-weekly cable TV show, 1004. *Address:* PO Box 961, Raleigh, North Carolina 27602, USA.

GLUBE Constance Rachelle, b. 23 Nov. 1931, Ottawa, Ontario, Canada. Chief Justice, Trial Division, Supreme Court of Nova Scotia. m. Richard H Glube, 6 July 1952. 2 sons, 1 daughter. *Education:* BA, McGill University, Montreal, 1952; LLB, Dalhousie University, Nova Scotia, 1955. *Appointments include:* Private law practice, 1964-68; Senior Solicitor, City of Halifax, 1969-74; City Manager, ibid, 1974-77; Appointed Puisne Judge, Trial Division, Supreme Court of Nova Scotia (ex-officio Appeal Court), 1977; Appointed Chief Justice, Trial Division, 1982. *Publications include:* Articles: Access-Family Law in Dimensions of Justice; Mediators, Resolve news magazine; Family Mediation of Canada; Professionals in Justice, The Role of the Judge; Justice Beyond Orwell; Les Editionsa Yvon Blais. *Memberships:* Executive, Canadian Judicial Council; Honorary Chairman, Nova Scotia Division, Canadian Mental Health Association; Advisory Council, Family Mediation of Canada; Board, Halifax Heritage Foundation; offices, Canadian Judges Conference; Past Regional Co-Chairman, Canadian Council of Christians & Jews, Board, 1979-82; Canadian Institute for the Administration of Justice. *Honours:* Tuition scholarship, Nova Scotia Barristers Soceity, 1954; Carswell Law Book Prize, 1954; Appointed Queen's Counsel, 1974;

Award of Merit, City of Halifax, 1977; Honorary LLD, Dalhousie University Law School, 1983. *Hobbies:* Reading (mystery and true crime); Knitting; Swimming; Classical music; Gardening. *Address:* Supreme Court of Nova Scotia, Trial Division Law Courts, PO Box 2314, Halifax, Nova Scotia, Canada B3J 3C8.

GLUCK Louise, b. 22 Apr. 1943, New York City, New York, USA. Author; Teacher. m. (1) Charles Hertz, (divorced), m. (2) John Dranow, 1 Jan. 1977, 1 son. *Education:* Sarah Lawrence College; Columbia University. *Appointments include:* Columbia University, 1979; Holloway Lecturer, University of California, Berkeley, 1982; Williams College, 1983-; Regents Professor, University of California, Los Angeles, 1985-87. *Publications:* Books: Firstborn, 1968, 1981; The House on Marshland, 1975; Descending Figure, 1980; The Triumph of Achilles, 1985; Ararat, 1990. *Honours:* Rockefeller Foundation Grant, 1968-69; NEA, 1969-70, 1979-80, 1988-89; Guggenheim Fellowship, 1975-76, 1987-88; American Academy and Institute Award in Literature, 1981; National Book Critics Circle Award, 1985; Melville Cane Award, Poetry Society of America, 1985; Sara Teasdale Memorial Prize, Wellesley College, 1986. *Address:* Creamery Road, Plainfield, VT 05667, USA.

GLYNN Carlin, b. 19 Feb. 1940, Cleveland, Ohio, USA. Actress; Teacher. m. Peter Masterson, 29 Dec. 1960. 1 son, 2 daughters. *Education:* Sophie Newcomb. *Appointments:* Has appeared in several films: The Trip to Bountiful released in 1986; Sixteen Candles; Continental Divide; Three Days of the Condor; Night Game, 1988. Played Mona Stangley in The Best Little Whorehouse in Texas on Broadway and London; Played in Winterplay for the Second Stage off Broadway; Played Vera Simpson in Pal Joey, Goodman Theatre, Chicago; Alterations for the Whole Theatre Company and Outside Wacor for the Hudson Theatre Guild; Resource Director for Sundance Institute, created by Robert Redford to promote independent films; Teaches Acting in New York City and London, England; Hosts talk shows, including her own: Today's Health; Teacher, Columbia University, Graduate Division of the film school. *Memberships:* The Actors Studio; Screen Actor;'s Guild; Actors Equity Association; American Federation of Television and Radio Actors. *Honours:* Antoinette Perry (Tony) for the Best Little Whorehouse in Texas; The Society of West End Theatres (SWET) (Lawrence Olivier Award) The Best Little Whorehouse in Texas; Theatre World Award; The Actors Studio Award the DUSE; Won Joseph Jefferson award for Best Actress in a musical. *Address:* 1165 5th Avenue No 15-A, New York, NY 10029, USA.

GODDARD Paula Oppermann, b. 26 July 1944, Washington, District of Columbia, USA. Specialist in international development; Policy maker; Public speaker; Educator. m. D Andrew Goddard, 7 June 1969, divorced 1987. 2 daughters. *Education:* BA, University of Wisconsin, Madison, 1966; MEd, Boston University, Boston, Massachusetts, 1967. *Appointments:* Volunteer in Kenya, 1969-72; US Peace Corps, Washington DC, 1972-78; Food and Agriculture Organization of the United Nations, Rome, Italy, 1982-83; US Agency for International Development, Washsington, DC, 1979-. *Publications:* Contributions to: Foreign Service Journal; Peace Corps Programming and Training Journal; The Bridge magazine; Author of USAID Project Impact Evaluation No 22, Rural Electrification in Costa Rica; drafted OECD/DAC guiding Principles to Member Countires on Women in Development. *Memberships:* First Elected President 1984-85, Board member 1984-88, Association for Women in Development; Returned Peace Corps Volunteers Association, 1985-88; Delta Gamma Sorority, Chapter Vice President, 1965-66. *Honours:* Women's Foreign Policy Council Director, Guide to Women's Foreign Policy Specialists; Superior Achievement Award and Meritorious Honour Award, Peace Corps, 1977 and 1978. *Hobbies:* Ballet; Jazz and tap dancing; Piano. *Address:* 5365 28th Street NW, Washington, DC 20015, USA.

GODDIN Margaret Ann, b. 27 Feb. 1928, Elkins,

USA. College Professor/Administrator. m. W. L. Goddin, 3 June 1950. *Education:* BA, Davis & Elkins College, 1950 MA, 1959, Ed.D., 968, West Virginia University; Postdoctoral study, various Universities. *Appointments:* Instructor, various schools & colleges, 1950-64; Assistant Professor, 1966-68, Associate Professor, 1968-75, Vice President, Dean of Faculty, Professor, 1975-80, Professor, 1980-83, English & Education, Director, Academic Resources Centre, 2nd Non Traditional Programs, 1983-, Davis & Elkins College. *Publications:* Know Your Schools, radio show, 1963; Co-author, Augusta Heritage Arts Workshop Grant Proposal, 1973; articles in various journals. *Memberships:* Numerous professional organisations including: American Association of University Professors; Association of College English Teachers. *Honours:* Recipient, various honours & awards. *Hobbies:* Hunting; Blueberry Cultivation; Gardening; Piano. *Address:* Rt. 1, Box 9, Elkins, WV 26241, USA.

GODENNE Ghislaine Dudley, b. 2 June 1924, Brussels, Belgium. Physician; Psychiatrist; Psychoanalist. *Education:* BS, 1948; MD, 1952. *Appointments:* Director, Adolescent Psychiatry Services, Johns Hopkins Hospital, 1964-73, Director, Counselling, Psychiatry Services, 1973-; Director, Health Services, 1978-88; Professor Psychiatry, Psychology, Pediatrics and Mental Hygiene. *Creative Works:* Sculptures: Mother & Child; Flame; Stairway to the Sun. *Memberships:* Fellow: American Society Adolescent Psychiatry (President 1981-82); American College of Physicains; American Psychiatric Association; American Ostheopsychiatric Association; American Public Health Association; Member, International psychoanalytic Association. *Honours:* Fulbright, 1952; Recipient various other honours and awards. *Hobbies:* Photography; Travel; Flying; Orchids. *Address:* Johns Hopkins University, 3400 N. Charles Street, Baltimore, MD 21218, USA.

GODFREY Ellen Rachel, b. 15 Sept. 1942, Chicago, USA. Company President; Author. m. William David Godrey, 25 Aug. 1963, 1 son, 1 daughter. *Education:* BA, History, Stanford University, 1963. *Appointments:* Teacher, Cape Coast, Ghana, 1963-65; Freelance Editor, 1970-74; General Manager, 1974-79, President, 1979, Press Porcepic Limited, and Softwords. *Publications:* The Case of the Cold Murderer; Murder Among the Well-to-Do; Murder Behind Locked Doors, 1988; By Reason of Doubt, (non fiction), 1982; Common or Garden Murder, short story. *Memberships:* Sectoral Advisory Group on Free Trade, Computers and Communication; Instructional Technology of the National Research Council; Board of Directors, Advanced Technology Association. *Honour:* Special Award, Mystery Writers of America, Edgar Allan Poe Award, 1982. *Address:* 4252 Commerce Circle, Victoria, BC, Canada V8Z 4M2.

GODFREY Joan Estelle, b. 9 Dec. 1922, Brisbane, Australia. Historical Researcher; Former Nurse. *Education:* General Nursing Certificate, Greenslopes Military Hospital, Cairns Base Hospital, 1947; Midwifery, Ryde District Soldiers' Memorial Hospital, Sydney, 1948; Mothercraft & Infant Welfare, Karitane, Sydney, 1949; Diploma, Nursing Education, Royal College of Nursing, Australia, 1955; BEd 1970, MA Educational Administration 1977, University of Queensland. *Appointments:* Sister Tutor 1949-51, 1956-60, Sister-in-Charge 1951-53, Royal Brisbane Hospital; Staff Tutor 1960-64, Assistant Director 1965-66, Branch Principal, 1967-77, Royal College of Nursing, Australia (Queensland); Head, Nursing Studies, School of Health Science, Queensland Institute of Technology, 1978-84; Consultant, Nurses' Higher Education, JEG Consultancy Services, 1984-88. Also: Various statutory appointments including: Chair, Education Committee, 1980-86: Nursing Research Committee; Board of Nursing Studies. *Publications:* Papers in state, national & international journals. *Memberships:* Offices including President 1982- 83, Royal College of Nursing, Australia; Offices, Australian Nursing Federation; Florence Nightingale International Nurses Association; Zonta Club, Brisbane; Past President, Brisbane chapter,

Alpha Delta Kappa; Australian Army Medical Women's Services, 1943-46; Honorary Officer, Royal Australian Army Nursing Corps, 1957-77. *Honours:* Florence Nightingale scholarship, 1955; Commonwealth University scholarship, 1967-69; Officer, Order of British Empire, 1984; Distinguished Nursing Service Medal, 1986. *Hobbies:* Theatre; Opera; Ballet; Australian wines; Biographical research. *Address:* 18/44 Brisbane Street, Toowong, Queensland 4066, Australia.

GODFREY Winifred M. (Winnie), b. 21 Nov. 1944, Philadelphia, Pennsylvania, USA. Artist; Painter. *Education:* BS 1966, MFA 1970, University of Wisconsin. Previous studies, Marycrest College, Art Institute of Chicago, University of California Los Angeles, University of Arizona Guadalajara, Mexico. *Appointments:* Artist-in-Residence, Rochester Art Centre, Minnesota, 1970; Visiting Lecturer, University of Illinois, Chicago, 1975-76; Instructor, North Shore Art League, Winnetka, Illinois 1977-82, 1986, 1987, Evanston Art Centre 1980-84. *Creative work includes:* Portrait painting, 10 years; Floral painting, 10 years; Lithography, watercolour & drawing, 20 years; Over 200 oil portraits, 400 oil flower paintings. *Memberships:* Artists Equity; Illinois Arts Alliance; Chicago Artists Coalition; North Shore Art League; Council on Foreign Relations. *Honours include:* Museum Publications Award 1987, Flora Exhibition awards 1986, 1988, Chicago Botanic Garden; 1st prize, floral competition, Artists magazine, 1986; 2nd prizes, Festival of the Masters, Orlando, Florida 1985, New Horizons in Art, Chicago 1978; 1st prizes, Arthur Baer Competition, Chicago 1983, Milwaukee Lakefront Festival 1985. *Hobbies:* Spanish language & history; Snorkeling & diving; Travel. *Address:* 2647 North Orchard Street, Chicago, Illinois 60614, USA.

GODLESKI Barbara, b. 13 June 1938, Mineola, New York, USA. Kinergarten Teacher; Consultant. m. Vincent Godleski, 9 July 1960, 2 sons, 1 daughter. *Education:* BS, State University of New York, Oneonta, 1960; MEd Elementary Education 1986, MEd Administration 1987, East Stroudsburg University. *Appointments:* Teacher: 2nd Grade or Kindergarten, various schools, Vermont & New Jersey, 1960-68; Kindergarten, 1st, 2nd & 3rd Grades, Tewksbury Township, NJ, 1972-. Also: Consultant, speaker, Developmental & Early Childhood Education. *Publications:* Handbook, Museums & Other Resources for Education; Thesis, Effects of Self Concept Enhancing Activities on Self Concept Levels in 3rd Grade Students, ERIC. *Memberships include:* Offices, Tewksbury Education Association; Phi Delta Kappa; Association for Supervision & Curriculum Development; Association of Childhood Education International; National Association for Education of Young Children. *Honour:* Excellent Teacher Award, Tewksbury Township Schools, 1986. *Hobbies:* Gardening; Swimming; Gourmet Cooking; Knitting; Aerobics; Researching development & early childhood issues. *Address:* Box 29, RD 5, Califon, New Jesey 07830, USA.

GOEKEN Sandra Kay, b. 18 Sept. 1958, Joliet, USA. *Education:* Joliet Junior College, 1976-77; Kendall County College, 1977-78. *Appointments:* Coporate Director: Goeken Communications Inc., 1978-, AF Holding Company, 1980-, JDG Holding Company, 1981-; Managing Director, Airfone International Inc., 1981-; Vice President, Marketing, Scientific Flight Corporation, 1982-; Project Coordinator: Skytel Limited of Canada, 1982-, Railfone, Inc., 1983-; Adjunct Professor, Southern Illinois University, Carbondale, 1985-. *Memberships:* National Honor Society; St Francis College Board of Trustees; Southern Illinois University at Carbondale; Joliet Junior College Board of Directors. *Honours:* Recipient, numerous honours and awards including: Outstanding Young Women in America, 1984; Goeken Day, at Joliet Junior College, 1985; Saragusa Foundation Grant, 1986. *Hobbies:* Flying Piper Club; Showing & Breeding Arabian Horses; Preparing & presenting Speeches. *Address:* 2809 Butterfield Road, Suite 200, Oak Brook, IL 60522, USA.

GOERKE Annette Maureen, b. 8 Sept. 1938, Perth, Western Australia. Musician. m. Vincent Leonard Goerke, 20 Aug. 1960, 3 daughters. *Education:* A.Mus.A., Piano, 1958; L.Mus.A., Organ, 1964; Mus.B., Composition, University of Western Australia, 1971. *Appointments:* Organist, St Mary's Cathedral, Perth, 1956-; Frequent Recitals broadcast by ABC, 1965-; Soloist, Orchestral Organist, West Australian Symphony Orchestra, 1969-; Acting Organist, University of Western Australia, 1973; Director Music, St Mary's Cathedral, 1974; Recitalist, 1977 Festival of Perth; Organist, University of Western Australia, 1982-88; Examiner, Organ/Piano, Australian Music Examinations Board, 1982-; Specialist Teacher, Organ Performance, University of Western Australia, 1982- . *Honours:* Churchill Fellowship, 1971-72. *Address:* 53 Pandora Drive, City Beach, WA 6015, Australia.

GOETZ-STANKIEWICZ Marketa, b. Liberec, Czechoslovakia. Professor. m. W. J. Stankiewicz. *Education:* BA 1954, MA 1955, PhD 1957, University of Toronto, Canada. *Appointments:* Teaching faculty, University of British Columbia, 1957-. *Publications:* Author: The Silenced Theatre, 1979. Editor: Dramacontemporary: Czechoslovakia (anthology), 1985; Vanek Plays: Four Authors One Character (anthology), 1987. Editorial committee, Canadian Review of Comparative Literature. *Memberships:* CAUTG; CCLA; AAASS. *Honour:* Certificate of Merit, Excellence in Teaching, University of British Columbia, 1974. *Hobbies:* Hiking; Skiing. *Address:* Department of Germanic Studies, University of British Columbia, Vancouver BC, Canada V6T 1W5.

GOETZE Marian Engle, b. 30 June 1926, Towson, Maryland, USA. Executive. m. Robert C. Goetze, 21 June 1947, 2 sons, 2 daughters. *Education:* BA, Randolph-Macon Woman's College, 1947; MEd, Goucher College, 1962. *Appointments:* Executive Director, Baltimore, New Directions, 1973-84; Moderator, 2 radio shows, Women at Crossroads, 1976-84; President, Business Exchange, 1984-; Executive Vice President, International Alliance of Executive & Professional Women, 1984-. *Memberships include:* Past President, Greater Baltimore YWCA; Former Chair, Advisory Council on Vocational Education, Baltimore City; Founder & Board of Directors, National Alliance of Professional & Executive Networks; Founder, Executive Women's Network. *Honours:* Executive of Year, Personnel Association of Baltimore, 1983; Commencement Speaker, Randolph-Macon College, 1979; Governor's Citation, Maryland, 1983; Gubernatorial Appointee: Maryland Apprenticeship & Training Council 1980, Governor's Employment & Training Council 1983; Mentor, Greater Baltimore Leadership Programme, 1983, 1984; Presentation, Displaced Homemakers, White House, Washington DC. *Hobbies:* Travel; Sailing; Skiing. *Address:* International Alliance, 8600 La Salle Road, Suite 308, Baltimore, Maryland 21204, USA.

GOETZKE Gloria Louise, b. 26 Apr. Monticello, Minnesota, USA. Medical Social Worker; Income Tax Preparer; Instructor. *Education:* BA, University of Minnesota, 1964; MSW, University of Denver, 1966; MBA, College of St thomas, 1977. *Appointments:* Medical Social Worker, Virginia Medical Center, Los Angeles, California, 1980-; Income Tax Preparer and Instructor, H & R Block Santa Monica, California, 1980- ; Preceptor for graduate social work students at UCLA and University of Southern California. *Memberships:* National Association of Social Workers; National Association of Enrolled Agents. *Honours:* NASW Diplomate in Clinical Social Work; Enrolment to practice before the Internal Revenue Service. *Hobbies:* Crochet designing for some of the handcraft magazines; Food designing; Flowers. *Address:* California, USA.

GOFFEN Rona, b. 7 June 1944, New York City, USA. Art Historian; Author. *Education:* AB, cum laude, Holyoke College, 1966; MA 1968, PhD with Distinction, 1974, Columbia University. *Appointments:* Lecturer, Dept of Fine Arts, Indiana University, 1971-73; Lecturer 1973-74, Assistant Professor 1974-78, Dept of Art and Archaeology, Princeton University; Assistant Professor 1978-80, Associate Professor 1980-86, Professor 1986-88, Dept of Art and Art History, Duke University; Distinguished Professor, Rutgers University, 1988-; Co-editor Renaissance Quarterly, 1988-. *Publications:* Calouste Gulbenkian Museum, 1982; Piety and Patronage in Renaissance Venice, 1986; Spirituality in Conflict, 1988; Giovanni Bellini, 1989; Icon and Vision, 1975; Renaissance Dreams, 1988; numerous other articles. *Memberships:* College Art Association of America; Renaissance Society of America. *Honours include:* Guggenheim Foundation Fellowship, 1986-87; National Endowment for the Humanities, 1986; National Humanities Center Fellowship, 1986-87; Fellow 1976-77, grantee 1979, American Council of Learned Societies; Fellowship, I Tatti Harvard Univ Center for Italian Renaissance Studies, 1976-77; Visiting scholar, American Academy in Rome, 1976; Millard Meiss Publication Fund award for Spirituality in Conflict, 1988. *Address:* Department of Art History, Voorhees Hall, Rutgers University, New Brunswick, NJ 08903, USA.

GOFRANK Catherine Ann, b. 8 May 1951, Detroit, USA. Lawyer. *Education:* BA, University of Michigan, 1972; JD, Illinois institute of Technology, 1976. Managing Counsel, Gofrank & Kelman, 1979-. *Memberships:* American, Detroit, Oakland County Bar Associations; Board of Directors, Oakland General Entities Inc; Michigan Bar and Gavel Society; Women Lawyers Association. *Address:* Gofrank & Kelman, 26555 Evergreen Rd, Suite 322, Southfield, MI 48075, USA.

GOLD Rhoda Pearl Segal, b. 26 Jan 1928, Paterson, New Jersey, USA. Psychotherapist; Clinical Social Worker. m. Jack A Gold, 19 June 1955, 1 son, 2 daughters. *Education:* BA, New York University, 1948; MSW, Columbia University, 1952. *Appointments:* Senior Caseworker, Family Service of West Essex, 1961-67; Private Practice of Psychotherapy, 1967-; Psychiatric Social Worker, Montclair Guidance Centre 1967-82. *Memberships:* National Association of Social Workers; New Jersey Society for Clinical Social Work, Board Member; Institute for Psychoanalysis and Psychotherapy of New Jersey; New Jersey Association of Women Therapists; American Association of Marriage and Family Therapy. *Honours:* Board Certified Diplomate, American Board of Examiners in Clinical Social Work; Diplomate in Clinical Social Work, NASW; Board Certified in Clinical Social Work, National Board of Examiners in Clinical Social Work; Licensed Marriage Counselor, New Jersey. *Hobbies:* Reading; Theatre; Gardening, Music. *Address:* 35 Francis Place, Caldwell, NJ 07006, USA.

GOLD Sylvia, President, Canadian Advisory Council on the Status of Women. *Education:* BA 1967, MA 1981, McGill University. *Appointments Include:* Teacher, various elementary & secondary schools, 9 years; Executive Assistant, Montreal Teacher's Association, 1971; Director, Professional Development Services, Canadian Teachers' Federation, 1975-85; President, CACSW, 1985-. *Memberships:* various professional organisations. *Honours:* Auxiliary Professor, Administration & Policy Studies in Education, McGill University, 1987. *Address:* CACSW, 110 O'Connor St. 9th Floor, Box 1541, Station B, Ottawa, Ontario, Canada K1P 5R5.

GOLD-BIKIN Lynne M. Zapoleon, b. 23 Apr. 1938, New York, USA. Attorney. m. (1) Roy Gold, 20 Aug. 1956 (div. 1976), 2 sons, 2 daughters, (2) Martin Feldman, 28 June 1987. *Education:* BA summa cum laude, Albright College, 1973; JD, Villanova Law School, 1976. *Appointments:* Associate, Pechner, Dorfman, Wolffe, Rounick & Cabot, 1976-81; Partner, Olin, Neil, Frock & Gold-Bikin, 1981-82; President, Gold-Bikin, Devlin & Associates, 1982-. Also: Instructor, adjunct professor: Law Education Institute, Temple Law University, Institute for Paralegal Training on Family Law, Villanova Law School, Dickinson Law Forum, various periods, 1977-. *Publications:* Pennsylvania Marital Agreements, 1984; Chapter, Modification of Matrimonial Determiniations, in Family Law & Practice, 1985; Contemporary Matrimonial Law Issues, 2 volumes, 1985; Associate editor, Pennsylvania Family Lawyer, 1980-84; Various articles, legal journals, newspapers. *Memberships include:* Fellow, American Academy of Matrimonial Lawyers; Offices, Family Law Section, American Bar Association; Offices, Pennsylvania & Montgomery County Bar Associations. *Honour:* Honoured speaker, Allegheny Bar Association, 1987. *Address:* Gold- Bikin, Devlin & Associates, PO Box 869, 516 Dekalb Street, Norristown, Pennsylvania 19404, USA.

GOLD-FRANKE, Paula Christine, b. 24 June 1952, Kentucky, USA. Assistant Managing Editor; Journalist; Freelance Writer. m. Wallace Henry Franke, 28 Mar. 1977. *Education:* BA, 1982, MA, 1986, Governors State University. *Appointments:* Russell Publications, 1984- ; Adjunct Professor, Governors State University, 1987. *Publications:* 12 half hour tv scripts for children's programme, 1985-87; Columnist, Radiosporting Magazine; Editor, Technical Amateur Radio Magazine, The Quarterly. *Memberships:* National Writers Club; QRP-ARC, International Director; Beecher Lioness Club, 2nd Vice President; Beecher Historical Society, Director. *Honours:* Recipient, various honours *Hobbies:* Amateur Radio; History; Crafts; Folk Art; etc. *Address:* PO Box 873, Beecher, IL 60401, USA.

GOLDEN Jane Elizabeth Crossley, b. 22 Oct. 1941, Washington DC, USA. Physical Therapist; Teacher. m. Dennis J. Golden, 15 Sept. 1962, 2 daughters. *Education:* BS, Ohio State University, 1963; MS, Wright State University (WSU), 1986; PhD candidate, University of Iowa, current. *Appointments:* Physical Therapy Consultant, Tennessee Public Health (19 counties), 1965-67; Staff Physical Therapist, acting Chief Therapist, and/or Education Coordinator, Hospitals & Clinics, Arizona, Ohio, Minnesota, 1967-81; Assistant Professor, Physical Therapy, Sinclair Community College, Dayton, Ohio, 1980-83; National Centre for Rehabilitation Engineering (spinal cord research), WSU, 1984-85. *Creative work:* 5 professional journal articles, Cardiovascular & Exercise Physiology, Energy costs for Amputee Gaits, Peripheral Blood Flow, Impedance Cardiography; 4 papers presented, Professional conferences; Master's thesis, Central Haemodynamics of Children with Cardiac Septal Defects. *Memberships include:* American Physical Therapy Association (APTA); Cardiopulmonary & Research Sections, APTA; American College of Sports Medicine; Various local advisory groups, councils, *Honours:* Favourite Faculty Member, Sinclair Community College, 1983; Graduate Award, Department of Physiology & Biophysics, WSU, 1986. *Hobbies:* Reading; Writing; Quiet evenings with friends; Swimming; Golf. *Address:* Physical Therapy Education, 2600 Steindler Building, University of Iowa, Iowa City, IA 52242, USA.

GOLDEN Renata, b. 3 Nov. 1952, Chicago, Illinois, USA. Photographer; Writer. *Education:* BSc, Journalism, 1978. *Appointments:* Photographer, Arizona: Phoenix Gazette 1978, Mesa Tribune 1978-80; Owner, commercial photography business, Renata Golden Photography, 1980-; Instructor, Photography, City of Phoenix, 1983-87. *Creative work includes:* Solo exhibitions: Austin Gallery, Scottsdale; Crafts Gallery, Phoenix Public Library. Group exhibitions: Tucson Museum of Art; Scottsdale Centre for Arts; Southwestern Invitational Exhibition; West 1st Street Gallery, Mesa. Also various articles, national magazines & newspapers. *Address:* Phoenix, Arizona, USA.

GOLDENSOHN Lorrie, b. 23 Sept. 1935, New York, USA. Writer; Professor. m. 5 Aug. 1956. *Education:* BA, Oberlin College; PhD, University of Iowa, 1973. *Appointments:* Writing Literature Faculty, 1971-77, Field Faculty, 1977-78, Goddard College; Part-time Lecturer, University of Massachusetts, 1978; Visiting Assistant Professor: Mount Holyoke College, 1978-79, Hampshire College, 1979-81, Vassar College, 1982-.

Publications: Poetry: Dreamwork, 1980; The Tether, 1983; Poetry Articles in: Anthology of Magazine Verse; New American Poets of the 80's; Seattle Review; Poetry Northwest; Ploughshares; etc. *Honours:* NEH Summer Seminars for College Teachers, Berkeley, 1980; Witter Bynner Fellow, MacDowell Colony, 1983; Mellon Grant, 1983, 1985; Fellowship for College Teachers, NEH, 1985. *Address:* 11 Seward Street, Saratoga Springs, NY. 12866, USA.

GOLDFARB Phyllis, b. 9 Dec. 1955, Sandusky, Ohio, USA. Law Professor. *Education:* BA, Brandeis University, 1978; EdM, Harvard University, 1979; JD, Yale University, 1982; LLM, Georgetown University, 1985. *Appointments:* E Barrett Prettyman Fellow, Georgetown University Law Centre, graduate fellowship as supervisory attorney and instructor in Criminal Justice & Juvenile Justice Clinics, 1982-84; Professor, Northern Illinois University College of Law, 1984-86; Law Professor, Boston College Law School, 1986-. *Publication:* The Power of the Particular, 1985. *Memberships:* Bar memberships: Massachusetts, Washington DC; Member of Bar of United States Supreme Court; American Bar Association; American Association of Law Schools; Section on Legal Education, National College of Criminal Defense Lawyers. *Hobbies:* Music; Fiction; Jogging. *Address:* Boston College Law School, 885 Centre Street, Newton,. MA 02159, USA.

GOLDIN Augusta, b. 28 Oct. 1906, New York City, USA. Columnist; Author. m. Oscar Goldin, 25 Oct. 1933. 1 son, 1 daughter. *Education:* BA, Hunter College, 1927; MS, Education, College of City of New York, 1929; EdD, Columbia University Teachers College, 1947. *Appointments:* Teacher, Elementary and Junior High, New York City, 1927-42; Principal Grades K-8, New York City, 1942-72; Assistant Professor Education, St Johns University, 1972-75, New York City; Columnist, The Staten Island Advance, 1968-. *Publications:* Published 16 books and over 1,000 articles on Education and the Environment for the Staten Island Advance. *Memberships:* Author's Guild; American Museum of Natural History; National Audubon Society; Space Studies Institute. *Honours:* Elected to the Hunter College Hall of Fame; President's Award for Science Education, Long Island University. *Hobby:* Gardening. *Address:* 590 Bard Avenue, Staten Island, NYC 10310, USA.

GOLDNER Janet, b. 6 June 1952, Washington DC, USA. Artist. *Education:* BA, Art, Antioch College, 1974; MA, Sculpture, New York University, 1981. *Creative Works:* One Person Shows Include: Washington Square East Galleries, New York City, 1980-81; Prehistoric Sites, Elmira College, Elmira, NY, Phoenix Gallery, NYC, 1983, 1984; Soho 20 Gallery, 1989; Group Exhibitions Include: Phoenix Gallery, New York City, 1981; Cable Artists, New York City, 1982; Warm Gallery, Minneapolis, 1986; Air Gallery, New York City, 1987; University of Georgia, Athens, 1988. *Memberships Include:* Women's Caucus for Art; College Art Association; International Scupture Centre. *Honours Include:* Fellowships: Millay Colony for the Arts, Austerlitz, 1981, Ossabow Island Project, Savannah, 1982 and 1988, Virginia Centre for the Creative Arts, 1982, Yaddo, Saratoga Springs, 1982; Award, Visual Arts Exchange, 1983; Artist in Residence, University of Georgia, 1987. *Hobbies and Interests:* Art; Archaeology; Anthropology; Textiles. *Address:* PO Box 947, Canal Street Station, New York City, NY 10013, USA.

GOLDOWSKY Barbara, b. 11 Nov. 1939, Dachau, Germany. Writer; Journalist; Radio Producer; Host-Annoucer. m. (1) Noah Goldowsky, 1961, dec. 1978, 2 sons, (2) M. Morman C. Pickering, 1979. *Education:* BA, Political Science, University ,of Chicago, USA, 1958. *Career:* Freelance Writer, local newspapers and national magazines; Volunteer, Public Radio WPBX-FM, Southampton, New York. *Publications:* Ferry to Nirvana, book, 1983; Many poems and articles published nationally; Journalism in various media. *Membership:* Poets and Writers. *Honour:* Scholarship, University of Chicago, 1957, 1958. *Hobbies:* Gardening; Archaeology;

History. *Address:* PO Box 663, Southampton, NY 11969, USA.

GOLDRING Nancy, b. 25 Jan. 1945, Oak Ridge, Tennessee, USA. Artist; Professor. m. N. Ubaldo Arregui, 16 May 1980. *Education:* BA, Art History, Smith College, Northampton, Massachusetts, 1967; Graduate research, University of Florence, Italy, 1967-68; MA, Fine Art (Sculpture, Graphics), New York University, 1970. *Career:* Instructor, English Literature/Language, University of Pisa, Italy, 1967-68; Lecturer, Public Art & Sculpture, School of Visual Arts, New York City, USA, 1970-71; Lecturer, Art History, Fashion Institute of Technology, State University of New York, 1971; Associate Professor, Drawing, Department of Fine Art, Montclair State College, New York, 1972-; Guest Professor, Art History, Lecturer, Contemporary Art, Rhode Island School of Design, 1974-75; Artist in Residence, Haverford-Bryn Mawr Colleges, 1978; New York Design Correspondent, Brava Casa, Corriere della Sera, Milan, Italy, 1984-85; Various lectures, workshops; Solo shows, Pennsylvania, Connecticut, New York, Israel, Italy; Participant, many group exhibitions: Missouri, Ohio, Massachusetts, New Jersey, Pennsylvania, New York; Rome, Italy, Bilbao, Spain, and Poland; Collaborator, Repertory Dance Ensemble, sponsored National Endowment for the Arts and Exxon, 1985, set design for Ode, Ze'Eva Cohen, 1987; Works appear in public collections, Paris, Milan, Israel, USA. *Publications include:* Peekskill Melt (co-author), 1971; Art in Public Places, 1973; Grant National Memorial: A Monument to the Living, 1974; Cover design for Landscape Views (symposium report),1979; Design for catalogue, poster, programme, Musica dei Caraibi: Film Rassegna, Milan, 1983; Recurrences (illustrated article), 1985; Cover design for Fleurs de Verite (Marie-Luce Dayer). *Honours:* Fulbright Fellowship, 1967-68; New York University Fellowship, 1969-70; Numerous grants, 1970-. *Address:* 436 West Street, Apt 1112A, New York, NY 10014, USA.

GOLDSMITH Barbara, b. 18 May 1931, New York City, USA. Author; Social Historian; Journalist. m. Frank Perry, 2 sons, 1 daughter. *Education:* BA, Wellesley College, 1953. *Career:* Contributor, NY Herald Tribune, Esquire Magazine, New York Times, 1957-64; Founder, Contributing Editor, NY Magazine, 1968-; Senior Editor, Harpers Bazaar magazine, 1970-74; Lecturer, New York University, 1969, 1975; Special writer, TV documentaries. *Publications include:* Straw Man, novel, 1975; Little Gloria, Happy at Last, non-fiction, 1980; Johnson v. Johnson, 1987. *Memberships:* Trustee, NY Public Library; Executive Board, PEN American Centre; Research Libraries Committee, NY Public Libraries; Guild Hall Academy of Arts; Founder, Centre for Learning Disabilities, Kennedy Centre, Albert Einstein College of Medicine; President's Council, Museum of the City of New York; Director, National Dance Institute, Goldsmith-Perry Foundation. *Honours:* Awards, Brandeis University Library Trust, 1980, 1981; Honorary doctorates, Syracuse University 1980, Pace University 1982; Elected, Guild Hall Academy of Arts, 1985; Spirit of Achievement Outstanding Woman Award, 1988; NY Public Library Literary Lions, 1988; Literary Market Place, First Annual Award, 1990. *Address:* Morton L. Janklow Association, 598 Madison Avenue, New York, NY 10022, USA.

GOLDSMITH Cathy Ellen, b. New York City, USA. Teacher. *Education:* BS, 1968, MA, 1971, MA, 1974, New York University. *Appointments:* Special Education Teacher, 1968-. *Publications:* Photography Collection - Around the Square; Bobst Library, New York University and an article; New York University - A Historical Perspective. *Memberships:* New York University Alumni Council, Secretary; Member Executive Board Jewish Association for College Youth; United Jewish Appeal Federation; Council for Exceptional Children; Association for Supervision and Curriculum Development; Orton Dyslexia Society; Past-President, Rho Chapter National Honor Society; Pi Lambda Theta; Foundation for Exceptional Children. *Honours:* Charles Oscar Maas Essay Award, American History, 1968; New York University Distinguished Service Award, 1987. *Hobbies:* Photography and Travel. *Address:* 3 Washington Square Village, New York, NY 10012, USA.

GOLDSMITH Karen Lee, b. 10 Jan. 1946, Bridgeport, Connecticut, USA. Attorney. m. (1)Michael Goldsmith, deceased 1979, 1 son, 1 daughter, (2)Jeffery S. Hooie, 13 June 1980. *Education:* BA, University of Central Florida, 1975; JD, University of Florida, 1978. *Appointments:* Associate, Pitts, Eubanks Ross, 1978-80; Associate, 1980-83, Partner, 1983-84, Dempsey & Slaughter; Partner, Dempsey & Goldsmith, 1984-. *Publications:* Articles in various journals and magazines. *Memberships:* Federal American, Florida, Orange County Bar Associations; National Health Lawyers Association. *Honours:* Outstanding Chairperson, Orange County Bar Association, 1982; Elected to Outstanding Young Women of the Year, 1983. *Hobby:* Breeding Dogs. *Address:* 605 East Robinson, Suite 500, Orlando, FL 32801, USA.

GOLDSMITH Lynn Natalie, b. 11 Feb. 1948, Detroit, Michigan, USA. Photographer; Director; Lyricist. *Education:* BA Honours, Secondary Teacher's Certificate, University of Michigan, 1968. *Appointments:* NBC Production Assistant, 1968; Publicity, Electra Records, 1969; Director, Joshua TV, 1971; Director, ABC TV In Concert, 1972; Creative consultant, 1973-75; President, Lynn Goldsmith Inc., photo agency and production company, 1976-. *Publications:* The Police, black & white book of photographs, 1983; Bruce Springsteen, colour book photographs, 1984. Director/Producer: Will Powers music videos; Adventures in Success; Kissing with Confidence; Smile Opportunity, 1983-86. *Memberships:* Directors Guild of America; American Society of Magazine Photographers; American Federation of Musicians; American Federation of Television & Radio Artists. *Honours:* 3rd Prize, Portrait, World Press Photo, 1985; Gold Medal, International TV & Film Festival of New York, 1983; Silver Medal, ibid, 1984, 1985; Monitor Award, 1984; Gold Award, Houston International Film Festival, 1985; Photographic Awards: NPC International, 1981/82; Lucien Clergue Award, 1986; NPC International, 1987. *Hobby:* Firewalking (unofficial record, 130' at 1600 degrees). *Address:* Lynn Goldsmith Inc., 241 West 36th, New York, NY 10018, USA.

GOLDSMITH Mary Ann, b. 12 Dec. 1952, San Antonio, USA. Lawyer. m. Ronald H. Fualkner, 30 Dec. 1978, 1 son. *Education:* BA, University of Texas, 1974; JD, University of Texas School of Law, 1979. *Appointments:* Associate Attorney, Sheppard Mullin Richter & Hampton, 1979-81; Assistant General Counsel, General Counsel, Vice President, Texas Energy Petroleum Corp., Houston, 1981-86; Private Practice, 1986-. *Publications:* Articles in: Texas Law Review. *Memberships:* State Bar of California; State Bar of Texas; Co-Founder, General Counsel, Texas Farm Foundation Inc. *Honours:* Numerous. *Hobbies:* Sailing. *Address:* PO Box 1896, Port Aransas, TX 78373, USA.

GOLDSTEIN Margaret Ann McNeill, b. 13 Mar. 1939, Sinton, Texas, USA. Cell Biologist; Professor. m. Alexander Goldstein, Jr, 14 Feb. 1959, 1 son. *Education:* BA magna cum laude 1965, PhD 1969, Rice University. *Appointments:* Teaching assistant, Rice University, 1965-69; Instructor, M. D. Anderson Hospital, University of Texas, 1969-70; Instructor, Cell Biophysics & Medicine 1970-73, Assistant Professor, Cell Biophysics & Medicine 1973-77, Medicine 1977-79, Associate Professor, Medicine & Cell Biology 1979-89, Professor, Medicine 1989, Baylor College of Medicine, Houston, Texas. *Publications:* Co-author, various professional papers. *Memberships include:* President, Charter Member, Texas Society of Electron Microscopy; American Association for Advancement of Science; American Society of Cell Biology; Biological Director 1990-1993, Electron Microscopy Society of America; Executive Committee, Basic Science Council, AHA; Biophysical Society. *Honours:* Rice Freshman Scholar, 1957; Alice G. Baker Distinguished Scholar, 1959; Predoctoral Fellow, US Public Health Service, 1965-69;

Elected, Sigma Xi, 1970; Established Investigator, American Heart Association, 1977; Research & career development award, National Institutes of Health, 1977-82. *Hobbies:* Music, including Vice President 1982-86, Texas Chamber Orchestra; Active participation, various professional & community organisations. *Address:* Department of Medicine, CVS, Baylor College of Medicine, One Baylor Plaza, Houston, Texas 77030, USA.

GOLLANCZ Livia Ruth, b. 25 May 1920, London, England. Chairman of Publishing Company. *Education:* ARCM, Solo Horn, Royal College of Music, 1940. *Appointments:* Professional Hornplayer, 1940-53; joined Victor Gollancz Ltd, as Junior Assistant, 1953, Director, 1954, Governing Director, Joint Managing Director, 1965-86, Chairman, 1983-. *Publications:* Editor, Introduction, Reminiscences of Affection, by Victor Gollancz, 1968. *Membership:* Alpine Club. *Hobbies:* Mountain Walking; Gardening; Music. *Address:* 14 Henrietta St., London WC2E 8QJ, England.

GOLTON Margaret Appel, b. 12 Jan. 1909, Cleveland, Ohio, USA. Social Psychotherapist. m. Eugene G. Golton, 15 Apr. 1934, dec. *Education:* BA, Mather College, Case Western Reserve University, 1931; MSW, 1945, DSW, 1964, School of Applied Social Sciences, Case Western Reserve University. *Appointments:* Public Welfare, 1933-47; Private Welfare: Foster Home Placement, Individual and Group Day Care, Institutional Placement of Emotionally Disturbed Children, 1947-59. *Publications:* Books: Unlock Your Potential: Know Your Brain and How It Works, 1982; Your Brain at Work: A New View of Personality and Behavior, 1983; Professional Potpourri: Seeds Are Sown, 1984; Insights in Poetry, 1987; Various contributions to International Conference for the Advancement of Private Practice in Social Work Proceedings, etc including; Criteria for Determining Competence in the Private Practice of Social Work, 1966; In Preparation for Immortality: How to Equip Children to Live 150 Years or More, 1971; Comprehensive National Health Insurance: What It May Mean to the Mental Health Practitioner, 1976; Basic Needs and Social Survival, 1978; Loss and Retrieval: How Spoouses Handle the Loss of a Partner (A Neural Network Approach), 1980; Newsletters. *Memberships:* National Association of Social Workers; National Directory of Clinical Social Workers; International Association for Advancement of Private Practice in Social Work. *Hobbies:* Writing non-fiction and poetry; Dressmaking by hand; Radio and TV talk shows. *Address:* 2628 Whiton Road, University Heights, OH 44118, USA.

GOMARD Kirsten, b. 4 Feb. 1945, Esbjerg, Denmark. Senior Lecturer in German and Women's Studies. m. Leif Hjorth-Hansen, 29 Dec. 1976. 1 daughter. *Education:* Cand mag. Major, German 1971, Minor, Art History 1973. *Appointments:* Lecturer in German 1972-76, Senior Lecturer 1976- 87, Senior Lecturer in German and Women's Studies, 1987-. *Publication:* Research on translation theory; The Early Socialist Women's Movement in Germany; Gender and Speech. *Membership:* Director of Dekvina, Women's Research Center of Aarhus. *Hobbies:* Biking; Gardening; Travelling abroad; Literature; Theatre; Film; Jazz. *Address:* Cekvina, Women's Research Center in Aarhus, Finlandsgade 26B, DK 8200 Aarhus N, Denmark.

GOMEZ Jill, b. Trinidad. Opera & Concert Singer. *Education:* Royal Academy of Music, Guildhall School of Music; Operatic Debut with Glyndebourne Festival Opera, 1969. *Appointments:* Leading Roles include: Mélisande, Calisto and Ann Truelove in The Rake's Progress; appeared with Royal Opera, English National Opera and Scottish Opera in roles including: Pamina, Ilia, Fiordiligi, the Countess in Figaro, Elizabeth in Elegy for Young Lovers, Tytania, Lauretta in Gianni Schicchi, and the Governess in The Turn of the Screw; created the role of Flora in Tippett's The Knot Garden, at Covent Garden, 1970 and of the Countess in Thea Musgrave's Voice of Ariadne, Aldeburgh, 1974; Sang title role in Massenet's Thais, Wexford, 1974, and Jenifer in The Midsummer Marriage with Welsh National Opera, 1976; created title role in William Alwyn's Miss Julie for radio, 1977, Tatiana in Eugene Onegin with Kent Opera 1977; Donna Elvira in Don Giovanni, Ludwigsburg Festival, 1978; title role in BBC world premiere of Prokoviev's Maddalena, 1979; Fiordiligi in Cosi fan tutte, Bordeaux, 1979; sang premiere of the Eighth Book of Madrigals, Zurich Monteverdi Festival, 1979; Violetta, Kent Opera's Production, La Traviata, Edinburgh Festival, 1979; Cinna, Lucio Silla, Zurich, 1981; The Governess in The Turn of the Screw, Geneva, 1981; Cleopatra, Giulio Cesare, Frankfurt, 1981; Leïla in Les Pêcheurs de Perles, Scottish Opera, 1982-83; Governess in The Turn of the Screw, English National Opera; Helena, Glyndebourne's production of Britten's A Midsummer Night's Dream, 1984; Donna Anna in Don Giovanni, Frankfurt Opera, 1985, Kent Opera, 1988; recitals worldwide. *Address:* 16 Milton Park, London N6 5QA, England.

GOMEZ Lynne Marie, b. 9 May 1952, Highland Park, Illinois, USA. Attorney. m. William J. Coffey II, 17 Dec. 1977, 1 son. *Education:* BA 1972, MA 1974, JD 1977, University of Texas. *Appointments:* Private law practice, Houston, 1978; Staff attorney, US District Court, Southern District of Texas, 1979-81; Judicial clerk, US District Judge Woodrow Seals, 1981-83; Associate attorney, Blackburn, Gamble & Henderson 1983-87, Ross, Banks, May, Cron & Cavin 1987-. *Publications:* Book review, American Journal of Criminal Law, 1976; Article, journal Comunidad (Mexico), 1975; Thesis, Use of Parental Attention-Getting Devices, 1974. *Memberships:* State Bar of Texas; Houston Bar Association. *Honours:* Phi Beta Kappa, 1972; Phi Kappa Phi, 1972; Alpha Lambda Delta, 1971. *Hobbies:* Bible study; Reading; Travel; Charity work. *Address:* c/o Ross, Banks, May, Cron & Cavin, 9 Greenway Plaza, 20th Floor, Houston, Texas 77046, USA.

GONCE Nancy Cummings, b. 21 May 1939, Birmingham, Alabama, USA. Librarian; Organizational Consultant. m. Robert L. Gonce, 26 Aug. 1961, 2 daughters. *Education:* BS, LS, University of Alabama, 1961; MS/LS, Peabody College, 1961. *Appointments:* International Womens Year, state delegate, national delegate; Reader's Advisor, Freidman Library, Tuscaloosa, 1960-61; Area Librarian, Field Representative, Alabama Public Library, 1961-67; Librarian, Riverbend Mental Health Center, 1972-78; White House Conference on Libraries and Information Sciences, 1979; Governor's Conference on Libraries and Information Sciences, 1979; Chamber of Commerce, Cultural Affairs Committee, Co-Chair Education Committee, Co-Chair Cooperative Campus Ministry, University of North Alabama, Chairman of Board; Alambama Reunion, Florence Celebration Committee, Co-Chair Finance Committee; Alabama Mountain Lakes Tourism Board, Board of Directors; Librarian, Webster Elementary School, 1982-83, 1984-; Owner, Consulting Firm, 1984-; Office Manager, W.C. Handy Music Festival, 1986-; American Association of University Women, various local and state offices. *Publications:* Editor, Qualified Women of Alabama. *Memberships:* Alabama Library Association, various offices; Music Preservation Society, Founding Board; Gingerbread Playhouse, Founding Board; Florence Ballet Company, Board of Directors. *Honours:* Recipient, many honours and awards. *Hobbies:* Music; Theatre; Hiking; Reading; Community Affairs. *Address:* 321 Palisade Drive, Florence, AL 35630, USA.

GONCERZEWICZ Maria Irena, b. 28 Aug. 1917, Brzeznica, Poland. Professor of Paediatrics. m. Zygmunt Goncerzewicz, 30 Dec. 1940, 1 son, 1 daughter. *Education:* MD, Medical College, Poznan University, 1949; PhD, 1959; Associate Professor, 1962; Professor, 1972. *Appointments:* Associate 1949-53, Senior Associate 1954-55; Tutor 1955-62 (research & didactic), Paediatric Clinic, Medical Academy of Poznan; Head, Department of Paediatric Propedeutics 1962-72, Vice Director 1970-76, Institute of Paediatrics; Chief Director, Children's Health Centre, Memorial Hospital, 1976-.

Publications: Numerous scientific articles, Polish & foreign journals. *Memberships:* Chair, Inborn Defects Commission & member, Commission of Man's Development, Polish Academy of Sciences; Polish, & International Paediatric Societies; Endocrynology Society; Polish Genetic Society. *Honours:* Award, perfect work in health service' 1963; Golden awards, contributions to towns: Zielona Gora 1967, Poznan 1974, Warsaw 1980; Bachelor's Cross 1974; Commander's Cross 1979; Order of the Banner of Labour, 1st Class, 1987. *Hobbies:* Reading books; Classical music; Water sports. *Address:* ul. Karowa 18a/5, 00-324 Warszawa, Poland.

GONNELLA Patricia Anne, b. 25 Nov. 1949, Philadelphia, Pennsylvania, USA. Scientist; Assistant Professor of Pediatrics. *Education:* PhD, Temple University, 1979; Postdoctoral Fellowship, Department of Anatomy, University of Pennsylvania School of Medicine, 1979-81; Postdoctoral Fellowship, Department of Anatomy, Harvard Medical School, 1982-85. *Appointments:* Instructor, 1986, Assistant Professor of Pediatrics, 1987-, Harvard Medical School; Assistant Anatomist, Children's Hospital, Boston, Massachusetts, 1986-; Assistant Biochemist, Massachusetts General Hospital, 1986-. *Publications:* Author of scientific publications in Journal of Cell Biology, Proceedings of the National Academy of Science, Blood, Thrombosis and Haematosis, Journal of Clinical Investigations; Journal of Cellular Physiology, Gastroenterology. *Memberships:* American Society for Cell Biology; American Association for the Advancement of Science, 1983-84. *Honour:* Recipient of National Research Service Award, 1982- 84. *Address:* Department of Surgery, Metabolism and Nutrition, Brigham and Women's Hospital, Boston, MA 02115, USA.

GONZALEZ Cristina, b. 9 Apr. 1951, Spain. Associate Professor. m. Richard A. Cohen, 8 Aug. 1979, 1 son. *Education:* MA, 1978, PhD, 1981, Spanish Literature, Indiana University, USA. *Appointments:* Assistant Professor, 1981-86, Director, Spanish & Portguese Graduate Programme, 1984-86, Purdue University; Assistant Professor, 1986-87, Associate Professor, 1987-, Director, Spanish & Portuguese Graduate Programme, 1987-, University of Massachusetts. *Publications:* El Cavallero Zifar y el reino lejano, 1984; book chapters; Annotated Edition: El Libro del Cavallero Zifar, 1983; articles in professional journals. *Honours:* Grant, University of Massachusetts, 1988; Research Fellowship, American Council of Learned Societies, 1984; Grant, Purdue University, 1983; *Address:* 135 Logtown Rd, Amherst, MA 01002, USA.

GONZALEZ Kimberly Regina Kramar, b. 5 Nov. 1964, Walnut Creek, California, USA. Controller; Treasurer. m. George Gonzalez, 30 May 1987. 2 sons. *Education:* BS, International Business Management, Woodbury University, Los Angeles, 1986. *Appointments:* Controller/Treasurer, Charisma in Missions Inc, Los Angeles (Non-profit/religious), 1986-; Associate Producer, Television Program, Alabaré, airing weekly in Los Angeles, CA, 1988-. *Memberships:* American Society of Professional & Exec Women; National Association for Femal Executives; American Management Assn; Republican National Committee; Catholic Communicators Association, Los Angeles. *Honours:* National Dean's List, 1984-85 and 1985- 86; Summa cum laude and Department Honours, International Business, 1986. *Interests:* Catholic evangelization; My children. *Address:* 629 Avenue A, Redondo Beach, CA 90277, USA.

GONZALEZ Raquel Maria, b. 1 June 1952, Veguitas, Oriente, Cuba. Pharmacist. *Education:* BS, Biology, Georgia College, 1974; BS, Pharmacy, Mercer University Southern School of Pharmacy, USA, 1977. *Appointments:* VA Hospital, South Nashville, 1979; VA Hospital, Decatur, 1979-81; Lewisburg Community HOspital, 1981-. *Memberships:* Ducks Unlimited; Atlanta Ski Club. *Honours:* Rho Chi Recognition Certificate, 1974-75; Certificate of Award, Metro Atlanta

Combined Federal Campaign, 1981; National Republican Senatorial Committee Certificate of Merit, 1986. *Hobbies:* Piano; White Water Rafting; Skiing; Snorkeling; Gardening; Canoeing. *Address:* PO Box 35, Belfast, TN 37019, USA.

GONZALEZ-LIMA Erika M, b. 9 June 1956, Caracas, Venezuela. m. Francisco Gonzalez-Lima, 9 Aug. 1981. *Education:* Licentiate, Catholic University Andres Bello, Caracas, 1978; M.Ed., University of Texas, Austin, USA, 1981; PhD Candidate, Texas A&M University. *Appointments:* Counsellor, Ponce, 1981-85; Programme Director, Grant DHHS Health Careers Opportunity Programme, Ponce, 1985; Graduate Assistant, Texas A&M University, 1986-. *Publication:* Santiago Ramon y Cajal, 1985. *Memberships:* Venezuelan Federation of Psychologists; American Association for Counselling and Development; Alzheimer's Disease Association, Programmes Chair, Bryan-College Station Support Group. *Honours:* Gran Mariscal de Ayacucho Scholarship, 1979-81; Don D. Albrecht Scholarship, College Station, 1988. *Hobbies:* Health Counselling; Languages; Fitness. *Address:* College Station, TX, USA.

GONZALEZ-MORENO Anna b. 12 Dec. 1956, New Delhi, India. Educationalist. m. Simon Gonzalez-Moreno, 12 July 1986. *Education:* Licence es Sciences Sociales, Sorbonne, Paris, 1977; MA, Anthropology, University College, London, 1979. *Appointments:* Stewart Wrightson, 1979-80; Clarkson Puckle Insurance Brokers, 1980-83; Hogg Robinson Insurance Brokers, 1983-87; Lloyd Thompson Ltd., 1987-89. *Memberships:* Insurance Brokers Council; Network Member; Bow Group. *Hobbies:* Skiing; Scuba; Reading. *Address:* Alphabet Nursery School, Chatham Hall, London SW11, England.

GONZALEZ-QUEVEDO Arnhilda Badia, b. 15 Nov. 1947, Havana, Cuba. University Associate Vice President. divorced. 1 son. *Education:* BA Education, Meredith College, Raleigh, North Carolina, 1968; MA, Spanish and Portuguese, 1969, PhD Romance Languages and Linguistics, 1971, University of North Carolina at Chapel Hill. *Appointments:* Instructor, University of North Carolina, Chapel Hill, 1969-71; Assistant Professor, Director of Foreign Languages in Elementary Schools Program, Winthrop College, Rock Hill, South Carolina, 1971-74; Assistant Professor, Supervisor of Foreign Languages in Elementary Schools Program, University of North Carolina, Charlotte, 1974-75; Assistant Professor, Multicultural Education, Pasco-Hernando Community College, Pasco, Florida, 1975-76; Assistant Professor, School of Education, University of South Florida, Tampa, 1975-77; Associate Professor, School of Education, Florida International University, Miami, Florida, 1980-; Director, Division of Sponsored Research and Training 1979-81, Associate Vice President, Academic Affairs, 1981-, Florida International University, Miami; State Representative, District 112, Florida House of Representatives, 1984-. *Publications:* Over 100 articles, documents and presentations made at major conferences and conventions dealing with educational developments, Global and International Awareness, Latin American and the Caribbean, Economic Trends and Foreign Policy. *Memberships include:* American Association of Teachers of Spanish and Portuguese; Modern Language Association; Southern Modern Language Association; Sociedad Hispanica Carolinesa; American Council on the Teaching of Foreign Languages; Florida Association of Teachers of English to Speakers of Other Languages. *Honours include:* Woman of the Year Award, Cuban Women's Club; Freshman of the Year Award, United Teachers of Dade, 1984; Freshman of the Year Award, Florida Educational Association, 1985; Freshman of the Year Award, Florida Student Government Association, 1984. *Address:* 600 Biltmore Way, Coral Gables, FL 33134, USA.

GONZALEZ-VILLAMIL Diana Cecilia, b. 14 May 1955, San Juan, Puerto Rico. Architect. m. Hector R. Lopez, 2 Apr. 1982, 1 son. *Education:* BArch., 1981. *Appointments:* Recreational Dev. Co., 1977-80; Marmol

Co., 1981-82; Jimenez & Rodriguez Barcelo, 1982-83; Private practice, 1983-. *Creative Works:* Equestrian Centre, San Juan, 1979; Playas de PR Tourist & Residential Development. *Memberships:* Puerto Rica Board of Architects; Florida Board of Architects; NCARB; AIA. *Honours:* Puerto Rico Olympic Commiittee Medal; Designated Olympic Rider, Pan American Games, 1979. *Hobbies:* Show Jumping; Alpine Skiing; Silk Screening. *Address:* 552 Waymouth Street, Suite C, Santurce, Puerto Rico 00907, USA.

GOOD Janet Gray Marshall, b. 4 Mar. 1921, Gargunnock, Stirlingshire, Scotland. Entrepeneur. m. (1)2 sons, (2)Edwin Good, 2 Nov. 1956, divorced, 1 son. *Appointments:* Domestic Service, 1934; Billeting Officer, 1943-45; Hotel Management Stirling, Royal Hotel Dundee and Harrington Hall, London, England, 1945-50; Ch Cashier, Statler Hotel, NY, 1950-53; Manageress, Blair Atholl Hotel, Duchess of Atholl's Estate, 1953-55; Controller, Meridian Films, Toronto, Canada, 1958; Controller, Kleinberg Studios, 1959-63; Founded, Canadian Motion Picture Equipment Rentals, 1963-. *Creative works:* Assisted many Canadian Filmmakers get started; Featured in film: The Woman Behind the Legend by Humber College, Ontario; Acted in Between Friends, Screwball Academy and Busted Up. *Honours:* Bill Hilson Trophy, Canadian Society of Cinematographers, 1983. *Hobbies:* Helping young filmmakers get started; Cooking; Motoring; Knitting. *Address:* Canadian Motion Picture Equipment Rentals Limited, 33 Granby Street, Toronto, Ontario M5B 1H8, Canada.

GOOD Mary Lowe, b. 20 June 1931, Grapevine, Texas, USA. Technology Management. m. Bill J Good, 17 May 1952. 2 sons. *Education:* BS, Chemistry, University of Central Arkansas, 1950; MS, Chemistry 1952, PhD, Inorganic Chemistry, 1954, University of Arkansas, Fayetteville. *Appointments:* Professor of Chemistry, Louisiana State University System, 1954-80; VP-Director of Research 1980-85, President-Director of Research 1985-, President-Engineered Materials Research 1986-88, Senior VP- Technology 19880-, Allied Signal Inc, Morristown, New Jersey. *Publications:* Books: Integrated Laboratory Sequence, Vol III, 1970; Biotechnology and Materials Science, Editor, 1988; About 100 articles in technical journals. *Memberships:* National Science Board, Chairman 1988-, Vice Chairman 1984; American Chemical Society, President 1987, Chairman, Board of Directors 1978, 1980; President Inorganic Division of IUPAC (International Union of Pure & Applied Chemistry), 1980-85. *Honours:* Delmar S Fahrney Medal, Franklin Institute, 1988; Gold Medal Award, American Institute of Chemists, 1983; Industrial R & D Magazine Scientist of the Year, 1982; American Chemical Society Garvan Medal, 1973; Elected to National Academy of Engineering, 1987; Recipient of numerous Honorary Doctorates. *Hobbies:* Music; Art; Fishing; Canoeing; Scottish History. *Address:* Allied-Signal Inc, P O Box 1021R, Morristown, New Jersey 07960, USA.

GOODENOUGH Judith Elizabeth Levrat, b. 28 Sept. 1948, Geneva, New York, USA. Education; Writer. m. Stephen Michael Goodenough, 21 Aug. 1971, 2 daughters. *Education:* BS, Wagner College, 1970; PhD, New York University, 1977. *Appointments:* Instructor, New York University, 1974; Lecturer, Staff Assistant, 1975-83, Lecturer, Staff Associate, 1983-, University of Massachusetts, Amherst. *Publications:* Laboratory Directions for Introductory Zoology, 5th edition; Mysterious Monthly Rhythms Natural HIstory, 1978; Animal Communication Carolina Bio. Reader, 1984; The Laboratory Collection, 1987; Supplement to the Laboratory Collection, 1988. *Memberships:* AAAS; Sigma Xi; Animal Behavior Society. *Honours:* Faculty Growth Grant for Teaching, 1976; Faculty Research Grant, 1980, 1982; Distinguished Teaching Award, 1986. *Hobbies:* Stained Glass; Needlework; Camping. *Address:* 16 Brookwood Dr., Florence, MA 01060, USA.

GOODFIELD June, b. 1 June 1927, Stratford-on-Avon, England. Author; TV Presenter. *Education;* BSc.,

Zoology, Honours, University of London, 1949; PhD, History & Philosophy of Science, University of Leeds, 1959. *Appointments:* Rebecca Bacarach Treves Professor of the History & Philosophy of Science, Wellesley College, 1966-69; Professor, Human Medicine and Philosophy, Michigan State University, 1969-78; Senior Research Associate, Adjunct Professor, Rockefeller University, 1977-82; President, International Health & Biomedicine Ltd., 1982-. *Publications:* Fom the Face of the Earth, 1985; An Imagined World, 1981; Reflections on Science & the Media, 1981; Playing God, 1976; The Siege of Cancer, 1975; Courier to Peking, 1973; 7 films either as writer, presenter or producer. *Memberships:* PEN; Royal Society of Medicine. *Honours:* Rockefeller Foundation Humanities Fellow, 1976-77; Gallatin Lecturer in Humanities, New York University, 1981; Nobel Lecturer, Gustavus Adolphus College, Minnesota, 1983; Osler Lecturer, McGill University, 1985; President, UN Association, London, 1986-87; Victoria Fellow, Contemporary Issues, Rutgers University, 1988. *Hobbies:* Music; Gardening; Walking; Driving Through France; etc. *Address:* The Manor House, Alfriston, East Sussex BN26 5SY, England.

GOODHART Celia McClare, b. 25 July 1939, England. Politican. m. William Howard Goodhart QC, 21 May 1966. 1 son, 2 daughters. *Education:* St Hilda's College, Oxford, 1957-60; BA Oxon 1960; MA Oxon 1982. *Appointments:* Assistant Principal and Principal, Ministry of Agriculture Fisheries and Food and HM Treasury, 1960-66; History Tutor, Queen's College, London, 1966-80; Appointed by Minister, Prices and Consumer Protection to Chairman, North Thames Gas Consumers Council, 1979-82; Member, Data Protection Committee appointed by Home Secretary; Member, Social Democratic Party; Worked in Headquarters, 1982-83; Stood for Parliament, Kettering Constituency, 1983; Stood for European Parliament for Northamptonshire, 1984. ssa 20*Memberships:* Elected Treasurer, SDP Candidates Association; Member, Executive Committee, Women for Social Democracy. *Address:* 45 Campden Hill Square, London W8 7JR, England.

GOODING Kathleen Mary Tinney, b. 2 Dec. 1911, Cardiff, Wales. Teacher; Writer. m. 7 Aug. 1937, 2 sons. *Education:* Qualified as Primary School Teacher, 1931. *Appointments:* Primary School Teacher, Berkshire, & Somerset, 1931-36. *Publications* Novels: The Venetians (prose version of The Merchant of Venice), 1973; Belfriere, 1970; The Rainbow Trail, 1983; Children's Novel: The Festival Summer, 1984; Other Publications: Approximately 40 stories broadcast on BBC Morning Story; Feature articles in The Guardian Newspaper; Bridge at Edenfall, political, historical novel, published in Woman's Own Journal, 1970; several articles in the Countryman and Pony Journals and in several different county magazines. *Memberships:* Society of Women Writers & Journalists; Weston-Super-Mare Writers' Workshop; Sidcot Society of Friends Meeting. *Honours:* Welsh Arts Council Commendation for Novel, The Rainbow Trail. *Hobbies:* Writing; Reading; Music; Crosswords; Current Affairs. *Address:* Woodside, Pilcorn Street, Wedmore, Somerset BS28 4AN, England.

GOODMAN Mary Anne (Spencer), b. 25 Oct. 1931, Gastonia, North Carolina, USA. Librarian; Musician; Music Teacher. m. Louis Goodman, 22 June 1969. 1 daughter, Henrietta Spencer Goodman. *Education:* BM, University of North Carolina at Greensboro, 1954; MM, Eastman School of Music, University of Rochester, 1956; Additional graduate courses in the School of Library Science, University of Southern California, 1962-65. *Appointments:* Freelance Musician and Private Instructor; Clarinetist, Greensboro Symphony Orchestra, N.C., 1950-54; Public School Music, Seattle, Washington, 1957-58; Public School Music, Washington County, Maryland, 1958-59; Reference Librarian, Los Angeles Public Library (Hollywood Regional Branch), 1963-73; World Book Encyclopedia sales representative, 1977-; Library Staff (Audio-visual, Reference and Periodicals) Gaston County Public

Library, North Carolina, 1982-. *Memberships:* Pi Kappa Lambda; American Federation of Musicians; Daughters of the American Revolution; Golden Chain. *Honours:* Fulbright Scholarship, 1954-55, Trinity College of Music, London England. *Hobbies and Interests:* Reading; Travel; Camping; Photography; Chamber Music; Musical Interpretation; Physical and Physiological aspects of Clarinet playing. *Address:* 514 West Third Avenue, Gastonia, North Carolina 28052, USA.

GOODMAN Sonya Gershowitz, b. 30 July 1940, USA. Businesswoman; Former Nurse. m. Jerome L. Goodman, 1 son, 1 daughter. *Education:* Sinai Hospital School of Nursing, 1960; AA, Cotonsville Community College, 1972; BSc 1973, MA 1978, University of Maryland. *Appointments:* Director of Nursing, Mount Sinai Nursing Home, 1963-64; Director, Nursing Multi-Medical, 1974-75; Owner, Chai Management, 1975-; Owner, Federal Hill Nursing Home, Lafayette Nursing Home, Great Pennsylvania Nursing Home, 1978- 84; Owner, Executive Director, Creative Health Services, 1984-. *Memberships include:* Board, Mount Washington Paediatric Hospital; President's Club, University of Maryland; American Nursing Association. *Honours:* Numerous. *Address:* Creative Health Services Consultants, 2115 North Charles Street, Baltimore, Maryland 21218, USA.

GOODWAY Martha Elizabeth, b. 27 Aug. 1934, Boston, USA. Archaeometallurgist. *Education:* SB, Engineering, MIT, 1958. *Appointments:* Metallurgical Engineer, Rayheon, 1958-59; American Science & Engineering, 1961-62; Self-employed 1963-70; Metallurgist, Smithsonian Institution, 1970; Consultant, various organisations. *Publications:* Co-author, The Metallurgy of 17th & 18th Century Music Wire, 1987; Corrosion & metal Artifacts, 1977; Contributor to various journals. *Memberships Include:* various professional organisations. *Honours:* Fellow, ASM International, 1988; Citation of Excellence, University of Southern California; Bausch & Loab Honorary Science Award. *Hobbies:* Archaeoastronomy; Sailing; Ice Dancing; Croquet. *Address:* Smithsonian Institution, Washington DC 20560, USA.

GOODWIN Susan Ann, b. 9 June 1944, Boston, Massachusetts, USA. University Administrator. *Education:* BA, Economics, Wellesley College, 1966; MA, Economics, Boston University, 1967; PhD, Economics, Tufts University, 1975. *Appointments:* Faculty, 1971, Special Assistant to President, 1977-78, Director of Information Systems, 1978-80, Acting Dean of Research, Acting Director of Research Foundation, 1980-81, Vice-President, Administration, 1981-84, Vice-President, Administration and Finance, 1984-. University of Lowell, Lowell, Massachusetts. *Publications:* Professional articles on economics and university administration. *Memberships:* Executive Committee, Greater Lowell Private Industry Council; Sub-Committee to construct and open day care centre; Board of Directors, Merrimack Valley United Fund, 1980-86. *Honours:* American Council on Education Fellow, 1977-78. *Hobbies:* Skiing; Piano. *Address:* University of Lowell, Lowell, MA 01854, USA.

GOOTNICK Margaret Mary, b. 14 Oct. 1951, Stamford, Connecticut, USA. Management Consultant. m. David E. Gootnick, 18 Sept. 1978. *Appointments:* Senior Partner, Associate Director, David Gootnick Associates, New York; Business Faculties: New York University's Business Management Institute, National Association of Accountants, American Management Associations, Marymount Manhattan College, Triton College Employee Development Institute. *Publications:* Co-Editor, Contributing Author, The Standard Handbook of Business Communication, 1984; Editor, The Insurance Primer for the Consumer, 1977; Management Columnist, Electronic Buyers News, 1982-84; Management Speaker, video cassette programme, National Association of Accountants, 1985; Poetry: The Treasure Drawer; There's Always Room in a Taxi; Looking Out My Window on 42nd Street; David; The Dining Room; Reflection; The Wedding Party. *Address:*

International Plaza, Suite 23B, 303 East 43rd Street, New York, NY 10017, USA.

GORDIMER Nadine, b. 20 Nov. 1923, Springs, South Africa. Author. m. Reinhold Cassirer, 29 Jan. 1954, 1 son, 1 daughter. *Publications:* 9 Novels; 8 Short Story Collections; 1 Collection Non-Fiction; numerous anthologies. *Memberships:* Vice President, International PEN; Patron, Congress of South African Writers; Fellow, Royal Society of Literature; Honorary Member: American Academy of Arts & Sciences, American Institute of Arts & Letters; Honorary Fellow, MLA. *Honours:* Numerous including: Booker Prize, 1974; Grand Aigle D'or, France, 1975; Nelly Sachs Prize, Germany, 1986; Malaparte Prize, italy, 1986; Bennet Award, USA, 1987; Hon. D.Litt, Harvard University, Yale University, USA, 1986, University of York, England, 1988; etc. *Address:* 7 Frere Road, Parktown West, Johannesburg 2193, South Africa.

GORDON Conni, b. New Britain, Connecticut, USA. Artist; Teacher; Entertainer. *Education:* Columbia School of Fine Art, 1945-48; Columbia Teachers College, 1945-48. *Appointments:* Originated use of art participation as form of entertainment, 1940; originator, Director, Hairdressers' Art Course for M. Louis Hair Design Institute, New York, 1946- 47; Conducted Audience participation Paint Parties, 1948-; Artist, Exhibitor, Palace of Fontainebleur, 1949; Founder, DDirector, Conni Gordon Art Schools, 1950-; Founder, Paint Party TV Shows, 1950-; Chairman, Board of Directors, Conni Gordon Inc., Florida, Miami Beach, 1959-; President, Palette Productions Inc., 1972-. *Honours:* Recipient, various honours and awards *Address:* 427-22 St., Miami Beach, FL 33139, USA.

GORDON Elaine, b. 8 Sept. 1931, New York, USA. Member, Florida House of Representatives. 2 sons, 1 daughter. *Education:* City University of New York; Miami-Dade Community College; Florida International University; Honorary Doctor of Laws, Barry University. *Appointments:* Past appointments include: Junior Accountant, Paul F Kretzschmar, Accountant; Executive Secretary, American Bankers Assurance Company; Executive Assistant and Property Manager, Kessler and Hess Real Estate and Development Holdings; Executive Secretary, Mass Mutual Life Insurance Company. Elected to Florida House of Representatives, 1972, re-elected every 2 years and now serving 9th term of office. Speaker Pro Tempore of House of Representatives, 1984-86; First woman to chair the Dade County Legislative Delegation. *Publications:* Encyclopedia Britannica; Annals of America Bicentonnial Edition, Article regarding The Equal Rights Amendment, 1977. *Memberships include:* Democratic Women's Club of Dade County; League of Women Voters, Metro-Dade; Founder, National and Florida Women's Political Caucus; B'nai B'rith Women; Women in Government Service; National Order of Women Legislators; American Business Women's Association, Biscayne Chapter; Regional Board Member, Anti-Defamation League. *Honours include:* Woman of the Year, Florida Women's Political Caucus, 1985; Nova University Honours Elaine Gordon for Distinguished Leadership, 1985; Na'amat Celebration of Women Award, 1986; Florida United Way, First Human Service Award, for Outstanding Leadership and Achievement, 1986; The Dade County League of Cities, Inc, Good Government Award, 1986. *Hobbies:* Fishing; Dancing. *Address:* 12100 N E 16th Avenue, North Miami, FL 33161, USA.

GORDON Ethel Edison, b. 5 May 1915, New York City, New York, USA. Writer. m. Heyman Gordon, 20 Sept. 1936, 1 son. *Education:* BA, Washington Square College, New York City, 1936. *Publications:* O'Henry Prize Stories, 1945; Best Short Stories, 1951; 5 Gothic novels published USA and Europe inluding Dell paperbacks: Freers Cove, The Chaperone, The Birdwatcher, Freebody Heiress, French Husband; Where Does The Summer Go?; So Far From Home; 100 stories in Redbook, Colliers, Ladies Home Journal, also Woman's Own, England, and Chatelaine, Canada.

Honour: Phi Beta Kappa, 1936. *Hobby:* Travel. *Address:* 105 Lake Drive, Hewlett Harbor, NY 11557, USA.

GORDON Hannah Campbell Grant, b. 9 Apr. 1941, Edinburgh, Scotland. Actress. m. Norman Warwick, 5 Feb. 1970. 1 son. *Education:* Certificate, Dramatic Studies, Glasgow University; Royal College of Music & Dramatic Art, Glasgow. *Performances:* Dundee Repertory Theatre, 1962; 1st Appearance, TV, 1965, then classic serials, many single plays. Notable TV successes including: My Wife Next Door, 1972; Upstairs, Downstairs, 1976; Telford's Change, 1979; Miss Morrison's Ghosts, 1980; The Day After The Fair, 1986. London Stage: The Killing Fame, 1980; The Jeweller's Shop, by Pope John Paul, 1982; The Country Girl, 1983-84; Light Up the Sky, 1985. Many radio plays including: Hedda Gabler; Macbeth, etc. *Honours:* James Bridie Gold Medal for Dramatic Art, Glasgow, 1962; Fellow, Royal Scottish Academy of Music & Drama, 1980. *Hobbies:* Tennis; Gardening; Cooking. *Address:* 200 Fulham Road, London SW10 9PN, England.

GORDON Marva Loretta, b. 12 Aug. 1945, Camden, New Jersey, USA. Professional Nurse; Medical Sociologist. m. 10 Oct. 1969. 1 son. *Education:* AAS, NYCCC, Brooklyn, New York, 1969; BA, ERichmond College, 1971; MA, Hunter College, 1972; MS 1975, BSN, C W Post, 1980, Long Island University; MPH 1980, PhD 1983, St John's University, New York. *Appointments:* Nursing Care Co-ordinator, St Albans Veterans Administration, New York, 1977-83; Assistant Chief, Nursing Service, Veterans Administration For Lyon, Colorado, 1983-84; Associate Chief Trainee for Nursing Home Care, 1984; Associate Chief, 1984-, Nursing Home Care and Nursing Research, Cleveland VA Medical Centre, Cleveland, Ohio. *Publications:* A Study of Weight Loss in Nursing Personnel, 1984; A Professional Challenge to make a Difference, 1986; Clinical Research and the Future of Nursing, 1986. *Memberships:* Ohio Nurses Association, Officer of the New Member Assembly; American Sociological Association; American Nurses Association; Medical Sociological Association; Midwest Nursing Research Association; American Public Health Association; New York Academy of Sciences. *Honours:* Summa cum laude, Richmond College, 1971; Selected as a Citizen Ambassador for the People to People Nursing Delegation to Republic of China, Japan, Inner Mongolia and Hong Kong, 1985. *Hobbies:* Minister of Music at a Church in the community; Public Speaking; Cats; Reading. *Address:* 8484 Brecksville Road, Brecksville, OH 44141, USA.

GORDON Tessa, b. 2 Feb. 1947, Johannesburg, South Africa. Professor. m. Philip Gordon, 8 Jan. 1967, 2 daughters. *Education:* BSc., Cape Town, 1966; PhD, Birmingham, England, 1972. *Appointments:* Assistant Professor, 1980-81, Associate Professor, 1982-87, Professor 1988-, Pharmacology, University of Alberta. *Publications:* The Role of Calcium & Magnesium Ions in the Response of Denervated Skeletal Muscle to Acetylcholine, 1972; Co-author: Nerve-Muscle Interaction, 1978; Co-Editor, The Current Status of Peripheral Nerve Regeneration, 1987; articles in numerous journals. *Memberships:* Society for Neuroscience; Canadian Physiological Society; Canadian Pharmacology Society; Canadian Association for Neuroscience. *Honours Include:* Class Medal, Physiology, University of Cape Town, 1966; Wellcome Foundation Scholarship, 1968-72; Medical Research Council Fellowship, 1972-75; J.F. Stevenson Visiting Professorship, Canadian Physiology Society, 1981; Medical Research Council of Canada Research Scholarship, 1982; Alberta Heritage Foundation for Medical Research Scholarship, 1987. *Hobbies:* My Children; Reading. *Address:* Dept. of Pharmacology, 9-36 Medical Sciences Building, University of Alberta, Edmonton, Alberta, Canada T6G 2H7.

GORDON-WALKER Ann Marguerite, b. 27 Feb. 1944, London, England. Scientific Administrator. m. Andrew Ball, 20 July 1968, divorced, 1983. 2 daughters. *Education:* BSc, Queen's College, Dundee, University

of St Andrew's, Scotland, 1966; DPhil, Oxford University, Oxford, England, 1969. *Appointments:* Assistant Editor, Biochemical Journal, 1972-74; Lecturer, University of Connecticut, 1978-79; Assistant Editor, University of Wisconsin Press, 1980-81; Lecturer, Edgewood College, Madison, 1980-81; Scientific Administrator, University of Wisconsin, 1981-. *Hobbies:* Travelling; Tennis; Reading. *Address:* 1230 University Bay Drive, Madison, WI 53705, USA.

GORE Myriam Kathleen, b. 28 June 1918, USA. Retired Teacher. m. C J Chandler, 16 Jan. 1942. *Education:* BA, MEd, University of Mississippi; Graduate Work, Florida State University, Mississippi State University, 3 art courses, Milsaps College, jackson; Tour, Art Galleries of Europe, 1960's; WPA Social Worker, 1 year, 1940's. *Appointments:* Teacher, Public Schools, High Schools, 1940's, 1950's, 1960's; Medical Records Secretary, Defence Plant, WWII; Secretary, Mississppi State Nurses Association, 1 year; head, File Room War Assets Administration, etc. *Publications:* Mississippi Miscellany; Englishings; Les Belles Lettres; various sketches on notepaper; 3 boxes Christmas Cards; One Man Art Show, Raymond Duncan Gallery, Paris. *Memberships:* Kappa Delta; Alpha Mu; Office, Hinds County Federation of Womens Clubs; President Boys Club Auxiliary, Jackson; Board of Directors, Family Service Association of Jackson; Jackson Civil War Round Table; American Association of University Women; League of Women Voters; Fondren Presbyterian Church; Jackson Council of Church Women; Mississippi Art Association; Mississippi Historical Society; Mississippi Poetry Society; Jackson Music Association. *Honours:* Winner, Prix de Paris One Man Art Show, Paris, 1960's; Awarded Experience Teacher, Fellowships to Florida State University, 1968-69. *Hobbies:* Writing; Painting; Sketching; Tennis; Bridge; Cooking; Housekeeping. *Address:* 808 North Jackson St., Houston, MS 38851, USA.

GORN Janet Marie, b. 29 Sept. 1938, Fond du Lac, Wisconsin, USA. Congressional Affairs Officer. m. Ronald Lee Braun, 20 June 1959, div. 20 Mar. 1980, 1 son, 1 daughter. *Education:* BA, Drew University, Madison, New Jersey, 1973; MA, San Jose State University, California, 1982; Post-Graduate, George Washington University, Washington DC, 1984-86. *Appointments:* Policy Analyst, City of San Jose, California, 1975-76; Research Assistant, Brookings Institution, 1977-79; Research Analyst, US Congressional Research Service, Library of Congress, 1978-79; Programme Analyst, Division of Radioactive Waste Management, 1980-82, Congressional Affairs Officer, Office of the Chairman, 1982-88, US Nuclear Regulatory Commission, 1988-. *Memberships:* Women in Energy, National Vice-President 1984-86; Nuclear Women in Energy; American Nuclear Society; American League of Lobbyists; US NRC Staff Alternate to Presidential Task Force, State Planning Council on Radioactive Waste Management, 1980-82; Prince William County Virginia Library Planning Committee, Subcommittee Chair 1987-88; City of Vienna Virginia Mayor's Advisory Commission, 1978-79; Chair, New Jersey State Ad Hoc Committee to Establish Bureau of Women and Advisory Board, 1971-72; San Jose California Bicentennial Commission, 1974-76; Peralta Adobe Restoration Commission, San Jose, 1974-76; American Association of University Women, Vice-President 1978-79; LWV, Vice-President 1966-67; International Order of DeMolay, Harold K Lind Chapter Mothers Club, President 1978-79; Morristown Junior Woman's Club, Vice-President 1972-73, President Designate; State Board, New Jersey Junior Woman's Club, 1969-73, Secretary 1972-73; Co-Organiser, Den Mother Coach, Pack 124 Cub Scouts, Morris-Sussex Area Council, Boy Scouts of America, 1969-73; Committee Member, Sanitary Landfill Oversight Committee, Prince William County Virginia, 1990; Commissioner, Commission on the Future Prince William Country Virginia, 1989-1991. *Address:* 15730 Cranberry Court, Eumfries, VA 22026, USA.

GORNA Christina, b. 19 Feb. 1937. Barrister. m.

1963. 1 son, 1 daughter. *Education:* LLB (Hons), University of Manchester, 1955-58; Diploma French Civilisation, Paris Sorbonne, 1958-60; British and European Council Scholar, International Law, University of Neuchatel, Switzerland; College of Law, Called to Bar, 1960. *Appointments:* Pupillage, Barry Chedlow, QC, 1960-61; Barrister, 1962; Examiner in Law, Council of Legal Education, 1964-68; Lecturer in Criminal Law, Leicester Polytechnic, 1969-70; Senior Lecturer in Law, Lanchester Polytechnic, Coventry, 1971-76; Barrister, Leicester, 1977-85; Member, Family Bar Association, 1983; Barrister, London, 1985-. *Creative works:* Books: Company Law; Questions and Answers on Company Law; Leading Cases on Company Law; Presented and Compiled Programme of Women's Poetry, The Haymarket Theatre, Leciester, 1977; Researched and Broadcast, BBC Radio Centenary Broadcast, You and Yours; Commissioned by BBC to script and present Legal Advice Phone-In Programme; BBC2 Contributor to Issues of Law (video available); Network Magazine regular column; Regular broadcaster on radio and television on legal issues. *Memberships include:* Network; 300 Club. *Hobbies:* Visual and performing arts; Literature; Communicating; Swimming. *Address:* 4 Paper Buildings, Temple, London EC4Y 7EX, England.

GOSS Donna Kay Richardson, b. 6 July 1953, Florence, Alabama, USA. Teacher. m. 25 May 1974, 1 son, 1 daughter. *Education:* BS, University of North Alabama, 1975. *Appointments:* Teacher, English and Computer Literacy, Colbert County Board of Education, Alabama, 1975-. *Memberships:* Sentinel, Order of the Eastern Star; National Alliance of English Teachers; Colbert County Teachers Association; Alabama Education Association; National Education Association; Leighton Middle Faculty; Secretary, National Honor Society. *Honours:* Senior Class Secretary, 1971, Senior Class Personality, Lexington High School; Outstanding Teenager of America, 1971; Top Ten Seniors, 1971; Daughters of the American Revolution Citizenship Award, 1971; Highest Academic Average in Business Education, University of North Alabama, 1975. *Hobbies:* Reading; Sports; Needlework; Computing; Politics. *Address:* 609 Pickwick Street, Sheffield, AL 35660, USA.

GOTHIA Sister Blanche, b. 27 Oct. 1930, Port Arthur, Texas, USA. Media Coordinator. *Education:* BA, Dominican College, 1960; MLS, Texas Women's University, 1973. *Appointments:* Teacher, Elementary Secondary Schools, Texas, 1950-69; Teacher 1964-67, Principal 1965-67, St Anthony's Cathedral School, Beaumont, Texas; Audio Visual Director 1967-69, Media Coordinator 1969-, St Agnes Academy, Houston *Memberships:* American Library Association; American Film Institute; Association of Education Communications and Technology; Catholic Library Association; Texas Association of Educational Technology; Texas Library Association; Area IV TAET; Bishop Byrne Unit of CLA; Texas Committee for White House Conference on Library and Information Sciences, 1978-79; Advisory Board, High School Section, National Catholic Library Association, 1979-83; Secretary, Young Adult Section, Texas Library Association, 1979-80; Administrator, Houston Area European Comparative Cultural Studies Program for International Travel Study Inc, 1984-; High School Advisory Board of CLA, 1988-93; various local and national committees. *Hobbies:* Fishing; Painting; Stamp Collecting. *Address:* St Agnes Academy, 9000 Bellaire Boulevard, Houston, TX 77036, USA.

GOTT Peggy S, b. 22 Feb. 1944, Williamson, West Virginia, USA. Associate Professor. *Education:* AA Biology, Stephens College, 1964; BA, Chemistry 1966, PhD Physiology 1971, University of Kentucky. *Appointments:* Research Fellow Psychobiology, California Institute of Technology, 1971-73; Clinical Neurophysiology Pediatrics, LAC-USC Medical Center, 1973-74; Director of Research and Training, West Virginia Department of Mental Health, 1974-75; Assistant Professor Neurology 1975-81, Associate Professor Neurology, 1981-, University of Southern

California School of Medicine. *Publications:* Numerous scientific publications in professional journals. *Memberships:* American EEG Society; International Neuropsychology Society; Society for Neuroscience; Sigma Xi; Society for Psychophysiological Research; LIV Independent Living Center; Adviersoty Committee Child Development; Div Intl Institute of Los Angeles. *Honours:* Alumnae Achievement Award, Stephens College, 1985; Successful Woman Award, Pasadena City College, 1984; Science Achievement Award Clinical Rubber Co, 1963; Curators Award, Stephens College, 1963; NASA Fellowship, 1966-69; Institute of Neurological Disease and sTroke Fellow, 1971-73. *Hobbies:* Travel; Music; Theatre. *Address:* Los Angeles County, University of Southern California Medical center, Department of Neurology Room 5640, General Hospital, 2025 Zonal Avenue, Los Angeles, CA 90033, USA.

GOTTLIEB Sherry Gershon, b. 6 Apr. 1948, Los Angeles, USA. Bookseller. m. David Gottlieb, 1971, divorced 1973. *Education:* AB, Dramatic Arts, University of California, 1969. *Appointments:* Owner, A Change of Hobbit, 1972-. *Publications:* Hell No, We Won't Go! Evading the Draft During Vietnam, 1989. *Memberships:* SFWA; SCBA; Dead Heads. *Honours:* Special Guest of Honour, Westercon, 1979. *Address:* Reading; Writing; Plays; Films. *Address:* c/o A Change of Hobbit, 1853 Lincoln Blvd., Santa Monica, CA 90404, USA.

GOTTSCHALK Jennifer Leigh, b. 15Feb. 1955, Bethesda, USA. Attorney. *Education:* BA, Universiy of Delaware, 1976; JD, Rutgers University, 1979. *Appointments:* Law Clerk, 1979-80; Assistant Prosecutor, Monmouth County, 1980-82; Assistant Counsel, New Jersey Casino Control Commission, 1983-84; Deputy Attorney General, New Jersey Division of Criminal Justice, 1984-. *Memberships:* Phi Alpha Delta, President 1978- 79; Monmouth Bar Association; Bar of US Supreme Court; Bar of NJ Supreme Court; Bar of Court of Appeals of MD; Bar of US District Court of NJ. *Honours:* Junior of the Year, Runner Up, Washington DC Metropolitan Area, Notre Dame Alumni Club, 1972; Kuskin Award, 1973. *Hobbies:* Monmouth Civic Chorus; Womens Softball; Bowling; Spectator Sports. *Address:* 118 Strathmore Gardens, Aberdeen, NJ 07747, USA.

GOUGEON Deborah J, b. 12 Mar. 1951, Scranton, Pennsylvania, USA. Associate Professor of Statistics. m. Dr Len Gougeon, 22 Feb. 1980. 1 son, 2 daughters. *Education:* BS 1973, MS 1974, University of Scranton; PhD, Walden University, 1979; Post doctoral work SUNY, 1981-82. *Appointments:* Instructor, Lackawanna Jr College, 1975-77, Instructor, Pennsylvania State University, 1977-79; Instructor, Statistics 1979-81, Assistant Professor of Statistics, 1981-88, Associate Professor of Statistics, 1988-, University of Scranton. *Memberships:* American Statistical Association; Mid-South Ed Research Association; Eastern Ed Research Association. *Honours:* University of Scranton Summer Research Grant, 1984; Omicron Delta Epsilon, Award in Economics, 1984. *Hobbies:* Floral arranging; Reading; Gardening. *Address:* Box 147 Glendale, Avoca, PA 18641, USA.

GOULD Carol Beth, b. 19 Sept. 1953, Philadelphia, Pennsylvania, USA. Photographer; Writer; Assistant to the Head of Drama, Anglia TV. *Education:* BA 1976, MA Coursework 1976-77, Temple University; MA thesis research, University of Kent, England, 1977-78. *Appointments:* Administrative aide, concert & theatre management, All Star Forum Inc, Philadelphia, USA, 1972-75; Administrator, The Almost Free Theatre, London, England, 1977-78; Special events coordinator, Shelter, 1979-80; Assistant to the Head of Drama, Anglia TV Ltd. Story Editor, Spitfire Girls, Cause Celebre, Menace Unseen, Tales of the Unexpected series, 1981-; Photojournalist-Contributor: World Tennis Magazine, 1986; Freelance theatre director, including: Raped Take Two, Kirk Foster, London, 1980; CG & Company Theatre Group (directed Public Property, Roger Newman & Barking to the Angel, 1979); Collecting Leaves, Frankie Finn, London, 1981; Then & Now, Polly Perkins, London,

1981; Summer Theatre programme, American School in London, 1980. *Publications:* Full length plays produced: Barking to the Angel, 1977 (London 1979); A Chamber Group, 1977 (produced Edinburgh Festival, 1980); Articles: The demons of Fleet Street; Tennis Camp (World Tennis 1986). Unproduced works: Virgo Rising, 1977; Red Hot Mama, 1977; Poor Marzelline (opera libretto), 1982; Book in preparation: Spitfire Girls (publ. Headline Ltd, 1989); Tennis Faces. *Memberships:* Association of Cinematograph, Television & Allied Technicians; Writers Guild of Great Britain; Phi Beta Kappa (USA); Fellow, International Biographical Association; Lawn Tennis Association; Honorary Member, Women's International Tennis Association. *Honours include:* Gold Key Award, Faculty Honours, 1972-73; Phi Beta Kappa Rho Chapter, 1976; President's Scholar , Temple University; BBC-Kodak Domesday Project Competition; Photographic Slides awarded inclusion on Domesday Project Video disc. *Address:* Drama Department, Anglia Television Ltd., 48 Leicester Square, London WC2, England.

GOVAN Patricia Burke, b. 11 Jan. 1933, Elizabeth, USA. Adjunct Professor. m. James Govan, 4 Apr. 1959, 2 sons. *Education:* BS, Newark State Teachers College, 1954; MA, Communication Sciences, Kean College of New Jersey, 1976. *Appointments:* Teacher, Hillside, 1954-60; Teacher, Resource Teacher, 1962-87; Adjunct Professor, Reading, Montclair State College, 1988-; Adjunct Professor, Kean College, 1988-. *Memberships:* Kappa Delta Pi; New Jersey Federation of Business & Professional Women, State Foundatiron Chair, 1987-88, President, Hillside BPW 1985-87; President, Elizabeth AAUW, 1985-87; Life Member, NJEA and NEA; President, St Catherines Booster Club, 1974; Charter Member, Union County Irish American Association. *Honours:* New Jersey Education Associatiron Teacher of the Month, 1979; NDEA Humanities Grant, 1974; NDEA Mathematics Grant, 1970. *Hobbies:* Reading; Literacy Training; Classical & Popular Music. *Address:* 918 Sterner Road, Hillside, NJ 07205, USA.

GOVE Barbara Evelyn, b. 26 Nov. 1935, Malden, Massachusetts, USA. Veterans Service Officer. *Education:* Nursing, Lynn General Hospital, Lynn, Massachusetts, 1953; Graduate, Woburn High School, Woburn Mass., 1953; Graduate, Marine Corps, Honor Platoon, 1954; Graduate, Aviation Training, Boston, 1955; Graduate, Cleveland Institute for Electronics, 1972; Doctor of Divinity, Kingsway Bible College, Iowa, 1983. *Appointments:* Electronics, 1st class FCC License, 1957-76; San Diego County Welfare for Elderly. *Creative works:* Painting: Charcoal, Rockport Massachusetts, 1951; Book: Art & Practice of Precision Wiring and Solding; Wrote song: To Dad at 88, 1960. *Memberships:* Chaplain, Service Officer, State of Florida, PRO, Marine Corps League, 1979-88; Women Marines Asso - PRO, 1980-86; President, Veterans Council Hillsborough County, Florida, 1987-88; Service Officer, Adjutant, Disabled American Veterans, 1977-79; National Adjutant & Treasurer WML Gove Sr Veterans Inc, 1979-88. *Honours:* Elks posture Award, 1953; Service to Civil Air Patrol, 1951; ALS, San Diego, 1974; Commanders Award, Disabled American Veterans, 1978; James A Haley Veterans Hospital, Tampa, 1982 and 1987; Veterans Council Hillsbrough County Florida, 1988; Personalities of the South, 1988. *Hobbies:* Photography; Painting; Reading; Crafts; Writing; Travelling; Mechanics; Electronics; Helping those in need; Helping veterans. *Address:* 2620 Hwy 60E Lot 81, Valrico, Florida 33594, USA.

GOVIER Katherine Mary, b. 4 July 1948, Edmonton, Canada. Writer. m. John Allen Honderich, 27 Feb. 1981, 1 son, 1 daughter. *Education:* BA, Honours, English, University of Alberta, 1970; MA, English, York University. *Appointments:* Visiting Lecturer, Creative Writing, York University, 1981-85 Visiting Research Fellow, Leeds, University, England, 1986. *Publications:* Random Descent, 1979; Going Through the Motions, 1981; Fables of Brunswick Avenue, short stories, 1985; Between Men, 1987; Before and After, 1989, short stories. *Memberships:* Writers' Union of Canada; PEN Canada. *Hobby:* Travel. *Address:* c/o Lucinda Vardey Agency, 297 Seaton Street, Toronto, Canada M5A 2E8.

GOWEN Marilyn Elizabeth Alley, b. 5 June 1953, Richmond, Virginia, USA. Physician (Pediatric Allergist/Pulmonologist); Teacher, Assistant Professor. m. Clarence William Gowen Jr., 8 Sept. 1984. 1 daughter. *Education:* BS cum laude Biology, University of Richmond, 1971-75; MD, Medical College of Virginia, Virginia Commonwealth University, 1975-79; Pediatric Residency, University of Louisville, 1979-82; Pediatric Allergy, Immunology and Pulmonology Fellowships, Duke University, 1982-85. *Appointments:* Director and Division Head of Pediatric Allergy, Immunology, Pulmonary Disease, East Carolina University, School of Medicine, 1985-. *Memberships:* American Medical Association; American Thoracic Society; American Academy of Allergy & Immunology; North Carolina Medical Association; Board of Directors/Member, American Lung Association, Eastern North Carolina; Board of Directors, Cystic Fibrosis Foundation, Carolinas Chapter; American Academy of Pediatrics. *Honours:* Chairman's Achievement Award, 1982; BS cum laude, 1975. *Hobbies:* Racquetball; Cooking; Stained Glass; Travelling. *Address:* East Carolina University, School of Medicine, PCMH W-260, Greenville, NC 27858, USA.

GOWING Margaret Mary, b. 26 Apr. 1921, London, England. Retired Professor. m. 7 June 1944. 2 sons. *Education:* Christ's Hospital, 1932- 38; London School of Economics, 1938-41. *Appointments:* Board of Trade, 1941-45; Historian, Cabinet Office, 1945-49; Historian and Archivist, UK Atomic Energy Authority, 1959-66; Reader in Contemporary History, University of Kent, 1966-72; Professor of History of Science, University of Oxford, 1972- 86; Fellow, Linacre College, Oxford, 1972-86. *Publications:* British War Economy (with W K Hancock), 1949; Civil Industry and Trade (with E L Hargreaves), 1952; Britain and Atomic Energy 1939-45, 1964; Independence and Deterrence, Volume 1 Policy, 1974; Making, Volume 2 Policy Execution, 1974. *Memberships:* Fellow, British Academy; Fellow, The Royal Society; Foundation Member, Academia Europea; Fellow, London School of Economics; Fellow, The Royal Historical Society; Trustee, National Portrait Gallery; Trustee, Imperial War Museum (resigned 1987 on introduction of entry charges). *Honours:* Honorary DLitt, University of Leeds 1976 and University of Leicester 1982; Honorary DSc, University of Manchester 1985 and University of Bath 1987; CBE, 1981. *Address:* Linacre College, Oxford.

GOZES Illana, b. 1 Mar. 1949, Jerusalem, Israel. Scientist. m. Jehoshua Gozes, 18 Sept. 1973. 1 daughter. *Education:* BSc, Biology, Tel Aviv University, 1972; PhD Neurobiology, Weizmann Institute, 1979; Postdoctoral studies, Mass. Institute of Technology, USA, 1979-80. *Appointments:* Research Associate, Salk Inst. 1981-82; Senior Scientist, Department of Hormone Research Weizmann Institute of Science, 1982- 87; Associate Professor, 1987 Visiting Scienctist, NIH Bethesda, Maryland, USA, 1988. *Publications include:* Over 40 articles in professional journals; Invited reviews and book chapters on molecular endocrinology. *Memberships:* Society of Neuroscience, 1979; New York Academy of Science, 1981; Israeli Society of Endocrinology, 1984; Scient. Council of Weizmann Institute, 1985; International Society for Development of Neuroscience, 1987; Editorial Board, Journal of Molecular Neuroscience, 1987. *Honours:* Landau Prize for excellent research, 1977; Chaim Weizmann Post Doctoral Fellowship, 1987-80; Jewish Agency Award, 1982-84; Bergmann Memorial Research Prize, 1982; Samuel O Freedman Career Development Chair, 1983-89; US Israel Binational Science Foundation grant award, 1982; National Institute of Health, NIH grant award, 1983. *Hobbies:* Reading; Films; Theatre; Travel. *Address:* Department of Hormone Research, The Weizmann Institute of Science, Rehovot 76100, Israel.

GRADIN Anita Ingegerd, b. 12 Aug. 1933, Hornefors, Sweden. Cabinet Minister for Foreign Trade.

m. Bertil Kersfelt. 1 daughter. *Education:* School of Social Work and Public Administration, Stockholm, 1960. *Appointments:* Journalist, 1958-60 and 1960-63; Social Worker, Stockholm Social Welfare Planning Committee and Secretary to Women's Affairs Committee, 1963-67; Member of Parliament, 1968-82; Cabinet Minister for Migration and Equality between Women and Men, 1982-86; Cabinet Minister for Foreign Trade, 1986-. *Publications:* Reports and articles on women's affairs, migration, social work, the situation of Jews in the Soviet Union, etc. *Memberships:* Delegate to the Council of Europe, 1968-82; Chairman of Council of Europe Committee on Migration, Refugees and Demography, 1978-82; Chairman, Stockholm District of National Federation of Social Democratic Women, 1968-82; Federation Executive Committee and Vice Chairman of the Federation, 1975-; Vice President, 1983-86, President, 1986-, Socialist International Women; Vice President, Socialist International, 1986-; Chairman, Swedish Association of Graduates from Schools of Social Work and Public Administration, 1968-79; Working Chairman, Swedish Council for Intercountry Adoptions, 1973-80; Delegate to Interparliamentary Union, International Planned Parenthood Federation, International Federation of Social Workers. *Honours:* The Council of Europe Pro Merito Medal, 1982. *Address:* Ministry for Foreign Affairs, Trade Department, Stockholm, Sweden.

GRAFTON Cathy (Catherine Lyn), b. 10 Apr. 1949, Aurora, Illinois, USA. Quiltmaker; Designer. m. Maurice E. Grafton, 26 Jan. 1974, 1 son, 2 daughter. *Education:* BA, American Studies, Knox College, Galesburg, Illinois, 1971; Graduate course with Michael James, Foundation in Colour and design for Quiltmakers, University of Wisconsin, 1984. *Appointments:* Teacher and Lecturer on Quilt topics, symposiums, guilds and festivals throughout USA, 1981-. *Creative works:* Articles in Professional Quilter, Quilt Magazine, Quilter's Newsletter Magazine, Patchwork Patter NQA; Quilts: Washington Island (designer Edward Larson), 1985; Flowerstar, 1986; Card design for Greene/Cross Co, 1987. *Memberships:* American Quilting Society; National Quilting Association; Hands All Around Quilt Guild of Central Illinois, Programme Chairman 1984, 1985, Challenge Quilts 1989, Raffle Quilt Designer 1991. *Honours:* Invitational shows including: Sinnissippi Quilters, Rockford,Illinois, 1985; McLean Arts Center Juried Show, 1986; National Quilting Association Shows, 1986, 1987, 1988; Greene/Cross Show, Attic Gallery, Portland, Oregon, 1987; Cedar Falls Arts Council, 1989. *Address:* 504 East Washington St., Pontiac, IL 61764, USA.

GRAH Karen Elizabeth, b. 10 Mar. 1953, Philadelphia, Pennsylvania, USA. US Naval Officer, 1 daughter. *Education:* BA, Psychology, Columbia College, 1979; Postgrad, Webster University, 1984-85. *Appointments:* Enlisted USN 1972, advanced through grades to Lieutenant, 1983; Admin Officer, Asst Intelligence Officer, Strike Fighter Squadron, Lemoore, CA, 1980-84; Personnel Officer, Service School Command, Great Lakes Naval Base, II, 1984-87; Chief Testing Management, El Paso, TX, Military Entrance Processing Station, 1987-; Executive Officer, Naval and Marine Corps Reserve Center, El Paso, TX, 1989-. *Memberships:* American Society for Personnel Administration; Northeast El Paso Civic Assocation; Non- Traditional Workers Speakers Bureau for Region XIX Education Service Center, El Paso. *Hobbies:* Volunteer English Teacher, El Paso Literacy Coalition (Amnesty Applicants); Amateur theatre; Crafts; Reading; Languages (speak French and Hungarian). *Address:* 5852 Devontry Drive, El Paso, TX 79934, USA.

GRAHAM Alison, b. 18 Dec. 1953, Stanford, California, USA. Management Consultant. m. Richard J. Messina, 8 Sep. 1984. *Education:* BA, Harvard College, 1975; MBA, Stanford University, 1979. *Appointments:* consultant, McKinsey & Co, 1980-83; Manager, MCI Communications, 1983-84; Vice-President, American Television Network, 1985-86; Vice-President, Messina & Graham, Management Consulting, 1986-. *Memberships:* Founding Member, Past President, The Charter 100; Founder, Board Member, Past President, Stanford Business School Alumni Association. *Honours:* Named Outstanding Young Woman of America, 1981- 82. *Hobbies:* Tennis; Skiing; gourmet cooking; Exotic vacations. *Address:* 6155 Callista Lane, McLean, VA 22101, USA.

GRAHAM Cheryl Lea, b. 18 Feb. 1957, Stockton, California, USA. Assistant Vice President; Appraisal Manager. m. Jeffrey Byron Fleming, 7 Mar. 1976, div. 1986. 1 son. *Education:* Salesperson License, California Real Estate, 1977; Private Pilots License, 1984; Four year college degree equivalent awarded by AIREA, 1985. *Appointments:* Real Estate Sales, 1977 and 1979-81; Central Bank Appraiser Asst. 1981-83; Appraiser, 1983-86; Cal. Fed. S&L Senior Income Property Appraiser, 1986-87; Cal Fed S&L Assistant Vice President & Regional Manager, No Calif. Income Property Appraisal Division, 1987-. *Memberships:* American Institute of Real Estate Appraisers: RM Designation, 1986; Regional Professional Standards Panel, 1987-; Admissions Committee Chapter 11, 1988-90; Vice-Chairperson/RM Committee Chapter 11, 1989; Co-Chairperson program Committee Chapter 11, 1989; Candidates Guidance Committee Chapter 11, 1987-88; Newsletter Committee Chapter 11, 1987; National Association of Female Executives, 1985-87. *Hobbies:* Cycling; Golf; Tennis; Hiking; Reading; Guitar; Snow Skiing; Water Skiing; Scuba Diving. *Address:* California Federal, 200 Pringle Ave, Ste. 340, Walnut Creek, CA 94596, USA.

GRAHAM Janelle Lear, b. 1 Feb. 1947, Melrose, Massachusetts, USA. Small Business Entrepreneur. m. (1)David W Hubbard, May 1969, 1 son, 1 daughter. (2)Edward B Graham, Dec. 1986. *Education:* Robie Secretarial, 1966; Notre Dame College, 1981; Writer's Digest School, non fiction writing, 1987; FAA private pilot instruction, 1983. *Appointments:* Secretary/Treasurer, Community Food Cooperative Program; Legal Secretary, 1981-87; FAA Basic Ground Instructor, Airplane, 1985; Small Business Entrepreneur, 1987-. *Publications:* Article to be published: Where Are Your Children? *Memberships:* Civil Air Patrol, USAF; International Organization of Women Pilots; Aircraft Owners & Pilots Association; American Boarding Kennel Association; Houston Cat Club, Texas; Moonport Cat Club. *Honours:* First prize, Miss Mitre bathing suit competition, 1968; Honourable Mention, On Your Own Time, 1981; Aerospace Education Award, CAP, 1984; Certificate of Proficiency Award, CAP, 1985; FAA Proficient Pilot Award, Phase II, 1986. *Hobbies:* Flying; Cats; Crafts; Civic Interests; Writing. *Address:* PO Box 219046, Houston, TX 77218, USA.

GRAHAM Nancy A, b. 10 May 1926, Milwaukee, Wisconsin, USA. Executive Director, Institute for Soviet American Relations. m. Richard A Graham, 21 Dec. 1949. 3 sons, 2 daughters. *Education:* BA University of Wisconsin, 1948; MA, Wellesley College, 1950. *Appointments:* Education Director, National Urban Coalition, 1970-73; Counsellor, Goddard College, 1974-76; Executive, Peace Corps, 1977-82; Executive Director, Peace Links, 1982-83; Executive Director, Institute for Soviet American Relations, 1983-. *Publications:* Recipes for Reading, Right-to-Read and Urban Coalition publication; 1983 Handbook on Organizations Involved in Soviet American Relations; 1986 Handbook on organizations Involved in Soviet American Relations; Surviving Together; Journal on Soviet American Relations. *Memberships:* National Women's Democratic Club; Parent-Teacher Association, several offices in 1960's. *Hobbies:* Sports; Reading. *Address:* 1608 New Hampshire Avenue NW, Washington, DC 20009, USA.

GRAHAM Patricia Albjerg, b. 9 Feb. 1935, Lafayette, Indiana, USA. Professor. m. Loren R Graham, 6 Sept. 1955. 1 daughter. *Education:* BS 1955, MS 1957, Purdue University; PhD, Columbia University, 1964. *Appointments:* Teacher, Deep Creek High school, Norfolk County, 1955-56; Maury High School, Norfolk, 1957-58; Chairman, History Department 1958-60, Part-time College Advisor 1961-63 and 1965-67, St Hilda's and St Hugh's School, New York City; Lecturer 1964-65, Assistant Professor 1965-66, School of Education, Indiana University, Bloomington; Assistant Professor 1965-68, Associate Professor 1968-72, Professor 1972-74, Barnard College, concurrently Assistant Professor, 1966-68, Associate Professor 1968-72, Professor 1972-74, History and Education, Teachers College, Columbia University, NY City; Distinguished Visiting Professor, Northern Michigan University, 1972; Professor, 1974-, Charles Warren Professor, History of American Education, 1979-, Dean of the Faculty, 1982-, Harvard University, Graduate School of Education. *Publications:* Books: Progressive Education: From Arcady to Academe, A History of the Progressive Education Association, 1967; Community and Class in American Education 1865-1918, 1974; Women in Higher Education, co-edited with W Todd Furniss, 1974; Numerous articles and reviews in professional journals and magazines. *Memberships include:* Josiah Macy, Jr Foundation, 1976-77 and 1979-; Northwestern Mutual Life Insurance Company 1980-; American Council of Learned Societies/USSR Ministry of Education Commission on Education, Chair, 1987-. *Honours include:* Recipient of numerous Honorary Degrees, scholarships and grants. *Address:* 7 Francis Avenue, Cambridge, Massachusetts 02138, USA.

GRAHAM Precious Jewel Freeman, b. 3 May 1925, Springfield, Ohio, USA. University Professor; Social worker; Lawyer. m. Paul N Graham, 8 Aug. 1953. 2 sons. *Education:* BA, Fisk University, 1946; Graduate Study, Howard University, 1946-48; MSSA, Case-Western Reserve University, 1952; JD, University of Dayton, 1979. *Appointments:* YWCA, Grand Rapids, Michigan, 1947-50; Dayton Receiving Home for Children, 1952-53; YWCA, Detroit, Michigan, 1953-56; Director, Antioch Program for Interracial Education, 1965- 69; Professor of Social Welfare, 1969-; Director, Institute of Human Development, 1984-; Antioch College, Yellow Springs, Ohio, 1964-. *Creative work:* Film: The Antioch Program for Interracial Education. *Memberships:* Ohio Bar; American Bar Association; Academy of Certified Social Workers; National Association of Social Workers; YWCA of the USA, National Board 1970-88, President, 1974-85; World YWCA, Executive Committee 1975-83, Vice President, 1979-83, President, 1987-91. *Honours:* Danforth Associate, 1971-; Antioch College Faculty Lecturer, 1979-80; Social Worker of the Year, Miami Valley NASW, 1975; Green County Womens Hall of Fame, 1982; Resolution by Ohio House of Representatives for Outstanding Leadership in YWCA of USA; Top Ten Women of Miami Valley, 1987; Ohio Women's Hall of Fame, 1988. *Hobbies:* Community service; Walking; Swimming; Cycling; Needlework. *Address:* Antioch College, Yellow Springs, OH 45387, USA.

GRAHAM-BRYCE Isabel, Dame, b. 30 Apr. 1902, Belfast, Northern Ireland. Retired. m. 25 Jan. 1934. 2 sons. *Education:* MA, Edinburgh University, 1926. *Appointments:* Investigator, Industrial Fatigue Research Board, 1926-27; HM Inspector of Factories, 1928-34; Research Fellow, Fatigue Lab, Harvard University, USA, 1943-44. Non-executive & voluntary posts include: Chairman, Oxford Regional Hospital Board; Chairman, National Staff Commitee, National Health Service; Chairman, National Nursing Staff Commitee, National Health Service; Nurses & Midwives Whitley Council; General Nursing Council; Public Health Inspectors Education Board; HM Prison Grendon Underwood Board of Visitors, Vice-Chairman; JP, City of Manchester; Independent TV Authority; ATV Network; British Transport Hotels; WVS Organizer, Manchester; WVS Ontario Division Director; WVS America, Technical Adviser; Association HMCS, Vice Chairman; Oxford Polytechnic Board; Radcliffe Infirmary, Oxford, League of Friends, President. *Publication:* Joint papers on Industrial Fatigue subjects. *Memberships:* Zonta International, Honorary Member Oxford; Oxford Member BFUW; Life Member Edinburgh; Princess Christian College, Vice President. *Honour:* Dame Commander of the British Empire, 1968. *Hobbies:* Music; Theatre; Ballet; Various types of embroidery and

tapestry. *Address:* 23 Russell Court, Woodstock Road, Oxford OX2 6JH, England.

GRALA Jane Marie, b. Philadelphia, USA. Securities Firm Executive; Account Executive. *Education:* BS, Rutgers University, Camden, 1976; MBA, Winthrop College, 1979; Postgraduate: American Management Association, New York City, 1980-82; American Instutute Real Estate Appraisers, Chicago, 1985. *Appointments:* Accounting Dept. Manager, NDI Engineering Co., 1968-72; Project Manager, 1972-76; Sales Representative, American Cyanamid, Wayne, 1976-80; District Manager, American Appraisal Association, 1980-86; Financial Advisor-Investments, Prudential-Bache Sec., Clearwater, 1986-. *Memberships:* Association of MBA Executives; National Association of Accountants; Business & Professional Womens Association; NAFE; Phi Chi Theta; Chi Delta. *Honours Include:* Deans List, 1972-73, 1974-75, Certificate Award, 1973, Rutgers University College; Student Council Vice President, Rutgers University College, 1972-73; Student Council President, Rutgers University College, 1973-74. *Hobbies:* World Travel; Archeology. *Address:* Prudential Bache Securities, 2920 US Highway 19 North, Suite 100, Clearwater, FL 34621, USA.

GRAMMER Elisa Joan, b. 5 Feb. 1952, Dover, New Jersey, USA. Attorney; Author. m. Fredric Davis Chanania, 17 May 1981, 1 son. *Education:* BA summa cum laude, Lafayette College, 1973; JD, College of William & Mary, 1976; LLM with highest honours, George Washington University, 1980; Admitted: District of Columbia State Bar; Virginia State Bar. *Appointments:* Attorney, General Accounting Office, 1976-78; Attorney, Nuclear Regulatory Commission, 1978-80; Associate, 1981-85, Partner, 1985-87, Pierson Semmes & Finley; Partner, Baller, Hammett, Williams, Grammer & Kissel PC, Washington DC, 1987-. *Publications:* LDC Bypass from End Users' and Marketers' Perspectives, 1986; The Legal Edge, monthly column in Petroleum Management Magazine, 1987-. *Memberships:* Women in Government Relations (Energy Task Force, Co-Chair, 1987-88); Federal Energy Bar Association; American Bar Association; Federal Bar Association; Women's Bar Association. *Honours:* Phi Beta Kappa, 1972. *Address:* Baller, Hammett, Williams, Grammer & Kisell, PC, 1225 Eye Street NW, Suite 1200, Washington, DC 20005, USA.

GRANDE Adele Irene, b. 2 Mar 1929, Indiana, Pennsylvania, USA. Multi-Linguist; Lecturer; Administrator; Educator; Sportswoman; Photographer; Teacher; Mother. m. Dr Harold Michael Grande MD, 6 Aug 1960, 1 son, 2 daughters. *Education:* BS 1951, MA 1952, Physical Education and Health, Teacher College, Columbia University, New York; Postgraduate Work, Advanced School of Education, Teachers College, Columbia University; Personal Administration & Youth Guidance/Physical Medicine and Rehabilitation, Kingsbridge Veterans' Hospital, 1952-58; Candidate for Doctoral Studies. *Appointments:* Teacher, Sacred Hearts of Jesus-Mary School, 1947-50; Teacher St Ambrose School, 1950-51; Coach, Women's Sports, Long Island University, 1950-51; Instructor, Physical Education and Health, Bayley Ellard Regional High School, New Jersey, 1951-52; Administrator/Director, Body Mechanics, Nursing Arts, Fordham Hospital, School of Nursing, 1952-57; Towson State Teacher's College, Baltimore, 1956-57; Miami Valley St Elizabeth's and Good Samaritan Hospitals, 1958; Professor, University of Dayton, 1968-; St Michael's School 1975-76. *Creative Works:* Producer/Director/Choreographer for amateur stage shows. *Memberships include:* World Health Organisation; AAHRE & Rec; American College of Sports Medicine; Kappa Delta Pi; Phi Delta Kappa; Brooklyn Historical Society; Business and Professional Women's Organisation; 1st Annual Trauma Anaesthesia and Critical Care Symposium, Wasgington DC; Board Member, 2nd and 3rd Annual Trauma Anaesthesia and Critical Care Symposia, Baltimore, Maryland; American Alliance for Health, Physical Education, Recreation and Dance; American International Youth Hostels 1952-58;

Payton Ski Club; Baltimore Ski Club; Mount Kenya Club. *Honours include:* Health Access (Lutheran Medical Centre) Hospital Walkathon 1988 Silver Medal; 1989 Gold Medal 1st place winner, Women and Men; 1983-89 Tap Dancing Guinness World Records; Holder of Certificates for Officials/Referees, Women's Sports Judging Events in Sports and Athletics as well as Dance, Bike riding events. *Hobbies:* Extensive World Travel; Climbing; Motor Racing; Photography; Languages; Costumes; Bicycling. *Address:* 61 Oliver Street, Brooklyn, NY 11209, USA. 138.

GRANDE Bernadette-Sylvia Joan Jeanne d'Arc, b. 21 Sept. 1963, Brooklyn, USA. Applied Sports Physiologist; Graduate Student. *Education:* BA, Natural Science and Psychology, (Double Major), Fordham University, 1985; MA, Applied Physiology, Columbia University, 1988; MS, Biology, New York University, 1989. *Appointments:* Pharmacist Assistant, Brooklyn VA Hospital, 1976-80; Medical, Office Assistant, Internal Medicine, 1980-88; Researcher, Thermogenesis, Mt. Sinai School of Medicine, 1987; Physiologist, Executive Fitness Faculty, Mobil Oil Corporation, 1988-. *Publications:* Articles in professional journals. *Memberships:* Phi Delta Kappa, 1988; Kappa Delta Pi, 1987; Womens Sports Foundation; American College of Sports Medicine, 1985. *Honours:* Recipient, various honours & awards. *Address:* 61 Oliver Street, Apartment 1C, Brooklyn, NY 11209, USA.

GRANDSTRAND Karen Louise, b. 14 Apr. 1955, Colorado Springs, Colorado, USA. Attorney. m. David Paul Grandstrand, 29 May 1976. *Education:* BA, summa cum laude, Concordia College, Moorhead, 1977; JD, Loyola University of Chicago, School of Law, 1982. *Appointments:* Law Clerk, Baker & McKenzie, Chicago, 1980-83; Attorney, Frankel & Mackay Ltd, Chicago, 1983-85; Senior Attorney, Federal Reserve Bank of Minneapolis, Minneapolis, 1988-; Legal Writing Instructor, University of Minnesota Law School, Minneapolis, 1986-. *Memberships:* American Bar Association; Minnesota State Bar Association; Ramsey County Bar Association. *Honours:* 1st place, Loyola Law School Appellate Advocacy Competition, 1981; National Moot Court Team, 1981; Little, Brown Student Award, 1982; Concordia College Merit Scholarship, 1975-76; Alliss Foundation Scholarship, 1975-76. *Hobbies:* Piano; Horseback riding; Travel. *Address:* Federal Reserve Bank of Minneapolis, 250 Marguette Avenue, Minneapolis, MN 55480, USA.

GRANGER Penelope Ruth, b. 14 July 1947, Norwich, England. Wife; Mother. m. Richard John Granger, 11 July 1970. 1 son, 1 daughter. *Education:* BA Hons Music, Sheffield University, 1966-69; PGCE, Homerton College, Cambridge, 1969-70. *Appointments:* Admin Assistant, WEA, Eastern District, 1971-73. *Publication:* Article in Grove's Dictionary of Music & Musicians. *Memberships:* General Synod of the Church of England, 1980-; Church Commissioner, 1983-; General Synod Standing Committee, 1985-; Lay Chairman, Ely Diocesan House of Laity, 1988-. *Hobbies:* Walking; Caravanning; Church Music; Singing; Dutch 17th Century and Impressionist Art. *Address:* 88 Queen Ediths Way, Cambridge, CB1 4PW, England.

GRANHOLM (Ester) Ann-Charlotte, b. 18 Nov. 1958, Gothenburg, Sweden. University Educator. *Education:* Dental School, 1978-80, Graduate School, 1980-85, Medical School, 1984-85, Doctor of Dentistry, 1985, Karolinska Institute, Stockholm; Postdoctoral Fellow, Department of Pharmacology, University of Colorado, USA, 1985-88. *Appointments:* Teaching Assistant, 1978-84, Lecturer, 1983-85, Department of Histology, Karolinska Institute, Stockholm; Assistant Professor, University of Linkoping, Linkoping, 1988-. *Publications:* 28 original papers in neurobiology; 5 review articles and book chapters; 25 abstracts to international meetings in neuroscience. *Memberships:* Amine Group, Department of Histology and Neurobiology, Karolinska Institute; European Neuroscience Association; American Neuroscience.

Honours: Graduate student scholarship, Karolinska Institute, 1980-84; BernadotteSwanson Scholarship for postdoctoral studies in USA, 1985; Daniel Heumann Fellowship for studies on neural regeneration, 1987. *Hobbies:* Active member of Arapahoe Basin Volunteer Ski Patrol; Volunteer assistant, schizophrenic mothers' therapy group; Writer and actor, amateur musical and theatre group; Oil painting; Silkscreen; Photography; Scuba diving. *Address:* Department of Cell Biology, University of Linkoping, S-581 85 Linkoping, Sweden.

GRANT Ellestine Johnson, b. 12 Dec. 1938, Baltimore, Maryland, USA. Administrator. m. 28 Aug. 1956, 1 son, 1 daughter. *Education:* BS, Coppin State College, 1964; MS, Morgan State University, 1972; APC, American University, 1973; EdD, Temple University, 1985. *Appointments:* Elementary Schoool Instructor, 1964-69; Director of Student Teaching, 1969-72; Educational Specialist, 1972-74; Project Manager, 1974-75; Coordinator/Supervisor, Baltimore, Maryland, 1975-89. *Publications:* Student and the Law; Handbook on School Volunteer Civics; An Analysis of the Attitudes of School Volunteers and Court Referred Community Service Volunteer-Urban Education (dissertation). *Memberships:* President, Las Companeras; President, Retiree Senior Volunteer Programme; Phi Delta Kappa; Mayor's Literacy Commission; 5 and 5 Democratic Association, Treasurer; Senatorial Resolution. *Honours:* Community Service, Baltimore City Police Department, 1974; Distinguished Educators Award, Governor of Maryland, 1975; Mayor's Excellence Citation for Leadership, 1975, 1976, 1977; Governor's Citation for Excellent Service, 1978, 1979; Senatorial Outstanding Educators Awards for Resolution, 1979, 1980, 1981; Mayor's Citation for Service on Literacy Commission, 1982-87; Baltimore City Health Department Citation, 1988- 89; State of Maryland Citation for Outstanding Leadership, 1988-89. *Hobbies:* Designing formal high fashion evening attire; Making handmade quilts; Reading; Travel; Singing sacred songs; Cooking (gourmet and exotic foods). *Address:* Office of Superintendent, 200 East North Avenue, Baltimore, MD 21202, USA.

GRANT Genelle Georgeanne, b. 16 Sept. 1949, Rochester, New York, USA. University Professor; Television Producer. m. Richard Patrick Shine, 1 May 1982, 2 sons. *Education:* BA, Psychology, Simmons College, Boston, 1971; MEd, Health Education, Plymouth State College, 1980; EdD, Health Communications, Boston University, 1982. *Appointments:* Instructor, Plymouth State College, New Hampshire, 1978-80; Director, TRADESWOMEN Workshops, 1979-81; President, Peer Productions, health/education TV, 1979-; Professor, Administrator, New Hampshire College, School of Human Service, 1983-86; Interamerican University, San Juan, Puerto Rico, 1986-. *Creative works:* Television: Tecnicas de Produccion, book; Director, documentaries: The Birth of Rachel; The Same Rights as Anyone (mental health); TRADESWOMEN; Historia de P.R. - Siglo XVIII; Pre-natal and Maternity Care. *Memberships:* MENSA International; Panamerican Coalition for AIDS Education; Board of Directors, New Hampshire Latin American Center, 1984-86; Founder, New Hampshire Media Women; New Hampshire Health Education Committee, 1983-85; Committee, New Hampshire Coalition Against Family Violence, 1983-85; National Federation of Local Cable (TV) Programmers. *Honours:* Honourable Mention by White House, College Competition, National Drug Abuse Prevention Campaign, 1979; Youth Advocate Award, New Hampshire Federation of Youth Services, 1980; Service Award, New Hampshire Future Homemakers of America, 1982; Outstanding Young Woman of New Hampshire for Outstanding Young Women of America, 1982; Outstanding Young Women of America, 1985. *Hobbies:* Painting; Swimming; Languages (Spanish); Metaphysics; Yoga and meditation; Video production; Community organising; Mothering; Ecofeminism. *Address:* Condominium La Arboleda 501, Guaynabo, Puerto Rico 00657, USA.

GRANT Jacquelyn, b. 19 Dec. 1948, Georgetown, South Carolina, USA. Assistant Professor, Systematic Theology. *Education:* BA, Bennett College, 1970; MDiv, Interdenominational Theological Center, 1973; Master of Philosophy, 1980; PhD, Union Theological Seminary, 1985. *Appointments:* Associate in Research, Harvard Divinity School, 1977-78 and 1978-79; Assistant Professor, Interdenominational Theological Center, 1980-. *Publications:* Contributing editor, Journal of Black Theology in South Africa; Editor, Women's Ministry, The Christian Recorder; Numerous articles in journals and magazines. *Memberships:* International Society of Theta Phi; National Association for Advancement of Colored People; American Academy of Religion; Ecumenical Association of 3rd World Theologians; World Council of Churches; Black Theology Project. *Honours:* Outstanding Alumni Award, Turner Seminary, 1988; The M L King Jr Ministerial Award, The Black Church Studies program of Colgate Rochester/Besley Hall/Crozer Theological Seminary, 1986; Merit Award, Women's Missionary Society, African Methodist Church, 1985, and many others. *Hobbies:* Playing the piano; Preaching and writing on concerns facing women in general, black women in particular and Theology. *Address:* Interdenominational Theological Center, 671 Beckwith Street SW, Atlanta, GA 30314, USA.

GRANT Josie, b. 4 June 1949, Los Angeles, California, USA. Artist: Muralist, Painter, Printmaker, California Visionary School. 1 daughter. *Education:* ABRA; BFA 1970, MFA 1972, Honours, San Francisco Art Institute; Lifetime Teaching Credential, California Community College, 1979. *Appointments:* Teacher, various schools; Board Member, SF Art Commission; Illustrator, various book publishers; Scene painter, colour consultant, various theatres; Own company, mural painting, Up Against the Wall. *Creative work includes:* Illustrations: 7 Circles that Danced the World, Childrens Bookpress, 1975; Cover, Ecology & Consciousness, North Atlantic Books, 1978; Wingbow-Diane Di Prima (Loba Part 1-8), 1975-76. Murals include: Zen Centre Guest House, 1976; Ping Yuen Housing Projects, 1978; Fort Help Counselling Centre, CETA Programme, 1980; NASA Space Mural, Mendocino Grammar School (with children), 1986; Keystone Korner Jazz Club, 1972. *Honours:* Awards, various art shows; Anthology - Art in SF Bay Area - T. Albright, 1945-80. *Hobbies:* Yoga; Skiing. *Address:* Box 537, San Anselmo, California 94960, USA.

GRANT Lois Margaret, b. 8 June 1937, Peoria, Illinois, USA. Architect. m. Keith F Weiland, 24 Aug. 1985. 1 son, 1 daughter. *Education:* BS, University of Illinois, 1959; BS Architecture, 1979; Bach of Architecture, Lawrence Technological Univ, Southfield, MI, 1980. *Appointments:* Minoru Yamasaki & Assoc, Troy, Michigan, 1978-79; Harley Ellington Pierce Yee Assoc, 1980-85; Stevens & Wilkinson Inc, Atlanta, Georgia, 1985-87; Rosser FABRAP International, Atlanta, GA, 1987-; URS Consultants, 1990, Atlanta, GA. *Publications:* Authored 48 documentary radio programmes for Mike Whorf, Inc; Kaleidoscope Radio Program WJR, Detroit, 1970-73. *Memberships:* American Institute of Architects; Chair, Women in Architecture; Long Range Planning Comm. *Hobbies:* Music; Photography; Metaphysics; Cats; Reading; Travel; Architectural history. *Address:* 4 Springlake Place NW, Atlanta, GA 30318, USA.

GRANT Tehmi Keki, b. 14 Apr. 1927, Karachi. President, National Council of Women in India. m. Keki Grant, 8 Jan. 1950, 1 son, 1 daughter. *Education:* BSc., honours, University of Bombay, 1947. *Appointments:* Lecturer, Microbiology, D J Sind College, Karachi, 1948-49; Hospital Laboratory, 1954-59; Adminstrator, Poona Medical Foundation, 1962-. *Publications:* Co-author, book on rose growing. *Memberships:* President, National Council of Women in India, 1987-1990; Regional Advisor, standing Committee on Home Economics. *Honours:* Recipient, various honours and awards. *Hobbies:* Gardening; Travel. *Address:* Poona Medical Foundation, Ruby Hall Clinic, 40 Sassoon Road, Poona 411 001, India.

GRASZ Lynne Anne Morian, b. 22 Sept. 1943, Los Angeles, California, USA. Broadcasting Executive. *Education:* BS, Certificate of Journalism, University of Nebraska, 1966; CBS School of Management, 1980; Women's Management Programme, Simmons College, 1983. *Appointments:* Michigan Newspaper Editor and Reporter, United Press International, Detroit, Michigan, 1966; Director, Promotion and Public Relations, KOLN-TV/KGIN-TV, Lincoln, Nebraska, 1966-76; Director, Creative Services, KMOX-TV, St Louis, Missouri, 1976-81; Director, Communications, 1981-83, Director, Special Projects, 1983-85, CBS/Broadcast Group, New York City; Manager Station Services, 1985-88, Executive Director, 1988-, Television Information Officer, New York City. *Creative Works:* Broadcast Advertising and Promotion, college textbook; Aliteracy; US Today, guest editorial; Television Worth Reading. *Memberships:* President, Broadcast Promotion and Marketing Executives, 1977; The Society of Professional Journalists, SDX; Founder, Broadcast Designers Association, 1977; International Radio and Television Society; Broadcast Pioneers; American Women in Radio and Television; Women in Communication, INC. *Honours:* Distinguished Journalist, 1979; Emmy, 1980, 1981; Headliner Award Winner, 1983; Outstanding Women in Communication, 1984. *Address:* Television Information Office, 745 Fifth Avenue, Suite 1701, New York City, NY 10151, USA.

GRATER Betsy, b. 29 Apr. 1933, Charlottesville, Virginia, USA. Business Owner. m. 26 Mar. 1960 (div. 24 June 1983), 2 daughters. *Education:* BA, Education, Kutztown University, Pennsylvania, 1955; MA, Education, George Peabody College, Vanderbilt University, 1958; Management Certificate, Goucher College, Women's Mangement Institute, 1981. *Appointments:* Public School Teacher, Pennsylvania, New Jersey, and Maryland, 1955-76; Member, Board of Education, Raleigh, North Carolina, 1971- 74; Development Coordinator, Maryland Committee for Children Inc, Baltimore, 1979-81; Sales/Marketing Intern Eskay Meat Packing Co, Baltimore, 1981; Manager, Marketing and User Services Inform, Maryland, 1981-83; Marketing Support Representative, Disc Inc, Baltimore, 1983-85; Owner, Operator, Amanda's Bed and Breakfast Reservation Service, Baltimore, 1985-; Owner, Operator, Betsy's Bed and Breakfast, Baltimore. *Memberships:* National Association of Women Business Owners; Executive Women's Network; National Association of Home Based Businesses; Baltimore Convention Bureau; Baltimore Attraction Association; American Bed and Breakfast Association; National Network of Bed and Breakfast; Bed and Breakfast WW.R.S.; Baltimore County Chamber of Commerce; Maryland Travel Council; Anne Arundel and Annapolis Chamber of Commerce. *Hobbies:* Needlework; Brass rubbing expert. *Address:* 1428 Park Avenue, Baltimore, MD 21217, USA.

GRAVES Alice, b. 7 Aug. 1942, Birmingham, Alabama, USA. Social Worker. m. Milton Graves, 9 Dec. 1961, divorced, 2 daughters. *Education:* BA, Wayne State University, 1977; MA, University of Detroit, 1979. *Appointments:* Management Consultant, Ed Ewell & Co., 1978-83; Schoolcraft College, Instructor, 1981-; Probation Officer, Wayne County Juvenile Court, 1987-. *Publications:* article in professional journal. *Memberships:* Michigan Educaiton Association; University of Detroit Alumni Association; etc. *Honour:* Outstanding Woman, Phy's Friday Bunch for Lunch, 1987. *Hobbies:* Swimming; Gardening; Reading. *Address:* 18400 Birwood, Detroit, MI 48221, USA.

GRAVES Joanne Marie, b. 12 Aug. 1960, Seattle, Washington, USA. Director of Personnel. m. David Lawrence Graves, 14 Feb. 1987. *Education:* BS honours, Hotel and Restaurant Management, University of Houston, 1983. *Appointments:* Yosemite National Park, 1981; Hotel Ibis, Boulogne-sur- Mer, France, summer 1982; The Mayflower, Stouffer Corporation Hotel, 1983-

84; Stouffer Dayton Plaza Hotel, 1984-88; Stouffer Concourse Crystal City Hotel, 1988. *Publications:* Applicability of the Lawrence and Lorsch Methodology to the Hotel's Front Office, 1983. *Memberships:* American Society of Personnel Administrators; Miami Valley Personnel Association. *Honours:* Professional Creativity, Stouffer Corporation, 1986; Outstanding Solicitor-Company Chairperson, Montgomery County United Way, 1987. *Hobbies:* Knitting; Sewing; Photography; Cycling; Gardening; Cooking; Dog obedience. *Address:* 2440 Corning Avenue, Fort Washington, MD 20744, USA.

GRAY Carol Lippert, b. 31 Mar. 1950, New York City, New York, USA. Magazine Editor. m. Lewis Gray, 5 Sept. 1970, 2 daughters. *Education:* BA, History, Douglass College, 1970; MS, Broadcast Journalism, Boston University, 1976. *Appointments:* Freelance Writer, 1976-; Managing Editor, Associate Editor, The Miniature Magazine and Creative Crafts, 1981-83; Managing Editor, Crochet Fantasy Magazine, 1984-88; Partner, Grayl Blanchard Enterprises, marketing, PR and consulting firm, 1988-; Editor, DAD and Care Giving, Creative Publishing Group Inc, Newton, New Jersey, 1989-. *Publications:* Freelance magazine and newspaper articles. *Memberships:* Past President, Sussex County Arts Council; Vice- President, Hilltop Country Day School Board of Trustees; New Jersey Press Women; National Federation of Press Women; Sussex County Medical Society Auxiliary. *Hobbies:* Travel; Theatre; Reading. *Address:* 65 Brookside Drive, Sparta, NJ 07871, USA.

GRAY Carol Patricia Hickson, b. 3 Jan. 1958, Atlanta, USA. Principal Production Engineer. m. Randy Lee Gray, 25 June 1983, 2 daughters. *Education:* BSc., Chemical Engineering, Georgia Institute of Technology. *Appointments:* Process Engineer, Day Foreman, 1979-83, Senior Process Engineer, 1983-86, Senior Production Engineer, 1986-87, Principal Production Engineer, 1988-, Air Products & Chemicals. *Memberships:* Society of Women Engineers, 1985. *Honours:* Co-Winner, Air Products 1985 Technology Symposium. *Hobbies:* Bicycling; Astronomy. *Address:* Air Products, Box 97, Calvert City, KY 42029, USA.

GRAY Constance Helen, b. 27 Feb. 1926, Medway, Massachusetts, USA. Professor of Biological Sciences. m. Reed A. Gray, 1951, div. 1976, 2 daughters. *Education:* BS, University of Massachusetts, 1947; MS, University of Hawaii, 1951; PhD, University of California, Berkeley, 1974. *Appointments:* Lecturer, Anatomy, University of California, Berkeley, 1974-76; Lecturer, Assistant Professor, Associate Professor, 1976-85, Professor, 1985-, California Polytechnic State University, San Luis Obispo. *Publications:* Scientific publications in anatomy and cancer education. *Memberships:* American Public Health Association; American Association for the Advancement of Science. *Interests:* Neuropathology; Health education. *Address:* Biological Sciences Department, California Polytechnic State University, San Luis Obispo, CA 93407, USA.

GRAY Donna Lea Chapman, b. 5 Sept. 1937, Ira, Texas, USA. Bookstore Owner & Operator. m. C. D. Gray Jr, 27 Dec. 1953, 2 daughters. *Education:* School of Cosmetology, Snyder, Texas, 1962. *Appointments:* Assistant Postmaster, Dunn, Texas, 1955-58; Clerk, J. C. Penny, Snyder 1958-59, Fabric Mart, Snyder 1959-60; Owner, operator, Donna's Beauty Shop, 1963-65; Owner, Manager, La Charme Health Spa 1968-75, Snyder Bookstore & Gift Shop 1978-. *Memberships:* Active: United Way, Heart Association, American Cancer Society, Snyder; District Chair 1984, March of Dimes; Board, Scurry County Fair Association; International Platform Association; Christian Booksellers Association; American Booksellers Association; American Business Women's Association; Snyder Retail Merchants Committee; Board, Snyder Chamber of Commerce. *Honour:* Notable Women of Texas. *Hobbies:* Oil Painting; Horseback Riding; Hiking; Water Skiing; Teaching Sunday School & Studying God's Word. *Address:* 2517 College Avenue, Snyder, Texas 79549, USA.

GRAY Dulcie Winifred Catherine, b. 20 Nov. 1920, Kuala Lumpur. Actress; Writer. m. 29 Apr. 1939. *Appointments:* Debut as an Actress: Her Majesty's theatre, Aberdeen, 1939; Most recent West End appearances: The Living Room (Theresa), 1987; 8 starring films; 400 broadcasts; numerous Television appearances including: Kate Harvey in Howard's Way, 4th year. *Publications:* 18 Crime Novels; 1 book of short horror stories; 3 novels; 1 book on the conservation of British Butterflies; Titles include: Baby Face, 1959; Murder in Mind, 1963; Ride on a Tiger, 1975; The Glanville Women, 1982; Mirror Image, 1987; 7 radio plays. *Memberships:* British Actors' Equity; Society of Authors; Fellow, Linnaean Society; Fellow, Royal Society of Arts. *Honours:* Queen's Silver Jubilee Medal, 1977; Times Educational Supplement Senior Information Award, for Butterflies on My Mind, 1978; CBE, 1983. *Hobby:* British Butterflies. *Address:* c/o Ronnie Waters, International Creative Managment, 388/396 Oxford Street, London W1N 9HE, England.

GRAY Ina Turner, b. 25 July 1926, Eagleville, USA. Executive Director. m. Wallace Gale Gray, 18 Dec. 1948, 2 daughters *Education:* BS, Central Methodist College, 1948; MA, Scarritt College, 1952; Postgraduate Studies, University of Hawaii, 1969. *Appointments:* Teacher, 1948-49; Director, Christian Education, 1st Methodist Church, Lawton, 1953-54, Winfield, 1957-58; Director, Commission on Archives & History, KSW Conference, 1960-78; English Teacher, Jo Gakuin Junior High, Hirohima, 1971-72; Executive Director, Pi Gamma Mu. *Publications:* Articles in: Methodist History; Kansas History. *Memberships:* Various professional organisations. *Honours:* Ina Turner Gray Award for Local Church History, instituted in January 1981. *Hobbies:* Church History; Travel. *Address:* 1717 Ames St., Winfield, KS 67156, USA.

GRAY Joanne S, b. 19 Dec. 1943, Headland, Alabama, USA. Teacher. m. Byron Kenneth Gray, 20 Aug. 1966. 1 daughter. *Education:* AA, Clinical Biology, Crane City College, 1965; BS, Biology, Chicago State Teachers College, 1970; MA, Science Teaching, Governors State University, 1978. *Appointments:* Teacher Aide 1965-66, Teacher 1971-, Chicago Board of Education; Chairperson, Science Department, 1984-; ECIA Government Funded Program Coordinator, 1986; Administrative Director, Summer Institute for Science and Mathematics Programs Ferm: National Laboratory, 1989. *Publications:* Life Science Curriculum Chicago Public Schools; Consultant Writer, Biological Science; Molecules To Man; Science Fair Success; Encouraging Females in Math/Science Activities. *Memberships include:* National Association of Biology Teachers; National Science Teachers Association, Presider/Presentator; Illinois Association of Biology Teachers, Presider/Presentator; Founding Member, Committee on Women and Minorities in Science, National Association of Biology Teachers; Writer, Newsletter, Phi Delta Kappa Fraternity in Education; Kappa Delta Pi. *Honours include: Recommended for Presidential Award for Excellence in Science Teaching, 1984; Celebrated Teacher, Sigma Pi Phi Fraternity, 1984; Governor's Master Teacher Award, 1984; Outstanding Biology Teacher Award, 1986; Recommended, Academy of Educators, Golden Apple Award, 1988; Recommended, Distinguished Teacher Award, Blackburn College, 1989.* *Hobbies:* Community Service; Writing; Singing; Speaking; Reading; Organizing; Physical fitness; Listening to classical music. *Address:* 11730 South Oakley, Chicago, Illinois 60643, USA.

GRCIĆ POLIĆ Jelena, b. 21 Sept. 1955, Trebinje, Yugoslavia. Lawyer; Teaching Fellow. m. Boris Polić, 2 Oct. 1982, 1 daughter. *Education:* LLB, Faculty of Law, University of Zagreb, 1978; LLM, Harvard Law School, USA, 1982; MA 1988, PhD candidate 1989-, Annenberg School for Communication, University of Pennsylvania. *Appointments:* Legal Department, RTV Zagreb, 1979; State Administration for International Coorporation, Croatia, Yugoslavia, 1980-84; Institute for Developing Countries, University of Zagreb, 1984-87; Annenberg School for Communication, Philadelphia, USA, 1986-

. *Publications:* Various articles, book chapters, international law, political economy of communications & national development. *Memberships:* Research Fellow, Institute for Developing Countries; Speech Communication Association; International Association for Mass Communication Research Union for Democratic Communications. *Honours:* Scholarships, fellowships, grants, Yugoslavia & USA; Expert member, Yugoslav delegation, 4th General Conference of Non-Aligned News Agencies Pool, Cuba, 1986; Invited seminar speaker, International Law Association, Belgrade 1985. *Hobbies:* Volleyball; Sailing; Swimming; Cross country skiing. Career interests: Teaching & consulting for international organisations & developing countries' administrations, areas of international law, communication, information. *Address:* Iva Vojnovica 79, 50000 Dubrovnik, Yugoslavia.

GREATHOUSE Patricia Ann Dodd (Pat), b. 26 Apr. 1935, Columbus, Georgia, USA. Counselor; Psychometrist. m. Robert Otis Greathouse, 4 July 1953. 2 sons. *Education:* BS, Education 1959, MEd 1966, Specialist Degree 1975, Auburn University; Psychometrist Certified by Alabama, 1975. *Appointments:* Teacher 4th grade 1961-62, 6th grade 1962-64, 7th grade 1964-66, 8th grade 1966-69, Counselor 1971-75 and 1975-80, County Psychometrist & Counselor 1983-89, Ladonia Elementary High School, Phenix City; Counselor 1969-71 Chavala High, Seale; Counselor 1980-82, Oliver School, Seale. *Publications:* Editor, Tiger Tales, 1973; Thesis, Gifted Children, 1966. *Memberships:* Russell County Education Association; Alabama Education Association; National Education Association; Alabama Personnel, Guidance Association; Alabama Association for Counselling and Development; Council for Exceptional Children. *Honours:* Honorary Life Membership, Ladonia PTA, 1967; Outstanding Elementary Teacher of America, 1972; Mardi Queen, Phenix City Moose Club, 1987; ABWA Woman of the Year, Phenix City Charter Chapter, 1987. *Hobbies:* Stamp collecting; Butterflies; Reading. *Address:* 1502 Nottingham Drive, Phenix City, AL 36867, USA.

GREDAL Eva, b. 19 Feb. 1927, Norresundby, Denmark. Social Worker; Former Cabinet Minister; Member, European Parliament. m. Otto Gredal. 2 sons, 2 daughters. *Appointments include:* Chairman, Danish Social Advisers Association, 1956; Vice Chairman, Board, Mental Health Association, 1967-71; Mental Hygiene Research Institute, 1968; Danish Womens Association, 1959; Member, Danish Parliament, 1971-; Minister for Social Affairs, 1971-73, 1975-78; Directly elected Member of European Parliament, 1979-, re-elected 1984-. Chairman, delegation for USA, 1979-84; Chairman, delegation for Canada, 1984-86; Chairman for delegation to New Zealand and Australia, 1986-89; Member, Environmental Committee & Economic Affairs Committee; Member, Executive Board, Danish Social Democratic Party. *Address:* Heisesgade 41-2000 Kobenham P, Denmark.

GREEN J Laura, b. 15 Nov. 1947, New York City, USA. Owner, Manager, Travel Agency; Radio talkshow hostess. m. Lawrence Ira Green, 28 Sept. 1969. 1 daughter. *Education:* BA, State University New York at Stony Brook. *Appointments:* International Transit Co, 1969-72; Wholesale Tours International, 1972-76; Travel With Laura Ltd; Empress Travel, 1976-; Two L's Ltd, 1984-88; Just Green Partnership, 1984-. *Publications:* Contributing writer to: Bucks County Magazine; The Jewish Post; The Travel Letter. *Memberships:* Secretary, Member Executive Board, Abrams Academy; Professional Women in Travel; Secretary, Empress Travel Franchise Assn; Bucks County Chamber of Commerce; Association of Retail Travel Agents. *Honours:* Travel Agent of the Year, Empress Franchise Association, 1986-87; Honoured by American Airlines, United Airlines, Carnival Cruises, Club Med, US Air for high achievement in production. *Hobbies:* Skiing; Scuba diving; Tour escort; Travel writing and speaking to groups about travel experiences; Photography. *Address:* 7006 Ely Road, New Hope, Pennsylvania 18938, USA.

GREEN Kay, b. 31 Dec,. 1927, Bradford, Yorkshire, England. Writer. m. 1 Oct. 1949, 1 son, 1 daughter. *Education:* Scholarship, Bolling High School for Girls. *Appointments:* Journalist, Bournemouth Echo; Self-employed writer. *Publications include:* Over 30 romantic novels, printed in over 70 editions. Also: 2 adventure/romance books; 1 Swiss Alps suspense/thriller teleplay. Screenplays: Phantom of the Osbert and Death from the Past, in process of production. *Memberships:* Society of Authors; Authors' Lending & Copyright Society; Screenwriters Guild. *Honours:* Featured, Authors of Year coast-to-coast promotion, Harlequin USA/Canada, & US National Honours Book; Outstanding Author, Harlequin's Who's Who of Romantic Authors, Canada; Books selected, training programmes, Canadian schools. *Hobbies:* Gardening; Walking; Reading. *Address:* Casa Mimosa, Santa Eugenia, Mallorca, Baleares, Spain.

GREEN Lennis H, b. 14 July 1940, Indiana, USA. Psychologist. m. Burdette L. Green, 11 Sept. 1965. *Education:* BSc., 1962, MA 1966, PhD, 1971, Ohio State University. *Appointments:* Psychologist, Consultant, 1968-. *Publicatirons:* Articles in professional journals. *Memberships:* American Psychological Association; Pacific Science Association; International Association of Crosscultural Psychologists; International Council of Psychologists; World Federation for Mental Health. *Honours:* Visiting Fellow, Health & Social Science Programme, 1985. *Hobbies:* Work Adjustment of Immigrants; Music; Arts. *Address:* 6290 Busch Blvd., Suite 10, Columbus, OH 43229, USA.

GREEN Linda Lou, b. 12 Sept. 1946, Cape Girardeau, Missouri, USA. Systems Engineer; Author; Lecturer. *Education:* BA 1967, MA 1969, East Carolina University; Postgraduate, University of Utah, 1969-70; Certificate in Collegiate Teaching, Virginia. *Appointments:* Assistant Professor of History, Jackson State University, Mississippi, 1970-72; Virginia State University, 1972-74; Commissioned 1st Lieutenant US Army, advanced to Major, reverted from active to reserve status, 1983; Logistics Engineer, Land Systems Div, General Dynamics Corp, 1983-84; Systems Engineer, Raytheon Service Co, 1984-86; President, Green & Assoc 1985-86; Systems Engineer, Applied Research Inc, 1986-. *Publications:* Author: Study Guides for American History; New Dimensions in Integrated Logistics; Contributor to Eighteenth Century Studies, 1980. *Memberships:* League of Women Voters; Society of Logistics Engineers, 1983-; Reserve Officer's Association, 1986-; Republican National Committee, 1986-; Board of Directors 1988-91, Local chapter of the Association of the US Army (AUSA); International Platform Association, 1989; National Association of Female Executives, 1989. *Honours:* Graduate Teaching Fellowship, 1967-69, East Carolina University; Honor Graduate, Naval War College, Newport, Rhode Island, 1985; Phi Alpha Theta, History Honor Fraternity, 1967; Military Awards: Overseas Service Ribbon, 1981; Service School Ribbon, 1981; Army Commendation Award, 1983; Army Reserve Forces Medal, 1988. *Hobbies:* Horseback riding; Racquetball; Needlepoint; Writing. *Address:* 708 Lily Flagg Road, Huntsville, AL 35802, USA.

GREEN Lucinda Jane, MBE, b. 7 Nov. 1953, London, England. Writer; Horserider (3-day events). m. David Green, 4 Dec. 1981. 1 son. *Publications:* Up, Up & Away; Four Square; Regal Realm; Cross Country Riding. *Membership:* Honorary member, Mount Kenya Safari Club. *Honours:* Member Order of the British Empire (MBE) 1970; 3-day Events: Badminton 1973, 1976, 1977, 1979, 1983, 1984; World Championship, 1982; European Championship, 1975, 1977. Olympic Silver Medal Team, Los Angeles, 1984. *Hobbies:* Skiing; Dirivng; Scuba diving. *Address:* Appleshaw House, Andover, Hampshire, England.

GREEN Marjorie Biller, b. 5 Nov. 1939, Boston, USA. Western States Education Director. m. Jason I. Green, 17 Mar. 1963, 2 sons, 1 daughter. *Education:* AB, 1961, AM, 1963, Boston University; PhD Candidate, University of California. *Appointments:* Co-ordinator, Wilshire Community Educational Complex, 1979-80; Executive Director, California Coalition for Public Education, 1985-87; Western States Education Director, Anti Defamation League, 1987-. *Publications:* Editor, Too Many Students: Not Enough Room, 1987. *Memberships:* Board, Community Relations Conference of Southern California; Board, Para los Ninos, 1984-; *Honours:* Phi Beta Kappa, 1961; Outstanding Service Award to LAUSD Students, 1981-82. *Address:* Anti-Defamation League of B'nai B'rith, 6505 Wilshire Blvd., No 814, Los Angeles, CA 90048, USA.

GREEN Mary Hester, b. 6 May 1941, Oxford, North Carolina, USA. Religious Counsellor; Nurse. m. Joe Lewis Green, 24 Dec. 1962, 1 son, 2 daughters. *Education:* Nursing Diploma, Essex Technical College, 1968; Surgical Nursing Certificate, 1971; AA, State University of New York, 1979; Diploma 1984, Certificate 1988, Christian Education. *Appointments:* Nurse: Newark City Hospital, 1967-69; Duke Medical Centre, 1969-; Lincoln Hospital, 1974-76; Durham County General Hospital, 1976-80. *Memberships:* Deaconess Board, Sunday School Teacher, Pine Grove Baptist Church; District 3 Missionary Club; Order of Eastern Star; American Society of Notaries; Girl Scout Leader. *Honours:* Certificate of Recognition, Durham YWCA, 1985; Service Award, Lincoln Hospital, 1976; Leader's Award, Girl Scouts, 1977. *Hobbies:* Reading; Singing; Music; Missionary work. *Address:* 5301 Whippoorwill Street, Durham, North Carolina 27704, USA.

GREEN Valerie Yvonne Crespi, b. 3 June 1950, Salford, England. Author; Nurse Practitioner. m. Juan Crespi Amengual, 10 May 1977, 1 son. *Education:* Victoria Home for Physically Handicapped Children, 1966-68; Staff Nurse, Mildmay Mission Hospital, Hackney, 1971; Royal Neurological Hospital, 1972; Clinica Juaneda Hospital, Mallorca, 1972-73; Policlinica Miramar Palma de Mallorca, 1973-77; Nurse Practitioner, Santa Eugenia, 1987-. *Publications:* Landscapes of Mallorca, 1983, in Spanish, German, French, Dutch, Norwegian & Swedish, 1989. *Memberships:* Walking Guide for British Journalists in Association with Mallorcan Tourist Board; Society of Authors; Affiliate Member, ALCS. *Hobbies:* Walking; Reading; Crochet; Swimming. *Address:* c/o Caidos 9/ 1, Santa Eugenia, Mallorca, Baleares, Spain.

GREENBERG Judith Lynn, b. 9 Feb. 1947, New York City, New York, USA. Social Worker; Psychotherapist; Mental Health Administrator. m. Michel P Méry, 12 Nov. 1987. *Education:* BA Education, with distinction, University of Michigan, 1967; MA, Social Work, University of Chicago, 1970, DSW pending, Adelphi University. *Appointments:* Health Ed in Vac Playgrounds & Art Teacher, NYC Board of Education, summers 1965-68; Teacher, Willow Run Public Schools, 1967-68; Urban Planner, Dept of Development & Planning, Chicago, 1970-71; Social Worker, St Luke's Hospital, New York City, 1972-73; Social Worker, Jewish Agency for Immigration and Absorption, Jerusalem, Israel, 1973-74; Social Worker/Student Supervisor, Family Life Educator, Jewish Board of Family & Childrens Servics, 1974-82; Faculty Instructor, St Joseph's College, Brooklyn, 1979-83; Faculty Instructor & Student Supervisor, Adelphi University School of Social Work, 1985-87; Director, Queens Family Court Preventive Services, Jewish Board of Family & Children's Services, 1982-. *Memberships:* National Association of Social Workers; Clinical Social Workers Registry; Academy of Certified Social Workers; American Association of Sex Educators, Counselors & Therapists; Society for Sex Therapy and Research; Board Certified Diplomate in Clinical Social Work. *Honours:* Mortaboard, Phi Kappa Phi Honorary Society, University of Michigan; Adelia Cheever Scholarship, University of Michigan, 1967; Child Welfare Grant, Dept of Health, Educ & Welfare, Children's Bureau, University of Chicago, 1970; Doctoral Grant, National Institute for Mental Health, Adelphi University, 1979. *Hobbies:* Art; Travel; Reading; Theatre; Movies. *Address:* 210 West 89 Street No 1C, New York, NY 10024, USA.

GREENBERG Karen J, b. 19 Sept. 1942, Baltimore, USA. School Administrator. m. George S. Greenberg, 26 June 1966. *Education:* BA, Adelphi University, 1964; MEd., Xavier University, 1967. *Appointments:* Chairman, Fine Arts, Duchesne Academy, 1974-; Assistant to headmaster, Isidore Newman School, 1976-. *Publications:* Lighting Design, Lincoln Centre; Stage Manager, Zizi, Broadway Theatre, 1965. *Memberships:* Cum Laude Association; Charter Member, Living History Institute; Vice President, Young Audiences NO Branch; Vice President, Youth Alternatives; Charter Member, Louisiana Shakespeare Festival. *Honours:* Kappa Delta Pi. *Hobbies:* Aerobics; Running; Reading. *Address:* 1116 Jena St., New Orleans, LA 70115, USA.

GREENBERG Marilyn Werstein, b. 29 Oct. 1937, Brooklyn, New York, USA, Professor. m. Eugene Greenberg, 29 Jan. 1956, 2 sons. *Education:* BA, Brooklyn College, 1960; MA, 1969, PhD, University of Chicago. *Appointments:* Librarian, Chicago Public Schools, Illinois, 1965-67; Instructor, University of Southern California, 1970-74; Professor, California State University, Los Angeles, 1974-. *Publications:* Monographs: Development Needs and Library Services, 1979; Media and the Young Adult (with Bernard Lukenbill and others), 1976; Ethnic Services Task Force Collection Evaluation Project, Report (with Patricia Tarin), 1982; Articles: A Study of Reading Motivation of Twenty-Three Seventh Grade Students, 1970; Desirable Outcomes of a Basic Course in Children's Literature, 1974; A New Librarym Services Credential Program, 1975; Se Habla Y.A. Aqui, 1976; Don't Underrate Service to Children (with Ryna Rothberg), 1976; Students Share Stories (with Joan Gardner), 1977; Challenges and Changes in Library Education, 1985; Measuring the Availability of Library Materials, 1986; Reviews; Editor, School Library Media Quarterly, 1985-88. *Memberships:* Councillor, American Library Association; Beta Phi Mu; California Library Association; California Media and Library Educators Assocaition; Board of Examiners, National Council for Accreditation of Teacher Education; Pi Lambda Theta; Southern California Council on Literature for Children and Young People. *Address:* 10661 Wilkins Avenue, Route 6, Los Angeles, CA 90024, USA.

GREENBERG Marya, b. 16 Sept. 1951, Bertha, Minnesota, USA. Chiropractic Physician. m. Jay M Greenberg, DC, 8 May 1977. 1 son, 1 daughter. *Education:* BA, University of Minnesota, Minneapolis, 1973; DC, Doctor of Chiropractic, St Paul, Minnesota, 1977. *Appointments:* Private practice (with husband, Dr Jay Greenberg), Red Wing Chiropractic Clinic, PA, Red Wing, Minnesota; Chiropractic Consultant. *Publications:* Articles. Live with your Success, 1983; The Referral Concept, 1984 in Success Express Magazine co-author with Dr Jay Greenberg; The Chiropractic Consultant: Why, What and When, Minnesota Chiropractic Association Journal, 1988. *Memberships:* American Chiropractic Association; Minnesota Chiropractic Association, Board of Directors, 1980-83; International Academy of Chiropractic Industrial Consultants, Board of Directors, 1985-86 and 1987-. Editor, International Newsletter, 1985-86; American Association of University Women; Business and Professional Women's Organisation; Faculty Preceptor, Northwestern College of Chiropractic; Student Body President, 1974-75; Red Wing City Council member, 1985-87; Red Wing Arts Association. *Honours:* John W Fisher Memorial Award for the Most Outstanding Chiropractic College Senior in the United States, 1976; Springwall Scholarship, 1976; Lifetime Honorary Member, Northwestern College of Chiropractic, Women Chiropractors of the American Chiropractic Association, conferred 1983; Appointed to Rehabilitation Review Panel, State of Minnesota Department of Labor and Industry, by Ray Bohn, Commissioner of Labor and Industry, 1988. *Hobbies:* Acting; Writing; Cycling. *Address:* Rt 3, Box 104, Red Wing, MN 55066, USA.

GREENE Adele Shuminer, b. 16 Sept. 1925, Newark, New Jersey, USA. Management Consultant (to corporations, non-profit groups, individuals). m. (1) Alan

Greene, 1948, div. 1953, (2) Bernard Burger, 1955, div. 1960, 1 son. *Education:* Juilliard School of Music, 1942-44; New York University, 1942-44; New School for Social Research, 1944-47; Management Programme, Harvard Business School, 1978. *Appointments:* Account Executive, 1964-66, Senior Associate, 1966-68, Vice-President, 1968-72, Senior Vice-President, 1972-76, Ruder & Finn Inc, New York City; Vice-President Public Affairs, Corporation for Public Broadcasting, Washington DC, 1976-78; President, Chief Executive Officer, Television Program Group, Washington DC, 1978-80; President, Greene and Associates, New York City, 1981-; Developer and Instructor, course in workplace politics. *Publications:* Teen-Age Leadership, 1971; Contributor to professional journals. *Memberships:* Public Relations Society of America; National Association of Educational Broadcasters; American Women in Radio and TV; Board Member: Union Settlement Association; The Acting Company; Duke Ellington School for the Performing Arts; American Craft Council, President and Chief Executive Council 1980-81; Coliseum Homeowners Corporation, Treasurer 1987-90. *Honours:* Silver Anvil, Public Relations Society of America, 1971; Teen-Age Leadership Citation, City of New York, 1973; Commendation, Corporation for Public Broadcasting, 1978; Gold Key Award, PR News, 1981. *Hobbies:* Music; Theatre; Literature. *Address:* 30 West 60th Street, New York, NY 10023, USA.

GREENE Ellin Peterson, b. 18 Sept. 1927, Elizabeth, USA. Educator; Consultant, Library Service to Children. m. K Richard Greene, 24 June 1962. *Education:* AB, Douglass College, 1953; EdD, Graduate School of Education, Rutgers University, 1979. *Appointments:* New York Public Library, 1959-67; Childrens Literature Specialist, National College of Education, & Visiting Professor, McGaw Graduate School, 1976-77; Associate Professor, Dean of Students, University of Chicago, 1980-85; Consultant and Project Director, The New York Public Library Early Childhood Project, 1986-89; Consultant and Guest Curator, Roger Duvoisin Retrospective Exhibition, Zimmerli Art Museum, Rutgers, The State University of New Jersey, 1986-89. *Publications:* Story Telling : A Selected Annotated Bibliography (with George Shannon); Storytelling : Art and Technique, (with Augusta Baker); A Multimedia Approach to Children's Literature (with Madalynne Schoenfeld); Midsummer Magic, stories for children; numerous articles in professional journals. *Memberships:* American Library Association; Association for Library Service to Children, various positions; Authors Guild; Society of Childrens Book Writers; Children's literature Association; Friends of the InternationalBoard on Books for Young People. *Honours:* Director, The Illustrator as Storyteller Project, 1984-85; Douglass Society Distinguished alumnae, 1981; Rutgers University Graduate Fellowship. *Hobbies:* Beachcombing; Gardening; Reading. *Address:* 113 Chatham Lane, Point Pleasant, NJ 08742, USA.

GREENE Freda H, b. 29 Mar. 1929, London, England. Author; International Correspondence. 1 daughter. *Education:* Regent Street Polytechnic, 1946-; Royal Society of Arts Certificate, The Sorbonne, Paris, France, 1948; Continuous education, University of California at Los Angeles, 1980. *Appointments:* Correspondent, China, Glass and Tableware, 1976-; Liaison consultant, California State University, Northridge, California, USA, 1977-81; Contributing editor, Big Valley Magazine, 1978, California Life, 1979; International Editor, Executive, Jeweler, 1984-85; Regional Editor, Changing Homes magazine; Freelance writer for various newspapers and magazines; Correspondent for various UK magazines and Hong Kong Standard News. *Publications:*How to get a job in Los Angeles; A Man for all Reasons; Organ Donation-The Ultimate Gift; Contributor to Europe Magazine and others. Television programme on organ transplants now used as a teaching medium for doctors and nurses in USA by University of California at Los Angeles. Frankly Female Show for Channel 9 in Los Angeles. *Memberships:* Moderator, Panelist for annual seminars, Activities chairman, American Society of Journalists and Authors;

Los Angeles Centre, Poets, Playwrights, Editors, Essayists and Novelists (PEN) International; Women's National Book Association; Book Publicists of Southern California; Women in Management. *Honours:* Foreign Press Award, MACEF, Milan, Italy, 1982; Writers Digest Award, Non-fiction, 1977, 1978. *Hobbies:* Art; Theatre; Music appreciation. *Address:* 6624 Newcastle Avenue, Reseda, CA 91335, USA.

GREENE Jo Ann, b. 11 Sept. 1938, Columbus, Ohio, USA. Director. m. Lawrance Greene, 17 June 1961, divorced 1966, 1 son. *Education:* Nursing Diploma, 1959; BSc., Nursing, 1969; MSc., Nursing, 1970; Graduate Studies Counseling Psychology, 1974-76; PhD in Progress, University of Southern California. *Appointments:* Staff Nurse, Ohio Univesity Medicla Centre, 1959-62; Staff Nurse, Paediatrics, Stanford Hospital, 1962-63; Staff Nurse, Hillhaven Convalescent Hospital, 1963-66; Staff Nurse, Psychiatry, 1966-69, Head Nurse, Mental Hygiene Clinic, 1970-72, VA Hospital, Palo Alto; Lecturer, San Jose State University, 1972-74; Director, Psychiatric Technician Programme, Misison College, 1974-. *Publications:* numerous articles in professional journals. *Memberships:* Alpha Kappa Alpha Sorority; Faculty Association of Certified Community Colleges; California Nurses Association; American Nurses Association; California Association of Psychiatric Technician Educators; ACLU; Advisory Committee, BVNPTE; Associate, College Educators, Vice President; Black Nurses Association; California Association of Health Careers Educators. *Honours:* L Society; Excelsior Society; National Honor Society; Florence Nightingale Award; Dean's List; President's Scholar; Sigma theta tau; Phi Kappa Phi. *Hobbies:* Sewing; Reading; Skiing; Art; Ice & Roller Skating. *Address:* 43512 Ocaso Corte, Fremont, CA 94539, USA.

GREENE Margaret Lyford, b. 12 Sep. 1942, New Rochelle, New York, USA. Central Banker; Economist. m. Edwin H. Yeo III, 30 Sep. 1978, 2 stepsons. *Education:* BA, Economics, Wellesley College, 1964; MA, Economics, 1966, PhD, Economics, 1972, Columbia University. *Appointments:* Research Assistant, International Economics Workshop, Columbia University, New York, 1964-66; Economist, International Research and Foreign Department, 1967-72, Chief, Financial Statistics Division, Statistics Department, 1972, Manager, Foreign Department, 1972; Assistant Vice-President, Foreign Department, 1974, Vice-President, Foreign Exchange, 1977-83, Senior Vice- President, Foreign Exchange, 1984-, Federal Reserve Bank of New York, New York City. *Publications:* Waiting Time: A Factor in Export Demand for Manufactures, 1975; The Last of the Mohicans, in Foreign Exchange Committee Annual Report, 1985. *Memberships:* American Economic Association; American Academy of Political Science; FOREX USA Inc; Council on Foreign Relations. *Honours:* Wellesley College Scholar, 1963, 1964; Faculty Scholar Award, 1964, 1965, Presidential Fellow, 1966-67, Columbia University; Research Assistantship, International Economic Workshop, 1964-66; Granville Garth Fellow, 1966-67; High Honour Roll; New York State Regents Scholarship; National Merit Certificate of Distinction. *Hobbies:* Sheep farming; Sailing; Classical music (piano and clarinet); Ballet; Photography; Skiing. *Address:* Foreign Exchange Function, 7th Floor East, Federal Reserve Bank of New York, 33 Liberty Street, New York, NY 10045, USA.

GREENE Susan, b. 1 Jan. 1955, Passaic, New Jersey, USA. Music Book Editor; Writer; Educational Consultant. *Education:* BA, Drew University, 1976; MA, New York University, 1978. *Appointments:* Senior Editor, Music Publications, 1976-, Chief Editor, Silver Burdett & Ginn Music, for the British Schools, 1985-88, Silver Burdett & Ginn Inc; Research Associate, Opera Orchestra of New York, 1978-; Research Assistant, Educational Materials, Metropolitan Opera, New York, 1980-; Vice-President, Education, New York City Opera Guild, 1985-. *Publications:* A Guide to Children's Opera; Teacher's Guides to Tannhauser and Arabella; Comedy in Puccini's Operas, 1984; Wozzeck and Marie: Two Outcasts in

Operas, 1984; Wozzeck and Marie: Two Outcasts in Search of an Honest Morality, 1985. *Memberships:* Music Critics Association; Music Library Association; Music Educators National Conference.*Hobbies:* Art; Literature; Theatre; Travel; Good food and wine. *Address:* 105 Ridgedale Avenue, Madison, NJ 07940, USA.

GREENSLATE Pamela S, b. Quincy, USA. Director; Pychotherapist. m. Roger W. Greenslate, 18 Oct. 1975, 2 sons. *Education:* BS, Iowa State University, 1970; Tulane University, Graduate School of Social Work, New Orleans, 1980; Diploma, Association Trainers in Clinical Hypnosis, 1982. *Appointments:* Peoria Childrens Home, 1971-79; Lutheran Social Service of Illinois, Supervisor, Child Abuse Programme, 1979-84; Founder, Director, Centre Against Sexual Assault, 1984-. *Memberships:* American Association for Counsellor Development; American Mental Health Counsellors Association; American Association for Hypnotherapy. *Address:* 2508 N. Sheridan Rd., Suite No 3, Peoria, IL 61604, USA.

GREENWALD Neva Elizabeth Farbizo, b. 24 May 1938, New Philadelphia, Ohio, USA. Physical Therapy Educator & Administrator. m. Edward Kenneth Greenwald, 27 Dec. 1959. *Education:* BA 1959, BS 1960, Ohio State University; MSPH, University of Missouri-Columbia, 1971. *Appointments:* Phys Therapist, United Cerebal Palsy, Columbis, Ohio; Assistant Director, Physical Therapy, Grant Hospital, Columbus, 1963-67; Senior Staff Member, Assistant Director, Physical Therapy, Duke University, Durham, 1967-68; Coordinator, Clinical Education, Instructor, Physical Therapy, University of Missouri, 1969-73l; Private Practice, Physical Therapy, New Philadelphia, 1973-74; Assistant Professor, Coordinator of Physical Therapy Clinical Education, University of Mississippi, 1976-79; Associate Professor, Chairman, Physical Therapy School of Health Related Professions, 1979-; Director, Physical Therapy, University Hospital, University of Mississippi Medical Centre, 1980-; Consultant, Missouri State Penitentiary, Jackson Ballet Co. *Memberships include:* Editorial Board, Topics in Geriatric Rehabilitation and Proceedings of Mississippi Association for Women in Higher Education Annual Meetings; American Physical Therapy Association (Sections on Administration, Education, Geriatrics and Community Health); Past President, Leagues of Women Voters of Jackson and Mississippi; Association for Women in Higher Education; Soroptimist International of Jackson; Past Secretary, Jackson, Mississippi Womens Political Caucus; Medical Center Womens Club; Jackson Symphony League; Past Chairman, Mississippi Alliance of Health Related Associations; Member, Advisory Committee, Mississippi Geriatric Education Center; Mississippi Museum of Art Auxillary; American Association of University Women; Friends of Mynelle Gardens; Consultant, International Ballet Competition 1979, 1982, 1986. *Honours:* Distinguished Service, Hinds County Human Resources Agency, 1986; Mississippi Equal Opportunity Officers Association Appreciation Award, 1983; Outstanding Woman of Achievement, 1985-86, Mississippi Association for Women in Higher Education; Joan Mills Award, Section on Geriatric American Physical Therapy Assn, 1988; Service Awards, Mississippi Chapter, American Physical Therapy Association, 1980, 1982. *Hobbies:* Needlework; Pug dogs; Leaded stained glass suncatchers; Indoor plants. *Address:* P O Box 4823, Jackson, MS 39216, USA.

GREER Birdia Marie, b. 2 Feb. 1952, Shreveport, Louisiana, USA. Attorney. *Education:* BA 1974, MA studies (psychiatric social work) 1975-76, Louisiana State University; JD, Southern University School of Law, 1980; Numerous postgraduate courses. *Appointments:* Teacher, counsellor, Caddo Parish Schools, 1976-77; Legal Assistant, Law Clerk, Withers & Withers law firm, Baton Rouge, 1979-80; Law Clerk, Committee on Health & Welfare, Louisiana State Legislature, 1979, 1980; Law Clerk (1st Judicial District Court) 1980, Assistant District Attorney 1981-, Caddo Parish District Attorney's Office; Assistant City Attorney, Shreveport, 1981-; Sole

practitioner, civil law practice, 1984-. *Memberships:* National, American, Louisiana, Shreveport Bar Associations; Shreveport Trial Lawyers Association & Association of Women Attorneys; National District Attorney's Association; Black Lawyers Association; National & Louisiana Child Support Enforcement Councils. *Honour:* Pro Bono Award, Northwest Louisiana Legal Services, 1987. *Hobbies:* Tennis; Billiards; Cycling; Travel; Gourmet cooking; Reading mysteries; Listening to music. *Address:* 414 Slattery Building, 509 Marshall Street, Shreveport, Louisiana 71101, USA.

GREGORIUS Beverly June, b. 21 June 1915, Ottawa, USA. Obstetrician, Gynaecologist. m. Hans Harvey Gregorious, 6 Apr. 1939, deceased 1977, 1 daughter. *Education:* BS, Madison College, 1935; Certified Medical Technologist, 1940; MD 1946. *Appointments:* Practice of Medicine, Specialist Obstetrics-Gynaecology, 1953-; Associate Clinical Professor, Obsetrics-Gynaecology, Loma Linda Univesity Medical School, 1956-; Associate Clinical Professor, Obstetrics-Gynaecology, 1956-85, Clinical Professor, 1985-, University of Soutern California; Programme Director, 1976- 81, Chairman, 1981-83, Obstetrics-Gynaecology, Glendale Adventist Medical Center. *Memberships:* Life Member, President 1984-85, Los Angeles Obstetrical & Gynaecological Society; Southern Obstetrics-Gynaecological Seminar; Fellow, American College of Surgeons; Fellow, International College of Surgeons; Fellow, American College of Obstetrics-Gynaecology. *Honours:* Graduated 1st in class of 94 at medical school. *Hobbies:* Travel; Photography. *Address:* 1530 East Chevy Chase Drive, Suite 101, Glendale, CA 91206, USA.

GREGORY Barbara Jean, b. 14 Mar. 1954, Geneva, New York, USA. Journal Editor. *Education:* BA, Alfred University, 1976; Offset Printing Workshop, Communiversity, Rochester, New York, 1977. *Appointments:* Editor, Fiat Lux student newspaper, Alfred University, Alfred, New York, 1974-75; Editorial Assistant, International Journal of Radiation Oncology, Biology and Physics, 1976, Assistant Medical Illustrator, School of Medicine and Dentistry, 1976-78, University of Rochester, Rochester, New York, 1976; Typesetter, Layout Artist, Type/Graphics, Syracuse, New York, 1979-80; Assistant Editor, Aeronautics Digest, United States Air Force Academy, Colorado Springs, Colorado, 1980-81, Editor, 1988-; Managing Editor, The Numismatist, American Numismatic Association, Colorado Springs, 1981-; Numismatic Consultant, The Random House Dictionary of the English Language, 2nd Edition, 1987. *Publications:* Articles in· 80 Microcomputing magazine, 1981; The Americana Annual, 1984, 1987; Le Club Francais de la Medaille Bulletin, 1986; Ideals magazine, 1988. *Memberships:* Society of Professional Journalists; Numismatic Literary Guild; Colorado Public Interest Research Group; Girl Scouts-Wagon Wheel Council Women's Work Volunteer Programme. *Hobbies include:* Victorian architectural restoration; Vintage British and American films; Early advertising and packaging; Art medals. *Address:* 452 W San Rafael, Colorado Springs, CO 80905, USA.

GREGORY Helen Jean Winfrey, b. 13 Feb. 1947, Richmond, USA. Ecologist; Educator. m. Ronald Alfred Gregory, 13 Dec. 1973. *Education:* BS, Biology, Mary Washington College, 1969; MS, Biology 1975; MA, Environmental Science, 1983. *Appointments:* Lab Specialist, Cardiovascular Division, Medical College of Virginia, 1969-70; Pollution Control Specialist, State Water Control Board, Richmond, 1970-77; Pollution Control Specialist, 1977-81; Adjunct Professor, Virginia Commonwealth Univesity, 1978-; Ecologist, 1981-85; Environmental Programme Manager, 1985-. *Memberships:* American Society Public Administration; North American Benthological Society; Ecologicla Society of America; American Planning Association; American Society Limnology and Oceanography; North American Lake Management Society. *Honours:* EPA Fellow, 1974-76. *Hobbies:* Crewel Embroidery; Herb

Gardening; Hiking; Reading; Writing. *Address:* State Water Control Board, Office of Environmental Research & Standards, PO Box 11143, 2107 Hamilton Street, Richmond, VA 23230, USA.

GREGORY Mary Ethel Coleman, b. 21 Sept. 1913, St Louis, Missouri, USA. AssociAtIon Official. m. Jesse Gregory, 27 Sept. 1941. *Education:* BS, Education, Miner Teachers College, 1935; MA, Sociology, Catholic University of America, 1941. *Appointments:* Programme Director, USO; Phyllis Wheatley YWCA, Washington, 1942-43; Associate Executive Director, 1945-50; Community Services Director, Urban League, Muskegon, 1954- 60; Adult Programme Dirctor, YWCA, Lansing, Michigan, 1960-. *Publications:* Papers and Personal Records presented to Library of Congress, Washington DC; Historic Documents presented to Bethune Museum and Archives. *Memberships Include:* American Association of Universiy Women; Adult Education Association; NAACP; National Association of Social Workers; National Urban League; Trustee, President Emeritus, Frederick Douglas Memorial and Historical Association; Budget Chairman, National Associaton Coloured Women, Washington 1950-54, Board of Directors, 1954-60; Vice President, Muskegon United Church Women, 1958-60; Lansing World Affairs Council, National Council Negro Women. *Honours:* Awards from YWCA and Interior Department, women's Service League; University of District of Columbia; NAACP and Urban League. *Hobbies:* International Travel; Black History; Civil Rights Associations; Historic Preservation. *Address:* 10594 Twin River Road, Columbia, MD 21044, USA.

GREIF Karen Faye, b. 11 Feb. 1952, New York, USA. Professor. *Education:* AB Human Biology, Brown University, 1973; PhD Psychobiology and Biochemistry, California Institute of Technology, 1978. *Appointments:* Postdoctoral Fellow, Dept of Physiology, University of California, San Francisco, 1978-82; Assistant Professor of Biology, 1982-88, Associate Professor of Biology, 1989-, Bryn Mawr College. *Publications:* Contributions of articles and abstracts to professional journals. *Memberships:* Society for Neuroscience, Chapters Committee, 1985-88; President, Philadelphia Chapter, 1987-88; AAS; AWIS; Soc for Develop Biology; Union of Concerned Scientists; NSF Neuroscience Oversight Review Committee, 1986. *Honours:* Alumnae Scholar for Western New Eng, Pembroke College, Brown University, 1970-71; NSF Summer Research Apprentice, Caltech, 1972; Fellow, Muscular Dystrophy Association of America, 1978-80. *Hobbies:* Active chamber musician; Amnesty International; Sierra Club. *Address:* Dept of Biology, Bryn Mawr College, Bryn Mawr, PA 19010, USA.

GREMM Judye Dyan, b. 24 Aug. 1953, Dallas, USA. Marketing Executive. *Education:* BBA, University of Colorado, 1974. *Appointments:* Sales Manager, Braniff International Airlines, 1974-82; Corporate Director, Tiffany & Co., 1982-85; Corporate Liaison, Baylor University Medical Centre, 1985-88; Business & Professional Institute, Counsellor, 1988-. *Publications:* Articles in professional journals. *Memberships:* American Association of Female Executives; American Marketing Association; Sales & Marketing Executives; American Association of University Women; American College of Healthcare Executives; American Red Cross; American Cancer Society. *Honours:* Sales & Marketing Executives Victor Award, 1979; Braniff Airlines Sales Manager of the Year, 1980. *Hobbies:* European Travel; Egyptology; Physical Fitness; New York Theatre. *Address:* 7621 Woodthrush, Dallas, TX 75230, USA.

GRENARD Nancy Carole, b. 17 July 1946, Lafayette, USA. Director. m. Bradley Ray Grenard, 1 Sept. 1972, 1 daughter. *Education:* BS, General Management, 1980, MS, Computer Science, 1985, Purdue University. *Appointments:* Assistant Director, Personnel, 1981-83, Manager, Users Information Centre, 1983-87, Director, Development & Alumni Information Systems, 1987-, Purdue Univesity. *Publications:* Articles in CUPA Journal. *Memberships:*

College & University Personnel Association; School of Science Alumni Advisory Board, 1987-; Data Processing Management Association; Board of Directors, Sycamore Audubon Society, 1988-; Wabash River Parkway Commission, 1988-. *Honours:* Co-winer, CUPA Achievement Award, 1983. *Hobbies:* Wild Flower Study; Reading; Computer Use; Nature Study. *Address:* RR2, Otterbein, IN 47970, USA.

GRESSITT Alexandra Susan, b. 11 Feb. 1953, Seattle, Washington, USA. Archivist. *Education:* BA, University of Puget Sound, 1975; MA History, University of Washington, 1977; MA Archival Management, North Carolina State University, 1985. *Appointments:* Assistant Reference Librarian, Vancouver Library, Washington, 1979-82; Archivist, St Mary's College, Raleigh, North Carolina, 1985-86; City Archivist, & Assistant University Archivist, University of Southern Mississippi, Hattiesburg, 1986-. *Publications:* Bibliographic Sources for Research on Women at NC State University, 1985; Guide to Papers of Harry C. Kelly 1882-1976, 1985; Co-Editor, Manuscript Processing Manual, McCain Library & Archives, 1988; Archives Manual: Policies, Procedures & Guidelines, 1988-. *Memberships include:* Board, Offices, Society of Mississippi Archivists; Office, Archivists Roundtable, University of Southern Mississippi; Member, other national & local professional bodies. *Honours:* Alumni Fellow, History, North Carolina State University, 1984-85; Phi Alpha Theta (history), 1985; Sigma Alpha Iota (music), 1974. *Hobby:* Scottish country dancing. *Address:* University of Southern Mississippi, Southern Station Box 5148, Hattiesburg, MS 39406, USA.

GREY Beryl Elizabeth, Dame.b. 11 June 1927, London, England. Prima Ballerina and Artistic Director. m. Doctor S.G. Svenson, 15 July 1950. 1 son. *Education:* Madeleine Sharpe, 1931-37; Sadlers Wells, 1937-41. *Appointments include:* Prima Ballerina, Sadlers Wells Ballet, now the Royal Ballet, 1941-57, dancing leading roles within first year; Freelance International Ballerina, 1957-66; 1st guest artisti to dance with Bolshoi Ballet, Moscow, 1957, with Peking Ballet, Peking, 1964; Director General Arts Educational Schools, Teacher Training College, 1965-67; Artistic Director, London Festival Ballet, 1967-79; Now freelance Director, Producer, Teacher, Lecturer, etc. *Publications:* Red Curtain Up, 1959; Through the Bamboo Curtain, 1965; My Favourite Ballet Stories, 1980. *Memberships:* Vice President and Member, Royal Academy of Dancing Executive Council; Chairman Imperial Society of Teachers of Dancing Governing Council; President Dance Council of Wales; Vice President Keep Fit Society; Vice Chairman London College of Dance and Drama; Trustee: London City Ballet, Royal Ballet Benevolent Fund, Vice Chairman Dance Teachers Benevolent Fund; Patron Dancers Resettlement Trust; Patron Benesh Institute.*Honours:* Hon. Doctor of Music, Leicester University, 1970; CBE 1973; Hon. Doctor of Literature, City of London, 1974; Dame Commander of the British Empire, (D.B.E.), 1988. *Hobbies:* Swimming; Painting; Piano Playing. *Address:* Fernhill, Priory Road, Forest Row, East Sussex, England.

GRIBBLE Carole L, b. 19 May 1940, Toppenish, Washington, USA. Executive. m. Vance Gribble, 19 May 1966. 1 son. *Education:* Attended Seattle Pacific College. *Appointments:* B F Shearer, Seattle, Washington, 1959-60; Standard Oil, Seattle, 1960-62; Seattle Platen, 1962-70; Co-owner, Cascade Golf, 1969-87; Co-owner, Waldorf Towers Apartments, 1970; Co-owner, Pacific Wholesale Office Equipment, Los Angeles & Seattle, 1972-87; Owner, Pacific Wholesale Office Equipments Los Angeles, San Pablo (San Francisco area office, DBA Bob Bianco Sales) and Seattle, 1988-; Owner, PAC Electronic Service, Seattle and San Pablo, 1988-; Owner, Waldorf Management Company, 1988-. *Creative works:* Created graphic arts catalogues for my business (wholesale office equipment catalogues). *Memberships:* Republican; Cedar Cross Methodist Church. *Hobbies:* Genealogy; Semi-classical music; Reading; Desk top publishing. *Address:* Mill Creek, Washington, USA.

GRIFFITH-SMITH Bella, b. USA. Opera Singer; Coach; Administrator. *Education:* Private tutors: Howard Thain, Franco Iglesias, Dr Paul Csonka. *Appointments include:* Debut, Civic Opera of Palm Beaches, Florida; Appearances with: Louis Quilico, Robert Merrill, Guiseppe Campora, etc. Madam Butterfly, Tosca, Cavaleria Rusticana, Pagliacci, Boheme, Suor Angelica, Il Tabarro, Faust, Carmen (Micaela), Cosi Fan Tutte (Fiordiligi), Tales of Hoffman (Antonia), Traviata, Handel's Messiah, Vivaldi's Gloria, Rossini's Stabat Mater; Guest soloist, Greater Miami Philharmonic, with Alain Lombard. Currently President, Coral Gables Civic Opera & Orchestra Inc. *Creative work includes:* Created concert-drama; Copyrighted own original scripts, to present historical events at concerts; Choreographed dance-drama for concerts. *Memberships include:* Offices, past/present: Coral Gables People to People Programme; Coral Gables Chamber of Commerce; Miami Conference, Women's Action for Progress in Caribbean & Central America. *Honours:* Scholarship, Greater Miami Opera Guild; Certificates of Appreciation, Dade County, Miami Lighthouse for Blind, Girl Scouts. *Hobbies:* Writing; Painting; Reading-research; History; Literature. *Address:* 700 Santander Avenue, Coral Gables, Florida 33134, USA.

GRIFFITHS Diana Margaret, b. 15 Feb. 1941, Neath, Glamorgan, Wales. Writer. m. Peter Mottley, 8 Aug. 1964, 1 daughter. *Education:* BA, Honours, English Language & Literature, University of Sheffield, 1962; Diploma in Education, University College of Wales, Cardiff, 1962-63. *Appointments:* Teacher, London, Berkshire, Bradford, 1963-87; Head, English, Downs School, Compton, 1977-83. *Publications:* Radio Plays: Set to Rites, 1988; Parents' Evening, 1986; The Hound of the Hgginbottoms, 1988; Poetry Anthologies compiled for BBC Radio 3 including: Great & Small; Awake & Asleep; Lies for Hire. *Hobbies:* Music; Viola Player - Played with National Youth Orchestra of Wales, 1957-60. *Address:* Haworth, West Yorkshire, England.

GRIFFITHS Helen, b. 8 May 1939, London, England. Church Secretary. m. Pedro Santos De La Cal, 17 Oct. 1959, deceased, 3 daughters. *Publications:* Horse in the Clouds, 1957; Wild & Free, 1958; Moonlight, 1959; Africano, 1961; The Wild Heart, 1963; The Greyhound, 1964; The Dark Swallows, 1966; The Wild Horse of Santander, 1966; Leon, 1967; Stallion of the Sands, 1968; Moshie Cat, 1969; Patch, 1970; Federico, 1971; Russian Blues, 1972; Just a Dog, 1974; Witch Fear, 1976; Pablo, 1977; The Kershaw Dogs, 1978; The Last Summer, 1979; Blackface Stallion, 1980; Love Forever, 1981; Dancing Horses, 1981; Hari's Pigeon, 1982; Rafa's Dog, 1983; Jesus as Told by Mark, 1983; The Dog at the Window, 1984; As Helen Santos: Caleb's Lamb, 1984; If Only..., 1987 *Honours:* Matthew Arnold Memorial Prize, 1952, 1953; Carnegie Medal, Commended, 1966; Daughter of Mark Twain, 1969; Dutch Silver Pencil Howad, 1978. *Hobby:* Classical Music. *Address:* c/o Century Hutchinson, Brookmount House, 62/65 Chandos Place, Covent Garden, London WC2N 4NW, England.

GRIGSON Jane, b. 13 Mar. 1928, Gloucester, England. Food Writer. m. Geoffrey Grigson, died 1985, 1 daughter. *Education:* BA, honours, Newnham College, Cambridge. *Appointment:* Cookery Correspondent, Observer Magazine, 1968-. *Publications:* Charcuterie & French Prok Cookery, 1967; Good Things, 1971; Fish Cookery, 1973; English Food, 1974, revised 1979; The Mushroom Feast, 1975; Jane Grigson's Vegetable Book, 1978; Food with the Famous, 1979; Jane Grigson's Fruit Book, 1982; Observer Guide to European Cookery, 1983; Observer Guide to British Cookery, 1984. *Memberships:* British Culinary Institute; Guild of Food Writers; Associate, Newnham College. *Honours:* Glenfiddich Trophy, 1978, 1982; André Simon Award, 1978, 1982. *Address:* Broad Town Farmhouse, Broad Town, Swindon, Wiltshire SN4 7RG, England.

GRIGSON Sophie, b. 19 June 1959, Wiltshire, England. Cookery Writer. *Education:* BSc., Honours, 1982. *Appointments:* Cookery Writer, London Evening Standard (Daily Column); Cookery Writer, Sunday Express Magazine. *Publications:* Food for Friends, 1987; Contributor to: Sunday Telegraph Magazine; Observer; Taste, TV Appearances: BBC-Food and Drink programme, Day Time Live, Granada-This Morning. *Membership:* Treasurer, Guild of Food Writers. *Address:* c/o London Evening Standard, 118 Fleet Street, London EC4, England.

GRIMES Rita Charlotte, b. 29 May 1923, San Francisco, California, USA. Publisher. m. Philip Stanford Grimes, 26 Dec. 1947. 2 daughters. *Education:* Graduate, Riverside Business College, 1941; Studied, University of California, Los Angeles, 1944-45; University of California at Berkeley, 1946-47. *Appointments:* Manager personal/financial affairs, Retired Naval Officer, 1978; Exec Dir, Occidental Pub Co, 1978; Coordinator, American Lives Endowment, 1980; Exec Sec, Health Organ Bus Systems, 1981; Consultant, Linwood Realty & Fina Services, 1982; Designer, Editor, Publisher, Portola Valley District Newsletter; Designer, Editor, Publisher, Medical & Dental Record Books. *Memberships:* Constituent Member, International Union for Health Education; Voting Member, National Council on Patient Information & Education; Participating Member, Viewer Advisory Council, San Francisco TV Channel 4 KRON. *Honour:* Action-in-Education, National School Boards Assn, 1962. *Hobbies:* Horses; Design; Gardening. *Address:* Medical Records Pub Co, Post Office Box 8545, Stanford, California 94309, USA.

GRIMMOND Arlene Patricia, b. 3 July 1944, Guyana. Physician. *Education:* BS, Zoology/Chemistry 1966-70, MD 1980, Howard University, Washington, DC, USA. *Appointments:* Teacher, Sacred Heart RC School, Georgetown, Guyana, 1962-66; Lab Asst, University of West Indies, Mena, Jamaica, West Indies, 1970-74; Intern in Surgery, DC General Hospital, Washington, DC, USA, 1980-81; Resident in Diag Radiology, Howard University Hospital, 1981-84; Resident in Nuclear Medicine, University of Connecticut; Affil Hospital of Connecticut, 1985-87. Private Practice, Washington DC, 1985- *Publications:* Numerous publications to professional journals. *Memberships:* American Assoc of Women Radiologists; American Medical Assoc; National Assoc of Female Executives; Society of Nuclear Medicine. *Honours:* Government Award, 1956; Alumni Scholarship for Medicine, Howard College of Medicine, 1977-78. *Hobbies:* Gardening; Sewing. *Address:* 1431 Crittenden St NW, Washington, DC 20011-4338, USA.

GRIMOND Laura Miranda, b. 13 May 1918, London, England. m. Joseph Grimond (now Lord Grimond of Firth), 31 May 1938. 3 sons, 1 daughter (1 son dec. 1966). *Education:* Private; Schwarzwald Gymnasium, Vienna, Austria, 1933-34; College Sevigne, Paris, France, 1934-35. *Appointments:* Contributed regular column, Guardian newspaper, 1965-69; Contested West Aberdeenshire, Liberal Party, 1970; Magistrate, Richmond, Surrey, 1954-59; Honorary Sherriff, Kirkwall, 1976; Member, Orkney Islands Council (rep. Harray of Firth), 1974-82; Chairman, Orkney Islands Council, Housing Committee, 1974- 76; Services Committee, 1979-81; Member, Ancient Monuments Board for Scotland, 1979; President, Women's Liberal Federation (England & Wales), 1984-86; Member SDP-Liberal Alliance Commission on Defence & Disarmament (Report 1986). *Address:* Old Manse of Firth, Kirkwall, Orkney, Scotland.

GRINDROD Muriel Kathleen, b. 4 Feb. 1902, Oxford, England. Writer; Translator. *Education:* BA Honours, Girton College, Cambridge, 1921-24; Sorbonne, Paris, France, 1925. *Appointments:* Staff, Royal Institute of International Affairs, 1927-29 and 1930-62. *Publications:* The Rebuilding of Italy, 1955; Italy, 1964, 1966; Italy, 1968. *Memberships:* Royal Institute of International Affairs; British-Italian Society, Executive Committee and Editor of the Society's periodical, Rivista. *Honours:* OBE 1962; Commandatore al Merito della Repubblica Italiana, 1973. *Hobby:* Travel, especially to

Italy. *Address:* 45 Lancaster Grove, London NW3 4HB, England.

GRISE Catherine Margaret, b. 30 Apr. 1936, Midland, Canada. University Professor/French Literature. m. Cameron Tolton, 15 Aug 1970, 1 daughter. *Education:* BA, 1959, MA 1960, PhD, 1964, University of Toronto. *Appointments:* Lecturer, 1964-65, Assisstant Professor 1965-70, Associate Professor 1970-77, Professor 1977-, University of Toronto. *Publications:* Two books; numerous articles in professional journals. *Memberships:* MLA; Canadian Association of University Teachers; University of Toronto Faculty Association. *Honours:* Canada Council Pre-Doctoral Fellowship, 1962-63; Recipient, various other honours & awards. *Hobbies:* Travel; Films. *Address:* University of Toronto, 7 Kings College Circle, Toronto, Ontario, Canada M6P 2U8.

GROBELNY Lori Jo-Ann, b. 14 June 1954, New Brunswick, New Jersey, USA. Manufacturing Executive. *Education:* BA, English Literature, Douglass College, Rutgers University, 1976. *Appointments:* Production Manager, North American Container Corporation (corrugated boxes), 1976-; Director, Housing Capital Corporation, 1984-; Director, Industrial Capital Corporation, 1985-. *Memberships:* Douglass College Alumnae Association; Republican National Committee. *Hobbies:* Classical music; Designing & working needlecraft & other crafts; Gourmet cooking; Model trains; Stock Market investments. *Address:* 1 Apple Street, Edison, New Jersey 08817, USA.

GROCEK Matilda A, b. 18 Feb. 1923, Hoboken, New Jersey, uSA. Library Director. m. 18 Nov. 1956, 1 son, 2 daughters. *Education:* AA, Honours, Orange County Community College, 1961; BA, Dinstinction, 1964, MLS, Honours, 1967, New York State University, Albany. *Appointments:* Director, Monroe Free Library, 1958-61; Director, Tuxedo Park Library, 1963-76; Library Consultant, Tuxedo Junior Free School, 1967-69; President, CEO, LRA Inc., Monroe, 1968-. *Publications:* Tuxedo Park Library: Social Aspects of Growth; Library Services for Committing Students; The Augusta Tract: A Historicla Survey; Benedict Arnold: Readers Guide & Bibliography; Orange County, NY: Readers Guide & Bibliography; Love is a Challenge: A philosophy. *Memberships:* Directors Association, RCLS, president 1967-70; Orange County Historical Society, Charter Member; many other professional organisations. *Honours:* Excellence in Scholarship Award, 1962; Idiom Poetry Award of the Year, 1965; Honorary Doctorte, Colorado State Christian College. *Hobbies:* Needlepoint; Country & Jazz Guitar; Biblical Studies; Philosophy; Reading. *Address:* Dunderberg Road, Monroe, NY 10950, USA.

GROGAN Valerie Margaret, b. 18 Sept. 1934, Sydney, Australia. District President, St John Ambulance Australia (NSW). m. Peter Rex Grogan, 21 Aug. 1959, 1 daughter. *Education:* BA, University of Sydney, Australia, 1956. *Appointments:* Secondary School Teacher, Presbyterian Ladies; College, Pymble, 1957-59; Syndey Church of England Girls' Grammar School, Redlands, 1960-61; New South Wales Supreme Court Associate to the Hon Mr Justice Jenkyn, 1965-69; President, St John Ambulance Brigade Headquarters Auxiliary, 1969-84; Member 1960-84, Vice President 1969-83, Deputy Chairman 1985-, St John Council for New South Wales; Vice-President, St John Ambulance Brigade New South Wales District Nursing Cadet Division, 1971-82, Cadet Divisions, 1982-84-; District President, St John Ambulance Australia, New South Wales District, 1984-; Member, Advertising Standards Council of Australia, 1986-. *Memberships:* Council Member, Pymble Ladies' College, Sydney, 1977-; President, Tibetan Friendship Group, Australian Section, 1968-; President, Vrindaban Research Institute, Australian Committee, 1975-; Vice President, Australia Tibet Society, 1975-; Vice-President, Australia Tibet Council, 1988-; Parish Council, St Swithun's Church of England, Pymble, 1980-81; Member 1960-79, Honorary Joint Public Relations Officer 1973-79, Sydney Opera House Appeal Fund, Ladies' Committee. *Honours:* SS StJ, 1970; OStJH, 1977; CStJ, 1984. *Hobbies:* Golf; Surfing; Opera; Civic and Charitable activites. *Address:* 39 Pymble Avenue, Pymble, New South Wales 2073, Australia.

GROHSKOPF Bernice, Editor/Writer, 1 daughter. *Education:* BA,MA 1954, English Literature, Columbia University. *Appointments:* Teaching Experience: Writer-in-Residence, Sweet Briar College, 1980-81, 1981-82; Creative Writing Teacher, Montclair Adult School, 1979-80; Writing Workshop, International Woman's Writing Guild, Fall 1979; Creative Writing Teacher, Piedmont Virginia Community College, 1983-84; Guest Speaker, University of Virginia Young Writer's Workshop, 1984; Highlands, North Carolina, Elderhostel, Oct 1984, Oct, Nov 1986, Oct 1987; Current employment: Editorial staff, William James Edition, Harvard University Press, The Correspondence of William James, University Press of Virginia, 1984-; Consulting Editor, Vol 1V United Nations Convention on the Law of the Sea, Center for Oceans Law and Policy, Jan-Apr 1988. *Publications:* Books: Seeds of Time, 1963; From Age to Age, 1968; The Treasure of Sutton Hoo, 1970, English publication 1971, paperback edition, revised 1973; Shadow in the Sun, fiction, 1975; Notes on the Hauter Experiment, 1975, German translation 1978, French edition 1979; Children in the Wind, fiction, 1977; Blood and Roses. 1979; Tell Me Your Dream, fiction, 1981; End of Summer, 1982; Saratoga, 1986. Numerous short stories and articles. *Memberships:* PEN; Authors Guild; Association for Documentary Editing; National Book Critics Circle; Poets and Writers. *Honours include:* Seeds of Time, American Library Association, Notable Book, 1963; The Treasure of Sutton Hoo, New Jersey State Teachers of English Award, 1970; MacDowell Colony Resident Fellowships, 1976, 1978, 1980; Virginia Center for the Creative Arts, Resident Fellowships, 1977, 1979. 1983, 1989; Karolyi Foundation, France, Resident Fellowships, 1979, 1980; New Jersey State Council on the Arts, Fellowship Award, 1980; Andrew Mellon Foundation Faculty Development Grant, 1981. *Address:* 116 Turtle Creek Road 11, Charlottesville, VA 22901, USA.

GRONOWETTER Freda, b. 10 Feb. 1918, Toronto, Canada. Concert Cellist; Teacher; Judge. m. George J. Herman, 15 Dec. 1945. *Publications:* In A Sacred Mood, cello, piano, orchestra; Manual, Basic Cello Instruction; series of films from elementary to artist performances, for teahers & students. *Memberships:* Vice President, Violoncello Society of New York; Chairman, Long Island Junior Cello Club; Music Director, Professor of Music, Southampton College of Long Island University; Music Director, Concert Series, New York; Long Beach Council on the Arts; Music & Art Foundation. *Hobbies:* Interior Decorating; Cooking; Writing. *Address:* 557 West Market St., Long Beach, NY 11561, USA.

GRONOWSKA-SENGER Anna Barbara, b. 26 May 1940, Poznan, Poland. University Professor. m. Marian Senger, 19 Oct. 1963, 1 son. *Education:* MSc in Human Nutrition, 1962; DSc, 1969; Dr.habil, 1976; Professor of Natural Science, 1986. *Appointments:* Assistant, 1963-65, Senior Assistant, 1965-67, 1968-70, Assistant Professor, 1970-77, Associate Professor, 1977-86, Department of Technology and Hygiene of Human Nutrition; Assistant, Department of Nutrition, Massachusetts Institute of Technology, USA, 1967-68; Professor, Institute of Human Nutrition, Warsaw Agricultural University, Warsaw, Poland, 1986-. *Publications:* Over 200 publications on vitamin A and carotene utilisation; 5 manuscripts in human nutrition. *Memberships:* President, Polish Society of Nutritional Sciences; GEN; FENS; Secretary, Human Nutrition Committee, Polish Academy of Sciences. *Honours:* Golden Badge of Merit and Golden Cross of Merit, Polonia Restituta. *Hobbies:* Modern paintings; Good music; Contact with nature. *Address:* Institute of Human Nutrition, Warsaw Agriocultural University, ul Nowoursynowska 166, 02-766 Warsaw, Poland.

GROSS Priva B, b. 19 June 1911, Wieliczka, Poland.

Art Historian (Retired). m. Feliks Gross, 1937. 1 daughter, Eva Helena Gross Friedman. *Education:* PhM, Jagiellonian University, Cracow, Poland, 1937; Postgraduate Study, New York University Institute of Fine Arts, USA, 1945-48. *Appointments:* Faculty, 1961-81, Co-chairman, Art and Music Department, 1966-68, Chairman, Art Department, 1968-74, Associate Professor of Art History, 1971-81, Director, College Gallery, 1968-77, Queensborough Community College, City University, New York. *Publications:* Series articles on Polish Artists in USA published in Nowy Swiat, 1941-42; Contributor to Slavonic Encyclopedia; Polish painting and Polish Sculpture, 1949-69; Some Aspects Mediaeval Church Architecture in Poland; Polish Review, 1967. Numerous Reviews and Articles in professional journals. *Memberships:* Board Directors, 1972-76, 1980-82, AAUW; College Art Association of America; Society Architectural Historians; Board Directors, Gallery Association, New York State, 1972-73; New York State Association Junior Colleges; Board Directors, Council, Gallery and Exhibition Directors, 1970-72; Polish Institute Arts and Sciences in America; American Association of University Professors. *Honours:* New York University Scholarship, 1945-47; SUNY Research Foundation Grant, 1967. *Hobby:* Painting. *Address:* 310 West 85th Street, New York, NY 10024, USA.

GROSSINGER Tania, b. 17 Feb. 1937, Evanston, Illinois, USA. Freelance Writer; Public Relations Consultant. *Education:* BA, Brandeis University, Waltham, Massachusetts, 1952-56. *Appointments:* Director of Broadcast Promotion, Playboy Magazine, 1963-69; Director of Broadcast Promotion, Rogers & Gowan PR, 1969-70; Director of Publicity, Stein and Day, Publishing, 1971-72; Self employed, Grossinger Associates, Public Relations, 1972-. *Publications:* Growing up at Grossinger's; Weekend (co-author); The Book of Gadgets; The Great Gadget Catalogue; Travel articles in Better Homes, Gardens, Ladies Home Journal etc. *Memberships:* American Society of Journalists and Authors (Executive Council, Public Relations Committee, Membership Committee). *Hobbies:* Travel writing; Parapsychology. *Address:* 1 Christopher Street, New York City, NY 10014, USA.

GROSSKURTH Phyllis Marguerite, b. 16 Mar. 1924, Toronto, Canada. Professor; Writer. m. Robert McMullan. 2 sons, 1 daughter. *Education:* BA, University of Toronto, Canada; MA, University of Ottawa; PhD, University of London, England. *Publications:* John Addington Symonds: The Woeful Biography, 1964; Havelock Ellis, 1980; Journals of John Addington Symonds, ed, 1984; Melanie Klein, 1986; Margaret Mead, 1989. *Memberships:* PEN International; Toronto Psychoanalytic Society; International Society for Political Psychology. *Honours:* Governor Generals Award for Non Fiction, 1964; Short listed for National Book Award, UK, 1981. *Hobbies:* Gardening; Opera. *Address:* New College, University of Toronto, Toronto, Ontario, Canada M5G 1A1

GROSSMAN Pauline Fried, b. 29 Sept. 1916, DeLray, Michigan, USA. Marriage Counsellor; Clinical Social Worker. m. Sol C. Grossman, 20 June 1939, 2 daughters. *Education:* BA, 1937, MSW, School of Social Work, 1941, Wayne State University; Diplomate, Clinical Social Work. *Appointments:* Senior Psychiatric Social Worker, Ypsilanti State Hospital, 1937-39; Senior Caseworker, Jewish Family Service, 1939-41; Private practice, 1946-; Admissions, School of Social Work, Wayne State University, 1966-68; Casework Supervisor, Oakland Family Service, 1966-86; Consultant, Attorney General Board of Social Workers, Lansing, Michigan, 1981-. *Memberships:* Scholarship Committee Chairman, National Council of Jewish Women, 1960-73; Board of Trustees, Michigan Association of Marriage and Family Therapists; President Elect, Michigan Interprofessional Association, 1987-88; Past President, Maimonides Medical Auxiliary; National Association of Social Workers; Michigan Association of Clinical Social Workers. *Honours:* Headliners Award, Women of Wayne State

University, 1971; Citation for Outstanding Community Service, State of Michigan, 1971; Citation of Recognition of Excellence, Michigan Association of Marriage and Family Therapists. *Hobbies:* Reading; Travel; Swimming. *Address:* 29614 Farmbrook Villa Court, South Field, MI 48034, USA.

GROVES Linda Jane Gamst, b. 30 May 1948, Staton Island, New York, USA. Teacher; Social Worker. m. Gary Lee Groves, 12 Apr. 1969, 1 daughter. *Education:* AA, 1975; BA, 1987. *Appointments:* Substitute Teacher, Chattanooga Public School System, 1980-83; Supervisor, Southern Opinion Associates, 1981-83; Psychiatric Research Associate, Cleveland Community Hospital, 1984-86; Director, Social Service, part-time; Teacher, new Avenue Education Centre, 1988-. *Publications:* Articles in professional journals. *Membership:* Menninger Foundation. *Honour:* National Leadership Award, 1989. *Hobbies:* Creaive Writing; Social Work; Teaching; Antiques. *Address:* 3053 Knollwood Avenue, La Verne, CA 91750, USA.

GROVES Sharon Sue Hodge, b. 25 Apr. 1944, Springfield, USA. Elementary Teacher. m. Donald L. Groves, 20 July 963. *Education:* AB, Drury College, 1966; MEd., Druce College, 1969. *Appointments:* Assistant Instructor, Drury College, 1969-76; Springfield Public Schools, 1966-. *Publications:* Booklet: Modeling Effective Practices: Geometry & Computation, 1987; papers, and articles. *Memberships:* Springfield Education Association, President; Missouri State Teachers Association; Association for Childhood Education International; Association for Supervision & Curriculum Development; National Council of Teachers of Mathematics. *Honours:* Honorary PTA Life Membership, 1981; Fremont Teacher of Year, 1989; Extra Mile Award for Springfield Public Schools, 1989. *Hobbies:* Horseriding; Showing Ccocker Spaniels; Sewing. *Address:* Rt. 7 Box 374, Springfield, MO 65802, USA.

GROWE Joan Anderson, b. 28 Sept. 1935, Minneapolis, Minnesota, USA. Minnesota Secretary of State. 3 sons, 1 daughter. *Education:* BS, St Cloud State University, 1956; Cert in Spl Edn, University of Minnesota, 1964; Executive Management Program State & Local Government, Harvard University, 1979. *Appointments:* Elementary Teacher Public School, Bloomington, Minnesota, 1956-58; Teacher for Exceptional Children, Elementary Public Schools St Paul, 1964-65; Special Education Teacher, St Anthony, 1965-66; Member, Minnesota House of Representatives, 1973-74; Secretary of State of Minnesota, 1975- *Memberships:* Executive Council Minnesota State Board Investment; Candidate US Senate, 1984; Board Member: Epilepsy Support Program (ESP), Great Minneapolis Council Girl Scouts USA; National Association Secs of State; Member: Democratic-Farmer Labor Party; Minnesota Equal Rights Alliance; League of Women Voters; Business & Professional Women, Inc; International Women's Forum, Women's Political Caucus. *Honours:* Recipient Minnesota School Bell Award, 1977; YMCA Outstanding Achievement Award, 1978; Distinguished Alumni Award St Cloud University, 1979; Charlotte Striebel Long Distance Runner Award, Minnesota NOW, 1985. *Hobbies:* Tennis; Skiing; Running. *Address:* Secretary of State's Office, 180 State Office Building, St Paul, MN 55155, USA.

GRUBB Kitty G, Lawyer. m. Larry L. Grubb. *Education:* JD, Cumberland School of Law, 1977; LL.M., Taxation, New York University, 1981. *Appointments:* Principal, McGehee & Grubb, PC, Knoxville, 1986-. *Publications:* Author, many articles in professional journals; TV and Radio appearances; Lecturer. *Memberships Include:* East Tennessee Association of Law Women; American, Tennessee, Alabama, Knoxville Bar Associations; Knoxville Zoological Society; many other professional organisations. *Honours:* Winner, Annie P Selwyn Award, 1986; Meritorious Award, Overlook Mental Health Centre Inc., 1986; Certificates of Appreciation, Matrix Inc., Knoxville Women's Centre;

many other honours and awards. *Hobbies:* Scuba Diving; Bridge. *Address:* 4034 Maloney Road, Knoxville, TN 37920, USA.

GRUEN Shirley Schanen, b. 2 Dec. 1923, Port Washington, Wisconsin, USA. Artist. m. Gerald Gruen, 1 Feb. 1947, 1 son, 2 daughters. *Education:* BS, Art Education, University of Wisconsin, 1945; Graduate studies, Los Angeles & Milwaukee. *Appointments:* Instructor, watercolour, portrait painting, Milwaukee Area Technical College, 1970-74; Professional artist, own studio, 1972-. *Creative work includes:* Paintings in 50 national juried shows, 1970-. Paintings in permanent collections: West Bend Fine Arts Museum; City of Milwaukee; West Publishing Company; Wausau Hospital Centre. *Memberships:* Wisconsin Painters & Sculptors; Wisconsin Watercolour Society. *Honours:* Watercolour awards, Chautauqua Art 1970, Pennsylvania Watercolour Society 1985; Purchase awards, Art & Law, St Paul, Minnesota 1980, Milwaukee Arts Commission 1983; 7 awards, Ozaukee Art, 1980-87. *Hobbies:* Sailing; Democratic Politics; Travel. *Address:* 103 East Grand Avenue, Port Washington, Wisconsin 53074, USA.

GRUMMON Phyllis Thompson Haight, b. 13 Oct. 1951, Syracuse, New York, USA. Organisational Psychologist. m. David S. Grummon, 5 Sept. 1981, 1 son, 3 daughters. *Education:* AB, Cornell University, 1973; PhD, University of Michigan, 1982. *Appointments:* Sole proprietor, Haight Associates, management consultants, 1981-87; Programme Manager, Workforce Development, State of Michigan, current. *Publications:* Numerous journal articles, organisational development in workplace. *Memberships:* Past local offices: American Society for Training & Development, Cornell Alumni Association; American Psychological Association; American Academy of Management; National Society for Performance & Instruction. *Honour:* Semi-finalist, international speech competition, Toastmasters International, 1985. *Hobbies:* Backpacking; Cross-country skiing; Baseball; Modern history. *Address:* 314 Kedzie Street, East Lansing, Michigan 48823, USA.

GRUNDY Joan, b. 17 Aug. 1920, Ulverston, Cumbria, England. University Teacher (retired); Professor Emeritus. *Education:* BA 1st class honours, English, 1943, MA, English, with distinction, 1947, University of London. *Appointments:* Assistant Lecturer in English, University of Edinburgh, Scotland, 1947-50; Lecturer in English, University of Liverpool, England, 1950-65; Reader in English, 1965-79, Professor of English Literature, 1979-80, Royal Holloway College, London. *Publications:* The Poems of Henry Constable (editor), 1960; The Spenserian Poets, 1969; Hardy and the Sister Arts, 1979; Contributions to Review of English Studies, Shakespeare Survey, Essays in Criticism. *Memberships:* Association of University Teachers; Thomas Hardy Society; Friends of Dove Cottage. *Honours:* Deccan Scholarship, Bedford College, University of London, 1939; Amy lady Tait Scholarship, Bedford College, 1945. *Hobbies:* Gardening; Walking; Listening to music. *Address:* Rose Cottage, Lamb Park, Rosside, Ulverston, Cumbria LA12 7NR. England.

GRUSOVIN Deirdre Mary, b. 1 Sept. 1938, Sydney, New South Wales, Australia. Deputy Leader of Opposition, NSW Legislative Council; Shadow Minister, Family & Community Services. m. Walter Sylvester Grusovin, 12 May 1962. 4 sons, 3 daughters. *Appointments:* Librarian-in-Charge, Mobile Library Service, Randwick Municipal Council, 1957-62; Managed family pharmacy business, 1962-78; Joined ALP, 1957-, Secretary, Youth Council, 1959-61; First Woman Chair, Legislative Council labour Caucus, 1984; Deputy Chairperson, Parliamentary Labour Caucus, 1985; Member, Federal Social Development Policy Committee, 1986; Member, NSW Administrative Committee; Minister for Consumer Affairs; Assistant Minister for Health; Deputy Leader, Legislative Council, 1986; Junior Vice President, ALP, NSW Branch, 1987; Minister for Small Business, 1987; Re-elected, Legislative Council, Deputy Leader of the Opposition in the Legislative Council, 1988-; Shadow Minister for Family and Community Affairs. *Address:* Parliament House, Macquarie Street, Sydney NSW 2001, Australia.

GU Zhi-Ping, b. 13 May 1937, Shanghai, China. Professor. m. Wang Hong, 26 Dec. 1967, 1 daughter. *Education:* MD, Shanghai First Medical University, 1960; PhD, 1964. *Appointments:* Shanghai Institute of Materia Medica, 1964-78, 1981-; Worcester Foundation for Experimental Biology, 1979; Population Council, Centre for Biomedical Research, 1979-81. *Publications:* Devloped New Contraceptive, Anordrin; Study on a Male Contraceptive, Gossypol; etc. *Memberships:* Society of Family Planning; China Medical Association, Standing Committee; Shanghai Society of Planned Parenthood Research, Deputy Secretary-General; Society of Reproductive Biology; Chinese Zoology Association, Council Member. *Honours:* Various awards from Planned Parenthood Committee of China. *Address:* Shanghai Institute of Materia Medica, Academia Sinica, 319 Yue-Yang Road, Shanghai, 200031, Peoples Republic of China.

GUENTHER Brenda Mae Ericson, b. 27 Mar. 1960, Kansas, USA. Financial Administrator. m. Eric Jerome Guenther, 3 Sept. 1983, 1 daughter. *Education:* BS, Kansas State University, 1982. *Appointments:* Koch Industries, 1982-83; Western Insurance Companies, 1983-86; Lincoln National, 1986-. *Memberships:* American Institute of CPA's; National Association of Accountants; Uniontown Future Farmers of America. *Honours:* Blue Key, 1981-82; Block and Bridle Senior Scholarship, 1982; CPA1985. *Hobbies:* Gardening; Sewing. *Address:* Route 1, Mapleton, KS 66754, USA.

GUERCIA Rosemarie C, b. 8 Mar. 1926, Brooklyn, New York, USA. Deputy Commissioner of Health; Physician. m. Anthony Thomas Guercia, 26 June 1949. 2 daughters. *Education:* BS, Queens College, Flushing, 1946; MD, NY Medical College, New York, 1950; MPA, CW Post College, LIU Greenvale, New York, 1979. *Appointments:* Assistant Pediatrician, City Hospital, Elmhurst, New York, 1955-58; Private Practice, Pediatrics, 1956-74; Physician, New York City Department of Health, 1953-74; Nassau County Department of Health, 1962-; Deputy Commissioner of Health, Nassau County, 1981-. *Memberships:* NY State Public Health Association; American Association of Public Health Physicians; American College of Preventive Medicine; American Public Health Association; American Red Cross, Nassau Chapter; Board of Directors, Health Systems Agency. *Honours:* Pi Alpha Alpha National Honour Society for Public Affairs and Administration, 1978-79; Citation, Office of the County Executive (Nassau County), 1987. *Hobbies:* Boating; Snorkelling; Skiing; Travelling. *Address:* 30 Birchwood Park Drive, Jericho, NY 11753, USA.

GUERON Judith Mitchell, b. 8 May 1941, New York City, USA. Economist. m. Henri Gueron, 29 Sept. 1963, 2 daughters. *Education:* BA summa cum laude, Radcliffe College, 1963; MA 1967, PhD 1971, Harvard University. *Appointments include:* Research Director 1974-78, Executive Vice President, Research & Evalution 1978-86, President 1986-, Manpower Demonstration Research Corporation. *Publications include:* Lessons from a Job Guarantee: Youth Incentive Entitlement Pilot Project, 1984; Lessons from Managing the Supported Work Demonstration, 1984; Reforming Welfare with Work, 1987. *Memberships:* American Economic Association; Association for Public Policy Analysis & Management; Boards of Directors: Alcoa, Independent Sector. *Honour:* Myrdal Prize, evaluation & practice, 1988. *Address:* 285 Central Park West, Apt. 8W, New York, NY 10024, USA.

GUILEY Rosemary Ellen, b. 8 July 1950, Fort Lauderdale, Florida, USA. Writer. m. 20 Mar. 1977. *Education:* BA Communications, University of Washington in Seattle, 1973. *Appointments:* Journalist, The Columbian (Vancouver), The Oregonian (Portland),

UPI (Dallas), 1973-78; Editor, Adweek Magazines, New York City, 1979-81; Editor, Internal Communications, IBM, White Plains, 1981-82; Self-employed Writer, 1982-. *Publications:* The Encyclopedia of Witches and Witchcraft, 1989; Psychic Spawn, 1987; Career Opportunities for Writers, 1985; Lovelines, 1983; Tales of Reincarnation, 1989. *Memberships:* American Society of Journalists & Authors; Authors Guild; Mystery Writers of America; American Society for Psychical Research; Society for Psychical Research; Academy of Religion & Psychical Research; Wainright House. *Hobbies:* Astronomy; Gardening; Opera; Animal rights; Zen; Yoga. *Address:* 9 Sanford Street, Rye, NY 10580, USA.

GUILFOYLE Margaret Georgina Constance, b. 15 May 1926, Belfast, Northern Ireland. Accountant. m. Stanley Martin Guilfoyle, 20 Nov. 1952, 1 son, 2 daughters. *Appointments:* Senator for Victoria, 1971-83; Minister for Education, 1975, Minister for Social Security, 1975-80, Minister for Finance, 1980-83, Government of Australia. *Memberships:* Fellow, Australian Society of Accountants; Associate, Chartered Institute of Secretaries & Administrators. *Honours:* Dame Commander of the Order of the British Empire, 1980. *Address:* 21 Howard St., Kew, Victoria 3101, Australia.

GUILL Margaret F Lou, b. 18 Jan. 1948, Atlanta, Georgia, USA. Physician. m. Marshall A Guill, 6 July 1973, 1 son, 1 daughter. *Education:* BA, AgnesScott College, 1969; MD, Medical College of Georgia, 1973. *Appointments:* Assistant Professor, 1981-86, Associate Professor, 1986- , Medical College of Georgia. *Memberships:* American Academy of Pediatrics, Fellow; American College of Allergy & Immunology, Fellow; American Academy of Allergy & Immunology, Fellow; Allergy/Immunology Society of Georgia, President; Southest Allergy Association. *Honours:* Alpha Omega Alpha, 1972; Mosby Book Award, 1973; Hall Davidison Award, 1985. *Hobbies:* Tennis; Swimming; Jogging; Family. *Address:* Dept. of Pediatrics, Allergy/Immunology Section, Medical College of Georgia, Augusta, GA 30912, USA.

GUINETTI Giuseppina, b. 9 May 1923, Milan, Italy. Business Executive. m. Paride Guinetti, 16 Nov. 1970, deceased. *Education:* Diploma, Rosa Stampa College, Vercelli, Italy; PhD, Universita Cattolica, Milan. *Appointments:* Founder, Managing Director, Tubi Acciaio E Derivati srl, Milan, Italy, 1950-55; President, TAD SpA, Milan, 1981-87; President, TAD FIN, Milan, 1987-; President, TQ Tubi Qualificati, Milan, 1972- ; Chairman of Board, TAD USA, Houston, Texas, USA, 1979-; Member of Board, TAD Holland, Amsterdam, 1984-; Member of Board, Ct Ceretti & Tanfani, Milan, Italy, 1987-; Member of Board, IPM, Milan, 1980. *Memberships:* Advisory Board, Peggy Guggenheim Collection, Venice; Association Mondiales Femmes Chefs d'Entreprise, Paris; Cercle Foch, Paris; Horticulture Society, London; Annabel's, London; Mark's London; Donne in Carriera, Milan. *Honour:* International Interpetrol prize, 1978. *Hobbies:* Garden and gardening; Music; Painting and art; Literature; Travel. *Address:* Casa Belmonte, Bigogno, 6927 Agra, Switzerland.

GUINN Suzanne Kay, b. 4 Mar. 1944, Kalamazoo, USA. Speech-Language Pathologist. m. Howard Christopher Guinn, 26 Apr. 1968, 1 son. *Education:* BS, Western Michigan University,1 966; MS, Univesity of Wisconsin, Madison, 1967. *Appointments:* Preschool Co-ordinator, Constance Brown Hearing & Speech Centre, 1967; Speech Pathologist, Alaska State Operated Schools, 1968; Speech Language & Preschool Co-ordinator, Fairbanks North Star Borough School District, 1974; Owner, Director, Communicaid, 1988- . *Memberships:* American Speech Language Hearing Association; Alaska Speech Language Hearing Association, President 1974, 1980; Council for Exceptional Children; League of Women Voters; Delta Kappa Gamma. *Honours:* Alpha Lamda Delta, 1968; Leaders of American Elementary & Secondary

Education, 1971; Di Carlo Award, 1983; Frank R. Kleffner Award, 1988. *Hobbies:* Cross Stitch; Antique Collecting; Cross Country Skiing. *Address:* 600 University Ave., Suite 110, Fairbanks, AK 99709, USA.

GULLIVER Pamela Mary, b. 10 Nov. 1942, Thirsk, Yorkshire, England. writes under pen-names Victoria Thirsk (fiction) and Mary Allerton-North (non-fiction). m. 17 Mar. 1962. *Education:* Chorleywood College, Hertfordshire; BA, Open University (Public Administration, 1977); History BA, Reading University, 1979; BA, History/Sociology, 1966. *Appointments:* Company Director; Director, Charity VARVES. *Publications:* Articles in professional journals; Book: Bosminster; Bosminster Callendar, (non-fiction); Biography of Gertie Millar. *Memberships:* Women in Management; Central Berkshire Chamber of Commerce. *Honours:* Bronze Medal, Public Speaking, 1966. *Hobbies:* Charity Work; Writing; Board Games. *Address:* The Neraldage, 35 Northcourt Avenue, Reading RG2 7HE, Berkshire, England.

GUNTHER Marita, b. 15 Sept. 1928, Leipzig, Germany. Voice Teacher; Actress; Singer. *Education:* Diploma, Translation & Interpretation, English, Leipzig Foreign Language College, 1948; Private study. *Appointments Include:* Founder Member, Alfred Wolfsohn Voice Research Centre, with Roy Hart, London, 1960; Founder Member, Roy Hart Theatre, London, 1969; Study & Work with Roy Hart, 1969-75; Actress & Singer, RHT Productions: The Baccae, and The Singer & the Song, Marriage de Lux; Director, Rilke's Cornet; Solo performance, Kurt Weill Songs; Translator, Alfred Wolfsohn's manuscripts, The Bridge, Orpheus; Historical Consultant, films; Teacher, Roy Hart Theatre Association, France, 1975-; Researcher, Teacher, Guest Teacher, theatre groups & individuals, Amsterdam, London, Berlin, Paris, San Francisco; Lecturer, Demonstrator, 7th Annual Conference, National Assocation for Drama Therapy, San Francisco, 1986. *Hobbies:* Literature; Piano; Swimming. *Address:* Roy Hart Theatre, Chateau de Maleragues, Thoiras, 30140 Anduze, France.

GUPTA Uma, b. 15 Feb. 1957, Meerut, India. Research Scientist. *Education:* BA (Hons) 1975, MA 1978, MPhil 1979, PhD 1983, Meerut University. *Appointments:* Research Fellow, UGC Project, 1983-84; Gen Research Fellow, ICSSR, 1986-88; Research Scientist, UGC, 1988-. *Creative works:* Books: Women, Work and Cancer, 1989; Kinesthetic After-Effect: Sex-Related Differences, 1990; Author of numerous research papers in scientific journals; Assistant Editor, Pharmacopsychoecologia, 1988-. *Memberships:* Indian Science Congress Association; Indian Psychological Association; Pharmacopsychoecological Association, Life member, Treasurer. *Hobbies:* Reading historical and literary novels; Singing; Listening to music; Cooking. *Address:* Department of Psychology, Banaras Hindu University, Varanasi 221005, India.

GURD Ruth Sights, b, 17 Sept. 1927, Chicago, Illinois, USA. Professor of Biochemistry. m. Frank Ross Newman Gurd, 12 June 1954, 1 son, 1 daughter. *Education:* BS, University of Michigan, Ann Arbor, 1949; MD, Washington University, St Louis, 1957; Postdoctoral Fellow in Physiology, Cornell University College of Medicine, New York, 1958; Senior Postdoctoral Fellow in Neurochemistry, Department of Chemistry, Indiana University, Bloomington, 1966-71. *Appointments:* Assistant Professor, Associate Professor, then Professor of Biochemistry, Emeritus Professor of Biochemistry Indiana University School of Medicine, Bloomington, 1972-88. *Publications:* Scientific articles in Journal of Biological Chemistry, Proceedings of National Academy of Sciences, Journal of Clinical Investigative Biochemistry, Biophysical Journal. *Memberships:* Biophysical Society; Society for Neuroscience; American Society for Biological Chemistry and Molecular Biology; American Diabetes Association; National Society of Arts and Letters; Kappa Kappa Gamma. *Honours:* Mortarboard, Wyvern, 1946, 1948; NSF Predoctoral Fellow, 1952; Graduate

Research Fellow, Kappa Kappa Gamma, 1952; Fellowship, Washington University School of Medicine, 1953; Life Insurance Medical Research Foundation, 1957. *Hobbies:* Music (keyboard, flute, bassoon); Gardening; Mountain walking. *Address:* 2032 Quail Run Drive, Albuquerque, NM 87122, USA.

GURKE Sharon Elizabeth Ann McCue, b. 4 Apr. 1949, Brooklyn, USA. Commander, US Navy. m. Lee Samuel Gurke, 1977, 2 daughters. *Education:* BA, Molloy College, 1970; MS, University of Southern California, 1977. *Appointments Include:* Various Naval Courses, 1970-74; Commander, naval Air Force Pacific Fleet, 1974-77; First Female Naval Officer Aeronautical Engineering-Duty Officer; Commander, Naval Air Force Pacific Fleet, San Diego, California, 1976-; Quality Assurance Division Officer, Naval Air Station, Miramar, San Diego, California, 1977-78; Avionics Division Officer, Aircraft Intermediate Maintenance Dept., 1978-; Officer in Charge, Naval Aviation Engineering Services Unit, 1980-; Officer in Charge, Naval Aviation Engineering Services Unit, 1980-82; Aircraft Intermediate Maintenance Dept., A/C Intermediate Maintenance Officer, 1982-84; Aircraft Intermediate Maintenance Dept. Naval Station, Rota, Spain, Aircraft Intermediate Maintenance Officer, 1984-; AIMD, Naval Station, Rota, Spain, 1984-86; Commander, Naval Air Systems Command, Air 411, 1986-88; Assistant Production Officer, Naval Air Rework Facility, North Island, San Diego, 1988-. *Publications:* Article in AED/AMD Quarterly; Contributor to All Hands Magazines; Lectures. *Membership:* International Organization of Women Pilots. *Honours:* Winner, Winnifred Quick Collins Award, 1980; Navy Commendation Medals, 1982, 1984; Meritorious Service Medal, 1986. *Hobbies:* Flying; Jogging. *Address:* 1386 Blue Falls Drive, Chula Vista, CA 92010, USA.

GURNEY Pamela Kay, b. 25 Sept. 1948, Joliet, Illinois, USA. Executive Girl Scouting. *Education:* BA, College of St Francis, 1971. *Appointments:* Teacher, Joliet Public Schools, 1972-73; Executive Girl Scouting, Trailways Girl Scout Council, Joliet, 1973-76; Executive Girl Scouting, Michigan Waterways Girl Scout Council, 1976-80; Executive Girl Scouting, Irish Hills Girl Scout Council, Jackson, 1980-. *Memberships:* American Society of Training Directors; American Association of University Women; Association of Girl Scout Executive Staff. *Honour:* Girl Scout Thanks Badge, 1973. *Hobbies:* Oudoor Activities; Sewing; Photography; Slide/Tape Shows. *Address:* 902 Gettysburg, Jackson, MI 49203, USA.

GUTIERREZ Olga, b. 29 Dec. 1928, Buenos Aires, Argentina. Psychiatrist/Consultant (Legal, Child, Adolescent, Adult); Medical Educator. widowed, 1 son. *Education:* PhD, Biochemistry, Pharmacy, 1954, MD, 1967, University of Buenos Aires; Postgraduate Fellow: Pasteur Institute, Paris, France, 1959-60; University of Southern California, USA, 1980-85; Certified Physician and Surgeon, American Board, 1980; Child and Adolescent Psychiatry, 1983, Legal Psychiatry, 1985, University of Southern California, USA; Diplomate, Psychiatry, American Board, 1987; Child and Adolescent Psychiatry, American Board, 1989. *Appointments:* Staff, School of Medicine, University of Buenos Aires, 1954-70; Researcher, Instituto Maranon Non, Madrid, Spain, 1970-71; Associated Researcher, 1971-74, University of Southern California, USA; Staff, Forensic Psychiatrist, Department of Mental Health, Los Angeles, California, 1985-; Child Psychiatrist, University of Southern California Child Clinic, Los Angeles, 1985-; President, Vth International Biochemical Meeting, Spain; Guest, TV medical and psychiatric educational programmes. *Publications:* Numerous scientific contributions to medical journals and presentations at international medical meetings. *Memberships:* Salegni College, University of Southern California; American Medical Association; ABA; Honorary Member: Association of Chemistry, Uruguay; Academy of Pharmacy, Argentina. *Honours:* University of Buenos Aires Award, 1952; School of Medicine Award, 1954; International Research Grant, Institute Pasteur, 1959; International

Grant, University of Buenos Aires, 1964; National Academy of Medicine Award, Argentina, 1966; Junior Chamber Award, 1969; Ford Foundation Grant, 1974; World Health Organization Grant, 1974; American Medical Association Award, 1988. *Hobbies:* Swimming; Sailing; Tennis; Music; Cinema; Theatre; Trips. *Address:* 746 W Adams Boulevard, Los Angeles, CA 90007, USA.

GUTKOWSKA Jolanta, b. 15 Sept. 1939, Warsaw, Poland. University Professor; Researcher. m. Jerzy Gutkowski, 30 Oct. 1964. *Education:* MSc, Warsaw University, 1966; PhD, Universite de Montreal, 1973. *Appointments:* Research Associate, Institute of Bioendocrinology, Montreal, Canada, 1973-75; Associate Director, Clinical Research Institute of Montreal, Laboratory of Biochemistry of Hypertension, 1975-. *Publications:* More than 200 scientific publications in the field of hypertension. *Memberships:* American Heart Association; American Association of Clinical Chemistry; New York Academy of Science; Canadian Clinical Chemist Association. *Honours:* Woman of the Year in Science, 1986; Fellow, Council for High Blood Pressure of American Heart Association, 1986. *Hobbies:* Gardening, growing roses; Travelling; Music. *Address:* Laboratory of Biochemistry of Hypertension, Clinical Research Institute of Montreal, 110 Pine Avenue West, Montreal, Quebec, Canada H2W 1R7.

GUTMAN Judith Mara, b. 22 May 1928, New York City, USA. Writer. m. Herbert Gutman, 18 June 1950, 2 daughters. *Education:* BA, History, Queens College, 1949; MS, Education, Bank St. College of Education, 1958. *Appointments:* Instructor, 1952-53, Consultant, 1953-55, University of Wisconsin; Director, Montefiore Hospital Nursery School, 1954-57; Lecturer, Education, Hunter College, 1958-60; Reporter, Clarkstown News, 1961-63; Script Writer, 1973-78; Consultant, 1976; Guest Curator, International Center of Photography, New York, 1981-82; Writer. *Publications:* Through Indian Eyes, 1982; Buying, 1975; Is America Used Up?, 1973; Lewis Hine: Two Perspectives, 1974; The Making of American Society, Volume I, 1972, Volume 2, 1973; Lewis W. Hine and the American Social Conscience, 1967; The Colonial Venture: An Autobiography of The American Colonies, 1966; articles in numerous magazines and journals ie: Connosseur, The New York Times, Washington Post Book World, After Image. *Memberships:* PEN; Society for Photographic Education; Organization of American Historians; Authors Guild. *Honours:* Recipient, various honours & awards. *Address:* 97 Sixth Avenue, Nyack, NY 10960, USA.

GUTTMAN Helene Nathan, b. 21 July 1930, New York City, USA. Microbiologist/Biochemist. *Education:* BA, Brooklyn College, 1951; AM, Harvard Medical School, 1956; MA, Columbia University, 1958; PhD, Rutgers University, 1960. *Appointments include:* Haskins Laboratories, NYC 1952-64, Goucher College, Maryland & Medical College of Virginia 1960-62; Faculties, New York University 1962-67, University of Illinois (Chicago) 1967-75; National Heart, Lung & Blood Institute, National Institutes of Health, 1975-79; Deputy Director, Science Advisory Board, US Environmental Protection Agency, Washington DC, 1979-80; Science Programme Administrator & Policy Coordinator, Policy Analysis & Coordination Staff Office, Science & Education Administration, U.S. Department of Agriculture, 1980-83; Associate Director, Beltville Human Nutrition Research Centre, Agricultural Research Service, 1983-. *Publications include:* Approx. 75 original scientific articles, book chapters, 2 books, 2 edited books. *Memberships include:* Fellow, American Society of Microbiology, American Association for Advancement of Science, American Institute of Chemists, American Academy of Microbiology, New York Academy of Sciences. *Honours:* Numerous awards, fellowships, scholarships, USA & abroad, including: Thomas Jefferson Murray Award, Theobald Smith Society, 1959; Special award, Deutscher Forschungs Gemeinschaft, 1960; Elected, Royal Society of Chemistry, UK, 1982. *Hobbies:* Gardening; Walking; Metaphysics; Oriental medicine; Photography. *Address:*

Beltsville Human Nutrition Research Centre, ARS/ USDA, BARC-East, Bldg. 308, Room 224, Beltsville, Maryland 20705, USA.

GUTTOWA Alicja Barbara, b. 12 Jan. 1924, Luck, USSR. Biologist. m. Jan Gutt, 25 June 1949, 1 son. *Education:* MSc., 1950, PhD, 1961, University of Warsaw. *Appointments:* Research Worker, University of Warsaw, 1947-50; Assistant, Agricultural High School, Warsaw, 1950-51; Assistant 1954-71, Professor, 1984-85, Director 1985-, Institute of Parasitology. *Publications:* 75 papers in professional journals. *Memberships:* Polish Parasitological Society, Chairman, Warsaw Section, 1964-69; Parasitological Committee of PAS, 1983-88; Editoral Board, Acta Parasitologica Polonica, 1982-88. *Honours:* Gold Service Cross, 1973; Polonia Restituta Cross, 1983; Medal, 25th anniversary of Polish Academy of Science, 1984. *Hobbies:* History; Biographies of Famous People. *Address:* Institute of Parasitology PAN, Pasteura 3, 00-973 Warsaw, Poland.

GUY Mildred Dorothy, b. 16 Apr. 1929, Grunswick, Georgia, USA. Retired Educator. m. Charles H. Guy, 9 Aug. 1956, divorced, 1 daughter. *Education:* BA, 1949; MA, Alanta Univesity, 1952. *Appointments:* Chairman, Social Studies, L.S. Ingraham H.S. Sparta, 1950-56; Tacher, North Junior H.S., 1958-84; Trustee, Pikes Peak Community College, 1976-83. *Publications:* Originator, Annual Minority Student Recognition Programme, School District NO. 11, 1979. *Memberships:* Life Member, NEA; ASALH; AAUW; NAACP. *Honours:* Recipient, numerous honours and awards. *Hobbies:* Reading; Hiking; Travel; Dancing; Singing; Piano. *Address:* 3132 Constitution Avenue, Colorado Springs, CO 80909, USA.

GUZMAN Loreto de Galinato, b. 13 June 1918, Urdaneta, Pangasinan, Philippines. Physician; Medical Mission Sister. *Education:* AA 1939,MD 1947, Santo Tomas University, Manila. *Appointments:* Resident Physician, Urdaneta Emergency Hospital 1948-50, Holy Family Hospital, Rawalpindi, Pakistan 1953-54; Doctor-in-Charge, St Michael's Hospital, Mymensingh, Bangladesh, 1955-60; Council, Philippine Foundation for Medical Mission Sisters, San Jose Batangas, Philippines, 1961-65; Pioneer, Holy Family Hospital, Bongao, Tawi-Tawi, Sulu, Philippines, 1966-75; College Physician, Minanao State University, Tawi-Tawi, 1971-75; Clinic Physician 1985-, In-Charge Nutrition Programme 1986-, Ephpheta Inc. for the Blind, Quezon City. *Memberships:* Society of Catholic Medical Missionaries; Philippine Medical Association; Philippine Women's Medical Association; PIMS Medic Club. *Honours:* Valedictorian, Vocation Department, Pangasinan Secondary School, 1937; Awards, Humanitarian Services, Government of Tawi-Tawi, Sulu 1975, Bagumbayan Barangay Council, Quezon City 1985; Tandang Sora Award, Banyaning Filipino Foundation, 1981. *Hobbies:* Gardening; Volleyball; Javelin throwing. *Address:* Medical Mission Sisters, 30 F. Collantes Street, Loyola Heights, Quezon City, Philippines 1108.

GWIAZDA Caroline Louise, b. 6 Jan. 1941, Cleveland, USA. Principal; Curriculum Consultant. m. Stanley John Gwiazda, 30 June 1962, 2 sons, 2 daughters. *Education:* BA, 1978; MEd., 982; EdD, 1988. *Appointments:* Teacher, 1977-79; Reading Consultant, 1979-85; Assistant Principal, Case School, 1985-87; Principal, Bolton School, 1987-89. *Publications:* Articles in professional journals. *Memberships:* Phi Delta Kappa; International Reading Association, Founder President IRA Cleveland Council; Cleveland Council of Administrators & Supervisors, Executive Board. *Honours:* Dedication of Yearbook, 1984; Founder, Greater Cleveland Chapter, Intenational Reading Association. *Hobbies:* Gardening; Reading; Exercising; History. *Address:* 8595 Broadview Road, Broadview Heights, OH 44147, USA.

GWIN Wiliviginia Faszhianato, b. 2 Feb. 1954, Mobile, Alabama, USA. Academic Counsellor; Advisor. *Education:* BA, 1975, MS, 1978, Alabama State University. *Appointments:* Director, Services, Upjohn Healthcare Services, 1979-80; Programme Director, American Cancer Society, 1975-79; Academic Counsellor, University of South Alabama, 1980-. *Publications:* Articles in professional journals. *Memberships:* Alpha Kappa Alpha; Kappa Delta Pi; Omicron Delta Kappa; Alabama Association of Counselling & Development. *Honours:* Alabama Literary Award, 1973. *Hobbies:* Jazz; Afro-American Art; History; Literature. *Address:* PO Box 5026, 3358 Clubhouse Road, Mobile, AL 36605, USA.

H

HABLUTZEL Margo Lynn, b. 16 Dec. 1961, St Louis, Missouri, USA. Attorney. *Education:* AB, University of Chicago, 1983; JD, Chicago-Kent College of Law, 1986. *Appointments:* Computer Consultant, 1984-89; Law Clerk, 1985; Legal Writing Instructor, University of Oregon School of Law, 1986-87; ABA/net Project Co-Ordinator, American Bar Association, Chicago, 1987-89; Judicial Clerk, Illinois Appellate Court, 1989-. *Publications:* Articles in professional journals. *Memberships:* Chair, Chicago Bar Association Young Lawyers Section Committee on Legal Services for the Disabled, 1987-89; Director, Chicago Bar Association Young Lawyers Section, 1989-; Illinois State, Chicago, Women's Bar and American Bar Associations. *Hobbies:* Reading; Sailing; Camping; Hiking; Swimming; Puzzles. *Address:* 211 East Ohio Street, Suite 710, Chicago, IL 60611, USA.

HACK Linda, b. 30 Nov. 1949, Chicago, USA. Divorced. *Education:* MA, Roosevelt University, 1975; JD, DePaul University, 1979. *Appointmnts:* Administrative Law Judge, Illinois Dept. of Labor, 1979-80; Litigation Associate, Law Offices F Ward Steinbach, 1981-83; Civil Litigation Partner, Hack & Derer, 1983-88; Magistrate, County of Dallas, 1987- *Publications:* Patent Law Annual, What is Alternate Dispute Resolution, 1983; articles in Mediation Quarterly. *Memberships:* National Conference of Women's Bar Association, Vice President; Academy of Family Mediators, Legislation Chair; National Woman's Lawyer Caucus; SPIDR Dallas Civil Service Board; American, Illinois Bar Associations; American Trial Lawyers Association; Judicature Society; State Bar of Texas. *Hobbies:* Theatre; Travel. *Address:* PO Box 595314, Dallas, TX 75359, USA.

HACKER Rose, b. 3 Mar. 1906, London, England. Writer; Lecturer. m. Mark Gould Hacker, 9 Sept. 1930, 2 sons. *Education:* Private, London, England. *Appointments:* Dress Designer, 1924-33; Marriage Guidance Counsellor, 1948-72; Greater London Councillor, 1973-77. *Publications include:* Books: Telling the Teenagers 1957, 1960, 1961, 1966, etc; The Opposite Sex, 1960, 1961, 1963, 1965, 1967, 1970; You and Your Daughter, 1964, and many others. *Memberships include:* Health Authorities; Social Service Committees; Education Authorities; Chair of School and Hospital Governing Bodies; Mental Health Charities, Founder of Camden MIND, 1968; President Progressive League, 1965-68, etc. *Hobbies:* Music; Art (sculpture); Travel. *Address:* 19 West Hill Court, Millfield Lane, London N6 6JJ, England.

HACKFORTH-JONES Penelope Beatrix, b. Connecticut, USA. Actress; Writer. *Education:* St Catherines, Toorak, Victoria, Australia; National Institute of Dramatic Art. *Appointments:* Has appeared in numerous productions on stage and television including: Sophy in Tom Jones, Perth Playhouse; Young Girl in Out of the Crocodile, Perth Playhouse; Bandwagon, Hobart Theatre Royal; Mrs Druge in The Audition, Hobart Theatre Royal; Contrabandits, ABC Television; Man of Property, Channel Seven; Love Story, ABC Television, Melbourne; Lead role of Jessica Johnson in Cash and Company and Tandara, Homestead Films; Sustaining role in A Country Practice, JNP Productions; Has appeared in several films. *Membership:* Actors Equity, Film sub-committee. *Honours:* Queen's Jubilee Medal for services to the Arts; Australian Film and Television Award, Best Lead Actress in a television series, 1976. *Hobbies:* Gardening; Ceramics. *Address:* c/o Shanahan Management, 72 Queen Street, Woollahra, New South Wales 2025, Australia.

HADEN-GUEST Jean (Lady), b. 1 Mar. 1921, New York, USA. Producer. m. Lord Haden-Guest, 29 Dec. 1945. 2 sons, 1 daughter. *Education:* New York

University, 1939-40; New York School of Social Research, 1940-42. *Appointments:* Production Assistant, The Playwrights Co (Frederick Brisson Prod.), 1953-55; Director, American National Theatre & Academy, 1955-69; Vice President, Wender & Associates (Talent Agency), 1970-76; Vice President, Talent & Casting, CBS, 1976-86. *Memberships:* TV Academy; Women in Film. *Honour:* Office Scientific Research & Development, 1941-42 for work on wartime poison gas project, Cornell Medical School at New York Hospital. *Address:* Apt 308, 122 Ocean Park Blvd, Santa Monica, CA 90405, USA.

HAEGER-ARONSEN Birgitta, b. 13 Oct. 1926, Malmo, Sweden. Professor. m. Karl-Fredrik Aronsen, 2 Oct. 1954, 1 son, 3 daughters. *Education:* MD, University of Lund, Sweden, 1960; Elected Professor, Occupational Medicine, University of Lund, 1980. *Appointments:* Various positions, University Hospitals of Malmo & Lund, 1953-70; Assistant Physician, Occupational Medicine, University Hospital of Lund, 1970-77; Consultant Physician, Labour Inspectorate, Malmo, 1973; Head, Occupational Medicine, Universiy Hospital, Malmo, 1977; Expert, Occupational Medicine, Insurance Court of Sweden, 1979; Member, Scientific Council, Swedish Board of Health & Welfare, 1981. *Memberships Include:* Swedish Medical Association; International Commission on Occupation Health; Swedish Association of Occupational Health Physicians. *Hobbies:* Art; Literature; Handicraft. *Address:* Ostanvag 62, S-216 19 Malmo, Sweden.

HAENDEL Ida, b. 15 Dec. 1928, Chelm, Poland. Concert Violinist. *Education:* Warsaw Conservatorium (Gold Medal, aged 7); private Teachers: Carl Flesch, & Georges Enesco. *Appointments:* British Debut: Queen's Hall, London, Brahms Concerto with Henry Wood, 1937; Performances with: Beecham, Celibidache, Solti, Klemperer, Szell, Barenboim, Mata, Pritchard, Rattle; accompanied British Orchestras on tours to China, Hong Kong, Australia, etc. *Publications:* Autobiography, Woman with Violin, 1970; Records for EMI. *Honours:* Huberman Prize, 1935; Sibelius Medal, Sibelius Society of Finland, 1982. *Address:* c/o Harold Holt Limited, 31 Sinclair Road, London W14 0NS, England.

HAFTER Daryl Maslow, b. 17 Jan. 1935, Elizabeth, New Jersey, USA. Professor. m. Monroe Z Hafter, 18 June 1957. 1 son, 1 daughter. *Education:* BA, Smith College, 1956; MA 1958, PhD 1964, Yale University. *Appointments:* Lecturer, University of Michighan, 1966-67; Assoc Professor 1976-81, Professor 1981-, Eastern Michigan University; Director of Women's Studies, 1982-84. *Publications:* Artisans, Drudges & The Problem of Gender in Pre-Industrial France, 1985. *Memberships:* Society for History of Technology, Executive Council 1985-90, Advisory Council 1980-85; American Historical Assn; Society for French History; Michigan Women's Studies Assn; Centre Internat D'Etude Des Textiles Anciens. *Honours:* National Science Foundation Research Grants, 1984-86; American Council of Learned Soc Grant-in-Aid, 1984; National Endowment for Humanities, Travel to Collections, 1984; Michigan Council for Humanities, 1983; American Philosophical Society Research Grant, 1975; Eleutherian Mills-Hagley Foundation Grant-in-Aid, 1974; Eastern Michigan University Faculty Research Grants, 1979, 1980, 1984, 1989. *Hobbies:* Travel; Art; Textiles; Early technology. *Address:* Department of History & Philosophy, Eastern Michigan Unviersity, Ypsilanti, Michigan 48197, USA.

HAGEMAN Anna Robbins, b. 24 May 1920, New York City, USA. Writer. m. William Charles Hageman, 7 July 1956, 2 daughters. *Education:* University of Pennsylvania, 1937-39; Beaver College, 1939-40. *Appointments:* Staff Head, KYW Feature Drug 1951-52; Market research analyst & Acting Research Director, Philadelphia Inquirer newspaper, 1952-56; Freelance writer & partner, Robbins & Hageman (Market and Editorial Research Co) 1956-; Panelist and Leader, writers symposia & workshops, Teen Arts Festivals, 1981-84. *Publications include:* Book, Love Myth, 1990.

Fiction including: Boat Club (Reader's Digest); Articles including Interfaith Laymen (NJ Living magazine), 1987; Making Contact (Women's Newspaper), 1987; Hearts in Crisis (Lady's Circle magazine), 1988. *Memberships:* University of Pennsylvania Alumni Association; Contact, USA & Gloucester County. *Hobbies include:* Publicity & telephone volunteer, Contact, national & local. *Address:* Sewell, New Jersey 08080, USA.

HAGER Susan, b. 19 Oct. 1944, Washington, District of Columbia, USA. Founder & President, Hager Sharp, Inc. m. C Eric Hager, 3 Nov. 1967. 1 daughter. *Education:* BA, Sociology, Brescia College, Owensboro, Kentucky, 1966. *Appointments:* Program Director, National Center for Voluntary Action, Washington, DC, 1971-73; Founder and President, Hager Inc, Washington, DC. *Creative work:* Guest Lecturer, Kennedy Institute of Politics, Harvard University; Keynote Speaker, Honours Convocation and Visiting Professor, Entrepreneurship Program, Brescia College. *Memberships:* National Association of Women Business Owners; Trustee, Democratic National Committee; National Advisory Council, US Small Business Administration; Member, Board of Directors, teh Greater Washington Board of Trade; Chairperson, Small Business Advisory Council, US Treasury; Member, Board of Directors, Leadership Washington. *Honours:* Businesswoman of the Year Award, National Association of Women Business Owners, 1985; Outstanding Young Woman of America, 1978-79; Advocate of the Year Award, National Association of Women Business Owners, 1987; Recipient, three leadership scholarships, Brescia College. *Address:* Hager Sharp Inc, 1101 17th Street NW Suite 1001, Washington, DC 20036, USA.

HAGERTY Polly Martiel Jerabek, b. 17 Aug. 1946, Joliet, Illinois, USA. Real Estate Commercial Banker. m. Theodore John Hagerty, 12 Feb. 1972. *Education:* BS, Elementary Education, Midland Lutheran College, Nebraska, 1968; MEd, University of Illinois, 1977; MBA, Finance, University of Texas, 1986. *Appointments:* Elementary school teacher, Michigan & Illinois, 1968-72, 1974-77; Systems clerk, US Army, Pentagon, Washington DC, 1972-74; Recruitment, SOHIO, Cleveland, Ohio, 1977-78; Real estate banker, Vice President NCN Bank, Texas, Houston, 1981-88; Real estate commercial banker, Vice president, Citibank (Arizona) Tucson, 1988-. *Membership:* National Association of Female Executives. *Hobbies:* Jazzercise; Needlework; Skiing. *Address:* 5921 North Oracle Road, 278, Tucson, Arizona 85704, USA.

HAGLUND Ann-Cathrine, b. 24 Aug. 1937, Sweden. Member of Parliament. m. Finn Haglund, 1957, 1 son, 2 daughters. *Education:* MA, languages. *Appointments:* Teacher, 1961-79; Member of Parliament, Moderate Party, 1979-. *Publications:* Political booklets & articles. *Membership:* President, Moderate Women's Association. *Address:* V Bangatan 24, 69235 Kumla, Sweden.

HAHS Sharon Kidwell, b. 9 Sept. 1947, Washington, Indiana, USA. University Dean. m. Billy G. Hahs, Jr, 1 Jan. 1969, 2 daughters. *Education:* BA, Chemistry, Illinois Wesleyan University, 1970; MS 1972, PhD 1974, Inorganic Chemistry, University of New Mexico. *Appointments:* Assistant, Associate, & full Professor of Chemistry 1974-84, Special Assistant to Vice President for Academic Affairs 1982-83, Metropolitan State College, Denver, Colorado; Academic Dean, School of Humanities & Sciences, University of South Carolina, Spartanburg, 1984-. *Creative work includes:* 8 publications, inorganic chemistry & chemical education; 9 presentations, regional & national conferences; 11 workshops, development of reasoning skills; 25 video tapes, chemical concepts. *Memberships:* American Chemical Society; National Science Teachers Association; Council 1986-89, Vice President 1989-, South Carolina Academy of Science; SC Science Council. *Honours:* Biographical recognitions. *Hobbies:* History of science; Music; Sewing; Gardening; Antiques. *Address:* School of Humanities & Sciences, University of South Carolina, 800 University Way, Spartanburg, SC 29303, USA.

HAIGHT Mary Rowland, b. 28 Feb. 1938, Los Angeles, California, USA. University Lecturer. *Education:* BA 1961, MA 1964, BPhil 1966, Oxford University; MA, University of California, USA, 1964. *Appointments:* Assistant Lecturer in Philosophy 1966-69, Lecturer 1969-, University of Glasgow, Scotland. *Publications:* Book: A Study of Self-Deception, 1980; Various articles in professional journals. *Memberships:* Mind Association (Great Britain); Aristotelian Society (Great Britain); British Society of Aesitiotics; Scots Philosophical Society; American Philosophical Association (International Associate). *Honour:* Woodrow Wilson Fellowship, 1961. *Hobbies:* Drawing, cartooning; Writing poetry; Designing games and puzzles; Travelling. *Address:* Dept of Philosophy, The University, Glasgow G12 8QQ, Scotland.

HAIKAL Fayza, b. 11 Apr. 1938, Cairo, Egypt. Professor of Egyptology. m. Dr Mohamed Abdel Halim, 10 Apr. 1965. 1 son, 1 daughter. *Education:* Bacchalaureat, Lycée Francais du Caine, 1956; BA, Egyptology, Faculty of Arts, Cairo University, 1960; DPhil, St Anne's College, Oxford, England, 1965. *Appointments:* Assistant Egyptologist, Centre of Documentation on Ancient Egypt, 1961-62; Assistant Lecturer, Associate Professor/Professor, Cairo University, 1962-84; Visiting Professor, American University in Cairo, 1984-89. *Publications:* Various articles on Ancient Egyptian Literary religious texts; Book: Two Hieratic Papyri of Nesmin, 2 vols, 1970 and 1972. *Membership:* Egypt Exploration Society, London. *Honours:* Nominated, but declined, Chairperson, Egyptian Antiquities Organisation, 1988; Chaired, vth International Congress of Egyptologists, Cairo, 29 Oct to 2 Nov, 1988. *Interests:* Art in General; Theatre; Cinema; Painting; Architecture. *Address:* The American University in Cairo, Department of Anthr Soc, 113 Kasr el Aimi Street, Cairo, Egypt.

HALE Christiane Bradford, b. 31 Aug. 1942, Boston, Massachusetts, USA. Professor; Consultant. m. (1) James G. Learning Jr, 1964, 1 daughter (divorced 1965), (2) Thomas L. Hale, 1973 (divorced 1978), (3) Irvin Emanuel, 1989. *Education:* BA Honours, History, Auburn University, 1971; MPH, Epidemiology, University of Alabama, 1974; PhD, Social Psychology & Demography, University of Cincinnati, 1978. *Appointments include:* Graduate programme, Community Health Planning & Administration, University of Cincinnati, 1977-78; Southern Research Institute, Birmingham, Alabama, 1978-80; Faculty 1980-, Associate Professor, Psychology 1987-; Director, Maternal & Child Health Training 1983-, Professor of Epidemiology 1986-, School of Public Health, University of Alabama, Birmingham (UAB); Visiting Professor, Universidad Cayatano Heredia, Lima, Peru, 1987-. *Publications:* 27 articles, 1 monograph. *Memberships:* American Public Health Association; Population Association of America; American Psychological Association; Southern Demographic Association. *Honours include:* Research Council grant, 1975, Taft Fellow 1975-76, 1976-77, 1977-78, University of Cincinnati; Award, National Endowment for Humanities, 1983; Biographical listing; Honour societies. *Hobbies:* Performing Arts; Yoga; Photography. *Address:* University of Alabama at Birmingham, School of Public Health, Room 231, Tidwell Hall, UAB Station, Birmingham, Alabama 35294, USA.

HALE Kaycee, b. 18 July 1947, Mount Hope, West Virginia, USA. Fashion Executive. *Education:* BA, Public Administration, California State University, Dominguez Hills. *Appointments:* Fashion model, 1967-77; Faculty 1971-77, executive director 1977-, museum director 1979-, Fashion Institute of Design & Merchandising (FIDM), Los Angeles. *Creative works:* Brochure, What's Your I. Q. (Image Quotient)?, Special Libraries Association; Audio tape, Image Builders, FIDM. *Memberships:* Various offices, Special Libraries Association; Public relations committee, Los Angeles

Fashion Group; Costume Society of America; California Media & Library Educators Association; Art Libraries of North America; American Marketing Association; American Association of Museums. *Hobbies:* Gardening; Writing. *Address:* Fashion Institute of Design & Merchandising, 818 West 7th Street, Los Angeles, California 90017, USA.

HALEVY Hilda Marie, b. 18 Oct. 1931, Havana, Cuba. Physician Anesthesologist. m. Simon Halevy, MD, 1968, 1 son. *Education:* BS, Instituto de Segunda Ensehanza de la Habana, Cuba, 1949; MD, University of Havana, 1957; Senior House Physician & Surgeon, Mother Cabrini Memorial Hospital, New York City, 1957-58; Resident, Anesthesiology, Metropolitan Hospital, New York City, 1958-60; Fellow, Anesthesiology, various New York City Hospitals, 1960-67. *Appointments:* Attending Anesthesiologist, Astoria General Hospital, 1967-; Visiting Scholar, Mexico, Holland, Israel, Music Consevatory (Piano), Habana, Cuba. *Memberships:* American Medical Association; Medical Society of State of New York; American Society of Anesthesiologists; New York State Society of Anesthesiologists; Medical Society County of Queens; American Society for Regional Anesthesia; American Society for Magnesium Research; Associaiton Internationale des Anesthesiolgoistes Reanimateurs d'Expression Francaise. *Honours:* AMA Physician's Recognition Award, 1977-. *Hobbies:* Classical Music; Travel. *Address:* Astoria General Hospital, Dept. of Anesthesia, 25-10 30th Avenue, Astoria LIC, NY 11102, USA.

HALL Bernice Lucia Edwards, b. 4 Mar. 1928, Bronx, USA. Minister of Music; Music Teacher; Soprano. m. Eugene Edward Hall, 28 July 1963. *Education:* BMus., 1949; M.Mus., 1955; HHD, Universal College, 1982; PhD, American College Religious Counsellors. *Appointments:* Soloist 1960-88. *Publications:* Author, Poems, Seeds of Hope, 1970; Education Editor, Urban Life Newspaper. *Memberships:* New England Music Alumni Association; Iota Phi Lambda; American Association of Religious Counsellors; Naional Association Key Women Inc; National Association Colored Womens Club; National Council Negro Women Inc. *Honours:* Recipient, many honours and awards. *Hobbies:* Writing; Needlework. *Address:* 2114 Lacombe Ave., Bronx, NY 10473, USA.

HALL Brenda Yvonne, b. 26 Sept. 1957, Tennessee, USA. Lawyer. m. 4 Sept. 1982, 1 son, 1 daughter. *Education:* AS Columbia State Community College, 1976; BA, 1978, JD 1980, University of Tennessee. *Appointments:* Tennessee Bar, 1981; Law Clerk, Meares & Meares, 1981; Partner, Gamble & Hall, Westburg, 1981-82; Partner, McDonald & Hall, Kingston, 1982- . *Publications:* Articles in Tennessee Law Review. *Memberships:* American, Tennessee Bar Associations; American Trial Lawyers Association; Tennessee Trial Lawyers Association; Roane County Bar Association, Secretary/Treasurer; Gamma Beta Phi; Phi Kappa Phi; Pi Delta Phi. *Hobbies:* Travel; Reading; Needlework. *Address:* 145 Court Square, Kingston, TN 37763, USA.

HALL Carolyn Susan, b. 22 May 1950, Bexley, England. Journalist. m. David John Hall, 3 Nov. 1973. 2 sons. *Education:* BS (Hons) French with Italian, University College London; MA, English Lit, Simmons College, Boston, Massachusetts, USA. *Appoinbtments:* Academy Editions, 1973-74; Harcourt Grace Jovanovich, 1977-78. *Publications:* Henry Fuseli, 1974; Henri Rousseau, 1976; William Blake: Selected Engravings, 1975; American Posters of the Turn of the Century, 1975; Odilon Redon, 1977; The Twenties in Vogue, 1983; The Thirties in Vogue, 1984; The Forties in Vogue, 1985. *Membership:* Fellow, Royal Society of Arts. *Address:* 106 Elgin Crescent, London W11 2JL, England.

HALL Helene W, b. 17 Sept. 1926, Centralia, Illinois, USA. Coordinator/Instructor. m. Dr W E Hall, 27 June 1948. 3 sons. *Education:* BSB 1966, MS 1969, EDS 1974, Emporia State University, Kansas. *Appointments:* Medical and Dental Assistant, 1944-66; Instructor, Emporia State University, 1966-69; Secretary, Roosevelt High School, ESU, 1969-70; Team Leader, Teacher Corps, ESU, 1970-73; Coordinator, Sec Sciences & Word Processing, Kansas City Community College, 1973-. *Publications:* Beginning Word Processing; Advanced Word Processing; Production Typewriting. *Memberships:* Association of Information Systems Professionals, Board of Directors; Classroom Educators Advisory Committee; National Education Association, NBEA; KBEA; AVA; KVA; Delta Pi Epsilon; Pi Omega Pi; Methodist Church, Financial Secretary, Board of Trustees. *Honours:* Outstanding KBOA Master Educator, 1981; Outstanding Service Award, OEA, 1981; Appreciation for Service Award, Classroom Educators Advisory Council, 1974-81. *Hobbies:* Camping; Skiing (water); Computers; Grandchildren. *Address:* 403 South Sixth, Osage City, KS 66523, USA.

HALL Jacqueline Dowd, b. 14 Jan. 1943, Pauls Valley, Oklahoma, USA. Professor of History. m. Robert H. Hall, 19 Aug. 1970 (div. 1982). *Education:* BA cum laude, Rhodes College, Memphis, Tennessee, 1965; PhD, Distinction, Columbia University, 1974. *Appointments:* Instructor, Columbia University, 1971; Instructor to Professor, & Director, Southern Oral History Programme, 1973-, Julia Cherry Spovill Professor 1989-, University of North Carolina, Chapel Hill. *Publications:* Author: Revolt Against Chivalry: Jessie Daniel Ames & Women's Campaign Against Lynching, 1979; Mind That Burns in Each Body, 1983; Disorderly Women, 1986; Second Thoughts, 1987. Co-author: Cotton Mill People, with R. Karstad & J. Leloudis, 1986; Women in the South, with A. F. Scott, 1985. Contributor: Like a Family: Making of a Southern Cotton Mill World, 1987. *Memberships:* Offices, past/present: American Studies Association; Organisation of American Historians; American & Southern Historical Associations; Centre for Research on Women, Duke University. *Honours:* Numerous awards & prizes, historical research & writing (social history, labour history). *Address:* Department of History, CB 3195 Hamilton Hall, University of North Carolina, Chapel Hill, NC 27599, USA.

HALL Laura Christine, b. 21 Sept. 1944, Buffalo, Texas, USA. Counselor. *Education:* BS, Paul Quinn College, 1966; Studied at California State University, 1966-69; MEd, Prairie View, 1970; Studied at University of Houston, 1985-86. *Appointments:* Teacher: Madisonville ISD, Texas, 1966; Orville, California, 1967; Los Angeles, California, 1968; Counselor: Houston, Texas, 1970; Waco, Texas, 1984-. *Memberships:* Vice President, Memberships Chairperson, Sigma Gamma Rho; Programs Chairperson, Delta Epsilon Phi; Volunterr in Politics; A Philip Randolph Voter Registration League; Precinct Chairman (Chairperson) No 3; Texas State Teachers Association; Texas State Counselor's Association. *Honours:* Outstanding Service Award, Sigma Gamma Rho Sorority, 1966; Personaltiy of the Year Award, Sigma Gamma Rho Sorority, 1983; Outstanding Service Award, NAACP, Los Angeles Chapter, 1967; Certificate of Appreciation, Volunteer In Politics, Houston, Texas; Outstanding Service Award, Delta Epsilon Phi, 1980; Outstanding Service, Voter Registration League, 1978. *Hobbies:* Bowling; Reading; Writing; Tennis. *Address:* 1626 Pecan Lane, Waco, Texas 76705, USA.

HALL Marcia Joy Stanton, b. 24 June 1947, Long Beach, California, USA. Administrator, Non-Profit Organisation. m. Stephen C. Hall, 29 Mar. 1969, 2 sons. *Education:* AA, Foothill College, 1967; BA, University of Washington, 1969. *Appointments:* Instructional aide, California, 1979-80; Market research interviewer, Massachusetts, 1981-83; Adult education instructor, 1982-83; Career information centre coordinator, 1983-86; Corporate Relations Director, 1985-86; NE Area Coordinator, YWCA, 1987-; NE Area Coordinator, YWCA, 1987-89; Executive Director, Chamber of Commerce, 1989-. *Creative works:* Vocal compositions published: If All The World, 1970; Two 17th Century Dance Songs, 1971. *Memberships:* Past President, Parent Teacher Organisation, California & Maryland;

Past President, Outriggers Toastmasters, Maryland; Past Member, American Association of University Women. *Honours include:* Winner, 1st Annual High School Composers Competition, Lewis & Clark College, Oregon, 1965; Valedictorian, high school 1965, college 1967; Music awards, Foothill College, 1966-67; Awards, Toastmaster International, 1987. *Hobbies:* Music composition; Volunteer work, activities for teenagers; Reading; Bridge; Walking. *Address:* 507 Devonshire Lane, Severna Park, Maryland 21146, USA.

HALL Marie Boas, b. 18 Oct. 1919, Springfield, Massachusetts, USA. Reader Emeritus in History of Science and Technology. m. A Rupert Hall, 10 June 1959. *Education:* AB, MA, Radcliffe College; PhD, Cornell University, 1949. *Appointments:* University of Massachusetts, 1949-52; Brandeis University, 1952-57; University of California at Los Angeles, 1957-61; Indiana University, 1961-63; Reader, 1963-80, Reader Emeritus in History of Science and Technology, University of London. *Publications:* Books: Robert Boyle & 17th Century Chemistry; The Scientific Renaissance; Robert Boyle on Natural Philosophy; All Scientists Now; Unpublished Scientific Papers of Isaac Newton, with A R Hall; The Correspondence of Henry Oldenburg, with A R Hall. *Memberships:* History of Science Society; British Society for the History of Science; Effective Member, Academie int. d'histoires des Science. *Honours:* Phi Kappa Phi; Phi Beta Kappa; Pfizer Award, History of Science Society, 1958; With A Rupert Hall, Sarton Medal, History of Science Society, 1981. *Hobbies:* Writing; Walking; Gardening. *Address:* 14 Ball Lane, Tackley, Oxford, OX5 3AG, England.

HALL Susan Dorothy, b. 17 Dec. 1942, Oldham, England. Scientific Editor. m. (1) P Feakin, 30 July 1966, div. 1983; (2) B D Hall, 5 June 1987. *Education:* BSc (2. 1), Agricultural Sciences, University of Nottingham, 1966. *Appointments:* Editor, Ministry of Overseas Development, 1966-73; Editor, Journal of Horticultural Science, 1973-75; Consultant, FAO, 1981-83; Research Editor, International Crops Research Institute for the Semi-Arid Tropics (ICRISAT), India, 1983-. *Publications:* Numerous scientific publications on Tropical agriculture, as Editor. *Memberships:* Association of Applied Biologists; Council of Biological Editors; European Association of Science Editors. *Hobbies:* Reading; Theatre, production and amateur acting; Wardrobe design and production (Bromley Little Theatre); Swimming; Travel. *Address:* The Manse, Hatch Beauchamp, Somerset, TA3 6TH, England.

HALLIDAY Mary Elizabeth, b. 20 Feb. 1909, Danefield, Kent. Housewife; Landowner. m. Ruthven John Wyllie Halliday, 4 Dec. 1935, died 1973, 1 son (deceased). *Education:* Abbots Bromley School, 1920-26; Mrs Hoster's Secretarial College, London; Diploma, Harcombe House. *Appointments:* Private Secretary to Mr J.P. Hedley, FRCS, FRCP, 1934-35. *Memberships:* JP, 1958; Borough Councillor, 1957-63; General Commissioner, Income Tax, 1971-80; Member, Council & Executive, Trinity College Carmarthen, 1971-80; Governing Body, Chuch in Wales, 1969-74; Council Member, Coleg Elidyr, 1973-87; Camarthenshire Executive Council NHS 1958-74, Chairman 1969-70; Dyfed Family Practitioner Committee NHS, 1974-81. *Honours:* Defence Medal, 1945; Chief Scouts Commendation, 1981; MBE, 1980; Royal British Legion Womens Section, Merit Award, 1987. *Hobbies:* Gardening; Music. *Address:* Llanfair House, Llandovery, Dyfed, SA20 0YF, Wales.

HALLIER Michele, b. 13 Oct. 1944, Oran, Algeria. 1 son, 2 daughters. *Education:* Graduate Gemologist, Gemological Institute of America, Los Angeles, 1984; Fellow, Gemmological Association of Great Britain, 1985; Senior Member, American Society of Appraiser (personal property), 1986; Master Gemologist Appraiser, Accredited Gemologists Association, 1986; Certified Gemologist Appraiser, American Gem Society, 1987; Certified Graphoanalyst, Chicago Graphoanalysis Society, 1986. *Appointments:* Secretary of French Consul in Bonn, Germany, 1964-65; Assistant Manager

and Vice President, Intercontinental Gemological Laboratory, 1984-88; Vice President, Jewels Replacement Co, 1985-; Vice President, Molina Fine Jewelers, 1986-. *Creative Works:* Speaker at Seminars on period jewellery, diamonds, different treatments on gemstones, origin of gemstones, 1986-88. *Memberships:* American Gem Society; American Society of Appraisers; Accredited Gemologists Association (Secretary of Governor Southwest Region, 1976-88; Secretary of Southwest Chapter GIA Alumni Association, 1985-88; Internal Revenue Service, Qualified appraiser; Expert, Better Business Bureau. *Hobbies:* Gemology; Mineralogy; Graphology; Dance, classic and modern; Raising children. *Address:* 4600 E Sparkling Ln, Paradise Valley, Arizona 85253, USA.

HALLMAN Viola, b. 8 Dec. 1944, Hagen, North Rhine Westphalia, Germany. President and Chief Executive officer. m. Olof Jon Hallman, 8 July 1971. 1 daughter. *Education:* MBA and PhD in Economics, Universities of Hamburg, Marburg, Federal Republic of Germany and Padua, Italy. *Appointments:* President and Chief Executive Officer, Friedr. Gustav Theis Kaltwalzwerke GmbH; Friedr. Gustav Theis GmbH & Co.; Chairman and Chief Executive Officer, Theis Precision Steel Corporation, Bristol, Connecticut, USA; Chairman of the Board and President, Theis of America, Inc., Wilmington, Delaware, USA. *Publication:* Entrepreneur - Profession without Future? 1975. *Memberships:* ASU - Working Association of Independent Business Entrepreneurs, Bonn; VvU - Association of Women Entrepreneurs, Cologne; Federal Committee of Business Economics (BBW) of the Rationalisation Curatorium of German Commerce (RKW), Eschborn. *Honour:* Manager of the Year, 1979. *Hobbies:* History; Literature; Riding. *Address:* Friedr. Gustav Theis Kaltwalzwerke GmbH, Bandstahlstr. 14-18, 5800 Hagen-Halden, Federal Republic of Germany.

HALLQVIST Berit V.E., b. 13 Dec. 1938, Stockholm, Sweden. Concert & Opera Singer; Professor. divorced 1 daughter. *Education:* Royal Academy of Music, Stockholm, 1957-65; MFA, 1963. *Appointments:* As Singer: Debut, Stockholm Concert Hall, 1966; several tours of Scandinavia; Concerts in France and USA; Radio & TV appearances; As Singing Teacher: State Academy of Music, Stockholm, 1965-; Guest Teacher, Copenhagen, 1969, Trondheim, Norway, 1983, Gustavus Adolphus College, St Peters, USA, 1986. *Memberships:* Association of Swedish Singing and Speech Teachers; Society of New Iden; Ring of Artists; Faculty of Singing Teachers, State Academy of Music, Stockholm. *Honours:* Edvin Rouds' Scholarship, 1963; Christine Nilsson Scholarship, 1903, Stockholms' Kulturnamund, 1985; Swedish Institute Award, 1986; etc. *Hobbies:* Singing; Travel; Aquarelle Painting; Gardening. *Address:* State Academy of Music, Valhallavag 103-109, 11531 Stockholm, Sweden.

HALSALL Maureen Patricia, b. 19 Jan. 1934, Hamilton, Ontario, Canada. Professor of English. *Education:* BA, McMaster University, 1957; MA, Radcliffe College, 1958; PhD, Harvard University, 1963. *Appointments:* Instructor, Wellesley College, 1962-65; Assistant Professor 1965-68, Associate Professor 1968-82, Professor 1982-, Associate Dean of Humanities 1974-82, Acting Dean of Humanities 1986-87, McMaster University. *Publications:* The Old English Rune Poem: A Critical Edition, 1981; Articles in professional journals. *Memberships:* Association of Canadian University Teachers of English; International Arthurian Society; International Society of Anglo-Saxonists; Mediaeval Academy of America; Modern Language Association of America. *Honours:* Woodrow Wilson Fellowship, 1957-58; Radcliffe College Fellowship, 1958-59; Phi Beta Kappa,. 1964; Canada Council Graduate Fellowships, 1959-61; Canadian Federation of University Women Fellowship, 1961-62; Canada Council Leave Fellowship, 1970-71; Canada Council Senior Leave Fellowship, 1977-78. *Hobbies:* Flying; Theatre; Travel. *Address:* Department of English, McMaster University, Hamilton, Ontario, Canada L8S 4L9.

HAMBLING Maggi, b. 23 Oct. 1945, Sudbury, Suffolk, England. Artist. *Education:* Ipswich School of Art; Camberwell School of Art, London; Slade School of Fine Art, London. *Creative Works:* Exhibitions: Morley Gallery, London, 1973; Warehouse Gallery, London, 1977; National Gallery, London, 1981; National Portrait Gallery, London, 1983; Serpentine Gallery, London, 1987; Arnolfini Gallery, Bristol, 1988; Public Collections include: Wakefield Art Gallery; Scottish National Portrait Gallery; Swindon Museum & Art Gallery; Harris Museum & Art Gallery, University College London; Arts Council of Great Britain; Birmingham City Art Gallery; British Council, British Museum; Eastern Arts Collection; European Parliament Collection; Gulbenkian Foundation; Imperial War Museum; National Gallery; National Portrait Gallery; Southampton Art Gallery; Scottish National Gallery of Modern Art; Tate Gallery; Whitworth Art Gallery. *Honours:* Boise Travel Award, New York, 1969; Arts Council Award, 1977; First Artist in Residence, National Gallery, London, 1980. *Address:* 1 Broadhinton Road, London SW4 0LU, England.

HAMBURGER Mary Ann, b. 25 Aug. 1939, Newark, New Jersey, USA. Medical Practice Management Consultant. 2 sons. *Education:* AA, University of Bridgeport, Bridgeport, Connecticut, 1960. *Appointments:* Medical Office Manager, Surgeons Office, 1970-84; Teacher, Adult School, Maplewood, South Orange Board of Education, New Jersey, 1975-83; Medical Management Consultant, Mary Ann Hamburger Associates, Maplewood, 1984-. *Membership:* Member, National Female Executive Association. *Hobbies:* Reading; Theatre; Needlepoint; Sports; Music. *Address:* 74 Hudson Avenue, Maplewood, NJ 07040, USA.

HAMILTON Eleanor, b. 6 Oct. 1909, Portland, Oregon, USA. Marriage Counselor; Author; Sex therapist. m. Albert E Hamilton, 11 Aug. 1932. 1 son, 3 daughters. *Education:* AB, University of Oregon, 1930; MA, Teachers College; PhD, Columbia University, 1955. *Appointments:* Director Girl Reserve Program, YWCA, 1930-32; Founder and Director, Hamilton School, New York City, 1933-48; Founder and Director, Hamilton School, Sheffield, Massachusetts, 1948-83; Director & Founder, Inverness Ridge Counseling Center, Inverness, 1984-. *Publications:* Partners In Love; Sex Before Marriage; Sex With Love - A Guide for Teenagers; 57 articles in Modern Bride Magazine; 196 columns in Pt Reyes Light (a weekly newspaper). *Memberships:* Society for the Scientific Study of Sex; American Federation of Television & Radio Artists; American Association of Sex Educators, Counsellors & Therapists; American Association of Marriage & Family Therapists; American Psych Association; American Society of Journalists and Authors; Humanists Counselors. *Honours:* American Library Award for Sex With Love, 1980; Annual Award of Society for the Scientific Study of Sex, 1980. *Hobbies:* Camping; Travel; Cooking; Carpentry; 6 Grandchildren. *Address:* 60 E Robert Drive, Inverness, California 94937, USA.

HAMILTON Madrid Turner, b. Georgia, USA. Clinical Therapist. m. Norman Woodrow Hamilton, deceased, 1 son. *Education:* AB, Spelman College, Atlanta, Georgia; MSN, Atlanta University; PhD, Union for Experimenting College, University of Cincinnati, University of Ohio. *Appointments:* Clinical Therapist, CASARC, Department of Public Health, San Francisco, California; President, M.T.Hamilton Enterprise Inc; Associate Professor, Sociology and Social Work: University of Redlands and San Francisco State University; Registered Representative, Family Service Association of America; Registered Director, Planned Parent, World Population; Columnist, Metro and Sun Reporter, San Francisco. *Publications:* Family Planning Prejudice and Politics; Rural Health Education; How to Give Health Fairs; Erosive Health: A Sociological Study of Health-Well-Being of Black Americans. *Memberships:* Vice-President, Treasurer, YWCA, San Francisco; Treasurer, YWCA, Redlands; Vice-President, National Board, YWCA of USA; Founding President, Spelman College Alumnae Association; Founding President, Coalition of 100 Black Women, North California; President, Democratic Women's Forum; Board of Directors, White Plains and Redlands United Way; National Association of Social Workers. *Honours:* Valuable Human Resource, American Heritage Foundation; Member, California Governor's Population Study Commission; Life Fellow, Medal of Honour, ABIRA; Grand Ambassador of Achievement, HE. *Hobbies:* Needlepoint and crewel work; Beekeeping; Writing; Volunteer work with social agencies. *Address:* 136 Geneva Avenue, San Francisco, CA 94112, USA.

HAMILTON Margaret Letitia, b. Galt, Ontario, Canada. Consultant, Thomson Newspapers Limited. m. *Appointments:* Past President and Chief Operating Officer; Consultant, Thomson Newspapers Limited; Director, Domtar Inc; Director, Montreal Trust Company; Director, Montreal Trust Co Inc; Director, Montreal Trust Company of Canada; Director, Credit Foncier; Director, Credit Foncier Trust Company; Governing Council, University of Toronto; Advisory Board, School of Usiness Administration, University of Western Ontario; Advisory Board, University of Toronto Press; Past Chairman and Director, Canadian Advertising Advisory Board and Advertising Standards Council; Past Vice President and Director, Canadian Press; Past Director, Metro Toronto Board of Trade; Past Director, Canadian Daily Newspaper Publishers Association; Past Co-Chairman, Task Force on Women in Advertising; Past Director, American Newspaper Publishers Association; Past Vice-Chairman, Advertising Bureau of Canadian Daily Newspapers; Past Advisory Committee to Secretary of State on Status of Women. *Memberships:* American Newspaper Publishers Association; Associated Press; Canadian Daily Newspaper Publishers Association; Inter-American Press Institute; International Press Institute; Commonwealth Press Union; Zonta International. *Address:* c/o Thomson Newspapers Limited, 65 Queen Street West, Toronto, Ontario, Canada M5H 2M8.

HAMILTON Nancy Jeanne, b. 1 Jan. 1959, Rochester, USA. Structural Engineer. m. Robert Edwards, 1 daughter. *Education:* BS, Architectural Engineering, California Polytechnic State University, 1981; MS, Civil Engineering, Massachusetts Institute of Technology, 1984. *Appointments:* Project Manager, KPFF Consulting Engineer, 1981-82, 1984-88; Project Manager, Ove Arup & Partners, 1988-. *Memberships:* American Concrete Institute; Earthquake Engineering Research Institute; Structural Engineers Association of Southern California. *Honours:* National Merit Scholar; Rotary Scholarship; Women's Architectural League Scholarship. *Hobbies:* Camping; Skiing; Reading; Sewing; Raising Her Daughter. *Address:* 9523 Lucerne Ave., Culver City, CA 90230, USA.

HAMILTON Susan Rebecca Owens, b. 8 July 1951, Birmingham, Alabama, USA. Attorney; Corporate Officer. m. 6 Aug. 1974. *Education:* BA, Auburn University, 1973; JD, Honours, Cumberland Law School, 1977. *Appointments:* Staff, house counsel to management, currently Assistant Vice President Administration, CSX Transportation Inc (& predecessors), 1977-. *Publications:* Various treatises, legal & trade journals. *Memberships include:* Professional: Alabama & Florida State Bars; US Supreme Court Bar; Federal Bar; American Bar Association. Civic: Past Director, Uptown Civitan Club; Past Club President, State Board member, Business & Professional Women; Office, United Way. *Honours:* Outstanding Young Career Woman, Louisville, Kentucky 1980, State of Florida 1982, Federation of Business & Professional Women. *Hobbies:* Singing (choir soloist); Sports; Reading. *Address:* 12154 Hidden Hills Drive, Jacksonville, Florida 32225, USA.

HAMILTON SCHAEFFER Barbara, b. 26 Apr. 1926, Newton, Massachusetts, USA. m. John Schaeffer, 7 Sept. 1946. 2 sons, 1 daughter. *Education:* Skidmore College, 1943-46; AB, Bucknell University, 1948; Montclair State University, 1950-51; Bank Street College of Education, 1961-62; Yeshwa University,

1962; Certificate Primary School, 1961; Certificate Secondary School, 1957. *Appointments:* Lecturer, Children's Art, 1959-70; Director, Pampton Plains School, 1959-61; Adviser, Episcopal School, 1968-70; Vice President, Deltona-DeLand Trolley Lines, 1980-81; President, Monroe Heavy Equipment Rentals, Inc, 1981- . *Publications:* Contributor of articles to professional journals; lectures on travel and guest lecturer in numerous schools. *Memberships:* Charter member, Small Business Development Regional Center, Stetson University Chapter; International Platform Association; DeLand Area Chamber of Commerce; Orange City Chamber of Commerce; Deltona Chamber of Commerce; American Society of Travel Agents. *Honour:* President's List of Scholars, Daytona Beach Community College, Daytona Beach, Florida, 1984. *Hobbies:* Restoring old home in Massachusetts; Writing; Grandmothering; Mothering; Painting; Piano. *Address:* 400 Foothill Farms Road, Orange City, FL 32763, USA

HAMMER Cheryl Lynn, b. 14 Dec. 1960, New Kensington, Pennsylvania, USA. Engineer. m. Edgar T. Hammer III, 28 May 1982. *Education:* BS, Honours, Management Engineering, Grove City College, Pennsylvania, 1982. *Appointments:* Engineer, Westinghouse Electric Corporation, Pittsburgh 1982-83, Consumers Power Company, Jackson, Michigan 1983-84; Manufacturing Engineer, General Motors Corporation, Lansing, Michigan, 1984-. *Memberships:* American Society for Quality Control; Consultant, Junior Achievement Project Business; Past offices, Grove City College, Tammany Hills Condominium Association; Various scholastic associations. *Honours:* Certified Quality Engineer, ASQC, 1987; Scholarship, National Presbyterian Agency, 1978. *Hobbies:* Physical fitness; Reading; Music (head organist, Plum Creek Presbyterian Church, 1976-78). *Address:* 2925 Staten Avenue no. 6, Lansing, Michigan 48910, USA.

HAMMER Helga, b. 20 July 1944, Miskolc, Hungary. Professor of Ophthalmology. m. Attila Dobozy, 5 Aug. 1966. *Education:* MD, 1968; CSc, 1979. *Appointments:* Professor of Ophthalmology, Department of Ophthalmology, Albert Szent-Gyorgyi Medical University, Szeged. *Publications:* Book: Uvea pigment and alpha-crystalline hypersensitivity in endogeneous uveitis (in Hungarian). *Memberships:* Hungarian Society of Ophthalmology; Hungarian Society of Immunology and Allergology. *Address:* Department of Ophthalmology, Albert Szent-Gyorgyi Medical University, Koranyi fasor 12, Szeged, Hungary.

HAMMOND Doris Blersch, b. 27 Jan. 1933. Cincinnati, Ohio, USA. Counsellor. Teacher m H. Ted Hammond, 30 May 1953, 3 daughters. *Education:* BS, Education, University of Cincinnati, 1954; MA, Counselling, Marshall University, West Virginia, 1975; PhD, Counselling, & Certificate in Gerontology, University of Georgia, 1979. *Appointments:* Elementary school teacher, various states, 1954-79; Associate Professor, Psychology and Director of Gerontology Graduate Program, Buffalo, New York, 1980-87; Adjunct Professor, University of South Carolina, & Guidance Counsellor, Aiken (SC), 1987-. *Publications:* Book, My Parents Never Had Sex: Myths & Facts of Sexual Ageing, 1987; Numerous journal articles; Contributing author, various books. *Memberships:* American Association for Counselling & Development; Gerontological Society; Regional Vice President, National School Volunteer Programme; Association for Gerontologists in Higher Education; Special Task Force, Understanding Ageing Inc. *Honours:* 1st place, intergenerational programming (national award), from Tupperware at National School Volunteer Programme Conference, 1983; Outstanding Faculty Member of Year, D'Youville College, Buffalo, 1986. *Hobbies:* Competitive tennis (Amateur Volvo League); Swimming, 1/2 mile per day; Writing. *Address:* 611 Medinah Drive, Aiken, South Carolina 29801, USA.

HAMMOND Karen Louise Smith, b. 20 Dec. 1954, Baton Rouge, Louisiana, USA. Journalist; Paralegal. m. 17 Dec. 1985. *Education:* BS, Journalism, University of Colorado, 1978; Paralegal Certificate, University of Texas, Arlington, 1981. *Appointments:* Editor, Ennis Press, Texas, 1981-82; Triex agent, Parkway Pontiac & GMC Truck, 1983-86; Marketing representative, Allnet Communications, Dallas, Texas, 1985-87; Sales representative, Legal Assistant Today magazine, 1987; Marketing representative, Call USA Corporation, 1987- ; Sales Representative, Paytel; Marketing Representative, Telecable, Richardson. *Publications:* Newspaper articles: Ennis Press, Mid-Cities Daily News, DeSoto News, Cedar Hill Journal. *Memberships:* Dallas Association of Legal Assistants; Women in Communications; Society of Professional Journalists. *Honours:* Scholarship to UTA, Dallas Association of Legal Assistants; Award, sales achievement, Allnet Communications; Biographical recognitions. *Hobbies:* Reading newspapers & business magazines; Voluntary work for political candidates; Films; Photography; Swimming. *Address:* 18809 Lina Street no. 2102, Dallas, Texas 75252, USA.

HAMMOND Ruth Fawns, b. 6 July 1920, Toronto, Canada. Public Relations Consultant. m. 7 Oct. 1950, 1 son, 1 daughter. *Education:* BA, Honours, University of Toronto, 1943; Specialist, English, Secondary School Teaching Certificate, 1945. *Appointments:* Teacher, 1943-45; Reporter, Womens Editor, Toronto Star, 1945-51; President, General Manager, Ruth Hammond Public Relations, 1950-. *Publications:* Public Relations for Small Business, co-author, 1979; numerous articles. *Memberships:* Director, Canadian Public Relations Society; International Association of Business Communicators. *Honours:* Life Member, Womens Press Club, Toronto, 1985, CPRS, 1988; President's Medal, Canadian Public Relations Society; The Award of Attainment, The Canadian Public Relations Society. *Hobbies:* Travel; Reading; Teaching. *Address:* Ste. 2410, 33 Elmhurst Ave., Willowdale, Ontario M2N 6G8, Canada.

HAMMONTREE Marie Gertrude, b. 19 June 1913, Indiana, USA. Writer. *Education:* AB, Butler University, Indianapolis, 1949. *Appointments:* Secretary, Bobbs-Merrill Co, 1934-42; Secretary, Indiana University Medical Center, 1942-48; Secretary, Travel Enterprises, 1949-50; Secretary, Federal Bureau of Investigation, 1950-75; Public Relations, Mayor's Office, 1978-. *Publications:* Books: Will and Charlie Mayo, Boy Doctors, 1954; A. P. Giannini, Boy of San Francisco, 1956; Albert Einstein, Young Thinker, 1961; Mohandas Gandhi, Boy of Principle, 1966; Walt Disney, Young Movie Maker, 1969. *Memberships:* Women in Communications; National League of American Pen Women, Indianapolis Chapter President, 1978-80; Society of Former FOB Women. *Hobbies:* Travel (visited 52 countries); Writing; Music; Cats. *Address:* 8140 Township Line Road 4303, Indianapolis, IN 46260, USA.

HAMPSHIRE Susan, b. 1942, London, England. Actress. m. Pierre Granier-Deferre, dissolved, 1974, 1 son, 1 daughter, deceased. (2) Eddie Kulukundis, 1981. *Appointments:* Stage Appearances: Expresso Bongo; Follow That Girl; Ginger Man; Fairy Tale of New York; She Stoops to Conquer; On Approval; The Sleeping Prince; A Doll's House; The Taming of the Shrew; Romeo and Juliette; Peter Pan; As You Like It; Arms and the Man; Miss Julie; The Circle; Man & Superman; Tribades; An Audience Called Edward; A Crucifier of Blood, a Sherlock Holmes Mystery; Night and Day; The Revolt; House Guest; Blythe Spirit; Married Love; Roles in TV Serials; Andromeda; Forsythe Saga; Vanity Fair; The First Churchills; The Pallisers; Dick Turpin; Barchester Chronicles; Leaving; Going to Pot. Films Include: During One Night; The Three Lives of Thomasina; Night Must Fall; Wonderful Life; Paris in August; Monte Carlo or Bust; Rogan; David Copperfield; Living Free; A Time for Loving; Roses and Green Pepper; Bang. *Publications:* Susan's Story; The Maternal Instinct; Lucy Jane; Lucy Jane II; Trouble Free Gardening. *Honours:* Honorary Doctor of Letters, City University, London, 1984; Hon.D.Litt, St Andrews University, Scotland, 1986. *Hobbies:* Gardening; Music; Study of Antique Furniture. *Address:* c/o Midland Bank Ltd., 92 Kensington High Street, London W8, England.

HAMPTON Carol Cussen McDonald, b. 18 Sept. 1935, Oklahoma City, USA. Historian; Church Worker. m. James Wilburn Hampton, 22 Feb. 1958, 2 sons, 2 daughters. *Education:* BA, 1957; MA, 1973; PhD, 1984. *Appointments:* Instructor, University of Oklahoma, 1977-81; Instructor, University of Sciences & Arts, Oklahoma, 1981-84; Associate Director, Graduate Opportunities for American Indians, University of California, Berkeley, 1984-86; National Field Officer, Native American Ministry, Episcopal Church, 1986-. *Publications:* Why Write History?, The Creative Woman, 1987; Opposition to Indian Diversity: Focus on Religion, UCLA; Peyote and the Law, Between Two Worlds, 1986. *Memberships:* Caddo Tribe of Oklahoma; Associate, American Indian Historians; Centre for the American Indian; Advisory Committee, Social Justice, Oklahoma State Regents on Higher Education; etc. *Honours:* Francis C. Allen Fellowship, Newberry Library, 1983; Oklahoma State Human Rights Award, 1987. *Hobbies:* American Indian History & Philosophy; Travel. *Address:* 1414 N. Hudson, Oklahoma City, OK 73103, USA.

HAMPTON Elizabeth A, b. 2 Dec. 1942, Baton Rouge, Louisiana, USA. Investments; Antique Business; Real Estate. *Education:* AA, 1962, BA, 1981, Stephens College, Columbia, Missouri (MO). *Appointments:* Vice President, Building Products Co., Baton Rouge, 1962-83; Head Teller, Louisiana National Bank, Baton Rouge, 1964-66; Supervisor, Office Manager, Simon Law Firm, Lafayette, 1966-80; Personal Investments & Real Estate, Breaux Bridge, 1980-; Assistant, Ray Cole Couturier Silks, New Orleans, 1984-; Co-Owner, Au Vieux Paris Antiques, 1985-. *Memberships:* Earthwatch, Louisiana Field Representative; National Foundation for Advancement in the Arts; Orangutan Project; Nature Conservancy; Greenpeace; African Wildlife Foundation; Amnesty International; World Wildlife Fund; League of Women Voters. *Honours:* World's Champion Equitation Rider, Walking Horses, 1960; Woman of the Year, Lafayette, American Business Women's Assocation, 1979. *Hobbies:* Travel; Photography; Bicycling; Aerobics. *Address:* 1127 Chartres Street, New Orleans, LA 70116, USA.

HAMRICK Karen Susan, b. 22 Nov. 1955, Charleston, West Virginia, USA. Attorney. *Education:* BA, Psychology, West Virginia University, 1977; MS, Industrial Relations, 1979; JD, 1982. *Appointments:* Associate, Fred F. Holroyd, Charleston, 1982-83; Partner, Holroyd & Hamrick, Charleston, 1983-85; Private Practice, Charleston, 1985-; Instructor, University of Charleston, 1983-; Hearing Examiner, WV Workers' Comp., Charleston, 1986-. *Memberships:* Vice President, Kanawha City Correction Officers Committee, Charleston, 1985-; Kanawha County Bar Association, Assistant Secretary. *Hobbies:* Jogging; Swimming; Horse Riding. *Address:* 237 Capitol Street, Charleston, WV 25301, USA.

HANAS Suzanne Elaine, b. 27 July 1950, Pittsburgh, Pennsylvania, USA. Sales Executive; Former Nurse. *Education:* RN Diploma, Shadyside Hospital School of Nursing, Pittsburg, 1971; BS, American University, 1976. *Appointments:* Nurse, Ohio, Virginia, Washington DC; Head nurse, cardio-vascular intensive care, Cleveland Clinic Hospital, 1971-73; Special duty nurse, Georgetown University Hospital, DC, 1973-75; Team Coordinator, Visiting Nurses Association, North Virginia, 1975-76; Ter Manager, Hollister Inc, Chicago, 1976-79; Senior Account Representative 1979-, Sales Trainer 1984-, 3M Company, West Caldwell, New Jersey. Also: President, Skyline Dance Studio Inc, Falls Church, Virginia; Instructor, Montgomery College, Maryland, 1977-80. *Memberships include:* Past delegate, Arlington County Civic Federation, Virginia Republican Convention; Past President, Fairlington Citizens Association; Past Member, Arlington County Republican Committee; American Cancer Society; American University Alumni Association; National Association of Female Executives; Federal City Republican Womens' Club, Regent 1989; Presidential Inaugural Committee 1984, 1988; Media operatioons, Campaign to Elect George Bush, President, 1988. *Honour:* Award, Order of Golden Scalpel, 3M Company, 1985. *Address:* 3122 Nestlewood Drive, Herndon, Virginia 22071, USA.

HANCOCK Sheila Cameron, b. Isle of Wight, UK. Actress; Director. m. (1) Alexander Ross (d. 1971), 1 daughter. (2) John Thaw, 25 Dec. 1973, 1 daughter. *Education:* Royal Academy of Dramatic Art. *Appointments:* 8 years repertory, Theatre Workshop, Stratford East, London; Associate Director, Cambridge Theatre Company, 1980-82; Artistic Director, Royal Shakespeare Company regional tour, 1983-84; Acting, directing, National Theatre, 1985-86; Director, Actors Centre. Performances Include: West End starring roles in: Rattle of a Simple Man, 1962; The Anniversary, 1966; A Delicate Balance, RSC, 1969; So What About Love? 1969; Absurd Person Singular, 1973; Deja Revue, 1974; The Bed Before Yesterday, 1976; Annie, 1978; Sweeney Todd, 1980; Winter's Tale, RSC, Stratford, 1981, Barbican, 1982; Artistic Director of RSC touring company, 1982-83; National Theatre, London & Chicago; Appeared in: The Duchess of Malfi; The Cherry Orchard. Directed, Sheridan's The Critic, 1985-86. Star, several successful reviews; Repeated stage role in film of The Anniversary; Broadway appearance, Entertaining Mr Sloan; Numerous television successes including own colour spectacular for BBC2, several comedy series. *Publications:* Ramblings of an Actress, 1987. *Honours:* Variety Club; London Critics; Whitbread Trophy (best actress, Broadway); Order of British Empire (OBE). *Hobbies:* Reading; Music. *Address:* c/o Jeremy Conway Ltd, Eagle House, 109 Jermyn Street, London SW1, England.

HANDY (Mary) Nixeon Civille, b. 5 Mar 1909, Ocean Park, California, USA. Retired Educator; Poet. m. Lawrence A Handy, 14 Feb 1932, 3 sons, 1 daughter. *Education:* BE, University of California at Los Angeles, 1930; ME, Central Washington University, 1958; Postgraduate studies: University of Washington, 1963, 1972, Claremont California School of Theology, summers 1969, 1971. *Appointments:* Placentia, California, Elementary School, 1931; Elementary School, Wenatchee, Washington, Instructor, Wenatchee VA Key College, Journalism, English, 1956-63, Dean of Women 1961-66; Director, Poets Workshop, 1961-66; Director, Released Time School, Visalia, California, 1945-46; YMCA Women's Director, 1949; Director, Summer YMCA Camp, Lake, Wenatchee, 1953-59; Adult Education Director, Sandpoint United Methodist Church 1979-81, Burien United Methodist Churchp 1970-71; Poetry Staff, Pacific NW Writers Conference, 1975-81; Contributing Editor, Fellowship of Prayer International 1978-83. *Publications:* Books of Poems: Do Not Disturb the Dance: Enter It; Earth House; Grandma Casey; A Little Leaven; Exhibitions of poems and photographs. *Memberships:* Poetry Society of America; Academy of American Poets; Washington Poets Association; Delta Kappa Gamma, State Editor, Chapter President, Speaker at Regional Conventions. *Honours:* Teacher of the Year, Wenatchee, Washington, 1954, 1956, Public Service Alpha Sigma Grant Poetry, University of Washington, 1972-73; King County Grant, Poetry in Libraries, 1980; Nixeon Civille Handy Poetry Prizes, University of Puget Sound, Tacoma, Washington, Annual since 1983; Various prizes for poetry. *Hobbies:* Collecting pitchers, Hats. *Address:* 19240 Tenth NE, Seattle, WA 98155, USA.

HANELL-KARLSSON Ingrid, b. 29 Mar. 1941, Lund, Sweden. Headmistress. m. (1) Sten Ingemar Hammar, 1 Dec. 1961, divorced 1975, 1 son, 1 daughter. (2) Chirster Karlsson, 16 July 1988. *Education:* Baccalaureate, Lund, 1960; Tourist Guide Diploma, Stockholm, 1963; Filosofie Magister, University of Lund and Stockholm, 1970. *Appointments:* Tourist guide Spain 1961-62, Tourleader of organized tours around USA, 1962-66, Nyman & Schultz Travel Agency; Teacher, High School, Partille, Sweden, 1966; Teacher, High School, Marsta and Jacobsberg, 1967-70; Founder and Headmistress, Ecole Reine Astrid, Brussels, 1973-; Founder, Swedish Club in Brussels, 1973. *Memberships:* Board member, Fonds Reine Astrid, Brussels, 1980-; Board Member, Svenska Klubben asbl,

1973-; Board member, SIMES SA, 1980-. *Honours:* PRIX Fonds Reine Astrid, 1976; Chevalier de l'Ordre de la Couronne Belgique, 1978. *Hobbies:* Literature education; Languages; Travelling. *Address:* Ecole Reine Astrid, Chee de Waterloo 280, B1640 Rhode-St-Genese, Belgium.

HANES Ursula Ann, b. 18 Jan. 1932, Toronto, Canada. Sculptor. m. (1) David John Fry, 30 Aug. 1956, divorced 1968, 2 sons and 2 daughters, (2) Daniel P. Guthrie, 1976, divorced 1981. *Education:* Cambridge School of Art & Crafts, 1951; Art Students League, New York, 1953; Columbia University, 1953; Diploma, University of Toronto, 1954. *Creative Works:* Several Sculpture & Batik Exhibitions in: Lanzarote, Canary Islands, Spain, 1969-75; exhibited at: Columbia University, New England Society of Artists, OSA, RCA, Stratford Festival, Young Canadian Contemporaries, Canadian National Exhibition; One Woman Show, Geneva, 1986. Commissioned to paint 4ft x 16 in wooden panels of the 21 California Mission Saints for town of San Juan Bautista, California, 1983; Various commissions in Bronze & Marble, Italy, 1985. *Memberships:* Sculptors Society of Canada, President 1964-66; Ontario Society of Artists; Royal Canadian Academy of the Arts. *Hobbies:* Reading; Theatre; Dance; Gardening. *Address:* Montemagno 43, Localita Casciana, 55040 Montemagno, Lucca, Italy.

HANEY Deborah Kay Onstad, b. 29 Jan. 1948, Minot, North Dakota, USA. Nurse Practitioner; Clinical Instructor. m. Thomas Marlin Haney, 25 July 1971. 2 sons. *Education:* BSN, University of North Dakota, College of Nursing, 1971; NP, UCLA Women's Health Care Nurse Practitioner Training Program, 1976; Certified OG Nurse Practitioner (NAACOG), 1980. *Appointments:* Staff Nurse float United Hospital, Grand Forks, 1971-72; Public Health Nurse 1972-74, Family Planning Nurse/Educator 1974-76, Nurse Practitioner 1976-77, First Dist Health Unit, Minot, North Dakota; Educator, Family Planning, North Dakota State Health Dept, 1978-79; Clinical Director, Dakota Family Planning Center, 1979-; Clinical Instructor, University of North Dakota School of Medicine, 1983-. *Publication:* Guide for Family Planning Nurses in North Dakota, 1974. *Memberships:* ANA (Cabinet of continuing education & Professional practice, 1981-83); ANA, Council of Primary Health Care Nurse Practitioners: NAACOG (Legislative Committee, 1980-87); NDPHA; Sigma Theta Tau. *Honour:* Named one of Outstanding Young Women of America, 1979. *Hobbies:* Volunteering, community youth organizations; Resource to Community Rape Crisis programme; Assistant, guest lecturer, Women's Issues course, University of Mary; Crochet; Embroidery; Crafts. *Address:* 908 Midway Drive, Bismarck, North Dakota 68501, USA.

HANFORD Patricia Atkins, b. 5 Dec. 1954, Oklahoma City, Oklahoma, USA. Corporate Management; Purchasing; Facilities; Administration. *Education:* BS Home Economics Education, Oklahoma State University, 1977; Purchasing Management Certificate, Tulsa Junior College, 1988. *Appointments:* Reservation agent, Supervisor 1978-79, Leasing Coordinator 1979-81, Staff Assistant 1981-83, Manager Purchasing & Admin Services 1983-86, Director Purchasing & Admin Services 1986-, Thrifty Rent-A-Car System, Inc. *Memberships:* Choir Secretary 1988-89, Choir Section Leader 1986-87, Asbory Methodist Church; Membership Chairman 1986-87, Vice President 1987-89, Tulsa International Facilities Management Association; Board of Directors, Theatre Tulsa, 1988-89. *Hobbies:* Sports; Reading; Piano; Choir; Sewing; Crafts; Restoration work; Friends and family; Art; Ballet; Theatre; Old movies; Exploring cities. *Address:* c/o Thrifty Rent-A-Car System, Inc, 4608 S Garnett, Tulsa, OK 74146, USA.

HANIN Leda, b. 3 Nov. 1940, Bronx, New York, USA. University Administrator. m. Israel Hanin, 6 Dec. 1960, 1 son, 1 daughter. *Education:* BA, University of California, Los Angeles, 1962; Marketing Certificate, 1978, MEd, 1984, University of Pittsburgh; Certified,

Public Relations Society of America, 1980. *Appointments:* Coordinator, 1974-75, Director, 1975-77, Office of Conferences & Communications, Western Psychiatric Institute & Clinic, University of Pittsburgh, Pennsylvania; Communications Coordinator, Museum of Art & Carnegie Museum of Natural History, Carnegie Institute, 1977-81; Account Executive, ARPR Public Relations Agency, 1981; Director, Public & Alumni Relations, Graduate School of Industrial Administration, 1981-86, Account Executive, College of Fine Arts, 1985-86, Carnegie-Mellon University; Director, Public Relations, Graduate School of Business, University of Chicago, Illinois, 1986-. *Memberships:* Board of Directors, Community Nursing Service, Oak Park, Illinois; Chicago Chapter, Public Relations Society of America (PRSA); American Assembly of Collegiate Schools of Business. *Honours:* Best of Category Awards, Exhibition of Western Pennsylvania Printing, Treasures of Early Irish Art brochure, 1979, Silver in American Life, 1980; 1st Place Public Relations, Matrix Awards, Pittsburgh Women in Communications, Treasures of Early Irish Art, 1979, Earth Week '80, 1981; Silver Anvil, Treasures of Early Irish Art, 1980, Merit Award, Introduction of a New Dean, East-Central Region, 1984, PRSA; Grand Prize, 1st Place, Victor Barkman Award, Introduction of a New Dean, Pittsburgh Chapter, PRSA, 1985; Silver Medal, Most Improved Public Relations, Council for Advancement & Support of Education, 1987; Silver Trumpet, Institutional Relations, Publicity Club of Chicago, 1987; President: Pittsburgh Chapter, PRSA, 1984-85; United Mental Health of Pittsburgh, 1984-86; APR, PRSA. *Hobbies:* Theatre; Opera; Baroque and chamber music; Travel; Snorkelling. *Address:* Oak Park, Illinois, USA.

HANKIN Elaine Krieger, b. 17 Oct. 1938, Scranton, USA. Psychologist. m. Abbe Hankin, 22 Dec. 1957, 2 daughters. *Education:* BA, 1979, MEd., 1980, Temple University; PhD, Bryn Mawr College, 1984. *Appointments:* Intern, Aldersgate Youth Service Bureau, 1975-84; Staff Psychologist, Bucks County Guidance Centre, 1981-84; Director, Partner, Abington Psychological Associates, 1984-. *Publications:* Articles in professional journals. *Memberships:* Phi Beta Kappa; American, Pennsylvania Psychological Associations; National Council on Family Relations; Pennsylvania Society of Behavioural Medicine & Biofeedback; Delaware Valley Group Psychotherapy Society. *Honours:* Phi Beta Kappa; President's Scholar, Temple University, 1979; Alumnae Scholar, Bryn Mawr College, 1984; Psi Chi. *Address:* Travel; Folk Music. *Address:* 242 Ironwood Circle, Breyer Woods, Elkins Park, PA 19117, USA.

HANNUN Kitty Sue, b. 10 Oct. 1954, San Antonio, Texas, USA. Airline Pilot, Instructor & Supervisor. m Candler Gareld Schaffer, 10 June 1976, div. 1983. *Education:* MusB cum laude, University of Miami, Florida, 1976. *Appointments:* Flight attendant, Eastern Airlines, Miami, 1977-84; Pilot, Instructor, Tibben Flight Lines, & Watham Flying Service, Iowa, 1981; Pilot, Mid-Continent Airlines, Iowa 1981-83, Cav Air/Jimmy Jet, Florida 1983, Airlift International Airlines 1983-84, Larken Inc, Iowa 1984, Life Investors 1984; Pilot, Flight Engineer 1984-, Instructor, Boeing 727 & Pilots' Supervisor 1985-, Co-Pilot 1986-, Check Airman 1987-, Eastern Airlines, Miami, Florida; Pilot Northwest Airlines, Minneapolis, Minnesota, 1989. Also speaker in field, 1st woman in many appointments. *Creative work:* Author, producer: Boeing 727 Emergency & Abnormal Training Video, 1988; Boeing 727 2nd Officer Cockpit Pre-Flight, 1989. *Memberships:* YWCA Women's Network; Airline Pilots Association; Aircraft Owners & Pilots Association; Smithsonian, Air & Space. *Honours include:* Business & Industry Young Women's Christian Association, 1984; Various honour societies, scholarships, biographical recognition. *Hobbies:* Music; Swimming; Walking; Reading. *Address:* 3420 Torremolinos Avenue, Miami, Florida 33178, USA.

HANSBURY Vivien Holmes, b. 5 Feb. 1927, Richmond, USA. Teacher. m. Leonard Hansbury, 28 Oct. 1962, 2 sons, 1 daughter. *Education:* BS, Virginia State

University, 1966; MEd., Temple University, 1970. *Appointments:* Teacher, Delaware County Intermediate Unit, 1966-69; Teacher, Counsellor, Pennsylvania State University, Oregon, 1969-74; Programme Manager, Preschool Programme, Instructional Advisor Teacher, School District of Philadelphia, 1974-. *Memberships:* Assault on Illiteracy NE Director; Pan Hellenic Council; Northeastern Federation of Women; Philadelphia Coalition of Federated Women, President; Sigma Pi Epsilon Delta, Chapter President; Top Ladies of Distinction, Chapter President. *Honours:* Recipient, many honours including: Special Educator of the Year 1986; Distinguished Service Award, Pennsylvania Federation of Women, 1987; Rose Linden Baum Teacher of the Year, 1988. *Hobby:* Sewing. *Address:* 2246 N. 52nd St., Philadelphia, PA 19131, USA.

HANSCOMBE Gillian Eve, b. 22 Aug. 1945, Melbourne, Australia. Writer. 1 son. *Education:* BA, Honours, Melbourne University, 1964-67; MA, Monash University, 1969; Certificate of Education, London University, 1974; D.Phil., St Hugh's College, Oxford University, 1979. *Appointments:* Lecturer, Tutor, College & 6th Form, 1969-74; Journalism, 1980-83; Freelance Writer, 1983-. *Publications:* Hecate's Charms, verse, 1976; Between Friends, novel, 1982, 1989; The Art of Life, literary criticism, 1983; Flesh and Paper, verse, with Suniti Namjoshi, 1986; Writing for Their Lives, literary criticism, with V. Smyers, 1987. *Memberships:* Australian Society of Authors; Writers Guild of Great Britain; Oxford Society. *Hobbies:* Founder, Jezebel Tapes & Books, 1986. *Address:* PO Box 12, Seaton, Devon EX12 2XH, England.

HANSEN Darlene Vivian Olga, b. 19 May 1949, Los Angeles, California, USA. Professional Hypnotist; Metaphysician; Speaker; Teacher. m. Jim Dennis Solum 12 June 1983, divorced 3 Apr. 1987. 1 daughter. *Education:* BA 1972, MA 1976, California State University, Long Beach, California. *Appointments:* Owner, The Numbers System-Organization, Employment counseling through Astrology and Numerology; Metaphysical work includes Astrology, Palmistry, Numerology and Tarot; Channeler; Writer, 1982-. *Publications:* Books: Secrets of the Palm, 1984; Power in Numbers - At Llewellyn New Times Now. Numerology articles for professional journals; Writer for Grunion Gazette and Beach Comber. *Memberships:* Treasurer, Numerology Association International, Inc; California Professional Hypnotist Association. *Hobbies:* Aerobics; Climbing; Running; Dancing; Working for world peace through higher awareness; Directing and producing documentaries related to the parapsychology field. *Address:* 5770 East 23rd Street, Long Beach, California 90815, USA.

HANSEN Elizabeth, b. 14 Sept. 1930, Redwood City, California, USA. Teacher; Writer; Antique Dealer. *Education:* Studied Law for 2 years at USC. *Appointments:* Owner, Shop, Monterey County, and Santa Cruz County, 1957; Founder and owner, Hansen's Academy, 1979-. *Publications:* Book of Marks; Furniture Manual, Volume I & II; History and Care of Antiques; Patterned & Art Glass Manual, Part I; Cut Glass Working Manual; Jewelry Manual, Volume I & II; Beading Manual; Appraisal Manual. *Contributions to:* Numerous articles to professional journals and magazines. *Hobbies:* Antiques; Writing; Decorating. *Address:* P O Box 1330, Freedom, CA 95079, USA.

HANSEN Kathryn G, b. 24 May 1912, Gardner, USA. *Education:* BS, 1934, MS 1936, University of Illinois. *Appointments:* Secretarial Positions, 1936-44; Personnel Assistant, 1944-46, Supervisor, Training, 1946-47, Personnel Officer 1947-52, Instructor, Psychology, 1947-52, University of Illinois; Executive Secretary, 1952-61, Secretary, 1952-68, Administrative Officer, 1961-68, Director, October 1, 1968-72, retired, University Civil Service System of Illinois. *Publications:* Editor: Illini Worker, 1945-52; Campus Pathways, 1952-61; Journal of College & University Personnel Association, 1955-73; newsletter, 1955-73; Civil Service Handbook, 1962-71. *Memberships:* College &

University Personnel Association; Delta Kappa Gamma; National League of American Pen Women Inc. *Honours:* Kappa Delta Pi; Kappa Tau Alpha. *Address:* Stipes Publishing Company, 10 Chester Street, Champaign, IL 61820, USA.

HANSEN Phyllis Jean, b. 28 Nov. 1934, Ames, Iowa, USA. Librarian. *Education:* AB, 1960, MS, 1961, University of Illinois; MA, California Polytechnic State University, 1984. *Appointments:* Librarian, Queensborough Public Library, New York City, 1961, Sean Leandro Public Library, 1962-63, California Polytechnic State University, San Luis Obispo, 1963-. *Publications:* Bibliographies: Vitamin C, 1980, revised 1984; Sex Role Stereotyping and Career Aspirations of Junior High and High School Students, grades 7-12, 1983; Sex Role Stereotyping in Career Literature for Adolescents & Young Adults. *Memberships:* American Library Association; California Library Association; Delta Kappa Gamma; American Association of University Women; San Luis Obispo County Historical Association. *Honours:* Graduated with Honours, University of Illinois, 1960; Delta Kappa Gamma; Alpha Lambda Delta. *Address:* Reading; Music - Playing and Listening. *Address:* 1241 Fredericks St., San Luis Obispo, CA 93401, USA.

HANSEN Virginia L., b. 13 Jan, 1944, New Jersey, USA. Business Owner. m. John L. Hansen (deceased 1987), 14 Aug. 1965, 1 son, 1 daughter. *Education:* RN, University of Pennsylvania, 1964; BS, Health Administration, Rutgers University, 1986; 18 credits towards MBA. *Appointments:* Registered Nurse, Paediatrics and Teaching; Health Care Auditing; Owner, Chief Executive Officer, Valley Distributors Inc. *Memberships:* New Jersey Association of Women Business Owners; Chamber of Commerce; American Association of University Women. *Hobby:* Alleviating homelessness and alcoholism. *Address:* 9F Chris Court, Dayton, NJ 08810, USA.

HANSEY Renee J. Payette, b. 24 Apr. 1927, Tacoma, USA. Media Specialist. m. (1) James B. Burgee, 1946, died 1950, (2) Orville Hansey, 1951, divorced 1987, 4 sons, 2 daughters. *Education:* BSc., St John's University, 1988. *Appointments:* Copywriter, Station KIT, 1943-44; Traffic Manager, Radio Station KRKO, 1944-45; Programme Manager, Radio Station King, Seattle, 1945-47; Advertising Manager, Sequim Press, 1967-76; Co-ordinary, Municipality of Anchorage, Producer, Radio KTVA CBS, 1976-86; Owner, Frontier Publishing, 1981-83; Director, Clallam-Jefferson, 1986-; Publisher, North Olympic Senior Voice, 1986-87. *Publications:* Go to Source; One Way to the Funny Farm; Northern Sights; Travel Alaska; articles in: Chicago Sun Times; Smithsonian Magazine; Sunet Magazine; Anchorage Daily News. *Memberships Include:* National Federation of Press Women; Alaska Press Women, Vice President; American Management Association. *Honours Include:* Many honours and awards. *Hobbies:* Travel; Photography; Swimming; Woodwork; Sewing; Tailoring; Knitting. *Address:* 235 N. Sunnyside, Sequim, WA 98382, USA.

HANSON Cheryl Jean, b. 8 Feb. 1954, Oakland, California, USA. Podiatrist. *Education:* AB/AB, Physiology & Physical Education 1976, MA Physical Education 1978, PhD Education (Exercise Physiology) 1981, University of California, Berkeley; DPM, Podiatry, California College of Podiatric Medicine. *Appointments:* Teaching & Laboratory Assistant, Reader, Research Assistant, Associate Instructor 1976-81, Visiting Lecturer 1981-83, University of California, Berkeley & Davis; Apartment Manager, 1984-; Reader, Teaching Assistant, California College of Podiatric Medicine, 1985-88; Resident, Podiatric Surgery, Kaiser Medical Centre, Santa Clara, 1988-89. *Publications:* Research Papers, Neuromotor Integration & Control, Podiatric Medicine & Surgery. *Memberships:* Student Chapter Research Director, American College of Foot Surgeons; American & California Podiatric Medical Associations; American College of Sports Medicine; Student Chapter Secretary, American Academy of Podiatric Sports

Medicine. *Honours:* Pi Delta National Honour Society, 1986-88; Scepter Award, 1988; Soroptimist Fellowship, 1980; Outstanding Young Women of America, 1985; Cahper Scholarship, 1975; Regents Scholar, Berkeley, 1972; Job's Daughters Scholarship, 1972. *Hobbies:* Stamp Collcting; Needlecrafts; Sports; Calligraphy; Diabetes Research. *Address:* 2533 Durant Avenue no. 21, Berkeley, California 94704, USA.

HANSON Leila Fraser, b. 26 May 1942, Chicago, USA. Senior Vice President. 1 son. *Education:* AB, 1964, MA, 1966, PhD, 1971, University of Illinois. *Appointments:* Teaching Assistant, Carleton University, Canada, 1967-68; Lecturer, Political Science, 1970, Assistant Director, Acting Director, Office International Programmes, 1970-72, University of Kentucky; Staff Associate, Assistant to Vice Chancellor, 1972-76, Assistant Vice Chancellor, 1976-77, University of Wisconsin, Milwaukee; Chief Administrator to Mayor, City of Milwaukee, 1977-82; Senior Vice President, Banc One Wisconsin Corporation, 1982-. *Honours:* Outstanding Achievement Award, YWCA, 1986. *Address:* 235 E Elm Grove Road, Brookfield, WI 53005, USA.

HARBIN Shirley M, b. 26 Dec. 1931, Santa Cruz, USA. Arts Administrator; Instructor. m. Dean Harbin, 2 sons. *Education:* BA, 1954, MA 1960, Theatre, University of Michigan; PhD, Theatre, Wayne State University. *Appointments:* High School Teacher, 1954-60; Arts Director, City of Detroit, 1963-; Part-time Creative Drama Instructor, Wayne State University, 1976-. *Creative Works:* Director, 4 International, 10 local festivals; Editor, Bravo Magazine; articles in numerous journals. *Memberships:* Past President, Young Audiences of Michigan; Michigan Theatre Association; American Community Theatre Association, Secretary General; North American Regional Alliance of International Amateur Theatre Association. *Honours:* Patron, American Association of Community Theatre, 1983; City of Detroit Most Outstanding Employee, Children's Theatre Association of America for Model Drama Work, 1984; Arts Award for Outstanding Graduate, 1985. *Hobbies:* Reading; Theatre; Clarinet; Swimming; Sewing. *Address:* 1008 Ferdinand, Detroit, MI 48209, USA.

HARBOTTLE Ann Woodley, b. 23 July 1956, Greenville, South Carolina, USA. Attorney. m. Scott Allan Harbottle, 6 Aug. 1983. *Education:* BA, Journalist/Political Science (Summa cum laude), University of Arizona, 1978; JD (cum laude), Arizona State University College of Law, 1981. *Appointments:* Judicial Law Clerk to the Honorable Carl A Muecke, Chief Judge, US District Court for the District of Arizona, 1981-83; Associate, Winston & Strawn, 1983-. *Memberships:* American Bar Association; American Trial Lawyers Association; District of Columbia Women's Bar Association. *Honours:* Phi Beta Kappa; Phi Kappa Phi. *Hobbies:* Mediator, District of Columbia Mediation Service; Arbitrator, District of Columbia Better Business Bureau. *Address:* Winston & Strawn, 2550 M Street NW, Suite 500, Washington, DC 20037, USA.

HARDER Heather Anne (Stacks), b. 2 Mar. 1948, Henderson, Tennessee, USA. Educational Consultant. m. Robert Alan Harder, 3 Apr. 1971, 2 daughters. *Education:* BS 1970, MS 1974, doctoral candidate 1988, Indiana University. *Appointments:* Elementary school teacher 1970-76, reading specialist 1976-79, Crown Point (Indiana) Community Schools; Faculties, Ball State, Purdue, Governor's State Universities, 1979-; Owner, Executive Director, Small World Child & Family Centre, 1979-; Founder, Human Resources Unlimited, 1982. *Publication:* Why Should I Read, mobile, produced Upstart Library Promotions, 1987. *Memberships include:* Validator, National Academy of Early Childhood Programmes; National Association for Education of Young Children; Indiana Association for Supervision & Curriculum Development; International Reading Association. *Honours:* Educational scholarship, Delta Kappa Gamma, 1987; Invited speaker, Subcommittee on Children's Issues, Indiana House of Representatives,

1986; Invited presentation, Blumberg Centre Colloquium, Indiana State University, 1987; Grants, training child care workers, Lake County Job Training Corporation, 1984-85. *Hobbies:* Reading; Painting; Watching old films. *Address:* 501 South Main Street, Crown Point, Indiana 46307, USA.

HARDESTY Sarah Elizabeth, b. 1 Dec. 1951, Fairmont, USA. Director of Communications. *Education:* BA, Duke University, 1972; MS, Northwestern University, 1973. *Appointments:* Copywriter, 1973-75; Reporter, Forbes Magazine, 1976-78; Acocunt Executive, 1978-80, Vice President, 1981-87, Hill and Knowlton; Senior Staff, Mobil Oil Corp., 1980-81; Director, Communications, Council for Advancement and Support of Education, 1987-. *Publications:* Co-Author, Success and Betrayal: The Crisis of Women in Corporate America, 1987. *Memberships:* Board, Horizons Theatre; National Council on Womens Studies. *Honour:* Outstanding Young Women in America, 1987. *Hobbies:* Reading; Writing; Theatre. *Address;* Suite 400, 11 Dupont Circle NW, Washington, DC 20036, USA.

HARDINGE Florence Elizabeth (Viscountess), b. 7 May 1957, Paris, France. Chairman, FHFC Holdings. m. Nicholas Henry Paul (5th Viscount), 11 Sept, 1982, deceased, 1 daughter. *Education:* Institute of Political Science, Paris, France, 1974-76; French Law Degree, 1979. *Appointments:* The Royal Bank of Canada, 1979-81; NMB Interunion, 1981-83; Chairman, FHFC Holdings, 1987-. *Hobbies:* Shooting; Riding; Skiing. *Address:* 5 Somerset Square, London W14 8EE, England.

HARDY Barbara Gladys, b. 27 June 1924. Professor. m. Ernest Dawson Hardy, deceased, 2 daughters. *Education:* BA, MA, University College, London. *Appointments:* Lecturer, Birbeck College, 1950, Professor of English, Royal Holloway College, 1965-70, Professor of English, Birkbeck College, 1970-. *Publications:* The Novels of George Eliot, 1959; The Appropriate Form, 1964; Editor, George Eliot: Daniel Deronda, 1967; Editor, Middlemarch: Critical Approaches to the Novel, 1967; The Moral Art of Dickens, 1970; Editor, Critical Essays on George Eliot, 1970; The Exposure of Luxury : Radical Thems in Thackeray, 1972; Editor, Thomas Hardy: The Trumpet Major, 1974; Tellers & Listeners: The narrative Imagination, 1975; Editor, Thomas Hardy: A Laodicean, 1975; A Reading of Jane Austen, 1975; The Advantage of Lyric, 1977; Particularities: Readings in George Eliot, 1982; Forms of Feeling in Victorian Fiction, 1985; Narrators and Novelists: collected essays, volume I 1987. *Honours:* Hon. D. Univ (Open), Hon. Member M.L.A. *Memberships:* Welsh Academy. *Address:* Birkbeck College, Malet Street, London WC1E 7HX, England.

HARFF Barbara, b. 17 July 1942, Kassel, Germany. Professor; Author. m. Ted Robert Gurr, 14 Jan. 1981, 1 son. *Education:* BA cum laude, 1975, MA summa cum laude, 1977, Northeastern Illinois University, USA; PhD, Northwestern University, 1981. *Appointments:* Senior Tutor, Department of Legal Studies, LaTrobe University, Melbourne, Victoria, Australia, 1981-82; Visiting Assistant Professor, Marquette University, 1982-83; University of Illinois, Chicago, USA, 1983-84; University of Colorado, 1985-86; Assistant Professor, then Associate Professor of Political Science, US Naval Academy, Annapolis, Maryland, 1986-. *Publications:* Genocide and Human Rights: International Legal and Political Issues, monograph, 1984; Genocide and State Terrorism, book chapter, 1986; Empathy for Victims of Massive Human Rights Violation, article, 1987; Victims of the State, article, 1989; Numerous others. *Memberships:* International Studies Association; Internet on the Holocaust and Genocide; Research Committee on Politics and Ethnicity, International Political Science Association. *Address:* Department of Political Science, US Naval Academy, Annapolis, MD 21402, USA.

HARGRAVES Maureen Eve, b. 4 Oct. 1938, Middleburg, Cape, South Africa. Managing Director/Bookseller. m. Michael John Hargraves, 10 Aug. 1963, 2 sons. *Appointments:* Managing Director, Exclusive Books (Cape) Pty Ltd, 1976-. *Memberships:* Chairman, Associated Booksellers of South Africa (Cape and Namibia); Vice-President, Associated Booksellers of South Africa; Vice-President, Book Trade Association (South Africa); Committee Member, Executive Women's Club (South Africa); President, 100 Club, South Africa; Soroptimists; Professional Culinary Circle. *Hobbies:* Reading; Cooking; Squash, *Address:* 230 Main Road, Claremont 7700, Republic of South Africa.

HARITOS Rosa, b. 7 July 1961, New York City, USA. Sociologist. *Education:* BA distinction Barnard College, 1983; MA 1984, MPhil 1986, Sociology, Columbia University. *Appointments:* Research Staff, Center for Social Sciences 1984-85, Research Assistant, Professor Robert K. Merton 1983-, Columbia University; Research Analyst, Center for Science & Technology Policy, New York, 1986-87; Instructor, State University of New York, Purchase, Summer 1987. *Creative work:* Dissertation in progress. *Memberships:* American Association for Advancement of Science; American Sociological Association; Society for Social Study of Science; History of Science Society; Socieyt for Women Sociologists. *Honours:* President's Fellowship 1983-85, Graduate Fellowship 1983-88, Columbia University. *Address:* c/o Columbia University, Box 58, 415 Fayerweather Hall, New York, NY 10027, USA.

HARJO Joy, b. 9 May 1951, Tulsa, Oklahoma, USA. Poet; Associate Professor. 1 son, 1 daughter. *Education:* HS, Institute of American Indian Arts, 1968; BA, University of New Mexico, 1976; MFA, Writer's Workshop, University of Iowa, 1978; Anthropology Film Center, Santa Fe, New Mexico, 1982. *Appointments:* Creative Writing Instructor, Institute of American Indian Arts, 1978-79, 1983-84; Assistant Professor, University of Colorado, Boulder, 1985-88; Associate Professor, University of Arizona, Tucson, 1988-. *Publications include:* What Moon Drove Me To This?, 1980; She Had Some Horses, 1983; Furious Light (taped reading), 1986; Secrets from the Center of the World, 1989; In Mad Love and War, 1990. *Memberships include:* Board of Directors, Native American Public Broadcasting Corporation; Modern Language Association; American PEN; American Film Institute; Writers Union. *Honours:* National Endowment Creative Writing Fellowship, 1979; Poetry Prize, Santa Fe Festival for the Arts, 1983; Richard Hugo Chair, University of Montana, 1985; Pushcart Prize for Poetry Anthology, 1987. *Hobbies:* Jazz; Saxophone; Painting. *Address:* Department of English, University of Arizona, Tucson, AZ 85721, USA.

HARKINS Mary Jane, b. 3 May 19051, Sheet Harbour, Canada. PhD Candidate. m. James J. Harkins, 15 Apr. 1974, 1 daughter. *Education:* BA, 1971; BEd., 1972; MA, 1983; Supervisor's Certificate, Post Masters, 1986. *Appointments:* Director of Preschool, 1983-86; Student Teaching Supervisor, 1984-87; Student Teaching Supervisor, Junior High School, Dalhousie University, 1988-89. *Memberships:* Kappa Delta Pi; National Association for Education of Young Childen; Dalhousie Association of Graduate Students, Executive Vice President. *Honours:* Kappa Delta Pi, 1983; Phi Kappa Phi, 1986; PhD Graduate Fellowship, 1987-. *Hobbies:* Playing Piano; Computer Programming; Gardening. *bb3Address:* 275 Huguenot Ave., Union, NJ 07083, USA.

HARKLESS-WEBB Mildred, b. 17 Aug. 1935, Texas, USA. Educator. m. James E Webb, 27 June 1981. *Education:* BA, Prairie View A & M University; MA, San Francisco State University. *Appointments:* Teacher & Head Sec, Texas, 1957-65; Subt Teacher, Texas, 1966-68; Teacher, California, 1968-; Cosmetics Consultant, 1976-79; Vice President, Webb's Pest Control, 1981-. *Memberships:* Commwealth Club of California; NEA; CTA; ISBE; WBEA; CBEA; ABE; NAACP; ELAC; SFABSE; TI; May Co; SFMA; NCPVA. *Honours:* Graduate Scholarship, Prairie View, 1953; Miss Homecoming,

High School, 1961; Grant, Newspaper Fund Inc, Wall Street Journal, 1964; Honorary Miss Homecoming, Prairie View, 1975; Outstanding Contributions, SFCTA, 1978-88; Selected to serve on Supt of San Francisco Sch Dist Program's Advisory Council, 1988-; Selected to interview Middle School Principals, 1988-. *Hobbies:* Travelling; Reading; Interior decorating; Helping and counselling youngsters and others. *Address:* 35 Camellia Pl, Oakland, CA 94602, USA.

HARMSWORTH Jessamine Cecile Marjorie Gordon (Lady), b. 14 Aug. 1910, London, England. Company Director. m. Michael Harmsworth, 2 Nov. 1937, 2 sons, 4 daughters. *Memberships:* Chairman, Multiple Sclerosis Society, Caithness County; President, Children's League, Caithness; Wick Choral Society; Save the Children Fund, Caithness; Vice-President, National Deaf Children's Society, Highland Region; Vice-President, Girl Guides, Caithness; Patron, Thurso Live Music, Caithness; Honorary Vice-President, Life Member, Red Cross Society, Caithness (Director 1968-85). *Honours:* Badge of Honour for Distinguished Service in Red Cross Voluntary Medical Service Medal, 1985; Citizen of the Year, 1988, Wick Rotary Club. *Hobbies:* Music (singing, organ-playing); Helping disabled; Being grannie to 22 grandchildren. *Address:* Thrumster House, Caithness, Scotland.

HAROLDSON Nancy Ann, b. 1 Sept. 1959, Summit, New Jersey, USA. President, Fabulous Foods Catering. m. Gregory Dell Haroldson, 10 Sept. 1983. *Education:* BA Biology, University of Colorado, 1981. *Appointments:* Flagstaff House Restaurant, 1979; Chef, Red Lion, 1980; 5 Star Restaurant Manager, Cafe Giovanni, 1981; Restaurant Manager, 1982; President, Fabulous Foods Catering, 1983-. *Memberships:* President, Denver Business Womens Network, 1983-; Programmes Chairman, 1986-87, Chairwoman-President, 1987-88, Denver Chamber of Commerce; Centennial Chamber of Commerce, 1985-; Chairman, National Caterers Roundtable, 1988; Denver Area Caterers Coalition, 1988; State of Colorado, Womens Economic Development Council Business Development Subcommittee, 1988. *Hobbies:* Skiing; Theatre; Camping; Cycling; Travel; Scubadiving; Sailing. *Address:* Fabulous Foods Catering, PO Box 239, Englewood, CO 80151, USA.

HARPER Monica Joka, b. 14 Sept. 1942, Cologne, Federal Republic of Germany. Attorney. *Education:* AB, Chestnut Hill College, USA, 1964; JD, University of Connecticut School of Law, 1976. *Appointments:* Teacher, 1964-68; Research Assistant, 1973, 1977-78; Associate, 1978-84, Partner, 1984-85, Rome, Case, Kennelly & Klebanoff, PC; Attorney, private practice, 1985-. *Memberships:* American, Connecticut & Hartford County Bar Associations; Connecticut Trial Lawyers Association; Hartford Women Attorneys Association, President, 1987-88; Hartford Women's Network; Connecticut Council of Divorce and Family Mediators Inc. *Hobbies:* Gardening; Racquetball. *Address:* 4001 South Street, Coventry, CT 06238, USA.

HYMAN Betty Francis Harpole, b. 20 Nov. 1938, Jasper, Texas, USA. Technical Equipment Consultant. m. Arthur Siegmar Hyman, 14 June 1957, deceased. *Education:* BA, Psychology, University of Texas, San Antonio, 1979. *Appointments:* Special project coordinator, Texas Stores, San Antonio, 1975-79; Communications consultant, Southwestern Bell Telephone, Midland, Texas and San Antonio, 1980-82; Technical Equipment Consultant, AT&T, San Antonio, 1983-85 and 1988-, Intelliserve Corp, Dallas, 1987-88; Consul

HARRELL Irene Burk, b. 10 Mar. 1927, Montcalm County, Michigan, USA. Publisher. m. Allen W. Harrell, 22 June 1952, 2 sons, 4 daughters. *Education:* BA summa cum laude, Ohio State University, 1948; BS, Library Science, University of North Carolina, Chapel Hill, 1949; Graduate, Famous Writers School, 1965. *Appointments:* Freelance Writer; Librarian, Westerville Public Library, Westerville, Ohio, 1949-52; Librarian, Sociology, Anthropology and City Planning Library,

University of North Carolina, Chapel Hill, 1952-53; Director, Halifax County Library, Halifax, North Carolina, 1953-54; Cataloguer, then Head Librarian, C.L.Hardy Library, Atlantic Christian College, Wilson, North Carolina, 1958-64; Editor, Writer, Logos International, Plainfield, New Jersey, 1970-79; President, Star Books Inc, Wilson, 1982-. *Publications:* 45 books including: Prayerables: Meditations of a Homemaker, 1967; Muddy Sneakers and Other Family Hassles, 1974; How to Live Like a King's Kid (with Harold Hill), 1974; Lord, How Will You Get Me out of This Mess? (with Kay Golbeck), 1978; China Cry (with Nora Lam), 1980, Re-released 1984; The General's Lady (with Charlene Curry), 1981; Divorced! (for BJ Smith), 1983; Isn't It Amazin'? A Book About the Love of God (with Tommy Lewis), 1983; Let Yesterday Go (with Mickey Jordan), 1984; A Heart Set Free (with Gloria Phillips), 1985; The Manufacturer's Handbook, Star Books 1987, Zondervan edition under title This Man Jesus, 1988; Articles, stories and poems in national magazines and area newspapers. *Memberships:* Living Faith Fellowship, Wilson, North Carolina; Advisory Board, Women in Leadership; Women's Aglow Fellowship; Authors Guild; Authors League of America; Phi Beta Kappa. *Honours:* Top honour graduate, Westerville High School, 1945. *Address:* 408 Pearson Street, Wilson, NC 27893, USA.

HARRELL Linda Darlyn, b. 29 Mar. 1949, Portsmouth, Virginia, USA. Certified Public Accountant - Tax. divorced. 1 son, 1 daughter. *Education:* Bachelor of Business administration, 1982-85, Master of Business Administration, 1985-87, University of Texas at San Antonio. *Appointments:* Controller, Liberto Specialty, San Antonio, Texas, 1975-76; Accounting Associate, Hardin, Wolff & Bradley, CPA's, San Antonio, 1976-77, Controller, Nicholas & Barrera, Attorneys, San Antonio, 1977-81; Deloitte Haskins & Sells, CPA's, San Antonio, 1981-84; Alexander Grant & Co, CPA's, San Antonio, 1984-85; Banking Administrator, USA, San Antonio, 1985-87; Touche Ross & Co, CPA's, New York, 1987-. *Memberships:* American Institute of CPA's; Texas Society of CPA's; SA Chapter, CPA's; National Association of Accountants; American Society of Women Accountants; Alliance for Women's Appointments; Beta Gamma Sigma; Alpha Chi. *Honours:* Summa cum laude, 1985; National Dean's List, 1984-85; Keynote Speaker, Annual Achiever's Award Breakfast; For Accomplishments, published in San Antonio Light. *Hobbies:* Aquarist; Crewel; Jazzercise; Hiking. *Address:* 35 Linden Lane, Farmingville, NY 11738, USA..

HARRHY Eiddwen Mair, b. 14 Apr. 1949, Trowbridge, Wiltshire, England. Soprano. m. Gregory John Strange, 23 Jan. 1988. *Education:* Royal Manchester College of Music. *Appointments:* Debut, Royal Opera House, Covent Garden in The Ring, 1974; English National Opera, 1975; Glyndebourne Festival Opera, Welsh National Opera, Scottish Opera, Teatro Colon, Buenos Aires; concerts in London, Australia, New Zealand, La Scala, Milan. *Creative Works:* Recordings for: EMI, Deutsche Grammph, Nimbus, BBC, etc. *Membership:* Friends of Musicians Benevolent Fund. *Honours:* Gold Medal, Royal Manchester College of Music, 1971; Miriam Licette Prize, 1972. *Hobbies:* Skiing; Walking. *Address:* c/o Athole-Still International Management Ltd., 113 Church Road, London SE19 2PR, England.

HARRIGAN Jinni Anne, b. 15 Nov. 1946, Cincinnati, Ohio, USA. Medical Educator. m. Dennis O'Connell, 17 Apr. 1982, 1 daughter. *Education:* RN, summa cum laude, St Elizabeth's Hospital, Covington, Kentucky, 1967; BA, summa cum laude, Psychology, 1975, MA 1977, PhD 1979, University of Cincinnati; Licensed Clinical Psychologist, Ohio. *Appointments:* University of Cincinnati: Surgical nurse, 1967-72; Teaching & research assistant, graduate studies, 1975-79; Instructor, Department of Education, 1979-80; Assistant Professor, Medical School, 1980-86; Postdoctoral Fellow, Clinical Psychology, 1984-87; Research Director, Department of Family Medicine, 1984-; Associate Professor, Medical School, 1986-. *Publications:* Contributions, various professional journals. *Memberships:* International Communication Association; American Anthropological Association; American Psychological Association; Society of Teachers of Family Medicine; Friends of Women's Studies; National Arbor Association. *Honours:* Grants, University of Cincinnati Research Council 1979, National Institute of Mental Health 1988. *Hobbies:* Photography; Pottery; Jewellery making. *Address:* University of Cincinnati, Department of Family Medicine, 231 Bethesda Avenue, Cincinnati, Ohio 45267, USA.

HARRINGTON Diana Rae, b. 25 Mar. 1940, USA. Professor. m. William Charles Harrington, 14 Oct. 1967. *Education:* BA, College of William & Mary, 1962; MSBA, Boston University, 1967; DBA, University of Virginia, 1977. *Appointments:* Director, SVCDF, 1972-74; Assistant Professor, University of Northern Iowa, 1973-74; Assistant Professor, Iowa State University, 1974-77; Professor, University of Virginia, 1977-. *Publications:* Case Studies in Financial Decision Making; Corporate Financial Analysis; Modern Portfolio Theory; The Capital Asset Pricing Model and Arbitrage Pricing Theory; The New Stock Market. *Memberships:* Financial Management Association, Board Member; Southern Finance Association, Board Member; Eastern Finance Association, Board Member, President. *Address:* Box 6550, Charlottesville, VA 22906, USA.

HARRINGTON Diane Gail, b. 5 Aug. 1963, Miami, USA. Owner; Administrator. *Education:* BBA, 1985, MBA 1988, University of Miami. *Appointments:* Marketing Representative, John Hancock Insurance Agency, 1985-86; Owner, Gold Seal Financial Inc., 1986-. *Memberships:* American Management Association; Centre of Fine Arts; Historic Preservation Society of America; Smithsonian Association; National Association of Female Executives. *Honours:* Dean's List, University of Miami, 1983; Outstanding Agent Award, John Hancock Mutual Insurance Co., 1985. *Hobbies:* Cooking; Interior Decorating; Old Films; Antiques. *Address:* 2620 NW 111 Street, Miami, FL 33167, USA.

HARRIS Beatrice, b. 18 Apr. 1938, Hartford, Connecticut, USA. Psychologist; Consultant. *Education:* BA, University of Connecticut, 1960; MS, Brooklyn College, 1965; PhD, New York University, 1970. *Appointments:* Research Associate, Graduate Center, CUNY, New York City, 1965-70; Associate Professor, Ferkauf Grad School, Yeshiva University, 1970-79; Partner, Harris, Rothenberg Associates, 1982-. *Memberships:* American Psychological Association; New York State Psychological Association, Occupational Clinical Psychology Committee; American Federation of Television & Radio Artists. *Honours:* US Office of education Research grant, 1969-70; New York University Founders Day Award, 1971; Education Honor Societies: Pi Lamda Theta 1960 and Kappa Delta Pi 1960; National Science Federation Research Grant in biochemistry, 1959; Fellowship, Department of Testing & Research, Brooklin College, 1964-65; Mortar Board, National Honor Society for sen college women, for leadership, scholarship and service. *Hobbies:* Fishing; Painting. *Address:* Harris, Rothenberg Associates, 99 Wall Street 8th Floor, New York, NY 10005, USA.

HARRIS Betsy Joyce, b. 5 Jan. 1915, Jamestown, Australia. Professional Farmer. m. William Thomas Harris, 10 Dec. 1935, 1 son, 1 daughter. *Education:* Teaching Certificate. *Appointments:* Professional Farmer. *Memberships:* Honorary Secretary, Kimba Henry George League. *Hobbies:* Knitting; Crochet; Tatting. *Address:* Box 286, Kimba, South Australia, Australia.

HARRIS Christie Lucy, b. 21 Nov. 1907, New Jersey, USA. Author. m. Thomas Arthur Harris, 13 Feb. 1932, 3 sons, 2 daughters. *Education:* Teachers Certificate, 1925. *Appointments:* Teaching, 1925-32; Freelance Scriptwriting & Broadcasting for CBC, Radio, 1935-63; Women's Editor, weekly newspaper, 1951-58. *Publications:* Approximately 300 scripts for CBC Radio, juvenile & adult plays, humour sketches, juvenile musical fantasies, adventure serial, women's talks, school broadcasts; 19 juvenile & young adult books. *Memberships:* Writers Union of Canada; Canadian Society of Children's Authors; Illustrators & Performers; Federation of BC Writers. *Honours:* Book of the Year for Children, Canadian Association of Children's Libraries Childrens Book of the Year, 1967 and 1977 ; Pacific NW Booksellers Award for Juvenile Fiction, 1967; BC Library Commission International Book of the Year Award, 1972; Vicky Metcalf Award, Canadian Authors Association, 1972; Order of Canada, 1980; Canada Council Children's Literature Prize, 1981. *Hobbies:* Walking; Mythology of the North West Coast Native Cultures. *Address:* No 1604, 2045 Nelson Street, Vancouver, BC V6G 1N8, Canada.

HARRIS Cynthia Coolidge Mead, b. 23 Feb, 1937, Yonkers, New York, USA. Editor. m. 29 Dec. 1962, widowed, Aug. 1966. *Education:* BA, Beaver College, 1959. *Appointments:* Copy Editorial Supervisor, Reinhold Publishing Corporation, 1963-67; Chief Copy Editor, Meredith Press, 1967-69; Editing Supervisor, Random House, 1969-71; Senior Production Editor, 1976-79, Editor, 1979-89, Executive Editor, 1990-, Greenwood Press, Westport, Connecticut. *Hobbies:* Hiking; Conservation; Travel. *Address:* Greenwood Press, 88 Post Road West, PO Box 5007, Westport, CT 06881, USA.

HARRIS Cynthia Lee, b. New York City, USA. Actress; Producer. *Education:* BA, Smith College. *Appointments:* Films Include: Been Down So Long It Looks Like Up to Me; Isadora; Up the Sandbox; I Could Never; The Tempest; Reuben Reuben; Three Men and a Baby; An Old Fashioned Story; TV appearances: Edward & Mrs Simpson, (as Mrs Simpson), Thames TV; Movies of the Week - The Princess and the Cabbie, Izzie and Moe, A Special Friendship, Pancho Barnes; Series, Sorotta's Court, Husbands, Wives & Lovers, LA Law; Guest appearances in: Kojak; Three's Company; Nurse; Hart to Hart; Bob Newhart Show; Plays Include: Member, Joseph Chaiken's Open theatre Company, 1968-71; America Hurrah, New York & London; Cloud Nine; Bad Habits; White House Murder Case; Hold Me; Festival; Shadow Box; etc; Co-Producer, Honky Tonk Nights. *Memberships:* Screen Actors Guild; American Federation of Television & Radio Artists; Actors Equity Association. *Address:* c/o STE, 888 Seventh Avenue, New York, NY 10019, USA.

HARRIS Dian (Helms), b. 18 Nov. 1951, Jackson, Tennessee, USA. Floral Designer. 1 son, 1 daughter. *Education:* Draughon's Business College. *Appointments:* Secretary, Holiday Inns, 1970-73; Manager, Flower Basket Inc 1972-88, Sheltons Flowers 1980-81; Owner, Designer Supply 1986-, Atlantic Imports 1987-. *Memberships:* Founding Director, Lexington Little Theatre, & Henderson County Chamber of Commerce; Member, Past Director, Westate Florists Association, & Tennessee State Florists Association; Member, American Institute of Floral Designers; Past Director, Southern Chapter, American Academy of Floriculture. *Honours:* National Symposium, American Institute of Floral Designers, 1984; Member, design teams (floral decorations), US Presidential Inaugral 1984, 1985 and 1989, Statue of Liberty Centennial 1986, Tennessee Governor's Inaugral 1986; Representative, Senatorial District's nomination, President's Volunteer Service Award, 1985. *Hobbies:* Local theatre, directing, producing & performing amateur productions; Producing pageants as preliminaries to Miss America pageant; Travel; Reading current periodicals. *Address:* PO Box 963, Lexington, Tennessee 38351, USA.

HARRIS Diane Barbara, b. 20 Aug. 1955, Santa Monica, California, USA. Psychiatrist. m. Michael S. Cheskes, 23 Apr. 1983. *Education:* BA magna cum laude, Pharmacology 1977, MA Biology 1978, University of California, Santa Barbara; MD 1982, psychiatry residency 1982-86, University of California Irvine (UCI) & California College of Medicine (CCM). Certificates:

National Board of Medical Examiners, 1983; Diplomate, American Board of Psychiatry & Neurology, 1988. *Appointments:* Private Practice, 1986-; Staff Psychiatrist, Veterans Administration Medical Centre, Long Beach, 1986-; Assistant Clinical Professor & Associate Physician, Management Programme, UCI Department of Psychiatry, 1986-. *Memberships:* Trustee, Associated Alumni, UCI-CCM; CME chair, Los Angeles Group Psychotherapy Society; American Psychiatric Association; Orange County Psychiatric Society; Association of Women Psychiatrists; Association for Transpersonal Psychology. *Honours:* Senior Award, Psychiatry & Human Behaviour, 1982; Service Awards, Associated Alumni, 1981, 1982; Certificate of Merit, Community Affairs Board, 1978; Dean's List Scholar, 1975-77. *Hobbies:* Eastern philosophies; Spiritual growth; Arts. *Address:* 11770 East Warner Avenue, Suite 110, Fountain Valley, California 92708, USA.

HARRIS Donna Elaine Meakins, b. 15 Nov. 1937, Minnesota, USA. Education Department Chairperson. divorced, 5 sons, 2 daughters. *Education:* BS, 1972, MSc, 1975, Ed.Spec., 1978, Winona State University; Ed.D., University of Wyoming, 1984. *Appointments:* Teacher, various schools, 1972-78; Elementary Principal, Hot Springs County, 1978-81; Adunct Professor, Educational Administration, Summers 1980, 1981, Adjunct Professor, 1985-87, Winona State Uiversity; Elementary Principal, St Mary's College Department of Education, 1987-. *Publications:* Articles in various journals. *Memberships:* Council for Exceptional Children; Association for Supervision and Curriculum Development; Phi Delta Kappa; Kappa Delta Pi; Delta Kappa Gamma; Orton Dyslexia Society. *Honours:* Recipient, various Grants, and Honours. *Hobbies:* Archery; Reading; Biking; Gardening; *Address:* 562 West Wabasha Street, Winona, MN 55987, USA.

HARRIS Eula Lee (Merry), b. 16 Mar. 1921, Chattanooga, Tennessee, USA. Freelance Photojournalist; Newspaper columnist; Feature writer. m. John Banks Harris Jr, 13 Sept. 1971. *Education:* Ventura College; LaVerne College; Imperial Valley College; San Diego State University; National Academy of Broadcasting, Magazine Institute. *Appointments:* Freelance Photojournalist, 1940-; Newspaper columnist, feature writer; Assistant Librarian; Social Worker. *Publications:* Books of poetry: Terse Verse; Melancholy Muse; Stars out of Heaven; Madigrals of a Modern Mystic; Even Such is Time; Poems in 80 Anthologies; Publishers; Cartoonist-illustrator publications. *Memberships include:* United Amateur Press Assn; Current Presidential Candidate, The Fossils; British Amateur Press Assn; Cherokee Historical Assn; Past Commander-Founder Paul Jones Memorial Chapter 25; Disabled American Veterans; Tenn Dava Child Welfare; Alpha Omega, College Literary Society; Business & Professional Women; Soroptimists; California Social Workers' Organization; National and California Press Women's Associations. *Honours:* Recipient of numerous honours and awards including: Citation for Meritorious Service to Disabled Veterans, National Commander Dav; Salvation Army Service Award; Service to Ventura College Award; District 14 and El Centro Pilots Club Disabled Woman of Achievement; First place National Award for writing on Traffic Safety. *Hobbies include:* Creative photography; Pen and ink sketching; Gardening; Designing clothes; Creative cookery; etc. *Address:* P O Box 25, Ocotillo, CA 92259, USA.

HARRIS Helen(a) Barbara Mary, b. 7 Feb. 1927, Dean Court, Buckfastleigh, Devon. m. Desmond John Harris, 18 Oct. 1952, dec. 1982. 1 son, 1 daughter. *Education:* National Diploma in Dairying, 1947. *Appointment:* Dairy Adviser, Ministry of Agriculture, 1948-56. *Publications:* The Industrial Archaeology of Dartmoor, 1968, revised 1986; The Industrial Archaeology of the Peak District, 1971; The Bude Canal (with Monica Ellis), 1972; The Grand Western Canal, 1973; Chapter on Dartmoor in The Duchy of Cornwall, 1987; Author of papers published in The Transactions of the Devonshire Association: Nineteenth Century Granite Working on Pew Tor and Staple Tor, Western Dartmoor, 1981; The Sourton Tors Iceworks, Northwest Dartmoor, 1988. Past contributor to numerous newspapers and magazines. *Memberships:* Devon History Society; Honorary editor, The Devon Historian, 1985-. *Hobbies and Interests:* The Countryside; Industrial Archaeology; Local History; Travel; My Family; Walking; Swimming (outdoor); Gardening; Photography; Dressmaking; Current and National affairs; The Church. *Address:* 22 Churchill Road, Whitchurch, Tavistock, Devon PL19 9BU.

HARRIS Irene Joyce, Air Cdre, b. 26 Sept. 1926, London, England. *Education:* SRN, Charing Cross Hospital; SCM, The London and Queen Mary's Maternity Home. *Appointments:* Nursing Service, Princess Mary's Royal Air Force, 1950-84 served in UK; Singapore; Germany; Cyprus; Group Captain Principal Matron, Princess Mary's Royal Air Force Nursing Service, 1978; Director Nursing Services, Royal Air Force; Matron-in-Chief, Princess Mary's Royal Air Force Nursing Service; Queen's Honorary Nursing Sister, 1981- 84. *Honours:* CB 1983; RRC 1976. *Hobbies:* Travel; Gardening. *Address:* Evdhimou, 51 Station Road, Haddenham, Ely, Cambs CB6 3XD, England.

HARRIS Jane Ellen, b. 26 Feb. 1945, New York City, USA. Director of Toxicology. m. 5 Sept. 1976, 1 son, 1 daughter. *Education:* BS, Cornell University, 1965; PhD, Yale University Medical School, 1971. *Appointments:* Assistant Professor, Pharmacology, Emory University, 1973-78; Toxicologist, Food and Drug Administration, 1978-84; Section Head, Environmental Protection Agency, 1984-86; Director, Toxicology, American Cyanamid Co., 1986-. *Memberships:* American Society of Pharmacology & Experimental Therapeutics; Society for Neuroscience. *Honours:* Merit Awards, FDA, EPA; National Institutes of Health Grants. *Hobbies:* Tennis; Theatre; Art; Dance; Music. *Address:* PO Box 400 ARD, American Cyanamid Co., Princeton, NJ 08540, USA.

HARRIS Janet Young, b. 3 Oct. 1952, Tupelo, Mississipi, USA. Nursing Administrator. m. Joseph MacDonald Hudspeth, 12 Mar. 1988, 1 son. *Education:* BSN, 1974, MSN in progress, University of Mississippi School of Nursing, Jackson; Courses in American Philosophy, Group Dynamics, Counselling Therapy, 1974-76; Registered RN. *Appointments:* Charge Nurse, Mississippi Baptist Hospital, Jackson, 1974-75; Instructor, University of Mississippi School of Nursing, Jackson, 1974-75; Head Nurse, Adult Intensive Care, 1975-79, Assistant Director of Nursing, 1979-84, Acting Associate Hospital Director, Nursing, 1984, Associate Hospital Director, Nursing, 1984-85, Associate Director of Nursing, 1985-86, University of Mississippi Medical Center, Jackson; Nursing Director, Cardiovascular and Critical Care Services, Mississippi Baptist Medical Center, Jackson, 1986-. Presentations at workshops, seminars. *Memberships include:* American Association of University Women; American Cancer Society, Past Chapter President; Business and Professional Women's Club Young Careerist Chairman for US, Member of National Planning Committee and Board of Directors, 1988; Mental Health Association; Sigma Theta Tau (Past Vice-President, Theta Beta Chapter); Board of Directors, Programme Planning Committee, President of Nursing Chapter, Finance and Recruitment Committee of Guardian Society, University of Mississippi Alumni Association; Charter Member, University of Mississippi School of Nursing Honor Society; Others; Numerous offices. *Honours:* Alumna of the Year, Nursing Alumni Chapter, University of Mississippi Alumni Association, 1983, 1985; Outstanding Young Woman of Jackson, 1985, Jackson Jaycees, 1985; Phi Kappa Phi, 1987; Biography Internationale, 1987; Numerous others. *Hobbies:* Dancing; Music. *Address:* 312 Longmeadow Drive, Ridgeland, MS 39157, USA.

HARRIS Jeanne Elizabeth, b. 4 July 1947, Detroit, Michigan, USA. Geologist. m. Robert John Groth, 30 Oct. 1982. 1 son. *Education:* BS 1968, MS 1975, MBA,

Graduate work in Computer Science, 1971-75, University of Michigan; Graduate work towards MBA, University of Denver, 1975-78. *Appointments:* Research Assistant and Computer Programmer, Seismological Observatory, 1970, and Geology Department, 1971-73 at the University of Michigan, Enviromental Research Institute of Michigan, 1973-74, and Great Lakes Research, 1975; Exploration Geophysicist and Geologist, Mobil Oil Corp, 1975-80; Project Manager, Team Leader, Natural Gas Corp of California, 1980-85; President and Consultant, G & H Production Company, 1986-87; Assistant Exploration Manager, Equity Oil Company, 1988-. *Memberships:* Alternate Delegate, 1983-86, Delegate, 1986-89, American Association of Petroleum Geologists; President 1987-89, Association for Women Geoscientists Foundation; Vice President 1985-86, Delegate 1981-85, Denver President 1982, Association for Women Geoscientists; Chaired several committees, Rocky Mountain Association of Geologists; Colorado State Treasurer 1984-85, National Organization for Women; President 1984-87, Lake Village Homeowner's Association; Advisor, University of Colorado at Denver Geology Dept; Wyoming Geological Society; Denver Geophysical Society; Society of Independent Professional Earth Scientists; Geological Society of America; YMCA; University of Michigan Alumni Association. *Honours:* Community Service Award, Pacific Gas & Electric, 1985; Denver Woman of the Year, Association for Women Geoscientists, 1984; Outstanding Young Women of America, 1983; Distinguished Service Award, Association for Women Geoscientists, 1988. *Hobbies:* Reading; Travel; History; Swimming; Bicycling; Riding; Most team sports; Motorcycles; Gardening; Building and repairs; Sketching. *Address:* 12803 Milwaukee Court, Thornton, CO 80241, USA.

HARRIS Kitty Scaling, b. 7 Mar. 1951, Lubbock, Texas, USA. Substance Abuse Therapist. m. Michael Benton, 10 Sept. 1988. *Education:* BS 1973, MS 1974, North Texas State University; PhD, Texas Tech University, 1983. *Appointments:* Private Practice, 1983-; Consultant Lubbock ISD, 1983-; Program Administrator, Adolescent Substance Abuse Unit, Charter Plains Hospital, 1985-; Consultant Educational Services Ct, 1987-. *Publication:* The Developmental Effects of Alcoholism In The Adolescent, 1983. *Memberships:* Board Member, Lubbock Council on Alcohol and Drug Abuse; National Association of Alcohol & Drug Abuse Counselors; Association for Medical Education and Research in Substance Abuse; Regional Networking Council for Substance Abuse Services; DWI Task Force. *Honours:* Counselor of The Year 1986-87, Lubbock Chapter, Texas Association of Alcohol and Drug Abuse Counselors; Texas Parent Teachers Association, Lifetime Membership Award, 1988. *Hobbies:* Running; Collecting antique books; Astronomy. *Address:* 801 N Quaker, P O Box 10560, Lubbock, TX 79408, USA.

HARRIS Linda Sue, b. 29 Mar. 1950, Des Moines, Iowa, USA. Computer Consultant. *Education:* BS, Women's Physical Education, University of Iowa, 1972. *Appointments:* Physical Education Teacher, Southeast Polk Community Schools, Runnells, Iowa, 1976-83; Owner-Operator, Harris Microcomputer Consultants, 1984-86; President, Harris Computer Services Inc, Des Moines, Iowa, 1987-. *Publications:* Poems: Sides of a Mountain, 1968; Scaling, 1971; Plez Gramma, Tie Shoe, 1975; A California Sunday, 1976; Upon Choice of a Pooh Character, 1977; An Apology, 1977; The Philanthropist Pie Lady, 1977. *Memberships:* American Association of Health, Physical Education and Dance; President, Chief Negotiator, Southeast Polk Educational Association; National Association of Women Business Owners. *Honours:* 1st woman to present a paper to Saudi Arabia National Computer Conference, Riyadh 1984. *Hobbies:* Cycling; Reading; Writing poetry; Jogging. *Address:* Harris Computer Services Inc, 4761 NE 46th Street, Des Moines, IA 50317, USA.

HARRIS Loretta Kelley, b. 20 Nov. 1935, Bryant, Mississippi, USA. Library Technical Assistant III. m. James J Harris, 20 June,. 1 daughter. *Education:*

Certificate, Vocational Technical Institute of Southern Illinois, University Carbondale, 1954; Certificate, Kennedy-King College, 1971; Diploma, Chicago Loop College, 1974; BA, Chicago State University, 1983. *Appointments:* Photographic Technician, University of Illinois, Library, 1957-59; Library Clerk, Southern Illinois University Library, 1959-68; Order Librarian, John Crerar Library, 1968-70; Library Technical Assistant III, University of Illinois at Chicago, Library of the Health Sciences, 1970-. *Memberships:* Council on Library/Media Technicians, Membership Chairperson, Constitution Chairperson; Ontario Association of Library Technicians; Midwest Chapter, Medical Library Association; Health Sciences Librarians of Illinois. *Honour:* Chicago State University Honor Society, 1982. *Hobby:* Reading Mysteries and Westerns. *Address:* 8335 S Colfax Avenue, Chicago, IL 60617, USA.

HARRIS Marion Rose, b. 12 July 1925, Cardiff, Wales. Author. m. Kenneth Mackenzie Harris, 18 Aug. 1943. 2 sons, 1 daughter. *Education:* Cardiff Technical College, 1941-43. *Appointments:* Freelance Journalist, 1953-63; Proprietor, Regional Feature Service, 1964-74; Editorial Controller, W Foulsham & Co Ltd, 1974-82; Author, 1982-. *Publications:* Books: Captain of Her Heart, 1976; Just a Handsome Stranger, 1983; The Queen's Windsor, 1985; Soldiers' Wives, 1986; Officers' Ladies, 1987; Nesta, 1988; forthcoming: Amelda, Megan. *Memberships:* Society of Authors; Romantic Novelists Association. *Hobbies:* Collecting Dragons; Reading; Research. *Address:* Walpole Cottage, Long Drive, Burnham, Slough SL1 8AJ, England.

HARRIS Martha Caldwell, b. 4 Dec. 1947, New Orleans, Louisiana, USA. Director. m. Scott A Harris, 2 Jan. 1982. *Education:* BA, Valparaiso University, 1969; MA Political Science 1979, PhD Political Science, 1981, University of Wisconsin, Madison. *Appointments:* Lecturer, University of Washington, Seattle, 1979-80; Project Director & Senior Analyst, Congressional Office of Technology Assessment, 1980-88; Director, Office of Japan Affairs, National Research Council, 1988-. *Publications:* Author of numerous reports; Articles to professional journals and to conferences. *Memberships:* Assoc of Asian Studies; International Institute of Strategic Studies, London, England. *Address:* Office of Japan Affairs HA 164, National Research Council, 2101 Constitution Ave NW, Washington, DC 20418, USA.

HARRIS Mary Ann Brooks, b. 10 June 1946, Moultrie, Georgia, USA. Project Associate, University of Michigan. m. John W Harris, 29 July 1972. 2 sons. *Education:* BS, Knoxville College, 1969; MA, Wayne State University, 1971; EdD, Nova University, 1986. *Appointments:* Case Western Reserve University, 1972-73; Cuyahoga Community College, 1974-81; Executive Director, Project Rainbow, 1983-85; Community Education Consultant, Ohio Division of Education, 1986-; Project Associate, University of Michigan, 1986-. *Publications:* Dissertation: The Development, Implementation and Evaluation of a Seminar to change selected perceptions of Black Youth toward Aging. *Memberships:* East Cleveland Board of Education; Ohio Caucus of Black School Board Members; Alpha Kappa Alpha Sorority; National Alliance of Black School Educators; NAACP; Friends of the East Cleveland Public Library; Cuyahoga County Advisory Council on Aging. *Honours:* Education/Leadership Award, Ohio State Senate and House of Representatives, 1987; East Cleveland Home Owners Association, 1986; Governor's Salute of Liberty Award, 1985; Cleveland Panhellenic Council, Community Service Award, 1984; Career Mother of the Year, Cleveland Call & Post Newspaper, 1984. *Hobbies:* Bowling; Sewing; Interior design; Writing; Landscaping. *Address:* 1326E 143 St, East Cleveland, OH 44112, USA.

HARRIS Muriel Diana Reader, b. 11 Oct. 1912, Hong Kong. Retired. *Education:* 1st class honours, English, London University. *Appointments:* Assistant Mistress 1934-43, House Mistress 1938-43, Headmistress 1950-75, Sherbourne Girls School; Staff, National Association of Girls Clubs, 1943-49. *Memberships*

include: Independent TV Authority, 1956-60; Panel on Broadcasting Church of England, 1975-86; King George's Jubilee Trust, 1955-67; Executive & Council, National Youth Mcbeha, 1976-79; President, Time & Talents, Northern hultre, British School Society; President, Churches Commission on Overseas Students; President, Church Missionary Society, 1969-72; Chairman, Christain Aid, 1978-83; President, Association of Headmistresses of Boarding Schools, 1960-62; President, Association of Headmistresses, 1964-66; Vice President, National Association of Girls Club, 1968-; Vice President, PHAB (Physically Handicapped-Able Bodied); Chairman, Outward Bound Girls Courses, 1954-59; Council, Outward Bound Trust, 1956-64; Women's National Commission, 1976-78; Women's Consultative Committee, 1958-77; Dorset Education, 1952-70; Committee on Agricultural Colleges Ministry of Agriculture, 1961-64; Archbishop's Council on Evangalism, 1966-68; Salsbury Arts Festival, etc. *Honours:* DBE 1972; Honorary Fellow, College of Preceptors, 1975. *Hobbies:* Reading; Travel. *Address:* 35 The Close, Salisbury, Wiltshire, SP1 2EL, England.

HARRIS R. Eleanor Murden, b. 28 July 1936, Cleveland, USA. Educator. m. Lawrence L. Harris, 5 Aug. 1961, 1 son. *Education:* BS, 1958, MEd., 1973, Bowie State Univesity; Ed.D., Nova University, 1985. *Appointments:* Teacher, 1958-70; Curriculum Specialist, 1970-73; Assistant Principal, 1973-75; Human Relations Co-ordinator, 1975-79; Administrative Assistant to Superinendent of Schools, 1979-. *Publications:* Unified Science K-12, 1970; Code of Student Rights & Responsibilities, 1976; Human Relations Comprehensive Guide, 1975; Interaction : Human Concerns in the Schools, 1986; Guide to Citiazen Advisory Committees, 1986. *Memberships Include:* Delicados, National President; Phi Delta Kappa, National President; American Association of School Executives. *Honours:* Recipient many honours & awards. *Address:* 1999 Forest Drive, Annapolis, MD 21401, USA.

HARRIS Shirley Darlene, b. 2 Feb. 1959, Brewton, Alabama, USA. Business Tax Product Manager. *Education:* BA, Accounting, University of West Florida, 1981. *Appointments:* Staff Accountant, 1981-82, Senior Accountant, 1983-84, Tax Supervisor, 1985-88, Robert A. Benz & Co., Accountants; Software Design Specialist, 1988-; Business Tax Product Manager, Convergent Professional Accounting Systems, 1989-. *Memberships:* American, Florida Institutes of CPA's; Phi Kappa Phi; New Members Committee, FICPA; Chairman, Public Relations, West Florida Chapter of FICPA. *Honours:* Elijah Watt Sells Silver Medal, 1981; Florida High Grade Award, 1981; Appointed to State Taxation Committee, Florida Institute of CPA's, 1985, 1986. *Hobbies:* Piano; Reading. *Address:* Route 3, Box 920, Jay, Fl 32565, USA.

HARRIS Zelema M, b. 12 Jan. 1940, Newton, Texas, USA. President, Penn Valley Community College. 1 son, 2 daughters. *Education:* BS, Prairie View A & M, 1961; MS 1972, EdD 1976, University of Kansas. *Appointments:* Director, Evaluation, 1976; Director District Services, 1978, Metropolitan Community College District; President, Pioneer Community College, 1980; President, Penn Valley Community College, 1987-. *Publications:* The Development and Field Testing of Vocational Education Model; A Method of Establishing Criterion Weights in the Evaluation of Vocational Education Programs. *Memberships:* AAWCJC; Presidents' Roundtable, AACJC; Central Exchange, NOW; Council of Black American Affairs; President, Kansas City Missouri Chapter NAACP, 1982-86; Board Member, Urban league and NCCJ. *Honours include:* Named one of Kansas City's Powerful Women, Kansas City Magazine, 1984; Jefferson Award, WDAF television, Channel 4, Kansas City's NBC affiliate, 1984; Service Award, Kansas City, Missouri, City Council, 1985; Citation Award as Protestant of the Year, National Conference of Christians & Jews, 1986; One of the Nation's Most Influential Black Women, Dollars & Sense Magazine, 1986; Black Achievers in Industry Award,

Southern Christian Leadership Conference; Kansas City Spirit Award, Gillis Center of Kansas City, 1987; One of 100 Most Influential Blacks in Kansas City, Kansas City Globe newspaper, 1987; One of 30 Women of Conscience, Panel of American Women, 1987, etc. *Hobbies:* Reading; Theatre; Walking. *Address:* Penn Valley Community College, 3201 Southwest Trafficway, Kansas City, MO 64110, USA.

HARRIS SMITH Joan A. Quigley, b. 14 Apr. 1933, Wilkes-Barre, Pennsylvania, USA. Administrator & Teacher, Dance, Voice & Drama. m. Joseph Michael Melchiona, 16 Nov. 1952, div. 1960, 1 son, 1 daughter, (2) Lynn Rynearson Harris, 14 Apr. 1962, div. 18 July 1971, 3 sons, 1 daughter, (3) Charles T. Smith, 14 Feb. 1984. *Appointments:* Actress, dancer, New York City, 1949-72; Owner, teacher, KLS Enterprises Inc, Edwardsville, Pennsylvania, 1967-72; Programme Director, College for Kids, King's & Wilkes College, Wilkes-Barre, 1976-79; Executive Director, Kids on Campus, Wilkes- Barre, 1979-80; Director, Marywood College, Scranton, 1981; Owner, Director, teacher, Joan Harris Centre for Gifted & Talented, Edwardsville, 1982- . *Publications:* Co-author, Creative Dance, 1977; Editor, books: 1st of 3 R's, Reason 1978, True Myths 1978, 1980, Tribute to Water 1979, Wheel 1979, Our Country 1979, Philosopher's Index 1981. *Memberships:* Republican National Committee; National Association for Gifted; Dance Educators of America; National Association of Female Executives; Offices, National Association for Gifted Children. *Honours:* 1st & 2nd place awards, talent contest, Youth Reserve Fund, 1984; Small Business Development Award, Greater Wilkes-Barre Chamber of Commerce, 1985; Certificate of Appreciation, OK Heart, 1985. *Hobbies:* Science, especially space; Greenpeace. *Address:* 185 Terrace Avenue, Trucksville, Pennsylvania 18708, USA.

HARRIS-EBOHON Altheria Thyra, b. 26 June 1948, Miami, Florida, USA. Educator; Businesswoman. m. Captain John Ikpomwenosa Ebohon, ALTP, 25 Dec. 1987. *Education:* AA, Miami-Dade Jr College, 1967; BA 1970, EdS 1976, Florida Atlantic University; MS, Morgan State University, 1972; EdD, Nova University, 1981. *Appointments:* Educator, Dade County Public Schools, 1970-73; Co-owner, Niam, Inc of Florida, 1988- . *Memberships:* New Mount Zion Missionary Baptist Church of Hialeah, Florida, 1955-; National Education Association, 1970-; Baptist Training Union (BTU), Directress, 1980; Florida General National Baptist Convention Association, 1985-; . *Honours:* Honoree at Governor's Banquet, 1986; Senator Bob Graham honored and congratulated each recipient, State of Florida on the launch of the official birthdate of Reverend Dr Martin Luther King, Jr, 1986; 1st place Art Exhibit, Miami-Dade Community College, 1967. *Hobbies:* Reading; Sewing; Cooking; Video taping; Cultivating green plants. *Address:* 475 N W 90th Street, El Portal, Miami, Florida 33150, USA.

HARRISON Daphne Duval, b. 14 Mar. 1932, Orlando, Florida, USA. Associate Professor. m. Daniel L. Comegys, 14 Jan. 1982, 1 son, 1 daughter. *Education:* BMus., 1953; MMus, 1962; DEd., 1971. *Appointments:* Instructor, Music: Ocala, 1953-54, Ft. Lauderdale, 1954-65; Television studio Teacher, 1966-68; Professor, Music, Benedict College, 1971-72, University of Maryland, Baltimore County, 1972-. *Publications:* Black Pearls: Blues Queens of the 1920s; articles in various journals. *Memberships:* Alpha Kappa Alpha; American Studies Association; Association for the Study of Afro-American Life & History; International Association for the Study of Popular Music; NAACP, etc. *Honours:* Recipient, various honours and awards including: Outstanding Black Woman of Maryland, 1985; Fulbright Award, 1986. *Hobbies:* Reading; Sewing; Cooking; Gardening; Museums. *Address:* Dept. of African American Studies, University of Maryland, 5401 Wilkens Avenue, Baltimore, MD 21228, USA.

HARRISON Gail Louise, b. 18 Aug. 1947, Danbury, Connecticut, USA. Government Relations Consultant. m. 2 Aug. 1987, 1 son. *Education:* BA, Government,

Cornell University, 1969. *Appointments:* Legislative Assistant to Senator Walter F. Mondale, 1969-76; Assistant for Issues Development, Vice-President W.F.Mondale, 1977-81; Government Relations Consultant, Senior Vice-President, Treasurer, Wexler, Reynolds, Fuller, Harrison & Schule Inc, 1981-; Director, State Mutual Assurance Company, 1986-; Elected Chairman, Committee on Audit, 1989. *Memberships:* Women at the Top. *Honours:* New York State Regents Scholarship, 1965; Dean's Scholarship, Cornell University, 1965-69; Alpha Lambda Delta, 1966; Phi Beta Kappa, 1969; Mortar Board, 1969. *Hobbies:* Tennis; Hiking; Travel. *Address:* 3825 No 37th Street, Arlington, VA 22207, USA.

HARRISON Kathleen (Mrs J H Back), b. Lancashire, England. Actress. m. John Henry Back, 1916. 2 sons, 1 daughter. *Education:* Clapham High School; Trained at RADA. *Creative Works:* Plays include: Badger's Green, Prince of Wales Theatre, 1930; Night Must Fall, Duchess, 1935; The Corn is Green, Duchess, 1938; Flare Path, Apollo, 1942; The Winslow Boy, Lyric, 1946; All for Mary, Duke of York's, 1955; Nude with Violin, Globe, 1956; How Say You? Aldwych, 1959; Watch it, Sailor!, Aldwych, 1960; The Chances, Chichester Festival, 1962; Norman, Duchess, 1963; Title role in Goodnight Mrs Puffin, New Theatre, Bromley; Harvey, Richmond Theatre, 1971; She Stoops to Conquer, Young Vic, 1972; Toured in All for Mary and Good Night Mrs Puffin, 1970. Films include: In Which We Serve; The Huggett films; Alive and Kicking; The Winslow Boy; Bank Holiday; Holiday Camp; Barabbas; West 11; Scrooge; The London Affair. Television includes: Martin Chuzzlewit serial (Betsy Prig); title role in Mrs Thursday series; Waters of the Moon; The Coffee Lace; Spring and Autumn, 1973; The Defence, in Shades of Greene, 1975; Mrs Boffin, in Our Mutual Friend, 1976; Danger UXB. *Address:* c/o T Plunket Greene, 91 Regent Street, London W1, England.

HARRISON Margaret Olson, b. 2 July 1930, Wichita, Kansas, USA. Business Executive. m. 22 June 1957, 2 sons, 1 daughter. *Education:* BS, University of Kansas, 1952. *Appointments:* Housewife, 1957-73; President, Pride Electric Co., 1973-. *Memberships:* National Electrical Contractors Association; Independent Electrial Contractors; Women's Business Owners Association; Denver Chamber of Commerce; Junior League of Denver Inc; Zonta. *Honours:* Business Woman of the Year, Colorado, 1982-83; US West Advisory Panel for Minority and Women Business Enterprises 1987-88. *Hobbies:* Reading; Travel; Sports. *Address:* Pride Electric Co., 4335 Cherokee, Denver, CO 80216, USA.

HARRISON Mary Styron, b. 7 Dec. 1949, Foley, Alabama, USA. Certified Public Accountant; Controller. m. Dale M Harrison, 1 May 1974. 1 son. *Education:* AS Business administration, Faulkner State College; BS Business Administration/Accounting, Troy State University, 1981. *Appointments:* Certified Public Accountant, Jerome Olsen, 1980-83; Certified Public Accountant, Johnson, Mongomery and Associates, 1983-84; UDA of S. Alabama, 1984-87; Lake Forest Yach & Country Club, 19887; Faulkner State College, 1983-. *Memberships:* American Institute of Certified Public Accountants; Alabama State Society of Certified Public Accountants; National Association of Accountants; Alabama Society of Women Accountants; Professional Women's Association. *Honour:* President's Award for Academic Excellence, 1981. *Hobbies:* Tennis; Running; Reading. *Address:* Rural Route 1, Box 89, Loxley, Alabama 36551, USA.

HARRISON Sarah, b. 7 Aug. 1946, Exeter, Devon, England. Writer; Broadcaster. m. Jeremy Richard Douglas Harrison, 7 June 1969, 1 son, 2 daughters. *Education:* BA, Engineering, Honours, London University, 1966. *Appointments:* Journalist, Woman's Own Magazine, 1967-70; Regular Contributor to Radio 4's Stop the Week with Robert Robinson. *Publications:* Novels: The Flowers of the Field, 1978; Flower That's Free, 1982; Hot Breath, 1985; An Imperfect Lady, 1988;

Children's Books: In Granny's Garden; The Laura From Lark Rise series; numerous short stories, articles, etc. *Hobbies:* Public Speaking; Long Distance Running; Theatre; Ballet. *Address:* Steeple Morden, Cambridgeshire, England.

HARROUN Dorothy Sumner, b. 29 Nov. 1935, El Paso, Texas, USA. m. Anthony Victor Parker, 20 June 1987. *Education:* Private Art lessosn with Roderick Mead, Carlsbad, 1944-53; BFA, University of New Mexico, Albuquerque, 1957; Fulbright Scholar, University of Paris, France, 1957-58; MFA, University of Colorado, Boulder, Colorado, USA, 1960. *Appointments:* Art Director, Wood-Reich Advertising Agency, Boulder, Colorado, 1960-61; Lecturer, University of Colorado, Boulder, 1961-62; Art Teacher, Langley-Porter Neuropsychiatric Institute of California Medical School, San Francisco, 1963-; Art Lecturer, San Francisco State College, 1963-65; Art Teacher, Center School, Albuquerque, 1975-79; Art teacher, University of New Mexico Continuing Education, 1980-84. *Publications and creative works:* Take Time to Play and Listen, 1963; Phun-y Physics; Set of 16 pen and ink drawings published in portfolio form; Pen and ink drawings used as chapter headings and cover of Historic Albuquerque Today; Illustrated the book, Mini Walks on the Mesa, 1989; Numerous One Person and Group Shows, most recently, Western Federation of Watercolour Societies, juried show, Tucson Museum of Art; Visions of Excellence, juried show, State Fair Fine Arts Gallery, Albuquerque; Invitational Show, Governor's Gallery, State Capitol, Santa Fe, New Mexico. *Honours include:* Recipient of numerous awards including most recently: Focus International, American Women in Art, United Nations World Conference on Women, Nairobi, Kenya, 1985; Art Contemporain, 1987; 1987 Show Galerie Hautefeuille, Paris, France. *Hobbies:* Masks; Stamps; Coins; Gardening; Languages; Travelling; Designing and building houses. *Address:* North Star Route, Box 982, Corrales, New Mexico 87048, USA.

HARROW Nancy, b. New York City, USA. Jazz Singer; Recording Artist. m. Jan Krukowski, 2 sons. *Education:* BA, Bennington College. *Appointments:* Vocalist, Tommy Dorsey Orchestra; various club dates and jazz festivals. *Creative Works:* Recordings Include: Wild Women Don't Have the Blues, 1961; You Never Know, 1963; Anything Goes, 1979; The John Lewis Album for Nancy Harrow, 1981; Two's Company, 1984; You're Nearer, 1986; Street of Dreams, 1989. *Address:* 130 East End Ave., New York, NY 10028, USA.

HARSHA Jacqueline Gayle, b. 30 Dec. 1946, Fargo, USA. Real Estate Research. *Education:* BA, English, Arizona State University, 1982. *Appointments:* Administrative Assistant, Centre for Environmental Studies, ASU, 1980-81; Market Analyst, Putte Home Corp, 1982-85; Director, Research, Putte Home Corp, 1985-. *Publications:* Co-author, A Proposal for the Cooperative Development by a a Water Conservation Programme. *Memberships:* Maricopu County Association Governments Water Quality Advisory Board; Board, Lagana Beach Chamber Music Society; AMA; BIA. *Honour:* Outstanding Service in the Community & Environment, Putte Hme Corp, 1985. *Hobbies:* Cello; Photography; Music. *Address:* 270 Newport Center Drive, Newport Beach, CA 92660, USA.

HART Helen P, b. 20 Feb. 1927, Fonda, USA. Manager. m. John J. Hart, 6 Sep. 1947, 2 sons, 1 daughter. *Education:* BS, Drake University, 1982. *Appointments:* Self Employed, 1947-74; Secretary, Treasurer, John Hart Engineering Inc., 1974-77; Secretary Treasurer, Weston Construction Co., 1977-80; President, The Hart Company, 1981-. *Memberships:* Associated General Contractors; Associated Builders & Contractors; Association of Women Contractors; National Association of Women Business Owners. *Hobbies:* ACBL - Life Master Bridge Player; Travel; Reading. *Address:* PO Box 4945, Des Moines, IA 50306, USA.

HART Jacquelyn D, Assistant Vice President. *Education:* BS, Lane College, 1959; MS, 1970, Ed.S, 1972, PhD, 1985, University of Florida, Gainesville. *Appointments:* Instructor, Santa Fe Community College, 1967; Instructor, State of Florida, 1972-74; Affirm. Actn. Officer, 1975-78, Affirm. Actn. Coord., 1978-86, Director, Affirm. Actn., 1986-88, Assistant Vice President, Minority affairs, 1988-, University of Florida. *Honours:* Alpha Phi Alpha, 1981; Administrative Leadership Award, City of Gainesville, 1986. *Hobbies:* Jogging; Biking; Reading; Bargain Shopping. *Address:* 1236 SE 13th Ave., Gainesville, FL 32601, USA.

HART Judith Constance Mary, b. 18 Sept. 1924, Burnley, Lancashire, England. Baroness Hart of South Lanark, member of the House of Lords (1988). m. Anthony Beruard Hart, 1946. 2 sons. *Education:* London School of Economics; BA Honours, London University. *Appointments:* Lecturer, Social Researcher and Journalist, 1946-59; Member of Parliament, Labour, Lanark and Clydesdale, 1959-87; Joint Parliamentary Under-Secretary of State for Scotland, 1964-66; Minister of State at the Commonwealth Office, 1966-67; Minister of Social Security, 1967-68; Paymaster General, Cabinet Minister, 1968-69; Ministry of Overseas Development, 1969-70, 1974-75, 1977-79; Member of United Nations Panel of Eminent Persons on Transnational Corporations, South Africa and Namibia, New York, 1985. *Publication:* Aid and Liberation, 1973. *Memberships:* Past Chairman, Labour Party; Past Chairman, Parliamentary Labour Party Committee on Latin and Central American and the Caribbean; Chair, ECOSA Committee, United Nations Association, UK; Honorary President of various organisations. *Honours:* DBE, 1979; Privy Councillor, 1967; Honorary Fellow, Institute of Development Studies, University of Sussex, 1984. *Hobbies:* Theatre; Gardening; Family. *Address:* 3 Ennerdale Road, Kew Gardens, Richmond, Surrey, England.

HART Kitty Carlisle, b. New Orleans, USA. Chairman. m. Moss Hart, deceased 1961. 1 son, 1 daughter. *Education:* Switzerland; France; London School of Economics, London, England; Royal Academy of Dramatic Arts, London. *Appointments:* Debut with the Metropolitan Opera, 1967; Metropolitan's series of Operas in the Park, 1973; American premiere of Benjamin Britten's Rape of Lucretia; 1st appearance on Broadway, Champagne Sec, most recently, On Your Toes, 1984. Films include: A Night at the Opera. Vice-Chairman, 5 years, Chairman, New York State Council on the Arts, 1976-. *Creative works:* Television series: Women on the Move; TV series sponsored by State University. *Memberships:* Visiting Committee, Board of Overseers, Harvard's Music School; Visiting Committee, Arts, Massachusetts Institute of Technology; Empire State College; Girl Scouts of Greater New York; Association Fellow, Timothy Dwight College, Yale University. *Honours:* Honorary Doctorates: College of New Rochelle; Hartwick College; Amherts College. *Address:* c/o New York State Council on the Arts, 915 Broadway, New York, NY 10010, USA.

HART Lois Borland, b. 15 May 1941, Syracuse, New York, USA. Consultant; Public Speaker; Publisher. m. 4 July 1969, 2 sons. *Education:* BS, University of Rochester, 1966; MS, Syracuse University, 1972; EdD, University of Massachusetts, 1974. *Appointments:* Administrative Assistant, East Lansing, Michigan, 1974-75; Field Service Coordinator, University of Michigan, Ann Arbor, 1975-77; President, Organizational Leadership, Lansing, 1977-79; Trainer, Mt States Employers Council, Denver, Colorado, 1979-80; President, Leadership Dynamics, Boulder, Colorado, 1980-. *Publications:* Conference and Workshop Planner's Manual, 1979; Moving Up! Women and Leadership, 1980; Learning from Conflict, 1981; The Sexes at Work, 1983; Saying Hello/Saying Goodbye, 1983; Are You Stuck, 1986; Survivors of Successful Sales, 1986; Taming Your Junk Jungle, 1986; A Woman's Complete Guide to Leadership (audio-cassette). *Memberships:* American Association of University Women; National Organization of Women;

American Society for Training and Development; Toastmasters International. *Honours:* Pi Lambda Theta; Phi Delta Kappa. *Address:* Leadership Dynamics, 3775 Iris Avenue, Suite 3B, Boulder, CO 80301, USA.

HARTLEY Marie, b. 25 Sept. 1905, Morley, Yorkshire, England. Author; Artist. *Education:* Leeds College of Art; Slade School of Fine Arts. *Publications:* Books with Ella Pontefract: Swaledale; Wensleydale; Wharfedale; Yorkshire Tour; Yorkshire Cottage; Books with Joan Ingilby: Old Hand-Knitters of the Dales; Yorkshire Village; Wonders of Yorkshire: Life and Tradition in the Yorkshire Dales; Life in the Moorlands of North-East Yorkshire; Life and Tradition in West Yorkshire; A Dales Heritage; Dales Memories. *Memberships:* Society of Authors; Yorkshire Archaeological Society; Society for Folk Life Studies. *Honours:* Honorary MA, Leeds University, 1968; Honorary MUniv, York University, 1986. *Hobbies:* Photography; Museums; Gardening. *Address:* Coleshouse, Askrigg, Leyburn, North Yorkshire, England.

HARTMAN Nancy Lee, b. 29 July 1951, Phillipsburg, Pennsylvania, USA. Physician. *Education:* AA, Medical Technology, Marcum Jr College, Bryn Mawr, 1969-71; BA, Biology, Lycoming College, Williamsport, 1972-74; MS, Medical Biology, Long Island University, Greenvale, 1975-77; MD, Medicine, American University of the Caribbean, Montserrat, West Indies, 1978-81. *Appointments:* Microbiology and Medical Technology Laboratory Experience in: Jersey Shore Hospital, 1974; New York Hospital and Cornell Medical Center, 1974-75; Drekter and Heisler Laboratories, New York, 1975; North Shore Laboratories, Inc, 1976-78; National Health Labs, Inc, 1982; CLI Labs Inc, 1982; North Shore University Hospital, 1982; Paramedic: Porta Medic, 1982; EMSI, 1984-85; Residency programmes, Interfaith Medical Center, 1983-84; Lenox Hill Hospital, 1986-87; Medical Consultant, Shapiro, Baines, Saasto & Shainwald, Mineola, New York, 1985-; Internal Medicine Program, Lenox Hill Hospital, New York, 1987-. *Publications:* Pocket Handbook of Infectious Agents and their Treatments, 1987; The Hospital and Clinic Infection Control Manual, in process. *Memberships:* American Medical Association; American Society of Clinical Pathologists; American Society for Microbiology; The International Platform Association; American Women's Medical Association. *Honour:* Allied Health Professions Traineeship Grant, 1976. *Hobbies:* Jogging; Scuba diving; Small plane flying; Tennis; Snow skiing. *Address:* P O Box 847, Glenwood Landing, NY 11547, USA.

HARTON Marsha Louise Tanner, b. 21 Apr. 1947, Columbus, Ohio, USA. Executive Director. m. Artie L. Harton, 11 Sept. 1968, divorced, 1981, 1 son. *Education:* BSc., Franklin University, Columbus, 1978. *Appointments:* United Negro College Fund Inc., 1974-78; New York Life Insurance Co., 1978-79; Banc Ohio National Bank, 1979-87; State of Ohio, Dept. of Development, 1987-. *Memberships Include:* Women's Advisory Committee, Ohio State University; National Association of Black Accountants; Delta Sigma Theta; American Institute of Banking; National Association of Bank Women. *Honours:* Outstanding Young Women of America, 1978. *Hobby:* Reading. *Address:* 2987 Baker Hill Road, Columbus, OH 43207, USA.

HARTSE Denise Yvonne Durfee, b. 5 Nov. 1951, Miles City, USA. Society Editor. m. Marcus R. Hartse, 16 June 1979. *Education:* BA, 1975. *Appointments:* Assistant Bills Co-ordinator, Montana House of Representatives, 1975; Assistant, H&T Quality Printing, 1975-76 and 1979-81; Advertising Representative, Larson Publications, 1976-79; Society and Page 2 Editor, Miles City Star, 1981-. *Publications:* Co-Editor, Culinary Artistry; numerous articles. *Memberships:* Miles City Branch, American Association of University Women, Secretary; Past President, Montana Press Women; President, Miles City Centennial Quilters: Miles City Concert Association. *Honours:* Sewing; Needlework; Ceramics; Piano. *Address:* PO Box 743, Miles City, MT 59301, USA.

HARTZLER Cheryl Elaine Somsel, b. 16 Feb. 1945, Kokomo, Indiana, USA. Financial Planner; Tax Preparer. m. Dr Edward W. Hartzler, 11 June 1967, divorced 1981, 1 son, 1 daughter. *Education:* BA, Indiana University, 1968; MBA, Southern Illinois University, 1985. *Appointments:* Elementary School Teacher, Indianapolis Public Schools, 1968-71; Sales & Inventory Work, Frederick & Nelson Department Store, Seattle 1971-72; Securities Registered Representative, University Securities, Seattle, 1983; Account Executive, Southmark Financial Services, 1984-; Financial Planner, Tax Preparer, C.E. Hartzler & Associates, 1985-. *Memberships:* International Association of Financial Planners; American Society of Women Accountants; Alpha Chi Omega. *Hobbies:* Skiing; Aerobics; Gardening; Travel. *Address:* c/o Southmark Financial Services, 1300 SE 114th Avenue, Suite 232, Bellevue, WA 98004, USA.

HARUTUNIAN Johar, b. 17 June 1923, Leninakan, Armenia, USSR. Museum Director. m. Sevoyan Nickolay, 7 Nov. 1946, 2 daughters. *Education:* Music School, Leninakan, 1929-36; Kara-Moorsa School of Music, Leninakan, 1936-39; Conductors' Faculty 1939-47, Assistant 1947-48, Yereva Conservatory. *Appointments:* Conductor: Tchaikovsky Music School 1948-50, Sayat-Nova Music School 1950-52, Director, Melikian School of Music, Yerevan, 1952-78; Founder & Director, Aram Khachaturian Museum, Yerevan, 1978-. *Creative works include:* Conductor, various symphony orchestras, 1948-78; Publisher, Aram Khachaturian's letters, Armenian & Russian, 1983. *Honours:* Honoured Teacher, 1965; Badge of Honour, 1971. *Hobbies:* Literature; Art. *Address:* Tumanian St 1, Ap. 12, Yerevan 375001, Armenia, USSR.

HARVEY Anne Berenice Lewis, b. 27 Apr. 1933, London, England. Writer; Editor; Actress; Presenter. m. Alan Harvey, 13 Apr. 1957, 1 son, 1 daughter. *Education:* AGSM, LGSM, Guildhall School of Music and Drama, London. *Appointments:* Director, Guildhall Players Summer Theatre, Perranporth. Cornwall, 1954-57; Freelance Drama Teacher, Lecturer, Examiner, Adjudicator, 1962-; Director, Pegasus Programmes, 1980-. *Publications:* Scenes for Two; Solo; Take Two; A Present for Nellie; Poets in Hand; Of Caterpillars, Cats and Cattle; In Time of War; Something I Remember; A Picnic of Poetry; The Language of Love 1989; Six of the Best 1989; Faces in a Crowd 1990; Headlines from the Jungle (with Virginia McKenna) 1990. *Memberships:* Examiner, Guildhall School of Music and Drama; Examiner, Board Member, Poetry Society; Central Board, British Federation of Music Festivals; Coordinator, Ealing Branch, National Schizophrenia Fellowship. *Hobbies:* Book collecting; Theatre; Walking; Reading; War poetry. *Address:* 37 St Stephen's Road, Ealing, London W13 8HJ, England.

HARVEY Barbara Fitzgerald, b. 21 Jan. 1928, Teignmouth, England. University Teacher. *Education:* BA, 1st Class Honours, 1949, BLitt, MA, 1953, Somerville College, Oxford. *Appointments:* Assistant, University of Edinburgh, Scotland, 1951-52; Lecturer, Queen Mary College, London, England, 1952-55; Tutor, 1955-, Fellow, 1956-, Somerville College, Oxford. *Publications:* Westminster Abbey and Its Estates in the Middle Ages, 1977; Articles in various Historical Journals. *Memberships:* Fellow, Society of Antiquaries of London, 1964; Fellow, Royal Historical Society; Vice President, 1986-; Fellow, British Academy, 1982. *Address:* Somerville College, Oxford, OX2 6HD, England.

HARVEY Denise Marie, b. 22 July 1954, Knoxville, Tennessee, USA. Doctoral Student. m. George J Roberson, Snr, 19 July 1986. *Education:* AA, Oxford College of Emory University, 1974; BA, George Peabody College for Teachers, Nashville, 1976; MSc, Social Work, University of Tennessee, 1978. *Appointments:* Research Fellow, 1978, Research Associate, 1978, National Institute of Public Management; Research Analyst, National Institute for Advanced Studies, 1978-80; Information Specialist, Howard University, 1980-81; Director of Affirmative Action, University of Tennessee,

1982-86; Southeastern Representative, Black Issues in Higher Education, 1988-. *Publications:* Articles: Demographics Dictates Access, Hodgkinson Warns; Strategies for Re-entry Outlined; Teacher Education Conference Promotes Professional Unity. *Memberships:* Southeastern Psychological Association; American Field Service (International Student Exchange Program). *Honours:* Teaching Assistantship, Department of Sociology, 1988-89, Graduate School Tuition Scholarship, 1988-89, Tulane University; Outstanding Young Women of America, 1981, 1982; National Institute of Public Management Research Fellow, 1978; State of Tennessee Legislative Intern, 1978, declined; Peabody in Denmark Exchange Student, University of Denmark, Copenhagen, 1975; American Field Service Exchange Student to The Netherlands, 1971. *Hobbies:* Reading; Writing; Vegetarianism; Outdoor sports; International travel. *Address:* 7621 Sandy Cove Drive, New Orleans, LA 70128, USA.

HARVEY Elaine Louise, b. 1 Mar. 1936, Riverside, California, USA. Artist. m. Stuart Herbert Harvey, 16 June 1957, 1 son, 2 daughters. *Education:* BA highest honours and distinction, Certificate in Elementary Education, San Diego State University, 1957. *Career:* Teacher, Cajon Valley Schools, California, 1957, 1958; Painter in watermedia, El Cajon, 1975-; Juror, art competitions, 1983-; Lecturing and demonstrating art, 1983-. *Creative works:* Tapestry Series, watermedia paintings; Seastone Series, watermedia paintings; Editor, Palette to Palate, 1986; Cover article in The Artist's Magazine, 1987. *Memberships:* President, San Diego Watercolor Society; Elected Member: Allied Artists of America; Artists Guild, San Diego Museum of Art, President; National Watercolor Society, Director; Watercolor West, Director; Rocky Mountain National Watermedia Society; West Coast Watercolor Society. *Honours:* McKinnon Award, American Watercolor Society, 1985; Winsor Newton Award, Midwest Watercolor Society, 1985; Creative Connections Award, Rocky Mountain National Exhibition, 1986; 1st Place, Juror's Award, San Diego International Watercolor Exhibition, 1986; Silver Recognition, San Diego Watercolor Society, 1986; Dassler-Nochs Award, Adirondacks Exhibition of American Watercolors, 1987; 1st Place, Inland Artists Exhibition, 1987. *Hobbies:* Choral singing; Natural history, *Address:* 1602 Sunburst Drive, El Cajon, CA 92021, USA.

HARVEY Elinor Beatrice, b. 11 Jan. 1912, Boston, Massachusetts, USA. Child Psychiatrist; Trainer; Brazelton Behavioural Neonatal Assessment. m. Donald K. Freedman MD, 2 July 1936, 2 sons. *Education:* BS cum laude, Jackson College, Medford, Massachusetts, 1933; MD, Tufts University Medical School, 1936. *Appointments include:* Consultant: SE Region Mental Health Clinic, Juneau, Alaska, 1975-79; Mars & Kline Psychiatric Clinic & Hospital, Port-au-Prince, Haiti, 1977-78; Navajo Area Indian Health Service, Gallup, New Mexico, 1980-; Brookside Hospital, San Pablo, California, 1985-. *Publications:* Co-author: Interaction Between Allergic Potential & Psycho-Pathology in Childhood Asthma (in Psychosomatic Medicine), 1946; Utilization of a Pychiatric-Social Work Team in an Alaskan Native Boarding School (Journal, American Academy of Child Psychiatry), 1976. Author: 3 articles in Psychiatric House Calls, 1988. *Memberships:* Life Fellow, American Psychiatric Association; Fellow, American Academy of Child Psychiatry, American Orthopaychiatric Association; International Association of Child Psychiatry; Past Secretary, E Bay Psychiatric Association; American Medical Womens Association; World Federation for Mental Health. *Honours:* Phi Beta Kappa, 1933; Grants, National Institute of Mental Health; Member, Advisory Committee, Emergency Maternal & Infant Care (EMIC) Children's Bureau, Washington DC. *Hobbies:* Hiking; Bird Watching; Music; Art; International Travel; Foreign cultures & languages. *Address:* 1547 Buckeye Court, Pinole, California 94564, USA.

HARVEY Leigh Kathryn, b. Abilene, Texas, USA. Attorney. m. Bert Gubbels, 28 Oct. 1983. *Education:* BA, cum laude, 1971, JD 1974, University of Texas, Austin. *Appointments:* Assistant City Attorney, San Angelo, Texas, 1974-77; Associate, Don Dorsey, Attorney, 1977; Assisant District Attorney, 1978; Private practice, 1978-. *Memberships:* Director, Tom Green County Community Action Association, 1975-77, President 1976; ABA; Texas Bar Association; Bell, Lampasas, Mills County Bar Associaton; Association of Trial Laywers of America; Travis Co Bar Association. *Honours:* Young Careerist Award Winner, Business and Professional Womens Club, 1977. *Hobbies:* Reading; Gardening. *Address:* PO Box 948, Lompasas, TX 76550, USA.

HARVEY Margie Ballard, b. 12 July 1910, Texas, USA. Poet; Homemaker. m. Walter Frank Harvey, 7 Jan. 1933, 1 son. *Career:* Housewife and freelance poet; Poetry column in Southeast Star newspaper, 3 years. *Publications include:* Contributor to young publications; 12 poetry anthologies; Clover Collection of Verse, vols 3 and 5; Most recent contributions to World of Poetry. *Memberships:* Poetry Society of Texas; World of Poetry; Life Fellow, World Literary Academy. *Honours:* Named Dame, Clover Publishing, 1970; Honorary Certificate of Merit, Honorary Member, Laural Publishing Symposium; Golden Poet Award, World of Poetry, 1985-87; 9 Certificates of Merit, 1986-87; Golden Poet Award, 1988 and 1989. *Hobbies:* Literature of all kinds especially poets and their work (modern and early American and English poets, Shakespeare); Long walks in the country. *Address:* 205 Water Street, Seagorville, TX 75159, USA.

HARVIE Alida Gwendolen Rosemary, b. 23 June 1910, London, England. Lecturer; Writer. m. John Keith Harvie, 3 Oct. 1950, died 1971. *Appointments:* Army Educational Corps, 1940-46; Staff Officer, Senior Commander ATS; Joined organising staff of the World Congress on Mental Health, 1947-48. *Publications:* Those Glittering Years; The Rationed Years; The Sundial Years; The Doom-Laden Years, 1980-85. *Memberships:* Kensington Borough Council, 1949-52; London County Council, 1949-55; Chairman, Schools for Blind and for Physically Disabled Children. *Honours:* Gold Cup, Public Speakers' Guild, 1931; Defence Medal, 1939-45; Oakleaf War Medal, 1939-45; Diploma, London Guide Lecturer, 1949. *Hobbies:* History Study; Historical Research; Classical Music; Reading; World Wild-Life; Fundraising for Tree Replacement. *Address:* 15 Brackens Way, Martello Rd South, Canford Cliffs, Poole, Dorset BH13 7HH, England.

HARVITH Susan Merryman Edwards, b. 13 Jan. 1946, Detroit, Michigan, USA. Museum Administrator & Curator; Film & Photography Historian. m. (1) John Dana Harvith, 15 June 1972. 1 daughter. *Education:* BA, Theatre, Wayne State University, 1968; Master, Museum Practice, University of Michigan, 1973. *Career:* Curator of Exhibitions, Director of Docent Programme, Cranbrook Academy of Art/Museum, Michigan, 1973-76; Freelance arts producer & curator, 1976; Gallery Director, Firelands Association for Visual Arts, Oberlin, 1981-89; Membership & Special Events Administrator, Allen Memorial Art Museum, Oberlin College, 1987-89; Executive Director, Sanata Cruz County Historical Trust, Santa Cruz, 1989-. *Creative works:* Co-author, books: Karl Struss, Man with a Camera 1976, Edison, Musicians & the Phonograph 1987. Co-Producer: Karl Struss Photography Portfolio, 1977-79. Co-organiser, co-curator: Karl Struss, Man with a Camera exhibition 1976-77, Struss centenary exhibition, Ohio State University 1987, & Hollywood, the Golden Years, Cleveland New Gallery for Contemporary Art, 1983. *Memberships:* American Association of University Women; Long-range Planning Commission, Lorain County Arts Council, Ohio, 1984-85; Past office, Oberlin College Women; Various clubs. *Honours:* Museum training grant, Henry Ford Museum & Greenfield Village, 1971-72; Winterthur Grant, Henry Francis du Pont Winterthur Museum, 1971. *Hobbies:* Art collecting; Women in the arts; Technology & arts. *Address:* The Octagon Museum, 118 Cooper St., Santa Cruz, CA 95060, USA.

HARWOOD Eleanor May Cash, b. 29 May 1921, Buckfield, Maine, USA. Librarian. divorced. 1 son, 1 daughter. *Education:* BA, American International College, 1943; BS, Southern Connecticut State University, 1955. *AppointmentsL:* Ensign to Lieutenant (JG) USNR (WAVES), World War II, 1943-46; Librarian, Rathburn Memorial Library, East Haddam, Connecticut, 1955-56; Assistant Librarian, Kent Boys' School, Kent, Connecticut, 1956-63; Consultant, Chester Public Library, Chester, Connecticut, 1965-71. *Publications:* Co-author, The Independent School Library and the Gifted Child, 1956; The Age of Samuel Johnson LLD, 1959; Remember When? Essay, 1985. *Memberships:* American Library Association; Connecticut Library Association; Society of the Descendants of the Mayflower; Trustee, Chester Historical Society, 1970-72; Disabled American Veterans; American Legion HIAC Post 97; Auxiliary, United Church of Chester. *Honours:* World War II Medals; Atlantic Theatre Medal; Victory Medal. *Address:* 10 Maple Street, Box 255, Chester, CT 06412, USA.

HARWOOD Vanessa Clare, b. 14 June 1947, Cheltenham, England. Ballerina. m. 14 June 1980. 1 daughter. *Education:* National Ballet School, 1959-64; Studied in London, Cannes, Russia and New York. *Appointments:* National Ballet Corps of Canada, 1965, Soloist, 1967, Principal 1970-86; Guest Artist in Europe, Australia, USA and Canada; Danced with Nureyev, A Godunov, P Bissell, S Jeffries and Schaufuss. *Creative Works:* Appearances in ballets as Queen in Swan Lake; Giselle and Myrtha in Giselle; Lise in La Fille Malgardee; Juliet in Romeo & Juliet; Swanhilda in Copellia; Kitri in Don Quixote; Aurora in Sleeping Beauty and The Sylph in La Sylphide; also coached the Canadian Olympic and World ice dance bronze Medalists, Tracey Wilson and Robert McCall, 1988. *Memberships:* ACRTA; Canadian Actors Equity Association. *Honours:* Officer of the Order of Canada, 1984. *Hobby:* Going to Formula One Car Racing. *Address:* 78 Woodlawn Ave W, Toronto, Ontario, Canada M4V 1G7.

HASEGAWA Lee Patton, b. 20 Nov. 1951, St Louis, Missouri, USA. Actress; Writer; Teacher. m. Clifton M Hasegawa, 28 July 1973. 1 son, 1 daughter. *Education:* BA, Acting and Directing, Washburn University; MA, Acting and Directing, University of Missouri at Kansas City. *Appointments:* Instructor, Acting for the Camera, Webster University, 1984-88; Acting teacher, M/STP and Theatre Project Company, 1979-83. Professional acting experience includes: Streetcar Named Desire; The Marriage of Bette & Boo; The Dining Room; The Birthday Party; Sister Mary Ignatius Explains It All for You; Cat on a Hot Tin Roof; Little Foxes: Singular Life of Albert Nobbs, etc; Numerous industrial films and TV/ Radio commercials. *Publications:* Storytheatre Pieces: Oriental Tales; Mystery and History; Ancient Honor; American Tall Tales; American Indian Tales. *Memberships:* Actors Equity Association; Screen Actors' Guild; American Federation of Radio and Television Actors; Equity Liaison Board; Co-Founder and Co-Chair of Center States Audition ASC; Union Avenue Christian Church, Pastoral Relations Committee, Religious Education. *Address:* c/o Talent Plus, 3663 Lindell, ST Louis, MO 63108, USA.

HASL, Hannelore Vera Margarete, b. 13 June 1955, Hersbruck, Bavaria, West Germany. Executive; Attorney; Lecturer. *Education:* AB, cum laude, Duke University, 1976; MBA, Cornell University, 1978; JD, Rutgers University, 1981. *Appointments:* Associate, Duncan, Allen & Mitchell, 1981-83; Attorney Advisor, Office of Gen. Counsel, US International Trade Commission, 1983-84; Vice President & Gen. Counsel, Alloy Tool & Mold Manfuacturing Corp and IML Technology Inc, 1984-. *Publications:* Editor-in-Chief, JD/MBA Quarterly, 1983; Contributed articles to Society of Plastics Engineers; Technical Association of Paper and Pulp Industry; Modern Plastics Encyclopedia. *Memberships:* Incorp. Director and Trustee, National Association of JD/MBA Professionals; American, Washington DC and New Jersey Bar Associations; International Platform Association; Admitted to practice law before Washington DC, State of New Jersey and Federal Courts. *Honours:* Phi Sigma Alpha, Political Science Honor Society, 1976; Winner of Best Oralist Award, Eastern Regional Jessup International Moot Court Competition, 1980. *Hobbies:* Sailing; International Business. *Address:* 854 Papen Road, Bridgewater, New Jersey 08807, USA.

HASLEGRAVE Marianne Huggard, b. 2 Nov. 1942, London, England. General Secretary, International Federation of Business & Professional Women. m. (1) David B Huggard, 31 Aug. 1968. divorced 1982, 1 son. (2) James Edward Haslegrave, 7 May 1982. *Education:* BA, Durham University, 1964; Diploma of Education, University of Newcastle upon Tyne, 1965; MA History, Queens College, City University of New York, USA, 1978. *Appointments:* Coordinator, NGO Forum for World Conference of UN Decade for Women; IGO/NGO Liaison Officer, UN Conference on New and Renewable Sources of Energy, 1981; Company Director, 1982-85; Consultant, 1985-88. *Publications:* Forward from Nairobi: Implementing the Nairobi Forward-looking Strategies; Chapter on Women's Rights in Human Rights, ed Peter Davies, 1988. *Memberships:* National Council of Voluntary Organizations, Women's Organizations Interest Group, Co-Chair, 1987-88; British Federation of University Women, Vice President, 1985-88; Institute of Directors. *Hobbies:* Women's Issues; Travel. *Address:* Braunston Manor, Church Street, Braunston-in-Rutland, Leics LE15 8QZ, England.

HASSI Satu, b. 3 June 1951, Helsinki, Finland. Writer. 2 daughters. *Education:* MS, Electrical EngiNeEring, 1979; Licentiate of Technology, 1985. *Appointments:* Design & Research Engineer, Oy Tampella, Tamrock, 1979-81; Teacher, Tampere University of Technology, 1981-85; Freelance Writer, 1985-. *Publications:* Poems: Magdaleena ei hapea enaa, 1984; Novel: Naaraskierre, 1986; Essays on Women and Technology; The Serpent and The Tree of Knowledge, 1987. *Membership:* Finnish Writers Union. *Honours:* Member, City Council in Tampere, 1985-. *Hobbies:* Women's Studies; Women's Peace Movement. *Address:* Paivolankatu 10B, Tamprere SF 33250, Finland.

HASTINGS Evelyn Grace, b. 25 May 1938, Seguin, USA. Elementary Teacher. m. Marvin Hastings, 9 Oct. 1982. *Education:* BS, Texas Lutheran College, 1960; MA, University of Texas, 1985. *Appointments:* Elementary Teacher, Seguin Independent School District, 1961-. *Memberships:* Guadalupe County Teachers Association; Texas Women Convention of Church of Our Lord Jesus, Historian, Correspondence Secetary, 1961-69; Texas State Armon Bearers Young People Union of Church of Our Lord Jesus Christ. *Hobbies:* 950 Elsik, Seguin, TX 78155, USA.

HASWELL Margaret Rosary, b. 22 June 1917, London, England. Rural Development Consultant; Author. *Education:* BLitt 1954, MA 1960, redesignated MLitt 1985 St Hilda's College, Additional Fellow 1970-80 St Hugh's College, Agricultural Economics, University of Oxford. *Appointments:* Manager, HM Yorkshire (East Riding) Flax Factory, 1940-45; Agronomist, Human Nutrition Research Unit, Colonial Medical Research Council, 1946-52; Agricultural Economist, Overseas Food Corporation, Tanganyika, 1954-55; Research, University of Cambridge, 1955-57; Leverhulme grantee, research, 1958; Agricultural Economics Research Institute, Oxford, 1959-67; University Lecturer, Oxford, 1967-80; Own consultancy, Margaret Haswell Associates, 1980-. *Publications:* Books: Economics of Development in Village India; Northeast Thailand; Tropical Farming Economics; Nature of Poverty; Energy for Subsistence. Monograph (Nuffield Foundation grant), Population & Change in a West African Ruaral Community: 40-Year Review, 1987. *Memberships include:* Society of Authors; Agricultural Economics Society. *Honours:* Leadership award, Deputy Governor, American Biographical Institute. *Hobbies:* Theatre; Travel Establishment of Yate-Genieri Link, between UK town & African village,

1987-. *Address:* The Deans, 3 Gibson Lane, Haddenham, Aylesbury, Buckinghamshire HP17 8AP, England.

HATCHFIELD Pamela Beth, b. 15 Dec. 1953, New York City, New York, USA. Conservator of Objects and Sculpture. m. Mitchell Owen Tunick, 1 Aug. 1980. *Education:* BA cum laude, Anthropology, Art History, Religion, Vassar College, Poughkeepsie, New York, 1975; MA, Art History, Diploma in Conservation, Institute of Fine Arts Center, New York University, 1984; Apprentice, Mario's Conservation Services, Washington DC, 1979-80; Internship, Textile Conservation Laboratory, Cooper-Hewitt Museum, New York, 1981. *Appointments:* Assistant, Sotheby Parke Bernet, New York and London, England, 1976-78; Interim Curator, Conservator, Grenada National Museum, Grenada, West Indies, 1980-82; Conservation Assistant, Metropolitan Museum of Art, New York City, 1981-84; Advanced Level Intern, Fogg Art Museum, Harvard University Art Museums, Cambridge, Massachusetts, 1984-85; Assistant Conservator, Research Laboratory, Museum of Fine Arts, Boston, 1985-; Associate Conservator, 1989; Consultant. *Publications include:* Scanning Electron Microscopic Examination of Archaeological Wood Microstructure Altered by Consolidation Treatment (with R.J.Koestler), 1987; Formaldehyde: How Great is the Danger to Museum Collections? (with J.M.Carpenter), 1987; The Use of Cellulose Ethers in the Treatment of Egyptian Polychromed Wood, 1988; Ancient Egyptian Gilding Methods, 1988. *Memberships:* American Institute for Conservation of Historic and Artistic Works; International Institute for Conservation; Canadian Group, International Institute for Conservation; New England Conservation Association. *Honours:* Hagop Kevorkian Fellowship in Conservation, 1983-84, Hebrew Technical Institute Fellowships, 1984-85, 1985-86, Institute of Fine Arts Conservation Center, New York University. *Hobbies:* Travel; Photography; Weaving; Environmental issues. *Address:* Museum of Fine Arts, Research Laboratory, 465 Huntington Avenue, Boston, MA 02115, USA.

HATFIELD Cordelia M, b. 6 May 1914, Michigan, USA. Retired. m. Hon Malcolm Hatfield, Judge, 19 Nov. 1948. 1 son, 1 daughter. *Appointments:* Formerly Registrar, Probate Court, Berrien County, Michigan, 20 years; Legal Assistant, Law firm, Butzbaugh, Page, Butzbaugh and Dewane, St Joseph, Michigan, retired. *Memberships:* Life Member, former board member, Memorial Hospital Womens Auxiliary, St Joseph; International Platform Association; Monday Musical; Economic Club; Antique Club; Former President, Garden Club; President Chapter Guild, Valparaiso University Chapter for Berrien County. *Honours:* Award from US Government for selling war bonds; Invitation to 48th Debutante Assembly New Years Ball, 1970 and 1971; Debutante European Holiday, 1970. *Hobbies:* Antiques; Gardening; Volunteer work. *Address:* 37788 Baywood Drive, Farmington Hills, MI 48024, USA.

HATTON Ragnhild Marie, b. 10 Feb. 1913, Bergen, Norway. Professor Emeritus. m. Harry Hatton, 23 June 1936. 2 sons. *Education:* Cand Mag degree Languages and History, Oslo University, 1936; Postgraduate work, University College, University of London, England, 1937; PhD History, 1947. *Appointments:* Assistant Lecturer 1949-50, Lecturer 1950-58, Reader 1958; Professor Intern. History, 1968-80, LSE, University of London; Frequent teaching assignments in USA, Canada and European countries. *Publications include:* Charles XII of Sweden 1968, in Swede, 1985; Europe in the Age of Louis XIV, 1969, 1979; Louis XIV and his World, 1972, 1984; George I, Elector and King, 1978, 1982; Numerous essays, articles and contributions; Editorship series Men in Office, Thames & Hudson. *Memberships:* Fellow, Royal Historical Society; Dean of the Faculty of Economics and Social Science, University of London; Institute of Historical Research. *Honours:* Gold medal Bergen Katedralskole, 1932; Honorary Member (first woman), American Hist Association; Corr. Member Swedish Vitterhets Academy; Honorary Doctorate

Humane Letters, USA, 1985; Medlicott medal for services to History, Historical Association, 1988; Knight (Ridder) 1st class, the Norwegian Royal Order of St Olav, 1983; Officier, French Ordre des Palmes Académiques, 1985; Commander, the Swedish Royal Order of the Northern Star, 1987. *Hobbies:* Travelling; Archive and museum research; Reading; Opera; Ballet; Music; Education; Friendship; Family relationships; Having fun. *Address:* 49 Campden Street, London W8 7ET, England.

HAUGHTON Rosemary Elena, b. 13 Apr. 1927, London, England. Writer; Lecturer; Voluntary Worker. m. Algernon Haughton, 19 June 1948, 7 sons, 3 daughters. *Career includes:* Caring for 2 foster-children; Currently member of team providing shelter and housing for the homeless. *Publications:* 35 books. *Honours:* 5 honorary doctorates from US universities; Avila Award, 1977. *Hobbies:* Painting; Embroidery; Gardening; Farming; Environmental science; Linguistics. *Address:* 5 Draper Corner, Heptonstall, Hebden Bridge, West Yorkshire, England.

HAUSER Marianne, b. 11 Dec. 1910, Strasbourg, France. Writer. 1 son. *Education:* University of Berlin, 1931; Sorbonne, Paris, 1934. *Appointments:* Lecturer, City University of New York, 1966-79; Literary Consultant. *Publications:* Novels: Monique, 1935; Indian Phantom, 1937; Dark Dominion, 1947; The Choir Invisible, 1958; Prince Ishmael, 1963; The Talking Room, 1976; The Memoirs of the Late Mr Ashley, 1986; Short Stories: A Lesson in Music, 1964; etc. *Memberships:* PEN; Union of Concerned Scientists, Poets & Writers; Fiction Collective. *Honours:* Fellow in Residence, Yaddo, 1947; Rockefeller Fellow, 1955; Nominee, Pulitzer Prize, Fiction, 1963; NEA, Creative Writing, 1977. *Hobbies:* Clean Environment; End to Racial Bias; Tai Chi Chuan; Swimming; Hiking; etc. *Address:* 2 Washington Square Village, Apt 13-M, New York, NY 10012, USA.

HAUSMANN Winifred Wilkinson, b. 1 Sept. 1922, Atlanta, Georgia, USA. Ordained Unity Minister (Retired). m. George R. Hausmann, 19 Dec. 1965, died, 1985. *Education:* BA, Agnes Scott College, 1946; Graduate, Unity Training School, 1958; Ordained, 1959. *Appointments:* Minister, Unity of Little Rock, Arkansas, 1957-58; Minister, Unity Center Church, Cleveland Heights, 1958-87; Minister Emeritus, Unity Center Church, 1988-. *Publications:* Focus on Living, 1967; Miracle Power for Today, 1969; Your God-Given Poetential, 1978; How to Live Life Victoriously, 1982; Dealing with Stress Through Spiritual Methods, 1985; A Guide to Love-Powered Living, 1986. *Hobbies:* Astronomy; Organic Gardening; Arts; Crafts. *Address:* 327 Katey Rose Lane, Euclid, OH 44143, USA.

HAUSSAMEN Carol Weil, b. 2 Dec. 1920, New York City, USA. Real Estate Owner; Philanthropist; Political Activist. *Appointments:* President, Carol W Haussamen, Carolyndale Foundations (housing rehabilitation specialists, Forty Central Park South Inc, (Owners and managers of luxury residential apartments); Board of Directors, Just One Break Inc, Manhattan Industrial Home for the Blind; Governors Committee on Scholastic Achievement. *Memberships:* Board Member, Community Board Five; First Womens Bank of New York; Urban Design Council; Citizens Housing and Planning Council; Democrats of New York State Senate; Delegate, Democratic National Finance Council; Honorary Commissioner, Department of Civic Affairs and Public Events; Elected Member: Democratic County Committee; Board of Directors, Fund for New Priorities. *Honours:* Recipient of numerous honours and awards most recently, Honoured on the occasions of International Women's Day, Fund for New priorities. *Address:* 40 Central Park South, New York, NY 10019, USA.

HAUTZIG Esther Rudomin, b. 18 Oct. 1930, Vilna, Poland. Author. m. Walter Hautzig, 10 Sept. 1950, 1 son, 1 daughter. *Education:* Hunter College, New York City, USA. *Appointments:* Publicity Assistant, Children's

Book Council, 1952-54; Director, Children's Book Promotion, T Y Crowell, 1954-59; Freelance Consultant, Children's Book Promotion, 1960-; Teacher, Children's Book Writing classes, 1960-. *Publications:* Let's Cook Without Cooking, 1955; Redecorating Your Room for Practically Nothing, 1967; The Endless Steppe, 1968; In the Park, 1968; At Home: A Visit in Four Languages, 1968; In School: Learning in Four Languages, 1969; Let's Make Presents, 1970; Let's Make More Presents, 1973; Cook Cooking, 1973; The Case Against the Wind, 1975; Life with Working Parents: Practical Hints for Everyday Situations, 1976; A Gift for Mama, 1981; The Seven Good Years, 1983; Holiday Treats, 1984; Make it Special, 1986; Christmas Goodies, 1989; Remeber Who You Are, 1990; Forthcoming: Riches; How We Get News. *Memberships:* President, Calhoun (New York) PTA, 1964; Authors Guild. *Honours:* Recognition for The Endless Steppe: Boston Globe/Horn Book Honour Book, 1968; Honour Book, Chicago Tribune/Washington Post Spring Children's Books Festival, 1968; Shirley Kravitz Award, Association of Jewish Libraries, 1968; Jane Addams Prize Book, 1969; Lewis Carroll Shelf Book, 1970. *Address:* 505 West End Avenue, New York, NY 10024, USA.

HAVENS Betty, b. 19 Oct. 1936, Omaha, Nebraska, USA. Provincial Gerontologist. *Education:* BA 1958, Secondary Education Certificate 1962, Downer College, Milwaukee; MA, Sociology, 1965, Postgraduate, 1967-70, University of Wisconsin. *Appointments:* Social Worker, Norquay Neighbourhood House, Winnipeg, Manitoba, Canada, 1958-62; Psychometric Technician 1962-63, Instructor Psychology & Sociology 1963-68, Assistant Dean, Instructional Resources, 1968-71, Area Technical College, Milwaukee, USA; Consultant, Research Methodology, Winnipeg, Canada, 1970-73; Research Director, Health & Soc Dev, Government of Manitoba, 1972-82; Assistant Professor, Community Health Sciences, Faculty of Medicine, University of Manitoba, 1980-; Provincial Gerontologist, Manitoba Health, 1982-. *Publications:* Author, with E Thompson, Aging in Manitoba, 10 volumes, 1973-78; Author, with others, Handbook of Research Instruments in Social Gerontology, 1984; and Social Bonds, 1985; Provincial Health Manpower Report, 1975, 1976, 1977 and 1978; Author, with others, Update Aging in Manitoba, 1979; with B Jacobs, Aging in Manitoba, 1983, 5 volumes forthcoming; Editor with E Rathbone-McCuan, North American Riders: Canadian and United States Perspectives, 1988-; Approximately 65 additional papers, briefs, reports and chapters; Articles and book reviews in professional journals. *Memberships:* Gerontology Society of America; Canadian and International Associations on Gerontology; Sociological Practice Section; Executive member, American Association on Sociology; Research Committee on Aging, International Sociological Assoc; Midwest Sociological Society; Midwest Council for Social Research on Aging; Canadian Sociology & Anthropology Association; Society for Study of Social Problems; Canadian Psychology Association. *Honours include:* Postgraduate fellowship, Midwest Council for Social Research on Aging, 1966-70; National Health grantee, 1974-78, 1978-; American Gerontology Society Travel Grantee, Israel, 1975; Cochair North American Regional Technical meetings for UN World Assembly on Aging, 1981; Expert Panel Member Health and Aging of WHO, 1982-; YWCA Professional Woman of the Year, 1984; Distinguished Service Awardee, University of Manitoba, 1984; Distinguished Service Award of Canadian Association of Gerontology, 1987; Citation Award, Canadian Association of Occupational Therapists, 1988. *Hobbies:* Camping; Canoeing; Cross-country skiing; Travel; Photography; Designing evaluation and research projects; Walking; Music. *Address:* 28 River Road, Winnipeg, Manitoba, R2M 3Y9, Canada.

HAWK Caroline, b. 2 Oct. 1933, Columbus, Ohio, USA. Manufacturing Company Executive. m. David Nelson Hawk, 13 June 1954, 2 daughters. *Education:* Ohio State University, 1951-54. *Appointments:* Owner, Manager, Hawk's Card & Hobby Shop, Canton, Ohio, 1967-75; Assistant to Vice President (Advertising), Citizen's Savings Association, Canton, 1967-70; Gift

buyer, Stern & Mann Company, Canton, 1970-72; Sales representative, Mutual New York Insurance Company, Akron, Ohio, 1972-75; President, owner, Timber Line Products Inc, Sugarcreek, Ohio, 1975-; Distributor, Lincoln Logs Ltd (log homes), Sugarcreek, 1979-. *Memberships:* Arbitrator, Better Business Bureau; Treasurer, American Women's Business Association; Tuscarawas County Chamber of Commerce. *Honour:* Boss of Year, American Business Women's Association, 1978. *Address:* Box 774, Sugarcreek, Ohio 44681, USA.

HAWKINS June, b. 9 June 1938, Jersey, Channel Islands. Physician. m. J Richard Kimmel, 10 Sept. 1976, 1 son, 1 daughter. *Education:* LRCP, MRCS, London, 1962; MB., BS, London, 1962; Diplomate, American Board Internal Medicine, 1972; Diplomate, American Board Allergy & Immunology, 1974. *Appointments:* House Surgeon, West London Hospital, 1962; House Physician, Internal Medicine, 1963; Medical Resident 1964-65; Assistant Professor, Baylor University, Micro Dallas Texas, 1968-69; Assistant Medical Director, 1969-70. *Publications:* Articles in numerous professional journals. *Memberships:* Oregon Medical Association; Oregon Society of Allergy & Immunology; American Academy of Allergy; American College of Allergy. *Hobbies:* Tennis; Scottish Country Dancing; Gardening; Hiking. *Address:* 5415 SW Westgate Drive, Portland, OR 97211, USA.

HAWKINS Linda Jean Parrott, b. 23 June 1947, Florence, South Carolina, USA. Teacher. m. Larry Eugene Hawkins, 15 Aug. 1970, 1 daughter. *Education:* BS, Business Administration, Univerity of South Carolina, 1969; M.Ed., Francis Marion College, 1978; Student, Specialist's Degree, Educational Administration, University of South Carolina, 1985-. *Appointments:* Teacher, 1969-70, Teacher, Department Chair, 1980-88, Lake City High School; Secretary, The Furniture Mart, 1972-73. *Publications:* Journal articles. *Memberships:* National Business Education Association; South Carolina Business Education Association; South Carolina Vocational Association. *Honours:* National Business Education Associations Secondary Teacher of the Year, 1989; South Carolina Business Education Association's Educator of the Year, 1988; many other honours and awards. *Hobbies:* Working with Young People; Reading; Cross Stitching; Softball. *Address:* Route 1, Box 225, Coward, SC 29530, USA.

HAWKINS Myrtle, b. 17 June 1923, Merritt, British Columbia, Canada. Artist; Lecturer. m. William E. Hawkins, 29 Mar. 1952, 1 son, 1 daughter. *Education:* Studied, 1944-45, AA, 1970, Hartnoll Collogo, USA; San Jose University, 1961, 1969; West Valley College, 1970, 1976, 1971; Studied art with Thomas Leighton, Meynard Steward and E.John Robinson. *Career:* Taught painting to the handicappped, 1969-71; Private Art Teacher; Judging art shows and lecturing, 1969-; Exhibited at Rosicrucian Gallery, Triton; Noted for portraiture and seascapes. *Creative works include:* Author, Art as Recreation, Rehabilitation and Therapy for the Handicapped; Illustrator, The Adventures of Mimi, books I and II; Paintings in public and private collections throughout the world. *Memberships:* Society of Western Artists; Triton Museum; National Museum of Women in the Arts. *Honours:* Over 60 awards mostly in art, 1960-; 1st Place, National Art Competition, Easter Seal Society, 1965; Gold Seal Award, 1965; Best of Show and Popular Vote, St Mark's, 1968; Le Foli Award, 1972; Woman of Achievement, 1973, 1974; Award of Merit, 1978; Honourable mention, Olive Hyde Art Center, 1982; Society of Western Artists Signature Award, 1986; Outstanding Senior Citizen of Santa Clara, 1987. *Hobbies:* Playing the mandolin; Cooking. *Address:* 646 Bucher Avenue, Santa Clara, CA 95051, USA.

HAWKINS Paula F, b. 24 Jan. 1927, Salt Lake City, Utah, USA. Politician. m. Walter E Hawkins, 5 Sept. 1946. 1 son, 2 daughters. *Education:* Utah State University; Honorary Doctorates: Utah State University, Humanities; Rollins College, Law; St Thomas University, Law; Bethune Cookman College, Law. *Appointments:*

Florida Public Service Commission, 1972-79, Chairman 1977-79; Air Florida, Vice President for Governmental Affairs, 1979-80; United States Senator, 1981-87. *Publication:* Children at Risk, 1985. *Memberships:* Florida Republican National Committeewoman, 1968-; National Republican Foundation Advisory Board; Appointments: Board of Visitors, US Military Academy at West Point; National Trust for Drug Free Youth; President's Child Safety Partnership; American Representative to Organisation of American States Drug Commission. *Honours:* 1985 Justice Department Child Advocate of the Year; 1985 American Academy of Pediatrics Excellence in Public Service award; 1985 American Legion Ladies Auxiliary Outstanding Woman of the Year Award; 1985 Grandparent of the Year Award; 1985 Albert Einstein College of Medicine Achievement Award for Government; 1983 Mother of the Year Award for Statesmanship; 1983 Israel Peace Medal; 1982 Utah Heritage Award; 1981 Republican Woman of the Year. *Hobbies:* Reading; Gardening; Stained glass. *Address:* Winter Park, FL 32790, USA.

HAWTHORNE Lucia Shelia, b. Baltimore, USA. Professor. *Education:* BS, Morgan State University, 1964; MAT, Washington State University, 1965; PhD, Pennsylvania State University, 1971. *Appointments:* Instructor, 1965-67, Morgan State University, 1967-69, Pennsylvania State University; Assistant Professor, 1969-71, Associate Professor, 1972-75, Associate Dean, 1974-75, Chairman, 1972-75, 1984-87, Morgan State University. *Memberships:* Speech Communication Association; Western, Eastern Communication Associations; Delta Sigma Theta; Alpha Kappa Mu; Phi Alpha Theta. *Honours:* Danforth Associate, 1971-76, ACE Fellow, 1974-75. *Hobbies:* Reading; Travel; Writing. *Address:* Speech Communication, Morgan State University, Baltimore, MD 21239, USA.

HAWTHORNE Susan, b. 30 Nov. 1951, Wagga Wagga, New South Wales, Australia. Writer; Editor. *Education:* Teaching Diploma (Primary), 1972; BA Honours, Philosophy, LaTrobe University, 1976; MA (Prelim), Ancient Greek, Melbourne University, 1981. *Appointments:* Tutor, University of Melbourne, 1980; Teacher, English as 2nd Language, Brunswick Neighbourhood House, 1983-84; Festival Organiser, Women 150, 1984-85; Tutor, Deakin University, 1986; Editor, Penguin Books Australia, 1987-. *Publications include:* Editor, Difference, 1985; Co-Editor, Moments of Desire, with Jenny Pausacker, 1989. Also contributor, various anthologies, newspapers, journals. *Memberships:* Management Committees: Feminist Book Fortnight, & Spoleto Melbourne Writers Festival 1988-89; PEN International; Women in Publishing; Fellowship of Australian Writers (Victoria); Australian Journalists Association. *Honours:* Joint winner (with J. Yowell), Barbara Ramsden Award, editing Stories from the Warm Zone, Fellowship of Australian Writers, 1988. *Hobbies:* Writing; Reading; Travel. *Address:* c/o Penguin Books Australia, 487 Maroondah Highway, Ringwood, Victoria 3134, Australia.

HAYASHI Darlene Midori, b. 15 Nov. 1944, Rohwer, Arkansas, USA. Chemist. *Education:* BSc, University of Southern California, 1968; MSc, State University of New York at Buffalo, 1973. *Memberships:* The American Institute of Chemists Incorporated; American Chemical Society; American Association for the Advancement of Science; International Union of Pure and Applied Chemistry; The Mathematical Association of America; The New York Academy of Sciences. *Honours:* Life Fellowship, International Biographical Association, 1987; Commemorative Medal of Honour, The American Biographical Institute, Inc., 1987. *Hobbies:* Playing the violin. *Address:* 3400 London Street, Los Angeles, CA 90026, USA.

HAYDON Julie, b. 10 June 1910, Oak Park, Illinois, USA. Actress; Author; Lecturer. m. George Jean Nathan, 19 June 1955. *Career:* Theatre: The Lady in Spectacles, Autumn Crocus, 1934; Titania, A Midsummer Night's Dream, 1934; Hope Blake, Bright Star, 1935; Brigid, Shadow and Substance, 1938; Kitty Duval, The Time of Your Life, 1939 and on tour 1940-41; Sweeney in the Trees, 1941; Patricia Carleon, Magic, double bill with Hello, Out There, 1942; Laura, World Premiere of The Glass Menagerie, 1944-45; Cecia Coplestone, The Cocktail Party, 1951; Total of 20 Films including Gora Moore in The Scoundrel (with Noel Coward), 1935; Radio and Television including: The Bells of Adano (with Robert Mitcham, Robert Montgomery); The Way of Hope, NBC 1953; Autumn Crocus, NBC 1954; The Grand Tour, ABC 1954; Alice Adams (Hallmark Hall of Fame); Recordings: Colette's Music Hall, Folkways Records; George Jean Nathan, New American Credo. *Publications:* Every Dog Has it's Day (Book), 1943; Still Shining Star (Town and Country Magazine), 1954. *Address:* c/o Patricia Angelin, 139 W. 28th Street, Suite 3E, New York, NY 10001, USA.

HAYES Doris Jean, b. 7 June 1946, Louisville, Kentucky, USA. Data Processing Manager. m. 30 Aug. 1974, 2 daughters. *Education:* BS summa cum laude, Mathematics, DePaul University, 1973; MBA with distinction, University of Michigan, 1984. *Appointments:* Teacher, Mathematics and Science, Junior High, Chicago Arch. School System, Chicago, Illinois, 1967-71; Systems Analyst, Sears Roebuck, Chicago, 1971-74; Systems Programmer, Blue Cross Blue Shield, Detroit, Michigan, 1974-78; Data Processing Manager, Electronic Data Systems (subsidiary of General Motors), 1978-. *Memberships:* Friends of Grosse Pointe Library; Sponsor, Foster Parents Plan; Founders Society of Detroit Institute of Arts; Michigan Humane Society; Nature Conservancy; Detroit Zoological Society; Environmental Defense Fund; Wayne State, WDET Supporters; WTVC, Channel 56 Supporters; Alumnae Associations: Holy Rosary Academy; St Catharine Junior College; University of Michigan. *Honours:* Full tuition scholarship to Holy Rosary Academy, 1960; Full tuition scholarship to Catherine Spaulding College, 1964; Pride in Excellence Award, Blue Cross Blue Shield, Michigan, 1977; Outstanding Performance Award, General Motors, 1983, 1984; Recognition Award, Electronic Data Systems, 1988. *Hobbies:* Alpine skiing; Cinema; Domestic mechanics; Natural science; White water rafting. *Address:* 750 Tower Drive, Troy, MI 48084, USA.

HAYES Lisa K. b. 11 June 1941, Ames, Iowa, USA. Reading Specialist. div. 1 son, 1 daughter. *Education:* AA, Marshalltown Community College, Iowa, 1962; BA, Sociology, Drake University, 1967; MA, American History, Northeast Missouri State University, 1974; MS, Reading Education, University of Nebraska, 1984. *Appointments:* 9th Physical Science Instructor, Trenton, Missouri, 1967-68; Acting Principal & Kindergarten Teacher, Laredo, MO, 1969-70; Kindergarten, Junior & Senior High School English & Social Studies, Cameron, MO, 1970-74; Adult Basic Education, Trenton, 1967-77; Home/Hospital Instructor, Council Bluffs, Iowa, 1980-83; Reading Specialist, Unified School District 501, Topeka, 1986-. *Publications:* Thesis: Use of Referendum To Destroy Legislation in Government-Hyde Tenure, Missouri 1920-22, 1974; Article, Infusion of Explicit Phonic-Linguistic Principles in an Elementary Whole Language Remedial Reading Program, 1987. *Memberships:* Contributor, Menninger Foundation, Topeka, Kansas; International Reading Association; National Education Association; Kansas Association for Supervision & Curriculum Development. *Honours:* 3.9 Grade Point Average (MA) 1974, 4.0 Average (MS) 1984; Elected, Phi Alpha Theta history society, 1973; Biographical recognitions. *Hobbies:* Family activities of all kinds; Dancing; Home repairs; Plans for own reading clinic, and study of use of coloured lenses to assist some learning difficulties. *Address:* 2428 Edgewater Terrace, Topeka, Kansas 66614, USA.

HAYES Martha B, b. 20 Oct. 1943, Cumberland County, USA. International Cosmetologist; Instructor. 12 sons, 5 daughters (9 adopted). *Education:* License, Cosmetology, Metropolitan Beauty School, Washington; North Capitol Beauty Institute; Graduate: Wake Forest University, North Carolina State University. *Appointments:* Owner, Martha's Beauty Salon, Fyetteville, 1968; Owner, Martha's Discounty Beauty

Salon, 1970; 2 salons in Arizona, 1970's; 2 salons under Martha's Beauty Salon, 1978; Founder, Cape Fear Beauty Institute & Hairweaving College. *Memberships:* National Association of Cosmetology Schools; North Carolina State Board of Cosmetic Art Examiners; First International Independent Hair Weavers Association Inc. *Honours:* Many awards including: Lee Iaccos, Chairman of Statue of Liberty-Ellis Island Centennial Commission, and Chairman of Chrysler Corporation, USA Black Gold, Hairweavers Specialist, 1986. *Hobby:* Working. *Address:* PO Box 0844, Fayetteville, NC 28302, USA.

HAYES Mary Phyllis Scott, b. 30 Apr. 1921, New Castle, Indiana, USA. Vice President & Corporate Secretary. m. John Clifford Hayes, 1 Jan. 1942. 1 son. *Education:* Attended: Ball State University; Indiana University; Standard, Merit & Graduate Diplomas, Institute of Financial Education (formerly American Savings & Loan Institute). *Appointments:* Teller, Henry County Savings & Loan Association, 1939-41; Executive Secretary, American National Bank, Nashville, 1943-44; Henry Co Savings Loan Officer 1951-62, Assistant Secretary-Treasurer, 1962-69, Secretary-Treasurer, 1969-73, Corp Secretary 1973-84, Vice President & Corporate Secretary 1984-, American Savings Bank; Secretary, HCSS Corp, 1984-. *Memberships:* Institute of Financial Education, East Central Indiana Chapter 233; Savins & Loan League of Indiana; International Platform Association; American Heart Association; American Red Cross; Henry Co Historical Society. *Honours:* Service Award, 1968; Gold Medallion, 1973 and 1978; 20 Year award, 1983; 25 Year award 1987, American Heart Association; Cub Scout Leader & Treasurer 4 years award. *Hobbies:* Music, pianist; Travel; Swimming; Gardening, roses; History. *Address:* 1405 H Avenue, New Castle, Indiana 47362, USA.

HAYES Melinda Kay, b. 24 Aug. 1953, Terre Haute, Indiana, USA. Librarian. *Education:* BA, German, 1980, MLS, 1982, University of California, Los Angeles. *Appointments:* Intern, Conservation, Huntington Library, 1982-83; Reference Cataloger, H.E. Huntington Library, 1983-85; Collection Development & Conservation Librarian, Hancock Library, University of Southern California, 1985-. *Publications:* articles in professional journals. *Memberships:* Americna Library Association; American Institute for Conservation; Western Associatiron of Art Conservators. *Hobbies:* Dance; Music; Needlework; Skiing; Reading. *Address:* Hancock Library of Biology & Oceanography, University of Southern California, Los Angeles, CA 90089, USA.

HAYES Nan DeVincentis, b. Pennsylvania, USA. Writer; College Teacher. m. James R. Hayes, June 1975, 2 daughters. *Education:* BS, Villa Maria College; MS, Duquesne University; PhD studies, University of Pittsburgh, University of Maryland, current; 6-year Writing Certificate, University of Rochester. *Appointments:* Freelance writer, 1979-; Adjunct teacher, literature, composition, journalism, Salisbury State University, 1985-. *Publications:* Non-fiction book, Move It!, 1988; Over 100 articles for magazines & newspapers including: Parade, People, Us, Brides, Grit, etc; Over 20 short stories; Novel under consideration. *Memberships:* Authors Guild; Writers & Poets; National Writers Club; Eastern Shore Writers Association; Salisbury-Wicomico Arts Council; Art Institute & Gallery. *Honours:* 4 endowment awards, writers' conferences including Bread Loaf; Selected 5 times as Fiction Judge, various state writing conferences; Dean's List graduate. *Hobbies:* Impressionist painting; Classical music; Boating; Reading. *Address:* 813 Riverside Drive, Salisbury, Maryland 21801, USA.

HAYES Rebecca Anne, b. 3 June 1950, Princeton, USA. Staff Manager. *Education:* AA, 1970; AB, University of Kentucky, 1972; MEd., University of Louisville, 1974. *Appointments:* Educator, Jefferson County Board of Education, 1972-78; Management Assistant, South Central Bell, Louisville, 1978-80; Engineer, 1980-82; Engineer, 1983-84; Assistant Staff Manager, 1984-87; Systems Consultant, Business

Markets Group, 1987-88; Staff Manager, BSD Sales Operations, AT&T, Basking Ridge, 1988-. *Memberships:* Kentucky Council of Teachers of Mathematics; Greater Louisville Council Teachers of Mathematics; National Council of Teachers of Mathematics. *Honours:* Mathematics Award, Midway College, 1970; Phi Teta Kappa; Directors Award, Engineering, 1983, Sales Vice President Award, Marketing, 1985, AT&T. *Hobbies:* Reading; Golf; Computer; Bridge. *Address:* Rm 33C02, 55 Corporate Drive, Bridgewater, NJ 08807, USA.

HAYLE Caludette Frederica, b. 24 Jan. 1955, Kingston, Jamaica, West Indies. President; Chief Executive Officer. divorced. 1 son, 1 daughter. *Education:* BSc Magna cum laude, Mathematics, York College, 1974-78; Certificate, Cornell University, 1981-82. *Appointments:* Supervisor Fin. Sys. 1980-81, Compensation Analyst, 1981-82, CBS Inc; Consultant, Citibank, Metro-North, AT&T, 1982-84; President, Chief Executive Officer, Goodman & Hayle Information Systems, 1984-. *Memberships:* Delegate, National White House Conference on Small Business; National Association of Women Business Owners; Trustee, Republican Presidential Task Force. *Honour:* Citation: Business Week's CAREERS, Entrepreneurial Women. *Hobbies:* Collecting Antique furniture; Writing; Travelling to historic cities; Horseback Riding; Sailing. *Address:* 245 East 63rd Street No 112, New York, NY 10021, USA.

HAYNES Eleanor Louise, b. 7 July 1929, Georgia, USA. Columnist; Director, Public Relations. m. Kenneth M. Thomas, 16 Jan. 1954, divorced 1963, 1 son. *Appointments:* Fashion designer, Petite Frocks, New York City, 1953-59; Reporter, New York Voice, 1968-; Designer, Sipkini Corp, New York City, 1969-74; Public Relations Director, Coler Hospital, New York City, 1978-; Editor, Coler Report. *Memberships:* National Association Media Women Inc.; National Association Female Executives; Edges Group Inc; Order Eastern Star. *Honours:* Recipient, numerous honours and awards most recent include: NAACP Community Service Award, 1988; Floyd H. Feake, Appreciation Award, 1988. *Hobbies:* Cooking; Travel; Entertaining Friends. *Address:* 231-16 126 Ave., Laurelton, NY 11413, USA.

HAYNES Lillie Nelson, b. 10 May 1951, Chicago, Illinois, USA. Psychologist. m. Carl Nelson, 22 June 1973. 1 daughter. *Education:* BA, Texas Woman's University, 1972; MA, Texas Southern University, 1976; Doctoral Student, Texas Woman's University, currently. *Appointments:* Teacher; Client Coordinator, Mental Health Mental Retardation Authority; School Psychologist, Dallas Independent School District. *Publications:* Skit: Therapy Role Induction; Prose Ebony Child. *Memberships:* Dallas Association of School Psychologists; American Assocaition for Marriage & Family Therapists; Texas Psychological Association; American Board of Medical Psychotherapists; Academy of Family Mediators; Dallas Society of Clinical Hypnosis; Dallas Psychological Association; National Association of Black Psychologists. *Honours:* Licensed Professional Counsellor; Certified Mediator, Dispute Mediation Service; Realtor; Associate School Psychologist; Rational Emotive Therapy, Primary Certificate; Southwest Family Institute Intern. *Hobbies:* Travelling; Swimming; Cooking; Meeting interesting people; Writing; Research. *Address:* 1541 Russell Glen Lane, Dallas, Texas 70232, USA.

HAYNES Mary Rapstine, b. 16 Jan 1945, Coral Gables, USA. Elected Official. m. Christopher Alan Haynes, 10 June 1967, 1 daughter. *Education:* BA, University of Texas, Austin, 1967; MA, University of Texas, El Paso, 1975. *Appointments:* Science Teacher, 1970-78; County Chairman, Democratic Party, 1978-80; Nominee, Democratic Party, 1980; El Paso County Commissioner, 1983-86, 1987-1990. *Publications:* Viral Electron Micro graphs of Wart Virus, 1975; Voters Guide and Directory of National State and Local Officials, 1979. *Memberships:* American Mensa; Alpha Epsilon Delta; Kappa Delta Pi; Delta Delta Delta. *Honours:* Faceless Childrens Award; Reach for Excellence Award.

Hobbies: British & American Literature; Skiing; Tennis; Travel; Hunting; Cooking. *Address:* 221 Silverwood, El Paso, TX 79922, USA.

HAYNES Renee Otiana, (Mrs Tickell), b. 23 July 1906, London, England. Writer. m. Jerrard Tickell, 1929, deceased 1966. 3 sons. *Education:* Lycee Francaise, UK, 1923-24; St Hugh's College, Oxford, 1924-27. *Appointments include:* Various posts, British Council, 1941-67; Editor, Vice President, Journal & Proceedings Society for Psychical Research, 1970-. *Publications include:* The Holy Hunger, 1935; Pan, Caesar & God, 1938; Hilaire Belloc, 1953; The Hidden Springs, 1961; Philosopher King, 1970. Contributions to numerous anthologies, magazines and journals. *Memberships:* Council Member, Society for Psychical Research; Alister Hardy Research Unit, Oxford. *Hobbies:* Cooking; Gardening; Swimming; Talk. *Address:* The Garden Flat, 41 Springfield Road, London NW8 0QJ, England.

HAYNES Sybille Edith, b. 3 July 1926, Leverkusen. Archaeologist; Writer. m. Denys Eyre Lankester Haynes, 18 Jan. 1951. *Education:* Universities of Frankfurt am Main, and Munich, 1947-52; Doctorate, summa cum laude, 1950. *Appointments:* Voluntary Assistant, Etruscology, Greek & Roman Dept., British Museum, London, 1951-76. *Publications:* Etruscan Bronze Utensils, 1965; Etruscan Sculpture, 1971; Land of the Chimaera, 1974; Zwischen Maander und Taurus, 1977; Die Tochter des Augurs, 1981; Etruscan Bronzes, 1985; The Augur's Daughter, 1987. *Memberships:* Istituto di Studi Etruschi ed Italici, 1965, Foreign member; Deutsches Archaeologisches Institut, 1985, Corresponding Member; Order of L'Ombra Della Sera at Volterra, 1981. *Honours:*MBE, 1976. *Hobby:* Travel. *Address:* Flat 17, Murray Court, 80 Banbury Road, Oxford OX2 6LQ, England.

HAYS Mary Katherine Jackson, b. Flora, Mississippi, USA. Civic Worker. m. (1) Herbert Puffer Oliver, 9 Aug. 1927 (deceased 1934), (2) Donald Osborne Hays, 30 Aug. 1937. *Appointments:* Secretary, various concerns, Texas & New York City, 1934-43. *Memberships include:* Music Club of Robston, Texas, 1933-34; Active, Little Theatre, Wilkes Barre, Pennsylvania, 1937-39; The Womans Club of Flora, 1943-45; Charter member, incorporator, Conference of State Societies, Washington, 1952; Member, The Womens City Club of Boston, 1953-54; Volunteer, American Cancer Society, Washington, 1956-; Women's Committee, volunteer USO, 1945-48, symphony sustaining committee drives 1957-66, National Symphony Association; Women's Committee, Corcoran Art Gallery, Washington, 1957-62; Pierce-Warwick Adoption Association, Washington Home for Foundlings; Volunteer, Washington Heart Association, 1959-66; DC Episcopal Home for Children, 1961-; DC Salvation Army Auxiliary, 1962-; Past secretary, Mississippi State Society, DC; Mississippi Women's Club, DC; Numerous offices, Daughters of American Revolution; Chapter Historian, UDC; The Washington Club 1970-; Executive Council and Membership Chairman, Johnstone Clan of America, 1982-84. *Hobbies:* Music; Antiques; Genealogy. *Address:* 4000 Massachusetts Avenue NW, Washington DC 20016, USA.

HAYTER Alethea Catharine, b. 7 Nov. 1911, Cairo, Egypt. Retired. *Education:*MA Oxon, Lady Margaret Hall, Oxford, 1929-32. *Appointments:*Editorial Staff, Country Life, 1930-38; Postal Censorship, Gibraltar, Bermuda, Trinidad, London, 1939-45; British Council, Athens, Paris, Brussels, London, 1945-71 (Cultural Attache, Brussels). *Publications:* Mrs Browning: A Poet's work and its setting, 1962; A Sultry Month: Scenes of London Literary Life in 1846, 1965; Elizabeth Barrett Browning, 1965; Opium and the Romantic Imagination, 1968; Horatio's Version, 1972; A Voyage in Vain, Coleridge's Journey to Malta in 1804, 1973. Ed. Confessions of an English Opium Eater, Thomas de Quincey, 1971; Melmoth The Wanderer, C R Maturin, 1977; Fitzgerald To His Friends, 1979. Numerous articles and reviews in Times Literary Supplement; Sunday Times; New Statesman, etc. *Memberships:* Society of Authors

Committee of Management, 1975-79; Royal Society of Literature; PEN. *Honours:* OBE 1970; W H Heinemann Award, Royal Society of Literature, 1962 for Mrs Browning; Rosemary Crawshay Prize, British Academy, 1968 for Opium and The Romantic Imagination; Fellowship, Royal Society of Literature, 1962; Leverhulme Research Award, 1966. *Address:* 22 Aldebert Terrace; London SW8 1BJ, England.

HAYWARD Victoria Clare, b. 28 May 1956, Worthing, Sussex, England. Writer; Book Editor. *Education:* Clare College, Cambridge University, 1974-77; BA, Historical Tripos Parts I and II. *Appointments:* Editor, Dorling Kindersley, 1977-79; Freeland Editor and Translator, New Hebrides, South Pacific, 1980-81; Senior Editor, Art and Illustrated Department, Weidenfeld & Nicolson, 1982-84; Freelance Writer and Editor, 1984-88. *Publications:* Non-fiction articles and contributions to magazines, newspapers and books. *Memberships:* National Union of Journalists; Guild of Food Writers. *Hobbies:* Travel; Swimming; Food; Dyslexia teaching; Music; Spain. *Address:* 8 Victoria Court, Cartwright Street, London E1 8LZ, England.

HAZELTINE Joyce, b. 16 July 1935, Pierre, USA. Secretary of State. m. David, 29 July 956, 2 sons, 1 daughter. *Education:* AA, Teaching. *Appointments:* Elementary Teacher; Office Management, various positions; Assistant Chief Clerk, House of Representatives; Secretary of the Senate, 10 years; Founder, Owner, Hazeltine Associates, 1974-86. *Memberships:* American Society of Legislative Clerks and Secretaries; National Association of Secretaries of State; Women Executives in State Government. *Honours:* Outstanding Jaycette Award, 1969; State Jaycette President, 1969-70. *Hobbies:* Working; Dancing. *Address:* State Capitol Building, 500 East Capitol, Suite 204, Pierre, SD 57501, USA.

HAZLEWOOD-BRADY Anne Felten, b. 22 Jan. 1925, Tuxedo, New York, USA. Poet. m. (1) Edward Hamilton Morgan, dec. 6 Nov. 1954, 2 sons, (2) Alfred F. Brady, 11 Aug. 1956, 3 stepsons adopted 1958. *Education:* BA, Vassar College, 1946; New York University and Columbia University, 1958-61; Studies with Babette Deutsch, Leonie Adams, Louise Bogan. *Appointments:* Executive Secretary to Director of Museum of Contemporary Crafts, New York City, 1969-70; Freelance Reviewer for Gannatt Newspapers, 1977-78; Poetry Editor, Maine Life magazine, 1979-85. *Publications:* Books of poetry: Steeps and Views: Unfinished Conversations; Unwritten Testament; The Cross, The Anchor and The Heart; One to the Many; A Year of Sundays. *Memberships:* Academy of American Poets; Founder Member, Maine Women in the Arts; Founder Member, Women's Interact Center, New York City; Commissioner, Maine Commission on the Arts. *Honours:* Publishers Award for Unfinished Conversations, 1969; Elected Delegate from Maine to National Women's Conference, 1977; Citation, Maine Women in the Arts, 1981. *Hobbies:* Photography; Wilderness trips by canoe; Gardening; Grandchildren; Surviving with a song worth singing. *Address:* Box 534, Kennebunkport, ME 04046, USA.

HEAD Audrey May, b. 21 Jan. 1924, Wonersh, Surrey, England. *Education:* St Catherine's School, Bramley. *Appointments:* Chartered Auctioneers & Estate Agents Institute, 1949-58; Hill Samuel Group 1958-86, Managing Director 1976-86, Director 1973-86, Hill Samuel Unit Trust Managers, Director, Hill Samuel Investment Management, 1974-86, Director, Hill Samuel Life Assurance, 1983-86; Part-time Member, Monopolies and Merger Commission, 1981-89; Director, Trade Union Unit Trust Managers, 1986-89. *Memberships:* Chairman, Unit Trust Association, 1983-85; Chairman of Governors, St Catherine's School; Governor, Cranleigh School; SW Surrey District Health Authority. *Honours:* Nominated as Business Woman of the Year, 1976; Queen's Silver Jubilee Medal, 1977. *Hobbies:* Golf; Gardening. *Address:* West Chantry, 4 Clifford Manor Road, Guildford, Surrey, England.

HEAD Fay Awtry, b. 11 Apr. 1949, Dallas, Texas, USA. Research Assistant/Education. m. Samuel Davies Head, 22 May 1971. 2 sons, 1 daughter. *Education:* BA 1971, MEd 1988, Texas Tech University. *Appointments:* Research Assistant, Lubbock Independent School District/Texas Tech University, 1987-; Cadre Trainer, Southwest Educational Development Lab, 1988- ; Graduate Assistant 1986-87, Summer Research Assistantship 1988, Texas Tech University; Teacher Training Board, 1980-85, New Dimensions in Childbirth. *Publications:* Numerous articles to professional journals. *Memberships:* Phi Kappa Phi; Phi Delta Kappa; Kappa Delta Pi; Sigma Delta Pi; Phi Gamma Nu; Alpha Lambda Delta; Association of Teacher Educators; Association of Supervision & Curriculum Development Council on Education & Anthropology; Southwest Educational Research Assn, National Council of Teachers of English; American Council on the Teacher of Foreign Languages; American Association of Teachers of Spanish & Portuguese; National Association for Bilingual Education; Texas Association of Teacher Educators. *Honours:* Texas Association of Teacher Educators Mentor Grant, 1989; Outstanding Master's Student (College of Education, Texas Tech University), 1988; Summer Research Assistantship Grant, Texas Tech University, 1988; Berlie J Fallon Memorial Scholarship, Texas Tech, 1986-89; LaVerne Faye Bumpass Bilingual Scholarship, 1987-88; Texas Tech University Scholarship, 1987-88. *Hobbies:* Horseback riding; Gardening; Walking; Camping; Reading. *Address:* P O Box 565, Wolfforth, Texas 79382, USA.

HEAD Mildred Eileen, b. 13 June 1911, Egham, Surrey, England. Retired. *Education:* MCSP, Chelsea College of Physical Education. *Appointments:* Teacher, PE, Northumberland, 1933-37; Lecturer, PE, Health Education, St Hilda's College, Durham, 1937-42; Organiser, PE, Essex County Council, 1942-50; Owner, Director, Partner, several furniture & drapery shops, 1950-82. *Publications:* Designed and promoted the Essex Agility Apparatus for Primary Schools, 1944. *Memberships:* UK Federation of Business & Professional Women, President 1966-69; Mayor, Borough of Sudbury, 1970-71; National Chamber of Trade, Board Chairman 1971-77, President 1977-79; International Federation of Business & Professional Women, President 1977-80. *Honours:* OBE, 1971; Member: Price Commission, 1977-77, various other commissions. *Address:* Rosebank, Ingrams Well Road, Sudbury, Suffolk CO10 6RT, England.

HEAD Violet Beryl, b. 30 Mar. 1922, S Marysburgh Twp, Pr Ed County, Ontario, Canada. Psychologist. *Education:* Certificate, Peterborough Teachers' College, 1041; DA, Queens University, Kingston, Ontario, 1958; AM, 1962; PhD, 1963, University of Chicago, Illinois, USA; Registered Certificate No 577, Ontario Board of Examiners in Psychology, 1965. *Appointments:* Elementary School Teacher, 1941-46; Various positions in business, 1946-56; Group services for immigrants, International Institute of Metro, Toronto, 1956-60; Psychologist, Toronto Psychiatric Hospital, 1963-65; Psychologist & Coordinator of Group Therapy, Addiction Research Foundation, 1965-70; Psychologist, Donwood Institute, Toronto, 1970-87; Private Practice, Toronto, 1987-; Consultant, Project Turnabout, Ontario Nurses Assis. Programme, 1987-. *Publications:* Articles: Research check list for scoring organicity from human figure drawings, 1972; An Impairment Rating Scale for Human figure Drawings, 1974; Experiences with Art Therapy in Short Term Groups of Day Clinic Addicted Patiets, 1975. Numerous articles presented to conferences. *Memberships:* Ontario Psychological Association; Founding Member, Ontario Group Psychotherapy Association; Canadian Group Psychotherapy Association, Toronto Section; Founding Member, Canadian Group Psychotherapy Association; American Group Psychotherapy Association; International Association of Group Psychotherapy; Art Gallery of Ontario; Royal Ontario Museum; Toronto Lawn Tennis Club. *Honours:* Fellow, Ontario Group Psychotherapy Affiliate of Canadian Group of Psychotherapy Association, 1975; Nominated for Ontario Psychological Association Award of Merit, 1986; Fellow, Canadian Group Psychotherapy Association, 1987. *Hobbies:* Painting; Drawing; Boating; Swimming; Entertaining; Music, piano; Theatre. *Address:* 34 Standish Avenue, Toronto, Ontario, M4W 3B1, Canada.

HEALY Anne Laura, b. 1 Oct. 1939, New York City, USA. Teacher; Sculptor. m. Richard Synek, 28 Feb 1960 (divorced 1962), 1 daughter. *Education:* BA, Queens College, City University of New York, 1962. *Appointments include:* Visiting artist, various establishments; Radio & TV broadcasts; Juror; Panelist; Lecturer, various colleges & universities; Board, & Head, Curatorial Committee, San Francisco Arts Commission Gallery, 1985-89; Arts Commissioner for Sculpture City of SF, 1989-; Associate Professor, UCB Sculpture, 1985-. *Creative work includes:* Numerous solo exhibitions throughout USA, 1971-; Participant, numerous group exhibitions throughout USA 1970-, international group exhibitions, France, Switzerland Japan, Sweden 1976-. Commissions, various universities, businesses, public buildings, 1971-, most recent include permanent sited sculptures: Squared Lightning, South Kitsap School District, Washington, 1985; Tumbling Shields, Litton Industries, Los Colinas, Texas, 1986. Work in numerous public collections including: Museum of Contemporary Crafts, New York City; Michigan State University; Wayne State University; Art Museum of South Texas; Chemical Bank, New York City; State of Washington Arts Commission. *Memberships:* Head, Visual Arts Committee, San Francisco Arts Commission for Sculpture; Board (from Artists' Committee), SF Art Institute. *Honours include:* Numerous awards, fellowships & grants. *Hobbies:* Dancing; Baseball; Horseback riding; Weight lifting. *Address:* Department of Art, Kroeber Hall, University of California, Berkeley, CA 94620, USA.

HEARD Chinita Ann, b. 7 Apr. 1961, Chambers County, Alabama, USA. Assistant Professor. *Education:* BS, Criminal Justice, Alabama State University, 1983; MS, Criminology, 1985, PhD, Criminology, 1988, Florida State University. *Appointments:* Assistant Professor, School of Public and Environmental Affairs, Indiana University, Fort Wayne, 1988-. *Memberships:* American Society of Criminology; Zeta Phi Beta Sorority Inc; Lambda Alpha Epsilon (American Criminal Justice Association). *Honours:* Excellence in Legal Studies Award, 1981-82; National Dean's List, 1981-83; Academic Excellence, College of Arts and Sciences Certificate, 1981-83; Pi Gamma Mu International Honour Society in Social Science, 1982; Alpha Kappa Mu, 1983; Graduate and Professional Study Followship, 1003-86; Outstanding Young Women of America Award, 1987. *Hobbies:* Reading; Travel. *Address:* 5124-10 Stonehedge Boulevard, Fort Wayne, IN 46835, USA.

HEARN Jean, b. 30 Mar. 1921, Launceston, Tasmania. Community Work. m. (1) Frederick Howe, 28 Sept. 1940, died 1956, 3 sons, 1 daughter, (2) Bevan Hearn. *Appointments:* Kindergarten Teacher, 1951-58; Work with children & youth, 1960-73; Member, Senate Australian Government, 1980-86. *Memberships:* Family Planning, Tasmania, Foundation Member, State Council, President 1985-; Inaugral Chairperson, Tasmanian Peace Trust, 1980-; State Secretary, Anthropological Society; etc. *Hobbies:* Peace; Music; Social Issues; Gardening; Cooking; etc. *Address:* 100 Balfour St., Launceston, Tasmania 7250, Australia.

HEARN Joyce C, b. Georgia, USA. Legislator. m. Thomas Harry Hearn. 3 daughters. *Education:* Graduated, Ohio State University, 1957; Advanced study, Finance, University of South Carolina. *Appointments:* House of Representatives, 1975-. *Memberships:* Chairman, State Real Estate Sub-Committee, Join Legislative Study Committee on Problems of the Handicapped; National Advisory Committee on Occupational Safety and Health; Labour and Commerce Committee; Workmen's Compensation Joint Legislative Study Committee; Study Committee on Alcohol & Drug Abuse; Board Member, Columbia Urban

League, Columbia College Board, National Federation of the Blind of South Carolina, Columbia Museum of Art, Columbia Women's Club. *Honours:* Outstanding Citizen Award, Columbia Rape Coalition, 1977; Distinguished Service Award, Claims Management Association of South Carolina, 1977; Distinguished Service Award, National Federation of the Blind, South Carolina, 1978; Order of the Palmetto, 1978; Distinguished Service Award, Columbia Urban League, 1983; Distinguished Service Award, MADD, 1985; Outstanding Legislator of the Year, Alcohol and Drug Abuse Association, 1980; Retarded Citizens Association, 1982, South Carolina Rehabilitation Association, 1984; Legislator of the Year Award, SC Association of the Deaf, 1987. *Address:* 1300 Berkeley Road, Columbia, SC 29205, USA.

HEARN Rosamond Ernst, b. 17 Sept. 1924, Boston, Massachusetts, USA. Music Service Executive. divorced. 1 son, 3 daughters. *Education:* Boston University, 1940-42; Longy Sch Music, 1947-49; Am Conservatory Music, 1966-71 and 1974-77; Music Fellow, University Colo, 1974-75. *Appointments:* Lab technician, Consol Rendering Co, Boston, 1942-52; Organist, choir director, Mass Conn and Ill, 1948-72; Assistant Conductor, accompanist, American Conservatory of Music, Chicago, 1970-73; Organist, choir director, Sacred Heart Ch, Lombard, Ill, 1973-78; Manager Music Store, Manhattan School of Music, 1978-79; Organist, Colesville Presbyn Ch Silver Springs, Md, 1979-; Gen Ptnr Manager, Allegro Music Service, Silver Springs, 1985-; Manager choral music dept, Lyon Healy Co, Chicago, 1975-78; Manager choral, vocal, organ depts, Harris Music Co, Rockville, Md, 1979-85; Columnist, Mitzi's Merit Series, 1984-. *Creative works:* Presentation of 26 Continuing Education Workshops to Mid-Atlantic Area Music Professionals, 1988. *Memberships:* American Guild Organists (board directors 1967-70); American Choral Directors Association (workshop coordinator); Music Educators National Conference; Choristers Guild; Music Industry Council; Silver Spring C of C; Delta Omicron; International Platform Association; International Federation for Choral Music; Business & Professional Women's Club. *Honour:* Outstanding Service to Music Profession, 1968. *Address:* Allegro Music Service, 1398 Lamberton Dr, Silver Springs, MD 20902, USA.

HEATH Bertha Clara, b. 22 July 1909, Middletown, Mon Co, New Jersey, USA. Retired Nurse; Humanitarian; Historian. *Education:* Diploma, Harlem Hospital School of Nursing, 1930; BS Public Health, New York University, 1948; MA Public Health, Columbia University, 1958. *Appointments:* Head Nurse, Ward Instructor, OPD Nurse, New York City Department of Hospitals, 1930-48; Clinician, Medical Center, Graduate School of Cancer Research, 1954-74; Teacher, New York City Board of Education, 1949-51; Established and Co Founder with Mon Co Park System, New Jersey Culture Center, Clinton P & Mary E Heath, 1974-80. *Memberships:* American Association of University Women, 1984; Harlem Hospital Alumni; Mon Co Historical Society; Commissioner, Middletown Human Rights Commission; NIAB Club, New Jersey; America Red Cross Nurse; National Association of Negro Nurses; New York Public Library Association; NAACP; President Trustee Clinton Chapel IAMEZ Church; Charter Member, Beltond Prayer Group. *Honours:* Proclamation, Human Rights, New Jersey, 1986; Proclamation, Afro American Black History (Mayoral), 1986; Honorary Member, National Police Officers Association of America; Honorary Mention United States Comm. Crime & Narcotics; Humanitqarian Award, N J State Federation of Colored Women; Humanitarian Award, National Association of Negro Business & Professional Women; Salutation, Masters of Philanthropy of N J, 1988; Hunger Task Force, Diocese of N J, 1988. *Hobbies:* Black History Research; National, International and Ancient research; Exercise/Health/Nutrition; Yoga; Sewing; Community activities; Church. *Address:* 179 Harmony Road, Middletown Mon Co, New Jersey 07748, USA.

HEATH Catherine Judith, b. 17 Nov. 1924, London,

England. Writer. m. Dennis F. Heath, 19 July 1947, divorced 1977, 1 son, 1 daughter. *Education:* BA, Honours, St Hilda's, Oxford, 1946. *Appointments:* University Lecturer, 1947-49; Journalism, 1949-52; Part-time Lecturer, 1955-64; Senior Lecturer, English, 1964-84; Theatre Criticism, 1983-. *Publications:* Stone Walls, 1975; The Vulture, 1974; Joseph and the Goths, 1975; Lady on the Burning Deck, 1977; Behaving Badly, novel & tv script, 1984, 1988. *Memberships:* Society of Authors; Pen; Amnesty International. *Hobbies:* Theatre; Conversation; Travel. *Address:* 17 Penarth Court, Devonshire Avenue, Sutton, Surrey SM2 5LA, England.

HEBERT Mary Eleanor (Ellie), b. 25 July 1959, Plaquemine, Louisiana, USA. Publisher & Editor, Women's News Magazine. *Education:* BA, Journalism, Louisiana State University, 1981. *Appointments:* Reporter, photograapher, Post/South & Times newspapers, Plaquemine, 1981-84; Editor, Times, & Associate Editor, Post/South, 1984-; Founder, owner, writer, editor, Louisiana Woman magazine, 1988-. *Publications include:* Various articles & photographs, regularly published, many subjects. *Memberships:* Seminar Chair 1989; YWCA Connections; Women Business Owners Association of Louisiana. *Honours include:* 26 awards, aspects of journalism, Louisiana Press Association, 1981-; 2nd place, best investigative story, National Newspaper Association, 1985. *Hobbies:* Sport; Photography; Outdoor activities. *Address:* c/o Louisiana Woman, 11931 Justice Street, Suite B, Baton Rouge, Louisiana 70816, USA.

HECKER Diane Clements, b. 28 Sept. 1945, Erie, Pennsylvania, USA. Administrator. divorced, 1 daughter. *Education:* BPS 1987, MBA 1988, Barry University, Miami, Florida. *Appointments:* Manager, Neiman Marcus department store, 1965-70; Consultant, Stout Fashions & Valerie's Retail Outlets, 1969-87; Flight attendant, Night Crew Scedule Manager, Braniff International Airways, 1976-82; Coordinator, Aids Research Laboratory, University of Miami Medical School, 1986; Facilities Engineering Administrator, 1987; ATC Supervisor 1988, Acting Manager Administrative & Technical Centre 1989-, Cordis Corporation. *Memberships:* National, & Southeast Academies of Management; American Management Association; American Society of Personnel Administration; National Association of Female Executives; Volunteer, adult literacy projects. *Honours:* Member, Mensa, 1987, 1988, 1989; Vice President, MBA Class, 1988; National Dean's List, 1987-88. *Hobbies:* Marathon running; Creating, designing & working own needlework; Piano playing; Reading. *Address:* 9151-6 Fontainebleau Boulevard, Miami, Florida 33172, USA.

HEDBERG Natalie Lancaster, b. 27 Sept. 1931, Riverhead, New York, USA. Professor of Communication Disorders and Speech Science. m. John Viking Hedberg, 18 Apr. 1954, 1 son, 2 daughters. *Education:* BS, Syracuse University, 1952; MA, Columbia University, 1960; PhD, Northwestern University, 1971. *Appointments:* Assistant Professor, State University College, New Paltz, 1963-68; Assistant Professor 1971-74, Associate 1974-80, Professor 1980-, Chair, Department of Communication Disorders & Speech Science 1986-, University of Colorado. *Publication:* Book, Narrative Analysis: Clinical Procedures, with Carol E. Westby, 1990. *Memberships:* Certification, American Speech-Language-Hearing Association; Colorado Speech-Language-Hearing Association; Orton Dyslexia Society. *Hobbies:* Skiing; Hiking; Tennis. *Address:* Department of Communication Disorders & Speech Science, Box 409, University of Colorado, Boulder, Colorado 80309, USA.

HEDER Tess, b. 8 Mar. 1941, Washington, USA. Businesswoman. m. Brian J. Miller, 24 Dec. 1986, 1 son. *Education:* BA, Radcliffe College, 1962; MArch., Harvard Graduate School of Design, 1969. *Appointments:* Architect, Tom Payette Associates, 1966-70, Benjamin Thompson & Associates, 1985-89;

Founder, President, Channel I Communications, 1986-. *Memberships:* American Institute of Architects; Boston Society of Architects; Cambridge Tenants Union. *Honours:* Templeton Kelly Award for Best Thesis, 1969; New England American Institute of Architects Award for Design of Cummings Office Building, Concord, 1970. *Hobbies:* Musical Composition; Playing Cello. *Address:* Channel 1 Communications, PO Box 338, Cambridge, MA 02238, USA.

HEDLEY (Gladys) Olwen, . 28 Apr. 1912, London, England. Author. *Education:* Various. *Appointments:* 1st woman, editorial staff, Windsor Slough & Eton Express, 1932-39; Hospital nurse, Windsor, 1939-45; Assistant to Royal Librarian, Royal Library, Windsor Castle, 1947-64. *Publications include:* Round & About Windsor & District, 1948; Windsor Castle, 1967, 1972; Royal Palaces, 1972; Queen Charlotte, 1975; Royal foundation of St Katharine, Ratcliffe, 1984. Numerous Pitkin Pictorials including: Princes of Wale, 1975; Queen's Silver Jubilee, 1977; (various French & German translations). Contributions: Official souvenir book, Royal Wedding, 1981; The Times (occasional historical articles), journals, reports; Editor, The Court Journals of Fanny Burney, 1786-91. *Honour:* Fellow, Royal Society of Literature, 1975. *Address:* 15 Denny Crescent, London SE11 4UY, England.

HEDLEY-WHYTE Elizabeth Tessa, b. 17 Jan. 1937, London, England. MD. m. John Hedley-Whyte, 19 Sept. 1959. *Education:* MB.BS, 1960; MD, 1976; Diplomate, American Board of Pathology, Anatomic 1966, Neuropathology, 1973. *Appointments:* Instructor,1968-70, Assistant Professor, 1970-76, Associate Professor, 1976-, Harvard Medical School; Neuropathologist, Massachusetts General Hospital. *Publications:* Papers in Scientific Journals. *Memberships:* Massachusetts Medical Society; American Association of Neuropathologists, Constitution Committee Chair 1974-76, Programme Committee, 1975-77, 1980-84, Membership Chair 1986-88, Councillor, 1987-9l; American Society for Cell Biology. bb3*Honours:* Consultant, National Institute of Health, 1976-81, 1982-86; Wellcome Research Fellowship, 1984-85; Guest Neuropathologist, Frank Walsh Society, 1987; Shields Warren Lecture, 1987. *Hobbies:* Research into Nervous System Diseases; Gardening; Needlework. *Address:* Massachusetts General Hospital, Boston, MA 02114, USA.

HEFFERNAN H (Helen) Patricia, b. 11 Apr. 1937, Brooklyn, New York, USA. Audiologist. 1 son, 1 daughter. *Education:* MA 1972, BA 1960, California State University, Los Angeles. *Appointments:* Audiologist, Los Angeles Otosurgical Group, 1962-72; Clinical Director, Hearing Clinics, California University, Los Angeles, 1972-74; Adviser, Early Childhood Education; Adjunct Professor, Whittier College; Adjunct Professor, 1974-78, California State University, Los Angeles; Director, Audiology, Otosurgical Group, Instructor, UCLA School of Nursing Extension, 1974-78; Private Practice, Hearing and Language Specialties; Director, Audiology, Tripod School for Deaf, 1978-. *Publications:* Temporary Increase in Sensorineural Hearing Loss with Hearing Aid Use, 1979; Contributer of articles and chapters to books; Has given several lectures on professional subjects. *Memberships:* Fellow, American Speech-Language-Hearing Association; Chair, Committee on Special Rules; AdHoc Committee on Provision of Audiologic Services; Nominating Committee, Legislative Councillor, 1977-; Chair, Sub-committee for National Convention; Fellow, California Speech-Language-Hearing Association, 1984; American Auditory Society. *Hobbies:* Gardening; Reading. *Address:* Hearing and Language Specialties, 9730 Wilshire Boulevard, No 212, Beverly Hills, CA 90212, USA.

HEFFLER Tara Francesca, b. 6 Aug. 1952, Paris, France. Manager, Sotheby Fine Art Auctioneers. m. Ross Heffler, 22 Apr. 1979. 1 son, 1 daughter. *Education:* Lycee Francais de Londres, 1956-66; Mayfield School, 1966-71; Kingston Polytechnic, 1974-76. *Appointments:* Organisation & Methods Analyst, British Gas, 1972-87; Manager, Sotheby Fine Art Actionneers, 1987-. *Address:* 146 Ramsden Road, London SW12 8RE, England.

HEFNER Christie, b. 8 Nov. 1952, Chicago, Illinois, USA. Company Chairman and Chief Executive Officer. *Education:* BA, Brandeis University. *Appointments:* Freelance Journalist, Boston Phoenix, 1974-75; Special Assistant to the Chairman, 1975-78, Vice President, 1978-82, Board of Directors, 1979-, Vice Chairman, 1986-88, Playboy Enterprises Inc; President, 1982-88, Chief Operating Officer, 1984-88, Chairman, 1988, Chief Executive Officer, 1988, Director, Playboy Foundation. *Memberships:* Direct Marketing Association, Board; American Civil Liberties Union of Illinois, Board; National Womens Political Caucus; Voters for Choice, Advisory Board; Young Presidents' Organization; Founding Member, Committee of 200; etc. *Honours:* Numerous awards, most recent include: Midwest Womens Center Founder's Award, 1986; Human Relations Award, American Jewish Committee, 1987; Harry Kalven Freedom of Expression Award, American Civil Liberties Union of Illinois, 1987; Spirit of Life Award, City of Hope, 1988. *Address:* Playboy Enterprises Inc., 919 N. Michigan Avenue, Chicago, IL 60611, USA.

HEILBON Vivien Sarah Frances, b. 13 May 1944, Glasgow, Scotland. Actress. *Education:* London Academy of Music & Dramatic Art, 1961-63. *Appointments:* Repertory Theatre, Dundee; Nottingham; Salisbury; Royal Lyceum Theatre, Edinburgh; Birmingham; A Heritage and its History, Phoenix Theatre, West End; Television: Sunset Song; Cloud House; Grey Granite; Target, BBC 1 Series; Tales of the Unexpected, Trilogy, BBC2 and Anglia; Take the High Road, STV; The New Statesman; Films: Kidnapped; Mysteries; 2 American Shakespeare Tours with the New Acter Company, Hamlet & Twelfth Night. *Honours:* Emmy Nomination for BBC Classic Serial, The Moonstone for Actress in Leading Role (Rachel Verinder). *Hobbies:* Reading; Classical Music; Theatre; Travel. *Address:* 121 Bishop's Mansions, Bishop's Park Road, London SW6 6DY, England.

HEIM Alice Winifred, b. 19 Apr. 1913, London, England. Psychologist (Retired). 1 son, 1 daughter (Adopted). *Education:* MA, Newnham College, 1935; PhD, Cambridge, 1939. *Appointments:* Experimental Psychology, Cambridge University, 1936-78, Selection RAF Pilots & Industrial, 1939-46, Research & Teaching, 1947-78, Weekly Clinic Children, Addenbrookes, 1949-62, Director, Psychology Studies, Newnham, 1960-78, Examiner, BPS Diploma, 1971-73. *Publications:* The Appraisal of Intelligence, 1954; Intelligence & Personality, 1970; Psychological Testing, 1975; Teaching in Higher Education, 1976; Barking Up the Right Tree; Thicker Than Water?, 1983; Understanding Your Dog's Behaviour, 1984; 12 Psychological Tests; 50 articles in journals. *Memberships Include:* Committee Member, BPS Education, 1967-70, Cambridge Women Research, 1968-71; Secretary, Science GP Newnham Associates, 1968-70; President, Cambridge Scientists' Lunch Club, 1970-73. *Honours:* Recipient, many honours & awards including: Smith-Mundt Fellow, Stanford, USA, 1951-52; Fellow, British Psychological Society, 1956; Official Fellowship, Clare Hall, Cambridge, 1972; President, Section J of British Association for the Advancement of Science, 1978-79. *Hobbies:* Music; Theatre; Film. *Address:* 8 Bateman Street, Cambridge CB2 1NB, England.

HEIM Kathryn Marie, b. 29 Sept. 1952, Milwaukee, USA. Registered Nurse Manager. m. (1) Vincent Robert Gouthro, 30 June 1970, divorced 1976, 1 son, (2) George John Heim, 17 Sept. 1977, divorced 1988. *Education:* AS, 1983; BS, Nursing, New York University, 1986; MS, Management, 1988; Certificate from American Nurses Association in Gerontological Nursing, 1986-91; Currently working on PhD. *Appointments:* RN Staff Geriatric Nurse, Clement Manor, Greenfield, 1983; Health Educator, Milwaukee

Boys Club, 1983-84; Nurse Manager, Milwaukee County Mental Health Complex, 1984-. *Publications:* articles in professional journals. *Memberships:* Director, Founder, local network, NAFE; Geropsychiatry Inpatient Advisory Committee, NEW; Nursing Research Committee; Chairperson of Sensory Deficit Committee Milwaukee County Mental Health Complex; Networking Executive Women; Member of Wellwoman Committee. *Hobbies:* Reading; Writing; Dance; Music. *Address:* 351 North 62nd Street, Milwaukee, WI 53213, USA.

HEIN Lucille Eleanore, b. 11 June 1915, Chicago, Illinois, USA. Freelance Writer. *Education:* BA, MA, PhD studies, English, Comparative Literature, Classical & Modern Languages, University of Wisconsin, 1933-40; Various courses, European Universities. *Appointments include:* Graduate Fellow & Teaching Aide, University of Wisconsin, 1938-40; Instructor, Wagner College, Staten Island, New York, 1940-44; Occasional teaching, various establishments, New York City, 1944-. Writer or editor, various organisations including: Camp Fire Inc; Lutheran Church; Ford Foundation; Boy Scouts; YMCA; International Reading Association; National Association for Mental Health; Inter-Agency Conference on Health Education. *Publications:* Wide variety of work, fiction/non-fiction, as author (stories for children, youth & adults) or editor. 14 books including: Enjoy Your Children, 1959; We Talk With God, 1968; Entertaining Your Child, 1971, 1972, Spanish 1973; My Very Special Friend, 1974; That Wonderful Summer, 1978; Thank You God, 1981. Editor, 5 books for young people; Author, numerous magazine articles, poetry. *Hobbies:* Travel; Outdoor life & nature; Hiking; Theatre; Music; Arts; Reading; Research. *Address:* 33 Central Avenue, Staten Island, New York 10301, USA.

HEINRICH Peggy, b. 20 Feb 1929, New York City, USA. Writer. m. Martin R Heinrich, 4 Apr 1952, 2 daughters. *Education:* BA, Hunter College, 1949. *Appointments:* Assistant Publicity Director, Doherty, Clifford, Steers and Shenfield, New York City, 1950-59. *Publications:* The Soul of Fire: How Charcoal Changed the World, with John Uhlmann,1987; A Patch of Grass,1984; Haiga-Haiku with Barbara Gray, 1982. *Memberships:* Poetry Society of America; Academy of American Poets; Haiku Society of America (Treasurer 1981-83). *Honours:* Poetry Society of Virginia, 1989; Japan Air Lines Haiku Contest, 1988; Hartford, Connecticut Poetry Contest, 1986; Connecticut Poetry Society, 1986; National League of American Pen Women, 1986; Blue Unicorn, 1985; Connecticut Writers League, 1985; North Carolina Haiku Society, 1984; Sri Chimney Award, 1980 etc. Editor, Connecticut River Review, 1985-87. *Hobbies:* Yoga; Tai Chi Chuan; Tennis; Dowsing; Holistic health. *Address:* 30 Burr Farms Road, Westport, CT 06880, USA.

HEJDUK Irena Krystyna, b. 27 Aug. 1949, Poland. Scientist; Economist. m. 6 July 1970, 2 sons. *Education:* B.Econ., 1972; PhD, Economics, 1979; 2nd Doctors Degree, 1987. *Appointments:* Academy of Economy, Wroclaw, 1972-; Transportation Management, 1976-. *Publications:* 57 scientific papers. *Memberships:* ASS; Polish Economical Society. *Honours:* Silver Award, 1979, Golden Award, 1983, TNOIK; Bronze Cross of Merit, 1984. *Hobbies:* Literature; Driving. *Address:* ul Komandorska 118/120, Instytut Ekonomiki Produkcji, 53345 Wroclaw, Poland.

HELFMAN Elizabeth S., b. 1 Aug. 1911, Pittsfield, Massachusetts, USA. Writer. m. 17 Sept. 1942, 1 son. *Education:* AB, Mount Holyoke College, 1933; MA, Radcliffe College, 1934; Bank Street College of Education, New York City, 1938-39. *Appointments:* Teacher, elementary grades, 1934-38, 1939-46; Teaching guide editor, Scholastic Magazines, 1959-66; Research & publications, Bank Street College, 1956-64. *Publications:* 19 books for children & young adults, including: Land, People & History; Our Fragile Earth; Signs & Symbols Around the World; Signs & Symbols of the Sun; Apples, Apples, Apples; Blissymbolics: Speaking Without Speech (awards); Celebrating Nature; etc. *Memberships:* Forum of Writers for Young People;

Society of Childrens Book Writers; Authors Guild (Authors League of America. *Honours:* Golden Kite award, non-fiction, Society of Childrens Book Writers, 1981; Selected, young Adult Literary Guild, 1981. *Hobbies:* Walking; Collecting rubber stamps; Helping the disabled. *Address:* 461-A Heritage Village, Southbury, Connecticut 06488, USA.

HELGERSON Marie-Christine, b. Lyon, France. Writer. *Education:* DES, Philosophy, University of Lyon, 1965; Study in Italy, 1966-67. *Appointments:* Worked with migrant children in California, USA, 1976-86. *Publications:* Histoires comme tu voudras, 1978; Quitter son pays, 1981; Claudine de Lyon, 1984; Dans les cheminées de Paris, 1985; Vers l'Amérique, 1986. *Honours:* Prix du meilleur livre Loisir-jeunesse for Histoires comme tu voudras, 1978; Selection 1000 jeunes lecteurs for Claudine de Lyon, 1984. *Hobby:* Yoga. *Address:* 334 E. Arrellaga St., Santa Barbara, CA 93101, USA.

HELGESON Eunice May, b. 21 Oct. 1947, Tracy, Minnesota, USA. Machine Tool Distribution Executive. *Education:* BA, Business Administration, magna cum laude, Augsburg College, 1969; Certificate, Credit and Financial Management, with high distinction, University of Minnesota, 1977; Certified Managerial Accountant, Institute of Certified Management Accountants, 1980. *Appointments:* Secretary, Tracy (Minn) Lutheran Church, 1964-65; Bookkeeper 1965-68, Office Manager 1968-70, Secretary/Treasurer 1970-, Milton Granquist Company. *Publications:* Helleson Family History, 1983; Helgeson Family History, 1984. *Memberships:* Board of Directors Treasurer, 1979-83, Boundary Creek Sixth (Homeowners) Association; Advent Lutheran Church; National Association of Credit Management (NACM); NACM, North Central; Credit Women's Group; American Society of Women Accountants; Sons of Norway. *Honours:* Associate Award with Distinction, 1972, Fellow Award with distinction 1977, NACM; Credit Master 1987; Certified Credit Executive (CCE), 1989. *Hobbies:* Genealogy; Family history; Sailing; Biking; Scandinavian culture. *Address:* 10943 105th Avenue North, Maple Grove, Minnesota 55369, USA.

HELLER Linda Joy, b. 25 July 1950, Peoria, Illinois, USA. Freelance Writer. *Education:* BA, University of Iowa, 1972. *Career:* Columnist, Writer, Mademoiselle Magazine, 1982-86; Freelance Writer, 1986- ; Currently Contributing Editor, Executive Female Magazine; Senior Scriptwriter for Cable TV Show, Fashion America, and other videos. *Publications:* Articles in The New York Times, Parade, Barrons, 6.Q, Redbook, Ms, Lears, Working Woman, Self, Mademoiselle. *Hobbies:* Collecting art; Viewing old films; Volunteering for political campaigns; Playing tennis. *Address:* 40 Harrison Street 16A, New York, NY 10013, USA.

HELLSTROM Pamela Donworth, b. 4 Apr. 1948, Bangor, Maine, USA. Founder & President, Human Resource Development Company. m. Michael Willard Hellstrom, 12 Oct. 1978, 1 daughter. *Education:* BA, English Education, Merrimack College, Massachusetts, 1970. *Appointments:* Assistant Director of Public Relations, employment counsellor, Extended Services for the Elderly, Seattle, Washington 1970-72; Social services assistant 1972-73, social work assistant 1974-81, Madigan Army Medical Centre, Tacoma; Mental health associate, American Lake Veterans Association Hospital, Tacoma, 1973- 74; GED Alternate Chief Examiner, L. H. Bates VTI, Tacoma, 1983-84; Founder & President, Growth Technologies Inc, 1984-. *Memberships:* Tacoma-Pierce County Chamber of Commerce; National Association of Female Executives; American Management Association; National Association for Training & Development. *Honours:* Awards, outstanding performance, 1977, 1978, 1980. *Hobbies:* Writing fiction, poetry, short stories, non-fiction; Sailing; Performing music; Horse riding; Camping; Swimming; Tennis; Research, design & implementation, human resource development; Travel. *Address:* 8918 Delores Court Northeast, Olympia, Washington 98506, USA.

HELMICH Pamela Jean Pence, b. 7 Feb. 1945, Weiser, Idaho, USA. Architect. m. David Michael Helmich, 3 June 1978, 1 son, 1 daughter. *Education:* California College of Arts & Crafts, 1961; University of California, Davis, 1962; BArch, University of California, Berkeley, 1972. *Appointments:* US General Services Administration, 1972-76; US Customs Service, 1976-77; Environmental planning & research, 1978-79; Owner, architect, CHYD Architects, 1979-. *Creative work includes:* Painting: Solo exhibition 1961, UC Berkeley 1972; Various published architectural projects. *Memberships:* American Institute of Architects; National Trust for Historic Preservation; State Bar Court; San Francisco Foundation for Architectural Heritage. *Honours:* Residential Remodelling, published 1981; Historic Preservation Award, City of West Hollywood, 1983; Design Excellence Award, 1985; Design Excellence Award, US Navy, 1985. *Hobbies:* Portrait painting; Cycling; Piano playing. *Address:* CHYD Architects Inc, 33 New Montgomery, Suite 950, San Francisco, California 94103, USA.

HELMS Mary Wallace, b. 15 Apr. 1938, Allentown, Pennsylvania, USA. Professor of Anthropology. m. James Van Stone, 1968 (div. 1980). *Education:* BA, Liberal Arts, Pennsylvania State University; MA Anthropology 1962, PhD 1967, University of Michigan. *Appointments:* Lecturer, Anthropology, Northwestern University, 1969-79; Professor of Anthropology, University of North Carolina, Greensboro, 1979-. *Publications:* Books: Asang; Middle America; Ancient Panama; Ulysses' Sail. Numerous articles, professional journals. *Memberships:* Past President, American Society for Ethnohistory, Southern Anthropological Society; American Anthropological Association; American Association for Advancement in Science. *Address:* Department of Anthropology, University of North Carolina, Greensboro, NC 27412, USA.

HEMING Diana Dean, b. 1 July 1940, Malmesbury, Wiltshire, England. Racehorse Trainer. m. Michael Peter Heming, 9 Jan. 1985. *Education:* BHSI, Crabbet Park Equestrian School; 1st Young Judge, Ponies of Britain, 1958. *Appointments:* Instructor, British Horse Society; National Judges Panel, South Africa; Racehorse Trainer 1971-. *Publications:* Articles for Farmers Weekly and Sunday Express; Weekly column for Sunday Express, South Africa. *Honours:* Leading Trainer, Trainer of the Year Award, 1978-79, 1979-80; Leading Transvaal Trainer, 1978-1987; Leading Trainer, South Africa, 1987. *Hobbies:* Reading; Writing; Travel; All animals, wildlife, birds, horses in general. *Address:* PO Box 23, Vildoens Drif, 9580 Orange Free State, South Africa.

HEMLOW Joyce, b. 30 July 1906, Liscomb, Nova Scotia, Canada. Greenshields Professor Emerita, retired. *Education:* BA 1941, MA 1942, Queen's University, Kingston, Ontario; AM 1944, PhD 1948, Radcliffe, Harvard, Cambridge, Massachusetts, USA. *Appointments:* Lecturer; Assistant Professor 1947-52, Associate Professor 1952-55, Professor 1955-, Greenshields Professor 1965, Emerita 1975, McGill University, Montreal. *Publications:* Biography: The History of Fanny Burney, 1958; Editor, Journals and Letters of Fanny Burney (Madame d'Arblay) 12 volumes. *Memberships:* Phi Beta Kappa; The Johnsonians; American and Canadian Associations; Studies in the 18th Century; ACUTE, and other professional societies; International Association of University Teachers of English. *Honours:* Guggenheim Fellow, 1951-52 and 1966-67; Fellow, Royal Society of Canada, 1960; British Academy Award, the Rose Mary Crawshay Prize, 1960; Distinguished Achievement Award, Radcliffe College, 1969; James Tait Black Memorial Book Prize, 1960; Governor General's Medal for academic non-fiction, 1958. *Hobbies:* Landscaping; Genealogical and archival research. *Address:* Liscomb, Nova Scotia, Canada, B0J 2A0.

HEMMINGS Margaret Elizabeth, b. 4 July 1941, Swansea, Wales. Head Teacher. m. Reverend V Blake Hemmings, 14 Aug. 1965. *Education:* BA, Honours, University College of Wales, Cardiff, 1959-62; Diploma, Education, Certificate, Biblical Studies, University College of Wales, Aberystwyth, 1962-63. *Appointments:* Head of Department, Grammar School for Girls, Bridgwater, 1963-65; Head of Department, Acting Deputy Head, High St Girls Secondary, Barry 1965-72; Lecturer, senior Lecturer, Glamorgan College of Education & Polytechnic of Wales, 1972-79; Examiner, University of Wales & Council for National Academic Awards, 1972-79; Deputy Headteacher, 1979-81, Head Teacher, 1981- , Lewis Girls' Comprehensive School, Mid Glamorgan. *Memberships:* Secondary Heads Association, Member Mid Glamorgan Executive; President, 1989, Welsh Secondary Schools Association; Court of Governors, University College, Cardiff; Joint Secondary Committee for Wales; Secondary Examinations Council, by invitation of Secretary of State for Education & Science, and Secretary of State for Wales; Vice Chairman Curriculum Council for Wales, by invitation of the Secretary of State for Wales. *Hobbies:* Reading; Classical Music; Theatre; Gardening. *Address:* Lewis Girls' Comprehensive School, Oakfield Street, Ystrad Mynach, Hengoed, Mid Glamorgan CF8 7WW, Wales.

HENARD Elizabeth Ann, b. 9 Oct. 1947, Providence, Rhode Island, USA. Businesswoman. m. John B. Henard Jr, 19 Oct. 1974, 2 sons. *Education:* Jacksonville University, 1966. *Appointments:* Secretary, Southern Bell T&T, Jacksonville, Florida, 1964-69; Office Manager, Gunther F. Reis Associates, Tampa, 1969-71; Executive Secretary, Ernst & Ernst, 1971-72; Executive Secretary to President, Lamalie Associates, 1972-74; Executive Secretary, Arthur Young & Company, Chicago, Illinois, 1975; Administrative Assistant, Irving J. Markin, 1975; Controller, Vice President & Corporate Secretary, Henard Associates Inc, Dallas, Texas, 1983-. *Membership:* Treasurer, Dallas Investors Group. *Hobbies:* Golf; Photography; Reading; Crafts. *Address:* 5706 Thames Court, Dallas, Texas 75252, USA.

HENDERSON Mary Elizabeth (Betty) Park, b. 12 Apr. 1921, Canada. Retired. *Education:* BA, 1941, MA, 1943, Library Science, University of British Columbia; BLS, University of Toronto, 1944. *Appointments:* Cataloguer, University of British Columbia 1944-49, University of Wales 1950-51; Technical Services Librarian, Province of Saskatchewan, 1952-59; Chief Librarian, University of Saskatchewan, Regina, 1960-66; Assistant Librarian, Prince of Wales College, PEI, 1967-69; Associate Professor, Professor, Dean, Library Science, University of Alberta, 1970-82. *Publications:* Planning the Future by the Past, 1969; Editor, Saskatchewan Library Bulletin, 1974-75; articles in journals. *Memberships:* American Library Association; Canadian Library Association, President 1974-75; Canadian Association University Teachers; Canadian Research Institute for Advancement of Women; etc. *Honours:* University Essay Prize, 1941; LLD, University of PEI, 1975; Alberta Achievement Award, 1976; Canadian Library Association Outstanding Service to Librarianship Award and Hon. Life Member, 1985; etc. *Hobbies:* Travel; Politics; Collecting Books; Art Work; Cats. *Address:* Rice Point, PEI, Canada.

HENDERSON Robbye Robinson, b. 10 Nov. 1937, Morton, Mississippi, USA. Director of the Library. 1 daughter. *Education:* BA, Tougaloo College, 1960; MSLS, Atlanta University, 1968; PhD, SIU, 1974-76. *Appointments:* Librarian, Patton Lane High School, 1960-66; Librarian, Utica Jr College, 1966-76; Librarian, MS Industrial College, 1967-68; Acq Librarian 1968-69, Director of Technical Services 1969-72, Director 1972-, MS Valley State University. *Publications:* A survey of Patton Lane High school, Rules and regulations governing book thefts in predominately black colleges and universities; HELP (Hurry Emergency Library Plea). *Memberships:* American Library Association; Mississippi Library Association; American Association of University Women; Alpha Kappa Alpha Sorority, Inc. *Honours:* Cum Laude Fellowship, 1974; Phi Delta Kappa, 1975; Recipient Fellowship, Mellon ACRL Interproject, 1974-75; Recipient Fellowship, Library Administrators

Development Program, 1974; Recipient Fellowship, Developing Leaders in Developing Institutions, 1974-76. *Hobbies:* Sewing; Metaphysics; Fishing; Reading; Fashion. *Address:* James Herbert White Library, Mississippi Valley State University, Itta Bena, Mississippi 38941, USA.

HENDERSON Stephanie, b. 3 Mar. 1932, Basildon, Essex, England. Medical Doctor. m. Frank Henderson, 14 Apr. 1962. *Education:* B.Med, 1954, MD, 1957, University of Edinburgh; FRCS (Scotland), 1958. *Appointments:* Junior Houseman, Strathclyde Central Hospital, 1958-60; Staff Consultant, Southern Area Health Authority, 1961-65; Senior House Consultant, Victoria Hospital of East Anglia, 1965-. *Creative Work:* Numerous articles for medical journals with Dr Ernest Haafsteiner on child mortality in urban areas. *Honours:* Monroe Prize for Medical Article, The Urban Crisis in Europe, 1958. *Hobbies:* Fishing; Reading; Ornithology. *Address:* 42 Duck Lane, Haddenham, Ely, Cambs CB6 3UE, England.

HENDLEY Edith DiPasquale, b. 5 Sept. 1927, New York City, USA. Professor of Physiology & Biophysics, and of P:sychiatry. m. Daniel Dees Hendley, 21 Apr. 1952. 1 son, 2 daughters. *Education:* AB, Hunter College of City of New York, 1948; MS, Ohio State University, Columbus, 1950; PhD, University of Illinois College of Medicine, Chicago, 1954. *Appointments:* Instructor, Physiology, University of Chicago, 1954-56; Assistant Lecturer, University of Sheffield, England, 1956-57; Instructor, Ophthalmology 1963-66, Research Assoc, Dept of Pharmacol Exper Ther 1966-72, Johns Hopkins University School of Medicine; Assoc Prof then Professor, Physiology & Biophysics, University Vermont Coll Med, 1973-. *Publications:* 37 papers and 5 book chapters in scientific journals and books. *Memberships:* Amer Physiol Soc; Soc Neuroscience; Amer Soc Pharmacol Exp Ther; Sigma XI; AAAS; Assoc Women in Science (elected Treasurer 1972-74, Executive Comm and Membership Chairperson). *Honours:* Phi Beta Kappa, 1948, Hunter College of City of New York; Scholarship, Ohio State University, 1948; Recipient of research grants from: National Institutes of Health; National Science Foundation; Vermont Heart Assoc; The Sugar Assoc Inc. *Hobbies:* Music; Art; Literature; Cinema; Opera; theatre. *Address:* Department of Physiology and Biophysics, University of Vermont, College of Medicine, Burlington, Vermont 05405, USA.

HENDRICKS-STERLING Dorothy, b. 13 Apr. 1940, West Virginia, USA. Social Services Administrator; Training & Consultation Specialist. m. Howard Thomas Sterling, 25 Aug. 1973. 1 son. *Education:* BS, Home Economics, Cheyney State College, 1965; MS Counseling, University of Pitts, 1971; Cert Group Specialist, 1971; PhD Counseling Education, Adolescent Psychology, 1974. *Appointments:* Teacher, Pitts Board Education, 1965-69; Counselor, U Pitts, 1969-71; Counselor Assistant Professor, Clarion State College, 1971-73; Youth Specialist, Met YWCA, Cleveland, 1973-82; Associate Executive Director, 1982-84; Chief Executive Officer, Center for Human Relations Inc, 1984-; Cons Trainer, Urban League, Cleveland, 1973-75; Spanish Am Commn, Cleveland, 1975-80; National Board, YWCA, NYC, 1982-; Trainer, Girl Scouts US; President Board Directors, Teen Fathers Program, Cleveland, 1983-; Board Directors, Frances Hollingsworth Calgie Found, Cleveland, 1983-; Cleveland Area Board Realtors, 1984-; Women Space, Cleveland, 1985-. *Creative Works:* Developed the Pact Program, pregnancy prevention program, Peer Approach Counseling by Teens, 1977. *Membership:* YWCA of US. *Honours include:* PACT Award, 1983; 5 Years Service Certificate, Metropolitan YWCA, 1982; Nominee Outstanding Toastmistress, 1981; International Toastmistress Clubs Speech Contestant: 1st place Club Level, 1980; 1st Place Council Level, 1980; 3rd Place Regional Level, Toronto, Canada, 1980; Service Award, Clarion State College, 1972; Literary Arts Award for Poetry, 1963 and 1964; Ile Elegba-Black Community Award, 1971. *Hobbies:* Reading; Fashions; Working with Youth; Writing poetry. *Address:* Center for Human

Relations, Inc, 12001 Shaker Blvd, Cleveland, Ohio 44118, USA.

HENDRICKSON Susan La Boon, b. 10 May 1948, Atlanta, Georgia, USA. Systems Programmer. m. William B. Hendrickson, 26 Aug. 1972, divorced, 1976. *Education:* AA, Psychology, 1986. *Appointments:* US Marine Corps, 1968-73; Dept. of Administrative Services, 1973-. *Memberships Include:* Veterans for Peace, National Board of Directors, 1986-87; Vietnam Veterans of America; Life Member, Women Marines Association; Life Member, Marine Corps Association. *Honours:* Certificate of Recognition, Vietnam Veterans of America, 1987; National Service Medal, Veterans for Peace, 1987. *Hobbies:* Volunteer Work; Theatre; Music; Reading; Sewing; Crochet; Travel. *Address:* 1621 Carter Road, Decatur, GA 30032, USA.

HENDRY Joy McLaggan, b. 3 Feb. 1953, Perth, Scotland. Writer; Broadcaster; Editor. m. Ian David Montgomery, 25 July 1986. *Education:* Mental Philosophy, Honours, Edinburgh University; Diploma in Education. *Appointments:* Teacher, English, Knox Academy, Haddington, 1977-84; Freelance Writer, 1984-; TV & Radio Broadcaster. *Publications:* Editor, Chapman, 1972-; Books: Scots: The Way Forward; The Land for the People; Critical Essays; articles in professional journals. *Memberships:* Scottish PEN; Scottish Association of Magazine Publishers, Convener, 1976-78; Scottish Poetry Library Association, Deputy Convener, 1983-88; Committee for the Advancement of Scottish Literature in Schools, Convener, 1981-84; Advisory Council for the Arts in Scotland. *Hobbies:* Philosophy; Scottish Politics; Theatre; Literature; Womens Affairs. *Address:* 15 Nelson Street, Edinburgh, EH3 6LF, Scotland.

HENES Donna, b. 19 Sept. 1945, Cleveland, Ohio, USA. Urban Shaman; Writer; Artist; Teacher. *Education:* Ohio State University, 1963-66; BS 1970, MS 1971, City College, New York. *Appointments:* Self employed for past 15 years, designing & producing public, participatory celebrations & events, in museums, universities, parks & plazas, in over 50 cities, 9 countries. *Creative works include:* Books: Dressing Our Wounds in Warm Clothes, 1982; Noting the Process of Noting the Process. Also: Numerous articles, magazines & professional journals; Editor, Celebration News. *Memberships:* Board of Directors, Centre for Celebration; Foundation for a Community of Artists; National Association of Female Executives. *Honours:* Fellowships: National Endowment for Arts 1982, New York Foundation for Arts 1986; Project grant, Jerome Foundation, 1985; Interarts grant, NEA. *Hobbies:* Travel; Dance; Hiking; Swimming. *Address:* Old PS 9, 279 Sterling Place, Brooklyn, New York 11238, USA.

HENKIN Roxanne Lee, b. 4 Jan. 1951, Chicago, USA. Teacher; Consultant. *Education:* BSEd., 1972, MS, Ed., 1983, Northern Illinois University. *Appointments:* Teacher, Barrington District, 1974-88; Writing Co-Ordinator, Elmhurst District, 1988-. *Publications:* Numerous articles in magazines & books. *Memberships:* National Council of Teachers of English; International Reading Association; Association for Supervision & Curriculum Development; International Reading Council; Young Authors Conference, Site Chair, 1987; Parents & Reading Committee. *Honours:* Kappa Delta Pi; Illinois Master Teacher Award, 1984. *Hobbies:* Reading; Travel. *Address:* 223 Country Dr., Bartlett, IL 60103, USA.

HENLEY Sylvia N, b. 5 Feb. 1940, El Dorado, Arkansas, USA. Coordinator of Guidance and Counselling. m. Dr Ed Henley, 26 Dec. 1981. 1 son, 1 daughter. *Education:* BA, Ouchita Baptist University, 1961; MA, Guidance and Counselling, Louisiana Tech University, 1975; Postgraduate studies, Southern Arkansas University, Ouchita Baptists University, University of Arkansas, Fayetteville. *Appointments:* El Dorado Public Schools: Southside Elementary 6th Grade 1962-63, Art & Social studies 1963-64, Art 1971-76,

Rogers Junior High; Counselor, Barton Junior High, 1976-80; Director, Guidance and Counseling, 1987-; Counselor, Camden High School, 1980-87; Arkansas Licensed Professional Counselor, 1983-. *Memberships:* American Association for Counseling, Guidance and Development; American School Counselor Association; Arkansas Association for Counseling, Guidance and Development, Board Member, 1980-83; Arkansas School Counselors Association, President, 1982-83; Southwest Arkansas School Counselors Association, President 1982, Secretary 1981; Secondary School Advisory Council, State Department of Education, 1978-; Louisiana Tech University Alumni Board, 1981-83; Delta Kappa Gamma Society; Phi Delta Kappa; Gifted and Talented Advisory Council, Camden Public Schools, 1983-87; Six-Year Goals Committee, Camden Public Schools; Six-Year Goals Committee, Smackover Public Schools. *Address:* Counseling Center, El Dorado High School, 501 Timberlane, El Dorado, Arkansas 71730, USA.

HENNESSY Darlene Lenore (Dean), b. 2 Nov. 1927, Macomb, Illinois, USA. Addictions and Family Therapist; Forensic Documents Examiner. divorced, 1 son, 2 daughters. *Education:* BA, Sociology, 1977, MA, Social Science, 1978, Northeastern Illinois University; MS, Counselling, Psychology, George Williams College, 1984; Certifications include: Alcoholism, Grant Hospital; Family Counsellor, Family Institute; Certified Medical Psychotherapist (Fellow and Diplomat), American Board of Medical Psychotherapists. *Appointments:* Casework Supervisor, Department of Public Aid, State of Illinois, 1972-77; Counsellor, Social Worker, Alcoholism Unit, Resurrection Hospital, 1977-79; Coordinator, Family Recovery Programmes, Addiction Treatment Center, Alexian Bros Medical Center, 1979-88; Addiction Recovery Corporation, Director of Outpatient Services, 1988-; Private Practice in Forensic Document Examination, 1982-; Private Practice in Therapy, Hoffman Estates and Research, Illnois, 1984-. *Publications:* Making the Write Personnel Selections Using Graphoanalysis; How We Learn to Write: The brain and the process; Alcoholic Women and Non-Alcoholic Women; Childhood Deprivations of Alcoholics. *Memberships:* American Association of Counseling and Development; National Employment Counselors Association; World Association of Document Examiners; Pan American Association of Forensic Sciences; Association of Forensic Document Examiners; Illinois Alcoholism Certification Board; Past President, Past Vice-President, Illinois Chapter, International Graphoanalysis Society. *Honours:* Individual Recognition Programme, International Graphoanalysis Society, 1985. *Hobbies:* Gardening; Stained Glass Photography; Birdwatching. *Address:* 214 West Des Plaines Lane, Hoffman Estates, Illinois 60914, USA.

HENNESSY Helen Adele, b. 5 June 1905, Duluth, USA. Homemaker; Writer; Genealogist. m. Harold Richard Hennessy, 24 July 1930, 1 son, 3 daughter. *Education:* BA, Carleton College, 1927. *Publications Include:* Co-author: Weinke, Krueger, Lounsberry Relationships, 1975; The Hennessy Sketch, 1979; Helen Lounsberry Hennessy's Lineage Data, 1980; Ousman, Hennessy and Allied Families, 1980; Colonel Clement A. Lounsberry, 1982; Ebenezer Hoskins, 1982; Lineage Laroy N. Castor, PhD, 1983; The Hennessy Immigrants 1850, 1984; Our Grand-Children's Great Grand Parents, 1985. *Memberships Include:* DAR; National Society Daughter of Founders & Patriots of America; General Society, Mayflower Descendants; National Society Magna Charta Dames; many other professional organisations. *Honours:* Clan Stewart Award, Duluth, 1922; many other honours. *Hobbies:* Writing; Needlework; Travel. *Address:* 10 East Hawthorn Parkway, Apt. 422, Vernon Hills, IL 60061, USA.

HENNIGAN Lura Taylor, b. 1 Dec. 1916, Bryceland, Louisiana, USA. Ordained Minister. m. Clarence Roland Hennigan, 5 May 1933. 3 sons, 1 daughter. *Education:* Powder Puff Beauty School, 1938; Certified, US School of Music, 1962; Studied piano under Eddi Kozak at Centenary College, 1974; English at Louisiana State University, 1974-75; Art at Lytles, 1980. *Appointments:* Operated Lura's Beauty Shop, 1939-44; Piano teacher, Webster Parish Public Schools, 1958-85; Ordained Minister, United Gospel Tabernacle, 1973-. *Creative works:* Painting of state flower, Magnolia, hanging in Webster Parish Courthouse; Several other paintings in public offices; Weekly column, Abundant Life in Minden Press-Herald. *Membership:* Former member, Piano Guild. *Honours:* Has been featured in numerous newspaper articles. *Hobbies:* Painting; Music; Flower arranging. *Address:* 604 Nella, Minden, LA 70155, USA.

HENRIKSON Lois Elizabeth Wessling, b. 10 Nov. 1921, Lytton, Iowa, USA. Photojournalist. m. Arthur Allen Henrikson, 3 July 1943. 3 daughters. *Education:* BS, Northwestern University, 1943; Certificate of Membership Marketing, American Society of Association Executives, 1986. *Appointments:* Administrative Assistant, Vice President, Director of Operations, ITT Telecommunications Corp, Business Communications Division, Des Plaines, 1980-82; Administrative Assistant, Executive Vice President, 1982-84; Membership Services Coordinator, 1984-88, Wholesale Stationers' Association, Des Plaines; Midwest Correspondant, Office World News Magazine, Hearst Business Communications Inc., Garden City, New York, 1988-. *Memberships:* American Society of Association Executives; Chicago Society of Association Executives; National Association for Female Executives; American Society of Professional & Executive Women; Social Chair, 1983-84, Newsletter Editor, 1984-85 and 1988-, American Association of University Women; Northwestern Club of Chicago; The Art Institute of Chicago; American Association of Editorial Cartoonists Auxiliary; Diaconate Board, First Congregational Church, United Church of Christ; National Society of Magna Charta Dames; Americans of Royal Descent; Alpha Gamma Delta Sorority. *Hobbies:* Photography; Art; Theatre; Music. *Address:* 27 North Meyer Court, Des Plaines, Illinois 60016, USA.

HENRITZE Bette Joan, b. 23 May 1924, Betsy Layne, Kentucky, USA. Actress. *Education:* BA, English and History, University of Tennessee, 1946; Virginia Intermont College, 1941-43; American Academy of Dramatic Arts, 1947. *Appointments:* Numerous appearances on Broadway including: Macbeth; Here's Where I Belong; Man and Superman; The Ballad of the Sad Cafe; Much Ado About Nothing; The White House; Jenny Kissed Me. Off-Broadway: New York Shakespeare Festival; Phoenix Repertory Theatre in 8 plays; 2 seasons at American Shakespeare Theatre; Television appearances include: Another World, NBC; The Doctors and Nurses; East Side, West Side; CBS Repertory Theatre; with Laurence Olivier in The Power and the Glory; with Irene Worth and Christopher Plummer in Omnibus; As the World Turns, CBS. Films: Brighton Beach Memoirs; Heartburn; World According to Garp; The Hospital; Rage; The Happiness Cage. *Memberships:* Actors Equity; Screen Actors Guild; AFTRA. *Honour:* OBIE Award, 1967. *Address:* Triad, 888 Seventh Avenue, New York City, NY 10019, USA.

HENRY Janice Lu Sirles Schoen, b. 31 July 1946, Herrin, Illinois, USA. Associate Professor. m. (1) Paul G. Schoen, 11 June 1967, div. Jan. 1985, 1 daughter, (2) James F. Henry, 15 Aug. 1987. *Education:* BS, 1968, PhD, 1987, Southern Illinois University; MEd, University of Illinois, 1970. *Appointments:* Special Needs Coordinator, Southern Illinois University, 1968; Instructor, Champaign Central High School, Champaign, Illinois, 1968-70; Instructor, John A. Logan College, Carterville, Illinois, 1970-75; Instructor, Southern Illinois University, 1974-79; Assistant Professor, Southern Illinois University, Carbondale, 1979-87; Associate Professor, College of Technical Careers, Southern Illinois University, 1987-. *Publications:* Business Education World, 1985; Index to Doctoral Dissertations in Business Education (co-author); Nontechnical Business Competencies in Delta Pi Epsilon Journal (co-author), 1987. *Memberships:* American Vocational Association; National Business Education Association; Illinois Vocational Association; Illinois

Business Education Association; Southern Illinois Business Education Association; Delta Pi Epsilon; Omicron Tau Theta; Phi Delta Kappa; Pi Omega Pi; Phi Kappa Phi; Alpha Lambda Delta. *Honours:* William E. Nagel Award, Vocational Education Studies, 1985, Outstanding Dissertation, from Vocational Education Studies, 1988, Southern Illinois University; Teacher of the Year Award, Southern Illinois Business Education Association, 1987; Outstanding Dissertation, Lambda Chapter, Omicron Tau Theta, 1988. *Hobbies:* Cooking; Waterskiing. *Address:* 615 Terrace Drive, Carbondale, IL 62901, USA.

HENRY JoAnne Schmitt, b. 10 Feb. 1942, Covington, USA. Educator; Writer. m. Robert A. Henry, 28 Dec. 1966, 1 son. *Education:* BA, 1964, MA, 1984, Georgetown College. *Appointments:* English Teacher, Department Head, Boone Co., Kentucky Board of Education, 1977-. *Publications:* Poems: Remembrance - Anthology of Southern Poets; Educational Research Papers. *Memberships:* National Council Teachers of English; Kentucky Council Teachers of English; National, Stae, Local Education Associations; Pi Lambda Theta; Alpha Psi Omega; Beta Sigma Phi. *Honours:* Kentucky Colonel, 1984; Kentucky Star Teacher, 1975. *Hobbies:* Reading; Travel; Painting; Photography; Writing. *Address:* PO Box 6392, Florence, KY 41042, USA.

HENRY Judith Euliss, b. 25 May 1940, Hickory, North Carolina, USA. Nursing Home and Reitrement Home Owner and Administrator. m. Je DeWitte Henry, 19 Mar. 1983. 1 daughter. *Education:* Clevenger Business College, 1958-60; Caldwell Community College and Technical Institute, 1980-82; University of North Carolina, 1985; Various seminars and courses on Ageing. *Appointments:* President, Camelot Manor Retirement Home, 1978-; President, Camelot Manor Nursing Care Facility, Inc, 1985-; President, Camelot Manor Comprehensive Outpatient Rehabilitation Facility, 1985-; President, Camelot Manor Retirement Village, 1986-. *Creative Works:* Numerous paintings hanging in the public areas of the facilities. *Memberships:* Caldwell County Lenoir Chamber of Commerce; Caldwell Community College, Nursing Department Advisory Board; South Caldwell High School, Health Occupations Advisory Board; Past President, Granite Falls American Field Service. *Honours:* Woman of the Year, Granite Falls Business and Professional Women, 1984; Nominee Distinguished Women of North Carolina, 1984 & 1985; Distinguished Leadership Award for Outstanding Service to Nursing Care Facilities, 1987; Distinguished Leadership Award for Outstanding Service to the aged, 1987. *Hobbies:* Oil Painting; Tennis; Swimming; Cooking; Dancing; Entertaining; Gardening; Working with the Underpriveleged, handicapped and most of all, working with the elderly. *Address:* Camelot Manor Nursing Care Facility, Inc, 100 Sunset Street, Granite Falls, NC 28630, USA.

HENRY Martha, b. 17 Feb. 1938, Detroit, Michigan, USA. Artistic Director; Actress; Director. 1 daughter. *Education:* Graduate, National Theatre School, Montreal, Canada. *Career:* Repertory with Murray Davis, Crest Theatre, Toronto, 1959-60; Played Manitoba Theatre Centre, 1961 & later including Hedda Gabler, 1973; Many Shakespearean & other roles, Stratford Festival, 1962-80, including Elizabeth Proctor, The Crucible, 1975, Elena, Uncle Vanya, 1978; Other roles include: Pegeen Mike, The Playboy of the Western World; Title role, Antigone, Olivia, Twelfth Night, Georgina, Narrow Road To The Deep North, Elizabeth Proctor, The Crucible, at Lincoln Center, New York; Starred in Affairs of Anatol, Centaur Theatre, Montreal, 1976; Marguerite Gauthier, The Lady of the Camellias world premiere, 1979; Mrs Simpson, Pal Joey; Final stage role, Beckett's Happy Days, Theatre Plus, Toronto, 1986; CBC TV roles include with Franchot Tone in The Master Builder and opposite Bruno Gerussi in The Present (The Newcomers series); The Wars, 1981, Dancing in the Dark, 1985; Glory Enough For All, 1987; Director: Brief Lives, Stratford; Moon for the Misbegotten; The Grace of Mary Traverse; Top Girls;

Brighton Beach Memoirs; Biloxi Blues; Others; Musical work includes Pierrot Luniere (Schoenberg) the Edith Sitwell-William Walton Façade with Toronto Symphony; Currently Artistic Director, Grand Theatre, London, Ontario; Teaching, National Theatre School, University of Windsor, Maggie Bassett Studio (Tarragon). *Memberships:* Board, Canada Council. *Honours:* Officer, Order of Canada, 1982; 3 Best Actress Genie Awards (The Present, The Wars, Dancing in the Dark), Academy of Canada Cinema; 2 Best Actress Gemini Awards, Canadian Television; 2 honorary doctorates. *Address:* Grand Theatre, 471 Richmond Street, London, Ontario, Canada N6A 3E4.

HENRY Nancy Twyman, b. 18 July 1940, Somerville, USA. Company President. Divorced, 2 sons. *Education:* Rutgers University, 1958-60. *Appointments:* Executive Assistant to Vice President, Johnson & Johnson, 1959-77; Special Assistant to Governor, State of New Jersey, 1978-79; Director of Resources & Community Participation, State of New Jersey, 1979-81; Purchasing Manager, Scanticon Princeton, 1982-84; President, Henry's Construction Inc. *Membership:* National Council of Negro Women. *Honours:* Recipient, various honours and awards. *Hobbies:* Reading; Jogging; Tennis. *Address:* 15 Dewald Avenue, Somerset, NJ 08873, USA.

HENRY Susan Bennett, b. 21 Feb. 1960, St Andrews, Scotland. Metphysical Practitioner; Astrologer; Tarot Consultant; Lecturer. *Education:* BSc, Speech Pathology, 1981; Diploma Clinical Hypnotherapy, 1986. *Appointments:* Speech Pathologist, Alfred Hospital, Melbourne, Australia, 1981-85; Founder, Director, Practitioner & Lecturer, Delphi Centre, 1985-. *Memberships:* Past secretary, Victoria branch, Australian Association of Clinical Hypnosis; Past secretary, Social Committee, Australian Association of Speech & Hearing. *Address:* c/o Delphi Centre, 1st Floor, 319 Clarendon Street, South Melbourne, Victoria 3205, Australia.

HENSCHEL Elizabeth Georgie, b. London, England. Writer; Stud Owner; Riding Instructor. *Appointments:* Singer, 1928-36; BBC, 1940-46; Stud Owner, 1957-. *Publications:* Well Dressed Woman, 1955; Careers with Horses, 1966; numbers of equestrian books, 1980-. *Memberships:* Society of Authors; British Equestrian Writers Association; British Horse Society; British Actors Equity; National Pony Society; Highland Pony Society. *Honours:* Cubitt Award for Services to Pony Club. *Hobbies:* Reading; Travel. *Address:* Ballintean, Kincraig, Kingussie, Scotland PH21 1NX.

HENSLEY Betty Austin, b. 12 Oct. 1923, Missouri, USA. Flutist. m. Cline D. Hensley, 13 May 1944, 3 sons. *Education:* BA, Chemistry, University of Kansas, 1944; Graduate Study, Flute, Illinois State University, 1976; others. *Appointments:* Self-employed Teacher, Performer, 1955-; Touring Performer for Kansas Arts Commission, 1980-; Owner, Performer, Flutes of the World. *Memberships:* Life Member, National Flute Association; Board Member, American Musical Instrument Society; Life Member, National Federation of Music Clubs; Past President, Wichita Musical Club. *Honours Include:* Citation for Distinguished Service to Music, Kansas Federation of Music Clubs, 1979; many other honours and awards. *Hobbies:* Travel; Music; Reading; Hiking. *Address:* Flutes of the World, PO Box 8642, Wichita, KS 67208, USA.

HENSON Margaret Swett, b. 3 Jan. 1924, Chicago, Illinois, USA. Retired History Professor; Writer. m. (1) W. A. Nowotny, 2 Oct. 1943; (2) J. Scott Henson, 14 Oct. 1951, 3 sons, 2 daughters. *Education:* BSE, 1962, MA, 1969, PhD, 1974, University of Houston. *Appointments:* Teaching Fellow, University of Houston, Texas, 1969-71; Instructor, University of Houston Downtown, 1971-72; Instructor, Houston Community College, 1972-74; Archivist, Houston Metropolitan Archives, 1974-76; Assistant Professor, University of Houston, Clear Lake, 1977-85. *Publications:* Samuel

May Williams, Texan Entrepreneur, 1976; Juan Davis Bradburn, 1982; Anahuac in 1832, 1982; Anglo American Women in Texas, 1982; A History of Baytown, 1986; A Pictorial History of Chambers County, 1988. *Memberships:* Texas State Historical Association, Editorial Board; East Texas Historical Association, Board of Directors; Harris County Historical Commission; Chair: Govermental entities, Summerlee Commission on Texas History, 1990. *Honours:* Summerfield G.Roberts Award for Best Texan History, 1976; Fellow, Texas State Historical Association; Fellow, East Texas Historical Association; T R Fehrenbach Award, Best County History, 1989. *Hobbies:* Sailing. *Address:* 6723 Richwood, Houston, TX 77087, USA.

HEPBURN Audrey, b. 4 May 1929, Brussels, Belgium. Actress. m. (1) Mel Ferrer, 1954, dissolved 1968, 1 son. (2) Dr Andrea Dotti, 1969, 1 son. *Education:* Arnhem Conservatoire; studied dancing in Amsterdam and London. *Career:* Ballet appearances in London. Stage appearances in Gigi (New York), 1951; Ondine (New York), 1954. *Creative Works:* Films include: Laughter in Paradise, 1951; The Lavender Hill Mob, 1951; Roman Holiday, 1953; Sabrina, 1954; War and Peace, 1956; Funny Face, 1957; Love in the Afternoon, 1957; The Nun's Story, 1959; Green Mansions, 1959; The Unforgiven, 1960; Breakfast at Tiffany's, 1961; The Children's Hour (called The Loudest Whisper in Britain), 1962; Charade, 1963; Paris When it Sizzles, 1964; My Fair Lady, 1964; How to Steal a Million, 1966; Two for the Road, 1966; Wait Until Dark, 1967; Robin and Marian, 1976; Bloodline, 1978; They All Laughed, 1980; Here a Thief (TV film), 1987. *Honours:* Tony award for Film acting, 1968; Commdr. Ordre des Artes et des Letters; Academy Award. *Address:* c/o Kurt Frings, 328 South Beverly Drive, Beverly Hills, CA 90212, USA.

HEPBURN Katharine, b. 8 Nov. 1909, Hartford, Connecticut, USA. Actress. *Education:* Bryn Mawr College. *Appointments:* Started Screen Career, 1933 with a Bill of Divorcement; Films include: Litle Women; Spitfire; The Little Minister; Alice Adams; Sylvia Scarlett; Mary of Scotland; A Woman Rebels; Quality Street; Stage Door; Bringing Up Baby; Holiday; Woman of the Year; Keeper of the Flame; Dragon Seed; Without Love; Song of Love; State of the Union; Adam's Rib; Sea of Grass; African Queen; Pat and Mike; Summertime; Iron Petticoat; The Rainmaker; Desk Set; Suddenly Last Summer; Long Days Journey into Night; Guess Who's Coming to Dinner; Lion in Winter; The Madwoman of Chaillot; The Trojan Women; A Delicate Balance; Rooster Cogburn; Oilly Olly; Oxen Free; On Golden Pond Awards (Oscars). *Address:* PO Box 17-154, West Hartford, CT 06117, USA.

HERBST Margaret Mary, b. 1 July 1917, New York City, USA. Public Relations Consultant. *Education:* BA, Hunter College, 1937. *Appointments:* Assistant, John Scheeper Inc, New York City, 1937-38; Public Relations Chief, Associated Bulb Growers of Holland, 1938-40; Assistant, Press Department, Information Bureau, 1940-46; Owner, Margaret Herbst Public Relations, 1951-. *Publication:* Collaborator, Lion Rampant. *Memberships:* President: Agricultural Relations Council, Garden Writers Association, Zonta International; Phi Beta Kappa; Publicity Club of New York; Advertising Women of New York. *Honours:* Phi Beta Kappa, 1936; Knight, Order of Leopold II, Belgium, 1963; Insigne Merito, Institut Agronomique de Gembloux, 1966. *Hobbies:* Swimming; Dancing. *Address:* 642 Locust Street, Mount Vernon, New York 10552, USA.

HERMAN Joan Elizabeth, b. 2 June 1953, New York City, USA. Actuary; Insurance Executive. m. 16 July 1977. *Education:* AB, Barnard College, 1975; MS, Yale Univerity, 1977; Fellow, Society of Actuaries, 1982. *Appointments:* Acturial student, Metropolitan Life Insurance Company, 1978-82; Assistant actuary 1982-83, associate actuary & Director, Underwriting Research 1983-84, 2nd Vice President 1984, Vice President 1985-89; Senior Vice President 1989-, Group Underwriting and Administration,Phoenix Mutual, Group Underwriting, Phoenix Mutual. *Memberships:*

Risk Classification Committee, American Academy of Actuaries; Home Office Life Uunderwriters of America; Member Risk Classification, American Council of Life Insurers; Group Underwriters Association of America. *Honour:* Fellow, American Leadership Forum, 1988-89. *Hobbies:* Theatre & dance; Jogging; Swimming; Aerobics. *Address:* c/o Phoenix Mutual Life Insurance Company, 100 Bright Meadow Boulevard, Enfield, Connecticut 06082, USA.

HERMANN Mary Kevin Howard, b. 26 Oct. 1934, Kentucky, USA. professor of Nursing. m. Robert R Hermann, 2 Feb. 1957, deceased. 2 sons, 2 daughters. *Education:* RN Diploma, St Mary's School of Nursing, 1955; BSN 1970, MA 1972, MSN 1974, University of Evansville; EdD, Indiana University, 1984. *Appointments:* St Mary's Medical Center, Evansville, 1955-68; Assistant Professor, Associate Professor, 1970-84, Professor of Nursing 1984-, University of Evansville. *Memberships:* American Nurses' Association; American Association of Critical Care Nurses; Indiana State Nurses' Association; ISNA District 4; North American Nursing Diagnosis Association; ISNA Delegate. *Honours:* Sigma Theta Tau; Psi Chi; Pi Lambda Theta; Phi Kappa Phi, Scholastic Honorary; BSN cum laude, University of Evansville. *Address:* 8011 Maple Lane, Newburgh, IN 47630, USA.

HERMARY-VIEILLE Catherine, b. 8 Oct. 1943, Paris, France. m. Jean Vieille, 15 Dec. 1962, 1 son, 1 daughter. *Education:* Baccalaureat; Classical Arabic, National School of Oriental Languages, France. *Appointments:* Assistant to Ambassador of Cyprus in Paris; Cypriot Embassy, 1967-68. *Publications:* Le Grand Vizir de la Nuit; L'Epiphanie des Dieux; La Marquise des Ombres; L'Infidele; Romy; One Scenario with Alain jessuah, France; One Scenario with Gilles Carles, Quebec. *Memberships:* PEN Club International; Associaiton of French-speaking Writers; Association Islam-Occident; Chevalier, French Order of Arts and Letters. *Honours:* Femina Award, 1981; Ulysse Award, 1983; Georges Dupau Award, Academie Francaise, 1981; RTL Award, 1986. *Hobbies:* Sport including Tennis, Sailing, Golf. *Address:* 7 Rue Auguste Blanqui, 94600 Choisy le Roi, France.

HERNANDEZ Christine, b. 23 July 1951, San Antonio, Texas, USA Educational Consultant. *Education:* BA, Sociology, Our Lady of the Lake College, 1973; MA, University of Texas, 1981. *Appointments:* Teacher, San Antonio Independent School District, 1974-83; President, San Antonio Federation of Teachers, 1983-86; Educational Consultant, Bexar County Federation of Teachers, 1986 . *Publications.* articles in various journals & magazines. *Memberships:* American Federation of Teachers; National Womens Forum; San Antonio 100; Hispanic Womens Network of Texas Board; etc. *Honours:* Numerous honours including: Hispanic Woman of the Year, 1984; Notable Woman of Texas, 1984, 1985; Leadership San Antonio, 1986-87; John Ben Shepperd Leadership Forum, 1987; Community Leaders of America, 1987; Leadership America, 1988. *Hobbies Include:* Travel; Dropout Prevention. *Address:* PO Box 9571, San Antonio, TX 78204, USA.

HERNANDEZ Wanda Grace, b. 23 Apr. 1942, Detroit, Michigan, USA. Vocational Rehabilitation Counsellor. m. Ignacio Herberto Hernandez, 25 Nov. 1969, divorced 1979. 1 son. *Education:* BSc, Wayne State University, 1969-73; MA, 1975-78; Natural Institute of Health Science, 1988- pursuing PhD in Homeopathic Medicine. *Appointments:* Substance Abuse Counsellor, Boniface Community Action Corp, 1972-73; Vocational Rehabilitation Counsellor, State of Michigan, Dept of Education Vocational Rehabilitation Services, 1974-. *Memberships:* Michigan Rehabilitation Association; Natural Foods Associates; Natural Heralth Science Associates; The American Natural Hygiene Society, Inc; Smithsonian Associates; Natural Institute of Health Science. *Honour:* 1987 Honoree of The National Distinguished Service Registry, Library of Congress No 86-51240. *Hobbies:* Music, classical and modern jazz; Writing, poetry; Reading and studying the

Holy Scriptures; Art, paintings; Piano. *Address:* 9056 Patton, Detroit, MI 48228, USA.

HEROLD Mary Ann, b. 15 Nov. 1949, Colorado, USA. Founder, President, Technical Research Institute. *Appointments:* Self-employed Author, Lecturer, 1971-; Corporate Secretary/Treasurer, Timing Light Inc., Denver, 1981-85. *Publications:* Technical Research Institute Research Files in Three Volumes; A Basic Guide to the Occult for Law Enforcement Agencies; The Delusion of Inherent Divinity; Pantheism and Theism: World Views in Collision. *Memberships:* Director, Dept. of Occult Research for Christian Research Associates, Denver. *Honours:* 1st, 2nd Places, for Crocheted Sweaters, 1979. *Hobbies:* Crochet; Knitting; Portrait Drawing; Writing. *Address:* Technical Research Institue, Post Office Box 2095, Arvada, CO 80001, USA.

HERRICK Stella, b. 4 May 1946, Gangkofen, Germany. Pedorthist. m. Richard Thomas Herrick, 2 sons, 1 daughter. *Education:* BS, Medical Sociology, 1971. *Appointments:* Histologist, 1964-76; Teacher, 1972-73, 1975-76; Personnel Manager, 1974-75; Athletic Trainer, 1976-83; Clinical Pedorthist, 1980-; Medical Clinic Administrator, 1980-. *Publications:* articles in professional journals. *Memberships:* IPF; ACSM; AMWA; USPF; PFA; FAISF. *Honours:* National Art Awards,1961, 1962, 1963, 1964. *Hobbies:* White Water Kayaking; Slalom Skiing; Sculpture; Travel; Powerlifting. *Address:* 2000 Waverly Parkway, PO Box 4160, Opelika, AL 36803, USA.

HERROLD Rebecca M., b. 29 Sept. 1938, Warren, Pennsylvania, USA. Professor of Music. m. Stephen Herrold, 1960. *Education:* BMus with honours, 1960; MA, San Jose State University, 1968; Doctor of Musical Arts, Stanford University, 1974. *Appointments:* Assistant Professor, Ohio State University, Youngstown, 1975-76; Assistant Professor, Oregon State University, 1976-80; Associate Professor, 1980-84, Professor, 1984-, San Jose State University, San Jose, California; Performances as Pianist aboard MS Sagafjord; Performances with Santa Clara Trio, Santa Clara University. *Publications:* New Approaches to Elementary Music Education, college text, 1980, 2nd Edition, 1988. *Memberships:* College Music Society; International Society for Music Education; California Council on Music Teacher Education, Executive Board 1985-87; Music Educators National Conference. *Honours:* Honoured by League of American Penwomen, 1985; Grantee for development of computer-assisted music instruction, Apple Co, Atari Inc. *Hobbies:* Languages; Art History; Gourmet cooking; Travel. *Address:* c/o Music Department, San Jose State University, San Jose, CA 95192, USA.

HERSHEY Linda Ann, b. 15 Jan. 1947, Marion, Indiana, USA. Physician; Scientist; Teacher. m. Charles O Hershey, 1 May 1976. 2 sons, 1 daughter. *Education:* BS, Biology, Purdue University, 1968; PhD, Neurobiology, 1973, MD 1975, Washington University. *Appointments:* Residency in Neurology, Washington University, 1976-78; Fellowship, University of Rochester, 1978-80; Assistant Professor, CWRU, 1980-86; Associate Professor, SUNYAB, 1986-; Chief of Neurology, VAMC of Buffalo, 1986- *Publications:* 32 journal articles; 7 book chapters; 28 invited scientific presentations. *Memberships:* Fellow, American Academy of Neurology; Society for Neuroscience; American Society for Clinical Pharm & Therapeutics; Fellow, Stroke Council of AHA; Central Society for Neurological Res; Movement Disorder Society; American Society for Neurological Investigation. *Address:* Department of Neurology (127), 3495 Bailey Avenue, Buffalo, NY 14215, USA.

HERSOM Naomi Louise, b. 4 Feb. 1927, Winnipeg, Canada. President. *Education:* BA, 1947; BEd., 1955; MEd., 1962; PhD, 1969. *Appointments:* Professor, Centre for the Study of Administration in Education, 1979; Professor, Dean, College of Education, University of Saskatchewan, 1981; President, Vice Chancellor, Mount Saint Vincent University, 1986-. *Memberships:* President, Canadian Education Association, 1988-89; President, Canadian Society for the Study of Higher Education, 1987-88; Canadian Society for the Study of Education, President; UNESCO Status of Women Sub-Commission, 1984; Delta Kappa Gamma International, President. *Honours:* Honorary Advisor, Education, Canadian Committee, Organization Mondiale pour l'Education Prescholarie, 1984-86; Grand Dame of Merit, Knights of Malta, 1987; Fellow, Canadian College of Teachers; Hon. Degree, McGill University, 1988, University of Manitoba, 1989. *Hobbies:* Bird Watching; Kite Flying. *Address:* The Meadows, Mount Saint Vincent University, Halifax, Nova Scotia B3M 2J6, Canada.

HERTWECK Alma Louise, b. 6 Feb. 1937, Moline, Illinois, USA. Professor. m. E. Romayne Hertweck, 16 Dec. 1955, 1 son. *Education:* AA, Mira Costa College, 1969; BA, 1975, MA 1977, PhD, 1982, University of California, San Diego. *Appointments:* Part-time Professor, Mira Costa College, Oceanside, 1983-87, 1988-; Part-time Professor, United States International University, 1985-; Vice President, Executive Director, El Camino Preschools Incorporated, Oceanside, 1985-. *Publications:* Handicapping the Handicapped, with Hugh Mehan; Contributor to: Discourse and Institutional Authority; Constructing the Truth and Consequences: Educators Attributions of Perceived Failure in School, PhD Dissertation. *Memberships:* American Education Research Association; American Sociological Association; National Council on Family Relations; National Association of the Education of Young Children. *Honours:* Life Member, Alpha Gamma Sigma; Graduated Summa Cum Laude, University of California. *Hobbies:* Foreign Travel; Sailing; Photography; Golf; Bicycling. *Address:* 2024 Oceanview Road, Oceanside, CA 92056, USA.

HESKETH Phoebe, b. 29 Jan. 1909, Preston, Lancashire, England. Writing poetry. m. William Aubrey Martin Hesketh, 30 Sept. 1931. 2 sons, 1 daughter. *Education:* Birkdale and Cheltenham Ladies College, 1918-26. *Appointments:* Woman's Page Editor, Bolton Evening News, 1942-45; Tutor General studies, Women's College, Bolton, 1967, 1968, 1969; Creative Writing Tutor, Bolton School, 1978-79; Creative Writing Group Tutor, University of the Third Age, 1984-. *Publications:* Poetry: Lean Forward, Spring, 1948; No Time for Cowards, 1952; Out of the Dark, 1954; Between Wheels and Stars, 1956; The Buttercup Children, 1958; Prayer for Sun, 1966; A Song by Sunlight, 1974; Preparing to Leave, 1977; The Eighth Day, 1980; Over the Brook, 1986; Netting the Sun, 1989. Prose: My Aunt Edith, 1966; Rivington, 1972; What Can the Matter Be? 1985. *Memberships:* Society of Authors; PEN; Fellow Royal Society of Literature; Member of Executive Committee, 1960-81, Council for the Protection of Rural England, (Retired). *Honours:* Greenwood Prize for Poetry, Poetry Society, 1948 and 1966; National Poetry Federation, 1st Prize, 1988. *Hobbies:* The Countryside and Environmental subjects; Poetry; Writing in general; Horses; Painting. *Address:* 10 The Green, Heath Charnock, Chorley, Lancs PR6 9JH, England.

HESS Beth B., b. 13 Sept. 1928, Buffalo, New York, USA. Professor of Sociology. m. Richard C. Hess, 25 Apr. 1953, 1 son, 1 daughter. *Education:* BA magna cum laude, Political Science, Radcliffe College, 1950; MA, 1966, PhD, Rutgers University. *Appointments:* Various positions to Professor, County College of Morris, Randolph, New Jersey, 1967-; Adjunct Professor, Graduate Center, City University of New York, 1979; Visiting Professor, Boston University Gerontology Center, 1980-81; Lecturer, Douglass College, 1981. *Publications:* Growing Old in America (editor), 1976, 3rd Edition, 1985; Sociology (with Elizabeth Markson and Peter J. Stein), 1982, 3rd Edition, 1988; Analyzing Gender (with Myra Marx Ferree), 1988; Various others mainly in field of aging; Book reviews in Social Forces, Contemporary Sociology, Journal of Marriage and the Family, The Gerontologist; Society, Sociology and Social Research, Public Welfare; Associate Editor, several journals. *Memberships:* American Sociological Asociation, Section on Aging, Nominations Committee 1980, Newsletter Editor 1982-84, Secretary 1985-87; Sociologists for Women in Society, Treasurer 1982-85, Editor 1984-86, President 1987-89; Eastern Sociological Association, Chair, Committee on the Status of Women, 1977, Executive Secretary 1978-81, Vice-President 1984-85, President 1988-89; Association for Humanist Sociology, President 1986-87; National Council on Family Relations; New Jersey Council on Family Relations, President, 1987; Society for the Study of Social Problems, Division Chair 1979-81; Director 1981-84; Behavioural and Social Science Section, Gerontological Society of America, Secretary 1979-81, Member-at-Large 1984-86, Chair 1987-88; Groves Conference on Marriage and the Family. *Honours:* Fellow, Gerontological Society of America, 1978; Peter I.Gellman Distinguished Service Award, Eastern Sociological Society. *Address:* 2 Hampshire Drive, Mendham. NJ 07945, USA.

HESS Frances Aaron, b. 16 Jan. 1933, Pittsburgh, Pennsylvania, USA. Professional Volunteer. m. Robert Lee Hess, 9 Apr. 1960. 3 sons, 1 daughter. *Education:* BA, Vassar College, 1953; MA, Teaching, Harvard-Radcliffe, 1954. *Appointments:* 8th Grade English and History teacher, Mt Diablo Unified School District, Concord, 1954-56; History Teacher, Taylor Allerdice, Jr-Sr High School, Pittsburgh, PA, 1956-60; Consultant, Carnegie Tech Advanced Placement Program, 1960-61; Professional volunteer: First Lady, Brooklyn College, 1980-; League of Women Voters of Glencoe, Il; American Jewish Committee, NY Chapter; Hebrew-Union College, Jewish Institute of Religion, Board of Overseers for New York School; North American Board of World Union for Progressive Judaism; Congregation Beth Elohim, Board Member; Alumnae and Alumni, Vassar College: Board Member 1973-79, President, 1983-86, Trustee of Vassar College. *Honours:* Phi Beta Kappa, 1953; Honorary Vassar College Fellowship, 1953-54; Robert L Payton Award for Voluntary Service, given by District II of CASE (Council for the Advancement and Support of Education), 1987. *Address:* 115 Westminster Road, Brooklyn, NY 11218, USA.

HESS Kären Jo Matison, b. 11 Apr. 1939, Austin, Minnesota, USA. Author; Instructor; Consultant; CEO. m. Sheldon Thomas Hess, 21 July 1962. 1 son, 1 daughter. *Education:* BS 1961, BA 1961, MA 1963, PhD 1968, University of Minnesota. *Appointments:* Instructor, Normandale Community Co, 1969-; CEO, Innovative Programming Systems, 1971-; CEO, Institute for Professional Development, 1987-; CEO, Information Age Communications, 1987-. *Publications:* Author or co-author: Criminal Investigation; Creating the High Performance Team; Aftershock, Introduction to Private Security; Introduction to Law Enforcement; For the Record: Report Writing in Law Enforcement. *Memberships:* National Council of Teachers of English; American Association of University Women; Phi Delta Kappa; Phi Beta Kappa, Textbook Author's Association; Bloomington Chamber of Commerce; International Society for General Semantics; National Society for Programmed Instruction; Association for Supervision and Curriculum Development. *Honours:* BS with high distinction; BA, magna cum laude, Phi Beta Kappa; General Motors Scholarship; American Association of Unviersity Women Fellowship. *Hobbies:* Reading; Writing; Tennis; Bridge. *Address:* 9001 Poplar Bridge Road, Bloomington, MN 55437, USA.

HESTER Patricia Lane O'Quinn, b. 20 Jan. 1942, USA. Educator. m. Clyde R. Hester. *Education:* BA, Campbell University, 1964; MA, 1984, EdS, 1987, East Carolina University; Doctorate in progress. *Appointments:* Teacher, Raleigh/Wake County Schools, North Carolina, 1964-69; Teacher, Ravenscroft School, Raleigh, 1969-73; Consultant, University Learning and Literacy, Emporia, Virginia, 1973-75; Teacher, Pinecrest/Moore County Schools, Southern Pines, North Carolina, 1975-76; Teacher, Member of Administrative Council, Wayne County Schools, Goldsboro, North Carolina, 1976-79; Instructional Coordinator/Supervisor for Communication Skills, 1979-; Consultant in educational field. *Publications:* Teacher...Why?; Teacher...; Bulletin Boards and Boxes; Book Boxes; Poems etc in The Christian Adventurer, Warrior, New York Anthology of Poetry. *Memberships:* Alpha Delta Kappa; Association of Supervision and Curriculum Development; National Council of English Teachers; National Education Association; North Carolina Council of English Teachers; North Carolina Teachers Association. *Honours:* American Legion Award; Alpha Delta Scholar; Teacher of the Year. *Address:* 805 Mill Road, Goldsboro, NC 27530, USA.

HETH Diana Sue Abraham, b. 25 Sept. 1948, Robinson, Illinois, USA. Health Executive. m. (1) Kenneth L. Greider, 16 Aug. 1970 (divorced 1985), 1 son, 2 daughters, (2) Harold E. Heth, 7 July 1985, 1 son, 1 daughter. *Education:* BS, Education, Eastern Illinois University, 1970; MSW, University of Illinois, 1984. *Appointments:* Executive Director, National Association for Downe's Syndrome, 1978-79; Director, Coordinator, Heartland Hospice, Lincolnland, 1983-. *Publication:* One Gift to the Next, anthology on death. *Memberships:* National Association for Downe's Syndrome; National Hospice Organisation; National Association for Home Care; Past Board, Compassionate Friends; Past President, Newcomers; Nominating Committee, Illinois State Hospice Organisation. *Honour:* Award, community service, Modern Woodmen of America, 1986. *Hobbies:* Bridge; Gardening; Cooking; Travel. *Address:* 200 N. Third, Effingham, Illinois 62401, USA.

HETZLER Susan Elizabeth, b. 18 Mar. 1947, USA. Instructor. m. Jeffrey David Hetzler, 23 Aug. 1986, 1 son, 1 daughter. *Education:* BSc. Ed., 1971; MSEd., 1978, CAS/ABD, 1984, Northern Illinois University; PhD Candidate. *Appointments:* Elementary Classroom Teacher, 1970-87; Owner, Small Business, 1978-82; Ski Instructor, 1980-87; Iowa State University Instructor, 1987-. *Publicaitons:* Elementary practicum in Teacher Education, 1988; Learning Centres for Teachers, 1988, 2nd edition 1989. *Memberships:* Association of Supervision & Curriculum Development; American Association of University Professors; NEA; Association of Teacher Educators; Delta Kappa Gamma. *Honours:* Outstanding Elementary Teachers of America Award, 1974. *Hobbies:* Reading; Walking; Cooking; Skiing; *Address:* N106 Lagomarcino Hall, Iowa State University, Ames, IA 50011, USA.

HEUGES Margaret Mary, b. 11 Apr. 1940, Sharon, Pennsylvania, USA. Dean of Admissions; Artist. m. 23 June 1962. 2 sons, 2 daughters. *Education:* BFA, Moore College of Art, 1962; MFA, Tyler School of Art of Temple University, 1978. *Appointments:* Director of Admissions, Tyler School of Art, 1979-86; Dean of Admissions, The University of the Arts, Philadelphia, 1986-. *Creative Works:* Paintings; Drawings; Prints. *Membership:* National Museum of Women in the Arts. *Honours:* Judith Sekowitz Fine Arts Inc Award, New York City, 1982; Purchase Prizes: Salisbury State University, 1980; Beaver College, 1977; Delaware Art Museum, 1987; Collections: Insurance Co of North America; Home Insurance Company; ARA Services; Delaware Art Museum. *Hobby:* Mycology. *Address:* 2039 Jenkintown Road, Glenside, PA 19038, USA.

HEUN Gisela Maria, b. 4 Aug. 1944, Stuttgart, Federal Republic of Germany. Administrative Manager. m. Hartmut Heun, 9 Jan. 1969. *Education:* BBA, College of Business Administration, Frankfurt, 1964. *Appointments:* Executive Assistant, VDO Instruments, Frankfurt/Main, 1962-68; Assistant to General Manager, VDO Instruments, Detroit, Michigan, USA, 1968-69; University of Michigan, Ann Arbor, 1971-; Translator/Editor, Language and Language Behaviour Abstracts Journal, 1971-72; Administrative Assistant, Germanic Languages and Literature, 1972-73; Business Manager, College of Literature, Science and the Arts, 1973-79; Administrative Manager, Medical School Department of Physiology, 1979-. *Publications:* Translations and editing of foreign abstracts for language research journal; Translating and researching literature on history of local families' chronicles throughout Europe; Translator and Interpreter for German/English; Attended International Automobile Shows as Interpreter until 1968; Translating and Interpreting in fields of business and natural sciences. *Memberships:* American Association of Medical Colelges, Group on Business Affairs, 19890-; Translators of The University of Michigan, 1971-; Commissioned Notary Public, County of Washtenaw, State of Michigan, 1985. *Honour:* Naturalized US Citizen, 1985. *Hobbies:* Travel; World history; Art. *Address:* The University of Michigan Medical School, 1331 Catherine Street, 7744 Medical Science II, Ann Arbor, MI 48109-0622, USA.

HEWETT Kathleen A, b. 20 Aug. 1954, St Paul, USA. Information Management Executive. m. Charles W. Hewett, 26 Nov. 1983, 1 son. *Education:* BA, College of St Catherine, 1981; M in Scientia Bibliothecaria, University of Wales, 1983. *Appointments:* Reference Librarian, Hamline University, 1979-80; Technical Services Reference Librarian, 1981; Library Manager Rider Bennett Egan & Arundel, 1982; Manager, Informatiron Systems, Dorsey & Whitney, 1982-. *Publications:* Articles in professional journals. *Memberships:* American Management Association; Society of Indexers; Minnesota Associaitron of Law Librarians; Minnesota Online Users Group. *Hobbies:* Birding; Hiking; Fishing; Ice Skating; Reading. *Address:* 1258 Fairmount Ave., St Paul, MN 55105, USA.

HEWITT Heather Agnes, b. 14 July 1934, Victoria, Australia. Academic. m. John R. Hewitt, 30 Dec. 1959, 2 sons, 1 daughter. *Education:* BA, Dip.Ed, University of Melbourne, 1955. *Appointments:* Officer in Charge Counselling Guidance, Clinical Services, Victorian Education Dept., 1957-79; Psychologist, Royal Children's Hospital, 1960-63; Lecturer, Institute Early Childhood Development, 1978-80; Lecturer, Victorian College Advanced Education (Burwood Campus), 1979-80; Lecturer Lincoln Institute Health Sciences 1966-70; Principal, University College, University of Melbourne, 1980-. *Publications:* Articles in professional journals; Editorial Board, International Journal of Rehabilitation Research, International Journal of Visual Impairment & Blindness. *Memberships Include:* Executive Member, International Association of Deaf/Blind; Executive Member, International Council for Education of Visually Impaired, 1987-; Australian Psychological Society; Australian College of Education. *Hobbies:* Music; Gardening. *Address:* University College, University of Melbourne, College Crescent, Parkside, VIC 3052, Australia.

HEWSON Donna Walters, b. 28 Mar. 1947, Columbia, USA. Real Estate Executive. m. James Robert Hewson, 1983, divorced 1986, 1 son. *Education:* Studies: Hollins College, 1971-72, Virginia Western College, 1972, Virginia Polytechnic & State University, 1972-73, University of South Carolina, 1978-79, 1984, 1985. *Appointments:* Sales Representative, 1969-71, Broker, 1971-72, Russell-Jeffcoat Realtors; Administrative Assistant, Roanoke Valley Psych. Centre, 1975-76; Sales Representative, Moore Business Forms, Columbia, 1976-79; Project Sales Manager, Continental Mortgage Investors, Columbia, 1979-80; Broker, Project Sales Manager Tom Jenkins Realty, Columbia, 1980-81; Sales Manager, Broker, RELM Inc., 1982-83; Sales Manager, So. US Realty/US Shelter, Columbia, 1983-84; President, Walters Hewson Co. Inc., Columbia, 1984-. *Memberships:* Many professional organisations including: Columbia Chamber of Commerce, Committee Chairman, 1987-; Greater Columbia Chamber of Commerce; National Association Real Estate Appraisers; State Association Realtors; National Association Realtors, Columbia Board. *Hobbies:* Piano; Historic Preservation; Fine Art. *Address:* Walters Hewson Co. Inc., 1600 Park Circle, Suite 104, PO Box 967, Columbia, SC 29202, USA.

HEYDEN Cheryl Martha, b. 28 Nov. 1954, Elmhurst, Illinois, USA. *Education:* BSc Psychology, Elmhurst College, 1976; Master Social Work, Jane Addams College of Social Work, University of Illinois, Chicago, 1982. *Appointments:* Director of Campus Programmes, residential and diagnostic services, Maryville Academy, City of Youth, 1976-; Field Instructor: Northeastern Illinois University, 1980-; Western Illinois University, 1983-; National College of Education, 1982-; George Williams College, 1981-83; Mundelein College, 1983-84; University of Illinois, Chicago, 1984-; Illinois State University, 1987-; Denisons University, 1988; Loyola University, 1983-. *Publications:* Article: Tools of the Trade: The Challenge of Partnership, Charities USA Magazine, 1988. *Memberships:* Certified Social Worker, State of Illinois; Academy of Certified Social Workers; National Association of Social Worker; National Teaching Family Association; Phi Kappa Phi Honour Society; Psi Chi National Honour Society in Psychology; Omnicron Delta Kappa. *Honours:* The Key Award for distinguished service to youth, 1988; Commemorative Medal of Honour, 1988. *Hobbies:* Needlework; Music, play the French Horn; Travel. *Address:* 15 Glenbrook Drive, Prospect Heights, Illinois 60070, USA.

HEYHOE FLINT Rachael, b. 11 June, 1939, Wolverhampton, England. Sportswoman; Journalist; Broadcaster. m. Derrick Flint, 1 Nov. 1971. 1 son. *Education:* Diploma, Physical Education, Dartford College of Physical Education, 1960. *Appointments:* Head of PE, Northcote School, Wolverhampton, 1960-62; Municipal Grammar School, 1962-64; Journalist, Express and Star, Wolverhampton, 1965-72; Sports Editor, Wolverhampton Chronicle, 1969-72; Marketing Executive, St George Assurance Company; Public Relations Executive, Europa Hotels and Leisure, 1982-. *Publications:* Just for Kicks, Hockey Goalkeepers Booklet; Women's Hockey, Pelham Instructional Series; Fair Play, Story of Women's Cricket; Heyhoe, Autobiography. *Memberships:* Womens Cricket Association; England Cricket Team, 1960-83; England Hockey Team, 1964; Staffordshire County Squash Player, 1961-65; Sportswriters Association; Institute of Journalists. *Honours:* MBE 1972; Guild of Professional Toastmasters After Dinner Speaker of the Year, 1972; Daily Express Sportswomen of the Year, 2nd, 1974; Honorary Lady Taverner, 1982. *Hobbies:* Sports; Driving. *Address:* Danescroft, Wergs Road, Tettenhall, Wolverhampton, West Midlands, England.

HEYMAN Sally Anne, b. 10 Nov. 1954, Baltimore, USA. Crime/Loss Prevention Specialist; Politician. *Education:* BA, University of Florida, 1975; MSc., Criminal Justice, Nova University, 1981. *Appointments:* Juvenile-Community Involvement Specialist, Miami Police Dept., 1977-81; Owner, Consultant, Crime Gopher It Inc., 1981-; Investigator, Bureau of Crimes Compensation, Florida, 1983; Councilwoman, North Miami Beach, 1987-. *Publications:* Author, Street Safety - A Working Woman's Handbook; articles in journals. *Honours:* Alumni-Florida Crime Prevention Training Institute; Jaycees, Director; Women on the Way, Vice President. *Honours Include:* Miami Police Department Employee of Month, 1980; Outstanding Young Woman of America, 1981; Focus: Successful Woman, 1983; Jaycees Distinguished Service Award, 1985; Lions Club International, Citation of the Year 1988; Professional Womens Council, Woman of Year, Athenia Award 1989. *Hobbies:* All Water Sports; Lecturing; Skiing; Travel; Bicycling; Films. *Address:* 1579 NE 171 Street, North Miami Beach, FL 33162, USA.

HEYZER Noeleen, b. 26 Apr 1948. Sociologist. *Education:* Graduate, Sociology, 1969-71, Master of Sociology, 1972-73, University of Singapore; PhD Sociology, University of Cambridge, England, 1978. *Appointments:* Bank Officer, The Chartered Bank, Singapore, 1971-72; Researcher/Tutor, Sociology, University of Singapore, 1972-73; Industrial Worker, Textile Factory, Singapore, 1974; External Researcher, International Labour Office, Geneva, Switzerland, 1978; Research Officer, Visiting Fellow, Institute of Development Studies, University of Sussex, England, 1979-82; Social Affairs Officer, Social Development Division, Economic and Social Commission for Asia and the Pacific, Bangkok, Thailand, 1982-84; Programme

the Pacific, Bangkok, Thailand, 1982-84; Programme Coordinator, Asian and the Pacific Development Centre, Kuala Lumpur, Malaysia, 1984-. *Publications:* Missing Women: Development Planning in Asia and the Pacific, (ed), 1985; Working Women in South East Asia: Development, Subordination and Emancipation, 1986; Women Farmers and Rural Change in Asia, (ed), 1987; Daughters in Industry: Work, Skills and Consciousness of Women Workers in Asia, (ed), 1988. Numerous articles to professional journals. *Honours:* Book prize for top Sociology student, University of Singapore; Research Scholarship, University of Singapore; Ford Foundation Scholarship, University of Singapore; Postdoctoral Fellowship, Social Science Research Council, New York, USA. *Address:* Asian & Pacific Development Centre, Pesiaran Duta, P O Box 12224, 50770 Kuala Lumpur, Malaysia.

HIATT Florence Ellen, b. Elwood, Indiana, USA. Musician. m. Frank A. Robertson, 1 Sept. 1948, 1 son, 1 daughter. *Education:* Cincinnati Conservatory of Music, University of Cincinnati, 1945-49; BMus, Auburn University, Alabama, 1964; Diploma, Ecoles d'Art et Musique, Fontainebleau, France, 1961; MM, Indiana University, 1972; Doctoral studies, Florida State University, 1984-85. *Appointments:* Current: Organist, St Luke United Methodist Church; Keyboard specialist, Columbus Symphony Orchestra; Music Director, Temple Israel; Concert organist; Musical Direction staff, Springer Opera House. *Publications:* Articles, Music Magazine, The Choral Journal, various other music & church journals. *Memberships:* Past Dean, American Guild of Organists; Royal College of Organists, UK; Regional Coordinator, Planetary Society. *Honour:* Mortar Board award, Auburn University, 1964; Honorary Fellow, Wessex Theological College, England. *Hobbies & Interests:* History; Reading; Travel; Astronomy & planetary sciences; Archaeology; Writing. *Address:* 2801 Gardenia Street, Columbus, Georgia 31906, USA.

HIBBLER Meril Edwards, b. 13 Feb. 1931, Clarence, USA. Community Consultant; Retired Teacher. m. Alphonso Hibbler, 31 Jan. 1959. *Education:* BA, 1955, MA, 1975, Southern University. *Appointments:* Elementary Teacher, Natchitoches Parissh, 1955-67, Caddo Parish, Shreveport, 1967-77; Self-employed Consultant Firm, 1980-. *Publications:* Positive Approach - On Being You; On Being Yourself; The Turning Point, newsletter. *Memberships:* National Association of Educators; Association of Classroom Teachers, President; Director, Women in Community Service; National Association of University Women, President; National Council of Negro Women, Vice President; Phi Delta Kappa Beta Alpha, Treasurer, etc. *Honours:* Recipient various honours and awards including: US Census Award, 1970; Women In Community Services Award, 1983; National Council of Negro Women Service Award, 1985; Zeta Gamma Rho Humanitarian Award, 1987; etc. *Hobbies:* Reading; Writing; Counselling. *Address:* 5802 Buncomb Road, Shreveport, LA 71129, USA.

HICKERNELL Thresa Elizabeth Kerr, b. 20 Sept. 1931, Altus, Oklahoma, USA. Special Education Teacher. m. Frederick Slocum Hickernell, 25 June 1954, 3 sons, 1 daughter. *Education:* BA, Education, 1953; MA, 1984. *Appointments:* Teacher: 1st Grade, Montebello School, Alhambra District, Phoenix, Arizona, 1953-54; Kindergarten, Awase School, Sukiran, Okinawa, 1955-56; Special education for mildly handicapped, Phoenix, Arizona, 1976-. *Memberships:* Kappa Delta Pi; Pi Lambda Theta; Association for Childhood Education; Membership Chair, Council for Exceptional Children. *Honours:* Award, Association for Childhood Education, 1953; Teacher of Year, Arizona Federation, Council for Exceptional Children, 1988-89; Biographical recognition. *Hobbies:* Tennis; Jogging; Cycling; Church activities, Board of Christian Education, Deaconess; World Travel. *Address:* Tonalea Elementary School, 6801 East Oak Street, Scottsdale, Arizona 85257, USA.

HICKS Grenetta McKinstry, b. 10 Oct. 1947,

Birmingham, Alabama, USA. Microbiologist. 1 son. *Education:* AB, Stillman College, Tuscaloosa, 1968; MA, Indiana University, Bloomington, 1970; PhD, Ohio State University, Columbus, 1979; Postdoctoral studies: Max-Planck-Institut fur Molekulare-Genetiks, West Berlin, Germany, 1979 and Ohio State University, Columbus, Ohio, USA, 1979. *Appointments:* Researcher, Eli Lilly Pharmaceutical Company, Indianapolis, 1970-72; Technical Assistant, Microbiology Department, Ohio State University, Columbus, 1972-76; Scientist, Microbial genetics, Abbott Laboratories, Chicago, 1979-85; Senior Microbial Geneticist, Oak Ridge Research Institute, Inc, Oak Ridge, 1985-87; Senior Microbiologist, Peer Consultants, PC, Oak Ridge, Tennessee, 1987-. *Publications:* Author of numerous articles and abstracts to professional journals and to conferences. *Memberships:* American Society for Microbiology, National and Illinois Branch; American Association for Advancement of Science; Association for Women in Science; Sigma Xi; New York Academy of Sciences; American Phytopathological Society; Alpha Kappa Alpha, Sorority, Inc, Secretary. *Honours:* Graduate Cum Laude, Stillman College, 1968; Graduate student representative, Committee for the selection of Dean, College of Biological Sciences, Ohio State University, 1978-79; Graduate student representative, Microbiology Department Graduate Committee, 1978-79; Abbott Laboratories Presidential Award, 1982. *Hobbies:* Reading; Tennis; Aerobics. *Address:* 116-B Arcadia Lane, Oak Ridge, TN 37830, USA.

HICKS Maureen Patricia, b. 23 Feb. 1948. Member of Parliament. m. Keith Hicks, 28 Apr. 1973, 1 son, 1 daughter. *Appointments:* Teacher, Drama & English, 1969-70; Marks & Spencer Management, 1970-74; Assistant Area Education Officer, NW Surrey, 1974-76; Director, Stratford-upon-Avon Motor Museum, 1976-82; Member of Parliament for Wolverhampton, North East, 1987-. *Hobbies:* Amateur Dramatics; Travel; Music; Golf. *Address:* House of Commons, London SW1A 0AA, England.

HIERHOLZER Joan, b. 26 Sept. 1928, Texas, USA. Artist. m. 2 sons. *Education:* BFA, Univerity ofTexas, 1952 MFA, Rutgers University, 1969. *Appointments:* Teacher, Summit Art Centre, Summit, New Jersey, Chatham Public Schools, New Jersey, and Summit Public Schools, Fashion Illustrator; Frost Brother's San Antonio, Texas, and Scarbrough, Austin, Texas; Solo Exhibitions, AT & T Basking Ridge, New Jersey; Drew Chemical Corporation, World Headquarters Boonton, New Jersey; Phoeni Gallery, New York City; Educational Testing Service, Princeton, New Jersey; Exxon Company, USA, Linden, New Jersey; Marion Kooglor McNay Art Institute; Lectures & Demonstrations; Private & Corporate Collections & Commissions. *Memberships:* Trustee, Hunterdon Art Centre, Clinton, New Jersey; National Arts Club, New York City. *Hobbies:* Portraits; Travel. *Address:* PO Box 380, RD3, Pittstown, NJ 08867, USA.

HIGONNET Margaret Randolph, b. 2 Oct. 1941, New Orleans, Louisiana, USA. Professor. m. Patrice Louis-Rene Higonnet, 14 Aug. 1974, 1 daughter. *Education:* BA, Bryn Mawr College, 1963; PhD, Yale University, 1970. *Appointments:* George Washington University, 1967-69; University of Connecticut, Storrs, 1970-. *Publications:* Horn of Oberon, 1970; The Cricket and the Ant, 1975; The Representation of Women in Fiction, 1983; Behind the Lines: Gender and the Two World Wars, 1987. *Membership:* English Institute, Secretary 1975-79. *Honours:* DAAD, 1963-64; Fulbright, 1966-67; Rockefeller, 1985; NEH, 1988; Visiting Scholar, Juan March Institute, 1987. *Address:* Department of English, University of Connecticut, Storrs, CT 06269, USA.

HILARY Jennifer, Actress. *Education:* Elmhurst Ballet School; Royal Academy of Dramatic Art, 1959-61. *Career includes:* Appearances in: Becket, film, 1963; The Rehearsal, on Broadway, 1963; Wings of a Dove, stage, 1964; A Scent of Flowers, stage, 1964; The Heroes of Telemark, film, 1965; A Month in the Country, stage 1965; The Idol, film, 1965; The Woman in White, BBC TV serial, 1966; Ivanov, 1966, Broadway & USA Tour; A Roof Over Their Mouths, 1966, ATV Play; Relatively Speaking, stage, 1967; Avanti, stage Broadway, 1968; Pig in a Poke, 1969, LWT; One Brief Summer, film, 1969; The Lady's Not for Burning, stage, 1970; Man and Superman, stage, 1971; Sam, Granada TV, 1974-75; Something for the Time Being, TV, 1975; Z Cars, BBC, 1976; Dear Daddy, stage, 1976-77; Alphabetical Order, Granda TV, 1978; Crown Court, TV, 1978; Speed King, TV, 1979; North Sea Hijack, film, 1979; Tales of the Unexpected, Anglia TV, 1980; Jackanory Playhouse, BBC TV 1980; I Have Been Here Before, stage, 1980; The Gentle Touch, LWT TV, 1981; Macbeth, stage, 1982; Betrayal, stage, 1982; Five Days One Summer, film, 1982; The Last Elephant, stage, 1982; Miss A and Miss M, 1982; Sufficent Carbohydrate, stage, 1983-84; Me and My Girl, TV, 1984; Some of My Best Friends Are Husbands, stage, 1985; Bouncing, Five Play Bill, Stage, 1985; Wild Honey, stage, 1986; Barnaby and the Old Boys, stage, 1987; Double First, BBC TV, 1988. *Address:* c/o London Management, 235/241 Regent Street, London W1, England.

HILBERT Virginia Lois, b. 6 Apr. 1935, Detroit, Michigan, USA. President, Computer Training and Consulting Firm. m. James R. Hilbert, 22 Nov. 1958, 2 sons, 2 daughters. *Education:* BA with honours, University of Michigan, 1957. *Appointments:* Government Analyst, Personnel Officer, City of Detroit, Michigan, 1957-60; Owner, President, Professional & Technical Development Inc/dba Lansing Computers Institute, Lansing, Michigan, 1979-. *Memberships:* Chamber of Commerce, Small Business Section; Governor's Conference on Small Businesses; Governor's Workgroup for MOC; NBEA; Pro Symphony; ASTD; GLTP. *Honours:* College honours. *Address:* Lansing Computer Institute, 501 North Marshall Street, Lansing, MI 48912, USA.

HILDEBRANDT Marie-Christine, b. 2 Sept. 1942, Southwest Africa-Namibia. Businesswoman; Road Transport Consultant. m. 24 Nov. 1974, 1 son, 2 daughters. *Education:* Lucie Clayton School for Professional Models, London, UK; Current studies, University of Namibia. *Appointments include:* Lucie Clayton, London, 1962; Vogue Academy, Capetown, South Africa, 1964; Franco Grillo, Rome, Italy, 1967; Fantasy Boutique, Capetown 1968, Cape Province 1974; Ricki's Charm School, Windhoek, 1975; Owner, Director, SWA Peruiits, 1982-; Lecturer, charm, modelling, Extravagansa Modelling School, various other organisations. *Memberships:* Vice President, Professional Business Club; Federation of Business & Professional Women, Namibia. *Honour:* Director, African Controlling Company. *Hobbies include:* Sailing (owner, yacht in Mediterranean); Horse riding; Painting; Cooking; Dressmaking. *Address:* PO Box 11441, Klein-Windhoek, Namibia.

HILDEBRAND Verna Lee, b. 17 Aug. 1924, Dodge City, Kansas, USA. University Professor. m. John R. Hildebrand, 23 June 1946, 1 son, 1 daughter. *Education:* BS 1945, MS 1957, Kansas State University; PhD, Texas Woman's University, 1970. *Appointments include:* Assistant Professor, Texas Tech University, 1962-67; Faculty 1967-, Professor of Family & Child Ecology 1974-, Michigan State University. *Publications include:* Introduction to Early Childhood Education, & accompanying workbook, 4th editions, 1986; Guiding Young Children, 4th edition, 1989; Parenting & Teaching Young Children, 3rd edition 1989; Management of Child Development Centers, 2nd edition 1989; China's Families: Experiment in Societal Change, 1981; Over 100 articles, professional journals. *Memberships:* National Association for Education of Young Children; American Home Economics Association; Women in International Development; World Association for Early Childhood Education; Women's Studies Association. *Honours:* Faculty awards, 1986, 1988; Outstanding Service, Michigan Association for Education of Young Children. *Hobbies:* Writing; Speaking; Swimming.

Address: Department of Family & Child Ecology, Michigan State University, East Lansing, MI 48824, USA.

HILEY Carole Shirley, b. 25 Aug. 1931, London, England. Managing Director; Qualified Nursery Nurse. m. Stanley S Cowan, 17 Aug 1952, divorced. Remarried 6 June 1975. 1 son, 1 daughter. *Education:* Nursery Nurse Qualification, Brighton Training College. *Appointments:* Founder and Managing Director, Beck Kindergarten, 1959-80; Founder and Managing Director, Kindergartens for Commerce, 1966-80; Founder and Managing Director, Our Childrens World Limited, 1980-86, name only sold in 1986, renamed World of Children Limited. *Creative works:* In 1977 research and development into the leisure industry created the need for professional child care at exhibitions, Airports and shopping centres. Since 1959 pioneered the development of over 30 private and industrial day centres and cared for over one million children throughout the UK. *Memberships:* Network; Institute of Directors; Phylis Court, Henley; PPA. *Honours:* Winston Churchill Travelling Fellowship (4 months) throughout USA and Europe studying child care. *Hobbies:* Children; Animals; Gardening; Writing childrens stories; Travelling. *Address:* Pankridge Manor, Bledlow Ridge, Bucks, HP14 4AE, England.

HILL Beverly Ellen, b. 20 May 1937, Albany, California, USA. Director, Medical Educational Resource Program and Adjunct Professor. *Education:* BA, College of Holy Names, 1960; MS, Dominican College, 1969; EdD, University of Southern California, 1978. *Appointments:* Producer/Director Health Services, TV, University of California, Davis, 1966-69; Coordinator Health Sciences TV 1969-73, Assistant Director IMS 1973-76, Assistant Director Continuing Education and Director Biocommunications, 1976-80, University of Southern California, Los Angeles. *Creative works:* Presenter, Catholic University, Nijmegen, Netherlands 1980, 1981; European Symposium on Clinical Pharmacy, Brussels, 1982, Barcelona, Spain, 1983; Contributor of articles to professional journals. *Memberships:* Board of Directors, 1985-, Association Biomedical Communications Directors; Board of Directors, 1976-79, Health Sciences Communicators Association; Association for Educational Communications and Technology. *Honours:* Recipient first place in rehabilitation category, 4th Biannual John Muir Medical Film Festival, 1980; International Media Award for Best Nursing Electronic Medica in 1987, presented by Sigma Theta Tau, the International Nursing Honorary. *Hobbies:* Painting; Travel; Archaeology; Music; Tennis; Swimming. *Address:* Medical Educational Resources Program, Indiana University School of Medicine, 1226 West Michigan Street BR 156, Indianapolis, Indiana 46223, USA.

HILL Bridget Teresa, b. 1 Oct. 1942, March, England. Cancer Research Scientist. *Education:* BSc., Honours, Chemistry & Zoology, London University, 1965; PhD, Biochemistry, London University, 1968; FRSC; FIBiol. *Appointments:* Wellcome Postdoctoral Fellow, London, 1968-72; Ludwig Fellow, Temple University Medical School, USA, 1972-73; Staff Member, 1974-, Head, Cellular Chemotherapy, 1985-, Imperial Cancer Research Fund Laboratories. *Publications:* Over 200 articles in professional journals; co-editor, 5 books. *Memberships:* Fellow, Royal Institute of Chemistry; Fellow, Institute of Biology; Biochemical Society; American Association for Cancer Research; American Society of Clinical Oncology; British Association for Cancer Research; New York Academy of Sciences. *Honours:* Recipient, various honours & awards including: Boehringer-Manheim Travel Fellowship, Manitoba Cancer Foundation, Canada, 1972; William Waldorf Astor Foundation Fellowship, University of Toronto, 1974; Visiting Professorship, Commonwealth of Virginia, 1977; MRC Visiting Fellow, Ontario Cancer Institute, 1987. *Hobbies:* Reading; Traditional Jazz; Classical Music; Piano; Photography; Walking. *Address:* Imperial Cancer Research Fund Laboratories, London WC2, England.

HILL Cherry, b. 5 Nov. 1947, Detroit, Michigan, USA. Writer; Horse Show Judge; Lecturer. m. Richard Klimesh, 25 Mar. 1975. *Education:* BS, Animal Science, Iowa State University. *Appointments:* Equine Science Instructor, Olds College, Alberta, Canada, 1975-77; Highland College, Freeport, Illinois, USA, 1979-83; Colorado State University, Fort Collins, CO, 1983-85; Author/Judge/Lecturer, 1976-. *Publications:* Books: The Formative Years, 1988; From the Center of the Ring, 1988; Horsekeeping on a Small Acreage, 1990. Contributing Editor: Chronicle of the Horse; Horsecare; Quarter Horse Journal; Appaloosa Journal; Horseplay. *Memberships:* Authors Guild; National Writers Club; Writers of the Round; American Quarter Horse Association; Appaloosa Horse Club; American Horse Shows Association; United States Dressage Federation. *Honours:* Sentinal magazine First Place Fiction, 1980; Writers of the Round, First Place Fiction, 1985. *Hobbies:* Dressage (riding); Cooking; Photography. *Address:* P O Box 140, Livermore, CO 80536, USA.

HILL Elizabeth Starr, b. 4 Nov. 1925, Lynn Haven, Florida, USA. Writer. m. Russell Gibson Hill, 28 May 1949, 1 son, 1 daughter. *Education:* Finch Junior College; Columbia University. *Career:* Freelance Writer since teenage years; Conducting fiction writing workshops and seminars, adult education programmes; Speaking to children's groups. *Publications:* Stories and articles in leading magazines including Reader's Digest, Harper's Bazaar, Cricket, Seventeen, The New Yorker; Books for young people including Evan's Corner, Ever-After Island; Education materials for Encylopedia Brittanica Educational Corporation and others; Excerpts and adaptations of work in textbooks and readers; When Christmas Comes. *Address:* c/o Harold Ober Associates Inc, 40 East 49th Street, New York, NY 10017, USA.

HILL Fannie Ezelle, b. Americus, Georgia, USA. Teacher. m. Benjamin Harrison Hill, 1932, 1 son. *Education:* BA, Paul Quinn College. *Appointments Include:* Teacher, States of Georgia, Mississippi & Oklahoma; Director, Young People of the 12th Episc. District, 20 years; Associate Director, RSVP for 6 years & currently. *Publications:* Contributor To: Poets Corner, 1968-78; Editor, The Vernon Newsette, 1950-72. *Memberships Include:* Salvation Army, N. Mabel Ctr. Advisory Board, Secretary; Governors Status on Women; Director, Christian Education, Vernon A. MECh; NAACP; YMCA; various community & charity organisations. *Honours:* Liberty Bell Award; Violet Anderson Award; Golden Age Fellowship Award for Outstanding Contributions in the field of Civil & Religious Activities; Humanitarian Award to Tulsa Youth; etc. *Hobby:* Making People Happy, *Address:* 3004 N. Cinn. Ave., Tulsa, OK 74106, USA.

HILL Hulene Dian, b. 17 Mar. 1948, Salisbury, North Carolina, USA. Certified Public Accountant. 1 son. *Education:* BS, Accounting, University of North Carolina, 1971. *Appointments:* Audit Staff, 1971, Tax Dept., 1973-74, Peat, Marwick, Mitchell, Charlotte; Tax Senior, Arthur Anderson, Charlotte, 1974-76; Tax Dept., Clarkson Harden & Gantt, 1976-78; Tax Manager, 1979, Partner, 1983-, Touche Ross. *Memberships:* Past President, College of Business Administration Alumni Interest Group; Past President, Women Executives *Address:* Touche Ross, One Independence Centre, Suite 1600, Charlotte, NC 28246, USA.

HILL Kathryn H. b. San Antonio, Texas, USA. Communications Consultant. m. Dr Richard N Hill, 10 Apr. 1964. 2 sons, 1 daughter. *Appointments:* Owner, Aries Enterprise International Consultant Corp. *Memberships:* United States Capitol Historical Society; American Association of University Women; National Association for Female Executives. *Honours:* Board of Directors: Mercury Control Systems, Chatswood, Sydney, Australia, 1986; Board of National Literacy Association, 1986; US Congress, Washington, 1987; US Capitol, Washington, 1987; Hawaii State Society, Washington; Business & Professional Womens Association National Convention, Milwaukee, 1985.

Address: 7519 Manulele Place, Honolulu, Hawaii 96825, USA.

HILL Lorna, b. 21 Feb. 1902, Durham City, England. 1 daughter. *Education:* Le Manoir, Lausanne, Switzerland; Durham University, England. *Publications:* Sadlers Wells Ballet Books; Dancing Peel Books; Patience Books; Marjorie & Co; Vicarage Children. Novels: The Other Miss Perkin; The Scent of Rosemary; Biography: La Sylphide (Taglioni). *Membership:* Society of Authors. *Address:* c/o Pan Books Ltd, Cavaye Place, London, England.

HILL Pamela, b. 26 Nov. 1920, Nairobi, Kenya. Writer. *Education:* Glasgow School of Art, 1939-43; University of Glasgow, 1947-53. *Publications:* Flaming Janet, 1954; Shadow of Palaces, 1955; Marjory of Scotland, 1956; Here Lies Margot, 1957; Maddalena, 1963; The Cherrycake Death, 1967; Forget Not Ariadne, 1965; Julia, 1967; The Devil of Aske, 1972; The Malvie Inheritance, 1973; The Incumbent, 1974; Norah Stroyan, 1976; Whitton's Folly, 1975; The Green Salamander, 1977; Tsar's Woman, 1977; Strangers' Forest, 1978; Daneclere, 1978; Daughter of Midnight, 1979; Homage to a Rose, 1979; A Place of Ravens, 1980; Fire Opal, 1980; Knock at a Star, 1981; This Rough Beginning, 1981; The House of Cray, 1982; The Fairest One of All, 1982; Duchess Cain, 1983; The Copper-Haired Marshal, 1983; Bride of Ae, 1983; Children of Lucifer, 1984; Still Blooms the Rose, 1984; The Governess, 1985; Sable for the Count, 1985; Venables, 1986; The Sisters, 1986; Digby, 1987; Fenfallow, 1987; The Sutburys, 1988; Jeannie Urquhart, 1988; forthcoming: The Woman in the Cloak; Trevithick; Artemia etc. *Address:* 89A Winchester Street, Pimlico, London SW1 V4NU, England.

HILL Patricia (Pat) N, b. 17 Aug. 1932, Delta, Louisiana, USA. High School Teacher; Writer; Entertainer. m. 10 Sept. 1949. 1 son, 1 daughter. *Education:* BA, MA, University of Mississipi; Post graduate studies at several universities. *Appointments:* School Teacher, 1977-; Freelance Writer, 1970-; Entertainer, 1983-. *Publications:* Poetry: Fix Life in the Eye; How to Help your Child in School, Booklet. *Contributions to:* Pegasus; Column in two newspapers. *Memberships:* Phi Delta Kappa, Newsletter Editor; Delta Kappa Gama, Newsletter Editor; President, Mississipi Association of Educators; President; Itawamba Junior College Alumni Association; Worthy Matron, Order of the Eastern Star; North East Mississipi Writers Association. *Honours:* Plaque, Appreciation for promoting education, Itawamba Junior College, 1979-80; Teacher of the Year, Pontotoc Co School, 1980; Monetary Award for 2nd Best Tall Tale Teller in the State of Mississipi, 1987; Endorsement of Teachers in State Senate Race. *Hobbies:* Reading; Writing; Entertaining and travel. *Address:* Rt 3, Box 54, Houlka, MS 38850, USA.

HILL Rosalind Mary Theodosia, b. 14 Nov. 1908, Neston, Cheshire, England. Professor Emeritus. *Education:* BA, 1st class honours, 1931, BLitt 1937, MA 1936, St Hilda's College, Oxford. *Appointments:* Assistant Lecturer, University of Leicester, 1932-37; Lecturer, Westfield College, University of London, 1937-56; Reader, 1956-72, Professor, 1972-77, London University. *Publications:* Editions of the Rolls and Register of Bishop Sutton (8 volumes); Register of Archbishop Melton (2 volumes proceeding); Anonymi Gesta Francorum; Numerous articles. *Memberships:* Historical Association; Society of Antiquaries of London; Royal Society of Arts; Canterbury and York Society (Vice President); Ecclesiastical History Society (past President); Lincoln Record Society. *Hobbies:* Mountain climbing; Gardening; Archaeology; Cats; Embroidery; Medieval History. *Address:* 7 Loom Lane, Radlett, Hertfordshire, WD7 8AA, England.

HILL Sylvia I. Bennett, b. 15 Aug. 1940, Jacksonville, Florida, USA. University Professor; Political Activist. 1 daughter. *Education:* BS, 1963; MS, 1966; PhD, 1971;

Nationally Certified Counsellor, 1984. *Appointments:* Professor, Macalester College, 1971-74; Professor, University of District of Columbia, 1974-; Professor, Union for Experimenting Colleges and Universities, 1978-. *Memberships:* Founding Member and Member of Steering Committee, Free South Africa Movement; Co-Chairperson, Southern Africa Support Project; Board Member, TransAfrica and TransAfrica Forum. *Honours:* Who's Who in Black America, 1984. *Hobbies:* Community activist for political empowerment and human rights domestically and internationally. *Address:* PO Box 50103, Washington, DC 20004, USA.

HILL-BEUF Ann Harper, b. 1 Oct. 1938, Philadelphia, Pennsylvania, USA. Professor of Sociology; Director of Women's Center. m. 21 Mar. 1955. 2 sons, 1 daughter. *Education:* AB 1969, MA, Sociology 1971, PhD, Sociology 1972, Bryn Mawr. *Appointments:* Assistant Professor of Sociology 1972-81, Director, Women's Studies 1976-81, University of Pennsylvania; Professor of Sociology 1981-, Director, Women's Center 1983-, Cedar Crest College; Instructor, Medical College of Pennsylvania, 1987-. *Publications:* Books: Red Children in White America, 1977; Biting Off the Bracelet: Hospitalization and Children, 1979; Biting Off the Bracelet: A Study of Children in Hospitals, 2nd edition, 1988; numerous articles to professional journals and to conferences. Poetry: About Authenticity; Friendly Dunce; Genesis I; Son; Knight. *Memberships:* American Soc Association, Minority Fellowship Committee; Pennsylvania Soc Society; National Womens Studies Association; National Womens Centers Association, Coordinating Board; Editor of Newsletter; YMCA, Board of Directors, Allentown. *Honours:* Ford Foundation Dissertation Grant, 1971-72; NIH Research Grant, 1976-80; Fulbright/Hayes Teaching Grant, Waikato, New Zealand, 1983; Lindback Award for Distinguished Teaching, 1981; Special Recognition, Cedar Crest College, 1987; Honourable mention, American Poetry Association for poem, Friendly Dunce. *Hobbies:* Photography; Painting; Travel; Poetry; Music. *Address:* Cedar Crest College, Allentown, PA 18104, USA.

HILLER Wendy, Dame, b. 1912. Actress. m. Ronald Gow, 1937. 1 son, 1 daughter. *Education:* Winceby House, Bexhill. *Career:* Manchester Repertory Theatre; Sir Barry Jackson's tour of Evensong; Sally Harcastle in Love on the Dole, London and New York; leading parts in Saint Joan and Pygmalion at Malvern Festival, 1936. *Creative works:* Plays include: Twelfth Night; Cradle Song; The First Gentleman; Tess of the d'Urbervilles; The Heiress; Ann Veronica; Waters of the Moon, 1951-53; The Night of the Ball, 1955; Old Vic Season, 1955-56; Moon for the Misbegotten, 1957; Flowering Cherry, 1958; Toys in the Attic, 1960; Aspern Papers, 1962; The Wings of the Dove, 1963; The Sacred Flame, 1967; When We Dead Awaken, 1968; The Battle of Shrivings, 1970; Crown matriomonial, 1972; John Gabriel Borkman, 1975; Lies! 1975; Waters of the Moon, 1977, 1978; The Old Jest, 1980; The Importance of Being Earnest, 1981; The Aspern Papers, 1984; Devil and Miss Davey, Apollo Theatre, 1988. Films: Pygmalion; Major Barbara; I Know Where I'm Going; Outcast of the Islands; Separate Tables; Sons and Lovers; Toys in the Attic; A Man for All Seasons; David Copperfield; Murder on the Orient Express; The Elephant Man. Television: When We Dead Awaken, 1968; Peer Gynt, 1972; Clochemerle, 1973; Last Wishes, 1978; Richard II, 1979; Miss Morison's Ghosts, 1981; The Kingfisher; Witness for the Prosecution; Attracta, 1982; The Comedy of Errors, 1983; Death of the Heart, 1985; Darley's Folly; All Passion Spent; The Importance of Being Earnest, 1986. *Honours:* Academy Award; Honorary LLD, Manchester, 1984; OBE 1971; DBE 1975. *Address:* c/o ICM, 388/396 Oxford Street, London W1N 9HE, England.

HILLMAN Carol B, Company Vice President. *Education:* BA, University of Wisconsin, 1961; MA, Cornell University Graduate School, 1966. *Appointments:* Assistant Editor, Holt Rinehart & Winston, 1965-66; Staff Associate, Public Relations, 1966-74, Eastern Airlines; Manager, Public Affairs, Squibb Corp., 1974-75; Assistant Director, 1975-77, Director, 1977-80, Vice President, 1980-82, Public Relations, Burlington Industries; Vice President, Corporate Communications, Norton Co., 1982-90; National Director, Public Relations and Communications, Deloitte and Touche, 1990. *Memberships:* Boston Cluub, Womens Economic Forum; various other professional organisations. *Address:* 299 Belknap Road, Framingham, MA 01701, USA.

HILLS Julia Margaret, b. 3 Apr. 1957, Nottingham, England. Actress. *Education:* BA Honours, Drama/English, University of Bristol, 1975-78. *Creative Works:* Theatre work includes: York Theatre Royal, 1978-79; Phantom Captain Theatre Company, 1979; Bristol Old Vic, 1979-80, 1980-81; Royal Shakespeare Company, 1981-83 in The Winter's Tale; All's Well That Ends Well; Our Friend's in the North; Poppy. Manchester Library Theatre, 1983; Bristol Old Vic, Christmas 1983-84; Emily, Leicester Haymarket, 1984; The Hired Man, Astoria Theatre, London. Television work includes: The Lost Tribe, BBC 1980; Reith, BBC 1983; Winter Harvest, BBC 1983; Who Dares Wins, Channel 4, 1984. *Membership:* Equity-Actors' Union, Deputy for RSC, 1981-83. *Honours:* Special Recommendation for Practical Work in Theatre, Drama Department, University of Bristol, 1978; Nomination for Laurence Olivier Award for Best Actress in Musical, The Hired Man. *Hobby:* Cooking for fun. *Address:* c/o Astoria Theatre, Charing Cross Road, London WC2, England.

HILL SMITH Marilyn, b. 9 Feb. 1952, Carshalton, Surrey, England. Soprano. m. Peter Kemp, 7 Dec. 1974. *Education:* Guildhall School of Music; AGSM (Distinction in Recital Diploma), Young Musician of Year, 1975. *Appointments:* Cabaret, Pantomime, Concerts, 1971-74; Toured Australia, New Zealand, USA, Canada, 1974-76; Principal Soprano, English National Opera, 1978-84; Debut: Royal Opera, Covent Garden, 1981; Appears regularly with English Bach Festival, Aldeburgh Festival, European Festivals; Debut with Welsh National Opera, 1987, Scottish Opera, 1988; appeared with Canadian Opera & New Sadlers Wells Opera; Frequent broadcasts BBC Radio; Commercial recordings of operetta. *Memberships:* Associate, Guildhall School of Music. *Hobbies:* Gardening; Cooking; Sleeping! *Address:* c/o Music International, 13 Ardilaun Road, Highbury, London N5 2QR, England.

HILSENBECK Susan Galloway, b. 24 Feb. 1952, Wilmington, USA. Biostatistician. m. Charles E Hilsenbeck, 23 Mar. 1974, divorced 1987. *Education:* BS, 1974, MS, 1977, PhD, 1989, University of Miami. *Appointments:* Biostatistician, Papanicolaan Comprehensive Cancer Centre, 1977-; Instructor, University of Miami, 1986-. *Publications:* Co-author, Quality Control for Cancer Registers, 1985; articles in professional journals. *Memberships:* American Statistical Association; Biometric Society; Society for Clinical Trials. *Honours:* Magtag Fellowship, 1974-77; Wilson Prize, Wilson Ornithologicla Society, 1978; University of Miami Fellowship, 1984-87; University of Miami Phi Lambda Pi Award. *Hobbies:* Gardening; Quilting. *Address:* PO Box 016960 D8-4, Miami, FL 33101, USA.

HILT Diane Elaine, b. 3 Jan. 1944, Gadsden, Alabama, USA. Teacher; Computer Specialist. m. James H. Hilt Jr, 13 Mar. 1968. *Education:* BS, Jacksonville State University, 1965; MEd, Georgia State University, 1972. *Appointments:* Teacher: Trinity Private School, 1968; Phoenix City School System, 1969; Post Dependent School System, 1970-. *Memberships:* Professional Educators' Association; Association for Curriculum & Development; National Council for Teachers of Mathematics; Secretary, Benning Education Association; Georgia Education Association; Delegate, National Education Association. *Honours:* Danforth Foundation, 1961; Participant, NASA Teacher-in-Space programme, 1986. *Hobbies:* Bridge; Shopping; Travel. *Address:* 3301 Tewson Drive, Columbus, Georgia 31909, USA.

HILTON Donnette L, b. 14 Sept. 1935, Minneapolis, Minnesota, USA. Projects Director, US Senator Rudy Boschwitz. m. Michael J Hilton. *Appointments:* President/owner, Mattison Processing Service, 1973-81; Projects Director for US Senator Rudy Boschwitz, 1981-; Vice President, Hilton Fire Brick Co. *Memberships:* Womens Political Caucus; Minneapolis Legal Secretaries Association, Past President; National Association of Legal Secretaries; American Swedish Institute; Pet Haven; Minnesota Vice Chairwoman Republican Party, 1979-81; Minnesota Republican State Central Committee, 1979- *Hobbies:* Volunteer American Red Cross; Advisor to political campaigns. *Address:* 4322 Kaufmanis Way, Eagan, Minnesota 55123, USA.

HILTON (Annie) Winifred, b. 26 July 1919, Scotland House, Tansley, Matlock, Derbyshire, England. Wife, Lord Lieutenant of Derbyshire; Voluntary Worker. m. Peter Hilton, 8 Jan. 1942, 2 sons. *Education:* Private governess; Diploma, National Domestic Science Training College, London, 1936; ATCL, Elocution, Drama, History, Trinity College of Music, London, 1938. *Appointment:* Teacher, Drama, History, English & Games, Rose Lea School for Girls, Hillam, Yorkshire, 1938-39; Director 1940-86, Chairman 1965-86, James Smith (Scotland) Nurseries Ltd, Tansley, Derbyshire (holders, Royal Warrant to Queen, Nurserymen); County President, St John Ambulance, 1969-; County Chairman 1977-, East Midlands Vice President 1981-, National Vice-President, 1981-, Women's Section, Royal British Legion; County Organiser, Women's Royal Voluntary Service (WRVS), 1973-86; President, East Midlands, Home & Leisure Safety, 1979-. *Memberships:* County Chairman, County Vice President, British Heart Foundation; Chairman, Mid & West Derbyshire, National Society for Prevention of Cruelty to Children (NSPCC); Arthritis & Rheumatism Council; County Committees, War Pensions, Royal Society for Prevention of Cruelty to Animals; President Derbbyshire Royal Infirmary League of Friends, 1979-; Vice President, Citizens Advice Bureau, Derby, 1989; Chairman, Derbyshire RNLI Appeal. *Honours:* Serving Sister, Officer Sister, Commander Sister, Dame, St John Ambulance; National Golden Award, National Vice President, Women's Section, Royal British Legion; National Council, NSPCC; County Award, Derbyshire Girl Guides Association; Long Service Medal and 2 Bars (50 years' service), WRVS. *Hobbies include:* Gardening; Community service. *Address:* Alton Manor, Idridgehay, Derbyshire, England.

HIMES Joanna Dee Saunders, b. 2 Aug. 1952, Huntington, West Virginia, USA. Interior Designer; Sales Executive. m. Robert Curtis Himes, 25 Mar. 1972, 1 con, 1 daughter. *Education:* BA, University of Kentucky, Lexington, 1978; Passsed Examination of National Council for Interior Design Qualification, 1982. *Appointments:* President, Himes Designs, Paintsville, Kentucky, 1978-83; President, Commercial Design Center Inc, Destin, Florida, 1985-87; Vice-President, Interstate of Florida, Division of Missco Corporation, Destin, 1987-. *Membership:* Professional Member, American Society of Interior Designers. *Hobbies:* Reading; Sewing; Knitting; Scuba-diving; Travel; Her children. *Address:* 215 Mountain Drive, Suite 110, Destin, FL 32541, USA.

HINCKLEY Barbara, b. 12 Aug. 1937, Boston, USA. Professor. 2 daughters. *Education:* AB, magna cum laude, Mt. Holyoke College, 1959; PhD, Cornell University, 1968. *Appointments:* Assistant Professor, Cornell University, 1970-72; Professor, University of Wisconsin, Madison, 1972-87; Professor, New York University, 1987-. *Publications:* 7 books including: the Symbolic Presidency; Stability & Change in Congress; Congressional Elections; Coalitions & Politics; The Seniority System in Congress; 2 dozen articles in journals; Consultant ABC News for congressional elections. *Memberships:* American Political Science Association, past Vice-President; Midwest Political Science Association, Past Vice President; Legislative Studies, past President. *Honours:* Phi Beta Kappa; Guggenheim Fellow, 1974; LLD, Hon., Mt. Holyoke College, 1984. *Address:* 29 Washington Square West No 4CN, New York, NY 10011, USA.

HINCKLEY Helen (Jones), b. 12 Apr. 1903, Provo, Utah, USA. Writer; Lecturer; Teacher. m. Ivan Charles Jones, 29 June 1938. 2 daughters,. *Education:* BS 1924, MS 1928, Brigham Young University; Studied at: Stanford, Utah State, University of California at Berkeley and Cambridge. *Appointments:* Teacher, Junior High and High School, 1924-38; College Teacher, 1951-75; Instructor of private classes, 1978-85. *Publications:* Translations into Swahili, Hindi, Turkish, Urdu: Mountain Arc Mine, 1946; Persian Village, 1953; A Wall and Three Willows, 1967; Israel, 1986; children's poems and numerous other books. *Memberships:* Authors Guild, Inc; PEN International; Society of Children's Book Writers; California's Council on Literature for Children and Young People. *Honours:* Distinctive Achievements in the Arts, Ira Nathaniel Hinckley Family; Distinguished Service Alumni Award, Brigham Young University; Distinguished Contribution to the Field of Children's Literature, SCCLCYP; Heritage Award, California; Distinguished Services Award. *Address:* 1191 East Mendocino Street, Altadena, CA 91001, USA.

HINDS Sallie Ann Chriscaden, b. 8 June 1930, Saginaw, Michigan, USA. Sims Township Treasurer. m. James F Hinds, 25 Aug. 1951. 2 daughters. *Education:* MacMurray College for Women; Speciality classes, Michigan State University. *Appointments:* Research Secretary, 1949-51; Television Traffic Manager, 1951-59; TV Model, 1951-59; Township Treasurer, 1980-; Elected two terms, up for re-election, 1988. *Publications:* Book: Bits & Pieces of Nature's Seasons; Several poems published. *Memberships:* US Coast Guard Auxiliary, Public Relations; Arenac County Historical Society, President, Vice-President, Secretary, Board of Directors; Northeast Michigan Arts Council, Board of Directors; Michigan Mutual Treasurers Association; St Joseph Hospital, Development Council. *Honours:* Designer: Saginaw Township Seal, 1976; Northeast Michigan Arts Council Logo, 1983; Omer Sucker Festival Logo, 1984; Omer Chamber of Commerce Logo, 1985; Michigan Airways, Inc Logo, 1987; Arenac County Homemaker of the Year, 1980; 1st 1986, 2nd 1987, Dress a Doll for Needy; World of Poetry: Silver Poet Award, 1986, Golden Poet Award 1987; Many awards for Artwork: Copper, Watercolour, Pastels, Charcoal and coloured pencil. *Hobbies:* Writing; Needlework; Artwork with copper; Sculpting; Sketching; Cross country skiing; Hiking; Nature study. *Address:* 767 Crescent Drive, Point Lookout, Au Gres, Michigan 48703, USA.

HINEMAN Nancy L, b. 23 Mar. 1951, West Chester, USA. Company Owner. 1 son. *Appointments:* Cosmetologist, Owner, Beauty Salon, Media, 1969-74; Detective & Polygraphist, Criminal Investigation Division, Delaware County District Attorneys Office, 1975-78; Co-owner, Urella's Detective Bureau, 1975-; Attended US Monetary War College, 1988. *Memberships:* Pennsylvania Polygraph Association; National Detective Association; National Association of Female Executives. *Honours:* Selected Liaision Officer for Women Against Rape Organization, 1975-78; First Woman Detective in 50 year History of the District Attorney's Office; First Woman Polygraphist in Delaware County. *Hobbies:* Tennis; Skiing; Horse Riding; Volleyball; Swimming. *Address:* 160 Paxon Hollow Road, Media, PA 19063, USA.

HINES Lyla Mae, b. 20 Apr. 1935, Cliff, New Mexico, USA. Paralegal. m. (1) William Thomas Jackson, 26 Sept. 1953, divorced 1970, 1 son, 4 daughters. (2) Charles Luther Hines, 12 Mar. 1971, 1 daughter. *Memberships:* Director, National Federation of Paralegal Associations, 1987-89; Secretary 1984-86, President Elect 1986-89, President 1987-88, Dallas Association of Legal Assistants; Advisory Board, Legal Assistants Program, Southern Methodist University, Dallas, Texas; Advisory Board, Southeastern Paralegal Institute, Dallas, Texas; Legal Assistants Division, State Bar of Texas. *Address:* 5206 Chestnut Place, Garland, TX 75043, USA.

HINMAN Myra M, b. 11 Jan. 1926, Saginaw County, Michigan, USA. Professor of English Literature. m. Charlton J K Hinman, 1968. 1 son. *Education:* Michigan State University, 1943-46; BS, Columbia University, 1947; MA 1954, PhD 1959, University of Florida. *Appointments:* Department of English, Assistant Professor, Memphis State University, 1959-61; Instructor, 1961-63, Assistant Professor, 1963-68, Associate Professor, 1968-, University of Kansas. *Creative works:* A Finding List in English and American Literature, 1970; Contributor to: Shakespeare Quarterly; Folklore; Bibliographic Bulletin, International Arthurian Society; Papers: International Arthurian Congress - Caen, France 1966 and Leuven, Belgium 1988; MLA New York, Comp Literature, 1966; MLA Editing Seminar, 1975; MLA Shakespeare's Diction, 1979; International Shakespeare Congress, Stratford- upon-Avon, England, 1981; Assistant Textual Editor, Hinman Shakespeare; Work on John Le Carré, in progress; (Paper on Malozy and Charles Williams' Grail Masses and Role of Evangelists). *Memberships include:* MLA; Midwest MLA; Kansas Folklore Society; International Arthurian Society; Shakespeare Association of America; United Burmese Cat Fanciers. *Honour:* Phi Kappa Phi; ACLS Travel Grant, 1966. *Hobbies:* Clothing design; Breeder of Burmese cats. *Address:* 1932 Maine Street, Lawrence, KS 66046, USA.

HINSON Catherine Louise Brewer, b. 3 Aug. 1951, Guilford County, North Carolina. Administrative Assistant. m. Tampa Bryant Hinson, 24 Aug. 1972, 2 sons, 2 daughters. *Education:* BA, High Point College, 1973; MEd., University of North Carolina, 1979. *Appointments:* Teacher, HP College, 1973-76; Independent District, Meadow Fresh Farms, 1981-83; The China Lion Collection, 1983-85; Market Management Association Inc., 1985-; Touch of Beauty Inc., 1985-88; IMSI Inc., 1989. *Memberships:* Certified Contractor, Carpet appearance Management; Specialist, Chemspec Inc; Association of Specialists in Cleaning & Restoration. *Honours:* Recipient, various Certificates and Awards. *Hobbies:* Karate; Weight Training; Art; Piano; Organ; Voice. *Address:* 1925 Chestnut Street, High Point, NC 27260, USA.

HIOTIS Helene, b. 16 Jan. 1951, Petra, Greece. m. Leandros Hiotis, 1 son, 1 daughter (twins). *Publications:* Articles in numerous magazines & journals. *Memberships:* Council Member, Equality, 1984-85, General Secretary 1985-. *Honours:* Verona & Mazgo, 1986; International Prize of Agriculture, 1988. *Hobby:* Family. *Address:* Petra Lesros, Greece 81109.

HIRANO Arlene Akiko, b. 24 Oct. 1962, Los Angeles, California, USA. Graduate Fellow. *Education:* BS, cum laude, University of California, Irvine, 1980-84; The Rockefeller University, 1984-. *Memberships:* American Association for the Advancement of Science; Society for Neuroscience. *Honours:* University of California Regents' Scholar, 1980-84; University of California President's Undergraduate Fellowship, 1983-84; UCI School of Biological Sciences Excellence in Research, 1984; Alpha Epsilon Delta Pre-Medical Honor Society, 1982-84; The Rockefeller University Graduate Fellowship, 1984-90; Lucille P Markey Charitable Trust Graduate Fellow, 1984-89. *Address:* Laboratory of Neurobiology, The Rockefeller University, 1230 York Avenue, New York, NY 10021, USA.

HIRD Thora, b. 28 May 1914, Morecambe, Lancashire, England. *Education:* The Nelson School, Morecambe. *Creative Works:* Films include: Screen debut 1940; The Black Sheep of Whitehall; Street Corner; Turn the Key Softly; Personal Affair; The Great Game; Storks Don't Talk; Shop Soiled; For Better or Worse; Love Match; One Good Turn; Quatermass Experiment; Simon and Laura; Lost; Sailor Beware; Home and Away; Good Companions; The Entertainer; A Kind of Loving; Term of Trial; Bitter Harvest; Rattle of A Simple Man; Some Will, Some Won't; The Nightcomers. Television: The Winslow Boy; The Bachelor; What Happens to Love; The Witching Hour; So Many Children; The Queen Came By; Albert Hope;

All Things Bright and Beautiful; Say Nothing; Meet the Wife; Who's A Good Boy Then? I AM!; Dixon of Dock Green; Romeo & Juliet; The First Lady; Ours is a Nice House; The Foxtrot; Seasons; She Stoops to Conquer; Villa Maroc; When We Are Married; In Loving Memory; Flesh and Blood; Your Songs of Praise Choice; Hallelujah; Happiness; Thats the Main Thing; Intensive Care; In Loving Memory; Praise Be; Last of the Summer Wine; The Fall. *Address:* c/o Felix de Wolfe, Manfield House, 376 The Strand, London WC2R OLR, England.

HIRSCH Arlene, b. 18 Mar. 1951, Chicago, Illinois, USA. Career Counsellor. *Education:* BA English, University of Iowa, 1973; MA Counselling Psychology, Northwestern University, 1983. *Appointments:* Supervisor, Neighbourhood Development, Council for Jewish Elderly, 1983-84; Instructor, Discovery Center, 1984-; Private Practice, Career Counselling and Psychotherapy, 1983-; Instructor, De Paul University, 1986-. *Publications:* Numerous articles in professional journals, magazines and newspapers. *Memberships:* Women Employed; YWCA; Association of Labor; Management Consultants on Alcoholism; American Association of Counseling and Development. *Honours:* Marcus and Therese Levie Foundation Scholarship, 1983. *Hobbies:* Aerobics; Racquetball. *Address:* 850 North State Street Suite 27K, Chicago, Illinois 60610, USA.

HIRSCH Ilona Ruth, b. 5 Apr. 1954, St Louis, Missouri, USA. Orthopaedic Surgeon. *Education:* BS, University of California, 1975; MD, Stanford University Medical School, 1979; Internship and Residency, Stanford University Hospital. *Appointments:* Private Practice, 1985-. *Memberships:* Candidate Member, American Acadmy of Orthopaedic Surgery; Sports Medicine Committee, Los Angeles County Medical Association; Los Angeles County Womens Medical Association. *Honours:* Ethel Terry McCoy Award. *Hobbies:* Former professional Ballet Dancer. *Address:* 9001 Wilshire Blvd., Suite 205, Beverly Hills, CA 90211, USA.

HIRSHMAN Carol Ann, b. 12 Aug. 1944, Montreal, Canada. Anesthesiologist; Professor. m. John Hirshman, 31 Jan. 1970, 1 son. *Education:* BSc, 1965, MD, 1969, McGill University; Resident, 1970-72, Fellow, 1972-73, University of Colorado, Denver, USA. *Appointments:* Instructor, 1974, Assistant Professor, 1974-75, University of Colorado, Denver; Assistant Professor, 1976-80, Associate Professor, 1980-82, Professor, 1982-86, University of Oregon; Professor, Johns Hopkins University and Hospital, Baltimore, Maryland, 1986-. *Publications:* 20 book chapters; 79 original manuscripts; 100 abstracts. *Memberships:* Alpha Omega Alpha; Association of University Anesthesiologists; American Society of Anesthesiologists; American Physiological Society; American Thoracic Society. *Address:* Department of Anesthesiology, Johns Hopkins Hospital, 600 North Wolfe Street, Baltimore, MD 21205, USA.

HITCHENS Marilynn Giroux, b. 14 Dec. 1938, Detroit, Michigan, USA. Instructor; Historian. m. Benjamin Franklin Hitchens, 17 Aug. 1974, 2 daughters. *Education:* BA, History, 1960; MA, History, 1975; PhD, History, 1979. *Appointments:* Jefferson County Schools, 1960-65, 1970-; Pan American, 1965-67; USA Congress, 1967-69; Instructor, University of Denver, 1984-85; Instructor, Loretta Heights College, 1985-86. *Publications:* Germany, Russia & the Balkans: Prelude to the Nazi Soviet Non-Agression Pact, 1939; The World: A Television History Contributing Authors. *Memberships:* World History Association, President; American Historical Association; American Council of Teachers of Russian. *Honours:* Scholarship Award, Colorado Congress of Foreign Language Teachers; Phi Beta Kappa; NDEA Language Institutes. *Hobbies:* Travel; Hiking. *Address:* 720 Josephine, Denver, CO 80206, USA.

HITE Linda Susan, b. 31 Aug. 1956, Camp Le Jeune,

North Carolina, USA. Senior Administrative Dietitian. *Education:* BS, Erskine College; MS, University of Alabama, Birmingham. *Appointments:* Registered Dietitian, Trainee, Centre for Developmental & Learning Disorders, 1980-81; Biology Instructor, Alabama Christian College, 1981-82; Food Service Supervisor, 1982-83, Administrator, 1983-84, Senior Administrator, University of Alabama Hospital. *Memberships:* Birmingham, Alabama & American Dietetic Associations (President Birmingham Dietetic Associatiron 1988-89); many other organisations. *Honours:* Biology Award, AAUW, 1976, 1977; William Ellison Biology Award, 1977. *Hobbies:* Jogging; Cycling; Drums; Sports. *Address:* 306 St. Charles St., Birmingham, AL 35209, USA.

HJORTH Noela Jane, b. 5 Dec. 1940, Melbourne, Australia. Artist. *Education:* Prahran Institute of Technology and RMIT, Melbourne, Australia, 1958-62; Chelsea School of Art, London, England, 1969-71. *Appointments:* Lectured part-time, Caulfield Institute of Technology, 1973-74; In charge of Printmaking, Box Hill Technical College, 1975-79; Vice-President, The Print Council of Australia, 1976; Founder Member and Co-Ordinator, Victorian Printmakers Group and Workshop, 1976-80; Established own etching studio, 1972-; Artist-in-Residence, Riverina College of Advanced Education, 1980. *Creative Works include:* One Woman Exhibitions: The Gallery, Hornsey London and Gallery 273, London, England, 1970; Battersea District Library, London, 1971; Warehouse Gallery, Melbourne, Australia, 1972; Swan Hill Regional Gallery, Victoria, 1973; Victor Mace Gallery, Brisbane, 1977; Solander Gallery, Canberra 1978, 1984; Robin Gibson, Sydney, 1978; Salamanca Place Gallery, Tasmania, 1979; Burnie Art Gallery, Tasmania, 1979; Greenhill Gallery, Adelaide, 1979; Fremantle Arts Centre, 1980; Powell Street Gallery, Melbourne, 1980; Riverina College of Advanced Education, 1980; Silpakorn University, Thailand, 1980; Hawthorn City Art Gallery, Melbourne, 1980; Wagga Regional Gallery, 1980; Kalamunda Gallery of Man, Perth, 1982; Tynte Gallery, Adelaide 1982, 1984; Niagara Galleries, Melbourne, 1984; Hogarth Galleries, Sydney, 1983; Northern Territory Museum of Arts and Sciences, 1988. Group Exhibitions: Leveson Street Gallery, Melbourne; Hawthorn City Gallery, Melbourne; Morley Art Gallery, London, England, 1970; South London Art Gallery, London, 1981; Australian Printmakers Impression Gallery, Melbourne, 1978; Melbourne Printmakers Bookshelf Gallery, Melbourne; Print Council of Australia, Travelling Exhibitions including the 1977 Japan Print Association 45th Exhibition; Victorians Printmakers Workshop Travelling Exhibition, CAS Adelaide; Susan Gillespie Galleries, Canberra; Naracoorte Regional Gallery, SA; Brisbane Civic Centre; Gallerie Dusseldort, Perth; Blackfriars Gallery, Sydney; Caulfield Arts Centre, 1978-80; Fifteen Australian Printmakers Queensland Arts Council, 1980. Collections: Australian National Gallery, ACT; Art Gallery of NSW; WA State Gallery; Tasmanian State Gallery; Swan Hill Regional Gallery; Burnie Regional Gallery, Tasmania; Stanthorpe Regional Gallery, Queensland; Wagga Wagga Regional Gallery; Latrobe Valley Arts Centre; Western Australian Institute of Technology; Riverina College of Advanced Education, Wagga Wagga; Box Hill Technical College, Victoria; Gainsborough Collection, London; Art Gallery of South Australia; Northern Territory Museum of Arts and Sciences; National Gallery of Victoria; Newcastle Region Art Gallery; other private and public collections. Book: Lasting Impressions by Pat Gilmour. *Honours:* Directory of Australian Printmakers 1976; Artists and Galleries of Australia and New Zealand, Lansdowne Editions 1980; Noela Hjorth, Granrott Press, Clarendon SA; Printmaking film Needle, Gouge and Crayon purchased by the State Film Centre; Australian Print Prize, Westmead. *Address:* PO Box 6, Clarendon, 5157 South Australia.

HLAVA Marjorie Maxine Kimmel, b. 9 June 1946, Manistee, Michigan, USA. Company President. m. Paul Frank Hlava, 2 Sept. 1967, 2 daughters. *Education:* BS, Botany, Secondary Education, University of Wisconsin, 1970; Graduate study, Botany, Information Science, University of New Mexico, 1974-76. *Appointments:* Information Scientist, Technology Application Center, 1973-76, Manager of Information, Technology Application Center, 1976-78, Information Director, National Energy Information Center Affiliate, Department of Energy, 1978, University of New Mexico, Albuquerque; Founder, President, Marketing Director, Access Innovations Inc, Albuquerque, 1978-. *Publications:* The Solar Energy Information Explosion (with Geoffrey Bell), 1978; The NASA Information System, 1978; Effective Search Strategies (with D.RKnox), 1979; Online Identification, Verification, and Ordering of Conference Publications, Conference Literature: Its Role in the Distribution of Information, 1981; Private File Creation/Database Construction: A Proceeding with Five Case Studies, 1984; Other journal contributions; Running Your Own Business (book chapter), 1984. *Memberships:* Special Libraries Association, Past Chapter President; Southwest Library Association, Past Online Bibliographic User Group Chair; National Online Circuit, Past Chair; New Mexico Library Association; Greater Albuquerque Library Assocaition; Western Information Network of Energy; New Mexico Online User Group, Past Chair; Association for Information Dissemination Centers, Chair 1985, President 1985-86, 1986-87; American Society for Information Science, Board Member 1986-87; Information Industry Association; Numerous committees and offices. *Honours:* Numerous. *Hobbies:* Needlework; Gardening; Birding; Sewing; Theatre, symphony and opera. *Address:* 4000 Smith SE, Albuquerque, NM 87108, USA.

HLAVAY Sarah Inez (Sally) Wood, b. 10 Dec. 1942, Corvallis, Oregon, USA. Management Consultant; Fund Raiser. m. Joseph Francis Hlavay, 3 Aug. 1985. *Education:* BS, University of Georgia, 1964; MA Teaching, Emory University, 1965; Ford Foundation Fellowship; MBA, Pepperdine University, 1979. *Appointments:* Social Studies Coordinator/Teacher, Holy Innocents' Parish Day School, Altanta, Georgia, 1965-68; Administrative Assistant/Copy Trainee, Dorothy Freedman and Associates, 1969; Regional Promotion Manager, Milliken Inc, New York (Agilon Division); Assistant Regional Sales Manager, Great Southwest (Kex Division); Regional Sales Manager, Pacific Northwest, USA and Canada (Kex Division) Los Angeles, 1969- 74; Account Executive, Clinique Laboratories Inc, Southern California, Los Angeles, 1974-75; Area Manager, Norton Simon Inc, Orlane Division, Great Southwest, Los Angeles, 1975-79; Area Representative, Payot (ITT), Los Angeles, 1979; Management Consultant/Fund Raiser, 1979-; Teacher of English as a Second Language, Beverly Hills Adult school, California, 1000-01, Regional Representative, St Jude Children's Research Hospital (Mid-Atlantic Region), Arlington, Virginia, 1982-83; Associate Director of Alumni Giving, Associate Director of Alumni Relations, Emory University, Atlanta, Georgia. *Memberships include:* National Society of Fund-Raising Executives, Georgia Chapter, Treasurer; National Charity League-Beaux Arts, Vice Chairman; National Society Daughters of the American Revolution, Beverly Hills Chapter, Vice Regent; Colonial Dames of America. *Honours:* Athens Pilot Club Award, 1962, 1963, 1964; Most Oustanding Alumna in support of Delta Alpha Chapter, Alpha Gamma Delta, 1976; Alpha Gamma Delta Honour of Epsilon Pi, 1977; Juvenile Diabetes Foundation, Award of Distinction, 1981. *Hobbies:* Doll collecting; Dancing; Reading; Needlepoint; Gourmet cooking; Travel; Historic preservation; Piano; Art; Riflery. *Address:* 94 Willow Park Green SE, Calgary, Alberta, Canada T2J 3L1.

HO Sylvia, b. 27 Jan. 1952, Hong Kong. Concert Pianist. m. Kam- Yung Lau, 30 June 1979. *Education:* BMus 1974, MMus 1976, Temple University, Philadelphia, USA; Postgraduate studies, Juilliard School of Music, New York, 1976-78. *Appointments:* Faculties: Settlement Music School, Philadelphia, 1974-79; Columbia Basin College, Pasco, Washington, 1979-80; University of Texas, El Paso, 1982-83; El Paso Community College, 1987-88. Performances include: New York debut, Carnegie Hall, 1977; Lincoln Centre;

TV broadcasts; Coast-to-Coast US tour, 1986. *Memberships:* Co-founder, East-West Piano Duo; National Guild of Piano Teachers; Music Teachers Association, California; Juilliard School Alumni Association. *Honours:* Award, Pi Nu Epsilon, 1969; Music scholarship, Philadelphia Board of Education, 1970; Elmer Yarnall scholarship, graduate studies, 1974; Scholarship, Juilliard School, 1976; Winner, Artists International Competition, New York, 1977. *Hobbies:* Reading; Gourmet cooking. *Address:* 20556 Avis Avenue, Torrance, California 90503, USA.

HOANG T K Trang, b. 10 Mar. 1950, Vietnam. Cancer Research Scientist. m. Khoi Huynh, 20 Oct. 1978. *Education:* Diploma of Pharmacist, 1972; Certificate of Biochemistry, 1974; PhD, Experimental Haematology, 1980. *Appointments:* Research Assistant, Swiss Cancer Institute, 1975-80; Research Fellow, Department of Pathology, Cambridge University, Cambridge, England, 1981-82; Research Fellow, Ontario Cancer Institute, Canada, 1983-85; Laboratory Director, Clinical Research Institute of Montreal, 1986-; Assistant Professor, Department of Medicine, University of Montreal. *Publications:* Union Medicale du Canada, 1988; Blood, 1988; Journal of Experimental Medicine, 1988. *Memberships:* Canadian Biochemical Society; American Society of Hematology. *Honours:* Fellowship, European Molecular Biology Organization, 1980-82; Fellowship, Leukemia Research Fund (UK), 1982; Research Scholar, National Cancer Institute, Canada, 1987-93. *Hobbies:* Music; Literature; Cinema. *Address:* Clinical Research Institute of Montreal, 110 Pine Avenue West, Montreal, Quebec H2W 1R7, Canada.

HOBACK Florence Kunst, b. 26 Oct. 1922, Grafton, USA. Psychiatrist. m. John Holland Hoback, 27 Oct. 1945, 1 son, 1 daughter. *Education:* BA, West Virginia University, 1944; MD, University of Maryland, 1948. *Appointments:* Private Practice, Psychiatry, Huntington. *Publications:* Editor, Psychiatry West Virginia, 1968, 1972, 1976, 1986. *Memberships:* West Virginia, Cabell County, Medical Societies; AMA; AMWA, Medical Committee President; Past President, Secretary, News Letter Editor, West Virginia Branch, American Psychiatry Association; League of Women Voters; American Association of University Women; Flower and Field Garden Club. *Hobbies:* Gardening; Writing. *Address:* 2658 3rd Avenue, Huntington, WV 25702, USA.

HOBDEN Sheila Muriel, b. 15 Feb. 1937, Gillingham, Kent, England. Headteacher. *Education:* Teachers Certificate, Birmingham Training College, 1957; Certificate in RE, Westminster College, London, 1958; ACP, 1973; BA, Open University, 1977. *Appointments:* Assistant Teacher, Ford Secondary Modern School, Plymouth, 1958-59; Baskerville School for P.H. Pupils, Birmingham, 1960-64; HQ Staff, Christian Education Movement, London, 1964-69; Head of Department, Burnt Mill School, Harlow, 1969-71; Deputy Head, Joseph Whitaker Comprehensive School, Rainworth, 1971-74; Deputy Head, Arnold Hill Comprehensive School, 1974-82; Head Teacher, Margaret Glen-Bott Comprehensive School, Nottingham, 1982-. *Publications:* Explorations in Worship, 1970; Further Explorations in Worship, 1974; Mother Teresa, 1973; George McLeod, 1975. *Memberships:* CEM General Council & Executive, Vice Chairman, 1986-. *Hobbies:* Fell Walking; Music; DIY. *Address:* The Margaret Glen Bott School, Sutton Passeys Crescent, Wollaton Park, Nottingham NG8 1EA, England.

HOBHOUSE (Mary) Hermione, b. 2 Feb. 1934, Castle Cary, Somerset, England. Urban Historian. *Education:* Honours Degree, Modern History, Oxford, 1954. *Appointments:* Researcher/Scriptwriter, Granada TV, 1958-68; Freelance Writer, 1964-; Tutor in Architectural History, Architectural Association, London, 1973-78; Secretary General, Victorian Society, 1976-82; Organiser, Prince Albert, Life and Work Exhibition, 1982-83; General Editor, Survey of London, 1983-. *Publications:* Thomas Cubitt: Master Builder, 1971; Lost London, 1971; History of Regent Street,

1975; Oxford & Cambridge, 1980; Prince Albert: His Life and Work, 1983; Editor, Volume 42, Survey of London, Southern Kensington, 1986. *Memberships:* Royal Archaelogical Institute; Victorian Society; Clapham Society; *Honours:* Member of the Order of the British Empire (MBE), 1981; GLC Conservation Medal, 1981. *Hobbies:* Gardening; Looking at old buildings. *Address:* Westcombe Stables, Evercreech, Somerset, England.

HOCH Jeanne Marie, b. 18 Feb. 1949, South Dakota, USA. Educator. *Education:* BA, South Dakota State University, 1967-71; Eberhard-Karls-Univ. Tubingen, 1973-75; MA 1971-73, PhD 1976-79, Vanderbilt University. *Appointments:* Teaching Associate, Vanderbilt University, 1979-80; Berea College Assistant Professor, 1980-85, Associate Professor, 1985-, Chairperson of Department of Foreign Languages, 1985-. *Memberships:* American Association of Teachers of German; American Association of Teachers of German, Kentucky Chapter Treasurer, 1981-85; Kentucky Council on the Teaching of Foreign Languages; Modern Language Association. *Honours:* Senior Teaching Fellowship, 1978-79, Teaching Fellowship, 1971-73, 1976-78, Vanderbilt University; Fulbright-Hayes Grant, 1973; Greater South Dakota State Fellowship, BA magna cum laude; Mortar Board, Delta Phi Alpha, Sigma Lambda Sigma, Alpha Lambda Delta, Phi Kappa Phi. *Hobby:* Travel. *Address:* 37 Cherry Lane, Berea, Kentucky 40403, USA.

HOCKING Mary Eunice, b. 8 Apr. 1921, London, England. Novelist. *Publications include:* Most recent novels: Good Daughters; Indifferent Heroes; Welcome Strangers; An Irrelevant Woman; plus 16 other novels. *Memberships:* Society of Authors; Royal Society of Literature; PEN. *Honour:* Fellow, Royal Society of Literature. *Hobbies:* Theatre; Walking. *Address:* 3 Church Row, Lewes, E Sussex, BN7 2PU, England.

HODGE Delma Griffith, b. 20 Aug. 1941, St Thomas, US Virgin Islands. Governmental Purchasing (Procurement) Commissioner. m. Arthur S. Hodge Sr, 28 Sep. 1961, 2 sons. *Education:* Diploma in Commercial Study, Charlotte Amalie High School, 1958; BS, Business and Economics, Illinois Institute of Technology, USA, 1971; MA, Business Administration, College (now University) of the Virgin Islands, 1980. *Appointments:* Various positions, 1958-65, Executive Secretary, 1965-68, Adminstrative Officer, 1968-72, Director of Procurement and Supply, 1972-87, Designated Acting Commissioner of Property and Procurement, 1987, Commissioner of Property and Procurement, 1987-, Department of Property and Procurement, Government of the Virgin Islands. *Memberships:* Charter Member, International Personnel Management Association; President, Eta Phi Beta Sorority, Alpha Chi Chapter; State Convention Secretary, Business and Professional Women's Club; League of Women Voters; National Association of Female Executives; SOHGC, Order of the Eastern Star, State of New York (District Deputy Grand Matron, 12th District). *Honours:* National Secretaries Association (International) Award for Outstanding and Dedicated Service in Property and Procurement, 1981; Citation for contribution as Instructor on the G.V.I. Accounting System 22-26 Feb. 1982, Association of Governmental Accountants, 1982; Ann Porter Award for Outstanding Achievement in Procurement, Eta Phi Beta, 1942. *Hobbies:* Gardening; Travel; Dancing; Music appreciation; Reading in a wide range of general and business publications. *Address:* Agnes Fancy No 97A, PO Box 2021, Veterans Drive Station, Charlotte Amalie, St Thomas, VI 00803, USA.

HODGE Jane Aiken, b. 4 Dec. 1917, Boston, Massachusetts, USA. Author. m. Alan Hodge, 3 Jan. 1948, deceased May 1979. 2 daughters. *Education:* BA Hons, English, Somerville College, Oxford, 1935-38; AM, Radcliffe College, Cambridge, Massachusetts, USA, 1938-39. *Appointments:* Assistant British Board of Trade, Washington DC, USA, 1942-44; British Supply Council, 1944-45; Research, Time Inc, New York City,

1945-47; Life Magazine, London, England, 1947-48. *Publications:* Books: Maulever Hall; The Adventurers; Watch the Wall, My Darling; Here Comes a Candle; The Winding Stair; Marry in Haste; Greek Wedding; Savannah Purchase; Strangers in Company; Shadow of a Lady; One Way to Venice; Rebel Heiress; Runaway Bride; Judas Flowering; Red Sky at Night; Last Act; Wide is the Water; The Lost Garden; Secret Island; Polonaise; First Night. Non-fiction: The Double Life of Jane Austen; The Private World of Georgette Heyer. *Memberships:* Society of Authors; Writers Guild of America; Authors' Lending & Copyright Society; Lewes Monday Literary Club. *Hobbies:* Theatre; Music; Opera; Walking; Conservation; Politics; Travel; Archaeology; My family. *Address:* 23 Eastport Lane, Lewes, East Sussex, BN7 1TL, England.

HODGES Janice Kay, b. 11 Sep. 1945, Miami, Oklahoma, USA. University Professor; Concert Pianist. m. Donald A. Hodges, 13 Aug. 1967, 1 son. *Education:* BMus, University of Kansas, 1967; MMus, Temple University, 1970; DMA, University of Texas, Austin, 1974. *Appointments:* Lecturer, Temple University, 1968-70; Assistant Instructor, University of Texas, Austin, 1971-74; Lecturer, University of South Carolina, 1974-77; Lecturer, Southern Methodist University, 1977-80; Associate Professor, University of Texas, San Antonio, 1980-. *Recordings:* Trombone and Piano Music (with John Kitzman, trombone), Crystal Records; Music from Meadows, Redwood Records. *Memberships:* 1st Vice-President, San Antonio Music Teachers Association; Board of Directors, Texas Music Teachers Association; Tuesday Musical Club; Phi Kappa Phi; Pi Kappa Lambda. *Honours:* Artist Teacher for National Piano Foundation, 1985; Awards: Most Notable Women in Texas; Outstanding Young Women of America; International Directory of Distinguished Leadership. *Hobbies:* Dance; Ballet; Reading; Travel. *Address:* 3007 Clearfield, San Antonio, TX 78230, USA.

HODGES Margaret, b. 26 July 1911, Indianapolis, USA. Professor Emeritus. m. Fletcher Hodges, 10 Sept. 1932, 3 sons. *Education:* AB, Vassar College, 1932; MLS, Carnegie Institute of Technology, 1958. *Appointments:* Radio & TV Storytelling, Carnegie Library of Pittsburgh, 1953-64; Children's Librarian, CLP, 1958-64; Story Specialist, Pittsburgh Public Schools, 1964-68; Storyteller, WQED-TV, 1965-68; Faculty, School of Library & Information Science, University of Pittsburgh, 1965-77. *Publications:* One Little Drum, 1958; What's for Lunch Charley?, 1961; The Wave, 1964; Hayching of Joshua Cobb, 1967; Lady Queen Anne, 1969; Making of Joshua Cobb, 1971; Hopkins of the Mayflower, 1972; Fire Bringer, 1972; Other World, 1973; Knight Prisoner, 1976; High Riders, 1980; Saint George and the Dragon, 1984. *Membership:* Distinguished Daughters of Pennsylvania, 1970. *Honours:* Best Book for Young Adults by Indiana Author, 1970; Outstanding Juvenile Book, New York Times, 1971; ALA Notable Children's Book, 1972; Caldecott Award, 1985; others. *Hobbies:* Storytelling; Folklore; Travel. *Address:* 5812 Kentucky Avenue, Pittsburgh, PA 15232, USA.

HODGMAN Vicki Jean, b. 22 May 1933, Joliet, USA. Special Education Supervisor. m. Leonard L Hodgman, 8 Aug. 1954, divorced 1975, 1 son, 2 daughters. *Education:* B.Ed., 1954, M.Ed., 1970, Illinois State University. *Appointments:* Teacher, Will County Schools, 1954-55, Joliet, Lockport, Bolingbrook, Rockdale, 1958-68, Baltimore County Schools, 1955-56; Special Education Teacher, Southern Will Co. Co-Op. for Special Education, 1969-79, Supervisor, Co-ordinator, 1979-. *Memberships:* Secretary, 1983-86, Pulse; Chicagoland Special Education Supervisors; Council Exceptional Children; Illinois Council Exceptional Children; etc. *Honours:* Scholarships, Special Education Grant, summer 1969; NDEA Grant, 1982-83. *Hobbies:* Sewing; Quilting; World Travel. *Address:* 310 Reedwood Drive, Joliet, IL 60436, USA.

HODGSON-BROOKS Gloria Jean, b. 28 Nov. 1942, Hartford, Connecticut, USA. Psychotherapist; Visual Artist. m. Peter C Brooks, 1 Jan. 1983. 2 stepsons.

Education: BA, Bennett College, 1965; Gestalt Body Centred Psychotheraphy, Hartford Family Institute, 1976-83; Masters Degree, Social Work, Smith College School of Social Work, 1979; NASW, Academy of Certified Social Work, 1983; Certified Independent Social Work, State of Connecticut, 1986; Board Certified Diplomate in Clinical Social Work, 1988. *Appointments:* Social Worker, Child & Family Services Inc/Inter Agency Services, 1974-77; Intern private practice Psychotherapist 1976-78, Associate 1978-85, Hartford Family Institute; Clinical Social Worker, Child & Family Services, 1979-80; Director, Dr Issiah Clark Family & Youth Clinic, 1980-81; Staff training, Directions Unlimited, 1982-85; Workshop leader, goal setting, PRO Disabled Entrepreneurs, 1985-86; President, psychotherapy and art, Brooks & Brooks Ltd, 1985-; Psychotherapist/partnership, Psychotherapy & Counseling Associates, 1985-; Staff training, Sander Sales Institute, 1986; Administrative Consultant, Connecticut Center for Human Growth and Development, 1986. *Creative Works:* Visual Arts: Handweaving Wallhanging: Untitled, 1974; Sculpture: Unfolding, 1987-88; Awakening, 1987-88; Untitled, 1987-88. Paper Collages, 1987-88. Publication: An Exploratory Study of the Diagnostic Process in Gestalt Therapy, 1979. *Memberships:* Connecticut Handweavers Guild, 1973-76; New England Handweavers, 1974-76; National Association of Black Social Workers, 1972-; Program Function Member, Commission to Study the Consolidation of Children's Services Mandate of the 1974 Session of the Connecticut General Assembly; National Association of Social Workers, 1977-; Connecticut Caucus of Black Women for Political Action, 1984-86; PRO Disabled Entrepreneur, Association, 1985-86; The Smithsonian Association, 1980; Farmington Valley Arts Center, 1986-88; Charter Member, The National Museum of Women in the Arts, 1988; Professional Level Member, International Sculpture Center, 1988; American Craft Council. *Honours:* Outstanding Young Women of America, 1972; Social Worker for Justice Award, Smith College School for Social Work, 1979; Juried Art Exhibits, New England Handweavers Guild, 1974; ECKANKAR Creative Arts Festival, Chicago, Sculpture, 1987; ECKANKAR Creative Arts Festival, Washington DC, Sculpture, 1988; ECKANKAR 2nd Collage, Lift Off, 1988. *Hobbies:* Reading; Sclarology; Dermaglyphics. *Address:* 483 West Middle Turnpike, Suite 217, Manchester, CT 06040, USA.

HOEHNE Felicia V Harris (Felder), Reference Librarian. m. Paul A Hoehne, 2 Jan. 1979. *Appointments:* Teacher, J L Cook High School, Athens, Tennessee; Receptionist, 1960-63, Assistant to the Director of Public Relations 1963-65, Head Circulation Librarian, Alumni Library, 1966-69, Knoxville College, Knoxville; Graduate Library Assistant, Trevor Arnett Library, Atlanta University, 1965-66; Instructor 1969-74, Assistant Professor, 1974-79, Associate Professor 1979-85, Professor 1985-, The University of Tennessee, Knoxville. *Publications include:* Drama Criticism Guide for English 1020: A Bibliography 1976, 1979, 1981, 1983, 1985, 1988; Death of a Salesman: A Bibliography and Sources for Criticism, 1980; Martin Luther King, Jr: A List of Sources by and about Martin Luther King, Jr, in The University of Tennessee/Knoxville Libraries, 1979; Parents without Partners: the Single- Parent Family, A Bibliography, 1978; A Selected List of Guides to Current Education Free and Inexpensive Materials, 1979; A Brief Historical Sketch of Payne Avenue Baptist Church, 1983; Numerous articles to professional journals. *Memberships include:* American Library Association; Tennessee Library Association; East Tennessee Library Association; Charter Member, The National Museum of Women in the Arts; Librarian-in-Residence, EXCEL Program, Austin-East High School; Charter Member, Beck Cultural Exchange Center; Member, The University of Tennessee Student Publication Board; Knoxville College Alumni Association; Board of Directors, Knoxville Roundtable of the National Conference of Christians and Jews; Knoxville Nativity Pageant Choir; Knoxville Community Chorus; President, Spring Place Neighborhood Association; Library Consultant, Austin-East High

School; Volunteer, Greater East Tennessee Chapter March of Dimes; Board of Directors, U T Federal Credit Uniion, PR Director, CAZE, Concerned Association of Residents East; etc. *Honours include:* Certificate for Outstanding Contributions to Library Service and Education, Jack and Jill of America, Inc, 1976; Certificate of Appreciation, Interdenominational Concert Choir, 1976; Chancellor's Citation, Extraordinary Community Service, University of Tennessee, 1978; Certificate of Appreciation, Radio Station WJBE, 1978; Religious Service Award, National Conference of Christians and Jews, 1976; Citizen of the Year Award, Order of the Eastern Star, 1979; Certificate of Appreciation, Knoxville's International Energy Exposition/The 1982 World's Fair; Public Service Award, University of Tennessee National Alumni Association; Payne Avenue Baptist Church, etc. *Address:* 5413 Spring Place Circle NE, Knoxville, Tennessee 37924-2174, USA.

HOEL Arline Alchian, b. 26 Apr. 1943, Fresno, California, USA. Economist. m. Carlton H Hoel, 16 Jan. 1972. 2 sons, 2 daughters. *Education:* BA, Stanford University, 1964; MA 1965, PhD 1973, University of California at Los Angeles. *Appointments:* Economist, Federal Reserve Bank of New York, 1973-77; Senior Research Fellow, Law & Economics Center, University of Miami, 1978-84; Economist, Foundation for Research in Economics & Education, 1984-. *Publications:* Economics Sourcebook of Government Statistics, with K W Clarkson & R L Miller, 1983; Media/Economics Sourcebook, with R L Miller, 1982. *Membership:* American Economics Assoc. *Address:* 7817 Scotia Drive, Dallas, TX 75248, USA.

HOEMAN Shirley A. Pollock, b. 15 Oct. 1942, St Charles, Missouri, USA. Healthcare Consultant; Assistant Professor. m. Richard D. Hoeman, 7 June 1964, 3 sons. *Education:* RN, 1964; BSN, 1964; PNA, 1974; MPH, 1974; MA, 1982; PhD, 1984; CNAA, 1986; CRRN, 1987. *Appointments:* Assistant Professor, Rutgers State University, 1979-81; Private Practice, Health Systems Consultations (own firm), 1981-; Director, Education and Research, Kessler Rehabilitation Institute, 1983-88; Assistant Professor, Columbia University, 1983-. *Publications:* Ethnographical study of a Hospital Home Health Agency, Counting Whatever Counts, 1984; A System Designed for Paradox, 1988; Grants for Federal Funding; Book: Rehabilitation Care in Home and Community, 1988; Presentations for professional conferences. *Memberships:* Research Committee Chairman, Association of Rehabilitation Nurses and Rehabilitation Nurses Foundation; American Public Health Association; Medical Anthropology Society; American Nurses Association; Sigma Theta Tau; Council on Nurses and Anthropology. *Honours:* National Science Foundation Scholarship, University of Missouri, 1960-64; USPHS Title II Traineeship for MPH studies, University of Minnesota, 1972-64; Life Member, Sigma Theta Tau, 1974. *Hobbies:* Herb gardening; Cross cultural and international studies/work and travel. *Address:* 6 Camp Washington Road, Long Valley, NJ 07853, USA.

HOFFBERG Judith A., b. 19 May 1934, Connecticut, USA. Editor; Publisher; Lecturer; Librarian; Archivist. *Education:* BA cum laude, Political Science, 1956; MA, Italian Language & Literature, 1960; MLS, Honours, Library Science, 1964. *Appointments:* Cataloguer, Bologna Centre, Johns Hopkins University, Italy, 1964-65; Cataloguer, Prints & Photographs (Special Intern), Library of Congress, 1965-67; Fine Arts Library, University of Pennsylvania, 1967-69; Librarian, Brand Art Centre, Glendale, California, 1971-73; Founder, Executive Secretary 1973-77, Art Libraries Society of North America; Director, Umbrella Associates (information brokers, publishing), 1978-. *Memberships include:* Life honorary, Art Libraries Societies, USA & UK; College Art Association; International Council of Museums; American Library Association; Friends of Photography; American Printing History Association. *Honours:* Grants: Italian Government 1960-61, Kress

Foundation 1972, National Endowment for Arts 1980, 1981, Australia & New Zealand Arts Council 1982, Dutch Government 1982, British Council 1983, Fulbright, New Zealand 1984; Fluxus Research Fellow, Sonja Henie & Niels Onstad Foundation, Oslo, Norway; Various honour societies. *Hobby:* Collecting objects, ephemera & other items relating to umbrellas. *Address:* PO Box 40100, Pasadena, California 91114, USA.

HOFFECKER Pamela Ruth Hobbs, b. 29 Dec. 1942, Washington DC, USA. Freelance Writer. m. W. Andrew Hoffecker, 24 Aug. 1963, 3 sons. *Education:* University of Pennsylvania Presbyterian School of Nursing. *Appointments:* Freelance writer, national magazines, 1982-; Editor, Service Israel, 1985-; Videoscript Writer, US Air, 1987-. *Publications include:* Articles in: Woman's Day, Parents, Tennis, Highlights for Children, Christian Writer; Book: Christopher Columbus! Yes I Can! in press; Videoscripts. *Membership:* American Society of Journalists & Authors. *Hobbies:* Tennis (played in US Open) with Family Equitable, 1987; Foxhunting; Bible Study. *Address:* 538 Craig Street, Grove City, Pennsylvania 16127, USA.

HOFFLEIT Ellen Dorrit, b. 12 Mar. 1907, Florence, USA. Astronomer. *Education:* AB, 1928, MA 1932, PhD 1938, Radcliffe College. *Appointments:* Assistant, Harvard College Observatory, 1929 to Astronomer, 1956; Mathematician, Ballistic Research Lab., Aberdeen Proving Ground, 1943-48; Research Associate 1956 to Senior Research Astronomer, 1983, Yale University; Director, Maria Mitchell Observatory, 1957-78. *Publications:* Some Firsts in Astronomical Photography, 1950; Yale Bright Star Catalogue, 3rd edition, 1964, 4th edition 1982; about 300 articles. *Memberships:* International Astronomical Union; American Astronomical Society; American Association of Variable Star Observers; American Association of Variable Star Observers; American Association for the Advancement of Science; Meteoritical Society, Editor, 1957-68; American Geophysical Union; Phi Beta Kappa; Sigma Xi; Nantucket Historical Society; Nantucket Maria Mitchell Association. *Honours:* Caroline Wilby Prize, Radcliffe, 1938; Radcliffe Graduate Society Medal, 1964; Radcliffe Alumnae Recognition award, 1983; DSc., Smith College, 1984; Asteroid Dorrit named in her honour, 1987; Georges Van Biesbroeck Award, University of Arizona, 1988. *Hobbies:* Encouragement of Amateurs; Reading; Walking. *Address:* 255 Whitney Avenue, New Haven, CT 06511, USA.

HOFFMAN Darleane Christian, b. 8 Nov. 1926, Terril, Iowa, USA. Professor of Chemistry. m. Marvin Morrison Hoffman, 26 Dec. 1951, 1 son, 1 daughter. *Education:* BS, 1948, PhD, 1951, Iowa State University, Ames. *Appointments:* Chemist, Oak Ridge National Laboratory, Tennessee, 1952-53; Staff Member, 1953-71, Associate Leader, Radiochemistry Group, 1971-79, Division Leader, Chemistry-Nuclear Chemistry Division, 1979-82, Division Leader, Isotope and Nuclear Chemistry Division, 1982-84, Los Alamos National Laboratory, New Mexico; Professor of Chemistry, University of California, Berkeley, 1984-; Faculty Senior Scientist, Lawrence Berkeley (California) Laboratory, 1984-. *Publications:* Numerous articles in field to professional journals. *Memberships:* Panel Leader, Speaker, Los Alamos Women in Science, 1975, 1979, 1982; Subcommittee on Nuclear and Radiochemistry, NAS-NRC, 1978-84, Chairman 1982-84; Chairman, Commission on Radiochemistry and Nuclear Techniques, International Union of Pure and Applied Chemistry, 1987-; Fellow, American Institute of Chemists; Fellow, American Physical Society; American Chemical Society, Chairman, Nuclear Chemistry and Technology Division, 1978-79, Commission on Science 1986-88, Executive Committee, Division of Nuclear Chemistry and Technology, 1987-89; New Mexico Institute of Chemists, President 1976-78; American Association for the Advancement of Science. *Honours:* NSF Fellowship, 1964-65; Guggenheim Foundation Fellowship, 1978-79; Alumni Citation of Merit, College of Sciences and Humanities, Iowa State University, 1978; John Dustin Clark Award, Central New Mexico

Section, American Chemical Society, 1983; Award for Nuclear Chemistry, American Chemical Society, 1983; Distinguished Achievement Award, Iowa State University, 1986; Jarvan Medal, American Chemical Society, 1990. *Address:* 2277 Manzanita Drive, Oakland, CA 94611, USA.

HOFFMAN Gloria L, b. 8 Feb. 1933, Norfolk, Virginia, USA. Writer; Products Designer. m. Frank Katz Hoffman, 18 Sept. 1954, deceased 1982, 2 sons, 1 daughter. *Education:* BA, University of Wisconsin, 1954. *Appointments:* Freelance Writer; Lyricist; Actress; President, Creative Concepts in Communications Ltd, Peoplehood Products by: I Belong to Me. *Honours:* Recipient, various honours and awards. *Address:* Peoplehood Products, 1250 West 63rd Street, Kansas City, MO 64113, USA.

HOFFMAN Mabel, b. 14 July 1923, Dawson, USA. Business Manager. m. Frenis, 16 July 1939, 1 son, 1 daughter. *Appointments:* Supervisor, McCrory Stores, 1950-54; Claims Examiner, Allstate Insurance, 1954-57; Administrative Secretary, 1957-74, Business Manager, 1974-82, Montgomery County Schools. *Publications:* 3 magazine articles in National FFA Magazine, and Farm Wife News. *Memberships:* Everett Lioness, Treasurer, President; Civil Air Patrol; Daughter of the Nile; Business Professional Women; Association of Retired Persons; etc. *Honours:* Ms Pennsylvania senior America, 1986; Ms Senior America, 1987; various honours. *Hobbies:* Reading; Civil War History; Antiques; Writing; Gardening; Flying. *Address:* Route 3, Box 247, Clearville, PA 15535, USA.

HOFFMAN Nancy Yanes, b. 2 July 1929, Boston, Massachusetts, USA. Author. m. Marvin J Hoffman, MD, 15 Feb. 1948. 1 son, 2 daughters. *Education:* BS, Magna cum laude, 1950, MA 1968, University of Rochester. *Appointments:* Associate Professor of English, St John Fisher College, Rochester, 1979-86; President, NYH Healthcare Associates, 1985-. *Publications:* Author: Change of Heart: The Bypass Experience, 1985; Breast Cancer: A Practical Guide to Diagnosis, 1989. *Memberships:* National Association Science Writers; American Medical Writers Association; Authors Guild; American Society of Journalists & Authors; American Diabetes Educators Association; NY State Task Force on Breast Cancer. *Honours:* Phi Beta Kappa, 1950; Instructor of Excellence, NY State English Council, 1982; National Endowment for Humanities, Summer Stipend, 1978; Hoffman Cavanaugh-Rothberg Scholarship/Lectureship, established by Former Students, 1986. *Hobbies:* Travel; Work it's fun! *Address:* 77 Southern Pkwy, Rochester, NY 14618, USA.

HOFFMAN Patricia, b. 1 Jan. 1925, Paragon, Indiana, USA. Professor; Psychologist. m. Paul Hoffman, 27 Jan. 1945, 2 sons, 3 daughters. *Education:* BA, Carleton College, 1945; MS, St Cloud State University, 1964; PhD, Union Graduate School, 1982. *Appointments:* Social Worker, 1964-66; Professor, Psychologist, St Cloud State University, 1966-; Private Practice. *Publications:* articles in professional journals. *Memberships:* American Psychological Association; Advanced Feminist Analysis Institute; Psychologicla Association. *Hobbies:* Bridge; Reading; Antiques. *Address:* 33 Highbanks Pl., St Cloud, MN 56301, USA.

HOFFMAN Ruth Irene, b. 23 Mar. 1925, Denver, Colorado, USA. Director, Mathematics and Computer Laboratory; Professor of Mathematics and Computer Science. *Education:* BA 1946, MS 1947, EdD, Mathematics Education, 1953. *Appointments:* Principal, Counsellor, Dean, Denver Public Schools, Denver, Colorado, 1947-63; Mathematics Lecturer, University of Colorado, 1956-63; Professor of Mathematics and Computer Science, University of Denver, 1963-. *Publications:* Microcomputers and Teachers, 1982; Mathematics System, 1979; International Math on Keys, 1977. Author of numerous journal articles. *Memberships:* Phi Beta Kappa; New York Academy of Science; Mathematical Association of America; Phi

Delta Kappa; Pi Mu Epsilon; National Council of Teachers of Mathematics. *Honours:* Honorary Distinguished Professor, Teachers College, Columbia University, New York; Leadership, Phi Delta Kappa; Outstanding Educators of America. *Hobbies:* Music; Travel. *Address:* Mathematics and Computer Science Department, University of Denver, Denver, CO 80208, USA.

HOFFMANN Ann Marie, b. 6 May 1930, Abingdon, Berks, England. Writer. *Education:* Diploma, St Godric's College, Hampstead, London, 1947-48. *Appointments:* Various, publishing, United Nations, conference organising, 1948-66; Principal, Authors' Research Services, 1966-87. *Publications:* The Dutch: How They Live and Work, 1971, 2nd edition 1973; Research: A Handbook for Writers and Journalists, 1975, 2nd edition 1979, 3rd edition new title, Research for Writers, 1986; Bocking Deanery, 1976; Lives of the Tudor Age, 1977; Majorca, 1978. *Memberships:* Society of Authors; PEN (English Centre); Society of Women Writers & Journalists; English Speaking Union. *Hobbies:* Travel; Theatre; Cooking. *Address:* Baixada Del Rei 8, Carretera De Las Cuevas, Capdepera, Mallorca (Baleares), Spain.

HOFFMANN Georgianna Grace S, b. 8 Dec. 1933, Flint, Michigan, USA. Psychotherapist; Coordinator, Family Stress Clinic. m. Louis G Hoffmann, ScD, 4 Nov. 1955. 2 daughters. *Education:* Diploma, Church Home & Hospital School of Nursing, Balto, 1955; BS, Nursing, cum laude, The Johns Hopkins University, Balto, 1959; MA, University of Iowa, 1970. *Appointments:* Nursing Instructor, Church Home & Hospital, 1956-59; Psychotherapist, Mid-Eastern Iowa Community Mental Health Center, 1970-82; Coordinator, Family Stress Clinic, Department of Family Practice, University of Iowa, 1982-; Private Practice, Psychotherapist, 1973-. *Publications:* Sexual health care in R W Rakel (Ed) Textbook of Family Practice, with C E Driscoll, 3rd Edition, 1984; Relaxation Tape: Time Out of Mind, in production. *Memberships:* American Nurses' Association (Certified Specailist Psychiatric/Mental Health Nursing); American Association Marriage & Family Therapy (Clinical Member & Approved Supervisor); American Asso Sex Educators, Counselors & Therapists (Certified Sex Therapist & Approved Supervisor); Society for Teachers of Family Medicine; Sigma Theta Tau. *Honours:* Listed, International Directory of Distinguished Psychoterapists, 1981; Approved Fellow in Sex Counseling & Therapy, International Council of the American University, Washington DC, 1981; Teacher of the Year Award, Dept of Family Practice, University of Iowa, 1984; Elected, New York Academy of Sciences, 1987. *Hobbies:* Jewellery making; Knitting; Cooking international ouisine; Gardening; Dancing. *Address:* 1016 East College Street, Iowa City, Iowa 52240, USA.

HOFMAN Lindsay Fiske, b. 5 July 1941, New York, USA. Clinical Chemist. m. 21 June 1968, 2 sons. *Education:* BA, Smithcollege, 1963; PhD, University of Washington, 1970; DABCC, American Board of Clinical Chemists, 1976. *Memberships:* AAAS; American Chemical Society; American Association Clinical Chemists; North Carolina Association Clinical Chemists, Chairman Elect, 1989-. *Honours:* AACC Endowment Award, 1983. *Hobbies:* Elementary School Science Education. *Address:* State Laboratory of Public Health, PO Box 28047, 306 North Wilmington St., Raleigh, NC 27611, USA.

HOFMANN Reva Butler, b. Illinois, USA. Engineering Consulting Firm Executive. 1 son, 1 daughter. *Education:* BS, Business, University of Missouri, 1967. *Appointments:* President, Owner, Executive Sales, St Louis Missouri, Butler Packing Co., California, 1976-82; President, CEO, Owner, HTS International, California, 1982-. *Memberships:* First Woman Sponsor, Newport Classic Pro-Am Golf tournament; Sponsor, numerous golf tournaments for Cystic Fibrosis; Fund Raising Drives for Muscular Dystrophy; March of Dimes; American Management Association, Board of Directors; National Employment Association. *Honours:* SME's Entrepreneurial of the

Year, 1987. *Hobbies:* Golf; Sailing; Gourmet Chef; Jazz; Travel. *Address:* HTS International Inc., PO Box 6840, Laguna Niguel, CA 92677, USA.

HOGAN Carolyn Ann Hogan, b. 13 July 1944, New Orleans, Louisiana, USA. Workers' Compensation Representative; Psychologist. *Education:* BA, Dillar University, 1962-66; MA, Fisk University, 1966-69; Studied for PhD, Southern Illinois University, 1973-74. *Appointments:* Instructor, Dillar University, 1969-73; Psychologist, Orleans Parish school Board, 1974-75; Evaluation Specialist, City of New Orleans, 1976-79; Researcher, National Opinion Research CTR, 1980-82; Researcher, National Testing Service, 1981; Benefits Specialist, Transit MGMT of Southeast LA, 1985-86; Workers' Compensation Representative, 19876-. *Publications:* A Black Woman's Struggles in Racial Integration; In Defense of Brown, in Integrateducation in 1980 and 1984 for the Horace Mann Bond Center for Equal Education. *Memberships:* Association of Black Psychologist, former member, 1969-73; President, McDonogh Neighborhood Historical Organization, 1978-79; New Orleans Neighborhood Anti-Crime Council, 1983-86; Scholarship Comm. Crescent City Chapter, Conference of Minority Transportation Officials, 1986-87. *Honours:* Graduate Fellowship, Fisk University, 1966-69; Researcher for President's Civil Advisory Commission, 1969; APA-ABPSI National Science Foundation Visiting Scientist in Psychology, 1971; US Public Health Traineeship in Clinical Psychology at Southern Illinois University, 1973-74; Commendation for Excellence in Job Performance, Finance Division and the Workers' Compensation Recommendation Committee of Transit Management of Southeast Louisiana, 1988. *Hobbies:* Reading; Walking; Listening to music; Listening to professional and grown awareness cassette tapes; Taking long drives by car in the country; Cooking; Listening to, sharing with and guiding my nieces and nephew and aiding the growth of friends and colleagues. *Address:* 1334 Pacific Avenue, New Orleans, Louisiana 70114, USA.

HOGAN Fannie Burrell Whipple, b. 6 Apr. 1923, New Orleans, Louisiana, USA. Librarian (Head Curriculum Materials Center). m. 11 June 1974. 2 daughters. *Education:* Diploma, Gilbert Academy, 1941; MSLS 1950, MA English 1978, EdD 1985, Atlanta University. *Appointments:* English Teacher, Gilbert Academy, 1945-49; English Teacher, Claflin College, 1950-54; Head Librarian, Atlanta University, Summers, 1957-61; Librarian, Reference, Circulation & Reserves, Clark College, 1954-81; Head Librarian, AUC Robert W Woodruff Library, 1981-. *Publications:* Poem: All Ages Can Learn; Dissertation: A Study of Staff Development Programs in College and University Libraries in the State of Georgia. *Memberships:* American Library Association, College and Research Libraries Division; Metro Atlanta Library Association; Ben Hill United Methodist Church, Crusaders Class Teacher. *Honours:* Oratorical Contest Winner, 1944; All expense paid trip to Poland from Clark College Scholarship, United Methodist Board of Education, 1981, 1982; Scholarship, Atlanta University School of Education, 1983. *Hobbies:* Reading; Sewing; Writing; Photography. *Address:* 1981 Valley Ridge Drive, SW, Atlanta, Georgia 30331, USA.

HOHN Hazel, b. Brooklyn, New York, USA. Writer. m. Werner Hohn, 26 July 1960, 2 sons, 2 daughters. *Education:* AA; Commercial Pilot with Multi-Engine, Instrument & Seaplane Ratings. *Publications:* The King Who Could Not Smile; Stories in 1st & 4th Grade Textbooks; Articles and poems in most major juvenile publications; Articles in adult magazines & newspapers. *Memberships:* Aviation/Space Writers Association; Experimental Aircraft Assocation; Ninety Nines; etc. *Honours:* Hazel Hohn Collection, University of Southern Mississippi, 1960's-; Recipient, several prizes, poetry contests. *Hobbies:* Reading; Sports; Wildlife; Poetry; Music. *Address:* 2750 Dickerson Rd, Unit 1, Reno, NV 89503, USA.

HOIT-THETFORD Sarah Elizabeth, b. 7 Sept. 1948, Selma, Alabama, USA. Program Specialist/ Administrator in Adult Continuing Education. m. Richard R Thetford, 10 Aug. 1979. 1 son. *Education:* BS 1972, EdD 1986, East Tennessee State University, Johnson City; MEd 1982, EdS 1984, William Carey College, Hattiesburg. *Appointments:* Owner, Fireside Handcrafts, 1973-76; Project Director, Mississippi Arts Commission, 1974-76; Secondary Teacher, Jackson County Schools, Mississippi, 1977-84; Doctoral Fellow, East Tennessee State University, 1984-86; Instructor, Hawaii Pacific College, 1986-88; Program Specialist, Kapiolani Community College/University of Hawaii, 1988-. *Publications:* On the Horns of a Moral Dilemma: An Anatomy of the Hawkins County, Tennessee, Textbook Controversy, 1988; Videotape, The Single Weave and Double Weave Baskets of the Mississippi Choctaws as Demonstrated by Isbie Gibson, 1976; Play: And if They Are Not, 1970. *Memberships:* Hawaii Chapter, American Society for Training and Development; Hawaii Council of Teachers of English (Newsletter Editor 1987-88); National Council of Teachers of English; South Atlantic Philosophy of Education Society; Tennessee Audiovisual Association (Newsletter Editor, 1985-86); Women in Academic Administration. *Honours:* Finalist, Distinguished Dissertation Awards Competition (KDP), 1987; Kappa Delta Pi, 1985; Phi Delta Kappa, 1985; Alpha Psi Omega, 1970. *Hobbies:* Working with community theatre; Judging high school speech tournaments; Collecting antiques, books and coins; Black & white photography; Arts and crafts. *Address:* University of Hawaii/Kapiolani Community College, Office of Community Services, 4303 Diamond Head Road, Honolulu, Hawaii 96816, USA.

HOLDSWORTH Janet Noott, b. 25 Dec. 1941, Evanston, Illinois, USA. Registered Nurse. 2 sons, 1 daughter. *Education:* BSN, High Distinction, University of Iowa, 1963; MN, University of Washington, Seattle, 1966. *Appointments:* Staff Nurse, University of Colorado Hospital, Denver, 1963-64; Presbyn Hospital, Denver, 1964-65; Grand Canyon Hospital, Arizona, 1965; Assistant Professor, University of Colorado School of Nursing, 1965-71; Counselling Nurse, Boulder Polydrug Treatment Centre, 1971-77; Private Duty Nurse Nurse's Official Registry, Denver, 1973-82; Nurse Health Educator, Teenage Patent Programme, Boulder Valley Schools, 1980-. *Publications:* Vicarius Experience of Reading a Book in Changing Nursing Students' Attitudes, in Nursing Research, 1968; A Creative Approach to Curriculum Development, in Journal of Nursing Education, 1969. *Memberships Include:* American, Colorado Nurses Associations; Society of Adolescent Medicine, Council High Risk Prenatal Nurses; Council Interacultural Nurses, 1983-; Board of Directors, Treasurer, Nott's Travel Aurora, 1980-; Advisory Board, Boulder County LaMaz Inc., 1980-; Child Find and Parent Family, Boulder 1981-; Colorado Organisation Adolescent Pregnancy and Parenting, 1985-. *Honours:* Sigma Theta Tau, 1966-; Outstanding Young Women of America, 1976; Outstanding Volunteer Work, Mile High Chapter, American Red Cross, 1980; Alpha Lambda Delta, 1980. *Hobbies:* Presbyterian Elder; Chairperson, Refugee Resettlement Committee; Camping; Hiking. *Address:* 1550 Findlay Way, Boulder, CO 80303, USA.

HOLETS WHITTEMORE Vicky Rae, b. 19 Mar. 1955, Cedar Rapids, USA. Assistant Professor. m. Scott R. Whittemore, 13 May 1984, 1 son. *Education:* BS, Zoology, Iowa State University, 1977; PhD, Anatomy, University of Minnesota, 1982. *Appointments:* Postdoctoral Fellow, University of California, Irvine, 1982-84; Fogarty Research Fellow, Karolinska Institute, 1984-86; Assistant Professor, University of Miami, 1986-. *Publications:* 20 papers in scientific journals; co-author 9 book chapters. *Memberships:* Society for Neuroscience; IBRO; Association of Women in Neuroscience; International Society of Developmental Neurobiology; National Tuberous Sclerosis Association, President. *Honours:* Arnold P. Lazarow Memorial Award, University of Minnesota, 1980; Grass Fellowship, 1980; Baccaner Award forOutstanding Doctoral Dissertation, University of Minnesota, 1983; Outstanding Young Alumnus, Iowa State University, 1989. *Hobbies:* Reading; Tennis; Hiking; Bicycling; Birdwatching; Music.

Address: University of Miami School of Medicine, Dept. of Neurological Surgery, The Miami Project to Cure Paralysis, 1600 NW 10th Ave (R-48), Miami, FL 33136, USA.

HOLLAN Susan R, b. 26 Oct. 1920, Budapest, Hungary. Professor of Haematology, Director General. m. Gyorgy Revesz, MD. 1 son, 1 daughter. *Education:* University Medical School, Budapest; Professor of Haematology, Postgraduate Medical School, 1970. *Appointments:* Internist, Rokus Hospital, Budapest, 1945-50; Research Fellow, University Medical School, Budapest, 1950-54; Science Adviser, Institute for Experimental Med Research, 1954-; Director 1959-85; Director General, 1985-, National Institute of Haematology and Blood Transfusion. *Publications:* Editor-in-Chief, Hung Med Encyclopaedia & Haematologia (quarterly); Basic Problems of Transfusion, 1965; Haemoglobins and Haemogllobinopathies, 1972; Genetics, Structure and Fuction of Blood Cells, 1980; over 200 papers in Hungarian and international medical journals. *Membership:* Hungarian Academy of Science, 1982-. *Honours:* Hungarian Acad Award, 1970; State Prize, 1974; Socialist Hungary Medal. *Hobby:* Fine arts. *Address:* National Institute of Haematology and Blood Transfusion, P O Box 44, H-1502 Budapest, Hungary.

HOLLAND Carolsue, b. 29 Oct. 1938, Easton, Pennsylvania, USA. University Professor. m. Gerald R. Garrett, 13 Oct. 1979. *Education:* BS, East Stroudsburg College, 1961; MA, Lehigh University, 1962; PhD, University of Pennsylvania, 1967. *Appointments:* Assistant Professor, Point Park College, 1967-71; Assistant Professor, York College, City University of New York, 1971-75; Lecturer, University of Maryland, 1975-76; Lecturer, Boston University, Boston, Massachusetts, 1976-80; Professor, Troy State University, 1980-. *Publications:* Instructors manuals in Western civilisation, ideas and issues in geopolitics and political geography; Articles in periodicals. *Memberships:* International Political Science Association; American Political Science Association; Academy of Criminal Justice Sciences; Armed Forces and Society Research Group. *Honours:* West German Government Grantee, 1965-67; Visiting Research Scholar, Wellesley College, 1988-89. *Hobbies:* Canine handling; Bridge; Sailing; Music. *Address:* Box 6837, APO, NY 09633, USA.

HOLLAND Jane Carolyn, b. 30 May 1952, Solihull, England. Public Relations Consultant. m. Colin Roy Holland, 18 Aug. 1973, divorced, (2) Clarence Poirier, 1 daughter. *Education:* BA, Honours, French, Bristol University, 1973; Diploma, Education, Birmingham University, 1974; Diploma, Arts Administration, Harvard University, USA, 1978. *Appointments:* Founder, President, Lewis Carroll Public Relations, Toronto, Canada, 1982-88; Founder, President, Lewis Carroll Communications, 1988. *Memberships:* Co-Chairman, Publicity, Juvenile Diabetes Foundation, Toronto. *Honours:* Recipient, Wintario Award, 1978. *Hobbies:* Modern Dance; Tennis. *Address:* 6 Green Valley Road, Toronto, Ontario, Canada M2P 1A5.

HOLLAND Mary, b. 22 Dec. 1931, London, England. Actress. m. Paul Antony Ciappessoni, 14 Feb. 1953, 3 sons, 1 daughter. *Education:* Gold Medal, LAMDA Acting & Elocution, 1952. *Appointments:* Theatre: Dear Charles, 1953; Tiger at the Gates, 1956; The Deep Blue Sea, 1956; Black Comedy, 1983; Wait Until Dark, 1983; TV: Little Lord Fauntleroy; The Last of Mrs Cheyne; The Rebel Heiress; Gaslight, 1984; Stars on Sunday; Here Today; 18 years as Katie in TV Advertisement for Oxo Cubes. *Honours:* Book of Records for 18 years Life with Katie. *Hobbies:* Sailing; Painting. *Address:* c/o Julia MacDermot Limited, 14 Leamore Street, London W6, England.

HOLLAND Mirabai, b. 28 Jan. 1951, Chicago, USA. Life Fitness Programs Company President. *Education:* BA, Education, University of Denver, 1972; MFA, Dance, New York University, 1980. *Appointments:* Exercise Program Director, Atrium Club, 1984-; Exercise Program Director Athletic & Swim Club, Equitable Club, 1988-. *Publications:* Contributing Editor, New Body Magazine; Fitness Column, Fit Beat; Teaching Technique, Moving Free. *Memberships:* American College of Sports Medicine, Examiner; IDEA; AFAA. *Honours:* Best Aerobics Teacher in New York City, New York Magazine; Member, National Advisory Board for Reebok. *Hobbies:* Dance; Poetry Writing; Writing; etc. *Address:* 206 A County Road, Tenafly, NJ 07670, USA.

HOLLAND Patricia Ann, b. 25 Mar. 1933, Indianapolis, Indiana, USA. Physical Therapist; Owner/Operator of Restaurant. m. Oliver L Pipkin, 8 Sept. 1986. *Education:* BS Physical Therapy, St Louis University, 1955; MS Ed and Psych, Butler University, 1968. *Appointments:* Long Hospital, IU Med Center, Indianapolis, 1955-64; St Mary's Child Center, 1964-68; Indy VA Hospital HBHC Hosp Based Home Care, 1979- 86; Norrell Home Health Care, 1987-88. *Memberships:* American Physical Therapy Association; Indianapolis Urban League; Women's International League for Peace & Freedom. *Honours:* Merit Award, Volunteer Secretary for Coalition for Adequate Transportation in Indianapolis, 1970-75; Award, volunteer teacher, pre & post natal exercises, St Elizabeth's Home for Unwed Mothers, 20 years, 1965-85; Best for Jazz, Indianapolis Monthly, 1985, 1987; Best Place to Hear Jazz, Indianapolis Magazine, 1985, 1986, 1987. *Hobbies:* Yoga; Swimming; Volunteer, Rental Gallery Indianapolis Museum of Art; Volunteer Chairman Indiana Black Expo Jazz Concert; Volunteer, Committee for Wes Montgomery Jazz Concert Free in City Park. *Address:* 4605 Washington Blvd, Indianapolis, IN 46205, USA.

HOLLAND Sandra Gunter, b. 12 Jan. 1952, Mount Airy, North Carolina, USA. Freelance Writer; Public Stenographer; Businesswoman. m. Gasper O. Holland, 14 Feb. 1981, 2 sons. *Education:* BSc, Virginia Commonwealth University, 1973; Graduate work, various universities. *Appointments include:* Former newspaper & radio stringer, newsletter editor; Publicity writer; Freelance article & essay writer; Owner, home-based secretarial service, 1982-. *Publications include:* Nationwide monthly 2-page trade newsletter, Typing Service Newsletter, 1986-; Family newsletter; Business column, Brush Country Advertiser; Numerous contributions, Income Opportunities magazine, Grit newspaper, Women's Circle, Woman's World, San Antonio Light. Also speeches, professional concerns, various schools, clubs, *Memberships:* Military Reserve, 1977-; Offices: 1st Baptist Church, Poteet, Atascosa County Republican Women's Club, & American Red Cross; Member: Friends of Library, Mensa; National Arbor Day Foundation; American Society of Notaries. *Honours:* Honourable mention, short story contest; Danforth I Dare You Award; Various awards, US 5th Army; 2 awards, Freedoms Foundation, Valley Forge; Publicity award, Civil Air Patrol Squadron; Tribute, Texas Federation of Republican Women; Biographical recognitions. *Hobbies:* Reading; Research, family tree; Improving home library; Civic work; Children; Letters to editor, editorials; etc. *Address:* Holland Secretarial Services, 529 Oakhaven, Pleasanton, Texas 78064, USA.

HOLLAND-HOGAN Yvonne Anita, b. 24 Oct. 1937, Bay City, Texas, USA. Professor. 1 son. *Education:* BS, 1958, MS, 1960, PhD, 1981, Zoology, Howard University. *Appointments:* Instructor, Biology: El Camino College, 1969-70, Texas Southern University, 1970-74; Assistant Professor, 1974-81, Associate Professor, 1983-, Biology, Texas Southern University. *Publications:* Articles in professional journals. *Memberships:* Sigma Xi; Beta Beta Beta; Texas Academy of Science; American Society of Zoology; National Association & Texas Association of Advisors for Health Professions. *Honours:* Smith-Noir Scholar, 1958-59; Howard University Doctoral Fellowship, 1961-62. *Hobbies:* Reading; Bridge; Walking; Travel. *Address:* Dept. of Biology, Texas Southern University, 3100 Cleburne, Houston, TX 77004, USA.

HOLLANDER Jean, b. Vienna, Austria. Poet; Teacher. m. Robert B. Hollander, 23 Apr. 1964, 1 son, 1 daughter. *Education:* MA, PhD pending, Columbia University, USA. *Appointments:* Teacher of Literature (part-time), Princeton University, USA, 1966-; Director, Annual Writers Conferences, Trenton State College. *Publications:* Crushed into Honey, book of poems, 1986; About 100 poems in various journals. *Membership:* Poetry Society of America. *Honours:* Poetry Fellowship Awards, 1980, 1984; 1st Prize, Billie Murray Denny Award for poem, 1982; Eileen W Barnes Award for book of poems, 1986. *Hobby:* Hiking, Address: RR2, Box 177, Hopewell, NJ 08525, USA.

HOLLAWAY Loretta Jean, b. 6 Oct. 1938, Eldon, USA. Elementary Teacher. *Education:* BS, Fort Hays State University, 1963; MS, Emporia State University, 1970; Studies, various other universities. *Appointments:* Pleasant Valley Rural School, Ellinwood, 1958-61; Countryside Rural School, Great Bend, 1961-73; Park School, Great Bend, 1973-89. *Creative Works:* Numerous training workshops conducted. *Memberships Include:* National Education Association; Great Bend National Education Association; Kansas National Education Association; International Reading Association. *Honours:* Recipient, many honours & awards including: Delegate to NEA Convention, Seattle; GBNEA Master Teacher of the Year Award, 1988. *Hobbies:* Reading; Oil Painting; Violin; Piano; Tennis; Volleyball; Travel. *Address:* 405 East Fourth, Ellinwood, KS 67526, USA.

HOLLERAN Constance, b. 19 June 1934, Manchester, New Hampshire, USA. Nurse. *Education:* Nursing Diploma, Massachusetts General Hospital, 1956; BS, Teachers College, Columbia University, 1958; MSN, Catholic University of America, 1965. *Appointments:* Various nursing positions in hospitals in USA, 1956-58; Faculty Member, Massachusetts General Hospital, 1958-63; Chief, Projects, Division of Housing HEW, 1965-70; Director, Washington Office, ANA, 1971-81; Executive Director, International Council of Nurses, Geneva, Switzerland, 1981-. *Memberships:* American Nurses Association; NLN; Womens Political Caucus; American International Club, etc. *Honours:* Outstanding Alumnae Award, MGH School of Nursing Centennial, 1973; Honorary Award, Teachers College Alumnae, Columbia University, 1982; Fellow, American Acadmey of Nursing, 1983; Outstanding Achievement Award, The Catholic University of America, 1984. *Address:* 121 Rue de Lausanne, 1202, Geneva, Switzerland.

HOLLEY Barbara, b. 14 Apr.1 936, Rockville Centre, USA. Editor; Publisher; Producer; Writer. m. Joseph Holley, 1 June 1956, 3 sons, 4 daughters. *Education:* BS, Business Management, Columbia University, 1 964. *Appointments:* Editor, Publisher, Earthwise Poetry PBNS, 1978-; Producer, CATV Show, Impromptu, 1982-. *Publications:* Pieces of Woman, 1982. *Memberships:* Founder, Earth Chapter, FSPA; NLAPW; FSPA Inc; Former President, Member, Laramore Reader Poets; South Florida Institute of Poetry, former President. *Honours:* Virginia Commonwealth University Award, 1979; Directors Award, 1980; Nominee, Pulitzer prize, 1982. *Hobbies:* Reading; Writing; Racing. ssa 20Address: 21 NW 203 Terrace, Apt. B-1, Miami, FL 33169, USA.

HOLLINGSHEAD Melinda Gay, b. 18 Dec. 1953, Huntsville, Alabama, USA. Research Immunologist. *Education:* BS, Biology, University of Alabama, 1976; MT(ASCP), Huntsville Cooperative School of Medical Technology, 1976; DVM, Auburn University College of Veterinary Medicine, 1981; PhD, North Carolina State University, 1986. *Appointments:* Medical Technologist, 1976-77; Veterinary Surgeon (small animals), 1981-82; Visiting Instructor, North Carolina State University, 1985-86; Staff Immunologist 1986-87, Section Head, Research Immunology 1987-, Southern Research Institute. *Memberships:* American Veterinary Medical Association; American Association for Advancement of Science; New York Academy of Sciences. *Honours:*

Dean's Award, President's Award, National Dean's List, 1981; Phi Zeta, Phi Kappa Phi, 1980; Outstanding Young Women of America, 1987. *Hobbies:* Hiking; Woodwork, furniture re-finishing; DIY; Music; Photography. *Address:* 4024 Sherborne Road, Birmingham, Alabama 35210, USA.

HOLLINGSWORTH Margaret Blanton (Husson), b. 30 Jan. 1920, Manhattan, New York, USA. Writer; Author; Lecturer. m. Willard Revelle Hollingsworth, 23 June 1950, 2 sons. *Education:* BA, Furman University, Greenville, South Carolina, 1941; Certified Secondary Teacher, Florida, 1944; Portrait, landscape, with Guy Wiggens, 1944-45; Flower Show School for Judges, 1955-56; Biblical Prophets, 1974. *Appointments:* Teacher, English, Latin, Spanish, St John's County, Florida, 1944-45; Editor, Illustrator, The Angler, 1947-50; English Tutor, 1953, 1962; Staff, Managing Editor, The Gordonia, 1954-57; Taught Art, St Mark's Episcopal, Duval County, Florida, 1973. *Creative works include:* Architectural model, Furman University permanent exhibition; Photographs in 1-man exhibitions: Ponce de Leon Hotel, 1946, Jacksonville Art Museum, 1961; Newspaper articles, 1953-63; St Augustine Cookery (layout, design), 1954; Author, producer, director, 4 play/pageants for 350 children, 1966-70; Lectures, church, ancient history, Bible (with Mary E Husson), 1967-69; What Child is this?, Script for large choirs, 1972; Floral design; Art. *Memberships:* Co-Founder with Mary E Evans, The Sports Fishing League (marine conservation), St Augustine; St Augustine Art Association; American Association of University Women, Art Chair 1954-56; Charter Founder, St Mark's Episcopal Day School; National League of American Penwomen, Historian 1989; President, Women of St Mark's Episcopal Board, 1968, 1969; Life Member, Board, Garden Club of Jacksonville; Many others. *Honours:* Medal, Ringo, National Humane Society Youth Short Story Contest, 1934; Tapped, NYC Debutante Committee for Debutante Coterie, 1940; USAF Certificate, Meritorious Service, 1946; Letters of Commendation, campaign windows design and execution, American Red Cross, 1949; Silver Trophy, ACS Certificate, Tricolor, floral design, Southeastern Camellia Show, 1963; 1st woman on Vestry, St Mark's Episcopal, 1970-72; Numerous others including many blue ribbons for floral design, horticulture, photography. *Hobbies:* Gardening; Reading. *Address:* 1426 Edgewood Circle, Jacksonville, FL 32205, USA.

HOLLINGSWORTH Peggie J, b. 7 Mar. 1936, Toledo, Ohio, USA. Biomedical Research Scientist. m. Charles B Smith, 1 June 1979. 1 son. *Education:* BS Biology & Chemistry, University of Toledo, 1959; MA Molecular Biology, Bowling Green State University, 1970; PhD Toxicology, University of Michigan, 1983. *Appointments:* Chief Research Technologist, Inst of Med Res, Toledo, Ohio, 1963-70; Research Associate, College of Engr, 1972-81; Assistant Research Scientist, Pharmacology, Medical School, University of Michigan; Toxicology, School of Public Health, University of Michigan, 1983-88. *Publications:* 19 articles in professional journals; chapters in books; over 35 Abstracts. *Memberships include:* Coalition for the Advancement of Blacks in Biomedical Sciences; Michigan Regional Chapter, Society of Toxicology; American Society of Clinical Pathologists; American Society of Medical Technologists; Sigma Xi, International Society; Sigma Xi, University of Michigan Chapter; Electron Microscopy Society of America; Microbeam Analysis Society; Michigan Electron Microscopy Forum; Tri-Beta National Biology Honor Society; University of Michigan School of Public Health Alumni Association; University of Michighan Alumni Association Reunion for Black Graduates Committee; Bowling Green State University Alumni Association; Delta Sigma Theta Sorority, etc. *Honours:* Black Scientist of Southeastern Michigan Salutee, 1984; Jesup W Scott High School Hall of Fame Inductee, 1984; Rackham Graduate Studies Scholarship for Minority Students, 1978; Continuing Education for Women Scholarship, 1978; National Institute of Health Predoctoral Training Grant, 1970; Alpha Kappa Alpha Scholarship, 1953. *Hobbies:* Photography; Improved status of women in academic environments; Increased representation of women and minorities at colleges and universities; Improved communication between scientists and the public. *Address:* Department of Pharmacology, M6428 Medical Science I, The University of Michigan Medical School, Ann Arbor, Michigan 48109, USA.

HOLLIS Jocelyn, b. 3 June 1927, New York City, USA. Writer. m. Raymond E Hollis, 2 May 1948, divorced 1970. 1 son, 2 daughters. *Education:* City College of NY, 1946-47; Monmouth Junior College, 1946; BA 1960-73, MA 1973-79, University of Delaware; University of Pennsylvania, 1985; Temple University, Philadelphia, PA, 1986-88. *Publications:* Chopin and Other Poems; Love and the Universe; Vietnam Poems: The War Poems of Today; Bridal Song; Another Eden: A New Paradise; Poems of the Vietnam War; Elizabethan Love Sonnets; A Planet Probable: A One-Act Poetic Play; Sonnets of Jocelyn Hollis; Paradise Lost: A Continuation; Peace Poems; Modern Metaphysical Lyrics; Vietnam Poems II: A New Collection; Twentieth Century Sonnets; Beirut and Other Poems; The Foundations of Paradise, A Prose- Poem; Collected Vietnam Poems and Other Poems; Collected Poems, Volume Two; Plowshares: Poems for Nuclear Disarmament; Collected Poems: Volume Three. *Honours:* 1st Prize, Philadelphia Writers' Conference, Modern Poetry Contest, 1978; 1st Prize, First State Writers Bicentennial Poetry Contest, 1976; 1st Prize, The DeKalb Literary Arts Journal Poetry Contest, 1969; 1st Price, The Lyric Foundation of Traditional Poetry Award, 1962; First Award, California Olympiad of the Arts for One Act Poetic Play, Marble and Gold Plaque, 1964. *Hobby:* Reading. *Address:* P O Box 2013, Upper Darby, PA 19082, USA.

HOLLIS Sheila Slocum, b. 15 July 1948, Denver, Colorado, USA. Attorney. m. John Hollis, 27 July 1967, 1 daughter. *Education:* BSc cum laude, Journalism, University of Colorado, 1971; JD, University of Denver, 1973; Various senior courses, government & management; Admitted, Bars of Colorado 1974, District of Columbia 1975, US Court of Appeals (DC & 5th Circuits) 1975, US Supreme Court 1980. *Appointments:* Trial attorney, Federal Power Commission, Washington Dc, 1974-75; Associate attorney, Wilner & Scheiner, Washington DC, 1975-77; Director, Office of Enforcement, Federal Energy Regulatory Commission, 1977-79; Partner, Butler & Binion 1980-84, Broadhurst, Brook, Mangham & Hardy 1984-87, Vinson & Elkins, Washington DC, 1987-; Professorial Lecturer in Law, George Washington University National Law Centre, 1980-; Member, chair, various professional committees. *Publications:* Co-author, books: Energy Decision Making 1983, Energy Law & Policy 1988; Numerous articles, energy law & policy Also: Frequent speaker, legal, consumer, government & industrial audiences, energy matters. *Honours include:* Various scholarships & education awards; Delegation leader, People to People Studies, Women in Legal System, People's Republic of China 1985, South America 1987; One of top 20 US energy lawyers, National Law Journal, 1984. *Memberships include:* Local, national & international bar associations; Washington Foreign Law Society; Federal Energy Bar; National Press Club. *Address:* 2415 Sandburg Street, Dunn Loring, Virginia 22027, USA.

HOLLOWAY Cindy Tannenbaum, b. 8 Aug. 1960, Queens, New York, USA. Loan Officer. m. David Milton Holloway, 1981, 1 son. *Education:* BA, California State University, 1981; Licenced Real Estate Broker, 1989. *Appointments:* Waitress, Bob's Big Boy, 1984-85; Receptionist, 1985; Processor, 1985-88, Loan Officer, 1988-, Quality Mortgage. *Memberships:* San Bernardino Board of Realtors; National Trust for Historic Preservation; Cantree Committee, 1989; Special Events Committee, Board of Realtors: Board of Realtors, Communications Committee, 1990. *Hobbies:* Reading; Cooking; Writing. *Address:* 1074 Waterman Canyon Road, PO Box 3187, Crestline, CA 92325, USA.

HOLMA Salme Tellervo, b. 21 Jan. 1936, Finland. Managing Director. m. Matti Holma, 1963, 1 son, 1 daughter. *Education:* MA, Agriculture & Forestry,

University of Helsinki, 1961. *Appointments:* Editor, 1962-67; Farmer, 1967-72; Managing Director, Krapihovi Oy. *Publications:* articles in magazines. *Memberships:* Vicechairman, Marttaliitto, 1971-75, Chairman, 1975-79, President, 1983-; Board Member, Finnish Population & Family Welfare Federation, 1975-79; Zonta International, 1988. *Honours:* Golden Badge of Merit of Marttaliitto, SLR rm. *Hobbies:* Skiing; Golf. *Address:* Krapi, 04310 Tuusula, Finland.

HOLME Barbara Lynn, b. 24 May 1946, Long Beach, California, USA. Writer; Editor. m. Howard Holme, 16 June 1968, 1 son, 1 daughter. *Education:* BA, Stanford University, 1967; Graduate work, Coro Foundation; Internship in Public Affairs. *Appointments:* Urban Consultant, Connecticut and Denver, Colorado, 1968-74; Director, Metro Denver Urban Coalition, 1969-71; Housing Assistant, Denver Housing Administration, 1972-74; State Senator, 1974-84; Editor, Writer, 1985- . *Creative works:* Laws against redlining; Establishing consumer advocate office; Providing more state aid for Denver schools. *Memberships:* Metro Air Quality Council, 1984-86; Colorado Common Cause Board, 1987-; Legislative Liaison, Denver Association for Gifted and Talented; Committee Member, Rocky Mountain Planned Parenthood. *Honours:* 1 of 50 women legislators chosen nationally to attend Washington Institute of Women in Politics, May 1978; Award for Outstanding Democratic Senator, Colorado Social Legislation Committee, 1979, 1980; Award for Outstanding Citizenship, Colorado Common Cause, 1984. *Hobbies:* Protecting the environment especially from air pollution; Improving schools especially for gifted children; Reading; Yoga; Bike riding. *Address:* 1243 Fillmore, Denver, CO 80206, USA.

HOLMES Barbara Ware, b. 2 Sept. 1945, Roanoke, USA. Writer. m. David Jeffrey Holmes, 30 Nov. 1968, 1 daughter. *Education:* BA, Springfield College, 1967; MA, Northeastern University, 1969. *Appointments:* Elementary School Librarian, Connecticut 1969-70, Alaska, 1970-72; Assistant to Editor, Independent School Bulletin, 1973-74. *Publications:* Childrens Books: Charlotte Cheetham: Master of Disaster, 1985; Charlotte the Starlet, 1980; Third Charlotte book due for publication, 1989; Short Stories in: Redbook; Samisdat; Moving Out; Pig Iron Magazine. *Memberships:* Board of Directors, PTA, 1981-84. *Hobby:* Speaking at Schools. *Address:* 322 Collings Ave , Collingswood, NJ 08108, USA.

HOLMES Joan, b. 6 Sept. 1935, Gunnison, Colorado, USA. Project Director. m. Edward M. Holmes, 21 June 1966, divorced 16 June 1971. *Education:* BA, Psychology, University of Colorado, 1957; MA, Psychology, San Francisco State University, 1964; Pupil Personnel Credential - Psychology and Supervisor. *Appointments:* School Psychologist, Belmont School District, California, 1964-68; Educational Consultant, Seattle, Washington, 1968-71; Director, Title III Project, The Humanistic Approach to Psychological Services, 1971-74; Lecturer, Supervisor, California State University Graduate School, Hayward, 1971-75; Director, Title III Project, Parents as Partners, 1974-75; Currently Global Executive Director, The Hunger Project, New York City. *Publication:* Ending Hunger: An Idea Whose Time Has Come, 1985. *Memberships:* USAID Advisory Committee on Voluntary Foreign Assistance; Interaction: The American Council for Voluntary International Action, Board, Executive Committee, 1984-87, 1988-; Trustee, International Development Conference; Director, Overseas Development Council. *Address:* The Hunger Project, One Madison Avenue, New York, NY 10010, USA.

HOLMES Lucille Martin, b. 9 Jan. 1921, Tylertown, Mississippi, USA. Teacher; Designer. m. Donald Holmes, 23 Apr. 1940. 1 daughter, deceased. *Education:* Design Schools: New Orleans, 1967; Miami, 1968; Mobile, Ala., 1969. *Appointments:* Owned and operated Grocery Store, 1956-60; Owner, Tylertown Florist and Taught Florist Design to students, 1960-88. *Memberships:* Mississippi Florist Association; Louisiana Florist

Association; Alabama Florist Association; Southeastern Florist Association. *Honours:* Gold Key Award, 1987; Hall of Fame Award, 1978. *Hobbies:* Reading; Travelling; Dancing; Camping. *Address:* 425 Beulah Avenue, Tylertown, Mississippi, USA.

HOLMES Nancy Ruth, b. 19 Jan. 1948, Grand Junction, Colorado, USA. Forester; Administrator. *Education:* BS, Outdoor Recreation, Colorado State University, 1971; MS, Resource Utilisation, University of Maine, 1979; MBA, International Business, Fairleigh Dickinson University, 1988. *Appointments:*Various jobs, forestry & environment, 1969-75; Resident Manager, Dyer Long Pond, Maine, 1975-77; Wood Energy Specialist, Maine Office of Energy Resources, 1978-85; Fuels & Utilities Contracts Manager, Time Energy Systems Inc, 1985; Senior Environmental Manager, Cogeneration Partners of America, 1986-90; President, NRH Associates, Inc, 1990-. *Publications:* 12, wood energy; 3, alternate energy. *Memberships:* National, & New England Division, Society of American Foresters; National Association of Female Executives; Past President, offices, Crises & Counselling Centres; Past Secretary, Maine Pilots Association; Senior member, National Ski Patrol; Board, Sam Ely Land Trust. *Honours:* Walter Priff Memorial Award, Colorado State University, 1971; Committee (Maine), Research Needs & Priorities, Intensive Forest Harvesting, 1984-85; Mass Transit Advisory Committee, Fairbanks North Star Borough, Alaska, 1975; 3rd place, spot landing, International Seaplane Pilots' Fly-In, Maine, 1982. *Hobbies & interests:* Private Pilot (single engine), land & sea; Downhill & cross-country skiing; Jogging; Sewing; First aid; International forestry & wood energy. *Address:* 206 West Shore 2, Grand Isle, Vermont 05458, USA.

HOLMES Susan Lesley, b. 8 Aug. 1945, Sydney, Australia. General Manager. m. Dr David Smith, 3 Oct. 1986. *Education:* Dip Phys Ed, University of Melbourne, 1965; BEd 1972, BPsych 1975, MPsych (Clin) 1977, University of Western Australia. *Appointments:* General Manager, Small Business Development Corporation 1988-, Senior Chairman, Promotions Appeal Board, Department of Premier and Cabinet 1987-88, Assistant Director, Ministry of Consumer Affairs 1985-86, Assistant Director, Senior Executive Service Management, Office of the Public Service Board, 1983, State Government of Victoria; Senior Consultant, W D Scott & Co, Management Consultants, Western Australia, 1981-82; Consulting Psychologist, Private Practice, Western Australia and USA, 1979-80; Employed by the Mental Health Services of Western Australia, 4 years; University of Western Australia, 2 years; Teacher, Schools in Australia and the United Kingdom, 4 years. *Memberships:* Australian Psychological Society; Board of Directors, Urban Land Authority, State Government of Victoria; Course Advisory Committee, School of Business Administration, Royal Melbourne Institute of Technology (RMIT); Management Education Liaison Committee (MELC); Board of Directors, Business in the Community (BCL); Women Chiefs of Enterprises, International; Trustee, Committee for Economic Development of Australia (CEDA); Representative of the Premier of Victoria on the Merit Promotion and Equal Employment Opportunity Consultative Committee. *Hobbies:* Farming; Modern art; Ballet; Theatre; Poetry; Travel; Languages. *Address:* Post Office Box 233, Abbotsford, Victoria 3067, Australia.

HOLMES Yvonne L Durr, b. 25 July 1947, Gary, Indiana, USA. Instructor. m. 11 Dec. 1971, divorced, 1979. *Education:* BA, Education, 1965; Diplomas, Computer Programming, ICS, 1984. *Appointments:* School Corporation of Gary, 1969-. *Publications:* Our World's Most Cherished Poems. *Memberships:* Smithsonian National Institution; Alpha Kappa Alpha; American Film Institute; etc. *Honours:* Golden Poet Award, World of Poetry, 1985; Presidential Trust, 1987, 1988. *Hobbies:* Fashion Designing; Writing; Interior Design; Music; etc. *Address:* 1529 Delaware St., Apt. 1, Gary, IN 46409, USA.

HOLMSTEN Victoria Lynn, b. 27 Nov. 1953, Hinsdale, Illinois, USA. English instructor. m. Donald Glen Allen, 18 Aug. 1984. *Education:* BA, Macalester College, MN, 1975; MA, University of New Mexico, Albuquerque, 1980; MA, Bread Loaf School of English, Middlebury College, Vermont, 1985. *Appointments:* US Peace Corps Liberia, 1975-77; English teacher, Laguna-Acoma HS, New Mexico, 1981-85; Languate Arts Instructor, Shiprock, New Mexico and Ft Wingate, New Mexico, 1985-88; English Instructor, San Juan College, Farmington, New Meixco, 1987-. *Publications:* Numerous articles in professional journals, magazines and newspapers; Chapter in Reclaiming the Classroom. *Memberships:* National Council of Teachers of English; New Mexico Council of Teachers of English, President 1986-87, Executive Secretary 1987-; American Association of University Women; Rio Grande Writers Association. *Honours:* Kathleen Downey Scholar, Bread Loaf School of English, 1985; Outstanding Young Women of America, 1985. *Hobbies:* Writing; Travelling; Southwestern history; Music; Hiking; Cross-country skiing. *Address:* 11 Road 6407 NBU 36, Kirtland, New Mexico 87417, USA.

HOLT Gloria Joan, b. 20 June 1940, Texas, USA. m. Scott A. Holt. *Education:* BS, Biology, 1964; MA, Biology, University of Texas, 1972; PhD, Fisheries, Texas A & M University, 1976. *Appointments:* Research Scientist, Associate, 1977-83, Research Scientist, 1983-, University of Texas, Austin. *Publications:*Articles in various journals including: Estuaries; Marine Ecology. *Memberships:* American Fish Society, ELHS President 1986-88; American Society for Icthy and Herpe; Estuarine Research Federation; Gulf Estuarine Research Society. *Hobbies:* Bird Watching; Scuba Diving; Marine Tropical Fish. *Address:* University of Texas at Austin, Marine Science Institute, PO Drawer, 1267, Port Aransas, TX 78373, USA.

HOLT Gwendolyn Kay Hill, b. 27 Jan. 1952, Louisa, Virginia, USA. Master Scheduling Specialist. m. Robert Dillard Holt, 3 July 1971, divorced 1984, 1 daughter. *Appointments:* Secretary, Louisa County Publishers, 1968-70; Medical Receptionist, Virginia, 1970-71, Univesity of Virginia, 1971; Secretary, Charlottesville Public Schools, 1970-79; Secretary, General Electric Co., 1979-81; Transportation Analyst, GE Fanuc Automation, 1981-88; Income Tax Preparer, Antique Dealer. *Memberships:* Various professional organisations including: NAACP. *Honours:* At Your Service Award, 1980, Employee of the Month, 1984, Cost Improvement Awards, 1985-88, General Electric Company; Top Fund Raiser, National Association of Advancement of Coloured People, 1986. *Hobbies:* Restoring & Selling Antiques; Carpentry. *Address:* 2717 Brookmere Road, Charlottesville, VA 22901, USA.

HOLTZMAN Elizabeth, b. 11 Aug. 1941, New York City, New York, USA. District Attorney. *Education:* AB magna cum laude, Radcliffe College; JD, Harvard Law School, 1965. *Appointments:* Staff Attorney, Wachtell, Lipton, 1965-67; Assistant to Mayor, New York City, 1968-70; Staff Attorney, Paul Weiss et al, 1970-72; Member, US Congress, 16 CD, 1973-81; Visiting Professor, New York University, 1981-82; District Attorney, Kings County, New York, 1982-. *Publications:* Numerous articles in newspapers, magazines and other periodicals. *Memberships:* New York State Bar Association; Board of Advisors, National Women's Political Caucus; Lawyers Commission on International Human Rights; Board of Overseers, Harvard University, 1976-82; President's Commission on US Observance of International Women's Year. *Honours include:* Athena Award, New York City Commission Status of Women, 1985; Meritorious Service Award, Jewish War Veterans, 1986; Women's Equality Award for Overall Achievement, NOW, 1987; Certificate of Appreciation, Messiah Baptist Church, 1987; Award of Honour, United Jewish Appeal, 1988; Distinguished Public Service Award, Anti-Defamation League, 1988; Outstanding Service to State and National National Women's Political Caucus. *Hobbies:* Swimming; Biking; Riding; Tennis;

Reading. *Address:* 210 Joralemon Street, Brooklyn, NY 11201, USA.

HOLYER Erna Maria, b. 15 Mar. 1925, Weilheim, West Germany. Writer; Artist; Educator. m. Gene Wallace Holyer, 24 Aug. 1957. *Education:* AA Degree, 1964; Lifetime California Teaching Credential, 1970; DLitt, 1984. *Appointments:* Freelance Artists, 1958; Freelance Writer, 1960; Teacher, San Jose Metropolitan Adult Education Programme, 1968. *Publications:* As Ernie Holyer: Reservoir Road Adventure, 1982; Sigi's Fire Helmet, 1975; The Southern Sea Otter, 1975; Shoes for Daniel, 1974; Lone Brown Gull, 1971; Song of Courage, 1970; At the Forest's Edge, 1969; A Cow for Hansel, 1967, 2nd edition 1979; Steve's Night of Silence, 1966; Rescue at Sunrise, 1965; Contributor to anthologies and to 80 publications. Published in Kyoto and Tokyo, Japan, 1984-87; Newspaper correspondent, 1988. *Memberships:* California Writer's Club; American Federation of Teachers; World University Roundtable; ABI Research Institute; ABI Research Board of Advisors. *Honours:* Various one-woman art exhibits and art awards, 1965-80; Lefoli Award for Excellence in Adult education Instruction, 1972; Woman of Achievement Certificate, 1973, 1974, 1975; Commemorative Medal of Honor, ABI, 1986; Woman of Achievement Nomination, Santa Clara County Commission on the Status of Women and San Jose Mercury News, 1987; Medal of Congress, IBC, 1988. *Hobbies:* Walking; Swimming; Bicycling. *Address:* 1314 Rimrock Drive, San Jose, California 95120, USA.

HOME Anna Margaret, b. 1938, London, England. Television Executive. *Education:* BA, Honours, Oxford University. *Appointments:* Director, Producer, Executive Producer in Charge of Children's Drama, BBC, 1960-80; Controller of Programmes, Head of Children's and Young Peoples' Programmes, TV 5, 1980-86; Head of Childrens Programmes at the BBC, 1986-. *Memberships:* British Association of Film and TV Arts; Fellow of Royal TV Society. *Honours:* Pye Television award for Distinguished Services to Children's TV, 1985. *Hobbies:* Reading; Theatre; Gardening; Cooking. *Address:* BBC, Television Centre, Wood Lane, London W12 7JR, England.

HONG Sookja, b. 25 July 1933, Seoul, Korea. President, Koean National Council of Women. Divorced, 1 son, 1 daughter. *Education:* BA, 1955, PhD, 1975, Tong Guk University; MA, Ewha Womens University, 1957; MA, Poston University, USA, 1958; PhD Credit work, New School for Social Research, 1967-69; Carnegie Fellow, Columbia University, USA, 1962-63. *Appointments:* 1st Woman Diplomat, Assistant to Foreign Minister; Protocol Office, 1962; Vice-Consul, New York, USA, 1965; UN Mission Advisor, 1967; Professor, Tong Guk University, 1972; organised feminist movement, 1975; President, KNCW, President, ICW, FAWA, 1985; International Council of Women; Federation of Asian Womens Associations. *Publications:* Hong's Essays, 1969; Feminism in Korea, 1975. *Membership:* Former Vice President, KAUW; President, KNCW; President, ICW; Vice President, FAWA. *Honours:* Korean National Medal of Merit, Dong B for service to the welfare of women and society. *Hobby:* Travel. *Address:* 132-9 Yunhi-dong, Seoul, Korea.

HOOD Morag MacLeod, b. 12 Dec. 1942, Glasgow, Scotland. Actress. *Education:* MA, French, English, Economics, Glasgow University. *Appointments:* Performances with: Roundup, TV curent affairs programme, 1962-65; Repertory theatre, Bristol, Dundee, Liverpool, Edinburgh, 1965-68; TV Films include: War & Peace, Persuasion, Wuthering Heights, 1968-73; Theatre including: West End Productions, Streetcar Named Desire, 1974-85; National Theatre Productions: Campello, Volpone, Amadeus, Lady from Maxims, etc; wrote BBC Radio Production, after Many Cares & Bitter Sorrows, Charlotte Brontë. *Hobbies:* Gardening; Travel. *Address:* c/o Marmant Management, Langham House, Regent Street, London W1, England.

HOOK Georgia Delis, b. 23 Apr. 1930, Lorain, Ohio, USA. Trustee; Homemaker. m. John B. Hook, 9 Feb. 1958, 1 son, 1 daughter. *Education:* BA Honours, Business Administration, Baldwin-Wallace College, Berea, Ohio, 1952; MBA, Marketing, Indiana University, 1956. *Appointments:* Manager, Retailing, Halle Brothers, 1952; Flight Attendant, New York City & Los Angeles, American Airlines, 1953-55; Professor of Marketing, Butler University, Indianapolis, 1957. *Memberships:* Vice President, Delta Mu Delta, national commerce honorary society; Trustee 8 years, & National President 1986-87, Alumni Association, Baldwin-Wallace College; Executive Committee 1975-77, Great Lakes Shakespeare Festival, Cleveland, Ohio; Sang in the church choir for twenty-five years. *Honours:* Delta Mu Delta; Women's Council, WVIZ-TV, PBS Channel 25, Cleveland, 1984-88; Biographical listings. *Hobbies:* Travel, USA & worldwide (41 countries, 49 US states); Tennis; Golf; Skiing; Hiking. *Address:* 435 Bates Drive, Bay Village, Ohio 44140, USA.

HOOKER Morna Dorothy, b. 19 May 1931, Beddington, Surrey, England. University Professor. m. W David Stacey (Revd Dr), 30 Mar. 1978. *Education:* BA 1953, MA 1956, University of Bristol; University of Manchester, 1957-58; PhD 1967; MA Oxon, 1970; MA Cantab, 1976. *Appointments:* Research Fellow, University of Durham, 1959-61; Lecturer in New Testament, University of London, King's College, 1961-70; Lecturer in Theology, University of Oxford, 1970-76; Lady Margaret's Professor of Divinity, University of Cambridge, 1976-. *Publications:* Jesus and the Servant, 1959; The Son of Man in Mark, 1967; Pauline Pieces, 1979; Studying the New Testament, 1979; The Message of Mark, 1983; Continuity and Discontinuity, 1986, etc. *Memberships:* Studiorum Novi Testamenti Societas, President, 1988-89; Society for Old Testament Studies. *Honours:* Visiting Professor, McGill University, 1968; Visiting Fellow, Clare Hall, Cambridge, 1974; Fellow, King's College, London, 1979; Honorary Fellow, Linacre College, Oxford, 1980; Visiting Professor, Duke University, 1987. *Hobbies:* Molinology; Music; Walking. *Address:* The Divinity School, St John's Street, Cambridge, CB2 1TW, England.

HOOPER Anne Caroline Dodge, b. 16 July 1926, Groton, Massachusetts, USA. Associate Professor of Pathology. m. 17 June 1952. 3 daughters. *Education:* AB 1947, MD 1952, Washington University; Rotating Internship, VA, Mason, Seattle, 1952-53; Internal Medicine, Hartford, Connecticut, 1953-54; Pathology, New Britain, Connecticut, 1954-57; Certified American Board Path: Anatomic 1958, Forensic, 1960 and Clinical Pathology, 1061. *Appointments:* Medical Examiner Office, Philadelphia, 1958-60; Medical Examiner, Vermont, 1967-71; Medical Examiner, Raleigh Co, 1977-; VA Hospital, Coatesville, Pennsylvania, 1960-66; Kerbs Hospital, St Albans, Vermont, 1966- 71; Appalachian Regional Hospital, 1971-76; West Virginia School of Osteopath Med, 1977-. *Publications:* Numerous articles in professional journals. *Memberships:* AMA; WV State Soc; Raleigh Co Medical Society; American Society Clinical Pathologists; American Academy Forensic Sciences; College of Amerrican Pathologists; Int Academy of Pathology; American Women's Med Association; National Association Medical Examiners. *Honour:* Borden Award, 1952. *Hobby:* Playing viola. *Address:* 104 Elmridge Court, Beckley, WV 25801, USA.

HOOPER Susan Jeanne, b. 4 Aug. 1950, Rapid City, South Dakota, USA. Nurse-Midwife. m. Robert E Hooper, 21 Feb. 1981. 1 son, 1 daughter. *Education:* RN Diploma, Presbyterian Medical Center School of Nursing, 1971; BS, University of Dubuque, 1973; Certificate Family Nurse Midwife, Frontier Nursing Service School of Family Nurse Midwifery, 1975; Family Nurse Clinician, MSN, Vanderbilt University, 1979. *Appointments:* Staff RN, Assistant Head Nurse, Presbyterian Medical Center, 1971-72; Director, Student Health Service, University of Dubuque, 1972-73; Family Nurse Practitioner/ Clinical Instructor, Frontier Nursing Service, 1973-75; Staff RN, St Joseph Hospital, 1975-76; PNP & Home

Health Programme, Custer County Health Dept, 1976; Staff Nurse-Midwife, 1976-78, FNC 1979, Ft Campbell; Staff Nurse Midwife, Ft Hood, 1979-83; FARMC Staff Nurse-Midwife, 1983-86; Head Nurse, Ft Riley, 1986-. *Publications:* Numerous presentations and booklets. *Memberships:* American Nurses Association; Colorado Nurses Association; American College of Nurse Midwives; Nurses Association of American College of OB-BYN. *Honours:* Spotlight on Staff, DACH, 1979; ARCOM, 1978; IOLC, 1976; MSM, 1982; 1st Oak Leaf Cluster 1986. *Hobbies:* Sewing; Reading; Gardening; Cross stitch. *Address:* Manhattan, KS 66502, USA.

HOOPER Virginia Fite, b. 23 Sept. 1917, Byhalia, Mississippi, USA. Republican National Committeewoman. m. James F Hooper, 29 Jan. 1943, 2 sons, 1 daughter. *Appointments:* Republican National Committeewoman, 1963-76. *Memberships Include:* President, Charter Member, City Garden Council; President, Cherokee Garden Club, 1955; Lowndes County Chowder & Marching Society; Advisory Board, Southern Debutante Association; Mississippi Heart Association; National Association of Junior Auxiliaries; Lowndes Historical Society; Lowndes County Society for the Preservation of Antiquities; Advisory Board, Contact; Executive committee, Lowndes County Youth Court Committee; Advisory Board, Touch; RSUR Committee. *Address:* 800 North 8th Street, Columbus, MS 39701, USA.

HOPE Akua Lezli, b. 7 June 1957, New York City, USA. Writer; Poet. m. 9 Sept. 1987. *Education:* BA, Williams College, 1975; MBA 1978, MSJ 1977, Columbia University. *Appointments:* Public Relations Associate, AT&T Network Systems, 1979-85; Senior Public Relations Specialist, Corning Incorporated, 1985-. *Publications:* Editor New Heat, 1989-; Shard, 1989. *Memberships:* Founder and coordinator, Corning Elmira Amnesty International, 1988-; Public Relations Coordinator, Partners of the Americas; Founding Member, New Renaissance Writers Guild; Poets and Writers; Poetry Society of America. *Honours:* Sterling Brown Award, 1975; Finalist, Walt Whitman Prize, 1983; Poetry Fellowship, New York Foundation for the Arts, 1987-88; National Endowment for the Arts Creative Writing Fellowship, 1990; Finalist in Barnard New Women Poets Series, 1990; Finalist in MacDonalds Literary Achievement Award Competition, 1989. *Hobbies:* Fiction; Music, jazz singing; Film; Oral history; Human rights. *Address:* P O Box 33, Corning, NY 14830, USA.

HOPGOOD Debra Jo Kendrick, b. 26 June 1958, Mount Vernon, Illinois, USA. Businesswoman. m. Joseph Hopgood, 9 Jan. 1981, 1 daughter. *Education:* Eastern Illinois University, 1976-79. *Appointments:* Chief Executive Officer, Kendrick Paper Stock Company, 1979-; Owner, Balloons n Tunes. *Memberships:* Jefferson County Crime Stoppers, 1984-85; Board, Mount Vernon Civic Centre Authority, 1984-86; Board of Education, Mount Vernon Township High School, 1986-87; Advisory Boards, Good Samaritan Hospital, Women's Crisis Centre; Jefferson County Board; Respresentative-at-large, Greater Egypt Regional Planning & Development Commission; Jefferson County Extension Education Building Association; National Association of Female Executives; American Institute of Professional Bookkeepers. *Honours:* Business Grant, Illinois Department of Energy & Natural Resources; Certificate of Recognition, efforts in waste reduction & recycling, Governor Thompson, Illinois; Biographical recognition. *Hobbies:* Reading; Watching old films; Collecting coins & antiques. *Address:* 204 North 16th Street, Mount Vernon, Illinois 62864, USA.

HOPKINS-PRICE Patricia Louise, b. 26 Dec. 1949, New Orleans, USA. Exercise Physiologist; Assistant Professor. m. David Stuart Price, 18 Dec. 1982. *Education:* BA, Economcs, 1971; BA, Physical Education, 1978; MS, 1980; PhD, 1986. *Appointments:* Accountant, Shell Oil Co., 1971-73; Tourguide, New Orleans, 1973-82; Swim Coach, New Orleans & Baton Rouge, 1976-82; Researcher, 1987; Research Associate, 1987-88; Exercise Physiologist, Memorial Medical Centre, 1987-88; Exercise Physiologist, Assistant Professor, Elmhurst College, 1988-. *Publications:* Articles in various journals. *Memberships:* Kappa Delta Pi; Society of the Founders of the City of New Orleans; American College of Sports Medicine; American Alliance of Health, Physical Education, Recreation and Dance. *Honours:* Recipient, various honours and awards. *Hobbies:* History of Louisiana and New Orleans; Swimming; Cycling. *Address:* 425 Naperville Road, Wheaton, IL 60187, USA.

HOPKINSON Betty Constance, b. 11 Mar. 1920, Coventry, England. Portrait Painter; Art Teacher. m. George Stanley Hopkinson, 23 Mar. 1940, 1 son, 2 daughters. *Education:* Studied part-time under Bernard Hailstone, Maidstone College of Art, 1952-57; Goldsmiths College of Art, 1957-63. *Career:* Professional Portrait Painter, 1964-; Teacher of Art, Portrait Painting, St Albans College of Further Education, 1967-; Teacher of Art, Portrait Painting, Hendon College of Further Education, 1984-. *Creative Works:* Portraits of Actors & Actresses including: Tom Conti; Beryl Read; Portraits of Poets: Adrian Mitchell, Peter Porter, Anne Clarke; Portraits of Queen Alexandria's Nurses from the Queen Elizabeth Hospital, Woolich; A Gordon Highlander, Cornet Player Pupil at Kneller Hall Military School of Music, Twickenham; Provencal landscapes painted in oils; Prints include woodcuts, linocuts, relief etchings, lithographs and screenprints. *Memberships:* Maidstone Art Society, 1952-; Founder, Secretary, 1958-61, Chairman, 1961-66, Hon. Member, 1966-, Harpenden Arts Club; Chairman, 1973-80, Vice President, 1980-, Milldon Art Society, Mill Hill; Chairman, 1983 and 1986-, President, Contemporary Portrait Society; Hampstead Artist Council, 1967-; National Society of Painters, Sculptors and Printmakers, elected 1986. *Honours:* Awards for portraits in oils from the Societe des Artistes Francaise, Paris Salon, Grand Palais; Honorable mention for Mr Mears, 1964, Medaille d'Argent for Hommage to Bonnard, 1967, Medaille d'Or for Someone in the Kitchen, 1971; City of London Polytechnic Certificate in Fine and Applied Art (Printmaking), 1984-86. *Hobbies:* Gardening; Antiques; Bird Watching; Cats; Creative Knitting; Butterflies; Wild Flowers. *Address:* 2 Lindhurst Avenue, Mill Hill, London NW7 2AB, England.

HOPPER Sherry Leigh Morris, b. 26 Mar. 1954, Cincinnati, Ohio, USA. Director of Communications (university advancement/fundraising). m. John Edward Hopper Jr, 29 Apr. 1983, 1 stepson, 1 stepdaughter. *Education:* BS, Journalism, Bowling Green State University, Bowling Green, Ohio, 1976. *Appointments:* Director of Publications, 1979-83, Communications Director, 1984-, The University of Cincinnati Foundation, Cincinnati, Ohio; Assistant Manager, B.Dalton Booksellers (Florida), 1983-84. *Publications:* Over 1000 short stories, poems and articles for religious youth/ teen market, USA and foreign readers. *Memberships:* Cincinnati Editors Association; National Writers Club; Council for Advancement and Support of Education; Public Relations Society of America; Women in Communications Inc; International Fund for Animal Welfare. *Honour:* Scripps Howard Journalism Scholarship Award, Bowling Green State University, 1974. *Hobbies:* Herb gardening; Raising bassett hounds; Reading (fantasy and science fiction); Classical music; Collecting pewter unicorns. *Address:* 4613 Brookview Drive, Batavia, OH 45103, USA.

HOPSON Joyce Sue, b. 14 May 1950, Kentucky, USA. Businesswoman; Adjunct Professor. *Education:* BA, Lincoln Memorial University, 1970; MA, Union College, 1973; Ed.D., University of Tennessee, 1978. *Appointments:* Special Education Teacher, 1970-75; Guidance Counsellor, 1975-77; Research Assistant, University of Tennessee, 1977-78; Career Education Director, 1979-83; Adjunct Professor, 1980-88; Congressional Aide, 1983-. *Publications:* Articles in professional journals. *Memberships:* Chairman, Claiborne County Democratic Party, 1981-88; Delegate to the 1988 Democratic National Convention; East

Tennessee Cerebral Palsy Board of Directors. *Honours:* Highest History Award, Lincoln Memorial University, 1970. *Hobbies:* Golf; Tennis; Boating; Reading. *Address:* Route 2, Box 52, Tazewell, TN 37879, USA.

HORE Marlene Carole, b. 7 Aug. 1944, Montreal, Quebec, Canada. Vice Chairman, National Creative Director, Canada. m. Ron Hore, 7 July 1968, 2 daughters. *Education:* BEd., McGill University, 1964. *Appointments:* Writer: CFCF TV & Radio, 1966-69; Writer, Vickers & Benson, 1969-71; Writer, 1971-75, Group Creative Director, 1975-77, M & L Creative Director, 1977-83, National Creative Director, 1983-, Vice Chairman, National Creative Director, 1987-, JWT. *Memberships:* Founding Member, Agency Creative Directors Association; Member Arts Directors' Club of Toronto. *Hobbies:* Skiing; Reading. *Address:* c/o J. Walter Thompson, 160 Bloor St - E, Toronto, Ontario M4W 3P7, Canada.

HORN Karen Carol, b. 12 Sept. 1957, Perth Amboy, New Jersey, USA. Science Educator. m. Russell Charles Horn, 4 Oct. 1980. *Education:* BSc 1979, Biological Science Certification, Comprehensive Science Certification 1980, Fairleigh Dickinson University. *Appointments:* Substitute Teacher, Board of Education, Woodbridge, NJ, 1978-79; Substitute Teacher, Nutley NJ, 1980; Dental Asst, Endodontic Assocs, 1980; Educator, Biology and Chemistry, Freehold Regional High School District, 1980-; Gymnastics Coach, 1987-; Vice President, RDI Promotions, 1983-. *Memberships:* Cousteau Society; National Geographic Society; Smithsonian Institution, Washington; Assoc Member, American Museum of Natural History, New York. ssa 20Honour: Certificate of Recognition, USA Army, 1983. *Hobbies:* Needlepoint/embroidery; Coin/plate collector; Wood refinishing. *Address:* 117 Park Place Avenue, Bradley Beach, New Jersey 07720, USA.

HORNE June M, b. 23 Feb. 1936, Chicago, Illinois, USA. Psychiatric Tech; President of company. m. Brazell Horne, 6 Oct. 1955. 1 son. *Education:* Graduate, Northern High. *Appointments:* Psychiatric Tech, VA Hospital; President, Browder & Watts Inc, 1985-. *Creative Work:* Invention: Escape apparatus, US Patent No 4498557, 1985. *Membership:* NAACP. *Hobbies:* Dancing; Listening to good music; Modelling; Politics. *Address:* 1713 W 90th Street, Chicago, ILL 60620, USA.

HORNE Shirley Beverley, b. 6 Sept. 1921, Melbourne, Australia. Social Researcher; Writer. m. Allen Valentine Horne, 14 Sept. 1951. *Education:* B.Com 1944; Diploma, Public Policy, 1070. *Appointments:* Research Officer, Commonwealth Dept. of Social Services, 1944-61; Tutor, Lecturer, part-time, Social Studies, 1962-84, Associate, Social Work, 1980-, University of Melbourne. *Memberships:* President, YWCA, Melbourne, 1962-65; President, YWCA, Victoria, 1977-80; Life Member, Melbourne Family Care Organisation; Australian & Victorian Councils of Social Service; National Council of Women of Victoria; Australian Federation University Women; Victorian Council on the Ageing. *Honours:* AM. *Hobbies:* Family History; Walking; Countryside & Seaside. *Address:* 2/401 Alma Road, North Caulfield, VIC 3161, Australia.

HORNER Matina Souretis, b. 28 July 1939, Boston, Massachusetts, USA. College President Emerita; Executive Vice President, Tiaa-Cref. m. Joseph L. Horner, 25 July 1961, 2 sons, 1 daughter. *Education:* AB cum laude, BrynMawr College, 1961; MS, 1963, PhD, 1968, University of Michigan; LLD, Dickinson College. *Appointments:* Teaching Fellow, 1962-66; Lecturer, Motivation/Personality, 1968-69, University of Michigan; Lecturer, Social Relations, 1969-70, Assistant Professor, Clinical Psychology Department, 1970-72, Harvard University; President, Radcliffe College, Cambridge, Massachusetts, 1972-89. *Publications:* Contributor of psychological articles on motivation to professional journals. *Memberships:* Director: Time Inc; Boston Edison; Trustee: 20th Century Fund, Massachusetts Eye & Ear Informary; American

College of Greece; Yale-China Association; Board of Directors, Revson Foundation, Women's Research and Education Institute. *Honours:* Roger Baldwin Award, Massachusetts Civil Liberties Union foundation, 1982; Citation of Merit, Northeast Region NCCJ, 1982; Career Contribution Award, Massachusetts Psychological Association, 1987; Radcliffe Medal, 1988; Honorary degrees: University of Massachusetts, 1973; Mount Holyoke, 1973; University of Pennsylvania, 1975; Tufts University, 1976; Smith College, 1979; Wheaton College, 1979; University of Hartford, 1980; University of New England, 1987; Claremont University Center and Graduate School, 1988. *Address:* 38 Oakley Road, Belmont, MA 02178, USA.

HORNYOLD-STRICKLAND Angela (Dowager Countess Della Catena), b. 31 May 1928, Ipswich, England. m. Lt Commander Thomas Henry Hornyold-Strickland RN, 20 Jan. 1951. 4 sons, 3 daughters. *Education:* New Hall Convent, Essex; St Mary's Convent, Ascot. *Memberships:* President of Cumbrian (formally Westmorland) British Red Cross Society, 1972-; Vice President Cumbrian Assoc of Boys Clubs, 1975-; Director, Catholic Caring Services (Diocese of Lancaster). *Honour:* Deputy Lieutenant, County of Cumbria. *Address:* Sizergh Castle, Kendal, Cumbria, LA8 8AE, England.

HOROWITZ Esther, b. 17 Dec. 1920, New York City, USA. Retired Professor. *Education:* BA, Brooklyn College, 1940; MA, University of Wisconsin, 1949; PhD, Columbia University, 1959; Certificate: University of London, 1950, University of Miami, 1958. *Appointments:* Speech Clinician, Queens College, 1944-46; Teacher, Speech Improvement, New York City Schools, 1946-50; Speech Instructor, Central Michigan University, 1949; Instructor, Assistant Professor, Associate Professor, Professor, Speech, Hofstra University, 1950-80; Director, Hofstra Speech Clinic, 1953-67. *Publications:* Co-author, Guidelines for Better Speech in the Schools, 1965; Articles in various journals including: Speech Teacher; Journal of Speech Disorders. *Memberships:* Chairman, Sub-Committee, American Speech Correction Association, 1958; Secretary, Sigma Kappa Alpha, 1965-66; Secretary, Hofstra Branch, American Association of University Professors, 1965-67; Consulting Editor, Speech Science, 1971-72. *Honours:* US Government Traineeship Grants, 1958, 1963, 1964; Sigma Kappa Alpha; Sigma Pi. *Hobbies:* Music; Theatre; Handicrafts. *Address:* 147-07 Charter Road, Jamaica, NY 11435, USA.

HORSMAN Lenore Lynde, b. 21 Apr. 1931, Zilwaukee, USA. Soprano; Researcher; Voice Teacher. m. 1 son, 2 daughters. *Education:* BS, MA, Indiana University. *Appointments:* Post Graduate Studies Italy Accademia Chigiana (Sienna) Mozarteum Salzburg Virgiliana Accademia Italy (Mantua); Director, School of Music, Voice Teacher, Mu Phi Epsilon School of Music, Chicago, 1976-81; Teacher, Director, Northshore Theatre, 1978-80; Teacher, Director, Shorewood Studios of Music, 1986-; Chicago Studio of Belcanto, 1987-; Over 30 roles in opera, operetta, musicals & plays; Performances & concerts in USA, Italy, Austria & Germany; Sang in premier TV performance of Greed Under a Tree; Director, Italian Bel Canto Institute, 1989. *Memberships:* National Association of Teachers of Singing; Mu Phi Epsilon; Theta Alpha Pi; First President, Wisconsin Women in the Arts, Milwaukee, 1973-76; Board, International Women's year Festival, Milwaukee, 1975; Chicago Music Teachers Association. *Honours:* Career Achievement Award, Milwaukee Panhellenic Association, 1978; Singer's Medal of Honour, Amici della Lirica of Mantova, Italy, 1981. *Hobbies:* Bel Canto; Languages; Costume Designing. *Address:* 3548 North Hackett, Milwaukee, WI 53211, USA.

HORTON Enobia Anastasia Lady, b. 3 July 1947, New York City, USA. US Army Retired. m. Adam Asenbrook Horton-Highsmith, 1 July 1968, 5 sons, 2 daughters. *Appointments:* Viet-Nam Military Police, 1968-71; Germany, recovering from wounds, 1971-72;

Spain, Foreign Training, 1972-73; Puerto Rico Advisement, 1974-75; Korea Reinforcement Training, 1976-78; Hawaii Training School, 1978-83. *Publications:* Byline, Army Times, 1983-86; Editorial Guard Life, 1986-87. *Memberships:* various professional & civic organisations. *Honours:* Commissioned First Lieutenant, US Army, 1968; Battlefield, Promotion to Captain First Class, 1968; Promoted to Major First Grade, 1975; First Class Field Training and Survival Award, 1976; Special Education, JAG Office, 1983; Promoted to Lieutenant Colonel, Field Action Duty, 1983. *Hobbies:* Dress Designing; Scuba Diving; Target Practice. *Address:* c/o Whales Audio/ Video Recording Studio Inc., Sixteen Wegman Parkway, Jersey City, NJ 07052, USA.

HORVATH Aniko, b. 7 May 1947, Gyor, Hungary. Harpsichordist. m. Antal Vadasz, 10 Oct. 1970, 2 daughters. *Education:* Béla Bartók Music Secondary School, Budapest, 1961-67; Ferenc Liszt Academy of Music, Budapest, 1967-72; Academy of Music, Bratislava, Czechoslovakia. *Career:* Soloist, Philharmonic Society of Hungary, 1977-; Member of Bach-Trio, Budapest; Horvath-Peteri harpsichord duo; Harpsichordist, Concentus Hungaricus chamber orchestra; Gave master courses, Staufen, Federal Republic of Germany, 1977-85; Professor of Harpsichord, Academy of Music, Budapest, 1985-. *Recordings:* Scheidt: Tabulatura nova - Excerpts, Hungaraton SLPX 11848; Kuhnau: Stories from the Bible illustrated in music, Hungaraton SLPX 12459-60. *Honours:* Winner, 2nd Grand Prix, International Harpsichord Competition at Festival Estival, Paris, France. *Address:* Solyom L.u.7/B, 1022 Budapest, Hungary.

HOSKING Barbara Nancy, b. 4 Nov. 1926, Penzance, Cornwall, England. Advisor, Yorkshire Television. *Appointments:* Secretary to Town Clerk, Council of the Isles of Scilly, & Local Correspondent, BBC & Western Morning News, 1945-47; Editorial Assistant, The Circle, Odeon and Gaumont Cinemas, 1947-50; Assistant to Information Officer, Labour Party, 1952-55; Assistant to General Manager, Uruwira Minerals Ltd., Tanzania, 1955-57; Research Officer, Broadcasting, Labour Party, 1958-65; Science Press Officer, DES, 1965; Press Officer, Ministy of Technology, 1967; Press Officr, 10 Downing Street, 1970; Principal Information Office, DoE, 1972; Private Secretary to Parliamentary Secretaries, Cabinet Office, 1973; Chief Information Office, DoE, 1974-77; Controller of Information Services, IBA, 1977-87; Advisor, Yorkshire TV, 1987- . *Publications:* Contributor To: Punch, New Scientist, Spectator, BBC Radio 4. *Memberships:* Various professional organisations. *Honours:* Special Citation, New York City, American Womens Forum, 1983; OBE, 1985; Fellow Royal Society of Arts, 1986; Fellow Royal Television Society, 1988. *Hobbies:* Opera; Leider; Watching Politics; Watching Sport. *Address:* 9 Highgate Spinney, Crescent Road, London N8, England.

HOSPITAL Janette Turner, b. 12 Nov. 1942, Melbourne, Australia. Writer. m. Clifford G Hospital, 5 Feb. 1965, 1 son, 1 daughter. *Education:* BA, University of Queensland, Australia, 1965; MA, Queen's University, Canada, 1973. *Appointments:* High School Teacher, Queensland, Australia, 1963-67; Librarian, Harvard University, USA, 1967-71; Lecturer in English, St Lawrence College and elsewhere, Kingston, Ontario, 1973-82; Full time writer, 1982-; Writer-in-Residence, MIT, Cambridge, Massachusetts, USA, 1985-86, 1987, 1989; Writer-in-Residence, University of Ottawa, Canada, 1987; Writer-in-Residence, University of Sydney, Australia, 1989; Writer-in-Residence, La Trobe University, Melbourne, 1989. *Publications:* The Ivory Swing, 1982; The Tiger in the Tiger Pit, 1983; Borderline, 1985; Charades, 1988; Dislocations, 1986; Contribution of short stories, articles or reviews to numerous magazines and journals. *Memberships:* PEN International; Writers' Union of Canada; American Authors' Guild; Amnesty International. *Honours:* An Atlantic First, The Atlantic Monthly (USA) for short story Waiting, 1978; Canada's $50,000 Seal Award for The

Ivory Swing, 1982; 1st prize, Magazine Fiction, Foundation for the Advancement of Canadian Letters, 1982; Winner $10,000 short story prize, Ladies Home Journal, USA, 1986; Short Story Prize, CBC Literary Competition, Canada, 1986; 1988 Fiction Award for Dislocations, Fellowship of Australian Authors; Listed in Canada's Ten Best Young Fiction Writers, 1986. *Address:* c/o Charlotte Sheedy, Literary Agent, 41 King Street, New York, NY 10014, USA.

HOSSAIN Suraiya, b. 15 Jan. 1940, Barisal, Bangladesh. Medical Specialist. m. Dr A S M T Hossain, 1 Feb. 1963. 1 son, 1 daughter. *Education:* Lic State Medical Fac, East Pakistan, 1959; DPH, St Andrews, 1966; MD, Berne, 1970; MSc, Edinburgh, 1970. *Appointments:* House Surgeon, Mitford Hispital, Dhaka, 1959; Medical Officer, Family Planning Association, Barisal, Bangaldesh, 1959-60; Medical Officer, Azim-Aman Cocoanut Industries Ltd, Barisal, 1960-62; General Practitioner, Barisal, 1962-63; Junior Hospital Medical Officer, Children's Disease Unit, Royal Infirmary, Dundee, Scotland, 1966-67; MRC Research Assistant, Department of Pathology, University of Edinburgh, 1968-70; Research Associate, Department of Pathology 1971, Registrar in Clinical Pathology 1971-72, London Chest Hospital, London, England; Specialist Physician, Dhaka, Bangladesh, 1972-75, 1976-78 and 1980-; Research Associate (Histopathology), Cholera Research Laboratory, Dhaka, 1975-76; Deputy Project Director (Clinical) Family Planning Model Clinic & Research centre, Mohammadpur, Dhaka, 1978-80. *Publications:* Barvabati Ma O Shishur Kotha (an informative book on maternal and child health care in Bangla), 1977; Co-Author, Quick Medical Diagnosis Treatment, 1987; Essentials of Clinical Medicine, 1988. *Memberships:* Associate Fellow, American College of Pathologists; American College of Chest Physicians. *Honour:* WHO Fellowship, 19789. *Hobby:* Reading. *Address:* c/o Ramitasu, GPO Box No 3497, Dhaka 1000, Bangladesh

HOTCHNER Beverly June, b. 13 July 1928, St Louis, USA. Psychologist; Consultant. m. 22 Nov. 1951, 2 sons. *Education:* BS, University of Illinois, 1950; MA 1964, PhD 1972, Washington University. *Appointments:* Assistant Publicity Director, Edison Bros. Stores, 1951-52; Instructor, Washington University, 1970-85; A founder St Louis Women's Counseling Center, 1970-76; Assistant Professor, Southern Illinois University, School of Dental Medicine, 1973, Acting Chairperson, Behavioural Medicine, 1974; Founder, Executive Director, Centre for Human Concern, 1975-82; President, Beverly Hotchner Inc., 1979-; Consultant, St Luke's Hospital, 1979-. *Memberships:* American Association of Sex Therapists, Counselor and Educator; Plain States Regional Chairperson, 1976-78; Society for Sci. Study of Sex; Board Member 1986-89 and Chairperson Continuing Education; American, Missouri, St Louis Psychology Associations; American Association Marriage & Family Therapists; Society for Scientific Study of Sex, Board Member, 1987-89. *Honours:* Alpha Lambda Delta; Phi Beta Kappa; Kappa Delta Pi. *Hobbies:* Cartoon Creation; Gardening; Canoeing. *Address:* 7206 Cornell, St Louis, MO 63130, USA.

HOTTEL Althea K., b. 16 Oct. 1907, Lansdale, Pennsylvania, USA. Retired Educator. m. A. Stauffer Hottel Jr, 5 Apr. 1941. *Education:* BS Education, 1929; MA, Sociology, 1934; PhD, Sociology, 1940. *Appointments:* Social Science Teacher, Wilmington, Delaware, 1929-30; Staff, Social Service Department, Graduate Hospital, 1930-33; Dean of Instruction, Professor of Education, Queen's College, Charlotte, North Carolina, 1935-36; Dean of Women, Lecturer in Sociology, University of Pennslyvania, 1936-59; Director, Commission on the Education of Women, American Council on Education, 1953-55; US Representative, Social Commission, UN Economic and Social Council, 1955-61. *Publications:* Prosecution and Treatment of Women Offenders and the Economic Crisis: Philadelphia 1925-1934, 1940; How Fare American Women? 1955. *Memberships:* American Association of University Women (National President

1947-51); International Federation of University Women (President 1965-68); Pennsylvania Association of Deans of Women (President 1941-43). *Honours:* Phi Beta Kappa, 1935; Philadelphia Gimbel Award, 1947; Award of Merit, University of Pennsylvania Alumni, 1950; Distinguished Daughter of Pennsylvania, 1950; World Affairs Council and Board of Trade of Philadelphia, 1959; Honorary Doctor of Laws: Cedar Great College, 1947; Juniata College, 1948; Elizabeth Town College, 1952; Miami University, 1956; University of Pennsylvania, 1959; Thomas Jefferson University, 1975; Honorary Doctor of Letters: Beaver College, 1947; Alabama College for Women, 1954; Douglas College, Rutgers University, 1958; Women's Medical College, Pennsylvania, 1960; Honorary Associate of Letters, Community College of Philadelphia, 1989. *Hobbies:* Photography; English literature; World affairs. *Address:* 74 Pasture Lane, Apr 201, Bryn Mawr, PA 19010, USA.

HOUGHTON-ALICO Doann, b. 3 Aug. 1940, Mount Kisco, New York, USA. Company President. m. C. Samuel Haines IV, 1960 (divorced 1974), 2 sons, 1 daughter. *Education:* BA, Cedar Crest College, Allentown, Pennsylvania, 1971; Qualified Expert Witness (Technical Writing), US District Court. *Appointments:* Public interest lobbyist, legislative analyst, Environmental Action Inc, Washington DC, 1971-73; Newspaper editor, publisher, Telluride, Colorado, 1974-75; Project consultant (communications), Denver, CO, 1975-79; Founder, President, TIA/Technical Information Analysts Inc (computer systems), Denver, 1980-. *Publications include:* Books: Fuel from Farms: Guide to Small-Scale Ethanol Production, co-author, 1981; Alcohol Fuels: Policies, Production & Potential, 1982; Creating Computer Software User Guides: From Manuals to Menus, 1985; Side-by-Side: A Model for Simultaneous Documentation and System Development in Perspectives on Software Documentation: Inquiries and Innovations; Amityville NY: Baywood Inc; co-author: Effective Support for Shop Floor Automation in Production and Inventory Management Review, 1990. Manuals, various commercial projects; Numerous articles, reports, papers, including 4-part series, software documentation management, in Software News, 1984. Also: Audio-visual training programmes. *Memberships:* Computer Society, Institute of Electrical & Electronics Engineers; Senior Memeber; Society for Technical Communication (STC); Association for Computing Machinery; Human Factors Society; Colorado Authors League. *Honours:* Awards, STC 1984, 1985, Colorado Authors League 1983. *Hobbies:* Sailing; Scuba diving; Skiing; Hiking. *Address:* TIA/Technical Information Associates Inc, 600 South Cherry Street, Suite 1100, Denver, Colorado 80222, USA.

HOULT Jennifer Ann, b. 31 July 1961, Pasadena, California, USA. Harpist; Software Engineer. *Education:* BM, Manhattan School of Music, 1982; BA, Computer Science & Religion, Barnard College, 1986. *Appointments:* Performances with The Boston Symphony Orchester, GBYSO; The Trenton Symphony; The Manhattan Philharmonic; Cognitive Systems, 1986-87; Chemical Bank, 1987-. *Memberships:* Local 802 (American Federation of Musicians); Association for Computational Linguistics; American Harp Society; VOICES, Victims of Incest Can Emerge Survivors. *Honours:* Youth In Concert Competition Winner, 1977; Hobin Harp Competition, 1st Prize, 1980; Manhattan School of Music Concerto Competition Winner, 1981. *Hobbies:* Ballet; Painting; Cycling; Reading; Volunteer work with Incest Survivors. *Address:* 299 Riverside Dr 3A, New York, NY 10025, USA.

HOUSE Faye Riggins, b. 2 June 1938, Dickson County, Tennessee, USA. Clinical Dietitian. m. Kenneth Neil House, 5 June 1959. 1 son, 1 daughter. *Education:* BS, Austin Pery State University, 1960; Certificate, Dietetic Internship, Vanderbilt University Medical Center, 1961; MS, Human Development Counselling, George Peabody College of Vanderbilt University, 1980. *Appointments:* Clinical Dietitian, Vanderbilt Medical Center, 1961-71; Research Dietitian, Vanderbilt School

of Medicine, 1971-75; Private Practice, Nutrition Counsultant with a private practice with Medical Internists, 1975-76; Nutritionist, Tennessee Dept of Public Health, 1976-83; Clinical Dietitian, Nashville Memorial Hospital, 1983-; Consultant to Sandoz Nutrition, Minnesota, 1988-. *Publications:* Book: Food Acceptances/Attitudes of Elderly, 1974; Nutritional Deficiencies in Disadvantaged Children: Their Relationship to Mental Development, 1971; Editor, Dietetic Section, Nashville Cookbook, 1975-76; Ask the Dietitian column, Nashville Tennessean Newspaper, Editor, 1976-78. *Memberships:* Nashville District Dietetic Association, Secretary and Chairs of Various committees, 1960-88; Tennessee Dietetic Association, 1960-88, President 1986; Legislation Chairman, Legislative Network coordinator; American Diabetes Association, Board of Directors, 1987-89; American Dietetic Association, 1960- (ADA State Advisory Committee, 1986). *Honours:* Outstanding Young Women of America, 1973; American Dietetic Association, Meade Johnson Award for Advanced Graduate Study, 1979; Outstanding Dietitian of Year, Nashville District Dietetic Association, 1986; Outstanding Dietitian of Year, Tennessee Dietetic Association, 1986; Chairman, State of Tennessee Board of Dietitian Examiners, 1988; State of Tennessee Advisory Committee on Diabetes, 1988. *Hobbies:* Crossword puzzles; Sewing; Needlework; Clothing design; Art and painting; Antiques; Animals, especially English Springer Spaniels and cats; Human personalities and behaviour; Genealogy; Food anthropology. *Address:* 822 Riverside Drive, Nashville, Tennessee 37206, USA.

HOUTKOOPER Linda Kathryn, b. 15 May 1949, Mitchell, South Dakota, USA. Nutrition Specialist. m. 11 Aug. 1973. *Education:* BS, 1971; MS, 1976, PhD, Nutritional Sciences, 1986. *Appointments:* Teacher, Minnesota, 1971-74; Dietition 1976-83, Research Associate (Department of Family & Community Medicine) 1984, Nutrition Specialist 1986-, University of Arizona. *Publications:* Books: Nutrition Super Stars 1982, Sports Nutrition 1983; Articles, Swimming World magazine 1983-, Swim magazine 1986-; Videotapes, Winning Sports Nutrition, 1988. *Memberships:* American College of Sports Medicine; Society for Nutrition Education; American, Arizona, & Southern Arizona Dietetic Associations; Nutrition Council of Arizona; Association for Women Faculty. *Honours:* Omicron Nu, 1971; Chi Omega sorority, 1969-71; Graduate Scholarship, Arizona Dietetics Association; Registered Dietician; Ruth Cowden Scholarship, 1984. *Hobbies:* Various sports; Research, interactions of exercise & nutrition, body composition assessment; Music; Theatre, Dance, Reading; Writing for professional journals & popular magazines. *Address:* 105 Sierra Vista Drive, Tucson, Arizona 85719, USA.

HOWARD Constance Mildred (Mrs Parker), b. 8 Dec. 1910, Northampton, England. Retired Principal Lecturer; Freelance Artist and Lecturer. m. Harold Wilson Parker, 15 Dec. 1945, deceased 4 Aug. 1980. 1 daughter. *Education:* ARCA 1931-34, ATD 1934-35, Royal College of Art. *Appointments:* Lecturer, Cardiff School of Art, 1935-37; Lecturer, Eastbourne School of Art, 1937-39; Lecturer, Kingston-on-Thames School of Art, 1939-47; Lecturer, Goldsmiths School of Art; Godsmith's College; Senior Lecturer, Principal Lecturer, Head of Textiles, University of London, 1947-75. *Publications:* Design for embroidery from traditional English sources, 1956; Inspiration for embroidery, 1966; Embroidery and Colour, 1976; Textile Crafts (editor) 1978; Constance Howard's Book of Stitches, 1979; Twentieth Century Embroidery in Great Britain, for Volumes up to 1984, published 1981-86; Commissions for Public and Private Buildings etc, 1980-84. *Memberships:* Art Workers' Guild; Fellow, Society of Designer Craftsmen; Embroiderers Guild; Costume Society. *Honour:* MBE 1975, Services to Art Education. *Interests:* Visiting the USA to teach and visit places and people; Design for textiles, collage, embroidery, wrapping thread over card for wall decorations. *Address:* 43 Cambridge Road South, Chiswick, London W4 3DA, England.

HOWARD Deborah Janet, b. 26 Feb. 1946, Westminster, England. Architectural Historian. m. Prof Malcolm Sim Longair, 26 Sept. 1975. 1 son, 1 daughter. *Education:* BA (Hons) 1968, MA 1972, Cambridge; MA, 1969, PhD 1973, Courtauld Institute of Art, London University. *Appointments:* Leverhulme Research Fellow, Clare Hall, Cambridge, 1972-73; Lecturer, History of Art, University College, London, 1973-76; Visiting Lecturer, Yale University, London, 1977 and 1980; Lecturer, Department of Architecture, Edinburgh University, Scotland, 1982-. *Publications:* Books: Jacopo Sansovino: Architecture & Patronage in Renaissance Venice, 1975 and 1987; The Architectural History of Venice, 1980 and 1987. Numerous articles to professional journals. *Memberships:* Royal Fine Art Commission for Scotland; Fellow, Society of Antiquaries; Editor, Journal of the Architectural Heritage Society of Scotland (on regional and national committees); Scottish Drawings Working Group; Scottish Arts Council Lecturing Panel; Governor, St Margaret's School, Edinburgh. *Honours:* Ashdown Travel Scholarship, 1963; County Major Scholarship, 1964-68; College Exhibition, Newnham College, Cambridge, 1964-66; State Studentship, 1968-69 and 1970-72; Leverhulme European Studentship, 1969-70; Gladys Krieble Delmas Fellowship, 1981-82. *Hobbies:* Music especially chamber Music & Opera; Hill walking; Skiing; Gardening; Photography. *Address:* Department of Architecture, University of Edinburgh, 20 Chambers Street, Edinburgh, Scotland, EH1 1JZ.

HOWARD Elizabeth Jane, b. 26 Mar. 1923, London, England. Author. m. Peter Scott, 28 Apr. 1941, divorced 1948, 1 daughter. (2) Kingsley Amis, 1964, divorced 1982. *Publications:* Novels: The Beautiful Visit; The Long View; The Sea Change; After Julians; Odd Girl Out; Something in Disguise; Getting It Right; Short Stories: Mr Wrong; We Are for the Dark, with Robert Ankerman; Biography: Bettina (with Arthur Helps); 14 TV plays; 3 film scripts. *Memberships:* Writers Guild; Authors Lending & Copyright Society; Royal Horticultural Society; National Trust. *Honours:* John Llewellyn Rhys Memorial Prize, 1950; Yorkshire Post Prize, 1978. *Hobbies:* Gardening; Cooking; Arts. *Address:* c/o Jonathan Clowes, 22 Prince Albert Road, London NW1, England.

HOWARD Elizabeth Fitzgerald, b. 28 Dec. 1927, Baltimore, Maryland, USA. Associate Professor of Library Science. m. Lawrence C Howard, 14 Feb. 1953. 3 daughters. *Education:* AB, Radcliffe College, 1948; MLS 1971, PhD 1977, University of Pittsburgh. *Employment:* Children's Librarian, Boston Public Library, 1951-56; Resource Librarian, Episcopal Diocese of Pittsburgh, 1972-74; Reference Librarian, Pittsburgh Theological Seminary, 1974-77; Visiting Lecturer, University of Pittsburgh, 1977-78; Assistant Professor 1978-85, Associate Professor of Library Science, 1985-, West Virginia University. *Publications:* The Train to Lulu's, 1988; America as Story: Historical Fiction for Secondary Schools, 1988; Chita's Christmas Tree, 1989. *Memberships:* Co-chair of Teachers of Children's Literature Group, American Library Association; Beta Phi Mu, Library Science Honor Society; President, Pittsburgh Chapter; National Secretary, Children's Literature Association; Society of Childrens Book Writers; International Board on Books for Youth. *Honours:* President of Senior Class, 1948; President of Class of 1948, 1948-73, Radcliffe College. *Hobbies:* Children's books; Writing; Symphony; Theatre; African folklore; French; Travelling. *Address:* 919 College Avenue, Pittsburgh, PA 15232, USA.

HOWARD Helen Addison, b. 4 Aug. 1904, Missoula, Montana, USA. Historian; Author. m. Ben Overland, 24 Apr. 1946. *Education:* BA, English, University of Montana, 1927; MA, English, University of Southern California, 1933. *Publications:* Feature Writer-Reporter, Daily Missoulian, 1923-29; Freelance magazine Writer, 1934-; Radio TV Monitor Editor, Radio Reports, Los Angeles, 1943-56; Staff Book Reviewer, Journal of West Los Angeles, 1943-69; KS St. U, Manhattan, 1970-; Editor, Advisory Board, 1978-. *Publications:* War Chief Joseph, 1941-58; Contributing Editor, frontier Omnibus, 1962; Northwest Trail Blazers, 1963; Saga of Chief Joseph, 1965; American Indian Poetry, 1979-; American Frontier Tales, 1982; The UX Ranch, 1989. *Memberships:* Life Member, Alumni Association, University of Montana, 1927-; Historical Society. *Honours:* Recipient, various honours and awards. *Hobbies:* Classical Music; Bicycle Riding; Horse Riding. *Address:* 410 South Lamer St., Burbank, CA 91506, USA.

HOWARD Joan Alice, b. 28 Apr. 1929, New York, USA. Artist; Choreographer. m. Robert Thornton Howard, 26 June 1949, 3 sons, 1 daughter. *Education:* Hunter College, 1947-48; University of California, Los Angeles, 1967-68; Valley College, LA, 1970-71. *Appointments:* Director, Choreography, Academy of Dance, Floral Park & Forest Hills, New York, 1947-57; Director of Dance, Catholic Parochial Schools, NYC, Brooklyn, Floral Park, 1948-55; Chairman, Dance Department, Molloy College, 1958-67; Self-employed artist, Station KNEC-TV, Los Angeles, 1967-74; Numerous exhibitions, various locations, 1974-. *Creative work includes:* Numerous paintings, oil, acrylic; Drawings, watercolours; Choreographer, various ballets, 1960-. *Memberships include:* Auxiliary, American Watercolour Society; Dance Educators of America; Women's Sailing Committee, US Yacht Racing Association; Manhasset Art Association. *Honours include:* Silver Award, acrylic painting, Great Neck House Gallery, 1986; Gold Award, Hutchins Gallery, C. W. Post College, Long Island University. *Hobbies:* Racing sail boats; Rally cars. *Address:* 19 Autumn Ridge Road, South Salem, New York 10590, USA.

HOWARD Kathleen, b. 3 Nov. 1947, Norman, USA. Computer Analyst. m. Norman Edio Gibat, 16 Oct. 1971. *Education:* University of Oklahoma, 1966-68. *Appointments:* Typesetter, Selenby Press, Norman, 1968-72; Owner, President, Noguska Industries, Fostoria, Ohio, 1973-; Consultant, Bechtel Corp, 1980-86. *Publications:* Co-Autho, Illustrator, The Lore of Still Building, 1972; Co-Author, Making Wine, Beer and Merry, 1973; Co- Author, 3 journals: Best printers Gazette, Beverage Communicator, Crafty Winemaker; Co-Author, Computer Comix Magazine; Author, many business management software packages. *Memberships:* Altrusa Club of Fostoria, Secretary, 1984-86, President, 1986-88; Altrusa District Five, Chairman ASTRA Committee; Better Business Bureau; National Federation of Independent Business; Chamber of Commerce; Founder, Home Wine Merchants Association, 1976. *Honours:* Distinguished Service Award, Bechtel Corporation, 1983; Founders Award, HWBTA, 1976. *Hobbies:* Painting; Graphics; Travel; Reading. *Address:* 1030 Columbus Avenue, Fostoria, OH 44830, USA.

HOWARD Linda Gordon, b. 7 Aug 1949, Richmond, Virginia, USA. Attorney-at-Law. *Education:* BA, Reed College, 1970; JD, University of Virginia, 1973. *Appointments:* Staff Attorney, US Department of Transportation, 1973-74; Legislative Assistant to US Senator Lloyd Bentsen, 1974-75; Assistant Professor, Associate Professor, Ohio State University College of Law, 1975-81; Director, Interdepartmental Task Force on Women, White House, Washington DC, 1980-81; Counsel to the President, Hunter College, City University of New York, New York City, 1981-89; Senior Counsel, Office of the Corporation Counsel, City of New York, NY 1989-. *Publication:* Hazardous Substances in the Workplace: Implications for the Employment Rights of Women, University of Pennslyvania Law Review, 1981. *Memberships:* Board of Trustees, Reed College, Portland, Oregon; Alumni Council, University of Virginia; Citizens Union, New York City; President, Reed College New York Alumni Chapter; Virginia Bar Association; New York Bar Association; Association of the Bar of the City of New York. *Hobbies:* Swimming; Crime novels; Singing. *Address:* Office of the Corporation Counsel, The City of New York, 100 Church Street, New York, NY 10007, USA.

HOWARD Patricia, b. 18 Oct. 1937, Birmingham, England. Musician. m. David Louis Howard, 29 July 1960, 2 daughters. *Education:* BA, 1959, MA 1963, Oxford University; PhD, Surrey University, 1974. *Appointments:* Lecturer, Tutor, Music, Open University, 1976-. *Publications:* Gluck and the Birth of Modern Opera, 1963; The Operas of Benjamin Britten: An Introduction, 1969; Haydn in London, 1980; Mozart's Marriage of Figaro, 1980; C.W. Gluck: Orfeo, 1981; Haydn's String Quartets, 1984; Beethoven's Eroica Symphony, 1984; Christoph Willibald Gluck: A Guide to Research, 1987; Music in Vienna, 1790-1800, 1988; Beethoven's Fidelio, 1988. *Honours:* Susette Taylor Travelling Fellowship, 1971; Leverhulme Research Award, 1976; British Academy Research Award, 1988. *Address:* Stepping Stones, Gomshall, Surrey, England.

HOWARTH Margaret Anne (Duchesse de Corinth), b. 22 Mar. 1930, Manitou, Manitoba, Canada. m. George, Duke of Corinth, 18 Sep. 1966, 1 son, 1 daughter. *Education:* Chilliwack High School. *Memberships:* Sovereign Dynastic Hospitalier Order of St John, Knights of Malta; Constantinian Order of St George; Sovereign Order of the Oak. *Honours:* Dame Grand Cross, Knights of Malta; Dame Grand Cross, Constantinian Order of St George; Dame Grand Cross, Sovereign Order of the Oak; Commanders Cross, Polonia Restituta. *Hobbies:* Dress and gown designing; Gourmet cooking. *Address:* 20 Stanford Drive, Rancho Mirage, CA 92270, USA.

HOWE Florence, Director, The Feminist Press. *Education:* AB, Hunter College, 1950; AM, Smith College, 1951. *Appointments:* Teaching Assistant, University of Wisconsin, 1951-54; Instructor, English, Hofstra University, 1954-57; Lecturer, English, Queens College, 1956-57; Assistant Professor English, Goucher College, 1960-71; Professor, Humanities, & American Studies, University of New York, 1971-87; Professor, English, City College, City University of New York, 1987-. *Publications:* The Conspiracy of the Young, 1971; No More Masks, 1973; Women and the Power to Change, 1975; Seven Years Later, 1976; Women Working, 1979; Everywoman's Guide to Colleges & Universities, 1982; Myths of Co-Education, 1984; With Wings: An Anthology of Literature By and About Women with Disabilities, 1987; Women & Higher Education, 1988; Monographs, articles. *Memberships Include:* Teachers & Writers Collaborative; American Historical Association. *Honours:* Recipient, many honours & awards. *Address:* 201 East 87 Street, Apt. 11D, New York, NY 10128, USA.

HOWELL Gailyn A, b. 24 Apr. 1942, Trent, Texas USA. Neuroscientlst. m. Eddie Howell, 25 May 1963. 1 son, 1 daughter. *Education:* BS, Nursing/Psychology, 1964; MS, Human Development, 1980; PhD, Communication Disorders, 1983. *Appointments:* Public Health Nurse, 1965-70; Research Assistant, 1978-83; Adjunct Professor, Lecturer, Stress Management Consultant, Research Scientist, University of Texas at Dallas, 1984-. *Publications:* Neurobiology of Zinc, 1984; Article in Nature Magazine, 1984. *Memberships:* Neuroscience Society; Women in Neuroscience; American Women in Science; Biofeedback Society. *Honours:* Valedictorian of High School, 1960; Bausch & Lamb Science Award, 1960; Alpha lambda Delta, 1964; Co-organizer of the International Neurobiology of Zinc Symposium, Boston, USA, 1983. *Hobbies:* Watercolour and Oil Painting; Weaving; Music, Indian flute and drums; Gardening. *Address:* PO Box 1000-265, McKinney, TX 75069, USA.

HOWELL Mary Elizabeth, b. 19 Feb. 1942, Galesburg, USA. Business Owner. m. Murrell D. Howell, 22 Dec. 1969, 3 sons, 1 daughter. *Education:* Business Administration Degree, University of Redlands, 1985. *Appointments:* General Manager, Gravel Products, 1978-80; Comptroller, Bluebird Int., 1981-83; Owner, President, Magnetic Power Systems, 1984-. *Publications:* Etching, Thin Graille of Insanity, 1983; Patent, Pitch Controlled Ground Effect Vehicle, 1984; Patent, Rail Mounted Camera System, 1986; Developer,

Cosmetic Cream. *Memberships:* National Association of Accountants; National Association of Executive Women; Rose Parade Decorating Committee. *Honours:* Letter of Commendation, VA, 1977; various civic awards. *Hobbies:* Needlework; Domestic Arts; Outdoor Activities. *Address:* Magnetic Power Systems, PO Box 1115, Huntington Beach, CA 92647, USA.

HOWES Barbara, b. 1 May 1914, New York, USA. Poet; Anthologist. m. William Jay Smith, 1 Oct. 1947. 2 sons. *Education:* BA, Bennington College, 1937. *Publications:* Editor, Chimera, 1943-47. Poetry: The Undersea Farmer, 1948; In the Cold Country, 1948; Light & Dark, 1959; Looking up at Leaves, 1966; The Blue Garden, 1972; A Private Signal: Poems New & Selected, 1977; Moving, 1983. Short Stories: The Road Commissioner & Other Stories, 1983. Anthologies Edited: 23 Modern Stories, 1963; From the Green Antilles: writings of the Caribbean, 1966, England, 1967 and 1971; The Sea Green Horse with Gregory Jay Smith, 1970; The Eye of the Heart: stories from Latin America, 1973, 1974, England, 1988. *Honours:* Guggenheim Fellowship, 1955; Brandeis University Creative Arts Poetry Grant, 1958; Award in Literature, National Institute of Arts and Letters, 1971; Golden Rose Award, New England Poetry Club, 1973; Christopher Award for The Eye of the Heart, 1974; Bennington Award for outstanding contributions to poetry, 1980. *Hobbies:* Seeing friends and talking; Reading; Living in the country; Working in my field. *Address:* Brook House, North Pownal, Vermont 05260, USA.

HOY Judith Cathryn, b. 4 Sept. 1941, Minneapolis, Minnesota, USA. Consultant. m. Kenneth R Levinson, Jr, 21 May 1967. divorced 1982. *Education:* BA, University of Minnesota, 1964; MA, Queens College, 1973; EdD, Columbia University Teachers College, 1988. *Appointments:* Counselor, New York State Youth Services, 1965-70; Assistant Co-ord. Academic Advisem, Queens College, 1970-76; Consultant in organizational effectiveness, 1976-. *Publications:* Writing Workbook; Learning in the Work Place: A Study of Women Executives. *Memberships:* Conference Director, 1986, National Organization Development Network; Steering Committee Member, Organization Dev. Network of Greater New York; ASTD; Officer, Business & Professional Women. *Honours:* Various College Awards and Scholarships. *Hobbies:* Music; Film; Jogging; Health. *Address:* 156 West 77th Street, New York, NY 10024, USA.

HOYOUNG Lana Wyomie Conner, b. 15 Jan. 1951, Anguilla, British West Indies. Administrator. m. Leroy Carlton Hoyoung, 0 July 1900, 2 daughters. *Education:* Certificate, Teacher Education, 1973; Diplomas, Social Studies 1972-74, Science Education, 1974; Certificates, Social Administration 1981, Social Work 1985, Women's Work 1986. *Appointments:* Teacher: Untrained 1968-73, trained 1973-74, specialised 1974-80; Assistant then Acting Community Development Officer, 1980-83; Coordinator, Women's Affairs, 1982-. *Creative work includes:* Founder, Anguilla Craft Centre (marketing outlet), 1982. *Memberships:* Founder, National Women's Council, 1982; Girl Guide Leader, 6th Anguilla; Organist, Maranatha Methodist Church, 21 years; Anguilla branch, Soroptimist International; Executive, WAND, 1982; Executive, Caribbean Womens's Association, 1985. *Honour:* Outstanding G-ite on Hall, 1985. *Hobbies:* Music; Drama (play writing); Cooking; Sewing. *Address:* Charomo Cottage, South Hill, Anguilla, British West Indies.

HOYTT Eleanor Hinton, Teacher; Author. *Education:* BA, SpelmanCollege, 1964; MA, Atlanta University, 1967. *Appointments:* Librarian, 1964-69; Faculty Member, School of Library & Information Studies, 1969-85, Co-Director, Africana Womens Centre, 1983-85, Atlanta University, Georgia; Conference Co-ordinator, National Womens Studies Association, 1985-87; Grants & Fellowship Co-ordinator, 1987-88, Emory University; Director, PEER, Washington DC, 1988-. *Publications:* Articles in professional journals; papers. *Memberships:* Association of Black Womens Historians; National

Alumnae Association of Spelman College; National Black Womens Health Project, Chair, Board of Directors. *Address:* 1570 Ivystone Court, Silver Spring, MD 20904, USA.

HRIBSEK Marija, b. 18 Jan. 1943, Cacak, Yugoslavia. University Professor. *Education:* Electrical Engineering, University of Belgrade, 1961-66; Dipl.Ing., 1966; MS, Electrical Engineering, University of Belgrade, 1974; PhD, University of Maryland, USA, 1976. *Appointments:* Electronics Industry, 1966-68; Electrical Engineering Dept., 1968-76, Assistant Professor, 1980-87, Associate Professor, 1987-, University of Belgrade; University of Maryland, 1974-76. *Publications:* Electronics I, 3rd edition 1986, in Serbo-Croat. *Memberships:* ETAN; MIDEM; Yugoslav Society of University Professors, Board Member, 1977-79; Sigma Xi, 1975; IEEE, 1976. *Honours:* Recipient, various honours and awards including Fulbright Grant, 1974. *Hobbies:* Knitting; Crochet; Classical Music; Reading; Concerts; Theatre. *Address:* 80 Nova 12, 11030 Belgrade, Yugoslavia.

HSU Ying, b. 16 Dec. 1935, China. Author; Instructor; Teacher. m. 2 Sept. 1961, 1 son. *Education:* BA, English Literature, Foreign Languages Institute, Beijing, 1958; MA, TESL, 1983, MA, Education, 1985, PhD Candidate, 1986, University of Utah, USA. *Appointments:* Translator, Beijing, 1958-80; Teacher, 1980-84; Teacher, Education, University of Utah, 1985-. *Publications:* Text Book in English, Speaking Chinese in China, 1983; 6 sets of audio cassettes, Speaking Chinese in China, 1983. *Hobbies:* Basketball; Piano. *Address:* English Section, Foreign Languages Press, Beijing, China.

HU Sue Irene King, b. 7 Nov. 1938, USA. Elementary Education. m. Richard Chee Chung Hu, 2 July 1960, 1 son, 1 daughter. *Education:* BS, Towson State University, 1960; MA, Marymount University, 1987. *Appointments:* Elementary Teacher: Harford County, 1960-61, Baltimore Co., 1961-63, Arlington Co., 1977-; School Science Co-ordinator, 1986-. *Publications:* Articles in professional journals. *Memberships:* Council for Elementary Science Intern.; National Science Teachers Association; Virginia Association of Science Teachers; National Association of Biology Teachers. *Honours:* Kappa Delta Pi; Delta Epsilon Sigma. *Hobbies:* Hiking; Gardening; Travel; Cooking. *Address:* 2326 North Tuckahoe Street, Arlington, VA 22205, USA.

HUBBARD Josephine Jacquelyn Brodie, b. 11 May 1938, Tampa, Florida, USA. Assistant Education Services Officer. m. Ronald C. Hubbard, 9 June 1962, 1 son, 1 daughter. *Education:* BSc., Honours, 1958; MEd., Honours, 1968. *Appointments:* Various Teaching positions, 1958-65; Special Services Director, Academic Advisor, University of South Florida, 1971-72; Academic Advisor, Wright State University, 1973; substitute Teacher, 1974-75; Education Services Officer, Landstuhl, Germany, 1980-81; Federal Women's Program Manager, Nellis Air Force Base, 1983-; Assistant Chief, Education Services, Nellis Air Force Base, 1987-. *Publications:* Counseling the Disadvantaged Pre-College Student, 1971; Heal & Energize Yourself Naturally, 1988. *Memberships:* Various professional organisations including: American Association of Counselling & Development. *Honours Include:* Kappa Delta Pi, 1968; Military Mother of the Year, Las Vegas, 1985. *Hobbies:* Sewing; Writing; Cooking; Holistic Health; *Address:* 5781 Brisbane Place, Las Vegas, NV 89110, USA.

HUBBARD Miriam, Lady, b. 12 Dec 1924, London, England. Retired. m. Lt. Cdr. Peregrine Hubbard, 19 Apr. 1952, 2 sons, 3 daughters. *Memberships:* Chairman, East Region, Riding for the Disabled; Chairman, St Nicholas Hospice, Bury St Edmunds; Chairman, Catholic Womens League, Bury St Edmunds; President, NSPCC, West Suffolk. *Hobbies:* Riding; Walking; Sailing. *Address:* Thurston Croft, Bury St Edmunds, Suffolk, England.

HUDDY Mary Ellen, b. 5 Aug. 1922, Fresno, California, USA. Musician; Medical Transcriptionist. m. Emil, 14 Feb. 1968. *Education:* BA, Pacific Union College, 1947; Cert. Medical Transcriptionist, 1979; Accred. Record Tech. 1980. *Appointments:* Instructor, Southern College, Tennessee, 1947-49; Pacific Union College, 1949-52; Music Studio, Fresno, 1952-63; North Fork, 1963-88; Instructor Music and English, Fresno Union Academy, 1958-59; Forest lookout and Receptionist, US Forest Service, Fresno, 1955-56; Med Office Manager, 1956-73; Med, Transcriptionist/Supr Valley Children's Hospital, 1973-87. *Publications:* The Youth's Instructor, 1955-58; Poems: National Poetry Anthology, 1959, 1960. *Memberships:* American Guild of Organists; American Medical Record Association; Beta Sigma Phi, president North Fork, 1969-70; American Association Medical Transcriptionists, Sgt at Arms, Fresno, 1980-81; American Bell Association. *Hobbies:* Gardening; Photography; Oil painting; Avid reader; Travel; California history; Collecting bells. *Address:* 54451 Road 200, North Fork, CA 93643, USA.

HUDSON Anne Hart, b. 5 May 1958, Grenada, Mississippi, USA. Auditor. *Education:* BBA Finance, Delta State University, 1980; Studies in Real Estate Principles, Real Estate Law, Holmes Junior College. *Appointments:* Teller, Bookkeeper, summers 1976-80, Bookkeeper, Research Department Operations, 1980-82, Management Trainee, Student Loan and Audit, 1982, Internal Auditor, 1985-, Sunburst Banking System. *Appointments:* Co-Chairman, Grenada's Sesquecentennial Celebration, 1096; Grenada Business and Professional Women's Club: Historian, Corresponding Secretary, Treasurer, 1st Vice-President, President-Elect, President; Mississippi Business and Professional Women's Club: Young Career Woman Chair and Board of Directors; Chairman of Production, Miss Grenada County Pageant; Former Recording Secretary and Social Chairman, Phi Mu Sorority. *Honours:* Selected as Young Career Woman, 1983, Member of the Quarter, spring 1986, spring 1988, Grenada Business and Professional Women's Club. *Hobbies:* Sewing and needlework; Dancing; Water sports; Coordinating various social and business affairs/conventions, banquets; Home interior designing; Other creative handiworks. *Address:* 1033 Mound Street, Grenada, MS 38901, USA.

HUDSON Margaret Stover, b. 27 Sept. 1947, Roanoke, USA. Business Manager. m. John Davidson Hudson, 1 Mar. 1974, 1 step-son. *Education:* BBA, Roanoke College, 971. *Appointments:* Cashier, Bookkeeper, 1965-74, Controller, 1974-79, Director of Finance & Administrative Services, 1979-84, Business Manager 1984-, Roanoke College; Customer Relation Representative, National Cash Register, Roanoke, 1974. *Memberships:* Director, National Association of Accountants, 1984; National Association of College & University Business Officers; College & University Personnel Association; Southern Association of College & University Business Officers; Virginia Dressage Association; US Dressage Association; Rotary Club of Salem. *Honours:* Cum Laude; Andrew Lewish High School, 1965; Roanoke College, 1971; Golden Key, Delta Mu Delta Upsilon Chapter, 1970. *Hobbies:* Dressage; Piano; Reading. *Address:* 6539 Laban Road NW, Roanoke, VA 24019, USA.

HUDSON Mary, b. Athens, Texas, USA. Chairman, Hudson Oil Company and Hudson Refining Company. 1 daughter. *Education:* College Extension Courses, University of Kansas and University of Oklahoma. *Creative Works:* Has given over 20 speeches between 1961 and 1983. *Memberships:* Consul of Republic of Colombia, 1959-84 (retired); Dean of Consular Corps of Kansas City, 1977-84 (Retired); International Platform; Women's Kansas City Association for International Relations and Trade, President, 1971-79; World Petroleum Congress; Director; Department of Energy, National Petroleum Council; Director, National Petroleum Refiners Association; American Petroleum Institute; Director, American Petroleum Refiners Association; Independent Gasoline Marketers Council,

1973-; Oil Men's Club of Kansas City; Society of Independent Gasoline Marketers of America; Empire State Bank, Former Director; United Missouri Bank, Former Director; Committee of 200; Director, American Academy of Achievement; Board of Governors, American Royal Association; Former Trustee, Baptist Memorial Hospital, Kansas City, Missouri; Chamber of Commerce of Greater Kansas City; Conservatory of Music, Board of Trustees, Historic Kansas City Founcation; Kansas City Art Insdtitute; Kansas City Museum of History and Science; Kansas City Philharmonic Association; Society of Fellows, Nelson-Atkins Galleries; Honorary Director, Rockhurst College; Kansas City Performing Arts Theatre, Director, and Kansas City (Women's Council), University of Missouri. *Honours include:* Ambassador of Good Will Arkansas Traveller; Business Week, 100 Top Corporate Women 1976; Honorary Citizen of Kansas City, Missouri, 1961; Honorary Citizen of New Orleans, Louisiana, 1965; Outstanding Woman in the Petroleum Industry, Desk & Derrick Club of St Louis, Missouri, 1964; Twenty Five Year Club of the Petroleum Industry, 1977 (first woman to the admitted to membership); Horatio Alger Award, 1981; Entrepreneur Babson College, 1983, etc. *Hobbies:* Travel. *Address:* Box B, Kansas City, KS 66208, USA.

HUGGAN Jean Isabel, b. 21 Sep. 1943, Ontario, Canada. Author. m. Robert David Huggan, 31 Dec. 1970, 1 daughter. *Education:* BA, English, Philosophy, University of Western Ontario, 1965. *Appointments:* Copy Editor, Macmillan Publishing, 1965-67; Teacher of English and Theatre, 1968-72; Reporter, Columnist, 1973-76; Teaching of Creative Writing, University of Ottawa, 1985-87. *Publications:* The Elizabeth Stories. *Honours:* 1st Prize (for women scriptwriters) for film script, National Film Board of Canada, 1977; New Voice of the Year Award (Joe Savage New Voice Award), Quality Paperback Award Book Club, New York, 1987; Alan Swallow Literary Award, Denver Quarterly, Denver 1987. *Hobbies:* Book reviewing; Reading; Walking; Music. *Address:* Box 30677, Nairobi, Kenya.

HUGHES Abbie Angharad, b. 28 Mar. 1940, St Helens, Lancashire, England. Research Scientist; Educator. 2 sons. *Education:* BA 1963, MA 1968, Pembroke College, Oxford University; DIC, Imperial College, London University, 1966; PhD 1968, DSc 1982, Faculty of Medicine, University of Edinburgh. *Appointments:* Assistant Lecturer, Edinburgh University Medical School, 1964-68; Demonstrator, Physiology, Oxford University, 1968-72; Extraordinary Lecturer, New College, Oxford, 1969; Postdoctoral Fellow 1972-74, Senior Research Fellow 1974-87, John Curtin School for Medical Research, Australian National University; Professor & Director, National Vision Research Institute, Australia, 1983-. *Publications include:* Numerous contributions, vision research, scientific literature. *Memberships:* Australian Medical Writers Association; American Academy of Optometry; Australian Neurosciences Society; Australian Physiological Pharmacological Society; Optical Society of America; Physiological Society (London); Society for Neurosciences (USA). *Honours:* Fellow: Optical Society of America 1986-, American Academy of Optometry 1982-; Editorial Boards: Behavioural Brain Research 1984-, Clinical Vision Sciences 1986-, Vision Research 1987-; Honorary Secretary, National Vision Research Foundation, 1984-. *Hobbies:* Antiquarian books; Reading; Personal computing; Dinner parties. *Address:* National Vision Research Institute, 386 Cardigan Street, Carlton, Victoria 3053, Australia.

HUGHES Anne, b. 23 Mar. 1925, New York, USA. Portrait Artist. *Education:* BA, McGill University, 1945; MA, Columbia University, 1956. *Appointments:* UN Chief of Official Records, Editing Section, 1980-82; UN, Chief of Editorial Service, 1982-85 (retired); Portrait Artist, 1985-. *Publications:* Portraits of: Joseph Nugent, Clarissa Lapoff, Nadia Chang, Maria De Freitas, Violet Bell, Annebeth Rosenboom, Thomas De Jong. *Memberships:* Salmagundi Club; Circumnavigators Club; Association of Former International Civil Servants; National Academy of Design; Metropolitan Museum of

Art. *Hobbies:* Cooking; Reading. *Address:* 300 East 40 Street, New York, NY 10016, USA.

HUGHES Betty Ann, b. Eau Claire, Wisconsin, USA. Public Relations Director. m. Arthur John Hughes, 2 Oct. 1954, 2 daughters. *Education:* University of Wisconsin; Harper College. *Appointments:* Weber-Stephen Products Company, Palatine, 1967-. *Publications:* Barbecuing the Weber Covered Way; Developed and Directed production, Barbecue Basics; Developer of Recipes; Author, Editor, all Weber Product Cookbooks and Demonstration Guide; Editor, Weber-Stephen Products Company News, 1974-78; articles in professional journals; Prepared and presented over 400 cooking classes; Spokesperson for Weber-Stephen Products Company, appearing on over 350 TV and radio programmes in the US, Canada and New Zealand; numerous newspaper interviews nationwide. *Memberships:* Electrical Women's Roundtable; Chicago Chapter Chairman, Vice Chairman, Scholarship Chairman, Hospitality Chairman, Membership Chairman, Newsletter Co-Chairman, Electrical Women's Roundtable; Mount Prospect Business and Professional Women's Club; National Association for Female Executives. *Hobbies:* Travel; Cooking; Golf; Collecting Cookbooks; Antiques; Reading. *Address:* Weber-Stephens Products Company, 200 E Daniels Road, Palatine, IL 60067, USA.

HUGHES Judith Lee Johnson, b. 23 Nov. 1940, Florida, USA. Owner, Ballet Studio. m. 26 Dec. 1966, 1 son, 1 daughter. *Education:* Adelphi College and St Petersburg Junior College. *Appointments:* Founder, Judith Lee Johnson Studios, 1961-; Instructor, Eckerd College, 1965-68; Started 2nd business 1987-. *Publications:* Pre-School Dance, 1977. *Memberships:* Advisor, Co-Director, City Centre Ballet Co; Artistic Advisor, St Petersburg Civic Ballet Inc; Artistic Advisor Florida, West Ballet Co; Board Member, Founder, Pinellas County Dance Teachers Association; State Dance Association of Florida. *Honours:* Woman in the Arts Award, St Petersburg Symphony Guild, 1967; Competition Judge, Dance Masters of America, Florida Chapter. *Hobbies:* Genealogy; Water Sports. *Address:* 2033-54 Avenue North, St Petersburg, FL 33714, USA.

HUGHES Judith Markham, b. 20 Feb. 1941, New York, New York, USA. Historian; Professor. m. H Stuart Hughes, 26 Mar. 1964. 1 son. *Education:* BA, Swarthmore College, 1962; MA 1963, PhD 1970, Harvard University. *Appointments:* Teaching Fellow, 1965-66 and 1967-70; Assistant Professor of Social Studies, 1970-75, Harvard University; Associate Professor of History, 1975-84, Professor of History, 1984-, University of California, San Diego. *Publications:* To the Maginot Line: The Politics of French Military Preparation in the 1920's, 1971; Emotion and High Politics: Personal Relations at the Summit in Late Nineteenth-Century Britain and Germany, 1983; Reshaping the Psychoanalytic Domain: The Work of Melanie Klein, W R D Fairbairn and D W Winnicott, 1989. *Memberships:* American Historical Association; North American Conference on British Studies; Group for the Use of Psychology in History; Membre correspondant, Association Internationale d'Histoire de la Psychanalyse; Western Association of Women Historians Article Prize Committee, 1985; Editorial Board, Diplomatic History, 1976-78. *Honours:* Phi Beta Kappa; Woodrow Wilson Fellowship, 1962-63; West European Studies Fellowship, Harvard University, 1972-73; National Endowment for the Humantities Fellowship, 1974. *Address:* Department of History, C-004, University of California, San Diego, La Jolla, CA 92093, USA.

HUGHES Libby (Vera Elizabeth Pockman), b. 11 Aug. 1932, Pittsburgh, Pennsylvania, USA. Author; Playwright; Freelance writer. m. R John Hughes, 20 Aug. 1955, divorced 1988. 1 son, 1 daughter. *Education:* BA, University of Alabama, 1954; MFA, Boston University, 1955. *Appointments:* Actress in USA, Kenya, South Africa, 1954-59; Freelance writer from Asia, 1964-70; Assistant Publisher, 1977-81, Publisher,

1981-85, Hughes Newspapers, Inc; Drama critic, interviewer, 1977-86; Playwright, 1977-. *Publications:* Bali, 1969; Margaret Thatcher, 1989; Edited Ginger Rogers' autobiography, 1989; Authored biography on Benazir Bhutto, 1990; Author of 20 unpublished plays. *Memberships:* Board, National Society of Arts & Letters; Protocol Officer, NSAL, 1984-88; President, Cape Cod Chapter, NSAL, 1984-86; Board of Wisdom Institute, 1984-86; Board of Cape Cod Museum, 1984-86; Board of Alabama Wildlife Rescue Service, 1988-;. Dramatists Guild, 1982-. *Honours:* Maxwell Anderson Playwrights Series for Cabbie, 1984; One Act Play contest for, The Opening, ATA in NYC, 1985; Honorable Mention for Mask of Summer, Theatre Southwest, 1985; Four plays produced off Broadway, 1984-88. *Hobbies:* Theatre; Art; News; Research and writing about alcoholism; Proust; Wildlife. *Address:* 2523 Mountain Brook Circle, Birmingham, Alabama 35223, USA.

HUGHES Margaret Eileen, b. 22 Jan. 1943, Saskatoon, Canada. Dean of Law. m. James R. Hughes, 21 May 1966, 2 daughters. *Education:* BA, 1965, LL.B., 1966, University of Saskatchewan; MSW, 1968, LL.M, 1968, University of Michigan. *Appointments:* Assistant Professor, Law, 1968-71, Associate Professor, 1971-75, Law, University of Windsor; Executive Interchange, Justice Dept., Otawa, 1975-77; Council, Dept. of Justice, 1977-78; Professor, Law, University of Saskatchewan, 1978-84; Dean, Law, Calgary, 1984-. *Publications:* Articles in professional journals. *Memberships:* Law Societies of Upper Canada and Saskatchewan; Calgary, Canadian Bar Associations; Canadian Association of Law Teachers. *Address:* Faculty of Law, University of Calgary, Calgary, Alberta, Canada T2N 1N4.

HUGHES Monica Mary, b. 3 Nov. 1925, Liverpool, England. Writer. m. Glen Hughes, 22 Apr. 1957, 2 sons, 2 daughters. *Publications:* Crisis on Conshelf 10; Earthdark; The Tomorrow City; Ghost Dance Caper; Beyond the Dark River; Keeper of the Isis Light; The Guardian of Isis; The Isis Pedlar; Hunter in the Dark; Ring Rise, Ring Set; Space Trap; Devil on my Back; The Dream Catcher; Sandwriter; Blaine's Way; Log Jam (Spirit River). *Memberships:* Writers' Union of Canada; Writers Guild of Alberta, Secretary; CANSCAIP; PEN International. *Honours:* Vicky Metcalf Award, 1981; Alberta Juvenile Novel Award, 1981; Canada Council Prize for Childrens Literature 1981, 1982; Ibby Certificate of Honour, 1982; Library Association Young Adult Novel Award, 1983; Runner-up for Guardian Award, 1983; Writers Guild of Alberta R. Ross Annett Award, 1983, 1984, 1987; The Silver Feather, Germany, 1986; Book Lion, Belgium, 1987. *Hobbies:* Swimming; weaving; Reading; Travel. *Address:* 13816 110A Avenue, Edmonton, Alberta Canada T5M 2M9.

HUGHES Selma Elizabeth, b. 3 May 1926, Cardiff, Wales. Professor. m. Nathan Hughes, 4 Dec. 1954, 2 sons, 1 daughter. *Education:* BCom, 1945, BSc(Econ), 1946, London University; MEd Southern Methodist University, Dallas, Texas, USA, 1970; Doctoral Teaching Fellow, 1973-74, PhD, Special Education, 1974, Texas Women's University. *Appointments:* Assistant Statistician, Ministry of Food, London, England, 1947-50; Statistician, National Coal Board, Cardiff, 1950-54; Teacher, Language/Learning Disabilities, Dallas, Texas, USA, 1970-74; Assistant Professor, Special Education, 1975-82, Associate Professor, 1982-, East Texas State University, Commerce. *Publications:* Child's Age Affects Bilingual Program, 1978; Another Look at Task Analysis, 1982; Toward Non-Sexist Education, in The Education of Young Children, 1982; Chapter in Sex Role Attitudes and Cultural Change, 1982; Math Activities for Primary Children (with Rose Kolstadt), 1984; Perceptual and Cognitive Disabilities in Leanring Disabled Adults, 1984; Reading Problems of the Learning Disabled College Student, 1985; Representation of Minority Students in Special Education Classes (with Philip Chinn), 1987; Several other articles. *Memberships:* World Federation for Mental Health; Internal Council of Psychologists; Council for Exceptional Children; International Reading Association; National Council of Teachers of

Mathematics; Association for Children and Adults with Learning Disabilities; American Association of University Professors; Texas Association of College Teachers; Association for Supervision and Curriculum Development; Pi Lambda Theta. *Address:* 1117 Shadyglen Circle, Richardson, TX 75081, USA.

HUGHES Suzanne Helen, b. 11 May 1944, Detroit, USA. Educator. m. Richard L. Hughes, 22 June 1968, 1 son, 1 daughter. *Education:* BA, Wayne State University, 1966; Teacher Certification, University of Michign, 1988. *Appointments:* Personnel Specialist, US Government, 1966-73; High School Educator, Lakeville Community Schools, 1988-. *Memberships:* Kappa Delta Pi; Pi Sigma Kappa. *Honours:* One of Five Outstanding Young Women in Michigan, 1981. *Hobbies Include:* Volunteer: Civic, Church & Politics. *Address:* 8530 N. State Road, Otisville, MI 48463, USA.

HUH Grace Byung-yul, b. 17 Jan. 1926, Seoul, Korea. Teacher; Editor. *Education:* Kyun Sung Woman's Teachers College, 1942-44; Tong Kook University, 1958-59; BS, George Peabody College, 1960; MS, Bank Street College, 1969. *Appointments:* Teacher, Korea & America, 1945-; Principal, Korean School of New York, 1973-; Editor, Children, Korea News, 1977-; Instructor, Korean, Columbia University, 1978-80. *Creative Works:* Story Book, Tong Gu Ra Me; Korean Textbook, 6 volumes; Teacher's Essays, Anthology; Solo Art Show, New York City; Writer, Director, Producer, Plays, Children, Off Broadway. *Memberships:* President, National Association Korean Schools, 1988; Advisor, PTA, Korean School; International P.E.N., Korea, 1988. *Honours:* Most Outstanding Teacher Award, Junior Chamber of Commerce, 1969, Secretary of State, Korea, 1977, Minister of Education, Korea, 1983; Ethnic New Yorker Award, New York City, 1984; Sopa, 1985. *Hobbies:* Writing; Painting; Plays; Reading; Photography. *Address:* 25 Boerum Street, Apt. 2C, Brooklyn, NY 11206, USA.

HULFORD Denise Lovona, b. 24 Oct. 1944, Christchurch, New Zealand. Composer; Singer; Accountant. m. R.F. Hulford, 2 Jan. 1965, 1 son, 1 daughter. *Education:* Studies, Professional Accountancy Degree, Auckland Technical Institute, 1962-65; ATCL (Performance Piano), 1965; BMus, Victoria University, 1982; MMus, Honours, Composition, Auckland University, 1986. *Appointments:* Piano Teacher, Australia, 1968-69; Choir Member & Singing Student with Joan Howard, 1972; Member, Wellington Regional Opera Company 1973-75, Holy Trinity Cathedral Choir 1976; Office Manager, Prince & Partners, Chartered Accountants, 1987-; Musical Director, composr, Young Company, current. *Compositions:* Evolution; Cantata: A Disciple Dreams; Psalm 121; Sonata for String Orchestra; Plus 50 Years; Pyramids. *Memberships:* NZ Society of Music Education; Business & Professional Women's Association; Committee, Composers Association of NZ. *Honours include:* Runner-up, piano scholarship, 1960-61. *Hobbies:* Weaving; Opera; Music Education; Orchids. *Address:* c/o 5B Fieldstone Court, North Park Estate, Howick, Auckland, New Zealand.

HULL Ann, b. 28 June 1949, Enid, Oklahoma, USA. Pharmacist. m. Mitchell Ray Hull, 24 June 1972, 2 daughters. *Education:* BS, Pharmacy, 1972. *Appointments:* Paul's Clinic Pharmacy, 1972-73; Relief pharmacist, 7 retail pharmacies, 3 hospitals, 2 veteran centres, 1973-85; Grade IV pharmacist 1985, Director of Pharmacy Services 1986-, Pauls Valley General Hospital. *Memberships:* Offices, Oklahoma Hospital Pharmacists Association, American Society of Hospital Pharmacists. *Honours:* Upjohn Achievement Award, 1972; Historical Pharmacy Award, 1972. *Hobbies:* Golf; Gardening. *Address:* 918 East 7th, Sulphur, Oklahoma 73086, USA.

HUMAN Linda, b. 18 Dec. 1950, Lincolnshire, England. University Lecturer; Researcher; Company Consultant. m. Dr Piet Human, 27 Oct. 1979, 2 sons, 1 daughter. *Education:* BA, honours, University of

London, 1972; MA, 1978, D.Litt, 1980, University of South Africa. *Appointments:* Social Worker, UK, 1974-75; Senior Researcher, HSRC, South Africa, 1976-82; Senior Researcher, University of South Africa, 1980-84; Research Co-ordinator, University of Witwatersrand, 1984-86; Academic Programmes Manager, Centre for African Management, University of Capetown, 1986-; Associate Professor, University of Cape Town, 1988-. *Publications:* The Chinese People of South Africa: Freewheeling on the Fringes, 1984; Black Managers in South African Organisations, 1985; numerous journal articles. *Hobbies:* English Literature; Walking. *Address:* Weltevreden Lodge, 16 Riesling Road, Constantia, Cape Town 7800, South Africa.

HUMBLE Joan Irene, b. 23 Apr. 1938, Birmingham, England. Artist. m. Dr John Edmund Humble, 26 Dec. 1959, 1 son, 1 daughter. *Education:* ALCM, 1960. *Appointment:* Landscape Artist, Tutor, private classes & adult education, Hobart. *Publications:* Eight One Woman Shows; 2 joint shows and many group shows including: Boston Symphony Orchestra Exhibition, Kennedy Library, Boston, MA, 1979, Australian International Art Fair, Sydney, 1988, Australian Bicentennial Exhibition, London, 1988. *Membership:* Art Society of Tasmania. *Honours:* Tourist Award, Kingborough Council, 1976; Olliebolen Festival, 1976-78, 1980, 1981; 1st prize, Acton Art Society, Massachusetts, 1979; Highly Commended, Circular Head Arts Festival, Tasmania, 1984. *Hobbies:* Photography; Violin; Bush Walking; Gardening. *Address:* 101 Channel Highway, Taroona, Tasmania 7053, Australia.

HUMPHREY Linda, b. 13 Nov. 1952, Cheverly, Maryland, USA. Cardiac Anaesthesiologist. m. Michael John Humphrey, 6 Dec. 1982. *Education:* BS honours, Biochemistry, Virginia Polytechnic Institute and State University, 1974; MD, University of Virginia School of Medicine, 1977; Internship/Residency: General Surgery, 1977-78, Orthopaedic Surgery, 1978-79, Anaesthesiology, 1979-81; Diplomate, American Board of Anesthesiology, 1983. *Appointments:* Assistant Professor, Associate Chief, Division of Cardiac Anesthesia, The Johns Hopkins Medical Institutions, Baltimore, Maryland, currently. *Publications:* Immediate enhancement of left ventricular relaxation by coronary artery bypass grafting; intraoperative assessment (co-author), 1988; Book chapters: Anesthetic Management of the Transplant Patient; Echocardiography. *Memberships:* American Society of Anesthesiologists; Society of Cardiovascular Anesthesiologists; International Anesthesia Research Society; American Medical Association; American Heart Association. *Honours:* Outstanding Undergraduate Award, Pi Lambda Upsilon, 1074. *Hobbies:* Cycling; Triathlon; Skiing. *Address:* Department of Anesthesiology and Critical Care Medicine, The Johns Hopkins Medical Institutions, 600 N Wolfe Street, Baltimore, MD 21205, USA.

HUMPHREY Sandra Faye, b. 27 Jan. 1945, Australia. Chief Executive. m. Graham Humphrey, 7 June 1969. *Education:* BA, Honours, 1965, PhD, 1972, MEd., 1982, University of Sydney; Dip.Ed., Univesity of New England, 1970. *Appointments:* Special Project Officer, Australian Dept. of Trade & Industry, 1963-65; Reseearch Officer, Reserve Bank of Australia, 1965-68; Tutor, Lecturer, University of Sydney, 1969-74; Principal, Petersham College of TAFE, 1979; Principal, East Sydney Technical College, 1980; Director, Planning, Research & Information, NSW, TAFE, 1983; Principal, Sydney Technical College, 1986; NSW Education and Trainig Foundation, PM Ltd, 1989. *Memberships:* various professional organisations, state and national training boards. *Honours;* Fulbright Grantee, 1984-85. *Hobbies:* Swimming; Reading; Travel. *Address:* 25 West St., Balgowlah Heights, Sydney 2093, Australia.

HUMPHRIES Joan Ropes, b. 17 Oct. 1928, Brooklyn, New York, USA. Psychologist; Educator. m. Charles C. Humphries, 4 Apr. 1957, 2 daughters. *Education:* BA,

University of Miami, Florida, 1950; MS, Florida State University, 1955; PhD, Louisiana State University, 1963. *Appointments:* Psychological consultant, East Louisiana State Hospital, 1961-62; Instructor, Psychology Department, University of Miami, Coral Gables, 1964-65; Associate Professor, Behavioural Studies, Miami-Dade Community College North Campus, 1966-. *Publication:* Principal author, Application of Scientific Behaviourism to Humanistic Phenomenon, 1975, revised 1979. *Memberships:* Board, International Platform Association; Past Vice President, 1986-88, Florida Conference, President Miami-Dade Community College Chapter, American Association of University Professors; New York Academy of Sciences. *Honours:* Certificate, dedicated service, Tamiami branch, American Association of University Women, 1977; Founder's Plaque 1976, appreciation award 1987, Phi Lambda, Miami-Dade North Campus. *Hobbies:* Biofeedbck research & practice; Camping; Swimming; Fishing. *Address:* 1311 Alhamabra Circle, Coral Gables, Florida 33134, USA.

HUMPHRIES Judy Lynn, b. 20 Nov. 1946, Charleston, West Virginia, USA. Attorney. m. Michael A. Grant, 29 Dec. 1971, 1 son, 2 daughters. *Education:* BSN, West Virginia University, 1968; MS, Psychiatric Nursing, University of Maryland, 1970; JD, Marshall-Wythe School of Law, College of William and Mary, Virginia, 1977; Bar admissions: West Virginia, Virginia, District of Columbia. *Appointments:* Assistant Professor, School of Nursing, West Virginia University, 1970-72; Nurse Clinical Specialist, Veterans Administration Hospital, Cincinnati, Ohio, 1972-73; Assistant Professor, West Virginia University, 1977-78; Assistant Prosecuting Attorney, Monongalia County, Morgantown, West Virginia, 1979-81; Assistant Prosecuting Attorney, Marion County, Fairmont, West Virginia, 1986-88. *Memberships:* American Bar Association; League of Women Voters of Marion County (Secretary 1986-88). *Honours:* Inducted, Sigma Theta Tau, 1970; Awarded full scholarship for Marshall-Wythe School of Law Summer Law School, University of Exeter, England, 1976; Inducted, St George Tucker Society, Marshall-Wythe School of Law, College of William and Mary, 1977. *Hobbies:* Sailing; Reading; Needlework. *Address:* 1160 Avalon Road, Fairmont, WV 26554, USA.

HUNGERFORD Mary Jane, b. 30 Aug. 1913, Chicago, Illinois, USA. Retired Marriage & Family Counsellor. m. Charles H. Lawrance, 22 Nov. 1947, 2 sons, 1 daughter. *Education:* MA, Columbia University, 1935; PhD, Teacher Education, Columbia University, 1947; studies & courses, various other Universities and Colleges. *Appointments Include:* Instructor, various colleges & universities, 1934-47; Member, Eleanor King Modern Dance Group, 1945-46; Associate Professor, PE, New Haven State Teacher College, 1948-53; Counsellor, American Institute of Family Relations, 1954-81; Private Practice, 1981-. *Publications:* Many articles in professional journals; short stories and poetry. *Memberships:* American Association of Sex Educators Counsellors and Therapists; Founder, President, Childbirth Education Association of Los Angeles; Society for the Scientific Study of Sex; AAMFT; American Institute of Family Relations. *Honours:* Recipient, numerous honours & awards. *Hobbies:* Folk Dancing; Square Dancing; Dancing; Writing & Public Speaking. *Address:* 1340 Kenwood Road, Santa Barbara, CA 93109, USA.

HUNNICUTT Virginia Gayle, b. 6 Feb. 1943, Texas, USA. Actress. m. 1 Oct. 1978, 2 sons. *Education:* BA, Honours, Regent Scholar, University of California, Los Angeles, 1966. *Appointments:* Theatre Appearances Include: A Ride Across Lake Constance; Twelfth Night; The Tempest; Dog Days; The Admirable Chrichton; A Woman of No Importance; Hedda Gabbler; Peter Pan; Macbeth; Uncle Vanya; Exit the King; So Long on Lonely Street; The Big Knife; TV appearances include: BBC: The Goden Bowl; The Ripening Seed; The Fall of Eagles; Humbolt's Gift; Dylan Thomas; LWT: Affairs of the Heart - Flora; Switch; The Ambassadors; Lorimar: Man Called Intrepid; Granada: The Ladykillers; Sherlock Holmes;

others include: Marlow, Private Eye; Tales of the Unexpected; Kiss Inc; Films Include: New Face in Hell; Eye of the Cat; The Little Sister; Fragment of Fear; Freelance; Running Scared; Scorpio; Legend of Hell House; The Spiral Staircase; The Sell-Out; Once in Paris; One Take Two; Target; etc. *Publications:* Health & Beauty in Motherhood, 1985. *Memberships Include:* Kappa Kappa Gamma; Theatre Trust, Trustee; Medan Society; SOS; Think British. *Hobbies:* Gardening; Travel. *Address:* c/o William Morris Agency, 31-32 Soho Square, London W1, England.

HUNSINGER Rhonda P, b. 18 Aug. 1965, Norfolk, Virginia, USA. Assistant Editor. m. 15 June 1985, 1 daughter. *Education:* Graduate, Valencia Community College, 1987; Currently, Junior, University of Central Florida. *Appointments:* Editorial Assistant, International Journal of Applied Philosophy, 1985-86; Staff Writer, Florida Foliage Magazine, 1986, 1987; Assistant Editor, Florida Foliage Magazine, 1988-. *Memberships:* Treasurer, Student Government, Indian River Community College, 1986. *Honours:* 1st Place, General Merchandising, DECA, 1982; Certificate of Merit, Florida Foliage Association, 1987. *Hobbies:* Music; Writing. *Address:* 4439 Scenic Lake Drive, Orlando, FL 32808, USA.

HUNT Anita M. Heard, b. 14 Oct. 1943, Sayre, Oklahoma, USA. Health Care Marketing Executive; Consultant; Agent. m. Virgil Eugene Medley, 27 Mar. 1959, div. 1970, 3 sons, 1 daughter. *Education:* AS, Medical Technology, Sayre College, Oklahoma, 1972; BS, Technical Education in Health Careers, Oklahoma State University, Stillwater, 1974; MPH, Health Administration, University of Oklahoma Health Science Center, 1985. *Appointments:* Laboratory Director, Edmond Medical Center, Oklahoma, 1974-77; Provider Relations Representative, Oklahoma Blue Cross and Blue Shield, 1977-78; Medical Technologist, Kern Medical Center, Bakersfield, California, 1979; Practice Management Consultant, Medical Management Group, 1980-81; Clinical Laboratory Supervisor, South Community Hospital, 1982-88; Adjunct Assistant Professor, Medical Technology Programme, Oklahoma University Health Science Center, 1983-85; Director of Sales, Mational Medical Enterprises, Santa Monica, California, 1988-89. *Publications:* Author of papers in field. *Memberships:* American Medical Technologists, 1972-86; Secretary, Board of Directors, Institute for Education, 1976-77; National Standards Committee, 1976-77; Oklahoma Society of Medical Technologists, Vice-President 1976-77; MENSA; Toastmasters; National Credentialing Agency; Clinical Laboratory Scientist; National Association of Female Executives; Oklahoma Public Health Association; American College of Health Care Executives. *Honours:* Scientific Products American Medical Technology Scholarship, 1973; American Medical Technologists Distinguished Achievement Award, 1977. *Hobbies:* Piano and vocal music; Yachting; Water and snow skiing; Photography. *Address:* Marketing, National Medical Enterprises, 2901 28th, Box 2140, Santa Monica, CA 90406, USA.

HUNT Nancy Louise, b. Bathurst, Australia. Writer. m. Walter Gibbs Hunt, 18 Nov. 1967, 1 stepson, 2 stepdaughters. *Education:* Secretarial Diploma, 1935. *Appointments:* Stenographer, Western Stores & Edgeleys Ltd., Bathurst, 1935-43; WAAAF, 1943-46; Secretary, various employers, Sydney, 1946-67. *Publications:* Novels: As N.L. Ray: Roma Mercedes & Fred; The Everywhere Dog; The Pow Toe; There Was this Man Running; Nightmare to Nowhere; As Nan Hunt: Never Tomorrow; Pictures Books as Nan Hunt: Whistle Up the Chimney; An Eye Full of Soot & an Ear Full of Steam; Wild & Woolly; Rain, Hail or Shine; When Ollie Spat on the Ball; Prisoner of the Mulligrubs; The Junk Eaters; A Rabbit Named Harris; The Show; Collection of Stories: We Got Wheels, Man. *Honours:* New South Wales Premier's Literary Award, Best Children's Book: Whistle up the Chimney, 1982, A Rabbit Named Harris, 1987. *Hobbies:* Reading; Writing; Gardening; People; Music. *Address:* 219 Peel Street, Bathurst 2795, Australia.

HUNT Patricia Joan, b. Sefton Park, Liverpool, England. Freelance Writer. *Education:* Altrincham County High School, Altrincham, Cheshire. *Appointments:* Town & Country Planning, Cheshire County Council, 1945-79; Freelance Writer, 1979-. *Publications:* Author of 20 books including: Children's books on religion; Guide book to Knutsford; History of the Parish Church, Knutsford. Articles in various journals. *Membership:* Secretary, Chester Diocesan Children's Committee. *Hobbies:* Gardening; Reading; Collecting miniature objects; History; Architecture; The Church, particularly as it affects children. *Address:* 54 Bexton Road, Knutsford, Cheshire, WA16 0DS, England.

HUNT Wanda H, b. 22 Mar. 1944, Mitchell County, USA. State Senator; Account Executive. divorced, 1 daughter. *Education:* Appalachian State University. *Appointments:* 3 years Public Relations Consultant; 13 years in State Government; 2 years as Public School Employee; 9 years in private business; Corporate Secretary, Computer Business; Political activities include: North Carolina Department of Transportation, Purchasing Officer, 1979-82; North Carolina General Assembly, 1983-; Resorts of Pinehurst Inc., 1984-87. *Memberships Include:* North Carolina State Government Employees Association; League of Women Voters; Women in State Government; Moore County Democratic Women; North Carolina Status of Women; North Carolina Heart Fund Association; etc. *Honours:* Social Service Award, 1978-81; 1984 Nominee, Distinguished Women of North Carolina; etc. *Hobbies:* Reading; Travel. *Address:* PO Box 1335, Pinehurst, NC 28374, USA.

HUNTER Betty Lou Smith, b. 23 Nov. 1938, Shafter, California, USA. Marietta City Council Member. m. Randall Earnest Hunter, 20 Oct. 1961, 3 sons. *Education:* BS, North Georgia College, 1960; Graduate, Charity Hospital school of Medical Technology, 1961. *Appointments:* Marietta City Council, 1981, Mayor Protem, 1988. *Publications:* Columnist, The Little Bit. *Memberships:* President Cobb Municipal Association; President, Evangelical Methodist Women, 1984-88; Chairman, Board of Stewards, Evangelical Methodist Church, 1987-88; PTA president. *Honours:* Honourary Life Member, Georgia PTA, 1976; City of Marietta Distinguished Citizen Award, 1985-86; PTA Founders Award, 1988. *Hobbies:* Genealogy; Water Skiing; Fishing; Travel. *Address:* 253 Lakewood Drive, Marietta, GA 30060, USA.

HUNTER Kim, b. 12 Nov. 1922, Detroit, Michigan, USA. Actress. m. (1) William A Baldwin, 11 Feb. 1944, divorced 1946, 1 daughter. (2) Robert Emmett, 20 Dec. 1951, 1 son. *Education:* Student acting with Carmine Lantaff Camine, 1938-40, Actors Studio. First stage appearance, 1939; Broadway debut in A Streetcar Named Desire, 1947. *Creative Works:* Stage: Two Blind Mice, 1950; Darkness at Noon, 1951; The Chase, 1952; They Knew What They Wanted, 1952; The Children's Hour, 1952; The Tender Trap, 1954; Write Me a Murder, 1961; Weekend, 1968; The Penny Wars, 1969; And Miss Reardon Drinks a Little, 1972; The Glass Menagerie; The Women, 1973; In Praise of Love, 1975; The Lion in Winter, 1975; The Cherry Orchard, 1976; The Chalk Garden, 1977; Elizabeth the Queen, 1977; Semmelweiss, 1977; The Belle of Amherts, 1978; The Little Foxes, 1980; To Grandmother's House We Go, 1981; Another Part of the Forest, 1981; When We Dead Awaken, 1982; Ghosts, 1982; Territorial Rites, 1983; Death of a Salesman, 1983; Cat on a Hot Tin Roof, 1984; Life With Father, 1984; Sabrina Fair, 1984; Faulkner's Bicycle, 1985; Antique Pink, 1985; The Belle of Amherst, 1986; Painting Churches, 1986; A Delicate Balance, 1986. Films: The Seventh Victim, 1943; Tender Comrade, 1943; When Strangers Marry, 1944; You Came Along, 1945; A Canterbury Tale, 1949; Stairway to Heaven, 1946; A Streetcar Named Desire, 1951; Anything Can Happen, 1952; Bermuda Affair, 1957; The Young Stranger, 1957; Money, Women and Guns, 1958; Lilith, 1964; Planet of the Apes, 1968; The Swimmer, 1968; Beneath the Planet of the Apes, 1970; Escape from the Planet of the Apes, 1971; Dark August, 1975;

The Kindred, 1986. Television: Numerous TV appearances include: Edge of Night, 1979-80; FDR's Last Year, 1980; Skokie, 1981; Scene of the Crime, 1984; Private Session, 1985; Three Sovereigns for Sarah, 1985; Hot Pursuit, 1985; Martin Luther King, Jr: The Dream and the Drum, 1986; Drop-out Mother, 1987. Recordings: From Morning 'Til Night (and a Bag Full of Poems), RCA Victor, 1961; Come, Woo Me-United Audio Classic, 1964. *Honours:* Recipient Donaldson Award for best supporting acress in A Streetcar Named Desire, 1948, also on Variety NY Critics Poll, 1948, for film version, 1952; Winner Academy award; LOOK award; Hollywood Foreign Corrs. Golden Globe award; Emmy nominations for Baretta, 1977, Edge of Night, 1980; Carbonnell award for Big Mama in Cat on a Hot Tin Roof, So Florida, 1984.

HUNTER Pamela, Dame, b. 3 Oct. 1919, Sunderland, England. m. Gordon Lovegrove Hunter, 5 Sept. 1942. 1 son, 1 daughter. *Education:* Westonbirt School (Matriculation, London University Board) & Eastbourne School of Domestic Economy, 1937. *Appointment:* Served WRNS, 1942-45. *Memberships:* Conservative Party: Vice President 1985-, Chairman National Union 1984-85, Chairman Women's National Advisory Committee, 1978-81; Northumbrian Water Authority, 1973-77; Berwick-Upon-Tweed Borough Council, 1973-83; Chatton Parish Councillor, 1987-; Chairman, Glendale Branch of RNLI and NSPCC; Vice Chairman PCC of Chatton with Chillingham 1989. *Honour:* DBE, 1987. *Hobbies:* Politics; Antiques. *Address:* The Coach House, Chatton, Alnwick, Northumberland NE66 5PY, England.

HUOTARI Bernice Martha, b. 3 Oct. 1940, Nisula, Michigan, USA. Ontonagon County Clerk and Register of Deeds. m. Waino Alfred Huotari, 6 June 1959. 1 son, 5 daughters. *Education:* Governmental Accounting Course, Michigan Technological University, 1965; Participating in Continuing Educational Forum, Michigan State University. *Appointments:* Greenland Township Clerk, 1963-76; Vice Chair, Michigan Board of Sanitarians, 1985-; Ontonagon County Clerk and Register of Deeds, 1977-. *Publication:* Poem: World Peace, 1958. *Memberships:* President 1988-89, Michigan Association of County Clerks; President 1986, Upper Peninsula Association of County Clerks; Secretary 1970-80, Upper Peninsula Horseshoe Pitchers Association; Chairman 1983-86, Vice Chair 1987-, Ontonagon County Democratic Party; Executive Committee, Western Upper Peninsula Substance Abuse Agency Board. *Honours:* Upper Peninsula Horseshoe Pitchers Women's Champion, 1970 and 1971, 1974-80; Award for Devotion to Association, 1980; Nominated by County Board of Commissioners for Excellence in Government Award, 1987. *Hobbies:* Gardening; Knitting; Crocheting; Fishing. *Address:* 395 Mud Creek Road, Mass City, Michigan 49948, USA.

HUPALO Kathleen Rose Fixsen, b, 21 Jan. 1945, Sheridan TWSP, Redwood County, Minnesota, USA. Attorney; Human Rights Enforcement Officer. m. Ivan Hupalo, 24 May 1964, 1 son. *Education:* BA, Sociology, University of Minnesota, 1976; JD, Law, University of Minnesota Law School, 1981. *Appointments:* Civil Rights Attorney, 1982; Juvenile Delinquency and Criminal Defence Attorney, 1984-85; Enforcement Officer, Minnesota Department of Human Rights, 1985-88. *Publications:* Numerous writings and speeches on human rights law including Sexual Harassment, and Employment Discrimination. *Memberships:* American Bar Association; Minnesota State Bar Association; Ramsey County Bar Association; Lex Alumnae; Minnesota Alumni Association; Minnesota Women Lawyers, Inc; National Association of Human Rights Workers; International Platform Committee. *Honours:* L.M.Fuhr Memorial Citizenship Award, 1963; Outstanding Achievement Award, Minnesota Department of Human Rights, 1987. *Address:* 684 Delaware Avenue, St Paul, MN 55107, USA.

HURD Deborah LaVerne, b. 18 Nov. 1944, New York City, USA. *Education:* BA Psychology, Pace College,

1969; MS Guidance & Counseling, Long Island University, 1974. *Appointments:* Teacher, St Joseph's School, 1969-70; Teacher, Our Lady of Sorrows, 1970-73; Counselor, College of Staten Island, 1973-76; Partner, Deboria Educational Consultants, P/T, Counseling, Educational Evaluations and Program Evaluations, 1987-; Assistant Principal, Holy Name School, 1982-. *Memberships:* New York State Association for Counseling and Development; Association for Counselor Educ & Supervision; National Catholic Education Association; School Counselors Association; Ass for Measurement & Evaluation in Guidance. *Hobbies:* Travel; Reading. Interests: Developing educational partnerships between Higher Education and Elementary Schools. *Address:* 58 St Marks Avenue, Brooklyn, New York 11217, USA.

HURLEY Mary Joann Moureen, b. 16 Apr. 1921, Dunkirk, New York, USA. Biodietetion; Teacher, Nursery school, Kindergarten. m. Victor William Kebort, 7 Apr. 1943. 2 daughters. *Education:* BS, Dietetics, Villa Maria College, Erie, 1942; MED, University of State of New York at Buffalo, 1961; Teacher certification; Studied at: Cornell University, Florida State University, Pima College and University of Arizona. *Appointments:* Dietitian Intern, Morrisania Hospital, Bronx, New York; Assistant Head Dietitian, Columbus State Hospital, Columbus, Ohio; Dietitian, Roswell Memorial Cancer Research Hospital, Buffalo, New York; Charge, Quality Control Cereal Plant, General Mills, Inc, Buffalo; Director, Home Management House, Florida State University, Tallahassee; Graduate assistant, Early Childhood Education Dept, University State of New York, Buffalo; Teacher, Harris Hill Elementary School, Clarence; Director, Clarence Cooperative Nursery; Teacher, Indian Oasis School District, Sells, Arizona; Substitute teacher, Marana School District; Substitute teacher, Mary Dill School District, Three Points; Library Research on Gluten Sensitive Enteropathy, University of Arizona. *Creative works:* Publication: Gluten Intolerance, with Beatrice Trum Hunter, 1987; Organized Lay Support Group, State of Arizona Chapter, Celiac Sprue Association. *Memberships:* American Dietetic Association; Associate Member, American Academy of Environmental Medicine; Associate Member, International Academy of Nutrition-Preventive Medicine; Celaic-Sprue Association of USA. *Honours:* Recipient of numerous awards and scholarships. *Hobbies:* Travel. *Address:* 5738 W Box R Street, Tucson Estates, Tucson, AZ 85713, USA.

HUSSEIN Carlessia Amanda, b. 1 Sept. 1936, Baltimore, Maryland, USA. Public Health Administrator/ Health Planner. divorced 1 daughter. *Education:* RN, Freedmen's Hospital Nursing School, 1957; BS, Nursing, 1966, MS Public Health Nursing, University of California, San Francisco; DPH, University of California, Berkeley, 1977. *Appointments:* Health Planner, California, 1975-76; Evaluation Consultant, Hypert. CA, 1975-77; Executive Director, Health Planning, 1977-80; Executive Director, LA Health Planning, 1980-83; Deputy Health Director, Fire Dept. 1984; Director, State Health Planning, 1984-. *Publications:* 4 Area Health Plans. *Memberships:* American Public Health Association; American Health Planning Association; Bay Area Black Nurses Association; Johns Hopkins International Health Board. *Honours:* Recipient, various honours & awards. *Address:* 3001 Veazey Terrace NW No 922, Washington, DC 20008, USA.

HUSTON Anjelica, b. 8 July 1951, California, USA. Actress. *Education:* London, England. *Appointments:* Director, & Starring Role in A Walk with Love and Death, Vienna, 1969; Hamlet, Roundhouse, London; Swashbuckler, Universal Pictures, California; Postmen Always Rings Twice, California; Short film, A Rose for Emily, PBS, California; Ice Pirates, MGM, California; starred in, Tamara, on stage, Los Angeles; Prizzi's Honour, 1986; Co-Star, Gardens of Stone, 1986. *Memberships:* Academy of Motion Picture Arts & Sciences; SAG; AFTRA; Women in Film; Smithsonian Institute; AIDS Foundation; Amnesty International.

Honours: All for Prizzi's Honour: Best Supporting Actress, New York Film Critics, La Film Critics, Nomination for Golden Globe, National Board of Review, Academy Award, Nomination for Golden Apple, National Society of Film Critics, Nomination British Academy Awards, for Best Supporting Actress, 1986; Dramalogue Award for Tamara, 1986. *Hobbies:* Languages & Dialects; Horse Riding (Jumping); Skiing; Painting & Drawing. *Address:* c/o Toni Howard, William Morris Agency, Los Angeles, California, USA.

HUSTON Anne Clark Marshall, Professor. m. James Alvin Huston, 5 June 1983. *Education:* AB, 1963, MEd., 1967, College of William & Mary; Ed.D., University of Virginia, 1977. *Appointments:* Teacher, Elementary Schools, 1963-68; Reading Consultant, Coordinator, Williamsburg-James City County Public Schools, 1968-70; Consultant, Education, various Virginia Public School Systems, 1968-; Lecturer in Education, College of William and Mary, 1968-70; Visiting Assistant Professor of Education, University of Virginia, 1977; Professor of Education, Lynchburg College, 1970-; Distinguished Faculty Scholar Award, 1988. *Publications:* Common Sense About Dyslexia, 1987; Co-editor, Symposium Readings: Classical Selections in Great Issues, 1982; Under the Double Cross, 1989. Articles in various professional journals; Numerous papers read and professional workshops at State, National, International and WWorld Conferences on Reading. *Memberships:* Phi Eta Sigma; Kappa Delta Pi; Phi Delta Kappa; etc. *Hobbies:* Travel; Reading; Writing; Gourmet Cooking; Riding Horses; Tennis. *Address:* School of Education and Human Development, Lynchburg College, Lynchburg, VA 24501, USA.

HUTCHEON Wilda Vilene Burtchell, b. 9 Sept. 1919, Maine, USA. Creative Artist. m. Philip S. Hutcheon, 26 Mar. 1955. *Education:* Federal Design School Graduate, 1944; Studied with various Artists. *Appointments:* Colour Consultant; Studio Receptionist, 1955-56; Superintendant, Art, State Exhibition, 1959; Curator, Fine Arts, Nylander Museum, 1959. *Creative Works:* Paintings include: Surge of the Sea; Tree Top Tapestry; Twilight Tapestry; Eventide Nova Scotia; Hillside Hermitage; Edge of the Sea; Keith Jensen; Hills of Canada; Kathy Kay. *Memberships Include:* National Museum of Women in the Arts; American Biographical Institute Research Association; International Platform Association; Past President: Art Society, Womens Literary Club, Garden Club; *Honours:* Recipient, many honours & awards including International Platform Association Best of Show Gold Medal Award, 1988; Commissioned as Kentucky Colonel (for Special Achievement), 1989. *Address:* 51 Prospect St., Caribou, ME 04736, USA.

HUTCHINS Jeanne Bahn, b. 12 Mar. 1922, Rochester, USA. Legislator. m. Frank M. Hutchins, 24 Aug. 1945, 4 daughters. *Education:* BA, Wells Cllege, 1943; MPA, SUNY, 1980. *Appointments:* Bacteriologist, Chemist, Manhattan project Atomic Energy, University of Rochester, 1943-45; Library Assistant, Fort Benning, 1946-47, Dartmouth College, 1947-48; Town Board, Legislator, Town of Brighton, Rochester, 1976-; Notary Public, County of Monroe, 1976-; Trustee, Monroe Savings Bank, 1978-; Trustee, Wells College; President, JR League of Rochester, 1957-59; Trustee, Colgate Rochester Divinity School, 1984-; Trustee, Bexley Hall Seminary, 1984-; Trustee Center for Governmental Research; Warden St Pauls Episcopal Church, 1987- *Memberships:* Numerous professional & civic organisations including: Family Service America; President, Rochester Female Charitable Society, 1983-85; Planned Parenthood. *Address:* 75 Indian Spring Lane, Rochester, NY 14618, USA.

HUTCHISON Kay Bailey, b. 22 July 1943, Galveston, Texas, USA. Attorney; Businesswoman. m. Ray Hutchison, 16 Mar. 1978. *Education:* University of Texas at Austin, 1961-64; University of Texas School of Law, 1964-67; Admitted, State Bar of Texas, 1967. *Appointments include:* Television news reporter, political correspondent, 1969-71; Member, Texas House of Representatives, 1972-76; Vice Chair, National Transportation Safety Board, 1976-78; Assistant Professor, University of Texas at Dallas, 1978-79; Senior Vice President & General Counsel, 1st Republican Bank Corporation, 1979-81. Currently: Owner & Chair, McCraw Candies Inc; Owner, Bailey-Hutchison Company Ltd; Counsel, Hutchison Price, Boyle & Brooks law firm; Boards, Lomas Mortgage Corporation, Windsor Financial Corporation, Fidelity National Bank, Dallas. *Memberships include:* Offices, Texas & American Bar Associations, various other professional bodies; Advisory boards/committees, Texas Transportation Institute, YWCA, Goodwill Industries, Dallas Womens Foundation, Communities Foundation of Texas, University of Texas School of Social Sciences; Director, offices, numerous other community activities, past/present. *Honours include:* Awards, recognitions, from: Women's Centre of Dallas, 1987; Texas Republican Women's Federation, 1983; Dallas Young Republicans, 1986; 'D' Magazine, 1984; Glamour Magazine, 1977; Houston Baptist University, 1977; Houston Young Lawyers Association, 1977. *Hobbies:* Reading; Skiing; Antiques. *Address:* 3900 First City Center, Dallas, Texas 75201, USA.

HUTCHISON Margaret Mary, b. 11 Feb. 1926, Carterton, New Zealand. Chartered Accountant. *Education:* BCom, Canterbury College, University of New Zealand. *Appointments:* S. P. Godfrey & Company, Christchurch, 1945-48; Christ's College, Christchurch, 1948-49; Price Waterhouse, London, UK, 1950-51; Rowley, Gill, Hobbs & Glen, Wellington, NZ, 1952-61; Cook, Craig & Company, Wellington, 1963-70; Partner, Spicer & Oppenheim, 1970-; Human Rights Commissioner, 1978-85. *Memberships:* NZ Society of Accountants; Past President (Wellington), various offices, Federation of University Women; Past President, NZ branch, Royal Scottish Country Dancing Society. *Honour:* Fellow, NZ Society of Accountants. *Hobbies:* Scottish Country Dancing; Tennis; Bird watching; Travel. *Address:* 1 Glasgow Street, Wellington 5, New Zealand.

HUTTON Susan Pawlias, b. 20 July 1957, Rochester, USA. Attorney. m. Noel C. Hutton, 21 June 1980, 1 daughter. *Education:* BA, Drake University, 1978; JD, Honours, Drake University, 1982. *Appointments:* Law Clerk, Peddicord, Simpson & Sutphin PC, Des Moines, 1980-82; Associate, Dobson & Dobsen, Greenville, 1982-. *Publications:* Case Note: The Derrogation of Parental Immunity in Iowa, 1982. *Memberships:* South Carolina Pro Bono Lawyer; Girl Scouts of America; American, Iowa, South Carolina & Greenville County Bar Associations; Greenville County Legal Auxiliary. *Honours:* Phi Sigma Iota; Phi Beta Kappa; Omicron Delta Epsilon; Order of the Coif; Judge Rich Moot Court Team, 1982; etc. *Hobbies:* Girl Scout Leader; Foreign Language Enthusiast. *Address:* PO Box 1923, 1306 South Church Street, Greenville, SC 29602, USA.

HUXLEY Elspeth Josceline, b. 23 July 1907, London, England. m. 12 Dec. 1931. 1 son. *Education:* Dip Agr, Reading University; Special Course, Cornell University, USA. *Appointments:* Press Officer, Empire Marketing Board, London, 1928-32; BBC News Department, 1941-43. *Publications:* White Man's Country: Lord Delamere and the Making of Kenya (2 vols), 1935; Murder at Government House, 1937, 1987; Red Strangers, 1939; Murder on Safari, 1939, 1986; The African Poison Murders, 1939, 1986; Atlantic Ordeal, 1943; Race and Politics in Kenya (with Margery Perham), 1944; The Walled City, 1948; The Sorcerer's Apprentice, 1948; I Don't Mind if I Do, 1951; Four Guineas, 1954; A Thing to Love, 1954; The Red Rock Wilderness, 1957; The Flame Trees of Thika, 1959; A New Earth, 1960; The Mottled Lizard, 1962; The Merry Hippo, 1963; Forks and Hope, 1964; A Man from Nowhere, 1964; Back Street New Worlds, 1965; Brave New Victuals, 1965; Their Shining Eldorado, 1967; Love Among the Daughters, 1968; The Challenge of Africa, 1971; Livingstone & His African Journeys, 1974; Florence Nightingale, 1975; Gallipot Eyes: A Wiltshire Diary, 1976, 1988; Scott of the Antarctic, 1977; Nellie: Letters from Africa, 1980; Out in the Midday Sun, 1985. Numerous articles to newspapers and journals. *Memberships:* BBC Advisory Council, 1952-59; Justice of the Peace, Wiltshire (Malmesbury), 1945-77. *Honour:* Commander of the British Empire (CBE), 1962. *Hobbies:* History and current events in Kenya; Gardening; Reading. *Address:* Green End, Oaksey, Malmesbury, Wiltshire, SW16 9TL, England.

HUXLEY Laura Archera, b. 2 Nov. 1914, Turin, Italy. Author; Foundation Director. m. Aldous Huxley, 19 Mar. 1956, widowed 22 Nov. 1963. *Education:* Music & Violin Studies. *Appointments:* Concert Violinist, 1927-38; Associate Producer, Documentary Films, 1944-49; Film Editor, RKO, 1950-51; Psychotherapy, private practice, 1952-70; Author, 1963-; Founder, Director, Our Ultimate Investment, 1978-. *Publications:* You Are Not the Target, 1963; This Timeless Moment, 1968; Between Heaven and Earth, 1975; Oneaday Reason to Be Happy, 1988; The Child of Your Dreams, co-author, 1987. *Honours:* DHS, Sierra University, 1961; Honoree, UN, 1978; Maharishi Award, World Government of the Age of Englightenment, 1981. *Hobbies:* Education. *Address:* 6233 Mulholland Highway, Los Angeles, CA 90068, USA.

HUZAR Eleanor Goltz, b. 15 June 1922, St Paul, Minnesota, USA. Professor of History. m. Elias Huzar (deceased), 21 June 1950. *Education:* BA, University of Minnesota, 1943; MA, 1945, Phd, 1948, Cornell University. *Appointments:* Instructor in History, Stanford University, Palo Alto, Calfornia, 1948-50; Assistant Professor of Classics, University of Illinois, Urbana, 1951-55; Associate Professor of History, South East Missouri State College, Cape Girardeau, Missouri, 1955-59; Professor of History, Michigan State University, East Lansing, 1960-. *Publications:* Mark Antony, a Biography, 1978; Articles in Aufstieg und Niedergang der Romischen Welt and Classical Journal; Book reviews in professional journals. *Memberships:* American Philological Association; American Historical Association; Archaeological Institute of America (President, Central Michigan Society); Classical Association of the Middle West and South (President 1984-85); American Catholic Historical Association (Nominating Committee 1983-86). *Honours:* George Boldt Fellow, 1947-48; Classical Jury, Prix de Rome, 1978-80; Council for International Exchange of Scholars, 1979-81; National Endowment for the Humanities Selection Committee, 1979-84; Michigan Committee of Selection for Rhodes Scholarships, 1981-84. *Hobbies:* Reading; Hiking; Travel; Skiing. *Address:* Department of History, Michigan State University, East Lansing, MI 48824, USA.

HWONG (Moroy) Nai-Ching, b. 12 Mar. 1957, Taiwan, China. Music Specialist; Music Therapist. m. Wan-Chu Kung, 11 July 1981, 1 daughter. *Education:* Teacher's Diploma, Voice, 1979; BS, Music Therapy, 1981, MA 1983, Music Education; PhD, Education, University of Minnesota, 1986. *Appointments:* Vocal Instructor, Louisiana State University, Laboratory School, 1989-; Music Specialist, Music Therapist, Minneapolis Public School, 1985-89; Music Therapy Research Assistant, University of Minnesota, 1985. *Memberships:* Music Educators National Conference, Active Research Member; National Association for Music Therapy; Pi Kappa Lamda; Mu Phi Epsilon. *Honours:* Paul Oberg Award, 1986; Finalist, 1986 Schubert Club Graduate Voice Competition. *Hobbies:* Reading; Music; Painting. *Address:* 2245 College Dr. No 123, Baton Rouge, LA 70808, USA.

HYDE Elizabeth Phebean, b. 10 Apr. 1924, Freetown, Sierra Leone. Educator; Curriculum Developer. m. Jonathan Hyde, 8 Dec. 1954, deceased, 1 son, 3 daughters. *Education:* Institute of Education, Bristol University, 1968; MA.Ed., 1974, MA, TESL, 1976, University of Illinois, USA. *Appointments:* Assistant Teacher, MGHS, 1945-50; Senior Teacher, acting principal, St Andrews Secondary School; Inspector of Schools, Ministry of Education; Curriculum Adviser in English; Director of Studies, Lebenese International School, Freetown, Sierra Leone. *Publications:* Practice

Papers in English for Secondary Selection; Sierra Leone Primary English. *Memberships:* African Womens Association, President 1972-74; Sierra Leone Association of University Women, Founder, 1st President 1976-78; YWCA. *Honours:* Honorary Life Member, Sierra Leone Association of Adult Education, 1988. *Hobbies:* Reading; Public Speaking; Literacy Work with Women; Early Childhood Education. *Address:* 89B Regent Road, Lumley, Freetown, Sierra Leone, West Africa.

HYDE Miriam Beatrice, b. 15 Jan. 1913, Adelaide, Australia. Composer; Pianist. m. 26 Dec. 1939, 1 son, 1 daughter. *Education:* AMUA, LAB, University of Adelaide, 1928; B.Mus., 1931; Studied at Royal College Of Music, London; ARCM; LRAM. *Appointments:* Kambala School, Sydney, 1937-41; Elder Conservatorium, 1942-45; Private Teaching, Sydney, 1945-; Examiner, Australian Music Examinations Board, 1945-82, Advisory Board, 1958-83; over 50 years of recitals for Australian Broadcasting Corportion; Lectures; etc. Compositions: 2 Piano Concertos; numerous works for Piano and Woodwind; 25 Own works recorded for Cherry Pie, Sydney, 1987; Autobiography completed, 1988; Special broadcasts, 75th birthday. *Memberships:* Hon. Life Member, Councillor, 1960-, Music Teachers Association of New South Wales & Victoria; Life Member, Australian Musical Association, London; Patron, Music Teachers Association of South Australia; Fellowship of Australian Composers; Australasian Performing Right Association; OBE Association, NSW Branch. *Honours:* Sullivan, Farrar, Cobbett Prizes, RCM, 1932-35; Anzac Song prizes, 1951, 1952, 1955; ABC-APRA Prizes, 1952, 1954-55; OBE, 1981. *Hobbies:* Writing; Gardening; Italian; Scrabble. *Address:* 12 Kelso Street, Enfield, NSW 2136, Australia.

HYDE Pauline Patricia, b. Brighton, Sussex, England. Company Director. m. (1) R M Pickford, 1946. (2) Anthony Hyde, 1963, 1 son. *Education:* Brighton & Hove Girls Public Day School; Royal Academy of Dramatic Arts (RADA). *Appointments:* Assistant to MD, Binder Hamlyn Fry, 1951-63; Founder, Forty-Plus Career Development Centre, 1978-82; CEO Pauline Hyde & Associates, 1982-; Director, Scottish TV, 1988-. *Creative works:* Founded charity, Forty-Plus Research Fund, to study the problems of mid-career crisis; Study together with Cranfield School of Management entitled The 'N' Factor in Executive Survival, 1986 has been widely reported. *Memberships:* Fellow, Institute of Directors; Companion, British Institute of Management; Member, Institute Personnel Management. *Hobbies:* Theatre; Fashion; Antiques. *Address:* 38 Lower Belgrave Street, London SW1W 0LN, England.

HYDEN Dorothy Louise, b. 19 July 1948, Ft Collins, Colorado. Executive Vice President, Hyden, Hyden & Associates. m. Howard E Hyden, 17 July 1976. 1 son, 2 daughters. *Education:* BA, University of California at Santa Barbara, 1970; MBA, Pepperdine University, 1980. *Appointments:* Teacher 1974-75, Admissions Rep 1975, Head Teacher, 1976, Sawyer Business College, Anaheim, California; Marketing Specialist, Anthony Schools, Orinda, California, 1976-77; Administrative Director, 1977-78; Private practice consulting, 1979-87; Executive Vice President, Hyden, Hyden & Associates Consulting/Training Services, 1988-. *Publication:* Co-author of Training in Excellence. *Memberships:* President Colonels Coeds, Chi Omega Sorority; Business/Professional Advertising Association; National Association for Female Executives; University of California at Santa Barbara Alumni Association; Episcopal Church. *Honours:* UCSB Chimes Award, Outstanding Woman Student of the Quarter Fall 1969; Outstanding Employee Award, Sawyer Business College, 1976. *Hobbies:* Travel; Foreign Languages; Guitar; Piano; Jumping Horses; Bridge. *Address:* 7415 Hyde Park Drive, Minneapolis, Minnesota 55435, USA.

HYMAN Betty Francis Harpole, b. 20 Nov. 1938, Jasper, Texas, USA. Technical Equipment Consultant.

m. Arthur Siegmar Hyman, 14 June 1957, deceased. *Education:* BA, Psychology, University of Texas, San Antonio, 1979. *Appointments:* Special Project coordinator, Texas Stores, San Antonio, 1975-79; Communications Consultant, Southwestern Bell Telephone, Midland Texas and San Antonio, 1980-82; Technical Equipment Consultant, AT&T, San Antonio, 1983-85 and 1988-, Intelliserve Corp, Dallas, 1987-88; Consultant, IMS Group, San Antonio, 1985-87. *Memberships:* Devel Com, San Antonio Spl Olympics, 1988-; San Antonio World Affairs Council, 1985-; Board of Directors, South Texas Childrens' Habilitation Center, San Antonio, 1985-87; American Business Women's Association (Program com 1987-88); Texas Tennis Association (ranked player 1976-). *Hobbies:* Tennis; Scuba Diving; Aerobics. *Address:* 108 Clubwood Court, Ashville, NC 28803, USA.

I

IACONETTI Joan E, b. 11 Sept. 1947, Racine, USA. Write; Psychotherapist. *Education:* BA, English Literature, University of Dayton, 1969; MS, Illinois University, 1976. *Appointments:* Psychotherapist, Family Service, 1976-80; Management Consultant, National Centre for Public Productivity, 1981-83; Freelance Writer, 1983-. *Publication:* First Time Manager, 1985; articles in magazines. *Memberships:* American Society of Journalists & Authors; Associate Member, American Society of Magazine Photographers; Clinical Membr, American Association for Marriage & Family Therapy. *Hobbies:* Scuba Diving; Yoga; Travel. *Address:* 215 W. 16 St., No 5RN, New York, NY 10011, USA.

IBRAHIM Zainab Malik, b. 1944, Billiri, Bauchi State, Nigeria. Educationist; Administrator. m. Mr Ibrahim, Jan. 1964, 1 son, 1 daughter. *Education:* Teacher's Grade II Certificate, 1970; Teacher's Grade I Certificate, 1973; BEd, 1976; MEd, Educational Administration and Planning, 1982. *Appointments:* Class Teacher, Primary School, 1963-68; Principal, Teachers College, 1978-84; Sole Administrator, Local Government, Alkaleri, 1984-87; Secretary, Establishment Department, Governor's Office, Bauchi State, 1988-. *Memberships:* President, National Council of Women's Societies, Bauchi State Branch; Affiliate, International Council of Women. *Honour:* Alkaleri Local Government Council received Governor's Award (an ambulance) for achieving 3rd place out of 16 in examination during her term of office, 1986. *Hobbies:* Gardening; Sewing; Reading; Travel; Meeting new faces. *Address:* No 1 Guru Close, New G.R.A. Bauchi State, PMB 1438, Nigeria, West Africa.

IDDINGS Kathleen Ann, b. Ohio, USA. Author; Editor; Publisher; Public Relations. divorced, 1 son, 3 daughters. *Education:* BS.Ed., Miami University, 1968. *Appointments:* Elementary Teacher, 1962-73; Author, editor, Publisher, 1973-. *Publications:* Poetry: The Way of Things, 1984; Invincible Summer, 1985; Promises to Keep, 1987. *Memberships:* Poetry Society of America; PEN; Academy of American Poets; La Jolla Press Inc; San Diego Poets Press; La Jolla Poets Press, Originator, Editor. *Honours:* NEA/COMBO Fellowship, 1968; Nominee, Pushcart Prize by Pulitzer Winner, Carolyn Kizer. *Hobbies:* Travel; Theatre; Symphony; Opera; Lectures; Photography. *Address:* PO Box 8638, La Jolla, CA 92038, USA.

IENEI Aurora, b. 28 Apr. 1939, Romania. Pianist; Professor. m. Dragos Tanasescu, 20 Aug. 1976. *Education:* Graduate, Ciprian Porumbescu Music Conservatory, 1960. *Appointments:* Profess, Piano, Music High School, Bucharest, 1960-68, Music Conservatory Ciprian Porumbescu, 1968-. *Creative Works:* Concert performances, records & recordings at home & abroaad. *Memberships:* EPTA; ATM. *Honours:* Various young artists prizes and awards. *Hobbies:* Reading & Writing Poetry. *Address:* Str. Dionisie Lupu No. 53, etj.V, Apt. 22, Sector I, 70183 Bucharest, Romania.

IFILL Wendy Ann, b. 10 July 1944, Trinidad & Tobago, West Indies. Writer; Video Producer. 1 daughter. *Education:* Certificate, Journalist, Thomson Group, 1963; Marketing & Advertising, NCK, 1968; Certificate, University of Chicago Social Development Centre, 1985; Midwest Centre for the Study of Oriental Medicine, Chicago, USA, 1988-. *Appointments:* Journalist, Trinidad Publishing Co, 1963-66; Advertising Copywriter/Radio TV Producer, NCK Advertising, 1966-70; Creative Director, NCK, 1970-74; Asst Editor, Arte Man Magazine, 1970-72; Man Editor, Imprint, 1975; Columnist, Trinidad Express, 1975; Creative Advertising Director, 1976- 82; Founder & Owner, Starr Productions, 1983-. *Publications:* Author of numerous articles for magazines and newspapers; Researcher/ Writer/Designer/Producer of numerous videos. *Membership:* Teleproduction Association of Trinidad and Tobago, 1st Elected President. *Honours:* Winner Best Television Series (1985) National Awards, Your Lifetime is The Right Time, and 1987 for Gold Comes to Gold. *Hobbies:* Walking; Hiking; Healing; Herbology; Philosophyl; Mysticism; Metaphysics; Wholistic Health. *Address:* c/o Starr Productions Ltd, 35 Cipriani Boulevard, Port-of-Spain, Trinidad & Tobago, West Indies.

IGNATESCU-PRUNNER Margareta Rose-Maria, b. 29 Oct. 1940, Bucharest, Romania. Harpist; Professor. m. Ignatescu Constantin, 19 Dec. 1962. 1 son, 1 daughter. *Education:* Music Lyceum, 1946-58; Music Conservatoire Bucharest, 1958-63; Diploma Professor First Degree. *Appointments:* Teacher of Piano and Harp, George Enescu School of Arts, 1963-; Solo recitals, radio recordings, television appearances and concerts with orchestras. *Creative works:* Studies and articles about harp and a biography of my grandfather, Josef Prunner, one the great double bassists in Romania and abroad. *Memberships:* Professoral Association of George Enescu school of Artts; World Harp Congress, USA. *Honours:* Diploma of Honour, Fourth International Harp Contest, Israel, 1970; National prizes and distinctions. *Hobbies:* Literature; Film; Ballet; Travelling. *Address:* Str Frumoasa No 54 et II apt 10, 78116 Bucharest I, Romania.

IKERMAN Ruth C, b. 4 Sept. 1910, Redlands, California, USA. Freelance Writer. m. Lawrence Howser Ikerman, 12 Jan. 1947. *Education:* BA, 1931, Hon. PhD, 1979, University of Redlands. *Appointments:* Co-Owner, Larry's Paint House, Redlands, 1955-71. *Publications:* Author, 16 Devotional books including: Cooking by Heart; Devotional Thoughts from the Holy Land; A Heart Trimmed Christmas. *Memberships:* National League of American Pen Women, Chaplain, San Bernardino Valley Branch. *Honours:* George Washington Honour Medals, Freedom Foundation, Valley Forge (3). *Hobbies:* Cross Stitch. *Address:* 11 Panorama Drive, Redlands, CA 92374, USA.

IKRAMULLAH Shaista Subrawarsky, b. 22 July 1915, Calcutta, India. Retired. m. Mahamad Ikramullah, 17 Apr. 1933, 1 son, 3 daughters. *Education:* Lareto House, Calcutta; SOAS, London; BA(Hons), Calcutta University; PhD, London University. *Appointments:* Member, Constituent Assembly of Pakistan, 1947-53; Delegate to United Nations, 1948, 1956-80, Leader of Delegation, 1956. *Publications:* Survey of the Urdue Novel and Short Story; Purdah to Parliament; Letters to Noona; Behind the Veil; Koohiah Ai Natamam; Naik Bi Bian. *Memberships:* Founder Member, 1st International Secretary, All Pakiston Women's Association; Pakistan Red Cross; All Pakistan TB Association; UNICEF; Syndicate and Board of Studies, University of Karachi. *Honours:* Gold Medal, Founders of Pakistan Award, 1987; Gold Medal, Business and and Professional, 1987. *Hobbies:* Reading; Writing; Walking; Entertaining. *Address:* Kashana, 117 Clifton, Karachi, Pakistan.

ILG Ruth Merkle, b. 29 July 1945, Konstanz, West Germanmy. Freelance Writer; Photographer; Painter. *Education:* Accounting & Tax Law; Economy; Languages & Linguistics; Literature and Drama. *Appointments:* Tax Consultant Officer; Foreign Correspondent; Trilingual Interpreter. *Publications:* Book of Poetry: Reflections; Poetry in numerous journals and magazines. *Memberships:* Anderson County Arts Council, past pres; Anderson Writers' Guild, past pres; SC Poerrtry Society, past director; Palmetto Writers' Conf, Past director; Foothills Authors' Guild, past pres; NC Poetry Society; The Writers' Workshop; Anderson Arts Association. *Honours:* AWG Poetry, Short Story, essays and Article Awards, USA; Foothills Authors Guild Poetry, Short Story, Essays & Article Awards, USA; Language Award, Royal Society of Arts, London, England and Cambridge University, England; Outstanding Young Woman of America Award, USA; KINSA International Photo Award; South Carolina Poetry Society Award,

Charleston, USA; BASF Photo Contest Awards. *Hobbies:* Philosophy; Psychology; Ancient studies; Mythology; Theatre; Music; Ballet. *Address:* P O Box 2323, Anderson, SC 29622, USA.

ILIC Marija, b. 11 Feb. 1951, Yugoslavia. University Professor. divorced. 2 sons. *Education:* Dipl Ing, 1974, MEE 1977, University of Belgrade, Yugoslavia; MSc, Washington University, 1978; DSc, St Louis, 1980. *Appointments:* Cornell University, 1982-84; University of Illinois, Urbana, 1984-87; Associate Professor, MIT, Laboratory for Electromagnetic and Electronic Systems, 1987-. *Memberships:* IEEE; Sigma Xi; AAAS. *Honours:* First Presidential Young Investigator (PYI) Award, 1984-89; Xerox Faculty Award, University of Illinois, 1986; University Scholar, 1987- 90, University of Illinois. *Hobbies:* bb3Jogging; Basketball; Folk dancing. *Address:* MIT, Laboratory for Electyromagnetic and Electronic Systems, Bldg 10-059, 77 Massachusetts Avenue, Cambridge, MA 02139, USA.

INAN Huricihan, b. 25 Dec. 1947, Istanbul, Turkey. Economic Historian. m. Kemal Inan, 29 Sept. 1980. 1 daughter. *Education:* BA Economics, 1967, PhD 1969, University of Chicago; MA Econ. History, 1972, PhD Economic History, 1979, University of Wisconsin. *Appointments:* Teaching Assistant, 1967-69, Research Associate 1972-74, University of Chicago; Teaching Assistant, University of Wisconsin, 1969-72; Lecturer, 1975- 79, Associate Professor, 1979-80, Middle East Technical University, Ankara; Visiting Professor, University of Lal, Santa Cruz, 1980-81; Research Asst in Agricultural Economics, University of California, Berkeley, 1981-82; Editor in Chief, Toplumve Bilim (Society and Science), Turkey, 1982-85; Visiting Professor, Development Economics, University of California, 1985-. *Publications:* Ottoman Empire and World Economy, 1987; Articles on the economic history of the Ottoman Empire Annales, 1987; Review 1977 and 1978; Review of Middle East Studies. *Memberships:* Joint Committee on Near and Middle East, Social Science Research Council, 1987-; Editorial Board, Historical Sociology; Editorial Board, Toplumve Bilim (Society and Science). *Honours:* Summa Cum Laude, 1967; University Fellowships at the University of Chicago; Dissertation grants from University of Wisconsin, Madison. *Address:* 3141 College Ave, Apt 1, Berkeley, California 94705, USA.

INDICK Janet, b. 3 Mar. 1932, Brooklyn, New York, USA. Sculptor; Teacher. m. Benjamin P. Indick, 23 Aug. 1953, 1 son, 1 daughter. *Education:* BA, Hunter College, New York, 1953; New School, NY, 1961- 62. *Appointments:* Director, Teaneck Jewish Centre Nursery School, New Jersey, 1964-; Arts Advisory Board, Teaneck Township. *Creative work includes:* Sculpture commissions: Tree of Life wall sculpture 1981, Menorah sculpture 1983, Temple Beth Rishon, Wyckoff, New Jersey; October War Memorial sculpture, Jewish Centre, Teaneck, 1973. Sculptures & paintings in numerous private collections, also Bergen Community Museum, Paramus, New Jersey. *Memberships include:* Juror 1988-, National Association of Women Artists; Vice President 1988-, Sculptors Associates, NJ; New York Society of Women Artists; Women's Caucus for Art, New Jersey-New York. *Honours:* IFFRA Award of Merit, 1984; Fellowship grant, NJ State Council on Arts, 1980-81; Sculpture prize, Art in the Park, Paterson, NJ, 1978; Sculpture prize, National Association of Women Artists, 1974. *Hobbies:* Painting; Music. *Address:* 428 Sagamore Avenue, Teaneck, New Jersey 07666, USA.

INGHAM (Ann) Mary, 13 Feb. 1947, Chesham, Bucks, England. Writer. m. David W. Lister, 15 Mar. 1985. *Education:* BA, Honours, Social Science, University of Liverpool, 1968; Diploma, London College of Printing, 1974. *Appointments:* Social Worker, 1968-73; Editorial Work, Freelance Writer, 1973-. *Publications:* Now We Are Thirty, 1981; Men: The Male Myth Exposed, 1984; Facing Our Forties, in press. *Membership:* NUJ. *Hobbies:* Furniture Restoration; Genealogy; Womens Issues; Conservation; Ecology;

Films. *Address:* c/o Anthony Sheil Associates, 43 Doughty Street, London WC1N 2LF, England.

INGLE Susan Mary, b. 23 Apr. 1955, London, England. TV Presenter; Director. *Education:* BSC., Botany, Durham University, 1974-77. *Appointments:* Presenter, Wildtrack, BBC 1978-85; Presenter, Tomorrow's World, 1978-82; Don't Ask Me, YTV, 1978-; Secrets of the Coast, TSW, 1981-83; Good Food Show, C4, 1982-83; E.Y.E Watch, Anglia, 1987; Director, films for Tomorrows world, 1987; Radio Reports from Operation Raleigh Pacific Crossing. *Publications:* Secrets of the Coast; What Can I Do? *Honours:* Bronze Award TV Series Secrets of the Coast, International Film & TV Festival of New York, 1983; Associate Producer & Presenter of Series, Sid Roberts Award, The Boat Show, TVS, 1985. *Hobbies:* Photography; Wildlife; Sailing; Skiing; Squash. *Address:* c/o Arlington Enterprises, 1-3 Charlotte Street, London W1P 1DH, England.

INGLETT Betty L, b. 6 Oct. 1930, Richmond County, USA. Director. *Education:* BS, Georgia State College for Women, 1953; MA, Georgia Southern, 1980; Ed.D., Nova University, 1988. *Appointments:* Elementary Teacher; Secondary Teacher; Elementary Media Specialist, 1975-80; Elementary Principal, 1980-86; Director, Media Services Richmond, 1986-. *Memberships:* AAUW, Vice President; GAE Public Relaitrons Committee; RCAE Recording Secretary; GAE; GAEL; GAIT; GLMD. *Honours:* Administrator of the Year, Richmond County, 1988. *Address:* 3148 Lake Forest Drive, Augusta, GA 30909, USA.

INGRAMS, Doreen Constance, b. 24 Jan. 1906, London, England. Writer. m. William Harold Ingrams, 3 June 1930, 2 daughters. *Education:* Private Schools, England & Switzerland. *Appointments:* BBC Arabic Service, 1956-68. *Publications:* The Social & Economic Condition of the Aden Protectorate; A Time in Arabia; Palestine Papers 1917-1922: Seeds of Conflict; The Awakened: Women of Iraq; Bachlor in Arab World - Reviews, Articles. *Memberships:* Founder Member, Council for the Advancement of Arab-British Understanding; Executive Committee, United Nations Association; Amnesty. *Honours:* Lawrence medal, Royal Central Asian Society, 1939; Founders Medal, Royal Geographical Society, with husband, 1940. *Hobbies:* Reading; Travel. *Address:* 3 Westfield House, Tenterden, Kent, TN30 6JL, England.

INGSTAD Anne Stine, b. 11 Feb. 1918, Norway. Archaeologist. m. H. Ingstad, 21 May 1941, 1 daughter. *Education:* MA 1960, PhD, 1978, University of Oslo; Dr. hc, University of St John, Newfoundland, 1979. *Appointments:* Keeper, Norwegian Museum for Games, Woods and Fisheries, 1960-61; Participant in Husband's 8 expeditions to Greenland & Newfoundland, 1961-68; Leader of the archaeological excavations on husbands expeditions at L'Anse aux Meadows, Newfoundland, Canada where a norse site dating from about 1000 AD was found. *Publications:* Numerous articles in professional journals; The Discovery of a Norse Settlement at L'Anse aux Meadows, Newfoundland, 1975. *Memberships:* Norwegian Archaeological Society; State Scholar (with a fellowship granted by the Norwegian Government). *Honours:* Franklin L. Burr Award, 1964; Wahlberos Gold Medal, Swedish Geographic Society, 1968; The Royal Order, 1st Class, St Olaf, 1979; Fridtjof Nansen Prize, 1985. *Hobby:* Nature. *Address:* Vettalivein 24, 0309 Oslo, Norway.

INNES Patricia Kim Sturgess, b. 29 Mar. 1955, Ottawa, Canada. Business Executive. m. William Campbell Innes, 12 May 1984. *Education:* BSc., Queen's University, 1977, MBA, Distinction, University of Western Ontario, 1984. *Appointments:* Engineer, National Energy Board, 1977-78; Engineer, Esso Resources Canada Ltd., 1978-83; Consultant, McKinsey & Co., 1984-88; Vice President-Assistant to President, Greyhound Lines of Canada Ltd., 1988-. *Memberships:* Board of Trustees, Queen's University, Kingston; University Council, Queen's University. *Honours:*

Dolasco Entrance Scholarship, 1973; H.G. Conn Award, 1977; Faculty of Graduate Studies Scholarship, 1983. *Hobbies:* b3Skiing; Cycling; Hiking. *Address:* Box 1 Site 32, RR12, Calgary, Alberta, Canada T3E 6W3.

IOVITU Mariana, b. 10 Apr. 1949, Bucharest, Romania. Economist; Professor in Economics. m. Iovitu Viorel, 10 June 1972. 1 daughter. *Education:* Graduate, Economic Science Academy, 1972; Political Training classes for Professors in Political and Social Sciences, 1972-73. *Appointments:* Professor, Social Sciences, University, Bucarest, 1972- 76; Membership in professoriate, teaching economics and health economics, Medicine Institute, 1976-. *Publications:* Author of many essays, articles, contributions to textbooks in professional journals and to conferences; Many broadcasts. *Memberships:* Institute of Economic Researchs. *Hobbies:* Literature; Plants, flowers; Music; Philosophy. *Address:* 712314 Calea Grivitei No 5 Ap 1, Bucarest 1, Romania.

IRELAND Jill, b. 1936, London England. Actress. *Career:* Music Halls in England at age of 12; Singing, dancing and entertaining at London's Palladium, in cabarets and a tour of the continent in ballet. Began acting in West End repertory; signed to major film studio contract at 16 by J Arthur Rank. Screen debut as ballet dancer in Oh, Rosalinda, first of 16 feature films for Rank. *Creative Works:* Films include: Three Men in a Boat; Hell Drivers; Robbery Under Arms; Carry On, Nurse; Raising the Wind; Twice Round the Daffodils; Villa Rides; Rider on the Rain; Cold Sweat; The Family; Someone Behind the Door; The Mechanic; The Valdez Horses; The Valachi Papers; Breakout; Hard Times; Breakheart Pass; From Noon Till Three; Death Wish II; Assassination. Television: Shane (series); The Man from U.N.C.L.E.; Ben Casey; Night Gallery; Daniel Bonne; Mannix; Star Trek (series). *Address:* PO Box 2644, Malibu, CA 90265, USA.

IROLA Wanda J, b. 11 June 1928, Erick, Oklahoma, USA. Retired. m. 26 Feb. 1965. 1 son, 2 daughters. *Education:* American Institute of Ben King, 1946. *Appointments:* Accounting Supervisor, Fresno Guarantee Savings, 1956-59; RE Sales & Finance, 1964-84; Amcar of No. Calif., Finance, 1984-86. *Memberships:* Commonwealth of San Francisco, 1970-72; La tiende Guild, 1969-; Sunnyside Co Club, 1974-76; Kings Country Club, 1976-79. *Address:* 3725 N Fruit, Suite C, Fresno, California 93705, USA.

IRVIN Regina Lynette, b. 13 Sept. 1963, Columbia, Mississippi, USA. Attorney. *Education:* BA, Alcorn State University, 1985; JD, Thurgood Marshall School of Law, Houston, Texas, 1988. *Appointments:* Law clerk, Burney, Coggins & Hartsfield, Houston, 1987; Intern, Federal Magistrate Karen K. Brown, Houston, 1988; Attorney, Department of Navy, Office of Central Counsel, Washington DC, 1988-. *Publications:* Comment, bankruptcy law 1986, staff 1986-87, book review editor 1987-88, Thurgood Marshall Law Review. *Memberships include:* National Bar Association; President, Phi Alpha Delta & member, various honour societies. *Honours include:* Houston Barrister's Scholarship, 1986-87; National Dean's List, 1987-88; Dean's List, 1981-85; Presidential Scholar, 1984; Alpha Kappa Alpha scholarship, 1981. *Hobbies:* Reading; Bowling; Tennis; Cooking. *Address:* 1212 Maxwell Street, Columbia, Mississippi 39429, USA.

IRWIN Constance H Frick, b. 11 May 1913, Evansville, Indiana, USA. Author. m. W.R. Irwin, 15 June 1954, 1 stepson. *Education:* AB, 1934, MA, 1941, Indiana University; BS, Columbia University, 1947. *Appointments:* Librarian, Reitz High School, Evansville, 1937-42, 1947- 54; Librarian, University of Evansville, 1946; Book Editor, Columbia Uiversity Press, 1947-50; Assistant Professor, Library Science, University of Iowa, 1961-67. *Publications:* As Constance Frick: The Dramatic Criticism of George Jean Nathan, 1943; As C H Frick: Tourney Team, 1954; Five Against the Odds, 1955; Patch, 1957; The Comeback Guy, 1961; As

Constance Irwin: Jonathan D, 1959; Fair Gods and Stone Faces, 1963; Gudrid's Saga, 1974; Strange Footprints on the Land, 1980. *Memberships Include:* Authors League of America; National League of Americn Pen Women, Past President, Iowa City Branch; American Association of University Women, Past President, Evansville Branch. *Honours:* Phi Beta Kappa, 1934; Black Hawk Award, Midland Booksellers Association, 1964; Dobbs National Biennial Award, 1965. *Hobbies:* History; Archaeology; Paleoanthropology; Gardening; Reading. *Address:* 415 Lee Street Iowa City, IA 52246, USA.

IRWIN Miriam Dianne Owen, b. 14 June 1930, Columbus, Ohio, USA Book Publisher; Author. m. 5 June 1960, 1 son. *Education:* BS, Home Economics, Ohio State University, 1952. *Appointments:* Editorial Assistant, American Home Magazine, 1953-56; Salesman, Owen Realty, Dayton, 1957-58, Clevenger Realty, Phoenix, 1958-59; Home Economist, Columbus & South Ohio Elec. 1959-60; Owner, Mosaic Press, 1977-. *Publications:* Lute and Lyre, 1977; Forty is Fine, 1977; Miriam Mouse's Survival Manual, 1977; Miriam Mouse's Costume Collection, 1977; Miriam Mouse's Marriage Contract, 1977; Miriam Mouse, Rock Hound, 1977; OSHA Specs : re the Fetus, 1979; Silver Bindings, 1983; Editor, Tribute to the Arts, 1984; Illustrator, Corals of Pennekamp, 1979. *Memberships:* Daytime Crew Chief, Wyoming Life Squad, 1966-71; International Guild of Miniature Artisans; President, Miniature Book Society; American Philological Association; Daughters of the American Revolution. *Honour:* Writer in Residence, Holy Cross Monastery, West Park. *Hobby:* Book Collector. *Address:* 358 Oliver Road, Cincinnati, OH 45215, USA.

ISAAC Eva Mae Nash, b. 24 July 1936, Louisiana, USA. Teacher; Public Speaker. m. Will Isaac, 1 July 1961, died, 1970. *Education:* BA, 1974; MSc., Counsellor, 1979; MSc., Educaiton, 1979; PhD, 1985. *Appointments:* Teacher, Oakland Public Schools, 1974- ; Counsellor: Garfield School, Oakland, 1976-77, Roosevelt Junior High School, Oakland, 1977-78; City College, San Francisco, 1978-79. *Publications:* Introducing Vocational Skill Training in an Elementary School: A Case Study in Social & Educational Change; Author, Advertisement for Radio & TV. *Memberships:* Phi Delta Kappa; California Association for Counselling & Development; Association for Supervision & Curriculum Development; NAFE; International Reading Association; NAACP. *Honours:* Recipient, various honours & awards. *Hobbies:* Tennis; Dancing; Chess; Hiking. *Address:* 920 Felton Street San Francisco, CA 94131, USA.

ISAAC Teresa Ann, b. 3 July 1955, Lynch, Harlan County, Kentucky, USA. Law Professor; Prosecutor. m. James Isaac Lowry IV, 30 Dec. 1978. 1 son, 1 daughter. *Education:* Transylvania University Abroad, study in Spain, England, France, Italy, Austria and Hungary, 1973; BA, Pre-Law and History, magna cum laude, Transylvania University, 1976; JD, University of Kentucky, 1979. *Appointments:* US Senate Aide, 1974; Private Law Practice, 1979- 86; Director, Kentucky Sports Equity Project, 1987-88; Associate Professor, Eastern Kentucky University, Department of Legal Studies, 1983-88; Prosecutor, Fayette County Attorney's Office, 1986-88. *Publications:* Article: Free Speech Rights for Public Employees, 1988; Sports-The Final Frontier: Sex Discrimination in Sports Leadership, 1987; Manual: Sex Equity in Sports Leadership: Implementing the Game Plan in Your Community, 1987. *Memberships:* Chairperson, American Bar Association Committee on Delivery of Legal Services to Women, 1987-88; Board of Editors, Kentucky Bar Association Journal, 1983-85; Task Force on Gender Bias in Kentucky Courts, 1987-88; Lead Counsel in Sex Discrimination Cases for the American Civil Liberties Union of Kentucky, 1983-86; Vice President, Kentucky Women's Heritage Museum, 1987-88; Treasurer, Kentucky Women Advocates, 1987-88. *Honours:* Merit Award, Kentucky Women's Intercollegiate Conference, 1988; White House Fellow Nominee, 1981; Leadership

America, 1988; Transylvania Bicentennial Award, 1980; American Bar Association Silver Key Award, 1979; University of Kentucky Moot Court Board, 1978; Omicron Delta Kappa Leadership Honorary, 1977; Most Outstanding Senior Award, 1976; Transylvania Student Government Service Award, 1975; Most Outstanding Sophomore Award, 1974; Most Outstanding Freshman Award, 1973. *Hobbies:* Running marathons; Politics; Travel; Reading. *Address:* 335 Garden Road, Lexington, Kentucky 40502, USA.

ISELIN Sally Cary, b. 16 June 1915, Massachusetts, USA. Freelance Writer. m. Lewis Iselin, 14 June 1935, 2 daughters. *Appointments:* Magazine Researcher, Newsweek Magazine, 1942-45; Editor, Town & Country, 1942-45; Reporter, Life Magazine, 1945-48; Columbia Broadcasting System in TV, 1948-51; Writer, 1951; Fashion Editor, Women's Home Companion, 1956; Freelance Author. *Publications:* Articles in various journals including: Atlantic Monthly; Vogue; Show; Harper's Bazaar; Passport Travel Newsletter. *Memberships:* Colony Club; Fashion Group. *Hobbies:* Photography; Sailing; Reading. *Address:* Belfast Road, Camden, ME 04843, USA.

ISHEE Dixie Kay White, b. 3 Dec. 1955, Raymond, Missouri, USA. Attorney. m. Jerry Ervin Ishee, 10 Oct. 1978. *Education:* AD, Nursing, 1975; BS, Anesthesia, University of Missouri, 1978; JD, Memphis State University, 1985. *Appointments:* RN Hinds General Hospital, 1976-77; RN, St Dominics Hospital, 1977-78; Staff Anesthetist, Baptist Hospial, 1978-85; Partner, Lucketts Law Firm, Memphis, 1985-88; Partner, Manire, Ishee, Bing & Shea, 1989-present. *Publication:* Medical Evidence in Back Pain, 1989. *Memberships:* American, Shelby County, Tennessee, Mississippi, Bar Associations; American Trial Lawyers Association; Tennessee Trial Lawyers Association; Association of Women Attorneys; Tennessee & American Nurse Anesthesia Associations. *Honours:* Outstanding Young Woman of Germantown, 1985; Woman on the Move, 1985; Memphis Metro Tennis Champion, Singles, 1988. *Hobbies:* Tennis; Skiing; Biking; Collecting Rare Books. *Address:* 1775 Lindell Circle, Germantown, TN 38138, USA.

ISRAEL Vivianne Winters, b. 29 Mar. 1954, Inglewood, California, USA. Registered Nurse. m. 29 May 1976, divorced 1985, 1 daughter. *Education:* ADN, 1976; California State University, Northridge, 1976- 78. *Appointments:* Registred Nurse, Northridge Medical Centre, 1977-79; St Joseph's Medical Centre, 1979-80; RN, Intensive Care, Mercy Medical Centre, 1980-85; St Francis Medical Centre, 1985-. *Publication:* Tender Moments, 1989. *Memberships:* Publishers Marketing Association; Publicists of Southern California; Publicists of San Diego; Walters International Speakers Associatiron; Womens International Network; many other professional organizations. *Hobbies:* Wildlife Conservation; Exotic Animal Handling/Training; Fitness. *Address:* Pacific Coast Publishers, 710 Silver Spur Road, Suite 126, Rolling Hills Estates, CA 90274, USA.

ISRAELOV Rhoda, b. 20 May 1940, Pittsburg, USA. Financial Planner; Writer. divorced, 3 sons. *Education:* BS, Hebrew Education, Herzlia Hebrew Teacher's College, 1961; BA, English Language & Literature, University of Missouri, 1965; Certified Financial Planner. *Appointments:* Hebrew Teacher, 1961-79; Insurance Agent, Conn. Mutual Life, 1979-81; Financial Planner, E. F. Hutton, Indianapolis, 1981-, Vice President, 1986-; Instructor, Mutual Fund Licensing Exams, Pathfinder Securities School, 1983-; Weekly Financial Columnist, IBJ; Weekly WTVX radio call in show, and weekly spot on the news show of Channel 6 TV, Indianapolis. *Memberships:* Financial Planning Practitioners Registry; International Association for Financial Planners; National Association of Professional Saleswomen; National Board of Directors, American Society of Chartered Life Underwriters; National Speakers Association; etc. *Honours:* Business Woman of the Year, 1986; Woman of the Year, Runner Up,

Indianapolis Woman Magazine, 1987; Gold Medal Award, Personal Selling Power, 1987; others. *Hobbies:* Piano; Folk & Square Dancing; Needlepoint; Theatre. *Address:* Shearson Lehman Hutton, 201 N. Illinois St., Suite 400, Indianapolis, IN 46204, USA.

ISSER Natalie, b. 12 July 1927, Philadelphia, Pennsylvania, USA. Professor of History. m. Leonard Isser, 15 June 1947. 3 sons, 1 daughter. *Education:* BA 1947, AM 1948, PhD 1962, University of Pennsylvania. *Appointment:* Pennsylvania State University, Ogortz Campus, 1962-. *Publications:* Books: The Second Empire and the Press, 1974; The American School and the Melting Pot, co-author, 1986; History of Conversion and Contemporary Cults, co-author, 1988. Numerous articles. *Memberships:* American Historical Association; Western Society French History. *Address:* Pennsylvania State University, Ogontz Campus, Abington, PA 19001, USA.

ITALIANO Marilynn Joanne, b. 2 Oct. 1942, East Orange, New Jersey, USA. Professor. m. 26 June 1965. 2 sons. *Education:* BA 1962, MA 1964, Michigan State University; PhD, University of Colorado, Boulder, 1974. *Appointments:* Eastwood Local Schools, Migrant School, Ohio, 1979-84; Woodmore Local Schools, 1984-86; Findlay College, Findlay, Ohio, 1986-. *Publications:* International Journal of Women's Studies, 1977; Reviews for Small Press Review. *Memberships:* Vice President, AAUW; Delta Kappa Gamme; OFLA. *Honours:* National Merit Semi-Finalist, 1960; Tower Guard, 1961; Sigma Delta Pi, 1964; Honours College, 1961-64; Phi Kappa Phi, 1964; BGSU Reading (Harmon) Award, 1980; Travel Scholarship Delta Kappa Gamma, 1987; Faculty Development Grants, 1987, 1988. *Hobbies:* Yoga; Travel; Hawaiian quilting. *Address:* 215 West Poe Road, Bowling Green, Ohio 43402, USA.

ITANI Frances Susan, b. 25 Aug. 1942, Belleville, Canada. Writer; Professor. m. Tetsuo Itani, 28 Dec. 1967, 1 son, 1 daughter. *Education:* BA, University of Alberta, 1974; MA, University of New Brunswick, 1980; RN. *Appointments:* Nursing, 1960-75; Freelance Author, 1974-; Teacher, University of Ottawa, 1985-; Guest Lecturer/Speaker. *Publications:* Radio work for CBC, 1974-; No Other lodgings, 1978; Linger by the Sea, 1979; Rentee Bay, 1983; Coming Attractions 3, 1985; Pack Ice, 1989; Truth or Lies, 1989; articles in journals & magazines. *Memberships:* ACTRA; Writers Union of Canada; Big Sisters Association; Amnesty International. *Honours:* Recipient, many honours & awards. *Hobbies:* Music; Tai Chi; Travel; Teaching English to New Immigrants. *Address:* c/o The Writers Union of Canada, 24 Ryerson Avenue, Toronto, Ontario, Canada M5T 2P3.

IVENS Virginia Ruth, b. 27 July 1922, Decatur, Illinois, USA. Associate Professor, retired. *Education:* BS, University of Illinois, 1950. *Appointments:* Assistant 1950, Instructor 1956, Assistant Professor 1971, Associate Professor 1979-88, College of Veterinary Medicine, University of Illinois. *Publications:* Co-Author, Principal Parasites of Domestic Animals in the United States-Biological and Diagnostic Information, 2nd edition 1981; Plato Lessons, 1974; Identification of Arthropods Important in Veterinary Medicine in the US, 1 Lice, 2 Fleas, 3 Fly Larvae, 4 Adult Flies, 5 Mosquitoes, 6 Mites, 7 Ticks; Articles in professional journals including: Journal Parasitology; American Journal Veterinary Research; Journal Protozoology; American Journal Veterinary Research; Eimeria; Monographs; Translations from Russian and Czechoslovakian. *Memberships:* American Society of Parasitologists; Society of Protozoologists; Entomological Society of America; American Institute of Biological Sciences; Phi Zeta; Sigma Xi; Chairperson, 9th Annual Conference on Coccidiosis, 1972; University Senate Member, various Committeess & Offices. *Hobbies:* Photography; Travel; Theatre; Business & Finance. *Address:* University of Illinois, College of Veterinary Medicine, Dept of Veterinary Pathobiology, 2001 South Lincoln Ave, Urbana, IL 61801, USA.

J

JAANUSSON Hille, b. 24 Dec. 1922, Tallinn, Estonia. Archaeologist (Antiquarian). m. Valdar Jaanusson, 26 Sep. 1945, 1 son. *Education:* Fil.kand, Uppsala University, Sweden, 1963; Fil.dr, Stockholm University, 1981. *Appointments:* Amanuensis, Institute of Archaeology, Uppsala University, Uppsala, Sweden, 1963-67; Antiquarian, Central Office of Antiquities, Stockholm, 1967-71; Curator, Museum of National Antiquities, Stockholm, 1971-88. *Publications:* Numerous papers mostly on Bronze Age; Dissertation: Hallunda. A Study of Pottery from a Late Bronze Age Settlement in Central Sweden, 1981. *Memberships:* Swedish Archaeological Society; Swedish Association of Museum Curators; Estonian Learned Society; Institutum Litterarum Estonicum. *Address:* Grindstorpsv. 25VII, S-183 32 Taby, Sweden.

JABLON Elaine Georgallas, b. 8 Dec. 1950, New York, USA. Education Specialist. m. 23 June 1976. *Education:* B.Ed., 1973; M.Ed., 1974. *Appointments:* Teacher, Broward County Public School, 1974-76; Transition Teacher, Orange County Public Schools, 1976-77; Education Specialist, Central Florida, 1977-. *Publications:* Contributor, Co- Compiler, What's Available for the Learning Disabled College Students in Florida. *Memberships:* Business & Professional Womens Club; President, Education Foundation; American Association of University Women; American Business Women Association. *Honours:* Citation, Kissimmee, & State National Business & Professional Womens Clubs for Education Foundation Work, 1983-86. *Hobbies:* Swimming; Rebating; Walking; Reading. *Address:* 808 Hastings Drive, Kissimmee, FL 32743, USA.

JACK Martha Louise, b. 23 July 1945, Detroit Michigan, USA. Engineer/Biomechanical Research. *Education:* BS, University of North Carolina at Greensboro, 1967; MS, Ball State University, 1975; PhD, Washington State University, 1981; *Appointments:* Physical Education Teacher, Indian Ridge Elementary School, 1968-74; Exercise Physiology Subject and Graduate Assistant, Ball State University, 1974-75; Biomechanics Laboratory Teaching Assistant, Washington State University, 1976-78; Engineer, Westinghouse Hanford Company, 1982-89; Researcher, NIKE Sports Research Laboratory, 1989-. *Publications:* Distribution of Cycling-Induced Saddle Stresses, 1981, Characteristics of the Badminton Smash Stroke, 1979; Selected Aspects of the Overarm Stroke in Tennis, Badminton, Racquetball and Squash, 1979; The Effects of Revolution Rate on Cycling Efficiency, 1975; An Analysis of the Angle of the Trunk in Relation to Other Variables While Cycling, 1974; Little Known Olympic Sports Series: Cycling, 1972. *Memberships:* Presenter, International Society of Biomechanics; Charter Member, American Society of Biomechanics; Presenter, American College of Sports Medicine; American Alliance for Health, Physical Education and Recreation; American Society of Mechanical Engineers; American Society for Testing and Materials; Human Factors Society; Awards Chairman, National Management Association; American Federation of Musicians; League of American Wheelmen; Leader, Bikecentennial; Official and competitor, United States Cycling Federation; United States Philatelic Society; North Shore Concert Band; WSU Wind Symphony; Treasurer, Columbia Basin Concert Band; The Mid-Columbia, Yakima, and Walla Walla Symphony Orchestras; Founder and Manager of Cascade Clarinets, Chamber Music Plus; Chairman, Bicycle Advisory Committee to the Washington State Department of Transportation; Treasurer, Bicycle Federation of Washington; Oratorio Chorus; Librarian, Good Shepherd Lutheran Church Choir. *Honours:* Outstanding Young Woman of America, 1982; Honorarium from Phi Epsilon Kappa Professional Sorority for Superior Dissertation; National Honors Society from Lyons Township High School; Numerous trophies, medals, certificates, plaques for Bicycle Racing Throughout the United States; Certificate of Completion and Leadership from Bikecentennial; Outstanding Achievement Award for Service to UNC Nuclear Industries National Management Association; Quality Achievement Award Certificate of Merit in Professional Category from Westinghouse Hanford Company. *Hobbies:* Mechanics; Bicycle racing and riding; All Sports; Bicycle mechanics; Out-of-Doors; Playing Bass Clarinet, etc. *Address:* Nike Sport Research Laboratory, 9000 S W Nimbus Drive, Beaverton, Oregon 97005, USA.

JACK Sheila Beryl, b. 26 Sept. 1918, Waterloo, Liverpool, England. Poet. m. Robert Lawrence Jack, 31 Jan. 1942, 1 son, 1 daughter. *Education:* Teachers' Certificate and Archbishops' Certificate for teaching of Religion, Derby Diocesan Training College for Teachers; Wolverhampton Teachers College, TESL. *Appointments:* Wrockwardine Parish Council (School Manager), 1953-66; Salop County Council, 1963-69, serving on the Children's Boarded and Fostered Out Committee and Welfare Committee; Supply Full-time Teaching, Shropshire Education Committee, 1953-63; Civil Servant, COD Donnington, 1963-65; Teacher, English as a Second Language, Woden Road, Wolverhampton, 1965-74; English Teacher, Deansfield High School, 1974- 75; Supply Full-time, Wolverhampton Education Committee, Priority Area Schools, 1975-78. *Publications:* 32 Poems, 1962; Another 32 Poems, 1973; contributor to various journals, and anthologies; Script: Footsteps from our Past; Documentary Book: To Save a Castle. *Memberships:* Attingham Writers Club; Anglo-Welsh Poetry Society; Poetry Society; Centro Studi e Scambi Internazionali; Fellow, World Literary Academy. *Honours:* Honorary Vice President, Centro Studi e Scambi Internazionali, 1978, Book of the Month, 1981; 1st Prize, Anglo-Welsh Poetry Society Competition, 1986; American Biographical Institute's Commemorative Medal of Honour, 1987. *Hobbies:* Travel; Painting; Politics. *Address:* Longacre, Wrockwardine, Nr. Telford, Shropshire, England.,

JACKANIN Albina Veronica Boblinski, b. 22 Dec 1924, New York City, New York, USA. Community Service Representative; Editor. m. Joseph M Jackanin, 6 Nov 1948, 2 sons, 3 daughters. *Education:* Public schools. *Appointments:* Employed at People's Fire House, Inc, 1978 -. *Publications:* People's Firehouse Bulletin (previously published monthly, now on a three-monthly basis. *Memberships:* Chairperson of the Neighbourhood Advisory Board of Dr Catherine White Residence. *Hobbies:* Art collecting; Photography; Reading. *Address:* 93, North 8 Street, Brooklyn, NY 11211, USA.

JACKLIN Anna, b. 17 May 1923, Heidelberg, Germany. Housewife; Investor. m. Dr Duane Elsworth Jacklin, 17 Jan. 1931. 2 sons, 2 daughters. *Education:* BS Business 1943; MS Business 1946. *Appointments:* Owner, Grocery Store Chain, 1980-; Investor: Art, Antiques, Coins, Real Estate, 1970-. *Memberships:* American Ex POW's; Disabled American Veterans; International Platform Association; President, Demolays Mothers. *Honours:* Demolay Mother of the Year, 1974 & 1975; Dav Women of the Year, 1977 & 1978. *Hobbies:* Art; Coins; Antiques; Jewellery. *Address:* 2108 W Manana Blvd, Clovis, New Mexico 88101, USA.

JACKSON Anna Marie, b. 22 Apr. 1942, Nampa, Idaho, USA. Educational Consultant; Teacher. m. James W. Jackson, 2 June 1960, 2 sons. *Education:* BA, Northwest Nazarene College, 1965; MA, University of Colorado, 1976; PhD, University of Denver, 1984; Post-Graduate, Colorado State University, 1985. *Appointments:* Littleton Colorado School District, 1968-70; Jefferson County, Colorado, 1970-; Assistantship, University of Denver, 1982; Supervisor, Student Teachers, University of Denver, 1982; Co-ordinator, Gifted & Talented Educational Programmes, 1985-; Metro State College, Colorado, 1988-. *Publications:* Holiday Heritage Curriculum, 1978; Communication with Parents of Gifted Children, 1984; WINGS Programme Development, 1985; Wings Landing Vistas, 1986; Wilmot Instructional System for Enrichment, 1987; Stewardship Adventure, Cook, 1987. *Memberships:* Phi Delta Kappa; Jefferson County Association for Gifted and Talented, President; World Counsel for Gifted Children; National Association for Gifted Children; Colorado Association for Gifted and Talented; American Association of University Women. *Honours:* State & International Judge, Olympics of The Mind, 1984-86; Various Teaching Recognitions; Governors Award for Excellence in Education, 1987; Teacher of the Year, 1988, Colorado Association for Gifted and Talented; L E Wesche Award, 1988, Northwest Nazarene College. *Hobbies:* International Travel; Public Speaking; Doll Collection. *Address:* PO Box 651, Evergreen, CO 80439, USA.

JACKSON Barbara Ann Garvey, b. 27 Sept. 1929, Normal, Illinois, USA. Professor of Music; Editor and publisher. m. Kern C Jackson, 29 Mar. 1970. 4 stepsons. *Education:* BM, University of Illinois, 1950; MM, Eastman School of Music, 1952; PhD, Stanford University, 1959. *Appointments:* University of Arkansas, 1952-54; Los Angeles Elementary Schools, 1956-57; Arkansas Tech University, 1957-61; University of Arkansas, Fayetteville, 1961-; Founder of ClarNan Editions, 1984. *Publications:* As Barbara Garvey Seagrave: Songs of the Minnesingers, with Wesley Thomas, 1966; The Songs of the Minnesinger Price Wizlaw of Rugen, with Wesley Thomas, 1968. As Barbara Garvey Jackson: editor, Sonatas for Violin Solos and Violoncello and with Cembalo, Giovanni Antonio Piani (from the original Paris Edition of 1712), 1975; trans. Hubert Le Blanc's Defense de la Viole, 1973, 1974, 1975; Journal of Viola da Gamba Society of America; Florence Price: Composer; Perspectives in Black Music, 1977; editor and violinist, Music for the Mass by Nun Composers, Leonardo Production (Recordings) 1982; ed. Sonata Duodecima from opus 16 (1693), by Isabella Leonarda, 1983; The ASTA Dictionary of Bowing Terms for String Instruments, 3rd edition, with Joel Berman and Kenneth Sarch, 1987; Practical Beginning Theory: A Fundamentals Worktext, with Bruce Benward, 6th edition, 1987; editor and publisher, Messa Prima from op 18 (1696), 1981; Quam dulcis es from op 13 (1687), 1984; Dori e Fileno, 1984; Il Sacrifizio di Ambramo (1708), 1984; S Beatrice d'Este (1707), 1986; Arias from Oratorios by Women composers of the eighteenth centure Volume 1, 1987; Lieder by Women Composers of the Classic Era, Volume 1, 1987, Volume II, 1987; Trois Sonates pour Harp ou Piano-forte avec Accompagnement de Violin (1785), 1988; Entries in Anthologies and Dictionaries. *Memberships:* Past President, South Central Society for 18th Century Studies; Reviewer for American String Teachers Association; Viola da Gamba Society of America; American Musicological Society; Early Music America; International Congress of Women in Music, etc. *Honours:* Honorary member, Sigma Alpha Iota, 1969; Master Teacher Award, Fulbright College of Arts and Sciences of the University of Arkansas, 1988. *Hobbies:* Gardening; Cooking; Wildflowers. *Address:* 235 Baxter Lane, Fayetteville, Arkansas 72701, USA.

JACKSON Betty Eileen, b. 9 Oct. 1925, Denver, Colorado, USA. Musician; Teacher. *Education:* BMus 1948, MMus 1949, BMusEd 1963, University of Colorado; Studies, Indiana University, 1952-55; Hochschule fur Musik, Germany, 1955-56. *Appointments include:* Vocal teacher, accompanist, graduate assistant, various schools & universities, 1948-69; Private voice studios, Riverside & Rialto, CA, 1963-; Lecturer, Music, California State University, San Bernardino, 1967-76. *Creative work:* (All performances, leading roles): Chorister, Central City Opera Company, Colorado, summers 1948, 1949; Performer, University of Colorado 1946-49, Denver Grand Opera Company (CO) 1950-52, Indiana University Opera Theatre 1952-55, 3 tours, West Germany 1956-59, Rialto Community Theatre, 1983-; Performer, coach, accompanist, University of Colorado, Boulder, 1961-69; Performer & accompanist, Riverside Opera Company 1964-75, West End Opera Company 1966-78; Performer & Music

Director, Fontana Mummers 1980-, Riverside Community Players 1984-. *Memberships include:* Offices, past/present: National Association of Teachers of Singing; American Association of University Women; San Bernardino Valley Concert Association; San Bernardino Cultural Taskforce; Inland Theatre League. Member, numerous other music associations, community organisations. *Honours:* Fulbright scholar, 1955-56; Outstanding Performer, Inland Theatre League, 1982, 1983, 1984. *Hobbies:* Community theatre; Opera; Travel; Collecting porcelain. *Address:* 230 East Valencia, PO Box 885, Rialto, California 92377, USA.

JACKSON Daphne Frances, b. 23 Sept. 1936, Peterborough, England. Professor. *Education:* BSc., Physics, University of London, 1958; ARCS, Physics, Battersea College, 1958; PhD, Theoretical Nuclear Physics, Imperial College, 1962; DSc., Nuclear Physics, 1970, University of London. *Appointments:* Lecturer, Physics, Battersea College of Technology, 1960-66; Reader, Nuclear Physics, 1967-71, Professor, Physics, 1971-, Dean, Physics, 1984-88, University of Surrey, Guildford. *Publications:* Nuclear Reactions, 1970; Concepts of Atomic Physics, 1971; Nuclear Sizes & Structures, with R C Barrett, 1977; Imaging with Ionizing Radiations, co-author, 1982; Imaging with Non-Ionizing Radiations, Ed Jackson, 1983; 80 papers & articles on Nuclear Physics; 43 papers on Medical Physics; 27 articles on education & the position of women. *Memberships:* Fellow, Institute of Physics; Fellow, Institute of Electrical Engineers; Senior Member, Institute Electrical & Electronic Engineers; Fellow, Royal Society of Arts; Womens Engineering Society, Hon Sec., 1988-, Vice President 1981-83, President 1983-85. *Honours:* OBE; Hon D. Univ., Open University; Hon DSc. Exeter University; Visiting Professor, University of Maryland, USA, 1970, University of Louvain, Belgium, 1972, University of Lund, Sweden, 1980-82. *Hobbies:* Writing; Encouraging Girls & Women in Science & Engineering. *Address:* 5 St Omer Road, Guildford, Surrey, GU1 2DA, England.

JACKSON Geneva, b. 30 Dec. 1931, Philadelphia, USA. Epidemiology Case Investigator. *Education:* BA, 1966; Registered Cytotechnologist, 1967; MPH, 1981; DHSc., 1982. *Appointments:* Therapeutic and Rehabilitative Services for the Elderly, 1980-86; Extensive Volunteer Work, 1971-; Associate Director, Health Club for Inner City Youth; Blood Pressure Screenings, Stop Smoking Programmes. *Publications:* Author, Illustrator, exercise Book for Senior Citizens; instructional manual for students interested in teaching the elderly. *Memberships:* American College of Sports Medicine; American Public Health Association; American Society of Clinical Pathologists; American Association for Physical Health Education Recreation & Dance. *Honours:* Beta Kappa Chi, 1974. *Hobbies:* Composing; Writing Poetry; Wood & Paper Crafts. *Address:* 3330 N. 18th Street, Philadelphia, PA 19140, USA.

JACKSON Glenda, b. 9 May 1936, Birkenhead, Cheshire, England. Actress. m. Roy Hodges, 1958, divorced 1967. 1 son. *Education:* Royal Academy of Dramatic Art. *Career:* Royal Shakespeare Company roles included Ophelia in Hamlet and Charlotte Corday in Marat/Sade (in London and New York); played Queen Elizabeth I in television series Elizabeth R. *Creative Works:* Plays include: Marat/Sade, New York and Paris, 1965; The Investigation, 1965; Hamlet, 1965, US 1966; Three Sisters, 1967; Collaborators, 1973; The Maids, 1974; Hedda Gabler, 1975; The White Devil, 1976; Antony and Cleopatra, 1978; Rose, 1980; Strange Interlude, 1984; Phaedra, 1984, 1985; Across from the Garden of Allah, 1986; Strange Interlude, 1986; The House of Bernardo Alba, 1986. Films include: Marat/Sade, 1966; Negatives, 1968; Women in Love, 1969; The Music Lovers, 1970; Sunday, Bloody Sunday, 1971; The Boy Friend, 1971; Mary, Queen of Scots, 1971; The Triple Echo, 1972; Bequest to the Nation, 1972; A Touch of Class, 1973; The Romantic Englishwoman, 1975; The Tempter, 1975; The Incredible Sarah, 1976;

The Abbess of Crewe, 1976; Stevie, 1977; Hedda, 1977; House Calls, 1978; The Class of Miss McMichael, 1978; Lost and Found, 1979; Hopscotch, 1980; The Return of the Soldier, 1982; Giro City, 1982; Summit Conference, 1982; Great and Small; 1983; And Nothing But the Truth, 1984l; Turtle Diary, 1985; Beyond Therapy, 1985; Business as Usual, 1986. Television appearances include: Sakharov, 1984. *Memberships:* President, Play Matters (formerly Toy Libraries Association), 1976-; Director, United British Artists, 1983-. *Honours:* Honorary DLitt (Liverpool), 1978; Academy Award (Oscar) for Women in Love, 1971; A Touch of Class, 1974. *Hobbies:* Gardening; Reading; Listening to Music. *Address:* c/o Crouch Associates, 59 Frith Street, London W1, England.

JACKSON Jurel (DeShazer), b. 28 July 1923, Ravenwood, Missouri, USA. Retired Teacher; Politician. *Education:* BSc 1965, MSc 1968, Northwest Missouri State University; Degree, Education Specialist, Eastern Illinois University, 1972; Postgraduate, University of Missouri, 1977-78. *Appointments:* Teacher: Language Arts, Savannah Junior High School 1965-66, Journalism & English, Senior High School 1966-68; Counsellor, administrator, Eastern Illinois University, 1968-74; Counsellor, Special Services Coordinator, Mexico Junior HS, Missouri, 1974-84; Educational consultant, 1984-. *Publications:* 2 books including family history with genealogy; Freelance writing, various periodicals & newspapers, 30 years. *Memberships:* Life member, past Legislative Chair, American Association of University Women; Life member, Beta Sigma Phi, National Education Association; Active, Phi Delta Kappa. Also: St Gregory Barbarigo Catholic Church; Rosanna Chapter 262, Order of Eastern Star. *Honours:* Counsellor of Year, Mid-Missouri Guidance Association, 1984; President, 6th Congressional District, Women's Democratic Clubs, 1962-63; 1st woman elected (full term), Maryville City Council, 1985-88; Mayor pro-tem, Maryville, 1986, 1987. *Hobbies:* Writing; Travel; Fishing; Handicrafts, various; Reading; Gardening. Political involvement including: Chair, Nodaway County & 12th Senatorial District Democratic Committees; Secretary, 6th Congressional District. *Address:* 624 West Thompson Street, Maryville, Missouri 64468, USA.

JACKSON Lucy (Deirdre Ruth), b. 13 Apr.1 930, Bridgewater, Somerset, England. Teacher. m. Ian Jackson, 12 Sept. 1970, 2 sons, 1 daughter. *Education:* Bedford College, 1948-51; Medau Diploma, 1954. *Appointments:* Movement & Dance Teacher, 35 years; Courses in many countries including: Sultanate of Oman, Egypt, USA, Iceland, Ireland (Eire) & France. *Publications:* Videos; articles in books and magazines. *Memberships:* Medau Society; laban Guild; slimnastics; Asset; AFTA; League of Health & Beauty; Irish Terrier Society. *Hobbies:* Birdwatching; Irish Terriers; Breeding Canaries; Music; Literature. *Address:* 23 Springfield Road, London NW8 0QJ, England.

JACKSON M Kate, b. 23 Apr. 1938, Sevierville, Tennessee, USA. Real Estate Sales. m. Ernest W Jackson, Jr, 10 Feb. 1967. 2 sons, 1 daughter. *Education:* Assoc degree, Draughons Business College, 1956; Graduate & License, Shannon & Luchs Academy of Realestate, 1986; GRI Designation, Realtors Institute, 1988. *Appointments:* Adm Asst to President, Cherokee Textile Mills, 1959-63; Adm Asst to US Congressman James W Quillen, 1963-68; Exec. Asst to Congressman James C Cleveland, 1969-80; Adm Asst to U S Congressman Judd Gregg, 1981-88; Real Estate Sales, Shannon & Luchs, 1986- 88. *Memberships:* National Association of Realtors, Virginia Association of Realtors, PW County Board of Realtors on two Committees, RPAC & P & GA; Capitol Hill Adm Assts Association; Republican Women of Capitol Hill. *Honours:* Rookie of the Year Award, Realtor, 1987-88; First year Licensee, P W Bor, Million Dollar Club, 1987; Shannon & Luchs Executives Club, 1987; Shannon & Luchs Presidents Club, 1988. *Hobbies:* Painting; Reading; Camping; Travel; Architecture. *Address:* 9720 Loudoun Avenue, Manassas, VA 22110, USA.

JACKSON Nora, (Tennant), b. 7 July 1915, London, England. m. 27 July 1957. *Education:* Furzedown Training College, 1932-34; Associate, College of Preceptors; Member, Royal Society of Teachers. *Appointments:* Whitelman School, Harrow, 1934-44; Senior Geography Specialist, Headstone, Harrow, 1944-57; Senior Mistress and Head of Geography, Hillcrest School, Dudley, West Midlands, 1957-60; Head of Geography Department, Vauxhall Manor, London, 1960-66; Deputy Head, Langley County Secondary School, Buckinghamshire, 1966-76. *Publications:* Dictionary of Natural Resources; A Groundwork of Physical Geography; A Groundwork of World Wealth; Groundwork Geographies (series of four books on the British Isles, Europe, North America, Asian and the Southern Continents); Articles for the World Encyclopaedia on the British Isles; Editorial work on Geography Textbooks. *Memberships:* Royal Geographical Society; National Trust; Pinner Local History Society; Royal Society Protection of Birds. *Hobbies:* Travel; Writing; Gardening. *Address:* 58 Hill Road, Pinner, Middlesex, HA5 1LE, England.

JACKSON Sally Ann, b. 9 July 1951, Springfield, Illinois, USA. Director. *Education:* BSc, Administrative of Justice, 1973; MSc, Administrative of Justice, 1975. *Appointments:* Faculty, Law Enforcement, Western University, Illinois, 1973-76; Budget & Program Analyst, Illinois Bureau of Budget, 1976-77; Asst to Director, Illinois Department of Law Enforcement, 1977-80; Asst to Governor, State of Illinois, 1980-83; Director, Illinois Department of Employment Security, 1983-. *Memberships:* Illinois Job Training Coordinating Council; Prairie State 2000 Authority; Chicago Private Industry Council; Interstate Conference Employment Security Agencies; Women Executives in State Government; International Association of Personnel in Employment Security. *Honours:* Fellowship to JFK School of Govt, Harvard University, RJR Nabisco, 1987; US Dept of Justice, Immigration and Naturalization Services Award for Project Save; Mortor Board, National Honorary for Women, Honorary Charter Member, Western Illinois University Chapter, 1976; Graduate Research Assistantship in Administration of Justice, Southern Illinois University, 1973; Phi Kappa Phi, National Honor Society; Order of Isis, Greek Women's Honorary, Southern Illinois University; Thompson Point Order of the Scroll, Residential Area Honorary, Southern Illinois University; Alpha Lambda Delta, National Freshman Women's Honorary. *Hobbies:* Jogging; Sewing; Downhill skiing; Cycling; Travel. *Address:* 1719 N. Fremont, Chicago, Illinois 60614, USA.

JACKSON-COLON Denise Cassandra, b. 2 Jan. 1952, New York City, New York USA. President, CEO, Colon Telecommunications Consultants Inc. m. 6 June 1970, divorced 1988. 2 daughters. *Education:* Student, Marymount College, New York, 1982. *Appointments:* Cons telecommunications various co, New York City, 1980-82; President, Chief Exec Officer, Colon Telecommunications Consultants Inc, New York City, 1982-; Cons, US Dept Labor US, 1986-87; Permanent Mission Guinea to UN HEM Saliou Coumbassa, 1985-87. *Publication:* Author: Controlling Corporate Telecommunications Costs, 1985. *Memberships:* Am Mgmt Assn; Soc Telecommunications Cons; Nat Assn Female Execs; Double Image Theatre. *Address:* Colon Telecommunications Consultants Inc, 47-28 210th St, Bayside, NY 11361, USA.

JACOB Carolina, b. 20 Jan. 1940, Bucharest, Romania. Painter. m. Stefan Alexandru, 27 Nov. 1969. 1 daughter. *Education:* BA, Plastics Art Institute. *Appointments:* Self employed painter. *Creative works:* Numerous solo exhibitions, Bucharest, 1967, 1972, 1977, 1979, 1982 and 1986; Collective exhibitions: Calgary, Canada; Haga, Moscow, Helsinki, Peking, Athens, Geneva, Stuttgart. *Membership:* Plastic Artists Union, Romanian Socialist Republic. *Honours:* Pioneers Award, 1981 and 1985. *Address:* Aghives 4 Apt 4, Bucharest Section 2, Cod 71452, Romania.

JACOB Karen Ann Hite, b. 14 Feb. 1947,

Wilkensburg, Pennsylvania, USA. Musician. m. John B. Jacob, 23 Mar. 1973, 1 son. *Education:* BM, Greensboro, 1969, MAT, Chapel Hill, 1970, University of North Carolina. *Appointments:* Central Piedmont Community College, 1971-75; Community School of the Arts, 1971-86; Artistic Director, Creator, Carolina Pro Musica, 1977-; St Johns Episcopal, 1981-. *Publications:* Compositions: Miscellaneous anthems, music arrangements; Author: The American Organist, Newsletter of Southeastern Historical Keyboard Society, Editor. *Memberships:* Founding Member, Southeastern Historical Keyboard Society; Registrar, Charlotte Chapter, American Guild of Organisists. *Honours:* Mu Phi Epsilon, 1967; Honorary Citizen, New Orleans, 1983; Music Ensemble Opens America's 400th Anniversary, 1984. *Hobbies:* 13- 18th Century Cooking & Recipes; Gardening; Sailing. *Address:* PO Box 32022, Charlotte, NC 28232, USA.

JACOB Lois Marie, b. 24 Mar. 1950, Chicago, Illinois, USA. Toxicologist/Consultant. m. Merle G Galbraith, Jr, 25 Mar. 1978. *Education:* BA, Honours Chemistry, University of Illinois, 1971; MS, Environmental & Industrial Health, University of Michigan School of Public Health, Ann Arbor, 1974. *Appointments:* Research Assistant, Toxicology Department, University of Michigan, Ann Arbor, 1974-76; Toxicologist, Office of Pesticides & Toxic Substances, 1976-78, Toxicologist and Science Advisor, 1978-81, USEPA Office of Enforcement, Washington; Senior Health Specialist, Toxic Substance Control Commission, Lansing, 1981-85; Consultant, 1985. *Publications:* Research Results & Recommendations for Environmental & Occupational MBOCA Levels; Citizen's Guide for Community Health Studies, 1985. *Memberships:* New York Academy of Science; American Association for the Advancement of Science; Michigan Society of Toxicology; American Chemical Society; American Public Health Association; American Conference of Governmental Industrial Hygienists; American Youth Hostels; North Cape Yacht Club; Seven Seas Cruising Association. *Honours:* Certificate of Appreciation, Michigan Association of Environmental Professionals, 1984; *Fellowships:* National Institutes of Health and Atomic Energy Commission, 1972- 74, 1970. *Hobbies:* Ocean sailing; Figure skating; Travel; International Cuisine; Music performance; Painting & design; Women's financial and career issues. *Address:* PO Box 2096, Chicago, Illinois 60690, USA.

JACOBS Alma R., b. 27 July 1924, Philadelphia, Pennsylvania, USA. Consultant, Ageing & Human Services. m. J. Alexander Jacobs, 4 June 1955. *Education:* Bryn Mawr College, 1942-43; University of Pennsylvania, 1967-68. *Appointments:* District Manager, Public Affairs, Bell of Pennsylvania, 1946-84; Secretary, Ageing Commonwealth of Pennsylvania, 1985- 86; Consultant, Ageing & Human Services, 1987-. *Memberships:* President, Women for Greater Pennsylvania; Secretary-Treasurer, Montgomery County Community College Foundation; Chair, Pennsylvania Federation of Business & Professional Women (PFBPA); Past Chair, Pennsylvania Commission for Women. *Honours:* Woman of Year, PFBPA, 1980; Awards, Chapel of 4 Chaplains, 1976, 1980; Hall of Fame, Seneca Falls, New York, 1976; Presidential Award, Greater Philadelphia Chamber of Commerce, 1982; Distinguished Daughter, Pennsylvania, 1982; Medal, Sons of American Revolution, 1984. *Hobbies:* Gardening; Politics. *Address:* 435 Holly Road, Blue Bell, Pennsylvania 19422, USA.

JACOBS Rita Goldman, b. 15 Jan. 1927, New York City, New York, USA. Physician (Anaesthesiologist). m. David J. Jacobs, 28 Nov. 1952, 2 daughters. *Education:* BA, New York University, 1947; MD, Woman's Medical College of Pennsylvania, 1951; Intern, Queens General Hospital, 1951- 52; Resident in Anaesthesiology, Columbia Presbyterian Medical Center, New York City, 1952-54; Diplomate, American Board of Anesthesia, 1957. *Appointments:* Attending in Anaesthesia: Columbia Presbyterian Medical Center, 1954-58; Memorial Sloan-Kettering Cancer Center, New York

City, 1958-71; Berkshire Medical Center, Pittsfield, Massachusetts, 1971-; Chairman, Department of Anaesthesia, 1975-84, Medical Director, Ambulatory Surgery, 1984-, Berkshire Medical Center. *Publications:* Numerous articles in medical journals and 3 chapters in medical books, mostly concerning use of nerve blocks in treatment of pain. *Memberships:* American Society of Anesthesiologists; American Medical Association; Massachusetts Medical Society; Massachusetts Society of Anesthesia; Secretary, Past Vice-President, Berkshire District Medical Society. *Honours:* 1st Prize for Scientific Exhibit, Use of Microhematocrits in Monitoring Changes in Blood Volume During and After Surgery, Postgraduate Assembly of New York State Society of Anesthesiologists. *Hobbies:* Needlework and crafts; House plants; Chamber music; Theatre. *Address:* Berkshire Medical Center, 725 North Street, Pittsfield, MA 01201, USA.

JACOBSON Debra Ann, b. 20 Mar. 1952, Kingston, New York, USA. Attorney. m. David Edward Jacobson, 10 Aug. 1975, 1 son. *Education:* BA summa cum laude, Environmental Studies, University of Rochester, 1974; JD, honours, National Law Centre, George Washington University, 1977. *Appointments:* Legislative assistant, US Congressman Bob Eckhardt, Washington DC, 1977-79; Counsel, Subcommittee on Oversight & Investigations, Committee on Energy & Commerce, US House of Representatives, 1979-. *Publications:* Author or co-author, several Congressional reports. *Memberships:* Director-at-large, Womens Council on Energy & Environment, 1981-83; New York State & District of Columbia Bar Associations; Nature Conservancy. *Honour:* Award, Delta Laboratories, 1972. *Hobbies:* Hiking; Cycling. *Address:* 2323 Rayburn House Office Building, Washington DC 20515, USA.

JACOBSON Phyllis C. b. 4 Sep. 1929, Irwin, Idaho, USA. University Educator. *Education:* BS, Elementary Education, 1953, MS, Physical Education, 1954, Utah State University; Graduate Study, Pennsylvania State University, 1963-64; PhD, University of Utah, 1971. *Appointments:* Elementary Teacher, Irwin, Idaho, 1949-50; Junior High Teacher, Jerome, Idaho, 1950-52; GTA, Logan, Utah, 1953-54; High School Teacher, Las Vegas, Nevada, 1954-57; Graduate Teaching Assistant, Pennsylvania State University, 1963-64; Instructor, 1957-, Professor, 1971, Chairman, Department of Physical Education-Dance, currently, Brigham Young University, Provo, Utah. *Publications:* Fund Skills in PE, 1977; Move It!, 1979; Fitness Manual for Lady Missionaries; A Sensible Course in Physical Fitness; Hooked on Aerobics, 1982; Hooked on Aerobics, TV Series for National PBS, 1982-90. *Memberships:* Alliance for Health, Physical Education, Rec and Dance, SW District; Utah Alliance for Health, Physical Education, Rec/Dance; Western Society for Physical Education; National Association for Physical Education in Higher Education; Membership Director, Dance Committee, National Dance Association; Smithsonian Institute; President, Utah Alliance HPERD; Dance Division Chairman, SW District HPERD; Charter Member, Utah Governors Council for Health and Fitness. *Honours:* Phi Kappa Phi Scholastic Rec Award; Master Teacher, Brigham Young University, 1971; Outstanding Educators of America Citation, 1972; Service Award, 1972, Honour Award, 1973, Karl G Maeser Distinguished Teaching Award, UAHPERD, 1978; Honour Award, AAHPERD, SW District, 1977. *Hobbies:* Skiing; Hiking; Cycling; Dancing; Riding; Camping; Running; Racquetball; Knitting; Crocheting; Farming. *Address:* Department of Physical Education-Dance, Brigham Young University, 296 RB, Provo, UT 84602, USA.

JACOBSON Ruth Blanche, b. 18 Aug. 1941, London, England. Artist; Painter; Printmaker. 2 sons, 1 daughter. *Education:* DFA, Slade School of Fine Art, London, 1959-63; Post Graduate Teaching Course, Manchester, 1963-64. *Appointments:* Part-time teaching in Adult Education, 1963-64; Returned seriously to art in 1972 exhibiting solo and in group shows. *Creative Works:* Solo Exhibits include: La

Comedie Humaine, Poole Arts Centre and Camden Arts Centre, 1985; Songs of my People, Zionist Confederation House, Jerusalem, 1986. Group shows include: Agnews, 1963; Wildensteins, 1974; Royal Festival Hall, 1982 & 1986; Gallerie Hanenhof, Geleen, Holland, 1984 & 1986; Barbican Centre, London, 1986; Drawings of Laboratory Technicians & Researchers used to illustrate: Faculty of Science & Engineering Research Report, 1985. Work in public collections includes: Panstwowe Muzeum Oswiecim Brzezinka, Poland; Yad Vashem Museum, Jerusalem; Ben Uri Art Gallery, London. *Honours:* Commission to paint a portrait of HM Queen Elizabeth, The Queen Mother, for presentation to the Museums Association of Great Britain; 1st prize, Dorothy Copsey Memorial Watercolour Competition, 1987, etc. *Hobbies:* Music, classical & folk; Travel; Study of Foreign Languages; History & Literature in general and especially of the Jewish people; Stained glass. *Address:* 25 Holne Chase, London N2 0QL, England.

JACOBSON-WIDDING H. Anita, b. Stockholm, Sweden. Professor of Cultural Anthropology. m. Lars Widding, 1975 divorced 1987. 1 son, 1 daughter. *Education:* MA 1961, PhD 1968, Uppsala University. *Appointments:* Journalist, Dagens Nyheter, 1968-69; Feature editor, Swedish Radio, 1969-72; Ass.Professor, 1973-77, Professor of Cultural Anthropology (Chair), 1977-, Uppsala University. *Publications:* Marriage and Money, 1967; Forsorjerskan: Kvinnai Kongo, 1977; Red-White-Black as a Mode of Thought, 1979; Identity: Personal and Socio-Cultural, 1983; African Folk Models, 1984; Culture, Experience and Pluralism, 1989. *Membership:* Royal Swedish Academy of Letters. *Honour:* Elin Wagner Award, 1963. *Address:* Department of Cultural Anthropology, Uppsala University, Tradgardsgatan 18, 75220 Uppsala, Sweden.

JACOBY Diane Marie Wentland, b. 6 Aug. 1958, Buffalo, New York, USA. Exercise Physiologist. *Education:* First Class of Women, United States Military Academy at West Point, 1976-78; BA Sociology, Psychology, Methodist College, North Carolina; MS Exercise Physiology, University of Michigan. *Appointments:* Manager, The Sports Center, North Carolina, 1980-84; Assistant Director, National Youth Fitness Survey/Fitness for Youth, University of Michigan, 1984-86; Fitness Director, Liberty Sports Complex, Michigan, 1986-. *Publications:* National Youth Fitness Survey, 1986; Norms for American alliance for Health, Physical Education, Recreation and Dance, 1986; Design fitness programs and create activities for schools and clubs to educate people about making fitness a lifelong habit *Memberships:* American Collogo of Sports Medicine; American Alliance for Health, Physical Education, Recreation and Dance. *Honours:* Honorary Member, President's Council on Physical Fitness and Sports, 1985; Sports awards: President Girls Athletic Association, 2 years; Most Valuable Player, Soccer, 1979, 1980; Volleyball, 1978, 1979, 1980; All Division Team/All Tournament Team, 1979. *Hobbies:* Own Professional Housewatch, House-sit, Pet-sit, Kid-sit, etc; Designing, assembling and packaging medical filters for preventing the spread of contamination and disease; Coach, Teach and/or play: Soccer; Softball; Volleyball; Weight training; Aerobics. *Address:* P O Box 2615, Ann Arbor, MI 48106, USA.

JACOBY Teresa Michelle, b. 12 Feb. 1956, El Dorado, Arkansas, USA. Ranch Owner; Breeder; Animal Behaviourist. m. Max Mason Jacoby, 30 Aug. 1976, 2 daughters. *Education:* BA, Animal Psychology, Pennsylvania State University, 1980. *Appointments:* Para-legal & executive secretary, 1980-1982; Self-employed ranch owner & breeder, 1981-. *Creative works:* Various articles, Pit Bull Gazette; Television & radio interviews, cable TV debates. *Memberships:* National spokesperson, show judge, American Dog Breeders Association; President, charter member, Southwest Pit Bull Association; Secretary, Lone Star State Pit Bull Club; American Quarterhorse Association; National representative, Endangered Breed Association; Founding member, Responsible Dog Owners of Texas;

North Texas Pit Bull Club. *Honours include:* Several champion awards, canine shows & weight pulls; Several awards, horsemanship. *Hobbies:* Horses & dogs; Hiking & high country back-packing; Bowling; Horse racing; Flying. *Address:* Rocking 'J' Ranch, PO Box 717, Emory, Texas 75440, USA.

JAEGER Sharon Ann, b. 15 Jan. 1945, Douglas, Arizona, USA. Poet; Editor; Translator. *Education:* BA, summa cum laude, University of Dayton, 1966; MA, English, Boston College, 1971; DA, English, State University of New York at Albany, 1982. *Appointments:* Editor, Intertext, 1982-; Co-editor, Sachem Press, 1980-; Freelance Writer and editor, 1980-; Fulbright Lecturer, Universidade Nova de Lisboa and Universidade de Aveiro, 1983-84; Visiting Asst Professor, Haverford College, 1987-88; Visiting Lecturer, University of Pennsylvania, 1988. *Publications:* Articles in books and magazines; numerous poems in journals and magazines. *Memberships:* Poetry Society of America; Academy of American Poets; American Literary Translators Association; Rhetoric Society of America; Society for Critical Exchange; Northeast Modern Language Association; COSMEP; Fulbright Alumni Association; Associated Writing Programs; American Studies Association. *Honours:* Fulbright lectureship to Portugal, 1983-84; Presidential Fellowship, State University of New York at Albany, 1979-82; 1st place, Ezra Pound Competition for Literary Translation, 1988; Honorable Mention, William Carlos Williams Awards, Academy of American Poets at University of Pennsylvania, 1988; Alpha Sigma Tau Honor Key, 1966; Austrian Government scholarship for German Study, Universitat Salzburg, 1966; Chaminade Award for Excellence, 1966. *Address:* P O Box 100014 DT, Anchorage, AK 99510, USA.

JAFFE Lorna S, b. 1941, Memphis, Tennessee, USA. Historian. *Education:* BA, with Honors, History, Newcomb College, Tulane University, 1963; MA, History 1965, PhD, History 1982, Yale University. *Appointments:* Instructor in History 1968-71, Academic Adviser 1971-72, Temple University; Historian, US Army Materiel Command, 1984-85; Historian, US Army Center of Military History, 1985-87; Historian, Joint Chiefs of Staff, 1987-. *Publication:* The Decision to Disarm Germany: British Policy towards Postwar German Disarmament, 1914-1919, 1985. *Memberships:* Society for History in the Federal Government, Executive Council 1989-, Chair, Program Committee 1987-88, Nominating Committee 1987-88; US Commission on Military History, Chair, Nominating Committee 1988-89; Office of Sec Defense Senior Professional Women's Association. Executive Board, 1989. *Honours:* Phi Beta Kappa, 1963; Woodrow Wilson National Fellowship, 1963-64; Yale University Fellowships and Grants, 1964-68 and 1979; Chi Omega Prize in History, 1963; Tulane Fellow, 1963. *Address:* Historical Division, Joint Staff, Washington, DC 20318, USA.

JAFFE Marcia Joan, b. 23 June 1934, Brooklyn, New York, USA. Education. m. Stanley Jaffe, 23 Nov. 1957. 3 sons. *Education:* BA, Education, 1956; MA, Education, 1977; Certificate in learning disabilities/behaviour disorders. *Appointments:* East Meadow School District, New York, 1956-59; Shaker Heights School District, Ohio, 1975-89; Founder/Adviser Student Group on Race Relations (SGORR), 1985-; Founder/Adviser, Continuum of Learning (COL). *Memberships:* Natl Cncl of Teachers of English (NCTE); Internatl Rdg Association, (IRA); Assoc for Supervision and Curriculum Development (ASCO); Human Relations Commission (Shaker Heights). *Honours:* Cum laude, Honours in Education, 1956; Kappa Delta Pi (Education Honour Society), 1956; Governor's Peace Award, 1986; National School Board Association, 100 winning curriculum ideas, 1987. *Hobbies:* Race Relations; Theatre; Children's literature; Human relations. *Address:* 2729 Rochester Road, Shaker Heights, Ohio 44122, USA.

JAFFE Nora, b. 25 Feb. 1928, Urbana, Ohio, USA. Artist. m. Joseph Jaffe, MF, 16 Jan. 1952. 1 son, 1 daughter. *Creative works:* Numerous Solo and Group Exhibitions including: Pastoral Gallery of Art, East Hampton, 1983; Vassar College, Poughkeepsie, 1979; Open Studio Gallery, Rhinebeck, New York, 1978; Gallery Lasson Modern Art, London, England, 1970; AM Sachs Gallery, New York City, 1965; Village Art Center, New York City, 1963; Montclair State College, Montclair, 1986; AIR Gallery, New York City, 1983 and 1984; Women Artists '78, Graduate Center, CUNY, 1978; Albin-Zeigler Gallery, New York City, 1973; Couturier Gallery, Stamford, 1973; New School Art Centre, New York City, 1973; Benefit for CCCU, New York City, 1972; Artists Equity Association, New York City, 1972; Two-person show, Orpheus Ascending, Stockbridge, 1971; Finch College Museum, New York City, 1971; Thorne Gallery, Keene, 1970; American Painting, 1970, The Virginia Museum of Fine Arts, Richmond, 1970. Works in permanent collections in Philadelphia, New York City and Berkeley. *Publications:* Sulfur 5, 1982; Sulfur 4, 1982; the Name Encanyoned River, 1977; Realignment, 1974; Caterpillar 13, 1970; Caterpillar 11, 1968; Snapshots of a Daughter-in-Law, 1967. *Honours:* Gymnasium Show I, 1964; MacDowell Colony Grant, 1969 and 1970. *Address:* 285 Central Park West, New York City, NY 10024, USA.

JAFFE Sylvia Sarah, b. 16 May 1917, Detroit, Michigan, USA. Collector of Art; Former Medical Technologist. m. David Jaffe, 8 Nov. 1942. *Education:* Internship, Wisconsin General Hospital, Madison, 1939-40; BS, Medical Technology, University of Wisconsin, Madison, 1940. *Appointments:* Medical Technologist, Watts Hospital Laboratory, Durham, North Carolina, 1940-45; Research Haematology Technologist, Sloan Kettering Memorial Hospital Laboratory, New York, 1946-47; Chief Medical Technologist, Arlington Hospital, Virginia, 1948-55; Chief Medical Technologist, Diagnostic Haematology, Georgetown University Hospital, Washington DC, 1959-70; Collector of 19th Century Art, 1970-. *Publications:* 2 Scientific Papers based on original research, Thrombocytopenic Purpura in the Newborn; Predetermination of Sex in the Unborn Child. *Memberships:* American Society of Medical Technologists; American Women in Science; American Society of Clinical Pathologists, Associate member; Smithsonian Resident Programme; Corcoran Gallery of Art; Wisconsin Alumni Association; Pennsylvania Academy of Fine Arts. *Hobbies:* Gardening; Attending Art Lectures; Gourmet Cooking. *Address:* 1913 S Quinty Street, Arlington, VA 22204, USA.

JAFFEE Kay, b. 31 Dec. 1937, Lansing, Michigan, USA. Musician; Musicologist. m. Michael Jaffee, 24 July 1961. *Education:* BA, University of Michigan, 1959; MA, New York University, 1965. *Appointments:* Founder, member and Associate Director of The Waverly Consort; Performer with that ensemble on Renaissance wind and keyboard instruments, harps, psalteries, percussion, program annotator, 1964-. *Publications:* Articles and reviews in professional journals; Six recordings on CBS Masterworks; 2 recordings on Vanguard Records. *Memberships:* American Musicological Society (performance committee, annual meetings, 1986-87, Chair, 1986); American Musical Instrument Society; American Recorder Society (Editorial Board, The American Recorder); Early Music America. *Address:* 305 Riverside Drive, New York, NY 10025, USA.

JAFFER Nazira Azam, b. 16 Dec. 1958, Kisumu, Kenya. Hospital Administrator. m. Azam Sadrudin Jaffer, 14 Mar. 1981, 1 son. *Education:* BSc., Honours, 1983; MHA, University of Ottawa, Canada, 1985. *Appointments:* Administrative Resident, North York General Hospital, Toronto, 1984; Assistant Director, Aga Khan Hospital, 1985-. *Publications:* Articles in professional journals. *Memberships:* American College of Health Care Executives; Canadian College of Health Services Executives; Canadian Organisation for Advancement of Computers in Health. *Honours:* Grand Prior Award, 1977; President's Award, Ontario Hospital Association, 1984. *Address:* PO Box 10536, Nairobi, Kenya.

JAGAN Janet, b. 20 Oct. 1920, Chicago, USA. Politican; Writer. m. Cheddi Jagan, 5 Aug. 1943, 1 son, 1 daughter. *Education:* University of Detroit, 1938-39; Wayne State University, 1939-40; Michigan State College, 1940-41; Cook County School of Nursing, 1941-43. *Appointments:* Founder Member, Peoples Progressive Party, General Secretary 1950-70; Editor, Thunder (party organ), 1950-56; First Woman Elected to Georgetown City Council, 1950- 52; Deputy Speaker, House of Assembly, 1953; Politicla Prisoner, 1954; Minister of Labour, Health & Housing, 1957-61; Minister of Home Affairs, 1963- 64; Member, National Assembly, 1976-; Editor, Mirror Newspaper, 1974-; President, Womens Progressive Organisation; President, Guyna Union of Journalists, Executive Secretary, 1983-, Peoples Progressive Party. *Publications:* History of the People's Progressive Party; The Struggles of the PPP for Guyana's Independence; Army Intervention in 1973 Elections in Guyana. *Memberships:* Bureau of Womens International Democratic Federation. *Address:* 41 Robb Street, Georgetown, Guyana.

JAHN Norma Jean, b. 17 Sept. 1926, Galveston, Texas, USA. Actress; Singer; Musician; Dancer. m. (1)Lester A. Balaski, divorced 1957, 2 daughters, (2)Charles F. Brass, 12 Dec. 1957, divorced 1959. *Appointments:* Warner Bros Records Inc., 1973-; Stage-TV Film, 1929-currently, 1980-88. *Memberships:* Screen Actors Guild; American Federation Television & Radio Artists; American Federation of Musicians; American Film Institute. *Honours:* Recipient, many honours & awards including: Alma Donna King Conkling Award; Alma Bravo Award; Honorary Citizen of New Orleans; Key to the City, New Orleans. *Hobbies:* Genealogy; Research; Rifle Range; Aerobics; Cycling; Swimming. *Address:* PO Box 2243, Toluca Lake, CA 91610, USA.

JAKUBIAK-LUPTON Paula Sue, b. 2 May 1951, Worcester, USA. Conservator, Works of Art on Paper. m. Bradshaw Babb Lupton, Jr., 12 June 1981, 1 son. *Education:* BFA, University of Massachusetts, 1973. *Appointments:* American Antiquarian Society, 1973-76; New England Document Conservation Centre, 1976-79; Yale British Art Centre, & Yale Art Gallery, 1980-81; Private Consulting Conservator, 1981-. *Publications:* Community TV Producer, Shrewsbury Public Access, Ice Cream Social, 1987, Boy Scout Jamboree 75th Anniversary, 1987, 200 Anniversary of the US Constitution, 1988, An Evening with Gail Sheehy, 1989. *Memberships:* American Institute for Conservation; New England Conservation Association; Worcester Foundation for Experimental Biology Auxiliary, Executive Board; History of Shrewsbury Education Project Steering Committee. *Hobbies:* Battery Operated Robots; Reproduction of Early American Furniture Finishes; Early Photographic Processes. *Address:* 227 Maple Avenue, Shrewsbury, MA 01545, USA.

JALOVICK Judith May, b. 27 May 1944, Neptune, New Jersey, USA. Elementary School Principal. *Education:* BS, Home Economics, Douglass College, 1966; EdM, Administration 1970, EdD, Administration 1977, Rutgers University. *Appointments:* HS Teacher of Home Economics, Sayreville, New Jersey, 1966-70; Jr High Teacher of Home Economics, Freehold Township, NJ, 1970-79; Associate Professor, Rutgers University, 1977-78; Elementary Principal Freehold Twp, 1979-. *Publications:* Articles in professional journals. *Memberships:* Association of Supervision & Curr Development, Principals & Supervisors Assoc; NJ School Masters. *Honours:* Kappa Delta Pi, 1973; Steering Committee for Principals' Institute; NJ Academy for the Advancement of Teaching & Management. *Hobbies:* Piano; Sewing. *Address:* 261 Pond Road, Freehold, NJ 07728, USA.

JAMES Dorothy Buckton, b. New York City, New York. USA. College Provost and Dean. m Judson L. James, 1 daughter. *Education includes:* PhD, Columbia University, 1966. *Appointments:* Lecturer, Assistant Professor, Associate Professor, Hunter College, City

University of New York, to 1974; Professor, Head of Government Department, VPI and State University, to 1980; Dean, School of Government and Public Administration, The American University, to 1988; Currently Provost and Dean of Faculty, Connecticut College, New London. *Publications:* The Contemporary Presidency; Poverty, Politics and Change; Outside, Looking In; Analyzing Poverty Policy; Numerous articles and chapters. *Memberships:* President, Policy Studies Organization; Executive Council, American Political Science Association; Executive Council, American Society for Public Administration. *Honour:* Outstanding Contribution to Policy Studies, Policy Studies Organization. *Hobbies:* Sailing; Canoeing; Chinese and Japanese art. *Address:* Office of the Provost, 202 Fanning Hall, Connecticut College, New London, CT 06320, USA.

JAMES Gillian Hilma, b. 6 Dec. 1934, Launceston, Tasmania. Member of Parliament. m. Peter Wilson James, 27 Jan. 1961, deceased 1983, 1 son. *Appointments:* Secretary to Senator Justin O'Byrne, 1953-61, while he was President of the Senate, 1975-76; Secretary to Hon. Lance Bernard, also whilst he was Deputy Prime Minister & Minister for Defence, 1962-75; Member, Tasmanian House of Assembly for Division of Bass, 1976-; Opposition Whip, 1982-; Deputy Chairman, Committees, 1976-79, Chairman, 1979-82; Minister for Public Health & Mental Health, Consumer Affairs & Administrative Services, 1980-82; JP; Honorary Advocate for Ex-Service Personnel, 1967-. *Memberships:* Commonwealth Parliamentary Association; Member, several Committees. *Honours:* Represented Tasmanian Parliament, Commonwealth Parliamentary Assocation Conference, Isle of Man, 1984. *Hobbies:* Sailing; Gardening. *Address:* 26a Gascoyne Street, Launceston, Tasmania.

JAMES Muriel M, b. 14 Feb. 1917, Berkeley, California, USA. Author; Psychotherapist; Independent Scholar; International Lecturer. m. Ernest Brawley, 2 sons, 1 daughter, 2 stepsons, 2 stepdaughters. *Education:* BA, 1956, EdD, 1964, University of California; M.Div., Church Divinity School of the Pacific, 1958. *Publications:* Author or Co-Author: 14 books including: Born to Win, 1971; Born to Love, 1973; Winning with People, 1973; Transactional Analysis for Moms and Dads, 1974; The Power at the Bottom of the Well, 1974; The OK Boss, 1975; The People Book, 1975; The Heart of Friendship, 1976; Techniques in T.A. For Psychotherapists and Counselors, 1977; A New Self, 1977; Marriage is For Loving, 1979; Breaking Free With Self-Reparanting, 1981; Winning Ways in Health Care, 1981; Its Never Too Late to be Happy, 1985. *Memberships:* President, International Transactional Analysis Association; American Group Psychotherapy Association; International Group Psychotherapy Association; International Logotherapy Association. *Honours Include:* Eric Berne Scientific Award in Transactional Analysis, 1983. *Hobbies:* Work; Family; Friends; Sewing; Amnesty and international concerns. *Address:* Box 356, Lafayette, CA 94549, USA.

JAMES Peggy Anne, b. 7 Nov. 1946, Burlington, Iowa, USA. Physician (Anaesthesiology, Critical Care Medicine). m. Christopher James, 6 May 1985, 2 sons, 1 daughter. *Education:* RN, St Vincent's Hospital School of Nursing, 1968; BS, Biology, Florida State University, 1975; MD, University of Florida Medical School, 1978; Internship, Residency, Wake Forest, Bowman Gray Hospital, 1978-81; Fellowship, ICU, Shands Hospital, University of Florida, 1982; Diplomate, American Board of Anesthesiology, 1984; Fellow, American College of Chest Physicians, 1986. *Appointments:* Nursing Coordinator, Surgical-Coronary Care Unit, Orlando Regional Hospital, Orlando, Florida, 1968-70; Nursing Supervisor, Coronary Care Unit, Mercy Hospital, Orlando, 1970-71; Emergency Room Physician, Glen Frye Hospital, Hickory, North Carolina, 1980-81; Faculty, Anaesthesiology, 1981-; Clinical Unit Chief, Jerome Johns Hyperbaric Facility, 1983-85, Shands Hospital, Gainesville, Florida; Assistant Professor, Department of Anaesthesiology, University of Florida College of Medicine, Gainesville, 1983-. *Publications:* The near-drowned victim (with J.H.Modell) in Current Therapy of Respiratory Disease, 1984; Large-volume crystalloid resuscitation does not influence extravascular lung water, 1985; Several presentations. *Memberships:* Alachua County Medical Society; American College of Chest Physicians; American and Florida Societies of Anesthesiologists; Anesthesiology Alumni Association of Florida Inc; Committee of a Thousand; Florida Medical Association; Society for Ambulatory Anesthesia; International Anesthesia Research Society; Physicians for Social Responsibility; Society of Critical Care Medicine; Undersea Medical Society; Education Committee, Central Florida Heart Association, 1968-71. *Honours:* Janet Glasgow Award, American Medical Women's Association. *Hobbies:* Gourmet cooking; Jogging; Cross country skiing; Reading. *Address:* J. Hillis Miller Health Center, Box J254, University of Florida College of Medicine, Gainesville, FL 32606, USA.

JAMES Sandra Elaine, b. 26 Feb. 1956. m. Vincent. *Education:* BS, California State University, 1979. *Appointments:* Sales, Fashion Co-ordinator, Display Manager, Broadway Department Store, Long Beach, 1973-79; Adminstration Assistant, 1979-, Director, V&CB, Executive Director, 1985, Ashland Chamber of Commerce. *Memberships:* Ashland Soroptimist; oregon Chamber Executives; Oregon Association of Visitor & Convention Bureaus; Southern Oregon State College Regional Advisory Board; Oregon Tourism Institute Board; Oregon Society of Associate Executives; American Society of Associate Executives. *Address:* 1237 Ashland Mine Rd., Ashland, OR 97520, USA.

JAMES Virginia Stowell, b. 9 July 1926, New Britain, Connecticut, USA. Elementary Teacher. m. William Hall James, 24 June 1950, 1 daughter. *Education:* BA, Middlebury College, Vermont, 1947; MA, Yale University, 1955; PhD, University of Connecticut, 1988; Studies, art education, Southern Connecticut State University. *Appointments:* Teacher, elementary grades: Wilton 1950-53, Westport 1953-58, Wallingford 1959-Connecticut. Also: Art, Wallingford Junior High, 1963-77; Talented & gifted children, 1977-81. *Publications:* Various articles, professional journals. *Memberships:* State President, offices, Delta Kappa Gamma International (DKGI); National Art Education Association; National Association for Gifted Children; Association for Supervision & Curriculum Development. *Honours:* State scholarship, Connecticut branch, DKGI; International scholarship, DKGI; Various honour societies, 1985-86. *Hobbies include:* Arts activities; Natural history, nature study, environmental interests, local church affairs; Writing; Active, Delta Kappa Gamma. *Address:* PO Box 234, Northford, Connecticut 06472, USA.

JAMESON Grace Klein, b. 19 Oct. 1924, Baltimore, USA. Psychiatrist. m. Henry E. Jameson, 2 May 1943, 2 sons, 2 daughters. *Education:* BA, High Honours, University of Texas, Austin, 1945; MD, University of Texas, Galveston, 1949. *Appointments:* Various Internships, Residencies, 1949-53; Private practice, 1953-; Instructor, Psychiatry, 1953-54, Clinical Assistant Professor, 1956-67, Clinical Associate Professor, 1967-84, Clinical Professor, 1984-, Psychiatry, University of Texas; Medical Director, Adult Psychiatric Units, St Mary's Hospital, Galveston, 1987-. *Publications:* Articles in various journals. *Memberships Include:* American Psychiatric Association, various offices; Galveston County, Texas, American Medical Association; etc. *Honours:* Phi Beta Kappa; Mortar Board; etc. *Address:* 200 University Blvd, Suite 620, Galveston, TX 77550, USA.

JAMESON Louise, b. 20 Apr. 1951, London, England. Actress. 2 sons. *Education:* RADA Degree. *Appointments:* TV work includes: Leela in Dr Who; Anne in the Omega Factor; Blanche in Tenko; Theatre includes: 3 years with Royal Shakespeare Company. *Memberships:* Board Member, Oxford Playhouse; RADA. *Hobbies:* Children; Cooking Vegetarian Food;

Playing Guitar. *Address:* c/o Jeremy Conway, Eagle House, 109 Jermyn Street, London SW1Y 6HB, England.

JAMIESON Alison Mary, b. 11 May 1952, Dundee, Scotland. Writer. m. Nigel Jamieson, 2 May 1981. *Education:* Honours Degree in French Language and Literature (2.1), St Andrew's University, 1970-74. *Appointments:* Teacher of English, Paris, France, 1974-75; Research Assistant, Economists Advisory Group, 1976-77; Assistant to Director, Council for International Contact, 1977-78; Security Consultant, Zeus Security Consultants, Control Risks Group, 1978-81; Co-owner, The Village Delicatessen, London, 1981-84; Writer & Researcher, Italian Terrorism, 1984-. *Publications:* The Heart Attached; Terrorism and Conflict in the Italian State, 1989; numerous articles for professional journals. *Memberships:* Secretary, European Chapter, The American Society for Industrial Security, 1978-80. *Hobbies:* Theatre; Opera; Reading. *Address:* Castiglione del Lago, Italy.

JAMISON Jennifer Rosemary, b. 28 Oct. 1947, Johannesburg, South Africa. Education/Medical Health Care. *Education:* BSc., 1968, MB BCh 1971, DTM & H, 1974, MSc., 1975, DPH 1976, University of the Witwatersrand, South Africa; BA, University of South Africa, 1979; MEd., La Trobe University, Melbourne, 1982. *Appointments:* Lecturer, Physiological Chemistry, University of Witwatersrand, 1973-74; Registrar, School of Pathology, S A Institute for Medical Research, 1975-77; Senior Lecturer, School of Applied Science, 1978-81; Head, Diagnostic Sciences, Phillip Institute of Technology, 1982-. *Publications:* Man Meets Microbes, 1978, 2nd edition 1984; Holistic Health Care, 1984; Health Pursuit, 1985; The Practitioners Handbook of Disease Intervention, 1984; many journal articles. *Memberships:* Orthomolecular Medical Association; International Academy of Nutrition; Course Advisory Committee on Osteopathy, Chiropractic, Natural Therapies. *Hobbies:* Reading; Health Promotion. *Address:* WO36 Glendower Hts., 10 Malais Street, Bedfordview, South Africa 2008.

JAMMAL Laila, b. 2 Apr. 1942, Acre, Palestine. Activist, Freelance Journalist. *Education:* BS, Computer Programming, Bedford College, Toronto, Canada, 1970; Diploma, TV Production, Ontario College of Art; Worked on MA, University of California, Berkeley, USA in International Relations. *Appointments:* Assistant Director, Beit Hagefen, Haifa, 1967; Super. EDP at PVO, SF, 1976; PR & Informatiron Director, Arab League, Washington, DC, 1979; Acting Director, Arab Information Centre, SF, 1981; Director, Middle East Public Relations, 1988. *Publications:* Contributions by Palestinian Women to the Nat'l Struggle for Liberation, 1985; Poems by an Exiled Child, 1988; Poetry: Arabic Poetry Novel, Alwassiya, 1978; Contributions to various journals and magazines. *Memberships:* Arab Club, Toronto; ACC-SF, 1973; AAUG; AWC: NAAA; ADC; PHRC; UHLF; FPC; GUPW; GUPWJ. *Honours:* Recipient, various honours and awards. *Hobbies:* Writing; Poetry; Painting; Filming; Folkdancing; Acting; Travel; etc.

JANES Violeta, b. Argentina. Artist. *Education:* Regent Street Polytechnic School of Art; Watford School of Art; City & Guilds School of Art. *Appointments:* Freelance Childrens Illustrator; Directed Art Studies, Alma College, Ontario, canada; Freelance, Showcards, Textile Designs, Portraits in Pastels & Oils, Flower Paintings & Landscapes. *Publications:* The Fiddler; Red River New Mexico; The Old Shepherd; Rosemary Cottage; The Cockney Character; Carmelita; The Village Green, etc. *Memberships:* United Society of Artists; Institute of linguists; The Milldon Art Society, London. *Honours:* One Man Shows, Broomfield Museum, 1975, Mayfair Art Gallery, London; numerous other galleries at home and abroad. *Hobbies:* Travel; Music; Languages; Antiques. *Address:* 2, Salisbury Avenue, Harpenden, Herts, AL5 2QQ, England.

JANICKI Agnes Colette, b. Illinois, USA. Advertising Writer. *Education:* BA, English Education, Western Illinois University, 1971; Course certificate, Medical editing, University of Chicago, 1985; Credit program, School of the Art Institute of Chicago, 1986. *Appointments:* Advertising writer, Sears, Roebuck and Co, Chicago, 1973-; Proofreader, Star-Courier newspaper, Kewanee; English teacher grades 10-11, Alwood High School. *Creative works:* Poetry; Numerous sketches and paintings. *Membership:* American Society of Professional and Executive Women. *Honours:* Student-at-Large Merit Scholarship, School of the Art Institute of Chicago, 1986; Speedwriting Certificate, Sears, Roebuck and Co, 1974; Federal Education Grant; Illinois State Teacher's Scholarship, 1967-71; Dean's List, Western Illinois University; Commencement Honor Guard, Western Illinois University, 1970; Commencement speaker, Bradford Township High School, 1967. *Hobbies:* Theatre; Ballet; Art; Films; Interior decorating; Gardening; Classical music; Horseback riding; Antique collecting. *Address:* P O Box 1787, Chicago, IL 60690, USA.

JANZ Millie. b. 4 Oct. 1928, Brooklyn, USA. m. Abraham Alan Janz, 25 Feb. 1950, 3 sons. Writer; Playwright; Teacher; Director; Consultant. *Appointments:* Director, New Theatre, North Jersey; Consultant, Modern Writing & the Arts, Brooklyn Township Schools. *Creative Works:* Producer, Piaf; Producer, Barrymore; Producer, George Sanus. *Memberhips:* Dramatists guild; Authors League. *Honours:* Cited by Governor of New jersey for Shakespeare Week; NEA Grant. *Address:* 19 Foothills Drive, Pompton Plains, NJ 07444, USA.

JARDINE Alice Ann, b. 7 May 1951, New York City, USA. Educator. *Education:* BA, Comparative Literature, OSU, 1973; MA French 1977, MPhil Comparative Literature 1980, PhD 1982, Columbia University. Special study, University of Paris VII, France. *Appointments:* Assistant Professor 1982-85, Associate Professor 1985-89; Professor 1989-, Romance Languages & Literatures, Harvard University. *Publications:* Books: Gynesis: Configurations of Woman & Modernity, 1985; Co-editor, Future of Difference, with H. Eisenstein, 1985; Co-editor, Men in Feminism, with P. Smith, 1987; Editor, journal, Copyright. *Membership:* Modern Language Association. *Honours:* Grants, National Endowment for Humanities, Summer Institute on Avant- Garde, 1987, 1989; Fulbright Senior Research Fellow, 1985-86; Fellow, American Council of Learned Societies, 1985-86; Giles Whiting Fellow, Columbia University, 1980-81; Woodrow Wilson Fellow, 1980; Pensionnaire, Ecole Normale Superieure, Paris, 1979-80. *Hobbies:* Music; Film; Photography; Writing. *Address:* Department of Romance Languages & Literatures, 218 Boylston Hall, Harvard University, Cambridge, Massachusetts 02138, USA.

JARIYA Chalida Peat, b. 24 Jan. 1958, Bangkok, Thailand. Graphic Designer Executive. m. Somkiat Petchsrisom, 24 Aug. 1984. 1 son, 1 daughter. *Education:* BA, Chulalongkorn University, Bangkok, Thailand, 1979; MFA, University of Houston, Texas, USA, 1984. *Appointments:* Graphic Designer, William Burwell Inc, 1981-82; Graphic Designer, 3D International, 1982-83; Design Director, Mel Anderson Communications, 1983-86; Owner, Peat Jariya Design, 1986-. *Memberships:* International Association of Business Communicator; Women in Communication; Art Directors Club of Houston; Art Directors Club of Los Angeles. *Honours:* Award of Excellence, Art Directors Club of Houston, 1983 and 1988; Creativity Award of Excellence, NY Art Direction Magazine, 1984 and 1986; 2 Awards of Excellence, Gem Award, Houston Advertising Federation, 1985; Matrix Award of Excellence, Women in Communications, 1985 and 1986; NY DESI Award of Excellence, Graphic Design USA, 1985, 1986 and 1989; Print Magazine Design Award of Excellence, 1985; Society of Technical Communication Award of Excellence, 1986, 1987 and 1989; Gold Addy Award, Houston Advertising Federation, 1988; 2 Award of Excellence, Public Relations Society of America, 1989; Lantern Award, B/

PAA, 1989. *Hobbies:* Reading; Swimming; Travel. *Address:* 303 Electra, Houston, TX 77024, USA.

JARRETT Deborah Lee, b. 9 Sept. 1961, High Point, North Carolina, USA. Habilitation Specialist I. *Education:* Associate Degree Early Childhood Specialist, Guilford Technical Community College, 1983; BS, Special Education, Western Carolina University, 1986. *Appointments:* Habilitation Specialist, Guilford County Mental Health, Greensobor, NC, teach developmentally delayed 2-5 year olds; Guilford County Mental Health, High Point. *Memberships:* WCU Student Council for Exceptional Children, President; NCSCEC, Pan Representative; GTCC Child Care Club, President; Watt Residence Hall Council WCU, Vice President; Child Care Education Committee. *Honours:* United Way Campaign Achievement Award, 1988; Outstanding Contributions to University Housing WCU, 1984 and 1985; Award of Outstanding Accomplishments Student Council for Exceptional Children WCU, 1986; Certificate of Achievement, Campus Leadership WCU, 1985; Outstanding Member, North Carolina Student Council for Exceptional Children, 1986; Outstanding Contribution GTCC Child Care Club 1982 and 1983. *Hobbies:* Cross-stitch needlepoint; Quilting; Reading books; Collecting teddy bears; Paper cutting. *Address:* 127 Buena Vista, High Point, North Carolina 27260, USA.

JASHARI Kaqusha, b. 16 Aug. 1946, Pristina, Yugoslavia. Engineer. m. 23 June 1969, 3 daughters. *Education:* Constructive Section, Secondary Technical School; Constructive Dept., Engineering Faculty. *Appointments:* Technical Manager, T. Grkovic, 1970-75; President, Trade Union Board of Construction Workers of Kosovo, 1975-82; President, Council of Trade Unions of Kosovo, 1985-86; Principal Committee, League of Community of Kosovo, President, Provincial Committee, 1988. *Publications:* Paintings in 2 solo exhibitions. *Memberships:* Association of Painters of Pristina, Gnjilane, 69 Group. *Honours:* Medal of Merit for People, 1979; Medallion, Peoples Defence of Kosovo, 1980; Goldon Badge of Trade Unions of Constructive Workers, 1982. *Hobbies:* Painting; Sports. *Address:* ul Goleska 4/6, 38000 Pristina, SAP Kosovo, Yugoslavia.

JAY Thelma Allen, b. 13 May 1923, Paonia, Colorado, USA. m. Robert A Jay, 27 Dec. 1942. 1 son, 4 daughters. *Education:* Friends University, Wichita, 1941-42; Diploma, Beginning Christian Writer, 1955; Diploma, Christian Fiction Writing, 1965; Photography Course, Pratt Community College, 1974; Photography & Creative Writing Course, Friends Bible College, Haviland. *Appointments:* Wrote for the Junior High Sunday School Quarterly for George Fox Press, 1960-65; Homemaker and Freelance Writer. *Publications:* Numerous articles and fiction in Sunday School Papers and magazines. *Memberships:* Leader local Loyal Temperance Legion, 1958-; Executive Director, Loyal Temperance Legion for Kansas, 1958-70, 1977-; Kansas Author's Club, 1966-; Kansans for Life at It's Best, 1968-; Local WCTU, 1957-; National Writers Club, 1978-. *Honours:* 1st, Kansas Authors Club writing contests, 1966, 1968, 1969, 1971, 1974, 1975, 1976; 2nd, 1966, 1968, 1971, 1974, 1975; 3rd, 1970; 1st Honorable Mention, 1966, 1973, 1977, 1979; 2nd Honorable Mention, 1975, 1978, 1986, 1987; Writers Digest Magazine Honorable Mention, 1968, 1975, 1981; Ada Mohn Landis Writing Contest, Honorable Mention, 1971. *Hobbies:* Genealogy; Painting; Crafts. *Address:* Box 351, Haviland, KS 67059, USA.

JAYAWEERA Swarna, b. 21 Sept. 1927, Colombo, Sri Lanka. Consultant, Education and Women's Studies; Coordinator, Centre of Women's Research. m. Claude S. V. Jayaweera, 26 Aug. 1955, 1 daughter. *Education:* BA(Hons) 2nd class upper division, History, University of London, England, 1950; Diploma in Education with distinction, University of Ceylon, 1954; MA, Education, 1957, PhD, Education, 1966, Institute of Education, University of London. *Appointments:* Lecturer, Associate Professor, 1958-74, Professor, Education, Head, Department of Social Studies, 1974-81, University of Ceylon, Peradeniya, 1958-74; UNESCO Adviser, Teacher Training, Equal Access of Girls and Women to Education, Nepal Project, 1980-82; UNICEF Consultant, Nepal Project, 1982-83; International Consultant, UNESCO, UNICEF, UNIDO. *Publications:* Human Resources Development in Sri Lanka: Analysis of Education and Training (with J.I.Lofstedt and A.Little), 1985; Modern Sri Lanka - A Society in Transition; Women in Asia (with H.Goonatilake); The Integration of Women in Development Planning in Sri Lanka (with K.Jayawardene). *Memberships:* Council of Management, National Institute of Education; Sub-Committee on Social Science, University Grants Commission; Consultant, Open University, Sri Lanka; Board Member, Natural Resources Energy and Science Authority, Chairman, Social Sciences Working Committee; Coordinator, Centre for Women's Research, Colombo. *Honours:* Khan Gold Medal for Education, University of Ceylon, 1954; British Council Scholarship for Education to UK, 1955-56; Agnes M.Allen Postdoctoral International Fellowship, American Association of University Women Educational Foundation, 1973-74; Visiting Scholar, Teachers College, Columbia University, New York; Zonta Woman of Achievement in International Recognition, 1989. *Hobbies:* Reading; Research; Travel. *Address:* 12 1/1 Ascot Avenue, Colombo 5, Sri Lanka.

JEFFERSON-BRAMHALL Rona Lee, b. 26 Nov. 1900, Tennessee, USA. Professional Tax Preparer. m. (1)William Thurman Tanner, 1922, died 1936, 1 daughter, (2)1949, divorced 1962, (3)Ray Carlton Bramhall, 24 Dec. 1982. *Education:* University of Southern California, 1937-40. *Appointments:* Professional Parliamentarian, 1961-; Industrial Specialist, USAF, 1965-70; Executrix of Estates, 1972-89; Enrolled Agent, Internal Revenue & professional Tax Preparer, 1978-89. *Publications:* Editor, Safety Sun, 1943-45. *Memberships Include:* California, National Associations of Parliamentarians; Research Council of Scripps Clinic; *Honours:* Recipient, many honours & awards. *Hobbies:* Travel; Dancing; Stamp Collecting. *Address:* 5537 Littlebow Road, Palos Verdes, CA 90274, USA.

JEFFORDS Lynn Redding, b. 5 Sept. 1957, New Jersey, USA. Lighting Designer; Architect. m. John Dobson Jeffords, 20 Sept. 1986. *Education:* BArch, Pratt Institute, 1980; Licensed Architect, State of New Jersey. *Appointments:* Architecture: Part of 4-person production team, WCCO-TV, Joyce Theatre for Hardy Holzman & Pfeiffer Associates, 1980-81. Lighting design: Project Manager, Jacob Javits' Convention Centre New York Public Library, Ellis Island Los Angeles Central Library, Seattle Art Museum, for Jules Fisher & Paul Marantz Inc, 1981-1990. *Memberships:* International Association of Lighting Designers (IALD); Illuminating Society of Engineers (IES); American Institute of Architects (AIA). *Honours:* Lumen Award, New York Public Library, 1986; AIA Award, WCCO-TV, 1985. *Hobbies:* Harp; Celtic studies; Knitting & needlework; Drawing & painting. *Address:* 2830 East 13th Avenue, Denver, CO 80206, USA.

JEHAN Sardar, b. 1 June 1932, Madras, India. Forensic Pathologist. m. Dr (Haji)S M Kabiruddin, 2 Oct. 1954. 2 sons, 2 daughters. *Education:* Fellow of Arts, Govt Arts College for Women, Madras, 1949- 51; MBBS, Madras Medical College, 1951-57; Diploma in Criminology and Forensic Sciences, Madras University, 1964-65; Clinical Attachment, University of Glasgow, Scotland, 1972; Diploma in Medical Jurisprudence, Apothecaries of London, England, 1974. *Appointments:* Houseman, Madras Medical College, 1957-58; Civil Assistant Surgeon: Govt Royapettah Hospital, Madras, 1959-60; Kasturba Grandhu Hospital, 1960-61; Police Hospital, Madras, 1961-64; Women & Children's Hospital, Madras, 1964-65; Lecturer, Forensic Dept: Stanley Medical College, Madras and Madras Medical College, 1965-68; Lecturer, Forensic Dept, University Hospital, Kuala Lumpur, Malaysia, 1968-72; Consultant in Forensic Medicine 1973-78, Acting Head of Dept of Pathology 1974-76, General Hospital, Kuala Lumpur;

Forensic Pathologist, General Hospital, Kuching; State Pathologist, Sarawak. *Creative works:* Numerous articles to professional journals and magazines. *Memberships:* Society of Pathologist of Malaysia; Malayan Medical Association; Perkin, W Malaysia; Perkis, E Malaysia; British Medical Association. *Honour:* Perkis Award for Excellent Services Rendered, 1989. *Hobbies:* Writing articles of medico-legal importance; Cooking; Gardening. *Address:* Meranti, Rodway Road, Kuching, Sarawak, East Malaysia.

JELLIFFE Rowena Woodham, b. 23 Mar. 1892, Albion, Illinois, USA. Retired. m. Russell Wesley Jelliffe, 28 May 1915. 1 son. *Education:* AB 1914, LLD 1944, Oberlin College; AM, University of Chicago, 1915; HHD, Western Reserve University, 1951; LHD, Cleveland State University, 1966. *Appointments:* Founder, Executive Director, Karamu House, 1915-63; Founder, Executive Director, Karamu Foundation, 1963-75; Delegate for Cleveland Branch, NAACP to Second Pan-African Congress, Paris, France, 1921. *Publications:* Study of the Arts, Boston, 1963; Study of the Arts, St Louis, 1965; Study of the Arts, Indianapolis, 1966; Arts & Education, Canton, Ohio, 1967. *Memberships:* Study of Co-Education Committee, Oberlin, 1987-; Legislative Committee, Astronomical Soc of Cleveland, 1982-; Legislation Committee, Audubon Society, 1986-; Board of Trustees, Willoughby School of Fine Arts, 1968-; Board of Trustees, East Cleveland Community Theatre, 1968-; Life Member, NAACP. *Honours:* Honored, Greater Cleveland Women's History Week, 1985; Special Citation, Women's City Club, 1963; Distinguished Service Award, NAACP, 1976; Honr & Recognition, The Ohio Story, Bell Telephone Co, 1963; Human Relations Award, B'nai Brith, 1963; Hon Award, City of Cleveland, 1960; One of Ten Outstanding Citizens, 1958; Honor Award, Cleveland Urban League Women's Guild, 1956. *Hobbies:* Theatre and the Arts; Environmental concerns; Cleveland Orchestra concerts; Cleveland Museum of Art, Fellow for Life. *Address:* Cleveland Heights, Ohio, USA.

JENG Helene Wu, b. 23 July 1938, Taipei, Taiwan, China. Librarian. m. Bih-Jing Jeng, 27 Nov. 1971, 1 son, 1 daughter. *Education:* BA, Soochow University; MLS, Appalachian State University, USA, 1968. *Appointments:* Head Librarian, Lancaster Reg. Campus, University of South Carolina, 1968-73; Director, Head Librarian, Learning Resources Center, Villa Julie College, 1973-78; Librarian, Mt Wilson State Hospital Library, 1978-81; Reference Librarian, Medical Library, US Army Medical Research Institute, 1981-83; Librarian, Maryland office of Planning Library, 1983-. *Memberships:* Maryland Library Association; Special Library Association; Council of Planning Librarians; Baltimore/Columbia, Maryland, Chapter, Taiwanese American Association (President 1986-87); Board Member, Baltimore Taiwanese Christian Church, 1988-90. *Hobbies:* Reading; Art appreciation; Gardening; Performing arts; Travel and sightseeing; Charity work. *Address:* 16 Woodholme Village Court, Pikesville, MD 21208, USA.

JENKINS Shirley Mae Lymons, b. 9 Aug. 1936, Pine Apple, Alabama, USA. Teacher. m. Henry Jenkins, 29 Feb. 1964. *Education:* BS, Knoxville College, 1958; MA, Atlanta University, 1969; AA Certificate, University of Alabama, Birmingham. *Appointments:* Boykin High School, Boykin, Alabama, 1959-62; Camden Academy, Camden, Alabama, 1962-68; Leeds Elementary School, Leeds, Alabama, 1968-89; Treasurer, Birmingham Chapter, Knoxville College National Association Alumni Association, 1989-; Chairperson, Students Affairs, Board of Trustees, Knoxville College. *Publications:* Curriculum Writer in Reading for Jefferson County of Education, 1972-73 (Title III Programme). *Memberships:* Golden Life Member, Delta Sigma Theta Sorority Inc; Past Treasurer, Birmingham Alumnae Chapter, Delta Sigma Theta Sorority Inc; Nu Chapter of the National Sorority of Phi Delta Kappa Inc; Board of Trustees, Knoxville College; American Federation of Teachers; Negro Council of Black Women; Past Regional Director, Knoxville College; National Alumni Association Inc; Past,

National Alumni President, Knoxville College Alumni Association Inc; Usher, Sixth Avenue Baptist Church; Life Member, Knoxville College Alumni Association Inc. *Honours:* Citation, American Federation of Teachers; Outstanding Regional Director, 1978-84; President's Distinguished Service Award, Knoxville College, 1979-82; Hostess of Year Award, Imperial Club, 1983; Outstanding Service Award, Southern Region of Delta Sigma Theta Sorority, 1984; Alumnus of Year, Knoxville College, Equal Opportunity in High Education, 1986; Soror of Year, Nu Chapter, National Sorority of Phi Delta Kappa, Inc, 1989. *Hobbies:* Reading; Travelling; Television. *Address:* 2692 20th Street West, Birmingham, Alabama 35208, USA.

JENKINS-EARLEY Helen L, b. 21 May 1935, Philadelphia, USA. Vocal Music Specialist; Lecturer. m. Paul L. Earley, 2 July 1988, 4 sons. *Education:* BA,Mus.Ed., Temple University, 1973; MMus.Ed., 1984; DMA Choral Conducting, 1987. *Appointments:* Culural Organizer, 1967-69; Vocal Music Specialist, 1973-. *Publications:* Various papers & articles in professional journals. *Memberships:* MENC; Delaware Valley Chapter, JSU Alumni, Vice President; PFT; AME Church. *Honours:* Phi Kappa Phi; Paths Research Fellow, 1988. *Address:* 3901 Conshocken Avenue, 4109, Philadelphia, PA 19131, USA.

JENNER Ann Maureen, b. 8 Mar. 1944, Ewell, Surrey, England. Ballet Teacher; Former Ballet Dancer. m. Dale Robert Baker, 16 Jan. 1980, 1 son. *Education:* Royal Ballet School, 1954-61. *Appointments:* Joined 1961, Soloist 1967, Principal 1970-78, Royal Ballet; Principal Dancer, 1978-80, Ballet Teacher, 1980-, Australian Ballet; Guest Teacher San Francisco Ballet Company, USA, Queensland Ballet Company; Ballets Dnced include: Giselle, Sleeping Beauty, Romeo and Juliet, Coppelia, Cinderella, Spartacus; Don Quixote; La Fille Mal Gardee; Mayerling; Anna Karenina; Les Deux Pigeons; Les Sylphides; Guest Teacher, Australia Ballet Co; Guest Teacher, Sydney Dance Co; Director, National Theatre Ballet School, 1988-. *Hobby:* Music. *Address:* National Theatre, CNR Barkly and Carlisle St., St Kilda, VIC 3182, Australia.

JENNINGS Diane Bonnie, b. 14 July 1953, Cedar Rapids, Iowa, USA. Certified Public Accountant. *Education:* Mount Mercy College, 1974-75. *Appointments:* Senior Accountant, Bell & Van Zee PC, 1975-81; Controller, 1981-82, Assistant Treasurer, 1982-83, Vice President, Chief Financial Officer, 1984-88, Vice President, Information Management, 1988-, Lease America Corp. *Publications:* Articles in journals. *Memberships:* AICPA; IA-CPA's; AWSCPA; NAA, Director, Member Relations, 1983-84; NAFE. *Honours:* Outstanding Young Woman State of Iowa, 1986; Winner, National Association of Accountants Chapter Storm Award, 1987. *Hobbies:* Running; Bicycling; Golf; Reading; Walking; Racquetball. *Address:* Cedar Rapids, IA, USA.

JENNINGS Shirley Kathryn, b. 28 Feb. 1931, Nipawin, Saskatchewan, Canada. Psychologist. m. Warren David Jennings, 27 Dec. 1952, divorced 1970, 2 sons (1 deceased), 1 daughter. *Education:* BA, Honours, 1967, MA, 1970, University of Toronto. *Appointments:* School Psychologist, Metro Toronto School Board, 1968-69; Research Assistant, Ontario Institute for Studies in Education, Toronto, 1970; Psychologist, Consultant, Madame Vanier's Children's Services of London, Ontario, 1970-74; Superviser, preschool Programme, mental Health Services, 1974-80; Childrens Consultant, Psychologist, Alberta Mental Health Services, Edmonton, 1980-86; Psychologist Consultant, Edmonton Public School Board, 1986-. *Memberships:* Psychologists Association of Alberta; Canadian Register of Health Service Providers in Psychology; many other professional organisations. *Honours:* Governor General's Award, 1967; Scholarship Award, 1Street & 77 A Avenue, Edmonton, Alberta T5R 5X6, Canada.

JENS Salome, b. 8 May 1935, Milwaukee, USA. Actress; Teacher; Director. *Education:* University of Wisconsin; Northwestern University. *Appointments:* As an Actress: Broadway Leads: Far Country; Night Life; the Disenchanted; I'M Soloman; First One Asleep Whistle; Patriot for Me; Lie of the MInd; Appearances with the Lincoln Center Repertory Company of New York, and Off Broadway performances; Films include: Angel Baby; Seconds; Me Natalie; Foolkiller; Just Betwen Friends; Clan of the Cave Bear; From Here to Eternity; Killer in the Family; Sharon, Portrait of a Mistress; Barefoot in Athens; 3 by Tennessee; Grace Kelly Story; Tomorrow's Child; Glitter Palace; A Matter of life and Death; TV Series include: Mary Hartman, Falcon Crest; Guest Star: Hart to Hart; Gunsmoke; Bonanza; Naked City; Cagney and Lacey; Macqyver; Trapper John, MD; Blue Knight; I Spy; etc. *Hobbies:* Hunger Project. *Address:* 1716 Redesdale Ave, Los Angeles, CA 90026, USA.

JENSEN Carol Ann, b. 22 Apr. 1951, California, USA. Vice President, Micon Wind Tubines Inc. *Education:* BA, History 1973, BA, Art History 1974, University of California, Santa Barbara; MBA, University of California, Los Angeles,. 1976. *Appointments:* Budget Analyst, Lawrence Berkeley Laboratory, Berkeley, California, 1976-79; Financial Analyst, Transactions Services Division, Tymshare Inc, Fremont, 1979-80; Senior Consultant, Management Advisory Services, Price Waterhouse, San Francisco, 1980-82; Manager, Financial Systems, Cambridge Plan International, Monterey, 1982-83; Manager, Information Systems, Transamerica Corporation, San Francisco, 1983-86; Controller, A-I Cal Leasing Corporation, Burlinghame, 1986; Vice President, Micon Wind Tubines, Inc, Livermore, 1986-. *Memberships:* Beta Gamma Sigma, National Business Honor Society; UCSB Alumni Assoc, Director & Past Treasurer; Bay Area Lawyers for the Arts.

JENSEN Carolyn Eastman Remington, b. 23 May 1912, Central Falls, Rhode Island, USA. Psychiatric Social Worker. m. Wesley Frederic Jensen, 11 July 1959. 1 son. *Education:* BA, Wellesley College, 1929-33; BS, Simmons College School of Social Work, 1934; Psychiatric Social Work Certificate, New York School of Social Work, 1940; Gerontological Counselling, Framingham State College, 1986. *Appointments:* Case Worker 1934-37, 1940-42, Family Society, Providence, Rhode Island; Hartford Family Society, 1937-39; Publications Dept, American National Red Cross, Washington DC, 1942- 44, 1944-45; First Mental Health Clinic of the US Public Health Service, 1944; Publicity Work, 1948-57; Case Supervisor, Greater Bridgeport, Child Guidance Clinic, 1957-60. *Publications:* Booklet for American National Red Cross on Social Work, Let's Talk It Over; Articles in professional journals. *Memberships:* National Association of Social Workers, Publicity Chairman RI Chapter, 1947-48; Publicity Chairman and Secretary, Connecticut Chapter. *Honours:* 5th International Award for poem Atlantic Storms; Wrote words to the 1933 Wellesley College Class Marching Song; Wrote a paper on The Returning Serviceman given to the National Conference of Social Work, 1945; Co-author of write-up on community project given to International Congress of Child Psychiatry, 1961. *Interests:* Giving Seminars on mental health; Conducted training course for secretaries interested in volunteer work; With husband started The Shoreline Unitarian Universalist Fellowship. *Address:* 928 Washington St, Holliston, MA 01746, USA.

JENSEN Regina Bunhild, b. 26 Oct. 1951, Bredsted, Germany. Psychotherapist. m. Benny Hvitfelt Jensen, 31 July 1976, 2 stepdaughters. *Educaiton:* BS, Physiotherapy, Krankengymanstik Schule, Tubingen, 1971; MA, Counselling Psychology, Vt. College, 1983; PhD, Human Behaviour, Ryokan College, 1984; PhD, Clinical Psychology, Sierra University, 1987. *Appointments:* Physiotherapist, Urban Krankenhaus, Berlin, 1971-73; Staff Physiotherapist, Werner & Beck, Santa ynez, 1982-; Consultant, Jensen Enterprises, Solvang, 1975-, Alexander & Jensen Associates, Los Angeles, 1983- 85; Health Consultant, Santa Ynez, 1982-; Adolescent Crisis Counsellor, Santa Ynez Valley High School, 1984-86; Tutor, Programme Coordinator, Sierra University, 1985. *Publications:* Education for the Medical Consumer, 1983; To Liberate or to Enslave, 1985; How To Buy Back Your Soul, 1987; Publisher, Fully Alive Publications, 1988-; Contributor to journals. *Memberships:* American psychology Association; California Association for Marriage & Family Therapists. *Address:* 2880 Baseline Ave B, Santa Ynez, CA 93460, USA.

JESESEKE Ellen Frances, b. 9 Mar. 1954, Saddlebrook, USA. Computer Programmer. *Education:* William Paterson College, 1972-76. *Appointments:* Assistant to Associate Professor of Art Education, William Paterson College, 1972-76; New Jersey Art Educator, 1976-79; Visual Merchandising Artist, Hahne's & Co., 1979-80; Health Aid & Art Therapy Assistant, John F. Kennedy Rehabilitation Center, 1980-81; Interior Designer, Carriage House, 1981-82; Mainframe Programmer, Data Processing Technical Writer, 1982-, Christian Salvesen. *Memberships:* National Computer Graphics Association; Digital Equipment Computers Users Society; National Association of Desktop Publishers; National Association of Female Executives; American Management Association. *Honours:* Recipient, various honours & awards. *Hobbies:* Aerobics; Swimming; Bowling; Racketball; Photography. *Address:* 260 Fourth Street, Saddle Brook, NJ 07662, USA.

JESKALIAN Barbara Jean, b. 12 Apr. 1936, Oakland, California, USA. Music Librarian. divorced. 1 son. *Education:* AB, University of California, Berkeley; MSLS, University of Southern California; Graduate Theological Union, Berkeley; MA, Philosophical and Systematic Theology. *Appointments:* Music Librarian, San Jose State University, Clark Library, 1967-. *Publications:* Article and Chapter on Hildegard of Bingen; Article on Margaret Avery Rowell. *Memberships:* Intl Hildegard of Bingen Society; National Music Library Association; Guild for Psychological Studies; Chamber Music America. *Honour:* Meritorious Performance and Professional Promise, San Jose State University, 1986. *Hobbies:* Study of violoncello with Margaret Avery Rowell; Collecting icons; Jungian psychology; Hiking; Gardening; Playing chamber music. *Address:* Clark Library, San Jose State University, San Jose, CA 95192, USA.

JESSEL Joan Betty, m. (1)2nd Baron Russell of Liverpool, 1933, 1 daughter, (2)Sir George Jossel BK.MC, 1948. *Membership:* Army & Navy Club. *Hobbies:* Gardening; Music. *Address:* Ladham House, Goudhurst, Kent TN17 1DB, England.

JESSEN Joel Anne, b. 7 Sept. 1940, Seattle, Washington, USA. Artist; Educator. *Education:* Research work, University of California, Santa Barbara, 1961; BA 1962, MFA 1964, University of Washington. *Appointments:* Instructor, Cornish College of the Arts, Seattle, 1965- 76; Instructor, University of Washington, Seattle, 1970; Instructor, Highline College, Burien, 1970; Research Work, Self employed, Seattle, 1976-. *Publications:* Graphics: Lift-Off 2000AD, 1968; The Universe Foursquare, 1969; The Transformation of Man, 1972. Books: The Imperative Step, 1972; The Physical, The Mental, The Spiritual, 1978. Lecturer on: The Science of Being, 1976-. *Memberships:* University of Washington Alumni Association, Seattle; President, Kappeler Institute, Wilmington. *Honours:* Purchase Award, International Printmakers, Seattle, 1961; Purchase Award, The Achenbach Foundation for Graphic Art, San Francisco, 1965; Patrick Gavin Memorial Prize, Boston Printmakers, 1965. *Hobbies:* Antiques. Interests: Research into ever advancing ideas in Science and Art. *Address:* 3555 27th Place West No 224, Seattle, Washington 98199, USA.

JESTER Janice May, b. 4 Jan. 1941, Muncie, Kansas, USA. Registered Nurse. *Education:* Completed

High school, 1952; Bethany Hospital School of Nursing, 1962; Texas Woman's University, Rehabilitation Nursing (4 hours/4 weeks), 1967; Enterostomal Therapy, Nursing Course, Grand Rapids, Michigan, 6 weeks, 1974. *Appointments:* Staff Nurse 1962-65, Head Nurse 1965-70, Rehabilitation Coordinator 1970-74, Rehabilitation and Enterostomal Therapy Nurse Specialist, 1974-, Bethany Medical Centre. *Memberships:* Board of Directors, Cancer Action Inc, Kansas City, Kansas, 1974-88, President of Board 1981-83; Board of Directors, Hospice Care Mid America 1975-86; United Cancer Council Inc, 1984, Member of National Board; Make Today Count National Board, 1986-; Director, Children's Department for Faith Temple Family Worship Centre, Kansas City, Kansas; United Ostomy Association, Advisor to Local Chapter, 1974-; Board of Directors National, 1984-87; World Council for Enterostomal Therapy, International Association for Enterostomal Therapy (Board of Directors 1977-84, Treasurer 1980-84). *Honours:* Named Woman of the Year, Business and Professional Women, Kansas City, Kansas, 1984; Sam Penneys Dubin Award from National United Ostomy Association, 1985; Golden Rule Award. *Hobbies:* Sing in Gospel Music Group; Chairman, National Youth Rally for Young Persons with Ostomy Surgery, held annually. *Address:* 34144 S 53rd Street, Kansas City, KS 66106, USA.

JETER-SYLVESTER Felicia Renee, b. 7 Dec. 1948, Atlanta, Georgia, USA. Broadcast Jornalist; Lecturer; Communication Consultant. m. Jon H Sylvester, 7 June 1984. *Education:* BA, Psychology and Social Science, Mundelein College, 1970; Graduate School of Broadcast Journalism, Columbia University, 1972; Broadcast Management Institute, University of Southern California, 1982. *Appointments:* Assistant Director of Broadcast Division, Vince Cullers Advertising Agency, Chicago, 1970-72; Radio Show Host/Producer/Disc Jockey/Interviewer, WAOK, Atlanta, 1972-74; Television Correspondent/Anchor/Producer, WAGA-TV, Atlanta, 1972-74; Television Achor/Reporter, Magazine Show Host, KNBC-TV, Los Angeles, 1974-80; Television Magazine Show Host, NBC Network, Los Angeles, 1980; Television Anchor/Interviewer, KHJ-TV, Los Angeles, 1980-81; President, Jetcom Enterprises, Los Angeles, 1981-; Television Correspondent/Anchor/Interviewer, CBS Network News, New York, 1982-84. *Publications:* Various articles and critiques in magazines and journals; Career Memorabilia & taped Autobiography part of Permanent Archives, Houston Public Library, Houston, Texas. *Memberships:* American Federation of television and Radio Artists; Screen Actors' Guild; National Association of Black Journalists; National Society of Professional Journalists, Sigma Delta Chi. *Honours include:* Emmy, Academy of Television Arts and Sciences; Associated Press Award, for Outstanding Broadcast Journalism; Image Award, NAACP; Citation of Merit, University of Southern California; Mayoral Citation, City of Los Angeles; Role Model Salute, West Los Angeles College; Certificate of Appreciation, Los Angeles County, USC Cancer Center; Judge, Sixth Annual Robert F Kennedy Journalism Awards, Washington DC. *Hobbies:* Travel; Yoga; Gardening; Youth counselling; Cooking; Theatre; Dance; Film criticism; Public speaking; Community Education. *Address:* 1909 Morgan Street, Houston, Texas 77006, USA.

JEVNE Ronna Fay, b. 24 Nov. 1948, Wetaskiwin, Alberta, Canada. Associate Professor; Psychologist. m. Allen C Eng, 1 Aug. 1981. 2 sons, 2 daughters. *Education:* BEd Education 1970; MA Educational Foundations 1974, PhD Counselling Psychology, 1978, University of Calgary. *Appointments:* Teacher, 1969-71; School Counsellor, 1972-75; Counsellor Educator, 1979-; Senior Psychologist, 1981-86, Research Associate, 1986-, Cross Cancer Institute. *Publications:* Managing the Stress of Cancer, 1987; Numerous articles in the field of counsellor education/health psychology/stress management. *Memberships:* ATA Guidance Council; Psychologist Association of Alberta; Special Interest Group on Counselling, PAA; Canadian Guidance and Counselling Association; Psychologists for Peace; Canadian Mental Health Association;

Canadian Society of Clinical Hypnosis, Edmonton Chapter; American Society of Clinical Hypnosis; Sons of Norway; Pain Interest Group; Chairperson of Examinations, Universities Council; Founding member/ Director, Canadian Association of Psychosocial Oncology. *Honours:* Recipient of numerous grants; Excellence in Teaching, Educational Psychology Department, 1988. *Hobby:* Photography. *Address:* Department of Educational Psychology, University of Alberta, 6-102 Education North, Edmonton, Canada, T6G 2G5.

JHABVALA Ruth Prawer, b. 7 May 1927, Cologne, Germany. Writer. m. C S H Jhabvala, 1951. 3 daughters. *Education:* Hendon Co School; London University. *Career:* Refugee to England, 1939; lived in India, 1951-76; in USA, 1975-. *Publications:* Novels: To Whom She Will, 1955; Nature of Passion, 1956; Esmond in India, 1958; The Householder, 1960; Get Ready for Battle, 1962; A Backward Place, 1962; A New Dominion, 1971; Heat and Dust, 1975; In Search of Love and Beauty, 1983; The Nature of Passion, 1986; Short story collections: A Stronger Climate, 1968; An Experience of India, 1970; How I Be came a Holy Mother, 1976; Out of India: Selected Stories, 1986; Three Continents, 1987. Film scripts: (for James Ivory), Shakespeare Wallah, 1965; The Roseland, 1977; Hullabaloo over Georgie and Bonnie's Pictures, 1978; Jane Austen in Michigan, 1980; Quarter, 1981; Room with a View, 1986. *Honours:* Neill Gunn International Fellowship, 1979; Booker Award for best novel, 1975; MacArthur Foundation Award, 1984. *Address:* c/o Harper and Row, 10 East 53rd Street, New York, NY 10022, USA.

JIAGGE Annie Ruth, b. 7 Oct. 1918, Lome-Togo. Retired Judge; President, Court of Appeal, Ghana. m. Fred K A Jiagge, 10 Jan. 1953. *Education:* Achomota Teacher Training College; LLB, London School of Economics, England, 1950; Lincoln's Inn, 1947-50. *Appointments:* Teacher-Headmistress, 1939-46, Heta Presbyterian Girls School, Ghana; Barrister at Law, Accra, 1950-54; Magistrate, 1957-59; Judge, High Court, 1961-69; Judge, Appeal Court, 1969-83; President, Court of Appeal, 1980-83. *Memberships Include:* Member, Executive Committee World YWCA, 1949-62; Ghana's Representative, UN Commission on Status of Women, 1962-72, President, 1968; Chairman, Commission on Investigation of Assets, 1966-69; Ghana Council on Women & Development; President, World Council of Churches, 1975-83; Moderator, World Council of Churches' Programme to Combat Racisim, 1984-; Chairman Ghana Committee on Churches Participation in Development, 1985-. *Honours:* Grand Medal, Ghana, 1969; Gimbles International Award, 1969; Hon. LLD, University of Ghana, 1974. *Hobbies:* Music; Gardening; Crafts. *Address:* Ebenezer House, Plot NO. 10 Roman Ridge, PO Box 5511, Accra North, Ghana.

JIE Zhang, b. 27 Apr. 1937, Beijing, Peoples Republic of China. Writer. m. Y Y Sun. 1 daughter. *Education:* Graduate, People's University, Beijing. *Publications:* Leaden Wings, 1981, translated into German, French, English, Sweden, Norwegian, Finnish, Dutch, Danish, Russian, Brazilian, Spanish and Portuguese; The Ark (also translated); Numerous short stories (also translated). *Memberships:* Council Member, China Writers Association; Vice President, Beijing Writers' Association; Beijing Political Consulting Conference; International PEN. *Honours:* 3 national awards for short stores, 1978, 79, 83; 1 national award for novelette, granted every 2 years, 1983-84; Mao Dong Prize, 1983-85, granted every 3 years; A number of other awards including People's Literature Award. *Hobby:* Music. *Address:* Peijing Writers Association; Beijing, Peoples Republic of China.

JOACHIM Margaret Jane, b. 25 June 1949, Brighton, England. Computer Services Sales Executive; Feminist; Politician. m. Paul Joseph Joachim, 2 July 1970, 1 daughter. *Education:* BA 1970, MA 1974, Geology, Oxford University; PhD, Geology, University of Birmingham, 1978. *Appointments:* School teacher, full-time 1971-73, part-time 1973-76; University Research Fellow, 1976-79; Various positions, computer services, 1979-. *Publications:* 2 academic papers, pleistocene entomology. *Memberships:* Chair 1984-87, Fawcett Society; 300 Group; Women's Liberal Federation; Liberal Party (fought 3 General Elections); Joint Coordinator, Women into Public Life campaign; Associate Member, Institution of Geologists; FRES; Reform Club; Chair, Working Group to establish a European Women's Lobby, 1988-; Chair, SLD Women's Organisation, 1989; Member, City Women's Network. *Hobbies include:* Political: Scientific & technological issues; Environment; Nuclear energy; Equal rights; Constitutional reform. Feminist: Achievement of genuine sexual equality; Encouragement of women into politics, top jobs, public appointments; Women writers. General: Sailing; Singing; Walking; Reading; Visiting traction engine rallies; Florentine embroidery; Making jam. *Address:* 8 Newburgh Road, London W3 6DQ, England.

JOHN Mary Elizabeth, b. 21 Dec. 1940, Standish, England. University Senior Lecturer. m. John Michael Croxen, 7 Nov. 1964, divorced 1977, 2 sons. *Education:* BA, Honours, Psychology; PhD, Psychology. *Appointments:* Lecture, Psychology: University of Bristol, 1965-66, University of Exeter, 1966-69, Open University, 1974-. *Memberships:* Associate Fellow, British Psychological Society. *Honours:* State Scholarship, 1959; Medical Research Council Scholarship, 1962. *Hobbies:* Painting; Drawing; Theatre. *Address:* The Open University, Southern Region, Foxcombe Hall, Boars Hill, Oxford OX1 5HR, England.

JOHN Patricia Spaulding, b. 16 July 1916, Canton, Illinois, USA. Harpist; Composer. m. Frank Geoffrey Keightley, 1 Mar. 1957, 2 daughters. *Education:* Mills College, California 1934; Curtis Institute of Music, Philadelphia, Pennsylvania, 1936; BA, Rice University, 1941. *Appointments:* Principal Harpist, Springfield Civic Symphony, 1947, Galveston Civic Symphony, 1952; Associate Harpist, Houston Symphony Orchestra, 1956; Houston Baptist University, 1976-80; Guest Artist, International Harpweek, Holland, 1973; Y Delyn, Wales, 1976; Wm. Marsh Rice University, Houston, Texas, 1975; Ernest Read Music Association, England, 1977; Stowe Summer School of Music, England, 1978. *Publications:* Compositions: Sea Changes, 1968; Aprille, 1969; Mnemosyne, 1969; Henrietta, 1974; Let's Play Series; Tachystos; Americana Suite; Sea Anemones; Wind Rose, 1983; Voyage of the Elissa, 1985; The Gothic Harp, 1988; Prelude to Summer, 1989. *Memberships:* American Harp Society; American Musical Instrument Society; American Recorder Society; Curtis Institute of Music Alumni Association; Association Internationale des Harpistes France; International Folk Harp Society; Welsh Harp Society of America; many others. *Honours:* Guest of Honour, various Harp Competitions & Festivals. *Address:* 2525 Eastside Lane, Houston, TX 77019, USA.

JOHNS Glynis, b. Pretoria, South Africa. Actress. m. (1) Anthony Forwood, dissolved, 1 son. (2) David Foster, DSO, DSC and Bar, dissolved. (3) Cecil Peter Lamont Henderson. (4) Elliott Arnold. *Education:* Clifton and Hampstead High Schools. *Creative works:* Roles include: Sonia in Judgement Day, Embassy and Strand, 1937; Miranda in Quiet Wedding, Wyndham's, 1938; Quiet Weekend, Wyndham's, 1941; Peter in Peter Pan, Cambridge Theatre, 1943; Fools Rush In, Fortune; The Way Things Go, Phoenix, 1950; Gertie (title role), New York, 1952; Major Barbara (title role), New York, 1957; The Patient in Too True to be Good, New York, 1962; The King's Mare, Garrick, 1966; Come as You Are, New, 1970; A Little Night Music, New York, 1973; Ring Round the Moon, Los Angeles, 1975; 13 Rue de l'Amour, Phoenix, 1976; Cause Celebre, her Majesty's, 1977; Hayfever, UK; The Boy Friend, Toronto. Films include: South Riding; 49th Parallel; Frieda; An ideal Husband; Miranda (the Mermaid); State Secret; No Highway; The Magic Box; Appointment with Venus; Encore; The Card; Sword and the Rose; Personal Affair; Rob Roy; The Weak and the Wicked; The Beachcomber; The Seekers; Poppa's Delicate Condition; Cabinet of Dr Caligari; Mad

About Men; Josephine and Men; The Court Jester; Loser Takes All; The Chapman Report; Dear Bridget; Mary Poppins. Television includes: Star Quality; The Parkinson Show (singing Send in the Clowns); Mrs Amworth (USA); All You Need is Love; Across a Crowded Room; Little Gloria; Happy at Last; Sprague; Love Boat; Murder She Wrote; The Cavanaughs. *Honours:* Tony Award for Best Musical Actress; Best Actress Award, Variety Club. *Address:* c/o Gottlieb, Schiff, 555 5th Avenue, New York, NY 10017, USA.

JOHNS Sonja Maria, b. 13 May 1953, Washington, USA. Physician. m. George L. Wheeler, 18 Sept. 1979, divorced 1982, 1 son, 3 daughters. *Education:* BS, Harvard University, 1976; MD, Howard University, 1978; Internship, Residency, various Hospitals. *Appointments:* National Health Plan Inc., Physician, 1981-82; Warners Medical Centre, Family Practitioner, 1985; District of Columbia Air National Guard, Chief Hospital Services, 1983-; Warsaw Medical Centre, Family Practitioner, 1983-. *Memberships:* Many professional organisations. *Honours Include:* Outstanding Young Woman of America, 1981, 1984, 1985, 1986, 1988; US Air Force Major, DC Air National Guard, 1985. *Hobbies:* Music; TV Sports; Films. *Address:* 404 Main Street, Warsaw VA 22572, USA.

JOHNSEN Vina Lee, b. 7 Sept. 1941, Shawnee, USA. Sales. m. 15 Apr. 1968, 2 daughters. *Education:* Studies, various Universities & Institutes. *Appointments:* Executive Assistant, Databank, 1980-84; Sales, A. Gathering of Eagles, 1982-85; President, Thee Beginning, Inc., 1987; Vice President, Thee Touch of the Master Inc., 1986-90. *Publications:* Articles in various journals. *Memberships:* National Federation Business & Professional Women; National Office Products Association. *Honours:* Recipient, many honours & awards. *Hobbies:* Christian Counselling; Fashion Designing; Oil Painting; Photography. *Address:* 1313 N. Park, Shawnee, OK 74801, USA.

JOHNSON Catherine Brady Grymes, b. 19 Feb. 1952, Oklahoma City, Oklahoma, USA. Sales Professional; Researcher, Child Development. m. R. Dale Johnson, 26 Nov. 1977, 1 son, 1 daughter. *Education:* University of Tennessee, 1970-71; Memphis State University, 1971-74. *Appointments:* Car rental agent, insurance clerk, sales representative, 1974-76; Department Manager, International Harvester Credit Corporation, 1976-81; Customer Service Manager, American Wallcoverings (division, Arton Group), 1981-82; Manager, retail store, 1985-86; Sales representative, Arton Group, Memphis, 1985-. *Publications:* Poetry: Career of Being a Mother; Children Are Our Greatest Gift; It Hurts To Say Goodbye. *Memberships:* Treasurer, New Beginnings Club; Pi Beta Phi; City President, Kings Daughters; American Society of Interior Designers; Construction Specifications Institute. *Honours:* Scholastic scholarship, University of Tennessee Alumni Association, 1970; Chosen (by Memphis State University) member, Angel Flight, US Air Force/ROTC. *Hobbies:* Writing poetry; Needlepoint; Child development; Management. *Address:* 7188 Larkfield Cove, Olive Branch, Mississippi 38654, USA.

JOHNSON Christina Kathleen, b. 6 Dec. 1949, London, England. Editor. m. Lee Johnson, 5 Aug. 1972, 1 daughter. *Education:* BA, Honours, English & American Literature, University of Kent, Canterbury, 1971. *Appointments:* Teacher, English, Jamaica & Trinidad & Tobago, 1972-81; Assistant Co-ordinator, Rape Crisis Centre, Trinidad & Tobago, 1985-87; Editor, Cafra News. *Memberships:* Founding Member, The Group. *Hobbies:* Reading; Writing; Film; Travel. *Address:* PO Bag, 442, Tunapuna, Trinidad & Tobago.

JOHNSON Deborah Ann, b. 4 Dec. 1950, Los Angeles, California, USA. Gem Broker. *Education:* AA, Theatre Arts, Santa Monica College (SMC); BA (Motion Pictures & TV), MA (Theatre Arts), University of California, Los Angeles (UCLA). *Appointments:* Bookkeeper, Meryl Lynch Pierce Fenner & Smith, 1968;

Artist, Hanna Barbara, 1969; TV bibliographer, UCLA, 1978; Owner, Gem Hunters International 1985, Red Moon Productions 1985, Book Nook 1988, Heavenly Herbs 1986. *Creative work includes:* Screenplays: Secrets; Lady Finger Aura; Once in a Blue Moon. Painting: Obsession. *Publications:* Books: Price for Freedom; Position of Trust; Just Another Wet Dream. *Memberships:* Thespian President, SMC; Daughters of American Revolution; UCLA Alumni Association. *Honours:* Scholarship, San Francisco Art Academy, 1968; Patron Scholarship, 1972; June Taylor Award, SMC, 1975; Undergraduate scholarship & grant 1976-78, Jim Morrison Best Film 1980, Clifton Webb Award 1981, UCLA; Honourable Mention, Samuel Goldwyn Screenplay Award, 1980; Grant & scholarship, Graduate Advancement Programme, 1982. *Hobbies include:* Acting; Collecting autographed 1st editions; Dance; Video production; Gemstones; Investigative research; Psychology; Human relationships & interaction; Meditation; Herbology. *Address:* 34 Brooks Avenue, Venice, California 90291, USA.

JOHNSON Diana Gillian Amanda, b. 5 May 1948, London, England. Equestrian Manager; Writer; Farmer. m. (1) David Huntington Williams, 23 Aug. 1969, 2 sons, (2) Harry Edward Johnson, 6 Apr. 1984, 2 daughters. *Education:* Diplome Alliance Francaise (honours), Institut d'Alpin Videmanette, Switzerland, 1965; BA Hons, Georgetown University, USA. *Appointments:* Jack Tinker and Partners, Advertising, New York, USA, 1967; Copywriter, McCann Erikson Advertising, London, England, 1968; Public Relations, Universal Health Sports, Bahamas, 1972-; Manager, West Haddon Farms and Red House Farm Stables, currently. *Memberships:* National Farmers' Union; Country Landowners Association; Lyford Cay Club, Bahamas; Pytchley Hunt lub; Warwickshire Hunt Club; Offchurch Bury Polo Club; National Light Horse Breeding Society. *Hobbies:* Foxhunting; Scuba diving; Skiing; Polo. *Address:* Red House Farm, Campion Hills, Leamington Spa, Warwickshire, England.

JOHNSON Dorothy Phyllis, b. 13 Sep. 1925, Kansas City, Missouri, USA. Art Therapist; Mental Health Counselor. m. Herbert Eugene Johnson, 1945. 2 sons. *Education:* BA 1975, MS 1976, MA 1979. *Appointments:* High Plains Com., Community Mental Health Center, 1974-76; Sunflower Mental Health Center, 1976-81; Pawnee Mental Health Center, 1981-84. *Creative Works include:* Murals and Paintings; Sculptures in Banks and private collections in USA. *Memberships:* Phi Delta Kappa; Kansas Association of Art Therapists; AM; Art Therapy Association; Phi Kappa Phi; Kansas Association for Counseling and Development; Treasurer, Kansas Mental health Counselors Association, 1986-87; Association of Humanistic Psychologist; Secretary of Board, Swedish America State Bank. *Honours include:* Wire sculpture featured in Look Magazine and Designers Handbook. *Hobbies:* Reading; Wheel-thrown ceramics; Horticulture; Sculpting; Painting. *Address:* Box 200, Courtland, KS 66939, USA.

JOHNSON D'Elaine Ann Herard, b. 19 Mar. 1919, Puyallup, Washington, USA. Artist; Lecturer; Educator; Critic. m. John Lafayette, 22 Dec. 1956. *Education:* BA, Central Washington State University, 1954; MA, Uiversity of Washington, 1958. *Appointments:* Art Professor, 1954- 78; Art Crtic; Lecturer. *Creative Works:* Exhibitions Include: Seattle Art Museum, 1959, 1965, 1973-75; Henry Gallery, Archives, 1972-74; Touring collection, Canadian Maritime Provinces & Newfoundland, 1971-72; Shoreline Historical Museum, 1978, 1979, 1980; numerous in universities, commercial galleries, etc. *Memberships Include:* Kappa Pi; International Society for Artists; National Artists Equity; President, Edmonds Arts Roundtable; President, Mount Olympus Estate Preserve for Arts & nature. *Honours:* Scholarships: Music, 1950-54, Art 1950-54; Muncie Award, Central Washington University, 1953; Purchase Award, Nova Scotia Art Museum, Permanent Collections: Vancouver Maritime Museum; Whatcomb Museum; Edmonds Art Commission & others. *Hobbies:*

Violin; Writings on Creativity; Scuba Diving; etc. *Address:* 16122 72nd Ave. West, Edmonds, WA 98020, USA.

JOHNSON Elizabeth B, b. 21 Dec. 1936, Atlantic City, new Jersey, USA. Broker/Owner. m. Wesley E Johnson Jr, 9 Sept. 1961, deceased. 3 sons, 1 daughter. *Education:* RN, 1957; Real Estate Broker, 1982. *Appointments:* Staff Nurse/Head Nurse 1958-59; Real Estate Salesperson, 1978-85; Owner/Broker, Betty Johnson Real Estate Inc, 1985-. *Memberships:* Aclon City Board of Realtors, General Committee Member; Atlantic County Board of Realtors, Harbor Lites Founding Member; Soroptomist International; Association of American Business Women; American Society of Female Executives. *Honours:* Million Dollar Salesperson, 1985-89; Mother of the Year, Rosco D Brown Youth Organisation, 1976. *Hobbies:* Antiques; Opera; Travelling; Skiing. *Address:* 7 North Swarthmore Ave, Ventnor, NJ 08406, USA.

JOHNSON Ellen Randel, b. 9 May 1916, Canton, Mississippi, USA. Real Estate Broker. m. Floyd E. Johnson, 1 Jan. 1936, 1 son, 1 daughter. *Appointments:* Various office positions, 1951-66; Freelance Feature Writer, Columnist, Yazoo Herald, 1969-74; Real Estate Sales, Ted Russell Real Estate, 1976; Owner, Broker, Ellen Johnson Realty, 1977; Real Estate Broker Associate, Phyllis Waltman Realty, 1978; Real estate Broker owner, Ellen Johnson Realtors, Hattiesburg, 1980-88. *Publications:* Credit Union Manual for Operations, 1966; Editor, Publisher, Cookbook, The Dining Table for Candida patients, 1988. *Memberships:* various professional organisations. *Honours:* Realtor of the Year, Hattiesburg Womens Council of Realtors, 1981, 1984, Mississippi Womens Council of Realtors, 1984; Realtor of the Year, Hattiesburg Board of Realtors, 1984; Omega Tau Award from National Board of Realtors, 1984. *Hobbies:* Reading; TV; Writing; Cooking; Piano. *Address:* 1302 Estelle, Hattiesburg, MS 39402, USA.

JOHNSON Geraldine Esch, b. 5 Jan. 1921, Steger, Illinois, USA. Language Specialist. m. (1) Richard William Esch, 12 Oct. 1940, deceased 1971, 2 sons, 1 daughter. (2) Henry Bernard Johnson, 23 Aug. 1978, deceased 11 Feb. 1988. *Education:* BSBA 1955, MA Education, 1958, MA Speech Pathology, 1963, University of Denver; Vocational Credential, University of Northern Colorado, 1978; Additional courses, University of Colorado, Metropolitan State College. *Appointments:* Teacher of Music, Judith St John School of Music, Denver, 1946-52; Teacher, West High School, Denver, 1955-61; Chairman, Business Education Department, 1958-61; Reading Specialist, 1977-78, West High School, Denver; Speech Therapist and Founder, South Denver Speech Clinic, 1965-71; Teacher, Educationally Handicapped Resource Room, Denver, 1971-74; Diagnostic Centre, The Belmont School, Denver, 1974-77; Speech-Language Specialist in Elementary and Junior High Schools, Denver, 1978-86; Lecturer, Speech Pathology and Learning Disabilities, Colorado Education Association, 1971-73; Home Language Teacher, Early Childhood Education, Denver, 1975; Member, Educational TV Advisory Committee, Colorado; Secretary, Central Business Education Committee, Colorado; Teacher, Letter Writing Clinics, Local Businesses, Denver, 1960-; Retain Lifetime Certification in Counselling and Guidance, Vocational Credential, Care and Guidance of Children; Counsellor, Parents and Students in Pre School, Elementary and Junior/Senior High Schools, Denver and throughout Colorado, 1955-. *Memberships:* Speech-Language-Hearing Association (Cert); University of Denver School of Business Alumni Board; Beta Gamma Sigma; Kappa Delta Pi; Delta Pi Epsilon. *Honours:* Recipient Special Education Award, Denver Public Schools, 1986; Finalist, Mrs Colorado Contest, 1956; OVR Grant to Study Speech Pathology (with 3-month internship at Craig Rehabilitation Center), 1961-62; Clinical Traineeship Grant, 1965; Nomination for Denver Public Schools Outstanding Teacher Award, 1965, Brown School 1966, University Park 1967.

Hobbies: Music; Play piano and theatre organ; Ice skating; Ice dancing; Reading; Swimming. *Address:* Denver, CO, USA.

JOHNSON Linda Avriemma, b. 4 June 1949, Orange, New Jersey, USA. Interior Architect. m. Jan. 1 1978. *Education:* BFA, 1971, BArch, 1972, Rhode Island School of Design. *Appointments:* Senior Planner, Warwick Department of City Planning, Rhode Island, 1973-74; Junior Draughtsperson, Residential Projects, Gredig Design Consultancy, Abbott Howard Architects, London, England, 1974-76; Job Captain, Residential and Institutional Projects, James Goldstein & Partners, Kachadourian Cahill, New Jersey, USA, 1978-79; Intermediate Designer, Residential, Commercial and Institutional Projects, Warner Burn Joan Lunde Architects, New York City, 1979; Project Architect, Residential and Commercial Projects, Munselle Brown, Jemston Shehl Architects, Los Angeles, California, 1980-83; Job Captain, Hilton Hawaiian Village, Honolulu, Pan Pacific, Vancouver, Hirsch Bedner & Associates, Santa Monica, California, 1983-86; Project Manager, Designer, Hyatt Regency, Dallas, Fort Worth International Airport, Outrigger Reef Hotel, Honolulu, Decorator, Sheraton, Anchorage, Barry Design Associates, Los Angeles, California, 1986- 87. *Creative works:* Acrylic paintings on paper, sold, 1985; Textured paper triptych; Abalone paper sculptures nos 3, 5 and 6; Paper cut out triptych. *Membership:* American Institute of Architects. *Honour:* Service Award from Councilman Marvin Braude as member of Citizens Advisory Committee, 1986. *Hobbies:* Fine art painting; Cooking. *Address:* 16076 Sunset Boulevard, Pacific Palisades, CA 90272, USA.

JOHNSON Lois Munselle, b. 3 Oct. 1909, Chicago, USA. Marriage & Family Therapist; Consultant. m. (1)Charles J. Seward, 21 Sept. 1936, divorced 1951, 1 daughter, (2)Roy F. Johnson, 15 May 1961, divorced 1962. *Education:* AB, Bradley University, 1933; MA, Western Michigan University, 1964. *Appointments:* Copywriter, WKMI, Kalamazoo, 1952-60; Executive Director, County Council of Churches, Kalamazoo, 1960-62; Adjunct Faculty, Lake Michigan College, 1962-72; Director, Michigan Centre for TA & Gestalt, 1972-80; Consultant to Weight Watchers of Central Florida & N. Alabama, Director of People Changers, Inc., 1983. *Publications:* Stakes of Mistakes, 1950; I'm Gonna Fly, 1969; Meditations for Inspired Living, 1970; *Memberships:* COETM Transactional Analysis; Marriage & Family Therapists; Radix Teachers Association; Orange City Mental Health Association; *Honours:* Trencher Award, 1929; Recipient, many other honours & awards. *Hobbies:* Writing; Golf; Knitting; Reading. *Address:* 1003 Inland Seas Blvd., Winter Garden, FL 32787, USA.

JOHNSON Lynne Ann Courtright, b. 16 May 1960, Los Alamos, New Mexico, USA. Architect. m. Richard Alan Johnson, 10 Oct. 1987. *Education:* BArch, Arizona State University, 1983. *Appointments:* HOK, 1983-86, 1987; Pierce, Goodwin, Alexander, 1986-87; Askew, Nixon, Ferguson & Wolfe, 1988-. *Memberships:* American Institute of Architects; Associate Director 1986, Dallas Women in Architecture. *Hobbies:* Running; Cycling; Playing piano. *Address:* PO Box 1193, Munford, Tennessee 38058, USA.

JOHNSON Margaret Anne (Meg), b. 29 Dec. 1947, New York City, New York, USA. Educator; Homemaker. m. Douglas E. Johnson, 7 Feb. 1970, divorced 18 May 1989, 2 sons, 2 daughters. *Education:* BA, Psychology, University of Colorado, Boulder, 1969; MA, Special Education, Kean College, Union, New Jersey, 1970; William Paterson College, Wayne, New Jersey, 1975-76; New Jersey Elementary and Special Education Certificates, 1976; MA candidate, Counselling, Psychotherapy, Rivier College, Nashua, New Hampshire, 1986-. *Appointments:* Team Teacher, 1970-71; Instructor, 4 children at home, 1976-; Counsellor/Consultant, Manager/Coordinator, advising and assisting families worldwide in children's home education, 1979-, Director, 1980-, Home Education Resource Center, Mont Vernon, New Hampshire, 1979-; Public speaker on home education. *Publications:* Editor/author, Home Education Resource Center Bulletin (quarterly), 1980-85; A Preliminary Guide for Preparing to Teach Children at Home, 1980; Contributing author: Home Spun Schools, 1982, The Home School Manual, 1984, 1986, other education, home education and family periodicals. *Memberships:* Active member in numerous community, political and church organisations, 1971-. *Honours:* Graduate Fellowship, Special Education, Kean College, 1969-70; National Home Schooling Award, Lewisville, Texas, 1983. *Hobbies:* Accomplished pianist, writer, public speaker; Needlework; Skiing; Swimming. *Address:* PO Box 124, Mont Vernon, NH 03057, USA.

JOHNSON Margaret M. Joyce, b. 17 Oct. 1948, Detroit, Michigan, USA. Lawyer. m. Steven M. Johnson, 11 Aug. 1972, 1 son, 1 daughter. *Education:* BS magna cum laude, German, Mathematics majors, 3 minors: Science, Philosophy and Theology, Siena Heights College, 1970; Eberhard Karl University, Tuebingen, West Germany, 1971-72; MA with honours, German Literature and Linguistics, University of Colorado, 1973; JD high honours, University of Montana, 1980; Admitted: Montana State Bar, 1980; US District Court, Montana, 1980; US Court of Appeals, Ninth Circuit, 1984; US Supreme Court, 1984. *Appointments include:* Various teaching positions, Siena Heights College; University of Colorado, Denver and Boulder; Wilhelmshaven, West Germany, 1969-76; Associate, Hughes, Bennett, Kellner and Sullivan, Helena, Montana, USA, 1980-82; Assistant Attorney General, Department of Justice, State of Montana, Helena, 1982-85; Associate, Church, Harris, Johnson & Williams, Great Falls, Montana, 1985-88; Partner, Church, Harrison, Johnson & Williams, Great Falls, Montana, 1989-. *Publications:* Criminal Procedure Survey (co-author), 1980; translation of Alfred Schmid's Traktat Ueber das Licht-eine gnostiche Schau, as The Marvel of Light: An Excursus (co- translator), 1984. *Memberships include:* State Bar of Montana including Eastern Director, Women's Law Section, Alternative Dispute Resolution Committee and Continuing Legal Education Institute); American and Montana Trial Lawyers Associations; American Bar Association; Montana Defense Trial Lawyers Association; Order of Barristers; International Platform Association; Board, Montana Christian Conciliation Service, 1983-85; Christian Legal Society; National Head Injury Foundation; Board, Montana Head Injury Association; League of Women Voters; Alumni Associations: Universities of Colorado and Montana, Siena Heights College. *Honours:* President, Siena Heights College Science Club, 1969-70; Delta Epsilon Sigma; Kappa Gamma Pi; Sigma Kappa Alpha; Fulbright Scholar, 1971-72. *Hobbies:* Family; Travel; Reading; Foreign languages; Singing; Hiking; Backpacking; Canoeing; Fishing; Camping; Downhill and cross-country skiing; Racquetball; Walking; Cinema; Softball; Volleyball. *Address:* Church, Harris, Johnson & Williams, PO Box 1645, Great Falls, MT 59403, USA.

JOHNSON Marlene, b. 11 Jan. 1946, Braham, Minnesota, USA., Lieutenant Governor, State of Minnesota. *Education:* BA, Macalester College, St Paul, Minnesota, 1968. *Appointments:* Community Organizer, Ramsey Action Programs, St Paul; President and Founder, Split Infinitive, Inc, St Paul, 1970-82; Elected Lieutenant Governor, State of Minnesota, 1982-. *Memberships:* Board Member, National Child Care Action Campaign; Executive Committee and Midwestern Region Chair, National Conference of Lieutenant Governors; Founder and Past Chair, National Leadership Conference for Women Executives in State Government; Past President, Founder and Past President Minnesota Chapter, National Association of Women Business Owners; Vice Chair, Minnesota Task Force on Small Business, 1978; Co-Chair, Minnesota Delegation, White House Conference on Small Business, 1980; Chair, Minnesota Women's Political Caucus, 1973-74. *Honours:* Distinguished Service Award for Community Service, St Paul Jaycees' 1980; One of Ten Outstanding Young Minnesotans, Minnesota

Jaycees; Outstanding Achievement Award, St Paul YWCA, 1980; Distinguished Citizen Citation, Macalester College, 1982; One of Ten Outstanding Women in Government, United States Women Jaycees, 1983; Distinguished Contributions to Families Award, Minnesota Council on Family Relations, 1986; Honor from Minnesota Sportfishing Congress, 1986. *Interests:* Swedish Culture and History; Women's Athletics. *Address:* State of Minnesota, USA.

JOHNSON Mertha Ruth, b. 10 Oct. Jackson, Mississippi, USA. Educator; Consultant; Writer; Lecturer. 1 daughter. *Education:* BS Social Science, Jackson State University, Jackson; MA Education, Masters of Public Administration, University of San Francisco. *Appointments:* District Teacher, San Matio High School, 1983-85; Atlanta Schools, 1986; Executive Director, Neighbourhood Housing Services, 1982-83; Administrator/Teacher, OICW; Administrator, Manpower Training Program; Teacher, Chicago Public School. *Publications:* Black History Study Manual; US History Guide; Geography Resource Book; Articles on education, religion, philosophy. *Memberships:* American Federation of Teachers; Atlanta's Ministry to International Students; National Council of Negro Women; NAACP-SCLC (Women's organization); Literary Guild. *Honours:* Oak Tree Award, Outstanding Teacher of the Year, 1988; Consultant, Literacy project, Georgia Black Caucas, Master Teacher; Lecturer, Multicultural Education; Poetry award; Writer, Martin Luther King currciulum for High School. *Hobbies:* Writing poetry, short stories; Professional singer; Collector of rare books and manuscripts. *Address:* 1445 Monroe Dr, NE, Atlanta, GA 30324, USA.

JOHNSON Nancy L, b. 5 Jan. 1935, Chicago, USA. Member of Congress. m. Dr Theodore Johnson, 1958, 3 daughters. *Education:* University of Chicago; Graduated, cum laude, Radcliffe College, 1957. *Appointments:* Active in Community affairs, 17 years; Elected, 6th District, State Senate, 1976-; Served as Member on Appropriations, Finance, Education, State Planning & Development, Government Administration & Policy, Human Rights & Opportunities Committees; Chairman, Bipartisan Review & Investigations Committee. *Memberships:* House Wednesday Group; Ripon Society; House Republican Research Committee; Republican Policy Committee; Congressional Caucus for Womens Issues; New England Caucus; Northeast-Midwest Coalition; Chairman, Education Task Force; Committee on Ways and Means; Health Sub-committee, Sub-committee on Human Resources. *Address:* 119 Cannon Building, Washington, DC 20515, USA.

JOHNSON Nancy Lucille Hill, b. 29 July 1918, Carrolton, Mississippi, USA. Teacher. m. Leon Johnson, 19 Jan. 1939, 2 daughters. *Education:* AA, Compton College, 1958; BA, University of California, Los Angeles, 1973; MA, Antioch College, 1977; Doctorate, Psychology, Lawrence University, 1978. *Appointments:* Teacher, Plaza de la Raza, 1967-83; Retired Substitute Teacher, Lynwood Unified School District, 1985-. *Creative work includes:* 7 children's books, unpublished. *Memberships:* American Association of University Teachers; Womens Ways & Means Committee, National Council of Negro Women; Past Vice President, Compton College Advisory Committee; Women's Programme Committee, American Business & Professional Women. *Honours:* Outstanding Community Mother & Good Neighbour, City of Los Angeles Council; Congressional Recognition, community service; Awards, Good Neighbour Council, City of Compton; All, 1987. *Hobbies:* Writing; Crafts; Politics Chair, Los Angeles County Democratic Central Committee; Treasurer, LA Girls Club; Past Chair, Federal Grants Advisory Committee, Compton; Elder, 1st Christian Church; Bellflower Region Board, Christian Church, Disciples of Christ. *Address:* 1207 West 127th Street, Compton, California 90222, USA.

JOHNSON Norma J, b. 30 Aug. 1925, Dover, Ohio, USA. Specialty Wool Grower and Farmer. m. Robert B Covey, 7 Oct. 1951, divorced 1960. 1 daughter.

Education: Certificate of Drafting Techniques, Case School Applied Scinece, 1944; Western Reserve University, 1945-47; Ohio State University, 1951; Muskingham College, 1965; AA, General Studies, Kent State University, 1979; Buckeye Joint Vocational School, 1979-84. *Appointments:* Instructor, Arts and Crafts, University Settlement House, Cleveland, Ohio, 1944; Mechanical Draftswoman, National Association Civil Aeronautics, Cleveland, 1944-46; Manufacturer's Representative, National Spice House, 1947- 49; Teacher, Mathematics, Home Economics, Economics, History, English, High School, Tuscarawas County School System, New Philadelphia, 1962-69; Owner, Manager Operator, Sunny Slopes Farm, Producer of Speciality Wools and Grain, 1967-. *Memberships:* Teacher, Methodist Sunday School, 1936-61; Chaplain, Winfield Parent-Teacher Association, 1960; Program Director, Brandywine Grange, 1960-62; Troop Leader, Girl Scouts, 1961-70; Tuscarawas County Ohio Jail Committee, 1981-87; American Angus Association, 1976-; Mid-States Wool Growers, 1967-; American Tree Farm System, 1988. *Honours:* Scholastic Honourable Mention, State of Ohio, 1939; Herbster Oration Award, 1943; Certificate Volunteer Trainer, Girl Scouts, 1967; Certificate of Merit, Tuscarawas County Ohio Schools, 1965; Ohio Wildlife Conservation Award, Tuscarawas County, 1972; First and Third Premiums, Handspinning fleece, Ohio State Fair, 1984; 8th and 10th Premiums, Handspinning fleece, Michigan State Fair, 1985. *Hobbies:* Carpentry, designed and built my home; Cooking; Gardening; Sewing. *Address:* Dover, Ohio, USA.

JOHNSON Shirley May Hill, b. 10 Mar. 1947, Virginia, Minnesota, USA. Psychologist. divorced. 2 sons. *Education:* BA Psychology/Biology, 1969; MA Clinical Psychology, 1972; State Licensing Exam, 1980. *Appointments:* Psychologist, Mesabi Regional Medical Center, 1977-. *Publications:* Developed workshops: After Cinderella: Women in the 80's; Cinderella and the Prince: A Workshop on Love and Intimacy; Women and Food. *Membership:* Minnesota Licensed Psychologists. *Hobbies:* Racquetball; Reading; Writing. *Address:* Health Promotion Department, Mesabi Regional Medical Center, Hibbing, MN 55746, USA.

JOHNSON-HILL Joyce Kalt, b. 4 Oct. 1932, New Jersey, USA. Practitioner of Postural Integration.. m. Irving Hill, 29 Oct. 1982, 3 sons, 1 daughter. *Education:* MA, 1975; PhD, Psychophysical Therapy, International College, 1977. *Appointmeents:* Memorial Hospital, Tampa, 1972-74; Private practice, Tampa, 1974-; Tampa Heights Hospital, 1977-84; Hickory Memorial Hospital, 1986-; Cabinet de psychologie Humaniste, 1986-88. *Publications:* Author, text, Detailed Description & Techniques for the Ten Sessions of Postural Integration. *Memberships:* American Dance Therapy Association; Association of Humanistic Psychology; National Rehabilitation & Counselling Association. *Honours:* Recipient, various honours & awards. *Hobbies:* Indian Art; Tennis; Dance. *Address:* 5837 Mariner Drive, Tampa, FL 33609, USA.

JOHNSON-REINIER Karen Louise, b. 15 Oct. 1956, San Bernardino, California, USA. Student; Parent. m. 4 May 1975 (div. 1979), 1 son, 1 daughter. *Education:* BA, Political Science (Russian minor) 1986, Certificate, Secondary Teaching (language arts & social studies) in progress, University of New Mexico. *Appointments:* Single parent, 1979-; Full- time student, 1981-. *Memberships:* American Political Science Association; Academy of Political Science; Association of Reform Zionists of America; Slavic Studies Association, 1984-86. *Honours:* Dean's List, College of Arts & Sciences, University of New Mexico, 1985, 1986; National Dean's List, 1987-88. *Hobbies:* Reading, finding interesting material for students; Library research, political science, literature, history. *Address:* PO Box 10356, Albuquerque, New Mexico 87184, USA.

JOHNSTON Donna Faye, b. 16 Oct. 1941, Stromsburg, Nebraska, USA. Lithographer/Colour Consultant. m. Robert C Johnston, 2 May 1964, divorced

1965. 1 daughter. *Education:* BFA, Kansas City Art Institute, 1963; Journeyman Certificate, GAIU, 1980; Colour Correction Certificate, 1980. *Appointments:* Production Manager, Oliver Advertising, 1972-73; Prod & Colour Correx, Vile Goller/Fine Arts, 1973-79; Colour Correction Artist, K&A Litho, 1979-80; Colour Correx Artist, Chromagraphics, 1980-81; Head, Colour Department/QC, Orent Graphics, 1981-86; Head, Colour Department, Epsen Hillmer Graphics, 1986-. *Creative works:* Editor, Newsletter American Singles, 1986; Design-logo, American signles, 1986; Design-logo, Dimples KCMO, 1978. *Memberships:* Omaha Club/Printing House Craftsmen, Board of Directors; International Association of Printing House Craftsmen; National Association for Female Executives; Graphic Arts International Union; American Singles, Board of Directors; Parents without Partners, Amigo; Perfect Strangers. *Honours:* Outstanding Service, Parents without Partners, 1986; Honourable mention, Woodcut, KC Lawn/Garden Invitational Art Show, 1980. *Hobbies:* Wood cut printing; Watercolour; Theatre; Dancing; Shesha embroidery; Costuming; Music; Literature. *Address:* Epsen Hillmer Graphics, 2000 California, Omaha, NEB 68102, USA.

JOHNSTON Janis Clark, b. 5 Jan,. 1947, South Bend, Indiana, USA. Psychologist/Consultant. m. Mark Emmett Johnston, 14 June 1969. 1 son, 1 daughter. *Education:* BA with Distinction, Manchester College, 1969; MEd, 1970, EdD, 1974, Boston University. *Appointments:* School Psychologist, Lexington Public Schools, 1972-78; Psychological Examiner, Harvard Pre-school Project, Cambridge, 1973-74; Instructor, Boston University, 1974-75; Professor & Psychologist, Hahnemann Medical College and Hospital, Philadelphia, 1978-81; Therapist, Acorn, Philadelphia, 1979-81; Psychologist, Oak Park & River Forest High School, 1981-; Family Therapist, Private Practice, 1984-. *Publications:* Author of numerous articles to professional journals. *Memberships:* American Psychological Association; Psychologists for Social Responsibility; National Association of School Psychologists; Illinois School Psychologists Association; Mental Health Private Practitioners of Oak Park & River Forest; National Organization for Women; League of Women Voters. *Honours:* School Psychology Practitioner of the Year (Region 1, Illinois), 1984; Title IV Fellowship, Boston University, 1969. *Hobbies:* Aerobics; Tennis; Reading. *Address:* 539 N Ridgeland Avenue, Oak Park, IL 60302, USA.

JOHNSTON Jennifer, b. 12 Jan. 1930, Dublin, Ireland. Writer. m. Ian Smyth, 1951, 2 sons, 2 daughters, (2) David Gilliland, 1976. *Education:* Trinity College, Dublin. *Publications:* Books: The Captains & The Kings; How Many Miles to Babylon; Shadows On Our Skin; The Old Jest; The Christmas Tree; The Railway Station Man; Fool's Sanctuary. Plays: The Nightingale & Not The Lark; The Porch; The Invisible Man; Christine & Billy; Triptych. *Honours:* Short-listed, Booker Prize, 1977; Whitbread Prize, 1979; Honorary DLitt, University of Ulster, 1985; Giles Cooper Award, 1990. *Address:* Brook Hall, Culmore Road, Derry, Northern Ireland.

JOHNSTON Lucile W., b. 22 Aug. 1914, Dallas, Texas, USA. Television Lecturer. m. 28 Feb. 1937, 2 sons, 2 daughters. *Education:* Graduated: Tekarkana College, 1934; Miss Wylie's Business College, 1935. *Appointments:* HOLC Regional Office, Memphis, Tennessee, 1935-36; TVA, 1936-41; Advertising Manager, WLA Radio, 1942; Co-Founder 1944, Sales Manager 1944-46, Johnston Conecrete Products Company; Lecturer, TV 30 minutes historical programmes, current. *Publications:* Books: Space Secret of the Universe; Will We Find our Way? - A Space-Age Odyssey; Celebrations of a Nation. *Memberships:* President, Huntsville Garden Club; Vice President, Parent-Teacher Association; Chairman, Media for Huntsville; National Chaplains Committee, Mothers of America; Elder, Central Presbyterian Church; Concerned Women of America; International Women in Leadership; President, Johnston Bicentennial Foundation. *Hobbies:*

Golf; Gardening. *Address:* 1701 Governors Drive SE, Huntsville, Alabama 35801, USA.

JOHNSTON Patricia Kahleen b. 21 May 1936, Seattle, USA. Associate Professor. m. Edward Paul Johnston, 3 Sept. 1955, 1 son, 1 daughter. *Education:* BA, Walla Walla College, 1958; MPH, Loma Linda University, 1978; MS, University of Washington, 1979; DPH, Universiy of California, 1987. *Appointments:* Instructor, 1979-81, Assistant Professor, 1981-88, Associate Professor, 1988-, Director, DPH Programmes, 1987-, Director, Nutrition Program, 1990-, Loma Linda University. *Publications:* Co-Editor, Poceedings First International Congress on Vegetarian Nutrition; Co-Chair, First International Congress on Vegetarian Nutrition; Chairman, Second International Congress on Vegetarian Nutrition, Chairman, Editorial Board, LLU School of Public Health Newsletter. *Memberships:* American Dietetic Association; American College of Nutrition; American Society of Bone & Mineral Research; American Public Health Association; Society for Nutrition Education; California Nutrition Council. *Honours:* Gladys Emmerson Award, UCLA, 1985;Honored Student Award, Greater Los Angeles Nutrition Council, 1985; National Merit Award, Delta Omega, 1985. *Hobbies:* Hiking; Reading; Writing; Public Speaking. *Address:* School of Public Health, Loma Linda University, Loma Linda, CA 92350, USA.

JOHNSTONE Paula Sue, b. 5 July 1947, Springfield, USA. *Education:* BSc., Southwest Missouri State University, 1969. *Appointments:* Teacher, Glidewell Baptist Church, 1972; Director, Church Training, 1984-85, Chairman Budget & Finance Committee, 1986-87. *Publications:* Contributor to various journals & magazines. *Hobbies:* Reading; Knitting; Houseplants. *Address:* Route 5, Box 495 C, Greensleeves, Springfield, MO 65803, USA.

JOHS Anna (Ann) C., b. 5 June 1934, Los Angeles, California, USA. City Councillor and Mayor Protem; Businesswoman. m. Anthony (Tony) Johs, 6 Aug. 1955, 2 sons. *Education:* High School Diploma, 1952; University of Southern California, 1952-55. *Appointments:* Owner, Oxnard Music Store, Oxnard, California, 1955-88; Owner, Liaison Personnel, 1957-67; Member, 1985-90, Mayor Pro tem, 1986-88, Oxnard City Council, also appointed to Economic Development, 1985-90, Oxnard-Port Hueneme Regional Waste Water Treatment Authority, 1985-90, Housing Authority, 1985-90, Redevelopment Agency, 1985-90, Incubator Committee, 1985-87, World Trade Center, 1986-87, Southern California Coastal Water Research Project, 1000-90 (Vice-President 1987-88), Southern California Association of Government, Transportation and Communications Committee, 1988-90, California League of Cities, Police Services Sub-Committee, 1988-90. *Memberships:* Oxnard Chamber of Commerce, Board of Directors 1977-81, 1984-85, Vice-President 1978, President 1980; Former Member, Oxnard Advisory Committee, Executive Board 1976-85, Chair 1979; Board of Directors, Oxnard Convention Bureau, 1978-79; Chair, Oxnard Merchants Fair, 1978-79; Board of Directors, Oxnard-Port Hueneme Community Action, 1979-82; Past Treasurer, Kappa Delta Alumnae Association of Ventura County; Founding Member, Oxnard School District Educational Foundation 1983-85; Various others. *Honours:* Proclamation for Oxnard Merchants Fair, City of Oxnard, 1978; Woman of the Year, Soroptimist International, Oxnard, 1980; Oxnard Trophy, Greater Oxnard Chamber of Commerce, 1980; Resolution, California State Assembly, 1981; Plaque, Oxnard Peace Officers Association, 1985; Certificate of Appreciation, El Concilio del Condado de Ventura; Resolution for Keep The K-9 Dinnrs Night, State Legislature, 1987. *Hobbies:* Fishing; Boating; Feeding wild animals at her mountain hide-away. *Address:* City of Oxnard City Council, 1828 Saviers Road, Oxnard, CA 93033, USA.

JOLLEY Elizabeth, b. 4 June 1923, Birmingham, England. Writer; Lecturer. m. Leonard Jolley. 1 son, 2 daughters. *Appointments:* Nursing Training, 1940-46;

Nursing, 1962-66; Teaching in Colleges and Prisons, 1974-88; Lecturer, School of English, Curtin University of Technology, 1978-88. *Publications:* Novels: Palomino; The Newspaper of Claremont St; Mr Scobie's Riddle; Miss Peabody's Inheritance; Foxybaby; Milk and Honey; The Well; The Sugar Mother; My Father's Moon; Collections of short stories; Radio plays. *Memberships:* Fellow, Australian Fellowship of Writers; Australian Society of Authors, President, 1985, 1986. *Honours:* The AGE Book of the Year for Mr Scobie's Riddle, 1983; Premier of NSW Award for fiction for Milk and Honey, 1985; The Miles Franklin Award for The Well, 1987; Honorary Doctorate, Curtin University, 1987; Officer, Order of Australia, 1988; Citizen of the Year in the Arts Culture and Entertainment, 1987; Prize for Radio Drama, Two Men Running, 1982. *Hobbies:* Orchardist; Goose farmer; Grandchildren; Reading. *Address:* 28 Agett Road, Claremont, Western Australia 6010, Australia.

JONAS, Ann, b. 15 July 1919, Joplin, Missouri, USA. Poet. m. Walter H. Jonas, 30 Mar. 1944, 1 daughter. *Education:* Graduate, Goodman Theatre, Chicago, 1939. *Appointments:* (As Ann Hubert) WHAS, Louisville, Kentucky, Radio Commentator, Actress, Writer, Producer, 1942-47; WAVE, Louisville, Radio & TV Interview Host, Actress, Writer, 1947-54. *Publications Include:* Poetry in Anthologies: Dark Unsleeping Land, 1960; Kentucky Harvest, 1968; Ipso Facto, 1975; The Kentucky Book, 1979; Lawrence of Nottingham, 1985; Dan River Anthologies; Poetry appears in numerous journals including: Adena; Carolina Quarterly; Colorado Quarterly; Latitudes; Orbis; The Quest; Southern Review; The Poetry Review; Skylark; Haiku Journals: American Haiku; Haiku (Canada); etc. *Memberships:* Poetry Society of America; American Civil Liberties Union. *Honours:* Recipient, various honours and awards. *Hobbies:* The Arts; Travel. *Address:* 2425 Ashwood Drive, Louisville, KY 40205, USA.

JONES Adrienne, b. 28 July 1915, Atlanta, Georgia, USA. Writer; Lecturer. m. 18 Aug. 1939. 1 son, 1 daughter. *Publications:* Thunderbird Pass, 1952; Where Eagles Fly, 1957; Ride the Far Wind, 1964; Wild Voyageur: Story of A Canada Goose, 1966; Sail, Calypso!, 1968; Another Place, Another Spring, 1971; The Mural Master, 1974; So, Nothing Is Forever, 1975; The Hawks of Chelney, 1978; The Beckoner, 1980; Whistle Down A Dark Lane, 1982; A Matter of Spunk, 1983; Street Family, 1987. *Memberships:* International PEN Center; Writers in Prison Committee; Society of Children's Book Writers; So California Council on Literature for Children and Young People; The Authors Guild of America; Orange County Authors for Children and Young People; American Civil Liberties Union. *Honours:* Best Children's Book, University of California at Irvine, 1969, 1973, 1975, 1979; Notable Book Award, Southern California Council on Literature for Children and Young People, 1972; Distinguished Work of Fiction Award, Southern California Council on Literature for Children and Young People, 1975; Included in 3 top American Library Asso. lists: Booklist, Notable Books and Best Books for Young Adults, for The Hawks of Chelney and Best Books for Young Adults for A Matter of Spunk; USA West Award, PEN International Center, 1988; Body of Work Award, Southern California Council on Literature for Children and Young People, 1984. *Hobbies:* Environmentalist, Member of the Sierra Club; Hiking; Beach walking; Golf; Mountain climbing, first woman to make both the ascent and descent of Mt Whitney's East Face. *Address:* 24491 Los Serranos Drive, Laguna Niguel, CA 92677, USA.

JONES Annie Eugenia Minter, b. 10 Sep. 1944, Knoxville, Tennessee, USA. Insurance Group Administrator; Community Volunteer. m. Casey C. Jones, 29 Apr. 1967, 1 son, 2 daughters. *Education:* BA, Knoxville College, 1968; Tennessee Insurance Systems, University of Tennessee Continuing Education. *Appointments:* Substitute Teacher, City Schools, 1969; Psychiatric Coordinator, Lake Shore, 1971; Mother's Co-op Assistant, 1974, Mother's Co-op Coordinatory, K.C.D.C; Administrator, Child Care Services, 1976; Co-owner, Secretary/Treasurer, Casey

C. Jones Insurance Group Inc, 1983- *Memberships:* Chairman, Black Family Achievement Awards, Delta Sigma Theta; 2nd Vice-President, Board of Directors, Knoxville YWCA, 1983; University of Tennessee Chancellor's Associates, 1986; Board of Directors, Secretary, United Way, 1986; Leadership Knoxville Class, 1988; Women's Day Chairman, Mt Olive Baptist Church, 1987. *Honours:* Loyal and Dedicated Service, Phyllis Wheatley Branch, YWCA, 1984; Volunteer of the Year, YWCA, 1985; AKA Award, Negro Women Achievers, 1985; University of Tennessee Chancellor's Associates Award in recognition of services, 1986; Certificate of Achievement, Leadership Knoxville, 1988. *Hobbies:* Travel; Golf; Reading; Walking; Volunteering for community causes. *Address:* 4504 Plymouth Road, Knoxville, TN 37914, USA.

JONES Beryl L, b. 30 July 1932, England. m. (3) Jeffrey Mackin, 9 Aug. 1987. 2 sons, 1 daughter. *Education:* Dip. Teach. Units in BEd. *Appointments:* Teacher of English, Speach/Drama, High School, 1975-88; Member of Parliament, 1986-. *Membership:* Councillor Local Government, Armadale City Council, 1981-86. *Address:* 12 Stainton Place, Leeming, WA 6155, USA

JONES Carolyn, b. 18 Apr. 1943, Vancouver, British Columbia, Canada. Actress. m. Jeremy P Mason, 19 Sept. 1970 (separated). *Education:* Graduated, Honours, London Academy of Music & Dramatic Art. *Appointments Include:* Several repertory productions including: A Midsummer Night's Dream, Exeter; A Day in the Death of Joe Egg, Bath; She Stoops to Conquer, Glasgow; A Cool Million, Glasgow; Cat on a Hot Tin Roof, Watford, etc; Joined National Theatre & appeared in: A Bond Honoured; Black Comedy; Much Ado About Nothing; West End Appearances include: The Royal Hunt of the Sun; Oh Calcutta; Black Comedy; More recent stage appearances include: Cranford; The Merchant of Venice; The Elephant Man; Outside Edge; Andy Capp; Stepping Out. Best Known for her many TV appearances including; Great Expectations; The Rivals of Sherlock Holmes; Marked Personal; The Pallisers; Canterbury Tales; Softly Softly; Z Cars; Within These Walls; Sharon Metcalf in Crossroads. Films include: Morgan, A Suitable Case for Treatment; The Sweeney. *Membership:* Canadian and British Actor's Equity. *Honours:* Memorial Drama Award, London Academy of Music & Dramatic Art. *Hobbies:* Aqua Diving, BSAC 3rd Class; Gardening. *Address:* Andrew Manson, 288 Munster Road, London, SW6 6BQ, England.

JONES Charlotte Ann, b. 27 May 1927, Jonesboro, Arkansas, USA. Museum Director; Associate Professor of Art. *Education:* BA, 1962;I Master of Secondary Education, 1970; DPhil, 1978. *Appointments:* 7th/8th Grade Teacher, ST Andrew's School, Little Rock, 1947-51; Teacher/Principal, Holy Souls School, Little Rock, 1951-61; Teacher/Principal, Sacred Heart High School, Muenster, 1962-69; Instructor in Art 1972-77, Assistant Professor 1978-84, Associate Professor/Museum Director 1984-, Arkansas State University. *Publications:* Essays: A Sister Considers Chastity; The Wellspring of Dylan; Women and Art; Extra-ordinary Art Classes. Museum Catalogue: Arkansas Treasures: Looking Back, then Forward. Short stories: Sunflower Petals; Noontime. *Memberships:* American Association of Museums; National Art Education Association; Arkansas Art Educators; Arkansas Museums Association; Arkansas Womens History Institute; Arkansas Council on Women in Higher Education; Association of American Colleges. *Honours:* Outstanding Art Educator, 18-State, Western Region, National Art Education Association, 1983; Outstanding Art Educator, Arkansas, 1983; Service to Art Education Award, Arkansas Art Educators, 1988; BA, magna cum laude, 1962. *Hobbies:* Reading; Canoeing; Watercolour painting; Restoring architecture; Travelling; Writing. *Address:* 1112 South Main Street, Jonesboro, AR 72401, USA.

JONES Clare L, b. Birmingham, England. Musician.

Education: ARCM, 1963; MA, Oxon. *Appointments:* International Recitalist in Universities & Music Establishments; Sighted Braille Music Expert; Director, New Hampstead Ensemble. *Publications:* Co-Compiler, Portraits in Music and Verse, And If Thou Wilt, Remember; Author, Co-Compiler, Oxford Sarabande. *Memberships:* Royal Society of Musicians of Great Britain; Concert Artistes Association. *Honours:* Hon.D.Phil.Mus., World University. *Hobby:* Cycling. *Address:* 40C Petherton Road, London N5 2RE, England.

JONES Claudella Archambeault, b. 25 Sept. 1930, Holgate, Ohio, USA. Director, National Institute for Burn Medicine. m. Christopher Jones, 23 Jan. 1971, divorced 1988. 2 sons, 1 daughter. *Education:* Diploma, Mercy School of Nursing, Toledo, 1956-59; University of Michigan, 1964-72. *Appointments:* Head Nurse, Burn Unit, University of Michigan Hospital, 1966-68; Research Associate and Burn Nurse Specialist, University of Michigan Medical School, 1968-76; Director of Education and Research Associate, 1976-81, Director of Education and Acting Executive Director 1981-83, Administrator, 1983-, National Institute for Burn Medicine. *Publications:* Author of numerous articles to professional journals, chapters in books and to conferences. Books: Nursing the burned patient, 1973; Procedures for nursing the burned patient, 1975; Teaching basic burn care, 1975; Emergent care of the burn victim, 1977; Psycho-social aspects of a severe burn: a review of the literature, 1979. *Memberships:* National Committee on Burn Foundations, 1985-; Consultant, Burn Care Facilities in US, Management and Delivery of Care, 1969-; American Burn Association; Michigan Nurses Association; American Nurses Association; Association of Critical Care Nurses; International Society of Burn Injuries. *Honours:* Distinguished Service Award, Associate Membership, American Burn Association, 1978. *Address:* 914 Lincoln St, Ann Arbor, Michigan 48104, USA.

JONES Doris Moreland, b. 25 Mar. 1927, Mt Vernon, Illinois, USA. Director, Counseling Center Meth Hospital. m. Harry Wilmont Jones, 22 Mar. 1945. 1 son, 1 daughter. *Education:* BA, KY Wesleyan, 1966; MDiv, Meth Theol School, Ohio, 1969; STM, Christian Theol Seminary, 1971. *Appointments:* Pastor, Churches in Louisville & Ohio Confs, 1961-69; Director, Buchanan Counseling Center, 1969-76; Dir, Bd Hg Ed & Min, 1976-80; Director, Counseling Center, 1980-. *Publications:* Books: Co-Author, New Witnesses: UM Clergywomen; Clergywomen Problems & Satisfactions. Editor Guidebook: Interviewing, Psych Testing & Pastoral Evaluation. *Memberships:* Diplomate, Am Assoc Pastoral Counselors; Fellow, College of Chaplains; Clinical Member, Am Assoc of Marriage & Family Therapists; Clinical Pastoral Education; Society for Pastoral Theology. *Honours:* Awarded Dr of Divinity, KY Wesleyan College, 1981; Graduate, magna cum laude, Christian Theol Seminary, 1971; International Society of Theta Phi, 1971; Keynote Speaker, 2nd Quad Clergywomens Conference, 1979. *Hobbies:* Writing; Travelling; Gourmet cooking; Rug hooking; Pets; Humour. *Address:* Counseling Center Meth Evang Hospital, 227 Medical Towers South, 234 E Gray St, Louisville, KY 40202, USA.

JONES Elizabeth R, b. 14 Oct. 1942, Atlanta, Georgia, USA. Nutritionist. m. Donald Lee Jones, 21 Feb. 1987, 1 son. *Education:* BA, Psychology, 1965. *Appointments:* Intake Screening, Public Mental Health Centers, 1965-75; Developed Nutrition Counselling Services, 1975-83; Director, Nutrition, Pacific West Sports & Racquet Clubs, Puget Sound Area, 1983-86; Founder, Owner, Nutrition Education Services, Seattle, Washington, 1985- , Austin, Texas, 1987. *Publications:* What is Good Nutrition. *Memberships:* International Academy of Nutrition & Preventive Medicine; Well Mind Association. *Hobbies:* Skiing; Tennis; Reading; Writing; Gardening. *Address:* 11006 D-K Ranch Road, Austin, TX 78759, USA.

JONES Gwyneth, b. 7 Nov. 1936, Pontnewynydd, Wales. Soprano. m. Till Haberfeld, 1 daughter.

Education: Royal College of Music, London; Accademy Chigiana, Sienza, Zurich International Opera Centre. *Appointments:* With Zurich Opera House, 1962-63; Royal Opera House, Covent Garden, 1963-; Vienna State Opera House, 1966-; Guest Performances in numeorus opera houses throughout the world including: La Scala, Milan; Rome Opera; Berlin State Opera; Munich State Opera; MET New York, San Francisco; Paris Opéra. *Address:* PO Box 556, CH 8037 Zurich, Switzerland.

JONES Jacqueline Antoinette, b. 24 Sep. 1948, Knoxville, Tennessee, USA. Radio Producer. *Education:* BA, Political Science, 1980, BA, Psychology, 1981, University of Tennessee. *Appointments:* Radio Producer, WUOT-FM, University of Tennessee Department of Radio Services, Knoxville, 1984-. *Creative works:* Producer/engineer/host, public and community affairs programmes for WUOT-FM. *Memberships:* Founder, President, Black Professional Women's Support Group, 1985-88; Continuing Education Black Staff Advisory Council, University of Tennessee Institute for Public Service; Knoxville Women's Center (Board Member 1984-85). *Honours:* Outstanding Leadership Award, Central Programme Council, University of Tennessee, 1982-83; Outstanding Young Woman of America, 1985. *Hobbies:* Films; Book collecting; History; Metaphysics; Cats. *Address:* Department of Radio Services, 232 Communications Building, Knoxville, TN 37996, USA.

JONES Jeannie Cromeans, b. 19 Jan. 1949, Arkansas, USA. Co- Founder/Co-Owner, DeSoto County Tribune & Publishing Co. m. Douglas Wendell Jones, 7 May 1971, 1 son, 1 daughter (deceased). *Appointments:* Commercial Artist, Bradfield Printing Co.; Branch Smith Publishing co.; Founder, Owner, DeSoto County Tribune & Publishing Co. Inc., & Home Market Magazine, Vice President, Freelance Writer & Photographer. *Publications:* various features in Newspapers. *Memberships:* Olive Branch Jaycettes; Mississippi Press Association; Greenpeace; Humane Socities. *Honours:* Recipient, various honours and awards presented to DeSoto Co. Tribune. *Hobbies:* Herbology; Yoga; Metaphysics; Reading. *Address:* 8141 Hunters Hill Cove, Olive Branch, MS 38654, USA.

JONES Katherine Elizabeth, b. 19 Mar. 1936, New York, New York, USA. Education Consultant. m. Hubert Jones, 7 Dec. 1957. 2 sons, 6 daughters. *Education:* BA, Mt Holyore College, 1957; MS, Simmons College, 1967; EdD, Harvard University, 1980. *Appointments:* Teacher, Boston Public Schools, 1958-59; Coordinator, Newton Public Schools, 1966-73; Instructor, Simmons College, 1067-G9, Instructor, Wheelock College, 1976-77; Supervisor, Cambridge Public Schools, 1978-81; Adjunct Professor, Roxbury Community College, 1986-. *Publication:* Dissertation: School Consolidation in Newton, 1980. *Memberships:* Board of Directors Metco, 1966-74; Board of Trustees Mt Holyoke, 1973-78; Minority Affairs Comm, National Association of Independent Schools, 1984-88; Board of Directors, Family Service Association, 1976-; Board of Directors, Boston Childrens Services, 1984-; Newton School Committee, 1979-86 (Fist Black person elected to this City wide office). *Honours:* Scholarship, Katherine E Jones, awarded to Black student of Newton Public Schools by Black Citizens of Newton, 1976; Service to Metco Awarded by City of Newton, 1976; Contribution to Integrated Education, Boston Metco Staff, 1976; Appreciation Award, Boston Metco Parents, 1976; Service Above Self, Newton Chamber of Commerce, 1974; Citizens Who Make A Difference, Mass. Association of Mental Health, 1982; Newton Metco Program Award, Vision Commitment, 1987; African Meeting House, 350 Black contributors to black community of Massachusetts, 1988. *Hobbies:* Swimming; Tennis; Reading; Theatre. *Address:* 1087 Commonwealth Avenue, Newton, Massachusetts, USA.

JONES Mary Della, b. 2 June 1949, Clarksville, USA. Accountant. m. James D. West, 31 Dec. 1981, 1 daughter (deceased). *Education:* BA, University of Pittsburgh, 1989; AS, Coommunity College of Allegheny

College, 1990. *Appointments:* Sales Clerk, Sears Roebuck & Co., 1967; File Clerk, Blue Cross/Blue Shield, 1967-68; Recruiter, Bookkeeper, Bidwell Training Centre, 1968-69; Receptionist, Homewood Brushton Health Center, 1969-70; Accountant, Volkswagen of America, Inc., 1978-88; St. Accounting Clerk, University of Pittsburgh, 1971-78. *Memberships:* Past President: Phi Chi Theta, National Associatiron of Business & Professional Womens Clubs Inc; Pittsburgh Young Adult Chapter; NAFE. *Honours:* Homewood-Brushton Community Service Award; Young Adult Club Award, 1979; Letter of Commendation for Academic Achievement, 1985, 1987, 1988; College Board Talent Roster, 1988. *Hobbies:* Singing; Sewing; Reading; Sports; Cooking. *Address:* 104 Old Farm Drive, Pittsburgh, PA 15239, USA.

JONES Mary Elizabeth, b. 31 Oct. 1942, Aberystwyth, Wales. Lecturer. *Education:* BA, 1966, MA 1969, Sheffied University. *Appointments:* Lecturer, English, New University of Ulster, Coleraine, Northern Ireland, 1969-. *Publication:* Resistance, 1985. *Honours:* Welsh Arts Council Fiction Prize, 1986. *Address:* English Dept, University of Ulster, Coleraine, Northern Ireland.

JONES Mary Louise Jordan, b. 10 May 1916, Fredericksburg, USA. Writer; Painter; University Lecturer, Retired. m. Charles Ingram Jones, 16 Aug. 1941. *Education:* BA, Texas Womens University, 1939; MA, Columbia University, 1946; PhD, Sorbonne and Exp. Colleges & Universities, 1983; University of Oxford, External Studies, 1987. *Appointments:* Principal, Aransas Pass, Texas, 1937-39; Adult Education Art, 1939-45; Adult Education, Baytown, 1946-51; Adult Art Education, Baytown, 1970-75; Professor, Art History University of Maryland, 1975-86. *Publications:* Five History of Art Books for Children; Woody Watches the Masters; Exhibitor of Paintings; Lecturer. *Memberships:* President, Baytown Art League, 1971-72; Lee College Foundaiton; Amis de Louvre; Board, Trustees Texas Fine Arts Association; Life member, Delta Kappa Gamma. *Honours:* Scholarship to Sorbonne for Doctoral Study, 1968; Award for Oil Painting, Clouds; many other honours & awards. *Hobbies:* Swimming; Golf; Bridge; Travel. *Address:* Baytown, Texas, USA.

JONES Mildred Josephine, b. 29 Jan. 1927, Calhoun County, Alabama, US. Realtor. *Education:* Howard College, Birmingham, Alabama. *Appointments:* Retail & secretarial positions, 1948-65; Area, then district manager, Field Enterprises Educational Corporation, 1965-71; Founder, owner, Southland Realty, Montgomery, Alabama, current. *Memberships:* National Association of Realtors; Farm & Land Institute; Montgomery Board of Realtors; Trinity Presbyterian Church; Alpine Bay Country Club. *Honours:* Numerous sales awards, Field Enterprises Educational Corporation, 1965-71. *Hobbies:* Gardening; Hiking; Crafts; Travel. *Address:* 3024 Biltmore Avenue, Montgomery, Alabama 36109, USA.

JONES Thelma, b. 8 Nov. 1937, New York City, USA. Physician. m. Josua Sack, 19 Nov. 1967, 2 daughters. *Education:* BA cum laude, Barnard College, 1959; MD cum laude, Downstate Medical Centre, State University of New York, 1963. *Appointments:* Intern, Jewish Hospital, Brooklyn, 1963-64; Resident, Montefiore Medical Centre, Bronx, NY, 1964-67; Chief, Haematology Section, & Attending Physician, Medicine & Haematology, White Plains Hospital, NY, 1982-. Also: Associate Attending Physician, Montefiore Hospital; Assistant Attending Physician, Internal Medicine, St Agnes Hospital, White Plains, NY. *Memberships:* Past President, Central Westchester, American Cancer Society; Fellow, American College of Physicians; NY State & American Societies of Internal Medicine; American Medical Association; American Medical Women's Association; NY State Medical Society; NY Academy of Medicine; Westchester County Medical Society. *Address:* 105 Garth Road, Scarsdale, New York 10583, USA.

JONES Yvonne Harris, b. 15 Sept. Florida, USA. Assistant Vice President, Employee Relations. m. Alan C Jones, 4 May 1988. *Education:* BA, CCNY, 1970; MA, New School for Social Research, 1976. *Appointments:* Training Specialist, NY Life Ins Co, 1968-72; Snr Training Specialist, Federal Reserve Bank of NY, 1972-76; Assistant Vice President, American Stock Exchange, 1982-. *Memberships:* NANBPW, NY Club; Coalition of 100 Black Women; Zeta Delta Phi Sorority Inc (President, 1970-76); Board of Directors, United Neighborhood Houses and Battery Dance Company. *Honours:* Black Achievers in Industry, 1979; NANBPW Corporate Award, 1985; Urban League Black Executive Exchange Program, 1976; Friend of Murray Bergtraum H S, 1980; Committee on Minority Affairs Award, 1986. *Hobbies:* Jogging; Tennis; Harlem YMCA Mentor Program. *Address:* 29 Winthrop Drive, Peekskill, NY 10566, USA.

JONES-DEMARR E. Yvonne, b. 23 Aug. 1923, Dayton, Ohio, USA. Retired Teacher; Consultant; Lecturer; Historian; Community Activist. m. W. L. Jones div, 3 daughters. *Education:* BA 1947, MA 1954, Hunter College, New York City. *Appointments:* Community Organisation Secretary, White Plains Urban League, 1947-50; Psychiatric group worker, Blythedale Children's Hospital, 1950-54; Teacher, Union Free School District 9, 1954-84. *Creative work includes:* Curriculum guide, black history; Organised, directed & produced annual black history performing arts, written by students; Articles published, various educational bulletins. *Memberships include:* President: Local branches, National Association for Advancement of Coloured Peoples, Association for Study of Afro-American Life & History; Chair, Elmsford-Greenburgh Community Action Programme; National Council of Negro Women; Westchester Women's Support Network; Board, Westchester Coalition; Executive, Westchester Community Opportunity Programme. *Honours include:* Awards & Recognitions from: Operation PUSH, Westchester; Westchester Club, National Association of Business & Professional Women; Westchester Black Women's Caucus; Key Women of Westchester; NAAC Prisoners of Woodbourne Correctional Facility. *Hobbies:* Swimming; Sewing; Reading; Historical Research. *Address:* 118 North Evarts Avenue, Elmsford, New York 10523, USA.

JOOS Irene R Makar, b. 18 Oct. 1945, Pittsburgh, Pennsylvania, USA. Faculty. m. 18 Nov. 1967. 1 son. *Education:* Diploma, Shadyside Hospital School of Nursing, 1966; BSN, Pennsylvania State University, 1970; MN 1974, PhD 1981, MIS 1988, University of Pittsburgh. *Appointments:* Staff Nurse 1966-70, Instructor 1970-72, Shadyside Hospital School of Nursing; Faculty, University of Pittsburg, 1974-. *Publications:* Man, Health, Nursing: Basic Concepts & Theories, with Nelson & Lyness; Foundations of Nursing Teacher's Manual; Use of game and simulations in teaching; Numerous artibles in professional journals. *Memberships:* Board Member, North American Simulation & Gaming Association; National League for Nursing/PA Leagter Nursing Pennsylvania state Alumni Association; Assoc for Development of Computer based Instructional Systems, ADCIS. *Honours:* Outstanding Junior Award, 1969; Sigma Theta Tau, National Nursing Honor Society, 1974. *Hobbies:* Reading; Computers; Games/Simulations; Ukranian Egg Painting; Walking; Travelling. *Address:* 5997 Irishtown Road, Bethel Park, PA 15102, USA.

JORDAN Alma Theodora, b. 29 Dec. 1929, Tunapuna, Trinidad, Trinidad and Tobago. University Librarian. m. Lennox Jordan, 20 Oct. 1962. *Education:* BA(Hons), London, 1951; ALA, 1955; ARCM, 1957; MS, 1958, DLS, 1966, Columbia University, USA. *Appointments:* Regional Librarian, Central Library of Trinidad and Tobago, and Librarian in Charge, Carnegie Free Library, San Fernando, Trinidad, 1955-56; Librarian, Industrial Development Corporation, 1959-60; Campus Librarian, University Librarian, The University of the West Indies, St Augustine, Trinidad, 1960-. *Publications:* The development of library service in the West Indies through inter-library cooperation,

1970; The English-speaking Caribbean: a bibliography of bibliographies, 1984. *Memberships:* Past President, Library Association of Trinidad and Tobago; Past President, ACURIL; Past President, SALALM; Library Association, Great Britain; American Library Association. *Honours:* Grolier Society Fellow, Columbia University, 1957-58; Beta Phi Mu, 1958; ACURIL IV Dedicatory Honour, 1972. *Hobbies:* Music; Gardening. *Address:* 28 Gilwell Road, Valsayn Park, Trinidad, Trinidad and Tobago.

JORDAN Barbara Leslie, b. 30 Sept. 1915, New York, USA. Poet. m. John Yellott, 2 June 1951, 2 sons by previous marriage, 1 stepson, 1 stepdaughter. *Appointments:* City Editor for New York, 1933-34; Treasurer, John Yellott Engineering Associates Inc., 1958-86, Elected President, 1987. *Publication:* Web of Days, 1949; Comfort the Dreamer, 1955; Silver Song. *Memberships:* Poetry Society of America; National Society of Arts & Letters; Member, The Newcomen Society of the U.S., 1987-. *Honours:* Bronze Medal, 1987; 3 Critics Awards, New York Women Poets. *Address:* 901 West El Caminito Drive, Phoenix, AZ 85021, USA.

JORDAN Deirdre Frances, b. 18 Sept. 1926, Loxton, South Australia. Chancellor, The Flinders University of South Australia. *Education:* BA 1946, DipEd 1948, MEd 1968, Adelaide; MA 1975, PhD 1983, London. *Appointments:* Teacher 1947-53, Principal 1954-63, St Aloysius College; Senior Lecturer, University of Adelaide, 1968-88; Chancellor, The Flinders University of South Australia, 1988-. *Memberships:* International Sociological Association; Australian College of Education. *Honours:* Fellow, Australian College of Education, 1968; MBE, 1969; AC (Companion of Australia), 1989; Zonta Woman of the Year, 1989; DLitt (Flinders University), 1986. *Hobbies:* Reading; Bush walking; Camping. *Address:* 23 Victoria Street, Prospect, South Australia 5082, Australia.

JORDAN Judith V, b. 28 July 1943, USA. Clinical Psychologist; Educator. m. William Redpath, 11 Aug. 1973. *Education:* BA, Brown University, 1965; MA, 1968, PhD, 1974, Harvard University. *Appointments:* Psychologist, McLean Hospital, 1973-; Instructor, Harvard Medical School, 1973-; Visiting Scholar, Wellesley College, 1984-; Director, Women's Studies Programme, Mclean Hospital, 1988-. *Publications:* Contributor to: Work in Progress; Change & Continuity in Infancy; Presentations. *Memberships:* Phi Beta Kappa; American, Massachusetts Psychological Associations; Diplomate, Clinical Psychology, American Board of Professional Psychology; *Honours:* Magna cum Laude, Phi Beta Kappa, Brown University; Elisha Benjamin Andrews Scholar, Brown University. *Hobbies:* Reading; Travel; Eastern Philosophy. *Address:* Psychology Dept., McLean Hospital, 115 Mill St., Belmont, MA 02178, USA.

JORDAN June, b. 9 July 1936, USA. Poet; Essayist; Dramatist; Professor of English. m. 5 Aug. 1955, div. 1966, 1 son. *Education:* Barnard College, 1953-55, 1956-57; University of Chicago, 1955-56. *Appointments include:* English Faculties, Connecticut College 1968, Yale University 1974-75, Sarah Lawrence College 1971-75, City College of New York 1967-70, 1972-75, 1977-78; Associate Professor of English 1978-82, Professor 1982-, Director, Poetry Centre & Creative Writing Programme 1986-, State University of New York, Stony Brook. Also: Visiting Poet, Poet-in- Residence, Visiting Professor, various locations. *Publications:* Books including poems, essays: Who Look At Me, 1969; Things That I Do In The Dark, selected poems 1954-77, 1977, 1981; Passion, New Poems 1977-80, 1980; Civil Wars, Selected Essays 1963-80, 1981; Kimalo's Story, 1981. Also: Editor, co- editor, various books; Contributions, essays, reviews, criticism, poetry, numerous anthologies, journals, newspapers; Keynote speeches, poetry readings. *Memberships include:* Boards: Poets & Writers Inc; PEN American Centre 1980-84; American Writers Congress; Centre for Constitutional Rights; New York Foundation of the Arts. Member, various other organisatins. *Honours:* Numerous grants, fellowships; Judge, various prizes, poetry & creative writing; Achievement award, international reporting, National Association of Black Journalists, 1984. *Address:* Department of English, SUNY at Stony Brook, New York 11794, USA.

JORDAN Ruth, b. 19 June 1926, Haifa, Palestine (now Israel). Writer; Translator; Lecturer. m. N. J Kivity, 7 Feb. 1955, 1 son, 1 daughter. *Education:* Teacher's Diploma, training college, Jerusalem; BA, Arabic Language & Literature, Hebrew University, Jerusalem; BA Honours, French Language & Literature, Phonetics, University of London, UK. *Appointments:* Newsreader, drama producer, documentary writer, BBC External Services, 1950-68; Voluntary tutor, adult literacy, 1964-72; London correspondent, Yediot Ahronot (Tel-Aviv daily), 1968-84; Lecturer, Spire Institute, London, 1986-. *Publications include:* Biographies (UK & USA): Sophie Dorothea (also radio adaptation); Berenice; George Sand (also German translation); Nocture: Life of Chopin (also cassettes, Australia); Daughter of the Waves (autobiography). Numerous radio features, TV adaptations, translations. *Memberships:* Society of Authors; Institute of Translation & Interpreting; Chelsea Harmonic Society; Association des Amis de George Sand, Paris. *Honours:* Present Tense Literary Award, USA; Certificate of Merit, Societe Frederic Chopin, Warsaw. *Hobbies:* Music; Theatre; English & Hebrew literature; Foreign travel. *Address:* 63 Peterborough Road, London SW6 3BT, England.

JORDAN-DELAURENTI Mary Agnes, b. 7 Dec. 1937, West Pittston, Pennsylvania, USA. Businesswoman. m. Robert DeLaurenti, 4 Oct. 1974, 1 daughter, 1 step-son, 2 step-daughters. *Education:* BA, Marywood College, 1964; PhD, Education, University of Notre Dame, 1970. *Appointments:* Project Administrator, General Motors Institute, Flint, Michigan, 1973-74; Manager, Management Education, Martin Marietta Aerospace, Orlando, Florida, 1974; Adjunct Professor, University of Michigan, 1973-77; Founder & President, Jordan-DeLaurenti Inc, 1975-. *Memberships include:* Co-Chair, North Texas Council on Small Businesses; Past President, National Association of Women Government Contractors; 1st woman, CEO Club, Dallas; Offices, Dallas Chamber of Commerce; Dallas Regional Chair, Steering Committee, Governor's Conference on Small Business, 1987; White House Conference on Small Business, 1986. *Honours:* Small Business Person of Year, Dallas Chamber of Commerce, 1989; Leadership Texas, 1988; Leadership America, 1989; Outstanding Educator of Year; Selected for inclusion, book Women, Naim Attallah, 1987. *Hobbies:* Reading; Writing; Music; Skiing. *Address:* 7800 Stemmons Freeway, Suite 300, Dallas, Texas 75247, USA.

JORDON Deborah Elizabeth, b. 24 June 1951, Pittsburgh, USA. General Attorney. *Education:* BA, Brown University, 1972; JD, Yale Law School, 1975. *Appointments:* Law Clerk, Presiding Justice, US District Court, 1975; Associate, Paul Weiss Rifkind Wharton & Garrison, New York City, 1977-79; Assistant to Mayor, New York City, 1979-82; Counsel to President, CCNY, 1982-84; Senior Attorney, 1984-87, Assistant General Attorney 1987-88, General Attorney 1988-, NBC. *Memberships:* Chairman, Board of Directors, Harlem legal Services corp, 1986-88; Board, Bennett College, 1985-; Board, Meropolitan Assistance Corp, 1986-; Bar Associations of Pennsylvania & New York. *Honours:* Special Awards NBC 3rd & 4th Quarters, 1987, 4th Quarter, 1988; Phi Beta Kappa; Harlem YMCA Achievers in Industry in America, 1988; Thomas Swan Barristers Union Board, Yale Law School. *Hobbies:* Photography; Sailing; Writing. *Address:* 200 West 79th Street, New York, NY 10024, USA.

JOSEPH Shirley T, b. 13 Dec. 1925, Buffalo, USA. Director, Women's Commission. m. Norman C. Joseph, 20 Oct. 1946, 3 sons. *Education:* BA, Political Science, University of Michigan, 1947. *Appointments:* Instructor, State University of New York, Buffalo, 1977; Area

Representtive, American Jewish Committee, 1980-82; public Policy Co-ordinator, Jewish Federation of Buffalo, 1984-87. *Memberships:* Delegate, US national Womens Conference, 1977; President, Jewish Federation Housing; Vice Chair, US National Commission, UNESCO. *Honours:* Hannah G. Solomon Woman of the Year, 1978; Distinguished Leadership & Community Service, United Jewish Federation of Buffalo, 1977. *Address:* Commission on the Status of Women, 95 Franklin Street, Buffalo, NY 14202, USA.

JOSHI Kumud, b. 31 Jan. 1934, Kathwada, Ahmedabad, India. Governor Andhra Pradesh. *Appointments:* Member, Parliament, Rajya Sabna 1973-85, Deputy Minister for Information & Broadcasting, Deputy Minister for Health & Family Welfare until 1984. *Memberships:* General Secretary, State Congress Committee, Gujarat, 1972-78; Govenor, Gujarat Pradesh Congress Committee, 1974-75. *Address:* Raj Bhavan, Hyderabad 500 041, India.

JOWELL Kate, b. 9 Jan. 1940, Coventry, England. University Lecturer; Managemen Consultant. m. Neil Ian, 7 Oct. 1970, 2 daughters. *Education:* BSc., 1960, MBA, 1973, University of Cape Town. *Appointments:* Income Tax Assessor, Federal Government of Rhodesia & Nyasaland, 1956-57; Financial Journalist, London, 1961-63; Junior Lecturer, University of Cape Town, 1964; Editor, Assistant Editor, Fair Lady Magazine, 1964-72; Graduate School of Business, University of Cape Town, 1974-. *Publications:* Co-Editor, Milton Friedman in South Africa, 1976; Co- author, Cases in South African Business Management. *Memberships:* International Industrial Relations Association, Geneva; Cape Chamber of Industries, Labour Affairs Committee. *Honours:* Recipient, various honours & awards. *Hobbies:* Food; Canoeing. *Address:* Graduate School of Business, Private Bag, University of Cape Town, Rondebosch 7700, Republic of South Africa.

JOWITT Juliet Diana Margaret, b. 24 Aug. 1940, Leamington Spa, England. Interior Decorator. m. (Frederick) Thomas Benson Jowitt, 12 Oct. 1963. 1 son, 1 daughter. *Education:* Educated in Switzerland, Spain and London. *Appointments:* Assistant Shopping Editor, Conde Nast, 1966-69; Proprietor, Wood House Design, 1971-; Director, Yorkshire Television PLC, 1987; Director, Yorkshire Television Holdings Ltd., 1989. *Memberships:* Independent Broadcasting Authority, 1981-86; Domestic Coal Consumers Council, 1985-; Potato Marketing Board, 1986-; Interior Decorators and Designers Association; Justice of the Peace, North Yorkshire, 1973-. *Address:* Thorpe Lodge, Ripon, North Yorkshire, England.

JOYCE Sheila M., b. 31 May 1953, Chicago, Illinois, USA. Partner in Executive Search Practice. m. James Franklin Verkamp, 29 Apr. 1979. *Education:* PhB, Human Resources Management, Northwestern University, 1976. *Appointments:* Avon, 1972-76; Supervisor of Employee Services, Johnson & Johnson, 1976-80; Senior Personnel Administrator, Verkamp-Joyce Associates, 1980-, Founder, Partner. *Memberships:* President, National Association of Women Business Owners, Chicago; Director, Oak Brook Association of Commerce and Industry; Executive Committee, President's Advisory Council for Illinois Benedictine College. *Honour:* Newswriter of the Year, 1976. *Hobbies:* Travel; Swimming; Investing. *Address:* Two Mid America Plaza, PO Box 1500, Oak Brook, IL 60522, USA.

JUDD Linda Marie, b. 30 Oct. 1939, Morrison, Oklahoma, USA. Lawyer. m. James F. Judd, 4 July 1970, 1 son. *Education:* Honours programme, Oklahoma State University, 1962-64; BA 1968, JD 1970, University of Idaho. *Appointments:* Partner, Judd & Judd, Post Falls, Idaho, 1970-81; Principal, Judd & Judd PA, 1981-87; Principal, Judd Law Firm PA, 1987-. *Creative work:* Contributor, Idaho Appellate Handbook, 1985; Drafting committees, Uniform State Laws: Uniform Notarial Act 1978-83, Uniform Marital Property Act 1979-83, Power

of Attorney Statutory Form Act 1985-88. *Memberships:* American, & Idaho State Bar Associations; Uniform State Laws Commission; Past Governing Board, Idaho Trial Lawyers Association; Past Governing Board, Kootenai County League of Women Voters; Past president, Post Falls Chamber of Commerce; Trustee, Post Falls Library. *Honours:* Phi Beta Kappa, Phi Kappa Phi, 1968; Commendation, International Academy of Trial Lawyers, 1970. *Address:* Post Falls, Idaho, USA.

JUDELSON Debra Ruth, b. 3 Oct. 1951, New York, USA. Physician; Cardiologist; Internist. m. A J Willmer, 15 May 1983. 2 daughters. *Education:* SB Metallurgy & Materials Science Engineering, MIT, 1969- 73; MD, Harvard Medical School, 1972-76; Harvard-MIT Joint Programme in Health Sciences & Technology, 1972-76; Residency, internal medicine, 1976-79; Cardiology Fellowship, 1979-81. *Appointments:* Cardiologist & internal medicine, Cardiovascular Medical Group of Southern California, 1981-. *Publications:* Editor, 3rd edition, 1986 and 4th edition 1989, Los Angeles County Medical Womens Association Directory of Women Physicians. *Memberships:* Los Angeles County Medical Womens Association, President 1987-; American Medical Womens Association, Chairman, Medical Ethics Committee, 1987-; American Medical Association, Los Angeles County Medical Association Chairman, Legislative Comm, Beverly Hills District; Fellow, American College of Cardiology; Fellow, American College of Chest Physicians. *Honours:* Morris Cohen Award, Outstanding Student in Metallurgy, Massachusetts Institute of Technology, 1972; Certificate of Appreciation, Los Angeles County Commission on Women, 1988; Chief of Staff, Westside Hospital, Los Angeles, 1988 and 1989. *Hobbies:* Computers; Piano; Accordion. *Address:* 414 North Camden Drive, Suite 800, Beverly Hills, California 90210, USA.

JUMONVILLE Susan Lynn, b. 12 May 1965, Encino, California, USA. Student; Legal Secretary (part-time); Ice Skating Champion. *Education:* California State University, Sacramento, 1985-86; CSU Northridge, 1983-85, 1986-. *Appointments:* Salesperson, 1984-87; Legal Secretary, Abrams Law Corportion, 1987-. *Memberships:* Ice Skating Institute of America; US Figure Skating Association. *Honours:* Gifted programme, Los Angeles School District, 1971-83; High school graduate as Silver Seal Bearer, 1983; Most Artistic Performer, Sierra-Nevada Ice Championships, 1982; Member, USFSA Ice Angels Drill Team, 1981-83; 19 trophies, 35 medals, competitive Ice Skating, 1976-83; Achievement award, poetry, 1980; 3rd runner-up, Miss Northridge Beauty Pageant, 1984; High School Homecoming Princess, 1983. *Hobbies:* Ice skating; Snow skiing; Dancing; Music; Travel. *Address:* 18427 Vincennes, no. 36, Northridge, California 91325, USA.

JUNKER Christine Rosetta, b. 6 Oct. 1953, Burlington, Iowa, USA. Swine Management Specialist. m. 3 Oct. 1977, 1 daughter. *Education:* AA, Animal Science, Hawkeye Institute of Technology, 1977; University of Iowa, 1984-86. *Appointments:* Designer, Confinement Specialist, 1973- 75; Herdsman, XL Pork, 1976-77; Livestock Specialist, Tasco Inc, 1977-81; Problem Accounting Specialist, IFG Leasing, 1981-86; President, owner, Pork Purveyors Ltd, 1986-88; General Manager, Pork Purveying Division, Doane Farm Management (merged company), 1988-89, (December 1989 company taken back to full ownership as Pork Purveyors Ltd); Produced Christian Children's Album, On Our Way to Hallelujah Station, wrote 5 of the songs. *Publications:* Several magazine articles, National Hog Farmer, Agri Business. *Memberships:* Parkersburg Chamber of Commerce; Pork Producers Association; Wool Growers Association; Mediator, Iowa Farmers Creditor Mediation Service; Hawkeye Institute Agricultural Advisory Committee. *Honours:* Outstanding 4-Her 1971, Outstanding Alumni 1979, Hawkeye; Featured, various magazines. *Hobbies:* Cross-stitch; Volleyball; Singing. *Address:* RR 2, Box 100, Parkersburg, Iowa 50665, USA.

JURICH Julie Ann, b. 18 June 1946, Toledo, Ohio, USA. Marriage and Family Therapist. m. 18 June 1971, div. 29 Dec. 1979. *Education:* BS cum laude, distinction in Home Economics, Ohio State University, 1968; MS, 1970, MEd, 1970, Pennsylvania State University; PhD, Kansas State University, 1978. *Appointments:* Family Therapist, Social Work Service, 1974-87; Family Therapist, Operation Bridge, 1987-88; Family Therapist, The Hudson Center, Omaha, Nebraska, 1988-. *Publications:* Articles in the area of self-concept, nonverbal expressions of anxiety, cognitive moral development, lost adolescence, variables related to therapy dropouts. *Memberships:* Approved Supervisor, American Association for Marital and Family Therapy; Board of Directors, Treasurer, Kansas Association for Marital and Family Therapy; Certified Supervisor, AASECT; American Psychology Association; AACD; Society of Pediatric Psychology. *Honours:* 4 undergraduate scholarships, Ohio State University, 1964-68; Title V(C) Fellowship, Pennsylvania State University, 1968-70; Exceptional Performance Awards, Community Mental Health Activity, 1975, 1980, 1983. *Hobbies:* Running; Tennis; Weightlifting; Skiing; Gardening; Cooking. *Address:* 2125 North 125 Circle, Omaha, NE 68164, USA.

JUTHANI Nalini V, b. 26 Jan. 1946, India. Physician; Psychiatrist. m. Virendra, 29 Mar. 1970, 1 son, 2 daughters. *Education:* MBBS, 1971; Certified: American Board of Psychiatry & Neurology, 1980, Committee of Administrative Psychiatrists, 1983. *Appointments:* Attending Psychiatrist, Broak Lebanon Hospital, 1978-79; Director, Residency Training, Psychiatry, Bronx Lebanon Hospital, 1979-; Assistant Professor, Psychiatry, Albert Einstein College of Medicine. *Memberships:* Fellow, American Psychiatric Association; APA; AADPRT; Examiner, ABPN. *Honours:* Recipient, various honours & awards. *Address:* 17 Pheasant Run, Scarsdale, NY 10583, USA.

K

KACLIK Debi Louise, b. 15 May 1953, Pittsburg, USA. Chief Executive Officer. *Education:* BA, West Liberty State College, 1975. *Appointments:* Programme Director, YMCA, Pittsburgh, 1975-78; Regional Supervisor, URLIC, 1977-80; Physical Therapy Assistant, Verlund Foundation, 1980-81; Estimator, PPS Enterprises Inc., 1981-83; Manager, Wild Sisters Restaurant Inc., 1983-84; VP & Project Manager, Kreisle Masonry, 1984-85; Partner, Construction Manager, Mastco Inc., 1986-88; CEO/President, Brick People Inc., 1988-. *Publications:* Presenter, News Special, KDKA TV, 1977; Guest Speaker: WTAE TV, 1978, WBTW TV 1987. *Memberships:* American Red Cross; Board, North American Riding for the Handicapped; March of Dimes; American Subcontractors Association. *Honours:* Most Outstanding Senior Athlete, 1971. *Hobbies:* Sailing Running; Reading; Photography; Camping. *Address:* 28 Bay Drive, Salters Cove, Garden City, SC 29576, USA.

KADER Nancy Stowe, b. 29 May 1945, Ogden, Utah, USA. Registered Nurse; Management Consulting. m. Omar Kader, 25 Jan. 1967. 4 sons. *Education:* BSc Nursing, Brigham Young University, 1967. *Appointments:* Critical Care Nursing: Utah Valley Hospital, Provo, Utah: LDS Hospital, Salt Lake City; Glendale Adventist Hospital, Glendale, California; US Army Hospital, Wiluzburg, Germany, 1967-84; Government Consulting, MESA Corporation, 1984-85; Health Management Strategies Utilization Management, 1985-88. *Memberships:* Vice President, 1976-80, Governor's Commission on the Status of Women, State of Utah; Vice President, 1977-83, Utah Women's Legislative Council; American Nurses Association; Vice Chair, 1979-83, Utah State Board of Nursing. *Political Activities:* Chair of Utah County Democratic Party, 1977-81; Campaign Manager, Gubernatorial Candidate, 1976; Campaign Manager, Senatorial Candidate, 1980; National Delegate to Democratic Convention, represented Utah, 1980; Virginia State Delegate, 1984-88. *Address:* 11401 Tanbark Drive, Reston, Virginia 22091, USA.

KAEL Pauline, b. 19 June 1919, Sonoma County, California, USA. Film Critic. *Education:* University of Berkeley, California, 1936-40. *Appointment:* Film Critic, New Yorker Magazine. *Publications:* I Lost it at the Movies, 1965; Kiss Kiss Bang Bang, 1968; Going Steady, 1970; Raising Kane, in The Citizen Kane Book, 1971; Deeper into Movies, 1973; Reeling, 1976; When the Lights Go Down, 1980; 50001 Nights at the Movies, 1982; Taking It All In, 1984; State of the Art, 1985; articles in numerous magazines & newspapers. *Honours Include:* Guggenheim Fellow, 1964; George Polk Memorial Award for Criticism, 1970; National Book Award, 1974; Front Page Awards, Newswomen's Club of New York, 1974, 1983. *Address:* c/o The New Yorker, 25 West 43rd Street, New York, NY 10036, USA.

KAHLOW Barbara Fenvessy, b. 26 June 1946, Chicago, Illinois, USA. Statistician, US Government. m. Ronald Arthur Kahlow, 28 Sept. 1985. *Education:* BA, Vassar College, 1968; Professional Statistician, US Public Health Service, 1969. *Appointments:* Dept. of HEW/National Centers for Educational & Health Statistics, US Government, 1968-72; Office of Management & Budget, US Government, 1972- , Chief of Grants Management, 1982-. *Publications:* Motor Vehicle Accident Deaths in the United States: 1950-67; various articles in professional journals. *Memberships:* American Statistical Association; various community & charity organizations. *Honours:* New York State Regents Scholarship; Quality Award, US Government, Dept. of HEW, 1971; Special Performance Award, US Government, Office of Management & Budget, 1982. *Hobbies:* Sports; Travel; Church Outreach Activities; etc. *Address:* 2555 Pennsylvania Avenue, NW 404, Washington, DC 20037, USA.

KAIL Martha Alice, b. 12 Feb. 1937, Spiro, Oklahoma, USA. Nurse- Radiological. m. Norman H. Kail, 29 Aug. 1962. *Education:* Diploma, Sparks Hospital School of Nursing, Fort Smith, 1955-58; BS, Psychology, Emmanuel College, Boston, 1978; MSN, Anna Marie College, Paxton, 1987. *Appointments:* Staff Nurse, OR-Ochsner Foundation, New Orleans, 1958-60; OR Presbyterian Hospital, San Francisco, 1960, OR Harbor General, Torrance, 1960-61; Supervisor, Sparks Hospital, 1961-62; Head Nurse, Peter Bent Brigham Hospital, Boston, 1962; Staff Nurse, US Naval Hospital, 1962-65; Head Nurse, Radiology, Massachusetts General Hospital, 1971. *Publications:* Author, Chapter, Interventional Radiology & Abdomen, 1981, 1984; papers presented. *Memberships:* Co-Founder, American Radiological Nurses Association, President Elect, 1981-83, President, 1983-84, Founded New England Chapter, 1982, President 1983-84, Nominating Chairman, 1984-85; Editor, ARNA Images, 1985-87. *Address:* Olde Gordon Road, RFDI, Exeter, NH 03833, USA.

KAJTOCHOWA Anna, b. 21 July 1928, Brzozow, Poland. Journalist; Novelist; Poetess. m. Jacek Kajtoch, 1 Dec. 1951. 1 son, 1 daughter. *Education:* Studied journalism, Jagielloian University, 1948-51. *Appointments:* Journalist, Gazeta Krakowska, 1951-59, 1959-64; Spokesman for Youth Organizations in Cracow, 1964-72; Editor of monthly Gtos Mtodzieźg, 1972-82; Editor of bi-weekly, Student, 1982-85; Editor of weekly ''Te Mi'', 1985-retired. *Publications:* Sercem i mysla, collection of essays, 1959; Babcia, a novel, 1982; Sytuacje, collection of poems, 1983; Krawedz, collection of poems, 1986; Wiersze gorczanskie, anthology, 1987; Wsamym srodku zycia, anthology, 1986. *Memberships:* Polish Journalists Union, 1953-82; Polish People's Republic Journalists Association, 1983; Polish Literary Union, 1984; Literary group Nadskawie, 1981-88. *Honours:* Knight Cross of the Restoration of Poland Order, 1977; Silver Cross of Merit, 1957; 30th Anniversary of Polish People's Republic Medal, 1974; Janek Krasicki Silver Award, 1975; Gold Medal and Honorary Diploma, 30th Annivery of Polish Journalists Association, 1981; Gold Medal for over 30 years as a journalist, 1985. *Hobbies:* Literature and art, especially historical and psychological novels; Italian cinema (Fellini); Literary criticism. *Address:* ul Barska 10/5, 30-307 Krakow, Poland.

KALAYJIAN Anie Sanentz b. Syria, Armenia. Educator; Psychoanalytic Psychotherpaist. m. Shahe Navasart Sanentz, 16 Dec. 1984. *Education:* BS, Long Island University, 1979; RN, The University of the State of New York, 1979; EdM, Teachers College, Columbia University, New York (in mental health and Psychosocial Gerontology), 1981; EdD, Education in Mental Health and Psychotherapy, Columbia University, New York, 1985; Courses at The American Institute for Psychoanalysis and William Alanson White Institute Dream Interpretation Change Theory and Issues in Transference Countertransference, 1986-87; Photography, Pratt Institute, 1977-79. *Appointments:* Registered Professional Nurse, 1979-81; Part-time Registered Professional Nurse, 1981-; Manhattan Bowery Project Alcoholic Detoxification Programe; RN Psychiatric Pavillion, Metropolitan Hospital, NY, 1981-84; Instructor, Hunter College, NY, 1980-82; Lecturer, Jersey City State College, New Jersey, 1985; Assistant Professor, Bloomfield College, New Jersey, 1984-85; Assistant Professor, Teaching Graduate and Undergraduate Levels, Seton Hall University, New Jersey, 1985-87; Associate Professor, Graduate level, 1987-present; Private Practice, Psychotherapy, New Jersey 1984-, New York City, 1986-. *Creative works:* Photography: One Woman Exhibition, Salina Gallery, Long Island University, 1978; Exhibition, One World Festival, NYC, 1982. *Memberships include:* The American Orthopsychiatric Association; American Nurses Association; American Nurses Foundation; The Associates of the Training Institute for Mental Health Practitioners; The Association of University Professors; Council on Psychiatric and Mental Health Nursing; Council on Continuing Education; The Institute for Psychodynamics and Origins of Mind; NY State Nurses Association, District 13; Chairperson of Education

Committee New York State Nurses Association; Society for stress and traumatic studies; East-coast coordinator of the Mental Health Outreach to Soviet Armenia; Founder and President of the Armenian-American Society for Studies on the Genocide and other stresses. *Honours include:* Scholarship, Clark Foundation, 1985; Endowed Nursing Education Scholarship, 1984-85; Kappa Delta Pi, 1981; Sigma Theta Tau, Alpha Zeta Chapter, 1981; Fellow, American Orthopsychiatric Association, 1988. *Hobbies:* Acting; Travelling. *Address:* 130 West 79th Street, New York, NY 10024, USA.

KALECHOFSKY Roberta, b. 11 May 1931, Brooklyn, New York, USA. Writer and Publisher. m. Robert Kalechofsky, 7 June 1953, 2 sons. *Education:* BA, Brooklyn College, 1952; MA 1956, PhD 1970, New York University. *Appointments:* Instructor in English, School of General Studies, Brooklyn College, 1956-59, 1962-63; Contributing Editor to Feminist Journal on Medical Issues for Women, On The Issues; Publisher and General Editor of Micah Publications. *Publications:* Justice, My Brother, novel, 1972; George Orwell, monograph, 1973; Stephen's Passion, novella, 1975, reprinted 1984; Orestes in Progress, novel, 1976; La Hoya, novella, 1976; Solomon's Wisdom, collection of short stories, 1978; Rejected Essays and Other Matters, collection of essays, 1980; Haggadah For The Liberated Lamb: A haggadah for a vegetarian seder, 1985, Hebrew/English edition, 1988; The 6th Day of Creation: a philosophical poem, 1986; Bodmin, 1349: An Epic Novel of Christians and Jews in the Plague Years, 1988. *Memberships:* Authors' Guild; National Writers' Union; Committee of Small Press Editors and Publishers; Association of Jewish Publishers; Jews for Animal Rights, Founder and President. *Honours:* Literary Fellowship from the National Endowment for the Arts, 1982; Literary Fellowship from the Massachusetts Council on the Arts, 1988; Honorary Mention in Best American Short Stories. *Hobbies:* Physical activity - walking, aerobics. Writing and lecturing on the Animal Rights Movement and on vegetarianism. *Address:* 255 Humphrey Street, Marblehead, MA 01945, USA.

KALIN Heather Lee, b. 13 Nov. 1952, Detroit, Michigan, USA. Clinical Director; Head Nurse. *Education:* BS, Microbiology major, Arizona State University, 1974; ADN, Nursing Major, Scottsdale Community College, 1978. *Appointments:* Medical/ Surgical Nurse, Pulmonary Function/Respiratory Therapy Technician, then Nurse Clinican, Special Care Unit, Scottsdale Memorial Hospital, Scottsdale, Arizona; Clinical Director, Head Nurse, Scottsdale Memorial Hospital, 1983-. *Memberships:* American Association of Clinical Nurses; ARNA; AARC; NAFE; American Association of Business and Professional Women; Norsemans Federation (past Board of Directors); Sons of Norway (former Trustee). *Honours:* CNRN, 1981-86; CCRN, 1982-. *Hobbies:* Crafts; Skiing; Figure skating; Travel; Photography. *Address:* 8602 East Laredo Lane, Scottsdale, AZ 85253, USA.

KALLIR Jane Katherine, b. 30 July 1954, New York, USA. Art Dealer; Writer. m. Gary Cosimini, 25 Jan. 1985. *Education:* BA, Brown University, Providence, 1976. *Appointments:* Assistant to Director, Lefebre Gallery, New York, 1976; Galerie St Etienne, New York, 1977-79, Co- Director, 1979-. *Publications:* Gustav Klimt/ Egon Schiele, 1980; Austria's Expressionism, 1981; The Folk Art Tradition, 1981; Grandma Moses, 1982; Arnold Schoenberg's Vienna, 1984; Viennese Deisgn & The Weiner Werkstaette, 1986. *Membership:* Art Dealers' Association of America. *Honours:* Art Libraries Society Awards for Arnold Schoenberg's Vienne, 1985; The Folk Art Tradition, 1982. *Address:* Galerie St Etienne, 24 West 57th Street, New York, NY 10019, USA.

KAMM Josephine Mary, b. 30 dec. 1905, London, England. Writer. m. George Kamm, 4 Apr. 1929, 1 son. *Appointments:* Ministry of Information, London, 1939-45; Senior Information Officer, Central Office of Information, 1945-46. *Publications:* Including: How Different from Us, 1958; Out of Step, 1962; Hope Deferred, 1965; Young Mother, 1965; Rapiers and Battleaxes, 1966; Explorers into Africa, 1970; John Stuart Mill in Love, 1977; The Slave Trade, 1980. *Memberships:* Executive Committee, London Centre, International PEN, 1965-69; Committee of Management, Fawcett Library, 1967-75; National Book League. *Honours:* Isaac Siegel Memorial Juvenile Award, USA, 1963. *Hobbies:* Reading; Listening to Music. *Address:* Flat 39, 67 Elm Park Gardens, London SW10 9QE, England.

KAMM Judith Mary Brown, b. 19 Oct. 1948, Somerville, Massachusetts, USA. Associate Professor of Management. m. Roger D Kamm, 1 Sept. 1974. 1 son, 1 daughter. *Education:* BA, English Literature, Emmanuel College, Boston, MA, 1970; MA, English Literature, University of Colorado, 1971; DBA, Harvard University Graduate School of Business Administration, Boston, MA, 1980. *Appointments:* Research Associate, Harvard Business School, 1972-75; Casewriter, Simmons College Graduate Program in Management, 1975-76; Assistant Professor of Management 1979-88, Associate Professor of Management 1988-, Bentley College. *Memberships:* Academy of Management; Organizational Behavior Teaching Society; Wellesley College Center for Research on Women; North American Case Research Association; Eastern Casewriters' Association; Harvard Business School Association of Boston; US Association of Small Business and Entrepreneurship. *Honours:* Harvard Business School Division of Research Fellowship, 1978-79; Bentley College Publication Award 1983 and 1988. *Hobbies:* Gardening; Birdwatching; Tennis; Bridge; Children's theatre. *Address:* Bentley College, Graduate Center 320, 175 Forest Street, Waltham, MA 02154, USA.

KAMM Phyllis S, b. 12 July 1918, Philadelphia, USA. Journalist. m. Herbert Kamm, 6 Dec. 1936, 3 sons. *Education:* Cleveland (Ohio) College of Jewish Studies, 1983-84. *Appointments:* Legal Secretary, 1936-42; Special Assistant to C. O. von Kienbusch, Art Collector, 1962-65; Syndicated Freelance Journalist, Author, 1965-; Theatre & Book Critic, San Luis obispo Co. Telegram-Tribune; Co-author: About Mourning Support & Guidance for the Bereaved. *Address:* 147 River View Drive, Avila Beach, CA 93424-2307, USA.

KANE Julie Ellen, b. 20 July 1952, Boston, Massachusetts, USA. Technical Writing Consultant; Poet. m. Gerard Evans Wimberly, Jr, 29 Nov. 1975 (div. 1978). *Education:* BA, English, distinction all subjects, Cornell University, 1974; MA, Boston University, 1975. *Career:* Planning Department Director & programme writer, Baton Rouge Association for Community Action, 1976-78; Editorial Supervisor & technical writer, Exxon Nuclear Company, 1978-84; Technical writing consultant, 1984-; President, Red Fox Documentation Inc, 1987-. *Publications:* Poetry: Two Into One, 1982; Body & Soul, 1987. *Memberships:* Past officers, Cornell Club, New Orleans; Society for Technical Communication; Poets & Writers Inc; American Poetry Society. *Honours:* Participant Reader Award, Napa Valley Poetry Conference, 1983; George Bennett Fellowship, writing, Phillips Exeter Academy, New Hampshire, 1975-76; 1st prize, college poetry competition, Mademoiselle magazine, 1973; Graduate scholarship, Boston University, 1974-75. *Hobbies:* Writing poetry; Running; Palmistry; Cajun cooking; Bridge; Blues & New Orleans rhythm & blues music; Reading. *Address:* 7111 Walmsley Avenue, New Orleans, Louisiana 70125, USA.

KANELY Edna Agatha, b. 24 Sept. 1910, Baltimore, Maryland, USA. Library Administrator, retired. *Education:* Honour Student, High School Diploma, City College, Baltimore, 1933; BS, Business Management, magna cum laude, University of Baltimore, 1958; MS, Library Science, Catholic University Washington, 1975, all education obtained in night school and college at night, while working full-time during the day. *Appointments:* Checkgirl, sewing machine operator, Faultless Nightwear Corp., Baltimore, 1925-29; Typist, Assistant Supervisor, Statistical Clerk,. Instructor, Montgomery Ward & Co, Baltimore, 1929-41; Typist,

Stenographer, Supervisor, Assistant Chief of Section, 1951-65; Chief, Customers Service Section, 1965-69; Assigned to Library Section, 1969; Promoted to Library Administrator, 1970, retired 1973; US Government Printing Office, Washington DC 1941-73; Trained personnel at Inverness Branch, Scotland, Carrollton Press Inc, 1973-75. *Creative works:* Baltimore and Ohio Railroad Employees 1842 & 1852; 1855 & 1857, published in 1982; Cumulative Index to Hickcox's Monthly Catalogue of US Government Publications 1885-1894 (3 volumes), 1981; Cumulative Subject Index to the Monthly Catalogue of US Government Publications, 1895-1899 (2 volumes), 1977; Cumulative Subject Guide to US Government Bibliographies 1924-73 (compiled by Edna A Kanely), 1976 and 1977 (7 volumes); Cumulative Subject Index to the Monthly Catalogue of US Government Publications 1900-1971 (15 volumes) compiled by William W Buchanan and Edna A Kanely; Directory of Maryland Church Records, compiled and edited by Edna A Kanely, 1987; Many other articles published. *Memberships include:* National Geographic Society; American Library Association, AdHoc Subcommittee on Federal Depository Legislation, 1976-77; Maryland Library Association; Special Library Association; Genealogical Council of Maryland, Chair; Maryland Church Records Project, 1983-; Maryland Genealogical Society, Librarian, 1981-; Baltimore County Genealogical Society, Vice-Preisdent, 1983-84; Delaware Genealogical Society; Maryland Historical Society, Committee on Genealogy, Publications Committee. *Honours include:* Honour Student Graduate, City College, Baltimore, 1933; Citation, US Treasury Department for Co-operation on behalf of the Savings Bond Programme, 1946; BS in Business Management, Magna Cum Laude, University of Baltiimore, 1958; Performance Awards, US Government Printing Office, Washington, 1964, 1969, 1972; Outstanding Volunteer Award, Enoch Pratt Free Library, 1977; Award of Merit, Maryland Genealogical Society, 1982; Award, Federation of Genealogical Societies, 1988. *Hobbies:* Computer; Reading; Genealogical and Historical Research; Library Volunteer Work. *Address:* 3210 Chesterfield Avenue, Baltimore, MD 21213, USA.

KANG Bann Chung, b. 4 Mar. 1939, Kyung Nam, Korea. Professor; Medical Director. m. U Yun Ryo, 30 Mar. 1963. *Education:* MD, Kyungpook National University, 1959; Fellowships: University of Michigan Medical Centre, USA, 1972-73, Henry Ford Hospital, 1971-72, St Joseph Hospital, 1970-71; Residency, 1967-69, Intern, 1963-64, Kyungpook National University; Intern, Long Island Jewish Hospital, 1964-65. *Appointments:* Instructor, Clinical Medicine, University of Michigan, 1972-73; Assistant Professor, Chicago Medical School, 1973-74; Acting Chief, Allergy & Clinical Immunology, Mt Sinai Hospital, 1973-76; Assistant Professor, 1975-84, Associate Professor 1984-86, Rush Medical College; Chief, Allergy & Clinical Immunology, Mt Sinai Hospital, 1976-86; Associate Professor 1987-, Chief, Allergy & Clinical Immunology, 1987-, University of Kentucky, Lexington. *Publications:* Over 50 scientific articles and abstracts. *Memberships:* Institutional Review Board, Mt Sinai Hospital; Faculty Committee, Research, Rush Medical College; Committee on laboratory Animal Welfare, Mt Sinai Hospital; Experimental Organ Transplanation Advisory Board, State of Illinois; National Heart Lung and Blood Institute; American Federation of Clinical Research; American College of Physicians; American Medical Association; American Academy of Allergy; International Allergology Society; Illinois Society of Allergy, Secretary, Vice President, President. *Honours:* Fellow, American College of Physicians, 1977; American Academy of Allergology; Illinois Society of Allergy & Immunology; Fellowship Award, University of Michigan and National Cancer Institute, 1972; Rceipient, numerous other honours and awards. *Hobbies:* Tennis; Antique Celladon Collection. *Address:* Dept of Medicine, MN629, University of Kentucky, Medical Centre, 800 Rose Street, Lexington, KY 40536, USA.

KANG Kaffee, b. 2 June 1955, Keelung, Taiwan. Architect. m. Joseph McGill, 24 June 1978, 2 daughters. *Education:* BA magna cum laude, Harvard University, USA, 1975; MArch, University of Pennsylvania, 1978. *Appointments:* Turner Construction Company, 1977-78; Geddes Brecher Qualls Cunningham, 1978-79; Zimmer Gunsul Frasca, 1979-81; Shepley Bulfinch Richardson & Abbott, 1981-85; Associate Professor of Architecture, Wentworth Institute of Technology, 1985-; Principal, Kaffee Kang Architects, 1986-. *Creative works:* Buildings. *Memberships:* American Institute of Architects; Boston Society of Architects; Sudbury Design Review Board. *Honour:* Microtexture educational grant, AIAS, 1988. *Address:* 36 Austin Road, Sudbury, Massachusetts 01776, USA.

KANTARIS Sylvia, b. 9 Jan. 1936, Grindleford. Poet. m. Emmanuel Kantaris, 11 Jan. 1958. 1 son, 1 daughter. *Education:* BA (Hons) French, 1957, Cert Ed, 1958, Bristol University, England; MA 1967, PhD 1972, University of Queensland, Queensland, Australia. *Appointments:* School teacher, Bristol and London, England, 1958-61; Tutor in French, Queensland University, Australia, 1962-67; Tutor, Open University, 1974-84; Writer in the Community, Cornwall, England, 1986-. *Publications:* Collections of poetry: Time & Motion; The Tenth Muse; News from the Front (with D M Thomas); The Sea at the Door; The Airmines of Mistila (with Philip Gross); Dirty Washing: New and Selected. *Honours:* Numerous awards and prizes for poetry since 1967. *Hobby:* Poetry. Address: 14 Osborne Parc, Helston, Cornwall, TR13 8PB, England.

KANWISCHER Heidi Elfenbein, b. Santa Monica, California, USA. Concert Pianist; Teacher. m. Alfred Kanwischer, 24 July 1959. 1 daughter. *Education:* BA, University of California, Berkeley; Studied with Egon Petri, 8 years; Graduate Student, Bela Boszormenyi-Nagy, Boston University; Scholarship Award to Aspen Music Festival. *Career:* California Public Schools, 1954-62, Massachusetts Public Schools, 1962-67; Public Concerts: Lincoln Centre, New York; Jordan Hall, Boston; San Francisco; Florida; Concergebouw, The Hague; Salzburg; Sophiensaal, Munich; Wigmore Hall, London; National Theatre, Seoul, Korea; Banku Centre, Tokyo, Japan, 1967-86; Radio Broadcasts: WGBH-TV; Concerts throughout USA. *Recordings:* United Sound, Duo Piano Concert, Rachmaninoff, Liszt, 1975; Orion Records, Duo-Piano, Brahms, Debussy, Ravel, 1985, with Alfred Kanwischer. *Memberships:* New England Piano Teachers Association; California Teachers' Association, Southern California Representative; California Music Teachers Association; National Music Teachers Association; Co-Director, John Ringling Festival Concerts, Sarasota, Florida, 1972-76. *Honours:* Albert Kay Concert Artist Management, New York, 1970-; Recipient, various Scholarships. *Hobbies:* Performing Chamber Music; Reading; Editing Music Publications of Dr Kanwischer; World Wildlife Fund; Audubon Society. *Address:* Los Gatos, California, USA.

KANY Judy Casperson, b. 29 June 1937, Oak Park, Illinois, USA. Maine State Senator; Mayor. m. 16 Aug. 1958. 2 sons, 1 daughter. *Education:* BBA, Finance & Accounting, University of Michigan; MPA, Public Administration, University of Maine. *Appointments:* Investment Analysis, Carol National Bank, Portland, 1959-60; Accountant, H R B Surgin Inc, 1960-61; Maine State Representative, 1974-82; Main State Senate, 1983-; Mayor, City of Waterville, Maine, 1988-. *Address:* City Hall, Waterville, Maine 04901, USA.

KAPLAN Gisela T, b. 25 Aug. 1944, Federal Republic of Germany. Academic, Writer. 1 daughter. *Education:* BA, 1st Class Honours, 1974, DipEd, 1975, MA, 1978, PhD, 1984, Monash University, Melbourne-Clayton, Australia. *Appointments:* University Teacher 1976-; University Lecturer, 1983- (Monash University, Australian National University, University of New South Wales); Lecturer in Literature & Sociology, Research Fellow in Sociology; Leading Role for German in Victoria, 1975-84, Chairperson of Committees in Victorian Institute of Secondary Education, 1980-84; Convenor of Women's Affairs Committee, Ethnic Communities Council, Sydney, 1984-85. *Creative Works:* Editor (jointly) of a book called, Hannah Arendt : Thinking, Judgement, Freedom, Allen and Unwin, 1989; many chapters in sociological and feminist texts; poetry published widely in journals and anthologies including one book, Tightrope Dance, 1984. *Memberships:* Sociological Association of Australia & New Zealand, Executive Member, 1986-1988; Co-Convenor of the Women's Section, Editor of its Newsletter, 1986-88; Australian Language and Literature Association; Australian Poets Union; PEN Club International; Australian Society of Authors; elected co-editor of The Australian and New Zealand Journal of Sociology. *Honours:* Australian Commonwealth Study and Research Awards; International Prose Writing Award, IADM, 1977; Australian Poetry and Short Story Awards, SWAN, 1987. *Hobbies:* Opera Singing; French Horn Player; National Park Trekking; Fishing. *Address:* Dept. of Economic History, University of New England, Armidale, NSW 2351, Australia.

KARASIK Gita, b. 14 Dec. 1949, San Francisco, California, USA. Concert Pianist. m. Lee Caplin, 25 June 1975, 1 son. *Education:* Private study with Mme Rosina Lhevinne, Juilliard; Karl Ulrich Schnabel; Lev Schorr; San Francisco Conservatory of Music. *Career Debuts:* First American Pianist to make Official concert tour of the Peoples Republic of China, 1978; Guest Soloist, National Television/NBC, The Bell Telephone Hour, 1963; Guest Soloist, San Francisco Symphony, 1958, 1969, 1972, 1974; Los Angeles Philaharmonic, 1971; St Louis Symphony, 1974-75; Boston Pops Orchestra with Arthur Fiedler, 1975; Indianpolis Symphony, 1972, 1976; Atlanta Symphony, 1972; Singapore Symphony, 1980-81; Hong Kong Philharmonic, 1980-82; Milwaukee Symphony Orchestra, 1983; Tours of Latin America; Far East; Europe; USA. *Creative works:* Composition: Concerto for Gita Karasik, No 2 by Andrew Imbrie, as first prize Ford Foundation Artists Award, World Premier with Indianapolis Symphony for BiCentennial, 1976. Recordings: Phillips Collection Recital, 1977; Metropolitan Museum of Art Concert Series, 1978; 92nd St YMHA Recital, 1981; Dame Myra Hess Memorial Concert Series, Chicago, 1987. Film scores: Andy Warhol: Made in China, 1987; The Serpent and the Rainbow, Universal Pictures, 1988; To Die For, Skourds Pictures, 1989. *Memberships:* Artists for Nuclear Disarmament; Artists to End Hunger. *Honours:* Oakland Symphony Award, Oakland, California, 1962; Kimber Award, 1966; Young Concert Artists International Auditions Winner, 1969; San Francisco Symphony Foundation Prize, 1970; Ford Foundation Artists Award, 1973; Martha Baird Rockefeller Foundation Musicians Award, 1976; Pro Musicis Foundation Solo Artists Sponsorship, 1976- 84; National Endowment for the Arts Solo Artists Award, 1983; Xerox/Affiliate Artists Pianists Sponsorship, 1983-84; Bösendorfer Piano Sponsorship, 1979-. *Address:* c/o Lee Caplin Productions, Inc, 8274 Grand View Trail, Los Angeles, CA 90046, USA.

KARAVIA Lia (Hariclia) Hadzopoulou, b. 27 June 1932, Athens, Greece. Writer; Actress; Lecturer. m. Vassilis Karavias, 20 Sept. 1953. 2 sons. *Education:* English Literature, Pierce College, Athens, 1953; French Literature, French Institute, 1954; German Literature, Goethe Institut, 1961; Acting, Theatre School, 1962; Classics, University of Athens, 1972; PhD Thesis being prepared, Paris XII University. *Appointments:* Teaching English, Aidonopoulou School, 1967-70; Hourdaki School, 1970-76; Teaching Theatre, Cultural Centres, 1977-84; Public Schools of Nea Smyrni, 1984-; Freelance Writer and Translator. *Publications include:* Poems: Designs on Water, 1956; Gradations, 1957; Two Phases of Iron, 1960; The Fruit of The Bitter Tree, 1963; Harvest 1956-1963, 1963; The Signal, 1973; The Banner and The Signal, 1976. Poetic composition: The Children of Estreda Nada, 1961, 2nd edition 1979; To Antigone, 1975. Novels: Summer, 1959; The Wild River, 1963, 2nd edition, 1977; Kouros, 1965; Hypermnesia, 1979, 2nd edition, 1984. Story: The Silen Piano Keys, 1969, 2nd edition 1979, 3rd edition 1988; The Lion, 1973. Plays: Three Short Plays: Frost, Matchmakers, Isidore, 1974; Commedia Dell Arte, 1977; Tatsi-Pitsi-Mitsi-Kotsi, 1980; Esperanto Inn, 1988; Prince Mickey

(story and play), 1988; Riki, A Story for Blindmice of All Ages, 1979 script of 24 sequels for TV 1988-89, lyrics for 26 songs put to music by Dimitris Lekkas. Numerous translations and essays in French, Greek and English. *Memberships:* Institut International du Theatre; Actors' Union of Greece; Society of Greek Writers; World Academy of Arts and Culture; International Board of Books for the Young, Greek Branch. *Honours:* Acting Prize, Ithaka Festival 1977, 1978; Loudemis Prize for Hypermnesia, 1980; M Averof Prize for Riki, a story for Blindmice of All Ages, 1981; Philologues' Prize for The Censor, 1986; Women's Prize for Our Neighbourhood, 1986 and for Youngsters and Oldsters, 1988. *Hobbies:* Animating children's Groups for theatre work; Directing amateur theatre groups of adults; Reading radio plays, proposing them and eventually translating them to be broadcast; Scriptwriting; Composing lyrics for songs; Language learning; Comparative literature research. *Address:* 51 Aghiou Polycarpou Str, Nea Smyrni 17124, Athens, Greece.

KAROUSOS Despo, b. 20 Jan. 1930, Alexandroupolis, Greece. Writer; Poet. m. Dr Papanicolaou Nicos, 20 Feb. 1954. 2 sons, 1 daughter. *Education:* French Academy (University of Athens, 1949-54. *Appointment:* Commercial Bank of Greece, 1948-49. *Publications:* Novel: The Journey, 1949; Poems: Memories and presences, 1977; The Avenue and the Time, 1978; Brief lyrics (of love and life), 1980; Echoes of the Abyss, 1985; Lyric poems, 1981; Autobiography: A Girl Grow, 1978. *Memberships:* Association of Greek Writers; Association of Theacean Studies; Association of Leucadean Studies; Federation of Greek Women, Member of Executive Committee. *Honours:* Honoured twice by Ministry of Culture and Sciences of Greece fo Brief Lyrics (of love and life), 1980 and Echoes of the Abyss, 1985. *Hobbies:* Theatre; Literature; Nature. *Address:* Kiffisias 94, 11526 Athens, Greece.

KARPACS Joanne Mary, b. 2 Feb. 1945, Philadelphia, USA. Homemaker; Freelance Writer. m. 2 sons, 1 daughter by first marriage, (2) George M Karpacs, 26 Mar. 1983, 1 daughter. *Appointments:* Waitress, 1981-82; Bank Teller, 1982-83. *Publications:* Faith: The Essence of Happiness and Eartheena, (both forthcoming); 22 articles in magazines. *Memberships:* ABI Research Board of Advisors; Cornucopia; Writer's Sphere. *Honours:* Award of Merit, World of Poetry, 1983; Silver Poet Award, World of Poetry, 1986; Writing Award, Laurel Hill Bible Church, 1987. *Hobbies:* Christian Psychology; Rosebushes; Writing. *Address:* 523 Buckingham Drive, Sewell, NJ 08080, USA.

KARPAN Kathleen Marie, b. 1 Sept 1942, Rock Springs, Wyoming, USA. Secretary of State. *Education:* BS, Journalism, 1964, MA, American Studies, 1975, University of Wyoming; JD, University of Oregon, 1978. *Appointments:* Press Assistant, 1965, 1966, 1971, 1972; Administrative Assistant, US Rep 1973-74; Attorney Advisor, EDA Washington, 1978-80; Assistant Attorney General, 1983-84; Director, Health Department, 1984-86; elected Secretary of State, Nov 4th 1986. *Memberships:* National Association of Secretaries of State; National Conference of Lieutenant Governors; Council of State Government; Wyoming and Washington Bar Associations. *Hobby:* Reading. *Address:* State Capitol, Cheyenne, WY 82001, USA.

KARPEN Marian Joan, b. 16 June 1944, Detroit, Michigan, USA. Financial Executive. *Education:* AB, Vassar College, 1966; Additional studies at: The Sorbonne, Paris, France; MBA Program, New York University Graduate School of Business, 1974-77. *Appointments:* New England Correspondent, 1966-68, Parish Fashion Editor, Women's Wear Daily 1968-69, WWD & Fairchild Publications; Fashion Editor, Boston Herald Traveler (newspaper), lecturer & TV commentator, 1969-71; Nationally Syndicated Newspaper Columnist & Photojournalist, Queen Features Syndicate, NYC, 1971-73; Account Executive, Blyth Eastman Dillon, NYC, 1973-75; Account Executive, Oppenheimer & Co, NYC, 1975-76; Vice

President and Municipal Bond Coordinator, Faulkner Dawkins & Sullivan (merged into Shearson), NYC, 1976-77; National Manager, Becker Paribas Private Investor Services Municipal Bond Department, 1977-79; Senior Vice President and Principal, Becker Paribas (formerly Warburg Paribas Becker-AG Becker), 1977-84; Limited Partner-Senior Vice President 1984-86, Associate Director 1986-, Bear Stearns & Co, Inc. *Publications:* Numerous articles and photos in newspapers & magazines (worldwide) freelance, 1966-; Lectures/ seminars (financial), 1978-. *Memberships:* Women's Economic Roundtable, NYC; US Republican Senatorial Business Advisory Council; Vassar Club, Board Member; American Society of Professional & Executive Women; AAUW; English Speaking Union. *Honours:* Various journalism and professional awards/achievements; Fishing Club of America Angler's Honor Roll (Citation for prize-winning sailfish in 48th annual Met Fishing Tournament, 1983). *Address:* 233 East 69th Street, New York, NY 10021, USA.

KARR Phyllis Ann, b. Oakland, California, USA. Writer. *Education:* AB, Modern Languages, Colorado State University, 1962-66. *Appointments:* Branch Librarian, East Chicago (Indiana) Public Library, 1966-69; Shop Assistant, Hamill & Barker, Antiquarian Booksellers, 1970; Cataloguer, University of Louisville Library, 1971-76. *Publications:* Frostflower and Thorn; Frostflower and Windbourne; Idylls of the Queen; Wildraith's Last Battle; At Amberleaf Fair; Lady Susan; My Lady Quixote; Meadowsong; Perola; The Elopement (Novels); The King Arthur Companion (Non fiction); numerous stories, articles. *Memberships:* MFA; SFWA; ALTA; EETS; International Wizard of Oz Society; SCA. *Hobbies:* Flute; Gilbert & Sullivan; King Arthur; Oz; Solitaire; Poker; Various kinds of Needlework and other textile handicrafts; Horseback riding; Karate; Lifelong interest in Dreams. *Address:* 2219 Monroe Ave, Rice Lake, WI 54868, USA.

KARSEN Sonja Petra, b. 11 Apr. 1919, Berlin, Germany (US citizen 1945). Professor Emerita of Spanish. *Education:* Titulo de Bachiller, Bogotá, Colombia, 1937; BA, Carleton College, USA, 1939; MA, Bryn Mawr College, 1941; PhD, Columbia University, New York City, USA, 1950. *Appointments include:* Instructor, Lake Erie College, 1943-45, University of Puerto Rico, 1945-46, Syracuse University, 1947-50, Brooklyn College, 1950-51, Sweet Briar College, 1955-57; with UNESCO, Paris, France, 1951-54; Member UNESCO Technical Assistance Mission, Costa Rica; Chairman & Professor of Spanish, Department of Modern Languages and Literature, 1957-79, Professor of Spanish, 1979-87, Skidmore College, New York. *Publications:* Guillermo Valencia, 1951; Versos y prosas de Jaime Torres Bodet, 1966; Selected Poems of Jaime Torres Bodet, 1964; Jaime Torres Bodet, 1971; Educational Development in Costa Rica with UNESCO's Technical Assistance 1951-54, 1954; Editor, Language Association Bulletin, 1980-83; Ensayos de literatura e historia iberoamericana, 1988. *Memberships include:* AAUP; AAUW; NEMLA; MLA; AIH; New York State Association Foreign Language Teachers; Phi Sigma Iota; National Association of Self-Instructional Language Programs, Treasurer 1973-77, Vice President 1981-82, President 1982-83. *Honours include:* Chevalier dans l'Ordre des Palmes Academiques, 1963; Fulbright Lectureship, Freie Universit at Berlin, Germany, 1968; Leadership Award, New York State Association Foreign Language Teachers, 1973; National Distinguished Foreign Language Leadership Award, 1979; Spanish Heritage Award, 1981; Alumni Achievement Award, Carleton College, 1982; Capital District Distinguished Service Award, 1987. *Hobby:* Photography. *Address:* PO Box 441, Saratoga Springs, NY 12866, USA.

KASKET Esther, b. 16 Mar. 1930, Morocco. Stockbroker. m. Harold Kasket, 20 Apr. 1958, 1 son, 1 daughter. *Education:* BA, Newnham College, Cambridge, 1951; Institute of Actuaries. *Appointments:* Actuarial Dept., Messrs Mullens & Co., 1951-59; Mathematics Teaching & Examining, 1960-68; Executive, James Capel & Co., 1968-76; Executive,

1976-85, Partner, 1985-86, Director 1986-, Laurence Prust & Co. *Publications:* Artist, Portraits; Exhibitions at Hampstead Arts Centre, Stock Exchange Art Society. *Memberships:* ASIA; Stock Exchange; Women of the Year Association, Committee Member. *Hobbies:* Painting; Gardening; Horse Riding. *Address:* London, England.

KASPER Christine Eleana, b. 16 Mar. 1953, Chicago, Illinois, USA. Assistant Professor. m. Ramiro Jorgé Iturralde, 25 June 1978. *Education:* BSN, University of Evansville, 1975; Obstetrical Nursing, Harlaxton College, Grantham, Lincolnshire, England, 1973-74; MSN, Rush University College of Nursing, 1975-76; PhD, University of Michigan, Ann Arbor, 1977-82; Postdoctoral fellow, Department of Physiology, Rush Medical College, Chicago, 1982-84. *Appointments:* Assistant Professor, School of Nursing, University of Wisconsin-Madison; Assitant Professor, School of Nursing, University of California, Los Angeles, 1988-. *Publications:* Numerous articles to professional journals. *Memberships:* American College of Sports Medicine; American Nurses' Association; American Nurses' Association, Council of Nurse Researchers; American Physiological Society; American Society for Gravitational and Space Biology; Biophysical Society; Electron Microscopy Society of America; Midwest Nurses Research Society; New York Academy of Sciences; Sigma Theta Tau. *Honours:* Alpha Lambda Delta; Sigma Theta Tau. *Address:* UCLA School of Nursing; 10833 LeConte Ave, Factor Building, Los Angeles, CA 90024-6918, USA.

KASTIGAR Susan Marie Elizabeth, b. 25 Feb. 1959, Chicago, USA. Electro-Optics Engineer. m. 25 Nov. 1988. *Education:* BS, Physics, 1981, BS Mathematics, 1981, University of Illinois, Chicago; MS, Electrical Engineering, 1983, MS Physics, 1987, University of Illinois, Champaign. *Appointments:* Argonne National Lab, Summer 1979; Fermi National Lab, Summer, 1980; Westinghouse Electric, Summer, 1981; University of Illinois, 1981-83; McDonnell Douglas Atronautics Co., 1984-. *Publications:* Articles in: Journal of Applied Physics; Physics Review; etc. *Memberships:* American Institute of Aeronautics & Astronautics; Eta Kappa Nu; Optical Society of America. *Hobbies:* Reading; Volleyball; Baking; Hiking; Camping; Photography. *Address:* 9914 Hudson, Rock Hill, MO 63119, USA.

KATAYAMA Alyce Irene Coyne, b. 31 Mar. 1950, St Louis, Missouri, USA. Lawyer. m. K. Paul Katayama, 29 Apr. 1970, 1 son, 1 daughter. *Education:* BA, Goucher College, Baltimore, Maryland, 1972; JD, University of Maryland School of Law, 1974; Law-taxation, Georgetown University Law School, 1974-75. *Appointments:* Associate 1975-82, Partner 1982-, Quarles & Brady. *Publications:* Health Law Chapters, Wisconsin State Bar Annual Survey of Wisconsin Law, 1985-. *Memberships include:* Director, Meta House 1976-78; Past Director, Past President, Health Law section, Wisconsin Bar Association; President 1988-89, Wisconsin chapter, American Immigration Lawyers Association; Ad Hoc Advisory Committee, Adverse Reactions to Food Substances, US Food & Drug Administration, 1985-87; Wisconsin, Maryland, California & American Bar Associations; Forum Committee on Health Law, American Bar Association. *Honours:* Phi Beta Kappa, 1972; Order of Coif, 1984; Staff, Maryland Law Review, 1973-74. *Hobbies:* Classical Music; Playing Piano. *Address:* Quarles & Brady, 411 East Wisconsin Avenue, Milwaukee, Wisconsin 53202, USA.

KATCHUR Marlene Martha Gustavia Wilde, b. 20 Dec. 1946, Belleville, Illinois, USA. Registered Nurse. m. Raymond J Katchur, 1 son. *Education:* BSN, Southern Illinois University, 1968; CCN Certificate, Adult Critical Care Course, 1975, Louis Allen Certificate, Louis Allen Management Course, 1984, LAC/USC Medical Center; MS, California State University, 1982. *Appointments:* Staff Nurse, General Medicine Unit 1968-69, Critical Care Nurse 1969-73, Assistant Head Nurse 1974, Medical Intensive Care Unit, Head Nurse (Nurse

Manager), Intensive Coronary Care Unit 1975-78, Nursing Supervisor 1978-81, Associate Nursing Director 1981-83, Fiscal Analyst and Information Systems Coordinator 1983-89, Internal Medicine Nursing, Patient-Centered Information Systems Consultant, 1989-, LAC/USC Medical Center, Los Angeles. *Publication:* Article, High Finance in Heartbeats, 1985. *Memberships:* American Association of Critical Care Nurses; Greater Los Angeles Chapter, American Association of Critical Care Nurses; National Critical Care Institute of Education; American Heart Association; Life Member, Southern Illinois University Alumni Association, *Honours:* American Red Cross Scholarship, 1964; Participated in Federally Funded Blue Ribbon Task Force for the Central Area Health Education Center to determine educational needs for the Health Care Professional in central/South-West California, 1984. *Hobbies:* Reading; Crocheting; Embroidering; Gardening; Travel. *Address:* 912 Glenwick, Walnut, CA 91789, USA.

KATIMS Virginia Peterson, b. 15 Nov. 1922, San Francisco, California, USA. Cellist; Cello Teacher; Writer. m. Milton Katims, 7 Nov. 1940, 1 son, 1 daughter. *Education:* Girls High School, San Francisco; Cello study with Michel Penha, San Francisco, Sir Ivor James, Royal College of Music, London, England, Alfred Wallenstein and Emanuel Feuermann, New York City. *Career:* Cellist, New York World's Fair, 1939; Cellist, Columbia Artists Beaux Arts Trio (CAMI); Cellist, Soloist, touring with Bary Ensemble under auspices of CAMI, throughout USA and Canada, 1946-50; Appearances as Soloist with orchestra, choral groups, and in joint recital; Frequent Narrator with Seattle Symphony Orchestra; Frequent chamber music concerts with Milton Katims, Isaac Stern, Leon Fleisher, Claudio Arrau; Teaching cello; Gave chamber music concerts for school children, under the auspices of Young Audiences, Houston, Texas, 1976-84. *Publications:* Articles in Seattle newspapers on travels with conductor-husband; Articles on China music; Articles on Toscanini. *Memberships:* Seattle Symphony Women's Association; Seattle Tennis Club; Volunteer, Children's Hospital of Seattle, Washington. *Honours:* Cello scholarships for study with Michel Penha, symphony (solo cello) with Alfred Wallenstein (New York Philharmonic), with Ivor James, with Emanuel Feuermann; Extension Scholarship, Juilliard School of Music. *Hobbies:* Playing chamber music; Tennis; Race walking; Swimming; Politics; Poetry; Painting. *Address:* Fairway Estates, 8001 Sand Point Way (C44), Seattle, WA 98115, USA.

KATZ Andrea Lynne, b. 30 June 1961, Norfolk, Virginia, USA. Exercise Physiologist; Professional Racquetball Player. *Education:* BS Physical Education cum laude, Virginia Tech, 1983; MA Physiology of Exercise, University of Texas, 1986. *Appointments:* Exercise Physiologist, US Olympic Committee in charge of Athlete testing (Fellowship), 1985-86; Professional Racquetball Player on WPRA Tour, 1986-; Exercise Physiologist, UT Southwestern Medical Center, 1988-. *Publications:* Contributor of articles to: Medicine Science in Sports and Exercise; American Journal of Sports Medicine; Fitness Industry; National Racquetball; Journal of Applied Physiology; American Journal of Sports Physiology, 1986, etc. *Memberships:* American College of Sports Medicine; Women's Professional Racquetball Association, Board member and Chairman of Rules and Rankings Committee; Women's Sports Foundation, 1987-89. *Honours:* US National Doubles Racquetball Champ, 1981; VA State Racquetball Champion, 1979 and 1981; East Coast Region Judo Champion, 1975; 6 time Virginia State Judo Champion; 2nd degree brown belt; World Ranking of No 15 on Women's Professional Racquetball Association Tour. *Hobbies:* Backpacking; Cross country skiing; Bicycle touring; Imnpressionist art; Broadway theatre; Backgammon. *Address:* 138 Granby Park, Norfolk, VA 23505, USA.

KATZ Carole Sue Rosenfeld, b. 27 Nov. 1936, New York City, USA. Psychoanalyst. m. Arnold Mortimer Katz, 1955, 2 sons. *Education:* BA, 1968, MA, 1973, New York University; MSW, SUNY, 1974. *Appointments:* Private Practice, 1977-. *Publications:* Articles in various journals. *Memberships:* American Orthopsychiatry Association; New York Society Clinical Social Work; National Association of Social Workers; Academy of Clinical Social Workers. *Honours:* Institute of Mental Health Educaiton Outstanding Service Awards, 1986, 1987. *Hobbies:* Photography; Cross Country Skiing; Walking; Grandchildren; Reading; Politics. *Address:* 1125 Park Avenue, Apt. 6D, New York, NY 10128, USA.

KATZ Gloria, Producer; Writer. *Education:* University of California at Los Angeles Film School. *Appointments:* Editor, Universal Pictures; With Willard Huyck joined Francis Ford Coppola to write and direct for his newly created company, American Zoetrope. *Creative Works:* With Willard Huyck wrote script for American Graffiti for director Paul Lucas; Wrote Lucky Lady, 1975, produced with French Postcards in 1979. Films: Indiana Jones and the Temple of Doom (Co-s p); The Best Defense (Prod Co-s p); Howard the Duck (Prod co-s p).

KATZ Lee, b. 24 June 1930, Brooklyn, USA. College Vice President. m. Harold W. Katz, 27 Sept. 1947, deceased, 1 son, 1 daughter. *Education:* BA, 1951; MS, 1961; PhD, 1972. *Appointments:* Associate Dean, Academic Affairs, University of Michigan, Dearborn, 1975-78; Dean, Academic Development, State University of New York, Purchase, 1978-82, Vice President, External Affairs, 1982-84, Vice President External Affairs & Development, President of Purchase College Foundation, 1985-. *Publications:* Articles in: Fund Raising Management, CASE Currents. *Memberships:* Association of Development Officers; Council for Advancement & Support of Education; National Society of Fund Raising Executives; American Council on Education, Michigan Committee Chairperson; Association for Continuing Higher Education. *Honours:* Recipient, many honours and awards. *Hobbies:* Needlepoint; Hiking; Cycling; Swimming. *Address:* 10 Waters Edge, Rye, NY 10580, USA.

KATZ Martha Lessman, b. 28 Oct. 1952, Chicago, Illinois, USA. Attorney. m. Richard M. Katz, 27 June 1976, 1 daughter. *Education:* AB, Washington University, St Louis, Missouri, 1974; JD, Loyola University School of Law, Chicago, Illinois, 1977. *Appointments:* Associate, Fein and Hanfling, Chicago, Illinois, 1977-80; Associate, 1981-82, Senior Associate, 1984-, Rudick Platt & Victor, San Diego, California; Assistant Secretary and Counsel, Itel Corporation, San Francisco, California, 1982-84. *Memberships:* American Bar Association; Lawyers Club of San Diego; San Diego County Bar Association; Illinois State Bar Association. *Honours:* Phi Beta Kappa, 1974; Friends of the Mayor's Advisory Committee on Women; Co-Chair 3rd Annual Women's Conference, Career Women's Network of Congregation Beth Israel. *Address:* c/o Rudick Platt & Victor, 1770 4th Avenue, San Diego, CA 92101, USA.

KATZ Phyllis Alberts, b. 9 Apr. 1938, USA. Psychology; Professor. m., 2 children. *Education:* AB summa cum laude, Psychology, Syracuse University, 1957; PhD, Developmental and Clinical Psychology, Yale University; Clinical Intern, 1959-60; Clinical Trainee, 1960-61. *Appointments include:* Assistant Professor, Psychology, 1963-67, Associate Professor, Psychology, 1967-69, New York University; Associate Professor, 1969-72, Professor, 1973-76, Chair, Developmental Psychology Section, PhD Programme in Education, 1969-75, Acting Executive Officer, PhD Programme in Education, 1974-75, City University of New York; Visiting Research Associate, 1975-76, Adjunct Professor, 1987-, University of Colorado, Boulder; Director, Institute for Research on Social Problems, Boulder, 1975-. *Publications:* About 60 articles and book chapters including: Verbal discrimination performance in disadvantaged children: Stimulus and subject variables, 1967; Perceptual concomitants of racial attitudes in urban grade school children (with L.Sohn and S.R.Zalk), 1975; The development of female identity,

1979; Development of racial and sex-role attitudes, 1983; Children and social issues, 1988; Towards the elimination of racism (editor and contributor), 1976; Eliminating Racism (co-editor), 1982; Guest Consulting Editor, various journals. *Memberships:* Fellow, American Psychological Association, Council of Representatives, APA, 1989-1992, other committees etc; President, The Society for the Psychological Study of Social Issues, 1986-87; Society for Research in Child Development; American Association for the Advancement of Science; Sigma Xi; Association for Women in Science; Society for Experimental Social Psychology; Fellow, American Psychological Society; Board Member, Women's Foundation of Colorado. *Honours:* APA Women and Leadership Award, 1989; Numerous other research grants and other honours. *Address:* 1035 Pearl Street, 5th Floor, Boulder, CO 80302, USA.

KATZ Susan Arons, b. 3 Dec. 1939, New York City, USA. Poet; Writer; Teacher. m. Donald I. Katz, 20 June 1961, 1 son, 1 daughter. *Education:* BFA, Ohio University, 1961. *Appointments:* New York State Poets in Public Service, 1976-; Book Review Editor, Bitterroot Magazine, 1986-. *Publications:* The Separate Sides of Need, 1985; Two Halves of the Same Silence, 1985; articles, poetry, in over 50 magazines, newspapers & anthologies. *Memberships:* Poetry Society of America; AWP; Academy of American Poets; Fellow, International Academy of Poets. *Honours:* Nominee, Pushcart Prize, 1978; Walt Whitman Award, 1980; White Mountain Press Poetry Award, 1981; Mushroom Poetry Award, 1982. *Hobbies:* Skiing; Hiking; Sailing; Horse Riding; Urban Hiking; Conservation & Environmental Issues. *Address:* 12 Timothy Court, Monsey, Ny 10952, USA.

KATZ Vera, b. 3 Aug. 1933, Dusseldorf, Germany. Director; Speaker of Oregon House of Representatives. 1 son. *Education:* BA, MA Studies, Brooklyn College, New York. *Appointments:* Director, Development-Portland, Community College; Speaker, House, Oregon Legislature. *Memberships:* Carnegie Task Force on Teaching as a Profession; Fellow, American Leadership Forum; Vice Chair, Assembly on the Legislature/NCSL. *Honours:* Abigail Scott Duniway Award, Women in Communications, 1985; Jeanette Rankin First Woman Award, 1st Woman Speaker, 1985. *Hobbies:* The Arts; Ballet; Camping; Music. *Address:* 2068 NW Johnson, Portland, OR 97209, USA.

KATZ MURPHY Reva Lee, b. 12 Oct. 1952, Atlanta, Georgia, USA. Legal Administrator; Social Worker; Consultant. *Education:* BS, Social Welfare, 1978, MS, Urban Studies, 1982, Georgia State University, 1978; Edmund Walsh Graduate School of Foreign Service, Georgetown University, 1978; Paul Baerwald Graduate School of Social Work, Hebrew University, Jerusalem, Israel, 1979-80. *Appointments:* Coordinator, Criminal Justice Group, Urban Life Associates, 1971-72, Assistant, Foreign Student Advisor, 1976-77, Georgia State University, Atlanta; Field Service Supervisor, Save The Children Federation, Hazor, Israel, 1975-76; Caseworker, Truck Stop Youth Lodge, Atlanta, 1978; Social Worker, Association for Soldiers Welfare, Israel, 1979- 81; Member, Prime Minister's Committee on Status of Women, Israel, 1979-81; Director, Community Education, Hadassah Hospital, Jerusalem, 1981-81; US Committee for UNICEF, Atlanta, 1982-83; Social Services Administrator, Cong. Shearith Israel, Atlanta, 1982-83; Legal Administrator, Cohen & Cooper, Atlanta, 1985-88; Organiser for Sir Richard Attenborough, Martin Luther King Jr Center and UNICEF benefit premieres of Gandhi, 1982, Cry Freedom, 1987. *Publications:* When Johnny Comes Marching Home: A Study of Battlefield Neuroses in Israel, 1979; Endemic Disease Eradication: Nigeria, a case study, 1981; The Relationship of Water Provision and Disposal to Economic Development in the Third World: Calcutta, India, a case study, 1982; Malaria, Rabies and Trypanosomiasis: Effects on Developments in Africa, 1983; Native Housing Methods and the Economic Development of South America, 1984; Nuts and Bolts of Entertainment Law, 1987. *Memberships:*

Southeastern Center for International Studies; Atlanta Historical Society; Association of Legal Administrators; International Association of Personnel Administrators; Lambda Alpha Epsilon; IAMAT. *Honours include:* Israel Volunteers Medal, 1975. *Hobbies:* Old house renovation; Gardening; Writing; Reading. *Address:* 347 Eighth Street N E, Atlanta, GA 30309, USA.

KATZIR Pamela, b. 13 Mar. 1938, New York, USA. *Education:* BA, 1959, Queens College; MSEd., 1965. *Appointments:* Teacher, Dade County Schools, Miami; O.P. Instructor, Miami-Dade Community College, Miami; Teacher, Ministry of Education, Jerusalem, Israel; Teacher, East Meadow Public Schools. *Memberships:* Trainer, Law Related Education National Council for the Social Studies; National Council of Teachers of English; Alliance for Career Education; Council for Exceptional Education; Alternates for Special Education Instructor; Presenter, Middle States Social Studies Conference, 1989. *Honours:* Phi Delta Kappa; Alpha Delta Kappa; Foundation for Education Grant, 1986. *Address:* Apt 638, 16950 West Dixie Highway, Miami, FL 33160, USA.

KAUFFMAN Janet, b. 10 June 1945, Lancaster, Pennsylvania, USA. Writer; Teacher. m. James Borland, 17 Aug. 1968, 2 sons. *Education:* NBA, Juniata College, 1967; MA, 1968, PhD, 1972, University of Chicago. *Appointments:* Professor, Eastern Michigan University, 1988-. *Publications:* The Weather Book, poems, 1981; Places in the World a Woman Could Walk, stories, 1984; Collaborators, novel, 1986; Where the World Is, poems, 1988. *Honours:* National Endowment for the Arts Fellowship, 1985; Rosenthal Award for Fiction, American Institute of Arts and Letters, 1985. *Address:* 1321 Beecher Road, Hudson, MI 49247, USA.

KAUFFMAN Teresa Jo (Terry), b. 24 Aug. 1951, San Francisco, USA. University Lecturer; Writer; Artist. *Education:* BA, Journalism, University of California, Berkeley, 1974; MA, Communication, University of Texas, 1980; Graduate studies, other California universities. *Appointments include:* Teaching: Visiting Lecturer, University of North Carolina, 1985-86, 1988; Lecturer, Television, Video Scriptwriting, North Carolina State University, 1986-. Television & Video: Producer, Writer, Director, Set Designer, various productions, 1980-; Executive Producer, Raleigh Cable TV, 1987-. Public Affairs, News, Documentaries: Newswriter, TV Moderator, Producer, Anchorwoman, Reporter, Camera, Editor, various radio/tv stations, 1973-, (in USA and Canada); Executive Producer, public affairs programme, WLFL-TV, Raleigh, 1988-. Various other activities including political media coordinator, painting & drawing & photographer; Producer, Director and Music Composer (melody and lyrics), T.V. Show, Seasons of Change; Poetry, music/poetry, Secret Place - audio tape with illustrations. *Publication:* Book, I'm Clueless, 1988. *Memberships include:* Board of Directors, Texas Consumer Association, 1979-80. *Hobbies:* Composing music, Playing handbells; History; Art; Literature; Psychology; Endocrinology; Masterpiece Theatre; Weather; Travel; Snow skiing. *Address:* 405 Furches Street, Raleigh, North Carolina 27607, USA.

KAUFMAN Bel, b. 10 May, Berlin, Germany. Writer; Lecturer. Divorced, 1 son 1 daughter. *Education:* BA, magna cum laude, Hunter College, New York City; MA, First Honours, Columbia University, New York City; Doctor of Letters, Nasson College, Maine. *Appointments:* Teacher of English in New York City high schools; Assistant Professor of English, Adjunct Professor of English, City University New York; Creative writing workshops and seminars at several universities; Keynote speaker at teachers' conventions and Speaker on Jewish humour and Sholom Aleichem, my Grandfather. *Publications:* Novels: Up the Down Staircase (64 weeks on best-seller lists); Love, etc.; Numerous short stories and articles in national magazines; Lyrics for Peabody, TV play; Translations of Russian poetry. *Memberships:* Authors' League; Authors' Guild; PEN American Centre; English Graduate Union, Columbia University; Commission on Performing

Arts; Boardr Member, Sholom Aleichem Foundation; Advisory Board, Town Hall Foundation. *Honours:* 1983 Winner of short story contest sponsored by National Endowment for the Arts and PEN; 1980 Woman of the Year, Brandeis University; 1976, 1979; Awards from Educational Association of America for best articles on Education; 1972 Hunter College Hall of Fame; National School Bell Award; National Human Resource Award; UJA plaque; Paperback of the Year; Box Office Blue Ribbon. *Hobbies:* Writing light verse; Doodling; Crosswords, puzzles and doublecrostics; Bicycling. *Address:* 1020 Park Ave, New York, NY 10028, USA.

KAUFMAN Tina M, b. 13 Jan. 1959, Pasadena, California, USA. Research Fellow, Physiology and Biochemistry. *Education:* BA, Humboldt State University, 1982; PhD, University of California San Francisco, 1987. *Appointments:* Postdoctoral Fellowship, Research Biochemistry, Department of Pediatric Cardiology, University of Texas Southwestern Medical Center at Dallas, 1987-. *Publications:* Dissertation: The Effects of Heart Rate, Contractility and Preload on the Atrial Contribution to Stroke Volume in Newborn and One Month Old Lambs. *Memberships:* American Association for the Advancement of Science; American College of Sports Medicine; American Heart Association, Council on Basic Science. *Honours:* Magna cum laude, Humboldt State University, 1987; UC Regents Fellowship, 1982-83. *Hobbies:* Travelling; Skiing; Backpacking; Photography; Collecting and playing stringed instruments from around the world; Antique Lionel Train sets; Computers; Disney memorabilia. *Address:* Department of Pediatrics, University of Texas Southwestern Medical Center, 5323 Harry Hines Blvd, Dallas, Texas 75235, USA.

KAUFMAN Victoria Elizabeth, b. New York City, New York, USA. Journalist. m. 20 Aug. 1965, 1 daughter. *Education:* House in the Pine, Weaton College, Norton, Massachusetts; Kalani High School, Hawaii. *Appointments:* Professional Model, 1958-; National Linen Service, 1964; Retail Manager, 1970; TV Producer, Host for Georgia Speaks, 1980; Writer; Owner, Forrest & Company, Publisher, Management. *Creative works:* Writing: Memories In Silverplated Frames/I can't say Good-bye (to my father); Photographer, world and local events; Painter; Poet. *Memberships:* International Photographer, American Image News Service; American Platform Society; American Film Institute; Country Music Association. *Hobbies:* Photography; Reading; Writing; Watching and listening to people; Talking with special people; Riding; Water sports; Giving of her time; Travel. *Address:* 2396 Ledgewood Drive, Dunwoody, GA 30338, USA.

KAUGER Yvonne, b. 3 Aug.1937, Cordell, Oklahoma, USA. Justice. m. Ned Bastow, 8 May 1982, 1 daughter. *Education:* BS, magna cum laude, Southwestern State University, 1958; JD, Oklahoma City University, 1969. *Appointments:* Certified Mechical Technologist, St Anthony's Hospital, 1959, Medical Arts Lab., 1959-68; Associate, Rogers Travis & Jordan, Law Firm, 1970-72; Judicial Assistant, Oklahoma Supreme Court, 1972-84; Justice, Oklahoma Supreme Court, 1984-. *Creative Works:* Founder, Gallery of the Plains Indian Colony, Oklahoma. *Memberships:* Appellate Division, Court on Judiciary; State Capitol Preservation Committee; Dean's Advisory Committee, Oklahoma City University, School of Law. *Honours:* Outstanding Young Women in America, US jaycees, 1967; Byliner Honoree, Women in Communications, 1984; Judge of Year, Oklahoma Trial Lawyer's Association, 1987; Woman of the Year, Delta Zeta Sorority, 1988. *Hobbies:* Quilting; Indian Art; The Arts. *Address:* 204 State Capitol Building, Oklahoma City, OK 73105, USA.

KAUWELL Gail Patricia Abbott, b. 30 Aug. 1952, New York City, New York, USA. Assistant Professor of Clinical & Community Dietetics; Registered Dietitian. *Education:* BA Psychology 1974, BS Nutrition 1975, University of Maine; Dietetic Internship, Perth Amboy Med Center, New Jersey, 1976; MAg, Nutrition 1979, Doctoral Student, University of Florida. *Appointments:* Clinical Dietitian, Lee Memorial Hospital, 1976-78; Nutrition Consultant, Beacon Donegan Manor, 1976-78; Clinical Dietitian, Chesapeake General Hospital, 1980; Nutritionist I, Charleston County Health Department, 1980-81; Instructor/Clinical Nutrition Specialist, Clinical & Community Dietetics 1982-83, Assistant Professor and Interim Program Director, 1983-85, Assistant Professor, 1985-, University of Florida; Instructor, Santa Fe Community College, 1984-86. *Publications:* Author of numerous articles to professional journals; Co-developer, The Nutritional Management of Type II Diabetes Mellitus: A Computer Simulation, 1984. *Memberships include:* Gainesville District Dietetic Association; Dietetic Educators of Practitioners; Dietitians in Nutrition Support; Diabetes Care and Education Practice Group, American Dietetic Association; Florida Dietetic Association; Board of Advisors, Directions in Applied Nutrition newsletter; Eating Disorders Task Force, The University of Florida. *Honours:* Phi Kappa Phi, 1974; Phi Beta Kappa, 1974; Omicron Nu, 1975; Maine Dietetic Association Award and Scholarship, 1975; Allied Health Traineeship Award, 1978; The College Register, 1980; Teacher of the Year, College of Health Related Professions, University of Florida, 1984; Outstanding Young Women of America, 1985; American Dietetic Association Outstanding Service Award, 1987; Florida Dietetic Association Distinguished Dietitian, 1988. *Hobbies:* Swimming; Scuba diving; Health & physical fitness; Dogs. *Address:* Clinical & Community Dietetics, Box J-184 JHMHC, University of Florida, Gainesville, Florida 32610, USA.

KAVANAGH Cheryl Elizabeth, b. 30 May 1949, Marlborough, Massachusetts, USA. Investor. m. Richard P Kavanagh, 10 Nov. 1967. 2 sons. *Education:* Mount Wachusett College, 1972-74; Business Courses, 1988-. *Appointments:* Freelance Writer, 1969-; Real Estate Investor, Manager, 1973-; Chapter I Coordinator, Marlborough School Dept, 1985-87; Part-time Financial Consultant, 1985-. *Publications:* Author of magazine and newspaper articles, 1970-; Poetry, radio broadcasted, 1970; Editor and publisher newsletter for Chapter I Pgoram, 1982-87. *Memberships:* Chairperson, Parent Advisory Council, Marlborough School Dept, 1982-87; Paradise Island Golf & Tennis Club, 1985-. *Hobbies:* Real estate investing; Coin collecting; Reading; Nature walks; Cultural events. *Address:* 95 White Pond Road, Hudson, Massachusetts 01749, USA.

KAVIN Rebecca J, b. 29 June 1946, Dodge, Nebraska, USA. President, Provider Management Associates (Hospital, Physician Financial Consulting). m. 22 Apr. 1978. 1 son, 1 daughter. *Education:* Journalism Cert, Ohio University, 1963. *Appointments:* Claims Adjuster, San Diego Foundation for Medical Care, 1968-70; Administrative Assistant, Friendly Hills Medical Group, 1971-77; Office Manager, Robert M Peck and Sergio Blesa MD's, 1978-81; President, Provider Management Associates, 1981-. *Publications:* Prevention and Detection of Embezzlement, Physician's Management Magazine; Guest on World Vision telethon. *Membership:* American Guild of Patient Account Managers (speaker LA chapter 1986). *Honour:* Children's Institute International, A special gift of friendship. *Hobbies:* Reading; Knitting; Health care reimbursements. *Address:* Provider Management Associates, 2441 Honolulu Avenue Suite 130, Montrose, CA 91020, USA.

KAVUMA-KAYONGA Jane Samallie, b. 24 Aug. 1952, Mulago, Kampala. Medical Doctor. m. Christopher Kayonga, 21 Feb. 1981, 2 sons, 1 daughter. *Education:* MB.ChB, Makerere University Medical School, 1977; Obstetrics Diploma, 1983. *Appointments:* Internship, 1977-78, Medical Officer, 1979-81, Mulago Hospital; Medical Officer, Family Planning Association of Uganda, 1984-. *Memberships:* Executive Committee, Uganda Medial Association; Uganda Association of Women Medical Doctors. *Hobbies:* Reading; Gardening. *Address:* Family Planning Association of Uganda, PO Box 30030, Kampala, Uganda, East Africa.

KAWASJEE Flora, b. 4 Nov. 1948, Japan. Banker. m. Patrick Kawasjee, 20 Aug. 1980. 1 daughter. *Education:* BS, Marymount College, 1972; MS, Loyola University, 1974. *Appointments:* Saitama Bank, 1975-78; Banque del Union Europeonne AVP, 1978-81; Continental Bank, SVP, 1981-86; Senior Director and Deputy Representative, Continental Illinois Ltd, 1986-. *Membership:* American Chamber of Commerce in Japan. *Hobbies:* Skiing; Piano; Japanese History. *Address:* 4-1-16 Yakumo, Meguro- ku, Tokyo, Japan.

KAY Margaret Joan Brown, b. 16 Apr. 1951, Washington, District of Columbia, USA. Licensed Psychologist. m. 24 Nov. 1984. 2 daughters. *Education:* BA Psychology, Indiana University of Pennsylvania, Indiana, 1973; MA, Psychology, University of Waterloo, Waterloo, Ontario, Canada, 1977. *Appointments:* Research Psychologist Assistant, Department of Air Force, 1973; Management Trainee, Hamilton Bank, 1973-74; Psychologist, Reality Homes Services for Children, Ontario, Canada, 1976-77; Project Director 1977- 80, Vice President and Chief Psychologist, 1978-81, Pan Am Corporation, Hersey, Pennsylvania, USA; Self-employed Psychologist, 1981-. *Publications:* A Time Study of Job Tasks for Pennsylvania CLA Direct Service Staff, 1979; Demographic Considerations and Real versus Ideal Employment Functions of Pennsylvania CLA Direct Service Staff, 1979; The Advocacy Network, 1984; Academic Therapy, with E Hoffman and B Crosby, 1984; Parent Power; Understanding Right to Education Laws, 1980. *Memberships:* Fellow and Diplomate, American Board of Medical Psychotherapists; Associate, American Psychological Association; Orton Dyslexia Society; Lancaster Association for Children and Adults with Learning Disabilities; Lancaster Chamber of Commerce. *Honours:* Certificate of Appreciation, Lancaster Association for Children and Adults with Learning Disabilities, 1985; University of Waterloo Psychology Department Bursary, outstanding student status, 1975 and 1976. *Hobbies:* Swimming; Photography; Racquetball. *Address:* 2895 Kissel Hill Road, Lititz, PA 17543, USA.

KAYE Geraldine, b. 14 Jan. 1925, Watford, Hertfordshire, England. Writer. m. 16 Apr. 1948, divorced, 1975, 1 son, 2 daughters. *Education:* BSc., London University, 1949. *Appointments:* Teacher, Methodist Girls School, Paya Lebar, Singapore, 1953-55; Teacher, Mitford Colmer School, 1963-65; Children's Writer, 1965-. *Publications:* The Runaway Boy, 1969; Nowhere to Stop, 1972; Marie Alone, 1972; Kassim Goes Fishing, 1973; Kofi and the Eagle, 1974; Billy-Boy, 1975; A Different Sort of Christmas, 1976; The Day After Yesterday, 1981; Comfort Herself, 1985; A Breath of Fresh Air, 1987; Great Comfort, 1988. *Memberships:* Society of Authors; PEN; West Country Writer's Association; Royal Commonwealth Society; National Trust. *Honours:* The Oher Award, for Comfort Herself, 1985. *Hobbies:* Theatre; Walking; Countryside. *Address:* 39 High Kingsdown, Bristol BS2 8EW, England.

KAYE Shirley, b. 22 May 1925, New York, USA. President & Chief Executive Officer of 3 Companies. m. Aaron R Stern, 30 June 1949, deceased, 6 Apr. 1978. 1 son, 2 daughters. *Education:* BA, Pratt Institute; John Gnagy School of Art Advanced Studies; MA, Queens College; Advanced Studies Art Students League of New York; Advanced Studies, Woodstock School of Art. *Appointments:* Chief Art Design, US P.O., 1943-45; Designed Ladies Couteriere, 1945-46; President of Adv. Art & Design Studio, 1946-49; Senior Instructor, Queens Art Academy, 1955-65; President/Chief Executive Officer of the following companies: Shirley Kaye & Co, inc, 1967-; Printmedia, 1970-; Click Photography, 1978-. *Creative works:* Art Exhibitions: Portrait & General Art Commissions; Illustrator of Children's Educational Books through major book publishers; Designer of Fortune 500 Annual Reports; Logo Designer for more than 25 major corporations. *Memberships:* Art Students League of New York; County Committee Woman, Democratic Club; PTA President's Council; Board Member, Comedy Hall of Fame; Metropolitan Museum of Art; Horticultural Society of New York; National Museum of Women in the Arts. *Honours:* Commendations from: USO 1941-45; Red Cross, 1942-45; Boy Scouts of America, 1957-60; Girl Scouts of America, 1959-61; City of New York Police Department, Detective Division, 1967. *Hobbies:* Art, Music, Adult Education, Aerobics, Sports, World Travel. *Address:* 58 West 58th Street, Suites 4A & 4B, New York City, New York 10019, USA.

KAYE SARSON Evelyn Patricia, b. 1 Oct. 1937, London, England. Author; Independent journalist. m. Christopher Sarson, 25 Mar. 1963. 1 sonm, 1 daughter. *Education:* NLCS, Edgware, Middlesex, 1945-56. *Appointments:* Co-founder, first president, Action for Childrens Television (ACT), 1969-74; Reporter for The Guardian, Manchester, England; Reuters News Agency, Paris, France; Feature writer, Boston Globe, USA; New York Times and other newspapers. *Publications:* Books: College Bound: The Student's Handbook to Getting Ready, Moving In and Succeeding on Campus, with J Gardner, 1988; The Hole In The Sheet: A Modern Woman Looks at Orthodox and Hasidic Judaism, 1987; The Parents Going-Away Planner, with J Gardner, 1987; Write and Sell your TV Drama!, with A Loring, 1985; Relationships in Marriage and the Family, with Professors Stinnett and Walters, college textbook, 1984; Crosscurrents: Children, Families and Religion, 1980; How to Treat TV with TLC: the ACT Guide to Children's Television, 1979; The Family Guide to Cape Cod: what to do when you don't want to do what everyone else is doing, with B Chesler, 1979; The family Guide to Childrens Television: what to watch, what to miss, what to change and how to do it, 1975. *Membership:* American Society of Journalists and Authors, President 1983-84, Executive Council, 1981-87. *Address:* 147 Sylvan Avenue, Leonia, NJ 07605, USA.

KAZLE Elynmarie, b. 22 June 1958, Saint Paul, Minnesota, USA. Theatrical Producer; Stage Manager; Publisher. *Education:* Dale Carnegie Diploma, 1975; BFA, University of Minnesota, Duluth, 1982; MFA, Ohio University, Athens, 1984. *Appointments:* Pet Show; Cinderella; Time Flies When You're Alive; No Place Like Home, 1989; Time Flies..(tour), 1988; Dear Gabby, 1988; Bent (LA Production); Brooklyn Academy of Music, 1987; A Chorus Line, MPLS, 1986 PCPA Prod Stg Manager, 2 seasons), 1985; Old Globe Theatre, San Diego Opera, Opera Columbus, Assistant to L D Tom Skelton, GLSF, 1984. *Publication:* Editor & Publisher, The Ohio Network. *Memberships:* Stage Managers Association, 1985; United States Institute of Theatre Tech, Northern Boundary Section, Tech Production Commission, prod Mgt Commission, 1978; Century Club, UMD Alumni Donation; University of Mn, Alumni Association; Former President, Delta Chi Omega, also Social Chair, Secretary; Former President, Panhellenic Council; President, AIW Productions, publishing, producing concern. *Honours:* Bulldog Award 1976, Arrowhead Awards 1976, 1977, UMD; President of the Year 1978, Secretary of the Year 1976, Salesperson of the Year 1978, JA, St Paul, Minnesota; Phi Beta Phi Honor Society, Ohio Unviersity, 1984. *Hobbies:* Flying, small planes; Travel; History; Literature. *Address:* 6075 Franklin Suite 360, Hollywood, California 90028, USA.

KE Fu-jiu, b. 18 Oct. 1943, Chengdu, Peoples' Republic of China. University Teacher. m. Yi-long Bai, 24 Sept. 1972. 1 daughter. *Education:* Peking University, 1961-67. *Appointments:* Institute of Physics, Chinese Academy of Sciences, Beijing, 1973; Research Associate 1981-86, Associate Professor 1986-87, Associate Professor, 1987-, Beijing University of Aeronautics and Astronautics. *Publications:* Author of numerous articles to professional journals, magazines and to conferences. *Memberships:* China Association for Physics; China Association for Nuclear Physics; Bejing Associate for Plasma Physics. *Hobbies:* Music; Fine Arts. *Address:* Division of Physics, Department of Applied Mathematics and Physics, Beijing University of Aeronatucis and Astronautics, Beijing 100083, People's Republic of China.

KEADY Marie E (Betsy), b. 19 Jan. 1955, Springfield, Massachusetts, USA. Publishing. *Education:* BA, Holy Cross College, 1977. *Appointments:* Technical Publishing Co, 1977-79; Research Assistant 1979-80, Research Analyst 1980-81, Research Director 1981-83, Marketing Director 1983-86, Inc Magazine; Publisher, Intrapreneur Magazine, 1987-. *Membership:* MPA Research Committee, 1983. *Hobbies:* Athletics; The arts; Spirituality and personal growth. *Address:* 488 Beacon Street, Boston, MA 02115, USA.

KEANEY Marian, b. 26 Mar. 1944, Ireland. Librrian; Writer. *Education:* Fellow, Library Association of Ireland, 1969; FIBA, 1984; DLitt, World University Roundtable, Tucson, Arizona, USA, 1986. *Appointments:* County Librarian, 1974-; Tutor, bibliography. *Publications:* 5 books, contributions to about 20 other titles & numerous periodicals, mainly on Irish cultural & literary matters. *Memberships:* PEN Irish Section; Library Association of Ireland. *Hobbies:* Reading; Art; Nature; Current research mainly on life & achievements of Lt Col C. K. Howard-Bury, DSO, explorer, photographer, mountaineer (leader, 1st Everest expedition, 1921), politician & writer. *Address:* 24 Newlands, Mullingar, County Westmeath, Ireland.

KEATLEY Anne, b. 15 Aug. 1941, Pineville, Kentucky, USA. Administrator. div., 1 son. *Education:* BA, English, Stetson University, 1963; Yale-in-China Programme, Chinese University, Hong Kong; MPA, Kennedy School of Government, Harvard University, Massachusetts, 1980. *Appointments:* Director, Committee on Scholarly Communication with the People's Republic of China, Commission on International Relations, 1971-77; Programme Director, Panel on Advanced Technology Competition & The Industrialized Allies, Office of International Affairs, 1981-83; Director, Academy Industry Programme, 1983-; Director, Office of Government & Public Sciences, 1987-. *Memberships:* Council on Foreign Relations; National Committee on United State China Relations; American Association for the Advancement of Science. *Honours:* National Research Council Staff Award, 1979. *Hobbies:* Travel; Chinese and Japanese art. *Address:* National Academy of Sciences, 2101 Constitution Avenue NW, Room 181, Washington, DC 20418, USA.

KECK Judith M. Burke, b. 24 Feb. 1938, Springfield, Ohio, USA. Weapons System Programme Manager. m. James E. Keck, 18 Feb. 1978, 1 daughter. *Education:* BS, Management, Park College, 1983; MA, Management, Central Michigan University, 1985; PhD Candidate. *Appointments:* Billiting Officer, Zweibrucken AB, Germany, 1969-72; Commissary Officer, Boron AFS, Edwards AFB, 1972-74; Certified Government Contracting Officer, 1976-83; Programme Manager, B-IB Bomber Air Launched Cruise Missile, Artificial Intelligence, 1983-; Instructor, Air Force Institute of Technology, 1985. *Memberships:* various professional organisations *Honours:* Aeronautical Systems Division Commander's Award, 1982; Special Act Award, 1986-87; Defense Systems Management College Research Fellow, 1986. *Hobbies:* Big Game & Bird Hunting; Animal Protection Organisations; Prevention of Child Abuse *Address:* ASD/CY, Wright Patterson AFB, OH 45433, USA.

KEECH Diana, b. 29 May 1945, Kingston-upon-Hull, England. Teacher. *Education:* Royal College of Music, London, 1963-66; ARCM (PfteT), 1965; Bretton Hall College of Education, 1966-67; ARCM (Ob.T), 1966; GRSM, 1967 Cert.Ed, 1967. *Appointments:* Peripatetic Woodwind Teacher, Hull Authority, 1967-78; Part-time, O & A Level Music Teacher, St Marys High, 1969-71; Senior Woodwind Tutor, Hull, 1978-. *Publications:* Scherzo Rondoso, for Oboe & Piano, 1982. *Memberships:* ISM; Branch Chairperson Musicians Union; AMMA; Executive Council Member, Hull Musical Festival Society; Playing Member, Hull Philharmonic Society; Royal Scottish Country Dance Society. *Hobbies:* Scottish Country Dancing; Yoga; Swimming; Photography; Snooker; Playing for Amateur Operatics and Choral Societies. *Address:* 33 Burniston Road,

Bricknell Avenue, Hull HU5 4JX, North Humberside, England.

KEEFE Mary (Margo) Marguerite Fortier, b. 29 Oct. 1946, Old Town, Maine, USA. Director of Quality Control; Molecular Biologist. m. Timothy D Keefe, 29 June 1969, divorced. 2 sons. *Education:* BS, cum laude, Medical Technology, University of New Hampshire. *Appointments:* Virology Research Assistant, 1968-70; Medical Technologist, 1970-73; Organizer, Keefe Co Realtors, 1977; Technical Specialist 1982-84, Assistant Manager QC 1984-85, Assistant Director of Laboratory Operations 1985-86, Director of Quality Assurance 1986-, International Biotechnology Inc/Kodak. *Memberships:* National Association of Female Executives; Secretary, American Association of University Women; Phi Mu Alumni Association; Registered Medical Technologist, American Society of Clinical Pathologists; Executive Committee, North Madison Congregational Church. *Honour:* Elected to Alpha Epsilon Delta, 1966. *Hobbies:* Tennis; Needlework; Painting; Classical music. *Address:* International Biotechnology Inc/Kodak, 25 Science Park, 275 Winchester Avenue, New Haven, CT 06535, USA.

KEEFREY Patricia Gail, b. 22 Feb. 1955, Madison, Wisconsin, USA. Designer. *Education:* BS, Landscape Architecture, University of Wisconsin, Madison, 1977; Masters program, Landscape Architecture, North Carolina State University, School of Design, 1977-78. *Appointments:* Teaching Assistant, HCSU, Raleigh, 1978-79; Private practice in Design, 1980-84; Assistant to Director Phil Lewis, Environmental Awareness Center, Wisconsin, Madison, 1985-86; The Bruce Co Inc, 1987; Private practice, 1987-. *Creative works:* American Poetry Anthology, A Willow Now Tall, 1982; Copyright, Keep it together, a Calendar planner, 1987. *Memberships:* Alumni Association; American Society of Landscape Architects; National Association of Female Executives. *Honours:* Dean's List, University of Wisconsin, Madison, 1974, 1975; Honorable mention, University of Wisconsin, Department of Landscape Architecture, 1976; Special Talent Award, NCSU, 1978; Spring & Fall teaching Assistantship, 1978. *Hobbies:* Writing poetry and childrens' stories; Skiing; Biking; Sailing; Swimming; Photography; Design; Fashion. *Address:* 311 N Hancock Suite 112, Madison, WI 53703, USA.

KEEN Cynthia Elaine, b. 8 Sept. 1948, Long Beach, USA. Marketing Manager; Author; Publicist. *Education:* BA, Bates College, 1970; MBA, Finance, University of Denver, 1970. *Appointments:* Researcher, Institute for Policy Studies, 1970-72; Publicist, NSPE, 1972-74; Publicist, University of Denver, 1977-79; Manager, Cable Television, San Mateo & Millbase, 1980-82; Marketing Manager, Colorado Video Inc., 1982-. *Publications:* variety of technical articles. *Memberships:* American Electronics Association; American Marketing Association; International Teleconferencing Association; International Trade Association of Colorado. *Honour:* Academic Scholarship, University of Denver. *Hobbies:* Art Collector; Rare Book Collector; Pianist; Skiing. *Address:* Colorado Video Inc., Box 928, Boulder, CO 80306, USA.

KEENAN Retha Ellen, b. 15 Aug. 1934, Iowa, USA. Nurse Consultant; Author. m. Roy Vincent Keenan, 5 Jan. 1980. 2 sons. *Education:* BSc, Nursing, University of Iowa, 1955; MSc, Nursing, 1979, Certificate, Mental Health Nurse Practitioner, 1979, California State University, Long Beach. *Appointments:* Instructor, Mental Health Nursing, Los Angeles Community College, 1981-87; Instructor, Mental Health Nursing, El Camino Community College, Torrance, 1981-86; Nurse Consultant, Private Practice, 1980-; Instructor, Mental Health Nursing, Mount Saint Marys College, 1986-87. *Publications:* Contributing Author: American Journal of Nursing Question & Answer Book for State Board Review, 1984; Nursing Care Planning Guides for Adults, 1986; Nursing Care Planning Guides for Children, 1987; Nursing Care Planning Guides for

Critically Ill Adults, 1988; Psychiatric and Mental Health Nursing Care Planning Guides, 1988. *Memberships:* Sigma Theta Tau, International Nursing Honor Society; Phi Kappa Phi; American Association of University Women; American Nurses Association; California Nurses Association; American Nurses Association Council of Psychiatric & Mental Health Nursing; Delta Zeta; Phi Delta Gamma; Assistance League of San Pedro-Palos Verdes. *Honours:* National Institute of Mental Health Grantee for Graduate Study, 1977-79. *Hobbies:* Travel; Classical Music; Writing; Reading. *Address:* 27849 Longhill Drive, Rancho Palos Verdes, CA 90274, USA.

KEENE Eloise Dolores, b. 16 July 1952, Huntington, USA. Dietitian; Nutritionist. *Education:* BA, University of Miami, 1976; MSc., University of Florida, 1980. *Appointments:* Public Health Nutritionist, 1980-81; Instructor, Co-ordinator, Miami Dade College, 1981-; Nutritional Consultant, 1981-. *Publications:* Articles in professional journals. *Memberships:* American, Florida, Miami, Dietetic Associations; American, Florida, Dade County School Food Service Associations; American Home Economics Association. *Honours:* PhySci; Alpha Zeta. *Hobbies:* Reading; Weaving; Photography; Exercise. *Address:* The Nutrition Producers, 7936 SW 8th Street, Suite 16, Miami, FL 33144, USA.

KEENE-BURGESS Ruth Frances, b. 7 Oct. 1948, South Bend, Indiana, USA. Inventory Management Specialist. m. Leslie U. Burgess, 1 Oct. 1983, 2 sons, 1 daughter. *Education:* BSc., Mathematics, Arizona State University, 1970; MSc., Management, Fairleigh Dickinson University, 1978; Graduate, US Army Command And General Staff College, 1986. *Appointments:* Inventory Management Specialist, US Army Electronics Command, Philadelphia, 1970-74; US Communications Electronics Material Readiness Fort Monmouth, New Jersey, 1974-79; Chief Inventory Management Division, Cane Army Ammunition Activity, 1979-80; Supply Systems Analyst, HQ 60th Ordnance Group 1980-83; Chief Inventory Management Division, Crane Ammunition, 1983-85; Chief Control Division, Crane Army Ammunitions Activity, 1985-; Inventory Management Specialist, 200th Theatre Army Material Management Centre, Zweibruecken, Germany, 1985-88; Supply Systems Analyst, US Army Armament Munitions and Chemical Command, Rock Island, 1988-. *Memberships:* Association for Computing Machinery; Society of Logistics Engineers; American Association for the Advancement of Science; National Association for Female Executives. *Honours:* Outstanding Performaance Award, US Army Electronics Command, 1973; Letter of Appreciation, US Army Communication Electronics Material Readiness Command, 1978; Letter of Commendation, Crane Army Ammunition Activity, 1980. *Hobbies:* Photography; Sewing. *Address:* 4916 West Pincot Avenue, Phoenix, AZ 85031, USA.

KEENEY Marisa G, b. 11 Dec. 1927, Amarillo, Texas, USA. Psychologist. *Education:* AB, Trinity University, San Antonio, 1949; MRE, Princeton Seminary, New Jersey, 1952; PhD, Michigan State University, East Lansing, 1966. *Appointments:* Director of Education, Mt Lebanon Presbyterian Church, Pittsburgh, 1952-56; Director of Education, First Presbyterian Church, Ann Arbor, 1956-63; University Counsellor 1966-, Assistant Director, 1984-, Wayne State University, Counseling Services, Detroit. *Publications:* Poem: Frozen Stream, 1980; Workbook: Life Career Planning Dialog-Student Speaks; Counselor Responds, 1987. *Memberships:* American Psychological Association, 1968; Michigan Psychological Association, 1968; Michigan Women Psychologists, 1987-; American Assoication of University Professors, 1968-; Ecumenical Campus Center, Ann Arbor, Michigan; United Campus Ministries, Detroit. *Honours:* International Women's Year Award for Outstanding Leadership, Delta Kappa Gamma Alpha Iota Chapter, 1976; WSU President Proclamation for outstanding service to WSU as Chair, Commission on the Status of Women, 1977; Outstanding Service - 25 years, Ecumenical Campus Center, University of Michigan, 1987; Service award

from Michigan Women Psychologists as Founding Member and First President, 1988. *Hobbies:* Travel; Crafts; Music; Writing; Cooking. *Address:* 2228 Glencoe Hills Drive No 11, Ann Arbor, MI 48108, USA.

KEILANY Kamar, b. 18 Feb. 1932, Damascus, Syria. Author; Arab Writers Union Executive. *Education:* BA, Arabic Literature, 1953; Diploma in Education, 1954. *Appointments:* Professor, Arabic Language and Literature, Teaching Methodology, Damascus Teachers Institutes, 1954-75; Member, Executive Bureau, Arab Writers Union, 1975-82, 1985-; Member, UNESCO Syrian National Committee, Head, ALECSO Affairs, 1982-87. *Publications:* 22 books, novels, short stories and research papers about literature and Islamic philosophy; Numerous articles in Arab magazines and newspapers, 1955-; Weekly article in Syrian newspapers, 1966-85. *Memberships:* Secretary, Information Committee, Women's General Union; Afro-Asian Solidarity Committee; Executive Bureau, Committee for the Protection of the Revolution and Defence of the Country; Higher Committee for the Support of the Palestinian Resistance; Central Committee of Illiteracy Eradication; Associated Member, Journalists Union; Arab Writers Union; Story Society; High Studies Association. *Hobbies:* Writing; Reading; tourism; Collecting old books. *Address:* Abu-Romana, Al-Rashid Street, Hajjar Bld 44, Damascus, Syria.

KEILANY Lina, b. 29 Nov. 1957, Damsacus, Syria. Agricultural Engineer. *Education:* BSc, Agricultural Engineering; MSc, Agricultural Economics, American University of Beirut, 1985. *Appointments:* Agricultural Engineer, Arab Organization for Agricultural Development, League of Arab States, 1978-. *Publications:* 8 published books of short stories for children; Various articles and short stories for children in Arab and International magazines and newspapers. *Memberships:* Syrian Agricultural Engineers Syndicate; Confident, Syrian National Committee for Man and the Biosphere. *Hobbies:* Reading; Writing; Listening to music. *Address:* Abu-Romana, Al-Rashid Str, Hajjar Bld 44, Damascus, Syria.

KEILLOR Elaine, b. 2 Sept. 1939, London, Canada. Pianist; Professor. m. Vernon McCaw, 29 June 1963. *Education:* Associate, Royal Conservatory of Music, Toronto, 1951; BA 1970; MA 1971; PhD (Musicology) 1976, University of Toronto. *Appointments:* Private Music Teacher, Church Organist, 1954-77; Concert Pianist, 1953-; Lecturer, York University, 1975-76; Instructor, Queen's University, 1976-77; Assistant Professor, 1977-82, Associate Professor 1982-, Carleton University; Visiting Professor, McMaster University, 1984. *Publications:* Piano Music 1, 1983; Piano Music 2, 1986; Numerous articles in Encyclopedia of Music in Canada, 1981; The Canadian Encyclopedia, 1985/1988 and various periodicals. Record: Piano Music to Torontonians 1834-1984. *Memberships:* Canadian University Music Society; CUMR Business Manager, 1980-86; Canadian Musical Heritage Society, Director 1981-; Alliance for Canadian New Music Projects, 1979-87, Director; American Musicological Society; International Council for Traditional Music; Society for Ethnomusicology; International Musicological Society. *Honours:* Chappell Medal, 1958; University of Toronto Open Fellowship, 1972-73; Canada Council Doctoral Fellowship, 1973-74; SSHRCC Research Grants, 1983-84, 1987-88. *Hobbies:* Cycling; Swimming. *Address:* Department of Music, Carleton University, Ottawa, Ontario, Canada K1S 5B6.

KEITH Pauline Mary, b. 21 July 1924, Fairfield, Nebraska, USA. Artist; Author. m. Everett B. Keith, 14 Feb. 1957, 1 son. *Education:* George Fox College, 1947-48; Oregon State University, 1955. *Appointments:* Illustrator, Goldenstein Press 1934-36, Merlin Press 1980-81; Pacific NW Telephone Company, 1950-57; Self-employed, artist (illustrator, watercolourist) & author, 1981-. *Creative work includes:* One-woman shows: Forest Grove, Oregon, 1959; Corvallis Art Centre, 1960; Corvallis Human Resources Building, 1976. Publications: Editor, book, 4 Generations of Verse,

1979; Chapbooks: Christmas Thoughts 1980; Come Join the Festivities 1981, This Christmas Tide 1982, Noel 1984, Retelling the Story 1985; Contributions, Ezra Pound Anthology, Teen Power anthology, 1957; The Vandals, Amherst Society, 1989, Anthology; My Neighbors Tree is Clothed in Lacy White, National Library of Poetry, 1989, Anthology. Periodicals: Seven Devotionals in Fruit of the Vine, 1988; A Psalm, Lenten Booklet, 1989; Tracks in the Desert and Walking in Solitude, Patchworks, 1989; Untitled, Poem to the Koret Living Library, 1989. *Memberships:* Corvallis Art Guild; Chintimmini Artists; Chintimmini Writers; Oregon Association of Christian Writers; American Legion Auxiliary; Elder, 1st Christian Church, Disciples of Christ, 1985-89, 1990-; President 1988-89, Hostess Club of Senior Center, 1983-; President of Hostess Club, 1988-89; Music Leader and Poet, American Legion Auxillary, Post II, Corvallis, Oregon, 1990. *Honours:* 1st prizes 1982, 1983, 1988, 2nd prize 1987, 3rd prize 1984, watercolours (flowers, still life), Benton County Fair; 3 watercolours Rachel & Evan Remple collection, 5 in Starn's collection. *Hobbies include:* Travel, USA & Europe; Music; Nature walks; Camping; Singing, church choir. *Address:* PO Box 825, Corvallis, Oregon 97339, USA.

KEITH Penny Sue, b. 15 Sept. 1949, Louisville, Kentucky, USA. Educator. *Education:* AS, The University of Kentucky, 1974; BS 1978, MEd 1982, MEd 1984, The University of Louisville. *Appointments:* Education, South Oldham Middle School, 1980-; Special Education, 1988-; Advance Education, 1988-. *Publications:* Editor: Through The Eyes of Sixth Grader. Interview with famous People (Willard Scott, twice, Diane Sawyer; Tom Armstrong and Richard Mixon). *Memberships:* Nation Education Association; m Oldham County Education Association; Kentucky Municipal League; Kentucky Colonel. *Hobbies:* Playing the Cello and Ukelele; Collecting and reading books; Playing golf. *Address:* 850 Melford Avenue, Louisville, Kentucky 40217, USA.

KELLER Irene Barron, b. 13 Jan. 1927, Falkirk, Scotland. Editor; Writer. m. Dick Keller, 16 Nov. 1946. 2 sons, 1 daughter. *Education:* University of Chicago, USA, 1959-62. *Appointments:* Freelance Editor and Proofreader, 1963-69; Copy Editor, World Book Encyclopedia Year Book and Science Year, 1969-. *Publications:* The Thingumajig Book of Manners, 1981; The Thingumajig Book of Health and Safety, 1982; A Thingumajig Christmas, 1982; The Thingumajig Book of Do's and Don'ts, 1983; Benjamin Rabbit and the Stranger Danger, 1985; Benjamin Rabbit and the Fire Chief, 1986; Benjamin Rabbit's Bad Dream, 1986; Other People's Things, 1987; Contributor of poetry: Choice I, II; Gallery I, II; Port Chicago anthology; and others, Lucle la Trivie, 1981; Galopin le Lapin, 1981; Poison le Chaton, 1981; Sniff la Mouffette, 1981. *Address:* World Book Year Book, Station 40, Merchandise Mart, Chicago, IL 60654, USA.

KELLER-COHEN Deborah, b. 24 Dec. 1948, Detroit, Michigan, USA. Associate Professor of Linguistics; Director, English Composition Board. m. Evan Cohen, 6 June 1971. 1 son. *Education:* AB, with distinction, Russian, University of Michigan, 1970; MA, Slavic Lang & Lit, University of Colorado, 1972; PhD, Linguistics, State University of New York, Buffalo, 1974. *Appointments:* Assistant Professor of Linguistics 1974-80, Associate Professor of Linguistics 1980-, Director, English Composition Board 1985-, University of Michigan. *Publications:* Numerous articles in professional journals including: Redesigning a Telephone Bill; Literate Practices in a Credit Union. *Memberships:* Linguistic Society of America, Member Program Comm 1984-86, Chair Committee on Status of Women in Linguistics 1976, 1977; American Anthropolical Association; American Association of Applied Linguistics Nominating Committee, 1985; Modern Language Association; National Council of Teachers of English. *Honours:* National Endowment for the Humanities, grant, 1989; American Antiquarian Society, Grant, 1988; Industrial Labeling Practices, Principal Investigator, Collegiate Institute for Values &

Science, 1981; Rackham Faculty Fellowship, 1977, Children's Acquisition of English as a Second Language, Principal Investigator 1975-77, University of Michigan. *Address:* English Composition Board, 1025 Angell Hall, University of Michigan, Ann Arbor, Michigan 48109, USA.

KELLER-STRITTMATTER Lili Lioba, b. 10 Jan. 1942, Breisach. Publishing House Employee. m. Hansuli Louis, 29 Oct. 1966. 2 sons. *Education:* Home Economics School; Commercial Training. *Appointments:* Worker in The Publishing House, Bote vom Untersee and Printers, Louis Keller AG, Steckborn, Switzerland, in family ownership since 1900. *Creative works:* Besuche dich in der natur, poetry; Gedichte zum Verschenken, poetry; Wunder des Augenblicks, poetry, illustrated by Johannes Diem; Staubwölkchen, poetry; Vergißmeinnicht, Haiku-poetry; Geliebte Zuflucht, poetry; Entries in 60 anthologies. *Memberships:* Swiss Writers' Association, Zurich; FDA, Freelance German Authors' Association, Tubingen; German-speaking Authors' Interest Group, Weinstadt; Zurich Writers' Union; International Bodensee Club, Constance; Circle of Friends, Walchum; PEN, Suisse. *Honours:* AWMM, Poetry Prize, Luxembourg, 1985. *Hobbies:* Photography; Expressive dance. *Address:* zur Blume, Seestrasse 94, CH-8266, Steckborn/TG, Switzerland.

KELLEY Carol Williams, b. 10 Dec. 1946, Philadelphia, USA. Arts Administrator. m. Michael J Kelley, 31 Aug. 1968, divorced 1976. *Appointments:* Director, School Tours, Children's Librarian, Education Dept., Nelson Gallery-Atkins Museum, Kansas City, 1967-69; Tour Planner, Lecturer, Washington Inc., 1975-; Director's Receptionist, 1976-78, Assistant to Deputy Director, 1978-, National Gallery of Art. *Memberships:* Junior League of Washington, Board of Directors; American Association of Museums; Georgetown Children's House, Board of Directors; Museum Management Institute. *Hobbies:* Antiques; Quilts; Reading; Cooking; Swimming. *Address:* National Gallery of Art, Washington, DC 20565, USA.bblank

KELLEY Kathleen Marie (Kathe), b. 22 Oct. 1957, Harrisburg, Pennsylvania, USA. Exercise Physiologist; Swimming Professional; Cardiac Rehabilitator; Rehabilitation Specialist. *Education:* BS, Physical Education, College of William & Mary, Virginia, 1979; MS, PE/Exercise Physiology, University of North Texas, 1988; Teaching Certification K-12. *Appointments:* Assistant Swimming Coach, Southern Methodist University, Dallas, Texas, 1983-86; Aquatics Facility Manager, Canyon Creek Country Club, Richardson, TX summers 1984-; Cardiac Rehabilitation Assistant, Sports Medicine, Centre, Lewisville, 1987-89; Rehabilitation Specialist, Presbyterian Hospital of Dallas/The Finley Ewing Cardiovascular and Fitness Center, 1989-. *Memberships:* American Association of Cardiovascular & Pulmonary Rehabilitation; American Heart Association; American College of Sports Medicine; Association for Fitness in Business; National Strength & Conditioning Association; American Swimming Coaches Association; Aquatic Exercise Association, Council for National Cooperation in Aquatics. *Honours:* AIAW Collegiate All-American Swimmer, 1976-79; Certification, Preventive & Rehabilitative Exercise Test Technologist, 1987, Exercise Specialist, 1989, American College of Sports Medicine; Certification, Advanced Cardiac Life Support, American Heart Association, 1989; Certified Pool Operator, National Swimming Pool Foundation, 1988; League Commissioner 1986-89, Coach, League Championship Team 1988, Dallas Amateur Swimming Association. *Hobbies:* Swimming; Cycling; Running; Triathlons; Canoeing; Remote Control Boating; Animals; Nutrition; Physical Fitness. *Address:* 2601 St Albans, Carrollton, Texas 75007, USA.

KELLEY (N.) Jane H. b. 31 Aug. 1928, Abilene, Texas, USA. Professor of Archaeology. m. David H. Kelley, 11 June 1958, 2 sons (1 dec.), 2 daughters. *Education:* BA, Texas Technological College, 1949; MA, University of Texas, 1951; PhD, Harvard University, 1966.

Appointments include: Instructor 1953-54, 1957-58, Assistant Professor 1961-63, Texas Technological College; Associate Curator of Anthropology, Nebraska State Museum, 1964-68; Associate Professor 1968-77, full Professor 1977-, Head of Department 1981-87, Department of Archaeology, University of Calgary, Canada. *Publications include:* Yaqui Women: Contemporary Life Histories, 1978; Archaeology of Sierra Blanca Region, Southeastern New Mexico, 1984; Tall Candle, co-author, 1971, re-issued as A Yaqui Life 1977; Cihuatan, El Slavador: A Study in Intra-Site Variability, 1988; Law-Talk, Mobilization Procedures & Dispute Management in Yaqui Society, Kiva, 1989. Numerous contributions, professional journals. *Memberships include:* Past offices: Society for American Archaeology; American Anthropological Association. Member: Canadian Archaeological Association; Canadian Ethnological Society; Society of Women Geographers. *Honours:* Numerous research grants, various bodies including: National Science Foundation; Canada Council; University of Calgary. *Address:* Department of Archaeology, University of Calgary, 2500 University Drive NW, Calgary, Alberta, Canada T2N 1N4.

KELLY Anne Catherine Donohue, b. 6 Mar. 1916, Buffalo, New York, USA. Retired. m. Thomas E Kelly, 19 Apr. 1941. 3 sons, 2 daughters. *Education:* Classical Diploma with Honour, Mount Mercy Academy, 1934; State University of Buffalo, New York, 1936-38. *Appointments:* Teacher, South Buffalo Schools under Sisters of Mercy; Marriage Clerk, City Clerk's Office, 1964-67; Secretary to City Comptroller, George D O'Connell, 1967-70; Council Clerk, 1970-76; Senior Council Clerk, 1976-81; Retired 1981; 1st Vice-Chairman, Erie County Democratic Committee Women's Division, retired 1987; New York State Democratic State Committee Woman, 145th Assembly District, retired 1987. *Memberships:* Knights of Columbus, President, Monsignor Nash Guild, 1960-61, 1962-63; Mercy League of Buffalo Mercy Hospital, President, 1963-64, 1973-74; South Side Women's Democratic Club, President, 1965-67, 1968-70; St Teresa Parent-Teacher Club, Secretary; St Thomas Aquinas Mother's Club, Secretary; St Teresa Altar Society, Secretary; Active Member, Daughters of Erin of the Irish Club; Active Member, Women for Downtown Buffalo. *Honours:* Woman of the Year, South Side Women's Democratic Club, 1970; Felicitations of the Common Council of the City of Buffalo, 1981; Senior Democrat of South Side awarded by South Side Men's Democratic Club, 1982; Certificate of Award for Distinguished Achievement as New York State Committee Woman in 145th Assembly District. *Hobbies:* Reading; Swimming; Politics; Children; Grandchildren; Travel. *Address:* 45 Weyand Street, Buffalo, NY 14210, USA.

KELLY Kate, b. 3 Nov. 1950, Pueblo, Colorado, USA. Writer. m. George F Schweitzer, 8 Aug. 1974, 2 daughters. *Education:* BA, Smith College, 1973. *Appointments:* Associate Director, CBS Radio Network, 1973-76; Public Relations Consultant, 1976-78; Writer, 1978-. *Publications:* Organize Yourself, co-author, 1986; Jobs!, Ghost Writer, 1985; How to Set Your Fees and Get Them, 1982; The Publicity Manual, 1979. *Memberships:* American Society of Journalists & Authors, Council Member 1984-86, Secretary 1987-88. *Hobbies:* Child Rearing; Working; Reading. *Address:* 11 Rockwood Drive, Larchmont, NY 10538, USA.

KELLY Linda, b. 1 Oct. 1936, Kent, England. Writer. m. Laurence Kelly, 20 Apr. 1963, 1 son, 2 daughters. *Education:* Byarn Shaw School of Art, 1954-57. *Appointments:* Copywriter, Vogue, 1957-59; Travel Editor, 1959-63. *Publications:* The Marvellous Boy: The Life and Myth of Thomas Chatterton, 1971; The Young Romantics, 1976; The Kemble Era, 1980; Women of the French Revolution, 1987; Feasts (with Christian Bland), 1987; Proposals (with Lawrence Kelly), 1989. *Memberships:* PEN. *Address:* 44 Ladbroke Grove, London W11 2PA, England.

KELLY Mattie Caroline May, b. 12 Mar. 1912, Vernon, Florida, USA. Business Woman. m. (1)Coleman Lee Kelly, 1932, divorced 1971, 5 children, (2)Paul Sims, 1973, divorced 1979. *Education:* Rollins College, 1944-46, 1948-49; AB, Florida State University, 1952; Postgraduate Studies, 1970- 71. *Appointments:* Teacher, Public Schools, Florida, 1928-33, 1937; Co-Trustee, Co-Owner, The cole L Kelly Trust; Founder, Promoter and President, Mattie M Kelly Fine & Performing Arts Centre Incoroporated; Owner, President, Destin's First Radio Station, WMMk Gulfcoast Broadcasting Incorporated. *Memberships:* Appointed Trustee, New Destin Humana Hospital, 1986; Member, School of Music National Board of Advisors of Stetson University, 1983-; Okaloosa County Democratic Committee, 1958-; State Democratic Executive Committee Advertising Board, 1966-70; Delegate National Convention, 1968, 1972; Board of Directors, Destin Library, 1956; Florida League Arts, 1980-81; Board of Directors, Okaloosa County Chapter, American Red Cross, 1954-60, Chairman, 1957-58; Advertising Board, Diversified Coop Training, Chocawatchee High School, 1960-; Patron, Stagecrafters, Okaloosa County Symphony; American Camelia Society; national Writers Club; Genealogy Society. *Honours:* Awad, American Red Cross; Florida Governor's Award for the Arts, 1982; Nell and Ross Marler Annual Citizenship Award, 1982; Citation, Governor Graham and Cabinet Members for Gift of Land and Endowment, Mattie M Kelly Fine Arts Centre, 1983; 1983 Winner, Harmony Award, SPEBSQSA, 1983; Nominee to Florida's Women's Hall of Fame, 1984. *Address:* PO Box 425 Destin, FL 32541, USA.

KELSEY Virginia Wier, b. 30 Aug. 1960, Houston, Texas, USA. Architect; Lecturer. *Education:* BArch, University of Texas, 1983. *Appointments:* Adjunct Assistant Porofessor of Architecture, University of Houston; I M Pei & Partners, NY, 1983-85; 3/D International, Houston, 1985- 87; Founder, Virginia W Kelsey, AIA, 1987-. *Creative works:* Kelsey House; Abbott House. *Memberships:* American Institute of Architects; Residential Committee of TX Society of Architects. *Honour:* AIA Scholastic Award. *Address:* 5151 Hazard, Houston, TX 77098, USA.

KELTY Miriam Carol Friedman, b. 4 Nov. 1938, New York, New York, USA. Psychologist; Science Administrator. m. Edward John Kelty, 6 Nov. 1966. 1 son, 1 daughter. *Education:* University of Paris, France, 1957-58; Antioch College, Ohio, USA, 1955-58; BA 1960, MA 1962, The City College of New York; PhD, Rutgers University, 1965. *Appointments:* Lecturer, City College of New York, 1962-65; Research Scientist, Harvard School Public Health, Boston, 1966-68; Psychologist, National Institute of Mental Health, 1968-70; Administrative Officer for Scientific Affairs, American Psychological Association, Washington, 1970-74; Psychologist, National Commission for Protection of Human subjects of Biomedical and Behavioural Research, 1974-78; Assistant Chief, Behavior & Neurosciences Review, National Institute of Health, Div. Research Grants, 1978-86; Associate Director, National Institute on Aging, National Institutes of Health, 1986-. *Publications:* Author of numerous scientific articles. *Memberships:* American Psychological Association; Fellow, Past-president of Division of Psychologists in Public Services, Division of Population and Environmental Psychology; Secretary, Division of Health Psychology American Association for Advancement of Science; Fellow, Eastern Psychological Association; World Futures Society. *Honour:* Pre and Postdoctoral Fellow, National Institutes of Health, 1963-66. *Hobbies:* Swimming; Tennis; Reading; Art. *Address:* Associate Director, Extramural Affairs, National Institute on Aging, National Institutes of Health, Bldg 37, 5C-02, Bethesda, Maryland 20892, USA.

KEMALI-AGOSTINI Milena, b. 26 Mar. 1928, Cosenza, Italy. CNR Researcher. m. Dargut Kemali, 19 Sept. 1955. *Education:* Degree in Medicine, 1951; Specialization Anesthesiology, 1955. *Appointments:* Neuroanatomy Researcher, Cybernetic Section CNR, Theoretical Physics, Naples University, 1962-68; CNR Res Head, Neuroanatomy Section, 1968-; Head,

Neuroscience Department, Cybernetics Institute, CNR, 1980-. *Publications:* Atlas of the Frogs Brain, (in collaboration with V Braitenberg), 1969; Numerous international publications; Scientific international congresses. *Memberships:* European Neuroscience Association; IBRO International Brain Research Organization; Italian Neuroscience Association; Italian Electron Microscopy Association. *Hobbies:* Reading books; Listening to music; Painting; Embroidery. *Address:* Cybernetics Institute of CNR, 80072 Arco Felice, Naples, Italy.

KEMP Patricia Anne (Penn), b. 4 Aug. 1944, Strathroy. Writer; Editor. m. 2 June 1984, 1 son, 1 daughter. *Education:* MEd., University of Toronto, 1988. *Appointments:* Faculty, University of Western Ontario, 1979-85; Writer in Residence, various schools, and libraries, 1984- 86; Writer in Residence, Flesherton Public Library, 1988-89. *Publications:* Travelling Light, 1986; Some Talk Magic, 1986; The Epic of Toad and Heron, 1985; Incremental, 1984; Binding Twine, 1984; Animus, 1983; Angel Makers,1978; Tapes: Ear Rings, 1987; Animus; Cloud; Findhorn Spring Festival of the Arts, 1984. *Honours:* Ontario Arts Council Awards, 1976-87;Canada Council Type B Awards, 1980, 1981. *Address:* c/o Flesherton Public Library, Flesherton, Ontario, Canada NOC 1EO.

KEMPF Martine, b. 9 Dec. 1958, Strasbourg, France. Voice-Control Device Manufacturing Company Executive. *Education:* French Science Baccaulaureat, Athens, Greence, 1980; Student, Astronomy, Friedrich Wilhelm University, Bonn, Federal Republic of Germany, 1981-83. *Appointment:* Owner, Manager, Kempf, Sunnyvale, California, USA, 1985-. *Creative works:* Inventor Comeldir Multiplex Handicapped Driving Systems (Goldenes Lenkrad Axel Springer Verlag 1981); Katalavox speech recognition control system. *Honours:* Oscar, World Almanac Inventions, 1984, Prix Grand Siecle, Comite Couronne Francaise 1985; Recipient Medal for Service to Humanity Spinal Cord Soc, 1986; Street named in honour in Dossenheim- Kochersberg, 1985. *Hobbies:* Flying, hold private, instrument rating, multiengine and sea-plane rating licenses; Piano; Violin; Bassoon; Studying foreign languages, speak German, French, Japanese, English, Spanish, Italian and Modern Greek. *Address:* 1080 E Duane Ave Suite E, Sunnyvale, CA 94086, USA.

KEMPSTER Linda Sue Decker, b. 3 Jan. 1950, Washington, USA. Technical Marketing Consultant. m. Mark Andrew Kempster, 3 July 1976. *Education:* BSc., Arizona State University, 1972; MSc., Systems Management, University of Southern California, 1984. *Appointments:* Senior Technical Writer, National Cash Register, 1978-80; Systems Analyst, International Computer Co., 1980-81; Finance Systems Analyst, Northrop Aircraft Division, 1981-85; Optical Storage Consultant, SeeSystems Corp., 1985; Information Systems Engineer, Computer Technology Association, 1986-88; Technical Marketing Consultant, Wang Labs, 1988-. *Publications:* Articles in professional journals. *Memberships:* Association for Information & Image Management; International Society for Optical Engineering; Digital Image Access Group. *Hobbies:* Boating; Motorcycling; Sewing. *Address:* Wang Laboratories, MS 103-900, 7500 Old Georgetown Rd., Bethesda, MD 20814, USA.

KENDAL Felicity, Actress. m. Michael Rudman, 1 son. *Education:* various schools in India. *Appointments:* Appeared in numerous plays including: The Norman Conquests, 1974; Clouds, 1979; Amadeus, 1981; Othello, 1982; On the Razzle, 1979; The Second Mrs Tanqueray, 1980; The Real Thing, National Theatre, 1982-83; Jumpers, 1985; Made in Bangkok, 1986; TV Appearances include: The Good Life, series, 1975, 1976, 1977; Solo, series, 1982; The Mistress, series, 1984; Twelfth Night, 1979; Films include: Shakespeare Wallah; The Seven Who Were Hung; The Seven Percent Solution; Valentino. *Honours:* Variety Club Award, Best Actress for Clouds, 1979. *Address:* c/o Chatto & Linnit

Limited, Prince of Wales Theatre, Coventry Street, London W1, England.

KENDALL Dolores Diane Pisapia, b. 1 June 1946, Newark, New Jersey, USA. Artist; Author; Direct Mail Marketing Executive. m. Dominik Pisapia. *Education:* Graduate, Berkeley Business College, East Orange, New Jersey, 1965; Postgraduate: Middlesex County College, 1966-67; Rutgers University, 1967-69; Todd Butler Art Workshop, Edison, 1964-74; Art Institute Boston, 1976; Graham Art Studio, Boston, 1975-77; School Visual Arts, New York City, 1978; New York University, 1977; Advt Club New York, 1978. *Appointments:* Proofreader, Supervisor, New Jersey State Diagnostic Center, 1965-74; Apprentice, Instructor, Graham Art Studio, Boston, 1975-77; Director, Direct Marketing, Boardroom Reports Incorporated, New York City, 1977-82; President, Chief Operating Officer, Roman Managed Lists, New York City, 1982; Director, Direct Marketing, Mal Dunn Associates, New York City, 1983; Director, Lists and Card Deck Management, Warren, Gorham and Lamont Incorporated, New York City, 1984-86; Direct Marketing Consultant, 1986-87; Vice President, Marketry Inc, New York City, 1987-. *Publications:* Author: My Eyes are Windows (Poetry), 1972; Feelings and Thoughts, 1979; Exhibited in Group Art Shows in USA; Represented in numerous private collectsion throughout the USA. *Memberships:* Direct Mail Marketing Association, Echo Awards Board Judges, 1982-85, List Day. Lecturer, New York City; International Poetry Association; Direct Marketing Creative Guild; National Mail Order Association; National Association Female Executives; NOW; Direct Marketing Club, New York City. *Honours include:* Desi Award for Direct Mail Marketing Promotion Package, 1980; Poetry Award One Mag, 1972. International Certificate of Recognition for List Day, 1982; Danae in International Poetry Association since 1973. *Hobbies:* Painting; Sports; Music; Writing. *Address:* 530 Second Avenue, New York, NY 10016, USA.

KENDALL Carol, b. 13 Sept. 1917, Bucyrus, Ohio, USA. Writer. m. Paul Murray Kendall, died 1973, 2 daughters. *Education:* AB, Ohio University, 1939. *Publications:* Adult Books: The Black Seven, 1946; The Baby-Snatcher, 1952; Childrens Books: The Other Side of the Tunnel, 1956; The Gammage Cup, 1959; The Big Splash, 1960; The Whisper of Glocken, 1965; Sweet & Sour, Tales from China, retold with Yao-wen Li, 1978; The Firelings, 1981; Haunting Tales from Japan, 1985; The Wedding of the Rat Family, 1988; Adaptations: the Whisper of Glocken, 13 part series, BBC TV, 1980; The Gammage cup, Animation by Hanna-Barbera for CBS Storybreak, 1987. *Honours:* Newbery Honor Book Award, 1960, Ohioana Award, 1960; Parents Choice Award, 1982; Mythopoeic Fantasy Award, 1983. *Hobbies:* Travel; Hiking; Climbing; Chinese Language. *Address:* 928 Holiday Drive, Lawrence, KS 66044, USA.

KENDRICK Pamela Ann, b. 6 July 1943, Joplin, USA. Mathematics Educator. m. Anthony Eugene Kendrick, 9 June 1963. *Education:* EdB, Pittsburg State University, 1965; MS, 1969; Certified Teacher, Missouri; Kansas. *Appointments:* Computer Programmer, RCA Missile Test Project, Cape Canaveral Air Force Station, Florida, 1969-72; Statistician, NASA, 1972- 73; Engineer, Computer Analyst, Jet Propulsion Lab, 1973-74; Instructor, Mathematics, Florida Institute Technology, 1974-81; Assistant Professor, Brevard Community College, 1982-. *Memberships:* AAUW; Mathematics Association of America. *Honours:* Outstanding Alumni Award, Pittsburg State University, 1975-76; Named Florida Outstanding Young Woman, 1976-77. *Address:* 350 Coral Dr., Cape Canaveral, FL 32920, USA.

KENEPP Nancy Breed, b. 17 Aug. 1942, USA. Doctor of Medicine; Anaesthesiologist. m. Darwin Lee Kenepp, 10 July 1971, 3 sons, 1 daughter. *Education:* Mount Holyoke College, 1964; MD, Downstate Medical Centre, State University of New York (SUNY), 1968; Graduate training, University of Florida, Gainesville, & University of Philadelphia. *Appointments:* Assistant Instructor,

Department of Surgery, University of Florida School of Medicine, Gainesville, 1968-69; Instructor, Surgery, Graduate School of Medicine, University of Pennsylvania, 1969-72; Assistant Instructor 1976-78; Assistant Professor 1978-81, Associate Professor 1981-, Department of Anaesthesiology, Temple University Medical School. *Publications:* Various articles, professional journals. *Memberships:* American & Pennsylvania Societies of Anaesthesiologists; International Anaesthesia Research Society; Society of Obstetrical Anaesthesiologists & Perinatologists; Philadelphia Perinatal Society; Association of University Anaesthetists; Society for Education in Anesthesia. *Honours:* National Merit Scholarship, 1960; Student research award, SUNY Downstate Medical Centre, 1968; Diplomate, American Board of Anaesthesiology 1977, American College of Anaesthesiology 1979. *Hobbies:* Obstetric anesthesia; Resident education; Piano. *Address:* Department of Anaesthesiology, Temple University Hospital, Broad & Ontario Streets, Philadelphia, Pennsylvania 19140, USA.

KENLEY Elizabeth Sue, b. 10 Oct. 1945, Kansas City, Missouri, USA. Supervisor, Northern Area Projects/Administration. *Education:* BS, Political Science, Social Studies, History, 1968; MPA, 1972, University of Kansas. *Appointments:* Assistant City Manager, Winfield, Kansas, 1968; Assistant to Budget Officer, KC Missouri Policy Dept. 1971-73; Self Employed Consulting Firm, Lenexa, Kansas, 1973-74; Assistant Plant Buyer, 1974-75, Production Control Supervisor, 1975-77, Dupont, Topeka, Kansas; Regional Buyer, Dupont, Kingwood, Texas, 1977-79; Special Assignment responsible for material start-up, Dupont Plant Delisle, Mississippi, 1979; Regional Technical Buyer, Dupont, Kingwood, 1980-82; Project Procurement Representative, 1982-84, Supervisor, Refineries and Northern Area Projects, 1984, Administrator/Project Buyer, 1985, Quality Assurance Liaison to UTVE Preisdent, 1986-, Aramco. *Hobbies:* Music; Piano. *Address:* Aramco, POBox 4534, Houston, TX 77210, USA.

KENNA Kathleen Marie, b. 13 Aug. 1957, New York City, New York, USA. Physical Therapist; Athletic Trainer. *Education:* BA, University of Rochester, 1979; ATC, William Paterson College, 1981; Med, University of Virginia, 1982; BS Physical Therapy, Medical College of Virginia, 1984. *Appointments:* Lewis-Gale Hospital, Salem, Virginia, 1984-; Medtronic, Minneapolis, 1986-. *Publications:* The Diabetic Ahtlete, 1983; Trainer Malpractice-A Sleeping Giant, 1984; Weekly column in Salem Times Register, Salem, Virginia. *Memberships:* American Physical Therapy Association; National Athletic Trainers Association; American College of Sports Medicine; Virginia Physical Therapy Association; Virginia Athletic Trainers Association. *Honours:* Pi Lambda Theta, Education Honor Society, 1980; Merle Spurrier Award, 1979; Department of Rehabilitation Services Traineeship Award, 1983-84; Cum Laude Graduate, University of Virginia and Medical College of Virginia. *Hobbies:* Stamp collecting; Sports; Crafts, Needlework; Interior design; Work with children. *Address:* 2626 Bluefield Blvd SW, Roankoe, VA 24015, USA.

KENNEDY Cornelia Groefsema, b. 4 Aug. 1923, Detroit, USA. Judge. m. Charles S. Kennedy, 1 son. *Education:* BA, University of Michigan, 1945; JD, 1947; LLD, honours, North Michigan University, 1971. *Appointments:* Law Clerk, 1947-48; Associate, Elmer H. Groefsema, Detroit, 1948-52; Partner, Markle & Markle, Detroit, 1952-66; Judge 3rd Judicial Circuit, Michigan, 1966-70; District Judge, US District Court, Eastern District, 1970-79, Chief Judge 1977-79; Circuit Judge, US Court of Appeals, 6th Circuit, 1979-. *Memberships:* American, Michigan, Federal Bar Associations; American Judicature Society; National Association of Women Lawyers; American Trial Lawyers Association. *Address:* US Ct. of Appeals (6th Cir), 744 Fed Bldg US Courthouse, 231 W Lafayette St., Detroit, MI 48226, USA.

KENNEDY Elspeth Mary, b. 6 Aug. 1921, Newbury, England. Scholar; Lecturer. *Education:* Somerville College, Oxford, 1945-47; BA, Modern Languages, 1947; MA, DPhil, 1951. *Appointments:* Civilian Assistant, War Office, London and Blenheim, 1940-44; Lecturer, French Department, University of Manchester, 1954-66; Fellow, Tutor in French, 1966-87, Emeritus Fellow, 1987-, St Hilda's College, Oxford; Research on Medieval Literature; Lecture tours to North American universities, 1987-. *Publications:* Lancelot do Lac: The non-cyclic Old French Prose Romance, Vol I Text, Vol II Introduction, notes, 1980; Lancelot and the Grail: A Study of the Prose Lancelot, 1986; Articles and reviews contributed to British, French, Belgian, American, German learned periodicals, and international mélanges. *Memberships:* Fellow, London Society of Antiquaries; International Arthurian Society (International President 1987); Society for the Study of Medieval Languages and Literature (President 1985); Committee Member, Royal Academy of the Netherlands; Several other learned societies. *Hobbies:* Wine; Travel; Country walking; mediaeval and renaissance art and music; Russian literature and language. *Address:* The White Cottage, Upper Bucklebury, Reading, Berks RG7 6SG, England.

KENNEDY Ida Maud, b. 4 Apr. 1925, Rockhampton, Queensland, Australia. College Principal. *Education:* AASA 1942, LASA 1946, Australian Music Examinations Board; BA, 1963, BEd, 1966, Queensland; MACE, 1964. *Appointments:* Primary and Secondary School Teacher, Girls' Grammar School, Rockhampton, until 1959; Mistress-in-Charge, Moreton House Finishing Course and Teacher, Moreton Bay College, 1959-64; Principal, Clayfield College, Brisbane, 1964-. *Publications:* Author, articles in various magazines. *Memberships Include:* Queensland Board of Secondary School Studies, 1971-, Chairman, 1988-; AMEB Queensland Advisory Committee; Advisory Committee, ABC School Broadcasts & TV, 1964-71; Executive, Education Committees, Presbyterian & Methodist Schools' Association; President, Association of Heads of Indpendent Girls' Schools, Australia, 1981-83; Member, Principals' group visiting Peoples Republic of China, 1982, USSR 1985; Queensland Institute of Educational Administration; etc. *Honours:* Queen's Silver Jubilee Medal, 1977; Paul Harris Rotary Fellowship Award, 1985. *Hobbies:* Music; Charity Organisations. *Address:* Clayfield College, Gregory Street, Clayfield, Queensland 4011, Australia.

KENNEDY Laurie Ewing, b. 14 Feb. 1949, Hollywood, California, USA. Actress. m. D Keith Mano, 18 July 1980. *Education:* BA, Sarah Lawrence College, 1971. *Appointments:* Numerous appearances include: Lady Macbeth, 'Macbeth'; Major Barbara, 'Major Barbara'; Violet, 'Man and Superman'; Sonya, 'Uncle Vanya'; Irina, 'Three Sisters'; St Joan, 'St Joan'; Hannah, 'Night of the Iguana'; Stella, 'Streetcar Named Desire'; Pat Cawford, 'President Kennedy'. *Memberships:* Equity; SAG; AFTRA. *Honours:* Clarence Derwent Award, 1979; Theatre World Award, 1979; Tony Award Nomination, 1980. *Address:* 392 Central Park West No 6P, New York, NY 10025, USA.

KENNEDY Sheila, b. 23 Nov. 1957, Chicago, Illinois, USA. Architect. *Education:* BA, Wesleyan University, 1979; Ecole Nationale Superieure des Beaux Arts, Paris, 1980; MArch with distinction, Harvard University, 1984; Registered Architect, Commonwealth of Massachusetts. *Career:* Kallmann, McKinnell & Wood, Architects, Boston, Massachusetts, 1984-86; Founder, Principal, Kennedy Violich Architecture, Boston, 1986-; Assistant Professor, Architecture, Graduate School of Design, Harvard University, 1987-; National Technology Conference, A.C.S.C., 1989; U.S.C. Modulator, Architecture and The Culture of Industrial Production, National Technology Conference, A.C.S.A. 1990; Symposium Speaker on Architecture and The Machine, 1989; Exhibitions: Architecture in the Public Realm, Young Architects Forum, New York City, 1989; Light Vessels: 2 Architectural Installations, Massachusetts Artists's Foundation Fellowship Exhibition, 1989;

Recent work by Kennedy Violich Architects, New York City, 1989. *Publications:* Building and Machine, SOM Foundation Archives, 1984; Design work for Best of Lighting World International, Interiors, 1987; Design for Market: Los Angeles, Interior Design, 1988; Design work, Boston Globe Magazine, 1988; Industrial Design work, Architectural Record, 1988. *Memberships:* American Institute of Architects; Boston Society of Architects. *Honours include:* 1st Prize, National Design Travelling Fellowship Competition, Skidmore, Owings and Merrill Foundation, 1983-84; International Furniture Design Competition, Progressive Architecture, 1987; Edison Award, General Electric Co Inc, 1988; Finalist, Newsstand 88 National Design Competition, 1988; Massachusetts Artist's Foundation Fellowship, 1988; Young Architects Award, Architecture League of New York: International Competition for Public Work, 1989. *Hobbies:* Cross-country skiing; Mountain climbing; Beachcombing. *Address:* Kennedy Violich Architecture, 63 Endicott Street, Boston, MA 02113, USA.

KENNELLY Barbara B, b. 10 July 1936, Hartford, Connecticut, USA. Congresswoman. m. James J Kennelly, 1 son, 1 daughter. *Education:* BA, Economics, Trinity College, Washington; Master's Degree in Government, Trinity College. *Appointments Include:* Member, Hartford Court of Common Council, 1975-79; Secretary of the State of Connecticut, 1979-82; Elected to Congress as Representative of First District of Conneticut, 1982-. *Memberships:* House Democratic Cucus Committee on Organization, Study & Review and of the Democratic National Committee's Democratic Policy Commission; Steering Committee, Northeast-Midwest Congressional Coalition. *Honours:* Honourary Doctorates: Sacred Heart Univerity, Bridgeport, 1981, Mount Holyoke College, 1984, University of Hartford, 1985, St Mary's College, Notre Dame, Indiana. *Address:* Abraham Ribicoff Federal Building, 450 Main Street, Room 618, Hartford, CT 06103, USA.

KENT Eleanor, b. 20 May 1931, San Francisco, USA. Artist. divorced, 1 son. *Education:* BA, English, Harvard University, 1953; MA, Language Arts, San Francisco State University, 1965; various painting courses. *Appoinments:* Various Teaching positions, 1954-82; Computer Art Demonstrations, 1983; Workshops, Computer Art, 1984; Lecturer, Computer Art, San Francisco Art Institute, 1985; Lecturer, Computer Art, San Bernadino State College, 1986. *Creative Works:* Numerous solo exhibitions including: Manuelita's Gallery, Nathan Hart Gallery, New College Gallery, Noe Valley Library, Local Color, Colorcrane, Eureka Valley Library, San Francisco; Galeria de la Ciudad, Mexico; Group Exhibitions in Japan, Canada, Europe, Spain, USA. *Address:* 544 Hill Street, San Francisco, CA 94114, USA.

KENT May, b. 18 Aug. 1903, Emmett, Idaho, USA. Business Woman. m. Dalam Kent, 10 Feb. 1935. 1 son, 2 daughters. *Appointments:* Self employed since 1945. *Membership:* Chamber of Commerce. *Honour:* Outstanding business women of Town, 1985. *Hobbies:* Handwork; Needlework; Sewing. *Address:* 59 North 1st West, Tremonton, Utah 84337, USA.

KENWARD Elizabeth, b. 14 July 1906. Social Editor; Jennifer of Jennifer's Diary, Harpers & Queen. m. Captain Peter Trayton Kenward, 22 June 1932. 1 son. *Education:* Privately and Les Tourelles, Brussels, Belgium. *Appointments:* Tatler, 1944-59; Queen Magazine, 1959-70; Harpers & Queen, 1970-. *Honours:* MBE, 1986; Off Sister of St John, 1986. *Hobbies:* Flat racing; Theatre; Flying. *Address:* Harpers & Queen, 72 Broadwick Street, London W1V 2BE, England.

KENYON Karen Beth (Smith), b. 4 Sept. 1938, Oklahoma City, USA. Author; Journalist; Teacher. m. Richard B. Kenyon, 14 Feb. 1963, 1 son. *Education:* Undergraduate work, Art major, University of New Mexico, 1958-61; BA Honours 1977, MA 1987, English, San Diego State University, California. *Appointments:*

Instructor: Mira Costa College, 1981-; San Diego State College of Extended Studies, 1985-; Various courses, Californian Universities. *Publications:* Many Faces, poetry (self-published); Sunshower, 1981; Writing by Heart, under consideration; Over 500 articles, various journals including Newsweek, Redbook, LA Times. *Membership:* PEN International Writing Association. *Honours:* Certificate of achievement, poetry, Atlantic Monthly; Creativity award, San Diego Creativity Association. *Hobbies:* Watercolour painting; Batik; Listening to jazz music. *Address:* PO Box 12604, La Jolla, California 92039, USA.

KER (Alice) Ann Steele, b. 10 Nov. 1937, Warsaw, Indiana, USA. Teacher; Composer; Church Musician. m. Charles A. Ker, 8 Sept. 1957 (div. 1980), 3 daughters. *Education:* De Pauw University, 1955-57; Butler University, 1957-58; BME, Indiana University, 1974; MA, University of Notre Dame, 1987. *Appointments:* Organist, 1st Presbyterian Church, Warsaw, 1969-79; Faculty, Huntington College, Indiana, 1975-; Choirmistress, Central Christian Church, Huntington, 1980; Director of Music, Redeemer Lutheran Church, Warsaw, 1980-87; Elementary Music, Redeemer Lutheran School, 1985-87; Director, Music Ministries, Reformed Church of Palos Heights, Illinois, 1989-. *Creative work includes:* Published compositions: Hear This!, 1973; 3 Men on Camelback, 1982; One Glorious God, 1982; Softly, 1983; Ways to Praise, 1983; House of the Lord, 1984; Jesus the Saviour is Born, 1988. *Memberships:* International League of Women Composers; Past board member, American Guild of Organists; American Choral Directors Association; National Guild of Piano Teachers; American Guild of English Handbell Ringers. Also various community associations. *Honours:* 1st prize, composition, St Francis College, 1974; Festival Conductor, Lutheran Circuit, South Bend, Indiana, 1982-. *Hobbies:* Gardening; Golf. *Address:* 1607 North Springfield Road, Warsaw, Indiana 46580, USA.

KERBIS Gertrude Lempp, b. 23 Aug. 1926, Chicago, Illinois, USA. Architect; Professor of Architecture. 1 son, 2 daughters. *Education:* BS, University of Illinois; MA, Illinois Inst Tech; Postgraduate, Grad Sch Design, Harvard University, 1949-50. *Appointments:* Archtl designer, Skidmore, Owings & Merrill, Chicago, 1954-59; C F Murphy Assocs, Chicago, 1959-62 and 1965-67; Private Practice Architecture, Chicago, 1967-; Lecturer, University of Illinois, 1969; Professor, William Rainey Harper College, 1970-; Washington University, St Louis, 1977, 1982; Architectural Consultant, Dept Urban Renewal City of Chicago; Northeastern Ill Planning Commn; Open Land Project; Mid-North Community Orgn; Chicago Met Housing and Planning Council; Chicago Mayor's Commn for Preservation Chicago's Hist Architecture; Board Directors, Chicago School of Architectur Foundation, 1972- 76; The Cliff Dwellars, 1987-88; Trustee, Glessner House Found, Inland Architect Mag; Lecturer: Art Inst Chicago, University of New Mexico, Illinois Inst Tech, Washington University, St Louis, Ball State University, University of Utah. *Creative works:* Princ archtl works include: Webster-Clark Townhouses, Chicago, 1986. Exhibited at Chicago Hist Soc 1984, Chicago Mus Sci and Industry, 1985; Paris Exhbn Chicago Architects, 1985, etc. *Memberships include:* Fellow AIA; AAUP; ACLU; Women in Architectur, etc. *Honour:* Recipient outstanding achivement award, UWCA Met Chicago, 1984. *Address:* Lempp Kerbis Associates, 172 W Burton Pl, Chicago, IL 60610, USA.

KERN Sister Frances Marie, b. 27 Dec. 1950, St Louis, Missouri, USA. Development Directress. *Education:* AA, St Mary's College, O'Fallon, 1972; BS, Quincy College, 1976; MSA, University of Notre Dame, 1984. *Appointments:* Athletic Directress, Teacher, St Elizabeth Academy, 1976-80; Teacher, St Brendan's Grade School, 1980-81; Assistant Directress, Development, 1981-82, Development Directress 1982-85, St Mary's College of O'Fallon, Development Directress for entire Order, Sisters of the Most Precious Blood, 1985-. *Publications:* Author of fund-raising letters for Sisters of the Most Precious Blood, each one being an original. *Memberships:* O'Fallon chamber of Commerce; National Catholic Development Conference; National Society Fundraising Executives, NSFRE; Notre Dame Club, St Louis, Missouri; St Charles Deanery; Committee for Retired Religious Fund, St Louis; Advisory Development Council for Franciscans in St Louis. *Honours:* Outstanding Administration Award, Sty Mary's College, 1985. *Hobbies:* Bowling; Volleyball; Reading; Painting; Crafts. *Address:* Sisters of the Most Precious Blood, 204 N Main Street, O'Fallon, MO 63366, USA.

KERR Ann Marie Loughridge, b. 24 Mar. 1940, St Petersburg, USA. Attorney at Law. m. 20 June 1964, divorced 1968. *Education:* BA, 1962, JD, 1965, Tulane University. *Appointments:* Attorney at Law, Gibbons, Tucker, Smith, Coffer & Taub, Tampa, 1966-70; Sole Practitioner, Tampa & Clearwater Florida, 1970-. *Publications:* Editor, Multi-volume Book, Southeast Litigation Guide. *Memberships:* Hillsborough County, American, and Florida Bar Associations. *Honours:* Recipient, various honours and awards including: Moot Court Award, 1962; Outstanding Service Award; Hillsborough County Bar Association, Child Advocate of the year; Development of the Board of Psychiatric Center, University of South Florida, 1985-88; President Florida Chapter of the American Academy of Matrimonial Lawyers. *Hobbies:* Sailing; Reading; Travel. *Address:* 425 South Garden Avenue, Clearwater, FL 34616, USA.

KERR Catherine Spaulding, b. 22 Mar. 1911, Los Angeles, USA. Environmental Leader. m. Clark Kerr, 25 Dec. 1934, 2 sons, 1 daughter. *Education:* BA, Stanford University, 1932. *Appointments:* Managing Editor, Stanford Daily, 1931; Editor, Kensington Outlook, 1947-49; Adviser, University of California Mortar Board, Theta Sigma Phi, YWCA, 1952-67; Founder, University Foreign Student & Visitor Hospitality Programme, 1962. *Publications:* Co-Author, Saving San Francisco Bay, 1988. *Memberships:* Advisory Board, East Bay Regional Parks; Berkeley Town & Gown; Berkley Fellows; Stanford Cap & Gown; Phi Beta Kappa; Theta Sigma Phi. *Honours:* Berkeley Citation Award, 1974; Carnegie Foundation Advancement of Teaching Certificate, 1979; Sol Feinstone Environmental Award, 1981; California Council Landscape Architects Citation, 1982; Robert C. Kirkwood Award, 1985. *Hobby:* Gardening. *Address:* 8300 Buckingham Dr., El Cerrito, CA 94530, USA.

KERR Catherine Budd, b. 18 Aug. 1961, Livonia, Michigan, USA. Health Care Administrator. m. Thomas Edwin Kerr, 3 Oct. 1987. *Education:* BSc, Michigan State University, 1983; Master's Degree, Health Services Administration, School of Public Health, University of Michigan, 1985. *Appointments:* Central Office 1984, Great Lakes Region 1984-85, Chicago VA Medical Centre 1985-86, Analyst, Medical District 14 1986, Planner, Great Lakes Region 1986-, Department of Veterans Affairs. *Memberships:* American College of Healthcare Executives; American Public Health Association; University alumni associations. *Honours:* Various certificates, awards, Department of Veterans Affairs. *Hobbies:* Equestrian activities; Reading; Travel; Music. *Address:* 1026 Lincoln, Ann Arbor, Michigan 48104, USA.

KERR Deborah Jane, b. 30 Sept. 1921, Helensburgh, Dunbarton, Scotland. Actress. m. (1) Anthony Bartley, 1945, divorced 1960, 2 daughters. (2) Peter Viertel, 1960, 1 stepdaughter. *Education:* Rossholme Prepatory School, Weston-super-Mare, Northumberland House, Bristol. *Career:* Began career at Open Air Theatre, Regent's Park, 1939; First film Contraband, first major role in film Major Barbara; Went to Hollywood, 1946. *Creative Works:* Films include: Major Barbara, 1940; Love on the Dole, 1940; Penn of Pennsylvania, 1940; Hatter's Castle, 1941; the Day Will Dawn, 1941; The Life and Death of Colonel Blimp, 1942; Perfect Strangers, 1944; Black Narcissus, 1945; I See a Dark Stranger, 1945; The Hucksters, 1946; If Winter Comes, 1947; Edward My Son, 1948; The Prisoner of

Zenda, 1948; Young Bess, 1949; King Solomon's Mines, 1950; Quo Vadis, 1950; Rage of The Vulture, 1951; Dream Wife, 1952; From Here to Eternity, 1953; The End of the Affair, 1954; The Proud and the Profane, 1955; The King and I, 1956; Heaven Knows Mr Allison, 1957; An Affair to Remember, 1957; Separate Tables, 1957/58; The Journey, 1958; The Blessing, 1958; Beloved Infidel, 1960; The Sundowners, 1960; The Innocnets, 1961; The Chalk Garden, 1963; The Night of the Iguana, 1963; Marriage on the Rocks, 1965; Gypsy Moths, 1968; The Arrangement, 1968/69; The Assam Garden, 1984; Reunion at Fairborough, 1984. Plays: Heartbreak House, 1943; Tea and Sympathy, 1953 (USA tour 1954-55); The Day After the Fair (USA tour 1973-74); Seascape, 1974-75; Souvenir, 1975; Long Day's Journey Into Night (USA 1977); Candida (London 1977); The Last of Mrs Cheyney (USA tour 1978); The Day After the Fair (Australian tour 1979); Overheard (London and UK tour, 1981); The Corn is Green (London 1985). Television: A Song at Twilight, 1981; Witness for the Prosecution (TV film), 1982; Ann & Debbie, 1984; A Woman of Substance, 1984; Hold the Dream, 1986. *Honours include:* Four New York Drama Critics' Awards, 1947 (two), 1957, 1960; Hollywood Foreign Press Association Awards 1956 (for the King and I), 1958; Variety Club of GB Award, 1961; 6 Academy Award Nominations; Awards for plays include Donaldson and Sarah Siddons Awards for Tea and Sympathy. *Hobbies:* Painting; Gardening. *Address:* Wyhergut, 7250 Klosters, Grisons, Switzerland.

KERY Patricia A, b. 5 Sept. 1960, Connecticut, USA. Legislative Director. *Education:* BA, Political Science, University of Connecticut, 1982; MPA, George Washington University. *Appointments:* Intern, Connecticut State Dept. on Aging, 1982; Administrative Assistant, University of Connecticut, 1982; Legislate Assistant, 1982-84, Campaign Manager, 1984, US Rep. Ratchford; Legislative Director, US Rep Kaptor, 1985-88; Legislative Aide, US Rep Kennelly, 1988-. *Membership:* Pi Sigma Alpha. *Honours:* Connecticut Democratic Womens Club Scholarship, 1982; Government Career Development Scholarship, 1988. *Hobbies:* Travel; College; Basketball; Cooking. *Address:* 4831 36th St NW 309, Washington, DC 20008, USA.

KESSLER Jean S, b. 20 Oct. 1954, New Brunswick, New Jersey, USA. Certified Professional Secretary. m. Michael P Gutzan, 16 Sept. 1984. *Education:* Executive Secretarial Diploma, Taylor Business Institute, 1973; Sacred Music, New York Christian Institute, 1973-75; Secretarial Science, Associate in Applied Science, Highest Honours, Middlesex County College, 1981; Business Management, Edison State College, 1981; Studying for BSBA and ASM; Certified Professional Insurance Woman, 1988; Certificate in General Insurance, 1988. *Appointments:* Executive Secretary to Corporate Vice President, Regulatory and Scientific Affairs, 1978-80; Secretary to Director of Management Services, Carter Wallace Inc., Cranbury, 1977-; Executive Secretary to Vice President of Personal Lines, 1981, Senior Vice President of Domestic Operations, 1981-83, President of Agency Group, 1984-, Continental Insurance, Cranbury. *Memberships:* Professional Secretaries International, various offices; National Association of Insurance Women; National Association for Female Executives; American Mensa Ltd. *Honours:* Recipient, various honours and awards; Secretary of the Year Nominee, New Jersey Division, 1982-83. *Hobby:* Ballroom Dancing. *Address:* One Continental Drive, Cranbury, NJ 08570, USA.

KESSLER Muriel S, b. 31 July 1925, Brooklyn, New York, USA. Lawyer. m. Emanuel Kessler, 5 Sept. 1949. 1 son, 1 daughter. *Education:* AB, Hunter College of City of New York, 1945; JD, Cornell Law School, Ithaca, 1948. *Appointments:* Lawyer (Partner) Kessler & Kessler, 1949-; Adminis Law Judge, Parking Viol Bureau, New York City, 1971-82; Hearing Officer, NYS Dept Motor Vehicles Appeals, 1975-82; Arbitrator, Civil Ct, BX & NY Counties, 1971-82; Hearing Examiner Family Ct, NYS, 1978-80; Deputy Public Administrator, Bronx County, 1982-85; Chair of the New York State

Bar Association General Practice Section, 1989. *Publications:* Author of articles in professional journals. *Memberships:* President, Metro Women's Bar Association, 1970-72; President, Bronx County Bar Association, 1984-85; Sec & Executive Committee, NYS Bar Assoc Gen Practice Section, 1988; NY County Lawyerrs, 1979-; President, Sisterhood, Riverdale Jewish Center, 1974-77; Director, Riverdale Jewish Center, 1977-. *Honours:* Metropolitan's Women's Bar Association, 1972; Bronx County Bar Association, 1985; Silver Jubilee Award, United Jewish Appeal, Federation, 1973 and 1979; Woman of the Year, Sisterhood, Riverdale Jewish Center, 1979. *Hobbies:* Writing articles on legal topics; Lecturing. *Address:* 60 East 42nd Street, New York, NY 10165, USA.

KESTON Joan Balboul, b. 6 Feb. 1937, New York City, New York, USA. Administrator; Speaker; Writer; Executive Director. divorced 1986. 1 son, 2 daughters. *Education:* BA, NYU, 1958; Graduate work, Rutgers University, 1959; MPA, USC, 1981; Doctoral Candidate, USC, currently. *Appointments:* Manager, Social Security Administration, 1978-86; Executive Director, Public Employees Roundtable, 1986-. *Publications:* Co-author, How to Celerate Public Service Recognition Work, 1986, 1987, 1988, 1989 and 1990 (booklet); Editor, Unsung Heroes, 1986- (newsletter). *Memberships:* American Society Public Administration; American Foreign Service Assocation; International Personnel Manager Association; Federal Employed Women; American Policy Association; Federal Government Information Processing Councils; DPA; Association of USC (Treasurer). *Hobbies:* Travel; Theatre; Reading; Art; Music; Bicycling; Swimming. *Address:* 330 Lynn Manor Drive, Rockville, MD 20850, USA.

KETTLE Sally Anne Smiley, b. 2 Feb. 1938, Omaha, Nebraska, USA. Educator; Marketing Consultant. m. William F. Kettle, 20 July 1968 dec. 2 sons, 3 step-daughters. *Education:* BSc 1960, graduate studies, University of Nebraska. *Appointments:* Television teacher, University of Nebraska, 1967-69; Marketing consultant, Staff Marketing Services, 3M Company 1978-83, Sally Kettle & Company 1984-; Adjunct Professor: Metropolitan State University 1982-, University of Minnesota School of Journalism 1989; Public speaker & lecturer, current. *Publication:* Export Manual US companies exporting to Europe, for Normandale College. *Memberships include:* Offices, past/present: Minnesota Press Club; Minnesota Advertising Federation; American Advertising Federation; National Trade Press Advertising Day; Better Business Bureau; Women's Resource Centre. President, Nebraska Association for Children with Learning Disabilities. *Honours:* Outotandiny Young Women of America, 1967; 2nd place, national award, Advertising Federation of America, 1984; Phi Delta Gamma honour society, 1969. *Hobbies:* Reading; Entertaining; Gardening; Civic organisation management; Church volunteer work; Helping handicapped son become Minnesota's 1st handicapped Eagle Scout. (F)Address: 10321 Morris Road, Bloomington, Minnesota 55437, USA.

KEVLES Betty Anne Holtzmann, b. 20 Aug. 1938, New York City, USA. Writer; Editor. m. Daniel Kevles, 18 May 1961, 1 son, 1 daughter. *Education:* AB, Vassar College, 1959; MA, Columbia University, 1961. *Appointments:* Instructor, Radcliffe seminar 1982, University of California Los Angeles 1982; Art Center College of Design, 1989-; Editor, University of California Press 1983-87; Stanford University Press 1988-. *Publications:* Watching the Wild Apes, 1976; Listening In, 1980; Thinking Gorillas, 1981; Females of the Species, 1986. *Memberships:* Advisory Board, PEN American Centre; American Association for Advancement of Science; Pacific Division, National Association of Science Writers. *Honours:* Best Book awards, New York Academy of Sciences 1976, Boston Globe-Horn Book; Best non-fiction, 1977. *Hobbies:* Archaeology; Literature; Swimming. *Address:* 575 La Loma Road, Pasadena, California 91105, USA.

KEYSERLING Mary Dublin, b. 25 May 1910, New York City, USA. Consultant Economicst. m. Leon H. Keyserling, 4 Oct. 1940. *Education:* BA, Barnard College, 1930; LSE, 1931-32; Graduate School, Columbia University, PhD 1932-1933. *Appointments:* Professor, Economics, Sarah Lawrence College, 1933-38; Executive Director, National Consumers League, 1938-40; Co-ordinator, Hearings, House Com Defence Migration, 1941; Chief, Research Division Office of Civilian Defence, Assistant to Mrs Eleanor Roosevelt, 1942; Economist, then Chief, Liberated Areas Division Foreign Economics Administration, 1943-45; Director, International Economic Analysis Division, US Dept. Commerce, 1946-53; Associate Director, Conference on Economic Progress, 1953-63, 1969-88; Director, Womens Bureau, US Dept. of Labour, 1964-68; Economic Consultant, Lecturer, Writer, 1969-. *Publications:* Windows on Day Care; author, 2 other books; numerous chapters, over 400 articles. *Memberships Include:* Past President: National Consumers Commission on Research & Education; National Clearing House on Womens Issues; National Women's Democratic Club; DC Commission on Status of Women; National Child Day Care Association Board, National Consumers League; Health Security Action Council, LTC. *Honours:* Phi Beta Kappa; LLD, Bryant College; LHD Womens Medical College of Pennsylvania. *Hobby:* Piano. *Address:* 2101 Connecticut Avenue, NW, Washington, DC 20008, USA.

KEZER Pauline, b. 4 Feb. 1942, Boston, USA. Politician. m. Kenneth Kezer, 3 daughters. *Education:* BSc., Psychology, 1963; various courses, Central Connecticut State University, 1974-80. *Appointments:* Teacher, Science, Humanities, Teenage Parent Programme, New Britain Schools, 1964-78; State Representative, Connecticut House of Representatives, 1979-86, Assistant Leader 1981-86; Republican Nominee, Secretary of State, 1986, Vice Chairman Republican Party, 1987-89; Fellow, Harvard University Institute of Politics, doing a study group on voluntarism in the '90's: Reviving a call to Public Service, Jan-May 1990. *Memberships Include:* Republican Town Committee, 1976-; Natural Resources Committee, National Conference of State Legislators, 1979-81; Executive, Human Resources Committee, Council of State Government, 1981-86, President 1981-82, Connecticut Order of Women Legislators; National Board of Directors Girl Scouts/USA, 1984-1990; Chair, Communications Com/Girl Scounts/USA, 1987-1990. *Honours Include:* Thanks Badge, Girl Scouts, 1981; Legislative Award, Connecticut Coalition for Maternal & Child Health, 1984; Legislator of the Year, Connecticut Valley Girl Scouts, 1984; Legislative Award, Association of Child Caring Agencies, 1984; Women Helping Women Award, Hartford Soroptimists, 1984; Government Service Award, New Britain YWCA, 1986. *Hobbies:* Reading; Sewing; Cross Country Running. *Address:* 10 River Edge Court, Plainville, CT 06062, USA.

KHATUN Shafia, b. 15 Jan. 1931, Calcutta, India. Professor of Education; Member, Bangladesh Public Service Commission. *Education:* BA, Lady Brabourne College, Calcutta University, 1950; MA, University of Dhaka, 1953; BEd, Teachers' Training College, Dhaka University, 1960; MEd, Institute of Education & Research, Dhaka University, 1961; EdD, University of Northern Colorado, Colorado, USA, 1965. *Appointments:* Teacher 1953-54, Headmistress 1954-55, Muslim Girls' High English School; Headmistress, Morgan Girls' High English School, 1955-62; Instructor-in-Women's Programme, 1962, Pakistan Academy for Village Development; Instructor-in-Education 1965-66, Pakistan Academy for Rural Development (now BARD); Acting Director, Institute of Education & Research, Acting Provost, S N Hall 1971-72, Acting Provost, Ruquyyah Hall 1969, Chairman, Department of Educational Psychology & Guidance 1968-72 and 1977, Reader/Associate Professor 1966-84, Professor of Education, 1985; Member, Public Service Commission 1977-82; Adviser in charge, Ministry of Social Welfare & Women's Affairs 1982, Minister, Social Welfare & Women's Affairs 1982-85, Government of the People's Republic of Bangladesh; Member, Bangladesh Public

Service Commission, 1985-. *Publications:* Numerous papers in professional journals. *Memberships:* Foundation for Research on Educational Planning & Development (FREPD), 1978-; First Vice-President, Lioness Club, Greater Dhaka Dist 315; International Committee, Zonta Club; numerous other clubs and societies. *Honours:* Recipient of numerous honours and awards including: Government Scholarship, Calcutta University; Doctoral Member, Philosophy of Education, University Roundtable, Benson, Arizona, USA, 1987. *Hobbies:* Reading; Travelling; Listening to music; Gardening; Social work. *Address:* Uttara Model Town, HN11, Rd No 8, Sector 3, Dhaka, Bangladesh.

KHEEL Martha (Marti), b. 25 Aug. 1948, New York City, USA. Writer; Activist; PhD Student. *Education:* BA, University of Wisconsin, 1974; MA, Sociology, McGill University, Canada, 1980; MA, Women's Studies, Antioch University, 1986. *Appointments:* University Teaching Assistant, 1974-80; Interviewer, Survey Research Centre, University of California, 1980- 81; Facilitator, Evergreen Catholic Charities, 1981-83; Lecturer, Antioch University, 1985; Adjunct Faculty, San Francisco Bay Institute, 1987-. *Publications Include:* Articles in: Matrix; Between the Species; Creation; New Catalyst; Environmental Ethics; *Memberships:* Co-Founder, Feminists for Animal Rights; American Philosophical Association; American Academy of Religion; Between the Species, Contributing Editor; Woman Earth Feminist Peace Institute. *Honours:* Graduated, Honours, Distinction, University of Wisconsin, 1974; Research Grant, McGill University, 1979. *Interests include:* Philosophy, theology, history, ecology ethics, vegetarianism and feminist thought. She also has an interest in holistic health and is a certified acupressure massage technician. *Address:* c/o Feminists for Animal Rights, PO Box 10017, North Berkeley Station, Berkeley, CA 94709, USA.

KICKNOSWAY Faye, b. 16 Dec. 1936, Detroit, Michigan, USA. Poet; Educator. m. 11 Dec. 1959 (div. 1967), 1 son, 1 daughter. *Education:* BA, Wayne State University, 1967; MA, San Francisco State College, 1969. *Appointments:* Self-employed, 1979-85; Faculty, University of Hawaii, Manoa, 1986-. *Publications:* Books: Asparagus, Asparagus, Ah, Sweet Asparagus, 1981; She Wears Him Fancy in Her Night Braid, 1983; Who Shall Know Them?, 1985; All These Voices, 1986. *Memberships:* Poetry Society of America; Associated Writing Programme; Artists & Artisans Guild. *Honours:* National Endowment for Arts, 1985; PEN fiction award, 1986; Individual artist's grants, Michigan, 1985, 1981; Artist's achievement award, 1984; Award, Michigan Foundation for Arts, 1981; Prize, Academy of American Poets, 1969. *Hobbies:* Drawing; Reading; Walking. *Address:* English Department, Kuykendall 412, 1733 Donaghho Road, University of Hawaii at Manoa, Honolulu, Hawaii 96822, USA.

KIELY Barbara Ann, b. 8 May 1949, Clinton, Iowa, USA. Chairman and CEO. m. Eugene J Berens, Jr, 2 Aug. 1975. *Education:* BA, Luther College, Decorah, Iowa, 1971; MBA, Loyola University, Chicago, 1976; CPA Certificate, State of Illinois, 1978. *Appointments:* Media Buyer for various advertising agencies, 1971-76; Internal Auditor, Montgomery Ward, 1976-79; Director of Internal Audit, IDC Services, Inc, 1979-82; Freelance motion picture accountant, 1983-84; Chief Financial Officer, Zwiren & Wagner Advertising, Inc, 1984-85; Chairman & CEO, H & K Financial Services, Inc, 1985-. *Memberships:* American Institute of CPA's; Illinois CPA Society; American Society of Women CPA's; Chicago Society of Women CPA's; National Association of Women Business Owners; Reserve Officer Association; Naval Reserve Association. *Honours:* US Naval Reserve Services Medal, 1986; US Naval Reserve Overseas Medal, 1987. *Hobbies:* Skiing; Travel; Lieutenant Commander in US Naval Reserve. *Address:* P O Box 138116, Chicago, IL 60613, USA.

KIEREN Dianne Kathryn, b. 3 Sept. 1941, Virginia, USA. University Professor. m. Thomas E. Kieren, 22 June 1969, 1 son, 1 daughter. *Education:* BA, 1963;

MS, 1963, PhD, 1966, University of Minnesota. *Appointments:* Edina Public Schools, 1963-65; Academic, Professor, 1967-, Associate Vice President, 1988-,University of Alberta, Canada. *Publications:* Co-author, His & Hers: A Problem Solving Approach to Marriage, 1975; Co- Author, The Home Economist as a Helping Professional, 1984; Discovering Yourself, 1986; Growing through Knowing, 1988. *Memberships:* Canadian & American Home Economics Associations; International Federation of Home Economics, Canadian Council Member; National Council on Family Relations, Board Member, Publications Committee, International Chair. *Hobbies:* Music; Sports; Reading. *Address:* 3-2 University Hall, University of Alberta, Edmonton, Alberta, Canada.

KIETA Arlene b. Chicago, Illinois, USA. Actress; Broadcaster; Public Relations Executive. *Education:* Notre Dame University, 1950; Loyola University, 1954; School of Millinery and Crafts, Schurz School, 1958. *Appointments:* Model, Patricia Stevens Modeling Agency, 1950-60; Actress, Radio, TV, Summer Stock, Talent Inc., 1958-64; New Yorks 1st Female Disc Jockey, Metromedia Corporation, 1966-70; President, Kieta Enterprises, 1967-; Broadcaster, WKQW, 1971-; Actress in Voice-Overs, Soap Operas and Films; Directors of International Chili Society, East Coast. *Publications:* Sugar & Spice, 1966; Under the Kitchen Clock (cookbook), 1974. *Contributor to:* Various Media Nationwide. *Memberships:* International Radio & TV Society; Cath Apostolate of Radio & TV; Board Nuestros Pequenos Hermanos Orphanage & Young Women's Towne House Girls' Residence; Arrangements Committee, American Women in Radio & TV; Publishing Chairman, Polish Assistance Inc.; Secretary, New York Chapters, AIDA & Freedom from Hunger Foundation; Opera Index; American Wagner Association; Catholic Actors Guild; Navy League; New York Television Academy; Beaux Arts Society; Metropolitan Museum of Art; Lincoln Center; New York Public Library; The Asia Society and Dame of Justice, Knights of Malta. *Honours:* Numerous honours include: Best Actress Award, Rockland Co., New York, 1972; Best TV Public Service Film Award; Best Radio & TV Actress, 1976; Beaux Arts Society. *Hobbies:* Snow & water skiing; Skating; Tennis; Graphol.; Astrology. *Address:* 23 Park Avenue, Apt. 1B, New York, NY 10016, USA.

KILBOURNE Claire (Clara Anne), b. 3 Aug. 1939, Port Jervis, New York, USA. Teacher. m. Charles Warren Kilbourne, 17 June 1961, 1 son, 1 daughter. *Education:* BA, Education, Trenton State College, 1961. *Appointments:* Teacher, English, Hopewell Township, 1961-; Supplemental Instructor, Hamilton Township School System, 1973-78; Teacher of the Gifted, Grice Middle School, 1978-88. *Publications:* America Sings, 1960; Chimes, 1961; Best Loved Contemporary Poems, 1979; Gifted and Talented Program Guide Grades 6, 7 and 8th, 1984; articles in journals. *Memberships:* New Jersey Educators of the Gifted and Talented; Grice PTA; Partners of the Americas; Planetary Society; Archaeological Institute of America; NEA; HTEA; NJEA; Association for the Advancement of Gifted and Talented Education; *Honours:* Recipient: Certificate of Recognition for Participation in the NJ Writing Project, 1981; Certificate of Appreciation, New Jersey Reading Association, 1981; Grant, National Foundation for the Improvement of Education, 1983. *Hobbies:* Arts & Crafts; Reading. *Address:* 200 Carlisle Avenue, Yardville, NJ 08620, USA.

KILDE Sandra Jean, b. 25 June 1938, Eau Claire, Wisconsin, USA. Certified Registered Nurse; Anesthetist; College Instructor. *Education:* Diploma, Luther Hospital School of Nursing, 1959; Diploma, Minneapolis School of Anesthesia, 1967; BA, Metro State University, 1976; MA, College of St Thomas, St Paul, 1981; EdD, Nova University, Fort Lauderdale, 1987. *Appointments:* OR Supervisor, Midway Hospital, St Paul, 1963-66; Staff Anesthetist, North Memorial Medical Centre, Robinsdale, 1968; Programme Director, Minneapolis School of Anesthesia, 1968-; Adjunct Associate Professor, St Mary's College, Winona, 1982;

Education Consultant, Accreditation Visitor, Council on Accreditation of Nurse Anesthesia Education Programmes/Schools, Park Ridge, 1983-; Programme Director, St Mary's College Graduate Programme, CRNA MSc. Degree Programme, 1985- (New programme for which Dr Kilde wrote the curriculum). *Creative Works:* Articles in professional journals and presentations to various bodies. *Memberships Include:* Past President, Minnesota Association of Nurse Anesthetists; Past President, American Association of Nurse Anesthetists. *Honours:* Recipient, various honours and awards. *Address:* 11784 Madison Street, NE, Blaine, MN 55434, USA.

KILSON, Marion, b. 8 May 1936, New Haven, USA. Editor. m. Martin L. Kilson, 8 Aug. 1959, 1 son, 2 daughters. *Education:* BA, Radcliffe College, 1958; MA, Stanford University, 1959; PhD, Harvard University, 1967. *Appointments:* Associate Professor, Simmons College, 1969-73; Professor, Chair of Sociology, Newton College, 1973-75; Director, Research Director, Bunting Institute, Radcliffe College, 1975-80; Academic Dean, Emmanuel College, 1980-86; Associate Editor, Silver Burdett & Ginn, 1987-89; Dean, Arts and Sciences, Salem State College, 1989-. *Publications:* Kpele Lala : 60 Religious Songs and Symbols, 1971; African Urban Kinsonca, 1974; Royal Antelope & Spider, 1976. *Memberships:* , Massachusetts Board, 1983-; Corporator, New England Baptist Hospital, 1983-; Harvard Graduate Council, 1986-; American Association of University Women, Educational Foundation Panel, 1988-90. *Honours:* Phi Beta Kappa; Fellowship, National Institute of Mental Health; Research Grants. *Address:* 4 Eliot Road, Lexington, MA 02173, USA.

KIM Bong Hee, b. 16 Jan. 1927, Seoul, Korea. Director, Zion Nursery School. m. Won Dong Park, 3 Jan. 1946, 3 sons. *Education:* BA, Seoul National University Teacher's College, 1949; MBA, Yonsei University Graduate School of Business Management, 1967. *Appointments:* Professor, Sang Myong Teachers' College, Seoul Womens' College, 1965-75; Education Co-ordinator, Korean Government, 1975-77; Director, Zion Nursery School, 1982-. *Publications:* History of Korean Women's Development. *Memberships:* Chairman, Christian Federation of Korean Women in USA, 1978-; President, Korean-American Preschool Association, 1985-; Chairman, Korea Girl Scouts, 1960-76. *Honours:* Recipient, various honours & awards. *Hobbies:* Travel; Tennis. *Address:* 748 South Kingsley Drive, Los Angeles, CA 90005, USA.

KIMBELL Judy Weidner, b. 16 Aug. 1919, Iowa City, Iowa, USA. Housewife; Political Advisor. m. Marion J Kimbell, 18 Dec. 1946. 3 daughters. *Education:* BSc, Commerce, 1942. *Appointments:* Secretary and Dispatcher, Lockheed Aircraft, Burbank, California, 1942-46; Clerk, Broadway Department Store, Van Nuys, California, 1956. *Publications:* Advertising columns, Daily Iowan, Iowa City, 1939; Iowa City Press Citizen, 1940, 1941, 1942. *Memberships:* Delta Gamma; Phi Gamma Nu. *Honour:* Ballroom Dancing Trophy. *Hobby:* Christian Religion. *Address:* 22324 Ralston Court, Hayward, CA 94541, USA.

KIMBLE Bettye Dorris, b. 21 June 1936, Tulsa, USA. Educator; Musician; Composer; Lecturer. Divorced, 1 son, 1 daughter. *Education:* BME, Tulsa Oklahoma University, 1959; MA, 1976, MS, 1980, Pepperdine University. *Appointments:* Choral Director, Sapulpa Oklahoma Schools, 1959-61; Co-ordinator, Music, Hamlin, Kansas Schools, 1961-62; Music Instructor, Kansas City Missouri Schools, 1963-67; Music, Choral Director, Fine Arts Chair, Compton CA Schools, 1967-. *Publications:* Book of Songs, 1978; Compositions: We Shall Extol Him; The Great Coronation; Changes Must Come; Inner City Blues (choral arrangement); Trust Him; Spreading the Gospel. *Memberships:* National Association of Negro Musicians; Phi Delta Kappa; Southern California Mission Conference, Director; Kimble Community Choir, Founder, Director; National Academy of Songwriters; National Academy of Recording Arts & Sciences. *Honours:* Recipient, many honours & awards. *Hobbies:* Lecturing; Composing; Directing Choirs; Reading; Bowling. *Address:* Bedekay Publishing Co., PO Box 2451, Inglewood, CA 90305, USA.

KIMBLE Dolores, b. 6 Apr. 1935, Oklahoma, USA. Official Court Reporter. m. Roy H Kimble, 21 Nov. 1956, divorced 1978. 1 son, 1 daughter. *Education:* BS, Langston University, 1956; Bryan Court Reporting College, 1958. *Appointments:* Freelance Reporter, 1959; Hearing Reporter, 1960 and 1961; Superior Court Reporter, 1962-. *Memberships:* Los Angeles Court Reporters Assoc, 1962-; Calif Court Reporters Assoc, 1974-; Natl Shorthand Reporters Assoc, 1972-; NAACP, 1980-; Alpha Kappa Alpha Sorority, 1954. *Honours:* Certificate of Merit 1976, Certificate of Proficiency 1972, National Shorthand Reporters Assoc. *Hobbies:* Travel; Classical piano; Theatre; Reading. *Address:* 111 North Hill Street, Los Angeles, CA 90012, USA.

KINCAID Elsie Elizabeth (Schuetze), b. 29 Nov. 1929, Vernon, Texas, USA. Educational Psychologist. m. Richard Warren Kincaid, 1 June 1949, 2 sons, 2 daughters. *Education:* AA, Del Mar College, 1949; BS magna cum laude, Texas A&I University, 1976; MS, Corpus Christi State University, 1978; PhD, Columbia Pacific University, 1985. *Appointments:* Director, Diagnostician, Educational Therapist, Corpus Christi Academic Development Services 1979-80, Academic Development Service, Corpus Christi 1980-86; Diagnostician, Educational Therapist for Learning Disabilities, Corpus Christi, 1987-. *Publications:* Preschool Diagnostic Development Screening Test, 1987; Reasoning Process as Early Intervention for Reading Disability, 1985. *Memberships include:* Past Vice President, Samaritan Counselling Centre, Coastal Bend; Board, High Risk Infant Task Force; Advisory Board, project, Any Baby Can (affiliated, Ada Wilson Children's Hospital); Various community associations, honour societies. *Hobbies:* Golf; Tennis; Music; Art; Bible study; Growing succulent plants on patio. *Address:* 18 Lakeshore Drive, Corpus Christi, Texas 78413, USA.

KINDNESS Irene, b. 19 May 1940, Jakarta, Indonesia. Artist: Painter, Sculptor. 1 son, 1 daughter. *Education:* Central Technical Art School, Brisbane, Australia, 1963-66; Sheridan College School of Crafts & Design, Canada, 1980-83. *Appointments:* Teacher, various workshops, summer schools, seminars. *Creative works include:* 13 solo exhibitions, Canada & Australia, 1967-; Participant, numerous group shows, USA, Canada, Australia. Work in collections, various business enterprises, civic art galleries. *Honours:* Awards, Queensland juried shows including: Mackay Art Prize, 1976-78; Cunamulla Art Prize, 1976-79; Gympie Art Prize, 1974; Cairns Art Prize, 1974-79; Townsville Art Prize, 1974-79. Also: Caltex Oil Prize, 1976, 78, 79; Goondiwindi Art Prize, 1972; Cairns Art Society Prize, 1974, 1979; Tweed Mall Art Prize, 1974, 1979; Westfield Art Award, 1978; Sunnybank Art Group Competition, 1978; Bundaberg Art Society Award, drawing, 1978; McGregor Art Competition, Toowomba, 1979; Numerous highly commended awards. *Address:* 12 Ingham Avenue, Toronto, Ontario, Canada M4K 2W5.

KINDT Lois Jeannette, b. 22 Feb. 1927, Milwaukee, Wisconsin, USA. Retired. m. Warren F Kindt, 25 Feb. 1949. 1 son, 1 daughter. *Education:* BA Psychology, University of Wisconsin, 1948. *Appointments:* Waynesboro Republican Committee; Delegate to National Convention, 1976; Delegate to all District and State Conventions (13 years); Sixth District Committee; Campaign Committees: Coleman, Giesen, Roller, Dawbarn and others; Legislative Aide to Delegate A R Pete Giesen, 1976-79; Candidate for, House of Delegates 1977, State Senate, 1979. *Memberships:* Board of Directors, Waynesboro East Augusta Chapter of American Red Cross; Board of Directors, Jr Achievement; Chairman, Economic Profile Committee for revision of Waynesboro Comprehensive Plan, 1979; Waynesboro Community Hospital; Red Cross

Bloodmobile; American Associationof University Women; Mayor's Advisory Committee; Led Workshop in Laubach method of Teaching Adults to Read; Delegate, Governor's Conference on the Food Dollar; Grace Evangelical Lutheran Church; Board of Trustees, Virginia Synod Lutheran Homes, Inc; Delegate to Synodical Conventions, 1978, 1979; 1980 Synodical Convention, Arrangements Committee; Evangelical Outreach Task Force, World Missions, 1987; VA Synod Lutheran Board of Missions, Secretary, 1982-86. *Address:* 2205 Brambleton Avenue, Roanoke, VA 24015, USA.

KING Annette Faye, b. 13 Sept. 1947, Murchison, New Zealand. MP. Divorced, 1 daughter. *Education:* BA, Waikato University, 1981. *Appointments:* Trained as School Dental Nurse, Christchurch, 1965-67, worked in profession, 1967-70, 1973-82; Tutor, School for Dental Nurses, Wellington, 1982-; Elected Member of Parliament, 1984-; Under Secretary to Minister of Employment, Tourism, Youth and Social Welfare, 1987- . *Memberships:* National Vice President, New Zealand Stat Dental Nurses Institute; Central Committee of Dental Nursing Occupational Group in Public Service Association; Amnesty International; New Zealand Labour Party; Public Speaking Association. *Hobbies:* Reading; Travel; Films. *Address:* 9A Worcester Street, Levin, New Zealand.

KING Carol Soucek, b. 8 Sept. 1943, Los Angeles, California, USA. Editor-in-Chief & Vice President, Designers West Magazine. m. Richard King, 31 Jan. 1976. *Education:* BA 1966, PhD 1975, University of Southern California; Postgraduate, University of Cambridge, UK, summer 1962; MFA, Yale University, 1966. *Appointments:* Writer 1973-77, Editor 1977, Lifestyle Section, Los Angeles Herald Examiner; Editor-in-Chief, Designers West magazine. *Creative work includes:* Dissertation: Use of Theatre in US Government International Cultural Relations Abroad, 1976. *Memberships:* Institute of Business Designers (Press); American Society of Interior Designers (ASID) (Press); International Society of Interior Designers; International Furnishings & Design Association; Board of Directors, Network of Executive Women in Hospitality; Offices, UCLA Extension Interior & Environmental Design Programme; Various civic & philanthropic groups. *Honours:* Editorial award, Dallas Market Centre, 1983; 1st Partners in Excellence award, Southern California & Nevada chapters, ASID, 1987; Woman of the Year, Network of Executive Women in Hospitality, 1989; Numerous awards for Designers West, Western Publications Association, 1978-. *Hobbies:* Effect of art & design on human life; Service on panels & juries, regional & national, aspects of interior design; Travel, Asia & Europe. *Address:* Designers West; 8914 Santa Monica Boulevard, The Penthouse, Los Angeles, California 90069, USA.

KING Cynthia, b. 27 Aug. 1925, New York, USA. Writer. m. Jonathan King, 26 July 1944, 3 sons. *Education:* Bryn Maw College, 1943-44; University of Chicago, 1944-46; New York University, 1964-67. *Appointments:* Assistant Editor, Hillman Periodicals, 1946-50; Managing Editor, Fawcett Publications, 1950-55; Creative Writing Teacher: The Milam School, Houston, Texas, 1971-74; The Awty School 1974-75; Creative Writing Residencies, numerous schools in Michigan, 1976-86. *Publications:* In the Morning of Time, The Story of the Norse God Balder, 1970; The Year of Mr Nobody, 1978; Beggars & Choosers, 1980; Sailing Home, 1982; Short Stories in various journals & magazines; book reviews, etc. *Memberships:* Authors Guild; Detroit Women Writers, President 1979-81, Treasurer, 1978-79; Poets & Writers Inc. *Honours:* Michigan Council for the Arts, Creative Artists Grant, 1985-86; others. *Hobbies:* Art; Art History; Natural History. *Address:* 4 Marsh Hen Cove, Fripp Island, SC 29920, USA.

KING Dominique Desiree, b. 27 Jan. 1956, Michigan USA. Corporate Executive. *Education:* BA, 1983, MA, 1987, Wayne State University. *Appointments:* King

Centerless Grinding, 1974-, Vice President 1980-. *Memberships:* Madison Heights Chamber of Commerce, Board Member, 1984-, Secretary 1988-; Royal Oak Library Board, Member, 1986, President, 1988-. *Honours:* Outstanding Service Award, National Teenage Republicans, 1977; Campaign Manager Award, Michigan Federation of Young Republicans, 1981; Presidents Award, Madison Heights Chamber of Commerce, 1988. *Hobbies Include:* Antiques; Canoeing; Needlework; Reading; Music. *Address:* 3103 Sylvan, Royal Oak, MI 48073, USA.

KING Jean Anne Hutchins, b. 16 June 1938, Fords, New Jersey, USA. Registered Nurse. m. Peter King III, 28 Nov. 1975. *Education:* BSc, Nursing, Russell Sage College School of Nursing, 1959. *Appointments include:* Various hospitals, New York, Philadelphia, California, New Jersey, 1959-74; Head Nurse & Supervisor, Whittaker Corporation, Jeddah, Saudi Arabia, 1974-77; Nursing Consultant, AMI International Inc, Beverley Hills, California, 1978-79, 1980-81; Hospital Services Adviser, King Abdul Aziz Teaching Hospital, Riyadh University, Saudi Arabia, 1979-80; Assistant Director of Nursing, King Fahad Hospital, Al Baha 1981-83; Office Manager & Nursing Consultant 1984-86, AMI Saudi Arabia Ltd; Locum Director of Nursing, King Khaled Eye Specialist Hospital, Riyadh, 1986; Staff Nurse, Veterans Administration Medical Centre, Lyons, New Jersey, USA, 1987-. *Hobbies:* Photography; Travel; Embroidery; Reading. *Address:* 73 Village Circle, Bridgewater, New Jersey 08807, USA.

KING Linda Lou, b. 18 Mar. 1943, Lumberton, North Carolina, USA. Resource Room Teacher. *Education:* BS, Elementary Education 1967, Certified Teacher, Educable Mentally Handicapped 1975, Pembroke State University. *Appointments:* 3rd Grade Teacher: Cumberland County Public Schools, North Carolina 1967-68, St Paul's City Schools 1968-69, Greensville County Schools Emporia, Virginia 1969-70, Cumberland Christian School 1972-73, Marlboro County Public Schools 1973-; Resource Room Teacher, Marlboro County Public Schools, Bennettsville, SC, 1975-. *Creative work:* Paintings, religious songs. *Memberships:* Parent Teacher Organisation; Council for Exceptional Children; President, Bennettsville Lioness Club; Vice President SC Region, & local President, Association for Retarded Citizens; Charter member, Robeson County Civic Chorale; Vice President, King Clan; Ordained Minister. *Honours:* 2nd prize, oil painting, Fayetteville Museum of Art Show, 1973; 3rd place, oils & acrylics, Marlborough Arts Festival, 1976. *Hobbies* Playing piano; Singing & Listening to Gospel Music; Writing Music; Travel; Reading; Macrame; Painting Pictures. *Address:* Route 4, Box 1, Bennettsville, South Carolina 29512, USA.

KING Lynn, b. 19 Apr. 1944, Sudbury, Canada. Family Court Judge. m. M. T. Kelly, 2 sons. *Education:* BA, University of Toronto; MA, Fletcher School of Law & Diplomacy; LLb., University of Toronto Law School. *Appointments:* Partner, Law practice, Copeland & King, 1973-75; Lecturer, Osgoode Hall Law School, 1975-76; Partner, Law Practice, King & Sachs, 1976-85; Appointed Judge, 1985-. *Publications:* Law, Law, Law, 1975; What Every Woman Should Know About Marriage, Separation & Divorce, 1980; Women Against Censorship, Contributor, 1984. *Memberships:* Past Director, National Action Committee on Status of Women; Rape Crisis Centre; Women's Habitat. *Hobbies:* Canoeing; Cross Country Skiing; Hiking; Travel. *Address:* 311 Jarvis St., Toronto, Ontario, Canada M5B 2C4.

KING Rheta Lois Baron, b. 15 Dec. 1935, Los Angeles, California, USA. Vocational Rehabilitation Consultant. div. 1 son, 1 daughter. *Education:* AB cum laude, Psychology, Occidental College, Los Angeles, 1957. *Appointments include:* Director, Vocational Programmes, D. Freeman Memorial Hospital, 1981-86; Research Scientist, Human Interaction Research Institute, & co-owner, Institute for Professional Competency, 1986-. *Publications:* Book, Guide to Selective Placement of Workers with Disabilities;

Articles: Living Less Restrictively in Community, Low Back Pain, Rehabilitation Success for Recipients of Social Security Benefits. *Memberships:* California Governor's Women Appointees Council; Alumni Board of Governors, Occidental College; Advisory Board, Counselor Education Program, California State University, Los Angeles; California Governor's Committee on Employment of Disabled Persons. *Hobbies:* Jungian psychology; Burmese cats; The enneagram of personality. *Address:* 515 South Oakland Avenue, Apt. 5, Pasadena, California 91101, USA.

KING Sheryl Jayne, b. 29 Oct. 1945, East Grand Rapids, Michigan, USA. Teacher; Counsellor. *Education:* BS 1968, MA 1971, Central Michigan University. *Appointments:* Teacher, Newaygo Public Schools, Michigan, 1968-72; Interior decorator, Sue King Interiors, Grand Rapids, 1972- 73; Director, Girls' Unit, Dillon Family Services, Tulsa, Oklahoma, 1973-74; Manager, Fellowship Press, 1974-76; Teacher, Counsellor, Itasca Community College, Grand Rapids, 1977-81; Teacher, District 318, Grand Rapids, Minnesota, 1977-. *Creative work includes:* Published poetry, Frost, Northern Minnesota Writing Project 1986, 'Schism' World Treasury of Great Poems 1989; Photography show, Duluth Art Institute, 1989. *Memberships:* Offices, active: Marriage & Family Development Centre; YMCA; Northern Minnesota Citizens' League; Itasca County Women's Consortium; Women's Day Conference; Fellowship of Believers. *Honours:* Deaconess 1974-, Outstanding Service Awards 1974-79, 1981, 1985, Fellowship of Believers. *Hobbies:* Photography; Sailing; Tennis; Travel; Writing; Reading; Sport. *Address:* PO Box 33, Bigfork, Minnesota 56628, USA.

KING Thea, b. 26 Dec. 1925, Hitchin, Hertfordshire, England. Musician. m. Frederick J Thursotn, 1953. *Education:* Royal College of Music. *Appointments:* Sadler's Wells Orchestra, 1950-52; Portia Wind Ensemble, 1955-68; London Mozart Players, 1956-84; Currently: English Chamber Orchestra, Melos Ensemble of London, Robles Ensemble; Professor Royal College of Music, 1961-87; Guildhall School of Music, 1988- . *Publications:* Clarinet Solos (Chester Woodwind Series), 1977; Arrangement of J S Bach's Duets for Two Clarinets, 1979. *Honour:* OBE, 1985. *Hobbies:* Cows; Pillow-Lace. *Address:* 16 Milverton Road, London NW6, England.

KING (Mary) Susan Jay, b. 17 Sept. 1950, Chicago, Illinois, USA. Medical Doctor; Paediatrician. m. Walter M. Jay, 23 June 1973, 2 daughters. *Education:* BS magna cum laude, Loyola University, 1972; MD, University of Illinois, 1976; Residency, University of Chicago hospitals & clinics, 1976- 78; Fellow, Paediatric Rheumatology 1978-79 (Chicago), Adolescent Medicine 1979-80 (Stanford, California); Licensed, Illinois, California, Georgia, Arkansas. *Appointments:* Instructor 1980-81, Assistant Professor 1981- 85, Department of Paediatrics, Medical College of Georgia; Associate Professor & Director, Division of Adolescent Medicine, Department of Paediatrics, University of Arkansas for Medical Sciences, Arkansas Children's Hospital, 1985- . *Publications:* Numerous research papers, presentations. *Memberships include:* Offices: Society for Adolescent Medicine; American Academy of Paediatrics; Southern Society for Paediatric Research; Southeastern Society for Adolescent Medicine. Numerous committee memberships. *Honours include:* Robert Wood Johnson General Academic Paediatric Fellow, 1979-80; Teacher of Year, Paediatric Housestaff, Medical College of Georgia, Augusta, 1983; Delegate, National Invitational Conference on AIDS in Adolescents, Society for Adolescent Medicine, 1988; Visiting Professor, Kao- Hsiung Medical College, China, 1988; Biographical recognitions, awards, grants. *Address:* Sturgis Building, Room 444, 800 Marshall Street, Little Rock, Arkansas 72202, USA.

KING-JEFFERS Sharon, b. 17 Mar. 1940, Chelsea, Massachusetts, USA. Attorney at Law. 2 sons. *Education:* BSL, Western State University, Fullerton,

California, 1974; JD 1975. Bar: California, 1978. *Appointments:* Legal research supr, 1st Am Title Ins Co, Santa Ana, 1978-79; Sole practice, Norco, California, 1979-80, Riverside, California, 1982-. *Memberships:* Editorial staff, Western State University Law Rev, 1973-75; Trustee, Chaffey Community College, Alta Loma, 1977-82, Secretary 1977-79, Vice president 1979-80, President 1980-82; Trustee Charter Grove Psychiatric Hospital, Corona, California, 1982- , President 1984-86; Adv Bd Charter Med Network, 1983-84; Past president, Corona Music Theater Assn; Former Bd dirs, Pres, Charter mem, Vol Aux Kellogg Psychiatric Hospital; Inland Empire Cultural Arts Foundation, Riverside, San Bernardino, 1983-; International Toastmasters Riverside 7979, 1984-86; Formation Committee, Child Care Action Task Force, Riverside County, 1985-86; Riverside Master Chorale, 1981-82 and 1984-85; Treasurer, US Air Force Academy Parent's Club, Inland Empire Chapter, 1987-88; Riverside County Bar Association (estate planning, probate, trust sect, family law sect Public/Bar relations comm, Chairman Speakers Bureau, Law & media comm, medical/legal liaison comm); AAUW, 1977-84; Nu Beta Epsilon; Participant, Leadership America, 1988; Steering committee, Leadership California; Chairman, Women Helping Women, 1985; Chairman, Gold Key Comm, 1988. *Hobbies:* Writing; Singing; Music. *Address:* 2399 Mountain Avenue, Norco, CA 91760, USA.

KING-SHAW Ethel Marguerite, b. 16 June 1927, Vancouver, British Columbia, Canada. Professor Emeritus. m. John Charles Shaw, 15 Aug. 1981. *Education:* BEd, University of Alberta, 1949; MA, State University of Iowa, USA, 1950; PhD, University of Iowa, 1963. *Appointments:* Teacher, kindergarten & schools; Assistant Professor, Memorial University of Newfoundland, St John's, 1953-55; Lecturer, 1955-57, Assistant Professor, 1957-62, Associate Professor, 1962-67, Professor, 1967-85, Professor Emeritus, 1985-, University of Calgary; Advisor to Women Students, University of Alberta in Calgary, 1958-61; Visiting Lecturer, University of Alberta, 1954-57, University of British Columbia, 1958. *Publications:* General editor, Canadian Tests of Basic Skills. Forms 1 & 2, 1968, Forms 3 & 4, 1974, Forms 3M & 4M, 1983; Teacher's Guides; manuals for Administrators, Supervisors and Counsellors; Many research & professional articles; Book reviews. *Memberships include:* International Reading Association (Director 1968- 71, committees etc, Calgary & District Council Member); Former Director, Early Childhood Council; Fellow, Canadian College of Teachers (Past President, Calgary & District Chapter); Pi Lambda Theta; International Member, National Conference on Research in English; Organization Mondiale pour l'Education Prescolaire (Secretary, Canadian Committee, 1979-85); Association for Childhood Education International; National Council of Teachers of English; Canadian & Alberta Associations for Young Children; Early Childhood Education Council; Canadian Society for Study of Education; Canadian Association of Teachers of Education; Canadian Association of University Professors; Committees, Alberta Department of Education; Charter Member, Altrusa Club of Calgary. *Honours:* IODE Marshall Scholarship, 1954; Lord Strathcona Medal & Scholarship, 1946; George Croskery Memorial Award, Canadian College of Teachers, 1987; Various others. *Hobbies:* Travel; Photography; Collecting coins, stamps, china. *Address:* Department of Curriculum and Instruction, University of Calgary, Calgary, Alberta, Canada T2N 1N4.

KINGSLEY Dorothy, b. 14 Oct. New York, New York, USA. Writer. *Education:* Detroit Arts and Crafts Academy. *Appointments:* Radio writer for Bob Hope, 1938; Edgar Bergen, 1939-43. *Creative works:* Films include: Date with Judy; Neptune's Daughter; Two Weeks With Love; Angels in the Outfield; Texas Carnival; It's a Big Country; When in Rome; Small Town Girl; Dangerous When Wet; Kiss Me Kate; Seven Brides for Seven Brothers; Jupiter's Darling; Don't Go near the Water; Pal Joey; Green Mansions; Can-Can; Pepe; Half a Sixpence; Valley of the Dolls. Television: Created series, Bracken's World.

KINGSTON Mazine Hong, b. 27 Oct. 1940, Stockton, California, USA. Author. m. Earll Kingston, 23 Nov. 1963, 1 son. *Education:* BA, University of California, Berkeley, 1962. *Appointments:* English teacher, various schools, California & Hawaii 1965-69, Honolulu Business College 1969, Mid-Pacific Institute, Honolulu 1970-77; Professor of English, Visiting Writer, University of Hawaii, Honolulu, 1977; Thelma McCandless Distinguished Professor, Eastern Michigan University, 1986. *Publications:* Woman Warrior: Memoirs of a Girlhood Among Ghosts (awards), 1976; China Men (awards), 1981; Hawaii One Summer, 1987; Through the Black Curtain, 1988; Tripmaster Monkey, His Fake Books, 1989. Numerous short stories, articles & poems, various magazines & journals including Iowa Review, New Yorker, Ms, American Heritage, Redbook. *Honours include:* Awards: National Book Critics Circle 1976, Mademoiselle magazine 1977, Anisfield-Wolf 1978, Stockton Arts Commission 1981, Hawaii Award for Literture 1982; Writing fellow, National Endowment for Arts, 1980; Guggenheim fellow, 1981; Named 'Living Treasure, Hawaii, 1980; Woman of Year, Asian-Pacific Women's Network, 1981; Various citations. *Address:* 5425 Golden Gate Avenue, Oakland, California 94618, USA.

KINOSIAN Janet Marie, b. 20 June 1957, Los Angeles, California, USA. Journalist. *Education:* BA, Psychology, University of California, Los Angeles (UCLA), 1980; MA, Loyola University, 1987. *Appointments:* UCLA Daily Bruin, 1979-80; Intern, Los Angeles Magazine, 1981; Metropolitan News, 1981-84; Orange Coast Magazine, 1984-; President, JMK & Company, multifaceted writing company. *Publications include:* Numerous articles, regional, national & international publications; Internationally syndicated, North America Syndicates, New York Times Syndicate, Times of London. *Memberships:* Co-founder, International Women's Solidarity Coalition, & UCLA Campus Coalition for Peace; Orange County, Hollywood Women's, & Pacific Coast Press Clubs; Authors' Guild; National Organisation of Women; Amnesty International; Greenpeace. *Honours:* Best Reporter, Orange County Press Club, 1988; Best Magazine Feature Story, Pacific Coast Press Club, 1988. *Hobbies:* Films; Music; Art; Travel; Tennis. *Address:* JMK & Company, Studio One, 11692 Chenault Street, Apt. 103, Los Angeles, California 90049, USA.

KINS Andra, b. 5 Dec. 1952, Perth, Western Australia. m. Imants Kins, 12 May 1973, 1 son, 1 daughter. *Education:* B.Arch., Honours, Univerity of Western Australia, 1974; General Management Course, 1987. *Appointments:* Forbes & Fitzhardinge, Architects, 1975; Community Arts Officer, Mundaring Community Arts Centre, 1982-86; Executive Director, Crafts Council of Western Australia, & Director, Crafts Council Centre Gallery, 1986- 88. *Publications:* Paper Collages & Drawings exhibited, 1974, 1981, 1982. *Memberships:* President, Community Arts Network of Western Australia, 1985, 1986; Member Policy Committee, Crafts Council, Australia, 1987, 1988; Board Member, Mundaring Community Arts Centre, 1987, 1988; Curtin University of Technology, Board of the Arts, 1988; Chairperson, Katharine Susannah Prichard Foundation, 1988. *Hobbies:* Books; Films. *Address:* 66 Johnston Road, Parkerville, WA 6553, Australia.

KINSEY Jean Gordon, b. 11 Jan. 1933, Wellington, England. Dental Surgeon; Lecturer. m. Robert Moseley Kinsey, 4 Jan. 1958, 1 son, 2 daughters. *Education:* LDS, 1956, LDS RCS, 1956, Liverpool University. *Appointments:* House Officer, Liverpool Dental Hospital, 1956; General Dental Practice, Chester, 1956-58; Civilian Dental Officer, RAF, 1959-61; General Dental Practice, Sheffield, 1962-72; Hospital Appointments, 1966-; Student Dental Service, 1975-81; University Lecturer, Sheffield University, 1981-. *Publications:* Short Study Visits to Dental Schools in 5 EEC Countries, 1985; A Comparison of Attitudes to Geriatric Dentistry in 5 EEC Countries, 1986; lecture presentations at International Congresses. *Memberships:* British Society for the Study of Prosthetic Dentistry; International Association of Gerodontology; Federation Dentaire Internationale; Consultant to Commission on Dental Health Education. *Hobbies:* Foreign Travel; Sport; Girl Guide Association; Gardening; Natural History. *Address:* Townhead Farm, Townhead Road, Dore, Sheffield, South Yorkshire, England.

KINTNER Janet Ide, b. 25 Feb. 1944, Dayton, Ohio, USA. Judge. m. Charles F Kintner, 14 Sept. 1968. 2 sons, 1 daughter. *Education:* BA 1966, JD 1968, University of Arizona; Admitted to Arizona State Bar, 1968; Admitted to California State Bar, 1969. *Appointments:* Staff Attorney, Legal Aid Society of San Diego, Inc, 1969-70; Deputy City Attorney, San Diego, 1971-74; Private practice of law, 1974-76; Municipal Court Judge, 1976-. *Publications:* Published articles on civil law, criminal law and consumer law. *Memberships:* National Assn of Women Judges, charter member; California Women Lawyers; Calif Judges Assn; Lawyers Club; Honorary Member, Arizona State Bar. *Honours:* Certificate of Appreciation, First Annual Women's Conference, 1974; Outstanding Young Woman of America, 1974, 1978 and 1980; Honoured by San Diego Volunteer Lawyers Program for Training Programs, 1984-85. *Hobbies:* Music; Bridge. *Address:* County Courthouse, 220 West Broadway, San Diego, California 92101, USA.

KINZIE Jeannie Jones, b. 14 Mar. 1940, Great Falls, Montana, USA. Physician; Professor of Radiology. m. Joseph Kinzie, 26 Mar. 1965 (div.), 1 son. *Education:* BS, Montana & Oregon State Universities, 1958-61; MS, Washington University School of Medicine, St Louis, Missouri, 1965; Intern, surgery, University of North Carolina, 1965-66; Resident, oncology, Washington University, St Louis, 1968-71. *Appointments:* Instructor, radiology, Washington University, 1971-73; Assistant professor, Medical College of Wisconsin, 1973-74; Assistant, associate professor, University of Chicago, 1975-80; Associate professor, Wayne State University, 1980-85; Professor of Radiology & Director, Radiation Oncology, University of Colorado, 1985-. *Publications:* Numerous medical research articles, scientific journals; Numerous chapters, medical text books. *Memberships include:* American, Colorado & Denver Medical Societies; American College of Radiology; Rocky Mountain Oncology Society; American Society for Therapeutic Radiology & Oncology; American Association of University Professors; New York Academy of Sciences; Society of Head & Neck Surgeons. *Honours:* Phi Kappa Phi, 1961; Sigma Xi, 1976; Fellow, American College of Radiology, 1984. *Hobbies:* Skiing; Hiking; Stamp collecting; Rug latching. *Address:* Radiation Oncology, Box A031, 4200 East 9th Avenue, Denver, Colorado 80262, USA.

KINZIE Mary, b. 30 Sept. 1944. Educator. *Education:* BA, Northwestern University, 1967; MA 1972, PhD 1980, Johns Hopkins University. *Appointments:* Associate Editor 1968-69, Executive Editor 1975-78, Tri Quarterly; Instructor 1975-78, Lecturer 1978-85, Department of English; Director, English Major in Writing, 1979-; Associate Professor, Department of English, 1985-, Norwestern University. *Publications:* Poetry: The Threshold of the Year, 1982; Masked Women, forthcoming; Author of numerous essays and review articles. *Memberships:* PEN; Poetry Society of America; Society of Midland Authors. *Honours include:* Fulbright Scholarship, 1967-68; Winner, Devins Award for The Threshold of the Year, 1982; Illinois Arts Council Award in Poetry 1981, 1984 and 1988, in the Essay 1982; Artist Grant in Poetry, Illinois Arts Council, 1983; Guggenheim Fellowship in Poetry, 1986; Elizabeth Matchett Stover Memorial Award in Poetry for The Southwest Review, 1986; Celia B Wagner Award, The Poetry Society of America, 1988. *Address:* 8605 Keeler Avenue, Skokie, IL 60076, USA.

KIRBY Margaret Loewy, b. 5 June 1946, Ft. Smith,

Arkansas, USA. Anatomist. m. 26 June 1971, 1 son, 2 daughters. *Education:* AB, Manhattanville College, 1968; PhD, University of Arkansas, 1972. *Appointments:* Assistant Professor, University of Central Arkansas, 1973-75; Postdoctoral Fellow, University of Chicago, 1975-77; Assistant Professor, 1977-80, Associate Professor, 1980-85, Professor, 1985-87, Regents' Professor, 1987-, Medical College of Georgia. *Memberships:* Society for Neuroscience; Sigma Xi; Developmental Biology; American Heart Association. *Honour:* Established Investigator, American Heart Association, 1984-89. *Hobbies:* Music; Running; Biking. *Address:* Dept. of Anatomy, Medical College of Georgia, Augusta, GA 30912, USA.

KIRK Janine Anne, b. 26 Jan. 1953, Melbourne, Australia. Senior Trade Counsellor. m. George William Kirk, 30 June 1984. *Education:* BEcon, Monash University, 1973; Certificate, Australian Institute of Management, 1981; Export development studies, International Business Centre, 1988; Ashridge Management College, 1989. *Appointments:* Project officer, Australian Consolidated Industries, 1974-76; Market researcher, Business Intelligance Services, 1976-77; Research assistant, Australian Minister for Foreign Affairs, 1978-79; Executive assistant to Chief Executive 1979-82, Manager, Policy Secretariat 1982-85, General Manager, Executive Policy & Operations 1985-88, Senior Trade Counsellor 1988-, Australian Chamber of Manufacturers. *Memberships include:* Past President, Women in Management; Australian Institute of Management; Fellow, & Victorian Executive Committee, Society of Senior Executives; Economic Society of Australia & New Zealand; Ashridge College Association; Australian Secretary, Commonwealth Study Conferences. *Honours:* Life member, Women in Management, 1988; Foreign & Commonwealth Office scholarship, British Council, 1989; Group Leader, Duke of Edinburgh's 6th Commonwealth Study Conference, 1986. *Hobbies:* Fly Fishing; Golf; Tennis; Women in management. *Address:* PO Box 469, South Yarra, Victoria 3141, Australia.

KIRK-STAUFFER Melanie Ann, b. 16 May 1949, Tacoma, Washington, USA. Fitness Specialist. m. Lawrence Allen Stauffer, 30 Oct. 1983. *Education:* The Evergreen State College; Western Washington University; Columbia Pacific University; Specialized training in Dance, Royal Academy of Dance Ltd, Joffrey Ballet, San Francisco Ballet. *Appointments:* Professional dancer; Teacher; Businesswoman; President and manager, Stauffer & Associates, Inc, 1978-; Pacific Northwest Regional Licensing Executive For BMI, Broadcast Music Inc. *Publications:* Fit To Be Tried; Director and Choreographer for The Astralrhythmics, Jazz dance exercise performing company in the Pacific Northwest. *Memberships:* National Association of Female Executives; International Dance Exercise Association; American Holistic Medical Association; AVIA Professional Instructors Alliance; Associate Member, American College of Sports Medicine. *Honours:* Outstanding Woman of the Year in Sports and Fitness, Pierce County YWCA, 1986; AVIA Instructor's Award, 1987; Selected for lead role with Robert Joffrey in TV Documentary A Day in the Life of a Dancer, 1967; Multiple Scholarships in dance: Ford Foundation, San Francisco Ballet, 1963, 1964; Joffrey Ballet, 1965, 1966, 1967; Banff School of Fine Arts, 1964; Original scholarship with Pacific Northwest Ballet, 1967. *Hobbies:* Dancing; Choreographing jazz dance exercise; Computer science and graphic programs; Music; Reading; Community service activities for public assistance and in the arts. *Address:* 6909 Twin Hills Drive West, Tacoma, WA 98467, USA.

KIRKBRIDE Dorothy Mary Rees, b. 28 Nov. 1924, Wales. Painter. m. Kenneth Michael George Kirbride, 10 Oct. 1953. *Education:* NDD, St Martin's School of Art, London, 1951; History of Art, Courtauld Institue, London, 1954. *Appointments:* Public Lecturing, Painting, 1954-63; Lecturering, History of Art, Kumasi University, Ghana, 1964-66; Painting Privately, Travel, 1966-73; Painting Privately, Hong Kong, 1973-. *Creative*

Works: Works exhibited regularly in group shows; One Woman Exhibition, Arts Centre, Hong Kong, 1983; 2 persons Exhibitions: Hong Kong, 1976, Rotunda, Exchange Square, Hong Kong, 1987; 3rd Asian International Art Exhibition, Fukoru, Japan, 1988. *Hobbies:* Reading; Listening to Music; Talking. *Address:* 101 Rockymount, 39 Conduit Road, Hong Kong.

KIRKBY Elisabeth, b. 26 Jan. 1921, United Kingdom. Member, Legislative Council, NSW Parliament. m. J. D. Llewellyn-Jones, 2 sons, 1 daughter. *Appointments:* War Service, 1942-45; Actress, Scriptwriter, Producer, 1942-45; Various Roles, Theatre, TV, Radio, United Kingdom, 1945-52; Scriptwriter, Producer, Newsreader, Radio Malaysia, 1952-65; Australian Broadcasting Commission, 1965-72; Lucy Sutcliffe, No 96, 1972-75; Elected to Legislative Council, 1981. *Memberships:* Past International President, International Association of Women in Radio & TV; Former Vice-President, Australian Actors and Announcers Equity Association; Vice-President, Worldview International Foundation; Vice President, Amnesty International. *Hobbies:* Swimming; Sailing; Gardening; Riding; Trekking. *Address:* Awabakal, Martinsville, NSW 2265, Australia.

KIRKGAARD Valerie Anne, b. 18 Aug. 1940, Merced, California, USA. TV & Radio Producer & Show Host; Therapist. m. Lon Bryson Kirkgaard, 6 Oct. 1962 div. 1984, 1 son, 1 daughter. *Education:* BA, History, University of California, Los Angeles; MA, Transpersonal Psychology, Goddard University, 1982. *Appointments include:* Consultant & therapist, creating 'quantum shifts in consciousness' for individuals & corporations, 1975-; TV & Radio producer & host,1984-. Owner, art gallery, 1985-87. *Publication:* Article, Take Two Deep Breaths & Call Me In The Morning. *Membership:* Associate Coordinator Los Angeles N.D.W., California Association of Marriage & Family Therapists. *Honours:* 3rd prize, costume, masked ball, 1985; Olympic Torch Relay, Olympic Games, 1984. *Hobbies:* Art; Writing for children; Developing conversations of love & responsibility for individuals & our planetary family. *Address:* 3331 Ocean Park Boulevard, no. 102, Santa Monica, California 90405, USA.

KIRKPATRICK Jeane Jordan, b. 19 Nov. 1926, Duncan, Oklahoma, USA. Political Scientist. m. Evron Maurice Kirkpatrick, 20 Feb. 1955, 3 sons. *Education:* AA Stephens College, 1946; AB, Barnard College, 1948; MA, 1950, PhD 1968, Columbia University; French Government Fellow, U. Paris Inst. de Sci. Politique, Paris, France, 1952-53. *Appointments:* Research Analyst, Dept. of State, USA, 1951-53; Research Associate, George Washington University, 1954-56; Fund for the Republic, 1956-58; Assistant Professor, Political Science, Trinity College, 1962-67; Professor, Political Science, 1967-78; Leavey Professor of Government, 1978-, on leave 1981-85, Georgetown University; Senior Fellow, 1977-, on leave 1981-85, American Enterprise Institute; Member of Cabinet, 1981-85; USA Permanent Representative to UN, 1981-85. *Publications:* Leader and Vanguard in Mass Society: The Peronist Movement in Argentina, 1971; Political Woman, 1974; The Presidential Elite, 1976; Dismantling the Parties : Reflections on Party Reform and Party Decomposition, 1978; Dictatorships & Double Standards: Rational and Reason in Politics, 1982; The Reagan Phenomenon, 1983. *Memberships Include:* various professional organizations. *Honours:* Several honorary degrees; Award of the Commonwealth Fund, 1983; French Prix Politique for Political Courage, 1984; Department of Defense Distinguished Public Service Medal, 1985; Presidential Medal of Freedom, 1985. *Hobbies:* Swimming; Cooking; Reading. *Address:* American Enterprise Institute, 1150 17th Street NW, Washington, DC 20036, USA.

KIRTLEY Jane Elizabeth, b. 7 Nov. 1953, Indianapolis, USA. Attorney; Executive Director. m. Stephen Jon Cribari, 8 May 1985. *Education:* BSJ, 1975, MSJ, 1976, Northwestern University; JD, Vanderbilt University, School of Law. *Appointments:* Attorney, Nixon Hargrave Devans & Doyle, 1979-84; Staff

Attorney, Reporters Committee, 1984; Executive Director, Reporters Committee, Washington, 1985-. *Publications:* Articles in professional journals including: Dickinson Law Review, 1986; Government Information Quarterly, 1988; Chapter, Openness in Government, in Winning America, 1988; Editor, News Media & the Law, 1985-; Editor, First Amendment Handbook. *Memberships:* First Amendment Congress, Board Member; Libel Defense Resource Center; Center for Comm. Law Studies; Society of Professional Journalists; American, DC, and New York Bar Associations. *Honours:* Group Reporter, Ditchley Foundation Conference, 1987; Adjunct Faculty, American University, 1988-; University of Maryland, University College, 1987-; Guest Lecturer, various US Universities. *Hobbies:* Music; Theatre; Cinema. *Address:* Suite 300, 800 18th Street NW, Washington, DC 20006, USA.

KISARAUSKIENE Saulute Stanislava, b. 2 June 1937, Kaunas, Lithuania. Artist (Painter and graphic artist). m. Vincas Kisarauskas, 4 Oct. 1957. 1 son, 1 daughter. *Education:* Graduated High School, 1955; Lithuanian Art Institute in Vilnius, 1957-60. *Appointments:* Freelance Artist, 1960-73; Library's Graphic Art Department, taking care of Old Engravings, Vilnius University, 1973-84; Freelance Artist, 1984-. *Creative Works:* Exhibited in Lithuania, The Soviet Union, Europe, USA. Old Paintings include: Figura (figure), 1966; Aktas I (nude 1), 1967; Prie Stalo (by the table), 1968; Kaukes (Masks), 1969; Graiku tragediju motyvai (Motifs of Greek tragedy), 1979; Lapkritis-Langas I-IV (November, Window I-IV), 1980; Skrendanti Figura (flying figure), 1981; Tarp Juodo ir Balto (Between black and white), 1982; Svytejimas (radiance), 1983; Lietus (Rain), 1984, etc. Graphic prints include: Arlekinas (Harlequin), 1962; Sekspyro Dramu Temomis I- VII (Shakespeare drama themes I-VII), 1962; Karalius (King), 1964; Graiku tragedijos motyvais-Medeja (In the Greek tragedy motif-Medeja), 1972; Antigone ir Edipas (Antigone and Oedipus), 1972; Elektra (Electra), 1972-73; Antigone (Antigone), 1976; Elektra (Electra), 1976; Visisoje Tyloje I-V (In complete quiet I-V), 1976-78; Iliuzija (Illusion), 1977; Langas (window), 1981. Monotypes: Kompozicija (composition), 1974; Figura (figure), 1974; Lietus (rain), 1982; Rauda (Lament), 1982; Vejas ir Smelis I-IV (the wind and the sand I-IV), 1982; Zenklai Erdveje (signs/marks in space), 1984-86; Zenklai (signs/marks), 1987. *Membership:* Lithuanian Artists Union, 1969-. *Honour:* Received award in the 6th International Exlibris Biannual Exhibit in Malbork, Poland, 1974. *Hobbies:* Reading; Knitting; Gardening; Spiritualism. *Address:* 54-21 R Armijos Prospektas, Vilnius 232015, Lithuania, USSR.

KISSEL Susan Jo Steves, b. 17 Apr. 1943, Chicago, Illinois, USA. Associate Professor of English. m. Michael C C Adams, 11 July 1985. 2 sons. *Education:* BA 1964, BS Education 1965, MA 1967, PhD 1975, University of Cincinnati. *Appointments:* Instructor 1965-69, Asdjunct Assistant Professor 1975-77, University of Cincinnati; Assistant 1977-81, Associate Professor of English, 1985-, Women's Studies Program Director, 1981-85, Northern Kentucky University. *Publications:* The Story of the Pewter Basin, co-ed with Margery Rouse, 1981; Essays in Women's Personal Narratives, 1985; Walker Percy, 1980; articles in Studies in the Novel; The Southern Quarterly; Studies in Short Fiction; The Southern Literary Journal; Frontiers, etc. *Memberships:* Kentucky Philological Association; North Central Women's Studies Association, Past President, 1982- 84; South Atlantic Modern Language Association; Kentucky Commission on Women, Governor's Appointee as Honorary Member; Cincinnati Women's Conference Planning Committee. *Honours:* Phi Beta Kappa, 1964; Mortar Board, 1964; Alpha Lambda Delta, 1962; Honours in English, 1964; No Ky University Grand Marshal, 1982; Grant awards from Kentucky Humanities Council, 1982, 1983; National Endowment for Humanities, 1982-83; National Science Foundation, 1980- 81. *Hobbies:* Photography, developing slide/lecture programs on Cincinnati Women Writers and Artists, Southern Women Writers and Regional History. *Address:* Department of Literature and Language,

Northern Kentucky University, Highland Heights, KY 41076, USA.

KITCHEN Denise Michele, b. 1 Aug. 1958, Ballarat, Australia. Journalist; Editor. *Education:* ArtsDegree. *Appointments:* Travel Consultant, NT Government, Based in Melbourne, 1980; Journalist, NT Government, Darwin, 1981; Publicity Office, Yulara, Alice Springs, 1982; Partner, Territory Editorial, Darwin, 1983; Journalist, Associate Editor, Outback Australia, 1985-; Partner, True North Productions, 1985-. *Publications:* Editor, Producer, Territory Digest; Publisher, Editor, Outback Australia; Writer, Producer, This Way Up, Into the Outback, Tourism Video; Editor, Publisher, Tourism Guide to the Northern Territory. *Memberships:* Australian Journalist Association; Treasurer, Darwin Press Club. *Honours:* Winner, Print Media Section, Australian Tourism Awards, 1987; Winner, Print Media Section, Brolga Awards, 1987; Winner, Graphic Design, NT Printing Industries Craftsmanship Awards, 1987. *Hobbies:* Squash; Sailing; Photography; Licensed Lightweight Aircraft Pilot. *Address:* 7 Quarry Cres., Stuart Park, NT 0820, Australia.

KITLER Mary Ellen, b. 3 Nov. 1939, Williamsport, Pennsylvania, USA. Management Consultant, Health Care Industry and Pharmaceutical Industry. *Education:* BSc Pharmacy, 1961; MSc Medicinal Chemistry, 1962; PhD Clinical Pharmacology, 1967; Postdoctoral Fellow, NIH/NCI Biostatistics. *Appointments:* Recognized Scholar, Biomathematics, University of Oxford, 1978-80; Manager, Experimental Therapeutics, Zyma SA, Nyon, Switzerland, 1980-87; Independent Management Consultant, Health Care Industry and Pharmaceutical Industry, Europe/USA, 1987-. *Publications:* Numerous preclinical studies, clinical trials, statistics, therapeutics in the field of health care. *Memberships:* Fellow, American College of Clinical Pharmacology; American Society of Clinical Pharmacology and Therapeutics. *Honours:* Fellowship, American College of Clinical Pharmacology, 1976; Outstanding Young Women of America, 1961. *Hobbies:* Foxhunting; Tennis; Downhill skiing. *Address:* Maison des Truites, CH-1182 Gilly, Switzerland.

KITT Eartha, b. 26 Jan. 1928, Columbia, South Carolina, USA. Actress; Singer. *Appointments:* Professional career started as dancer in Katherine Dunham Group; toured USA, mexico & Europe with group, then opened night club in Paris; in Orson Welles stage production of Faust for European tour; New York Night Clubs; Stage in US, New Faces; at Macambo Hollywood, 1953. *Publications:* Thursday's Child; On Screen, 1954; New Faces, 1958; The Maker of the Hawk, St Louis Blues, Anna Lucasta, 1987; Dragonard. *Address:* De Jager/Burrichter Public Relations, 752 West Ave., 15J New York, NY 10025, USA.

KITTOCK Claudia, b. 3 May 1952, Rochester, Minnesota, USA. College Professor. m. Richard Kittock, 23 Dec. 1978. 2 sons. *Education:* AA, 1972; BA, 1974; MA, 1977; PhD, 1986. *Appointments:* Choral Teacher, High School, 1974-76; Private Music Teacher, 19676-77; Choral Teacher, High School, 1977-81; Consultant, E/BD, 1981-85 and 1986-87; Professor of Education, 1985-86; Professor of Child Psychology, 1987-. *Publications:* Perception of Teachers, Students and an Observer in Selected Choral Classrooms, 1986. *Memberships:* MENC; Phi Delta Kappa; MEED; MEA. *Hobbies:* Reading; Gardening; Bicycling; Swimming. *Address:* Cambridge Community College, Highways 95 and 70, Cambridge, MN 55008, USA.

KITZINGER Sheila Helena Elizabeth, b. 29 Mar. 1929, Taunton, England. Writer; Childbirth Educator; Anthropologist. m. Uwe Kitzinger, 1952, 5 sons. *Education:* Ruskin College, St Hugh's College, Oxford University; M.Litt., University of Edinburgh, 1954. *Publications:* Giving Birth: Choice in Childbirth; Giving Birth: How it Really Feels; The Experience of Childbirth; Education & Counselling for Childbirth; Women as Mothers; Birth at Home; The New Good Birth Guide;

The Experience of Breastfeeding; Pregnancy & Childbirth; Birth over Thirty; Woman's Experience of Sex; Being Born; A Celebration of Birth; Freedom and Choice in Childbirth; The Midwife Challenge; The Crying Baby. *Memberships:* Adviser, NCT; Management Committee, Midwives Information & Resource Service; Patron, Seattle School of Midwifery; Adviser, ICEA, USA; President, Oxford Branch, Royal College of Midwives; Editor, Issues in Women's Health, Pandora Press; Editorial Board, Montessori Today. *Honours:* MBE, 1982; American Health Book Award for Birth over Thirty, 1985; American Hornbook Award for Being Born, 1987; Times Educational Supplement Award for Being Born, 1987. *Hobby:* Painting. *Address:* The Manor, Standlake, Nr. Witney, Oxon OX8 7RH, England.

KIVETT Vira Rodgers, b. 18 May 1933, Augusta, Georgia, USA. Professor. m. Allen E. Kivett, 17 Aug. 1957, 1 son, 1 daughter. *Education:* BSHE, Woman's College, 1955, MSHE, 1960, PhD, 1976, University of North Carolina at Greensboro. *Appointments:* Vocational Home Economics Teacher, South Pines, North Carolina, 1955-57; Dietitian, Woman's College, 1957-59, Research Instructor, 1960-76, Assistant Professor, 1976-81, Associate Professor, 1981-87, Professor, 1987-, University of North Carolina, Greensboro. *Publications:* Contributions in area of gerontology in Journal of Gerontology, The Gerontologist, Family Relations, The Journal of Rural Studies, and International Journal of Aging and Human Development; Book chapters on families and aging. *Memberships:* Executive Committee, Gerontological Society of America; National Council on Family Relations; Southern Gerontological Society; International Association of Sociology. *Honours:* Distinguished Service Award, Piedmont Triad Council of Governments, Greensboro, 1978; US Community Services Administration Award, Washington DC, 1980; Certificate of Appreciation, State of North Carolina State Goals and Policy Board, 1983; Certificate of Recognition, Committee of the Status of Women, North Carolina, 1983; Distinguished Academic Gerontology Award, Southern Gerontological Society, 1988. *Hobbies:* Travel; Study of family relationships in later life. *Address:* 1316 Clover Lane, Greensboro, NC 27410, USA.

KIZER Kathryn W., b. 2 Nov. 1924, Greenville, South Carolina. Editor. m. Lawton E. Kizer Jr, 12 June 1948, 2 sons. *Education:* BA, Winthrop College, Rock Hill, South Carolina, 1945; Graduate studies: University of South Carolina, Columbia, 1946, 1947; Union Theological Seminary, New York, 1963. *Appointments:* Elementary School Teacher, 1945-47; Church Youth Director, 1947-49; Church Kindergarten Director, 1950-54; Pre school/Children's Director, 1961-76; Editor, Woman's Missionary Union of Southern Baptist Convention, Birmingham, Alabama, 1981-. *Publications:* Books: Circus Tent Summer; The Harley Shields: Alaskan Missionaries; Sunday School Challenge: Reaching Preschoolers; 200 Ideas for Teaching Preschoolers; Mission Friends Leader Manual; 200 Games and Fun Activities for Teaching Preschoolers. *Memberships:* Southern Association for Children Under Six; NAEYC. *Honours:* Best All-Round Student, High School; President, Baptist Student Union, Winthrop College; President, Georgia Religious Education Association. *Hobbies:* Reading; Collecting recipes; Entertaining. *Address:* Woman's Missionary Union, PO Box 830010, Birmingham, AL 35283, USA.

KJOS Victoria Ann, b. 17 Sept. 1953, Fargo, North Dakota, USA. Lawyer. *Education:* BA cum laude, Social Science, Minot State University, 1974; JD, University of North Dakota, 1977. *Appointments:* Lawyer, Jack E. Evans Ltd, 1977-78; Sales representative, Pacific Mutual Life Insurance, 1978-79; Deputy State Treasurer, North Dakota, 1979-80; Consultant, 1980-82; Assistant Vice President, Trust Department Manager, Great Western Bank, 1982-84; Associate lawyer, Robert A. Jensen PC, 1984-86; Shareholder, lawyer, Jensen & Kjos PC, 1986-. *Publications:* Various legal articles, professional journals. *Memberships include:* Offices: State Bar of Arizona, & Maricopa

County Bar Association; Family Law & Litigation Sections, American Bar Association; American, & Arizona Associations of Trial Lawyers; Western Pension Conference; Board, Central Arizona chapter, Arthritis Foundation; Arizona Democratic Council. *Hobbies:* Weight training; Downhill skiing; Reading. *Address:* 3246 North 16th Street, Phoenix, Arizona 85016, USA.

KLAHR Myra B, b. 16 Apr. 1933, New York, USA. Founder, Exec Dir, Poets in Public Service. divorced. 1 son, 3 daughters. *Education:* BA 1954, MS, Education 1959, Queens College. *Appointments:* Classroom Teacher, El School (Sub & Reg), 1954-70; Poet/Poet in Classroom, 1972-76; Founded, Poets in Public Service (aka NYS Poets in the schools), 1973-. *Publications:* The Waiting Room, 1972. *Memberships:* NYS Alliance for Arts Ed, Bd Member; Institute for Educ Leadership. *Honours:* Phi Beta Kappa; Dylan Thomas Poetry Prize, 1970. *Hobbies:* Swimming; Reading; Walking. *Address:* One Union Sq No 612, New York, NY 10003, USA.

KLECZKOWSKA Krystyna Felicja Maria, b. 24 June 1932, Stanislawow, Poland. Writer. m. Antoni Kleczkowski, 14 Oct. 1953. 1 son. *Education:* MA, History of the Arts, Jagiellonian University, Krakow, 1953. *Publications:* Books: Tomorrow I Will not Be a Mystery, 1959; The Four Walls of the World, 1964; A Visit to the Day Before Yesterday, 1968; The Little Partisan, 1969. *Membership:* Association of Polish Writers. *Honours:* Award, Contemporary Play Contest, 1963; Award, Polish Radio's Play Contest, 1982. *Hobbies:* Growing plants; Listening to music; Intellectual talk with friends; Literature; Politics. *Address:* ul Grunwaldzka 21/2, 31-524 Krakow, Poland.

KLEIN Kay Janis, b. 22 Aug. 1942, Detroit, Michigan, USA. Registered Nurse (RN). 2 sons, 1 daughter. *Education:* C. S. Mott Community College, 1960-62; Michigan State University, 1962-64; AA, ASc Nursing (Honours), St Petersburg Community College, 1975-78; BSc Nursing, University of South Florida, in progress; National Certification, Perioperative Nurse. *Appointments:* Display Manager 1960-62, layout artist & illustrator 1966-67, artist & varitypist 1967-70, Flint, Michigan; RN, 1976-; Staff Nurse, Intensive Care, Suncoast Hospital, Largo, Florida, 1976-78; Staff Nurse & Team Leader, Oncology Unit, Inservice Education Instructor & Director, Video Department, HCA Largo Medical Centre Hospital, 1978-81; Associate Director of Nursing, Roberts Home Health Services, 1982-84; Staff Nurse, Outpatient Surgery 1985-87, Surgical Services 1987-, HCA Largo Medical Centre Hospital; Medical illustrator, various publications, United Howmedica division, Pfizer Laboratories. *Publications include:* Editor & illustrator, books: Some Questions & Answers About Chemotherapy, Thoughts for Today; Illustrator, 2 cookery books. *Memberships:* Offices, past/present: American Business Women's Association, Union of American Hebrew Congregations; Phi Theta Kappa; Association of Operating Room Nurses; Hospital Corporation of America, Good Government Group. *Honours include:* Various awards, art work, 1961-; Chemotherapy book chosen for publication, American College of Surgeons, 1980. *Hobbies:* Painting & drawing; Tennis; Scuba diving. *Address:* 122 Palmetto Lane, Largo, Florida 34640, USA.

KLEIN Norma, b. 13 May 1938, New York City, USA. Writer. m. Erwin Fleissner, 27 July 1963. 2 daughters. *Education:* Graduate, Barnard College, 1960; Master's degree, Slavic Languages, Columbia, 1963. *Publications:* For Adults: Love and Other Euphemisms, 1972; Give Me One Good Reason, 1973; Coming to Life, 1974; Sunshine, 1975; Girls Turn Wives, 1976; It's Okay If You Don't Love Me, 1977; Love is One of the Choices, 1978; Domestic Arrangements, 1981; Wives and Other Women, 1982; Sextet in A Minor, 1983; Beginners' Love, 1983; The Swap, 1983; Lovers, 1984; Give and Take, 1985; American Dreams, 1987; That's My Baby, 1988. For Young Adults: Mom, the Wolf Man and Me, 1972; It's Not What You Expect, 1973; Confessions of an Only Child, 1973; Taking Sides, 1974; What It's All About, 1975; Hiding, 1976; Tomboy, 1978;

BrEaKing Up, 1980; A Honey of a Chimp, 1980; Robbie and the Leap Year Blues, 1981; The Queen of the What Ifs, 1982 Bizou, 1983; Barishnikov's Nutcracker, 1983; Angel Face, 1984; Snapshots, 1984; The Cheerleader, 1985; Family Secrets, 1985; Going Backwards, 1986; Older Men, 1987; My Life as a Body, 1987; Now That I Know, 1988; No More Saturday Nights, 1988. Picture books for Younger children: Girls Can Be Anything, 1973; Naomi in the Middle, 1974; If I Had My Way, 1974; A Train for Jane, 1974; Dinosaur's Housewarming Party, 1974; Blue Trees, Red Sky, 1975; Visiting Pamela, 1979. *Address:* 27 West 96th Street, New York City, NY 10025, USA.

KLEINROK Maria, b. 21 Mar. 1932, Tarnowskie Gory, Poland. Dentist. m. Zdzislow Kleinrok, 23 July 1953. 1 son. *Education:* Graduate, Stomatological Faculty, Silesian Medical Academy, Zabrz, 1955; Doctoral dissertation, 1966; Habil diss, nomination for professor, 1984. *Appointments:* Assistant, Dept of Prosthodontics, Silesian Med Ac, 1955-69; Stom Clinic, Lublin, 1969-75; Head of Dept of Prosthodontics, Medical Academy, Lublin, 1975-. *Publications:* Author of 140 articles; Book: Diagnostik und Therapie von Okklusionsstörungen, 1984; 16 patents. *Memberships:* Polish Stomotological Association; European Prosthodontic Association. *Honours:* Prizes awarded from Minister of Health in Poland for research, 1984 and 1987; Golden Honour Medal, Polish Stomatological Association; Winner, Best patent in health service, Poland, 1984; Membership, Bene Meritus, Polish Stomatological Association. *Hobbies:* Patents; Travelling; Prevention in Dentistry. *Address:* 20-534 Lublin, ul. Uśmiechu 21, Poland.

KLEINWORT Joan Nightingale, b. 3 Apr. 1907, London, England. Retired. m. Ernest Greverus, 29 Dec. 1932, died, 1 son, 1 daughter. *Appointments:* Private Secretary, Ellis Piers, 1931-32. *Memberships:* Vice President: WWF, UK, Wildfowl Trust; President, several local charitable organisations. *Honours:* MBE, 1945; JP, Chairman of Bench 972-77; DL, West Sussex, 1981. *Hobbies:* Conservation; Charitable Causes; Gardening. *Address:* Heaselands, Haywards Heath, W. Sussex RH16 4SA, England.

KLEJMENT Anne, b. 27 Apr. 1950, Rochester, USA. Professor. *Education:* BA, Nazareth College, Rochester, 1972; MA, 1974, PhD, 1981, State University of New York. *Appointments:* Instructor, History, Vassar College, 1978-79; Administrator, Historians in Residence, Cornell University, 1979-81; Assistant Professor, SUNY, 1981-83; Assistant Professor, History, 1983-88, Associate Professor, 1988-, College of St Thomas. *Publications:* The Berrigans: A Bibliography, 1979; Dorothy Day and the Catholic Worker: A Bibliography and Index, co-author, 1986. *Memberships:* Organization of American Historians, 1974; Catholic Historical Association; Women Historians of the Midwest, Steering Committee, 1987-88; Vice President, 1989-. *Honours:* New York State Regents College Scholarship, 1968-72; Nazareth College Competitive Scholarship, 1968-72; SUNY Foundation Fellowship, 1976-77; Senior Muriel Ford Lecturer, Briar Cliff College, 1986. *Hobbies:* Mediterranean & East Asian Cooking; Folk Music. *Address:* College of St Thomas, No. 4188, Dept. of History, St Paul, MN 55105, USA.

KLEMM Margaret Fae, b. 22 Sept. 1958, Ypsilanti, Michigan, USA. Professor. *Education:* AAS, Lansing Community College, 1988; BS, Arizona State University, 1978; MA, Western Michigan University, 1981; PhD, University of New Orleans, 1986. *Appointments:* Xavier University, New Orleans, Louisiana, 1984; Saginaw Valley State University, 1985-88; Northern Illinois University, DeKalb, 1989. *Publications:* A Look at Criminal Case Processing in Five Cities, 1986; A Comparison of Position Making and Controversy in Congress (with Steven A Shull), 1987; Criminal Law: Cases and Materials (with Craig Ducat), casebook forthcoming. *Memberships:* Academy of Criminal Justice Sciences; American Judicature Society; American Political Science Association; Law and Society Association; Midwest Political Science Association;

Midwestern Criminal Justice Association; Southern Political Science Association. *Honours:* Phi Theta Kappa; Phi Sigma Alpha. *Hobbies:* Flying (commercial pilot and flight instructor); Photography. *Address:* Department of Political Science, Zulauf Hall 410, Northern Illinois University, DeKalb, IL 60115, USA.

KLIMA Martha Scanlan, b. 3 Dec. 1938, Baltimore, Maryland, USA. Delegate to Maryland House of Delegates. m. James Patrick Klima, 8 Apr. 1961. 2 sons, 1 daughter. *Education:* AA, Villa Julie College, 1958. *Appointments:* Medical Stenographer, University of Maryland Medical School, Baltimore, 1958-63; Delegate, Maryland House of Delegates, 1982-. *Publication:* Maryland's Workers, Compensation System - Out of Control, 1986. *Memberships:* Maryland Spec Olympics, Board of Directors; The Exchange Club of Baltimore; Nat Republican Legislators Assoc; VP, Women Legislators of Maryland; Greater Baltimore Med Cent, Board of Directors; Maryland State Planning Commission; Amer Leg Exch Coun, State Chairman. *Honours:* Governor's Citation for outstanding services to the citizens of the State of Maryland; Woman of the Year, Towsontowne Bus & Prof Women's Club, 1988; Freshman of the Year, Award from the Speaker of the House of Delegates, 1983; Honorary Life Membership, maryland Congress of Parents and Teachers, Inc. *Hobbies:* Fishing; Walking. *Address:* 1403 Newport Place, Lutherville, Maryland 21093, USA.

KLINE Faith Elizabeth, b. 22 Dec. 1937, Louisiana, USA. Investment Broker. m. George Ellis Kline, 26 Nov. 1959, 1 son, 2 daughters. *Education:* BA, Southern Nazarene University, 1960; Northwestern University, 1963-64. *Appointments:* Executive Secretary to the President, Camp International Inc., 1980-85; Investment Counsellor, IDS/American Express, 1985-86; Investment Broker, A.G. Edwards & Sons Inc., 1986-. *Publication:* The Klines of Evanston: 1848-1968. *Memberships:* Trustee, Board of Education, Concord Community Schools; Executive Committee, Jackson County Republicans; Greater Jackson Chamber of Commerce; etc. *Hobbies:* Antique Restoration; Piano; Genealogy. *Address:* 9023 Hammond Road, Concord, MI 49237, USA.

KLINE Robin Leone Berglund, b. 13 Jan. 1920, Vermillion, South Dakota, USA. Teacher. m. Otis E Kline Snr. 3 sons, 1 daughter. *Education:* University of South Dakota, 1937-39; BA, Elementary Education, 1960-66, MA, Audiovisual, 1968-75, Arizona State University; SS University of Hawaii, 1968; Model Rocketry-Estes, University of North Colorado, SS, 1982; Space Down To Earth-NASA, USAF, CAP, San Jose State University, 1983; University of Arizona SS; Travel all over the world. *Appointments:* Teacher: 2nd Grade, Kiva Scottsdale School District, 1970; 1st Grade, Kiva Scottsdale School District, 1970-87; 7th Grade Literature, Kiva, 1978-79; Gifted Grades 1-8, Kiva, 1979-84; 1st Grade, Tonalea, Scottsdale School District, 1984-. *Creative Works:* Phenomenon and Strategic Minerals-The Invisible War; The Teaching of Composition: First Grade Children Can Compose; AECT Student 8mm Film Festival-1st Place Award TV Documentary, School Days. *Memberships:* Alpha Phi International Fraternity; Pi Lambda Theta Beta Kappa National Honour and Prof Ass in Ed; Phi Delta Kappa Professional Ed. Fraternity, Research Chr; Delta Kappa Gamma Society International Corresponding Secretary, 2nd Vice-president, Membership; 1st Vice-president, Programme; President; Junior League of Phoenix-Sustainer Advisor for HELP forerunner of Crisis Nursery; Olympics of the Mind-Phoenix Chapter-Secretary; Abiding Saviour Lutheran Church, Church Council and Sunday School Teacher; President of 2 different PTA's; Cub Scout Den Mother, 6 years; Rank of Captin, Wing Unit Civil Air Patrol, 1988. *Honours:* Scottsdale Honours Teacher, 1982, 1984, 1985, 1986, 1987, 1988; State winner of the USA Federal Aviation Administrator's Award for Excellence in Education, 1987; Teacher-In-Space Finalist from Arizona; Recipient of A Scott Crossfield Aerospace Education Teacher of Year Award at National Congress on Aviation and Space Education, 1986; Phi Delta Kappa Outstandign Educator,

Scottsdale Chapter, 1986. *Hobbies:* Hot Air ballooning; Model Rocketry; Teach English to 4 Cambodian Families; Sponsors Child from Bolivia; Collects shells from all over the world; Travel; Cooking. *Address:* 5226 North 69th Place, Scottsdale, AZ 85253, USA.

KLINK Karin Elizabeth, b. 12 NOv. 1937, New York City, USA. Freelance Medical Writer. m. Fredric J. Klink, 28 Nov. 1958, divorced 1979, 2 sons. *Education:* BA, Geology, Barnard College, 1958; MFA, Columbia University, 1963; MSc., Art Therapy, University of Bridgeport, 1977; Graduate Certificate, Corporate Video, Fairfield University, 1983. *Appointments:* Director, Creative Therapies & Rehabilitation Dept., Hall-Brooke Hospital, 1978-83; Manager, editorial Development, Wilcom Ltd., 1984-85; Editorial Director, Logical Communications Inc., 1985; President, Creative Word & Image, 1985-. *Creative Works:* Director, Animator, film, The Stage Evolves, 1964; Author, series of films, Land Biomes of the World, 1968; Author, various medical films and videotapes, various one person shows of drawings. *Memberships:* American Art Therapy Association; Women in Communications; Arts Institute, Silvermine Guild of Artists, Board of Directors. *Honours:* Best in Show Award, 20/20 vision (60th Anniversary Show), Silvermine Guild of Artists, 1982; Invited to paint Easter Egg for White House Easter Egg Collection at Smithsonian Institution, 1986; various prizes. *Hobbies:* Painting; Drawing; Photography; Sailing; Reading. *Address:* 13 Sammis Street, Rowayton, CT 06853, USA.

KLYMAN Cassandra, b. 1 Jan. 1938, New York City, USA. Psychiatrist; Psychoanalyst. m. 20 June 1960, 2 sons. *Education:* BA, Barnard College, 1958; MD, University of Michigan, 1962; Residency, various hospitals. *Appointment:* Private Practice, 1966-. *Publications:* Articles in professional journals. *Memberships:* AMA; American Psychiatric Association, Fellow; American Psychoanalytical Association. *Honours:* Recipient, Certificate of Appreciation for Outstanding Teaching, Sinai Hospital, Detroit, 1975; Service Certificates, Michigan Psychiatric Society. *Interests:* Tennis; Travel; Art. *Address:* 3060 Chickering Lane, Bi. Hills, MI 48013, USA.

KMET Rebecca Eugenia Patterson, b. 17 June, 1948, Ellisville, Mississippi, USA. Pharmacist; Community Activist. m. Joseph Paul Kmet, 29 Mar. 1969. *Education:* BSc, University of Arizona, Tucson, Arizona, 1971; Master's Degree in Business Administration, National University, San Diego, California, 1980. *Appointments:* Star Drugstore, Tucson, 1971-72; Santa Monica Prof Pharmacy, 1972-73; Wadsworth Veteran's Admin Hosp, West Los Angeles, 1973-74; US Navy, Naval Hospital, San Diego, 1975-78; Kaiser Medical Center, San Diego, 1979-82. *Publications:* Article on Military Women in Amphibious Warfare Review, Summer 1988. *Memberships include:* US Senatorial Club; Smithsonian Associates; Navy League, Union Mission Ministries; Naval Historical Foundation; Marine Corps Historical Foundation; Daughters of the American Revolution. *Honours:* Presidential Achievement Award, (Republican Party) National Congressional Committee, 1987; Current Strategy Forum Participant, 1981; Rho Chi Pharmacy Scholastic Honorary, 1968. *Hobbies:* Theology; Needlepoint; Bicycling; Gardening; Student of government; Literature; Anthropology; Piano playing; Community service lecturer. *Address:* 6155 Rolfe Avenue, Norfolk, Virginia 23508, USA.

KNAACK Twila Jean, b. 22 Mar. 1944, Iowa, USA. Writer. m. Scott A. Kuklin, 12 Apr. 1986. *Education:* Minneapolis Business College, 1963; AA, Pasadena City College, 1973. *Appointments:* Secretary, Billy Graham Evangelistic Association, Minneapolis, 1964-69; Administrative Assistant, World Wide Pictures, Burbank, California, 1970-88. *Publications:* I Touched A Sparrow, 1978; Special Friends, 1980; Promise Me Forever, 1983; Touched By Diamonds, 1984; Always & Forever, 1985. *Memberships:* Jubilate (Chairperson 1985); Walter Hoving Home Auxiliary (Chairperson 1985-87). *Honours:* Angel Award for book Special

Friends, Religion in Media; Bronze Halo Award for Outstanding Contribution to the Entertainment Industry, Southern California Motion Picture Council. *Hobbies:* Sculpturing; Tennis; Skiing; Swimming; Biking; Travel (visited 15 European countries, 3 Middle Eastern countries, Soviet Union, Hong Kong, Australia). *Address:* 13171 Bromont, Sylmar, CA 91342, USA.

KNAUF Suzanne Wood, b. 14 Feb. 1948, Camp Pendleton, California, USA. Judge of the Municipal Court. m. Charles B Flood III, 5 Apr. 1979. *Education:* BA, UCSB. 1969; JD, California Western School of Law, 1972. *Appointments:* Private Law Practice: Kimball and Mitchell, Encinitas, California, 1972-75; Feist, Vetter, Kanuf & Loy, Oceanside, California, 1975-78; Judge of the Municipal Court, Vista, California, 1978-. *Memberships:* North County Bar Association, Board of Directors; San Diego County Bar Association, Director of Lawyers Referral Services; California Bar Association; California Judges Association; San Diego County Judges Association; National Association of Women Judges; North County Concert Association; Carlsbad Girl's Club, Board of Directors; San Diego County Alcohol Task Force; Rotary International; TriCity Christian School, Board of Directors; Lawyers Club; California Women Lawyers; Presiding Judge and Assistant Presiding Judge, North County Municipal Court; Community Colleges Credential for Instructor in Law. *Hobbies:* Antiques and Collectibles; Travel; Gardening; Montana. *Address:* North County Municipal Court, 325 S Melrose Drive, Vista, CA 92083, USA.

KNIGHT Alanna, b. County Durham, England. Novelist; Biographer. m. Alexander Harrow Knight, 2 sons. *Appointments:* Lecturer, Creative Writing, Workers' Educational Association, 1971-75; Organiser, Meet the Author, Aberdeen, 1973-75; Tutor, Arvon Foundation, Lumb Bank, July 1982. *Publications:* Novels: Legend of the Loch, 1969; The October Witch, 1971; This Outward Angel, 1971; Castle Clodha, 1972; Lament for Lost Lovers, 1972; The White Rose, 1974; A Stranger Came By, 1974; The Wicked Wynsleys, 1977; Historical Novels: This Passionate Kindness, 1974, 1980; A Drink for the Bridge, 1976, 1977, 1986; The Black Duchess, 1980, 1983; Castle of Foxes, 1981; Colla's Children, 1982; The Clan, 1985; Estella, 1986; Crime Novels: Enter Second Murderer, 1988; Blood Line, 1989; Non Fiction: The Robert Louis Stevenson Treasury, 1985; R L S in the South Seas, 1986; Plays; The Private Life of R L S; Girl on an Empty Swing, 1977; numerous articles, short stories & serials in journals and magazines; Radio plays, etc. *Memberships:* Scottish Arts Council's Writers in Schools; Writers in Public; Society of Authors, Scottish Pen, Radiowriters Association; Crime Writers; Romantic Novelists Association; Founder, Chairman, Aberdeen Writers' Workshop. *Honours:* RNA First Novel Award, Legend of the Loch; Pitlochry SAW Award, Girl on an Empty Swing, 1977. *Hobbies:* Walking; Music; Painting; Creative Knitting. *Address:* 24 March Hall Crescent, Edinburgh EH16 5HL, Scotland.

KNIGHT Gloria Delores, b. 4 Jan. Jamaica, West Indies. General Manager, Urban Development Corporation. m. Marcel Knight 1 June 1960. 1 son, 4 daughters. *Education:* BA General, University of the West Indies, 1950-53; Special course in Public Administration, Oxford University, England, 1955-56; Postgraduate course in Sociology, McGill University, Canada, 1962-64; MSc Applied Behavioural Science, Johns Hopkins University, USA, 1982-84. *Appointments:* General Manager, Urban Development Corporation. *Memberships:* Mona Campus Council; Director: Mutual Life of Jamaica; National Hotels & Properties Limited; Alprojam Limited. *Honours:* One of 5 distinguished women, University Guild of Graduates, Mona Campus in celebration of International Women's Year, 1975; Order of Distinction (Commander), 1977; Certificate of Honour for Distinguished Service, 1980; Distinguished Service, International Decade for Women; Plaque in recognition of contribution to HABITAT and to the organization of the 8th Session, 1985; Pelican Award, Guild of Graduates, 1986; Order of Jamaica,

Independence Day National Honours and Awards, 1987. *Hobbies:* Reading; Badminton. *Address:* c/o Urban Development Corporation, 12 Ocean Boulevard, Kingston Mall, Kingston, Jamaica, West Indies.

KNIGHT Jill Joan Christabel, b. 9 July 1927, Bristol, England. Member of Parliament. m. James Montague Knight, 14 June 1947, died 1985, 2 sons. *Appointments:* County Borough Councillor, 1956-66; Member Parliament, Birmingham, Edgbaston, 1966-; Member, Council of Europe, 1977-88; Member, Western European Union, 1977-88. *Publications:* various press articles. *Memberships:* Numerous. *Honours:* MBE, 1964; DBE, 1984. *Address:* House of Commons, London SW1A 0AA, England.

KNIGHT Kathleen (Kit) Duell, b. 21 Sept. 1952, North Kingston, Rhode Island, USA. Writer. m. Arthur Winfield Knight, 25 Aug. 1976. 1 daughter. *Education:* BA, communications, California University of Pennsylvania, 1975. *Appointments:* Co-publisher, The Unspeakable Visions of the Individual, 1976-; Columnist, Russian River News, 1988-. *Publications:* A Marriage of Poets, co-author with Arthur Knight, 1984; The Beat Vision, c-edited with Arthur Knight, 1987; Kerouac and The Beats, co- edited with Arthur Knight, 1988. *Membership:* American Bison Association. *Honours:* Fels Award, 1977; Pushcart Press prize, 1978. *Hobbies:* Hand-sewing; The American buffalo. *Address:* P O Box 439, California, PA 15419, USA.

KNIGHT Lindsay Margaret, b. 25 Mar. 1948, England. Writer; TV Producer (documentaries). *Education:* St Anne's College, Oxford, 1965-68; BA(Hons), English Literature and Language. *Appointments:* Assistant Editor, New Internationalist, 1970-72; Production Assistant, New Society, 1972-74; Feature Writer, Community Care magazine, 1974-77; Editor, Mind Out, 1977-80; TV Producer, Well Being and other documentaries including Channel 4's Nov 1988 series on cities and health, also Director, Holmes Associates independent production company, 1980-. *Publication:* Talking to a Stranger - A Consumers Guide to Therapy, 1986. *Honours:* Mind/Allen Lane Award for Talking to a Stranger, 1986; TV Award, 1986, Award for Talking to a Stranger, 1987, Medical Journalists Association. *Address:* 70 Rokeby Road, London SE4 1DF, England.

KNIGHT Virginia Frances, b. 12 Oct. 1918, Fort Dodge, Iowa, USA. Writer; Historian (California). m. (1) C. Lyle Carlson (killed in action 1944), 28 June 1940, (2) Honorable Goodwin J. Knight (dec. 1970), 2 Aug. 1954. *Education:* Graduated Los Angeles High School, 1937. *Career:* Fashion Model, Warner Bros, theatres, radio, 1937-42; Pioneer TV programmes, KHJ, Don Lee Network, 1937; Accommodation sales and emergency procurement, Douglas Aircraft; Civic and veterans rehabilitation work and entertainment for veterans hospitals; Victory House, Pershing Square; War bond drives, World War II; Associate Producer/Participant, TV Tele-Forum and Freedom Forum, 1947-54; First Lady of California, 1954-58; Official Hostess, National Republican Convention, San Francisco, 1956; Planted Virginia Knight Camellia, Capitol Park, 1958; Established collection of portraits of California First Ladies; Owner/ Operator, Elephant-Eagle Gold Mines, Mojave, currently. *Publications:* The Golden Heritage of Goodwin Knight, 1975; Series of oral history interviews, Bancroft Library, UCB, 1977-80; Reflections on Life with Goodwin J. Knight; Virginia Knight California's First Lady, 1954- 58, 1987; Numerous poems including: A Tribute to the Unknown Soldier, dedicated to General Douglas MacArthur, 1988; Caressing Rain, 1989. *Memberships:* Past President, American Legion Auxiliary; Honorary Member, VFW Auxiliary; Edwin Markham Poetry Society; Founder, The Music Center Building Fund Committee; Society of Arts and Letters (National Advisory Council 1956-58); Ettie Lee Homes for Youth (National Advisory Committee); Stanford University Libraries; Life Member, Navy League; Fellow, American Institute of Fine Arts; Society of Literary Designates, Washington DC; Life Member, International

Clover Poetry Association. *Honours:* Various awards and honours including: Honorary Poet Laureate, State of Delaware, 1955; Dame Commander, Order of the Crown of Thorns, 1977; Golden Poet Award, World of Poetry, 1988-89. *Hobbies:* Writing verse; Swimming; Tennis; Recreational sports events; Television; Cinema. *Address:* 540 South Arden Boulevard, Los Angeles, CA 90020, USA.

KNOTT Kim, b. 25 May 1955, Watford, England. Lecturer. *Education:* BA, Honours, 1976, MA, 1977, PhD, 1982, Religious Studies. *Appointments:* Research Fellow, 1982-88, Lecturer, 1988-, University of Leeds. *Publications:* Hinduism in Leeds, 1986; My Sweet Lord: The Hare Krishna Movement, 1986. *Memberships:* British Association for the History of Religions, Bulletin Editor; International Association for the History of Religions; Association of University Teachers. *Address:* Dept. of Theology & Religious Studies, The University, Leeds LS2 9JT, England.

KNOTTS Wynelle Harrison, b. 5 May 1927, Ocala, Florida, USA. Retired School Librarian. m. (1)George Neal MacMullen, 21 Mar. 1948, div. 1970, 1 son, 2 daughters; (2)Thomas Knotts, 17 Apr. 1980, 1 son, 1 daughter. *Education:* Stetson University, 1945-47; BS, Florida State University, 1947-49; Jacksonville University, 1956; Florida Southern College, 1964; Emory University, 1970. *Appointments:* 2nd grade Teacher, Jacksonville, Florida, 1956-60; 3rd grade Teacher, Ft Lauderdale, Florida, 1960-61; 5th and 3rd grade Teacher, St Petersburg, Florida, 1961-66; Jr High Audio-Visual Coordinator, St Petersburgh, Florida, 1966-68; DeKalb County Adult Education Librarian, Atlanta, Georgia, 1968-72; Elementary School Librarian, Ocala, Florida, 1972-80; Elementary/Jr High Librarian, Yankeetown, Florida, 1980-81. *Publications:* Compiled Bibliographjy, International Geophysical Year, 1957; Handbook for School Librarians, 1976. *Memberships:* National Education Association; Florida Education Association; Florida Library Association; Georgia Teachers Association; Georgia Library Association; South Eastern Library Association; American Library Association; Florida Free Lance Writers Association; Florida Historical Society; Histopical Association of South Florida. *Hobbies:* Reading; Editing; Needlepoint. *Address:* 13499 Biscayne Blvd, Apt 1609, North Miami, Florida 33181, USA.

KNOWLES Barbara B, b. 27 Feb. 1937, New York City, New York, USA. Professor of Microbiology. *Education:* AB, Middlebury College, 1958; MS 1963, PhD 1965, Arizona State University. *Appointments:* Postdoctoral Research Fellow, University of California at Berkeley, 1965-66; Research Associate 1967-76, Wistar Associate Professor 1976-82, Wistar Professor 1983-, The Wistar Institute of Anatomy and Biology; Faculty 1977-, Vice Chairman, Immunology Graduate Group 1984-87, University of Pennsylvania; Visiting Professor, Hahnemann Medical College, 1980-84; Wistar Professor of Pathology and Laboratory Medicine, Wistar Professor of Microbiology, University of Pennsylvania School of Medicine, 1984-; Senior Visiting Scientist, Cold Spring Harbor Laboratory, 1987-88. *Publications:* Author of 132 papers to professional journals. *Memberships:* Editorial Board, Immunogenetics, 1977-80; Cancer Research Manpower Review Committee, NCI, 1980-84; Editorial Board, Molecular and Cellular Biology, 1984-89; Consultant, Cancer Information Dissemination Analysis Center, 1976-89; Editorial Board, Differentiation, 1988-; Board of Scientific Counselors National Institute of Dental Research, 1989-. *Honours:* Recipient of numerous grants and fellowships. *Address:* The Wistar Institute, 36th Street at Spruce, Philadelphia, PA 19104, USA.

KNOWLES Dorothy, b. 28 Mar. 1906, Johannesburg, South Africa. University Teacher (Retired); Literary Historian, Modern French Theatre. m. J. S. Spink, 27 July 1940. *Education:* LRAM, 1926; BA Honours 1928, DipEd 1929, MA 1931, University of Leeds, UK; Docteur ès Lettres en Sorbonne, Paris,

France, 1934. *Appointments:* Lecturer, French, Liverpool University, 1934-68; ABCA Lecturer (French politics, ballet demonstrations), 1940-46; Honorary Research Fellow, Bedford College (now RHBNC), University of London, 1968-. *Publications:* Author: La Réaction Idéaliste au Théâtre depuis 1890, 1934; Censor, Drama & Film 1900-34, 1934; French Drama of Inter-War Years 1918-39, 1967; Armand Gatti in the Theatre: Wild Duck Against the Wind, 1989. Co-author, Forces in Modern French Drama, 1972. *Memberships:* Past President, Association of University Teachers of French; BBC's 51 Society, 1951-58. *Honours:* Award for book 1935, Officier 1948, Académie Française; Medal, French play production, French Consul General, 1966. *Hobbies:* Former solo ballet performances; Productions, French drama (in French), 1952-66; Former competitive fencer (fenced solo in Moscow, twice). *Address:* 48 Woodside Park Road, London N12 8RS, England.

KNOWLES Susan Christine, b. 10 Apr. 1951, Brisbane, Australia. Senator. *Appointments:* Sales & Marketing Manager, 1971-84; Senator, Western Australia; Opposition Deputy Whip in the Senate. *Memberships:* Liberal Party of Australia; Life Member, Young Liberal Movement; Australian Parliamentary Association for UNICEF; Amnesty International Parliamentary Group; Australia UK Parliamentary Friendship Group; Interparliamentary Union; Foundation Member, Sales Executive Society of Australia. *Hobbies:* Photography; Gardening; Sports. *Address:* Suite 2, 2 Richardson Street, West Perth, Western Australia, 6005 Australia.

KNOWLES Wyn, b. 30 July 1923, Southbourne, England. Part-time Teaching Auxiliary; Volunteer, London Zoo; Various Charity Committees. *Appointments:* Room 055 War Office, 1941-45; Secretarial, 1945-57; BBC Drama Producer, 1957-59; Producer, Woman's Hour, 1960-65; Assistant Editor, 1965-67; Deputy Editor, 1967-71, Editor, 1971-83 (retired), Woman's Hour. *Publications:* Co-Editor, The Woman's Hour Book, 1983. *Memberships:* Intenational PEN; 300 Group; Network. *Hobbies:* Oil Painting; Travel; Food & Wine; Container Gardening. *Address:* 80 A Parkway, Regent's Park, London NW1 7AN, England.

KOCAK (Ayce) Nur, b. 14 Dec. 1941, Istanbul, Turkey. Artist. m. Ali Bahir Guran, 1965 (div. 1969). *Education:* Diploma, State Academy of Fine Arts, Istanbul, 1960-68; Further studies (state scholarship), painting, Paris, France, 1970-74. *Appointments:* Draughtsman, Lausanne, Switzerland, 1964-67; Assistant professor, State Academy of Fine Arts, Istanbul, 1975-81. *Creative work includes:* Paintings: Series, Femmes Objets et Objets Fetiches 1974-79, 1987, From the Family Album 1979-86; Drawings, series, Souvenirs de Bonheur, 1981; Contributions, art magazines, Turkey & abroad. *Honours:* High achievement prize, Children of Turkey exhibition, 1979; Gold Medal (1st prize), 3rd Istanbul Art Festival, New Tendencies in Art exhibition, 1981; Honourable mention, 20th Art Exhibition, DYO, 1986. *Hobbies:* Cinema; Interior decoration; Photography; Literature. *Address:* Ferit Tek Sok. 40/12, Moda, Istanbul, Turkey.

KOCH Adrienne Jeanne, b. 14 July 1935, Johannesburg, South Africa. Member, President's Council. m. Arnim Rolf Dixi Koch, 16 Apr. 1956, 2 sons, 1 daughter. *Appointments:* Member, Paarl Municipality, 1963-77; Mayor, Paarl, 1971-73; Member, South African Senate, 1977-80; Member, First President's Council, 1981-. *Hobbies:* Literature; Theatre; Cinema; Art; Swimming; Walking. *Address:* 6 Ave. Le Sueur Sea Point, Capetown 8001, Republic of South Africa.

KOCH Carole (Capman) Jackson, b. 25 Feb. 1951, Evergreen Park, Illinois, USA. Human Resources Executive. m. (1) Donald Charles Jackson, 24 Sept. 1976 (dec. 1984), (2) Curtis Gerard Koch, 28 Aug. 1987. *Education:* BA Honours, German Language & Linguistics, University of Illinois, 1972. *Appointments:*

Assistant to Dean & Manager, Language Laboratory 1972-73, Job Analyst, Personnel Department 1973-76, Personnel Coordinator 1976-80, Associate Director 1980-83, Director of Personnel (Hospitals & Clinics) 1983-, University of Illinois, Chicgo. *Memberships:* College & University Personnel Association; American Management Association; American Society for Personnel Administration; American Society for Healthcare Human Resources Administration; International Personnel Management Association; Women's Health Executive Network. *Honours:* Appointed, Human Resources Council, Metropolitan Chicago Healthcare Council, 1987-; Chair, United Way/Crusade of Mercy campaign, University of Illinois, Chicago, 1982. *Hobbies:* Playing piano; Sailing; Gardening. *Address:* University of Illinois Hospital, 1740 West Taylor, Suite 1400, Chicago, Illinois 60612, USA.

KOCH Ursula, b. 7 Aug. 1944, Plauen, Germany. Professor. m. Rudiger Koch, 1966 (div), 1 son. *Education:* Sociology Diploma 1970, Dissertation, Social Science Research Methodology 1974, Free University, Berlin. *Appointments:* Assistant Professor, Free University, Berlin, 1970-75; Professor, Fachhochschule Ostfriesland, 1975-; Social Scientist, World Health Organisation, Geneva, Switzerland, 1986-87. *Publications:* Books & articles, social science methodology, information technolocy in human services, studies on the elderly, professionalisation in human sevices. *Memberships:* National Board, Pro Familia; German Association for Educational Sciences. *Hobbies:* Violin; Classical music. *Address:* Fachhochschule Ostfriesland, D-2970 Emden, Federal Republic of Germany.

KOCHAN Miriam Louise, b. 5 Oct. 1929, London, England. Freelance Writer & Translator. m. Lionel Kochan, 23 Dec. 1951, 2 sons, 1 daughter. *Education:* BSc, Economics, London University, 1950. *Career:* Sub-editor, Reuters News Agency, 1950-54; Assistant sub-editor, Past & Present historical studies journal, 1977-81; General Editor, Berg Women's series, current. *Publications:* Life in Russia Under Catherine the Great, 1968; Last Days of Imperial Russia, 1976; Prisoners of England, 1980; Britain's Internees in Second World War, 1983; Numerous translations from French. *Hobby:* Knitting. *Address:* 237 Woodstock Road, Oxford OX2 7AD, England.

KOCHANSKY-KATZ Rosalie, b. Bayonne, New Jersey, USA. Writer; Artist. m. Eli Katz, 21 July 1949. *Education:* BA, Brooklyn College, 1960; MA, City University of New York, 1963; Doctoral Equivalency, NYU, 1967. *Appointments:* Buyer-Merchandiser to 1954; Freelance Artist, 1954-; Teacher; New York City & State Certified, 1962-70. *Publications:* Editor, YANK, 1943-46; Kinesthetic & Visual Learning, 1964; Katz Game Test, 1964; International Gourmet Ultimate Cookbook, 1980. *Memberships:* American Board, Weizmann Institute, 1986-88; American Board, ALYN (Jerusalem based Children's Hospital for Physically Handicapped; American Board, AMIT (for education of Orphan's Israel). *Honours:* Most Promising Artist, Village Art Show, 1955; Docent Brooklyn Museum of Contemporary Art, 1980-82. *Hobbies:* Travel; Music; Art; Ballet; Theatre; Swimming. *Address:* 311 W. 24 St. (5C), New York, NY 10011, USA.

KODIS Mary C, b. 17 Dec. 1927, Chicago, Illinois, USA. Retail Home Centre Executive; Consultant, Retail Stores. *Education:* San Diego State College, 1945-47; Latin American Institute, 1948. *Appointments:* Controller, Division Administration Manager, Fed Mart Stores (discount), 1957-65; Controller, Administration Manager, Gulf Mart Stores (Division of Diana Stores), 1965-67; Corporation Budget Director, administration Manager, Diana Stores (discount stores, dress shops, clothing stores), 1967-68; Founder, Treasurer, Controller, Handy Dan Stores (Home Centres), 1972-76; Senior Vice President, Treasurer, Handy City Stores (division of W R Grace and Co), 1976-79; Consultant, Retail Home Centres Stores, Restaurants, Real Estate & Construction, 1979-; President, Hal's HDW and

Lumber Stores, Milwaukee, Wisconsin, 1982-83. *Memberships:* Board of Directors, Treasurer, Watsonville, YWCA; Santa Cruz County Grand Jury, 1984-85. *Honours:* Soroptomist Scholarship, International Relations, 1945; 1st tribute to Women in International Industry, 1978; Woman of the Year, 1985. *Hobby:* Needlepoint. *Address:* 302 Wheelock Road, Watsonville, CA 95076, USA.

KOENIG Marie Harriet King, b. 19 Feb. 1919, New Orleans, Louisiana, USA. Public Relations; Fund Raising; Research, American History. m. Walter W Koenig, 24 June 1956. 2 daughters. *Education:* BSc, University of La Vaerne; Pre-Law School, Loyola University of the South; School of Music, Louisiana State University, Baton Rouge. *Appointments:* Executive Director, Research Consultants Associates, 1979-; Staff Assistant for Development (Fundraising); Republican Party of Los Angeles County. *Publications:* Research Project, Does the National Council of Churches Speak for You?; Lectures; etc. *Memberships:* American Conservative Union; Republican Presidential Task Force; United States Senatorial Committee; National Federation of Republican Women; American Academy of Political and Social Science; Greater Los Angeles Press Club; Publicity Club of Los Angeles; Wilshire Business and Professional Women's Club, Chairman, Public Relations, 2 years; Women in Communication Inc; Pasadena Opera Guild; Pasadena Area Opera Trust; Charter and Life Member, Los Angeles County Chapter, Freedoms Foundation at Valley Forge; Friends of the Huntington Library; Los Angeles World Affairs Council; Town Hall of California; Charter Member, Gene Autry Western Heritage Museum; Member, National Trust for Historic Preservation; Honorary Citizen, Colonial Williamsburg; Sustaining Member, Republican National Committee; Member, Republican Women's Club of San Marino; Associate Member, East Pasadena Republican Women Federated. *Honours:* Recipient, Commendations for Political Activities & Help on Fund Raising Benefits. *Hobbies:* Research; Reading; Opera. *Address:* 205 Madeline Drive, Pasadena, CA 91105, USA.

KOENIG Sandra Gladys, b. 21 May 1959, Chicago, Illinois, USA. Senior Word Processing Operator II. *Appointments:* Extra Help Assistance, University of Illinois, Business Affairs Office, 1976; Clerk Typist I, 1977, Clerk Typist II, 1978, Clerk Typist III, 1981; Senior Word Processing Specialist, University of Illinois, School of Public Health, 1984-. *Memberships:* NAW/IPS, Secretary, Committee on Committees, 1985-; Non-Academic Award Committee. *Honours:* Recipient, various honours and awards including Nomination for Non-academic Award, 1987. *Hobbies:* Collecting Dolls. *Address:* 4709 West Race Avenue, Chicago, IL 60644, USA.

KOERNER JoEllens Goertz, b. 13 Aug. 1946, Sioux Falls, USA. Nursing Administrator. m. Dennis Koerner, 17 Feb. 1967, 1 son, 1 daughter. *Education:* SVH Diploma, 1967; BSN, Mount Marty College, 1980; MSN, South Dakota State University, 1982; Management Certificate, University of Pennsylvania. *Appointments:* CCU Staff Nurse, Medical Head Nurse, SVH, Sioux Falls, 1967-70; Licensed Physician Assistant, Freeman, 1973-75; Director, Nursing Dept., Freeman Junior College, 1975-82; Nursing Education Consultant, South Dakota Board of Nursing, 1982-83, Executive Secretary, 1983-84; Vice President, Patient Services, Sioux Valley Hospital, 1984-. *Publications:* Articles in journals & magazines. *Memberships Include:* American Nurses Association, various offices; South Dakota Board of Nursing, Vice President 1981-82; Sigma Theta Tau; Phi Kappa Gamma; Delta Kappa Gamma; American Organization of Nurse Executives. *Honours Include:* Golden Heart Award, United Way, 1985; Fellow, Wharton School of Management of Nurse Executives, University of Pennsylvania, 1986; South Dakota Nurses Association President's Award. *Hobbies:* Playing Organ & Piano; Reading; Weaving; Skiing. *Address:* Rural Route 1, Box 146, Freeman, SD 57029, USA.

KOHLSTEDT Sally Gregory, b. 30 Jan. 1943, Ypsilanti, Michigan, USA. Historian; Educator. m. 27 Dec. 1966, 2 sons. *Education:* BA, Valparaiso University, 1965; MA, Michigan State University, 1966; PhD, University of Illinois, 1972. *Appointments:* Instructor 1971-72, Assistant Professor 1972-75, History, Simmons College; Assistant Professor 1975-78, Associate Professor 1978, Women's Studies Director 1980-82, Professor 1986-88, History, Syracuse University; Visiting Professor, History of Science, Cornell University, 1989; Professor, History of Science & Associate Dean, Institute of Technology, 1989-, University of Minnesota. *Publications include:* Books: Author, Formation of American Scientific Community: American Association for Advancement of Science, 1976; Co-editor, Historical Writing on American Science, 2nd series, 1, 1985, 1986. Numerous articles, major essays, various professional & learned journals. Also: Reviews, professional presentations. *Memberships include:* Offices, past/present: American Association for Advancement of Science; American Historical Association; Berkshire Conference of Women Historians; History of Science Society; International Congress for History of Science; Organisation of American Historians. *Address:* 102 Walter Library, University of Minnesota, Minnepolis, MN 55455, USA.

KOHRING Dagmar Luzia Anna Dorothea, b. 8 Mar. 1951, Lage, Federal Republic of Germany. Fundraiser. m. Arthur Gingrande Jr, 29 Dec. 1976 (div. 1982). *Education:* BA 1972, MA 1974, American University; Certified Fund Raising Executive, 1986. *Appointments:* Assistant Director, Development, Harvard Art Museums, USA, 1981-83; Campaign Officer, Harvard Campaign, 1983-85; Senior Consultant, C. H. Bentz Associates, 1985-88; Vice President, Brakeley, John Price Jones Inc, 1988-. *Membership:* National Society of Fund Raising Executives. *Honour:* Fellow, National Endowment for the Arts, 1983. *Hobbies:* Yoga; Swimming. *Address:* 36 Hancock Street, Apt. 7A, Boston, Massachusetts 02114, USA.

KOLASA Kathryn, b. 1949, Detroit, Michigan, USA. Professor. m. Patrick Noud Kelly, 3 Jan. 1983. *Education:* BS, Michigan State University, 1970; PhD, University of Tennessee, 1975. *Appointments:* Test Kitchen Home Economist, Kellogg Company, 1970; Assistant, Associate professor, Dept Food Science and Human Nutrition, Michigan State University, 1974-83; Chairman, Food Nutrition and Institution Mgt, 1983-86, Professor, Dept Family Medicine, 1986-, East Carolina University. *Publications:* More than 100 publications and presentations, including three book chapters, several video tapes and training films. *Memberships:* American Institute of Nutrition; Society of Teachers of Family Medicine; American Dietetic Association; Society for Nutrition Education, president 1984-85; Institute of Food Technologists. *Honours:* General Foods Fellow, 1970-73; Kellogg National Leadership Fellowship, 1985-88; Outstanding Alumni Award, College of Human Ecology, Michigan State University, 1986. *Hobbies:* Gardening; Golf; Photography. *Address:* 3080 Dartmouth Drive, Greenville, NC 27858, USA.

KOLBER Sandra Diane, b. 7 June, 1934, White Plains, New York, USA. Writer and Film Consultant. m. Senator E Leo Kolber, 8 Sept. 1957. 1 son, 1 daughter. *Education:* BA, McGill University, 1955. *Appointments:* Wrote for Anglo-Jewish press, 1968-74; Head of Story Department, Sagittarius Productions Inc, 1970-73; Consultant, Canadian Film Development Corporation (now Telefilm Canada), 1972-79; Director, Creative Development, Astral Film Productions Ltd, 1979-83; Vice President, Canadian International Studios Inc, 1983-86. *Creative Works:* 2 books of poetry: Bitter Sweet Lemons and Love, 1967; All There Is of Love, 1968. *Memberships:* PEN International Writers' Organization; CAPAC (Composers, Authors, Publishers Association of Canada); Academy of Canadian Cinema & Television; Vice President, Member of Executive Committee, Co-President of Honorary Council, Orchestre symphonique de Montreal. *Honours:* Tel Aviv University for Israel/

Canada Co-Production of feature film, Tell Me That You Love Me, 1983; Board of Directors of Cineplex Odeon Corporation. *Address:* 100 Summit Circle, Westmount, Quebec, H3Y 1N8, Canada.

KOLENDA Pauline, b. 4 Feb. 1928, Manchester, New Hampshire, USA. Professor of Anthropology. m. 9 June 1962. 1 son. *Education:* BA, Wellesley College, 1949; Cornell University, 1955. *Appointments:* University of Arizona, 1959-61; Oakland University, 1961-62; University of Houston, 1963-. *Publications:* Caste in Contemporary India; Caste, Cult and Hierarchy; Regional Differences in Family Structure. *Memberships:* American Anthropoligcal Association; Association for Asian Studies. *Honours:* Phi Kappa Phi, 1953; Scholar at Bellagio Study Center of Rockefeller Foundation, 1985; National Science Foundation Visiting Professor to Rice University, 1988-89. *Address:* Department of Anthropology, University of Houston, Houston, Texas 77004, USA.

KOLINSKA-SECHACZEWSKA Krystyna, b. 23 Dec. 1923, Czechoslovakia. Writer. m. (1) 1950, (2) Wlodzimierz Sechaczewski, 23 Dec. 1971, 1 step-daughter. *Education:* MA, Polish Philology & Philosophy. *Appointments:* Publishers editor, 1950-64; Journalist, literary & cultural problems, 1964-81. *Publications include:* Secrets for Sale; Black & White Ladies; Mysteries & Women; Sienkiewicz & Beautiful Inhabitant of Great Poland; Enchanted; Stachu, His Women, His Children; Castle on Tricky Papers; Luck in Luck; Letters to Not-Lowed; Emil & Mary; Kill Darkness; Young Heart of the Elder Women; Mr Gustav. (All in Polish). *Memberships:* ZAIKS; Association of Polish Writers. *Honours:* Literary award, for Black & White Ladies; 1st prize, literary competition, for Kill Darkness. *Hobbies:* Meetings & conversations with friends & interesting people; Collecting antique letters & photos; Small collection, personal letters from famous writers & artists (contemporary). *Address:* Warsaw, Poland.

KOLLER Marita Ann, b. 6 June 1955, Chicago, Illinois, USA. Accounting Associate. *Education:* BA, History/Political Science- Education, Western Illinois University, 1976; MPA, Public Administration, American University, Washington, 1980. *Appointments:* US Congress Legislative Assistant, Congressmen Jim Leach, Iowa and John Porter, Illinois, 1977-80; Actuarial Assistant, Towers, Perrin, Foster & Crosby, 1981-85; Baxter Travenol Laboratories, 1985-88; Accounting Associate, UOP, Inc, 1988-. *Creative Works:* Developed computer training materials for adults. *Memberships:* League of Women voters, President; Des Plaines Chapter, Voters Service Chair; American Business Women's Association; American Association of University Women; Association of Female Executives. *Honours:* Congressional Intern, Congressman Abner Mikua, 1975; Congressional Intern, Congressman Tom Railsback, 1976; Outstanding Young Woman of America, 1985; Who's Who among Professional and Business Women, 1987, 1988. *Hobbies:* Writing Short Stories, Magazine Articles; Folkmusic, Dulcimer, Guitar; Needlework; Public Speaker on League of Women Voters and Voter Education Issues; Calligraphy. *Address:* 934 Forest Av, Des Plaines, ILL 60018, USA.

KOMISAR Lucy, b. 8 Apr. 1942, New York City, USA. Journalist. *Education:* BA, History, Queens College, City University of New York, 1964. *Appointments:* Associate Editor, The Hatworker, 1966; Special Assistant, Speech Writer, Deputy Administrator, New York Ciy Human Resource Administration, 1967-68; Reporter, The Bergen Record, 1978-80; Radio Commentator, 1971, 1974, Washington DC; Associate Producer, Researcher, News & Public Affairs Shows, NET; Commentator, WNET TV, 1979-; Freelance Journalist, 1981-. *Publications:* Books: Corazon Aquino: The Story of a Revolution, 1987, 1988; Down and Out in the USA, 1973; The New Feminism, 1972. Contributor of articles to: Miami Herald; New York Times; San Francisco Chronicle; San Diego Union; many others. *Memberships:* National Vice President, Public Affairs, National Organisation for Women, 1970-71; Executive

Board, Pen American Centre, 1976-. *Honours Include:* Grant, Ploughshares Fund, 1985; various other honours & awards. *Hobbies:* Tennis. *Address:* 100 West 12 Street, New York, NY 10011, USA.

KONTOGOURIS Venetia, b. 16 Apr. 1951, Athens, Greece. Businesswoman. m. Zoran Djokic, 16 Aug. 1982, 1 son, 1 daughter. *Education:* BA, Political Science, Northeastern University, USA, 1974; MA, International Relations 1975, MBA 1977, University of Chicago. *Appointments:* IBM, 1977-79; AT&T, 1979-80; Kingsley, Boye, Southwood, 1980-83; Vice President, Venture Capital, Dun & Bradstreet, 1983-. *Memberships:* Direct Marketing Association; Information Industry Association; Bank Marketing Association; ADAPSO. *Honour:* Women in Industry Award, business achievement, 1988. *Hobbies:* Antiques; Gardening; Cycling. *Address:* 10 Old Hyde Road, Weston, Connecticut 06883, USA.

KOON Helene Wickham, b. 14 Oct. 1925, Minneapolis, Minnesota, USA. Professor of English. m. Charles Koon, 6 Apr. 1946, 5 sons. *Education:* BFA, University of Iowa, 1946; MA, Drama, Pasadena Playhouse, 1948; MA, English, Immaculate Heart College, 1965; PhD, University of California, Los Angeles, 1969. *Appointments:* Actress, 1948-62; Lecturer, California State University (CSU) Northridge, 1968-70; Assistant Professor 1970-73, Associate Professor 1973-78, Professor 1978-, CSU San Bernardino. *Publications:* Translation, The Late Lionel (Scribe), 1966; Female Spectator, 1977; Essays on Death of a Salesman, 1980; Eugene Scribe, 1983; Colley Cibber, 1986; Articles, reviews. *Memberships:* Modern Language Association; Society for Theatre Research; Society for 18th Century Research; California Classical Society. *Honours:* Member, Academy of American Poets, 1966; Director, NEH grant on writing, 1978-82. *Hobbies:* Music; Painting; Chess; Travel. *Address:* 6316 Ivarene Avenue, Hollywood, California 90068, USA.

KOONTZ Eva Isabelle, b. 3 Feb. 1935, Kansas, USA. *Education:* BS, Natural Sciences, Sterling College, 1957; Certificate, Medical Technology, University of Kansas, Medical Center, 1958. *Appointments:* Medical Technologist, Group Practice, 1958-60; Supervisor, Chemistry, Bethany Hospital, Kansas City, 1960-64; Research Assistant, University of Kansas Medical Centre, 1964-72; R&D Staff, Technologist, Providence St Margaret Health Care Centre, 1972-74; Hormone Laboratory Technologist, St Luke's Hospital, 1974-79; Laboratory Supervisor, Manager, Quincy Research Centre, 1979-80; Staff Medical Technologist, Lakeside Hospital, 1980-82; Supervisor, Clinical Laboratory, Midwest Research Institute, 1982-88; Toxicology Supervisor, Clinical Reference Laboratory, Lenea, 1988-. *Memberships:* American Society for Medical Technology; Missouri Society for Medical Technology; American Association for Clinical Chemistry. *Hobbies:* Sports Cars; Musical Instruments; Reading. *Address:* 10251 Cedarbrooke Lane, Kansas City, MO 64131, USA.

KOOPMANN Reta Colene, b. 27 Feb. 1944, Oklahoma City, USA. Company Vice President. m. 3 Jan. 1987, 1 daughter. *Education:* BS, 1987, MBA Candidate, California Coast University. *Appointments:* Vice President, Bakery, Kash & Karry Food Stores, 1983-. *Publication:* Store Manager Training Manual, Bakery/ Deli Merchandising Training Manual, 1984. *Memberships:* International Deli/Bakery Association; Board, Jim Borck Educational Endowment Foundation; National Association for Female Executives. *Hobbies:* Golf; Fishing; Gardening. *Address:* Kash & Karry Food Stores, 6422 Harney Road, Tampa, FL 33610, USA.

KOPLEY Margot B, b. 10 Oct. 1952, Boston, Massachusetts, USA. Psychologist. *Education:* BA, University Rochester, 1974; MS, University of Miami, 1976; MS 1982, PsyD 1983, Pace University; Lic psychologist New York 1984, California 1985; Cert. Sch Psychologist, California 1984, New York 1985. *Appointments:* Graduate fellowship Mailman Center,

Miami, Florida, 1975-76; Psychology intern White Plains Public Schools, 1980-81; Psychology extern Childrens Village, Dobbs Ferry, New York, 1981-82; Psychology intern Bergen Pines Co Hospital, Paramus, New Jersey, 1982-83; Psychologist Ladson Coastal Center, South Carolina, 1977-78; Putnam Assn for Retarded Citizens, New York, 1979-80; Psychologist/Clin dir. Greystone House Ince, Poughkeepsie, 1981-84; School Psychologist, Board of Cooperative Education, Valhalla, 1983-84; Private practice, consultant therapist, Westchester, 1980-84; Private practice Psychologist, North San Diego Co, 1984-; Volunteer therapist, Parents/Daughters/Sons United, North Coastal Chapt, 1985-87; Adj faculty National University, San Diego, 1987. *Publication:* Evaluation of Effects of Residential Placement Upon Psychosocial Competence and Self-Esteem, CASP/NASP, 1985. *Memberships:* American Board of Med Psychotherapists (diplomate and fellow); American Psychological Association; National Association of School Psychologists; Acad SD Psychologists (legislative/women's coms); North San Diego County Psychology Association (President 1985-86); SD Com Child Abuse Coord Council (board, co-chair res. com. 1986-88); North Co Child Abuse Coalition (child abuse rev. com); Volunteers in Probation Inc, 1986-87 (bd, 1986-87). *Honours:* Recipient appreciation awards: San Diego Comm Child Abuse Council, 1986-87; S D Dept Social Services, 1985, 1986; North County Assn Retarded Citizens, 1984. Listed National Register Health Social Services Providers Psychol. 1985, 1986, 1987, 1988. *Hobby:* Sailing. *Address:* 162 S Rancho Santa Fe, Suite B-50, Encinitas, CA 92024, USA.

KOPP Nancy Ann Kornblith, b. 7 Dec. 1943, Coral Gables, Florida, USA. Member of Maryland State House of Delegates. m. Robert Kopp, 5 May 1969, 1 son, 1 daughter. *Education:* BA, Honours, Wellesley College, 1965; MA, University of Chicago, 1968; PhD work, 1967-70. *Appointments:* Legislative Staff, rep. Edith Green (D Oregon), 1964-69 Passim; Graduate Management Inten, US Office of Education, 1967; Instructor, University of Illinois, 1968-69; Committee Staff, US House of Representatives, 1970-71; Legislative Staff, Montgomery Delegation to Annapolis, 1971-74. *Publications:* Delivered speeches & papers at the invitations of various Associations & Universities. *Memberships:* American Political Science Association; Policy Studies Association; National Advisory Panel, National Centre for Postsecondary Governance & Finance, 1986-; Trustee, Maryland Centre on Aging, 1983-. *Honours:* Outstanding Service to Education Award, Maryland Independent Colleges & Universities Association, 1984; Outstanding Service to the Handicapped Award, 1984; Betterment for United Seniors, etc. *Address:* 6301 Dahlonega Road, Bethesda, MD 20816, USA.

KOR Eva, b. 31 Jan. 1935, Portz, Romania. Realtor; Lecturer on the Holocaust. m. Michael Kor, 27 Apr. 1960. 1 son, 1 daughter. *Education:* Indiana State University, USA. *Appointments:* Draftsperson, Israeli Army, 1952-60; Draftsperson, Ewing Miller Architects, 1960-61; Draftsperson, Construction Engineering Serv, 1965-77; Realtor, Johnson Barcus Inc, 1977-79; Realtor, Calico Realty, 1979-82; Realtor, Williams & Assoc, 1982-. *Creative works:* Founded CANDLES, 1983, initiator dir, CANDLES mock trial of Dr Mengele in Jerusalem, 1985; ICH Holocaust Conference on Prej, 1981-82; Freedom Petition for Soviet Jews, 1976-77. *Memberships:* Past president, Hadassah; Past President, Federation of Jewish Women; Women in Terre Haute, 1983-; Executive director, CANDLES; National Board of Realtors. *Honours:* Jewish Activism Award, Jewish News & Views, New York, 1985; Honoured by Indiana House of Representatives for Humanitarian work, 1987. *Interests:* Political activism; History and historical books and movies; Nazi hunter for Truth and Justice. *Address:* 24 West Lawrin Blvd, Terre Haute, Indiana 47803, USA.

KORTE-VAN HEMEL Virginie Norbertina Maria, b. 8 May 1929, Bergen op Zoom. State Secretary for Justice. m. Harmannus Wolbertus Korte, 19 Apr. 1955, 3 sons, 1 daughter. *Education:* LLD, 1955.

Appointments: Lawyer, 1955-82; Muncipality Bussum, 1966-78; Alderman Bussum, 1971-74; MP, Christian Democratic Party, 1977-82; State Secretary for Justice, 1982-. *Hobbies:* Horseriding; Reading; Listening to Classical Music. *Address:* Dept. of Justice, PO Box 20301, 2500 EH The Hague, The Netherlands.

KOSTICH Shirley Ann, b. 3 June 1944, Milwaukee, Wisconsin, USA. Health Services Administrator. m. Nikola P, 28 May 1969. 1 son, 1 daughter. *Education:* BSc, University of Wisconsin, 1967. *Appointments:* Case worker and Assistant to Admin, Milwaukee Unicare Health Care Facilities, Inc, 1967-69; Residential Care Consultant, Madison Unicare Health Care Facilities, Ibnc, 1969-70; After care team, Medical College of Wisconsin, 1979-80; Administrative Coordinator-Medical Services, Milwaukee County Mental Health Complex, 1981-. *Publications:* Editor, Milwaukee County Mental Health Complex newsletter, The Communicator; Author: How to Organize and Conduct Your Own Combined Giving Campaign; Co-author, Combined Giving Campaign video, 1988. *Memberships:* Chi Sigma Lambda Sorority (Vice President); Alliance for the Mentally Ill; Mental Health Association of Wisconsin; National Association for Female Executives; National Association of Medical Staff Coordinators; Sinai Samaritan Sexual Assault Treatment Center Advisory Council, President 1987-; Combined Health Appeal of Wisconsin Advisory Board. *Honours:* Editor's Forum Writing Awards, 1987 and 1988; Combined Giving Campaign, Silver Award, 1987 and 1988; Combined Giving Campaign Chairman's award, 1987. *Hobbies:* Gardening; Reading; Walking; Pet care and animal rights; Environmental issues; Cooking; Community volunteer projects. *Address:* 3715 North Lake Drive, Shorewood, WI 53211, USA.

KOTKER (Mary) Zane, b. 2 Jan. 1934, Waterbury, Connecticut, USA. Writer. m. Norman R Kotker, 7 June 1965. 1 son, 1 daughter. *Education:* BA, Middlebury College, 1952-56; MA, Columbia University, 1959-60. *Appointments:* Editor, Harcourt, Brace & Jovarovich, 1966-69; Guest Assoc Professor, Mt Holyoke college, Spring 1983; Guest Professor, University of Massachusetts, Amherst, Autumn 1983. *Publications:* Novels: Bodies in Motion, 1972; A Certain Man, 1976; White Rising, 1981. *Memberships:* Former: PEN; Author's Guild; Founding member, Bay State Writers. *Honours:* National Endowment for the Arts fiction grant, 1974; The MacDowell Colony Fellow, 1979, 1982, 1984, 1987, 1989; Yaddo Fellow, 1989; Judge, Illinois Council Arts, Fiction, 1984. *Hobbies:* Swimming; Hiking. *Address:* 45 Lyman Road, Northampton, MA 01060, USA.

KOWALCHYK Gayle, b. 6 June 1955, Tyler, Texas, USA. Keyboard Editor; Piano teacher. m. E L Lancaster, 28 Dec. 1980. *Education:* BM, Ohio University, 1973; MM, Northwestern University, 1979; Doctorate of Education, Teachers College, Columbia University, 1989. *Appointments:* Special Instructor of Music, Oklahoma Baptists University, 1981-87; Adjunct Instructor, University of Oklahoma, 1981-87; Independent Piano Studio, 1981-; Keyboard Editor, Alfred Music Pub Co Inc, 1988-; Editor, Keys Piano Music Magazine, 1986-. *Publications:* Sight reading and ear training books, primer, levels 1-4 for David Carr Glover Musicianship Series. *Memberships:* Music Teachers National Association; Oklahoma Music Teachers Association; National Guild of Piano Teachers; Accredited Music Teachers Association of Central Oklahoma. *Honours:* Teaching Assistantship, Teachers College, Columbia University, 1987-88; Graduate Assistantship, Northwestern University, 1977-78. *Hobbies:* Travel; Reading. *Address:* 3923 Pine Tree Circle, Norman, Oklahoma 73072, USA.

KOZAK Ellen M, b. 5 Feb. 1944, Ft. Jackson, South Carolina, USA. Attorney; Author. *Education:* AB, Barnard College, 1966; JD, University of Wisconsin Law School, 1969. *Appointments:* General Attorney, FCC, 1969; Law Clerk, Federal District Court, 1970-71; Private General Practice, Law, 1971-; Published Writer,

1972-. *Publications:* Over 250 articles in print; 2 pseudonymous science fiction novels, 1984; Every Writers Practical Guide to Copyright Law, 1985. *Memberships:* Science Fiction Writers of America; State Bar of Wisconsin, Chair, Patent Trademark & Copyright Section, 1987-88; American Bar Association; Authors Guild. *Address:* PO Box 380, Milwaukee, WI 53201, USA.

KRACUN Mary Dolores, b. 23 Nov 1959, Hazleton, Pennsylvania, USA. Registered Professional Nurse. *Education:* Associate in Applied Science, Northampton Community College, 1975; BSc, Nursing, Gwynedd Mercy College, 1979; MSc, Nursing, University of Pennsylvania, 1980; DPhil, Nursing, Texas Woman's University, 1988. *Appointments:* Assistant Professor of Nursing, Allentown College of St Francis de Sales, Center Valley, Pennnsylvania, 1981-1989; Registered Nurse, Muhlenberg Hospital Center, Bethlehem, Pennsylvania, 1975-89. *Publications:* When the Problem is ICU Psychosis, RN Magazine, Jun 1972; Social Support and Anxiety in Adult Emergency Department Patients, Doctoral Dissertation, Aug 1988. *Memberships:* American Association of Critical Care Nurses; American Nurses' Association, Sigma Theta Tau International Honor Society of Nursing. *Hobbies:* Reading; Needlecraft; Travel; Movies. *Address:* Coopersburg, PA, USA.

KRAMER Gilda Lea, b. 16 July 1954, New York City, USA. Attorney. *Education:* BA, Swarthmore College, 1976; JD, University of Virginia, 1979. *Appointments:* Pepper, Hamilton & Scheetz, 1979-81; Assistant City Solicitor 1981-83, Deputy City Solicitor 1983-84, City of Philadelphia Law Department; Schnader, Harrison, Segal & Lewis, 1984-89; Sole practice, Gilda L. Kramer Esq, 1989-. *Memberships:* American, Pennsylvania & Philadelphia Bar Associations. *Address:* 1500 Walnut Street, Suite 1100, Philadelphia, Pennsylvania 19102, USA.

KRAMER Jeannette Ross Kramer, b. 11 May 1922, Belle Center, Ohio, USA. Family Therapist; Assistant Professor. m. Charles H. Kramer, 15 Sept. 1946, 5 sons, 1 daughter. *Education:* BA, University of Illinois, 1944; Basic Hospital Administration, School of Public Health and Adminstrative Medicine Continuing Education, Columbia University, 1962; 2-year Training Programme, Family Institute of Chicago, 1972-73. *Appointments:* Co-Owner, Administrator, Plum Grove Nursing Home, Palatine, Illinois, 1953-73; Coordinator of Special Projects, Family Institute of Chicago, Institute of Pychology, 1973-88, currently Assistant Professor, Department of Psychological and Behavioural Sciences, Northwestern University Medical School, Chicago; Private Practice in Family Therapy, 1973-. *Publications:* Basic Principles in Long-Term Care: Developing a Therapeutic Community (with C H Kramer), 1976; Family Interfaces: Transgenerational Patterns, 1984; 27 articles in Nursing Home and Family Therapy. *Memberships:* President, Illinois Home Association, 1963-64; Fellow, American College of Nursing Home Administrators; Charter Member, American Family Therapy Association; Board of Trustees, Family Institute of Chicago. *Honours:* Salutatorian, University of Illinois; Phi Beta Kappa; Phi Kappa Phi; Mortar Board; Better Life Award, Illinois and American Health Care Associations, 1970; Winner (as co-author), Book of the Year Award in Psychiatric Nursing and Book of the Year Award in Geriatric Nursing, American Journal of Nursing, 1976. *Hobbies:* Photography; Sailing; Reading. *Address:* 417 North Kenilworth Avenue, Oak Park, IL 60302, USA.

KRAMER Karen Ruoff, b. 3 Dec. 1945, Long Beach, California, USA. College Teacher; Administrator; Writer. m. David Kramer, 23 July 1966, 1 son, 1 daughter. *Education:* BA 1969, PhD 1984, Stanford University; MA, Free University, Berlin, Germany, 1976. *Appointments:* Fachhochschule fur Sozialarbeit, Germany, 1972-73; University of Maryland, USA, 1976-80; Instructor & Administrator, Berlin Study Centre, Stanford University, 1980-; Director, ibid, 1984-.

Creative works: New Subjectivity: Third Thoughts on a Literary Discourse, 1984; e.g. Scenes from the Life of Emma Goldman, musical, with L. Lehrmann, 1986; Numerous poems & articles. *Memberships:* Modern Language Association; Dramaturgische Gesellschaft; Forderverein der Theatermanufaktur; Internationaler Verein der Germanistik. *Hobbies:* Bicycle touring; Cello playing. *Address:* Stanford in Berlin, Pacelliallee 18-20, D-1000 Berlin 33, Federal Republic of Germany.

KRAMER Leonie Judith, (Dame), b. 1 Oct. 1924, Melbourne, Australia. Professor. m. Harold Kramer, 2 Apr. 1952, 2 daughters. *Education:* BA, University of Melbourne 1945; D.Phil, University of Oxford, England, 1953. *Appointments:* Tutor, Lecturer, University of Melbourne, 1945-49; Tutor, Postgraduate Student, St Hugh's College, Oxford, 1949-52; Lecture Senior Lecturer, Associate Professor, University of New South Wales, 1958-68; Professor, Australian Literature, University of Sydney, 1968-; Visiting Professor, Chair of Australian Studies, Harvard University, USA 1981-82; Deputy Chancellor, University of Sydney Senate, 1989-. *Publications:* Henry Handel Richardson & Some of Her Sources, 1954; A Companion to Australia Felix, 1962; Editor, Coast to Coast 1963-64, 1965; Myself When Laura : Facts & Fiction in Henry Handel Richardson's School Career 1966; Henry Handel Richardson, 1967; Editor, Hal Porter : Selected Stories, 1971; Language & Literature: A Synthesis, co-author, 1976; A Guide to Language & Literature, co-author, 1977; A D Hope, 1979; Oxford History of Australian Literature, edited & introduced, 1981; The Oxford Anthology of Australian Literature, co-editor, 1985; My Country Australian Poetry & Short Stories - 200 years, 2 volumes selected by L Kramer, 1985; James McAuley: Poetry, Essays and Personal Commentary, edited by Leonie Kramer, 1988. *Memberships:* numerous professional organisations. *Honours:* Dame of the Order of the British Empire, 1983; Britannica Inaugural Award, 1986. *Address:* Dept. of English, University of Sydney, NSW 2006, Australia.

KRANTZ Hazel, b. 29 Jan. Brooklyn, USA. Freelance Writer; Teacher. m. Michael Krantz, 7 June 1942, 2 sons, 1 daughter. *Education:* BS, New York University, 1942; MS, Hofstra University, 1959. *Appointments:* Advertising Copywriter, 1942-45; Elementary Teacher, 1957-68; Editor, True Frontier Magazine, 1970-76; Copy Editor, The Sound Engineering Magazine, 1977-83. *Publications:* Juvenile: 100 Pounds of Popcorn; Freestyle for Michael; The Secret Raft; Teen: Tippy; A Pad of Their Own; Pink & White Striped Summer; None but the Brave; Daughter of My People : The Story of Henrietta Szold; Adult: Guide to Success & Happiness. *Memberships:* Society of Children's Book Writers; Brandeis University National Womens Committee; International Emissary Foundation. *Hobbies:* Handweaving; Photography; Tennis; Reading; 3 Grandchildren. *Address:* 1306 Stoney Hill Dr., Ft. Collins, CO 80525, USA.

KRASILOVSKY Alexis Rafael, b. 5 July 1950, Juneau, Alaska, USA. Filmmaker; Assistant Professor. 1 son. *Education:* BA, Yale University, 1971; MFA, California Institute of the Arts, 1984. *Appointments:* Owner, Rafael Film, 1973-; Publisher, The Street Agency, 1983-; Assistant Professor, Radio TV Film, California State University, Northridge, 1987-; Otis/Parsons, Instructor, 1988-89. *Publications:* Some Women Writers Kill Themselves; Some Men; Films: Exile; Just Between Me & God; End of the Art World; Blood; Videos Directed: Beale Street; Mr Boogie Woogie; Inside Story. *Memberships:* University Film & Video Association; Behind the Lens; Founding Member, Association of Independent Video & Filmmakers; etc. *Honours:* Various honours including: CAPS Film Grant, 1973-74; NEA Video Production Grant, 1977-78; Walter Lantz Productions Inc. Scholarship for Cal Arts, 1983-84. *Hobbies:* Swimming; Poetry; Cooking; Blues. *Address:* Dept. of Radio Television Film, California State University, Northridge, CA 91330, USA.

KRAUS Anna Josephine, b. 11 Apr. 1927, Brookville,

Pennsylvania, USA. Registered Medical Record Administrator. *Education:* BA, Medical Record Administration, 1959; AA, Registered Nurse, 1969; MPH, 1972; MA, Teacher Preparation for Allied Health Professions, 1974. *Appointments:* Medical Record Assistant and Director and Consultant in hospitals and nursing homes, Los Angeles, California area, 1960-69; Director, St Joseph Medical Center, Burbank, 1969-72I; Short-term, Medical Record Consultant, World Health Organ, Nassau, Bahamas, 1976 and 1977; Director & Assistant Professor Medical Record Administration Program, Alderson Broaddus College, Philippi, WV, 1976-81; Assistant Director for like program, York College of Pennsylvania, 1974-75; Director Medical Records, Clarion Hospital, Clarion, PA, 1983-. *Memberships:* Calif Med Record Assoc, 1962-72, Past district President, Treasurer, Chairman, various committees and Board of Directors; West Virginia Med Rec Assoc, Past President, 1980-81; Legislative Comm, West VA Nurses Assoc, 1978-80; Am Assoc Univ Women, Treasurer; Penna Med Rec Assoc; Penna Nurses Assoc; Amer Hosp Assoc; American Legion Auxiliary, Recording Scy. *Honours:* American Legion Art Award, 1944; Leadership and Service Award, Student Nurse Association, Pasadena City College, Calif, 1969. *Hobbies:* Swimming; Travel; Organ and piano playing; Working with plants. *Address:* P O Box 437, Fetzer Street, Brookville, PA 15825, USA.

KRAUS Joanna Halpert, b. 7 Dec. 1937, Portland, Maine, USA. Playwright; Professor. m. Ted M. Kraus, 1 Apr. 1966, 1 son. *Education:* BA, Sarah Laurence, 1959; MA, University of California, Los Angeles, 1962; Ed.D., Columbia University, 1973. *Appointments:* Professor, Co- ordinator, Interdisciplinary Arts for Children, State University of New York, 1979-. *Publications:* Plays: The Ice Wolf, 1965; Mean to Be Free, 1967; Vasalisa, 1972; Circus Home, 1978; The Last Baron of Arizona, 1987; Kimchi Kid, 1987; Books: The Great American Train Ride, 1975; Two Plays from the Far East 1978; Sound and Motion Stories, 1980; The Night the Elephants Marched on New York, 1984; articles in numerous magazines, journals, etc. *Memberships:* AAE; ASSITES; Dramatists Guild. *Honours:* Charlotte B Chorpenning cup, 1971; Creative Artists Public Service Fellowship, 1976; MCA-ESIPA Award, 1983; Fellowship, Playwriting, Virginia Center for the Creative Arts, 1984. *Address:* Dept. of Theatre, State University of New York, Brockport, NY 14420, USA.

KRAUSZ Susan Lavinsky, b. 4 Mar. 1953, Brooklyn, USA. Psychotherapist. m. Moshe Krausz, 7 Dec. 1972, deceased 1981, 1 daughter, (2) Laszlo Papp, 19 Aug. 1984. *Education:* BA, Brooklyn College, 1973; CSW, 1975; MSW, 1975; DSW, Adelphi University School of Social Work, 1982. *Appointments:* Social Worker, 1975-78; Psychotherapist, Private Practice, 1979-; Assistant Professor, NYU School of Social Work, 1981-87; Family Therapy Consultant, Eating Disorders Center, 1983-87; Adjunct Associate Professor, New York University School of Social Work, 1987-. *Publications:* Numerous publications on Loss, Group Therapy & Couples Therapy. *Memberships:* American Orchopsychiatric Association; National Association of Social Workers; Fellow, New York State Sociaty of Clinical SW Psychotherpist. *Honours:* Board Certified Diplomate in Clinical Social Work; Mary Richmond Award, National Society of Clinical Social Work Psychotherapists, 1980. *Address:* 108 East 66 Street, Suite 1A, New York, NY 10021, USA.

KRAVIS Lillian Panzer, b. 8 Dec. 1920, USA. Physician. m. Irving B Kravis, 22 June 1941. 2 sons, 2 daughters. *Education:* BA 1940, MD Med School 1943, University of Pennsylvania, Philadelphia; Resident Physician, Garfield Mem Hosp, Washington DC, 1944; Chief Resident Physician 1945-46, Epidemiologist in Training 1950-53, Children's Hosp, Philadelphia, Pennsylvania; Neonatology Resident, Penna Hospital, 1950. *Appointments:* Virologist 1950-53; Associate in Pediatrics 1964-66, Asst Prof Ped 1966- 77, Associate Prof Ped 1977-86, Clin Prof Ped 1986-, Children's Hospital, Philadelphia, Pennsylvania; Consultant

Allergist, Children's Sea Shore Home, 1964-. *Publications:* 38 articles in professional journals; Chapters in: Practice of Pediatrics, Brenneman, 1968 and 1974; Allergy-Immunology in Children, Speer Dockhorn & Shira, 1973; Pediatric Clinics of N America, 1969. *Memberships:* Amer Academy Pediatrics; Phila College of Physicians; Amer Academy Allergy/Clinical Immunology. *Honours:* Grant-in-Aid, Penna Tuberculosis & Health Society, 1968-69; Mead-Johnson Clinical Scholar Award, 1988. *Hobbies:* Gardening; Music; Hiking. *Address:* Children's Hospital of Phila, 34 St & Civic Center Blvd, Phila, PA 19104, USA.

KRAVITCH Phyllis A, b. 23 Aug. 1920, Savannah, Georgia, USA. Judge. *Education:* BA, Goucher College, 1941; LIB, University of Pennsylvania, 1943; LLD, Hon., Goucher College, 1981. *Appointments:* Law Practice, Savannah, 1944-76; Judge, Superior Court, Eastern Judicial Circuit of Georgia, 1977-79, US Court of Appeals, 5th Circuit, Atlanta, 1979- 81, US Court of Appeals 11th Circuit, 1981-. *Memberships:* Fellow, American Bar Foundation; American Bar Association; Savannah Bar Association, President 1976; State Bar of Georgia; American Judicature Society; American Law Institute. *Address:* 30 E. 53rd St., Savannah, GA 31405, USA.

KREAMER Karen S, b. 13 May 1956, Montgomery, Alabama, USA. Licensed Professional Counselor. *Education:* BS, Auburn University, 1978; MA, University of Alabama in Birmingham, 1979. *Appointments:* Director of Public Relations, Womens Medical Center, Birmingham, Alabama, 1978-79; Director of Counseling, Summit Medical Center, Birmingham, 1979-81; Private Practice Therapist, Vestavia Counseling Center, Birmingham, 1981-82; College Instructor, Southern Institute, Birmingham, 1982; Director, Campus Counseling Center to the University of Alabama in Birmingham, 1982-84; Private Practice Therapist, Birmingham Professional Counseling Services, 1986-; Private Practice Therapist, Kreamer and Associates, PC, 1984-. *Publications:* Holisit Weight Loss; Poetry. *Memberships:* American Mental Health Counselors Association; American Association for Counseling and Development; Auburn Allumni Association; AAUW; National Federation of Business and Professional Women; Alabama Mental Health Counselors Association; Alabama Association for Counseling and Development; Alabama Coalition for Mental Health Providers. *Honour:* Special Citation, American Red Cross, 1985. *Hobbies:* Writing Poetry; Painting; Collecting antiques; Composing music; Native American Spiritualism. *Address:* 956 Montclair Road, Suite 115, Birmingham, Alabama 35213, USA.

KREBS Kay E, b. 27 Aug. 1946, Wisconsin, USA. Owner, Business Management Consulting Firm. *Education:* BS, University of Wisconsin, 1970; MBA, University of Chicago, 1980. *Appointments:* Director of Exploratory Products, Kimberly-Clark Corporation, 1968-86; Owner, Krebs & Associates, 1986-. *Memberships:* AATCC, Tampon Standards Committee; AAUW, Alumni Association of the University of Wisconsin. *Honours:* High School Valedictorian, 1964; Sigma Epsilon Sigma Honorary Fraternity; Phi Kappa Phi Honorary Fraternity; Beta Gamma Sigma Honorary Fraternity. *Hobbies:* Sailing; Skiing; Barbershop singing; Woodworking. *Address:* 5130 I Ah May Tah, Oshkosh, WI 54901, USA.

KRECIC Marjeta, b. 27 Mar. 1925, Ljubljana, Yugoslavia. Clinical Psychologist. m. Vladislav Krecic, 3 Aug. 1946. 2 sons, 2 daughters. *Education:* BA, Certified Nurse, 1951; BS, 1962; Masters, Clinical Psychology, 1968. *Appointments:* Health Care Unit, Yugoslav Railway System, Ljubljana, 1950-57; Blood Bank, Ljubljana, 1957-62; University Clinical Centre, Clinical Psychiatric Hospial, Ljubljana-Polje, 1963-81 (Retired). *Publications:* Research on Epilepsy, 4 volumes, 1970-79; Research on Exogenious and Endogenious Superstructure of Mentally Retarded Persons, 3 volumes, 1983-85. *Honour:* Order of Labor with Silver Wreath, Presidency of the Socialist Federal Republic of Yugoslavia, 1983. *Hobbies:* Music; Literature; Art. *Address:* Titova 115, Ljubljana 61000, Yugoslavia.

KRELL Helen Louise, b. 27 Nov. 1944, Freeland, Pennsylvania, USA. Psychiatrist. m. Michael Krell, 28 June 1968. 2 daughters. *Education:* BS, St Univ of New York, 1962-66; MD, UC Med School, San Francisco, 1966-70; Internship, Herrick Memorial Hospital, 1970-71; 2 year Adult Psychiatry Residency, University of Vermont Medical School, 1971-73; 2 year Child Psychiatry Fellowship, Darmouth Medical School, 1973-75. *Appointments:* Externship-physicals, St Joseph's Hospital, 1968-69; Assistant Professor, Psychiatry, 1975-81, Assistant Professor, Maternal & Child Health, 1980-81, Associate Professor, Clinical Psychiatry & Maternal/Child Health, 1981, Dartmouth Medical School; Associate Clinical Professor Psychiatry, UC Davis Medical School, 1981-. *Publications:* Articles in numerous professional journals. *Memberships:* American Psychiatric Association; Central California Psychiatric Association; American Academy of Child Psychiatry; Central Calif Regional Organization of Child Psychiatry. *Address:* 433 F Street, Davis, CA 95616, USA.

KREPS Juanita Morris, b. 11 Jan. 1921, Lynch, Kentucky, USA. Economist; Educator. m. Clifton H. Kreps Jr, 11 Aug. 1944, 1 son, 2 daughters. *Education:* AB, Berea College, 1942; MA, 1944, PhD, 1948, Duke University. *Appointments:* Instructor, Economics, Denison University, 1945-46; Assistant Professor, 1948-50, Faculty, 1955-77, Associate Professor, 1962-68, Professor, Economics, 1968-77, Assistant Provost, 1969-72, James B Duke Professor, 1972-77, Vice-President, 1973-77, Duke University, Durham, North Carolina; US Secretary of Commerce, 1977-79; Director: Eastman Kodak Co; Armco Inc; UAL Inc; J C Penney Co Inc; AT&T; Chrysler Corporation; Deere & Co; Zurn Industries Inc; Trustee, Duke Endowment, Berea College, 1979-. *Publications:* Principles of Economics (with C E Ferguson), 2nd Revised Edition, 1965; Lifetime Allocation of Work & Income, 1971; Sex in the Marketplace: American Women at Work, 1971; Sex, Age & Work, 1975; Others. *Memberships:* Vice-President, American Economic Association, 1983-84; President, Southern Economic Association, 1975-76; Former Chairman, Commission on Academic Affairs, American Council on Education; President-Elect, American Association for Higher Education, 1975-76; Chairman, Board of Trustees, Educational Testing Service, 1975-76; Past Vice-President, Gerontological Society; Phi Beta Kappa; Director, Council on Foreign Relations, 1983-89; Trilateral Commission, 1980-86; Trustee, TIAA Stock, Member, CREF, 1985-. *Honours:* Various awards and recognitions for achievement in field, Address: 3511 Cambridge Road, Durham, NC 27707, USA.

KRESCH Sandra Daryl, b. 13 Sept. 1945, New York, USA. Communications. m. Samuel H Hagler, 6 Jan. 1973, 2 step-daughters. *Education:* BS, University of Pennsylvania, 1966. *Appointments:* Research Associate, Simat Helliesen & Eichner Inc., New York, 1966-67; Research Associate, Study Director, 1968-69, National Analysts Inc., Phialdaelphia; President, Sandra D Kresch Consulting Services, Atherton, 1969- 70; Vice President, Manager, Market Research, National Analysts, Chicago, 1970-75; Booz, Allen Venture Management Inc., New York, 1976-78; Corporate Development, New York, 1978-80, Booz Allen & Hamilton Inc., 1980-82; Senior Vice President, Marketing, Vide Group, 1983-84; Director, Strategic Planning, magazine Group, 1984-86, Time Magazine, 1986-; Time Inc., New York. *Memberships Include:* Board Directors, Spence Chapin Services to Families & Children; Personnel & Pension committee Chairman, Study Policy Committee; Jose Limon Dance Foundation Inc., President, Board Directors, Executive Committee, Chairman, Nominating Committee Chairman; Volunteer Consulting Group, Board Candidate Service Advisory Committee Chairman, Development Committee Vice Chairman, Salary & Administrative Committee; etc. *Honours:* Tribute to Women in International Industry,

1978. *Address:* 14 East 75th Street, New York, NY 10021, USA.

KRETSCH Josephine Ann McKasy, b. 27 May 1920, St Paul, USA. Social Worker. m. J R Kretsch, 11 Oct 1943, 4 sons, 2 daughters. *Education:* BSW, St Catherine's College, 1976. *Appointments:* Geriatric Social Worker, 1977-80. *Memberships:* President, St Therese Catholic Church Guild, 1962; Founder, 1977, President 1981, Secretary/Treasurer, 1982, Vice President, Treasurer, Director, 1983-86, Closed Head Injury Group, Family Interest Group-Head Trauma; President, Psi Psi Psi, 1980-82; Board Member, Benilde High School; Josephine Kretsch Resource Library on Brain Injury, est. 1985. *Hobbies:* Music; Tennis; Swimming; Skiing; Reading; Dancing. *Address:* 2805 McKenzie Pt. Rd, Wayzata, MN 55391, USA.

KREUSCHER Irene Katz, b. 20 Jan. 1954, New York City, USA. Hospital Administrator. m. Douglas J. Kreuscher, 26 June 1977, 1 son, 1 daughter. *Education:* BS, State University of New York, Albany, 1975; MBA, Baruch College, Mount Sinai School of Medicine, 1977. *Appointments:* Various positions, Albany Medical Centre 1975, Beth Israel Medical Centre 1976-78, New York University Medical Centre 1980-82, New York; Director of Planning 1983-83, Associate Administrator, Clinical Information Services 1983- , Memorial Sloan-Kettering Cancer Centre, NY. *Memberships:* American College of Health Care Executives; American Hospital Association. *Honours:* Scholarship, academic excellence, Equitable Life Assurance. *Hobbies:* Travel; Skiing; Gardening. *Address:* Memorial Sloan- Kettering Cancer Centre, 1275 York Avenue, New York, NY 10021, USA.

KRIENKE Carol Belle, b. 19 June 1917, Oakland, California, USA. m. Oliver Kenneth Krienke, 4 June 1941, 3 daughters. *Education:* BS, University of Minnesota, 1940. *Appointments:* Demonstrator, General Foods Corporation, Mineapolis, 1940; Youth Leadership, 1940-41; War Production Worker, 1944; Teacher, Los Angeles City Schools, 1945-49; Realtor, DBA Ethel Purdon, Manhattan Beach, 1949; Buyer, Purdon Furniture & Appliances, 1950-58; Realtor & Appraiser, O.K. Krienke Realty, 1958-. *Memberships Include:* Board of Directors, South Bay Council Girl Scouts USA, 1957-62; Chairman, United Way, 1967; Friends of Library; National Association of Real Estate Appraisers; El Redondo Chapter, 1971-; New England Women, (Poppy Calong), 1972-; Life Member, California Retired Teachers Association, 1988. *Address:* 924 Highview Ave., Manhattan Beach, CA 90266, USA

KRISHNARAJ Maithreyi, b. 1 Aug. 1931, India. Teacher; Researcher. m. 6 Aug. 1964, 1 son, 1 daughter. *Education:* B.Ed., MA, University of Delhi; MSc., Education, State University of New York; PhD, SNDT. *Appointments:* Lady Irwin Higher Secondary School, New Delhi, 1961-63; Kendriya Vidyalaya, Bombay, 1964-70; Gandhi Shikshan Bhavan College of Education, Univesity of Bombay, 1970-75; Research Associate, 1975-82, Associate Director, 1982-86, Director, 1986-, Women Studies, SNDT Womens University. *Publications:* Poetry; Watercolours; 4 books; over 30 papers and over 30 articles. *Memberships:* Executive Secretary, National Association Innovative Teaching; Life Member, Science Forum; Indian Women Scientists' Association; Life Member, Indian Association Women Studies; Music Society; World Wildlife Fund, India. *Honours:* Recipient, various honours and awards including: Fulbirgh Grants, 1963, 1979-80; New York University Exchange Scholar, 1987. *Hobbies:* Sketching; Music; Literature; Hiking. *Address:* 7 Manohar Mahal, 252 Mogul Lane, Mahim, Bombay 400016, India.

KRIZ Marjorie M, b. 2 May 1920, Evanston, Illinois, USA. Author; Writer. m. Jack Jerome Kriz, 8 May 1954, deceased. 1 son, 1 daughter. *Education:* BS 1942, MA 1943, Northwestern University; Seminar, University of Wisconsin, 1985; Seminar, Christ Church College, Oxford, England, 1985. *Appointments:* Director

Publicity, NU Theatre, 1942-43; Cry Havoc, Theatre Guild, 1943; BWR Theatre Wing, 1943; City News Bureau of Chicago, 1944-54 and 1967-72; Assistant Public Affairs Officer, Federal Aviation Administration, Great Larez Realtor, 1972-88. *Publications:* Various newspapers and US Government publications. But We don't Eat the Lemons, autobiography As told to Me. *Memberships:* Board Member, Chicago Press Veterans Association; Chicago Newspaper Reporters Association; Aviation/Space Writers Association; Board Member, Mitchell Gallery of Flight (Milwaukee Aviation Museum); Zeta Phi Eta. *Honours:* Various plaques and certificates from Federal Aviation Administration. *Hobbies:* Travel; Photography; Research writing. *Address:* 3306 Hayes Street, Evanston, IL 60201-1832, USA.

KROLL Evelyn Brennan, b. 5 Oct. 1927, New York City, USA. Marketing Executive. m. John L Kroll, 29 Dec. 1966, 2 sons, 1 stepdaughter. *Education:* Student, Hunter College, 1949-57. *Appointments:* Teacher, Public Schools, New Jersey, 1952-53; Advertising Representative, The New York Times, 1954-60; Assistant Director, School & Camp Advertising, 1960-65; Principal, Sanmarev Advertising Agency, Stamford, 1965-67; Director, Advertising & Public Relations, Jayfro Corp, Waterford, 1968-72; Vice Presidnet, Marketing & Public Relations, 1972-79; President, 1979-86; President, Kroll Associates, 1987-; Founder, Owner, Fun Stuff Division, 1982-; Co-Founder, Director, National Catalogue Distribution Corp, 1973; Co-Founder, Nanaging Editor, National Trade Newsletter, 1973-; Founder, Kroll press Publishers and Advertising Co, Waterford, 1978. *Publications:* Author with John L Kroll and Frank Smith, It Doesn't Pay to Work Too Hard, 1977; Editor, Blueprint for Safety in Sports and Recreation, 1978; Regular Marketing and Salesmanship Columnist: The Sporting Goods Dealer Magazine, 1974-80; contributor to other journals & magazines. *Memberships Include:* Tustee, Eugene O'Neill Theatre Centre, Waterford; National Sporting Goods Association; National School Supply and Equipment Association, Board of Directors 1983-85; American Sports Education Institute; Southeastern Ct. Chamber of Commerce, Board of Directors, 1983-86; Eastern Ct. Symphony Orchestra, Board of Directors, 1985-87. *Hobbies:* Gourmet Cooking; Bio-Chemistry. *Address:* c/o Kroll Associates, 535 Pequet Avenue, New London, CT 06320, USA.

KROLL Natasha, b. 20 May 1914, Moscow, USSR. Television & Film Designer. *Education:* Reimann School of Art, Berlin, 1932-35. *Appointments:* Teacher, Window Display, Reimann School of Art, London, England, 1936-40; Display Manager, Rowntrees, Scarborough & York, 1940-52; Display Manage, Simpson, Piccadilly Ltd., 1942-55; Senior Designer, BBC TV, 1955-66; Freelance Designer, 1966-. *Publications:* Window Display, Studio publicaiton, 1954; BBC TV Programmes include: Monitor; Panorama; Science Programmes; Lower Depths; Death of Danton; The Duel; Ring Round the Moon; La Traviata; Day by the Sea; Sponge Room; Freelance Work includes; The Seagull; Family Reunion; Eugen Onegin; The Soldiers Tale; La Vida Breve; Mary Stuart; Doll's House; Three Sisters; Cherry Orchard; Rasputin; Wild Duck; Loves Labours Lost; Film Designer of: Music Lovers; The Hireling; Absolution. *Memberships:* RDI; FSIAD. *Honours:* The Hireling, FTA Film Award for Best Art Direction, 1973. *Hobbies:* Painting; Entertaining. *Address:*.5 Ruvigny Gardens, London SW15, England.

KROLOWNA Krystyna, b. 12 Nov. 1939, Sosnowiec, Poland. Actress. m. August Kowalczyk, 1979 (div. 1985). *Education:* Master of Theatrical Arts, State College of Theatrical Arts, 1963. *Appointments:* Polish Theatre, Bielsko Biala, 1963-65; J. Slowacki Theatre, Krakow, 1965-68; Polish Theatre, Warsaw, 1969-83; National Theatre, Warsaw, 1983-. *Creative work includes:* Theatre: Threepenny Opera; As You Like It; Anthony & Cleopatra; Pygmalion. Films: Peasants, by Reymont; Pastorale Heroica. *Memberships:* Polish Actors Association; Monuments Preservation Society. *Honours:* Awards: Chairman, Committee of Polish Radio

& TV, 1974, 1983; Ministry of Culture & Arts, 1979; Ministry of National Defence, 1982. *Hobbies:* Collecting old books; Reading biographies; Care of animals. *Address:* ul. Sobieskiego 6-65, 02-954 Warsaw, Poland.

KRONEGGER Maria Elisabeth (Marlies), b. 23 Sept. 1932, Graz, Austria. Professor. *Education includes:* Equivalents, French agregation & American MA, Romance Languages & Literatures, Philosophy, Karl-Franzens University, Graz, 1950-53; Sorbonne, Paris, 1953-54; MA, Kansas University, USA, 1958; PhD, Florida State University, 1960. *Appointments include:* School teacher, Reims, France, 1956-57; Instructor, Florida State University, USA, 1958-60; International College, St Gallen, Switzerland, 1961- 62; Hollins College, USA, 1962-64; Assistant Professor 1964-67, Associate Professor 1967-70, Professor 1970-, French & Comparative Literature, Michigan State University. *Publications include:* James Joyce & Associate Image Makers, 1968; Impressionist Literature, 1973; Life Significance of French Baroque Poetry, 1989. Also Editor, Phénoménologie et littérature. L'Origine de l'oeuvre dart, Sherbrooke, Naaman, 1985; Phenomenology and Aesthetics: New Approches to Comparative Literature. Analecta Husserliana, XXXIII, Dordrecht: Kluver, 1990. *Memberships include:* President, International Society of Literature & Phenomenology; Board, Literature & Phenomenology, World Institute of Phenomenology, Boston; US, Rocky Mountain, & South Atlantic Modern Language Associations; Federation Internationale des Langues et Litteratures Modernes; International Association of Philosophy; International Comparative Literature Association, etc. *Honours include:* Numerous scholarships, grants, awards, fellowships, Europe & USA. *Hobbies:* Skiing; Swimming; Opera. *Address:* Wells Hall 502, Michigan State University, East Lansing, Michigan 48824, USA.

KRONICK Doreen Relly, b. 9 Nov. 1931, Winnipeg, Canada. Author; Psychoeducational Consultant; Lecturer. m. Joseph Kronick, 7 Sept. 1950, 2 sons. *Education:* BA, Skidmore College, 1974; MA, York University, 1976. *Appointments:* Professional Director, Integra Foundation, 1970-76; Teacher Trainer, 1978-, Ontario Ministry of Education; Associate Professor, York University, 1979-87. *Publications:* I Need You Who Needs Me, 1989; Toward Productive Living, 1988; New Approaches to Learning Disabilities, 1988; Social Development of Learning Disabled Persons, 1981; Three Families, 1976; Involving Impaired, Disabled and Handicapped Persons in Regular Camp, 1976; What About Me?, 1975; A Word or Two About Learning; Learning Disabilities, 1969; They Too Can Succeeed, 1969; numerous book chapters & articles in journals & magazines. *Memberships:* President, Learning Disabilities Association of Ontario, 1966-68, 1971-72; Vice President, US Association for Children with Learning Disabilities, 1965-66; Secretary, International Academy for Research in Learning Disabilities, 1989. *Honours:* Recipient, various honours & awards. *Hobbies:* Writing; Reading; Art; Travel; Cooking; Music. *Address:* 8 Rollscourt Drive, Willowdale, Ontario, Canada, M2L 1X5.

KRONIN-BUDD Bernadette Smith, b. 23 Feb. 1948, New York, USA. Educator; Publisher. m. Thomas Witbeck Budd, 4 July 1988. 4 daughters. *Education:* BA, History, English, Bucknell University, Lewisburg, Pennsylvania; MA, State University of New York, Stony Brook; EdM, Teachers College, Columbia University. *Appointments:* Owner Editor, Publisher, Community Journal Newspaper, 1978-; Editor, Shoreham Wading River School District Newsletter, 1978-; Advertising Executive, Public Relations Consultant, 1978-; President, CJ Typesetting & Printing. *Publications:* Editorials, news stories, layout, compolsition of a weekly commercially supported Newspaper; Creation of a monthly newsletter for Shoreham Wading River School District; Production of Labor & Employment Law Newsletter for Management Law Firm of Clifton Budd, Burke & Demaria, New York City. *Memberships:* Sigma Delta Chi; Suffolk County Business and Professional

Women's Association; NYS Press Club; Long Island Press Club; Kappa kappa Gamma; Editor, Chamber of Commerce Director, Rocky Point; Board of Directors, Wading River Chamber of Commerce; President, Wading River Parent Teachers Association; Vice-President, Special Education PTA; Suffolk County Human Rights Commission; Women's Equal Rights Congress; Member, NYS Press Association. *Honours:* Distinguished Service Award, American Cancer Society, 1982-84; Award of Merit, NYS Public Relations Association, 1983; Award of Honour, National School Public Relations Association, 1984; Board of Directors, Rocky Point Chamber of Commerce, 1986-89. *Hobbies:* Breeding and Showing Golden Retriever Dogs; Art Appreciation; Tennis; Golf; Jogging. *Address:* Box 619, Wading River, NY 11792, USA.

KROONENBERG Nancy C., b. 20 June 1948, Newton, Massachusetts, USA. French Teacher; Modern Language Department Head. m. Joseph A. (Bob) Kroonenberg, 9 July 1972. *Education:* University of Nice, France, 1968- 69; BA, Northwestern University, Illinois, 1970; MA, 1971, Additional study, 1989-, Columbia University, New York. *Appointments:* Teaching positions: Norwalk High School, Connecticut, 1971-72; International School of Amsterdam, Netherlands, 1974-76; Hong Kong International School, 1977-. *Publications:* Booklets: Things French, vols 5 and 8; Let Your Students Talk and Teach; Be There!. *Memberships:* American Association of Teachers of French; Association of French Teachers of Hong Kong; American Council on the Teaching of Foreign Languages. *Honours:* Rockefeller Foundation Fellowship, 1986; Chevalier, Ordre des Palmes academiques, 1988; Joseph Klingenstein Fellow, Columbia University, 1989-. *Hobbies:* Travel; Reading. *Address:* 142 Tin Hau Temple Road, Skyscraper Mansion F/12, Hong Kong.

KRUCHTEN Marcia Helen Chambers, b. 15 Aug. 1932, Orleans, Indiana, USA. Writer; Poet; Artist; Medical Records Administrator. m. Malcolm Newland Kruchten, 18 Sept. 1954, 2 sons, 2 daughters. *Education:* Indiana & Indiana State Universities, 1950-52; Graduate, commercial art, Famous Artists' School, 1967; Graduate, AMRA Medical Records Technician, 1972. *Appointments:* Director, Medical Records, Dunn Memorial Hospital 1962- 71, Bedford Medical Centre 1971-78; Muralist (various shops & restaurants) & illustrator, freelance, 1967-; Author, poetry, children's books, educational materials, short stories, 1973-. *Publications:* Children's books: Ghost in the Mirror, 1985; I Don't Want To Be Like Her, 1986; Skyborn, 1989. Poetry book: Catwalk, 1986. Poetry contributions, various publications; Short stories *Memberships:* American Medical Records Association; Society of Children's Book Writers. *Honours:* Golden Poet Award, World of Poetry, 1987; Reading at poetry film, Indiana University, 1975; Placing, Writer's Digest poetry competition, 1974. *Hobbies:* Reading; Baking bread; Walking; Painting rural scenes & wild flowers. *Address:* 1515 16th Street, Bedford, Indiana 47421, USA.

KRUGER Barbara, b. 6 Aug. 1944, Corpus Christi, Texas, USA. Audiologist. m. 19 June 1966. *Education:* BA, psychology 1967, MA Speech Pathology, 1970, Queens College, City Univerity of New York; PhD, Audiology & Hearing Science, CUNY Graduat School, 1975. *Appointments:* Speech Pathologist, audiologist, researcher, Audiological Consultant, prior to 1975; Assistant Professor, Audiology & Director, hearing Research, 1975-78; Adjunct Professor, 1979-82; Teachers College, Columbia University, New York; Assistant Professor, otlaryngology & Director, Audiology, Speech Language Pathology, Albert Einstein College of Medicine, Yeshiva University, 1978-87; Director, Kruger Associates. *Publications:* Articles in professional journals. *Memberships:* Acoustical Society of America; American Speech Language Hearing Association (member several committees); Phi Beta Kappa; Sigma Alpha Eta; psi Chi. *Honours Include:* Fellow, ASLHA, 1985; Deans List, New York State Regents Scholarship. *Address:* Kruger Associates, 37 Somerset Drive, Commack, NY 11725, USA.

KRULEWICH Helen Dworetzky, b. 6 Apr. 1948, New Jersey, USA. m. 2 Sept. 1973. 1 son, 1 daughter. *Education:* BSc, Syracuse University, Syracuse, New York; JD, Suffolk University Law School, Boston, Massachusetts; Student Insurance Institute, Northeastern University, Boston, 1982-83; Tufts University Special Student, 1988-89. *Appointments:* Title Examiner, Clerk 1971-74, Nutter, McClennan and Fish, Boston; Conveyancing, Rackemann, Sawyer & Brewster, Boston, 1974-76; Private Practice, Boston, 1976-78; Assistant Regional Counsel 1978-81, Associate Regional Counsel 1981-85, The Prudential Insurance Company of America, Boston; Karger and Arnowitz, Boston, 1986-. *Memberships:* American Bar Association; Massachusetts Bar Association; Boston Bar Association; Historic Neighborhood Foundation, Board of Trustees; New England Women in Real Estate; Urban Land Institute; Cultural Organizations; Friends of Public Garden; Museum of Fine Arts; Museum of Modern Art; Society Preservation new England Antiquities; MASS Association Women Lawyers; League of Women Voters; Women's Bar Association. *Hobbies:* Reading; Decorative arts; Arts; Travel; Cities; Museums. *Address:* 153 Woodchester Drive, Chestnut Hill, Massachusetts 02167, USA.

KRUMLAUF Frances Ann, b. 30 July 1952, Milwaukee, Wisconsin, USA. Exercise Physiologist; Director of Exercise. m. Lloyd Russell Krumlauf, 31 Dec. 1987. *Education:* BA Exercise Physiology, North Central College, Naperville, 1984. *Appointments:* Lecturer, instructor 17 years; Sportsmed Center for Fitness, 1986-; Director of Exercise/Exercise Physiologist, Humana Hospitals; Prenatal Exercise Consultant/Instructor. *Memberships:* American College of Sports Medicine; Association of Health, Physical Education & Recreation; International Dance-Exercise Association; Reebok Professional Advisory Panel. *Honours:* Richter Fellowship Research Grant, Exercise and Pregnancy, 1984; Beta Beta Beta, Honorary Society, 1984; Outstanding Senior, Physical Education, 1984. *Hobbies:* Distance running; Snow skiing; Race cars. *Address:* 1001 Oswego Road, Naperville, Illinois 60540, USA.

KRUPANSKY Blanche E, b. 10 Dec. 1925, Cleveland, Ohio, USA. Judge. m Frank W. Vargo, 30 Apr. 1960. *Education:* AB, Flora Stone Mather ollege, 1947; JD, 1948, LLM, 1966, Case Western Reserve University. *Appointments:* Admitted to Ohio Bar, 1949; General Law Practice, 1949- 61; Assistant Attorney General of Ohio, (3 1/2 years); Assistant Chief Counsel to the Bureau of Workers' Compensation (2 Years); Judge, Cleveland Municipal Court, 1961-69; Judge, Common Pleac Court, 1969-77, Judge, Court of Appeals of Ohio, 1977-81; Justice, Supreme Court of Ohio, 1981-83; General Law Practice, 1983-84; Judge, Court of Appeals, Ohio, 1984-. *Memberships Include:* Ohio State Bar Association; Bar Association of Greater Cleveland; Cuyahoga County Bar Assocation; National Association of Women Lawyers; National Association of Women Judges, Charter Member. *Honours:* Recipient, numerous honours and awards including: Outstanding Accomplishments in Law, Women Space, 1984; Margaret A. Ireland Award, 1985. *Address:* 18846 North Valley Drive, Fairview Park, OH 44126, USA.

KRUSICK Margaret Ann, b. 26 Oct. 1953, Milwaukee, USA. State Representative. *Education:* BA, Certificate in Law Studies, University of Wisconsin, Milwaukee, 1978; Masters Studies, Public Administration, University of Wisconsin, Madison, 1978-82. *Appointments:* Paralegal, Milwaukee Law Office, 1973-78; Teaching Assistant, University of Wisconsin, 1978-79; Staff Member, Governor's Ombudsman Programme for the Aging & Disabled, 1980; Administrative Assistant, Higher Educational Aides Board, 1981; Legislative Aide, 1982-83; Elected State Representative, 1983, re- elected 1984, 1986. *Publications:* Wisconsin Youth Suicide Prevention Act. *Memberships:* Wisconsin Democratic Party; CESA Children at Risk Task Force; Chair, Suicide Prevention; UWM Alumni Association, Board of Trustees; Milwaukee Womens Court & Civic Converence; Jackson

Park Assocation; etc. *Honours:* Milwaukee Area Girl Scouts Appreciation Award, 1984; Milwaukee Police Retirees Award, 1985; Wisconsin Chiefs of Police Statesmen for Law Enforcement Award, 1986; Clean 16 Environmental Award, 1986; etc. *Hobbies:* Horse Riding; Travel; Camping; Basketball; Biking; Swimming; Tennis; Aerobics. *Address:* 6832 West Morgan Avenue, Milwaukee, WI 53220, USA.

KRYNICKI Margaret, b. 8 Nov. 1953, Long Beach, California, USA. Manager, Industrial Relations. *Education:* BA, 1975, MA 1982, California State University; Teaching Credential, University of California, Los Angeles, 1976; Certified School Audiometrist, 1975. *Appointments:* Corporate Personnel Administrator, Mattel Inc., 1978-79; Personnel Administrator, TRW, 1979-82; Manager, Human Resources, Rockwell Int., 1982-88; Manager, Industrial Relations, Rockwell Int., 1988-. *Memberships:* National Management Association; Mensa. *Hobbies:* True Crime/Mystery; Writing. *Address:* 628 Daisy No 412, Long Beach, CA 90802, USA.

K-TURKEL Judi (also known as Judi Kesselman-Turkel), b. 3 Jan. 1934, Bronx, New York, USA. Author. 2 sons. *Education:* BA, Brooklyn College, New York, 1951-55. *Appointments:* Editor, Managing Editor and Editor in Chief, various New York film and confession magazines, 1955-68; Project Editor, Wisconsin Center for Public Policy, 1979; Co-author and Co-editor, CPA Micro Report newsletter, 1982-83, 1984-86, 1988; Editor, Computer Insider Newsletter, 1983; Co-author and Co-syndicator, twice weekly national newspaper column, 1983-. *Publications:* 22 books including: Stopping Out: A Guide to Leaving College and Getting Back In, 1975; Good Writing, 1980; Test Taking Strategies, 1981; The Author's Handbook, 1982, 1987; The Grammar Crammer; Research Shortcuts; Note-Taking Made Easy; The Vocabulary Builder; The Magazine Writer's Handbook, 1983, 1987; Getting It Down: How to Get your Ideas on Paper; Spelling Simplified; Study Smarts; Over 100 newspaper articles and over 1,000 national magazine articles. *Memberships:* American Society of Journalists and Authors, 1974-; Authors Guild, Authors League, 1978-; National Press Club, 1979-. *Honours:* Jesse H Neal Editorial Achievement Award (American Business Press Association), 1977; Citation for Excellence in Consumer Journalism, National Press Club, 1984; First Prize for Excellence in Consumer Journalism, National Press Club, 1985. *Hobby:* Travel. *Address:* P/K Associates Inc, 3006 Gregory Street, Madison, WI 53711, USA.

KUBLER-ROSS Elisabeth, b. 8 July 1926, Zurich, Switzerland. Thanatologist. 1 son, 1 daughter. *Education:* MD, University of Zurich, 1957. *Appointments Include:* Various Internships, Residencies, 1963-65; Acting Chief, Associate Chief, Psychiatric Inpatient Service, 1965-67; Chief, Consultation & Liaison, LaRabida Childrens Hospital, 1969-70; President, Ross Medical Associates, SC, 1973-78; President, Elisabeth Kubler-Ross Center, 1977-. Clinical Professor, University of Virginia, 1985-. *Publications:* On Death and Dying, 1969; Questions & Answers on Death & Dying, 1974; Death - The Final Stage of Growth, 1975; To Live Until We Say Goodbye, 1978; Letter to a Child with Cancer, 1979; Working it Through, 1981; Living with Death & Dying, 1981; Remember the Secreet, 1982; On Children and Death, 1983; Uber Den Tod Und Das Leben Danach, 1984; Aids: The Ultimate Challenge, 1987; books chapters; numerous articles. *Memberships Include:* American Medical Association; American Association for Advancement of Science; Founding Member, American Holistic Medicla Association; many others. *Honours:* Recipient, many honours & awards. *Address:* Elisabeth Kubler-Ross Center, South Route 616, Head Waters VA 24442, USA.

KUDLACIAK Helena Bronislawa, b. 3 Sept. 1932, Kety, near Bielsko- Biala, Poland. Writer; Teacher. m. Alojzy Kudlaciak, 26 Dec. 1952, 1 daughter. *Education:* Graduate, Teachers' College, 1951. *Appointments:* Boys' primary school, Lipiny, 1951; Primary school, Bielsko, 1953. *Publications:* Writer, books, 1966-. Titles include: Poem, Pasjans ze Sloncem; Novel, Poza Otwartym Oknem, Poem, Rytualne Medytage. *Memberships:* Inter-Provincial Writers Club, Katowice; Teachers' Writers Club, Bielsko- Biala; Folk Writers Group 'Gronie' Zywiec; Association of Polish Authors. *Honours:* Golden Cross of Merit, 1977; Mark of Distinction, Bielsko Province, 1987; Golden Mark of Distinction, Polish Teachers Association, 1988. *Hobbies:* Sculpture in rope; Graphic art; Prose; Satire; Mountaineering stories. *Address:* 43-300 Bielsko-Biala, ul. Piechy 20, Poland.

KUEHL Nancy L, b. 22 May 1947, Lufkin, Angelina County, Texas, USA. Certified Shorthand Reporter. m. (1) Jack B Ely, 13 Mar. 1966, divorced, 1 daughter. (2) W A Kuehl, Jr, 23 Sept. 1972. 1 son, 1 daughter. *Education:* BA, 1981; Postgraduate studies; Certification, Shorthand Reporter, State of Texas. *Appointments:* Paralegal, Harvill & Hardy, 1976-77; Litigation Supervisor, Fenley & Bate, 1977; Legal Assistant, Forrest G Braselton, 1977-78; Hill-Mace Reporting Agency, 1982-87; Kuehl Reporting Service, 1987-. *Publications:* The Glass Staircase, 1982; How to Set Up a Successful Typing Service, 1982; A Seale Anthology, Volumes I, II, 1985; Henry Seale, The King's Bookseller, 1989. *Memberships:* Phi Alpha Theta; Pi Sigma Alpha; Sigma Tau Delta; Nacogdoches Writer's Group; NSVRA (National Stenomask Verbatim Reporting Association); International Platform Association. *Hobbies:* Travel; Art; Genealogy; Music; History. *Address:* P O Box 4165, Bryan, TX 77805, USA.

KUENZLI Gwen Lee, b. 30 Nov. 1936, Bucyrus, Ohio, USA. College Professor; Speech Pathologist. m. David P. Kuenzli, 6 June 1958, 2 sons, 1 daughter. *Education:* BFA, 1958, MFA, 1959, Ohio University; Postgraduate studies, Bowling Green State University, 1975-76, 1986-88. *Appointments:* Speech Pathologist, Syracuse Public Schools, Syracuse, New York, 1959-60; Speech Pathologist, Worthington Public Schools, Ohio, 1961-62; Speech Pathologist, Hancock County Board of Health, Findlay, Ohio, 1977- 80; Ohio Northern University, Ada, 1979-80; Speech Pathologist, Blanchard Valley Hospital, 1980-84; Findlay College, 1980-. *Publication:* Registry of Ohio Clinical Services. *Memberships:* Speech Communication Association; Writing Centers Association; Women's Caucus, Central States Speech Association; Executive Board, Aphasiology Association of Ohio; Ohio Speech Communication Association; Executive Board, Ohio Speech and Hearing Association; Board of Trustees, Hancock Family Services; Scholarship Chairman, Zonta International; International Communication Association; Staff Consultant, Training and Research Center for Language and Multicultural Studies, Society for Intercultural Education. *Honours:* Director, Honours Programme; Nomination as Outstanding Speech Teacher, Ohio. *Hobbies:* International students. *Address:* 5163 Twp Road 79, Rawson, OH 45881, USA.

KUHN Sarah, b. 24 June 1952, Boston, Massachusetts, USA. Consultant; Teacher. m. Ralph E. LaChance, 29 Aug. 1987. *Education:* BA, Harvard University, 1974; PhD, Massachusetts Institute of Technology (MIT), 1987. *Appointments:* Instructor, researcher, MIT, 1980-84; Researcher, Cambridge, Massachusetts, 1984-87; Private practice, consultant, 1987-; Project Manager, Stone Centre, Wellesley College, 1987-88. *Publications:* Author: Computer Manufacturing in New England, 1982. Co- Author: Retail Revolution, 1981: Mass High Tech: Promise & Reality, 1984. *Memberships:* Association of Computing Machinery; American Planning Association; Computer Professionals for Social Responsibility; Women's Economic Literacy Project. *Honours:* Fellow, Harvard-MIT Joint Centre for Urban Studies, 1982-83; Eastern women's rowing champion, National Women's Rowing Association, 1974. *Hobbies:* Swimming; Gardening; Home renovation; Fabric sculpture. *Address:* 340 Winter Street, Framingham, Massachusetts 01701, USA.

KUKU Felicia Ostfunke, b. 6 Mar. 1944, Lagos, Nigeria. Research Scientist; Ogun State Commissioner of Commerce & Industry. m. Ao Kuku, 28 Dec. 1968, 4 daughters. *Education:* BSc., 1968, MSc., 1974, PhD, 1986, Ibadan. *Appointments:* Research Officer, 1968-72; Senior Research Officer, 1973-76; Principal Research Officer, 1977-81; Chief Research Officer, 1982-87; Commissioner of Commerce & Industry, 1987-. *Honours:* Corresponding Secretary, Zonta International, Ibadan, 1985-87; Vice President, Horticultural Society of Nigeria, Ogun State Branch, 1987-; Vice President, Better Life for Rural Women, Ogun State, 1987-. *Hobbies:* Reading; Ballroom Dancing. *Address:* Ogun State Commissioner of Commerce & Industry, Ogun State, Abeokuta, Nigeria.

KULP Marilyn J, b. 28 July 1941, Philadlephia, USA. Association Executive Director. m. Louis F Kulp, 2 July 1966, 1 son, 3 daughters. *Education:* various colleges. *Appointments:* Quality Control, Paramount Packaging Co., Chalfont, 1963-64; Electrical & design Engineering, Selas Corp., 1964-66; Assistant Staff Director, Willow Grove, 1966-69; Abington Associates, 1973-79; Executive Director, 1979-, Association for Multi Image International Inc., 1974-. *Publications:* numerous articles in professionaljournals. *Memberships:* International Communications Industry Association; Association for education Communications & Technolgoy; Visual Communications Congress; American Society of Association Executives; International Association of Business Communicators; International Film Producers Association. *Hobbies:* Sports; Gradening; Sewing; Music; Travel; Crafts. *Address:* Association for Multi Image International Inc., 8019 North Himes Avenue, Suite 401, Tampa, FL 33614, USA.

KULYK KEEFER Janice Lynn, b. 2 June 1952, Toronto, Canada. Writer. m. Michael, 1 Sept. 1972, 2 sons. *Education:* BA, English Literature, University of Toronto, 1974; MA, Modern Literature, 1976, D.Phil, English Literature, 1983, Sussex University, England. *Appointments:* Lecturer, English, Universite Sainte Anne, 1981-82; Assistant Professor, English,, Universite Sainte Anne, 1983-84; SHRCC Post-Doctoral Fellowship, 1984-86; SSHRCC Research Fellowship, 1987-88. *Publications:* The Paris- Napoli Express, 1986; White of the Lesser Angels, poetry, 1986; Transfigurations, 1987; Under Eastern Eyes: A Critical Reading of Maritime Fiction, 1987; Constellations, 1988; Reading Mavis Gallant, 1989. *Memberships:* Nova Scotia Writers Federation, Executive Council, 1986-88; Advisory Member, Canadian Centre for Studies in Publishing, 1987-88. *Honours:* Recipient, many honours and awards. *Address:* The Colbert Agency, 303 Davenport Road, Toronto, Ontario, Canada M5R 1K5.

KUMAR Mary Louise, b. 23 Jan. 1941, Chicago, Illinois, USA. Associate Professor, Dept of Pediatrics; Chief, Ped Infectious Diseases. m. Dr Unni Kumar. 2 sons, 2 daughters. *Education:* BA, University of Colorado, 1958-62; MD, Western Reserve University, 1963-67. *Appointments:* Assist Pediatrician, Infectious Diseases, 1971-78, Assoc Dir 1978-79, Chief 1979-, Ped Infectious Diseases, Director, Viral Diagnostic Laboratory 1979-, Metro-Health Medical Center; Associate Professor, Case Western Reserve Univversity School of Medicine, 1985-. *Publications:* Numerous articles for medical journals. *Memberships:* American Academy of Ped; Northern OH Ped Society; Society for Ped Research; Midwest Society for Ped Research; American Society for Microbiology; Pan American Group for Rapid Viral Diagnosis; American Society for Virology; American Veneral Disease Association; Association for Practitioners in Infection Control; American Medical Women's Association. *Hobbies:* Gardening; Health care of children. *Address:* MetroHealth Medical Center, 3395 Scranton Road, Research Building 311, Cleveland, OH 44109, USA.

KUMAR Smita Rajeev, b. 12 Apr. 1959, Kerala, India. Paediatric Allergist. m. Rajeev Kumar, 13 Jan. 1981, 1 son. *Education:* MB,BS, 1982. *Appointments:* Assistant Professor of Paediatrics, Cornell University Medical College, New York, USA, 1988-. *Memberships:* American Academy of Paediatrics; American Academy of Allergy & Immunology; American College of Allergists. *Honour:* Fellowship, Allergy, Immunology & Pulmonary Diseases, Cornell University Medical College, 1985-88. *Hobbies:* Reading; Painting. *Address:* 107 Lakeview Avenue, Scarsdale, New York 10583, USA.

KUMIN Maxine Winokur, b. 6 June 1925, Philadelphia, Pennsylvania, USA. Freelance writer. m. 29 June 1946, 1 son, 2 daughters. *Education:* AB 1946, AM 1948, Radcliffe. *Appointments:* Woodrow Wilson Visiting Fellow 1979-84, Hurst Professor 1975, Brandeis University; Consultant in Poetry, Library of Congress, 1981-82; Visiting Lecturer, Princeton University, 1981-82; Visiting Professor 1984, Visiting Writer 1986-87, MIT. *Publications:* Poetry: Halfway, 1961; The Privilege, 1965; The Nightmare Factory, 1970; Up Country, 1972; House, Bridge, Fountain, Gate, 1975; The Retrieval System, 1978; Our Ground Time Here will be Brief, 1982; The Long Approach, 1985; Nurture, 1989. Novels: Through Dooms of Love, 1965 in England A Daughter and Her Loves, 1965; The Passions of Uxport, 1968; The Abduction, 1971; The Designated Heir, 1974, 1975. Short stories: Why Can't We Live Together Like Civilized Human Beings?, 1982; Essays: In Deep: Country Essays, 1987, 1988; To Make a Prairie: Essays on Poets, Poetry and Country Living, 1980; Numerous children's books. *Memberships:* PEN; Authors Guild; Poetry Society of America; National Writers Union. *Honours:* Recipient of several honorary degrees; Levinson Prize, Poetry Magazine, 1986; American Academy & Inst Arts & Letters Award, 1980; Academy of American Poets Fellowship, 1985; Pulitzer Prize in Poetry, 1973; Tietjins Prize, Poetry Magazine, 1972. *Address:* RD1 Box 30 Joppa Road, Warner, NH 03278, USA.

KUNSTLER-LANGNER Danuta, b. 21 Apr. 1959, Poland. University Lecturer. m. Boguslaw Langner, 4 Jan. 1985, 1 son. *Education:* PhD, Nicolai Copernici University, Torun, 1981. *Appointment:* Lecturer, 1982-. *Publications:* Poetry: Nikt nie klamie, 1980; Wrozba pieciopalczasta, 1981; Cztery strony swiatla, 1986. *Memberships:* Union of Polish Writers; Learned Society of Torun. *Honour:* Klemens Janicki Prize, 1988. *Address:* ul. Goscinna 2 m 9, 85-792 Bydgoszcz, Poland.

KUNTZ Dolores (Sister), b. 4 Dec. 1925, London, Ontario, Canada. Educator. *Education:* BA, University of Western Ontario, 1946; MA, University of Detroit, Michigan, USA, 1962; PhD, Queen's University, Kingston, Ontario, 1968. *Appointments:* Secondary school teacher, Ontario, 1947- 59; University teacher, psychology, Brescia College, London, Ontario, 1959-; Principal & Dean, ibid, 1977-. *Memberships:* Ursuline Religious of the Chatham Union; Ontario Psychological Association. *Honours:* Canada Council, 1965-66; Ontario Graduate Fellowship, 1965-68. *Address:* Brescia College, 1285 Western Road, London, Ontario, Canada N6G 1H2.

KUNZMAN Carolyn Fern, b. 29 Aug. 1940, Nokomis, Saskatchewan, Canada. Musician. m. Glen G. Kunzman, 28 Dec. 1984. *Education:* ARCT, Royal Conservatory of Toronto, Piano Performance, 1967; BEd, University of Saskatchewan, 1970; Orff Certificate, Toronto, 1978; Orff Institute (Mozarteum), Salzburg, Austria, 1976-77; MEd, University of Manitoba, 1983; Musikhochschule, Freiburg, Germany, 1985-86. *Appointments:* Public School Teacher, especially music, gifted classes, Orff Schulwerk, recorder, choir, handbells, Renaissance dance; Orff music programme & certificate courses, preparatory studies, recorder ensembles, early childhood music, University of Manitoba. *Creative works include:* Medieval Feast I & II, Waterloo; Renaissance Banquet, Schott; Elementares Blockflötenspiel for English-Speaking Schools, Ostinato, AOSA Echo; Member, Prairie Consort (early music performing group). *Memberships:* Carl Orff Music for Children, Manitoba

& Canada (Offices); Manitoba Music Educators Association; American Orff-Schulwerk Association; American Recorder Society; Syllabus Committee, Associated Manitoba Arts Festivals. *Honour:* 1 of 25 outstanding graduates, Orff Institute (Mozarteum), Salzburg. *Hobby:* Travel, especially Germany & Austria. *Address:* c/o School of Music, University of Manitoba, Winnipeg, Manitoba, Canada R3T 2N2.

KURIANSKY Judy, b. 31 Jan. 1947, New York, USA. Radio talk host; Broadcaster; TV personality; Psychologist; Author. m. Edward Jay Kuriansky, 24 Aug. 1969. *Education:* BA, Smith College, 1968; EdM, Boston University, 1970; PhD, NYU, 1980. *Appointments:* Columbia Medical Center, 1970-76; Talk Show, WB2-TV, Boston, 1980-81; News Reporter, WABC-TV, 1980-82; News Reporter, WCBS-TV, 1982-85; Talk Show, WOR Radio, New York, 1985-86; Talk Host, WABC Radio, 1986-. *Publication:* Book: Sex: Now that I got your attention, let me Answer Your Questions, 1984. *Memberships:* American Women in Radio & TV (Vice Chair, Foundation); Television Academy, Board of Governors; Amer Psychol Assoc; International Radio & TV Society. *Honours:* Mercury award, 1987; Maggie Award, 1984; Freedoms Foundation Award, 1986; Olive Award, 1986; Civilian Commendation, Police Department. *Hobbies:* Travel; Movies; Tennis; Theatre. *Address:* c/o WABC Radio, 1330 Avenue of Americas, New York, NY 10019, USA.

KURTH Carol Joan Weissman, b. 18 May 1959, New York City, USA. Architect; Developer. m. Peter Kurth, 1 Aug. 1982, 1 son, 1 daughter, 1 stepson. *Education:* Bronx High School of Science, 1976; BS magna cum laude (Architecture) 1980, BArch 1981, School of Architecture, City College of New York (CCNY). *Appointments:* Employee 1979-88, partner 1984-88, Milowitz-Kurth Associates, Architects; Adjunct Assistant Professor, CCNY School of Architecture, 1981-85; Vice President & partner, Kurth & Kurth Architects, 1988-. *Memberships:* American Institute of Architects, National Council of Architectural Registration Boards; Society of American Registered Architects. *Honours:* Medal, student leadership in architecture, Alpha Rho Chi, 1980; Henry Adams Gold Medal, architecture (student), 1981; Matthew del Gaudio Total Design Award (student), New York Society of Architects, 1981; Award of Excellence, Descending Deck (Bedford, NY), 1986; Women in Architecture award, AIA, 1988. *Hobbies:* Architectural product design; Fashion; Gardening; Arts & crafts with children. *Address:* Bedford, New York 10506, USA.

KURTZ Katherine Irene, b. 18 Oct. 1944, Coral Gables, Florida, USA. Author. m. Scott Roderick MacMillan, 9 Apr. 1983, 1 son. *Education:* BS, Chemistry, University of Miami, 1966; MA, History, University of California, Los Angeles, 1971; D.D., American Apostolic University, 1989. *Appointments:* Instructional Designer, Los Angeles Police Department, Los Angeles, California, 1969-81. *Publications:* Deryni Series of fantasy novels, several editions: Deryni Rising, 1970; Deryni Checkmate, 1972; High Deryni, 1973; The Chronicles of the Deryni (3 books in 1 vol), 1985; Legends of Saint Camber, several editions: Camber of Culdi, 1976; Saint Camber, 1978; Camber the Heretic, 1981; Histories of King Kelson: The Bishop's Heir, 1984; The King's Justice, 1985; The Quest for Saint Camber, 1986; The Heirs of Saint Camber Trilogy: The Harrowing of Gwynedd, 1989; The Deryni Archives, short story collection, 1986; Lammas Night, mainstream novel, paperback 1983, hard cover, 1986; The Legacy of Lehr, science fiction, hard cover 1986, paperback 1987; Short stories; Many works translated into German/Italian/Swedish/Dutch. *Memberships:* Chevaliere, Order of the Temple of Jerusalem; Dame of Honour, Hospitaller Order of St John of Jerusalem; Commander, The Military and Hospitaller Order of St. Lazarus of Jerusalem; Fellow, Augusten Society; Dame, Noble Company of the Rose; Fellow, Octavian Society; Society of Descendants of the Latin Kingdom of Jerusalem. *Honours:* Edmund Hamilton Memorial Award for Camber of Culdi, 1977; Saint Camber nominated for Gandalf Award for Best

Book Length Fantasy, 1978; Balrog Award for Camber the Heretic, 1982; The Legacy of Lehr cited in Best Science Fiction Titles, Voice of Youth Advocates, 1986. *Hobbies:* Heraldry; Needlework; Costuming; History. *Address:* Holybrooke Hall, Kilmacanogue, Bray, Co. Wicklow, Republic of Ireland.

KURYLOWICZ Ewa Maria, b. 4 Dec. 1953, Warsaw, Poland. Architect; University Lecturer. m. Stefan Kurylowicz, 16 Sept. 1976, 2 sons. *Education:* MSc, Architecture, 1977; PhD, Architecture, Warsaw Technical University, 1982. *Appointments:* Assistant Lecturer, 1977-78, Senior Assistant Lecturer, 1978-86, Lecturer, 1986-, Architectural Department, Warsaw Technical University; Designer, Owner, Architectural Studios SE, Warsaw, 1984-; Exchange Professor, University of Detroit, Detroit, Michigan, USA, 1986. *Creative works:* Designs: Church in Grodzisk Mazowiecki; Resort Centre, Lansk; International Air Terminal No 2, Warsaw; Church and Parish Centre, Lomza; Interiors; Designing with the Disabled in Mind, book, 1990; Several articles and reports. *Membership:* Association of Polish Architects. *Honours:* 2nd Prize, Competition for School Design, Warsaw, 1980; Honourable Prize for PhD Dissertation, Rector of Warsaw Technical University, 1982; 1st Prize, Competition for Church in Lomza, 1987; 2nd Prize, Competition for Pullman Hotel in Warsaw, 1989. *Hobbies:* Music; Aerobics. *Address:* Tarnowiecka 3, Apt 71, 04174 Warsaw, Poland.

KUSHNER Rose, President and Exectuvie Director, Breast Cancer Advisory Center. *Education:* Pre-Med, Johns Hopkins University, McCoy College, 1946-47; Pre-Med, Baltimore Junior College, 1950-51; Pre-Med, Montgomery College (Maryland), 1963-65; Experimental Psychology 1965-68, BS Journalist 1968-72, University of Maryland. *Publications:* Alternatives: New Developments in the War on Breast Cancer, 1984, 1985; Why Me? Rewritten and Updated for the Eighties, 1982; A Breat Cancer Manual Every Woman Should Have, 1980, 1981; If You've Thought about Breast Cancer.., 1979, 1980, 1981, 1983, 1985, 1987; What to Do If..You Find Something That Suggests Breast Cancer, 1979; Why Me? What Every Woman should know about Breast Cancer to Save Her Life, 1977; Breast Cancer: A Personal History & an Investigative Report, 1975; Contributions to magazines and journals. *Membership:* National Cancer Advisory Board (Presidential appointment), 1980-86. *Honours include:* First Award for Distinguished Medical Writing, American Medical Writers' Association, Mid-Atlantic Chapter, 1980; Volunteer of the Year Award, National, 1982; National Consumers' League Activist Award, 1983; Research and lecturing regarding breast cancer, National Cancer Institute of the People's Republic of China, 1985; Award for Excellence in Biomedical Writing, American Medical Writers' Association, Mid-Atlantic Chapter, 1985; Award, Oustanding Service in Cancer Control, American Cancer Society, District of Columbia Division, 1985; Washington Woman of the Year, Washington Woman Magazine, 1986; Medal of Honor and Medal of Courage, American Cancer Society, 1987; Ladies Home Journal: 100 Most Importan tWomen in America, 1988; American Legion Auxiliary, Public Spirit Award, 1989. *Address:* 9607 Kingston Road, Kensington, Maryland 20796, USA.

KUUSKOSKI-VIKATMAA Eeva Maija Kaarina, b. 4 Oct. 1946, Aura. Member of Parliament. m. Juha Vile Vikatmaa, 1973, deceased, 1 daughter, deceased. *Education:* Licentiate in Medicine, 1972; Specialist in Paediatrics, 1982. *Appointments:* Physician, Turku Health Centre, 1973; Assistant Physician, Clinic of Paediatrics, Helsinki University Central Hospital, 1976-80; Member of Parliament, 1979-; Minister of Social Affairs & Health in the Cabinet, 1983-87. *Memberships:* Turku City Council, 1973-80; Chairman, Council for Equality, 1981-87; Governing Body, State Alcohol Monopoly ALKO, 1983-; Chairman, Finnish Opera Association, 1985-; Chairman, Finnish Association for Allergic Diseases, 1985-; Vice Chairman, Finnish Red

Cross, 1988-. *Address:* Toolonkatu 1 C22, SF 00100 Helsinki, Finland.

KWIATKOWSKA Barbara, b. Sopot, Poland; Dutch nationality, 1986. Associate Professor, Public International Law. m. 1976, divorced 1982. *Education:* LLM, Faculty of Law, Jagiellonian University, Cracov, Poland, 1969; PhD, Political Sciences, Polish Institute of International Affairs, Warsaw, Poland, 1979. *Appointments:* Faculty of Law, University of Gdansk, Poland, 1970-71; Associate Professor, Dept of International Law & Theory of Int. Relations, Polish Institute of International Affairs, Warsaw, 1971-81; Associate Professor, Faculty of Law, Limburg University, Maastrich, Netherlands, 1982-85; Associate Director NILOS, Faculty of Law, University of Utrecht, Netherlands, 1985-. *Publications:* Exclusive Economic Zone in the New Law of the Sea, 1989; Transboundary Air Pollution, International Legal Aspects of the Co-Operation of States, Co-editor, 1986; International Organizations and the Law of the Sea - NILOS Documentary Yearbook, Co-editor, 1987; NILOS Yearbook is continuous publication. Author of about 50 articles/studies on international law of the Sea/ environmental law; Published under the name of B Kwiatkowska-Czechowska, 1976-82. *Memberships:* International Law Association; Law of the Sea Institute, Honolulu; International Council for Environmental Law, Bonn; American Society of International Law; Netherlands Association of International Law; Association of Attenders and Alumni of the Hague Academy of International Law; Netherlands Branch of International Commission of Jurists; Co-Project-Leader between NILOS and: Indian Ocean Marine Affairs Cooperation Conference, Colombo, Sri Lanka; Southeast Asian Programme on Ocean Law & Management, Bangkok, Thailand; Indonesian Centre for the Law of the Sea, Bandung, Indonesia; Representative, International Ocean Institute, Malta to the UN Preparatory Commission for the International Sea-Bed Authority and the International Tribunal for the Law of the Sea (PrepCom), since 1988. *Hobbies:* Painting; Theatre; (Auto)biographies. *Address:* Faculty of Law, University of Utrecht, Janskerkhof 3, 3512 BK Utrecht, Netherlands.

KWIATKOWSKI Carole Monaco, b. 13 Feb. 1943, Columbus, Ohio, USA. Science, Social Studies Educator. m. William F Kwiatkowski, 20 Aug. 1981. 4 sons, 1 daughter. *Education:* BS Education, Ohio State University, 1965; Masters of Christian Ed, International Theological Seminary, 1984. *Appointments:* Wolford Elem 1965; Oakwood, Edwin D Smith, 1965-66; Whispering Hills Christian Academy, 1975-76; Oneco Elem, 1977-. *Publications:* High School Homecoming Program Covers; Painting: Fruit of Spirit for Mr Rossi, President, Tropicana; Instruction manual for Florida History Costumed Celebration; Viedo for Children, Science Projects. *Memberships:* Founder/President, Women Aglow, Greenville; Secretary, Women Aglow, Nashville; President, Vice President, Secretary, Music Director, Bradenton, Florda, Women Aglow; Federation of Social Studies Teachers; Federation of Science Teachers; President, Teachers for Christ. *Honours:* Social Studies Teacher of the Year, Plaque Trophy, 1984; Florida Teacher of the Year Nominee, 1988. *Hobbies:* Speaker/Lecturer; Singer; Painting; Drawing; Sewing; Designer, home decorating; Missionary; Marketing representative. *Address:* 411-63rd Street Northwest, Bradenton, Florida 34209, USA.

KYD Marilyn Joyce Gratton, b. 26 Jan. 1948, Wichita, Kansas, USA. Writer. m. Charles William Kyd, 25 Mar. 1984. *Education:* AA, Pasadena City College, 1967; BA, English, University of California, Los Angeles, 1969; Standard Secondary Teaching Credential, life, California State College, Long Beach, 1970. *Appointments include:* Teacher, employment counsellor, personnel agency owner, engineering writer, California, 1970-80; Logistics analyst & writer, Vitro Laboratories, California, 1980-81; Documentation Manager, Computer Data Corporation, 1981-83; Marketing Director, KPS Inc, 1983-84; President,

CashMaster Business Systems Inc, Seattle, Washington, 1984-; Freelance writer, 1984-. *Publications include:* Books: It's A Good Thing I'm Not Married, 1975; The Quest fore Caper: A Nosmo King Mystery, 1991. Also: Numerous articles, columns, short stories, various magazines & journals. *Memberships:* National Writers Club; Mensa. *Honours:* Honorable Mention, articles contest, National Writers Club, 1987; Young Careerist, Business & Professional Women's Club, 1974. *Address:* c/o CashMaster Business Systems Inc, 12345 Lake City Way NE, Suite 220, Seattle, Washington 98125, USA.

KYLE Mary, b. St Paul, Minnesota, USA. Freelance Writer; Newspaper Publisher. m. Earl F. Kyle Sr (dec.), 12 Nov. 1927, 2 sons, 2 daughters. *Education:* University of Minnesota; University of Minnesota Extension; Croydon Institute of Writing, Illinois; Palmer Institute of Writing, California. *Appointments:* Publisher, Editor, Twin Cities Courier Newspaper Division, 1967-87; President, 1967-, Minnesota Sentinel Publishing Co; Editorial Commentator, KMSP-TV, 1969-79; Talk Show Host, WLOL AM/FN, 1969-79; Freelance Writer, 1987-; Book Reviewer. *Memberships include:* Minnesota and National Newspaper Associations; National Newspaper Publisher's Association; Press Women of Minnesota; National Press Women; Minnesota and National Business Leagues; Sigma Delta Chi; Greater Minneapolis Chamber of Commerce; American Rehabilitation Foundation; Minnesota Council on Economic Education; Trustee, Minnesota Society of Fine Arts; Minnesota Chapter, National Council of Christians & Jews; SBA Regional Council; Former Member: Minnesota State Board of Law Examiners; National Advisory Council on Status of Women; Boards of Directors: Norwest Bank, North American Office; KTCA-TV, Minneapolis; Urban League; Metropolitan YMCA of Greater Minneapolis; National Association for the Advancement of Colored People (Life Member); Minnesota Press Club (President 1975-76). *Honours:* Herman Roe Memorial Award for Editorial Writing; Frank Murray Award in Journalism, St Thomas College; Human Rights Award, Jewish Labor Committee; Alpha Phi Alpha Journalism Award; Journalism and Human Rights Award, NAACP; Bishop Allen Journalism Award; Urban League Civic and Service Award; Community Service Award, African American Cultural Arts Center; Minnesota Governor's Citation of Honour; Numerous other awards and citations. *Address:* 3637 4th Avenue S, Minneapolis, MN 55409, USA.

L

LABOVITCH Carey Elizabeth, b. 20 Apr. 1960, London, England. Publisher; Company Director. *Education:* BA, Honours, Modern Languages, St Hilda's College, Oxford, 1982. *Appointments:* Founder, Publisher, Blitz Magazine, 1980; Director, Jigsaw Publications Ltd; Founder, Publisher, beat Magazine, Director, beat Productions Ltd; Founder, Publisher, The Magazine Book, Managing Director, The Cadogan Press, 1984. *Honours:* 1st Guardian for Best Graphics Award, Blitz, 1981; Publishing Entrepreneur of the Year Award, 1984, Highly Commended; BBC Award for Small Business, 1985; Veuve Cliquot Business Woman of the Year Finalist, 1986. *Hobbies:* Cartooning; Cinema. *Address:* 40-52 Newman Street, London W1P 3PA, England.

LACOUNT Jill Marie Thorn, b. 17 Aug. 1961, Rochester, Minnesota, USA. Financial Analyst; Accounting Professor. m. David William LaCount, 26 Dec. 1987, 2 son. *Education:* BS, Accounting, Illinois Wesleyan University, 1984; MBA, Finance, Sangamon State University, 1986; JD, National University School of Law, 1990; DBA, Finance, US International University, expected 1991. *Appointments:* Accountant, Central Illinois Public Service, 1984-86; Financial Analyst, Property & Overhead Accounting, Space Systems Division, General Dynamics, 1986-87; Professor, Accounting & Finance, National University, & Financial Analyst II, Northern Telecom Electronics, 1987-. *Memberships include:* President, Telemasters-Toastmasters; Treasurer, NUSL Alumni Association; American & National Management Associations; American Bar Association; Trial Lawyers Association; National Association of Accountants. *Honours:* Judge Michael Brennan Memorial Law Scholarship; Leadership Award, National University; William H. Chamberlain Scholarship; CMA; Biographical listings. *Hobbies:* Water skiing; Reading; Sewing; Camping & Hiking; Photography; Travel. *Address:* 10836 Whitehill Road, San Diego, California 92124, USA.

LACY Lucile P, b. 1 July 1909, Waco, Texas, USA. Forensic Document Examiner. m. George J. Lacy, 30 Nov. 1944. *Education:* BS, University of Houston. *Appoinments:* Private Practice, Forensic Document Examiner, 1956-. *Publications:* Articles in journals including: Texas Bar Journal, Washington and Lee Law Review, The Journal of Criminal Law, Criminology and Police Science. *Memberships:* Secretary, Vice President, President ASQDE; Fellow, AAFS. *Honours:* First Woman Member, American Society of Questioned Document Examiners, 1954. *Hobbies:* Travel; Sewing; Bridge. *Address:* 1432 Esperson Building, 808 Travis, Houston, TX 77002, USA.

LACY Suzanne, b. 21 Oct. 1945, Wasco, California, USA. College Dean; Artist; Producer. *Education:* AA, honours, Premedical Sciences, Bakersfield College, 1965; BA, honours, Zoological Sciences, University of California, Santa Barbara, 1968; Psychology, Fresno State College, 1969-71; MFA, Social Design, California Institute of the Arts, 1972. *Career:* Teaching: Fresno State College, Fresno, California, 1969-70; California Institute of the Arts, Los Angeles, 1971-72; Feminist Studio Workshop, Woman's Building, Los Angeles, 1974-79; University of California, Los Angeles, 1974, San Diego, 1976, 1977, 1979, Irvine, 1982; Minneapolis College of Art & Design, 1985-86; School of the Art Institute of Chicago, Illinois, 1986; Dayton Hudson Distinguished Visiting Artist, Carleton College, 1987; Dean, School of Fine Arts, California College of Arts & Crafts, 1987-; Lectures, workshops; Many exhibitions, USA (California, New York, Seattle, Chicago, Minneapolis, abroad (Bologna Arts Fair, 1977, Amsterdam, 1978, Bonn, also Festival de la Rochelle, France, 1982, Banff Art Centre, 1985, Havana, 1986, Vancouver, Toronto, 1988); Many performances including: The Dark Madonna, UCLA, 1986; The Whisper Minnesota Project/Crystal Quilt, Minneapolis, 1987. *Publications:* Books: Rape Is, 1972; Falling Apart, 1976; Three Love Stories, 1978; Three Weeks in May, 1982; Travels with Mona, postcard series, 1977; Contributor, journals and magazines; Film/video: Learn Where the Meat Comes From (writer, performer), 1976; Director and/or producer: In Mourning and In Rage, 1978; Sofa, 1984; Whisper, the Waves, the Wind, 1986; The Crystal Quilt, 1987. *Memberships:* College Art Association; Former Member: Board of Directors, The Woman's Building; National Advisory Board, Women's Caucus for Arts. *Honours:* Honourable Mention, San Francisco International Film Festival, 1988; Chris Bronze Plaque, Columbus International Film Festival, 1988; Honourable Mention, Crystal Quilt sound- track, National Federation of Community Broadcasters, 1988; Many fellowships, grants. *Address:* 1151 Mountain Boulevard, Oakland, CA 94611, USA.

LADERMAN Carol C, b. 25 Oct. 1932, Brooklyn, New York, USA. Associate Professor of Anthropology. m. Gabriel Laderman, 2 Dec. 1953. 2 sons. *Education:* BA, Hunter College, 1972; MA 1974, MPhil 1975, PhD 1979, Columbia University. *Appointments:* Adj Asst Professor, Hunter College, 1978-80; Visiting Lecturer and Research Scholar, Yale University, 1980-82; Associate Professor of Anthropology, Fordham University, 1982-. *Publications:* Wives and Midwives, 1983; Techniques of Healing In Southeast Asia (a special issue of Social Science and Medicine), 1988; Numerous articles and book chapters. *Memberships include:* Assoc for Asian Studies, Advisory comm, Women in Asian Studies; Council on Nutrition Anthropology, Exec Board and Chair, Curriculum Committee; American Anthropological Association; Society for Medical Anthropology; American Ethnolog Society; Royal Asiatic Society; NY Women's Anthro Conference. *Honours include:* Bellagio Foundation, 1989; John Simon Guggenheim Memorial Fellowship, 1987; National Endowment for the Humanities Interpretive Research Fellowship, 1987; National Endowment for the Humanities Translation Award, 1982; Nat Inst for Mental Health Fellowship, 1975-78; Danforth Foundation Fellowship, 1972-75 and 1978; Social Science Research Fellowship, 1975-77. *Hobbies:* Music; Art. *Address:* 760 West End Ave, New York, NY 10025, USA.

LAFAVE LeAnn Kay Larson, b. 31 May 1953, Ramona, South Dakota, USA. Attorney. m. (1)Richard Curtis Finke, 19 May 1973, div. 1978, 1 son, (2)Dwayne Jeffery LaFave, 31 May 1981, 1 son, 1 daughter. *Education:* BS, Psychology/Communication, 1974, JD honours, School of Law, 1977, University of South Dakota; Admitted: State Bar of South Dakota; State and Federal Courts, South Dakota; US Court of Appeals, 8th Circuit. *Appointments:* Associate Attorney, Bjella Neff Rathert & Wahl, Williston, North Dakota, 1978-79; Assistant Attorney-General, State of South Dakota, 1977-81; Attorney, Tobin Law Offices PC, Winner, South Dakota, 1981- 83; Associate Dean, 1983-86, Associate Professor of Law, Director of Continuing Legal Education (for State Bar of South Dakota), 1983-89; Partner, Aho & LaFave, 1990-; Member, South Dakota Board of Pardons and Paroles, currently. *Publications:* Articles in South Dakota Law Review. *Memberships:* American Bar Association; South Dakota Trial Lawyers Association; National Association of Counsel for Children; ACE/NIP State Planning Council; South Dakota Volunteer Lawyers for the Arts; Commercial Arbitrator, American Arbitration Association. *Honours:* Distinguished Service Award, Williston ND Jaycees, 1978; South Dakota Woman Attorney of the Year, 1985; Attorney General's 1st woman appointee to South Dakota Board of Pardons and Paroles, 1987. *Hobbies:* Family; Sailing; Camping; Reading; Needlework. *Address:* 518 Main, PO Box 767, Brookings, SD 57006-0767, USA.

LA FOUREST Judith Ellen, b. 10 Jan. 1938, Indianapolis, Indiana, USA. Adjunct Faculty. 1 son, 1 daughter. *Education:* BA, English, IU, Indianapolis; MA, English, IU, Bloomington. *Appointments:* Educational

Administrator and Lead Pre-Voc Instructor, Opportunities Industrialization Center, 1972-76; Instructor, Professional Careers Institute, (part-time), 1972-76; Editor, publisher Womankind, 1977-83; Editor Creative Writer, Bio-Feedback, 1977-80; Associate Faculty, IUPUI, 1979-; Adjunct Faculty, Butler University, 1984-. *Publication:* Womankind, 1977-83. *Memberships:* National League of American Pen Women; Sigma Tau Delta; National Organization for Women, State Secretary Ind Chapter, 1978-80; School of Liberal Arts Alumni Assoc. *Honours:* Ind Univ School of Liberal Arts, Distinguished Alumnus Award, 1980; Honoured by Women's Community and various groups, Indpls/Ind for Womankind 1981, with an original play performed in editor's /founder's honour. *Hobbies:* Reading; Walking; Old films; Gifted children; Women writers. *Address:* Butler University, English Department, 4600 Sunset, Indianapolis, IN 46208, USA.

LAING Gertrude Mary, b. 13 Feb. 1905, Tunbridge Wells, Kent, England. Retired Teacher. m. Stanley Bradshaw Laing, 16 June 1930, 2 sons. *Education:* BA, University of Manitoba, Canada, 1925; Postgraduate studies, University of Paris, France, 1926-27. *Appointments:* (Canada) Teacher, French, Riverbend School for Girls, 1928-33; Lecturer, French, University of Manitoba, 1944-47; Sessional Lecturer, Department of Political Science, University of Calgary, 1976-80. *Publications:* A Community Organises for War: History of Voluntary Services in Winnipeg, 1948; Face to Face, political commentary, with Solange Chaput-Rolland, 1974. *Memberships:* Royal Commission on Bilingualism & Biculturalism, 1963; Canadian Radio-TV Commission, 1968-72; Chair, Canada Council for Arts, 1975- 79; Canadian delegation, UNESCO, 1978. *Honours:* French Government bursary, 1927; Honorary doctorates: Universities of Calgary 1973, British Columbia 1977, Ottawa 1978, Manitoba 1980; Officer, Order of Canada, 1972. *Hobbies:* Music; Art; Reading; Voluntary social welfare. *Address:* No. 405, 220 26th Avenue SW, Calgary, Alberta, Canada T2S 0M4.

LAIR Jacqueline Carey, b. 1 Mar. 1930, Minnesota, USA. Writer; Editor. m. Jesse K Lair, 7 July 1949, 3 sons, 2 daughters. *Education:* College of Saint Katherine and Universiy of Minnesota. *Appointments:* Freelance Author, Lecturer, Editor. *Publications:* Co-Author: Hey God, What Should I Do Now?; Author: I Exist I Need, I'm Entitled; Von Mir Aus Nennt es Wahnsinn, in collaboration with Walther H Lechler; I Don't Know Where I'm Going But I Sure Aint Lost; How to Have a Perfect Marriage with Your Present Mate, in collaboration with Jesse K. Lair; numerous magazine articles. *Hobbies and Interests:* Womens Rights; Birth Control Issues; Equal Pay; Women in Politics, Women in the Catholic Church. *Address:* PO Box 249, Bozeman, MT 59715, USA.

LAJOS Judith, b. 21 Dec. 1941, Pecs, Hungary. Head of Blood Group Serology. m. 21 Aug. 1965. 1 son, 1 daughter. *Education:* Dipl Chemist, 1964; Candidate of Acad Sci, 1974. *Appointments:* Serobacteriological and Research Institute, Human, Budapest; Ophthalm Hospital of Medical University of Budapest; National Institute of Haematology and Blood Transfusion, Budapest. *Memberships:* Hungarian Haematological Association; Hungarian Immunological Association; Hungarian Microbiological Association. *Interests:* Immunology; Serology. *Address:* Filler u.22, Budapest II, 1026 Hungary.

LAKE Barbara R. b. 18 Apr. 1947, Ogdensburg, New York, USA. Attorney. div., 4 daughters. *Education:* AA, Liberal Arts, Mater Dei College, 1975; BS, St Lawrence University, 1979; JD, Syracuse University, 1978. *Appointments:* Legal Secretary, Brown & Silver, 1965-76; Private Attorney in General Practice, 1979-; Assistant District Attorney, 1982-84, Chief Assistant District Attorney, 1984-, St Lawrence County, New York. *Memberships:* New York State Bar Association; St Lawrence County Bar Association (Chairman of Grievance Committee, Executive Committee, Law Day Committee); Association of Trial Lawyers of America;

The Order of Barristers; Vice-President, Board Member, Morristown Foundation; Charter Member, Central New York Women's Bar Association; Phi Theta Kappa. *Honours:* Winner, Edmund H Lewis Moot Court Competition, Syracuse University, 1978. *Hobbies:* Music; Dance. *Address:* Route 1, Box 342, Hammond, NY 13646, USA.

LAKEMAN Enid, b. 28 Nov. 1903, Hadlow, Kent, England. Editorial Consultant. *Education:* BSc, London, 1926. *Appointments:* Several posts in Chemical Industry, 1927-41; War Service, WAAF, 1941-45; Staff, 1945-, Director, 1959-79, Consultant, Electoral Reform Society. *Publications:* When Labour Fails; How Democracies Vote; Power to Elect; Numerous pamphlets. *Memberships include:* Vice President, Electoral Reform Society; Liberal (now Social & Liberal Democratic Party); United Nations Association; Royal Institute of International Affairs; International Political Studies Association. *Honour:* OBE 1980. *Hobbies:* Travel; Languages; Gardening. *b3Address:* 37 Culverden Avenue, Tunbridge Wells, Kent, TN4 9RE, England.

LA MARCHE Judith Ann, b. 11 May 1947, Oak Park, Illinois, USA. Licensed psychologist. m. Robert D Stainback, 7 Oct. 1983. 1 son, 1 daughter. *Education:* BA 1968, MS 1970, University of Wisconsin, Madison; PhD, Utah State University, Logan, 1984. *Appointments:* Teacher, Milton Union High School, 1968-69; Teacher, Irving Crown High School, 1969-70; Instructor, Harper College, Palatine, 1977-79; Instructor, College of Lake County, 1978-79; Consultant, Hoffman Estates Youth & Family Services, 1978-79; Facilitator, Women's Resource Center, 1979; Counselor, USU Counseling & Testing Center, 1980; Director, Information-Referral Helpline, Utah State University, 1980-81; Clinical Psychology Intern (Neuropsychology), 1981-82, Research Assistant, Neuropsychology Laboratory, Salt Lake City Veterans Administration Medical Center, 1981-82, 1982-84; Clinical Psychologist, Hertage Center, Lloyd Noland Hospital, 1984-85; Instructor, University of Alabama, 1985, 1987; Pastoral Consultant, Christ Church United Methodist Church, 1987-; Sales, 1982-85, Co-chairman, Board of Directors, 1985-, La Marche Manufacturing Company. *Publications:* Articles in professional journals. Presentations to conferences. *Memberships include:* American Psychological Association, Division 40, Clinical Neuropsychology; Alabama Psychological Association; Birmingham Regional Association of Licensed Psychologists; Licensed Psychologist, Alabama; American Board of Medical Psychotherapists; Association for the Advancement of Psychology, etc. *Honours:* Dean's Letter of Commendation for Scholarship, 1979-81; Guest Speaker, LDS Institute Second Annual Women's Conference, 1980; Practicum Supervisor of Graduate Group Psychotherapists, 1980; Relaxation Trainer, Dysmenorrhea Research, 1980. *Hobbies:* Tennis; Golf; Sports. *Address:* 3304 Tartan Circle, Birmingham, Alabama 3524, USA.

LAMB (Angela Marie) Ann Marie Cammalleri, b. 14 Oct. 1938, Throggs Neck, Bronx, New York City, USA. Research Associate; Rehabilitation Research & Training Centre. m. Jackson L Lamb, 15 Dec. 1964, divorced Sept 1980. 2 daughters. *Education:* BS, SUNY, Cortland, New York, 1960; MEd 1969, PhD in process, Mississippi State University; Southeastern Drug & Alcohol Studies, University of Georgia, Athens, 1975. *Appointments:* Teacher, Several States Girls Physical Education Health Recreation, 1960- 68; Director, Psychological & Guidance Services, Noxubee County schools, 1968- 74; Regional Coordinator State Department, Mental Health Division of Drug Misuse, 1974-75; Director, Mental Health Services for School Age Children, 1975-78; Executive Director, 3 Rivers Area Health Services, Inc, 1978-81; Counselor, Financial Aid, Mississippi State University, 1983-87. *Publications:* Presentation: Results of Alcohol Survey including Students living in Residence Halls, Mississippi State University, Mississippi Counseling Association, Jackson, 1986; Contributor: Technical Research Report, 1985, predicting work status outcomes of blind/severely visually impaired clients of State Rehabilitation Agencies; Professional Journals, 1988, 1989; Education of Deaf-Blind Youth; I Learning Tasks & Teaching Methods; II Teacher Characteristics & program Issues. *Memberships:* Secretary, Faculty Women's Association; Phi Delta Kappa; Mississippi Association of Psychologists in Schools; National Association of School Psychologists; Council on Exceptional Children; The National Federation of Business and Professional Women's Clubs, Inc; Mississippi Counseling Association; Association for Psychological Types; American Association of University Women; Association for Education and Rehabilitation; Mississippi Registry of Interpreters for the Deaf; Mississippi Association of Women in Higher Education; Clay County Democratic Executive Committee Vice Chairman, 4 years. *Honours:* President's Commission on the Status of Women; Women's Week Panelist: E Type Women: E is for Everything. *Hobbies:* Cooking, Needlepoint; Antiques; Reading; Political involvement and activities; Entertaining friends and colleagues. *Address:* RRTC/MSU/Low Vision and Blindness, P O Box 6189, Mississippi State University, MS 39762, USA.

LAMB Elizabeth Searle, b. 22 Jan 1917, Topeka, Kansas, USA. Writer; Poet; Editor (formerly Harpist). m. F Bruce Lamb, 11 Dec 1941, 1 daughter. *Education:* BA 1939, BMus 1940, University of Kansas, Lawrence, Kansas, USA. *Appointments:* Harpist and Harp Teacher (Kansas City) Music Conservatory, 1940-41; Personnel Clerk, Walsh-Driscoll Construction Co, Trinidad, British West Indies, 1942-43; Temporary clerk, US Consulate, Belem, Brazil, 1943. *Publications:* Lines for my Mother, Dying, 1988; Casting into a Cloud, 1985; 39 Blossoms, 1982; Picasso's Bust of Sylvette, 1977; In This Blaze of Sun, 1975; Inside Me, Outside Me, 1974; Today and Every Day, 1970; The Pelican Tree and Other Panama Adventures, 1953, co-author; Numerous poems and articles. *Memberships:* Haiku Society of America, President 1972; Editor of quarterly journal, Frogpond, 1984- ; Poetry Society of America; Phi Beta Kappa; Pi Kappa Lambda; Mu Phi Epsilon; National League of American Pen Women; New York Women Poets; Haiku Canada; Haiku International Association (Japan). *Honours:* Ruben Dario Memorial Award (OAS) 1967; National League of American Pen Women Biennial Awards, 1965,68,72,76,78,80; Henderson Memorial Haiku Award, 1978, 81; High/Coo Press Publication Award, 1982; Haiku Society of America Biennial Book Awards 1979, 83; Wind Chimes Press Publication Award, 1988; Mainichi Daily News (Tokyo) 1988 Traditional Haiku Award; Poetry Society of Japan Haiku Contest 1987; KO Poetry Association (Nagoya, Japan) 1987 Award; Modern Haiku Association of Japan, 1987 Award. *Hobbies:* Collecting haiku materials of all kinds - books, pamphlets, articles, miscellany; Chamber Music; History of New Mexico, particularly Santa Fe and the northern New Mexico villages. *Address:* 970 Acequia Madre Street. Santa Fe, NM 87501, USA.

LAMBERT Nadine Murphy, b. 21 Oct. 1926, Ephraim, Utah, USA. Professor. m. Robert E. Lambert, 29 Dec. 1956, 1 son, 1 daughter. *Education:* BA, University of California, 1948; MA, Los Angeles State University, 1956; PhD, University of Southern California, 1965. *Appointments:* School Psychologist, 1952-53; Guidance Consultant, 1953- 58; Research Consultant, California State Dept. of Education, 1958-64; Professor, University of California, Berkeley, 1964-. *Publications:* Educationally Retarded Child, 1974; Moral Development and Socialization, 1979; over 100 published papers; Tests; etc. *Memberships:* California Association of School Psychologists, President 1963; American Psychological Association, Board of Directors, 1984-87; American Education Research Association; American Orthopsychiatric Association. *Honours:* Distinguished Service Award, School Psychology, American Psychological Association, 1980; Sandra Goff Award for Contributions to School Psychology, 1985; American Psychological Association award for Distinguished Contributions to Applied Psychology as a Professional Practice, 1986. *Address:* School of Education, University of California, Berkeley, CA 94720, USA.

LAMBERT Patricia, b. 16 Mar. 1926, Hull, East Yorkshire, England. Company Director. m. George Richard Lambert, 1 Oct. 1949, dissolved 1983. 1 son, 1 daughter. *Education:* Nottingham & District Technical College. *Appointments:* BSI Consumer Standards Advisory Committee (renamed Consumer Policy Committee 1987), 1972; Member, National Consumer Council, 1978-82; Chairman, Consumer Standards Advisory Council, Member BSI Board, 1980-86; National House Building Council, 1980; Unit Trust Association Consumer Affairs Panel, 1981; Director, Direct Mail Services Standards Board, 1983; Director & Vice Chairman, Think British Campaign, 1983; Public Interest Director, Life Assurance & Unit Trust Regulatory Organisation, 1986; Member BSI Quality Assurance Board, 1986; Chairman of several BSI technical committees. *Honour:* OBE, 1980. *Hobbies:* Crosswords; Glass engraving; Calligraphy. *Address:* 42 Tollerton Lane, Tollerton, Nottingham NG12 4FQ, England.

LAMBERT Phyllis, b. 24 Jan. 1927, Montreal, Canada. Architect. *Education:* BA, 1948; MS, 1963; Doctorates hc, various Universities. *Appointments:* Director, Centre Canadien D'Architecture/Canadian Centre for Architecture Projects; Consultant to Fairview & Toronto Dominion Bank, Toronto Dominion Centre, 1962; Founder, Director, Curator's Office, Joseph E. Seagram & Sons Inc., New York, 1972; Board Chairman, Principal, Ridgway ltd., Los Angeles, 1972-84; Director, Groupe de recherche sur les batiments en pierre grise de Montreal, 1973; Founder, Director, Centre Canadien d'Architecture, Montreal, 1979I President, Societe d'Amelioration Milton Parc, 1979-85; Project Director, renovation of Ben Ezra Synagogue, Cairo, Egypt, 1981. *Creative Works:* Author, Co-Author, various publications including: Court House: A Photographic Document, and Photography and Architecture, 1839-1939; numerous articles in professional journals and magazines. *Memberships Include:* American Institute of Architects; Royal Canadian Academy of Arts; American Jewish Congress National Womens Division; Fellow, Royal Architecture Institute of Canada. *Honours:* Recipient, numerous honours and awards. *Address:* 1440 St Catherine St. W, Montreal, Quebec H3G 1R8, Canada.

LAMBERT Verity Ann, b. 27 Nov. 1935. Owner and Chief Executive Cinema Verity Limited. *Appointments:* Secretary, ABC TV, 1961; Production Assistant, ABC TV; Producer, BBC, Dr Who, The Newcomers, Somerset Maugham BAFTA Award Winner, 1969; Adam Adamant; Detective; For London Weekend TV, Budgie; Between the Wars; BBC, Shoulder to Shoulder; Controller of Drama, Thames TV, responsible for Rock Follies; Rooms; Rumpole of the Bailey; Edward & Mrs Simpson; The Naked Civil Servant; Last Summer; The Case of Cruelty to Prawns; No Mama No; Chief Executive of Euston Films, 1976 developing series: Fox; Out; Danger UXB; Minder; The Flame Trees of Thika; Thames Director of Drama, 1982; Member, Board of Thames TV, 1982; Director of Production, Thorn EMI Screen Entertainment, 1982-85; Formed own Film and Television Production Company, Cinema Verity Limited, 1985-; Produced A Cry in The Dark, 1988; May to December, (a six part situation comedy), for the BBC, 1989. *Hobbies:* Good Books; Good Food. *Address:* The Mill House, Millers Way, 1A Shepherds Bush Road, London W6 7NA, England.

LAMBERTI Marjorie, b. 30 Sept. 1937, New Haven, Connecticut, USA. Professor of History. *Education:* BA, Smith College, 1959; Freie Universitat, Berlin, Federal Republic of Germany, 1962-63; PhD, Yale University, 1965. *Appointments:* Various positions, Middlebury College, Middlebury, Vermont, 1964-. *Publications:* Jewish Activism in Imperial Germany, 1978; State, Society and the Elementary School in Imperial Germany, 1989; Articles in Yearbook of the Leo Baeck Institute. *Memberships:* American Historical Association; German Studies Association. *Honours:* Elected to Phi Beta Kappa, 1959; Ford Foundation Fellowship, 1962-63; National Endowment for the Humanities Fellowships, 1968-69, 1981-82; Charles A Dana Professorship, 1985; German Academic Exchange

Research Grant, 1988. *Address:* History Department, Middlebury College, Middlebury, VT 05753, USA.

LAMONT Frances Bailey, Peg, Stiles, b. 10 June 1914, Rapid City, South Dakota, USA. Homemaker; Former State Senator. m. William Mather Lamont, 6 Oct. 1937, dec. 1973, 2 sons, 2 daughters. *Education:* BA Journalism, high honours 1935, MA Political Science 1936, University of Wisconsin. *Appointments:* McCalls Magazine, New York, 1936-37; Homemaker, 35 years; Lecturer, Presentation College, 1967-68; Elected State Senator Republican, South Dakota, 1974-88; Consultant on ageing, 1977-79. Service included: Appropriations, Health & Welfare, Education Committees; Chief sponsor, bills on child abuse, child safety, victims of crime, female juvenile work therapy, protection of elderly. *Memberships:* Federal Council on Ageing, 1982-; Past State President, American Association of University Women ; Past Chairman, Governor's Advisory Council on Ageing; Past Delegate, White House Conference on Ageing; Numerous other community associations. *Honours:* Numerous awards & recognitions including: Gerontologist of Year, 1977; Governor's Award, contributions to ageing, 1979; State Award, contributiosn to mental health, 1980; National honour, civic contribution, AAUW, 1981. *Hobbies include:* Historical preservation; History; Legislation & politics; Development programmes & legislation for elderly & handicapped. *Address:* PO Box 1415, Aberdeen, South Dakota 57402, USA.

LAMOUREUX Gloria Kathleen, b. 2 Nov. 1947, Billings, USA. USAF Officer; Registered Nurse. *Education:* BSc., Nursing, University of Wyoming, 1970; MSc., Nursing Administration University of Maryland, 1984. *Appointments:* Maternal Child Health Co-ordinator, 1980-82; Chief Nurse, USAF Clinic Eielson, 1984-86; Chief Nursing Services, AFSC Hospital, Edwards AFB, 1986-. *Memberships:* Sigma Theta Tau; Association of Military Surgeons of the USA; Air Force Association; Nurses' Association of America. *Honours:* Air Foce Commendation Medal, 1976; Meritorious Service Medal, 1984; Outstanding Student in Nursing Administration 1984; Meritorious Service Medal, First Oak Leaf Cluster, 1986. *Hobbies:* Music; Reading; Photography; Hiking. *Address:* AFSC Hospital Edwards/SGN, Edwards AFB, CA 93523, USA.

LAMPE Annacarol, b. 30 Sept. 1951, Indianapolis, Indiana, USA. Research Communications Specialist. m. Peter J Florzak, 11 Dec. 1985. 1 daughter. *Education:* BS, Communications 1973, MS English, Drama 1974, MS Communications, 1975, Indiana University; MBA, Management. Rockhurst College, 1981. *Appointments.* Faculty, Eastside High School, Butler, Indiana, 1974-77; Student Activities Director, Penn Valley Community College, Kansas City, 1977-78; Sales Representative, Fisher Scientific, Kansas City, 1978-80; Associate Director, Kaleidoscope 1981-83; Research Communications Specialist 1984-89, Hallmark Cards, Inc.; Communications/Training Manager, 1989-, Hallmark Cards, Inc.; Manager of Technical Publications, Martin Marietta, Oak Ridge, Tennessee, 1983-84. *Creative works:* Professional Speaker on approximately 100 occasions. *Memberships:* Junior League of Kansas City, 1986-; Board of Directors, Kansas City Westport Ballet, 1985; Board of Directors, Oak Ridge, Tennessee Art Center, 1984; Board of Directors, Oak Ridge, Tennessee Arts Council, 1983; Conference Leader, Midwest Regional Conference, Women in Business, 1980. *Honours:* Semi-finalist, North American Open Poetry Competition, 1989; 75 Women of Achievement, Girl Scouts of America, 1987; Outstanding Young Women in America, 1985; Key to the City: Johnson City, Tennessee, 1982; MBA Executive Semester, Rockhurst College, 1981; Northern Indiana's Young Careerist Award, Business and Professional Women, 1977. *Address:* 9627 N. Bradford, Kansas City, Missouri 64154, USA.

LAMPERT Lynn Karen Rosen, b. 17 June 1951, Philadelphia, Pennsylvania, USA. Psychologist. m. Lawrence David Lampert, 15 Aug. 1983, 1 son, 1 daughter. *Education:* BS, Pennsylvania State University, 1972; MEd 1974, PhD 1982, Temple Universty. *Appointments:* Counsellor: elementary schools, 1973-76, Rebecca Gratz School for Adolescent Girls 1979-80; Psychotherapist, Norristown Life Centre, 1980-83; Private practice, Pennsylvania & Florida, 1983-. *Memberships:* State Representative, Pennsylvania Guidance Association; American, & Florida Psychological Associations; American Association of Marriage & Family Therapists; Charter Member, American Association for Specialists in Group Work. *Hobbies: include:* Music; Sewing; Reading; Aerobics; Weight training; Dining; Theatre; Dance. *Address:* 22497 Ensenada Way, Boca Raton, Florida 33433, USA.

LAMPERT Shirley, b. Baltimore, Maryland, USA. Marriage & Family Therapist; College Instructor. m. Seymour Lampert, 2 sons, 1 daughter. *Education:* BA, 1970, MA, 1971, California State University. *Appointments:* College Instructor: Orange Coast College, 1975-82, Irvine Valley College, 1984-87, Fullerton College, 1987-; Psychotherapist, Private Practice, 1976-. *Publication:* Human Sexuality Workbook for College Students. *Memberships:* American Association of Sex Educators, Counsellors & Therapists; American Association of Marriage & Family Therapists; California Association of Marriage & Family Therapists; President, Southern California Section, AAEECT, 1986-. *Honours:* Programme Chair: Western Regional Conference, American Association of Sex Educators, Counsellors & Therapists, 1985, 1986, 1987. *Hobbies:* Travel; Bridge; Performing Arts. *Address:* 1101 Dove St., Ste. 260, Newport Beach, CA 92660, USA.

LAMPSATIS Alisa Raminta, b. 11 Mar. 1950, Chicago, USA. Professor; Pianist; Musicologist. Divorced. *Education:* B.Mus., 1971; BA, German Literature, 1971; Dr.Phil, Musicology, 1978. *Appointments:* Assistant Professor, Art Song & Opera, 1978-82, Professor, 1982-, Hamburg Musikhochschule; Master Classes, Chamber Music, Accompanying & Interpretation in Lithuania. *Publications:* Dodekaphone Werke von Balsys; Juzeliūnas und der jüngeren Komponistengeneration Litauens, 1978; Festschrift fur Ferry Gebhardt, 1985; TYLA: The Composer Osvaldas Belakauskas, 1988. *Memberships:* Liszt Society; Pfitzner Society, Competition Committee; Ciurlionis Foundation; Jury Member, Oscar-Vera Ritter Stiftung; Hamburg Womens Academic Council; University Association of Women. *Honours:* State Guest, Soviet Union, 1986, 1987, 1988; Accompanist, numerous vocalists. *Hobbies:* Art; Comparative Literature. *Address:* 2000 Hamburg 13, Böttgerstr. 1C, Federal Republic of Germany.

LANCASTER Rita, High School Principal. *Appointments:* Principal, Luray High School. *Memberships Include:* Page County Education Association, President 1974-76; Virginia Education Association Personnel Policies Committee; Northwest Virginia Health Association; President, Beta XI. *Address:* Luray High School, 14 Luray Avenue, Luray, VA 22835, USA.

LANCOUR Karen Louise, b. 2 June 1946, Cheboygan, Michigan, USA. Science Teacher. *Education* AA summa cum laude, Alpena Community College, 1966; BA magna cum laude 1968, MS 1970, Eastern Michigan University. *Appointments:* Graduate teaching & research fellowship, Eastern Michigan University, 1968-70; Teacher, secondary science, Utica Community Schools, Michigan, 1970-. *Publication:* State & National Code of Ethics, Science Olympiad. *Memberships:* National Rules Committee, National Event Supervisor (Bio-Process), Science Olympiad; National Science Teachers Association; National Association of Biology Teachers; Smithsonian Institution; National Education Association; National Wilflife Federation; National Geographic Society; Edison Institute. *Honours include:* Numerous honour societies. *Hobbies & interests:* History; Literature; Art; Conservation & recycling; Drug education; Travel, culture & world affairs; Sports; Crafts. *Address:* Henry Ford II High School, 11911 Clinton River Road, Sterling Heights, Michigan 48078, USA.

LANDA Martha, b. 8 Nov. 1958, Brockton, Massachusetts, USA. Physical Therapist. *Education:* BS, Ithaca College, 1980; MSc, Health Care Management, Lesley College, 1985. *Appointments:* Sportscare, Weymouth Public Schools; Private Home Care, & Children's Hospital Medical Centre, Boston; Director of Physical Therapy, Sports Medicine Centre, 1987-. *Memberships:* American Physical Therapy Association; American College of Sports Medicine. *Honour:* Dean's List. *Honour:* Aerobic Dancing; Weight Lifting; Skiing. *Address:* 5425 Connecticut Avenue NW, Washington DC 20015, USA.

LANDAZURI Colleen Ann, b. 8 Sep. 1950, Fond du Lac, Wisconsin, USA. Public Health Nurse; Spuervisor/Programme Director. m Gabriel Landazuri, 26 Oct. 1974, 3 sons. *Education:* BSN, College of Nursing, Marquette University, 1972. *Appointments:* District Staff Nurse, 1972-75, Staff Nurse, Lady Pitts School-Age Parent Programme, 1975-76, District Supervisor, 1976-79, Programme Director, Prenatal Education and Assessment Programme, 1979-, Nursing Bureau, City of Milwaukee Health Department, Milwaukee, Wisconsin. *Memberships:* Past Co-Chair, Greater Milwaukee Committee on Unmarried Parent Services; Past Co-Chair, Milwaukee Public Schools Critical Health Problems, Curriculum Advisory Committee; Past Co-Chair, South-Eastern Wisconsin Parent-Child Nursing Organization; Milwaukee Urban League Health Services Resource Committee; Lady Pitts/School-Age Parent Programme Advisory Committee; Family Hospital Teen Pregnancy Service Advisory Committee; North Shore Junior Woman's Club; Organization of Twin-Blessed Mothers (Secretary 1984); Nurse Advisory Committee, Community Services Committee, March of Dimes Milwaukee Chapter; Time of Your Life Programme Network Programme Committee, Family Service; Sherman Park Community Association. *Honours:* Federal Nurse Traineeship, 1976-77. *Hobbies:* Golf; Bridge; Needlework; church choir. *Address:* 3368 North 44th Street, Milwaukee, WI 53216, USA.

LANDOR Rosalyn, b. 1958, London, England. Actress. *Education:* Royal Ballet School, 1969-72; Tolworth Girls School, 1972-76. *Appointments:* Performances in: Devil Rides Out, film, 1965; Jane Eyre, film, 1969; Amazing Mr Glunden, film, 1972; Divorce His/Divorce Hers, film, 1972; Hammer : Guardian of the Abyss, TV film, 1978; Love in a Cold Climate, TV serial, 1979; Arthur the King, film, 1982; Arms & the Man, theatre, 1983; Little Gloria Happy at Last, mini-series, 1983; Hay Fever, theatre; Rumpole of the Bailey, TV series, 1983; Speckled Band, TV Sherlock Holmes series, 1984; Oxbridge Blues, TV play, 1984; C.A.T.S. Eyes, TV series, 1985; Putting on the Ritz, pilot, 1986. *Memberships:* Music, Varied; Antiques & Paintings, Collecting; Clothes (fashion); Reading; Dogs. *Address:* c/o 84 Kings Drive, Surbiton, Surrey, KT5 8NH, England.

LANDRY Jane Lorenz, b. 112 Feb. 1936, San Antonio, Texas, USA. Architect. m. 8 Sept. 1956, 4 daughters. *Education:* University of Texas, 1952-55; Yale University, 1956; B.Arch. University of Pennsylvania, 1957. *Appointments:* Wade, Gibson & Martin, Corpus Christi, Texas, 1958-59; O'Neil, Ford & Associates, San Antonio, 1959-65; Duane Landry (Arch), San Antonio 1965-68, Dallas 1968-76; Meyer, Landry & Landry, Dallas, 1977-80; Landry & Landry, 1980-. *Memberships:* Fellow, American Institute of Architects; Texas Society of Architects. *Honours:* Design Awards: Texas Society of Architects 1969, 1981, Dallas Chapter, American Institute of Architects 1970, 75, 76, 77, 80; IFRAA, 1985, 1989. *Address:* Landry & Landry, Architects & Planners, 1925 San Jacinto, Dallas, Texas 75201, USA.

LANDRY Monique, b. 25 Dec. 1937, Verdun, Canada. Minister of External Relations. m. Jean Guy Landry, 13 Oct. 1958, 3 sons, 1 daughter. *Education:* Graduate, Physiotherapy & Occupational Therapy, School of Rehabilitation, University of Montreal. *Appointments:* Physiotherapist, 1957-63; Publicist, 1957-80; Co-Owner, Vice President, Cordevin

International, 1980-84; Elected to House of Commons, 1984; Parliamentary Secretary to Secretary of State, 1984; Parliamentary Secretary to Minister for International Trade, 1985; Minister for External Relations, 1986-. *Memberships:* Canada-Europe Parliamentary Association; Canada France Inter-Parliamentary Association; Canada NATO Parliamentary Association. *Hobbies:* Golf; Tennis; Reading. *Address:* House of Commons, Confederation Building, Room 582, Ottawa, Canada K1A 0A6.

LANE Carolyn, b. 4 June 1926, Providence, Rhode Island, USA. Playwright. Author; Playwright. m. M Donald Lane, Jr, 28 May 1951. 1 son. *Education:* BA, Connecticut College, 1948. *Creative Works:* Books, Juvenile: Uncle Max and the Sea Lion; Turnabout night at the Zoo; The voices of Greenwillow Pond; The Winnemah Spirit; Princess; Princess and Minerva; Echoes in an Empty Room; Ghost Island. Plays, Juvenile: Turnabout night at the Zoo; The Wayward Clocks; The Runaway Merry-go-Round; Tales of Hans Christian Andersen; The world of the Brothers Grimm; The ransom of Emily Jane. Plays, Adult: The last Grad; Child of Air; The Scheme of the Driftless Shifter. *Memberships:* The Authors Guild; Society of Children's Book writers; The Dramatists Guild. *Honours:* Annual Merit Award, Community Children's Theatre of Kansas City, 1963 for Turnabout Night at the Zoo; Best Children's Play of 1969, Pioneer Drama Service for The Wayward Clocks; First Prize, Annual Playwriting Contest, Theatre Guild of Webster Groves, 1969 for The Last Grad; Second Prize, Annual Playwriting Contest, Theatre Guild of Webster Groves, 1980 for The Scheme of the Driftless Shifter; Senior Adult New Play List, American Theatre Association, 1982 for Child of Air; First Prize, Weisbrod One-Act Playwriting Contest, Alexandria, 1982 for Cousin Ernestine. *Hobbies:* Illustration (3 books); Cover & set designs (5 plays). *Address:* 40 Skyline Drive, Mumford Cove, Groton, CT 06340, USA.

LANE Gloria Carolyn Julian, b. 6 Oct. 1932, Chicago, Illinois, USA. Organizational Administrator/Educational Consultant. 1 daughter. *Education:* BS, Education, Central Missouri State University, 1958; MA, Communications, Bowling Green State University, 1959; PhD, Communications, Northern Illinois University, 1972. *Appointments:* Asst Professor, William Jewell College, 1959-60; Director of Forensics, Coral Gables High School, 1960-64; Director of Theatre, Chicago City College, 1964-65; Assistant Professor, Northern Illinois University, 1965-72; National University, 1979-. *Publications:* Books: Positive Concepts for Success; Project Text for Effective Communication; Project Text for Executive Communication; Editor, Who's Who Among San Diego Women. *Membership:* Founder, CEO, President, Women's International Center. *Honours:* Woman of the Year, Girls Club of San Diego, 1986; Independence Award, Community Center for the Disabled, 1986; Woman of Accomplishment, Soroptimist International, San Diego, 1986; Woman of Achievement, Pressident's Council, 1986; Many awards of Appreciation. *Hobbies:* Computers; Writing; Creating. *Address:* Women's International Center, 6202 Friars Road 311, San Diego, CA 92108, USA.

LANE Patricia Anne, b. 26 Jan. 1945, Waterloo, New York, USA. Professor of Biology; President and Director, environmental consulting company. 1 son, 3 daughters. *Education:* BA, Biology, Hartwick College, Oneonta, 1964; MA Biology, State University of New York at Binghamton, 1966; PhD, Ecology, State University of New York at Albany, 1971. *Appointments:* Assistant, Associate, Full Professor of Biology and Chair of Senate, Dalhousie University, 1973-; Visiting Associate Professor, Harvard School of Public Health, 1980-82; President and Director, P Lane and Associates Limited, 1983-. *Publications:* Over 50 publications including scientific journal papers, technical reports and abstracts. *Memberships:* American Society of Naturalists, 1976; National Foundation for the Environment (elected Director), 1985; United Nations Association of Canada, 1985; Director, The Rawson Academy of Aquatic

Sciences, 1987; The Rawson Academy of Sciences (elected Director), 1988-89. *Honours:* Predoctoral Fellowship (NDEA), 1969-71; Ford Foundation Grant, Postdoctoral Fellowship, 1971-73; Environmental Science and Engineering Fellowship (AAAS), 1984; Senior Ecologist Certification, Ecological Society of America, 1985; One of Top Ten Outstanding Campus Achievers, Campus Canada, 1985. *Interests:* Ecology; Sustainable development; Cumulative environmental impact assessment; Risk assessment; Limnology; Marine pollution. *Address:* 1046 Barrington Street, Halifax, Nova Scotia, Canada B3H 2R1.

LANE Sarah Marie, b. 27 July 1946, Conneaut, Ohio, USA. Newspaper-in-Education Coordinator; Freelance Writer. m. Ralph Donaldson Lane, 28 May 1977. 1 son, 1 daughter. *Education:* BS Education, Kent State University, 1977; MS Education, College of Mount St Joseph, 1988. *Appointments:* Newspaper-in-Education Coordinator 1988-, Newspaper Correspondent 1986-, Warren Tribune Chronicle; Tutor, MacArthur Foundation project, 1988-. *Memberships:* Bazetta Historical Society, Vicepresident, 1985-87; Cortland Community Concert Band. *Honour:* George Record Scholar, 1964-65. *Hobbies:* Nature study; Reading; Historical and genealogical research. *Address:* 298 Corriedale Drive, Cortland, Ohio 44410, USA.

LANE Shari Luanne, b. 13 July 1945, Cleveland, Ohio, USA. Psychotherapist; Consultant. 1 daughter. *Education:* BA, Arts & Sciences, USC, 1967; Certificate, Secondary Education, UNC, 1969; MEd., University of Houston, 1978; Certified Alcoholism and Drug Abuse Counsellor, 1986. *Appointments:* Teacher, Consultant, Broadcaster, 1969-78; Instructor, Univesity of Huston, 1978-79; Director, New Options Counselling Centre, 1977-79; Director, Management & Training, Austin MHMR, 1979-81; Consultant, Management Training, Director, Consulting Sus. MOHR Development Inc., 1981-83; Psychotherapist, Consultant in area of co-dependency & substance abuse, 1983-. *Publications:* Book: For Giving, 1983; various professional articles. ssa 20Memberships: NOW, Chapter President, Vice President; AACD; TAADAC; LWV; MHA; Speakes Bureau Speaker; ALMACA. *Hobbies:* Tennis; Swimming; Snorkelling; Music; Meditation; Yoga; Tai-Chi; Travel; Reading. *Address:* 6666 Harwin, Suite 400, Houston, TX 77036, USA.

LANE Sylvia, b. 26 May 1916, New York City, USA. Professor Emerita; Economist. m. Benjamin Lane, 2 Sept. 1932. 2 sons, 1 daughter. *Education:* AB, Economics 1934, MA, Economics, 1936, University of California; Columbia University, 1937; PhD, Economics, University of Southern California, 1957. *Appointments:* Lecturer, Assistant Professor 1947-60, Visiting Professor Summer 1967, University of Southern California; Associate Professor, Economics, Associate Professor, Finance, San Diego State University, 1961-65; Associate Professor, Finance, Associate Director, Center for Economic Education 1965-69, Chairman, Dept of Finance 1967-69, California State University at Fullerton; Professor, Agricultural Economics, 1969-82, Professor Emerita 1982-, University of California, Davis; Visiting Professor, University of Missouri, Summer 1974; Delegate, White House Conference on Inflation, 1974; Visiting Scholar, Stanford University, 1975-76; Professor Emerita, Berkeley Agric and Resource Economics, 1982-. *Publications include:* 70 publications including: Personel Finance, 1963, revised 1969 1973. *Memberships include:* Omicron Delta Epsilon, International Economics Honorary, Past President, Board of Trustees 1976-78; American Agricultural Economics Association, Board of Directors; American Real Estate and Urban Economic Association. *Honours include:* Recipient of numerous honours and awards including Fellow, American Agricultural Economics Association, 1982; Fellow in Economics, University of Chicago, 1968. *Address:* Dept of Agricultural and Resource Economics, University of California, Berkeley, CA 94720, USA..

LANEY Victoria, b. 18 July 1951, Montgomery

County, Maryland, USA. Product Manager. *Education:* BA English 1975, MA Management 1977, Brigham Young University, Utah. *Appointments:* Missionary, France & Belgium, Church of Jesus Christ of Latterday Saints, Mormons, 1972-74; Personnel Analyst, IBM, Armonk, New York, 1977-79; Employment Manager 1979-81, Sales Trainer 1981-83, Product Development 1984-85, IBM, Boca Raton, Florida; IBM Faculty Loan, University of Utah, Salt Lake City, 1983-84; Product Manager, IBM, Atlanta, Georgia, 1986-. *Memberships:* President 1989-, Alumni Board, Mariott School of Management, Brigham Young University; President 1987-, National Laney Clan; President 1988-89, Chimney Lakes Garden Club; National Trust for Historic Preservation; American Mensa; International Platform Association. *Honours:* Biographical recognition. *Address:* 3351 Lake Crest Lane, Roswell, Georgia 30075, USA.

LANG Jean McKinney, b. 6 Nov. 1921, Cherokee, Iowa, USA. Freelance Writer; Adjunct Professor. m. (2)Thomas Edward Greef, 12 Nov. 1988, 1 stepdaughter. (1)1 stepson, 1 daughter. *Education:* BS, Iowa State University, 1946; MA, Ohio State University, 1969; Post Master's studies, University of South Florida, 1972, 1973, 1981. *Appointments:* Merchandiser, Rike-Kumler Co, 1952-59; Metropolitan Co, Dayton, Ohio, 1959-64; Teacher, De Vilbiss High School, Toledo, Ohio, 1966-67; Chairman, Retailing Department, Webber College, Babson Park, Florida, 1967-72; Associate Editor 1972-75, Wet Set Illustrated, Pleasure Boating, Executive Editor 1975-80, Senior Editor 1980-84; Prof, St Petersburg Jr College, 1976-88; Ed, Suncoast Woman, 1987-88; Freelance Writer, 1988-. *Publications:* Articles published in magazines. *Memberships:* National Boating Safety Advisory Council; Greater Tampa Chamber of Commerce; American Marketing Assn; Sales & Marketing Executives; International Platform Assn; Florida Freelance Writers Assn; The Fashion Group; National Retail merchants Association; American Association University Women; Tampa Yackt and Country Club; Florida Council of Yacht Clubs; Chi Omega. *Honours:* First woman to cruise solo from Florida to Lake Erie in a single-engine inboard, 1969; Recipient of recognition, US Power Squadron 1976 and 1978; National Retail Merchants Association, 1971; President's Award Sales & Marketing Executives, 1973; Webber College Certificate of Appreciation, 1972; Nominee 1987 for making greatest contribution to understanding of fashion in Western Florida. *Hobbies:* Yachting; Travel; Reading; Gourmet cooking. *Address:* P O Box 402, Largo, FL 34649, USA.

LANGE Katherine J, b. 8 Feb. 1957, Wyandotte, Michigan, USA. Writer; Artist manager in music; Vice President, TSJ Productions Inc. *Education:* Degree in ASLAM, Normandale College, 1980-82; Degrees in English and Math, Control Data Corporation, 1981. *Appointments:* Freelance writer, 1970-; Vice President and Management, TSJ Literary Agency, 1973-; Vice President & Artist Manager, The TSJ Productions Inc, 1975- ; Agent, TSJ booking Agency, 1980-; Assistant Editor/Author, Songwriter USA magazine, Atlanta, 1986-87; Staff Writer, Music Management and International Promotion Magazine, Copenhagen, Denmark, 1983-. *Publications:* Author of numerous articles to newspapers and magazines, including Analysing what you're doing wrong; Women in Music, 1984; Artists and Trademarks, 1985; The Moody Blues, an interview with Patrick Moraz, 1989. *Memberships:* The Christian Children Fund, Inc, 1973-88; AFM American Federation of Musicians, 1980-; The National Association of Female Executives, 1983-; ASCAP, 1975-; The Planetary Society, 1989-. *Honours:* Award from Fine Arts Press for Excellence in Poetry, 1988; Certificates from NAFA 1983, The AFM 1980. *Hobbies:* Building model ships (clippers); Painting; Space; History; Pool playing; Computers; Collecting books of notable quality. *Address:* 422 Pierce Street, North East, Minneapolis, Minnesota 55413, USA.

LANGER Laura Lynn Noddings, b. 11 July 1952, New Jersey, USA. Manager of Reservoir Engineering.

m. Erick Detlef Langer, 25 June 1978, 2 sons, 2 daughters. *Education:* BA, Mathematics, 1975, MA, Mathematics, 1977, University of Colorado; MS, Petroleum Engineering, Stanford University, California, 1979; MA, Secondary Education, Duquesne University, Pennsylvania, 1986. *Appointments:* Various positions to Senior Reservoir Engineer, Southern California Gas Company, 1979-84; Manager of Gas Storage and Production, Equitable Gas Co, 1985-87; Manager of Reservoir Engineering, Equitrans Inc, Pittsburgh, Pennsylvania, 1988-. *Memberships:* Association for Women Geoscientists Foundation (President 1989-91); Underground Storage Committee (First Vice Chairman), Computer Capabilities Task Group Chair, American Gas Association; Supply and Storage Committee, Chairman, 1989-90, Pennsylvania Gas Association. *Honours:* Scholarship in Petroleum Engineering, Standard Oil Co of California and Chevron Companies, 1978-79; Outstanding Young Woman of America, 1983; Leadership Award, Los Angeles YWCA, 1984; Distinguished Service Award, Association for Women Geoscientists, 1987; Outstanding Troop Leader Award, Girl Scouts USA, 1987. *Hobbies:* Gardening; Cooking; Reading. *Address:* Equitrans Inc, 4955 Steubenville Pike, Pittsburgh, PA 15205, USA.

LANGER Sandra (Cassandra), b. 18 Dec. 1941, Montecello, New York, USA. Independent Scholar; Art historian; Critic; Author. *Education:* BA 1967, MA 1969, University of Miami, PhD, New York University, 1974. *Appointments:* Miami Magazine, 1973-74; Florida International University, 1973-78; University of South Carolina, Columbia, 1978-87. *Publications:* New York: Empire City In The Age of Urbanism 1875-1945 - Biographical Sketches, 1989; Co-author, The Healing, MS Magazine, 1989; An Anthology of Feminist Art Criticsm, 1988; Art and Impressionism/Post Impressionism-Biographical Sketches, 1988. *Memberships:* College Art Association of America; International Association of Art Critics; Association of Authors and Journalists; Women's Caucus for Art; National Women's Studies Association; New York Feminist Art Institute. *Honours:* Phi Kappa Phi honor society; Smithsonian Post Doctoral Fellow, 1984; New York State Council of the Arts Grant, Fine Art, 1989. *Hobbies:* Horseback riding; Gardening; Hiking; Chess; Reading; Opera; Cooking; Poetry. *Address:* One Irving Place 3-21 H, New York, NY 10003, USA.

LANGER Susanne Mary, b. 19 Aug. 1955, Red Wing, Minnesota, USA. Cosmetologist; Salon Owner; Educator. *Education:* Graduate, Ritters Beauty College, 1974; Graduate, 3year Study Programme, bruno's college, 1978. *Appointments:* Junior Instructor, 1974-75, Cosmetologist, 1974-75, Ritters professional Salon; Cosmetologist, Assistant Manager, then Manager, scot Lewis Salon, St Paul, 1975-79; Cosmetologist, My Kind of Place, St Paul, 1979-80; Co-Owner, Charpentier's Hair Design, 1980-85; Owner, Someone's Looking Inc., St Paul, 1985-. *Memberships:* St Paul Cosmetologist Association, Director, President (2 years); Minnesota and National Cosmetology Associations; Hair America; Elite International; Salon America; Minnesota Cosmetology Educaiton Committee. *Honours:* Recipient, numerous honours and awards. *Hobbies:* Travel; Singing; Dance. *Address:* Someone's Looking Inc., 151 Endicott Arcade, St Paul, MN 55101, USA.

LANGHAM Gay Patterson, b. 1 Nov. 1945, Beaumont, Texas, USA. Corporate Consultant. m. Lindsay L Langham, 28 Jan. 1978, 1 step-daughter. *Education:* BS, University of Texas, 1968. *Appointments:* Red Cross Hospital Volunteer Southeast Asia, 1969-72; Image Consultant, 1972-75; Department Head, Tyler Junior College, 1975-78; Owner, New You Workshop, 1978- 83; Owner, Executive Profiles Inc., 1983-. *Publications:* Growing Up at 33, 1989; Assessing Your Patients Behaviorally, 1987; Stress & Wellness Management, 1983. *Memberships:* North American Nutrition & Preventive Medicine Association; American Society of Training & Development; National Health Federation; Junior League of San Antonio; National Museum of Women in the Arts (Charter); Centre for

Science in the Public Interest. *Honours:* Recipient, various honours and awards. *Hobbies:* Volunteer Worker; Sogetsu Degrees in Ikebana Flower Arrangement; Biking; Classical Piano Playing; Day Hiking. *Address:* 5909 Luther Lane NO 1807, Dallas, TX 75225, USA.

LANGLEY Dorothy A, b. 8 July 1953, Brockton, Massachusetts, USA. Attorney. m. Bryan S O'Neill, 22 June 1985. *Education:* AA, Massasoit Community College, 1977; BA, Boston University, 1979; JD, Washington University School of Law in St Louis, 1982; MBA expected, Harvard University Graduate School of Business Administration, 1989. *Appointments:* Chief of Civil Law, Area Defense Counsel, Tyndall Air Force Base; Judge Advocate General Officer, Captain, 1983-87, US Air Force; Attorney, Posternak, Blankstein & Lund, 1988. *Publications:* Drug Testing: The Right to Privacy vs. The Right To Test, 1988; numerous articles in professional jounrals and magazines. *Memberships:* Society of Scholars and Fellows at Boston University; Massachusetts Bar; Admitted to practice of law before Massachusetts Supreme Judicial Court; US District Court for District of Massachusetts; US Court of Military Appeals; US Tax Court; VITA; Washington University's High School Law Project; Harvard Business School's Management Consulting and Marketing Clubs. *Honours:* Air Force Commendation Medal, 1987; Air Force Oustanding Unit Award, 1985; Combined Federal Campaign's Silver Award, 1983; Finkelnburg Scholarship, Washington University School of Law, 1982; Phi Delta Phi, 1981-83; Boston University Trustee Scholarship, 1977-79; Psi Chi, 1979; Apha Nu Omega, 1977. *Hobbies:* Writing; Jogging. Interests: Finance; Business law; Workplace privacy issues. *Address:* 114 High Street, Everett, MA 02149, USA.

LANK Heather Powell, b. 8 Oct. 1962, Arvida, Quebec, Canada. Sociologist. m. Peter T Fortier, 9 Aug. 1986. *Education:* BA, Sociology, Anthropology, Middlebury College, Vermont, USA, 1980-83; MA, Sociology, 1984-85, Studying PhD, Sociology, 1985-, University of Toronto, Canada. *Appointments:* Teaching Assistant, 1984-88, Lecturer, 1988-, University of Toronto, Canada. *Publications:* Coming Home: An Inquiry Into The Re-entry Experiences of Students Who Study Abroad, Association of Departments of Foreign Languages Journal, 1985; Patterns of Labour Participation of Older Female Workers in Victor W Marshall (editor), Aging in Canada, 2nd edition, Toronto, 1987. *Membership:* American Sociological Association. *Honours:* Doctoral Fellowship, Social Sciences and Humanities Research Council of Canada, 1985-89; Connaught Scholarship, 1984- 85; Graduated from Middlebury College as Valedictorian with Summa Cum Laude, Phi Beta Kappa and Highest Honours in Sociology, Anthropology, 1983; George C Catlin Award. *Hobbies:* Sports; Squash; Skiing; Cycling; Swimming; Travel; Cooking; Films; Collecting coins; Playing the guitar; Reading. *Address:* 25 avenue du Lignon, 1219 Geneva, Switzerland.

LANSBURY Angela Brigid, b. 16 Oct. 1925, London, England. Actress. m. (1) Richard Cromwell. (2) Peter Shaw, 1949. 1 son, 1 daughter, 1 stepston. *Education:* South Hampstead High School for Girls; Webber Douglas School of Singing and Dramatic Art, Kensington; Feagin School of Drama and Radio, New York. *Career:* With Metro-Goldwyn-Mayer, 1943-50. *Creative Works:* Films included: Gaslight, 1944; National Velvet, 1944; Dorian Gray, 1944; Harvey Girls, 1946; Till the Clouds Roll By, 1946; If Winter Comes, 1947; State of the Union, 1948; Samson and Delilah, 1949; Kind Lady, 1951; the Court Jester, 1956; The Long Hot Summer, 1957; The Reluctant Debutante, 1958; Summer of the 17th Doll, 1959; A Breath of Scandal, 1959; Dark at the Top of the Stairs, 1960; Blue Hawaii, 1962; All Fall Down, 1962; The Manchurian Candidate, 1963; In the Cool of the Day, 1963; The World of Henry Orient, 1964; Out of Towners, 1964; Harlow, 1965; Bedknobs and Broomsticks, 1972; Black Flowers for the Bride, 1972; Death on the Nile, 1978; The Lady Vanishes, 1979; The Mirror Crack'd, 1980; The Pirates of Penzance, 1983; The Company of Wolves, 1984. Plays include: Hotel Paradiso, 1957; A Taste of Honey, 1960; Anyone can Whistle, 1964; Mame, 1966-68; Dear World, 1969; Gypsy, 1973; Hamlet, 1975; The King and I, 1978; Sweeney Todd, 1979. TV Series: Murder She Wrote, 1984. *Honours:* Tony Award for best actress in a Broadway Musica, for Mame; Tony Award, for Dear World; Tony Award; Chicago, Sarah Siddons Award, 1974 for Gypsy; Tony Award for Sweeney Todd, 1979; Golden Globe Award, 1984, 1986; NY Drama Desk Award, 1979; Sarah Siddons Award, 1980, 1983; inducted Theatre Hall of Fame, 1982. *Address:* c/o William Morris Agency, 1350 Avenue of the Americas, New York, NY 10019, USA.

LANSBURY Angela, b. 16 Mar. 1946, London, England. Travel Writer; Journalist. m. Trevor Sharot, 11 June 1978, 1 son. *Education:* BA Honours, University College, London, 1967. *Appointments:* Freelance travel correspondent, Mayfair Times, London; Contributor, numerous publications including Northern Echo; Magazine articles, broadcasting, honeymoons, family holidays & outings, Royalty, romance, 4-posters; Speaker, Radio & TV, BBC & Independent (UK), public radio & independent radio & TV, USA. *Publications include:* Unforgettable British Weekends; Etiquette for Every Occasion; See Britain at Work; A to Z of Shopping by Post; Enquire Within Upon Travel & Holidays; Wedding Speeches & Toasts; How To Be the Best Man; Wedding Etiquette; The Wedding Planner. *Memberships:* Institute of Journalists (Freelance & Travel Writers sub-group); Guild of Jewish Journalists. *Hobbies:* Playwriting; Romantic destinations; Inspecting hotels with 4-poster beds; Photography (travel & honeymoon suites). *Address:* 6 Hillview Road, Hatch End, Pinner, Middlesex HA5 4PA, England.

LAPALMA Marina de Bellagente, b. 10 Jan. 1949, Arcisate, Milan, Italy. Writer; Poet; Freelance Critic; University Professor; Lecturer. m. Rich Gold. *Education:* BA, Music, Poetry, Recording Media, Mills College, Oakland, California, USA, 1980; MFA, Art, University of California, San Diego, 1984; PhD programme, Comparative Literature, Graduate Center, City University of New York, 1987-. *Appointments:* Freelance Writer, 1978-; Adjunct Professor, Research Assistant, University of California, San Diego, USA, 1981-83; Otis Parsons Professor, 1984-87; Lecturer, Communications Department, Hunter College, New York City, 1987-88. *Publications:* Contributions to Artweek, High Performance, L.A.Weekly; Poetry books: Neurosuite, 1976; Casablanca, Carousel, 1978; Grammars for Jess, 1981; 22 Cropped Sets, 1981; Facial Index, 1983; Works in several anthologies, 1970's-; Radio and other readings, USA, Canada, Australia, Italy; Several record compilations. *Memberships:* Southern California Art Writers; AICA. *Honours:* State Scholarships and Levi Fellowship, University of California, Berkeley, 1967-69; Ina Coolbrith Poetry Award, 1977; California STate Poetry Award, 1978; Regents Fellowship, University of California, 1981; Louis Mayer Award, 1982; Chancellor's Grants, 1983; Creative Writing Fellowship, National Endowment for the Arts, 1984; University Fellowship, Graduate Center, City University of New York, 1987, 1988, 1989. *Address:* 815 N Gardner Street, Los Angeles, CA 90046, USA.

LAPIDOS Joan Sylvia, b. England. Company Director. div, 1 son. *Education:* Girls High School, Salisbury, Rhodesia (now Zimbabwe). *Appointments:* Managing Director, South African companies: Fuses International (Pty) Lt, previously Fuses LRS (Pty) Ltd, founded with partner, 1981; LRS Properties (Pty) Ltd, founded with partner, 1984; LRS Components (Pty) Ltd, founded with partners, 1980. Previous owner, supermarket & hairdressing salon, Rhodesia. *Membership:* Wanderers Club, Johannesburg. *Hobby:* Horse Riding. *Address:* 6 Lanzerac, Benmore Road, Morningside-Sandton, Republic of South Africa.

LAPIDUS Gail Warshofsky, b. 6 Apr. 1939, New York City, New York, USA. Professor of Political Science. 1 son. *Education:* BA, 1960, MA, 1963, Radcliffe College; PhD, Harvard University, 1974. *Appointments:* Assistant Professor of Political Science and Sociology, 1979-81, Associate Professor, 1981-85, Professor of Political Science, 1985-, University of California, Berkeley. *Publications:* Women in Soviet Society, 1978; Gorbachev and the Reform of the Soviet System, 1987; State and Security: Toward the Emergence of Civil Society in the USSR, 1988. *Memberships:* Chair, Berkeley-Stanford Programme on Soviet International Behaviour; Council on Foreign Relations; American Political Science Association; American Association for the Advancement of Slavic Studies. *Honours:* Fellow, The Kennan Institute, Woodrow Wilson International Center for Scholars, 1983- 84; Senior Fellow, The W Averell Harriman Institute for Advanced Study of the USSR, Columbia University, 1984-85; Fellow, Center for Advanced Study in the Behavioral Sciences, 1986-87. *Address:* Center for Slavic and East European Studies, University of California, Berkeley, CA 94720, USA.

LAPOTAIRE Jane Elizabeth Marie, b. 26 Dec. 1944, Ipswich, Suffolk, England. Actress. 1 son. *Education:* Bristol Old Vic Theatre School. *Appointments:* Member, National Theatre of Great Britain; Prospect Theatre Co; Compass Theatre Co; Bristol Old Vic theatre Co; Freelance, TV, Films & Radio Work. *Publication:* Grace and Favour, 1989. *Memberships:* Hon. President, Bristol Old Vic Theatre Club; Hon. President, Friends of Southwark Globe; Visiting Fellowship, University of Sussex. *Honours:* Variety Club of Great Britain Award, 1979; Best Actress, SWET, 1980; London Critics Award, 1980; Best Actress, Tony Award, USA, 1981. *Hobbies:* Writing; Cooking; Gardening; Looking After Son. *Address:* c/o William Morris Inc., 31-32 Soho Square, London W1V 5DG, England.

LARBALESTRIER Deborah Elizabeth, b. 17 July 1934, Pittsburgh, Pennsylvania, USA. Paralegal Manager, Legal Profession. *Education:* BA cum laude, History & Sociology, Storer College, West Virginia; Studies, Robert H. Terrell law School, Washington DC; Certificates, paralegal studies; Various other courses. *Appointments include:* Legal assistant, general practice specialising litigation, approx. 16 years; Paralegal instructor, Southland Career Institute , Los Angeles, 1985-88; Paralegal Manager, Lynberg & Watkins, attorneys, Los Angeles, 1988-. Also: Senior Deputy Auxiliary Police Officer, Volunteer, Crime Prevention Specialist, Member Wilshire Community Police Council, 1984-. *Publications:* 3 text/reference books, 1981-85, 1 with cassettes; Various articles, pamphlets; Statement on use, training & education of legal assistants before staff attorneys, US Congressional Record, 1974. *Memberships include:* Past President, American Paralegal Association; Advisory Board, School of Paralegal Studies, University of West Los Angeles; Founder, National Chairman, American Inmate Paralegal Association, Missouri State Penitentiary. *Honours include:* President's Award, American Paralegal Chapter Presidents, 1975; Nominee, Lay Board, California State Bar Board of Governors, 1976, 1977; Nominee, Memberships Republican Senatorial Inner Circle, 1984, 1985; Biographical recognition. *Address:* 1321 1/2 South Sycamore Avenue, Los Angeles, California 90019, USA.

LARIVE Jessica Elisabeth Stephanie, b. 24 Nov. 1945, Voorburg, Netherlands. Member of European Parliament. m. Jan Julius Groenendaal, 25 June 1976, 1 daughter. *Education:* Universities of Leiden and Amsterdam. *Appointments:* Lawyer, Editor in Chief, Benelux, 1974-78; Political Assistant, Liberal & Democratic Fraction, European Parliament, 1978-79; Head, Mr Bangemann's Cabinet, 1979-84; Elected Member, European Parliament, 1984-. *Publications:* Reports for European Parliament. *Memberships:* Dutch Liberal Group; European Liberal Group; Vrouwen in de VVD. *Hobbies:* Tennis; Swimming; Reading; Writing Poems; Indonesian Cooking; Gardening; Interior Decorating. *Address:* European Parliament, Liberal & Democratic Group, 97-113 rue Belliard, 1040 Brussels, Belgium.

LARKIN Mary Ann Connors, b. 31 May 1935, Pittsburgh, Pennsylvania, USA. Writer; Poet. m. Daniel D. Cronin, 23 July 1960 (div. 1976), 2 sons, 1 daughter. *Education:* BA, Sociology, Duquesne University, 1957; MA, English, St Louis University, 1960. *Appointments include:* English teacher, various schools & colleges, 1960-86; Director of Trustees, Independent School of East Cleveland, 1973-76; Director, Early Childhood Enrichment Centre, 1974-77; Freelance writer, 1977-; Writer, Editor, Corporate Giving Watch, & Foundation Giving Watch, 1985-89; Director of Major Donor Relations, Africare, 1989-. *Publications include:* Books of poems: Coil of the Skin, 1982; White Clapboard, 1988. Freelance writing: Book on Mammals, National Geographic Society; American Author series, National Public Radio, DC; Pamphlets, Department of Health & Human Services, National Institutes of Science; Vice President, Development, Watershed Foundation. *Memberships:* Big Mama Poetry Troupe; Poets & Writers; Writers Centre, Maryland; Capitol Hill Poetry Group; Washington Writers' Publishing House, DC. *Address:* 221 Channing Street NE, Washington DC 20002, USA.

LARON Eve, b. 13 Feb. 1931, Budapest, Hungary. Architect. m. George Laron, 17 May 1949. 1 son. *Education:* BA, Architecture and Anthropology. *Appointment:* Principal, Eve Laron & Associates, Architects. *Creative works:* Many buildings: Houses, high-rise home units, town houses. *Memberships:* FRAIA; ARIBA; Founder, Constructive Women (Ass of Women Architects and Planners). *Honour:* Excellence in Building & Environmental Design, 1979. *Interests:* Feminism; Design. *Address:* 18 Monash Ave, Killara 2071, Australia.

LARSEN Jenniece Beryl, b. 9 Aug. 1942, Bassano, Alberta, Canada. Professor and Director, School of Nursing. divorced. 1 son, 1 daughter. *Education:* Diploma, Psychiatric Nursing, 1964; RN, 1968; BScN, 1970; Master of Education in Educ Admin, 1976; PhD, Educational Administration, 1984. *Appointments:* Instructor, School of Nursing, 1970-72; Instructor, Department of Nursing, 1972; Chairperson, Allied Health Dept, 1973-76; Assistant Professor 1978-82, Associate Professor 1982-85, University of Alberta; Professor and Director, School of Nursing, University of Manitoba, 1985-. *Publications:* Canadian Nursing Faces the Future: Development and Change, Co-editor; Chapters in professional journals. *Memberships:* Canadian Research Institute for the Advancement of Women; Canadian Assoc of Univ Schools of Nursing, Pres Elect; Canadian Nurses Association; Academic Women's Association, University of Alberta; Manitoba Assoc of Reg Nurses, Board of Directors. *Honours:* Certificate of Merit for distinguished services to Medicine, 1986; Dissertation of the Year Award, Canadian Society for the Study of Higher Education, 1984; Undergraduate Teaching Award, Fac of Nsg, University of Alberta, 1982. *Hobbies:* Hiking; Reading; History; Biographies; Political activites at local and government levels. *Address:* School of Nursing, University of Manitoba, Winnipeg, Manitoba, R3T 2N2, Canada.

LARSEN Karen Marie, b. 14 July 1954, Cheyenne Wells, Colorado, USA. Attorney; Financial Planner; Investment Adviser. *Education:* BA, University of Denver, 1976; JD, Hamline University School of Law, 1979. *Appointments:* Private Law Practice, 1979-83; General Counsel, AEI Real Estate Funds, 1983-87; Owner, President, Larsen Financial Services, 1987-. *Memberships:* American Bar Association; Colorado Bar Association; Southeast Colorado Bar Association; National Assoc for Female Executives; International Association for Financial Planners; Twin City Association for Financial Planners. *Honours:* Outstanding Woman in Colorado, 1983; Special Service Award, Womens Library Association, University of Denver, 1976. *Hobbies:* Recreational and Competitive Sports; Travel. *Address:* 3601 Minnesota Drive, Suite 880, Bloomington, Minnesota 55435, USA.

LARSON Mabel Howell, b. 5 Sept. 1939, Trenton, Kentucky, USA. Chairperson of Board, Larson Enterprise. m. Howard E Larson, deceased. 1 son, 1 daughter. *Education:* BS, Western Kentucky State University; MA and PhD, Vanderbilt University, Nashville; HU Degree, McDonald's Hamburger University, Oak Brook. *Appointments:* Vice President 1962-84, President and Chairman of Board, 1984-, Larson Enterprise; President of McDonald's Mid- TN Co-op; Owner and Operator, Seven McDonald's Restaurants; Member, Mid-Tn Co- Op Advertising and Public Relations Committee; Chairperson on Public Relations, Ronald McDonald House; Owner, Larson's Register Black Anges Cattle Farm. *Creative work:* Founder and supporter of Howard Larson Art Museum. ssa 20Memberships: Clarksville Area chamber of Commerce; Clarksville-Montgomery County Tourist Commission; United Way; Leadership Clarksville; Member, Board of Directors, Austin Peay State University Foundation. *Honours:* Present, Mayer's Certificate for Community and Civic Affairs; Outstanding Business Person of the Year, Clarksville, 1987; Served on Governor Ned McWhorter Steering Committee; Active in local legislation with the State Representatives; Honorary Kentucky Colonel. *Hobbies:* Golf; Travel. *Address:* 1000 Sandy Drive Clarksville, TN 37043, USA.

LARSON, Muriel Koller, D.R.E. b. 9 Feb. 1924, Orange, New Jersey, USA. Author; Lecturer; Musician. m. Alfred J. Larson, 3 Nov. 1942, 2 daughters. *Education:* MRE, 1988. *Appointments:* Professional Writer, 1969-; Teacher, Christian Writers Conferences; Church Organist, 1981-. *Publications Include:* Devotions for Women's Groups, 1967; Devotions for Children, 1969; The Bible Says Quiz Book, 1976; Joy Every Morning, 1979; Are You Real, God?, 1976; I Give Up God, 1978; Living by Faith/Study on Romans, 1984; Praise Every Day, 1984; Me and My Pet Peeves, etc. *Hobbies:* Child Evangelism; Gardening; Swimming; Camping; Music; Reading. *Address:* 10 Vanderbilt Circle Greenville, SC 29609, USA.

LARUE Monique, b. 3 Apr. 1948, Montreal, Canada. Writer; Professor. m. 1968, 2 sons, 1 daughter. *Education:* B.Ph., University of Montreal; MPh., Doctorate, University of Paris, France. *Appointment:* College Edouard Montpetit, Longuevil, Quebec. *Publications:* Novels: Copie Conforme, 1988; Les Faux Fuyants, 1982; La Cohorte Fictive, 1979; Short stories in various journals & magazines. *Memberships:* Union of Writers of Quebec; Association of French Professors of Quebec. *Honours:* Prix du Concours de Dramatiques Radiophoniques de Radio Canada. *Hobbies:* Swimming; Children; Arts in General. *Address:* 764 Avenue Stuart, Outremont, Quebec, Canada H2V 3H5.

LASKA Vera, b. 21 July 1928, Kosice, Czechoslovakia. Professor; Lecturer; Columnist; Author. m. Andrew J. Laska, 5 Nov. 1949, 2 sons. *Education:* MA, History, MA, Philosophy, Charles University, Prague; Phd, History, University of Chicago, USA, 1959. *Appointments:* Foreign Student Counsellor, University of Chicago, Illinois, USA, 1954-59; Consultant, Institute of International Education, New York, 1964-65; Professor, Regis College, Weston, Massachusetts, 1966-. *Publications:* Remember the Ladies: Outstanding Women of American Revolution, 1976; Czechs in America, 1979; Franklin and Women, 1979; Benjamin Franklin, the Diplomat, 1982; Women in the Resistance and in the Holocaust, 1983, 2nd Edition, 1988; Nazism, Resistance & Holocaust: A Bibliography, 1985; Over 100 articles, reviews. *Memberships include:* American Historical Association; New England Historical Association; President, Weston Historical Society; Massachusetts Bicentennial Commission; Pan-American society; National Association of Foreign Student Affairs; Czech Academy of Arts & Sciences in America. *Honours:* Masaryk Scholar, 1945, 1946; International House Fellow, University of Chicago, 1947-49; Fellow, Institute of International Education, 1947-48; Outstanding Educator of America, 1972; Grantee, National Endowment for the Humanities, 1974; Kidger Award for Excellence in History, 1984;

Grantee, American Historical Association and others, 1985. *Hobbies:* People; Travel; Reading. *Address:* 50 Woodchester Drive, Weston, MA 02193, USA.

LASSITER Mary Leslie, b. 27 Dec. 1949, Moultrie, Georgia, USA. Manager. *Education:* BSc, George Mason University, 1979; Masters of Business Administration, George Washington University, 1983; Advanced Management Program, Claremont Graduate School, 1988. *Appointments:* Foreign Affairs Officer, Department of State, 1978-83; Legislative Analyst, TRW, Inc, 1983-85; Manager, Legislative & International Affairs, Jet Propulsion Laboratory, 1985-. *Memberships:* Women in Defense, National Secretary; National Space Club, General Chairman; Women in Aviation; California Aerospace Alliance; World Affairs Council. *Honour:* Women at Work Medal of Excellence, 1987. *Hobbies:* Reading; Bicycling; Cooking. *Address:* 321 3rd Street, Manhattan Beach, CA 90266, USA.

LAST Joan Mary, b. 12 Jan. Littlehampton, Sussex. Professor of Piano; Composer; Author; Lecturer; Teacher. *Education:* Godolphin School, Salisbury, 1918-25; Piano with Mathilde Verne, 1926 (Accident to hand terminated study as Concert Painist); York Bowen, 1940; LRAM (Teacher), 1925; ARCM (Performer), 1940. *Appointments:* Piano Teacher, Dorset House, Littlehampton, 1926-28; Teacher, eventually Director of Music, Rosemead, Littlehampton, 1926-53; Director of Music, Warren School, Worthing, 1940-62; Professor, Royal Academy of Music, 1959-83. *Creative Works:* Over 120 Albums of Educational Piano Music. Books: The Young Pianist, 1954; Interpretation in Piano Study, 1961; Freedom in Piano Technique, 1988. ssa 20Memberships: Composers Guild; PRS Society; Incorporated Society of Musicians (Chairman Brighton Centre, 1978-85). *Honours:* Honorary ARAM, 1965; Honorary RAM, 1975; OBE, 1988. *Hobbies:* Photography; Contributor to Cassette Magazines for the blind. *Address:* Sury, 11 St Mary's Close, Littlehampton, W Sussex BN17 5PZ, England.

LAST Marian Helen, b. 2 July 1953, Los Angeles, California, USA. Division Manager, Elderly, Psychotherapist. *Education:* BA, 1975; Postgraduate work, USC, 1975-84; MS, 1980; Marriage & Family Therapist, 1982; Vocational Educator, 1989. *Appointments:* Consultant, Sexual Assault, 1971-80; Coordinator, Information Referral, 1975-76; Project Director, Nutrition, Social Service, 1977-; Psychotherapist, 1982-; Division Manager/Elderly, 1982-; Educator, 1988-. *Publications:* Editor, Alternatives/Institutionization, 1976-87; Author, Thesis; Community Response Rape, 1980; Co-author, Training Guide-Rape Survival, 1971. *Memberships:* Clinical Member, California Association o Marriage/ Family Therapist, 1982- ; American Society on Aging, 1975-; California Association of Senior center Directors, 1987-. *Honours:* Commendation, Elderly programs, Los Angeles County Board of Supervisors, 1987; Commendation, Women's Programs Los Angeles County Board of Supervisors, 1983; Susan B Anthony National Organization for Women, Pomona, 1976. *Hobbies:* Golf; Softball; Investments; Advocacy for older Americans; Public speaking. *Address:* 3372 Rowena Dr, Rossmoor, CA 90720, USA.

LATTEA Charlene Marie, b. 26 May 1959, Clarksburg, USA. Writer. *Education:* BSJ, 1982, MA in Progress, West Virginia University. *Appointments:* Editor, Salem College, 1978-79; Office of Legislative Information, WV State Legislature, 1982; Preston Co. News, 1983-84; WVU Health Sciences Centre, Writer, 1984-89; WVU School of Medicine, Co-author of History, 1987. *Memberships:* West Virginia Writers Inc; National Trust for Historic Preservation; WV Historical Society; Smithsonian Associates; National Trust for Historic Preservation. *Honours:* Recipient, various honours & awards. *Hobbies:* Archaeology; Antiques. *Address:* 963 Chestnut Ridge Road, Morgantown, WV 26505, USA.

LAUBER Anne, b. 28 July 1943, Switzerland. Composer; Teacher; Conductor. 1 son. *Education:* Baccalaureat, Conservatory of Music, Switzerland, 1968; Master's degree, 1982, Doctorate, 1986, University of Montreal. *Appointments:* Quebec University, 1986-87, 1988, Montreal, Canada; UQAM, Concordia, Montreal, 1986-87. *Creative works:* Over 35 works premiered; Numerous radio broadcasts; 2 records; Film music. *Memberships:* Canadian Music Center; Canadian League of Composers; Guilde des Musiciens. *Honours:* Numerous grants and commissions, Canadian Arts Council, Quebec Ministry of Culture, Les Amis de l'Art, 1978-. *Hobby:* Reading. *Address:* c/o Canadian Music Center, 430 rue St-Pierre, Montreal, Quebec, Canada K1P 5V8.

LAUENSTEIN Ann Gail, b. 8 Nov. 1949, Milwaukee, Wisconsin, USA. Corporate Librarian. m. Mark Robert Lauenstein, 16 Aug. 1986. *Education:* BA English 1971, MA Library Science 1972, University of Wisconsin. *Appointments include:* Assistant librarian, University of Wisconsin, Wausau, 1972-73; Catalogue librarian, MacMurray College, Jacksonville, Illinois, 1973-76; Corporate librarian, Anheuser-Busch Company Inc, St Louis, Missouri, 1976-. *Memberships include:* Offices, past/present: Women in Business Network; Special Libraries Association; Advisory Council, School of Information Sciences, University of Missouri; American Association of University Women; Anheuser-Busch Quality Circle; Friends of Kirkwood Library. *Honour:* Gift Scholar, American Association of University Women, 1984. *Hobbies:* Cooking; Reading; Ice skating; Aerobics; Enology; Stamp collecting. *Address:* Corporate Library, Anheuser-Busch Company Inc, One Busch Place, St Louis, Missouri 63118, USA.

LAUER Elizabeth, b. 2 Dec. 1932, Boston, Massachusetts, USA. Musician; Composer and performer. m. Louis Lauer, 18 Feb. 1960. 1 son, 2 daughters. *Education:* BA, Bennington College, 1953; MA, Columbia University, 1955; Staatliche Hochschule fur Musik, Hamburg, Germany. *Appointments:* Assistant to president, 1957-62, Associate Producer, Masterworks, 1962-63, Columbia Records; Lecturer, Teacher on opera, symphonic music, theory, composition, New York tri-state area, 1970-. *Compositions:* Musical compositions include: 1 opera; orchestral works; Many chamber pieces; Choral works; Many songs; Solo instrumental pieces; Ballet scores; Music for theatre and cabaret; Many arrangements for chamber groups and for piano, 4-hands and two pianos. *Memberships:* American Composers Alliance; Sigma Alpha Iota; Connecticut Composers Inc, Board Member. *Honours:* AL Walters scholarship, Bonnington College, 1949-53; Ellis Fellowship, Columbia University, 1954; Fulbright Scholarship, 1955-57; American Penwomen Composition Awards, 11; Composer-in-Residence, Chamber Music Conference, Vermont, 1983, 1984 and 1985. *Hobbies:* Tennis; Cooking; Reading; Correspondence; Walking. *Address:* 26 Juniper Place, Wilton, CT 06897, USA.

LAUFMAN Leslie Rodgers, b. 13 Dec. 1946, Pittsburgh, Pennsylvania, USA. Physician. m. 1 son, 1 daughter. *Education:* BA Chemistry, Ohio Wesleyan University, Delaware, 1964-68; MD, University of Pittsburgh School of Medicine, 1968-72; Postgraduate training: Medicine Internship, 1972-73, Medical Residency, 1973-74, Montefiore Hospital; Fellowship in Hematology/Oncology, Ohio State University, 1974-76. *Appointments:* Central Ohio Medical Clinic, 1976-77; Principal Investigator, Southwest Oncology Group Satellite, 1977-79; NSABP, Principal Investigator for Grant Hospital, 1982-83; Medical Advisory Committee of American Red Cross of Central Ohio, 1981- 82; Board of Trustees, Columbus Cancer Clinic, 1985-; Vice President, Board of Trustees, Columbus Community Clinical Oncology Program, 1983-; Investigator, OSU CC Phase I Grant, 1986-; Clinical Scientific Review Committee, Ohio State University, 1983-; Director, Medical Oncology Unit, Grant Medical Center, 1977-; Clinical Assistant Professor of Medicine, Ohio State University, 1976-. *Publications:* Author of Book

Chapters, Articles and Abstracts to professional journals. *Memberships:* American Society of Clinical Oncology; American Medical Women's Association, Branch Secretary Treasurer, 1986, President 1987. *Honours:* Phi Society, Achievement Scholar, Chi Gamma Nu, Chemistry Honorary, Pi Mu Epsilon, Mathematics Honorary, Ohio Wesleyan University; Student Advisor, Pennsylvania Air Pollution Commission, 1969. *Hobbies:* Tennis; Sailing; Travel. *Address:* 340 East Town Street 8-300, Columbus, Ohio 43215, USA.

LAUREL Deborah Spring, b. 7 Feb. 1948, Washington, DC, USA. Personnel Management Consultant. m. Don Robbins, 1 son, 1 daughter. *Education:* BA, Clark University, 1971; MA, University of Wiconsin, 1973. *Appointments:* Personnel Officer, Wisconsin State Government, 1976-85; President, Laurel & Associates, Madison, 1985; Instructor, Small Business Development Centre, Madison, 1987-. *Publications:* Plays: Empty Space Blues, 1972; Women Alone Together, 1973; Zounds, There's A Sound, 1974; Poetry: A Collection, 1968. *Memberships:* Chair, Training, State Employees Combined Campaign; Americna Society of Training & Development. *Honours:* NEA Grantee, 1974, 1975; Governor's Award, 1987. *Hobbies:* Running; Walking; Swimming; Theatre; Music; Gardening. *Address:* 917 Vilas Avenue, Madison, WI 53715, USA.

LAURIE Rona, b. 16 Sept. 1916, Derby, England. Actress. m. Edward Lewis Neilson, 28 Aug. 1961. *Education:* BA, Honours, Birmingham University; LRAM, LGSM, Royal Academy of Dramatic Art. *Appointments Include:* Numerous stage appearances; Professor, Examiner, Guildhall School of Music & Drama, 1957-, Head, Drama, Tutor, Postgraduate Course, 1972-79; Examiner, Gold Medal, Poetry Society, 1986; Drama Coach, Opera School, Royal College of Music, 1986-. *Publications:* Adventures in Group Speaking, 1967; Speaking Together, 1966; Scenes & Ideas, 1967; A Hundred Speechers from the Theatre, 1966, USA 1973; Festivals & Adjudication, 1975; Auditioning, 1985; Mrs Tiggy-Winkle & Friends, 1986. *Memberships:* Former Chairman, Society of Teachers of Speech & Drama, Guild of Drama Adjudicators; Central Board, British Federation of Music Festivals; Drama Board, Guildhall School of Music & Drama. *Honours:* Principal's Medal, Royal Academy of Dramatic Art, 1941; Fellow, Guildhall School of Music & Drama, 1967. *Hobbies:* Theatre; Birdwatching; Walking. *Address:* 2 New Quebec Street, London W1H 7DD, England.

LAUTZENHEISER Barbara J., b. 15 Nov. 1938, LaFeria, Texas, USA. Actuary; Insurance and Management Consultant. *Education:* BA with high distinction, Nebraska Wesleyan University, 1960. *Appointments:* Actuarial Trainee, 1960-64; Programmer, Systems Analyst, 1964-65, Assistant Actuary, 1965-69, Associate Actuary, 1969-70, Actuary, 1970-80, 2nd Vice-President, 1970-72, Vice-President, 1972-80; Senior Vice-President, Phoenix Mutual Life Insurance Company, Hartford, Connecticut, 1980-84; President, Chief Operating Officer, Montgomery Ward Insurance, Schaumburg, Illinois, 1984-85; Principal, Lautzenheiser & Associates, Hartford, 1986-; Testified on insurance issues, US Senate and House committees/commissions and state legislatures. *Publications:* Articles on risk classification, 1974-, effect of social trends on insurance, 1978-. *Memberships:* Fellow, Society of Actuaries (President 1982-83, Board 1975-80, 1981-85, Vice-President 1978-80, Administration and Finance Committee Chair 1981-82, Education Policy Committee Chair 1978-80, Reorganization Committee 1976-78, Actuarial Restructuring Committee 1976, Election Committee 1974-75); American Academy of Actuaries (Board 1974-77, Risk Classification Committee 1978-81, Publications Chair 1980-81); Nebraska Actuaries Club Board, 19697-, 1971-74 (President 1972-73, Chair 1973-74, Secretary/Treasurer 1971-72); Nebraska Wesleyan University Board, 1977-82; Corporate Finance Planning Committee of LOMA, 1974-81 (Chair

1976-78); American Council of Life Insurance Risk Classification Committee, 1973-81; National Policies Panel, Greater Hartford Chamber of Commerce, 1980-84; Former Member: Salvation Army Advisory Board; Government Research Institute Board; Lincoln Electric Systems Board; Lincoln Chamber of Commerce; Chair, National Committee for Fair Insurance Rates. *Honours:* Corporate Woman Award, Women Business Owners of New York, 1983. *Address:* 17 Huntingridge Drive, South Glastonbury, CT 06073, USA.

LAVIN Louise Miller, b. 20 May 1947, Altoona, Pennsylvania, USA. Nurse Therapist. m. Justin P. Lavin, 18 Aug. 1974, 4 sons, 1 daughter. *Education:* BSN with distinction, University of Rochester, 1969; MSN, Psychiatric Nursing, University of Pennsylvania; Diplomate, American Board of Medical Psychotherapists. *Appointments:* Clinical Nurse Specialist, Director of Nursing Staff Development, Philadelphia Psychiatric Center, Pennsylvania, 1971-73; Psychiatric Nurse Specialist, Medical College of Pennsylvania, 1973-79; Instructor, Graduate Division of Nursing, University of Pennsylvania, 1975-79; Instructor, Graduate Division of Nursing, University of Cincinnati, Cincinnati, Ohio, 1979-81; Nurse Psychotherapist, Akron, Ohio, 1983-88. *Memberships:* Ohio Nurses Assocaition; American Nurses Association; Charter Member, Advanced Practitioners of Psychiatric-Mental Health Nursing; Childbirth Educator, Childbirth Education Association. *Honours:* Pi Lambda Theta; Sigma Theta Tau. *Hobbies:* Music; Computers; Travel; Skiing; Embroidery. *Address:* 2166 Ridgewood Road, Akron, OH 44313, USA.

LAW Beulah Enfield (Boo), b. 15 Sept. 1922, Lemoyne, Nebraska, USA. Nurse; Educator. m. Melvin J. Law, 1 Jan. 1949, 1 son, 2 daughters. *Education:* Teaching Certificate, University of Nebraska, Curtis, 1941; Pre-Nursing, Glendale College, California, 1944-45; RN, Los Angeles County General Hospital School of Nursing, 1949; Public Health Nursing, University of Maryland, 1961-63; PhD, College of Life Science, Austin, Texas, 1984. *Appointments:* Elementary School Teacher, 1941, 1942, 1943; General Assembler, B17s Lockheed, Burbank, California, 1943-46; Delivery Rooms, Los Angeles County General Hospital, California, 1946-50; Prudential Life Insurance Co, Los Angeles, 1950-51; National Institutes of Health, Bethesda, Maryland, 1959-61; Holton-Arms School, Bethesda, 1961-70; Johns Hopkins Hospital, Baltimore, Maryland, 1975-77; Army Distaff Hall, Washington DC, 1970-75, 1977, currently. *Memberships:* Life Member: Reorganized Church of Jesus Christ of Latter Day Saints; Girl Scouts of America; American Youth Hostels; Antique Automobile Club of America; Cohasset Garden Club, all offices, President 1966, Editor; Los Angeles County General Hospital Alumni Association; Natural Hygiene Century Club; Member: Boy Scouts & Explorers, many offices; Professional Nurses Club of Maryland; Sigmas of Sigma Chi, President 1968; National Travel Club; Travelers Century Club. *Honours:* Certificate, Outstanding Service, 1969; Thanks Badge, 1972, Golden Trefoil Award, 1982, Girl Scouts of America; Certificate of Recognition, Girl Scout Council of Nation's Capital, 1971; Service Award Plaque, Boy Scouts of America, 1972; International Who's Who on Community Service Award, 1979. *Hobbies:* Canoeing; Sailing; Gardening; Orcharding; Antique cars; Quilts; Patchwork; Camping; Hiking; Travel; Dancing; Herbs (culture, medicinal use); Nutrition and metabolism; Youth and its preservation; Gerontology; Health (Life Science philosophy). *Address:* Ogallala, 7603 Winterberry Place, Bethesda, MD 20817, USA.

LAWER Betsy, b. 27 July 1949, Anchorage, Alaska, USA. Banker. *Education:* BA, Economics, Duke University, 1971; Marketing studies, California State University, Sacramento. *Appointments include:* Executive Officer & Senior Vice President, Marketing Division, 1st National Bank of Anchorage, current. *Memberships include:* Director, 1st National Bank of Anchorage, Providence Health Care Foundation, Providence Hospital Advisory Board; Trustee, Alaska

Council on Economic Education; American Institute of Banking; Past Officer, numerous other Community Organisations. *Honours include:* Outstanding Young Woman of America, 1982; Listing, several biographical publications. *Address:* 1st National Bank of Anchorage, 646 West 4th Avenue, PO Box 100720, Anchorage, Alaska 99510, USA.

LAWRANCE June Cynthia, b. 3 June 1933, Manchester, England. Head Mistress. m. Rev. David Lawrance, 27 June 1957, 3 daughters. *Education:* BA, 1954, MA 1957, Oxford University. *Appointments:* Assistante, Lycee Fenelon, Paris, 1954-55; Lecturer, British Institute, Paris, 1955-57, British Council, Cyprus, 1957-58; Ahlyya School, Amman, Jordan, 1958-61; Counthill school, Oldham, 1962-64; Deputy Head, Chadderton Grammar School, Oldham, 1965-70; Headmistress, Broughton High School, Salford, 1971-74; Headmistress, Harrogate Ladies College, 1974-. *Memberships:* NAHT; SHA; GSA. *Hobbies:* Music; Reading; Chess. *Address:* 21 Clarence Drive, Harrogate, North Yorkshire HG1 2QG, England.

LAWRENCE Frances Elizabeth, b. 26 Feb. 1925, Glendale, California USA. Educator. m. Vester Blount-Lawrence, 2 Apr. 1955, 1 son, 2 daughters. *Education:* AA, Pasadena Junior College, 1945; BA, Whittier College, 1949. *Appointments:* Victor School District, 1944--56; Adelanto School District, 1965-. *Memberships:* Adelanto District Teachers Association; California Teachers Association; National State Association for the Education of Young Children; Association of Early Childhood. *Hobbies:* Travel; Grandchildren. *Address:* 18258 Symeron Road, Apple Valley, CA 92307, USA.

LAWRENCE Glorija Kathleeŋ, b. 20 Apr. 1945, Auckland, New Zealand. Astrologer; Writer; Lecturer; Researcher. m. Lionel Arthur Lawrence, 22 Aug. 1964, 1 son, 1 daughter. *Education:* Certificate, Child Care Studies, New Zealand Play Centre, 1973; Certificate, Cosmobiology Academy. *Appointments:* Childcare Directress, Kelgallie Centre, 1979-84; Publishing Assistant, Regulus Publications, 1985-87; Lecturer, astrology, Council Adult Education, 1988-. *Memberships:* Toastmasters International; Mornington Club, Past President, Educational President, Secretary & Treasurer, District 73 Area; Federation Australian Astrologers; Editor, Regulus Ebertin Newsletter. *Honours:* Competent Toastmaster; Able Toastmaster. *Hobbies:* Astrological Research Specialising in Horse Racing Personalities; Humanitarian & Social Issues. *Address:* PO Box 463, Mornington, VIC 3931, Australia.

LAWRENCE Joan Margaret, b. 14 Dec. 1933, Gordonvale, North Queensland, Australia. Psychiatrist. m. Michael John Lawrence, 1 Sept. 1967. *Education:* MB,BS, University of Queensland, 1957; DPM (AAP-ANZCP), 1963; FRANZCP; FRCPsych. *Appointments:* Resident Medical Officer & Registrar, Royal Brisbane Hospital (RBH), 1958-61; Medical Director, Youth Welfare & Guidance Clinics, 1962-64; Supervisor, Psychiatry Department 1964- 70, Visiting Consultant 1970-, RBH; Consultant (various hospitals), part-time lecturer, private practice, 1970-. *Memberships:* President 1986-87 (2nd woman), Queensland branch, Australian Medical Association; President 1987-89 (3rd woman), Royal Australian & New Zealand College of Psychiatrists. *Honours:* Jean & Joyce Stobo Prize, 1957; Fellow, Australian Medical Association, 1988. *Hobbies:* Breeding Afghan Hounds & Lowchens; Sailing. *Address:* 225 Wickham Terrace, Brisbane, Queensland 4000, Australia.

LAWSON Deloris Sharpe, b. 2 Aug. 1941, Franklin, Virginia, USA. Special Needs Counsellor. 1 daughter. *Education:* Diploma, Hayden High School, 1959; BS in Education (Major: English), Central State University, Wilberforce, Ohio, 1963; MEd (Major: Learning Disabilities), Georgia State University, Atlanta, Georgia, 1979. *Appointments:* English, Journalism and Reading Instructor, Peabody High School, Petersburg, Virginia,

1963-66; English and Journalism Instructor, Jane Addams Vocational High School, Cleveland, Ohio. 1966-68; Reading and Journalism Instructor, Fayette County High School Fayetteville, Georgia, 1968-69; English Instructor, Academic Specialist, Special Needs Counsellor, Atlanta Area Technical School, Atlanta, Georgia, 1969-. *Memberships:* Sphinx Chapter of the American Business Women's Association, Vice-President; Georgia State University Chapter of Phi Delta Kappa, Vice-President; Council for Exceptional Children; Improved Benevolent Protective Order of Elks of the World; Georgia Association for Children and Adults with Learning Disabilities (Adult Advisory Committee); Association on Handicapped Student Service Programs in Postsecondary Education; Georgia Alliance for the Mentally Ill; Central State University Chapter of Alpha Phi Gamma, President. *Honours:* Salutatorian of High School Graduating Class, 1959; Named to the Adult Advisory Committee for the Georgia Association of Children and Adults with Learning Disabilities, 1982; Selected to participate in the Georgia State University Expanding Leadership Skills in Vocational Education Workshop, 1987; World Who's Who of Women in Education. *Hobbies:* Public speaking; Reading; Meeting people. *Address:* 1183 Kimlie Lane, Decatur, GA 30035, USA.

LAWSON Sarah Anne, b. 4 Nov. 943, Indianapolis, USA. Writer; Translator. m. Alastair Pattigrew, 8 Apr. 1969. *Education:* BA, Indiana Univerity, 1965; MA, University of Pennsylvania, 1966; PhD, Glasgow University, 1971. *Publications:* translation of Christina de Pisan, The Treasure of the City of Ladies, 1985; Poetry Introduction 6 (with seven other contributors), 1985. Booklet of poems: Dutch Interiors, 1988; Dutch Poems & Articles in many journals & magazines. *Memberships:* PEN; Poetry Society. *Honours:* C. Day Lewis Fellowship, 1979-80; Runner Up, Redcliffe National Poetry Competition, 1983. *Hobbies:* Classical Music; Jazz; Swimming; Cycle Touring. *Address:* 186 Albyn Road, London SE8 4JQ, England.

LAYMAN Barbara Jean, b. 22 Apr. 1944, Terre Haute, Indiana, USA. Clinical Psychologist. *Education:* EdD, Oklahoma State University, 1975; PhD, San Diego Professional School of Psychological Studies, 1986. *Appointments:* Private practice, 1976-; Psychology Instructor, Eastern MI University, 1987-; Psychology Instructor, LIT, 1978-. *Memberships:* President Elect, Membership Chair, Research Chair, Michigan Women Psychologists; Women's Issue Chair, MI Psychological Assoc; AAMFT; APA, Pres subdivision association. *Honour:* Charter Member, Michigan Women Psychologists *Hobbies:* Tennis; Golf; Biking; Walking; Aerobics. *Address:* 31584 Schoolcraft Road, Livonia, MI 48150, USA.

LAYSON June, b. 6 June 1932, London, England. University Lecturer. *Education:* Teachers Certificate (Dist), University of London; Diploma, I M Marsh College of PE, Liverpool; Advanced Certificate, Laban Art of Movement Centre, Surrey; Diploma in Advanced Studies in Education, MEd, University of Manchester; PhD, University of Leeds. *Appointments:* Teacher, Primary School, 1952-55; Teacher, Secondary School, 1955-60; Lecturer/Senior Lecturer, I M Marsh College of PE, 1960-66; Principal Lecturer, Anstey College of PE, 1968-71; Lecturer, University of Leeds, 1971-81; Director of Dance Studies, Director of National Resource Centre for Dance, University of Surrey, 1981-. *Publications:* Co-author, Teaching Gymnastics, 1965, 2nd edition 1980; Co-author, Dance History: a methodology for study, 1983; PhD thesis, Isadora Duncan: her life, work and contribution to Western theatre dance. *Memberships:* Calouste Gulbenkian Foundation National Inquiry into Dance in Education, Committee member, 1975-80; CNAA Dance Board, 1975-81; DES APU Working party on Aesthetic Development, 1977-81; Arts Council of Great Britain Dance Advisory Panel, 1982-86; Central School of Ballet, 1982-; Royal Opera House Education Advisory Council, 1982-88; Society for Dance Research, Executive Committee, 1982-88; Standing Conference on Dance in Higher Education, Executive Committee, 1982-89; Brighton Polytechnic Council Member, 1984-; Benesh Institute Council, 1986-; Labanotation Council, 1986-; South East Arts Association Dance Panel member 1983, Chairperson 1986. *Hobbies:* Theatre; Hill Walking; Ornithology. *Address:* Dance Studies, University of Surrey, GU2 5XH, England.

LEAKE Brenda Louise Henry, b. 10 Oct. 1949, Cleveland, Ohio, USA. University Professor. m. Donald Oneal Leake, 7 July 1972. 1 son. *Education:* BSE, 1971; MA, Education, 1979; PhD, Education, 1987. *Appointments:* Intern, Natl Teacher Corps, 1969-71; Teacher, St Ann's School, Toledo, Ohio, 1971; Teacher, Columbus Public Schools, 1972-85; Professor, Youngstown, State University, 1985-88; Professor, University of Wisconsin-Milwaukee, 1988-. *Publications:* An Expectancy Analysis of Academically Successful and Unsuccessful Black Early Adolescents; Numerous articles, papers, presentations. *Memberships:* American Association of Colleges for Teacher Education; Association for Supervision and Curriculum & Develop; Natl Assoc of Black school Educators; National Middle School Association; Phi Delta Kappa; Phi Lambda Theta; National Education Association. *Honours:* Outstandign Freshman Woman of the Year, University of Toledo, 1968; Outstanding Teacher of the Year, Columbus, Ohio, 1975; Martha Holden Jennings Scholar, 1980-81; Outstanding Young Woman of America, 1983. *Hobbies:* Reading; Tennis; Music. *Address:* University of Wisconsin-Milwaukee, School of Education, P O Box 413, Milwaukee, WI 53201, USA.

LEALMAN Brenda, b. 12 June 1939, Yorkshire, England. Religious Educator. *Education:* BA, Honours, Birmingham, 1961; Postgraduate Studies, Education, University of London, 1962. *Appointments:* Religious Education Teacher, Staffordshire School, 1963-69; Head, Religious National Education Adviser, Christian Education Movement, London, 1979-; Consultant, Dictionary of Religious Education, SCM Press, London, 1982-83; Co-Director, International Project, CEM/Religious Experience Research Unit, London, 1982-86. *Publications:* Co-Author:The Image of Life, 1980, Knowing and Unknowing, 1981, The Mystery of Creation, 1982; Christ Who's That?, 1983; Anybody There?, 1985; Editor, Questions About Religion, series, 1982-; Questions About Religious Education, series, 1984-; Contributor, various professional publications; Photographic Exhibition, Earth Water, 1987. *Memberships:* Association Professionals and Researchers in Religious Education; Professional Council of Religious Education; International Seminar on Religious Education and Values; SEC A Level RS Committee. *Honours Include:* Walter Pothecary Award, Court of Clothworkers, 1962; Goldsmiths Co. Travel Scholar, 1978; St Luke's Foundation Grantee, 1982-85; Guest Lecturer, University of Nova Scotia, 1987, Theological College of the Arctic, Baffin Island, 1987. *Hobbies:* Arts; Writing Poetry; Counryside; Travel; Islands. *Address:* CEM Lancaster House, Borough Road, Isleworth, Middlesex TW7 5DU, England.

LEATHERMAN Janie Lee, b. 15 Nov. 1959, Toledo, Ohio, USA. Political Scientist; Educator. *Education:* BA, Peace Studies, Spanish, Manchester College, 1982; MA, International Politics, Graduate School of International Studies, 1985, PhD Candidate, University of Denver. *Appointments:* Assistant Director, Brethren College Abroad, University of Barcelona, Barcelona, Spain, 1982-83; Instructor, University of Helsinki, Helsinki, Finland, 1988; Instructor, University of Denver, Colorado, 1989; Instructor, University of Colorado, Denver, 1989; Visiting Assistant Professor of Political Science (International Politics), Macalester College, 1989-. *Publications:* International Negotiation Simulation: Bringing 'Reality' into the Classroom, in Politiikan Tutkimus ja Yhteiskunta (Finland), 1988; International Negotiation and the Politics of Neutrality: Finland and Sweden in the Conferences on Security and Cooperation in Europe, dissertation. *Memberships:* Finland Society; Arms Control Association; International

Studies Association; American Political Science Association; Church of the Brethren. *Honours:* John Allen Fellowship, University of Denver Graduate School of International Studies, 1984-85; West German Government Fellowship as GSIS Exchange Grantee to University of Tubingen, 1985-86; American Scandinavian Foundation Dissertation Fellowship for University of Helsinki, 1987-88; Fulbright Travel Grant and Full Summer Extension Grant for Finland, 1987-88. *Hobbies:* Personal: Oil painting; Sculpting; Classical piano and guitar; Tennis; Cross-country skiing; Academic: International politics; Peace studies; Western Europe and American foreign and defence policy; International negotiation; Cross-cultural communication; Foreign language study especially Romance and Germanic languages and Finnish. *Address:* 29074 Bradner Road, Millbury, OH 43447, USA.

LEDEANU Alina, b. 24 Oct. 1948, Bucharest, Romania. m. Vladimir Schor, 20 June 1972. 1 son. *Education:* Dance School, Bucharest, 1963; Master of Arts, Bucharest, 1972. *Appointments:* Editor, French Department and Dance Department, 20th Century (Secolul 20) Magazine, Bucharest, 1972-. *Publications:* Translations from the French Literature, (Pau Valéry, Francis Ponge, Nathalie Sarraute, Marcel Schwob etc.); dance chronicles. *Hobbies:* Music; Theatre; Painting. *Address:* Secolul 20, Calea Victoriei 115, Bucharest 1, Romania.

LEDERBERG Victoria, b. 7 July 1937, Providence, Rhode Island, USA. State Senator; Professor; Attorney. m. Seymour Lederberg, 15 Mar. 1959, 1 son, 1 daughter. *Education:* AB, 1959, AM, 1961, PhD, 1966, Brown University; JD, Suffolk University, 1976. *Appointments:* Professor, Psychology, Rhode Island College, 1968-; State Representative, 1975-83, State Senator 1984-; Attorney at Law, 1977-. *Publications:* Articles in scientific journals. *Memberships:* Sigma Xi; American, Rhode Island Bar Associations; New England, Rhode Island Psychological Associations. *Honours Include:* Outstanding Educator of America, 1973; Award for Community Service, 1978; Legislator of the Year, Rhode Island Media Association, 1980. *Hobbies:* Archaeology; Art; History; Travel. *Address:* Dept. of Psychology, Rhode Island College, 600 Mt. Pleasant Ave., Providence, RI 02908, USA.

LEDIG-JENKINS Claire, b. 2 July 1924, Minneapolis, USA. R.N.; P.H.N.; Educator; Counsellor. m. (1)Jerome Brown, 1944, divorced 1954, 1 son, 1 daughter, (2)Vincent Ledig, 1955, divorced 1975, 1 son, (3)Robert Garfield Jenkins, 1979, 3 step-sons, 1 step-daughter. *Education:* AA, Nursing, 1969; BSc., Nursing, San Jose State University; MA, Psychology, University of Santa Clara, 1981. *Appointments:* General Hospital: Charge Nurse, Spinal Cord, Head Injury, and Stroke Units; Seminars to Professional persons; In-house Corporated Seminars regarding mental and physiological health. *Publications:* Articles in various professional journals. *Memberships:* California Public Health Association; San Jose State University Alumni Association; California Association of Marriage & Family Counsellors; American Association for Counselling & Development; Clinical Associate, American Board of Medical Psychotherapists; etc. *Hobbies:* Photography; Gardening; Swimming. *Address:* Route 36, Los Gatos, CA 95032, USA.

LEE Amy Elaine, b. 7 June 1960, Knoxville, Tennessee, USA. Senior Project Coordinator. *Education:* AA, Science & Music, Cumberland College, 1978-80; Computer Science, University of Tennessee, 1980-82. *Appointments:* Employee 1982-, Customer Software Department Representative 1983-84, Project Manager 1985-86, Senior Project Coordinator 1986-, American Software Inc. *Creative work includes:* Systems Integration Handbook, Elizabeth Arden; Currently writing children's book. *Memberships:* National Association of Female Executives; French Elephants, private executive women's club. *Honours:* Numerous Recognitions, Professional Merit, American Software

Inc. *Hobbies:* Poetry; Painting; Travel; Body Building; Large Jigsaw Puzzles; Aquarist; Gardening; Unusual toys. *Address:* 2402 Summerlake Drive, Dunwoody, Georgia 30350, USA.

LEE Bobbie Jean Grice, b. 2 Apr. 1947. Social Service Eligibility Specialist. *Education:* Prairie View A&M College, 1965-69; Houston Community College, 1985-86. *Appointments:* Quality Control Inspector 1969-70; Texas Instrument Food Service Supervisor, State & Texas Children's Hospital, 1970-73; Interviewer, Texas Employment Commission, 1973-74; Social Service Worker, Texas Department of Human Services, 1974-. *Memberships:* National Republican Congressional Committee, Sponsor, 1984-; National Association of Female Executives; Communication Workers of America; Smithsonian Institute. *Hobbies:* Sewing; People Watching; Fishing. *Address:* PO Box 14582, Houston, TX 77221, USA.

LEE Catharine Anne, b. 27 Apr. 1940, Beverley, Yorkshire, England. Educator; Researcher. m. John N Lee, 12 July 1964, divorced 1984. 2 daughters. *Education:* BA, MA, Cambridge University, 1959-62. *Appointments:* School Teacher, 1962-66; Tutor, Open University, 1977- 82; Tutor, Frome College, 1982-. *Publications:* Articles in Literary journals on Fanny Burney, Jane Austen, etc. Poems and stories in Granta etc. *Memberships:* Professional Associations; Women's Groups (Local and national); Women's Study Group 1660-1825. *Hobbies:* Music; The arts; Ballet; The Countryside; Dressmaking. *Address:* Yew Tree Farmhouse, Prestleigh, Shepton Mallet, Somerset, BA4 4NL, England.

LEE Dorothy Ann Hicks, b. 22 Jan. 1925, Columbia, Missouri, USA. Professor of English & Comparative Literature. m. George E. Lee, 18 June 1950, 1 son, 1 daughter. *Education:* BA (French) 1945, MA (English) 1947, Wayne State University; MA, Comparative Literature, Radcliffe College, 1948; PhD, Radcliffe & Harvard University, 1955. *Appointments:* Instructor & Assistant Professor, 1950-51, 1955-57, 1957-63, Wayne State University; Instructor, Henry Ford Community College, 1963-72; Assistant, Associate, full Professor, University of Michigan, Dearborn, 1972-88. *Publications:* Scholarly articles, journals including: Michigan Quarterly Review, Black American Literature Forum, Journal of Spanish Studies, Critique, Modern Drama, Black Women Writers. *Memberships:* Modern Language Association; American Association of University Professors; Your Heritage House Museum for the Arts (for children). *Honours:* Various scholarships, 1942, 1943-45, 1947; Award, French fluency, 1946; Susan B. Anthony Award (contributions to progress of women), & Distinguished Teaching Award, University of Michigan, 1985; Distinguished Faculty Award, Michigan Association of Governing Boards of Colleges & Universities, 1987. *Hobbies:* Gardening & house plants; Needlework; Reading. *Address:* 4775 Fullerton, Detroit, Michigan 48238, USA.

LEE Josephine Christine, b. 23 Jan. 1926, Michigan, USA. Philosopher; Lecturer; Writer; Music Theorist. m. Melvin Lee, 10 Jan. 1948. *Education:* BA; MA; PhD. *Appointments:* Teacher, Holochwost Music Conservatory, 1947-48; Teacher, American School of Music, 1948-50; Director, Instructor, Music Manor Conservatory, 1951-72; Media Lecturer, Assistant Librarian, St Ignatius College, 1977-88; Freelance Lecturer, 1974-88. *Creative Works:* Presented papers, various congresses. *Memberships:* National Society for Women in Philosophy; American Federation of Musicians; Society for General Semantics. *Honours:* Congreso Internacional Extraordinario de Filosofia, Universidad Nacional De Cordoba, 1987. *Hobbies:* Composing Music; Lapidary Art & Sculptor; Languages. *Address:* N15545 Rd, D1, Wilson, Michigan 49896, USA.

LEE Pali Jae, b. 26 Nov. 1929. Publisher; Author. m. (1)Richard H W Lee, 4 July 1945, divorced 1978.

(2)John K Willis, 1 May 1978. 5 daughters. *Education:* University of Hawaii, 1944-46; Michigan State University, 1961-65. *Appointments:* Librarian, 1960-74; Researcher, Bishop Museum, 1974-82; Author, 1982-; Publisher, 1987-; President, Night Rainbow Pub, 1988-. *Publications:* Books: Giants, 1967; Winemaking, 1958; Kane 'Ohe: History of Change, 1974; Tales from the Night Rainbow, 1984, 1987; View from the Mt, 1988. Movie: Big Hawaii, 1978. *Memberships:* AFSC 1961-77; Kameekua 'Ohana 1983-; Paia-Kapela-Willis 'Ohana 1982-; President, Lee Hui, 1981-; ALA, 1960-87. *Honour:* Mother of the Year Award, 1960. *Hobbies:* Plants; Grandchildren; Travel. *Address:* c/o Night Rainbow Pub, P O Box 10706, Honolulu, Hawaii 96816, USA.

LEE Peggy, (Norma Egstrom), b. 26 May 1920, Jamestown, North Dakota, USA. Singer; Actress. *Career:* Night Club Vocalist in Fargo; Radio singer, WDAY; With Sev Olsen, bandleader, Minneapolis; Will Osborne; Benny Goodman; Colaborated with Dave Barbour, popular songs, Manana; It's a Good Day; What More Can a Woman Do?; Leading feminine vocalist. Y V & records: screen debut in Mr Music (Bing Crosby); singer on Bing Crosby programme, CBS, TV appearances. *Creative Works:* Films include: Jazz Singer; Pete Kelly's Blues; Act., collaborator songs, Lady and the Tramp. *Address:* c/o 812 N Roxbury Drive, Beverly Hills, CA 90046, USA.

LEE (Maureen) Sylvia, (Mrs M S Bough), b. 21 June 1949, Brighton, England. Writer; Educational Administrator. m. Tony Bough, 4 May 1974, 1 son, 2 daughters. *Education:* Studying for BA English. *Appointments:* Community Programmer, Lakeland College, Vermilion, Alberta, Canada, 1985-. *Publications:* Numerous non-fiction articles published on many topics in variety of Canadian and American magazines. Two books in progress, one, Ever to Excel - The History of Lakeland College, due June 1989. *Memberships:* Secretary, Writers Guild of Alberta; Periodical Writers Association of Canada; Canadian Science Writers Association; MENSA; Historical Society of Alberta. *Hobbies:* Art; Music; Literature; Archaeology; Photography; Psychology; Science and Medicine. *Address:* Box 1470, Cold Lake, Alberta, Canada, T0A 0V0

LEEK Gladys Elnora, b. 8 Nov. 1933, Clarksburg, West Virginia, USA. Instructor in Sociology. m. Ardell C Leek, 26 Mar. 1954. 2 sons. *Education:* AA, Sociology, Parkersburg Community College, West Virginia, 1982; Regents BA, Glenville State College, West Virginia, 1983, MA, Sociology, Ohio University at Athens, 1985. *Appointments:* Instructor in Sociology, Parkersburg Community College, Parkersburg Campus, Jackson County Campus, Ripley, 1985-86; Alerson-Broaddus College, Philippi, West Virginia, 1986-87. *Memberships:* American Sociological Association; West Virginia Sociological Association; Women in Higher Education. *Interests:* Volunteer Services: Church work; Mentally retarded; International exchange services. Hobbies: Sewing; Jigsaw puzzles; History and culture Amerindian. *Address:* Happy Valley Road, Cedar Grove, Parkersburg, West Virginia 26101, USA.

LEEMING Jan Dorothy, b. 5 Jan. 1942, Kent, England. Broadcaster. Divorced, 1 son. *Education:* Ewell Technical College; Open University, 1974. *Appointments:* Varied work, stage & television, New Zealand & Australia, 1962-66; Varied work, television, regionally & nationally, ITV & BBC, currently News-Reader, BBC News. *Publications:* Working in Television, Batsford series, Careers 1980; Chapter, Korean Cooking, in Encyclopaedia of Asian Cooking, 1980; Simply Looking Good, Barker, Health, Make-up, Clothes the Practical Way. *Honours:* TV & Radio Industries Award for Newsreaders, 1981, 1982; Pye TV Award, TV Personality, 1982. *Hobbies:* Theatre; Travel. *Address:* c/o IMG, 14-15 Fitzhardings Street, London W1H 9PL, England.

LEENHOUTS Lillian May (Scott), b. 2 June 1911, South Milwaukee, Wisconsin, USA. Architect. m. 21 July 1943. 1 daughter. *Education:* Leyton School of Art, 1929-32; University of Illinois, 1932-35; BS, Architecture, University of Michigan, 1936. *Appointments:* Architect, Office of Harry Bogner, 1936-42; Power Plant, Naval Building and Fairchild Aircraft drawings, World War II, 1942-45; Partner with Husband in own Architectural Office, 1945-. *Publications:* Regional Guidelines for Building Passive Conserving Energy Homes, one chapter. *Memberships:* American Institute of Architects; Wisconsin Society of Architects; Society of Women Engineers. *Honours:* Elevated to Fellowship, American Institute of Architects, 1975; Elevated to Fellowship, Society of Women Engineers, 1980; Award of Excellence, Wisconsin Women in the Arts, 1976; Sacajawea Award of Professional Dimensions, 1986. *Hobbies:* Photography; Watercolour painting; Sketching; Biking; Canoeing. *Address:* 3332 N Dousman Street, Milwaukee, Wisconsin 53212, USA.

LEES Marjorie B., b. 17 Mar. 1923, New York, USA. Biochemist. m. Sidney Lees, 17 Sept. 1946, 3 sons. *Education:* BA, Biology, Hunter College, 1943; MS, Biology, University of Chicago, 1945; PhD, Medical Science, 1951. *Appointments:* McLean Hospital & Harvard Medical School, 1953-62; Senior Research Associate, Pharmacology, Dartmouth Medical School, 1962-66; Harvard Medical School, Mclean Hospital, 1966-76; Biochemist, E.K. Shriver Center & Massachusetts General Hospital, 1976-; Professor, Biochemistry in Neurology, Harvard Medical School, 1985. *Publications:* Over 90 scientific articles & book chapters. *Memberships:* American Society of Biological Chemists; International Society for Neurochemistry; American Society for Neurochemistry; American Association of Neuropathologists; Society of Neuroscience, New York Academy of Sciences; Radcliffe Graduate Society, Chairman, 1978-80; New York Academy of Sciences. *Honours:* Phi Beta Kappa; Principal Investigtor on NIH Grants, 1962-; Javitz Neuroscience Investigator Award, 1984-1990. *Address:* Biochemistry Dept., E.K. Shriver Center, 200 Trapelo Road, Waltham, MA 02254, USA.

LEESS Lynelle, b. 26 Sept. 1954, Kingston, New York, USA. Creative Consultant. m. Jonathan Leess, 26 Apr. 1980. 2 sons. *Education:* BA/BS English & Business, Skidmore College, 1976. *Appointments:* Revlon, 1976; L'Oreal/Lancome, 1979; Ted Bates, 1980; Senior VP/ Creative Group Head, Benton & Bowles, 1982; Creative Consultant, 1986-. *Publications:* ABCs of Pregnancy; numerous articles for magazines. *Memberships:* Skidmore Club; ORT; Board Member, Creative Playcare. *Honours:* Several Effie's. *Hobbies:* Painting; Writing poetry; Skiing and water sports. *Address:* 7 Patricia Lane, Briarcliff Manor, NY 10510, USA.

LEFEVER Maxine Lane, b. 30 May 1931, Illinois, USA. Professor of Bands. m. Orville J Lefever, 18 Aug, 1951, deceased. 1 son. *Education:* BA, Western State College of Colorado, 1958; MS 1964 Advanced Studies, 1965, Purdue University. *Appointments include:* Elementary Teacher, Mancos County Public Schools, 1954-57; Elementary Teacher, Cortez County Public Schools, 1956-60; Graduate Teaching Assistant, Prudue University Bands, 1962-65; Professor of Bands, Purdue University Bands, 1965-; Numerous positions throughout USA and Canada adjudicating bands, band and percussion clinics and lectures; numerous performances with bands and symphony orchestras; considerable work with music/travel companies; Vice President and Executive Secretary, The John Philip Sousa Foundation, 1978-. *Publications include:* Numerous articles in professional musical journals; 31 percussion ensembles. *Memberships include:* Executive Secretary Treasurer, 1969- 72, Indiana Percussive Arts Society; Editor, National Band Association Journal, 1970-78; Editor, National Band Association Directory, annual 1966-78; numerous committee chairmanships; Delegate, National Band Association; numerous conferences. *Honours include:* Citation of Excellence, National Band Association, 1977; Honorary Member,

Kappa Kappa Psi, 1977; US Navy Band Association, 1971; Star of the Order, John Philip Sousa Foundation, 1983. *Hobbies include:* Foreign travel; President, American Bands Abroad. *Address:* P O Box 2454, West Lafayette, IN 47906, USA.

LEGGE Diane, b. 4 Dec. 1949, Englewood, New Jersey, USA. Architect. 1 son. *Education:* Wellesley College, 1967-69; BA, Stanford University, 1972; MArch, Princeton University, 1975. *Appointments:* The Ehren Krantz Group, New York, 1975-77; Partner, Skidmore, Owings & Merrill, Chicago, Illinois, 1977-89; Partner, Decker & Kemp Associates, Chicago, 1989- . *Creative works:* Arlington International Racecourse; Boston Globe Printing Plant; Manufacturer's Hanover Plaza Office Building; Expansion to McCormick Place Exhibition; Olympia Center mixed-use. *Memberships:* American Institute of Architects; National Council of Architectural Registration Boards; Urban Land Institute; American Society of Landscape Architects. *Honours:* Masonry Institute Awards, 1983, 1984; 1st Award, Progressive Architecture, 1984; Young Architect Award, 1984, Distinguished Building Award, 1985, Certificate of Merit, Interiors Award Programme, 1989, Chicago Chapter, American Institute of Architects, 1984; Edison Award, Certificate of Merit for Lighting Design, 1986; 40 Under 40, published in Interiors, New York Architectural League, 1986; Illinois Chapter, ASHRAE Energy Awards Programme, 1986; Waterfront Honour Award, 1988; Honour Award, Illinois Chapter, American Society of Landscape Architects, 1988; Honour Award, Friends of Downtown-Best New Open Space, 1988. *Hobbies:* Skiing (telemarking and downhill); Swimming; Sailing; Contemporary arts; Flute, piano and cello. *Address:* Decker and Kemp Associates, 410 South Michigan Avenue, Chicago, IL 60605, USA.

LEGINSKI Janet, b. 23 Jan. 1949, Oak Park, Illinois, USA. Businesswoman; Systems Analyst. *Education:* Roosevelt University, 1969- 79. *Appointments:* Secretary 1968-70, programmer 1970-80, Programming Supervisor 1980-83, Senior Systems Analyst 1983-, Borg-Warner Corporation; President, Femline Designs Inc, 1981-. *Memberships:* Chicago Zoological Society; Art Institute of Chicago; AAU/Illinois Physique Association. *Honours:* Body building: 1st place, novice, Illinois short class, 1985; 5th place, Central USA, short class, 1985. *Hobbies:* Body building; Writing; Art; Gardening; Animals. *Address:* 6907 Roberts Road, Bridgeview, Illinois 60455, USA.

LEGRANDE Margaret Estella, b. 28 May 1931, Richmond, Virginia, USA. Teacher, Nursing, Registered Nurse; Health Educator, Adjunct Lecturer. m. Floyd Posby, 20 Aug. 1960, divorced 1986. 1 son, 1 daughter. *Education:* BS, Nursing, VA Commonwealth University, 1957; Columbia University, 1972; Yeshiva University, 1985; MPS, New School for Social Research, 1987. *Appointments:* Supervisor, Mt Sinai Hospital, New York City, 1958; Private duty Nurse, Hosp for Joint Diseases, 1959-65; Head Nurse Dept Health, 1965-66; Dir Staff Development, Call View Nursing Home, 1966-72; Supervisor, Jewish Home and Hosp for Aged, 1972-77; Supervisor, Concord Nursing Home, Brooklyn, 1977-78, 1982-85; Tch Coordinator 1985-89, Teacher 1989, Adj Lecturer Physical/Health Education, Borough of Manhattan Community College, New York City, 1988- . *Memberships:* American College of Health Care Administrators; Association for Supervision and Curriculum Development; American Management Association; National Association for Female Executives, Inc; Chi Eta Phi Sorority; Alpha Kappa Alpha Sorority. *Honours:* Recipient Sojurner Truth Award, Harlem Women's Committee, New Future Foundation, 1988; Special Mother of the Year Award, ABG Cable TV, 1988; Recognition Award, Mio-Manhattan School of Practical Nursing, 1988. *Interests:* Volunteer for numerous organisations including: Harlem Hospital Community Board, Harlem Teams for Self Inc. *Address:* 626 Riverside Drive, Apartment 24G, New York, NY 10031, USA.

LEHANE Maureen, Concert Singer; Singing Teacher.

m. Peter Wishart, 26 May 1966. *Education:* Guildhall School of Music & Drama. *Appointments:* Has sung numerous leading roles with Handel Opera Societies of England and America, in London and in Carnegie Hall, New York, also in Poland, Sweden & Germany; Given number of Master Classes; Festival appearances include: Stravinsky Festival, Cologne; City of London; Aldeburgh; Cheltenham; Three Choirs; Bach; Oxford Bach; Göttingen Handel Festival, etc; Toured USA, Australia and Far and Middle East; appears regularly on BBC and in Promenade Concerts; numerous recordings. *Publication:* Co-editor, Songs of Purcell. *Hobbies:* Cooking; Gardening; Reading. *Address:* Bridge House, Great Elm, Frome, Somerset, BA11 3NY, England.

LEHMAN Yvonne, b. 3 Apr. 1936, South Carolina, USA. Writer. m. Howard N Lehman, 28 Sept. 1958. 1 son, 3 daughters. *Education:* BA English Literature, University of North Carolina at Asheville; Currently enrolled in Master's Degree Program, English Literature, Western Carolina University. *Publications:* Red Like Mine, 1970; Dead Men Don't Cry, 1973; Verliebt in Einen Farbigen-Was Nun? 1978; Fashions of the Heart, 1981, 1983; In Shady Groves, 1983; Smoky Mountain Sunrise, 1984; Taken by Storm, 1984; More than a Summer's Love, 1985. Articles to magazines and journals including: The Pen Woman; Marriage and Family Living; Cumerlands; The Christian Writer; The Writer, etc. *Memberships:* Founder/Director, Blue Ridge Christian Writers Conference, 1976-; The National League of American Pen Women; Romance Writers of America, Carolina Chapter; Appalachian Writers Association. *Honours:* Dwight L Moody Award for Excellence in Christian Literature, 1968; First Place novels category, Biennial Contest sponsored by The National league of American Pen Women for Dead Men Don't Cry, 1974; Winner in articles category Writers Digest Contest, 1977; Third place novels category, Pen Women for Fashions of the Heart, 1982; Writers Digest Contest articles category (Inspirational Romance Writing), 1983; Inspirational Award (first in nation), Romantic Times Booklovers Conference, New York, 1984. *Address:* P O Box 188, Black Mountain, North Carolina 28711, USA.

LEHR Ursula Maria, b. 6 May 1930, Frankfurt, Germany. Gerontologist. m. Helmut Lehr, 14 Mar. 1950, 2 sons. *Education:* Dr phil 1954, Habilitation (venia legendi Psychology) 1968, University of Bonn. *Appointments:* Research Assistant 1955-60, Assistant Professor 1960-69, Associate Professor 1969-71, Professor of Psychology & Director, Department of Psychology 1975-86, University of Bonn; Director, Institute for Gerontology, University of Heidelberg, 1986-. *Publications:* Numerous professional articles & reports. *Memberships:* Past Vice President, German Society of Gerontology; International Society of Applied Psychology; Deutsche Gesellschaft fur Psychologie; Honorary member: Schweizer Gesellschaft fur Gerontologie, Mexican Society of Gerontology & Geriatrics; American Society of Gerontology *Honours:* Max-Burger Prize, Deutsche Gesellschaft fur Gerontologie, 1973; Bundesverdienstkreuz, 1st Class, 1987. *Hobbies:* History of arts; Literature; Paintings of middle ages. *Address:* Institut fur Gerontologie, Ruprecht-Karls University, Akademiestrasse 3, 6900 Heidelberg 1, Federal Republic of Germany.

LEIBOWITZ Sarah Fryer, b. 23 May 1941, White Plains, USA. Neurobiologist; Research Scientist. m. Martin Lewis Leibowitz, 25 June 1966, 3 sons. *Education:* BA, 1964, PhD, 1968, New York University. *Appointments:* USPHS Postdoctoral Fellow, Quest Investigator, 1968-70, Assistant Professor, 1970-78, Associate Profesor, 1978-, Rockefeller University. *Publications:* 125 articles in scientific journals & books. *Memberships:* AAAS; American Psychological Association; New York Academy of Science; American Society Pharmacology & Experimental Therapeutics; Society Neuroscience. *Honours:* Phi Beta Kappa; Yetta Karen Hirsch Award, 1968; Sigma Xi, 1968; First Award, Psychopharmacology, APA, 1969; Alfred P. Sloan

Foundation Award, 1977-79; Fellow, APA, 1980. *Hobbies:* Music; Sports; Travel. *Address:* The Rockefeller University, 1230 York Avenue, New York, NY 10021, USA.

LEIGH-HUNT Barbara, b. 14 Dec. 1935, Bath, Somerset, England. Actress. m. Richard Edward Pasco, CBE, 18 Nov. 1967, 1 stepson. *Education:* Bristol Old Vic Theatre School, 1952-54. *Appointments:* Old Vic Company, 1954, 1957-60; Bristol Old Vic Company, 1960-63, 1963-66, 1967-70; Prospect Theatre company, Nottingham Play House, West End Theatres, 1964, 1967, 1983; BBC Radio broadcasting from age of 12 years. *Creative Works:* Films: Hitchcock's, Frenzy, 1971; A Bequest to the Nation, 1972; Wagner, 1982; Royal Shakespeare Company, 1974-. *Memberships:* Associate Artist, Royal Shakespeare Company; Board Member, English Chamber Theatre; Committee Member, Theatrical Ladies Guild. *Honours:* Bristol Evening Post Award to Most Promising Student of Bristol Old Vic Theatre School, 1953-54; Clarence Derwent Award, Best Supporting Performance as Gertrude in Hamlet, Royal Shakespeare Company, 1981-82. *Address:* c/o Michael Whitehall Ltd., 125 Gloucester Road, London SW7 4TE, England.

LEINBERGER Joan H. Schmidt, b. 28 Nov. 1942, Bay County, Michigan, USA. Business Manager. m. Kenneth E. Leinberger, 14 Oct. 1961, 1 son, 1 daughter. AA, Bay de Noc Community College, 1971; BS, 1973, MS, 1977, Northern Michigan University. *Appointments:* Dow Chemical Co, 1960-61, 1962-68; Briggs Manufacturing, 1961-62; Rust Engineering, 1970; Instructor, Bay de Noc Community College, 1973-76; Substitute Teacher, Gladstone Schools, 1073-76; George D.Maniaci Center, 1976-. *Memberships:* Vice-President of Programme, Secretary, American Association of University Women; American Society of Public Administrators; Board Member, Community Concert Association; Escanaba City Planning Commission. *Honours:* Outstanding Business Education Student, 1974; Pi Omega Pi; Phi Kappa Phi; Dean's List, Bay de Noc Community College; Meritorious Service Citation, Public Service Credit Union, 1988. *Hobbies:* Camping; Bowling; Travel; Civic service: Volunteer, American Cancer Society and March of Dimes. *Address:* 3601 Eighth Avenue South, Escanaba, MI 49829, USA.

LEITH Prudence Margaret, b. 18 Feb. 1940, Cape Town, South Africa. Managing Director of own Group of Companies. m. Rayne Kruger, 1974. 1 son, 1 daughter. *Education:* University of Cape Town; Cordon Bleu Advanced; Diplome de la Cours de la Civilization Francaise, Sorbonne, Paris, France. *Appointments:* Own small outside catering service, 1960-65; Founded Leith's Good Food, commercial catering, 1965; Founded, Leith's Restaurant, 1969; Founded, Leith's School of Food and Wine, 1975; Added Leith's Farm, 1976. *Publications:* Leith's All Party Cook Book, 1972; Parkinson's Pie (co-authored with Michael Parkinson), 1974; Cooking for Friends, 1978; The Best of Prue Leith (co-authored with Jean Reynaud), 1979; Leith's Cookery Course (co-authored with Caroline Waldegrave), 1979; The Cook's Handbook, 1981; Cooking Around The World (60 min video), 1981; Masterclass-a chapter contribution, 1982; Dinner Parties, 1984; Leith's Cookbook (co-authored with Caroline Waldegrave), 1985; Leith's Cookery School, co-authored with Caroline Waldegrave, 1985; Entertaining With Style (co-authored with Polly Tryer), 1986; The Good Food Cookbook (90 min. video), 1988. *Memberships:* Restaurateurs' Association of Great Britain; Association Culinaire; Royal Society of Arts; Museum of Modern Art; British Gastronomic Academy; Guild of Food Writers. *Honours:* Cordon Bleu Diploma; Corning Award, 1981; Finalist, Veuve Clicquot Business Woman of the Year Award, 1984; President's Prize, Royal Borough of Kensington & Chelseam, 1986. *Hobbies:* Riding; Tennis; Old cookbooks; Kitchen antiques; Modern painting and architecture; Gardening. *Address:* 195 The Colonnades, 34 Porchester Square, London W2 6AR, England.

LELAND Joy Hanson, b. 29 July 1927, Glendale,

California, USA. Research professor of Anthropology. m. Robert Leland, 6 May 1961, deceased 24 Oct 1986. 1 stepson. *Education:* BA, English Literature, Pomona College, 1949; MBA, Business Administration, Stanford University, 1960; MA, Anthropology, University of Nevada, Reno, 1972; PhD Anthropology, University of California, Irvine, 1975. *Appointments:* Research Associate 1966-75, Assistant Research Professor 1975-77, Associate Research Professor 1977-79, Research Professor 1979-, Social Sciences Center; Desert Research Institute, University of Nevada System, Reno, 1961-. *Publications include:* Firewater Myths: Indian Drinking and Alcohol Addiction, 1976; Women and Alcohol in an Indian Settlement, 1978; Foreword and Literature Review Chapter in P Mail and D McDonald (compilers), Tulapai to Tokay: an annotated bibliography of alcohol use and abuse among Native Americans of North America, 1980; Sex roles, family organization and alcohol abuse, 1981; The context of Native American drinking: what we know so far, 1981; Gender, drinking and alcohol abuse, 1982; Alcohol use and abuse in ethnic minority women, 1984; Demography of Great Basin Indians, 1873-1980, 1986. Numerous papers to professional journals and conferences. *Memberships include:* American Anthropological Association; Southwestern Anthropological Association; Society for Medical Anthropology; Society for Applied Anthropology; Society for Psychological Anthropology; Alcohol and Drug Study Group, etc. *Hobbies:* Horticulture; Music. *Address:* 6126 Carriage House Way, Reno, Nevada 89509, USA.

LEMAY Charlotte Zihlman, b. 30 June 1919, Fort Worth, Texas, USA. m. Jack Evans LeMay, 29 July 1944, 2 sons, 1 daughter. *Education:* AB, Christian University, 1940; MA, Physics, Mount Holyoke College, 1941; PhD, Physics, Louisiana State University, 1950. *Appointments Include:* Various Teaching Positions, 1941-50; Engineer, Texas Instruments Inc, 1951-53; Research Physicist, Stanford Research Inst., 1953-54; Engineer, Texas Instruments Inc., 1955-57; Engineer, Westinghouse Electric Corp., 1957-60; Research Physicist, IBM, 1960-63; Professor, Western Connecticut State University, 1963-; Member China-US Scientific Exchange, 1986. *Publications:* Articles in: Echo; Journal of Applied Physics; Electromechanical Technology; Journal of Chemical Physics; several Patents. *Memberships:* various professional organisations including: American Physical Society; American Association of Physics Teachers; American Society of Engineering Education; Institute of Electrical and Electronic Engineers; Optical Society of America. *Honours:* Recipient, various honours & awards. *Address:* 60 Chestnut Ridge Road, Mt. Kisco, NY 10549, USA.

LEMBERGER Norma, b. 21 July 1944, Monticello, New York, USA. Financial Executive. *Education:* BSc, summa cum laude, Brooklyn College, 1965. *Appointments:* With IBM, Armonk, N.Y. 1965-; various technical, marketing, finance and management positions including positions in New York City and Paris, France, 1965-84; Director Special Financing IBM Credit Corporation, Stamford, Connecticut, 1985; General Manager Rolm Credit Corporation IBM, Santa Clara, California, 1985-87; President Rolm Credit Corporation and Director Financing Programs IBM Credit Corporation, Stamford, 1987-88; Treasurer IBM Americas Group, Mount Pleasant, N.Y., 1988-89; Program Director Investor Relations, IBM Corporation, Armonk, N.Y., 1989-. *Memberships:* Women's Economic Roundtable. *Hobbies and Interests:* Photography; Cooking; Personal Computing; Gardening. *Address:* 34 Limestone Road, Armonk, NY 10504, USA.

LEMELIN Louise, b. 7 Oct. 1946, St Romuald, Quebec, Canada. Laywer. m. Hamel Pierre, 1 May 1976. *Education:* BA, College F X Garneau, 1966; LLB, Laval University 1969; Admission to the Bar, 1970. *Appointments:* General practice, Moisan Bellavance, Aubert and Associates, 1970-81; Teacher, CEGEP, Victoriaville, 1971-76; President Arbitral councils, Canada Manpower and Immigration Commission, 1981; Commissioner, 1981-86, Senior Advisor and Researcher, 1987-, Law Reform Commission, Canada; Director General, Executive Services within the Secretariat of Solicitor General, Canada. *Memberships:* Counsel for Arthabaska Division, Quebec Bar Association, 1979; Chamber of Commerce, Victoriaville and Arthabaska; Canadian Bar Association; Association des Juristes de Langue française. *Honours:* Recipient of Lacroix Award (Criminal Procedure), 1969; Named Queen's Counsel (QC), 1982. *Address:* 130 Albert Street, Ottawa, Canada, K1A 0L6.

LEMER-KORNEY Ellen Terry, b. 27 Dec. 1943, Brooklyn, USA. Interior Designer; Art Consultant. m. 25 Dec. 1988, 1 daughter, previous marriage. *Education:* BA, Hofstra University, 1965; Cert. Prog., New York School Interior Design, 1971. *Appointments:* President, Ellen Terry Lemer Ltd., 1971-; Instructor, Parsons School of Design. *Publications:* Manhattan Living, 1963; The Designer Magazine, cover May 1979; Home Entertainment, 1986; House Beautiful, 1987; Very Small Living Spaces, 1988. *Memberships:* American Society of Interior Designers, Board Member, Metropolitan Chapter; Co-Chairperson, Design Service Corps; Chairperson, Special Events Committee; Special Events Committee. *Honour:* Dean's List, Ithaca College, 1961. *Hobbies:* Skiing; Tennis. *Address:* 120 East 81st Street, New York, NY 10028, USA.

L'ENGLE Madeleine, b. 29 Nov. 1918, New York City, USA. Author. m. Hugh Franklin, 1946, 3 children. *Appointments:* Faculty, University of Indiana, 1965-66, 1971; Writer in Residence, Ohio State University, 1970, University of Rochester, 1972, Wheaton College, 1976-. *Publications Include:* A Cry Like a Bell; Many Waters; A Stone for a Pillow; And It Was Good; A Severed Wasp; Walking on Water; The Other Side of the Sun; A Circle of Quiet; A Winter's Love; Ilsa; The Small Rain; Books for Younger Readers: A House Like a Lotus; The Sphinx at Dawn; A Ring of Endless Light; A Swiftly Titling Planet; Prayers for Sunday; Everyday Prayers; Dragons in the Waters; A Wind in the Door; Dance in the Desert; The Young Unicorns; The Moon by Night; A Wrinkle in Time; The Anti-Muffins; Meet the Austins; Camilla; And Both Were Young. *Honours:* American Library Association Newberry Medal, 1963; University of Southern Mississippi Award, 1978; American Book Award, for Paperback, 1980; Logos Award, 1981. *Address:* Crosswicks, Goshen, CT 06756, USA.

LENGYEL Laura La Foret, b. 20 Aug. 1946, Bridgeport, Connecticut, USA. Artist (Sculptor/Painter). m. June 1968, 1 son. *Education:* Aspen Art School, 1965; BA, Art, Hills College, 1967; Stanford University, summers 1964, 1966; Academy of Art College, San Francisco, 1974. *Career includes:* Painting since age 11; Owner, Operator, Gallery West Inc, Mendocino, California, 1968-73; Building design and renovation, 1975-80; Life drawing workshops, Fairfax, California, 1979-82; Art Instructor, Carden Marin School, San Anselmo, California, 1981-82; Lecture series, Oakland Museum, 1982; Invited Instructor, etching, Mendocino, 1986-88; Sculpture workshops, 1987; Participant, over 40 group exhibitions, Houston, Texas, Ashland, Oregon, throughout California, 1968-; 15 solo exhibitions, San Francisco, Los Angeles, San Rafael, California, 1980-. *Creative works:* Sculptural works, wood carving, stained glass, prints and etchings, silkscreen, painting (oil, watercolour, acrylic), drawing; Traditional human figures, modern classic realism, plants, animals, abstracts; Commissioned works in painting and sculpture; Numerous works in private collections; Unpublished writing on aesthetic poetry. *Memberships:* International Sculpture Society; San Francisco Fine Art Museums; San Rafael Chamber of Commerce; Mills College Alumni Association, Marin County Branch President 1988, 1989-90; Artists Equity Association; Bay Area Art Conservationists Guild; Marin Arts Guild. *Honours include:* Merit Award in Printmaking, Ross, California, 1986; Select commissions: Harrah's Casino Hotel, Lake Tahoe, California; Annabel Candy Co; Mountain Lion Preservation Fund; Cafe Renoir, Cafe Monet; Windward Traders; Nomura, Babcock & Brown. *Hobbies:* Music (plays violin and piano); Dance; World affairs; Women's issues; Plants, animals and the natural world; Photography; Sports; Travel; International art; Writing poetry. *Address:* 193 Mill Street, San Rafael, CA 949401, USA.

LENOIR Gloria Irma Cisneros Flores, b. 18 Aug. 1951, Monterrey, Nuevo Lean, Mexico. Business Owner/Manager. m. Walter Frank Lenoir, 6 June 1975, 2 daughters. *Education:* French and Art Studies, Institute for American Universities, Aix-en-Provence, France, 1971-72; BA, 1973, MA, 1974, French, Art, Austin College, Sherman, Texas, 1973; French Studies, University of Strasbourg, 1976; MBA, University of Texas, Austin, 1979. *Appointments:* Teacher, French, Sherman High School, Sherman, Texas, USA, 1973-74; Teacher, French, Spanish, 1974-77, Chair, Foreign Languages Department, 1975- 77, Lyndon Baines Johnson High School, Austin, Texas; Legislative Aide, Texas State Capitol, Austin, 1977-81, 1983; Stockbroker: Merrill Lynch, Pierce, Fenner & Smith Inc, Austin, 1981-83; Schneider, Bernet & Hickman Inc, Austin, 1983-84; Business Manager/Owner, Holleman Photographic Laboratories Inc, Austin, 1984-87, 1988-present; Stockbroker, Eppler, Guerin & Turner Inc, Austin, 1987-88. *Creative works:* Reparation to Victims of Crime, report for State Representative, 1977; Photographs published in Women in Space, 1979, Review, 1988; Photographs exhibited throughout Texas, 1979, 1988-. *Memberships:* Austin Investment Association; Austin College Volunteer Liaison Leads Programme; Central Presbyterian Church, Elder, Class of 1990, Co-Chair, Finance Committee, 1988, Clerk of the Session, 1989; Austin Chamber of Commerce, Participant in Advantage Austin 1988; American Cancer Society, Neighborhood Captain, Austin, 1982-86. *Honours:* Scholarship, Institute for American Universities, 1971-72; Brinegar Fellowship, Austin College, 1973- 74; Night on the Town Award, IBM, Austin, 1978; J.L.Mosle Scholarship, University of Texas, 1979; Volunteer Award, Hispanic Chamber of Commerce, Austin, 1986. *Hobbies:* Reading; Needlepoint; Embroidery; Walking; Writing; Travel. *Address:* 1202 West 29th Street, Austin, TX 78703, USA.

LENZER Irmingard I, b. 3 Sept. 1938, Munich, West Germany. Psychologist. 1 son, 1 daughter. *Education:* BA, 1964; Phd, 1969. *Appointments:* Teacher, Psychology, St Mary's University, 1969-; Neuropsychological Consultant, Nova Scotia Hospital, 1986-. *Publications:* Articles in professional journals. *Memberships:* New York Academy of Sciences; International Neuropsychological Society. *Address:* 1232 Edward Street, Halifax, NS, Canada, B3H 3H4, NS.

LEO Jacqueline, b. 19 Oct. 1946, New York City, USA. Editor. m. John Leo, 21 Jan. 1978, 3 daughters. *Education:* City University of New York, 1963-65. *Appointments:* Teacher, American International School, Duesseldorf, 1970-71; Senior Editor, Modern Bride, 1972-86; Editor in Chief, Child, 1986-88; Editor in Chief, Family Circle, 1988-. *Publications:* The New Woman's Guide to Getting Married, 1982. *Membership:* American Society of Magazine Editors. *Honours:* Mossesm Award for Editorial Excellence. *Hobbies:* Sports; Reading; Literacy Programmes for Adults & Children. *Address:* 20 Fifth Avenue, New York City, NY 10011, USA.

LEON Tania Justina, b. 14 May 1943, Havana, Cuba. Composer; Conductor. *Education:* MA, Music Education, Havana National Conservatory, 1965; BS Music Education 1973, MA Composition 1975, New York University, USA. *Appointments include:* Conductor, orchestras throughout USA, Central & South America, Italy, France, UK; Founder, Orchestra, Music Department (Music Director 1968-79), Dance Theatre of Harlem; Family Concert Series, Brooklyn Philharmonic Community, 1977-; Alvin Ailey American Dance Theatre 1983-; Whitney Museum Contemporary Music Concert series 1986-; Teaching Artist 1982-, Resident Composer 1985, Lincoln Centre Institute; Artistic Director, Composers Forum, New York, 1987;

Associate Professor of Composition, Brooklyn College, 1987; Various boards, panels. *Creative work includes:* Commissions, organisations including Brooklyn College, American Composers Orchestra, Affiliate Artists Inc, Whitney Museum, Brooklyn Philharmonic, Queen's Symphony Orchestra. *Memberships:* American Society of Composers, Authors & Publishers (ASCAP); American Music Centre Inc; Local 802, AFL-CIO. *Honours:* Awards from: National Endowment for Arts, 1975; CINTAS, 1976, 1979; National Council of Women, USA, 1980; Byrd Hoffman Foundation, 1981; City of Detroit, 1982; Queens Council on Arts, 1983; Meet the Composer, 1978-88; ASCAP, 1978-88; Dean Dixon, 1985; Manhattan Arts, 1985. *Address:* 35-20 Leverich Street, Jackson Heights, New York 11372, USA.

LEONARD Carolyn Marie, b 20 Nov. 1943, Portland, Oregon, USA. Educational Administrator. m. 8 Dec. 1962, 2 daughters. *Education:* BS, Business Administration, 1976; MS, Education, Portland State University, 1979. *Appointments:* Research Assistant, 1979-80, Evaluator, 1980-85, Co-ordinator, Multicultural/Multiethnic Education, 1985-, Portland Public Schools. *Publications:* Editor, African American Baseline Essays; Co-Author, Uniform Guidelines for Productivity and Workforce Utilization; Co-Producer, Videotape, Moving Toward Multicultural Education; Co-Author, Wole Soyinka, 1986. *Memberships:* National Council for Black Studies, President, Pacific NW Region; Chairperson, Oregon Commission on Black Affairs; Research Chairperson, Metropolitan Human Relations Commission; Oregon Black Resource Centre, President; many other professional organisations. *Honours:* Recipient, many honours and awards. *Hobbies:* Reading; Writing; Roller Skating. *Address:* Portland Public Schools, PO Box 3107, Portland, OR 97208, USA.

LERMAN Lisa Gabrielle, b. 4 Apr. 1955, Denver, Colorado, USA. Law Professor. m. Philip Gordon Schrag, 29 Dec. 1985, 1 son. *Education:* BA, Barnard College, Columbia University, 1976; JD, New York University School of Law, 1979; LLM, Georgetown University Law Center, 1984. *Appointments:* Staff Attorney, Center for Women Policy Studies, 1979- 81; Advocacy Fellow, Georgetown Law Center, 1982-84; Visiting Assistant Professor, West Virginia University School of Law, 1984-85; Associate, Lobel, Novins, Lamont & Flug, 1985-87; Visiting Assistant Professor, Catholic University Law School, Washington DC, 1987-. *Education:* Articles in Maryland Law Review; Harvard Women's Law Journal; Harvard Journal on Legislation, etc; Many publications on domestic violence law. *Memberships:* American Bar Association; Women's Legal Defense Fund; Women's Bar Association: New York University Public Interest Law Foundation; DC Coalition of Battered Women's Advocates. *Hobbies & Interests:* Travel; Sports; Film; Art history. Domestic violence; Family law; Legal ethics. *Address:* The Catholic University of America, Columbus School of Law, Washington, DC 20064, USA.

LERMAN Rhoda, b. 18 Jan. 1938, New York City, New York, USA. Writer. m. Robert Lerman, 1 son, 2 daughters. *Education:* BA, University of Miami, Coral Gables, Florida. *Appointments:* Visiting Professorships: University of Colorado, Hartwick College, Syracuse University and University of Buffalo; Eduard H Butler Chair in English Literature, SUNY at Buffalo, Spring 1990. *Publications:* Novels: Call Me Ishtar; The Girl That He Marries; Eleanor, A Novel; Book of the Night; God's Ear. *Memberships:* New York State Council on the Arts; PEN; Writers Guild of America. *Honours:* National Endowment of the Arts Grantee; Yaddo Fellowships; National Endowment for the Humanities; Distinguished Professor; Ampart, State Department Appointee, 1982, 1984. *Hobby:* Raising Newfoundlands. *Address:* c/o Owen Laster, Wm Morris Agency, 1350 Avenue of the Americas, New York, NY 10019, USA.

LESLIE Eloise Myretta Williams, b. 10 Sept. 1943, Louisiana, USA. EMployment Supervisor. m. Peyton H. Leslie, 2 sons, 2 daughters. *Education:* BS, 1961 *Appointments:* Bookkeeper, DRAG, 1975-76; Intake

Analyst, City of Kansas City, 1979-83; Employment Supervisor, 1983-. *Memberships:* Secretary, Human Relations Commission; Democratic Womens Federation; Board, Democracy Inc; Intenational Personnel Managers Association; *Honours:* Recipient various honours including: City of Kansas City Mayors Merit Award, 1987; Supermom Nominee, KMBC TV, 1988. *Hobbies:* Outdoor Sports; Reading; Craft. *Address:* 5720 Georgia Avenue, Kansas City, KS 66104, USA.

LESSING Doris (May), b. 22 Oct. 1919, Persia. Author. m. (1) Frank Charles Wisdom, 1939, dissolved 1943, 1 son, 1 daughter. (2) Gottfried Anton Nicholas Lessing, 1945, dissolved 1949, 1 son. *Publications:* The Grass is Singing, 1950 (filmed 1981); This Was the Old Chiefs Country, 1951; Martha Quest, 1952; Five, 1953; A Proper Marriage, 1954; Retreat to Innocence, 1956; Going Home, 1957; The Habit of Loving, 1957; A Ripple from the Storm, 1958; Fourteen Poems, 1959; In Pursuit of the English, 1960; The Golden Notebook, 1962; A Man and Two Women (short stories), 1963; African Stories, 1964; Landlocked, 1965; Particularly Cats, 1966 (non fiction); The Four-Gated City, 1969; Briefing for a Descent into Hell, 1971; The Story of a Non-Marrying Man and the Habit of Loving , 1972 (short stories); The Summer Before the Dark, 1973; The Memoirs of a Survivor, 1975 (filmed 1981); Collected stories: Vol 1, To Room Nineteen, 1978; Vol II, The Temptation of Jack Orkney, 1978; Canopus in Argos: Archives: Re Plant 5, Shikasta, 1979; The Marriages Between Zones Three, Four and Five, 1980; The Sirian Experiments, 1981; The Making of the Representative for Planet 8, 1982; The Sentimental Agents in the Volyen Empire, 1983; The Diaries of Jane Somers, 1984 (Diary of a Good Neighbour, 1983; If the Old Could...1984 published under pseudonym Jane Somers); The Good Terrorist, 1985; Prisons We Choose to Live Inside (non-fiction), 1986; A Sport of Nature, 1987; The Wind Blows Away Our Words (non-fiction), 1987; The Fifth Child, 1988 (novel); Play: Play with a Tiger, 1962. *Memberships:* Associate Member, AAAL, 1974; National Institute of Arts and Letters (US), 1974; Institute for Cultural Res, 1974; Honorary Fellow, MLA (America), 1974. *Honours:* Austrian State Prize for European Literature, 1981; Shakespeare Prize, 1982; Somerset Maugham Award, Society of Authors, 1954; Prix Medicis, 1976 for French translation, Carnet d'or; W H Smith Literary Award, 1986; Palermo prize, Premio Internazionale Mondello, 1987. *Address:* c/o Jonathan Clowes Ltd, 22 Prince Albert Road, London NW1 7ST, England.

LEVI-SCHAFFER Francesca, b. 14 Jan. 1955, Milan, Italy. Lecturer; Scientist. m. Jacob Schaffer, 11 July 1976, 1 daughter, 1 son. *Education:* Pharm. Doctor, University of Milan, 1978; PhD, Immunology, Weizmann Institute of Science, Removot, Israel, 1984. *Appointments:* Research Fellow, Immunology, Harvard Medical School, Boston, 1984-86; Lecturer, Assistant Professor, Hadassah Men School, Jerusalem, 1986-; Visiting Professor, Pharmacology, University of Milan, Italy, 1987-. *Publications:* several papers in professional journals. *Memberships:* Association of Italian Pharmacists; American Academy of Allergy & Clinical Immunology; Israeli Society of Immunology; Israeli Society of Allergy and Clinical Immunology; International Society for Immunopharmacology. *Honours:* Haim Weitzmann Fellowship, 1984. *Hobbies:* Music; Art; Philosophy. *Address:* Dept. Pharmacology, Hadassah Medical School, The Hebrew University of Jerusalem, Jerusalem, Israel.

LEVICK Myra Friedman, b. 20 Aug. 1924, Philadelphia, Pennsylvania, USA. Psychologist; Art Psychotherapist; Author. m. Leonard J. Levick, 26 Dec. 1943, 3 sons. *Education:* BFA, Moore College of Art, 1963; MEd, Temple University, 1967; PhD, Bryn Mawr College, 1982. Licensed Clinical Psychologist. *Appointments:* Art Therapist, Psychiatric Unit, Albert Einstein Medical Centre, Philadelphia, 1963-67; Professor & Director, Graduate training, art, music & dance therapy, Hahneman University, Philadelphia, 1967-86; Professor, Consultant, 1986-. *Creative works include:* Books: They Could Not Talk & So They Drew,

1983; Mommy, Daddy, Look What I'm Saying, 1986. Also: Various articles, refereed journals; Editor- in-Chief, Arts in Psychotherapy international journal; Paintings exhibited, juried shows. *Memberships:* Founder, 1st President, Honorary Life Member, American Art Therapy Association; American & Pennsylvania Psychological Associations; Ortho Psychiatric Association; American & International Societies for Expression of Psychopathology. *Honours:* Myra Levick Scholarship Fund, Hahnemann University & American Art Therapy Association; Outstanding Alumni, Moore College of Art; Humanitarian Award, Bruce Nippon Society; Honorary Associate Member, Hahneman University Alumni Association; Graduate Faculty Award. *Hobbies:* Painting; Sculpture; Research, Child Development & Children's Drawings. *Address:* 21710 Palm Circle, Boca Raton, Florida 33433, USA.

LEVIN Vera, b. 27 Apr. 1929, Harbin, China. Lawyer. 1 son, 2 daughters. *Education:* BA 1979, LLB 1983, University of New South Wales, Australia. *Appointments:* Australian Legal Aid Office, 1983-86; Legal Aid Commission, Victoria, 1986-. *Publication:* Chapter, You'll Be Fifty Anyway, in Different Lives, ed. Jocelyn A. Scutt. *Memberships:* Law Society of New South Wales; Law Institute of Victoria. *Hobbies:* Songwriting; Music; Reading; Public speaking; Travel; Adviser & concert manager to daughters, Aura & Liana Levin. *Address:* Apartment 3, 35 Narong Road, Caulfield, Melbourne, Victoria 3161, Australia.

LEVINE Judith Dee, b. 2 Sept. 1950, New York, USA. Attorney. *Education:* BA, Kirkland College, 1972; JD, University of Denver, 1975. *Appointments:* Brownstein Hyatt Farber & Madden, 1975-78; Krupman, Fromson, Bownas & Selcer, 1979-80; Guren, Merritt, Feibel, Sogg & Cohen, 1980-84; Benesch, Friedlander, Coplan & Aronoff, 1984-. *Publications:* Articles in journals & magazines. *Memberships:* Chairman, ABA Subcommittee on Mortgage Loan Commitments for Lenders & Borrowers; Women Lawyers of Franklin County; American, Ohio & Columbus Bar Associations. *Honours:* Order of St Ives, 1974. *Hobbies:* Skiing; Tennis; Photography. *Address:* 88 East Broad Street Suite 900, Columbus, OH 43215, USA.

LEVINE Rosalind P, b. 20 Aug. 1936, Bridgeport, Connecticut, USA. Architect. m. Robert S Levine, 30 Aug. 1959. 2 daughters. *Education:* Bachelor of Architectur, Syracuse University, New York, 1959; Ecole des Beaux Arts, Fontainebleau, France, 1957. *Memberships:* American Institute of Architects; Connecticut Society of Architects. *Hobbies:* Painting; Graphics; Crafts. *Address:* 16 Wayfaring Road, Norwalk, Connecticut 06851, USA.

LEVINE Suzanne Marin, b. 28 June 1951, New York City, USA. Podiatric Surgeon. m. 28 Oct. 1972, 2 daughters. *Education:* BA, City University, New York, 1971; MS, Columbia University, 1972; Doctor, Podiatric Medicine, New York College of Podiatric Medicine, 1977. *Appointments:* Private Practice, 1978-. *Publication:* My Feet Are Killing Me, 1983. *Memberships:* New York College of Podiatric Medicine; Albert Einstein School of Medicine, Founder. *Honours:* Cum Laude, Brooklyn College, 1971; Diplomate, American Board of Podiatric Surgery, 1985. *Hobbies:* Skiing; Tennis; Writing; Playing Piano. *Address:* 930 Fifth Avenue, Apt. 10B, New York, NY 10021, USA.

LEVINE Janice Ruth, b. 4 Mar. 1954, Cleveland, Ohio, USA. Psychologist. m. Brian Richard Igoe, 31 Aug. 1980, 1 son, 1 daughter. *Education:* BA, cum laude, Yale University, 1976; MA, 1979, PhD, 1983, Harvard University. *Appointments:* Freshman Counsellor, Yale University, 1976-77; Advisor, Psychology, Harvard Univesity, 1979-81; Private Practice, Lexington, 1981-; Staff Psychologist, Herbert Lipton Community Mental Health Centre, 1983-85. *Publications:* Articles in professional journals. *Memberships:* American Psychological Association; Massachusetts Psychological Assocation; National Register of Health

Service Providers in Psychology; American Board of Medical Psychotherapists; etc. *Honours:* Recipient, various honours and awards. *Hobbies:* Violin Performance; Tennis; Skiing; etc. *Address:* 76 Bedford St., Suite 32, Lexington, MA 02173, USA.

LEVY Anne, b. 29 Sept. 1934, Perth, Australia. Member of Parliament. m. Keith Percival Barley, 4 May 1957, deceased 1975. 1 son, 1 daughter. *Education:* MSc, University of Adelaide, 1962. *Appointments:* Tutor in Genetics 1959-64, Senior Tutor in Genetics 1965-75, University of Adelaide; Elected Member of Legislative Council of South Australia, 1975, re-elected 1982; President, Legislative Council of South Australia, 1986 (First woman to be a presiding officer in Any Australian Parliament). *Memberships:* Patron, Humanist Society of South Australia; Officer bearer, Family Planning Assoc of Sth Aust; Abortion Law Repeal Assoc of Sth Aust; Australian Labour Party (Sth Aust Branch); Council for Civil Liberties (Sth Aust); Council of University of Adelaide. *Honour:* Australian Humanist of the Year Award, 1986. *Hobbies:* Theatre; Women's issues; Tennis. *Address:* Parliament House, Adelaide, South Australia, Australia.

LEWIN Rebecca, b. 5 May 1954, Dover, New Jersey, USA. Writer. *Education:* AB, Syracuse University, 1977; MA, City College of New York, 1981. *Career:* Columnist, Fiction Writer, Playwright; Readings of plays presented at HB Playwrights Foundation, 1984, and American Renaissance Theater, 1988; Artist; Participated in group exhibits of paintings, Ceres Gallery and Grey Art Gallery, New York City. *Publications:* Contributions in Newsday, Journal of Commerce, San Francisco Chronicle, New York Native (columnist), The Advocate, Jewish Daily Forward, Poets and Peace International, Ikon. *Memberships:* Feminist Writers Guild, New York Chapter Steering Committee; National Writers Union; International Platform Association; Dramatists Guild; Authors League of America; Coalition for a Nuclear-Free Harbor, Political Strategy Committee. *Honours:* Bennett Cerf Award, Columbia University, 1981; Goodman Fund Prize for Extended Fiction, City College of New York, 1983; Winner, PEN/National Endowment for the Arts Syndicated Fiction Competition, 1985; Included in Pushcart Prize: Best of the Small Presses anthology's list of outstanding writers, 1988. *Address:* 203 West 107th Street 5B, New York, NY 10025, USA.

LEWIS Anne McCutcheon, b. 15 Oct. 1943, New Orleans, Louisiana, USA. Architect. m. Ronald B. Lewis, 2 Oct. 1971, 2 sons. *Education:* BA, Radcliffe College, 1965; MArch, Harvard University Graduate School of Design, 1970. *Appointments:* Skidmore, Owings & Merrill, 1969-72; Keyes Lethbridge & Condon, 1972-75; Anne McCutcheon Lewis AIA, 1976-81; McCartney Lewis Architects, 1981-. *Creative works include:* Many residences (new houses & additions), Washington DC area. *Memberships include:* Design Committee 1986-, American Institute of Architects; Awards Chair 1981-82, Washington Chapter, AIA; Alumni Council, Harvard Graduate School of Design, 1979-82. *Honours:* 1st award, & citation, historic preservation, Washington Chapter AIA, 1983; Merit award, Mayor Barry's Environmental Design Awards, 1989. *Hobbies include:* Board, Friends Non-Profit Housing Inc. *Address:* McCartney Lewis Architects, 1503 Connecticut Avenue NW, Washington DC 20036, USA.

LEWIS Janet, b. 17 Aug. 1899, Chicago, Illinois, USA. m. Yvor Winters, 22 June 1926, 1 son, 1 daughter. *Education:* AA, Lewis Institute, 1918; PhB, University of Chicago, 1920. *Appointments:* Instructor, Lewis Institute, 1921; Lecturer in English, Stanford University, Stanford, California, 1960, 1969, 1970; Lecturer in English, University of California at Berkeley, 1978. *Publications:* The Invasion, novel, 1932; The Wife of Martin Guerre, 1941; Against a Darkening Sky, 1942; The Trial of Soren Quist, 1946; The Ghost of M. Scarron, 1959. *Memberships:* American PEN; National Association for the Advancement of Colored People; ACLU. *Honours:* Shelley Award, 1946; Guggenheim

Fellow, 1951; Robert Kirsch Award, 1985. *Address:* 143 West Portola Avenue, Los Altos, CA 94022, USA.

LEWIS Jenny, b. 17 Oct. 1945, Macclesfield, England. Fashion Designer. Divorced, 1 son, 1 daughter. *Education:* Virgo Fidelis Convent, 1957-61. *Appointments:* Managing Director, Jenny Lewis Fashions Limited. *Memberships:* Foreign Correspondents Club. *Hobbies:* Textile Art; China; Inspired People; History; Future Vision; World Peace. *Address:* Swire House, Chater Road, Hong Kong.

LEWIS Kathleen S., b. 4 Dec. 1944, Greeenville, South Carolina, USA. Writer; Rehabilitation Counsellor. m. 29 Jan. 1966, 2 sons. *Education:* BSN, Vanderbilt University School of Nursing, 1966; Pastoral Care, Georgia Baptist Medical Center, 1981; MS, Rehabilitation Counselling, 1986, Doctoral study, Family Sociology, 1988, Georgia State University; Registered Nurse; Certified Medical Psychotherapist. *Appointments:* Staff/Charge Nurse: Vanderbilt University Hospital, Nashville, Tennessee, 1966; Methodist Evangelical Hospital, Louisville, Kentucky, 1966-67; Clinical Instructor, Kentucky State University School of Nursing, Frankfort, 1968-73; Assistant Director, Medco Nursing Home, Frankfort, 1973; Language Missionary, Baptist Home Mission Board, Baltimore, Maryland, 1973-75; Field Nurse, Instructive Visiting Nurse Association, Baltimore, 1974-75; Rehabilitation Specialist, International Rehabilitation Association, Norcross, Georgia, 1975-76; Field Nurse, Area Supervisor, Metro Atlanta Visiting Nurse Association, Atlanta, Georgia, 1976-78; Freelance Writer, 1978-; Editorial Board, Humane Medicine, 1984-; Private volunteer counselling practice, 1985-; Advisory Committee: Arthritis Today, 1987-88; Masters Rehabilitation Counselling Programme, Georgia State University, Atlanta, 1987-; Lectures, workshops, media appearances. *Publications:* Successful Living with Chronic Illness...Celebrating the Joys of Life, 1985; Various articles concerning psychological problems of chronic illness especially arthritis. *Memberships:* Arthritis Foundation Allied Health Professionals Association; Georgia Arthritis Health Professionals; American Board of Medical Psychotherapists; Committees, Arthritis Foundation; Board of Directors, offices, Lupus Foundation of America Inc; Chaplain, Georgia Baptist Hospital, Atlanta, 1980-81. *Honours:* 1st Place, National Rehabilitation Association Literary Contest, 1983; American Lupus Society Hall of Fame, 1985; Hardee's Hometown Hero, 1986. *Address:* 1651 Northlake Springs Court, Decatur, GA 30033, USA.

LEWIS Lesley Lisle, Lady, b. 4 July 1924, Dunedin, New Zealand. Housewife. m. Anthony Lewis, 12 Sept. 1959. *Education:* St. Hilda's Collegiate School, Dunedin; New Zealand School of Physiotherapy, 1943-45. *Appointments:* Physiotherapist, New Zealand, 1945-51; Queen Elizabeth Hospital, 1951-59. *Memberships:* several Charity committees. *Honours:* Hon. FRAM. *Hobbies:* Golf; Travel; Gardening. *Address:* High Rising, Holdfast Lane, Haslemere, Surrey, England.

LEWIS Patricia Sue, b. 11 May 1952, Milwaukee, Wisconsin, USA. Public Relations Executive. *Education:* BA, Ripon College; CEP, Institut D'Etudes Politiques, Paris, France; MS, Northwestern University. *Appointments:* Manager, PR, General Dynamics Corporation, 1975-80; Account Executive, Public Communications Inc., 1980-81; Director, Public Relations, The Marketing Centre, 1983-84; Principal, Public Relations Services Consulting, 1985-. *Publications:* Editor, A Mother Goose in Stitches; Contributor to: Public Relations Journal, other professional journals. *Memberships:* Public Relations Society of America; Director, Hospice Care Inc; Board of Directors; Northside Centers Inc., 1988. *Honours:* Accredited Public Relations Society of America, 1984; Honour, Institut D'Etudes Politiques, 1973. *Hobbies:* Weight Training; Floral Arrangement. *Address:* Public Relations Services, 3314 Henderson Blvd., Ste. 106, Tampa, FL 33609, USA.

LEWIS Victoria, b. 16 Aug. 1945, Jacksonville, Florida, USA. Educator; Counsellor. m. Rodney Lewis, 5 Jan. 1976, 3 sons, 2 daughters. *Education:* AA, Los Angeles Valley College, 1975; BA, Immaculate Heart College, 1977; MS, Education, Mount St Mary's College, 1982. *Appointments:* Computer programmer & operator, 1964-71; Administrator, grant writer, group counsellor, 1978-81; Marriage, family & child counsellor, 1981-84; Secondary teacher, Los Angeles Unified Schools, 1984-. *Publication:* Effects of Multi-Modality Therapy Program on Learning Disabled Juvenile Delinquents, professional study. *Memberships:* Parent Committee, Van Nuys Teen Centre; National Education Association; National Council of Teachers of English; California Association for Marriage & Family Therapists; California School Counselling Association; California Personnel & Guidance Association. *Honours:* 2 education scholarships, Mount St Mary College, 1981-82; Certificate of Completion, Grantsmanship Writing, 1980; Grant, scholarship, Immaculate Heart College, 1976-77; 2-year Scholarship, Upper Division, Ford Foundation, 1975. *Hobbies:* Writing music lyrics; Oil painting; Crafts; Gardening; Camping; Yoga. *Address:* PO Box 2094, Van Nuys, California 91404, USA.

LEWIS-SMITH Anne Elizabeth, b. 14 Apr. 1925, London, England. Editor; Publisher; Poet. m. Charles Peter Lewis-Smith, 17 May 1944, 1 son, 2 daughters. *Education:* BSc. *Appointments:* Feature writer, Stamford Mercury, Northampton Life, various other magazines, 1962-; Editor, Aerostat 1971-76, Crownline 1977-80, BAFM Yerbook 1983-, Envoi 1983-; Publisher & owner, Envoi Poets public. *Publications:* Seventh Bridge, 1963; The Beginning, 1964; Flesh & Flowers, 1967; Dandelion Flavour, 1971; Dinas Head, 1980; Places & Passions, 1986; In the Dawn, 1987. *Memberships:* Chair, Poetry Day, London, 1967, 1970; Committee, BBAC; Steering Committee, East of England Arts Council, 1969-70; Fellow, PEN; Honorary member, Balloon Federation (USA), Pioneer Balloon Club (South Africa), Balloon Club (Dublin); Council, BAFM. *Honours:* Services to aviation; Tissandier Award, 1978; Debbie Warley Award, 1983; Ballooniana Priset, Sweden. *Hobbies:* Poetry; Ballooning; People; Islands. *Address:* Pen Ffordd, Newport, Pembrokeshire, Dyfed SA42 0QT, Wales.

LEWIS-SMITH Jennifer Susan, b. 4 Sept. 1949, Stamford, Lincolnshire, England. Illustrator; Managing Director. m.(1) Wayne Parkin, 25 Nov. 1972, div 22 Nov. 1988. 2 sons, 1 daughter. m.(2) Richard d'Alton, 11 Aug. 1989. *Education:* Northampton School of Art, 1966-68; Winchester School of Art, 1968-70. *Appointments:* John Lewis Partnership, 1970-72; Unilever, 1972; Own company, Berkshire Buffets (Outside Catering), 1984-86; Public Relations Officer, Henley Distance Learning, 1986-87; now runs succesful design studio called Design Matters. *Address:* Chaucers, Oare, Hermitage, Nr Newbury, Berkshire RG16 9SD, England.

LEWISON-SINGER Rita Kirschner, b. 3 May 1939, New York City, New York, USA. Business Owner; Professional Development Specialist. m. Lawrence Edward Singer, 24 May 1987, 1 son, 3 daughters. *Education:* University of California, Los Angeles, 1956-57; BA, American Civilisation, 1960, MEd, English, 1969, Doctoral course work, Linguistics, 1969-76, University of Miami, Coral Gables; Several Human Potential training courses. *Appointments:* Faculty, Miami-Dade Community College, Miami, Florida, 1973-83; Faculty, University of Miami, Coral Gables, Florida, 1973-83; President, Lewison & Shapo Inc., 1978-87; President, Rita Lewison-Singer & Associates Inc., Professional Development Specialists, 1987-; Speaker and Presenter, workshops and seminars; Co-Host, Educational Cable Television Series. *Creative works include:* Written materials for Exxon Corporation: English Language Diagnostic Portfolio, E I A Language Instruction Policy Suggestions for Evaluating English Proficiency Levels (report) and Guidelines for Research Report Writing (instructional package); Executive producer: 10-minute fundraising video, 1986.

Memberships: Women in Communications; National Association of Women Business Owners; Phi Delta Kappa. *Hobbies:* Tennis; Skiing; Music; Dance. *Address:* 9700 South Dixie Highway, Suite 610, Miami, FL 33156, USA.

LEWITAN Rachelle Ann, b. Tel Aviv, Israel. Barrister At Law. m. Dr George Levy, Feb. 1985. 2 sons. *Education:* BA; LLB (Hons), 1974. *Appointments:* Associate, Corr & Corr (Solicitors), 1974-77; Admitted to Victorian Bar, Australia, 1977; Barrister, 1977-; Member, University Council, Monash University, 1984; Lieutenant Royal Australian Navy (Royal Australian Naval Legal Reserve Panel). *Membership:* Victorian Bar Association. *Honours:* First Woman elected to Victorian Bar Council (for 100 years); Served on Bar Council, 1982-85. *Hobbies:* Skiing; Reading; Languages; Cooking; Cycling. *Address:* Owen Dixon Chambers, 205 William Street, Melbourne, Victoria, Australia 3000.

LEY Alice Chetwynd, b. 12 Oct. 1913, Halifax, Yorkshire, England. Novelist. m. Kenneth James Ley, 3 Feb. 1945. 2 sons. *Education:* Diploma in Sociology, London University, 1962. *Appointments:* Birmingham Municipal Bank, 1930's; Tutor in Creative Writing, Social History and Sociology (part-time), Harrow Education Committee, College of Further Education, 1963-82. *Publications:* 19 historical novels published in UK, USA and other countries. Masquerade of Vengeance to be published in 1989. *Memberships:* Chairman, 1970-72, Romantic Novelists' Association; Society of Women Writers & Journalists; Jane Austen Society. *Honour:* Gilchrist Award, London University. *Hobbies:* Reading; Music; The Theatre; Foreign travel; Walking; Gardening; Family. *Address:* 42 Cannonbury Avenue, Pinner, Middx HA5 1TS, England.

LEYIMU Hilda Osilelume, b. Ibadan, Nigeria. Exercise Physiologist. m. Olatubosun Leyimu, 14 Nov. 1988. *Education:* BEd Physical Education, University of Benin, 1985; MSc, Exercise Physiology, University of Ibadan, 1987. *Appointments:* Sports Secretary, Rivers State Sports Council, 1986; Volunteer Worker to Lesotho, 1988 (Teacher at Sefika High School); Physical Education Teacher and Sports Coach, National University of Lesotho. *Publications:* A comparative study of the fitness level of athletes and non athletes; The effects of Physical Fitness on Abdominal Fitness; A Comparative Study of the Physical Fitness of Children from Different Socio-Economic Status. *Memberships:* National Association of Health, Physical Education and Recreation; Association of Sports Medicine and Exercise Physiologists, Nigeria. *Honours:* National Honours Award, Nigeria, 1986; Presidential National Service Award, 1986; State Honours Award, 1986. *Hobbies:* Jogging; Squash; Running a physical fitness programme and class. *Address:* No 30 Oshuntokun Avenue, Bodija, Ibadan, Nigeria.

LI Fang-hua, b. 6 Jan. 1932, Hong Kong. Professor. m. Fan Hai-fu, 1 May 1960. 1 son, 1 daughter. *Education:* BSc, Department of Physics, Leningrad University, USSR, 1956. *Appointments:* Assistant, 1956; Research Associate, 1962; Associate Professor, 1979; Professor, 1986-, Institute of Physics, Chinese Academy of Sciences. *Publications:* About 100 published papers on electron diffraction, electron microscopy, crystallography, quasi crystals, etc. *Memberships:* The Chinese Physics Society; Vice President, The Chinese Electron Microscopy Society. *Honours:* Award (3rd grade) of achievement on science and technology, The Chinese Academy of Science, 1979; Award (2nd grade) of Achievement on science and technology, The Chinese Academy of Science, 1985. *Address:* Institute of Physics, Academia Sinica, Beijing, Peoples Republic of China.

LIANG Vera Beh-Yuin Tsai, b. 29 July 1946, China. Physician. m. Hanson S. Liang, 6 Nov. 1971, 2 sons. *Education:* MB,BS, Faculty of Medicine, University of Hong Kong, 1969. *Appointments:* Intern, Hong Kong 1969-70, Massachusetts, USA 1970-71; Resident, Long

Island Jewish Medical Centre, New York, 1971-73; Fellow, Albert Einstein College of Medicine, NY, 1973-75; Instructor, Downstate Medical Centre, State University of New York (SUNY), 1975-79; Assistant Professor, SUNY Stonybrook, 1979; Medical Director, Hillside Eastern Queen's Clinic, NY, 1978-. *Memberships:* American Psychiatric Association; Nassau Psychiatric Society; American Academy of Child Psychiatry; American Medical Women's Association. *Interests include:* Eastern religion. *Address:* 96-09 Springfield Boulevard, Queen's Village, New York 11429, USA.

LIBISZOWSKA Zofia, b. 18 Feb. 1918, Krakow, Poland. Professor of Modern History. m. Stefan Libiszowski, 23 June 1943. 2 sons, 1 daughter. *Education:* Undergraduate, University of Lwow, 1936-39; Master of Arts, University of Warsaw, 1942; Phil Dr, 1950, Docent 1956, Professor extraord 1972, Professor ord, full, 1980-. *Appointments:* University of Lodz, Poland 1945- positions include: Head, Section of Modern History 1973-81, Vice Dean, Faculty of Phil and Hist, 1981-84; Dean of the Faculty, 1984-87; Professor Emeritus, part-time employed, 1988-. *Publications:* Selected books in Polish language: Polish Opinion on the American Revolution in XVIII c, 1962; Polish Mission in London 1769-1795, 1967; Polish Life in London, 1972; The Sun King, 1967; France in the Time of Encyclopaedia, 1973; Thomas Paine, 1976; Thomas Jefferson, 1984; Louis XV-th in print; 250 articles and studies in French and English. *Memberships:* T. Paine Society, Nottingham; European Association for American Studies; EAAS; Scientific Society in Lodz; Member of the Board, Polish Historical Society; Member of the Committee of Historical Science, Polish Academy; Poland-US Society; Polish-French Friendship Society and others. *Honours:* Decorations: Knight 1973, Officer 1986, of the Cross of the Polish People's Republic; Awards, Minister of Education, No II, 3 times, No 1, 1988; Scientific Award, City of Lodz, 1985; Many prizes from University of Lodz. *Hobbies:* History; Travel. *Address:* Armii Ludowej 29/7, 90 248 Lodz, Poland.

LICENCE Dianne Elizabeth Watson, b. 21 Apr. 1941, Danbury, Connecticut, USA. Store Manager; Office Manager; Interior Decorator. m. Edward Albert Licence, 30 Sept. 1961, 1 son. *Education:* Graduate, Bookkeeping/Business, Danbury High School Adult Education, 1959; Certificates, Small Business Association 1975, Brookfield High School 1976, West Connecticut State College 1989. *Appointments:* Laboratory technician, Barden Corporation, 1959-61; Owner, World of Fabrics, 1964-65; Office Manager, Sperry Controls 1965-67, Licence HTG & CLG 1973-; Newtown Color Center 1978-87; Store Manager & Interior Designer, Newtown Color Center, 1987-. *Memberships:* Small Business Association; Public Relations Director 1987-88, Chamber of Commerce; Offices Chairman, Brookfield Youth Committee, 1985, 1986, 1987-. *Hobbies:* Watercolour painting work in private collections; Reading; Needlework, crochet, sewing; Home decorating; Travel; Meeting people. *Address:* 11 Powder Horn Hill Road, Brookfield Center, Connecticut 06804, USA.

LICHTENBERG Jacqueline, b. 25 Mar. 1942, Flushing, Long Island, New York, USA. Writer. m. 11 Sept. 1966. 2 daughters. *Education:* BS Chemistry, University of California at Berkeley, 1964. *Publications:* Sime/Gen Universe: House of Zeor, 1974; Unto Zeor, Forever, 1978; First Channel, with Jean Lorrah, 1980; Mahogany Trinrose, 1981; Channel's Destiny, with Jean Lorrah, 1982; RenSime, 1984; Zelerod's Doom, with Jean Lorrah, 1986. Kren Universe (Book of the First Lifewave): Molt Brother, 1982; City of a Million Legends, 1985. Dushau University: Dushau, 1985; Farfetch, 1985; Outreach, 1986. Those of My Blood, 1988; Star Trek Lives!, with Sondra Marshak and Joan Winston, 1975. numerous short stories in magazines. *Memberships:* Science Fiction Writers of America Speakers' Bureau; Board of Directors, North American Time Festivals, Inc; Founder, Star Trek Welcommittee. *Honours:* Romantic Times Award, Best Science Fiction

Writer, 1985. *Address:* PO Box 290, Monsey, New York 10977, USA.

LIEBERMAN Rochelle Phyllis, b. 27 June 1940, Brooklyn, New York, USA. Relocation Company Executive. m. Melvyn Lieberman, 10 June 1961, 2 sons. *Education:* AB, Brooklyn College, 1961; MEd, Duke University, 1977; Certificate, Bacon & Company School of Real Estate, 1978; Real Estate Licensed Broker, North Carolina, 1978. *Appointments:* Teacher, Brooklyn Public Schools, 1961-64; Instructor, Carolina Friends' School, Durham, NC, 1967-70; Graduate intern 1974-75, faculty adviser 1975-76, Duke University; Sales associate, Kelly Matherly, Durham, 1978-81; President, Shelli Inc, 1981-. *Memberships:* Past Secretary, Durham Chapter, Women's Council of Realtors; Past Treasurer, Duke Forest Association; Durham Business & Professional Womens Club; League of Women Voters; National Association of Female Executives; Durham & Chapel Hill Board of Realtors; Duke University Eye Center Advisory Board. *Honour:* Kappa Delta Pi, education honour society, 1977. *Hobbies:* Piano; Walking; Literature; Knitting; Writing. *Address:* 1110 Woodburn Road, Durham, North Carolina 27705, USA.

LIEBES Raquel, b. 28 Aug 1938, El Salvador, Central America. 2 sons, 1 daughter. *Education:* BA, Sarah Lawrence College, 1960; MEd., Harvard University, 1961; MA, Yale University, 1962; Oxford University, 1989. *Appointments:* Spanish Instructor: Sarah Lawrence College, 1958-60; Yale University, 1964-65. *Publications:* Glossary of Spanish Medical Terms, 1967-. *Memberships:* Founding Member, John F. Kennedy Center. *Honours:* Honourary Consul, Government of El Salvador, 1977-80; Lecturer, American University, 1989-90; Lecturer, University Georgetown, both in Washington, DC, USA. *Hobbies:* History of Great Britain; European History; Comparative Literature; Art; Music. *Address:* 700 New Hampshire Ave., NW, Washington, DC 20037, USA.

LIEBHABER Josephine Gorliss, b. 2 Feb. 1917, Thelan, North Dakota, USA. Lecturer; Workshop Director; Poet; Freelance Writer. m. Louis J Liebhaber, 19 June 1960. *Education:* BS, Winona State University, 1953; MS, Mankato State University, 1956; EdD, Teachers University, 1974; University of Minnesota; University of Minnesota, Duluth; University of Northern Colorado; Northwestern University; University of Hawaii. *Appointments:* Saleslady, Dayton's Minneapolis; Receptionist, Deavid Shearer, Attorney, Minneapolis; Teacher, High School English, College Bound, Wells, Minnesota, 1945-82. *Publications:* Play: Touches of Heritage. Poetry: The Song Alone; American Poetry Anthology, 1983; The Mocassin; Our World's Best Loved Poems, 1984; A Treasure of Lyric Poetry; Spotlight Review; Lite News, 1988. *Memberships:* One of Founders, Southern Minnesota Poetry Society, Mankato; Founder, Home and School Association; PTA President and Secretary; Founder, Wells Hospital Student Loan Fund; Founder, Wells Blue Birds Campfire Groups; Secretary, Graduate Women; Auxiliary, American Legion; Founder, Local Girls State, American Association of University Women; Minnesota Council of Teachers of English. *Honours include:* Honorary Doctor of Divinity for outstanding contribution to world peace, Church Council; Invitational Audience with Pope Pius, Castle Gondolfo, Rome, Italy, 7 Aug 1957; MFT Citation and Life Membership, 1982; Golden Poetry Award, 1985; Silver Poet Award, 1986; CTE Legislative Committee, Publication Evaluation; NCTE Speaker Committee, Award of Merit; Commemorative Medal of Honour; 1987 Presidential Achievement Award; Honorary Fellow, John F Kennedy Library Foundation; Minnesota Science Fair Judge; Ronald Reagan Presidential Foundation Library; Scholarship Committee AAUW; Private White House Reception and Spring Meeting, 1988. *Hobbies:* Creative Writing; Freelance Writing; Fishing; Reading; Sports; Music. *Address:* 36½ Franklin W, Wells, MN 56097, USA.

LIEBLING-KAHAN Rochelle, b. 5 Sept. 1939, Chicago, USA. Lawyer; Pianist. m. Barry Kahan, 22 Sept.

1962, 1 daughter, Kara. *Education:* BA, 1959, JD, Northwestern University School of Law, 1963. *Appointments:* Attorney, Treasury Department Washington DC; Currently, President Educational Planning Incorporated, makers of College Decision. *Appearances:* Piano Soloist, Chicago Symphony, North Side Symphony, Community Symphony, Benton Harbour Symphony, Rockford Symphony, Evanston Symphony; Recitals in Midwest; Appeared on Jack Benny, Milton Berle, Arthur Godfrey; Currently part of a duo piano team, Liebling-Kahan and Trawick, featured at Houston Festival, 1982. *Memberships:* President, Evanston Junior Music Club; President, Chicago Woman's Council; Kidney Foundation; President, Kappa Beta Phi; Tuesday Musical Club; Historian, 1989. *Honours:* Woman of the Day, WAIT Radio; Recipient, numerous music awards including, Stillman Kelly. *Hobbies:* Art. *Address:* 4 Rain Hollow, Houston, TX 77024, USA.

LIEBRENZ-HIMES Marilyn Louise, b. 3 Aug. 1944, Minneapolis, Minnesota, USA. Associate Professor of Business Administration; Author; Consultant. m. James W Himes, 13 Oct. 1986. 4 sons. *Education:* BA, Wheaton College, 1966; MA 1973, PhD 1980, Michigan State University. *Appointments:* Teacher, Illinois, Hawaii, Thailand, 1966-68; Journalist, Iran, Italy, 1968-70; Editor, Law Library of Congress, USA, 1970- 72; Program Coordinator, Michigan State University, 1972-80; Professor of Business admin, GWU, 1980-. *Publications:* Books: Transfer of Technology: US Multinationals and Eastern Europe, 1982; International Business, 1985; Study Guide to Advertising, 1989. *Memberships:* Program Chairperson, International Collegiate Conference 1985, Vice President, Programs for Metro Washington DC Chapter 1984-86, American Marketing Association; Academy of International Business, Local Arrangements Chair, 1984; MacroMarketing Group, Conference Chair, 1985. *Honours:* Invited guest lecturer/foreign expert, Beijing University of International Business and Economics, 1984; Awarded, GWU Dilthey Fellowship for interdisciplinary study, 1982; Awarded, GWU Summer Research Grant, 1981. *Hobbies:* Sailing (racing); Writing; Skiing; Tennis; Photography; Gold. Interests: International management and marketing. *Address:* 783 Ruxshire Drive, Arnold, Maryland 21012, USA.

LIEBSCHUTZ Sarah Fisher, b. 24 Nov. 1934, Pennsylvania, USA. Professor of Political Science & Public Administration. m. Sanford J. Liebschutz, 26 Aug. 1956, 1 son, 1 daughter. *Education:* AB, Mount Holyoke College, 1956; PhD, Political Science, Universty of Rochester, 1971. *Appointments:* State University of New York, 1970-75, 1977-; Brookings Institution, 1975-77. *Publications:* Books: Federal Aid to Rochester, 1984; Bargaining Under Federalism, 1991. Monographs, articles, book chapters, over 30 on American intergovernmental relations. *Memberships:* American Political Science Association; American Society of Public Administration. *Honours:* Phi Beta Kappa, 1956; Fellowship, Rockefeller Institute, 1985; Grant, Ford Foundation, 1987; Alumnae Medal of Honour, Mount Holyoke College, 1986. *Address:* Department of Political Science, State University of New York, Brockport, NY 14420, USA.

LIEF Nina R, b. 12 Feb. 1907, Liberty, New York, USA. Director, Early Childhood Development Center. m. Dr Victor F Lief, 31 May 1932. 1 daughter. *Education:* AB, Barnard College; MD, New York University Medical School. *Appointments:* Assistant Professor, Child Psychiatry, Tulane Medical School, New Orleans, 1959-63; Director, Child Psychiatry, New York School Psychiatry, 1963-68; Associate Professor, Clinical Psychiatry, New York Medical College, 1963-. *Publications:* First Year of Life; Second Year of Life. *Memberships:* American Medical Association, Life Fellow; American Academy Pediatrics, Fellow; American Academy Child Psychiatry; American Academy of Science. *Honours:* Board Certified in Pediatrics, 1944; Board Certified in Psychiatry, 1961; Board Certified in Child Psychiatry, 1965. *Hobbies:*

Theatre; Music; Politics. *Address:* 61 Signal Hill Road, Wilton, Connecticut 86097, USA.

LIER Nancy Jean, b. 21 Sep. 1942, Breckenridge, Michigan, USA. Director of Medical Technology; Medical Educator. m. James William Lier, 20 June 1964, 1 son. *Education:* BS, Medical Technology, Madonna College, Livonia, Michigan, 1964; Postgraduate work, University of Kansas, Kansas City, Missouri, 1976-77; MS, Science Administration, Central Michigan University, Mt Pleasant, 1985. *Appointments:* Supervisor, Immunohaematology, 1964-66, 1967-69, Supervisor, Microbiology, 1968-69, Director, School of Medical Technology, 1967-, St Mary's Medical Center, Saginaw, Michigan; Staff Technologist, Flint Medical Laboratory, 1966-67; Various academic appointments, Grand Valley State University, Allendale, Central Michigan University, Mt Pleasant, University Center, Saginaw Valley State University, Aquinas College, Grand Rapids, Lake Superior State College, Sault Ste Marie, Nazareth College, Kalamazoo, Madonna College, Livonia, Michigan State University, East Lansing, Michigan Technological University, Houghton, 1967-; Adjunct Faculty, University Center, Saginaw Valley State University, Michigan, 1987-. *Memberships:* Medical Technology, American Society of Clinical Pathologists; Clinical Laboratory Scientists, American Society of Medical Technology. *Hobby:* Volunteer, Boy Scouts of America, Frankenmuth, Michigan, 1972-83. *Address:* 9112 East Curtis, Frankenmuth, MI 48734, USA.

LIGTERMOET-EBBINGE Henny (Hinderkien Jantien), b. 8 Dec. 1921, Franeker, The Netherlands. Antenatal Teacher. m. Gerrit Ligtermoet, 14 Oct. 1946, deceased 1987. 4 sons. *Appointments:* Started Midwifery contact centre, 1956-83; Established Homebirth Australia in 1978, Co-ordinator, 1982- 84. *Publications:* Book: Responsible Home Birth, 1977; Booklet: Thoughts on Women's Issues, 1986. Film: Birth Rediscovered, 1985; Numerous articles on Childbirth; Organised two Childbirth Conferences. *Memberships:* Life Member, National Childbirth Trust, UK; International Childbirth Education Association, USA; National Association for Parents and Professionals for Safe alternatives in Childbirth. *Hobbies:* Stamp Collecting; Swimming; Walking; Childbirth and Women's right to choose the manner and place of birth. *Address:* 1A Shoalwater Road, Shoalwater, WA 6169, Australia.

LILLIKER Shelley Lerner, b. 17 Feb. 1945, Chicago, Illinois, USA. Psychotherapist. *Education:* BA, Washington University, 1963-66; MA, Psychological Counseling, So East Mo State University, 1978. *Appointments:* Social Worker, Anna Mental Health Ctr, 1967-82; Psychotherapist, Private practice, San Antonio, Texas, 1982-. *Publication:* Prevelance of Diabetes in a Manic-Depressive Population, 1980. *Memberships:* Amer Assoc of Couns & Devel; Texas Assoc of Couns & Devel; San Antonio Prof Singles, Treasurer; Amer Ment Health Council Assoc; Texas Ment Health Council Assoc. *Honours:* Diplomate & Fellow, American Board of Medical Psychotherapists, 1987; Lic Professional Counselor, Texas, 1982; Certificate of Academic Distinction, Southeast Missouri State Univ, 1978. *Hobbies:* Reading; Gardening; Cooking. *Address:* Alamo Mental Health Group, 4242 Medical Dr, San Antonio, TX 78229, USA.

LIMBO Rana K, b. 27 Oct. 1946, Nebraska, USA. Director, Resolve Through Sharing. *Education:* BSN, St Olaf College, 1968; MS, University of Colorado, 1969; Doctoral Student, Indiana University. *Appointments:* University of Nebraska College of Nursing, 1972-75; Viterbo College, La Crosse, 1979-82; Lutheran Hospital, La Crosse, 1980-. *Publications:* When a Baby Dies: A Handbook for Healing and Helping, with Sara Rich Wheeler; numerous articles on grief. *Memberships:* Wisconsin Nurses Association; Sigma Theta Tau; NAACOG. *Honours:* Teacher of the Year, 1973; WI Nurses Foundation Research Award, 1984; Nurse of the Year, 1987. *Address:* Resolve Through Sharing, Lutheran Hospital, La Crosse, WI 54601, USA.

LIMET Elizabeth, b. Canada. Writer; Poet; Painter; Musician. *Education:* Trained as singer, Canada, postgraduate at Academie de Musique, Belgium, with Henri Delvaux & Paul Gilson; Painting studies, Ecole de Beaux Arts, Montreal, & studios of Georges Bracque, & sculptor Daost, France. *Appointments include:* Many years' professional singing (operatic soprano), as Sonia Lear; Appearances with Maria Dina Ricci, Attilio Dell'Orso (tenor) in Canada, Marcelle Sippell in Paris & Casa Blanca; Numerous performances, Europe, South Africa, Canada; One of 1st Canadian opera singers to record with RCA, New York, early 1950's; Founder, own choral group, La Cantate (specialising classical songs, opera & poetry), 1962; Invited singer, Expo' 67. *Creative work includes:* 5 published books: La Voix de mes Pensees, 1958; Le Phare des Amants, 1969; Gel de Feu, 1972; J'aime l'Espace, 1980; Rosetendre, 1980. 9 solo art exhibitions, Canada, Spain, France, USA (styles, classical to abstract); Composer, over 75 pieces of music including many songs, French & English. *Memberships include:* Societe des Gens de Lettres, France; Auteurs Quebecois; Fellow, World Literary Academy; Union des Peintres Europeens; Union des Artistes. *Honours include:* 1st prizes, piano & singing, Academie de Musique; Various literary commendations; Finalist, Governor General's Award (literature), Canada, 1985; Various biographical recognitions. *Address:* 2300 St Matthew, Apt. 303, Montreal, Quebec, Canada H3H 2J8.

LIN Sharon Shiang Chien, b. 22 Aug. 1933, Nanjing, Jiangsu, People's Republic of China. Librarian. m. Duo-Liang Lin, 8 June 1963. 1 son, 1 daughter. *Education:* BA, Foreign Languages/Literature, National Taiwan University, 1956; MA, Library Science, University of Minnesota, USA, 1960; Public librarian's professional certificate, State Education Department, University of State of New York, 1980. *Appointments:* Cataloger/Snr Cataloger, Yale University Library, New Haven, 1960-64; Head, Periodical Department, State University College, Buffalo, 1965-67; Visiting Librarian, Stanford University Library, Palo Alto, 1966; Visiting Staff, Oxford University Library, Oxford, England, 1970; Visiting Librarian, Qinghua University, Beijing, People's Republic of China, 1978; Serials Cataloger, State University of New York, Buffalo, USA, 1978-; Visiting Lecturer, Shanghai Jiao Tong University, Shanghai, People's Republic of China, 1985; Visiting Lecturer, China University of Science & Technology Library, Hefei, Anhui, 1987; Visiting Lecturer, Over 20 Chinese university libraries and library schools. *Publications:* Elementary Particles (cotranslator from English to Chinese), 1967; Contemporary physics (co-translator from English to Chinese), 1970; Chinese Libraries and Librarianship, 1986. Numerous articles in professional journals. *Memberships:* American Library Association, 1981-; Officer, ALA Resources & Technical Services Div, Committee on Cataloging Asian & African Materials, 1983-85; ALA Chinese-American Librarian's Association, 1983-; Secretary, Chinese Club of Buffalo, 1979-80; Treasurer, Chinese Club of Western NY, 1984-85. *Honours:* Distinguished Achievement Award, 1973; Research/Study Grant, 1985, 1987, NY State/United University Professions, Professional Development and Quality of Working Life Committee. *Hobbies:* Gardening; Travel. *Address:* 152 Northington Drive, East Amherst, New York 14051, USA.

LINCOLN Catherine Ruth, b. 29 Apr. 1941, Fulmer, Buckinghamshire, England. Direct Marketing Executive. m. 19 Feb. 1968, 2 sons. *Education:* BA Hons, Modern History, 1962, MA, 1972, Oxford University. *Appointments:* British Diplomatic Service, London, England, New Delhi, Calcutta and Madras, India, Ankara, Turkey, 1962-68; Capital Campaign Director, Head of Richmond Office, Saint Paul's Episcopal College, Lawrenceville, Virginia, USA, 1977-79; Account Executive, then Vice-President (Creative), The Viguerie Company, 1979-87; Regional Manager, Ed Burnett Consultants, 1987-. *Publications:* The Care and Feeding of Donors. *Memberships:* Direct Marketing Association of Washington (President 1986, President of Education Foundation 1988-90); Board Member, St Paul's College Associates; Board Member, Indo-Chinese Refugees

Social Services, 1980-82; Board Member, Women's Direct Response Group, 1988-89. *Honours:* Scholarship to Oxford, Oxford and Cambridge Society of East Africa. *Hobbies:* Lively arts (theatre, opera); Fine arts; Family history. *Address:* 7389 Hallcrest Drive, McLean, VA 22102-2909, USA.

LIND Marilyn Marlene Thiem, b. 15 Aug. 1934, New Ulm, Minnesota, USA. Artist; Writer; Researcher; Lecturer; Publisher. m. Charles Richard Lind, 22 Aug. 1952, 1 son, 2 daughters. *Publications:* Thiem, Christoph & August - A Dream & A Promise, 1981; Researching & Finding Your German Heritage, 1984; Using Maps & Aerial Photography in Your Genealogical Research, 1984; Beginning Genealogy & A Guide to Continuing Research & Introduction to Foreign Research, 1984; Immigration, Migration & Settlement in the US, 1985; Supplement to Using Maps & Aerial Photography in Your Genealogical Research, 1985; Looking Backward to Sweden - And the Lind/Bure Family 1000 to 1986, 1986; Using Maps & Aerial Photography in Your Genealogical Research, Revised & Enlarged Edition, 1986; Continuing Your Genealogical Research in Minnesota, 1986; Printing & Publishing Your Family History, 1986; contributor to various professional journals. *Memberships:* Independent Republicans of Minnesota, Carlton County/Senate District No. 14 Chairwoman; Genealogical Society of Carlton County, President, Chairman of the Board; Duluth Art Institute. *Address:* 1204W. Prospect, Cloquet, MN 55720, USA.

LINDAY Linda Anne, b. 16 June 1949, New York City, USA. Medical Doctor; Inventor. m. 23 Aug. 1975, 1 son, 1 daughter. *Education:* BA, Barnard College, 1970; MD, College of Physicians & Surgeons, Columbia University, 1975. *Appointments include:* Assistant Professor, Pharmacology & Paediatrics, Cornell University Medical Centre, 1981-82; Director, Medical Affairs, Knoll Pharmaceutical Company, 1982-84; Associate Director, Clinical Research, Ayerst Labortories, 1984-87; President, Dr Pockets Inc, 1987-. *Creative work:* 14 articles, medical journals including: American Journals of Cardiology, Paediatrics, Clinical Pharmacology & Therapeutics, Inventor: The Connection (TM), licensed to Cherubs Collection; The Carry Rite (TM), licensed to Pansy Ellen Products Inc. *Memberships:* American Federation for Clinical Research; American Society for Clinical Pharmacology & Therapeutics; American Society for Pharmacology & Experimental Therapeutics; *Honours:* Mary Putnam Jacobi Fellowship, Women's Medical Association, NYC, 1979; Fellowships, Pharmaceutical Manufacturers Association, 1981-83; Fellow, American Collogo of Cardiology 1982, American Academy of Paediatrics 1983. *Hobbies:* Tennis; Music. *Address:* 340 West 55th Street, Suite 9A, New York, NY 10019, USA.

LINDE Maxine Helen, b. 2 Sept. 1939, Chicago, USA. Lawyer; Corporate Executive. m. Ronald K. Linde, 12 June 1960. *Education:* BA summa cum laude, University of California, Los Angeles, 1961; JD, Stanford University, 1967. *Appointments:* Applied mathematician, research engineeer, Jet Propulsion Laboratory, Pasadena, California, 1961-64; Law clerk, US District Court, North California, 1967-68; Admitted, California Bar, 1968; Member, California law firms, Long & Levit, San Francisco 1968-69, Swerdlow, Glikbarg & Shimer, Beverly Hills 1969-72; Secretary, general counsel, Envirodyne Industries Inc, Chicago, 1972-. *Memberships include:* Order of Coif; Phi Beta Kappa; Pi Mu Epsilon; Alpha Lambda Delta. *Address:* c/o Envirodyne Industries Inc, 142 East Ontario Street, 10th Floor, Chicago, Illinois 60611, USA.

LINDEN-WARD Blanche M.G., b. 4 July 1946, Battle Creek, Michigan, USA. College Professor. m. (1)Thomas Lindow, 1968, divorced 1976, 1 son, 1 daughter, (2)Alan Ward, 1982. *Education:* BA, University of Michigan, 1968; MA, University of Cincinnati, 1976; PhD, Harvard University, 1981. *Appointments:* Instructor, American Sudies, Brandeis University, 1979- 81; Visiting Assistant Professor, Middlebury College, 1981-82;

Assistant Professor, Brandeis University, 1982-85; Assistant Professor, Co-ordinator, American Culture & Communication, Emerson College, 1985-. *Publicaitons:* Silent City on a Hill: Landscapes of Memory and Boston's Mount Auburn Cemetry, 1989; documentary video, Nature by design, 1987. *Memberships:* American Historical Association; Organization of American Historians; American Studies Association; American Culture and Popular Culture Association. *Honours:* Bradford Williams Medal, American Society of Landascape Architects, 1985. *Hobbies:* Photography; Travel. *Address:* 73 Union Street, Watertown, MA 02172, USA.

LINDFORS Viveca, b. Uppsala, Sweden. Actress. m. George Tebori, 4 July 1954, 3 children. *Appointments:* Came to USA, 1946, Naturalised 1950; Joined Royal Dance Theatre, Sweden, 1935; Appeared in Plays in Sweden; Swedish films include: Think If I Marry the Minister, 1940; Anna Lens, 1941; The Two Brothers, 1941; In Death's Waiting Room, 1942; Plays in the USA Include: I've Got Sixpence, 1953; Anastasia, 1954; King Lear, 1955; I Am a Woman, 1973; Films in USA include: Four Men in a Jeep; Run for Cover, 1953; Captain Drayfus, 1956; Weddings & Babies, 1956; Sylvia, 1964; Brainstorm, 1965; The Stronger; The Jewish Wife; An Actor Works; The Way We Were, 1972; Welcome to LA 1975; A Wedding, 1978; Voices, 1979; TV Appearances include: Ben Casey, 1964; The Nurses, 1964. *Memberships:* Founder, Berkshire Theatre *Address:* 172 E. 95th Street, New York, NY 10028, USA.

LINDSTEIN Marit Ingrid, b. 16 June 1948, Hudiksvall, Sweden. Lawyer. m. Stephan, 28 Aug. 1976. 2 sons, 1 daughter. *Education:* Student, Hudiksvall, 1967; Master of Law, Upsala 1972. *Appointments:* CFD Estate Data System, 1972; Department of Justice, 1974; Estate Office of Stockholm, 1975; ADB Assistant, Consultant, 1977-84; Lawyer and Consultant in EDB, Systemjurdik, 1984-. *Publications:* Open Door Project, a model for leading EDB Projects with full awareness of the users will by legal contracts. *Memberships:* Swedish Liberals, 1967-82; Board member of local communities, 1972-76; 3-d suppl. of Parliament, 1975-81; Green Party in Sweden, 1982-; Greenpeace, 1985-; Right Livelihood Foundation in Sweden, 1987-; Womens Network in Tyreso, 1987-; ESEC European Society for Ecology and Culture chairperson, 1988-; Board member of the Regional Community of Stockholm läns landsting. *Hobbies:* Politics; Economics; Environment; Nature; New Technics. *Address:* Lonnv 5A, S-13552 Tyreso, Sweden.

LINDSTROM Linda Little, b. 9 Sept. 1948, mt Sterling, Kentucky, USA. Educator. m. William Allen Lindstrom. 1 son, 5 daughters. *Education:* AB 1969, MA 1971, Morehead University; Cert. School Superintendent; High school & elem Prin; high school & elem teacher; director of pupil personnel, 1985. *Appointments:* Teacher, Mapleton Elementary School, Mt Sterling, 1969-73; Teacher, Foreign Embassy students, Iranamis International School, Tehran, Iran, 1976-77; Instructor, Iranamis University, Iran, 1976-77; Teacher, Camargo Elementary, Mt Sterling, 1977-. *Memberships:* Phi Delta Kappa; Honorable Order of Kentucky Colonels; Scandinavian Heritage Society; Women's Fellowship; Democratic Party; Presbyterian Church. *Honours:* Recipient School Community Award, Montgomery County Schools, Mt Sterling, Kentucky, 1986. *Hobbies:* Foreign travel; Hiking; Reading; Watching sunsets; Studying school systems in other countries first-hand. *Address:* 15 Trojan Avenue, Mt Sterling, Kentucky 40353, USA.

LINGARD Joan Amelia, b. 8 Apr. 1932, Edinburgh, Scotland. Author. 3 daughters. *Education:* Teaching Diploma, Moray House Training College, Edinburgh. *Publications:* 11 adult novels including: Liam's Daughter, 1963; A Sort of Freedom, 1968; Second Flowering of Emily Mountjoy, 1979; Greenyards, 1981; Sisters by Rite, 1984; Reasonable Doubts, 1986; The Women's House, 1989. 19 children's books including: 12th Day of July, 1970; Across the Barricades, 1972;

Into Exile, 1973; Hostages to Fortune, 1976; File on Fraulein Berg, 1980; Winter Visitor, 1983; Freedom Machine, 1986; Rags & Riches, 1988; Tug of War, 1989. *Memberships:* Past Chair, Society of Authors in Scotland; Scottish PEN. *Honours:* Buxtehuder Bulle, West Germany, 1987; Preis der Lesenrater (shared), ZDF, 1986. *Hobbies:* Reading; Travel. *Address:* c/o David Higham Associates Ltd, 5/8 Lower John Street, Golden Square, London W1R 4HA, England.

LINGENFELTER Sharon Marie, b. 17 June 1947, Nyssa, Oregon, USA. Vice President. Divorced, 2 sons. *Education:* George Fox College, 1966; Portland State University, 1968. *Appointments:* Editing consultant, 1983; Administrative Assistant, Century Data Inc., 1983-85; Office Systems Analyst, Business Prospector, 1985-87; Vice President, Administration, Century Data Inc., 1985-; General Manager, Business Prospector, 1988-; Chief Operations Officcer, Business Prospector, Inc, 1989-. *Publications:* Personal collection of poetry & paintings. *Memberships:* National Association of Female Executives; American Management Association; American Society of Professional and Executive Women. *Honours:* Poet Laureate of George Fox College, 1966. *Hobbies:* Skiing; Writing; Reading; Travel. *Address:* 14862 SW 109th Ave., Tigard, OR 97224, USA.

LINNEHAN Kathryn Joan Richards, b. 14 Nov. 1930. Entrepreneur; Writer. m. William Francis Linnehan III, Esquire. *Education:* Duke University; Oxford University, England; Harvard University, Cambridge. *Appointments:* Research & Development Division, Wyeth Laboratories Inc., 1960-77; Founder, President, Linnehan Associates, 1977-. *Publications:* numerous professional and technical publications. *Memberships:* Phi Beta Kappa; American Medical Writers Association; Regulatory Affairs Professional Society; Historical Society of Hingham. *Honours:* 1st Recipient, Distinguished Service Award, Public Radio of Boston; The International Who's Who of Intellectuals; Honorary Appointment to the Research Board of Advisors of the American Biographical Institute; Certificate of Merit for Distinguished Services in the First Edition of the International Who's Who of Professional and Business Women; Shareholder (together with William F. Linnehan) of the Boston Athenaeum. *Hobbies:* Breeding Irish Wolfhounds; Sailing; Writing; Gardening; American Folk Art. *Address:* 303 Gardner Street, Hingham, MA 02043, USA.

LINSE Bonnie Jean K Hartley, b. 26 July 1923, Chicago, Illinois, USA. Nurse Clinician; Educator and Health Service Administrator. m. (1)Robert W Hartley MD, 23 June 1949, divorced 1961, 2 sons. (2)Howard A Linse, 10 June 1978, deceased 18 Nov. 1985. 1 stepson, 1 stepdaughter. *Education:* BS Nursing, St Xavier College, Chicago, 1945; Certification in Secondary Education through Equivalency Program, Portland State College, Portland, 1965; MS Nursing Education, University of Oregon, School of Nursing, Portland, 1972; Certificate, College Health Nurse Practitioner Program, Brigham Young University, Provo, Utah, 1976; Registered Nurse, State of Illinois, 1945; Registered Nurse, State of Oregon, 1962-. *Appointments:* Faculty (Nursing) St Xavier College, Chicago, 1945-47; Head Nurse, Zoller Memorial Clinic, University of Chicago Clinics, Chicago, 1947-48; Nurse Researchers, Newborn Neurology, University of Oregon Medical School, Portland, 1961; Coordinator and instructor, Dental Assistant Program, Biology Instructor and Science Instructor, Medical Assistant Program, Portland Public Schools, 1965- 67; College Health Centre Clinician/Administrator, Clackamas Community College, Oregon City, 1970-84. *Creative works:* Submitted papers/surveys/questionnaires concerning: Student perceptions of college health services; Use of College Health Services for treating the community's Medically indigent population; Alcoholism on college campuses. *Memberships:* American Nurses' Association; State of Oregon Nurses Association; Clackamas County Nurses Association; State of Oregon College Health Service Directors Association, 1970-84;

President, Oregon College Health Nurses Special Interest Group, 1976-78; Pacific Coast College Health Association, 1970-, Program coordinator for annual regional meeting, 1980; Northwest Oregon Health Systems (a Federal health planning agency); Clackamas County Sub-Area Advisory Council, 1979-86, Vice president, 1984. *Honours:* United States Public Health Service grantee, 1968; Recipient of Recognition for Outstanding Service Award, Clackamas Community College, 1984; Sabbatical Leave granted to attend Australian and New Zealand Student Services Association Triennial Conference, Christchurch, New Zealand, 1979. *Hobbies:* Travel; Playing piano; Choral singing; Swimming; Writing humorous poetry. *Address:* 18633 Roundtree Drive, Oregon City, OR 90745, USA.

LINTERMANS Gloria, b. 11 May 1947, Brooklyn, New York, USA. Columnist. m. Eric Lintermans, 15 June 1968, divorced 1981, 2 sons. *Appointments:* Newspaper Columnist: Inter-Continental Press Syndicate, Glendale, California, 1978-82; Universal Press Syndicate, KansasCity, Missouri, 1982-; Internationally syndicated newspaper columnist, Editors Press, New York City, 1980; Radio Host, 1982-; Television Host, 1983-; Author, Capistrano Press Limited, Long Beach. *Publications:* The Professional Babysitter's Guide, 1980; Internationally Syndicated Newspaper column: Gloria Lintermans Looking Great, 1978-; Star: Syndicated TV andRadio Shows, Looking Great with Gloria Lintermans, 1982--; Publisher, Gloria Lintermans Looking Great newsletter, monthly 1986-; Spokesperson, Foster Parents Plan, Los Angeles; etc. *Memberships:* Fashion Group Incorporated; Society of Professional Journalists; Sigma Delta Chi; Greater Los Angeles Press Club; Women in Communications Inc; American Federation of Television and Radio Artists. *Hobbies:* Cooking; Gardening; History of the Art in China. *Address:* 12439 Magnolia Blvd., Suite 215, North Hollywood, CA 91607, USA.

LIPHAM Mary Catherine, b. 16 Sept. 1947, Bowdon, USA. Data Processing Co-ordinator. *Education:* BA, West Georgia College, 1969; MA, University of Georgia, 1971. *Appointments:* Maryland Hall of Records, 1972-79; Residential Assessor, 1979-84, Commercial/Industrial Trainee, 1984-86, Commercial Industrial Assessor, 1986, Data Processing Co- ordinator, 1987-, Maryland Dept. of Assessments & Taxation. *Memberships:* International Association of Assessing Officers; Maryland Association of Assessing Officers, Parliamentarian 1982-87; National Trust for Historic Preservation. *Honours:* Ford Foundation Graduate Fellowship, 1969-70. *Hobbies:* Ballroom Dancing; Square Dancing; Mixology. *Address:* 1567 Ritchie Lane, Annapolis, MD 21401, USA.

LIPKA Judy Ann, b 28 Dec. 1960, Detroit, Michigan, USA. Chiropractor. m Stephen J Scott, 5 Oct. 1985. *Education:* AA, Arts, High Honours, Macomb College, Warren, 1979; Doctor of Chiropractic, magna cum laude, Life Chiropractic College, Marietta, 1982. *Appointments:* Private Practice, Mobile, 1983-; Diplomate National Board of Chiropractic Examiners; Licensed to practice Chiropractic in Alabama, Michigan & Virginia. *Memberships:* American Chiropractic Association; Alabama State Chiropractic Association; Baldwin Chiropractic Society, Secretary/Treasurer,1987-88; Life Chiropractic Alumni Association; Parker Chiropractic Research Foundation; Mobile Chamber of Commerce. *Honours:* Pi Tau Delta, 1982; National Dean's List, 1982-83; WWAX Working Woman of the Day, 1983 *Hobbies:* Free Weights; Music; Swimming. *Address:* 2501 Dauphin Island Parkway, Suite C, Mobile, AL 36605, USA.

LIPMAN Maureen Diane, b. 10 May 1946, Hull, Yorkshire, England. Actress. m. Jack Rosenthal, 18 Feb. 1973, 1 son, 1 daughter. *Education:* LAMDA, 1965-67. *Appointments:* First Roles: he Knack, Palace Theatre Watford; Fay in Loot; Film, Up the Junction; tage Appearances include: Chapter II, Lyric, Hammersmith; The Front Page; Candida; Outside Edge; Night and Day; Design for Living; Meg and Mog; On Your Way Riley;

TV appearances include: numerous Quiz and Chat Shows; Smiley's People; Rolling Home; Outside Edge; Agony (3 series); The Little Princess; Absurd Person Singular; Absent Friends; Shiftwork; Executive Yarns; Films: Educating Rita; Water; Recent Theatre: Messiah; See How They Run; Muscal: Wonderful Town; Re:Joyce, co-wrote and starred in at the Fortune Theatre. *Honours Include:* Best Comedy Performer for Agony; BAFTA Best Actress in comedy for Outside Edge, 1983, and Best Supporting Actress, Educating Rita, 1984; Recipient, Best Comedy Performer in See How they Run, 1984, and Best Actress Royal Variety Club of Great Britain; Wonderful Town, Variet Club Best Musical Actress, 1987; TV Times Award for Best Actress in a comedy for All at No. 20, 1988. *Address:* Anne Hutton, 200 Fielham Rd., London SW10, England.

LIPPINCOTT Barbara Sue Barnes, b. 27 Oct. 1934, Raleigh, Illinois, USA. Research Biologist. m. James Andrew Lippincott, 2 June 1956, 2 sons, 1 daughter. *Education:* AB, 1955, MA, 1957, PhD, Molecular Biology and Zoology, 1959, Washington University, St Louis, Missouri. *Appointments:* Postdoctoral Fellow, Laboratoire de Genetique Physiologique, Centre National de la Recherche Scientifique, Gif-sur-Yvette, France, 1959-60; Research Associate in Biological Sciences, 1960-80, Senior Research Associate in Biochemistry, Molecular Biology and Cell Biology, 1980-, Northwestern University, Evanston, Illinois, USA. *Publications:* About 60 technical publications; Invited contributions to about 10 books. *Memberships:* American Society for Microbiology. *Honours:* Phi Beta Kappa, 1955; Sigma Xi, 1955; Fellow, Jane Coftin Memorial Fund for Medical Research, 1959-60; Visiting Scientist, University of California, Berkeley, 1970-71; Visiting Scientist, University of Heidelberg, Federal Republic of Germany, 1974. *Address:* Department of Biochemistry, Molecular Biology and Cell Biology, Northwestern University, Evanston, IL 60208, USA.

LIPPINCOTT Sarah Lee, Astronomer; Observatory Director Emeritus; Professor Emeritus; Graphologist. m. Dave Garroway, dec. *Education:* BA, University of Pennsylvania, 1942; MA, Swarthmore College, 1950. *Appointments:* Research Assistant, 1942-51, Research Associate, 1951- 72, Lecturer, 1961-77, Director, 1972-81, Professor of Astronomy, 1977-81, Director Emeritus, Professor Emeritus, 1981, Research Astronomer, 1981-, Sproul Observatory, Swarthmore College, Swarthmore, Pennsylvania; Participant, astronomical research: Lick Observatory, University of California, 1949, Harvard College Observatory, 1952, Paris Observatory, Meudon, France, 1953-54: French Solar Eclipse Expedition to Oland, Sweden, 1954, Sacramento Peak Observatory, New Mexico, 1955; Visiting Associate, California Institute of Technology, 1977; Invited Participant, colloquia, conferences, Currently Graphologist. *Publications:* Point to the Stars (with Joseph M Joseph), 1963, Revised 2nd Edition, 1976; Philadelphia, the Unexpected City (with Laurence LaFore), 1965; Papers in scientific journals, USA, Netherlands, France, Canada, 1945-. *Memberships:* Past Secretary, Rittenhouse Astonomical Society, 1946-48; American Astronomical Society; Vice President, 1970-73, President, 1973-76, International Astronomical Union: Commission 26; Vice President, 1959, President, 1959-60, Secretary, 1968-77, Sigma XI Swarthmore Chapter; Executive Committee, 1988-, Treasurer, 1988-, American Society of Professional Graphologists. *Honours:* Lectureship, Visiting Professors Programme, National Science Foundation and American Astronomical Society, 1961-80; Kappa Kappa Gamma Achievement Award, 1966; Distinguished Alumna Award, Springside School, 1971; National Lecturer, Sigma Xi, 1972; Honorary DSc, Villanova University, 1973; Member, 1976, Secretary, Executive Committee, 1988-, Distinguished Daughters of Pennsylvania. *Hobbies:* Photography; Ornithology; Art; Golf; Gardening. *Address:* 507 Cedar Lane, Swarthmore, PA 19081, USA.

LIPSMAN Paulee, b. 19 July 1947, Davenport, Iowa, USA. Deputy Secretary of State. *Education:* BS,

Northwestern University, 1969. *Appointments:* Reporter: KSTT Radio, 1972-77, WQAD TV, 1977-78; Sales Representative, KSTT/WXLP Radio, 1978-80; Sales Manager, KSTT/WXLP Radio, 1980-84; Political Consultant, 1985-86; Deputy Scretary of State, Iowa, 1986-. *Memberships:* Jewish Federation of Greater Des Moines; Iowa Network for Women, Steering Committee; American Civil Liberties Union; People for American Way; Handgun Control; NAACP; Planned Parenthood; NOW; etc. *Honours:* Sales Manager of the Year, Guy Gannet Broadcasting Company, 1983. *Hobbies:* Reading; Bridge; Politics. *Address:* 3407 Grand Avenue No 305, Des Moines, IA 50312, USA.

LISTAnneliese (née Pfenninger) (Pseudonym Alice Pervin), b. 6 Jan. 1922, Heroldsberg, Soubrette. m. Huldreich List, 29 Feb. 1945, deceased. *Education:* State Examination, Dancer, Munich, 1939; Dancing Training, Opera House, Nuremberg, 1926-38. *Appointments:* Dancer: Municipal Theatre, Guben, 1939-41; Soubrette: Municipal Theatre of Landsberg/Warthe, 1941-42, Municipal Theatre, Thorn, 1943, 1944, Municipal Theatre, Elbing, 1944, 1945; Clerk: US European Exchange System, 1954; Secretary: Refugee & Migration section, Field Office Nuremberg, American Consulate General, US Embassy Escapee Program 1955-60; Clerk in Charge: Foreigners Office of the City of Nuremburg, 1960-82. *Publications:* The Tree, 1973; The Luck behind the Mountains, 1978; Magazine articles in various publications including: Frau Aktuell; True Stroies; Zenit; Last Publication 1986; etc. *Memberships:* World Literary Academy. *Honours:* 2nd Prize, Contest for Best Story in True Stories Magazine, 1975. *Hobbies:* Reading; Theatre; Cinema/TV; Travel. *Address:* Ritter-von-Schuh-Platz 15, 8500 Nuerenberg 40, Federal Republic of Germany.

LISTER Moira, b. Capetown, South Africa. Actress. *Education:* Holy Family Convent, Johannesburg. *Appointments:* Stage debut at 6 years in Vikings of Heligoland; screen debut in Shipbuilders, 1943. Numerous TV appearances. *Creative Works:* Films include: Love Story; Wanted for Murder; Don Chicago; Uneasy Terms; So Evil My Love; Another Shore; Once a Jolly Swagman; Run for Your Money; Pool of London; White Corridors; Something Money Can't Buy; Cruel Sea; Grand National Night; Limping Man; Trouble in Store; John and Julie; Deep Blue Sea; Seven Waves Away; The Yellow Rolls Royce; Joey Boy; Double Man; Stranger in the House; Murder on Safari; The Choice. *Address:* c/o Richard Stone Partnership, 18-20 York Buildings, London WC2N 6JU, England.

LITCHFIELD Ruby Beatrice, Dame, b. 5 Sept. 1912, Australia. m. Kenneth Litchfield, 1940 (deceased 1976). 1 son. *Education:* N Adelaide PS; PGC Glen Osmond SA. *Career:* Dir Festival City Broadcasters Ltd SA, 1975-86; Trustee, The Adelaide Festival Centre Trust SA, 1971-82; Member, Board of Governors Adelaide Festival of Arts, 1966- (committee member 1960-); Vice President and Board Member, Queen Victoria Maternity Hospital, 1953-72 (life member 1972); President, Sportswoman's Association, 1969-74; Mayoress of Prospect SA, 1954-57; Board Member, The Adelaide Repertory Theatre, 1951-68 (life member 1967); Member, Div Cncl Red Cross Soc (SA), 1955-71; Cllr Royal District Bush Nursing Soc, 1957-64; Board Member, Crippled Children's Association, 1976-; Board Member, Kidney Foundation, 1968-; Council Member, Sudden Infant Death Syndrome Research Foundation, 1979-; Honorary Life Member, Spastic Paralysis Welfare Assn Inc; Chair, Board of Carclew Youth Performing Arts Centre, 1972-88; Board Member, South Australian Housing Trust, 1962-70; Board Member, Telethon Channel 9, 1961-86; Member, South Australian Davis Cup Committee, 1952-63-68; Member, SA Committee Royal Academy of Dancing, 1961-66; Chair, Families, Religion, Cultural Committee, SA Jubilee Committee, 1981-86. *Membership:* Royal Commonwealth Society. *Honours:* Queen's Silver Jubilee Medal, 1977; Awarded DBE for services to the performing arts and the community; Advance Australia Award, 1985; South Australia Great Award, 1987; Life Member, Adelaide

Festival Arts, 1988. *Hobby:* Tennis (hardcourt tennis champion 1932-35). *Address:* 33 Hallett Road, Burnside, S Australia 5066, Australia.

LITTLE Anna Denise, b. 2 May 1954, Montclair, USA. Businesswoman. *Education:* BA, Florida State Univesity, 1980. *Appointments:* Funk & Wagnalls Inc., 1981-84; Editor, Media Co-ordinator, Hotel's Travel Index, Murdoch Magazines, 1984-86; Window Shopping Editor, House Beautiful magazine, 1986; Promotion/ Editorial Manager, Direct Response Group, 1986-88; Hearst Co-orperation Magazines, 1986-. *Memberships:* National Association of Female Executives; National Academy of Arts & Sciences. *Honours:* Blue Ribbon Panel for Daytime Emmy Awards, 1987. *Hobbies:* Horticulture; Music; Photography; Writing; Asian Studies. *Address:* Eight Mission Street, Montclair, NJ 07042, USA.

LITTLE Flora Jean, b. 2 Jan. 1932, Taiwan, Republic of China. Children's Writer. *Education:* BA, Victoria College, University of Toronto, Canada, 1955; Course in Special Education, University of Utah, 1958. *Appointment:* Teacher, Class for physically disabled children, 1958-62. *Publications:* Books: Mine for Keeps, 1962; Home From Far, 1965; Spring Begins in March, 1966; When the Pie Was Opened, 1966; Take Wing, 1968; One to Grow on, 1969; Look Through My Window, 1970; Kate, 1972; Stand in the Wind, 1975; From Anna, 1972; Listen for the Singing, 1977; Mama's Going to Buy You a Mocking Bird, 1984; Lost and Found, 1985; Different Dragons, 1986; Hey World Here I Am, 1986; Little By Little: A Writer's Education, 1987; Upcoming: Jess Was the Brave One, 1989; In progress: Stars Come Out Within; Once Upon a Golden Apple. *Memberships:* Writers' Union of Canada; Can SCAIP, Corresponding Secretary,(Canadian Society for Children's Authors, Illustrators and Performers). *Honours:* Little Brown Canadian Children's Book Award, 1961; Vicky Metcalf Award, 1974; Canada Council Children's Literature Award, 1977; Ruth Schwartz Award, 1985; Canadian Library Assoc Children's Book of the Year Award, 1985; Boston Globe Horn Book Honor Book, 1988; Deutscher Jugendliteratur Award, 1981. *Address:* 198 Glasgow Street North, Guelph, Ontario, Canada N1H 4X2.

LITTLEDALE Freya (Lota), Writer. 1 son. *Education:* BS, Ithaca College; English, New York University Graduate School of Arts & Science. *Appointments:* Freelance Writer, 1965-; Adjunct Professor, Creative Writing for Children, Fairfield University, Fairfield, Connecticut, 1984-90; Juvenile Book Editor, Parents Magazine Press, New York City; Associate Editor: Maco Magazine Corp, New York City: Ridge Press and Rutledge Books, New York City; Editor, South Shore Record, Hewlett, Long Island, New York; English Teacher, Willsboro Central School, Willsboro, New York. *Publications:* The Magic Fish, 1967, newly illustrated edition, 1985; Timothy's Forest (co-author), 1969; King Fox and Other Tales, 1971; The Boy Who Cried Wolf, 1975; The Elves and the Shoemaker, 1975; Seven at One Blow, 1976; The Snow Child, 1978, newly illustrated, 1989; I Was Thinking, poems for young children, 1979; The Magic Plum Tree, 1981; Snow White and the Seven Dwarfs, for beginning readers, 1981; Sleeping Beauty, 1984; The Farmer in the Soup, 1987; The Twelve Dancing Princesses, 1988; Peter and the North Wind, 1988. Editor: A Treasure Chest of Poetry, 1964; Andersen's Fairy Tales, 1966; Thirteen Ghostly Tales, 1966; Ghosts and Spirits of Many Lands, 1970; Strange Tales from Many Lands, 1975; Adaptations: Pinocchio, 1979; The Wizard of Oz, 1982; Frankenstein, 1983; The Little Mermaid, 1986; King Midas and the Golden Touch, 1989; Plays including: Stop That Pancake, 1975; The King and Queen Who Wouldn't Speak, 1975; The Giant's Garden, 1975; The Big Race, 1976; The Magic Piper, 1976; Contributor: The Scribner Anthology for Young People, 1976; A New Treasury of Children's Poetry, 1984. *Memberships:* PEN; Authors Guild; Society of Children's Book Writers. *Honours:* 2 IRA Children's Choices; 1 of 70 Favourite Paperbacks, Children's Book Council/IRA Liaison Committee, 1986; Peter and the North Wind, recommended by Faith McNulty 12 Dec. 1988 edition of The New Yorker in her annual round-up of books for children. *Hobbies:* Drawing; Dance; Music; Theatre; Reading. *Address:* c/o Curtis Brown Inc, Ten Astor Place, New York, NY 10003, USA.

LITTLEJOHN Joan Anne, b. 20 Apr. 1937, London, England. Creative Artist. *Education:* Royal College of Music (RCM), 1955-59; Postgraduate study, including tuition from Howells, Fricker, Berkeley, Hopkins, Boulanger, Ruth Dyson. *Appointments:* Freelance composer, poet, photographer, musicologist, 1959-; Piano teacher, Orpington Grammar School 1958-59, Harrow School 1972-73; Administrative staff, RCM, 1960-83; Assistant to British composers including Fricker & Howells', reassembled Howell's Requiem, 1980, collated & edited some of his works, 1980's. *Creative work includes:* Approx. 300 songs, including 20 song cycles; Approx. 200 poems; Music manuscripts deposited, various archives, UK, Austria, USA; Works commissioned, broadcast and published. *Memberships include:* Adjudicator, British Federation of Music Festivals; Performing Rights Society; Life member, Women's Corona Society, Bronte Society; Founder member, RCM Staff Association; 1st elected Chair, London Music Colleges Branch, National Association of Local Government Officers (NALGO), 1978-81. *Honours:* Scholarships, James Allen & Christ's Hospital, 1948; Patron's Fund awards, 1970's; RVW Trust awards, 1970's; Recipient, Howells' composing piano (Steinway grand), 1984; Golden Poet Award, USA, 1985; Silver Poet, 1986; Biographical recognition in UK, USA, India, S. Africa and Internationally. *Hobbies include:* Animals; Gardening. Interests include: Preparing own papers for the nation, including manuscripts, letters, memorabilia from 20th century personalities; Autobiography; Diaries since 1946; Family history. *Address:* Chanterhayes, Bow, near Crediton, Devon EX17 6HR, England.

LIU Katherine Chang, b. China. Artist; Lecturer; Juror. m. Yet- Zen Liu, 1 son, 1 daughter. *Education:* MS, Biochemistry, University of California, Berkeley, USA. *Career:* 28 solo shows: Louis Newman Galleries, Los Angeles, California, USA (7); Riverside Art Museum, California; Roanoke Museum of Fine Arts, Virginia; State University of New York; Utah State, East Texas State, Pennsylvania State and Florida A&M Universities; Lung Men Gallery, Taipei, Taiwan; Competitive/invitational shows include: National Watercolor Society Annuals, 1979-87; Allied Artists of America, 1980, 1986, 1987; Butler Institute of American Art, Youngstown, Ohio, 1982; National Society of Painters in Casein & Acrylic, 1985, 1986; Los Angeles Artcore Invitational, 1988; Invited Juror/Lecturer, over 60 national and regional exhibits and organisations including: Rocky Mountain National, Texas Watercolor Societies, 1984; Arizona Aqueous, National Watercolor Societies (Jury Chairman), 1985; Watercolor West National, San Diego International, Ohio Watercolor Societies, Western Federal Exhibit (Houston), 1986; New Jersey Watercolor Society, Arizona Watercolor Association, 1987; Pittsburgh Aqueous National and Oregon Watercolor Societies, 1988; Invited Faculty: University of Virginia Extension, Longwood College; Roanoke Museum; Conejo Valley Art Museum, California. *Memberships:* Life, National Watercolor Society (President 1983-84); Watercolor USA Honor Society; Allied Artists of America; National Society of Painters in Casein & Acrylic; Rocky Mountain National Watermedia Society; West Coast Watercolor Society. *Honours:* Grants: Travel Show, National Endowment for the Arts, 1979-80; Artist-in-Residence, Virginia Commission of Arts & Humanities, 1978-80; 51 national/regional awards including Top Award, National Watercolor Society Membership Show, 1984; Gold Medal of Honor, 1986, Mary Lou Fitzgerald Memorial Award, 1987, Allied Artists of America. *Address:* 2872 East Panamint Court, Westlake Village, CA 91362, USA.

LIU Zhenqi, b. 13 Jan. 1933, Liaoning, Peoples Republic of China. Professor of plant physiology. m. Liu Zhenye, 20 Aug. 1957. 2 sons. *Education:* Graduate,

Northeast Agricultural University, Department of Agromomy, 1954. *Appointments:* Translator Russian to Chinese, Ministry of Forestry, China, 1954-55; Assistant, Lecturer, Associate Professor, Professor, Guizhou Agricultural College, 1957-. *Publications include:* 47 Books and papers including: A study of the photosynthetic characteristics of different plant types in rice, 1980; A study of some photosynthetic charaters of rice, 1982; A study of relationship between chlorophyll content and photosynthetic rate in rice, 1984; Genetic and breeding for photosynthesis, 1984; Rice collection of Guizhou Agricultural College, 1985; Scientific survey of the Hundred Li Rhododrendron, Forest area in Guizhou, China, 1987. *Memberships:* Director, Chinese Society of Plant Physiologists; Director General, Guizhou Society of Plant Physiologists; Member, Guizhou Association of Science and Technology. *Honours:* Advanced prizes, Guizhou Science and Technology, 1980 and 1987; Advanced prizes, China Association of Science and Technology, 1985; Distinguished Educationist of China and Awardee of May Day Labour Medal of China, 1988; Model worker of Guizhou province, 1988. *Hobby:* Music. *Address:* Guizhou Agricultural College, Huaxi, Guiyang, Guizhou, Peoples Republic of China.

LIU-ZALOGA Anna Yalan, b, 1 Sep. 1923, Harbin, China. Educator, Fine Arts. m. Igor Liu, May 1949, div. 1980, 1 son, 1 daughter. *Education:* Graduated, Moscow High School, USSR, 1944; Graduated, Surikov Arts Institute, Moscow, 1950. *Appointments:* Tutor, Academy of Arts, Beijing, People's Republic of China, 1950-51; Tutor, Faculty of Painting, Pedagogical University of China, Beijing, 1951-62; Professor, Department of Fine Art, Beijing Teachers College, 1962-80. *Publications:* Editor, 7 volumes of Biography of Outstanding Russian Artists. *Creative works include:* 2 paintings in Chinese Artists Association; 2 paintings in Chinese Art Gallery. *Memberships:* Chinese Artists Association; Australian Chinese Community Association, Australia; Royal Art Society of New South Wales. *Honours:* Her personal exhibition in Beijing was 1st art exhibition after Cultural Revolution, 1979; Elected to 4th Conference of Literary and Arts Workers Representative Council of China, 1979; Elected to Conference of Literary and Arts Workers Representative Council of Beijing, 1980; Biography included in Dictionary of Chinese Artists, 1981; 3 major prizes for still-life and landscapes, Beijing. *Hobbies:* Literature; Gardening; Chinese brush painting. *Address:* PO Box 255, Pendle Hill, New South Wales 2145, Australia.

LIVELY Penelope Margaret, b. 17 Mar. 1933, Cairo, Egypt. Writer. m. Jack Lively, 27 June 1957, 1 son, 1 daughter. *Publications:* Fiction: The Road to Lichfield, 1977; Nothing Missing But the Samovar, 1978; Treasures of Time, 1979; Judgement Day, 1981; Next to Nature, Art, 1982; Perfect Happiness, 1983; Corruption, 1984; According to Mark, 1984; Pack of Cards, Stories 1978-86, 1986; Moon Tiger, 1987; Non-Fiction: The Presence of the Past: An Introduction to Landscape History, 1976; Childrens Books: Astercote, 1970; The Whispering Knights, 1971; The Wild Hunt of Hagworthy, 1971; The Driftway, 1972; The Ghost of Thomas Kempe, 1974; The House in Norham Gardens, 1974; Going Back, 1975; A Stitch in Time, 1976; The Voyage of QV66, 1978; The Revenge of Samuel Stokes, 1981; The Stained Glass Window, 1976; Boy without a Name, 1975; Fanny's Sister, 1976; Fanny and the Monsters, 1978; Fanny and the Battle of Potter's Piece, 1980; Fanny and the Monsters, 1983; Univited Ghosts, 1984; Dragon Trouble, 1984; Debbie and the Little Devil, 1987; A House Inside Out, 1987. *Memberships:* Fellow, Royal Society of Literature; PEN; Society of Authors. *Honours:* Arts Council National Book Award; Southern Arts literature Prize; Shortlisted for the Booker Prize: The Road to Lichfield, According to Mark; Carnegie Medal; Whitbread Award; Booker Prize, and shortlisted for the Whitbread Award, Moon Tiger. *Address:* c/o Murray Pollinger, 4 Garrick St., London WC2E 9BH, England.

LIVESAY Dorothy K. M., b. 12 Oct. 1909, Winnipeg,

Canada. Poet; Editor. *Career:* Freelance poet, many years; Journalist, editor and broadcaster; Engaged in social work; Writer-in-Residence, several universities. *Publications:* Prose editing: Raymond Knister Selected Poems, 1949; 40 Women Poets of Canada, 1971; Woman's Eye: 12 B. C. Poets, 1974; Alan Crawley and Contemporary (foreword), 1976; Room of One's Own: The Dorothy Livesay Issue, 1979; The Papers of Dorothy Livesay: A Research Tool, 1986; Poetry: Green Pitcher, 1928; Signpost, 1932; Day and Night, 1944; Poems for People, 1947; Call My People Home, 1950; New Poems, 1955; Selected Poems, 1957; The Colour of God's Face, 1964; The Unquiet Bed, 1967; The Documentaries, 1968; Plainsongs, 1969, 1971; Disasters of the the Sun, 1971; Collected Poems, The Two Seasons, 1972; Nine Poems of Farewell, 1973; A Winnipeg Childhood, 1973; Ice Age, 1975; Beginnings: A Winnipeg Childhood, 1976, new edition, 1989; Right Hand Left Hand, 1977; The Woman I Am, 1977; The Raw Edges, 1981; The Phases of Love, 1983; Feeling the Worlds, 1984; The Self-Completing Tree, 1986; The Husband (Novella), 1990. *Memberships:* Founding Member, The League of Canadian Poets. *Honours:* Winner, Governor General's Medal for Poetry, 1944, 1947; Honorary Doctorates: DLitt, University of Waterloo; DLitt, McGill University; LLD, Simon Fraser University, 1987; DLitt, University of Toronto, 1987; DLitt, University of British Columbia, Vancouver, 1990; Person's Case Award for work on behalf of feminism and peace, 1984; Officer, Order of Canada, 1987. *Hobbies:* Reading; Radio; Swimming. *Address:* 607 Cornwall Street, Victoria, British Columbia, Canada V8V 4L2.

LIVIA Anna, b. 13 Nov. 1955, Dublin, Ireland. Publisher; Writer. *Education:* Schools, Swaziland & Ireland; BA Honours, French, University College, London, UK, 1979; PCGE TESL, St Mary's College, 1982. *Appointments:* Lectrice, Avignon University, France, 1979-80; Editor, Onlywomen Press, 1983-. *Publications:* Relatively Norma, novel; Accommodation Offered, novel; Incidents Involving Warmth, stories; Bulldozer Rising, novel. Also co-editor, Gossip, journal of Lesbian ethics. *Memberships:* Writers Guild. *Honours:* 2nd prize, Hackney poetry competition, 1973; Stewart Headlam Award, spoken English, 1972. *Hobbies:* Politics; Radical feminism; Linguistics. *Address:* c/o Onlywomen Press Ltd, 38 Mount Pleasant, London WC1X 0AP, England.

LIVINGSTON Myra Cohn, b. 17 Aug. 1926, Omaha, USA. Poet; Critic; Educator. m. Richard Roland Livingston, 14 Apr. 1952, 2 sons, 1 daughter. *Education:* BA, Sarah Lawrence College, 1948. *Appointments:* Senior Lecturer, Poet in Residence, Beverly Hills Unified School District, 1967-84, University of California Extension; Consultant, Harcourt Brace Jovanovich, Silver-Burdett & Ginn, others, 1964-. *Publications:* 57 published books including: Worlds I Know and Other Poems, 1985; Sea Songs, 1986; Earth Songs, 1986; Higgledby Piggledy, 1986; I Like You, if You Like Me, 1987; New Year's Poems, 1987; Space Songs, 1988; Poems for Mothers, editor,1988; There Was a Place and Other Poems, 1988; over 60 articles in professional journals including: Horn Book; Top of the News; New York Times; SLJ. *Memberships:* International Reading Association; PEN; Authors Guild; International Board on Books for Young People; National Council of Teachers of English. *Honours:* Recipient, various honours & awards. *Hobbies:* Rare Book Collecting; Bookmark Collecting; Gardening. *Address:* 9308 Readcrest Drive, Beverly Hills, CA 90210, USA.

LLOYD Leonia Jannetta, b. 6 Aug. 1949, Detroit, Michigan, USA. Attorney. *Education:* BS, Wayne State University, 1971; JD, Wayne State Law School, 1979. *Appointments:* Senior Law Partner, Lloyd and Lloyd; Co-Owner, Double L Management Company,1985-. *Memberships:* Wolverine Bar Association; Mary Mcleod Bethune Association; American Bar Association; American Trial Lawyers Association; Michigan Trial Lawyers Association; Past Co-Chairperson, Political Task Force of Women's Conference of Concerns; State Senator Virgil Smiths' Community Advisory Cabinet,

1988; Optimist International Club. *Honours:* Fred Hampton Image Award, Mayflower, Illinois, 1984; Certificate of Appreciation, Mayor Coleman Young, 1977; Exhibition, Black Women in Michigan, 1985; Black Woman Hall of Fame, Kizzy Image and Achievement Award, Chicago, Illinois, 1985; National Coalition of 100 Black Women Award, 1986; Wayne County Community Service Award, 1986; Association of Black Business Students Minority Business of the Year, 1985-86; Merit Award, Black Students Law Association, University of Detroit, 1986. *Hobbies:* Listening to Music; Concerts; Plays. *Address:* 600 Renaissance Centre, Ste 1400, Detroit, MI 48243, USA.

LLOYD Leonora, b. 16 Nov. 1940, Cape Town, Republic of South Africa. Campaign Coordinator. m. 4 Apr. 1963 (div. 1974), 1 son, 1 daughter. *Education:* Thomas Huxley College of Education, England, 1972-75. *Career:* Involved, National Joint Action Campaign Committee for Women's Equal Rights, 1968-70; Editor, Socialist Women, 1970-74; Presented paper on Equal Pay Bill at 1st Women's Liberation Conference, Oxford, 1971; Joint Treasurer, Women's National Coordinating Committee, 1971-75; Member, 1st Women's Committee, National Union of Students, 1974; Co-founder, Ad-Hoc Committee Against SPUC; Founding Member, 1975-, National Coordinator, 1984-, Editor, NAC News, 1986-, National Abortion Campaign; NAC Delegate to conferences and meetings all over Europe, including Mid-Decade of Women Conference, Copenhagen, Denmark, 1981. *Publications:* Books for Women's Liberation, 2 editions, 1969-70; Women Workers in Britain, 1971; Numerous articles in Socialist Women and NAC news. *Hobbies:* Politics (Vice- Chair, Ealing Acton Labour Party, 1987-88); Dressmaking; Bridge; Walking. *Address:* National Abortion Campaign, Wesley House, 4 Wild Court, London WC2B 5AU, England.

LOBANOV-ROSTOVSKY Roxane, Princess, b. 3 Oct. 1932, Athens, Greece. m. Prince J. Lobanov-Rostovsky, 22 Jan. 1956, divorced, 1980, 2 sons, 1 daughter. *Creative Works:* Paintings and Sculpture in Watercolours. *Memberships:* Society of Women Artists. *Hobbies:* Sailing; Philosophy; Religion; Gardening; Sculpture; Travel; Languages. *Address:* Swallowdale, 67 Woodruff Avenue, Hove BN3 6PJ, England.

LOCK Margaret M., b. 26 Feb. 1936, Bromley, Kent, England. Professor of Medical Anthropology. m. Richard Lock, 2 May 1965, 1 son, 1 daughter. *Education:* BSc, University of Leeds, 1961; Japanese Language Diploma, Stanford Inter-University Center, Tokyo, Japan, 1973; PhD, University of California, Berkeley, USA, 1976. *Appointments:* Assistant Professor of Anthropology, 1977-81, Associate Professor of Anthropology, 1981-86, Professor of Anthropology, 1987-, McGill University, Montreal, Quebec, Canada. *Publications:* East Asian Medicine, 1980, Revised Edition, 1984, Japanese Edition, 1990; Health, Illness, and Medical Care in Japan (editor with E.Norbeck); Biomedicine Examined (editor with D. Gordon). *Memberships:* International Association for the Study of Traditional Asian Medicine; Fellow, Canadian Sociological and Anthropological Association; Canadian Asian Studies Association; Fellow, American Anthropological Association; Fellow, Association, Association for Asian Studies; Society for Medical Anthropology; Groupe Inter-Universitaire de Recherche en Anthropologie Medicale et en Ethnopsychiatrie. *Honours:* Japan-Canada Bilateral Exchange Fellow, 1982; Sigma Xi National lecturer, 1988-90. *Hobbies:* Tennis; Skiing; Gardening. *Address:* McGill University, Department of Humanities and Social Studies in Medicine, 3655 Drummond Street, Montreal, Quebec, Canada H3G 1Y6.

LOCKARD Bonnie Elam, b. 4 Apr. 1943, Brent, Alabama, USA. Professor. m. William Winston Lockard, 6 Sept. 1964. 1 son, 1 daughter. *Education:* BSN 1965, MSN 1973, University of Alabama; Pediatric Nurse Practitioner Certificate, 1973; EdD, Mississippi State University, 1982. *Appointments:* Instructor, Druid City Hospital School of Nursing, 1965-73; Assistant

Professor 1973-82, Associate Professor 1982-86, Professor 1986-, Mississippi University for Women. *Publications:* Articles in professional journals. *Memberships:* Sigma Theta Tau, Nursing Honorary Society; Phi Delta Kappa, Education Honorary; Association for Death Education & Counselling; Mid-South Educational Research Association; National League for Nusring; Professional Advisor, The Compassionate Friends and GTRMC Hospice Program. *Honours:* Award for Excellence in Nursing Education, Zeta Rho Chapter of Sigma Theta Tau, 1986. *Hobby:* Reading. Interests: Death Education Research; Presenting Death Education Programmes. *Address:* 412 Forrest Ct, Columbus, MS 39702, USA.

LOCKE Rosanna, b. 9 Feb. 1964. Actress. *Education:* BFA, University of California, 1982; BA, Theatre Arts, University of California, Los Angeles, 1984; Milton Katselas Acting Workshop; Delia Salvi Actor/Director Workshop. *Appointments:* Extensive Acting Career; Designer, Manager, Guavas Surfwear. *Creative Works:* TV and Films: La Bamba; The President's Wife; Knott's Landing; T J Hooker; Changing Times; But It's Not My Fault; The Last Convertible; Episode II; One Day at a time; Chips; And the Fourth Commandment is Love; The $5.20 An Hour Dream; Panic in Echo Park; Love Trap; Instinct for Survival; Curse of the Black Widow; Only When I Laugh; The Diary of Anne Frank; Murder at the Vicarage; A Midsummer Night's Dream; Feiffer's People. *Memberships:* Student Body President, Corvallis. *Honours:* Teen Miss California. *Hobbies:* Flying Kites; Singing; Dancing; Playing Piano; Volleyball. *Address:* Studio City, CA, USA.

LOCKE Theresa Ann, b. 27 Sept. 1950, Ozark, Alabama, USA. Military Education Counsellor. 1 son. *Education:* BS, Alabama State University, 1972; MEd, Auburn University, 1976. *Appointments:* Classroom teacher, Andalusia School System, 1972-74; Classroom Teacher, Eufaula School, 1974-78; Teacher, Ozark Schools, Alabama, 1978-80; Music/Theatre Director, Ft Rucker, Alabama, 1980-82; Military Education Counsellor, Army Education Center, 1982-. *Publications:* The Forgotten Sacred Harp, Negro History Bulletin; College Credit for the Aviation Warrant Officer, Aviation Digest; Mother of Black Aviation and Father of Black Aviation, Negro History Bulletin and Army Flyer. *Memberships:* Tau Beta Sigma National Honorary Band Sorority; Military Educators and Counselors Association (Nat Secretary); Blacks in Government, American Assoc for Counseling and Development; Zeta Phi Beta Sorority. *Address:* 507 Hull Street, Ozark, Alabama 36360, USA.

LOCKHART-MUMMERY Elizabeth Rosamund, b. 16 May 1947, London, England. Interior Designer. m. 4 Sept. 1971. 1 son, 2 daughters. *Education:* MA, St Andrews University, Scotland, 1965-69; MA, Art History, Oxford University, 1969-70; MA 1970-71, DipEd 1971-72, London University, Courtauld Institute. *Appointments:* Teacher, All Saints' Fulham, London, 1972-73; Tutor & Counsellor, Open University, 1973-83; Interior Designer, own building and decorating firm, 1986-. *Hobbies:* Reading; Listening to music; Walking; Theatre. *Address:* 52 Argyll Road, London W8 7BS, England.

LOCKWOOD Betty, (The Baroness Lockwood of Dewsbury) b. 22 Jan. 1924. m. Lt. Col. Cedric Hall, 25 Apr. 1978. *Education:* Ruskin College, Oxford. *Appointments:* Local Government Employment; Constituency and Regional Organiser, Chief Women's Officer and Assistant National Agent, Labour Party 1948-75; Chairman, Equal Opportunities Commission, 1975-83. *Memberships:* President, Birkbeck College, 1983-; Council Member, Pro Chancellor, Bradford University, 1983-; Council, Leeds University, 1985-; Advertising Standards Authority, 1983-; Leeds Urban Development Corporation, 1988-; Deputy lord Lieutenenant, West Yorkshire. *Honours:* Hon.D.Litt.; Bradford University; Hon. LID, Strathclyde University; Hon. Fellow, UMIST; Hon. Fellow, Birkbeck College; Fellow, Royal Society of Arts. *Hobbies:* Country Life;

Music; Gardening. *Address:* House of Lords, London SW1, England.

LODER Lorraine L, b. 22 Nov. 1952, Glendale, California, USA. Attorney. *Education:* AB cum laude, 1974, JD, 1977, University of Southern California. *Appointments:* Associate, 1979-84, Partner, 1985- 87, Demetriou, Del Guercio & Lovejoy, Los Angeles, California; Principal, Lorraine L Loder, 1987-. *Publication:* Co-author, Punitive Damages, 1988. *Memberships:* President, Women Lawyers Association of Los Angeles, 1988-89; Trustee, Los Angeles County Bar Association Board of Trustees; Board of Governors, California Women Lawyers, 1987-88; National Association of Women Business Owners; American Association of University Women. *Honours:* President's Award, California Women Lawyers, 1987; Dean's List, University of Southern California, 1970-74; Alpha Kappa Delta Honor Society, 1974. *Hobbies:* Tennis; Photography; Drawing. *Address:* 811 West Seventh Street, Eleventh Floor, Los Angeles, CA 90017, USA.

LOFAS Jeannette, President, Counselor, Lecturer. *Education:* BA, University of Michigan. *Appointments:* Co-Founder, Associate Editor, Atlas Magazine, 1960-61; Reporter, Radio Free Europe, New York City, 1961-69; Co-Founder, New American Film Service, Whitney Museum, 1970; Independent Producer, Ivan Tors Films, 1970-71; TV Reporter, Film Critic, KWTV, 1971-72; Executive Director, Snowmass Arts Foundation, Aspen, 1973; Founder, President, Stepfamily Foundation Inc., 1975-. *Publications:* Living In Step, co-author, 1977; Step-parenting, co-author, 1985; Everything You Always Wanted to Ask About Step Kids But Were Afraid to Know, 1987. *Honours:* Honorary PhD, University of Oklahoma, 1972; Southwest Film Award, 1972; Woman of the Month, Good Housekeeping Magazine, 1977; Keynote Speaker, Family Service Centre, Naval Academy, Annapolis, 1982; Speaker, White House conference on the Family, 1983; Keynote Speaker, The State of the Family, US Armed Forces in Europe, Heidelberg, 1988. *Address:* c/o Stepfamily Foundation Inc., 333 West End Avenue, New York, NY 10023, USA.

LOGAN Carolyn Elizabeth Ferguson, b. 9 May 1943, Pontotoc County, Mississippi, USA. Financial Manager; Assistant General Manager. m. John W Logan, 28 Nov. 1963. 2 sons, 1 daughter. *Education:* BBA, University of Mississippi, 1981. *Appointments:* Production Worker, Rivera Inc, 1965- 72; Asst Manager, Buckhorn General Store, 1976-81; Financial Manager, L & M Frames Inc, 1982-81; Secretary/Treasurer/Assistant to General Manager, L & M Corporation, 1982- *Memberships:* Pontotoc County Democratic Committee; Pontotoc County Advisory Council; South Pontotoc PTO; South Pontotoc Bond Boosters; 4-H Volunteer Leader; Fund raiser for Heart Association, Lung Association and Mississippi Boys and Girls Ranches. *Honours:* 5 year Pin for County Volunteer Work, 1987; Nominated, Ole Miss Mortar board, 1981; National Dean's List, 1981-82. *Hobbies:* Reading; Tours; Sewing; Horses; Club work; Charity work. *Address:* Rt 1, Box 185, Rondolph, MS 38864, USA.

LOGAN Joanne, b. 14 Aug. 1954, Boston, Massachusetts, USA. Assistant Professor. m. 26 July 1986. 1 son. *Education:* BS, University of Connecticut, 1976; MS 1981, PhD 1984, University of Nebraska. *Appointments:* Peace Corps Volunteer, Ecuador, 1976-79; Graduate Research Assistant 1979-84, Assistant Professor 1985-87, University of Nebraska; Assistant Professor, University of Tennessee, 1987-. *Publications:* Various research reports, bulletins and journal articles. *Memberships:* Secretary, East Tenn PC Users Group; Amer Society Horticultural Science; Agronomy Society of America; American Meteorological Society; Sigma Xi; Graduate Women in Science. *Honour:* Volunteer recognition award, Lincoln, Nebraska, 1981. *Hobbies:* Computers; Fitness walking; Bicycling; Tennis; Reading; Science fiction. *Address:* P O Box 1071, Dept Plant & Soil Science, University of Tennessee, Knoxville, TN 37901, USA.

LOGAN Lillian May, b. 14 Dec. 1909, Sy Keston, North Dakota, USA. Professor Emerita. m. 30 Sept. 1946. *Education:* BS, Education, Eastern Michigan University, 1939; MS, Education, 1950, PhD, 1952, University of Wisconsin. *Appointments:* Teaching, Public Schools, Michigan, Ohio, Indiana, 1934-48; Professor of Education, University College, Lincoln, Nebraska, 1948-54; Evansville College, 1954-62; Professor of Education, Findlay College, 1962-65; Professor of Education, Brandon University, 1965-78. *Publications:* Teaching the Young Child, 1960; Teaching Elementary Child, 1962; Creative Communications, 1967; Creative Teaching, 1972; Framework for Learning Resources, 1987. *Memberships:* National Vice President, Pi Lambda Theta, 1961-63; Editor of Spectram, 1970-73, Canadian Speech Association; Membership Chairman, Association Childhood Education, 1965-75; OME. *Honours:* Award for Excellence in field of Speech, Canadian Speech Association, 1987; Research award, Pi Lambda Theta, 1963. *Hobbies:* Organist; Gardening; Concert pianist; Writing. *Address:* 602 15th Street, Brandon, Manitoba, R7A 4W5, Canada.

LOGAN Rose-Marie Fox, b. New Haven, Connecticut, USA. Investment Banker. *Education:* BFA, Manhattanville College; MBA, Finance, Wharton School, University of Pennsylvania, 1983. *Appointments include:* Financial Manager, AT&T, 1975-83; Vice President Corporate Finance, Prudential Bache Securities, 1983-84; Senior VP Corporate Finance, Lehman Brothers, 1984-89; President, Compass Group (investment banking, mergers & acquisitions) 1989-. *Creative works:* Oil paintings; Poetry. *Memberships:* Metropolitan Club, New York City; Boards (NYC): United Neighbourhood Houses, Playschools Association, Roundabout Theatre; Chair, Associate Guild, NY City Opera. *Hobbies:* Skiing; Tennis; Opera; Theatre; Painting; Reading. *Address:* 354 East 50th Street, New York, NY 10022, USA.

LOIS Wendy Harper, b. 7 July 1964, Worcester, Massachusetts, USA. Wellness Coordinator (Health Educator). m. Glenn F Lois, 27 Aug. 1988. *Education:* BA, Biology, Physical Education & Dance, Skidmore College, 1982-86; MS, Health Promotion/Wellness Management, Springfield College, 1986- 88. *Appointments:* Health and Fitness Coordinator, Prime Computer Inc, Framingham, Massachusetts, 1986-88; Welness Coordinator/ Department Head, The Kingston Hospital, Kingston, 1988-. *Publications:* Undergraduate thesis: Effects of ballet & modern dance on selected measures of College females; Edited/assisted in writing a Wellness Manual with Professor F Wolcott, Springfield College; Masters thesis: The Influence of nutrition and exercise intervention on Physiologic, Anthropometric and behavioral measure of corporate employees. *Memberships:* American Alliance for Health, Recreation Physical Education and Dance; American College of Sports Medicine; Association for Fitness in Business. *Honours:* Excellence Award, Prime Computer Inc, 1988; Fellowship Award, Springfield College, 1986-88; All College Scholarship Award, Skidmore College for Academics, 1986-88; Periclean Honor Society, Skidmore College, 1986; Selected student representative, Dept Physical Ed & Dance Skidmore College for College Government Association, 1985- 86; Various awards for Road Race Running; Dancing, 1980-88. *Hobbies:* Skiing; Ballet, modern and jazz dance; Running; Aerobics; Teach health education classes/ aerobics/gymnastics; Landscaping; Sketching; Attending auctions; Writing poetry; Music (appreciator of every type). *Address:* RD1 Box 104A, Lake Katrine, NY 12449, USA.

LOLLOBRIGIDA Gina, b. 4 July 1927, Sibiaco, Italy. Actress. m. Milko Skofic, 1949. 1 son. *Education:* Liceo Artistico, Rome. *Career:* First screen role in Pagliacci, 1947. *Creative Works:* Films include: Campane a Martello, 1948; Cuori senza Frontiere, 1949; Achtung, banditi! 1951; Enrico Caruso, 1951; Fanfan la Tulipe, 1951; Altri Tempi, 1952; The Wayward Wife, 1952; Les belles de la nuit, 1952; Pane, amore e fantasia, 1953; La Provinciale, 1953; Pane, amore e gelosia, La Romana, 1954; Il Grande Gioco, 1954; La Donna piu Bella del Mondo, 1955; Trapeze, 1956; Notre Dame de Paris, 1956; Solomon and Sheba, 1959; Never so Few, 1960; Go Naked in the World, 1961; She Got What She Asked For, 1963; Woman of Straw, 1964; Le Bambole, 1965; Hotel Paradiso, 1966; Buona Sera Mrs Campbell, 1968; King, Queen, Knave, 1972. *Publication:* Italia Mia (Photography), 1974. *Hobby:* Photography. *Address:* Via Appia Antica 223, 1-00178 Rome, Italy.

LOMAX-SIMPSON Josephine Mary, b. 11 Mar. 1925, London, England. Consultant Psychotherapist; Consultant Psychiatrist; Psychoanalyst; Large Group Therapist. *Education:* MB, ChB, Aberdeen University, 1948; Diploma of Psychological Medicine, 1953. *Appointments:* Psychiatrist, Children's Home, Roehampton, 1953-67; Consultant Psychiatrist, Family Therapist, East Grinstead Family Consultation Centre, Sussex, 1963-88; Founder, Therapeutic Adviser, Messenger House Trust, Wimbledon, London, 1970- 88. *Publications:* The Large Group as a Vehicle for Change, Maturation & Therapy, article, 1978; The Therapeutic Large Group, Comment, Channel 4 TV. 1985. *Memberships:* Vice-President, Association for Workers with Maladjusted Children; Society of Group Analysis; Associate Member, The Institute of Psycho-Analysis. *Honours:* 2nd Prize for Mental Health, Aberdeen University, 1947; Foundation Lecturer, Cairnmiller Institute, Melbourne, Australia, 1967; Sir Cyril Black for Service to Community, Wimbledon, 1979; Fellowship, Royal College of Psychiatrists, 1984. *Hobbies:* Travel abroad; Lecturing; Theatre; Ballet. *Address:* Flat 5, Raymond Court, Raymond Road, Wimbledon, London SW19 4AR, England.

LONG Bettye Virginia, b. 13 July 1924, Bernice, Louisiana, USA. Business Management. m. H. L. Long, 20 Oct. 1946, 4 sons. *Education:* AA, Kilgore College, 1943; Bachelor of General Studies, University of Texas at Tyler, 1980. *Appointments:* Managing Trustee, 1954-78, Joint Manager, 1978-, The Long Trusts; Secretary-Treasurer, Rusk County Well Service Co, 1970-; President, Cherokee Oil Traders, 1979-. *Memberships:* Texas Historical Commission, Vice-Chairman 1983-85, 1986-88; President, Kilgore Improvement and Beautification Association, 1987-89; Co-Chairman, Civic Affairs Committee, Kilgore Chamber of Commerce, 1982-84. *Honours:* Nominee, Texas Women's Hall of Fame, 1984; First Lady of Kilgore, selected by Beta Sigma Phi Sorority, 1985. *Hobbies:* Travel; Collecting antiques. *Address:* 2902 Royal Drive, Kilgore, TX 75662, USA.

LONG Dorothy Valjean Shepherd, b. 10 Mar. 1928, Paducah, USA. Company President. m. Earl Wallace Long, 16 Sept. 1944, 2 sons. *Appointments:* Keypuunch Supervisor, IBM Corp, 1950-54; SW Region Terminal Service Manager, Control Data Corp, 1966-80; President, CEO, Keypeople Resources Pesonnel Agency, 1980-. *Memberships:* Houston Area Association; Texas Association of Personnel Consultants; ABW. *Memberships:* Life Member, PTA, Houston; Life Member, Womens Society of Christian Service. *Hobbies:* Reading; Dancing; Camping; Bride; Politics; Church Leadership. *Address:* Keypeople Resources Inc., 200 W. Loop S., 1620, Houston, TX 77027, USA.

LONG Joan Dorothy, b. Victoria, Australia. Film Producer. m. Martin Merrick Long, 31 Dec. 1953, 3 sons (2 stepsons), 1 daughter. *Education:* BA, Melbourne University. *Appointments:* Editor, director, Film Australia, 1948-53; Home Occupations, 1954-63; Freelance Scriptwriter, 1963-67; Scriptwriter, Director, Film Australia, 1967-73; Feature Film Producer, Screenwriter, 1974-. *Publications:* Films: The Pictures That Moved, 1968; The Passionate Industry, 1972; Paddington Lace, 1970; Caddie, 1976; The Picture Show Man, 1977; Puberty Blues, 1981; Silver City, 1984; Emerald City, 1988. *Memberships:* Australian Writers Guild, President, 1972-73; Screen Production Association of Australia; Australian Film Institute;

Women in Film & Television; Sydney Film Festival. *Honours:* Australian Writers Guild Awards, 1970, 1971, 1973; Vittoria de Sica Award, 1980; Order of Australia, 1980; Critics Circle Award, Best Film Silver City, 1985. *Hobbies:* Reading; History. *Address:* 81 Bent Street, Lindfield, NSW 2070, Australia.

LONG Rose-Carol Washton, b. 1 Mar. 1938, New London, Connecticut, USA. Art Historian. m. Carl D. Long, 28 Mar. 1970, 1 son. *Education:* BA, Wellesley College, 1959; MA 1962, PhD 1968, Yale University. *Appointments:* Museum Lecturer, Guggenheim Museum, 1964-67, CUNY Queens College; Lecturer 1967-69, Assistant Professor 1969-78, Queens College, Associate Professor 1978-83, Professor, Department of Art 1983-, Queens College & Graduate Centre, City University of New York, Executive Officer 1980-81, 1985-, Department of American History Graduate Centre. *Publications include:* Book, Kandinsky: Development of an Abstract Style, 1980, Co-editor, Life of Vasilii Kandinsky in Russian Art, 1980; Catalogues: Editor, 20th Century Prints from Godwin-Ternbach Museum, 1983. Essays & articles, various publications including Art Journal, Art Bulletin; Papers & lectures. *Membership:* College Art Association of America. *Honours:* John Simon Guggenheim Fellow, 1983-84; Grants-in- aid, ACLS 1972-73, 1982-83; Younger Humanist Fellow, National Endowment for Humanities, 1972-73; Reviewer, various professional bodies, 1976-. *Address:* CUNY Graduate Centre, 33 West 42nd Street, New York, NY 10036, USA.

LONG Virginia Love (Mariposa), b. 21 Aug. 1941, Roxboro, North Carolina, USA. Poet. 2 sons. *Education:* Catawba College 1958-61. *Appointments:* Active journalist, including columnist, reviewer, women's news editor, book page, Roxboro Courier Times, 1963-75; Typographer, Medical Illustration & Photography School of Medicine, University of North Carolina, Chapel Hill, current. *Publications include:* After the Ifaluk & Other Poems; Gallows Lord; Upstream; Squaw Winter. In press: All Roads Lead to Bushy Fork; Blue Butterfly. Co-author, with Rochelle L. Holt: Letters of Human Nature; Shared Journey. *Memberships:* Past offices: North Carolina Poetry Society, Poetry Council of NC. Member: Byron Society; Academy of American Poets; Feminist Writers Guild. *Honours:* Pulitzer nominee, 1975, 1987; Awards, NC Press, 1969, 1973; 1st places, free verse contests, NC Poetry Council, 1975, 1988; Yadkin Arts Council, 1975; 1st place, Greensboro Writers Poetry Contest, 1964; Featured writer, Forum for Universal Spokesmen, 1987; recipient of 1988 Oscar Arnold Young Book Award for Best Volume by N.C. Poet in 1987. *Hobbies:* Pre-Columbian cultures; Feminist history; Nahuatl & Russian poetry & languages; Animal rights & preservation of endangered species; Flowers; Professional wrestling. *Address:* Route 2, Box 54, Hurdle Mills, North Carolina 27541, USA.

LONGFORD Elizabeth, b. 30 Aug. 1906, London, England. Writer. m. Hon. Frank Pakenham (now Earl of Longford), 3 Nv. 1931, 4 sons, 4 daughters (1 deceased). *Education:* MA, Oxford University. *Appointments:* Advisory Board, British Library; Vice President, London Library. *Publications Include:* Jameson's Raid, 2nd edition 1982; Victoria RI, 1964; Wellington: Years of the Sword, 1969; Wellington: Pillar of State, 1972; Pilgrimage of Passion, 1979; Churchill, 1974; Eminent Victorian Women, 1981; Elizabeth R, 1983; contributor to Literary Review; etc. *Honours:* James Tait Black Memorial Prize, 1964; Yorkshire Post Book of the Year, 1972; Honorary DLitt, Sussex University; CBE. *Address:* 18 Cheshil Court, Chelsea Manor Street, London SW3 5QP, England.

LONGLEY Ann Rosamund, b. 5 Mar. 1942, St Austell, Conwall, England. Headmistress. m. Stephen Roger Longley, 1964, died 1979, 1 son, 2 daughters. *Education:* MA, Edinburgh University, 1964; PGCE, Bristol University, 1981. *Appointments:* Teacher, Toorak College, Australia, 1964-65; Assistant Housemistress, Peninsula C of E School, Australia, 1966-67; Residential Teacher, Choate School, Connecticut, USA, 1968-73;

Teacher, Webb School, California, 1975-79; Founding Headmistress, Vivian Webb School, California, 1981-84; Headmistress, Roedean School, England, 1984-. *Hobbies:* Tennis; Swimming; Fishing; Walking. *Address:* Roedean House, Roedean School, Brighton, E. Sussex BN2 5RQ, England.

LONGLEY Bernice, b. 27 Sep. 1923, Moline, Illinois, USA. Painter; Graphic Artist; Sculptor. 1 daughter. *Education:* Graduate, The Art Institute of Chicago, 1945; Instituto de Allende, San Miguel de Allende, Guanajuato, Mexico, 1971; Sculpture, Bronze Casting, Santa Fe School of Arts and Crafts, 1975. *Career:* Numerous one-woman shows, 1947-: Museum of New Mexico; Knopp-Hunter Gallery, College of Santa Fe, Canyon Road Art Gallery, Gallery Five, Summer Gallery, Santa Fe East, Santa Fe, New Mexico; Appleman Gallery, Denver, Colorado; VanDieman-Lillienfield Galleries, New York; Gallery A, Taos; Lars Laine Gallery, Palm Springs, California; Cushing Galleries, Dallas, Texas; Governor's Gallery, New Mexico State Capitol; Santa Fe East, Austin, Texas; Women's Bank, Denver, Colorado; Hickory Museum of Art, Hickory, North Carolina; Participated in exhibitions, Chicago, Denver, Santa Fe, California, San Francisco, 1946-. *Creative works include:* Mural for private home, Santa Fe, 1959; Mural, La Fonda Del Sol Restaurant, Time Life Building, New York, 1960; Oil and watercolour paintings; Lithographs; Bronze sculpture; Works in several public collections including Museum of New Mexico; Bernique Longley - A Retrospective (book), 1982. *Honours:* Bryan Lathrop Foreign Travelling Fellowship, Art Institute of Chicago, 1945; Honourable Mention for Sculpture, Denver Art Museum, 1948; Honourable Mention, International Watercolour Show, Art Institute of Chicago, 1948; Purchase Prize, Museum of New Mexico, 1953; 1st Prize for Figure Painting, New Mexico State Fair, 1953; Honourable Mention, Museum of New Mexico, 1965. *Address:* 427 Camino Del Monte Sol, Santa Fe, NM 87501, USA.

LONNETT BURGESS Maria Josephine, b. 28 June 1957, Philadelphia, USA. Doctoral Student. m. William Burgess, 5 Aug. 1988. *Education:* BS, Penn State University, 1981; MS, University of Pittsburgh, 1988; Currently, PhD Candidate, University of South Carolina. *Appointments:* Interpreter for Deaf, Pittsburgh, 1981-86; Sign Language Teacher, Pittsburgh, 1985; Phlebotomist, Presbyterian Hospital, 1985-86; Teacher of Deaf, Western PA School for Deaf, 1985. *Publications:* Abstracts; articles in professional journals. *Memberships:* American College of Sports Medicine; National Registry for the Deaf; Professional Teachers Association, Programme Chair. *bbJHonours:* Research Award, Graduate School, University of South Carolina; Research Award, University of Pittsburgh. *Hobbies:* Muscular Dystrophy Research; Bicycling; Walking; Playing the Piano; Church Group Participation. *Address:* Blatt Physical Education Center, University of South Carolina, Columbia, SC 29205, USA.

LONTZ Mary Belle, b. 1936, Williamsport, Pennsylvania, USA. Historian; Genealogist; Historic Site Searcher. *Education:* BS, Elementary Education, Bloomsberg; MS, Secondary Education, Bucknell University; PhD, Education, 1987. *Career:* Worked on properties in Nevada and Utah; Research in North Carolina. *Publications:* Index to 1957 Edition of Otzinachson, 1963; Union County, PA, 1966; Tombstone Inscriptions of Union County, Pennsylvania, 1967; Our German, Pilgrim, Quaker Ancestors, 1968; Index to History of Northumberland, Huntingdon, Mifflin, Center, Union, Columbia, Juniata and Clinton Cos, PA, 1970; Index to Vols 1, 2, 3 of Now and Then; Miller Family of Union County, 1970; Hoover Family of Union & Lancaster Cos, PA, 1970; Earlywine Family of East and Midwest, 1970; Crouse Family, 1970; Grimes Family, 1970; Wills of Centre County, Pennsylvania, 1970; The Narehood Family, 1971; The Ruhl Family, 1972; The Davidson/Davisson Family, 1972; The Berkheimer Family, reprint, 1972; Tax List for Union & North'd Cos, PA, 1974; Logan and Shikellamy; Milton, Penna; 1850 Census of Union Co, PA, 1978; The Noll

Family of Union Co, PA, 1979; Revolutionary War Soldiers of Union & Snyder Cos, PA, 1980; Tombstone Inscriptions of Snyder Co, reprint, 1981; Index to Annals of Buffalo Valley (Linn); Chillisquaque, (PA), 1983; Rev John Bryson, 1983; Tombstone Inscriptions of Center County, PA, 1984; One Room Schools of Union Co, PA; Deaths and Marriages from Old Newspapers and Books (Central Pennsylvania); Tombstones Inscriptions of Union County. *Memberships:* Daughters of the American Revolution; Daughters of the American Colonists; Sons and Daughters of the Pilgrims; Indiana Society of Pioneers. ssa 20Honours: Medal of Appreciation and Martha Washington Award, Sons of the American Revolution. *Address:* 608 Broadway, Milton, PA 17847, USA.

LOPER Candice Kay, 29 Oct. 1953, Subliette, USA. Computer Systems Analyst/Consultant. *Education:* Diablo Valley College, 1988. *Appointments:* Owner/ Operator, Candi's for Beautiful Hair, 1974-78; Data Clerk, Adia Temporary Services, 1979-80; Systems Project Librarian, 1980, Analyst, 1981, Systems Analyst, 1981-82, Senior Systems Analyst, 1982-83, Bank of America; Consultant, Bank of America, 1984; Project Manager, Wells Fargo Bank, 1984-86; Advisory Systems Engineer, Bank of America, 1988-; Owner, Manager, Lper Comp-u-Pix, Concord, 1988-; Policyholder Service Corporation, Kansas City, Missouri, 1989-. *Membership:* American Quilters Society. *Hobbies:* Crochet; Quilting; Photography. *Address:* 3419 So. Home, Independence, Missouri 64052, USA.

L'ORANGE Helen, b. 20 Aug. 1942, Australia. First Assistant Secretary. divorced. 2 sons. *Education:* Teachers certificate, Armidale Teachers College, 1961. *Appointments:* Infant Teacher 1962-68, Deputy Headmistress 1969, NSW Education Department; Executive Director, International Year of the Child, 1978-80; Director, Women's Coordination Unit, NSW Premier's Department, 1980-89; Head, Office of the Status of Women, Department of the Prime Minister and Cabinet, Commonwealth Government, 1989-. *Current Memberships:* Standing Committee, Commonwealth/State Government Women's Advisers; Inaugural Chairperson, National Working Party on the Portrayal of Women in the Media; Chairperson, Commonwealth/State Task Force for Naltional Domestic Violence Education Program; Inaugural Chairperson, Commonwealth/State Task Force on Non-English Speaking Background Women's Issues. *Hobbies:* Bike riding; Reading; Tapestry. *Address:* Office of the Status of Women, Department Prime Minister and Cabinet, 3-5 National Circuit, Barton, ACT 2600, Australia.

LORBER Charlotte, b. 11 Apr. 1952, Brooklyn, New York, USA. Publisher. *Education:* Seminar on China Studies, National Chengehi University, 1972; BBA, University of Miami, 1975. *Appointments:* Director Special Events, Third Century USA Dade County Bicentennial Organization, 1975-76; Promotion Director, Donato Advertising, 1977-78; President/ Publisher, Towne Publishing & Advertising Co, 1979-89. *Publications:* Publisher of award winning publications. *Memberships:* Greater Miami Chamber of Commerce, Trustee; Coral Gables Chamber of Commerce, Life Member; Miami Beach Chamber of Commerce, Trustee, Board Member; World Trade Center; American Chamber of Commerce Executives; North Dade Chamber of Commerce; Rotary Club of Coral Gables. *Honours:* American Chamber of Commerce Executives: Award of Excellence for New View of our City Magazine, Greater Miami Chamber, 1987 and 1988; Award of Excellence for New View of our City Directory, Greater Miami Chamber, 1987; Award of Merit for Directory, Greater Miami Chamber, 1988; Award of Merit for Direct Mail Brochure, Greater Miami Chamber, 1988. Award of Merit for Magazine, Printing Industries of South Florida Greater Miami Chamber, 1989; Recipient Merit Award, City of Hialeah. *Hobbies:* Pilot; Scuba diver; Race car driver; Cooking. *Address:* Towne Publishing & Advertising Co Inc, 4203 Salzedo Street, Coral Gables, Florida 33146, USA.

LORD Catherine, b. 8 Mar. 1959, Dartford, Kent, England. Classical Violinist. *Education:* Royal College of Music, London, 1975-79; ARCM, Performers, Honours, 1976; Juilliard School, New York, 1979-82; Diploma, 1982. *Appointments:* Recitalist, Concerto Soloist with various orchestras including: London Chanticleer Orchestra, Royal Philharmonic Orchestra, Bach Players, New York; many recordings for radio & TV, 1984-85; Associate Concertmaster, New Orleans Symphony Orchestra, 1985-87; Professor, Violin, University of New Orleans & Member, Faculty Piano Trio. *Honours:* Associated Board Scholarship, 1975; Beatric Montgomerie Prize, 1978; Stoutzker Prize, 1979; Martin Scholarship, Countess of Munster Award, Boise Scholarship, South East Arts Award, Seymour Whinyates Prize, juilliard Scholarship, 1980; Juilliard Scholarship, 1981; Royal Society of Arts Scholarship. *Hobbies:* Jazz; Reading; Travel; Horse Riding; Cats. *Address:* 59F Netherhall Gardens, Hampstead, London NW3 5RE, England.

LORD Mia W, b. Dec. 1920, New York City, New York, USA. World Peace Activist for Abolition of War and Armaments. m. Robert P Lord. 2 daughters. *Education:* BA cum laude, Liberal Arts, Brooklyn College, New York City, USA; currently graduate student working toward second baccalaureate in Fine Arts, San Francisco State University, San Francisco, California. *Appointments:* Honorary Secretary, Commonwealth of World Citizens, London, England; Life Member, Secretariat of World Citizens, USA; Membership Secretary, British Association for World Government, London, England; Secretary, Group 68, Americans in Britain for US Withdrawal from SE Asia; Organiser, Vietnam Vigil to End the War, London, England; Honorary Secretary and National Excecutive Committee Member, Association of World Federalists, UK; Founder and Director, Crusade to Abolish War and Armaments by World Law; Founder and President, Let's Abolish War!, the San Francisco State University Chapter of the World Federalist Association, USA. *Publications:* The Practical Way to End Wars and Other World Crises: the Case for World Federal Government, 1984 Edition of World Peace through World Law and in Strengthening the United Nations, 1987; War-the Biggest Con Game. *Memberships:* Association of World Federalists, USA; World Government Organization Coordinating Committee; World Federal Authority Committee; Campaign for UN Reform; Citizens Global Action; World Constitution and Parliament Association; World Public Forum; International Registry of World Citizens. *Honours:* Nominated for the Nobel Peace Prize, 1975; Officially invited to Vietnam, 1973; Recipient of four Merit Awards from the President of San Francisco State University, San Francisco, California. *Address:* 174 Majestic Avenue, San Francisco, California 94112, USA.

LOREN Sophia, b. 20 Sept. 1934, Rome, Italy. Actress. m. Carlo Ponti, 1957. 2 sons. *Education:* Scuole Magistrali Superiori. *Career:* First screen appearance as an extra in Quo Vadis. *Creative Works:* Films include: E Arrivato l'Accordatore, 1951; Africa sotto i Mari (first leading role); La Tratta delle Bianche; La Favorita, 1952; Aida, 1953; Il Paese dei Campanelli; Miseria e Nobilta; Il Segno di Venere, 1953; Tempi Nostri, 1953; Carosello Napoletano, 1953; L'Oro di Napoli, 1954; Attila, 1954; Peccato che sia una canaglia; La Bella Mugnaia; La Donna del Fiume, 1955; Boccaccio, 1970; Matrimonio All'Italiana; The Pride and the Passion, 1955; Boy on a Dolphin; Legend of the Lost, 1956; Desire Under the Elms, 1957; That Kind of Woman, 1958; Houseboat, 1958; The Key, 1958; The Black Orchid, 1959; It Started in Naples; Heller in Pink Tights, 1960; The Millionairess, 1961; Two Women, 1961; El Cid, 1961; Madame Sans Gene, 1962; Yesterday, Today and Tomorrow, 1963; The Fall of the Roman Empire, 1964; Lady L, 1965; Operation Crossbow, 1965; Judith, 1965; A Countess from Hong Kong, 1965; Arabesque, 1966; More than a Miracle, 1967; The Priest's Wife, 1970; Sunflower, 1970; Hot Autumn, 1971; Man of La Mancha, 1972; Brief Encounter (TV), 1974; The Verdict, 1974; The Voyage, 1974; The Cassandra Crossing, 1977; A Special Day, 1977; Firepower, 1978; Brass Target, 1979; Blood Feud, 1981. *Publications:* Eat with Me, 1972; Sophia

LOREN on Women and Beauty, 1984. *Membership:* Chair, National Alliance for Prevention and Treatment of Child Abuse and Maltreatment. *Honours:* Venice Festival Award for The Black Orchid, 1958; Cannes Film Festival Award for Best Actress (Two Women), 1961. *Address:* Chalet Daniel, Burgenstock, Lucerne, Switzerland.

LORING Ann, b. 17 Jan. 1915, New York City, USA. Actress; Writer; Teacher. 2 sons. *Education:* BA, Brooklyn College, 1935. *Appointments:* Worked in all major radio & tv shows for 25 years; Producer, WOR, Barry Farber Talk Show & Panellist more than 500 times; Lead on daytime drama, Love of Life, 13 years. *Publications:* Author, 4 novels; contributor, lead articles in professional magazines. *Memberships:* Trustee, Governor, many times and currently, National Academy of TV Arts & Sciences; President, New York American Federation of Television and Radio Artists Union; President of American Federation of TV and Radio Artists, for five terms; Member, MWA. *Honours:* Award, Best Daytime TV Actress, 1957-58, 1958- 59. *Hobbies:* Swimming; Water Skiing. *Address:* AFTRA, 260 Madisin Avenue, NYCV, NY 10016, USA.

LORRIMER Claire, b. 1 Feb. 1921, Hove, Sussex, England. Author. m. Donald Campbell Clark, 4 Mar. 1948, divorced 1982. 2 sons, 1 daughter. *Education:* Swiss Institute, Munich University. *Appointments:* Sub Editor, Woman's Illustrated Magazine, 1937-39; Flight Officer, WRAF, 1939-46; Author, 1946-. *Publications:* Pseudonym Patricia Robins, 1944-73: To the Stars; See No Evil; Three Loves; Awake My Heart; Beneath the Moon; Leave My Heart Alone; The Fair Deal; Heart's Desire; So This is Love; Heaven in Our Hearts; One Who Cares; Love Cannot Die; The Foolish Heart; Give All to Love; Where Duty Lies; He is Mine; Love Must Wait; Lonely Quest; Lady Chatterley's Daughter; The Last Chance; The Long Wait; The Runaways; Seven Loves; With all My Love; The Constant Heart; Second Love; The Night is Thine; There is But One; No More Loving; Topaz Island; Love Me Tomorrow; The Uncertain Joy; The Man Behind the Mask; Forbidden; Sapphire in the Sand; Return to Love; Laugh on Friday; No Stone Unturned; Cinnabar House; Under the Sky; The Crimson Tapestry; Play Fair with Love; None But He; Verse: Seven Days Leave; Children's fiction: The Adventures of The Three Baby Bunnies; Tree Fairies; Sea Magic; The Heart of a Rose; The 100 Reward. As Claire Lorrimer, 1967-88; A Voice in The Dark; The Shadow Falls; Relentless Storm; The Secret of Quarry House; Mavreen; Tamarisk; Chantal; The Chatelaine; The Wilderling; Last Year's Nightingale; Frost in the Sun. A Cameo: The Garden. Biography: House of Tomorrow. Short stories in numerous magazines. *Memberships:* Society of Authors; RAF Club. *Hobbies:* Gardening; Travel; Skiing; Golf; Reading; Entertaining. *Address:* Chiswell Barn, Edenbridge, Kent, England.

LOSCHIAVO Linda Ann, b. New York City, USA. Author. m. Sergei Brozski, 3 Sept. 1977, divorced 1987. *Education:* BA, 1971, MA, 1976, Hunter College; PhD Candidate, New York University. *Appointments:* Managing Editor, various magazines, 1968-75; Freelance Writer, 1975-; Adjunct Professor, Hunter University, 1976-78; Adjunct Professor, New York University, 1978-80. *Publications:* Articles in numerous magazines & journals on five continents; contributor to: Writer's Markets, 1985; Writer's Handbook, 1987, 1988. *Memberships:* Sigma Tau Delta; American Mensa Ltd; Authors Guild; American Society of Journalists & Authors; American Bromeliad Society. *Honours:* Marquis Award, 1964; Mensa Journalism Award, 1977, 1978; Mensa OWL Award, 1978; Writer's Digest Annual Writing Contest, Winner: 1978, 1985, 1987, 1988. *Hobbies:* Writing; Breeding Bluepoint Siamese Cats; Breeding Bromeliads. *Address:* 24 Fifth Avenue, New York, NY 10011, USA.

LOSEY Beverley Isabella Brown, b. 25 July 1948, Seattle, Washington, USA. Lawyer; Public speaker. m. Robert F Losey, Jr 12 Feb. 1988. *Education:* BS, Nursing, University of Maryland, Walter Reed Army Institute of Nursing Extension, 1970; Juris Doctor, University of Puget Sound School of Law, 1984. *Appointments:* Nurse, Department of Army, 1970-77; Nursing Supervisor, State of Wyoming, 1977-81; Solo practitioner, law firm of Beverley Brown Losey, 1985-. *Publications:* Articles in Medical Bulletin of US Army, Europe; Nursing Outlook. *Memberships:* Major, US Army Reserves; Psi of Zeta Tau Alpha Building Corp; Board of Directors and Treasurer, 1986-88; Reserve Officers Association, Tacoma Area Chapter, Past Secretary, Treasurer and Past Vice President, Army; Phi Delta Phi Legal Fraternity. *Honours:* American Jurisprudence Award for study of trusts and estates, 1983; Juris Doctor, cum laude. *Hobbies:* Reading; Swimming. *Address:* 3425 So 176th Street, No 132, Seattle, WA 98188, USA.

LOSINSKA Kathleen Mary (Kate), b. 5 Oct. 1924, Croydon, England. Retired Trade Union President. m. Stanislaw Losinski, 24 Dec. 1942, 1 son *Appointments:* Office of Population Censuses & Surveys, 1964-74; Civil & Public Services Association, 1976, 1979-82, 1983-86, Trade Union General Council. *Publicaitons:* Articles in journals & magazines. *Memberships:* Council Civil Service Union; Ruskin College Governor; European Christian TU Movement; Peace Through NATO; Amnesty International. *Honours:* Queens Jubilee Medal, 1977; OBE, 1986; Knight Commander, Order of Polonia Restituta, 1988. *Hobbies:* Journalism Research; Travel; Music. *Address:* Ballinard, Herbertstown, County Limerick, Southern Ireland.

LOTEMPIO Julia Matild, b. 14 Oct. 1934, Budapest, Hungary. Accountant; Educator. m. Anthony Joseph LoTempio, 11 Mar. 1958. *Education:* AAS, 1967; BS, 1970; MS, 1973; BBA, 1983; Permanent Teaching Certification, 1985. *Appointments:* Senior Analyst, Industrial Researcher, 1967-71; High School Science Mathematics English Teacher, 1973-77; College Instructor, Applied Chemistry, 1979; Administrator, Accountant, 1979-81; Business Consultant, 1981-85; Accountant, CPA Firm, 1986-87; Accountant, Private Practice, 1988-; Board of Directors, Beechwood Residence Inc., Beechwood Nursing Home, Inc., The Blocher Homes, Inc., 1988-. *Publications:* Teaching Film: The Periodic Table, 1971; Teaching Tapes & Workbooks for the Intermediate Science Curriculum, 1975. *Memberships:* National Association of Accountants; National Association for Female Executives Inc; National Federation of Business & Professional Womens Club Inc; International Platform Association. *Honours:* All Degrees, Summa Cum Laude; Academic Proficiency Award, 1967; Womens Club Award, 1967; Academic Proficiency Award, 1970. *Hobbies Include:* Public Speaking; Walking; Travel; Reading; Computero. *Address:* 1026 Ridge Road, Lewiston, NY 14092, USA.

LOTHROP Gloria Ricci, b. 30 Dec. 1934, Los Angeles, California, USA. University Professor; Writer. m. David L. Levering, 27 June 1982. *Education:* BA, 1956, MA, 1963, Immaculate Heart College; PhD, University of Southern California, 1970. *Appointments:* Adjunct Professor, University of Southern California, 1970; Professor of History, California State Polytechnic University, Pomona, 1970-. *Publications:* Recollections of Flathead Mission (editor), 1977; California Women, A History (co-author), 1987; Pomona, A Centennial History, 1988; A Guide to the History of California (co-editor), 1989; Over 60 articles and reviews. *Memberships:* American Historical Association; Organization of American Historians; Western History Association; Californian Historical Society; Souther Californian Historical Society; Phi Alpha Theta; Kappa Gamma Pi. *Honours:* Fulbright Fellowship, 1963; Oakley Graduate Fellowship, 1965- 67; Haynes Dissertation Fellowship, 1967-68; Huntington Library Fellowship, 1986; Award of Merit, Daughters of the American Revolution; Teaching Award, Daughters of Colonial Wars; Distinguished Alumna Award, 1981; Outstanding Professor, California Polytechnic, 1981; Outstanding Italian-American Award, 1982; Outstanding Feminist, Pomona Valley National Organization for Women. *Hobbies:* Cardening; Drama; Antiques; Lecturing. *Address:* 880 Paige Drive, Pomona, CA 91768, USA.

LOTT Felicity Ann Emwhyla, b. 8 May 1947, Cheltenham, England. Opera Singer. m. Gabriel Woolf, 19 Jan. 1984, 1 daughter. *Education:* BA, Honours French, Royal Holloway College University of London, 1969; Royal Academy of Music, 1969-73. *Appointments:* Principal roles with: Glyndebourne Festival Opera, English National Opera, Covent Garden (Royal Opera), Scottish & Welsh Operas; appearances in: Paris, Hamburg, Chicago, Zurich, Munich; Recitals in: London, Paris, Brussels, New York, Hong Kong. *Honour:* FRAM, 1987. *Hobby:* Keeping Up with a 4 Year Old. *Address:* c/o Lies Askonas Ltd., 186 Drury Lane, London WC2B 5RY, England.

LOTT-BERNARDONI (Sarah) Katheryn, b. 23 Nov. 1952, San Antonio, Texas, USA. Architect. m. John Michael Bernardoni, 22 May 1981, 1 son. *Education:* BArch, Honours, University of Texas at Austin, 1974. *Appointments:* Martin & Ortega, Architects, 1974-76; 3-D International Architects, 1976-79; Lundren & Associates, 1979-80; American Design Group Inc, 1981-88; Own practice, Katheryn Lott, Architect, 1988- . *Memberships:* Past Secretary, Austin Chapter, American Institute of Architects; Texas Society of Architects; Trustee: American Institute for Learning & Creative Rapid Learning Centre. *Hobbies:* Skiing; Sailing; Swimming. *Address:* 2216 River Hills Road, Austin, Texas 78733, USA.

LOUCHEUX-LEFEBVRE Marie-Henriette, b. 22 Jan. 1934, Saint-Pol/Ternoise, France. Scientist. m. Claude Loucheux, 30 Apr. 1957. 1 son, 1 daughter. *Education:* Ingenieur, Ecole Nationale Superieure de Chimie de Lille, 1955; These d'Etat, University de Strasbourg, 1962. *Appointments:* Centre de Recherches sur les macromolecules, Strasbourg, 1955-68; Montreal University, Canada, 1965-66; Lille Universite des Sciences, 1968-74; Unite 124 INSERM, 1974-, Head of the Unite 124 INSERM, 1985-. *Publications:* 100 scientific publications. *Memberships:* Societe francaise de biophysique; European Association for Cancer Research; European Environmental Society; Association Franco-Japonaise de Biologie; President, CSCRI (Conseil Scientifique Consultatif Regional INSERM). *Hobby:* Music. *Address:* Unite 124 INSERM, Institut de Recherches sur Le Cancer de Lille, Cite Hospitaliere, 59045 Lille Cedex, France.

LOUDON Prudence Katharine Patton, b. 30 Aug. 1913, London, England. Retired Voluntary Worker. m. F. W. H. Loudon, 22 Dec. 1936, 1 son, 2 daughters. *Education:* Diploma, Theology, 1981. *Appointments:* Past Chairman, National Council for the Unmarried Mother; Chairman, Ashford School, Kent; Trustee, Burrswood, Tunbridge Wells; Council, University of Kent; Governing Body, Christ Church Teachers' Training College, Canterbury; Justice of Peace, Juvenile Courts, London & Kent. *Hobbies:* Travel, Reading, Sketching. *Address:* Little Olantigh, Wye, Ashford, Kent TN25 5DH, England.

LOUDOVA Ivana, b. 8 Mar. 1941, Chlumec n c, Czechoslovakia. Composer. m. Milos Haase 16 Aug. 1973. 1 son. *Education:* Prague Conservatory, 1961; Diploma, Academy of Musician Arts, Prague, 1966; Postgraduate study, Academy, 1968-72. *Appointments:* Comp study by M. Kabelác, E. Hlobil and T.O. Messiaen and André Jolivet, Paris, France, 1971; Composer in residence by American Wind Symphony Orchestra, Pittsburgh, USA, 1980; Freelance Composer, 1972-. *Creative works:* Compositions: Over 95 works including two symphonies; Rhapsody in Black; Chorale; Hymnos; Spleen-Hommage a Ch. Baudelaire; Concerto for Perc, Organ and Wind orchestra; Dramatic concerto for Solo percussion and Wind orchestra; Luminous voice for English horn and wind orchestra. Chamber music: Suite for Solo Flute, Per Tromba; Gnomai-trio for soprano, flute and harp; Solo for King David, harp solo; String quartet No 1, 2; Air; Aulos; Agamemnon; Nocturne for viola and Strings; Soli e Tutti, Partita in D; Musica Festiva; Hukvald's Suite; Trio in B; Trio Italiano. Numerous vocal and choral works, many instructive works for children, film and theatre music. *Honours:*

Several prizes in comp contests in Czechoslovakia; 2nd prize, Culture Ministry Contest, CSSR, for Concerto for Percussion, organ and wind orchestra, 1976; 1st prize, Inter. Comp. Contest, Guido d'Arezzo for Sonetto, 1978; 2nd prize, Compt Contest OIRT, Moscow, for Little Christmas Cantate, 1978. *Hobbies:* Tennis; Skiing. *Address:* Aubrechtove 3100, 106 00 Praha 10, Czechoslovakia.

LOUGHLIN Mary Anne Elizabeth, b. 30 July 1956, Biddeford, Maine, USA. Television News Anchor. *Education:* BS, Communications, Florida State University, Tallahassee, 1977. *Appointments:* Reporter, WFSU-FM, Tallahassee, 1976; News Anchor & Producer, WECA Television 1977-81; Programme Host & Producer, WTBS-TV Atlanta, Georgia, 1981-84; News Anchor, CNN Atlanta, 1983-. *Memberships:* American Women in Radio and Television; Women in Cable; Women in Communications. *Honours:* Women at Work Broadcast Award, National Commission on Working Women, 1982; AWRT Woman of Achievement, (Nominated 1983), 1984. *Hobbies:* Photography; Piano. *Address:* 1050 Techwood Drive NW, Atlanta, GA 30318, USA.

LOVE Christa Maria (Carolyn Maude White), b. 10 Feb. 1940, Providence, Rhode Island, USA. Development Expert; Author; Artist; International Educator; Executive. *Education:* BA, University of Virginia, 1962; MA, Columbia University, 1968; Studied Abroad: Columbia University French Program, Paris, France; Universita di Firenze and Accademia di BelleCurti, Florence, Italy; Université de Geneve and Ecole des Beaux-arts, Geneva, Switzerland; research for MA Thesis in Japan. *Appointments:* Chairwoman, International Executive Board, Director, CEO, Quest for Peace, Inc., New York, 1984-; Consultant, Observer to UN, including to UN Non-Proliferation Treaty Review Conference, Geneva, Switzerland, 1975-, UN Law of Sea Conference, and development, education, peace-related work, Field Work, Research, India, 1973-74; Assistant to President, Kent State University, Ohio, 1972-73; Program Administration, Overseas Programs, Institute of International Education, 1069-71; Organizer of Conferences on Development, 1968, 1972. *Publications:* Composer, Lyricist, Anthem and Hymn for Our New Earth, 1983; Author, Code of Universal Development Principles, UN, 1984; Author, Essays on Development, 1989; additional publications. *Memberships Include:* American Academy of Political & Social Science; US Representative, Recontres Creatives Internationales, Geneva, 1985-; Chairwoman, International Employment Service, Society for International Development/NY, also member, 1981-; Chairwomen, UN Action Team, The Business Initiative, 1983-86; Chairwomen, Art Exhibits, 1989-; Member, The Authors Guild and Authors' League of America, 1987-; numerous charities and other memberships. *Honours:* Distinguished Leadership Award, and numerous meritorious citations, 1986-89. *Hobbies:* Family; Friends; Painting; Poetry; Sports, especially alpine skiing, swimming, figure skating (USFSA), hiking/trekking. *Address:* PO Box 1000, Rockefeller Centre, New York, NY 10185, USA.

LOVE-BLECKER Jean Olivia, b. 27 Feb. 1920, South Carolina, USA. Retired Professor of Psychology. m. Albert William Blecker, 9 Nov. 1984. *Education:* BA, Erskine College, Due West, South Carolina, 1941; MA, Winthrop College, Rock Hill, SC, 1949; PhD, University of North Carolina, 1953; Postdoctoral study, Clark University, Massachusetts. *Appointments:* Professor of Psychology, Lebanon Valley College, Pennsylvania, 1954-85. *Publications:* Books: Worlds in Consciousness; Virginia Woolf: Sources of Madness & Art. 2 further works in progress. *Honour:* Penelope McDuffie Fellow, American Association of University Women, 1966-67. *Hobby:* Painting, including several juried shows (local & regional), several solo exhibitions. *Address:* 217 West Sheridan Avenue, Annville, Pennsylvania 17003, USA.

LOVELACE Carey, b. 21 Aug. 1952, Los Angeles, California, USA. Writer; Art Critic; Editor. *Education:*

BFA, Music, California Institute of the Arts, 1975; MA, Journalism, New York University, 1984. *Appointments:* Editor for Ralph Goings, Associate Editor for Verve, Harry N. Abrams Inc, currently. *Publications:* articles in numerous periodicals including Harpers, Arts and Artnews. *Memberships:* International Association of Art Critics. *Hobbies:* Music; Theatre. *Address:* 480 Broome Street, New York, NY 10013, USA.

LOVING Pamela Yvonne, b. 28 Sept. 1943, Detroit, Michigan, USA. Assistant to the President, GMI Engineering. m. William Copeland, 14 Feb. 1981. 1 son, 1 daughter. *Education:* Associate Degree, Applied Science, 1967; Bachelor's Degree, University of Detroit, 1978; Graduate study, Central Mich University. *Appointments:* Butcher, Cashier, Technical Aide, 1964-67; Team Leader, Pediatrics, St Joseph's Hospital, Flint, 1967-69; Public Health Nurse, Flint, 1969-72; Nurse, Health Centre 1972-74, Head Nurse &RN) 1974-76, Coordinator, Health Services 1976-79, Salaried Personnel Rep 1979-81, Manager, Personnel Services 1981-82, Director of Personnel 1982-88, GMI; Assistant to the President, GMI Engineering & Management Institute, 1988-. ssa 20Memberships: President, Young Adult Negro Business & Professional Women Inc; Vice President, Flint Area Personnel Association; Vice President & Charter Member, Top Ladies of Distinction Inc, Flint Chapter; Director, Minority Women in Higher Education. *Honours:* Exceptional Volunteer, Huron Valley Women's Prison, 1987; Human Relations Commission, City of Flint, Youth Award, 1988; Youth Award, Masjid of Al-Islam, City of Flint, 1988; Outstanding Service to Flint Area Personnel Assoc, 1986. *Interests:* Prison ministry; Young people; Education. *Address:* 914-D Glenbrook Circle, Flint, Michigan 48503, USA.

LOVINGER Sophie L, b. 15 Jan. 1932, New York City, USA. Clinical Child Psychologist. m. Robert Jay, 18 June 1957. 2 sons. *Education:* BA, Brooklyn College, 1954; MS, City College of New York, 1959; PhD, New York University, 1967. *Appointments:* Therapy Trainee, Jamaica Ctr for Psychotherapy, 1964-67; Asst Prof, Hofstra University, 1967-70; Professor, Central Michigan University, 1970-. *Publications:* Child Psychotherapy: A Developmental Approach, in process; Learning Disabilities and Games, 1978; Multiple Personality: A Theoretical Approach in Psychotherapy, 1983. Author of numerous articles to professional journals, magazines and to conferences. *Memberships:* Div 37 of APA; American Psychological Association; Michighan Psychological Association; Michigan Psychoanalytic Council; ISMPD/DS. *Hobbies:* Noodlwork; Cooking. *Address:* 405 South Main St, Mt Pleasant, MI 48858, USA.

LOW Barbara Wharton, b. 23 Mar. 1920, Lancaster, England. Professor of Biochemistry and Molecular Biophysics. *Education:* BA, Chemistry, 1942, MA, Chemistry, 1946, DPhil, Chemistry, 1948, Oxford University, England. *Appointments:* Research Fellow, Dept of Chemistry, California Institute of Technology, 1947-48; Research Associate 1948, Associate 1948-70, Assistant Professor of Physical Chemistry related to Medicine and Public Health, 1950-56, Harvard University; Associate Professor of Biochemistry, Columbia University, 1956-66; Professor Associe, Faculte des Sciences, University of Strasbourg, France, 1965; Professor of Biochemistry 1966-85, Professor of Biochemistry and Molecular Biophysics, 1985-, Columbia University, USA. *Publications:* Numerous publications in professional journals; Chapters in books on Penicillin, proteins, snake venoms and Neurotoxin protein structure. *Memberships:* American Academy of Arts and Sciences; American Association for the advancement of Science; American Crystallographic Association; American Institute of Physics; American Society of Biological Chemists; Biophysical Society; Chemical Society (London); Harvey Society; International Society of Toxicology; Seminar on the Archaeology of the Eastern Mediterranean Eastern Europe and the Near East. *Honours:* Scholar, Somerville College, Oxford University, 1939-43; Rose Sidgwick

Memorial Fellow, AAUW, 1946; Rockefeller Foundation Fellow, 1948; Elected Fellow, American Academy of Arts & Sciences, 1953; Visiting Professor, Japan Society for the Promotion of Science, Tohoku University, 1975; Invited Lecturer, Chinese Academy of Sciences, 1981 and Soviet Academy of Sciences, 1988. *Interests:* History of Medicine; Snake bites and their treatment; Symmetry in art; Gardening. *Address:* Department of Biochemistry and Molecular Biophysics, College of Physicians and Surgeons of Columbia University, 630 West 168 Street, New York, NY 10032, USA.

LOWDEN Rafaela Joaquin de, b. 25 Nov. 1940, Dominican Republic. Professor. m. Richard M. Lowden, 27 June 1970, 1 son, 2 daughters. *Education:* BA, Education, University Catolica Madre y Maestra, 1969; MA, Education, Ohio State University, USA, 1971. *Appointments:* Secondary School Teacher, Liceo Domingo Faustino Sarmiento, Moca, 1971-78; Professor, Universidad Catolica Madre y Maestra, Santiago, 1972, Dean, School of Education, 1978-79, Associate Professor, 1979-. *Publication:* Constitution Education; articles in professional journals. *Memberships:* Alumni Society, Universidad Catolica Madre y Maestra; Alumni Association, Ohio State University. *Honours:* Recipient, various honours & awards. *Hobbies:* Writing; Swimming; Reading; Cooking. *Address:* Pontificia Universidad Catolica Madre y Maestra, Dept. de Educacion y Psicologia, Santiago, Dominican Republic.

LOWE Cylvia Archer, b. 31 Octy. 1927, Hartford, Connecticut, USA. Author; Writer. 1 daughter. *Education:* BA 1981, MA 1986, University of Healing Campo, CA; Rose Croix Univ, San Jose, CA, 1971-72; Human Services, New Hampshire College, 1985; Connecticut Certified Nurse Assistant, Gr Hartford Community College, 1987; Certificate, Secretarial Skills, Hartford College for Women, 1989. *Appointments:* Manager/Distributor, Fuller Products Co, Chicago, 1957-70; Account Representative, Barbara Walden Cosmetics, Los Angeles, CA, 1971-73; Flori Roberts Cosmetics, New Jersey, 1973-74, Company Representative and make-up artist; Writer, Reporter, Manager, Northend Agent's Newspaper, 1974-89; Secretary, BKKPR, North Hartford Sr Ctr, Hartford, CT, 1983-84; Secretary/Receptionist, Sand Corp Hartford, CT, 1984-86. *Publications:* Words of Wisdom from The Masters, 1976; Create and design pocket affirmation booklets, design flyers, newsletters, stationery. *Memberships:* North Hartford Churches for Aging, Secretary, Board of Directors; A-on-o Ctr of Light, Founder, Pastor, Metaphysology Teacher; Teacher; Greater Hartford Senior Citizen's Council, White Eagle Lodge, New Lands, Liss, Hampshire. *Honours:* Honorary Degree, Doctor of Humanities, 1984; Recipient Appreciation Award, Hartford Pronaos, 1977. *Hobbies:* Sewing; Crochet; Teaching; Travel; People in general. *Address:* P O Box 241, Hartford, CT 06141, USA.

LOWTHER Susan Ann (The Hon), b. 7 Oct. 1934, London, England. Retired Social Worker. m. (1)1 son, 1 daughter. (2)The Hon Timothy Lancelot Edward Lowther, 8 Mar. 1977. 1 daughter. *Education:* The Court House, Painswick, Ellerslie, Malvern; LAMDA. *Appointment:* 1st Councillor, The Guernsey Council on Alcoholism. *Hobbies:* Theatre; Sailing; History; Social Work; Countryside. *Address:* Ivy Stone House, Rue de la Croix, St Clement, Jersey, Channel Islands.

LOZBA Marcela, b. 8 July 1935, Ungurehi, County of Botosani, Romania. Associate Professor. m. Mihai Lozba, 19 July 1963. 2 sons. *Education:* Botosani Foreign Languages Institute, 1954-58; Postgraduate Studies, Moscow, 1962-65; PhD, Moscow University. *Appointments:* Assistant Lecturer, University of Bucharest, 1958-65; Lecturer 1965-74, Associate Professor, 1974-, Deputy Dean, Faculty of Philology 19077-80, Head of Dept of Slavonic Languages 1982-85, University of Iasi, Romania. *Publications:* Glagoly dvizernija v russkom i rumynskom jazykah, 1965; Limbe rusa, 1974; Limba ruso, 1979; Limba rusa Vol I II, 1982. *Memberships:* International Association, Teachers of

Russian (MAPREAL); Romania Society of Philological Sciences. *Hobbies:* Reading; Education; Travelling; Foreign languages and cultures. *Address:* St Ciurchi 107, Bloc F4, Sc F et IV apt 3, Iasi 6600, Romania.

LU Mary, b. 3 Aug. 1954, Uchitomari, Okinawa, Japan. Contract Auditing. *Education:* BA, History, University of Virginia, 1977; Accounting, George Mason Univerity, Fairfax, 1978. *Appointments:* Auditor, Naval Audit Service, 1979-82; Project Manager, Dept. of Defense Inspector General, 1982-. *Memberships:* Association of Government Accountants; Association of the Institute for Certified Computer Professionals; National Contract Management Association. *Honours:* Certified Public Accountant, 1985; Certified Systems Professional, 1985; Office of the Secretary of Defense Executive Leadership Demonstration Programme, 1987. *Hobbies:* Skiing; Bicycle Riding; Horse Riding; Hiking. *Address:* 400 Army Navy Drive, Arlington, VA 22202, USA.

LUBER Diana Litz, b. 21 Apr. 1942, Syracuse, New York, USA. Physical Fitness Trainer; Coporate Energizer. m. Robert John Luber, 17 June 1961, 2 sons, 1 daughter. *Appointments:* Aerobic Dance Instructor, Westvale Clubhouse, Syracuse, 1978-81; Manager, Director of Fitness, Pine Grove Fitness Centre, Camillus, 1981-84; Director, Health Promotion Services, YWCA of Syracuse & Onondaga County, 1984-88; Owner, Founder, Body Management, Camillus, 1988-. *Memberships:* Association for Fitness in Business; Master/Charter Member, International Dance Exercise Association; Aerobics and Fitness Association of America; Womens Sports Foundation; RPIA; CCPI. *Honours:* People to People Citizen Ambassador Programme's Fitness Delegation to China, 1988; YMCA Community Fitness Award, 1987. *Hobbies:* Skiing; Culinary Arts; Breeding Begonias & Christmas Cacti. *Address:* Orchard Village, 102 North Way, Camillus, NY 13031, USA.

LUBIC Ruth Watson, b. 18 Jan. 1927, Bristol, Pennsylvania, USA. Voluntary Health Agency Director; Nurse-Midwife. m. William James Lubic, 2 May 1955, 1 son. *Education:* Nursing Diploma, Hospital of The University of Pennsylvania, 1955; BS, 1959, MA, 1961, EdD, 1979, Teachers College, Columbia University; Certificate in Nurse-Midwifery, State University of New York/Maternity Center Association, 1962. *Appointments:* Staff to Head Nurse, Memorial Hospital for Cancer and Allied Diseases, 1955-58; Faculty, Graduate School of Nursing, New York Medical College, 1963; Parent Educator, 1964-67, General Director, 1970-, Maternity Center Association, New York City. *Publications:* Childbearing: A Book of Choices (with Gene Hawes), 1987. *Memberships:* American College of Nurse-Midwives; National Association of Childbearing Centers, President 1984; Fellow, American Association for the Advancement of Science; American Public Health Association, Governing Councillor 1986-88; Fellow, Society for Applied Anthropology. *Honours:* Elected Member, Institute of Medicine, National Academy of Sciences, 1971; Member, 1st Official American Delegation to People's Republic of China, 1973; Fellow, American Academy of Nursing, 1978; Rockefeller Public Service Award, Woodrow Wilson School of Public and International Affairs, Princeton University, 1981; The Hattie Hemscheyer Award, American College of Nurse- Midwives, 1983. *Hobbies:* Travel; Home decoration; Languages. *Address:* 48 East 92nd Street, New York, NY 10128, USA.

LUBICH Chiara Silvia, b. Trent, Italy, 1920. Religious Worker. *Appointment:* Founder, President, Director, Focolare Movement (also called Work of Mary). The Movement's spirituality is unity, ie, the entire Gospel seen in light of Jesus' Testament, May they all be one, God is Love; Unifying belief is (as Pope John Paul II declared during his visit in 1984), evangelical radicalism of love. Consists of over 69,000 intern members, over 1 million adherents; Activities include annual Mariapolis Gatherings, 7 small cities (permanent Mariapolis), where members strive to bear witness to what the world would be if it lived the Gospel; Centre of Focolare organises international conventions in Rome; On-going dialogue with men & women of good will who are non-believers; Own university (Marian Popular University). *Publications:* Own publishing house, Citta Nuova Editrice; Bi-monthly cultural magazine, Nuova Umanita, & bi-weekly, Citta Nuova, both translated many languages. Books by Chiara Lubich: Scritti Spirituali, 4 volumes, 1978- 81; L'Unita e Gesu Abbandonato (Unity & Jesus Forsaken), 1984; Diario 1964-65, 1985; Incontri con l'Oriente (Encounters with the Orient), 1986. *Address:* Via di Frascati 306, 00040 Rocca di Papa, Rome, Italy.

LUCAS Helen Cecilia, b. 23 Oct. 1938, Bristol, England. Publicity Consultant; Writer. m. Ian Skidmore, 20 Oct. 1971. *Education:* BA Honours Degree, Modern History, 1958-61, MA, St Hilda's College, Oxford. *Appointments:* Editorial Assistant, George Rainbird, London, 1962-65; Art Editor, W H Allen, Publishers, 1965-66; Researcher, Daily Mail, London, 1966-68; Reporter, Daily Mail, Manchester, 1968-71; Partner, Skidmore Agency, Chester, 1971-76; Director, Public Relations Consultancy, 1976-. *Publications:* Prisoners of Santo Tomas, 1974; Paperback, David & Charles, 1988; Steel Town Cats, children's novel, 1987. *Memberships:* Society of Authors; National Union of Journalists; Anglesey Golf Club. *Honours:* Tir Na N-og Award for Children's Novel, Steel Town Cats, 1988. *Hobbies:* Golf; Walking with dog. *Address:* Virgin & Child Cottage, Brynsiencyn, Llanfairpwll, Gwynedd, LL61 6UA, Wales.

LUCE Marcia R, b. 25 July 1944, Sterling, Colorado, USA. Education Administrator; Staff Development, Gifted/Talented, Wellness Coordiantor. *Education:* AA, Northeastern Junior College, 1964; BA 1967, MA 1970, Adams State College; Post graduate studies, Santa Clara University, Colorado State University and University of California, Los Angeles. *Appointments:* Resident Advisor, Clinton Job Corps for Women, 1968; Teacher, 6th Grade, Hagen Elementary School, 1969-74; History Teacher, Coach 1974-77, Asst Dean of Students 1977-80, Asst Principal 1980-86, Sterling High School; Administrative Offices; Staff Development, Gifted/Talented, Wellness Coordinator, 1986-. *Publication:* Women can turn the World upside Down, contributing writer. *Memberships:* South Platte Education Association, President; Colorado Education Association; National Education Association; Colorado Association of School Executives; Valley Association of School Executives; American Association of School Administrators; National Association of Secondary School Principals; National Staff Development Council. *Honours:* Sterling City Council Councilwoman Ward III, 1973-; Outstanding Young Educator, Jaycees; Distinguished Service Award, Jaycees; Notable Americans. *Hobbies:* Boating; Fishing; Golf; Walking; Bodybuilding; Travel; Reading; Painting; Gardening; Writing. *Address:* 332 Platte St, Sterling, Colorado 80751, USA.

LUCERO Elthia (Fia), b. 19 Sept. 1949, Albuquerque, New Mexico, USA, Isleta Pueblo Indian. President; Business owner; Instructor. m. 9 Dec. 1978. 2 daughters. *Education:* BUS, University of New Mexico, 1982. *Appointments:* Indian School Counselor, Albuquerque, 1976-77; Program Manager, Sterling Institute, 1977-79; Program Manager, Management Concepts, 1979-81; Owner, American Training & Technical Assistance, 1981-. *Publications:* Books: Skills for Secretaries; Records Management; Filing Techniques; Managing the Front Desk; Office Administration; Family Planning for Native Americans; Telephone Techniques. *Memberships:* Association of Records Managers and Administrators; National Organization of Native American Women; North American Indian Women's Association; Professional Secretaries Association; New Mexico Indian Business Association. *Hobbies:* Travel; Languages (Spanish & North American Indian); Human relations type work; Skiing; Tennis; Running. *Address:* 2400-B Comanche NE, Albuquerque, NM 87107, USA.

LUCEWICH Sandra J, b. 23 July 1955, Worcester, Massachusetts, USA. Student; Part-time Graduate Assistant. *Education:* AA, 1986; BSE, 1988; Full-time Graduate student Florida International University, N. Miami, Florida, pursuing Master of Public Health. *Published works:* Dieting is Fattening, The Public Health Chronicle, 1989. *Memberships:* American College of Sports Medicine; National Alumni Association; Phi Theta Kappa; Alpha of Florida; Florida Atlantic Alumni Association. *Honours:* Deans List: Palm Beach Junior College, 1985, 1986; President's Honour List, Florida Atlantic University, 1988, Deans List, 1988. *Hobby:* Karate. *Address:* 2520 S. Federal Hwy., Boynton Beach, FL 33435, USA.

LUDLOW Christy Leslie, b. 7 June 1944, Montreal, Canada. Speech Pathologist. m. 7 Sept. 1968. *Education:* BSc., 1965, MSc., 1967, McGill University; PhD, New York University, 1973. *Appointments:* Speech Pathologist, New York University Medical Centre, 1967-70; Poject Manager, American Speech-Language Hearing Association, 1973-74; Health Scientist, 1974-87, Chief, Speech & Voice, 1987-, NIDCD. *Publications:* The Neurological Bases of Language Disorders in Children, 1980; various articles in professional journals. *Memberships:* Academy of Aphasia; Society for Neuroscience; International Medical Society for Motor Disturbances; International Academy for Research in Learning Disabilities. *Honours:* Walter A. Anderson Doctoral Fellowship, 1970- 72; Founders Day Awad, 1973; NIH Director's Award, 1977. *Hobbies:* Philosophy of Science. *Address:* Speech & Voice Unit, Intramural Research, National Institute on Deafness and Other Communication Disorders, Bldg. 10, Rm. 5N226, Bethesda, MD 20892, USA.

LUDWIG-BECKER Marsha McMahon, b. 29 May 1945, St Louis, Missouri, USA. Associate Program Manager. 2 sons. *Education:* AB History, magna cum laude, University of Missouri, 1967; MEd Admst & Supervision, Stetson University, 1980. *Appointments:* Admst Asst, University of Missouri, St Louis, 1964-69; Teacher, Writer, Brevard Ct Schools, Cocoa Beach, 1971-81; Safety proposals 1981-84, Ind Engineer 1984-85, Project Administrator, 1985-87, Program Management, 1987-89, Associate Program Manager, 1989-, Rockwell International. *Publication:* Author 1972-80, curriculum guides: history, reading, environmental science. *Memberships:* Cape Canaveral Citizens Association, 1972-75; Phi Delta Kappan, 1980-; Silver Kellog/CA Polytech University, Pomona, 1987-; Charter Member, University of Missouri, St Louis Alumni Association, 1967-; American Society for Quality Control, 1985-; VP Special Events, VP Programo, National Management Association, Anaheim, Newport. *Honours:* Outstanding Young Women of America, 1972; Certified Manager, 1987-. *Hobbies:* Reading; Travelling. *Address:* 1262B S Diamond Bar Blvd., Diamond Bar, CA 91765, USA.

LUI Alice Yee-lai, b. 7 Oct. 1948, Hong Kong. University Lecturer. m. Lui Hau Tuen, 3 July 1976, 2 daughters. *Education:* BSocSc, University of Hong Kong, 1970; MSc, London School of Economics (LSE), University of London, UK, 1975. *Appointments:* Lecturer: Hong Kong Polytechnic, 1975- 82; Chinese University, Hong Kong, 1982-. *Publications:* Book, Interview Techniques. Journal articles: Non-financial Incentives in Motivation; The Peter Principle: A Follow-Up; Personnel Management in Hotels in Hong Kong; Business Ethics; Theory Z as Applied to Business Management in Hong Kong. *Memberships:* British Institute of Management; Hong Kong Management Association; International Commissioner, Hong Kong Girl Guides Association; Friends of LSE in Hong Kong. *Honour:* 5-year good Service Award & Certificate, Hong Kong Girl Guides Association, 1988. *Hobbies:* Reading; Antique Collecting; Music Appreciation; Swimming; Squash. *Address:* Department of General Business Management & Personnel Management, Chinese University of Hong Kong, Sha Tin, New Territories, Hong Kong.

LUKE Ruth Regina Gladys, b. 19 Aug. 1919, Freetown, Sierra Leone. JP; Commissioner of Oaths. m. William A Fashole-Luke, 5 Apr. 1942, 3 sons, 2 daughters. *Education:* Women Teachers College, 1936-38; Queen Elizabeth College, London University, 1968-69. *Appointments:* Headmistress, 1961-64; Lecturer, 1970-84; JP, 1975-. *Publications:* Cookery: The Sierra Leone Way; Infant Feeding; Vegetable Cookery; Biblical Plays; Thesis: Technological Developments in Home Economics, Academic Postgraduate Diploma, Queen Elizabeth College. *Memberships:* Vice President, Association of Justices of the Peace; National Federation of Sierra Leone Womens Organisation, National General Secretary, Coordinator; Freetown Secondary School for Girls, Board of Trustees; YWCA. *Honours:* Appointed JP, 1975; Recipient, various other honours and awards. *Hobbies:* Gardening; Reading; Writing; Broadcasting. *Address:* PO Box 811, Freetown, Sierra Leone, West Africa.

LUM Jean L. J., b. Honolulu, Hawaii, USA. Professor, Nursing. *Education:* BS, University of Hawaii, Manoa, 1960; MS, University of California, San Francisco, 1961; MA 1969, PhD 1972, University of Washington, Seattle. *Appointments:* Instructor to Professor 1961-, Department Chair 1973-76, Acting Dean 1982, Dean 1982-89, School of Nursing, University of Hawaii at Manoa; Project Co-Director, Analysis & Planning Project, Western Interstate Commission on Higher Education, 1978. *Publications:* Numerous articles & book chapters, aspects of nursing. *Memberships:* Past President, American Pacific Nursing Leaders Conference; Offices, National League for Nursing, & Western Council on Higher Education for Nurses; American & Hawaii Nurses Associations. *Honours:* Awards & recognitions: National Academies of Practice 1986, University of Hawaii School of Nursing 1984, Hawaii Nurses Association 1982, St Andrew's Priory 1983; Fellow, American Academy of Nursing, 1977; Women's Honours, Public Service, 1986. *Hobbies:* Reading; Photography. *Address:* School of Nursing, University of Hawaii at Manoa, Webster 409, 2528 The Mall, Honolulu, Hawaii 96822, USA.

LUND Julie A., b. 26 Aug. 1946, Annapolis, Maryland, USA. Interior Designer. 2 daughters. *Education:* Russell Sage College, Troy, New York, 1964-66; Philadelphia College of Art, 1970-74; BS, Housing and Interior Design, Central State University, Edmond, Oklahoma, 1977; Interior Design Practicum Student, Myers Haus Interiors, Edmond, 1977. *Appointments:* Head Interior Designer, John G Gann, Builder, Huntsville, Alabama, 1975; Interior Designer, Myers Haus Interiors, Edmond, Oklahoma, 1070-79, Freeland design consultation, Aug 1982; Senior Staff, Interior Designer, Exclusively Contemporary, Charlotte, North Carolina, 1982- 85; Owner, Senior Designer, Julie A Lund Associates, Atlantic Highland, New Jersey, 1985-. *Creative works:* Southern Living Shows, 1983, 1984, 1985; Charlotte Symphony Design House, 1984-87; Kitchen and Bath Business, 1987; International Collection of Interior Design, 1988. *Membership:* American Society of Interior Designers. *Honours:* Recognised for services to design profession. *Hobbies:* Riding; Cycling; Running; Sailing; Tennis; Skiing. *Address:* 3023 Shallowood Lane, Matthews, NC 28105, USA.

LUNDGREN Clara Eloise, b. 7 Mar. 1951, Temple, Texas, USA. Deputy Public Affairs Officer. *Education:* B.Journalism, University of Texas, 1973; MA, Columbia Pacific University, 1986. *Appointments:* Reporter, Temple Daily Telegram, 1970-72; News Editor, Austin American-Statesman, 1972- 75; Managing Editor, Stillhouse Hollow Pub. Inc., Belton, Texas, 1975-77; Public Affairs Officer, Darnall Army Community Hospital, 1978-80; Editor, Ft. Hood Sentinel III Corps & Ft. Hood, 1980-85; Command Information Officer, III Corps & Ft. Hood, 1985-87; Community Relations Officer, 1987-88; Deputy Public Affairs Officer, III Corps & Ft. Hood, 1988-. *Memberships:* National Organization of Women; Texas Press Women; Association of US Army; Jaycees. *Honours:* National Observer Journalistic

Achievement Award, 1971; Community Relations Award of Excellence, Dept. of Army, 1988. *Hobbies:* Racquetball; Film; Bicycling. *Address:* 1305 S. 13th St., Temple, TX 76504, USA.

LUNDY Sadie Allen, b. 29 Mar. 1918, Milton, Florida, USA. Purchasing Manager and Corporate Secretary. m. Wilson T Lundy 17 May 1939 (d 1962). 4 sons, 1 daughter. *Education:* Degree in accounting, Graceland College, 1938. *Appointments:* Acct Powers Furniture Co, Milton, Florida, 1939-40; Lundy Oil Co, Milton, 1941-52; Controller, First Fed Savs & Loan, Kansas City, Missouri, 1953-55; Herald Pub Co, Independence, 1956-58; Manager, Baird & Son Toy Co, Kansas City, 1959-62; Regional Manager, Emmons Jewelers of NY, Kansas City, 1963-65; Owner, President, Lundy Tax Service, Independence, 1965-85; Acct 1974-85, Manager 1985-, Optimation, Inc, Independence; Vice President, Lundy Oil Co, Milton, 1941-52. *Publications:* Contributor of articles to professional journals. *Memberships:* Com Neighborhood Council, Indpendence, 1985; Am Bus Women's Assn; Independence C of C (mem com 1965-85). *Hobbies:* Counselling; Swimming; Bicycling. *Address:* PO Box 520238, Independence, MO 64052, USA.

LUNSFORD Cin Forshay, b. 2 May 1965, New York, USA. Author; Lecturer. *Education:* Queens College, 1985-88. *Publications:* Novel: Walk Through Cold Fire; Articles in various journals. *Honours:* Delacorte Press Prize, 1985; 1986 Books for Young Adults Poll of University of Iowa. *Hobbies:* Reading; Music; Theatre; Art; Ballet; Mystic Arts. *Address:* 2929 Longbeach Road, Apartment A, Oceanside, NY 11572, USA.

LUO Shenyi, b. Hangzhou, Peoples Republic of China. University Professor, French Linguistics. m. Baoyi Chen, 26 Nov. 1957. 2 daughters. *Education:* Maitrise de langue et de civilisation francaises, Peking; 1957; Licence de Linguistique, Grenoble, 1979; Diplome superieur d'Aptitude a l'Enseignement du Francais, langue etrangere, Grenoble, 1979; Equivalence DEA 1981, Ecole des Hautes Etudes en Sciences Sociales, Paris, France. *Appointments:* Professor, Beijing Foreign Studies University, 1957-; Chargee de cours, University of Beijing, 1984; Chef de travaux, EHESS, Paris, France, 1981-83; Directeur d'Etude, Maison des Sciences de l'Homme, 1986; Directeur de Recherche, CNRS, Paris, 1986-87. *Publications:* Manual of French, 1962; Le Francais (1-4), 1980; Le Francais Niveau II, 1988; Putong Yuyanxue Gangyao, chinese version of Elements de Linguistique Generale, 1988; Homage to Luo Changpei, 1984. *Memberships:* Association of Linguists, Beijing; Editorial staff, Linguistics abroad, 1987; Directeur de Recherche associe, Guangzhou Foreign Languages Institute, 1988-90. *Hobbies:* Singing; Swimming. *Address:* French Department, Beijing Foreign Studies University, Beijing, Peoples Republic of China.

LURIE Nancy Oestreich, b. 29 Jan. 1924, Milwaukee, Wisconsin, USA. Curator of Anthropology. m. Edward Lurie, 11 Aug. 1951, div. 1963. *Education:* BA, University of Wisconsin, 1945; MA, University of Chicago, 1947; PhD, Northwestern University, 1952. *Appointments:* Teaching Anthropology: University of Wisconsin, Milwaukee, 1947-49, 1951- 53, 1963-72; University of Michigan, 1956-63; Fulbright Lecturer, University of Aarhus, Denmark, 1965-66; Curator of Anthropology, Milwaukee Public Museum, 1972-. *Publications:* Over 100 articles and monographs including: Mountain Wolf Woman; Wisconsin Indians; A Special Style: The Milwaukee Public Museum 1882-1982; North American Indian Lives, 1985. *Memberships:* American Anthropological Association, President 1983-85; American Association for the Advancement of Science; American Association of Museums; American Ethnohistorical Society; Central States Anthropological Society, President 1967; Council for Museum Anthropology; Wisconsin Academy of Sciences, Arts and Letters. *Honours:* Woman of the Year, Milwaukee Municipal Women's Club, 1975; Honorary Doctorate of Letters, Northland College, Ashland, Wisconsin, 1976; Merit Award, Alumni Association, Northwestern University, 1982; Merit Award for A Special Style, State Historical Society of Wisconsin, 1984; Fellow (1 of only 50), Wisconsin Academy of Sciences, Arts and Letters, 1987. *Address:* Anthropology Section, Milwaukee Public Museum, 800 West Wells Street, Milwaukee, WI 53233, USA.

LUSH Adaline Lincoln, b. 15 July 1899, Van Buren, Arkansas, USA. Teaching. m. 20 Dec. 1923. 1 son, 1 daughter. *Education:* BA, University of Arkansas, 1916; MA, University of Chicago, 1917; Graduate study of Latin, 1920-22. *Appointments:* Teaching, Marysville High School, Marysville, Kansas, 1918-20; Augusta High School, August, Kansas, 1918-20. *Publications:* Treasure Hunt (Poetry), 1982; What Next? (Autobiography), 1984; Triumph Or Disaster, 1987; Women Are People. *Memberships:* National Board, General Federation of Women's Clubs; Leader of thirteen tours of Europe. *Address:* 2200 Hamilton Drive, No 406, Ames, Iowa 50010, USA.

LUSKACOVA Marketa, b. 29 Aug. 1944, Prague, Czechoslovakia. Photographer. m. Franzwurm, 1971, divorced. 1 son. *Education:* Social Science Degree (Sociology of Culture), Charles University, Prague, 1967. *Appointments:* Freelance Photographer. *Creative works:* Numerous commissions; Work in public collections; Numerous exhibitions including: The Women in photography, San Francisco Museum of Arts, 1975; Exhibition (One Woman Show), Victoria & Albert Museum, 1983; Group show, Palais de Tokyo, Paris 1987 (travelling Europe in 1987, 1988); Mexico City, 1987; National Centre of Photography, Paris, Touring Europe 1987; Impressions Gallery, York, 1987; London, 1987; One Woman show, Museum of Childhood, 1989. *Honours:* British Arts Council, 1975, 1976; GLA, 1984. *Hobbies:* Photography; Art; Literature. *Address:* 63 Blenheim Crescent, London W11 2EG, England.

LUSTIG Eugenia Saccidote, b. 9 Nov. 1910, Turin, Italy. m. Maurizio Lustig, 5 Sept. 1937, 2 sons, 1 daughter. *Education:* MD, University of Turin, Italy; MD, University of Buenos Aires, 1959. *Appointments:* Italian medical Doctor, Turin, 1936; Argentine Medical Doctor, 1959; Head, Virology, National Institute Microbiology, 1951-58; Professor, Cell Biology, Buenos Aires University, 1958-66; Head, Research, Oncology Institute, Buenos Aires, 1966-86; Member, Scientific CONICET, 1966- 88. *Publications:* 150 published papers in the field of experimental embryology and oncology; Tissue Culture book, in spanish. *Memberships:* Tissue Culture Association; New York Academy of Science; Adviser, ASARCA; *Honours:* 7 Scientific Argentine Prizes, Medical National Academy, 1971-86. *Hobbies:* Reading; Gardening. *Address:* Virrey Loreto 1830 6B, Buenos Aires 1426, Argentina.

LUTHER Susan Militzer, b. 28 May 1946, Lincoln, USA. Poet; Scholar; Teacher. m. Robert N Luther, 18 July 1971, 1 stepson, 1 stepdaughter. *Education:* BA, Louisiana State University, Baton Rouge, 1969; MA, University of Alabama, 1976; PhD, Vanderbilt University, 1986. *Appointments:* Various public commercial college & college teaching appoinment, 1967-79; Assistant Editor, Poem, 1985-; Lecturer, English, University of Alabama, 1986-. *Publications:* Wordsworth's prelude Vi 592-616 (1850) in The Wordsworht Circle, 1981; Christabel as Dream-Reverie, Monograph, Salzburg, 1976; Sidney's Astrophil and Stella, Sonnet 29, in Explicator, 1975; Poems in numerous journals including: Negative Capability, Malahot Review; etc. *Memberships:* MLA; South Atlantic Modern Language Association; Board Member, Poetry Workshop Leader, Huntsville Literary Association. *Honours:* Sigma Tau Delta, 1974; Phi Kappa Phi, 1969. *Hobbies:* Music; Travel; Reading; Walking; Jogging; Decorative Arts; Antiques; Aviator (Spectator, Passenger, Sometime Navigator). *Address:* Huntsville, AL 35803, USA.

LUTTRELL Elizabeth Hermione Lady, b. 3 Dec 1923, London England. Housewife. m. John Fownes Luttrell,

24 Oct. 1959, 1 son. *Appointments:* WRNS, 1942-46; various secretarial posts until marriage. *Memberships;* Arts Diocesan Associaiton, 1953-55; Past Member: Anglo-Arab Association, English Speaking Union, Royal Central Asian Society. *Hobbies:* Architecture; Gardening; Music; Travel. *Address:* Waterwynch, Itchen Abbas, Nr. Winchester, Hants SO21 1AX, England.

LUTZ Linda Ann, b. 11 July 1947, Waco, Texas, USA. Anesthesiologist. m. John Page, 1 Jan. 1975, 1 son, 1 daughter. *Education:* BA summa cum laude, Trinity University, San Antonio, Texas, 1968; MD, University of Texas Medical School, San Antonio, 1972; Rotating and Anesthesia Internship, Walter Reed General Hospital, Washington DC, 1972-73; Residency, Anesthesiology, Parkland Memorial Hospital and affiliated institutions, Dallas, Texas, 1973-75; Fellow, American College of Anesthesiologists, 1976; Diplomate, American Board of Anesthesiology, 1978. *Appointments:* Private Practice specialising in Anesthesiology, Garland, Texas, 1975-. *Memberships:* American Medical Association; Texas Medical Association; Dallas County Medical Society; American Society of Anesthesiologists; Texas Society of Anesthesiologists; Dallas County Society of Anesthesiologists; Founding Member, Ophthalmic Anesthesia Society. *Honours:* Salutatorian, Richfield High School Graduating Class, Waco, 1965; Honour Scholarship, Trinity University, 1965-68. *Hobbies:* Swimming; Ice-skating; Skiing. *Address:* PO Box 38344, Dallas, TX 75238, USA.

LUXEMBOURG Charlotte, (Grand Duchess) b. 23 Jan. 1896, Berg Castle, Luxembourg. Grand Duchess of Luxembourg. m. Prince Felix of Luxembourg, 6 Nov. 1919, 2 sons, 4 daughters. *Appointments:* Princess of Luxembourg; Grand Duchess of Luxembourg, after abdication of elder sister, Grand Duchess Marie Adelaide 1919-; Abidcated in favour of eldest son Jean, 1964. *Address:* Grand Ducal Palace, L 1728, Luxembourg.

LYALL Katharine Culbert, b. 26 Apr. 1941, Lancaster, USA. University Professor/Administrator. *Education:* BA, Economics, 1963, PhD, Economics, 1969, Cornell University; MBA, New York University, 1965. *Appointments:* Economist, Chase Manhattan Bank, 1963-65; Assistant Professor, Syracuse University, 1969-71; Deputy Assistant Secretary, Economic Affairs, US Dept. of Housing, 1977-79; Professor, Economics, Johns Hopkins University, 1971-81; Executive Vice President, University of Wisconsin, 1982-. *Publications:* Micro Economic Issues of the 1970's; Reforming Public Welfare. *Memberships:* Ameican Economic Association; Editorial Board, Land Economics; Editorial Board, Evaluation Quarterly. *Honours:* Phi Beta Kappa, 1963; Phi Kappa Phi, 1984. *Hobbies:* Sailing; Tennis. *Address:* 4018 Council Crest, Madison, WI 53711, USA.

LYLE Emily Buchanan, b. 19 Dec. 1932, Glasgow, Scotland. Research Fellow. *Education:* MA, 2nd Class Honours, English Language & Literature, St Andrews University, 1954; DipEd, Glasgow University, 1955; PhD, Leeds University, 1967. *Appointments:* English teacher, various schools, 1955-61; Lecturer, English, Ripon College, 1961-65; Senior Lecturer, Neville's Cross College, 1965-68; Research Fellow, School of Scottish Studies, Edinburgh University, 1970; Visiting Lecturer, Folklife, Stirling University, 1979-82. *Publications:* General Editor: Greig-Duncan Folk Song Collection (8 volumes) 1981-, Cosmos (journal); Editor: Andrew Crawford's Collection of Ballads & Songs 1975, Ballad Studies 1976, Shadow (journal); Author: Articles, Scottish ballads & traditional cosmology and Macbeth. *Memberships:* President, Traditional Cosmology Society; Secretary, Scottish Text Society; Folklore Society; International Arthurian Society; British Society for Study of Religion; Association for Social Study of Time. *Honours:* Fellowships: Bunting Institute, Harvard University 1974-75, Humanities Research Centre, Australian National University 1976, Institute for Advanced Studies in Humanities, Edinburgh University 1977; Coote Lake Medal, Folklore Society, 1986.

Hobbies: Establishing traditional cosmology as a field of study; Reading; Travel. *Address:* School of Scottish Studies, University of Edinburgh, 27 George Square, Edinburgh EH8 9LD, Scotland.

LYLE Virginia Reavis, b. 19 Apr. 1926, Nashville, USA. Archivist; Genealogist. m. John Reid Lyle, 25 Sept. 1943, 1 daughter. *Education:* BA, Vanderbilt University, 1974; MLS, 1975; Certified Genalogist. *Appointments:* Administrative Officer, Commerce, Union Bank, Nashville, 1961-70, 1975-78; Research Assistant, RCH Matthews, 1970-75; 1978-79; Genealogist, Nashville, 1980; Archivist, Metro Nashville Davidson County archives, 1981-. *Memberships:* Tennessee Archivists; Association Records Manages & Administrators; National Genealogical Society; *Hobbies:* Geanlogical Research. *Address:* Metro Archives, 1113 Elm Hill Pike, Nashville, TN 37210, USA.

LYLES Marjorie A., b. 9 Jan. 1946, New York, USA. Professor of Strategic Management. 1 son, 1 daughter. *Education:* BS, Carnegie- Mellon University, 1969; MLS, 1971, PhD, 1977, University of Pittsburgh. *Appointments:* Assistant Professor, Business Administration Department, University of Illinois, 1982-87; Visiting Professor, European Institute of Business Administration, Fontainebleau, France, 1984; Associate Professor, Management Science Department, Ball State University, Muncie, Indiana, USA, 1987-. *Publications:* Over 50 articles and presentations including: Organizational Learning in JV Sophisticated Firms; Strategic Problem Formulation; Managing the Planning Process. *Memberships:* Academy of Management (Editorial Board, Review, 1984-87); Institute for Decision Sciences; Editorial Board, Journal of Management, 1983-87; National Academy of Management (Executive Committee, Policy Division, 1982-85, Co-chair, Doctoral Student Consortium, Business Policy Division, 1984). *Honours:* Stanley K.Lacy Executive Leadership, Indianapolis Chamber of Commerce, 1978-79; Young Women to Watch in the 1980s, Indianapolis Magazine, 1979; Sigma Iota Epsilon; 1 of 6 speakers to address 60th Anniversary Celebration, National Chengchi Strategic Management Symposium, Taiwan, 1987. *Hobbies:* Travel; Tennis; Gardening; Wine. *Address:* 4401 N Pennsylvania, Indianapolis, IN 46205, USA.

LYNCH Patricia Gates, b. 20 Apr. 1926, Newark, USA. US Ambassador. m. Mahlon Eugene Gates, 19 Dec. 1942, divorced 1972, 1 son, 1 daughter, (2)William Dennis Lynch. *Appointments:* Broadcaster, 1958-68; Education (Public) TV Host WETA, Washington, 1967-68; Staff Assistant to First Lady, The White House, 1069-70; Host, Breakfast Show, Morning Show, 1970-85; US Ambassador to Madagascar, 1986-. *Publicaitons:* Author of stories on America for English Teaching Dept., Radio Sweden, 1967-68; others. *Memberships:* Member, various professional organisations. *Honours:* Grantee, USIA, 1983; others. *Address:* US Embassy, Antananativo, Madagascar.

LYNDEN-BELL Ruth Marion, b. 7 Dec. 1937, Welwyn, Hertfordshire, England. University Teacher; Chemist. m. Donald Lynden-Bell, 1 July 1961, 1 son, 1 daughter. *Education:* Newnham College, University of Cambridge; BA, 1959, MA, PhD, 1962, ScD, 1989, University of Cambridge. *Appointments:* Fellow and Lecturer, 1962-65, 1972-, Vice-President, 1978-83, New Hall, University of Cambridge, 1962-65, 1972-; Lecturer, University of Sussex, 1965- 72. *Memberships:* Royal Society of Chemistry. *Address:* 9 Storey's Way, Cambridge CB3 0DP, England.

LYNN Donna Maria, b. 4 Oct. 1945, Hollywood, California, USA. Public Relations Executive. m. Dennis D. Schreffler, 1965 (div. 1973), 1 son, 1 daughter. *Education:* University of California, Los Angeles, 1963-65; University of Utah, 1965-68; BA, Universty of Arkansas, 1970; Law studies, Baltimore College of Law, Maryland, 1973-74. *Appointments:* Legislative Chair, teacher, Arkansas Education Association, Little Rock, 1970-73; Lobbyist, UniServ Director, National Education

Association, Washington DC, 1970-77; Manager, Media Relations, Perrier/Great Waters of France, New York, 1978-79; Accounting Group Supervisor, Daniel J. Edelman, NY, 1979-81; Senior Consultant, Nestle Company, White Plains, Washington DC, 1979-83; Deputy Director, Sports Division, Hill & Knowlton, NY, 1983-85; Manager, Public Relations, Avon Products Inc, NY, 1985-86; President & Chief Executive Officer, Lynn Associates Inc, Westport, Connecticut, 1977-. *Publications:* Author, various features & articles, newspapers & magazines; Features editor, Flight Attendant magazine, 1986-87. *Memberships:* American Management Association; Fashion Group; Public Relations Society of America; Life member, National Education Association; Board, National Downes Syndrome Society; Past Commissioner, Maryland Commission for Women; Past President, Annapolis Summer Garden Theatre. *Honours include:* Phi Alpha Theta; Biographical recognition. *Hobbies:* Sailing; Skiing; Horses; Tennis. *Address:* Lynn Associates Inc, 2 Burnham Hill, Westport, Connecticut 06880, USA.

LYNNE Gillian, b Bromley, Kent, England. Director; Choreographer. m. Peter Land, 17 May 1980. *Education:* Arts Educational School, Royal Academy of Dance Awards. *Appointments Include:* Solo Dancer, Lead Dancer, Guest Principal Dancer; Choreographer; Director, Films, Musicals, TV etc; Title include: Wonderful Life, film, 1964; Every Day's A Holiday; Three Hats for Lisa; Roar of the Greasepaint; Pickwick; The Match Girls, 1966; Bluebeard, Sadlers Wells Opera, 1966; Half a Sixpence, film, 1966-67; Love on the Dole, 1970; Muppet Show, series, ATV, 1976-80; New Ice Dance, John Curry, 1977; Morte D'Arthur, 1983; Mr Love, 1984; European Vacation, 1984; Alice in Wonderland 1985; Cafe Soir, new ballet, Houston; Cabaret, stage, 1986; Phantom of the Opera, musical, 1986; etc. *Memberships:* Director Guild of Great Britain; Equity; Society of Sage Directors Choreographers. *Honours:* Olivier Award, 1981; Austrian Order of Merit, 1984; Samuel G Engel Award, 1985. *Hobby:* Making Homes. *Address:* c/o London management, 235 Regent Street, London W1, England.

LYON Christina Margaret, b. 12 Nov. 1952, Liverpool, England. Professor of Law; Head of Department; Solicitor to the Supreme Court. m. Adrian Pierre Lyon, 29 May 1976, 1 son, 1 daughter. *Edcucation:* LLB(Hons) 1st Class, Faculty of Law, University College, London, 1974; Solicitor's Part II Qualifying Examinations, 1975. *Appointments:* Tutor in Law, University College, London, 1974-75; Tutor in Law, 1975-77, Lecturer in Law, 1977-80, Liverpool University; Lecturer in Law, Sub-Dean, Manchester University, 1980-86; Professor of Law, Head of Department of Law, Keele University, 1987-. *Publications:* Butterworth's Family Law Service; Cohabitation without Marriage; The Law of Residential Homes and Day Care Establishments; The Domestic Jurisdiction of Maginstrates Courts. *Memberships:* Council Member, Society of Public Teachers of Law; International Society of Family Law; Joint Editor, Journal of Social Welfare Law. *Honour:* Maxwell Law Prizewoman, University College London Law Faculty, 1974. *Hobbies:* International travel; Riding; Going to the opera, ballet, concerts and theatre. *Address:* 54 Cromptons Lane, Calderstones, Liverpool LI8 3EX, England.

LYON Elinor Bruce, b. 17 Aug. 1921, Guisborough, Yorks, England. Housewife. m. Peter Wright, 19 Apr. 1944, 2 sons, 2 daughters. *Education:* lady Margaret Hall, Oxford University. *Publications:* Children's Books: Hilary's Island; Wishing Water-gate; The House in Hiding; We Daren't Go a-Hunting; Run Away Home; Sea Treasure; Dragon Castle; The Golden Shore; Daughters of Aradale; Ridder's Rock; Cathie Runs Wild; Carver's Journey; Green Grow the Rushes; Echo Valley; The Dream Hunters; Strangers at the Door; The Day that Got Lost; The Wishing Pool; The King of Grey Corrie; The Floodmakers. *Honours:* Chair (1st Prize), Welsh Prose, Learners' Eisteddfod, Merioneth, 1982. *Hobbies:* Writing; Music; Gardening; Walking; Grandchildren.

Address: Bron Meini, Harlech, Gwynedd, Wales LL46 2YT.

LYSTER Jenifer Jo (Joie), b. 13 Nov. 1953, Lansing, Michigan, USA. Exercise Physiologist. m. Mixchael John Lyster, DO, 5 Sept. 1981. *Education:* BS Medical Technology 1976, MS Anatomy 1982, Michigan State University. *Appointments:* Research Lab, Michigan State University, 1976-79; Cardiac Rehabilitation, Borgess Medical Center, Kalamazoo, Michigan, 1979-81; Founded, Health & Fitness Program, Pontiac, Michigan, 1982-83; Founded Future Health Wellness Program, Kansas City, Missouri, 1983-87; Director, Cardiac Rehabilitation/Life Trends Wellness Program, Mt Clemens General Hospital, 1987-. *Publications:* American College of Sports Medicine, National Convention Presentation, 1980; Muscle Fiber Differentiation in Newborn Rats, Journal of Embryology, 1982. *Memberships:* American College of Sports Medicine; American Heart Association; American Cancer Society; United States Figure Skating Association. *Honours:* Employee of the Month, Trinity Lutheran Hospital, March 1986; Honored Speaker at several Civic functions in Kansas City, Missouri and Macomb County Michigan. *Hobbies:* Figure Skating Judge, United States Figure Skating Association; Bicycling; Cross country skiing. *Pets. Address:* 31151 Reid Drive, Warren, Michigan 48092, USA.

LYSTER Reiko B, b. 21 Mar.1934, Tokyo, Japan. Chief Executive Officer. m. E. William Lyster, 3 Oct. 1973, 1 daughter. *Appointments:* Film Actress, 1956-60; Training Supervisor, Max Factor, Japan, 1960-65; Product Manager, Coty Div., Pfizer Corp., Japan, 1966-69; Account Co- ordinator, Estee Lauder Inc., 1970-71; National Training Director, Shiseido America, 1971-72; Executive Director, International Beauty Institute, 1972-74; Division Director, Revolon, KK, 1974-76; President, Orlane Japon KK, 1976-79; President, Elle International Co. Ltd., 1979-. *Publications:* Articles in professional journals. *Memberships:* American Chamber of Commerce. *Hobbies:* Reading; Travel. *Address:* 4-4-11-501, Higashi, Shibuya-ku, Tokyo 150, Japan.

M

MA L. Eve Armentrout, b. 28 Dec. 1943, Greenville, South Carolina, USA. College Professor; Consultant. Divorced, 2 sons, 1 daughter. *Education:* BA, San Francisco State College, 1968; MA, California State University, Hayward, 1972; PhD, University of California, Davis, 1977. *Appointments Include:* Various Research & Writing positions, 1978-83; Legal Research, Condie and Lee, Attorneys at Law, 1988; Translator, Berlitz Translation Services, 1988-; Teaching Positions include: Teaching Assistant, 1974-77, Assistant Professor, 1980, University of California, Davis; Lecturer, Japanese History, California State University, 1988-. *Publications:* American Army Engineers in an Asian Setting, Historical Background and Development of Japan Engineer District, 1956-84, (in press); Revolutionaries, Monarchists and Chinatowns: Chinese Politics in the Americas, 1893-1911, (in press); Editor, One Day, One Dollar: Locke, California and the Chinese Farming Experience in the Sacramento Delta, 1984; The Chinese of Oakland: Unsung Builders, co-author, 1982; numerous articles in professional journals; Editor, Bulletin of the Chinese Historical Society of America. *Memberships:* Association for Asian Studies; Chinese Historical Society of America; etc. *Honours:* Recipient, various honours and awards. *Address:* 1355 Arlington, El Cerrito, CA 94530, USA.

MABRY Sharon Lee Cody, b. 16 July 1945, Newport, Tennessee, USA. Professor of Music; Professional Classical Singer. m. George Louis Mabry, 18 June 1967. *Education:* BMusEd, Florida State University, 1967; MMusEd 1970, DMA 1977, George Peabody College for Teachers. *Appointments:* Instructor to full Professor, Austin Peay State University, 1970-. *Creative works include:* Recordings: New Music for Mezzo-Soprano (Owl label), Music by Women Composers (Coronet); Numerous recitals, USA & Europe. *Memberships:* Mid-South Regional Governor, National Association of Teachers of Singing; International Congress on Women in Music. *Honours:* Graduate Fellowship, National Defence Education Act, 1969; Scholarship, Franz-Schubert Institute, Austria, 1979; Touring Grant, Tennessee Arts Commission, 1976-79; Richard Hawkins Award, creativity, 1979; Solo recitalist fellowship, National Endowment for Arts, 1988. *Hobbies:* Gourmet Cooking; Writing Poetry. *Address:* 315 Fairway Drive, Clarksville, Tennessee 37043, USA.

MACARTHUR Sally Ann, b. 22 Sept. 1950, Bombala, New South Wales, Australia. Musicologist; Educator. *Education:* DipMusEd, Sydney Conservatorium, 1972; BMus, Adelaide University, 1977; PhD studies, School of Creative Arts, James Cook University, current. *Appointments:* Mosman High School, 1973; Demonstration teacher, South Australia Department of Education, 1973; Director of Music, various schools, 1974-80; Part-time teacher, various schools & colleges 1981-86, NSW State Conservatorium 1981-; Teacher, Music-Theatre, La Rochelle, France, 3 months 1985-86. *Publications:* Various scholarly contributions, professional journals; Guest Editor, Sounds Australian, Autumn 1989; Book, Australian Women Composers 1900-, in progress. *Memberships:* Choirs: NSW Conservatorium, 1969-72; St James Singers, 1970-72; Bach Choir, Adelaide University, 1976; Adelaide Chorale Society, 1975-76. Societies: Various professional associations. *Honours:* Composition prize, Abbotsleigh Girls' School, 1968; Teachers college scholarship, 1969-72; Most Promising Music Direction (production, Sound of Music), Australia Council, 1978. *Hobbies:* Attending concerts, plays, art exhibitions; Reading; Writing; Sculpture; Bush walking; Listening to music; Conservation; Animals including pets, 1 dog, 3 cats. *Address:* 10 Corniche Road, Church Point, New South Wales 2105, Australia.

MACAULAY Jacqueline Huquenin Ramsey, b. 2 Aug. 1932, Racine, USA. Lawyer. m. Stewart Macaulay, 20 Mar. 1954, 2 sons, 2 daughter. *Education:* AB, Stanford University, 1955; PhD, 1965, JD, 1983, University of Wisconsin. *Appointments:* Researcher, University of Wisconsin, 1965-75; Agitator, 1975-82; Lawyer, 1983-. *Publications:* Articles in professional journals. *Memberships:* Association for Women in Psychology; Implementation Collective. *Honours:* Distinguished Publication Award, Association for Women in Psychology, 1978. *Hobby:* Radical Feminism. *Address:* 314 Shepard Terrace, Madison, WI 53705, USA.

MACCARTHY Karin Mary, b. 18 Nov. 1942, Sutton, Surrey, England. Actress. m. 9 Dec. 1976. *Education:* Private school; Trained as a dancer at Arts Educational School, Sadlers Wells, Central School of Speech and Drama, London. *Appointments:* Leading parts in repertory companies including: Liverpool, Glasgow, Edinburgh, Windsor, Guildford, West End performances include: Virginia Crawford, The Right Honourable Gentleman at Her Majesty's Theatre; Clara in The Watched Pot by Saki at The Mermaid Theatre; Goneril in King Lear for the Oxford Playhouse Theatre Co; Viola in Twelfth Night at St George Theatre, London; Sarah in Harold Pinter's The Liver at The King's Head Theatre, Islington, London, 1986. Television parts in: War and Peace; Nicholas Nickleby; Pride and Prejudice; Man of Straw; The Pallisers; The Professionals; Carol in Eric Chappell's long-running series, The Squirrels. *Honours:* The Madge Kendal Award for Shakespeare; The Associated Rediffusion scholarship and The Rodney Millington Award, all at the Central School of Speech and Drama. *Hobbies:* Music; Ballet; Painting. *Address:* Chiswick, London, England.

MACCINI Margaret Agatha, b. 6 Dec. 1931, Manhattan, New York, USA. Local Government Official. m. Arthur Maccini, 25 Sept. 1955, 2 sons, 1 daughter. *Education:* New York University; City College, New York; Department of Government Services, Rutgers University; Management & Supervision, New Jersey Civil Service; Certified Municipal Clerk, 1982. *Appointments:* Executive Secretary, Universal-International Pictures Company, NY & Hollywood; Administrative Assistant, Chipman Chemical Company, New Jersey; Corporate Treasurer 1964-73, President 1979-82, Pyramid Bindery Inc, New York; Administrative Assistant to County Administrator, & Executive Secretary 1973-75, Deputy Clerk 1975-76, Clerk 1976-, Board of Chosen Freeholders, County of Somerset, New Jersey. *Memberships include:* Past President: New Jersey Association of Freeholder Board Clerks, Somerset County Municipal Clerks Association. Offices, past/present: NJ Munipal Clerks Association, International Institute of Municipal Clerks, NJ Association of Counties, National Association of Counties. Numerous community associations. *Honours:* Biographical recognitions. *Hobbies:* 38 Murray Drive, Neshanic, Hillsborough, New Jersey 08853, USA.

MACDONALD Charie, b. 9 Sept. 1935, Chicago, Illinois, USA. Chef; Owner. m. James D MacDonald, 8 Apr. 1961. 2 sons, 1 daughter. *Education:* BA, Manhattanville College, 1957. *Appointments:* Delta Air Lines, Chicago, 1956-65; Charie's Kitchen, Wilmette, 1973-; Charles Martine Imports, Chicago, 1977-79; Foodstuffs, Glencoe, 1979-81; Owner, Beautiful Food, Inc, Winnetka, 1982-. *Memberships:* Founding President, Association of the Junior League Chicago Culinary Guild, 1982-87; International Association of Cooking Professionals; Society for Cuisine in America; Association of Specialty Food Trade. *Hobbies:* Gardening; Travelling; Cross country skiing; Cooking. *Address:* 2111 Beechwood Avenue, Wilmette, Illinois 60091, USA.

MACDONALD Eleanor Catherine, b. 1 Sept. 1910, Wanstead, Essex. Management Consultant. *Education:* BA (Hons) Sociology, London University. *Appointments:* Staff Controller, Selfridges, 1945-47; Manager then Director, Unilever Ltd, 1947-69; Director, own consultancy, EM Courses, 1969-. *Publications:* Books: Live by Beauty; Why a Secretary; The Successful

Secretary; An Autobiography of a Pioneer Business Woman - Nothing by Chance. Tapes: Building Personal Effectiveness Follow-Up; Building Confidence. Broadcasting Radio and Television; Numerous articles. *Memberships:* Companion, British Inst of Management; Fellow, Institute of Personnel Management; Royal Institute of International Affairs; British Federation of University Women; European Women's Management Development; Associate, Associates of St George's House, Windsor; Fellow, Association of Business Executives; Institute of Marketing; Royal Society of Arts; Fawcett Society. *Honour:* MBE 1945. *Hobbies:* Antiques; Ballet; Opera; Gardening; Art; Music; Ornithology; Theatre; Wildlife Conservation; Travel; Reading; Writing. *Address:* 4 Mapledale Avenue, Croydon, CRO 5TA, England.

MACDONALD Elizabeth Jean Hutton, b. 3 Dec. 1926, Minneapolis, Minnesota, USA. Artist-Designer. m. Edward H. MacDonald, 15 Sep. 1951, 2 sons, 2 daughters. *Education:* Pennsylvania Academy of Fine Arts, 1943-48; BFA, University of Pennsylvania, 1948, Graduate studies, 1949, University of Pennsylvania. *Appointments:* Freelance commercial artwork, 1948-49; Interior Decorator, rooms for magazine advertisements, TV commercials, Armstrong Cork, 1949-51; Artist-Designer, designing/painting needlework canvases, The Needlework Studio, Bryn Mawr, Pennsylvania, 1949-77; Teacher of Painting, 1954-65; Artist, Co-Owner, Bryn Mawr Needlework, 1977-80; Self-employed Needlework Designer, 1980-. *Creative works include:* Kneelers for Grace Church, Providence, Rhode Island, St Columba Church, Detroit, Michigan, Christ Methodist Church, Charleston, West Virginia, St Thomas Church, Roxborough, Pennsylvania, All Saints Church, Wynnewood, Pennsylvania, Incarnation of Holy Sacrament, Drexel Hill, Pennsylvania, Holy Trinity Lutheran Church, Narberth, Pennsylvania, Church of Atonement, Morton, Pennsylvania; Altar, pulpit, lectern falls, acolyte kneelers for Trinity Cathedral, Miami, Florida. *Memberships:* Philadelphia Art Museum (Art Goes to School 1974-85); Plastic Club, Art Club for Women (Teacher 1982-85, Admissions Committee Chairman 1984-85, Exhibit Committee Chairman 1985-89); Fellow, Pennsylvania Academy of Fine Arts; Embroiderers Guild of America (Newsletter Editor, Past Secretary and Vice-President, Philadelphia Chapter); International Old Lacers; Girl Scout Leader, 1964077; Delaware County and Chester County Art Leagues, 1988. *Honours:* Silver Medal, Watercolours, 1952, 1980, Gold Medal, Watercolours, 1981, Plastic Club; Winner, 1st place, 1983, 2nd place, 1987, Embroiderers Guild, Philadelphia Area. *Hobbies:* Making bobbin lace; Birdwatching; Gardening; Creative cookery. *Address:* 205 Woodside Avenue, Narberth, PA 19072, USA.

MACDONALD Virginia Brooks, b. 17 July 1918, Denver, Colorado, USA. Architect. m. (1) Paul Brooks, 1941 (divorced), 3 sons, 1 daughter. (2) Gordon Macdonald, 1975, (deceased), (3) Russ Apple, 1983. *Education:* BArch (5-year degree), Western Reserve University, 1946. *Appointments:* Director, Timberline Camp, 1962-67; Planner, State of Hawaii, 1969-78; Licensed Architect, 1978-. *Publications:* State of Hawaii Trail Law; West Hawaii; Na Ala Hele; Ala Kahakai. *Memberships:* American Institute of Architects (AIA); President, Hawaii Section, AIA; Board, Hawaii Sierra Club; President, Hawaii Conservation Council. *Honours:* State & National Energy Award, 1984. *Hobbies:* Hiking (through Switzerland); Cycling (China, 1988); Snorkling (Great Barrier Reef, 1981). *Address:* Box 47, Hawaii National Park, Hawaii 96718, USA.

MACFADYEN Cornelia Vera, b. 3 Aug. 1953, New York, USA. Artist; Office Manager; Sales Agent. *Education:* BFA, Pratt Institute, 1976. *Appointments:* Art Director, Truut & Ries Advertising, 1977-80; Graphic Designer, CVMdesigns, 1980-84; Office Manager, Netter Real estate, 1984-86; Assistant to President & Chairman, Urban Capital Corp, 1986-. *Creative Works:* Paintings include: Alone, 1987; The Vision, 1987; The Highway, 1986; Lady in the Garden, 1986; Under the Sea, 1986; Man on the Move, 1985; Father & Son,

1985; The Happy Aphorist, 1976; The Hallway, 1976; Blue Nude, 1979; Yellow Nude, 1979; The Inferno 1976. *Memberships:* Society of Illustrators; Society of Professional & Executive Women; New School for Social Research; National Association for Female Executives. *Honours:* Desi Award, 1979; Effie Award, 1980. *Hobbies:* Painting; Drawing; Writing. *Address:* 95 Christopher Street, Apt 5A, New York, NY 10014, USA.

MACGRAW Ali, b. 1 Apr. 1938, Pound Ridge, New York, USA. Actress; Top fashion model. *Creative works:* Films include: Goodbye Columbus; Love Story; The Getaway; Convoy Players; Just Tell Me What You Want. Television: The Winds of War; China Rose. *Address:* c/o 31108 Broad Beach Road, Malibu, CA 90265, USA.

MACGREGOR Jackie D, b. 10 July 1940, Boise, Idaho, USA. Managing Director. Divorced. *Education:* BA, Queens College, Flushing, 1981; PhD Programme, City University of New York. *Appointments:* Office Manager, Robert Lamb Hart, New York City, 1972-76; Vice President, Chief Operations Officer, Soras Fund Management, New York City, 1977-86; Vice President, Managing Director, Citco St Thomas Inc., 1986-. *Memberships:* National Association Female Executives; New York Academy of Sciences; Alpha Sigma Lambda. *Honour:* Graduated, summa cum laude, Departmental Honours, 1981. *Hobbies:* Walking; Snorkelling; Tennis; Gardening. *Address:* 160 West End Avenue, New York, NY 10023, USA.

MACHISKO Diana Michelle Sweeney, b. 21 Feb. 1961, Ft Thomas, Kentucky, USA. Mental Health Therapist. m. David William Machisko, 29 Septy. 1984. *Education:* BA, Psychology, College of Arts & Science 1978-82, MEd, Counseling, College of Education 1982-84, University of Cincinnati. *Appointments:* Director & Founder, Creative Afterschool Program, St Pius Latchkey, 1985-86; Senior Program Director for Youth Programs, Community Resources, Conselor Training, YMCA, 1986-87; Mental Health Therapist, Chairman Afterschool Committee, Adviser for Battered Womens Shelter, Moundbuilders Guidance Center, 1987-. *Memberships:* American Association of Counseling and Development; Association for Specialists in Group Work; Association for Measurement & Evaluation in Couns & Dev; Kappa Kappa Gamma, Advisor 1985-; United Methodist Women Representative & Officer; International Platform Association. *Honours:* National Deans Merit List, 1984; Coached first place, 1985, second place 1987, Intermediate Girls Softball; Student Social Studies Finalist, 1978; Tri-M Member, 1978; Silver Dollar Sales Award 1980, Gold Courtesy Award 1981, Friendly Restuarants; 3 quarters 1980, 2 quarters 1981, Deans List. *Hobbies:* Softball; General psychology and counselling; Reading; Golf; Physical Fitness/Nutrition; Cards; Darts; Pets; Female psychology (womens issues). *Address:* 385 Swallow Court, Pickerington, Ohio 43147, USA.

MACIUSZKO Kathleen Lynn, b. 8 Apr. 1947, Nogales, Arizona, USA. Librarian. m. 11 Dec. 1976. 1 daughter. *Education:* BA, Eastern Michigan University, 1969; MA, Kent State University, Kent, Ohio, 1974; PhD, Case Western Reserve University, Cleveland, Ohio, 1987. *Appointments:* Cataloguer, Kent State University, 1970-74; Director, Jones Music Library, Baldwin-Wallace College Conservatory of Music, 1977-85; Reference Librarian, Baldwin-Wallace College Ritter Library, 1974-77; Manager, Harcourt Brace Jovanovich Publications, Cleveland, Ohio, 1985-89; Staff Assistant to Executive, Director, Cuyahoga County Public Library, Cleveland, 1989-. *Publication:* Book: OCLC: A Decade of Development, 1984. *Memberships:* Special Libraries Association, Chairman, Public Relations Division, 1966-, President 1988-90, Cleveland Chapter; Baldwin-Wallace College Faculty Women's Club, President, 1979. *Honours:* Plenum Scholarship Winner, 1986; Hilbert T Ficken Award for Library Development, Baldwin-Wallace College, 1985; PhD Dissertation listed in Current Research in Library and Information Science, 1987. *Address:* Cleveland, OH 44017, USA.

MACK Onita, b. 27 Apr. 1938, Memphis, Tennessee, USA. Administrative Assistant, Radio-TV Broadcasting. *Education:* Diploma 1956; AA Liberal Arts, 1979; BA Radio/Television broadcasting, 1985. *Appointments:* Secretary, 1985-86; Administrative Assistant to Chief of Anesthesiology, 1986-87; Administrative assistant, 1986-. *Membership:* Phi Theta Kappa Honor Fraternity. *Hobbies:* 35mm photography; Sewing; Crocheting; Knitting; Needlepointing; Reading. *Address:* P O Box 190237, Chicago, IL 60619, USA.

MACKAY Macha Eirene, b. 10 Nov. 1938, Falmouth, Cornwall, England. Psychologist; Counsellor. m. Elmer MacKay, 1961, divorced 1974. 2 sons, 2 daughters. *Education:* BSc, Home Economics, 1960; MEd, Counselling, 1978; Registered Psychologist, Nova Scotia, 1984-. *Appointments:* Director Adult Training Workshop, 1977; Psychologist/Counsellor, Dalhousie University, Halifax, Nova Scotia; Acadia University, 1978-79; Psychologist/Counsellor, Wolfville, Nova Scotia, 1979-. *Publications:* Research: Job Related Stress & Burnout in Female Mental Health Professionals, 1983. Papers: Beyond Nairobi Slide/tape, 1986; Making the Connections: Women in Development, 1988; Women Helping Women: MATCH Model, 1987. Workshop: Women & Health an International Concern, San Jose, Costa Rica, 1987. *Memberships:* Association of Psychologists of Nova Scotia (APNS); Women's Health Education/Network (WHEN), Past President; MATCH International Centre, Ottawa, Past President; Atlantic Association of College & University Student Services (AACUSS); Latin American Information Group (LAIG), Founding Member; National Action Committee on the Status of Women (NAC); Partnership Africa Canada, Boardmember, 1988-89; Canadian Research Institute for the Advancement of Women (CRIAW), 1988-89. *Interests:* Women and health, especially feminist counselling; Travel; Global Feminism; Interest in African recovery and development education. *Address:* Acadia University Counselling Centre, Wolfville, Nova Scotia, Canada, B0P 1X0.

MACKENZIE Sarah Isabel MacWalker, b. 8 Jan. 1920, East Point, Prince Edward Island, Canada. Barrister; Solicitor (Semi-Retired). m. Stanley Ellis Mackenzie, 3 July 1942, 2 sons, 1 daughter. *Education:* BA, 1940; B.ED, 1941, Acadia University, Wolfville, Nova Scotia; LLB, Dalhouse University, Halifax, Nova Scotia. *Appointments:* School Teacher, 1941-42, 1950-51, 1953-62; Teacher Exchange to Scotland, 1962-63; Curriculum Development Committee, 963-69; Dalhousie Legal Aid Services, 1974-86. *Publications:* Articles & pamphlets. *Memberships:* Canadian College of Teachers; Nova Scotia Bar Association; etc. *Honours:* Weldon Meritorious Public Service Award, 1905. *Hobbies:* Reading; Church Activities; Travel. *Address:* 7020 Bayers Road, Halifax, Nova Scotia B3L 2B9, Canada.

MACKEY Mary Lou, b. 21 Jan. 1945, Indianapolis, Indiana, USA. Novelist; Poet; Critic; Professor of English. *Education:* BA, Harvard/Radcliffe College, 1966; PhD, French, English, Spanish Comparative Literature, University of Michigan, 1970. *Appointments:* Poet, 1960-; Novelist, 1972-; Professor of English, California State University, Sacramento, 1972-; Writer-in-Residence, 1972-. *Publications:* Split Ends, 1974; McCarthy's List, 1979; The Last Warrior Queen, 1984; A Grand Passion, 1986; The Dear Dance of Eros, 1987; The Kindness of Strangers 1988; Work published in 11 languages including Japanese and Finnish. *Memberships:* Writers Guild of America; Co-Founder, West Feminist Writers Guild; Bay Area Reviewers Association (Poetry Committee); PEN. *Honours:* Research Fellowships, California State University, Sacramento, 1986-1988. *Hobbies:* Hiking; Swimming; Travel. *Address:* PO Box 8524, Berkeley, CA 94707, USA.

MACKINNON Cinda Crabbe, b. 28 Dec. 1948, USA. Environmental Consultant; Geologist. m. Thomas C. MacKinnon, 25 Oct. 1976, 2 sons. *Education:* BA, Geology, Environmental Science minor, UCSB, 1977; MS, Geology, CSULB, 1984. *Appointments:* Scientist, Regional Water Board, New Zealand, 1977-80; Lecturer, Earth Science, California State University, 1981-84; Hydrologist, California consulting firm, 1985-87; Principal, CCM Environmental Consulting, 1987-. *Publications:* Geologic Wonders of the Southwest. *Memberships:* Registered Geologist, State of California; Board of Directors, Association for Women Geoscientists; Association of Ground Water Scientists and Engineers. *Interests:* World peace; Fight against poverty; Children's rights; Ground water pollution; Languages (English and Spanish). *Address:* 2834 San Antonio Drive, Walnut Creek, CA 94598, USA.

MACKINNON The MacKinnon of, b. 13 Feb. 1955, Taunton, Somerset, England. Occupational Therapist. m. Allan Jeffery, 19 Dec. 1981. 2 sons. *Education:* St Loyes School of Occupational Therapy, 1973-76. *Appointments:* Musgrove Park Hospital, Taunton, Somerset, 1976; Bridgwater General Hospital, 1977; East Reach Hospital, Taunton, 1983; Ivy House Day Hospital; Cheddon Road Hospital, Taunton Bridgewater Social Services; locum posts. *Membership:* British Association of Occupational Therapists. *Hobbies:* Yoga; Badminton; Family. *Address:* 16 Durleigh Road, Bridgwater, Somerset TA6 7HR, England.

MACLAINE Shirley, b.24 Apr. 1934, Richmond, Virginia, USA. Actress; Writer; Film director. m. Steve Parker. 1 daughter. *Education:* Grammar school; Lee High School, Washington. *Career:* Former Chorus Girl and Dancer. *Creative Works:* Films include: The Trouble With Harry; Artists and Models; Around The World in 80 Days; Hot Spell; The Matchmaker; Can-Can; Career; The Apartment; Two For The Seesaw; The Children's Hour; Irma La Douce; What A Way To Go; The Yellow Rolls-Royce; Gambit; Woman Times Seven; The Bliss of Mrs Blossom; Sweet Charity; Two Mules For Sister Sara; Desperate Characters; The Possessions of Joel Delaney; The Turning Point, 1977; Being There, 1979; Loving Couples, 1980; The Change of Seasons, 1981; Slapstick, 1981; Terms of Endearment, 1984; Out on a Limb, 1987; Steel Magnolias, 1989. Revues: If My Friends Could See Me Now, 1974; To London With Love, 1976, London 1982. Produced and co-directed: The Other Half of the Sky-A China Memoir, 1973. Producer and Star: Amelia, 1975. *Publications:* Don't Fall Off the Mountain, 1971; The New Celebrity Cookbook, 1973; You Can Get There From Here, 1975 (volumes 1 and 2 of autobiography); Out on a Limb (volume 3 of autobiography), 1983; Dancing in the Light, 1985. *Honours:* Star of the Year Award, Theater Owners of America, 1967; Best Actress Award for role in Desperate Characters, Berlin Film Festival, 1971; Academy Award for Best Actress, 1984. *Address:* c/o International Creative Management, 8899 Beverly Boulevard, Los Angeles, CA 90048, USA.

MACLEAN Barbara Barondess, b. New York, USA. Actress. *Appointments:* Broadway Plays Include: Gay Paree, 1926, Crime 1927, Riddle Me This, Garden of Eden, Topaze, 1929-31, A Thousand Summers, death Takes a Holiday, 1932, Faithfully Yours, 1951; Films Include: Rasputin; Hold Your Man; Merry Widow; Tale of Two Cities; Plot Thickens; Easy Money; Queen Christina; Soldiers of the Storm; When Strangers Maryr; TV Film, Open Cage, 1982; Columnist, Morning Telegraph, 1929-31; Created Column, Little Bo Peep on Broadway; Interior Designer, Designer of Textiles, 1938-78. *Publications:* Cooking on the Run; One Life is Not Enough; Timing, 1986. *Memberships:* Equity; SAG; AFTRA; ASID; Authors League; Dramatists League. *Address:* 630 Park Ave., New York, NY 10021, USA.

MACLEOD Jean Sutherland, b. 20 Jan. 1908, Glasgow, Scotland. Novelist. m. Lionel Walton, 1 Jan. 1935, 1 son. *Appointments:* John Leng and Company; People's Friend, Dundee; Woman's Own, London; IPC Magazines, London; Mills and Boon Limited, Publishers, London. *Publications:* Author of 160 novels up to 1986; short stories in various magazines; author, 10 novels under the name of Catherine Airlie; 2 historical novels.

Memberships: St Andrew Society of York, Past President, 1st Lady President of Society; Romantic Novelists of Great Britain. *Honour:* Cartland Historical Award, 1962. *Hobbies:* Sailing; Painting; Gardening. *Address:* Rose Garth, The Stonebow, Thornton-le-Beans, Northallerton, North Yorkshire, England.

MACMAHON Clare, b. 26 Nov. 1924, Downpatrick, Northern Ireland, Retired College Deputy-Principal. *Education:* BSc 1st Class Honours, Zoology, Queen's University, Belfast, 1946; MIBiol, 1982. *Appointments:* School Teacher, 1946-48; Museum Education Officer, 1948-52; Lecturer, College of Education, 1952-59; Vice Principal, Leeds Day College, 1959-63; Vice Principal, Deputy Principal, Stranmills College of Education, 1963-85. *Memberships:* Institute of Biology; Linnean Society; Royal Society of Arts; National Trust; Royal Society for Protection of Birds; Past Northern Ireland President, Soroptimists International; Convenor, Membership Committee, International Federation of University Women. *Honours:* Officer, Order of British Empire, 1982; 1st woman Pro-Chancellor, Queen's University, Belfast, 1987; 1st woman Chair, Fire Authority for Northern Ireland, 1979-81. *Hobbies include:* Field Botany; Bird Watching; Walking; Music; Knitting. *Address:* 7 Kimscourt, 21 Kensington Road, Belfast BT5 6NH, Northern Ireland.

MACMARTIN Marie, b. 5 Sept. 1914, Hamilton, Ontario, Canada. Health Educator;. m. James MacMartin, 31 Mar. 1956. *Education:* Registered Nurse, Elyria Memorial Hospital, Elyria, Ohio, USA, 1940; AA with honourable mention, University of Berkeley, California, 1955; Nutrition Consultant, North American College of Natural Health Sciences, San Rafael, California, 1981; Able Toastmaster, Toastmasters International, Santa Maria, California. *Appointments:* Dog Trainer; Nurse, Cleveland City Hospital, Ohio, USA; Flight Leader, Civil Air Patrol; Charge Nurse, various hospital wards, USA and overseas, 1945-49, Flight Nurse, Pacific and Alaska routes, 1949-52, USAF; Served to Captain; Publicity Chairman, Alameda County Women's Bowling Association, California, 1960s; Co-Organizer, Independent Order of Foresters State Bowling Tournament, 1969-79; Nutrition Consultant, Lecturing and radio appearances, 1987-. *Publications:* Does Your Pet Itch? (The Real Cause of so-called Fleabite Allergy), 1986; Articles in health-oriented magazine. *Memberships:* Women's International Bowling Association; Toastmasters International; Secretary, Bulletin Editor, Independent Order of Foresters, Santa Maria Chapter; President, Organizer, Central Coast Chapter, National Health Federation. *Honours:* Numerous dog training awards including as Owner/ Trainer of 1st Shetland Sheepdog in history of American Kennel Club to win all 3 training titles, 1930s; Civil Air Patrol Fliers Wings, 1943; Certificate of Appreciation for contribution to student speakers, Lions Club. *Hobbies:* Photography; Organic gardening; Semi-classical music. *Address:* 859 Juniper Street, Nipomo, CA 93444, USA.

MACNAB Iona Gayle, b. 14 June 1961, Melbourne, Australia. Barrister and Solicitor; Swimming Teacher. *Education:* BA, Honours, 1986, LLB, 1986, Melbourne University. *Appointments:* Part-time Researcher, Victorian Law Reform Commission, 1984, 1985; Barrister, Solicitor, Gargan & Roache, Geelong, 1986-. *Publications:* Surrogate Mothering: An Annotated Bibliography, 1984. *Memberships:* Law Institute of Victoria; Chairman, Ormond College Students Club, University of Melbourne, 1983; Co-Chairman, Inter-Collegiate Council, University of Melbourne; Secretary, National Association of Australian University Colleges, 1983-85. *Hobbies:* Outdoor Activities; Camping; Bagpipes; Cooking; Bulldogs; Swimming; Rowing; Running. *Address:* c/o 49 Alandale Road, Blackburn, VIC 3130, Australia.

MACVEAN Jean Elizabeth, Writer. m. James Wright 11 Oct. 1952, divorced. 1 son, 1 daughter. *Education:* Girls' Grammar School, Bradford, England; College d'Hulst, Versailles, France. *Appointments:* Passport Control Department, Foreign office, 1941-45; American Informationa Department, Foreign Office, latterly Head of Pressland Radio, 1945-51. *Publications:* Poems: Ideas of Love; Eros Reflected; Novel: The Intermediaries; Plays: The Image of Freedom; Flight of the Swan; The Adjacent Kingdom. *Memberships:* Fellow, International PEN; National Poetry Society. *Hobbies:* Study of Art; Cookery. *Address:* 21 Peel Street, London W8 7PA, England.

MACWILLIAMS Margaret E., b. 26 May 1929, Osage, Iowa, USA. Nutritionist; Educator. 1 son, 1 daughter. *Education:* BS 1951, MS 1953, Iowa State University; PhD, Oregon State University, 1968. *Appointments:* Faculty, Iowa State University, 1951-53; Faculty 1961-, currently Professor of Food & Nutrition, California State University, Los Angeles. *Publications:* Food: Experimental Perspectives; Food Fundamentals; Nutrition for the Growing Years; Living Nutrition; Understanding Food; Nutrition for Good Health; Experimental Foods Laboratory Manual; Illustrated Guide to Food Preparation; Parents' Nutrition Book; World of Nutrition; Food for You; Modern Food Preservation. *Memberships:* American Dietetic Association; Institute of Food Technology; Society for Nutrition Education. *Honours:* Fellowships: American Home Economics Association, Phi Upsilon Omicron; Various awards: California State University, Iowa State University (2). *Hobbies:* Violin; Photography; Classical music; Hiking. *Address:* PO Box 220, Redondo Beach, California 90277, USA.

MACY Janet Kuska, b. 9 Nov. 1935, Omaha, Nebraska, USA. Broadcaster; Educator. *Education:* BS, University of Nebraska, Lincoln, 1957; MS, Kansas State University, Manhattan, 1961; MEd, South Dakota State University, Brookings, 1970. *Appointments:* Producer/ Interviewer, Station KSAC, 1957-61; Producer/ Interviewer, KUON-TV, 1961-62; Producer/Interviewer, WOW-TV, 1962-67; Producer/Interviewer, KESD-TV, 1967-70; Producer/Interviewer, KUOM-AM, 1971-88. *Creative work:* Video Documentary on Head Start Interactive Video Disc-Level 1 on Family Intervention. *Memberships:* Faculty Women's Advisory Committee, Council for University Women's Progress, Secretary-Treasurer, Campus AAUP; Twin Cities Assembly; University Senate; American Women in Radio-TV; American Home Ec Association. *Honours:* Nutrition Communication Award, AWRT, 1977; Masters Program, University of Nebraska, 1973; School Bell Awards, MEA, 1979, 1980, 1982, 1983. *Interests:* Interactive video disc; Women's issues; Documentaries for radio and TV. *Address:* 6852 Bethany Park Drive, Lincoln, NE 68505, USA.

MADDEN Kathryn Wood, b. 27 Dec. 1949, Washington DC, USA. Actress; Singer; Writer. m. Ronald Madden, 11 Feb. 1984. *Education:* BA, cum laude, Speech and Theatre Education, University of Maryland. *Appointments:* The role of Grace Farrell in Annie, New York, Los Angeles and major originating 2 companies. *Publications:* Anthology edited by John Campbell, Our Western World's Greatest Poems; Poem, Sausalito. *Memberships:* Kappa Delta Pi, Election Honorary, 1972; Phi Honorary for top 10% graduating class, University of Maryland, 1972; Actor's Equity Association; Screen Actor's Guild; American Federation of Radio and Television Artists. *Honour:* Honorary Citizen Award of Kansas City, 1982. *Hobbies:* Writing children's stories; Collecting antiques; A progressive study of religion and depth psychology. *Address:* 210 W 101st Street, New York, NY 10025, USA.

MADDEX Diane R., b. 14 June 1943, Riverside, California, USA. Book Publisher. m. Robert Lucien Maddex Jr, 11 June 1965, 1 daughter. *Education:* Antioch College, 1961-62; BA, English, Northwestern University,, 1965. *Appointments:* Editorial assistant, National Association of Mutual Insurance Agents, 1965-67; Index Editor, Bureau of National Affairs, 1967-68; Editor, Preservation News, 1968-72; Managing Editor, National Trust for Historic Preservation, 1971-72; Micronesian correspondent, Pacific Daily News, 1973-74; Director, Preservation Press, National Trust for

Historic Preservation, 1974-90; President, Archetype Press, 1990-. *Publications include:* Author: Historic Buildings of Washington DC; (Text) Architects Make Zigzags. Editor: All About Old Buildings; America's Forgotten Architecture; Industrial Eye; Archabet; Built in the USA; I Know That Building!. *Memberships:* Design Review Board, Reston, Virginia; Chair, Publications Committee, US/ICOMOS General Assembly; Founding member, DC Presevation League. *Honours:* Numerous awards including: Federal Design Achievement, 1984; American Institute of Graphic Arts, 1986, 1987, 1980; Art Directors Club, Metropolitan Washington, 1985; Type Directors Club, New York, 1985; American Society of Interior Designers, 1989. *Hobbies:* Architecture; Fine arts; Photography; Collecting glass & pottery. *Address:* 11785 Indian Ridge Road, Reston, Virginia 22091, USA.

MADISON Vivian L, b. 6 Mar. 1956, Lake Charles, Louisiana, USA. Attorney. *Education:* BA, Loyola University, New Orleans, 1978; JD, Loyola University School of Law, 1981. *Appointments:* Jones Walker, Waechter, Positevent, Carrere & Denegre. *Publications:* Harris v McRae : The Court Retreats from Roe v. Wade, Loyola Law Review, 1980. *Memberships:* Louisiana State, Federal, American & New Orleans Bar Associations; Association for Women Attorneys; Louisiana Hospital Association; New Orleans Association of Defense Counsel. *Honours Include:* Dean's List; Academic Scholarship; Pi Sigma Alpha; Louisiana Trial Lawyers' Association Award for Appellate Advocacy, 1979. *Hobbies:* Scuba Diving; Skiing; Tennis. *Address:* 201 St Charles Avenue, Place St Charles, New Orleans, LA 70170, USA.

MADRID Donna Kay, b. 29 May 1937, Mount Ayr, Iowa, USA. Businesswoman. m. George C. Madrid, 21 June 1954, 2 daughters. *Education:* AA, Interior Designers Guild, 1978. *Appointments:* Owner-Manager, part-time house cleaning service, 1970-79; Designer, Beam Interiors, 1979-80; Owner-Manager, Innovative Interiors, 1980-81; Assistant Vice President, Office Manager, Personnel Director, Jardine Emett & Chandler, Insurance Brokers. *Memberships:* Personnel & Industrial Relations Association; National Association of Female Executives; Westside Executive Network; Women's Referral Service; Insurance Personnel Management Forum. *Hobbies:* Interior Design; Horseback Riding; Water Skiing. *Address:* 3627 Summershore Lane, Westlake Village, California 91361, USA.

MADSEN Patricia Anne, b. 17 Feb. 1949, Chicago, Illinois, USA. Judge. *Education:* BA, Loretto Heights College, 1973; JD, University of Denver, Colorado, 1976. *Career:* Director, US CU Legal Service, 1976-77; Clinical Fellow, Antioch School of Law, 1977-78; Referee: Denver County Court 1978-79; Denver District Court 1980-83; Judge, Denver County Court, 1983-. *Memberships:* Past Board member, Colorado Women's Bar Association; Committee Chair, Colorado Bar Association; Denver Bar Association; American Judicature Society; Interamerican Bar Association; Amnesty International. *Honour:* 50th Anniversary Award, Colorado Chapter, National Lawyers Guild, 1987. *Hobbies:* Theatre; Arts; Reading. *Address:* City & County Building, Room 108, Denver, Colorado 80202, USA.

MAGALLANES Deborah Jean, b. 22 May 1951, Gary, Indiana, USA. General Manager; Project Management. m. Gary Allen DeBardi, 15 May 1975. *Appointments:* Marketing Assistant, VMC Corporation, 1975-76; Personnel Consultant, Business Mens Clearing House, 1976-79; General Manager, Cypress Steel, 1979-; President and General Manager, Magallanes Inc, 1979-; Founded Hug'M Messengers, 1980-; Founded, Ace Entertainment, 1981-. *Publication:* Money In Love Relationships, with Margaret Samuelson, 1988. *Memberships:* Bellevue Leaders, Board 1982-88, President 1984-86, Treasurer 1987; Soroptimist International, Director 1986-88, Chair Archives Committee 1988-89; Womens Business Exchange, Board of Advisors 1981-84, Life Member;

MIT Alumni Association, Honorary, 1975-; Friends of Youth, Board of Directors, 1984-89, Vice President, 1986-88; Up With People Alumni Association, 1970-; Girl Scouts of America. *Honours:* Up With People Cast Member, 1969-70; Networker of the Year, 1983, Womens Business Exchange; Nominee, Distinguished Women Award, 1987, The Womens Network; Community Service Anaeird, 1987, Totem Girl Scout Council. *Hobbies:* Canoeing; Downhill and cross country skiing; Fishing. *Address:* 405-114th Ave SE No 300, Bellevue, WA 98004, USA.

MAGEAU Mary, b. 4 Sept. 1934, Milwaukee, Wisconsin, USA. Composer; Harpsichordist; Composition teacher. m. Kenneth Luton White, 26 Dec. 1974. 2 sons. *Education:* BMus, DePaul University, 1963; MMus (Composition), University of Michigan, 1969; Composers Fellowship Programme, Berkshire Music Centre, 1970. *Appointments:* Assistant Professor, Scholastica College, Duluth, Minnesota, 1969-73; Lecturer, Brisbane College of Advanced Education, Australia, 1974-85; Lecturer, Queensland Conservatorium of Music, 1986-90. *Creative works:* Montage; Indian Summer; Concerto Gross, for symphony orchestra; Contrasts; Sonate Concertate; Doubles; Piano Trio; Fantasy Music; Timepieces; Lacrimae; Pacific Ports; Ragtime; Three Pieces for Organ; Forecasts; Soliloquy. *Memberships:* American Society of Composers, Authors and Publishers; Fellowship of Australian Composers; International League of Women Composers. *Honours:* Louis Moreau Gottschalk Centenary Competition (silver medal), 1970; ASCAP Standard Award, annually since 1981; Commission Grants, Australia Council Music Board, 1980, 1985, 1988 and 1989; Fellowship to attend, International Dance Course for Professional Composers and Choreographers, Melbourne, Victoria, 1984; Minnesota Composers Competition, 1972. *Hobbies:* Sailing; Travel; Astronomy. *Address:* 57 Ironside Street, St Lucia, Queensland, Australia 4067.

MAGEE Maureen Elizabeth Bowie, b. 24 Nov. 1949, Niagara Falls, Ontario, Canada. Traveller. m. Anthony Peter Magee, 30 Dec. 1972, divorced 1988. *Education:* Management Development for Arts Administrators, Banff School of Management, 1983; BFA, Theatre, University of Victoria, British Columbia, 1984. *Appointments:* Teacher Aide, Winnifred Stewart School for Retarded, Edmonton, 1973-76; Director of Education, Bastion Theatre, Victoria, 1982-83; Co-ordinator, Association of Cultural Executives, Toronto, 1985-88. *Memberships:* Association of Cultural Executives; The Globetrotters. *Hobbies:* Rock climbing; Dance; Theatre; Travel; Billiards; Needlework. *Address:* c/o 149 Hanson Street, Toronto, Ontario, M4C 1A5, Canada.

MAGGIO Rosalie, b. 8 Nov. 1943, Victoria, Texas, USA. Writer; Editor. m. David C. Koskenmaki, 28 Dec. 1968, 1 son, 2 daughters. *Education:* BA, College of St Catherine, 1965; Certificates, University of Nancy, France, 1966. *Appointments:* Editor, International College of Surgeons, 1967-70; Public relations assistant, French Consulate General, Chicago, 1971; Self-employed writer & editor, 1971-. *Publications:* Books: Travels of Soc, 1985; Nonsexist Word Finder, 1987; Music Box Christmas, 1990; How to Say It, 1990; La Fiancee du Danger, in press. Articles & stories, all major US children's magzines including Jack & Jill, Cricket, Highlights for Children, Young American, Children's Playmate. Total, over 700 stories & articles in magazines & educational publications. *Honours:* Children's writing award, Northwind Story Hour, 1985; Author of Month, Highlights for Children magazine, 1987; Society of Childrens Book Writers Magaazine Merit Award (non-fiction), 1988. *Hobbies:* Genealogy; Peace activism; Travel; Stamps. *Address:* 1297 Summit Avenue, St Paul, Minnesota 55105, USA.

MAGGIORE Susan, b. 14 Mar. 1957, Newark, New Jersey, USA. Geophysical Oceanographer. m. Stephen Paul Garreffa, 21 Oct. 1989. *Education:* BS, Geoscience, Montclair State College, 1978; Postgraduate Studies in Geophysics, University of New Orleans and University of Southern Mississippi. *Appointments:* Supervisor, Research and Communications, The Cousteau Society, 1979-81; Geophysicist, Geomagnetics Dept, Naval Oceanographic Office, 1981-85; Marine Research Specialist, NECOR (NE Consortium of Oceanographic Research), 1985-86; Oceanographer, AT&T Bell Laboratories, 1986-. *Publications:* Researcher, The Cousteau Almanac Of The Environment, 1981; Columnist, Cousteau's Newsletter, The Dolphin Log; Articles; Technical manual for AT&T, 1989. *Memberships:* Marine Technology Society; American Geophysical Union; National Association of Female Executives. *Honours:* Exceptional Contribution Award 1987 and 1988, Award for Excellence 1988 and 1989, from AT&T Bell Laboratories. *Hobbies:* Singing; Musical instruments (piano, guitar, mandolin, violin); Reading; Gourmet Cooking. *Address:* A&T Bell Laboratories, 1 Whippany Road, Whippany, NJ 07981, USA.

MAGNO Marcelita Coronel, b. 3 Dec. 1939, Orion, Bataan, Philippines. Chemistry Education Specialist. m. Ruperto C Magno, 22 June 1963. 3 sons, 1 daughter. *Education:* BS, Chem, Mapua Inst of Tech, 1959; MS, Chem, Lehigh University, 1962; PhD (Chem) Ateneo de Manila University, 1986. *Appointments:* Research Assistant, Lehigh University, 1961-62; Faculty Member, Mapua Institute of Technology, 1959-75; Science Education Specialist, Senior Lecturer, University of the Philippines, 1975-. *Publications:* Chemistry for a Better Life, 1988; Science and Technology III, 1987; Dangerous Drugs A Resource Book for Teachers and Students, 1984; Chemistry in Our Environment, 1980; various modules and articles. *Memberships:* Phi Lambda Theta; American Electroplaters Society; Phil Fulbright Association; Phil Ass of Chemistry Teachers; Society of Sigma Xi. *Honours:* Outstanding Mapuan Award, Nat Ass of Mapua Alumni, 1987; First Place, Outstanding Paper, First Nat Chemistry Congress, 1985; Honorary Visiting Fellow, Univ of New South Wales, Australia, 1984; Most Outstanding Silver Jubilarian, Mapua Institute of Technology CHE-CHEM Alumni Association, 1984; Outstanding Mapuan Award, 1979; Fulbright-Hays Educational Leadership Development Grant, Lawrence Hall of Science, University of California, Berkeley, 1978; Kentile Inc Research Fellowship, 1961-62. *Hobbies:* Reading; Swimming; Sewing; Cooking. *Address:* University of the Philippines, Institute for Science and Mathematics Education Development, Diliman, Quezon City, Philippines.

MAGNUSDOTTIR Torunn, b. 12 Dec. 1920, Iceland. Historian; Teacher. m. (1) 29 June 1940, (2) 24 Sept. 1954, 1 son, 4 daughters. *Education:* B.Ed., Kennarahaskola Islands, 1982; Cand. Mag. in History from Universitiet of Iceland, 1982. *Appointments:* Teacher, 1971-82 Research Work, 1983; ASI, 1986-87. *Publications:* Ungverjaland og Rumenia, 1977; Sjosoken Sunnlenskra Kvenna..., 1984; Sjokonur a Islandi, 1988. *Memberships:* Writers Association of Iceland; Union of Teachers with Academic Degrees. *Honours:* Recipient, various honours and awards. *Hobbies:* Literature; Travel. *Address:* Hofsvallagata 17, 101 Reykjavik, Iceland.

MAGNUSSEN Karen Diane, b. 4 Apr. 1952, Vancouver, British Columbia, Canada. Professional Skater and Teacher. m. Robert Anthony Cella, 23 July 1977. 1 son. *Education:* Simon Fraser University, 2 years of Kinesology. *Appointments:* Ice Capades Star, Canada, US, Hawaii, Japan, 1973-77; Founder, Karen Magnussen Foundation, 1973; Started Karen & Friends, Ice Show Annual Events, 1974; Coaching from 1974; Show Karen and Friends televised 1973, 1974 and 1975. *Publications:* Karen, with Jeff Cross, 1973. *Honours:* British Columbia Sports Hall of Fame and Canadian Sports Hall of Fame, Canadian Amateur Hall of Fame, Ottawa North Shore Hall of Fame, Athlete of the Year, 1971; Sportsman's Merit Award, 1971; Canadian Women Athlete of the Year, 1972; Special Achievement Award from The Sons of Norway, Members of North America; Vanier Award; CBC's Sport Award; CFSA Award of Merit; Ice Skating Queen of America; Order of Canada Medal. *Hobbies:* Golf;

Swimming; Skiing; Collects Skating Figurines, Plates. *Address:* 33 Old Farm Road, Reading, MA 01867, USA.

MAHLAB Eve, b. 30 May 1937, Vienna, Austria. Director. m. 19 Dec. 1959, 1 son, 2 daughters. *Education:* LLB(Melbourne), Australia. *Appointments:* Director, Mahlab Group of Companies, Member, State Training Board, Director Walter and Eliza Hall Institute of Medical Research Chairperson, Co-Founder, Know-Biz (Business Education) Project. *Memberships:* Womens Electoral Lobby. *Honours:* Australian Businesswoman of the Year, 1982; Order of Australia, 1988. *Hobby:* Status of Women. *Address:* 81 City Road, South Melbourne, Victoria 3205, Australia.

MAHONEY Colleen Ann, b. 14 June 1956, Petaluma, California, USA. Architect. *Education:* AA, University of London (UK) & Santa Rosa Community College, California, 1976; BA, University of California, Berkeley, 1978; Graduate studies, University of Hawaii. Licensed, California, Arizona, Hawaii. *Appointments:* Gensler & Associates, San Francisco, 1978-80; Ossipoff, Snyder, Rowland & Goetz, Honolulu, 1980-81; Callister, Gately & Bischoff, Tiburon, California, 1982-84; Princeton Group, San Francisco, 1984- 86; Self-employed, own practice, 1987-. *Creative works:* Dozens of buildings. *Memberships:* American Institute of Architects; National Council of Architectural Registration Boards; Organisation of Women Architects; Rotary, Tiburon-Belevedere; Pacific Association of Women Martial Artists. *Honours:* Builders Choice Award, 1986; Gold Nugget Award, Pacific Coast Builders Conference, 1987; Biographical recognition. *Hobbies:* Black Belt, Korean Martial Art Tae Kwon Do; Horseback riding, Water & Snow Skiing; Speaking engagements, women's groups. *Address:* 773 Tiburon Boulevard, Tiburon, California 94920, USA.

MAHONEY Joelle Katherine Marguerite Dennis, b. 6 Jan. 1948, Amiens, France. Astrologer. m. John William Christopher Mahoney, 14 Aug. 1971. *Education:* AA, Manhattan Community College, 1970; BA, Adelphi University, 1982; MBA, Hofstra University. *Appointments:* Founding President, Astrological Research Centre & Training Institute, Ltd, 1974-84; Mahoney Associates, Ltd, International Practice for Astrological Counselling, 1974-. *Publications:* The Concepts I, II and III; In Search of Time; numerous articles in professional journals. *Memberships:* President, Astrologers Guild of America, 1980-83 and 1988-; American Federation of Astrologers, Inc; Association for Research & Enlightenment (ARE). *Hobbies:* Equitation; Painting (Oils); Gardening (Flowers); Wildlife Conservation; Nutrition; Physical Fitness; Writing. *Address:* Route 116, RR No 1, North Salem, New York 10560, USA.

MAIER Donna Jane Ellen, b. 20 Feb. 1948, St Louis, Missouri, USA. Professor of History; Author. m. Stephen J. Rapp, 3 Jan. 1981, 1 son, 1 daughter. *Education:* BA, History, College of Wooster, Wooster, Ohio, 1969; MA, History, 1972, PhD, History, 1975, Northwestern University, Evanston, Illinois. *Appointments:* Acting Assistant Professor, University of Texas, Dallas, 1975-78; Assistant Professor, 1978-81, Associate Professor, 1981-86, Professor, 1986-90, University of Northern Iowa, Cedar Falls, Iowa. *Publications:* Priests and Power, 1983; History and Life, 1986; Asante War Aims, in The Golden Stool, 1987; Slave Labor/Wage Labor in German Togoland, in Germans in the Tropics, 1987; Article: The Dente Oracle, 1981. *Memberships:* African Studies Association; American Historical Association; American Association of University Women; Quota Club. *Honours:* Fulbright Hays Research Fellowship, 1972; American Philosophical Society Grant, 1978; Fulbright Hays Summer Fellowship, Egypt, 1987. *Address:* Department of History, University of Northern Iowa, Cedar Falls, IA 50614, USA.

MAIHLE Nita Jane, b. 4 June 1955, Mansfield, Ohio, USA. Scientist. m. Jeffrey L. Salisbury, 3 Sept. 1982, 1 daughter. *Education:* BA, MS, Botany, Miami

University, 1977; MS, PhD, Cell Biology, 1983, Albert Einstein College of Medicine. *Appointments:* Instructor, Histology, Albert Einstein College of Medicine, 1980-81; Scientific Consultant, Encyclopedia of Life Sciences, 1981; Case Western Reserve University, Mayo Clinic, 1989. *Publications:* Articles in: Journal of Cell Science; Journal of Cell Biochemistry. *Memberships:* American Association for the Advancement of Science; American Association of Biological Chemists; American Association of University Women; American Society for Cell Biology; American Society of Microbiologists. *Honours Include:* Ohio Board of Regents Scholarship, 1973-76; Outstanding Young Women of America Award, 1983; Muscular Dystrophy Association Fellowship, 1984-85; NIH Fellowship, 1985-87; American Fellowship, 1987-88. *Address:* Dept. of Biochemistry and Molecular Biology, Mayo Graduate School of Medicine, Rochester, MN 55905, USA.

MAILLART Ella (Kini), b. 20 Feb. 1903, Geneva, Switzerland. Freelance Journalist. *Appointments:* Swiss & French Newspapers, dailies, weeklies & monthlies; lecture tours in France, Switzerland, England; Sent by Paris newspapers to Russia, China, Manchuria, Afghanistan, Nepal & India. *Publications:* Parmi la Jeunesse Russe, 1932; Des Monts Celestes aux Sables Rouges, 1934; Oasis Interdites, 1937; Gipsy Afloat, 1942; Cruises & Caravans, 1942; The Cruel Way, 1947; Ti-Puss, 1952; The Land of the Sherpas, 1955; In English: Turkestan Solo; Forbidden Journey; The Cruel Way; Gipsy Afloat, all with reprints in English, French and German. *Memberships:* Honorary Member, Ski Club Great Britain; Kandahar Ski Club; Fellow, RGS, London; Royal Society for Asian Affairs; Club des Explorateurs; Ti-Puss, Alpine Club. *Honours:* Schiller Foundation, 1942; Sailed for Switzerland, Olympic Games of 1924; Sir Percy Sykes Medal, Royal Central Asian Society, 1955; Prix Ville de Geneve, 1987. *Hobbies:* Skiing; Sailing; Gardening. *Address:* 10 av. Vallette, 1206 Geneva, Switzerland.

MAINE Virginia Louise Mottorn, b. 24 Mar 1937, Pennsylvania, USA. Consultant. m. John Groves Maine, 21 Dec. 1967, 2 sons, 1 daughter. *Education:* BA, Sociology, Pennsylvania State Univesity, 1959; MSW, Honours, University of Pittsburgh, 1963. *Appointments Include:* Various positions in social work, 1959-69; Project Co-ordinator, Child Abuse Prevention Programmes, Family Service Centre, Houston and Harris County, 1973-81; Self-employed Consultant, 1981-. *Publications:* Co-Author, Presentor, A Unique Family Centred Approach for Child Abuse Prevention, 1977; articles in professional journals. *Memberships:* American Association of University Women, Treasurer, 1984-86; PEO; National Association for Social Workers; American Society for Hospital Social Work Directors. *Honours:* Mental Health Association Outstanding Service Award, 1970; Larue D Carter Meritorious Service, 1967. *Hobbies:* Oil and Acrylic Painting; Spinning Yarns; Knitting; Travel. *Address:* Silverbrook, RT1 Box 33A, Rochester Mills, PA 15771, USA.

MAIR Sylvia Lorraine, b. 2 Sept. 1948, Wangaratta, Victoria, Australia. Artist. m. Robert Ian Mair, 1970. 1 daughter. *Education:* BSc (Hons), 1970; PhD, 1974. *Appointments:* Physicist, CSIRO, 1974- 87, (Principal Research Scientist, 1986-87); Artist, Printmaker, 1987-. *Creative works:* Publications: Numerous papers in professional journals like Journal of Physics; Acta Crystallographica. Exhibition of Prints: Raw Pressure, Roar 2 Studios, Melbourne, 1989. *Memberships:* American Physical Society, 1977-87; Australian Institute of Physics, 1975-88; Society of Crystallographers in Australia, 1975-88; Australian Print Council, 1988-. *Hobbies:* Japanese language; Terrestrial orchids (native to region); Equal opportunity for women. *Address:* Apartment 603-Homat Governor, 5- 17 Roppongi 1-Chome, Minato-Ku, Tokyo 106, Japan.

MAITLAND Olga Helen (Lady), b. 23 May 1944, New York, USA. Journalist. m. Robin William Hamilton Hay, 19 Apr. 1969. 2 sons, 1 daughter. *Education:* School of St MAry & St Anne, Abbots Bromley, 1956-60; Lycee Francais de Londres, 1960-62. *Appointments:* Trainee Reporter, Blackheath & District Reporter, Fleet Street News Agency, 1964-67; Sunday Express, 1967-; Columnist, television and radio broadcaster. *Publication:* Margaret Thatcher - First Ten Years, 1989. *Memberships:* Families for Defence, Chairman 1983-; WHY Campaign against Offensive Weapons, Deputy Chairman, 1986-; Parliamentary Candidate, Bethnal Green & Stepney, 1986; ILEA Candidate Holborn & St Pancras, 1985; Bow Group. *Honour:* Nominated, United Nations Media Peace Prize, 1984. *Hobbies:* Family; Travel. *Address:* 21 Cloudesley Street, London N1 0HX, England.

MAITLAND Sara Louise, b. 27 Feb. 1950, London, England. Writer. m. The Reverend Donald Lee, 24 June 1972. 1 son, 1 daughter. *Education:* BA (Hons) English Language and Literature, St Anne's College, Oxford, 1971. *Publications include:* Numerous books including: Daughter of Jerusalem, 1978; Tales I Tell My Mother, 1978; Map of the New Country, 1983; Virgin Territory, 1984; A Book of Spells, 1987; Arky Types, 1987. Over 16 anthologies etc, radio and television interviews and appearances. Lectured on Theology, women's history and contemporary literature; Gave paper at Zimbabwe National Book Fair Conference, Harare, 1985, etc. *Membership:* Writers Guild. *Honour:* Somerset Maugham Award, 1979 for Daughter of Jerusalem. *Interests:* Socialist feminism; Anglo Catholocism; Radical Theology; Friendship; Gardening. *Address:* St Chad's Vicarage, Dunloe Street, London E2 8JR, England.

MAJUMDER Madhuri, b. 8 Mar. 1933, Malaysia. Dermatologist. *Education:* MBBS, Calcutta; Diploma in Dermatology (London), 1967; MRCP, Edinburgh, 1968; FRCP, Edinburgh, 1982. *Appointments:* Government Service, 1960-65; Government scholarship to specialise in Dermatology, 1966-68; 1st Female Consultant Dermatologist in Malaysia, 1968-81; Private consultant, Ipoh Specialist Centre, 1981-. *Publications:* Articles in Australian Medical Journals; Conference papers read at ASEAN Dermatology Conferences in Singapore, Penang, Bangkok and Tokyo. *Memberships:* Life Member, President 1981-82, Perak Malaysian Med. Association. Founder Member, Academy of Medicine, College of Physicians, Surgeons, General Practitioners; President, Dermatology Society of Malaysia, 1982-84; Associate Member, Dermatology Society of Singapore and India; President, Perak Society for Promotion, Mental Health; Committee and Life Member, Perak Medical Practitioners Society. *Honours:* AMP, awarded by Sultan of Perak for services to the state, 1978; PMP awarded by Sultan of Perak for voluntary ocrvices, 1987; Public Service Award, Rotary Club of Ipoh, 1987; Vice-President, Society for Prevention of Cruelty to Animals; Swimming; Music; Theatre; Fine Arts. *Address:* 9 Jalan Hang Tuah, Ipoh 31400, Malaysia.

MAJWER Eva, b. 6 Jan. 1933, Stanislawow, Poland. Poet; Novelist. *Education:* Bachelor of Literature, 1955, Doctor of Literature, 1971, Poznan University. *Appointments:* Teacher of Polish, 1955-79; Publishing poetry and prose, 1958-. *Publications:* Poetry: Lightcuts; The Art of Non-Loving; Herbs are Flying Away; Puppets and Demons; The Sentence Passing on Vineyard; Fox Bridges; The Seventh Book of Verses; Prose: Dardzielanie; Eyes With no Eyelids; A Dancer in Red. *Memberships:* Union of Polish Writers, 1965-83; Solidarnosc, 1980-; Komitet Porozumiewawcry Srodowisk Tworcrych, 1980-81; Archbishop's Council of Social Matters; Participant, underground movement for independent culture; Polish PEN Club. *Honours:* Peleryny (Pelerine) Award, Gdansk, 1966. *Hobbies:* Lectures; Gardening; Ornithomantia; Radiaesthesy. *Address:* Os Kraju Rad 26 m 16, 61-697 Poznan, Poland.

MAKGILL Diana Mary Robina, The Honourable, b. 4 Jan. 1930, London, England. Civil Servant. *Education:* Stathcona Lodge School, Vancover; Nursery Nurses Examination, 1948. *Appointments:* Ceremonial Officer, Protocol, Foreign Office, 1961-70; Foreign & Commonwealth Office, London, 1970-79. *Membership:*

Honorary Steward, Westminster Abbey, London, 1977-89. *Honours:* Royal Victorian Order Member, 1972, Lieutenant, 1983; Jubilee Medal, 1977; Recipient, various other honours and awards. *Hobbies:* Reading; Riding; Gardening. *Address:* 15 Iverna Court, Iverna Gardens, London W8 6TY, England.

MAKI Susan Kay, b. 29 Nov. 1947, Virginia, USA. Attorney. *Education:* BS, University of Minnesota, 1970; jD, William Mitchell College of Law, 1979. *Appointments:* Attorney, Minnesota State Public Defenders Office, 1979-. *Publications:* Articles in professional journals. *Memberships:* American Bar Association; Minnesota Public Defenders Association, Secretary 1986-87; National Association of Counsel of children. *Hobbies:* Aerobic Dancing; Cross Country Skiing. *Address:* 95 Law Center, University of Minnesota, Minneapolis, MN 55455, USA.

MALENOIR S Andree M, b. 13 Mar. 1950, London, England. Hypnoanalyst. *Education:* Diploma, Hypnotherapy, Psychology, HCB, Bournemouth; Hypnohealing Diploma, Advanced, W Atkinson-Ball College of Hypnotherapy. *Appointments:* Hypnotherapist, 1985-; Hypnohealer, 1988-. *Publications:* Series of painted greetings cards, Gilbert & Sullivan Operetta Characters, & British Flowers. *Memberships:* Institute of Analytical Hypnotherapists; International Association of Hypnoanalysts; Associate, British Association of Therapeutical Hypnotists; International Guild of Natural Medicine Practitioners; Society for Primary Cause Analysis; Fellow, International Biographic Association; Association of Natural Medicine. *Honour:* Smythe Prize for Scripture, 1964. *Hobbies:* Music; Keep Fit; Reading; Disco Dancing; Animals. *Address:* 102 Harley Street, London W1N 1AF, England.

MALEY Robin Anne, b. 26 Feb. 1955, Lake Charles, USA. Insurance Executive. *Education:* BS, 1976, Skidmore College; MPH, Columbia University, 1981. *Appointments:* Staff Nurse, Massachusetts General Hospital, 1976-78; Staff Nurse, Lenox Hill Hospital, 1979-81; Risk Manager, Beth Israel Medical Centre, 1981-85; Assistant Vice President, Johnson & Higgins, 1985-87; Vice President, Continental Ins. Healthcare, 1987-. *Publications:* Articles in: Risk Management; Perspectives in Healthcare Risk Management. *Memberships:* Columbia University School of Public Health, Board; Metropolitan Health Administrators Association; Association of Healthcare Risk Management. *Honours:* Johnson & Higgins Recognition for Article. *Hobbies:* Skiing; Reading; Travel. *Address:* 433 East 51st Street, 2F, New York, NY 10128, USA.

MALKANI Roma Vaswani, b. 4 June 1949, India. President, Information Systems and Networks Corporation. m. Preem Malkani, 18 Apr. 1971. 1 son, 1 daughter. *Education:* MS 1969-71, PhD 1973-74, George Washington University; BS, Madison College, 1967-68; BS 1966-67, BS 1968-69, University of Virginia. *Appointments:* National Aeronautics and Space Administration, 1971-73; House of Representatives, 1975-79; President, Information Systems and Networks Corporation, 1980-. *Membership:* American Management Association. *Honours:* Best All Round Student, 1968; Dean's List on numerous occasions. Address: Information Systems and Networks Corporation, 10411 Motor City Drive, Bethesda, MD 20817, USA.

MALLINSON (Elizabeth) Anne, b. 19 Jan. 1929, St Albans, England. Bookseller. m. John Mallinson, 18 Aug. 1955, divorced 1967. *Education:* The Triangle Secretarial College, London, 1949. *Appointments:* Bookkeeper, The Royal Ocean Racing Club, 1951; Estate Secretary to late Sir Richard Sharples, Chawton, 1961; Created The Selborne Bookshop, Hants, 1968-. *Publications:* Author, Director, Jane Austen's Village, 1967, Chawton Pageant, 1975; sundry magazine articles; Creator, Mallinson Collection of Rural Relics, 1988. *Memberships:* 1st Chairman, Edward Thomas

Fellowship, 1980-88. *Hobbies Include:* Research; Nature. *Address:* The Selborne Cottage Shop, Selborne, Alton, Hampshire GU34 3JH, England.

MALLIS Stephanie Elaine, b. 14 Sept. 1945, Brooklyn, USA. Architect. *Education:* MArch, Harvard Univerity, 1978; BFA, honours, Pratt Institute, 1967. *Appointments:* Designer, Skidmore, Owings & Merrill, 1967-70; Parnter, Kahn & Mallis, 1971-76; Director, Interiors & Associate, Rogers, Butler & Burgun, 1972-76; Director, Interiors & Associate, I M Pei and Partners, 1979-86; President, Stephanie Mallis Inc., 1986-. *Memberships:* American Institute of Architects; American Society of Interior Designers. *Honours:* Fulbright Scholar, India, 1978-79; AIA Certificate of Merit, 1978; NSID Award, 1967. *Hobbies:* Travel; Painting. *Address:* 405 Lexington Avenue, New York, NY 10174, USA.

MALMFORS Lena Ann-Mari, b. 10 Feb. 1943, Stockholm, Sweden. Consultant, Management & Business Development. m. Torbjorn Malmfors, 14 Feb. 1979. *Education:* Swedish Student Exam, 1962; Economist, Stockholm School of Economics, 1970. *Appointments:* Skandinaviska Banken (bank), 1967-70; Moller & Company (food industry), 1970-77; Personnel manager, Distr AB Dagab (food), 1974-79; Personnel director, Vitrum AB (pharmaceutical) 1979-84; Management development, Asea Stal AB, 1984-86; Consultant, President of Vaxt Verket AB, 1986-. *Memberships:* Past chairman, Swedish Association of Personnel Managers; Board, Newthinkers. *Hobbies:* Music; Theatre; Art; Italy; Dogs. *Address:* Blidovagen 17, S-18245 Enebyberg, Sweden.

MALMGREN René Louise, b. 14 Nov. 1938, Minneapolis, USA. Academic Arts Administrator. m. Donald Elwin Malmgren, 27 Dec. 1958, 2 sons, 2 daughters. *Education:* BA, Colorado Womens College, 1966; MA, University of Colorado, 1981; Certificates. *Appointments:* Cultural Arts & Understanding Programme, Denver, 1970-72; Creative Drama, APS, Colorado, 1972-78; Teacher, Colorado Womens College, 1974-75; Educational Director, Colorado Children's Theatre Co., 1977-86; Coordinator, Curriculum, APS Colorado, 1982-85; Assistant Director, Instruction/Fine Arts, Tucson Unified School District, 1985-. *Publications:* Articles in professional journals. *Memberships:* President, Arizona Theatre Educators, 1988-89; Arizona Alliance for Arts Education; Tucson Symphony Education Board; Southern Arizona Opera Guild; Arts Genesis Board. *Honours:* Arizona Dept. of Education Certificate of Recognition, 1988; Phi Delta Kappa. *Hobbies:* Rape Assistance & Awareness Programme; Peacekeeper. *Address:* Tucson Unified School District, Lee Instructional Resource Centre, 2025 East Winsett Street, Tucson, AZ 85719, USA.

MALONE Mary Patricia, b. 1 June 1961, New York City, New York, USA. Health Care Consultant. *Education:* BS, Biology, 1983, BA, Anthropology, 1983, University of Notre Dame; MS, Health Systems Management, Rush University, 1985. *Appointments:* Project Assistant, Rush-Presbyterian St Luke's Medical Center, Chicago, Illinois, 1983-85; Senior Consultant, 1985-87; Director of Health Care Communications, 1987-, Laventhal & Horwath, Chicago. *Publications:* Professional articles and presentations. *Memberships:* Rush University Health Systems Management Alumni Association, President 1988; American College of Health Care Executives; Healthcare Financial Management Association. *Honour:* Lambda Alpha Honor Society, 1983. *Hobbies:* Sailing; Reading; Travel. *Address:* Laventhol & Horwath, 1845 Walnut Street, Philadelphia, PA 19103, USA.

MAMER Louisan, b. 28 Aug. 1910, Hardin, Illinois, USA. Writer; Editor; Advisor; Retired Home Electrification Specialist. m. Arthur C Hagen, 20 Mar. 1954. *Education:* AB, University of Illinois, 1931; USDA Graduate School, George Washington University, Adult Education; Washington School of Gemology, 1953-54;

Certified Gemologist; Certified Home Economist. *Appointments:* Women's Editor, Daily Illini & Illinois Agriculturist, 1930-31; Secondary, adult, Extension & College teaching, at Erie, Morrison & DeKalb, Illinois, 1931-35; Home Electrification, Information & Youth Club Liaison jobs & Trainer, Rural Electrification Administration, Washington, 1935-81. *Publications:* Personal Regimen lessons for NYA youths, electric co-op consumer folders, 1935-36; Leader's Guide and 6 lessons each on small appliances, lighting & co-op practices; Major equipment manuals; Articles in 33 state rural electric magazines. *Memberships:* American Home Economics Association, 1931-89; Electrical Women's Round Table, Inc, 1948-89; National Capitol Area EWRT Founder & Chair, 1968 and 1988; Illuminating Engineering Society, 1947-89; International Federation for Home Economics; International Federation of University Women; Phi Beta Kappa, Omicron Nu, Phi Upsilon Omicron (Washington Alumni Chair, 1946 and 1961); President's Council, University of Illinois, 1985-89; American Council of Consumer Interests; American Association of University Women; Business & Professional Women; Consumers Federation of America; League of Women Voters; National Consumers League; National Rural Electric Women's Association; Organization of Professional Employees of the (US) Department of Agriculture; Women's Council on Energy & the Environment; World Future Society. *Honours:* Scholarship Cup, 1924; National Honor Society, 1927; University of Illinois Scholarship Plaque, Alpha Lambda Delta, 1928; Orange and Blue Feathers Activity Honorary & Jr Illini Editor, 1929; Omicron Nu, Phi Beta Kappa, Phi Upsilon Omicron, Torch & Sr Illini Ed, 1930; Illinois Home Economics Teachers' Program & Publicity Award, 1935; Administrator's Commendation: Co-Founder REA National Farm Tour, 1938; USDA-REA Merit Award Salary Increase for youth & women's work, 1952; 50 year Service Awards: AHEA, Omicron Nu, Phi Upsilon Omicron, 1985-87. *Hobbies:* Collecting, grinding & appraising gems and rock specimens; Reading, clipping and writing on electric equipment; Collecting Hovsep Pushman prints, Oriental china, art objects; Fencing; Riding. *Address:* 2853 Ontario Road NW, No 422, Washington DC 20009, USA.

MAMONOVA Tatyana, b. 10 Dec. Jaroslavl, USSR. Writer. m. G Shikarov, 9 Jan. 1973. 1 son. *Education:* Leningrad Institute of Pharmacology, 1964. *Appointments:* Television Journalist, Leningrad, 1967-68; Literary Fellow & Critic for Magazine Aurora Leningrad, 1969-72; Editor-in-Chief, Almanac Woman and Russia, 1979; Lectured World-wide, 1980-; Scholar in Residence, Harvard University, USA, 1984; Scholar in Residence, University of Michigan, 1986; Scholar in Residence, CUNY Graduate School, 1989. *Publications:* Books: Woman and Russia; Russian Women's Studies; Sexism in Soviet Culture. *Memberships:* Sisterhood is Global, NYC; PEN, NYC; Women's Institute for Freedom of the Press, Washington DC; Contemporary Authors, Detroit. *Honours:* F Magazine Paris, One of Five Top Women of the Year, 1980; Elle Magazine Paris, One of Top Books of the Year: Woman and Russia, 1982; Top Award for Painting Sono Art Festival, 1988. *Hobbies:* Painting; Poetry writing. *Address:* c/o Margaret Maxwell, 81 Charles Street, New York, NY 10014, USA. 3.

MANCHEE Jane Walker, b. 28 Sept. 1960, Toronto, Ontario, Canada. Set Decorator & Dresser. *Education:* Honours Grade 13, Canadian Junior College, 1978; Fine Art & Film, Concordia University, 2 years; Film, Ryerson Polytechnic, Toronto, 4 years, graduated 1986. *Appointments:* Set dresser: Anne of Green Gables: The Sequel, 1986; Captain Power & Soldiers of the Future, 1987; Alfred Hitchcock Presents, 1987-88. Set decorator, Where the Spirit Lives, 1988. *Creative work includes:* Experimental documentary film, In the Eye of the Hunter (58 minutes, shown cable TV several times), with M. Lindsay Holton, 1984-86. *Memberships:* Association of Canadian Film Craftspeople; Royal Canadian Yacht Club. *Hobbies:* Film; Photography; Skiing (alpine, telemarking, cross-country, water); All water sports, sailing, swimming; Reading; Travel; Gardening; Music; Politics; History; Environment;

Family-Psycho; Dogs; Hiking; Outdoors; Stargazing. *Address:* 105 Withrow Avenue, Toronto, Ontario, Canada M4K 1C8.

MANCINI Elaine, b. 21 Sept. 1953, Chicago, Illinois, USA. Public Relations Executive. m. Alan G. Morrice, 14 Aug. 1974. *Education:* BA, University of Illinois, 1975; MA, 1977, PhD, 1981, New York University. *Appointments:* Assistant Professor, School of Visual Arts, College of Staten Island, St John's University, 1980-86; Director, Film Archive and Film Library Services, 1980-86; Vice-President, GCI Group, 1986-. *Publications:* The Free Years of the Italian Film Industry, 1985; Luchino Visconti: A Guide to References and Resources, 1986; D. W. Griffith and the Biograph Company, 1986. *Honours:* Key Pin and Scroll, Outstanding Woman Graduate, New York University, 1981; Fulbright Grant, Teaching Fellow, University of Bologna, Italy, 1982-83. *Hobbies:* Skiing; Tennis; Swimming. *Address:* 84 Pinewood Road, Hartsdale, NY 10530, USA.

MANDEL Carola Panerai Bertini. Skeet Shooter. m. Leon Mandel, 1938. *Publications:* Contributor of various articles on shooting. *Memberships:* Women's Board, North Western Memorial Hospital, Chicago; Trustee, Carola and Leon Mandel Fund, Loyola University, Chicago; Everglades Club; The Beach Club, Palm Beach, Florida. *Honours:* Captain, All American Skeet Team, 1952, 1953, 1954, 1955, 1956; Winner, Skeet Shooting 20 Gauge Men's Championship, 1954; Highest Average in World over Man in 12 gauge gun, 1956; European Women's Target Shooting Championship, Torino, Italy, 1958; European Women's Live Bird Shooting Championship of the World, Sevilla, Spain, 1959; Skeet Shooting Hall of Fame, 1970; Chevalier, Confrerie des Chevaliers du Tastevin. *Hobby:* Bridge, ACBL Life Master. *Address:* 324 Barton Avenue, Palm Beach, FL 33480, USA.

MANDELLI Gina Elizabeth, b. 12 Feb. 1957, Montreal, Canada. Costumer. *Education:* BA, Trent University, 1975, 1979. *Appointments:* Costume Designer, 1812, TV Movie, 1983; Video Costuming, Starscope, 1986; Wardrobe Assistant, Adderly, TV Series, 1986-88; War of the Worlds, TV series, 1988-89. *Publications:* Articles in professional journals. *Memberships:* ACFC; Costuming Society of Ontario; Military Heritage Society, Director, Costuming & Authenticity. *Hobbies:* Historical Costuming & Re-enacting; Writing; Theatre; Music; Travel; Hiking. *Address:* 1691 Gerrard St. E., Apt. 402, Toronto, Ontario, Canada M4L 2B1.

MANERO Victoria, b. 23 Apr. 1942, Cuba. Education Administrator. *Education:* BA. Spanish, Mercy College, Dobbs Ferry, New York, USA, 1970; MA, Spanish Literature, New York University, New York City, 1973; MS, Bilingual Education, Hunter College, New York City, 1977. *Appointments:* Clerk, American Express, New York City, USA, 1966-69; International Adjustments, The Chase Manhattan Bank, New York City, 1969-72; Teacher, PS 65 Bronx, 1972-77; Supervisor of Bilingual and Second Language Programmes, District 5M, 1977-, New York Board of Education. *Memberships:* National Association for Bilingual Education; Association for Supervision and Curriculum Development; International Reading Association. *Hobbies:* Reading; Foreign films; Opera; Ballet; Travel. *Address:* 433 West 123rd Street, New York, NY 10027, USA.

MANGIAMELE Rosemary Grace, b. 19 Oct. 1943, Melbourne, Australia. Occupational Therapist. m. Giorgio Mangiamele. *Education:* Diploma of Occupational Therapy; Bachelor of Applied Science; Graduate Diploma in Evaluation. *Appointments:* Sole Occupational Therapist, Gippsland Base Hospital, 1964-66; Occupational Therapist, Royal Children's Hospital, Melbourne, 1967-70; Chief Occupational Therapist, St Vincent's Hospital, 1971-77; Consultant Occupational Therapist, Papua New Guinea, 1979-82; State Adviser, Dept Community Services & Health, 1988-90.

Publication: Occupational Management of the Cardiac Patient, Co-author with M DiMasi, N Rose, 1986. *Memberships:* Victorian Association of Occupational Therapists, Secretary 1967-68, Vice President 1969; Ergonomics Society of Australia & New Zealand, Credited Member; Victorian Artists Society; Australian Malacological Society. *Honours:* Appointed Expert Adviser to the World Federation of Occupational Therapists, 1984; Australian Association of Occupational Therapists' Nominee to the Australian International Development Assistance Bureau, 1988. *Hobbies:* Watercolour painting; Singing; Music; Opera; Films; Italian language; Theatre; Tai Chi; Malacology. *Address:* 312 Nicholson Street, Fitzroy 3065, Melbourne, Australia.

MANLEY (Ellis) Elizabeth, b. 21 Mar. 1943, Jacksonville, Florida, USA. Marriage & Family Therapist; Family & Divorce Mediator. *Education:* BA, Carson-Newman College, 1965; MEd, Georgia State University, 1974; JD, Woodrow Wilson College of Law, 1980. *Appointments:* Juvenile Court Probation Officer, Fulton County, 1970-79; Private practice, therapy, mediation, training, 1979-; Adjunct Professor, Georgia State University, 1980- ; Consultant, Southern Bell Employee Assistance Programme, 1982-85. *Memberships include:* President, Georgia Association for Marriage & Family Therapy; Offices, past/present, American Association for Marriage & Family Therapy, Academy of Family Mediators, Planned Parenthood, Georgia Juvenile Services Association. *Honours:* Twice nominated, Harold K. Ables Award, juvenile justice work, 1974, 1976. *Hobbies:* Gourmet cooking; Spending time in mountains; Travel, USA & world; Cross-country skiing; Whitewater rafting. *Address:* 150 East Ponce de Leon Avenue, Suite 460, Decatur, Georgia 30030, USA.

MANLEY Nancy Jane, b. 13 Sept. 1951, Fort Smith, Arkansas, USA. Deputy Base Civil Engineer; Environmental Engineer. *Education:* BSc., Engineering, Purdue University, 1974; MSc., Engineering, University of Washington, 1976; Executive Leadership Demonstration Programme; Air Command & Staff College. *Appointments:* Sanitary Engineer, US Environmental Protection Agency, Minnesota Dept. of Health, 1976-77, Chicago, 1977; Leader Water Supply Primacy Unit, US EPA, Atlanta, 1977-79; Leader Groundwater Technical Assistance Team, US EPA Atlanta, 1979-82; Chief Environmental & Contract Planning Branch, Moody Air Force Base, Georgia, 1982-84; Deputy Base Civil Engineer: Carswell Air Force Base, Texas, 1984-86, Scott Air Force Base, Illinois, 1986- . *Publications:* Book chapter, Water System Supervision, 1979. *Memberships Include:* National Society of Professional Engineers; American Society of Civil Engineers; National Association of Female Executives; Society of Women Engineers; American Military Engineers. *Honours Include:* First Female Deputy Base Civil Engineer in Air Force, 1984; Distinguished Government Service Award Dallas Fort Worth Federal Executive Board, 1986. *Hobbies:* Photography; Hiking. *Address:* RR 1, Box 65, Lebanon, IL 62254, USA.

MANN Grace Carrol, b. Berkeley, USA. Ballerina; Teacher; Choreographer. *Education:* BA, University of California, Berkeley, 1941. *Appointments:* San Francisco Ballet & Opera Ballet, 1939-41; Kosloff Ballet, 1942-46; Principal Dancer, Original Ballet Russe; Appearances at Covent Garden, London, England, 1947-48; Danced in the Film the Specter of the Rose, 1945; Opened Studio of the Dance, 1951-70; Formed Ballet Valmann with her brother, 1955; Choreographer. *Creative Works:* Choreography includes: Concerto in D, Poulenc; Allegro Brilliante, Mendelssohn; Concerto, Mendelssohn. *Honours:* Delta Epsilon. *Hobbies:* Reading; Music; Collecting Paintings. *Address:* 5960 Margarido Drive, Oakland, CA 94618, USA.

MANN Jessica, b. 13 Sept. 1937, London, England. Writer. m. Professor Charles Thomas, 1 July 1959. 2 sons, 2 daughters. *Education:* MA, Newnham College, Cambridge; LLB, Leicester University. *Appointments:* Member, Carrick District Council, 1972-78; Member,

Cornwall & Isle of Scilly Area Health Authority, 1976-78; Member, South West Regional Health Authority, 1979-84; Member, Cornwall & Isle of Scilly Family Practitioner Committee, 1985-88; Member, Medical Practices Committee, 1981-87; Member, Industrial Tribunals, 1977-. *Publications:* Fiction: A Charitable End, 1971; Mrs Knox's Profession, 1972; The Only Security, 1973; The Sticking Place, 1974; Captive Audience, 1975; The Eighth Deadly Sin, 1976; The Sting of Death, 1978; Funeral Sites, 1982; No Man's Island, 1983; Grave Goods, 1985; A Kind Of Healthy Grave, 1986, 1987; Death Beyond The Nile, 1988. Non Fiction: Deadlier Than the Male (An Investigation into Feminine Crime Writing), 1981; Numerous book reviews, prefaces and articles. Speaker at seminars and symposiums including those organised by the DHSS; Institute of Contemporary Art and The British Council. *Address:* Lambessow, St Clement, Cornwall, TR1 1TB, England.

MANN Nancy Tucker Wilson, b. 24 Feb. 1912, Williamsburg, Virginia, USA. Freelance writer. m. (1) John Metcalf Drewry, 22 Dec. 1938, 2 sons, 1 daughter. (2) James Mann, 2 May 1970. *Education:* BA, French, Sweet Briar College, 1932; Graduate Course, International Relations; Cert Teacher of French 1966, ME Deaf or Hard of Hearing 1969, University of Virginia. *Appointments:* TB Association, Washington DC, 1951; Alexandria Housing Assoc 1952; Secretary to Law office, Anna Hedrick, 1953-56; Secretary, National Red Cross, 1956-59; Willcox Law office, 1959-62; VA Beach Schools, 1964-66; Teacher of French & English, 1968-69; Teacher of Deaf and Heard of Hearing children, 1969-71. *Publications:* Book: Tylers and Gardiners on the Village Green; Poetry, published in anthologies and magazines under Nancy Tucker Wilson; Paintings in oil, pastel and watercolours accepted in 3 juried shows. *Memberships include:* Poetry Society of VA; Poetry Society of America; Poetry Society of Florida; VA Writer's Club; Jamestowne Society; l'Alliance Francaise of Norfolk; Tidewater Artists Assoc. *Honours include:* 2nd prize, NFSPS; Golden Poet, 1985 and 1987; Silver Poet, 1986; *Hobbies:* Gardening; Writing; Poetry; Biochemistry and inventions (reading only). *Address:* 214 Sixty-Sixth Street, Virginia Beach, VA 23451. USA.

MANN Patricia (Trish) Anne, b. 22 Oct. 1946, Berkeley, California, USA. Consultant; Social Worker. m. Lonnie Mann, 7 June 1969, 1 daughter. *Education:* BA, St Andrews Presbyterian College, 1968; MSW, University of North Carolina, 1970; Licensed Clinical Social Worker, Florida. *Appointments include:* Day Treatment Director, Clinical Social Worker, Clinical Supervisor, Mental Health centres North Carolina, Florida, 1970-80; Programme Supervisor, Outpatient Mental Health Services 1980-84, Training Facilitator 1984-85, Apalachee Community Mental Health Services, Florida; Private Consultant, Trainer & Therapist, 1985-. *Publication:* Join Other Mothers, Leaders' Manual, groups. *Memberships:* National Association of Social Workers; Academy of Certified Social Workers; Various offices, Florida Council for Community Mental Health; Past National Secretary, Workshop Institute for Living-Learning; American Group Psychotherapy Association; Invited Fellow, American Orthopsychiatric Association; Leon County Steering Committee, Youth at Risk. *Honour:* Fellow, Florida Council for Community Mental Health, 1985. *Hobbies:* Travel; Crafts; Enjoying Nature. *Address:* 1120 Windwood Way, Tallahassee, Florida 32301, USA.

MANNING Catherine Marie, b. 10 Nov. 1938, Bradford, Pennsylvania, USA. Sister of Saint Joseph, 1956. Healthcare Administration: Vice President Patient Affairs. *Education:* BS, Elementary Education, 1966; MEd with Concentration in Counselling, 1971; MA, Theology, 1981. *Appointments:* Principal, Cathedral Center, Erie, Pennsylvania, 1966-73; Director of Admissions, Villa Maria College, Erie, 1973-76; Medical Social Service Caseworker 1976-79, Vice President Patient Affairs 1985-, Saint Vincent Health Center, Erie; Sociology & Psychology Instructor, Swampscott, Massachusetts, 1981-82; Academic Dean, Marymount International School, Rome, Italy, 1982-85.

Memberships: American College of Healthcare Executives, 1985-; European Council of International Schools, 1982-85; Pax Christi, USA, 1980-; American Association of University Women, 1975-; Governing Board, US Federation of Sisters of St Joseph (SSJ), 1989; Board of Directors, SSJ of Northwestern Pennsylvania, 1989. *Interests:* St Mary's Home of Erie, Board of Trustees; Minority Health Education Delivery System Inc, Board of Directors; Travel. *Address:* 1014 Weschler Avenue, Erie, Pennsylvania 16502, USA.

MANNING Jane Marian, b. 20 Sep. 1938, Norwich, England. Concert Singer (Soprano). m. Anthony Payne, 24 Sep. 1966. *Education:* Royal Academy of Music, London, 1956-60; LRAM, 1958; GRSM, 1960; ARCM, 1962; Scuola di Canto, Cureglia, Switzerland, 1964. *Career:* Specialises internationally in 20th century music (soprano); Concerts at leading halls and festivals, UK, Europe, North America, Australasia; London debut, 1964; US debut, 1981; Appearances with Brussels Opera and Scottish Opera; Over 300 world premieres; Tours, Australia, 1978, 1980, 1982, 1984, 1985, 1986, 1990; Visiting Professor, Mills College, Oakland, California, USA, 1981, 1982, 1983, 1986; Founder and Artistic Director, Own Ensemble, Janes Minstrels, 1988. *Publications:* The Voice, chapter in How Music Works; New Vocal Repertory, 1986. *Memberships:* Vice-President, Society for the Promotion of New Music; Member, Executive Committee Musicians Benevolent Fund. *Honours:* Special Award, Composers Guild of Great Britain, 1973; FRAM, 1982; DUniv (York), 1988. *Hobbies:* Ornithology; Cinema; Cookery; Philosophy. *Address:* 2 Wilton Square, London N1 3DL, England.

MANNO Barbara Annette Reynolds, b. 16 Mar. 1936, Columbus, Ohio, USA. Professor; Toxicologist. m. Joseph E. Manno, 17 Aug. 1968, 2 sons. *Education:* BS, Otterbein College, 1957; MS, 1968, PhD, 1970, Indiana University. *Appointments:* Consultant, VA Medical Centre, Clinical Lab & Nuclear Medicine, 1975-; Co Director, Toxic Laboratory, LSU Medical Centre, 1976-; Executive Director, LA Regional Poison Centre, 1977-84; Professor, Louisiana State University Medical Centre, 1980-. *Publications:* 81 scientific publications & abstracts; 12 invited book chapters. *Memberships:* Society of Toxicology; American Academy of Forensic Sciences; Fellow, American Society for Pharmacology & Experimental Therapeutics; Southwestern Association of Toxicologists, President 1988-89. *Honours:* Diplomate, American Board of Forensic Toxicology, 1977; Editorial Board, Journal of Analytical Toxicology, 1980. *Address:* Louisiana State University Medical Centre, Dept. of Pharmacology and Therapeutics, PO Box 33932, Shreveport, LA 71130, USA.

MANSFIELD Tobi Ellen, b. 4 Oct. 1949, Miami Beach, Florida, USA. Psychologist. 1 daughter. *Education:* BA, University of Miami, 1974; MA, Norwich University, Vermont, 1982; PhD, Union Graduate School, Cinn, 1988. *Appointments:* Jackson Memorial Hospital, Miami, 1975-78; South Dade Comm Mental Health, Miami, 1978-80; Miami Psychotherapy Institute, 1980-86; Director, Miami Wellness Center, 1986-89; Private Practice; Adjunct Faculty Nova University and Miami Dade College, 1988-. *Publications:* Some Observations Relating Tattoos to the Potential for Violence in Clients in a Drug Treatment Clinic, 1978; The Psychology of Illness, 1986. *Memberships:* Clinical Associate, American Board of Medical Psychotherapists. *Hobbies:* Scuba diving; Paranormal phenomenon; Extensive travel. *Address:* 1390 South Dixie Highway, No 1208, Coral Gables, Florida 33146, USA.

MANSION Gracie, b. 22 Oct. 1946, Braddock, Pennsylvania, USA. Gallery Owner and Director. *Education:* Clarion State College, Clarion Pennsylvania, 1964-66; BA, Fine Art, Montclair State College, Montclair, New Jersey, 1979. *Appointments:* Owner, Director, Gracie Mansion Gallery, New York City, 1981-; Numerous lectures. *Publications:* Articles in New York Woman, New York Talk and New Art Examiner. *Honours:* Participant, numerous panel discussions including:

Whitney Museum of American Art at Fairfield County, Hirshhorn Museum, Baltimore Museum of Art, New Museum, School of Visual Arts and New York University; Currently: Member, Advisory Board, New York Woman magazine and Art Advisor, New School for Social Research, New York. *Address:* Gracie Mansion Gallery, 532 Broadway, New York, NY 10012, USA.

MANSMANN Carol Los, b. 7 Aug. 1942, Pittsburgh, Pennsylvania, USA. US Circuit Judge, Court of Appeals for the Third Circuit. m. J Jerome Mansmann, 27 June 1970. 2 sons, 2 daughters. *Education:* BA, Duquesne University, Pittsburgh, 1964; JD, Duquesne University School of Law, Pittsburgh, 1967; Honorary LLD, Seton Hill College, 1985. *Appointments:* Assistant DA, Allegheney City, Pennsylvania, 1968-72; Special Assistant Attorney General Cmth, Pennsylvania, 1974-79; Associate, Law firm McVerry, Baxter and Mansmann, Pittsburgh, 1973-79; Associate Professor of Law, Duquesne University, School of Law, Pittsburgh, 1973-82; US District Judge for Western District of Pennsylvani, 1982-85; US Circuit Judge, US Court of Appeals for the Third Circuit, 1985-. *Memberships:* American Bar Association; PA Bar Association; Allegheny County Bar Association, Board of Governors, 1982-85; Pennsylvania Criminal Procedural Rules Committee, Member 1972-78; Pennsylvania Bar Institute, Board of Directors 1985-; Villanova University School of Law, Board of Consultors, 1985-; National Association of Women Judges. *Honours:* St Thomas More award, 1983; Honorary Phi Alpha Delta, 1978; Honorary Order of the Barrister, 1971. *Address:* 402 USPO and Courthouse, Pittsburgh, PA 15219, USA.

MANUEL Vivian, b. 6 May 1941, Queens County, New York, USA. Public Relations Executive. *Education:* AB, Wells College, Aurora, New York, 1963; MA, Political Science, University of Wyoming, Laramie, 1965. *Appointments:* Management Analyst, Department of Navy, Washington DC, 1966-68; Account Supervisor, General Electric News Bureau, 1968-72; Business and Finance Representative, General Electric Company, USA, 1972-76; Director, Corp Comm. Standard Brands, 1976-78; Consultant, 1978-80, President, 1980-, V M Communications Inc. *Publication:* A Crisis is Coming! A Crisis is Coming!, 1983. *Memberships:* Trustee, Wells College, Aurora, New York, 1984-; Women Executives in PR; NY Women in Communications, Board Member 1982-84; Matrix Awards Chair, 1985; NY Professional PR Chair, 1985; Women Business Owners of New York; Association of University Women; Women's Economic Roundtable. *Honours:* Sustained Superior Performance Award, Department of the Navy, 1967; General Electric Management Award, 1972. *Hobbies:* Art; Theatre; Reading; Painting; Gardening. *Address:* 501 East 79th Street, Suite 17B, New York, NY 10021, USA.

MANZ Beatrice Forbes, b. 21 Nov. 1947, Boston, Massachusetts, USA. Historian. m. Robert D Manz, 30 Dec. 1972. 2, daughters. *Education:* BA 1970, PhD 1983, Harvard University; MA, University of Michigan, 1974. *Appointments:* Fellow, Russian Research Ctr and Ctr for Middle Eastern Studies, 1983-85; Assistant Professor, History of the Middle East and Inner Asia, Tufts University, 1985-. *Publications:* The Rise and Rule of Tamerlane, 1989; Articles in professional journals and magazines. *Memberships:* Affiliate, Harvard Center for Middle Eastern Studies, 1983-; Fellow, Russian Research Center, Harvard. *Honour:* Middle East Studies Association Dissertation prize in the Social Sciences, 1983. *Address:* 7 Spafford Road, Milton, Massachusetts 02186, USA.

MAPONDERA Esinet Ndayiteyi, b. 22 June 1926, Chinhoyi Western Province, Zvimba Communal Land, Zimbabwe. Manager Welfare/Social Worker. 2 sons, 4 daughters. *Education:* Advanced Diploma in Social Work, Oppenhiemer College of Social Work, Lusaka, Zambia; Master Degree in Social Work, Wurzweiler School of Social Work, Yeshiva University, New York, USA, 1969. *Appointments:* Domestic Science Teacher, 1951-62; Welfare Officer then Assistant Personnel

Officer, 1964-76, Chilanga Cement, Zambia; Self employed commercial market gardener, 1976-79; Teacher, School of Social Work, Harare, Zimbabwe, 1980; Volunteered to prepare a program for female ex-combatants at their training centre, 1980; Appointed to serve on the Riddell Commission, Terms of Reference, 1980-81; Manager Welfare, Posts and Telecommunications Corporation, 1981-. *Creative works:* Contributor of articles to internationl conferences. *Memberships:* Local Preacher, Trinity Methodist Church, 1982-; Chairperson and founder, Zimbabwe Women's World Banking affiliate, Zimbabwe Women's Business Promotions (Pvt) Ltd, 1982-; Inter University Consortium for International Social Development, 1982-; Chairperson, National Steering Committee on Women in Development in Zimbabwe, Ministry of Women's Affairs. *Hobbies:* Working on the land; Visiting the needy when time permits. *Address:* 10 Meredith Drive, Eastlea, Harare, Zimbabwe.

MARCH Connie Lee, b. 9 Nov. 1951, Albuquerque, New Mexico, USA. Company President. m. Douglas B. March, 3 June 1972, 1 son, 1 daughter. *Education:* Graduated, Albuquerque Public Schools, 1969; *Appointments:* Collections Supervisor, Pitney Bowes, 1972-73; Started own business, 1974; President, Doug March Enterprises Inc, 1979-. *Publications:* Several business in-house publications (handbooks, computer operation manual); Full-length novel, in progress. *Memberships:* Balloon Federation of America; British Balloon and Airship Club; National Aeronautic Association; Federation Aeronautique Internationale. *Honour:* Current Holder of Women's World Altitude Record for size AX-4 Hot Air Balloons, set 2 Mar. 1980. *Hobbies:* Reading; Writing; Miniatures; Needlework. *Address:* 9305 Seabrook Drive NE, Albuquerque, NM 87111, USA.

MARCHAK Maureen Patricia Russell, b. 22 June 1936, Lethbridge, Canada. Professor. m. William Marchak, 31 Dec. 1956, 2 sons. *Education:* BA, Sociology, 1958, PhD, 1970, University of British Columbia; FRSC, 1987. *Appointments:* Assistant Professor, 1972-75, Associate Professor, 1975-80, Professor, 1980-, Head, Anthropology & Sociology, 1987-, University of British Columbia; Visiting Professor, Carleton University, 1985. *Publications:* Ideological Perspectives on Canada; In Whose Interests; Green Gold, The Forest Industry in British Columbia; Editor: The Working Sexes; Co-Editor, Uncommon Property, The Fishing and Fish Processing Industry in BC; others. *Memberships:* Canadian Sociology & Anthropology Association, President, 1979; Canadian Political Science Association; International Sociology Association; Association for Canadian Studies. *Honours Include:* Research Council of Canada, Research Grants, 1977, 1981, 1987; Fellow, Royal Society of Canada, 1987; Shastri Indo Canadian Institute, Government of India, Canadian Scholar, Lecture Tour, 1987; John Porter Memorial Award for Green Gold, 1986-87. *Hobbies:* Walking her Dog; Swimming; Skiing; Painting. *Address:* Dept. of Anthropology & Sociology, University of British Columbia, 6303 NW Marine Drive, Vancouver, BC, Canada V6T 2B2.

MARCUM Billye Jean, b. 10 Nov. 1946, Lincoln, Nebraska, USA. RN; Director of Education. Divorced, 1 daughter. *Education:* Nursing Diploma, Methodist Hospital, 1967. *Appointments:* Phoebe Putney Memorial Hospital, 1967-70; Dr Ames Coffer, 1970-71; Bothwell Memorial Hospital, 1971-72; M U Medical Centre, Columbia, 1972-76; Lake Ozart Clinic, 1976-81; Director of Education, 1981. *Memberships:* Americna Business Womens Association; Missouri Association for Health Care Education. *Honours:* Woman of the Year, ABWA, 1986. *Hobbies:* Antiques; Hiking; Sports; Animals. *Address:* Rt 1 Box 128 E, Linn Creek, MO 65065, USA.

MARCUS Helen, b. New York City, New York, USA. Photographer. *Education:* BA, Smith College. *Appointments:* Casting Director, CBS, 1951; Associate Producer, Beat the Clock, Goodson-Todman Television Productions, 1958-61; Associate Producer, Number Please, 1961; Casting Director, To Tell The Truth, 1962-68; Photographer, 1975-; Executive Director, 1988-. Exhibitions, Overseas Press Club, Asia Society, New York Public Library. *Creative works include:* Works in George Eastman House Photography Collection, Rochester, New York, and International Center of Photography. *Memberships:* American Society of Magazine Photographers (President, 1985-88, President, Founder, New York Chapter, 1981-83, 2nd Vice-President, 1984, 1st Vice-President, 1985), Advisory Board, International Photography Congress in Rockport, Maine; Board of Governors, Catskill Center of Photography. *Hobbies:* Tennis; Travel; Biography. *Address:* 120 East 75th Street, New York, NY 10021, USA.

MAREK Dagmar Irene, b. 30 Mar. 1944, Karlsruhe, Federal Republic of Germany. Head of Bureau of National & International Relations. m. Josef, 30 Mar. 1972. *Education:* Diplomat, Bibliothekar. *Appointments:* Universitatsbibliothek, Konstanz, 1966-69; Fachinformationszentzyum Energie Physik Mathematik, Eggenstein-Leopoldshafen, 1969-; Lecturer at several documentation & information educational institutions. *Publications:* Glossar zum Bereich Informationswesen in Bibliothek Forschung u. Praxis, 1981; Zwei Jahre Online Input in Fachinformationszentrum Energie Physik Mathematik GmbH, 1983; Internationale arbeitsteilige Informationssysteme: Erfahrungen aus dem Fachinformationszentrum Karlsruhe, 1986. *Memberships:* Verein d. Diplom-Bibliothekare an dt. Bibl.; Eagle Board of Management; Eagle Technical Committee; Verein Deutscher Dokumentare; Alternate Member of ICSTI; Alternate INIS Liaison Officer. *Hobbies:* Travel; Languages. *Address:* Murgstr. 11, 7514 Eggenstein-Leopoldshafen 2, Federal Republic of Germany.

MAREKA (Jeannie) Dorothy Jean Mareka Bollinger, b. 25 Apr. 1952, Fort Jackson, South Carolina, USA. Company Owner. m. Donald B Bollinger, 22 Sept. 1979, 1 daughter. *Education:* BS, Pembroke State University, 1974; MS, Florida International University, 1977. *Appointments:* Counsellor, Beaufort Co. Technical Institute, 1974; Group Treatment Leader, Pentland Hall, 1974-77; Marketing Research Assistant, Miami, 1976; Group Home Specialist, Miami, 1977; Assistant Scuba Instructor, Atlanta, 1977; Sales, J C Penny Inc., Atlanta, 1977-78; Director, Robeson Co. Youth Services, 1979-81; Senior Clerk, Gulf Oil, 1982; Owner, Organization One, Houston 1983-; Executive Director, Greater Houston Committee for Prevention of Child Abuse, 1984-87. *Memberships:* Executive Member, North Carolina Juvenile Services Association; American Personnel & Guidance Association. *Honours:* OAR Good Citizen; many others. *Hobbies:* Gardening; Reading; Calligraphy; Exercise. *Address:* 12714 Skyknoll Ln, Houston, TX 77082, USA.

MARGIE Joyce Daly, b. 29 May 1940, Washington, District of Columbia, USA. Nutritionist; Writer; Consultant. m. Robert P. Margie, 18 May 1968, 2 sons. *Education:* BS, College of Saint Elizabeth, 1962; University of Paris, France, 1963-64; MS, University of Maryland, 1972. *Appointments:* Dietitian, Washington Hospital Center, 1962-63, 1965-66; Dietitian, District of Columbia General Hospital, 1967-68; Research Nutritionist, Mayo Clinic, Rochester, Minnesota, 1968-72; Consultant to government and industry on development of health and nutrition programmes, 1973-; Editor, Dialogues in Nutrition, Health Learning System, Linhurst, New Jersey, 1974-79; Editor, The Clinical Viewpoint, McGraw-Hill, New York City, 1981-83. *Publications:* The Mayo Clinic Renal Diet Cookbook (co-author), 1975; The Hypertension Diet Cookbook (with J.C.Hunt), 1978; Living Better: Recipes for a Healthy Heart (co-author), 1980; Finding Your Thin Self (with T.B.Van Itallie), 1982; Nutrition and The Cancer Patient (with A.Block), 1983; The Complete Diabetic Cookbook (with P.J.Palumbo), 1988; The All-In-One Diabetic Cookbook, 1989; Contributor to: Present Knowledge in Nutrition, 1977; Proceedings, 1st International Congress on Nutrition and Renal Disease, 1977; Hypertension Update: Mechanisms, Epidemiology, Evaluation and Management, 1980; Chronic Renal Disease, 1985. *Memberships:* Authors Guild; American Dietetic Association; Nutrition Education Society. *Honours:* Xavier Award for Outstanding Alumnus, 1987. *Hobbies:* Travel; Skiing; Sailing; Working with Community Food Bank of New Jersey feeding the hungry and homeless; Working with Summit Area Gerontology Endevors helping the elderly. *Address:* 135 Rotary Drive, Summit, NJ 07901, USA.

MARGOLIS Lesle Stewart, b. 11 Dec. 1950, Marshall, Minnesota, USA. Real Estate Management. m. Herbert A Margolis, 11 Feb. 1979. 1 son. *Education:* BS, Fashion Merchandising, University of Wisconsin; MBA, University of Minnesota, 1989. *Appointments:* Vice President, General Manager, Jack and Jill Stores Inc, 1973-85; Vice President, Accent Real Estate Co Ltd, 1987-. *Memberships:* Vice President, Zonta Club of Minneapolis; Zonta International; NCJW Professional Women; National Association for Executive Women. *Honour:* Grete Waitz Award, Highest Achievement, Kaiser Roll Foundation, 1984-86. *Hobbies:* Reading; Jogging; Civic work; Gourmet cooking; Entertaining; Needlepoint; Music; Travelling. *Address:* 14601 Minnehaha Place, Wayzata, MN 55391, USA.

MARGOLYES Miriam, b. 18 May 1941, Oxford, England. Actress. *Education:* LGSM & D, 1959; BA, Honours, Newnham College, Cambridge, 1963. *Appointments:* BBC Drama Radio Repertory, 1965; Repertory, Traverse, Edinburgh, 1966; Phoenix Leciester, 1967; Girls of Slender Means, BBC TV, 1974; Baroness in Freud, BBC TV, 1984; film, Little Dorritt, 1988. *Memberships:* British Actors Equity Councillor, 1979-80, 1982-84. *Hobbies:* Politics; Property. *Address:* c/o Kate Feast, 43a Princess Road, London, NW1, England.

MARINELLI Ada Santi, b. 27 July 1942, Borgo a Mozzano, Italy. Real Estate Specialist; Principal, US Postal Service. m. Rudolph Marinelli, 12 July 1964. 2 daughters. *Education:* Rivier College, Nashua, 1962-63; George Washington University, 1963; AA, Prince George's Community College, 1980. *Appointments:* Secretary, Post Office Dept, Washington, DC, 1961-70; Administrative Secretary, US Postal Service, Washington, 1970-80; Real Estate Specialist Trainee, 1980-82; Realty Management & Acquisition Analyst, 1982-84; Real Estate Specialist, 1984-, Principal, 1986-; Associate Broker, 1977-, Larry Eul Realty and Alvin Turner Real Estate. *Publication:* Editor and translator of book, Adventures of an Illegal Alien by Rudolph Marinelli, 1975. *Memberships:* Federal Real Porperty Association; Orsogna Club, Washington DC, President 1965-66; Alumnae Association, Rivier College, Nashua. *Honours:* Special Achievement Award, US Postal Service, 1987; Graduated with High Honours, Prince George's Community College 1980; Dean's List, Rivier College, Nashua, 1963. *Hobbies:* Walking on the beach, Ocean City, Maryland; Relaxing in the mountains, West Virginia; Reading; Travelling; Sewing. *Address:* 7006 Sheffield Drive, Camp Springs, Maryland 20748-4149, USA.

MARINESCU Mihaela, b. 3 June 1951, Bucharest, Rumania. Musicologist. *Education:* Conservatory of Music, Bucharest, 1970-74; Diploma, Musicology, 1974. *Appointments:* Music Professor, 1974-77; Music Secretary, Librarian, Musicologist, Union of Composers of Bucharest, 1977-. *Publications:* Instrumental Romanian Contemporary Concerto, 1983; Contributor to Dictionary of Musical Terms, 1984; Faust in 8 Musical Hypostases, 1985; Modal Column by Theodor-Grigoriu - Investigation in Romanian Musical Ethos, 1986; Contributions to History of Trio in A Minor by George Enescu, 1987; George Enescu's String Quartet in C Major, Written in 1906, 1987; Studies, essays and articles in Musica, Atheneum, Romanian Life. *Memberships:* Composers' Union of SSR Rumania. *Hobbies:* Painting; Poetry. *Address:* Str Dr Sion nr 1-9 sc 2 ap 70 sect 1, 70737 Bucharest, Rumania.

MARINKO Monica Marie, b. 26 Feb. 1948, Cleveland, Ohio, USA. School Psychologist. *Education:* BA, University of Detroit, 1970; MA, John Carroll University, 1975; School Psychology Certification, 1975; School Psychology Licensure for Private Practice, 1980. *Appointments:* Willoughby Eastlake Schools, 1974-75; Ashtabula Area City Schools, 1975-. *Memberships:* Ohio School Psychologists Association; National Association of School Psychologists; Associate, Society for Personality Assessment; Support Group Leader, American Chronic Pain Association. *Hobbies:* Classical Piano; Tennis; Golf. *Address:* 12321 Norton Drive, Chesterland, Ohio 44026, USA.

MARJANSKA Ludmila, b. 26 Dec. 1923, Poland. Translator; Poet; Novelist. m. *Education:* MA English Philology, Warsaw University, 1961. *Appointments:* Translator, Poet, Novelist, Editor, Polish Radio, 1959-79. *Publications:* Volumes of poetry: Clouded Windows, 1958; The Hot Star, 1964; Rivers, 1969; The Second Journey, 1976; In the Crown of a Tree, 1979; The Scar, 1987. Novels: Come Back to Love, 1971, 1972; Foot of the Third Grace, 1980; First Snows, First Springs, 1986; Your Own Life, 1988. Translations of Drama: John Ford, Tis pity She is a Whore; William Luce, The Belle of Amherst. Translations of poetry: Theodore Roethke, The Far Field; Elizabeth Browning, Selected Poems 1976, 1987; Marianne Moore, Selected Poems, 1980; Richard Wilbur, The Mind-Reader and Other Poems, 1981; Edwin Arlington Robinson, Selected Poems, 1986; William Butler Yeats, Selected Poems, 1976, 1987; Walt Whitman, Robert Frost, Henry Longfellow, Christina Rosetti and others in the Anthology of English Poetry (four volumes). Translation of Prose: Margaret Forster, Mr Bone's Retreat, 1973; John Bierhorst, The Red Swan, Myth and Tales of American Indians, 1984; Several books for children. *Membership:* Writer's Union, dissolved 1983. *Address:* Ul. Raszynska 15, m.44, Warsaw 02-026, Poland.

MARK Marilyn Sabetsky, b. Brooklyn, New York, USA. Fine Art Sports Painter; Exhibition Coordinator; Author; Lecturer. m. 17 May 1953. *Education:* Graduate, Thomas Jefferson High School, 1947; Self-taught, Fine Art Painting. *Career:* Coordinated exhibitions nationally, 1976-; Art sales in public spaces, late 1970s-; Delivered lecture On Your Mark with Marilyn, Iowa State University, Ames, 1988; Presented manuscript From an Expansion of Line to Doane College, Crete, Nebraska, 1989. Works in public collections: Hidden Secrets, Stuhr Museum of the Prairie Pioneer, Grand Island, Nebraska; Free Spirit and Triangle, National Art Museum of Sport, Indianopolis; C'mon John! Kick It! Soccer, American Sport Art Museum, US Sports Academy, Alabama; And You're Going the Wrong Way, National Soccer Hall of Fame. *Memberships:* Board Member, Burr Artists, New York City; Associate Trustee, The National Art Museum of Sport, Indianapolis, Indiana; President, Founder, Visual Individualists United; Network Director, National Association for Female Executives. *Honours:* Citation for Effective Leadership as Network Director, National Association for Female Executives, 1988; Participant, national tour of National Contemporary Exposition of Artists of Achievement, Visual Individualists United, 1988-89. *Hobbies:* Walking; Travel; Books; Music; Playing the electric organ; Singing; Films; Theatre. *Address:* 2261 Ocean Avenue, Brooklyn, NY 11229, USA.

MARKEL Geraldine, b. USA. Educator; Psychologist. *Education:* PhD. *Appointments include:* Reading Consultant, Junior & Senior High Schools, Belleville, Michigan, 1964-66; Evaluator, Office of Research & Evaluation, Ann Arbor Public Schools, 1971-72. University of Michigan: Instructor, Assistant Psychologist, Research Assistant 1970-72, Social Science Research Associate, Institute for Human Adjustment 1982-, Reading & Learning Skills Centre; Workshop Faculty (Instructional Design), Division of Management Education, Graduate School of Business Administration, 1972-; Assistant Professor, Special Education, 1974-82; Health Science Senior Research Associate, Departments of Community Dentistry &

Educational Resources, School of Dentistry, 1982-86. *Publications include:* Articles, professional journals: Achieving Writing Improvement Through Information Feedback; Dental Health Promotion in the Classroom; Helping Students with Learning Disabilities Do Their Best with the SAT; Crisis Intervention, Greenbaum and Markel, 1989; Exceptional Children in the Schools, Markel and Greenbaum, 1990. Also: Training manuals; Study guides; Various slide/tape programmes. *Address:* University of Michigan Reading & Learning Skills Centre, 1610 Washtenaw Avenue, Ann Arbor, Michigan 48104, USA.

MARKHAM Kika, Actress. m. Colin Redgrave, 5 Oct. 1985, 2 sons. *Education:* Guildhall School of Music & Drama. *Creative Works:* Theatre: Viola in Twelfth Night, at Royal Court; Abigail in Time Present, at Royal Court & Duke of York; Nina, in The Seagull, Nottingham Playhouse; Katharine, in The Taming of the Shrew, Edinburgh; Played Lady MacBeth at Leaherhead, Bianca in the Taming of the Shrew, at the Haymarket, & Portia in Julius Caesar at the Young Vic; TV Appearances: Gloria in You Never Can Tell, BBC; Double Dare & Blade on the Feather, Dennis Potter, BBC & LWT TV; Clouds of Glory, Ken Russell, Granada; Freda Dudley Ward in Edward & Mrs Simpson, Thames; Jane Morris, The Love School, BBC; Black Silk, BBC2; Films: Anne & Muriel, Francois Truffault, Carol in Outland, Peter Hyams, Mrs Dobson, The Innocent, J McKenzie; Helen in A Very British Coup, Channel 4; Agnes in A Bright Room called Day, The Bush Theatre; Catherine in Arms and the Man, BBC TV. *Membership:* Equity. *Hobbies:* Singing; Playing the Piano; Cooking; Drawing. *Address:* 20 Elmfield Road, London SW17, England.

MARKHAM Marion Margaret, b. 1 June 1929, Chicago, Illinois, USA. Writer. m. R. Bailey Markham, 30 Dec. 1955, 2 daughters. *Education:* BS, Northwestern University, 1953. *Appointments:* Lecturer, Fiction Writing, various schools. *Publications:* Books: Escape from Velos; Halloween Candy Mystery; Christmas Present Mystery; Thanksgiving Day Parade Mystery; Birthday Party Mystery. *Memberships:* Past office, Mystery Writers of America; Past Board Member, Society of Midland Authors; Past President, Northbrook Public Library, Board of Trustees. *Hobbies:* Involvement with Writers & Writers' Organisations; Bird Watching; Grandchildren's Company; Reading about Science, Mysteries. *Address:* 2415 Newport Road, Northbrook, Illinois 60062, USA.

MARKLINGHAUS Michele, (Shelley Bruce) b. 5 May 1965, New Jersey, USA. Actress; Accounts Clerk. *Appointments:* Kate in the original cast of Annie, 1977-78, title role, 1978; Actress and Accounting Clerk for Bank. *Publication:* Autobiography, Tomorrow is Today. *Memberships:* Chairperson, Make a Wish Foundation; National Leukemia Association; National Spokesperson, American Cancer Society. *Honours:* various junior achievement awards, 1977-79; National Cancer Courage Award, 1984, Presented by Nancy Reagon at the White House. *Hobbies:* Swimming; Bicycling; Racquet Ball; Games. *Address:* Box 261 East Rutherford, NJ 07073, USA.

MARKOVA Alicia, b. 1 Dec. 1910, London, England. Prima Ballerina Assoluta; Professor. *Education:* Hon.DMus., Leicester, 1966; Hon. D.Mus., East Anglia, 1982. *Publications:* Giselle & I, 1960; Markova Remembers, 1986. *Honours:* CBE, 1958; DBE, 1963. *Hobby:* Music. *Address:* c/o Royal Ballet School, London W14, England.

MARKS Linda Susan, b. 25 Nov. 1958, Boston, Massachusetts, USA. Author; Psychotherapist; Social Entrepreneur. *Education:* BA Music, cum laude, Yale University, 1980; MSM, Management, Sloan School of Management, MIT, 1982. *Appointments:* Management and consulting positions-organization and business development, Digital Equipment Corporation, 1979-85; Life Integration Training, 1985-86; Co-founder, partner, The Marks-Miller Collaborative, 1986-89. *Publications:*

New Visions for our Work, our Organizations and Our World, 1986; Living with Vision: Reclaiming the Power of the Heart, 1989. *Memberships:* American Holistic Medical Foundation, Healer's Resource Centre; Co-op America; Action Linkage; Institute for Gaean Economics (co-founder, Board Member); Living with Vision Partnership (founder). *Hobbies:* Dance; Singing/songwriting; Holistic healing; Body-centered psychotherapy; Relationships; Nature; Travel; Adventure. *Address:* 785 Centre Street, Newton, MA 02158, USA.

MARKS Tracy, b. 26 Sept. 1950, Miami, Florida, USA. Writer; Psychotherapist; Humanistic Astrologer. *Education:* BA, magna cum laude, 1968, MA 1972, Tufts; Postgraduate work in psychology and social work, Boston University and Lesley College, 1981-87. *Appointments:* Workshop leader/Teacher, 1973-; Author, 1977-; Psychotherapist, 1983-. *Publications:* Books include: Your Secret Self; Planetary Aspects; Art of Chart Interpretation; Astrology of Self-Discovery; How to Handle Your T-Square; The Twelfth House; Transits; New Moon Full Moon; Turning Squares into Trines; 12 booklets. *Memberships:* International Women's Writing Guild; Endometriosis Association. *Honours:* Carnegie Fund for Authors, 1978; Ford Foundation Grant, 1978 and 1988; Tufts University Poetry Prize, 1973; Greater Miami Poetry Festival First Prize, 1967 and 1968; American Penwomen Writing award, 1967. *Hobbies:* Psychology of dreams; Women's identity issues; Mythical role models for women. *Address:* Box 252, Arlington, Mass 02174, USA.

MARKS Virginia Pancoast, b. 2 Sept. 1940, Philadelphia, Pennsylvania, USA. Professor; Concert Pianist. m. Edward J. Marks, 4 June 1961 (divorced 1987), 1 son, 1 daughter. *Education:* BS, Music, Temple University, 1961; MA, American University, 1965; Advanced piano study, various teachers. *Appointments:* Piano Instructor, Cornell University 1966-67, Temple University 1968-69, National Music Camp, Interlochery, Michigan 1980-82; Professor of Performance Studies & Coordinator, Keyboard Studies, Bowling Green State University, Ohio, 1972-. *Creative works:* Recordings, Educo Records; Recitals, major US cities; Soloist, Philadelphia Orchestra, Richmond Symphony, Boston Pops, Atlanta Symphony, Spoleto Music Festival (Italy). *Memberships:* National Executive, Music Teachers National Association; Vice President, Ohio Music Teachers Association; Mu Phi Epsilon international music fraternity; Friday Morning Music Club, Washington DC. *Honours:* 1st prizes: Mu Phi Epsilon International Competition, 1964; Richmond Symphony Young Artists, 1965; Brevard Young Artists, 1965; Concert Artists Guild, New York City, 1964; Philadelphia Orchestra Young Artists. Distinguished teaching awards, Bowling Green University, 1980, 1982. *Hobbies:* Gardening; Finance; Reading. *Address:* College of Musical Arts, Bowling Green State University, Ohio 43403, USA.

MARLOW Carol Ann, b. 30 Mar. 1941, Takoma Park, Maryland, USA. Educator. m. Paul W. Marlow, 19 Aug. 1962, 1 son, 1 daughter. *Education:* BS, Elementary Education, Southern Missionary College, 1962; MPH, Loma Linda University, 1978; Special Student, Epidemiology, University of Michigan, 1988. *Appointments:* Teacher, Touchet WN Public School, 1962-64; Teacher, Berrien Springs MI Public School, 1964-66; Practical Pulpit Instructor, 1967-85; Co-ordinator, Montana Lay Nutrition Instructors, 1975-79; Teacher, Glendive MT Seventh-Day Adventist School, 1979-80; Teacher, Chilhouse MO Public School, 1981-82; Director of Education, Memorial Hospital, Manchester, 1985-. *Publications:* Produced materials for Leaders of children's Bible schools, 1967, 1976; Wrote church news articles for newspaper, 1967-; Director choral & instrumental church music groups, 1967-; Editor, Contributor, Nutrition Team Newsletter, 1975-78; Editor, Vital Signs, 1988-. *Memberships:* Director of Exchange, 1964-65, President, Graduate Guild, 1965-66, Andrews University; Delta Omega; American Society for Healthcare Education & Training.

Honours: 1st Place, 1960, Grand Award, 1961, Pen League, V.I.P. Award, Clay County Board of Education, 1985. *Hobbies:* Studying; Music; Photography. *Address:* Memorial Hospital, 401, Memorial Drive, Manchester, KY 40962, USA.

MARLOW Joyce Mary, b. 27 Dec. 1929, Manchester, England. Author. m. Patrick Connor, 24 July 1955. 2 sons. *Education:* Bradford Civic Theatre School, 1947-49. *Appointments:* Actress, 1949-66; Author 1964-. *Publications:* Peterloo Massacre; Tolpuddle Martyrs; Captain Boycott and the Irish; The Uncrowned Queen of Ireland; Mr and Mrs Gladstone; Kessie; Sarah; Anne (trilogy). *Membership:* Society of Authors. *Honour:* Elizabeth Goudge Award for Kessie, 1985. *Hobbies:* Gardening; Cricket; Theatre. *Address:* 3 Spring Bank, New Mills, via Stockport, SK12 4AS, England.

MARMER Ellen Lucille, b. 29 June 1939, Bronx, New York, USA. Pediatric Cardiologist, private practice. m. Harold O Shapiro, MD, 5 June 1960. 2 daughters. *Education:* BS Chemistry, University of Alabama, Tuscaloosa, 1957-60; MD, University of Alabama Medical College, Birmingham, 1960-64; Straight Pediatric Internship 1964-65, Pediatric Residency 1965-66, Upstate Medical Center, Syracuse; Fellowship-Pediatric Cardiology, Babies Hospital, Columbia Presbyterian Medical Ctr, New York, 1967-69. *Appointments:* Examining Pediatrician for Child Development Program 1967, Instructor-Pediatrics 1967-69, Columbia Presbyterian Medical Center; Practicing Pediatric Cardiologist, Vernon and Great Hartford Area, Connecticut, 1969-; Director of Pediatric Cardiology Clinic, St Francis Hospital, 1970-80; Assistant State's Medical Examiner, Tolland County Connecticut, 1974-79; Sports Physician, Rockville High School, 1976-; Pediatric Cardiologist, Rockville General Hospital, 1969-; Dept of Pediatrics, Dept of Cardiovascular Medicine, St Francis Hospital, 1970-; Consulting Staff, Manchester Memorial Hospital, 1970-; Courtesy Staff, Dept of Pediatrics, Hartford Hospital, 1987-; Courtesy Staff with Assignment, Dept of Pediatrics, Mount Sinai Hospital, 1969-, and Newington Children's Hospital, 1969-; Clinical Instructor, Dept of Pediatrics, University of Connecticut Health Center, 1969-; Consulting Staff, New Britain General Hospital, 1972-. *Publications:* Articles in professional journals. *Memberships:* Fellow, American Academy of Pediatrics; American Heart Association (Council of Cardiovascular Disease in the Young); Heart Association of Greater Hartford. *Honours:* Life Member, Tolland County Chapter of Hadassah; Temple B'Nai Israel Congregation and Sisterhood. *Address:* 351 Merline Road, P O Box 2340, Vernon, CT 06066, USA.

MARQUARDT Diana Lee, b. 4 Oct. 1954, LaCrosse, Wisconsin, USA. Physician; Immunologist. m. John Rodney Franklin, 15 Dec. 1984. *Education:* BA, Chemistry, David Lipscomb College, 1975; MD, Washington University, 1979. *Appointments:* Assistant Profesor, Medicine, University of California, San Diego, 1984-. *Publications:* over 30 articles, review articles and book chapters. *Memberships:* American Federation for Clinical Research; American Association of Immunologists; American Academy of Allergy & Immunology. *Honours:* John and George Hartford Foundation Fellowship, 1986; AFCR Award for Trainees in Clinical Research, 1983; Robert Brookings Prize for Medical Research, 1979. *Hobbies:* Running; Soccer. *Address:* c/o UCSD Medical Centre, H-811-G, 225 Dickinson Street, San Diego, CA 92103, USA.

MARQUART Grafin Flaustine Antoinette Von, Baroness, b. 9 Oct. 1944, Houston, Texas, USA. Merchant Banker; Wholesale Diamonds & Precious Gems. m. Gary Stewart Sossamon Pardue, 26 June 1971, 1 daughter. *Education:* BA, University of Houston, 1967; Postgraduate work in historical finance. *Appointments:* Merchant Banker, House of Marquart, Fugger, Wittelsbach and Arnim, 1963-. *Publications:* Poetry, various magazines. *Memberships:* Phi Beta; United Methodist Church. *Honours:* Ambassador at Large, La Communaute Musulmane Universelle, 1971-. *Hobbies:* Painting; Writing; Dancing. *Address:* Suite 317 San Jacinto Building, 911 Walker Avenue, Houston, TX 77002, USA.

MARRINER-TOMEY Ann, b. 25 Jan. 1943, Nebraska, USA. Professor. m. (1) Gerald Marriner, 7 Feb. 1964, divorced 1985, 1 son, 1 daughter, (2) H. Keith Tomey, 14 Feb. 1987. *Education:* BS, 1967, MS, 1970, PhD, 1975, University of Colorado. *Appointments:* Instructor, University of Texas, 1970-71; Assistant Professor, NYSU, 1971-72; Lecturer, Humboldt State University, 1973-74; Lecturer, University of California, 1974-75; Associate Professor, 1975-80, Chairperson, 1976-77, Graduate Faculty, 1977-80, University of Colorado; Professor, 1980-, Indiana University; Visiting Professor, University of Evansville, 1985; Visiting Professor, Georgia College, School of Nursing, 1988-89. *Publications:* The Nursing Process: A Scientific approach to Nursing Care, 1975, 1979; Guide to Nursing Management, 1980, 1984, 1988; Guide to Teaching Nursing Management, 1980, 1984, 1988; Nursing Theorist and Their Work, 1986, 1989; Dimensions of Nursing Administration, 1989-; Editor, Current Perspectives in Nursing Management, Volume I, 1979; Book chapters; articles. *Memberships:* various professional organisations. *Hobbies:* Reading; Writing; Cooking. *Address:* RR 2, Forest Lane, Trafalgar, IN 46181, USA.

MARSAL Maria-Merce Serra, b. 13 Nov. 1952, Barcelona, Spain. Teacher of Catalan Literature and Writer (Poetry). 1 daughter. *Education:* BA, Classical Philology. *Appointments:* Teacher of Catalan Literature, High School, Barcelona, 1977-88. *Publications:* Cau de Llunes (Burrow of Moons), 1977; Bruixa de Dol (Witch In Mourning), 1979; Sal Oberta (Open Salt), 1982; Terra de Mai (Neverland), 1982; La Germana, L'Estrangera (The sister, the foreigner), 1985. *Honours:* Carles Riba, Barcelona (Poetry), 1976; Flor Natural-Jocs Florals, Barcelona (Poetry), 1981; Lopez-Pico (Poetry), 1985; Award to Literary Creation, Spanish Cultural Ministry, 1986-87. *Address:* Trullols 7, Atic, Barcelona 08023, Spain.

MARSANICO Linda, b. 24 Nov. 1946, Queens, New York, USA. Psychotherapist; Social Psychologist. m. Luke Byrne, 22 Oct. 1971, 1 son, 2 daughters. *Education:* BSc., Ramapo College, 1979; M.Ed., Vanderbilt University, 1981; PhD, Loughborough University, Leicestershire, England, 1987. *Appointments:* Alcoholism Therapist, Arapohoe House, 1982; Private practice, Toronto, Canada, 1984-86; Private Practice, Counselling Psychotherapy, New York City, 1987-. *Publications:* Human Relations Training between Black & White Adults to Reduce Prejudice, in press. *Memberships:* American Association for Counselling & Development; Student Member, British Psychological Society; Psychotherapists of Park Slope. *Hobbies:* Karate; Raising Children. *906 President St., Brooklyn, NY 11215, USA.*

MARSCHALL Marlene Elizabeth, b. 20 Oct. 1936, St Paul, Minnesota, USA. Medical Center Executive. m. George Marschall, 6 Aug. 1973. *Education:* Diploma, Ancker School of Nursing, 1958; BS, Viterbo College, 1965; MA, University of Iowa, 1972. *Appointments:* Director of Nursing, 1976-77, Associate Director, 1977-80, Senior Associate Director, 1980-84, Hospital Director, 1984-85, Executive Director, 1985-86, President, Chief Executive Officer, 1986-, St Paul-Ramsey Medical Center, St Paul, Minnesota. *Memberships:* American College of Health Care Executives; American Hospital Association; Minnesota Hospital Association Chair Elect, 1990, Chair, 1991; Sigma Theta Tau; Rotary International; Minnesota Safety Council Board of Directors, Chair 1990; St Paul Chamber of Commerce Board of Directors, Treasurer, 1990; Council of Hospital Corporations, Chair, 1989/90. *Honours:* Air National Guard Recognitiion for Business and Industry Leaders within the United States, 1977; Spurgeon Award, 1986. *Address:* St Paul-Ramsey

Medical Center, 640 Jackson Street, St Paul, MN 55101, USA.

MARSENGILL Kathy, b. 5 Dec. 1960, Columbia, South Carolina, USA. Freelance Writer. *Education:* Psychology, Florida Junior College, Jacksonville, 1978-80. *Appointments:* Publicist, Consultant: Patricio Apey (tennis coach/manager), Apey Management Corporation, Gabriella Sabatini (tennis player), 1984-. *Publications include:* Articles: Sabatini, Giant Killer 1984, Key Biscayne's Little Brazil 1985, World Tennis Magazine; Consultant to: Para Ti, & Gente magazines, Argentina. *Memberships:* Florida Freelance Writers Association; National Guide to Writers Association; Cousteau Society; National Geographic Society; Greenpeace; People for Ethical Treatment of Animals. *Honours:* Creative writing award, 1977; Award, best short story, 1978; Emily Dickinson Award, 1979. *Hobbies include:* Racquetball; Reading; Art; Shakespeare. *Address:* 2800 NW 56th Avenue, Fort Lauderdale, Florida 33313, USA.

MARSH Shirley Mac, b. 22 June 1925, Benton, USA. State Senator, 1973-89. m. Frank Irving Marsh, 5 Mar. 1943, 4 sons, 2 daughters. *Education:* BA, 1972, MBA, 1978, University of Nebraska. *Appointments:* Placement Assistant, University of Nebraska, 1966-70; Caseworker Practicum, Lancaster Co. Welfare Dept., 1971-72; Visiting Instructor: NE Wesleyan University, Lincoln, 1978, Doane College, Crete, 1979; State Senator, Nebraska, 1979-. *Publication:* A Standard of Need for the State of Nebraska Relating to aid to Dependent Children. *Memberships:* National Order of Women Legislators, President, 1977-78; National Federation of Business & Professional Women, 1973-; PEO; Nebraska Wesleyan University, Board of Trustess. *Honours:* Recipient, various honours & awards. *Hobbies:* Reading; Cooking; Canoeing. *Address:* 2701 South 34th Street, Lincoln, NE 68506, USA.

MARSHAL Nellie Jean, b. 30 Jan. 1933, Pulaski, USA. Company Chairman. m. James E Taze, 1 son, 1 daughter. *Education:* University of California, 1955-63 (part-time). *Appointments:* Owner, Trailestate Realty, Reno, 1957-60; Vice President, Bank Mortgage Loan Co., Los Angeles, 1960-66; Manager, First Trust Deed Dept., Union Home Loans, Los Angeles, 1966-69; Chairman, Golden State Holding Company Inc. *Memberships:* National Association of Review Appraisers & Mortgage Underwriters; World Affairs Council; Kentucky Colonels; Santa Monica Board of Realtors; Santa Monica Chamber of Commerce; National Association of Female Executives; Women in Business. *Honours:* Recipient, various honours and awards. *Address:* 2701 Ocean Park Blvd. Suite 131, Santa Monica, CA 90405, USA.

MARSHALL Clare Mary Philomena, b. India. Actress; Broadcaster. m. Kenelm Clevely Marshall, 30 July 1960, 3 daughters. *Education:* Studied Drama, LCC, London; Signing, Brierly School, Lancashire, England. *Appointments:* Actress, Singer, Dancer, D'Arcy Richards, Blackpool, Lancs., 1956-57; Fashion Model, Geo. White Creations Rhodesia, 1957-58; Broadcaster, Newsreader, DJ, Rhodesian Radio & TV, 1965-74; PRO, TA Group, Tobacco Floors, 1972-73; Actress, Broadcaster, Freelance, 1975-. *Creative Works:* Stage Productions in Rhodesia: Gentlemen Prefer Blondes; Guys & Dolls; Oklahoma; Gypsy; Blythe Spirit; Hay Fever; 40 Love; On Golden Pond; A Tribute to Lili Lamont; Noises Off; etc; TV Productions: In Confidence; Cry of the Peacock; Miss Candida; Valley of the Vines; The Settlers Westgate; Town Guard; People Like Us; International Films: Zulu Dawn; Hostage; Murphy's Fault; Purgatory; Nuclear Legacy. *Honour:* Hon. Cert., Classical Singing/Voice, 1956. *Hobbies:* Ballroom Dancing; Singing; Cooking; Gardening; Art; Reading. *Address:* PO Box 781781, Sandton 2146, Johannesburg, South Africa.

MARSHALL Doreen, b. 22 Dec. 1922, Los Angeles, USA. Property Manager. m. Robert J. Marshall, 24 Nov.

1946. *Education:* BA, University of California, Los Angeles, 1944. *Appointments:* National Bureau of Economic Research, New York City, 1944-45; Newell-Emmett Advertising Agency, New York City, 1945-56; A.D. Smiley Public Accountant, Orange, 1948-52; Councilman, City of Newport Beach, 1962-70; Mayor, City of Newport Beach, 1968-70; Foreman, Orange County Grand Jury, 1971; Executive Assistant, County of Orange, Board of Supervisors, 5th District, 1979-85; Property Manager, Director, Coastal Municipal Water District, 1987-. *Memberships:* Newport Harbor Art Museum, Trustee, 1970-76; Assistance League of Newport Beach. *Hobbies:* Swimming; Travel; Music. *Address:* 367 Via Lido Sound, Newport Beach, CA 92663, USA.

MARSHALL Evelyn (pseudonym Jean Marsh), b. 2 Dec. 1897, Pershore, Worcestershire, England. Author; Broadcaster. m. Lt Eric Marshall, MGC, 26 June 1917. 1 son, 1 daughter. *Education:* Teaching Certificate. *Appointment:* Teacher, 1915-1919. *Publications:* Shore House Mystery, 1931; Murder Next Door, 1933; Death Stalks the Bride, 1943; Adventure at Castle Rock Zoo, 1946; Secret of the Pygmy Herd, 1947; The Island of Singing Frogs, 1948; Trouble for Tembo, 1949; On the Trail of the Albatross, 1950; Identity Unwanted, 1951; Death Visits the Circus, 1953; The Pattern is Murder, 1954; Death Amongst the Stars, 1955; Death at Peak Hour, 1957; Adventure with a Boffin, 1962; Valley of Silent Sound, 1963; Sand Against the Wind, 1973; Unbidden Dream, 1977; Loving Partnership, 1978; Bewdley, Sanctuary Town, 1979; Sawdust and Dreams, 1980; Family at Castle Trevissa, 1980; Mistress of Tanglewood, 1981; Unbidden Dream, 1981; Rekindled Flame, 1982; This Foolish Love, 1983; Divided Heart, 1983; Sanctuary for Louise, 1984; Quest For Love, 1984; Destiny at Castle Rock, 1985; Pride of Vallon, 1985; The Golden Parakeet, 1986; Island of Dreams, 1987; Mission to Argana, 1988. 13 Children's Hour Serials; Radio Adult Dramas: Helen Had a Daughter, 1953; The Small Beginning, 1955. *Memberships:* Society of Authors; Broadcasting Association; Bewdley Civic Society. *Hobbies:* Gardening; Care of animals. *Address:* Bewdley, Worcestershire, England.

MARSHALL Louise Hanson, b. 2 Oct. 1908, Perrysburg, Ohio, USA. Science Administrator; Neuroscientist. m. Wade Hampton Marshall, 31 Dec. 1934, 1 son, 1 daughter. *Education:* BA, 1930, MA, 1932, Vassar College; PhD, University of Chicago, 1935. *Appointments:* Instructor in Physiology, Vassar College; Research Physiologist, National Institutes of Health; Professional Associate, National Research Council, Washington DC; Managing Editor, Experimental Neurology; Associate Director, Neuroscience History Programme, University of California, Los Angeles. *Publications:* Research reports in professional journals of biomedical science and history. *Memberships:* Education Committee, American Physiological Society; 1st Secretary-Treasurer, Society for Neuroscience; Society of American Archivists; American Association for the History of Medicine; Oral History Association; Council of Biology Editors. *Address:* Brain Research Institute, UCLA, Los Angeles, CA 90024, USA.

MARSHALL Thelma Elaine Hodge Larsen, b. 30 June 1929, Idaho Falls, Idaho, USA. General Contractor, specializing in Terrazzo and Epoxy floors. m. Don, 15 Oct. 1953. 2 sons, 1 daughter. *Appointments:* Co-owner, Floor Doctor, Honolulu, Hawaii, 1961-73; Owner, Laines Contracting Inc, Tacoma, Washington, 1976-. *Membership:* Associated General Contractors, Chairman, Membership Committee, Open Shop Committee. *Honours:* 2 awards, Associated General Contractors; Recipient Medal of Honour, American Biographical Institute, 1988. *Hobby:* Plate collecting. *Address:* 6112 East N Street, Tacoma, WA 98404, USA.

MARSHALL, Rosalind Kay, b. Dysart, Scotland. Historian. *Education:* MA, 1959, Dip.Ed., 1960, MA, Honours, Scottish Historical Studies, 1966; PhD, 1970, University of Edinburgh. *Appointments:* Teacher,

History, 1961-64; Assistant Editor, Dictionary of The Older Scottish Tongue, 1970-71; Historian, Scottish National Portrait Gallery, 1973-. *Publications:* The Days of Duchess Anne, 1973; Mary of Guise, 1977; Virgins & Viragos: A History of Women in Scotland, 1983; Queen of Scots, 1986; Bonnie Prince Charlie, 1988; many scholarly articles & reviews. *Memberships:* Chairman, First Division Association, Scottish National Galleries & Museums Branch; Member, Council of the Society of Antiquans of Scotland; Scottish History Society; Scottish Records Association; Scots Ancestry Research Society; Costume Society; Scottish Record Society; Company of Scottish History; etc. *Honours:* Senior Dobson Morpeth Prize, 1966; Senior Hume Brown Prize, 1971; Jeremiah Dalziel Prize, 1971; Scottish Arts Council New Writing Award, 1974; Fellow, Royal Society of Literature, 1974. *Address:* Scottish National Portrait Gallery, 1 Queen Street, Edinburgh, Scotland.

MARTIN (Mary) Blanche, b. 21 Feb. 1920, Malta. Retired British Civil Servant, Ministry of Defence, Navy. *Education:* GCE, St Joseph's Convent School, 1926-39; Teacher Training Centre, 1940-41; Tailoring Certificates, City & Guilds of London Institute, 1957-58; Diploma, Meeting Procedures, Centre for Social Leadership, 1971. *Appointments:* Establishedd Civil Seravant, Malta Government, 1940-41; Established Civil Servant, Ministry of Defence Navy, Malta, 1943-78; Retired 1978 *Memberships:* President 1978-82, numerous offices, National Council of Women (Malta); Benefactress, Offices, Din I'Art Helwa (This Fair Land) National Trust, Malta; Offices, Maltese Byron Society; British Culture Association; Women Corona Society; Active, wide range of community work. *Honours include:* Investiture, Knight Grand Dame of Grace, OSJ, 1982; International PRO, Knight Grand Dame, 1984; Sovereign Order, St John of Jerusalem; Knights of Malta; International and Ecumenical Priorate of the Holy Trinity of Villedieu; HQ Auberge de la Chaste, Valleta, Malta. *Hobbies:* Charitable & philanthropic work; Reading; Sewing; Travel, International Conferences & Seminars. *Address:* 19 Balluta Buildings, St Julians, Malta GC.

MARTIN Catherine Anne, b. 6 Apr. 1952, Chicago, USA. Child Psychiatrist. m. John Woodring, 27 Aug. 1977, 2 sons. *Education:* BS, 1972, MD, 1976, University of Kentucky; General Psychiatry Resident, 1978; Child Psychiatry Fellowship, 1980. *Appointments:* Assistant Professor, 1980-86, Assistant Director, Residency Training, 1980-81, 1981-82, Associate Professor, Pscyhiatry, 1986-, University of Kentucky. *Memberships:* American Psychiatric Association; Kentucky Psychiatric Association, President Elect; American Medical Women's Association. *Honours:* Outstanding Young Woman of America, 1983. *Address:* Dept. of Psychiatry, University of Kentucky Medical Centre, 820 South Limestone, Lexington, KY 40536, USA.

MARTIN Diana Joan, b. 18 June 1949, Jackson Heights, New York, USA. University Administrator. m. Thomas David Creola, 26 Apr. 1981. *Education:* BA Honours, 1971; MEd, 1976; PhD, 1986. Various certificates, graduate study. *Appointments:* Teacher, Vanguard High School, 1971-73; Director of Admissions & Career Programme Director, Prospect Hall College, Fort Lauderdale, Florida, 1973-79; Assistant to President & Director of Development, Webber College, Babson Park, Florida, 1979-84; Director of University Development, University of North Florida Jacksonville 1984-86, Trinity University, San Antonio 1986-. *Publication:* Public/Private Partnership Philanthropy: Phase I, McKnight Foundation Projects, Florida, 1986; Events in Support of the Annual Fund, 1990. *Memberships include:* American Association of Higher Education; American Personnel & Guidance Association; Leadership Consortium; National Associations of Female Executives; The National Association of Fund Raising Executives; Offices, Program Board Education Council, Funding Centre, & San Antonio Chamber of Commerce. *Honours:* Bovier

Award, academic excellence, 1968; Phi Kappa Phi, 1971; Fellowship award, Newspaper Fund, 1972; Scholar's Award, USF Multi-Campus Alumni, 1983. *Address:* 434 Countrywood Lane, San Antonio, Texas 78216, USA.

MARTIN Elaine Pauline, b. 8 Jul 1947, Chicago, Illinois, USA. Educational Consultant. *Education:* AA, Education, Morton College, 1967; BS, Elementary Education, 1969, MS, Education, 1971, Northern Illinois University; Ed.D., Education, Texas A & I University, 1984. *Appointments:* Teacher, Cicero Public School District, 1969-79; Bilingual and High School Reading Resource Teacher, Broward County Public School District No 6, 1979-82, 1984-. *Publications:* Articles in professional journals. *Memberships:* TESOL; International Reading Association; Florida Reading Association; Broward County Reading Council; Florida Freelance Writers Association; etc. *Honours:* Recipient, various honours & awards. *Hobbies:* Writing; Swimming; Tennis; Dancing; Basketball. *Address:* 5810 NW 12th Street, Apt. B, Sunrise, FL 33313, USA.

MARTIN Gwendolyn Rose, b. 12 Dec. 1926, Cleveland, Ohio, USA. Director, Illinois Department of Labor. m. Aaron Martin, 3 Apr. 1953. 1 son. *Education:* Ohio State University, Columbus; Western Reserve University, Cleveland. *Appointments:* Service Rep., Ohio Bell Telephone, 1967-72; Communications Workers of America AFL-CIO-Administrative Assistant, Regional Representative, Illinois Director, 1972-87; Director, Illinois Department of Labor, 1987-. *Memberships:* Executive Board Member, WESG, 1987-88; Executive Board Member, NAGLO, 1988; Vice President, Illinois AFL-CIO, 1978-87; Vice President, Leadership Council Metro Open Communities, 1976-78; Board American Red Cross, Mid America Chapter; United Way; ERA Illinois Executive Board; League of Women Voters, Education Advisory Board; Illinois Statewide Health Coordinating Council; Democratic National Committee, 1980-84; Democratic National Platform Committee, 1976, 1980; Illinois Commission on Status of Women, Labor Union Womens' Committee, Coalition of Labor Union Women. *Honours:* Resolution of Commendation, Illinois House of Representatives, 1978; Coalition of Labor Union Women's Florence Criley Award, 1980; CBTU Harriet Tubman Award, 1975; Sojourner Truth Award, Michigan Women Trial Lawyers Association, 1974. *Hobbies:* Travel; Photography. *Address:* Arlington Heights, Illinois 60004, USA.

MARTIN Jane Roland, b. 20 July 1929, New York City, USA. Professor of Philosophy. m. Michael Lou Martin, 15 June 1962. 2 sons. *Education:* AB 1951, PhD 1961, Radcliffe College; EdM, Harvard University, 1956. *Appointments:* University of Colorado, 1963-65; Harvard Graduate School of Education, 1965-70; University of Massachusetts, 1972-. *Publications:* Reclaiming a Conversation: The Ideal of the Educated Woman, 1985; Science in a Different Style. *Memberships:* American Philosophical Association; Philosophy of Education Society (past president); Society for Women in Philosophy. *Honours:* John Simon Guggenheim Fellowship, 1987-88; University of Massachusetts Chancellor's Distinguished Scholarship Award, 1987; National Science Foundation Fellowship in the History and Philosophy of Science; Research Associate, Bunting Institute. *Address:* Department of Philosophy, University of Massachusetts, Harbor Campus, Boston, MA 02125, USA.

MARTIN Julie Warren, b. 4 Jan. 1943, Knoxville, Tennessee, USA. Sculptor. m. William F. Martin, 15 Mar. 1975, 2 sons, 2 daughters. *Education:* BFA, Sculpture, University of Tennessee (1st awarded there), 1965. *Creative work includes:* Numerous works in metal & marble, latest commission for Glaxo (pharmaceuticals), to be a plaza of 3 stones from 60 tons of New Mexico travertine. 11 solo exhibitions, Tennessee, Florida, Georgia, Alabama, Kentucky, 1969-; Numerous group & invited exhibitions, as above. *Memberships:* International Sculpture Association; Board, Knoxville Museum of Art. *Honours:* Numerous awards, various exhibitions; Outstanding Tennessee Woman, University of Tennessee Panhellenic Council, 1974; Artist of Year, Knoxville Arts Council, 1984; Finalist, YWCA Tribute to Women, 1986; Tennessee Treasure, 1986; Biographical recognitions. *Hobbies include:* Walking; Entertaining friends; Anything associated with the arts; Building project, Knoxville Museum of Art. *Address:* 6006 Walden Street, Knoxville, Tennessee 37919, USA.

MARTIN Lequita Jerelene, b. 22 July 1933, Montrose, USA. Assistant Principal. m. 3 Juy 1955, 2 daughters. *Education:* BS, 1954, MS 1967, University of Southern Mississippi. *Appointments:* Teacher: Gulfport City Schools, 1954-57, Huntsville City Schools, 1958-60; Hattiesburg Public School System, 1960-67; Houston Independent School District, 1967-70; Charleston City Recreation Dept., 1970-73; Teacher, Lillie Burney, 1973-74, Thames Junior High School, 1974-87; Assistant Principal, 1987-, Rowan Junior High School. *Memberships:* President, South Mississippi Science Teachers Association; President, HCTA, 1978; President, Mississippi Association of Classroom Teachers, 1980; etc. *Honours:* Recipient, various honours and awards. *Address:* 1717 Mamie Street, Hattiesburg, MS 39401, USA.

MARTIN Lorraine Margaret, b. 6 Apr. 1941, Brisbane, Australia. Principal & Managing Director. m. Ronald D. Paul, 1979, 2 sons. *Education:* BA, University of Queensland, 1977; Diploma, Institute of Personnel Consultants, 1981. *Appointments:* Private Secretary, Inns of Court, Brisbane, 1957-61; Principal, Lorraine Martin Commercial College, Australian Business Academy, Martin College of Management and Queensland English Language Centre, 1976-; Managing Director, Lorraine Martin Personnel Agency. *Publication:* From Office Wife to Office Manager, 1986. *Memberships:* Fellow, Commercial Education Society of Australia; Institute of Personnel Consultants; Commercial Teachers Society of Queensland; Institute of Professional Secretaries of Australia; Australian Council of Independent Business Colleges, Queensland President, 1982-. *Honours:* 1st Prize, Shorthand Writer's and Bookkeepers, Queensland, 1957; Fellow, Commercial Education Society of Australia, 1984. *Hobbies:* Golf; Bridge; Beach Walks. *Address:* Lorraine Martin Commercial College, 7th Floor, The Professional Suites, 138 Albert Street, Brisbane, Queensland 4000, Australia.

MARTIN Mary Evelyn, b.23 Dec 1958, Lexington, Kentucky, USA. Creative Director of Advertising; University Teacher. *Education:* BA, English Literature, magna cum laude, Lindenwood College, St Charles, Missouri, 1980; MA candidate in English Literature, University of Kentucky. *Appointments:* Assistant to President, Park Place Country Homes, 1985-87; Creative Director of Advertising, Park Place Country Homes, 1987-89; Founder, Good Help Consulting Service, Louisville, Kentucky, 1989. *Creative Works:* Pilot for TV comedy for TBS network (as yet untitled). *Memberships:* National Association of Female Executives; International Platform Association; American Film Institute; Kentucky Film Coalition; People for the American Way; Greenpeace; Kentucky Philological Association. *Honours:* Honor Scholarship, Lindenwood College, 1976-80; National Observer Social Studies Award, Eastern High School, 1976; Richard C Spahmer Creative Writing Award, Lindenwood College, 1979; Outstanding Senior Award, Lindenwood College, 1980; Haggin Fellowship for Graduate Study in English Literature, University of Kentucky, 1987; Nominated for English Speaking Union Scholarship to England, 1989; Nominated for University Open Competition Fellowship, University of Kentucky, 1989. *Hobbies:* Theatre; Screenwriting; Weaving; Producing Radio and Television commercials; Multitrack Sound Recording; Tennis; Renaissance Art; Architecture; Shakespeare's plays; Study of Romance Languages; Mystery and detective novels; Swimming. *Address:* P O Box 23282, Anchorage, KY 40223, USA.

MARTIN Maureen Ann, b. 4 June 1962, Oak Park,

Illinois, USA. Commercial Real Estate Agent. *Education:* BA, magna cum laude, St Mary's College, Notre Dame, Indiana, 1984; Candidate, Certified Commercial Investment Member, Realtors National Marketing Institute, current. *Appointments:* Employee, Rubloff Inc, full service real estate organisation, 1984-; Director of Leasing, JMD/Urban Devlopmenmt Co, Philadelphia, major retail, office, hotel and mixed use property developer, 1989-; Formerly Vice-President of Corporate Real Estate Services, Rubloff Inc, 1984-89. *Memberships:* Chicago Real Estate Organisation; YWCA. *Honours:* Thomas More Award, Humanistic Studies, St Mary's College, 1984; Rubloff National Awards, 1987. *Hobbies:* Travel; Piano; Theatre; Sailing. *Address:* c/o JMB/Urban Development Co, One Logan Square, Philadelphia, PA 19103, USA.

MARTIN Millicent, Actress; Singer. *Career:* Toured USA in The Boy Friend, 1954-57. *Creative Works:* Stage: Expresso Bongo; The Crooked Mile; Our Man Crichton; Tonight at 8; The Beggars Opera; Puss 'n' Boots; The Card; Absurd Person Singular; Aladdin; Side By Side By Sondheim; Move Over Mrs Markham; Meet Mr Stewart; 42nd Street (NY & LA); Two Into One (NY); Follies (London). Television: International Detective Series; Millie; That Was the Week That Was; Harry Moorings; own series Mainly Millicent; Kiss Me Kate; 1966 own series, Millicent TV; 1967 London Palladium Colour Show, USA, Danny Kaye, Piccadilly London; From a Bird's Eye View (own series); Tom Jones show; Englebert Humperdinck show. Films include: The Horsemaster; The Girl on the Boat; Nothing But the Best; Alfie; Stop the World I Want to Get Off. *Address:* London Management, 235-241 Regent Street, London W1A 2JJ, England.

MARTIN Patricia Jean, b. 3 Apr. 1945, Kilcoy, Australia. *Education:* RN, 1971; Midwifery, 1972; Dip. Nursing Admin, 1976; Grad. Dip. Health. Sc., 1980; M. App. Sc., 1981. *Appointments:* Deputy of Nursing, Alfred Hospital Melbourne, 1983-88; Director of Nursing, King Edward Memorial Hospital for Women, 1988-. *Publications:* Articles in: Australian Nurses Journal. *Memberships:* Fellow, College of Nursing, Australia; Royal Australian Nursing Federation; Australian Administrative Staff College Association; Curtin University Alumni. *Honours:* Kellogg Foundation Fellowship, 1981; Royal Melbourne Hospital Past Trainers Association, Jane Bell Scholarship, 1979. *Hobbies:* Ballet; Theatre; Golf. *Address:* Director of Nursing, King Edward Memorial Hospital for Women, Subiaco, WA 6008, Australia.

MARTIN Rhona Madeline, b. 3 June 1922, London, England. Author; Miniature Artist. m. Peter Wilfrid Alcock, 9 May 1941 (divorced), 2 daughters. *Education:* West of England College of Art, Bristol. *Career:* Stage designer, various theatres & costumiers. *Publications:* Novels: Gallows Wedding (award), 1978; Mango Walk, 1981; Unicorn Summer, 1984; Goodbye, Sally, 1987. Non-fiction: Writing Historical Fiction, 1988. *Memberships:* Society of Authors; Society of Women Writers & Journalists; Romantic Novelists Association; Society of Limners. *Honour:* Georgette Heyer Historical Novel Award, 1978. *Hobbies:* Music; Travel; T'ai Ji; Exotic cats (former breeder, Siamese & Burmese). *Address:* c/o Campbell, Thomson & McLaughlin, Literary Agents, 31 Newington Green, London N16 9PU, England.

MARTIN Roxanne, b. 12 May 1947, Salina, Kansas, USA. Registered Nurse; Diabetes Educator. m. William Scott Martin Jr, 29 Nov. 1969, 1 daughter. *Education:* Baccalaureate 1969, MSc 1980, Nursing, Northwestern State University, Louisiana; Certified Diabetes Educator, 1988. *Appointments:* Charge Nurse, Obstetrics, 1969-75; Instructor, Northwestern State University, 1975-80; Education Instructor 1980-88, Diabetic Education Consultant 1981-, Acting Co-Supervisor, Education Department 1984-86, Schumpert Medical Centre. *Creative work includes:* Developed & Implemented present Diabetes Patient Education Programme, Schumpert Medical Centre, 1980. *Memberships:*

American Nurses Association; Sigma Theta Tau; Offices, Shreveport District Nurses Association, American Diabetes Association; American Business Woman's Association; Arthritis Foundation; Diabetes Camp Nurse 1986, 1988, American Association of Diabetes Educators; Chairman, Annual Workshop for Diabetics & Families, 1984-88. *Hobbies:* Cross-stitch; Photography; Girl Scouts. *Address:* PO Box 21976, Shreveport, Louisiana 71120, USA.

MARTIN Sherilyn Jones, b. 5 Apr. 1952, Atlanta, Georgia, USA. Educator. m. John Noel Martin, 14 June 1986. *Education:* BSc, Sociology, University of Georgia, 1974; MA History 1979, PhD candidate 1986-, Georgia State University. *Appointments:* Instructor, Dekalb College 1983-85, Georgia State University 1986-. *Creative work includes:* Paper, Robespierre The Incorruptable As Seen Through Historians Eyes, Annual Conference, Georgia Association of Historians, 1989. *Memberships:* President, Phi Alpha Theta; Alpha Chapter, Phi Beta Kappa; American Historical Association; Georgia Association of Historians; Smithsonian Associates. *Honours:* Award for paper, National Archives, Georgia Association of Historians, 1988; Biographical recognition; Honour societies. *Hobbies:* Sailing; Painting; Nazi Germany, French Revolution, & Napoleonic Era; Art History. *Address:* c/o Georgia State University, University Plaza, History Department, Atlanta, Georgia 30305, USA.

MARTIN Shirley M, b. 15 Apr. 1944, Tekamah, Nebraska, USA. *Education:* Diploma, Edmonds High School, 1962; Everett Junior College, 1962; Diploma, Bell & Howell School of Accounting, 1974. *Appointments:* Finance Coordinator, Continental Ins. Co, 1963-70; Audit Reviewer, 1975-80, Premium Field Auditor, 1975-80, Home Ins. Co; Owner, Insurance Agency, Martin & Assoc. 1980-88; Author/Publisher/Speaker, S M Martin Co, 1986-88. *Publications:* Author and publisher of the 15 Minute System, simplified record keeping for businesses, 1986. *Memberships:* National Association of Premium Auditors, 1975-88; National Association, Life Underwriters, 1986-88; National Association Female Executives, 1985-88; Whatcom County Chamber of Commerce, 1986-88. *Honours:* Number One Female Insurance Producer in the Nation INA Life Insurance Company, Philadelphia, 1985-86; Number One Insurance Producer in the Pacific Northwest INA Life Insurance Company, Philadelphia, 1985-86. *Hobbies:* Hiking; Camping; Horses; Superb Restaurants. *Address:* 2801 Superior Street, Bellingham, Washington 98226, USA.

MARTIN Wilma Jean Queen, b. 30 July 1937, Logan County, USA. Nursing Home Administrator; Social Worker; Hospital Administrator. m. James P Martin, 1 Feb. 1977, 2 sons. *Education:* BA, West Virginia State College, 1987. *Appointments:* Registered Medical Secretary, 1957; Hospital Administrator, 1960-70, 1970-85; Licensed Nursing Home Administrator, 1983; Licensed Social Worker, 1987. *Honours:* Summa Cum Laude, West Virginia State College, 1987. *Hobbies:* Swimming; Cooking; Travel; Golf. *Address:* 171 Nighbert Ave., Logan, WV 25601, USA.

MARTIN-CROSA Ana Maria, b. 6 May 1933, Argentina. Professor. *Education:* B.Ed., 1952; BA, Drawing, 1958; MA, 1967. *Appointments:* Adjunct Professor, Painting, Universidad Nacional de la Plata, 1968-73; Adjunct Professor, Painting, La Plata National University, 1972-77; Design Professor, Social Communications College, 1969-73; Painting Professor, Public School of Arts, Magdalena, 1977-; Founder, Director, Taller de Creatividad Integral, Buenos Aires, 1981. *Creative Works:* Collages, 1968-69; Femina 72, 1970-72. *Honours:* Recipient, various honours & awards. *Address:* 61 No 471 1/2 A, 1900 La Plata (Bs As), Argentina.

MARTINEZ-RODGERS Victoria Neoma, b. 27 Mar. 1938, Alburquerque, USA. New Impressionist. m. Clarence Rodgers, 23 May 1957, 1 son, 2 daughters.

Appointments: Self-employed Artist, 1958-. *Creative Works Include:* Orchids in Space, series; Universe, series; American & European Garden, series; Sea Life, series; etc. *Memberships:* Society of Layerists in Multimedia; Museum of Albuquerque; Museum of Natural History. *Honours:* Recipient, various honours and awards. *Hobbies:* Tennis; Gardening; Sailing. *Address:* 1410 Goff Blvd, SW, Albuquerque, NM 87105, USA.

MARX Gertie F., b. 13 Feb. 1912, Frankfurt/Main, Germany. Professor of Anaesthesiology. m. Eric P. Reiss, 26 Sept. 1940 (deceased 1964). *Education:* Medical School, University of Frankfurt, 1931-36; MD, University of Bern, Switzerland, 1937. *Appointments:* Intern, Resident, Attending Anaesthesiologist, Beth Israel Medical Centre, New York, USA, 1939-55; Assistant Professor 1955-60, Associate Professor 1960-70, Professor 1970-, Albert Einstein College of Medicine, Bronx, NY. *Publications:* 4 books, obstetric anaesthesia; 133 original contributions, refereed journals including Anaesthesiology, Obstetrics & Gynaecology; 26 Letters to Editor. *Memberships:* Professional bodies including: American Society of Anaesthesiologists; Founding member, Society for Obstetric Anaesthesia & Perinatology; New York Academy of Sciences; New York Academy of Medicine; *Honours:* Best Teacher, Albert Einstein College, 1974; We Salute, Gold Medal, Obstetric Anaesthetists Association, 1980; Award of Merit, NY State Society of Anaesthesiologists, 1985; Honorary Dr med, Johannes Gutenburg University, Mainz, Germany, 1986; Distinguished Service Award of the Ameriacan Society of Anesthesiologists, 1988; Distinguished Service Award of the American Society of Regional Anesthesia, 1990. *Hobbies:* Outdoors; Classical music, especially baroque. *Address:* Department of Anaesthesiology, J-1226, Albert Einstein College of Medicine, Bronx, New York 10461, USA.

MARYFIELD Pamela, b. 4 Mar. 1935, Earby, West Riding, Yorkshire, England. Sixth Form College Principal. m. F. G. G. Maryfield, 26 Aug. 1967. *Education:* Girton College, Cambridge, 1953-56; BA Hons, Historical Tripos, 1956; MA Cantab, 1959. *Appointments:* Teaching posts: Heathfield School Ascot, 1956; St Albans High School, 1959; Southampton Girls School, 1960; Vice-Principal, Hill College, Southampton, 1975-85; Principal, Strode's College, Egham, Surrey, 1985-. *Memberships:* Secretary, Southampton branch, Historical Association; President, Hampshire, Assistant Masters and Mistresses Association; Justice of the Peace, Southampton bench, to 1981; Chairman, Hampshire Teachers' Liaison Panel. *Honours:* Schoolteacher Fellow, Lady Margaret Hall, Oxford, 1968. *Hobbies:* Music; Cricket; Gardening. *Address:* Strode's College, Egham, Surrey, England.

MARZI Ninas Alessandra, b. 16 May 1921, Krasnodar, Russia. Therapist. m. (1) Boris Milenko, 6 Aug. 1949, (2) Omero Marzi, 15 July 1966. 1 son. *Education:* College Diploma, Tientsin Business School, 1938-40. *Appointments:* Secretary, Solicitor, Sydney, Australia, 1940-43; Own Clothing Business, 1943-47; Own Guest House, 1947-; Health Centre, 1947-; Dr James' Drugless method of Treating Asthma. *Publications:* Dr A James, Biography. *Memberships:* Charter Member, Zonta Club; International Training in Communication, Orana; International Member of Salesman With a Purpose; Wollongong City Library Listing Public Speaking, Guest Speaker. *Honours:* Arthur Murray Latin American Dance Championship, 1960; Humanitarian Smith Family, 1973. *Hobbies include:* Dancing; Theatre; Painting; Gardening; Social Work; Socialising; Cooking; Function Organiser; Reading; Physical Culture; Swimming. *Address:* 18 Kembla Street, Wollongong 2500, NSW, Australia.

MASCOLO Donna M, b. 13 Jan. 1955, Lakewood, USA. Director. *Education:* BA, Susquehanna University, 1976; MBA, Lehigh University, 1979. *Appointments:* Credit Manager, Commercial Consultant, Midlantic Banks Inc., 1976-78; Operations Research Analyst, Air Products & Chemicals, 1978-79; Teaching Assistant,

Lehigh University, 1979; Systems Engineer, Bell Labs., 1979-81; Business Planning Advisor, Exxon Corp., 1981-85; Director, Planning, Burger King Corp., 1985-88; Director, Planning & Analysis, Jack Eckerd Corp., 1989-. *Memberships:* Director, Community Development, United Way; Director, Stratigic Planning, Greater Miami Chamber of Commerce. *Hobbies:* Golf; Organ & Guitar Playing. *Address:* 757 Tomoka Drive, Palm Harbor, FL 34683, USA.

MASHAM Susan Lilian, (Baroness) (Countess of Swinton) OF ILTON Primrose Cunliffe-Lister, b. 14 Apr. 1935. Peer of the Realm. m. Lord Masham, now 2nd Earl of Swinton, 8 Dec. 1959, 1 son, 1 daughter (adopted). *Education:* London Polytechnic. *Publications:* The World Walks By, 1986. *Memberships Include:* President, North Yorkshire Red Cross; President, Yorkshire Association for the Disabled; Yorkshire Regional Health Authority; Chairman, Board of Directors, Phoenix House; President, Spinal Injuries Association; Board of Visitors, Youth Custody Centre, Wetherby; Member, Parliamentary Aids Group; Member, Vice-Chairman, Parliamentary Drug Misuse Committee; Patron, Disablement Income Group; Trustee, Spinal Research Trust; Vice President, Disabled Drivers Assocation; Vice President, Action for Dysphasic Adults; Winston Churchill Trust; Patron, Yorkshire Faculty of General Practitioners; President, Papworth & Enham Village Settlements; etc. *Honours:* Honourary Fellowship, Royal College of General Practitioners, 1981; Honorary MA, Open University; Honorary MA, York University, 1985; Honorary LLD, Leeds, 1988; Honorary Fellowship, Bradford & Ilkley Community College, 1988. *Hobbies:* Health & Disability Problems; Penal Affairs; Drug & Alcohol Abuse Matters; Breeding Highland Ponies; Swimming; Table Tennis; Fishing; Gardening. *Address:* Dykes Hill House, Masham, Nr Ripon, North Yorkshire HG4 4NS, England.

MASON Bobbie Ann, b. 1 May 1940, Mayfield, Kentucky, USA. Writer. m. Roger Rawlings, 12 Apr. 1969. *Education:* BA, English, University of Kentucky, 1962; MA, English, State University of New York, Binghamton, 1966; PhD, English, University of Connecticut, 1972. *Publications:* Shiloh and Other Stories, (short stories), 1982; In Country, (novel), 1985; The Girl Sleuth, Criticism (children's literature), 1975; Nabokov's Garden, criticism (PhD dissertation), 1974; Spence & Lila (novel), 1988; Love Life (stories), 1989. *Memberships:* Author's Guild; PEN. *Honours:* Shiloh and Other Stories: Hemingway Foundation Award for best first fiction, 1982; Nominated for PEN-Faulkner Award; national Book Critics Circle Award; American Book Award. *Address:* c/o Amanda Urban, International Creative Management, 40 W 57th Street, New York, NY 10019, USA.

MASON Joan Ellen Fritz, b. 29 June 1947, Reading, Pennsylvania, USA. Professor Nurse/Clinical Editor. m. 12 Feb. 1977. *Education:* Temple University Hospital School of Nursing, 1965-68; BSc., Nursing Education, 1971; Master, Health Education, 1981, Temple University; Posgraduate Courses, University of Pennsylvania. *Appointments:* Staff Nurse, Medical/Dermatology Unit, Temple University Hospital, 1968; Instructor/Class Advisor, Philadelphia General Hospital School of Nursing, 1971-76; Staff Education Co-ordinator, Memorial Hospital, Roxborough, 1976; Clinical Editor, Professional Book Department, Springhouse Corporation, 1984. *Creative Works:* Chapters: Plasma Cell, Moncycle and Macrophage Disorders: Myeloma and Other Problems, in Nurse Review; Schizophrenic Disorders, in Nurse Review, etc. *Memberships:* Victorian Society; American Bed & Breakfast Association; American Nurses Association; Profesional Nursing Development; Board of Governors, University City Historical Society; mid Atlantic Centers for the Arts. *Hobbies:* Bed and Breakfast Inns; Victoriana; Meeting People. *Address:* 430 South 42nd Street, Philadelphia, PA 19104, USA.

MASON Pamela, Actress; Broadcaster; Author. m. James Mason, divorced, 1 son, 1 daughter. *Publications:* 4 novels; bi-weekly columnist, Movieline; TV appearances. *Address:* c/o 9021 Melrose Ave., No 207, Los Angeles, CA 90069, USA.

MASOPERH Elizabeth Regina Naa Norkai, b. 12 May 1938, Christiansborg, Accra, Ghana. Dental Surgeon. m. Joseph Amate Masoperh, Dec. 1966, 2 sons, 2 daughters. *Education:* Cambridge School Certificate Exam, 1957; Pharmacy, University of Science & Technology, 1958 (unfinished); Cambridge HSC, Aburi Girls' Secondary School, 1960; Certificate, German, Goethe Institute, Kochel, Germany, 1962; Staatsexamen, Dental Surgeon, Free University of Berlin, 1962-69; Fellowship for Developing Countries, Oro-Facial Surgery, 1969-70. *Appointments:* Appointed Dental Surgeon, Ministry of Health, 1971; Posted, Cape Coast, 1971-74; Transferred, Ridge Hospital & Labadi Polyclinic, Accra, 1974; Senior Dental Surgeon with training programme, Dental Nursing Assistants, 1976; Resigned from Civil Service, 1978; Private Dental Surgeon, 1979-. *Memberships include:* Ghana Medical & Dental Council; Ghana Medical Association; OSU Medical Foundation; Medical Women International Association; Current President, & Ghana representative, Berlin International Conference 1978, Society of Ghana Medical & Dental Women (affiliate, MWIA); Medical Women's Representative 1978-86, Vice President 1984-86, Women's Committee, Christian Council of Ghana; Elder, Osu North Presbyterian Church; Women's Representative, Synod Committee, Presbyterian Church of Ghana, 1983-86. *Honours:* Numerous school prizes & awards; Certificates of honour from various church choirs, Moderator, & Youth Guilds, Ghana Presbyterian Church, 1983-. *Hobbies:* Gardening, orchids & roses, floral arrangements; Church work. *Address:* Maabs Dental Clinic, PO Box 0565, Osu, Ghana.

MASSEVITCH Alla Genrikhovna, b. 9 Oct. 1918, Tbilissi, Russia. Astronomer. m. Joseph Fziedlander, 1942, 1 daughter. *Education:* Studied, Moscow University; Dr.Phys.Mathem.Sc. *Appointments:* Senior Scientific Research Worker, Astronomical Institute of Moscow University, 1945-48; Professor, Astrophysics, Moscow University, 1948-70; Astronomical Council, USSR Academy of Sciences, 1952-; Professor, Satellite Geodesy, Moscow Technical University, 1970-76. *Publications:* 133 scientific papers; Articles in professional journals; books: Observations of Satellites for Geodesy, 1979; Physics and Evolution of Stars, 1972, 1981, 1988. *Memberships:* Vice President: USSR Peace Committee, USSR-USA Friendship Society; Moscow Club for Scientists. *Address:* Astronomical Council, USSR Academy of Sciences, 48 Piatnitskaya Street, 10917 Moscow, USSR.

MASSEY Doris Eunice, b. 1 Dec. 1930, Florida, USA. Real Estate Broker. m. John Max Massey, 12 Dec. 1956, deceased, 2 sons. *Education:* Studies various colleges & institutes. *Appointments:* Teller, Loan Officer, Acting Secretary-Treasurer, First Federal Saving & Loan of NS, 1948- 57; Owner, Manager, Massey Ranch Airpark, 1950-; Real Estate Salesperson, 1957- 58; Owner, Edgewater Loan Service, 1957-70; Real Estate Broker, 1959-; Secretary, City of New Smyrna Beach, 1972-77; Managing Partner, Massey Enterprises, 1981-. *Memberships:* New Smyrna Beach Board of Realtors, Vice President, 1989; New Smyrna Beach Chamber of Commerce, Secretary & Director, 1987-1990; Women's Council of Realtors, Secretary, 1988/89; many other professional organisations. *Honours:* American Business Women's Association, Woman of the Year Award, 1976, 1987; Realtor of the Year Award, 1984. *Hobbies:* Art; Aviation; Travel. *Address:* 541 Skyway Dr., Edgewater, FL 32032, USA.

MASSEY Jamila, b. 7 Jan. 1934, Simla. Actress; Writer. m. Reginald Massey, 6 Dec. 1961, 1 son. *Education:* BA, King's College, University of London, 1959. *Appointments:* Actress, Writer, 1959-; has worked in Repertory, Fringe and Legit Theatre & appeared in various films & tv series including: Jewel in the Crown; Crossroads; Albion Market; Langley Bottom & Mind Your Language; Books: (Co-author with Reginald Massey):

The Immigrants; The Music of India; The Dances of India. *Membership:* Equity. *Hobbies:* Wine Making; Gardening; Painting. *Address:* Bryndu Canol, Tylwch, Llanidloes, Powys SY18 6JJ, Wales.

MASSOUD Mary M F, b. Cairo, Egypt. Head, Department of English. *Education:* BA, Hons, English, Cairo University; MA, Eng Lit, Columbia University, New York City, USA; MRE, Union Seminary, New York City; PhD 1967, DLitt, Ain Shams University, Cairo, Egypt. *Appointments:* Assistant Lecturer 1961-67, Lecturer in English 1967-73, Associate Professor of English Lit, 1973-78, Professor of English Lit, 1978- and Head, Department of English 1983-, Ain Shams University, Cairo. *Publications:* Book: Translate to Communicate; 90 plays mostly in Arabic, few in English including Our Father translated into ten languages; Several critical works on English Literature. *Memberships:* Served on Committee for translating the Bible into a more contemporary Arabic, 1968-72; Representing the Middle East, Global Executive Committee of World Day of Prayer, 1986-90; Co-Chairman, Women's Ecumenical Fellowship of Egypt, 1975-78. *Honours:* Ain Shams University Prize for best research work, 1976; Fellowship, Selly Oak, Birmingham, England, Dorothy Cadbury Lecturer, 1978; Fulbright Visiting Professor, University of Utah, Salt Lake City, USA, 1980-81; Exchange Visiting Professor, Indiana University, Pennsylvania, 1982-83. *Hobbies:* Reading; Music; Swimming; Producing plays. *Address:* 29 Emad El Dine Street, 2nd floor flat 7, Cairo, Egypt.

MASSURA Eileen Kathleen, b. 25 July 1963, Chicago, USA. Professor. m. Alfred Massura, 30 Aug. 1963, 3 sons, 2 daughter. *Education:* BS, Nursing;; RN. *Appointments:* Director, Nurses Franklin Blvd., Hospital, Chicago, 1958-62; Administrator, 1958-62, 1962-64, Michigan Hospital; Instructor, St Xavier College, Chicago, 1972-81; Family Therapist, Oak Lawn, 1978-; Professor, Nuring Governors State University, 1981-. *Publications:* 4 Audio-Tutorial Lab Books for Junio College Nursing Courses, co-author, 1973-74. *Memberships:* American Nurses Association, Nominating Committee, 1982-; Illinois Nurses Association, Programme Committee, 1980-84; American Asosciation Marital and Family Therapists; Sigma Theta Tau. *Honours:* Sigma Theta Tau; Mental Health Grants. *Hobbies:* Crewel & Needlepoint. *Address:* 4537 W. 105th St., Oak Lawn, IL 60453, USA.

MASTERMAN-SMITH Virginia, b. 18 Nov. 1937, New York City, New York, USA. Teacher; Writer. div., 2 sons. *Education:* BA, Elementary Education, English, Philosophy, Georgian Court College, Lakewood, New Jersey, 1969; MS, Education, Teacher of the Handicapped, Monmouth College, West Long Branch, New Jersey, 1988. *Appointments:* Various positions as Resource Room Teacher, Elementary, Middle & Grammar School Teacher, Special Education Teacher, Business English, Professional Development and College Survival Teacher, 1959-, Long Branch Middle School, Long Branch, New Jersey, currently; President, Director, Photo-Trax, 1972-; Consultant in Reading and Language Arts, In-service workshops, school districts, New York, New Jersey, Pennsylvania, Writing workshops; District Newswriter for Long Branch School System; Reporter, Feature Writer, The Daily Register and The Daily Record; Guest speaker. *Publications include:* Juvenile novels: The Treasure Trap, 1979; The Haunted Mansion Mystery; The Great Egyptian Heist, 1982; Our Life, musical (story and book), 1983; Contributing Editor, Monmouth Business Talk; The Grandich Letter (editor); Magazine and newspaper articles; Video industrial, promotional films, brochures. *Memberships:* American Mensa Ltd; Authors' Guild East; Society of Children's Bookwriters; American Federation of Teachers; National Council of Teachers of English; Monmouth College Library Association; Georgian Court Alumni Association. *Honours:* Certification of Merit, New Jersey Reading Association, 1980, 1986; Author Citation, New Jersey Institute of Technology, 1981. *Hobbies:* Growing flowers; Learning programmes for IBM compatible and Apple computers;

Theatre; Writing for fun; Dancing; Crossword puzzles and brain teasers; Bridge; Listening to classical, soft rock and country music. *Address:* 1237 Eatontown Boulevard, Oceanport, NJ 07757, USA.

MASTERSON Patricia, b. 15 May 1952, Worcester, USA. Publications Editor. *Education:* BFA, Emerson College, 1974; MA, Goddard College, 1980. *Appointments:* Reporter, Photographer, Patriot Newspaper, 1975- 77; Public Relations Director, Mount Pleasant Hospital, 1980-84; Publications Editor, Ocean Spray Cranberries Inc., 1984-89; Marketing Communications Coordinator, Groundwater Technology, 1989-. *Publications:* Articles in: Worcester Telegram & Gazette; South Shore Business Journal; Bay State Business Journal; Equal Times; The Communicator; numerous others. *Memberships:* Women in Communications; Cooperative Communications Association; South Shore A Club; volunteer, Rosie's Homeless Shelter, 1987-; Board of Directors; YWCA, 1980-84. *Honours:* Recipient, various honours & awards. *Hobbies:* Sports; Writing; Flute; Volunteer; Army England Award for Outstanding Volunteer, 1984. *Address:* 132 Union Street, Rockland, MA 02370, USA.

MASTROLIA Lilyan Spitzer, b. 28 Mar. 1934, Brooklyn, New York, USA. Teacher; Writer. m. Edmund J Mastrolia, 28 Aug. 1956. 2 sons. *Education:* BS Cum Laude, Brooklyn College, 1955; Post graduate, University of Southern California, 1955-56; MEd, California State College, Los Angeles, 1957; Post graduate, California State University, Sacramento, 1959-60 and 1980-81. *Appointments:* Teacher, LA Unified School Dist, 1957-58; Folsom Unified School Dist, 1958-63; San Juan Unified School Dist, 1967-89; Science Chairman, Barrett Intermediate School, 1970-84, History Leader, 1987- 88; Science Chairman, Mills Jr High School, Rancho Cordova, 1959-63. *Publications:* Book: Teachers' Guide to Physical Science; Poetry book: Observations from the Back Room; over 45 poems. Sculpture: Dog-eared Cat; Needlepoint: Antique Roses; Painting: Go-Kart. *Memberships:* National League of American Penwomen; National Teachers Association; National Writers' Club; Computer Writers Association; California Writers' Club; American Medical Writers Association; International Food, Wine & Travel Writers' Association; American Society of Journalists & Authors. *Honours:* Honorable Mention, Chaparral Poets, 1972; Outstanding Teacher, 1979, 1980; National Science Foundation Grantee, 1960, 1983, 1984; American Cancer Society Grantee, 1984. *Hobbies:* Tennis; Needlepoint; Computers; Reading. *Address:* 4706 Cameron Ranch Drive, Sacramento, CA 95841, USA.

MATALAMAKI Margaret Marie, b. 10 May 1921, Hampton, Iowa, USA. Educator. m. William Matalamaki, 11 Sept. 1942, deceased 1978, 1 son, 1 daughter. *Education:* AA, Itasca Community College, 1941. *Appointments:* High School Instructor School District 1, Bigfork, 1942- 45, University Minnesota School Agriculture, Grand Rapids, 1955-58, high school Substitute School District 318 Grand Rapids, 1967-69; Vocational Instructor, Itsaca Community College, Grand Rapids, 1970-78. *Memberships Include:* Board, Christus Home, Grand Rapids; Board, Itasca Memorial Hospital, 1975-85, Itasca County Nursing Home, 1975-85, N. Itasca Nursing Home, 1982-85, Itasca County Social Services, 1975-85; University of Minnesota Institute of Agriculture, Forestry and Home Economics Advisory Council, Vice Chair, 1980-; County Commissioner, Itasca County, 1981-85; Lutheran Social Services of Minnesota, Vice Chair, 1985-. Board, Blandin Foundation, Grand Rapids, Trustee 1981-, Vice President, 1985-87, Chairman, 1988-; Director, University of Minnesota National Alumni Association, 1987-; University of Minnesota, No. Central Station Foundation, 1987-; Board of Trustees, Gustavus Adolphus College, 1988-; Trustee: University of Minnesota: 4H Foundation, 1988-. *Honours:* Good Government Award, 1977; WCCO Radio Good Neighbour Award, Grand Rapids Chamber of

Commerce, 1977. *Hobbies:* Cross Country Skiing; Canoeing; Travel. *Address:* 727 Mishawaka Shores Drive, Grand Rapids, MN 55744, USA.

MATANOSKI Genevieve Elizabeth Murray, b. 26 Aug. 1930, Salem, Massachusetts, USA. Professor of Epidemiology. 4 sons, 1 daughter. *Education:* AB Chemistry, Radcliffe College, 1951; MD Medicine 1955, MPH Epidemiology 1962, DrPH Epidemiology 1964, Johns Hopkins School of Hygiene and Public Health; Certified, Specialist in General Preventive Medicine American Board of Preventive Medicine, 1973. *Appointments:* Research Assistant, Johns Hopkins School of Medicine, 1955; Intern, Pediatrics 1955-56, Assistant Resident, Pediatrics, 1956-57, Pediatrician, Out-Patient Department, 1957-, Johns Hopkins Hospital; Research Assistant, Epidemiology 1957-59, Instructor, Epidemiology, 1959-64, Assistant Professor, Epidemiology, 1964-69, Associate Professor, Epidemiology, 1969-76, Coordinator and Evaluator of Special Projects, 1970-73, Professor, Epidemiology, 1976-, Program Director, Occupation and Environmental Epidemiology, 1978-, Johns Hopkins School of Hygiene and Public Health; Instructor, Preventive Medicine 1967-69, Associate Professor, Preventive Medicine 1970-, Associate Professor, 1970- , University of Maryland. *Publications include:* Over 60 articles in professional journals. *Memberships:* American Association for the Advancement of Science; American Public Health Association; New York Academy of Sciences; Society for Epidemiological Research; International Epidemiological Association; Association of Teachers of Preventive Medicine; American College of Preventive Medicine; Society for Occupational and Environmental Health; Air Pollution Control Association; Member, American Epidemiological Society, 1983. *Honours:* Training Fellowship in Public Health, Johns Hopkins School of Hygiene and Public Health, 1962-64; Fellow, American College of Preventive Medicine, 1975; Alpha Chpater, Delta Omega Honorary Society, 1980. *Address:* The Johns Hopkins University School of Hygiene and Public Health, Department of Epidemiology, Room 6019, 615 North Wolfe Street, Baltimore, MD 21205, USA.

MATEJKA Jacquelin Rae Cranfill, b. 21 Dec. 1928, New Kensington, Pennsylvania, USA. University Professor. m. Robert Earl Matejka, 9 Sept. 1949, 2 sons, 1 daughter. *Education:* BA 1978 (Colorado Springs), MA 1979 (Boulder), University of Colorado; PhD, University of Texas, 1983. *Appointments:* Journalist, Black Forest News, 1977; Instructor, University of Colorado, 1983-84; Instructor 1984-88, Assistant Professor 1988- 89, Colorado Baptist University; Assistant Professor, Southwest Baptist University, Missouri, 1989-. *Creative work includes:* Devotionals for College Students; Understanding the Bible Through Middle Eastern Culture. (Not yet published.) *Memberships:* American Political Science Association; Centre for Study of Presidency; Middle East Institute; Academy of Political Science; Concerned Women of America. *Hobbies include:* Numerous activities, Baptist church work. *Address:* Southwest Baptist University, Bolivar, Missouri 65613, USA.

MATHESON Theresa B. (Teri), b. 14 July 1953, Nash County, North Carolina, USA. Mortgage Broker. m. 30 May 1976, 1 daughter. *Education:* BS, Recreation Resources Administration, North Carolina State University, 1975; Licence, Real Estate Sales, 1985; Mid-Management School, University of North Carolina School of Banking, 1983-85. *Appointments:* Marketing operations, 1979-85; Property manager, Woodland Associates, 1985-86; Marketing officer, 1st American Savings Bank, 1986-87; Mortgage officer, D&N Mortgage 1987, NC Federal Savings & Loan 1988, Fairfield Financial 1989-. *Creative work:* Designed & built own home. *Memberships:* Local branches; Womens Council of Realtors, Home Builders Association, Board of Realtors; Ambassador, Cary Chamber of Commerce. *Honour:* Ambassador of Year, Cary Chamber of Commerce, 1988. *Hobbies:* Horseback riding, breeding, showing; Snow skiing; Reading;

Gourmet cooking; Travel; Volleyball. Volunteer coordinator, Cary Olympic Festival, 1987; Various offices, community welfare organisations. *Address:* Route 5, Box 402, Salem Church Road, Apex, North Carolina 27502, USA.

MATHEW Rae, b. 7 Jan. 1944, Tasmania. Businesswoman. 1 son, 1 daughter. *Education:* BA, Honours. *Appointments:* Assistant Lecturer, Russian, University of Canterbury, New Zealand, 1965; Lecturer, Russian Language, University of Melbourne, 1969-78; Executive, Trading House, 1979-84; Top Drawer Business Accessories, 1984-. *Publications:* Co-Editor, Essays to Honour Nina Christesen; The Steel Bird & Other Stories, (Translator); The Directory of Women. *Memberships:* ADMA; BPW; ALSA; Chamber of Commerce; Entrepreneurs Network; Women in Management. *Honours:* Nominated for Advance Australia Award, 1987. *Hobbies:* Reading; Music; People. *Address:* PO Box 250, Albert Park, VIC 3206, Australia.

MATHEWS Marilynn Cash, b. New York, New York, USA. President of Management Consulting Firm. *Education:* BA 1977, MA 1979, PhD 1984, University of California at Santa Barbara. *Appointments:* Professor, Dept of Political Science, Washington State University, 1984-87; Lecturer, Department of Management and Organization, University of Washington, 1988-; President, International Consulting and Executive Development, 1987-. *Publications:* Book: Strategic Intervention in Organizations: Resolving Ethical Dilemmas, 1988; Numerous articles in professional journals. *Memberships:* Academy of Management; Society for Business Ethics; American Society of Criminology. *Address:* International Consulting and Executive Development, 1220 N 173rd Street, Seattle, WA 98133, USA.

MATHEWS Mary Kathryn, b. 20 Apr. 1948, Washington, USA. Federal Agency Administrator. *Education:* BS, 1970, MBA, 1975, American University. *Appointments:* Deputy Chief, Department Services & Special Programmes, Dept. of Transportation, 1978-81; Assistant Director, Administrative Division, Farm Credit Administration, 981-84; Division Director, Farm Credit Administration, 1984-86; Division Chief, Administrative Services, Farm Credit Administration, 1987-88; Deputy Staff Director, Management, US Commission on Civil Rights, 1988-. *Memberships:* American Society of Professional & Executive Women; National Trust for Historic Preservation; Charter member, National Museum of Women in the Arts; Delta Gamma. *Honours:* Special Act Award, 1988. *Address:* 6420 Franconia Court, Springfield, VA 22150, USA.

MATHEWS Susan Caroline Porteous, b. 6 Jan. 1948, Essex, England. Managing Director. *Education:* BA, Honours, London School of Economics, 1983. *Appointments:* Assistant to Head of Training & Development, Hong Kong Bank, 1970-73; Personnel Manager, National Mutual, 1973-76; Training Manager, Uniroyal, 1977-80; Managing Director, Training by Design, 1980-. *Publications:* Articles in: Craft Art; Canberra Times; She; Personnel News; Daily Mail; British Heritage. *Memberships:* Institute of Personnel Management; Associate Institute of Employment Consultants. *Hobbies:* Horse Riding; Walking; History; Writing; Music; Theatre; Travel. *Address:* 6 Spencer Road, London W3 6DN, England.

MATHIS Marsha Debra, b. 22 Dec. 1953, Detroit, Michigan, USA. Marketing Executive. *Education:*)BSc, Florida State University, 1978; MBA, Mississippi College, 1982. *Appointments:* Florida Department of Safety, 1973-76; Tallahassee Federal Savings & Loan, 1976-78; Sales engineer, Prehler Inc, 1978-82; Marketing Manager, Norand Corporation, 1982-87; Vice President, Marketing & Sales, Professional Datasolutions Inc 1987-88, Target Systems 1988-90, Vice President, Marketing and Sales, Professional Datasolutions, Inc., 1990-, Vice President, Marketing and Sales . *Publications:* Various articles, professional subjects, C-Store News. *Memberships:* National Association of Convenience Stores; National Advisory Group; Adviser, American Diabetes Association; National Republican Committee. *Honours:* Sales achievement, 1st place 1980, 2nd 1981, 1st 1982. *Hobbies:* Reading; Coin collecting; Tennis; Softball. *Address:* 600 Eagle Nest, Irving, Texas 75063, USA.

MATHIS-EDDY Darlene Fern, b. 19 Mar. 1937, Elkhart, Indiana, USA. Professor of English; Poetry Editor. m. Spencer Livingston Eddy Jr, 23 May 1964. *Education:* BA summa cum laude, Goshen College, 1959; MA, 1962, PhD, 1964, Rutgers University. *Appointments:* Instructor in English, Douglass College, 1962-64; Instructor, Rutgers University and University College, Rutgers University, summers 1964, 1965; Assistant Professor, 1967-71, Associate Professor, 1971-75, Professor of English, 1975-, Ball State University, Muncie, Indiana; Poetry Editor, Forum; Poet-in-Residence, Ball State University, 1989-. *Publications:* The Worlds of King Lear, 1970; Leaf Threads, Wind Rhymes, 1985; Weathering, 1989; Poetry in Snowy Egret, Calyx, Pebble, Cottonwood, Blue Unicorn, Amelia; Articles in American Literature, English Language Notes, Green River Review and others. *Memberships:* Modern Language Association; American Association of University Professors; National Council of Teachers of English; Associated Writing Programs; Shakespeare Association. *Honours:* Woodrow Wilson National Fellow, 1959-62; Rutgers University Graduate Honours Fellow, 1964-65; Rutgers University Dissertation Honours Grant, 1966; Numerous creative arts, creative teaching, and research grants, Ball State University. *Hobbies:* Reading; Gardening; Music; Photography; Needlepoint. *Address:* RB 248, Department of English, Ball State University, Muncie, IN 47306, USA.

MATJASICH Carol Ann, b. 27 Mar. 1955, USA. Marketing Communications & Design Executive. *Education:* BFA, Northern Illinois University, 1977. *Appointments:* Designer 1977-80, Executive Vice President 1980-81, Design Investigation Group, Chicago; Owner, Executive Vice President, Porter/ Matjasich & Associates, 1981-. *Memberships:* Director, National Association of Women Business Owners; Chicago Association of Commerce & Industry; Women in Design; APDF; STA. *Honours:* Design-related awards. *Address:* Porter/Matjasich & Associates, 154 West Hubbard, Suite 504, Chicago, Illinois 60610, USA.

MATJASKO Jane, b. 22 Nov. 1942, Pennsylvania, USA. Physician. m. Shao-Huang Chiu, 8 July 1971, 1 son. *Education:* BA, Mercyhurst College, 1964; MD, Medical College of Pennsylvania, 1968. *Appointments:* Instructor, Department of Anesthesiology, 1972-73, Chief, Section of Neurological Anesthesia, 1972-, Assistant Professor, 1973-76, Associate Professor, 1976-, Associate Clinical Professor, Department of Surgery, 1984-, Acting Chairman, Department of Anesthesia, 1986-, University of Maryland, Baltimore. *Publications:* Controversies in Neuroanesthesia & Neurosurgery; Anesthesia and Neurosurgery; Neurologic Emergencies Recognition and Management chapter on Applied cardio-respiratory physiology; Systemic Effects of Head Trauma, in Handbook of Neuroanesthesia. *Memberships:* Refresher Course Committee, Self-Evaluation Examination Committee, Refresher Course Lecturer, American Society of Anesthesiologists; Association of University Anesthetists; Examiner, American Board of Anesthesiology; Society of Neurosurgical Anesthesia and Neurologic Supportive Care (President 1982-84); Society of Academic Anesthesia Chairmen. *Honours:* Alpha Omega Alpha, 1968; Prizes for Excellence in Medicine and Surgery, Medical College of Pennsylvania, 1968; Outstanding Alumni AWard, Golden Anniversary Year, Mercyhurst College, 1976. *Address:* Department of Anesthesiology, University of Maryland, 22 South Greene Street, Baltimore, MD 21201, USA.

MATLHARE Nkele Sarah, b. 31 Oct. 1941, Soweto, Johannesburg, South Africa. Lecturer; Associate Editor.

m. Dr M A C Matlhare, 8 Dec. 1967. 1 son. *Education:* University, 1981-84; Post University Degree, 1985-89. *Appointments:* Registered Nurse and Midwife, Baragwanath Hospital, 1965-69; Nursing Sister, Husband's Medical Practice, 1969-80; Managing Director, Salon Four Queens (self owned), 1986-89; Lecturer in Paediatrics School of Nursing, Kanye Hospital, Botswana, recently. *Creative works:* Compiled handbook for Women's Missionary Society African Methodist Episcopal Church; Translated WMS Constitution into different African Languages. *Memberships:* National President, Women's Missionary Society of the African Methodist Episcopal Church, South Africa & Namibia, 1979-84; Director of Overseas work in AME Church, 1984-87; Associate Editor, Missionary Magazine, Women's Missionary Society AME Church. *Honours:* Public Speech Award, International Toastmistress Clubs, 1980; Episcopal President's Award, New Orleans, USA, 1980; AME, Women of Distinction Award for Social Services and Religious Affairs, 1983; Episcopal Presidents Award for consecrated service, 1983; AME Merit Award for Consecrated Missionary Service, 1987. *Hobbies:* Reading; Entertaining; Aerobics; Tennis. *Address:* P O Box 222, Jwaneng, Botswana, Southern Africa.

MATSUI Dorothy Nobuko, b. 9 Jan. 1954, Hawaii, USA. Educator. *Education:* BEd., 1979, MEd., 1986, University of Alaska. *Appointments:* Clerical Assistant, University of Hawaii, 1974-76; Passenger Service Agent, Japan Air Lines, Anchorage, 1980; Bilingual Tutor, Anchorage School District, 1980; Anchorage School District Educator, 1980-. *Memberships:* NEA; Alaska Education Association; National Association for Female Executives; Smithsonian National Associate Programme. *Hobbies:* Reading; Volleyball; Baseball; Basketball; Downhill Skiing; Music. *Address:* 2271 Belmont Drive, Anchorage, AK 99517, USA.

MATSUMOTO Chiyoe, b. 1 Jan. 1920, Nara, Japan. Professor Emeritus; Author. m. Masakatsu Gunji, 4 Apr. 1970. *Education:* Teacher's Certificate. *Appointments:* Lecturer, 1952, Professor 1963-70, Tokyo University of Education; Professor 1971-85, Professor Emeritus, 1985-, Ochanomizu University. *Publications:* The Search for Beauty of Dance; A Complete Guidebook to Dance Learning; Dance Expression; Films: Dance Research - Problem Situation & Problem Solving, 1, 2, & 3. *Memberships:* Japan Associatiron of Physical Education for Women, President; International Association of Physical Education & Sports for Girls & Women, Vice President; Japanese Society for Dance Research, Vice President. *Honours:* Letter of Thanks from Minister of Education, 1980. *Hobbies:* Travol; Composing Waka; Theatre; Art. *Address:* 2-4-8- 1108 Otsuka, Bunkyo-ku, Tokyo 112, Japan.

MATSUNAGA Alicia Catherine Orloff, b. 25 May 1937, Livermore Valley, California, USA. Buddhist Theologian. m. Daigan Lee Matsunaga, 14 Apr. 1965. *Education:* AB, University of California, Davis, 1958; MA, University of Redland, 1960; Graduate study, Otani University, Kyoto, Japan, 1962-64; PhD, Claremont Graduate School, 1964. *Appointments:* Professor of Oriental Languages, University of California Los Angeles (UCLA), 1965-76; Editor, Directory of Buddhist Books, 1976-87; Director, Eikyoji Institute of Buddhist Studies, Japan, 1988-. *Publications include:* Author: Buddhist Philosophy & Assimilation, book, 1969 (award); Yuki: Temple Dog, 1987. Co- author: Buddhist Concept of Hell, 1972, Foundation of Japanese Buddhism, 3 volumes, 1972, 74, 76. Co-translator, various books; Contributor, Monumenta Nipponica. *Membership:* Sapporo Director, Buddhist Books International. *Honour:* Cultural award, Japanese National Broadcasting Company, 1970. *Hobbies:* Dogs; Computers. *Address:* Eikyoji Institute of Buddhist Studies, Tadoshi, Fukagawa, Hokkaido, Japan 074-01.

MATTEUCCI Sherry Jean Scheel, b. 17 Aug. 1947, Columbus, Montana, USA. Attorney. 2 sons. *Education:* Graduated with honours, University of Montana School of Law, 1979; Admitted State Bar of Montana.

Appointments: Clerk, Datsopoulos, McDonald & Lind, Missoula, pre-1979; Comment Editor, Montana Law Review, pre-1979; Associate, 1979-85, Partner, 1985-, Crowley, Haughey, Hanson, Toole & Dietrich law firm. *Memberships:* Yellowstone County Bar Association (President 1987-88); Judicial Polling Committee, State Bar of Montana (Chairman 1984-87); Committee on Evaluation of Judicial Performance, Judicial Performance Committee, State Bar of Montana; Women's Law Section, State Bar of Montana (Chairman 1985); Billings City/County Library Board (County Representative 1982-88); Board of Visitors, University of Montana School of Law; Secretary/Treasurer, State Bar of Montana; Former Chairman, Former Director, Billings Unitarian Universalist Fellowship; Legislative Affairs Committee, Leadership Billings Committee, Chamber of Commerce; Montana Association for Female Executives; Chairman, Billings Community Cable Corporation; Montana Lawyers for Peace; Big Brothers and Sisters (Director 1982-84); Allocations Panel, United Way. *Honours:* Outstanding Young Women in America, 1983. *Hobbies:* Golf; Racquetball; Politics; Reading; Music. *Address:* 500 Transwestern Plaza II, 490 North 31st Street, PO Box 2529, Billings, MT 59103, USA.

MATTHEWS Carol Joyce, b. 8 Nov. 1942, Vancouver, British Columbia, Canada. Associate Dean of Instruction; Registered Social Worker. m. Michael Matthews, 6 Nov. 1965. 1 daughter. *Education:* BA, English 1984, MA, English 1987, University of Victoria; RSW, BC Assoc of Social Workers, 1973. *Appointments:* Counsellor, Forward House, Montreal, 1965-70; Social Worker, Nanaimo Hospital, 1972-77; Executive Director, Nanaimo Family Life Association, 1977-82; Sessional Instructor 1982-88, Associate Dean of Instruction 1988-, Malaspina College, University of Victoria. *Publications:* Saturday's Cook, with S Knowles TV show; Matrix: The Story of Women in Dialogue, Editor with P Keays; Contributions to professional magazines. *Memberships:* Director-Social Planning & Research Council of British Columbia, 1988-; Director, Nanaimo Women's Resources Society, 1988-89; Executive, BC Assoc of Social Workers, 1985-87; Executive, BC Council for the Family, 1979-82; Executive, CVI Community Music School, 1983-85; Executive, Nanaimo Community Employment Advisory Society, 1982-86. *Honours:* BC Year of the Child and the Family Achivement Award, 1979; University of Victoria President's Award, 1984; University of Victoria Fellowship for Graduate Study, 1984; Social Science & Humanities Research Council of Canada Special MA Scholarship, 1985. *Hobbies:* Women's studies; Literature of old age; Community development; Music. *Address:* 730 Brechin Road, Nanaimo, British Columbia, Canada V9S 2X2.

MATTHEWS Judith Ann, b. 20 Jan. 1952. Lecturer; Open University Tutor. *Education:* BA, University of Leicester; PGCE, University of Bristol; PhD, University of Sheffield. *Appointments:* Assistant Teacher of Geography, Ashton Park School, Bristol, 1974-76; Lecturer in Geography, College of St Paul & St Mary, Cheltenham, 1981-82; Lecturer in Geography & Social Science, Director of Research, Rolle College, Exmouth, 1982-. *Memberships:* Institute of British Geographers; Committee Member, Social Geography Study Group, 1981-85; Planning & Geography Study Group, 1985-. *Hobbies:* Singing; Swimming; Business and Professional Women's Federation. *Address:* Plymouth Polytechnic, Rolle Campus, Rolle Road, Exmouth, EX8 2AT, England.

MATTHEWS Patricia Anne, b. 1 July 1927, San Fernando, California, USA. Writer. m. (1) Marvin Owen Brisco, Dec. 1946, div. 1961, 2 sons, (2) Clayton Hartly Matthews, Nov. 1971. *Education:* Pasadena Junior College; California State University, Los Angeles. *Appointments:* Various positions to Office Manager for Associated Students, California State University, Los Angeles, 1959-77; Freelance Writer, as P.A.Brisco, Patty Brisco, Laura Wylie and Patricia Matthews. *Publications include:* 20 historical romances, most recently Gambler in Love, 1985, Tame the Restless Heart, 1986, Enchanted, 1987, Thursday and the Lady, 1987, The Dreaming Tree, 1989, Sapphire, 1989; Juvenile books, Gothics, suspense, fantasy and occult fiction; Love's Many Faces, poetry, 1979; Poetry in The Oregonian, The American Bard, Ladies Home Journal, Statement Magazine, Cosmopolitan, Ellery Queen's Mystery Magazine; Short stories in Escapade Annual, 1960, Alfred Hitchcock's Anthology, 1980, Microcosmic Tales - 100 Wondrous Science Fiction Short Stories, 198l; The Death of Love, 1990; Short stories - Magazine of Fantasy & Science Fiction, 1989, Ellery Queen's Mystery Magazine, 1990, Alfred Hitchcocks Mystery Magazine, Mike Shayne Mystery Magazine; Miniature Mysteries - 100 Malicious Little Mystery Stories, 1982; Romania is a Good Choice for Health Spa Visit, article, 1986; Romantic Romania, article, 1986. *Memberships:* Mystery Writers of America; Romance Writers of America, Novelists' Ink. *Honours:* Porgie Awards, West Coast Review of Books: Silver Medal for The Night Visitor (occult), 1979; Silver Medal for Empire, 1983; Bronze Medal for Flames of Glory (historical romance), 1983; Team Writing Award (with Clayton Matthews), Romantic Times, 1983; Reviewers Choice Awards for Best Historical Gothic, Enchanted, 1986-87. *Hobbies:* Reading; Playing the piano; Songwriting; Singing; Guitar; Theatre; Painting; Swimming; Tai Chi Chuan.

MATTHEWS Wanda Miller, b. 15 Sept. 1930, Barry, Illinois, USA. Artist-Printmaker. m. Eugene Edward Matthews, 14 Sept. 1952, 2 sons. *Education:* BFA, Bradley University, Peoria, Illinois, 1952; MFA, University of Iowa, Iowa City, 1957. *Career:* Special Services Artist, US Army, Fort Riley, Kansas, 1954-55; Graduate Research Assistant in Printmaking, University of Iowa, Iowa City, 1956-57; Self-employed Artist with own studio and press, Boulder, Colorado, since 1961; Solo exhibitions at various venues including: Lehigh University, Bethlehem, Pennsylvania, 1973; American Center Gallery, Belgrade, Yugoslavia, 1982; Oxford Gallery, Oxford, England, 1982; Jane Haslem Gallery, Washington DC, 1982 & 1990; UMC Gallery, University of Colorado, Boulder, 1985; Group exhibitions: International Print Biennales, Bradford, England, 1970, 1979; International Graphic Art Exhibition, Ljubljana, Yugoslavia, 1975; International Print Biennales, Cracow, Poland, 1976, 1978, 1980, 1984, and 1986; International Print Exhibition, Taipei, Taiwan, Republic of China, 1988; C.S.P. Exchange Show, Brandts Klaedefabrik Museum, Odense, Denmark, 1989. *Creative works include:* Prints in many collections including Library of Congress, Washington DC, Philadelphia Museum of Art, Boston Public Library, Portland Art Museum, Oregon, Los Angeles County Museum of Art, Bytow National Museum, Bytow, Poland. *Memberships:* Society of American Graphic Artists, New York City; California Society of Printmakers. *Honours:* Grants in Graphic Arts, Tiffany Foundation, New York City, 1957, 1958; B.Spruance Prize, National Print Exhibition, The Print Club, Philadelphia, 1971; Purchase Award, Society of American Graphic Artists National Exhibition, New York, 1979; Drabkin Award, American Color Print Society, Philadelphia, 1981; L.Sawyer Memorial Award, National Association of Women Artists Exhibitiion, New York City, 1986. *Address:* 3066 7th Street, Boulder, CO 80304, USA.

MATTOON Sara (Sally) Halsey, b. 8 July 1947, Bronxville, New York, USA. Businesswoman. *Education:* BS, Education & Sciences, Southern Connecticut State College, 1969; MA, Education & Humanistic Psychology, California State University, Chico, 1976. *Appointments:* Teacher, San Diego School District 1969-72, Montgomery Creek 1972-73, California; Founder, teacher, Director, Chico Youth Development Center, 1973- 80; President, Executive Excellence, La Jolla, California & Weston, Connecticut (business & professional communications consultancy, 1980-. Teacher, facilitator, classes in business, stress reduction, various establishments & events. *Creative work includes:* 3 Books, publication pending, business, self help, fiction. *Memberships:* President, American Association of Professionals Practising Transcendental Meditation, San Diego Chapter; Greater San Diego Chamber of Commerce; Founding member, MIT

Enterprise Forum, San Diego; Board of Governors, World Plan Executive Council (WPEC). *Honours:* Information & Inspiration Award, WPEC, 1985; Guest lecturer, various colleges & universities; Master of Ceremonies, various major business events. *Hobbies:* World peace projects; Stress reduction; Volunteer counselling, substance abuse. *Address:* Executive Excellence, 7555 Miramar Avenue, La Jolla, California 92037, USA.

MATTSON Laura Ann, b. 16 Jan. 1966, Middleboro, USA. Graduate Student. *Education:* BA, English, Spanish, Philosophy, summa cum laude, Salve Regina College, 1987; Currently studying for PhD in Politics, Brandeis University. *Appointments:* Teaching Assistant, Philosophy, Salve Regina College, 1986-87; Technical Services Assistant, Spanish Civil War Collection, brandeis Library, 1987-88. *Honours:* Trinity Scholarship, 1985-86; Mellon Fellowship, 1987-1992; Department Awards, Salve Regina College, 1987. *Hobbies:* Ragtime Piano; Portrait Painting; Sketching; Tennis; Reading. *Address:* 345 Sandwich St., Plymouth, MA 02360, USA.

MAUGHAN Anne Margery, b. Darlington, Co. Durham, England. Company Director; Writer. *Education:* Queen Ethelburga's School, Harrogate, Yorkshire. *Publications:* Monmouth Harry, 1956; Young Pitt, 1974; The King's Malady, 1978. *Hobbies:* Exploration of castles, country houses and cathedrals; Cricket. *Address:* 2 Ryton Square, Sunderland, Tyne and Wear SR2 7UF, England.

MAUGHAN Joyce Bowen, b. 26 June 1928, Rupert, Idaho, USA. Psychologist; Educator; Writer; Sculptor. m. Dean L. Maughan, 4 Nov. 1949 (div.), 1 son, 5 daughters. *Education:* BS, University of Idaho, 1958; MA, MCounselling, Arizona State University, 1974. *Appointments:* Teacher, Elementary Schools, Spokane, Washington, 1958-64; Columnist, Thoughts in Passing, Sun Valley Newspaper, California, 1968-69; Sculptor, portrait busts, 1969-; Instructor, Maricopa County Community College, 1973-88; Coordinator/ Psychologist, Kyrene School District, Tempe, Arizona, 1975-81; Private Practice in Psychology, 1981-88. *Publications:* Talks for Tots, Vol. I, 1964, Vol. II, 1967; Talk Themes for Sub-Teens, 1964; Stories You'll Want to Remember, 1969; Stories That Never Grow Old, 1965; Unicornucopia - Guidebook for Gifted and Talented (co-author), 1977. *Memberships:* Arizona Personnel Guidance Association; American Personnel Guidance Association; National League of American Pen Women (President 1975-76); Council for Exceptional Children; Association for the Gifted, California; Association for the Gifted, Arizona; International Platform Association. *Address:* 735 E 3rd Street, Mesa, AZ 85203, USA.

MAUGHAN Sharon Patricia, b. Liverpool, England. Actress. m. Trevor Eve, 1 Mar. 1980, 1 son, 1 daughter. *Education:* Diploma, Royal Academy of Dramatic Art. *Appointments:* Appearances in Hamlet as Ophelia, 1972; in TV production, Shabby Tiger, 1973, Habeas Corpus, The Main Chance, 1975, Huggy Bear, 1978, Filvmena, 1978, Plenty, 1978, The Enigma Files, 1979, Keats, 1980, The Flametrees of Thika, 1982, Dombey & Son, 1983- 85, By the Sword Divided, 1983-85. *Hobbies:* Sports; Reading; Sewing; Talking to Friends & Family. *Address:* London, England.

MAULE Annabel, b. 8 Sept. 1922, London, England. Actress; Play Director; Theatre Manager. *Education:* Lycee de Londres, London, England. *Appointments:* Debut on London Stage, Winter Garden Theatre, 1934; numerous appearances before enlisting in the WRNS & serving in England & Germany; returned to acting profession in 1946; First appeared in theatre created by her parents, Kenya, 1952; Worked in Nairobi, 1962-64; Stage, Radio & TV Roles in England, returned to Kenya, 1968; Took over theatre after parents' retirement, Managing Director, 1971-79, The Donovan Maule Theatre. *Honours:* MBE, 1975. *Hobbies:* Work. *Address:* PO Box 42333, Nairobi, Kenya, East Africa.

MAVRODIN Alice, b. 4 Nov. 1941, Bucharest, Romania. Musicologist. *Education:* Bucharest Music Academy, 1960-65; Courses of musical analysis with Igor Matkevitch, St Cezaire, France. *Appointments:* Music Editor, Romanian Radio, Bucharest, 1965-; Served intermittently as musicological assistant to Igor Markevitch in the preparation of his encyclopaedic edition of Beethoven Symphonies, 1969-80. *Creative works:* Publications: Monographs on G Verdi, 1970 and J Ph Rameau, 1974; Articles to professional journals. Over 250 broadcasts on Romanian composers; music history; art of conducting. *Membership:* Romanian Union of Composers and Musicologists, 1977-. *Hobby:* Philately. *Address:* Romanian Radiotelevision, Calea Dorobantilor 191, 79757 Bucharest, Romania.

MAXWELL Alice Stubing, b. 2 Nov. 1924, New York, USA. Writer; Appraiser. m. Robert W., 8 Sept. 1945, 2 sons, 1 daughter. *Education:* BA, Barnard College, 1945. *Appointments:* Editorial Assistant, New York Times, 1943-46; Writer Stringer, Associated Press, Asia, 1950-53; TV Moderator, World Affairs Council, 1955-57; Columnist Advisor, 1967-1974; Freelance Writer. *Publications:* Articles for Holiday, Travel, American Weekly, Mclean's, Atlantic Monthly Magazines; Books: Asia Revisted, 1953; Virago, Story of Anne Newport Royall, 1985. *Memberships:* Asia Society; National Decorative Arts Trust, Board Member, 1968-82; American Society of Appraisers, Senior Associate, 1978-; New Jersey & National Federation of Republican Women, PR Officer. *Honours:* New Jersey Institute of Technology Author's Citation, 1987. *Hobbies:* Books; Stamps; Netsukes; Chinese Porcelains. *Address:* 5253 SE Sea Island Way, Stuart, FL 34997, USA.

MAXWELL Judith, b. 21 July 1943, Kingston, Ontario, Canada. Chairman, Economic Council of Canada. m. Anthony Maxwell, 8 May 1970, 1 son, 1 daughter. *Education:* BCom, Dalhousie University, Halifax, Nova Scotia, 1963; Postgraduate Studies, London School of Economics, England, 1965-66. *Appointments:* Researcher, Combines Investigation Branch, Cons. & Corp. Affairs, Ottawa, 1963-65; Economics Writer, Member of Editorial Board, Financial Times of Canada, Montreal, 1966-72; Director, Policy Studies, C D Howe Institute, Montreal, 1972-80; Consultant, Esso Europe Inc., London, England, 1980-82; Consultant, Economist, Coopers & Lybrand, Montreal, 1982-85; Chairman, Economic Council of Canada, 1985-. *Publications:* 7 issues of the C D Howe Institute's Policy Review & Outlook; Economic Realities of Contemporary Confederation, with C Pestieau; Partnership for Growth : Corporate University Education in Canada, with S Currio. *Memberships:* Member, Ontario Premier's Council, 1988; Member New Foundland and Labrador Science and Technology Advisory Council, 1988; Director Institute for Research on Public Policy, 1987-88; Director, Canadian Foundation for Economic Education, 1985-88; President, Canadian Association for Business Economics, 1976-77; President, Montreal Economics Association, 1975-76. *Address:* PO Box 527, Ottawa, Ontario, Canada K1P 5V6.

MAXWELL Katherine Gant, b. 27 Nov. 1931, El Paso, USA. Author; Poet; School Psychologist. m. Dr Fowden G Maxwell, 14 July 1955. 2 sons, 1 daughter. *Education:* BS, Psychology, Abilene Christian University, 1955; MS, Sociology, 1962; PhD, Educational Psychology, 1974, Mississippi State University. *Appointments:* College teaching assistantships, Elementary Education Department, Mississippi State University, 1968-72; Administered psychological tests, 1972-77; School Psychologist, Dixie Co, Florida, 1977-79. *Publications:* Book: What Makes Bosses Tick; 8 poems published, most recently The Little Angel Who Came to Earth. *Memberships:* 1st Vice President, 1985; 2nd vice president, 1986, Secretary, 1987; President, 1988-89, Extension Service Club; Newsletter Chairman 1985, College Station Branch, American Association of University Women; OPAS Sponsor; Programme Chairman, Opas Gala, 1987; Yearbook Chairman, 1988-89, OPAS Guild; Yearbook Chairman, 1987, Bryan/

College Station Business and Professional Women's Club; Treasurer, 1987-89, Humana Hospital Auxiliary; Secretary- Treasurer, 1988-89, Braxos Unit, American Cancer Society; 3rd Vice president, 1988-89, Tex. A&M Social Club; President, 1988-89, Campus Study Club; Corresponding Secretary, 1988-89, Friends of the Association of the Symphony Orchestra. *Honours:* Phi Delta Kappa, 1975-; Associate Member, American Pen Women. *Hobbies:* Playing organ; Interior decorating; Music. *Address:* POBox 10027, College State, Texas 77842, USA.

MAXWELL Marina Ama Omowale, b. 10 Nov. 1934, Trinidad, West Indies. Writer; Lecturer; TV Producer. m. John William Maxwell, 15 Aug. 1959, 1 daughter. *Education:* BA; MSc. *Appointments Include:* Lecturer, various High Schools, and Colleges, 1954-64; Teacher, London, England, 1966-69; College of Arts & Science & Technology, Jamaica, 1973-79; Scriptwriter, Ministry of Education Schools Broadcasting Series; Head of Department, Cipriani Labour College, Trinidad, 1976-; Video Producer, ETV/ITV Consultant, WALCO/ OMNAMEDIA, Trinidad, 1983-. *Publications:* Plays; Articles; Books; Novel, Chopstix in Mauby. *Memberships:* Founder, Yard Theatre, Jamaica; Founder, Writers Union of Trinidad & Tobago. *Honours:* Recipient, various honours and awards. *Hobbies:* Reading; Swimming; Yoga. *Address:* 4 Plum Avenue, Santa Rosa Heights, Arima, Trinidad, West Indies.

MAXWELL Mary Delene Brownlee, b. 29 Aug. 1910, St Louis, Missouri, USA. Marriage & Divorce Consultant. m. Raymond J. Maxwell, 4 Apr. 1933, 1 daughter. *Education:* AB, University of Illinois, 1934; MS, Academy of Social Workers, St Louis University, 1951; Postgraduate study, various universities. *Appointments:* Counsellor, St Louis Children Count, 1940-43; Child Welfare Worker, Douglas County Welfare, Omaha, Nebraska, 1943-65; Director, District Court Conciliation Court, 1965-80; Private practice, Dispute Resolution Inc, 1980-. *Publications:* Pamphlets: Parents Are Forever; Children of Divorce. *Memberships include:* Board 1966-75, Legal Aid Society, Omaha; Various offices, Omaha Association for Retarded Children; American Association of University Women; National Association of Social Workers; American Academy of Certified Social Workers. *Honours:* National Honour Society, 1928; Alpha Kappa Delta, 1934. *Hobbies:* Republican; Episcopalian; Travel; Photography; Drama; Music; History. *Address:* 5511 Blondo, Omaha, Nebraska 68104, USA.

MAXWELL Mary Winifred, b. 14 July 1922, St Helens, Tasmania. Artist. *Education:* Diploma of Fine Art; Diploma of Commercial Art; East Sydney Technical College, 1946; Goldsmith College, London, 1949; etc. *Appointments:* Launceston Technical College, 1953-58; Taroona High School, Hobart, 1959-62; School of Art, Hobart, 1962-66; Teachers College, Hobart, 1966-71; Huonville High School, 1972-78. *Publications:* One Man Exhibitions at Lloyd Jones Gallery, 1965, Franklin House Gallery, Launceston, 1966, Don Camillo Gallery, 1970, 1971, Salamanca Place Gallery, 1972; Saddlers Court Gallery, 1976; Art Centre Gallery, 1980. *Memberships:* Tasmanian Group of Painters, 1954-65; Secretary, Contemporary Art Society of Tasmania. *Hobbies:* Paper Making; Travel; Gardening; Spinning; Tapestry. *Address:* 10 Red Knights Road, Sandy Bay 7005, Tasmania, Australia.

MAXWELL Patricia Anne, (Pen Name: Jennifer Blake) b. 9 Mar. 1942, Winn Parish, Louisiana, USA. Writer. m. 1 Aug. 1957, 2 sons, 2 daughters. *Education:* GED Diploma, 1963. *Appoinment:* Writer in Residence, Northeast Louisiana University, 1983. *Publications:* As Patricia Maxwell: Secret of Mirror House, 1970; Stranger at Plantation Inn, 1971; The Bewitching Grace, 1974; Court of the Thorn Tree, 1974; Dark Masquerade, 1974; Bride of a Stranger, 1974; Notorious Angel, 977; Sweet Piracy, 1978; Night of the Candles, 1978; As Elizabeth Trehearne: Storm at Midnight, 1973; As Patricia Ponder: Haven of Fear, 1977; Murder for Charity, 1977; As Maxine Patrick: The Abducted Heart,

1978; Bayou Bride, 1979; Snowbound Heart, 1979; Love at Sea, 1980; Captive Kisses, 1980; April of Enchantment, 1981; As Jennifer Blake: Love's wild Desire, 1977; Tender Betrayal, 1979; The Storm and the Splendor, 1979; Golden Fancy, 1980; Embrace & Conquer, 1981; Royal Seduction, 1983; Surrender in Moonlight, 1984; Midnight Waltz, 1985; Fierce Eden, 1985; Royal Passion, 1986; Prisoner of Desire, 1986; Southern Rapture, 1987; Louisiana Dawn, 1987; Perfume of Paradise, 1988. *Memberships:* North Louisiana Branch, American League of American Penwomen; Romance Writers of America; Delta Kappa Gamma. *Honours:* Historical Romance Author of the Year, 1985; Best Historical Romance with a Southern Background, 1985, 1987; Golden Treasure Award, Romance Writers of America, 1987. *Hobbies:* Travel; Gardening; Antiques; Historical Preservation. *Address:* Route 1, Box 133, Ouitman, LA 71268, USA.

MAY Phyllis Jean Irvine Kent, b. 31 May 1932, Flint, Michigan, USA. Accountant. m. (1)Gordon Kent Jr, 10 Dec. 1955. 3 2ons. (2) John W May, 24 Apr. 1971. *Education:* Teachers Certificate, Mott Junior College, 1955; Student, Dorsey School of Business, 1957; Accounting, International Correspondence School, 1959; Seminar Tax & Accounting and Micromatics, New York University, 1963; MBA, Michigan University, 1970; National Tax Institute, 1978. *Appointments include:* Office Manager, Commercial Construction Co, 1962-68; Business Manager, New and Used Car Dealership, Controller for 6 Corporation (Cemeteries) in 4 counties, 1970-75; Fiscal Director, Rubicon Odyssey, Drug Rehabilitation non-profit, 1976-; Academic Consultant, Detroit Institute of Commerce, 1981. *Creative works:* Written a manual on Practical Accounting Procedures, 1981. *Memberships include:* Volunteer Federation of the Blind, 1974-76; Past Board Member, MacKenzie Area Prevention Project; Director; Professional Female Executive Network, 1981; American Business Women's Association, Treasurer 1981, Secretary 1982, Vice President 1983; President of Board, Accounting Designs, 1982; Tau Alpha Gamma National Sorority, 1983; Citizens Advisory Board, Northville Regional Psychiatric Hospital, 1987-88. *Honours include:* Excellent Performance and High Achievement Rubicon Odyssey, 1981; Woman of the Year, 1982; Meritorious Services Rendered on behalf of the Genesee County Probate Court Juvenile Division, 1974-76. *Hobbies:* Semi classical Music (Piano); Bowling; Dance (ballet and tap). *Address:* 12050 Barlow, Detroit, MI 48205, USA.

MAY, Gita, b. 16 Sept. 1929, Brussels, Belgium. Professor. m. Irving May, 21 Dec. 1947. *Education:* BA, Hunter College, 1953; MA 1954, PhD, 1957, Columbia University. *Appointments:* Assistant Professor, 1958-61, Associate Professor, 1961-68, Professor, 1968-, Chairman, 1983-, French, Columbia University. *Publications:* Diderot et Baudelaire, 1957; De J.J. Rousseau a Madame Roland, 1964; Madame Roland and the Age of Revolution, 1970; Stendhal and the Age of Napoleon, 1977; numerous essays, articles & book reviews. *Memberships:* Modern Language Association of America, Executive Council, 1980-83; Northeast American Society for 18th Century Studies, President, 1981-82; American Society for 18y Century Studies, President, 1985-86; Societe Francaise d'Etude du 18e Siecle. *Honours:* Guggenheim Fellowship, 1964; Fulbright Grant, 1965; NEH Senior Fellowship, 1971; many other honours and awards. *Hobbies:* Phtography; Painting; Travel. *Address:* 404 West 116th Street, New York, NY 10027, USA.

MAYER Adele, b. 21 Feb. 1942, Glenridge, New Jersey, USA. Psychotherapist. widowed, 1 son. *Education:* High School Diploma, Ecole Internationale, Geneva, Switzerland, 1960; BA, University of Chicago, 1964; MC, Arizona State University, 1978; PhD, Columbia Pacific University, 1983. *Appointments:* Director of Outpatients, PreHab of Arizona, 1978-83; Programme Director, Phoenix Center Against Sexual Assault, 1983-84; Private Practice in Psychotherapy, Valley E. Couseling, Mesa, Arizona, 1984-. *Publications:* Books: Incest, 1983; Sexual Abuse, 1985; Sex

Offenders, 1988; Continuing Education course on sex abuse. *Memberships:* Former Chair, Sexual Abuse Subcommittee, Maricopa County Child Abuse Council; American Association of Counseling and Development; American Association of Artist-Therapists; Member, Clinical Associate, American Board of Medical Psychotherapists. *Hobbies:* Fine and commercial arts; Travel. *Address:* 7432 E. Century Drive, Scottsdale, AZ 85253, USA.

MAYER Ann Elizabeth, b. 5 May 1945, Seguin, Texas, USA. Associate Professor of Legal Studies. *Education:* JD, University of Pennsylvania, 1975; Certificate in Islamic and Comparative Law, School of Oriental and African Studies, University of London, England, 1977; PhD, University of Michigan, USA, 1978. *Appointments:* Assistant Professor, 1977-82, Associate Professor of Legal Studies, 1982-, Department of Legal Studies, The Wharton School, University of Pennsylvania, Philadelphia. *Publications:* Articles including: Islamic Resurgence or New Prophethood, 1982; Editor, Property, Social Structure and Law in the Modern Middle East, 1985. *Memberships include:* American Bar Association; American Branch, International Law Association; American Research Center in Egypt; American Society for Political and Legal Philosophy; Middle East Studies Association of North America. *Honours:* National Defence Foreign Language Fellowships, 1973-75; Gowan Prize Fellowship, University of Pennsylvania Law School, 1975- 77; Fellowship, Society for Libyan Studies, 1978; Fellowship, American Research Center in Egypt, 1980; Fellowship, American Institute for Pakistan Studies, 1982; Phi Beta Kappa. *Hobbies:* Opera; Foreign travel; Skiing; Swimming; Writing. *Address:* Department of Legal Studies, The Wharton School, University of Pennsylvania, Philadelphia, PA 19104, USA.

MAYER Eve Reuss, b. 4 Feb. 1930, Berlin, Germany. Psychotherapist. m. Ferd S Mayer, 20 June 1951, deceased. 2 sons. *Education:* BA, Brooklyn College, 1949; MSW, University of Pennsylvania, 1951; Am Inst for Psychotherapy/Psychoanalysis, 1967; PhD, Columbia Pacific University, 1983. *Appointments:* Children's Counselling Center, New York City, 1951-53; Family Service of Lower East Side, New York City, 1955-58; Chief Psychiatric Social Worker, Brooklyn Community College, 1958-63; Private Priactice, New York City, 1963-68; Private Practice, Scottsdale, Arizona, 1968-; Faculty, Tulane University, 1984-87; Faculty, Metropolitan University of the Southwest, 1985-; Faculty, Pacific Western University, 1987-. *Publications:* Books: Let's Stay Lovers; A Handbook for Keeping Love Relationships Alive, 1981; Good Love: Dad Love, 1989. Papers: Use of Dreams in the Treatment of Schizophrenics; Early Deprivation in the Mother-Daughter Relationship: A Factor in the Development of the Narcissistic Personality; Marital Separation - Another Chance at Achieving Individuation; Some Dynamics of an Ongoing Couples Group; Treatment of the New Woman; Some Insights into the Treatment of Female Homosexuals; Some Insights into an All Women's Group; Touching in the Dark; Some Implications of Current Psychoanalytic Thinking as it Applies to Therapy with Women. *Memberships:* Council of Psychoanalytic Psychotherapists; Fellow and Diplomate, American Board of Medical Psychotherapists; American Group Psychotherapy Association; National Registry of Health Care Providers in Clinical Social Work; Board Certified Diplomate in Clinical Social Work; Fellow/Past President, Arizona Society for Clinical Social Work and Psychotherapy; National Association for Social Workers; Arizona State and National Women's Political Caucus; Arizona Representative to the National Fedceration of Societies for Clinical Social Work; Fellow, International Conference for the Advancement of Private practice in Social Work and Psychotherapy. *Honours:* Arizona Representative, British American Conference for Clinical Social Work, Oxford, England, 1979; Recognition of Service Award, International Conference for the Advancement of Private Practice in Social Work and Psychotherapy, 1986. *Hobbies:* Modern art;

Chamber music; Jazz. *Address:* 3337 N Miller Road, Suite No 106, Scottsdale, Arizona 85251, USA.

MAYER Gisela, b. 30 Oct. 1931, Germany. Manageress; Town Councillor. m. Curt Mayer, 28 Oct. 1955, 2 sons, 3 daughters. *Appointments:* Manageress, Law Firm, 1955-; Town Councillor. Honorary judge on administrative court, Stuttgart, Official expert for structures. *Memberships:* Land Womens Council, Baden-Wurttemberg; Law Committee, German Frauenring. *Honours:* Peter Haag Prize, 1980; Prize, Land of Baden-Wurttemberg, 1984; Foundress of Womens Lists, Federal Republic of Germany, 1979. *Hobbies:* Womens Politics. *Address:* Marktplatz 18, 7090 Ellwangen, Federal Republic of Germany.

MAYER Susan Martin, b. 25 Oct. 1931, Atlanta, USA. Artist; Educator. m. 9 Aug. 1953, 1 daughter. *Education:* BA, University of North Carolina, 1953; MA, Arizona State University,1966. *Appointments:* Artist in Residence, Norfolk, Virginia, 1966; Co-ordinator, Education, Huntington Art Gallery, University of Texas, 1971. *Creative Works:* Paintings in many private collections & public places including: The Museum; 5 Books, 10 articles, 12 musuem catalogues for children; Co-author, Texas, 1987. *Memberships:* National Art Education Association, Board; Texas Art Education Association, Board; American & Texas Associations of Museums. *Honours:* Museum Educator of the Year, Texas Art Education Association, 1986; Museum Educator of the Year, National Art Education Association, 1987. *Hobbies:* Painting; Writing. *Address:* Dept. of Art, University of Texas at Austin, Austin, TX 78712, USA.

MAYESKA Irena, b. Poland. Actress. *Education:* BA, Queens University, Kingston, Canada. *Appointments:* Has spent over 20 years in the theatrical profession in Great Britain & North America. *Hobbies:* Tennis; Sculpture; Bridge. *Address:* 53A Primrose Mansions, Prince of Wales Drive, London SW11 4EF, England.

MAYHAR Ardath Frances (Hurst), b. 20 Feb. 1930, Timpson, Texas, USA. Author; Instructor in Fiction. m. Joe Earl Mayhar, 7 June 1958, 2 sons, 2 stepsons. *Education:* Self-educated after secondary school. *Appointments:* Instructor in Short Fiction, Writer's Digest School; Lectures, workshops, private instruction. *Publications:* Novels: How the Gods Wove in Kyrannon, 1979, Paperback, 1982; Seekers of Shar-Nuhn, 1980, Paperback, 1982; Texas Gunsmoke (as Frank Cannon), 1988; Soul Singer of Tyrnos, 1981, Paperback, 1983; Warlook's Gift, 1982, Runes of the Lyre, 1982, Paperback, 1983; Lords of the Triple Moons, 1983, Paperback, 1984; Khi to Freedom, 1983; Golden Dream: A Fuzzy Odyssey, 1983; The Absolutely Perfect Horse, 1983, Paperbacks, 1983, 1987; Exile on Vlahil, 1984; The Saga of Grittel Sundotha, 1985; The World Ends in Hickory Hollow, 1985; Medicine Walk, 1986, Danish Edition, 1987; Carrots and Miggle, 1986; Feud at Sweetwater Creek (as Frank Cannon), 1987; Makra Chorla, 1987; BattleTech: The Sword and the Dagger, 1987; Trail of the Seahawks (with Ron Fortier), 1987; The Wall, Space & Time, 1987; A Place of Silver Silence, 1988; Bloody Texas Trail (as Frank Cannon), 1988; Monkey Station (with Ron Fortier), 1989; Numerous short stories including: Night of the Cougar, 1987; Narrative poetry and short verse; Journey to an Ending, South and West, (poetry chapbook), 1965; Articles and reviews. *Memberships:* Western Writers of America; Science Fiction Writers of America; MENSA. *Honours:* Prizewinner, Pineywoods Writers Conference Poetry Book Competition, 1965; Balrog Award for Poetry in the Fantasy Field, 1984; Finalist, Spur Award for Short Story, Western Writers of America, 1987; Numerous award lists. *Hobbies:* Reading; Natural history; Archaeology; Ancient history; Psychology; Computers. *Address:* PO Box 180, Chireno, TX 75937, USA.

MAYNARD Nancy Gray, b. 18 Apr. 1941, Middleboro, Massachusetts, USA. Marine Biologist. m. Conrad Dennis Gebelein, 22 Jan. 1969 (div, 1977), 1 daughter. *Education:* BS, Mary Washington College, 1963; MS, University of Miami, Florida, 1967; PhD, Rosenstiel School of Marine & Atmospheric Science, University of Miami, 1974. *Appointments include:* Research Assistant, various projects, 1963-76; Expert Witness, effects of oil on marine life, American Petroluem Institute, & Consultant, Bermuda Government, 1976; Environmental Studies Field Coordinator, US Bureau of Land Management, Alaska, 1976-78; Oil Spills Scientific Support Coordinator, Alaska 1978-80, Southeastern USA 1980-82; Fellow, Department of Commerce, Science & Technology, Washington DC, 1982-83; Policy Analyst, Office of Science & Technology Policy, 1982-83; Staff Director, Board on Ocean Science & Policy, National Academy of Sciences, 1983-85; National Research Council Resident Research Associate, Jet Propulsion Laboratory & Scripps Institution of Oceanography, California, 1985-87; Branch Head, Oceans & Ice, NASA Goddard Space Flight Centre, Maryland 1987-. *Publications include:* Numerous research articles, scientific journals. *Memberships:* Professional bodies including: American Association for Advancement of Science; American Polar Society; American Geophysical Union. *Honours:* Postdoctoral Fellow, Harvard University, 1975-76; Public Service Commendation, US Coast Guard, 1979; Various prestigious appointments, as above; Certificates of recognition. *Hobbies:* Skeet; Sailing; Languages; Skiing; Fishing. *Address:* NASA Goddard Space Flight Centre, Code 671, Oceans & Ice Branch, Greenbelt, Maryland 20771, USA.

MAYNARD Nancy Kathleen Brazier, b. 25 June 1910, Maidenhead, England. Author. m. Geoffrey Mansfield Maynard, 17 Sept. 1939, 1 daughter. *Publications:* This is My Street, 1962; Weep Not, My Wanton, 1964; The Bawdy Wind, 1965; Flesh and Blood, 1967; All Sauce for the Gander, 1968; The Wayward Flesh, 1969; Almost An Affair, 1969; A Fig for Virtue, 1970; Strumpet Voluntary, 1970; Rings for Her Fingers, 1971; When the Devil Drives, 1972; Leaf in the Wind, 1973; A Crumb for Every Sparrow, 1974; Red Roses Dying, 1974; If You Can't Catch, Don't Throw, 1976; A Grief Ago, 1976; Losers Weepers, 1977; Table 21, 1978; Not Quite Summer, 1980; The Last Dawn, 1981; One for the Stairs, 1982; Too Near the Sun, 1983; Springtime of Tear 1984; The Distance and the Dark, 1984; Silence and Tears, 1985; Big Girls Don't Cry, 1985; Love is a Green, Green Apple; And then the Rain Stopped; As Long as the Birds Still Sing. *Address:* Morven House, 5 Keble Road, Maidenhead, Berkshire SL6 6BB, England.

MAYNE Lucille S, b. 6 June 1924, USA. University Professor. divorced, 3 daughters. *Education:* BSc., University of Maryland, 1946; MBA, Ohio State University, 1949; PhD, Business Finance, Northwestern University, 1966. *Appointments:* Instructor, Utica College, Syracuse University, 1949-50; Lecturer, Roosevelt University, 1961-64; Various positions, Pennsylvania State University, 1965-70; Professor, 1971-, Dean, Graduate Studies, 1980-84, Case Western Reserve University. *Publications:* Articles in numerous journals and magazines. *Memberships:* American Finance Association; Financial Management Association, Board, 1982-83; Midwest Finance Association, 2nd Vice President 1988-; Beta Gamma Sigma; Phi Kappa Phi. *Address:* 3723 Normandy Road, Shaker Heights, OH 44120, USA.

MAYO Virginia, b. 30 Nov. 1920, St Louis, Missouri, USA. Actress. m. Edward Francis Michael O'Shea, 5 July 1947, 1 daughter. *Education:* The Alice Jones Wientge School of Dramatic Expression, St Louis, 1926-35. *Appointments:* Samuel Goldwyn Studio, 1943-48; Contract with Warner Bros Studio, 1948-58; Actress in 45 films with numerous starring roles; starred in numerous stage productions. *Creative Works:* Painting - numerous works have been sold. *Memberships:* Daughters of America Revolution, Missouri; Screen Actors Guild; Equity; AFTRA. *Honours:* Top Ten Box Office Award, 1952, 1953, 1954. *Hobby:* Painting in Oils. *Address:* Thousand Oaks, California, USA.

MAYROECKER Friederike, b. 20 Dec. 1924, Wien, Austria. Poet; Writer. *Education:* Teacher's Exam, 1946. *Appointments:* Teacher, Vienna, 1946-69; Freelance Writer, 1969-. *Publications:* First book 1956; Author, 50 books including: Poetry, novels, radio plays, childrens books, experimental prose texts; most recent: Winterglück; Magische Blatter II; Mein Herz mein Zimmer mein Name. *Memberships:* Österreichischer Kunstsenat; Kurie fur Wissenschaft und Kunst; Akademie der Kunste, Berlin; Deutsche Akademie fur Sprache und Dichtung; Internationales Kunstlergremium; Grazer Autorenversammlung. *Honours:* Horspielpreis der Kriegsblinden 1968; Östereichischer Wurdigungspreis, 1975; Preis der Stadt Wien, 976; George Trakl Preis, 1977; Groszer Österreichischer Staatspreis, 1982. *Hobbies:* Reading; Walking; Drawing; Nature; Arts. *Address:* Zentagasse 16/40, A 1050 Wien, Austria.

MAZIBUKA Niomb'Fikile, b. 22 Dec. 1951, South Africa. Company Director. 1 son. *Education:* BA, Social Work, Honours, University of Zululand; BA, Communications, University of South Africa; Diploma, Public Relations. *Appointments:* Social Worker, 1973-74; Community Development Officer, 1975-78; Programme Co-ordinator, 1979; Project Co-ordinator, Sociology Tutor, 1980-83; Director, Mzarno Child Guidance Clinic, 1983-86; Director, Home & Family Life Division. *Publications:* Manual on Community Development; articles in professional journals. *Honours:* South African Black Social Workers Association, National Secretary; Steering Committee on Welfare Policy; Founder Member, FOYSA. *Honours:* Recipient, many honours & awards. *Hobbies:* Reading; Travel; Theatre; Jazz. *Address:* AA 952 Umlazi Township, Natal, South Africa 4031.

MAZUR Dorothy E., b. 7 Apr. 1947, Fairbury, Nebraska, USA. Clinical Social Worker. m. David J. Mazur, 3 Nov. 1977, 2 daughters. *Education:* BS, Nebraska Wesleyan University, 1969; MSW, University of Kansas, 1973; Psychiatric Social Work Fellowship, Menninger Foundation, 1975; Diplomate of Clinical Social Work. *Appointments:* Clinical social worker: Family Service & Guidance Centre, 1972-75; Menninger Foundation, 1975-85; Psychiatric Consultation Services, 1985-. *Publications:* Article, A Starving Family: Interactional View of Anorexia Nervosa, in Bulletin of Menninger Clinic 1977, Women in Mental Health (ed. Howell & Bayes) 1981. *Memberships:* National Association of Social Work; National Association of Marriage & Family Therapy. *Hobbies:* Knitting; Needlepoint; Snow & water skiing; Reading; Swimming. *Address:* Psychiatric Consultation Services, 825 Parchment, Grand Rapids, Michigan 49546, USA.

MAZUR Gail Beckwith, b. 11 Oct. 1937, Cambridge, Massachusetts, USA. Writer; Teacher; Arts Administrator. m. Michael Mazur, 28 Dec. 1958. *Education:* BA, Smith College, 1959; MA, Lesley College, 1983. *Appointments:* Director, Blacksmith House Poetry Centre, 1973-; Writer-in-Residence, Emerson College, 1979-80; Visiting Lecturer, University of Massachusetts 1985, Wellesley College 1986; Visiting Associate Professor, University of Houston, 1988-89. *Publications:* Books of poems: Nightfire, 1978; Pose of Happiness. *Memberships:* New England Vice President 1988-, Poetry Society of America; Board 1983-, New England PEN; Co-Director 1983-, New England Writers for Survival. *Honours:* Creative Writing Award, National Endowment for Arts, 1978; Bread Loaf Fellowship, 1978; Gertrude B. Clayton Prize, Poetry Society of America, 1980. *Address:* 5 Walnut Avenue, Cambridge, Massachusetts 02140, USA.

MAZUR Suzan Christine, b. 1 Nov. 1947, Newark, New Jersey, USA. Journalist. *Education:* AAS, Apparel Design, Fashion Institute of Technology, New York City, 1973; BSEd, English, Bloomsburg University, Bloomsburg, Pennsylvania, 1969. *Career:* Freelance Writer specialising in foreign policy, science and technology, status of women, Middle East and Latin America affairs. *Publications:* Writing credits: The

Economist, The Connoisseur, Forbes, The New York Times, Omni, Geo, Solar Age, Science 84, Archaeology, Medical Herald, Gentlemen's Quarterly, Attenzione, Islands, Ambiance, Popular Mechanics. *Memberships:* Sponsor, Women's Foreign Policy Council; Chair, Benefit for Battered Women, Sponsor, National and New York State Coalitions against Domestic Violence, 1985; Press Coordinator for Special Events, Friends of Mario M Cuomo, 1986. *Honours:* Listed, Outstanding Young Women of America, 1982; Profiled, Women's Foreign Policy Council, 1987; Fellow, Bloomsburg University, 1987. *Address:* 40 Harrison Street, New York, NY 10013, USA.

MAZZAROPPI Loretta Lucrezia, b. New Jersey, USA. University Professor. m. Russell Clayton Thomas, 27 Aug. 1988. *Education:* BS, 1968; MBA, 1969; PhD, 1976. *Appointments:* Professor, business, Clinton Community College, 1969-73; Graduate Teaching Fellow, Louisiana State University, 1974-76; Professor, Management, Fairleigh Dickinson University, 1976-. *Publications:* Articles in professional journals. *Memberships:* Academy of Management; American Assocation of University Women; NAFE; US Association for Small Business/Entrepreneurship. *Honours:* Lambda Sigma Tau; Beta Gamma Sigma. *Hobbies:* Reading; Gardening; Bicycling. *Address:* 780 Morningside Drive, Millbrae, CA 94030, USA.

MCALEER Donna G, b. 24 Nov. 1948, Hartford, Connecticut, USA. Long Term Care Administration; Executive Director. m. A Gordon McAleer, 6 Dec. 1985. 2 stepsons, 2 stepdaughters. *Education:* BS, Skidmore College, 1979; MS, Hartford Graduate Center, 1982; Licensed Nursing Home Administrator, States of New York and Connecticut. *Appointments:* Admin Asst 1973-79, Admin Residency 1979-80, Hartford Hospital; Asst Administrator, Jefferson House, Div Hartford Hospital, 1980-84; Executive Director, Arden Hill Life Care Center, 1984-; Consultant Administrator, Mercy Community Hospital's Nursing Home, 1988-. *Memberships:* Board of Directors, Arden Hill Life Care Center; Board of Directors; Arden Hill Hospital; Board of Directors, Arden Hill Foundation; New York Assoc. of Homes & Services for Aging; American Assoc. of Homes for the Aging; Orange County Citizens Foundation; Goshen Historic Track. *Honours:* New York Association for Services for the Aging; Thomas Clarke Memorial Award for Young Administrator of the Year, 1988. *Hobbies:* Raising Gordon Setters; Skiing; Tennis. *Address:* Arden Hill Life Care Center, Harriman Drive, Goshen, NY 10924, USA.

MCALPINE Phyllis Jean, b. 29 Aug. 1941, Petrolia, Ontario, Canada. Professor. *Education:* BSc. Honours, University of Western Ontario, 1963; MA, University of Toronto, 1966; PhD, University of London, England, 1970. *Appointments:* University of Manitoba, & Children's Hospital of Winnipeg, Canada, 1972-. *Publications:* Numerous scientific articles. *Memberships:* Canadian College of Medical Geneticists, Board of Directors, 1984-88; Genetics Society of Canada, Secretary, 1981-84; American Society of Human Genetics; American Society for the Advancement of Science; Consultant to Howard Hughes Medical Institute Human Gene Mapping Library. *Honours:* Gold Medal, University of Western Ontario, 1966. *Hobby:* Performing Arts. *Address:* Dept. of Human Genetics, University of Manitoba, 770 Bannatyne Ave., Winnipeg, Canada R3E 0W3.

MCARTHUR Janet Ward, b. 25 June 1914, Bellingham, Washington, USA. Physician. *Education:* AB magna cum laude 1935, MS 1937, University of Washington; MA 1941, MD 1942, Northwestern University Medical School. *Appointments:* Instructor, Clinical Associate, Assistant Clinical Professor, Professor of Obstetrics & Gynaecology 1950-84, Professor Emerita 1984-, Harvard Medical School; Clinical Professor, Boston University School of Medicine, 1984-. *Publications:* Co-author, book, Functional Endocrinology from Birth Through Adolescence; Co-editor, book, Statistics in Endocrinology; Author or co-author, over 180 research papers, endocrinology, various professional journals. *Memberships include:* Diplomate, American Board of Internal Medicine; Fellow, American College of Physicians; Council, Endocrine Society; Massachusetts Medical Society; President, Pre- Journal Club; Aesculapian Club. *Honours:* Phi Beta Kappa, Sigma Xi, 1935; Alpha Omega Alpha, 1940; H. P. Walcott Fellow, Clinical Medicine, Harvard Medical School, 1945-47; Honorary ScD, Mount Holyoke College, 1962; Distinguished Alumnus, Northwestern University Medical School, 1980. *Hobbies:* Travel; Photography. *Address:* Sargent College of Allied Health Professions, Boston University, 36 Cummington Street, Boston, Massachusetts 02215, USA.

MCBETH Sara Lucile Grimes, b. 15 Sept. 1942, Rock Island, Illinois, USA. Caseworker. m. Jerry McBeth, 29 May 1967 (div. 1976), 1 son, 1 daughter. *Education:* Graduated, Hannibal-LaGrange, Missouri, 1964; Central Methodist College, Fayette, Missouri. *Appointments:* Teacher, various high schools, Missouri, 1964-74; Ewing Law Firm, tax seasons 1972-75; Caseworker, State of Missouri, 1975-. *Creative work:* Member: Nevada (Missouri) Theatre Association, 1972-75; Task Force to Make Nevada an All- Missouri Certified City, 1976. *Memberships:* Nevada President, American Association of University Women, & Benton School Parent Teacher Association; Offices, various honour societies. *Honours:* Member, Kappa Mu honorary mathematics society; Certificate, increase in membership while President, Benton School PTA. *Hobbies:* Drawing & painting; Breeding quail; Reading. *Address:* 119 State Fair Boulevard, Sedalia, Missouri 65301, USA.

MCBROOM LANDESS Marcia Leanne, b. 6 Aug. 1947, New York City, USA. Actress; Model; Social Activist. *Education:* BA, Hunter College, 1973; Graduate credits from NYU and New York Theological Seminary. *Appointments:* Starred in Beyond the Valley of the Dolls appeared in 5 other major films and numerous commercials; Organized and mounted The Rights of the Child art show for UNICEF, Lever House and the Federal Building; Coordinated week of cultural activities at the United Nations during Special Session on Africa, 1986, New York; Member, Board of Directors, New York Metropolitan Committee for UNICEF, United Nations Association-New York Chapter, Religious Education Association Rod Rodgers Dance Co; Founder, For our Children's Sake Foundation, Inc.; Community Board No. 6 in Manhattan, started the first human rights committee on a community board in the history of New York City; Created Breastfeeding poster which she donated to UNICEF. Poster distributed to fifteen countries; Member of Speakers Bureau of the US Committee for UNICEF, Member of historic goodwill delegation of 18 African American Women who toured Japan, 1989; Advisory Council for Central Amercia for La Leche League International; Board of Directors, Paul Robeson Family Medical Center of Harlem; Originator of the Apartheid Project for high school students. *Hobbies:* Collecting American Indian and African art; Russian icons; Netsukes. *Address:* 305 East 24th Street, New York City, NY 10010, USA.

MCBURNEY Annetta, b. Northern Ireland, UK. Consultant Psychologist. m. 1 daughter. *Education:* Academic Diploma in Education; MA; PhD. *Appointments:* Education Officer, Aden & South Arabia Federation; Assistant Professor, Faculty of Medicine, Division of Neurology; Assistant Professor, Psychology. *Publications:* Co-author, books: Neuropsychology of Learning Disorders; Child Neurology; Neurological & Ophthalmological Outcome of Low Birth Weight. Also: Various articles in learned journals. *Memberships:* British Psychological Society; Canadian University Service Overseas; Academic Women's Association; Fulham Psychological Foundation. *Address:* 35 Piccadilly, Suites 101-110, London W1V 9PB, England.

MCBURNEY Margot, b. Lethbridge, Canada. Chief Librarian. m. 4 Sept. 1954, 1 son, 1 daughter. *Education:*

Principia College; MSc., University of Illinois. *Appointments:* Reference Librarian, 1971-72, Serials Cataloguer, 1973-74, Head, Acq., 1974-77, Chief Librarian, 1977-, University of Alberta. *Memberships:* American Society of Info Science; Association of Reference Librarians, Director 1978-81; Canadian Association of Reference Librarians; American Library Association; Ontario Council of University Librarians, Secretary 1982-83. *Hobbies:* Dressage Riding; Tennis; Swimming; Skiing. *Address:* Landmark, 165 Ontario Street No 607, Kingston, Ontario K7L 2Y6, England.

MCCABE Sarah Frances, b. 28 Feb. 1913, Glasgow, Scotland. Criminologist. m. Edward McCabe, 12 Apr. 1942, 1 daughter. *Education:* MA, Classics, University of Glasgow, 1934; Diploma, Public & Social Administration, 1943; B.Litt, University of Oxford, 1964. *Appointments:* HM Inspector of Taxes, 1936-45; Research Assistant, Senior Research Officer, Criminological Research Centre, University of Oxford, 1951-81. *Publications:* Young men in Detention Centres, co-author, 1964; Three Studies on the English Jury, 1972-74; Crime & Insanity, co-author, 1973; Defining Crime 1978; Juvenile Justice in the UK, 1983; The Police, Public Order & Civil Liberties, co-author, 1988. *Memberships:* British Society of Criminology; Howard League; National Association for the Care & Resettlement of Offenders. *Honours:* Jane Stewart Bursary, 1930-34; Emeritus Fellowship, Leverhulme Trust, 1984- 86; Member, Parole Board for England & Wales, 1981-84. *Hobbies:* Gardening; Walking; Reading. *Address:* 1 Stoke Place, Old Headington, Oxford, OX3 9BX, England.

MCCAFFERY, Margo, b. 29 Sept. 1938, Corsicana, Texas, USA. Consultant, Nursing Care of Patients with Pain. m. John Richard Brewer, 19 July 1986, 1 daughter. *Education:* BS, Nursing, Baylor University, 1959; MS, Nursing, Vanderbilt University, 1961. *Appointments Include:* Various nursing positions, 1958-63; Assistant Professor, Pediatric Nursing, University of California, Los Angeles, 1965-70; Clinician, Unit Manager, Pain Management, Centinela Hospital Medical Centre, Inglewood, 1983- 84; Self-employed Consultant. *Publications:* Articles in professional journals including: American Journal of Nursing; Pediatric Nursing; etc; chapters in books; reviews; lectures. *Memberships Include:* American Academy of Nursing, Fellow 1980- ; American Pain Society, Charter Member 1977; Hospice Organization of Southern California, 1979-86; International Association for the Study of Pain, Founding Member; etc. *Honours:* Recipient, various honours and awards. *Hobby:* Dancing. *Address:* 1458 Berkeley St., Apt. 1, Santa Monica, CA 90404, USA.

MCCALL Mabel Bunny, b. 6 Feb. 1923, Bronx, New York, USA. Retired. m. Theodore R Ross, 31 Oct. 1947, deceased. *Publications include:* Poems: My trip to the Holy Land, 1984; The Night my Spirit took Flight, 1984; Christmas Wish, 1984; The Reason for Dying, 1984; Did I Pass You God?, 1983, Crucifixion, 1983; Dear Bereaved Mothers of Atlanta, 1981; The Spirits of the First American; An eagle feather on my bed; The Trail of Tears; A Tribute to my Indian Ancestors; My Reincarnation; Shalom; The Rape of the Lady called Harlem; Too Late; The Last Will and Testament of Jesus Christ; The Holy Shroud of Turin; Ode to the Statue of Liberty; I'm Going on a Diet..by and by; Africa...Sings; She walked to the Tune of a Different Drummer; Carnival Time; A full moon in the West Indies; Ode to a rose of a darker hue; Sweet memories of Dixie Land; The chosen one; The Rapture of God, etc; Lyrics for songs: The Chosen One; When to harvest love. *Memberships:* World of Poetry; American Poetry Association; Chorale Ensemble, singer and wardrobe mistress, Harlem Hospital Centre. *Honours:* Recipient of numerous honours. *Hobbies:* Writing; Poetry; Artist; Gown and Hat Designer; Gourmet cooking; Egyptology. *Address:* 41-12 10th Street No 4F, Long Island City, New York 11101, USA.

MCCALLISTER Lynn Weiss, b. 17 Oct. 1956, Jefferson City, Missouri, USA. Postdoctoral Fellow;

Medical Research Scientist. m. Larry D McCallister, 19 May 1979. *Education:* BS, Life Sciences, University of Missouri, 1979; PhD, Physiology, University of Texas, Southwestern Medical Center, Dallas, 1988. *Appointments:* Chemist, US Army, 1980-81; Predoctoral Fellow 1983-88, NIH Postdoctoral Fellow, 1988-, UT Southwestern Medical Center, Dallas, Texas. *Publications:* The Peripheral and Central Neural Control of Airway Caliber in Dogs (Dissertation), 1988; Research articles in professional journals. *Memberships:* Society for Neuroscience; American Association for the Advancement of Science, 1984-86. *Honours:* US Army Official Commendation, 1981; Honorable Mention, National Science Foundation Graduate Fellowship Competition, 1984. *Hobbies:* Biblical studies; Flute; Piano; Voice; Travel; Languages; Interior design; Animals; Reading. *Address:* 200 Cinnamon Lane, Euless, Texas 76039, USA.

MCCALLUM Valerie Lane, b. Huntington, West Virginia, USA. Assistant Food Service Director; Dietitian. m. Edward Lee McCallum, Jr, 13 May 1978. 1 son, 1 daughter. *Education:* BSc Biology, James Madison University, 1979; MSc Nutrition, Clemson University, 1986. *Appointments:* Cytotechnologist, 1979; Greenhouse Manager, 1981; Veterinary Technician, 1982; Graduate Research Assistant, 1984; Clinical Dietitian, 1986; Assistant Food Service Director, 1987- . *Publication:* Thesis: Zinc Bioavailability and the use of Photon Absorptiometry as a measure of zinc bioavailability from soy isolate. *Memberships:* American Business Women's Association, 1980; American Dietetic Association, 1985-, Public Relations Chairman of Piedmont Chapter, 1988-89; American Society for Parenteral and Enteral Nutrition; American Society for Hospital Food Service Administration, Secretary Palmetto Chapter, 1989. *Honours:* Athletic Letter Track & Field & Gymnastics, 1972 and 1975; Athletic Letter Gymnastics, 1973; Letter Gymnastics, 1974; Collegiate Athlete Gymnastics 1976 and 1977; Dean's List James Madison University, 1978. *Hobbies:* Reading; Scrimshaw; Aerobics; Biking; Knitting. *Address:* 67 Washington Drive, Piedmont, South Carolina 29673, USA.

MCCANN Mary Cheri, b. 29 July 1956, Pensacola, Florida, USA. Medical Technologist; Horse breeder and trainer. m. Robert Lee Spencer, 20 July 1977, divorced Nov. 1983. *Education:* AA, Pensacola Jr College, 1975; University of Maryland, 1977-78; BS, Biology, Troy State University, 1979; Postgraduate, University of Florida, 1979. *Appointments:* Med Technologist, Cape Fear Valley Med Ctr, Fayetteville, NC, 1981-85; Doctors Diagnotisc Centre, Fayetteville, 1985-86; Sales Rep, Waddell & Reed, Fayetteville, 1985-85; Med Technologist, Roche Biomed Lab, Burlington, NC, 1986-88; Contract Mawnaged Lasb, Cumberland Hosp, Fayetteville, Roche Biomed, 1988-; Served with US Army, 1976-77. *Memberships:* Am Soc Clin Pathologists (Registrant); Nat Assn Female Execs; Am Quarter Horse Assn; Appaloosa Horse Club; Pinto Horse Assn Am; Republican. *Hobbies:* Horses; Karate; Guns; Oil painting. *Address:* Route 2 Box 571, Hope Mills, NC 28348, USA.

MCCANN Mary Colleen, b.8 Oct 1934, Johnstown, Pennsylvania, USA. President of Foodservice Management Consulting Firm; Registered Dietitian. *Education:* BS, Dietetics, Seton Hill College, 1956; MPH, Nutrition, University of Pittsburgh, 1964; Dietetic Internship, Shadyside Hospital, 1957. *Appointments:* Director of Dietary Department, 1957-63, Lawrence Flick Hospital; Director, Dietetic Internship, Pennsylvania State University, 1964- 67; Assistant Professor and Director, Institution Food Research/ Service Program, PS University, 1967-77; Director, Bureau of Foodservice Management of Pennsylvania, 1977-80. *Publication:* Pennsylvania Diet Manual 1964 and 1967. *Memberships:* American Dietetic Association; Commission on Dietetic Registration, Chair; Pennsylvania Dietetic Association, President; Central Pennsylvania Dietetic Association, President; American Correctional Association; American Correctional

Foodservice Association; American Management Association; Pennsylvania Nutrition Council; Society for Nutrition Education. *Honours:* Distinguished Dietitian, Pennsylvania Dietetic Asscoiation, 1987; Keystone Award, Pennsylvania Dietetic Association, 1981; Distinguished Service, American Correctional Foodservice Association, 1979. *Hobbies:* Watercolour painting; Reading; Travel. *Address:* PO Box 1913, Harrisburg, PA 17105, USA.

MCCARTHY Jan Elizabeth, b. 19 July 1954, Albany, USA. Marketing Manager. m. Gerald Michael McCarthy, 4 June 1983. *Education:* Dental Assistant Certification, Atlanta Area Technical School, 1972; Real Estate Agent's License, Atlanta Institute for Real Estate, 1977; Graduate, Marketing & Intrnational Business, University of Colorado, 1986. *Appointments:* Account Executive Manager, American Bankers, 1978-80; Account Executive, Sci-Pro Inc., 1980-82; Marketing Director, Manager, MLM/Wind River, 1982-85; Marketing Manager, Winds of Change Magazine for American Indians in Science & Technology, 1985-. *Memberships:* National Association of Professional Saleswomen, Programme Co-ordinator; Professional Women's Association. *Honours:* Miss Tartan (winner in Contest for Miss Yearbook), 1972; Junior Homecoming Representative, 1971; Top Sales Producer for Wind River, 1984-85. *Hobbies:* Scuba-diving; Golf; Skiing. *Address:* 1411 Westview Drive, Boulder, CO 80303, USA.

MCCARTHY Karen P, b. 18 Mar. 1947, Massachusetts, USA. State Representative, Missouri General Assembly. *Education:* BS English/Biology, 1969, MBA 1985, University of Kansas; Masters Degree English Education, University of Missouri at Kansas City, 1976. *Appointments:* State Representative, Missouri General Assembly, 1987-88; Research Analyst, Stern Brothers and Company, 1984-85; Associate Analyst, Midwest Research Institute, 1985-86; Consultant, Governmental Affairs Department, Marion Laboratories, 1986-. *Memberships include:* National Conference of State Legislatures, Vice Chairman, State Federal Assembly, 1988; Chairman, Federal Budget and Taxation Committee, 1987; Federal Taxation, Trade and Economic Development Committee, 1985-86; Energy Committee, 1978-84; Delegation on Trade and Economic Development to West Germany, Bulgaria and Japan, 1987; National Democratic Institute for International Affairs instructor in Northern Ireland, 1988; Member of the Council, American Council of Yough Political Leaders, 1981-87, etc. *Honours:* Outstanding Young Woman of America Award, 1977; Missouri Start Recipient, 1978; Outstanding Woman of Missouri Award, Phi Chi Theta, 1978; Woman of Achievement Award, Mid-Continent Council of Girl Scouts, 1983, 1987; Civil Liberties Award, American Civil Liberties Union of Western Missouri, 1983; Conservation Legislator of the Year, Conservation Federation of Missouri, 1987; MOVA Award for Meritorious Service, Missouri Victim Assistance Network, 1988; Phi Delta Kappa Education Honorary. *Address:* 1111 Valentine Road, Kansas City, MO 64111, USA.

MCCARTHY Mary, b. 21 June 1912, Seattle, Washington, USA. Writer. m. James Raymond West, 15 Apr. 1961. 1 son. *Education:* Annie Wright Seminary, Tacoma, Washington, 1929; AB, Vassar College, 1933; LittD, Syracuse University, 1973; LittD, University of Hull, 1974; LittD, Bard College, 1976; LLD, University of Aberdeen, 1979; LittD, Bowdoin College, 1981; LittD, University of Maine, Orono, 1982; Litt. D., Smith College, 1988. *Appointments:* Editor, 1937-38, Drama Critic, 1937-62, Partisan Review, New York City; Instructor in Literature, Bard College, Annandale-on-Hudson, New York, 1945-46; Instructor in English, Sarah Lawrence College, Bronxville, New York, 1948; Northcliffe Lecturer, University College, University of London, England, 1980; Literature, Bard College, 1986-. *Publications:* The Company She Keeps, 1942; The Oasis, 1949; The Groves of Academe, 1952; A Charmed Life, 1955; Venice Observed, 1956; Memories of a Catholic Girlhood, 1957; The Stones of Florence, 1959; The Group, 1963; Birds of America, 1971; Cannibals and Missionaries, 1979; Ideas and the Novel, 1980; Occasional Prose, 1985; How I Grew, 1987. *Memberships:* National Institute of Arts and Letters; National Institute of Arts and Sciences; Authors League of America; Phi Beta Kappa. *Honours:* Vassar College President's Distinguished Visitor Medal, 1982; National Medal for Literature, 1984; Officer, French Institute of Arts and Letters, 1983; National Academy of Arts and Letters, 1988. *Address:* 141 rue de Rennes, 75006 Paris, France.

MCCARTNEY Marjorie Anne, b. 20 Jan. 1954, Hartford, Connecticut, USA. Neuropharmacologist. m. Ross W Silver, 28 Dec. 1984. *Education:* BS, Michigan State University, 1975; MS, Pharmacology and Physiology, University of Chicago, 1977; PhD, Neurosciences, University of Illinois, 1989. *Appointments:* Sr Research Assistant 1979-80, FDA Compliance Auditor 1980-81, Lab Supervisor and Research Associate, Toxicology, 1981-85, Baxter Labs, Deerfield; Physiology Instructor, Triton College, Illinois, 1982-83; Teaching Assistant, University of Illinois, 1985-89. *Memberships:* Soc Neuroscience; American Association for Adv Science; American Women in Science; Women in Neuroscience. *Honours:* Women in Neuroscience Award, 1987; American Soc of Pharmacology and Experimental Therapeutics Award, 1987; Graduate Student Council Representative, 1983-88; Tri Beta Membership; American Baptist Scholarship. *Hobbies:* Music; Travel; Photography; Swimming; Dance. *Address:* 348 Laurelwood Dr., Rochester, NY 14626, USA.

MCCLATCHEY Diana Parry, b. 10 July 1920, Malvern, England. Deaconess, Church of England. m. Alfred Henry Bailey McClatchey, 28 Dec. 1945, 1 son, 2 daughters. *Education:* MA, DPHil, 1948, Lady Margaret Hall, Oxford; Diploma, Biblical and Religious Studies, London University, 1969. *Appointments:* Tutor, County Organiser, Workers Educational Association, Norfolk, 1941-45; History Teacher, Adult Education, Nigeria, Ireland, England; Ordained Deaconess, by Bishop of Durham, 1971; Diocesan Adviser for Womens Ministry in Durham, 1970-74, in Worcester 1974-83; Minister, in Charge, Parish of Wilden, Worcestershire, 1981-85; Vice Moderator of Movement for the Ordination of Women, 1983-85, Moderator, 1985-. *Publications:* Oxfordshire Clergy 1770--870, 1960; 1300 Years - People of Worcester and Their Church, 1980, Joint editor. *Memberships:* Anglican Group for Ordination of Women, Secretary, 1975-78; Representative of Laity of Diocese of Worcester, General Synod, Church of England, 1975-. *Hobbies:* Wild Flowers; Local History. *Address:* 10 Bellars Lane, Malvern, Worcestershire, WR14 2DN, England.

MCCLEAN Celeita Ann, b. 14 Dec. 1956, Huntington, West Virginia, USA. Army Program Manager; Captain/Pilot/Test Pilot, US Army. *Education:* BSEd, cum laude graduate, West Virginia State College, 1980; Masters in Aviation Management, Embry-Riddle Aeronautical University, 1985. *Appointments:* Officer/Pilot/Test Pilot/Maintenance Officer, Lieutenant through to Captain, US Army, 1980-84; USA Reserves, 1984-; Marketing Representative, GE Aircraft Weapons, 1984-87; Army Programs Manager, GE Aerospace, Washington, 1987-. *Creative works:* Sculpture: Boat People, 1980; Acrylic on Canvas: Beach and Sunset, 1980; Numerous works of fine art in various museums. *Memberships:* Alpha Kappa Mu Honour Society; Whirly Girls, Inc, International Women Helicopter Pilots; Aviation Association of America; Association of US Army; Association of US Reserve; American Defense Preparedness Association; American Helicopter Society; Marine Corps Aviationa Association; Naval Helicopter Association. *Honours:* DA Superior Cadet, 1978; Excellence in Scholarship, 1979; Distinguished Military Graduate, 1980; First woman to fly and test fly The 4H-60 Helicopter, 1981; Miss Pershing, 1981; Army Aviator Wings, 1981; Army Service and Overseas Service Ribbon, 1983; Army Achievement Medal, 1983;

Army Commendation Medal, 1984; Army Meritorious Service Medal, 1984; Expert Riflemen Badge, 1984; Expert Badge for Pistols, 1981; Commercial Pilots License, 1981; Sikorsky Helicopter Rescue Award, 1986; Included in Smithsonian Institutes Aire & Space Museum Exhibit on 'Women in Aviation' 1986. *Hobbies:* Basketball; Volleyball; Baseball; Football; Tennis; Cyhcling; Track and field; Dance; Performing Arts; Fine Arts; Flying; Weapons; Travelling; Cars; Interior Design; The Mislitary; Animals; Children. *Address:* 1300 Crystal Drive No 608, Arlington, Virginia 22202, USA.

MCCLEARY Linda Sue Caldwell, b. 26 Dec. 1948, Indianapolis, Marion County, Indiana, USA. Librarian; Genealogist. m. James E. McCleary Jr, 6 Oct. 1979. *Education:* BS, 1971, MLS, 1973, Ball State University; Certificate in Genealogical Research, Brigham Young University, 1986. *Appointments:* School Librarian, Randolph Eastern School Corporation, 1971-73; Medical Transcriber, Good Samaritan Hospital, 1973-76; Assistant Bookkeeper, Receptionist, Elizabeth Arden Salon, 1976-79; Law Library Librarian, 1979-80, Genealogy Librarian, 1980-, Arizona State Library. *Publications:* Many articles for genealogical publications. *Memberships:* American Library Association; Arizona State Library Association, Secretary, Special Libraries Division; Mountain Plains Library Association, Chairman of Preservation Division; National Genealogical Society; Director, 1st Vice-President, Sun City Genealogical Society; Genealogist, Family History Society of Arizona. *Honours:* Distinguished Sister, Gamma Sigma Sigma Sorority, Ball State University, 1971; Distinguished Service Award, National Genealogical Society, 1989. *Hobbies:* Genealogical research; Stamp collecting; Reading. *Address:* 945 East Denton Lane, Phoenix, AZ 85014, USA.

MCCLELLAN Catharine, b. 1 Mar. 1921, York, Pennsylvania, USA. m. John Thayer Hitchcock, 6 June 1974. *Education:* AB, Bryn Mawr College, 1942; PhD, University of California, Berkeley, 1950. *Appointments:* Various Teaching positions 1946-56; Assistant Professor, Anthropology, Chairman, Anthropology, Barnard College, 1956-61; Associate Professor, 1961-65, Professor, 1965-73, Bascom Professor, 1973-83, Professor Emeritus, 1983-, University of Wisconsin, Madison; Visiting Distinguished Professor, University of Alaska, 1987. *Publications:* The Girl Who Married the Bear, 1971; My Old People Say: An Ethnographic Survey of Southern Yukon Territory, 1975; Part of the Land, Part of the Water, 1987; numerous articles in professional journals, book reviews, etc. *Address:* Anthropology Dept., University of Wisconsin, Madison, WI 53704, USA.

MCCLELLAN Gloria E, Mayor, City of Vista. *Appointments:* Police Matron; Businesswoman, 1974-82; Mayor, City of Vista, 1984-. *Memberships:* Numerous organisations including: Womens Auxiliary Associate Membership of Boys Club; Vista Rotary; American Red Cross Advisory Board, 1987-88; Life Member, Beta Sigma Phi; Vista Emblem Club; Vista Woman's Club; Vista Hlstorical Society; American Legion Auxiliary; VFW Auxiliary; etc. *Honours:* League of California Cities, 1988; Proclamation: Congressman Packard, 1988, Board of Supervisors, 1988; Resolution: Senator Craven, 1988, Assemblyman Frazee, 1988; many others. *Address:* 1426 Alta Vista, Vista, CA 92084, USA.

MCCLUNEY Joan T., b. 13 Oct. 1929, Chicago, Illinois, USA. Marriage and Family Therapist. m. 17 Mar. 1952 (widowed), 2 sons, 2 daughters. *Education:* AA, 1971; MA, Rehabilitation Counselling, 1973; Certified Sex Therapist, 1979; Licensed Marriage and Family Therapist, Florida, 1982; Certified Supervisor of Sex Therapists, 1988. *Appointments:* Adjunct Instructor, Eckerd College, St Petersburg Junior College, 1978; Counsellor, Marriage and Family Therapy to Supervisor, Sexuality Programme to Director of Sexuality Programme, 1978-88; Director of Clinical Services, Family Service Centers, Clearwater, Florida, 1988-.

Creative works: Photography. *Memberships:* Faculty of Family Institute-Family Service Centers; American Association of Sex Educators, Counselors and Therapists; American Association of Marriage and Family Therapists; Florida Council of Sexual Abuse Services; Pinellas Association of Marriage and Family Therapists. *Honour:* Outstanding Woman of the Year, Pinellas County Chapter, NOW, 1981-82. *Hobbies:* Camping; Boating; Photography; Gardening; Travel. *Address:* Family Service Centers, 2960 Roosevelt Boulevard, Clearwater, FL 34620, USA.

MCCOLLOUGH Lucille H, b. 30 Dec. 1905, Michigan, USA. State Commission on Aging. m. Clarence McCollough, 16 June 1925. 2 sons, 1 daughter. *Education:* State Teachers Certificate, 1924; Extra College courses in Public Speaking. *Appointments:* Teacher, 1924-25; Secretary, 1925-48; Elected City Councilman, 1949-54; Elected State Representative, 1954-82; Appointed by Governor Blanchard to State Commission on Aging, 1982-88. *Memberships include:* National Order Women Legislators; League of Women Voters; Women in the Moose VFM; Ladies Auxiliary State Commissioner on Aging. *Honours:* Named in Guinness Book of World Records as only State Legislator to serve 28 consecutive years with 100% perfect attendance record at all sessions; Honorary Member, Neighborhood Group; First Woman to serve as Chairman of Michigan House of Representatives Committee on Education. *Hobbies:* Volunteer work in many local and State organizations, in particular, Senior Citizen groups. *Address:* 7517 Kentucky, Dearborn, Michigan 48126, USA.

MCCOMBS Susan Brooks, b. 2 June 1957, Mississippi, USA. Interior Designer. m. David Louis McCombs, 20 Sept. 1986, 1 daughter. *Education:* BFA, Mississippi University for Women, 1979. *Appointments:* Interior Designer, Marlene Dibrell & Associates, 1979-81; Interior Designer, Assistant Manager, Larry Robert Taylor & Associates, 1981-84; Interior Designer, Commercial & Residential Design Director, Marcia Capps & Associates, 1984-87; Project Designer, Perry & Plummer Design Associates, 1988-89; Brooks Design Associates, 1989-. *Memberships:* American Society of Interior Designers; Smithsonian Associates; North Carolina, Dallas Museums of Art; Dallas Sales & Marketing Association; Dallas Home & Apartment Builders Association; Texas Association for Interior Designers. *Hobbies:* Needlework; Reading; Water Skiing; Biking. *Address:* 4112 Joshua Lane, Dallas, TX 75287, USA.

MCCONNELL Jo Ann, b. 3 Aug. 1944, Ft. Sill, USA. Health Scientist Administrator. m. Allen Charles Stoolmiller, 19 Dec. 1985, divorced 1988. *Education:* BS, Biology, Florida State University, 1965; PhD, Anatomy, University of Arizona, 1977. *Appointments:* Research Technician, Emory University, 1965-66; Research Technician, 1966-68, Research Assistant, 1968- 71, University of Virginia; Clinical Assistant, Holland, 1971-72; Assistant Professor, University of Texas Medical School, 1977-84; Administrator, neurology review Group, 1984-. *Publications:* 17 research articles; 6 book chapters; Videotape series. *Memberships:* American Association of Anatomists; Cajal Club; American Society for Neuroscience. *Honours:* National Honour Society, 1962; National Research Service Award, 1979-81. *Hobbies:* Computer Information Exchange; Car Repair; Horse Riding; Sailing; Skiing. *Address:* NEUB-1 Study Section, NIH/DRG, Westwood 152, 5333 Westbard Avenue, Bethesda, MD 20892, USA.

MCCORMACK Elizabeth Calfee, b. 11 Aug, 1940, Jackson Heights, New York, USA. College Instructor. m. Joseph John McCormack. 2 sons. *Education:* BA, University of Connecticut, 1962; MA, Southern Connecticut State University, 1977. *Appointments:* Teacher, New Haven School System, 1966-77; Instructor, Southern Connecticut State University, 1979-; Instructor, University of Bridgeport, 1982-. *Memberships:* American Association of University

Professors; Elected to New Haven Board of Aldermen, 1988; Legislation Committee, Community Development, Drug Committee, Board Representative to Arts Council, Justice of the Peace, 1989-; Mayor's Task Force for Edgewood Park, 1989; Supporters of Connecticut Hospice, 1988-89; Captain, New Haven Black Watch Association, 1982-*Honours:* Co- chairwoman, Mayor's Inauguration, 1986; Master Teacher, New Haven School System, 1975-76; Whalley Avenue Special Services District Outstanding Achievement Award, 1989. *Interests:* Neighbourhood improvements; Safer neighbourhoods. Hobbies: Antiques; Reading. *Address:* 66 Pendleton St, New Haven, Connecticut 06511, USA.

MCCOY Elaine Jean, b. 7 Mar. 1946, Brandon, Manitoba, Canada. Member of the Legislative Assembly for Calgary West; Minister of Alberta Consumer and Corporate Affairs; Responsible for Women's Issues. m. Miles Hudson Patterson, 19 Apr. 1988. *Education:* Degrees in Political Science and Law, 1968 and 1969; Admitted to Bar, 1970. *Appointments:* Alberta Government-Member of the Legislative Assembly & Cabinet Minister, 1986-; Barrister with Black & Company of Calgary, specializing in Regulatory Law; Alberta Government, Senior Legal Counsel to Public Utilities Board in Edmonton. *Publication:* Article: Technical Owners and the Public Utilities Board. *Memberships:* Founding trustee, Angela Cheng Musical Foundation; Law Society; Canadian Bar Association. *Address:* 104 Legislature Building, Edmonton, Alberta, Canada, T5K 2B6.

MCCRAY Evelina Williams, b. 1 Sept. 1932, Plaquemine, Louisiana, USA. Research Librarian. m. John S McCray, 7 Apr. 1955. 1 daughter. *Education:* BA, Southern University, 1954; MSLS, Louisiana State University, 1962; Diploma in Journalism, Newspaper Institute of America, 1969. *Appointments:* Librarian, Iberville High School, 1954-70, Plaquemine Junior High School, 1970-75, Local Day Care Centre, 1978-79; Volunteer Service, Allen J Nadler Branch, Iberville Parish Library, 1980-82. *Publications:* Bibliography on books for the gifted child; unpublished biographical data, Iberville High School, 1961-67; Poem: The Road of Life, New American Poetry Anthology, 1988. *Memberships:* American Library Association; National Retired Teachers Association; Louisiana Retired Teachers Association; Iberville Retired Teachers Association, Director, Informative and Protective Services, 1981-. *Honours:* Outstanding Secondary Educators Award, 1975; Library Consultant for Evaluation and Capitol High School, 1964, Iberville Parish Educators Workshop, 1980; Consultant, Louisiana Retired Teachers Workshop, 1986; Outstanding Service to Louisiana Retired Teachers, 1986; Merit Award for Poem, My Search for Sanity, 1988. *Hobbies:* Reading; Cooking; Sewing; Freelance writing. *Address:* PO Box Q, Plaquemine, LA 70765, USA.

MCCULLOUGH Elayne K, b. 16 May 1926, Staten Island, New York, USA. Division Manager-Billing. m. A Stewart McCullough, 3 Nov 1956. *Education:* BA, University of Delaware, 1946. *Appointments:* Division Manager-Billing, New York Telephone Company, 1948-. *Membership:* Vice President, Colisium Tenants' Association. *Hobbies:* Real Estate Management; Economic trending; Music; Arts. *Address:* 30 West 60th Street, New York, NY 10023, USA.

MCCURRY Sandra Louise, . 23 Sept. 1949, La Grange, Georgia, USA. Banker. m. Nathan Harsh Brown Chitty, 21 Dec. 1985. *Education:* BA, Florida State University, 1971; Graduate studies, Universities of Mississippi & Central Florida. *Appointments:* English teacher, secondary high schools, Florida, Mississippi, 1972-83; Staff (currently Vice President), American Pioneer Savings Bank, 1983-. *Publications:* Articles: American Pioneer Savings Bank Introduces Wealth Care, & Wealth Care, Prescription for Sound Financial Management, in Central Florida Physician, 1987. *Memberships:* Offices, past/present: Delta Zeta sorority, Junior League of Orlando; Member, Financial Institutions Marketing Association. *Honours:* William

Danforth I Dare You leadership award, 1967; One of 20 People to Watch, Orlando Magazine, 1986. *Hobbies:* Bridge; Interior design; Antique furniture; French Impressionist paintings; Renaissance art & architecture. *Address:* 2192 Woodbridge Road, Longwood, Florida 32779, USA.

MCDANIEL Phila Lou, b. 4 Dec. 1931, Los Angeles, California, USA. Lecturer, Teacher, Researcher, Chinese Folk Art. m. 10 Apr. 1964, 1 son, 2 daughters. *Education:* BA, Pepperdine University, 1953; MA, California State University, 1971; Graduate work, California & Arizona. *Appointments:* Teacher, art & art history, various California schools, 1954-. *Creative works:* Photography, Chinese people & country; Book, Influence of Zen on Kannon in Japanese Art, 1971; Television documentaries, China, Chinese symbolism; Exhibitions, Ventura Historical Museum 1988, Wing Luke Asian Museum, Seattle 1989; Book, Minority People of China & Tibetan Tribes, in progress. *Memberships include:* China Exploration & Research Society; Museum Textile Associates; Pacific Asia Museum Association of Asian Scholars; Wing Luke Asian Museum; President, offices, Los Angeles County Museum of Art. Various honour societies. *Honours include:* Bravo Award, Music Centre of Los Angeles County (Education Division), 1989; Recognition, work in art education, California State Senate Rules Committee 1989, Los Angeles County Board of Supervisors 1988, 1989; Woman of Achievement, Gardena chapter, Soroptimist International, 1989. *Hobbies:* Travel & Research in Asia, particularly rural China & minority tribes; Photography, rare tribal people & art; Collecting beads, artifacts, costumes, Chinese minority tribes; Making documentary films; Conducting tours, Chine & SE Asia; Making cultural exchanges & museum exhibitions. *Address:* 2462 Rue Le Charlene, Rancho Palos Verdes, California 90274, USA.

MCDERMOTT Renee R, b. 26 Sept. 1950, Danville, USA. Lawyer. m. James A. McDermott. *Education:* BA, 1970, MA, 1972, University of South Florida; JD, Indiana University-Bloomington, School of Law, 1978. *Appointments:* Associate, 1980-84, Partner, 1985-, Barnes & Thornburg. *Publications:* Articles in professional journals. *Memberships Include:* American, Indiana State & Indianapolis Bar Associations; Editor-in-Chief, Indiana Law Journal, 1977-78; Fellow, Indiana Bar Foundation, 1986-; Presidential Citation, Indiana State Bar Association. *Hobbies:* Horse Riding; Scuba Diving; Water Sports; Reading; Music. *Address:* Barnes & Thornburg, 1313 Merchants Bank Building, 11 South Meridian Street, Indianapolis, IN 46204, USA.

MCDONALD Barbara Black Robertson, b. 7 Mar. 1951, New Jersey, USA. Design Consultant. *Education:* Western New England College, 1969- 70; Fashion Institute Technology, New York City, 1970-71; School of Visual Arts, New York, 1971-72. *Appointments:* Designer, Unique Studios, New York City, 1972-74; Associate Art Director, CBS, New York City, 1974-77; Creative Director, Remco Toys, New York City, 1977-80; Senior Design Manager, Lever Bros, New York City, 1980-81; Owner, B. McDonald, New York City, 1981-. *Creative Works:* Creation and marketing strategies of a new line of educational science products & their packaging; market strategies & design for new lines of health product (condoms); Redesign & positioning of soap products; development & creation of numerous toys & their packaging; Conceptual design & repositioning for RCA video tapes; Design & creation of new producs for a line of consumer work gloves, dental gloves & surgical gloves. *Memberships:* Graphic Arts Guild; Package Designers Council; National Association of Female Executives; Canvasser, Recruiter Re-election Ed. Koch, New York City. *Honours:* Awarded Recognition for Excellence for Design by Package Designers Council, 1979, 1980. *Hobbies:* Wind Surfing; Racquetball; Canoeing; Writing; Reading. *Address:* 1123 Broadway, Suite 817, New York, NY 10010, USA.

MCDONALD Eva Rose, b. 30 Mar. 1909, Harlesden, London, England. Novelist. *Education:* St John's Girls

Church of England School, Penge, London; Scholarship to South London Commercial College, Anerley. *Publications:* Author of 38 novels including: House of Secrets; Chateau of Nightingales; The Runaway Countess; The Captive Lady; Dark Enchantment; The Lady from Yorktown; Lord Byron's First Love; Shelley's Springtime Bride; Napoleon's Captain. *Membership:* Society of Authors. *Hobbies:* Playing the piano; Listening to music. *Address:* Wyldwynds, 105 Bathurst Walk, Iver, Bucks, SLO 9EF, England.

MCDONALD Marie L, b. 21 Oct. 1927, Seattle, Washington, USA. Elevator Consultant/Contractor. m. John R McDonald, 4 Oct. 1969, 1 son, 4 daughters. *Appointments:* With various accounting and construction firms, California, 1946-54; Office Manager, Dwan Elevator Co., San Francisco, 1955-62, Assistant to President, 1963-68, Sales Manager, 1968-76; President, McDonald Elevator Co., San Francisco, 1976-; incline elevator cons., 1970-; Board of Directors, Ind. Living Project of San Francisco, 1977-. *Memberships:* Women Entrepreneurs; North California Elevator Industry Group, etc. *Honours:* First Woman in State of California to obtain Elevator Contractors License, 1962; First Woman in USA to start elevator contracting business, 1976, elevator inspection business, 1982; First Woman in US to become Certified Elevator Inspector, 1987; Woman Entrpreneur of the Year San Francisco Chamber of Commerce, 1988. *Hobbies:* Gardening; Reading; Travel; etc. *Address:* 51 Lusherm Court, Walnut Creek, CA 94596, USA.

MCDONNELL Ann Elizabeth Alexander, b. 22 July 1938, San Francisco, California, USA. Fundraising/Public Relations Executive. m. Joseph Anthony McDonnell, 23 Dec. 1962, div. May 1983, 3 daughters. *Education:* Smith College, 1955-56; BA, Lawrence College, 1959; Accademia delle Bell'Arte, Florence, Italy, 1959-60; Graduate Realtors Institute (GRI), 1979- 79. *Appointments:* English Teacher, Instituto Americano, Florence, Italy, 1960-61; Real Estate Broker, Vincent and Whittemore Real Estate, Bedford, New York, 1976-83; Director of Development, Westchester Association for Retarded Citizens, White Plains, New York, 1983-89; Executive Director, New Canaan CARES, Inc., 1989. *Publications:*, Numerous pamphlets and articles for professional journals. *Memberships:* Board of Visitors, Governor's Appointment, 1973-81; Board Member, President, Westchester Association for Retarded Citizens, committees including Chairman, Nominating Committee, 2 years; Director Emeritus, Association for Mentally Ill Children, Board Member 1973-88, Chairman, Nominating and Legislative Committees; Corresponding Secretary, Chairman Public Relations Committee, Community Advisory Board, Harlem Valley Psychiatric Center; Board of Directors, Westchester County Medical Center; Westchester County Board of Realtors; Association of Development Officers; Women in Communications Inc; United States Masters Swimming Inc; Empire State Masters Swimming; Class Secretary, Lawrence College Class of 1959. *Honour:* Elected Member, Emeritus Board of Directors, Association for Mentally Ill Children, 1988. *Hobbies:* Swimming; Tennis; Gardening; Reading; Painting. *Address:* Old Pound Road, Pound Ridge, NY 10576, USA.

MCDONOUGH Sheila Doreen, b.13 Dec. 1928, Calgarary, Canada. Professor. Divorced, 1 son, 1 daughter. *Education:* BA, 1952; MA 1955; PhD, 1963. *Applications:* Kinnaird College, 1957-60; Concordia University, Montreal, 1964-88. *Publications:* The Authority of the Past, 1970; Jinnah, Maker of Modern Pakistan, 1970; Muslin Ethics & Modernity, 1985; articles in journals. *Memberships:* Resident Director, Shastvi Indo-Canadian Institute, New Delhi, 1971; Secretary, Canadian Society for the Study of Religion, 1968-70. *Hobby:* Star Trek. *Address:* Dept. of Religion, Concordia University, Montreal, Canada H3G 1M8.

MCDOUGALL Barbara, Minister of Employment & Immigration, Minister Responsible for the Status of Women. *Education:* BA, Honours, Political Science & Economics, University of Toronto, 1960; Chartered Financial Analyst, 1973. *Appointments:* Investment Analyst, 1964-74; Manager, Portfolio Investments, North West Trust Company, 1974-76; Vice President, Dominion Securities Ames Ltd., 1976-81; Executive Director Canadian Council of Financial Analysts, 1982-84; Elected to Parliament, 1984-, appointed Minister of Employment & Immigration, 1988-. *Memberships:* Counsellor, Oakhalla Provincial Prison for Women; Vice Chairperson, Elizabeth Fry Society of British Columbia; etc. *Address:* Office of the Minister of Employment and Immigration, Place du Portage, Phase IV, Hull, Quebec K1A 0J9, Canada.

MCDOWELL Cecelia Marie, b. 8 Aug. 1952, Jacksonville, Florida, USA. Corporate Supervisor, Human Resources. *Education:* Journalism, University of Georgia, 1969; BS cum laude, Psychology & Special Education, Armstrong State College, 1972; Graduate study, Comparative Science, Washington State University, 1984; JD Honours, University of Texas School of Law, 1986. *Appointments:* Assistant Accounting Supervisor, Palmetto Elec Coop, 1972-75; Employee Interviewer, State of Georgia, 1975-79; Corporate Supervisor, Human Resources, Gulfstream Aerospace Corporation, 1979-; Self- employed antique dealer, 1979-; Co-owner, Rayce Enterprises & Easy Does It Mobile Home Service, 1984-86. *Creative works include:* Freelance writer, numerous labour textbooks; Painter; Pianist; Poet. *Memberships include:* Advisory Council, Savannah Area Voc-tech School 1981-87, Displaced Homemaker Programme 1984-; Trustee, Savannah Voc-Tech Foundation; Instructor, Labour Law, Women in Management, 1984; Advisor, Governor's Councils, Special & Vocational Education, 1983-85. *Honours:* Phi Beta Kappa, Dean's List, other scholastic honours, 1969-86; AP Scholarship, 1969; Miss Navy, 1971. *Hobbies include:* Environmental lobbyist, SC Environmental Coalition, 1972; Educational lobbyist, SC Comm, Adv Education, 1984; Acting Director, Tidelands Comm School for Exceptional Children, 1971; Music, various instruments; Dance; Antiques. *Address:* 608 East 49th Street, Savannah, Georgia 31405, USA.

MCDOWELL Jennifer Loventhal, b. 19 May 1936, Albuquerque, USA. Playwright; Author; Composer; Sociologist. m. Milton Loventhal, 2 July 1973. *Education:* BA, 1957; MA, 1958; MLS, 1963; PhD, 1973. *Appointments:* Teacher, English, Abraham Lincoln High School, 1960-61; Freelance Editor, Soviet field, 1961-63; Research assistant, Sociology, University of Oregon, 1964-66; Editor, Publisher, Merlin Papers, san Jose, 1969-, Merlin Press, 1973-. *Publications:* Poems, essays, short stories, book reviewers to literary magazines; Writer, Song, Money Makes A woman Free, 1976; 3 songs featured in Parade of American Music; Co-creator, musical comedy, Russia's Secret Plot to Take Back Alaska, 1983; Play (off-off Broadway), The Estrogen Party to End War, 1986. *Honours:* Recipient, 8 awards, American Song Festival, 1976-79; AAUW Doctoral Fellow. *Hobbies:* Tennis; Hiking; Native Plants & Animals. *Address:* PO Box 5602, San Jose, CA 95150, USA.

MCDOWELL Johanna Susan, b. 31 Jan. 1952, Solihull, England. Managing Director. m. Stephen McDowell, 21 May 1977, divorced 1984, 1 son. *Education:* HND Business Studies, Twickenham College of Technology. *Appointments:* Bentalls, 1972-74; United Biscuits, 1974; SSC & Blintas, 1974-79; Grey Phillips Advertising, 1979-86; Brookes & Vernons, 1986- 88; Managing Director, Grey Phillips, South Africa, 1988-. *Memberships:* IMM; Marketing Society; network, Midlands Branch, Founder Chairman, 1988. *Honour:* Marketing Student of the Year, 1974. *Hobbies:* Bride; Theatre; Network; My Son; Home Decorating. *Address:* 3 Tana Road, Linden, Johannesburg, South Africa 2195.

MCDUFFIE Deborah Jeanne, b. 8 Aug. 1950, Manhattan, USA. Music Producer; Composer. 2 sons. *Education:* BA, Western College Women. *Appointments:* Music producer, composer, McCann-Erickson Advt, Inc, New York City, 1971-81; Music director, Mingo-Jones Advt, 1981-; President, Jana Prodns, Inc, Janee Music

Co, Great Music Management Co, New York City, 1977-; Professional singer, composer, arranger, producer. *Creative works:* Vocal arranger: I'd Like to Teach the World to Sing, 1972; composer producer Miller High Life campaigns, 1980-83; album: I Am an Illusion, 1981; Damaris, 1984; Composer, Hooray for Love; producer We Shall Overcome by Roberta Flack, 1986; Producer, Simon Estes, Polydor; Cindy Valentine, Secret Rendezvous, Polydor; Al Green, A & M Records. *Memberships:* ASCAP; Screen Actors Guild; AFTRA; Am Fedn Musicians, Nat Acad Rec Arts and Scis; Nat Assn Female Execs. *Honours:* Recipient numerous advt awards. *Address:* 69 W 89th St, New York, NY 10024, USA.

MCEACHERN Phyllis W., b. 8 Dec. 1959, Atlanta, Georgia, USA. Certified Public Accountant (CPA). m. Gregory S. McEachern, 11 Apr. 1981, 1 daughter. *Education:* ASc, Business Administration, Abraham Baldwin Agricultural College, 1979; BBA, Accounting, Valdista State College, 1981; CPA, 1986. *Appointments:* Baker & Rentz, CPA's, 1981-, now Senior Accountant. *Memberships:* American Institute of CPA's; Georgia Society of CPA's; Sherwood Baptist Church. *Hobbies:* Gardening; Needlework & other crafts. *Address:* 1536 Westwood Drive, Albany, Georgia 31707, USA.

MCELROY Colleen (J)ohnson, b. 30 Oct. 1935, St Louis, Missouri, USA. Writer; Professor of English. div., 1 son, 1 daughter. *Education:* BS, 1958, MS, 1963, Kansas State University; PhD, University of Washington, 1973. *Appointments:* Director, Speech and Hearing Clinic, Western Washington University, 1966-72; Talkshow Moderator, KVOS/CBS, 1968-71; Professor of English, 1973-, Director, EOP Freshman English, 1973-82, Director, Creative Writing, 1984-87, University of Washington, Seattle, Washington. *Publications:* Poetry: Music from Home, 1976; Winters Without Snow, 1979; Lie and Say You Love Me, 1981; Queen of the Ebony Isles, 1984; Bone Flames, 1987; Jesus and Fat Tuesday (fiction), 1987; Driving Under the Cardboard Pines (fiction), 1990; Follow the Drinking Gourd (play), 1987. *Memberships:* Writers Guild of America, East; Authors Guild; Dramatists Guild. *Honours:* Bridgman Scholars, Breadloaf Writers Conference, 1974; Pushcart Prize for Poetry, 1975; NEA Fellowship (poetry), 1978; CALLALOO Award for Fiction, 1981; MacDowell Colony Residency, 1984, 1986; 1st Place for Poetry, Cincinnati Review, 1984; Fulbright Fellowbright for Creative Writing, Yugoslavia, 1988; Washington State Governor's Award for fiction and poetry, 1988. *Hobbies:* Visual art (pen and ink). *Address:* Department of English GN-30, University of Washington, Seattle, WA 98109, USA.

MCEWAN Geraldine, Actress. m. Hugh Cruttwell. 1 son, 1 daughter. *Education:* Windsor County Girl's school. *Appointments:* Career began at the Theatre Royal Windsor, 1949-51, numerous appearances on stage including: Who Goes There, Vaudeville Theatre and Duke of York's Theatre, 1951; For Better, For Worse, Comedy Theatre, 1953; Love's Labour's Lost, Stratford, 1956; A Member of the Wedding, Royal Court Theatre, 1957; The Entertainer, Palace Theatre, 1957-58; Twelfth Night, Pericles, Much Ado About Nothing, Stratford, 1958; Much Ado About Nothing, Hamlet, Stratford, 1961; The School for Scandal, Haymarket Theatre and USA, 1962; The National Theatre, 1965-71; Armstrong's Last Goodnight; Love for Love; A Flea in Her Ear; Dance of Death; Edward II; Home and Beauty; Rites; Way of the World; The White Devil; Amphitryon. Chez Nous, Globe Theatre, 1974; On Approval, Haymarket Theatre, 1975-76. The National Theatre, 1980-81: The Browning Version; Harlequinade; The Provok'd Wife. The National Theatre, 1983-84: The Rivals; You Can't Take it With You. A Lie of the Mind, Royal Court Theatre, 1987; Lettice and Lovage, Globe Theatre, 1988-89. Numerous television roles, The Prime of Miss Jean Brodie, 1977; L'Elegence, 1982; The Barchester Chronicles, 1982; Mapp and Lucia, 1984-85. Films include: the Dance of Death, 1968; Henry V, 1989. *Address:* c/o Marmont Management Ltd, 308 Regent Street, London W1R 5AL, England.

MCEWEN Margaret Mary, b. 11 Aug. 1917, London, England. General Secretary and Co-Founder of charity. *Education:* Various training courses, 1936-38; Diploma in German, Vienna University, 1938-39; Student, St Omer, France. *Appointments:* Censorship, Ministry of Information, 1940-43; Secretary, US Signal Section, London, 1943-44; Children's charity, London working mainly for relief of war affected Dutch children, 1944-47; General Secretary and Co-Founder, International Help for Children, 1947-89, now helping medical cases in the Third World. *Honours:* United States Medal of Freedom, 1947; Gold Medal Greek Red Cross, 1969; Presentation of book on Dutch painters, The Netherlands Ambassador, 1988, at reception given in her honour at the Royal Netherlands Embassy, London; The Margaret McEwen Trust (charitable trust) activated in 1989. *Hobbies:* Painting in oils, watercolours and pastels.

MCEWEN Mary Anne, b. 9 July 1945, Toronto, Ontario, Canada. Writer; Producer; Director; Editor. *Education:* BA, University of British Columbia, 1967; Film Workshops, Simon Fraser University, 1970-72; Professional Photography Diploma, Little Falls, New Jersey, USA, 1977. *Appointments:* Senior Writer 1969-70 and 1980-82, Hayhurst Communications; Creative Director/Audio Visual Department Manager, Creative House Ltd, 1973-77; President, Forward Focus Productions Ltd, 1977-. *Creative works:* Books: Ocean Odyssey; Universal Lotto Manual (with Ivan Dimitrov); Magazine: Ocean Breezes; Newsletter: Sex Success Over Forty (current). Videos: It Feels Great; Who Killed Alfred Hitchcock?; Diabetes: the Goal is a Cure; Magic Summer; God, Gays and the Gospel; Anything Goes (rock video); The Joy of Four Wheel Driving; Apprenticeship (series); Celebration '90; NGV: Driving Force of the Future (series). Cablevision series: founding producer Gayblevision (Vancouver, San Francisco); W.O.W. (Women's Show); West End Edition; The Seniors Show. Film: Paving for People; An Inheritance from Salt; Burnout; Hawaii '74; CP Air's Mexico; Garden of Eden; Sounds of Silence; Legacy. Multi-media: This One's for You; The Beat Goes On; Great Moments in Sport; A World of Wood; Eurocan's Kitimat; See You in Court; A Service to Ourselves; A Safe Start; Flying in Formation; BP Academy Awards (comedy). *Memberships:* British Columbia Motion Picture Association; Women in Film; Canadian Academy of Cinema and Television. *Honours:* Gold Medal, Graphica 1971, Montreal (Book); Certificate of Merit, LA Advertising Women, 1971; Award of Merit, The West Coast Show, LA 1974 (Radio) and 1975 (Brochure); Certificate of Excellence, The Graphics Gallery, Mass., 1975; Certificate of Merit, Television Bureau of Canada, 1981; Certificate of Appreciation, Canadian Diabetes Assn, 1984 and 1985 (Television). *Hobbies:* Photography; Feature film scriptwriting - Kickstart; Celebration '90 volunteer; Travelling. *Address:* Postal Box 33954 Station D, Vancouver, BC, Canada V6J 4L7.

MCFADDEN Mattie Florence, b. 22 Mar. 1918, West Windsor, Vermont, USA. Engineer; Author. *Education:* Graduate, Art Institute of Pittsbugh, 1939; CVA Scholar, Aeronautical Engineering, New York Univesity, 1943. *Appointments:* Assistant Engineer, Design & Materials Engineer, Chance Vought Aircraft Stratford, 1943-46; Manager, Materials & Processes, Norden Company, 1951-54; Missile Systems Division, Ragtheon Company, 1954-81; Manager, Materials & Standards, 1954-71, Technical Staff, Product Assurance, 1971-79, Manager, Corporate Engineering Standards, 1979-81, Technical Staff, to Manager of Operations, 1979-81. *Publications:* Contributing author: Materials Handbook, volume 2, 8th edition, 1964; Metal Selector, software programme, 1984; over 35 technical papers. *Membershis Include:* American Society for Metals; Standards Engineers Society, Public Relations Director 1983-84; American Institute of Aeronautics & Astronautics, Materials Committee, 1978-79; Aerospace Materials Specifications, Chairman; National President, Women Flyers of America, 1950-54; President, Boston Section, Society of Women Engineers. *Honours:* 59th Anniversary of Powered Flight, under Lt. Gen. Doolittle, 1953; Delegate to: 1st & 2nd

Metallurgical Congresses, Europe, 1955, USA 1957, SAE Achievement Award, 1977; SWE Past Chairman Award, 1985; SWE Fellow, 1986. *Hobbies:* Travel; Reading; Writing. *Address:* 24 Holly St., PO Box 257 South Dennis, MA 02660, USA.

MCFADDEN Rosemary, b. 1 Oct. 1948, Scotland. President, New York Mercantile Exchange. m. Brian Doherty, 26 May 1973. *Education:* BA 1970, MBA 1974, Rutgers University, USA; JD, Seton Hall Law School, New Jersey, USA, 1978. *Appointments include:* Executive Director, Hudson Health Systems Agency, NJ, 1976-81; Associate Legal Counsel, 1981-82, Executive Vice President, 1982-84, President, 1984-, New York Mercantile Exchange. *Memberships:* Board, Jersey City Medical Centre, 1985; Dean's Advisory Council, Rutgers University, 1985; Editorial Advisory Board, Petroleum Management Magazine, 1985; American & New Jersey Bar Associations; American Petroleum Institute; Society of Independent Gasoline Marketers; Institute of Petroleum; Rutgers & Alumni Association. *Honours:* Honorary Doctorate, Humanities, St Elizabeth's College, Convent Station, NJ, 1985; Alumna of the Year, Rutgers University, 1985. *Hobbies:* Travel; Collecting Antiques. *Address:* New York Mercantile Exchange, 4 World Trade Center, New York, NY 10048, USA.

MCFARLAND Violet Sweet Haven, b. 26 Feb. 1908, Seattle, Washington, USA. Author; Teacher. m. Glen W McFarland, 28 July 1958, divorced 1965. *Education:* BA, Washington State University, 1928; MA, Columbia University, New York City, 1933. *Appointments:* Teacher, Hawaiian Island 1928-30; Teacher, American School, Tokyo, Japan, 1930-31; Society Editor, Japan Times, Tokyo, 1930-31; Editorial Assistant Department of Justice, Washington, District of Columbia, USA, 1934-43; Society Editor, Hong Kong Telegraph, Hong Kong, 1940. *Publications:* As Violet Sweet Haven: Many Ports of Call; Gentlemen of Japan; Hong Kong for the Weekend. *Memberships:* Delta Zeta; National Board of Realtors; Past Member, Pen and Brush, New York City. *Honours:* Fellow, International Institute of Arts and Letters, Geneva and Zurich, 1965; Life member, National Press Club, Washington DC, 1986. *Hobbies:* World travel; Curator of oriental art. *Address:* PO Box 872, Lake Elsinore, CA 92330, USA.

MCFARLIN Leona Margaret, b. 19 Mar. 1944, New Orleans, Louisiana, USA. Office Education Coordinator. m. 24 Aug. 1968. 1 daughter. *Education:* BBA, Texas Western College, 1965; Teaching Certificate 1966, Vocational Certification 1972, University of Texas at El Paso. *Appointments:* Secretarial Teacher, Manpower Development Training Program, 1965; Business Teacher, Coronado High School, 1965-70; Vocational Office Ed Lab Teacher, 1972-80; Office Education Coordinator, Jefferson High School, 1980-. *Memberships:* Volunteer, America Heart Asso; American Vocational Association; Texas Vocational Consortium; Texas Vocational Assoc; State Board for Voc Of Ed Teachers of Texas; Parent Teacher Asso; Sponsor of Business Professionals of America. *Honours:* Outstanding Leadership Award, Conference Co-chairperson, OEA Leadership Conference, 1982; Outstanding Service Award, OEA of Texas, 1981; Certificate of Recognition, OEA, 1988. *Hobbies:* Swimming; Reading; Working with young people. *Address:* 9200 El Dorado, El Paso, TX 79925, USA.

MCFERREN Martha Dean, b. 25 Apr. 1947, Henderson, Texas, USA. Librarian; Poet. m. Dennis Scott Wall, 21 May 1977. *Education:* BS (Education) 1969, MLS (Library Science) 1971, North Texas State University; MFA (Creative Writing), Warren Wilson College, Swannanoa, North Carolina, 1988. *Appointments:* Jefferson Parish Library System, Metairie, Louisiana, 1976-81; New Orleans Public Schools, 1984-85. *Publications:* Books of verse: Delusions of a Popular Mind, 1983; Get Me Out of Here!, 1984; Contours for Ritual, 1988. *Memberships:* Poetry Society of America; Poets & Writers; New Orleans Poetry Forum. *Honours:* Finalist, AWP Anniversary Awards, 1982; Artist Fellowship, Louisiana State Arts Council,

1983-84; Poetry Prize, Deep South Writers, 1985; Yaddo Fellowship, 1985. *Hobbies:* Collecting Victorian & Edwardian children's books, books on Japan & China. *Address:* 2679 Verbena Street, New Orleans, Louisiana 70122, USA.

MCGARA Bonnie, b. 28 Aug. 1946, San Angelo, Texas, USA. Author. *Education:* University of Texas, Austin, 1970-72. *Publications:* Poetry in: New Hope INternational; Spokes; Matrix; Prospice; Forum; Short Story, The Blue Room, Karamu, 1988. *Address:* Austin, TX, USA.

MCGAUGHEY Miriam, b. New York, USA. Musician. m. Elvin Samuel McGaughey, 22 Apr. 1938. *Education:* BM cum laude, Music Education 1954, MM Music Education, 1959, University of Southern California, Los Angeles; Colleagues and Fellows degrees, Music Teachers' Association of California; Credentials, California Department of Education; Studied piano with: Adelaide Trowbridge Perry; Homer Simmons; Earle C Voorhies; Calvin B Cady. *Career:* Concert debut at age of 8; Toured as member of a duo-piano team, 1936-40; Soloist twice with Glendale, California Symphony Orchestra; Teacher of Music, Los Angeles Unified School District, 1954-74; Master Teacher, Occidental College, Los Angeles; Lecturer, pre-concert reviews, Glendale Symphony Association; Master classes and workshops; Los Angeles City Schools at Occidental College, 1960-61; Private Studio Teacher, 1932-. *Memberships include:* Sigma Alpha Iota; Adjudicator, Southwest Youth Music Festival; District Chairman, California Association of Professional Music Teachers; President, Elvin Samuel McGaughey Music Foundation, Inc. *Honours:* Won Highest Honours in California for Fellow's Thesis; Full Piano Scholarship, University of Southern California; Pi Lambda Theta, 1953; Alpha Chi Alpha, 1954. *Hobbies:* Gardening; Reading; Collecting Baroque recordings and books relevant to Baroque performance practices; Fine porcelain figurines. *Address:* Glendale, CA 91202, USA.

MCGEER Edith G., b. 18 Nov. 1923, New York City, New York, USA. Professor. m. Patrick L. McGeer, 15 Apr. 1954, 2 sons, 1 daughter. *Education:* BA, Swarthmore College, 1944; PhD, University of Virginia, 1946, *Appointments:* Researcher, 1946-54, E.I.DuPont de Nemours; Research Associate, 1954-74, Associate Professor, 1974-78, Acting Head, 1976-78, Professor 1979-, Head, 1983-88, Division of Neurological Sciences, University of British Columbia, Vancouver, Canada. *Publications:* Kainic Acid as a Tool in Neurobiology, 1978; Molecular Neurobiology of the Mammalian Brain, 1978, 2nd Edition, 1987; Over 300 papers in refereed journals. *Memberships:* Editorial Advisory Boards: Neurobiology of Aging; Journal of Developmental Neuroscience; Brain of Research; Neuroscience Letters; Alzheimer's Disease and Associated Disorders (international journal); Executive Committee, World Federation for Neurological Research, Group on Dementias; Canadian Biochemical Society; International Neurochemical Society; American Neurochemical Society; Society for Neuroscience; Canadian Federation of Biological Societies. *Honours:* Phi Beta Kappa, 1944; DuPont Fellow, 1945-46; Lychnos Society, 1946; Citation, Delaware Section, American Chemical Society, 1958; Honorary Fellow, North Pacific Society of Neurology and Psychiatry; Teaching Award, 1st Year Residents in Psychiatry, Faculty of Medicine, University of British Columbia, 1982; Distinguished Science Lecturer, Faculty of Medicine, University of British Columbia, 1982; Eccles Lectureship, 1st Canadian Symposium on the Organic Dementias, 1986; Honorary DSc, University of Victoria, 1987. *Hobbies:* Golf; Skiing; Swimming. *Address:* University of British Columbia, Division of Neurological Sciences, 2255 Wesbrook Hall, Vancouver, British Columbia, Canada V6T 1W5.

MCGHEE Nancy Bullock, b. 19 Mar. 1913, High Point, North Carolina, USA. Emeritus Professor of English. m. Samuel C. McGhee, 9 Nov. 1955. *Education:* AB, Shaw University, 1930; MA, Columbia University,

1931; PhD, Chicago University, 1942. *Appointments:* Teacher: Faulty Hampton Institute, Virginia, 1945; Louisville Municipal College, & summer session, Lincoln University, Jefferson City, Missouri, 1955; Director Pre-College Training, Instructor in Humanities 1964-69, Professor of Humanities 1968-79, Professor Emeritus 1978-, Director Faculty Seminar 1969, Chair, Department of English 1967-73, Avalon Foundation. *Publications:* Langston Hughes, Poet in the Folk Manner (in Langston Hughes Black Genius), 1971; Visit to Mexico, 1976; Hampton Institute Revisited: A Humanist Returns; History of Hampton Institute, currently commissioned by president. *Honours:* Honorary DH, Shaw University, 1973; Emeritus Professor, 1968; Distinguished Alumni, Shaw University, 1964; Distinguished Teacher, Hampton Institute, 1965. *Address:* 20 Gayle Street, Hampton, Virginia 23669, USA.

MCGIBBON Pauline Emily Mills (The Honorable), b. 20 Oct. 1910, Sarnia, Ontario, Canada. Former Lieutenant-Governor, Province of Ontario. m. Donald Walker McGibbon, 26 Jan. 1935. *Education:* BA, University of Toronto, 1933; LLD, Universities of Alberta, 1967, Western Ontario, 1974, Queens, 1974, Toronto, 1975, McMaster, 1981, Carleton, 1981, University of Windsor, 1988; DU, University of Ottawa, 1972 and Laval University, 1976; DHumL, St Lawrence University, Canton, New York, USA, 1977; DLittS, Victoria University, 1979; BAA Theatre, Ryeson Polytechnical Institute, 1974. *Appointments:* Lieutenant-Governor of the Province of Ontario, 1974-80; Boards of George Weston Limited, Mercedes-Benz of Canada, IBM, Canada, Retired, 1974; Imasco Limited, Retired, 1974. *Memberships:* Chairman, Board of Womens College Hospital, 1970-74; National Arts Centre, Ottawa, 1980-84; Member, Vice-President of Board of Governors, Roy Thompson Masssey Hall; Honorary Chairman, du Maurier Council in the Arts; Chairman, National Theatre School of Canada, Montreal, 1955-59; Canada Council, 1968-72; Chairman, Ontario Selection Committee/ Rhodes Scholarship, 1984-; Chancellor, University of Toronto, 1971-74 and University of Guelph, 1977-83. *Honours:* Canadian Centennial Medal, 1967; Dame of Grace, Order of St John of Jerusalem, 1974; 1st Canadian Woman to be appointed Honorary Colonel of a Regiment, 25 Toronto Service Battalion, 1975-83; Jubilee Medal, 1977; Honorary Fellow, Royal College of Physicians and Surgeons of Canada, 1977; Eleanor Rosenthal Humanities Award, 1978; Companion Order of Canada, 1980; Dame Grand Cross, Order of St Lazarus of Jerusalem, 1982; Grand Prior, 1982-1985. *Hobbies:* Theatre; Music; Ballet. *Address:* 20 Avoca Avenue, Apt 2004, Toronto, Ontario, Canada M4T 2B8

MCGILCHRIST Erica Margaret, b. 10 Feb. 1926, South Australia. Artist; Teacher. m. George Pilley, 16 Oct. 1953, divorced 1963. *Education:* South Australian School of Arts & Crafts, 1944; Adelaide Teachers College, 1945-46; Royal Melbourne Institute of Technology, 1950-52; Akademie der bildenden Kuenste, Munich, 1960, 1961. *Appointments Include:* Teacher, various schools & colleges, 1947-77; Teacher, Swinburne Technical College, 1977-80; Teacher, Holmesglen College of Technical & Further Education, Melbourne, 1982-86; Outer Eastern College of Technical & Further Education, 1987. *Creative Works Include:* 34 solo exhibitions in Australian Cities, London and Munich, 1951-; numerous group exhibitions; Commissions include postage stamp designs for Australia Post; theatre designs for Ballet Guild, Victoria & Australian Ballet; Helena Rubinstein Mural for Womens University College, Melbourne; decorated tram for Victorian Ministry for the Arts, Melbourne. *Memberships:* Contemporary Art Society; Womens Art Register. *Honours:* Recipient, various honours and awards. *Address:* 2 Daniell Crescent, Caulfield, VIC 3162, Australia.

MCGONIGAL Pearl Kathryn, b. 10 June 1929, Melville, Saskatchewan, Canada. Former Lieutenant-Governor of Manitoba, 1981-86. m. 3 Nov. 1949. 1 daughter. *Education:* Secondary School, Saskatchewan.

Appointments: Merchandising Representative, 7 years; Bank Employee, 9 years; Councillor, Deputy Mayor, City of Winnipeg, Manitoba, 1969-71; Lieutenant-Governor of Manitoba, 1981-86. *Publication:* Frankly Feminine. *Memberships:* St James Business and Professional Women's Club; Past President, Winnipeg Lionelles; Former Chairman, St James Assinoia Inter-faith Immigration Council; Former Member of the Vestry, St Andrew's Anglican Church; Former Volunteer, Lions Manor, Sherbrook Day Centre. *Honours:* Honorary LLD, University of Manitoba; Honorary Colonel, 735 Communication Regiment; Toastmasters International Communications Leadership Award; Dame of Grace, Order of St John; 1984 B'nai B'rith National Humanitarian Award; Canadian Corps of Commissionaires' Corps Silver Medal. *Hobbies:* Fishing; Gourmet cookery; Writing; Member of various Boards. *Address:* 51-361 Westwood Drive, Winnipeg, Manitoba, Canada R3K 1G4.

MCGOVERN Ann, b. 25 May 1930, New York City, New York, USA. Writer; Lecturer. m. Martin Scheiner, 6 June 1970. 3 sons, 1 daughter. *Education:* University of New Mexico, 1948-49. *Appointments:* Editor and Copywriter in various publishing houses including Western Publishing, Scholastic, Inc; Macmillan, etc., 1953-67. Freelance writer 1953-. *Publications:* Author of 43 books for young people including: Little Whale, 1979; Mr Skinner's Skinny House, 1980; Elephant Baby, 1982; Nicholas Bentley Stoningpot, III, 1982; Night Dive, 1984; Eggs on Your Nose, 1987; Down Under: Adventures on the Great Barrier Reef, 1989, etc. Numerous magazine articles. *Memberships:* Fellow, The Explorers Club; PEN; Authors Guild; Society of Journalists and Authors; Society of Women Geographers; International Food, Wine & Travel Writers. *Honours:* Best Science Book Award, National Science Teachers Association for Sharks, 1976, Shark Lady, 1979 and Night Dive, 1984; Author of the Year, Scholastic Books, 1978. *Hobbies:* Travel; Scuba diving; Photography. *Address:* 42 Usonia Road, Pleasantville, NY 10570, USA.

MCGOWAN Sherry A., b. 11 May 1946, Richmond, Virginia, USA. Realtor; Lecturer; Author. m. Richard W. Benson, 2 Sept. 1976. *Education:* BA, Ottawa University, 1976; Study, Washburn University School of Law, 1977-80. *Appointments:* Legal assistant to Chief Counsel, Kansas Department of Social & Rehabilitation Services, 1980; Executive Director, Breakthrough House Inc, 1980-82; Administrator, Kansas Mental Health & Retardation Services, 1982-86; Realtor, Re/Max Associates of Topeka, 1986-. *Publications:* Author: Go! Go! Get Organised, training manual, 1984; Reaching Out to Chronically Mentaly Ill, 1984; Individual's Right to Power, monograph & lecture (presented, various conferences); My Rap Group - in the Beginning, 1983; Developing Psychosocial Rehabiliatation Services, & Editor, Support Services for Long Term Mentally Ill, 1985; Golden City: Celebrating Good Life in Topeka, book, calendar, 1989. *Memberships:* Offices, Kansas Democratic National Committee, Topeka Board of Realtors, National Association of Realtors; Member, Kansas Association of Realtors; Ambassador, Topeka Sizzlers CBA Basketball Team. *Honours:* Member: Million Dollar Club, Topeka, 1987, 1988; President's Club, Re/Max Midwest Region, 1987, 1988. *Hobbies:* Politics; Season ticket holder, KC Royals (baseball), Topeka Sizzlers (basketball); Walking 4 miles per day; Hostess, social gatherings. *Address:* 2621 SW College, Topeka, Kansas 66611, USA.

MCGRAW Eloise Jarvis, b. 9 Dec. 1915, Houston, Texas, USA. Writer. m. William Corbin McGraw, 29 Jan. 1940. 1 son, 1 daughter. *Education:* BA, Principa College, Elsah, Illinois, 1937. *Appointments:* Teacher of portrait and figure painting, Oklahoma City Unviersity, 1942, 1943; Teacher of Fiction writing, Lewis and Clark College, Portland OR, 1966, 1967; Haystack summer sessions, Cannon Beach for Oregon University Dept of Continuing Education and Portland state University, 1970- 78; Teacher and/or speaker, numerous writers' workshops, conferences. *Publications:* Books: Sawdust in His Shoes, 1950; Crown Fire, 1951; Moccasin Trail, 1952, 1986; Mara, Daughter of the Nile, 1953, 1986; Pharoah, 1958; Techniques of Fiction Writing, 1961; The Golden Goblet, 1961, 1986; Merry Go Round in Oz (with Lauren Lynn McGraw), 1963; Greensleeves, 1968; Master Cornhill, 1973, 1987; A Really Weird Summer, 1977; Joel and the Great Merlini, 1979; The Forbidden Fountain of Oz, with Lauren Lynn McGraw, 1980; The Money Room, 1981; Hideaway, 1983; The Seventeenth Swap, 1986, 1988; The Trouble with Jacob, 1988. *Memberships:* Oregon Freelance Club; Author's League. *Honours:* Recipient of numerous awards most recently, Nominee, Western Writers of American Golden Spur Award, 1983; Evelyn Sibley Lampman Award, 1983; L Frank Baum Memorial Award, 1983. *Hobbies:* Printmaking; Drawing; Sewing (dressmaking); Breadmaking; Oenology; Travel; History. *Address:* 1970 Indian Trail, Lake Oswego, OR 97034, USA.

MCGREGOR Iona, b. 7 Feb. 1929, Aldershot, England. Writer. *Education:* Schools in India, Scotland, Wales, England; BA Honours, Bristol University, 1950. *Appointments:* Sub-editor, Dictionary of the Older Scottish Tongue, School of Scottish Studies, Edinburgh University, 1952- 57; Classics teacher, various schools, England & Scotland, 1959-85. *Publications:* An Edinburgh Reel, 1968, 4th edition 1986; Popinjay, 1969, 1979; The Burning Hill, 1970; Tree of Liberty, 1972; Snake & the Olive, 1974, 1978; Edinburgh & Eastern Lowlands: Lothian, Fife & Borders, 1979; Wallace & Bruce, 1986; Oscar Wilde: Importance of Being E. , 1987; Huckleberry Finn, 1988; Death Wore A Diadem (feminist-historical crime novel), 1989. *Hobbies:* Hill walking; Scottish history; Do-it-Yourself; Siamese cats. *Address:* 9 Saxe Coburg Street, Edinburgh EH3 5BN, Scotland.

MCGUIRE Sondra Lee Whitehurst Shumate, b. 9 Nov. 1941, Columbus, Ohio, USA. President, CEO, Auto Trimmer's Supply. m. (1) Brandt Shumate, 2 June 1958, divorced 1978, 2 sons. (2) Clyde McGuire, 29 May 1982. *Education:* University of Arizona, 1975-76; Pima College, 1977-81. *Appointments:* Sales Audit and Payroll, Levy's Department store, 1960-61; Office Manager, Shumate's Custom Interiors, 1962-78; President and CEO, Auto Trimmer's Supply, Inc, 1978- . *Publications:* Numerous articles for Auto Trim News, a trade publication. *Memberships:* So Arizona Executive Women's Council; Automotive Service Industry Assoc (Member of executive committee, 7 years and National Chairman 2 years, program chairman 2 year); Industrial Fabric Association. *Honours:* Certificate of Appreciation, Beacon Foundation, 1984; Certification of Appreciation, Automotive Service Industry Association, 1985, 1986, 1987; Hall of Fame Plaque, Automotive Service Industry Association, 1986. *Hobbies:* Dancing; Swimming; Sewing; Crochet; Reading. *Address:* 8900 Bear's Path, Tucson, AZ 85749, USA.

MCILVAIN Helen Eugene Roberts, b. 17 Nov. 1942, Kansas City, Missouri, USA. Medical Educator; Medical Psychotherapist; Behavioural Medicine Researcher. m. Robert Jeffrey McIlvain, 24 Mar. 1964, div. 1974, 1 son. *Education:* BA, Social Science, Kansas State Teachers College, Emporia, 1965; MSE, Counsellor Education, 1974, PhD, 1977, Kansas State University, Manhattan; Doctoral Internship, University of Kentucky Medical Center, Lexington, 1976-77. *Appointments:* Counsellor, Belleville Area College, Belleville, Illinois, 1977-81; Medical Educator, Psychotherapist, Researcher, University of Nebraska Medical Center, Omaha, 1981-. *Publications:* Various articles including: The effects of sexism on female achievement, 1976; Type A personalities: How can they change? (with J C Buell and R S Eliot), 1982; Application of the MRFIT smoking cessation program to a healthy mixed-sex population (with M E McKinney, A V Thompson, G L Todd), 1987; Screening for blood pressure hyperreactivity to stress (with J C Glass, M E McKinney, H Ruddell, J C Buell, R S Eliot), 1988; Several abstracts; Stress Management Techniques for Care Givers of the Elderly, educational TV programme, 1983.

Memberships: Board of Directors, American Lung Association of Nebraska; American Psychological Association; American Mental Health Counselors Association; American Board of Medical Psychotherapists; Society of Behavioral Medicine; Association for the Behavioral Sciences and Medical Education. *Honour:* Phi Kappa Phi, 1973. *Hobbies:* Riding; Snorkelling and scuba-diving; Skiing; Hiking; Travel; Reading mysteries; Southwest Indian culture. *Address:* University of Nebraska Medical Center, 42nd and Dewey, Omaha, NE 68105, USA.

MCINTOSH Edith Marie, b. 3 Aug. 1931, Beaumont, Texas, USA. Clinical Psychologist. m. Jesse McIntosh, 19 Mar. 1954. 2 sons, 1 daughter. *Education:* BS, Stephen F Austin University, 1953; MEd 1968, MA 1977, University of Texas at El Paso; PhD, Florida Institute of Technology, 1982. *Appointments:* Teacher, El Paso Schools, 1953-77; Associate Psychologist, Ysleta Schools, 1978-82; Part-time Faculty, University of Texas at El Paso, 1981-83; Paediatric Psychologist, WBAMC, 1982; Private Practice, Clinical Psychologist, El Paso, 1983-. *Creative Works:* Unpublished Manuscripts: Validity of clinical judgement of Adjustment from drawings of emotionally distrubed and normal children; Sources of Diagnostic Error in the Detection of Maladjusted Children using Human Figure Drawings. *Memberships:* American Psychological Association; Texas Psychological Association; El Paso Psychological Association; Academy of Psychologists; American Board of Medical Psychologists; Mental Health Association of El Paso and Texas; American Society of Clinical Hypnosis; American Association of Professional Hypnotherapists; American Association of Marriage and Family Therapy; Psi Chi; World Organization for Mental Health. *Honours:* Outstanding Citizen, 1985; One of 10 member Task Force for State of Texas on Parenting, 1986; *Hobbies:* Reading; Gourmet Cooking; Drawing or Painting; Biking. *Address:* 413 Stewart Drive, El Paso, Texas 79915, USA.

MCINTOSH Kinn Hamilton, b. 20 June 1930, Huddersfield, England. Author. *Education:* Honorary MA, University of Kent, 1986. *Publications:* Under pseudonym, Catherine Aird: The Religious Body; A Most Contagious Game; Henrietta Who?; The Complete Steel; A Late Phoenix; His Burial Too; Slight Mourning; Parting Breath; Some Die Eloquent; Passing Strange; Last Respects; Harm's Way; A Dead Liberty. *Memberships:* Former Chairman, UK Finance Committee, Girl Guides Association; Assistant Treasurer, World Association Girl Guides and Girl Scouts; Committee Member Crime Writers Association; South East Arts Literature Panel. *Honour:* MBE, 1988. *Hobby:* Bridge. *Address:* 1 Sturry Hill, Sturry, Canterbury, Kent, CT2 0NG, England.

MCINTOSH Margaret Vance Means (Peggy), b. 1 Nov. 1934, New York City, New York, USA. Educator; College Administrator. m. Kenneth McIntosh, 28 Mar. 1965, 2 daughters. *Education:* BA summa cum laude, English, Radcliffe College, 1956; University of London, England, 1956-57; MA, English, 1961, PhD, English, 1967, Harvard University. *Appointments:* English Teacher, The Brearley School, New York City, 1957-60; Teaching Fellow in English, Harvard University, 1962-64; Assistant Professor of English, Trinity College, Washington DC, 1966-69; Assistant Professor of English, University of Denver, 1970-79; Honorary Visiting Lecturer in American Studies, University of Durham, England, 1976-77; Programme Director, 1980-87; Associate Director, 1987-, Wellesley College Center for Research on Women, Wellesley, Massachusetts; Visiting Associate Professor of Women's Studies, Wellesley College, 1981-82. *Publications include:* Varieties of Women's Studies (with Elizabeth Minnich), 1984; Women's Studies International at Nairobi, 1986; Rethinking Women, Education, and Leadership, 1987; White Privilege and Male Privilege, 1988; New Knowledge for a New Age, 1989; Contributing editor, Women's Studies Quarterly, 1981-; Consulting editor, Sage: A Scholarly Journal on Black Women, 1988-. *Memberships:* Co-Founder, Board Vice-President Rocky Mountain Women's Institute, Denver, 1975-81; Board of Directors: The Feminist Press, 1981-87; Greenwood Music Camp; Trustee Associate, Bryn Mawr School, Baltimore; Advisory Board: Princeton (NJ) Friends' School; Black Women's Studies Institute, Medgar Evers College, Brooklyn. *Honours:* Phi Beta Kappa, 1956; Outstanding Academic Advisor, University of Denver, 1979; Chair, Radcliffe College Class of 1956, 1981-85; President, Radcliffe Graduate Society, 1983-84; Honoree, Celebration of Women, Council for Women in Independent Schools, 1985; Educational Leadership Award, North-East Coalition of Educational Leaders Inc, 1988; Foundation grants, 1983-. *Hobbies:* Gardening; Music; Mountain hiking; Correspondence; Travel. *Address:* Wellesley College Center for Research on Women, Wellesley, MA 02181, USA.

MCINTYRE Marilyn Rose, b. 23 May 1949, Erie, Pennsylvania, USA. Actress. *Education:* Guilford College, 1967-69; BFA, North Carolina School of the Arts, 1969-72; Rose Bruford College of Speech & Drama, Kent, England, 1970; Pennsylvania State University Acting Programme, 1972-75. *Appointments:* Arena Stage, Washington DC 1975-77; New York, Shakespeare Festival, 1976, 1984; Roundabout Theatre, New York City, 1978; Circle in the Square, New York City, 1981; Broadway, Gemini, 1980-81; Virginia Museum Theatre, 1981; The Alley Theatre, Houston, Texas, 1985-86; Daytime TV Contract Roles on: Loving; One Life to Live and Search for Tomorrow, 1977-84; Coach Privately, Teacher, Weist Baron School of Acting. *Memberships:* Phi Kappa Phi. *Honours:* Nancy Reynolds Merit Scholarship, North Carolina, School of the Arts, 1971. *Hobbies:* Scuba Diving; Swimming; Downhill Skiing; Visiting Historical Districts of Cities; Coaching Teenagers Acting. *Address:* c/o Don Buchwald Ass., 10 E 44th St., New York, NY 10017, USA.

MCINTYRE Vera Lynette, b. 4 June 1949, Havana, Florida, USA. Consultant. 3 daughters. *Education:* AA, Tallahassee Community College, 1967-70; BA, Social Welfare and Criminology, 1970-71, Master's Degree, Urban and Regional Planning, 1972-80, Florida State University. *Appointments:* Teacher, Gadsden County School Board, 1969-74; Researcher, Division of Youth Services, Bureau of Statistics, 1970; System Analyst, Parole and Probation Commission, 1975; Manpower Planning Specialist I, Balance of State Prime Sponsor, 1977-79, Manpower Management Planning Specialist II, Governor's Special Grants, 1979, Employment and Training Administrator I, Governor's Special Grants Unit, 1979-81, Employment and Training Administrator II, Research Development and Evaluation Section, State Job Training Coordinating Council, 1981-84, Unemployment Compensation Executive II, Division of Unemployment Compensation, 1984-87, Chief, Bureau of Placement, Division of Labor, Employment and Training, 1987-88, Department of Labor and Employment Security; President, McIntyre and McIntyre Marketing, Inc, 1988-. *Creative work:* Founder of Black Families of America, Inc (National Organization, non-profit). *Memberships:* American Business Women Association (President); Black Families of America, Inc (President); March of Dimes, Executive Board Member. *Honours:* National Alliance of Business Award; Young Adult Conservation Corp, Certificate of Merit; Distinguished Service Award, Frontiers International, Inc; Leadership Award, State of Florida; Woman of the Year, American Business Women Association; Mt Lion AME Church Missionary Society Special Recognition. ssa 20Hobbies: Public speaking; Writing; Interior decorating; Gardening. *Address:* Route 1, Box 721, Havana, Florida 32312, USA.

MCKELLAR Marie Therese, b. 28 Mar. 1940, Chicago, Illinois, USA. Professor of Mathematics. m. Archie C. McKellar, 26 Aug. 1967. *Education:* BA cum laude, Mathematics, St Mary's College, Notre Dame, Indiana, 1962; MA, Mathematics, University of Illinois, 1964; EdD, Mathematics Education, Rutgers University, 1972. *Appointments:* Instructor, Mathematics, Mundelein College, Chicago, Illinois, 1964-66; Assistant Professor, 1970-73, Chair, Department of Mathematics and CIS, 1971-86, Associate Professor, 1973- 78,

Professor, 1978-87, Mercy College, Dobbs Ferry, New York; Member, Graduate MBA Faculty, Long Island University, New York, 1978-87; Visiting Professor of Mathematics, Temple University, Tokyo, Japan, 1987- . *Memberships:* National Council of Teachers of Mathematics; Mathematical Association of America; Women and Mathematics Education; Association for Women in Mathematics; Pi Mu Epsilon. *Honours:* Kappa Gamma Pi, 1962; Graduate Assistantship, Mathematics Department, University of Illinois, 1962-64; Graduate Assistantship, Mathematics Department, Rutgers University, 1966-68. *Hobbies:* Opera; Wine-collecting; Scuba-diving. *Address:* 4-2-12 Aobadai, Meguro-ku, Tokyo 153, Japan.

MCKENNA Rachel Mary, b. 2 July 1956, Dublin, Ireland. Research Scientist. m. James Christopher Gough, 20 July 1983, 1 daughter. *Education:* BA Mod, Honours, Microbiology, Trinity College, Dublin, 1977; PhD, National University of Ireland, 1981; Postdoctoral fellowships, Departments of Immunology & Medicine, University of Manitoba, Canada, 1982-85. *Appointments:* Assistant Professor of Medicine, Assistant Professor of Microbiology, University of Manitoba, 1985-. *Publications:* Over 30 papers, immunogenetics, immunologically mediated diseases of brain & joints, mechanism of transplant rejection. *Memberships:* Canadian Transplant Society; Canadian Society of Immunology; American Society of Histocompatibility & Immunogenetics. *Honours:* Research grants, various bodies including Medical Research Council, 1983-. *Hobbies:* Active, Canadian Council on Status of Women (particular interest, problems in science & medicine); Medicine; Part-time lecturer, Women's Studies, University of Manitoba. *Address:* 116 Brock Street, Winnipeg, Manitoba, Canada R3N 0Y4.

MCKENZIE Tracey Perrier, b. 10 Aug. 1960, Hartford, Connecticut, USA. Fisheries Biologist. *Education:* BS, Pitzer College, Claremont Colleges, 1983; MS Zoology, University of Rhode Island, 1989. *Appointments:* Biologist 1983-87, Fisheries Biologist 1987-, NOAA Fisheries, UAS Department of Commerce, Narragansett, Rhode Island. *Publications:* Articles to professional journals. *Memberships:* American Fisheries Society; Society for Marine Mammology; Northeast Estuarine Research Association; National Estuarine Programe, Alternate Technical Committee. *Honours:* Sustained Superior Performance, 1987; Certificate of Recognition, 1985. *Hobbies:* Scuba diving; Travelling; Reading. *Address:* NOAA Fisheries, Narragansett Laboratory, South Ferry Road, Narragansett, RI 02882, USA

MCKEOWN Judy Lynn, b. 18 Dec. 1948, Mobile, Alabama, USA. Marriage and Family Therapist. m. Dr Douglas O'Neal McKeown, 24 Aug. 1974. 2 sons. *Education:* AA, Gulf Coast Community College, 1970; BA 1972, MA 1974, University of West Florida; PhD work, Florida State University, 1986. *Appointments:* Northwest Florida Mental Health Center, 1972-82; Holmes-Washington Guidance Clinic, 1972-82; Psychological Specialties of Dothan, 1982-. *Creative works:* Conducted seminars and public speaking dealing with psychological issues. *Memberships:* Clinical Member, American Association for Marriage and Family Therapy; Alabama Psychological Association; Licensed Professional Counselor; Licensed Marriage & Family Therapist; Registered Psychological Assistant; Alabama Counseling Association. *Honours:* Florida Blue Key Award, 1970; Presidential Scholarship Award, 1970; Journalism Award, 1969-70. *Hobbies:* Public speaking; Modelling; Walking; Biking; Volunteer work for local school systems; Gardening. *Address:* 704 South Second Street, Chipley, Florida 32428, USA.

MCKERNAN Llewellyn Teresa, b. 12 Jul 1941, Hampton, Arkansas, USA. Poet and Children's Book Writer. m. John Joseph McKernan, 3 Aug 1967, 1 daughter. *Education:* BA, English, cum laude, Hendrix College, 1963; MA, English, University of Arkansas, 1966; MA, Creative Writing, Brown University, 1976.

Appointments: English Instructor, Georgia Southern College, 1966-67; Reporter, Herald-Dispatch, 1979-80; Adjunct English Professor, Marshall University, 1980-87; Writing Specialist, Marshall University Writing Centre, 1988. *Publications:* Short and Simple Annals: Poems About Appalachia, Ist ed 1979, 2nd ed 1982; More Songs of Gladness: Psalms for Children, Concordia, 1987; Bird Alphabet, An ABC in Verse, Standard Publications, 1988. *Memberships:* West Virginia Writers, Appalachian Writers Association; Appalachian Writers Co-operative; Society of Children's Book Writers; International Women's Writing Guild. *Honours:* 1978-79 AAUW Publication Grant; 1981 West Virginia Arts and Humanities Commission Fellowship; 1982 West Virginia Humanities Foundation Publication Grant; Poet and Writers Reading Grant 1984; First Prize, Poetry, West Virginia Writers Contest, 1982, 1986, 1988, 1989; Third Prize, Poetry, 1982 National Poetry Competitiion; First Prize, California State Poetry's Society Summer 1985 Dial-A-Poem Contest; First Prize, Artemis magazine 1988 Poetry Contest. *Hobbies:* Painting; Singing; Playing the Autoharp; Reading; Walking. *Address:* 1012 Chesapeake Court, Huntington, WV 25701, USA.

MCKIERNAN Susan, b. 30 June 1947, Barberton, Ohio, USA. Art Educator. m. Brian D. McKiernan, 1967 (div. 1980), 1 son, 1 daughter. *Education:* BFA, Metalsmithing 1977, Certificate, Higher Education Administration 1987, MS Education 1987, University of Akron. *Appointments:* Instructor, Metalsmithing & Enamelling 1979-80, Assistant to Head, Department of Art 1980-86, Art History Teacher 1986-, Assistant Director, School of Art 1987-, University of Akron. *Creative work includes:* Walking tours, Peninsula (Ohio), downtown Akron. *Memberships:* Trustee, Medina County Historical Society; Charter member, Museum Contemporaries of Akron Art Museum, & Progress Through Preservation; Past President, Hower House Victorians; National Council of Arts Administrators; Ohio Association of Women Deans & Administrators; Ohio Association for Counselling & Development. *Hobbies:* Antiques; Travel; Architecture; History; Genealogy. *Address:* 3306 South Weymouth Road, Medina, Ohio 44256, USA.

MCKINNEY Tatiana Ladygina, b. Smolensk, Russia. Artist; Instructor; Lecturer. m. Samuel Henry McKinney, 12 Sept. 1928, 2 sons, 1 daughter. *Education:* Private tutors, Russia; Certificate, Vinogradov Academy of Art, Latvia; Painting technique, Escola Nacional de Belas Artes, Brazil; Certificate, New College Fine Arts Institute, Sarasota, Florida, USA. *Appointments:* Private teaching, Brazil 1954-57, Greece 1960-63; Programme Director, Venice Art League, Florida, USA, 1967-70; Instructor, Venice Art League 1968-, Painting in the Mountains School, North Carolina 1984-. Also: Painting demonstrations, lectures, art show judging, Florida, North Carolina, Washington DC, 1963-. *Creative work includes:* Paintings in permanent collections: Dartmouth College, New Hampshire; New College, Florida; Fine Arts Society, Sarasota, Florida; Roman Catholic Diocese, Venice, FL; Vatican. Religious works commissioned by & used in many churches; Christ the King, Wisconsin; Resurrection painting, private collection of Pope John Paul II. *Memberships:* Artists Equity; Florida Artists Group; National League of American Pen Women; Vice President, Venice Area Art League; President, Women's Guild, Holy Spirit Orthodox Mission. *Honours include:* Awards, USA, Belgium, 1967-71; Numerous solo exhibitions, Brazil, Greece, USA, 1955-; Invited Guest, Grand Salon, Union Feminine Artistique et Culturelle, Charleroi, Belgium, 1986; Brussels Belgium, 1987; Kobi, Japan, 1989. *Hobbies:* Gardening; Culinary arts. *Address:* 409 Darling Drive, Venice, Florida 34285, USA.

MCKINNEY WHITFIELD Megan, b. Columbia, Missouri, USA. Journalist. m. Robert William Whitfield (divorced), 1 daughter. *Education:* BA, University of Missouri. *Appointments:* Writer, TV Guide, New York; Senior press representative, CBS-TV, New York; Vice President, Frank Sullivan & Associates, Chicago; Public Relations Director, Swedish Covenant Hospital, Chicago; Columnist, Pulitzer-Lerner Newspapers; Editor, Avenue M magazine. *Publications include:* Numerous articles, TV Guide & Avenue M magazines; Snapshots column, Pulitzer-Lerner newspaper & Avenue M; Fiona Cavendish column, Avenue M; Editorials, Philadelphia Inquirer & Chicago Sun-Times newspapers. *Memberships:* Director 1988-, President Woman's Board 1988-90, Northwestern Memorial Hospital, Chicago; Past President, Art Resources in Teaching; Board of Governors, English-Speaking Union; Council, Shakespeare Globe Theatre. *Address:* 1100 North Dearborn, Chicago, Illinois 60610, USA.

MCKINSTRY Grenetta, b. 10 Oct. 1947, Birmingham, Alabama, USA. Senior Microbiologist. 1 son. *Education:* AB cum laude, Biology, General Science, Stillman College, Tuscaloosa, Alabama, 1968; MA, Microbiology, Indiana University, Bloomington, 1970; PhD, Microbiology, Ohio State University, Columbus, 1979; Postdoctoral work, Max Planck Institute for Molecular Genetics, Berlin, Federal Republic of Germany and Ohio State University, Columbus, 1979. *Appointments:* Researcher, Eli Lilly Pharmaceutical Company, Indianapolis, Indiana, 1970-72; Technical Assistant, Microbiology Department, Microbial Genetics Laboratory, Ohio State University, Columbus, 1972-76; Scientist, Microbial Genetics, Abbot Laboratories, Chicago, Illinois, 1979 77-85; Senior Microbial Geneticist, Oak Ridge Research Institute Inc, Oak Ridge, Tennessee, 1985-87; Senior Microbiologist/Enviromentalist, PEER Consultants, 1987-89; Career Consultant. *Publications include:* Maltose Transport in Escherichia coli, thesis, 1970; Genetic Evidence for Circularity for the Bacillus subtilis chromosome (with J.C.Copeland), 1974; Protoplasts of Gibberella fujikuroi, 1982; Amplification of Heavy Metal Resistance of Pseudomonas Syringae O2 after Addition of Ampicillin or Penicillin V to Synthetic Growth Medium (with T.Osborne, S.Ebong, S.Benson, C.Hadden, N.Revis, 1986. *Memberships:* American Society for Microbiology, National and Illinois Branch; American Association for Advancement of Science; Association for Women in Science; New York Academy of Sciences; American Phytopathological Society. *Honours:* Graduate Student Representative, Committee for Selection of Dean, College of Biological Sciences, Ohio State University, 1978-79; Full Membership, Sigma Xi, 1978; Abbott Laboratories Presidential Award, 1982. *Hobbies:* Reading; Aerobics; Tennis. *Address:* Gene Amplification Inc, PO Box 568032, Atlanta, GA 30356, USA.

MCLACHLIN Beverley Marian, b. 7 Sept. 1943, Pincher Creek, Alberta, Canada. Chief Justice. Widow, 1 son. *Education:* BA, 1965, MA, 1968, LLB, 1968, University of Alberta. *Appointments:* Admitted to Alberta Bar, 1969, British Columbia Bar, 1971; Lawyer, Wood Moir Hyde & Ross, Edmonton, 1969-71; Lawyer, Thomas Herdy Mitchell & Co., Fort St. John, 1971-72; Lawyer, 1972-75, Associate, 1974-75, Bull Housser & Tupper; Honorary Lecturer, 1974-75, Associate Professor, 1975-78, 1978-, University of British Columbia; Appointed Judge, County Court of Vancouver, 1981; Justice, Supreme Court of British Columbia, 1981; Appointed Justice, British Columbia Court of Appeal, 1985; Appointed Chief Justice, Supreme Court of British Columbia, 1988. *Publications:* Articles in various journals; The American Bill of Rights - Implications for Canada, 1967; Consumer Protection, 1976; Co-author, Materials in Civil Litigation, 1977; Co-Author, British Columbia Practice, 1979, 3 volumes; Co-author, British Columbia Court Forms, 1985, 3 volumes; Co-Author, Canadian Law of Architecture & Engineering, 1987, 1 volume. *Address:* The Law Courts, 800 Smithe Street, Vancouver, BC, Canada V6Z 2E1.

MCLARTY Velma Corrine, b. 9 Nov. 1930, Kingston, Jamaica. Company President. m. Horace George McLarty, 1957, 1 son, 2 daughters. *Education:* BA, University of West Indies. *Appointments:* Under Secretary Ministry of Mining & Natural Resources, 1972-73; Director, Personnel, Ministry of Public Service, 1974; Managing Director, Sugar Industry Housing Ltd., 1975-77; Managing Director, National Housing Tru,

1977-80; Managing Director JNIP, 1983-88; President, Jampro Ltd., 1988-. *Memberships:* National Sugar Co. Workers Savings & Loan Bank; Workers Bank Trust Co; Agricultural Development Corp; Jamaica Industrial Development Corp. *Hobbies:* Reading; Theatre; Gardening. *Address:* Jampro Ltd., 35 Trafalgar Road, Kingston 10, Jamaica, West Indies.

MCLEOD Iris Helena, b. 9 Oct. 1946, Ellenville, New York, USA. m. David J McLeod, 31 May 1968. 2 sons. *Education:* AA, BA, Psychology, Thomas A Edison State College, Trenton, 1985; Currently studying at Fielding Institute, Santa Barbara, California. *Appointments:* Department of Psychiatry, 1970-73, Nationally Certified Operating Room Technologist, Scrub and Circulating Surgical Nurse, 1973-76, Montefiore Hospital and Medical Center, New York; Adolescent Suicide Awareness Program, South Bergen Mental Health Center, Inc; Inservice Training Programme, Bergen Regional Counselling Center, Hackensack, N.J., 1981-. *Memberships:* American Orthopsychiatric Association, Inc; Fellow and Diplomate American Board of Medical Psychotherapists; Institute for the Advancement of Health; American Association for Counseling and Development; American Mental Health Counselors Association; New Jersey Professional Counselors Association; National Hemophilia Foundation; Hemophilia Association of New Jersey; Narcolepsy Network; American Association of Suicidology; Phobia Society of America; New York Milton H. Erickson Society for Psychotherapy; Associate Fellow, Institute for Rational-Emotive Therapy; American Group Psychotherapy Association; New Jersey Group Psychotherapy Society; New Jersey Association for Specialists in Group Work; Respiratory Health Association; New York Academy of Sciences; Humor Project of the Saratoga Institute; American Society of Professional and Executive Women; Parents Anonymous of New Jersey, Inc; Parents United. *Honours:* National Deans List, 1983-84 and 1985-86; Phi Theta Kappa, Bergen Community College, 1984 and 1985; Certificate of Award, 1983, 1984, 1985, 1986, Bergen Regional Counselling Center; Certiciate of Award, 1986, South Bergen Mental Health Center, Inc; Certificate of Achievement, Award for Dedication and Loyal Service, Montefiore Hospital and Medical Center. *Address:* 667 Grant Terrace, Teaneck, New Jersey 07666, USA.

MCLEOD Ruth Mary, b. 27 Nov. 1951, Oldham, England. Director, Homeless International, U.K. m. Michael McLeod, 1 Mar. 1975. 1 son, 1 daughter. *Education:* BA (Hons) 1973, MA 1976, Cambridge; Dip Ed, University West Indies, 1977. *Appointments:* Founder of Women's Construction Collective, Jamaica, 1983; First Director, Construction Resource & Development Centre, 1983-89; Director, Oasis UK, 1989-. *Publications:* The Women's Construction Collective-Seeds Publication, 1985; Papers on low income shelter for USAID, Organisation of American States and others. *Membership:* Habitat International Coalition. *Hobby:* Photography. *Address:* 39 Rushton Road, Rothwell, Kettering, Northants, England.

MCMAHAN Celeste Tina, b. 4 Jan, 1948, Denver, Colorado, USA. Architectural Manager. m. George Cardinal Richards, 2 Dec. 1977. *Education:* BS Urban Studies 1976, MS Urban and Regional Planning 1977, Postgraduate in Architecture 1977, University of Colorado; Licensed Real Estate Salesman, Colorado; Certified Lymphologist, International Academy of Lymphology, Utah, 1985. *Appointments:* Housing Sales Coordinator, Great Western United, Colorado City, 1970-74; Director of Parks and Recreation, City of Edgewater, 1975-76; Intern, WICHE, 1976; Intern Planner, City of Aurora, 1976-77; Project Manager/Architect, Stanford University, Palo Alto, California, 1977-79; Designer, Facilities Planner, Sacramento Savings, Sacramento, 1979-80; Owner, McMahan Associates, Vallejo, 1979-; Project Manager, Crocker Bank, San Francisco, 1980-81; Manager of Design and Construction, Bank of America, San Francisco, 1981-. *Publications:* A Market Analysis of Downtown, 1976;

Housing Market and Population Projections, 1976; Tales from the Old Country, photographer, 1984. *Memberships include:* Organization of Women Architects; American Institute of Architects; National Association of Women in Construction; National Association of Corporate Real Estate; Trustee, Grace Cathedral; Board of Directors, Friends of the Arts; Board of Directors, Bay Area Lawyers for The Arts; Board of Directors, Natural Systems. *Honours:* All City Orchestra, Educators Association Ensemble, Colorado, 1965; 1st Place Award Music Educational Grantee and Honours Student, Unviersity of Colorado, 1974-77; Exceptional Performance Award, Bank of America, San Francisco, 1985. *Address:* 550 Battery No 406, San Francisco, CA 94111, USA.

MCMAHON Leonie Jean, b. 26 Feb. 1941, Brisbane, Australia. Chiropractor; Osteopath; Acupuncturist. m. Peter Francis Egan, 11 Jan. 1969, 1 son. *Education:* Diploma, Naturopathy, 1963; DR, Chiropractic, 1969; Dip. Acupuncture, 1973. *Appointments:* Private Practice, Acupuncturist, Osteopathy, 1963-. *Publications:* Magazine articles; radio & TV appearances. *Memberships:* Federal Secretary, Austrlian Acupuncturists Federation; President, Acupuncturist Association of Australia, 1984-; Director, Sydney College of Chiropractic; Director, Academy of Natural Healing; Australian Society of Authors; Opera Autitions Committee. *Honours:* Award of Honour, Outstanding Service to the Chiropractic Profession, 1983. *Hobbies:* Singing; Opera; Classical Music. *Address:* 23 Beaumont Road, Killara 2071, NSW, Australia.

MCMASTER Juliet Sylvia, b. 2 May 1937, Kenya. m. Rowland Douglas McMaster, 10 Apr. 1968, 1 son, 1 daughter. *Education:* BA, Honours, Oxford University, 1959; MA, 1962, PhD, 1965, English, University of Alberta. *Appointments:* Assistant Professor, 1965-70, Associate Professor, 1970-76, Professor, 1976-86, University Professor, 1986-, University of Alberta. *Publications:* Thackeray: The Major Novels, 1971; Trollope's Palliser Novels, 1978; Jane Austen on Love, 1978; The Novel from Sterne to James, co-author, 1981; Dickens the Designer, 1987. *Memberships:* Modern Language Association; Victorian Studies Association of Western Canada, Founding President; Royal Society of Canada, 1980; Jane Austen Society of North America, Board Member, 1982; Dickens Society, Board Member, 1987; *Honours:* Canada Council Post-Doctoral Fellowship, 1969-70; Alberta Woman Athlete of the Year; Guggenheim Fellowship, 1976-77; McCalla Professorship, 1982-83; Killam Research Fellowship, 1987-89. *Hobbies:* Art, Fencing; Riding; Guitar. *Address:* Dept. of English, University of Alberta, Edmonton, Alberta, Canada T6G 2E5.

MCMASTER Mary Jane, b. 15 Feb. 1943, New York, USA. College Professor. *Education:* BS, Math & Sic, SUNY, Oswego, 1965; MS, Math, University of Oregon, Eugene, 1970; PhD, University of Wisconsin, Madison, 1975; Graduate work, Puskkin Institute, Leningrad and University of Moscow, Russia, 1975. *Appointments:* Maths Teacher, Goshen New York High School, 1966-69; Teaching Assistant, University of Wisconsin, 1970-74; Professor, University of Northern Iowa, Cedar Falls, Iowa, 1974-75; Mathematics Professor, LA Valley College, 1979-80; Professor, Mathematics, West LA College, Culver City, 1980-; Professor, Mathematics, Compton College, 1986-. *Creative works:* Research in math learning problems of disadvantaged and minority students, 1986-. *Memberships:* Cal Com College Math Teachers Association; LA Math Teachers Association; Wilderness Society; Sierra Club; Canyon Explorers Club. *Honours:* National Science Foundation Grant, 1969-70; Presenter, Nat Council of Math Teacher Meetings, Iowa, 1975. *Hobbies:* Run four marathons yearly; Participant in several triathlons; Backpack the 215 mile John Muir trail in Sierra's; Rode bicycle across the USA in 1985; Lead weekend bike trips for CEC; 3rd female finisher in world's highest altitude marathon, Rocky Mountina Marathon, Colorado, 1986. *Address:* Compton College, 1111 Artesia Ave, Compton, California 90221, USA.

MCMEEKIN Dorothy, b. 24 Feb. 1932, Boston, Massachusetts, USA. Plant Pathologist; Professor. *Education:* BA, Biology, Wilson College, 1953; MA, Botany, Wellesley College, 1955; PhD, Plant Pathology, Cornell University, 1959. *Appointments:* Assistant Professor, Upsala College, 1959-64; Assistant Professor, Bowling Green University, Bowling Green, 1964-66; Professor, Natural Science 1966-89; Botany and Plant Pathology, 1989-, Michigan State University, East Lansing. *Publications:* Diego Rivera: Science and Creativity in the Detroit Murals; Numerous articles on Downy Mildew Peronospora parasitica in cabbage in science periodicals. *Memberships:* Botanical Society of America; American Phytopathological Society; American Mycological Society; National Science Teachers Association; Michigan Women's Studies Association. *Honours:* Sigma Xi; Phi Kappa Phi. *Hobbies:* Gardening; Hiking; Sewing; Art. *Address:* Department of Botany and Plant Pathology, Michigan State University, 335 N Kedzie, East Lansing, MI 48824, USA.

MCMILLAN Ruth Elaine, b. 16 June 1952, Cookeville, USA. Counselor. m. Phillip Edward McMillan, 31 Aug. 1985. *Education:* BS, 1976; MA, 1982; Ed.S., 1984. *Appointments:* Tennessee Department of Human Services, 1978-80; Graduate Assistant, 1984-; Counselor, Tennessee Technological University. *Membership:* Pi Lambda Theta, Secretary; Kappa Delta Pi. *Hobbies:* New Age Spiritual Movement; Reading; Music; Golf. *Address:* Tennessee Technological University, Counseling Centre, Box 5094, Cookeville, TN 38505, USA.

MCMILLIAN Josie Anderson, b. 21 Oct. 1940, Childersburg, USA. President, New York Metro Area Postal Union. divorced, 1 son, 2 daughters. *Education:* Cornell University, 1977. *Appointments:* Sector Aide, Chief Steward, Shop Steward, 1969, Executive Director of Clerk, 1975, Original Vice President, 1976, Executive Vice President, 1979, President, New York Metro Area Postal Union. *Memberships Include:* Labor Advisory Council, New York National Urban League; Coalition of Labor Union Women; National Organisatiron of Women; NYC Black Trade Leadership Commission; United Way of New York City; Life Member, NAACP. *Honours:* Recipient, numerous honours and awards. *Address:* New York Metro Area Postal Union, 460 West 34th Street, 9th Floor, New York, NY 10001, USA.

MCNAIR Rita Hadley, b. 8 Aug. 1939, Mobile, Alabama, USA. University Lecturer. m. Donald Wesley McNair, 21 Dec. 1968, 2 sons, 1 daughter. *Education:* BEd, National College of Education, 1968; MEd, University of Southern Alabama, 1982; EdD, Auburn University, 1985. *Appointments:* Elementary Teacher, Glen Ellyn School District 41, 1972- 77; Doctoral Teaching Fellow, 1982-83; Faculty 1982-86; Lecturer,1986-, University of South Alabama; Director, Curriculum & Education, South Alabama Institute, 1984-87. *Publications:* Curriculum Guide for Remedial Learners; Micro-computer Curriculum Guide for Adult Learners; Child Care Worker Training Curriculum Guide. *Memberships:* Association for Supervision & Curriculum Development; Alabama Council for Computers in Education; Alabama Reading Association; Alabama Association for the Young Child; International Reading Association; National Association for Education of the Young Child; National Association for Early Childhood Teacher Educators; Southern Association for Children Under Six. *Honours:* Phi Lamda Theta, 1985. *Hobbies:* Antiques; Theatre; Reading. *Address:* PO Box 173, Magnolia Springs, AL 36555, USA.

MCNEELA Bernice Ann, b. Chicago, USA. Social Worker. *Education:* BA, 1947, DePaul Univeristy, 1947; MSW, Loyola University, 1952. *Appointments:* Social Caseworker, Catholic Charities, Chicago, 1952-86. *Publications:* numerous articles in journals and magazines. *Memberships:* International President, St Joan's International Alliance, 1986-; Past President, US Section, St Joan's International Alliance; National Association of Social Workers; Academy of Certified Social Workers. *Honours:* Recipient, many awards. *Address:* 1212 A Carol St., Park Ridge, IL 60068, USA.

MCNEILL Brandy Rachele, b. 16 Aug. 1956, Washington, DC, USA. State Agency Official. m. Paul Spurgeon McNeill, 23 Sept. 1982. *Education:* BSc., Towson State College, 1979; Certificate, Shepard-Pratt School of Mental Health, 1979; MA, Adelphi University, 1981. *Appointments:* Trainer, Sports Training Institute, New York City, 1982; Exercise Physiologist, New York Nephology, 1982-83; Supervisor, Printing House Fitness Centre, New York City, 1983; Director, Fitness Centre, St Bartholomew's Community Club, New York City, 1984-85; Director, Wellness Programmes, State of Missouri, Jefferson City, 1985-; Executive Director, Physical Fitness, Jefferson City, 1985-. *Memberships:* American Association of University Women; American College of Sports Medicine; Association of Fitness and Business; etc. *Hobbies:* Swimming; Dogs. *Address:* PO Box 809, Jefferson City, MO 65102, USA.

MCPHERSON Alice Ruth, b. 30 June 1926, Regina, Canada. Ophthalmologist. m. Anthony Mierzwa. *Education:* BS, 1948, MD 1951, University of Wisconsin; Diplomate, American Board Ophthalmology. *Appointments Include:* Intern, Resident, various hospitals, 1952-55; Ophthalmologist, Davis and Duehr Eye Clinic, Madison, 1956-57; Clinical Instructor, University of Wisconsin, 1956-57; Fellow, Retina Service, Massachuesttes Eye; and Ear Infirmary, 1957-58; Ophthalmologist, Scott & White Clinic, Temple, 1958-60; Private Practice, 1960-. *Publications:* Board of Editors: Ophthalmology, 1981-; Survey of Ophthalmology, 1982-; Journal of Ophthalmic Surgery, 1983-; American Journal of Ophthalmology, 1984-; Articles in numerous journals and magazines. *Memberships Include:* American Academy of Ophthalmology; Fellow, Ameriacan College of Surgeons (FACS); Fellow, International College of Surgeons (FICS); many other professional organisations. *Honours Include:* Recipient, numerous honours and awards most recent, Senior Honor Award, American Academy of Ophthalmology, 1986; Kathryn J. Whitmire, Mayor, City of Houston Proclaims Saturday March 12, 1988 as Alice R. McPherson Day; Woodlands Medal, Community of the Woodlands, Texas, 1988. *Address:* 6560 Fannin, Suite 2200, Houston, TX 77030, USA.

MCPHERSON Karen Michel, Radio Producer and Sound Designer. *Education:* Study in Sculpture and Ceramics, San Francisco Art Institute, San Francisco, California, 1965; BA, Visual Arts, San Francisco State College, 1967; MEd, Cross-Cultural Education, University of Alaska, Fairbanks, 1980. *Appointments:* Project Co-ordinator, Alaska Native Oral Literature Project, 1973-75; Director, Bilingual/Bicultural Language and History Program for the Nulato, Alaska City Council, 1975-76; Video Producer, clients included: Tanana Chiefs Video Center, the University of Alaska and KUAC-TV, 1976-79; Executive Director, Institute of Alaska Native Arts, 1979-81; President, Educational Media Services, New York City, clients include: Canadian Broadcasting Corporation, National Public Radio, Alaska Public Radio, Mabou Mines, New York Theatre Workshop; Artist-in-Residence, Museum of Holography, also Artist-in-Residence, PASS/ Harvestworks, New York City, 1986. *Memberships:* Steering Committee, 1985-86, Board of Directors, 1987-88, Association of Independents in Radio, New York City; Board Member, Alaska Association for the Arts, 1982-84, Chair, Visual Arts Committee; Media Arts Panel, Alaska State Council for the Arts, 1983. *Honours:* Grants: Corporation for Public Broadcasting (Satellite Program Developmernt Fund) 1983, 1985; National Endowment for the Arts (Media Arts) 1981, 1982, 1983, 1985; Alaska State Council on the Arts (Fellowselta Chi) (Society of Professional Journalists) 1981-84; Various Radio awards, Alaska Press Club, 1981-84; Nominee, Oustanding Young Women of America, 1982, 1983; Public Radio Program Award, Corporation for Public Broadcasting, 1987; US-Japan Creative Artists Fellowship, 1988. *Address:* 167 Congress Street No 4F, Brooklyn, NY 11201, USA.

MCQUEEN Sandra Marilyn, b. 30 Nov. 1948, Greenville, South Carolina, USA. Educator. *Education:* BA, Presbyterian College, 1970; MA, Presbyterian School of Christian Education, 1972; PhD, Georgia State University, 1987. *Appointments:* Director of Christian Education, Rock Spring Presbyterian Church, 1972-74; Primary Teacher 1974-80, Teacher, Gifted Children 1980-89, Atlanta Board of Education. *Creative work includes:* Development of Evaluation Model & Instrument for Non-Residential Education Programmes for Older Adults, 1984; Middle School Curriculum for Gifted Children, Atlanta Public Schools, 1989. *Memberships:* Association of Supervision & Curriculum Development; Kappa Delta Pi; Atlanta & Georgia Associations of Educators; National Education Association; Church Teachers; Various community organisations. *Honours:* Teacher of Year, Sutton Middle School, 1984; Apple Corp Award, 1986. *Hobbies:* Working with re-settlement of refugees; Travel; Reading. *Address:* 4360 Powers Ferry Road NW, Atlanta, Georgia 30327, USA.

MCQUILLEN Eleanor, b. 26 Dec. 1934, Boston, USA. Chief Medical Examiner. m. James Barrie McQuillen, 12 Sept. 959, 3 sons, 2 daughters. *Education:* BA, University of Massachusetts, 1956; MD, Boston Univerity School of Medicine, 1956; DABP, 1971; DABP, 1976. *Appointments:* Massachusetts Dept. of Health, 1960-62; Resident, Pathology, Boston City Hospital, 1963-64, Robert Packer Hospital, 1965-71; Staff, Robert Packer Hospital, 1971-74; Resident, Forensic Pathology, University of Rochester, 1974-75; State of Vermont, 1976-. *Publications:* Issues Related to the Medical Certification of Death: A Physician Survey, co-author; articles in various journals. *Memberships:* National Association of Medical Examiners, President Elect, 1983-84, President 1984-85, Chairman of Board, 1985-86; American Academy of Forensic Sciences; College of American Pathologists. *Honours:* Distinguished Alumna Award, 1988. *Hobbies:* Early American Decoration; Furniture Refinishing. *Address:* Box 506 Shelburne, VT 05482, USA.

MCRAE Sandra Frances, b.4 Dec 1956, Ottawa, Canada. Historian of Medicine; Museum Curator. 1 son. *Education:* BSc, Biology, Carleton University, 1977; MA, History of Science, University of Toronto, 1981; MLS, Science Librarianship, McGill University, 1983; PhD, History of Science, University of Toronto, 1987. *Appointments:* Associate Curator of Medical Technology, National Museum of Science and Technology, 1987-. *Memberships:* American Association for the History of Medicine; Canadian Society for the History of Medicine; Canadian Society for the History and Philoophy of Science; Canadian Science and Technology Historical Association; Toronto Academy of Medicine, History of Medicine Museum (Museum Committee Member). *Address:* National Museum of Science and Technology, PO Box 9724, Station T, Ottawa, Ontario, Canada K1G 5A3.

MCREYNOLDS Mary Maureen, b. 15 July 1940, Tacoma, USA. Environmental Management. m. Gerald A McReynolds, 10 Dec. 1964. *Education:* BA, Biology, University of Oregon, 1961; PhD, Zoology, University of Chicago, 1966. *Appointments:* Research Associate, Stanford University, 1968-71; Chemist, Syva Co., Palo Alto, 1972; Environmental Specialist, San Diego, 1973-75; Chief Environment Officer, Office of Environmental Resource Management, Austin, 1976-85; Manager, Water Quality, Water Utility, Austin, 1985-. *Publications:* Technical Papers in: Nature, Genetics, Biochimica et Biophysica Acta. *Memberships:* American Water Resources Association; Water Pollution Control Federation; Texas Water Pollution Control Association; American Planning Association; American Association for Advancement of Science; Association of Environmental Professionals; National Association for Female Executives; etc. *Honours:* Recipient, various honours and awards. *Hobbies:* Reading; Sailing; Gourmet Food & Wine. *Address:* Water & Wastewater Utility, City of Austin, PO Box 1088, Austin, TX 78767, USA.

MEAD Harriet Council, b. Franklin, Virginia, USA. Writer/Librarian. m. Berne Matthews Mead, Jr, 2 Dec. 1940. 2 sons. *Education:* BA, College of William and Mary, Williamsburg, Virginia, 1935; Writers Workshops, 1948, 1950 and 1980; Postgraduate Courses: Rollins College, Winter Park, Florida, 1966, 1970 and 1984; University of Florida, Gainesville, Florida, 1959-62; Postgraduate, Florida State Univesity, Tallahassee, Florida, 1962-63. *Appointments:* County Librarian, Carroll Co, Virginia, 1935-36; City Librarian, Suffolk, Virginia Schools, 1936-41; Librarian, Cathedral Church of St Luke, 1959-61; Media Specialist and Librarian, Orange County schools, Orlando, Florida, 1961-80. *Publications:* The Irrepresible Saint, Biography of C Bertram Runna, Priest, 1983; A Family Legacy (History), 1987; Magazine article: The History of The Order of St Luke, 1984. *Memberships:* Orange County School Librarians, President, 1968-69; Hispanic Institute, Rollins College, Board of Directors, 1968-69; Orange County Historical Society, 1987; Morse Gallery of American Art Associates, 1987; Rollins College Cornell Gallery Associates, 1987; Junior League of Orlando, Winter Park, Florida, 1987; National Society of Colonial Dames, 1987. *Honour:* Nominated for Volunteer of the Year for Work with Blind, 1983. *Hobbies:* Watercolour painting; Historical research. *Address:* 500 East Marks Street, Orlando, FL 32803, USA.

MEAD Vaila Elizabeth, b. 19 Aug. 1948, Brisbane, Queensland, Australia. Painist. *Education:* BM 1975, MM 1976, Juilliard School of Music, New York, USA; DSCM (Performers) Diploma, State Conservatorium of Music, Sydney, Australia, 1970; LMusA, 1968, AMusA 1965, Sydney University, 1966-67. *Career:* Debut, Wigmore Hall, London, England, 1977; Alice Tully Hall Lincoln Center, New York, USA, 1979. First public performance, Australian Broadcasting Commission, aged 11; Radio broadcasts, telecasts, numerous concerts & recitals including appearances as concerto soloist, 1962-70; Recitals: Australia House, London, 1977, 1979; St Martins-in-the-Fields, London, 1978; Australian Consulate, New York, USA, 1979; Alice Tully Hall, 1979; Australian Tour, New South Wales, Queensland And ACT, 1979; Victoria, South Australia, Tasmania, Northern Territory, 1980; Stamford Arts Centre, England, 1980; American Church in Paris Concert Series, 1981; Beaulieu Abbey, England, Summer Series, 1981; Special Concert, Palace House, Beaulieu, 1981; National Gallery of Victoria, Melbourne, Australia, 1982; University of Hawaii, Honolulu, Recital and Master Class, 1982; Hephzibah Menuhin Memorial Scholarship Recital, Sydney, 1983; Adjudicator, City of Sydney Eisteddfod, 1983; broadcasts including ABC and 2MBS-FM Australia. Teaching: Conservatorium of Music (Newcastlo branch), 1983-84; Sydney University, 1984-85; Central Coast Music Centre, Gosford, NSW, 1984-87; Cranbrook SChool, Sydney, 1986-; Sisters of Charity Music Centre, Edgecliff, Sydney, 1986-. *Honours:* Numerous honours and awards including: 1st prize, ABC Annual Awards for Composition, 1958-63; Winner, Dante Alighieri Piano Competition, 1970; Linda Joan Israel Memorial Scholarship (Juilliard School of Music New York), 1975-76, etc. *Hobbies:* Legal studies; Test cricket. *Address:* Unit 42, Kilburn Towers, 1 Addison Road, Manly, New South Wales 2095, Australia.

MEAGER Jill, b. 4 Dec. 1957, Leeds, England. Actress. m. Barnaby Spurrier, 1 Dec. 1984. *Education:* Studied Honours French & Italian, Trinity Hall, Cambridge University, 1977. *Appointments:* Assistant Stage Manager, Hampstead Theatre, 1978-79; Appearances in Funny Man, TV, 1979; Liberty Hall, Greenwich Theatre, 1979-80; Ronnie Corbett Show, BBC TV, 1980; Time and Time Again, Oxford Playhouse, 1980-81; Wilfred and Eileen - A Love Story, BBC TV, 1981; Goodbye Mr Kent, BBC TV 1981; The Old Men at the Zoo, BBC TV, 1982; East Lynne, BBC TV, 1982; Never Say Never Again, film, 1983; Under the Hammer BBC TV, 1983; Goodbye Mr Chips, BBC TV; The Secret Servant, BBC TV, 1984; Cards on the Table, Churchill Theatre, Bromley, 1985; Bergerac, BBC TV 1985; Taggart, STV 1986; Truckers, BBC 1987; Agatha Cristie: Miss Marple, BBC 1987; Hannay, Thames TV 1988, 1989; Translator & Interpreter. *Hobbies:* Writing;

Drawing; Sailing. *Address:* c/o Duncan Heath Assoc., 162 Wardour Street, London W1, England.

MEANS Jacqueline A, b. 26 Aug. 1936, Peoria, Illinois, USA. Episcopal Priest. 3 sons, 1 daughter. *Education:* Indianapolis School of Practical Nursing, 1969; Indiana University, 1970-82; Christian Theological Seminary, Indianapolis, 1986. *Appointments:* Senior Citizens Chaplain, Riley Lockerbie Ministerial Association, 1974-76; Assoc Priest, All Saints Episcopal Church, 1974-81; Assoc Priest, St John's Episcopal Church, 1981-84; Director Prison Ministries, Episcopal Diocese of Indianapolis; Rector, St Mark's Episcopal Church, Plainfield. *Creative works:* Developed programme for chaplaincy of Marion County Juvenile Court; One-to-One Programme for Prison Ministries; Founder of Craine House for Women Ex-offenders; Television series on ACOA; Originator and Chairperson, Coalition Against Capitol Punishment for Juveniles (included a debate aired on Good Morning America); Angel Fund for Ronald McDonald House; Founder of St Mark's Shelter Programme. *Honours:* Kentucky Colonel, 1980; Ordination voted number one Newsowrthy Story, 1976 and 1977; Article about ordination in World Book 1978 Year Book; YWCA Woman of the Year, 1977. *Hobbies:* Hiking; Canoeing; Numerous outdoor activities. *Address:* 213 Sheffield Drive, Danville, IN 46122, USA.

MEDFORD-ROSOW Traci, b. 6 June 1955, Alexandria, USA. Attorney. m. Joel Rosow, 12 Aug. 1978, 1 son, 1 daughter. *Education:* BS, Virginia Polytechnic Institute, 1977; JD, Brooklyn Law School, 1980; LLM, International Law, New York University Law School, 1984. *Appointments:* Manager, Health Care Programme, Pfizer Inc., 1980-84; Corporate Counsel, Europe Pfizer Inc., 1984-87; Corporate Council, International Patent Litigation, Pfizer Inc., 1987-. *Memberships:* New York, Washington, American Bar Associations; Phi Beta Kappa. *Honours:* Elected to Fortune Magazines People to Watch Column, 1986. *Hobbies:* Chess; Swimming; Children. *Address:* 2 Candlewood Ct., Scarsdale, NY 10583, USA.

MEDLEY Nancy May, b. 8 Oct. 1948, Knoxville, Tennessee, USA. Head Nurse, Cardiac Care Unit. *Education:* RN, Riverside City College, 1970. *Appointments:* Staff Nurse in Medicine, Riverside General Hospital, 1970-71; Staff Nurse, Neo-natal Unit, Kaiser Permanente Hospital, Hollywood, California, 1972; Critical Care Nurse, Neuro Unit, Harbor UCLA Medical Center, 1978-. *Membership:* American Heart Association. *Hobbies:* Gardening; Swimming; Jogging; Bike riding. *Address:* 636 Manhatten Avenue No C, Hermosa Beach, California 90254, USA.

MEEKS Carol Jean, b. 9 Mar. 1946, Columbus, Ohio, USA. Associate Professor. *Education:* BS, 1968, MS, 1969, PhD, 1972, Ohio State University. *Appointments:* Assistant Professor, Extension, University of Massachusetts, 1972-74; Assistant Professor, 1974-78, Associate Professor, Consumer Economics & Housing, 1978-80, Cornell University; Supervisory Economics, Housing Section Head, US Dept. of Agriculture, Economic Research Service, 1980-85; Associate Professor, Housing, Home Management & Consumer Economics, University of Georgia, Athens, 1985-. *Publications:* Textbook, Housing, 1980; journal articles in various journals. *Memberships:* American Association of Housing Educators; American Home Economics Association; American Council on Consumer Interests; American Real Estate & Urban Economics Association. *Honours Include:* Young Professional Achievement Award, 1979; Phi Upsilon Omicron; Omicron Nu; Epsilon Sigma Phi. *Address:* 270 Davis Estates Road, Athens, GA 30606, USA.

MEEKS Esther MacBain, b. 17 Feb. 1921, Council Bluffs, Iowa, USA. Freelance Writer. m. Wilkison Windfield Meeks, 23 Feb. 1946, 2 daughters. *Education:* AA, Stephens College, Columbia, Missouri; BA, University of Iowa. *Appointments:* Staff script writer, WSAY Radio, Rochester, New York, 1944-45; Radio show writer, B. Ellis, New York City; Freelance documentary programmes, ASCAP & NBC Recording Division, NYC, 1946-47; Freelance writer (also workshops, speaker) children's fiction, 1960-. *Publications include:* Childrens books: Jeff & Mr James' Pond, 1962; Web of Winter, 1967, 1972, 1983. Text, Canticles for Christmas, 1968. *Memberships:* Society of Children's Book Writers; Children's Reading Roundtable, Chicago. *Honours:* Chosen, Junior Literary Guild Author, 1962; Runner-up, award, Distinguished Writing for Children, Indiana University, 1963. *Address:* 2911 Oak Street, Terre Haute, Indiana 47803, USA.

MEGGERS Betty J, b. 5 Dec. 1921, Washington, USA. Anthropologist; Archaeologist. m. Clifford Evans, 13 Sept. 1946. *Education:* AB, University of Pennsylvania, 1943; MA, University of Michigan, 1944; PhD, Columbia University, 1952; Doctor, HC, University of Guayaquil, Ecuador, 1987. *Appointments:* Instructor, American University, 1950-51; Research Associate, Smithsonian Institution, 1954-; Executive Secretary, American Anthropological Association, 1959-61. *Publications:* Ecuador, 1966; Amazonia, 1971; Prehistoric America, 1972; numerous articles in professional journals. *Memberships:* Anthropological Society of Washington, Treasurer 1955-60, Vice President 1965-66, President 1966-68; American Athropological Association; Society for American Archaeology; Association for Tropical Biology; American Association for the Advancement of Science. *Honours:* Recipient, various honours & awards including: Gold Medal, 37th International Congress of Americanists, 1966; Order Al Merito, Government of Ecuador, 1966; Order Bernardo O'Higgens, Government of Chile, 1985; Secretary's Gold Medal for Exceptional Service, Smithsonian Institute, 1986; Order Andres Bello, Government of Venezuela, 1988. *Address:* NHB-112, Smithsonian Institution, Washington DC 20560, USA.

MEIER-VOTIK Barbara Ellen, b. 10 Apr. 1944, Clearwater, USA. District Sales Manager. m. John Carl Votik, 21 Sept. 1986, 1 son, 1 daughter. *Education:* BS, James Madison University, 1965. *Appointments:* CIA, 1965-67; Prince Wm. Co. Schools, 1967-68, 1971-75; Greensville County Schools, 1976-77; Waver's Business Machines, 1982-83; Market Support Representative, Brother International Corp, 1984-85; Sales Development Manager, BIC, 1985-86, District Sales Manager, 1986-. *Publications:* Brother Dealer Guide, How to Sell Me; How to Sell Brother, series. *Memberships:* Toastmasters; NAFE. *Honours:* Recipient, many awards & honours. *Hobbies:* Snorkelling; Reading; Hiking; Swimming; Photography. *Address:* 882 N. Fig Tree Lane, Plantation, FL 33317, USA.

MEILACH Dona Z, b. Chicago, USA. Author; Lecturer. m. Melvin Meyer Meilach, 15 Feb. 1948, 1 son, 1 daughter. *Education:* MA, Art History, Northwestern University, 1969; PhB, University of Chicago, 1942. *Appointments:* Contributing Editor, Computer Graphics Today; Teacher, University of California, San Diego. *Publications Include:* Computer Books: Before You Buy Word Processing Software; Before You Buy a Used Computer; Before You Buy a Computer; Dynamics of Presentatiron Graphics; Better Business Presentations; Art-Craft Books: A Modern Approach to Basketry; Basketry Today; Box Art: Assemblage & Construction; Collage and Found Art; Creating with Plaster; Creating Modern Furniture; Ethnic Jewelry; Papercraft; Cookery Books: Homemade Cream Liqueurs; Marinade Magic; Homemade Liqueurs; Exercise-Health Books: How to Relieve Your Aching Back; Jazzercise; The Art of Belly Dancing; A Doctor Discusses Pregnancy; A Doctor Discusses Menopause; Radio & TV appearances. *Memberships Include:* Authors Groups, various positions; Art Groups, various Positions; Art Commissioner, City of Carlsbad. *Address:* 2018 Saliente Way, Carlsbad, CA 92009, USA.

MEISENHEIMER Erma B., b. 4 June 1909, Farnham, New York, USA. Book Reviewer; Travel Lecturer; Campaigner, Legislation for Elderly. m. Charles

Meisenheimer, 13 Aug. 1954. *Education:* Teaching Certificate, State University of New York, Fredonia, 1930; BS, Education, English, University of Buffalo; Graduate work, Columbia University. *Appointments:* Teacher, English, Social Studies, Orchard Park High School, Orchard Park, New York, 1930-31; Chairman, Department of English, Hamburg Senior High School, Hamburg, New York, 1931-72; Currently working on state/federal legislation for the elderly, Albany & Washington DC; Lecturer, Buffalo Museum of Science; Book Reviewer, many years. *Publications:* How does a Teacher of Language Arts Grow? 1957; Many original poems, speeches, legislative statistics, sermons. *Memberships:* Chairman of Legislation, Nominating, Resolutions Committees, New York State Teachers Association; President, Parliamentarian, Hamburg Women's Club & Hamburg Garden Club; President, Life Member, New York State Retired Teachers Association Inc; Life Member, National Education Association; National Chairman, Legal Rights of the Elderly; Member, 4-man Team on Hospital Cost Containment, appointed President Carter; National Advisory Committee to American Association of Retired Persons Chapters; Executive Committee, Legislative Chairman, Executive Committee, Buffalo Federation of Women's Clubs; Substitute Minister, Choir Member, St James United Church of Christ, Hamburg. *Honours include:* Certificate of Merit, Dedicated Service, Town of Hamburg; Outstanding Key Award, University of Buffalo; Citation, Exceptional Service, New York State Retired Teachers Association, Western Zobe; Woman of the Year, Women's Business and Professional Club, 1989; Member, Legislative Chairman, Delta Kappa Gamma; 1st woman chair, Joint State Legislative Committee. *Hobbies:* Golf; Duplicate bridge; Travel (USA, Europe, Africa, South America, Asia). *Address:* 79 Milford Street, Hamburg, NY 14075, USA.

MEISTAS Mary Therese, b. 22 July 1949, Grand Rapids, USA. Physician; Endocrinologist. *Education:* BS, Chemistry, 1971; MD, 1975, University of Michigan; Endocrinology Fellow, Cleveland Clinic, 1978-79; Paediatric Endocrinology Fellow, Johns Hopkins Hospital, 1979-81. *Appointments:* Associate, Medicine, Diabetes Consultant, Researcher, Brigham and Women's Hospital, Joslin Diabetes Centre, Boston, 1981-86; Practice, Internal Medicine, Endocrinology, Diabetes Researcher, Massachusetts General Hospital, Harvard Medical School, 1986-. *Publications:* contributor to: Journal of Clinical Investigation; American Journal of Physiology. *Memberships:* American Diabetes Association; American Federation for Clinical Research; American College of Physicians; Endocrine Society. *Honours:* BS, magna cum laude, 1971; MD, honours, 1975; Mary K. Iacocca Award, 1982. *Address:* Massachusetts General Hospital, AOG 617, Fruit Street, Boston, MA 02114, USA.

MELCHIORI Marie Varrelmare, b. 25 July 1935, Camden, New Jersey, USA. Certified Genealogical Record Searcher. m. Robert Thomas Melchiori, 19 Apr. 1958. 1 son, 2 daughters. *Education:* BS Nursing, Rutgers University, Newark, 1957; Certified Genealogical Record Searcher, 1980. *Appointments:* Professional Genealogical Record Searcher specializing in Civil War Records, 1979; Assistant Director, National Institute on Genealogical Research, 1988, 1989, 1990; 1st Level Coordinator, George Mason University, American History & Genealogy Institute, 1987, 1988; Fairfax Co Adult Education, 1983-; Lecturer, NGS Conferences in 1988, 1989, 1990; Lecturer, FGS Conference, 1988. *Creative works:* Lecturer Civil War Roundtables; Genealogical Societies; Historical Societies. *Memberships:* Association of Professional Genealogists; Fairfax Genealogical Society, President 1982-83; Secretary 1979-81; National Genealogical Society; National Institute on Genealogical Research Alumni. *Address:* 121 Tapawingo Rd SW, Vienna, VA 22180, USA.

MELECKI Sherry Miller, b. 13 Oct. 1950, Brownfield, Texas, USA. Coordinator of Management Training. m. Thomas G Melecki, 27 May, 1978. 2 daughters. *Education:* MEd, Texas Tech University, 1972; BA, Angelo State University, 1971. *Appointments:* Coordinator of Management Training 1984-; Coordinator of Women's Residence Halls 1981-84; Assistant to Director of Housing and Food Service 1978-81, University of Texas at Austin; Coordinator of Resident Life, Southern University, 1977-78. *Memberships:* American Society for Training and Development, Austin Chapter Nominating Committee, 1986; Intergovernmental Training Council, Communication Committee Chairperson, 1986-87; Mentor Committee, Chairperson, 1985-86; Personnel Administrators of Texas Senior Colleges and Universities, 1984-; American College Personnel Association, Commission III Directorate Body Member, 1981-84; Southwest Association of Colleges and University Housing Officers, Secretary, 1983-84. *Honours:* Recognition Service Award, University of Texas at Austin Housing and Food Service, 1983; Service Award from Disabled Students in Action, Ball State University, 1976; Outstanding Young Women of American, 1980, 1984. *Hobbies:* Reading; Baking; Piano; Conflict management. *Address:* 3607 Ambleside, Austin, TX 78759, USA.

MELEKA Agia Hanna, b. 11 June 1943, Cairo, Egypt. Professor. 1 daughter. *Education:* BA, 1963, MA, 1971, American University, Cairo; MPA, 1975, PhD, 1979, University of Southern California. *Appointments:* Management Consultant, 1969-; Lecturer, University of Southern California, 1975-81; Professor, California State University, Northridge, 1981-. *Publications:* several articles in: World Affairs; International Journal of Business; Journal of Public Adminisration. *Memberships:* Academy of Management; European International Business Association; Academy of International Business Management; International Studies Association; Human Resources Management Association. *Honours:* Meritorius Performance Award for California State University, Northridge, 1984, 1986; Bryn Mawr Fellow for Women in Higher Education Administration, 1986. *Hobbies:* Classical Music; Art History; Decorative Art; Swimming. *Address:* Dept. of Management, California State University, Northridge, CA 91330, USA.

MELICH Tanya Marie, b. 23 Apr. 1936, Utah, USA. Political Issues Consultant/Analyst. m. Noel L. Silverman, 28 Dec. 1962, 1 son, 1 daughter. *Education:* BS, University of Colorado, 1958; MA, Columbia University, 1961. *Appointments:* Nelson Rockefeller Research Writer, 1973-74; Associate Director, Public Policy Unit, 1975-; Director, CBS Inc., 1978-81; Political Issues Management, Provident, 1982-. *Publications:* Articles in: Newsday; The Ripon Forum. *Memberships:* Executive Director, New York State Republican Family Committee, 1985-; National Womens Political Caucus, Advisory Committee, 1988; National Womens Education Fund, President 1980-83; *Honours:* Recipient, various honours including: Commission on Judicial Nomination, 1983-; Outstanding Woman Award, Manhattan Womens Political Caucus, 1986. *Hobbies:* Gardening; Theatre. *Address:* 115 East 9th St., New York City, NY 10003, USA.

MELISSANO Rita Rosaria, b. 4 Feb. 1956, Campi Salentina (LE) Italy. Marriage & Family Therapist. *Education:* BA 1975, MA 1979, Psychology, University of Padua; Diploma, Family Counselling, CISF, Milan, 1982; Diploma, Family Therapy & Communication, School of Family Communication, Aviano, 1985; PhD candidate, Marriage & Family Therapy, Brigham Young University, Provo, Utah, USA, 1985-; Doctoral residency, Marriage & Family Counselling Service, Rock Island, Illinois, USA, 1988-89; PhD, Predicting Desired Change from Intimacy om Married Couples: A Regression Study, 1990. *Creative work:* Research, Yoga Techniques for Prevention & Control of Anxiety, 1979; Research projects in progress: Empirical Measurement of Therapeutic Double Bind, Intimacy & Change in Married Couples; Clinical case presentation, UAMFT Conference, USA, 1988; Yoga teacher, Italy, 1981. *Membership:* Clinical member, American Association for Marriage & Family Therapy. *Hobbies:* Speaks Italian, English, French, Spanish, some Mandarin Chinese & modern Greek; Studied Latin & ancient Greek, several years; Interests in oriental culture, western & eastern mysticism, meditation, yoga; Alternative medicine, vegitarianism; Music, plays piano & guitar; Horseback riding; Travel; Astrology, numerology & divinatory sciences. *Address:* 512 Safety Building, Rock Island, Illinois 61201, USA.

MELL Gertrud Maria, b. 15 Aug. 1947, Ed, Sweden. Composer; Sea Captain; Organist. m. Ned Stanley Sernhag, 15 Aug. 1985. *Education:* Studied Conducting of Orchestra, Conservatory, 1965-67; Ped Kyrkokantorsex, Stockholm, 1968; Mate's exam (sea officer) ships mechanic, 1979, Sea captain exam (master mariner) 1981, Telephone operator (for ships), 1982, Engineer of Ships exam, 1985, Gothenburg. *Appointments:* Organist, Tofledal, 1967-76; Music Teacher, Ed, 1969-71; Bengfors, 1972-76; Private music teacher, 1967-76; Leader and founder of 3 choirs and 2 orchestras, Ed; Able Seaman, Transatlantic Ships, 1976-78; Organist, Pater Noster Church, Gothenburg, 1982. *Creative works:* 4 symphonies for orchestra, 1964-67; 1 symphonic poem, 1980; 1 string quartet, 1969; Numerous compositions for piano, organ, chamber, pop and orchestra. *Memberships:* STIM; KMR. *Honours:* Alvsborgs Lans Landstrings Kulturstipendium, as composer, 1975; Award from Dalslands Gille as composer and Church musician, 1988. *Hobbies:* Nature; Photographs. *Address:* Krokegatan 9, 41318 Goteborg, Sweden.

MELLICHAMP Josephine Weaver, b. 30 Sept. 1923, North Carolina, USA. Writer; Historian. m. (1) F M Stafford Smith, 15 Dec. 1944, divorced 1959, (2) Stiles A Mellichamp, 16 Dec. 1961, 2 stepsons. *Education:* AB, Emory College, 1943; Studies at Emory University Graduate School, University of Georgia, 1951. *Appointments:* Teacher, High Schools, 1943-50; Price Comparer, Macy's New York City, and Clerical Worker, Idu Pont de Nemour, Wilmington, 1944; Editorial Assistant, Emory University Office of Public Information, 1951-53; Newspaper Librarian, Atlanta Journal, 1957-79; Writer, Historian, 1979-. *Publications:* Senators from Georgia, 1976; Georgia Heritage, Volumes in progress; articles in various journals, newspapers & magazines. *Memberships Include:* Deputy Director General, International Biographical Centre; Deputy Governor, National Adviser, American Biographical Institute Research Association; Life Member, World Institute of Achievement; Fellow, World Literary Academy; etc. *Honours:* Recipient, many honours and awards. *Hobbies:* Reading; Writing; Sewing; Cooking; Fishing; Stamp Collecting; Travel; Homemaking. *Address:* 1124 Reeder Circle, NE, Atlanta, GA 30306, USA.

MELLOR Gail McGowan, b. 8 July 1942, Louisville, Kentucky, USA. President, Writer's Inc. m. Steven Anthony Friend Weller, 13 Mar. 1988. 2 sons, 1 daughter. *Education:* BA, Political Science, cum laude & distinction, BA, Middle American Studies, cum laude & distinction, Newcomb College, 1964; NDEA Fellow, Graduate School of Political Science, Tulane University, 1968; ME, Manhattanville, 1972. *Appointments:* Upper School Coordinator, Paedeia (experimental) School, Armonk, New York, 1972; Co- founder, Administrator and Upper school Coordinator, Lakewood Community School, Dallas, 1973-74; Professor of English, Postgraduate School of Education, Toluca, Mexico, 1974-75; Assistant Planetarium Director, Orlando Science Center, 1976-77; Freelance medical journalist, 1978-79; President, Writer's Inc, 1980-; Senior Editor, Louisville Today Magazine, 1981; Contributing Editor, Beaux Arts Magazine, 1980; Research Consultant, American College of Emergency Physicians, 1981; Technical writing consultant, General Electric, FMAC and Concord Casting, 1984; Medical writing consultant, NKC Inc and Louisville Hand Surgery, 1986-87. *Publications:* The First Hundred Years, 1988; Articles in numerous magazines and journals. *Memberships include:* MENSA; Society for Technical Communicators; American Medical Writers' Association. *Honours*

include: Pulitzer Nomination, Investigative Reporting, 1979; Ky Hos Ass Excellence in Writing, 1989; Distinguished Technical Communication, 1990. *Hobbies:* Travel; Children; Reading; Adventure. *Address:* Writer's Inc, 2407 Lime Kiln Lane, Louisville, Kentucky 40222, USA.

MELNICK Sharon Kay, b. 3 May 1956, Billings, Montana, USA. Psychiatrist; Professor; Analyst. *Education:* BA, Brandeis University, 1978; MD, University of Washington School of Medicine, 1982; Psychiatry residency, UCLA/Sepulveda VA, 1982-86; Chief resident, 1987; Board Certified, American College of Psychiatry and Neurology, 1988; Analytic Training, C G Jung Institute of Los Angeles, 1988-. *Appointments:* Private practice of general psychiatry and psychotherapy, 1986-; Assistant Chief Residency Education UCLA/San Fernando Valley Program, 1987- . *Memberships:* C G Jung Institute, Los Angeles; APA; SCPS; AK Rice; AADRTP; AMWA; WIP; PSR; IPPNW. *Honours:* US/USSR therapist exchange leader, 1988; Citizen diplomat to USSR, 1987. *Hobbies:* Aboriginal and matriarchal religions; Painting; Poetry. *Address:* 16550 Ventura Blvd, Suite 420, Encino, CA 91436, USA.

MELROSE Margaret Elstob Jackson, b. 2 May 1928, Birmingham, England. County Councillor; Drapers Company Scholarship to Girton College, Cambridge. m. Kenneth Ramsay Watson, 19 June 1948, 1 daughter. *Appointments:* Secretary to Consultant Psychiatrist, Crumpsall Hospital, Manchester, 1961-62; Secretary to Consul for Lebanon for N. England, Scotland & N. Ireland, 1962-63; Vice Counsul for Lebanon, 1963-67. *Memberships Include:* Cheshire County Council, 1967- , Chairman, 1984-85, 1986-87; Chief Whip, Conservative Group, 1973-84; Chairman, Tatton Park Management Committee, 1985-; Cheshire Rural Community Council, Chairman, 1987-; President, Macclesfield Conservation Association; Chairman, Manchester Airport Consultative Committee, 1985-; Chairman, NW Regional Children's Planning Committee, 1977-81; Member, E Cheshire Hospital Management Committee, 1967-71; Member, Cheshire Area Health Authority, 1971-74; Member, Mersey Regional Health Authority, 1974-76; Member, Runcorn New Town Development Corporation 1974-80; General Commissioner for Taxes, 1985-, Vice President Cheshire Agricultural Society, Vice-President Cheshire Ploughing and Hedgecutting Society. *Honours:* Deputy Lieutenant, County of Cheshire, 1987; Cheshire Woman of the Year, 1986; North of England Woman of the Year, 1985. *Hobbies:* Golf; Sailing; Skiing; Horses; Bridge; Country Life. *Address:* Merryman's Cottage, Great Warford, Alderley Edge, Cheshire SK9 7TP, England.

MELVIN Marilee Ann, b. 20 Aug. 1950, Hinsdale, Illinois, USA. Educational Administrator; Writer. *Education:* BA, Philosophy, Wheaton College, 1972; MA, University of Chicago, 1974. *Appointments:* Assistant to Chairman, Frigidmeats Inc, Chicago, 1973-76; Assistant to President, NLCPI, Washington DC, 1977-79; Stenographer, White House, Washington DC, 1979-81; Assistant to Counsellor to President, 1981-85; Assistant to Attorney General, Department of Justice, 1985-88; Vice president Alumni Relations, Wheaton College, Illinois, 1988-; Columnist, Wheaton College's Alumni Magazine. *Publications:* Contributor: (Prose) Give Us This Day Our Daily Bread, (ghost writer), C. T. Evans, 1980; (Poetry) Sightseers into Pilgrims, 1973. *Memberships:* National Association of Female Executives; Centre for Study of Presidency. *Honour:* Achievement Award, US Department of Justice, 1987. *Hobbies:* History; Calligraphy; Quilting; Public Administration. *Address:* 233 Union Avenue, Batavia, IL 60510, USA.

MENDOZA June Yvonne, b. Melbourne, Australia. Portrait Painter. m. Keith Mackrell, 1 son, 3 daughters. *Education:* St Martin's School of Art, London, England; period of Commercial Art. *Creative Works:* Portraits Include: H.M. Queen Elizabeth; Prince & Princess of Wales; Princess Royal; Mrs Margaret Thatcher; Prime Minister of Fiji; President of Iceland; President of

Philippines; Prime Minister of Australia; works academic, regimental, governmental, theatrical, medical, sport, etc and private, in collections internationally, Multiple of House of Commons in Session, (440 portraits), also for House of Representatives, Canberra. *Memberships:* Royal Society of Portrait Painters; Royal Institute of Oil Painters; Hon. Member, Society of Women Artists. *Honours:* Hon.D.Litt., Bath University, 1986. *Address:* 34 Inner Park Road, London SW19 6DD, England.

MENDOZA Lolita Rachel, b. 9 Aug. 1920, DeKalb, Texas, USA. Retired Teacher; Local Board of Education Member. m. John T. Mendoza, 26 May 1952, divorced, 1 son, 3 daughters. *Education:* Bookkeeping Certificate, Draughron's Business College, 1941; BA, Elementary Education, East Texas State University, 1964; Master's degree in Sociology, 1970. *Appointments:* Bookkeeper, Gordon Jewelry, Houston Texas, 1941-43; Served to F/Sergeant, WAC, 1943-52; Teacher, John F.Kennedy Elementary School, Elcia, Texas, 1964; Teacher, Will Rogers Elementary School, Hobbs, New Mexico, 1964-67; Teacher, Palm Vista Elementary School, Morongo Unified School District, Twentynine Palms, California, 1967-82; Substitute Teacher, 1982-85; Member, Board of Education, Morongo Unified School District, 1985-89. *Creative works:* 3 plays for elementary schools. *Memberships:* National Education Association; State and local teachers organisations; Advisory Commission Board, 29 Palms Park and Recreation District; American Business Women's Association, Past President, Chemehuevi Charter Chapter; Phi Delta Kappa; Disabled American Veterans; Retired Teachers Association; Hi-Desert Tract Owners Association, 29 Palms; American Legion; Non-Commissioned Officers Association; 29 Palms Chamber of Commerce. *Honours:* Meritorious Achievement Award for WAC-WAF Recruitment, 1951-52, 1952; Other routine military awards; First Lady of the Year, Beta Sigma Phi Sorority, Hi-Desert Area Council, 1978; Award for Service, American Legion, 1979. *Hobbies:* Arts and crafts; Sewing; Reading; Working on projects for the school district and communities of the Morongo Basin; Sports including riding. *Address:* 74593 Cactus Drive, 29 Palms, CA 92277, USA.

MERCER-CARTER Ethel, b. 13 Sept. 1947, Ashland, Kansas, USA. Writer. m. Floyd Carter, 2 July 1987. 2 sons, 2 daughters. *Education:* Friends Bible College, 1971-72; Sam Houston State University, 1973; Bookkeeping Machines Diploma, Salt City Business College. *Appointments:* President, Women's Missionary, Rocky Mountain Yearly Meeting of Friends Churches, 1982-83. *Publications:* A Child of the King, 1988; Images, 1985. *Honour:* Golden Poetry Award for Images, 1985. *Hobbies:* Writing; Religions study; Poetry. *Address:* Box 314, Ashland, KS 67831, USA.

MERCHANT Donna Rae, b. 29 Aug. 1948, Wichita, USA. Sales & Marketing Manager. m. Christopher Wayne Merchant, 31 Aug. 1968, divorced 1973, 1 daughter. *Education:* Wichita State University, 1966-68. *Appointments:* Administrative Assistant, 1974-80; Acting Co-ordinator, Wesley Medical Centre, 1980-84; Manager, Support Services, Farm Credit Services, 1984-88; Sales & Marketing Manager, Greater Oregon Travel Consulting, 1988-. *Memberships:* President, Great Plains Business Administraton Group, 1988; Wichita Convention & Visitors Bureau; Delta Gamma; Eugene Chamber of Commerce; American Marketing Association. *Hobbies:* Writing; Skiing; Water Skiing; Cmaping; Interior Decorating. *Address:* 87 E. 33rd, Eugene, OR 97405, USA.

MERK-GOULD Linda Emmy, b. 11 Aug. 1952, Providence, Rhode Island, USA. Art Conservator. m. Robert F. Gould, 13 June 1987, 1 daughter *Education:* BA, Honours, Wellesley College, 1974; MA, Conservation, Queen's University, Canada, 1977. *Appointments:* Objects Conservator: Los Angeles County Museum of Art, 1977-78, Indianapolis Museum of Art, 1978-82; Director, Conservation, Peabody Museum, Harvard, 1980-82; President, Fine Objects

Conservation Inc., New York City, 1982-. *Publications:* Articles in professional journals. *Memberships:* Fellow: American Institute for Conservation, International Institute for Conservation; National Institute for Conservation; New York Conservation Association, Dire or; Conservators in Private Practice, Director, 1986-87. *Honours:* Graduated, Wellesley College, BA honours, Wellesley College Scholar, 1974; Samuel H. Kress Foundation Fellow, 1977. *Hobbies:* Skiing; Aeroplane Pilot's Licence; Sailing; Flower Gardening. *Address:* 3 Meeker Road, Westport, Connecticut 06880, USA.

MEROLA ROSCIANO Giovanna, b. 1 Dec. 1947, Padua, Italy (nationality, Venezuelan). University Lecturer & Researcher. m. Makram Haluani, 1 Nov. 1984, 1 daughter. *Education:* BA, Biology, 1971; Graduate studies, ecology, 1972; MA, Sociology, 1972-74; PhD, Urbanism, in progress. *Appointments:* Researcher, Human ecology, Ministry of Environment, 1977-79; Lecturer, researcher, environmental conditioning, Faculty of Architecture & Urbanism, Central University of Venezuela, 1979-; Project consultant, landscaping design. *Publications:* Books: In Defence of Abortion in Venezuela, 1979; Medicinal Plants for Women, 1987; Relationship Man-Vegetation in the City of Caracas, 1987; Guide for Women, in progress. Also: Numerous articles; Editor, director, diagrams & layout, own feminist publication, La Mala Vida, also various calendars. *Memberships:* Venezuelan Association of Cinematographic Critics; Association of Graduates in Sciences; Ecological group, Eco-Accion; Universal Park of Peace Foundation; Commission for Classification of Public Entertainment (films). *Honours:* Honorary mention, Municipal Prize for Literature, 1986; Scholarship, studies in Paris, French Government, 1971-74; Scholarship, Brazil, Getulio Vargas Foundation-IDB, 1985. *Hobbies:* Reading; Music; Cinema; Drawing & painting; Architecture & landscape design; Gardening; Medicinal plants; Botany; Arts; Activism for peace, disarmament, feminism & ecological issues. *Address:* Calle la Colina, Edf. la Colina, Ap. 24, Las Acscias, Caracas 104, Venezuela.

MERRICK Beverly Georgianne Childers b. 20 Nov. 1944, Troy, Kansas, USA. Writer; Poet; Teacher. m. John Douglas Childers, 10 July 1964. 1 son, 2 daughters. *Education:* BA 1980, Masters of Journalism 1982, Marshall University, Huntington; Masters of Creative Writing 1986; Women Studies Certificate 1984; Doctor of Philosophy, Mass Communication, 1989, Ohio University. *Appointments:* Pres, Southern Ohio Improvement League, 1973-76; Pres of Board, Pine Creek Conservancy, 1976-82; Writer/Consultant/ Poet/Teacher, 1984-88. *Publications:* Navigating the Platte; Ishbel Ross, On Assignment with History; Grasshoppers on the Platte, Poetry; The Pruning of a Rose; Poems: The Spoon; Red Cloud; We Park by the Crossing Now; The Chosen; Numerous articles to magazines and newspapers. *Memberships:* President, New Mexico State Poetry Society; National Membership Committee, Business & Professional Women; Albuquerque Business & Professional Women; Sigma Tau Delta English Honorary; Sigma Delta Chi Professional Journalism Society; Kappa Tau Alpha Scholastic Honorary. *Honours:* Southern Hills Sportsman of the Year, 1973; Grand prize winner, Sewing, Ohio State Fair, 1973; Community Betterment Award, Sears & Roebuck, 1973; 1 of ten top Homemakers of Ohio, 1974; Silver Clover 4-H Leader, 1977; Jesse Stuart Award, 1978 and 1979; Reader's Digest Travel Grant to Plains, Georgia, 1980; Aviators/ Space Writers Midwest Writing Award, 1981; Full Tuition to National Women's Studies Institute, Ann Arbor, Michigan, 1983; Reader's Digest Travel Grant to Rutgers University, 1984; Scripps-Howard Scholarship, 1984; First Place, National Writing/ Research Award, Assoc of Educators in Journalism, 1984; Past President's Award, Ntional Federation of State Poetry Societies, 1986; Nominee, Chirsta McAliffe Congressional Fellowship, 1987. *Hobbies:* Sewing; Knitting; Reading; Community betterment; Conservation projects; Gardening; Flower arranging; Reading about trials and legalese; Politics. *Address:* 655 Spur Road, Rio Rancho, New Mexico 87124, USA.

MERRIL Judith, b. 21 Jan. 1923, New York City, USA. Writer; Editor; Broadcaster. Divorced, 2 daughters. *Appointments:* Writer, 1945-; Anthology Editor, 1952-; Teacher, 1962-; Speaker Lecturer, 1968-; Radio & TV Documentaries, 1971-81; Performer, 1971-. *Publications:* 4 novels; 3 novellas; 50 short stories; translations; poetry; criticism; Edited 20 anthologies. *Address:* 40 St George St., Toronto, M5S 2E4, Canada.

MERRILL Jean Fairbanks, b. 27 Jan. 1923, Rochester, New York, USA. Writer. *Education:* BA, Allegheny College, 1944; MA, Wellesley College, 1945; Fulbright Fellow, University of Madras, India, 1952-53. *Appointments:* Feature Editor, Scholastic magazines, 1947-50; Editor, Literary Cavalcade 1956-57, Publications Division, Bank Street College of Education 1964-65. *Publications:* Numerous children's books including: Henry the Hand-Painted Mouse, 1951; Song for Gar, 1960; Emily Emerson's Moon, 1960; High Wide & Handsome, 1964; The Pushcart War, 1964; Red Riding, 1968; How Many Kings Are Hiding On My Block?, 1971; The Toothpaste Millionaire, 1973; Maria's House, 1974. Short stories (in anthologies) including: Grandpa Fix, 1968; Tiger Who Played the Guitar, 1968; Dirty Boys, 1972; Shadow, 1972; Greatest Liar, 1972; etc. Opera libretto, Mary Came Running, 1982. *Memberships:* Authors Guild; Dramatists Guild; League of Vermont Writers; Vermont Arts Council; North American Mycological Association; Vermont Institute of Natural Science; Phi Beta Kappa; Society of Childrens Book Writers. *Honours:* Book award, Boys Club of America, 1965; Lewis Carroll Shelf Awards, 1963, 1965; Dorothy Canfield Fisher Memorial Children's Book Award, 1975-76; Sequoyah Award, 1977. *Hobbies:* Reading; Theatre; Mycology. *Address:* Angel's Ark, 29 South Main Street, Randolph, Vermont 05060, USA.

MERRITT Diane Frances, b. 14 Jan. 1949, Cleveland, Ohio, USA. Obstetrician; Gynaecologist. m. Sandor J Kovacs MD PhD, 16 Apr. 1983. 2 sons; 1 daughter. *Education:* BA, Miami University; MD, New York University School of Medicine. *Appointments:* Internship and Residency, Washington University School of Medicine; Faculty, Washington University, 1981-89; Director of Pediatrics and Adolescent Gynaecology. *Memberships:* Diplomate American Board of Obstetrics and Gynecology; American College of Obstetricians and Gynecologists; The American Fertility Society; North American Society of Pediatric and Adolsecent Gynecology. *Hobbies:* Scuba diving; Photography. *Address:* Dept of Obstetrics and Gynecology, 4911 Barnes Hospital Plaza, St Louis, MO 63110, USA.

MERRY Marilyn Diana Hoover, b. 28 July 1946, St Louis, USA. Cartographer. m. Allan Preston Merry, divorced 1978, 1 son, 1 daughter. *Appointments:* Clerk Typist, US Mobility Equipment Command, St Louis, 1968-70; Supply Clerk, US Troop Support Command, St Louis, 1970-71; Clerk Typist, Institute Heraldry, Alexandria, 1971-72; Med. Intelligence, Washington 1972-73; Office Manager, Yodi Enterprises, 1973-74; Secretary, Defense Mapping Agency, Washington, 1974-79; Cartographic Technician, 1979-82, Cartographer, 1982-. *Memberships Include;* American Cancer Society, Secretary 1985-87; Black Trade Unionist; Washington Area Labor Committee on Central America and the Caribbean. *Honours:* Outstanding Performance Award, 1978; Presidential Award, American Cancer Society, 1985; Golden Poet Award, World of Poetry, 1988; A. Philip Randolph Award, Southern Christian Leadership Conference, 1988. *Address:* 5803 Falkland Pl., Capitol Heights, MD 20743, USA.

MERSCHER Hannelore Karin, b. 9 Aug. 1941, Berlin, Germany. Teacher; Translator. m. Jakob Merscher, 19 June 1965, 2 sons, 1 daughter. *Education:* BA, Interpreting & Translation, 1984; Graduate diploma, Education, 1985. *Appointments:* Typist & book-keeper, private health insurance, 1959-62; Clerk, Der Tagesspiegel, Berlin, 1962-64; Book-keeper, Leslie Service Centre, Toronto, Canada, 1965-67; Clerk, electrical wholesale, 1978; Teacher, Kelmscott High School, Australia, 1986; Translator, self- employed, 1985-. *Memberships:* Western Australian Institute of Translators & Interpreters; Modern Language Teachers Association of WA; English Teachers Association of WA. *Hobbies:* Reading; Films; Nature; Swimming; Culture. *Address:* 16 Woburn Way, Kelmscott, WA 6111, Australia.

MESSINGER Carla J S, Founder, President and Museum Director. 1 daughter. *Education:* Masters degree, Lehigh University. *Appointments:* Presented multi-media prgrams on Lenape cultural heritage, 15 years; Consultant and Speaker for Native Culture for Senior Citizens, St Francis de Salles College, 1981 and 1982; Consultant, Agape Dancers Inc; Consultant and speaker, Agape project Lenni Lenape Indians: A Regional Culture, 1983-84; special Constulant, Philadelphia School District; Participant, William Penn Tricentennial, 1982; Founder and President, Lenni Lenape Historical Society. *Honours:* Recipient, President's Volunteer Action Award, 1985; Award of Merit, Pennsylvania Federation of Historical Societies, 1986; Semi-finalist, Jefferson Award, 1987. *Address:* 1819- 1/2 Linden St, Allentown, PA 18104, USA.

METCALF Sheila Margaret, b. 14 Mar. 1934, Airdrie, Scotland. General & Child Psychiatrist. m. Arnold Metcalf, 24 Mar. 1962, 2 sons, 1 daughter. *Education:* MB,ChB, Commendation, St Andrews University, 1957; DCH 1959, DPM 1961; MRANZCP 1970; FRANZCP 1978; FRCPsych, 1986. *Appointments:* Senior House Officer, Psychiatry Registrar, Royal Dundee Hospital, 1960-62; Registrar, Child Psychiatry, Royal Alexandra Hospital for Children, Glasgow, 1962; Private practice, adult & child psychiatry, Australia, 1968-. *Publications:* Contributions to: Psychiatry for the Non-Psychiatrist; Modern Medicine. *Memberships:* Founder member, Royal College of Psychiatry; Association of Child Psychology & Psychiatry; Faculty of Child Psychiatry, Royal Australian & New Zealand College of Physicians; American Academy of Child & Adolescent Psychiatry. *Honours:* Margaret Fairlie Prize, John Kynock Scholarship, University Medal in Obstetrics, 1957. *Hobbies:* Travel; Tennis; Food & Wine; Gardening. *Address:* The Ellard Practice, 2 Greenwich Road, Greenwich, New South Wales 2065, Australia.

METCALFE Alexandra Naldera, Lady, b. 20 Mar. 1904, London, England. m. 15 July 1925, 1 son, 2 daughters. *Memberships:* Vice President, Save the Children; Royal Geographical Society; Royal Asian Society. *Honours:* CBE; Cross of Merit of the Sovereign Military Order of Malta; Commander, Order of St John of Jerusalem. *Hobbies:* Save the Children Fund; Travel; Other Charities. *Address:* 65 Eaton Place, London SW1, England.

METGE Alice Joan, b. 21 Feb. 1930, Auckland, New Zealand. Writer. *Education:* BA 1951, MA 1952, New Zealand; PhD 1958, London. *Appointments:* Junior Lecturer Geography, Auckland University College, 1952; Fieldwork and Doctoral Study, New Zealand and London, 1953-61; Lecturer, University Extension, University of Auckland, 1961-64; Senior Lecturer 1965- 67, Associate Professor, 1968-88, Anthropology, University of Wellington; Captain James Cook Fellow, 1981-83. *Publications:* A New Maori Migration, 1964; The Maoris of New Zealand, 1967 revised 1976; Talking Past Each Other (with Patricia Kinloch), 1978; In and Out of Touch, 1986. *Memberships:* Royal Anthropological Institute; Association of Social Anthropologists of the Commonwealth; New Zealand Association of Social Anthropologists, Chairman 1982-83 and 1986-88; New Zealand Federation of University Women; New Zealand Association of Women in Science; Polynesian Society; Science and Technology Advisory Committee. *Honours:* Hutchinson Medal, London School of Economics, 1959; Elsdon Best Memorial Medal, 1987; Dame Commander of the British Empire, 1987. *Hobbies:* Drama; Music; Literature. Interests: Continuing education; Prevention of violence; Work trusts and co-operatives. *Address:* 8 Paisley Terrace, Karori, Wellington 5, New Zealand.

METZGER Deena, b. 17 Sept. 1936, New York, USA. Writer; Psychotherapist. m. (1) H Reed Metzger 26 Oct 1957, 2 sons. (2) Michael Ortiz Hill, 20 Dec. 1987. *Education:* BA, cum laude, Literature and Philosophy, Brooklyn College; MA, English and American Literature, UCLA; PhD, Creative Writing and Education, International College. *Appointments:* Therapist and healer, 20 years; Faculty, California Institute of the Arts; Los Angeles Valley College; Feminist Studio Workshop; Founder, The Writing Program, Woman's Building, Los Angeles; Tutor, International College. *Creative works:* Publications: Skin: Shadows/Silence, novel, 1976; The Book of Hags, radio drama, 1977; Dark Milk, poetry, 1978; The Axis Mundi Poems, 1981; The Woman Who Slept With Men to Take the War Out of Them, dramanovel, 1981; Tree, 1983, 1978; What Dinah Thought, novel, 1989; Looking For the Faces of God, poetry, 1989, author of poetry, prose articles and critical studies in many journals, periodicals and anthologies. Leader of workshops; Co-writer and co-producer, documentary film, Chile: With Peosm & Guns; Plays: Not As Sleepwalkers, 1977; Dreams Against the State, 1981. *Memberships:* Pen American Center, International PEN. *Honours:* First Academic Freedom Award, California Federation of teachers, 1975; First annual Vesta Award in Writing, Womans' Building, Los Angeles. *Address:* Topanga, CA 90290, USA.

MEYER Carol Frances, b. 2 June 1936, Berea, Kentucky, USA. Physician, Allergy/Immunology. *Education:* AA, University of Florida, Gainesville, 1955; BA, Duke University, Durham, North Carolina, 1957; Research Fellowships, summers 1964, 1965; MD, 1967, Pediatric Intern, 1967-68, Fellow, Pediatric Respiratory Disease, 1969-71, Medical College of Georgia, Augusta; Resident, Pediatrics, Gorgas Hospital, Republic of Panama, 1968-69. *Appointments:* Pediatric Research Technician, 1962-63, Instructor, Pediatrics, 1971-72, Medical College of Georgia, Augusta; Medical Officer, Pediatrics, Allergy/Immunology, Gorgas Hospital, Arcon, Republic of Panama, 1972-89; Assistant Professor, Allergy-Immunology, Medical College of Georgia. *Publications:* Scientific contributions (with B B J Wray) to Journal of Southern Medical Association, 1970, Proceedings of NCB, Ent Society of America, 1971; Co-author, contributions to Revista Medica de Panama, 1980, 1984. *Memberships:* Medical Association of Panama Canal Zone, President 1978, Vice-President 1977, Secretary-Treasurer 1976, Delegate to American Medical Association 1979, 1980; Former Member and President, Canal Zone TB & Respiratory Disease Association; Fellow, American Academy of Pediatrics; American College of Allergy & Immunology; American Academy of Allergy & Immunology; Society of Leukocyte Biology; American Medical Womens Association; Panama Audubon Society; Museum of Natural History; Florida and National Audubon Societies; Smithsonian Association; Life Member: Nature Conservancy; Royal Society for the Protection of Birds. *Honours:* J Hillis Miller Scholar, University of Florida, 1954; Alpha Omega Alpha, 1966; Merck Award, Medical College of Georgia, 1967; Outstandingm Young Women of America, 1971; Certificate of Exceptional Performance, Gorgas Army Community Hospital, 1986. 1987. *Hobbies:* Music especially cello (member, Curundu Chamber Ensemble); Nature; Reading. *Address:* 2523 Tupelo Drive, Augusta, GA 30909, USA.

MEYER Deanna Marie Arras, b. 9 July 1937, New Britain, Connecticut, USA. Realtor; Corporate Executive. m. (1) Nee Yuhas, 1 son, 1 daughter, (2) Richard A. Meyer, 19 July 1986. *Education:* Syracuse University, 1957; Ryder College, 1958; Licensed Realtor, California, 1980. *Appointments:* Media Centre Director, Librarian, Chino Unified School District, 1973-80; Realtor, Partner, ERA American Diversified Realty, Chino, 1980-; Partner, Fashion Artistry by Ka-Dee, 1989-; Administrative Assistant, San Bernardino County Sup, 4th District, 1983-86; Chair, Governor's Committee, Neighbourhood Watch, San Bernardino County, 1985; Executive Director, Prado Tiro Grand Prix Corporation, 1986-88; Secretary, Treasurer, Prado Tiro Foundation; Executive Director, American Outdoor Sports Associates Inc (Decathlon Championship), 1989. *Memberships:* Various offices: Inland Empire West Board of Realtors, Soroptomist International (Chino), Chino Community Hospital; Corporate Challange Executive Committee, 1990; Citizen Board World Cup, USA, 1990; Chino Family YMCA Board of Mgr. Chair. *Honours:* Paul Harris fellowship, Rotary, 1987; Honorary Life Service award, Parent Teacher Association. *Hobbies:* Golf; Travel. *Address:* 778 Via Montevideo, Claremont, California 91711, USA.

MEYER Joan Marie, b. 15 July 1956, Peoria, Illinois, USA. Research Scientist. m. Timothy Robert Meyer, 13 Nov. 1982, 1 son, 1 daughter. *Education:* BA, Biology, 1978, BA, Psychology, 1978, St Mary's College; MS, 1982, PhD, 1986, University of Illinois. *Appointments:* Unit Manager, St Francis Hospital, Peoria, 1979-80; Research Assistant, University of Illinois, 1980-86; Research Scientist, The Procter & Gamble Company, 1986-. *Publications:* Numerous articles in professional journals including; Journal of Neurochemistry; Clinical & Experimental Hypertension; American Journal of Physiology. *Memberships:* Society for Neuroscience; Women in Neuroscience; New York Academy of Science. *Honours:* National Research Service Award, National Institute of Health Pre-doctoral Fellowship, 1984-86. *Hobbies:* Singing; Aerobics; Reading; Cooking. *Address:* The Procter & Gamble Company, Miami Valley Laboratories; PO Box 398707, Cincinnati, OH 45239, USA.

MEYER Michele Jean Landers, b. 10 June 1949, Coral Gables, Florida, USA. Marriage and Family Therapist. m. Frank Meyer, 1 son, 1 daughter. *Education:* University of South Florida, 1967-70; BS, Early Childhood, K-6, 1972, MS, Community Counselling, 1981, Florida International University; Parent Effectiveness Training, LaVerne University, 1977; Certified Family Life Educator; Licensed Marriage and Family Therapist, State of Florida. *Appointments:* Co-Owner, Operator, Famous Restaurant, Miami Beach, Florida, 1969-76; Executive Assistant to Actor, Producer, Richard Boone Develop Repertory Company, State of Florida, 1978-79; Marriage and Family Therapist in private practice, 1978-; Assistant Director, Intensive Counseling Services, 1980-82; Director of Social Services, Clinical Supervisor and Administrator, Pius XII Youth and Family Services, 1982-87; Site Supervisor, PINs Meditation and Diversion Unit, 1987-. *Memberships:* American Association for Marriage and Family Therapy, President New York Association for Marriage and Family Theraphy, Westchester/Mid-Hudson Chaptor; American Personnel and Guidance Association; National Board of Certified Counselors, Town of Newcastle; Chairman, Drug Abuse Prevention Council; AACD, Certifed Family Life Educator, National Counsel on Family Relations. *Honour:* Kappa Delta Pi. *Hobbies:* Theatre; Art. *Address:* 45 Brevoort Road, Chappaqua, NY 10514, USA.

MEYER Patricia Morgan, b. 23 June 1934, Delaware, Ohio, USA. Emeritus Professor. m. Donald R. Meyer, 31 Dec. 1957, 1 daughter. *Education:* BA, Ohio Wesleyan University, 1956; MA, 1958, PhD, 1960, Ohio State University. *Appointments:* Research Associate, 1960-76; Professor, 1976-85, Emeritus Professor, 1985-, Ohio State University. *Publications:* About 60 articles and book chapters. *Memberships:* American Psychological Association; Fellow, Board of Scientific Affairs; Chairman, Animal Care Panel; Society for Neuroscience; Psychonomic Society. *Honours:* Career Development Award, NIMH, 1966-76; NTMH Small Grants Subchairman, 1970-74; NIMH IRG Chairman Committee, 1971-74; Board for Scientific Affairs Representative to Neuroscience Council Meeting, 1974-76; Section Editor, Comparative and Physiological Psychology, JSAS, 1980-81; Editor, Physiological Psychology Journal, 1980-85; Invited Consulting Editor and outside Reviewer, BSF and NIMH. *Hobby:* Videography. *Address:* 476 Overbrook Drive, Columbus, OH 43214, USA.

MEYER Roberta, b. 27 July 1936, San Francisco, USA. Communication Consultant; Alcohol Educator; Author. m. G. William Sheldon, 22 Sept. 1965, 2 daughters. *Education:* University of Utah, 1976; San Francisco State Uiversity. *Appointments Include:* Owner, Director, Ballet Arts of San Francisco, 1965-79; Founder President, Communication Experiences & Creative Communications Consultants, 1977-; Instructor, Communicating with the Addict, San Francisco State University & Probation Department, 1983-. *Publications:* The Parent Connection, How to Communicate with Your Child about Alcohol and Other Drugs, 1984; Facts About Booze, 1980; Power of Hearing, 1977; Hearing with the Heart, 1987. *Memberships:* National Speakers Association; San Francisco Chamber of Commerce; American Arbitration Association; Republican Presidential Task Force Member; Board Member, National Council on Alcoholism; etc. *Honour:* Recipient, various honours and awards. *Hobbies:* Ballet; Reading; Ice Skating. *Address:* 1300 Quarry Court, No 301, Point Richmond, CA 94801, USA.

MEYEROWITZ Patricia, b. 29 Mar. 1933, London, England. Artist. m. Jacob, 27 Oct. 1957. *Education:* Studied techniques of jewellery making, Central School of Arts and Crafts, London, England, 1959-60. *Career:* Making Jewellery, 1962-; Sculpting in metal and wood, 1962-; Writing, 1965-. *Creative works:* Sculpture: Shown at galleries in London and Oxford, England; New York and Washington, USA; collections with Joseph H Hirshhorn; McGraw-Hill; Zimmcor Company; Sano-Rubin Construction Co. Jewellery: Exhibitions in London, Coventry, Nottingham and Oxford, England, 1962-69; Vienna, Austria, 1969; New York City, USA, 1972, 1974, 1975, 1976; private collections in many parts of the world bought by Cartier Inc; Georg Jensen Inc; Undertaken lectures and a film, Simply Making Jewelry, 1977. Writing: Author of: Jewelry and Sculpture through Unit Construction, 1967, republished, 1972, 3rd edition, 1978; And A Little Child, 1982; Introduction to: How to Write (Gertrude Stein), 1975. Editor of: Gertrude Stein: Writings and Lectures 1909-1945, 1967, republished 1971. *Honour:* Certificate of Excellence for Outstanding Achievement in Sculpture, International Art Competition, New York, 1988; Certificate of Excellence in Sculpture, Art Horizons, New York, 1988. *Address:* P O Box 8, Easton, PA 18044, USA.

MEYERS Beth, b. 30 Aug. 1911, Neutral Bay, New South Wales, Australia. Artist. m. Edward L Meyers, 1 son, 2 daughters. *Education:* Sculpture Course with 1st Class Honours and Bronze Medal, East Sydney Technical College. *Creative works:* Selected part-time exhibitions since 1962 and numerous one man shows in 1982; Over 90 paintings sold; Sculptures; plastic; Bronze and woodcarving. *Memberships:* Royal Art Society of New South Wales; Desiderius Orban Studio, New South Wales. *Honours:* 2 first class awards in painting at Robertson Centennary Exhibition, New South Wales; Highly commended and commended in exhbitions in New South Wales and Victoria; Hung in highly selected Blake Prize, Sydney. *Address:* Sydney, New South Wales 2093, Australia.

MEYERS Christine Laine, b. Detroit, USa. Publishing Executive/Consultant. 1 daughter. *Education:* BA, University of Michigan. *Appointments:* Editor, Industrial Relations Diesel Div., General Motors Corp, 1968; National Advertising Manager, J.L. Hudson Co. Detroit, 1969-76; President, Owner, Laine Meyers Associates, Troy, 1978-. *Memberships:* various professional organisations including: International Association Business Communicators. *Honours:* Recipient, many honours and awards including: Named One of AD Age's 100 Best & Brightest, 1987. *Address:* 3645 Crooks Road, Troy, MI 48084, USA.

MGBOJIKWE Rose Uzoamaka, b. 30 Mar. 1946, Ogoja, Nigeria. Education Administration. *Education:* BA English, University of Nigeria, Nsukka, Nigeria, 1965. *Appointments:* Acting Editor, Women's Page, Eastern Nigeria Outlook Newspaper, 1965-76; Education Officer, Republic of Zambia, Central Africa, 1972-75; Chief Education Officer, Federal Republic of Nigeria, Federal Ministry of Education, Centre for Educational Measurement, Kaduna, 1975-. *Publications:* Contributor of numerous articles on women to the newspaper Outlook. *Memberships:* English Association of Nigeria; Nigerian Union of Civil Servants. *Honours:* Commendation by British Council for Outstanding Contribution to Course attended in Exeter, England, 1985. *Hobbies:* Swimming; Reading; Socialising; Travelling. *Address:* Centre for Educational Measurement (CEM), PMB 2291, 5A Dawaki Road, Kaduna, Nigeria.

MICHAELS Joanne, b. 30 Dec. 1950, New York City, New York, USA. Publisher; Author. m. Stuart Alan Ober, 20 Sept. 1981, 1 son. *Education:* BA, University of Connecticut, Storrs, 1972. *Appointments:* Aquisitions Editor, St Martin's Press, New York City, 1977-78; Director of Marketing, Beekman Publishers, New York City, 1978-82; Editor-in-Chief, Hudson Valley Magazine, 1982-86; Publisher, JMB Publications, Woodstock, New York, 1986-. *Publications:* Living Contradictions: The Women of the Baby Boom Come of Age, 1982; The Best of the Hudson Valley and Catskill Mountains, 1988; Famous Woodstock Cooks, 1988; Lets Take the Kids! Great Places to Go With Children in New York's Hudson Valley. *Memberships:* Authors Guild; Women in Communications; Secretary, Board of Trustees, Woodstock Library. *Honour:* Article nominated for American Society of Magazine Editors Journalism Award for Investigative Reporting, 1986. *Hobbies:* Photography; Running; Skiing; Hiking. *Address:* PO Box 888, Woodstock, NY 12498, USA.

MICHEL Mary Ann, b. 1 June 1939, Evergreen Park, Illinois, USA. Dean, College of Health Sciences; Professor of Nursing. m. May 1974. *Education:* Diploma, School of Nursing, 1960; BSN Nursing, 1964; MS Community Mental Health, 1968; EdD Educational Psychology, 1971. *Appointments:* Instructor, Little Company Mary Hospital, Evergreen Park, 1964-67; Instructor Assistant Professor, No Illinois University, 1968- 71; Chair/Department of Nursing 1971-73, Professor of Nursing, 1976-, Dean College of Health Sciences, 1973-, University of Nevada, Las Vegas. *Publications:* Keynote address published in the Journal for the Society of Otorhinolaryngology and Head Neck Nurses, Inc. *Memberships:* Treasurer, 1988-90, Chair, Secy Awards Comm, 1982-83, Chair, National By- Laws Comm, 1985-87, American Soc Allied Heal Assoc; chair, 20th Annual Convention, 1987, NV Donor Organ Referral Services (DORS) Secretary/Treasurer 1988-89; Phi Kappa Phi, Chapter 100, Secretary 1981-83, President, 1984-85. *Honours:* Honorary Member, Alpha Beta Gamma Honor Society, Radiological Sciences, 1981; Outstanding Alumni Award, Loyola University, School of Nursing, 1983; Las Vegas Chamber of Commerce, Women of Achievement Award, Category of Education, 1988. *Hobbies:* Reading; Knitting; Swimming. *Address:* 4163 W Warm Springs Road, Las Vegas, Nevada 89118, USA.

MICHEL Rosmarie Louise, b. 16 Aug. 1931, Zurich, Switzerland. Entrepreneur. *Education:* Studies, Diploma, Swiss Hotel School, Lausanne, 1956-59. *Appointments:* Partner, Managing Director, Family Company, 1956-; Board of Directors 1976-; Chairperson, Food & Beverage Firm SFV, 1979-; Chairperson, Building Society, 1985-. *Memberships:* International Federation of Business and Professional Women, President 1983-85; Womens World Banking, Trustee, 1986-; Association Management-Syposium for Women, President, 1988-. *Hobbies:* Music; Travel. *Address:* Niederdorfstr. 90, CH 8001 Zurich, Switzerland.

MICHELS Eileen Phyllis, b. 27 Mar. 1926, Fargo, North Dakota, USA. Professor of Art History. m. Joseph Michels, 9 Mar. 1955. 1 son. *Education:* BA, magna cum laude 1947, MA 1953, MA 1959, PhD 1971, University of Minnesota; Sorbonne, Paris, France, 1956-

57; Institute of Fine Arts, NYU, 1950-51. *Appointments:* Art Librarian, University of Minnesota, 1948-50, 1951-53; Curator, University of Minnesota Gallery, 1954- 56; Asst Professor Art History, Wisconsin State University, River Falls, 1966- 70; Visiting Asst Prof, Stanford University, 1972-73; Assoc Prof & Chair, Dept of Art History 1978-88, Professor 1989-, College of St Thomas. *Publications:* Book: A Landmark Reclaimed, the Old Federal Courts Building, 1971; Numerous articles and papers on architectural history. *Memberships:* Society of Architectural Historians, Director 1976-79, Secretary 1982-86; College Art Association; Women Historians of the Midwest; Treasurer, Minnesota Society of Architectural Historians, 1973-86; State Review Board of Minnesota, 1976-; Heritage Preservation Commissions St Paul, 1982-85. *Honours:* Phi Beta Kappa, 1947; Fulbright Scholarship to Paris, 1956-57; Delta Chi Delta, 1947. *Hobbies:* Collect studio ceramics and glass; Architectural in USA and Europe. *Address:* 2183 Hendon Avenue, St Paul, Minnesota 55108, USA.

MICHELSON Lorelle Naomi, b. 28 Jan. 1950, New York City, USA. Plastic Surgeon. m. Jacob Jay Lindenthal, 16 Sept. 1984. *Education:* BA, City College, City University of New York, 1970; MD, State University of New York, 1974; Paediatric Residency: New York-Bellevue Hospital Centre, 1974-75, 1975-76; General Surgery Residency, Lenox Hospital, 1976-79; Plastic Surgery Residency, Albany Medical Centre Hospital, 1980-81; Aesthetic Surgery Post-Graduate Fellowship, Manhatten Eye, Ear & Throat Hospital, 1982. *Appointments:* Assistant Instructor, Albany Medical College, 1980-81; Instructor, 1982-84, Assistant Professor, 1984-85, Clinical Assistant Professor, 1985-, UMDNJ; Associate Attending Staff, Beth Israel Hospital, Passaic, 1985-. *Publications:* Articles in professional journals including: Clinics in Plastic Surgery; Aesthetic Plastic Surgery; etc. *Memberships:* American Society of Plastic & Reconstructive Surgery; New York Regional Scoiety of Plastic & Reconstructive Surgery; Passaic County Medical Society; American Medical Society, many other professional organisations. *Honours:* Recipient, various honours and awards. *Address:* 250 Gorge Road, Apt 23J, Cliffside Park, NJ 07010, USA.

MICHIE Janet Ray, b. 4 Feb. 1934, Balmaha, Scotland. Member of Parliament for Argyll & Bute. m. 11 May 1957. 3 daughters. *Education:* Edinburgh School of Speech Therapy. *Appointments:* Speech Therapist, MOD, BAOR 1960-63; Far East 1966-68; Area Speech Therapist, Argyll & Clyde Health Board, 1977-87. *Memberships:* Scottish NFU; Scottish Crofters Union; Rural Forum; An Comunn Gaidhealach; CSA. *Honours:* Member of Parliament Argyll & Bute, 1087-. *Hobbies:* Swim; Golf; Watching rugby. *Address:* Tigh an Eas, Glenmore Road, Oban, Argyll, Scotland.

MICKELSON Norma I, b. 5 Nov. 1926, Victoria, Canada. Professor. m. Harvey P. Mickelson, 12 Aug. 1946, 1 son, 1 daughtr. *Education:* BEd., University of British Columbia, 1963; MA, University of Victoria, 1968; PhD, University of Washington, USA, 1972. *Appointments:* Teacher, 1945-60; Supervisor of Instruction, 1961-66; Professor, University of Victoria, 1968-. *Publications:* Monographs; Book chapters; TV Series: Reading; Whole Language; Articles in various journals. *Memberships:* International Reading Association; Educational Research Association; PEO. *Honours:* Denton Memorial, 1945; Dirks Gold Watch, 1961; Ethel Buchanan Award, 1989; Recipient, various fellowships & awards. *Hobbies:* Japanese Flower Arranging; Bridge. *Address:* 2010 Ferndale Road, Victoria, BC V8N 2Y7, Canada.

MIDDLEBROOK Diane, b. 16 Apr 1939, Pocatello, Idaho, USA. University Professor; Author; Lecturer. m. Carl Djerassi, 21 June 1985, 1 daughter. *Education:* AB, magna cum laude, University of Washington, Seattle, 1961; MA 1962, PhD 1968, Yale University. *Appointments:* Assistant Professor of English, 1966-74, Associate Professor 1974-79, Associate Dean of Undergraduate Studies, 1979-82, Professor of Englilsh

1983- Howard H and Jessie T Watkins University Professor 1985-90, Stanford University. *Publications:* Walt Whitman and Wallace Stevens, 1974; Worlds Into Words: Understanding Modern Poems, 1980; Gin Considered as a Demon, chapbook of poems, 1983; Coming to Light: American Women Poets in the 20th Century, essays, edited with Marilyn Yalom, 1985; Selected Poems of Anne Sexton, ed. with an introduction by Diane Wood Middlebrook and Diana Hume George, 1988; Anne Sexton: A Biography, 1991. *Memberships:* Director, Center for Research on Women, Stanford University, 1977-79; Trustee, Djerassi Foundation, 1980-82, 1984-; Modern Language Association; Virginia Woolf Society; Wallace Stevens Society. *Honours include:* University Fellow, Stanford, 1975-77; Dean's Award for Distinguished Teaching, Stanford, 1977; NEH Fellowship for Independent Study and Research, 1982-83; Fellow of the Bunting Institute, Radcliffe College 1982-83; Fellow of the Stanford Humanities Center 1983-84; Pew Foundation Faculty Research Grant, 1987; Walter J Gores Award for Excellence in Teaching, Stanford, 1987; John Simon Guggenheim Memorial Foundation Fellowship, 1988-89. *Hobby:* Collecting Art. *Address:* 1101 Green Street, San Francisco, CA 94109, USA.

MIDLARSKY Elizabeth, b. 29 Apr. 1941. University Professor; Psychotherapist. m. 25 June 1961, 1 son, 2 daughters. *Education:* BA, Brooklyn College, 1961; MA, 1966, PhD, 1968, Northwestern University. *Appointments:* Assistant Professor, University of Denver, 1968-73; Associate Professor, Director Psychology Training, Metro State College, 1975-77; Associate Professor, 1977-83, Chairperson, 1978-81, Professor 1983-, University of Detroit; Director, Center for the Study of Development & Aging, 1981-. *Publications:* Numerous articles, book chapters; Editor, Academic Psychology Bulletin, 1982-86. *Memberships:* American Psychological Association, Fellow; Gerontological Society of America; Society for the Psychology Study of Social Issues; Michigan Psychological Association, Executive Council. *Honours:* Various honours & awards. *Hobbies:* Poetry; Piano; Singing. *Address:* Dept. of Psychology, University of Detroit, 4001 W. McNichols Road, Detroit, MI 48221, USA.

MIDLER Bette, b. 1 Dec. 1945, Honolulu, Hawaii, USA. Actress; Singer. m. Martin von Haselberg. *Education:* University of Hawaii. *Creative Works:* Debut as actress in film Hawaii, 1965. Stage appearances: Fiddler on the Roof, 1966-69; Salvation, 1970; Tommy, 1971; Nightclub concert performer on tour, USA 1972-73; Palace Theatro, New York City, 1973. Television includes: David Frost Show; Tonight Show; Clams on The Half-Shell Revue, New York City, 1975; Recorded The Divine Miss M, 1972; Bette Midler, 1973; Broken Blossom, 1977; Live at Last, 1979; New Thighs and Whispers, 1979; New Depression, 1979; Divine Madness, 1980; No Frills, 1984; Mud Will Be Flung Tonight, 1985. Films: The Rose, 1979; Jinxed, 1982; Down and Out in Beverly Hills, 1986. *Publication:* A View from Abroad, 1979; The Saga of Baby Divine, 1983. *Honours:* After Dark Ruby award, 1973; Grammy award, 1973; Special Tony Award, 1973; Tony award for One Woman Show on Broadway, 1974; Emmy award, 1978; Grammy award, 1981; Golden Globe awards (2), 1980; Walk of Fame Star on Hollywood Boulevard. *Address:* c/o Atlantic Records, 75 Rockefeller Plaza, New York, NY 10019, USA.

MIEL Alice Marie, b. 21 Feb. 1906, Six Lakes, Michigan, USA. Retired Educator. *Education:* Life Certificate, Teaching, 1924; BA 1928, MA 1931, University of Michigan; EdD, Teachers College, Columbia, 1944. *Appointments:* Elementary and Secondary Teacher, Michigan Public Schools, Vicksburg, Farmington, Rogers City and Ann Arbor, 1924-37; Elementary School Principal, Ann Arbor, 1937-39; Curriculum Coordinator, Mt Pleasant, 1939-42; Instructor, Asst Professor; Associate Professor; Full Professor, Teachers College, Columbia University, 1942-71. *Publications:* Democracy in School

Administration, 1943; Changing the Curriculum, 1946; Cooperative Procedures in Learning, 1952; More Than Social Studies, 1957; Creativity in Teaching, 1961; Educating the Young People of the World, 1970; Supervision for Improved Instruction, 1972. *Memberships:* Ex Secretary, 1973-77, World Council for Curr. and Instruction; President, 1953-54, Assoc. for Supervision & Curr. Dev; Assoc for Childhood Ed, Int. *Honours:* Honorary LLD, Central Michigan University, 1954; 75th Anniversary Award, Central Michigan University, 1968; Award, National Ed Assoc, Com on Civil and Human Rights, 1968; Teachers College Medal for Distinguished Service, 1978; Election to Laureate Chapter of Kappa Delta Pi, 1984. *Hobbies:* Golf; Bridge; Cooking; Reading; Writing; Travel; Community service. *Address:* 1649 NW 19th Circle, Gainesville, FL 32605, USA.

MILAM Mary June Matthews, b. 27 Mar. 1931, Preston, Georgia, USA. Insurance Agent. m. Walker H. Milam, 15 June 1957, 2 sons, 2 daughters. *Education:* BA, Louisiana State University, 1949. *Appointments:* New York Life Ins. Co., 1966-. *Publications:* Articles for Nylic Review and Life Association News. *Memberships:* New Orleans and Louisiana State Associations of Life Underwriters; Board of Battered Womens Programme; etc. *Honours:* Recipient, various honours and awards including: Appointed to Jefferson Parish Economic Development and Port Commission, 1988; Outstanding Volunteer, Battered Women's Programme, 1986. *Hobbies:* Cooking; Politics; Fundraising. *Address:* 3333 W. Napoleon Ave., Ste. 200, Metairie, LA 70001, USA.

MILES Angela Rose, b. 17 SEpt. 1946, England. University Professor. m. Anthony Graham Miles, 4 Oct. 1969, divorced 1978. *Education:* BA Hons 1968, MA 1970, Leeds University, England; PhD, University of Toronto, Canada, 1979. *Appointments:* Lecturer, Atkinson College, York University, Toronto, 1971-81; Asst Professor 1981-84, Associate Professor 1984-88, St Francis Xavier University, Antigonish, Canada; Associate Professor, Ontario Institute for Studies in Education, Toronto, 1988-. *Publications:* Books: Feminism in Canada (co-editor with Geraldine Finn), 1982; Feminist Radicalism in the 1980s, 1985; Feminism: From Pressure to Politics, (main editor with Geraldine Finn), 1988. *Memberships:* Antigonish Women's Assoc, Board; Can Assoc for the Study of Adult Education; Canadian Women's Studies Association; Canadian Sociological & Anthropological Association; Canadian Pol Sci Assoc; Atlantic Association of Sociological & Anthrops; Canadian Society for Women in Phil; Canadian Res Instit for the Study of Women; Canadian Congress of Learning Opportunities for Women; Match Intl Centre. *Hobbies:* Reading; Walking; Cycling; Tai Chi. *Address:* Adult Education, OISE, 252 Bloor Street W, Toronto, Ontario, Canada M5S 1V6.

MILES Dori Elizabeth, b. 3 Jan. 1953, Brooklyn, USA. Attorney. *Education:* BA, New York University, 1974; JD, Southwestern University School of Law, 1982. *Appointments:* Fonda & Garrard, 1982-85; MeMel Jacobs Pierno Gersh & Ellsworth. *Publications:* Erisa: A Gleaming Shield for the HMO Industry, Contract Healthcare. *Memberships:* Admitted to Practice: California Supreme Court, US District Court for the Central District of California, US Court of Appeals for the Ninth Circuit. *Hobbies:* Music; Film; Art. *Address:* 1815 Glendon Ave., No 103, Los Angeles, CA 90025, USA.

MILES Joanna, b. 6 Mar. 1940, Nice, France. Actress. m. (1) William Burns, 23 May 1970 (divorced 1977), (2) Michael Brandman, 29 Apr. 1978, 1 son. *Education:* Graduated, Putney School, Vermont, 1958. *Career:* Member, Actors Studio, New York City, New York, USA, 1966; Member, Los Angeles Classic Theatre, California, 1986; Filmed in: The Way We Live Now, 1969; Bug, 1975; The Ultimate Warrior, 1975; Golden Girl, 1978; Cross Creek, 1983; As Is, 1986; Blackout: Rosencrantz and Guildenstern are Dead, 1990; Numerous TV films including: In What America, 1965; My Mother's House, 1968; Glass Menagerie, 1974; Born Innocent, 1974;

Aloha Means Goodbye, 1974; The Trial of Chaplain Jensen, 1975; Harvest Home, 1977; Fire in the Sky, 1978; Sophisticated Gents, 1979; Promise of Love, 1982; Sound of Murder, 1983; All My Sons (PBS), 1986, 1987; The Right To Die, 1987; Appeared in numerous TV series episodes including Barney Miller, Dallas, St Elsewhere, The Hulk, Trapper John, Kaz, Cagney and Lacey, Studio 5B, 1989, Star Trek The Next Generation, 1990; Stage play roles in: Walk-Up, 1962; Once in a Life Time, 1963; Cave Dwellers, 1964; Home Free, 1964; Drums in the Night, 1968; Dracula, 1968; One Night Stands of A Noisy Passenger, 1972; Dylan, 1973; Dancing for the Kaiser, 1976; Debutante Ball, 1985; One Flew Over the Cuckoos Nest, 1988; Growing Gracefully, 1989; Performed in radio shows, Once in a Lifetime, 1987, Babbit, 1987, The Grapes of Wrath, 1989, Sta KCRW; Playwright, Vice-President, Brandman Productions. *Memberships:* Academy of Motion Picture Arts and Sciences; Academy of TV Arts and Scientists; Dramatists Guild. *Honours:* 2 Emmy Awards (Glass Menagerie), 1970; American Women in Radio and TV Award, 1974; Actors Studio Achievement Award, 1980. *Address:* 2062 North Vine Street, Suite 5, Hollywood, CA 90068, USA.

MILES Sarah, b. 31 Dec. 1941. Actress. *Education:* Royal Academy of Dramatic Art, London, England. *Career:* First film appearance, Term of Trial, 1962; With National Theatre Company, 1964-65; Shakespeare stage season, 1982-83. *Creative Works:* Films include: Those Magnificent Men in Their Flying Machines, 1964; I Was Happy Here, 1966; The Blow-Up, 1966; Ryan's Daughter, 1970; Lady Caroline Lamb, 1972; The Hireling, 1973; The Man Who Loved Cat Dancing, 1973; Great Expectations, 1975; Pepita Jiminez, 1975; The Sailor Who Fell From Grace With the Sea, 1976; The Big Sleep, 1978; Venom, 1981.

MILGRAM Gail Gleason, b. 14 June 1942, USA. Professor. m. 6 Aug. 1966, 2 daughters. *Education:* BS, Georgian Court College, 1963; M.Ed., 1965, Ed.D., 1969, Rutgers University. *Appointments Include:* Associate Professor, 1971-82, Executive Director, Summer School of Alcohol Studies, & New Jersey Summer School of Alcohol & Drug Studies, 1982-, Professor, Director, 1982-, Education & Training, Center of Alcohol Studies, Rutgers University. *Publications:* Books Include: Coping with Alcohol, 1987; What, When and How to Talk to Students About Alcohol & Other Drugs: A Guide for Teachers, co-author, 1986; What, When and How to Talk to Your Children About Alcohol and Other Drugs, A Guide for Parents, 1983; Alcohol Education materials, 1980-81, 1979-80, 1978-79, 1973-78, 1980, 1950-73, 1975; Your Career in Education, 1976; The Teenager and Sex, 1974; The Teenager and Smoking, 1972; The Teenager and Alcohol, 1970; etc; Pamphlets, and numerous articles in professional journals. *Memberships:* Numerous professional organisations. *Honours Include:* Distinguished Service Award, Middlesex County Alcohol Association, 1983; Presidential Award, Distinguished Public Service, Rutgers University, 1988. *Address:* Center of Alcohol Studies, Busch Campus, Smithers Hall, Rutgers University, New Brunswick, NJ 08903, USA.

MILLARD Wenda Harris, b. 7 Sept. 1954, Alexandria, Virginia, USA. Publisher. m. William John Millard, 8 Oct. 1983. 1 son. *Education:* BA, English, Trinity College, Hartford, CT, 1976; MBA, Harvard Business School, 1983. *Appointments:* Promotion Manager, American Home Magazine, 1976; Promotion Manager, Ladies Home Journal, 1977-79; Sales Development Director, New York Magazine, 1979-81; General Manager, Wishing Woman Ventures, 1983-85; Publisher, Adweek Magazine, 1985-. *Publications:* Various articles in numerous magazines. *Memberships:* Advertising Club of New York (Chairman ANDY Awards); Advertising Women of New York; Women in Communications; Harvard Club; Trinity College Alumni Association, VP. *Honours:* One of Good Housekeeping's 100 Young Women of Promise, 1985; Natl Commission on Working Women Radio Award, 1984; International Assoc of Business Communicators Award, 1980. *Hobbies:*

Squash; Skiing; Sailing; Film; Theatre. *Address:* 60 Echo Drive North, CT 06820, USA.

MILLER Adele Engelbrecht, b. 31 July 1946, Jersey City, USA. Educator. m. William A. Miller, 21 Dec. 1981. *Education:* BS, 1968, MBA, 1974, Fairleigh Dickinson University. *Appointments:* Business Education Teacher, 1968-73, Co-ordinator, Cooperative Education Programme, 1973-, Chairman, Cooperative Education Advisory Board, 1978-, Acting Vice Principal, 1985-86, Principal, 1986, Dickinson High School, Jersey City; Parents Council Trustee, 1986-. *Memberships:* Jersey City Womens Club Scholarship Chairman, 1978-; President, College Club, Jersey City, 1982-84; American Association of University Women, Education Chairman, 1984-, Recording Secretary, 1985-, New Jersey Division; Jersey City Rotary Club, 1987-; Jersey City State Community Orchestra, Vice President 1988-, Secretary 1986-1988, Trustee, 1978-; Jersey City YWCA Trustee, 1988-. *Hobbies:* Boating; Gourmet Cooking; Playing the Piano; Theatre; Travel. *Address:* 91 Sherman Place, Jersey City, NJ 07307, USA.

MILLER Agnes Marie, b. 1 Apr. 1922, Blacksher, Alabama, USA. Retired. m. Russell W. Miller, 26 July 1947, 3 sons. *Education:* Wayne State University, 1942-43, 1977-78; Loretta Heights College, 1973; University of Michigan, 1974. *Appointments:* Equal Emloyment Opportunity Counsellor, 1978-83; Community Services Advisor, Dept. of HUD, 1978-83; Consumer Affairs Representative, 1980-83; Volunteer Community Services Advisor & Community Social Worker. *Publications:* Roots: Some Student Perspectives Readings in Black History & Culture. *Memberships:* Society of Consumer Affairs Professionals in Business; Iota Phi Lambda; Museum of African-American History; Inter-Collegiate Council, President; etc. *Honours Include:* Testamnial Resolution, Detroit City Council, 1983; Proclamation, Wayne County Executive, William Lucas; etc. *Hobbies:* Writing; Lecturing; Reciting own Poetry Compositions. *Address:* 7121 Linsdale Street, Detroit, MI 48204, USA.

MILLER Anne Small, b. 15 Sept. 1907, Calham, Colorado, USA. Teacher of oral-aural deaf, retired. m. Purviance Miller, 14 Aug. 1932, 1 daughter. *Education:* BA, Colorado College, 1926; MA, Smith College, 1927; Teacher Training Course, Clarke School for the oral-aural deaf, 1928. *Appointments:* Teacher, Clarke School, 1928-74; Clarke School Summer Institute; International Congress for the Deaf, Manchester, England, 1958; Northampton, Massachusetts, USA, 1967; Stockholm, Sweden, 1970. *Creative works:* Articles in professional journals; Television appearances; Workshops on speech, language, curriculum, sex education. *Memberships:* Teachers' Union; Phi Beta Kappa; Alexander G Bell Association for the Deaf; Unitarian Director; Cape Ann Speech and Lip Reading Services, 1974-87. *Honours:* Phi Beta Kappa, cum laude, 1926; Trustee Fellowship, Smith College, 1927. *Hobbies:* Historical and biographical books; Antiques; Horseback riding; Sailing. Interests: Teenage problems; Development of self worth; Environmental problems. *Address:* 4 Cathedral Avenue, Rockport, Massachusetts 01966, USA.

MILLER Barbara (Bobbi) A, b. 3 Feb. 1955, Fort Bragg, North Carolina, USA. Independent Writer/Editor. m. 28 May 1983, 2 daughters. *Education:* BA, Mass Media Communications, Univerity of Colorado; AA, Journalism, Pikes Peak Community College; Honours Certificates in Fiction & Advanced Writing, Writers Digest School, LaSalle Extension University. *Appointments:* Assistant Editor, Scribe Newspaper, 1981-82; Editor, Memo Placement Newsletter, 1982-83; Graphic Designer, 1983-84; Associate Editor, local magazine, 1983; Independent Writer/Editor, 1983-. *Publications Include:* 2 photo exhibits, 1980; Collegiate Career Woman; Aztec peak; Netwrok Magazine for Colorado Women; Christian Writer; Professional Communicatorp Community Bank President; Woman Engineer. *Memberships:* National Writers Club; Women in Communications Inc; International Womens Writers

Guild. *Honours:* 1st Place, General Overall Excellence, Rocky Mountain Collegiate Press Association, 1980; 10th Place, Short Story, Science Fiction Writers of Earth, 1986. *Address:* 1514 North El Paso, Colorado Springs, CO 80907, USA.

MILLER Bonnie Mary, b. 21 July 1956, Aurora, Illinois, USA. Editorial Director. *Education:* BA, English Literature, Mundelein College, Chicago. *Appointments:* Editorial Director, Dialogue Publications, Berllyn, Illinois, 1986-; Freelance Writer, Beacon News, Northern Star News, Mainstream Magazine, Tollers Magazine, Rhino Magazine, Career World Magazine. *Publications:* Chicago's Authors Celebrate Chicago; A Fire in the Snow. *Memberships:* Past President, Alpha Pi Chapter, Sigma Tau Delta; Chicago Women in Publishing. *Honours:* 1st Place, Josephine Lusk Award for Poetry, 1982; 2nd Place, Josephine Lusk Award for Short Story, 1982; Mundelein College Writing Scholarship, 1982. *Hobbies:* Gardening; Fencing; Theatre; Riding; Photography. *Address:* c/o Dialogue, 3100 South Oak Park Avenue, Berwyn, IL 60402, USA.

MILLER Cheryl Renee Harrison, b. 24 Sept. 1952, Peru, Indiana, USA. Independent Writer. m. Garry L Miller, 24 Apr. 1983. *Education:* AB Journalism, Indiana University, Bloomington, 1975. *Appointments:* Editorial Assistant, 1975-76, Columnist & Staff writer, 1979-80, Clearwater Sun; Reporter, 1976-77; Feature Editor, 1977-78, Chronicle-Tribune; Staff Writer, Evening Independent, St Petersburg, 1980-82; Associate Editor, Tampa Magazine, 1982-83; Promotion Co-ordinator, Times Publishing Co, St Petersburg, 1983-86; Editor, Art Product News, St Petersburg, 1986-87. *Membership:* Florida Freelance Writers Association. *Honours:* 35 awards including: 1st Direct mail/ Brochures/Consumer appeal, 2nd, Black & White Institutional print advertising campaigns, National Federation of Press Women, 1987; 1st Newspaper self-promotion, American Advertising Federation, 1986; 1st direct mail/brochures/consumer appeal, 1st newspaper advertising campaigns, 3rd 4-colour brochures for profit, National Federation of Press Women, 1986; 1st print media advertising campaign, National Federation of Press Women, 1985; 2 awards of merit, Athena/Creative newspaper competition, 1984; Sales and Marketing Management's Selling with Data Award, 1984; Hoosier Scholar, 1970-74. *Hobbies:* Travel; Photography; Reading; Psychology. *Address:* 251 16th Avenue NE, St Petersburg, FL 33704, USA.

MILLER Elly, b. 5 Mar. 1928, Vienna, Austria. Publisher. m. Harvey Miller, 4 June 1950, 1 son, 2 daughters. *Education:* Oxford High School for Girls, England; Somerville College, Oxford University (MA Oxon), 1946-49; Typography, Central School of Art, London, 1952-53. *Appointments:* Research assistant (Times' History), The Times, 1949; Oxford University Press, New York, USA, 1949-50; Editor, Phaidon Press, London, 1950-72; Editorial Director, Harvey Miller Publishers, 1972-. *Creative work includes:* Initiator & editor, definitive art history publications, especially medieval art, eg, Survey of English Illuminated Manuscripts; Translations from German, works of Wilhelm Busch, eg, Mac & Murray (Max und Moritz), published Canongate, 1986. *Hobbies:* Art; Book design; Music, especially opera; Piano playing; Song writing. *Address:* Harvey Miller Publishers, 20 Marryat Road, London SW19 5BD, England.

MILLER Emilie Feiza, b. 11 Aug. 1936, Chicago, Illinois, USA. Senator. m. Dean E. Miller, 26 June 1958, 1 son, 1 daughter. *Education:* BS, Business Administration, Drake University, 1958. *Appointments:* Retail Management, Fashion Buying: Woodward & Lothrop, Washington DC; Carson, Pirie, Scott & Co, Chicago, Illinois; Jordan Marsh, Boston, Massachusetts; Legislative Aide, Senator Adelard L.Brault, 1980-83; TV Host, Producer, Channel 61; Legislative Consultant, Virginia Federation of Business & Professional Women, 1986-87; State Senator, 34th Senate District, Virginia, 1988-. *Creative Works:* Paintings; Silkscreens; Editorials; Political columns. *Memberships include:*

Board of Directors, SCAN & Mental Health Association, Northern Virginia, 1988; State Mental Health & Mental & Retardation Board, 1982-88 (Chairman, Evaluation Committee, Block Grants Commission, 1982-86); Child Abuse Prevention Task Force, 1984-87; Past Chairman, Fairfax Falls Church Community Services Board; Past Chairman, Virginia Association of Community Services Boards (Chairman 1980-82); Northern Virginia Association of Community Boards; Executive Committee, International Children's Festival, Vice-President, Fairfax County Arts Council; Community Advisory Board, WNVC Channel 56; Fairfax Committee of 100; Executive Board, Mantua Citizens Association; Business & Professional Women's Club; National Alumni Board, Junior Achievement; BRAVO, Advisory Committee for 1st Governor's Arts Awards, Virginia, 1979-80; Lay Teacher, Religious Education; Phi Gamma Nu; National Organization of Women; Member, Mantua Precinct, Chair, 1976-80, Fairfax County Democratic Committee; Chair, Virginia Association of Democratic County & City Committee Chairmen; Virginia Democratic State Central Committee; Board of Governors, Past Vice-President, Women's National Democratic Club. *Honours:* Awards for paintings/silkscreens; Phi Gamma Nu Award, 1958; Distinguished Graduate Award, Junior Achievement, 1973; Woman of Achievement Award, 1982; Victims Assistance Network Service Award, 1988. *Hobbies:* Artist; Tennis. *Address:* 8701 Duvall Street, Fairfax, VA 22031, USA.

MILLER Erica T, b. 17 Oct. 1950, Laramie, Wyoming, USA. Aesthetician; Company President. *Education:* Sophia University, Tokyo, Japan; University of Maryland, 1969-70; Christine Shaw School of Beauty, 1972; Sothys Institute, Paris, 1972. *Appointments:* Instructor, Researcher, Kanebo Cosmetics, Tokyo, Japan, 1973-76; Aesthet Inernational, 1976-79; President, Correlations Inc., 1979-; Beauty Director, Greenhouse, 1980-82; Associate Publisher Editor, Aesthetics World Magazine, 1980-84. *Publications:* Articles in professional journals. *Memberships:* National Cosmetology Association; Esthetics America, Former Skin Care Director; Aesheticians International Association, Vice President, Director of Education; NACMAD, Vice Chairman; Texas Cosmetology Association. *Honours:* Executive Directors Award, American Institute of Esthetics, 1984; CIDESCO, USA, 1984; etc. *Hobbies:* Animals; Music; Stained Glass; Literature; History. *Address:* 4803 W. Lovers Lane, Dallas, TX 75209, USA.

MILLER Geraldine Blanche, b. 30 Sept. 1917, Johnstown, USA. Private Piano Teacher. m. Wale R. Miller, 18 Sept. 1942, 1 son, 1 daughter. *Education:* BA, Languages, Ursinus College, 1939; BMus., Philadelphia Conservatory of Music, 1964. *Appointments:* Teacher, Lancaster PA Conservatory of Music, 1959-62; Private Piano Teahcer, 1962-. *Memberships:* Philadelphia Music Teachers Association, Vice President, Publicity Chairman, Programme Chairman; TriCounty Concerts Association, Vice President; Musical Coterie of Wayne, Junior Coterie Chairman; Music Study Club of Bryn Mawr. *Honours:* Student, First Prize Winner, TriCounty Youth Festival, 1968; Student Second Prize Winner, Pennsylvania Music Teachers Association, 1982. *Hobbies:* Decorating; Gardening; Sewing. *Address:* 314 Kent Road, Bala Cynwyd, PA 19004, USA.

MILLER Harriet Evelyn, b. 4 July 1919, Idaho, USA. Company President. *Education:* BA, 1941, DHL, hc, 1979, Whitman College; MA, University of Pennsylvania, 1949. *Appointments:* Executive Director, American Association of Retired Persons, 1976-77; Management Consultant, 1977-79; Executive Director, US Occupational Safety & Health Review Commission, 1979-81; Management Consultant, 1981-84; President, HMA Inc., 1984-; Member, Santa Barbara City Council, 1987-. *Publications:* Author, numerous articles. *Memberships:* Commissioner, Santa Barbara County Parole Commission, 1981-84; Board of Directors, Family Service Agency, 1982-84; many other professional organisations. *Honours:* Phi Beta Kappa, 1941; Phi Kappa Phi; Psi Chi; Honorary Member, Blackfeet Indian

Tribe, 1960; Associated Press Woman of the Year, Montana, 1961. *Hobbies:* Politics; Hiking; Reading. *Address:* Box 1346, Santa Barbara, CA 93102, USA.

MILLER Judith Ann Oyster, b. 27 Nov. 1939, Bertha, Minnesota, USA. Teacher; Writer; Researcher; Therapist. m. Charles P Miller, 24 Feb. 1964. 2 Stepsons, 1 daughter. *Education:* BS, Home Economics, 1971, MS, Child Dev. & Family, 1978, Colorado State University, Ft Colorado; PhD, Human Development & Family, University of Nebraska, 1981. *Appointments:* Research Associate, Colorado State University; Director Area Agency on Aging; National Director, Women's Ed. Ser. Association; Executive Director, Home Health Care; Teacher (self employed); Wilderness Awareness. *Publications:* Flood Recovery of Big Thompson Flood; The Value of Children. Numerous research articles in Family Journals. Play: Red Feather, The Princess & The Land. *Memberships:* American Association of Marriage & Family Therapy; Colorado Association of Marriage & Family Therapy; World Congress on Women; National Women in Development. *Honours:* Scholarships, Grants and Assistantships for study on Masters and PhD Programmes; Presented papers at 1st and 2nd International Interdisciplinary Congress on Women, Hiafa, Israel and Holland. *Hobbies:* Horses and nature; Native American Rituals and Symbols; Reading; Writing. *Address:* PO Box 967, Bavria, CO 81428, USA.

MILLER Leslie Beth, b. 29 Oct. 1951, New York, USA. Judge. m. Sean Connelly, 1 July 1985. *Education:* BA, Goucher College, Baltimore, 1973; JD, Saint Louis University Law School, 1976. *Appointments:* Atorney, Whilehill, Karp, Berger & West, Tucson; Assistant Public Defender, Pima County, Tucson; Magistrate City of Tucson; Judge, Pima County Superior Court, Tucson. *Memberships:* Arizona Women Lawyers; Board of Directors, Pima County Bar Association, 1982-, President Elect 1988-89; American Bar Association; National Association of Women Judges; Board of Governors, State Bar of Arizona, 1983-85; President, Young Lawyers Division, 1983-84. *Honours:* Outstanding Young Women in America. *Hobbies:* Travel; Camping. *Address:* Division 7, 110 W. Congress, Tucson, AZ 85701, USA.

MILLER Linda B., b. 7 Aug. 1937, USA. Professor of Political Science. *Education:* Diploma cum laude, Emma Willard School, 1955; AB cum laude, Radcliffe College, 1959; MA, 1961, PhD, 1965, Columbia University. *Appointments:* Lecturer, Department of Government, Harvard University, 1968-69; Instructor, Assistant Professor, Department of Government, Barnard College, Columbia University, New York City, 1964-67; Associate Professor, 1969-75, Professor, 1975-, Chair, 1985-89, Department of Political Sciences, Wellesley College; Various research positions including: Research Fellow, Center for International Affairs, 1967-71, Center for Science & International Affairs, 1976-81, Harvard University; Senior Fellow, Marine Policy & Ocean Management Programme, Woods Hole Oceanographic Institution, 1979-80, 1982-85; Research Associate, Few Diplomatic Training Initiative, School of International Affairs, Columbia University, 1986-88. *Publications:* World Order and Local Disorder: The United Nations and Internal Conflicts, 1967; Dynamics of World Politics: Studies in the Resolution of Conflict (editor, co-author); Monographs: Cyprus: The Law and Politics of Civil Strife, 1968; Internal War and International Systems (with George A Kelly), 1969; The Limits of Alliance: America, Europe, and the Middle East, 1974; Various articles, book chapters, reviews. *Memberships:* National Executive Committee, Vice-Chairman, American Professors for Peace in the Middle East; International Institute for Strategic Studies; Northeast Vice-President, International Studies Association; British International Studies Association; North American Council, International Peace Academy, 1976-78; American Political Science Association; International Council on the Future of the University, 1976-83; Editorial Board, Polity, 1980-83; Council for European Studies; Phi Beta Kappa. *Honours:* Recipient of several research fellowships. *Address:* Box 415, South Wellfleet, MA 02663, USA.

MILLER Mary Rita, b. 4 Mar. 1920, USA. Professor. 1 son. *Education:* BA, University of Iowa, 1941; MA, University of Denver, 1959; PhD, Georgetown University, 1969. *Appointments:* Instructor, Assistant Professor, 1962-65, Regis College; Assistant Professor, Associate Professor, Professor, 1968-, University of Maryland. *Publications:* Children of the Salt River, 1977; Place Names of the Northern Neck of Virginia, 1983; over 12 articles; numerous book reviews. *Memberships:* Southeastern Conference on Linguistics, President 1984; American Name Society, President, 1988; American Dialect Society, Executive Committee, 1987-88; Linguistic Society of America; American Association Applied Linguistics; Society for Caribbean Linguistics. *Honours:* NDEA Fellow, 1965-67. *Hobbies:* Travel; Boating; Antiques; Old Houses. *Address:* English Dept., University of Maryland, College Park, MD 20742, USA.

MILLER Phoebe Amelia, b. 13 Jan. 1948, Evanston, Illinois, USA. Computer Software Marketing Consultant. *Education:* BA Honours, Mathematics, University of Wisconsin, 1970; Graduate work, Civil Engineering, Stanford University, 1973; MBA work, Golden Gate University, 1978; ICP Sales Training, 1979. *Appointments:* Optics Analyst, Coherent Radiation, Palo Alto, California, 1970-72; Engineer, Bechtel Inc, 1972-77; Assistant Division Manager, Rand Information Systems, San Francisco, California, 1977-79; Senior Marketing Representative, Computer Sciences Corporation, San Francisco, 1979-81; Senior Marketing Consultant, 1981-84, Manager, Distributor Sales, 1984-86, Cognos Corporation, Walnut Creek, California; President, P.A.Miller & Associates Inc, San Francisco, 1986-. *Publications:* Computer Input/Output Methods Useful for Engineers, 1976. *Honours:* Bechtel Award of Merit, 1977; Marketing Representative of the Year, CSC Infonet Division Northwest District, 1981; New Account Leader, 3rd quarter, CSC Infonet Northwest District, 1981; New Account Leader, 1st quarter, CSC Infonet Western District, 1981; Most New Accounts, Most Registered Accounts and Most Quality Accounts, CSC Infonet Division, 1981; Vice-President, CSC Infonet Achievement Club, 1981; Cognos Sales Honour Roll, 1982, 1983, 1984; Cognos President's Award, 1982, 1983; ICP Million Dollar Super Seller AWard, 1983. *Address:* 101 Lombard, San Francisco, CA 94111, USA.

MILLER Rosamund Augusta, b. 15 Apr. 1936, Exeter, Devon, England. Director of Music. *Education:* Guildhall School of Music, 1954-57; AGSM, ARCM (Piano teachers); Teachers Training, Course Certificate. *Appointments:* Assistant Muoic Mistress, Downe House, Newbury, 1957-61; Assistant Music Mistress 1961-69, Housemistress 1961-69, Sherborne School for Girls; ESU Exchange to The Masters School, Dobbs Ferry, NY, USA, 1966-67; Chorus Mistress, Dorset Opera, 1974-; Chorus Mistress, Sherborne Musical Society, 1974-89. *Memberships:* Music Masters & Mistresses Association, President 1985-86; Incorporated Society of Musicians; Association British Choral Directors. *Honours:* Choral Conductor, won 1st Prize, National Choir Competition, 1979; Churchill Fellow to study choral training and opera in USA, 1981. *Hobbies:* Bridge; Travelling; Reading; Painting; PHAB summer schools in Sherborne and Austria; Adjudicating. *Address:* Monks Newell, Green Hill, Sherborne, Dorset DT9 4EP, England.

MILLER Susan Wise, b. 1 Feb. 1941, Cambridge, USA. Career Counsellor; Consultant. m. Joseph M. Miller, 29 Dec. 1963, 2 daughters. *Education:* BS, Wheelock College, 1963; MA, University of California, 1965. *Appointments:* Instructor, Trainer, 1966-; Career Counsellor, Private Practice, 1977-. *Memberships:* American Vocational Association; Catalyst, Nationwide Network of Career Resource Ceters, 1979-; American Society for Training & Development, 1980-. *Honours:* Recipient, many honours and awards including: Counsellor of the Month, Los Angeles Personnel and Guidance Association, 1981. *Address:* Vocational Training Consulting Services, 6363 Wilshire Blvd., Suite 210, Los Angeles, CA 90048, USA.

MILLER Trudy Joyce, b. 17 Oct. 1939, Chicago, Illinois, USA. Retail Executive; Publisher. m. William Robert Miller, 8 Oct. 1960, 3 sons, 1 daughter. *Education:* Interior Design Student, Marycrest College, Prairie State College. *Appointments:* Writer, Hammond Times, 1968-74; Owner, The Emporium, 1975-76; Writer, Village Press, 1975-76; President, Second Thoughts, 1976-88; Designer, The Contemporary Shop, 1978-79. *Publications:* Guide to Suburban Resale & Thrift Shops, 1983; Where to Find Everything for Practically Nothing in Chicago, 1984, updated version, 1987. *Memberships:* National Association of Resale & Thrift Shops, Co-Founder, Secretary, Board of Directors Women in Publishing; South Suburban Association of Commerce & Industry. *Honours:* Recipient, various honours and awards. *Hobbies:* Writing; Travel; Speaking; Collecting Antique Womens Clothing. *Address:* Second Thoughts Inc., 153 Halsted, Chicago Heights, IL 60411, USA.

MILLER-SHAIVITZ Patricia, b. 29 Jan. 1943, Philadelphia, USA. Instructor. m. Stephen A Shaivitz, 16 June 1966, 2 sons. *Education:* RN, St Agnes Hospital, 1964; AS, Palm Beach Junior College, 1976; BA, 1980, MA, 1986, Florida Atlantic University; PhD Candidate, University of South Florida. *Appointments:* Nurse: Philadelphia General Hospital, 1964; Bronx St. Hospital, 1966; Instructor: South College, 1982, Palm Beach Junior College, 1986, University of South Florida, 1988-. *Publications:* Articles in professional journals. *Memberships:* American Anthropological Association; American Association of Physical Anthropology; American Academy of Forensic Sciences; Sigma Xi. *Honour:* Grant, Sigma Xi, 1986. *Hobbies:* Ancient Disease Systems; Use of Cadavers in Scientific Research. *Address:* 252 Jamaica Lane, Palm Beach, FL 33480, USA.

MILLIN-MOORE Melanie, b. 27 May, 1949, Johannesburg, South Africa. Group Public Relations Executive. m. Randall Jay Moore, 30 Oct. 1986. *Education:* Matriculated 1966, Secretarial and Business Course 1967, Damelin College, Johannesburg; PRISA accredited, 1987. *Appointments:* Press Office Superviser, Ster-Kinekor, 1967-71; Publicity and PR for RPM Records, Deemillin, Brooke Theatre, 1971; Press Officer then Director of publicity/advertising, MGM, 1972; Founded own PR company, 1974-81; In charge of PR and Promotions for Southern Sun Hotels, 1981-83; Group PR and Promotions Manager 1983 87, Group PR Executive 1987-, Sun International. *Creative works:* Campaigns publicising wide range of international films, theatre, entertainment, cosmetics, food, fashion, advertising, education, art, corporate and personal images. *Membership:* Accredited Public Relations Practitioner (PRISA). *Hobbies:* Wildlife; Movies; Theatre; Classical music; Reading; Animal anticruelty organisation; Largest collection of owls (artificial variety) in South Africa; Real owls sponsored at Johannesburg Zoo. *Address:* P O Box 781571, Sandton 2146, South Africa.

MILLN Susan Margaret, b. 18 Feb. 1931, Darlington, England. m. Peter Lindsay Milln, 8 May 1954, 1 son, 3 daughters. *Appointments:* Catering Employment, 1949-53. *Memberships:* British Horse Society's Bridleways Officer for Cornwall. *Hobbies:* Horse Riding; Sailing; Painting; Antiques; Gardening. *Address:* Bosinver Farm, St Austell, Cornwall PL26 7DT, England.

MILLONIG Marsha Katherine, b. 3 Oct. 1959, Minneapolis, Minnesota, USA. Pharmacist; Administrator. *Education:* Baccalaureat, Pharmacy, University of Minnesota, 1982; MBA, University of Maryland, 1988. *Appointments:* Executive resident, American Society of Hospital Pharmacists, 1982-83; Manager 1983-85, Director 1985-88 (Professional Affairs), Director (Pharmacy Affairs) 1988-, National Association of Chain Drug Stores (NACDS).

Memberships: Past offices, Montgomery County Democratic Party, American Pharmaceutical Association; Kappa Psi pharmaceutical fraternity; American Society of Hospital Pharmacists. *Honours:* Honour societies: Beta Sigma Gamma 1988, Rho Chi 1982, Mortar Board 1982; President's scholarship & leadership award, 1982; Biographical listings. *Hobbies:* Politics; Art; Antiques; Theatre; Skiing; Skating. *Address:* 881 Azalea Drive, Rockville, Maryland 20850, USA.

MILLOTT Christina Jane, b. 4 June 1948, Buckinghamshire, England. Psychotherapist; Speech Therapist. m. Richard John Millott, 26 Oct. 1974, 1 son, 3 daughters. *Education:* Licentiate of Australian College of Speech Therapists, 1968; MSc., 1973. *Appointments:* Senior Speech Pathologist, Prince Henry's Hospital, Victoria, 1974-76; Private Practice, 1976-. *Memberships:* Australian Association of Speech & Hearing; Australian Association of Group Psychotherapists; American Group Psychotherapy Association. *Honours:* Commonwealth Advanced Education Scholarship, 1966. *Hobbies:* Horse Riding; Sailing; Art; Music. *Address:* 99 Princess St., Kew 3101, Victoria, Australia.

MILLS Hayley, b. 18 Apr. 1946, London, England. Actress. m. Ray Boulting, 1971, divorced 1977, 2 sons. *Appointments:* Debut, Tiger Bay, 1959; Pollyanna, 1960; Signed Disney Contract, 1960; Films include: The Parent Trap; Whistle Down the Wind; The Castaways; Summer Magic; The Chalk Garden; The Moonspinner; The Truth About Spring; Sky West and Crooked; Trouble with Angels; The Family Way; Pretty Polly; A matter of Innocence; Twisted Nerve; Take a Girl Like You; Sillouettes; What Changed Charley Farthing; The Diamond Hunters; That Darn Cat; Forbush and the Penguins; Endless Night; Appointment with Death; TV: The Flame Trees of Thika; Parent Trap II; Amazing Stories; Illusion of Life; Good Morning Miss Bliss (NBC series). *Honours:* Silver Bear Award, Berlin Film Festival, 1958; British Academy Award; Special Oscar, USA. *Hobbies:* Riding; Reading; Children; Cooking; Scuba-diving. *Address:* c/o James Sharkey Associates, 90 Regent Street, London W1, England.

MILLS Juliet, b. 21 Nov. 1941, London, England. Actress. *Creative Works:* Made stage debut at 14 in Alice Through the Looking Glass. Pictures: So Well Remembered; The History of Mr Polly; No, My Darling Daughter; Twice Around the Daffodils; Nurse on Wheels; Carry on Jack; The Rare Breed; Wings of War; Oh, What a Lovely War!; The Challengers; Avantil; Beyond the Door; The Second Power; The Last Melodrama. Television: Movies: Wings of Fire; The Challengers; Letters from Three Lovers; QB VII; Once an Eagle; Alexander; The Other Side of Dawn; The Cracker Factory etc. *Address:* 9714 Oak Pass Road, Beverly Hills, California 90210, USA.

MILNER Teresa Ann, b. 1 Dec. 1956, Santa Monica, California, USA. Assistant Professor in Neurology. *Education:* BS, Biological Sciences, University of California, Irvine, 1978; PhD, Neuroscience, University of California, San Diego, 1982; Postdoctoral Fellow, Cornell University Medical College, 1982-85. *Appointments:* Research Assistant, Department of Phychobiology, University of California, Irvine, 1978; Tutor in Basic Medical Neurology, University of California, San Diego, 1978-82; Instructor, Department of Neurology, 1985-87, Assistant Professor in Neurology and Neuroscience, 1987-, Cornell University Medical College, New York City, New York. *Memberships:* Society for Neuroscience; New York Society of Electron Microscopists. *Honours:* Regents Fellowship, 1978, Regents Dissertation Fellowship, 1981-82, University of California, San Diego; NSF Predoctoral Fellowship, Honourable Mention, 1978; NIH Postdoctoral Fellowship, Cornell University Medical College, 1983-85. *Hobbies:* Cinema; Sewing; Embroidery. *Address:* Division of Neurobiology, Cornell University Medical College, 411 East 69th Street, New York, NY 10021, USA.

MILOVANOVIC-BERTRAM Smilja, b. 7 Jan. 1948, Maribor, Yugoslavia. Architect; University Professor. m. F Stefan Bertram, 9 June 1972, 1 son, 1 daughter. *Education:* BA, 1970, BArch, 1972, Rice University, USA; MArch, Graduate School of Design, Harvard University, 1974. *Appointments:* Project Manager, Barnes Landes Goodman Youngblood, USA, 1979-83; Lecturer, University of Texas, Austin, 1983-; Principal, MB Design, Austin, 1984-. *Creative works:* St Francis/ St George, TAC, 1980; For Barnes Landes Goodman Youngblood: Bureau of Economic Geology, 1981; South Plains Hospital and Clinic, 1981; San Marcos Baptist Academy; Employers Insurance of Texas, 1983; Breed & Co, MB Design, 1986. *Memberships:* American Institute of Architects; Texas Society of Architects; Austin Chapter, American Institute of Architects; Architektonsko, Belgrade, Yugoslavia. *Honours:* Design Award for Breed & Co, Austin Chapter, American Institute of Architects, 1988; Design Excellence Award for Breed & Co, City of Austin, 1988; Excellence in Teaching Award, Ex-Students Association of Texas, 1988. *Hobbies:* Photography; Serbo-Byzantine Architecture. *Address:* 4503 Twisted Tree Cove, Austin, TX 78735, USA.

MINCHINTON Robyn Myra, b. 5 June 1954, Melbourne, Australia. Chief Scientist. m. Stephen George Perry, 28 June 1980. *Appointments:* Medical Scientist, Immunolgy Dept., University of Melbourne, 1972-75; Medical Scientist, Haematology Dept., Royal Melbourne Hospital, 1975-77; Research Officer, St Bartholomew's Hospital, London, 1977-83; Lecturer, Haematology, Royal Melbourne Institute of Technolgoy, 1984-88; Chief Scientist, Red Cross Blood Transfusion Service, Queensland, 1988-. *Publications:* over 30 published scientific papers. *Memberships:* Fellow, Australian Institute of Medical Laboratory Scientists; Haematology Society of Australia; Australian Society of Blood Transfusion; Australian Society for Medical Research; Foundation Member, Women in Medical Science. *Honours:* Commonwealth High School Scholarship, 1969; Commonwealth Scholarships of Advanced Education, 1971; Ames Student Travel Award, 1976; AIMLS Top Graduate Student Award, 1976; Top Haematology Student Award, AIMLS, 1976; Inaugural Cliff Francis Award, AIMLS, 1985. *Hobbies:* Golf; Reading; Cinema; Photography; Downhill Skiing. *Address:* Red Cross Blood Transfusion Service, Queensland Division, 480 Queen Street, Brisbane, 4001, Australia.

MINER Valerie Jane, b. 28 Aug 1947, New York, New York, USA. Novelist. *Education:* BA 1969, Masters degree 1970, University of California, Berkeley. *Appointments:* Novelist, essayist, critic, journalist 1970-, for many journals including TLS, NY Times, Village Voice, The Nation, The New Statesman, Spare Rib, The LA Times, Conditions, Saturday Night, Maclean's. *Publications:* Trespassing (story collection) 1989; All Good Women (novel), 1987; Winter's Edge (novel) 1984; Murder in the English Department (novel) 1982; Movement (novel) 1982; Blood Sisters (novel) 1981; Competition: A Feminist Taboo? (anthology co-editor) 1987; Tales I Tell My Mother (co-author) 1978; More Tales I Tell My Mother (co-author) 1987; Her Own Woman (co-author) 1975. *Memberships:* PEN; National Book Critics Circle; National Writers Union; Feminist Writers Guild. *Honours:* 1988 Australia Council Literary Arts Grant; 1986 PEN Syndicated Fiction Prize; Other writing and teaching prizes. *Hobbies:* Hiking; Reading; Travelling; Swimming. *Address:* Undergraduate Studies, 301 Campbell Hall, University of California, Berkeley, Berkeley, CA 94720, USA.

MINNELLI Liza, b. 12 Mar. 1946. Actress; Singer. m. (1) Peter Allen, 1967, divorced 1970. (2) Jack Haley Jr, 1974, divorced 1979. (3) Mark Gero, 1979. *Creative Works:* Films: Charlie Bubbles, 1968; The Sterile Cuckoo, 1969; Tell Me that You Love Me Junie Moon, 1971; Cabaret, 1972; Lucky Lady, 1976; A Matter of Time, 1976; New York, New York, 1977; Arthur, 1981. Television Specials: Liza, Liza with a Z, 1972; Goldie and Liza Together, 1980; Baryshnikov on Broadway,

1980; A Time to Live, 1985. Theatre: Best Foot Forward, 1963; Flora, the Red Menace, 1965; Chicago, 1975; The Act, 1977-78; Liza at the Winter Garden, 1973; The Rink, 1984. Recordings: Liza with a Z, Liza Minnelli; The Singer, Liza Minnelli; Live at the Winter Garden; Tropical Nights; The Act, Liza Minelli; Live at Carnegie Hall, The Rink. *Honours:* Academy Award for Best Actress, 1972; The Hollywood Foreign Press Golden Globe Award; The British Academy Award; David di Donatello Award, Italy; Emmy Award, 1972; Two Golden Globe Awards; Two Tony Awards; Special Tony Award. *Address:* c/o PMK, One Lincoln Plaza, 2nd Floor, New York, NY 10023, USA.

MINNETTE Rhonda Williams, b. 10 Oct. 1952, Evansville, Indiana, USA. Sales Representative, Glaxo, Inc. m. Timothy Lee Minnette, 11 July 1982. 2 daughters. *Education:* BS, Education, Indiana State University, 1974; MA, Curriculum & Instruction in Early Childhood, 1979. *Appointments:* Teacher, Broward County Schools, 1974-81; Sales Rep, Breon Labs, 1981-82; Sales Representative, Glaxo, Inc. 1982-. *Publication:* 1977 Writing Team for Broward County Schools, wrote new program guidelines. *Honours:* Number one Sales Representative in nation for Glaxo, Inc, 1987; Representative of Region, 3 times. *Hobbies:* Running; Aerobics; Dogs, Siberian huskies. *Address:* 5841 NE 20th Terrace, Ft Lauderdale, FL 33308, USA.

MINNICK Anna Jean, b. St Mary's, West Virginia, USA. Educator. m. Clay Tallman (divorced). *Education:* BS, MS 1964, West Virginia University; PhD, New York University, 1970. *Appointments include:* Professor, Health & Physical Education & General Studies 1963-, Director, Academic Advisement, Davis & Elkins College; Varsity field hockey coach, 1963-83; Leader, overseas study tours, 1970-. *Memberships:* American, & West Virginia Alliances of Health, Physical Education & Dance; Past President, Alpha Delta Kappa. *Honours:* Lois Latham Award, teaching, 1988; Recognition award, West Virginia Sports Writers Association; Biographical listings. *Hobbies:* Sports; Marine biology; International travel. *Address:* Davis & Elkins College, Elkins, West Virginia 26241, USA.

MINSHEW Janiz, b 14 Oct. 1948, Texas, USA. Doctor of Chiropractic. m. Bernard Justin Shur, 6 Nov. 1988. *Education:* BS, Anatomy; MSc., Biochemistry; DC, 1980. *Appointments:* Private Practice; Associate Professor, Special Lectures, Beiijing Medical University. *Memberships:* American Council on Neurology; New York Academy of Science; International Academy of Preventative Medicine; International College of Applied Nutrition; American Council of Sports Injuries. *Honours:* Team Physicians, Summer Olympic Games, Seoul, Korea, 1988. *Hobbies:* Lecturing; Travel. *Address:* 301 West 53rd Street, New York City, NY 10019, USA.

MINTY Judith, b. 5 Aug. 1937, Detroit, USA. Writer; Professor. m. Edgar Minty, 19 June 1957, 1 son, 2 daughters. *Education:* BS, Ithaca College; MA, Western Michigan University, 1974. *Appointments:* Assistant Professor, Central Michigan University, 1977-78; Associate Professor, Syracuse University, 1979; Visiting Poet in Residence, Interlochen Centre for Arts, 1980; Visiting Lecturer, University of California, Santa Cruz, 1981-82; Visiting Poet in Residence, University of Oregon, 1983; Associate Professor, Humboldt State University, 1982. *Publications:* Poetry: Lake Songs & Other Fears; Yellow Dog Journal; Letters to My Daughters; In the Prescence of Mother; Counting the Losses; numerous poems in anthologies. *Memberships:* Poets & Writers; PEN; Associated Writing Programmes; Poetry Society of America. *Honours:* US Award, International Poetry Forum, 1973; John Atherton Fellowship, 1974; 2 PEN Syndicated Fiction Awards, 1985, 1986; PEN/Head Foundation, Fiction CA Award, 1986. *Hobbies:* PO Box 1128, Trinidad, CA 95570, USA.

MISCHE Patricia Mary (Schmitt), b. 14 Aug. 1939, Shakopee, Minnesota, USA. Teacher; Writer; Editor. m. Gerald F. Mische, 18 Apr. 1964, 3 daughters. *Education:*

BA, 1961; MA, 1969; EdD, 1989. *Appointments:* Teachers for East Africa, 1961-63; Association for International Development, 1963-67; Riverside Church Nursery School, 1969-70; Essex Community College, 1971-72; Seton Hall University, 1973-78; Founder, Global Education Associates, 1973-. *Publications:* Co-author, with Gerald Mische, Toward A Human World Order: Beyond the National Security Strait Jacket, 1977; Book, Star Wars & the State of Our Souls, 1985; Do the Soviets Cheat at Arms Control?, 1985; Women Power & Alternative Futures; Global Spirituality; Over 100 articles, various global issues. *Memberships include:* American Association of University Women; Amnesty International; Consortium on Peace Research, Education & Development; Board, Exploratory Project on Conditions for Peace; Advisory Board, Fellowship of Reconciliation. *Honours:* Honorary doctorates, St Rose College, Albany 1982, Marian College 1986; Pope John XXII Award, Viterbo College; Franciscan International Award, 1984; Marian Award, Caldwell College, 1977; International Women's Year Award, College of St Benedict, 1975. *Hobbies:* Hiking; Mountain climbing; Poetry; Cooking. *Address:* c/o Global Education Associates, Suite 456, 475 Riverside Drive, New York, NY 10115, USA.

MITCHELL Cheryl Elaine, b. 27 Dec. 1951. President, Mitchell & Associates. *Education:* BA History 1973, BA Political Science 1973, Hartwick College; Studied for PhD Social Science, Syracuse University, not completed. *Appointments:* Staff, Udall for President, 1975-76; Reporter, Syracuse Record, 1976-78; Assoc Natl Dir Public Relations, Cushman & Wakefield, Inc, 1978-81; Senior Accounts Executive, J P Lohman, 1981-84; Vice President, SPGA Group, 1984-86; President, Mitchell & Associates, 1986-. *Publications:* Numerous professional articles, promotional brochures. *Memberships:* Commercial Real Estate Women (CRW); National Association of Female Executives. *Honours:* ANDY Award (Art Directors of New York Award), 1984; Champion Paper Award, 1984; 43rd Annual Graphic Arts Exhibition, 1986; 150 East 52nd Street leasing brochure; The Minskoff Corporation, 75th Anniversary Brochure; Brochures featured in Design Communications. *Hobbies:* Architectural photography; Clothing and textile design. *Address:* Mitchell & Associates, 11th Floor, 36 West 20th Street, New York, NY 10011, USA.

MITCHELL Johanna, b. 14 June 1917, Germany. Business Executive & Owner. Divorced, 2 sons, 1 daughter. *Education:* Max Reinhardt Seminar, Vienna, Austria 1936-38. *Appointments:* Director, 1941 Overseer, Vancouver, British Columbia, Canada Operations, 1963, President 1970, Chairman, Chief Executive Officer, 1976-, Intercontinental Packers Limited, Saskatoon, Saskatchewan, Canada. *Creative Works:* Starred in film, 3 Stripes in the Sun, with Aldo Raym, Chuck Connors and Richard York, 1954; currently working on Autobiography. *Memberships:* Riviera Country Club; Riverside Golf and Country Club; Saskatoon Board of Trade; Mendel Art Gallery. *Honours:* Registered Owner of the horses, Fuersten Brauch, winner of Hungarian Derby, 1937, of Puczur, winner of Hungarian Derby, 1939, of Melvynm, winner of the Hungarian Oaks, 1939 and of Credo who won many important races during this period; Appointed Honorary Chairman, Mendel Art Gallery. *Hobbies:* Art Collecting; Writing; Travel; Cattle Breeding; Swimming. *Address:* F Mendel Ranch, P.O. Box 850, Saskatoon, Saskatchewan, Canada S7K 3V4.

MITCHELL Martha, b. 19 Sept. 1921, Talladega Springs, Alabama, USA. Historian; State Bureau Administrator. 2 daughters. *Education:* BA, University of Montevallo, Montevallo, Alabama, 1943; MA, 1946, PhD, University of Chicago. *Appointments:* Chair, Department of History and Political Science, 1964-71; Director, Bureau of History, Michigan Department of State, Secretary, Michigan Historic Commission, and State Historic Preservation Officer, Michigan, 1971-. *Publications:* Article in Negro History Bulletin, 1970; Conquistadors, Voyageurs, & Mississippi, 1973;

Michigan/Mississippi: Comparative Histories of Two States, 1980; Michigan chapter, in Heartland: Comparative Histories of the Midwestern States, 1988; Chapter in Leadership for the Future: Changing Directorial Roles in American History Museums and Historical Societies, 1989. *Memberships:* President, AASLH, 1978-80; Organization of American Historians; Michigan Historical Society; National Association of State Archives and Records Administrators. *Honours:* Graduated 1st in class, University of Montevallo, 1943; Tuition Fellowship and Julius Rosewald Scholarship, 1943-44; Julius Rosewald Fellowship, 1945-46. *Address:* Bureau of History, Department of State, 717 West Allegan, Lansing, MI 48918, USA.

MITCHELL Sophy Mae Jr, b. 10 Oct. 1931, Sebring, Florida, USA. Food Service Director/Specialist. *Education:* BS, Floriculture, University of Florida, 1953; MS, Business Hotel and Restaurant Administration, Florida State University, 1959. *Appointments:* Supervisor, Welcome Wagon Inc, 1953-57; Manager, Morrison's Food Services, 1959-62; Food Service Specialist, Interstate United Corp, 1962-71; Assistant Professor, School of Business, Hotel and Retaurant Administration, Florida State University, 1971-75; Food Service Specialist, Interstate United Corp, 1976-81; Food Service Director, Interstate United State, University of New York Maritime College, Bronx, New York, 1981-85; Food Service Director, Interstate United, Bowery Savings Bank, New York City, 1985-. *Publications:* Vending Times, Creative Food Packaging, 1975; Proper Garnish adds Buy-Appeal to Vended Foods, 1975; The Personalization of Frozen Foods, Vending Times, 1982. *Memberships:* International Food Service Executives Association, President, New York Branch, New York City Restaurant Association, Secretary-Treasurer; New York State Restaurant Association, Director; Research and Development Associates for Military Food and Packaging Systems Inc, National Treasurer; International Food Technologists; Council of Hotel, Restaurant and Institutional Educators; American Business Women's Association; Director (National Board) Roundtable for Women in Food Service, etc. *Honours:* Sebring's Outstanding Girl Scout, 1947; Best All Round Sebring Senior Class Superlative, 1949; University of Florida Gator band's Most Outstanding Freshman, 1950; Phillip Connelly Evaluating Team Chairman for US Army's Best Large Dining Facility, 1981; Edward Ney Evaluating Team Alternative for US Navy's Best Food Service, 1984, 1985; Edward Ney Evaluating Team, 1986. *Hobbies:* Travel; Sea Stories; Cook Books. *Address:* 888 Eight Avenue, Apt 1-B, New York, NY 10019, USA.

MITCHELL Velda J, b. 27 July 1937, Alton, USA. Employee Relations Supervisor. m. (1) Spencer Middleloff, 1958, 1 son, 1 daughter, (2) Robert E. Mitchell, 31 May 1986. *Education:* Studying for BA, Business Management, Sinclair College, Dayton. *Appointments:* Secretary, Sinclair Refining Co., Hartford, 1955-58; Executive Secretary, Laclede Steel Co., Alton, 1958-71; Personnel Specialist, Fram Corp., Greenville, Ohio, 1974-80; Personnel Administrator, Bendix Fram Division, Greenville, 1980-83; Supervisor, Human Resources, 1983-84, Employee Relations, 1984-, Allied Corporation, Fram Division, Greenville. *Memberships:* Advisory Board, Blue Cross/Blue Shield, South West Ohio; Advisory Board, Ansonia High School, Business Education; Greenville City Schools Business Education; Darke County Chamber of Commerce, Industrial Management Association Education Committee; Job Sharing Program Act (JTPA); Local and Regional Private Industry Council; Advisory Board, Edison State College; National Association of Female Executives; Personnel Association of Western Ohio. *Hobbies:* Antiques; Collectibles; Flea Markets. *Address:* 110 South Broadway, Greenville, OH 45331, USA.

MITCHELL (Emily) Jane, b. 3 May 1956, Toronto, Canada. Research Scientist. m. Luis Horacio Martin, 15 Aug. 1981, 1 daughter. *Education:* BSc (high distinction) 1979, PhD, Cell Biology, 1984, University of Toronto. *Appointments:* Adjunct Lecturer, University of Waterloo,

Canada, 1983; Visiting Scientist, Laboratory of Molecular Biology, Medical Research Council, Cambridge, UK, 1984-87; Research Associate, Biotechnology Research Institute, National Research Council of Canada, Montreal, 1987-. *Publications:* 6 articles, professional journals. *Memberships:* Associate, Department of Pharmacology & Therapeutics, McGill University; Canadian Society of Cell Biology; International Cell Cycle Society; Canadian Association for Women in Sciences. *Honours:* Postgraduate scholarships, Natural Sciences & Engineering Research Council, Canada, 1979-83; Ramsay Wright Scholarship, Outstanding Graduate Student, 1983; Visiting Fellowship, Clare Hall, University of Cambridge, UK, 1985; Postdoctoral fellowships, Medical Research Council, Canada, 1984-87. *Hobbies:* Family; Travel; Fitness. *Address:* 4685 Trenholme Avenue, Montreal, Quebec, Canada H4B 1X8.

MITCHELL (Sibyl) Elyne Keith, b. 30 Dec. 1913, Melbourne, Australia. Author; Grazier. m. Thomas Walter Mitchell, 4 Nov. 1935, 2 sons, 2 daughters. *Publications:* Adult Books: Australia's Alps, 1942; Speak to the Earth, 1945; Soil and Civilization, 1946; Images in Water, 1947; Flow River, Blow Wind, 1953; Black Cockatoos Mean Snow, 1956; Light Horse, The Story of Australia's Mounted Troops, 1978; The Snowy Mountains, 1983; Discoverers of the Snowy Mountains, 1985; A Vision of the Snowy Mountains, 1988; Novelization of the films, Man from Snowy River, 1982; Chauvel Country, 1984, The Light Horse Men, 1987; Childrens Books: Silver Brumby Series including; Silver Brumby, 1958; Silver Brumby's Daughter, 1960; Silver Brumbies of the South, 1965; Silver Brumby Kingdom, 1966; Silver Brumby Whirlwind, 1973; Snowy River Brumby, 1980; Brumby Racer, 1981; Other Childrens Books: Kingfisher Feather, 1962; Winged Skis, 1964; Moon Filly, 1968; Jinki, Dingo of the Snow, 1970; Light Horse to Damascus; etc. *Memberships:* Australian Society of Authors. *Honours:* Silver Brumby commended Children's book Week Awards; Winged Skis, Highly Commended. *Hobbies:* Skiing; Tennis; Birdwatching; Bush Walking; Swimming; Art; Travel; etc. *Address:* Towong Hill, Corryong, Victoria 3707, Australia.

MITCHISON Naomi, b. Edinburgh, Scotland. Writer. m. Dick Mitchison. 3 sons, 2 daughters. *Education:* Dragon School, Oxford, England; St Anne's College, Oxford. *Appointments:* Argyll County Council, 1945-64; Highland Panel, 1945-64; Highland and Island Advisory Council, 1965-75; contested Scottish Universities Parliamentary constituency for Labour. *Publications:* Author of about 80 books, including: The Corn King and the Spring Queen; Blood of the Martyrs; The Bull Calves; The Big House; Lobsters on the Agenda; Five Men and a Swan; Cleopatra's People; three volumes of autobiography, The Cleansing of the Knife; Images of Africa; Early of Orcadia. *Address:* Carradale House, Carradale, Campbeltown, Argyll PA28 6QQ, Scotland.

MITCHISON Rosalind Mary, b. 11 Apr. 1919, Manchester, England. Retired. m. J M Mitchison, 21 June 1947. 1 son, 3 daughters. *Education:* MA, Oxford University. *Appointments:* Assistant Lecturer, Manchester University, 1943-46; Tutor, Lady Margaret Hall, Oxford, 1946-47; Assistant 1954-58, Lecturer, 1967-76, Reader, 1976-81, Professor, 1981-86, Edinburgh University; Assistant, 1962-63, Lecturer, 1966-67, Glasgow University. *Publications:* Agricultural Sir John, 1962; A History of Scotland, 1970; British Population Change Since 1860, 1977; Life in Scotland, 1978; Lordship to Patronage: Scotland 1603-1745. *Memberships:* Scottish History Society; Royal Historical Society; Scottish Economic and Social History Society; Historical Association; Economic History Society. *Address:* Great Yew, Ormiston, East Lothian, EH35 5NJ, Scotland.

MITNICK Mindy Faith, b. 10 Oct. 1950, Miami Beach, Florida, USA. Psychologist. m. Carl Marquit, 17 Aug. 1979. *Education:* BA, Bryn Mawr College, 1972; Ed.M, Harvard University, 1973; MA, University of Minnesota, 1986. *Appointments:* Psychology Fellow,

Hennepin Co. Medical Center, 1977-78; Court Psychologist, 1978-83; Psychologist, Uptown Mental Health Centre, 1980-. *Publications:* Identification & Treatment of Child Incest Victims; The Reality of Sexual Abuse; Child Sexual Abuse; The Joint Custody Experience; Family Sexual Abuse & Custody Evaluation. *Memberships:* Minnesota Women Psychologists; Minnesota Licensed Psychologists, Executive Board of Directors; Minnesota Committee for Prevention of Child Abuse, Board. *Hobbies:* Cooking; Travel; Needlepoint; Aerobics. *Address:* 2215 Pillsbury Ave., Minneapolis, MN 55404, USA.

MITSON Eileen Nora, b. 22 Sept. 1930, Langley, Essex, England. Housewife; Writer. m. 22 Sept. 1951, 1 daughter. *Education:* Secretarial College, Cambridge. *Appointments:* Regular Columnist, Christian Woman Magazine, 1982-. *Publications:* 3 Childrens Novels; 3 Adult Novels; 3 Religious Non-Fiction Works: Beyond the Shadows, 1968, Inside Room, 1973,Reaching to God, 1978. *Hobbies:* Dressmaking; Reading. *Address:* 39 Oaklands, Hamilton Road, Reading, Berks RG1 5RN, England.

MITTAL Kamla, b. 3 Mar. 1937, India. Professor of History. *Education:* BEd, MA; PhS, Indian History; Study visits (History of American Civilization), USA. *Appointments:* Teaching, 20 years; Graduate and Postgraduate degree classes, Barkat Ulia University; Currently Professor of History (British, Modern European and Indian History), Bhopal University. *Publications:* History of Bhopal, thesis, in press; Articles in newspapers on topics related to history of India, America and Britain, also social problems; Radio talks. *Memberships:* Indian History Congress; M.P.History Society; American Historical Association, USA. *Address:* F-124/20 Shivaji Nagar, Bhopal (M.P.), India.

MITZEN Nancy Elizabeth, b. 5 May 1955, Pittsburg, USA. Senior Graphic Designer. *Education:* BA, Graphic Design, Columbia College, 1983; MA, Communication Arts, Honours, New York Institute of Technology, 1987. *Appointments:* Production Co-ordinator, ASN Publishing, Chicago, 1981-83; Freelance Designer, Computer Artist, Mitzen Graphics, Huntingdon Valley, 1983-; Senior Graphic Designer, Technical Advertising Service, Bryn Athyn, 1983-88; Art Director, Mainstream Advertising and Design, Audubon. *Memberships:* American Film Institute; Society of Typographic Arts; American Institute of Graphic Arts; Women in Design Chicago. *Hobbies:* Sports; Reading; Painting. *Address:* 1810 Autumn Leaf Lane, Huntingdon Valley, PA 19006, USA.

MITZO Karen Lynn, b. 16 July 1962, Lakewood, Ohio, USA. Industrial Engineer. m. Gregg Wesley Hilderbrand, 14 Apr. 1989. *Education:* BSIE, Purdue Univerity, 1985. *Appointments:* Industrial Engineer, Moore Business Forms, 1985-87; Project Engineer, Sedlak Management, 1987-88; Industrial Engineer, Alvey Inc., 1988-; President, Twin Sisters productions, 1988-. *Publications:* Writer, vocals, producer, Recorded, Rap with the Facts, audiocassette for children. *Memberships:* Institute Industrial Engineers; Society Women Engineers; Whitehouse Educational Research Council; National Association Female Executives. *Hobbies:* Piano; Skiing; Swimming; Racquetball; Singing; Yoga. *Address:* 1722 Forest Hllls Dr., St. Charles, MO 63303, USA.

MOBLEY Sybil C., b. 14 Oct. 1925, Shreveport, Louisiana, USA. University Dean. m. James Otis Mobley, 6 Apr. 1947, 2 sons, 1 daughter. *Education:* BA, Bishop College; MBA, University of Pennsylvania; PhD, University of Illinois; CP, State of Florida. *Appointments:* Current Dean, School of Business & Industry, Florida A&M University; Director: Anheuser-Busch Companies, Champion International Corporation, Hershey Foods Corporation, Sears Roebuck & Company. Former: Special consultant in Senegal, Nigeria, Zaire & Kenya, & team leader, consultant services to industrialists in Cameroon, Ivory Coast & Liberia, US Agency for International Development State Department; Member, President's Commission on Industrial Competitiveness. *Publications include:* Numerous articles, accountancy; Official reports & development plans; Book chapters; reviews. *Memberships include:* American Assembly of Collegiate Schools of Business; International Association of Black Business Educators; Overseer, Wharton School, University of Pennsylvania; Director, National Junior Achievement. *Honours:* Robert Russa Moten Leadership Award, National Business League; Honorary doctorates, Wharton School, Babson College, Bishop College, Hamilton College; Florida Hall of Fame; National Achievement Award, National Council of Negro Women. *Hobbies:* Reading; Travel; Home entertaining. *Address:* School of Business & Industry, Florida A&M University, Tallahassee, FL 32307, USA.

MODRICK Jeanette Marie, b. 2 Sept. 1952, Ann Arbor, Michigan, USA. Clinical Psychologist. m. James Eugene Klutho, 23 May 1988. *Education:* BA, Human Relations 1978, MA, Special Studies 1983, University of Kansas; PsyD, University of Denver, 1986. *Appointments:* Bethesda Mental Health Center, 1982-86; Profile Employee Assistance Program, 1986-87; Swedish Hospital Employee Assistance Program, 1987-89; Private Practice Clinical Psychologist, 1987-. *Memberships:* American Psychological Assoc; Colorado Psychological Assoc; Executive Board Member, Colorado Women Psychologists; Employee Assistance Professionals Association. *Honours:* Sigma Phi Omega National Honor Society, 1982; Phi Beta Kappa National Honor Society, 1978; Phi Kappa Phi National Honor Society, 1978; Hilden Gibson Award for Most Outstanding Senior in Social Sciences, 1978, Speech and Human Relations Departmental Award for Academic Excellence 1978, University of Kansas. *Hobbies:* Dogs; Lap swimming; Parakeets; Fantasy fiction. *Address:* 2305 E Arapahoe Road Suite 216, Littleton, CO 80122, USA.

MOHNS Grace Updegraff Bergen, b. 20 Nov. 1907, Dubuque, Iowa, USA. Composer; Pianist; Recitalist; Organist; Lecture-Recitals on American Indian. m. Rev Dr Edward A Mohns, 28 June 1930. 1 son, 1 daughter. *Education:* BA, magna cum laude, University of Minnesota, 1930; Juilliard School of Music, New York City, 1930; McPhail School Music, 1931; Southern Methodist University Music Dept, Dallas, Texas, 1968-69. *Appointments:* Private Piano Theory Teacher, 1930-; Teacher of Piano, Composition and Theory, Private School, St Paul, 1930-32; Organist, Choir Director in Churches, New Jersey, Michigan, Washington, Oregon; Recitalist, Piano Performance, 1937-; Professional lecturer, Recitals on the American Indian, 1949-. *Creative works:* Songs, word and music; Piano compositions; Songs: Thine is the Power; Maid of Spring; Mysteries of Life; L'Armistice; Nocturne; Firemist; In God We Trust; Sea Suite; Love is God's Gift; Sands of the Desert; Dawnmist; Gaelic Hornpipe; Christ is Risen; Easter Bells; Old Love is Best; Music Everywhere; At Bethany; He is Saving Some Glory for Me; Sing Toys, Sing; Oregon Coast Sunset, Poem. *Memberships include:* Delta Gamma, Treasurer, Anchora Correspondent, 16 yrs; Sigma Alpha Iota, Chaplain, 12 years; Texas Composers; Michigan Composers; Oregon Composers Society; California Assoc Music Teachers. *Honours:* 1st Prize, Senior High Piano Composition, Minneapolis, 1922, 1924, 1925; Juilliard Fellowship Award, Composition, 1930; International Honorary Member, Beta Sigma Phi, 1980; Piano Competition Award Winner, McPhail School Music, Minneapolis, 1931. *Hobbies:* Swimming; Reading; Travel; History. ssa 20Address: 12705 SE River Road Apt 405-S, Portland, Oregon 97222, USA.

MOHNSEN Rosalind E, b. 9 Oct. 1942, Nebraska, USA. Organist; Church Musician. *Education:* BME, University of Nebraska, 1964; MM, Indiana University, 1966; Performer's Certificate, Indiana University, 1968; Study in Paris with Jean Langlais. *Appointments:* Faculty, Westmar College, 1967-75; Director, Music: St Joseph's, Belmont, 1975-83, Immaculate Conception, Malden, 1983-88. *Creative Works:* Recording: A Pfeffer

Odyssey. *Memberships:* American Guild of Organists; Organ Historical Society; Sigma Alpha Iota; Pi Kappa Lambda. *Honours:* Iowa State Arts Council Grant, 1974. *Hobbies:* Gardening; Swimming; Reading; Travel. *Address:* 410 Pleasant St., Malden, MA 02148, USA.

MOJEKWU Victoria Ifeyinwa, b. 29 Sep. 1933, Port Harcourt, Nigeria. Educational Planner. divorced, 2 sons. *Education:* Queen's College, Lagos, 1948-52; SRN, School of Nursing, University College Hospital, Ibadan, 1958; SCM, British Hospital for Mothers and Babies, Woolwich, England, 1958; Ward Sister's Certificate, 1959, STD distinction, 1964, Royal College of Nursing, London; BS magna cum laude, 1968, MS, 1969, Boston University, USA; EdD, Educational Planning, Harvard University, 1973; Senior Management Course Certificate, Nigerian Institute of Management, 1974. *Appointments include:* Staff Nurse, then Ward Sister, 1956-62; Sister Tutor, School of Nursing, 1964-66; University College Hospital, Ibadan; Chief Nursing Officer, Kano State, 1972-75; Assistant Chief Planning Officer, Federal Ministry of Health, Lagos, 1975-79; Regional Officer, Health Manpower Administration, World Health Organization, 1979-. *Publications:* BMET Program Review, 1971; Education and Training Implications of a New Rural Health Care Delivery System, 1972, The Future Community Midwives, 1974; Paediatric Education for Nigerian Nurses, 1975; Problems of Rural Health Care Delivery in Nigeria, 1975; Trainer's Guide for Health Management (with Adjou Moumouni, Bula-Bula, Helfenbein and Kinzounza), 1985. *Memberships:* Nigerian Academy of Arts, Science and Technology; Nigerian Institute of Management; Life Member, Family Planning Council of Nigeria; Nigerian Paediatric Association; Fellow, West African College of Nursing. *Honours:* Rockefeller Foundation Fellowship; Women's International Fellowship, American Association of University Women; Sinclair Kennedy Travelling Fellowship. *Hobbies:* Swimming; Traditional Dancing; Yoga. *Address:* World Health Organization, BP 99, Bamako, Mali.

MOLHO Laura, b. 22 Mar. 1933, Thessaloniki, Greece. Physician (Pathologist). m. Joseph Theodore Sard, MD, 24 June 1960, deceased 1982. 1 son, 1 daughter. *Education:* MD, Medical School, University of Thessaloniki, Greece, 1956; Certified, American Board of Pathology (Anatomic Pathology), 1962. *Appointments:* Assistant Pathologist, Long Island Jewish Hospital, New Hyde Park, NY, 1962-64; Staff Pathologist 1965-84; Associate Director, Department of Pathology 1984-, Queens Hospital Center, Jamaica, New York. *Publications:* Co-author of numerous scientific papers. *Memberships:* American Medical Association; Medical Society of The State of New York; New York Pathological Society; International Academy of Pathology; American Society of Clinical Pathologists; Fellow, College of American Pathologists. *Hobbies:* Music; Theatre; Arts; Travel. *Address:* Dept of Pathology, Queens Hospital Center, 82-68 164 Street, Jamaica, NY 11432, USA.

MOLT Cynthia Marylee, b. 1 Nov. 1957, Sierra Madre, USA. Author; Publisher. *Education:* BA, California State University, 1980. *Appointments:* Managing Editor, 1981-87, Authenticator, 1981-, Publisher, Senior & Managing Editor, 1987-, Associated Graphics, Arts & Letters. *Publications:* Correspondent, The Monrovia Review; Correspondent, GWTW Collectors Newsletter, 1979-82; Author, Editor: Magazines: The Wind, 1981-, California Film, 1987-; Author, Gone with the Wind: A complete Reference, 1989. *Memberships:* President: Gone with the Wind Society, 1985; Clark Gable Fan Club; Grace Kelly Fan Club; Vivien Leigh Fan Club. *Honours:* Dean's Honour List, California State University, 1975, -78. *Hobbies:* Breeding Yorkshire Terriers, Silkies & Poodles; Photography. *Address:* Associated Graphics, Arts, and Letters, 364 North May Avenue, Monrovia, CA 91016, USA.

MON Lourdes Gagui, b. 6 March 1944, Philippines. School Administrator. m. Francis Mon, 17 July 1968.

Education: BSc., Education, University of the East, Manila, 1963; M.Ed., Loyola University, USA, 1976. *Appointments:* Faculty Member, San Sebastian College, St Joseph's College, Beloit Schools, Philippine Public Schools, Immaculate Conception Schools, 1963-83; Principal, St Josaphat School, Chicago, USA, 1983-. *Publications:* Senior Editor, Columnist, VIA Times; Contributing Editor, TM Herald Newspaper; Columnist, Maynila Magazine. *Memberships:* Association of Supervision & Curriculum Development; Asian Human Services, First Filipino President; Filipino American Womens Network, Illinois Chapter, Charter President; etc. *Honours:* Outstanding Asians Award, 1985; etc. *Hobbies:* Amateur Stage Actress; Volunteer, US Immigration Service. *Address:* 8447 Harding Avenue, Skokie, IL, USA.

MONAHAN Marie Terry, b. 26 June 1927, Milford, Massachusetts, USA. Attorney at Law. m. John Henry Monahan, 25 Aug. 1951. 2 sons, 4 daughters. *Education:* AB, Radcliffe College, 1949; JD, New England School of Law, 1975. *Appointments:* Teacher, French and Spanish, Holliston High School, Massachusetts, 1949-52; Practice of Law, 1977-. *Memberships:* American Bar Association; Massachusetts Bar Association; Massachusetts Academy of Trial Attorneys; Massachusetts Association of Women Lawyers, Treasurer, Secretary, Vice President, President 1986-87. *Honour:* Special Commendation, National Conference of Christians and Jews, Northeastern Region, 1966. *Hobbies:* Reading; International Affairs; Foreign Travel. *Address:* 34 Foster Street, Newtonville, MA 02160, USA.

MONCHEK Lana Teri, b. 17 Sept. 1947, New York City, USA. Administrator; Researcher; Attorney. *Education:* BS.Ed., State University College at Buffalo, 1968; MEd., 1969, JD, 1981, University of Miami; Ed.S., 1974, Phd, 1982, University of Florida. *Appointments:* Teacher, Broward County, 1969-81; Attorney, 1981-; Teacher, Dade County, 1983; Assistant Director, 1983-85, Director, 1985-, Development Research, University of Miami. *Publications:* A Model for linking General and Special Education, 1982; Service of Process in Florida - a Manual, 1981. *Hobby:* Reading. *Address:* 4617 West Hawthorne Circle, Hollywood, FL 33021, USA.

MONTE Elisa, b. 23 May 1946, New York, USA. Choreographer; Dancer. m. David A. Brown, 14 June 1982, 1 daughter. *Education:* St John University, 1964-66; American College, Paris, 1966-67. *Career:* Dancer: Pearl Lang Dance Co, 1971-72; Lar Lubovitch Dance Co, New York City, New York, 1972-73; Martha Graham Dance Co, 1974-82; Pilobolus Dance Theatre, Washington, Connecticut, 1978; Artistic Director, Elisa Monte Dance Co, 1981-; Television appearances: Dance in America, with Martha Graham Dance Co; Guest Choreographer: Maryland Dance Theatre, 1980; Alvin Ailey American Dance Theatre, 1981, 1982; Gulbenkian Ballet, Lisbon, Spain, 1983; New York University, 1983; San Francisco Ballet, 1984; La Scala Ballet, Milan, Italy, 1985; Les Greems Ballet Canadienne, 1986; North Carolina Dance Theater, 1986; Sun Dance Institute, 1987. *Creative works:* Choreographed Treading, 1979, Pell Mell, 1980, Pigs and Fishes, 1981, White Dragon, 1982, Life Time, 1983, Indoses, 1984, Orfeo and Euridice, St Louis Opera, Dreamtime, 1986, Anima, 1986, Audentity, 1987, Turtles East Bones, 1988. *Memberships:* Panelist, New York State Council on the Arts, 1985-87; Dance USA. *Honours:* Fellowship, National Endowment for the Arts, 1982, 1985; American Express Award, International Festival of Dance, Paris, 1983; NEA/Esson Choreographic Project, 1985; Alumni Award, Professional Children's School, 1988. *Address:* 39 Great Jones Street, New York, NY 10012, USA.

MONTEIRO-RIVIERE Nancy Ann, b. 5 Sept. 1954, New Bedford, Massachusetts, USA. Assistant Professor of Anatomy and Toxicology. m. Jim E. Riviere, 31 May 1976, 2 sons. *Education:* BS cum laude, Stonehill College, 1976; MS, 1979, PhD, 1981, Purdue University; Postdoctoral studies, Pathology and Toxicology,

Chemical Industry Institute of Toxicology, 1982-84. *Appointments:* Postdoctoral Fellow in Pathology and Toxicology, 1982-84; Assistant Professor of Anatomy, Graduate Faculty for Toxicology, School of Agriculture and Life Sciences, North Carolina State University, College of Veterinary Medicine, Raleigh, North Carolina, 1984-. *Publications:* Contributor of numerous articles, book chapters and investigations in professional works. *Memberships:* Society of Toxicology, North Carolina SOT; American Association of Anatomists; American Association of Veterinary Anatomists; World Association of Veterinary Anatomists; Southeastern Electron Microscopy Society; North Carolina Society for Electron Microscopy and Microbeam Analysis; Society for Toxicologic Pathology; Electron Microscopy Society of America; National Audubon Society. *Honours:* Science Forum Award, 1976; Sigma Xi Scientific Research Society, 1981; Postdoctoral Fellowship Award, Chemical Industry Institute of Toxicology, 1982; International Life Sciences Institute Harvard Travel Scholarship, 1984; International Life Sciences Institute Pathology Expert, 1986; Reviewer for Toxicology and Applied Pharmacology, 1986. *Hobbies:* Birdwatching; Sculpture; Swimming; Tennis; Piano. *Address:* North Carolina State University, College of Veterinary Medicine, 4700 Hillsborough Street, Raleigh, NC 27606, USA.

MONTEMAYOR Rosa, b. 29 July 1952, Chicago, Illinois, USA. Podiatrist. *Education:* BS, Medical Technology, 1974; Bachelor Basic Medical Science, 1982; Doctor of Podiatric Medicine, 1984; Residency, VAMC, Denver Co, 1985. *Appointments:* Private practice, Podiatry, 1985-. *Memberships:* American Podiatric Medical Assoc, 1986; Colorado Podiatric Medical Assoc, 1986. *Honours:* President, Student Chapter, Podiatric Students Medical Ethnic Minority Organization 1982, Treasurer Class of 84, 1983, President Class of 84, 1984, California College of Podiatric Medicine; Member of Student Council, 1982-84; Treasurer, Women in Podiatry, 1981-82. *Hobbies:* Biking; Weight lifting; Gardening; Walking; Racketball; Softball. *Address:* 205 S Garrison St, Lakewood, CO 80226, USA.

MONTESA Linda, b. 12 Sept. 1940, Manila, Philippines. Concert Pianist; Teacher. m. Claro L Pio Roda, 27 Jan. 1968, 2 sons, 2 daughters. *Education:* B.Mus., University of Sto. Tomas, Philippines, 1963; M.Mus., 1965, Artist Diploma, 1968, Peabody Conservatory of Music, USA. *Appointments:* Faculty Member, Piano, Peabody Institute, 1965-; Private Piano Studio, 1972-. *Creative Works:* Piano Cocnerts, with orchestras throughout the USA, Philippines, Europe; Guest Artist, Radio Broadcasts, USA & Philippines; Piano Festival Adjudicator. *Memberships:* National Guild of Piano Teachers; American College of Musicians; Maryland State Music Teachers Association; Music Teachers National Association; Baltimore Music Club; etc. *Honours Include:* University Scholarships, 1960-63, 1965-68; Winner, various Piano Competitions; Most Distinguished Alumna in Music Award, College of the Holy Spirit, Manila, 1978. *Hobbies:* Travel; Music; Arts. *Address:* 1805 Blakefield Circle, Lutherville, MD 21093, USA.

MOODY Elizabeth Anne, b. 29 Oct. 1948, Portland, Maine, USA. Physicist. *Education:* AB Physics/Art History, Simmons College, 1971; Graduate work, Astrophysics, Harvard University, 1973. *Appointments:* Data Analyst, Smithsonian Astrophysical Observatory, Cambridge, Massachusetts, 1969; Research Consultant, Massachusetts Institute of Technology, Instrumentation Laboratory, Cambridge, 1973-74; Research Consultant, Independent Consultants, Boston, 1975-76; Research Scientist, Aerodyne Research, Burlington, 1977-78; Research Scientist, Science Applications, Bedford, 1979-80; Research Scientist, US Air Force Geophysics Laboratory, Bedford, 1981; Design and Development Engineer, Raytheon Co, Bedford, 1981-. *Publications:* Scientific and Civil Liberties articles in professional journals; Truth and Freedom in Science and Art, book in progress; Painting expressing science

in modern art. *Memberships include:* American Astronomical Society; American Physical Society; Astronominand Society of the Pacific; Association for Women in Science; American Civil Liberties Union; Anti-Defamation League; National Association for the Advancement of Coloured People; National Organization for Women; People for the America Way/Citizens for the constitution; Memorial Society of New England; Harvard Alumni Kirkland Cosmology Club. *Honours:* Woman of the Future Citation, Massachusetts Department of Education, 1965; Award for Courage, Honor, Leadership, Patriotism, Scholarship and Service, American Legion, 1966; Community Service Commendation, United Community Services of Massachusetts, 1965; Scholastic Achievement Award, Massachusetts Department of Education, 1970. *Hobby:* Studying the evolution and origin of the universe. *Address:* PO Box 5546, Beverly Farms, MA 01915, USA.

MOOKHERJEE Sheila, b. 6 Sept. 1933, India. Professor. m. Rangnath, 1965, 1 daughter. *Education:* BA, 1953, MA 1955, Banaras Hindu University; DSSA 1957; PhD, 1978. *Appointments:* Lecturer, Institute of Social Sciences, Varanasi, 1957, Delhi School of Social Work, 1958-61; Teenage Summer Camps Supervisor, New York, 1962, 1963; Director, summer research project, Forest Neighbourhood House, 1964; Social Worker, Salvation Army, New York, 1964-65; Professor, Social Work, Kashi Videyapith. *Publications:* Numerous articles in professional journals. *Memberships:* Life Member, Red Cross Society; many womens organisations. *Honours:* Recipient, many honours and awards. *Hobbies:* Social Work; Music; Art; Poetry; Travel; Photography. *Address:* P8/3 Lane No. 16 Ravindrapuri, Varanasi 221 005, India.

MOONAN Gloria Jean, b. 3 Nov. 1950, Bowling Green, Kentucky, USA. Businesswoman. m. Michael Clive Moonan, 1 Aug. 1967 div. 1988, 1 daughter. *Appointments:* General Manager, Alexander Wall Coverings, 1976-81; Decorator 1982-84, sales representative 1984-85, architectural representative 1985-86, Director, Architectural Department 1986-, Duron Paints & Wallcoverings. *Memberships:* National Association of Female Executives; Interior Design Society; Construction Specification Institute; Washington Sales & Marketing Council; Women's Republican Club. *Hobbies:* Interior Design; Cooking; Reading; Vineyards & Fine Wines. *Address:* 7488 Tangier Way, Manassas, Virginia 22110, USA.

MOORE Carole Rinne, b. 15 Aug. 1944, Berkeley, California, USA. Librarian. m. Thomas Moore, 2 sons. *Education:* AB, Stanford University, 1966; MS, Columbia University, 1967. *Appointments:* Reference Librarian, Columbia University Libraries, 1967-68; Reference Librarian, 1968, Assistant Head, Reference Department, 1973-74, Head, Reference Department, 1974-80, Head, Bibliographic Processing Department, 1980-86, Associate Librarian, Tech. Services, 1986-87, Chief Librarian, 1986-, University of Toronto, Canada. *Publications:* Editor, Labour Relations and the Librarian, 1974; Canadian Essays & Collections Index 1972-73, 1976. *Memberships:* Canadian Library Association; American Library Association; Association of Research Librarians; Canadian Association of Research Librarians (Director 1988-). *Honours:* Columbia University School of Library Service Centenary Distinguished Alumni Award, 1987. *Address:* 5 Albemarle Avenue, Toronto, Ontario M4K 1H6, Canada.

MOORE Debbie, b. 31 May 1946, Manchester, England. Businesswoman; Fashion Designer. 1 daughter. *Appointments:* Current Chairman, Managing Director & fashion designer, Pineapple Ltd. *Publications:* Pineapple Dance Book, 1983; When A Woman Means Business, 1989. *Honours:* Veuve Clicquot Business Woman of Year, 1983; Institute of Directors Award, 1983; Business Woman of Year, Variety Club of Great Britain, 1983; 1st & only female Chairman allowed on Stock Exchange floor, at Pineapple's placing, Unlisted Stock Market, 1982. *Address:* Pineapple, 7 Langley Street, London WC2H 9JA, England.

MOORE Dianne Susan, b. 11 Jan. 1946, Brooklyn, USA. Businesswoman; Nurse-Midwife; Researcher. m. Frederick A Gonzalex, 16 Dec. 1978, 2 sons. *Education:* BS, Hunter College, 1960; MN, 1970; CNM, Downstate Medical Centre, 1978; PhD, New York University, 1981; MPH, Columbia University, (in progress). *Appointments Include:* Various Nursing Positions, 1968-79; Assistant Professor, University of California, Los Angeles, 1981-83; Associate Professor, Pace University, 1984-85; North Central Bronx Hospital, CNM, 1985; President, Mooreinfo, 1986-; Associate Professor, H H Lehman College, 1988-. *Publications:* Numerous articles in professional journals including: Nursing Research; Journal of Nurse-Midwifery; Topics in Clinical Nursing; Professional Nurse Quarterly; etc. *Memberships Include:* American College of Nurse-Midwives; American Nurses Association; New York State Nurses Association; Council of Nurse Researchers; American Public Health Association; International Childbirth Education Association, etc. *Honours:* Recipient, numerous honours and awards. *Hobbies:* Theatre; Art; Travel; Interior Design. *Address:* 54 Butterwood Lane West, Irvington on Hudson, NY 10533, USA.

MOORE Georgina Mary, b. 8 Apr. 1930, Oxford, England. Principal, St Hilda's College, Oxford. m. Anthony Ross Moore, 30 Aug. 1963, 1 son. *Education:* BA, MA, Modern History, Lady Margaret Hall, Oxford University, 1948-51. *Appointments:* HM Foreign (later Diplomatic) Service 1951-63; British Legation, Budapest, 1954-56, UK Permanent Mission to the UN, New York, 1956-59, Promoted to Rank of First Secretary, 1961; JP, 1977-82; Principal, St Hilda's College Oxford, 1980-; Trustee, British Museum, 1982-; Member, The Rhodes Trust, 1984-. *Publications:* (As Helena Osborne) The Arcadian Affair, 1969 (in USA The Yellow Gold of Tiryns); Pay-Day, 1972 (in USA My Enemy's Friend); White Poppy, 1977; The Joker, 1979; TV Plays: The Trial of Mme Fahmy (one of the Ladykillers Series), Granada, 1980; Radio Plays: Plays for Radio 4. *Membership:* University Women's Club. *Address:* St Hilda's College, Oxford, England.

MOORE Jean K, b. 11 June 1936, Chicago, USA. Neuroanatomist. m. 24 May 1969, divorced 1988, 3 sons, 1 daughter. *Education:* BS, Marquette Univesity, 1957; PhD, University of Chicago, 1971. *Appointments:* Therapist, various hospitals, 1957-62; Research Assistant, Psychology, University of Illinois, 1962-63; Predoctoral Trainee, University of Chicago, 1963-64, 1967-69, University of Oslo, Norway, 1968-69; Instructor, Anatomy, University of Chicago, 1971-72; Lecturer, 1979-80, Assistant Professor, 1980-83, Research Assistant Professor, 1983-, Anatomical Sciences, State University of New York, Stony Brook. *Publications:* Articles in professional journals. *Memberships:* Society for Neuroscience; American Association of Anatomists; Association for Research in Otolaryngology; Sigma Xi. *Hobbies:* Piano; Choral Music; Running; Tennis. *Address:* Port Jefferson, NY 11777, USA.

MOORE Jellether Marie, b. 9 Apr. 1949, Sacramento, California, USA. Computer Systems Manager. 1 son, 1 daughter. *Education:* BA, Washburn University, Topeka, Kansas, 1973; California State University, Sacramento; Sacramento City College; Cosumnes River College, Sacramento; University of California, Davis. *Appointments:* Programmer/Analyst, Computer Software Applications, State of California, 1976-84; Land and Water Use Analyst/Computer Systems Manager, Farmland Mapping and Monitoring Programme, Department of Conservation, State of California, 1984-; Partner, Mooncraft/Minds Eye Images. *Memberships:* California Association of Professional Scientists; Association of Women Entrepreneurs; Chamber of Commerce, Sacramento; Better Business Bureau, Sacramento; Reviewer, Digital Cartographic Standards; Correspondence Secretary, Women's Civic Improvement Center. *Honours:* Superior Accomplishment Award for Excellence in Information Management, Office of Information Technology, State of California, 1988; Sustained Superior Accomplishment, Department of Conservation, State of California, 1988. *Hobbies:* Photography; Computers; Storytelling; Crafts; Esoteric interests; Graphics. *Address:* State of California - Farmland Mapping and Monitoring Program, 1516 Nineth Street, Room 400, Sacramento, CA 95814, USA.

MOORE Marjorie, b. 7 May 1937, Waukegan, Illinois, USA. Minister; Teacher; Doctor of Oriental Medicine. 1 son. *Education:* BS, 1960, MEd., 1965, Ball State University; BS, South Baylo University, 1983; OMD Post graduate Institute of Oriental Medicine, Hong Kong, 1989. *Appointments:* Minister, Mental Physics Tibetan Church, 1984; Director, Acucare Holistic Health Centre, 1985-89; Instructor, South Baylo University, 1986; Examiner, State Medical Board of Quality Assurance, Acupuncture Section, 1987, 1988, 1989. *Memberships:* California Acupuncture Alliance; American Foundation of Traditional Clinical Medicine. *Honours:* Deans List: Ball State, 1957-60, South Baylo, 1982-84. *Hobbies:* Travel; World Religions. *Address:* 1034 E. Irvine Blvd., Tustin, CA 92680, USA.

MOORE Mary Ann, b. 11 Feb. 1940, Potlach, Idaho, USA. Administrator. m. Gary Aerni Moore, 19 July 1963. 2 sons, 2 daughters. *Education:* Diploma, St Luke's School of Nursing, Spokane, 1961; BS 1980, MS, Health Care Administration 1981, Columbia Pacific University; Masters, Public Health, University of Minnesota, 1982. *Appointments:* Assistant to Nursing Administrator 1975-78, Assistant Administrator 1978-81, Alaska Hospital and Medical Center; Independent Consultant, Denver, CO, 1981-82; Associate Executive Director, Humana Hosp, Alaska, 1982; Associate Administrator, Virginia Mason Medical Center, Seattle, 1983-. *Creative works:* Author of numerous articles to professional journals, magazines and numerous conference presentations and speaking engagements. *Memberships include:* American College of Medical Group Administrators; American Nurses Association; American Public Health Association; American Academy of Ambulatory Nursing Administration; American Organization of Nurse Executives; American College of Healthcare Executives; Medical Group Management Association; National League for Nursing; Washington Organization of Nurse Executives. *Honours:* Washington Organization Nurse Executives, board member, 1989; American Academy of Ambulatory Nursing Administration, President, 1990-91; Kellogg Fellow, Public Health Nursing/Nursing Administration; Sigma Theta Tau, National Honor Society for Nursing. *Hobbies:* Gardening; Skiing; Hiking. *Address:* 17248 NE 125th Street, Redmond, WA 98052, USA.

MOORE Mary Tyler, b. 29 Dec. 1937, Brooklyn, New York, USA. Actress. m. (1) Richard Meeker, 1 child deceased. (2) Grant Tinker, 1963, divorced 1981. (3) Robert Levine, 1983. *Creative Works:* Television: Richard Diamond; Private Eye, 1957-59; Dick Van Dyke Show, 1961-66; Mary Tyler Moore Show, 1970-77; Mary, 1978; Mary Tyler Moore Hour, 1979; Mary, 1985-; Love American Style, 1969; Run a Crooked Mile, 1970; First You Cry, 1978; How to Survive the Seventies, 1978; Heartsounds, 1984; Finnegan Begin Again, 1984. Films include: X-15, 1961; Thoroughly Modern Millie, 1967; Don't Just Stand There, 1968; What's So Bad About Feeling Good?, 1968; Change of Habit, 1969; Ordinary People, 1980; Six Weeks, 1982; Just Between Friends, 1986. *Memberships:* Chairman of Board, MTM Enterprises Inc. *Honours:* Academy Award nominee for Best Actress, 1981; Recipient Emmy award, National Academy TV Arts and Scis, 1964, 1965, 1973, 1974, 1976; Golden Globe Award, 1965, 1981; Elected to TV Hall of Fame, 1985. *Address:* c/o MTM Enterprises, 4024 Radford Avenue, Studio City, CA 91604, USA.

MOORE Maureen, b. 8 Dec. 1953, Wallingford, Connecticut, USA. Actress. m. Barry Vener, 27 Mar. 1978. *Education:* BFA, Carnegie Mellon University, 1972. *Appointments:* Appeared in leading lady role in numerous Broadway Shows including: Godspell, 1973-74; Gypsy, 1973-74; Unsung Cole, 1977; By Strouse, 1978; I Love My Wife, 1979; The Mooney Shapiro

Songbook, 1981; Amadeus, 1982; Big River, 1984-85; Song and Dance, 1985; Films: The Circus, 1972; The Goodbye Girl, 1976; The Pope of Greenwich Village, 1982; National Tours of Cabaret, Gypsy, Shenendoah and Al Jolson Tonight. *Memberships:* Screen Actors Guild; Actors Equity Association; American Federation of Radio & TV Association; Carnegie Mellon Honour Society; Theatre World. *Address:* New York, NY, USA.

MOORE Maurine, b. 27 Feb. 1932, Lamar, Colorado, USA. Writer; Graphologist. m. Robert T. Moore, 12 Sept. 1954 (divorced 1970), 2 daughters. *Education:* BS, University of Colorado; MS, University of Wyoming; Certified Graphologist (CGA), 1974; Master Graphologist (MGA), 1975. *Appointments:* Teacher, Wyoming, 1970-73; Grapholegal consultant, Wyoming, Florida, California, 1973-. *Publications:* Books: Sex in Handwriting, 1978; Income Graphology, 1978; Who Could I Tell: Examination of Child Sexual Abuse, 1985; Overcoming A Life Of Abuse, 1988. *Memberships:* International Graphoanalysis Society; American Handwriting Association; Western Writers of America; National Writers Club. Alumni associations. *Honours:* Gold Pen Award, journal editor, Colorado chapter, IGAS. *Hobbies:* Swimming; Parlour games; Water skiing. *Address:* 200 S Glenn Drive 55.D, Camarillo, CA 93010, USA.

MOORE Peggy Sue, b. 16 June 1942, Wichita, Kansas, USA. Corporate Executive; Executive Vice President/Chief Financial Officer. *Education:* Famous Writers School, Westport, 1959-61; Business Major,1961-63, Continuing Ed Programs: Managerial Psych; Lotus 1-2-3, 1980-86, Wichita State University; Business Degree, Wichita Business College, 1962-64. *Appointments:* Controller, Mears Electric Co., Midwest Division, Wichita, Kansas, 1965-69; Executive Vice President, Corp Secretary, Chief Financial Officer; Board of Directors, Executive Committee, Company Co-Founder and Stockholder, CPI Corporation, Wichita, 1969-. *Memberships:* International Platform Association, 1987-88; National Association Female Executives, 1982-88; Republican National Committee, 1984-88; Republican Task Force, 1986-88; American Biographical Institute, 1987; Sedgwick County Zoological Society, 1986-88; Wichita Chamber of Commerce, 1979-88. *Honours:* Fringe Benefits Design, Kansas City, Trustee, 1985-88; Women's National Bowling Association Publicity Chairman, 1969-76; Board Member, Good Shepherd Lutheran Church, 1977-81. *Hobbies:* Golf; Bowling; Hiking; Fishing; Skiing; Crafts; Woodcarving; Painting. *Address:* 130 Longford Court, Wichita, KS 67206, USA.

MOORE Sherry Gail (North), b. 20 May 1937, St Louis, Missouri, USA. Administrator. m. Edward Russell Moore Jr, 26 May 1961, 2 sons, 1 daughter. *Education:* Louisiana State University, 1956-58; McNeese State University, 1957; Charity Hospital School of Nursing, 1959-61. *Appointments:* Medical Receptionist, Nurse, Bookkeeper, E. Russell Moore MD, 1961-75; Administrator, Calcasieu Parish Coroner's Office & Forensic Facility, 1981-. *Publications:* Articles, Boxer Review. *Memberships:* Deputy Sheriff, Calcasieu Parish, Louisiana; District Attorney's Task Force on Substance Abuse, 1984-; National Commission on Correctional Health Care, 1985-; Louisiana State Coroner's Association. *Honour:* Featured, Flair magazine (Lake Charles American Press), Aug. 1986. *Hobbies:* Cooking; Walking; Writing; Reading; Painting; Sketching; Woodwork; Raising Boxer Dogs; Family. *Address:* 221 Madison, Sulphur, Louisiana 70663, USA.

MOORE Shirley Beaham, b. 28 July 1934, Tucson, Arizona, USA. Realtor. m. Jack K Moore, Jr, 30 June 1956, divorced 1969. 1 son, 1 daughter. *Education:* BA, Scripps College, Claremont, California, 1956. *Appointments:* Civic Worker, Tucson, Arizona, 1958-89; Executive Director, Arizona Kidney Foundation, Tucson, 1977-81; Realtor, Tucson, 1982-. *Memberships:* Junior League of Tucson, 1959-89, served on Board of Directors 1962-73; Board of Directors, Planned Parenthood, 1960-65, Vice President & President 1962-

64; Board of Directors, Silver & Turquoise 1963-73, Chair 1968; Board of Directors, St Luke's Board of Visitors 1968-78, Baile Ch 1972, VP 1974, Pres 1975; Board of Directors, St Luke's in the Desert, Inc, 1975-86; St Luke's Planning Com, 1984-89; Area Ch American Red Cross, 1964; Co-Ch, US Senatorial Campaign, Pima County, 1972; Invitations & General Arrangements Ch, Tucson Symphony Cotillion, 1974-75; Arizona Town Hall, 1975; Arizona Academy, 1975-84; Board of Directors, Alcoholism Council of Tucson, 1977-87; Alumnae Admissions Representative Scripps College, 1975-84; University of Arizona President's Club, 1975-; PEO, 1958-. *Hobbies:* Politics; Travel; Gardening; Hiking; Genealogy. *Address:* 7000 E Calle Arandas, Tucson, AZ 85715, USA.

MOORE Susan Evelyn, b. 20 July 19054, Mobile, Alabama, USA. Electron Microscopist, Chemist. *Education:* BS, Mobile College, Alabama, 1976; Graduate work, University of South Alabama, Mobile. *Appointments:* Research Assistant, University of South Alabama, 1977- 79; Technical Director, Alabama Eye Bank, 1979-81; Chemist, Industrial, Merck Co, 1981-84; Chemical Sales Representative, Drew Chemical Co, 1984-85; Electron Microscopist, University of Alabama, Birmingham, 1985-. *Memberships:* National Association Female Executives; Electron Microscopy Society of America; Alabama Electron Microscopy Society; National Sports Officials Association; Alabama High School Athletic Association; Birmingham Basketball Officials Association and Football Officials Association; Greater Metro Umpires Association; National Federation Interscholastic Officials; Amateur Softball Association. *Honours:* Natural Science Divisional Award, 1976I; SGA Environmental Research Grant, 1977-78; In-House Faculty Research Grant, 1977-78; State Slowpitch Softball Championship, 1979; Outstanding Woman Graduate of Mobile College, 1976. *Hobbies:* Coach, Ladies Slowpitch softball team; Tennis; Officiating high school football and basketball; Adult choir, Shades Mountain Baptist Church; Refinishing and restoring antique furniture. *Address:* 1219 I Beacon Parkway East, Birmingham, AL 35209, USA.

MOORE-STOVALL Joyce Geneva Arnell, b. 5 Nov. 1948, Washington, USA. Radiologist. m. Arthur J. Stovall, 25 June 1979, 2 sons. *Education:* BA, Fisk University, 1970; MD, Meharry Medical College, 1974. *Appointments:* Veteran's Medical Centre, Leavenworth, 1979-80. *Publications:* Articles in: Journal Kansas Medical Society; Journal National Medical Association. *Membership:* National Medical Association. *Honours:* Dean's List; Chief Resident of General Radiology Residency Programme, 1978; American Medical Association Physician Recognition Award, 1981, 1985, 1988. *Hobbies:* Reading; Travel; Art Museums; Painting; Writing. *Address:* 3707 Lakeview Drive, Leavenworth, KS 66048, USA.

MOOREHEAD Caroline Mary, b. 28 Oct. 1944, London, England. Writer; Journalist. m. 27 May 1967, 1 son, 1 daughter. *Education:* BA Hons, Psychology and Philosophy, London University. *Appointments:* Time Magazine, 1969-70; The Times, 1971-88; The Independent, 1988-. *Publications:* Hostages to Fortune, 1980; Letters of Freya Stark (editor), 1982-83; Sidney Bernstein: A Biography, 1983; Freya Stark: A Biography, 1985; Troublesome People: Enemies of War 1916-1918, 1987; Over the Rim of the World: Letters of Freya Stark (editor), 1988; Betrayal: Child Exploitation in Todays World, 1989; Contributor to Spectator, Times Literary Supplement, Departures, Traveller, The Literary Review. *Honours:* Valiant for Truth Award, 1985. *Address:* c/o Anthony Sheil, 43 Doughty Street, London WC1, England.

MOORMAN Helen Louise, b. 5 Dec. 1940, Chicago, Illinois, USA. Lawyer. m. G Edward Moorman, 28 Dec. 1960, divorced 1983. 1 son, 1 daughter. *Education:* AB, University of Chicago, 1962; JD, Washington University School of Law, St Louis, Missouri, 1972; Postgraduate study, London School of Economics, England, 1982-83. *Appointments:* Judicial Clerk, Illinois Appellate Court;

Public Defender, Madison County; Land of Lincoln Legal Assistance Foundation; Marion-Polk Legal Aid Service, 1984-86; Hyatt Legal Services, 1986; Natkin & Associates, PC, 1987-88; Senior Assistant Public Defender, Juvenile Division Lake County, IL , 1988-. *Memberships:* American Bar Assoc; Illinois State Bar Association (Juvenile Committee 1978-82); Association of Women Attorneys; Missouri Bar Association; Oregon State Bar Association; Mensa (Pres St Louis Chapter 1973, 1974); Vice President, Board of Directors, Oasis Women's Center, Alton, 1977-84; Board of Directors, YWCA, Quincy, 1979-81; Board of Directors, Mid-Valley Women's Crisis Service, Salem, 1984-86. *Honours:* Westinghouse Science Talent Search, Hon Mention, 1958; Scholarship, University of Chicago, 1958-62; Mortar Board Scholarship, 1960; George Marsalek Scholarship, 1969-72; Mensa Education and Research Foundation Scholarship, 1982; English Speaking Union Travel Grant, 1982; American Friends of London School of Economics Scholarship, 1982-83. *Hobbies:* Travel; Theatre; Camping; Cross country skiing; Bicycling; Hiking; Photography. *Address:* 445 S Cleveland Ave, Apt 301, Arlington Heights, IL 60005, USA.

MORA Juana M, b. 27 Oct. 1953, Jalisco, Mexico. Health Researcher and Planner; Lecturer. *Education:* BA Linguistic, University of California at Santa Cruz, USA, 1976; MA Sociolinguistics 1977, PhD Education 1984, Stanford University. *Appointments:* Faculty, University of California at Santa Barbara, 1981-84; Adjunct Faculty, National Hispanic University, Oakland, 1987; Associate Research Scientist, Prevention Research Center, Berkeley, 1986-87; Research Analyst, Los Angeles County Department of Health, 1987-. *Publications:* Alcohol Problem Prevention among Mexican-Americans; Alcohol Consumption Among Mexican-American Husbands and Wives; Alcohol and Drugs are Women's Issues: Issues for Latinas. *Memberships:* National Hispanic Health & Human Services Organization; Comision Femenil of Los Angeles; Stanford Hispanic Alumni Association; Board Arroyo Vista Family Health Center. *Honours:* Ford Foundation Graduate Fellowship, 1976-81; ABD Teaching and Research Fellowship, University of California at Santa Barbara, 1981-82; National Chicano Council on Higher Education, Dissertation Grant, 1981. *Hobbies:* Latin American Theatre and Literature; Travel. *Address:* 6015 El Mio Dr, Los Angeles, California 90042, USA.

MORAGNE Lenora, b. 29 Sept. 1931, Evanston, Illinois, USA. Editor; Publisher. *Education:* BS, Dietetics, Iowa State University, Ames, 1954; MS, Foods, Management, PhD, Education, Nutrition, Cornell University. *Appointments:* Assistant Professor, Cornell University; Assistant Professor, North Carolina College, Durham; Professor, Hunter College, New York City; Head, Nutrition Education and Training, USDA; Professional Staff Member, US Senate Agriculture Committee; Nutrition Adviser, Nutrition Coordinating Office, DHHS; Chief Executive Officer, Nutrition Legislation Services; Currently Founding Editor and Publisher, Nutrition Legislation News, Nutrition Funding Report, and Congressional Black Monitor. *Publications:* Baby's Early Years (with Rudolph Moragne); Focus on Food (Junior H.S. Nutrition textbook). *Memberships:* President, Society for Nutrition Education; Chairperson, Food and Nutrition Section, American Public Health Association; Board of Directors, American Dietetic Association; Chairperson, Cornell University Federal Government Relations Committee. *Honours:* Elected Member, Cornell University Council, 1981; Distinguished Alumni Citation, Iowa State University, Ames, 1983; Nominee, Cornell University Board of Trustees, 1984; Inducted into Gamma Sigma Delta Agriculture Honor Society, 1987. *Hobbies:* Tracking legislation in US Congress concerning nutrition and minority set-asides; Serving on advisory committees at Cornell University School of Human College, University of Maryland, and Center for Nutrition, Meharry Medical College, Nashville, Tennessee. *Address:* 607 Fourth Street SW, Washington, DC 20024, USA.

MORAITIS Karen Karl, b. 28 Sept. 1943, Orange, Texas, USA. Real Estate Broker. m. George Reynold Moraitis, 14 Aug. 1965, 1 son, 1 daughter. *Education:* BS, University of Florida, 1965; MEd, Florida Atlantic University, 1968; EdS, 1974. *Appointments:* Real Estate Broker, Karen Moraitis Realty Inc., Ft. Lauderdale, 1978-. *Publications:* Editor, Official Florida Publications, 1966. *Memberships Include:* Ft Lauderdale Board of Realtors; National and Florida Associations of Realtors. *Honours:* Recipient, various honours and awards. *Address:* 631 Middle River Dr., Fort Lauderdale, FL 33304, USA.

MORAN Janet Elaine, b. 21 July 1954, Croydon, Surrey, England. Actress; Director. *Education:* CSSD, Distinction, Certificate of Education, Distinction, BEd., English, Drama, Honours, Central School of Speech & Drama. *Appointments:* 5 seasons, including leading parts in Terson's Zigger Zagger, National Youth Theatre, 1971-76; Director, Three Sisters, Dome Theatre, Montreal, Canada, 1976-77; Formed, The Ruddles Theatre Company, Directed, Acted, Toured, Midlands, 1978-79; Proprietor, A-One Theatre Company, Rutland, 1980-81; Associate Director, Highway Theatre Company, 1981; Nance, in Gaslight, 1982; New Shakespeare Company, Nottingham Playhouse, 1982; Appearances, Nottingham Playhouse, 1982-83; BBC Schools Radio, All in the Dark, 1984. *Creative Works:* Seven Ages of Women, video film, written, acted, directed, edited with Carrie Humphries, 1984. *Address:* 14 Birchwood, Orton Goldhay, Peterborough, Cambridgeshire, England.

MORAN Joann Hoeppner, b.12 May 1944, Eau Claire, Wisconsin, USA. Professor of History. m. Theodore H Moran, 7 Aug 1966, divorced 1987, 2 sons. *Education:* BA, Radcliffe College, Harvard University, 1966; MA 1969, PhD 1975, Brandeis University. *Appointments:* Assistant Professor of History, 1978-84, Associate Professor of History, 1984-, Georgetown University. *Publications:* Education and Learning in the City of York, 1300-1560, 1979; The Growth of English Schooling 1340-1548, 1985; Co-editor,Recently Published Articles, 1980-85; Co-editor, British Studies Intelligence, 1986-; Articles published in Northern History, History of Education Quarterly, Manuscripta, Journal of Ecclesiastical History, Modern Fiction Studies. *Memberships:* Medieval Academy of America; North American Conference on British Studies, Council Member; American Historical Association; Fellow, Society for Values in Higher Education; Renaissance Society of America; History of Education Society. *Honours:* Woodrow Wilson Graduate Fellowship, 1966-67; Woodrow Wilson Dissertation Fellowship, 1970-72; ACLU Grant; Radcliffe College, Bunting Institute Fellow, 1982-84; John Nicholas Brown Prize, Medieval Academy of America, 1989. *Address:* 4945 Allan Road, Bethesda, MD 20816, USA.

MORANI Alma Dea, b. 21 Mar. 1907, New York, New York, USA. Emeritus Professor of Plastic Surgery. *Education:* BS, NYU, 1928; MD, Woman's Medical College, Pennsylvania, 1931; DHL (Hon), Chestnut Hill College, Philadelphia, 1974; DMedSci (Hon), Medical College, Pennsylvania, 1976; Diplomate: Am Bd Surgery. *Appointments:* Intern, St James Hospital, Newark, 1931-32; Resident surgery, Womens Medical Hospital, Philadelphia, 1932-35; Fellow, Plastic Surgery, University of Washington Medical School, St Louis, 1946-47; Specializing plastic surgery, Philadelphia, 1948-; Assoc Surgeon, Roxborough Hospital, 1940; Chief Plastic Surgeon, St Mary's Hospital, Philadelphia, 1964-; Consultant, Philadelphia VA Hospital, 1955-; Professor, Clinical Surgery, Womens Medical College, 1950-82. *Publications:* Contributed numerous articles to medical journals. *Memberships:* Fellows ACS; International College Surgeons; American Society Plastic & Reconstructive Surgery; Robt H Ivy Society Plast Sg, Philadelphia; College Physicians; American Physicians Art Association; American Medical Womens Association; Alumnae Association Womens Medical College; Med Womens Internat Association; British Med Womens Fedn; Philadelphia County Med Soc; Chinese Medical Society; Philippine Medical Society; Royal

Society Medicine, England; Philadelphia Academy Surgery; Military Surgeons, USA. *Honours:* Professor Emeritus, Medical College of Pennsylvania, 1982; Consultant to Department Humanitites in Art Med Col of Pennsylvania, 1985; Vol Vis Prof, Nat Def Med Center, Taipei, Taiwan, 1964; President Am Womens Hsps Service Inc, NYC, 1967; Order Sons Italy, 1955; Order Merit Cavaliere Ufficiale Republic Italy, 1967; recipient Alumnae Achievement Award, Woman's Med College, 1964; Achievement Award S Philadelphia Lions Club, 1965; Friendship Fete Fame Award, 1968; Award distinction Soroptimist Fed Am, 1970; Parliamentarian of American Womens International Association, 1984; Humanitarian Award, Chapel of Four Chaplins, 1988; Ivy Society of Plastic Surgeons of Pa, as Founder, 1988; Eliz Blackwell Am Med Womens Assn, 1972; Dist Daughters of Pa Award, 1973; Citation HEW 1976; Tribute in Congl Record, 1974. *Hobbies:* Art and humanities; Sculpture and photography; Founded Morani Art Gallery, Medical College of Pennsylvania; Importance of Art in Medical Education; Donated art collection of 35 years to Medical College of Pennsylvania Morani Art Gallery. *Address:* 3665 Midvale Avenue, Philadelphia, PA 19129, USA.

MORAWSKI Mariola T J, President, M & M Consulting Services. *Education:* BM, Academy of Music, Warsaw, Poland, 1967; Master of Law, specialization in Public Administration and Corporate Law 1975, Postgraduate Studies, Journalism Science 1975, Warsaw University, Poland; Bachelor of Management, Canadian School of Management, Toronto, Canada, 1983; Master of Business Administration, 1989; Candidate for Doctor of Law. *Appointments:* Junior Judge, Warsaw Provincial Court, Poland, 1975; Law Assistant/Administrative Manager, Singer's Legal Office, Johannesburg, Republic of South Africa, 1977-79; Director, Student Affairs Department 1980-88, Associate Dean Student Affairs 1988-, Canadian School of Management, Toronto, Canada; Director, Advisory Board, Executive Business Education Inc; Vice President, Institute of Certified Administrative Managers of Ontario; Vice President, Balfour Institute for International Management; President, M&M Consulting (Training & Education); President, Elliott International University. *Memberships include:* Canadian Institute of Certified Administrative Managers, Secretary; Canadian Association of Women Executives; Royal Commonwealth Society; Empire Club of Canada. *Honour:* Fellow, Canadian Institute of Certified Administrative Managers. *Hobbies:* Travelling; Music; fashion; Decorative arts and design; Charity work. *Address:* 19 Knoll Drive, Etobicoke, Ontario, Canada M9A 4G9.

MORCH Dea Trier, b. 9 Dec. 1941, Copenhagen, Denmark. Graphic Artist; Writer. 1 son, 2 daughters. *Education:* Royal Academy of Fine Art, Copenhagen; Postgraduate Studies, Warsaw, Cracow, Belgrade, Leningrad & Prague, 1964-67. *Creative Works:* Exibitions: West-East Europe, North-South America, Middle East; Books: Bittersweet Socialism, 1968; Poland, 1970; Winter's Child, 1976; A Triangle, 1977; Into the World, 1977; Chestnut Avenue, 1978; Inner City, 1980; Evening Star, 1982; Morning Gift, 1984; When I Discovered America, 1986; The Ship in the Bottle, 1988. *Memberships:* Union of Danish Writers; Union of Danish Artists. *Honours:* Elected Danish Author, 1977; Government Stipend for Life, 1985; Hvass Foundation, 1985; Peter Sabroe Children's Prize, 1987; Tagea Brandts Travel Stipend, 1988. *Hobbies:* Art; Literature. *Address:* Jens Juelsgade 7, 2100 Kobenhavn, Denmark.

MORELLA Constance Albanese, b. 12 Feb. 1931, Somerville, USA. Congresswoman. m. Anthony C Morella, 21 Aug. 1954, 2 sons, 1 daughter. *Education:* AA, 1950, AB, 1954, Boston University; MA, American University, 1967. *Appointments:* Teacher, Montgomery County Public Schools, 1956-60; Instructor, American University, 1968-70; Professor, Montgomery College, Rockville, 1970-; Delegate, Maryland General Assembly, Annapolis, 1979-86; Congresswoman, US

House of Representatives, Washington, 1987-. *Publications:* The Female Alcoholic in American History, Culture and Jurisprudence, The Alcoholism Digest, 1974. *Memberships Include:* Committees in US Congress; Montgomery County Commission for Women, President 1973-74; Womens Institute Advisory Council; American Association of University Women; etc. *Honours:* Distinguished Alumna Award, American University, 1980, 1982; Woman of the Year, Zona International, 1984; Distinguished Legislator Award, Maryland Victims Advocacy Network, 1985; etc. *Hobbies:* Theatre; Tennis; Reading. *Address:* US House of Representatives, 1024 Longworth House Office Building, Washington, DC 20515, USA.

MORELLI Jill K., b. 23 Dec. 1949, Iowa, USA. Architect. m. Patrick T. Morelli, 26 Feb. 1972, 1 daughter. *Education:* BArch, Iowa State University, 1971. *Appointments:* Various architectural firms, Tulsa, Oklahoma, 1971-78; Haller & Larson Inc, Denver, Colorado, 1978-83; Cambridge Development Group, Denver, 1983-. *Creative works include:* Project Manager for: Hewlett-Packard-Greeley, Masonic Building, Neusteter's Building, Denver. *Memberships:* Denver Chapter, American Institute of Architects; Women in Architecture; President, Capitol Hill United Neighbourhoods Inc; Denver Victims Advisory Board. *Honours:* Numerous awards, various bodies, most recent include: Best Exterior Signage, & Best Leasing Office, Apartment Association of Metro Denver, 1988; Fellow (highest honour), Women in Architecture (Colorado). *Hobbies include:* Developing & participating in schools' environment education, Kindergarten to 12th Grade, using architecture to integrate curriculum. *Address:* 540 Franklin, Denver, Colorado 80218, USA.

MORENO Rosemarie Lillian Traina, b. 7 Aug. 1957, New York, USA. Stockbroker; Art Consultant. m. George Moreno Sr, 21 Oct, 1984, 1 son. *Education:* Bachelor's degree cum laude, Hunter College, City University of New York, 1980; Master's degree, Fordham University, 1981. *Appointments:* Owner, Freelance Art Consultant, R.T.Moreno & Co; Institutional Sales Assistant, Nesbitt Thompson Securities Inc, 1981-83; Registered Representative, Broker, Shearson Lehman Bros Inc, 1983-87; Administrative Manager, R.L.Renck Holdings Inc, 1987-88. *Publication:* Employment Techniques, article, 1984. *Memberships:* Public Relations Society of America; Publicity Club of New York; National Association of Female Executives; National Honor Society of America; Democratic Club; National Italian-Americans Association. *Honours:* Italian-American Teachers Association, 1972; Certificate of Merit, Honours, 1975; Dean's List, 1975; Honor Society, High School of Art and Design, 1975; Distinguished Investment Achievement, 5000 Personalities of the World, 1987; Outstanding Service, 2000 Notable American Women, 1987; Distinguished Investment Achievement, Who's Who in Professional and Executive Women, 1987; Certificate of Achievement, Who's Who in American Women, 1988. *Hobbies:* Art collecting; Philatelist; Photography; Writer of Childrens Stories. *Address:* 3555 Bruckner Boulevard, Bronx, NY 10461, USA.

MOREY Robin, b. 14 Apr. 1924, Detroit, Michigan, USA. Fibre Artist. m. (1) Thomas E. Nichols, 23 Mar. 1942, divorced 1946, (2) Charles T. Morey, 23 Nov. 1948, divorced 1972, 4 sons, 1 daughter. *Education:* John Herron Art Institute, Indianapolis, 1945-48; Black Mountain College, North Carolina, 1948-49; C. G. Jung Institute, Zurich, Switzerland, 1980-81. *Appointments include:* Private instruction, own studio, 1956-. Teacher, part-time: Clay modelling, Dartmouth College, 1956-57; Sculpture & quilt-making, St Clair College, Windsor, Ontario, 1973-80; Lectures & workshops, Quilt Guilds, USA & Canada, 1983-. *Creative work includes:* Commissions, purchases, bronze portraits & quilted textiles, USA, Canada, UK, Poland; Work featured, various journals & magazines. *Memberships:* Board, Arts Council, Windsor & Region; Women's Economic Forum, Windsor; Ontrio Crafts Council. *Honours include:* Louise Vonnegut Memorial Award, John Herron Art

Institute, 1946; Textile award, Art in the Park, Windsor, 1976; Prize, work in fibre, Windsor Art Gallery, 1983; Projects grant 1985, materials grant 1987, Ontario Arts Council; Co-curator & contributor, catalogue, touring exhibit, Fibre: Tradition/Transition, Windsor Art Gallery, 1988. *Hobbies:* Growing cacti & succulents; Work in machine-shop; Sewing large canvas boat covers; Carpentry; Fast driving; Manx cats; Reading; Good films. *Address:* RR 1, Harrow, Ontario, Canada N0R 1G0.

MORGAN Audrey, b. 19 Oct. 1931, Neenah, Wisconsin, USA. Architect. divorced. 1 son, 3 daughters. *Education:* BA, Architecture, University of Washington, Seattle, 1955; NCARB Certification, 1979; Architect Licensed, Washington, 1978. *Appointments:* Edmonds Comm College Inst, 1978-79; Austin Co Proj Dir/Med Planner, 1972; NBBJ Group Med Facilities Arch, 1975; WA State Division of Health, 1979; John Graham Co Med Planner, 1981; Private Consultant, practice, 1983-. *Publications:* Contributor to professional journals; Participant in review and writing of state and federal health care facility codes, standards and guidelines. Significant works: Quality Assurance coordinator design Phase Madigan Army Medical Center, Fort Lewis, WA; Rockwood Clinic Spokane WA; Comprehensive Health Care Clinic Yakima Indian Nation, Toppenish, WA. *Memberships:* American Institute of Architects; Comm on Arch for Health, sub comm Codes & Standards, Vice Chairman Mental Health Sub comm; Founding member and past chair, Arch for Health Panel (Pacific NW Component); SAVE; AHA; AWA; WSHA; NFPA; Totem G S Council. *Honours:* AHP recognition award for service to AHP & CAH, 1985; SW WA Chapter AIA Award for service to chapter, 1984. *Hobbies:* Sailing, member of Coronado 25 Fleet 13 Seattle WA and Seattle Women's Sailing Association; Swimming; Camping; Hiking; Beachcombing; Arts and crafts; Reading; Music and theatre; Travel; Pinochle; Working with children and youth, Member of 25 plus Club Totem Girl Scout Council; Member, Audubon Society. *Address:* 4216 Greenwood Avenue North, Seattle, WA 98103, USA.

MORGAN Cheryl Eileen, b. 12 Aug. 1951, Atlanta, Georgia, USA. Architect. *Education:* AS with highest honour, Kennesaw Junior College, 1971; BS with highest honour, BArch with highest honour, Auburn University, 1974; MArch with highest honour, University of Illinois. *Appointments:* Instructor, Auburn University, 1974-75; Assistant Professor, Georgia Institute of Technology, 1976-79; Designer, Environmental Planning and Research, San Francisco, California, 1979-80; Designer, Genster and Associates, San Francisco, 1980-81; Designer, Gruzen Partnership, Instructor, CCAC, San Francisco, 1981-82; Associate Professor, Oklahoma State University, 1982-87; Architect, ELS Architects, Berkeley, California, 1987-. *Publications:* Firmitas, Utilitas, Venustas: Architecture and Society (with David Hanser); The Sketch Problem, 1986. *Memberships:* NCARB; American Institute of Architecture; Treasurer, NCOC-AIA, 1986-87. *Honours:* Phi Kappa Phi, 1973; Senior Achievement Award, Phi Beta Kappa, Auburn University, 1974; Alpha Rho Chi, Auburn, 1974; President's Award, Auburn, 1974; American Institute of Architecture Award, Auburn, 1975; Creative and Performing Arts Fellowship, University of Illinois, 1975; Halliburton Excellent Young Teacher, CEAT, Oklahoma State University, 1986. *Hobbies:* Travel with sketch books and journals; Reading. *Address:* 259 Page Street, San Francisco, CA 94102, USA.

MORGAN Helen Gertrude Louise, b. 11 Apr. 1921, Ilford, Essex, England. Author. m. Tudor Meredydd Morgan, 1954, 3 daughters. *Education:* Royal Normal College for the Blind, 1938-42. *Publications:* The Little Old Lady, 1961; Meet Mary Kate, 1963; Tales of Tigg's Farm, 1963; A Mouthful of Magic, 1963; The Tailor, the Sailor & the Small Black Cat, 1964; Two in the Garden, Two in the House, Two on the Farm, Two by the Sea, 1964-67; A Dream of Dragons, 1965; Satchkin Patchkin, 1966; Mary Kate & the Jumble Bear, 1967; Mrs Pinny & the Blowing Day, 1968; Mrs Pinny & the Sudden Snow, 1969; Mary Kate & the School Bus, 1970;

Mother Farthing's Luck, 1971; Mrs Pinny & the Salty Sea Day, 1972; The Sketch Book Crime, 1980; Contributions to journals and magazines. *Memberships:* Society of Authors. *Hobbies include:* Reading. *Address:* c/o Barclays Bank, Calverley Road, Tunbridge Wells, Kent, England.

MORGAN Lila, Public Relations Executive/Consultant. *Education:* Scholarships, University of California, Los Angeles, 1966; Royal Academy of Dramatic Arts, London, England, 1967. *Appointments:* Administrative/Operations Manager, Arizona, 1966-71; Legal Administrative Assistant, California, 1971-72; Charter Tour Director, C & L Services, California, 1972-84; Traffic Manager/Secretary, Board of Directors, LUCX, Inc, LUC Leasing, Inc, California, 1972-79; Property/Operations Manager, J. Allen Radford Co and College Park Realty Co, California, 1979-80; Management Consultant/Partner, C & L Office Efficiency Services, California, 1980-83; Marketing Director/Operations Manager, CMS/Robinson Insurance Brokers, Inc., Corner Arcades, Inc., Jewelart, Inc, DNB Manufacturing, Inc/Riffler Services, Co., California, 1980-82; Management Consultant/Executive Recruiter, Corporate Management Services Inc, California, 1982-84; Executive Manager, Reseda Chamber of Commerce, California, 1983-84; Director of International Development, Sephardic Educational Center, California, 1984-85; Magazine Journalist, The Golden Chef Magazine, California, 1985-86; Newspaper Columnist, Coast Media Newspapers, California, 1985-86; Chamber of Commerce Consultant, within California, 1983-; Executive Director, Greater Rancho Park Chamber of Commerce, California, 1985-87; Newspaper Editor/Publisher, The Rancho Round-up Newspaper, California, 1986-; Public Relations Executive/Consultant, Kress-Morgan & Associates, California, 1978-. *Memberships:* Affiliated to: Executive Vice President/General Manager, Hawthorne Chamber of Commerce, California, 1988-; National Federation of Press Women, Inc; California Association of Chamber of Commerce Executives; Women in Management; National Association of Women Business Owners; The National Notary Association; Public Relations Chair, California Federation of Business & Professional Women, 1988-89; 1st Vice President, California Press Women, Los Angeles District, 1987-89; 2nd Vice President, Public Relations, Memberships Expansion Chairs, California Federation of BPW, Los Angeles District, 1985-89; Association of Westside Chambers of Commerce, 1985-87; President, Vice President, Legislative & Program Chairs, Culver City Business & Professional Women, 1981-88; Los Angeles County Commission on the Status of Women, 1984. *Honours include:* Culver City Business & Professional Women, 1986; Los Angeles County Supervisor Michael D Antonovich, 1985; California Republican Assembly, 1984, etc. *Address:* 904 W. Huntington Drive No. 8, Arcadia, California 91006, USA

MORGAN Marabel, b. 25 June 1937 Crestline, Ohio, USA. Author. m. Charles O. Morgan Jr, 25 June 1964, 2 daughters. *Education:* Ohio State University. *Appointments:* President, Total Woman Inc, Miami, 1970-; Public speaker. *Publications:* Total Woman, 1973, Total Joy, 1976; Total Woman Cookbook, 1980; Electric Woman, 1985. *Address:* c/o Total Woman Inc, 1300 NW 167th Street, Miami, Florida 33169, USA.

MORGAN Marion Nora Eluned, b. 21 June 1942, Woodford Green, Essex, England. Ecumenical worker. *Education:* BA (Hons), Bristol University, 1971-74; Diploma in Pastoral Theology, Heythrop College, 1974-75. *Appointments:* Ministry of Pensions and National Insurance and Department of Health and Social Security, 1960-71; Executive Secretary, Bristol Council of Christian Churches, now known as Greater Bristol Ecumenical Council, 1980-. *Publications:* Will You Walk a Little Faster? (with Rupert Davies), 1984; Prayer for Our Time, 1986. *Membership:* Catholic Theological Association. *Hobbies:* Music, singing and piano; Foreign travel. *Address:* 4 Dover Place, Clifton, Bristol BS8 1AL, England.

MORGAN Mary Holliday (Reverend), b. 11 Mar. 1912, Summerton, South Carolina, USA. Retired Elementary Teacher; Minister of Religion; m. Rev. Clifton Morgan, 7 Sept. 1940, 2 adopted daughters. *Education:* BA, South Carolina State College, 1951; MA, Religion, Bale State University, 1975; MA, Religion, Christian Education, Anderson University School of Theology, 1979. *Appointments:* South Carolina Elementary Schools, 1935- 40; Missionary to India, 1960-70; Working with school for our Church and other organizations, 1970-82; Teacher, Anderson Communities Schools. *Publications:* Small book: The Christian's Defence-Faith, Fasting, Prayer; Thesis: The growth and development of the Church of God Sunday School, USA. *Memberships:* Women Minister's Fellowship; West Middlesex, Pennsylvania, Sec Ladies Aux; Chaplain, NAACP; Board of Directors, CCV, Citizens of Communities Values; Board of Directors, YWCA, Membership Comm Member. *Honours:* Sunshine Award, 1982; Meadowbrook School Faithful Christian Service to Community and Church, 1971-78; Award for Years of Youth, MSPTO, 1978; NAACP Ladies Aux Award, Love and Work, 1987; Faithful Service to the Church of God Award, Ohio State, 1985; Award, Ladies Aux, 1986; Certificate for help, Church of God, East Africa; Certificate to Christian Ministry, 1984. *Hobbies:* World travel; Reading. *Address:* 2011 Arrow Ave, P O Box 2041, Anderson, Indiana 46018, USA.

MORGAN Natasha, b. 8 Nov. 1945, London, England. Actress; Writer; Theatre Director. *Education:* BA, English, St Hughs College, Oxford, 1967. *Appointments:* OUDS, Oxford; Northcote Theatre; The Women's Theatre Company; the People Show; Shoulder to Shoulder; Glittering Prizes; Beyond the Pale BBC TV; That's Not It, Theatre Company, 1980-86; Gertrude Stein and A Companion, England, Australia & USA; The House Of Bernardo Alba, The Globe Theatre, 1987. *Publications:* Plays for Theatre: Room; Mothers Arms; By George; Ariadne's Afternoon; An Independent Woman. *Honours:* Writers Award for By George, Arts Council of Great Britain, 1982, and An Independent Woman, 1984. *Address:* That's Not It Theatre Company, 5 Arminger Road, London W12 7BA, England.

MORGAN Sharon Haf, b. 29 Aug. 1949, Wales. Actress. 1 son. *Education:* 2nd Class Honours Degree, History, University College of Wales, Cardiff, 1970. *Appointments:* Arts Council Training Scheme, Cwmni Theatr Cymru, 1970-71; Theatre work, Caricature Theatre Company; Cambian Theatre Company; Cardiff Open Air Theatre; Casson Studio Theatre; Became Associate Actress with Cwmni Theatre Cymru, 1974-76; Founder Member, Theatre Bara Caws, 1977; Theatr Hwylg Fglag, 1982; Theatr Clwyd, 1977 70; Under Mllk Wood, Mayfair Theatre, London; TV work includes: Grand Slam, BBC Wales, 1978; Thomas and Sarah, LWT, 1979; Henry IV Part 1, BBC, 1979; Versweworse and Baby Grand, BBC Wales, 1979; Lloyd George, BBC Wales, 1980; Coronation Street Granada; Nye, BBC Wales, 1981; The Gentle Touch, LWT, 1982; The Citadel, BBC, 1982; Never the Twain, Thames, 1983; The Magnificent Evans, BBC, 6 episodes Sitcom series; many programmes in Welsh; Tour, House of America, The Company, 1987-88; Radio work,etc. *Membership:* Equity. *Hobbies:* Reading; Music. *Address:* 80, Plasturton Avenue, Pontcanna, Cardiff, Wales.

MORGENTHAL Becky Holz, b. 5 Aug. 1947, Altadena, USA. Businesswoman. m. Roger M. Morgenthal, 12 Aug. 1972. *Education:* AA, Goldey Beacon College, 1967; Continuing Education, Wilson College, 1986-. *Appointments:* Clerk, Hercules inc., 1969-71; Accountant, Beth Products, Lebanon, 1971-72; Administrative Assistant, Legal Services, Carlisle, 1973-76; Office Manager, Cemi Corp, 1976-77; Accountant, Tressler Luth Svcs., 1978-79; Accountant, Benatec Associates, 1979-80; Financial Analyst, Electronic Data Systems, 1983-87; Owner, BHM Busienss Services, 1982- *Memberships:* President, Carlisle Junior Civic Club, 1979-80; Active Diocese of Harrisburg, 1985-88. *Hobbies:* Riding; Flying; Cooking. *Address:* 1311 Windsor Court, Carlisle, PA 17013, USA.

MORIMOTO Akiko Charlene, b. 2 May 1948, Los Angeles, California, USA. Teacher. *Education:* BA, California State University, 1971. *Appointments:* Los Angeles Unified School District, 1972-77; Vista Unified School District, 1977-; Consultant, San Diego Area Writing Project, 1981-; Instructor, University of California, San Diego, 1983-85. *Publications:* Contributor: A Syllabus for Art Education, Ronald Silverman, 1972; Learning About Art, 1981; Editor, Visions of our Youth, 1986, 1987. *Memberships:* Greater San Diego, National Councils of Teachers of English; Association of San Diego Educators of the Gifted; California Association of the Gifted; California Reading Association. *Honours:* Recipient, various honours and awards. *Hobbies:* Theatre; Arts; Graphic Arts. *Address:* 704 C-6 Regal Road, Encinitas, CA 92024, USA.

MORITZ Amy, b. 9 Nov. 1958, Pittsburgh, Pennsylvania, USA. Director of Public Policy Foundation. *Education:* Economics, University of Maryland at College Park, 1977-81. *Appointments:* Reagan-Bush for President, 1980; Western Gools Foundation, 1980-81; Deputy Director, College Republican National Committee, 1981-82; Executive Director, The National Center for Public Policy Research, Washington DC, 1982-. *Publications:* Articles in professional journals; Editor, Liberation Bulletin, National Policy Watch, and Liberty Letter, foreign affairs newsletters; Several public policy papers published by private foundations; Other newsletters and articles. *Memberships:* Council on National Policy; Board Chairman, The Liberty Institute Inc; Board of Trustees, The National Center for Public Policy Research; Board of Directors, American Freedom Institute; Various other Boards of Directors and Advisors. *Honour:* William Paca Award, Maryland Republican Party, 1978. *Hobbies:* History; Foreign affairs; Skiing; Travel. *Address:* 300 Eye Street NW, Suite 3, Washington, DC 20002, USA.

MORLEY Barbara Jane, b. 14 Oct. 1946, Cleveland, Ohio, USA. Neurochemist; Senior Staff Scientist; Professor. m. Edward H. Patterson, 19 July 1985. *Education:* BA, MacMurray College, Jacksonville, Illinois, 1968; PhD, University of Maine, Orono, 1973; Postdoctoral Fellow, University of Alabama Medical School. *Appointments:* Assistant Professor, University of Alabama Medical School, 1978-80; Associate Professor, 1980-85, Professor, 1985-, Creighton University Medical School; Staff Scientist, Boys Town National Institute, Omaha, Nebraska, 1980-. *Publications:* 44 articles in scientific journals; 5 book chapters. *Memberships:* American Association for the Advancement of Science; Sigma Xi; Phi Kappa Phi; Psi Chi; Society for Neuroscience; New York Academy of Sciences. *Honours:* Nellie Beatrice Yarman Scholarship for Academic Excellence, 1966-68. *Address:* 555 North 30th Street, Boys Town National Institute, Omaha, NE 68131, USA.

MORREAU Jacqueline Carol, b. 18 Oct. 1929, Milwaukee, Wisconsin, USA. Artist; Author; Lecturer. m. Patrick Morreau, 31 Oct. 1959, 2 sons, 2 daughters. *Education:* Studied Art at Chouinard Art Institute and with Rico Lebrun, Jepson Art Institute; Diploma in Medical Illustration, University of California Medical School, San Francisco, 1958. *Career:* 1st exhibited, Frank Perls Gallery, Beverly Hills, California, 1951; Major exhibitions: Women's Images of Men (also co-organiser and spokeswoman), Institute of Contemporary Arts, and tour; Power Plays, 1983-84; Pandora's Box, 1984; Jacqueline Morreau: Myth and Metaphor touring show, 1988-89. *Creative works:* Major works: Children's Crusade, 1980-81; Persephone: A Season in Hell, 1983; Lessons of History, 1987-88; Publications: Women's Images of Men (with Sarah Kent), 1985, Revised Edition, 1989; Jacqueline Morreau: Drawing and Graphics, 1986; Jacqueline Morreau: Myth, History and the Construction of Gender, 1988. *Honours:* Purchase Award, Arts Council of Great Britain, 1983; Greater London Arts, 1987. *Hobbies:* Mythological studies; Travel; Music. *Address:* c/o Odette Gilbert Gallery, 5 Cork Street, London W1, England.

MORRIS Anne G., b. 12 Aug. 1938, Cleveland, Ohio, USA. Director, Centre for Logistics & Transportation. *Education:* BS, Ohio State University, 1960; MA, Columbia University, 1970; PhD, Fordham University, 1977. *Appointments:* Policy Analyst, US Department of Transportation, 1979-81; Committee to Re-Elect Senator Moynihan, 1982; Field Director & Senior Researcher, New York State Department of Education Evaluation, 1983; Director, Centre for Logistics & Transportation, Graduate School & University Centre, City University, New York (CUNY), 1984-. *Memberships:* Council of Logistics Management, Consumer Advisory Board, Taxi & Limousine Committee, NYC; Co-Chair & Founder, Taxi Educators Workshop. *Hobbies:* Art; Film. *Address:* Centre for Logistics & Transportation, Graduate Centre, CUNY, 33 West 42nd Street, New York, NY 10036, USA.

MORRIS Janet Ellen, b. 25 May 1946, Boston, Massachusetts, USA. Novelist; Author; Editor. m. Christopher Crosby Morris, 31 Oct. 1970. *Publications:* High Couch of Silistra, 1976; Golden Sword, 1977; Wind from the Abyss, 1978; Carnelian Throne, 1979; Dream Dancer, 1980, 1981; Cruiser Dreams; Earth Dreams, 1982; I, The Sun, 1983, 1984; Beyond Sanctuary, 1984; Active Measures, 1984; Beyond the Veil, 1985; Beyond Wizardwall, 1986; Warlord!, 1987. With Chris Morris: The Forty Minute War, 1985; MEDUSA, 1986, 1987; The Little Helliad, 1987; Outpassage, 1988. Editor, Heroes in Hell; Rebels in Hell; Crusaders in Hell; Angels in Hell; Masters in Hell; War in Hell; Prophets in Hell; Afterwar, 1985. Co-author with David Drake, Kill Ratio; Target, with C J Cherryh, Gates of Hell, Kings in Hell. *Memberships:* Science Fiction Writers of America; (Pseudonymously) Mystery Writers Guild; National Intelligence Study Center; BMI; AAAS; Planetary Society. *Honours:* Hellva Award for Best Novel, 1985, Forty Minute War (with Chris Morris); 3ditor, Afterwar, 1985, one of LOCUS 10 Best of Year; editor of Rebels in Hell, a story from which won the 1987 Hugo Award; Heroes in Hell was one of five Nebula Award Finalists, 1987; Selected for the Rolex/Yacht Fiction Program. *Hobbies:* 2nd Millenium BC; Philosophical problems of space and time; Aerospace development programmes; Foreign intelligence issues with concentration on Near East/South Asia. *Address:* c/o Perry Knowlton, Curtis Brown Ltd, 10 Astor Place, New York, NY 10003, USA.

MORRIS Jean, b. 15 Jan. 1924, Sevenoaks, Kent, England. Author; Dramatist. 1 daughter. *Education:* BA (Hons), London, 1960. *Creative works:* Television and radio drama; Adult novels; Children's novels; Crime novels under pseudonym Kenneth O'Hara. *Hobby:* Sussex local history research. *Address:* Flat 1, 56 Pevensey Road, Eastbourne, BN21 3HT.

MORRIS Jill, b. 25 June 1931, New York, USA. Psychoanalyst. *Education:* BA, MA, English, New York University; Certified Psychoanalyst, Center for Modern Psychoanalytic Studies, New York City, 1981; PhD, California Graduate Institute, 1981. *Appointments:* Woman's Editor and/or Feature Writer, Steelways, US Camera, Image, Scholastic Roto, Pageant, Camera 35, and Mademoiselle, 1959-68; Painter, 1968-; Self-employed in Private Practice of Psychoanalysis, 1976-; Instructor, Creativity and the Unconscious, Cooper Union, 1984-; Adjunct Professor, Dreamwork, New York University, 1987-. *Publications:* Creative Breakthroughs, forthcoming; The Dream Workbook, 1985, also in paperback, also Netherlands, Italy, Denmark, Sweden editions; Feature articles in national magazines including Good Housekeeping. *Memberships:* National Accreditation Association of Psychoanalysts; American Examining Board of Psychoanalysis; Center for Modern Psychoanalysis Alumni Association; Association for Humanistic Psychology. *Hobbies:* Painting; Writing; Reading; Collecting antiques; Theatre; Concerts; Travel. *Address:* New York City, New York, USA.

MORRIS Katharine, Novelist. *Publications:* Novels: New Harrowing; Country Dance; The Vixens Cub; The House by the Water; The Long Meadow. *Memberships:* International PEN; English Speaking Union. *Hobbies:*

Sculpture; The French Language; Music. *Address:* Little Dower House, Bleasby, Nottingham, NG14 7FX, England.

MORRIS Miranda Sexton, b. 17 Sept. 1957, Georgia, USA. Account Executive. divorced, 1 son. *Education:* BA, University of Kentucky, 1979. *Appointments:* Spa Technician, Assistant Manager, 21st Century Health Spa, 1981; Staff Counsellor, Physicians Weight Loss Centre, 1981; Sales Rep., Lou. Automobile Club, 1982; Assistant Manager, Lerner Shops Inc., 1982; Assistant Director, Funskool & Gagel Ebm, 1983-; Kindergarten Teacher, 1984; Sales Rep., Columbia Sussex Corp, 1984-86; Account Executive, Naegele Outdoor Advertising, 1986-. *Memberships:* various organisations. *Honours:* Recipient, various honours & awards. *Hobbies:* Jogging; Piano. *Address:* 10801 Cherry Grove Court, Louisville, KY 40299, USA.

MORRIS-YAMBA Trish, b. 9 Jan. 1943, Binghamton, New York, USA. Day Centre Director. m. A. Zachary Yamba, 11 Apr. 1987, 1 son, 3 daughters. *Education:* BA, Livingston College, New Jersey, 1973; MEd, Rutgers University, New Jersey, 1974. *Appointments:* Executive Director, The Chen School, Newark, New Jersey, 1973-81; Executive Director, Newark Day Center, 1981-. *Publications:* Booklet: Educational Survival Techniques. *Memberships:* President, National Political Congress of Black Women, Metro-Newark; President, TRZ Associates Inc; President, Federation of Youth Services Inc; WISE Women's Advisory Board, Essex County College. *Honours:* Black Achiever, 1980; Professional Woman of the Year Award, 1982; Community Leadership Award, 1985; Outstanding Child Care Advocate Award, 1988; Jerseyan of the Week Award, 1988; Community Service Award, 1989. *Interests:* Working with youth and the elderly; Community work; Women's issues; The arts. *Hobby:* Music. *Address:* Newark Day Center, 43 Hill Street, Newark, NJ 07102, USA.

MORRISON Debra Lynn, b. 26 Mar. 1956, Mercer, Pennsylvania, USA. Certified Financial Planner. *Education:* BS, Bus Admin, Messiah College, Grantham, PA, 1974-78; Certified Financial Planner Designation, College for Financial Planning, Denver, Colorado, 1987-88. *Appointments:* Claims Adjuster, Nationwide Ins, 1978-; Special Rep, 1978, Insurance/Investment Consultant 1979-80, John Hancock Companies; Director of Tax Advantaged Investments, Manzi & Assoc, 1980-86; Certified Financial Planner, The Financial Network, 1986-87; Certified Financial Planner, Stockbroker and General Securities Principal, Financial Roadmaps, Inc., 1989-. *Memberships:* French Creek Baptist Youth Association, President; Messiah College Senior Class President; New Jersey Leaders Association; Million Dollar Round Table; Passaic-Bergen Life Underwriters Association, Vice Pres Membership & Education, President; National Association of Life Underwriters; International Association for Financial Planning, Inc; National Association for Female Executives. *Honours:* Junior Associate of the Year 1979, 100% Persistency Award 1979, President's Honor Club 1979-85, John Hancock; Life Underwriter of the Year, Passaic/Bergen Life Underwriters Association, 1985; Lincoln National President's Club 1987, Cabinet 1988; Admitted to The Registry of Financial Planning Practitioners, 1988. *Hobbies:* Racquetball; Water and snow skiing; Volunteer service with Special Olympics, New Jersey; Make-A-Wish Foundation. *Address:* 11 Yearling Trail, Hewitt, NJ 07421, USA.

MORRISON Kerry, b. 15 May 1959, New Zealand. Environmental Consultant. *Education:* BA, Geography, University of New South Wales; Diploma of Environmental Studies, Macquarie University, Sydney. *Appointments:* Assistant Geographer, currently Senior Environmental Planner, Dames & Moore, 1981-. *Memberships:* Institute of Australian Geographers; International Association for Impact Assessment; Australian Conservation Foundation. *Interests:* Environmental Management and Conservation; Public participation in Decision making. *Address:* 23 Probert Street, Camperdown, Sydney, NSW 2050, Australia.

MORRISON Lillian, b. 27 Oct. 1917, Jersey City, USA. Poet; Anthologist; Editor. *Education:* BS, Douglass College, Reutgers University, 1938; BS, Library Service, Columbia University Graduate School, 1942. *Appointments:* Librarian, New York Public Library, 1942-47; Vocational High School Specialist, 1947-52; Assistant Co-ordinator, YA Services, 1952-68, Coordinator 1968-82; General Editor, Crowell Poets Series, & Poems of the World Series, 1963-74. *Publications:* Poetry: The Ghosts of Jersey City, 1967; Miranda's Music, with J. Boudin, 1968; The Sidewalk Racer, 1977; Who Would Marry a Mineral?, 1978; Overheard in a Bubble Chamber, 1981; The Break Dance Kids, 1985; Anthologies: Yours Till Niagara Falls, 1950; Black Within and Red Without, 1953; A Diller, A Dollar, 1955; Touch Blue, 1958; Remember Me When This You See, 1961; Sprints & Distances, 1965; Best Wishes, Amen, 1974; Rhythm Road, 1988; articles in various journals. *Memberships:* Poetry Society of America; Authors Guild; PEN. *Honours:* Phi Beta Kappa; Grolier Award, American Library Association, 1987. *Hobbies Include:* Sports; Reading; Films; Dance; Music; Language. *Address:* 116 Pinehurst Ave., New York, NY 10033, USA.

MORRISON Mable Renee, b. 22 May, 1935, Tunica, Louisiana, USA. Educator. *Education:* BS, Xavier University of NO, Louisiana, 1958; Master of Music Degree, DePaul University of Chicago, Illinois, 1960. *Appointments:* Delaware State College, Dover, Delaware, 1962-, currently Associate Professor, 1988-. *Creative works:* Performed piano recitals in Pennsylvania, Delaware, Ohio, Illinois, Louisiana, USA, Liberia and Sierre Leone, West Africa, 1973. *Memberships:* National Music Teachers Association; National Piano Teachers Guild; Mu Phi Epsilon, International Professional Sorority; Alpha Kappa Alpha Sorority. *Honours:* Certificate, L'Academie Internationale D'Ete, Nice, France, 1962; Government of France Grantee, 1962; Certificate, National Music Teachers Association; US Intercultural Grant for performance in Sierre Leone, West Africa; B Sharp Music Club scholar; Louisiana Weekly Educational Fund Scholar. *Hobbies:* Reading; Travelling; Meeting people; Helping community causes. *Address:* Delaware State College, Box 63, Dover, Delaware 19901, USA.

MORROW Nancy Susan, b. 18 Dec. 1961, Lewisburg, Pennsylvania, USA. Physiological Psychologist, researcher/teacher. *Education:* BS, Juniata College, 1983; MS 1986, PhD 1988, Kansas State University. *Appointments:* Research Assistant 1985-88; Instructor in Psychology, 1987-88. *Publications:* Numerous research publications in professional journals. *Memberships:* Society for Neuroscience; American Psychological Association. *Honour:* 1st prize, Graduate Research at 6th Annual Kansas Students' Contributions to Psychology Convention and Paper Convention, 1986. *Hobbies:* Cooking; Photography. *Address:* Department of Psychology, Bluemont Hall, Kansas State University, Manhattan, KS 66506, USA.

MORSE Carmel Lei (Lindgren), b. 15 June 1953, Spokane, Washington, USA. Film Maker; Author. m. Scott Morse, 21 June 1980, 1 daughter. *Education:* BFA, magna cum laude, Motion Picture Production, Wright State University, Ohio, 1979; *Appointment:* General manager, Brookline Visual Arts Services Inc, 1983-. *Creative work:* Book, Audio-Visual Primer; Screenplay, Murder is a Negative Act; Producer, director, various short films & commercials. *Honours include:* Nominee, Danforth graduate scholarship, 1979. *Address:* 130 Watervliet Avenue, Dayton, Ohio 45420, USA.

MORSE Hazel, b. 19 June 1937, Bar Harbor, Maine, USA. Business Consultant. 2 sons, 1 daughter. *Education:* Broward Community College, 1969; Certificate, Real Estate, University of Connecticut, 1979; BBA, Nova University, 1986; Registered Stockbroker, Securities Exchange Examination, 1987; Diploma, Travel Industry, ACT Travel School, 1988. *Appointments:* Office Manager 1968-70, club receptionist 1970-71, accountant 1971-75, Fort Lauderdale, Florida; Admissions Supervisor, Nova University, 1975-79; Film actress 5 films, 1978-; Billing Registrar, health maintenance organisation, Connecticut, 1979-80; Internal Auditor, Hotel, Fort Lauderdale, 1980-82; Payroll Coordinator, North Broward Medical Centre, Pompano Beach, 1982-87; Print-ad model, brochures, newspaper, 1984-; Mutuals Cashier, Pompano Race Track, 1986-; Stockbroker, 1st Investors Corporation, Fort Lauderdale, 1987; Business Consultant, 1988-. *Memberships include:* Offices, past/present: Nova University Alumni Association, North Broward Medical Centre, Fort Lauderdale Republican Party, United Way; Mensa; National Association of Female Executives. *Hobbies:* Reading; Stock Market; Research; Modelling; Films. *Address:* 1111 Northeast 30th Drive, Fort Lauderdale, Florida 33334, USA.

MORSE Marie Rudisill, b. 2 Dec. 1927, Birmingham, Alabama, USA. Political Director. m. William Allen Morse, 6 Apr. 1955. 2 sons. *Education:* BS, Florida State University, 1949; Law School, University of Miami, Florida, 1953-55; San Jose (CA) State University, 1978-79. *Appointments:* Teacher, Public Schools in Georgia and Florida, 1950-57; President, Morse Decorating, San Francisco, 1970-73; Assistant to Treasurer, Carter/Mondale Campaign, Washington, 1979-80; Director of Corporate Development, Broward Federal Savings & Loan, Sunrise, Florida, 1982; Fundraising Coordinator, Mondale for President, Washington, 1983; Finance Director, Exon for Senate, Washington, 1983-84; Dixon for Senate Committee, Washington, 1985-87; Sam Beard for US Senate, Wilmington, 1987-88; Political Director, National Women's Political Caucus, Washington, 1988-. *Memberships:* Secretary/Acting Director, South Florida Crippled Children's Clinic, Ft Lauderdale, 1960-64; Board of Directors, Broward County Girl Scouts of America, Ft Lauderdale; Board Member, Chairman of the Promenade, Beaux Arts of Ft Lauderdale Museum of the Arts, 1962-72. *Honour:* Woman of the Year, Beaux Arts of Ft Lauderdale Museum of the Arts, 1967. *Hobbies:* Aerobics; Running. *Address:* 3321 N Street NW, Washington, DC 20007, USA.

MORTMAN-FRIEDMAN Beth-Lynn, b. 17 Dec. 1950, New Jersey, USA. Graphic Designer; Art Director; Art Teacher, Special Education. 1 daughter. *Education:* AAS, Queensborough Community College; Hofstra University; New York University; BS, Buffalo State College; MS, Pratt Institute. *Appointments include:* Student teacher/teacher: Cerebral Palsy Association, Buffalo, New York, 1972-74; Albert Einstein Medical Centre, Bronx, 1977-78; Human Resources School, Albertson, & Great Neck School District, Long Island, 1974-75; Lowell School, Queens, New York, 1978-82; Nassau BOCES, Long Island, 1982-. Also commercial work: Mercury Neon Signs Inc, & Time, Space & Light Art Galery, NYC, 1968-72; Transhigh Corporation, NYC, 1975-76; Visual Persuasion Studio (own studio), 1981-. *Creative work includes:* Master's thesis, Artists For Sale, publication pending; Graphic design work, numerous magazines & journals. *Memberships:* American Institute of Graphic Artists; New York State Teachers Association; Graphic Artists Guild; Alumni Association, State University of New York, Buffalo. *Honours include:* Various awards, paintings; Award-winning students, Lowell School, 1978-82; Biographical recognitions. *Hobbies:* Abstract art painting; Dancing; Music; Body Building; Children; Travel; Reading; Theatre. *Address:* c/o Visual Persuasion Studio, Jericho, New York 11753, USA.

MORTON-ROBINSON Shelley Annette, b. 4 June 1960, Missoula, USA. Director. m. Josh Robinson, 2 Nov. 1985, 1 son, 1 daughter. *Education:* BA, University of Montana, 1982. *Appointments:* Teacher, Kake, 1982-83; Teacher, Missoula, 1983-84; Consultant, Chisholm, 1984-86; Director, Facility for Developmentally Disabled

Adults, 1987-. *Publication:* Positive Parenting Programme, co-author. *Memberships:* Psi Chi, Life Member; AAUW, Cherperson, Clinic Organisation. *Honours:* Scholar/Athlete Award, NE Region, 1980; Dean's List, 1982; High Honours Graduate, 1982. *Hobbies:* Reading; Skiing; Knitting. *Address:* 820 17th Ave. NW, Grand Rapids, MN 55744, USA.

MORYADAS Virginia Hill, b.28 Nov 1937, New York, New York, USA. Realtor; Instructor. m. 17 Sept 1962, 2 sons, 1 daughter. *Education:* BA, University of Maryland, 1959; MURP, George Washington University, 1974; PhD, Candidate in Geography, University of Maryland. *Appointments:* Planner, Prince George's County, Maryland, 1969-76; Planner, Southern Maryland Health Systems Agency and Prince George's County, Office of Comprehensive Health Planning, 1976-77; Consultant, Medical Service Consultants, Inc, 1978-79; Independent Consultant and Realtor 1977-81; Realtor and Associate Broker 1981-. *Memberships:* Prince George's Board of Realtors, Director 1984-86; Maryland Association of Realtors, Director 1986; Health Plus, an HMO Corporate Secretary, 1980-84; Greenbelt Homes Inc, Director, 1976-82. *Hobbies:* Hiking; Reading. *Address:* 11-J Ridge Road, Greenbelt, MD 20770. USA.

MOSER Sarah Gunning, b. 17 Sept. 1953, Seattle, USA. Business Owner; Engineer. m. Lawrence Herman Moser, 18 May 1985, 1 daughter. *Education:* BA, Evergreen State College, 1975. *Appointments:* Clerk, Assistant Department Manager, Safeway Corp, Seattle, 1977-79; Manufacturing Engineer, Boeing Co., 1980-82; Manufacturing Engineer, Senior Manufacturing Engineer, McDonnell Douglas Helicopter Co., Mesa, 1982-87; Co-Owner, Custom Services, Tempe, 1985-87; Co-Founder, Moser Design Associates, 1988-. *Publications:* Songs: Feelin All Right Again, 1973; Winged Victories, 1977; Song for Carla, 1980; Love's Pure Light, 1983. *Memberships:* National Association of Female Executives; International Executive Development; American Institute of Aeronautics & Astronautics; Society of Manufacturing Engineers. *Honours Include:* Campaign Manager, Bellevue, City Council Race, 1970; Soloist, Unity Chuch of Truth, Seattle, 1978-82. *Hobbies:* Singing; Organic Gardening; World Peace. *Address:* 14105 SW 240th Street, Vashon, WA 98070, USA.

MOSS Kathleen Susan, b. 21 Dec. 1950, Washington DC, USA. Attorney. m. Dale Thomas Moss, 1 Jan. 1980, 1 son. *Education:* BS, Genetics, University of California, Berkeley, 1971; MA, George Washington University, 1978; English law studies, University of Virginia, 1978; JD, George Mason University School of Law, 1978; Polish law, American University, Warsaw, 1979. *Appointments:* Scientific research, George Washington University, 1971-75; Law Clerk, 1976; Attorney Adviser, Food & Drug Administration, 1976-79; Associate, Cotten, Day & Doyle 1971-80, Bernard & Brown PC 1980-81; Patent Examiner, US Patent Office, 1981-85; Freelance Patent Prosecution, firms in Washington DC, 1985-87; Patent Attorney, US Navy, 1987-; Patent A Horney, University of California, 1988-. *Publications:* Various scientific research articles, 1974-78. *Memberships:* DC Bar; US Patent Bar. *Hobbies:* Piano; Drawing. *Address:* c/o Dr Janet McCowin, 285 32nd Avenue, San Francisco, California 94121, USA.

MOSS Rose, b. 2 Jan. 1937, Johannesburg, South Africa. Management Consultant; Writer. m. Stanley Felix Moss, 30 Apr. 1964, 1 son. *Education:* BA, University of Witwatersrand, 1957; BA, Honours, English, University of Natal, 1959; MBA, Honours, Boston University, USA, 1983. *Appointments:* Wellesley College, 1972-82; Cambridge Meridien Group, 1983; Synectics Inc., 1984-87; Rose Moss Associates, 1987-. *Publications:* The Terrorist/The Schoolmaster, 1979; The Family Reunion, 1974. *Membership:* PEN. *Honours:* Various honours including: Mellon Fellow, 1980; Quill Prize, Massachussets Review; Phelps Stokes Scholar, 1988. *Address:* 580 Walnut St., Newtonville, MA 02160, USA.

MOTTER (Roberta L) Robbie, b. 8 Mar. 1936, Honolulu, Hawaii, USA. Businesswoman. divorced. 1 son, 2 daughters. *Education:* Personnel Management Course, Cornell University, 1956; Informationa Management, George Washington University. *Appointments:* Director of Personnel, Hawaiian Village Hotel, Honolulu, 1956-59; Office Manager, Fisher Construction Company, Honolulu, 1960-61; Paymaster Computer Specialist, Gate City Steel, Omaha, Nebraska, 1961-64; Accounts Receivable Supervisor, Mayflower Hotel, Washington, 1966-67; Computer Specialist and Personnel Director, Alan M Voorhees & Associates, Mclean, Virginia, 1968-71; Administrative Manager, Planning Research Company Computer Center, 1972-73; Conversion Specialist, Accounts Payable, Meenco, Inc, Houston, 1973-74; Personnel Director and Office Manager, Summit Insurance Company of New York, Houston, 1974-75; Director of Administrative Services, New York State Insurance Department Liquidation Bureau, New York, 1975-80; Supervisory Procurement Analyst, General Services Administration, Arlington, 1980-84; President, Contacts Unlimited, Inc, 1985-. *Memberships:* Women in Information Processing, American Society of Personnel Administrators; Administrative Management Society; Washington DC Purchasing Management Association; International Platform Association, Hawaii State Society; National Association of Professional Saleswomen, Sacramento Chapter; Community Entrepreneurs Organization, Sacramento; Sacramento Womens Network; Sacramento Valley Marketing Association; National Procurement Management Association; Sales Marketing Services Association. *Honours:* Featured in New York Metropolitan Magazine, 1976; Woman of the Year, Delta Kappa Chapter of Beta Sigma Phi, 1979, 1981; Xi Gamma Beta Chapter, 1985; Xi Gamma Alpha Chapter, 1986, etc. *Address:* 9198 Greenback Ln, Ste 116, Orangevale, CA 95662, USA.

MOTZ Annabelle, b. 13 June 1920, Milwaukee, USA. Professor Emerita. m. Joseph Motz, 25 Mar. 1945, divorced 1978, 1 son, 1 daughter, (2) Joseph Blum, 24 June 1984. *Education:* BS, 1941; MA, 1943; PhD, 1950. *Appointments:* Scholar in Residence, USACE, 1977-78; Director, Institute in Sociology for Secondary School Social Science Teachers; Visiting Scholar, Environmental Protection Service, Israel, 1981-82. *Publications:* Social Research for Policy Decisions, co-author, 1980; numerous articles in professional journals. *Memberships:* American Sociological Association; DC Sociological Associaiton; AKD; Sigma Xi; AAAS. *Honours:* Recipient, various grants and honours. *Hobbies:* Reading; Volunteer Work; Travel. *Address:* Dept. of Sociology, American University, Washington, DC 20016, USA.

MOULD Daphne Desiree Charlotte Pochin, b. 15 Nov. 1920, Salisbury, England. Author. *Education:* BSc 1st class honours, Geology, 1943; PhD Geology 1946, Edinburgh University. *Appointments:* Freelance author and photographer. *Publications:* The Roads from the Isles, 1950; West-over-Sea (The Outer Hebrides), 1953; Scotland of the Saints, 1952; Ireland of the Saints, 1953; Irish Pilgrimage (the traditional pilgrimages), 1955; The Rock of Truth, 1953; The Irish Dominicans, 1957; The Celtic Saints (Celtic spirituality), 1956; Peter's Boat, 1959; The Angels of God, 1960; The Irish Saints (critical biographies), 1964; St Brigid, Dublin, 1965; The Aran Islands, 1972; Ireland from the Air, 1972; The Mountains of Ireland (2nd edition), 1976; The Monasteries of Ireland, 1976; Valentia: Portraits of an Island, 1978; Captain Roberts of the Sirius, 1988; Discovering Cork. An exploration of the county, 1989. Contributor to numerous magazines and radio programmes. *Memberships:* Aircraft Owners & Pilots Association; Maritime Institute of Ireland. *Hobbies:* Flying, holder of private pilot's licence and flying instructor's rating; Aerial photography; Archaeological survey flying; Hill walking; Keeping German shepherd dogs and assorted cats. *Address:* Aherla House, Aherla, Co Cork, Eire.

MOULTON Joy Wade, b. 30 November 1928,

Oxnard, California, USA. Genealogist; Writer. m. Edward Quentin Moulton, 2 Jan. 1954, 2 sons, 2 daughters. *Education:* AB, University of California, Berkeley; MS, Wellesley College. *Appointments:* Part-time Instructor, Ohio State University, 1954-66; Professional Genealogist, 1973-; Lecturer, Ohio State University Continuing Education, 1973-83; Columnist, Find Your Ancestors, Columbus Dispatch, Columbus, Ohio, 1975-; Lecturer, Capital University, 1977. *Publications:* Ancestors and Descendants of Burt F. Moulton, 1976; Genealogical Resources in English Repositories, 1988; Editor, International Society for British Genealogy and Family History Newsletter, 1986-. *Memberships:* President, International Society for British Genealogy and Family History, 1989; President, Council of Genealogy Columnists, 1989-; Ohio Historical Society (Trustee 1976-79); New England Historic Genealogical Society (Trustee 1979-81); Association for Professional Genealogists (Trustee 1985-88). *Honours:* 1st Prize in Class 2, National Genealogical Society Newsletter Competition, 1986. *Interests:* English genealogical research 16th century onwards. *Hobbies:* Tennis; Antiques. *Address:* 1303 London Drive, Columbus, OH 43221, USA.

MOUNTBATTEN OF BURMA Patricia Edwina Victoria (Countess), b. 14 Feb. 1924, London, England. Peer of the Realm; Magistrate. m. Lord Brabourne, 26 Oct. 1946, 5 sons (1 deceased), 2 daughters. *Education:* Educated in Malta, PNEU London, & New York City, USA. *Appointments:* Voluntary Employment; Magistrate for Kent, 1971; Deputy Lieutenant for Kent, 1973; Vice Lord Lieutenant for Kent, 1984. *Memberships:* numerous societies & committees. *Honours:* CD, 1976; JP, 1971; DL, 1973; D St J, 1981; Colonel-in-Chief of Princess Patricia's Canadian Light Infantry . *Address:* 39 Montpelier Walk, London SW7 1JH, England.

MOURA Maria Lucia Seidl de, b. 6 June 1946, Rio Grande Do Sul, Brazil. Psychologist. m. Flavio Joppert De Moura, 16 Dec. 1967, 1 son, 1 daughter. *Education:* Doctor in Psychology, Fundaçao Getulio Vargas, 1987. *Appointments:* Elementary School Teacher, 1964-69; Research Work, Professor, Graduate School of Psychology, Fundaçao Getulio Vargas, 1973-88. *Memberships:* Board of Directors, 1st Secretary, 1976-80, Associacao Brasileira de Psicologia. *Address:* Av. 13 de Maio, 23 Sala 1236, Rio de Janeiro, Brazil.

MOURA CASTRO Bridget Mary de, b. 11 Aug. 1941, Yorkshire, England. Musician. m. Luiz de Moura Castro, 1966, 4 daughters. *Education:* BA, Honours, Music, Reading University; ARCM; M.Mus., Piano Performance, texas Christian University, USA *Appointments:* Clarinet Teacher, 1967-69; Pro Arte Seminarios de Musica, Universiy Catholica, Rio de Janeiro; Tarrant County Junior College, Texas Christian University, USA, 1970-79; Staff, Hartt School of Music, University of Hartford, 1980-; Pianist, Hartford Symphony. *Creative Works:* Arrangements of liturgical hymns, carols, mass settings; contributor to ICS. *Memberships:* Vice President, Hartford Chapter, Music Teachers National Association; Secretary, Pi Kappa Lambda, University of Hartford; Musicians Union; etc. *Honours:* British Council Scholarship to Hungary; Best Female Artist of Year, Rio de Janeiro, 1968; etc. *Hobbies:* Reading; Theatre; Travel. *Address:* 38 East Woodhaven Drive, Avon, CT 06001, USA.

MOUTAFIAN Helena (The Princess), b. 2 May 1930, Austria. Social Welfare (Voluntary). m. 14 Jan. 1955. 2 daughters. *Appointment:* Director, Moutafian Commodities Ltd. *Voluntary work:* Deputy President, St John Ambulance Brigade; Hon Vice President, Women's Council; Patron, Kingston & District Charity; Life Patron, NSPCC; Patron: Alexandra Rose Day Ball; Animal Vigilantes; Institute for Complimentary Medicine; KIDS (for deprived & handicapped children); World Farm Trust; Yoga Foundation for Health; Sponsor, Friends of Royal Academy. *Memberships:* English Speaking Union; Honorary Member, Commonwealth Countries League; Life Member, Jersey Wildlife Preservation Trust; Freelance Member, Institute of Journalists; Fellow,

Fauna Preservation Society; Fellow, Royal Geographical Society; Fellow, Soil Association; Fellow, Zoological Society; British Association of Women Entrepreneurs; President Ladis Comm, Help the Aged; President Ladies Comm, World Wide Fund for Nature; Vice President, European Atlantic Group, and many others. *Honours:* MBE, 1976; Grande Medaille de Vermeil de la Ville de Paris, 1977; Etoile Civique; Croix de Chevalier (Ordre de la Courtoisie Francaise). *Hobbies:* Reading; Art; Music. *Address:* 12 Greenwaway Gardens, Hampstead, London NW3 7DH, England.

MOYER Ellen Louise Oosterling, b. 12 Feb. 1936, Camden, New Jersey, USA. Municipal Government Official; Teacher. m. Roger W. Moyer (divorced), 4 sons, 1 daughter. *Education:* BA, Pennsylvania State University, 1958; MEd, Goucher College, 1961; Graduate School of Social Work & Community Organisation, University of Maryland, 1963-66. *Appointments:* Field Director, Girl Scouts, 1958; Area Director, YWCA, 1962; Teacher; Executive Director, Maryland Commission for Women, 1976; Coordinator, Government Relations & Political Action, Maryland State Teachers' Association, 1978; Elected (currently Alderman), Annapolis City Council, 1987. *Creative work includes:* Award-winning urban parks & paths plan; 1st municipal environmental trust; 1st municipl maritime preservation act. *Memberships include:* Annapolis Conservancy Board; Maryland Citizen Action Board; Founder, Maryland Hall for Creative Arts; President, Annapolis Summer Garden Theatre; Elected, Democratic State Party; Numerous other community activities. *Honours:* Awards: Maryland Recreation & Parks Department, 1988; YWCA, 1986; Various others including Girl Scouts, Board of Education, Recreation Department. *Hobbies:* Walking & hiking; Swimming; Camping, Canoeing; Horseback riding; Reading; History, & exploring small towns; Travel. *Address:* Box 3172, Annapolis, Maryland 21403, USA.

MTERO Betty Flora, b. 16 May 1929, Zimbabwe. National Executive Director. m. James Charles Mtero, 24 Aug. 1950, 1 son, 3 daughters. *Education:* Teacher Education Certificate, 1945; Social Work Diploma, 1955; Community Development Diploma, 1960; Adult Education Diploma, 1969; Associateship, Institute of Education, 1973. *Appointments:* School Teacher, 1947; Social Welfare Officer, 1959; Community Development Officer, 1964; Community Development Training Officer, 1966; Director, Community Projects, 1980; National Executive Director, 1988-. *Publication:* Dissertation, Training Needs of Women Community Workers/Advisors. *Memberships:* YWCA, Public Relations Officer; Womens Church Association; Hospital Advisory Board, Chairperson; Children's Helping Society, President, etc. *Honours:* Citation, Ministry of Internal Affairs, 1977. *Hobbies:* Women & Childrens Educational Activities; Voluntary Welfare Work; TV. *Address:* 657 Glenwood Drive, PO Chisipite, Glenlorne, Harare, Zimbabwe.

MUELLER Anne Elisabeth, b. 15 Oct. 1930, India. Second Permanent Secretary, HM Treasury. m. J H Robertson, 1958, divorced 1978. *Education:* MA, Somerville College, Oxford University, 1958; Diploma, Management Studies, 1968. *Appointments:* Entered Ministry of Labour and National Service, 1953; Served with Organisation for European Economic Co-Operation, 1955-56; Treasury, 1962; Department of Economic Affairs, 1964; Ministry of Technology, 1969; Department of Trade & Industry, 1970; Cabinet Office, Management & Personnel Office, 1984; HM Treasury, 1987. *Memberships:* Director, European Investment Bank, 1978-84; Council Member, Institute of Manpower Studies, 1981-; Board Member, Business in the Community, 1984-; Council Member, Templeton College, Oxford, 1985-, Manchester Business School, 1985-; Trustee, Whitechapel Art Gallery, 1985-; Trustee, Duke of Edinburgh's Commonwealth Study Conferences, 1986-; Vice-President of the Industrial Participation Association, 1986-; Council Member, London Education Business Partnership, 1988-; Board Member, Leicester Polytechnic, 1988-. *Honours:*

Companion of the British Institute of Management, 1978; CB, 1980; Honorary Fellow, Somerville College, 1984; Honorary DLit, Warwick, 1985; Fellow of the Institute of Personnel Management, 1986; DCB, 1988. *Address:* HM Treasury, Parliament Street, London SW1P 3AG, England.

MUELLER Betty J Compton, b. 13 May 1930, St Louis, Missouri, USA. Director. m. Charles A. Mueller, 20 Nov. 1954, 1 son, 1 daughter. *Education:* BA, 1952; MAT, 1983; MA, 1989. *Appointments:* Professional Actress, 1948-89; Theatre Coordinator, City of Trenton, 1975-80; Lecturer, 1981; Assistant Director, ISC Lecturer, 1982-87; Director, International Student Center, Webster University, 1987-; Lecturer Theatre, 1988-89, UG & MAT. *Publications:* Paintings: Doll in Garden, 1970; Slocum Truax Ham, 1973. *Memberships:* Soroptimists International; Trenton Theatre Guild; Michigan Cancer Society. *Honours:* Cultural Achievement Award, 1975; Best Supporting Acress in a Musical, 1979; Mayor's Special Award, 1980. *Hobbies:* Painting; Acting; Singing; Needlework; Tennis; Swimming. *Address:* International Student Centre, Webster University, 470 East Lockwood, St Louis, MO 63119, USA.

MUELLER (Peggy) Jean, b. 14 June 1952, Austin, Texas, USA. Dance Teacher; Choreographer; Rancher; Trail Boss. m. John Yerby Tarlton, 24 June 1972. divorced 1983. *Education:* BS, Home economics, Child Development, University of Texas at Austin, 1974. *Appointments:* Dance Teacher, 1972-; Shirley McPhail School of Dance, 1972-75; Jean Mueller School of Dance, 1975-; Dance Teacher, Sul Ross State University, 1975-77; Dance Teacher, Texas A & M University, 1977-80; Dance Teacher, University of Texas at Austin, 1980-. *Memberships:* Texas Assn Teachers of Dancing; Trail Ride Chairman, Austin-Travis County Livestock Show & Rodeo, 1986-; Pres/Trail Boss, Austin Founders Trail Ride, 1986-; Pres 1986-90, Vice Pres 1985-86, Austin Women's Tennis Assn; Treasurer 1987-89, Panhellenic Vice President 1989-90, Social Advisor 1982-87, Zeta Tau Alpha Austin Alumnae; Women's Symphony League of Austin; Junior Austin Woman's Club; The Settlement Club of Austin; Austin Chamber of Commerce. *Honours include:* Texas First Lady Trail Boss honoured by Governor Mark White, Mayor Frank Cooksey and Austin City Council, 1986; Judge Bill Aleshire & Travis County Commissioners Court, 1989; Outstanding Trail Rider of the Year, Oklahoma Wild Horse Trail Ride, 1984; Outstanding Intramural Sports Team Manager, Texas A&M University 1978-79. *Hobbies:* Dance; Theatre; Piano; Drums; Tennis; Racquetball. *Address:* 1506 Hardouin Avenue, Austin, Texas 78703, USA.

MUELLER Kathleen A, b. 7 May 1950, St Ann, Missouri, USA. m. Roy D. Mueller, 12 Oct. 1977, 2 sons, 1 daughter. *Education:* AA, 1983. *Appointments:* Assistant Cash Manager, Consolidated Alumninium Corp., 1979-80; Assistant to VP Finance, CMC Corp., 1981; Special Documents co-ordinator, McCarthy Brothers, 1981-83; Word Processing Manager, American Soybean Association, 1983-86; Consultant, Owner, la debug, St Louis, 1986-. *Publications:* Articles in St Louis Manager; St Louis Computing. *Memberships:* DPMA; National Association Female Executives; Board, St Louis Users Group for IBM PC. *Honours:* Nominee, American Biographical Institute Award, 1989. *Address:* 9544 Roslan Place, St Louis, MO 63114, USA.

MUELLER Virginia Rumely, b. 22 May 1949, Detroit, Michigan, USA. Senior Analyst. m. 22 Nov. 1986, 1 son, 1 daughter. *Education:* BA cum laude, DePauw University, Greencastle, Indiana, 1971; MA, Teaching, Northwestern University, Evanston, Illinois, 1972; MEd, University of Illinois, Chicago, 1978. *Appointments:* Educator, Chicago Board of Education, 1971-82; Programming Trainer, 1982-83, Programmer, 1983, Parogrammer Analyst, 1983-84, Zurich Insurance Co; Systems/Programming Analyst, Miles Labs Inc, 1984-86; Senior Analyst, User Development Center (information center), Miles Inc, 1986-. *Publications:* The

Post-Withdrawal Effect of Sodium Pentobarbital in Maze-Learning of Rats, 1971; Reading Fantastics: A Handbook of Games and Activities. *Memberships:* Programme Chairperson, Association for Systems Management; Elkhart Personal Computer Users Group; Frank Lloyd Wright Home and Studio Foundation (Volunteer for Saturday Walking Tour); Mothers of Twins Club; Sigma Gamma. *Honours:* Ford Foundation Scholar, 1971-72. *Hobbies:* Golf; Tennis; Swimming. *Address:* 420 Court of the Royal Arms, South Bend, IN 46637, USA.

MUHLNICKEL Isabelle Q, b. 11 May 1931, Strong, Colorado, USA. Executive Director. m. Ludwig A Muhlnickel, 13 Jan. 1952, 1 son, 2 daughters. *Education:* BA, Sociology, Metropolitan State College, Denver, 1980. *Appointments:* Education Loan Officer, Lowry Federal Credit Union, 1972-76; Manager, Teamsters Credit Union, Denver, 1980-81; State of Colorado, Licensed Psychiatric Technician, 1981-; Executive Director, Founder, Fathers Crisis Centre, 1984-. *Honours:* Colorado Scholars Award, Metropolitan State College, 1977, 1978, 1979. *Hobbies:* Oil Painting; Photography; Travel. *Address:* Rt 7, 2190 Colorado 72, Golden, CO 80403, USA.

MUIR Isabella Helen Mary, b. 20 Aug. 920, India. Director, Kennedy Institute. *Education:* MA, 1944; D.Phil, 1947; DSc., 1973; DSc., Hon. Edinburgh, 1982; DSc., Hon., Stratchlyde, 1983 *Appointments:* Research Fellow, University of Oxford, 1947-48; National Institute of Medical Research, 1948-54; Empire Rheumatism Council Fellow, Medical Unit, St Mary's Hospital, London, 1954-58; Pearl Research Fellow, St Mary's Hospital Medical School, & Honorary Lecturer, Chemical Pathology, 1959-66; Head, Biochemistry, 1966-87, Director, 1977-, Kennedy Institute of Rheumatology; Trustee, Wellcome Trust, 1982-. *Memberships:* President, Heberden Society; Vice President, Charing Cross Medical Research Centre Appeal; Arthritis & Rheumatism Council Research Sub-Committee; Medical Research Council; Royal Society; etc. *Honours Include:* Heberden Orator & Medallist, 1976; Fellow, Royal Society, 1979; Feldberg Foundation Award, 1977; Bunim Medal, American Arthritis Association, 1978; Honorary Fellow, Somerville College, Oxford, 1978; Volvo International Prize, 1980; Ciba Medal, Biochemical Society, 1981; CBE, 1981; Neil Hamilton Fairley Medal, Royal College of Physicians, 1981; etc. *Hobbies:* Gardening; Music; Horses; Natural History; Ballet. *Address:* The Kennedy Institute of Rheumatology, 6 Bute Gardens, Hammersmith, London W6 7DW, England.

MUKA Betty Loraine Oakes, b. 30 Jan. 1929, McAlester, Oklahoma, USA. Wife; Mother; Attorney; Scientist; Businesswoman; Civic Leader. m. Arthur Allen Muka, 6 Sept. 1952, 2 sons, 3 daughters. *Education:* BS, University of Oklahoma, Norman 1950; MS, Cornell University, Ithaca, 1953; MBA, Finance and Accounting, Cornell University, 1970; JD, Syracuse University Law School, 1980. *Appointments Include:* Hostess and Dining Room Manager, Anna Maudes Cafeteria, Oklahoma City, 1950-51; Faculty Dining Room Manager, VPI Blacksburg, Virginia, 1955-56; Owner/Manager, The Cottae Restaurant, Ithaca, 1959-60; Lecturer, Laboratory Instructor, Food Preparation & Organic Chemistry, Cornell University, 1961; Owner, Manager, Student Housing, 1965-68; Junior Accountant, Maxifield Randolph & Carpenter, CPA's, 1970-71; Tax Consultant and Preparer, H & R Block, Ithaca, 1971-73; Attorney Pro-Se, 1972-; Holiday Inn Hostess, Public Relations Officer, Bookkeeper, 1972-73; Salesperson, Investors Diversified Services, IDS, 1972-73; Agent, Inventory Control Co., 1975-78; Law Clerk, 1978-79; Sole Practitioner, 1983-. *Publications:* Songwriter, Stars of the Sky, 1947; Monticello Cuties, Class of '48 Class Song, 1946. *Memberships:* Delta Delta Delta; Omicron Nu; Mortar Board; Sigma Delta Epsilon; American Home Economics Association; National Association of Security Dealers; Phi Delta Phi; New York State Bar Association; American Bar Association; Rhode Island Bar Association; Rhode Island

Trial Lawyers Association; Association of Trial Lawyers of America; RI Bar, 1983; US District Court Bar, 1984. *Honours:* Oklahoma University's Letzeiser Medal, 1950; Phi Delta Phi's J Mark McCarthy Award, 1980; Oklahoma City Bachelor's Club Debutante, 1949. *Hobbies:* Sports; Music; Leader of Youth Group Activities. *Address:* 113 Kay St., Ithaca, NY 14850, USA.

MULDNER-NIECKOWSKA Malgorzata Anna, b. 15 Mar. 1948, Tarnow, Poland. Artist sculptor; Jeweller. m. Dr Piotr Muldner-Nieckowski, 8 Apr. 1970. 1 son, 1 daughter. *Education:* Graduated, Sculpture Department, Fine Arts Academy, Warsaw, Poland, 1974. *Appointments:* Founded studio of Jewellery, Medal-making and Sculpturing, 1977-. *Creative works:* Hundreds of sets of original style hand-made jewellery, best known series: Black and White; Special Stones; Fluid Line; For You; You and He; Green; Style; Light Silver; Soft Gem. Minted medals: Prof S Konopka; Anniversary of Polish Hygiene Society. Small sculpts series: The Body. *Memberships:* Polish Society of Artists, dissolved 1982; Fine Arts Co-op; Polish Art Institute, 1975-. *Honours:* 1st prize in Competition for Artistic Management, Town Department, Warsaw, 1974; 3rd prize in Competition for Commemorative Medal of Polish Army, 1977; 3rd Prize and special award, Competition for Subject in Silver, Warsaw, Poland, 1985; Individual exhibitions: Sculpts, Medals and Drawing, Warsaw, 1979; Silver Jewellery, Warsaw, 1983. Group exhibitions in Poland and the West; Work included in many official and personal collections all over the world. *Hobby:* To compose, sing and play music, especially songs. *Address:* ul. Zeganska 24 B m. 1, 04-713 Warsaw, Poland.

MULFORD Philippa Clarke Greene, b. 29 May 1948, New York City, USA. Writer. m. R Edward Mulford, 29 Sept. 1978. 1 stepson, 1 stepdaughter. *Education:* BA, Psychology, Skidmore College. *Appointments:* Feature Writer, Clinton Courier, 1971-72; Ex Director, Central NY Community Arts Council, 1971-78. *Publications:* If It's Not Funny, Why Am I Laughing?, 1982; The World is My Eggshell, 1986; Everything I Hoped For, to be published. *Honour:* The World Is My Eggshell named Outstanding Book of 1987 for Young Adults by University of Iowa Writers Program. *Hobby:* Downhill skier. *Address:* Rd 41, Norton Avenue, Clinton, NY 13323, USA.

MULFORD Ruth Sorlie Stomne, b. Chicago, Illinois, USA. Musician; Educator. m. David Barbour Mulford, 30 June 1954, 5 sons, 3 daughters. *Education:* BA, Vassar College; MA, Yale Graduate School; Yale Music School; Westminster Choir College, City College of New York; Graduate study, various universities, USA & Norway. *Appointments include:* Music Director, radio stations (New Haven, Connecticut), various churches (Delaware & Maryland); Teacher, various private & public schools; Music faculty, University of Delaware (current, including lecture series, Masters of Romantic Period); Member, New Jersey, New Haven, Yale, Salisbury and Dover Symphony Orchestras; Concert Master, Eastern Shore Symphony Orchestra. *Memberships include:* Local President, American Association of University Women; American Musicological Society; College Music Society; Music Educators National Conference; American String Teachers Association; Suzuki Association; Hardanger Fiddle Association; Music Education for Handicapped. *Honours include:* Order of 1st State, services to music & education, 1985; Special awards, participation, Arts Festival for Handicapped, 1985-86; Citation, performances & lectures, Methodist Manor House, Seaford, Delaware, 1985. *Hobbies:* Chamber groups (violin); Research, women in music; Playing Norwegian folk fiddle (Hardingfele), dulcimer & hammered dulcimer; Lecturing, Norwegian music; Teaching music to pre-schools, handicapped, senior citizens; Director, choral groups & handbell choir. *Address:* 1910 Concord Road, Seaford, Delaware 19973, USA.

MULLEN Margaret Jean, b. 3 Dec. 1955, Milwaukee, Wisconsin, USA. Attorney. m. Terry Campton, 31 Mar. 1977, 1 son, 1 daughter. *Education:* Graduated, Illinois State University, Normal, 1977; John Marshall Law School, Chicago, Illinois, 1980. *Appointments:* Clerk to Hon. Presiding Judge George W. Lindberg, Illinois Appellate Court, 1981; Assistant State Attorney, County of Dupage, 1982; Chief, Juvenile Division, Lake County State Attorney's Office, 1987; Associate, Tressler, Soderstrom, Maloney & Priess. *Publications:* Comment, Wrongful Life, Birth Control Spawns A Tort, 1980. *Memberships:* American Bar Association; Illinois State Bar Association; Lake County Bar Association; Association of Women Attorneys; Guild of St Mary's. *Honours:* Order of John Marshall, 1980; Commendation, Lake County Merit Commission, 1984; Commendation, Libertyville Police Department, 1985; Commendation, Lake County Fire Inspectors, 1986. *Hobbies:* Waterskiing; Riding; Gardening. *Address:* 128 West Madison Street, Waukegan, IL 60085, USA.

MULLENSKY Elizabeth Ann, b. 12 Dec. 1946, Los Angeles, California, USA. Health Care Administration. m. (1) Lee A Buckingham, 19 July 1969, divorced 1978, 1 son, 1 daughter. (2) Steven Mullensky, 12 Apr. 1981. *Education:* BS, St Mary's College, Los Angeles, 1969. *Appointments:* Charge Nurse, University Hospital of San Diego, 1970-72; Public Health Nurse, San Diego County Health Department, 1972-73; Public Health Nurse/Discharge Planner, Southern California Permanent Medical Group, 1973-79; Discharge Coordinator, Alvarado Community Hospital, 1979-81; Department Manager 1981-85, Director, Alternative Hospital Services, 1985-, Kaiser Foundation Hospital. *Memberships:* YWCA Twin Forum; California Association for Health Services at Home Education Committee; Nominee, American College of Health Care Executives; Member, Board of Directors 1987-88, Families Against Drugs. *Honours:* YWCA Twin Awardee, 1985; Kaiser Permanente Exceptional Contribution Award, 1986. *Hobbies:* Skiing; Biking; Walking; Reading. *Address:* P O Box 2199, La Jolla, CA 92038, USA.

MULLER Marcia, b. 28 Sept. 1944, Detroit, Michigan, USA. Writer. *Education:* BA English, 1966; MA Journalist, 1967, University of Michigan. *Appointments:* Freelance Journalist, 1971-78; Partner, Invisible Ink, San Francisco, 1978-82; Full time writer 1982-. *Publications:* There Hangs the Knife, 1988; Eye of the Storm, 1988; The Lighthouse (with Bill Pronzini), 1987; Beyond the Grave (with Bill Pronzini), 1986; The Cavalier in White, 1986; There's Nothing to Be Afraid Of, 1985; The Legend of the Slain Soldiers, 1985; Double (with Bill Pronzini), 1984; Leave a Message for Willie, 1984; Games to Keep the Dark Away, 1984; The Tree of Death, 1983; The Cheshire Cat's Eye, 1983; Ask the Cards a Question, 1982; Edwin of the Iron Shoes, 1977. Anthologies (with Bill Pronzini): The Deadly Arts, 1985; The Wickedest Show on Earth, 1985; Kill or Cure, 1985; She Won the West, 1985; Dark Lessons, 1985; Chapter and Hearse, 1985; Witches' Brew, 1984; Child's Ploy, 1984; The Web She Weaves. Criticism: 1001 Midnights: The Aficionado's Guide to Mystery and Detective Fiction (with Bill Pronzini), 1986. Short Stories to numerous magazines. *Honour:* Mystery Writers of America Scroll, 1986. *Hobbies:* Book collecting; Miniature building. *Address:* PO Box 1349, Sonoma, CA 95476, USA.

MULLIGAN Carolyn Littlejohn, b. 12 Dec. 1927, Spartanburg, South Carolina, USA. School Social Worker. m. Charles Ray Mulligan, 29 June 1949. 1 son, 1 daughter. *Education:* BA, Limestone Colelge, 1949; Graduate work, University of North Carolina, Charlotte, 1956-57; South Eastern school of Alcoholism, 1963; Graduate work in Social Work, 1965-66, University of Georgia, Arthur. *Appointments:* Case worker with adults and children, Supervisor of Public Association Workers, Department of Social Services, 1949-59; Specialised case worker to families and children, Chief Welfare Supervisor, Department of Social Services, 1962-66; School Home Visitor, 1966-87; Title I Coordinator for Parents Advisory Council, 1980-86. *Creative works:* Talks and lectures to various community, church and civic organisations. *Memberships:* South Carolina School Social Workers Association; Spartanburg County

Mental Health Association; First Baptist Church; Limestone College Alumnae for Child Abuse and Neglect; Former Board Member, Services to Family; Mountain View Nursing Home; Spartenburg Mental Health Association; International Platform Association; Child Welfare League of America, 1988, Children's Campaign; American Association of Retired People (AARP); Spartanburg County Association for Retarded Citizens. *Honours include:* Limestone College Hall of Fame, 1948-49; Title I, Coordinator for Parents Advisory Council School Home Visitor, 1966-87. *Hobbies:* Reading; Gardening; Music; Attending seminars relating to working with people. *Address:* 221 Connecticut Avenue, Spartanburg, SC 29302, USA.

MULLIN Mary Veronica, b. 1 June 1941, Dublin, Ireland. Director. *Appointments:* W.R. Grace & Co., New York, 1966-67; Kilkenny Design Workshops, Ireland, 1967-78; Chartered Society of Designers, London, 1978-81; Director, M V Mullin Associates, 1981-. *Publications:* Industrial Design in Mexico, Columbia, Brazil & Argentina, 1978; Design for Tourism, 1977; articles in various journals. *Memberships:* Chairman, London Region Design & Industries Association; Association of British Professional Conference Organizers. *Honours:* Fellow, Royal Society of Arts; Community Award, London, 1980. *Address:* PO Box 398, London W11 4UG, England.

MUMMA Emily Jean Metzger, b. 1 Apr. 1933, Pike Township, Ohio, USA. Administrative Assistant. m. Luke Richwine Mumma, 30 Aug. 1952, 1 son, 1 daughter. *Education:* Conflict Management, Epicenter, 1979; Mediation Training, 1986; Advanced Mediation, Elgin, 1988. *Appointments:* Co-owner, Manager, Mumma Appliance Service, 1960-68; Interim Director, Pastoral Placement & Congregational Concerns, 1979; First Person Licensed to Ministry of Reconciliation, Church of the Bretheren, 1987. *Publications:* Youth Club Manual, 1977; articles for Messenger. *Memberships:* Moderator, District of Florida, 1977-78; General Board, Church of the Brethren, 1982-87; various other organisations. *Honours:* Recipient, many honour & awards. *Hobbies:* Reading; Sewing; Gardening; Maintenance Jobs. *Address:* 860 Corvette Dr., Largo, FL 34641, USA.

MUNDELL-PIGOTT Christeen, b. 15 July 1948, Dunoon, Scotland. Clinical Director. m. Dr Francis Pigott, 10 Dec 1988. *Education:* Glasgow Royal Infirmary; Queen Mother's Hospital, Glasgow; RGN; SCM. *Appointments:* Staff Nurse, Surgical Unit, 1971; Sister, Night Duty Surgical Area, 1971-72, Senior Sister in Charge, University Department of Surgery Wards, 1972-77, Nursing Officer in Charge, University Dept. of Surgery Wards, Acute Receiving Wards & Urology Wards, 1977-83, Glasgow Royal Infirmary; Director, Nursing, 1983-85, Director, Clinical Services, 1985-86, Director of Hospital Services, 1986-88, Ross Hall Hospital, Glasgow, Clinical Director, Health Care Group Plc, Schaw Medical Centre, Bearsden, Glasgow, Jan. 1989-. *Publications:* Nutritional Support-the Role of a Surgical Nutritional Advisory Group, 1984. *Memberships:* European Society for Parental and Enteral Nutrition; American Society for Parental & Enteral Nutrition; Royal College of Nursing; Soroptomist International of Paisley. *Hobbies:* Travel; Reading; Horse Riding. *Address:* 6 Buchanan Drive, Newton Mearns, Glasgow, Scotland.

MUNGAI Evelyn Karungari, b. 14 May 1944, Lower Kabete, Kenya. Company Executive. m. 2 Jan. 1965. 1 son, 1 daughter. *Education:* Chura Primary School; Mary Leakey Girls School; Kianda College. *Appointments:* Private Secretary, Assistant Recruitment Officer, EA Common Services; Personal Assistant, Firestone EA; Editor-in-Chief/Publisher, Presence Magazine; Founder and Executive Director, Evelyn College of Design; Director, Kenya Film Corporation. *Publications:* Kenya Women Reflections, co-author. *Memberships:* President, 1978-81, Board Member, 1976-, Business and Professional Women's Club, Nairobi; Vice President, National Council of Women of Kenya, 1980-; Kenya National Chamber of Commerce; Founder Member, Networking Group, Kenya; Kiambu Institute of Science and Technology, 1987-; President, Kenya Women Entrepreneurs Association. *Hobbies:* Swimming; Cooking; Reading. *Address:* PO Box 10988, Nairobi, Kenya.

MUNROE Donna Louise Scott, b. 28 Nov. 1945, Cleveland, Ohio, USA. Data Processing Strategic Planning & Management Consulting. m. Peter Carlton Munroe, 14 Feb. 1981, 1 daughter. *Education:* BS, Sociology, 1976; BS, Philosophy, 1978; MS, Sociology, 1983. *Appointments:* University Lecturer, 1979-81; Writer, Editorial Consultant, 1979-80; Statistical Consultant, 1979-82; Manager, Data Proc, 1982-87; Management Consultant, Strategic Planner, 1987-. *Memberships:* Sigma Xi; American Management Association. *Honours:* Outstanding Undergraduate Scholar, Sociology, 1974; Outstanding Graduate Scholar, Sociology, 1978; Election to Sigma Xi, 1981. *Hobbies:* Reading; Philosophy; Soccer. *Address:* 1435 SW Harrison, Portland, OR 97201, USA.

MUNSKI Mary-Margaret, b. 9 Sept. 1950, Flint, Michigan, USA. Architect. *Education:* BSc, Architecture, 1972, March 1974, University of Michigan; Registered Architect, 1979. *Appointments:* Tomblinson & Harburn Architects, Flint, 1974-75; Architonics Architects, Jackson, Michigan, 1975-82; Project Manager, Steel Case, Grand Rapids, 1982-. *Memberships:* Past Treasurer, Grand Rapids Chapter, American Institute of Architects; National Affirmative Action Committee, AIA, 1981-83; Past Co-President, University of Michigan Alumnae Association; Past Board, Michigan Department of Licensing & Regulation of Architects. *Hobbies:* Tennis; Travel; Skiing; Cycling; Gardening; Art; Architecture. *Address:* 2220 Anderson Drive SE, East Grand Rapids, Michigan 49506, USA.

MUNSON Nancy K, b. 22 June 1936, Huntington, New York, USA. Attorney at Law. *Education:* Hofstra University, 1959-62; JD, Brooklyn Law School, 1965. *Appointments:* Law Clerk to E Merritt Weidner, Huntington, New York, 1959-66; Sole Practitioner, Huntington, New York, 1966-. *Memberships:* American Bar Association; New York State Bar Association; Brooklyn Bar Association; Suffolk County Bar Association; Past President, Soroptimist; Trustee, Huntington Fire Dept Death Benefit Fund; Chairman of Board, Brooklyn Home for Aged Men Foundation; Legal Advisory Board of Chicago Title Ins Co. *Honours:* Surrogate Rubinstein Prize for excellence in study of Wills & Administration of Estates, 1965. *Hobbies:* Cooking; Photography; Tennis; Boating. *Address:* 197 New York Avenue, Huntington, NY 11743, USA.

MUNTS Mary Lou, b. 21 Aug. 1924, Chicago, USA. Commissioner. m. Raymond Munts, 1 son, 2 daughters. *Education:* MA, University of Chicago, 1947; JD, University of Wisconsin and Bar admission, 1976. *Appointments:* Research Assistant, US Treasury, Paris, France, 1947-48; Instructor, School of Business, Wilkes College, 1949-50; Assisant Congressman Robert Kastenmeier, 1960; Economic Research Assistant, Robert Nathan Association, Washington, DC, 1964-66; Administrative Secretary, 1964-66; State Representative, Democrat Wisconsin Assembly, 1972-84; Commissioner, WI Public Service Commission, Madison, 1985-. *Publications:* Co-Editor, Future of Small Business; Co-Editor, Measuring Fiscal Capacity. *Memberships:* Conservation National Association Regulatory Commissioners, 1985; National Sea Grant Review Panel, 1978-81; Natural Resources & Environmental Committee of the National Conference of State Legislature, 1978-82. *Honours:* Phi Beta Kappa. *Address:* 4802 Sheboygan Ave., PO Box 7854, Madison, WI 53707, USA.

MUNZER Martha E, b. 22 Sept. 1899, New York City, USA. Retired Teacher; Writer. m. (1) Edward Munzer, 15 June 1922, 1 son, 2 daughters, (2) Isaac Corkland, 30 Mar. 1980. *Education:* BS, MIT, one of the first women graduates from MIT, 1922. *Appointments:* Chemistry Teacher, Fielston School, 1930-54; Staff: The Conservation Foundation, 1954-68, Wave Hill Center for Environmental Studies, 1968-72, Watson Ecology Workshops, 1969-. *Publications:* Teaching Science through Conservation, co-author, 1960; Unusual Careers, 1962; Planning Our Town — A Primer of City Planning, 1969; Pockets of Hope - Studies of Land & People, 1966; Valley of Vision - The TVA Years, 1969; Block by Block, Rebuilding City Neighborhood, co-author, 1973; New Towns - Building Cities from Scratch, co-author, 1974; Full Circle, Rounding Out a life, 1978; the Three R's of Ecology. *Memberships:* Various professional organisations. *Honours:* Oscar R Foster Award, Chemistry Teachers Club of New York, 1947; Fellow, Society of Women Engineers, etc. *Hobbies:* Reading; Knitting; Swimming; Hiking. *Address:* 4411 Tradewinds Ave E, Lauderdale by the Sea, FL 33308, USA.

MURAK Teresa, b. 5 July 1949, Kielczewice, near Lublin, Poland. Visual Artist. div. 1 son. *Education:* MA, Academy of Fine Arts, Warsaw, 1976. *Creative work includes:* Performance Art: Procession, Easter Carpet (living plants), 1974; Coming of Verdune, Cradle, 1975; Lady's Smock, 1976; Desire, Action, Vigilance, 1987. Exhibitions, Installations: Lund, Sweden, 1974; Warsaw & Italy, 1976; Amsterdam, 1979; Balbao, Spain, 1982; West Germany, 1984, 1987; Italy, 1985; Warsaw & Canada, 1988. Work in Collections; National Museum, National Library, Warsaw; City Art Gallery, Lublin; Private collections throughout Europe. Materials have included: Plants, seeds, grain, bread dough, river mud & silt, also drawings. *Address:* ul. Orla 8/20, Warsaw, Poland.

MURDOCK Pamela E, b. 3 Dec. 1940, Los Angeles, California, USA. Corporate Executive. 2 daughters. *Education:* BS, University of Colorado, 1962. *Appointments:* Manager, Snelling & Snelling, 1969-70; Owner/President, Dolphin Travel, 1972-87; Owner/President, Mile Hi Tours, 1974-; Owner/President, M H International, 1987-. *Memberships:* American Society of Travel Agents; Colorado Association of Commerce & Industry; Always Buy Colorado; Federal of Independent Businessmen; Republican Part; Kappa Kappa Gamma. *Honours:* Las Vegas Wholesaler of the Year Award, 1984, Las Vegas Visitors Convention Authority. *Hobbies:* Travelling; Reading. *Address:* 2120 S Birch, Denver, CO 80222, USA.

MURDY Louise Baughan, b. 28 Sept. 1935, Dover, New Hampshire, USA. Associate Professor. m. William George Murdy, 23 Aug. 1958, 1 son, 1 daughter. *Education:* BA, Honours, Political Science, 1957, PhD, English, 1962, University of Florida; MA, English, University of North Carolina 1958. *Appointments:* Instructor, Humanities, Florida State University, 1962-63; Part-time Assistant Professor, 1963-70, Part-time Associate Professor, 1970-76, Associate Professor, 1976-, English, Winthrop College. *Publications:* Sound and Sense in Dylan Thomas's Poetry, 1966; Dylan Thomas, Encyclopedia Americana, 1971-. *Memberships:* South Atlantic Modern Language Association; Southeastern 19th Century Studies Association. *Address:* The Department of English, 319 Kinard Building, Winthrop College, Rock Hill, SC 29733, USA.

MURDY Silvia Vega de, b. 21 Aug. 1950, Mexico City, Mexico. Conservation and restoration of paintings and murals. m. Carson Neff Murdy, 5 Apr. 1975. 1 son. *Education:* Diploma, Centro Escolar Universtario, Mexico, 1970; Tecnico Restaurador, Instituto Nacional de Bellas Artes y Literatura, Mexico, 1972; Diploma in Deterioration of Materials 1973, Diploma in Restoration of Monuments 1974, Sociedad Mexicana de Arquitectors Restauradores AC, Mexico. *Appointments:* Restoration of museum and paintings, Pinacoteca Virreinal de San Diego, Mexico, 1972; Projects 1973, Supervision of restoration of mission buildings, Sierra Gorda, Queretaro, Departamento de Monumentos Coloniales de la Republica, Mexico; Restoration of mural

paintings by Diego Rivera, National Palace, Mexico, 1974-75; Restoration of paintings, private practice, California, USA, 1975-76; Private Practice, State College, Pennsylvania, 1976-. *Creative work:* Poster, Uniting the World, Community International Hospitality Council, State College, Penhnsylvania, 1977. *Memberships:* International Institute for Conservation of Historic and Artistic Works; American Institute for Conservation of Historic and Artistic Works. *Hobbies:* Batik; Ceramics; Collecting fossils; Collecting ethnographic textiles. *Address:* 409 Carpenter Building, University Park, Pennsylvania 16802, USA.

MUREZ Melanie Goodman, b. 11 May 1954, Los Angeles, USA. President, Translation Company. m. James D Murez, 20 Sept. 1986. 1 son. *Education:* BA, French 1974, MA, Romance Ling & Lit 1977, PhC, Romance Linguistics & Literature 1981, UCLA. *Appointments:* Hebrew, French, Spanish Tutor, 1968-82; French Instructor, UCLA, 1976-81; Manager, Language Services, LA Olympic Organizing Comm, 1982-84; President, Language Services International, 1984-. *Memberships:* SCATIA (So Calif Translators & Interpreters Association: Citroen Car Club; Alpha Mu Gamma; La Bordeaux Sister City; President, UCLA Romance Ling & Lit Grad Student Assoc; President, UCLA Communications Council. *Memberships:* UCLA Alumni Award for Academic Distinction, 1981; University Grants, 1985-88; Teaching Assistantships, 1976-81; BA, cum laude, 1974. *Hobbies:* Reading; Movies; Antique cars; Travelling. *Address:* 804 Main Street, Venice, CA 90291, USA.

MURIO Jay, b. Louisiana, USA. Soprano. *Education:* BA, Arkansas College; Mus M, BM, American Conservatory; MA, University of Chicago, 1933. *Appointments:* Feature Story Write, trade Journals, 1933-36; Soprano Soloist, World's Fair (Century of Progress, Merrie England), Chicago, 1933-34; Soloist, Texas Centennial, 1936; Concerts in Latin America, 1937-42; member, Civi Opera, Chicago; National Opera, Mexico; tours in Latin America and USA. *Publications:* El Siglo Pitagorico y Vida de Don Gregorio, by Enriquez Gomez; As a Source of a Journey from this World to the Next; Jonathan Wild, by Henry Fielding. *Memberships:* President, Chicago Chapter, Board Member, National Society of Arts and Letters; Board Member, Illinois Opera Guild; UDC; Daughters of the American Revolution; Associate Member, Lyric Opera of Chicago; President, Delta Omicron Fraternity. *Hobbies:* Owner, Wild Animal Refuge, Fish Hatchery, and Lake for Gese and Cranes, Central Wisconsin. *Address:* PO Box 678, Oak Park, IL 60303, USA.

MURPHY Betty Jane Southard, b. East Orange, New Jersey, USA. Lawyer. m. Cornelius F. Murphy, 1 May 1965, 1 son, 1 daughter. *Education:* AB, Ohio State University; Postgraduate, Alliance Francaise, & Sorbonne University, Paris, France; JD, American University, 1958; Admitted, DC Bar, 1958. *Appointments:* Correspondent, freelance journalist, Europe & Asia, UPI, Washington; Public Relations Counsellor, Capital Properties Inc of Columbus (Ohio), Washington; Attorney, Appellate Courts br, National Labour Relations Board, Washington, 1958-59; Practised, Washington, 1959-74; Member, McInnis, Wilson, Munson & Woods (& predecessor firm), 1959-70; General partner, Wilson, Woods & Villalon, 1970-74; Adjunct Professor of Law, American University, 1972-; Deputy Assistant Secretary, Administrator, Wage & Hour Division, Department of Labour, 1974-75; Chairman, member, NLRB, 1975-79; Partner, Baker & Hostetler, 1980-. *Memberships:* Boards, committees, including: Conciliators Panel, International Centre for Settlement of Investment Disputes, 1974-85; US Administrative Conference, 1976-80; Public Service Advisory Board, 1976-79; Human Resources Committee, National Centre for Productivity & Quality of Working Life, 1976-80. *Honours include:* 4 honorary doctorates, 1975-87; Ohio Governor's Award, 1980; Various fellowships; Outstanding Public Service, US Information Service, 1987; Residential appointments.

Address: Baker & Hostetler, 1050 Connecticut Avenue NW, Washington DC 20036, USA.

MURPHY Brenda, b. 12 May 1950, Beverly, Massachusetts, USA. College Professor. *Education:* AB, University of Dayton, 1971; PhD, Brown University, 1975. *Appointments:* Assistant Professor, 1975-80, Associate Professor, 1980-87, English, Associate Dean, Academic Affairs, 1985-87, Professor, English, 1987-, St Lawrence University, Professor, English, Univesity of Connecticut, 1989-. *Publications:* American Realism and American Drama 1880-1940, 1987; John Hay - Howells Letters, with George Monteiro, 1980. *Memberships:* Board of Directors, American Drama Society, 1987-89; MLA; American Studies Association; Henry James Society; American Society for Theatre Research; Eugene O'Neill Society. *Honours:* National Merit Scholarship, President's Scholarship, University of Dayton, 1968-71; University Fellowship, Brown University, 1971-72; American Council of Learned Societies Fellow, 1981-82; National Humanities Center Fellow, 1981-82; NEH Summer Stipend 1980, 1987. *Address:* Dept. of English, University of Connecticut, Storrs, CT 06268, USA.

MURPHY Diana E, Judge. m. 2 sons. *Educated:* BA, magna cum laude, University of Minnesota, 1954; JD, magna cum laude, 1974; Fulbright Scholar, Johannes Gutenberg University, Mainz, Germany, 1954-55. *Appointments:* Staff 1972-73, Editor 1973-74, Minnesota Law Review; Legal practice, Minneapolis, 1974-76; Judge, Hennepin County Municipal Court, 1976-78; Judge, Minnesota District Court Fourth Judicial District, 1978-80; Instructor, Trial Practice 1977-79 and 1983, Student Practice Trials 1979-84 and Appellate Moot Court Judge 1979 and 1982, University of Minnesota School of Law; Lecturer, Federal Practice Seminars, Federal Bar Association, 1979-84; Lecturer, US Attorney General's Advocacy Institute, 1982 and 1983; Judge, US District Court, District of Minnesota, 1980-. *Publications:* Minneapolis Works for Equal Opportunity, 1965; An Effort to Revise the Minnesota Bill of Rights, 1973. *Memberships include:* Fellow, American Bar Foundation; Board of Directors, Federal Judges Association, 1982-; American Judicature Society, 1982-; Hennepin County Bar Foundation (Board of Directors 1981-, President 1983-84); Minnesota Women Lawyers (Fourth Judicial District Coordinating Committee); Eighth Judicial Circuit Judges Association (Program Committee 1981-82); National Association of Women Judges; American Law Institute. *Honours:* Recipient Amicus Founder's Award, 1980; Outstanding Achievement Award, YWCA, 1981 and University of Minnesota, 1983. *Address:* 670 US Courthouse, 110 South Fourth Street, Minneapolis 55401, USA.

MURPHY Edrie Lee, b. 4 Dec. 1953, Redwood Falls, USA. Hospital Laboratory Manager. m. David Joseph Murphy, 28 July 1984. *Education:* Registered Medical Technologist, 1976; BS, Medical Technology, summa cum laude, Mankato State University, 1976; MBA, College of St Thomas, 1984. *Appointments:* Medical Technologist, Children's Hospital, St Paul, 1976-81; Chemistry Supervisor, 1981-85; Laboratory Manager, 1985-. *Publications:* Co-author, several research articles in professional journals. *Memberships:* American & Minnesota Societies of Medical Technologists; American Association Clinical Chemists; Clinical Laboratory Management Association; Phi Kappa Phi. *Honours:* Charles H. Cooper Scholar, 1976. *Hobbies:* Photography; Sailing; Tennis; Skiing; Travel. *Address:* Childrens Hospital of Saint Paul, 345 N Smith, St Paul, MN 55102, USA.

MURPHY Kay Ann, b. 28 Sept. 1942, Paris, Illinois, USA. Writer; Teacher. m. Ted Drake Murphy, 17 Feb. 1962, div. 1971, 2 sons, 1 daughter. *Education:* AA, Danville Community College, 1974; BA, Eastern Illinois University, 1976; MFA, Goddard College, 1980. *Appointments:* Instructor of English, Danville Area Community College, 1979-84; Instructor of English, University of English, New Orleans, Louisiana, 1984-; Associate Director of Writing Programmes, New Orleans Center for Creative Arts, 1987-. *Publications:* The Autopsy, poetry collection, 1985; Individual poems, stories, reviews, memoirs, essays in Ascent, Black Warrior Review, St Andrews Review, Poetry, New York Quarterly, Seneca Review. *Membership:* Associated Writing Program. *Hobbies:* Reading; Listening to jazz; Running; Films. *Address:* 4315 Perrier Street, New Orleans, LA 70115, USA.

MURPHY Lillian Sybil, b. 27 July 1920, London, England. Freelance Writer (non-fiction articles); Retired Executive Secretary. m. (2) William C. B. Murphy, 21 Dec. 1965. 1 son, previous marriage. *Education:* Writing course, London School of Journalism, 1977-79. *Career:* Secretary, Thames Bank Iron Company, London, 1936-42; Secretary, Supervisor, Executive Secretary, various firms, San Francisco, USA, 1956-80. *Publications:* Freelance non-fiction articles, numerous national magazines including syndicated & government publications, UK & USA, 1936-. *Membership:* (Current) Professional member, National Writers Club, Aurora, Colorado. *Honour:* Volunteer of Month (hospital work), Travellers Aid Society, San Francisco, 1964. *Hobbies include:* Extensive travel, worldwide; Baking & cooking contests; Writing for magazines. *Address:* PO Box 1571, Rohnert Park, California 94928, USA.

MURPHY Margaret Pauline, b. 26 June 1936, Carlow, Ireland. University Lecturer. m. John Donall Murphy, LLB, 22 Oct. 1962. 1 son, 3 daughters. *Education:* BComm, 1st class Honours, 1956, Higher Diploma in Education, 1957, NUI; Diploma in Guidance and Counselling, 1978; Fellowship in Adult Education, 1979, Ulster Polytechnic; On-going DPhil, University of Ulster. *Appointments:* Lecturer, Cookstown Technical College, 1957-58; Head of Social Science Department, St Louise's College, Belfast, 1958-64, and 1974-78; Head of Community Education, St Louise's College, 1979-85. Chief Examiner 'O' Level Economics, N I Schools Council, 1984-87; Chief Reviser GCSE Economics, 1987-; Director, EC Project, Women & Information Technology, 1987-90. *Publications:* Articles on Community/Adult Education in ICEA; Community Education Worldwide Journal, 1983, 1986; International Interdisciplinary Congress on Women, 1987, articles on Women, Work & New Technology. Reports: Co-Author, A Cry for Learning, 1984; Community Education for Waht, 1986; Guidance for Adult Learners in NI, 1986; NRI EC Project, Women and Information Technology, 1988. Book: Voluntary Schools going Community, 1987. Paper: Women, Work & Information Technology, Women's Studies Association of Ireland, Conference Report, 1987. *Memberships:* Executive Member, Northern Ireland Council for Continuing Education, 1983-86 and 1987-88; Chairperson, NICCEd Working Party of Guidance & Counselling in Adult Education in Northern Ireland; Founder and Chairperson, NI Community Education Association, 1983-88; NI Representative on ICEA; Member of Governing Body, Newtownabbey Technical College; Member of Management Committee, Ulster People's College; Member of Editorial Panel, Adult Education in Ireland Journal. *Hobbies:* Community Education for change; Women's Education; Drama/Media/Communications; Music; Singing; Innovatory projects. *Address:* 120 Harberton Park, Belfast 9, Northern Ireland.

MURPHY Mary Reynolds, b. 15 Nov. 1948, Utica, New York, USA. Audit Manager. m. D Paul Murphy, Jr, 2 July 1977. *Education:* BA, Washington State University, 1970; MS, Management, Houston Baptist University, 1987; Certified Internal Auditor, 1980; Certified Public Accountant, 1985. *Appointments:* Accountant, Verne Eng Co, Detroit, Houston, 1971-76; Auditor, ICI Americas Inc, Bayport, Texas, 1976-78; Audit Manager, Aramco Services Co, Houston, 1978-. *Memberships:* Institute of Internal Auditors; American Institute of Certified Public Accountants; Texas Society of Certified Public Accountants; President, PC Users Group, Aramco Services Co. *Hobbies:* Scuba diving; Snow skiing. *Address:* 115 Pine Manor, Conroe, Texas 77385, USA.

MURPHY Sharon Funcheon, b. 8 Jan. 1954, Lafayette, Indiana, USA. Attorney. m. Daniel Ralph Murphy, 14 June 1980, 1 daughter. *Education:* BA, University of Dallas, Texas, 1976; JD, Indiana University, 1982. *Appointments:* High school teacher, English, 1976-79; Locke, Reynolds, Boyd & Weisell, 1982-84; Dibble, Bartlett & Robb, 1984-87; Sole practitioner, 1987-89; Lowe Gray Steele and Hoffaman, 1989-. *Memberships:* Secretary, Tort & Insurance Practice Section; Past Chair, Appellate Advocacy Committee, Tort & Insurance Practice Section, American Bar Association; Past Treasurer, Tippecanoe County Bar Association; Diocesan Advocate, Roman Catholic Diocese of Lafayette. *Honour:* 1st place, National Appellate Avocacy Competition, 1982. *Hobbies:* Duplicate bridge; Tennis; Golf; Volleyball; Piano. *Address:* One Indiana Square, Suite 3130, Indianapolis, IN 46204, USA.

MURPHY Susan L, b. 12 Dec. 1951, Flint, USA. Marketing Consultant. m. 29 Dec. 1975, 1 son, 1 daughter. *Education:* BS, University of Michigan, 1974. *Appointments:* Vice President, Marr Marketing Consultants, 1974-80; President, Owner, Murphy Marketing Inc., 1981-88; Secretary, Andrews Imports Inc., 1985-88; Owner, President, QV Corporation, 1986-88; President, Owner, Kelker Co., 1987-88; Marketing Consultant, Bonneville International, 1988-. *Memberships:* Elder, Presbyterian Church, USA; Dame de la Chaine des Rotisseurs; NAFE; Les Amis du Vin; Utah Advertising Federation, etc. *Hobbies:* Skiing; Outdoor Sports; Reading; Bicycling; Cooking; Wine Tasting. *Address:* 4092 Gary Road, SLC, UT 84124, USA.

MURRAY Joan, b. 12 Aug. 1943, New York City, USA. Art Gallery Director, Author, Artist. *Education:* BA, University of Toronto, 1965; MA, Columbia University, 1966. *Appointments:* Research Curator, Art Gallery of Ontario, 1969; Visiting Lecturer, York University, 1970-71, 1973-75; Curator, Canadian Art, Art Gallery of Ontario, 1970-73, Acting Chief Curator, 1973; Director, Robert McLaughlin Gallery, Oshawa, 1974-. *Publications:* The Beginning of Vision: The Drawings of Lawren S. Harris; Letters Home: 1859-1906, The Letters of William Blair Bruce, 1982; Kurelek's Vision of Canada, 1983; Frederick Arthur Verner, The Last Buffalo, 1984; Daffodils in Winter, 1984; The Best of the Group of Seven, 1984; The Best of Tom Thomson, 1986; The Best Contemporary Canadian Art, 1987; The Life and Letters of Pegi Nicol MacLeod; over 70 catalogues and 200 articles. *Address:* 400 St John Street West, Whitby, Ontario, Canada.

MURRAY Lorene F, b. 6 Nov. 1953, Evergreen Park, Illinois, USA. Attorney. m Thomas J Shanahan, 29 Nov. 1985. 1 stepson, 2 stepdaughters. *Education:* BA, Political Science, Urban Studies, St Mary's College, Notre Dame, 1975; JD, Lewis Univ College of Law, Glen Ellyn, Illinois, 1978; Licensed to practice, November 1978. *Appointments:* Dir General Law, Chicago Transit Authority, 1979-87; Attorney, Naphin, Banta & Cox, Chicago, Illinois, 1987-. *Memberships:* American Bar Association; Chicago Bar Association. *Honours:* ALMACA, 1982, 1985; APTA, 1983. *Hobbies:* Swimming; Skiing; Reading. *Address:* 55 West Monroe Street, Xerox Centre, Suite 2800, Chicago, Illinois 60603, USA.

MURRAY Sonya Lever, b. 12 Aug. 1939, Philadelphia, Pennsylvania, USA. Financial Planner; Jewellery Designer. 1 son, 1 daughter. *Education:* BA, Mills College, 1961. *Appointment:* Account Executive, Investment Network of America, 1988-. *Creative work:* Numerous jewellery creations, also paintings, ceramics, mixed media works. *Memberships:* Bravo Chapter, Orange County Chamber Orchestra; Mensa; International Association of Financial Planners. *Honours:* Outstanding sales achievements, 1989; Million Dollar Club, 1989. *Hobbies:* Cultural events; Travel; Art exhibitions; Swimming; Sailing; Reading; Theatre; Dining out. *Address:* PO Box 2097, Laguna Hills, California 92654, USA.

MURRELL Janice Marie, b. 29 Nov. 1937, St Louis, Missouri, USA. Concert Opera Singer, Mezzo Contralto. *Education:* Diploma, Sumner High School, 1956; Certificate, Washington University, 1961; Degree, The Kroeger School of Music, 1962; Certificate, Bernard U Taylor Institute, New York City, 1966. *Appointments:* St Louis Board of Education permanent position; Music Teacher, Central Visual Performing Arts High School, 1975-78; Municipal Opera Co, St Louis, 1972-75; Stephan Foster Drama, Bardstown, Kentucky, 1972. *Publications:* Poetic Anthologies - Worldwide distributed, Sands of times, Dreams-Wishes-Poetic Forum Inspirational, 1987-88; Sparrowgrass Poetry Forum, 1988. *Memberships:* St Louis Symphony Orchestera's Woman's Association; Friends of Placido Domingo, American Symphony Orchestra League, Washington DC; Conductors Guild, Washington DC; American Music Centers Concert Presenter, New York City; World Concern, Washington DC. *Honours:* The Louise Kroeger Scholarship award, 1980; Stephan Foster Drama Trophy, 1972; St Louis Symphony Young Artist Award, 1958; American Music Award, 1952. *Hobbies:* Writing Poetry, Short Stories, Painting, Sketching, Sculpture, Designing. *Address:* 5556 Riverview Blvd., St Louis, MO 65120, USA.

MUSAFIA Judith N, b. 14 Mar 1941, North Hollywood, California, USA. Freelance Writer; Musician. m. Julien Musafia, 7 Jun 1962 (divorced 1977) 2 sons. *Education:* BA Creative Writing, California State University, 1974. *Appointments:* Journalist, California newspapers; Music critic and columnist for San Luis Obispo Telegram-Tribune 1983-; Food Columnist, New Times, San Luis Obispo, 1989-; Contributor of essays to Christian Science Monitor (Boston) 1981-. *Creative Works:* Novel (unpublished) 1986; Screenplay (unproduced) 1988; Poetry (few publications); Cookbook (in progress); Music, various recital appearances. *Honours:* International Fellowship, Music Critics Association of US and Canada, 1976; Short Story Prize, Santa Barbara Writers Conference, Santa Barbara, California, 1981; Golden Poet's Award, Poetry World, Sacramento, California, 1989. *Hobbies:* Cooking; Hiking; Camping. *Address:* 758 Evans Road, San Luis Obispo, CA 93401, USA.

MUSGRAVE Susan, b. 12 Mar. 1951, Canada. Author. m. Stephen Reid, 1986, 2 daughters. *Publications:* The Charcoal Burners, 1980; Hag Head, 1980; The Dancing Chicken, 1987; Poetry Books: Songs of the Sea Witch, 1970; Entrance of the Celebrant, 1972; Grave Dirt & Selected Strawberries, 1973; Gullband, 1974; The Impstone, 1976; Kiskatinaw Songs, 1977; Selected Srawberries & Other Poems, 1977; Becky Swan's Book, 1978; A Man to Marry, a Man to Bury, 1979; Tarts & Muggers: Poems New & Selected, 1982; Cocktails at the Mausoleum, 1985; Non-fiction: Speculating on the Sex Lives of People in Elevators, 1989; pamphlets; poetry in journals & magazines. *Honours Include:* Canada Council Short Term Grants, 1969, 1983; Canada Council Arts B Grant, 1972, 1976, 1979; Canada Council A Grant, 1985. *Address:* Box 241, Sidney, BC V8L 3Y3, Canada.

MUSOKE Rachel Nandawula, b. 8 Feb. 1944, Mityana, Uganda. Paediatrician. m. Apollo Musoke, 18 Dec. 1976, 1 son, 1 daughter. *Education:* MB.ChB, 1969; M.Med., 1974. *Appointments:* Internship, 1969-70; Senior House Officer, 1970-74; Senior Registrar, 1974-76; Special Training, Neonatology, 1977; Lecturer, 1978-83, Honorary Consultant, 1983-; Senior Lecturer, 1983-88. *Memberships:* Kenya Medical Association; Kenya Paediatric Association; Association of Physicians of East & Central Africa; Breastfeeding Information Group; Nairobi Music Society. *Honours:* Heinz Fellowship, British Paediatric Association, 1986. *Hobbies:* Singing; Dress Making. *Address:* PO Box 48066, Nairobi, Kenya.

MUSSO Judy G, b. 20 Aug. 1938, San Diego, California, USA. Word Processing Service Specialist. *Education:* San Diego State University, 1957-59. *Appointments:* Sales Manager, Sheraton Inn, Tulsa,

1969-71; Owner, Real Estate Agent, Stanley Investments, Tulsa, 1969-71; Marketing Consultant, Standard & Poor's Corporation, New York, 1972-73; Word Processing Specialist, Norrell Services, Dallas, Texas, 1982-86; Legal Assistant, City Attorneys Office, City Hall, Dallas, Texas, 1986-. *Memberships:* Secretary-Treasurer, Apollo Investment Club. *Honours:* Honourable Order of Kentucky Colonels, 1972-73, Chamber 44, 1944; Best Public Relations for the MKO States, 1968; Daughter of the American Revolution. *Hobbies:* Oil Painting; Reading; Computer. *Address:* 2206 Walraven Lane, Dallas, TX 75235, USA.

MUSZYNSKA-ZAMORSKA Danuta-Maria, b. 14 May 1931, Sroda, Poland. Painter; Artist. m. Zamorski, 15 Mar. 1955. *Education:* Diploma, Academy of Art, Lodz, 1958. *Appointments:* Teacher of Drawing, 1959-67; Designer of Texture and tapestry, Textile industry, 1967-74; Painter-Artist, mainly in water-colour, 1974- . *Creative works:* Paintings mainly in water-colour; Favourite subject of pictures are portraits of children and Mother and child. *Membership:* Polish Trade Union of Artists and Graphic Artists. *Honours:* Honour in Drawing, Lodz, 1958, 1961, 1965, 1968, 1971, 1972; First prize, painting, Lodz, 1973; Reward of audience in The International Competition, Maidoneck 85 Against the War, 1985; Gold Order of Merit for the creation in Art, 1986. *Hobbies:* Travelling; Reading biography and diary of famous people; Designing clothes. *Address:* Wierzbowa Str 24/26 Apt 13, Lodz 90-245, Poland.

MYERS Carole Ann Wade, b. 14 June 1938, Henderson, Kentucky, USA. Owner, Myers Ambulance Service; Certified Paramedic. m. Lawrence W. 28 Dec. 1957, deceased 1980, 1 son, 3 daughters. *Education:* Emergency Medical Technician, 1971; Paramedic Degree, Butler University/St Francis Hospital, 1979. *Appointment:* Owner, Myers Ambulance Service, Inc., 1966-. *Memberships:* Indiana Ambulance Association: Secretary 1981-83, President 1983-85, Treasurer, 1987-88; American Ambulance Association: Secretary, 1983-84, Treasurer, 1985-86, Vice President, 1987-88, President Elect. *Honours:* Woman of the Year, American Ambulance Association, 1983; Distinguished Hoosier Award, Governor of Indiana, 1984; Appointed as Commissioner, Indiana Emergency Medical Service Commission, 1986; Distinguished Service Award from the commission, March, 1988. *Hobbies:* Travel; Reading. *Address:* 150 N. Madison Ave., Greenwood, IN 46142, USA.

MYERS Gretchen Hardy Godar, b. 6 Dec. 1958, Webb City, Missouri, USA. Lawyer. m. Daniel Joseph Myers Godar, 11 Oct. 1985. *Education:* AB, 1981, JD 1984, University of Missouri. *Appointments:* Federal Judicial Clerkship, The Honorable James H Meredith, US District Court, 1984-85; Lawyer, Associate, Hullverson, Hullverson & Frank, 1985-. *Publications:* A Separate Course of Action for Contribution Among Joint Tort Feasors, 1983; Contributing Author, Antitrust Textbook, 1983. *Memberships:* Bar memberships: Missouri; California; Illinois; US District Court for Eastern & Western Districts, 1984; Missouri Association of Trial Attorneys, Board of Governors, Student President, 1982-83; Continuing Legal Education Co, Legislative Co, Fundraising Co; Missouri Bar, Special Co on Dispute Resolution, Tort Law Committee, Civil Practice Committee; Lawyers Association of St Louis, Bar Association of Metropolitan St Louis, Judicial Facilities Co; Women Lawyers Association of Greater St Louis. *Honours:* Missouri Law Review, 1982-84; Outstanding Young Woman of America; Outstanding Greek Woman, MU, 1980; Mortar Board; Speaker, The Vocational Expert, 1988; A Career in Law, 1989; Moderator and Coordinator, Personal Injury - Winning Trial Notebooks, 1989; Premises Liabilty: The Theory of Winning, 1989. *Hobbies:* Swimming; Tennis; Reading. *Address:* 7130 Maryland, St Louis, MO 63130, USA.

MYERS Marilyn Gladys, b. 17 July 1930, Nebraska, USA. Physician. m. Paul Frederick Motzkus, 24 July 1957. *Education:* BA, University of Omaha, 1956; MD, University of Nebraska College of Medicine, 1959;

Internship, Residencies, 1950-62; Fellow, Orange County General Hospital, 1962-64. *Appointments:* Director, Outpatient Clinic, 1964-72, Director, Hematology & Oncology, 1964-80, Childrens Hospital, Orange County; Associate Director, Leukapheresis Unit, 1971-80; Private Practice, Oncology, 1980-. *Publication:* Articles in Cancer; various other medical journals. *Memberships Include:* American Medical Association; California, Orange County Medical Associations; Orange County Pediatric Society; Los Angeles Pediatric Society. *Honours:* Grants for Clinical Research, American Leukemia Society, 1963, American Heart Association, 1964-66. *Hobbies:* Reading; Knitting. *Address:* 2220 East Fruit Street, Suite 217, Santa Ana, CA 92701, USA.

MYERS Mary Athena, b. 7 Apr. 1914, Edmonton, Alberta, Canada. Minister; Teacher; Writer; Poet. m. 25 Apr. 1937, 3 sons, 1 daughter. *Education:* Business Diploma, D.Div. *Appointments:* Secretary; Teacher, Physical Education, Foreign Language & Journalism, University of Maryland; Leader, Minister, International Organization, 18 years. *Publications:* My Truth; My Peace; The Higher Meaning of the 10 Commandments; The Path of Light; Here Comes the Sun. *Memberships:* various professional organisations. *Honours:* Recipient, various honours and awards. *Address:* 3427 Denson Place, Charlotte, NC 28215, USA.

MYERS-WALLS Judith Ann, b. 21 Aug. 1952, Roaring Spring, Pennsylvania, USA. Professor. m. Richard A. Myers-Walls, 11 Sept. 1977, 1 son, 1 daughter. *Education:* Lehrerseminar Zofingen, Switzerland, 1970-71; BA with high distinction, Psychology, Manchester College, 1974; MS, Child Development, 1977, PhD, Child Development, 1979, Purdue University. *Appointments:* Programme Director, Vernon Manor Children's Home, Wabash, Indiana, 1974; Houseparent, Fort Wayne (Indiana) Children's Home, 1975; Materials Development Specialist, 1975-76, Graduate Assistant, 1976-79, Assistant Professor, Associate Professor, Extension Specialist, 1979-, Purdue University, West Lafayette, Indiana. *Publications:* A Child in Your Life videotapes and publications for teen parents, 1984-88; Young Peacemakers Project Book (with Kathleen Fry-Miller), 1988; Book chapters, journal articles and publications for parents. *Memberships:* National Council on Family Relations; Indiana Council on Family Relations, President 1983-87; Society for Research on Child Development; National and Indiana Associations for the Education of Young Children; Indiana Council on Adolescent Pregnancy; National Organization on Adolescent Pregnancy and Parenting; Family Resource Coalition. *Honours:* Gamma Sigma Delta, 1977; General Foods Fellowship, Omicron Nu, 1978; Lilly Endowment Leadership Education Programme, 1987-88. *Hobbies:* Camping; Spending time with family. *Address:* Department of Child Development and Family Studies, Purdue University, West Lafayette, IN 47907, USA.

MYRICK Suellen, b. 1 Aug. 1941, Tiffin, Ohio, USA. President, Myrick Advertising; Mayor of the City of Charlotte. m. Edward Myrick, 11 Sept. 1977. 3 sons, 2 daughters. *Appointments:* President and Chief Executive Officer, Myrick Advertising; Board of Directors, Sister Cities International; Advisory Board, Housing and Urban Development; Elected Mayor, City of Charlotte, 1987-; At-large Member, Charlotte City Council, 1983-85; Board of Directors, NC Institute of Politics; Advisory Council, US Small Business Administration; Vice Chair, Transportation Committee, United States League of Cities; Secretary, National Conference Republican Mayors and Municipal Elected Officals; Founder and Coordinator, Charlottes volunteer tornado relief effort in lower North Carolina and upper South Carolina; Member, Charlotte Mecklenburg Citizens Forum; Executive Officer, Carolinas Council on World Affairs. *Memberships:* National Association of Female Executives; Advisory Board, United States Conference of Mayors; Director of the Alliance, Ohio, Office of the Stark County Court of Juvenile and Domestic Relations; Executive Secretary to the Mayor

and City Manager of Alliance, Ohio; Secretary,
Department of the Army, Erie Ordinance Depot, Port
Clinton, Ohio; Executive Committee, Muscular
Dystrophy Association; March of Dimes; Jaycettes; Elks
Auxiliary; Charlotte-Mecklenburg Republican Women's
Club; Charlotte Women's Political Caucus; League of
Women Voters; Public Relations Chair, Mecklenburg
Republican Executive Committee, etc. *Address:* 505
North Poplar Street, Charlotte, North Carolina 28202,
USA.

N

NAADIMUTHU Amirtha, b. 4 June 1951, Madras, India. Physician. m. Govindasami Naadimuthu, 17 Aug. 1975, 1 son, 1 daughter. *Education:* MBBS, Kilpauk Medical School, Madras, 1973; Various Residencies & Internships, 1974-79; Fellowship, Paediatric Hematology & Oncology, University of Medicine & Dentistry, Newark, USA, 1979-81. *Appointments:* Private Practice, General Medicine, Madras, 1975; Associate Medical Director, American Cyanamide Co., New York, 1981-82; Associate Medical Director, 1982-85, Senior Associate Medical Director, 1985-86, Director, Endocrinology & Fertility Control Section, 1987-, Berlex Labs Inc., Cedar Knolls. *Publications:* Several reports of clinical research studies; articles in professional journals incuding: Journal of Urology; American Journal of Rhinology. *Memberships:* American Academy of Allergy & Immunology; Joint Council of Allergy & Immunology; Asthma & Allergy Foundation of America. *Honours:* Certificate of First Honour, Anatomy, 1970, Physiology 1970; Gold Medal, Pharmacology, 1971; Certificate of First Honour, Surgery, 1973; Merit Scholarship, etc. *Hobbies:* Gardening; Cooking; Sewing; Music. *Address:* 669 Franklin Lake Road, Franklin Lakes, NJ 07417, USA.

NAGY Biserka, b. 27 June 1944, Zagreb, Yugoslavia. Cell & Molecular Biologist. m. Zvonimir Nagy, 22 Dec. 1971. *Education:* BS, Faculty of Natural Sciences, Zagreb, 1968; MS 1971, PhD 1973, Professor 1985, University of Zagreb. *Appointments:* Institute R. Boskovic, Zagreb, 1968-71; Paterson Laboratories, Christie Hospital, Holt Radium Institute, Manchester, UK, 1971-72; Central Institute for Tumours, Zagreb, 1973-89; Argonne National Laboratory, Illinois, USA, 1984-88; Department of Molecular Biology, University of Zagreb, 1988-. *Publications:* 45 original scientific papers in worldwide journals: subjects radiation biology, mutagenesis & cancerogenesis, interaction of radiation & drugs, role of plasminogen activator in metastasis, DNA damage & repair. *Memberships:* Treasurer, European Association for Cancer Research; European Society for Radiation Biology; Cell, Tissue & Organ Culture Study Group, New York Academy of Science. *Honours:* Fellowship to Institute of Molecular Biology, Paris, France, from European Molecular Biology Organisation, 1972; Fellowship, Italian Society of Biophysics & Molecular Biology, 1986; Eleanor Roosevelt Award, American Cancer Society, 1987. *Hobbies:* Geography; Art; Music. *Address:* Department of Molecular Biology, Biology Division, Faculty of Natural Sciences, Zagreb, Rooseveltov trg 6, 41000 Zagreb, Yugoslavia.

NAKHOST Zahra, b. 14 Aug. 1948, Tehran, Iran. Scientist. m. Ahmadreza Kamarei, 24 Aug. 1971. 1 son, 1 daughter. *Education:* BS, College of Nutrition and Food Science, Tehran, Iran, 1970; MS, Tehran University School of Agriculture, Karaj, Iran, 1975; MS, MIT Food Science and Technology, Cambridge, MA, USA, 1979. *Appointments:* Food Sci. Officer, Department of Food & Bev., Tehran, Iran, 1970-72; Project Officer, Agricultural Dev. Bank of Iran, 1975; Research Specialist, MIT, Dept of Nutrition & Food Science, 1979-86; Research Associate, MIT, Dept of Applied Biological Sciences, 1986-. *Publications:* Chapter in book: Fluorescence Analysis in Foods (Ed. L Munck). Contributed numerous articles to profesional journals includingFood Biotechnol; Adv. Space Res; Society of Automotive Engineers, Inc; Journal of Food Science. *Memberships:* Institute of Food Technologists; American Chemical Society; American Association for the Advancement of Science; New York Academy of Science. *Honours:* Letter of scholastic recognition, Imperial Court of Iran, 1968; 2 Grants, Phalavi Foundation, 1969 and 1970. *Hobbies:* Interest in art (impresionists and expressionists paintings); Social and outdoor activities. *Address:* Dept of Applied Biological Sciences, Massachusetts Institute of Technology, 77 Massachusetts Avenue, Cambridge, MA 02139, USA.

NALEPKA Joyce Dee, b. 24 Mar. 1936, Friendsville, Maryland, USA. Founder/President own company. m. Raymond, 19 Jan. 1963. 2 sons. *Education:* West Virginia University, 1954-57; Waynesburg College, 1957; American Society of Association Executives. *Appointments:* Founder/President, National Federation of Parents for Drug-Free Youth, 1980-86; Founder/President, Interstate Movement Moms Against Drugs (I'm MAD). *Publications:* Author: You Can Do It, Stop the Drug Epidemic in Your Community; Numerous articles in newspapers. *Memberships:* National Assoc Female Executives; National Assoc Broadcasters Drug Alcohol Advisory Board; McDonald's Corp Drug/Alcohol Advisory Bd; International Commission on Drug & Alcohol Prevention. *Honours:* Internatl Award for Pioneering & Developing Parent Organization for Drug-Free Youth, 1986; Jefferson Award for Public Service, 1982; Maryland State Senate Resolution Award, 1982; Outstanding Service to the Youth of America, 1983. *Hobbies:* Reading; Skiing. *Address:* 1805 Tilton Drive, Silver Spring, Maryland 20902, USA.

NAMMACK Marta Frimann, b. 8 Aug. 1957, Madrid, Spain. Fisheries Biologist. m. Ichirou Nakamura, 14 July 1984, divorced 22 Jan. 1988. 1 son, 1 daughter. *Education:* BS, Biology, College of William & Mary, 1979; MA, Marine Science, Virginia Institute of Marine Science (VIMS), 1982. *Appointments:* Summer Aide, VIMS, 1977; Turtle Observer 1980, Foreign Fisheries Observer, 1982-83, NMFS; Fisheries Biologist, Washington DC Government, 1986-88; Fisheries Biologist, Point No Point Treaty Council, Port Angeles, 1988-. *Memberships:* American Fisheries Society; American Fisheries Society, International Fisheries Section, Secretary/Treasurer; American Fisheries Society, Potomac Chapter, Treasurer; World Fisheries Congress Steering Committee. *Hobbies:* Scuba; Volleyball; Springboard diving; Photography; Stamp collecting; Tennis. *Address:* 4012 Newell Road, Apt C-1, Port Angeles, WA 98362, USA.

NANDI Anita, b. 12 June 1951, India. Senior Crown Councel; Lawyer. m. Panna Lal Nandi, 15 Aug. 1974, 2 daughters. *Education:* BA, Honours, Economics, 1971; LLB, Honours, 1975. *Appointments:* Assistant Crown Counsel, 1978-80, Crown Counsel, 1980-84, Senior Crown Counsel, 1984-, Attorney-General's Chambers, Hong Kong. *Memberships:* Law Society of Hong Kong; Solicitor, Supreme Court of Hong Kong; Solicitor, Supreme Court of England and Wales; Barrister & Solicitor, Supreme Court of Victoria, Melbourne, Australia. *Hobbies:* Reading; Travel; Music; Theatre. *Address:* Attorney General's Chambers, Queensway Government Offices; Queensway, Hong Kong.

NAPELLO Dolores Irene Walters, b. 4 Sept. 1950, Middletown, New York, USA. Educational Administrator. m. Ronald N. Napello, 29 May 1971. *Education:* AA, Orange County Community College, New York, 1979; BS, Fairleigh Dickinson University, New Jersey, 1981; MS 1985, CAS 1986, State University of New York (SUNY), New Paltz. *Appointments:* Executive secretary, Orange-Ulster BOCES, Goshen, NY, 1979-81; School Business Manager, West Park Union Free School District 1981-84, New Paltz Central School District 1984-86, NY; Assistant Superintendent, Personnel & Finance, Pocantico Hills Central School District, Tarrytown, NY, 1986-. *Publication:* Article, School Business Affairs journal, 1988. *Memberships:* Offices, including workshop presenter 1985-87, NY State Association of School Business Officials; International Association of School Business Officials; Southeastern Zone, & Southern Westchester Business Officials Associations; Association of Women Administrators, Westchester. *Honours:* Philip J. Moore Memorial Scholarship, 1984; Lynn Davis Memorial Scholarship, 1985. *Hobbies:* Travel; Dancing; Swimming; Bowling. *Address:* 1 Robalene Drive, Goshen, New York 10924, USA.

NARBUTIENE Ona, b. 26 Oct. 1930, Kaunas, Lithuania. Music Educator. m. 20 Aug. 1954, 1 son, 1 daughter. *Education:* Conservatoire of Vilnius, 1960. *Appointments:* Teacher of Music History, M.K.Ciuzionis Art School, Vilnius, 1969-. *Publications:* Monographs on Lithuanian composers Y. Naujalis, K. Brundzaite, E. Balsys, S. Valniunas and Y. Indra. *Memberships:* Union of Lithuanian Composers. *Honours:* Merited Arts Figure of the Lithuanian SSR, 1988. *Hobbies:* Broadcasting and telecasting. *Address:* Y. Kupalos 3Y-16, 232004 Vilnius, Lithuanian SSR.

NASH Mary, b. 10 Jan. 1947, Limerick, Ireland. Historian; University Professor. m. (1) Robert Tomas, 15 July 1970. (2) Richard Bristow, 19 July 1986. 1 daughter. *Education:* BA, National University of Ireland, 1967; Diploma European Studies, Turin, Italy, 1968; MA 1975, PhD 1977, University of Barcelona, Spain. *Appointments:* Founder and Director, Centre for Research on Women's History, University of Barcelona; Associate Professor, Department of Contemporary History, University of Barcelona. *Publications:* Mujeres Libres: Espana 1936-39, 1976; Femmes Libres. Espagne 1936-39, 1977; Mujeres Libres: Die Freien Frayuen in Spanien 1936-39, 1979; Mujer y movimiento obrero en Espana 1931-39, 1981; Mujer, familia y trabajo en Espana 1875-1936, 1983; Presencia y protagonismo: aspectos de la historia de la mujer, 1984; Mes enlla del silenci. Historia de les dones a Catalunya, 1988. Numerous articles in professional journals. *Memberships:* Board member, Centre for International Historical Studies, University of Barcelona; Regional representative for Spain, Women's Studies International Forum; Editorial board, Historia Social; President, Spanish Commission International Federation of Societies for Research in Women's History. *Hobbies:* Reading; Classical music and opera; Swimming. *Address:* CIHD, Calle Brusi 61, Barcelona 08006, Spain.

NATANAEL Christine Ann Gipson, b. 18 July 1963, Chicago, Illinois, USA. Freelance Rock Journalist. m. 30 Aug. 1984 (div. 1987). *Education:* Anthropology, John Jay College of Criminal Justice, New York City, 1985-86; Certificate, Ornamental Horticulture & Herbology, 1987. *Appointments:* Computer operator's assistant, International Business Machines (IBM), 1980-81; Beauty consultant, Merle Norman Cosmetics, 1981; Brokerage secretary, Union Mutual Insurance, 1982; Marketing consultant, OPC Associates Inc, 1984; Freelance rock journalist, 1985-. Contributor to magazines: Powerline; Reflex; Rock Scene; Concert Shots; Rock in the 80's; Metal Mania; Spin; Details; Whole Life; Easyrider's Tattoo; Thrash Metal. *Creative works:* 2 unpublished volumes of poetry; Numerous unshown sketches & portraits; Science fiction short stories. *Memberships:* National Beta Club, National Honour Society, 1980-81; Delegate: College Music Journal Seminar, Concrete Foundations Forum, New Music Seminar, 1988-89; Daughters of American Revolution. *Hobbies:* Studio 24 track production, Artist development & management; Artist marketing & publicity; Amer-Indian anthropological research; Occult research; Music theory & composition; Flute; Guitar; Photography. *Address:* One Penn Plaza, Suite 100, New York, NY 10119, USA.

NATCHEZ Gladys, b. 13 Nov. 1915, New York City, USA. Psychotherapist. m. Ben Nastchez, 29 Apr. 1939. 2 sons, 1 daughter. *Education:* MA, New College, Columbia University, 1939; PhD, New York University, 1958; Postdoctoral Psychoanalysis & Psychotherapy, 1968; Certified Psychologist, New York State; Professor Emeritus, City College, 1980. *Appointments:* New York University Reading Inst, 1953; Board of Coop Ed Sucs, Valhallah, New York, 1953-55; Westchest Children's Association, 1962; Ackerman Family Institute, New York (Staff), 1972-74; Payne Whitney Clinic, New York City Hospital, Staff Member, 1974-79. *Publications:* Basic Books: Reading Disability, 1964-88, 4th edition in print; complete, Gideon A Boy who hates Learning in School, 1975; Children with reading Problems, 1968; Personality Patterns & Reading, 1959. *Memberships:* American Adacemy of Psychotherapists; American Psych Association; American Orthopsychiatric Association; Jubinath Reading Association; NY State Psych Association; North Eastern Division of AAP; American Association of University Professors. *Honour:* Published PhD Thesis, Personality Patterns and Oral Reading, 1959. *Hobbies:* Gardening; Baking; Travel. *Address:* 263 West End Ave, New York City, NY 10023, USA.

NATUSCH Sheila Ellen, b. 14 Feb. 1926, Invercargill, New Zealand. Writer. m. Gilbert Gardner Natusch, 28 Nov. 1950. *Education:* C- Certificate, Dunedin Teachers College, 1945; MA, University of Otago, 1948. *Appointments:* Primary School Teacher, Dunedin, 1945-46; Library work, National Library, 1949; Secondary School Teacher, New Zealand Correspondence School, Wellington, 1960s. *Publications:* Stewart Island (with N.S.Seaward); Native Plants (also illustrator); Animals of New Zealand (also illustrator); Brother Wohlers; Native Rock (also illustrator); On the Edge of the Bush; The Cruise of the Acheron; Hell and High Water; Southward Ho!; William Swainson, FRS (with G.M.Swainson); A Bunch of Wild Orchids (also illustrator); A Pocketful of Pebbles (also illustrator); Illustrator: Mere's Adventures (Adele Schater); Aotearon (Olive Baldwin); Gardens Full of Wings (Jean Lawrence); Granny Gurton's Garden (with Lois Chambers). *Memberships include:* Royal Society of New Zealand; Royal Astronomical Society of New Zealand; New Zealand Ship and Marine Society; Goethe Society; Friends of the Turnbull Library; Hutt Valley Tramping Club; New Zealand Alpine Club. *Honours:* MacMillan Brown Prize, Otago University, 1946; Hubert Church Award, PEN, 1970. *Hobbies:* Painting and sketching; Travelling about on foot, by boat, bicycle and public transport; Staying at home by fireside in winter, outside in summer. *Address:* 46 Owhiro Bay Parade, Wellington 2, New Zealand.

NAUJALIS Jurate Irena, b. 29 Mar. 1935, Lithuania. Medical Technologist. m. 4 May 1957, after a tragic car accident was widowed and left a partial paraplegic, 7 May 1957. *Education:* AIMLS, 1970; FAIMLS, 1977 by Thesis. *Appointments:* Senior Hospital Scientist in charge of Coagulation Laboratory, The Queen Elisabeth Hospital. *Publications:* Co-author: Von Willebrand's Disease Type III, 1979; Congenital Anti-Thrombin III Deficiency with Mesenteric Vendus Thrombosis-Functional and Immunological Estimations, 1984; Fitzgerald Factor Deficiency in an Australian Aborigine, 1987; Simple Aggregometry to confirm Heparin induced Thrombocytopenia and Thrombosis Syndrome (HITTS), 1988; Warfarin-Induced skin Necrosis, Lupus like Anticoagulant (LLA) and Antiphospholipid Antibodies (PLA), 1988. *Membership:* Fellow, Australian Institute of Medical Laboratory Scientists. *Hobbies:* Music; Opera; Symphony Orchestra; Ballet; Cooking; Gardening; Swimming; Travel. *Address:* 156 Seaview Road, Tennyson 5022, South Australia, Australia.

NAVE Cynthia Webster, b. 10 Mar. 1951, Whittier, CA, USA. Artist; Photographer; Lecturer. m. Roy L. Nave, 12 Oct. 1974. *Creative Works:* Shows at: Kentucky Derby Museum; Animal Imagery; Thoroughbred-Bluegrass Style; Lexington Fine Arts Gallery; Paintings include: Pastoral; The Late Foal; Remembrance; Bold Forbes; The Meadow; Angle Light; Grace; Autumn Morning; Sunlight & Shadow; Sentinel; Waiting. *Memberships:* American Academy of Equine Art Association; Professional Photographer of America; Kentucky Professional Photographers Association. *Honours:* Kentucky Professional Photographers Association Artist of the Year, 1987 & 1988; American Artist Talent Search Top 100 Finalist, 1988. *Hobbies:* Horseriding; Sea Kayaking; Camping. *Address:* 30 Richmond Avenue, Lexington, KY 40502, USA.

NAVIAUX LaRee DeVee, b. 8 Aug. 1937, Nebraska, USA. Psychologist. m. Frank D'Abreo, 16 June 1973. *Education:* BSc., University of Nebraska, 1959; MSc., Iowa State University, 1963; PhD, Duquesne University, 1973. *Appointments Include:* Graduate Faculty, Carnegie Mellon University, 1966-69; Assistant

Professor, Psychology, West Georgia College, 1969-73; Regional Director, WV Dept. of Childen's Mental Health Services, Charleston, 1973-77; Regional Director, Children's Mental Health Services, Therapist & Educator, 1977-82; Private practice, 1982-. *Publications:* Articles in professional journals; book chapter. *Memberships Include:* American, West Virginia Psychological Associations; Association of Humanistic Psychology; Mental Health Association. *Honours:* Recipient, various honours & awards. *Hobbies:* Sewing; Decorating; Landscaping; Weaving; Travel; Reading. *Address:* 3500 Staunton Avenue, Charleston, WV 25304, USA.

NEAL Marie Augusta, b. 22 June 1921, Brighton, Massachusetts, USA. Teacher; Researcher; Member, Sisters of Notre Dame de Namur. *Education:* AB, Emmanuel College, Boston, 1942; MA, Boston College, 1953; PhD, Harvard University, 1963. *Career:* High school teacher, 1946-53; Faculty 1953-, Professor of Sociology 1963-, Emmanuel College; Visiting Professor, University of California 1968, Harvard Divinity School 1972-75. *Publications:* Books: Values & Interests in Social Change, 1965; A Socio-Theology of Letting Go, 1977; Catholic Sisters in Transition 1960's to 1980's, 1984; Just Demands of Poor, 1987; From Nuns to Sisters, 1990. *Memberships:* Past President: Society for Scientific Study of Religion & Association for Sociology of Religion; Member, American Sociological Association. *Honours:* Honorary degrees: Notre Dame University, Southbend, Indiana 1985, Our Lady of Elms College 1979, St Michael's College, Vermont 1987; Isaac Hecker Social Justice Award, Paulist Centre, Boston, 1977; Pope John XXIII Award, College of New Rochelle, 1985; Distinguished Teaching Award, American Sociological Association, 1986. *Hobbies include:* Effective metods for teaching social justice; Reading alternate media; Working for liberation of peoples. *Address:* Emmanuel College, 400 The Fenway, Boston, Massachusetts 02115, USA.

NEALE Marie Draga, Consultant Psychologist; Emeritus Professor. 1 son, 1 daughter. *Education:* Teaching Certificate, Auckland & Otago Teacher colleges, 1942; Diploma of Educaiton, 1945, MA, 1945, University of Auckland; PhD, University of Birmingham, England, 1956. *Appointments:* Foundation Professor, Chair, Special Education, Monash University, 1970- 87; Research Professor, Studies of Exceptional Children, 1982-87; Emeritus Professor, Education, Monash University, 1988-; Consultant Psychologist, 1988. *Publications:* numerous tests and papers on child development, reading skills. *Memberships:* Fellow, British Psychological Society; Fellow, Australian Psychological Society. *Honours:* Postgraduate Scholarship Travel Award, British Council, 1946; Pageant Pioneer Women, New South Wales, 1970; Rosemary F Dybwad Award in Mental Retardation, 1972; Mona Tobias Award, Australian Remedial Association; OBE, 1980. *Hobbies:* Reading; Music; Swimming; Dance; Film. *Address:* PO Box 141 Elwood, VIC 3184, Australia.

NEDEAU Janet Elaine Fryer, b. 3 May 1953, Port Chester, New York, USA. Sculptor; Photographer; Teacher. m. Christopher Alan Nedeau, 17 May 1983, 2 sons, 1 daughter. *Education:* BFA, Sculpture, 1977; MFA, 1983; Teacher's Credential, secondary single subject, Art, 1987. *Appointments include:* High school art teacher, San Francisco, 1979-81; Assistant Director, 20 x 20 Gallery, 1981-83; Substitute teacher, 1987-. *Creative work includes:* 4 solo exhibitions, San Francisco, 1983-; Numerous group exhibitions, California, Texas, London (UK), 1977-; Work reviewed, various magazines & journals; Also window displays, slide registry. *Membership:* Historic researcher, Buena Vista North Association, San Francisco. *Honours:* Awards: San Francisco Art Exposition Competition, 1982; Hill County Arts Foundation (Texas), East Texas International Photographic Competition, & Crocker-Kingsley Competition (Sacramento, California), 1984; Sacramento Regional Arts Council Festival, & Arco Centre Photo Competition (1st Place), California, 1985;

2nd Place, East Texas International Photographic Competition, 1988. *Hobbies:* Archaeology; River rafting; Skiing. *Address:* 102 Baker Street, San Francisco, California 94117, USA.

NEEDHAM Sheila June, b. 22 June 1937, Wallington, Surrey, England. Managing Director. *Appointments:* Various Secretarial Appointments, London, New York, California, 1955-71; Executive Director, Scribe-Ex Ltd., 1971-74; Founder, Managing Director, Needham Pritners Limited, 1974-. *Memberships:* Liveryman, Worshipful Company of Stationers & Newspaper Makers; Fellow, Royal Society for the Encouragement of Arts Manufactures & Commerce; President, Farringdon Ward Club, 1984-85; Freeman, City of London, 1977-; President, NE District, London Printing Industries Association, of British Printing Industries Federation; Fellow, BIM; Chairman, London Groups, Management Research Groups, 1986-. *Hobbies:* Travel; Theatre; Church; Hill Walking; Sailing; Sunshine. *Address:* Needham Printers Limited, Titchfield House, 69-85 Tabernacle Street, London EC2A 4BA, England.

NEEDLE Susan Judith, B. 18 June 1941, Newark, New Jersey, USA. Makeup Specialist. m. Robert Joseph Henderson, 14 Sept. 1985. *Education:* BEd, Secondary Education, University of Miami, Florida, 1962; MA, Human Resources and Public Affairs, University of Houston, Texas, 1979. *Appointments:* Event Manager, The Summit, Houston, Texas, 1975-83; Associate Professor, College of the Mainland, Texas City, 1983-85; Vice- President Operations, Total HELP Inc, Houston (Ushering Service), 1984-86; President, Colorific Inc, Houston, 1978-; Behaviour Counsellor, Nutri System, Ft Myers, 1987-; Assoc Professor, Edison Community College, Ft Myers, 1987-88; President, RJH & Assoc Inc, Cape Coral, 1987-88; Owner, Cosmetic & Skin Care Center, Cape Coral, 1988-; Distributor RCMA (professional makeup) for State of Florida, 1988-; Zonta International, 1988-; Department Head of Makeup, Hair and Wardrobe, Naples International Studio, 1988; Consultant to Walt Disney Studios, Florid, and Universal Studios, Florida, 1988; Executive Vice President Florida Motion Picture and Television Association, 1989. *Publications:* Fashion Impact (Create Your Own Fashion Style), 1986; Clear Lake Voice, Beauty and Fashion Editor. *Memberships:* American Business Womens Association, President, Bay Area Chapter, 1984- 85, Vice-President, 1985-86; Association of Fashion and Image Consultants, Charter Member; Professional Image Consultant's Association International, Charter Member; International Platform Association; American Association of University Women; Alpha Epsilon Phi; Florida Motion Picture & TV Assoc, 1987- 88; Public Relations Chairman, Zonta International, 1987-88. *Honours:* Award of Excellence, American Institute of Esthetics, 1983-85. *Hobbies:* Ceramics; Knitting; Boating; Reading. *Address:* 1417 Del Prado Blvd, Suite 480, Cape Coral, FL 33915, USA.

NEFF Bonita Dostal, b. 16 Aug. 1942, Grinnell, Iowa, USA. Communication Developmental Facilitator. m. 27 Apr. 1974. 1 daughter. *Education:* BA Communication 1964, MA Communication 1966, University of North Iowa; PhD Communication, University of Michigan, 1973; AA, Dance Career, Cum Laude, Lansing Community College, 1980. *Appointments:* Policy Analyst and Fellow, Institute for Educational leadership, Washington, 1975-76; Specialist, Cooperative Extension, 1977-80, Co-Investigator, Institute for Family and Child Studies, 1980-82, Michigan State University; Assistant Professor, Purdue University, 1982-87; President, Public Communication Associates, 1986-. *Publications:* Numerous articles to professional journals and magazines. *Memberships include:* International Communication Association; Speech Communication Association; World Communication Association; Women in Communication, Inc; International Society for the Intercultural Education, Training and Research; Institute for Educational Leadership. *Honours:* Recipient of numerous honours and awards. *Hobbies:* Dance; Piano; Reading; Professional clown. *Address:* Public

Communication Associates, 8320 Greenwood, Munster, Indiana 46321, USA.

NEFF Francine Irving, b. 6 Dec 1925, Albuquerque, New Mexico, USA. Corporate Director. m. Edward John Neff, 7 June 1948, I son, I daughter. *Education:* AA, Cottey College, Nevada, Missouri, 1946; BE, University of New Mexico, Albuquerque, 1948. *Appointments:* Treasurer of United States and National Director, US Savings Bonds Division, 1974-77; Member, Board of Directors, E-Systems, Inc, Dallas, Texas, 1978-; Member, Board of Directors, Hershey Foods Corporation, Hershay, Pennsylvania, 1978-; Member, Board of Directors, Louisiana-Pacific Corporation, Portland, Oregon, 1984-. *Memberships:* Past President: Republican Women's Federal Forum, District of Columbia, Albuquerque Federated Republican Women, Albuquerque City Panhellenic, Albuquerque Mortar Board Alumnae, Albuquerque Alpha Delta Pi Alumnae; Auxiliary to the New Mexico Society of CPAs; Chapters L and AL, PEO, New Mexico; Republican National Committeewoman for New Mexico. *Honours:* US Department of Treasury, Exceptional Service Award, 1976; Horatio Alger Association of Distinguished Americans Award, 1976; Outstanding Alumni Award, National Phi Theta Kappa, 1976; Distinguished Alumnae Citation, Cottey College, 1975; Outstanding Alumna Award, Grand Chapter,Alpha Delta Pi, 1974; University of New Mexico Lobo Award, 1974; Honorary degrees: Mount St Mary's College, Newburgh, New York, 1974; American International College, Springfield, Massachusetts 1975; New Mexico State University, Las Cruces, New Mexico. *Hobbies:* Republican politics; Reading; Bridge; Episcopal Church; PEO Sisterhood. *Address:* 1509 Sagebrush Trail SE, Albuquerque, NM 87123, USA.

NEGLEY Kathleen Ruth, b. 4 Feb. 1954, Pennsylvania, USA. Health Care Administrator. *Education:* BSc., 1976, MSc., 1982, MHA, 1986, University of Pittsburgh. *Appointments:* Numerous positions in Physical Therapy & Rehabilitation Administration, 1976-80; Director, Rehabilitation, Allegheny General Hospital, 1980-83; Assistant Vice President, Corporate Communications, 1983-. *Publications:* Co-author, Professional Responsibility for the Welfare of Poetential Life, 1988. *Memberships:* American College of Healthcare Executives, Nominee; William H. Ford Fellowship Selection Committee. *Honours:* Omicron Chapter, Delta Omega, 1986; William H. Ford Fellowship in Health Administration (1st Awardee), 1984; Foster G. McGaw Scholarship, 1984. *Hobbies:* Travel; Reading; Dance; Piano. *Address:* 3811 O'Hara Street, Pittsburgh, PA 15213, USA.

NEIMAN Tanya Marie, b. 28 June 1949, Pittsburgh, Pennsylvania, USA. Attorney; Directory of Legal Services Programme. *Education:* AB, Mills College, 1970; Juris Doctor, Hastings College of the Law, University of San Francisco, 1974. *Appointments:* Law Associate, Boalt Hall School of Law, 1974-76; California State Public Defender, Criminal Appellate Practice & Statewide Training Director, 1976-82; Associate General Counsel, Bar Association of San Francisco and Director of Volunteer Legal Services Programme, 1982-. *Publications:* Teaching Woman Her Place: The Role of Public Schools in the Development of Sex Roles in 24 Hastings Law Review, 1972. *Memberships:* State Bar of California, Legal Services Section Executive Committee, Secretary; Horizons Foundation, Vice President of Grantmaking & Director; National Lawyers Guild; Bay Area Lawyers for Individual Freedom; American Bar Association. *Honours:* American Bar Association, Harrison Tweed Award, 1985; Hastings College of Law Law Review. *Hobbies:* Scuba Diving; Flower Arranging; Politics. *Address:* Bar Association of San Francisco, Volunteer Legal Services Programme, 685 Market Suite 700, San Francisco, CA 94105, USA.

NELMS Sheryl Lynne, b. 3 Dec. 1944, Marysville, Kansas, USA. NCOA Counsellor; Writer. m. Danny Clayton Pennington, 3 June 1986, 2 sons, 1 daughter. *Education:* BS, South Dakota State University,

Brookings, 1979; Graduate work, MFA programme, University of Texas, Arlington, 1980. *Appointments:* Freelance Writer, 1979-; Insurance Adjustor, 1983-86; Insurance Sales, 1986-; Counsellor, Non-Commissioned Officers Association. *Publications:* Books of poetry: Their Combs Turn Red in the Spring; The Oketo Yahoos; Strawberries and Rhubarb; Over 2500 poems in literary and commercial magazines. *Memberships:* National League of American Pen Women (Letters Chairman); Oklahoma Writers Federation (Vice-President 2 years, Secretary 2 years); Society of Southwestern Authors; Western Writers of American; Dallas Writers Workshop; Dallas/Fort Worth Writers Workshop (President, Vice-President); Board of Directors, Head of Humanities Division, Trinity Arts Council; Tucson Poetry Society; Arizona Poetry Society. *Honours:* Phi Upsilon Omicron, 1977; Pi Gamma Mu, 1979; Kappa Delta Pi; 1st Place Schultz-Wyerth Research Award, 1978; Over 150 poetry prizes, 1978-. *Hobbies:* Painting; Weaving; Tennis; Camping; Cycling; Photography. *Address:* PO Box 31745, Tucson, AZ 85751, USA.

NELSON Beryce Ann, b. 10 Jan. 1947, Brisbane, Australia. Member of Parliament. m. John Arthur Nelson, 24 Aug. 1968. 1 son, 2 daughters. *Education:* Diploma in Radiography, 1967. *Appointments:* Radiography, Royal Brisbane Hospital, Royal Children's Hospital and private practice in Sydney, 1967-71; Public Relations Officer, Downs Syndrome Association, 1979-80; Member of Legislative Assembly of Queensland, 1980-83; Senior Public Relations consultant, Eric White Associates, 1983; Private Practice, Beryce Nelson Public Relations, 1983-; Endorsed as National Party candidate and Elected as Member for Aspley to the Legislative Assembly Queensland, 1986-; Chairman, Natural Resources/Economic Development Advisory Committee, 1987; Chairman, Brisbane River Committee, 1987; Chairman, Intellectual Handicap Services Task Force, 1988. *Memberships:* Institute of Radiography; PRIA. *Honour:* Justice of the Peace. *Hobbies:* Reading; Opera; Music; Art; Tennis. *Address:* 19 Retreat Street, Bridgeman Downs 4035, Queensland, Australia.

NELSON Eleanor Frances, b. 7 May 1944, Edinburgh, Scotland. Barrister. m. Dr E J Williams. 1 son, 1 daughter. *Education:* LLB, University of Adelaide, Australia, 1962-66. *Appointment:* Barrister, 1967-. *Memberships:* Chairman, Parole Board of South Australia, 1983-; Member of the Council of the South Australia College of Advanced Education, 1988-; Board of Examiners Supreme Court of South Australia, 1975-. *Honour:* Appointed one of Her Majesty's Counsel, 1982. *Address:* 140 Fullarton Road, Rose Park, South Australia 5067.

NELSON Elizabeth, b. Birmingham, Alabama, USA. Elementary Teacher. *Education:* BS, Alabama State Teachers College, 1939; ME, Wayne State Uiversity, 1948; Advanced Study: New York, & Heidelberg Universities, 1950; Michigan State University, 1961; University of Maryland, 1964, 1969; University of Paris, 1965, 1967; University of Switzerland, 1969, 1971. *Appointments:* Teacher, 1945-55, Principal, 1955-58, Curriculum Co-ordinator, 1959, George Washington Carver School; Teacher, Bad Kreznach Elementary School, Germany, 1962; Teacher, Vassincourt American Elementary School, France; Teacher, Verdun American Elementary School, France, 1966; Teacher, SHAPE International School, Belgium, 1967-84; Teacher, City of Ferndale, Michigan, UsA, 1984-88. *Memberships Include:* Organized, Carveer Federationo Teachers, Ferndale, 1947, President 1947-54; Organised, Inkster Federation of Teachers, 1950-51; Michigan Federation of Teachers; Zeta Phi Beta; District Chairman, Association for Childhood Education International; many others. *Honours Include:* Governors Award, Notable Contributions to Education & the People of Michigan, 1955; Zeta of the Year, Zeta Phi Beta, 1960; Honoured with a programme, This is Your Life, by the Crver School Teachers; Recipient, of many other honours. *Hobbies:* Gardening; Music; Languages. *Address:* PO Box 03887, Detroit, MI 48203, USA.

NELSON Jo, b. 5 Feb. 1946, Del Nonte, Colorado, USA. Antiquarian bookseller; Realtor; Author. *Education:* BA, German, 1968. *Appointments:* Teacher, Maryland, 1968-70; Teacher, Colorado, 197-72 and 1975; Office Manager, Wolf Creck, 1972-74; Owner, Chef La Mariposa, 1974- 80; Realtor, 1980-; Bookseller, 1987-. *Publications:* Poetry published in dozens of small poetry and regional magazines also several short stories. *Memberships:* Pacific Northwest Writers Assoc; National Association of Realtors; Board Trustees, Crede Repertory Theater, 1975-79; Board Directors, South Fork Water District, 1978-79; Board Member, Hillside Free Clinic, 1971- 72. *Hobbies:* Piano; Gardening; Art. *Address:* 3518 NE 147, Seattle, Washington 98155, USA.

NELSON Joni Lysett, b. 3 June 1938, Michigan, USA. Lawyer. m. Alden Arnold Nelson, 21 June 1965, deceased, 2 sons. *Education:* BA, cum laude, Michigan State University, 1959; JD, Harvard Law School, 1962. *Appointments:* Lawyer, New York City, 1962-; Partner, Rogers & Wells, 1977-. *Publications:* New Euromarket Products, NIFs and Eurocommercial Paper, 1986; The Inconvenient Kitchen, 1972; Editor, International Ship Finance, 1981, 1983, 1984. *Memberships Include:* Fellow, Institute of Directors, London; Fellow, Economic Club of New York; Advisory Board, World Trade Institute; American, International Bar Associations; Bar Association of the City of New York; Founder, City Women's Network. *Hobbies:* Running; Tennis; Sailing; Gardening; Quilting. *Address:* Rogers & Wells, 200 Park Avenue, New York, NY 10166, USA.

NELSON Lynn Anne, b. 12 June 1952, Panama City, USA. Businesswoman. m. Ron Nelson, 5 Sept. 1971, divorced 1978, 1 son, 1 daughter. *Appointments:* Microfilm Technician, Microfilm Services, Corona, 1970- 71, Blue Cross Blue Shield of Minnesota, 1972-73, Customer Services Representative, 1973-76; Regional Sales Reprsentative, 1978-83, General Manager, 1983-85, Vice President, 1985-, MicroD International. *Memberships:* Minneapolis Society of fine Arts; Board of Directors, Neoteric Arts Inc. *Hobbies:* Drawing; Illustration; Painting; Golf; Fishing; Hunting. *Address:* 1212 Hillside lane, Burnsville, MN 55337, USA.

NELSON Marilyn, b. 19 Aug. 1939, Minneapolis, Minnesota, USA. Vice President, Carlson Holdings. m. 30 June 1961. 1 son, 2 daughters. *Education:* BA, Intl Econ, Smith College, 1961. *Appointments:* Carlson Companies, 1963-. *Memberships:* President, Citizens State Bank of Waterville, MN; Bd of Dir, Carlson Companies Inc; First Bank System; First Trust Company; US West Communications; Minneesota Orchestral Assnl; United Way of Mpls; Plymouth Music Series; Women's Economic Roundatble (Founder); United Way of America. *Honours:* Member, Royal Order of the North Star First Class, King Carl Erik XVI Gustaf and Queen Silvia of Sweden; Order of the White Rose, Officer First Class, President of Finland; Honorary Degrees: Doctor of Humane Letters, College of St Catherine; Doctor of Humane Letters, Gustavus Adolphus College; Extraordinary Leadership, Greater Mpls Chamber of Commerce. *Hobbies:* Water psorts; Downhill and cross country skiing. *Address:* Carlson Companies Inc, Carlson Parkway, P O Box 59159, Minneapolis, MN 55459, USA.

NELSON Martha J, b. 13 Aug. 1952, Pierre, South Dakota, USA. Editor. *Education:* BA, magna cum laude, Barnard College, 1976. *Appointments:* Managing Editor, Signs, Journal of Women in Culture & Society, 1976-1980; Editor, MS magazine, 1980-85; Editor in Chief, Women's Sports and Fitness, Palo Alto, 1985-. *Publication:* Women in the American City, Editor, 1980. *Memberships:* American Society of Magazine Editors; Media Alliance. *Address:* Women's Sports & Fitness, 310 Town & Country Village, Palo Alto, CA 94301, USA.

NELSON Mary Ellen Dickson, b. 24 Mar. 1933, Minneapolis, Minnesota, USA. Actuary. m. David Aldrich Nelson, 25 Aug. 1956. 2 sons, 1 daughter. *Education:* BA, Vassar College, 1950-54; Fellow, Society of Actuaries, 1970. *Appointments:* North American Life & Casualty Co, 1955-56; John Hancock Mutual Life Insur Co, 1956-58; Actuary, David R Kass & Assoc, 1973-74; President, Nelson & Co, 1975; President, Conrad, Nelson & Co, 1975-81; President, Nelson & Co, 1981-; Director, Blount, Inc, 1986-. *Memberships:* Fellow, Society of Actuaries; American Academy of Actuaries; Enrolled Actuary (Joint Board, Department of Labor/Treasury Department); Cincinnati Actuaries Club; Midwest Pension Conference (Vice Chairperson Ohio Valley Chapter). *Honours:* Phi Beta Kappa, 1953; Fulbright Scholarship to Cambridge University, England, 1954-55. *Address:* Nelson & Co, 105 West Fourth Street Suite 1120, Cincinnati, Ohio 45202, USA.

NELSON Merle Chandler, b. 30 June 1908, Nicholson, Georgia, USA. Real Estate. m. Ealton L. Nelson, 2 Dec. 1938, 2 daughter. *Education:* Studies: American University, George Washington University, 1938. *Appointments:* Executive Secretary, Civil Aeros. Bd., Washington, 1938- 41; Real Estate Broker, North Virginia Board Realtors, Fairfax, 1957-87; President, Nelson Realty Inc., Arlington, 1957-87. *Memberships:* Arlington County Democratic Committee Lake Barcroft Civic Association; Northern Virginia Board of Realtors. *Hobbies:* International Travel; Civic Associations; Political Activity. *Address:* 3816 Lakeview Terrace, Falls Church, VA 22041, USA.

NELSON Toni Gaylord Cooke, b. 9 Sept. 1949, Houston, USA. Marketing Director. m. 27 Nov. 1970, 1 son, 1 daughter. *Education:* Texas Technical University, 1967-70; University of Houston, 1970-71. *Appointments:* Market Research Field Supervisor, Higginbotham Associates, 1971-76; Realtor, LaGuarda, Gavrel & Kirk, 1983-84; Realtor, Gary Greene Realtors, Better Homes & Gardens, 1984; Manager, Marketing Director, Gary Greene Realtors, Better Homes & Gardens, 1984-. *Publications:* Articles in professional journals. *Memberships:* Ft. Bend County Board of Realtors, President 1988; Texas Associatiron of Realtors, Board, 1989-; Ft. Bend County Chamber of Commerce, 1989-90; Greater Ft. Bend Economic Development Council. *Honours:* Realtor of the Year, Ft. Bend County Board of Realtors 1987. *Hobbies:* Economic Development; Governmental Affairs/Legislation; Tennis. *Address:* 1418 Sugar Creek Blvd., Sugar Land, TX 77478, USA.

NELSON Victoria Elizabeth, b. 14 Sept. 1953, St Louis, Missouri, USA. Health Care Executive. *Education:* BA, 1975; MA, Health Administration, 1977. *Appointments:* Acting Chief Executive Officer & Associaate Administrator, St Louis City Hospital, 1983-85; Executive Vice President & Chief Operating Officer, St Mary's Hospital, East St Louis, 1985-. *Memberships:* American College of Health Care Executives; Hospital Association, Metropolitan St Louis; Illinois Hospital Association; Catholic Hospital Association; St Louis Association, Women in Health Care Administration. *Honours:* Yes I Can Award, special achievement, business & industry, 1987; Biographical recognitions. *Hobbies:* Collecting antique Kodak cameras; Sewing & fashion design. *Address:* 5058 Northland Avenue, St Louis, Missouri 63113, USA.

NELSON-HUMPHRIES Tessa, b. Yorkshire, England. Professor of English Literature; Writer; Poet. m. (1) Kenneth N Brown, 1 June 1957, deceased 1962. (2) Cecil H Unthank, 26 Sept. 1963, deceased 1979. *Education:* BA, University of London; MA, University of North Carolina; PhD, University of Liverpool. *Appointments:* University, New Mexico, 1960-63; Head of English, Walsall, Staffordshire, England; Director of English, Windsor College, Buenos Aires, Argentina; Professor of English, Cumberland College, Kentucky, USA, 1964-. *Publications:* Poetry published in Blue Unicorn; Z-Miscellaneous; Outposts etc. Articles and children's stories in Cats Magazine; Child Life; Let's Live and others. *Memberships:* Mensa; Society of Children's Book Writers; National Writers' Club; Society Women Writers and Journalists; Vegetarian Society of United

Kingdom, etc. *Honours:* Best Actress Awards, 1962, 1979; Julia Cairns Silver Trophy for Poetry, London, 1978; Article and Short story Prizes, London, 1975, 1986, 1987, 1988; Poetry Prize, London, 1988; Fulbright Fellow, 1955-56; AAUW Fellow, 1972-73; Mellon Awards for Travel/Study China, Iberia, 1981, 1987, 1988; James Still Fellow, 1983; Nominated 3 times for Excellence in Teaching Award, most recent, 1988. *Hobbies:* Travel; Gourmet Vegetarian Cooking; Animal Welfare; King Charles Spaniels and Golden Retriever Owner; Reading; Music. *Address:* York Cottage, Florence Avenue Box 944, Williamsburg, KY 40769, USA.

NEMET Stella, b. 14 Mar. 1905, Cracow, Poland. Musician. m. Paul Nemet, 10 July 1932. 1 daughter. *Education:* MA, University of Cracow, Poland, 1925; Diploma from the Liszt Ferenc Academy of Music in Budapest, Hungary, 1930; Diploma in Music, Conservatorium of Cracow, 1924. *Appointments:* Concert and Radio solo performances in Poland, Austria, Hungary and Australia, 1925-82; High School Teacher, Melbourne, Australia, 1967-790; Leader of the Victorian Chamber Players; Member of Orion Trio; Official adjudicator at Eisteddfodds and Competitions. *Publication:* History of the Musical Society of Victoria, 1861-1981, 1982. *Memberships:* President, Council of the Musical Society of Victoria, 1972-79; Patron, Musica Viva Australia. *Honours:* Prize winner, Polish Radio Violin Contest, 1929; Queen Elizabeth II's Silver Jubilee Medal, 1977; Honoured by Queen Elizabeth II with MBE 1980. *Hobbies:* Languages; Reading. *Address:* Mt Waverley, Victoria, Australia.

NESBIT Phyllis Schneider, b. 21 Sept. 1919, Newkirk, USA. District Judge. m. Peter Nicholas Nesbit, 14 Sept. 1939. *Education:* BS, chemistry, 1948; LLB, 1958; JD, 1969. *Appointments:* Partner, Wilters Brantley and Nesbit, 1958-74; Sole Practice, 1975-76; Municiple Judge, Daphne, 1964-76; Municiple Judge, Silverhill, 1969-76; City Attorney, Loxley, 1975-76; District Judge, 1977-89. *Memberships:* Alabama, Baldwin County Bar Associations; Phi Delta Delta; Alabama Women Lawyers Association; Alabama Municiple Judges Association. *Honours:* Recipient, various honours and awards. *Hobbies:* Sewing; Sailing; Gardening. *Address:* 302 Creek Drive, Fairhope, AL 36532, USA.

NESVAN Geraldine Ann, b. 28 June 1927, Council Bluffs, Iowa, USA. Clinical Psychologist; Nationally Certified School Psychologist. *Education:* Intern, Child Service Study, 1958-60, BA, Psychology, 1959, MA, Psychology, 1960, University of Nebraska, Omaha; Special Education and Psychology degree UNL, and additional graduate work, 1968. *Appointments:* Director, Child Study Service, University of Nebraska, Omaha, 1960-67; Director, Psychological Services, Omaha Public Schools, 1960-76; Consultant, Powell School for Handicapped, Red Oak, Iowa, 1966-81; Consultant, Richard Young Memorial Hospital, 1970-73; Consultant, Nebraska School for the Deaf, 1976-82; Director, Psychological Services, Children's Memorial Hospital, Omaha, Nebraska, 1976-84; Consultant, Chemical Dependency Unit, Methodist Midtown, 1980-82, 1986; Private Practice, Omaha Children's Clinic PC, Omaha, 1981-; Consultant, Iowa School for the Deaf Council Bluffs, Iowa, 1983-86. *Memberships:* American Psychological Association; Nebraska Psychological Association; Nebraska Society of Professional Psychologists; Fellow, American Association on Mental Deficiency Past Chairman 1975 and 1985 Region VIII, General Division Chair 1987-88); National Association of School Psychologists (Past State Representative, Past National Publicity Chairman); Council for Exceptional Children (Past President Omaha Chapter). *Honours:* PTA Scholarship Award, 1960; Board Member, Past President & President 1989-91 Vice-President, Edwards Foundation; President, 1975, 1986-90, Special Advisor, 1988-89, Zonta, Omaha Area Club; Nebraska School Psychology Founders Award, 1984; Board Member, 1985, Vice-President, 1988-89, Nebraska Committee for Children and Youth; Appointed Education Advisory Committee, Senator Kannes, Nebraska, 1988-89.

Address: 7040 Rainwood Road, Omaha, NE 68152, USA.

NETSCH Dawn Clark, b. 1926, Cincinnati, Ohio, USA. State Senator; Professor of Law. m. Walter A. Netsch. *Education:* BA, distinction, Northwestern University, 1948; JD, magna cum laude, Northwestern University School of Law, 1952. *Appointments:* Staff, league of Female Voters of Cook Couny, 1949; Private Practice, 1952-54; Law Clerk to Federal Judge Julius J Hoffman, US District Court, Northern District of Illinois, 1954-56; Private Practice, Snyder, Chadwell, Keck, Kayser & Ruggles, Chicago, 1957-61; Aide to Governor Kerner, 1961-65; Professor, Northwestern University School of Law, 1965-; Senator, Illinois State Senate, 1972-. *Publications:* State and Local Government in a Federal System, with D R Mandelker, 1977, 2nd edition with D R Mandelker & P Salsich, 1983; several articles on State constitutional issues. *Memberships Include:* American, Illinois State & Chicago Bar Associations; Board of Directors, Illinois Division, American Civil Liberties Union; many other professional organisations. *Honours Include:* 5 Awards, Ehel Parker Best Legislator Award, Independent Voters of Illinois, 1973-81; 4 awards, Environmental Legislators of the Year Award, 1975-81. *Address:* 561 West Diversey, Suite 211, Chicago, IL 60614, USA.

NEU Margaret Jane, b. 13 Oct. 1951, Wisconsin, USA. Library Director. *Education:* BA, 1973, MLS, 1974, University of Wisconsin, Madison. *Appointments:* Alice Public Library, Alice, Texas, 1974-76; Corpus Christi Public Libraries, Corpus Christi, Texas, 1976-80; Lewis & Clark Library, State of Montana Energy Project, Helena, Montana, 1980-82; Director, Caller-Times Library, Corpus Christi, 1982-. *Publications:* Articles in several professional newsletters and journals. *Memberships:* Texas Library Association (state and district); Special Libraries Association (Chair of several committees). *Honours:* Lecturer in numerous workshops. *Hobbies:* Aerobics; Gardening; Needlecrafts; Women writers, especially published by small presses and feminist presses. *Address:* 409 Atlantic, Corpus Christi, TX 78404, USA.

NEU Marlene (Marnie) Theresa Trossen, b. 2 Dec. 1947, St Cloud, Minnesota, USA. Anchor/Reporter. m. David Leo Neu, divorced, 2 sons. *Education:* BA, Wichita State University, Kansas, 1975. *Appointments:* Reporter Kard TV, Wichita, 1975; Staff Writer, Wichita Talk, 1976-77; Education Services Advisor, USAF Kalkar, Federal Republic of Germany, 1977-79; Reporter, KWKH Radio, Shreveport, Louisiana, USA, 1979-80; Reporter, Anchor, KTAL TV 1980-84; Public Relations & Marketing Director, Shreveport Eye Research Foundation, 1984-86; Anchor, Reporter, KTAL TV, Shreveport, 1986-. *Memberships:* Society of Professional Journalists; Women in Communications Inc.; Public Relations Society of America; Shreveport chapter, American Medical Advertising Federation; Marketing & Public Relations; American Hospital Association; Louisiana Society for Hospital Public Relations & Marketing; Medical Group Management Association. *Honours:* Pelican Award for TV Public Service Announcements, Pelican Award for Print Advertising, Louisiana S Hospital, 1985. *Hobby:* Theatre. *Address:* 3405 Nathan Circle, Shreveport, LA 71108, USA.

NEUBERT Joan S., b. USA. Operation Systems Analyst. *Education:* BSIE, Pennsylvania State University, University Park; MBA, Drexel University, Philadelphia. *Appointments:* Industrial Engineer Trainee, US Postal Service, Washington, District of Columbia, 1981-83; Industrial Engineer, Staff, 1983-85, Maintenance Officer, 1985-86, Operations Systems Analyst, 1986-, US Postal Service, Philadelphia, Pennsylvania. *Memberships:* Institute of Industrial Engineers, President 1986-87, Treasurer 1985-86, 1987-88; National Association of Female Executives; Career Counsellor, Pennsylvania State University Alumni Association; Drexel University Alumni Association. *Honours:* Recipient of Beta Gamma Key Award for

Academic Excellence, Drexel University. *Address:* PO Box 8601, Philadelphia, PA 19197, USA.

NEUGARTEN Bernice Levin, b. 11 Feb. 1916, Norfolk, Nebraska, USA. Social Scientist. m. Fritz Neugarten 1 July 1940, 1 son, 1 daughter. *Education:* BA, University of Chicago, 1936; PhD, 1943; DSc., (hon), University of Southern California, 1980, University of Nigmegen, Netherlands, 1988. *Appointments:* Research Associate, Committee on Human Development, 1948-50, Assistant Professor, 1951-60, Associate Professor, 1960-64, Professor, 1964-80, Chairman, 1969-73, Professor, Social Service Administration, 1978-80, University of Chicago; Professor, Human Development and Social Policy, Northwestern University, 1980-88; Rothschild Distinguished Scholar, University of Chicago, 1988-. *Publications:* Articles in various journals; Editor, Middle Age & Aging, 1968; Co-Editor, Age Discrimination, 1981; Editor, Age or Need? Public Policies for Older People, 1982. *Memberships:* Numerous professional organisations. *Honours:* Recipient, many honours and awards. *Address:* 5801 Dorchester Ave., Chicago, IL 60637, USA.

NEUMAN Shirley Carol, b. 10 Oct. 1946, Edmonton, Canada. Professor; Literary Critic. m. (1) Paul Swartz, 10 Oct. 1967, divorced 1979. (2) Jorge Frascara, 8 Apr. 1982. *Education:* BA English 1968, MA English 1969, PhD English 1976, University of Alberta. *Appointments:* Sessional Lecturer 1976; Assistant Professor 1977-86; Professor, 1986-; Chair, Women's Studies Program, 1987-, University of Alberta. *Publications:* Gertrude Stein: Autobiography and the Problem of Narration, 1979; Some One Myth: Yeats Autobiographical Prose, 1982; Labyrinths of Voice: Conversations with Robert Krdetsch, co-author, 1982; Co-editor, A Mazing Space: Writing Canadian Women; Co-editor, Gertrude Stein and The Making of Literature, 1988. *Honours:* Social Sciences & Humanities Research Council of Canada, 1982; Gabrielle Roy Essay Award, 1985; Fellow of the Royal Society of Canada, 1989. *Interests:* Canadian Literature; 20th Century Literature; Women's Literature; Feminist theory. *Address:* Dept of English, University of Alberta, Edmonton, Alberta, Canada T6G 2E1.

NEUMEYER-HUTCHINGS LeAnne von, b. USA. Communication Executive & Consultant; Administrator. m. 1962-85, 5 sons, 1 daughter. *Education:* Humanities, Brigham Young University. *Appointments:* Administrative Director, Pasadena Genealogical Library, California, 1975-82; Design Consultant, Office Systems Management, Harvey Malkin Jewellers, Los Angeles, 1981-; Director, Community Relations, Southern California Public Communications Council, Church of Jesus Christ of Latter-Day Saints, 1981-; Director, Corporate Relations, Seminar Coordination, REDI Preparedness Inc, 1981-; Vice President, Development, Steenhoek, Neeley, von Neumeyer & Associates, 1985-; Executive Associate, California Bicentennial Foundation for US Constitution, 1987; Legislative Committee on Child Pornography; Chair, Public Relations Committee, LA County Commission on Obscenity & Pornography, 1988-. *Publications:* Former freelance journalist, columnist, Foothill Intercity News, Arcadia, California. *Memberships include:* Various professional associations. *Honours include:* Best of Show, Sculptors Workshop West, 1983; Masterworks Chorale, LA Symphonic Chorale, 1982; Mother of Year, Church of Latter-Day Saints, 1979; Merit award, violin, National Institute of Music & Arts; Numerous biographical recognitions. *Address:* 17 La Sierra Drive, Arcadia, California 91006, USA.

NEUWIRTH Gloria S, b. 16 Aug. 1934, New York City, USA. Attorney. m. Robert S. Neuwirth, 9 June 1957 (divorced), 1 son, 3 daughters. *Education:* BA, Hunter College, 1955; JD, Yale Law School, 1958. *Appointments:* Associate Director, joint research project on Court Calendar Congestion, Columbia Uiversity project for Effective Justice, 1958-61; Partner, Kridel Slater & Neuwirth, New York, 1978-82; Associate, Kaye Scholer, Fierman, Hays & Handler, New York, 1982-84; Associate, Graubard Moskovitz McGoldrick Dannett

& Horowitz, New York, 1984-86; Partner, Kridel & Neuwirth, 1986-. *Publications:* Who Sues in New York City? A Study of Automobile Accident Claims, with R. B. Hunting, 1962; How to Protect Lifetime Transfers from Being Included in the Estate of the Transferor, Taxation for Lawyers, 1982; Steps a Client Can Take to Plan for Future Medical Treatment Decisions, Estate Planning, 1985; Estate planning for the Surving Spouse, Prentice Hall, 1988. *Memberships:* Committee on Immigration & Nationality Law, 1972-75, Committee on Trusts, Estates & Surrogates Courts, 1979-82, New York City Bar Association; Trusts & Estates Law Section, New York State Bar Association; American Bar Association; Florida Bar; etc. *Honours:* C La Rue Munson Prize, Yale Law School, 1958; Fellow, American College of Probate Counsel. *Address:* 630 West 254th Street, Riverdale, NY 10471, USA.

NEW Suzan Wynn, b. 19 May 1956, Linden, Texas, USA. Registered Nurse. m. 15 Oct. 1983, 1 daughter. *Education:* Dallas Baptist College, 1978; Management programme, Baylor University Medical Centre, 1982. *Appointments:* Operating room staff nurse, doctors' health facilities, Dallas, 1978-81; Staff nurse (operating room) 1982-84, charge nurse grade III (education) 1984-86, Education Supervisor 1986-, Operating Room Services, Baylor University Medical Centre. *Creative works:* Author, educational video programme & study guide, 3 Techniques in the Art of Communication. *Memberships:* Treasurer, Dallas Association of Operating Room Nurses; Audio-Visual Committee, National Association of Operating Room Nurses. *Honours:* Plaque, video production; CNOR certification, 1985. *Hobbies include:* Singing: Performances with Dallas Civic Chorus 1983- 84, Mesquite Civic Chorus 1986. *Address:* Baylor University Medical Centre, 2 Roberts Operating Room Education, 3500 Gaston Avenue, Dallas, Texas 75246, USA.

NEWBY Karen Smith, b. 7 Apr. 1959, Blue Island, USA. Accountant. m. Thomas P. Newby, 24 Dec. 1981. *Education:* BA, Augustina College, 1981; MBA, Keller Graduate School of Management, 1986. *Appointments:* Reservation Sales Agent, Northwest Airlines, 1981-84; Travel Consultant, Arthur Andersen & Co., 1984-87; Accountant, Peaelzer Brother, 1987-. *Membership:* American Management Association. *Honours:* BA, 1981; MBA, Distinction, 1986. *Hobbies:* Trombone Playing; Piano; Golf; Gardening; Sewing; Cooking; Reading. *Address:* 4037 W. 99th Place, Oak Lawn, IL 60453, USA.

NEWLIN Margaret Elizabeth Rudd, b. 27 Feb. 1925, New York City, New York, USA. Writer; Critic; Poet; Artist. m. Nicholas Newlin, 2 Apr. 1956, 4 sons. *Education:* BA, Bryn Mawr College, 1947; PhD, University of Reading, England, 1951. *Appointments:* Admissions, 1948, teaching, 1953, Bryn Mawr College; Teaching, Harcum Junior College, 1953; Teaching, Washington College, 1955-56; Various freelance seminars. *Publications:* Under Rudd: Dividid Image, 1953; Organiz'd Innocence, 1956; Under Newlin: Poetry: The Fragile Immigrants, 1971; Day of Sirens, 1973; The Snow Falls Upward, 1976; The Book of Mourning, 1982; Collected Poems, 1986. *Memberships:* Poetry Society of America; Authors League; Authors Guild. *Honours:* Gerowld O and M C Thomas Awards, Bryn Mawr, 1947; Fellowships, American Association of University Women and American Philosophical Society, 1948-51; Greenwood Prize, 1969, 1971; NBA nomination in poetry, 1977; Fellow, National Endowment for the Arts, 1977; Honorary DLitt, Washington College, 1980. *Hobbies:* Swimming; Raising orphaned wild birds and animals; Cooking. *Address:* Shipley Farm, Secane, PA 19018, USA.

NEWMAN Andrea, b. 7 Feb. 1938, England. Writer. *Education:* BA, 1960, MA 1972, London University. *Publications:* A Share of the World, 1964; Mirage, 1965; The Cage, 1966; Three into Two Won't Go, 1967; Alexa, 1968; A Bouqet of Barbed Wire, 1969; An Evil Streak, 1977; Another Bouquet, 1977; Mackenzie, 1980; A Sense of Guilt, 1988; 45 TV plays including series;

contributor to: She; Woman's Own; Woman's Realm. *Address:* c/o A D Peters, 10 Buckingham Street, London WC2, England.

NEWMAN Anita Nadine, b. 13 June 1949, Honolulu, Hawaii, USA. Assistant Professor, Dept of Surgery. m. Frank Ellis Burkett, 30 Dec. 1978. 3 sons, 1 daughter. *Education:* AB, Stanford University, 1971; MD, Dartmouth Medical School, 1975; Intern, Surgery, 1975-76; Resident, Surgery, otolaryngology, 1976-78, Northwestern Memorial Hospital, Chicago; University of California Los Angeles, 1979-83. *Appointments:* Staff Surgery, Wadsworth VA Hospital, Los Angeles, 1982-84; Assistant Professor, Department of Surgery, UCLA, 1982-84 and 1987-; Neurotology Fellow, Postdoctoral Scholar, UCLA, 1984-87; Physician Specialist, Harbor-UCLA Medical Center, 1987-88. *Publications:* Numerous articles in medical journals. *Memberships:* Am Acad Otolaryngology, Head and Neck Surgery; LA Medical Women's Assoc; American Medical Women's Assoc. *Honours:* National Honor Society, 1966- 67; American Field Service, Exchange Student in Brazil, 1966; Stanford Women's Honor Society, 1971-72; Stanford Dean's List, 1970-72; Honor's program in Dept of Philsophy, Stanford University, 1970-71; Resident Research Award, Northwestern Hospital Dept of Otolaryngology, 1978; Shirley Baron Research Award, Triologic Society, 1986. *Hobbies:* Music, violin, piano; Sports, running, skiing; Wilshire YMCA, Board of Directors. *Address:* UCLA School of Medicine, Dept of Surgery, Division of Head & Neck, 10833 le Conte Avenue, Los Angeles, CA 90024, USA.

NEWMAN Anne Temple, b. 25 Jan. 1947, Minden, Louisiana, USA. Teacher; Student Council Sponsor. divorced. *Education:* BA, East Texas Baptist University, 1972; MA, Stephen F Austin University, 1979. *Appointments:* Teacher, Honours US History; Sponsor, Student Council, Marshall Independent School District, 1974-. *Publications:* Articles in Texas Youth Safety Newsletter; Student Advocate. *Memberships:* Texas Council for Social Studies; National Council for Social Studies; National Assn of Workshop Directors; National Assn of Student Activity Advisers; Texas Classroom Teachers Assn; Regional Planning Committee on Secretarial Initiative on Youth Alcohol Abuse and Treatment Conference. *Honours:* Top Ten Teacher in Texas, 1988; Southern Methodist University Award for Excellence in Teaching, 1988; PTA Lifetime Membership, 1983; Energy and Environmental Education Award, Texas Education Agency, 1983, 1984; Community Service Award, East Texas Council on Alcoholism and Drug Abuse, 1982. *Hobbies:* Photography; Travel; Reading; Working with teens. *Address:* 1900 Maverick Dr, Marshall, TX 76670, USA.

NEWMAN Janice Marie Swindler, b. 11 Aug. 1951, New York City, USA. Attorney; Public Relations Consultant. *Education:* BA, 1973; JD, 1980. *Appointments:* Public Information Officer, 1974-82, Assistant Communications Director, 1982-86, City of Newark; President, J.M. Newman & Associates, 1986-; Legislative Liaison, Division on Women, State of New Jersey. *Publications:* Magazine articles; weekly radio programme, Newark Report. *Memberships:* New Jersey Women Lawyers Association, President 1986-88; National Association of Media Women, National Secretary, 1986-87; New Jersey State Bar Association; Secretary, Women's Rights Section 1989-; N.J. Women's Political Caucus, Secretary, 1989-. *Honours:* Public Service Award, New Jersey Voice Newspaper, 1977; Achievement Award, 1982; Media Woman of the Year - New York, 1985; Young Lawyer's Service to the Community Award, 1989. *Hobbies:* Sewing; Needlework; Cooking; Weightlifting; Swimming. *Address:* PO Box 6070, Newark, NJ 07106, USA.

NEWMAN Laura Lindsay Eager, b. 30 Jan. 1928, Jacksonville, Florida, USA. Counselling Psychology. m. E Gustave Newman, Jr, 29 Dec. 1948. 1 son, 3 daughters. *Education:* Queens College, Charlotte, 1944-46; AB, Duke University, 1946-48; MEd 1962-64, PhD 1965-75, University of Florida. *Appointments:* Counselling Association, 1969-72; Consultation & Guidance, 1972-75; Brevard Comm, MHC, 1975-76; Gustave Newman, MD, 1976-77; Consultation Guidance, 1977-81; Alternatives Unlimited, 1981-88; Laura E Newman Association, 1988-. *Publications:* Personality Types of Therapist and Client and Their Use in Counseling, Research in Psychological Type, Vol II, 1979. *Memberships:* FMCHA (Florida Mental Health Counselors Association); AMHCA (American Mental Health Counselors Association); AACD (American Association for Counseling & Development); AAMFT (American Association for Marriage and Family Therapy; FAMFT (Florida Association for Marriage and Family Therapy); AASECT (American Association of Sex Educators, Counselors and Therapists). *Honours:* Queen's Scholar, 1945; Phi Beta Kappa, Duke, 1948; Phi Kappa Phi, UF, 1964; Kappa Delta Pi, UF, 1964; Pi Lambda Theta, UF, 1965. *Hobbies:* Growing plants; Knitting; Crocheting. *Address:* Laura E Newman Assoc, 4001 Newberry Road B-3, Gainesville, FL 32607, USA.

NEWMAN Lea Bertani Vozar, b. 3 Aug. 1926, Chicago, Illinois, USA. Professor of English. m. (1) Cam Vozar, 21 Sept 1947, 2 sons, 3 daughters, (2) Meredith Newman, 10 Jan. 1976. *Education:* BEd, Chicago Teachers College, 1947; MA, Wayne State University, 1966; PhD, University of Massachusetts, 1978. *Appointments:* Macomb Community College, 1965-66; Pennsylvania State University, Schylkill, 1966-68; North Adams State College, Massachusetts, 1968-. *Publications:* Reader's Guide to Short Stories of Nathaniel Hawthorne, 1979; Reader's Guide to Short Stories of Herman Melville, 1986. *Memberships:* President 1989-90, offices, Nathaniel Hawthorne Society; Melville Society; Poe Studies Association; American, & Northeast Modern Language Associations. *Honours:* Fulbright Lecturer, University of Bologna, Italy, 1973-74; Grant, National Endowment for Humanities, 1980-82. *Address:* 120 Imperial Avenue, Bennington, Vermont 05201, USA.

NEWMAN Leslea, b. 5 Nov. 1955, Brooklyn, New York, USA. Writer. *Education:* BS, Education, University of Vermont, 1977; Certificate in Poetics, Naropa Institute, 1980. *Appointments:* Self-employed Writer, Teacher and Lecturer. *Publications:* Good Enough to Eat, novel; Love Me Like You Mean It, poetry; A Letter To Harvey Mills, short stories; Heather Has Two Mommies, children's book; Secrets, short stories; Bubbe Meisehs by Shayneh Maidelehs: An Anthology of Poetry by Jewish Grandaughters About our Grandmothers. *Memberships:* Writers Guild; Poets and Writers; Feminist Writers Guild. *Honours:* 2nd Place Finalist, Raymond Carver Short Story Competition, 1987; Massachusetts Artists Fellowship in Poetry, 1989. *Address:* 20 Orchard Street, Northampton, MA 01060, USA.

NEWSON Eula M, b. 27 Dec. 1931, Fruitland Park, Florida, USA. Alcoholism Counselor; Business woman; Writer. *Education:* AA, Correction Administration, John Jay College of Criminal Justice, New York, 1978; BA, Psychology, City University of New York, 1979; Journalism Certificate, London School of Journalism, 1983; Paralegal Certifgicate, 1986; Master's degree in process. *Appointments:* President, The House of Great Creations; Design of the Year Club, 1959-; Alcoholism Counsellor, 1987-. *Creative works:* Invetor: Designed 20th Century Antique Music box; Wrote articles on antiques and collectibles; Book: Do You want a boy first or a girl, now you may choose. *Memberships:* American Association of Museums; NY Zoological Society; National Writers Club; National Council of Negro Women; NFAC; Alcoholism Awareness Services. *Honours:* International Gold and Silver Medals for inventions, 1969; Bronz International medal for inventing an electronic eye device for certain blind persons, 1989. *Hobbies:* Reading; Visiting museums and zoos; Inventing; Writing. *Address:* 175 W 137th Street, New York, NY 10030, USA.

NEWSON Olive Winifred, b. 1 Oct. 1918, London, England. Retired. *Education and Training:* LCC College of Physical Education, 1937-38. *Appointments:* Local Government Officer, School Health Service, Middlesex, 1938-47; Assistant Secretary, Central Council of Physical Education, 1947-55; Head, PE & Social Activities, Regent Street Polytechnic, London, 1956-63; Principal Officer, International Affairs & Special Events, The Sports Council, 1964-83. *Publications:* Skipping, 1964; Fitness for Women, 1962; Contributor to Feel Fit Come Alive, 1979. *Memberships Include:* Founder Secretary, Life Member, The Keep Fit Association; Hon. Life Member, British Ski Federation, British Amateur Gymnastics Association; Council Member, Lawn Tennis Foundation; Council, Imperial Society of Teachers of Dancing; Sports Aid Foundation; Governor, London College of Dance; many other professional organisations. *Honours:* Various honours and awards.

NEWTON Elaine M Lister, b. 10 Mar. 1935, Toronto, Canada. Professor. Divorced, 1 son, 2 daughters. *Education:* BA, 1954, MA 1955, Psychology, University of Toronto; MA, English, York University, 1965. *Appointments:* Psychologist, YMCA, 1953-56; Book Critic, Globe & Mail, 1956-70; Teacher, North York Board of Education, 1962-66; Assistant Professor, 1967-72, Associate Professor, 1972-, York University; Visiting Professor, various universities. *Publications:* Mirror of a People; articles in various journals & literary magazines. *Memberships:* MLA; Canada Institute for American Studies; Senate, York University; Board, National Council of Jewish Women; Board, Holy Blossom Temple; Consultant, North York Board of Education. *Honours:* Reuben Wells Leonard Award, 1950; Margaret Anna Brock Scholarship, 1950; Governor General's Award, 1954; Pan Hellenic Award, 1954; OCUFA University Teaching Award, 1972; Toronto Life University Teaching Award, 1980. *Hobbies:* Reading; Theatre; Music; Tennis; Hiking; Travel. *Address:* c/o Dept. of Humanities, York University, Keele Campus, 323 Fonders College, Downsview, Ontario, Canada.

NEWTON-JOHN Olivia, b. 26 Sept. 1948, Cambridge, England. Singer; Actress. m. Matt Lattanzi, 1984. 1 daughter. *Creative Works:* Recordings include: Let Me Be There; If You Love Me; Let Me Know; Clearly Love; Come On Over; Don't Stop Believin'; Making a Good Thing Better; Totally Hot; Physical. Film appearances include: Grease, 1978; Xanadu, 1980; Two Of a Kind, 1983. Television appearances: Numerous, including It's Cliff Richard (BBC-TV series). *Honours:* Order of the British Empire (OBE); numerous awards and honours. *Hobbies:* Horse riding; Song writing; Cycling; Astrology; Conservation; Animals. *Address:* c/o Roger Davies Management, 3855 Lankershim Boulevard, North Hollywood, CA 91604, USA.

NG Fae Myenne, b. 2 Dec. 1956, San Francisco, California, USA. Writer. m. Mark Covells, 28 Dec. 1984. *Education:* English Literature, University of California, Berkeley, 1979; MFA, Columbia University, New York, 1983. *Appointments:* Lecturer: Expository Writing, University of California, Berkeley, 1986; Creative Writing, UC Santa Cruz, 1987. *Publications include:* Contributions, literary magazines: Pushcart Prize XII; Best of Small Presses; City Lights Review; American Voice, Calyx, Crescent Review, PEN Syndicated Fiction Project. Short fiction, Harper's Magazine. *Honours:* D. H. Lawrence Fellowship, University of New Mexico, 1988; Creative Writing Fellow, Mary Ingraham Bunting Institute, Radcliffe College, 1987-88; Fiction Fellowship, Masschusetts Artists' Foundation, 1988; Joseph Henry Jackson Award, San Francisco Foundation, 1988. Artists' Colony Residencies: MacDowell Colony 1988, Yaddo Corporation 1987, Djerassi Foundation 1985. *Address:* c/o Bunting Institute, Radcliffe College, 34 Concord Avenue, Cambridge, Massachusetts 02138, USA.

NGUYEN Anne Allain, b. 15 June 1942, France. Director of School for Adults. *Education:* BA summa cum laude, Literature, City University of New York, USA; MA, TESOL, Teachers College, Columbia University. *Appointments:* Coordinator, Writing Centre, Hunter College, New York City, 1976; Teacher, English for Speakers of Other Languages, 1978; Founder, Director, Riverside Adult Learning Centre, 1979-; Founder, Riverside Language Programme, 1983. *Publications:* Various articles in professional journals. *Memberships:* International TESOL; New York Society of TESOL, Executive Board Member, Founder, Applied Linguistics Special Interest Group; Language Innovations Inc, Board Member, President; New York City Coalition of Adult Providers. *Honours:* Award for service on Executive Board, New York Society of TESOL; Named Outstanding Programme in New York State, Riverside Adult Learning Centre. *Hobbies:* Photography; Skiing. *Address:* 490 Riverside Drive, New York, NY 10027, USA.

NICHOLAS Carol Lynn, b. 28 July 1938, Berkeley, California, USA. Attorney. m. Donald Herrick Maffly, 24 Aug. 1958, divorced 1973. 2 sons, 1 daughter. *Education:* BA, University of California, Berkeley, 1971; JD, University of San Francisco, San Francisco, 1975; LLM, Georgetown University, Washington, 1983. *Appointments:* Staff Attorney, Securities and Exchange Commission, San Francisco, 1976-79; Attorney, Crocker National Bank, San Francisco, 1979-81; Attorney, Federal Home Loan Bank of San Francisco, San Francisco, 1983-84; Attorney, Rosen, Wachtell & Gilbert, Los Angeles, 1984-86; Attorney, Lewis, D'Amato, Brisbois & Bisgaard, Los Angeles, 1986-88; Attorney, Gaston & Snow, San Francisco, 1988-. *Publications:* Review, Modern Investment Management and the Prudent Man Rule by Bevis Longstreth, 1988; FIRA: Emerging Patterns on Director Liability, 1986; review of The Transformation of Wall Street by Joel Seligman, 1984; The Integrated Disclosure System and Its Impact Upon Underwriters' Due Diligence, 1983. *Memberships:* Committee on Developments in Investment Securities and Subcommittee on Broker-Dealer Matters of the Federal Regulation of Securities Committee, American Bar Association. *Address:* 2738 Webster Street, Berkeley, California 94705, USA.

NICHOLAS Gwendolyn Smith, b. 27 Jan. 1951, San Francisco, California, USA. Social Worker. m. Alvin Nicholas, 28 Aug. 1984. *Education:* BA, Sociology, 1972; MSW, 1974. *Appointments:* Supervisor, Allstate Insurance Company, 1974-76; Business Systems Analyst, Fireman's Fund Insurance Company, 1976-77; Psychiatric social worker, West Oakland Mental Health Department, 1977-78; Psychiatric social worker, Mental Health Programme Specialist, California Department of Mental Health, 1978-83; Licensing Programme Analyst II, Department of Social Services, California, 1984-. *Memberships include:* Advisory Board, Centre for Black Concerns; Various offices, Links Inc; Alpha Kappa Alpha; Oakland founder member, Soroptimist International; Board, Bay Area Association of Black Social Workers. *Honours:* Biographical listings, 1983, 1988. *Hobbies:* Networking, problem solving; Conference planning; Dancing; Travel; Meeting new people; Puzzles; Music (jazz, soul, classical); Spending time with family & friends. *Address:* PO Box 8581, Oakland, California 94662, USA.

NICHOLLS Dominie, Lady, b. 30 Dec. 1911, Liverpool, England. Retired. m. Sir John Nicholls, GCMG, OBE, 2 Sept. 1935, 1 son, 2 daughters. *Appointments:* Served in Athens, 1935-36; Portugal 1943-44, Australia 1946; Minister's Wife in Russia, 1949-51, Ambassador, Israel 1954-57, Yugoslavia 1957-600, Belgium 1960-63, South Africa 1966-70. *Publications:* Pantomime: Envoy Extraordinary; 2 Plays: Bloodshed in Bled, and Evil Counsellors. *Memberships:* Friend, Royal Academy; Supporter, Society for Animal Welfare in Israel; Greek Animal Welfare. *Honours:* Recipient, various honours and awards. *Hobbies:* Gardening; Reading; Writing; Collecting Antiques; Walking; Sailing. *Address:* The Burgh House, 15 London Road, Saffron Walden, Essex, England.

NICHOLLS Judith Ann, b. 12 Dec. 1941, Westwoodside, Lincolnshire, England. Writer; Writer in Schools. m. John Richard Nicholls, 9 Sept. 1961, 1 son, 2 daughters. *Education:* Cert. in Education, 1974; BEd.,

Honours, 1983. *Appointments:* Secretary, 1959-62; Teacher, 1974-85; Writer, Writer in Schools 1985-. *Publications:* Magic Mirror & Other Poems for Children, 1985; Midnight Forest & Other Poems, 1987; Wordspells, Compiler; Popcorn Pie, 1988; What on Earth......?, 1989. *Hobbies:* Reading; Walking; Swimming. *Address:* c/o Faber & Faber, 3 Queen Square, London WC1N 3AU, England.

NICHOLS Elizabeth Grace, b. 1 Feb. 1943, Tehran, Iran. Professor. m. Gerald Ray Nichols, 20 Nov. 1965, 1 son, 1 daughter. *Education:* BS, San Francisco State College, 1969; MS, 1970, DNS, 1974, University of California. *Appointments:* University of California, 1974-82; Idaho State University, 1982-85; University of Wyoming, 1985-. *Publications:* Transitions in a Woman's Life, co-author; articles in professional journals. *Memberships:* Gerontological Society of America, Chair, Clinical Medicine, 1987; Western Institute of Nursing, Board Member, Chair Elect, 1989; American Nurses Association. *Honours:* Fellow, American Academy of Nursing, 1982, Gerontological Society of America, 1982; St Paul's Hospital Alumnae Award for Academic Achievement. *Hobbies:* Skiing; Sewing; Gardening; Travel. *Address:* Box 3065 University Station, Laramie, WY 82071, USA.

NICHOLS Sharon M. b. 12 Oct. 1949, Detroit, Michigan, USA. Consultant; Trainer. *Education:* BA Psychology, The University of Michigan, Ann Arbor, 1971; MA Guidance & Counseling, Eastern University, Ypsilanti, 1976; International Business Student, American University under study. *Appointments:* Consultant and trainer on human relations and behavioural health care issues nationally, 1980-; Program Director, Hillcrest Medical Center, Tulsa, 1983-; Assistant Director, Alcohol and Drug Abuse Services Inc, Des Moines, Iowa, 1976-. *Memberships include:* Tulsa Chamber of Commerce, Small Business Association, 1986-; Advisory Board Member, Hillcrest Women's Health Center, 1985-; Advisory Board Member, Junior League of Tulsa Pediatric Enrichment Program, 1985-; National Association of Female Executives, 1985-; Board Member, Oklahoma Drug, Alcohol & Mental Health Advisory Board, 1984-; Program Committee & Public Relations Committee, Leadership Tulsa, 1984-; Advisory Board, University of Tulsa Women's Center, 1983-85; Co-Chair Commission on Women, Alcohol & Drug Problems Assoc. of North America, 1982-84; Executive Committee Member & Chair of Family Life Committee, Tulsa City PTYA, 1982-84; Board Member: South Tulsa Mental Health Center, 1982-84; Tulsa Mental Health Coordinating Council, 1982-84; Treatment Alternatives to Street Crimes, Dept of Corrections, 1982-83; Oklahoma Department of Mental Health, Alcohol & Drug Merger Task Force, 1981; Oklahoma Dept of Mental Health Legislative Task Force,. 1981-83; Oklahoma Alcohol & Drug Assoc. 1981-84; Tulsa Alcohol & Drug Abuse Committee, 1981-84; Civitan 1981; Executive Women's Forum, 1981-84; Community Service Council Women's Concern Forum, 1981-84, etc. *Honours:* Oral History Archives, Women's Center, University of Tulsa, 1987; One of the Ten Outstanding Young Women in America, 1985; Outstanding Program Achievement, Behavioural Medical Care, 1985 & 1984; Outstanding Unit Achievement, Hillcrest Medical Center, 1985; Leadership Tulsa, 1983; White House Fellowship Regional Finalist, 1983; Outstanding Young Women in America, 1983; Civitan, VIP Award, 1981; Graduate Student Instructor, Group Dynamics, 1976; University of Michigan Regent's Alumni Scholarship, 1967-71; Michigan Higher Education Assistance Authority Scholarship, 1967-71. *Hobbies:* Reading; Ballet; Music; Travelling. *Address:* 6130 East 61st Street, Tulsa, Oklahoma 74136, USA.

NICHOLSON Emma Harriet, b. 16 Oct. 1941, Oxford, England. Politician. m. Sir Michael Harris Caine, 9 May 1987. *Education:* LRAM, ARCM, Royal Academy of Music. *Appointments include:* Computer Programmer, Programming Instructor, Systems Analyst, Computer Consultant, General Management Consultant, various firms, 1963-74; Employee 1974-85, Director of Fund Raising 1977-85, Save the Children Fund; Deputy Chair, Duke of Edinburgh's Award 30th Anniversary Tribute Project 1986, International Project 1987. Political: Vice Chair, Conservative Party, 1983-87; Member of Parliament (Conservative), Devon West & Torridge, 1987-. Community commitments include: Chair, Friends of Duke of Edinburgh Award; Trustee, Suzy Lamplugh Trust; President, Hatherleigh District, Save the Children Fund; President, Plymouth & West Devon Cassette Talking Newspaper; Council, Howard League; Trustee, Ross McWhirter Foundation; Vice President, Small Farmers Association; Advisory Board, Women of Tomorrow Awards; Chair, Advisory Committee, Carnegie UK Trust Venues Improvement Programme (access for disabled, arts venues & libraries); Director, Cities in School; Patron, North Devon Hospice Care Trust. *Memberships:* Centre for Policy Studies, Royal Institute of International Affairs; Fellow Elect, Industry & Parliament Trust; Patron, Devon Care Trust; Reform Club. *Hobbies:* Music; Walking. *Address:* c/o House of Commons, London SW1A 0AA, England.

NICHOLSON Rosemary Thomas, b. 10 Feb. 1941, Meridian, Mississippi, USA. Civil Servant. m. Donald R. Graft, 10 Aug. 1985 (div. 1987). 2 sons, 1 daughter, previous marriage. *Education:* Georgia State University, 1976-77; Edison Community Collge, Fort Myers, Florida, 1981, 1987- 88. *Appointments:* Staff 1965-, Assistant District Manager, Lakeland Florida 1979-80, District Manager, Fort Myers 1980-, Social Security Administration. *Memberships include:* Various offices: Lee County Community Coordinating Council, American Business Women's Association (ABWA), Florida Association of Health & Social Services, Atlanta Regional Management Association, Zonta International. Past/present member, various other civic or professional organisations. *Honours:* Numerous awards including: Southside Charter Chapter Woman of Year, ABWA, 1978; Superior performance awards, Social Security, various occasions; Biographical recognition. *Hobbies:* Swimming; Reading; Sewing. *Address:* PO Box 277, Cape Coral, Florida 33910, USA.

NICOLAU Graziella Yvonne, b. 29 Apr. 1936, Bucharest, Romania. Research Scientist. *Education:* Baccalaureate, 1953; Diplomate in Biology, 1958, Diplomate in Chemistry, 1968, PhD (Biology), 1974, University of Bucharest. *Appointments:* Junior Scientist, 1958-73, Senior Scientist 1974-82, Principal Scientist, 1982-; Head Department of Chronobiology, 1974-, CI Parhon, Institute of Endocrinology of the Romanian Academy of Medical Sciences. *Publications:* 150 articles in scientific journals; 16 Chapters in books; 65 Presentations at International Scientific Meetings; 42 Presentions at Regional Meetings. *Memberships:* Romanian Society of Endocrinology; Romanian Association of Scientist; Union des Societes des Sciences Medicales de la Romanie (USSM); International Society of Chronobiology; European Society of Chronobiology; Endocrine Society (USA). *Honours:* Invention Certifications, Romanian University of Agriculture and Food Industry, 1982; Victor Babes Prize, Romanian Academy of Sciences, 1983. *Hobbies:* Music; Dance. *Address:* Head, Chronobiology Department, C I Parhon Institute of Endocrinology, Bd Aviatorilor 34-36, R- 79600, Bucharest, Romania.

NIELSEN Diane Tappen, b. 4 July 1947, Manhattan, New York City, New York, USA. Mathematician; Natural Resources. *Education:* BA Applied Mathematics, George Washington University, Washington DC, 1983; BA, Sociology, American University, Washington DC, 1969. *Appointments:* Computer Specialist, 1972-79, Mathematician, 1979 and 1985-, US Geological Survey, Reston, Virginia; Assistant to Natural Resources Adviser, Inter-American Development Bank, Washington DC, 1979-85. *Publication:* In Search of Oil with B F Grossling, 1985. *Memberships:* Society of International Development, 1980-83; George Washington University Club, Mathematical Association of America, 1981-85; International Association Mathematical Geology, 1981-86; Society of Industrial and Applied Mathematics, 1981-; International Assn Energy Economists, 1988-; National Computer Graphics Association. *Hobbies:* Travel; Piano; Swimming; Tennis. *Address:* 4890 Battery Lane No 215, Bethesda, MD 20814, USA.

NIEMANN Christi Cay, b. 5 Oct. 1956, Valparaiso, Indiana, USA. Paralegal/Workers Compensation Specialist. m. Richard R Niemann, 1 Nov. 1980. 1 son, 1 daughter. *Education:* BA Psychology, Bethany College, 1978; California Teachers Credential, 1979; Graduate Classes at Ak Pacific University. *Appointments:* Teacher, Foothill Christian School, 1978-79; Account Executive, Murray Bradley Public Relations, 1979-81; Claims Adjuster, Providence Washington Ins Co, 1981-82; Workers Compensation Claims Supervisor, American International Adj Co, 1982-83; Paralegal, Staley, DeLisio, Cock & Sherry, 1983-84; Paralegal/Workers Compensation Specialist, Mason and Griffin, 1985-. *Publications:* Co-editor, Lighter Than Air Cookbook; Photographs have appeared in Anchorage Newspapers and other regional publications. *Memberships:* Public Relations Society of America; Advertising Federation of Alaska; Alaska Adjuster's Association; Alaska Association of Legal Assistants; Alaska Public Interest Research Group; Abbott Loop Community Council, Board Member. *Honour:* Board of Trustees Scholarship, 1976. *Hobbies:* Photography; Travel; Camping; Reading; Music. *Address:* 7015 Henderson Loop, Anchorage, AK 99507, USA.

NILSSON Torborg Birgitta, b. 4 Oct. 1939, Gothenburg, Sweden. Company President. m. Lars Tage Nilsson, 12 Apr. 1960, 2 daughters. *Education:* Fil. lic (Doctor), Psychology. *Appointments:* Swedish Occupational Council, 1962-64; University of Gothenburg, 1967-70; Modokem, 1970-74; Berolkemi, 1974-89; Life Work Limited, 1989-. *Publications:* Book, Personnel Administration. Also numerous lectures, universities, public meetings. *Memberships:* Chairman, New Thinkers Group; Member of the Board, Creseutia Ltd; Health Council, Stenungsund; Nilco Promotion Ltd; Human Dynamics Association. *Hobbies:* Philosophy; Music; Spiritual development. *Address:* Berol Nobel, Box 851, 44400 Stenungsund, Sweden.

NISBET Florence Mary, b. 29 Oct. 1931, Monifieth, Angus, Scotland. Nurse. m. 18 Sept. 1954. 1 son, 4 daughters. *Education:* Open University Certificates, The Handicapped in the Community and The Ageing Population, 1976, 1977. *Appointments:* Nursery Nurse, Dundee Public Health Authority, 1950; Registered General Nurse, Edinburgh Royal Infirmary, 1954; Staff Nurse, Western General Hospital, 1973; Health Visitor, Midlothian Health Board, 1974-76; Nursing Officer Community, Borders Health Board, 1976- 86. *Creative works:* Children's Stories published 1970, 1978; Nursing articles published 1985, 1986; Editor of Scottish Christian Writers Magazine; Regular writer for teenagers for Release Publications magazine, Manchester Press. *Memberships:* Health Visitors Association (Scotland) Chairman 1980, Secretary 1982, Treaasurer 1986; Age Caoncern Scotland, Executive Committee 1984-86; Arthritis Care, Peebles, Chairman 1977-79; Muscular Dystrophy Peebles, Chairman 1978-86; Member of Tweedale Voluntary Organisations 1976-86; Member, Borders Health Board, 1983-86. *Honours:* 1st prize for articles, Scottish Association of Writers, Pitlochry, 1980; 2nd Prize for children's story, Edinburgh Writers Club, 1978; Appearance on BBC Television, Songs of Praise 1985 and on Borders Television for Age Concern, 1986. *Hobbies:* Writing (research in nursing); Reading; Animal charities; Walking; Children (Duke of Edinburgh Awards). *Address:* Strathairlie, 4 Edinburgh Road, Peebles, EH45 8DZ, Scotland.

NISSENSON Norma, b. 18 Nov. 1917, Frankfurt, Kentucky, USA. Clinical Psychologist. m. Marc Nissenson, 6 July 1940, 2 daughters. *Education:* BS magna cum laude 1938, MA magna cum laude 1948, Psychology, Northwestern University, Illinois. *Appointments:* Executive Director, guidance agency,

1946-52; General practice, clinical psychoiogy (individual psychotherapy, marital counselling), Nissenson Associates Ltd, 1962-; Associate Professor, Graduate Education, Roosevelt University, 1962-70; Vocational Expert (Consultant), US Department of Health & Human Services, 1962-88. *Memberships:* Fellow: American Orthopsychiatric Association, International Council on Sex Education & Parenthood; American Association of Marriage & Family Therapists; American & Illinois Psychological Associations; Past President, Chicago Psychological Association; American Association for Counselling & Development. *Honours:* Life member, Delta Sigma Rho; Member, State Advisory Council, Illinois Commission on Human Relations; Boards, Moraine Council of Girl Scouts, & local Parent-Teachers Associations; President, North Shore Film Society. *Hobbies:* Volunteer activities (other than above) including founder, director, Operation HEP (Higher Education Pays), programme of music & career planning for inner city schools; Lecturer, TV, radio, platform, various topics related to interpersonal relationships. *Address:* 966 Princeton Avenue, Highland Park, Illinois, USA.

NISSMAN Blossom S, b. 23 Feb. 1928, Yonkers, New York, USA. Superintendent of Schools. 1 son, 1 daughter. *Education:* BS, Ed, Temple University, 1951; MA, Guidance and Counseling, Trenton State College, 1969; EdD, Social and Philosophical Foundations of Ed, Rutgers University, 1975. *Appointments:* Elementary Teacher, Cheltenham Township Schools, PA, 1951-53; Elementary Teacher, Pennsbury School District, 1953-57; Teacher Counselor, Learning Consultant, Willingboro Board of Ed, New Jersey, 1966-72; Regional Director, Central Region, Burlington, 1972-87; Principal/Superintendent, Long Beach Island Schools, 1987-. *Publications:* Books: Elementary Guidance; Middle school Guidance; Over 50 articles in periodicals and many booklets on education. *Memberships:* New Jersey Association of School Admin; American Assoc of School Ad; South Jersey School Ad; Delta Kappa Gamma Society International; Long Beach Island Parent Assoc. *Honours:* Temple University Scholarship, 1948; Emma Johnston Scholarship, 1950; Outstanding Senior Award, Temple University Blazer, 1951; Women of the Year Award, Willingboro ORT, 1965; Delta Kappa Gamma State Scholarship Award 1972, International Scholarship Award, 1974; Camp Council Award of Distinction, 1974; Mt Holly Outstanding Educator's Award, 1987. *Hobbies:* Writing; Needlepoint; Painting. *Address:* c/o Long Beach Island School District, 20th and Central Avenue, Ship Bottom, NJ 08008, USA.

NIVEN Barbara Susanna, b. 24 Jan. 1927, Greytown, Natal, South Africa. Research Mathematician. *Education:* BSc, Mathematics, Physics, University of South Africa, 1946; MSc, Mathematical Statistics, Witwatersrand University, 1961; PhD, Mathematics, Zoology, University of Adelaide, Australia, 1968. *Appointments:* Statistician, Chamber of Minese Research Laboratories, Johannesburg, 1955-58; Lecturer, Mathematics Department, Witwatersrand University, 1959-60; Visitor and Assistant, London University, England, 1961-62; Lecturer, Mathematics Department, University of Western Australia, 1963-65; Senior Lecturer, Waite Institute, University of Adelaide, South Australia, 1966-79; Senior Consultant, Food and Agriculture Organisation, Philippines, 1976, 1979; Honorary Senior Fellow, Griffith University, 1980-. *Publications:* Articles in scientific journals. *Memberships:* Australian Mathematical Society; American Mathematical Society; Statistical Society of Australia (Foundation Secretary, Western Australia, 1963-65, Foundation Secretary, South Australia, 1967). *Honours:* Fellowship to University of Illinois, Chicago Circle, National Science Foundation, USA, 1973; Australian Research Grants Committee, Griffith University, 1982; Griffith University Research Grants, 1981, 1984, 1985, 1986. *Hobby:* Astronomy. *Address:* PO Box 233, Annerley, Queensland, 4103, Australia.

NIX Clara Margaret, b. 1 Aug. 1923, Edmonton, Canada. Media Resources Consultant. m. James Ernest

Nix, 16 Apr. 1946, 2 sons, 2 daughters (1 deceased). *Education:* AB, Edmonton, 1939. *Appointments:* Programme & Resource Officer, Montreal Presbytery, The United Church of Canada, 1976-78; Media Resources Consultant, Communication, United Church of Canada, Toronto, 1978-. *Memberships:* Ontario Film Association Inc., President, 1986-88. *Hobbies:* Music; Handicrafts; Outdoors. *Address:* 4112 Pheasant Run, Mississauga, Ontario, Canada L5L 2C1.

NIXON Carol Holladay, b. 25 Dec. 1937, Salt Lake City, Utah, USA. Arts Council Director. m. William L. Nixon, 9 Sept. 1958, 3 sons, 3 daughters. *Education:* Brigham Young University. *Appointments:* Assistant: Senator Herman Welker, R-Idaho, 1956-57; Senator Henry Dworshak, R-Idaho, 1959-62; Senator Len Jordan, R-Idaho, 1962-64; Senator Orrin Hatch, R-Utah, 1977-80; Executive Director, Utah Arts Council, State Division of Fine Arts, Salt Lake City, 1985-. *Memberships:* Utah Co-Chair, Women for Reagan-Bush, 1984; National Federation of Republican Women, 1984-85; President, Utah Federation of Republican Women; Utah Symphony Board, 1983-84; President, Utah Symphony Guild, 1983-84; Pioneer Theatre Board, 1985-87; Salt Palace/Fine Arts Board 1985-88; Utah Alliance for Arts Education; Western States Arts Federation Board. *Honour:* Special Service Award, Utah Music Educators Association, 1988. *Hobbies:* Arts; Reading; Skiing; Golf; Fishing. *Address:* Utah Arts Council, 617 East South Temple, Salt Lake City, UT 84102, USA.

NOAKES Vivien, b. 16 Feb. 1937, England. Writer. m. Michael Noakes, 19 June 1960. 2 sons, 1 daughter. *Appointments:* Guest Curator of the major exhibition, Edward Lear, 1812-1888, at the Royal Academy, London and the National Academy of Design, New York, 1985; Philip and Frances Hofer Lecturer, Harvard University, 1988. *Publications:* Edward Lear: The Life of A Wanderer, 1st edition 1968, 2nd edition 1979, 3rd edition 1985; Edward Lear 1812-1888, catalogue of the Royal Academy Exhibition, 1985; The Selected Letters of Edward Lear, 1988. *Address:* 146 Hamilton Terrace, London NW8 9UX, England.

NOCHLIN Linda, b. 30 Jan. 1931, Brooklyn, New York, USA. Distinguished Professor, Art History. m. (1) Philip Nochlin, deceased, 1 daughter, (2) Richard Pommer, 1 daughter. *Education:* BA, Vassar College, 1951; MA, English, Columbia University, 1952; PhD, Art History, New York University. *Appointments:* Associate Professor, Graduate School of Art History, Columbia University, 1967-68, 1975-76; Pofessor, Art History, Vassar College, 1969-71; Visiting Profesor, Art History, Stanford University. *Publications:* Realism, 1977; Gustave Courbet: A Study of Style & Society, 1976; Women, Art & Power and Other Essays, 1988. *Memberships:* College Art Association; Societe des Amis de Gustave Courbet Institute for the Humanities Fellow. *Honours:* Arthur Kingsley Porter Prize, 1967; Frank Jewett Mather Prize, 1977; Woman of the Year Award, Mademoiselle Magazine, 1977; Honorary Doctorate, Colgae University, 1987. *Hobbies:* Race Walking; Recorder Playing. *Address:* PhD Programme in Art History, Box 110, The Graduate Centre, City University of New York, 33 West 42nd Street, New York, NY 10036, USA.

NOEL Claudine, b. 4 Apr. 1938, Houilles, France. Directeur de Recherche (CNRS). m. Michel Noel, 18 July 1960, 2 sons, 1 daughter. *Education:* ESCIL Engineer, 1960; Licence es Sciences Physiques 1961, Doctorat d'Etat es Sciences Physiques 1966, University of Paris, France. *Appointments:* Stagiaire de Recherches 1960, Attachee de Recherches 1961, Chargee de Recherches 1967, Maitre de Recherches 1979, Directeur de Recherches 1987-, CNRS. *Publications:* Contribution to Atlas of Polymer Morphology, 1989; Siole-chain liquid Crystal Polymers, 1989. *Memberships:* Groupe Francaise d'Etudes et d'Applications des Polymeres; Titular Member, IUPAC Commission on Macromolecular Nomenclature; Membre de la commission du GFP. *Honours:* Prix Langlois for research in the area of synthetic membrances for reverse osmosis and ultrafiltration, 1979; Prix Langlois, for research in the area of thermotropic liquid crystalline polymers, 1987. *Hobbies:* Stamp collector; Tapestry. *Address:* ESPCI, 10 Rue Vauquelin, 75231 Paris Cedex 05, France.

NOEL Tallulah Ann, b. 21 Oct. 1945. Nursing Agency Administration. 2 daughters. *Education:* BS, 1983. *Appointments:* Research Clinician, Mt. Sinai Medical Centre, 1976-81; Head, nurse, MacNeal Memorial Hospital, 1982-84; Director, 1984-87, Vice President, 1987- 88, Professional Services, Vice President, Operations, 1988-, Nursefinders. *Publications:* Oil Painting, westrn Scene; articles in journals. *Memberships:* National League of Nursing; National Association of Orthopaedic Nurses; Chicago Heart Association; Illinois Health Care Association; Women in Health Executives Network; Women in Management; NAFE. *Honours:* Women of Achievement Award, 1987; Outstanding Leadership & Achievement Award, 1987. *Hobbies:* Skiing; Reading; Horse Riding; Oil Painting. *Address:* 136 N. Delaplaine Road, Riverside, IL 60548, USA.

NOLAN (Rosenthal) Karen Lori, b. 18 Nov. 1958, Paterson, NJ, USA. Businesswoman. m. Timothy Reynolds Nolan, 24 June 1984. *Education:* BS, Business Administration, Montclair State College, Upper Montclair, NJ, 1981; MBA Candidate, Marketing, Fairleigh Dickinson University, Teaneck, 1981-. *Appointments:* Advertising Manager, Meadox Medicals Inc., Oakland, New Jersey, 1980-83; Account Executive, McGovern Advertising Inc., Red Bank, New Jersey, 1984-86; Account Manager, Allen Consulting Inc., Holmdel, 1986-87; Manager, Advertising & Public Relations, Tarkett Inc., 1987-. *Memberships:* Business/ Professional Advertising Association, New Jersey Chapter, Board Member, 1981-; American Business Associates; American Marketing Association; Montclair Athletic Commission, Board 1979-80. *Hobbies:* Bicycling; Skiing; Antique Refinishing; Reading. *Address:* 46 Lathrop Avenue, Madison, NJ 07940, USA.

NOLAND Patricia Hampton, b. New Orleans, Louisianna, USA. Writer. *Education:* BA, University of Houston, 1981; Postgraduate Studies, Rice University, 1987-88. *Appointments:* Founder, President, International Poetry Institute, 1969-80. *Publications:* Poems; poetry in numerous anthologies. *Memberships:* International Platform Association; Smithsonian Institution; Junior League Luncheon Club; Metropolitan Opera Guild. *Honours:* Recipient, various honours & awards. *Hobbies:* Music; Art; Fashion Design, Book Collecting; Travel. *Address:* 2400 Westheimer Road, Apt. 215 W, Houston, TX 77098, USA.

NONHEBEL Clare, b. 7 Nov. 1953, London, England. Author. m. Robin Nonhebel, 30 Aug. 1975. *Education:* BA (Hons), University of Warwick, 1971-74; Postgraduate Bilingual Secretarial Certificate, Ealing Tech. *Appointments:* Social Work, 1974-75; Public Relations, 1976-81; Freelance Journalism, 1980-. *Publications:* Novels: Cold Showers; The Partisan; Incentives. Short Story: Popcorn in 1987 Winter's Tales Anthology. *Honour:* Betty Trask Award, 1984. *Hobbies:* Gardening; Dressmaking; Painting. *Address:* Ealing, West London, England.

NORDLINGER Angela Marion, b. 28 Oct. 1943, Inverell, New South Wales, Australia. Lawyer. m. Robert Haines Nordlinger, 18 Mar. 1967. 2 daughters. *Education:* BEc, University of Sydney, 1964; LLB (Hons), 1982, Diploma in Commercial Law 1988, Monash University; FRMIT (Management) (RMIT), 1977. *Appointments:* Computer Programmer, IBM (UK) and BHP (Australia), 1964-67; Systems Analyst, C & A Modes, UK, 1967-68; Lecturer on Management, Melbourne, Australia, 1974-79; Solicitor, Melbourne, 1982-. *Publications:* Various legal publications. *Memberships:* Commercial Law Association of Australia, Chairman; Royal Children's Hospital, Member of Committee of Management. *Hobbies:* Private flying;

Contemporary art. *Address:* 28 Berry Street, East Melbourne, Victoria 3002, USA.

NORFLEET Janet, b. 14 Aug. 1933, Chicago, Illinois, USA. Postal Services Executive. m. Junious Norfleet, 2 Nov. 1984. 1 son. *Education:* AA, Olive Harvey College, 1977. *Appointments include:* US Postal Service: Staff, 1958-; Superintendent, Customer Service Repairs, 1978; Manager, Retail Sales & Services 1979, Delivery & Collections 1980, North Suburban Facility 1985; Field Division General Manager/Postmaster, South Suburban Division 1986, Chicago Division 1987-. Responsible: Chicago Post Office (largest postal facility in world under one roof), Chicago Bulk Mail Facility, & O'Hare Airport Mail Facility. *Memberships:* National Association of US Postmasters; Chicago Womens Network; Board of Directors, corporate level, Carsons. *Honours:* Numerous awards & recognitions including: Shirley Chisholm Government Award, 1987; Woman of Year, Veterans Group WW II, 1987; Outstanding Community Service Award, Joint Negro Appeal, 1987; American Black Achievement Award (Business & Professional), 1987; President's Distinguished Alumni Award, Olive Harvey College, 1988. *Hobbies:* Cooking; Cycling; Music. *Address:* 433 West Van Buren Street, Chicago, Illinois 60607, USA.

NORMAN Dorothy, b. 28 Mar. 1905, Philadelphia, Pennsylvania, USA. m. Edward A Norman. *Education:* University of Pennsylvania, 1923-25. *Appointments:* Research, American Civil Liberties Union; Worked with Margaret Sanger, early Planned Parenthood movement; with NY League of Women Voters; NY Citizens Union; Chairman first Civil Liberties Committee, Women's City Club of NY; Member, Board of Directors, New York Urban League; Hamilton House; United Neighborhood Houses; Women's Archives; Member Board of Directors: National Urban League; City-Wide Citizens Committee on Harlem; NY City Committees Against Discrimination in Employment and Housing; India League and numerous other civic organizations; Active with Citizens Union; Chairman SOS Committee (Save Our Schools; Founder and Chairman, American Emergency Food Committee for India; American Citizens Committee for Economic Aid Abroad; Citizens Committee to Support US Economic Aid for India. *Publications:* Poetry: Dualities, 1933; Editor and publisher, Twice A Year, 1938-48, 1967; Columnist, A World To Live In, New York Post, 1942-49; contributor of numerous poems, reviews, articles and photographs to various publications USA and abroad. *Address:* 124 East 70 Street, New York City, NY 10021, USA.

NORMAN Janice Maureen Doris, b. 23 Oct. 1937, Norwich, Englnd. Headteacher. *Education:* BA, Honours, History, University of London, 1958; PGCE, University of Southampton, 1959. *Appointments:* Deputy Head, Hewett School, Norwich, 1973-82; Head Teacher, Heartsease School, Norwich, 1982-. *Memberships:* National Union of Teachers; Secondary Heads' Association. *Hobbies:* Education Research; Adult Education (WEA); Travel; Theatre; Gardening. *Address:* Heartsease School, Marryat Road, Norwich NR7 9DF, Norfolk, England.

NORMAN Jessye, b. 15 sept. 1945, Augusta, Georgia, USA. Soprano; Concert & Opera Singer. *Education:* BM cum laude, Howard University; Peabody Conservatory, 1967; MMus., University of Michigan, 1968. *Appointments:* Operatic Debut: Deutsche Oper, Berlin, 1969, La Scala, Milan, 1972, Royal Opera House, Covent Garden, 1972, New York Metropolitan Opera, 1983; American Debut, Hollywood Bowl, 1972, Lincoln Centre, 1973; tours include: North & South America, Europe, Middle East, Australia, Israel, Japan; many international festivals. *Honours:* Grand Prix Du Disque, 1973, 1976, 1977, 1982, 1984; IRCAM Record Award, 1982; Grammy, 1985; Hon. Member, Royal Academy of Music, London, 1987. *Address:* c/o Shaw Concerts Inc., 1900 Broadway, New York, NY 10023, USA.

NORMAN Lilith, b. 27 Nov. 1907, Sydney, Australia.

Author. *Education:* Associate, Library Association of Australia, 1962. *Appointments:* Librarian, City of Sydney Public Library, 1956-70; Assistant Editor, NSW Dept. Education, School Magazine, 1970-76, Editor 1976- 78; Freelance Author, 1978-. *Publications:* Climb a Lonely Hill; The Shape of Three; The Flame Takers; Mocking-Bird Man; My Simple Little Brother; A Dream of Seas; The Brown and Yellow; The Laurel & Hardy Kids. *Memberships:* Children's Book Council, Treasurer, 1968-70; Library Association of Australia, Branch Councillor; President, LAA Children's Libraries Section. *Honours:* Queen's Silver Jubilee Medal, 1977; Hans Christian Handerson Honours Book for Australia, 1980. *Hobbies:* Reading; Old Films; Cats. *Address:* Curtis Brown (Aust) Pty Ltd., PO Box 19, Paddington, NSW 2021, Australia.

NORMAN Patricia, b. 3 Sept. 1947, New York City, USA. Chief Financial Officer. *Education:* AAS, Junior College, 1966; BS, Business Administration, St John's University, New York, 1975. *Appointments:* Hospital for Jint Diseases & Medical Centre, 1967-79; North General Hospital, 1979-. *Memberships:* Hospital Financial Management Association, Advanced Member; National Oblate Sisters of Providence Alumni Association. *Hobbies:* Music Appreciation; Photography. *Address:* North General Hospital, 1919 Madison Avenue, New York, NY 10035, USA.

NORMAN Priscilla (Baroness), b. 20 Mar. 1899, Brussels, Belgium. Retired Voluntary & Local Government Worker, London, UK. m. (1) Alexander Koch de Gooryend, 1921, div. 1929, 2 sons, (2) 1st Baron Norman, 1933. *Appointments include:* Member: London County Council, 1925-33; Chelsea Borough Council, 1928-31; Bethlem Royal & The Maudsley Hospital Board, 1951- 75; South East Metropolitan Regional Board, 1951-74; Honorary President, World Federation for Mental Health, 1972; Vice Chairman, Women's Voluntary Services for Civil Defence, 1938-41; Vice President, Royal College of Nursing. *Publication:* In the Way of Understanding, 1983. *Honours:* Commander, Order of British Empire, 1963; Justice of Peace, 1944. *Address:* 67 Holland Park, London W11 3SJ, England.

NORRIS Barbara Jean, b. 19 Nov. 1937, San Francisco, California, USA. University Administrator. m. William H. Cowie Jr. 1 daughter, previous marriage. *Education:* AB, Vassar College, 1938. *Appointments:* Time Inc, 1960-62; Press aide, Democratic National Committee, 1964-67; Public affairs consultant, 1967- 70; Vice President, Media Relations, Daniel J. Edelman Inc, 1970-74; Director, Public Affairs, Johns Hopkins Medical Institutions, 1974-82; Vice President, Communications & Public Affairs, Johns Hopkins University, 1982-89. *Memberships:* Council for Advancement & Support of Education; Association of American Medical Colleges; Vassar Alumni Association; Yale University Council. *Honour:* 1st woman Vice President. *Hobbies:* Sailing; Tennis; Art History; Italian culture; Films; Gardening. *Address:* 1408 Ruxton Rod, Baltimore, Maryland 21204, USA.

NORRIS Deborah Ann Olin, b. 24 Mar. 1957, Bethesda, MD, USA. Administrator; Psychologist. m. Jon William Norris, 25 Sept. 1982. 2 daughters. *Education:* BA, The Collorado College, 1979; MA 1984, PhD 1988, The American University. *Appointments:* Administrative Director, 1981-84, Vice President, 1986-, Olin Conservation, Inc; Adjunct Assistant Professor, 1984-86, Assistant to the Dean of Students, 1984-86, The American University. *Memberships:* Sigma Xi Society; Phi Kappa Phi Society; Society for Neurosciences. *Honours:* National Science Foundation Fellowship, 1974; Graduate Student Research Support Grant, 1983-84; The American University Doctoral Dissertation Fellowship, 1986-87. *Hobbies:* Naturalist; Diver; Ballet Dancer. *Address:* 3515 Nimitz Road, Kensington, Maryland 20895, USA.

NORRIS Deborah Jane, b. 27 Jan. 1966, Slough, England. Actress. *Appointments:* Tessie in Annie,

Victoria Palace Threatre; Royal Gala Performance, Coliseum; Orphan in Barnardo, Royalty Theatre; Maud in schoolgirl Chums, BBC TV; Queenie in The Baker Street Boys, 8 part BBC TV Series; Sarah in By the Sword Divided, BBC TV Series; Mavis in Jonny Briggs, BBC TV series 13 part serial, second 20 part serial; Mary in The Verger, Tales of the Unexpected, Anglia TV. *Memberships:* Imperial Society of Teachers of Dancing; Womens League of Health and Beauty. *Honours:* Winner, All England Sunshine Dancing Competition, 1977; 30 Trophies, 200 medals and over 400 certificates for dancing and drama. *Hobbies:* Playing Piano; Swimming; Stamp Collecting. *Address:* St James's Management, 22 Groom Place, London SW1X 7BA, England.

NORRIS Donna Marie, b. 28 May 1943, Columbus, Ohio, USA. Child Psychiatrist. m. Dr Lonnie Norris, 16 June 1966. 1 son, 1 daughter. *Education:* BA, Fisk University, 1964; MD, Ohio State University College of Medicine, 1969. *Appointments:* Judge Baker Children's Center & Children's Hospital Medical Center, 1974-; Boston Juvenile Court Clinic, 1973-88. *Memberships:* Sr Rep Mass APA Assembly, 1986-; Exec Comm, Mass Psych Society, 1986-; Treasurer, Middlesex Chap Links, Inc, 1987-89; Treasurer, Mass Assn Psych, 1987; American Acad of Child & Adol Psychiatry, 1975-; American Coll of Psychiatrists, 1987-. *Honours:* Falk Fellowship; Fellow, American Psychiatry Association, 1985; American College of Psychiatrists, 1988; Board of Trustees, University of Lowell, 1988. *Hobbies:* Historical fiction/non-fiction; Charities. *Address:* 295 Longwood Ave, Boston, MA 0215, USA.

NORRIS Frances (McMurtray), b. 27 Mar. 1946, Jackson, Mississippi, USA. Government Administrator. m. Stephen Leslie Norris, 8 Oct. 1981. *Education:* BS, 1967, School of Law, 1973, University of Mississippi; MSLS, University of Kentucky, 1970; Postgraduate study, University of Tennessee, 1971. *Appointments:* Legal Assistant to Representative G. V. Montgomery, 1974-78; Assistant to Representative Trent Lott, US House Committee on Rules, 1979-80; Assistant to Republican Whip, US House of Representatives, 1981-83; Director, Legislation Liaison, 1983, Deputy Assistant Secretary, 1983-86, Assistant Secretary for Legislation, 1986-88, US Department of Education; Director, Congressional Relations, Office of National Drug Control Policy, 1989-1990. *Memberships:* Federal City Republican Women; Former President, Mississippi Society of Washington DC; Bravo Opera Society; University of Mississippi Alumni Association. *Honours:* US Government Fellowship for Graduate Study, 1965-70. *Address:* Executive Office of the President, The White House. Washington, DC 20500, USA.

NORRIS Patricia A., b. 1 Nov. 1932, Minneapolis, Minnesota, USA. Research Psychologist. m. Steven Lee Fahrion, 1 son, 1 daughter. *Education:* BA, Clinical Psychology, University of California, Santa Barbara, 1954; Graduate work, University of California, Los Angeles, and New York University; Clinical Psychology Intern, Brooklyn Psychiatric Centers Inc, 1968-69; PhD, Psychology of Consciousness, Union Graduate School, 1976. *Appointments include:* Elementary School Teacher, New York City Public Schools, 1969-70; Clinical Psychologist, Kansas Reception & Diagnostic Center, Topeka, 1970-74; Director, Biofeedback Seminars/Workshops, Assistant Research Psychologist, Voluntary Controls Programme, 1974-77, Associate Director, Biofeedback Research, and Psychophysiological Therapy, Voluntary Controls Programme, 1977-79, Clinical Director, Biofeedback & Psychophysiology Center, 1980-, The Menninger Foundation, Topeka. *Publications:* Working with prisoners, or, there's nobody else here, 1976; Preliminary observations on a new non-drug method for control of hypertension (with E E and A M Green), 1979; On the status of biofeedback and clinical practice, 1986; I choose life: The dynamics of visualization and biofeedback (with G Porter), 1987; Current conceptual trends in biofeedback and self-regulation, in Eastern and Western approaches to healing; Articles in Biofeedback

& Self-Regulation; Hypertension: The Mind/Body Connection (co-author), film, 1981. *Memberships:* Board of Directors: Institute of Behavioral Medicine; Institute for Adjunctive Cancer Therapy; Associate Editor, Biofeedback & Self-Regulation, 1982-85; Biofeedback Society of America, President 1984, Board of Directors 1978-81, Applied Division Chair 1980-81; Association of Humanistic Psychologists; Transpersonal Psychologists Association. *Hobbies:* Sailing; Skiing; Opera; Reading. *Address:* Biofeedback and Psychophysiology Center, Menninger Clinic, PO Box 829, Topeka, KS 66601, USA.

NORRIS Phyllis Irene, b. 7 May 1909, Salisbury, Wiltshire, England. Author. *Appointments:* Civil Service, 1939-49. *Publications:* The Nasturtium Club; The House of the Ladybird; The Polkerrin Mystery; The Cranstons at Sandly Bay; Meet the Kilburys; The Mystery of the White Ties; The Duffers' Brigade; The Harlands Go Hunting; Short stories etc. *Memberships:* Former Member of Society of Authors; West Country Writers' Association. *Hobbies and Interests:* Reading; Art; Gardens; Historical Houses; Antiques. *Address:* Salisbury, Wiltshire, England.

NORRIS-SHORTLE Carole, b. 19 Sept. 1949, Rush County, Indiana, USA. Social Worker; Family Therapist. m. David R. Shortle, 14 Feb. 1975, 1 son. *Education:* BS, Purdue University, 1971; Master's degree in Social Work, University of Maryland, Baltimore, 1974; Master's degree in Liberal Arts, Johns Hopkins Evening College, 1979; Diplomate in Clinical Social Work, 1987; Board Certified in Clinical Social Work, 1987. *Appointments:* Director of Training, Family Studies Center, Huntington, New York, 1981- 84; Clinical Coordinator, Center for Infant Study, University of Maryland School of Medicine, 1984-89. *Publication:* Strategic Home Visits, in Social Casework professional journal. *Memberships:* National Association of Social Workers; ACSW; Charter Member, Local Baltimore Chapter, Association for Infant Mental Health; American Association for Marriage and Family Therapy. *Hobbies:* Gardening; Family farm. *Address:* Baltimore, Maryland, USA.

NORTH Joan Marian, b. 15 Feb. 1920, Hendon, England. Writer. m. C A Rogers, 13 Feb. 1952, 2 daughters. *Publications:* Books: Emperor of the Moon, 1956; The Cloud Forest, 1965; The Whirling Shapes, 1968; The Light Maze, 1972. *Membership:* Society of Authors. *Address:* 8 Grey Close, London NW11 6QG, England.

NORTH Woesha Cloud, b. 7 Sept. 1918, Wichita, Kansas, USA. Educator. m. Robert Carver North, 14 Aug. 1943. 1 son, 4 daughters. *Education:* BA Art Hist/Allied Arts & Sociology, Vassar College, 1940; MA, Representation/Design, Ohio University, 1944; MA, Art Education, Stanford University, 1972; PhD, History & Philosophy of Education, University of Nebraska, 1978. *Appointments:* Instructor, US Indian Service, 1940-42; Art/Drama Teacher (Secondary), 1961-69; Instructor, Native American Studies, College level, 1970-79 and 1984-87; Assistant Professor, Native American Studies and English, 1979-84. *Publications:* Articles on Native American subjects, 1971-84; Painting Exhibits, 1966-87; American Indian Artists Association, 1966-69; Heard Museum, 1969-74; Gov. Brown Minorities, Native American, 1975; Sioux Indian Art/Crafts Museum, 1983; Scottsdale, 1988. *Memberships:* Chair, Relig. Ed. Committee, Unitarian Church, 1966-69; Officer, Native American Women's Action Council, 1970-74; Lincoln (NE) Indian Center Board, 1979-84, Chair, 1983-84; Board, Fresno Amer. Indian Council, 1985. *Honours:* Ford Foundation Postdoctoral Fellowship for Minorities, 1980-81. *Hobbies:* Creative Writing; Camping, walks in park and wilderness areas; Arts (fine arts, drama, crafts); World Peace Advocate. *Address:* 3051-C N West Ave, Fresno CA 93705, USA.

NORTON-TAYLOR Judy, b. 29 Jan. 1958, Santa Monica, California, USA. Actress. *Appointments:* Acting Debut, 1965; Films: Hotel, 1967, Valentine, 1978; TV

Film: Homecoming, 1971; TV Series, The Waltons, 1972-81; Stage Appearances: Cinderella, Annie Get Your Gun, I Ought to be in Pictures, Perfect Pitch, Times of Your Life, Social Security. *Memberships:* Screen Actors Guild; AFTRA; Equity. *Honours:* Womens World Record, Skydiving, 1986 (60 way); World Record, Skydiving (120 way), 1986. *Hobbies:* Skiing; Tennis; Horse Jumping; Skydiving; Waterskiing. *Address:* c/o Tillman, 10965 Fruitland Drive No. 314, Studio City, CA 91604, USA.

NORWOOD Barbara Mann (Bobbie), b. 2 Sept. 1946, Ft McPherson, USA. Account Executive; Uniform Sales Retail. m. Mar 1982. 2 sons, 1 daughter. *Education:* Marketing; Psychology; Office Management; Business. *Appointments:* John Mann's Uniforms, 1959-76; Martins Service Uniforms, 1976-79; Banner Uniforms, 1979-; First female Road Salesman in this business. *Publications:* How to deal with the man who fixes your car, 1973; How to live in a mans world, 1972. *Memberships:* Sales & Marketing Executives; WDTM; NOW; National Assoc of Executive Women; GMTA. *Honours:* Lieut Colonel Aide de Camp to Governor, 1979-; Deputy Sheriff, Cobb City, 1976-; Deputy Sheriff, Putnam City, 1979. *Hobbies:* Political Campaigns; Community Vol work; Fund Raisers. *Address:* 919 Woodward Cir, Mableton, GA 30059, USA.

NORWOOD Janet L, b. 11 Dec. 1923, Newark, New Jersey, USA. Economist, US Commissioner of Labor Statistics. m. Bernard Norwood, 25 June 1943. 2 sons. *Education:* BA, Douglass College, Rutgers University, 1945; MA 1946, PhD 1949, Fletcher school, Tufts University. *Appointments:* University teaching, Wellesley College and Research Associate, Fletcher School, 1949-57; Economist/Division Chief 1963-73, Deputy Commissioner 1973-79, Commissioner 1979-, US Bureau of Labor Statistics. *Publications:* Numerous articles in professional journals and to conferences. *Memberships:* President, American Statistical Assocaition; American Economic Association; Member Executive Board, Industrial Relations Research Association; National Academy of Public Administration; International Statistical Institute; American Association for Advancement of Science; International Association for Official Statistics. *Honours:* LLD (Honorary) Carnegie Mellon University, 1984; Florida International University, 1979; Fellow, Royal Statistical Society; National Association of Business Economists; American Statistical Association; Member, Alumni Hall of Fame, Rutgers University, 1986; National Public Service Award, 1984; Julius Shiskin Award, Washington Statistical Society, 1986; Elmer B Staats Award, American Society for Public Administration, 1982; Department of Labour, Philip Arnow Award, 1979. *Address:* US Bureau of Labor Statistics, Washington, DC 20212, USA.

NOVAK Kim, b. 13 Feb. 1933. Actress. m. Richard Johnson, 1965, divorced 1966, (2)Dr Robert Malloy, 1976. *Education:* Wright Junior College. *Appointments:* Model, Chicago, Hen with the Caroline Leonetti Modelling Agency in Hollywood; Film Debut in the French Line, 1954; Films include: Five Against the House; Picnic; Man with the Golden Arm; Pal Joey; Middle of the Night; Bell Book and Candle; Vertigo; Pepe; Strangers When We Meet; He Notorious Landlady; Boys' Night Out; Of Human Bondage; Kiss Me, Stupid; The Amorous Adventures of Moll Flanders; The Legend of Lylah Clare; The Great Bank Robbery; Tales that Witness Madness; The White Buffalo; The Mirror Crack'd; TV: Falcon Crest. *Address:* c/o The Agency for Performing Arts, 120 West 57th Street, New York, NY 10019, USA.

NOVOTNY Deborah Ann, b. 23 Sept. 1964, Oak Lawn, USA. Marketing Analyst. *Education:* BA, Economics, Northwestern University, 1986; MBA, Candidate, 1989-. *Appointments:* Consultant, Northwestern, 1983-86, Microcomputer Consultant, 1986; Senior Consultant, Sara Lee Corporation, 1986; Lante Corp., 1987-88; Graduate Management Development Programme, IDS Financial Services Inc., 1988-. *Publications:* Poetry published in Invision.

Memberships: National Association of Female Executives; Chi Omega Rho; Smithsonian Institute. *Honours:* National Honour Society, 1979-82; Illinois State Scholar, 1982. *Hobbies:* Flying; Bowling; Reading; Baking; Massage; Nature; Travel. *Address:* 14424 West Avenue, Orland Park, IL 60462, USA.

NOWAK Carol A, b. 5 Mar. 1950, Buffalo, New York, USA. Pension Clerk, City of Buffalo. *Education:* AAS, Business Administration, 1986; BS, Business Management, State University of New York at Buffalo, in process. *Appointments:* Wire Operator, Liberty/Norstar Bank, 1968-70; Various Positions, Personnel Admin/Labor Relations 1970-74, Administrative Assistant, Administration & Finance Dept 1974-82, Pension Clerk, City Clerk's Office 1982-, City of Buffalo, New York. *Creative works:* Designer of Seasonal Xmas Cards, 1982-; Macrame Designs, have appeared in area art shows, 1973-74. *Membership:* National Association of Female Executives, 1988, 1989. *Honour:* Graduated with Highest Honors, AAS Degree, Erie Community College, 1986. *Hobbies:* Art; Antiques; Fashion design; Greeting card design; Gardening; Sports. *Address:* 422 Dingens Street, Buffalo, New York 14206, USA.

NOWAKOWSKA Wanda, b. 29 May 1929, Lodz, Poland. Art Historian; Scientific Worker. Divorced. *Education:* PhD, Humanities, Lodz, 1965; Doctor Habilitatus, Art History, Jagiellonian University, Cracow, 1983. *Appointments:* Museum of Art, Lodz, 1953-55; Head, Publications, Lodz Scientific Society, 1956-59; Lecturer, History of Art, State College of Theatrical & Film Arts, 1959-65 State College of Plastic Arts & State College of Music; Professor, Head of Art History, University of Lodz, 1965-. *Publications:* 30 publications including 3 books: Stanislaw Witkiewiez-Art Theoretician; Stanislaw Witkiewicz about Art; National Function of Art in Polish Art Criticism 1863-1890. *Memberships:* Assocation of Art HIstorians; President, Scientific Soction, Charter Member, Lodz; Board, Third University Age, Lodz; Editorial Staff, Aesthetical Studies, PAN. *Honours:* Recipient, many honours and awards. *Address:* Mazurska 23 m 6, 93-149 Lodz, Poland.

NOYES Elisabeth Joyce (van Epen), b. 15 Oct. 1940, Hilversum, Netherlands. University System Administrator. m. Arnold Eugene Noyes, 2 Sept. 1961, 2 sons. *Education:* USA Postgraduate, Middlebury College, 1961; MA, University of Massachusetts, 1962; MEd, Salem State College; EdD, Nova University, 1976; Postdoctoral, League for Innovation, Executive Leadership Institute, 1988. *Appointments include:* Faculties: White Pines College, New Hampshire, 1965-70; North Shore Community College, Massachusetts, 1972-74; Bunker Hill Community College, 1976-78, 1978-83. Academic Programme Officer, Massachusetts Board of Regents of Higher Education, 1983-87; Director, Academic Planning & Programme Development, University System of New Hampshire, 1987-. *Creative work includes:* Research & commentary, importance of Job's wife in William Blake's Job, in progress. *Memberships:* Numerous professional & community organisiations including: New Hampshire Postsecondary Education Commission; Stat Higher Education Acdemi Officers' Association; NH State Council for Vocational-Technical Education. *Honours:* Grant, Fund for Improvement of Secondary Education, American Association of Community & Junior Colleges, 1981-82; Grant, College Administrators, International Education Consortium, 1978. *Hobbies include:* Much time devoted to community services, including Moderator, Town of Shirley, annually elected 1983-, also offices with schools, hospitals. *Address:* University System of New Hampshire, Dunlap Centre, Durham, New Hampshire 03824, USA.

NSHAIWAT Naila Awad Mijalli, b. 20 May 1942, Amman, Jordan. Assistant Professor. m. Emile E. Shuwayhat, 2 July 1961, 4 sons. *Education:* BA, Philosophy & Psychology, Beirut University, 1973; PhD, Research Librarianship, Indiana University, USA. *Appointments:* Practitioner, Main Library, University of Jordan, 1980-81; Librarian, Library of Central Bank of

Jordan, 1981-82; Librarian, Library of International School of American Consulate, Dharan, Saudi Arabia, 1982-83; Head Librarian, Information Centre, Queen Alia Social Welfare Funds, 1983-84. *Publications:* Library Cooperation and its Importance for Jordanian Libraries; Al-Husein Bibliography; Book Reviews, articles, etc. *Membership:* Pi Lambda Theta; Jordan Library Association; American Library Association; Special Libraries Association; American Society for Information Science; Indiana University Libraries Association. *Honours:* First Woman in Jordan to receive PhD in Library & Information Science, 1983; many other honours & awards. *Hobbies:* Swimming; Tennis; Theatre; Painting; Travel; Family. *Address:* PO Box 5640, Amman, Jordan.

NUNLEY Lorene Weddington, b. 5 May, Magoffin County, Kentucky, USA. Professional Mental Retardation. *Education:* BS, Texas Woman's University, 1970; Currently Graduate Student, University of Cincinnati. *Appointments:* Teacher, Aubrey High School, 1974-75, Clermont co. High School, 1975-77; Pofessional Mental Retardation, Clerco Inc., 1977-83; Rehabilitation Counsellor, RSC Ohio Division, 1983-. *Creative Works:* Innovative Programming and Planning for Mentally Retarded Clients also implementation. *Memberships:* ORSC; AHEA; Texas Division; PAR, Ohio Division. *Honours:* Dean's List, Texas Woman's University; Dean's List UC (Cincinnati, Ohio). *Hobbies:* Bridge; Needlepoint; Reading; Astrology; Golf; Travel; Pattern Design; Square Dancing; Swimming; Weekly Meditation Group. *Address:* 6047 Wayside Avenue, Cincinnati, OH 45230, USA.

NUSBAUM Adele H., b. Toronto, Canada. Government Official, Communications. *Education:* BA magna cum laude, University of Rochester, USA, 1940; MA, Columbia University, 1942; Postgraduate study, American University, 1971. *Appointments:* Information Specialist, US Department of Agriculture, New York City, 1942-45; Staff Associate: C.M.Bayer Public Relations, New York City, 1945-47; Sally Dickson Associates, New York City, 1947-49; United Jewish Appeal Federation, New York City, 1950-55; Director of Public Relations, United Jewish Federation, Pittsburgh, Pennsylvania, 1955-64; Director of Public Relations, 1964-68, Communications Consultant for Urban Affairs, 1968-69, B'nai B'rith Women, Washington DC, 1964-68; Senior Writer, Bureau of Health Manpower, 1969-71, Director, Federal Women's Programme, 1971-74, National Institute of Health, Bethesda, Maryland; Programme Director, Communications Development, 1974-82, Special Assistant, 1982-88, Programme Analysis Officer, 1988-, National Cancer Institute, Bethesda. *Memberships:* Public Relations Society of America; National Press Club; National Association of Government Communicators; American Public Health Association; American Society for Public Administration. *Address:* National Cancer Institute, NIH, 3 Executive P, Rockville, MD 20892, USA.

NUTTA Joyce Watson, b. 22 Jan. 1963, St Petersburg, Florida, USA. Language Co-ordinator. m. Giorgio Nutta, 20 Sept. 1981, 1 daughter. *Education:* AA, St Petersburg Junior College, 1979; BA, Mass Communications, 1981, MA, Linguistics, 1988, University of South Florida. *Appointments:* English Instructor, American Language Academy, University of Tampa, 1982-83; Marketing Manager, Suncoast Property Investments, 1983-85; Informaitron Specialist, University of South Florida, 1985-87; President, Town & Country Real Estate Services, 1986-88. *Publications:* Articles in journals & magazines. *Memberships:* Florida Department of Education Adult ESOL Advisory Committee; CALICO; TESOL; AAIS; PAVE. *Hobbies:* Western Pleasure Horse Riding; Cooking; Australian Shepherd Dogs. *Address:* 484 45th Avenue North, St Petersburg, FL 33703, USA.

NYAMBE Prisca Matimba, b. 31 Dec. 1951, Lusaka, Zambia. Legal Counsel to Bank of Zambia. m. Mohamed Ismail Hassan, 17 Aug. 1973, divorced 1983, 1 son, 1 daughter. *Education:* LLB, Univerity of Zambia, 1975.

Appointments: Resident Magistrate, Central Province Lusaka, 1978-80; Senior Magistrate, Zimbabwe, 1981-84; Deputy Legal Counsel, 1984-87, Legal Counsel, 1987-, Bank of Zambia. *Memberships:* Magistrates Association of Zambia; Law Association of Zambia, Council Member; Commonwealth Lawyers Association; International Bar Association. *Honours:* Recipient, various honours and awards. *Hobbies:* Reading; Gardening; Music. *Address:* c/o Bank of Zambia, PO Box 30080, Lusaka, Zambia, Central Africa.

O

OAKLEY Ann Rosamund, b. 17 Jan. 1944, London, England. Sociologist; Writer. 1 son, 2 daughters. *Education:* MA, Oxford University, 1965; PhD, London University, 1974. *Appointments:* Research Officer, Bedford College, London 1974-79, Oxford 1979-84; Deputy Director, Thomas Coram Research Unit, Institute of Education, London, 1985-. *Hobbies:* Music; Politics; Gardening. *Address:* Thomas Coram Research Unit, 41 Brunswick Square, London WC1N 1AZ, England.

OBERHAUSEN Joyce Wynn, b. 12 Nov. 1941, Plain Dealing, Louisiana, USA. Aircraft Executive Artist. m. James J Oberhausen, 15 Oct. 1966. 1 son, 2 daughters. *Education:* High School, Plain Dealing, Louisiana, 1954-57; Ayers Business School, Shreveport, Louisiana, 1962-63; Seminars worldwide; Various art courses, University of Alabama, 1974-75. *Appointments:* Stenographer, Secretary, Lincoln National Life, Shreveport, 1959; Secretary, Baifield Industries, Shreveport, 1963-66; International Art Teacher Artist, Huntsville, Alabama, 1974-; Vice-President, Co-owner, Precision Speciality, Huntsville, 1966; Vice President, Co-owner, Military Aircraft, Huntsville, 1979-; President, Owner, Wynnson Enterprises, Wynnson Galleries, Private Collection, Limited Edition Prints, Florist, Gifts, Wynnson Enterprises, Military Packaging Company, President, Sole Proprietor, Huntsville, currently. *Creative works:* Oil painter; Tole painter; Water colourist; Pastels and mould and patent porcelain; Designed and built home, swimming pool and tennis court; Represented International Porcelain Art Teachers also Europe including East Germany and Mexico. *Memberships:* International Teacher, International Porcelain Guild; National Association Female Executives; People to People; International Teacher, Porcelain Portrait Society; National Museum Women in Arts; United International Artists Association; National Trust for Historic Preservation; American Society of Professional and Executive Women; Chamber of Commerce; Better Business Bureau; Republican Senatorial Inner Circle; Huntsville Art League & Museum Association; Association of Community Artist; Historical Society-Smithsonian. *Honours:* Life & Achievements in Personalities of America; Community Leader of America of 1988; Hall of Fame for Outstanding Achievements as an Aircraft Executive, 1987; Commemorative Distinguished Life-Long Achievements Medal of Honor; Commemorative Medal of Honour; Outstanding Achievements and Dedication to Personal Professional Goals; Excellence in Business Art. *Hobbies:* Gardening; Rug hooking; Refinishing furniture; Collecting pewter; Snow skiing; Water skiing; Tennis; Gourmet cooking; Decorating; Photography; Crewel embroidery; Crochet; Antique collecting; Jewellery designer; Sewing. *Address:* 156 Spencer Drive, P O Box 440, Meridiansville, AL 35759, USA.

OBERMAYER Judith Barbara Hirschfield, b. 7 May 1935, Pittsburgh, Pennsylvania, USA. President, Obermayer Associates. m. Arthur S. Obermayer, 23 June 1963, 2 sons, 1 daughter. *Education:* BS with high honours, Mathematics, Carnegie-Mellon University, 1956; AM, Mathematics, 1957, PhD, Mathematics, 1963, Harvard University. *Appointments:* Assistant Professor of Mathematics, Wellesley College, 1963-66; Vice-President, Technical Management, Research & Planning Inc, 1978-81; Vice-President, 1978-85, Chairman, 1985-, Moleculon Research Co; President, Obermayer Associates, 1982-; Director of Corporate Planning, Corporation Secretary, Director, Moleculon Inc, 1987-88. *Publications:* Case Studies Examining the Role of Government R&D Contract Funding in the Early History of HiTechnology Companies; The Role of Patents in the Commercialization of New Technology for Small Innovative Companies; Small HiTechnology Companies and National Objectives during a Period of Severe Debt and Equity Shortages. *Memberships:* Executive Committee, Massachusetts Institute of Technology Enterprise Forum; National Board of Governors, President, NE Region, President, Boston Chapter, American Jewish Committee; American Mathematical Society; American Women in Science; Director, National Association for the Self-Employed. *Honours:* National Science Foundation Fellow, 1956-50; Phi Kappa Phi, 1956; Tau Beta Pi, 1956; Sigma Xi, 1956; Phi Beta Kappa, 1963. *Address:* 239 Chestnut Street, West Newton, MA 02165, USA.

OBI Dorothy Schmidt, b. 29 Apr. 1931, Washington DC, USA. Librarian. m. Ogbuhukwu Fidelis Obi, 11 Sept. 1954, 2 sons, 2 daughters. *Education:* BA, Art, Berea College, 1953; MLS, Columbia University, 1957; PhD, University of Pittsburgh, 1974. *Appointments:* Cataloguer Trainee, NY Public Library, 1954-57; Cataloguer, Eastern Nigeria Library Board, 1957-60; Assistant Librarian, UN Economic Commission for Africa, 1960-61; Assistant Librarian, University of Nigeria, Enugu, 1962-63; Sub Librarian, 1963-74, Senior Librarian, 1974-77, Deputy Librarian, 1977-. *Publications:* numerous articles in professional journals; Manual for School Libraries on Small Budgets. *Memberships:* Chairman, Anambra State Chapter, Nigerian Library Association, 1980-84; Secretary, United Church Women of Nigeria, 1976-; Beta Phi Mu. *Honours:* MLS, Honours, Columbia University, 1957; Research Fellow, Council of Library Resources, 1973. *Hobbies:* Writing Poetry; Oil Painting; Reading. *Address:* Enugu Campus Library, University of Nigeria, Enugu, Nigeria.

O'BRIEN Claudine Michele, b. 24 July 1953, Wilmington, USA. Attorney; Financial Counselor. *Education:* BA, University of Delaware; JD, LL.M, Taxation, Villanova University Law School. *Appointments:* Independent Legal Work, 1979-; Financial Counsellor, Connecticut General in Philadelphia, 1981-82; Staff Attorney, CIGNA, 1983-85; Financial Design Counsel, Southwest Financial Group, 1985-. *Publications:* large scale murals for restaurants; exhibited art at MIT. *Memberships:* English Speaking Union; Alliance Francaise; American Bar Assocciation; Texas Bar Foundation; Pennsylvania Bar Association; Houston Bar Association. *Honours:* Senior Diploma, Piano, 1971; National Historical Society Essay Award, 1973. *Hobbies:* Art Work; Swimming; Skiing; Sailing. *Address:* 1400 Post Oak Boulevard, Suite 300, Houston, TX 77056, USA.

O'BRIEN Darlene Anne, b. 14 July 1955, Cleveland, Ohio, USA. Attorney. m. Thomas Carey O'Brien, 2 Feb. 1984, 1 son, 1 daughter. *Education:* BA, Political Science, University of Toledo, 1977; JD, Notre Dame Law School, 1980. *Appointments:* US Bankruptcy Court Northern District of Indiana Law Clerk, 1980-81; Associate, Smith and Brooker, PC, 1981-84; Partner, O'Brien & O'Brien, 1984-. *Memberships:* American, Michigan Bar Associations; Women Lawyers Association of Michigan. *Honours:* University of Toledo Best Essay of the Year Award, 1976; Summa Cum Laude, 1977; Barristers Midwest Regional Moot Court Trial Competition, 1980. *Hobbies:* Piano; Literature. *Address:* O'Brien & O'Brien, 300 North Fifth Avenue, Suite 150, Ann Arbor, MI 48104, USA.

O'BRIEN Katharine Elizabeth, b. Amesbury, Massachusetts, USA. Educator; Writer. *Education:* AB, Bates College, 1922; AM, Cornell University, 1924; PhD, Brown University, 1939. *Appointments:* Mathematics, College of New Rochelle, 1925-36; Mathematics, Deering High School, 1940-71; Lecturer, University of Maine, Portland Campus, 1962-73; Lecturer, Brown University, summers 1962-65, 1967. *Publications:* Books: Sequences, 1966; Excavation, 1967; Composition: When I Set Out for Lyonnesse, chorus for women's voices, 1947; Member of master-class in Piano with Sigismond Stojowski, New York City; Numerous poems in professional journals, magazines and newspapers. *Memberships:* Phi Beta Kappa; Sigma Xi; New York Academy of Sciences; Mathematical Association of America; Poetry Society of America; Society of Bowdoin Women; Bates Key. *Honours:*

Honorary degrees: ScDEd, University of Maine, 1960; LHD, Bowdoin College, 1965; Deborah Morton Award, Westbrook College, 1985. *Hobbies:* Mathematics; Poetry; Piano. *Address:* 130 Hartley St, Portland, Maine 04103, USA.

O'BRIEN Maureen, b. 29 June 1943, Liverpool, England. Actor; Writer. m. Michael Moulds, 1968. *Education:* Teaching Diploma, Central School of Speech and Drama, London, 1961-64. *Appointments:* Everyman Theatre, Liverpool, England, 1964-65; First TV, Vicki in Dr Who BBC Television, 1965-66. *Creative Works includes:* Theatre: Celia in Volpone, Oxford Playhouse/Garrick Theatre; Dorinda in The Beaux Stratagem and Sibley in The Farmer's Wife, Chichester, 1967; Miranda in The Tempest, Chichester, 1968; Isabelle in Ring Round The Moon, Haymarket Theatre, London; Portia in The Merchant of Venice and Imogen in Cymbeline, Stratford, Ontario, Chicago; Nina in The Seagull, Chichester, 1973/Greenwich; Vivie in Mrs Warren's Profession and Rosalind in As You Like It, Crucible, Sheffield; Portia in The Merchant of Venice and Amanda in The Relapse, Old Vic Theatre, London, 1980; Bertha in Exiles, Bristol Old Vic; Candida in Candida, British American Drama Academy Tour and Kings Head Theatre & Arts Theatre, 1988; Maya in The Archbishop's Ceiling, Theatre Royal/Bristol; Mary in The Garden Girls, Bush Theatre, 1987. Television: Alayne Whiteoak in The Whiteoaks of Jalna, CBC Series, 1972; Florence Bravo in The Poisoning of Charles Bravo, BBC Trilogy, 1974; Lizzie in The Duchess of Duke Street, BBC Series; Skittles, Victorian Scandals, Granada; Mary Barrie in The Lost Boys, BBC Trilogy; Electra in The Serpent Son (The Orestaia), BBC Trilogy; Nora in The Doll's House, BBC; Morgan Le Fay in The Legend of King Arthur, BBC 8 part serial; Linda in On the Shelf, Central, 1986; Elizabeth Straker in Casualty, BBC series, 1987. Author of: The Great Gobstopper Show (Childrens Play); Going On (Play); Close Up On Death (Novel). Directed Getting-In by Mike English, Kings Head Theatre, London. Films: Joan in She'll be Wearing Pink Pyjamas, 1985; Natalya in Zina, 1986. Numerous parts in Radio plays and serials. *Memberships:* British Equity; Canadian Equity; ACTRA; Friends of the Earth. *Honours:* Best Radio Actress, 1979 and 1984. *Hobbies:* Reading; Gardening; Looking at paintings. *Address:* c/o William Morris agency (UK) Ltd, 31/32 Soho Square, London W1V 5DG, England.

O'CONNELL Carmela Digristina, b. 8 Nov. 1925, Johnstown, Pennsylvania, USA. Businesswoman; Consultant. m. (2) Maurice F. O'Connell, 21 Sept. 1974. 2 sons, 1 daughter, previous marriage. *Education:* Business Diploma, Eastern Secretarial School, New York City, 1942; Interior Design School, NYC, 1952; Finance courses, New York University, current. *Appointments:* Typist to Secretary-Treasurer, Philip P. Masterson Company, NYC, 1942-72; Founder & President, New York Appraisal Corporation, 1971-80; Board member & Executive Vice President 1972-80, Consultant 1981-, Masterson & O'Connell Inc; Co-Founder & President, Park Avenue Appraisal Associates Inc, 1981-. *Memberships:* Offices, New York League, National Federation of Business & Professional Women; Amita Inc; Ladies of Charity. *Honour:* Business Woman of Year, Amita Inc, 1977. *Hobbies:* Parish Council member, fundraising activities, Church of Our Saviour; Opera (member Metropolitan Opera Guild); Needlepoint. *Address:* 80 Park Avenue, New York, NY 10016, USA.

O'CONNELL Susan Margaret, b. 17 Aug. 1946, Vermont, USA. Film Producer; Film Actress. 1 son. *Education:* University of California, Los Angeles. *Appointments:* Creator, Director, Video Studios Incorporated of Hollywood; Developed training & marketing programmes for institution and industrial clients, Video Cassette Industries Incorporated; Account Executive Media One; starred in TV series including: Hawaii Five-O, Emergency, FBI, Ironside, etc; currently co-founder, Godmother Productions; Currently CEO and President Pacific Film Fund. *Memberships:* President, founder, Northern California Chapter, Women in Films & Television; Advisory Board, Mill Valley Film Festival; Representative, Northern California Media Association.

Honours: Tell Me a Riddle Awarded Best Film, London Film Festival, England, 1980. *Hobbies:* Swimming; Crossword Puzzles. *Address:* 916 Kearney No. 201, San Francisco, CA 94133, USA.

O'CONNOR Maureen, b. 14 July 1946, San Diego, California, USA. Local Government Official. m. Robert O. Peterson, 1977-. *Education:* BA, Psychology, Sociology & Recreation, San Diego State University, 1970. *Appointments:* Instructor, counsellor, Rosary High School, San Diego, 1970; Elected Member, San Diego City Council, youngest ever in such office, 1971-79; Member 1976-81, Vice-Chair 1979-80, Chair 1980-81, Metropolitan Transit Development Board; San Diego Port Commissioner, 1980-85; 31st (1st woman) Mayor of San Diego, 1986-. Achievements include: Co-author, San Diego's 1st Growth Management Plan, 1971-79; Key role, construction of San Diego Trolley, light rail transit system, 1976-81; Budgeting for new convention centre, 1980-85; Projects concerning growth review, federal & state funding for sewage treatment system, links with twinned city (Tijuana, Mexico), drugs prevention, working relationship with US Navy, funds for AIDS research, 1986-. *Address:* City Administration Building, 202 C Street, San Diego, California 92101, USA.

O'CONNOR Patricia Ann Walker, b. 26 Apr. 1931, Memphis, USA. Professor. m. Anthony M. Paquariello, 11 Feb. 1978, 1 son 1 daughter by former marriage. *Education:* BA, 1953, MA, 1954, PhD, University of Florida. *Appointments:* Instructor, 1961-62, Assistant Professor, 1962-66, Associate Professor, 1966-72, Professor, 1972-, University of Cincinnati. *Publications:* Books: Gregorio y Maria Martinez Sierra; Cronica de una colaboracion; Women in Theatre of Gregorio; Martinez Sierra; Gregorio and Maria Martinez Sierra; Dramaturgas espanolas de hoy; and numerous articles plus two editions. *Memberships:* AAUP; MLA; Phi Beta Kappa; ITI; MMLA; Sigma Delta Pi. *Honours:* Rieveschl Award for Creative & Scholarly Work, 1982; Taft Grants, 1972, 1975, 1979, 1981; American Philosophical Society Grant, etc. *Hobbies:* Tennis; Music. *Address:* Dept. of Romance Languages & Literatures, University of Cincinnati, Cincinnati, OH 45221, USA.

O'CONNOR Teresa McCann, b. 23 June 1956, USA. Lawyer. m. William J O'Connor, 17 June 1978, 2 sons, 1 daughter. *Education:* BA, Political Science, Catholic University, 1977; MLS, JD, 1980. *Appointments:* Legal Intern, Enforcement Director, SEC, Washington, 1979-80; Librarian, US Senate Library, 1980; Staff Counsel, Lobbyist, Al A, Washington, 1900-81; Associate Law Offices, Robert Ryan, Billings, 1981-82; Deputy County Attorney, Yellowstone County, Billings, 1983-; County Attorney, Liaison Rape Task Force, Billings, 1983-; Sexual Abuse Task Force, 1984-. *Memberships:* ABA; ALA; Montana Bar Association; Yellowstone County Bar Association. *Address:* County Attorneys Office, Yellowstone County Courthouse, Billings, MT 59107, USA.

ODAGA Asenath Bole, b. 5 July 1938, Kenya. Writer; Editor. m. James Charles Odaga, 27 Jan. 1957, 2 sons, 3 daughters. *Education:* BA, Honours, Dip. Ed., 1974; MA, Literature, 1980. *Appointments:* School Teacher, 1957-63; Assistant Director, Curriculum Development, Centre of Christian Churches Education Association, 1974-75; Research Fellow, University of Nairobi, 1976-81; Editor, 1982-. *Publications:* Secrets of the Monkey Rock; Kip on the Farm; Kip at the Coast; Kip goes to the City; Look and Write I; Look and Write II; Jande's Ambition; The Tinda Stories; Novels: Between the Years; The Shade Changes; A Bridge in Time; Yesterday's Today: Study of Oral Literature; The Storm. *Memberships:* Secretary, Writers' Association of Kenya; International Board on Books for Young People; Chairman, Children's Literature Association of Kenya; Chairman, Business & Professional Women's Club; Association of African Scientific Editors; Chairman, Kenya University Women Association, Kisumu Branch. *Honours:* Prize, Best short story, Women's Voice, 1976.

Hobbies: Reading; Photography; Cooking. *Address:* PO Box 1743, Kisumu, Kenya.

ODAMTTEN Helen Mary, b. 14 Feb. 1938, Accra, Ghana. University Lecturer. *Education:* BA, English/History, University of Southampton, England, 1959; Postgraduate Diploma in Education, University of London, 1960; MA Applied Linguistics, University of Essex, 1971; Certificate in English Phonetics, University College, London, 1981; International Phonetic Association. *Appointments:* Tutor, English, History and Assistant Housemistress, Achimota School, Accra, 1960-62; Producer/programme Organiser, English, History & French programmes, for Secondary Schools and Training Colleges, 1963-66, Senior Programme Organiser/Assistant Controller of programmes in charge of radio programme training, 1966-74, Ghana Broadcasting Corporation; Research Fellow, 1974-84, Senior Research Fellow, 1984-, Co- ordinator, Study Skills Unit, Language Centre, 1988-, Language Centre, University of Ghana, Legon. *Publication:* Play: No place like Home under the pen-name Herma Dove, 1969. *Memberships:* University Teachers' Association of Ghana; Association of University Women; Linguistic Circle of Accra; West African Linguistic Society; The Historical Society of Ghana; The International Association of Women in Radio & Television; Teachers of English to speakers of other Languages. *Honours:* 6 months UNESCO Fellowship, 1970; 1 year Academic Staff Fellowship, Association of Commonwealth Universities, 1980-81. *Hobbies:* Tennis, Bridge, Reading, Writing plaChurch, Accra. *Address:* Betty House, D358/3, PO Box 438, Accra, Ghana.

O'DELL Deborah Ann, b. 11 Nov. 1957, Pottstown, USA. Assistant Professor. m. Marc S. O'Dell, 18 Mar. 1988. *Appointments:* BS, Ursinus College, 1979; PhD, State University of New York, 1985. *Appointments:* NIH Postdoctoral Fellow, 1985-87; Trevelyan Research Fellow, Selwyn College, Cambridge University, 1987; Assistant Professor, Indiana University Southeast, 1988. *Publications:* Articles in: Journal of Experimental Biology; Science. *Memberships:* Society for Neuroscience; American Society for Cell Biology; American Association for the Advancement of Science; Sigma Xi. *Honours:* NATO Student Travel Award, 1982; EMSA Presidential Scholarship, 1984. *Hobbies:* Knitting; Cooking; Travel. *Address:* Natural Sciences, Indiana University Southeast, 4201 Grant Line Road, New Albany, IN 47150, USA.

O'DELL June Patricia, b. 9 June 1929, Sliema, Malta. Director. m. Ronald Desmond O'Dell, 10 Feb. 1951, divorced 1963, 1 son, 2 daughters. *Appointments:* Negotiator, Estate Agents, 1963-65, Principal, 1965-88; Director, Property Co., 1988-. *Memberships:* Deputy Chair, Equal Opportunities Commission, 1985-; Northwood & Pinner Chamber of Trade, Vice President, 1971; UK Federation of Business & Professional Women, National President 1983-85; International Federaiton Business & Professional Women, Chairman, Employment Committee; Fellow, National Association of Estate Agents; Fellow, Royal Society of Arts. *Hobbies:* Opera; Theatre; Countryside; Literature; Writing; The Family. *Address:* Fir Tree Cottage, Buslins Lane, Chartridge, Bucks HP5 2SN, England.

O'DONNELL Elizabeth Mary, b. 30 Sept. 1953, Buffalo, New York, USA. Former Ice Skater; Handicapped Association Executive. *Appointments:* Competitive ice skater, 1958-71; Performer, Ice Capades, 1971-73; Director, recreational, power & figure skating, shop manager, coach & trainer, for ice hockey teams, 5 arenas, Western New York, 1973-77; President & Founder, Skating Association for Blind & Handicapped, Buffalo, 1976-; Producer, ice shows, local arenas, 1974-; US representative, World Professional Figure Skating Championships, Jaca, Spain, 1978; Producer, Ice Extravaganzas at Buffalo (with national skaters, media stars & numerous handicapped skaters), Buffalo Memorial Auditorium, 1979-; Speaker, leadership, voluntary work, sensory awareness, throughout USA; Various involvements, community affairs. *Publications:*

Author, Teaching the Handicapped Through Ice Skating, 1977; Co-author, Special Olympics Skating Manual, 1983; Writer, song, Dream Your Dream, 1984. *Membership:* US Figure Skating Award Association. *Honours:* Numerous freestyle club & interclub skating titles, Buffalo Skating Club & other regional competitions, 1958-71; Humanitarian of Year, 1983; Local & Tri-State awards, service to mankind, Sertoma, 1984; Citizen of Year, Buffalo News, 1985; Community Service Award, Medical Society of Erie County, 1987; Volunteer Spirit Award, United Way, 1988. *Hobbies:* Dancing; Sports; Sewing & designing; Reading. *Address:* 274 Ruskin Road, Amherst, New York 14226, USA.

OESTERLING Wendy L., b. 11 Oct. 1949, Circleville, Ohio, USA. Training and Education Executive. m. James S. Greene, 7 July 1979, 1 son, 2 daughters. *Education:* Connecticut College, 1967-68; BMus, Wittenberg University, 1972. *Appointments:* Information Control Systems, 1975-76; Alphatext Ltd, 1976-78; Vice-President, Federal Systems Division, Advanced Systems Inc, 1978-87; Vice-President, Federal Systems Division, Applied Learning International, 1987-. *Memberships:* Board of Directors, National Training Systems Association; American Society for Training and Development; Women in Government Relations; Coalition for Open Markets and Expanded Trade; Chairman, CCCE National Conference, 1983. *Hobby:* Music. *Address:* Falls Church, Virginia, USA.

O'FAOLAIN Julia, b. 6 June 1932, London, England. Writer. m. Laurd R Martines, 20 Nov. 1957. 1 son. *Education:* BA 1952, MA 1953, University College, Dublin, Ireland; Post graduate work at Rome University, 1952-53 and Sorbonne, Paris, 1953-55. *Appointments:* Instructor in French, Reed College, Portland, Oregon, USA, 1958-62; Teacher of interpreting in French, English and Italian, Scuola Interpreti, Florence, Italy, 1963-67. *Publications:* Fiction: We might See Sights! and Other Stories, 1968; Godded and Codded, 1970, 1971; Man in the Cellar (short stories), 1974; Women in the Wall, 1975; No Country for Young Men, 1980; Daughters of Passion (short stories), 1982; The Obedient Wife, 1982; The Irish Signorina, 1984. *Membership:* Society of Authors. *Hobby:* Karate, Black Belt, First Dan. *Address:* c/o Rogers, Coleridge & White Ltd, 20 Powis Mews, London W11 1JN, England.

OFORI-ATTA Grace Amoakoa, b. 10 Oct. 1930, Kibi, Akim Abuakwa, Ghana. Librarian. m. Isaac Emmil Osei-Bonsu, 11 Nov. 1962. 5 sons, 1 daughter. *Education:* ALA, Leeds College of Commerce, England, 1958; Certificate, Children's Library Work, Northwest London Polytechnic, 1960; Summer School, College of Librarianship, University of Wales, 1983. *Appointments include:* 1st lady teacher, Abuakwa State College, 1949; Pioneer staff, newly established Gold Coast Library Board (later Ghana Library Board), 1950-68; 1st National Organiser, Children's Library Work, 1958-68, 1973-. *Creative works:* Contribution: Notes on children's reading in Ghana to Library World, 1963; Seminars, lectures, talks, radio interviews throughout Ghana, publicising children's libraries. *Memberships:* Former Executive member, West African Library Association; Children's Literature Foundation, Ghana Book Development Council; Ghana Reading Association; Child Services Volunteers Group, Ghana National Commission on Children; Ministry of Education Committee, Community School Libraries for 1st Cycle Institutions; Chairman, Board of Directors, Regie's Creche & Kindergarten; Chairman, Kanda Schools Community School Library; Chairman, Greater Accra Regional Committee on Children, Ghana National Commission on Children. *Honours:* 1st woman from Ghana to qualify as professional librarian; Mentioned for praise in Parliament of 1st Republic of Ghana; US Government grant, tour of US libraries, 1960. *Hobbies:* Listening to traditional music; Collecting cartoons. *Address:* Ghana Library Board, PO Box 663, Accra, Ghana.

OHANIAN Rubina, b. 20 Dec. 1953, Iran. Associate Professor. m. Armen Tashchian, 17 Sept. 1978.

Education: BBA 1976, MBA 1981, PhD 1981, University of Texas at Austin. *Appointments:* Florida State University, 1980-85; Emory University, 1986-. *Publications:* Numerous articles in professional journals. Speaker, National Professional Conference, Broadcast Promotion and Marketing Executives, National Broadcast Association, Atlanta, 1987; Judge, Intercollegiate Business Competition and Conference, 1987; Participant, Direct Marketing Association Educators Conference, 1985, etc. *Memberships:* Board Member, Atlanta American Marketing Association Professional Chapter, 1987-88; Collegiate Affairs Committee, Atlanta American Marketing Association professional Chapter, 1987-88; American Marketing Association; Association for Consumer Research; American Academy of Advertising; Southern Marketing Association. *Honours:* Recipient of Grants 1983, 1984 and 1987; Educator Scholarship, American Association of Advertising Agencies, Inc, 1987; Ranked by Emory University Student Government Association publication The Key Hole as an outstanding faculty, 1987!; Second highest ranking among 18 faculty members in the Department of Marketing, Florida State University for 1982, 1983, 1984; Beta Gamma Sigma. *Hobby:* Artist, Painter. *Address:* Emory University, Rich Building, Atlanta, GA 30322, USA.

O'HARE Linda Parsons, b. 30 Nov. 1947, Robinson, Illinois, USA. Management Consultant. *Education:* BS, University of Illinois, 1972; Master's degree, Management, Northwestern University, 1983. *Career:* Leo Burnett Company Inc, 1972-75; Booz Allen & Hamilton Inc, 1975-81; President, The Bridge Organisation Inc, 1981-. *Memberships:* Offices, Chicago chapters, Institute of Management Consultants, National Association of Women Business Owners; Director, Chicago Finance Exchange, YWCA (Metropolitan Chicago); Chicago Health Executives Forum; Executive's Club of Chicago; Human Resources Advisory Council, Northeastern Illinois University; Northwestern University Kellogg Alumni Advisory Board; Advisory Council to Global Division, American Marketing Association; Boards of Directors, Chair-Audit Committee, All-American Bank of Chicago, Bridge Organisation Inc. *Hobby:* Arabian horses. *Address:* The Bridge Organisatin Inc, 33 North Dearborn Street, Suite 500, Chicago, Illinois 60602, USA.

O'HEARN Elizabeth, b. 9 Feb. 1959, New York City, USA. Physician. *Education:* BS, Yale University, 1981; MD 1985, Postdoctoral Fellow in Neuroscience 1986, Johns Hopkins University School of Medicine. *Appointments:* Residency, Internal Medicine, Yale University School of Medicine, Yale-New Haven Hospital, 1986 80; Residency, Neurology, Johns Hopkins University School of Medicine/Hospital, 1989-. *Publications:* Several articles in professional journals. *Memberships:* Physicians for Social Responsibility; Society for Neuroscience; Professionals' Coalition for Nuclear Arms Control; Union of Concerned Scientists. *Honours:* Wilton High School Outstanding Junior, 1976; Yale Book Award, 1976; Connecticut Scholar, 1977; Magna cum Laude, with distinction in Philosophy, Yale University, 1981; Semmler Prize, High scholarship in Russian, Yale University, 1981; Henry Strong Denison Award for Medical Research, Johns Hopkins University School of Medicine, 1985. *Hobbies:* Music: flute, recorder, trumpet player, conductor Yale Slavic Choir 1981; Athletics: track, rugby, field hockey, lacrosse, tennis, weightlifting. *Address:* 129 York St Apt 6-D, New Haven, Ct 06511, USA.

OKABE Marie Lorenz, b. 18 Aug. 1943, Copenhagen, Denmark. Musician/Flautist. m. Noriyuki Okabe, 1967, 1 daughter. *Education:* Diploma, Royal Danish Conservatory of Music, 1967; Studied with Marcel Moyse, William Bennett, Geoffrey Gilbert, Julius Baker; Graduate, Tokyo University of Fine Arts and Music, 1974. *Career:* 4 major solo recitals, Tokyo, Japan, 1978-85; Debut recital, Wigmore Hall, London, England, 1984; Appeared chamber music evenings, English-kan, Yokohama, Japan, 1976-82; Participant, Karuizawa Music Festival; Lecturer, Japan Flutists Association

Seminar; Performed as soloist with Tokyo Solisten, Ars Nova, Tokio Akademiker Ensembles and New Japan Philharmonic; Broadcast for NHK (Japan Broadcasting Corporation) and TV; Toured Denmark with Tokio Akademiker Ensemble, 1985; Appeared, Scandinavia Today Festival, Tokyo, 1987. *Memberships:* Japan Federation of Musicians; Japan Flutists Association. *Honours:* Tokyo recitals well-received by critics; Very good London Times review, Wigmore Hall debut recital, 1984. *Hobbies:* Sketching; Watercolour painting; Preservation of traditional Japanese domestic architecture. *Address:* Isshiki 2129-3, Hayama-machi, Kanagawa-ken, Japan 240-01.

O'KELLY Elizabeth, b. 19 May 1915, Manchester, England. Consultant in rural development programmes. *Education:* Diploma, Associate of the Royal Manchester College of Music; Selly Oak Colleges, Birmingham. *Appointments:* Second Officer, Women's Royal Naval Service, 1941-46; Member of Her Majesty's Overseas Civil Service seconded to Nigerian and Sarawak Governments, 1950-65; Acting Director, Asian Christian Service, South Vietnam, 1967-69; General Secretary, Associated Country Women of the World, 1969-72; Freelance Consultant overseas. *Publications:* Books: Aid & Self Help, 1973; Simple Technologies for Rural Women in Bangladesh, 1978; Rural Women, their integration in Development programmes, 1978; Processing & Storage of foodgrains, 1979. Numerous articles in specialist journals and several handbooks. *Memberships:* Associated Country Women of the World, UK; Intermediate Technology Group, UK; International Women's Tribune Centre, New York. *Honours:* Member of the Order of the British Empire (MBE) 1959; Order of the Star of Sarawak (Ahli Bintang Sarawak), 1964. *Hobbies:* Travelling; Walking; Music; Reading. *Address:* Flat 2 Downash House, Rosemary Lane, Flimwell, East Sussex TN5 7PS, England.

OLDAKER Trudy Anne, b. 8 May 1946, Australia. Writer; Factory Worker. 1 son, 1 daughter. *Appointments:* Columnist, Knox-Sherbrooke Gazette, 1973; Clerk, Public Service, 1975-78; Taxi Proprietor, 1979-85; Assistant Editor, Women's Movement, Childrens Literature Co-Op, 1982-85; Researching History of Taxis in Victoria, 1986. *Publications:* Poetry in magazines; Short Stories, articles in various journals & magazines; Book, The Plumber, 1983. *Memberships:* Society of Women Writers Australia; Society of Editors, Victoria; Eve Fortune Writers Group, Chairperson; Historian, Mt. Evelyn Horse Riding Club; etc. *Honours:* Recipient, various honours and awards. *Hobbies:* Researching Family Tree; Gardening; Music; British Comedy; Ghosts. *Address:* PO Box 45, Lilydale, VIC 3140, Australia.

OLDHAM Maxine Jernigan, b. 13 Oct. 1923, Whittier, California, USA. Realtor. m. Laurance M Oldham, 28 Oct. 1941. 1 son. *Education:* AA, San Diego City College, 1974; Western State University of Law, 1975; Business Law, La Salle Extension University, 1976; San Diego State University, 1981. *Appointments:* Pacific Telephone Co., 1951-58; US Civil Service Commission, 1957-58; Board of Education, San Diego District, 1958-59; Associate, Harig, Real Estate Office, 1966-70; Associate, Julia Cave, Real Estate, 1970-73; Realtor, Shelter Island Realty, 1974-. *Publications:* Jernigan-History, 1982; Mears Geneology, 1985; Sissoms, 1987. *Memberships:* National Association of Realtors, California Association of Realtors; San Diego Board of Realtors; Apartment Owners Association; FIABCI; International Real Estate; DAR; Linaries Chapter; Colonial Dames 17th Century native Daughters of the Golden West; International Federation of University Women; International Platform Speakers. *Honours:* Certificate, Outstanding Achievement, California Executive Women, 1984; Certificate First American Title, Outstanding Realtor, 1973. *Hobbies:* Painting; Music; Theatre; Continuing education; Geneology. *Address:* 3348 Lowell Street, San Diego, California 92106, USA.

OLDS Jacqueline, b. 1 Apr. 1947, Springfield,

Massachusetts, USA. Psychiatrist; Psychoanalyst. m. Richard S Schwartz, MD, 26 Aug. 1978. 1 son, 1 daughter. *Education:* Radcliffe College, 1963-67; Tufts Medical School, 1967-71; Adult psychiatry residency, Massachusetts Mental Health Center, 1971- 74; Child Psychiatry residency, Mclean Hospital, 1974-76; Graduated psychoanalyst, 1983. *Appointments:* Mclean Hospital, Belmont, 1974-; Beth Israel Hospital, Boston, 1979-; Private Practice, Cambridge, Massachusetts; Assistant Clinical Professor of Psychiatry, Harvard Medical School, 1984-. *Publications:* Various articles in psychiatric journals. *Memberships:* American Psychiatric Association; American Psychoanalytic Association; American Academy of Child Psychiatry; New England Council of Child Psychiatry; Massachusetts Psychiatry Society. *Hobbies:* Drawing; Music (piano); Cooking. *Address:* 115 Mill Street, Mclean Hospital, Belmont, MA 02178, USA.

O'LEARY Therese Anne, b. 10 Mar. 1955, Charters Towers, New South Wales, Australia. Editor. *Education:* Diploma of Film and Video Production, Honours, Australian Film, Television and Radio School; Short course in Computer Editing. *Appointments include:* Post Production Editor, Shame (feature), The Great Bookie Robbery (mini series), Ephemeral Desire (drama), SBS Television, 1986-. *Creative works:* Drawings; Screen printings. *Memberships:* Women in Film and Television. *Honours:* Award for Best Mini-Series Post Production, The Great Bookie Robbery, Australian Film Institute; Award for Best Short Drama Camera Crew, A Town Like This, Australian Film Institute. *Hobbies:* Theatre (drama and dance); Cinema; Wines. *Address:* GPO Box 4902, Sydney, New South Wales 2001, Australia.

OLES Laura Treadgold, b. 21 June 1956, Seattle, Washington, USA. Attorney. m. Douglas S Oles, 18 Dec. 1979. *Education:* AB, History (with distinction), with Honours in Humanities, Stanford University, 1978; JD, University of Washington, 1981. *Appointements:* Associate, Bogle & Gates, Seattle, 1981-83; Associate 1983-87, Member of Counsel 1987-88, Weinrich & Gilmore, Seattle; Member of Counsel, Davis Wright Tremaine, Seattle, 1988-89; Partner 1990-. *Publication:* The Scope of the Commerce Clause in International Commerce, 1980. *Memberships:* ABA; Washington State Bar Association; US District Court (WD Wash); Seattle-King County Bar Association; MIT Enterprise Forum of the Northwest (Board of Directors 1986-; Chairman 1989-90); Japanese-American Society for Legal Studies. *Honours:* Articles Editor, Washington Law Review, 1980-81; Japan Endowment Fund Fellowship 1980 and 1981; Phi Beta Kappa, 1978. *Hobbies:* Reading; Travel. *Address:* Davis Wright Tremaine, 2600 Century Square, 1501 Fourth Avenue, Seattle, WA 98101, USA.

OLIPHANT Nancy Elizabeth (Betty), b. 5 Aug. 1918, London, England. Artistic Director, Ballet. divorced 2 daughters. *Education:* Studied with Tamara Karsavina & Laurent Novikoff. *Appointments:* Founded Ballet School, Toronto, 1947; Ballet Mistress, National Ballet of Canada, 1951; Established National Ballet School, 1959, Director & principal, concurrently, Associate Artistic Director, National Ballet of Canada, 1969-75; undertook the reorganisaiton of the Ballet School of the Royal Swedish Opera, 1967; Reorganised Ballet School, Royal Danish Theatre, 1978. *Memberships Include:* Jury Member, 3rd Competition, 1977, and 4th in 1981, International Ballet Concours, Moscow; Jury Member, 2nd International Ballet Competition, Jackson, Mississippi, 1986; Fellow, Examiner, Imperial Society of Teachers of Dancing; Charter Member, Past President, Canadian Dance Teachers Association; Founding Member, Canadian Association of Professional Dance Organisations. *Honours:* Recipient, numerous honours & awards. *Hobbies:* Theatre; Music; Film .*Address:* National Ballet School, 105 Maitland Street, Toronto, Canada M4Y 1E4.

OLIVARES Frederica, b. 5 Sept. 1950, Milan, Italy. Marketing & Communication Consultant; Publisher. m. Mario Carlo Ferrario, 18 Oct. 1984. *Education:* PhD, Political Science, Milan State University, 1972; Various Courses. *Appointments:* Heidrick & Struggles International, Milan; Roland Berger & Partners, Milan; Owner, Chief Executive Officer, Olivares & Associates, Milan, Marketing Communication & Publishing. *Publications:* Women in Eastern Economies, 1975; Women and European Labour Markets, 1978; Women and Work : A Shifting Reality, 1981; Nothing to Fear: Career Women Today, 1987; Keine Angst, German Translation, 1988. *Memberships:* EWND; Founder, President, Italy's Womens Professional Network, Milan. *Honours:* President of the Republic, Mota Award, 1982; Paul Harris Fellowship, 1988. *Hobbies:* Quality of Working Life; Womens Professional Development. *Address:* 9 Via San Pietro All'orto, 20121 Milan, Italy.

OLIVARIUS-IMLAH Mary Pat, b. 25 Oct. 1957, Brooklyn, USA. President, Advertising Agency/Print Brokerage. m. Craig Alexander Olivarius-Imlah, 18 Sept. 1982. *Education:* BS, Business Administration and Contemporary Arts/Communications, Ramapo State College, 1979; MBA, Marketing & Management, Fairleigh Dickinson University, 1986. *Appointments:* Direct Mail Advertising Copywriter, Prenice-Hall Inc., New Jersey, 1979-81; Editor, Promotional Designer, Trade Show Manager, Beauty & Barber Supply Institute, New Jersey, 1981-83; National Director, Advertising & Public Relations, Emerson Radio Corp., New Jersey, 1983-85; President, Founder, Imagery Print & Advertising, New Jersey & Vermont, 1985-. *Memberships:* Board Member, Chittenden County Court Diversion Programme; National Association of Female Executives; Alumni Association of Ramapo College of New Jersey. *Honours:* Dean's List, 1978, 1979; Student Activities Award, Ramapo College of New Jersey, 1978, 1979. *Hobbies:* Painting; Singing; Swimming; Dancing; Crafts; Photography; Design. *Address:* RR1 Box 2862, Hinesburg, VT 05461, USA.

OLIVE Agnes Weatherall, b. 22 Mar. 1919, Havana, Arkansas, USA. Executive Director, Oklahoma Literacy Council. m. Wiley Robert Olive, 24 Jan. 1937. 1 son, 1 daughter. *Education:* Oklahoma City University, 1965-68. *Appointments:* Asst Banking Supervisor, Kerr-McGee Corp, 1953-74; Consultant, Oklahoma Dept of Libraries and Oklahoma Dept of Education, 1985- 87; Coordinator, Oklahoma Literacy Coalition, 1986-87; Executive Director, Oklahoma Literacy Council, 1987- . *Memberships:* Oklahoma City University Library Assoc; Oklahoma Opera and Musical Comedy Society; Nat'l Federation of Republican Women, Chmn 5th Dist Reagan Pres Campaign; Laubach Literacy International, Member of Nomination Committee; Zonta Club of Oklahoma City. *Honours:* Award for Meritorious Service, Community Council of Central Oklahoma, 1983; Award of Honour, Five Who Care, KOCO-TV, Channel 5, 1984; Certificate of Appreciation, Volunteer Action Committee, 1984; Legislative Citation, State of Oklahoma, 1986; Citizen Recognition Award, Oklahoma Library Assoc, 1987; American Library Trustee, Association Literacy Award, 1987; Outstanding Trainer Award, Laubach Literacy Action, Syracuse, New York, 1988. *Hobbies:* Theatre; Reading; Volunteering. *Address:* 10 Lytle Drive, Oklahoma City, Oklahoma 73127, USA.

OLIVEIRA JORGE Susana Maria Soares Rodrigues Lopes, b. 27 Feb. 1953, Lisbon, Portugal. Professor of Archaeology (Prehistory). m. Vítor Manuel Oliveira Jorge, 16 Sept. 1972. *Education:* Licentiate degree, History 1976, PhD, Prehistory and Archaeology 1986, Faculty of Arts, Porto. *Appointments:* Assistant (Lecturer), Prehistory, 1976-86, Professor, Prehistoric Archaeology 1986-, Faculty of Arts, University of Porto. *Publications:* Povoados da Pré-história Recente da Regiao de Chaves-Vila Pouca de Aguiar, 3 volumes, 1986; O Povoada do Bouça do Frade (Baiao) No Quadro do Bronze Final do Norte de Portugal, 1988. *Memberships:* President, Direction of Sociedade Portuguesa de Antropologia e Etnologia (Portuguese Society of Anthropology and Ethnology); Société Préhistorique Francaise; Associaçao dos Arqueólogos Portugueses. *Hobbies:* Classical music; Vocal music (sing soprano). *Address:* R Anibal Cunha 101-3o Dto Tras, 4000 Porto, Portugal.

OLIVER Adela, b. New York City, USA. Management Consultant. m. 2 daughters. *Education:* BA, Brooklyn College, 1959; MS, CCNY, 1966; PhD, Yeshiva University, 1973. *Appointments:* Assistant Professor, Psychology and Counseling, John Jay College, CUNY, 1971-76; Internal Human Resource Cons, Met Life Ins, Co, 1976-79; Vice President, Lee Hecht & Associates, New York City, 1979-82; Director, Human Resource Planning and Development, Coopers & Lybrand, 1983-84; President, Chief Executive Officer, Oliver Human Resource Cons, Inc, 1984-; Cons, Ford Foundation, US Army, Stamford Research Inst, Am. Inst Banking. *Memberships:* Met NY Assn Applied Psychology; Am Psychology Association; Human Resource Planning Soc; Soc for Indsl and Orgnl Psychology. *Honour:* NDEA Fellow, 1968-69. *Address:* 120 W 97th St, Apt No 11I, New York, NY 10025, USA.

OLIVER Joyce Anne, b. 19 Sept. 1958, Coral Gables, Florida, USA. High Technology Journalist; Editorial Consultant. *Educations:* BA, Communications, Honours, CSU Fullerton, 1980; MBA Candidate, 1989. *Appointments:* Corporate Editor, Norris Industries, Inc., 1979-82; President, J A Oliver Associates, La Habra Hts, 1982-. *Publications:* Special Feature Editor, The Electron, 1988; Contributing Editor to: Computer Dealer Magazine, 1987-88; Can. Elec. Eng. Mag.; Editorial Contributor to: Nomda Spokesman; PC Week; High-Tech Selling; etc. *Memberships:* President, International Association of Business Communicators; President, Communications Advisory Council, Fullerton; Treasurer, Orange Co., IABC Chapter, 1982; etc. *Honours:* Mathematics Scholarship, Miami Dade College, 1972-73; BA, Honours, 1980; etc. *Hobbies:* Sailing; Water Skiing; Travel. *Address:* 2045 Fullerton Road, La Habra Heights, CA 90631, USA.

OLIVER Patricia Belton, b. 10 Dec. 1947, San Diego, California USA. Architect; Educator. 1 daughter. *Education includes:* BA 1974, March 1977, University of California, Los Angeles (UCLA). *Appointments include:* Draftsperson, architectural designer, various firms, 1973-78; Architectural Designer, Interior Designer & Planner, Charles Kober Associates, 1978-81; Associate Professor, Department of Architecture, California State Polytechnic University (CSPU), 1981-87; Principal, Oliver, Kurze, Georges, 1982-87; Associate Dean, College of Environmental Design, CSPU, 1987-. Also numerous positions as guest speaker, visiting critic. *Creative work includes:* Participant, numerous architectural exhibitions, USA & abroad; Series, 6 half-hour television shows, design & construction of houses by non-designer, non-architect owners. *Publications:* Books: Floor Works, Wall Works, 1988; Articles, professional journals. *Memberships:* American Institute of Architects; Other professional bodies. *Address:* College of Environmental Design, California State Polytechnic University, 3801 W Temple Ave, Pomona, CA 91768, USA.

OLIVER Susan Mary, b. 15 Mar. 1951, Melbourne, Victoria, Australia. Strategic Planning Consultant. m. Brent David Taylor, 4 July 1983, 1 son. *Education:* Bachelor of Building (QS), Melbourne University, 1973. *Appointments:* Tutor, Assistant Lecturer, Melbourne University and Royal Melbourne Institute, 1974-76; Principal in Consulting Practice, Susan Oliver Building Economist, 1976-82; Manager, Ministry of Housing, Victoria, 1982-85; Director, Industry Development, 1985-87; General Manager, Investment and Industry, 1987, Victorian Government; Manager, Technology Strategy, Invetech Limited Australia, Clayton, Melbourne, 1988-. *Memberships:* Women in Management. *Honours:* British Council Scholarship to Templeton College, Oxford University, 1986. *Hobbies:* Opera; Modern art; Classical music; Technology and Design curriculum development in schools; Encouragement of women into non-traditional careers. *Address:* Invetech Limited, 35 Winterton Road, Clayton, Melbourne, Victoria 3168, Australia.

OLIVIER Jacoba Salomina (Joey), b. 26 May 1918, Storms River, Eastern Cape, South Africa. Director of Companies. m. 26 May 1941, widowed 1979, 1 daughter. *Appointments:* Own Secretarial Business, South Africa, Commercial Teacher, Tanskei; Manager, Michelsens SWA Limited, 1958-75; Director, Multi Engineering Contractors Pty Limited, & Thuringer Trust Pty Limited, 1976-. *Memberships:* Executive Member, Afrikaanse Sakekamer; Afrikaanse Damesclub; National President, Business and Professional Womens Club, 1972-74; Deputy Mayor, 1979-83; Treasurer Institute Marketing Management, 1982-88; Elected Mayor, 1984-87. *Hobbies:* People; Knitting. *Address:* PO Box 1521, Windhoek, Namibia, South West Africa.

OLLERENSHAW Kathleen Mary (Dame), b. 1 Oct. 1912, Manchester, England. Mathematician. m. Col Robert Ollerenshaw, ERD TD DI FRCS, 6 Sept. 1939, deceased. 1 son, 1 daughter deceased. *Education:* MA DPhil (Oxon), Somerville College, Oxford, 1931-34. *Appointments:* President, St Leonards School, 1968-; Chairman numerous local and national committees and governing bodies of education establishmetns; Deputy Pro-Chancellor, University of Lancaster, 1978-; Deputy Pro-Chancellor, University of Salford, 1982-. *Publications:* Numerous books, research papers etc on Girls' Education; Local Government Finance; Research Mathematics. *Memberships:* President, 1979-80, Institute of Mathematics and its Applications; President, 1983-84, Manchester Statistical Society; Lord Mayor of Manchester, 1975-76; Elected Member of Manchester City Council, 1954-80. *Honours:* Deputy Lieutenant, County of Greater Manchester, 1986; Freeman of the City of Manchester, 1984; Honorary Doctorates: Manchester University, Salford University; Council for National Academic Award; Companion Royal Northern College of Music; Dame of Order of British Empire, 1971; Dame of the Order of St John of Jerusalem, 1985; Honorary Fellow: Institute of Mathematics and its Applications, University of Manchester Institute of Science and Technology, City & Guilds of London Institute, Manchester Literary & Philosophical Association, Somerville College, Oxford. *Hobbies:* Mathematics; Music; Mountains. *Address:* 2 Pine Road, Manchester, M20 0UY, England.

OLLIF Lorna, b. 19 Mar. 1918, Stawell, Victoria, Australia. Writer; Lecturer. m. 19 Oct. 1946, 2 daughters. *Education:* State High School and Hassett's College, Melbourne; Bookkeeping, Shorthand, Secretarial Diplomas; Technical College courses. *Appointments:* Stenographer, Melbourne solicitors, 1933; Secretary, insurance company, 1937; Driver, Australian Women's Army, 1943; Stenographer to General Northcott, AWAS, 1944; Stenographer, Repatriation Department, Brisbane, Queensland, 1946; Secretary, commercial company, Sydney, New South Wales, 1948. *Publications:* Andrew Barton Paterson; There Must Be A River; Early Australian Crafts and Tools; Louisa Lawson; Women in Khaki; Colonel Best and Her Soldiers; Safari to the Centre; Gateway to Vision (Talking Book for the Blind); The Military Historical Society of New South Wales, 1968-88 (co-author, editor); George Henry Morling (with Ronald Rogers); Articles; Short stories; Essays; Reviews. *Memberships:* Vice-President, Military Historical Society of New South Wales; Committee Member, Baptist Historical Society of New South Wales; AWAS Association; North Shore Historical Society; Ashfield Historical Society Delegate to Royal Australian Historical Society. *Honours:* Numerous prizes including: 1st Prize, Children's Book Week Competition, Victoria, 1929; Prize, Year's Best Item, 1968, 1969, Trophy for winning 2 years running, 1969, View World magazine; 2nd Prize for story, Maryborough Wattle Festival, 1976; Government writing grant, 1977; Australian War Memorial military writing grant, 1979; Fellow, Military Historical Society of New South Wales, 1987; Certificate of Achievement, Royal Australian Historical Society, 1987; 3 books in Royal Library, Windsor Castle. *Hobbies:* Literature; Lecturing; Travel; Home; Grandchildren; Gardening; Fine needlework. *Address:* 41 Galston Road, Hornsby, New South Wales 2077, Australia.

OLORUNTIMEHIN Olufunmilayo Yetunde, b. 17 June 1941, Maiduguri, Nigeria. University Lecturer. m. 8 Apr. 1967, 1 son, 1 daughter. *Education:* BSc, Economics, University of Ife, 1966; MSc, Sociology, University of Ibadan, 1969; PhD Honours, Sociology, Marquis Guiseppe Scicluna International University Foundation, Malta, 1987. *Appointments:* Junior Research Fellow, 1968-70; Research Fellow, 1970-73; Lecturer, 1973-78; Senior Lecturer, 1978-83; Reader, 1983-. *Publications:* Man & Society in Africa, book, 1983; Study of Juvenile Delinquency in a Nigerian City, article (British Journal of Criminology), 1973. *Memberships:* Nigerian Association of Sociologists & Anthropologists; Offices, past/present, Nigerian Society for Criminologists, International Sociological Association. *Honours include:* Government scholar, Western Region of Nigeria 1961- 62, Federal Government 1963-66. *Hobbies:* Gardening; Listening to music; Voluntary work including Lioness Club International, National Ministry for Rehabilitation of Prisoners. *Address:* Sociology & Anthropology Department, University of Ife, Ile-Ife, Nigeria.

OLSEN Kathie Lynn, b. 3 Aug. 1952, Portland, Oregon, USA. Neuroscientist; Assistant Professor. *Education:* BS, Chatham College, 1974; PhD, University of California, Irvine, 1979. *Appointments:* Postdoctoral Fellow, Harvard Medical School, 1979-80; Research Associate, Long Island Research Institute, 1980-83; Assistant Professor, State University of New York, Stony Brook, 1982-; Associate Director, Psychobiology & Integrative Neural Systems Programmes, National Science Foundation, 1984-86. *Publications:* numerous articles & book chapters in scientific journals. *Memberships:* Society for Neurosciences; Women in Neurosciences; Animal Behavior Society; International Academy of Sex Research. *Honours:* Phi Beta Kappa, 1974; Edward A. Steinhaus Memorial Teaching Award. *Hobbies:* Squash; Running. *Address:* Dept. of Psychiatry & Behavioral Sciences, State University of New York, Stony Brook, NY 11794, USA.

OLSON Gayle A. b. 9 Jan. 1945, St Louis, Missouri, USA. m. Richard D. Olson, 26 Aug. 1967. *Education:* BA, Butler University, 1966; MS 1968, PhD 1970, St Louis University. *Appointments:* Assistant professor, St Mary's Dominican College, New Orleans, 1970-71; Assistant professor 1971-74, associate professor 1974-81, associate dean (graduate school) 1976-78, professor 1981-, University of New Orleans; Psychologist, De Paul Hospital, New Orleans, 1974-76. *Publications:* Co-author, book, Learning in the Classroom: Theory & Application; 50 articles & book chapters; Member, editorial advisory board, international journal. Also 22 presentations, professional meetings. *Memberships:* American Association for Advancement of Science; American Psychological Association; Society for Neuroscience; Psychonomic Society; Sigma Xi; Psi Chi; Southeastern Psychological Association. *Honours:* Teaching award, Amoco Foundation; Grant, Edward Schlieder Foundation; 5 university research awards. *Hobbies:* Gardening; Reading; Stained glass. *Address:* Department of Psychology, University of New Orleans, New Orleans, Louisiana 70148, USA.

O'MOORE Astrid Mona Elisabeth, b. 2 Mar. 1945, Oslo, Norway. Child and Educational Psychologist. m. Rory R L de Valmont O'Moore, 15 May 1969. 3 sons. *Education:* BA, Dublin University, Trinity College, 1966; MA, University of Nottingham, 1968; PhD, University of Edinburgh, 1977. *Appointments:* Assistant Lecturer in Developmental and Educational Psychology, University College, Cork, 1968-69; Child Psychologist, Institute of Child Psychology, London, 1975-77; Lecturer in Child and Educational Psychology, Dublin University, Trinity College, 1977- (also University Tutor). *Publications:* Numerous contributions to books and scientific journals in the area of childhood autism, psychology of childhood disability, special education and investigation and management of stress in infertility. *Memberships:* British Psychological Association; National Children's Bureau, London; British Association of Autogenic Training and Therapy; Psychological

Association of Ireland-Chairman of Committee on Teaching of Psychology in Schools. *Hobbies:* Photography; Music; Theatre; Cinema; Watersports. *Address:* Department of Teacher Education, Arts Building, Trinity College, Dublin 2, Republic of Ireland.

ONDEK Violet Cecilia Hughes, b. Philadelphia, Pennsylvania, USA. Residential Building Contractor; Company Director. m. Steve Michael Ondek, 1 son, 1 daughter by former marriage. *Appointments:* Newspaper Correspondent, Advertisement Dept., Gettysburg Times & News, 1951-53; Residential Contractor, 1953-72; Co-Founder, Secretary Treasurer, Director, Corporate Life Insurance Co., Corporate Investment Co., & Corporate Land Investment Co., 1970-, & 1972-, (Retired 1984). *Memberships Include:* Adams Co. Home Builders Association (Director); Pennsylvania Home Builders (Legis. Bd., many years); US Small Business Administration Advisory Council; Licenced Life Agent; numerous civic organisations. *Honours:* Recipient, numerous awards for home building, & as Life Agent. *Hobbies:* Painting in Oils; Writing; Public Relations. *Address:* 470 Guernsey Road, Biglerville, PA 17307, USA.

O'NEAL Harriet Roberts, b. 28 Dec. 1952, Kentucky, USA. Clinical Psychologist. *Education:* BA, 1974; JD, 1978, MA, Clinical Psychology, 1980, PhD, Clinical Psychology, 1982, University of Nebraska. *Appointments:* Staff Psychologist, Kaiser-Permanente Medical Cener, Walnut Creek, 1983-; Private practice, 1984-. *Publications:* Competency to Serve as a Witness in Mental Disability Law in Nebraska, 1978; Sterilization of the Mentally Retarded in Mental Disability Law in Nebraska, 1978. *Memberships:* American, California State Psychological Associations; Commonwealth Club of California. *Honours:* NIMH Fellow, 1974-79; Consultant, Nebraska Governors Commission, 1978. *Hobbies:* Dance; Swimming; Hiking; Travel. *Address:* 286 Park Lake Circle, Walnut Creek, CA 94598, USA.

O'NEAL Sheila Noreice Wiggins, b. 11 Oct. 1957, Jacksonville, Florida, USA. Registered Nurse. m. James Moody O'Neal, 2 Feb. 1980, 1 son. *Education:* Diploma, Georgia Baptist Hospital School of Nursing, 1978. *Appointment:* Clinical & data coordinator research, working with physician & drug company to find new medicine to reverse process of osteoporosis, also study of oestrogen-testosterone, Emory University School of Medicine, 1986-. *Memberships:* Secretary, local Parent-Teacher Association; Recorder, local School Advisory Committee. *Hobbies:* Walking; Sewing; Needlecrafts; Visiting family & friends; Assisting at son's school & extra-curricular activities. *Address:* 1365 Clifton Road NE, Room 5526, Atlanta, Georgia 30322, USA.

O'NEAL Tatum, b. 5 Nov. 1963, Los Angeles, California, USA. Actress. *Creative Works:* Films: Paper Moon; The Bad News Bears; Nickelodeon; International Velvet; Little Darlings; Prisoners; Certain Fury. *Honour:* Academy Award for debut performance in Paper Moon. *Address:* c/o 22240 Pacific Coast Highway, Malibu, CA 90265, USA.

O'NEILL Diane Weaver, b. 4 Feb. 1959, Miami, Florida. Therapist; Clinical Social Worker. m. James F O'Neill III, 29 Nov. 1986. *Education:* BSW, cum laude, University of Southern Florida, 1981; MSW, Florida State University, 1982. *Appointments:* Claims Rep Tr, Social Security Admin, 1979-81; Family Counselor, Coordinator of Admissions, Eckerd Family Youth Alternatives, 1981-88; Private Practitioner with Tampa Psychiatric Consultants, 1985-; Adjunct Professor, St Petersburg Jr College, 1988-. *Memberships:* Academy of Certified Social Workers; National Association of Social Workers; Phi Kappa Phi Honor Society; Themis National Honor Society. *Honours:* Diplomate designated by National Association of Social Workers; Listing in Clinical Register of Social Workers; Board certified Medical Psychotherapist by American Board of Medical Psychotherapist. *Hobbies:* Gardening; Racquetball;

Aerobics. *Address:* 1502 W Busch Blvd, Suite H, Tampa, FL 33612, USA.

O'NEILL JoAnne, Blanche, b. 2 Nov. 1946, Niagara Falls, New York, USA. Biochemist. m. John Charles O'Neill, 30 Mar. 1968. 1 son. *Education:* BA, 1968; MA, 1976; PhD, 1988. *Appointments:* Technician 1968-72, Chief of Virology 1972-74, Grand Island Biological Company, Grand Island, New York; Assistant Cancer Research Scientist, Roswell Park Memorial Institute, Buffalo, New York, 1974-78; Microbiologist, National Cancer Institute, Bethesda, Maryland, 1978-81; Technical Information Specialist, National Library of Medicine, Bethesda, 1982; Biologist, Laboratory of Neuropsychology 1982-87, Biologist, Laboratory of Brain Biochemistry 1987-, National Institute of Mental Health, Bethesda. *Publications:* Numerous articles and abstracts to professional scientific journals. *Memberships:* American Soc Microbiology; Society for Neuroscience; Graduate Women in Science. *Hobbies:* Photography; Sailing; Computers. *Address:* 8615 Bradmoor Dr, Bethesda, MD 20817, USA.

O'NEILL Patricia Enid, b. 30 June 1925, London, England. Racehorse Breeder. m. Frank O'Neill, 3 Dec. 1968. *Education:* Private education. *Hobbies and Interests:* Parrots; Wild Animals; Domestic Animals; Monkeys; Decorating; Rally Driving; Riding; Racehorse Training and Breeding. *Address:* Broadlands Stud Farm, PO Box 126, Somerset West 7130, Republic of South Africa.

O'NEILL Sallie Boyd, b. 17 Feb. 1926, Ft Lauderdale, Florida, USA. Educator; Business owner. m. (1)Roger H Noden, 8 July 1945. 1 son, 1 daughter. (2)Russel R O'Neill, 309 June 1967. *Education:* AA, Stephens College, 1945. *Appointments:* Course coordinator, UCLA Extension, 1960- 72; Academic appointment, 1972-83; HEW Women's Edn Equity grantee, 1976-77; Founder and Pres, Learning Adventures, Inc, 1983-85; VP and Chief Financial Officer, The Learning Network, Inc, 1985-86; Educational consultant; Professional Sculptor, 1987-. *Memberships:* Nat Univ Cont Ed Assoc; Friends of the Ctr for the Study of Women and Women's Studies UCLA; Women in Business Inc (vp and bd of Directors 1976-77 and 1986-87). *Address:* 15430 Longbow Dr, Sherman Oaks, CA 91403, USA.

ONG Janis Elaine, b. 15 Jan. 1939, Arizona, USA. Architect. *Education:* BS, 1965; Licensed architect, States of California and New Mexico. *Appointments:* President, director and general manager, Jaguar Ltd, 1984-; Principal and general manager, Stoller and Ong, Architects and Planner, 1978 84; Land planning and open space conservation consultant, Republic of South Africa, 1975-77; Guest Speaker, Univ of Cpaetown, 1976; Guest design critic, University of California, Berkeley, 1982-84. *Creative works:* Projects: Jane Fonda's Workout, San Francisco; Seven Springs Ranch, 110 ac solar subdivision, Cupertino; San Francisco Housing Authority headquarters; San Jose State Univ student housing; Masterplan 3 new townships: Port Zimbali, San Lameer, Mitchell's Plain, Republic of South Africa, acted as consultant on land planning and conservation. *Memberships:* American Institute of Architects; National Council of Architectural Registration Boards. *Honours:* State of California: Design Excellence, affordable housing, 1982; Pacific Gas and Electric Co, Design Excellence, energy efficiency, 1982; Design Excellence competition, 1981; San Francisco Housing Authority, Design Excellence Competition, 1983. *Hobbies:* Travel; Martial arts; World of mystery books. *Address:* P O Box 36172, Albuquerque, New Mexico 87176, USA.

ONISHI Aiko, b. 26 Nov. 1930, Tokyo, Japan. Pianist. *Education:* BM & Performer's Certificate 1953, Artist's Diploma 1956, Eastman School of Music, Rochester, New York, USA; Further study, Frank Mannheimer & Dame Myra Hess, London, UK. *Appointments:* Toho School of Music, Tokyo, Japan, 1957-64; San Jose State University, California, USA, 1966-88. *Creative work*

includes: Recitals, solo appearances, lecture-demonstrations, all major cities in Japan, over 60 US cities; Taught many prize-winning students, Japan & USA. *Memberships:* California Association of Professional Music Teachers; Music Teachers' Association of California; Mu Phi Epsilon. *Honours:* Honorary Citizen, San Jose, 1968; President's Annual Scholar, San Jose State University, 1977; Artist, Mu Phi Epsilon. *Hobbies:* Reading; Painting; Photography. *Address:* 53 Citation Drive, Los Altos, California 94024, USA.

OODIT Geeta, b. 19 Aug. 1948. Executive Director. *Education:* Diploma in Social Sciences, University of Mauritius, 1975-77; Diploma in Management Studies, University of California, 1980; MA, Population Research, University of Exeter, 1988-89. *Appointments:* Secondary School Teacher, Ideal College, 1969-72; Information and Education Officer 1973-79, Deputy Manager/Director of Programmes 1980-86, Executive Director 1986-, Mauritius Family Planning Association; Public Affairs Assistant, US Embassy, 1979-80. *Creative works:* Participation in numerous training courses. *Memberships:* Mauritius Alliance of Women; IPPF Africa Regional Task Force; INTRAH Technical Advisory Committee. *Address:* c/o Mauritius Family Planning Association, 30 SSR Street, Port Louis, Mauritius.

OPIE June, b. 27 June 1926, New Plymouth, New Zealand. Author; Lecturer; Broadcaster. *Education:* BA; Diploma Social Science. *Appointments:* Research in Cerebral Palsy; Psychologist, Education Department; HM Prison; Health Department; Private practice, Brain damage. *Publications:* Over my Dead Body, 1957; Portrait of a Painter, Documentary for BBC; Come and Listen to the Stars Singing, Pictorial biography of composer Priaulx Rainier, 1988; Numerous articles and short stories. *Memberships:* Penwith Society of Arts; Associat. Dis. Professionals (Editor of Quarterly, 1971-81); SIA; World Wide Fund for Nature. *Honours:* Fellow, Royal Society of Arts. *Hobbies:* All the arts (drama, painting, sculpture, music, etc); Natural Sciences; Space; Geology. *Address:* c/o Callender, 264A Annandale Street, Annandale, Sydney, 2038 NSW, Australia.

OPPENHEIM Sally, (The Right Honourable), b. Dublin, Ireland. Member of Parliament, England. m. (1) Henry M Oppenheim, deceased 1980, 1 son, 2 daughters, (2) John Barnes, 1984. *Education:* Royal Academy of Dramatic Art. *Appointments:* Elected, Member of Parliament, Gloucester, 1970; Member, BBC Advisory Council, 1971-79; National Vice President, Royal Society for Prevention of Accidents, Association of Townswomen's Guilds, National Mobile Homes Residents Association, 1974; Spokesman, Prices & Consumer Protection, Opposition Front Bench, 1974; Spokesman, Prices & Consumer Affairs, Opposition Shadow Cabinet, 1975; Minister of State, Department of Trade, Minister for Consumer Affairs, 1979-82; Member, Privy Council, 1979; Non-Executive Director, Board, Boots, Company plc, 1982; Chairman, National Consumer Council, 1987-. *Hobbies:* Bridge; Tennis.

ORAN Geraldine Ann, b. 27 June 1938, Burleson, Texas, USA. Teacher. m. Francis Larry Oran, 18 Dec. 1960, 1 son, 1 daughter. *Education:* AS, 1976, BS, 978, University of Tennessee. *Appointments:* IBM Instructor, Kelsey-Jenney Business College, 1958-61; Executive Secretary, Bendix Corp, 1961-62; Educational Administrator, South Harriman Baptist Church, 1964-74; Teacher, Midtown Elementary, 1979-. *Publications:* Oil paintings; Pen & Ink Drawings; Pencil Drawings; Wood Sculptures; Stone Sculpture. *Memberships Include:* various professional organisations. *Honours:* Gamma Phi Beta; Kappa Delta Pi; Phi Kappa Phi; Outstanding Service Award, Tennessee Education Association, 1985-86; Teacher of the Year, Roane County, 1987. *Hobbies:* Painting; Sculpting; Reading; Singing; Walking. *Address:* PO Box 917, Harriman, TN 37748, USA.

ORD Catherine Frances, b. 15 Nov. 1955, Ft. Lauderdale, Florida, USA, Canadian Citizen. Filmmaker. 1 son. *Education:* BFA, University of British Columbia; MFA, York University, 1988. *Appointments:* Director, Writer, Producer, Editor, Dear John, 1988. *Creative Works:* Films: No More Dick & Jane, 1983; Dirty Laundry, 1983; Hockey Night in Canada, 1984; Dear John, 1985. *Memberships:* Toronto Women in Film & Video; Ordinary Film Productions Inc. *Hobbies:* Film; Cycling; Drawing. *Address:* Apt. 121, 680 Queens Quay West, Toronto, Ontario M5V 2Y9, Canada.

ORDMAN Jeannette, b. Gemiston, Republic of South Africa. Artistic Director; Principal Dancer; Studio Director. *Education:* University Entrance Matriculation. *Appointments:* Rehearsal Director, Batsheva Dance Company, 1966; Artistic Director, Founder, Director, Bat-Dor Studios of Dance, 1967; Principal Dancer, Bat-Dor Dance Company, 1968-; Principal Dancer, Johannesburg Festival Ballet, and Soloist whilst still at school; BBC TV Engagements, 1952-. *Publications:* Choreographer, 4 works & numerous childrens ballets; Introduced Royal Academy of Dancing London Syllabus for Children to 17 teachers in Israel, and its first examiner to be sent to Israel annually, 1967-; introduced Pilates system of training Bat-Dor and Israel; instrumental in founding Israel Dance Medicine Centre. *Memberships:* Organising Secretary, Royal academy of Dancing, Israel Branch, 1965; Jury Member, International Ballet Competition, Jackson, Mississippi, USA, 1982, 1986; Chairman, Professional Advisory Committee, Israel Dance Medicine Centre. *Honours:* Guild Loyal Women Bursary, 1948; Recipient, various honours and awards. *Hobbies:* Reading; Music; Dogs. *Address:* c/o Bat-Dor Studios of Dance, 30 Ibn Gvirol Street, Tel-Aviv, Israel.

ORLIN Karen J., b. 2 Apr. 1948, Washington, USA. Lawyer. 1 daughter. *Education:* AB summa cum laude, Mathematics, University of Pennsylvania, 1969; JD, Harvard Law School, 1972. Bars: US Court of Appeals, 2nd Circuit, 1973; US District Courts, Southern & Eastern New York, 1973; New York State, 1973; Floria, 1982. *Appointments:* Associate Attorney, Kronish, Lieb, Weiner & Hellman, New York City, 1972-81; Senior Associate 1981-82, Partner (shareholder) 1982-83, Valdes-Fauli, Cobb, Petrey F. Bischoff, P.A., Miami, Florida; Senior Associate & Resident Corporation & Securities Attorney, Ruden, Barnett, McClosky, Smith, Schuster & Russell P.A., Miami 1983-85; Shea & Gould, Miami 1985-87; of counsel to Thomson, Bohrer, Werth & Razook, Miami, 1987-. *Publications:* Article, Women Lawyers in New York City, in Practicing Law in NYC, 1975; Various articles & contributions, Florida Corporations 1985 seminar, & related handbook, Florida Bar, 1985. *Memberships include:* Corporation, Banking & Business Law Section, American Bar Association; Various committees, The Florida Bar; Florida Association for Women Lawyers; Past office, The Association of the Bar of The City of New York Bar; YWCA Women's Network. *Honours:* Outstanding Young Woman of America, 1982; Biographical recognitions. *Address:* 1121 Sunset Road, Coral Gables, Florida 33143, USA.

ORLOCK Carol Elleen, b. 17 Feb. 1947, San Diego, California, USA. Author; Teacher. *Education:* BA, English, Pennsylvania State University, 1968; MA honours, English/Creative Writing, San Francisco State University, 1970. *Appointments:* Instructor, Olympic College, Bremerton, Washington, 1974-78; Extension Lecturer, 1976-88, Coordinator, Writing, 1982-88, University of Washington Extension. *Publications:* The Goddess Letters (novel), 1987. *Memberships:* Associated Writing Programs; Feminist Writers Guild; International Women Writers Guild. *Honours:* Literary Fellowship, Washington STate Arts Commission, 1985; King County Publication Project, 1985-86; Semi-finalist, Iowa Short Fiction Award, 1985; Governor's Award, State of Washington, 1987; Pacific Northwest Bookseller's Award, 1987. *Hobbies:* Reading; Computer programming; Gardening. *Address:* 920 2nd Avenue West, Seattle, WA 98119, USA.

ORR Helen Louise, b. 13 Apr. 1927, Denver, Colorado, USA. Electronic Consultant; Retired educator. *Education:* BA, Hastings College, 1947-51; MA, San Francisco Theological Seminary, San Anselmo, 1951-54; Calif General Secondary Teaching Credential, Calif General Elementary Teaching Credential, Calif Reading Specialist Teaching Credential, University of California, Riverside, 1963-65. *Appointments:* Owner, Quality Photos, Denver, 1947-54; Director of Christian Ed, St Andrews Pres Church, Newport Beach, 1954-58; Director of Christian Ed, First Presbyterian Church, Colton, 1958-59; Community Youth Director, YWCA, Riverside, 1959-64; Educator, Chino Unified School District, 1964-76; Board of Education, Chino, 1979-83; President, Orrtronics, Inc, Chino, 1979-. *Publications:* Johnny Can Read, A guide for teaching reading, 1970; English textbook (and workbook) for 11th grade English to be used in adult school, Chino Unified School District. *Memberships:* Life Member, National Education Association; Chino Business & Prof Women; Scholarship Chair, 1987-, Chino Valley Woman's Club; Scholarship Chairman, 1984-, Chino Community Hospital Auxiliary; Baldy View Regional Occupational Program; Advisory Council, Electronics & Microcomputer Repair, 1983-. *Honours:* Soroptimist Int (Chino) Women Helping Women Award, 1988; Outstanding Alumni, Hastings College, 1987; Friend of Magnolia, Magnolia Jr High School, 1988. *Hobbies:* Photography; Classical music; Travel; Needlepoint. *Address:* 12594 16th St, Chino, California 91710, USA.

ORR Kay A, b. 2 Jan. 1939. Governor of Nebraska. m. 26 Sept. 1957, 1 son, 1 daughter. *Education:* Attended, University of Iowa, 1956-57. *Appointments:* Executive Assistant to Nebraska Governor Charles Thone, 1979-81; Nebraska State Treasurer, 1981, 1982-86; Elected Governor of Nebraska, 1986-. *Memberships:* Chairman, National Governors Association Committee, Transportation, Commerce & Communications; Commission, Presidential Debates, 1988. *Honours:* Elected Delegate to Republican National Convention, 1976, 1980, 1984, 1988; Member, Republican National Platform Committee, 1976-80, Co-Chairman, 1984, Chairman, 1988; etc. *Hobbies:* Reading; Biking; Gardening. *Address:* Governor's Office, Nebraska State Capitol, Box 94848, Lincoln, NE 68509, USA.

ORRISON Brenda Lee Krebs, b. 3 Oct. 1954, Pottsville, Pennsylvania, USA. Attorney. m. John Irvin Orrison, 17 Mar. 1988. *Education:* BA magna cum laude, University of Tennessee, 1975; JD, University of Georgia School of Law, 1977; Admitted, Georgia, 1977; North Carolina, 1978; U.S.D.C.N.D.Geogia, 1981; U.S. Ct Appeals, 11th Circuit, 1981; Georgia Court of Appeals, 1986; Georgia Supreme Court, 1986; U.S.D.C.M.D.Georgia, 1988. *Appointments:* Associate, Redmond Stevens Loftin & Currie, Asheville, North Carolina, 1978-80; Senior Associate Counsel, Metropolitan Atlanta Rapid Transit Authority, Atlanta, Georgia, 1980-85; Senior Trial Counsel, Fireman's Fund Insurance Companies, Atlanta, 1985-; Speaker, seminar on South Carolina Construction Law, Charleston, South Carolina, Apr. 1988. *Memberships:* American Bar Association; North Carolina Bar Association; ABA Forum Committee on the Construction Industry; Panel of Construction Industry Arbitrators, American Arbitration Association. *Honours:* Alpha Lambda Delta, 1972. *Hobbies:* Skiing; Boating; Water-skiing; Golf. *Address:* 302 Perimeter Center North Suite 300, Atlanta, GA 30346, USA.

ORTEGREN Kerstin, b. 27 Oct. 1918, Goteborg, Sweden. Medical Doctor; Specialist, Ophthalmology. m. Olle Kjellgren, 14 Aug. 1943, 1 son, 3 daughters. *Education:* MD, Karolinska Institute, Stockholm, 1947; Specialist, Ophthalmology, 1956; Paediatric Ophthalmology, London, UK, 1979. *Appointments include:* Assistant physician, various hospitals, 1947-51; Ophthalmology Department, Goteborg, 1951-54; Assistant Neurol-Neuro- Perid, 1954-56; Assistant Physician, Ophthalmology, Goteborg, 1956-62; University of Umea, 1962; Senior Physician, Head,

Ophthalmology Department, University Hospital, Umea, 1968-83; Retired, 1983. *Memberships:* Swedish Association of Physicians; Swedish Association of Women Medical Doctors; Swedish Association of Doctors of Ophthalmology. *Hobbies include:* Working against war, for peace & sustainable environment, as member of International Physicians for Prevention of Nuclear War, & Women's International League for Peace & Freedom; Literature; Arts; Nature; Travel; Mountaineering. *Address:* Slojdgatan 1, S-902 48 Umea, Sweden.

ORTWEIN Linda, b. 27 Dec. 1956, Albuquerque, New Mexico, USA. Management Consultant. m. Thomas A. Ortwein Jr, 20 Aug. 1983, 1 daughter. *Education:* MBA, Harvard Business School, 1982; MA cum laude, Middlebury College, 1978. *Appointments:* Harcom Associates, 1978-80; Young and Rubicam, June-Aug 1981; Staff Consultant, 1982-84, Senior Consultant, 1984-87, Principal, 1987-, Kurt Salmon Associates. *Publication:* Organizing for Change, 1988. *Memberships:* Institute of Management Consultants; Harvard Business School Club, Vice- President 1984-86. *Honour:* Certified Management Consultant, 1989. *Hobbies:* Skiing; Running; Other sports; Handcrafts. *Address:* New York, USA.

ORY Marcia Gail, b. 2 Aug. 1950, Dallas, Texas, USA. Medical Sociologist; Gerontologist. m. Raymond J. Carroll, 13 Aug. 1972. *Education:* BA, University of Texas, Austin, 1971; MA, Indiana University, 1973; PhD, Purdue University, 1976; MPH, Johns Hopkins University, 1981. *Appointments Include:* Programme Director, 1981-86, Chief, Social Sciences Research on Aging, 1987-, National Institute on Aging. *Publications:* Author, numerous articles and edited volumes on Aging and Health. *Memberships:* American Public. Health Association, Governing Council, 1986-88; American Sociological Association, Medical Sociology Section Nominating Committee; Society for Behavioral Medicine, Public Health Tract Programme Chair. *Honours:* Phi Kappa Phi, 1974; Department of Health and Human Services Awards, 1984, 1985, 1988. *Hobbies:* Birdwatching; Biking; Bargain Hunting. *Address:* Behavioral & Social Research Program, National Institute on Ageing, Bldg. 31-5C32, Bethesda, MD 20892, USA.

OSBORNE Theresa Jo Pospichal, b. 22 Aug. 1945, Seattle, Washington, USA. Corporate Secretary/Investment Administrator. m. Herbert L Osborne, Jr, 3 June 1967, divorced 1987. 1 son, 1 daughter. *Education:* BFA, Art, Printmaking, University of Nebraska, Omaha, 1967; MFA, Performing Arts Management, Brooklyn College, 1982. *Appointments:* Consultant, Special Projects, City of NY Borough of Queens, 1978-81; Project Coordinator, Brooklyn Bridge Centennial Commission, 1981-82; Director, Cultural Affairs, City of New York, Borough of Queens, 1982-85; Corporate Secretary, Live Oak Realty Corporation, New York City, 1985-. *Memberships:* New York City Junior League (Board of Mgrs 1984-87); Chi Omega Sorority Alumni; New York Crama League; Women's City Club; Flushing Meadow Corona Park Corporation, Board of Directors, 1987-88. *Honour:* Citation of Honour, City of New York, Borough of Queens for outstanding cultural contributions, 1985. *Hobbies:* Growing orchids/roses; Performing and visual arts; Cross country skiing; Hiking. *Address:* 19 Ingram Street, Forest Hills Gardens, NY 11375, USA.

OSLEY-VERCZ Carol Ann, b. Herkimer, New York, USA. Writer. m. *Appointments:* Professional Freelance Writer for Magazines; Editor & Publisher of Monthly Magazine Writer's Guidelines. *Publications:* Creative Writing Workbook; The Soldier, America & Me; Life Through Verse; Helpful Hints for Writers; Getting around Writers Block; Writers Do's and Dont's. *Membership:* The National Writers Club. *Honours:* Authors parties; Television appearances including Books and You. *Hobbies:* Music; All sports; Horseback riding; Crafts. *Address:* Rd No 1, Box 71, Mohawk, NY 13407, USA.

OSTENSO Grace Laudon, b. 15 Sept. 1932, Tomah, Wisconsin, USA. Science and Technology Policy. m. Dr Ned A Ostenso, 29 June 1963. *Education:* BS, University of Wisconsin, Stout, 1954; MS 1960, PhD 1963, University of Wisconsin, Madison. *Appointments:* Food and Nutrition Service, US Dept Agriculture, 1970-78; Comm Science, Space, and Technology, US House of Representatives, 1978-. *Memberships:* American Dietetic Association; Institute of Food Technologists; American Association Advance Science; American Public Health Association; Society for Nutrition Education; American Institute of Nutrition; American Society of Clinical Nutrition. *Honours:* Alumni Distinguished Service Award, University of Wisconsin, 1970; Certificate of Merit, USDA, 1972; Medallion Award, American Dietetic Assoc, 1978; Cooper Memorial Lecturer and Award, American Dietetic Assoc, 1986; Leadership and Exemplary Service Award, State and Territorial Public Health Directors, 1986; Certificate of Appreciation, Food and Nutrition Section, American Public Health Assoc, 1986. *Hobbies:* Art; Antiques; Music. *Address:* 2871 Audubon Terrace NW, Washington, DC 20008, USA.

OSTERGAARD Lise, b. 18 Nov. 1924, Denmark. Professor of Human Studies. *Education:* PhD. *Appointments:* Academic Career: Doctor of Philosophy, 1962, Professor, Clinical Psychology, 1963-77, Professor, Human Studies in International development, 1984-, University of Copenhagen; Political Career: Membership, Danish Social-Democratic Governments, 1977-80; Vice Foreign Minister with special responsibility for overseas development, 1980-82; Minister of Culture, 1977-82; Minister of Nordic Affairs, 1980; Member of Danish Parliament, 1979-84. *Memberships:* Consultant, World Health Organization; Consultant, Danish International Development Agency; Vice President, UNESCO MONDIACULT Conference, 1982; Danish Refugee Council, Chairman, 1974-77; Chairman, Danish Government Commission for Young children, 1975-77. *Address:* Store Kongensgade 118, DK 1264 Copenhagen K, Denmark.

OSTMANN Barbara Gibbs, b. .25 Dec. 1948, Berryville, Arkansas, USA. Journalist. m. Wilfred C. Ostmann, 3 Apr. 1976. *Education:* AA Honours, Christian College, 1969; BJ 1971, MA 1974, University of Missouri; Postgraduate French, University of Neuchatel, Switzerland, 1973. *Appointments:* Bilingual secretary, International Union for Conservation of Nature, Morges, Switzerland, 1973; Teacher, journalism, English College of Chinese Culture, Taipei, Taiwan, 1974; Food Editor, St Louis Post-Dispatch, USA, 1975-; Judge, various cookery contests; Food Editors' Advisory Panel, Food Marketing Institute, 1982-84; Lecturer in field. *Publications include:* Co-editor with Jane Baker: Food Editors' Favorites Cookbook, 1983; St Louis Post-Dispatch Best Recipes Cookbook, 1983; Food Editors' Hometown Favorites Cookbook, 1984; Food Editors Favorites: Desserts, 1988. *Memberships include:* Women in Communications; Past President, offices, Newspaper Food Editors & Writers Association; Past Board Member, Women in Leadership Alumni Association; University of Missouri-Columbia Alumni Association; Smithsonian Institute; Past President, St Louis Culinary Society. *Honours:* 1st place, Vesta Award 1978, 1979, 1981, Certificate of Merit 1980, 1982, American Meat Institute; 1st Place, Golden Carnation Award, Carnation Company, 1981; Leadership Award, St Louis YWCA, 1986; Fellow, Rotary International, 1971-72; Mott Fellowship, 1973-74; First recipient, Pulitzer Fellowship, 1989; Visiting Professor, University of Missouri, 1989. *Address:* St Louis Post Dispatch, 900 North Tucker Boulevard, St Louis, Missouri 63101, USA.

OSTROWSKI-SKOLNICK Nancy Louise, b. 7 Aug. 1954, Erie, Pennsylvania, USA. Neuroscientist. m. Phil Skolnick, 17 Aug. 1985, 1 child. *Education:* BA, Psychology, Edinboro State University, Pennsylvania, 1976; MSc, Physiological Psychology, Rensselaer Polytechnic Institute, 1979; PhD, Psychobiology, University of Pittsburgh, 1984. *Appointments include:* Instructor, Psychology Department, University of

Pittsburgh, 1982-83; Pharmacology Research Associate Fellow, National Institute of General Medical Science (NIGMS), National Institutes of Health, 1984-86; Staff Fellow, Senior Staff Fellow 1986-89, Laboratory of Cerebral Matabolism, Section on Clinical Brain Imaging, National Institute of Mental Health (ADAMHA); Special Assistant to the Director, 1989-. *Creative works:* Author, co-author, numerous research papers, professional journals; Abstracts, Conference Presentations: Invited Lectures. *Memberships include:* American Association for Advancement of Science; International Narcotics Research Conference; American Psychological Association; Society for Neuroscience; Eastern Psychological Association; New York Academy of Sciences. *Honours:* Numerous Academic Awards, Scholarships, Fellowships, including: National Research Service Award, National Institute on Drug Abuse, 1981-83; Provost's Development Award, University of Pittsburgh, 1983-84; Travel award to Maui, Hawaii, American College of Neuropsychopharmacology-Mead Johnson, 1985; Authorised user, radionuclides, Radiation Safety Branch, NIH, 1986. *Hobbies:* Photography; Painting; Sailing. *Address:* Laboratory of Cerebral Metabolism, Section on Clinical Brain Imaging, Building 10, Room 4N-317, NIMH, 9000 Rockville Pike, Bethesda, Maryland 10892, USA.

OSTROY Joan Patsy, b. USA. Lawyer. m. Joseph Martin Ostroy, 24 May 1964, 1 son, 1 daughter. *Education:* Certificate, University of Paris France, 1963; BA honours, French Literature, 1964, honours seminar student, Political Science, University of Pennsylvania; London School of Economics and Political Science, England, 1972-73; JD cum laude, Loyola University School of Law, Los Angeles, California, 1976; Admitted: California State Bar, 1977; US District Court, Central District of California, 1977; US Court of Appeal, 9th Circuit, 1978. *Appointments:* Solo Practice, 1980- 84; Partner, Ostroy & Truby, Los Angeles, 1984-; Social Work, private/public agencies; Editorial Assistant, Northwestern University. *Publications:* HFH v. Superior Court-Another Perspective on the Dilemma of the Downzoned Property Owner, 1977. *Memberships:* Former Chair, Vice-Chair/Member, Executive Committee, Former Vice-Chair, Resolutions Committee, State Bar of California Conference of Delegates; Past President, Former Officer/Member, Board of Governors, Founder/Co-Chair, Oral History Project, Former Delegate, State Bar Conference, Volunteer Attorney, Harriett Buhai Family Law Center, Women Lawyers Association of Los Angeles; Officer, Executive Committee of Family Law Section, Mediation Panel of Central District Family Law Departments, Panel Arbitrator, Former Member, several committees, Los Angeles County Bar Association; Volunteer Mediator, Former Executive Committee Member, Family Law Section, Beverly Hills Bar Association; Steering Committee, Welfare & Institutions Code Section 317 Dependency Panel, 1981-83; Governing Board, Steppingstone Youth Crisis Shelter, 1984-86; Women's Legal Clinic Advisory Board, Co-Founder, Attorneys Against Discrimination. *Honours:* Scholarship; Teaching Assistantship; Dean's List; Editor, Loyola Law Review, 9th Circuit Board; Commendation, Los Angeles City Council, 1984. *Address:* Ostroy & Truby, 11601 Wilshire Boulevard, Suite 1830, Los Angeles, CA 90025-1754, USA.

OSTRY Sylvia, b. Winnipeg, Manitoba, Canada. Public Servant; Economist. m. Bernard Ostry. 2 sons. *Education:* BA 1948, MA 1950, McGill University; PhD, Cambridge University and McGill University, 1954. *Appointments:* McGill University, University of Montreal, Oxford University, 1954-64; Statistics Canada, Economic Council of Canada, 1964-72; Chief Statistician of Canada, 1972-75; Deputy Minister, Consumer and Corporate Affairs Canada, 1975-78; Chairman, Economic Council of Canada, 1978-79; Head, Department of Economics and Statistics, OECD, Paris, France, 1979-83; Deputy Minister, International Trade and Coordinator, International Economic Relations, 1984-85; Ambassador for Multilateral Trade Negotiations and the Prime Minister's Personal Representative for the Economic Summit, 1985-.

Publications: Co-author: International Economic Policy Coordination, 1986; over 80 publications on empirical and policy-analytic subjects. *Memberships include:* Fellow, American Statistical Association; American and Canadian Economic Associations; Royal Economic Society; Founding Member, Centre for European Policy Studies, Brussels; Group of Thirty. *Honours include:* 17 honorary degrees; Officer of Order of Canada, 1978; Government of Canada Outstanding Achievement Award and Per Jacobsson Foundation Lecture, 1987. *Hobbies:* Films; Theatre; Contemporary Reading. *Address:* Department of External Affairs, Lester B Pearson Building, 125 Sussex Drive, Ottawa, Ontario, Canada K1A 0G2

O'SULLIVAN Judith, b. 6 Jan. 1942, Pittsburgh, Pennsylvania, USA. Art Historian; Author; Museum Administrator. m. James P. O'Sullivan, 1 Feb. 1964, 1 son, 1 daughter. *Education:* BA, Art, Literature, Carlow College, 1963; MA, 1969, PhD, 1976, History of Art, University of Maryland. *Appointments:* Teacher: High School, 1964; Elementary School, 1965-66; Teaching Fellow, Instructor, University of Maryland Department of Art, 1967- 70; Editor, The American Film Institute, 1974-77; Associate Programme Coordinator, Smithsonian Resident Associate Programme, 1977-78; Director of Institutional Development, National Archives, 1978-79; Executive Director, Maryland State Humanities Council, 1979-84; Executive Director, Center for the Book, Library of Congress, 1981-82; Deputy Assistant Director, 1984-87, Acting Assistant Director, 1987-, National Museum of American Art, Smithsonian Institution, Washington DC; Adjunct Professor of Art, Trinity College, 1986-. *Publications include:* The Art of the Comic Strip, 1971; Workers and Allies: Female Participation in the American Trade Union Movement, 1975; The American Film Institute Catalog of Motion Pictures: Feature Films, 1961-1970, 1976; The Complete Prints of Leonard Baskin, 1984; The American Film Institute Catalog of Motion Pictures: Feature Films, 1911-1920, 1988; The Great American Comic, 1989. *Memberships:* American Association of Museums; Chairperson, Smithsonian Institution Women's Council; Mid-Atlantic Association of Museums; American Association of University Women. *Honours:* Prize for General Excellence for The Art of the Comic Strip, Printing Industries of America, 1971; Smithsonian Fellow, 1971; University of Maryland Museum Fellow, 1971. *Hobbies:* Mystery writer. *Address:* National Museum of American Art, Smithsonian Institution, Washington, DC 20560, USA.

O'SULLIVAN Maureen, b. 17 May 1911, Roscommon, Republic of Ireland. Actress. m. (1)John Farrow, 1936, deceased 1963, 7 children. (2)James E Cushing, 1983. *Creative Works:* Films include: Song o' My Heart; So This Is London; Just Imagine; The Princess and the Plumber; A Connecticut Yankee; Skyline; The Silver Lining; The Big Shot; Tarzan, The Ape Man; Fast Companions; Skyscraper Souls; Strange Interlude; Okay America; Payment Deferred; Robber's Roost; The Cohens and the Kellys in Trouble; Tugboat Annie; Stage Mother; Tarzan and His Mate; The Thin Man; Hide-Out; The Barretts of Wimpole Street; David Copperfield; West Point of the Air; Cardinal Richelieu; The Flame Within; Anna Karenina; Woman Wanted; The Bishop Misbehaves; The Voice of Bugle Ann; Tarzan Escapes; The Devil Doll; A Day at the Races; The Emperor's Candlesticks; Between Two Women; My Dear Miss Aldrich; A Yank at Oxford; Hold That Kiss; Port of Seven Seas; The crowd Roars; Spring Madness; Let Us Live; Tarzan Finds a Son!; Sporting Blood; Pride and Prejudice; Maisie Was a Lady; Tarzan's Secret Treasure; Tarzan's New York Adventure; The Big Clock; Where Danger Lives; Bonzo Goes to College; All I Desire; Mission over Korea; Duffy of San Quentin; The Steel Cage; The Tall T; Wild Heritage; Never Too Late; The Phynx. Television: The Crooked Hearts; The Great Houdinis.

OSWALD Angela Mary Rose, Lady, b. 21 May 1938, London, England. Woman of the Bedchamber to H.M. Queen Elizabeth the Queen Mother. m. William Richard Michael Oswald, C.V.O., 21 Apr. 1958, 1 son, 1 daughter. *Appointments:* Formerly Extra Woman of the Bedchamber to HM Queen Elizabeth, The Queen Mother; Woman of the Bedchamber, 1983-. *Address:* Flitcham Hall, King's Lynn, Norfolk PE31 6BY, England.

OUNJIAN Glenna Lorraine, b. 14 Aug. 1952, Toronto, Ontario, Canada. Paleoethnobotanist. *Education:* BA (Hons) Anthropology, Scarborough College, 1977, MA Anthropology, 1981, PhD Anthropology expected 1989, University of Toronto. *Appointments:* Floral Analysis of Coleman Site, Ontario, 1985; Ontario Heritage Foundation Research Grants for doctoral research, 1985-86 and 1986-87; Floral Analysis of Calvert Village, Ontario, 1987; Floral Analysis, McKeown Village, Ontario, 1988. *Memberships:* Ontario Archaeological Society; OAS London Chapter; Society for Economic Botany; Southeastern Archaeological Conference; Society of Ethnobiology; Federation of Ontario Naturalists; Royal Ontario Museum; Metropolitan Toronto Zoological Society; Planetary Society. *Honours:* Ontario Graduate Scholarship, 1980; Connaught Scholarship, 1981 and 1982; Eleanor Cate Allen Fellowship, 1983; Mary H Beatty Fellowship, 1984. *Hobbies:* Nature; Nature photography; Antiques; Needlepoint; Quilting; Gardening. *Address:* 16 Larchwood Place, Brampton, Ontario, Canada.

OUNJIAN Marilyn J, b. 24 Oct. 1947, Harrisburg, Pennsylvania, USA. Chairman & Chief Executive Officer. m. George E Ounjian, 31 July 1982. 1 son, 2 daughters. *Education:* University of Maryland, College Park. *Appointments:* President, Today's People, Philadelphia, 1973-81; Chairman, Careers USA and The Career Institute, Philadelphia, 1981-. *Memberships:* Governor's Club; Greater Philadelphia Chamber of Commerce; Pennsylvania State Chamber of Commerce; Center City Proprietors Association; National Association for Female Executives; National Association of Women Business Owners; Association of Venture Founders; Republican Senatorial Inner Circle. *Hobbies:* Swimming; Horseback riding; Gardening. *Address:* Careers USA, 1825 JFK Boulevard, Philadelphia, PA 19103, USA.

OVENDEN Juliet Ann, b. 9 Nov. 1959, Hitchin, Hertfordshire, England. Teacher of Ballet. *Education:* Various private dance teachers including Dame Merle Park, 1977-79; London College of Dance and Drama, Dip. LCDD AISTD, 1979-82; City Literary Institute, London (Drama Training), 1982-85. *Appointments:* Ballet Teacher, Holy Cross Convent, Gerrards Cross, Buckinghamshire, 1983-85; Teacher of Movement and Dance, London Academy of Performing Arts, 1986; Artistic Director, Link-up Dance Company (for deaf and hearing dancers), 1986-87; Teacher of Dance, Founder of Ballet Department, Queen's College, London, 1986-89; Ballet Teacher, Founder of Ballet Department, Cavendish School, London, 1988-; Principal, Marylebone Ballet School, London, 1990-. *Memberships:* Imperial Society of teachers of Dancing; Sacred Music-Drama Society. *Hobbies:* Music; Classical singing; Drama; Reading; Hospital voluntary work. *Address:* Flat 1A, 16 Maresfield Gardens, London NW3 5SU, England.

OVERHOLT Mary Ann, b. 15 Feb. 1935, Charleston, West Virginia, USA. Attorney. m. Walter Melvin Redman Jr, 14 Jan. 1981. *Education:* BA, Ohio University, 1956; JD, Salmon P. Chase College of Law, Cincinnati, 1964. *Appointments:* Personnel administration & engineering design, General Electric Company, Cincinnati, 1956-65; Assistant Counsel, Associate Counsel, Assistant Secretary, Inter-Ocean Insurance, 1965-77; Secretary & Director, Micrographix Data Services Inc, 1970-74; Adjunct Assistant Professor of Law, Salmon P. Chase College, 1973-75; Associate Counsel 1977-79, Vice President & General Counsel 1979-, Union Central Life Insurance Company, Cincinnati; Vice President & General Counsel 1988-, Manhattan National Corporation. *Memberships:* Past Chair, offices, Life Insurance Law Committee, American Bar Association; Boards, past/present, Association of Life Insurance Counsel, & Lawyers Club of Cincinnati; Ohio &

Cincinnati Bar Associations. *Honours include:* Career Woman of Achievement, Cincinnati YWCA, 1983. *Hobbies:* Sailing; Golf. *Address:* Union Central Life Insurance Company, PO Box 179, Cincinnati, Ohio 45201, USA.

OVESEN Ellis, b. 18 July, 1923, New Effington, South Dakota, USA. Writer; Artist. m. Thor Lowe Smith, 28 Aug 1949, 2 sons. *Education:* MA, cum laude, English, University of Wisconsin; California Teacher's Certificate, San Jose State University, San Jose, California. *Appointments:* Teacher of English, University of Wisconsin, 1945-47; Du Pont Company, Advertising Department, Wilmington, Delaware, 1948-49; Teacher of English, San Jose State University, 1963. *Publications:* 13 books of poetry; 2 books of prose; many paintings; prophesy sheets; essays on famous poets; cassette tapes. *Memberships:* National Writers Club, Professional Member; Founder and President, Peninsula Poets; Charter Member, President, Toyon Chapter, CFCP; Poetry Society of America; President, California State Poetry Society; Founder, Citizens United for Rural Environment, LAH; Pacific Art League, Palo Alto, California. *Honours:* Named Los Altos Hills Town Poet; Lives Touch (Poetry) National Award; A Time for Singing (Haiku, Self-Illustrated) Award by NLAPW; Honorary Doctorate of Literature, World Academy of Arts and Culture, 1986; Named Dame of Merit, Knights of Malta, 1988; Named World Poet 1989 by World Poetry Research Institute, 1989; Golden Poet Award, World of Poetry, 1988, 1989. *Hobbies:* Music; Gardening; Study of the Bible. *Address:* Box 482, Los Altos, CA 94023, USA.

OWEN Eirwen Mary, b. 24 Nov. 1914, Glamorgan, Wales. Retired. *Education:* BA, University College of Wales, 1936. *Appointments:* WVS Organiser for Wales, 1937-39; Deputy Regional Commissioner for Wales, 1939-44; Head, Overseas Dept., WVS, 1944-56; Director, Administration, Zoological Society of London, 1956-79. *Memberships:* Council, University of Wales; Royal Commission on the Press, 1947-50. *Honours:* OBE, 1946; CBE, 1973. *Hobbies:* Social History; Music; Gardening. *Address:* 4 Hope Cote Lodge, Church Road, Combe Down, Bath BA2 5JJ, England.

OWEN Patricia Jane, b. 2 Dec. 1948, Lawton, Oklahoma, USA. Administrative Assistant; Consultant. *Education:* BA, Oklahoma University, 1971. *Appointments:* Legislative Staff Member 1971-81, Legislative Assistant/Legislative Coordinator, 1981-87, to Senator Russell B Long; Administrative Assistant/Consultant, Jim Guirard Enterprises and Walden Associates, 1987-88. *Membership:* Women in Government Relations. *Honours:* 12 year Senate Pin and 16-year Certificate for service with United States Senate. *Hobbies:* Bicycling; Raquetball; Reading; Swimming; Needlework; Architecture; Travel. *Address:* 7820 Miracle Lane, North Richland Hills, Texas 76180, USA.

OWSIANY Ewa Barbara, b. 23 Jan. 1940, Rabka, Poland. Journalist. m. Wladyslaw Owsiany, 5 Sept. 1964, 3 daughters. *Education:* MA, Polish Philology, University of Cracow. *Appointments:* Gazeta Krakowska, 1964-85; Publicist, Przeglad Tygodniowy, 1985-. *Publications:* The Short Southern Shadow, 1979; The Line Under Tension 1983; To Cure the Life, 1986. *Memberships:* Polish Students' Association; Polish Journalists Association; The Association for The Relations with Poles Abroad, POLONIA. *Honours:* Silver Cross of Merit, 1973; Golden Cross of Merit, 1981; Golden Medal of Merit, City of Cracow, 1981. *Address:* ul. Komandosow 19A/7, 30-334 Krakow, Poland.

OWSNITZKI Gabriele Anna, b. 5 Mar. 1957, Osnabruck, Germany. Marketing/Brand Manager. *Education:* Part-time study for BS Degree, Marketing, Fairleigh Dickinson University, 1978-. *Appointments:* Office/Showroom Manager, Watches, Dynasty/Eterna Mido, 1975-77; Admin Asst, Leiser Katz Partners, 1977-78; Product Manager, Bridal/Fashion Jewelery, Art

Carved, 1978-83; Director of Merchandising, Hirsch USA, 1983-87; Brand Manager, Watches, Pulsar Time, 1987-. *Membership:* National Association for Female Executives, 1985-. *Honours:* Phi Betta Kappa; Delta Mu Delta; Phi Omega Epsilon. *Hobbies:* Country crafts; Needlework. *Address:* 144 West Stearns Street, Rahway, New Jersey 07065, USA.

OXLADE Zena Elsie, b. 26 Apr. 1929, London, England. Retired Regional Nursing Officer. *Education:* Nurse Tutor's Diploma, London University, 1954-56. *Appointments:* Registered Nurse 1950-52, Ward Sister 1952-54, Nurse Tutor 1956-63, Chase Farm Hospital, Enfield; Principal Nurse Tutor, W Suffolk Hospital, 1963-70; Chief Nursing Officer, West Suffolk Health Authority, 1970-78; Area Nursing Officer, Suffolk Area Health Authority, 1978-81; Regional Nursing Officer, East Anglia, 1981-87. *Publication:* Ear, Nose & Throat Nursing Textbook. *Memberships:* General Nursing Council, England & Wales, 1975-83, Chairman, 1977-83; UK Central Council for Nurses, Midwives & Health Visitors, 1983-88; Chairman, General Nursing Council Trust, 1983-. *Honour:* Commander of the British Empire, 1984. *Hobbies:* Motoring; Handicrafts; Countryside. *Address:* 5 Morgan Court, Claydon, Ipswich, Suffolk IP6 0AN, England.

OZAITA Maria Luisa Marques, b. 20 Apr. 1939, Baracaldo (Vizcaya), Spain. Composer (Spinetist). *Education:* Piano, 1958; Composition, 1971; Clavichord, 1981. *Appointments:* Lecturer in Music, IB Felipe II, Moratalaz, Madrid, 1961-. *Creative works:* La fuente del Halcon, 1961; La balada de Atta Trollm, 1963; Tres pequenas, piezas, 1968; Urte-berri Ametza dantza, 1971; Irurat bat, 1973; Pelleas y Melisanda, 1974; Aforismos, 1975; In Memorian, 1975; Trio Oh, 1981; Preludio Danza y Postludio, 1981; Aleluvas, 1982; Preludio y danza con 3 variaciones, 1982; Fantasia y fugueta, 1982; A modo de improvisacion, 1982; Homenaje a Gova, 1983; Tres canciones espanolas, 1983; Tema con 10 variaciones, 1984; Preludio y danza con variaciones, 1987; Fantasia,. 1987; Recordando, 1987; Triptico encadenado, 1987; Para chelo, 1988. *Memberships:* Member, Royal Basque Society of Friends of the Country; Spanish Symphonic Composers; Women in Music. *Honours:* Scholarships: International Courses, Music in Compostela, Spain, 1965-68; Royal Conservatory of Copenhagen, Denmark, 1967-68; Ruckers Genootschap de Amberes, Belgium, 1980, 1982; Composition, Darmstad, Germany, 1972. *Hobby:* Theatre direction. *Address:* Jose Sanchez Pescador-5-50E, Madrid 28007, Spain

P

PACK Lena Marie Hansen, b. 26 Nov. 1905, Brigham City, Utah, USA. Retired. m. Alvin Grabau Pack, 8 Sept. 1927, 4 sons, 1 daughter. *Education:* University of Utah; Brigham Young University; Utah State University. *Publications:* Famous Jewels; Famous Furniture Stories; Pioneer Stories; Organ Stories; Children are People; Marriage Clinic; Happy Family Life; Let's Go Calling; Maria Fontaine's Scrap Book; Room Recipes, all for radio; various multi media presentations; stage presentations; Author, Director, The Living Monument, Gods and Goddesses, It's Your Move; etc. *Memberships:* National League of American Pen Women, Vice President, Salt Lake City Branch, 1982, President, 1985-87; Chairman, National Mid-Administration Congress; Docent, Church Museum of History and Art. *Honours Include:* Recipient various honours, prizes and awards including: National PTA Award, 1943; Utah Woman Teacher of the Year, 1971; 1988 Hall of Fame, Salt Lake Council of Women; 1988 Hall of Fame, Utah Broadcasters. *Address:* 610 The Belvedere, 29 S. State, Salt Lake City, UT 84111, USA.

PACKARD Betty J, b. 1 Oct. 1937, Indianapolis, USA. Writer; Lecturer; Publisher; Management Consultant. m. Stephen M. Voris, 26 Sept. 1975, 1 son, 1 daughter. *Education:* BA, Franklin College, 1967. *Appointments:* Reporter, Indianapolis Star, 1954-57; Journalism Director, Ben Davis HS, 1967-69; Editor, Research & Review Ser. of America, 1969-75; Owner, President, Packard Consulting, 1975-; Publisher, Owner, Hoosier Hospitality, 1985-; Publisher, Owner, Reno Hospitality, 1987-. *Publications:* When Someone is Crying, 1975; I Love You, 1975; numerous articles. *Memberships:* National Federation of Press Women, Board, 1972-78; California Press Women, Board, 1985-; Northern California Press Women, President 1983-85. *Hobbies:* Motor Sports; Piano; Classical Music. *Address:* 1419 De Haro, San Francisco, CA 94107, USA.

PACKARD Sandra Podolin, b. 13 Sept. 1942, Buffalo, New York, USA. University Provost; Art Educator. m. Martin T Packard, 2 Aug. 1964. 2 daughters. *Education:* BFA, Syracuse University, 1964; MsEd 1966, EdD 1973, Indiana University. *Appointments:* Art Teacher, Public Schools, New York and Indiana, 1964-68; Assistant Professor of Art Education, State University College of New York at Buffalo, 1972-74; Associate Professor of Art Education 1974 80, Special Assistant to Provost 1979-80, Associate Provost for Special Programs, 1980-81, Miami University; Dean, College of Education, Bowling Green State University, 1981-85; Provost, The University of Tennessee at Chattanooga, 1985-. *Publications:* Book: The Leading Edge, over 60 articles in Scholarly Journals, Editorial Consultant, Journal of Aesthetic Education, 1984-; Editorial Board 1981-83, Co-Editor 1976-79, Senior Editor, 1979-81, Studies in Art Education. *Memberships:* American Association of Colleges for Teacher Education, 1982-85 (Chair, National Convention Committee, 1985); Council for Policy Studies in Art Education, 1982-; Evaluator, New York State Board of Education, 1985; Ohio Commission on Educational Excellence, 1982-83; National Art Education Association (Director of Higher Education Division, 1983-85, President, Women's Caucus, 1976-78); Teacher Education Council (Executive Board, 1983-86); American Art Therapy Association; State University Council of Education Deans, 1981-85. *Honours:* June King McFee Award for outstanding Leader in Art Education; Associate, Academic Affairs Resouce Center of the American Association of State Colleges and Universities, 1985; American Council on Education Fellow, 1978-79; Leadership Award, Bowling Green Chapter of Phi Delta Kappa, 1975; Golden Key Honorary Member, 1983. *Hobbies:* Sailing; Travel. *Address:* The University of Tennessee at Chattanooga, 615 McCallie Avenue, Chattanooga, TN 37403, USA.

PACKER Katherine Helen, b. 20 Mar. 1918, Toronto, Canada. Educator & Administrator, Library and Information Science, retired. m. William A Packer, 27 Sept. 1941. 1 daughter. *Education:* BA, University of Toronto, Canada, 1941; AMLS, University of Michigan, USA, 1953; PhD, University of Maryland, 1975. *Appointments:* Cataloguer, Wm L Clements Library, University of Michigan, 1953-55; Cataloguer, University of Manitoba Library, 1956-59; Cataloguer, University of Toronto Library, 1959-63; Head Cataloguer, York University Library, Toronto, 1963-64; Chief Librarian, Ontario College of Education, University of Toronto, 1964-67; Assistant Professor, Faculty of Library Science 1967-75, Associate Professor 1975-78, Professor & Dean 1978-84, Professor Emeritus, 1984-, University of Toronto. *Publications:* Early American School Books, 1954; Articles in professional journals. *Memberships:* American Library Association; Canadian Library Association; Association for Library & Information Science Education; IFLA; FID/ET. *Honours:* Howard V Phalin, World Book Graduate Scholarship in Library Science Award, 1972; Distinguished Alumnus Award, University of Michigan Library School, 1981; Phi Kappa Phi Honour Society. *Interests:* Literacy movement; Protection of the environment; Preservation of rain forests; Opposition to hunting in wildlife preserves in Ontario; Birdwatching. *Address:* 53 Gormley Avenue, Toronto, Ontario, Canada M4V 1Y9.

PADDIO-JOHNSON Eunice Alice, b. 25 June 1928, Crowley, Los Angeles, USA. Company President. m. John David Johnson Sr., 23 June 1984, 8 sons, 2 daughters. *Education:* BS, Grambling State University, 1949; MA, UCLA, 1960; MS, Cornell University, 1988. *Appointments:* Teacher, Counselor, Administrator, St. Helena Parish School Board, 1948-72; Director, SHARE, 1972-73; Administrator, Cornell University, 1973-85; Director, St Helena Head Start, 1986-87; CEO Paddio-Johnson Ent. Inc., 1987-. *Publications:* Creative Career Exploration Programme; Winning Behavior Skills; Genealogy. *Memberships:* AAUW; NCNW; AARP; NEA; LAE Delta Sigma Theta Sorority & St Helena Parish Association of Educators. *Honours:* Eunice Paddio-Johnson Foundation Inc., 1973; Outstanding Leader; Black & Gold Award. *Hobbies:* Writing; Singing; Roses. *Address:* PO Box 245, Hwy 87N, Greensburg, LA 70441, USA.

PADILLA Lorraine Marie, b. 24 Mar. 1952, New York City, USA. Insurance Company Executive. m. Samuel P. Padilla, 21 Aug. 1971, 1 son. *Education:* BS, Mathematics, New York University, 1973; Chartered Life Underwriter, 1980; Chartered Financial Consultant, 1984. *Appointments:* Contract'o Actuarial Specialist, North American Reassurance Company, 1973- 75; Regional Manager, Pension Sales, Phoenix Mutual Life Insurance Company, 1975-. *Memberships:* General Agents & Managers Association; National, Life, & Women Life Underwriters Associations. *Honours:* National Merit & Regents Scholarships, 1969; Management Executive Awards, Phoenix Mutual Life, 1979-84. *Hobbies:* Reading; Swimming. *Address:* 40 Mallow Street, Staten Island, New York 10309, USA.

PAGE Kathleen Reavette, b. 30 Jan. 1949, Tulsa, Oklahoma, USA. Architect. m. Michael D. Graves, 7 June 1975. *Education:* BA, Architecture, Washington University, St Louis, Missouri, 1971; MArch, Catholic University of America, 1976. *Appointments:* Rural Housing Alliance, 1972-75; Bairley & Maginniss Architects, 1976-77; Grossman, Martin, Chapman, 1977-78; Housing Authority, Louisville, 1978-80; Murray-Jones-Murray Architects, 1980-82; Kathleen R. Page, Architect, 1982-86; Page-Zebrowski Architects, 1987-. *Creative work includes:* Architect, Wallace residence, Creek County, Oklahoma. *Memberships:* Past President, Eastern Oklahoma, American Institute of Architects; Vice President 1989, Oklahoma Council of Architects; Past President, Preservation Tulsa; National Committee on Design, AIA; Board, Tulsa YWCA. *Honour:* Henry Adams Certificate of Merit, Catholic University, 1976; National winner, Helping Hands for Small Businesses, Working Woman magazine & Apple

Computers, 1989. *Hobbies:* Classical piano; Ballet; Gardening; Tennis; Skiing. *Address:* Page-Zebrowski Architects, 233 South Detroit, Suite 310, Tulsa, Oklahoma 74120, USA.

PAIETTA Elisabeth, b. 22 Nov. 1951, Klagenfurt, Austria. Biologist; Assistant Professor of Medicine. *Education:* PhD, University of Graz, 1975; Associate Professor, Tumor Biology, University of Vienna, Austria, 1984; Assistant Professor, Medicine, Albert Einstein College of Medicine, Bronx, New York, 1984. *Appointments:* Assistant Professor, Pharmacodynamics & Toxicology, University of Graz, Austria, 1975-76; Postdoctoral Research Fellow, National Jewish Hospital, Denver, 1976-77; Pharmacologist, Research Fellow, First Medical Dept., University of Vienna Medical School, austria, 1978-82; Exchange Research PhD, Oncology, Montefiore Medical Centre, Bronx, New York, USA, 1982-. *Publications:* Numerous abstracts & articles including: Activation-antigen (K1-1) expression on lymphocytes from patients with AIDS or AIDS-related complex (Letter) Ann int Med 104:890-891, 1986; unique antigen of cultured Hodgkin's cells: A putative sialyltransferase, J. Clin Invest 78:343-354, 1986. *Memberships:* Austrian Society of Biochemistry; American Association for the Advancement of Sciences; New York Academy of Sciences; American Federation for Clinical Research; American Society of Clinical Oncology; International Society of Experimental Hematology; etc. *Honours:* Hoechst AG Award, 1982; Max Kade Fellowship, 1982-84; Henry M and Lillian Stratton Foundation Grant, 1986-89. *Hobbies:* Antiques; Classical Music; Ballet; Travel. *Address:* Montefiore Medical Centre, Dept. of Oncology, 111 East 210th Street, Bronx, NY 10467, USA.

PAIGE Elaine Jill, b. 5 Mar. 1951, Barnet, England. Actress; Singer. *Appointments:* Appearances in: Roar of the Greasepaint, 1964; Hair, 1968; Rock Carmen, 1972; Jesus Christ Superstar, 1973; Nuts Revue, 1973; Grease 1974 Billy 1974; Evita, 1978; Cats, 1981; The Lady Killers, (Granada TV), 1980; Debut Concert, The Royal Festival Hall, 1981; Royal Variety Show, 1981; etc; numerous recordings, concerts, tours, and tv appearances. *Honours:* Show Business Personality of Year, Variety Club of Great Britain, 1978; Best Actress in a Musical, (Evita), Society of West End Theatre Managers; Silver Disc, Original Cast Album of Cats, 1981; Platinum Disc, Evita, Original London Cast Album, 1982; Silver Disc, 250,000 Singles of Memory, from the original cast album of Cats, 1982; Platinum Disc, Stages, 1984; Best Selling British Female Singer, 1984; Platenum Disc, Cinema; Rear of Year Award, 1984. *Hobbies:* Antiques; Architecture; Gardening; Biogrpahies; Tennis. *Address:* James Sharkey Associates, International Business Centre, 90 Regents Street, London W1, England.

PAINTER Charlotte, b. 24 May 1926, Louisiana, USA. Writer; Professor. *Appointments:* Lecturer, Stanford University, 1962-69, University of California, 1971; Professor, San Francisco State University, 1975-. *Publications:* Who Made the Lamb, 1969, 1988; Revelations: Diaries of Women, 1971; Confession from the Malaga Madhouse, 1971; Seeing Things, 1976, 1988; Gifts of Age, 1986. *Memberships:* PEN; Yaddo Foundation; MacDowell Colony. *Honours:* Radcliffe Institute, Fellow, 1965-67; NEA Grant, 1973; D.H. Lawrence Fellowship, 1975; Fulbright Summer Fellowship to India, 1985. *Address:* c/o Russell & Volkening Literary Agents, 50 W 29 St., New York, NY 10001, USA.

PALAEOLOGINA Patricia, Her Imperial Highness Princess, b. 3 July 1941, Carlisle, England. Official & Legal Regent of the Imperial House of Palaeologos and Sovereign Grand Master of The Imperial Constantinian Military Order of Saint George. m. His Imperial Highness Petros, The Prince Palaeologos, 12 Dec. 1985. *Education:* N.D.D., Special Level, Fine Art, Carlisle College of Art & Design 1963; A.T.D., London University, 1964. *Appointments:* Fine Art Specialist, Wyndham Comprehensive, Cumbria, 1964-67; Lecturer, Design,

Iran Girls College, Tehran, 1967-69; Fine Art Specialist, Wimborne Grammer School, Dorset, 1970; Fine Art Specialist, St Joseph's High, South Wales, 1970-75; Fine Art & Art History Specialist, Jedburgh Grammar, Scotland, 1975-85. *Publications:* Exhibited Paintings in Great Britain, France, Rome. *Memberships:* Many professional organisations. *Honours:* Dame Grand Cordon, Order of Polonia Restituta, 1987. *Hobbies Include:* Music; Writing; Research. *Address:* c/o Midland Bank PLC., 58 Main Street, Egremont, Cumbria, CA22 2DD, England.

PALEVSKY Lynda Louise, b. 17 Dec. 1943, Los Angeles, USA. Educator; Peace Activist. m. Max Palevsky, 1972, divorced 1983, 2 sons. *Education:* BS, 1966; MS, University of Southern California, 1969. *Appointments:* Teacher, Los Angeles City Schools, 1966-72; Mayor's Liaison to Los Angeles City Schools, 1973-74; Peace Activist, 1980-. *Memberships:* Board, Ploughshares Fund; National Advisory Board, Jane Addams Conference, Chicago; Women's Leadership Network; Peace Links. *Honours:* Founder's Award, Liberty Hill Foundation Los Angeles, 1988. *Hobbies:* Archaeology; Art; Dance. *Address:* 1431 Ocean Avenue, Suite B, Santa Monica, CA 90401, USA.bblank

PALEVSKY Sheila Lynn, b. 30 Jan. 1953, Bronx, New York, USA. Physician. *Education:* BA, New College, Hofstra University, 1973; MD, University of Pittsburgh, School of Medicine, 1978; MPH, Columbia University, 1986. *Appointments:* Pediatric residency, Children's Memorial Hospital, 1978-80 and Montefiore Hospital and Medical Center, 1980-81; Attending Physician, Harlem Hospital, 1981-86; Director Pediatrics, St Joseph's Medical Center, 1986-; Faculty, Columbia University, 1981-86; Faculty, New York Medical College, 1987-. *Publications:* Numerous articles and abstracts in professional journals. *Memberships:* Fellow, American Academy of Pediatrics; American Pediatric Association; American Public Health Association; Society of Teachers of Family Medicine; Board of Directors, Epilepsy Association of Westchester; Yonkers Academy of Medicine. *Honours:* Radiology Prize, University of Pittsburgh, 1978; Service Award, Community Service Council of Greater Harlem, 1983; Certificate of Appreciation, Physician Assistant Program, Harlem Hospital, 1984. *Hobbies:* Classical music; Hiking. *Address:* St Joseph's Hospital, 127 South Broadway, Yonkers, NY 10701, USA.

PALMER Beverly Blazey, b. 22 Nov. 1945, Cleveland, Ohio, USA. Professor; Psychologist. m. 24 June 1967, 1 son. *Education:* BA, Psychology, University of Michigan, 1966; MA, Counselling, 1969, PhD Counselling Psychology, 1972, Ohio State University. *Appointments:* Research Psychologist, University of California, Los Angeles, 1971-74; Professor, Department of Psychology, California State University, Dominguez Hills, 1973-; Private Practice in Clinical Psychology, Torrance, California, 1985-. *Publications:* Numerous publications in scientific journals. *Memberships:* American Psychological Association; American Association for Counselling and Development. *Honours:* Proclamation for Community Activities, 1972, for Public Health Activities, 1981, Board of Supervisors, Los Angeles County; Commissioner of Public Health, Los Angeles County, 1978- 81. *Address:* Department of Psychology, California State University, Dominguez Hills, Carson, CA 90747, USA.

PALMER Paige, b. Akron, Ohio, USA. Journalist; TV Personality, 3 sons. *Education:* BS Education, University of Akron; MS Physical Education, University of California, Berkeley; Journalism seminars; Dale Carnegie Course; Ann Delafield Success School, NYC. *Appointments:* TV programme, NYC, 1943-45; Foreign Fashion Editor, California Magazine, Los Angeles, 1945-47; The Paige Palmer TV Show: WEWS-TV, Cleveland, Ohio, 1947-73; WAKR-TV, Akron, 1955-65; KDKA-TV, Pittsburgh, Pennsylvania, 1950-54; The Paige Palmer Radio Show, WELW Radio, Cleveland, 1974-84; Wrote travel health, fitness features, Healthways Magazine, 1965-74; Fashion Writer, Lorain County (Ohio) Times

Newspaper, 1975-; Travel features/guidebooks, 1976-. *Publications include:* Travel Guide to North India - Bargain Travel Discovery of the 1980's; The Senior Citizen's Guide to Budget Travel in Europe, 1983, 1985, 1988, 1990, to Budget Travel in the US and Canada, 1981, 1982, 1986, 1988, 1989; Guide to the Best Buys in Package Tours, 1986, 1990; The Travel and Vacation Discount Guide, 1987; The Best of India from Budget to Luxury, 1987; Alaska On Your Own - By Car, 1989; Off the Beaten Path Destinations in Europe, USA, Canada, Asia and India, 1990. *Memberships include:* Charter Member, American Women in Radio & TV (Past President); National Federation of Press Women; Ohio Press Women; Akron Manuscript Club; Board, American Cancer Society, Summit County Unit; American Association of University Women; Ohioana Library Association; Western Reserve (Life Member) & Ohio Historical Societies; Friends of Crawford Auto Aviation Museum (Past President); Travellers Century Club; Fashion Press; Pacific Asia Travel Association (NE Ohio); National Association for Female Executives; Western Reserve Tourist Council Inc; Board, Cleveland Goodwill Industries; Highland Shop, Highlandview Rehabilitation Hospital; Aviation/Space Writers Association; World Association of Women Journalists/Writers; California Alumni Association of Berkeley; Akron University Alumni; National Trust; Cleveland Restoration Society; Cleveland Playhouse Club; Korea Cultural Society; English Speaking Union. *Honours:* Many awards for USA/worldwide articles; PATA Gold Awards 1988 Honour Roll. *Hobbies:* Travel; Art; Antiques including Ohio pottery/glass; Museums (world). *Address:* PO Box 255, Bath, OH 44210, USA.

PALMER Suzanne Lee Sawyer, b. 24 Mar. 1947, Crescent City, California, USA. Professor of Physical Therapy. m. Philip Wayne Palmer, 7 May 1983, 1 son. *Education:* AB, Biology, University of California, Santa Cruz, 1970; MA, Physiology, Behavioural Biology, San Francisco State University, 1975; PhD, Physiology, Biophysics, University of Washington, Seattle, 1982; Postdoctoral Fellowship, Veterans Administration Medical Center, Minneapolis, 1982-84. *Appointments:* Visiting Professor, Department of Biology, St Lawrence University, Canton, New York, 1984-85; Visiting Professor, Department of Exercise Science, University of Iowa, 1985-86; Assistant Professor, Departments of Kinesiology, Physiology and Biophysics, University of Illinois, Urbana-Champaign, 1986-89; Assistant Professor, Department of Physiology, Oral Roberts University School of Medicine, Tulsa, Oklahoma, 1989-90; Associate Professor, Department of Physical Therapy, Texas Technical University, Lubbock, 1990. *Publications:* 3 articles (with Fetz) in Journal of Neurophysiology, 1985; Exercise Therapy for Parkinson's Disease, 1986; Article (with Mortimer and Eisenberg) in Experimental Neurology, 1987; Article (with Kilani et al)in Human Movement Science, 1989. *Memberships:* American Physiological Society; American College Sports Medicine; Society for Neuroscience; International Brain Research Organization. *Honours:* Mark E.Reed Simpson Timber Scholarship, 1965; Herbert Tryon Scholarship, 1965, 1966. *Address:* Department of Physical Therapy, Texas Technical University Health Sciences Center, Lubbock, TX 79430, USA.

PALMER-PHELPS Rosemary, b. 14 Oct. 1943, Scott, USA. Director of Support; Registered Nurse. m. (1)Anthony Palmer, 1 son, 1 daughter, (2)Alvin Phelps, 13 June 1985, 4 stepsons, 1 step daughter. *Education:* RN, 1979. *Appointments:* Executive Director, Support, 1979-; Pittsburgh Nursing Specialist, 1988-. *Memberships:* Child Support Project, American Bar Association, Advisory Board, 1987-; Health & Welfare Association; Mayors Commission on Families. *Hobbies:* Needlework; Oil Painting; Macrame; Arts & Crafts. *Address:* Support, 429 Forbes Ave., Suite 1607, Pittsburgh, PA 15219, USA.

PANG Leila Mei, b. 14 May 1944, Honolulu, Hawaii, USA. Anaesthesiologist. m. Roger B. Lee, 12 Aug. 1979, 2 daughters. *Education:* BS, University of Hawaii, 1966; MD, Downstate Medical Center, State University of New York, 1970; Diplomate, American Board of Anesthesiology, 1975. *Appointments:* Assistant Professor of Anaesthesiology, then Associate Professor of Anaesthesiology, Columbia University College of Physicians and Surgeons, New York, 1976-. *Memberships:* American Society of Anesthesiologists; New York State Society of Anesthesiologists; American Physiological Society; American Thoracic Society; Society for Education in Anesthesia; Society for Pediatric Anesthesia. *Honours:* Mortar Board, 1965; Fellow, American College of Anesthesiology, 1976. *Address:* Columbia-Presbyterian Medical Center, 622 West 168th Street, New York, NY 10032, USA.

PANNAM Janette Margaret, b. 8 Oct. 1936, Sea Lake, Victoria, Australia. Solicitor (Partner). m. 8 Jan. 1960, divorced 2 Sept. 1968. 2 sons. *Education:* LLB, Melbourne University, 1971. *Appointments:* Cornwall Stodart, 1972-74; William Lasica & Co, 1974-76; Blake & Riggall, 1976-79; Stedman Cameron, 1979-. *Publications:* Numerous articles for Law Journals, Seminars and Conferences. *Memberships:* Law Institute of Victoria; Discipliniary Tribunal, Family Law Section (former Chairman); Family Lawyers Association; Women Lawyers (former President); Lyceum Club (Committee Member); Former Convenor of Laws and Status of Women; National Council of Women of Australia (Former Vice-President). *Hobbies:* Sewing; Gardening; Reading; Archaeology. *Address:* c/o Stedman Cameron, 143 Queen Street, Melbourne 3000, Victoria, Australia.

PAOLINI Shirley J, b. 29 July 1932, Cleveland, USA. University Dean; Professor of English. m. 10 Oct. 1955, 2 sons, 2 daughters. *Education:* BA, 1954; MA, 1966; PhD, University of California, 1973. *Appointments:* Dean Special Programmes, 1979-88, Dean, School of Arts & Sciences, 1988-, Barry University. *Publications:* Confessions of Sin & Love in the Middle Ages; articles in professional journals; Editor, studies in Interdisciplinarity, 1987-; Editor, North American School of Conservation, 1971-73. *Memberships:* American Comparative Literature Association; International Comparative Literature Association; American Association for Italian Studies; American Association for Australian Studies. *Honours:* Swiss Government Fellowship, 1955; Faculty Research Award, 1987. *Hobbies:* Tennis; Sailing; Skiing; Travel. *Address:* School of Arts & Sciences, Barry University, 11300 NE 2nd Ave., Miami Shores, FL 33161, USA.

PAPACHRISTOU Patricia Ann Towne, b. 16 Oct. 1946, Hartford, Connecticut, USA. Economist. m. Gerald C. Papachristou, 23 Aug. 1969, 1 son, 1 daughter. *Education:* BA cum laude, Political Science, Trinity College, District of Columbia, 1968; MA, Political Science, Duke University, 1970; MA, Economics, 1975, MBA, 1979, Memphis State University; Doctoral candidate, Economics, University of Mississippi; Internship, Kaiser-Permanente Health Services Research Center, Portland, Oregon, 1983-84. *Appointments:* Instructor, University of Mississippi, 1979-80; Assistant Professor of Economics, 1980-88, Associate Professor of Economics, 1988-, Christian Brothers College. *Memberships:* American Economics Association; Mid- South Academy of Economics; Missouri Valley Economics Association; Southern Economics Association; Eastern Economics Association. *Honours:* None-Service Fellowship, University of Mississippi, 1979; Jane Cassels Record Scholar AWard, 1984. *Hobbies:* Bridge; Camping; Canoeing. *Address:* 2858 Shelley Cove, Memphis, TN 38115, USA.

PAPAROZZI Ellen Theresa, b. 2 Nov. 1953, Passaic, New Jersey, USA. Associate Professor, Urban Horticulture. m. Walter J Stroup, 23 June 1984. *Education:* BSc, Cook College, Rutgers University, 1976; MSc 1978, DPhil 1980, Cornell University, Ithaca. *Appointments:* Salesperson-Designer, part-time, Schweinfurth Florist, New Jersey, 1971- 76; Graduate Assistant, 1978-80; Assistant Professor 1981-87, Associate Professor 1987-88, UNL; Visiting Professor, University of Tennessee, Knoxville, Utah, 1989-90.

Publications: 1 rose cultivar, Concetta, Patent ed 1989; 14 research articles; 25 research abstracts; 4 teaching publications. *Memberships:* American Association for Advancement of Science; American Society for Horticultural Science, numerous offices; Botanical Society of America; International Society for Horticultural Science; National Association of Women in Horticulture; Nebraska Academy of Sciences; Nebraska Association of Nurserymen; Nebraska Graduate Women in Science; Nebraska Statewide Arboretum; Sigma Delta Epsilon, National Graduate Women in Science. *Honours:* Cornell University Summer Fellowship, 1977; Alpha Zeta, agricultural honor and service fraternity, 1975; George H Cook Scholar, 1975- 76; Maplewood Garden Club Scholarship, 1975, 1976; Pi Alpha Xi, horticultural honor fraternity president, 1975-76; Hortus Society, vice-president 1974-76; Outstanding Teaching Assistant Award, 1979; Outstanding Young Women in America, 1981; Sigma Xi, Scientific Research Society, Full member, 1980; Finalist, Sigma Delta Epsilon Award for Excellence in Graduate Student Research, 1980; Selected as one of 30 Outstanding Faculty by the University Foundation, University of Nebraska, 1988-89. *Hobbies:* Refinishing and refurbishing furniture; Languages; Travel; Cooking; Swimming; Jazzercise. *Address:* Department of Horticulture, University of Nebraska, 377 Plant Sciences, Lincoln, NE 68583, USA.

PAPPAS Effie Vamis, b. 26 Dec. 1924, Cleveland, Ohio, USA. Teacher; Writer. m. Leonard G. Pappas, 3 Nov. 1945, 2 sons, 2 daughters. *Education:* BBA, Industrial Management, 1948; MA, Education, 1964; MA, English Literature, 1986; MA (PhD Pending 1988-89, English). *Appointments:* Public School Teacher, 1964-70; University Development (Public Relations), Office Manager, Editor-Writer, 1970-73; Feature Writer, Journalist, 1970-78; College Instructor, English & Business, 1978-. *Publications:* Will Ladislaw : Dorothea's Romantic Second Choice in George Eliot's Middlemarch, (Thesis), 1986; etc. *Memberships:* Charter Member, National Museum of Women in Arts; National Association for Female Executives; National Education Association; OEA; etc. *Honours:* Recipient, various honours including: Valedictorian, Mantle Orator & Scholarship, Drama Awards, 1943; Grant, Writing & Research Seminar, Carnegie Mellon University, 1982; Presented Paper on US Education at Fudan University, Shanghai, China, with first AIC Contingent, 1984. *Hobbies Include:* Reading; Writing Poetry & Short Stories; Performing; Reading & Attending Plays; Gardening; Sewing Designer Dresses; Cooking. *Address:* 8681 Brecksville Road, Brecksville, OH 44141, USA.

PAPPAS Leah Aglaia, b. 23 Mar. 1936, Ogden, Utah, USA. Political Consultant; Civic Worker. *Education:* BA, College of St Mary of Wasatch, 1959. *Political Campaigns:* Alternate delegate for Senator Robert F Kennedy, 1968, Chicago Convention; Supervisor Senator Edward M Kennedy Campaigns, Boston, Massachusetts, 1970-76; Campaign Worker, Senator Paul Laxalti, Las Vegas, 1974; Governor Jerry Brown campaign, Los Angeles, 1978; Office Manager, Reagan-Bush, 1984 campaign, Ogden. Civic work: Opera Guild; Heart Fund; City of Hope; Senior Citizen Groups; Prevention of Blindness; March of Dimes, numerous other charitable endeavours. *Hobbies:* Playing piano; Singing; Writing; Horseback riding; Opera; Broadway shows; Literary works. *Address:* 1323 Marilyn Drive, Ogden, Utah 84403, USA.

PAPPENHAGEN Nancy Carol Andrews, b. 9 July 1958, Halifax County, Virginia. Disability Determination Specialist. m. James David Pappenhagen, 29 Dec. 1983. *Education:* BA, Sociology, Mary Washington College, 1980; MEd, Guidance and Counselling, Loyola University, New Orleans, 1986. *Appointments:* Resident Hall Coordinator, Longwood College, Farmville, Virginia, 1980-83; Projects with Industry Coordinator, Goodwill Rehabilitation Center, New Orleans, 1987; Job Trainer/Supervisor with Volunteers of America, Community Living Center, New Orleans, 1987; Disability

Determination Specialist, State of North Carolina, Division of Social Services, Raleigh, 1988-. *Memberships:* American Association for Counseling and Development; American Mental Health Counselors Association; American Rehabilitation Counselors Association. *Honour:* Inducted, Kappa Delta Pi, National Education Honor Society, 1986. *Hobbies:* Reading; Walking; Music; Antiques. *Address:* 103-D Butterwood Court, Cary, NC 27511, USA.

PARADIS Carmen, b. 31 Mar. 1950, Edmonton, Alberta, Canada. Plastic Surgeon. *Education:* BSc 1968-70, MD Summa Cum Laude, 1970-74, University of Alberta, Edmonton, Canada. *Appointments:* Surgical Internship, Wellesley Hospital, University of Toronto, 1974-75; General Surgery Residency, Royal Victoria Hospital, McGill University, Montreal, 1975- 78; Plastic Surgery Residency, Case Western Reserve University Hospitals, Cleveland, USA, 1978-80; Emanual B Kaplan Fellowship in Hand Surgery, Hospital for Joint Diseases, New York, USA, 1980-82. *Memberships:* Certified, American Board of Plastic Surgery, 1983; Fellow, American College of Surgeons; American Society of Plastic & Reconstructive Surgeons; Plastic Surgery Educational Foundation; Ohio Valley Society for Plastic & Reconstructive Surgeons; Northeast Ohio Society of Plastic & Reconstructive Surgeons' Ohio State Medical Society; Academy of Medicine of Cleveland; Cleveland Medical Women's Society; Cleveland Surgical Society; Women's Faculty CWRU; Cleveland Medical Library Association; Geauga County Medical Society; Canadian Society of Plastic Surgeons. *Honours:* Birk Medal for Academic Excellence, 1965; Florence E Dodd Prize for Leadership, 1969; Pacesetter Award, Greater Cleveland's Enterprising Women, 1987. *Hobbies:* Gardening; Reading; Cooking; Swimming; Scuba diving. *Address:* Village Station, 401 South Street, 3-B, Chardon, OH 44024, USA.

PARE-WALSH Pierrette, b. 14 Sept. 1931, Quebec, Canada. Director, Chief Editor. m. Robert Walsh, 11 Feb. 1956. 2 sons, 1 daughter. *Appointments:* Founder, La Revue des Fermiers, magazine of Rural Women's Association of Quebec, 1974; World Vice President 1982-85, International President 1985-, Asociacion Mundial de Mujeres Periodistas Y Escritoras (World association of Women Journalists and Writers) (AMMPE). *Publication:* Book: Quand je vous regarde vivre. *Memberships:* AMMPE; Groupe Action Nord-Sud; Cercle des Femmes Journalists; ACWW, Associated Country Woman of the World. *Honours:* Named a member, Le Cercle des Batisseurs Molson, 1986; Woman of the Year, Salon de la Femme de Montreal (Women Universe), 1987; Nominated Honorary Member, Groupe Action Nord-Sud, 1988; Honoured by Mayor of the City of Laval, 1988; Elected, Woman of the Year, Cercle des Femmes Journalistes, 1988. *Hobbies:* Painting; Writing; Handcraft; Travelling around the world; Alpine ski competition (3 medals). *Address:* c/o World Association of Women Journalists and Writers, 3945 boul St-Martin ouest, Chomedey, Laval, Quebec, Canada H7T 1B7.

PARFITT Judy, b. 7 Nov, Sheffield, Yorkshire, England. Actress. m. Tony Steedman, 25 Aug. 1963, 1 son. *Education:* Notre Dame Convent. *Honours:* Voted most promising actress, 1966; nominated best Theatre Actress, best TV Actress, 1985. *Hobbies:* Walking; Drinking; Needlepoint; Eating. *Address:* c/o Jeremy Conway, Eagle House, Jermyn Street, London, England.

PARK Daphne Margaret Sybil Desiree, b. 1 Sept. 1921, Surrey, England. Principal, Somerville College, Oxford. *Education:* Rosa Bassett School, 1932-40; MA, Somerville College, Oxford, 1940-43; Certificate of Competent Knowledge (Russian), Newnham College, Cambridge, 1951-52. *Appointments:* Foreign office (The Diplomatic Service), 1948-79 including: UK Delegation to NATO, 1952; 2nd Secretary, Moscow, 1954; Foreign Office, 1956, 1961, 1967; Consul and 1st Secretary, Leopoldville, 1959; Lusaka, 1964; Consul-General, Hanoi, 1969-70; Honorary Research Fellow, University of Kent, 1971-72; Charge d'Affaires, Ulan Bator, 1972;

Foreign and Commonwealth Office, 1973-79; Pro Vice Chancellor, University of Oxford, 1985- *Memberships:* Governor of the BBC, 1982-87; British Library Board, 1982-; Council, VSO, 1981-84; Royal Institute of International Affairs; Royal Society of Arts; Royal Asian Society; Chairman, Legal Aid Advisory Committee to the Lord Chancellor, 1985-. *Honours:* OBE 1960; CMG 1971. *Address:* Somerville College, Oxford OX2 6HD, England.

PARK Zaida Ann Harris, b. 15 Apr. 1940, Lyons, New York, USA. Administrative Assistant; Registered Nurse. m. Roswell Park, 20 Apr. 1985, 1 son, 1 daughter. *Education:* RN, Genesee Hospital School of Nursing, 1962. *Appointments:* Nurse: Yung-Soo Pang, MD, 1975; Clifton Springs Hospital & Clinic, 1973-76; Lyons Emergency Room, part-time, 1976-78; Nurse Administrator, Borden Inc., 1976-86; Administrative Assistant, Park Packaging, 1986-. *Memberships:* ANA; AAOHN; TGH; Treasurer, United Way; Wayne County Unit; Instructor, American Red Cross; Co-Founder, Lyons Co-op Nursery School. *Hobbies:* Travel; Sailing; Needlepoint; Crafts. *Address:* PO Box 70, Lyons, NY 14489, USA.

PARKER Camille Killian, b. 28 June 1918, Columbus, Ohio, USA. Ophthalmologist. m. Francis W Parker Jr, MD, 7 Dec. 1958. 2 sons. *Education:* Premed, University of Chicago, 1942-43; BS 1945, MD 1946-47, University of Illinois; Intern, Wesley Memorial Hospital, 1946-47; Postgraduate Ophthalmology, Northwestern University, 1948; Resident, Ophthalmology Illinois Eye & Ear Infirmary, 1949-51. *Memberships:* Fellow, American Academy of Ophthalmology & Otolaryngology, 1952; Charter member, Society of Eye Surgeons, 1969; Indiana State Medical Association; Indiana Academy of Ophthalmology & Otolaryngology; American Medical Association; Mental Guidance Board, 1967-69; Diplomate, American Board of Ophthalmology; Memorial Hospital Medical Staff Secretary, 1959; Cass County Medical Society President, 1971; Chairman, Continuing Medical Education program and library Cass County Medical Society and Staff of Memorial Hospital; Vice President, Indiana Academy of Ophthalmology 1978; President, Indiana Academy of Ophthalmology, 1979; Altrusa Club; Culver Mothers Club; Logansport Council for Public Schools; Chamber of Commerce, Legislative Affairs Committee; Republican Women's Club; Methodist Chairman, Social Concerns. *Honours:* Service Award, Culver Military Academy, 1969; Physician Recognization Award 1971, 1976, 1979, 1982, 1985, 1988; American Medical Association. *Address:* 2500 E Broadway, Logansport, IN 46947, USA.

PARKER Carol Tommie Thompson, b. 10 Dec. 1928, Birmingham, Alabama, USA. Psychotherapist. m. John Albert Parker, 14 June 1948, divorced, 1976, 3 sons, 3 daughters (1 deceased). *Education:* BSW, 1977, MSW, 1978, University of Nebraska. *Appointments:* Family Psychotherapist, 1978-, University of Nebraska Medical Center, Meyer Children's Rehabilitation Institute, Adjunct Faculty. Dept. of Psychiatry, College of Medicine, U. of NE Medical Center; Private Practice, Omaha, 1980-. *Publications:* Articles in professional journals including: Family Therapy; Educational Resources Information Centr; Building Family Strengths. *Memberships:* American Association of Family Counsellors & Mediators; International Academy of Behavioural Medicine and Psychotherapy; American Board of Medical Psychotherapists; etc. *Hobbies:* Gardening; Travel; Decorating. *Address:* 5505 Dodge Street, Omaha, NE 68132, USA.

PARKER Nancy Winslow, b. 18 Oct. 1930, Maplewood, New Jersey, USA. Artist; Writer. *Education:* BA, Mills College, 1952; Studies, School of Visual Art, & Art Students' League, New York City. *Appointments:* Public relations executive, 1961-63; Art director, Appleton-Century- Crofts, NYC, 1968-70; Staff designer, Holt Reinhart & Winston, 1970-73; Freelance writer & illustrator, 1974-. *Creative work includes:* Author & illustrator, 10 children's books including: Man

With The Take-Apart Head, 1974; Mrs Wilson Wanders Off, 1976; Ordeal of Byron B. Blackbear, 1979; Spotted Dog, 1980; Bugs (co-author, non-fiction), 1987, also 3 Uncle Clyde books, 4 American history books. Illustrator, 8 children's books including: Warm as Wool, Cool as Cotton: Story of Natural Fibers, 1975; Willy Bear, 1976; No Bath Tonight, 1978; General Store, 1988, also 3 John Langstaff Song Books. *Honours:* Various awards, 1974-, including: Jane Tinkham Broughton Fellow, 1975; Christopher Awards, 1976, 1981; Notable Book, American Library Association, 1980. *Memberships:* Past Secretary, East 74th Street Block Association; Society of Illustrators; Graphic Artists Guild; Various clubs. *Address:* 51 East 74th Street, New York, NY 10021, USA.

PARKER Sharon, Consultant. *Education:* BA, Slavic Languages, University of California, Los Angeles, 1970; MA, Bilingual Education, Antioch Graduate School of Education, 1974. *Appointments:* Instructor, ESOL, Montgomery County Public Schools, 1974-75; Assistant Director, National Commission on Working Women, Washington, 1977-80; Programme Analyst, DC Office of Personnel, 1981; Consultant, 1981-. *Publications:* Articles in professional journals. *Memberships:* Chairman, National Institute for Women of Color, 1981- ; DC Private Industry Council Board of Directors; Women's Legal Defense Fund Board of Directors; Older Womens League, Board of Directors; Women of Color Task Force. *Address:* 1400 20th Street NW, Suite 104, Washington, DC 20036, USA.

PARKER Susan Brooks, b. 7 Nov. 1945, Newport, New Hampshire, USA. Chief Executive Officer, Human Services Department. m. (1)Allen Denslow Avery, 20 May 1967, divorced 1978, 2 sons. (2)Ole Martin Amundsen Jr, 29 Apr. 1989. *Education:* BS, English, French, University of Vermont, 1968; Master in Social Planning, Boston College, 1978. *Appointments:* Hotel Manager, Vermont Avery Inns, Fairlee, VT, 1968-74; Psychiatric Counselor, Orange County, VT M Health, 1974-76; Planner, MH Regional Office, Boston, MA 1976-78; Exec Dir, Grafton County (NH) Planning Council, 1978-80; Exec Dir, New Hampshire Disabilities Council, 1980-87; Commissioner, Dept of Mental Health, Maine, 1987-. *Publications:* Poetry Collection: Scheme, 1965-66; Journalism: Special Interest Stories, 1973-75; Poetry: Jamaican Studies, 1973- 74. *Memberships:* National Assoc of Developmental Disabilities, Council-Chairman of Planning and Program Committees, Board Member; Am Assoc on Mental Retardation; Natl Assoc of State Mental Health Program Directors. *Honours:* Elected to Executive Committee at Boston College School of Social Work, 1077 70; Elected to board by popular vote of peers, Massachusetts Association of Social Workers, Beacon Hill, Boston, 1977; Principal Investigator, Transition Grant, Office of Special Education, Washington DC, 1986. *Hobbies:* Outdoor sports; Canoeing; Mounting climbing; Skiing; Gardening; Music, listening and playing piano; Yoga; Meditation; Holistic health; Travel; Reading. *Address:* 73 Starboard Drive, Cape Elizabeth, Maine 04107, USA.

PARKINSON Antoinette, b. 1 Oct. 1943, Camden, USA. Public Relations Consultant. 1 son, 2 daughters. *Education:* BS, Public Relations, Pacific Western University; Peirce Schoolof Business Administration. *Appointments:* Instructor, Vice President, National Sales, President, Franchise, Canterbury Press; Community Liaison Co-ordinator, O'Brien Kreitzbrey; Director, Marketing, Consolidated Financial Mgt.; Owner, President, Parkinson Public Relations. *Publications:* Editor, Writer, Bookier Camden County Recycling Program; Videos. *Memberships:* Board: Robins Nest, Heart Association; Chairman, Camden County Library Committee; Chairman, Membership, South Jersey Development Council. *Honours:* Academic Achivement, Peirce School of Business Administration; Service Award, Garden State Rotary. *Hobbies:* Reading; Travel; Antiques; Spectator Sports. *Address:* 653 West Crystal Lake Avenue, Haddonfield, NJ 08033, USA.

PARKINSON Claire L, b. 21 Mar. 1948, Bay Shore,

New York, USA. Climatologist. *Education:* BA, Mathematics, Wellesley College, 1970; MA 1974, PhD 1977, Ohio State University. *Appointments:* Research Assistant, National Center for Atmospheric Research, Boulder, Colorado, 1976-78; Research Scientist in climatology and remote sensing, Goddard Space Flight Center (NASA), Greenbelt, Maryland, 1978-. *Publications:* Author: Breakthroughs: A Chronology of Great Achievements in Science and Mathematics, 1985; Co-author with W M Washington, Three-Dimensional Climate Modeling, 1986; Co-author with 5 others, Arctic and Antarctic sea ice atlases. *Memberships:* Assoc for the Philosophy of Mathematics; International Glaciological Society; American Polar Society; American Meteorological Society; (Chairman of Committee on the History of Atmospheric Sciences); Phi Beta Kappa; Sigma Xi. *Honours:* NASA Group Achievement Award, 1982; Goddard Exceptional Performance Award, 1979; Goddard Certificate of Outstanding Performance, 1983; Inclusion of book Breakthroughs in Library Journal's list of 100 outstanding science and technology books of 1985-86; Peer Award for leadership in the publication of an Arctic sea ice atlas, 1988. *Hobbies:* History of science; Astronomy; Space exploration; Polar exploration; Swimming; Jogging. *Address:* Code 671, Goddard Space Flight Center, Greenbelt, Maryland 20771, USA.

PARKS Thelma Reece, b. Muskagee, USA. Member, City Board of Education. 1 daughter. *Education:* BS, Elementary Education, Langston University; MS, Education, University of Oklahoma. *Appointments:* Teacher, Muskagee, 1949; Teacher, Oklahoma City, 1951-62; Teacher, English, 1960-70, High School Counsellor, 1970-71, Douglass High School; High School Counsellor, US Grant, 1971-887; Retired 1987. *Publications:* Guest Feature Writer, Ebony Tribune, 1988-; Black History Writer, Black Chronicle, 1979-80. *Memberships:* NEA; Phi Delta Kappa; Langston Universiy National Alumni Board; Kappa Alpha. *Honours:* Recipient, several honours & awards. *Hobbies Include:* Organizer/Programme Planner; Bridge; Reading; Writing. *Address:* 2804 NE18 Oklahoma City, OK 73111, USA.

PÅRLOG Hortensia, b. 27 July 1942, Timisoara, Rumania. Lecturer/Teacher of English. *Education:* MA, Faculty of Philology, University of Cluj, 1965; Summer schools of English, England: University of Reading, 1964; University of London, 1965; University of Durham, 1968; PhD, Center for Research in Ethnology and Dialectology, Bucharest, 1981. *Appointments:* Department of Germanic Languages, University of Iasi, 1965-68; Department of Germanic Languages, University of Timisoara, 1968-. *Publications:* The English Verb, 1982; The Sounds of English and Romanian (co-author), 1984; Dictionar de Termeni Lingvistici Englez-Roman (co-author), 1986; Ghid De Pronuntie A Limbii Engleze (co-author), a guide to the Pronunciation of the English language, 1989. *Memberships:* International Society of Applied Psycholinguistics; Rumanian Society of Philological Sciences. *Hobby:* Classical music. *Address:* str Narciselor 6, apt 104, 1900 Timisoara, Rumania.

PARRY Erika Anne Blackmore, International Designer; Author. m. Croose Parry, 2 daughters. *Creative Works:* Wild Tudor, Tableware & Giftware ranges for Aynsley China Ltd; Designer, 250 different items including kitchenware, wall coverings, textiles, stationery, collectors enamel boxes, silver wrought iron entrance gates, Busbridge Lakes Ornamental Waterfowl, Godalming. *Memberships:* Chartered Society of Designers; Burea of European Designers Association. *Hobbies:* Studying Wildlife; Horse Racing. *Address:* Rushbrooke, Wonersh, Surrey GU5 0QS, England.

PARRY Pamela Jeffcott, b. 6 Mar. 1948, Forest Hills, New York, USA. Library Executive. m. Ellwood C. Parry III, 21 Nov, 1971, 2 sons, 1 daughter. *Education:* BA, University of Arizona, 1969; MA 1972, MLS 1973, Columbia University. *Appointments:* Assistant Slide

Curator, Department of Art History & Archaeology 1969-72, Assistant Fine Arts Librarian 1972-76, Columbia University; Editorial Assistant, Archives of Neurology, 1976-78; Bibliographer, International Dada Archive, University of Iowa, 1979-81; Executive Director, Art Libraries Society of North America, 1980-. *Publications:* Contemporary Art & Artists, 1978; Photography Index, 1979; Print Index, 1983. *Memberships:* ARLIS/NA; American Society of Association Executives; Visual Resources Association; Association of Architectural Librarians; Society of American Archivists. *Address:* ARLIS/NA, 3900 East Timrod Street, Tucson, Arizona 85711, USA.

PARSONS Gail, b. 12 Mar. 1946, Salt Lake City, Utah, USA. Certified Public Accountant. m. Carl Anderson Heyes, 25 July 1975. *Education:* BA, Accounting, 1969. *Appointments:* Staff Accountant, Hansen, Barnett Maxwell CPA's, 1969-75; Controller, Timberhaus Ski Shops Inc, 1975-76; Self-employed Certified Public Accountant, 1976-. *Memberships:* American Institute of CPA's; Utah Association of CPA's; American Woman's Society of CPA's; Utah Woman's Society of CPA's. *Hobbies:* Gardening; Cooking; Doberman Pinschers. *Address:* 5641 Oakdale Drive, Salt Lake City, UT 84121, USA.

PASCAL Julia, b. 15 Nov. 1949, Manchester, England. Theatre Director; Writer. *Education:* BA, Honours, English, Upper Second, London. *Appointments:* First Woman Director, National Theatre, 1978. *Creative Works:* Author, BBC Drama Documentary, Char-lotte and Jane; Stage Play, Far Above Rubies. *Memberships:* National Union of Journalists; Directors Guild; Equity. *Address:* c/o Lodge Brisley Morris & Co., 2 Bow Street, London WC2, England.

PASSOS Adelaide, b. 23 Sept. 1947, Mozambique. International Tax Consultant. m. Jose Amilcar Passos, 17 Apr. 1965. 1 son, 1 daughter. *Education:* LLB, University of Lisbon, Portugal, 1972. *Appointments:* Advocate, Lisbon Supreme Court, 1973-75; Tax Consultant, Barclays National Bank, 1975-79; Partner, Arthur Andersen & Associates, international tax consultants, 1979-. *Publication:* Book, Tax Treaty Law, 1986. *Membership:* International Fiscal Association. *Hobbies:* Aerobics; Reading. *Address:* Arthur Andersen SA, 53 Route de Malagnou, CH-1211 Geneva 17, Switzerland.

PASTAN Linda, b. 27 May 1932, New York City, New York, USA. Poet. m. Ira Pastan, 14 June 1953, 2 sons, 1 daughter. *Education:* BA, Radcliffe College, 1954; MA, Brandeis University, 1957. *Publications:* A Perfect Circle of Sun; Aspects of Eve; The 5 Stages of Grief; Waiting for My Life; PM/AM; A Fraction of Darkness; The Imperfect Paradise. *Memberships:* PEN; Poetry Society of America. *Honours:* Dylan Thomas Award, 1955; Di Castagnola Award, 1978; Maurice English Award, 1985; Bess Hoken Prize, 1985. *Address:* 11710 Beall Mt Road, Potomac, MD 20854, USA.

PASTIZZI-FERENCIC Dunja, Director, UN, International Research & Training Institute for the Advancement of Women (INSTRAW). *Education:* Advanced University degrees in linguistics, foreign trade and economy, University of Zagreb, Yugoslavia. *Appointments:* Researcher, Scientific Project Co-ordinator, Africa Research Institute and Institute for Developing Countries in Zagreb, Yugoslavia; Director, International Research & Training Institute for the Advancement of Women, (INSTRAW), 1981-. *Memberships:* various professional organisations. *Address:* Calle César Nicolás Person No 102-A, Santa Domingo, Dominican Republic.

PATEL Marilyn Hall, b. 2 Sept. 1938, Amsterdam, New York, USA. United States District Court Judge. m. Magan C Patel, 2 Sept. 1966, 2 sons. *Education:* BA, Wheaton College, 1959; JD, Fordham University School of Law, 1963. *Appointments:* Trial Attorney, Benson & Morris, New York, 1962-64; Attorney, US Department of Justice Immigration & Naturalisation Service, San Francisco, 1967-71; Professor, Law (Adjunct Faculty), Hastings College of Law, San Francisco, 1974-76; Private Law Practice; Judge, municipal Court, Oakland Piedmont Judicial, State of California, 1976-80; US District Court, Northern California, 1980-. *Publications:* A 105 page course and instructional book for use at Hastings College of Law, Immigration & Nationality Law, 1974; articles in professional journals. *Memberships:* American Judicature Society; America Law Institute; Board of Visitors, Fordham University School of Law; American Bar Association; etc. *Address:* 450 Golden Gate Avenue, San Francisco, CA 94102, USA.

PATERIA Varlaxmi, b. 22 May 1947, Waltaire (Andhra Pradesh), India. University Teacher. m. Anil Kumar Pateria, 23 Nov. 1981. *Education:* BA, Government Girls College, Raipur, M.P., 1966; MA, Sociology, 1968, Research Fellow, 1968-72, PhD, 1974, Ravishankar University, Raipur. *Appointments:* Research Assistant, 1972-80, Lecturer, 1980-, Ravishankar University, Raipur. *Publications:* Many research papers in national and international professional academic journals. *Memberships:* International Human Science Research Society; Life Fellow, Indian Academy of Social Sciences; Indian Association for Women's Studies; Visiting Professor, M.P.Council of Child Welfare. *Honour:* Honoured for academic achievements, Andhra Association, Raipur. *Hobbies:* Singing; Reading; Cooking. *Address:* 24/248 Shankar Chowk, Nayapara, Raipur (M.P.) 492 001, India.

PATRICK Jennie R, b. 1 Jan. 1949, Gadsden, Alabama, USA. Research Engineering Manager; Chemical Engineer. m. Benjamin Glover. *Education:* BS, Chemical Engineering, University of California, Berkeley, 1973; PhD, Massachusetts Institute of Technology, 1979. *Appointments:* General Electric Co, 1979-83; Philip Morris USA, 1983-85; Rohm and Haas Co, 1985-. *Publications:* Supercritical Extraction (SCE) of Dixylene Sulfone (DXS), Supercritical Fluid Technology, 1985. *Memberships:* Sigma Xi; American Institute of Chemical Engineers (AIChE); National Organization for the Professional Advancement of Black Chemists and Chemical Engineers (NOBCChE). *Honours:* 1st African-American woman in US to earn a doctorate in Chemical Engineering, 1979; Outstanding Young Women of America, 1979; NOBCChE Outstanding Women in Science & Engineering Award, 1980; A principal in Ciba-Geigy Exceptional Black Scientist Poster Program, 1983. *Hobbies:* Gardening; Body building; Herbs and nutrition studies. *Address:* Post Office Box 1000, Bristol, PA 19007, USA.

PATTEN Maurine D, b. 30 Aug. 1940, Peoria, Illinois, USA. Clinical Psychologist, Private Practice. m. C Alfred Patten, 26 Aug. 1961. 1 son, 1 daughter. *Education:* BS, Bradley University, 1961; MS, Chicago State University, 1971; EdD, Northern Illinois University, 1977. *Appointments:* Teacher, 1961-63; Director, Southwest Cooperative Preschool, Chicago, 1970-74; Special education Teacher, 1974-78; Assistant Director, De Kalb County Special Education Association, 1978-80; Assistant Professor, Chicago State University, 1980-82; Consultant, Arthur Anderson & Co, 1982-; Licensed/Registered Psychologist, private practice, 1982-. *Publications:* Numerous articles in professional journals; Leader of workshops and training events. *Memberships:* American Psychological Association; Illinois Psychological Association; American Pain Society; American Society of Professional and Executive Women; International Association of Neuro-Linguistic Programming. *Hobbies:* Sewing; Canoeing; Reading. *Address:* 964 W State Street, Sycamore, IL 60178, USA.

PATTERSON Fiona Elizabeth Cameron, b. 14 Nov. 1942, Glasgow, Scotland. m. (1) David Cecil, 6 Aug. 1967, divorced 1971, (2) W. Garry Patterson, 5 Dec. 1973, 3 sons. *Appointments:* Kindergarten Teacher. *Memberships:* Welsh Pony Society. *Hobbies:* Golf; Tennis; Pony Breading; Riding for the Disabled. *Address:*

Kisbys Farm, Ecchinswell, Newbury, Berks RG15 8TS, England.

PATTERSON Lydia R., b. 3 Sept. 1936, Carrabelle, Florida, USA. Human Resources Manager; Administrator. m. (1) Edgar A. Corley, 1963 (dec.), 1 son, (2) Berman Patterson, 1981. *Education:* BA, Political Science, Hunter College, City University of New York, 1958. *Appointments include:* Regional Director & Manager, New York State Division of Human Rights, & Industrial Relations Specialist, US Energy Department, 1966-68; Vice President, Bankers Trust Company, 1976-87; President, Chief Executive Officer, Extend Consulting Services, 1985-; Vice President, Merrill Lynch & Company Inc, 1987-. Seminar leader & panelist, Columbia University, Wharton School of Business, University of Pennsylvania, Harvard & Duke Universities, Cornell University School of Industrial Relations. *Publication:* Article: Human Resources in Industry (Journal, Columbia University School of Industrial Social Welfare). *Memberships:* Board, Project Discovery, Columbia University; Advisory Board, NY Women's Centre; Financial Women's Association; American Society of Personnel Administrators; Employment Managers' Association. *Honours:* Ford Foundation/New York State Legislative Intern (1st female), 1961-62; Economic Justice Award, National Bar Association, 1989. *Hobbies:* Reading; Writing; Volunteer work with youth groups. *Address:* Merrill Lynch & Company Inc, World Financial Centre, South Tower, New York, NY 10080, USA.

PATTERSON Patricia Ann Wilson, b. 7 Jan. 1929, Kansas City, USA. Teacher. m. Dr John W. Patterson, 31 May 1950, 2 sons, 4 daughters. *Education:* BA, B Jones University, South Carolina, 1950; ME, Virginia Commonwealth University, 1981; Additional Studies, Escuela de Idiomas, San José Costa Rica; University of Texas, Arlington. *Appointments:* Professor, Foreign Language & Music, Seminario Teológico Bautista Internacional of Cali, Colombia, South America, 1957-67; Teacher, French & Spanish, Richmond, Virgina, USA, 1974-83; Teacher, French, Spanish, German, Fort Worth, Texas, 1983-85; Teacher, French, Newport News & Hampton, Virginia, 1985-86; Teacher, French and Spanish, Hampton, Virginia, 1987-89. *Hobbies:* Vocal Music; Church Work. *Address:* 104 Pamela Place, Yorktown, VA 23696, USA.

PAUL Dorothy Hayman, b. 6 Apr. 1941, Philadelphia, Pennsylvania, USA. Adjunct Associate Biology Professor; Sessional Lecturer. m. Miles Paul. 25 June, 1965. *Education:* BA, Harvard University, 1963; DES, University of Marseille, 1965; PhD, Stanford University, 1970. *Appointments:* Postdoctoral Fellow: Tufts University 1970-72, University of Victoria 1973-74, British Columbia Health Sciences Research Fellow, 1975; Ass Professor Oregon State University, 1976-78; Visiting Investigator, Hopkins Marine Station, 1978-79; Research Zoologist, U C Davis, 1979-81; Visiting Associate Professor, 1981-82, Associate Professor, 1983-, University of Victoria. *Publications:* Decremental Conduction of giant afferent processes in an arthropod, 1972; Role of proprioceptive feedback from nonspiking mechanosensory cells, 1976; Evolution of telson neuromusculature in decapod crustacea, 1985; Nonspiking local interneuron in the motor pattern generator of the crayfish swimmpret, 1985; Nonspiking stretch receptors of the crayfish swimmeret receive an efference copy of the central motor pattern for the simmeret, 1989; A Neurophylogenist's view of decapod crustacea, 1990. *Memberships:* Society for Neuroscience; International Society for Neuroethology. *Hobbies:* Music, mandolin and recorders; Ultramarathon distance running; Backpacking. *Address:* Biology Department, University of Victoria, Victoria, British Columbia, Canada, V8W 2Y2.

PAUL Ellen Louise, b. 18 Feb. 1948, Seoul, Korea. Writer. Public Relations Executive. *Education:* BA, 1969, MA, 1974, University of Maryland, USA. *Appointments:* The Grand Union Supermarket Corporation, 1970-73; Director of Communications, Salvation Army, 1973-77;

Director of Communications, American Association of Blood Banks, 1977-78; Assistant World Director of Communications, USO, 1978-81; Director of Direct Mail Marketing, USO World Headquarters, 1981-83; President, The Image Makers, 1983-88. *Publications:* Hundreds of articles in magazines, newspapers and journals. *Memberships:* Religious Public Relations Council (President, Washington DC Chapter, 1976); International Association of Business Communications (President, Washington DC Chapter, 1980); Public Relations Society of America; Direct Mail Marketing Association; Women in Direct Mail; Art Directors Club; Advertising Club; Washington Women in Public Relations. *Honours:* Hinkhouse Award for Editorial Writing, 1973, Hinkhouse/Derose Award for TV Production, 1975, Religious Public Relations Council; Citation from the Pentagon for Exceptional Service to the US Military, 1978; Toth Award and Silver Anvil Award for Non-Profit Public Relations, Public Relations Society of America, 1979, 1981; 1st place, Gilbert International Letterhead Design Competition, 1982. *Hobbies:* Writing; Gardening; Music. *Address:* 3500 Spring Lake Terrace, Fairfax, VA 22030, USA.

PAUL Grace, b. 12 Mar. 1908, Liberal, Kansas USA. Retired. *Education:* Graduate, Hutchinson High School, 1926; Evening courses, Tulsa University, 1930-36; Auburn University, 1 quarter, 1948; Evening courses, Columbia University, 1949-51. *Appointments:* Rural School Teacher, Kansas, 1926; Medical Technologist, St Johns Hospital, Tulsa, Oklahoma, 1930-36; Medical Technologist, private and government hospitals, 1937-48; Served Women's Army Corps, 1944-46; Plant Quarantine Inspector, US Department of Agriculture, New York City, 1948-51; Social Security Medical Evaluator, 1956-71; Freelance Writer. *Publications:* Your Future in Medical Technology; A Short Course in Skilled Supervision; Contributor to Environmental Engineer's Handbook; Contributions to local histories, Temple, Texas. *Memberships:* American Society of Medical Technologists; Entomological Society of America; Business and Professional Women; Presbyterian Church; International Platform Association. *Honours:* Unsung Hero in Baltimore, Maryland, 1968; 2nd place in Playwriting, Temple, 1974; Volunteer Serving Most Hours, Retired Senior Volunteer Program, 1981; Jefferson Award for Central Texas, 1983; Outstanding Church Volunteer of Temple, 1985; 1st place in Children's Literature, Temple, 1986. *Hobbies:* Writing; Walking; Crafts. *Address:* 18 Carlton Road, Hutchinson, KS 67502, USA.

PAUL Karen, b. 23 Sept. 1944, Jeffersonville, Indiana, USA. Associate Professor. 2 sons, 2 daughters. *Education:* BS, summa cum laude, 1969, MA 1971, PhD 1974, Emory University. *Appointments:* State University of New York, Brockport, 1974-80; Rochester Institute of Technology, 1980-88. *Publications:* Business Environment and Business Ethics, 1987; Sweden: Focus on Post-Industrialism, 1977. *Memberships:* Academy of Management & Social Issues; Academy of International Business; Society for Business Ethics. *Honours:* Phi Beta Kappa; Phi Kappa Phi; Woodrow Wilson Fellow, 1967; NEH Fellow; Fulbright Senior Research Award, 1988. *Address:* College of Business, Rochester Institute of Technology, Rochester, NY 14623, USA.

PAUL Sandra Koodin, b. 6 June 1938, New York City, New York, USA. Management Consultant. *Education:* BA Psychology 1958-62, MA Industrial Psychology 1962-65, Hunter College; ABD Industrial Psychology, City University of New York, 1965-70. *Appointments:* Management Consultant, J K Lasser & Co, New York City, 1960-64; Management Consultant, Shatzkin & Co, New York City, 1965-67; Various positions, Random House, Inc, New York City, 1967-78; President, SKP Associates, New York City, 1978-. *Publication:* Editor, Electronic Publishing Business. *Memberships:* Chairperson, National Information Standards Organization, 1983-85; President, Women's National Book Association, 1984-86; Secretary 1974-77, Chairperson 1977-78, Book Industry Systems Advisory Committee; President, Metropolitan Chapter,

Association for Systems Management, 1975-77; Co-Chair and Founder, Metropolitcan Information Systems Conference, 1979-; Certified Systems Professional, 1985; American Psychological Association; American Society for Information Science; American & New York and Special Libraries Associations; Independent Computer Consultants Association. *Honours:* Bookwoman, 1987; Systems Professional of the Year, 1977; Fannie Simon Award, Special Libraries Association, 1984. *Address:* SKP Associates, 160 Fifth Avenue, New York, NY 10010, USA.

PAYES Rachel Ruth Cosgrove, b. 11 Dec. 1922, Westernport, MD, USA. Writer. m. Norman M. Payes, 12 Sept. 1954, 1 son, 1 daughter. *Education:* BSc., West Virginia Wesleyan College, 1943. *Appointments:* Medical Technologist, Research Biologist, 1943-57. *Publications:* 41 Published Books to date including: Hidden Valley of Oz, 1951; O Charitable Death, 1968; Malverne Hall, 1970; Moment of Desire, 1978; Lady Alicia's Secret, 1986; Emeralds and Jade 1988. *Memberships:* SFWA. *Hobbies:* Reading; Crochet; International Travel. *Address:* 301 Green Tree Road, Brick, NJ 08724, USA.

PAYNE Deborah Anne Moser, b. 22 Sept. 1952, Norristown, Pennsylvania, USA. Medical Company Supervisor. m. Randall Barry Payne, 8 Mar. 1975. *Education:* AA, Liberal Arts, Northeastern Christian Junior College, 1972; BMus.Ed., Virginia Commonwealth University, 1979. *Appointments:* Driver, Social Assistant, Children's Aid Society, 1972- 73; Manager, Boddie-Noell Enterprises, 1974-79; Retail Food Saleswoman, Hardee's Food Systems, 1979-81; Supervisor, Cardiac Datacorp, 1981-. *Memberships:* NAFE; Delta Omicron; American Society of Professional and Executive Women. *Honours:* Leadership Award School of the Arts, 1979; Service Award, School of the Arts, 1979; Star of Delta Omicron, 1979. *Hobbies:* Politics; Sports; Music. *Address:* Cardiac Datacorp, 1429 Walnut Street 2nd Floor, Philadelphia, PA 19102, USA.

PAYNE Margaret Anne, b. 10 Aug. 1947, Cincinnati, Ohio, USA. Attorney-at-Law. *Education:* AB, University of Cincinnati, 1969; JD, Harvard Law School, 1972; LLM Taxation, New York University School of Law, 1976. *Appointments:* Summer Associate 1971, Associate Attorney, Trusts & Estates Department, 1972-75, Mudge, Rose, Guthrie & Alexander; Associate Attorney, Tax, Trusts and Estates Departments, Davis Polk & Wardell, 1976-78; Associate Attorney, Trusts and estates Department, Seltzer Caplan Wilkins & McMahon, 1978-79; Adjunct Professor, California Western School of Law, Estate Planning, 1980, 1981 and 1982; Adjunct Professor, University of San Diego, School of Law, 1979-; Judge Pro Tem, The Municipal Court of the San Diego Judicial District, 1983-; Partner, Trusts and Estates Department, Higgs, Fletcher & Mack, 1980-. *Creative work:* Prepared A Christmas Carol in dramatic form, 1982. *Memberships:* San Diego Historical Society; Library Association of La Jolla; The Artist Chamber Ensemble, Inc; YWCA; Charter 100; Charter 100 International. *Honours:* Phi Beta Kappa, University of Cincinnati; Mortar Board (National Senior Women's Honor Society), Guidon Society, (National Junior Women's Honor Society), University of Cincinnati; Nominated for Woodrow Wilson and Danforth Fellowships, University of Cincinnati; First Year Moot Court, Harvard Law School; Best Lawyers in America, 1987, 1988. *Hobbies:* Taekwondo; Antique automobiles; Classical music. *Address:* 1235 Virginia Way, La Jolla, Calfironia 92037, USA.

PAZ Lois Jean Blanton, b. 10 June 1949, Poplar Bluff, Missouri, USA. Electronics Engineer; Mathematician. m. Guido Paz, 10 Oct. 1980. 1 daughter. *Education:* BA, 1971; Master of Education, 1976. *Appointments:* Secondary Math Teacher, 1974-76; Reliability, Maintainability Division, Naval Sea Systems Command, 1979-84; Elec Eng, Naval Surface Warfare Center Planning and Assessment Division, 1984-88. *Memberships:* Association of Scientists and Engineers; Women in Science and Engineering; Bolivian Medical

Society Auxiliary; Society of Reliability Engineers. *Honours:* High School Salutatorian, 1967; Medals in English, Mathematics and Chemistry, 1967. *Hobbies:* Reading; Bicycling; Playing piano; Charitable and civic work. *Address:* 2105 Westview Terrace, Silver Spring, MD 20910, USA.

PEACOCK Elizabeth Joan, b. 4 Sept. 1937. Member of Parliament for Batley and Spen. m. Brian David Peacock, 1963. 2 sons. *Appointments:* Member Select Committee on Employment, 1983-87; Vice-Chairman Back Bench Party Orgn Commitee, 1984-86; Member Exec '1922' Commitee, 1987-; Secretary Yorkshire Conservative Members Group, 1983-87; Vice-President, Yorkshire Area Young Conservative, 1984-87; Member of Parliament (Conservative) Batley and Spen, 1983-. *Memberships:* North Yorkshire County Council; Magistrate, 1975; UK Fedn of Business and Professional Women, 1965-; National Association of Approved Driving Instructors; Vice-President, Yorkshire Conservative Trade Unionists, 1988-. *Hobbies:* Motoring; Dressmaking; Theatre. *Address:* House of Commons, London SW1A 0AA, England.

PEACOCK Molly, b. 30 June 1947, Buffalo, New York, USA. Poet; English Teacher. *Education:* BA, magna cum laude, Harpur College, Binghamton, New York, 1969; MA Honours, Johns Hopkins University, 1977. *Career:* Administrator, Lecturer in English, State University of New York, Binghamton, 1970-76; Lecturer, Johns Hopkins University, 1977-78; Poet- in-residence, Delaware Arts Council, Wilmington, 1978-81; Instructor, English, Friends Seminary, New York City, 1981-. Also: Lecturer, various colleges & universities; Visiting poet, NY State Poets-in-Schools programme, 1973-76; Director, Wilmington Writing Workshops. *Publications:* And Live Apart, 1980; Raw Heaven, 1984; Take Heart Random House, 1989. *Memberships:* Governing Board, Poetry Society of America; Fellows Committee, MacDowell Colony; PEN. *Honours:* Fellow: Danforth Foundation 1976, Yaddo 1980, 1982, Ingram Merrill Foundation 1981, 1986, New Virginia Revue 1983; Grants: Creative Artists Public Service Programme 1977, NY Foundation for Arts 1985. *Address:* Post Office Boc 1282, Peter Stuyevesant Station, New York, NY 10009, USA.

PEAK Lori M, College Instructor. *Education:* Charles Stewart Mott Community College, 1972-73; Religious Training Permit, Diocese of Lansing, 1973; Associate, Liberal Arts, henry Ford Community College, 1979; BSc 1982, Educational leadership 1987, Wayne State University. *Appointments:* Dental Technician, R M MacKenzie, Flint, 1969-75; US Navy, 1975-77; Sales Executive, Tiara Exclusives, 1978-79; District Sales Manager, Wright Air Lines Inc, Cleveland, 1982-85; Various Part-time Teaching Positions, 1982-85; Leasing Analyst, Stroh's Brewery, Detroit, 1985-86; General Manager, Advanced Copier Services Inc, Detroit, 1986-87; College Insructor, Dorsey School of Business, Roseville, 1986-87; Team Educational Coordinator, Boysville of Michigan, Inc, Detroit, 1987-. *Memberships:* Detroit Women in Travel Association; Detroit Passenger and Traffic Organisation; National Association for Female Executives; Detroit/Windsor Interline Club; District Area Sales Managers Association. *Honours:* Pi Lambda Theta, 1982; US Navy Honorary Plaque, Outstanding Work during service, 1977. *Hobbies:* Skiing; Weightlifting; Dancing; Camping; Theatre; Art Museums; Entertaining at Home. *Address:* 109 Fisher Ct, Clawson, MI 48017, USA.

PEAKE Felicity Hyde (Lady Peake), b. 1 May 1913, England. Air Commodore. m. (1) John Charles Mackenzie Hanbury, 1935 (dec. 1939), (2) Sir Harald Peake, 1952 (dec. 1978), 1 son. *Education:* England & France. *Appointments:* Joined ATS Company of RAF, 1939; Command WAAF 1939, served at home & Middle East; Director, Women's Auxiliary Air Force 1946-49, Women's Royal Air Force (from inception) 1949-50, retired 1950; Honorary ADC to King George VI, 1949-50; Trustee, Imperial War Museum, 1963-85, re-elected Governor London House 1978-. *Memberships:* Member

1946-, Vice President 1978, RAF Benevolent Fund; Founding Chair 1986-88, President 1988-, Friends of Imperial War Museum. *Honours include:* Member (MBE) 1941, Dame (DBE) 1949, Order of British Empire. *Address:* Court Farm, Tackley, Oxford OX5 3AQ, England.

PEAKE-JONES Tessa Mary, b. 9 May 1957, London, England. Actress. *Education:* Central School of Speech & Drama, 1975-78. *Appointments:* BBC Series, Telford's Change, 1978; Danedyke Mystery, Granada Series, 1979; A Year with Alan Ayckbourn at Stephen Joseph Theatre in the Round, 1980; The Bell, 1981; Season at Bristol Old Vice, 6 month tour of Sisterly Feelings, 1982; Tour with Cambridge TheatreCompany of Beaux Stratagem and The Vortex, 1984; Member, Tight Assets Theatre Company, 1986. *Honours:* British Fight Certificate, 1987. *Hobbies:* Cansta; Chess; Reading; House Decorating; Cooking. *Address:* c/o London Management, 235 Regent Street, London W1A 2JT, England.

PEARL Valerie Louise, b. 31 Dec. 1926, Newport, Gwent, Wales. College Head. m. 27 Aug. 1949. 1 daughter. *Education:* BA Hons 1949, MA, DPhil 1953, St Anne's College, Oxford University. *Appointments:* Research Fellow/Lecturer, Somerville College, Oxford, 1965; Reader, History of London 1968-76; Professor, History of London 1976-81, University College, London; President, New Hall, Cambridge, 1981-; Governor, Mus London, 1978-; Member, Royal Commission Historical 1983-; Syndicate, Cambridge University Library, 1982-; Cambridge University Press, 1984-. *Publications:* London and the Outbreak of the Puritan Revolution 1625-1643, 1961; History and Imagination,, Essays for Hugh Trevor-Roper, Ed-jointly, 1981; Founder, Editor, London Journal, 1975-78; Contributions to journals and books. *Memberships:* Literary Director, Royal Historical Society, 1975-77; Fellow, Soc of Antiquaries, 1976. *Address:* New Hall, Cambridge, England.

PEARSON P.A. Lee, b. 23 June 1939, Phoenix, Arizona. Marine Surveyor/Consultant. m. M. F. Pearson, 10 Oct. 1959, divorced, 1 son. *Education:* Yacht Design Institute, 1975-76. *Appointments:* Marine Surveyor, 1974-79, 1981-; Promotional Management, 1974-78; Purchasing Management, 1980-81. *Publications:* Lecturer on Marine Safety; Contributor to The Planimeter. *Memberships:* Society Naval Architects & Marine Engineers; American Boat & Yacht Council; Society of Small Craft Designers; Mensa; Instructor, USCG Auxiliary; Boat US Technical Exchange; Society of Accredited Marine Surveyors. *Honours:* Most Outstanding Art Award, 1954; National Honour Society. *Hobbies:* Boating; Reading; Travel; Photography. *Address:* Box 580547, Houston, TX 77258, USA.

PECK Marie Johnston, b. 15 Aug. 1932, New Haven, Connecticut, USA. Businesswoman. m. Austin Monroe Peck, 19 July 1952. *Education:* BA, distinction, Latin American Studies 1968, PhD Ibero-American Studies 1974, University of New Mexico. *Appointment:* Proprietor, Southwestern Images, Inc. *Publications:* Mythologizing Uruguayan Reality in the Works of Jose Pedro Diaz, 1985; Script editor, TV production, Brown v. Board of Education of Topeka: Case of the Century, 1986; PhD dissertation & various scholarly works on themes related to Latin America. *Memberships:* American Association of Teachers of Spanish & Portuguese; Fulbright Alumni Association; Kansas City International Trade Club; Silicon Prairie Technology Association; Kansas City International Trade Task Force. *Honours:* Phi Beta Kappa, 1968; Title VI National Defence foreign language fellow, US Government, 1967-71; Research fellow, Organisation of American States, Montevideo, Uruguay, 1970; Fulbright senior scholar, Uruguayan Fulbright Commission, 1981-82. *Hobbies:* Photography; Outdoor activities; Travel. *Address:* 209 Girard, S.E., No. 6, Albuquerque, NM 87106, USA.

PECK Marilyn Cecilia, b. 18 Sept. 1932, Melbourne,

Australia. Artist. m. Colin Henry Peck, 20 Sept. 1958, 1 son, 1 daughter. *Education:* Commercial Art, Caulfield Technical College. *Appointments:* Lithographic Artist, Fabric Designer until late 50's; Freelance Fabric Designer until late 60's; Professional Artist. *Creative Works:* Joint Shows Include: Gallery 8; Barbizon Gallery; Ku-Ring-Gai Art Gallery; Solo Shows Include: University of New South Wales; Ku-Ring-Gai Motor Yacht Club; Boronia House, Mosman. *Memberships:* Ku-Ring-Gai Art Society; Peninsula Art Society; Royal Art Society, New South Wales; Royal Art Society Queensland; North Shore Art Society; Australian Societies of Miniature Art: NSW (Foundation Member), Queensland (Foundation Member, President 1988). *Honours:* Sydney Boat Show Art Competition, 2nd Prize, 1977; Warringah Art Prize, Highly Commended, 1981; Ku-Ring-Gai Art Society: Helen Gero Award, 1981, Highly Commended, 1981, Artists Supplies Co. Award, 1985, Highly Commended, 1985; Royal Agricultural Society Easter Show, Australian Birds & Fellows, 1st, 1985; Nundle Art Exhibition, Highly Commended, 1985; Macquarie Award 1000, First Prize, 1985; Gulgong Art Exhibition, Highly Commended, 1986; Queensland Royal Art Society, Gold Coast Branch, Highly Commended, 1987; Willoughby Municipal Art Prize, Highly Commended, 1988. *Hobbies:* Living on 10 Acre Orchard; Growing Lychees and Macadamia Nuts; Writing Childrens Books; Tai Chi. *Address:* Buckenham, Darwalla Road, Mount Nathan, Queensland, Australia.

PECKENPAUGH Angela Hazelton Johnson, b. 21 Mar 1942, Richmond, Virginia, USA. Associate Professor of English. m. Clarence William Peckenpaugh, 27 Jul 1970, divorced 1981. *Education:* BA, Denison University, 1965; MA, 20th Century Literature, Ohio University, 1966; MFA, Writing, University of Massachusetts, 1978. *Appointments:* Lecturer, Ohio University, 1967; Instructor, University of Wisconsin, Milwaukee, 1968- 74; Co-ordinator of Freshman Seminars, University of Wisconsin, Milwaukee, 1975; Director of Development, MIAD, 1976-77; Director, Writing Program for Adults, University of Wisconsin Extension, 1978-82; Associate Professor of English, University of Wisconsin, Whitewater, 1982 -. *Publications:* Letters from Lee's Army, 1979; Discovering the Mandala, 1981; A Book of Charms, 1983; Refreshing the Fey, 1986. *Memberships:* Associated Writing Programs; Artist Book Works; Wisconsin Women in the Arts; Women's Art Caucus; Fellowship of Poets; Feminist Writers' Guild; Council of Wisconsin Writers; Wisconsin Designers and Craftsmen. *Honours:* All University Fellowship, University of Massachusetts, 1977-78; Honorable Mention, Council of Wisconsin Writers, 1979, 1983; Grants from Wisconsin Arts Bosrd, 1988; Wisconsin Hummanities Committee, 1987; 2nd place Edna Meudt Contest, Wisconsin Fellowship of Poets, 1989. *Hobbies:* Color Xerox art;; Needlepoint; Walking; Cats; Paganism; Ecological work; Sales of vintage clothing and poem notecards. *Address:* 2513 E Webster Place, Milwaukee, WI 53211, USA.

PEDERSEN Joy Susan, b. 6 Nov. 1955, Denville, New Jersey, USA. Success consultant; Trainer; Lecturer; Entrepreneur. *Education:* Dover Business College, 1974-75; Professional School of Business, 1975; County College of Morris, 1973-74; First School of Paralegal Studies, 1978; UCLA for PR Designation, 1980-82. *Appointments:* Alfred F Carolonza Jr, Paralegal, 1976-79; Television publicity, Paramount Pictures Corp, 1980-85; President, Pedersen Public Relations, 1985-86; Bureau Chief, PM Magazine, 1986-88; Owner, Express Success, 1981-. *Publications:* Express Success workshops, trainings and booklets. How to Master Wealth, workshops, tapes, booklets. *Memberships:* The Publicists Guild of America; Academy of Television Arts and Sciences; Women in Show Business (past Vice President); Book Publicists of Southern California; Institute of Noetic Sciences. *Honours:* National Honor Society, 1972 and 1973; Olympic Organizing Committee Recognition, 1984; Norwegian Jr Olympics Team pin for swimming, 1970. *Hobbies:* Polo; Swimming; Sailing; Hot air ballooning; Art, particularly French Impressionists; Travel; Writing;

World Peace. *Address:* 8539 Sunset Blvd, Suite 4-112, West Hollywood, California 90069, USA.

PEEBLES Mary Josephine, b. 21 Dec. 1950, LaJolla, California, USA. Clinical Psychologist. *Education:* BA, Wellesley College, 1972; PhD, Case Western Reserve University, 1977; Candidate, psychoanalytic training, Topeka Institute, 1980-. *Appointments include:* Child care worker, student social worker, trainee, clinical psychology intern, various establishments, Ohio, 1968-76; Staff Psychologist, Gulf Coast Regional Mental Health/Retardation Community Service Centre, Galveston, Texas, 1976-77; Postdoctoral Fellow, Clinical Child Psychology, University of Texas 1977-78, Menninger Clinic, Topeka, Kansas 1978-80; Staff Psychologist, Menninger Clinic, 1980-. *Creative work includes:* Author, co-author, various professional articles; Book reviews, Menninger Clinic Bulletin; Writer & speaker, educational videotapes. *Memberships:* Divisions, Psychoanalysis, Psychotherapy, Psychological Hypnosis, American Psychological Association; Board 1986-89, Kansas Psychological Association; Society for Clinical & Experimental Hypnosis. *Honours include:* David Rapaport Award, teaching, Menninger Clinic, 1985; Alumni professional writing award, Menninger Alumni Association, 1987; Publications award, Topeka Institute, 1987; Sherry K. & Harold B. Crasilneck Award, Society for Clinical & Experimental Hypnosis, 1987; Various scholarships, student honours. *Hobbies:* Classical piano; Ballet; Art history. *Address:* Menninger Clinic, PO Box 829, Topeka, Kansas 66601, USA.

PEEBLES-WILKINS Wilma, b. 21 Apr. 1945, Raleigh, USA. Social Work Educator. m. James A. Wilkins, 1 June 1984. *Education:* BA, North Carolina State Univerity, 1967; MSSA, Case Western Reserve University, 1971; PhD, University of North Carolina, 1984. *Appointments:* Cuyahoga County Division of Social Services, 1967-72; Case Western Reserve University, 1972-76; Eastern Kentucky University, 1976-77; NC Memorial Hospital, 1977-78; North Carolina State University, 1978-. *Publications:* Numerous articles on social work. *Memberships:* Academy of Certified Social Workers; Council on Social Work Education; Triangle Association of Black Social Workers; State Council for Social Legislation. *Honours:* Irene Sogg Gross Service Award, 1971; Swedish International Fellowship, 1980; Gubenatorial Appointee to NC Certification 1984, 1987; Ford Curriculum Development Award, 1988. *Hobbies:* Collector; Travel; Music. *Address:* 2620 Cottage Circle, Raleigh, NC 27613, USA.

PEEL Hazel Mary, b. 26 May 1930, London, England. Housewife; Writer. m. Roy Peel, 24 Oct. 1953. *Appointments:* Legal secretary/clerk. *Publications include:* Fury Son Of The Wilds, 1959; Pilot the Hunter, 1962; Pilot the Chaser, 1963; Easter the Showjumper, 1965; Jago, 1966; Night Storm the Flat Racer, 1966; Dido and Rogue, 1967; Gay Darius, 1968; Untamed! 1969; Land and Power, 1975; Law of the Wild, 1975; Pocket Dictionary of the Horse, 1977; Numerous articles in magazines. Currently working on historical novel. *Hobbies:* Reading contemporary fiction and selected Classics; Writing to pen friends; Gardener; Travelling. *Address:* England.

PELTIER Wanda Jo, b. 26 July 1933, USA. State Representative. m. Robert T Stapleton, 5 Aug. 1982, 2 daughters by previous marriage. *Education:* BA, Oklahoma Baptist University, 1963; MA, University of Kansas, 1965. *Appointments:* Graduate Assistant, English, University of Kansas, 1963-65; Instructor, English, State University of New York, 1966-67; Assistant Professor, Oklahoma Baptist University, 1968-73; Director, Native American Programmes, 1974-77; Owner, Peltier Pen Productions, 1977-86; State Representative, State of Oklahoma, 1986-. *Publications:* Author, Textbook used nationwide for vocational-technical schools displaced homemaker programmes. *Memberships:* Founder, 1st President, Mayor's Council on Ageing, Shawnee, Oklahoma, 1975; President,

Governor's Commission, Status of Women, 1978-79; President, Oklahoma Women's Political Caucus, 1980-84. *Honours:* Recipient, various honours and awards. *Hobbies:* Technical Writing. *Address:* 425 Southwest 51, Oklahoma City, OK 73109, USA.

PELTOMAKI Lea, b. 24 Jan. 1931, Finland. Director of Finance. Widowed, 1986, 1 daughter. *Education:* School of Social Studies, Helsinki. *Appointments:* Chief, Finance, City of Pori; Director, Finance, Satakunta Central Hospital, Pori, current. *Memberships:* President, Business & Professional Women in Finland, 1986-; President, BPW, Pori, 1985-86; President, UNIFEM, Pori, 1986-; Elected Member, Council, City of Pori, 1988-. *Hobbies:* Social Affairs; Womens Issues. *Address:* Liisankatu 17 A 17, 28100 Pori, Finland.

PELTON Virginia Lue King, b. 15 Apr. 1928, Utica, USA. Businesswoman. m. Harold M. Pelton, 11 July 1970, 2 daughters. *Appointments:* Bergdorf Goodman, Couture, 1951-53; Fashion Consulting, Titche's, Dallas, 1955, Charles Gallay, 1975-79; Buyer, Slavick's Jewelry, 1980-83; Owner, P.J. Secretarial, 1983-; Co-Owner, H.P. Financial, 1983-. *Memberships:* Professional Network, Secretary; Saddleback Chamber; Leukemia Society, Secretary, 1985-86; Republican Club. *Honours:* Valedictorian, 1946; Home Economics Scholarship Grant, 1946; Complete Costume Design Award, 1947; College Fashion Board, 1950-51; Rivera Cruise, 1981; Bahamas Fantasy Cruise, 1988. *Hobbies:* Gourmet Cookery; Art. *bb3Address:* 24942 Georgia Sue Drive, Laguna Hills, CA 92653, USA.

PELTZMAN Barbara Ruth, b. 12 Mar. 1950, Brooklyn, New York, USA. College Professor. *Education:* BS, Elementary Education, Mills College of Education, 1968; MS, Early Childhood Education, St John's University, 1969; EdD, Teachers College, Columbia University, 1975; Professional Diploma, Postdoctoral study, Reading, Hofstria Univerity, 1978. *Appointments:* Classroom Teacher, 1969-72; (doctoral study leave, 1972-75), Reading Specialist, 1975-85, New York City Board of Education, 1969-72; Adjunct Assistant Professor, 1973-85, Full-time Assistant Professor, 1985-, St John's University, New York. *Publications:* Books: Anna Freud: A Guide to Research, 1989; How Reading Problems Begin, in progress; Numerous journal articles and book chapters. *Memberships:* Vice-President, National Doctorate Association; World Organization for Early Childhood Education; International Reading Association; Council for Exceptional Children; Phi Delta Kappa (1 of 1st women members); Kappa Delta Pi; National Society for the Study of Education; Doctorate Association of New York Educators, Editorial Board, Conference Coordinator, 1985-89. *Honours:* Parents-Teachers Association, PS 118 Q Teachers of the Year, 1970; Laurel Wreath Award, Doctorate Association of New York, 1972; International Freud Fellowship, Freud Museum, London, 1988-89; Outstanding Educator of the Year, National Doctorate Association, 1989. *Hobbies:* 18th Century American Colonial antiques; Reading; Riding; Ballet; Needlepoint; Travel especially by ship and train. *Address:* Division of Education, Rosati Hall, Notre Dame College, St John's University, 300 Howard Avenue, Staten Island, NY 10301, USA.

PELZMAN Liliane Talita, b. 24 Mar. 1953, Amsterdam, Netherlands. Producer; Director; Editor. *Education:* BA, Tel Aviv, Israel, 1975; MA, Broadcast Journalism, University of Southern California, 1984. *Appointments:* Owner, Producer, Director, LP Productions, producing Hollywood Entertainment News for Netherlands, Chile, Peru and Germany, and commercials. *Creative Works:* China Images, documentary (producer, editor, writer), 1987. *Memberships:* International Documentary Association; Academy of Television, Arts and Sciences; Women in Film; Women Behind the Lens. *Honours:* Hometown USA Video Festival, 1988. *Hobbies:* Making films; Jogging; Windsurfing; Swimming; Writing. *Address:* 223 Strand Street, Suite K, Santa Monica, CA 90405, USA.

PEMBERTON Margaret, b. 10 Apr. 1943, Bradford, England. Author. m. Michael G pemberton, 18 Oct. 1968, 1 son, 4 daughters. *Publications:* Rendezvous with Danger, 1974; The Mystery of Saligo Bay, 1976; Vengeance in the Sun, 1984; The Guilty Secretary, 1979; Tapestry of Fear, 1979; Lion of Languedoc, 1981; African Enchantment, 982; Pioneer Girl, 1982; Devil's Palace, 1983; Flight to Verechenko, 1983; Forever, 1982; Harlot, 1981; The Flower Garden, 1982; Silver Shadows Golden Dreams, 1985; Never Leave Me; A Multitude of Sins, 1988. *Memberships:* Romantic Novelist Association; Crime Writers Association, Committee Member; PEN; Society of Authors. *Hobbies:* Jacobean Drama; Opera; Sailing. *Address:* 13 Manor Lane, London SE13 5QW, England.

PENCE Coralynn, b. Oregon, USA. Artist; Goldsmith. m. W. Ross (dec. 1950), 1 son (dec.). *Education:* Chouinard, Los Angeles, California; University of Washington, Seattle; Museum studies; Studied Gold Museum, Bogota, 1984, New Zealand, Australia, New Guinea, 1987. *Career:* Taught Jewellery and Metalsmithing, University of Washington, 1 year, Adult Education and Seattle Community College, Seattle, Washington, 16 years; Full-time work on commissions; Held 5 private jewellery shows, 1958, 1969, 1972, 1978, 1982; Exhibitions: Philadelphia Art Association, 1949; Decorative Arts, Wichita, Kansas, 1949, 1952, 1953; Art Today, Anchorage, Alaska, 1952; Walker Art Center, 1955; Jewellery and Related Objects, Smithsonian Institution, 1955, 1956; Designer-Craftsmen of West, De Young Museum, San Francisco, 1961; Designer-Craftsmen of Far West, Museum of Contemporary Crafts, New York, 1961; American Jewellery Today, Everhart Museum, Pennsylvania, 1963; World Craft Council Exhibition, New Zealand, 1966; Design Center, Philippines, US Information Service, 1977; Commissioned to create necklace for opening of Treasures of Tutankhamen, Seattle Art Museum, 1978; Invited by Fashion Group International to assist in establishing group in Bogota and Lima; Invited to show jewellery on 12 foreign trips and meeting goldsmiths, buying gems, 1956-87. *Creative works include:* Jewellery in 18 carat gold, signed and dated; Works presented in books, magazines and newspapers. *Memberships:* Seattle Art Museum; Pacific Northwest Arts Council; Charter Member, National Museum of Women in the Arts, Washington DC; World Craftsmen's Council; Fashion Group International. *Honours:* Theta Sigma Phi; Merit Award, American Craftsmen's Council, 1966; Great Designs in Jewellery Award, Austria, 1967; Awards, Henry Gallery, University of Washington; Many others. *Hobbies:* Gardening; Reading; Microwave; Artifacts. *Address:* 5009 48th NE, Seattle, WA 08105, USA.

PENDER Lydia Kathleen, b. 29 June 1907, London, England. Writer for Children. m. Walter G B Pender, 5 Mar. 1932, 2 sons, 2 daughters. *Education:* Studies at University of Sydney, 1925. *Appointments:* with E.S. Wolfenden, 1928-32. *Publications:* Marbles in My Pocket, 1957; Barnaby & the Horses, 1961; Dan McDougall & the Bulldozer, 1963; Sharpur the Carpet Snake, 1967; Poems to Read to Young Australians, with Mary Gilmore, 1968; Brown Paper Leaves, 1971; Barnaby & the Rocket, 1972; The Useless Donkeys, 1979; Morning Magpie, 1984; Lydia Pender's Australian Alphabet, verse, in press; contributor to anthologies of children's verse, Australia & abroad. *Memberships:* Australian Society of Authors; Childrens Book Council of Australia. *Honours:* Childrens Book Council of Australia Annual Picture Book Awards, Highly Commeded, 1968, Commended 1973, Commended, 1980; Lady Cutler Award for Distinguished Services to Australian Children's Literature, 1988. *Hobbies Include:* Fine Embroidery. *Address:* 10 Blenheim Road, Lindfield, NSW 2070, Australia.

PENNEY Jacqueline, b. 26 Mar. 1930, New York, USA. Artist; Teacher. m. Kenneth G Moore, 7 Sept. 1985. 1 son, 1 daughter. *Education:* Phoenix School of Design, New York; Black Mountain College, North Carolina, Institute of Design, Chicago; Art Student's

League, New York; Studied with: Charles Reid, Robert E Wood, Tom Hill, Miles Batt, Henry Fukuhara, Frank Webb, Paul Wood, Daniel Green, Mario Cooper and Barbara Nechis. *Creative works:* Solo Exhibitions: Gallery East, East Hampton, New York, 1980-88; William Ris Galleries, Stone Harbor, New Jersey, 1986; East End Arts Council, Riverhead, New York, 1980-84; Plandome Gallery, Plandome, New York, 1982; Quogue Library, Quogue, New York, 1987; Preusser Gallery, New Mexico, 1989. Numerous Group Exhibitions, Gallery Representation and Private Collections. Publication: NY Art Review by American References, 1988. *Honours:* William Meyerowitz Memorial Award, National Association of Women Artists Inc, New York, 1986; Nora Mirmont Hambeuchen Award, Huntington Township Art League, Hecksher Museum, Huntington, New York, 1985; First prizes and Honourable Mentions, East End Arts Council, Riverhead, New York, 1980-85; 1st Prize, Gallery 21 WLIW Channel 21, 1982. *Address:* 270 North Street, P O Box 959, Cutchogue, NY 11935, USA.

PENNINGTON Sheila, b. 8 Apr. 1932, Toronto, Canada. Psychotherapist. m. Ben Harrison, 14 June 1975, 3 sons, 1 daughter. *Education:* BA, 1955; MEd., 1966; PhD, 1982. *Appointments:* Research Dept., Board of Education, 1962-65; Crisis Intervention, Scarborough General Hospital, 1969-71; Private practice, 1971-87. *Publications:* Healing Yourself: Understanding How Your Mind Can Heal Your Body, 1988. *Memberships:* New York Academy of Sciences; Association of American Humanistic Psychotherapists; American Association of Marriage and Family Therapists; World Federalists of Canada; Amnesty International. *Honours:* Ontario Psychological Association Presidential Award, 1981. *Hobbies:* Swimming; Ballet; Bicycling; Baroque Music; Nature; Pets; Reading. *Address:* 491 Eglinton Ave W. No B2, Toronto, Ontario M5N 1A8, Canada.

PEPINO Nicholas Jane, b. 13 Apr. 1947, London, Canada. Lawyer. m. James D Pearson, 11 Oct. 1974, 1 son, 2 daughters. *Education:* LLB, 1970; LLM, 1971; Called to Bar of Ontario 1973. *Appointments:* Jarvis Blott Fejer Pepino, 1973-82; Aird & Berlis, 1982-. *Publications:* Articles in various professional journals. *Memberships:* Ontario Human Rights Commission, 1980-82; 1st Woman, Metro Toronto Police Commission, 1982-; Executive Member, Canadian Advisory Council on the Status of Women, 1985-; Board of Trustees, Metro Toronto United Way & Womens College Hospital Foundation. *Honours:* Recipient, various honours & awards. *Address:* c/o Aird & Belis, Suite 1500, 145 King St. W, Toronto, Canada, M5H 2J3.

PEPPERCORN Lisa M, b. 2 Oct. 1913, Frankfurt/ Main, West Germany. Brazilian citizen of German Origin. Musicologist. m. Lothar Bauer, 9 Apr. 1938 (deceased 1968). *Education:* Royal Conservatoire, Brussels, 1933-34. *Appointments:* London Music Correspondent, Neue Zurcher Zeitung and Basler Nachrichten, Writing Teachers Notes for The Robert Mayer Concerts for Children, 1934-38; Rio de Janeiro Music Correspondent, New York Times and Musical America, 1939-46; Specialist on Heitor Villa-Lobos, Brazilian Composer. *Publications:* H Villa-Lobos, Leben und Werk des brasilianischen Kompositen, Atlantis, 1972; Villa-Lobos, The Illustrated Lives of the Great Composers, 1989; The Villa-Lobos Letters, 1990; The Music of H. Villa-Lobos, 1990; contributor to New York Times; Bulletin of the Pan American Union; Latin American Music Review; Journal of Musicological research; Music Review; Monthly Musical Record; Musical Times; Music and Letters; Tempo; Ibero-Amerikanisches Archiv; Studi Musicali; Mens and Melodie; Neue Zurcher Zeitung; Revue Belge de Musicologie. *Address:* Schulhaus Strasse 53, 8002 Zurich, Switzerland.

PERCIVAL Millicent Gwendolyn, b. 13 Mar. 1927, St John's, Antigua, West Indies. Supervisor. m. Oswald Percival, 19 Oct. 1967. 1 daughter. *Education:* Clerical and Dentist's Help, 1942-58; Certificates, Pitmans College, London, England, 1959-64. *Appointments:* Legal Secretary, London, England, 1962-69; Legal Secretary, Antigua, West Indies, 1969-76; Legal Secretary, Hon. Attorney General of Antigua-Barbuda, 1976-81; Supervisor, Antigua Public Utilities Authority, 1981-. *Creative works:* Presented papers at seminars and home and abroad. *Memberships:* Secretary, YWCA, Antigua, 1970-74; Executive Member, Treasurer, Co-ordinating Council of Women, Antigua, 1971-81; Executive Member, Caribbean Women's Association, 1981-; Secretary, Womens Action Group, Antigua Labour Party, 1975-78; President, Womens Action Group, 1978-; Executive Member, Antigua Labour Party, 1973-; Executive Member, Antigua Trades & Labour Union, 1987. *Honours:* Member of the Senate, Antigua, 1984-; Member of Police Service Commission, 1976-78; Secretary, De La Bastide Commission of Enquiry into certain Government matters, 1978; Member of the National Awards Committee, 1988. *Hobbies:* Reading; Politics; Agriculture. *Address:* PO Box 598, St John's, Antigua, West Indies.

PEREZ Enriqueta Gonzalez, b. 10 Feb. 1941, La Feria, Texas, USA. Teacher. m. Jesus Salas Perez, 23 Mar. 1959, 3 sons. *Education:* BSc., 1973; MS, 1975; BE, 1975; MMA, 1985; PhD, 1987. *Appointments:* Teacher, Donna Independant School District, 1972-73, Mercedes ISD, 1973-75, 1977-78; Curriculum Director, Progreso ISD, 1981-85; External Supervisor, Indiana University, 1981-85; Bilingual Teacher, McAllen ISD, 1985-86. *Publications:* Legends of the Crying Lady in the Mexican Tradition; Family Life of Mexican American Children of South Texas; Bilingual Editor, Passport to Success; Perez Language Arts Skills Continuum System. *Memberships:* Pan American University American Humanics Association, Board; Pan American University Alumni Association; Indiana University Alumni Association. *Honours:* Citizen of the Week Award, 1981. *Hobbies:* Quilting; Gardening; Research Studies in Education. *Address:* Rt. 2 Box 117, Mercedes, TX 78570, USA.

PEREZ-WOODS Rosanne Harrigan, b. 24 Feb. 1945, Miami, Florida, USA. Nursing Educator; Child Development Consultant. m. 12 Apr. 1986. 3 sons. *Education:* BS, St Xavier College, Chicago, 1965; MSN, Indiana University, 1974; EdD, Indiana University, Bloomington, 1979; Cert. pediatric nurse practitioner, Nat Bd Pediatric Nurse Practitioners and Assocs. *Appointments:* Staff Nurse, Evening Charge Nurse, Mercy Hospital, Chicago, 1965-66; Nursing Educator, Chicago State Hospital, 1966-67; Pediatric Nurse Practitioner, Marion County Health and Hosp Corp, Indiannapolis, 1974- 75; Lecturer, Indiana University, 1974-75; Assistant Professor Nursing 1975- 77, Project Director perinanta nursing program, 1978-85, Associate Professor, 1980-82, Professor, Chairman of Dept Pediatrics, Family and Women's Health, School of Nursing, 1982-85; Adjunct Professor, Pediatrics School Medicine, 1982-85; Chief Nursing Sect, James Whitcom Riley Hosp Child Devel Prog, Indiannapolis, 1982-85; Niehoff Chair and Professor Maternal Child Health Nursing, 1985-. *Publications:* Author: Immunological Concepts Applied, 1978; Protocols for Perinatal Nursing Practice, 1981; Contributor of numerous articles to professional journals. *Memberships:* American Nurses Association, Illinois; State Nurses Association; Nurses Association of America Coll Ob-Gyn; National Perinatal Association; Adult Education Association of America; America Nurses Foundation; Indiana University Alumni Assoiciation; AAAS; Sigma Xi; Pi Lambda Theta; Sigma Theta Tau. *Honours:* Ednl Cons Named Nurse of the Year, March of Dimes, 1978. *Address:* 6525 N Sheridan Rd, DH 411, Loyola University, Chicago, Illinois 60626, USA.

PERLMAN Sophia Ina, b. 24 Jan. 1926, Bloemfontein, South Africa. Executive Director, Operation Hunger. m. Dr Michael Perlman, 4 Dec. 1947. 2 sons, 2 daughters. *Education:* Medicine Studies, University of Witwatersrand, not completed. *Appointments:* Finance Department 1972- 73, Southern

Transvaal Manager 1974-83, South African Institute of Race Relations; Executive Director, Operation Hunger, 1984-. *Memberships:* Black Sash; Executive Member, Action Committee to Stop Evictions, 1980-83; President, Northcliff Rotary Anns. *Honour:* Paul Harris Award, Rotary International. *Address:* Operation Hunger, P O Box 32257, Braamfontein 2017, Johannesburg, South Africa.

PERLMUTTER Marion A, b. 2 Sept. 1948, New York City, USA. Professor of Psychology; Research Scientist. *Education:* BS, Psychology, Syracuse University, 1970; MS, Educational Psychology, State University of New York, 1971; PhD, Developmental Psychology, University of Massachusetts, 1976. *Appointments:* Assistant Professor to Professor and Associate Director, Institute of Child Development, University of Minnesota, 1976-84; Visiting Scholar, Max Planck Institute for Psychological Study, Munich, West Germany, 1984; Professor, Department of Psychology, Research Scientist, Institute of Gerontology and Center for Human Growth and Development, University of Michigan, 1985-; Visiting Fellow, Center for Advanced Studies, Andrus Gerontology Center, University of Southern California, 1986; Visiting Fellow, Max Planck Institute, Berlin, West Germany, 1987. *Publications:* Books: New directions in child development: Children's Memory, 1980; Development and aging across adulthood, 1985; Child psychology today, 1986; Life long development, 1988; Late life potention (in press). *Memberships:* Fellow, American Psychological Association; Fellow, Gerontological Society of America; International Society for the Study of Behavioural Development; Society for Research in Child Development. *Honours:* Boyd McCandless Young Scientist Award, American Psychological Association, Division of Developmental Psychology, 1981; University of Minnesota Young Women Scholar, 1982; Brookdale Foundation, National Fellow, 1985-. *Hobbies:* Swimming; Biking; Reading; Dance; Music; Art; Cinema. *Address:* Institute of Gerontology, The University of Michigan, 300 North Ingalls Rm 935NW, Ann Arbor, MI 48109, USA.

PERLOFF Marjorie Gabrielle, b. 28 Sept. 1931. Vienna, Austria. Professor of English & Comparative Literature. m. Joseph K. Perloff, 31 July 1953, 2 daughters. *Education:* (USA) Oberlin College, 1949-52; AB magna cum laude, Barnard College, 1953; PhD, Catholic University, 1965. *Appointments:* Assistant Professor, Catholic University, 1965-69; Associate Professor 1969-72, full Professor 1972-77, University of Maryland; Florence Scott Professor of English, University of Southern California, 1977- 85; Professor, Stanford University, 1986-. *Publications:* Poetic Art of Robert Lowell, 1973; Frank O'Hara, Poet Among Painters, 1977; Poetics of Indeterminacy: Rimbaud to Cage, 1981; Dance of the Intellect, 1985; Futurist Moment, 1987; Poetic Licence, 1990. Editorial boards, various literary journals. *Memberships:* Executive, Modern Language Association; Advisory Council, American Comparative Literature Association. *Honours:* Phi Beta Kappa; Guggenheim Fellowship, 1981-82; Senior Fellowship, National Endowment for Humanities, 1985-86. *Address:* 1467 Amalfi Drive, Pacific Palisades, California 90272, USA.

PERLOV Dadie, b. 8 June 1929, New York, USA. Executive Director. m. Norman B Perlov, 30 May 1950, 3 daughters. *Education:* BA, New York University, 1950. *Appointments:* Executive Director, Operation Open City, New York, 1962-64; Director, Field Services, NCJW, New York, 1968-74; Executive Director, New York Library Association, 1974-81; Executive Director, National Council of Jewish Women, 1981-. *Publications:* Contributor of numerous articles in journals & magazines. *Memberships Include:* President, New York Society of Association Executives, 1985; Association Evaluator, American Society of Association Executives, 1980-; Board Member, Research Institute, Hebrew University, Israel, 1981-; Ameican Society of Association Executives, 1987-1990; etc. *Honours:* PEN Certificate for Legislation, New York Governor Carey, 1978; Award of Excellence, American Society of Association Executives, 1983; Named as one of America's 100 most important women by the Ladies Home Journal, 1988; many other honours and awards. *Hobbies:* Writing; Mycology; History; Music; Art. *Address:* National Council of Jewish Women, 53 W. 23 Street, New York, NY 10010, USA.

PERPINAN Norma (Sister Mary Soledad), b. 18 May 1937, Manila, Philippines. Religious of the Good Shepherd. *Education:* AB, BSE, St Theresa's College, Manila, Philippines, 1957; MS, Education, Fordham University, New York, 1959. *Appointments:* Asst Personnel Manager, 1958; Teacher, High School, College, Graduate School, 1962-74; Researcher/Writer, 1974-75; Editor, 1978-88; Lecturer/Consultant on Womens concerns, 1981-88; Counselling Psychologist, 1975-79; Coordinator of Third World Movement Against the Exploitation of Women (TW-MAE-W). *Publications:* Yielding; Flint and Fire; Editor, BALAI Asian Journal; Editor, IBON; Editor, ORION. Participant at numerous international conferences. *Membership:* IBON Databank, Corporate Secretary. *Honours:* Summa cum laude, Bachelor of Arts, 1957; Summa cum laude, Bachelor of Science in Education, 1957; Fulbright Scholar, Fordham University, 1958. *Hobbies:* Writing; Reading; Art; Nature. *Address:* Good Shpeherd Convent, 1043 Aurora Boulevard, Quezon City, Philippines.

PERRY Erma, b. Winthrop, Massachusetts, USA. Photo-Journalist. m. 29 Apr. 1939, 1 son, 1 daughter. *Education:* BS, Boston University, 1936; University of Pennsylvania, 1987-88. *Appointment:* Freelance photo-journalist. *Publication:* Carry-Out Cuisine, Philadelphia section. *Memberships:* American Society of Journalists & Authors; Society of American Travel Writers. *Honours:* Freelance photography awards 1979, 1980, 1st prize 1981, grand prize 1983, best travel sell 1987, Society of American Travel Writers. *Address:* 134 Greenwood Avenue, Jenkintown, Pennsylvania 19046, USA.

PERRY June Carter, b. 13 Nov. 1943, Texarkana, Arkansas, USA. Foreign Service Officer. m. 13 July 1968, 2 sons. *Education:* BA cum laude, Mundelein College for Women, Chicago, 1965; MA, University of Chicago, 1967. *Appointments:* Public Affairs Director, WGMS/RKO Radio, Washington DC, 1974-77; Community Services Administration, 1977-79; Peace Corps, Washington DC, 1979-82; US Embassy at Lusaka & Harare 1984-87, Desk Officer for Botswana & Lesotho 1987-89, Special Assistant to Deputy Secretary of State Lawrence Eagleburger, 1989-, Department of State, Washington DC. *Publications:* Articles: Ancient African Heroines, Washington Post 1983; Micronesia; Trip for Intrepid Traveler, Chicago Daily News 1968. *Memberships:* Founding Vice President 1975, Womens Institute, American University; American Foreign Service Association; Phi Alpha Theta. *Honours:* Awards: Department of State, 1985, 1987; Mundelein College, 1982; RKO Radio, 1974, 1975; Action Agency, 1981, 1982; Blacks in Industry, 1975. Woodrow Wilson Fellowship, University of Chicago, 1965. *Hobbies:* Classical music, role of African-American composers (produced radio series Soul of the Classics, 1974-77); African & American history (produced black history programmes, Zimbabwe & Washington DC). *Address:* 3017 Oregon Knolls Drive NW, Washington DC 20015, USA.

PERRY Kimberly, b. 8 Mar. 1955, Meadville, Pennsylvania, USA. Environmental Engineer. m. 17 Oct. 1987. *Education:* BA, Ecology-Conservation, Vassar College, 1977; MS, Virginia Tech, Environmental Sciences and Engineering; Additional studies, Washington University, Central Missouri State University and Southern Illinois University. *Appointments:* Research Assistant, Environmental Impact Sector, National Commission on Water Quality, Washington DC, summer 1975; Microbiology Research Assistant, Chesapeke Bay Center for Environmental Studies, Smithsonian Institution, Edgewater, Maryland, summer 1976; Research Assistant, Marine Protection Branch, Environmental Protection Agency, Washington

DC, summer 1977; Engineer, Environmental Division, Sverdrup & Parcel and Associates Inc, St Louis, Missouri, 1979-81; Quality Assurance Auditor, Department of Medicine and Environmental Health, Monsanto, 1981-86, Senior Environmental Engineer, Department of Engineering Technology, Monsanto, 1986-89, St Louis. *Memberships:* American Chemical Society; Society of Quality Assurance; Water Pollution Control Federation; Society of Women Engineers; First Unitarian Church of St Louis (President, Board of Trustees, 1986-87, Midwest Leadership School Graduate, 1986); Operation Clean Stream Trip Leader, 1984-85; Conference Panelist, Mathematics/Science Network of Greater St Louis, 1988. *Hobbies:* Singing; Biking; Golf. *Address:* Monsanto Krummrich, 500 Monsanto Avenue, Sarget, IL 62206, USA.

PERRY Mabel Josephine Bentley, b. 6 Aug. 1926, Jacksonville, Florida, USA. Educational Consultant. m. Claude A Perry, Sr, 1 son. *Education:* BA, University of Iowa, 1949; MA, Newark State College (presently Kean College) Union, New Jersey, 1966; Doctor of Education, Rutgers, The State University of New Jersey, New Brunswick, 1984. *Appointments:* Essex County Probation Department, 1954-62; Elementary/Secondary Teacher, Newark, New Jersey, 1962-67; Guidance Counsellor, Newark, 1967-71; Guidance Counsellor, Glen Rock, New Jersey, 1971-. *Memberships:* National Education Association; New Jersey Education Association; New Jersey Association of College Admission Counselors (NJACAC), Exeuctive Board member; New Jersey Association of Student Personnel Services; Glen Rock Education Association; Alpha Kappa Alpha Sorority. *Honours:* Alpha Kappa Mu Honorary Society; Associate Trustee, Bethune-Cookman College, Daytona Beach, Florida; President, Phyllis Wheatley Literary Club; Distinguished Award, Alpha Kappa Alpha Sorority; 100 Black Women. *Hobby:* Travel. *Address:* 4 Dellmead Drive, Livingston, New Jersey 07039, USA.

PERRY Margaret N, b. 23 Apr. 1940, Waynesboro, USA. University Chancellor. m. Randy L. Perry, 30 Oct. 1965, 2 sons. *Education:* BS, University of Tennessee, Martin, 1961; MS, 1963, PhD, 1965, University of Tennessee, Knoxville. *Appointments:* Assistant Professor, Food Science, University of Tennessee, Knoxville, 1966-69; Assistant to Dean, Assistant Dean, Associate Dean, Home Economics, 1966-73, Dean, Graduate School, 1973-79, University of Tennessee, Knoxville; Associate Vice President, Academic Affairs, Tennessee Technological University, 1979-86; Chancellor, University of Tennessee, Martin, 1986-. *Memberships:* IfT; AHEA; THEA; American Council on Education Commission on Women. *Honours:* Recipient, various honours and awards. *Hobbies:* Aerobics; Reading; Collecting Angels. *Address:* University of Tennessee, 325 Admin. Bldg., Martin, TN 38238, USA.

PERRY Marion Judith Helz, b. 2 June 1943, Takoma Park, Maryland, USA. Poet; Professor; Writer. m. Franklyn A H Perry, 17 July 1971. 1 son, 1 daughter. *Education:* BA, 1964; MA, 1966; MFA, 1969; MA, 1979; PhD, 1986. *Appointments:* West Liberty State College, 1966-68; Albright College, 1968-70; SUNY, 1970-79; Empire state College, 1979-82; Erie Community College, 1980-. *Publications:* Books: Dishes (poetry), 1989; Training of Professional Writers, 1986; Establishing Intimacy, 1982; The Mirror's Image, 1981; Icarus, 1980. *Memberships:* Poetry Society of America; Poets & Writers; Academy of American Poets; Phi Delta Kappa; Pi Lambda Theta; League of Women Voters, Vice President. *Honours:* All nations Poetry Contest Winner, 2 years; College Arts Poetry Contest Winner; Elected to members in Phi Delta Kappa, Pi Lambda Theta and Poetry Society of America. *Address:* Erie Community College-South, 4140 S W Blvd, Orchard Park, NY 14127, USA.

PERRY Nicolette Elizabeth, b. 4 Sept. 1949, Britain. Lecturer; Writer; Photographer. *Education:* BA, Open University; MA. *Appointments:* Course Leader, BA (Honours) Course in Photography, Film and Video,

Harrow College of Higher Education; GCSE Moderator; BTEC Moderator. *Publications:* Beyond Photography; Symbiosis: Close Encounters of the Natural Kind; Many articles in press. *Hobbies:* Travel; Reading; Gardening. *Address:* 53 Kirtle Road, Chesham, Buckinghamshire HP5 1AD, England.

PERRY Pauline, b. 15 Oct. 1931, Wolverhampton, England. Director, South Bank Polytechnic. m. George W. Perry, 26 July 1952, 3 sons, 1 daughter. *Education:* BA, Girton College, Cambridge 1952, MA, 1956. *Appointments:* Teacher, USA, Canada, UK, 1953-55, 1959-61; Lecturer, Philosophy, University of Manitoba, 1956-59, University of Massachusetts, 1961-62; Part-time Lecturer, University of Oxford & Exeter, 1963-70; In-Service Tutor, Berkshire LEA, 1966-70; HM Inspector, 1970; Staff Inspector, 1975; Chief Inspector, 1981-86; Freelance Journalist, Newspapers, Radio & TV. *Publications:* 3 Textbooks for training of teachers & youth workers; numerous articles in professional journals. *Memberships:* Economic and Social Research Council; Director, Institute of Development Studies; Education Advisory Committee, Independent Broadcasting Authority; Council of Open College; Examinations Council of Royal Society of Arts; Director, South Bank Technopark. *Honour:* Hon. Fellow, College of Preceptors, Fellow Royal Society of Arts. *Hobbies:* Music; Walking. *Address:* South Bank Polytechnic, Borough Road, London SE1 0AA, England.

PERVAN HEURTLEY Jasna, b. 24 Sept. 1914, Split, Yugoslavia. Simultaneous Court Interpreter. m. (1) John Ames, 1944; (2) Richard Heurtley, 1951. 1 son. *Education:* JD, University of Zagreb, Yugoslavia, 1941; MLS, Columbia University, New York, USA, 1955; MA Art History, Institute of Fine Arts, New York University. *Appointments include:* Librarian, New York Public Library, 1955-57; Metropolitan Museum of Art, 1957-65; The Parapsychology Foundation, New York City, 1965-67; Staff Librarian, New York Academy of Medicine, 1967-70; Librarian-documentalist, Dag Hammarskjold Library, United Nations, 1970-73; Chief translator, Federal Reserve Bank, New York City, 1974-78; Freelance Simultaneous Court Interpreter, 1978-. *Publications:* Numerous articles to professional journals. *Memberships:* Association des Professeurs Francais; the English Speaking Union; Special Libraries Association; American Association of Language Specialists. *Hobbies:* Swimming; Hiking; Jogging; World affairs; Music; Theatre; Children in Need. *Address:* 16 East 98th Street, Apt 5A, New York, NY 10029, USA.

PETEL Phyllis May, (nee Hawley), b. 16 Sept. 1910, Nottingham, England. International Civil Servant (retired). m. Max Petel, 25 May 1945. *Education:* BSc Economics, Honours, University of London; Private reading, 1941-45. *Appointments:* Civil Servant, POED Nottingham, 1926- 40; Assistance Board, 1940-45; Marshall Plan, US Embassy, Paris, France, 1949- 53; OEEC/OECD Administrator, 1955-75. *Publications:* Translation: Murder in Mexico by Julian Gorkin, 1948. *Memberships:* Committee 1955- 75, Vice President, 1967-70, 1972-75, President, 1970-72, OECD Staff Association; Vice President, 1975-77, President, 1977-, OECD Retired Staff Association; International Committee, Coordinated Staff Associations. *Hobbies:* Gardening; Sewing; Art; Travel; Languages. *Address:* 279 bis route de l'Empereur, 92500 Rueil Malmaison, France.

PETERMAN Donna Cole, b. 9 Nov. 1947, St Louis, Missouri, USA. Businesswoman. m. John A. Peterman, 7 Feb. 1970. *Education:* BJ, Journalism, University of Missouri, 1969; MBA. University of Chicago, 1984. *Appointments:* Manager, Employee Communications, Sears Merchandise Group, 1975-80; Director, Public Affairs & Marketing Communications, Serco Real Estate Group 1980-82, Corporate Communications 1982-85, Sears, Roebuck & Company; Senior Vice President & Director, Corporate Communications, Dean Witter Financial Services Group Inc, 1985-. *Publications:* Feature articles, Atlanta Magazine, 1975. *Memberships:* IABC; PRSA; Various community organisation. *Honours:*

Leadership Atlanta, 1978; Numerous IABC awards, chapter & region, 1976-80. *Hobbies:* Sailing; Skiing; Bridge; Reading. *Address:* Dean Witter Financial Services Group Inc, 101 Barclay Street, 22nd Floor, New York, NY 10007, USA.

PETERS Evelyn Jonez, b. 25 Mar. 1927, Anchorage, Alaska, USA. Artist; Painter. m. (1) Curtis Gordon Chezem, 29 Sept. 1945 (div. 1956), (2) Frederick W. Peters, 30 May 1958. 1 son, 1 daughter. *Education:* University of Oregon, 1945-50; Oregon State University, 1956. *Appointments:* Los Alamos Scientific Laboratory, 1958-70; EG&G, Los Alamos, 1970-71; Self-employed, home art studio, Taxas, 1971-; Official Coast Guard artist, 1988-. *Creative works include:* 800 paintings in private, corporate, museum, gallery collections, USA & abroad; Several limited edition prints (paintings), Forever Yesterday, Granbury Station, Journey to Yesterday, Prairie Peddler; Cover, Independent Cattlemen journal, 1983. *Memberships:* Past secretary, Highland Lakes Arts Council; Past board chairman, Buchanan Arts & Crafts Gallery; Past president, Highland Arts Guild; National Museum of Women in Arts; Texas Women Western Artists; Hill Country Arts Foundation; Llano Fine Arts; Emerald Empire Art Association; Cowboy Artists of America Museum. *Honours include:* 1st prizes, paintings, 1981, 1985 (2), 1987, 1988; 1st prize & purchase award, 1983 and 1988; Best of Show, 1981. Also: Olin-Matheson Marine Safety Award, 1968; Certificates of appreciation, US Coast Guard Auxiliary National Commodores, 1969, 1970. *Hobbies:* Amateur naturalist & historian; Boating; Fishing; Gardening; Reading; Continuing study of art; Giving demonstrations & workshops for art groups. *Address:* 406 North Lake Drive, Granite Shoals, Texas 78654, USA.

PETERS Frances Barbara, b. 8 Nov. 1936, Lowell, Massachusetts, USA. Research Textile Scientist. m. Frank C Peters, 6 Jan. 1963. 1 son, 1 daughter. *Education:* BS, Textile Chemistry, Lowell Technological Institute, 1961; Postgraduate study, University of Missouri, 1974-75; MS, Plastics, University of Lowell, 1978. *Appointments:* Technical Director, Testing Division, 1974-79, Visiting Lecturer, 1978-79, University of Lowell; Manager, Fabrics Laboratory, NIKE Inc, Exeter, New Hampshire, 1979-81; Research Textile Technologist, US Army Research & Development Laboratories, Natick, Massachusetts, 1981-85; Director, Finishes Fibre and Fabric, Foss Manufacturing Co, Haverhill, Massachusetts, 1985-86; Consultant, 1986-. *Publications:* Contributor of articles to professional journals. *Memberships:* Textile Institute, Manchester, England, 1982; American Association Textile Chemists & Colourists, Corporate Representative, 1970-77, ASTM, Senior Member, TAPPI; American Association for Textile Technology, ex-council, 1980-, Secretary, 1982-84, Chairman, 1984-86; Colonial Treasure Hunters Association, EDitor, 1983-. *Honours:* Sustained Superior Performance, US Army R & D Centre, 1983; Outstanding Service and Interest, AAT 1986; ASTM Frank W Reinhart Award, 1982; Textile Institute Chartered Textile Technologist, 1982. *Hobbies:* Metal detecting; Archaeology; Museums; Travelling. *Address:* 12 Blodgett Street, Lowell, MA 01851, USA.

PETERS Mary Elizabeth, b. 6 July 1939, Halewood, Liverpool, England. Managing Director, Health Club. *Education:* Diploma, Belfast College of Domestic Science. *Appointments:* Teacher, Domestic Science, Graymount Girls Secondary School, 1960-64; Managing Director, Mary Peters Health Club. *Publications:* Mary P, autobiography, 1974. *Memberships:* Sports Council (GB) 1987-; Sports Council of Northern Ireland; BBC Broadcasting Council for Northern Ireland; Team Manager, British Womens Athletics Team, 1979-84. *Honours:* MBE, 1973; DSc., Honorary, New UnIvErsity of Ulster, 1974. *Hobbies:* Home Crafts; Keeping Fit. *Address:* 37 Railway Street, Lisburn, County Antrim, Northern Ireland.

PETERSON Amelia Martha (Mickie) Wyckoff, b. 22 Feb. 1942, Tallapoosa County, USA. Professional I Teacher; City Council Lady. m. William Theodis Peterson Jr, 16 May 1964. 1 daughter, Patrice. *Education:* Tuskegee Institute, 1964 & 1972; Ball State University, 1979; Auburn University, 1987. *Appointments:* Tuskegee Institute, 1965; Alabama Industrial School 1966-67; Auburn City Schools, 1969-. *Memberships:* Auburn City Teachers Association, President; Alpha Kappa Alpha Sorority, Tamiouchous and Philacter; Kappa Delta Pi, National Honour Society; Clerk/ Treasurer, Mount Olive Missionary Baptist Church. *Honours:* Outstanding Young Women of America, 1974; Outstanding Elementary Teachers of America, 1974; Distinguished Educator, Tuskegee Institute School of Education, 1975. *Hobbies:* Playing Scrabble; Duplicate Bridge; Rook; Disco Dancing; Walking, daily 3-1/2 miles; Baking; Barbecuing; Reading. *Address:* 2805 Rainbow Drive, PO Box 150, Tuskegee, AL 36083, USA.

PETERSON CarolAnn, b. 13 Mar. 1949, Miami, Arizona, USA. Legislative Advocate. *Education:* Bachelor, Political Science, 1975; Master, Public Admin. 1983. *Appointments:* Corporate Fundraiser, Los Angeles National Organization for Women, Los Angeles, 1984; Executive Director, Gender Gap Action Campaign (Anti-Reagan Campaign), Los Angeles, 1984; Legislation Analyst, Los Angeles Commission for Women/ Legislation Committee, Los Angeles, 1987-; Legislative Advocate, California Federation of Business and Professional Women, Sacramento, 1987-; Group Administrator, Hughes Aircraft Company, El Segundo, California, 1985-. *Publications:* She Could Be Your Sister, Rape and the Paramedic Response, 1983; Loyola Marymount University, Brochure, 1983. *Memberships:* Business and Professional Women: District Legislation Chair, 1986-87, 1987-88; (Local Organization) President, 1988-89, 1st Vice President/President-Elect, 1987-88, 2nd Vice President/Program Chair, 1986-87, Legislation Chair, 1985-86, Charter Member of Local, 1985; National Organization for Women, Los Angeles Chapter Speaker's Bureau, 1981-84; YWCA; National Council of Jewish Women; Women For; Forward Looking Strategies Coalition; California Women in Higher Education, Vice President, Legislation, 1980; California Women in Government; American Civil Liberties Union; Planned Parenthood; Board of Directors, Westside Fair Housing Council, 1986-87. *Honours:* YWCA Outstanding Young Woman Recipient, 1987; Achievement Award, Hughes Aircraft, 1987. *Hobbies:* Golf; Tennis; Watching Pro Football and Pro Baseball; Flying; Playing Trivial Pursuit. *Address:* 8717 Delgany Ave., Playa del Rey, CA 90293, USA.

PETERSON CarolAnn, b. 13 Mar. 1949, Miami, Arizona, USA. Legislative Advocate. *Education:* AA, Liberal Arts, Marymount College, Palos Verdes, California, 1973; Bachelor's degree, Political Science, 1975, MPA, 1983, Loyola Marymount University, Los Angeles. *Appointments:* Corporate Fundraiser, Los Angeles National Organization for Women, California, 1984; Executive Director, Gender Gap Action Campaign, Los Angeles, 1984; Group Administrator, Hughes Aircraft Company, Electro-Optical and Data Systems Group, El Segundo, California, 1985-88; Legislative Advocate, California Federation of Business and Professional Women, Los Angeles and Sacramento, 1987-; Legislative Analyst, Los Angeles County Commission for Women, 1987-; Community Speaker, Proposition 100, Woodward and McDowell, San Francisco, California, 1988; Administrative Assistant, Graduate School of Education, University of California, Los Angeles, 1988-; California State Senate Task Force on Family Relations Court, Sacramento, 1989. *Publication:* She Could Be Your Sister: Rape and the Paramedic Response, 1983. *Memberships:* Business and Professional Women, various offices including local President 1988-89; National Organization for Women, Speaker's Bureau Chair 1981-84; YWCA; National Council of Jewish Women; Women For; Forward Looking Strategies Coalition; Coalition for Family Equity; California Women in Higher Education, Vice-President 1980; California Women in Government; League of Women Voters; California Abortion Rights Action League; Planned Parenthood; Westside Fair Housing Council, Board of Directors 1985-86; Board of Directors, Los Angeles Friends of the Los Angeles City Commission on the Status of Women. *Honours:* Outstanding Young woman, YWCA, 1987; Achievement Award, Hughes Aircraft Company, 1987. *Address:* 8717 Delgany Avenue, Playa del Rey, CA 90293, USA.

PETERSON CarolAnn, b.13 Mar 1949, Miami, Arizona, USA. Legislative Advocate. *Education:* AA, Liberal Arts, Marymount College, Palos Verdes, California, USA, 1973; BSc, Political Science, 1975, MPA, 1983, Loyola Marymount University, Los Angeles, California, USA. *Appointments:* Corporate Fundraiser, Los Angeles National Organization for Women, Los Angeles, Jan-Jun 1984; Executive Director, Gender Gap Action Campaign, Los Angeles, Jul-Dec 1984; Legislative Analyst, Los Angeles County Commission for Women, Legislation Committee, Los Angeles, 1987- ; Group Administrator, Hughes Aircraft Company, Electro-Optical and Data Systems Group, El Segundo, California, 1985-88; Board of Directors, Los Angeles City Commission on the Status of Women, Los Angeles, 1988-; Community Speaker, Proposition 100 (Nov 1988 Ballot) Woodward and McDowell, San Francisco, Calilfornia, 1988; Legislative Advocate, California Federation of Business and Professional Women, Los Angeles/Sacramento, 1987-. *Publication:* She Could Be Your Sister: Rape and the Paramedic Response, California Fire Chiefs Magazine, 1983. *Memberships include:* Business and Professional Women; National Organization for Women; YWCA; National Council of Jewish Women; League of Women Voters. *Honours:* YWCA Outstanding Young Woman Recipient, 1987; Achievement Award, Hughes Aircraft Company, 1987. *Hobbies:* Gourmet cooking; Flying; Tennis; Watching football and baseball; Reading mystery novels. *Address:* Peterson Consulting, 8717 Delgany Avenue, 202, Playa del Rey, CA 90293, USA.

PETERSON Charlotte M, b. 2 Sept. 1946, California, USA. Psychologist. m. Dr Carl Verner Peterson, 22 June 1974. 1 son, 1 daughter. *Education:* BA 1968, MA 1971, California State University, Long Beach; PhD, University of Oregon, 1980; Oregon Psychologist License, 1982. *Appointments:* Child Therapist, County Mental Health, 1975-76; Instructor and Senior Clinical Supervisor, University of Oregon, 1977-78; Child Therapist, Eugene Psychological Services, 1978-80; Psychologist, Private Practice, 1980-. *Publications:* Doctoral Thesis: The Impact of a Mother - Infant Group Experience on Maternal Adjustment. *Memberships:* Founding Member/President, Eugene Soviet Sister City Committee, 1986-88; Women's Action for Nuclear Disarmament; National organization of Women; International Physicians for Prevention of Nuclear War; Oregon Psychological Association. *Honours:* Invited by Soviet Mayor of Siberia, USSR to establish a sister city relationship between Eugene, Oregon and Irkutsk, USSR, 1988; Created the 25th Soviet-American Sister City Agreement, 1988; Mayor's Award for Outstanding Contributions to the City of Eugene, Oregon, 1989. *Interests:* How more positive parent-child relationships effect level of violence within a society; Observation of family practices, parent-child relationships and maternal infant attachment in 50 countries; Pursuing positive global relationhips to reduce the nuclear threat. *Address:* 1210 Pearl Street, Eugene, Oregon 97401, USA.

PETERSON Connie L, b. 19 Feb. 1946, Superior, Wisconsin, USA. District Court Judge. *Education:* BA, BS (Honours), University of Wisconsin, 1968; JD, University of Colorado, 1975. *Appointments:* Deputy District Attorney, Jefferson County, 1975-77; Assistant Attorney General, National Resources Section, 1979-82; Private Practice of Law, 1982- 84; District Court Judge, 1984-. *Publications:* The Houston Cases, Farm Bureau Magazine, 1983; Crisis in the Criminal Justice System, Esq Magazine, 1986. *Memberships:* Colorado Womens Bar Association, President 1980-81; Denver, Colorado Bar Associations. *Hobbies:* Sailing; Kyaking; Whitewater Rafting; Skiing. *Address:* Denver District Court, City & County Building, Denver, CO 80202, USA.

PETERSON Jeannie Ellen, b. 18 Feb. 1940, Traverse City, Michigan, USA. United Nations Officer. *Education:* BS, Journalism, Medill School of Journalism, Northwestern University, Illinois, 1962; MS, Journalism, 1963. *Appointments:* Freelance Travel Writer, Europe, 1963-67 and 1970-71; Advertising writer, McCann Erickson, San Francisco, 1968-69; Assistant Editor, AMBIO, International Journal of the Human Environment, Royal Swedish Academy of Sciences, Stockholm, 1972-77, Editor-in-Chief 1978-81; Deputy Chief, Information and External Relations, UN Population Fund, NYC, 1981-85, Senior Information Policy Officer, 1985-86; UNFPA Country Director (Philippines), Manila, 1986-; Director, Public Information Center on Consequences of Nuclear War, Washington, DC, 1984; Editor: The Aftermath: The Human and Biological Consequences of Nuclear War, 1983. *Publications:* Contributor of numerous articles to professional journals. *Memberships:* Advisory Committee, Conf Medical Implications of Nuclear War, US National Academy of Sciences, 1985; Swedish Sci Journalism Assoc, Chairman of organizing Committee, 1980; Club of Rome, 1984. *Hobbies:* Skiing; Scuba-diving; Photography; Travel. *Address:* UNFPA/UNDP, P.O. Box 7285, ADC, Mia Road, Pasay City, Manila, Philippines.

PETERSON Kathleen (Kathy), Marie James, b. 11 Apr. 1951, Burlington, Colorado, USA. Senior Vice President, Commercial Property Mangement Division. m. Kent M Peterson, 9 May 1981. 1 daughter. *Education:* Business Administration, Colorado State University, 1970-73; Real Estate & Business, Colorado University, 1979-81. *Appointments:* United Banks of Colorado, 1978-83; Silverado Banking, 1983-84; Property Manager 1984-85, Vice President-Leasing, 1985-86, Vice President, Property Mgt 1986-88, Senior Vice President 1988-, Field Real Estate Co. *Memberships:* BDMA-building Owners & Mgrs Assoc (Educational Cont, 1987-89); BOMI-Building Owners & Mgrs Intl; SORPA-Society of Real Property Admin; Denver Board of Realtors; Women in Commercial Real Estate. *Honours:* Governor Appointment to Colorado Business for Energy Conservation (Secretary), 1982-83; Board of Directors, Cherry Creek North, Executive Committee, Treasurer, 1989-91; Real Property Administrator (RPA), 1988. *Hobbies:* Porcelain painting; Home renovation; Antiques; Art collecting; Music, piano; Gardening. *Address:* 1150 Lafayette Street, Denver, Colorado 80218, USA.

PETERSON Marilyn Ethel, (Smith), b. 18 June 1926, Sutton. Freelance Writer. m. Donald R. Peterson, 18 June 1955, 2 sons, 2 daughters. *Education:* BA, Clark University, 1947; AM, Education, Clark University, 1968. *Appointments:* Reporter, Feature Writer, Worcester Telegram, 1945-56; Freelance Writer, 1959-. *Publications:* It's Nifty to Be Fifty, 1985; Sixty's Fine if You Look Thirtynine, 1987; articles in many newspapers, journals and magazines; Organizing co-ordinator, Oxford Ecumenical Food Shelf. *Memberships:* Professional Member, National Writer's Clulb, USA; Daughters of the American Revolution. *Hobbies:* Music; Costume Design; Gardening; Cooking. *Address:* North Oxford, MA, USA.

PETERSON Patti Lynn, b. 3 Nov. 1953, Stambaugh, Michigan, USA. Neurologist. m. John Holliday, 24 Aug. 1974 (div. 1985), 2 sons. *Education:* BSc, Northern Michigan University, 1975; MD, Wayne State University, 1980. *Appointments:* (Current) Assistant Professor, Neurology, Wayne State University; Chief of Neurology, Detroit Receiving Hospital. *Publications include:* Book, Basic Neurology; Numerous articles, papers. *Memberships include:* American Medical Association; American Medical Women's Association; American Academy of Neurology; American College of Physicians; American Medical Writers' Association; American Association for Advancement of Science; Society for Neuroscience; American Society for Neurologic Investigation; New York Academy of Sciences; Sigma Xi; American Society for Neurochemistry; Various other Professional Bodies. *Honours:* Outstanding Psychology Graduate & Board of Control Graduate Fellowship 1975,

Outstanding Young Alumni 1984, Northern Michigan University; Sandoz Award, 1984; Fellowship, Muscular Dystrophy Association, 1984-85; Fellow, American College of Physicians, 1988; Various honour societies. *Hobbies:* Metabolic Neurology; Portrait Drawing; Flute, Cello, Guitar. *Address:* Department of Neurology UHC 6E, 4201 St Antoine, Detroit, Michigan 48201, USA.

PETERSON Patti McGill, b. 20 May 1943, Johnstown, Pennsylvania, USA. University President. m. 31 Aug. 1968, 1 son. *Education:* BA, Pennsylvania University, 1965; MA, 1968, PhD, 1974, University of Wisconsin; Postdoctoral studies, Harvard University, 1977. *Appointments:* Vice- President, Academic Services and Planning, State University of New York, Oswego, 1977-80; President, Wells College, 1980-87; President, St Lawrence University, Canton, New York, 1987-. *Publications:* Numerous publications in the areas of political science, public policy, comparative education and higher education. *Memberships:* Vice-Chair, Consortium for Independent Colleges and Universities, 1982-85; Chair, Common Leadership Development and Academic Administration, American Council on Education, 1982- 84; Chair, National Women's College Coalition, 1983-85; President, Association of Colleges and Universities of the State of New York, 1984-86; Commission on National Challenges in Higher Education, 1986-88. *Honours:* Vilas Fellowship, University of Wisconsin, 1967; Carnegie Fellowship, Harvard University, 1977; Doctor of Humane Letters, LeMoyne College, 1983; Distinguished Alumna Award, Pennsylvania State University, 1989. *Hobbies:* Environmental preservation; Tennis; Cycling; Mountain climbing. *Address:* Office of the President, St Lawrence University, Canton, NY 13617, USA.

PETERSON Susan Vietzke, b. 13 Oct. 1960, Oklahoma, USA. Psychology Instructor. m. Alan Peterson, 21 May 1982. *Education:* BA, Sociology, University of Science & Arts, Oklahoma; MA, Human Relations, Univeristy of Oklahoma; PhD, Oklahoma State University. *Appointments:* Assistant Producer, KWTV Channel 9, Oklahoma City, 1981-82; Kindergarten Teacher, McAllen, 1986-87; Psychology Instructor, Texas State Technical Institute, 1987-88. *Creative Works:* Bilingual Guide: Human relations Activities for the Single Parent to Develop More Effective Parent/ Child Relations, 1988; Fear of Success and the Relationship Between Sex and Vocational Choice in Married Students, Doctoral Dissertation, 1984. *Membership:* American Home Economics Association. *Honours:* Outstanding USAO Freshman/Sophomore Student Award, 1978-79; Scholar Leadership Enrichment Programme, University of Oaklahoma, 1979. *Hobbies:* Public Speaking; Research & Grant Writing. *Address:* RR2 Box 100 H, Stratford, OK 74872, USA.

PETRA-BASACOPOL Carmen, b. 5 Sept. 1926, Sibiu, Romania. Composer. m. Alexandru Basacopol, 1962, 1 son. *Education:* BA, Philosophy, Bucharest, 1949; Academy of Music, Bucharest, 1949-56; Doctor of Musical Science, Paris Sorbonne University, 1976. *Appointments:* Professor, Composition, Music Academy, Bucharest, 1962-82; Member, Board of Composers Union, Bucharest, 1968-. *Publications:* L'originalite de la musique roumaine, 1978; Compositions: Concerto for Violin and Orchestra; Concertino for harp, string orchestra and kettle-drums; Chamber Music for: Piano, flute, harp, violin, cello; Sonata for harp and flute, etc; Vocal music; Ballet Music. *Memberships:* SACEM, Paris; Jury Member, Jerusalem 7th Harp Competition, 1979, ROMA Concorsi Internazionali di compozione, Valintino Buchi, 1986. *Honours:* Recipient, honours & awards. *Hobby:* Travel. *Address:* Avenue Dr., Petru Groza No. 14, et I, Bucharest 5, Romania.

PETRE Donna Marie, b. 21 Apr. 1947, Jolier, Illinois, USA. Municipal Court Judge. m. 4 Sept. 1971, 1 son, 1 daughter. *Education:* BA, Clarke College, Dubuque, Iowa; MA, Northwestern University, Evanston, Illinois; HD, Hastings College of Law, University of California, San Francisco. *Appointments:* Judicial Clerk, California

Court of Appeals, 1976-77; Criminal Appeals and Consumer Law, Attorney General's Office, San Francisco, California, 1978-83; Medical Fraud, Attorney General's Office, Sacramento, California, 1983-86; Judge, Yolo County Municipal Court, Woodland, California, 1986-88. *Memberships:* California Judges Association; Judicial Representative on Driving Under the Influence Advisory Committee for Department of Motor Vehicles; Women Lawyers of Sacramento; Association of American University Women, Davis, California; Business and Professional Women, Woodland, California. *Honours:* American Jurisprudence Award in Torts, 1974; Managing Editor, Constitutional Law Quarterly, 1975-76; 1st woman, Municipal Court in Yolo County , 1986; Planning Member and Seminar Leader, California Judges Conference for Municipal Court Judges, 1987; Chosen by Chief Justice of California to Advisory Committee for California Judicial Council on Administration of Justice in Rural Justice, 1988. *Hobbies:* Music (opera), Cross-country skiing. *Address:* Yolo County Municipal Court, 725 Court Street, Woodland, CA 95695, USA.

PETRIDES Charlotte Roberta Ackerman, b. 20 Sept. 1941, Miami, Florida, USA. Interior Designer. m. James T. Petrides, 26 Nov. 1959, 1 son, 2 daughters. *Education:* AA, Atlanta Area Technical School, 1974; AVA, Dekalb College, 1979; BVA, Georgia State University, 1981; Certified Professional Interior Designer, NCIDQ examination, 1983. *Appointments:* Owner, Forte Interior Design, 1974-; Senior project designer, Designers II Inc, 1980-. *Membership:* American Society of Interior Designers. *Honours:* 1st place, Hospitality Design Award, ASID/AMOCO Fibers, 1985; Finalist, ASID Georgia chapter awards, 1987. *Hobbies:* Art; Drawing; Nature studies. *Address:* Designers II Inc, 3690 North Peachtree Road, Suite 100, Atlanta, Georgia 30341, USA.

PETRIE Dorothea Grundy, b. Lawton, Oklahoma, USA. Film Producer. m. Daniel Petrie, 27 Oct. 1946, 2 sons, 2 daughters. *Education:* State University of Iowa, 1943-44; Columbia University, 1944-45; Northwestern University, 1947-48. *Appointments:* Producer, TV Films: Orphan Train, 1979, Angel Dusted, 1980, License to Kill, 1983, Picking Up the Pieces, 1985, Love is Never Silent, 1985; Foxfire, 1987; Producer of Theatre Production, Catholics, Citadel Theatre, Canada, & Hartman Theatre, Connecticut, 1981. *Publications:* Orphan Train, co-author with James Magnuson, 1977-78. *Memberships:* Writers Guild of America West; Producers Guild; Women in Film. *Honours:* Writers Guild, Christopher Award, Film and Advisory Board, Southern California Motion Picture Council for Orphan Train, 1979, Film Advisory Board, Southern California Motion Picture Council, for Angel Dusted, and License to Kill; Christopher Award; Emmy Award for Love is Never Silent. *Address:* Los Angeles, CA 90049, USA.

PETTIS Joyce Owens, b. 14 Mar. 1946, Columbia, North Carolina, USA. Teacher. 1 son. *Education:* BA, 1968; MA, 1973; PhD, 1983. *Appointments:* North Carolina Public Schools, 1968-72; Pitt County Community College, 1972-74; East Carolina University, 1974-85; Department of English, North Carolina State University, Raleigh, 1985-. *Publications:* Difficult Survival: Mothers and Daughters in the Bluest Eye, 1987; Margaret Walker, in Dictionary of Litarary Bibliography, 1988. *Memberships:* College Language Association; National Women's Studies Association; Area Chair for African-American Studies, Popular Culture Association; Board of Directors, North Carolina Writers Network; Modern Language Association. *Honours:* Minority Presence Fellowship, UNC-CH, 1978-80; North Carolina Humanities Committee Grant for Symposium, 1978; Danforth Associate, 1981; UNC Board of Governors Faculty Doctoral Study Award, 1981. *Hobbies:* Reading; Physical exercise; Contemporary jazz; Critical writing. *Address:* Department of English, North Carolina State University, Raleigh, NC 27695, USA.

PETTYJOHN Shirley Ellis, b. 16 Aug. 1935, Liberty, Kentucky, USA. Lawyer; Real Estate Executive. m. Flem

D. Pettyjohn, 24 Sept. 1955, 2 daughters. *Education:* BS 1974, JD 1977, University of Louisville; Admitted, Kentucky Bar, 1978. *Appointments:* President: Universal Development Corporation (Kentucky & Florida), Pettyjohn Inc. (KY & Indiana); Vice president, Continental Investments Group; Senior partner, Pettyjohn, Grant & Turner, 1987-. Also: Vice-chairman, Louisville & Jefferson County Planning Commission, 1971-75; Member, Governor's Conference on Education, 1977; Judicial nominee, 1981. *Memberships include:* American, Kentucky, Louisville Bar Associations; Women Lawyers Association; American Judicature Society; President, Arts Club of Louisville, American Institute of Planners; Past board, offices, Womens Chamber of Commerce; Louisville Ballet Guild; Metropolitan Louisville Womens Political Caucus; Shively Democratic Club; Past Vice President, Jefferson County Democratic Womens Club. *Honours include:* Mayor's certificate of recognition, 1974; Mayor's Fleur de Lys award, 1969-73; Woman of Achievement award, Council of Women Presidents, 1974; Honour societies. *Address:* 6924 Norlynn Drive, Louisville, KY 40228, USA.

PEVEHOUSE Dolores Ray Ferrell, b. 15 Sept. 1928, Corsicana, Texas, USA. Consultant: Peace, Education; Writer. m. Ben B. Ferrell, 2 Oct. 1952, 1 son, 1 daughter. *Education:* BA, Baylor University, 1948; JD, Western State University, College of Law, 1976. Art & design studies, California. *Appointments:* Teacher, Texas & California, 1948-68; President, Executive Director, Women's Law Centres, Orange County (California) & Dallas (Texas), 1975-79. *Creative work:* Books: I, the Christ; The Beloved Disciple; Single Parenting. Also: Pevehouse Programme for Dyslexic Children; Paintings. *Memberships:* Vice President, founder, Peacemakers Inc; President, founder, Sawdust Festival Corporation; Founder, Windward School of Art, Hawaii; Founder, Russian River Festival of Artists, California. *Honours:* High school valedictorian, 1945; Kappa Delta Pi, 1947; 1st prize, painting, Honolulu, 1962; Times Herald Award for Women, 1977; Achievement award, Sawdust Festival, 1967. *Hobbies include:* Founded Peacemakers Inc (Dallas, Texas) 1987, project director for Women's International Peace Meeting, Aug. 1988, Dallas; Painting pictures of the sea. Creating new avenues to peace on earth, 1989, Publishing a newspaper. *Address:* 901 South Main, New London, Texas 75682, USA.

PFAFF Lucie, b. 17 Sept. 1929, Stuttgart, Germany. Professor of Business & Economics. m. Hans Pfaff, 15 May 1954, deceased. 1 son. *Education:* BA, Pace University, 1968; MA 1970, PhD 1972, New York University; MBA, Fairleigh Dickinson University, 1981; DBA, International Graduate School, 1986. *Appointments:* Lecturer (German), New York University, Fairleigh Dickinson University, 1971-77; Academic Recorder, 1977-80, Lecturer (economics), 1980-82, Fairleigh Dickinson University; Associate Professor (Business & Economics), College of Mt St Vincent, 1982-. *Publications:* The Devil in TH Mann's Dr Faustus and P Valery's Mon Faust, 1976; The American and German Entrepreneur: Economic and Literary Interplay, 1988. *Memberships:* American Association of Teachers of German; Modern Language Association; Faust Society (Germany); American Marketing Association; American Marketing Educators; International Studies Association. *Honours:* University Scholarships, 1969-71, Valery's Day Award, 1973, New York University; Magna cum laude, Academic Excellence Award, 1968, Honor Society, Pace University. *Hobbies:* Tennis; Swimming; Skiing; Travel. *Address:* Department of Business/ Economics, College of Mt St Vincent, Riverdale, NY 10471, USA.

PFEUFFER Sylvia Reichel, b. 28 Feb. 1949, San Antonio, Texas, USA. Chief Executive Officer, Medical Record Consulting Service. m. 17 Dec. 1977. 1 daughter. *Education:* Accredited Record Technician, American Medical Record Association, 1975-77; BS, Business Administration, 1982; Post- graduate Work, South West Texas State University, 1983-84. *Appointments:*

Supervisor, Word Processing Center, 1972-76; Health Record Analyst 1976-78, Director, Medical Records 1978-84, Santa Rosa Medical Center; Division Director, San Antonio Children's Center, 1984-. *Publications:* Editor, Journal of the Tx Medical Record Association, 1983; National Publication of The Admitting Office and Diagnostic Related Groups, 1982; Back to the Basics, 1983. *Memberships:* Delegate for the State of Texas at: The National Quality Assurance Assoc Annual Meeting; Aermican Medical Record Association; Tx Medical Record Association, Editor of Monthly Journal and Committee Member for Public Relations; National Assoc of Quality Assurance Association, 1982- 84, Associate Editor of Monthly Journal. *Honours:* Honorary Judge, National History Fair, 1987; Career Day Representative, 1977-78; Lecture on Quality Assurance, Incarnate Word College, 1976; Management Practicum Instructor, Incarnate Word College, 1984; Speaker for Explorers Club, 1979-83; Instructor of Sanyo Program 1978-83; Dean's List for academic Achievement, 1980-82. *Hobbies:* Research on Texas history; Reading; Writing; Bowling and other sports. *Address:* 7335 Karankawa, San Antonio, TX 78223, USA.

PFLAUM Melanie Sophia, b. 12 Apr. 1909, St Louis, Missouri, USA. Novelist. m. 1 Feb. 1930. 3 sons. *Education:* PhD, University of Chicago, 1929; Cours de Civilization, University of Paris at Sorbonne, France, 1930; Honours Course, University of London, England. *Appointments:* Professor of English, Interamerican University, San German, Puerto Rico, 1959-69; Lecturer, Department of English, Northwestern University, Evanston, Illinois, 1958. *Publications:* 13 books, 12 novels. Bolero; Windfall; The Insiders; The Gentle Tyrants; Ready By Wednesday; The Maine Remembered; Lili; The Old Girls; Shadow of Doubt; A Walk-On Part (nonfiction). French editions: Fleuve Noire, Paris; German ed: Constanza, Hamburg. 25 short stories and articles in numerous magazines; NEA Correspondence (Scripps Howard Syndicate) in Europe; Educational films; Encyclopedia Britannica; Science Series for WLS (Chicago), This Wonderful World. *Memberships:* Arts Club, Chicago and London; Society of Women Geographers; American Association of University Professors; Soc Midland Authors. *Hobbies:* Travel; Swimming; Archaeology. *Address:* 323 El Tosalet, Javea (Alicante), Spain.

PFUND Rose Toshiko, b. 22 July 1929, Honolulu, Hawaii, USA. Associate Director. m. 24 Dec. 1954, divorced 1987. 2 sons, 3 daughters. *Education:* BA 1951, MEd 1978, University of Hawaii; PhD, University of Pittsburgh, 1985. *Appointments:* Scientific Technical Editor, Water Resources Research Center, 1966-73, Coordinator of Information, Sea Grant College Program, 1973-79, Acting Associate Director, Sea Grant College Program, 1979-84, Associate Director, Sea Grant College Program, 1984-, University of Hawaii. *Publications:* Contributor to numerous conference proceedings on coastal and ocean resources; professional journals; Marine education program for children, Makahiki Kai (festival of the sea); *Memberships:* American Society for Public Administration, Member National Council, Committees, Regional Liaison; Academy of Political Science; Western Government Res Association; Hawaii State PTA, President 1976-78; National PTA, Member Board of Directors, 1976-78; National Caucus Asian American Women, Founder, President 1977-80. *Honour:* Alumnus of the Year, Farrington High School Honolulu, 1967. *Hobbies:* Travel; Theatre; The arts. Research interests: Risk management of coastal and ocean recreation activities, fishery management. *Address:* University of Hawaii Sea Grant College Program, 1000 Pope Road, MSB 220, Honolulu, Hawaii 96822, USA.

PHELPS Edna Mae, b. 12 June 1920, Tulsa, Oklahoma, USA. Homemaker; Politician. m. Joe Elton Phelps, 10 Sept. 1942. 2 sons. *Education:* BA Journalism 1942, AA Liberal Arts 1940, Oklahoma State University; Graduate work, Oklahoma University, 1950. *Appointments:* Oklahoma Live Stock News, 1942-

45; Tulsa Chamber of Commerce, 1945-46; Freelance Writer. *Memberships:* President, Oklahoma Federation Demo Women, 1968-78; Ok's Demo National Committee Woman, 1973-84; Oklahoma State Election Board, Chair, 1969-76; Oklahoma Member Demo Charter Commission, 1972- 74; Delegate to Demo National Conventions, 1968, 1972, 1976, 1980, 1984; Delegate to Mid Term Demo Conventions, 1972, 1974, 1978. *Honours:* Oklahoma Presidential Elector, 1984; Oklahoma State University Board of Regents, 1983-88; Oklahoma Women's Hall of Fame, 1986; Oklahoma Centennial Commission, 1988-89; Named one of Women of the 80's in New York, 1976; Oklahoma Commission Status of Women, 1978-82; Co Chair, Oklahoma ERA, 1976-82. *Hobbies:* Collect Political Buttons; Fishing; Boating; Bridge; Reading; Promoting Library and Athletics at Oklahoma State University. *Address:* RT No 4, Box 298, Seminole, OK 74868, USA.

PHILIP Beverly Khnie, b. 27 Dec. 1948, New York, USA. Physician; Anesthesiologist. m. James Henry Philip, 12 Mar. 1972, 2 sons. *Education:* BA, Queens College, 1969; MD, Upstate Medical Centre SUNY, 1973; National Board Examiners, 1974; American Board of Anesthesiology, 1978; FACA, 1978. *Appointments:* Anesthesiologist: Boston Hospital for Women, 1977-80, Brigham and Women's Hospital, 1980-; Organization, Day Surgery Unit, BWH, 1980; Director, Day Surgery Unit, BWH, 1981-. *Memberships:* Massachusetts Medical Society; American Society of Anesthesiologists, Committee on Ambulatory Surgical Care, 1986-; Federated Ambulatory Surgery Association, Board of Directors, 1986-; Society for Ambulatory Anesthesia, 1st Vice President, 1985-. *Honours:* Editorial Board, Ambulatory Anesthesia; Recipient, various Research Grants; Assistant Professor, Anaesthesia, Harvard Medical School, 1985-. *Hobbies:* Skiing: Senior Member, National Ski Patrol; Scuba Diving; Dancing. *Address:* 75 Francis St., Boston, MA 02115, USA.

PHILLIPS Barbara Ruth, b. 30 Oct. 1936, Kansas City, Missouri, USA. Insurance Official. m. Wayne A. Phillips, 29 Feb. 1964, 1 son. *Education:* BS, Education, University of Missouri, 1961; Life Teaching Certificate, Missouri; Insurance Licence, California & Tennessee; Certified Professional Insurance Woman, 1986. *Appointments include:* Secondary school teacher, Missouri & California, 1958-68; Underwriting Liaison, San Francisco, 1963-64; Claim Examiner, Seattle, 1964-65; Claims Liaison 1965-66, Adjusters Casualty Claims 1968-70, Casualty Claims Administrator 1970-74, Los Angeles; Regional Assistant to Superintendent of Agencies, Republic National Life Insurance Company, LA, 1974-82; Corporate Risk Manager, Rogers Group Inc 1983-87, Director, Risk Management, Equicor Equitable HCA Corportion 1987-, Nashville, Tennessee. *Memberships include:* National Association of Insurance Women; American Society of Safety Engineers; Office, Risk Insurance Managers' Society; Republican National Committee; President, Encino Historical Society; Various other community organisations. *Hobbies:* Travel; Gardening; Arts; Writing; Reading. *Address:* Equicor Inc, 16th Floor, 1801 West End Avenue, Nashville, Tennessee 37203, USA.

PHILLIPS Cherry Ann, b. 8 Apr. 1942, Texas, USA. Manager. m. Paul Robert, 21 Nov. 1973, 2 sons, 1 step-son, 3 daughters, 3 step-daughters. *Education;* numerous management courses. *Appointments:* Field Underwriter, New York Life Ins. Co., 1973-81; Insurance Manager, New York Life Ins. Co., 1981-87; Financial Services Manager, Red River Federal S & L, 1987-. *Publications:* Numerous articles in professional journals. *Memberships Include:* National Association of Life Underwriters; Chairperson, Founder, Environmental Quality Advisory Board; Founder, President, Environmental Improvement Organization. *Honours Include:* Keep America Beautiful Award, 1971; Named to 8 Member Advisory Panels Advising Chief Executives of a Marketing Team. *Hobbies:* Swimming; Tennis; Volleyball; Bridge. Grandchildren. *Address:* 6931 NW Eisenhower Drive, Lawton, OK 73505, USA.

PHILLIPS Constance Anne Gaiser, b. 11 Jan. 1949, Toledo, Ohio, USA. Officer; Attorney. m. Ronald Edward Phillips, 20 Aug. 1988, 1 son, 1 daughter. *Education:* BS, Bowling Green State University, 1972; JD, University of Louisville, 1978; LL.M., 1988. *Memberships:* Kentucky Bar Association; Army Court of Military Review; Eastern Stars; Rouche de Bouche; Beta Lambda. *Honours:* Life Member, Pi Omega Pi, 1971; Army Achievement Medal, 1984; Meritorious Service Medal, 1987. *Hobbies:* Piano; Sports; Crafts; Reading. *Address:* Office of the Staff Judge Advocate, Fort Dix, NJ 08640, USA.

PHILLIPS Geneva Ficker, b. 1 Aug. 1920, Staunton, Illinois, USA. Editor. m. James Emerson Phillips, 6 June 1955, deceased 1979. *Education:* BS, Journalism, University of Illinois, Urbana, 1942; MA, English Literature, University of California, Los Angeles, 1953. *Appointments:* City Desk, Chicago Journal of Commerce, 1942-43; Editorial Assistant Patent Disclosures, Radio Research Laboratory, Harvard University, 1943-45; Assistant Editor, Administrative Publications, University of Illinois, 1946-47; Editorial Assistant, Quarterly of Film Radio and TV, University of California Press, 1952-53; Managing Editor, The Works of John Dryden, Dept. of English University of California, Los Angeles, 1964-. *Memberships:* Board of Directors, University Religious Conference, Los Angeles, 1979-; Association of Academic Women; Deans Council, College of Letters & Science; Renaissance Society of Southern California; Conference of Christianity and Literature; Friends of the Huntington Library; Friends of UCLA Library; Society of Mayflower Descendants. *Honours:* UCLA Teaching Fellow, English, 1950-53; UCLA Research Fellow, English, 1954-55. *Address:* Dept of English, 2225 Rolfe Hall, University of California, Los Angeles, CA 90024, USA.

PHILLIPS Jean, b. 20 Aug. 1949, Bishop Auckland, England. Writer; Writing Tutor. m. John Phillips, 21 Apr. 1976, 1 daughter. *Education:* BA, Durham University, 1970. *Appointments:* Director of Studies, Academy of Children's Writers. *Publications:* Writing for Children; various children's stories; sundry business guides. *Honour:* Fellow, World Literary Academy. *Address:* Brockerscliffe,, Witton Le Wear, Bishop Auckland, Co. Durham, England.

PHILLIPS Marlene Elaine, b. 25 Dec. 1939, Brooklyn, New York, USA. Psychotherapist; Hypnotherapist. 1 son, 2 daughters. *Education:* BA 1981, MS 1983, California State University, Fullerton; PhD, in progress, United State International University. *Appointments:* Private Practice, Paddlobook Counselling and Psychotherapy Associates. *Publications:* Articles published for Orange County South and South County News Magazines. *Memberships:* American Psychological Association; California State Psychological Association; Orange County Psychological Association; California Association of Marriage & Family Therapists; Am Soc of Clinical Hypnosis; Soc of Behavioural Medicine; Soc of Psychosomatic Medicine. *Honours:* BA degree with honours; Member of Psychology National Honour Society, Psi Chi. *Hobbies:* Music, choral singing; Horseback riding; Reading; Theatre going; Board member, Adam Walsh Child Resource Center. *Address:* 23521 Paseo De Valencia No 302A, Laguna Hills, California 92653, USA.

PHILLIPS Sian, b. Bettws, Wales. Actress. m. Robin Sachs, 30 Dec. 1979. *Education:* BA, honours, Cardiff College, University of Wales; Gold Medallist, Royal Academy of Dramatic Art; Fellow, University College, Cardiff, 1982; Hon.DLitt, University of Wales, 1984. *Appointments:* Films Include: Beckett, 1964; Young Cassidy, 1964; Laughter in the Dark, 1969; Goodbye Mr Chips, 1969; Murphy's War, 1970; Under Milk Wood, 1972; Dune, 1984; A Painful Case; Beyond All Reason; Valmont, 1988; West End Plays: Night of the Iguana; Man and Superman; Ride a Cock Horse; Pal Joey (Musical); Dear Liar; Major Barbara; Peg; Gigi (Musical); Thursdays Ladies, 1987; Gentle Jack; Maxibules; Hedda Gabler; You Never Can Tell; The Lizard on the Rock;

Epitaph for George Dillon; The Burglar; The Gay Lord Quey; Brel, musical, 1987-88; TV: Shoulder to Shoulder, BBC series; How Green Was My Valley, BBC series; Crime and Punishment, BBC series; Tinker Tailor Soldier Spy, and Smiley's People, both BBC Series; Barriers, Tyne Tees Series; Heartbreak House, BBC; Lady Windermere's Fan, BBC; Vanity Fair, Serial; I Claudius, BBC Serial; Boudicca, Thames TV Serial; Oresteia, BBC TV; The Garden of Loneliness, Granada; The Other Man, Granada; How Many Miles To Babylon, BBC; Sean, RTE Serial; Murder on the Exchange, serial; Shadow of the Noose, BBC, 1988; Snow Spider, HTV Serial, 1988; Records: Single, Bewitched, Bothered and Bewildered; LP, Pal Joey; LP, Peg; LP, Night of 100 Stars; LP, I Remember Mama. *Publications:* Sian Phillips's Needlepoint, 1987; contributor to various journals and magazines. *Memberships:* Welsh Arts Council; Governor, St David's Trust. *Honours:* BAFTA Best Actress; Royal TV Society Best Performer for I, Claudius; American Critics Circle Award and US Famous Seven Award, Goodbye Mr Chips; Hon. Fellow Polytechnic of Wales, 1988. *Hobbies:* Gardening; Canvas Embroidery. *Address:* c/o Saraband Limited, 265 Liverpool Road, London N1, England.

PHILLIPS Susan E., b. 23 June 1945, Cambridge, Massachusetts, USA. Executive. *Education:* BA, University of Massachusetts, 1967; Syracuse University, 1967-68; Certificate, Programme for Senior Managers in Government, John F. Kennedy School of Government, Harvard University; MBA, Virginia Polytechnic University, 1985. *Appointments:* Teacher, 1968-72, Chairman, English Department, 1970-72, Newton Public Schools, Newton, Massachusetts; Independent Representative, several textile manufacturers, New York, 1972-76; Director, Research and Publications, The Conservative Caucus Inc, and The Conservative Caucus Research, Analysis and Education Foundation Inc, 1976-82; Expert Consultant, Grants/ Contracts Management, 1982, Director, Intergovernmental and Interagency Affairs, 1982-83, US Department of Education, Washington DC; Director, Institute of Museum Services, Washington DC, 1983-85; Associate Director, Office of Presidential Personnel, The White House, 1985-88; Director of Development, The Corcoran Gallery of Art, Washington DC, 1988-. *Memberships:* National Board, Medical College of Pennsylvania; National Women's Economic Alliance; Executive Women in Government; Ball Committee, Hospital Relief Fund of the Caribbean; Former Member: Advisory Committee on Dependent's Education; Interagency Committee for Physical Fitness and Sports; Federal Advisory Committee on the Arts; President's Committee on the Arts and Humanities; Chairman, Interagency Committee on Women's Business Enterprise, 1986-88. *Address:* The Corcoran Gallery of Art, Seventeenth and New York Avenue, Washington, DC 20006, USA.

PHILLIS Marilyn Hughey, b. 1 Feb. 1927, Kent, Ohio, USA. Artist; Instructor; Juror. m. Richard Waring Phillis, 19 Mar. 1949, deceased 1987, 2 sons, 1 daughter. *Education:* BS, Ohio State University, 1949; Toledo Museum of Art, School of Design, 1961-62; Aquamedia Training with Fred Leach, Jeanne Dobie, Nita Engle, Edward Betts, Glenn Bradshaw, 1967-83. *Appointments:* Chemist, Battelle Memorial Institute, Columbus, 1949-53; Art Instructor, Edison State Community College, Piqua, 1976; Watermedia Instructor, Springfield Art Centre, 1976-84; Watercolour Instructor, Miami University, Oxford, 1982; Watermedia Instructor, Workshops in USA, 1982-. *Creative Works:* Featured in: Painting the Spirit of Nature, by Maxine Masterfield, 1984; Articles in magazines; Illustrator of Western Reserve Magazine, historic Piqua, An Architectural Survey, 1976; Commissions include designing and painting harpsichord soundboard for Ms. Rosalyn Schneider, Mezzo Soprano, Piqua. *Memberships:* various professional organisations. *Honours:* Recipient, many honours and awards including: Ohio Watercolour Society, Award of Excellence, 1986. *Hobbies:* Hiking; Reading; Geneology; Gardening; Music; Drama. *Address:* 72 Stamm Circle, Wheeling, WV 26003, USA.

PHIPATANAKUL Chintana Sirikoranun, b. 2 July 1941, Thailand. Physician. m. Supote, 16 June 1968, 1 son, 1 daughter. *Education:* MD, Chulalongkorn University, Medical School, 1965. *Appointments:* Assistant in Medicine, 1970-72; Medical Director, Student Health, 1972-75, Instructor, Medicine, 1972-77, Assistant Clinical Professor, Internal Medicine, 1977-, St Louis University Medical School, USA; Allergist, Private Practice, 1975-. *Publications:* Several oil paintings & sketches; articles in various journals & magazines including: Thai Naval Medical Journal; New England Journal of Medicine; Annals of Allergy, etc. *Memberships Include:* St Louis Metro Medical Society; Missouri State Allergy Association; Fellow, American Association of Certified Allergists; Fellow, American College of Physicians. *Honours:* Bronze Medal, Internal Medicine, Chulalongeorn University, 1965. *Hobbies:* 1125 Graham Road, Florissant, MO 63031, USA.

PICACHE-ENRIQUEZ Lina Sarah, b. 4 Mar. 1935, Manila, Philippines. Editor; Author. m. Felicisimo P Enriquez Jr, 12 Oct. 1959. 1 son, 5 daughters. *Education:* BSc, Education, University of the Philippines, 1955; MA, Columbia University, New York, USA, 1958; Summer Institute on Children's Literature, Simmons College, Boston, 1977. *Appointments:* President/ Manager, C M Picache Inc, Pawnshops, 1958-; Vice President/Editor, Bookman Publishing House, 1960-; Professor, PWU, 1958-64; Mapua Institute of Tech, 1958-59; University of the East, 1958-84; Director/ Treasurer, Multi-Concept Business, Inc., 1969-; Director/Treasurer, EDLER Universal Trade, 1980-; Director, Capitol Development Corp, 1981-. *Publications:* Editor, Philippine School Life Magazine, 1974-; Author, Easy Steps to English (Gr 3 & 4); Let's Learn Through English (Gr 5 & 6); Exercises in Reading Skills (Kindergarten Gr 6); Reading Skills Series, 1-4; Speech Improvement For More Effective Communication; Effective Communication in English; Acquiring Library Skills (workbook); Reading for Information & Interpretation Skills (workbook); Acquiring Study Skills (Workbook); Developing Skills in Reading (workbook); Interpretation & Critical Reading (workbook); Reading for Enjoyment (workbook); Developing Skills in Critical Reading (workbook). *Memberships:* Women's Management Association of the Philippines; Business and Professional Women's Association of the Philippines; Civic Assembly of Women of the Philippines. *Honour:* College Scholar, Unviersity of the Philippines, 1953. *Hobbies:* Reading; Drama (plays); Concerts; Travel; Music; Jewellery. *Address:* 373 Quezon Avenue, Quezon City, Philippines.

PICARD Barbara Leonie, b. 4 Dec. 1917, Richmond, Surrey, England. Author. *Education:* Matriculation, 1934. *Publications include:* Ransom for a Knight, 1956; Lost John, 1962; One is One, 1965; Young Pretenders, 1966; Twice Seven Tales, 1968; Three Ancient Kings, 1972; Tales of Ancient Persia, 1972; Iliad & Odyssey of Homer, 1986. *Hobbies:* Reading; Opera recordings; Collecting Japanese prints. *Address:* c/o Oxford University Press, Walton Street, Oxford, England.

PICHE Stephanie Emilie, b. 9 Dec. 1959, Hialeah, Florida, USA. Regional Sales Manager. 1 son. *Education:* BS, Univ Nevada, Las Vegas, 1981; Graduated Real Estate School, Utah, 1982; Business Women's Training Institute, 1987. *Appointments:* Lab Asst, Pathology Dept, Sunrise Hospital, Las Vegas, 1978-81; Nurse, Wasatch Med Center, Orem, Utah, 1981-82; Realtor Associate, Centeryzi, 1982-83; Marketing VP, Zion W W Ent, Provo, Utah, 1983-84; Telemarketing Sales 1984, Telemarketing Manager 1985, Outside Sales 1986, Registering 1987-, Digital Tech Intl, Orem, Utah. *Publication:* Article in professional journal, 1985. *Memberships:* Fundraiser, American Cancer Society, 1985; Organized Swimming lessons for local handicapped people, 1985; Director, National Association of Female Executives, 1986-. *Honours:* Honors Graduate from High School, 1977; Dean's List, University of Nevada, 1980-81; Top Sales Person of the Year, 1987 and 1988. *Hobbies:* Snow skiing; Camping; Tennis; Sailing; Reading; Travelling. *Address:* 1100

Hooksett Road Suite 414, Hooksett, New Hampshire 03106, USA.

PICKARD Linda Eileen, b. 22 May 1946, Toronto, Ontario, Canada. Management Consultant. m. Richard S. Laws, 28 Oct. 1978, 1 son, 1 daughter. *Education:* BSc honours, 1968, Diploma in Community Nutrition, School of Hygiene, 1971, MEd, 1977, PhD, Adult Education, Ontario Institute for Studies in Education, 1982, University of Toronto; Diploma in Dietetics, St Joseph's Hospital, 1968. *Appointments:* Therapeutic Dietitian, St Joseph's Hospital, London, Ontario, 1968-69; Research Home Economist, Canada Packers, 1969-70; Community Nutritionist, Etubicoke Health Department, 1971- 77; President, L.E.Pickard Associates, 1977-85; Senior Consultant, Sibson & Co, Toronto, 1986-. *Publications:* Taking Charge: Personal Responsibility for Health (doctoral dissertation), 1982; Unlocking the Potential to Compete in a Deregulated Environment, 1988. *Memberships:* Ontario Institute of Certified Management Consultants; Canadian Association of Women Executives; Canadian Association for Adult Education; Canadian Association for Research in Adult Education; Canadian Home Economics Association; Toronto Home Economics Association; Canadian Organization for Nutrition Education; Chairman, Toronto Nutrition Committee, 1974; Director, Ontario Organization for Nutrition Education, 1984-85; President, Trelawny Home Owners Association, Mississauga, Ontario, 1987-88. *Honours:* 4th Year Honour Award, Innis College, University of Toronto, 1968; Silver Jubilee Scholarship, Canadian Home Economics Association, 1978-79; Social Science and Humanities Research Council Fellowship, 1979-81. *Hobbies:* Tai Chi; Tae Kwon Do; Cross-country skiing; Latest trends in modern physics; Organizational development/business literature. *Address:* Sibson & Company, 40 Dundas Street West, Suite 421, Toronto, Ontario, Canada M5G 2C2.

PICKERING Ava Jane, b. 5 Nov,. 1951, New Castle, Henry County, Indiana, USA. Teacher; President and Administrative Director of Specialized Educational Programming Service Inc. *Education:* BA Social Studies Education, Purdue University, 1974; Certification, Special Education, Brigham Young University, 1976; MS Special Education 1983, PhD Special Education 1989, University of Utah. *Appointments:* Youth Agent, Indiana Cooperative Extensikon Service, 1970-74; CoDirector, Preschool for Gifted Children, 1970- 74; Resource Teacher 1975-77, Self-Contained LD Teacher 1977-85, Salt Lake City School District; Teacher, Granite Community Education, 1974-79; Co Director, Specialized Educational Programming Service, 1976-; Adjunct Clinical Instructor, University of Utah, 1985-88. *Publications:* The comprehension of cartoon humor in learning disabled and nonhandicapped boys, 1987; Test administration I, 1988; Test administration II, 1988; A review of the literature of humor and the learning disabled, 2988. *Memberships:* Council for Exceptional Children: Division of Learning Disabilities; Division of Childhood Communication Disorders; Division of Early Childhood; Division of Teacher Education. Association of Children and Adults with Learning Disabilities; Council for Learning Disabilities; The Orton Dyslexia Society; Delta Kappa Gamma Society International - Alpha Chapter. *Honour:* Fellowship, University of Utah, 1986-88. *Hobbies:* The Arts: Opera, Ballet, Plays etc; Travelling; Cooking. *Address:* 1595 South 2100 East, SLC, UT 84108, USA.

PICKERING EvaJean, b. 5 NOv. 1951, USA. Clinical Instructor; Teacher. *Education:* BA, Purdue University, 1974; MS, 1983, PhD, 1988, University of Utah. *Appointments Include:* Youth Agent, Indian Cooperative Extension Service, 1970-74; Co-Director, 1970-74, Preschool for Gifted Children; Resource Teacher, 1974-82, Self Contained LD Teacher, 1982- 85, Salt Lake City School District; Co-Director, Specialised Educational Programming Service, 1976-; Teacher Assistant, 1986-87, Adjunct Clinical Instructor, 1987-88, University of Utah. *Publications:* Articles in professional journals. *Memberships:* Council for Exceptional Children, various offices. *Honours:* University of Utah Fellowship, 1985-88. *Hobbies:* Singing; Travel; Cooking. *Address:* 1595 South 2100 East, Salt Lake City, UT 84108, USA.

PICKLES RAINER Sheila Maureen, b. 29 Oct. 1944, Hebden Bridge, Yorkshire, England. Managing Director. m. David Rainer, 24 Sept. 1981, 1 son, 1 daughter. *Education:* Penrhos College, Colwyn Bay, Wales, 1952-62; *Appointments:* Assistant to Franco Zeffirelli, 1965-70; Production Manager, BMB Products, 1971-72; Literary Agent, London Management, 1972-75; Managing Director, Penhaligon's Limited, 1975-. *Memberships:* Fellow, Royal Society of Arts. *Honours:* Recipient, Royal Society of Arts Presidential Award for Design Management, 1981. *Hobbies:* Antiques; Gardening; Reading. *Address:* 2 Canonbury Place, London N1, England.

PICMAN Anna Krystina, b. 3 Apr. 1948, Czechoslovakia. Research Scientist. m. Jaroslav Picman, 31 Mar. 1971, 2 sons. *Education:* Diploma, Charles University, Prague, 1971; MSc., 1977, PhD, 1981, University of British Columbia, Canada. *Appointments:* Postdoctoral Fellow, University of British Columbia, 1981; Research Associate, University of Ottawa, 1981; Research Scientist, Agriculture, Canada, 1982-. *Publications:* Over 25 articles in scientific journals. *Memberships:* Phytochemical Society of North America; American Phytopathological Society. *Address:* Plant Research Centre, Agriculture Canada, Ottawa, Ontario, Canada K1A 0C6.

PICONE Regina Maria, b. 27 Mar. 1959, Chicago, Illinois, USA. Lawyer. *Education:* BA magna cum laude, Education major, Spanish and English minor, Southern Methodist University, Dallas, Texas, 1981; JD, Loyola University, University of Chicago School of Law, 1984. *Appointments:* Law Clerk, 1982-84, Lawyer, 1984-86, Jay A.Baier Ltd, Chicago, Illinois; Lawyer, Kasdin & Nathansonson, Chicago, 1986-87; Lawyer, Peter D.Kasdin Ltd, Chicago, 1987-. *Memberships:* Legislatice Committee Member, Illinois Trial Lawyers Association; Tort Litigation Section, Chicago Bar Association; Illinois State Bar Association; ATCA; American Bar Association; Justinian Society of Lawyers. *Honours:* National Register of Outstanding College Graduates, 1977-81; Dean's List, 1977-81; Eastwood Scholarship, 1979-81; Southern Methodist University Academic Scholarship, 1979-81; Dad's Club Scholarship, 1980; Art School Senator, 1977-81, Student Advisor, 1978-79, Resident Assistant, 1978-81; Women's Trial Lawyers Council, 1987. *Hobby:* Tennis. *Address:* 1540 N. State Parkway, Apt 10c, Chicago, IL 60610, USA.

PIERCE Donna Lee, b. 8 Sept. 1950, Wichita Falls, Texas, USA. Research Consultant. *Education:* BA History 1972, MA Art History 1976, Tulane University; PhD, Art History, University of New Mexico (UNM), 1987. Studies, University of Warwick, UK, 1970. *Appointments:* Curator, Spanish Colonial Collections, Museum of International Folk Art, Santa Fe, New Mexico, 1983-87; Research Associate, Palace of Governors, Santa Fe, 1987-; Consultant: Minneapolis Institute of Art 1988-89, Metropolitan Museum of Art, New York 1988-; Faculty, Hispanic Culture Institute, Albuquerque, New Mexico, 1988-. *Publications:* Editor, Vivan Las Fiestas, 1985; Co-author with Eliot Porter, chapter Portraits of Faith, in book Mexican Churches, 1987; Co-author with E. Porter, Mexican Celebrations, book, in press. *Memberships:* Board, Assistant Curator, Spanish Colonial Arts Society; Membership Committee, Historical Society of New Mexico; Southwest Mission Research Centre; Board of Advisers, NM Community Foundation. *Honours:* Fellowships: Samuel H. Kress Foundation, 1978-79, 1979-80; American Association of University Women, 1980-81; Bainbridge Bunting Memorial, 1981- 82. Travel grant, Spain, Colonial New Mexico Historical Foundation, 1987. *Address:* PO Box 8442, Santa Fe, New Mexico 87504, USA.

PIERCE Hilda Herta, b. 8 July 1921, Vienna, Austria.

Artist (painter). m. (1)Charles Rubin, 21 Jan. 1941 (d. 1969), 1 daughter. (2)Norman Pierce, 11 Sept. 1970 (d. 1985). (3)Dr S Thomas Friedman, 1 Feb. 1988. *Education:* Art Institute of Chicago, 1942-44; Ray Vogue School of Design, 1945-46; Lake Forest College, Ill, 1960-62; Study with Oskar Kokoschka, 1962. *Appointments:* Self employed; Taught painting in Highland Park, Illinois; Surburban Fine Art Center, 1955-65; Oldtown Art Center, Chicago, Illinois, 1963-68; Sandburg Village Art Workshop, Chicago, Illinois, 1968-75. *Creative works:* Completed in May 1989, 1294 works on paper (monotypes); Oil paintings and murals for Superliner MS Fantasy of Carnival Cruise Lines, launch date December 1989; One woman and group shows include: Fairweather Hardin Gallery, Chicago; Marshall Field Galleries, Chicago; Old Orchard Art Festivals, Skokie, Ill; ARS Galler Art Institute of Chicago. Publications: Contributor to magazines and newspapers of articles and reproduction of paintings. *Memberships:* Artists Equity, Chicago; The Arts Club of Chicago; North Shore Art League, Wimvetka, Illinois; Owned and operated the Hilda Pierce Gallery, Laguna Beach, California, 1981-85. *Honours:* Exhibited in the ARS Gallery of the Art Institute of Chicago for 27 years; Numerous private and corporate collections in USA, Europe and Japan; Delivered art programs on cruise ships in the Caribbean and Mexican Riviera; Guest lecturer, Art tours to France, Italy, Switzerland and Austria, 1983-85. *Hobby:* Travel. *Address:* Post Office Box 7390, Laguna Niguel, California 92677, USA.

PIERCE Lisa, b. 5 Aug. 1948, Reading, Pennsylvania, USA. Consulting Company Executive. m. Mark L Rutledge, 1 Jan. 1983. *Education:* BA, Hood College, 1970; Postgrad, George Washington University Grad Sch Bus, 1974. *Appointments:* Trade specialist and Economist, Dept Commerce, Washignton, 1973-75; Vice President, George A Suter Associates Inc, Pittsburgh, 1975-81; President, Pierce Suter Associates Inc, Pittsburgh, 1982-. *Memberships:* Board Directors, GAM Lab Fittings Inc; Labomet Inc; Board Directors, Member of Rolling Rock Club. *Hobbies:* Fly fishing; Hunting; Scuba diving. *Address:* 246 Old Forbes Road, Ligonier, PA 15658, USA.

PIERCE Meredith Ann, b. 5 July 1958, Seattle, Washington, USA. Writer; Library Assistant. *Education:* AA, Liberal Arts 1976, BA, English 1978, MA, English 1980,. University of Florida. *Appointments:* Graduate teaching assistant, University of Florida, 1978-80; Bookseller, Bookland, Waldenbooks, 1981-87; Library Assistant, Alachua County Library District, 1987-; Writer, 1980-. *Publications:* Books: The Darkangel, 1982; A Gathering of Gargoyles, 1984; Birth of the Firebringer, 1985; The Woman Who Loved Reindeer, 1985; Where the Wild Geese Go, 1988; The Pearl of the Soul of the World, 1989. *Memberships:* Phi Beta Kappa; The Author's Guild; Science Fiction Writers of America (area coordinator of SFWA's Circulating Book Plan); Founder, The Writing Group. *Honours:* International Reading Association's Children's Book Award, 1982; American Library Association Best of the Best Books, 1970-82; New York Times Notable Children's Book, 1982; Parents' Choice Award Superbook, 1982; Jane Tinkham Broughton Fellow in Writing for Children, Bread Loaf Writers' Conference, 1984; Parents' Choice Book Award for Literature, 1985; American Library Association Best Book for Young Adults, 1985; Special Award for Children's Literature, State of Florida, 1987. *Hobbies:* Music (Piano, harp, voice, composition); Narrative arts (literature, cinema, drama, storytelling); Fiber arts (spinning, weaving, sewing, needlecraft); Visual arts (drawing, sculpture, design). *Address:* 703 NW 19th Street, Gainesville, FL 32603, USA.

PIERCE Patricia Jobe, b. 18 May 1943, Seattle, Washington, USA. Art dealer; Writer; Talent agent. m. Norman Pierce, 26 June 1965. 2 sons, 1 daughter. *Education:* BFA, Boston University, School of Fine & Applied Arts, 1965. *Appointments:* Actress, Boston, New York City, Los Angeles, 1958-68; Employment Manager, Kelly Services, Boston, 1965-67; President,

Pierce Galleries, Inc and Pierce Galleries Publishing, Inc, 1968-; Literary agent to Kahlil gibran, 1975-; Talent agent, 1981-. *Creative Works:* John Joseph Ennekini, American Immpresionist, 1972; The ten American Painters, 1976; Edmund C Tarbell & The Boston School of Painting, 1980; Richard Thomspon, An American Impressionist Painter, 1982; JWS Cox, The Watercolored World, 1981; Lightning Samurai (movie), 1984; Quarantine! (Novel), 1987; Victim Under Siege (Novel), 1988; Heads (movie), 1989; Secrets (play), 1989. Numerous articles for magazines. *Memberships:* Appraisers Assoc of America, 1974-; Museum of Fine Art, Boston; Archives of American Art, Advisory Board, Boston; International Platform Association; People for the American Way (donor), Washington DC; International Academy of Poets; World of Poetry, California; Karate Reference Association; Karate Illustrated Rules Committee; National Wildlife Foundation; Victorian Society; Smithsonian Institute. *Honours:* Golden Poet Award, World of Poetry, 1987-88; Certificate of Merit: World of Poetry 1987; Krane Association, 1985; Outstanding Young Woman of America, 1974; Certificates of Merit for Artistic Achievement in the Arts: El Paso Museum, Schenectady Museum, International Foundation of Poets, London. *Hobbies:* Writing novels, plays, screenplays; Karate (coaching world champions); Charitable community work with the handicapped; Civil Rights work. *Address:* 721 Main St, Hingham, MA 02043, USA.

PIERCE Phylis Ann, b. 25 Aug. 1937, Middlesboro, Kentucky, USA. Attorney. m. John Thomas Pierce, 20 Dec. 1959, 1 son, 1 daughter. *Education:* BA, Psychology, Berea College, 1960; MA, Reading, East Tennessee State University, 1973; JD, University of Tennessee College of Law. *Appointments:* Language arts teacher, Kingsport, Tennessee, 1966-68; Reading Specialist, Bristol, Virginia, 1974-76; Attorney Adviser 1980-84, Supervisory Attorney Adviser 1984-86, Social Security Administration, OHA, Kingsport; Private practice, law, 1986-88; Owner/broker, Pierce & Company, 1988-. *Memberships:* Tennessee 1st Vice President 1972-74, National Programme Development Committee 1975-77, American Association of University Women; Co-president, Board, Roller-Russ Group Home, 1984-87. *Honours:* Phi Kappa Phi, Psi Chi, 1960; American Jurispruence Award, Family Law, 1980. *Hobbies:* Travel; Collecting antiques. *Address:* PO Box 3762, Kingsport, Tennessee 37664, USA.

PIERCY Nancy Starr, b. 10 June 1948, Niles, Ohio, USA. Service Engineer; Technical Writer; Freelance Writer. m. Garvie G Piercy, 23 July 1977, 2 sons, 1 daughter. *Education:* BS, Indiana University, 1969; Postgraduate work, Purdue University, 1981-84. *Appointments:* Teacher, Public Schools, 1969-73; Restaurant & Retail Manager, 1973-76; Service Engineer, Senior Technical Writer, Allison Transmission Division, General Motors Corp, Indianapolis, 1977-; Freelance Writer, Editor, Publications Consultant, 1980-. *Creative Works:* 30 Transmission Repair Manuals (Books) for General Motors. *Memberships:* Campaign Chairman, local county government, Indiana, 1968; League of Women Voters; Indianapolis Chamber of Commerce. *Honours:* EEO Scholar, 1966-69. *Hobbies:* Gourmet Cooking; Reading; Women's Rights; Hiking; Jazz. *Address:* 1114 Woodpointe Drive, Indianapolis, IN 46234, USA.

PIERCY-PONT Ann Lisa, b. 15 Nov. 1951, Tacoma, WA, USA. Military Officer; Educational Technologist. m.(1)Larry Thomas Moore, 5 Feb. 1970, divorced Dec. 1972. (2)Steven Pont, 23 Nov. 1974. *Education:* AA, Florida State University, 1974; BA 1976; MA, California State University, Sacramento, 1981; Cert, USAF Training Instructor, 1978. *Appointments:* Commissioned 2nd Lieutenant, USAF 1976, advanced through grades to Major, 1987; Occupational Analyst, Occupational Measurement Center, Lackland AFB, 1976- 77; Instructional System Development Advisor, Training Evaluation Officer, 323 Flying Training Wing, Mather AFB, California, 1977-81; E-3 Systems Instructional System Development Training Advisor, 52

Airborne Warning and Control Wing, Tinker AFB, Oklahoma, 1981-85; Chief Exportable Education Board, Deputy Director, Nonresident Programs Division, School Systems and Logistics, Chief Evaluation and Technical Board, Chief Plans Division, Operations and Plans Directorate, Air Force Institute of Technical, Wright-Patterson AFB, Ohio, 1985-. *Memberships:* Air Force Association; American Society for Training and Development; National Society for Performance and Instruction; Association for Educational Communications and Technical; NOW, National Organization of Women (delegate 1980). *Honours:* Air Force Meritorious Service Medal, 1985; Air Force Commendation Medal, 1981. *Hobbies:* Poetry; Sports cars; Sewing; Gourmet cooking; Travel. *Address:* 1005 Meadowlark Drive, Enon, OH 45323, USA.

PIERUCCI Janet Barnett, b. 12 June. 1941, Bakersfield, California, USA. Psychotherpaist. m. Leo Pierucci, 18 Dec. 1965. 1 son, 2 daughters. *Education:* AA (Honours Graduate, Bakersfield College, 1971; BA, Magna Cum Laude, 1972, MS 1976, California State University, Bakersfield; MA, California School of Professional Psychology, Fresno, CA, 1986. *Appointments:* Program Coordinator, California State University, Bakersfield, 1976-79; Social Worker, Kern Medical Center, Bakersfield, 1979- 81; Owner/Partner, Westchester Counseling Center, 1981-. *Publication:* Duration of Participation of correctional volunteers as a function of Personal and situational variables, Journal of Community Psychology, 1980. *Memberships:* President, American Cancer Society, Kern Unit, 1985-86 and many other committees at local and state level; Member of many professional associations and organizations. *Honours:* Honours graduate, Bakersfield College, 1971; Magna Cum Laude Graduate, California State University, Bakersfield, 1972. *Hobbies:* Reading; Tennis; Walking; Volunteering. *Address:* 2012 E Street, Bakersfield, CA 93301, USA.

PIETIKAINEN Margareta, b. 28 Aug. 1940, Helsinki, Finland. Principal. m. Seppo Pietikainen, 27 Aug. 1966, 1 son, 2 daughters. *Education:* MSc., University of Helsinki, 1966; MSc., University of Southern California, 1974. *Appointments:* Vice Principal, Borga Medborgar-Institut, 1971-76; Principal, Finns Folkhogskola, 1980-. *Membership:* Chairperson, Womens Organization, Swedish Peoples Party, 1983-; Vice Chairperson, Swedish Peoples Party, 1987-. *Hobbies:* Politics; Education. *Address:* Finns Folkhogskola, 02780, Esbo, Finland.

PIFER Ellen Ina, b. 26 June 1942, New York, USA. University Professor. m. Drury L. Pifer, 30 Dec. 1962, 1 daughter. *Education:* Mills College, 1900-62; BA Distinction (English) 1964, MA (Comparative Literature) 1969, PhD 1976, University of California, Berkeley (UCB). *Appointments:* Acting instructor, UCB, 1974-76; Assistant professor (English) 1977-81, Associate Professor (English & Comparative Literature) 1981-89, Professor (English & Comparative Lit) 1989-, University of Delaware. *Publications include:* Books: Nabokov & the Novel, 1980; Critical Essays on John Fowles, 1986; Saul Bellow Against the Grain, 1990. Also: Numerous articles & reviews, professional & literary journals; Co-author, bi-weekly column, New West magazine, 1976-77; Theatre critic, San Francisco magazine & Berkeley Gazette, 1975-76. *Memberships:* Modern Language Association; Offices, Vladimir Nabokov Society; Saul Bellow Society. *Honours:* Nominated, teaching award, University of Delaware, 1986 & 1988; Research fellowship, Delaware Humanities Forum, 1987-88; General university research grants, 1978, 1981, 1986; National defence foreign language fellowship, University of California, 1968-71; Nominated, Woodrow Wilson Fellowship, 1964; Undergraduate scholarship, Mills College, 1960-62; George Stewart Prize, creative writing, 1961; Phi Beta Kappa outstanding freshman, 1961. *Address:* English Department, 204 Memorial Hall, University of Delaware, Newark, DE 19716, USA.

PIGOTT Irina V, b. 4 Dec. 1917, Russia. Educational Administrator. m. Nicholas Prischepenko, 11 Feb. 1945,

1 son, 1 daughter. *Education:* BA, Mills College, 1942; Certified Social Worker, Oakland, 1944; MA, New York Univesiy, 1951. *Appointments:* Director, Owner, Parsons Nursery, Flushing, 1951-59; Director, Montessori School, New York City, 1960-67; Director, Teacher, Day Care Center, 1967-68; Director, Owner, East Manhattan School for Bright & Gifted, New York City, 1968-; Director/Owner, The House for Bright and Gifted Children, Queens, NY, 1989-. *Memberships:* National Association for the Educatiron of Young Children; League of Women Voters, Vice President 1950-57. *Honours:* Distinguished Leadership; Community Leader of America. *Hobbies:* bb3Music; Dance; Theatre; Art; Sports. *Address:* 208 East 18th Street, New York, NY 10003, USA.

PILARSKI Laura Patricia, b. Niagara Falls, New York, USA. Journalist; Author. *Education:* BA, Syracuse University, 1948; University of Wisconsin, Milwaukee, 1958-59; Warsaw University, Poland, 1962- 63. *Appointments include:* General News Reporter, Milwaukee Journal, Wisconsin, 1949-60; Freelance Correspondent, from Europe including Poland, 1961-62; Assistant to Associated Press Correspondent, Warsaw, Poland, 1962-63; Freelance Correspondent from Switzerland, 1963-65; Chief Correspondent, McGraw-Hill World News, Zurich, 1965-88; Special Correspondent, McGraw-Hill Publications, New York City, New York, USA, 1988-. *Publications:* They Came from Poland, 1969; Tibet, Heart of Asia, 1974; Contributor to The Businessmen's Guide to Europe, 1965; Various journals, USA and abroad. *Memberships include:* Phi Beta Kappa; Sigma Phi. *Address:* Korneliusstrasse 3, 8008 Zurich, Switzerland.

PILGRIM Constance Maud Eva, b. 3 Dec. 1911, Thornton Heath, London. Retired. m. (1) Paul Cecil Smither, 29 Dec. 1934, (Egyptologist, Queen's College, Oxford). Died War Service 1943, 1 daughter b. 1935, 1 son b. 1942. (War Widow fo 14 years). m. (2) Richard W. Pilgrim, parish priest, 10 Sept. 1957, died 1979. *Educated:* Eastbourne G.P.D.S.T. Girls School and Eastbourne Art College, Oxford University and WEA Extension Department, 3 year course in English Literature. *Appointments:* Textile Designer, City of London, 1930-34; Trained by Professor of Egyptology at Queen's College, Oxford, Battiscombe Gunn, to write plates in Hieroglyphs for publications by Scholars at Oxford, and other European Universities and in USA, 1936-45. *Publications:* Dear Jane: A life of Jane Austen; biography, 1971; Contributor to Persuasions, 1987. *Memberships:* Jane Austen Society; Jane Austen Society of North America; Society of Authors; West Country Writers Association; Somerset Archaelogical and Nat. Hist. Society; Senior Wives Christian Fellowship. *Hobbies:* Reading; Writing. *Address:* 24 Withington Court, Abingdon, Oxfordshire, OX14 3QB, England.

PILLAERT E. Elizabeth, b. 19 Nov. 1931, Baytown, Texas, USA. Museum Curator. *Education:* BA, University of St Thomas, Houston, Texas, 1953; MA, University of Oklahoma, Norman, 1963; University of Wisconsin, Madison, 1962-67, 1970-73. *Appointments:* Assistant Curator, Archaeology, 1959-69, Education Liaison Officer, 1960-62, Stovall Museum, Norman, Oklahoma; Research Officer, University of Oklahoma, Norman, 1962; Research Assistant, University of Wisconsin, Madison, 1962-65; Curator of Osteology, 1965, Chief Curator, 1967-, University of Wisconsin Zoological Museum, Madison; Consultant for Archaeological Faunal Analysis, 1965. *Publications:* Contributions to Oklahoma Anthropological Society and The Wisconsin Archaeologist. *Memberships:* Society of Vertebrate Paleontology; Oklahoma Anthropological Society; The Wisconsin Archaeologist; Association of Systematics Collections; Ornithological Society of North America. *Address:* 216 North Prairie Street, Stoughton, WI 53589, USA.

PILLOW Rosemary T., b. 21 Apr. 1925, Homer, Louisiana, USA. City Court Judge. m. (1) J. A. Broussard, 1950 (div. 1974), 2 sons, (2) Raymond E. Pillow, 19

Feb. 1977, 4 step-children. *Education:* BA, Political Science, Louisiana State University, 1946; JD, Tulane University, 1949; Admitted Louisiana Bar, 1950. *Appointments:* Notary Public, 1951-; Law clerk, Baton Rouge, 1950-51; Research assistant, State Legislative Council, State Mineral Board, 1952-56; Right-of-way clerk, Baton Rouge, 1961-62; Assistant Parish Attorney, Baton Rouge, 1962-71; Council Administrator, 1971-79; Certified Municipal Clerk, 1975; City Court Judge, 1980-. Numerous civic & political activities. *Memberships include:* Louisiana & Baton Rouge Bicentennial Commissions, 1972-76; Board of Directors, Arts & Humanities Council 1971-79, Baton Rouge Community Correction & Research Centre 1972-75. Numerous professional associations including: American, Women Judges & Louisiana Judges Associations; Past President, Louisiana Municipal Clerks Association; Past Executive, International Institute of Municipal Clerks. *Honours:* Volunteer Activist, Baton Rouge Speech & Hearing Foundation 1985; Woman of Achievement, Baton Rouge YWCA, Finalist 1987, Winner 1988. *Hobbies:* Golf; Needlepoint; Reading. *Address:* 1561 Sherwood Forest Boulevard, Baton Rouge, Louisiana 70815, USA.

PINCKARD Terri Ellen (Pen names: T E Merritt and J M Parradee), b. 24 May 1930, Asbury Park, New Jersey, USA. Freelance Writer. m. G Thomas Pinckard, 14 July 1961. 1 son, 3 daughters. *Education:* AB, Monmouth Junior College; BS, UCLA. *Appointments:* Art layout and copy editor, Lynn-Western, Inc., 1952; Teacher, Adult Education, Professional Writing Course, Mentally Gifted Minor Program, 1970-75; Lecturer, 1960-; Founder and Creator with husband, Pinckard Science Fiction Writer's Salon, 1963-; Freelance Writer, 1950-. *Publications:* Collaborated CBS Weird Tales television series, 1955; Contributor of numerous non-fiction and fiction dramas to magazines and television in science fiction, fantasy, gothic, romance and mainstream, 1950-; Centennial Musical, The American Spirit, 1976; Official Co-Biographer with G Thomas Pinckard, Forrest J Ackerman, Mr Science Fiction. *Memberships:* Science Fiction Writers of America; World Science Fiction Writers Association; Academy of Science Fiction and Fantasy Films; Count Dracula Society; Praed Street Irregulars - Solar Pon Society; Madame Severance Society; The Little Green Miniature Men Society. *Honours:* Best Horror Story of the Year (English and US Editions), 1971; Solar Pons Mystery Society, Praed Street Penny Mystery Award, 1971; Count Dracula Gothic Literature Society, Mrs Ann Radcliffe Award, 1971; E E Evans, Big Heart Award, 1984. *Address:* Far Horizons, 2340 Lake Marie Drive, Santa Maria, CA 93455, USA.

PINCUS Helen Frances, b. 22 Oct. 1938, London, England. Fibre Artist; Lecturer. *Education:* Diploma, Adult Education, Nottingham University, 1979; Diploma, Embroidery Design, 1979, BA (Hons) 1982, Loughborough College of Art & Design. *Appointments:* Professional singer and actress; Artist; Lecturer; Engagements in music and films; numerous one person and mixed exhibitions including: Commonwealth Institute Art Gallery, London, 1980; Galerie 39, Barbican Centre (Sculpture Court); Cork St. Fine Art, Leighton House, 1983; Savaria Muzeum, Hungary, 1984; Bridport Gallery, Childerley's, Westminster Abbey, Loggia Gallery, Smith's Gallery, Shaw Theatre, University of Surrey, London, 1985; Contemporary Arts, Hong Kong, 1986; Bloomsbury Galleries, London, 1987; Hampton Court Palace, Guild Gallery, Heifer Gallery, London, 1988; Grove Gallery, Loggia Gallery, Bloomsbury Galleries, London, 1989; with further invitations to show in Hong Kong, Australia and Canada. *Creative works:* Numerous one person and mixed exhibitions including: Commonwealth Inst Art Gallery, 1980; Galerie 39; Barbican Centre (Sculpture Court); Cork St Fine Art; Leighton House, 1983; Savaria Muzeum, Hungary, 1984; Bridport Gallery, London; Childerley's; Westminster Abbey; Loggia Gallery; Smith's Gallery; Shaw Theatre; University of Surrey, 1985; Contemporary Arts, Hong Kong, 1986; Bloomsbury Galleries, London, 1987 and 1989; Hampton Court Palace; Guild Gallery; Heifer Gallery, 1988; Grove Gallery; Loggia Gallery; Textile panels also featured in books and magazines. *Memberships:* Free Painters and Sculptors (MFPS); Embroiderers' Guild; New Embroidery Group; Contemporary Applied Arts; The Textile Society; Fibre Art; Active Member, London Symphony Chorus. *Honours:* Many private commissions undertaken including showhouses in Harley Street, London; Work in permanent collection of the Embroiderers' Guild, Hampton Court Palace and The Savaria Muzeum, Hungary; Special Distinction, (for hand worked silk panel entitled Counterpoint Variation), Fourth Annual International Exhibition of Miniature Art, Toronto, Canada, 1989. *Hobbies:* Enthusiastic dog owner, owns rare long haired Weimaraner. *Address:* Lower Studio, 14 West Lodge Avenue, Acton Hill, London W3 9SF, England.

PINSKER Essie Levine, b. New York City, USA. Sculptor, former advertising and public relations executive. m. Sidney Pinsker. 1 son, 1 daughter. *Education:* BA, Brooklyn College, 1940; Postgraduate, Columbia University, New York University, New School for Social Research, Art Students League, 1955, Museum of Modern Art, New York, 1970-71, Cambridge University, England, 1985. *Appointments:* Former Fashion model/buyer, Ohrbach's, New York City, Arkwright, New York City; Former editor, Woman's Wear Daily, New York City; Former press director, American Symphony Orchestra, New York City; President, Essie Pinsker Advt Associates, Inc, New York City, 1960-82; Guest editor, Teen Merchandiser magazine, Infant's and Children's Rev; Editor travel, beauty and fashion Woman Golfer magazine; Lecturer, instructor, Fashion Inst of Tech; Contributing journalist, New York Times. *Creative Works:* One-woman shows include: Bodley Gallery, New York City, 1981; Vorpal Gallery, New York City, 1987. Exhibited in group shows at: Metropolitan Life, New York City, 1969; Huntington (NY) Art League, 1977; C W Post Center, Old Westbury, New York, 1978; North Shore Arts Centre, Manhasset, New York, 1980; Allied Artists of America, New York City, 1980; Lever Bros, New York City, 1982; Knickerbocker Artists, New York City, 1982; Cadme Gallery, Philadelphia, 1984; River Gallery, Westport, Connecticut, 1984; Clark Whitney, Lenox, Massachusetts, 1985; Images Gallery, South Norwalk, Connecticut, 1987; Arco International Art Fair, Madrid, 1988; Kontsmassan International Art Fair, Stockholm, 1988; Galleri Atrium, Stockholm, 1988; Galerie Atrium, Marbella, Spain, 1988; Nina Owen Ltd, Chicago, 1989; The Art Collector, San Diego, 1989; Galerie Isle Lommel, Leverkusen, West Germany, 1989. Represented in permanent collections: Everson Museum, Syracuse; Aldrich Museum Contemporary Art, Ridgefield, Connecticut; Oklahoma Art Center, Oklahoma City; Minnesota Museum of Art, St Paul; Museum of Arts and Sciences, Daytona Beach, Florida; Vassar Museum, Poughkeepsie, New York; National Museum, Warsaw, Poland; New School, New York City; Pace University, New York City; Necca Museum, Brooklyn; Lincoln Center, Fordham University, New York City; Hinkhouse Collection, Eureka (III) College. Represented in corporate collections: Robert D Scinto, Inc; Marriott Hotels, USA; Devon Inc, New York City; Judy Bond, Inc, New York City; Regina Porter, Inc, New York City; Paramount Group, Los Angeles; Joseph P Day Realty Corp, New York City; Rubenstein Planning Corp, New York City; Queensboro Steel Corp, Wilmington, North Carolina; Southerland Tours, St Croix. Executive producer film: Pupae. *Memberships:* National Museum of Women in the Arts; International Sculpture Society; Artist's Equity; Fashion Group NY; Advt Women NY; Fashion Coalition NY. *Honours:* Cine Eagle Award for film Pupae; Knickerbocker Artist's 24th annual exhibition sculpture award; Met Life sculpture award. *Address:* 8 Peter Cooper Road, New York, NY 10010, USA.

PINTO Jacqueline, b. 1927, London, England. Housewife; Children's Writer. m. Joel Pinto, 24 Oct. 1957. 1 son, 2 daughters. *Education:* St Paul's Girls' School, London. *Appointment:* Sub-Editor, Homes and Gardens Magazine, prior to marriage in 1957. *Publications:* As Jacqueline Blairman: Headmistress in Disgrace; Rebel at St Agatha's; Triplets at Royders. As

Jacqueline Pinto: Moses Mendelssohn, 1960; The School Dinner Disaster, 1983; The School Gala Disaster, 1985; The School Library Disaster, 1986; The School Outing Disaster, 1987; The School Donkey Disaster, 1988. *Address:* 89 Uphill Road, Mill Hill, London NW7 4QD, England.

PIPCHICK Margaret H, b. 14 Dec. 1942, Brooklyn, New York, USA. Clinical Specialist; Psychiatric Mental Health Nursing. m. Robert Pipchick, 13 June 1971. 1 son, 1 daughter. *Education:* BSN, Seton Hall University, 1968; MA, New York University 1974; Certificate Marriage & Family Therapy, Blanton-Peale Graduate Institute. *Appointments:* Various Staff Nurse Positions, 1968-71; Staff, Administration Faculty, Center for Counseling & Human Development, 1974-; Private Practice, New York and Cranford New Jersey, 1981-89. *Publications:* Contributing Author: Review Manual for State Board Examinations, 1980; Developing a Sense of Power School Age Child, 1976; Chapter in Foundations of Mental Health Nursing Practice. *Memberships:* American Nurses Association; NJS Nurses Assoc; American Association Marriage & Family Therapists; Society of Certified Clinical Specialists, Treasurer & Board Member; Advocates for Child Psychiatric Nursing; American Orthopsychiatric Association. *Honours:* Sigma Theta Tau, 1974; National Registry of Certified Nurses in Advanced Practice, 1987-88. *Hobbies:* Jogging; Sailing; Skiing. *Address:* 107 Lincoln Ave East, Cranford, NJ 07016, USA.

PIRTLE Klaire Beatrice Kaufman, b. 27 Aug. 1943, Brooklyn, New York, USA. Principal, Kingsbury Middle School. m. Jack Reginald Pirtle, 4 July 1966. 1 son, 3 daughters. *Education:* BA 1965, MEd 1969, PhD 1982, University of Arizona. *Appointments:* Teacher, Fountain Valley School District, California, 1965-68; Teacher, Los Ninos Elem, Tucson, 1968-71; Part-time Lecturer, University of Arizona, 1972-78; Teacher, Sunnyside High School, Tucson, 1979-81; Principal, Gardnerville Elementary School, 1982-88; Principal, Kingsbury Middle School, 1988-. *Creative works:* Film: Make a Might Reach, 1966; Chapter, Gardnerville Elementary School; Dissertation, Cross-Age Tutoring. *Memberships:* Douglas County Administration Association, Pres, 2 years; Nevada Association of School Administration, Professor Review Committee; Chairman, Nevada State Middle School Task Force; ASCD (Association Supervision & Curriculum Dev); NAESP (National Association of Elementary School Principals); Pi Lambda Theta; Board Member, Children's Museum, Carson City, Nevada. *Honours:* Awarded, US Elementary School Recognition Award for Gardnerville Elementary School, 1985-86; Nevada Top Education Award, Milken Foundation, 1988. *Hobbies:* Raising my children, spending time with husband; Vegetarian cooking; Aerobics and exercise; Member Beyond War; Chairman, Pastor-Parish United Methodist Church. *Address:* PO Box 263, 685 Pinto Circle, Gardnerville, Nevada 89410, USA. 15.

PITKIN Hanna Fenichel, b. 17 July 1931, Berlin, Germany. Professor of Political Science. m. Harvey Pitkin, 1953, div. 1957. *Education:* BA, Political Science, 1953, MA, Political Science, 1954, University of California, Los Angeles, USA; PhD, Political Science, University of California, Berkeley, 1961. *Appointments:* Teaching Assistant, 1956- 59, Associate, 1959-60, Instructor, 1962-64, Assistant Professor, 1966-68, Associate Professor, 1968-73, Professor, 1973-, University of California, Berkeley, USA; Instructor, San Francisco State College, California, 1961-62; Assistant Professor, University of Wisconsin, Madison, 1964-66. *Publications:* The Concept of Representation, 1967; Wittgenstein and Justice, 1972; Fortune Is A Woman, 1984. *Memberships:* American Academy of the Arts and Sciences. *Honours:* Phi Beta Kappa; SSRC Fellow, 1960-61; ACLS Fellow, 1967-68; Guggenheim Fellow, 1972-73. *Address:* Department of Political Science, 210 Barrows Hall, University of California, Berkeley, CA 94720, USA.

PITTENGER Karen D., b. 10 Oct. 1954, Nashville,

Tennessee, USA. Advertising & Direct Marketing Executive. m. Glenn Lewis Arnold, 15 Jan. 1977 dec. 1 son. *Education:* BA, Purdue University, 1976; MBA, Butler University School of Business, in progress. *Appointments:* Art Director, Art Emporium, 1975-76; President & Chief Executive Officer 1976-84, Pittenger Studio; Vice President, Special Projects, 1984-; Senior Vice President 1984-88, President 1988-, Haynes & Pittenger Direct. *Publications include:* Articles, Bereavement Magazine, Business Buys - Direct Marketing Editor. *Memberships include:* Agency Leader, Association of Direct Marketing Agencies; DMAI; Indiana Art Directors Club; Advertising Club of Indiana; Indianapolis Business Network. Also: Advisory Board President, Hospice Advisory Board Chairman, St Vincent Stress Centre. *Honours:* Various national & international Echo Awards including top Direct Marketing Award of Year, 1986, 1984-; Target Marketing Bronze Award, 1989; Various awards of excellence, 1979-; Indianapolis 500 Awards, Governors, Judges, Directors & Queens, 1979-84; Outstanding Young Woman of America, 1983. *Hobbies:* Outdoor living; Reading; Swimming. *Address:* 303 North Alabama Street, Suite 310, Indianapolis, Indiana 46204, USA.

PITTOCK WESSON Joan Hornby, b. 1 May 1930, Yorkshire, England. University Lecturer. m. Malcolm John Whittle Pittock, 1955, 1 son, divorced 1973 (2) Harry Chamberlain Wesson, 19 July 1974. *Education:* BA, 1st Class Honours, English Language & Literature, 1951, MA 1952, PhD, 1960, University of Manchester. *Appointments:* Temporary Lecturer, Teacher, various schools and universities, 1955-64; Lecturer, English, 1964-78, Senior Lecturer, 1978-, University of Aberdeen; Convener, Course Organiser, Cultural History Degree, 1985, 1986-. *Publications:* Ascendancy of Taste, 1973; Poems in: New Lines, 1987, 199 articles and reviews, Durham University Journal, English Studies, etc. *Memberships:* British Society for Eighteenth Century Studies, editor, Newsletter, Founder-editor, Journal, 1978; President 1980; International Research Fellow, Edinburgh University; Institute for Advanced Studies in Humanities, 1986; Visiting Research Fellow, Magdalen College, Oxford, 1986. *Address:* Dept. of English, University of Aberdeen, AB9 2UB, Scotland.

PLACKO Judy Hewitt, b. 21 July 1952, Detroit, Michigan, USA. Interior Designer; Space Planner. m. 18 July 1981, 2 daughters. *Education:* BA, American College of Switzerland, 1974; MS, Florida State University, 1977. *Appointments:* Designer, Brown & Deyo Architects, Bloomfield Hills, Michigan, 1978-81; Designer, Planner: Robert Corna, Architects, Westlake, Ohio, 1982; Dalton, Dalton, Newport, Shaker Heights, Ohio, 1983; S Rose Inc, Cleveland, Ohio, 1983-85; Owner, Hewitt Design Associates, Lakewood, 1985-. *Creative works include:* Exhibits at art shows, Les Diablerets, Switzerland, 1973, Montreux, Switzerland, 1974. *Hobbies:* Sports; Artwork. *Address:* 1642 Belle Avenue, Lakewood, OH 44107, USA.

PLATT Eleanor Frances, b. 6 May 1938, London, England. Barrister. m. 1963, 1 son, 1 daughter. *Education:* LLB, University College, London, 1959; Called to Bar, Gray's Inn, 1960. *Appointments:* Recorder, 1982; Queen's Counsel, 1982; Member, Matrimonial Causes Rule Committee, 1986-. *Memberships:* Family Law Bar Association; Chairman, Law and Parliamentary and General Purposes Committee, Board of Deputies of British Jews, 1988-; Chairman, Jewish Family Mediation Service, 1986-. *Hobbies:* The Arts; Travel; Skiing. *Address:* 6 Pump Court, Temple, London EC4Y 7AP, England.

PLATT Janice Kaminis, b. 27 Sept. 1936, St Petersburg, Florida, USA. Hillsborough County Commissioner. m. William R Platt, 8 Feb. 1962. 1 son. *Education:* BA, Florida State University, 1958; Postgraduate Studies, University of Florida School of Law, 1958-59; University of Virginia, 1962; Vanderbilt University, 1964. *Appointments include:* Field Director,

Girls Scouts, USA, 1960-62; Public School Teacher, Hillsborough County, Nashville, Tennessee; City Council, City of Tampa, Florida, 1974-78; Member, Hillsborough County BOCC, 1978-; Chairman: Hillsborough County Board of County Commissioners, 1980-81, 1983-34; Tampa Bay Regional Planning Council, 1982; West Coast Regional Water Supply Authority, 1985-; Agency on Bay Management, 1985-; Hillsborough County Environmental Protection Commission, 1981-82, 1985- 86; Hillsborough County Council of Governments, 1976, 1979; Sunshine Amendment Drive 7th Congressional District, 1976; Community Action Agency, 1980-81; 1983-34; Charter Revision Commission, 1975; Prison Siting Task Force, 1983; Tampa Housing Study Committee; Metropolitan Planning Organization, 1984; Board of Tax Adjustment, 1984; Appointed by Governor Askew, Constitution Revision Commission, 1977 and HRS District IV Task Force on Coastal Zone Management; Member: Arts Council of Tampa-Hillsborough County, 1983-86; Hillsborough County Expressway Authority; Drug Abuse Coordinating Council Organization; American Judicature Society; Board of Criminal Justice; Florida Council on Aging; Inebriate Task Force; Tampa Downtown Development Task Force; Tampa Sports Authority, 1984; Tampa Area Mental Health Board; Children's Study Commission; Taxicab Commission; Manahill Area Agency on Aging, etc. *Memberships:* Tampa Area Committee on Foreign Affairs; Athena Society; League of Women Voters; American Association of University Women; Florida Association of Counties; National Association of Counties. *Honours include:* Phi Beta Kappa; Phi Kappa Phi; Spessard Hollant Memorial Award, Tampa Bay Committee for Good Government, 1979; First Lady of the Year Award, Beta Sigma Phi, 1980; Women Helping Women Award, Soroptimist International of Tampa, 1983; Eliza Wolff Award, Tampa United Methodist Centers, 1982; Good Government Award, Tampa Jaycees and League of Women Voters, 1983; Foremost Women of the 20th Century, etc. *Address:* 4606 Beach Park, Tampa, Florida 33609, USA.

PLATT OF WRITTLE Beryl Catherine,(Baroness), b. 18 Apr. 1923, Leigh-on-Sea, Essex, England. European Engineer. m. Stewart Sydney Platt, 22 Oct. 1949, 1 son, 1 daughter. *Education:* Mechanical Science Tripos, Girton College, 1943. *Appointments:* Technical Assistant, Experimental Flight Test Department, Hawker Aircraft, 1943-46; Research & Development Section, British European Airways, 1946-49; Council of Local Education Authorities; Technician Education Council (later Vice-Chairman): London Regional Advisory Council for Technological Education (later Vice Chairman); Burnham Committee; House of Lords Select Committee of Science & Technology; 1983-88, chairman, Equal Opportunities Commission; Commission of European Advisory Committee on Equal Opportunities for Women and Men. *Memberships Include:* Past: Royal Aeronautical Society; Womens Engineering Society; Royal Society of Arts. Member: Council of City and Guilds of London Institute; Careers Research & Advisory Council; The Engineering Council, etc. *Honours:* CBE, 1978; MA; F.Eng; FRACS; Created Baroness, 1981; Deputy Lieutenant of the County of Essex, 1983; Hon.DSc., City University & Salford University, 1984; Hon. FIMech.E; Hon. D.Sc, Cranfield Insitute; Hon. D.Tech, Brunel University; Hon. D.Univ, Open University & Essex University; City & Guilds of London Institute Insignia Award, (Hon). *Hobbies:* Cooking; Gardening; Reading. *Address:* Equal Opportunities Commission, Overseas House, Quay Street, Manchester M3 3HN, England.

PLAYER Theresa Joan, b. 17 Nov. 1947, Great Lakes, Illinois, USA. Law Professor. *Education:* AB, San Diego State University, 1970; JD, UCLA, 1973. *Appointments:* Staff Attorney, Legal Aid Society of San Diego, 1974-78; Private Practice, San Diego, 1978-79; Law Professor, University of San Diego School of Law, 1980-. *Publications:* Contributing Author, Everywomans Legal Guide. *Memberships:* California State, American, San Diego County Bar Associations; Lawyer Club; California Attorney's for Criminal Justice. *Honours:* Service

Award, Womens Criminal Defence Bar, 1983; Outstanding Contribution to San Diego Volunteer Lawyers, 1985. *Hobbies:* Running; Cycling; Swimming; Skiing; Travel. *Address:* University of San Diego Law School, Alcula Park, San Diego, CA 92110, USA.

PLAZA DE GARCIA Norma. *Education:* LLD, Catholic University, Guayaquil, 1970; Master, Comparative Jurisprudence, New York University, USA, 1970. *Appointments:* Professor, Commercial Law, Catholic University, Guayaquil, 1971; Co-ordinator Professor, Catholic University of Guayaquil, 1971-72; Civil Law Professor, Writer, El Universo, 1973-75. *Publications:* Forms of Semirepresentative or Semidirect Popular Action: Referendum Popular Iniative, veto, Juries and Recall, 1970; Practice in Notary Law Nos 1, 2 and 3; Ecuadorian Legislation - Summary from 1970-87, 2 volumes. *Memberships:* Ex Vice President, School of Notaries, 1980-87; Vice President, Francisco de Orellana Foundation, 1987-88; School of Lawyers Guayqauil; etc. *Honours:* Literary Prize, Society Dr Aurelio Espinonza Polit SJ, 1963; Diploma Philanthropic Society of Guays, 1963-68; etc. *Hobbies:* Travel; Reading; Writing; Swimming. *Address:* Jose Salcedo 206 and Maracaibo, Guayaquil, Ecuador.

PLEASANCE Angela, b. Chapeltown, Sheffield, England. Actress. 1 son. *Education:* Pre-nursing, SRN, Chiswick Polytechnic; Diploma, Royal Academy of Dramatic Art. *Appointments:* Appeared as Titania in A Midsummer Nights Dream, Birmingham Repertory Theatre, 1984; London Theatre includes: Juliet in Romeo and Juliet; Miranda in Johnathan Miller's production of The Tempest; St Joan in St Joan; The Ha Ha Electra, The Hothouse, Pinter; The Entertainer, John Osborne; other theatres include: Ludlow Festival, Nottingham Playhouse, Chichester and Edinburgh Festivals. Television productions: Six Wives of Henry VIII; Marching Song; Charlotte Bronte; Mansfield Park; Barchester Chronicles; St Joan; Sila Marner; Anastasia. Films include: Tales from Beyond the Grave; Symptoms; Les Miserables; The Godsend; Numerous radio plays. *Membership:* Associate Board of Governors, Royal Academy of Dramatic Art. *Honours:* West End Critics Award for The Ha Ha, 1969 and The Bitter Tears Petra von Kant, 1977; various nominations include: Best Actress on radio. *Hobbies:* Allotment; Reading.

PLOTKIN Judith Adele, b. 3 Nov. 1949, Miami, Florida, USA. Scientist; Educator; Researcher. 2 sons, 2 daughters. *Education:* BS, 1969, Florida State University; MS, 1971, University of Chicago; PhD, Hebrew University, 1988. *Career:* Educator: Sciences, Maths, Statistics, Languages, Swimming and Safety; GMAT, LSAT, MCAT, GRE prep, 1967-. Research and Clinical: Georgia State University, 1983-84; Mercer University, 1984; Hebrew University, 1975-82; Israeli Ministry of Health, 1975; Hadassah Medical Center, 1973-74; Georgia Baptist Hospital, 1971-73; Mount Sinai, MB, 1968. *Publications:* Scientific; Poetic; Journalistic; For and About Kids. *Memberships:* American Chemical Society; Fellow, American Institute of Chemists; American Genetic Society; Genetic Society of Georgia; New York Academy of Science; Georgia Academy of Science; Village Writers; S.W. Writers; AWIS. *Address:* PO Box 2596, Springfield, VA 22152, USA.

PLOWDEN Bridget Horatia (Lady), Chairman Independent Broadcasting Authority, 1975-80. m. Baron Plowden, 1933, 2 sons, 2 daughters. *Education:* Downe House. *Appointments:* Director, Trust Houses Forte Ltd., 1961-72; Chaiman, Central Advisory Council for Education (England), 1963-66; Working Ladies Guild; Metropolitan Architectural Consortium for Education, 1968-79; MSC Area Manpower Board, North London, 1983-88; A Governor and Vice Chairman, BBC, 1970-75; Member, National Theatre Board, 1976-88; Member, Houghton Inquiry into Pay of Teachers, 1974; Chairman, Governors, Philippa Fawcett College of Education, 1967-76; Robert Montefiore Comp School, 1968-78; Co-opted Member, Education Committee, ILEA, 1967-73; Vice Chairman, ILEA Schools Sub-

Committee, 1967-70; President, Harding House Association; National Association of Adult Continuing Education, 1980-88; National Marriage Guidance Council; Professional Classes Advisory Committee, 1980-88, Advisory Committee for Education of Romany and Other Travellers, 1985-, The British Accreditation Council for Independent Further & Higher Education; President, College of Preceptors; Liveryman, Goldsmiths Company, 1979-; JP Inner London Area Juvenile Panel, 1962-71. *Honours:* Honorary LLD, Leicester, 1968; OBE, 1972; Honorary FCP, 1973, D.Univ. Open, 1974; Honorary D.Litt., Loughborough, 1976; FRTS, 1980. *Address:* 11 Abingdon Gardens, Abingdon Villas, London W8 6BY, England.

POGREBIN Letty Cottin, b.9 June 1939, New York City, USA. Writer; Editor. m. Bertrand B Pogrebin, Dec 1963, 1 son, 2 daughters. *Education:* BA, cum laude, Brandeis University, 1959. *Appointments:* Editorial Assistant, Simon & Schuster, 1957-59; Editorial Assistant, Coward McCann, 1959-60; Vice President and Director of Publicity, Advertising and Subsidiary Rights, Bernard Geis Associates, 1960-70; Columnist: Moment Magazine, 1990-; Ms magazine. Person to Person, 1988-89, Newsday, In Person column 1986, The New York Times, Hers column 1989, 1983, Ladies Home Journal, The Working Woman column 1971-81; Editor: Ms magazine, founder and editor 1971-87, Editor-at-Large 1988-89, Contributing Editor, 1990-. *Publications:* Books: Editor, Stories for Free Children, 1982; Author: How to Make It in a Man's World, 1970, Getting Yours, 1975, Growing Up Free, 1980, Family Politics, 1983, Among Friends, 1986, Deborah, Golda and Me, 1990. Contributor of articles to newspapers and magazines. *Memberships include:* Board of Directors or Advisory Boards: Action for Children's Television, American Friends of Peace Now, Authors Guild of America, Child Care Action Campaign, Ms Foundation for Education and Communication, Ms Foundation for Women, International Center for Peace in the Middle East. *Honours include:* Fellow, MacDowell Colony, 1989-90; Swedish Bicentennial Award Study Grant to Sweden, 1981; Matrix Award for Books, Women in Communications, 1981; Poynter Fellow in Journalism, Yale University, 1982; National Honorary Life Member, Pioneer Women, 1984; Fellow, Cummington Community of the Arts, 1985; Fellow, Edna St Vincent Millay Colony for the Arts, 1985; National Council on Family Relations Award, 1986. *Address:* 33 West 67th Street, New York, NY 10023, USA.

POHLER Sue, b. 5 Nov. 1955, Baumholder, Germany. Attorney. *Education:* BA Psychology 1975, JD 1985. *Appointments:* Director of Personnel, 1979-82; Self employed Taxplanner/preparor, 1903-, Assistant City Prosecutors, 1985-86; Assistant City Attorney, 1986-. *Memberships:* Columbus Bar Association, Member Justice Planning Committee; Assistant General Counsel Young Republican National Federation, 1985-87; Chairman, Ohio League of Young Republican Clubs, 1983-85; Director, Franklin County Republican Lawyers, 1987-; Deputy Chairwoman Franklin County Group, 1987-. *Honour:* Ohio Young Republican Woman of the Year, 1982. *Hobbies:* Raquetball; Reading. *Address:* 1075 Minerva Avenue, Columbus, Ohio 43229, USA.

POLAN Nancy Moore. b. USA. Fine Arts Painter. m. Lincoln Milton Polan, 1934. 2 sons. *Education:* AB, Marshall University, 1936; Huntington Galleries. *Appointment:* Self-employed Artist. *Creative works:* One-woman exhibitions: Charleston Art Gallery, 1961, 1967, 1973; Huntington Galleries, 1963, 1966, 1971; West Virginia University, 1966; Carroll Reese Memorial Museum, 1967; New York World's Fair, 1965; Exhibited in group shows: International Platform Association Art Exhibition, 1968-69, 1972, 1973, 1974, 1979, 1985, 1986, 1988; Allied Artists of America, National Arts Club, 1962-86; Pennsylvania Academy of Fine Arts, Opening of Creative Arts Centre, West Virginia, 1968-69; Joan Miro Graphics Barcelona, Spain, Travelling USA and Europe, 1970-71; American Watercolour Society Framed Travelling Exhibition, 1972-73; Paintings: Cover, La Revue Moderne, Paris, France,

1961-66; Talent Magazine, 1977. *Memberships:* Accademia Italia and Current; National Arts Club, New York City; Pen and Brush Inc, New York City; International Platform Association (Art Committee 1967-86); Centro Studie Scambi International (Honorary Vice President and Honorary Representative); American Federation Arts; Associate, Allied Artists of America; Associate, American Watercolour Society; Sigma Kappa; DAR; Allied Artists of West Virginia; Tri-State Art Association; West Virginia Watercolor Society, Charter Member; National Trust Historical Preservation; Vero Beach Florida Art Club. *Honorus:* Norton Memorial Award, National July Show Chautauqua, New York, 1960; Huntington Galleries Purchase Prize, Jurors, 1960; Watercolour, 1961; Grumbacher Award Pen and Brush Inc, 1978; National Arts Club Award, 1969; Gold Medal, Accademia Italia, 1979, 1986; Watercolour, Accademia Italia, 1985-86. *Hobby:* Fine Arts Collecting. *Address:* 2106 Club Drive, Vero Beach, FL 32963, USA.

POLAND Dorothy Elizabeth, b. 3 May 1937, Barry, South Glamorgan, Wales. Writer. m. George Poland. 20 Sept. 1969. 1 daughter. *Appointment:* Civil Servant, 1954-68. *Publications:* As Alison Farely novels include: Shadows of Evil; Plunder Island; High Treason; Throne of Wrath; Crown of Splendour; King Wolf; Last Roar of The Lion; Leopard From Anjou; The Cardinals Nieces; Tempestuous Countess; Archduchess Arrogance; Scheming Spanish Queen. As Jane Hammond novels include: Hell Raisers of Wycombe; Fire & The Sword; The Doomtower; The Golden Courtesan; Shadows of Evil; Witch of The White House; The Queen Assassin; The Admirals Lady; Secret of Petherick; Massingham Topaz; Moon in Aries. As Phillipa Greer, novels include: Santa Cruz; A Cold Eye of Destiny; A Daughter of Cornwall; Swim For Your Life. *Hobbies:* Swimming; Reading; Music; Gardening; Researching for writing. *Address:* Horizons, 95 Dock View Road, Barry, South Glamorgan, Wales CF6 6PA.

POLAND Marguerite Jean, b. 3 Apr. 1950, South Africa. Writer. m. Martin Ooshuizen, 27 Apr. 1973, 2 daughters. *Education:* BA, Rhodes University, 1970; BA Honours, Stellenbosch University, 1971; MA, Natal Univesity, 1977. *Appointments:* Assistant, Ethnology, South African Museum, 1972; Research Assistant, Centre for Applied Social Sciences, Natal University, 1973-75; Musicologist, Killie Campbell Museum, 1975. *Publications:* Mantis & The Moon, 1979; Once at Kwafubesi, 1981; Nqalu, The Mouse without Whiskers, 1979; The Bush Shrike, 1982; The Woodash Stars, 1983; Train to Doringdut, 1987; Th African History; Conservation; African Languages. *Address:* 54 Ronalds Rd, Kloof 3610, Natal, South Africa.

POLENSKE Karen Rosel, b. 20 Mar. 1937, Lewiston, Idaho, USA. Professor. *Education:* BA, Home Economics, Oregon State University, 1959; MA, Public Administration and Economics, Syracuse University, 1961; PhD, Economics, Harvard University, 1966. *Appointments:* Research Associate 1966-72, Instructor, Lecturer 1966-70, Harvard University; Senior Visitor, Faculty of Economics, University of Cambridge, England, 1970-71; Sabbatical Fellowship, Netherlands Institute for Advanced Study, 1980; Visiting Lecturer, University of Queensland, sT Lucia, Queensland, Australia, 1983; Associate Professor 1972-81, Professor 1981-, Massachusetts Institute of Technology, Department of Urban Studies and Planning. *Publications:* Books: Frontiers of Input-Output Analysis, Coeditor with Ronald E Miller and Adam Rose, 1989; Chinese Economic Planning and Input-Output Applications, Coeditor with Chen Xikang, forthcoming; The US Multiregional Input-Output Accounts and Model, 1980; Advances in Input-Output Analysis, Co-editor with Jiri V Skolka, 1976; State Estimates of technology 1963, co-author, 1974; Multiregional Input-Output Analysis, Editor, 1972, 1973; State Estimates of the gross National Product 1947, 1958, 1963, co-author, 1972. *Memberships:* American Economic Association; Regional Science Association; International Association for Research in Income and Wealth; International Input-Output Association. *Honours:* Visiting Scholar, Chinese

Academy of Science, Beijing, China, May-July 1986, August 1988; Visiting Professeur, Universite de Montpellier-I, Montpellier, France, May-June 1985. *Hobbies:* Birding; Photography. *Address:* 9-535 MIT, Cambridge, MA 02139, USA.

POLITE Carlene Hatcher, b. 28 Aug. 1932, Detroit, Michigan, USA. Author; Assoc Professor. divorced. 2 daughters. *Education:* Sarah Lawrence College, 1949; Martha Graham School of Dance, 1952. *Appointments:* Author: Editions Julliard, Paris, France, 1966; Farrar, Straus & Giroux, New York City, 1967-89; Assoc Professor, Department of English, State University of New York at Buffalo, 1971-; Dancer, 1952-72. *Publications:* The Flagellants, 1966, 1967, 1968; Sister X and the Victims of Foul Play 1975, 1988. *Memberships:* Panelist-Jury, New York State Council on the Arts, 1981-85; New York Foundation on the Arts; National Endowment on the Arts, Washington DC; Buffalo & Erie County Historical Society; Natl Trust for Historical Preservation; PEN; American Center. *Honours:* Pulitzer Prize Nominee, The Flagellants, 1967; National Endowments for Arts & Humanities, 1968; Rockefeller Foundation, 1969; Micheaux Library Collection, Harlem Schomburg Center for Research in Black Culture, 1968-89; Fisk Univ and Mugar Memorial Collection, Boston Univ; Centro Studi e Scambi Internazionale Accademia Leonardi da Vinci, Rome, Italy, 1980. *Hobbies include:* Raja yoga; Tai Chi Ch'uan; Egyptology; Landmarks and historical preservation socieites. *Address:* c/o Dept of English, State University of New York, Buffalo, NY 14260, USA.

POLK Edwina Rowand, b. 30 Jan. 1921, Lakeland, USA. Surveyor- Engineer. m. V.I. Polk, 2 Jan. 1949, 1 daughter. *Education:* BS, Maths, Florida Southern College, 1942; Postgraduate, The Citadel, 1943; Registered Land Surveyor, 1958. *Appointments:* Draughtsman, US Navy, Charleston, 1942-45; Teacher, Brandon High School, 1945-46; Draughtman, Food Mach., Lakeland, 1946-49; Draughtsman-Designer, 1949-63; Design, Polk County Bartown, Florida, 1963-76; Assistant County Engineer, 1976-; Teacher, Member, Technical Company, Polk Com. College, 1966-69. *Memberships:* American Association of University Women; Florida Society of Professional Land Surveyor, Ridge Chapter, Secretary, 1980. *Hobbies:* Antiques; History; Cooking; Music. *Address:* 302 Ariana Street, Lakeland, FL 33803, USA.

POLLAND Madeleine Angela, b. 31 May 1918, Kinsale, County Cork, Ireland. Writer. m. Arthur Joseph Polland, 10 June 1946 (dec. 1987), 1 son, 1 daughter. *Education:* Hitchin Girls' Grammar School, Hertfordshire, England (Matriculation), 1928-37. *Appointments:* Letchworth Public Library, Hertfordshire, 1938; Radar operator, Women's Auxiliary Air Force, 1942-45. *Publications:* Children's books: 19 titles including: Children of the Red King, 1960; Beorn the Proud, 1961; White Twilight, 1962; City of the Golden House, 1963; Flame Over Tara, 1964; Queen Without Crown, 1965; To Tell My People, 1968; Stranger in the Hills, 1968; A Family Affair, 1971; Prince of the Double Axe, 1976; etc. Adult books: 10 titles including: Thicker Than Water, 1964; Random Army, 1969; Double Shadow (as Frances Adrian), 1977; Sabrina, 1979; No Price Too High, 1983. Majority published UK & USA; All notes & manuscripts in Mugar Memorial Library, Boston University, USA; As it was in the beginning, (Runner-up Best Romantic Novel of the Year), 1987; Rich Man's Flowers, 1990. *Memberships:* Local community organisations, England & Spain. *Honours:* Numerous awards including: Citation, New York Herald Tribune, 1961; Various recommendations, American Library Association; Book of the Month (twice); Runner-up, Best Romantic Novel of Year, 1987. *Hobbies:* Family & friends; Reading; Lawn bowling. *Address:* Edificio Hercules 406, Avenida Gamonal, Arroyo de la Miel, Malaga, Spain.

POLLAND Rebecca Irene Robbins, b. 11 Jan. 1922, Philadelphia, USA. Foundation Administrator. m. Harry, 14 July 1946, divorced, 1 son, 2 daughters. *Education:*

BA, Bryn Mawr College, 1942; MA, 1957, PhD, 1971, University of California, Berkeley. *Appointments:* Budget Analyst, US Dept. of Agriculture, 1942-44; Economist, War Labour Board, 1944-46; Research Associate, Economics, 1946, Teaching Assistant, 1957-60, University of California; Associate Professor, Sacramento State University, 1974-75; Assistant Professor, Sonoma State University, 1975-78; Assistant Professor, Rutgers University, 1978-86; Foundation Administrator, 1984-. *Memberships:* White House Conference on Food, Nutrition and Health, 1969; World Food Conference, Rome, 1974; Consultant, Ford Foundation, London 1974-75; American Society for Tropical Medicine & Hygiene; Member, Board for International Food and Agricultural Development, 1979-82 . *Honours:* President, J F Kapnek Charitable Trust Inc. *Hobbies:* Walking; Swimming; Concertgoing. *Address:* 220 Locust St., Philadelphia, PA 19106, USA.

POLLOCK Ellen Clara, b. 29 June 1902, Heidelberg, Germany. Actress; Antique Dealer. m. (1) Captain Leslie Frank Hancock, RE; (2) James Proudfoot, RP ROI, 13 July 1944, 1 son. *Appointments:* Career includes: 1st Appearance, Everyman Theatre, 1920, as page in Romeo & Juliet; Baroness in The Melting Pot, The Big-eared Goblin and the Fairy Doll in Through the Crack & Herod's Son in an Old English Nativity Play in which she appeared with the late Ellen Terry Eliza in Pygmalion, 1944; joined the Donald Wolfit Company at Kings, Hammersmith, 1953; Audrey in As You Like It; Maria in Twelfth Night; Judith in the Wandering Jew; etc; Appeared in TV plays and series including The Forsythe Saga; The Palliser; Commenced film career, 1927; created part, Sweetie in Too True to be Good, GBS, The Albery Theatre, 1932; created part, Aloysia Brollikins in On the Rocks, GBS, The Winter Garden Theatre (now New London Theatre, Drury Lane); has played more Shavian Heroines than any other actress. *Membership:* President, Shaw Society. *Hobby:* Antiques Dealer. *Address:* 9 Tedworth Square, London SW3, England.

POLON Linda Beth, b. 7 Oct. 1943, Baltimore, Maryland, USA. Teacher; Writer; Illustrator; Educator. m. (1)Martin Polon, 18 Dec. 1966, divorced, (2)Robert Dorsey, 13 Apr. 1986. *Education:* BA, University of California, Los Angeles, 1966; Elementary Teaching Credential, 1967. *Appointments:* Elementary School Teacher, 1967; Writer/Illustrator, Children's Educational Books, 1974-; Book Reviewer, 1980-. *Publications:* Creative Teaching Games, 1974; Teaching Games for Fun, 1976; Paragraph Production, 1981; Stir Up a Story, 1981; Illustrated & Written: Making Kids Click, 1979; Write Up a Storm, 1979; Using Words Correctly, Grade 3/4 and 5/6; The Whole Earth Holiday Book, 1984; Whirlwind Writing, 1986; Magic Story Starters, 1987. *Memberships:* Society of children's Book Writers. *Hobbies:* Tennis; Jogging; Swimming; Drawing; Long Distance Walking; Gardening. *Address:* 1515 Manning Avenue No. 3, Los Angeles, CA 90024, USA.

PONSONBY RYBOT Doris Almon, b. 23 Mar. 1907, Devonport, England. Journalist. m. John Rybot, 30 Sept. 1933. *Publications:* As D.A. Ponsonby, & Doris Rybot: 32 novels; 3 biographies; 3 on Animals. *Memberships:* London Library; West Country Writers Association. *Hobbies:* Natural History; Animals. *Address:* c/o Curtis Brown, 162-168 Regent Street, London, England.

PONTIOUS Susan Anita, b. 19 Feb. 1951, Lynwood, California, USA. Arts Administrator (Public Art); Artist. m. Robert Saltz, 16 June 1973, 1 daughter. *Education:* BA magna cum laude, University of California, Irvine; MFA, University of Massachusetts, Amherst, 1976. *Appointments:* Artist, Publicist, Grant Writer, Hestia Art Collective, Northampton, Massachusetts, 1978-80; Art Instructor, Holy Names College, Oakland, California, 1981-83; Executive Director, Public Art Works, San Rafael, California, 1983-; Curator and Co-ordinator of the Art in Public Places program, San Francisco Art Commission, 1990-. *Creative works:* Hestia Mural Project, Northampton, 1980; Book: History of Women in Northampton, 1600-1980. *Membership:* Arttable.

Honour: Governor's Regional Design Award, Hestia Mural Project, 1986. *Address:* 45 Hyde Street, San Francisco, CA 94102, USA.

POOL Michelle Robin Rizer (Captain), Commissioned Officer, US Army. *Education:* BA, Biology, Talladega College, 1976; Officer Basic Course, 1980, Advance Course, 1984, Army Medical Department (AMEDD); MA, Management, 1983, MA, Public Administration, 1983, Webster University; Combined Arms Services Staff School, Command and General Staff College, 1988. *Appointments:* Teacher, Science and Mathematics, Mays Junior High School, Miami, Florida, 1977-78; US Army service, 1978-; enlisted, 1978, commissioned 2nd Lieutenant, 1980, currently Captain; Platoon Leader, 429th Medical Company (AMB), 1980-82, Training Officer, HQ, 44th Medical Brigade, 1982-84, Fort Bragg, North Carolina; Unit Commander, 32nd Combat Support Hospital, 1985-86, Company Commander, 557th Medical Company (AMB), 1986-88, Wiesbaden, Federal Republic of Germany; AMEDD Personnel Procurement Officer, Army Surgeon General's Office, Procurement Division, 1988-; Major exercise involvement: Bold Eagle, 1980; Life Line, 1983; Gallant Eagle, 1983, 1984; Grenada Conflict; Reforger, 1988. *Memberships:* Delta Sigma Theta Sorority Inc, 1973; American Legion Auxiliary 165, Miami, Florida; Associate Matron, Worthy Matron, Blanche M. Bruner Chapter No. 17, Order of the Eastern Star, Wiesbaden, Federal Republic of Germany; St Albans Congregational Church Choir, St Albans, New York; Heroines of Jericho, 1985. *Honours:* Army Good Conduct Medal, 1980; Expert Field Medical Badge, 1981; Army Achievement Medal, 1984; Army Commendation Medal and Oak Leaf, 1984, 1988; Meritorious Service Medal, 1988; Mainz Baptist Fellowship, Mainz, Federal Republic of Germany; Women's Day Speaker; Safety Officer of the Year, XVIII Airborne Corps, 1983; Member of the Year for the Order of The Eastern Star, 1986. *Hobbies:* Reading (mystics, mysteries, philosophy, religion and self-improvement books); Sports (cycling and weight-lifting); Letterwriting; Interior decorating; Landscaping; Writing poetry; Driving, especially European driving. *Address:* Post Office Box 4187, Bay Terrace, NY 11360-4187, USA.

POOL Nancy M, b. 4 Dec. 1920, St Louis, USA. Company President, Nancy Pool Developers. *Education:* BA, English, Washington University, 1941. *Appointments:* Partner, Vice President General Manager, KADI-FM, 1964-66; WIL-FM, 1966-69; KMOX FM, 1967-70; KSHE, 1970-84; KWK/KGLO, 1984-86; KXOK, KLTH, 1986-; President, Nancy Pool Construction Co. *Honours:* Citations for Community Service Awards. *Hobbies:* Golf; Tennis; Jogging; Yoga; Thoroughbred Racing. *Address:* 1801 South McKnight Road, Ladue, MO 63124, USA.

POOLE Josephine, b. 12 Feb. 1933, London, England. Writer. m. (1) Timothy Poole, 14 July 1956, divorced, 1974, 4 daughters, (2) Vincent Helyar, 29 Aug. 1974, 1 son, 1 daughter. *Publications:* A Dream in the House, 1961; Moon Eyes, 1965; The Lilywhite Boys, 1968; Catch as Catch Can, 1969; Yokeham, 1970; Billy Buck, 1972; Touch and Go, 1976; When Fishes Flew, 1978; Hannah Chance, 1980; Diamond Jack, 1983; Country Diary Companion, 1983; Three for Luck, 1985; Wildlife Tales, 1986; The Loving Ghosts, 1988; TV Scripts: Serial of Touch & Go, 1977; The Harbourer, 1975; Contributor to West Country Tales Series; Three in the Wild, 1985 (3 part series); Remedial Readers: The Open Grave; The Forbidden Room, 1979; Retold Golden Classics: Puss in Boots; The Sleeping Beauty, 1982. *Hobbies:* Conversation; Cooking; Travel; House, Garden. *Address:* Poundisford Lodge, Poundisford, Taunton TA3 7AE, England.

POPE Janet Coral Campbell, b. 24 Nov. 1953, Albuquerque, New Mexico, USA. Architect. m. Rodney Lee Pope, 14 June 1977. *Education:* BS (Architecture) 1975, MArch 1977, Georgia Tech; MS, Real Estate, College of Business, Georgia State University, 1989. *Appointments:* Assistant Planner, Marta, 1977-78;

Architectural Intern, Toombs, Amisano & Wells, 1978-80; Project Architect, Thompson, Ventulett & Stainback 1980-84, Dimery Corbett West, 1984; Architectural Renderer, Dan Harmon & Associates, 1984-85; Principal, Campbell Pope & Associates Inc, 1985-; Principal, Chantilly Properties, Inc., 1986-; Presently active as Architect, Renderer and one active Real Estate Development Project in Atlanta. *Creative work includes:* Painting exhibited, High Museum of Art, Atlanta, 1981. *Memberships:* Elected Member, from Atlanta Chapter to Georgia Board, American Institute of Architects (AIA), 1989 & 1990; Urban Land Institute; National Society for Historic Preservation. *Honours:* Cheesborough Pond Award (State Prize), watercolour painting, Georgia, 1967; Governor's Honors Program, Art, 1969; Swguoyan High School, Best Artist Awards, 1968-69 and 1969-70; High school graduation with honours, 1971; Completed one year Junior Enrollment Program for High School Students senior year of High School, 1970-71, to Dekalb Junior College, Clarkston, Georgia; Dean's List, Dekalb College, 1970-71; Art Editor, Dekalb College Yearbook, 1970-71; Firts JEPHS Student elected to Student Senate, Dekalb College, 1970-71; Beauty Pageant Sponsored Entry, Dekalb College, 1971; Scholarship, Georgia Tech, 1971; Dean's List, 1971-75; 3rd prize, Emerson Memorial Award, National Institute for Architectural Education, 1975; Award, Excellence of Studies in Housing, Graduate Program, Atlanta chapter AIA, 1977. *Hobbies:* Painting & drawing; Reading; Photography; Travel; Extracurricular studies. *Address:* Suite 1035, 3400 Peachtree Road, Atlanta, Georgia 30326, USA.

POPE Rose Iree Williams, b. 26 July 1916, Screven County, Georgia, USA. Judge of Probate Court, Richmond County, Georgia. m. Otto W Pope, 19 June 1938, deceased. 1 son, deceased. *Education:* Graduated, Screven County High School; Studied, Garrett Commercial School, Augusta, Georgia. *Appointments:* Typist 1943, Deputy Clerk 1943-47, Clerk 1947-57, Judge 1957-, Court of Ordinary (now Probate Court), Richmond County, Georgia; Director, Georgia Federal (now Commercial Bank), 1959-86. *Memberships:* Life Member, International Association of Probate Judges; Life Member, National Association of Probate Judges, 1972; Life Member, Augusta Geneological Society, 1981; Election Laws Study Committee under Governors Griffin and Vandiver; Constitutional Revision Committee, under Governor Sanders; Board of Directors, Augusta Richmond County Law Library, also Secretary-Treasurer; Advisory Board, Parents Without Partners, Greater August Chapter No 131; Past President, August Area Mental Health Association; Past Board Director ARC Homes Service Committee; Past Vice President, Local Democratic Party, Board Governors; Past Member, State Democratic Executive Commmittee; Past Member Advisory Committee, Half-Way House, Augusta Area Mental Health Association. *Honours:* Elected to Serve as A Member of the Board of Advisors at the Georgia Regional Hospital (Mental, Alcohol and Drugs), Augusta, Georgia, December 1989; First woman, State of Georgia elected Director of a Federal Savings and Loan Association or Banking Institution; Outstanding Citizen, Augusta Geneological Society, 1986; Bronze Plaque, County Officers Association of Georgia, 1987. *Address:* Richmond County Probate Court, 401 Municipal Building, 530 Greene Street, Augusta, Georgia 30911, USA.

POPELL Catherine Long, b. 16 Feb. 1941, San Diego, California, USA. Clinical Neuropsychologist; Psychologist and Registered Nurse. m. Steven David Popell, 9 Aug. 1969. 1 son, 1 daughter. *Education:* BA, St Joseph College, 1966; BS, San Diego State University, 1969; MS, University of California, San Francisco, 1970; PhD, Wright Institute, Berkeley, California, 1983. *Appointments:* Teacher/Registered Nurse, 1963-77; Hospital Clinical Psycholgist, Santa Clara Valley Medical Center, 1984; Consultant Clinical Neuropsychologist, Greenery Rehabilitation Center, 1987-88; Assistant Clinical Professor, University of California, 1986-; Private Practice, 1985-. *Publications:* Transition to a Modular Curriculum Design: A Challenge in Nursing Education, 1976; An Interpretive Study of

Stress and Coping Among Parents of School-Age Developmentally Disabled Children, 1983; Articles in professional journals. *Memberships:* International Neuropsychological Society; Neuropsychology Forum; American Psychological AssociAtIon; California Psychological Association; The Association for Persons with Severe Handicaps; Bay Area Coalition for the Handicapped, Director 1978- 87; United Cerebral Palsy Association of San Mateo/Santa Clara Counties Inc, Director 1979-84. *Honours:* Diplomate and Fellow, American Board of Medical Psychotherapy, 1987; Volunteer Recognition Plaque, United Cerebral Palsy San Mateo/Santa Clara Counties Inc, 1979; Sigma Theta Tau Honor Society 1970; Alpha Gamma Sigma Honor Society, 1966. *Hobbies:* Books; Gardening; Environment; Politics. *Address:* 201 San Antonio Circle, Suite 118, Mountain View, California 94040, USA.

POPRICK Mary Ann, b. 25 June 1939, Chicago, Illinois, USA. Clinical Psychologist. *Education:* BA, Psychology, Sociology, 1960; MA, General Psychology, 1964, DePaul University, Chicago, Illinois; PhD, General Experimental Psychology, Loyola University, Chicago, 1968; Registered Psychologist, State of Illinois, 1968; National Register of Health Service Providers in Psychology. *Appointments include:* Graduate Assistant, 1960-61, DePaul University, Chicago; Psychology Intern, 1961-62, Staff Psychologist, 1962, Elgin State Hospital, Elgin, Illinois; Staff Psychologist, Illinois State Training School for Girls, Geneva Illinois, 1962-63; Staff Psychologist, Mount Sinai Hospital, Chicago, 1963-64; Lecturer in Psychology, 1964-67, Graduate Assistant in Experimental Psychology, 1964, Research Assistant in Experimental Psychology, 1966, Loyola University, Chicago; Assistant Professor of Psychology, 1967-70, Chairman, Department of Psychology, 1968-72, Associate Professor of Psychology, 1970-75, Adjunct Associate Professor of Psychology, 1975, Lewis University, Lockport, Illinois; Private Clinical Practice, Associated with David Psychiatric Clinic Ltd, South Holland, Illinois, 1973-87; Scientific Staff, Department of Psychiatry, Christ Hospital, Oak Lawn, Illinois, 1983-; Private Independent Clinical Practice, South Holland, Illinois, 1987-. *Publications:* Master's thesis: Transfer of training as a function of complexity in a mirror-tracing experiment; Doctoral Dissertation: Risk taking behaviour: Risky and conservative shifts; Jointly: Effects of source credibility on the relationship between authoritarianism and attidue change, 1968. *Memberships include:* American Association for the Advancement of Sciences; American Psychological Association; Association for the Advancement of Psychology,; California State Psychological Association; various posts held in Illinois Psychological Association; Midwestern Psychological Association; Representative from Illinois to the American Psychological Association Council of Representatives, 1985-88. *Honours include:* Delta Epsilon Sigma; Kappa Gamma Pi; Psi Chi. *Hobbies:* Reading; Music. *Address:* 547 Marquette Avenue, Calumet City, IL 60409, USA.

PORRAS Juanita Ana, b. 11 Feb. 1955, Dallas, Texas, USA. Registered Nurse. *Education:* AA, Nursing, 1981; Medicallaw Associate legal assistance, 1984; BA, General Studies, 1986. *Appointments:* Tutorial Assistant, Acounting Laboratory, 1983-87; Registered Nurse, General Duties, 1987-. *Memberships:* Phi Theta Kappa national honour society; Dallas Association of Legal Assistants; American Red Cross Nurse. *Honours:* Humane Award, North Shore Animal League, 1978-79; Student Nurse Achievement Awards, American Red Cross, 1979, 1980; Student Leader Award, 1987. *Hobbies:* Nature walks; Reading; Music; Visiting museums & libraries. *Address:* 4710 Travis, Dallas, Texas 75205, USA.

PORTAL OF HUNGERFORD Rosemary Ann, Baroness, b. 12 May 1923, Denton, Lincolnshire, England. Retired Medical Secretary. *Appointments:* Medical Research Council Headquarters. *Memberships:* Fellow, Huguenot Society of London. *Honours:* created Baroness Portal of Hungerford, inherited under Special Arrangement through her father. *Hobbies:* Music;

English; Art; Garden Birds. *Address:* West Ashling House, Nr. Chichester, West Sussex, PO18 8DN, England.

POSEY Elsa, b. 27 June 1938, USA. Dance Educator. 2 sons. *Education:* Metropolitan Opera Ballet School; Ballet Russe de Monte Carlo School; American Ballet Theatre School; School of American Ballet. *Appointments:* Founder, Posey School of Dance Inc., 1953-; Founding Member, American Dance Guild, 1956; Co- Director, All About Dance Co., 1969-76; Director, Posey Dance Company, 1976- 79; Long Island Ballet, 1979-80; Artistic Director, Posey Dance Co., 1980-; Founder, Dance Ed. Services of L I Inc., 1969. *Publications:* At Ease with dance, 1979; Choreographer, It's Raining. *Memberships:* Congress on Research in Dance; Dance History Scholars; Dance Critics Association; Founding Member, President 1983-84, American Dance Guild; Chair, Professional Studio Teachers of Dance; National Dance Association; National Coalition Education in the Arts. *Hobby:* Sailing. *Address:* PO Box 254, Northport, NY 11768, USA.

POSNIAK Sallie Cecelia, b. 2 Mar. 1934, Appleton, Wisconsin, USA. Retail Designer. *Education:* Ray Vogue Art School, 1952-53; Chicago Art Institute, 1954-57. *Appointments:* Trimmer 1957-58, assistant designer 1958-61, designer 1961-67, Master Designer 1967-86; Manager, Central Design 1986-, Marshall Field, Chicago. *Honours:* Scholarships, 1952, 1954. *Hobbies:* Archaeology; Portrait & landscape painting; Sculpting; Gardening. *Address:* 5014 Greenwood, Skokie, Illinois 60077, USA.

POTASH Janice Sue, b. 24 Mar. 1955, Fort Knox, Kentucky, USA. Accounting Professor, Marian College. m. Steven R Potash, 28 May 1978. 1 daughter. *Education:* BS, Business, cum laude, Miami University, 1977; MBA, Xavier University, 1982. *Appointments:* Staff Accountant & Auditor, Arthur Andersen & Co, 1977-78; Accounting Supervisor, Children's Hospital Medical Center, 1978-81; Accounting Professor, Miami University, 1982-84; Accounting Professor, Marian College, 1985-89. *Memberships:* American Institute of CPAs; Ohio Society of CPAs; Indiana CPA Society; American Accounting Association; Accounting Research Association; American Women's Society of CPAs; American Society of Women Accountants. *Honours:* CPA, Ohio, 1982; Outstanding Young Women of America, 1983. *Hobbies:* Golf; Dancing. *Address:* 11123 Haverstick Road, Carmel, Indiana 46032, USA.

POTOCKA Maria Anna, b. 22 June 1950, Paczkow, Poland. Artist; Art Dealer; Photographer; Writer. m. (1) Jaroskaw Potocki, 1970, div. 1972, (2) Jozef Chrobak, 2 Sept. 1971, div. 1980, (3) Ryszard Ondrusz, 1980, div. 1988, 1 son. *Education:* Polish Philology, 1968-73, History of Art, 1972-74, Jagellonian University. *Appointments:* PI private gallery, 1972-80; DESA firm, Cracow, 1974; Pawilon Gallery, 1974; Photo-Video Gallery, 1979; Potocka Gallery, 1986. *Creative works:* Numerous works with photography and texts exhibited in Poland and Germany; Something Should Be For Blyn, thriller; Short stories and articles. *Memberships:* Internationale Kunstler; Gremium. *Hobbies:* Modern art; Cologne Cathedral; Tatra Mountains; Thrillers; Watching people. *Address:* ul Pijarska 19/4, 31- 017 Cracow, Poland.

POTTER Margaret (Newman), b. 21 June 1926, Harrow, Middlesex, England. Writer. m. 11 Feb. 1950, 1 son, 1 daughter. *Education:* St Hugh's College, Oxford University, 1944-47; MA (Oxon). *Publications:* As Anne Betteridge, 20 books including: Truth Game, Tiger & the Goat, Journey From A Foreign Land, novels; Time of Their Lives, Place for Everyone, short stories. As Anne Melville, 12 books for adults including: Lorimer Line, House of Hardie, Sirocco. As Margaret Newman: Murder to Music. As Margaret Potter, 2 adult books: Unto the Fourth Generation, Lochandar; 9 children's books including: Touch-&-Go Year, Sandy's Safari, Story of the Stolen Necklace, Tony's Special Place, Boys Who

Disappeared, Trouble on Sunday, Motorway Mob, Tilly & the Princess. *Honours:* Major scholarship, Modern History, St Hugh's College, 1944; Major award, Romantic Novelists' Association, 1966. *Hobbies:* Tennis; Bowls; Travel; Gardening; Reading. *Address:* c/o Peters Fraser & Dunlop, 5th Floor, The Chambers, Chelsea Harbour, Lots Road, London SW10 0XF, England.

POTTS Barbara J, b. 18 Feb. 1932, Los Angeles, California, USA. Radiology Technician. m. Donald A Potts, 27 Dec. 1953, 3 sons, 1 daughter. *Education:* AA, Graceland College, Lamoni, Iowa RT (Radiology Technician) Independence Sanitarium and Hospital. *Appointments:* Technician, Independence Sanitarium and Hospital, 1953, 1958-59; St Mary's Hospital, Baltimore, 1954-55; Council Member-at-Large, City of Independence, Missouri, 1978-82; Mayor, City of Independence, 1982-90. *Memberships:* Chair, Mid-America Regional Council, 1984, 1985; President, Missouri Municipal League, 1987-88; Missouri Committee on Local Government Co-operation, 1985, 1986, 1987, 1988, 1989; Human Development Policy Committee, National League of Cities, 1984, 1985; Board Member, Greater Kansas City Chamber of Commerce, 1984, 1985; President, Child Placement Services, 1972-; Board Member, Independence Regional Health Centre, 1982-. *Honours:* Woman of Achievement Award, Mid-Continent Council of Girl Scouts, 1983; Jane Adams Award, Hope House, Shelter for Battered Women, 1984; Community Leadership Award, Comprehensive Mental Health Services, 1984; 75th Annual Women of Achievement Award, Mid-Continent Council of Girl Scouts, 1987. *Address:* 111 E. Maple, City Hall, Independence, MO 64050, USA.

POULTON Donna Lee, b. 6 Sept. 1945, Columbus, Ohio, USA. CPA. *Education:* BS, Ohio State University. *Appointments:* Senior Manager, Ernst & Whinney, 1967-84; Director, of Internal Audit, Liebert Corporation, 1984-87; Director, of Accounting, Quest International, 1987-. *Memberships:* Zonta International, Treasurer; American Institute of CPA's; Ohio Society of CPA's, Columbus Chapter, Director; Institute of Internal Auditors. *Honours:* Recipient, various honours and awards. *Hobbies:* Golf; Tennis; Community Service. *Address:* 4860 Smoketalk Lane, Westerville, OH 43081, USA.

POWDERLY SUTTON Barbara K, b. 29 Oct. 1940, Scranton, Pennsylvania, USA. Marketing/Advertising/Management Consultant. m. Ronald Lewis Sutton, 7 Jan. 1984, divorced 1985. *Education:* Miami-Dade Junior College. *Appointments:* Director of Media, Marketing Systems International, Reno, 1981-82; Owner, Powderly Associates Consultants, Reno and Scottsdale, 1983-86; Owner, Dolphin Secretarial Services, Reno, 1983-88; President, Business-Promotional Services Inc, Reno, 1986-. *Publications:* TV: The Ultimate Marketing Tool, Workbook/seminar written and conducted; Advertising & Marketing for Small Business, workbook & 3 hour seminar, writer and presenter. *Memberships:* Board Member, Reno Entrepreneurial Women; National Association of Female Executives; National Association of Secretarial Services. *Honour:* Appointed by Mayor as Commissioner to the Reno Commission on the Status of Women. *Hobbies:* Sculpting; Writing; Teaching; Reading; Bridge; Auto racing. *Address:* 1555 Ridgeview Drive, No. 241, Reno, NV 89509, USA.

POWELL Annabelle Council, b. 23 Nov. 1953, Burlington, North Carolina, USA. President and Founder, Geoscience Resources, Inc. m. Russell Eugene Guy, 12 July 1986. *Education:* AB, Wellesley College, Wellesley, USA, 1975; DPhil, University of Oxford, England, 1980. *Appointments:* Assistant Curator, Natural History Museum, Basel, Switzerland, 1980-81; Assistant Professor, Rutgers University, New Brunswick, New Jersey, USA, 1981- 82; Founder & President, Geoscience Resources, Inc, 1982-. *Memberships:* Member of various geological organizations including: Palaeontological Association (UK); Geol Society of America; American Association of Petroleum

Geologists; Board of Directors, Love School of Business, Elon College, North Carolina. *Hobbies:* Private pilot (single engine); Playing ragtime piano and pipe organ. *Address:* P O Box 1992, Burlington, NC 27216, USA.

POWELL Bee Amabel Rhoda, b. 22 Nov. 1908, New Zealand. m. John Eric Nilson, 15 May 1937. *Education:* BHSc, University of New Zealand, 1931; Academic Diploma in Education, London University, England, 1959. *Appointments:* Municipal Electricity Department, Christchurch, New Zealand, 1932-35; Demonstrator and research, General Electric Co, London, England, 1935-39; Ministry of Food, London, 1943-46; Lecturer, N. Poly. London, 1948-68. *Publications include:* The Penguin Cookery Book; Cooking for Special Diets; ed. The Coeliac Handbook; Slimming Guide; ed. Womens Institute Diamond Jubilee Cookery Book; Best of Bee Nilson, etc. *Memberships:* British Dietetic Association; State Registered Dietitian; Home Economics Association; Society of Genealogists. *Honour:* Bronzemedaille-Gastronomische Akademie Deutschlands fur das Buch, Cooking for Special Diets, 1968. *Hobbies:* Gardening; Recording plants in pastel drawings; Researching the history of food in New Zealand/Polynesian to European/14th-19th Century; Researching the history of three families who emigrated to New Zealand in the 19th century. *Address:* 27 Betjeman Close, Pinner Road, Pinner, Middlesex HA5 5SA, England.

POWELL Carol Christine, b. 15 Feb. 1941, Seattle, Washington, USA. Restaurant Owner/Manager. m. (1) William F Roth, 8 Apr. 1961, divorced 1972, 1 son, 2 daughters, (2) George B Powell, 22 Dec. 1972, 1 son, 1 daughter. *Appointments:* Dishwasher, Happy Chef, 1978; Waitress, Cook, Dishwasher, 1978, Manager 1979-82; Owner, Operator, The Food Broker, Cherokee, 1983-. *Memberships:* Cherokee Chamber of Commerce; Cherokee Community School Advisory Committee. *Hobbies:* Piano; Reading; Arobics. *Address:* 320 North Sixth, Cherokee, IA 51012, USA.

POWELL Elizabeth, b. 17 May 1943, Thorpe, West Virginia, USA. Union Official. m. Vernis Harris, 28 Mar. 1964 (div. 1982), 2 sons, 1 daughter. *Education:* West Virginia State Collge, 1961-63; Arbitration Schools, Detroit, Michigan 1981, McClean, Virginia 1987. *Appointments:* Secretary-Treasurer 1972-76, Local President 1979-83, New York State Vice President 1980-83, National Business Agent 1983- (1st woman elected), American Postal Workers Union. Also: Teacher's Aide, Hempstead School District, New York, 1975-77. *Memberships:* National Council of Negro Women; National Association for Advancement of Coloured Peoples; Order of Eastern Star; Post Office Women Equal Rights Association; Coalition of Labour Union Women. ssa 20Honours: Salutarian, Aracoma High School, 1961; Image Award, POWERA, Houston, Texas, 1985; Academy of Women Achievers, New York YWCA, 1986; Service Awards, Western Nassau 1985, Hempstead 1986, APWU; Honour Award, NY State APWU, 1987; Special Lady Award, Hawaii APWU, 1987; Accomplishment Award, POWERA, 1986. *Hobbies:* Music; Dancing; Reading; Representing union members. *Address:* c/o American Postal Workers Union, 460 West 34th Street, 9th Floor, New York, NY 10001, USA.

POWELL Kerstin Marianne Burkhard, b. 30 Nov. 1944, Georgenswalde, Germany. US Citizen. Human Resources Administrator; Seminar Leader; Lecturer. m. Henry Edgar Powell, 29 May 1971, 1 daughter. *Education:* BA, Sociology, MA, Counselling, West Virginia University, USA. *Appointments:* Human Relations Consultant Anne Arundel County Public Schools, 1970-74; Programme Director, YWCA Woman's Centre, Annapolis, 1978-80; Director, Patient Services, Planned Parenthood of Maryland, 1980-83; Director, Human Resources, Anne Arundel General Hospital, 1983-87, Beebe Medical Centre, Lewes, 1987-. *Memberships:* Anne Arundel County Commission for Women, Chairperson, 1978; Mental Health Association of Anne Arundel County, Board of Directors; US Pony Clubs, Board of Directors; National Association for

Female Executives; Association of Delaware Hospitals; American Society of Personnel Administrators; American Society of Training & Development; American Society of Human Resource Administrators. *Honours:* Outstanding Young Annapolitan, 1978; Gubenatorial Commendatin for Public Service to the State of Maryland, 1978. *Hobbies Include:* Equestrian Sports. *Address:* 2548 Arbor Court, Davidsonville, MD, 21035, USA.

POWELL Sharon Lee, b. 25 July 1940, Portland, Oregon, USA. Executive Director. *Education:* BSc., Oregon State University, 1962 MEd., Seattle University, 1971. *Appointments:* Director, Outdoor Education, Mapleton Public Schools, 1962-63; Director Field Services, Assistant Director, Field Services, Field Director, Totem Girl Scout Council, 1963-72; Programme Director, GS Council of Tropical Florida, 1972-74; Esecutive Director, Homestead Girl Scout Council, 1974-78; Executive Director, Moingona Girl Scout Council, 1978-. *Membrships Include:* Association of Girl Scout Executive Staff, various offices including: National Treasurer 1987-90; AAUWS, Altrusa. *Honours:* Girl Scouts of America Thanks Badge, 1981; Sportsman of the Year Nominee, Des Moines Obedience Training Club, 1987; United Way of Central Iowa Volunteer Service Award, 1988. *Hobbies:* Dog Obedience & Conformation Showing; Sailing; Downhill Skiing; Gardening. *Address:* 10715 Hickman Road, Des Moines, IA 50322, USA.

PRABUCKA-FIRLEJ Anna, b. 8 Mar. 1950, Elblag, Poland. Academic Teacher; Artist Musician (Pianist). m. Jan Firlej, 20 Mar. 1971, 1 son. *Education:* Diploma with distinction, Music Lyceum, Gdansk, 1969; MA, (Instrumental Faculty), 1974, Doctor (Adiunkt qualification), 1980, Academy of Music, Gdansk; Habilitation (Docent qualification), Academy of Music, Lodz, 1987. *Career:* Debut as Piano Soloist with orchestra at age 11, 1961; Soloist, symphony concertos, recitals, chamber concerts, Poland, Finland, Sweden, UK, Federal Republic of Germany, Democratic Republic of Germany, Iceland, Austria, Greece, Czechoslovakia, Hungary, Bulgaria, USSR; Radio and TV recordings; Teaching: Lecturer, 1974, Adiunkt, 1980, Docent, 1987, Academy of Music, Gdansk; Guest Professor: Music master-classes, Mynamaki, Finland, 1976; Internationale Musikseminar der DDR, Weimar-GDR, 1984-89; Mattheiser Sommer-Akademie, Sobernheim-GFR, 1988. *Publications:* Realisation of the piano part of instrumental baroque sonatas on basis of selected contemporary editions, 1988; Remarks on realisation accompaniment for piano extract from the selected works of vocal-instrumental scores by J. S. Bach, 1989. *Membership:* Association of Polish Artist Musicians. *Honours:* Honour Diploma, VII International R Schumann Piano Competition, Zwickau, Democratic Republic of Germany, 1977; Distinction for Merit, Town of Gdansk, 1981; Special Award (highest grade) of Culture Minister, 1989; About 10 prizes for Best Accompanist, national and international competitions. *Hobbies:* Painting; Literature; History. *Address:* ul Leszczynskich 1 g 24, 80-464 Gdansk, Poland.

PRADHAN Uma, b. 28 Feb. 1946, Nepal. Educator. *Education:* MA, Home Science; Special, Community Development and Sociology and Nutrition, 1984; Numerous courses, workshops and seminars. *Appointments:* Instructor, Training, Women's Training Centre, 1972-78; Editing Officer, Training Material Production Centre, 1978-81; Training Incharge, Women Development Section, 1982-. *Publications:* Books: Nutrition, 1977; Food Preservation, 1979; Articles in joournals. *Address:* Ka 1, 426 Inbanal Jyatha, Kathmandu, Nepal.

PRASLICK Gail Fitzpatrick, b. 22 Jan. 1949, Bronx, New York, USA. Pension Executive. m. Edward D Praslick, 28 Oct. 1972. *Education:* BA Mathematics, Marymount College Tarrytown, New York, 1970; Courant Institute of Mathematics, New York University's Graduate School of Mathematics; Certificate-Pension Fund Money Management, University of Pennsylvania,

Wharton School, 1986. *Appointments:* Actuarial Student, 1971; Actuarial Financial Analyst, 1974; Supervisor, Actuarial Technical Services, 1977; Manager, Actuarial Financial Reporting, 1978; Manager, Pensions Actuarial Pricing, Contracts, Financial Experience, 1982; Assistant Vice President, Pensions Operations, 1983; Vice President, Pensions Clinet Relations, 1985; Vice President, Pensions Client Relations, Market Research and Administration, 1987-, Metropolitan Life Insurance Company. *Honours:* National Honor Society, 1962-66; Dean's List, Marymount College, 1966-70; YWCA, Woman Achiever, 1985. *Hobbies:* All sports; Piano. *Address:* 7 Trimbleford Lane, Middletown, NJ 07748, USA.

PRATT Jeanne Marie, b. 22 June 1965, Port Jefferson, New York, USA. Freelance filmmaker; Photographer; Clerk. *Education:* BFA, Honors diploma, 1988. *Appointment:* Clerk, United Parcel Service-Controlled Dispatch. *Creative work:* Editor, Metalstopheles, short film. *Memberships:* Women in Communications Inc; American Society of Prof & Exec Women; American Film Institute. *Honours:* Represented Long Island University/CW Post in England and Wales 1987 in an Adopt-A-Student Program for film students; Honors diploma, 1988, Honor Society 1984-88, Long Island University/CW Post. *Hobbies:* Black and white darkroom photography; Cinematography and film editing; Nature photography; Painting 25mm lead figures. *Address:* 89 Oakmont Ave, Selden, NY 11784, USA.

PRESTAGE Jewel Limar, b. 8 Dec. 1931, Hutton, USA. Dean. m. James J. Prestage, 8 Dec. 1953, 3 sons, 2 daughters. *Education:* BA, Political Science, Southern University, 1951; MA, 1952, PhD, 1954, Political Science, University of Iowa. *Appointments:* Associate Professor, Politicla Science, Prairie View College, 1954-55; Associate Professor, 1956- 57, 1958-62, Professor, Political Science, 1962-, Chairperson, Political Science, 1965-83, Dean, Public Policy & Urban Affairs, 1983-, Southern University. *Publications:* A Portrait of Marginality: The Political Behaviour of the American Woman, co-author, 1977. *Memberships:* President, outhwestern Society School Association, 1973-74; President, Southern Polical Science Associaiton, 1975-76; President, National Conference of Black Political Scientists, 1976-77; etc. *Honours:* Recipient, various honours and awards. *Address:* 2145 -77th Avenue, Baton Rouge, LA 70807, USA.

PRESTON, Ivy Alice, b. 11 Nov. 1913, Timaru, New Zealand. Writer. m. Percival Edward James Preston, 14 Oct. 1935, 2 sons, 2 daughters. *Publications:* Autobiography, Landscapes of the Past; Elizabeth Ward, Pioneer, biography; 39 romance novels in hardback & reprinted in over 130 different editions including paperbacks, large print, casettes & 9 languages. *Memberships:* South Canterbury Writers Guild, President Secretary; romantic Novelists Association, London; Romance Writers of America; New Zealand Women Writers Association; South Island Writers Association. *Hobbies:* Writing; Reading; Travel; Poetry; Drama; Crosswords; Genealogy. *Address:* 95 Church Street, Timaru, South Canterbury, New Zealand

PREUSS Mary H, b. 4 Aug. 1937, Ellwood City, Pennsylvania, USA. Associate Professor. m. Franklin A Preuss, 21 Mar. 1964. *Education:* BA 1959, MED 1965, Graduate Certificate Latin American Studies 1977, PhD Hispanic Literature 1981, University of Pittsburgh. *Appointments:* Lecturer in Spanish, Chatham College, Pittsburgh, 1978-80; Taught conversational Spanish to four executives of Magee Corporation, 1979-80; Lecturer in Spanish, Carlow College, Pittsburgh, 1979-81; Associate Professor, Geneva College, Beaver Falls, Pennsylvania, 1981-89; Head of Foreign Language Department 1983-89; Coordinator, Latin American Business Studies Programme; Translator for local business firms, 1983; Associate Professor, Pennsylvania State University, 1989-. *Publications include:* Los Dioses del Popol Vuh, 1988; Gods of the Popol Vuh: Xmukane, K'ucumatz, Tohil and Juracan,

1988; Journal articles, translations, book reviews, abstracts; numerous original research papers presented to conferences. Editor: Latin American Indian Literatures Journal, 1985-; Honorary Editorial Board, Mythologic (Argentina); Editor, Newsletter of LAILA/ALILA, 1982-84; Editorial Assistant, Latin American Indian Literatures, 1977-84; Editor, In Love and War: Hummingbird Lore and other selected papers of Lbila/Alila's 1988 Symposium, 1989. *Memberships:* Founding Member, Board of Directors, President 1982-87, Latin American Indian Literatures Association; Latin American Studies Association; Modern Language Association; Middle Atlantic Council on Latin American Studies. *Honours:* Delta Kappa Gamma, 1972; Served on interviewing committee for Fulbright Scholarships, 1977; Phi Sigma Iota, 1980; American Philosophical Society Research Grant, 1983; Reviewer of grants for Translation Program of NEH, 1984; International Research Fellowship, Delta Kappa Gamma Society, 1984; Reviewer predoctoral grants for NEH, 1985; Research Development Grant, Pennsylvania State University. *Hobbies:* Travel; Gardening; Oil painting; Classical guitar; Cats. *Address:* 145 Timberlane Drive, Pittsburgh, PA 15229, USA.

PRICE Betty Jean Griesenauer, b. 28 Sept. 1928, Newport News, Virginia, USA. Reading Consultant; Private Tutor. m. Robert Carroll Price, 14 June 1952, 2 sons. *Education:* Diploma, St Patrick's Catholic Academy, 1946; Diploma, Pan-American Business College, Richmond, 1947; BA, English 1983, MA Linguistics, 1985, Hollins College, Virginia. *Appointments:* Activities concerned with reading 1952-; Private Tutoring, 1970-. *Publications:* See Me Read and Discover the World, co-author; Rewrite of John Milton's Paradise Lost, a contemporary piece to appeal to 10-14 year old boys; Reading, An Analytical Survey; articles in: Reading Newsletter; Virginia Club Woman; Roanoke Times and World News. *Memberships:* President, Valley Junior Woman's Club; Virginia Frederation of Womens Clubs; General Federation of Womens Clubs; Contact Representative, Easter Seal Society and Camp Easter Seal; Chairman, Miss Virginia Pageant; President, Williamson Road Citizens' Committee; President, Ki-Wives of Williamson Road; International Reading Associatiron; Reading Reform Foundation; American Association of University Women. *Hobbies:* Reading; Painting; Music; Handicrafts; Cooking. *Address:* 542 Elden Avenue, NW, Roanoke, VA 24019, USA.

PRICE Carol Ann, b. 4 Apr. 1944, Detroit, Michigan, USA. Computer Science Manager. m. William Robert Price, 27 June 1964, 2 sons *Education:* BA, University of Florida, 1965; MA, Wayne State University, 1970. *Appointments:* Math programmer, Parke Davis & Co, Detroit, 1965-69; Mathematician advanced product and manufacturing engineering staff 1969-75, Staff Devel Engineer 1976-78, Senior Staff Project Engineer 1978-81, Supervisor 1981-85, General Motors Corp, Warren, Michigan; Regional Manager, Electronic Data Systems, Warren, 1985-; President, Emerald Lake Homeowners, Troy, Michigan, 1980-82. *Memberships:* IEEE; Michigan Professional Women's Network. *Hobbies:* Bridge; Travelling; Reading. *Address:* 6136 Sandshores, Troy, MI 48098, USA.

PRICE Lucile Brickner, b. 31 May 1902, Decorah, Iowa, USA. Retired College Administrator. m. (1) Maynard Wilson Brown, 2 July 1928, deceased 1937, (2) Charles Edward Price, 14 Jan. 1961, deceased 1983. *Education:* BS, Iowa State University, 1925; MA, Northwestern University. *Appointments:* Assistant Dean of Women, Kansas State University, 1925-28; Board Student Per. Adm., 1937-41, Northwestern University; Overseas Club Director, American Red Cross, England, North Africa, Italy, 1942-45; Director, Child Education Foundation, New York City, 1946-56. *Memberships:* American College Personnel Association; American Association of University Women; Winneshiek County Civil Service Commission, 1978-84; Board, Northeast Iowa Mental Health Centre, etc. *Honours:* Alumni Merit Award, Iowa State University, 1975; Gift to American

Association of University Womens Education Foundation in her name, 1977; Certificate of Appreciation, Winneshiek County Historical Society, 1984. *Hobbies:* Mental Health Services; Historic Preservation. *Address:* 508 West Broadway, Decorah, IA 52101, USA.

PRICE Nancy, b. 30 Mar. 1943, Dawlish, Devon, England. Freelance Writer. *Appointments:* Contributor To Magazine, English Art, 1966-67; Editor, English Art, 1967-78; Freelance Writer, 1978-. *Publications:* many articles in English Art, and all other art magazines & journals. *Memberships:* English Art Forum; Brush and Wash Club, London. *Hobbies:* Watercolours; Reading. *Address:* Wychelm, Walden Road, Hadstock, Essex, England.

PRIMAROLO Dawn, b. 2 May. 1954, London, England. Member of Parliament (Bristol South). m. Oct. 1972, separated. 1 son. *Education:* BA Hons, Bristol Polytechnic, 1981-84; PhD Research student, Bristol University, 1984-87. *Appointments:* Legal Secretary, Law Centre. Elected Member of Parliament, Bristol South, 1987-. *Address:* House of Commons, London SW1A 0AA

PRINCE Antoinette Odette, b. 18 Mar. 1946, Watertown, New York, USA. Visual Artist; Art Educator. m. George Mather Prince, 5 Aug. 1976, divorced 1981. *Education:* 5th yr. graduate, Boston Museum School, 1982; Degree Candidate, Harvard University Extension, 1986-. *Appointments:* Painting Instructor, Boston Museum School, 1981-82, 1986; Painting/Drawing Instructor, Tufts University Experimental College, 1986; Director, Loading Dock Gallery, 1982-83; Painting Instructor, Cambridge Art Association, 1983-85; Painting, Drawing, Art Instructor, Cambridge Centre Adult Education, 1984-89. *Memberships:* Board of Directors, Cambridge Art Association. *Honours:* Travelling Scholars Award, Museum of Fine Arts, 1982; Public Action for the Arts Grantee, 1985. *Hobbies:* Archaeology; Astronomy; Ballet; Opera; Travel. *Address:* 6 Vernon Street, Somerville, MA 02145, USA.

PRINCE Frances Anne Kiely, b. 20 Dec. 1923, Toledo, USA. Editor, Nebraska Garden News. m. 17 Aug. 1951. 1 son, 1 daughter. *Education:* AB, Berea College, 1951; Postgraduate, Kent School Social Work, 1951; Creighton University, 1969; MPA, University of Nebraska, Omaha, 1978. *Appointments:* Instructor, flower arranging Western Wyoming Jr College, 1965, 1966; Editor, Nebraska Garden News, 1983-. *Memberships:* Chairman, Lone Troop Council Girl Scouts USA, 1954-57, trainer leaders 1954-68, state camping com, 1959-61, bd mem Wyo state council, 1966-69; Chairman, Community Improvement, Green River, 1959, 1963-65; Wyo Fedn Women's Clubs State Library Services, 1966-69; Wyo State Adv Bd on Library Inter-coop, 1965-69; Bd Member Sweetwater County Library System, 1962-, pres bd 1967-68; Adv Council, School District 66, 1970-; Bd Dirs, Opera Angels, 1971, fundraising chairman 1971-72, vicepresident 1974-; Bod Dirs, Morning Musicale, 1971-; Bazaar com, Children's Hosp, 1970-75; Docent Joslyn Art Mus, 1970-; Nebr Forestry Adv Bd, 1976-; Citizens adv bd, Met Area Planning Agency, 1979-; Nebr Tree-Planting Commn 1980-; Commission, Bicentennial for US Constitution Committee, 1986-; Board, US Constitution Bicentennial Commission of Nebraska, 1987-; Board, Omaha Commission on the Bicentennial, 1987-; National Council of State Garden Clubs, Bd of Directors, 1979-; etc. *Honours:* Recipient Library Service award, Sweetwater County Library, 1968; Girl Scout Services award, 1967; Conservation award, US Forest Service, 1981; Plant Two trees award, 1981; Nat Arbor Day award, 1982; US Constitution Bicentennial Commission of Nebraska, 1987; Omaha Commission on the Bicentennial, 1987; President's Award, National Council of State Garden Clubs, 1986, 1987. *Address:* 8909 Broadmoor Dr, Omaha, NE 68114, USA.

PRINCE Helen Walter Dodson, b. 31 Dec. 1905,

Baltimore, Maryland, USA. Retired University Professor. m. Edmond L Prince, 24 Oct. 1956. *Education:* AB 1927, ScD (Hon) 1952, Goucher College; MA 1932, PhD 1933, University of Michigan. *Appointments:* Assistant Professor of Astronomy, Wellesley College, 1933-45; Professor of Astronomy, Goucher College, 1945-50; Member of Faculty, University of Michigan, 1947-76; Associate Director, McMath-Hulbert Observatory, 1962-76; Solar Consultant, Applied Physics Laboratory, Johns Hopkins University, 1976-82. *Publications:* Numerous research articles in professional journals. *Memberships:* American Astronomical Society; International Astronomical Union; Phi Beta Kappa; Sigma Xi. *Honours:* Prize, American Astronomical Society, 1954-55; Distinguished Faculty Achievement Award, University of Michigan, 1975. *Hobby:* Reading. *Address:* 4800 Fillmore Ave, Alexandria, VA 22311, USA.

PRINCIPAL Victoria, b. 3 Jan. 1945, Fukuoka, Japan. Actress. *Education:* Dramatic Studies with Max Croft, Springfield, and Al Sacks in Miami; went to New York to become a model. *Creative Works:* Film debut: The Life and Times of Judge Roy Bean, 1972; Films include: The Naked Ape; Earthquake; I Will, I Will....for Now; Vigilante Force; TV: Fantasy Island (pilot); Love Story; Love American Style; Greatest Heroes of the Bible; Dallas; Author: The Body Principal. *Address:* c/o Lorimar TV Public Relations, 3970 Overland Ave., Culver City, CA 90230, USA.

PROCTER Carol Ann, b. 26 June 1941, Oklahoma City, USA. Cellist. *Education:* Eastman School of Music, 1958-60; BM, 1963, MM, 1965, New England Conservatory of Music. *Appointments:* Boston Symphony Orchestra, 1965-; Boston Pops Orchestra, 1965-; Japan Philharmonic Cultural Exchange, 1969-70. *Creative Works:* Soloist, Boston Pops, 1980, 1987; New England Harp Trio Member, 1972-; Member, Curtisville Consortium, 1973-. *Membership:* Association of Responsible Communication. *Honours:* Fromm Fellowship, 1965; Fulbright Award, 1965. *Hobbies:* Aquarium; Seashell Collecting; Hiking; Canoeing; Early Music; New Music. *Address:* c/o Boston Symphony Orchestra, Symphony Hall, Boston, MA 02115, USA.

PROLO Barbara, b. 23 Nov 1958, Bay Shore, USA. Attorney. *Education:* BA, cum laude, Belmont Abbey College, Belmont, North Carolina, 1980; JD, Oklahoma City University, School of Law, Oklahoma City, Oklahoma, 1984. *Appointments:* Legal Intern, Associate, Richard L Hasley Attorney, 1982-86; In-house Counsel, Blue Diamond Investments, 1986-. *Memberships:* Oklahoma County Bar Association; Oklahoma Bar Association; American Bar Association; Big Brothers/Big Sisters of Greater Oklahoma; Legal Aid of Western Oklahoma. *Honours:* Young Professional Hall of Fame, Contributions to the field of Law. *Hobbies:* Tennis; Golf; Soccer. *Address:* 1101 Westchester Drive, Oklahoma City, OK 73114, USA.

PROUD Elizabeth Ann, b. 1 May 1939, Southampton, England. Actress; Writer. *Education:* Stockton-on-Tees and Cambridgeshire High School for Girls; BA (Cantab) English Literature, Girton College, Cambridge, 1959-61; Acted with Marlowe Society, ADC, Mummers, Footlights etc. *Appointments:* Worked in Radio, TV, Film and on Stage, 1961-. Started writing professionally late 1970's. *Creative works:* Numerous Radio and TV plays; Written work broadcast on Radio 4 and for BBC Radio Schools. *Memberships:* British Actors Equity Association, 1960-; Society of Authors, 1982-; Chairman of Broadcasting Group, 1984-86; Radio Academy; Member of Sony Radio Awards organising committee since 1982; Founder Member, Lyra Greek Dancer, Honorary Secretary, 1986-87. *Hobbies:* Reading; Gardening; Greek language and culture, including Greek traditional dancing. *Address:* London and Asini, Nauplion, Greece.

PROVIS Dorothy Smith, b. 26 Apr. 1926, Chicago,

Illinois, USA. Sculptor. m. William Harold Provis, 28 July 1945, 2 sons. *Education:* School of the Art Institute of Chicago, 1953-56; School of Fine Arts, University of Wisconsin, Milwaukee, 1967-68, 1969-70. *Appointments:* Self Employed Artist in home studio. *Creative Works:* Innovator of Fur Sculpture with many 2D and 3D sculptures; Author, Wisconsin Consignment Bill, signed to law by Governor Madison, Wisconsin, November, 1979. *Memberships:* Chaired Panel, on Art Advocacy, Women's Caucus For Art Conference, Rabb Hall, Boston Public Library, Massachusetts, 1987; Served on Panel, The Arts Speak for Women, National Womens Conference Committee, A Decade of Women on the Move 1977-87, Sheraton Hotel, Washington DC. *Address:* 123 East Beutel Road, Port Washington, WI 53074, USA.

PRZEWORSKA-ROLEWICZ Danuta, b. 25 May 1931, Warszawa, Poland. Professor of Mathematics. m. Stefan Rolewicz, 26 Dec. 1951. 2 sons, *Education:* MA, University of Warsaw, 1956; PhD 1958, DSc 1964, Institute of Mathematics of the Polish Academy of Sciences. *Appointments:* Assistant to Lecturer, Technical University of Warsaw, 1954-60; Lecturer, 1960-74, Associate Professor, 1974-, Institute of Mathematics of the Polish Academy of Sciences. *Publications:* Books: Equations in linear spaces, with S Rolewicz, 1968; Equations with transformed argument, 1973; Linear spaces and linear operators (Polish), 1977; Introduction to Algebraic Analysis and its Applications (Polish), 1979; Shifts and Periodicity for Right Invertible Operators, 1980; Algebraic Analysis, 1988. *Memberships:* Polish Mathematical Society; American Mathematical Society; Gesellschaft für Mathematik, Ökonometrie und Operations Research, Federal Republic of Germany; Union of Polish Teachers (several offices held in 1972-85). *Honours:* Stefan Banach Prize of Polish Mathematical Society (with S Rolewicz), 1968; Prize of the Sci Secretary of 3rd Branch of the Polish Academy of Sciences (with S Rolewicz), 1970; Price of the Sci Secretary of the Polish Academy of Sciences, 1972; Prize, Commander of Military Technical Academy, 1975; Common Prize, Akademie der Wissenschaften der DDR and Polish Academy of Sciences, 1978; Warsaw Uprising Cross, 1982; Gold Cross of Merit, 1985. *Address:* Sierpecka 6/23, 01-593 Warszawa, Poland.

PUCKETT Ruby Parker, b. 26 Nov. 1932, Dora, Alabama, USA. Nutritionist Manager. m. Larry Willard Puckett, 2 July 1955, 2 daughters. *Education:* BS, Food & Nutrition, Auburn University, 1954; MA, Education & Health Care, Central Michigan University, 1976. Also: Henry Ford Hospital, & University of Florida. *Appointments:* Dietitian, Houston, Texas, 1955-56; Sole dietitian, Meridian, Mississippi, 1957-58; Assistant Director, Jackson, Mississippi, 1960-61; Director, Dietetics, Knoxville, Tennessee 1961-63, Eustis, Florida 1963-68; Director Food & Nutrition Services, Shands Hospital, University of Florida, 1968-; President, Square One Inc, 1979-85. *Publications include:* Numerous diet manuals, nutrition guides, correspondence courses, training manuals. Most recent: Foodservice in Health Care Facilities, 1988. Also: Monologues, abstracts, papers. *Memberships include:* Numerous offices, American, Florida & Gainesville Dietetic Associations; Offices, various other professional bodies. *Honours include:* White House Conference, & Senate Select Committee on Food & Nutrition, 1976; Scholarship named in honour, 1976; Numerous awards, recognitions, honour societies; Biographical recognition. *Hobbies:* White water rafting; Hiking; Gardening; Reading; Writing; History; Religion. *Address:* Route 3, Box 108-B2, Gainesville, Florida 32606, USA.

PUFLETT Delmont, b. 8 Oct. 1921, Sydney, Australia. Gynaecologist. m. Roy Richard Purcell, 26 Jan. 1956, 2 sons, 2 daughters. *Education:* MB.BS, Sydney, 1945; MRCOG, London, 1952; FRCOG, 1976; FRACOG, MHP, 1977. *Appointments:* Senior Gynaecologist, Rachel Forster Hospital, 1968-; Senior Gynaecologist, The Womens Hospital, 1976-81; Senior Gynaecologist, St Margarets Hospital, 1981-. *Publications:* Articles in journals and magazines including, Australian Medical Journal. *Memberships:* Committee, NSW Branch, Royal College Obstetricians & Gynaecologists, 1975- 79; Chairman, Medical Advisory Board, Family Planning Association of Australia; National Council of Women, Convenor for Health, 1975-; Australian Govt. Consultant in Gynaecology, 1976-, To Australian Army, 1978-. *Honours:* AM, 1984. *Hobbies:* Gardening; Family; Music; Travel; Sewing; Boating. *Address:* 9/94 Wycombe Road, Neutral Bay, Sydney 2089, Australia.

PUGLISI Angela Aurora, b. 28 Jan. 1949, Messina, Italy. Naturalised American Citizen. University Lecturer; Artist. *Education:* BA, cum laude, Dunbarton College, 1972; MFA, 1974, MA, Language & Literature, 1977, MA, art History, 1976, PhD Comparative Literature, 1983, Catholic University. *Appointments:* Instructor, Art, Catholic University, 1974-84; Assistant to Dean, American University, 1988; Lecturer, Georgetown University, 1986-. *Creative Works:* Writer, Consultant, US Dept. of Education, 1983-85; Poetry: Woodland Revisited, 1988; Prelude, 1987; etc; artistic works in private collections in USA & abroad. *Memberships:* Founding Member, Casa Italiana; Board of Directors, Senese Education Ent.; Academician, Cath. Academy of Sciences; etc. *Honours:* Recipient, various honours and awards. *Hobbies:* Sculpting; Writing. *Address:* 3003 Merritt Ct., Berkshire, MD 20747, USA.

PUKHOVA Zoya Pavlovna, b. 24 Sept, 1936. Ivanovsky region, USSR. President, Soviet Women's Committee. m. Valentin Alekseyevich Pukhov, 7 Sept. 1957. 2 sons. *Education:* Textile Vocational School; Party Higher School. *Appointments:* Weaver, Weaving Mill, Ivanovo, 1952-73; Director, March Weaving Mill, 1973-85; Chairman, Executive Council, Soviet People's Deputies, Ivanovsky region, 1985-87; Elected President, Soviet Women's Committee, National Women's Conference, 1987-; Deputy 1966-, elected People's Deputy 1989-, of the USSR and of the Supreme Soviet of the USSR. *Memberships:* Vice-President, Women's International Democratic Federation; Presidium of All-Union Central Council of Trade Unions; Board Member, Soviet Children's Fund; Mercy and Health Fund. *Honours:* Hero of Socialist Labour; USSR State Prize winner. *Hobby:* Books. Address: Nemirovich-Danchenko Str 6, Moscow 103832, USSR.

PULLEIN-THOMPSON Josephine Mary Wedderburn, b. Wimbledon, England. Writer. *Publications:* Over 40 books published including: Gin and Murder, 1959; They Died in the Spring, 1960; All Change, 1961; Murder Strikes Pink, 1963; Proud Riders, 1973; Black Raven, 1982; Mystery on the Moor, 1984; Pony Club Challenge, 1984; Pony Club Trek, 1985; Suspicion Stalks the Moor, 1986; As Josephine Mann, A Place with Two Faces, 1972; with sisters: It Began with picotee, 1946. *Memberships:* General Secretary, English Centre, International PEN, 1976-; Crimewriters Association, Committee 1971-73; Children's Writers Group, Committee, 1973-79; Deputy Chairman, 1978-79; Pony Club Visiting Commissioner, 1960-68, District Commissioner, 1970-76. *Honours:* Ernest Benn Award, for All Change, 1961; MBE, 1984. *Hobbies:* Reading; Travel; Gardening. *Address:* 16 Knivet Road, London SW6 1JH, England.

PUMPHREY Janet Kay, b. 18 June 1946, Baltimore, Maryland, USA. Editor. *Education:* AA 1967, AA 1976, Anne Arundel Community College, University of Maryland, Indiana University. *Appointments:* Office Manager, Anne Arundel Community College, Truxal Library, 1964-; Managing Editor, American Polygraph Association, 1973-. *Publications:* Ten Years of Polygraph (with Albert Snyder), 1984; Justice and the Polygraph, with Norman Ansley, 1985; Love will Forever Flow, poem, 1985; House Full of Love, 1986; To Fly a Kite, poem, 1987; Mama, poem, 1988; A House Full of Love, novel, 1989. *Memberships:* American Polygraph Association, Honorary Member; Maryland Polygraph Association, Affiliate Member; National Association of Female Executives; Anne Arundel County Historical Society, Contributing Member; Alumni Association;

Anne Arundel Community College, Secretary for 8 years; International Platform Association. *Honours:* Young America Gardens, Teen Division, 1st Place, 1961; 1st Place, College Scholarship, 1962; American Polygraph Association Service Awards, 1976, 1986; American Polygraph Association Service Certificates, 1976-88; Golden Poet Award, World of Poetry, 1986, 1987. *Hobbies:* Travel; Creative writing; Gardening; Painting; Handicrafts. *Address:* 3 Kimberly Court, Severna Park, MD 21146, USA.

PUNNETT Audrey Frances, b. 25 Oct. 1947, Washington, USA. Psychologist. *Education:* BS, 1971, MS, 1975, University of Utah; PhD, 1981. *Appointments:* Clinical Coordinator, Mental Health Service, DOBP Valley Children's Hospital, 1985-; Assistant Clinical Professor, UCSF, 1985-. *Publications:* Articles in professional journals. *Memberships:* American Board of Medical Psychotherapists, Fellow, Diplomate; American Psychological Association; California, San Joaquin Psychological Associations. *Honours:* Nominated, Outstanding Alumni, 1973-1983. *Hobbies:* Bicycling; Tennis; Reading. *Address:* Valley Childrens Hospital, 3151 N. Millbrook Avenue, Fresno, CA 93703, USA.

PUNNETT Betty Jane, b. 15 May 1947, St Vincent, Caribbean. University Professor. m. Donald Wood, 12 May 1984. 1 son, 1 daughter. *Education:* BA, McGill University, 1968; MBA, Marist College, 1977; PhD International Business & Organizational Behaviour, New York University, 1984. *Appointments:* Organizational Design and Development, Eureka Management Consultants, 1984-; Associate Professor of Business, University of Windsor, 1985-. *Publications include:* Experiencing International Management, 1989; Numerous articles to professional journals; numerous papers presented at conferences. *Memberships:* Institute for International & Developmental Studies, Executive Council; Academy of International Business; Academy of Management; Administrative Sciences Associatin of Canada. *Honour:* Mevil Fellowship, 1983. *Hobbies:* Gardening; Camping; Sailing. *Address:* University of Windsor, Faculty of Business Administration, 401 Sunset Avenue, Windsor, Ontario, Canada N9B 3P4

PURCELL Sally Anne Jane, b. 1 Dec. 1944, Cheshire, England. Writer. *Education:* BA 1966, MA 1970, Lady Margaret Hall, Oxford. *Literary Appointments:* Honorary Secretary, Foundation for Islamic Culture, Oxford, 1969-. *Publications:* The Devil's Dancing Hour, 1968; Provençal Poems, translator, 1969; The Happy Unicorns. Poetry of the Under-25's, editor with L Purves, 1971; The Holly Queen, 1972; George Peele, editor, 1972; Monarchs and the Muse: Poems by Monarchs and Princes of England, Scotland and Wales, editor and translator, 1972; The Exile of James Joyce by Hélène Cixous, translator, 1972; Charles d'Orléans, editor, 1973; Dark of Day, 1977; By The Clear Fountain; Guenever and the Looking Glass, 1984-85; The Early Italian Poets, by D G Rossetti, editor, 1981; Gaspara Stampa, 1984-85; Lake and Labyrinth, 1985; Amorgos, by Nikos Gatos, 1986, translator. Contributions to numerous magazines and journals. *Honour:* Arts Council Grant. *Address:* c/o Anvil Press, 69 King George Street, London SE10 8PX, England.

PURDY Felicity Anne, b. 7 Aug. 1937, Sydney, Australia. Deputy General Manager, Royal Blind Society of New South Wales. m. Justice John S Purdy, 6 Dec. 1958. 2 sons. *Education:* BA, 1st Class Honours, Psychology, University of Sydney, 1958. *Appointments:* Vocational Guidance Officer, labour & Industry, 1958-62; tutor, Psychology, University of Sydney (part-time), 1959; Psychologist (part-time), 1968-74, Director, Childrens Services, 1974-76, Director, Client Services, 1976-84, Director, Planning & Development, 1984-87, Deputy General Manager, 1987-, Royal Blind Society of New South Wales, Australia. *Memberships:* Australia's Representative on Rehabilitation Internation's World Commission on Social Welfare, 1980-; Convenor, Australian National Council of and for the Blind Low Vision Sub-Committee, 1980-84; Australian Council for Rehabilitation of Disabled,, Chairman New South Wales Division, 1983-86, National Executive Committee, 1983-, Senior Vice President, 1986-. *Honour:* Lithgow Scholarship in Psychology, University of sydney, 1954. *Hobbies:* Scottish Country Dancing; Reading. *Address:* 26 Upper Serpentine Road, Greenwich, New South Wales 2065, Australia.

PURVES Daphne Helen (Dame), b. 8 Nov. 1908, Dunedin, New Zealand. Retired. m. Herbert Dudley Purves, 16 Dec. 1939. 1 son, 2 daughters. *Education:* University of Otago; MA 1st class Hons, English & French, University of New Zealand, 1931. *Appointments:* Secondary School Teacher, 1931-63; Lecturer 1963-66, Senior Lecturer 1967-73, Dunedin Teachers College. *Publications:* Various publications in educational journals, newspapers. Broadcaster. *Memberships:* Alliance Francaise (Committee member and Vice-President); Otago Institute of Educational Research; United Nations Association; Zonta International; Post-Primary Teachers Association (President DTC Branch); President, Friends of Olveston; NZ National Commission for Unesco, 1964-68; Executive Member, NZ National Commission for International Year of the Child; International Federation of University Women, President 1977-80, previously Vice President. *Honour:* Dame Commander of the Most Excellent Order of the British Empire (DBE), 1979. *Hobbies:* Promotion of the status of women; Reading; Bridge; Travel; Gardening; Croquet. *Address:* 12 Grendon Court, 36 Drivers Road, Dunedin, New Zealand.

PUSKAR Kathryn Rose, b. 7 Apr. 1946, Akron, Ohio, USA. Nurse; Educator. m. George Paul Puskar, 28 Aug. 1969, 1 daughter. *Education:* Diploma in Nursing, Johnstown Mercy School of Nursing, 1966; BS, Duquesne University, 1969; MS, Nursing, 1971, MPH, 1978, DrPH, 1981, University of Pittsburgh; RN; Certified Psychiatric Specialist. *Appointments:* Clinical Specialist, McKeesport (Pennsylvania) Hospital, 1971-73; Director, Mental Health Clinic, Frick Hospital, Mount Pleasant, Pennsylvania, 1974-76; Member, Faculty, University of Illinois, Chicago, 1976-78; Consultant, Westmoreland College, Greenburg, Pennsylvania, 1976; Assistant Professor, University of Pittsburgh, Pennsylvania, 1980- ; Consultant: Southwood Hospital, 1984-86, Veterans Administration Medical Center, Pittsburgh, 1985-. *Publications:* Articles in professional journals; Editor, professional journal. *Memberships:* Consultant, Newcomers Club, Pittsburgh, 1985-87; American Nurses Association; Pennsylvania Nurses Association; Sigma Theta Tau. *Honour:* NIMH Fellowship. *Hobby:* Golf. *Address:* 1795 Robson Drive, Pittsburgh, PA 15241, USA.

PYKE Sandra W, b. 9 Apr. 1937, Winnipeg, Canada. Professor; Dean of Graduate Studies. m. Dale Randolph Pyke, 19 Sept. 1959, 2 daughters. *Education:* BA, Hons., 1959, MA 1961, University of Saskatchewan; PhD, McGill University, 1964. *Appointments:* Adviser to President on Status of Women at York, 1978-79, Chairperson, Counselling & Development Centre, 1982-84, Co-ordinator, Women's Studies Programme, Professor Psychology & Programme Co-ordinator, Counselling & Development Centre, 1985-87, Dean, Graduate Studies, 1987-, York University. *Publications:* The Science Game, 4 editions with N. Agnew; numerous articles in professional journals. bb3*Memberships Include:* Canadian Psychological Association, Fellow, President 1981-82; American Psychological Association, Fellow; Registered Psychologist, Ontario; Canadian Guidence & Counselling; Canadian Research Institute for the Advancement of Women; Canadian Association of College & University Student Services. *Hobby:* Gardening. *Address:* York University, Toronto, Canada.

PYNE Natasha, b. 9 July 1946, Crawley, Sussex, England. Actress. m. Paul Copley, 7 July 1972. *Appointments:* Films: The Taming of the Shrew; One of Our Dinosaurs is Missing; Madhouse; The Idol; Father Dear Father; The Breaking of Bumbo; Devil Ship Pirates; TV Plays include: The Excavation, BBC; Hamlet, BBC; The Adventurer, ITV; Jason King, ITV; Tales of Mystery, ITV; Haunted, ITV; A Brush with My Porter on the Road to Edlorado, BBC; Father Dear Father, ITV; Theatre: Season with RSC; Three West End Seasons; Three Years work with Young Vic theatre Company including tours: Hong Kong and Madrid; plays at Leeds Playhouse, Birmingham Repertory and Manchester Royal Exchange; Bush Theatre A Party for Bonzo, Soho Poly Theatre; BBC Drama Company, 1985-88; Twelfth Night Tour of Iraq and Pakistan, 1988. *Hobbies:* Reading; Cooking; Biking; Chinese Art. *Address:* c/o Kate Feast, 43A Princess Road, London NW1, England.

Q

QIAN Zhengying, b. 4 July 1923, Shanghai, China. Government Administrator. m. Huang Xinbai, 7 Sep. 1951, 1 son, 2 daughters. *Education:* Civil Engineering Department, Datong University, Shanghai, 1939-42. *Appointments:* Deputy Director, Yellow River Administration, 1947-50; President, Hohai University, 1952-56; Vice-Minister of Water Conservancy (and Electric Power), 1952-74; Minister of Water Resources (and Electric Power), 1974-88; Vice-Chairman, National Committee of Chinese People's Political Consultative Conference, 1988-. *Publications:* The Problems of River Control in China, 1983; General reports on Water Conservancy (and Hydropower), 1956-88. *Honours:* Honorary President, Chinese Society of Water and Soil Conservation, 1986; Honorary Professor, Hohai University, 1988. *Hobbies:* Swimming. *Address:* National Committee of CPPCC, No 23 Tai Ping Qiao Street, Beijing, China.

QUALE (Gladys) Robina, b. 10 Jan. 1931, Manistee, Michigan, USA. College Professor of History. *Education:* BA Honours (Mathematics) 1952, MA (History) 1953, PhD (History) 1957, University of Michigan. *Appointments:* Albion College, Michigan, 1957-. *Publications:* Books: Eastern Civilizations, 1966, 1975; History of Marriage Systems, 1988. *Memberships:* American Historical Association; Association for Asian Studies; Middle East Studies Association; American Academy of Political & Social Science; World History Association; International Society for Comparative Study of Civilisations; Society for Asian & Comparative Philosophy. *Honours:* Fellowship, American Association of University Women, 1955-56; Fulbright-Hays travel grant, 1964; Distinguished Faculty, Michigan Academy of Science, Arts & Letters, 1968; Scholar of Year, Albion College, 1976; Postgraduate awards, University of Michigan, 1961-62, 1966-67, 1988-89. *Hobbies include:* Chair 1980-82, Commission on Ordained Ministry, Episcopal Diocese of Western Michigan; Senior Warden 1988-89, St James Episcopal Church; East Asia studies advisory groups 1962-, Great Lakes Colleges Association; President 1967-68, 1980-81, Asian Studies Section, Michigan Academy of Science, Arts & Letters. *Address:* Department of History, Albion College, Albion, Michigan 49224, USA.

QUARLES Denise Marie, b. 26 Jan. 1950, Detroit, Michigan, USA. Prison Warden. m. Alvin Whitfield, 11 May 1985. *Education:* BS Sociology, Eastern Michigan University, 1971; MA, Sociology, University of Detroit, 1977. *Appointments:* Probation Agent, 1971-74, Parole Agent, 1974-76, Community Liaison, 1976-77, Supervisor, Corrections Centre, 1977-79, Assistant Deputy Warden, Marquette Branch Prison, 1979-81, Administrator, Riverside Reception Centre, 1981, Deputy Director, Probation Services, 1981- 83, Prison Warden, Huron Valley Womens Facility, 1983-85, Prison Warden, Riverside Correctional Facility, 1985-87, Prison Warden, G Robert Cotton Correctional Facility, 1987-, Department of Corrections; Deputy Director of the Bureau of Field Services for the Michigan Department of Correction, 1988-. *Memberships:* Michigan Corrections Association, President 1979-80, Vice President 1978- 79, Secretary, 1977-78; American Corrections Association; National Association for Female Executives. *Honours:* Career Woman of the Year, Business & Professional Womens Club, Marquette, 1980. *Hobbies:* Photography; Sewing; Reading. *Address:* Michigan Dept. of Correcton, PO Box 30003, Larsing, Michigan 48909, USA.

QUESTED Rosemary K I, b. 19 Sept. 1923, Thanet, Kent, England. Historian. m. Sergei Olesov, 20 July 1952, 2 daughters. *Education:* BA, honours, London, 1949; MA, London, 1957; PhD, London, 1963. *Appointments:* War Service, ATS, 1942-46; British Foreign Service Branch 'A' 1949-52; Various part-time posts, 1952-64; Lecturer, History, University of Malaya,

1964-70; Lecturer, Senior Lecturer, Reader, History, University of Hong Kong, 1970-84. *Publications:* The Expansion of Russia in East Asia 1857-60, 1968; The Russo-Chinese Bank, 1977; Matey Imperialists?, The Tsarist Russians in Manchuria 1895-1917, 1982; A Short History of Sino-Russian Relations, 1984, reprinted 1986. *Memberships:* Fellow, Royal Historical Society; British Association for Slavonic & East European Studies; Institute of Historical Research. *Hobbies:* Travel; Language; Conservation; Walking. *Address:* Institute of Historical Research, University of London, Senate House, Malet Street, London WC1E, England.

R

RAAD Virginia, b. 13 Aug. 1925, Salem, West Virginia, USA. Concert Pianist; Musicologist. *Education:* BA, Wellesley College, 1947; Diplome, Ecole Normale de Musique, Paris, 1950; Doctorate with highest honours, University of Paris, 1955. *Appointments:* Artist in Residence, Salem College, 1957-70; Musician in Residence, North Carolina Arts Council & Community Colleges, 1971-72; Concerts, Lectures, Master Classes in major colleges, universities and preparatory schools throughout the USA and abroad. *Memberships:* Musicology Program Chairman, Music Teachers National Association; American & International Musicology Societies; Societe de Francaise Musicologie; College Music Society; American Society for Aesthetics . *Honours:* Recipient of two grants and numerous extensions from the Fench Government; American Council of Learned Societies, travel grant, awarded in conjunction with an invitation to the Debussy Clloque, an international commemorative event, organized by the Centre National de la Recherche Scientifique to celebrate the Debussy Centenary at the University of Paris; Delta Kappa Gamma: Outstanding West Virginia Woman Educator; Biography palced in the Arthur and Elizabeth Schlesinger Library, Radcliffe College. *Hobbies:* Gardening; Birding and bird watching; Amnesty International Urgen Action Network. ssa 20Address: 60 Terrace Avenue, Salem, WV 26426, USA.

RABINOWITZ Aija Solveiga Gabliks, b. 7 Nov. 1958, Newark, New Jersey, USA. Marketing Consultant. m. Dr Stuart Alan Rabinowitz, 12 Oct. 1980. 2 sons, 1 daughter. *Education:* BS, Mechnical Engineering, Tufts University, 1980; MBA, Marketing, Georgetown University, Washington, 1986. *Appointments:* Product Design Engineer, Raytheon Co, Bedford, Massachusetts, 1979; Task Manager/Packaging Engineer, AVCO Systems Division, 1980-82; Senior Analyst, Raytheon Co, Wayland, Massachusetts, 1982-84; Assistant to Marketing Director, American Red Cross National Headquarters, Washington DC, 1985-. *Memberships:* American Institute of Aeronautics and Astronautics, Board of Directors, New England Section; American Society of Mechanical Engineers; National Association of Female Executives; American Society of Professional and Executive Women. *Honours:* Certificate of recognition of excellent service performed while chairman of an AIAA branch, 1980; Certificate in recognition of outstanding efforts and accomplishments on behalf of an ASME section, 1980. *Hobbies:* Travel; Golf; Flying; Gourmet cooking; Reading. *Address:* 2104 Woodfork Road, Timonium, MD 21093, USA.

RABINOWITZ Ellen Saltz, b. 20 May 1958, Bronx, New York, USA. Registered Occupational Therapist & Gerontologist. *Education:* BS, New York University, 1980; MPS, New School for Social Research, 1987. *Appointments:* Gracie Square Hospital, New York City, 1980-83; Private Practice, New York City, 1983-86; New York Institute for Aging, New York City, 1984-86; Cedar Lodge Nursing Home, Center Moriches, New York, 1986-; Lawrence Nursing Home, Arverne, New York, 1986-88; Ross Nursing Home, Brentwood, New York, 1986-; LaGuardia Community College, Queens, New York, 1986-; Good Samaritan Home Health Agency, Babylon, New York, 1988-. *Publications:* Various professional articles published on The Role of Occupational Therapy with the Alzheimer's Disease Patient, 1985-86. *Memberships:* American Occupational Therapy Association; New York State Occupational Therapy Association; Alzheimer's Disease and Related Disorders Association; Gerontological Society of America; National Council on the Aging; American Society on Aging. *Hobbies:* Philately; Photography; Fishing. *Address:* 52 Wilshire Lane, No M-1, Oakdale, NY 11769, USA.

RACE Anne Rinker, b. 14 May 1925, Dallas, Texas, USA. Physician; Psychiatrist. m. George Justice Race, 21 Dec. 1946, 3 sons, 1 daughter. *Education:* BS, Southern Methodist University, 1946; MD, 1958, Resident, Psychiatry, Fellow, Child Psychiatry, 1966-70, University of Texas Southwestern Medical Center, Dallas; Intern, Internal Medicine, Baylor University Medical Center, Dallas, 1962-63; Diplomate, American Board of Psychiatry & Neurology, 1974. *Appointments:* Private Practice, 1970-; Director, Student Mental Health, Southern Methodist University, 1970-79; Assistant Professor, Psychiatry, Psychiatry in Obstetrics/Gynaecology, 1971-75, Associate Professor, Psychiatry in Obstetrics/Gynaecology, 1975-79, Associate Clinical Professor, Psychiatry, 1975-, Director, Student Mental Health, 1979-88, University of Texas Southwestern Medical Center, Dallas; Co-Host, Here's To Your Health TV show, PBS-TV, 1980, 1981. *Publications:* The Sex Scene: Understanding Sexuality (book), 1975. *Memberships:* Board, Baylor Research Foundation; Board, Family Guidance Center; Fellow, American Psychiatric Association; American Medical Association; Texas Medical Association (Chairperson, Mental Health & Retardation Committee, 1982-85); American Psychiatric Association; Texas Psychiatric Association; Board, Secretary, Texas Rehabilitation Commission, 1980-85; Texas Board Mental Health & Retardation, 1989-; Past Board Member: Dallas County Medical Society; American Cancer Society; Visiting Nurse Association; Analytic Psychology Association; Isthmus Institute in Dallas. *Honours:* National Honor Society, 1941; Most Outstanding Girl Blanket Award, Highland Park High School, Dallas, 1942; Mortar Board, Southern Methodist University, 1944; Dallas Junior League, 1960; Charter 100 of Dallas, 1980. *Hobbies:* Saltwater fishing; Gardening; Gourmet cooking; Viticulture; Flying. *Address:* 3429 Beverly Drive, Dallas, TX 75205, USA.

RACHELSON Joyce Ann, b. 8 Sept. 1946, Philadelphia, USA. Eastern Regional Director for Marketing. m. Harry Steven Lichter, 8 Aug. 1971, divorced 1973. *Education:* BA, History, Temple University, 1968. *Appointments:* Junior Porject Director, H Epstein, 1967-70; Senior Project Director, Dataprobe, 1970-73; Director, Research Services, Grey Adv., 1973-83; Director, Marketing & Sales Computers, Marketing Corporation, 1983-. *Publication:* Manual for Market Research Coding & Editing. *Memberships:* Hor Zion Young Adults, President 1968-69; American Marketing Association; Market Research Association. *Hobbies:* Foreign Language Study; European & Far Eastern Travel; Ancient HIstory & Foreign Culture Studies. *Address:* 245 E. 19th St., No 14 K, New York, NY 10003, USA.

RACHLIN Ann, b. 23 July 1933, Leeds, England. Musical Story-Teller; Actress; Writer. m. (1) Neville Ziff, 15 Dec. 1952, 1 son, 2 daughters, (2) Ezra Rachlin, 25 May 1969. *Appointmnts:* Started Fun with Music Sessions for Children, 1966; Performed series Funtasia Concerts for Children with London Symphony Orchestra, Barbican Centre. *Publications:* 18 Cassettes & Albums, 1985 released simultaneously by EMI, Fun with Music, Stories; Book, Sinbad & the Wizard Eagle. *Memberships:* Founder, Chairman, Beethoven Fund for Deaf Children; Actors Equity. *Honours:* OBE, 1986. *Hobbies:* Song & Lyric Writing; Jazz; Gardening; Stamps. *Address:* 2 Queensmead, St John's Wood Park, London NW8 6RE, England.

RADECKI Monica Marie, b. 19 Sept. 1952, South Bend, Indiana, USA. Conservator, Paintings. *Education:* Apprentice, conservation, Indianapolis Museum of Art, 1972-79; 3 years, John Herron Art School; Indiana University; Purdue University. *Appointments include:* General staff 1964-72, conservator 1979-, family framing & restoration business, Radecki Inc, est. 1958. *Creative work includes:* Watercolourist, printmaker, non-professional. *Memberships:* Past Secretary, Midwest Regional Conservation Guild; International, & American Institutes for Conservation; Conservators in Private Practice; American Association for State & Local History. *Hobbies include:* Painting & drawing; Metaphysical studies. *Address:* 721 East Jefferson Boulevard, South Bend, Indiana 46617, USA.

RADFORD Joan Treasure, b. 1 Mar. 1920, Australia. Retired Academic Chemist. *Education:* BSc., Honours, Melbourne University, 1939. *Appointments:* Analytical Chemist, 1940-43; Supervisor Spectrographic Laboratory & Physical Testing Laboratory, 1943-47; Spectroscopist, London, England, 1947-50; Spectroscopist, Lecturer, Senior Lecturer, Universities of Queensland and Melbourne, 1951-80. *Publications:* Contributor to various journals and magazines; Chemistry in Australia and New Zealand in 19th Century, Histories. *Memberships:* SCIV, 1940-47; MUCS, 1954-; Women in Chemistry network, 1984- . *Honours:* Recipient, various honours and awards. *Address:* 25, Hillcrest Avenue, Kew, VIC 3101, Australia.

RAE Barbara Joyce, b. 17 May 1931, Prince George, Canada. President; Chief Executive Officer. m. George Suart, 14 Feb. 1984, 3 sons. *Education:* MBA, Simon Fraser University. *Appointments:* President, Chief Executive Officer, ADIA Canada Ltd., 1952-. *Memberships:* Chancellor, Simon Fraser University; Judicial Appointments Committee, BC; National Advisory Council Imagine Campaign; Premier's Economic Advisory Council; Director: B.C. Telephone Company; Microtel, Seaboard Life Insurance Company; Royal Trust Company Limited. *Honours:* Simon Fraser University Outstanding Alumnae Award, 1985; Vancouver YWCA Business Woman of the Year Award, 1986; West Vancouver Achievers Award, 1987; BC Business Entrepreneur of the Year Award, 1987. *Hobbies:* Skiing; Hiking. *Address:* 3-2206 Folkestone Way, West Vancouver, BC, Canada V7S 2X7.

RAEBURN Antonia Dora, b. 27 Oct. 1934, London, England. Author; Teacher. m. Alan Jefferson, 24 Sept. 1976, 2 sons. *Education:* Bath Academy of Art, 1952-55; Art Teachers Diploma, Certificate in Education, Institute of Education, Bristol University, 1955. *Appointments:* Art Teacher, 1955-63; Warden, Lecturer, Graphics, Bath Academy, 1963-67; Author, Picture Researcher, Art Director, BBC TV, 1967-74. *Publications:* The Militant Suffragettes, 1973; The Suffragette View, 1976. *Memberships:* Suffragette Fellowship, White Eagle Lodge. *Hobbies:* Education through Art; Country Life; Social History. *Address:* Deviock Farmhouse, Deviock, Torpoint, Cornwall PL11 3DL, England.

RAGLAND-NJAU Phillda, b. New Jesey, USA. Photographer. *Education:* BA, English, Upsala Collee, 1961; New York Camera Club, 1967; School of Visual Arts, New York, 1967. *Publications:* Photographs in numerous magazines and journals; exhibitions, displays at: Schoenburg Museum; Interchurch Centro; National Council of Churches; Kibo Arts Gallery, Tanzania; Paa Ya Paa Gallery, Kenya. *Memberships:* Member various professional organisatirons. *Address:* Paa Ya Paa Gallery, PO Box 49646, Nairobi, Kenya.

RAILING Sharon Anne, b. 13 Sept. 1951, Wilmington, Delaware, USA. Systems Analyst. *Education:* College prep, Mount Vernon Seminary, 1969; BA, Theatre, Lycoming College, 1973. *Appointments:* Computer operator 1973-74, coordinator, user education 1974-80, University of Delaware, Newark; Junior systems analyst 1980-83, systems analyst 1983- , Delmarva Power, Newark. *Creative work includes:* Photographer, Corporate Systems magazine, 1977; Art show, Wilmington Drama League, 1983; Lighting design: Wilmington Drama League 1980-, Opera Delaware 1984, 1987, Brandywiners 1986-, Delaware Children's Theatre 1987-. *Memberships:* National Association of Female Executives; Past president, Delaware Association of Theatre Technicians; Offices, Wilmington Drama League; Brandywiners; Friends of Rockwood Museum; Past president, Delmarva Photo Colub. *Honour:* Honourable mention, Delmarva Photo Club contest, 1982. *Hobbies:* Theatre; Travel; Photography. *Address:* 505 Clearview Avenue, Woodside Hills, Wilmington, Delaware 19809, USA.

RAILTON Ruth (Dame), b. 14 Dec. 1915, Folkestone,

England. Musician. m. Cecil Harmsworth King, 1962. *Education:* Royal Academy of Music, London, England, ARAM, FRAM, FRCM, 1937-39. *Appointments:* Director of Music on Choral work for many shcools and socieites, 1937-49; Founder & Musical Director, The National Janios Music Shool & its Orchestra; The National Youth Orchestra of Great Britain, 1946-65; Adjudicator, Federation of Music Festivals, 1946-74. *Memberships:* Honorary Member, Royal Society of Musicians; Incorporated Society of Musicians. *Honours:* OBE, 1954; DBE, 1966; Honorary LLD, Aberdeen University, 1960; Honorary FRCM, 1965; Honorary FTCL, 1969; Harriet Cohen Prize for Bach; President, Ulster College of Music, 1960-; Vice President, Cork International Festival, 1960-80; Founder & President, Irish Childrens Theatre, 1978-81; Board of Directors, National Concert Hall, Dublin, 1981-86; Honorary Professor, Chopin Conservatoire, Warsaw; Honoary Professor, Conservatoire of Azores, 1972; Honorary Ward Sister, St Vincent's Hospital, Dublin. *Hobbies:* Ballet; History; Newspapers; Politics; Natural world; Animals; Teaching; Great art in all its forms. *Address:* 54 Ardoyne House, Pembroke Park, Dublin 4, Ireland.

RAINER Luise, b. 12 Jan. 1916. Actress. m. (1) Clifford Odets. (2) Robert Knittel, 12 July 1945. 1 daughter. *Education:* Studied drawing and Painting at Camden Institute, London. *Career:* Performances in: Spring Awakening; Phea; An American Tragedy; The Taming of the Shrew; Measure for Measure; Medmoisell; Six Characters in Search of an Author; A Kiss for Cinderella; St Joan; Joan of Lorraine; Lady From the Sea; Biography; The Sea Gull; Little Foxes; Doll's House. Films included: Escapade; The Great Ziegfeld; The Good Earth; The Emperor's Candlesticks; Big City; Toy Wife; The Great Waltz; Dramatic School; TV included: Stone Faces, BBC TV; Narrator of Judith with Pittsburgh Symphony Orchestra, 1973; Poem: Enoch Arden, The Library of Congress in Washington and New York, 1982, Los Angeles, 1983; 6 episodes for an International Television series, 1987. Painting: One-woman Show, London, England, 1978. *Honours:* Two consecutive Academy Awards, 1936 and 1937 for The Great Ziegfeld and The Good Earth; Grand Cross 1st Class, Order of Merit, German Federal Republic, 1985; Special Award, San Sebastian Film Festival, 1986. *Address:* Villa Isola, 6911 Vico Morcole, Swizterland.

RAMALEY Judith A Aitken, b. 11 Jan. 1941, Indiana, USA. Executive Vice Chancellor. m. Robert Folk Ramaley, 1966, 2 sons. *Education:* BA, Zoology, Swarthmore College, 1963; PhD, Anatomy, UCLA, 1966. *Appointments:* Assistant Vice President, Academic Affiars, 1072-02, University of Nebraska; Associate Dean, R & D, University of Nebraska Medical School, 1979- 81; Vice President, Academic Affairs, 1982-85, Acting President, 1984, Executive Vice President, Academic Affairs, 1985-87, SUNY, Albany; Executive Vice Chancellor, University of Kansas, Lawrence, 1987- . *Publications:* Articles in: Endocrinology; Steroids; Neuroendocrinology; Life Sciences; Journal of Andrology. *Memberships Include:* Endocrine Society, Chair, Education Committee, 1980-85, other offices; Society for the Study of Reproduction, Treasurer, 1982-85, other offices; Society for Neurosciences; American Physiological Society. *Honours:* A.C.E. Fellowship, University of Nebraska Medical School,1978-79; Mid American State University Association Lecturer, 1978; Elected Fellow, American Association for the Advancement of Science. *Hobbies:* Music; Theatre. *Address:* 231 Strong Hall, University of Kansas, Lawrence, KS 66045, USA.

RAMAROSAONA Zaiveline, b. 5 Apr. 1926, Antananarivo, Madagascar. Researcher. m. Emile Ramarosaona, 25 Nov. 1950. 5 sons, 2 daughters. *Education:* French degrees and diplomas: Baccalaureate; Master degree of Sociology; Doctor degree of Sociology. *Appointments:* Assistant of Ethnology, 1953-55; Senior official, Legislative Assembly of the French Union, Paris, France, 1955-57; Senior official, National Assembly of Madagascar, 1957-63; Senior official, Government of Madagascar,

1963-71; Sociological Researcher on family and on women, 1972-. *Publications:* Books and articles: Le lait frais a Tananarive, 1955; Le role de la femme dans la famille malgache, 1969; Les femmes dans le Fokonolona, 1979; Etude sur la condition de la femme et la legislation a Madagascar, 1984. *Memberships:* Corresponding Member, Malagasy Academy, Section of Moral Sciences; President, National Council of the Malagasy Women's Association; Founder and first President, Family Planning Association, Fianakaviana Sambatra; International Council, The World Movement of Mothers; International Alliance of Women. *Hobbies:* Raising livestock and poultry. *Address:* Boite postale 1737, 101 Antananarivo, Madagascar.

RAMIREZ-DE-ARELLANO Diana T C, b. 3 June 1919, New York City, USA. Writer. *Education:* BA, University of Puerto Rico, 1941; MA, Columbia University, 1946; Licenciate & Doctorate, University Central Complutense, Madrid, Spain, 1959. *Appointments:* Professor, Spanish Literature: University of North Carolina 1946-48; Rutgers University, 1948-58; City University of New York, 1958-84. *Publications:* Albatros Sobre el Alma, 1955; Angeles De Ceniza, 1958; Un Vuelo Casi Humano, 1960; Privilegio, 1965; Arbol en Visperas, 1987. *Memberships:* President, Josefina Romo- Arregui Memorial Foundation Inc.; Honorary President, Ateneo PR, New York; Royal Academy of Doctors of Madrid; Hispanic Society of America; Pen; MLA; AATSP. *Honours:* Recipient, many honours & awards. *Hobbies:* Astronomy & Astrology; Medicine; Sailing; Hunting; Travel; Reading. *Address:* 23 Harbor Circle, Centerport, NY 11721, USA.

RAMOS Linda Marie Vieira, b. 8 July 1961, San Jose, California, USA. Endoscopy Technician; Aerobic Instructor. m. John Bettencourt Ramos, 12 June 1982. *Education:* AA, De Anza College, Cupertino, California, 1986; BA, St Mary's College, Moraga, California, 1988. *Appointments:* Endoscopy Technician, O'Connor Hospital, San Jose, 1979-; Professional certification May, 1979, Certified Castrointestinal Clinician; Aerobic Instructor, 1st Lady Spas, Mountain View, 1986-. *Publications:* Articles, RN Magazine; Journal, Society of Gastrointestinal Assistants. *Memberships include:* American, & Northern California Societies of Gastrointestinal Assistants; Numerous offices including State Director, Youth Programs 1988-, Luso- American Fraternal Federation; Sociedade do Espirito Santo; Other community & political organizations. *Honours:* Distinguished Service Award 1978, Scholarship 1979, Luso-American Fraternal Federation; Biographical recognitions. *Hobbies:* Aerobic dance; Weight lifting; Piano; Sewing; Reading; Real estate investments. *Address:* 1101 Civic Center Drive, no. 10, Santa Clara, California 95050, USA.

RAMPERSAUD Olga Mavis, b. Trinidad, West Indies. Obstetrician; Gynaecologist and Community Medicine Consultant. *Education:* University of Liverpool, England; MRCPS, LRCP, London; DGO, Dublin, Ireland; LM Rotuda, Dublin, Ireland; LMCC, Toronto, Canada; FRCOG, London, England; DPH, University of Toronto, Canada. *Appointments:* Staff, Hexham General Hospital, England; Jessop Hospital for Women, Sheffield, 1954; University of West Indies, Jamaica, 1958; Specialist Consultant Obstetrician & Gynaecologist, Government of Trinidad and Tobago, 1960; Director of Medical Services, Dept of Public Health 1967, Associate Medical Officer of Health 1982, City of Toronto, Canada; Lecturer, Community Medicine, University of Toronto, 1982. *Memberships:* CPHA (Canadian Public Health Assoc); OPHA (Ontario Public Health Assoc); CARIPA (Caribbean Public Health Assoc); TECH (Tur East Gen Hospital). *Hobby:* Numismatics. *Address:* 18 Lower Village Gate, Suite 411, Toronto, Canada M5P 3N1.

RAMPLING Charlotte, b. 1946, London, England. Actress. m. (2) Jean-Michel Jarre. 2 sons. *Career:* Film debut, 1963. *Creative Works:* Films include: The Knack, 1963; Rotten to the Core; Georgy Girl; The Long Duel; Kidnapping; Three; The Damned, 1969; Skibum; Corky, 1970; 'Tis Pity She's a Whore; Henry VIII and His Six Wives, 1971; Asylum, 1972; The Night Porter; Giordano Bruno; Zardoz; Caravan to Vaccares, 1973; The Flesh of the Orchid; Yuppi Du, 1974-75; Farewell My Lovely; Foxtrot, 1975; Sherlock Holmes in New York; Orca-The Killer Whale; The Purple Taxi, 1976; Stardust Memories, 1980-82; The Verdict, 1983; Viva le vie, 1983; Beauty and Sadness, 1984; He Died with his Eyes Open, 1985; Max mon Amour, Max My Love, 1985. Numerous television plays. *Address:* c/o Olga Horstig Primuz, 78 Champs Elysees, Paris 75008, France.

RAMSAY June, b. 25 Jan. 1937, Greensburg, USA. Founder, Executive Director, Missing Persons International Humanatarian. m. 12 Ap. 1960, 2 sons, 3 daughters from previous marriage. *Appointments:* Founder, Canyon Country Emergency Services; Adoptee-Natural Parent, Locators International and Missing Persons International, Los Angeles. *Publications:* Letters to Lost People; Even the House is Crying; Journals of Search Techniques for Missing Persons, and video libraries materials. *Memberships:* various humanitarian organisations. *Honours:* Nominated for many awards. *Address:* Post Office Box 1337, Canyon Country, CA 91351, USA.

RAMUSACK Barbara Nell, b. 5 Nov. 1937, Gary, Indiana, USA. Professor of History. m. Larry L. Goodman, 29 June 1974. *Education:* BA, History, Alverno College, 1960; MA, History, 1962, PhD, History, 1969, University of Michigan. *Appointments:* Various positions, currently Professor of History, University of Cincinnati, Cincinnati, Ohio, 1967-. *Publications:* The Princes of India in the Twilight of Empire, 1978; Women in South and Southeast Asia, in Restoring Women to History, 1988. *Memberships:* American Historical Association, Nominating Committee, 1989-; Association for Asian Studies, Council of Conferences 1989-; Coordinating Committee of Women in the Historical Profession. *Honours:* Rackham-Woodrow Wilson Dissertation Fellow, University of Michigan, 1966- 67; Phi Beta Kappa, University of Michigan; Outstanding Alumnae Award, Alverno College, 1975; Fellowship, American Institute of Indian Studies, 1976-77; Fulbright-Hays Faculty Research Abroad Award in India, 1981-82; Fellowship at National Humanities Center, 1986-87. *Hobbies:* Travel; Gardening; Walking. *Address:* Department of History, University of Cincinnati, Cincinnati, OH 45221-0373, USA.

RANA Sangeeta, b. 31 Jan. 1959, Nepal. Project Manager. *Education:* Diploma, Shorthand and Typing, Typing Institute, Kathmandu, 1981; Diploma, French Language, French Cultural Centre, Kathmandu, 1982; BA, Loreto Convent, Lucknow, India, 1980; MA, Development Studies, Institute of Social Studies, The Hague, The Netherlands, 1987; Numerous courses, seminars and workshops. *Appointments:* Editor, Roop Rekha, magazine, 1980-82; Editor, Training Material Production Centre; Trainer, 1982-84; Project Manager, Women Development Section, Ministry of Panchayat and Local Development, 1985-. *Publications:* Author of numerous papers to professional journals, magazines and conferences. *Memberships:* Nepal Jaycees; Information Network on Women and Development; Community Service Coordination Committee; Society for International Development, Nepal Chapter; Nepal Netherlands Alumni Group. *Address:* Ka 1-273 Thapathali, Kathmaandu, Nepal.

RANDALL Rona, b. Cheshire, England. Novelist; Non-fiction Author. m. Frederick Walter Shambrook, FRICS. 1 son. *Appointments:* Journalist/Sub-Editor, IPC, 4 years; Assistant Editor, George Newnes, 1 year. *Publications include:* Non-fiction: The Model Wife, 19th Century Style, 1989; Jordan and the Holy Land (with a Foreword by H M King Hussein of Jordan), 1968. Novels: The Potter's Niece, 1987; The Drayton Legacy, 1985; Curtain Call, 1983; The Ladies of Hanover Square, 1981; The Mating Dance, 1979; The Eagle at the Gate, 1978; Watchman's Stone, 1976; Dragonmede, 1974; Glenrannoch, 1973; Broken Tapestry, 1971; Knight's Keep, 1966, etc. *Memberships:* Fellow, International PEN; Associate, South East Arts Association; Committee

Member, Society of Sussex Authors; Former Vice-Chairman, Women's Press Club of London; Society of Women Writers and Journalists. *Honours:* Awarded Exclusive Selection for Young Adult Division, US Literary Guild for Watchman's Stone; Awarded Alternate Selection, US Literary Guild and Exclusive Selection, Doubleday Book Club for Dragonmede; Joint Major Award Winner, British Romantic Novelists' Association for Broken Tapestry; Short-listed for Major Award, British Romantic Novelists' Association for Knights' Keep. *Hobbies:* Collecting antiques; Theatre-going; Ceramic Modelling, exhibiting and selling widely. *Address:* c/o Curtis Brown Ltd, Literary Agents, 162-168 Regent Street, London W1R 5TB, England.

RANDALL Margaret, b. 6 Dec. 1936, New York City, USA. Writer; Photographer; Professor; Lecturer. 1 son, 3 daughters. *Education:* University of New Mexico, 1954-55. *Appointments:* various positions in Latin America, Mexico, Cuba, & Nicaragua; Professor, Women's Studies, & American Studies & English, University of New Mexico, 1984-87; English, Trinity College, Hartford, CT 1987-88; Hubert H. Humphrey Professor of International Affairs, Macalester College, Saint Paul, MN, Spring 1989; Professor of English, Trinity College, Spring 1990. *Publications:* Books of Poetry: Giant of Tears, 1959; Ecstasy is a Number, 1961; Poems of the Glass, 1964; Small Sounds from the Bass Fiddle, 1964; October, 1965; This is About Incest, 1987; Memory Twenty-five Stages of My Spine, 1967; Getting Rid of Blue Plastic, 1967; Water I Slip into at Night, 1967; So Many Rooms Has a House but One Roof, 1967; Part of the Solution, 1972; Parte de la solucion, 1973; Day's Coming, 1973; With These Hands, 1974; We, New York City, 1978; The Coming Home Poems, 1986; This is About Incest, 1987; Memory Says Yes, 1988; Oral History: Cuban Women Now, 1974; Spirit of the People, Vietnamese Women Two Years from the Geneva Accords, 1975; Inside the Nicaraguan Revolution: The Story of Doris Tijerino, 1976; Risking a Somersault in the Air, Conversations with Nicaraguan Writers, 1984; Photography: Sandino's Daughters, 1981; Christians in the Nicaraguan Revolution, 1983; Women Brave in the Face of Danger, 1985; Nicaragua Libre!, 1985; The Rebellion on the Walls, 1985; Albuquerque: Coming Back to the USA, 1986; The Shape of Red: Insider/Outsider Reflections (with Ruth Hubbard), 1988 etc. *Hobbies and Interests:* Womens Issues; Poetry; World Affairs; Photography; Art; etc. *Address:* 50 Cedar Hill Rd. NE, Albuquerque, NM 87122, USA.

RANDOLPH Suzanne Marie, b. 4 Aug. 1953, New Orleans, Louisiana, USA. Psychologist; Educator. *Education:* BS, Psychology, Howard University, 1974; MA 1977, PhD 1981, Psychology, University of Michigan. *Appointments:* Research Coordinator & Assistant Professor, Paediatrics & Child Health, College of Medicine, Howard University, 1981-85; Research & Programme Development Association, American National Red Cross, 1986-88; Assistnt Professor, Department of Family & Community Development, University of Maryland, College Park, 1988-. *Creative work:* Book chapters, Howard University Normative Study, Health Problems & Hispanic Elderly; Slide tape, Behavioural Assessment of Black Newborns; Film/video, Culture without Consciousness: Bahia, Brazil; Research articles. *Memberships include:* National President 1989-, Association of Black Psychologists; President 1987-89, YWCA, National Capital Area; Past Chair, Black Caucus, Society for Research in Child Development; American Psychological Association. *Honours:* Phi Beta Kappa, 1974; Psi Chi, 1973; *Fellowships:* W. K. Kellogg Foundation (1985-88), Rockefeller Foundation, American Psychological Association. *Hobbies:* Racquet ball; Skiing; Collecting Black art, books, memorabilia; Travel; Maternal & child health; Black infants' development; Health, psychology & family relations. *Address:* University of Maryland, Department of Family & Community Development, College Park, MD 20742, USA.

RANJITSINGH-RAMPERSAD Indrani, b. 29 Dec. 1952, San Juan, Trinidad, West Indies. Lecturer; Writer; Social Worker; Hindu Activist. m. (1) Devindra Dookie, 24 Nov. 1977 div. 1983, (2) Mahindranath Rampersad, 10 July 1983. *Education:* BA Honours, Banaras Hindu University, India, 1976; Education Diploma 1982, MPhil studies current, University of West Indies. *Appointments:* Teacher, Trinidad, 1968-73, 1976-85; Editor, Jagriti magazine, Trinidad, 1985-88. *Publications:* Book, Towards a National Culture in Trinidad & Tobago, in press; Poems. *Memberships:* Trinidad & Tobago Teachers Union; 1st (current) President, Hindu Women's Organisation, Trinidad & Tobago; Caribbean Feminist Association. *Honour:* BA Honours Geography, 1st Prize, 1976. *Hobbies:* Reading; Writing; Human rights issues; Representing Hindu & Indian interests at national level; Culture & free expression of all peoples; Travel. *Address:* c/o Rambarran, Southern Main Road, Chase Village, Carapichaima, Trinidad, West Indies.

RANNARD Clytie Louise, b. 6 Aug. 1929, Adelaide, South Australia. Supervising Draftsman, retired. m. Alford Roy Wallace Rannard, 2 Sept. 1950. 2 sons. *Education:* Riverton High School, South Australia; Norwood High School, Adelaide, South Australia. *Appointments:* Tracer, Lands & Survey, Darwin, 1948; Draftsman, Grade 1, 1954; Draftsman Grade 2, 1968; Senior Draftsman, 1971; Supervising Draftsman, 1977-81. *Memberships:* Craft Council of NT; Australia British Society. *Honour:* Order of Australia Medal, 1981. *Hobbies:* Oil Painting; Reading; Northern Territory Nomenclature and Early History; Travel. *Address:* 38 Phillip Street, Fannie Bay, Darwin, Australia.

RANNEY Helen Margaret, b. 12 Apr. 1920, Summer Hill, New York, USA. Physician; Professor of Medicine. *Education:* AB, Barnard College, New York City, New York, 1941; MD, College of Physicians and Surgeons, Columbia University, New York City, 1947. *Appointments:* Professor of Medicine, Albert Einstein College of Medicine, 1965-70; Professor of Medicine, State University of New York at Buffalo, New York, 1970-73; Professor of Medicine, 1976-, Chairman, Department of Medicine, 1976-86, University of California, San Diego; Distinguished Physician, Department of Veterans Affairs, 1986-. *Publications:* 75 original scientific articles, 1951- 86; 30 invited scientific articles, 1958-87; 36 scientific abstracts, 1952-85; Books: Human Hemoglobins, 1977; Hemoglobinopathies, 1977. *Memberships:* Trustee, The Population Council, 1976-88; Director, Squibb Corporation; Director, NAXCOR; National Academy of Sciences; Institute of Medicine; American Association for the Advancement of Science; American Academy of Arts and Sciences. *Honours:* Phi Beta Kappa; Alpha Omega Alpha, 1982; Joseph Mather Smith Prize, 1955; Dr Martin Luther King Jr Medical Achievement Award for Outstanding Contributions in the Field of Sickle Cell Anemia, 1972; Mayo H Soley Award for Excellence in Research, Western Society of Clinical Investigation, 1987. *Address:* Veterans Administration Medical Center (11F), 3350 La Jolla Village Drive, San Diego, CA 92161, USA.

RANSOM Dorothy Ellen, b. 21 Jan. 1917, Perth, Western Australia. Teacher; Microbiologist; Manager, Property and Investment Trust. m. Aubrey Albert Turner Ransom, 18 Mar. 1942. 2 sons, 1 daughter. *Education:* BSc, Zoology & Geology, 1983; Diploma, Education, University of Western Australia, 1940. *Appointments:* Teacher, Mathematics and Science, 1938; Research Officer, Australian Wool Board, 1939; Microbiologist, Royal Perth Hospital, 1940-44; Private Company Director, 1969-82; Manager, Property & Investment Trust. *Memberships:* University of Western Australia, Senate, Chairperson of Buildings Committee, Convocation; Member Irwin Street Building and Appeal Committees; Australia Federation of University Women, numerous offices including, Vice President, 1969, 1970, 1985, 1986, Council Member, 1968-71, 1985-88, President WA Branch, 1969, 1970, 1985, 1986; Vice President 1988; Chairperson Headquarters Committee; Honorary Life Membership, Christ Church Grammar School Parents Association; Chairperson,

Subcommittee, Victoria League for Commonwealth Friendship, 1968-72; Council Member, Joint Commonwealth Societies, 1972-75; Chairperson, Women's Committee, Australian Lega Convention, Perth, 1973; Chairperson, Perth Modern School, Golden Jubilee Reunion, 1984; National Trust; Friends of Royal Perth Hospital; University House. *Hobbies:* Golf; Travel; Sport. *Address:* 72 The Avenue, Nedlands, WA 6009, Australia.

RAPAPORT Bertha K, b. 15 Apr. 1900, Ukrania. Citizen of USA. Attorney at Law. m. Dr Hyman Rapaport, 31 July 1921, 3 sons. *Education:* Diploma, Pittsburgh Training School, 1917; JD, Southwestern University School of Law, 1927. *Appointments:* Elementary School Teacher: Pittsburgh, 1915-1919, Los Angeles, 1920-21; Principal, Los Angeles School, 1921; Own Law Firm, Los Angeles, 1927-. *Publications:* Book of Published Poems, 1969; Composer, Musical Lyric, 1969; Oil Painter. *Memberships:* President, Hollywood Bar Association; President, Lawyers' Continuing Educatiron of the Bar, Hollywood; Chairman, Hollywood Courthouse Committee; Hollywood Chamber of Commerce. *Honours:* Scholarship, School of Engineering, 1914-197; Prizes, Lawyers Oil Paintings, 1970, 1972; Women Lawyers' Trophy of Lady Justice, 1982; Award for Outstanding Service, Hollywood Bar Associatiron, 1983. *Hobbies:* Research; Supporter of Youth Activities; Legal Aid to Indigents; Music; Oil Painting. *Address:* 7060 Franklin Avenue, Hollywood, Los Angeles, CA 90028, USA.

RAPHAELY Jane Patricia, b. 30 July 1937, Birmingham, England. Editor; Publisher. m. Michael David Raphaely, 24 Sept. 1961, 1 son, 3 daughters. *Education:* BSc., Sociology, Economics, London School of Economics; Columbia University Graduate Studies. *Appointments:* Copywriter, Van Zyl & Robinson, 1959-60; Account Executive, Bernstein Wilson, 1960-62; Manager, Public Relations, Bernstein Wilson, 1962-64; Founder Editor, Fair Lady Magazine, 1965-83; Managing Director, Jane Raphaely & Associates Pty Ltd., 1983-; Founder Editor, Publisher, Cosmopolitan Magazine SA, 1984-; Editor/Publisher, Femina Magazine, 1988-. *Publication:* Collected Last Words. *Memberships:* Various professional organisations. *Honours:* Rotary Foundation Fellowship; Star Women of Our Time, 1986; Business Woman of the Year, 1986; Sole South African invited to participate in United States Information Service 2nd Council Conference in Washington D.C. June 1988. *Address:* 2309 Golden Acre, Adderley Street, Cape Town 8001, Republic of South Africa.

RAPIN Lynn Suzanne, b. 26 Nov. 946, Sault St Marie, Michigan, USA. Psychologist; Educator. m. Robert K. Conyne, 26 July 1980, 1 son, 1 daughter. *Education:* BA, Psychology, Florida State University, 1970; MEd., Counselling, 1973, PhD, Counselling Psychology, 1973, University of Illinois. *Appointments:* Assistant Associate Professor, Illinois State University, Normal, 1973-80; Adjunct Associate Professor, University of Cincinnati, 1981-; Psychologist, Private Practice. *Publications:* Book Chapter, Organization Development: Quality Circle Groups in The Group Workers; Handbook, 1985; 20 articles in various journals. *Memberships:* American Psychological Association; American Association for Counselling & Development; American Society for Training & Development. *Honours:* Various honours. *Hobbies:* Cross Country & Downhill Skiing; Sailing; Needlepoint. *Address:* 1134 Cryer Avenue, Cincinnati, OH 45208, USA.

RAPP Lea Bayers, b. 19 July 1946, Brooklyn, New York, USA. Editor; Writer; Lecturer. m. Stanley J. Rapp, 3 Sept. 1968, 1 son, 1 daughter. *Education:* BA, Thomas A Edison College, 1989. *Appointments:* Author, Journalist, Magazine Writer, Lecturer, 1968-; Syndicated Columnist, Things for Free, The News Tribune, Woodbridge, New Jersey; Columnist, American Life, The Japan Times, Tokyo; Editor, Woman's Interest Magazine (Financial); Features Editor, Marketing Insights Magazine, 1989-. *Publications:* Put Your Kid in Show Biz; You Can Overcome Stuttering; Anthology of Diet Plans; How to Operate a Dating Service; Sensuality - It's Primal; How to Meet and Date Women; How to Earn Money in TV Commercials; Small Businesses You Can Start At Home; Your Step by Step Guide to Importing; Buying Bargain Land Overseas; 5,000 Things You Can Get For Free; Twelve Methods of Making Money in Real Estate; Job Opportunities in Alaska; Profiting from the Land Boom; Cheap Travel Around the World; Distress Property; Finding for Profit; Recycling - Oil and Rubber; The Solar Energy Boom; Articles in USA Today, Sunday New York Times, Sunday New York News, New York Post, Christian Science Monitor, Clarion Ledger (Jackson, Mississippi), Daily World Telephone (Bloomington, Indiana), Tribune Chronicle (Warren, Ohio), Business Journal of New Jersey Magazine, In Business Magazine, Playbill - The National Theatre Magazine, Greenville Woman Magazine, Complete Woman Magazines, Technical Photography Magazine, NJ Focus Magazine and Others. *Memberships:* Authors Guild; Society of Professional Journalists; National Press Women's Association; New York Business Press Editors; New Jersey Press Women. *Honours:* Feature Writing Awards, 1987, 1988; Business Writing Award, 1989; New Jersey Press Women; Award of Excellence, Society of Professional Journalists, 1988. *Hobbies:* Family; Entertaining; Theatre; Film; Music. *Address:* 82 Marsh Avenue, Sayreville, NJ 08872, USA.

RAPPE Jadwiga, b. 24 Mar. 1952, Torun, Poland. Singer. m. M. Niemirski, 9 June 1973, 1 son, 1 daughter. *Education:* Secondary School of Music, Warsaw; Graduated, Department of Slavic Languages, Warsaw University, 1975; Graduated, Wroclaw Music Academy, 1984. *Career includes:* Leading role in Handel's Amadigi, Warsaw Opera, 1983; Commenced collaboration with Concentus Musieus, Vienna, 1985; Sang Erola in Wagner's Nibelung Ring, Deutsche Oper, Berlin, 1986; Handel's Messiah, Royal Albert Hall, London, 1988. *Memberships:* Polish Musicians Association. *Honours:* 1st Prize and Gold Medal, International J.S.Bach Competition, Leipzig, 1980; Gold Medal, Young Soloist Festival, Bordeaux, 1981; 1st Prize for Distinguished Recordings, Polish Radio and TV. *Hobby:* Family life. *Address:* ul Mickiewicza 66, apt 150, Warsaw, Poland.

RATCLIFF Ruth, b. 19 Oct. 1905, Detmold. Writer; Translator. m. A.J.J. Ratcliff, 31 May 1952, deceased 1961. *Appointments:* Bookseller; Publisher; Journalism; Writer. *Publications:* Heritage of the Kaiser's Children, 1983; The Brothers Grimm, 1970; European Choice, 1977; several other; numerous translations. *Memberships:* Folklore Society; Europaische Marchengesellschaft. *Honours:* Several Arts Council Awards. *Hobbies:* Literature; Arts; Theatre; Cooking. *Address:* The Lang Hoose, East Saltoun, East Lothian, EH34 5EB, Scotland.

RATH Mari Kaye, b. 10 Sept. 1958, Elgin, USA. Litigation Consultant. *Education:* BBA, Western Illinois University, 1979. *Appointments:* Arthur Andersen & Co., Chicago, 1980-81; Peterson & Co., Chicago, 1981-. *Memberships:* American Institute of CPA's; Illinois Society of CPA's; Illinois Auctioneers Association, Secretary/Treasurer; National Auctioneers Association. *Honour:* CPA Certificate, 1980. *Hobbies:* Classic Automobiles; Horse Riding; Antiques; Travel. *Address:* 38W 196 Rt. 20, Elgin, IL 60123, USA.

RAVEN Kathleen Annie, b. 9 Nov. 1910, Coniston, Cumbria, England. Chief Nursing Adviser, Allied Medical Group. m. Professor John Thornton Ingram MD, FRCP, 12 Dec. 1959 deceased 1972. *Education:* SRN, St Bartholomew's Hospital, London, 1936; SCM, City of London Maternity Hospital, 1938. *Appointments:* Night Superintendent, Ward Sister, Assistant Matron, St Bartholomew's Hospital, London, 1938-48; Matron, General Infirmary, Leeds, 1948-57; Chief Nursing Officer, Ministry of Health, 1958-72; Chief Nursing Adviser, Allied Med Group, 1972-; Civil Service Chairman, Interviewing Panels, 1972-79. *Publications:* Many articles in professional journals; watercolours exhibited, Civil Service Exhibition, 2 occasions. *Memberships:* Officer, Order of Saint John, 1963; Fellow, Royal Society of Arts, 1970; Vice-President, Royal College of Nursing, 1972; Life Member, Royal Commonwealth Society. *Honours:* Recipient, various awards including: Fellow, World Health organisation, 1960; Dame Commander of the British Empire, 1968; Freewoman, Barber Surgeons Livery Company, 1981; Freeman, City of London, 1986; Fellow, Royal College of Nursing, 1986. *Hobbies:* Reading; Painting; Walking. *Address:* Jesmond, Burcott, Wing, nr. Leighton Buzzard, Beds LU7 0JU, England.

RAWLS Catherine Potempa, b. 19 Mar. 1953, Chicago, Illinois, USA. Commodities Trader. m. 30 July 1983, 1 daughter. *Education:* BA, Marquette University, Milwaukee, Wisconsin, 1975. *Appointments:* Financial Futures Analyst, Peavey Grain Co, 1977-82; Director of Research, Geldermann Inc, 1982-86; President, Tiare Trading Co, 1987-. *Memberships:* Art Institute of Chicago. *Honours:* Women in Communications Chapter, Marquette University, 1975. *Hobbies:* Scuba diving; Skiing; Race car driving; Wine collecting; Needlepoint. *Address:* 421 Sandhurst Circle, Glen Ellyn, IL 60137, USA.

RAY Dixy Lee, b. 3 Sept. 1914, Tacoma, Washington, USA. Retired. *Education:* BA 1937, MA 1938, Mills College; PhD, Stanford University, 1945. *Appointments:* Teacher, Oakland Public School and Pacific Grove Public Schools, California, 1939-42; Special Consultant, Biographical Oceanography, US National Science Foundation, 1960-63; Visiting Professor, Stanford University, 1964; Director, Pacific Science Center, Seattle, 1963-72; US Atomic Energy Commission 1972, Chairman 1973-75; Asst Secretary of State, Bureau of Oceans, International and Environmental and Scientific Affairs, US Government, 1975; Faculty, University of Washington, 1945-76; Governor, State of Washington, 1977-81. *Creative works:* 140 wood carvings, 3 exhibits. Book ed, Boring and Fouling Organisms; Numerous scientific papers, reviews and speeches. *Memberships:* Senior Scholar, Institute for Regulatory Science; Board Member, American Ecology Corp. *Honours include:* Institute of Electrical & Electronic Engineers, Centennial Medal, 1984; International Freedom of Mobility Award, Automobility Foundation, 1982; Outstanding Women in Energy Award, Nuclear Energy Women, 1981; Numerous other honours and awards. *Hobby:* Wood carving, Pacific Northwest Native Indian style. *Address:* 600 Third Avenue, Fox Island, Washington 98333, USA.

RAY Judith, b. 14 Sept. 1946, St Louis, USA. Univerity Professor. *Education:* ABED, 1968; MA, Ed., 1972, MS, 1979, Washington State University. *Appointments:* Graduate Assistant, 1970-72, 1975-79, Washington State University; York College, 1973-75; American Red Cross, 1973. *Publications:* Articles in various journals. *Memberships:* ASTM; AAHPERI; ASB; ASBS; AFA; AFCA; ISB. *Honours:* Recipient, various honours and awards. *Hobbies:* Travel; Languages; Tennis; Fencing; Sailing; Dancing. *Address:* West Chester University, No 307 South Campus, West Chester, PA 19383, USA.

RAY Rene (Irene Lilian), b. 22 Sept. 1917, London, England. Actress; Author; Painter. m. 2nd Earl of Midleton, 24 Apr. 1975. *Career:* Appeared in 46 films including: The Gallopping Major; Women of Twilight; The Good Die Young; Vicious Circle; The Strange World of Planet X. Radio Career included: The Road to Samarkand; Return of the Native. Stage Career included: Wonder Bar; The Dominant Sex; Private Company; Bees on the Boatdeck; Climbing; Yes and No; Three Blind Mice; Q. *Publications:* Play: The Tree Surgeon. Books: The Garden of Cahmohn; Angel Assignment; The Christmas Present; Wraxton Marne; Emma Conquest; A Man Named Seraphin; The Tree Surgeon; The Strange World of Plante X. *Membership:* Patron of The Jersey Film Society. *Honour:* Special Award for Painting, International Arts Guild, Palme D'Or Des Beaux Arts, 1969. *Address:* Martello Lodge, St Brelades Bay, Jersey, Channel Islands.

RAY Sandra Sue, b. 1 July 1944, Lincoln, Nebraska, USA. Financier; Former Social Worker. m. (1) Daniel A. Lenhart, 29 June 1963 (div. 1972), 1 son, 1 daughter, (2) Nazrie Ray, 11 June 1976 (div. 1982), 1 daughter. *Education:* BSc, University of Oregon, 1964; MSW, University of California, Los Angeles, 1966; Licensed Clinical Social Worker, 1975. *Appointments:* Deputy Probation Officer, Los Angeles County Probation Department, 1970-78; Associate Professor, California School of Professional Psychology, 1975-78; Guidance Manager, LA Job Corps, Hollywood, 1978-79; Clinical Director, Penny Lane, Sepulveda, California, 1980-83; Psychiatric Consultant, Clinical Director, I-ADARP Inc, San Fernando Valley, 1981-86; Clinician, Hathaway Home for Children, Lake View Terrace, 1983-85; Director, Residential Services, Calabasas Academy, 1985; Programme Director, Pasadena Community Hospital, 1986; Administrative Assistant, Prudential Insurance Company, 1987-88; Partner, Administrtor, V. S. Associates Financial Services, 1988-. *Memberships:* Alpha Kappa Delta, national sociology honour society, 1963-64; Past President, University of Oregon Chapter, AKD. *Hobbies:* Los Angeles Civic Light Opera; Swimming; Photography; Dancing. *Address:* 8111 Reseda Boulevard No. 208, Reseda, California 91335, USA.

RAYMOND Vicki Kathleen, b. 16 Nov. 1949, Daylesford, Victoria, Australia. Clerk. *Education:* BA (Hons), University of Tasmania, Australia, 1972. *Appointments:* Administrative Officer, University of Tasmania, Australia, 1974-80; Typist/Clerk, Australia House, London, England, 1981; Typist/Clerk, Victoria House, London, 1982; Clerk, Australia House, London, 1983-. *Publications:* Books: Holiday Girls and Other Poems; Small Arms Practice. Contributor to: Island Magazine; Quadrant; Agenda. Participant in: Struga Poetry Festival, Greenwich Festival, London Irish Festival, XVIth Poetry Biennial (Liege), Concerts at British Music Information Centre; Poetry readings at Commonwealth Institute London; Universities of Gothenberg & Lund, Sweden, University of Kent and for ABC Radio, Australia. Author of six lyrics set for piano and bass-baritone by composer Patrick Morris; Led Women Writers' Workshop at Commonwealth Institute, London. *Memberships:* The Performing Right Society, Great Britain; Australia House Staff Association; The Labour Party of Great Britain. *Honour:* British Airways Commonwealth Poetry Prize for First Volume, 1986. *Hobbies:* Flute; Hiking; Genealogy; Italian literature. *Address:* Department of Finance, Australia House, London W9 2AX, England.

RAYNER Claire Berenice, b. 22 Jan. 1031, London, England. Writer. m. 23 June 1957, 2 sons, 1 daughter. *Education:* SRN, Royal Northern Hospital, London, 1954; Midwifery Studies, Guy's Hospital. *Appointments Include:* Various nursing positions Royal Free Hospital; Sister, Paediatric Dept., Whittington Hospital; Author 1960-; Agony Aunt, Petticoat, several years, The Sun Problem Page, 7 years; Agony Aunt, The Sunday Mirror, 1980-88; Currently writing for Today Newspaper; Appearances on Woman's Hour, Schools, Today for radio; TV appearances include: David Frost Programme; Michael Parkinson Show; Russell Harty Show; Tuesday Documentary, etc; Presenter, Family Advice slot, Pebble Mill at One, 3 years; Co-Presenter,Kitchen Garden, 4 years; Claire Rayner's Casebook, 1980-84; weekly appearance on TV AM's Good Morning Britain in the After Nine Slot. *Publications Include:* Over 80 books including: 12 volume saga overall title is The Performers; other books include: Mothers & Midwives, 1962; Cottage Hospital, 1963; Your Baby, 1965; 101 Facts an Expectant Mother Should Know, 1967; Lady Mislaid, 1968; protecting Your Baby, 1970; A Time to Heal, 1972; Where Do I Come From?, 1973; Claire Rayner Answers Your 100 Questions on Pregnancy, 1978; Related to Sex, 1979; Everything Your Doctor Would Tell You If He Had the Time, 1980; Claire Rayners Lifeguide, 1980; Baby and Young Child Care, 1981; Death on the Table, 1983; Growing Pains, 1984; The Getting Better Book, 1985; The Virus Man, 1985; Woman, 1986; When I Grow Up, 1986; Safe Sex, 1987; Maddie, 1988; Claire Rayner Talking, 1988; The Don't Spoil Your Body Book,

1989; Clinical Judgements, 1989; The House on the Fen, 1989; etc; Contributor numerous articles to journals and magazine and was Ruth Martin of Woman's Own, 9 years, then her own by-line, 12 years; currently working for Woman Magazine. *Honours Include:* Hospital Gold Medal for Outstanding Achivement, Royal Northern Hospital, 1945; Admitted to, Freedom of the City of London, 1981. *Address:* c/o Desmond Rayner, Holly Wood House, Roxborough Avenue, Harrow-on-the- Hill, Middlesex HA1 3BU, England.

RAYNER Mary Yoma Grigson, b. 30 Dec. 1933, Mandalay, Burma. Author. m. Eric Rayner, 6 Aug. 1960, 1 daughter, 2 sons, divorced 1981, (2) Adrian Hawksley, 9 Mar. 1985. *Education:* MA, honours, English Language & Literature, University of St Andrews, Scotland, 1954. *Appointments:* Various London Publishing Houses, 1956-62; Freelance Author & Illustrator, 1972-. *Publications:* Author & Illustrator: The Witch Finder, 1975; Mr and Mrs Pig's Evening Out, 1976; Garth Pig and the Icecream Lady, 1977; The Rain Cloud, 1980; Mrs Pig's Bulk Buy, 1981; Crocodarling, 1985; Mrs Pig Gets Cross, 1986; Reilly, 1987; Oh Paull, 1988; Illustrator: The Boggart, by Emma Tennant, 1980; Daggie Dogfoot, by Dick King-Smith, 1980; The Dead Letter Box, by Jan Mark, 1982; The Sheep-Pig, by Dick King-Smith, 1983; Lost and Found, by Jill Paton Walsh, 1984. *Membership:* Society of Authors. *Address:* c/o Macmillan Childrens Books, 4 Little Essex Street, London WC2R 3LF, England.

RAZ Hilda, b. 4 May, 1938, Rochester, New York, USA. Editor. m. Dale Nordyke, 22 July 1980, 1 son, 1 daughter. *Education:* BA, Boston University, 1960. *Appointments:* Assistant Director, Planned Parenthood League of Massachusetts, 1960-62; Editorial Assistant, 1970-74, Contents Editor 1974-77, Poetry Editor 1980-87, Editor 1987-, Prairie Schooner. *Publications:* What Is Good, 1988; The Bone Dish, 1989; Contributions to North American Review, Poetry Miscellany, Denver Quarterly, New Letters, Hollins Critic. *Memberships:* President, Associated Writing Programs; Board of Governors, Center for Great Plains Studies, University of Nebraska; Board of Directors, Planned Parenthood League of Nebraska; Board of Directors, The Nebraska Literary Heritage Association. *Honours:* Literary Heritage Award, 1988; Bread Loaf Fellow, 1989; Bread Loaf Scholar, 1985; Fellow of the Center for Great Plains Study, 1987. *Address:* 960 South Cotner Boulevard, Lincoln, NE 68510, USA.

RAZINK Kristi Kay, b. 28 Dec. 1956, Minneapolis, USA. Media Director; Account Executive. *Education:* Studies: Marketing Certificate, University of Minnesota, 1976-82, Metro State University, 1982-; Minneapolis Community College, 1984. *Appointments:* Assistant Media Buyer, Capp Homes, 1975- 79; Media Planner, Buyer, Kamstra Communications, St Paul, 1979-82; Media Director, Clarke Livingston Associates, 1982-84; Jack Carmichael Advertising, 1984-85; John Miles Co., 1985-87; Creative Communication Consultants, 1987-88; Account Executive, Media Director, Roth Graham Inc., 1988-. *Memberships:* various professional organisations. *Address:* 4609 - 30th Avenue South, Minneapolis, MN 55406, USA.

READ D J, (Mrs Saint), b. 17 Apr. 1913, Norwood, Surrey, England. Writer. m. Douglas Edward John Saint, 26 July 1940. 1 daughter. *Education:* Homerton College, Cambridge, 1931-33. *Appointments:* Teacher, Middlesex, 1933-40; Supply Teaching, Rural Schools in Berkshire, 1947-52. *Publications:* 36 novels, the first: Village School, 1955. *Hobbies:* Theatre; Reading; Music. *Address:* c/o Michael Joseph Ltd, 27 Wrights Lane, London W8 5TZ, England.

READ Elfreida, b. 2 Oct. 1920, Vladivostok, Russia. Writer. m. George J. Read, 10 July 1941, 1 son, 1 daughter. *Appointments:* *Publications:* The Dragon and the Jadestone, 1958; The Magic Light, 1963; The Enchanted Egg, 1963; The Spell of Chuchuchan, 1967; Magic for Granny, 1967; Twin Rivers, 1968; No One

Need Ever Know, 1971; Brothers by Choice, 1974; The Message of the Mask, 1981; Kirstine and the Villains, 1982; Race Against the Dark, 1983; Growing Up in China, 1985; short stories in numerous journals and magazines; Poetry in various Anthologies. *Honours:* Canadian Centennial Contest for Children's Stories; Poetry in British Columbia. *Hobby:* Music. *Address:* 2686 W. King Edward Ave., Vancouver, BC, Canada V6L 1T6.

READ Sylvia Joan. Actress; Writer. m. (1) Peter Albery, 12 May 1945, deceased, 1 son, (2) William Fry. *Education:* Froebel Educational Institute; Kensington High School; Royal Academy of Dramatic Art; Diploma, RADA; LGSM Gold Medal, Poetry Society. *Appointments:* Worked with Nancy Price, Ashley Dukes, E Martin Browne in Theatre; Leading Actress for Theatre Roundabout, 1960; appeared in TV productions of Brother Francis, The Pilgrim's Progress, and numerous others; appeared in Celebration, film. *Publications:* Burden of Blessing; Cage of Arms; Travelling Actors; 'The Poetical Ark; Play, Harvest; Christian Theatre. *Memberships:* Co- Director, 1979-82, The Religious Drama Society of Great Britain; Director, Theatre Roundabout, 1965-. *Hobbies:* Walking; Architecture; Painting; Going to the Theatre. *Address:* 859 Finchley Road, London NW11 8LX, England.

REAMS-BUCK, Jacqueline Louise, b. 7 Apr. 1927, Des Moines, Iowa, USA. Teacher. m. Edward E. Buck, 1981, 4 sons, 2 daughters. *Education:* AA, Mount San Antonio College, 1956; BA, California State University, Fullerton, 1962; California State University, Los Angeles; University of California, Irvine; MEd, Whittier College, 1968; Administrative Credential, Whittier College, 1968; Work for MA, Geogrphy, finished at California State University of Los Angeles. *Appointmens:* Nursing: 1947-48, 1955-62; La Habra City Schools, Washington Junior High, Chairman, Science, Social Science Department; Imperial Junior High, Chairman, Science, Social Science; Washington Middle School, Social Science Department, 1962-87. *Publications:* Founder, editor, Association Newsaper, Reflections; History Advisor, Universal Studios, Rebels and Seekers; Advisor, Religious Films, Paulist Studios; MacMillan Publishers West Coast Advisor and Consultant for 8th Grade History Text. *Memberships:* President, Vice-President, Bargaining Chair, Legislative Chair, Editor, Association newspaper, La Habra Education Assn., Vice Chair, Orange County Service Center, elected 8 years to California Teachers Association and National Education Association for 7 years; National Science Association; National California and Orange County Social Science Associations; Mensa. *Honours:* WHO Award, California Teachers Association & La Habra Education Association, 1976; Business & Professional Women's Club, Silver Drum, 1976; Nke Award, 1977; Nominee, Outstanding Teacher of American History, Daughters of the American Revolution, 1987; Citizen of the Month, La Habra Chamber of Commerce, September 1987. *Hobbies:* Hot Air Ballooning; Music; Coin Collecting; Hunting; Fishing; Writing *Address:* 2300 East Nutwood Avenue, Fullerton, CA 92631, USA.

REBECK Pamela Joan, b. 24 Sept. 1949, Chicago, USA. Psychologist. m. James E. Clark, 5 Sept. 1981, 2 sons. *Education:* BA, Psychology & Education, 1971; MS, Psychology, 1973, PhD, Psychology 1977, Illinois Institute of Technology. *Appointments:* Governor State University, 1977-80; Associate, Chicago Stress Centre, 1977- Private practice, 1980-. *Publications:* Articles in: Creative Women. *Memberships:* American, Illinois Psychological Associations; National Register of Health Service Providers. *Honours:* Graduation, BA with Honours, 1971. *Hobbies:* Family; Sports; Travel; Photography; Reading. *Address:* 475 River Bend No 600, Naperville, IL 60540, USA.

REDDOCH Mildred Lucas, b. 1 Mar. 1916, Texarkana, Texas, USA. Writer; Artist. m. Elbert D Reddoch, 25 Sept. 1938 (d. 1956). 1 son, 1 daughter. *Education:* Texarkana College, 1934-36; BS 1963-64, Masters of Education 1968-69, Sam Houston State

Teachers University. *Appointments:* Houston In Schools, 1946-65; Texarkana, Arkansas Schools, 1967-70; Houston, Texas Ind Schools, 1970-75; Formed own business, The Think Business, 1981-; Professional writing; art. *Publications include:* Poetry book: Gems to be Polished; Novels: So White, The Lilies; Art: Scenic The Rippling brooks, displayed in Louvre Museum, Paris, France. *Memberships:* National Teachers' Assn, 1947-; National League of American Pen Women, Inc, President, Houston Branch, 1984-90, National Librarian, 1988-90; Delta Kappa Gamma Honor Society, Women Educators Program Chairman; Woodlands Art League; National Female Executives, Inc; National Institute of Business Management, Inc; MENSA; United States Senatorial Club; President Bush's Task Force; Council of Sustaining Members Campaigners; Charter Member, Ronald Reagan Republican Center. *Honours:* George Washington Award for Essay, A Symbol of Freedom Foundation, Valley Forge, 1965; Scholarship to attend Teachers' Seminar, Freedoms Foundation, 1967; Plaque and medal, Outstanding Teacher for State of Arkansas, Freedom Foundation, 1967; Golden Poet Award, World of Poetry (California), 1983-90; Invited to serve on the President of USA Trust Committee, 1988-89; Essay, I Shall Go Forward won 1st place, Holy Land Fellowship; Medal of Merit, received from President George Bush, 1990. *Hobbies:* Stamp collecting; Attending productions of music-orchestra and theatre; Sponsoring contests for children; Sustaining sponsor for the National Republican Party, USA. *Address:* 4434 Cherry Oak Lane, Houston, TX 77089, USA.

REDDY Helen, b. 25 Oct. 1942, Australia. Singer. *Career:* Began career at 4 years as singer. Appeared in hundreds of stage and radio roles with parents by age of 15. Came to New York in 1966, played nightclubs and appeared on TV. *Creative Works:* Films: Airport 1975 (debut); Pete's Dragon. Television: David Frost Show; Flip Wilson Show; Mike Douglas Show, etc; The Helen Reddy Show (Summer 1973, NBC); Permanent host of Midnight Special; Appearances on Tonight Show; Mac Davis Show. Hosted Merv Griffin Show; Sesame Street; Children's Workshop Prod.; Tonight Show; Muppet Show. Records: I Don't Know How To Love Him; Delta Dawn; Leave Me Alone; Angle Baby; Albums include: Love Song for Jeffrey; Free & Easy; No Way to Treat a Lady; I Don't Know How To Love Him; Music; Music; I Am Woman; Long Hard Climb; Helen Reddy's Greatest Hits. *Honours:* Grammy Award, 1973 for I Am Woman; Most Played Artist, Music Operators of America; American Music Award, 1974; Los Angeles Times Woman of the Year, 1975; No 1 Female Vocalist in 1975 and 1976; Record World, Cash Box and Billboard; One of the Most Exciting Women in the World, International Bachelor's Society, 1976. *Address:* c/o 820 Stanford, Santa Monica, CA 90403, USA.

REDGRAVE Lynn, b. 8 Mar. 1943, London, England. Actress. m. John Clark, 1967. 1 son, 2 daughters. *Education:* Queensgate School; Central School of Speech and Drama. *Creative works:* National Theatre of Great Britain, 1963-66 (Tulip Tree; Mother Courage; Andorra; Hay Fever, etc); Black Comedy, Broadway, 1967; The Two of Us; Slag; Zoo Zoo Widdershins Zoo; Born Yesterday, London 1968-71; A Better Place, Dublin, 1972; My Fat Friend; Knock Knock; Mrs Warren's Profession, Broadway, 1973-76; The Two of Us; California Suite; Hellzapoppin, US tours, 1976-77; Saint Joan; Chicago and New York, 1977; Twelfth Night, American Shakespeare Festival, Connecticut, 1978; Les dames du jeudi, Los Angeles, 1981; Sister Mary Ignatius Explains It All for You, Los Angeles, 1983; The King and I, N American Tour, 1983. Films include: Tom Jones; Girl with Green Eyes; Georgy Girl; Deadly Affair; Smashing Time; Virgin Soldiers; Last of the Mobile Hotshots; Every Little Crook and Nanny; National Health; Happy Hooker; Everyting You Always Wanted to Know About Sex; the Big Bus; Sunday Lovers; Don't Turn The Other Cheek; Morgan Stewart's Coming Home; A Woman Alone, 1988; Midnight, 1989; BBC Death of A Son (Centre Films), 1989; The Old Reliable, 1989; Getting It Right, 1989; Les Liaisosn Danereuses, 1989. USA television includes: Co-host of nationally televised talk-show, Not For Women Only; appearances in

documentaries, plays. The Muppets; Centennial; Beggarman Thief; The Seduction of Miss Leona; Rehearsal for Murder and series: Housecalls (CBS); Teachers Only (NBC); The Faint-Hearted Feminist (Arts & Entertainment Channel); Television Films include: The Turn of the screw; Gauguin the Savage; Anthony & Cleopatra; The Bad Seed; My Two Loves. *Honours:* New York Film Critics, Golden Globe and IFIDA Awards; Academy nomination for Best Actress. *Hobbies:* Cooking; Gardening; Horse-riding. *Address:* c/o John Clark, PO Box 1207, Topanga Canyon, CA 90290, USA.

REDGRAVE Vanessa, b. 30 Jan. 1937, London, England. Actress. m. Tony Richardson, 1962, divorced 1967. 2 daughters. *Education:* Queensgate School, London; Central School of Speech and Drama. *Creative Works:* Stage appearances: A Midsummer Night's Dream, 1959; The Tiger and the Horse, 1960; The Taming of the Shrew, 1961; As You Like It, 1961; Cymbeline, 1962; The Seagull, 1964, 1985; The Prime of Miss Jean Brodie, 1966; Daniel Deronda, 1969; Cato Street, 1971; Threepenny Opera, 1972; Twelfth Night, 1972; Anthony and Cleopatra, 1973, 1986; Design for Living, 1973; Macbeth, 1975; Lady from the Sea, 1976, 1979 (Manchester); The Aspern Papers, 1984; Ghosts, 1986. Films include: Morgan-A Suitable Case for Treatment, 1962; Sailor from Gibraltar, 1965; Camelot, 1967; Blow Up, 1967; Charge of the Light Brigade, 1968; Isadora Duncan, 1968; The Seagull, 1968; A Quiet Place in the Country, 1968; Dropout; The Trojan Women, 1970; The Devils, 1970; The Holiday, 1971; Mary Queen of Scots, 1971. Television: Katherine Mansfield, 1973; Murder on the Orient Express, 1974; Winter Rates, 1974; 7% Solution, 1975; Julia, 1977; Agatha, 1978; Yanks, 1978; Bear Island, 1979; Playing for Time, 1979, 1980; My Body My Child, 1981; Wagner, 1982; The Bostonians, 1983; Wetherby, 1984; Prick Up Your Ears, 1987. Produced and narrated documentary film The Palestinians, 1977. *Publication:* Pussies and Tigers, 1963. *Honours:* Evening Standard Award, Best Actress, 1961; Variety Club Award, 1961; Award for Best Actress, Cannes Film Festival, 1966 for Morgan-A Suitable Case for Treatment; Award for Leading Actress, US Nat. Soc. of Film Critics and Best Actress Award, Film Critics' Guild (UK) for Isadora Duncan, 1969; Academy Award (Best Supporting Actres) for Julia, 1978; Award (TV for best Actress) for Playing for Time, 1981; Laurence Olivier Award, 1984. *Membership:* Workers' Revolutionary Party (Candidate for Moss Side, 1979). *Interest:* Changing the status quo. *Address:* 1 Ravenscourt Road, London W6, England.

REED Barbara Joan, b. 25 Mar. 1937, St Catherines, Canada. Judge, Federal Court of Canada. m. Robert Barry Reed, 3 Sept. 1960, 2 sons, 1 daughter. *Education:* BA, University of Toronto, 1960; LLB 1968, LLM 1970, Dalhousie University; Called to Bar of Ontario, 1971. *Appointments include:* Assistant professor, Common Law, University of Ottawa, 1971-73; Legal officer, Department of Justice, Ottawa, 1973-74; Constitutional adviser, Privy Council Office (PCO) & Federal Provincial Relations Office (FPRO), 1974-80; Director, legal services, FPRO, 1980-82; Legal counsel, PCO, 1982-83; Judge, Trial Division, Federal Court of Canada & Chairman, Competition Tribunal, current. *Memberships:* Law Society of Upper Canada; Canadian & International Bar Associations; Canadian Institute for Administration of Justice. *Honour:* QL, 1982. *Hobbies:* Cross-country skiing; Volleyball; Photography; Drama; Needlework. *Address:* Federal Court of Canada, Supreme Court Building, Wellington Street, Ottawa, Ontario, Canada K1A 0H9.

REED Cynthia Rae, b. 3 Dec. 1956, Des Moines, Iowa, USA. Registered Nurse; Director, Psychiatric Services. m. Thomas Joseph Shea, 30 Aug. 1986. *Education:* BSc., Nursing, 1978, MA, Counsellor Education, 1981, University of Iowa. *Appointments:* Clinical Nurse Specialist, 1982-83, Director, Psychiatric Service, 1983-, St Lukes Hospital, Cedar Rapids; Project consultant, STC Health Resources, 1987-. *Publications:* Directed, The Development of the Award winning Psycho-Educational Programme, Patterns for Growth;

Co-author, Children & Adolescent Service System Programme Grant, 1987; Co-author, Gamblers Assistance Programme. *Memberships:* American, Iowa Nurses Associations; American & Iowa Organizations of Nurse Executives; Sigma Theta Tau. *Honours:* Suicide Outreach Project, 1983; Nominee for Women in Business & Industry, Woman of the Year Award, 1987. *Hobbies:* Photography; Bicycling; Canoeing; Camping; Hiking; Travel; Watersports. *Address:* 600 Carlton Road SE, Cedar Rapids, IA 52403, USA.

REED Jane Barbara, b. 31 Mar. 1940, Letchworth, England. Managing Editor. *Appointments:* Editor, Woman's Own, 1969-79; Publisher, Womens Monthly magazines Group, IPC Magazines Ltd., 1979-81; Editor in chief, Woman Magazine, 1981-83; Managing Director, Holborn Publishing Group IPC, 1983-85; Managing Editor, Today Newspaper, 1985-. *Publications:* Girl About Town, 1965; Kitchen Sink or Swim, 1981, co-author. *Memberships:* Committee, Public Understanding of Science, Royal Society; External Examiner, City University Post-Graduate Journalism Course. *Address:* London, England.

REEDY Patricia (Pat) M., b. 1 May 1940, Mt Vernon, New York, USA. Playwright; Actress. *Education:* Graduated, Berkeley School of Business, 1960; Advertising Certificate, Y & R School of Advertising, 1961; Courses at Hunter College, The Arts Students League, State University of New York at Purchase, Fairfield University. *Career:* As Actress/Singer: Fran, in Promises, Promises, Tydewater Dinner Theatre, Norfolk, Virginia, 1973-74; Anita, in Black Mountain, Lincoln Center Library, 1974; Wonder Women, in Paranoia Pretty, Theatre for the New City, 1975; Delores, in Sisters and Brothers, Women's Interart, 1976; Maggie, in It's Only Temporary, Gate Theatre, 1976; Irma, in Bagging It, American Theatre of Actors, 1981; Queen of France, in Cordelia, Wife, in Tynside, Composer, in Ever Wake Up, New York University, 1987; Soloist, various restaurants; Sang with band, SUNY-Purchase; TV appearances: Dick Lamb Show, Virginias and Carolinas, 1973; Another World, NBC, 1976; Stage Struck, CBS and 13, 1977; Hotline, Cable, New York City, 1978; Joe Franklin, ABC, 1979; Go For It, Westchester, Cable 3, 1982; Off-Off Broadway productions of her plays, 1976-81; Director, several performances including: A Step Beyond & The Pond, New York University, 1987; Terror Brokers, Theater at Americas Society, Inc., 1988; Off-Off Broadway, Trapped in the Basement, American Theatre of Actors Play Festival, 1983. *Creative works:* Plays: It's Only Temporary; A Bundle for Brunch; the Stop-Over; A Step Beyond; Bagging It. *Memberships:* Dramatists Guild; Actors Equity Association; Screen Actors Guild; American Federation of Television and Radio Artists; Smithsonian Institution. *Honours:* Cheer Leader, Vice-President of Class, President, Phi Pi Psi, High School; President, Entertainment Committee, Junior League, Westchester Women's Club; Vice-President, Our Town Club; Vice-President: Hi-Y (YMCA), Little Theatre, Dramatic Society; Champion Basketball Team; Many awards including 1st Prize for All State Skit Writing Competition, YMCA. *Hobbies:* Photography; Racketball. *Address:* PO Box 245, Westport, CT 06881, USA.

REES Barbara Elizabeth, b. 9 Jan. 1934, Worcester, England. Writer. m. Larry Herman, 1 Sep. 1967, div. 1978, 1 daughter. *Education:* Lady Margaret Hall, Oxford, 1953-56; BA Hons (Oxon); MA. *Appointments:* Fundraiser, 1985-, International Planned Parenthood Federation. *Publications:* Try Another Country, 3 short novels, 1968; Diminishing Circles, 1969; Prophet of the Wind, 1972; George and Anna, 1976; The Victorian Lady, 1978; Harriet Dark, 1979; many short stories. *Honours:* Arts Council of Great Britain Award, 1972; Creative Writer-in-Residence, North London Polytechnic, 1975-77. *Hobbies:* Countryside; Music; Politics. *Address:* 102 Savernake Road, London NW3 2JR, England.

REES Mina S(piegel), b. 2 Aug. 1902, Cleveland, Ohio, USA. University Administrator. m Leopold Brahdy.

Education: AB, 1923, ScD, 1973, Hunter College; AM, 1925, LLD, 1971, Columbia University; PhD, University of Chicago, 1931. *Appointments:* Instructor, Mathematics, 1926-32, Assistant Professor, 1932-40, Associate Professor, 1940-50, Professor, Faculty Dean, 1953-61, Hunter College; Professor, Dean of Graduate Studies, 1961, Provost, Graduate Division, 1968-69, President, Graduate School and University Center, 1969-72, President Emeritus, 1972-, City University of New York; Technical Aide, Administrative Assistant, Applied Mathematics Panel, National Defence Research Committee, Office of Scientific Research and Development, 1943-46; Head, Mathematics Branch, 1946-49, Director, Mathematical Sciences Division, 1949-52, Deputy Scientific Director, 1952-53, Office of Naval Research; Mathematical Division, 1953-56, Executive Committee, 1954-56, NRC; Advisory Boards, Panels: Department of Defence, 1957-61; Computation and Exterior Ballistics Lab, US Navy, 1958-61; National Bureau of Standards, 1954-58; NSF, 1955-58; School of Mathematics Study Group, 1962-64; NY Advisory Council on Graduate Education, 1962-72; Commission for Humanities, 1963-64; National Science Board, 1964-70; Chair, Council of Graduate Schools in US, 1970. *Publications:* Contributor to mathematical publications. *Memberships include:* Executive Committee, Trustee: Woodrow Wilson National Fellowship Foundation; Charles Babbage Institute for History of Information Processing; Fellow, Past Vice-President, President, Board Chairman, American Association for the Advancement of Science; New York Academy of Sciences; American Mathematical Society, Trustee 1955-59; Past 2nd Vice-President, Mathematical Society of America; Society for Industrial and Applied Mathematics, Director of Institute for Mathematics and Sociology 1973- 86; Sigma Xi; Phi Beta Kappa; Pi Mu Epsilon. *Honours:* 18 honorary doctorates; King's Medal for Service in Cause of Freedom, England; President's Certificate of Merit, US; Many other awards and honours. *Address:* City University of New York, 33 West 42nd Street, New York, NY 10036, USA.

REEVES A Sue Windsor, b. 1 Mar. 1947, Oxford, Mississippi, USA. Healthcare Executive. m. Johnny Lafayette Reeves, Jr, 1 Nov. 1969. 1 son, 2 daughters. *Education:* BAE, University of Mississippi, 1969; MEd, Louisiana State University of New Orleans, 1972. *Appointments:* Certified Teacher, Jackson, Mississippi Public Schools, 1969-71; Graduate Assistantship, Louisiana State University of New Orleans, 1971-72; Private School Teacher, Carrollton Presbyterian School, New Orleans, 1972-73; Professional Volunteer, National Association of Junior Auxiliaries, Slidell, Louisiana, 1979-89; Teacher, St Tammany Parish Schools, Slidell, 1981-83; Director of Infant/Youth Services 1984, Director of Community Relations 1984-85, Director of Women's Center and Physician Recruitment 1985-87, Director of Physician Services, Exeuctive Director Women's Health Foundation, 1987-, Slidell Momorial Hospital and Medical Center; Physician Recruitment Coordinator 1986-88, Executive Director of Women's Health Foundation of Louisiana 1987-88, American Medical International, New Orleans Network. *Creative works:* Designed State Grant Proposal, Volunteer Coordinating Center, 1982. *Memberships:* Phi Mu Fraternity, Chapter President, University of Mississippi 1968-69; Phi Mu National Carnation Queen, Denver, 1969; Regional Membership Advisor 1972-76; CoFounder, Slidell Alumnae Chapter, 1974; CoFounder, Slidell National Panhellenic Conference Sororities Assocaition, 1976; National Association of Junior Auxiliaries, Slidell Chapter, Associate Member, 1986-; Volunteer Coordinating Center, Slidell; National Association of Junior Auxiliaries, National Admissions Committeewoman, 1982-87; Women's Health Foundation of Louisiana, Slidell Regional Chapter, Founder 1985; Chapter Executive Director, 1988-; National Association of Female Exeuutives, 1987; National Association of Directors of Women Health Programs, Charter Member, 1988-; Louisiana Association of Business and Industry Healthcare Council, 1988; Women's Healthcare Executives Network, New Orleans, Founding Board

Member, 1988. *Honours:* Phi Kappa Phi, Louisiana State University of New Orleans, 1972; National Association of Junior Auxiliaries, Chapter President, receiving Martha Wise Award for oustanding new project in nation, 1984;I As President, National Association of Junior Auxiliaries (Slidell Chapter) received Louisiana State Grant for Volunteer Coordinating Center, 1982. *Hobbies:* Reading; Volunteer work; Coordinating children's activities; Needlework. *Address;* 163 West Pinewood Drive, Slidell, Louisiana 70458, USA.

REEVES Glenda Marie, b. 19 Nov. 1956, Nashville, Tennessee, USA. Dietitian. *Education:* ASc, Nashville Tech, 1976; BSc, David Lipscomb College, 1981; Diploma, Dietetic Internship 1982, MEd 1982, Vanderbilt University. Registered Dietitian (RD). *Appointments:* Junior Accountant, 1976; Computer Programmer, 1976-78; Dietary Aide, summer 1978; Food Service Supervisor, 1979-80; Dietitian's Assistant, 1981; Clinical Dietitian 1982-, Chief Clinical Dietitian, 1989-, Park View Medical Center, Nashville. *Memberships:* Past Chair, Education Division, Nashville District Dietetic Association; American & Tennessee Dietetic Associations. *Honours:* Scholarships: Gerber Products Company 1980, Tennessee Dietetic Association 1981, American Dietetic Association 1981; Home Economics Award, David Lipscomb College, 1981. *Hobbies:* People; Cooking; Nature; Sewing. *Address:* Park View Medical Center, 230 25th Avenue North, Nashville, Tennessee 37203, USA.

REHRMANN Eileen M, b. 30 Nov. 1944, Chester, USA. Member, Maryland House of Delegates. m. 7 Mar. 1965, 2 sons, 2 daughters. *Appointments:* Elementary School Teacher, 1963-66; Bel Air Town Commissioner, 1978-82; Maryland House of Delegates, 1982-. *Memberships:* President, Maryland Municipal League; former President, Harford County League of Women Voters; President Elect, Women Legislators of Maryland. *Honours:* Outstanding Standing State Legislator, Assembly of Goverrnmental Employees, 1984; Distinguished Service Award, Maryland Municipal League, 1985; Maryland Police Chief's Chief's Award, 1988; State Fireman's Association Appreciation Award, 1988. *Hobbies:* Child Care; Port of Baltimore; Golf. *Address:* 619 Dorsey Road, Bel Air, MD 21014, USA.

REID Beryl, b. 17 June 1920, Hereford, England. Actress. m. (2)Derek Franklin, divoced. *Appointments:* First professional engagement, Bridlington 1935; numerous appearances including: Educating Archie; The Belles of St Trinians; The Extra Day; Two Way Stretch; The Dock Brief; Henry Hall's Guestnight; Creator of 'Monica'; own series on TV; most recent London Play, Gigi, 1985. *Publications Include:* Autobiography, So Much Love, 1984, The Cat's Whiskers, 1986, Beryl Food and Friends, 1987, all with Eric Brown. *Honours:* OBE, 1986; numerous other awards. *Hobbies:* Gardening; Water Skiing; Raising & Caring for Cats. *Address:* c/o Eric Brown, 36 Michelham Gardens, Strawberry Hill, Twickenham TW1 4SB, England.

REID Bonnie Lee, b. 30 Jan. 1937, St Louis, USA. Junior High School Principal. m. (1) Thomas James Fitzsimmons, 16 Aug. 1958, divorced 1966, 1 son, 1 daughter, (2) Donald Francis Reid, 18 Nov. 1966, 4 step-sons, 1 step-daughter. *Education:* BE, University of Missouri, 1958; MA, Washington University, 1977; Certified Teacher, Missouri. *Appointments:* Teacher, Webster Groves High School, 1958-60; Teacher, Department Chairman, Parkway School District, Chesterfield, 1971-81, Assistant Principal, 1982-83, Associate Principal, 1984, Interim Principal, 1985; Principal, Parkway E. Junior High School, Chesterfield, 1986-. *Memberships:* National Middle School Association; Mortar Board; Missouri State Future Teachers; American, Parkway Ind. Community Teachers Associations; Delta Kappa Gamma; Kappa Alpha Theta; Pi Lambda Theta; Phi Sigma Iota; Kappa Epsilon Alpha; Sigma Rho Sigma. *Honour:* Award of Excellence, US Department of Education Secondary School

Recognition, 1987. *Address:* 14017 Agusta Dr. Chesterfield, MO 63017, USA.

REID Elspeth Margaret Georgina, b. 9 Apr. 1930, Blackheath, Kent, England. Sculptor. *Education:* City & Guilds of London Art School, 1956; Hammersmith College of Art. *Appointments:* Sculpture and woodcarving Tutor, London Boprough of Hillingdon Adult Education, 1976-. *Creative works:* Portrait of King George VI, 1958; Figure of St Alban- St Albans, 1967-68; Cruxifix, Sydenham, 1973-74. *Memberships:* Associate Royal Society British Sculptors (ARBS) 1979; Member Free Painters and Sculptors (MFPS), 1989. *Honours:* City & Guilds, Certificate of Merit, 1959; Second Prize for Sculpture, 1958; Beckwith Scholarship, 1961; London Certificate of Art & Design (LCAD), Hammersmith. *Hobbies:* Poetry; Music; Painting. *Address:* Northwood, Middlesex, England.

REID Frances Marion P., b. 18 Dec. 1910, LaGrange, Missouri, USA. Retired Teacher; Freelance Writer. m. Garth O. Reid, 27 Aug. 1940, 2 sons. *Education:* AB, Drury College, 1931; Graduate study, Northwestern University, 1935-40, University of Idaho, 1936, Boise State University, College of Idaho, 1968. *Appointments:* English Teacher: Diamond High School, Diamond, Missouri, 1931-32; Castleford High School, Castleford, Idaho, 1935-36; Filer High School, Filer, Idaho, 1936-39; Clinton Junior High School, Tulsa, Oklahoma, 1939-40; Borah High School, Boise, Idaho, 1958-76. *Publications:* Books: None So Small, 1958; Thy Word in My Heart, 1962; Walk a Rainbow Trail, 1974; In the Lee of Mountains, 1976; Given to Time, 1978; No Leave-Taking, 1982. *Memberships:* Idaho Writers League; American Association of University Women; Delta Kappa Gamma Society International; Christian Writers League; American Association of Retired Persons, NRTA Division; Idaho Retired Teachers Association; Boise Retired Teachers Association. *Honours:* Coe Foundation Fellowship, College of Idaho, 1968; Writer of the Year, Idaho Writers League, 1975; Hall of Fame, Idaho Retired Teachers Association; Poet of the Year, Idaho Writers League, 1983; Numerous prizes for prose and poetry in various contests. *Hobbies:* Wildflowers; Birds; Reading. *Address:* 6117 Lubkin, Boise, ID 83704, USA.

REID Heather Ann, b. 7 May 1941, Melbourne, Australia. Occupational Therapist; Health Educator. m. Robert Alton Reid, 23 Feb. 1963 (div. 1971), 2 daughters. *Education:* Bachelor, Applied Science (Occupational Therapy) 1979, Graduate Diploma (Health Education) 1986, Lincoln Institute of Health Sciences. *Appointments:* Secretarial work & home management, 1958-72; Marketing executive, Larwin Shiff Development Corporation Pty Ltd, 1972-74; Student, 1976-79; Occupational therapist, St Vincent's Hospital, 1979-83; Administrator, Community Services, Royal Victorian Institute for Blind, 1984-86; Private practice, 1987-. *Membership:* Executive 1980-81, Victorian Association of Occupational Therapists. *Honour:* Travelling scholarship, Lincoln Institute of Health Sciences, 1982. *Hobbies:* Ice skating; Travel, Asia & India; Ballet; Yoga; Theatre; Healthy Lifestyle. *Address:* 4 Victor Street, Beaumaris, Victoria 3193, Australia.

REID Margaret Elizabeth, b. 28 May 1935, South Australia. Senator. m. Thomas Reid, 25 Feb. 1967, 2 sons, 2 daughters. *Education:* LLB, 1961. *Appointments:* Solicitor, private practice, 1961-81; Senator, 1981-. *Memberships Include:* Adoptive Parents Association; ACT Athletic Association Inc; ACT Cricket, Croquet, Ice Hockey Marching, Rugby, Soccer Associations; Australian Cancer Foundation for Medical Research; Australian Water Ski Associaiton; Royal Life Saving Society of Australia; Young Liberal Movement of Australia, ACT Division; Amnesty International; Australia Day Council; Greening Australia; Law Asia; Liberal Party of Australia; National Press Club; Royal National Capital Agricultural Society. *Honours:* Queen Elizabeth Jubilee Medal, 1977; Order of Polonia Restituta, 1987. *Address:* Parliament House, Canberra, Australian Capital Territory 2600, Australia.

REID Nanci Glick Reid, b. 22 Sept. 1941, Brookline, USA. Health Care Professional. m. Raymond Augustus Reid, 15 Feb. 1985, 2 daughters. *Education:* BA, Liberal Arts, Harvard University, 1965; BS, Health Science, 1983; MBA Candidate. *Appointments:* Research Technician, 1961- 63; Senior Research Technician, Medical Technician, New England Medical Centre, Boston, 1963-65, 1967-69; Crtyogenticist Supervisor, Carney Hospital, Boston, 1969-84; Instructor, Medicine, Tufts Univesity Medical School, 1969- 86; Quality Control Manager, Oncolab Inc., 1988-89. *Publications:* Articles in professional journals. *Memberships:* Association Cytogenetic Technologists, President 1976-78; American Society Medical Technologists; Sigma Epsilon Rho, Vice President 1987-88; etc. *Honours:* Key Achievement Award; Dean's List, Northeastern University; etc. *Hobbies:* Sailing; Lobstering; Game Fishing; Cranberry Growing; Photography; Travel; Skiing. *Address:* 70 Flintlocke Drive, Plymouth, MA 02360, USA.

REID Sherri Jo Wells, b. 22 June 1941, Maquoketa, Iowa, USA. Tax Practitioner and Consultant. m. (1) Gary Harrison Hicks (dec. 1973), 2 July 1958, (2) Ronald D. Reid, 21 July 1977, 3 stepsons. *Education:* Numerous technical schools. *Appointments:* Proof Operator, Jackson (Iowa) State Bank, 1958-61; Co-Owner, Manager, Hicks TV & Appliance, Maquoketa, Iowa, 1961-72; Tax Practitioner, Schoenthaler, Schoenthaler, Roberg, Maquoketa, 1972-75; Owner, Tax Consultant, Sherri's Tax Service, Onslow, Iowa, 1975-; Owner, Computer Programmer, Reid Enterprises, Onslow, 1975-. *Publications:* Computer software: Red Ink; Inform; Repo. *Memberships:* National Association of Tax Practitioners; National Federation of Independent Businesses; National Association of Enrolled Agents; National Association of Public Accountants. *Honours:* Sales Award, Philco-Ford, 1966; Enrolled to Practice before IRS, 1980; Operation Pride Award, Maquoketa Chamber of Commerce, 1988. *Hobbies:* Geology; Science; Fishing; Crafts; Flower arranging; Bowling. *Address:* R.R. 1 Box 27, Onslow, IA 52321, USA.

REID Sue Titus, b. 13 Nov. 1939, Bryan, Texas, USA. Professor. *Education:* BS, Texas Womans University, 1960; MA, 1962, PhD, 1965, University of Missouri, Columbia; JD, University of Iowa, 1972. *Appointments:* Associate Professor, Law, University of Washington, 1974-78; Visiting Distinguished Professor, 1977-78, Professor, 1978-88, University of Tulsa; Dean, Professor, School of Criminology, Florida State University, 1988-. *Publications:* Crime & Criminology, 5th edition; Criminal Justice, Criminal Law, An Introduction to Corrections. *Memberships:* American Criminology Association; Academy of Criminal Justice Sciences. *Honours:* Beto Professor Criminal Justice, Sam Houston State University; Outstanding Alumnae, Texas Womans University. *Hobby:* Swimming. *Address:* School of Criminology, Florida State University, Tallahassee, FL 32306, USA.

REIJNEN Bess (Gijsbertha Cornelia Maria), b. 29 Oct. 1938, Eindhoven, The Netherlands. Senior Lecturer. m. Professor Dr Willem de Graaff, 14 Feb. 1978. *Education:* Graduated, Faculty of Law, 1973, PhD, 1976, Utrecht University. *Appointments:* Space Research Laboratory, 1969-78, Faculty of Law, 1978-, Utrecht University; Guest Professor, University of Amsterdam, 1988. *Publications:* Published 54 articles on space law in international legal journals. 4 books: Legal Aspects of Outer Space, 1976; Utilization of Outer Space and International Law, 1981, translated into Chinese, 1984; Space Law in the United Nations, co-authors M Benko and W de Graaff, 1985; The Pollution of Outer Space, in particular of the Geostationary Orbit, co-author W de Graaff, in press. *Memberships:* International Law Association, Dutch branch; Life member, International Institute of Space Law of the International Astronautical Federation, Paris, France; Deutsche Gesellschaft fur Luft-und Weltraumrecht (DGLR); Editor, Space Communication and Broadcasting Journal; Editor-in-Chief, Utrecht Studies in Air and Space Law Series; Legal Adviser, ESA/ESOC (European Space Agency/European Space Operations Centre, Space Debris Working Group). *Hobbies:* Classical music; Sculpture; Art history; Political history; 18th and 19th century English and French poetry; Bird watching; Country life in general. *Address:* Post Office Box 8324, 3503 RH Utrecht, The Netherlands.

REIN Catherine A., b. 7 Feb. 1943, Lebanon, Pennsylvania. Insurance Company Executive Vice-President; Lawyer. m. Barry B. Rein, 1 May 1965. *Education:* BA, Pennsylvania State University, 1965; JD cum laude, New York University School of Law, 1968. *Appointments:* Dewey, Ballantine, Bushby, Palmer & Wood, 1968-74; Continental Group, 1974-85; Senior Vice-President, Metropolitan Life, New York City, 1988-89. *Memberships:* Pennsylvania State University Alumni Association; Board of Visitors, Fairfield University; Board of Directors, Atlantic Legal Foundation; Board of Directors, General Public Utilities; Director, Bank of New York. *Hobbies:* Historic building restoration; Cooking; Travel. *Address:* Metropolitan Life, One Madison Avenue, New York, NY 10010, USA.

REIN Natalie, b. 5 Feb. 1932, London, England. Course Director, The Course Centre, London. m. Sydney Rein, 6 July 1952. 3 daughters. *Education:* Diploma in Social Administration, London School of Economics, University of London, 1971; MSc, School for Advanced Urban Studies. *Appointments:* Senior Management, London Borough of Islington, London, 1973-84; Course Director, The Course Centre, London, 1985-. *Publication:* Daughters of Rachel, 1980. *Memberships:* Group Analytic Society; Institute of Directors. *Hobbies:* Knitting; Hanging out with my children and their partners. *Address:* The Course Centre, 13 Loraine Road, London N7 6EZ, England.

REINERT Pamela Ann, b. 28 Dec. 1952, Pipestone, USA. Administrator. m. Roger Leo Reinert, 14 Mar. 1970, 2 sons, 4 daughters. *Education:* BA, Psychology, 1973; MS, Clinical Psychology, 1974; MA, Special Education, 1980. *Appointments:* Behaviour Consultant, REM, 1973; Teacher, pre-School, DAC, 1974; Special Education Co-ordinator, Head Start, 1975; Councellor, Crossroads, 1976; Executive Director, Building families Through Adoption, 1984-. *Publications:* Building Blocks - Adoption Jurnal Research Study; Need Analysis Post Legal Adoption Services. *Memberships:* Founder, Partners Aiding Children Today; Co-Founder, Project Love; Chairwoman, Tri State Ours; National Chairwoman, US Jaycettes; Regional Director, Jaycee Women. *Honours:* Outstanding Jaycee Woman, 1974; Outstanding National Officer, Jaycettes, 1975; Kay Woman, 1981; National Honour Outstanding Director, Jaycettes, 1982. *Hobbies:* Knitting; Needlepoint; Counted Cross Stitch; Dancing; Reading. *Address:* PO Box 550, Dawson, MN 56232, USA.

REINES Rena, b. New York City, USA. Administrator. *Education:* Certificates in: Physical Education; Elementary, Common Branch, & Special Education. *Appointments:* Teacher, New York City Public Schools, 1962- 67; Deer Park Public Schools; Buffalo Public Schools. *Memberships:* AWPENYS, President; NYSAHPER; ACLD; ARC, Public Relations Committee; NEA; NYEA, delegate; BTF. *Address:* 180 Linwood Avenue, Buffalo, NY 14209, USA.

REINHARDT Joann Hedden, b. 19 Oct 1960, Atlantic City, New Jersey, USA. Research Associate; Psychologist. m. Kenneth Reinhardt, 3I May 1986. *Education:* BA, Immaculata College, Immaculata, Pennsylvania, 1983; MA, Developmental Psychology, 1985, PhD, Developmental Psychology, 1988, Fordham University, Bronx, New York. *Appointments:* Graduate Teaching Fellow, Department of Psychology, Fordham University, Bronx, New York, 1984- 86; Adjunct Assistant Professor, The College of Staten Island, New York; Research Associate, The Lighthouse, New York, New York. *Publications:* Kinship versus friendship: Social adaptation in married and widowed elderly women (with C B Fisher) in L Grau and I Susser (Eds) Women in the Later Years: Health, Social and Cultural Perspectives 1988. *Memberships:* American Psychological Association, Associate Member; Member of Division 20 of American Psychological Association; Gerontological Society of America. *Honours:* Tuition Scholarship, Immaculata College, Immaculata, Pennsylvania, 1979-83; Graduate Assistantship, Fordham University, Bronx, New York, 1983-84; Graduate Teaching Fellowship, Fordham University, 1984-86; Brookdale Research Fellowship, Brookdale Research Institute on Aging, Fordham University, 1986-88. *Hobbies:* Reading; Music; Boating; Camping. *Address:* 104 Cebra Avenue, Staten Island, NY 10304, USA.

REINTOFT Hanne, b. 3 Mar. 1934, Copenhagen, Denmark. Social Worker. m. 1 daughter. *Education:* Examinations: Bookkeeper, 1955; Social Worker, 1957. *Appointments:* Journalist, Author, Lecturer; Social Worker; Co-Founder, Mother's Aid, 1983-; Leader, Danish Radio Programme, The Social Column. *Publications:* Rosa Luxemburg: Social Reform el.revol, 1969; Kvinden i Klassesamfundet, 1972; Two Manuals on Social Law, 1980; Om Forsorg, 1975; Om Familien I & II, 1977; Samfundsstotte, 1978; Den bedste forsorg i verden, 1980; Min ret og plight..., 1982. *Memberships:* Numerous. *Honours:* PH Prize, 1977; Ingrid Jespersens Legat, 1978; IKEA Prize, 1983; LO's Cultural Prize, 1983; Cavling Prize, 1983; Skjoldmo Prize, 1987. *Address:* Uraniavej 21, DK 1878 Frederiksberg C, Denmark.

REIS Lidia Maass, b. 26 Mar. 1959, Rio de Janeiro, Brazil. Biologist. m. Jose Fernando Jasmini Reis, 9 Mar 1984, 1 daughter. *Education:* BA, University of Brasilia, 1980; MSc., Auburn University, 1987. *Appointments:* Superintendency of Fisheries Development, 1980-81; FAC Centre, Sao Paulo State, 1982-; Superintendency, Fisheries Development, 1983-. *Hobbies:* Reading; Exercising. *Address:* Rua Elzira Vivacqua 526, J Camburi - Vitoria ES, 29090 Brazil, South America.

REISBY Kirsten Helen, b. 10 Feb. 1936, Valby, Denmark. Senior Lecturer. m. Niels Christian Reisby, 23 Mar. 1958. *Education:* Teacher Certification, 1958; Master's Degree of Education, 1970; Research Grant, 1975-77. *Appointments:* Comprehensive Public School, Valby, 1958-61; Experimental school, Emdrupborg, 1962-67; Teacher, Training College, Emdrupborg, 1967-69; The Royal Danish School of Educational Studies. *Publications:* Books: Undervisningsmal, 1972, skoledage 1 & 2 1978, Skoleliv-pigeliv 1987; Videoproduction: Klasse billeder tatloot jao jigorno 1987; Articles in books, journals. *Memberships:* Steering Group, President 1984-88, Nordic Association for Education Research; Co-editor, Nordisk Pedagogik, 1982-; The Innovation Council for Schools, 1986-88; The State Research Council for Humanities, 1988-. *Hobbies:* Paintings; Arts and handicraft; Women movements; Sex and gender in schools. *Address:* Danmarks Larerhojskole, Arhus Department, Rudolfgardsvej 1, Dk-8260 Viby J, Denmark.

REISMAN Judith A, b. 11 Apr. 1935, New Jersey, USA. Institute President. *Education:* MA, 1976, PhD, 1980, Case Western Reserve University. *Appointments:* Martze, Anthropology/Sociology, School of Education, Haifa Univeity, 1981-83; Principal Investigator, Science Ministry Grant, Israel, 1981; Research Professor, American University, Washington DC, 1983-85; Research Design Consultant, Drug Free Youth School Candidates, Dept. of Education, 1988; President, Executive Director, Institute for Media Education. *Memberships:* numerous professional organisations. *Honours:* Dukane Award, 1982; Gold Camera Award, 1982; Silver Screen Award, 1982; Filmstrip of the Year Award, 1982; Silver Plaque Award, 1982. *Address:* Time, PO Box 7404, Arlington, AA 22207, USA.

REITER-SCOTT Gayla Denise, b. 12 Sept. 1945, Beloit, Kansas, USA. Union President. m. Wilfred Joseph Scott, 4 July 1983. 1 daughter. *Education:* BS, Political Science, History and Speech, magna cum laude, Portland State University, 1967; Certificate, Psychology of Aging, 1972; Certificate, Labour Studies, 1985. *Appointments:* President, Council 147, American Federation of Government Employees, 1982-86; President, Local 3172, 1980-86; Executive Vice President, National Council, 220, 1980-; SSA Claims Authorizer, 1983-86; Public Affairs Specialist, 1981-82; Branch Manager, 1975-81; Supervisor, 1973-75; Field Representative, 1969-71. *Publications:* Editor, Union Line, Regional Union Newsletter; Numerous articles in newspapers, magazines; Congressional testimony with publication of text of testimony, TV Coverage; Exhibitions of arts and crafts; Sponsor of many bills (humanitarian) passed by US Congress. *Memberships include:* AFGE National Council 220, President, 1982-; Regional Council 147, President, 1980-86; Local 3172, 1980-86; National SIDS Foundation, Legislative Chairperson; AFGE National Legislative Chairperson, Northern Council of AFGE Locals, 1st Vice-President, 1980-84; Soroptomists; Phi Beta Kappa; Alpha Sigma Omega; Red Cross Club; San Mateo Labor Council; League of Women Voters, Redevelopment Committee, production of educational films. *Honours include:* Outstanding Young Woman of America, 1984; San Mateo Hall of Fame, 1985-86; Phi Beta Kappa Outstanding Young Woman, 1966; Governor's Award, 1971; National AFGE Leadership Award, 1982; Chairman, California SIDS Legislative Project, *Hobbies:* Masters swim program; Crocheting; Candlemaking; Arts and crafts; Antique collecting; World travel; Photography; Investigation of psychic phenomenum. *Address:* 240 Baker Street, Benicia, CA 94510, USA.

REITER-ZEDEK Miriam, b. 2 Apr. 1906, Russia. Psychologist; Teacher. m. 12 Aug. 1930, 1 son. *Education:* Teacher's Diploma 1928, kindergarten Teacher's Diploma 1929, Tel-Aviv, Israel (then Palestine); BS, School Psychology 1934, MA Psychology 1935, New York University, USA; Graduate Work, ibid, 1965-68; Doctor of Jewish Literature, People's University, New York, 1968. *Appointments:* Kindergarten Teacher, Israel, 1930-31; Public School Teacher, 1935-48; Teacher & Lecturer, Psychology, various Teachers' Colleges, Haifa, Tel-Aviv, Netaniah, Hadassian, 1951-56; Chief Examiner, Graduate Teachers of Psychology (& other subjects), Israeli Board of Education, 1957-69. *Publications include:* Book, Directory for Teachers Evaluating & Choosing Literature for Children in School Grades, 1951; Numerous Articles on Education, Psychology, Children's Literature, in various Educational Papers. Research works: Psychology of Hebrew Teachers' Writing, 1976; Development of a Child's Personality by Children's Literature, 1968. *Memberships:* Organisation of Psychologists, Israel; Founder, Heiker Ameinu (Study of Our People) Organisation, for study of Jewish problems, anti- semitic persecutions & Jewish responses); Tel Aviv; Board of Education, Jerusalem; B'nai B'rith, Tel-Aviv. *Honours:* Honour certificates from: B'nai B'rith, 1981; Mayor of Tel-Aviv, 1983; Heiker Ameinu, for Cultural & Social Activities, 1986. *Hobbies include:* Human Rights & Freedom; Reseach, Psychology of Jewish People. *Address:* 8 Maaleh Hazofim Street, Ramat-Gan 52483, Israel.

REIZES Judith Ann, b. 7 Jan. 1942, Sydney, Australia. Sculptor; Recycling Consultant; Writer. m. John Arthur Reizes, 8 Aug. 1964, 2 sons. *Appointments:* Reverse Garbage Truck Co-op Ltd., 1976-84. *Publications:* Articles in professional journals; Books: Ideas for Craft, 1978; Converting Containers; Fast Knitting, Weaving & Tyeing; The Big French Knitting Revolution; Reverse Garbage Christmas Book, 1980; The Woolly Look, 1983. *Hobbies:* Tennis; Bushwalking; Surfing; Australian History. *Address:* 154 Woodland St., Balgowlah 2093, NSW, Australia.

REMPEL Ursula Mikulko, b. 23 Jan. 1943, Perth, Scotland. Associate Professor of Music. m. W. John Rempel, 8 July 1967. *Education:* Certificate of Education, 1964, BMus, Music History, 1967, University of British Columbia, Canada; MA, Musicology, University of British Columbia, Canada; MA, Musicology, University of California, Santa Barbara, USA, 1979. *Appointments:* Lecturer, 1970-74, Assistant Professor, 1974-81, Associate Professor, 1981-, School of Music, University of Manitoba, Winnipeg, Manitoba, Canada. *Publications include:* New Light on a Member of the Krumpholtz Family: Fanny Krumpholtz and her Milieu, 1976; A Medieval Feast: Songs & Dances for Recorders and Orff Instruments (with Carolyn F.Ritchey), 1981; Méthodes de Harpes: An Introduction to Eighteenth- Century Tutors, 1982; A Medieval Feast: Children's Menu (Songs & Dances in Easy Arrangements for Voices & Orff Instruments) (with Carolyn Ritchey), 1984; Women & Music: Ornament of the Profession?, 1984; Medieval Music & Dance: or, What You can do with only One Line (with Carolyn R. Kunzman), 1986; The Complete Female: Musical Accomplishment in the late Eighteenth Century; Review, 3 books on American music (with W.John Rempel), 1981; Mosaic special issue (guest editor with W.John Rempel), 1985; Conference & workshop presentations on recorder consort music. *Memberships:* Board of Readers, American Harp Society; World Harp Congress; Canadian Society for Eighteenth-Century Studies; International Congress on Women in Music; Canadian Association of University Teachers; Canadian Universities Music Society; Carl Orff, Canada; Contributing Editor, Ostinato. *Honours:* Outreach Grants for performances with Prairie Consort early-music performing ensemble, 1980, 1981; Outreach Award for work with Prairie Consort, 1981, University of Manitoba; Instrumental Trophy for work with Prairie Consort, Canadian Music Industries, 1983. *Hobbies and Interests:* Antiques; Historical dance; The harp & its literature; Music & literature; Renaissance consort music; Women in Music. *Address:* School of Music; University of Manitoba, Winnipeg, Manitoba, Canada R3T 2N2.

RENDELL Joan, b. Launceston, Cornwall, England. Author; Lecturer. *Education:* Private Schools and Ealing School of Art. *Publications:* Collecting Matchbox Labels; Matchbox Labels; The Match, The Box & The Label; Collecting Out of Doors; Your Book of Corn Dollies; Your Book of Pressed & Dried Flowers; Country Crafts; Collecting Natural Objects; Flower Arrangement with a Marine Theme; Cornish Churches; Hawker Country; Lundy Island; Along the Bude Canal; The Story of the Bude Canal; Gateway to Cornwall; North Cornwall in the Old Days; Around Bude & Stratton; etc. *Memberships:* Hon. Secretary, Federation of Old Cornwall Societies, Launceston Old Cornwall Society, Dunheved Flower & Garden Group; Life Member, Hon. Editor, British Matchbox Label & Booklet Society; Life Member, Launceston Floral Art Group; Honorary Member, Japan Society of London. *Honours:* MBE, 1958; Queen's Silver Jubilee Medal, 1977; Bard of the Cornish Gorsedd, 1980. *Hobbies:* Collecting Matchbox Labels; Local History; Making Corn Dollies. *Address:* Tremarsh, Launceston, Cornwall, England.

RENEE Paula, b. Hackensack, New Jersey, USA. Artist. m. Robert F. Handschuh, 19 June 1954 (div. 1968), 2 daughters, (2) Thomas D. Murray, 4 Jan. 1969 (div. 1975), (3) Samuel R. Hazlett, 6 June 1978 (div. 1986). *Education:* Rockland Community College, 1970-71; Ramapo State College, 1973; Fairleigh Dickinson University, 1973-77; Thomas A. Edison College, 1978; AS degree, Empire College (SUNY), 1990. *Appointments include:* Self-employed artist, New Jersey 1978-87, New York 1987-; Artist-in-residence, Bergen Community College, Hackensack, 1978- 79. *Creative work includes:* Tapestry work featured, Shuttle, Spindle & Dyepot magazine, 1981-86. *Address:* Rivercrest, 103 Gedney Street 1H, Nyack, New York 10960, USA.

RENNEKAMP Rose Greeley, b. 14 Sept. 1949, Des Moines, Iowa, USA. Vice President, Product Marketing and Planning. m. Steven Rennekamp. 2 Aug. 1975. 1 son, 1 daughter. *Education:* BS 1971, MS 1973, Iowa State University, Ames, Iowa; MBA, Marketing, University of Iowa, Iowa City, 1978. *Appointments:* Product Home Economist, Laundry Products, Whirlpool Corporation, 1973-75; Research Home Economist;

Manager, Product Evaluation 1976-77; Manager, Sales Training 1977-78, Manager, Operations & Marketing 1981-82, Manager, Marketing Sales Promotions 1980-81, Major Appliance; Product Manager, Radarange(R) Microwave Ovens, 1978-80; Marketing Manager, 1983-85, Vice President, Product Marketing and Planning, 1985-, Amana Refrigeration; Visiting Professor, University of Iowa, 1982-. *Publications:* Numerous articles published in professional journals. *Memberships:* Association of Home Appliance Manufacturers (chairperson, Microwave Executive Board); International Microwave Power Institute (past education chairperson, symposium director, president, member of board); Home Economists in Business; American Home Economics Association (Certified Home Economist); Campbell Soup Company Microwave Advisory Board, 1980-82; American Council on Consumer Interests; Iowa State University; College of Family and Consumer Science Advisory Board; Society of Consumer Affairs Professionals. *Honours:* National Merit Special Scholar; Veishea Leadership Scholar; Alpha Lambda Delta; Phi Upsilon Omicron; Omicron Nu; Phi Kappa Phi; Mortar Board; Beta Gamma Sigma. *Hobbies:* Swimming; Walking; Foreign travel; Gourmet cooking; Public speaking. *Address:* Amana Refrigeration Inc, Amana, IA 52204, USA.

RENNINGER Mary Karen, b. 30 Apr. 1945, Pittsburgh, Pennsylvania, SA. Librarian. m. Christian Renninger, 3 Sept. 1965, divorced. 1 son. *Education:* BA 1969, MA 1972, MLS 1975, University of Maryland. *Appointments:* Teacher, English, Morehead City, 1969-70; Graduate Assistant Instructor, English, University of Maryland, 1970-72; Head, Network Services 1974-78, Assistant for Network Support 1978-80, NLS, Library of Congress; Chief, Library Division, Veterans Administration, 1980-. *Memberships:* Medical Library Association, Government Relations Committee; American Library Association; DC Library Association; Board of Regents of National Library of Medicine; Federal Library & Info Centre Committee, Executive Advisory Board; MDR Videodisc Consortium; Iota Chapter, Beta Phi Mu; Speaking for Ourselves Foundation, Executive Advisory Board; Fed Libns TF on White House Conf. *Honours:* Phi Beta Kappa; Alpha Lambda Delta; Beta Phi Mu; Library of Congress Meritorious Service Award 1974, Special Achievement Award 1976; VA Special Achievement Award 1986; Administrator's Commendation, 1985 & Performance Awards, 1982-87. *Hobby:* Tennis. *Address:* Rockville, MD, USA.

RENSHAW Domeena C., b. 20 July 1929, Douglas, Cape, South Africa. Psychiatrist; Physician. m. 13 June 1965. *Education:* MB,ChB, University of Cape Town; MD; FACP. *Appointments include:* Groote Schuur Hospital, University of Cape Town, 1961; Harvard Children's Hospital, Boston, Massachusetts, USA, 1962-63; Livingston Hospital, Port Elizabeth, South Africa, 1963-64; Medical Faculty 1965-, Director, Child Programme 1969-78, Director, Sex Clinic 1972-, Professor of Psychiatry 1977-, Loyola University, Maywood, Illinois, USA. *Publications include:* The Hyperactive Child, 1974, 1976, Spanish 1976; Incest: Understanding & Treatment, 1982, Portuguese. Also: Over 300 medical articles, book chapters. *Memberships include:* Fellow, American Psychiatric Association, American College of Psychiatry. *Honours:* Aescalupian Award, medical student teaching, University of Ottawa, Canada, 1978; Honorary Citizen, New Orleans, 1978; Special Teacher Award, Oregon Academy of Family Physicians, 1978. *Hobbies:* Photography; Gardening; Hiking. *Address:* Loyola University of Chicago, 2160 South First Avenue, Maywood, Illinois 60153, USA.

RENTOUMIS Ann Maria, b. 27 Apr. 1928, New Haven, Connecticut, USA. Psychotherapist. m. George Rentoumis, 27 June 1959. 1 son, 2 daughters. *Education:* BA, Vassar College, 1949; Boston University, School of Medicine, 1949-50; MS, Columbia University, 1952. *Appointments:* Foxboro State Hospital, 1950; Bellevue Hospital, 1951; Brooklyn Psychiatric Clinic, 1952-54; Community Service Society, 1955-58; Bleuler

Psychotherapy Center, 1959-60; Texas Children's Hospital, Psychiatric Clinic, 1976; Ft Lauderdale Psychiatric Group, 1978-. *Memberships:* American Association for Marriage and Family Therapy; Board Certified Diplomate in Clinical Social Work; Fellow, American Orthopsychiatric Association; American Group Therapy Association; Florida Association of Psychotherapists. *Honours:* President, Ft Lauderdale Philharmonic Society, 1988-89; First Vice President, 1987-88, Philharmonic Orchestra of Florida, 1988-89; ExeCutive Committee, Board of Governors; Board of Directors, Opera Society, 1988-89; Vice President; Board of Directors, Hospice Hundred, 1988-89; Board of Directors, Performing Arts Center, 1987-89; Board of Directors, Broward Community Foundation, 1987-89; Community Assessment Committee, Founder's Council Pine Crest School, 1980-88; President, Pine Crest Mother's Club, 1981-82; President, Houston Vassar Club, 1980-82; Board of Directors, Princeton Vassar Club, 1962-64. *Hobbies:* Piano; Tennis; Sailing; Travel. *Address:* 1535 East Lake Drive, Ft Lauderdale, FL 33316, USA.

RENTZEL Jean, b. 15 Nov. 1936,Hanover, USA. Design Engineer. m. Walter Rentzel, 13 Apr. 1953, 1 son. *Education:* Mesa College; Strategy Institute. *Appointments:* Ron Rowland Insurance, 1965-67; Adams Co. Construction & Oxford Construction Company, 1968-77; General Atomic and Subsidary, 1978-. *Publications:* Various operation and maintenance manuals. *Memberships:* American Nuclear Society; Institute of Industrial Engineers; National Association for Female Executives; Women Republican Federation. *Honours:* Certification of Merit, Ronald Reagan, George Bush, 1984, California Republicans Party, 1984; Citizen of the Year, Citizens Committee for the Right to Keep and Bear Arms, 1984. *Hobbies:* Home Repair & Decorating; Writing Poetry; Golf; Tennis. *Address:* 13114 Dana Vista, Poway, CA 92064, USA.

RESNICK Cynthia Bilt, b. 8 Mar. 1946, Brooklyn, New York, USA. Speech/Language Pathologist. m. Jerry Resnick, 1967, deceased 1972. *Education:* BA cum laude 1976; MS, Columbia University Teachers College, New York City, 1978. *Appointments include:* Therapist, New York City Board of Education, New York, 1978; Coordinator of Services and Therapist, Lorge School, New York City, 1978-80; Speech/Language Pathologist, Summit School, Forest Hills, New York, 1980; Forest Hills Nursing Home, Forest Hills, New York 1980-85; College Nursing Home, 1983-85; Private practice, Speech/Lanquage Pathologist, Rego Park, New York, 1981-. *Creative Works include:* Participant, Study to establish new norms on Test of Language Development for Speakers Black American English Dialect. *Memberships include:* New York Speech-Language-Hearing Association; American Speech-Language-Hearing Association; Massachusetts Speech-Language-Hearing Association. *Honours:* Honorary Mention for Academy Excellence in Speech Science, 1976; Citizenship Award, 1963. *Hobbies:* Needlepoint; Sculpting; Painting; Collage; Music; Sports. *Address:* 94-11 59 Ave, Suite A7, Rego Park, NY 11373, USA.

REULER Susan Lee, b. 25 Nov. 1952, Denver, Colorado, USA Executive Director; Nurse Entrepreneur. *Education:* AA Nursing, 1970; BA, Psychology, 1973; Cardiovascular Clinical Specialist, CVNS, 1976. *Appointments:* Head Nurse, Emergency Porter Memorial Hospital, 1977-79; Director, Nursing, St Lukes Hospital, 1979-80; Director, NSI Services Inc., 1980-82; President, Professional Nursing Associates, 1983-85; Executive Director, American Nursing Resources, 1985-. *Publications:* Articles in professional journals. *Memberships:* Colorado Nurses Association, Chairperson, Commission on Continuing Education; Nurse Consultants Association; Plaza III Association, Treasurer. *Honours:* NSI Manager of the Year, 1981; ANR Excellence Award, 1986; ANR Recognition Award, 1986; National Speaker, Career Evaluation, Nurse Owned Businesses, The Nurse Entrepreneur. *Hobbies:* Skiing; Needlwork; Bicycling; Fishing; Red Cross AID's

Educator. *Address:* 5250 Leetsdale Drive, Suite 125 Denver, CO 80222, USA.

REYNOLDS Debbie b. 1 Apr. 1932, El Paso, Texas, USA. Real name, Mary Francis Reynolds. Actress. m. (1) Eddie Fisher, 1955, divorced 1959, 1 son, 1 daughter. (2) Harry Karl, 1960, divorced 1975. *Education:* High school, Burbank, California. *Career:* Film debut in June Bride, 1948; With Warner Brothers, 1948-50; with MGM 1950-59; Musicals, 1950's; Nightclub work, 1961; Actress in The Debbie Reynolds Show, 1969-70; Star of Irene, Broadway, 1973; TV series, Aloha Paradies, 1981. *Creative works:* Films: June Bride, 1948; The Daughter of Rosie O'Grady, 1950; Three Little Words; Two Weeks with Love; Mr Imperium, 1951; Singin' in the Rain, 1952; Skirts Ahoy!; I Love Melvin, 1953; The Affairs of Dobie Gillis; Give a Girl a Break; Susan Slept Here, 1954; Athena; Hit the Deck, 1955; The Tender Trap; The Catered Affair, 1956; Bundle of Joy; Meet Me in Las Vegas; Tammy and the Bachelor, 1957; This Happy Feeling, 1958; The Mating Game, 1959; Say One for Me; It Started with a Kiss; The Gazebo; The Rat Race, 1960; Pepe; The Pleasure of His Company, 1961; The Second Time Around; How the West Was Won, 1963; My Six Loves; Mary, Mary; The Unsinkable Molly Brown, 1964; Goodbye Charlie; The Singing Nun, 1966; Divorce American Style, 1967; How Sweet It Is, 1968; What's the Matter with Helen? 1971; Charlotte's Web, 1972. *Honours:* Best Actress Academy nomination for The Unsinkable Molly Brown, 1964. *Address:* c/o 11595 La Maida, N Hollywood, CA 91602, USA.

REYNOLDS Jane Leslie, b. 21 Mar. 1952, Houston, Texas, USA. ARchitect. *Education:* BArchitecture, 1976 (Houston); BArts, 1974. *Appointments:* A/V Fakhro-Manama, Bahrain, 1974; Fumihiko Maki, Tokyo, Japan; Mordz Associated Consultants, 1983; E G Lowry, Houston, 1983-86; MPB Architects, Philadelphia, 1986-. *Creative works:* Quality Control Engineer-Menil Collection, 1983-89; Danger Rangerrette (painting, tryptich), 1985; Meshigene Chronicles. *Memberships:* American Institute of Architects, Secretary, West Jersey Society, 1989; Warwick Breakfast Club, Houston, President 1983, V President 1982. *Honours:* M N Davidson Travelling Fellowship for student travel to Japan, 1975; Silver Medallist, New Jersey Women's Roller Speed Skating Meet, 1988. *Hobbies:* Music, piano, clarinet; Sports, swimming, softball, roller speed skating; Spoon bending. *Address:* c/o MPB Architects, 262 S. 23rd Street, Philadelphia, PA 19103, USA.

REYNOLDS Margaret Ann Osborn, b. 9 Dec. 1920, York, Nebraska, USA. Retired Clery; School teacher (Retired). m. The Rev John M Reynolds, 27 June 1942. 2 sons. *Education:* BA, University of Nebraska, 1942; MA, Columbia University, NY, 1947; MDiv, Union Theol Sem, NY, 1948. *Appointments:* Director, Christian Ed First Congregational Church, Ft Wayne, Indiana, 1942-43; Nat Sec, Forerunners, NYC, 1943-45; Director, Youth Campaign Japan Intol Christian Uni, 1949-50; County Dir, Retarded and Handicapped Center, San Bernadino, 1966-67; Teacher, Colton, 1967-78; Assoc Minister, Neighborhood Congregational Church UCC Laguna Beach, CA, 1979-83. *Memberships:* Moderator Kern Assn UCC, 1963-64; Moderator, NJ Assn UCC, 1954-56; Bd Member, Foothill Assn UCC, 1989-90; Bd Member, Friends of Oak Park Cemetery Claremont, 1986-; Bd Member, Asilomar Missions Conf, 1989. *Honours:* Vestals of the Lamp, Univ of Nebraska, 1939; Merit Colton Unified School District, 1978; Del Oslo Christian Youth Conf, Norway, 1947; Life Membership, McKinley School, Colton, PTA, 1978; Minister emerita, Neighborhood Congregational Church UCC, Laguna Beach, 1983. *Hobbies:* Oil painting; Swimming; Travel; Reading. *Address:* 729 Plymouth Road, Claremont, CA 91711, USA.

REYNOLDS Margaret, b. 19 July 1941, Launceston, Tasmania, Australia. Cabinet Minister. m. Henry Reynolds, 1 son, 2 daughters. *Education:* Teacher training, University of Tasmania; Diploma, Special Education, James Cook University, North Queensland;

BA, Double Major, Government, University of Queensland. *Appointments include:* Primary teacher, special educator, UK & Queensland; Lecturer, teacher training, Queensland; Alderman, Townsville City Council, 1979-83; Elected to Australian Senate, for State of Queensland, 1983, 1984, 1987-; Parliamentary Secretary for Local Government, 1987; Minister for Local Government, 1987-; Minister Assisting Prime Minister for Status of Women, 1988-; Numerous parliamentary committees, overseas conferences & delegations. *Memberships:* Member 1971-, numerous offices including committees on Local Government, Aboriginal Affairs, Urban & Regional Development, Australian Labour Party; Past Chair, North Queensland Regional Advisory Committee, Australian Broadcasting Commission; Founding member, Womens Electoral Lobby; International Womens League for Peace & Freedom; Various community, welfare, education, environmental, planning & heritage organisations. *Address:* Parliament House, Canberra, ACT 2600, Australia.

REYNOLDS Pamela Kay, b. 1 Jan. 1948, St Louis, Missouri, USA. Pharmacist; Pharmacy Executive. m. Gary Keith Reynolds, 13 May 1972, 1 son, 1 daughter. *Education:* BS, Pharmacy, St Louis College of Pharmacy, 1972; Registered Pharmacist, Illinois and Missouri. *Appointments:* Manager, Pharmacist, Ross Drug, Mt Vernon, Illinois, 1972-74; Staff Pharmacist, Pine Street Pharmacy, Eldorado, 1974-75; Relief Pharmacist, Southern Illinois Area, 1976-79; Co-Owner, Operator, Reynolds Value-Rite Pharmacy, Mcleansboro, 1973-; Consultant, Oak View Nursing Home, McLeansboro, 1975-; Consultant, Life Care Centre, McLeansboro, 1984-; Relief Pharamcist for Hamilton County Memorial Hospital, 1987-88. *Memberships:* Assistant Cubmaster & Committee Chairman, 1987-88; Girl Scout Support Team Leader; Troop Leader; Cookie Chairman for Hamilton County, 1987-88; American Pharmacist Association; Illinois, Southern Illinois Pharmacists Associations (House of Delegates 1978-83, and 1986-88 of Illinois Pharmacist Association); Treasurer, Hamilton County Pharmacist Association; Beta Sigma Phi, Vice President McLeansboro Chapter, 1976-78, Chairman, Ways & Means Committee, St Louis Chapter, 1971-72. *Hobbies:* Reading; Sewing; Swimming; Rose Garden Research. *Address:* McLeansboro, IL 62859, USA.

REYNOLDS Susan Elizabeth, b. 12 December 1950, carlisle, USA. Branch Manager, IBM. *Education:* BS, Honours, Political Science, Western Michigan University, 1973. *Appointments:* Manager, Greco's Restaurant, 1973-77; Systems Engineer, Lansing, 1977-81, Advisory Market Support Rep., Southfield, 1982-83, Systems Engineering Manager, 1984-85, Resource Programmes Manager, 1986-87, Area Marketing Manager, 1987, Assistant to Vice President, 1987, Southfield, Branch Manager, Youngstown, 1988-89, IBM. *Publications:* Articles in: Retriever International; Dog World; Retriever Field Trial News. *Memberships:* Youngstown Chamber of Commerce, Board; Youngstown Rotary Club; Bukeye Retriever Club. ssa 20Honours: Grand Prize, National Photography Contest, Dogs USA, 1986; Multiple National Photography Awards, 1987, 1988. *Hobbies:* Retriever Field Trials; Photography; Judge of AKC Retriever Field Trials. *Address:* c/o IBM Corporation, 250 Federal Plaza East, Youngstown, OH 44503, USA.

RHODAS Virginia, b. Rhodas, Greece. Director; Poet; Writer. *Appointments:* Director, International Poetry Letter. *Publications:* Petals; Blossoms; Will Come a Day...and Other Poems; Brother Century XXI; Open Letter to Humanity; Listen to Me, Humanity. *Memberships:* YWCA; various other organisations. *Honours:* Recipient, awards from: World Poetry Society; World Academy of Arts & Culture; International Academy of Poets; DC, hc, Literature, World University. *Hobbies Include:* Theatre. *Address:* Rivadavia 2284, PB "J" (1034), Buenos Aires, Argentina.

RHODES Zandra Lindsey, b. 19 Sept. 1940,

Chatham, Kent, England. Textile & Fashion Designer; Artist. *Education:* Medway College of Art; Royal College of Art (DesRCA, 1964); RDI 1977; FSIAD, 1982. *Appointments:* With Alexander Macintyre, set up print factory and studio, 1965; sold designs to Foale and Tuffin and Roger Neslon; formed partnership with Sylvia Ayton & began producing dresses using her own prints 1966; Opened Fulham Road Clothes shop, 1967-68; took collection to USA 1969; wih Anne Night and Ronnie Stirling founded Zandra Rhodes (UK)Ltd., and Zandra Rhodes (Shops) Ltd., 1975- 86; Opening First shop in London, 1975; Licensees: Wamsutta, USA, 1976; CVP Designs, 1977; Regal Rugs, USA, 1977; Baar and Beard Inc., USA, 1978; Sari Fabics, 1979; Wagner Furs, 1979; Sabrina Coats, 1979; Jack Mulqueen, USA, 1980; Green & Makofsky, USA, 1980; Senko, Japan, 1980; Courtaulds, 1981; Lyle & Scott, 1982; Zandra Rhodes II Ready to Wear UK, 1984; Philip Hockley, 1986; Swarovski, 1987; Hilmet Ltd., 1988; Albany Fine China Ltd, 1988. *Creative Works Include:* One Man Exhibitions: Oriel, Cardiff, 1978; Texas Gallery, Houston, 1981; Otis Parsons, Los Angeles, 1981; La Jolla Museum of Contemporary Art, 1982; Barbican Centre, 1982; many others; Boo: The Art of Zandra Rhodes, 1984; The Zandra Rhodes Collection by Brother, 1988; articles in professional journals. *Honours:* Recipient, many honours & awards including: Designer of the Year, 1972; Royal Designer for Industry UK, 1977; DFA, HC, International Fine Arts College, Miami, 1986; DD, HC, Council for National Academic Awards, 1987; DRCA HC, Royal College of Art. *Address:* 87 Richford Street, Hammersmith, London W6 7HJ, England.

RIBEIRO Aileen Elizabeth, b. 15 Apr. 1944, Stoke-on-Trent, England. University Lecturer. m. 4 Sept. 1965. *Education:* BA Honours, History, King's College, University of London, 1965; MA 1971, PhD 1975, History of Art, Courtauld Institute. *Appointments include:* Head, History of Dress, Courtauld Institute of Art, University of London, 1975-. *Publications:* Dress in 18th Century Europe 1715-1789, 1984; Dress & Morality, 1986; Fashion in the French Revolution, 1988. *Address:* History of Dress Department, Courtauld Institute of Art, Somerset House, Strand, London WC2R 2LS, England.

RICCI Donna Seibert, b. 9 July 1947, St Louis, USA. International School Owner & Directress. m. Alfredo Ricci, 2 Aug. 1975, 1 son, 1 daughter. *Education:* BA, Pennsylvania State University, 1969. *Appointments:* Research Technician, US Embassy Rome, Italy, 1969-74; Owner, International Preschool, Greenwood Garden School, 1974-. *Memberships:* American Women's Association of Rome; Rome International Schools Association; National Association for the Education of Young Children. *Hobbies:* Travel; Piano. *Address:* Via Vito Sinisi, 47, 00189 Rome, Italy.

RICE Linda Jo, b. 11 Nov. 1952, Lexington, Kentucky, USA. Paediatric Anaesthesiologist. *Education:* BS, 1973; MD, 1977; ABA Certified, 1982. *Appointments:* US Navy, 1977-86; Children's National Medical Centre, Washington DC, 1986-. *Publications:* Chapters on Regional Anaesthesia; Association of Anaesthetists of Great Britain & Ireland; European Regional Anaesthesia Society; American Society of Regional Anaesthesia. *Hobbies:* Heraldry; Needlework; Medieval British history. *Address:* Department of Anaesthesia, Children's National Medical Centre, 111 Michigan Avenue NW, Washington DC 20010, USA.

RICE Mary Esther, b. 3 Aug. 1926, Washington, District of Columbia, USA. Biologist. *Education:* AB, Drew University, 1947; MA, Oberlin College, 1949; PhD, University of Washington, 1966. *Appointments:* Instructor Biology, Drew University, 1949-50; Research Associate, Columbia University, 1950-53; Research Assistant, National Institutes of Health, 1953- 61; Curator of Invertebrate Zoology and Director of Marine Station, Smithsonian Institution, 1966-. *Publications:* Co-editor, Biology of Sipuncula and Echiura, with M Todorovic; Co-editor, Settlement and Metamorphosis of Marine Invertebrate Larvae, with F S Chia; Over 50 articles in scientific journals. *Memberships:* Sigma Xi; American Institute of Biological Sciences; American Society of Zoologists, President, 1979; American Association for Advancement of Science, Member at Large, 1984-88. *Honours:* Fellow, American Association for Advancement of Science, 1978; Award in Science, Alumni Achievement, 1980; Phi Beta Kappa Honorary Society, 1988. *Address:* Smithsonian Marine Station at Link Port, 5612 Old Dixie Highway, Fort Pierce, Florida 34946, USA.

RICH Elaine Sommers, b. 8 Feb. 1926, Plevna, Indiana, USA. Writer; Adviser to International Students. m. Dr Ronald L Rich, 14 June 1953. 3 sons, 1 daughter. *Education:* BA, Goshen College, 1947; MA, Michigan State University, 1950. *Appointments:* Instructor in Speech and English, Goshen College, 1947-49; Instructor in Speech, Bethel College, 1953-56; Lecturer, International Christian University, Tokyo, Japan, 1971-78; Adviser to International Students, Bluffton College, Bluffton, Ohio, USA, 1979-. *Publications:* Books: Breaking Bread Together (ed), 1958; Tomorrow, Tomorrow, Tomorrow, 1966; Hannah Elizabeth, 1964; Am I This Countryside (poems), 1981; Mennonite Women 1683-1983: A Story of God's Faithfulness, 1983; Spiritual Elegance: A Biography of Pauline Krehbiel Raid, 1987. Contributor to Mennonite Weekly Review. *Memberships:* National Association for Foreign Student Affairs; Commission on Education of General Conference Mennonite Church; Life Member, AAUW; Women's International League for Peace and Freedom. *Address:* 3208-B, Shire Lane, Raleigh, NC 27606, USA.

RICHARD Emily, b. London, England. Actress. m. Edward Peherbridge, 25 Jan. 1981, 1 son, 1 daughter. *Education:* Webber Douglas Academy of Dramatic Art. *Appointments Include:* Recent Theatre: RSC Kate in Nicholas Nickleby, Broadway, New York, 1981; Admiral Bashville at Regents Park Theatre, 1982; Viola, Twelfth Night; RSC 1st small scale tour, British Council tour of Far East, 1982; RSC Princess of France in Loves Labours Lost, Stratford, 1984-85; TV: The Glittering Prizes, BBC 1975; Title Role in Lorna Doone, BBC, 1976; Enemy at the Door, LWT, 1977; An Affinity with Dr Still, BBC 1979; Irene in Trevor Nunn's production, Three Sisters, Stratford upon Avon and televised by Thames TV, 1981; Filmed Nicholas Nickleby at the Old Vic for Channel 4, 1981; The Cleopatras, BBC 1982; Dark Side of the Sun, BBC 1983; Oscar, BBC 1984; Member, BBC Radio Repertory Company, 1975; Film: Steven Speilberg's Empire of the Sun, 1987. *Hobbies:* Lace Making; Gardening. *Address:* Marmont Management, Langham House, 302-308 Regent Street, London W1R 3AL, England.

RICHARDSON Barbara Connell, b. 29 Dec. 1947, New York City, USA. Transportation Research Scientist. m. Rudy James Richardson, 23 Aug. 1970 (div. 1984), 1 daughter. *Education:* BA, State University of New York, Albany, 1969; SM, Massachusetts Institute of Technology, 1973; PhD, University of Michigan, 1982. *Appointments:* Programmer, analyst, Physical Review, Upton, NY, 1969-70; Transportation planner, Massachusetts Executive Office of Transportation & Construction, 1973-74; Transportation Research Officer, Greater London Council, London, England, 1974-75; Associate research scientist & Director, Transportation Planning & Policy, University of Michigan, 1975-86; President, Richardson Associates Inc, 1983-. *Publications:* Author, co-author, numerous research reports & articles, professional journals. *Memberships:* Transportation Research Board, National Academy of Science; Society of Automotive Engineers. *Honours:* Various honour societies, biographical listings. *Address:* Richardson Associates Inc, 325 East Eisenhower Parkway, Suite 106, Ann Arbor, Michigan 48108, USA.

RICHARDSON Fiona Jane, b. 23 Sept. 1965, Nottingham, England. Classicl Guitarist, Performer & Teacher. *Education:* Intermediate School, Royal Academy of Music (RAM), 1982-84; RAM, 1984-88; Professional Certificate RAM, LRAM Teacher's Diploma,

Certificate of Advanced Studies. *Appointments:* Private Guitar Teacher, 1982-; Member, English Guitar Quartet, 1987-88; Guitar Teacher, Inner London Education Authority Panel, 1987-; Editor, Guitar Music, Barry Brunton Music Publisher, 1986-; Guitar Teacher, Bryanston School, Dorset, 1988-; Fiona Richardson Promotions, 1988-; Recordings as Guitarist, Radio Trent. *Publications:* Articles, Guitar International Magazine. *Membership:* RAM Club, *Honours:* Recordings as Guitarist, Anglia Television, BBC Radio. *Hobbies:* Photography; Sport; Art; Music Arranging. *Address:* 36 Caroline House, 135 Bayswater Road, London W2 4RQ, England.

RICHARDSON Helen Hilda, Forbes- b. 26 July 1950, Detroit, Michigan, USA. Project Manager. 1 son. *Education:* BA, University of Detroit, 1972. *Appointments:* Substitute Teacher, Detroit Board of Education, 1972-75; Michigan Depart of Social Service 1975-: Assistant Payment Worker, 1975-77, Assistant Payment Supervisor, 1979-85, General Services Project Manager, 1985-. *Memberships:* Michigan County Social Services Association, Conference Planning Committee, 1988. *Honours:* National Honors Society, 1968; Spirit of Detroit Leadership Award, 1985. *Hobbies:* Reading; Sewing; Billiards. *Address:* 15718 Fielding, Detroit, MI 48223, USA.

RICHARDSON Joanna, b. London, England. Biographer. *Education:* MA, St Anne's College, Oxford. *Publications include:* Fanny Brawne, 1952; Rachel, 1956; Théophile Gautier: His Life and Times, 1958; Sarah Bernhardt, 1959; The Everlasting Spell: A Study of Keats & His Friends, 1963; Edward Lear, 1965; George IV: a Portrait, 1966; Creevey & Greville, 1967; Princess Mathilde, 1969; Verlaine, 1971; Stendhal: A Critical Biography, 1974; Victor Hugo, 1976; Zola, 1978. Contributor to BBC; Times Literary Supplement; Sunday Times; Spectator; New Statesman; Modern Language Review; New York Times Book Review; Washington Post, etc. *Memberships:* Fellow, Royal Society of Literature, 1959; Member of Council, Royal Society of Literature, 1961-86. *Honour:* Chevalier de l'Ordre des Arts et des Lettres, 1987. *Address:* c/o Curtis Brown Ltd, 162-168 Regent Street, London W1R 5TB, England.

RICHARDSON Joely Kim, b. 9 Jan. 1965, London, England. Actress. *Education:* Lycee Francais de Londres until 1977; St Paul's Girls' School, until 1980; Pinellas Park High School, Florida, until, 1981; The Tacher School, Ojai, California, graduated 1983; RADA, Lodnon, 1983-85. *Appointments:* Title Role in Miss Julio, Liverpool Playhouse, Sept. 1985; Role in beauty and the Beast, Liverpool Playhouse moved to Old Vic, Christmas, 1985; Role in Saxon Shore by David Rudkin, at Almeida Theatre, 1986; RSC Stratford, 1986; 4 plays including, A Midsummer Night's Dream, playing Helena and Worlds Apart playing Alicia; Film Role in Wetherby, directed by David Hare, 1984; Role in Peter Greenaway's Drowning By Numbers. *Honours:* Scholarship for one year at Harry Hopman's International Tennis School, Florida. *Hobbies:* All Sports including: Gymanstics, Skating, Horse Riding; Dance. *Address:* 36 Prebend Mansions, Chiswick, London W4, England.

RICHARDSON Lyndsey Vivien, b. 11 July 1958, England. Actress. *Education:* Advanced Ballet Executant, RAD; Advanced Modern Executant, ISTD; Advanced National Executant, ISTD; Advanced Ballet Executant, ISTD. *Creative works:* Theatre appearances: The Two Ronnies, 1982; played Brooke in Noises Off, 1984-86. Television appearances: Kelly Monteith, BBC; Morecambe and Wise, Thames; Benny Hill, Thames; Mike Yarwood, BBC; Super Troupers, Tyne Tees TV. *Memberships:* ARAD, Royal Academy of Dancing; MENSA. *Hobbies:* Winemaking; Swimming; Knitting; Playing clarinet; Walking. *Address:* c/o Liam Dale Associates Ltd, 59 Hampton Road, Croydon, Surrey, England.

RICHARDSON Mary Margaret Milner, b. 14 May 1943, Waco, Texas, USA. Attorney. m. John L.

Richardson, 22 July 1967, 1 daughter. *Education:* AB, Vassar College, 1965; JD, Honours, George Washington University, 1968. *Appointments:* Law Clerk, US Court of Claims, Washington DC, 1968-69; Tax Court Attorney 1969, Director Administrative Services Division, Special Assistant to Associate Chief Counsel 1977, Office of Chief Counsel, Internal Revenue Service; Attorney & Partner, Sutherland Asbill & Brennan, 1977-. *Memberships include:* DC & Virginia State Bars; American & Federal Bar Associations; Prentice Hall Federal Tax Advisory Group; Supreme Court of US Bar; US Court of Appeals for DC 4th, 5th & 7th Circuits; US Tax Court Bar; US Claims Court Bar; Commissioner's Advisory Group, Internal Revenue Service; Washington Area Lawyers for Arts; Past President, Friends of Superior Court; President, National Cathedral School Parents Association. *Honour:* Chief Counsel's Award, Internal Revenue, 1976. *Hobbies:* Foreign travel; Antique collecting; Skiing. *Address:* 5121 Tilden Street, Washington DC 20016, USA.

RICHARDSON Natasha Jane, b. 11 May 1963, London, England. Actress. *Education:* Lycee Francaise de Londres; St Pauls Girls School; Mander, Portman and Woodward; Central School of Speech and Drama, 1980-83. *Appointments:* Theatre: On the Razzle, 1983; Top Girls, 1983; Charley's Aunt, 1983, Leeds Playhouse; Midsummer Nights Dream, New Shakespeare Company, 1984; Hamlet, Young Vic Company, 1984; The Seagull, Lyric Hammersmith and Queens Theatre, China, Bush Theatre, 1985; High Society, Victoria Palace, 1986. Television: In The Secret State, 1983; Ghosts, BBC 1985; The Adventures of Sherlock Holmes, Granada, 1985. Films: Every Picture Tells a Story, 1984; Gothic, directed by Ken Russell, 1986; A Month in the Country, Euston Films, 1986; Patty hearst, direted by Paul Strader, 1987; Fat man and Little Boy, directed by Roland Joffee, 1988. *Honours:* Most Promising Newcomer, for role of Nina in the Seagull, London Theatre Critics Poll, 1986. *Hobbies:* Movies; Music; Books; Food. *Address:* London, England.

RICHARDSON Rosamond Ann, b. 18 Dec. 1945, Oxford, England. Author. divorced. 1 daughter, 2 adopted sons. *Education:* Diploma of Art and Design, St Martin's School of Art, London. *Appointments:* Freelance; Assistant to Susan Collier at Liberty's; Fabric design; Patchwork cottage industry. *Creative Works:* TV Series: Discovering Patchwork, 1978; BBC2, Discovering Hedgerows, 1982; Regional television and local radio. Books: Discovering Patchwork; Hedgerow Cookery; Discovering Hedgerows; Roses: A Celebration; Countryside Herbs; Exotic Spices; Many cookery books including 5 cookery books for Sainsbury's including: Vegetarian Meals; Seasonal Pleasures. *Hobbies:* Yoga; Painting; Photography; Cycling; Ballet; Theatre; Cinema; Reading. *Address:* Ivy Cottage, Arkesden, Saffron Walden, Essex, England.

RICHARDSON Valerie Jean Cooper Thomas, b. 21 Apr. 1948, Akron, Ohio, USA. Executive Director, Greater Cleveland Tutorial & Training Services Inc. m. 26 Sept. 1988. *Education:* Graduate, Akron School of Practical Nursing, 1968-69; BA, Social Sciences, Thomas A Edison College, 1969-73; MSW, University of Pittsburgh, 1974-76; PhD Social Work, Union Graduate School, 1976-78. *Appointments:* Interim Executive Director, Neocross, Inc, Youngstown, 1978-79; Executive Director, Gilliam Family Service Center, Youngstown, 1979-82; Executive Director, Cleveland Adult Tutorial Services, Inc, 1983-86; Associate Director, Georgian Allied Health Educational Services, 1986-89. *Publications:* Nursing magazine feature story; Editor, Heartbeat, Newsletter publication by the Akron District American Heart Association. *Memberships:* American Heart Association, Akron District; American Sociological Assn; American Association for University Women; Altrusa of Greater Cleveland, Ohio; Ohio Legal Services Commission. *Honours:* US Congressional Record, Washington DC, 1985; Local, state and national commendations and proclamations. *Hobbies and Interests:* Planning, developing and implementing medical technology training program; Social work

research with Population studies: Bowling; Tennis; Aerobics. *Address:* Crystal Towers, 16000 Terrace Road Apt No 212, East Cleveland, Ohio 44112, USA.

RICHESON Cena Rae Golder, b. 11 Apr. 1941, Oregon City, Oregon, USA. Author; Public Speaker. m. Jerry Dale Richeson, 3 June 1961. 2 sons. *Education:* AA, Diablo Valley College, 1962; BA English, California State University, Hayward, 1972; Graduate Studies, California State University. *Appointments:* College Instructor, Shasta College, Redding, 1974-76; Newspaper Columnist, Anderson Press, 1974-77; Writing Instructor, Liberty High School, Brentwood, 1984-85. *Publications:* As Velma Chamberlain: For Love's Skae, 1980. As Cyndi Richards: Love is Where You Find It, 1984; Verliebt in Einen Cowboy, 1987; Go For Broke, 1988. Book Reviews: Roundup; Tombstone Epitaph; the Californians; Horizons West. Numerous articles to magazines and journals. *Memberships:* Western Writers of America; Poets & Writers Inc, New York; Society of Children's Book Writers; California Writers Club; Zane Grey's West Society; Friends of the Library; Secretary, Calyton Community Club; Clayton Historical Society; Special frontier correspondent, The National Tombstone Epitaph, Arizona. *Honours:* Writer's Digest Nonfiction award, 1976; Willamette Writers Nonfiction award, 1976; Poet of the Year, 1975; Nominee SPUR Award, 1984; Nominee, Stirrup award, 1987; Judge, Biannual Writing Contest for California Writers Club, 1985; Judge, SPUR awards panel, Western Writers of American, 1987. *Hobbies:* Horses, especially black and white pintos; History of the American West; Cowboys; Rodeo; California Gold Rush; Singing; Playing guitar; Stagecoaches; Medicine and Health; Nutrition; Equine health. *Address:* PO Box 268, Knightsen, CA 94548, USA.

RICHMOND Fiona, b. 3 Mar. 1945, Hilborough, Norfolk, England. Writer; Actress. m. James Montgomery, 3 June 1983. 1 daughter. *Education:* Alfred Golfox School, Bradpole, Dorset. *Appointments:* Numerous appearances on stage including: Pyjama Tops, Whitehall Theatre, 1972; Let's Get Laid, Windmill Theatre, 1974; Come into my Bed, Whitehall Theatre, 1976; Women Behind Bars, 1977; Nationwide tours include: Yes we have no Pyjamas, 1979; Wot: No Pyjamas, 1981; Space in my Pyjamas, 1982; Appearances in films: Expose, 1975; Hardcore, 1976; Let's Get Laid, 1977; History of the World Part 1, 1981. *Publications:* Books: Fiona; Story of I; On the Road; The Good, The Bad and the Beautiful; Galactic Girl; From Here to Virginity; In Depth; Tell Tale Tits; articles for Punch, Sunday Telegraph, Evening Standard, Daily Mail; Travelogues for Time Off. *Memberships:* Equity; National Union of Journalists; Women of the Year Association. *Honours:* Bottom of the Year Award, 1977; Winner, Gold Award (Atlanta) for television documentary, What the Actress Said. *Hobbies:* Dress designing; Nutrition; Auditioning nude men. *Address:* Dorothy Solomon Associated Artists, 31a Bruton Place, London W1X 7AB, England.

RICHTER Harvena, b. 13 Mar. 1919, Reading, Pennsylvania, USA. Writer; University Professor. *Education:* BA, University of New Mexico, 1938; MA, 1955, PhD, 1967, New York University. *Appointments:* Advertising Copywriter, Copy Chief, Advertising Director, Saks Fifth Avenue, Macy's, Elizabeth Arden, and I. Miller, 1941-48; Lecturer, New York University, 1955-66; Visiting Professor (part-time), University of New Mexico, 1969-89. *Publications:* The Human Shore (novel); Virginia Woolf: the Inward Voyage; Edited The Rawhide Knot and Other Stories (Conrad Richter); Writing to Survive: The Private Notebooks of Conrad Richter (biography); Essays, articles, short fiction and poetry in various publications and anthologies. *Memberships:* Author's Guild; American Association of University Women. *Honours:* Katherine Mather Simms Prize in Poetry, 1938; American Association of University Women Fellowship, 1964-65; Residence grants at Yaddo, 1963-64, MacDowell Colony, 1965-66, Wurlitzer Foundation in Taos, 1968, 1973-1975, Virginia Center for the Creative Arts, 1983, 1985;

Founder's Day Award for Outstanding Scholarship, New York University, 1968. *Hobbies:* Travel to far places; Music; Gardens; Anything connected with the sea; Writing poetry. *Address:* 1932 Candelaria Road NW, Albuquerque, NM 87107, USA.

RIDDELL Alice Mary, b. 12 Aug. 1928, Queens, New York, USA. Educator/Field of expertise: Substance Abuse Prevention Intervention. m. Robert Lawrence Riddell, 17 Jan. 1948. 1 son. *Education:* BA 1963, MS 1966, Queens College, University of New York City; Certificate Narcotics Inst., Queens College, 1968; PD, St John's University, 1973. *Appointments:* School Secretary & Parish Secretary, Our Lady of Sorrows School, Queens, New York, 1957-59; Teacher, Consumer Education & Family Living, School Narcotics Coordinator, 9th Grade Advisor, JHS 218Q, 1963-70; Narcotics Coordinator, CSD 25, 1970-71; Director of Project 25, CSD 25's Drug Prev. Programme, 1971-; Professor, Queens College Child Development, 1988. *Publications:* Editor & Writer, The Quarterly; Co-author, A Handbook for School Staffs re: Alcohol, Drugs - Possession, Use, Abuse & Crisis, 1982; Editor, Newsletter of NYS Association of Drug & Alcohol Abuse Prevention Professionals; Article: Magic Markers, Alcohol Health & Research World, 1989. *Memberships:* Past President, NYS Assoc of Drug & Alcohol Abuse Prevention Professionals; Trustee & Board Member, Daytop Village Inc; Board Member, College Point Sports Association; NYS Advisory Council on Substance Abuse, 1978-83; Board of Regents Comm. for Prof. Assistance of NYS Aduc. Dept; Queens Borough President's Advisory Council on Substance Abuse; Volunteer USO 30 years. *Honours:* Phi Delta Kappa, St John's University, 1973; Frank DeSilva Memorial Award, Outstanding Contributions to the Field, 1982; Educator of the Year, NYC Board of Education Catholic Teachers Association, 1985; Congressional Delegate, White House, 1970; New York State Excellence Award for Drug Abuse Prevention, 1986. *Hobbies:* Piano; Organ; Travelling; Needlework; Sports. *Address:* 65-25 160th Street, Flushing, NY 11365, USA.

RIED Glenda Eileen Thompson, b. 20 June 1933, Toledo, Ohio, USA. Professor of Accounting. m. Richard Theodore Ried, 23 Mar. 1963, 1 son. *Education:* BBA cum laude 1955, MBA Highest Honours 1961, University of Toledo; CPA, Ohio, 1960. *Appointments:* Public accountant, Arthur Singer & Associates, 1955-58; Professor of Accounting, University of Toledo, 1959-. *Publications:* Editor, The Woman CPA (professional journal), 1983-86; Book, Careers in Accounting 1984; Article, Historical Perspective on Women in Accounting, in Journal of Accountancy, 1987. *Memberships:* National Vice President, Director, American Woman's Society of Certified Public Accountants; Ohio Regional Director, GNP Section, American Accounting Association; State Director, Ohio Society of CPA's; Toledo Chapter President, American Society of Women Accountants; American Institute of CPA's. *Honours:* Plaque; Honour societies. *Hobbies:* Genealogy; Travel; Gardening. *Address:* Accounting Department, University of Toledo, 2801 West Bancroft Street, Stranahan Hall, Toledo, Ohio 43606, USA.

RIFKIND Linda, b. 25 Jan. 1938, Glasgow, Scotland. Actress; Singer; Writer; Teacher. m. Dr Nathaniel Rifkind, 14 Oct. 1958. 2 daughters. *Education:* DipSD; DSD, Royakl Scottish Academy of Music and Drama, Glasgow. *Appointments:* Numerous appearances on television including: TuttiFrutti; Call me Mister; Sailing Away; Crossfire; Charles Rennie MacIntosh; Naked Video; The Campbell's; The Dark Room; Taggart; Leaving; The Blues; Bookie; Take the High Road; Christable; One Woman Shows; Numerous concerts, cabaret appearances for Glasgow Old People's Welfare Committee, Scottish Old Age Pensions Association, Strathclyde Regional Council, Churches *Publications:* Short stories. *Memberships:* Equity; Scottish Community Drama Association; Musicians Union; Spotlight-Actresses Directory. *Hobbies:* Work; Writing short sotires and poetry. *Addres:* Newton Mearns (Broom Estate), Glasgow G77 5DU, Scotland.

RIGG (Enid) Diana (Elizabeth), b. 20 July 1938, Doncaster, Yorkshire, England. Actress. m. (1) Menahem Gueffen 1973, divorced 1976. (2) Archibald Stirling, 1982. 1 daughter. *Education:* Fulneck Girls' School, Pudsey, Yorks; RADA. *Career:* Professional debut as Natella Abashwilli in The Caucasian Chalk Circle, York Festival, 1957; Repertory, Chesterfield and Scarborough, 1958; Dir. United British Artists, 1983-; Associate Artist of RSC, Stratford and Aldwych, 1959-64. *Stage Appearances include:* Troilus and Cressida; Ondine; The Devils; Becket; The Taming of the Shrew; The Art of Seduction; A Midsummer Night's Dream; Comedy of Errors; King Lear; The Physicists; Macbeth; Jumpers, 1972; Tis Pity She's A Whore, 1972; The Misanthrope, Washington and New York, 1973, 1975; Phaedra Britannica, 1975; The Guardsman, 1978; Abelard and Heloise, 1970, 1971; Pygmaloin, 1974; Night and Day, 1978; Colette, 1982; Heartbreak House, 1983; Little Eyolf, 1985; Antony and Cleopatra, 1985. Toured Eastern Europe, USSR, USA in King Lear; Comedy of Errors, 1964. Television Appearances include: Sentimental Agent, 1963; A Comedy of Errors, 1964; The Hothouse, 1964; Emma Peel (The Avengers) 1965-67; Women Beware Women, 1965; Married Alive, 1970; Diana (US series), 1973; In This House of Brede, 1975; Three Piece Suite, 1977; The Serpent Son, 1979; The Marquise, 1980; Hedda Gabler, 1981; Little Eyolf, 1982; King Lear, 1983; Witness for the Prosecution, 1983; Bleak House, 1984; Wildfire, 1986; Follies, 1987. Films include: A Midsummer Night's Dream, 1969; The Assassination Bureau, 1969; On Her Majesty's Secret Service, 1969; Julius Caesar, 1970; The Hospital, 1971; Theatre of Blood, 1973; A Little Night Music, 1977; The Great Muppet Caper, 1981; Evil under the sun, 1982. *Publication:* To Turn Unstoned, 1982. *Honour:* Plays and Players Award for Best Actress, 1975 and 1978. *Hobbies:* Reading; Writing; Cooking; Travel. *Address:* c/o London Management, 235 Regent Street, London W1A 2JT, England.

RIGGS Constance Kakavecos, b. 6 Apr. 1928, Indianapolis, USA. College Administrator. m. Kenneth Wesley Riggs, 4 Dec. 1947, deceased, 3 sons, 3 daughters. *Education:* BA, 1975. *Appointments:* Medical Education co-ordinator, St Vincent Hospital, 1967-72; Assistant to President, Wabash College, 1972-78; Assistant Vice President, St Mary of the Woods College, 1978-79; Assistant to President, Rollins College, Winter Park, 1979-. *Publications:* Sam Shue and the Seven Satchels, 1976; Editor, Montgomery County Remembers, 1976; Columnist, Orlando Sentinel, 1981-, Winter Park Outlook 1984-, Senior Voice 1985-. *Memberships:* Florida Freelance Writers Association; National Federation Press Women. *Address:* 200 St Andrews Blvd. Apt 3503, Winter Park, FL 32792, USA.

RIHOIT Catherine, b. 12 June 1949, Caen, France. Lecturer; Writer; Journalist. 1 son. *Education:* Agregation d'Anglais, 1972. *Appointments:* Lecturer, La Sorbonne, 1975-; Contributor to Marie Claire Magazine, 1978-. *Publications:* Portrait de Gabriel et Le Bal des debutantes; La Favorite les Abîimes du coeur; Triomphe de l'Amour; Soleil. Retourà Cythère; film scripts; biographies; essays; plays. *Hobbies:* Travel; Ballet; Gardening. *Address:* 39 rue Esquirol, 75013 Paris, France.

RILEY Bridget Louise, b. 1931. *Education:* Cheltenham Ladies College; Goldsmith's College of Art; Royal College of Art. *Career:* AICA Critics Prize and Prize of the John Moore's Exhibition, Liverpool, 1963; Peter Stuyvesant Foundation Travel Bursary to USA 1964; International Prize for Painting, XXXIV Venice Biennale 1968; Ohara Museum Prize, 8th International Print Biennale, Tokyo, 1972; numerous solo exhibitions and two international retrospective museum touring exhibitions, 1970-71 (Arts Council) and 1978-81 (British Council); Colour projects for Royal Liverpool Hospital 1980-83 and for St. Mary's Hospital, Paddington, 1987-88; Colour Moves for Ballet Rambert 1983; Trustee National Gallery, London, 1981-88. Represented in Major museums and art collections. *Address:* c/o Mayor

Rowan Gallery, 31A Bruton Place, London W1A 7AB, England.

RILEY Helene M Kastinger, b. 11 Mar. 1939, Vienna, Austria. University Professor; Author; Lecturer. m. (1)Edward R Riley, 6 Nov. 1957, divorced, 3 sons, 1 daughter. (2)Darius G Ornston, MD, 11 May 1983. *Education:* BA Music, University of North Texas, 1970; MA Germanics 1973, PhD Germanics 1975, Rice University. *Appointments:* Assistant Professor 1975-78, Associate Professor 1978-85, Yale University; Guest Professor, Middlebury College, 1976; Chair, Dept/ Foreign Languages, Washington State University, 1981-82; Professor, Clemson University, 1985-. *Publications:* Idee und Gestaltung, 1977; L.A.v. Arnims Jugend-u. Reisejahre, 1978; Achim von Arnim, 1979; Virginia Woolf, 1983; Romain Rolland, 1979; Das Bild der Antike, 1981; Clemens Brentano, 1985; Die weibliche Muse, 1986; A.v.Arnims Kritische Schriften, 1988; Numerous articles. *Memberships include:* President, American Association of University Professors (Clemson, 1988-89), Vice President, 1987-88; Modern Language Association. *Honours:* NEH Travel grant, 1986; SC Dept of Education grant, 1986; Deutsche Forschungsgemeinschaft grant, 1982; Hilles Fund, 1982; Holland Fund, 1982; Sr Fac Fellow, 1981-82; Hilles Grant, 1976, 1979; DAAD, 1979; Griswold, 1975-76, 1978; Morse Fellow, 1977-78; Rice Fellow, 1971, 1974; NDEA Fellow, 1972, 1973. *Hobbies:* Reading; Writing; Needlecraft; Painting, Piano; Singing; Sports. *Address:* Clemson University, Department of Languages, 201 Strode Tower, Clemson, SC 29634, USA.

RILEY Julie Moore, b. 2 Feb. 1958, Union City, Tennessee, USA. Dental Hygienist. m. James Patrick Riley, 29 May, 1982. *Education:* BSc, Dental Hygiene, University of Tennessee, Martin, 1976-78; University of Tennessee, Memphis, 1978-79. *Appointments:* Robert L Moore, DDS, Martin, 1980-82; Jerry G Brewster, DDS, Memphis, 1982-84; John R Maxwell, DDS, Memphis, 1983-87; H R & W W Manning, DDS, Memphis, 1984-87; William D Pierce, Dyersburg, 1987-. *Memberships:* American Dental Hygienists Association; Tennessee Dental Hygienists Association; Memphis Dental Hygienist's Assoc (Chairperson dental health program 1983-86, President 1985-86); Jaycette's; Zeta Tau Alpha Alumni Assoc (Pres 1980-81, Secretary 1981-82); Pilot Club; 7th District Dental Hygienist's Association, Trustee, 1980-81, 1988-90 and Memphis Dental Hygienist's Association, Secretary 1984-85. *Honour:* Outstanding Young Women of America, 1980. *Hobbies:* Swimming; Boating; Handwork, crocheting and knitting; Reading. *Address:* P O Box 923, Milan, TN 38358, USA.

RILEY Kathleen Ann, b. Evanston, Illinois, USA. Business Consultant. *Education:* BA, College of St. Thomas, 1986. *Appointments:* Partner, R-W and Associates, Minnetonka, 1980-; Consultant, Small Business Development Centre, St Paul, 1985-. *Memberships:* Sales & Marketing Executives; Pi Sigma Epsilon Sales & Marketing Association; Kimberwick Equestrian Club, Treasurer. *Honours:* Pi Sigma Epsilon. *Hobbies:* Training Doberman Pinschers; Equestrian; Tennis; Sailing; Writing; Gourmet Cooking. *Address:* 4615 Ellerdale Road, Minnetonka, MN 55345, USA.

RILEY Kathleen Ann, b. 30 Jan. 1945, Norfolk, Virginia, USA. International Pharmaceutical Marketing Manager. m. Wendell Earl Dunn III, 29 Mar. 1981, 1 daughter. *Education:* Sophie Newcomb College, 1962-64; BS, Chemistry, College of William & Mary, 1967; MS Chemistry 1970, postgraduate Pharmaceutical Chemistry (Medical Centre) 1970-72, University of Illinois; MBA, Northwestern University, 1977. *Appointments:* Pharmaceutical assistant 1970-73, Clinical Research Associate 1973-75, Senior Clinical Research Associate 1975-76, Abbott Laboratories, North Chicago; Consultant, Management Analysis Centre Inc, Northbrook, Illinois, 1976-77; Strategic Planning Manager, Agricultural Chemicals 1977-80, Phosphorus Chemicals 1980-81, FMC Corporation,

Philadelphia; Manager, New Compound Opportunities 1981-84, Market Planning & New Business Opportunities 1985-88, Smith, Kline & French International, Philadelphia; Associate Director, New Compound Evaluation, 1988-, Smith Kline Beecham Pharmaceuticals. *Creative work includes:* 3 patents, pharmaceutical compounds; Articles, pharmacologically active compounds, various professional journals, 1970-74. *Memberships include:* Sigma Xi; Advisory Board, European Foundation for Osteoporosis & Bone Diseases, 1987; Various offices, Philadelphia Women's Network; Offices, Evening Department, Haddon Fortnightly. *Honours:* National Honour Society, 1961; Iota Sigma Pi, 1966; Women to Watch in Delaware Valley, DV Business Magazine, 1979. *Hobbies:* Sailing; Gardening & landscaping; Cross country skiing; Travel; Reading. *Address:* 443 Gladstone Avenue, Haddon Field, New Jersey 08033, USA.

RING Diann Benningfield, b. 8 Jan. 1943, Dallas, Texas, USA. Advertising and Public Relations Consultant; City Councilwoman. m. Dr Robert Ring III, 28 Dec. 1963. 1 son, 1 daughter. *Education:* BA Journalism, University of Texas, 1961-63; Southern Methodist University, 1963-64; MA Public Policy Studies, Claremont Graduate School, 1974-76. *Appointments:* Writer/PR aide, WFAA-TV, Dallas, 1964-66; Teacher, Boston Area Schools, 1966-67; Editor/ Publisher, Bay Breeze Magazine, Seabrook, Texas, 1972-73; Political Consultant, California, 1978-82; Partner, Ring/Robinson & Assoc. Media Group, California, 1987-. *Publications:* Future Food Resources - A Challenge for Today, co- author, 1975; Claremont Hillsides Planning, co-author, 1977; I Did It My Way, diet cookbook, 1982; numerous articles for periodicals. *Memberships:* Local President, State, County & Local Budget Chair, Local Board, League of Women Voters, 1973-85; City Planning Commissioner, 1982-86; President & Board, Claremont High School PFA, 1982-88; President & Board, Community Friends of International Students, 1977-82; President & Board, Claremont Foothill Association, 1974-78; Soccer coach & Referee, 1977-84; Camp Fire Girls Leader, 1976-78. *Honours:* Elected to the City Council, Claremont, California, 1986-; Prism of Excellence Award, Jerry Voohris Democratic Club for Outstanding leadership in community and educatin. *Hobbies:* Cooking, especially for large charity fundraisers; Running; Travel; Political action; International relations. *Address:* 816 Peninsula, Claremont, CA 91711, USA.

RING Lucile Wiley, b. 2 Jan, 1920, Kearney, Nebraska, USA. Lawyer. m. John Robert Ring, 28 Mar. 1948. 3 sons. *Education:* AB, Kearney State College, 1944; JD, Washington University, 1946. *Appointments:* Barrister, Missouri, 1946; US District Court, (Eastern District), Missouri, 1946; US Court Appeals (8th Circuit), 1972; Attorney-adviser, Chief legal group adjudications br. Army Fin. Ctr., St Louis, 1946-52; Exec. dir. lawyer referral service, St Louis Bar, 1960-70; Sole practice, St Louis, 1960-88; Staff law clk, US Ct Appeals (8th circuit), st Louis, 1970-72; Exec. dir. St Louis Com. on Cts., 1972-85; Legal adviser, Missouri State Anat. Bd., 1965-88; Adj. prof. administrative law Webster College, Missouri, 1977-78. *Publications:* Author, editor: Guide to Community Services - Who Do I Talk To, 1974, 75, 1976-79; St Louis Court Directories, 1972, 73, 74, 75; Felony Procedures in St Louis Courts, 1975; Contributor of articles to professional journals. *Memberships:* Missouri Profl. Liability Rev. Bd., State of Missouri, 1977-79; Missouri Mental Health Authority, 1964-65; Board of directors, Vice President, Drug and Substance Abuse Council. St Louis, 1973-86; Adv. Council St Louis Agency on Training and employment, 1976-84; Mayor's Judicial Reform Subcom. St Louis, 1974-76; Vice President, 1975-76, Bar Assn. Met. St Louis; Vice President, 1978-79, Director Legal Services of Eastern Missouri, Inc; Board of Directors, 1977-78, Legal Aid Society of St Louis City and County; Commr. 1975, HUD Women and Housing Commn; Treasurer, 1959-60, President, 1960-61, Missouri Association of Women Lawyers. *Honours:* Washington University Sch. Law Scholar, 1944-46; 1st Missouri woman nominated for St Louis Ct Appeals, Missouri Appellate Commn. 1972;

Recipient letter of commendation Office of Chief of Finance, US Army 1952; Pi Kappa Delta; Sigma Tau Delta; Xi Phi. *Address:* 755 Catalpa Avenue, Webster Groves, MO 63119, USA.

RIOS-GONZALEZ Palmira N, b. 29 July 1953, Puerto Rico. Deputy Director. *Education:* BA, University of Puerto Rico, 1970; MA, Fisk University, 1975; PhD, Yale University, USA, 1988. *Appointments:* Lecturer, Sociology, State University of New York, 1982-83; Instructor, Puerto Rican Studies, Lehman College, 1983-87, Deputy Director, Centre for Immigrant & Population Studies, College of Staten Island, 1987-, CUNY. *Publications:* Book Chapter, La Mujer como productora cultural, 1988; articles in professional journals. *Memberships:* American Sciological Association; Asociacion Latinoamericana de Sociologia; Caribbean Studes Association; Caribbean Association for Feminist Research & Action; National Congress for Puerto Rican Rights. *Honours:* National Hispanic Scholarship Fund Scholar, 1977; Funacion Campos del Toro Fellow. *Hobbies:* Record Collecting. *Address:* Centre for Immigrant & Population Studies, College of Staten Island, 130 Stuyvesant Place, Rm. 1-932, Staten Island, NY 10301, USA.

RIPHAGEN Colleen Linda, b. 13 Aug. 1957, Kroonstad, South Africa. College Instructor. m. Derek, 2 Dec. 1978, 1 son. *Education:* BSc., 1978; PhD, 1987. *Appointment:* College Instructor, Mount Royal College, Calgary, 1988-. *Publications:* Scientific papers in professional journals. *Memberships:* Society for Neuroscience; Canadian Physiology Society. *Honours:* Alberta Heritage Foundation for Medical Research, Studentship Award, 1983-87; Medical Research Council of Canada Postdoctoral Fellowship Award, 1988; Canadian Heart Foundation Fellowship Award, 1988. *Hobbies:* Mountaineering; Travel. *Address:*Dept. of Chemical & Biological Sciences, Mount Royal College, 4825 Richard Road, Calgary, Canada T3G 6K6.

RIPPON Lesley Margaret, b. 10 Mar. 1936, Sydney, New South Wales, Australia. Artist. m. Ellis L. Rippon, 9 Feb. 1962, 1 son, 1 daughter. *Education:* Lynden Art School, 1968-76; Studied with Fred Martin, 1978, Margaret Wills, 1983; Full-time Art Certificate course, Meadowbank College, TAFE, 1979-80; Study/painting tours with Fred Bates, England and France, 1985, Robert Lovett, Greece, Yugoslavia and Italy, 1986, with Maxine Masterfield & Zoltan Szabo in Canada in 1988. *Appointments:* Art Teacher: YMCA, Epping, New South Wales, 1977; Willandra Art Centre, Ryde, 1981-86; Castle Hill Art Centre, 1902-03; Castle Hill Evening College, 1982- 83; Workshops throughout New South Wales. *Publications:* Article in The Australian Artist, 1985. *Memberships:* Royal Art Society of New South Wales; The Peninsula Art Society; Ryde Municipal Art Society; Art Gallery Society, New South Wales; Castle Hill Art Society. *Honours:* 1st Prize, Meadowbank College of TAFE full-time Art Certificate, 1979 & 1980; Many other awards in numerous art competitions, Australia. *Hobbies:* Travel; Embroidery; Photography; Gardening. *Address:* 12 Woods Street, North Epping, New South Wales 2121, Australia.

RISNES Marilyn Louise Neitzert, b. 22 Mar. 1935, Huron, USA. Elementary Educator. m. Lawrence Martin Risnes, 6 June 1959, divorced 1975, 2 sons, 1 daughter. *Education:* BS, 1963; MA, 1978; DCH, 1989. *Appointments:* Elementary Educator, 1954-57, Mound 1957-59, Roseville, 1959-60, Special School, District 1, 1968-. *Memberships:* National Education Association; Minneapolis Education Association; Minnesota Federation of Teachers; Educators for Social Reponsibility; American Civil Liberties Union. *Honours:* US Dept. of Education Study Grntee, Oxford University, 1972; Mentor Educator, Baldwin Girls School, Banglaore, India, 1980. *Hobbies:* Travel; Jewellery & Gemstones; Dancing; Fishing; Acting. *Address:* Tuttle-Marcy School, 1042 18th Ave. SE, Minneapolis, MN 55414, USA.

RITBLAT Jillian Rosemary, b. 14 Dec. 1942, Newcastle on Tyne, England. Chairman Patrons of New Art, Tate Gallery. m. (1)Ewea Zilkha, 21 Apr. 1966, divorced 1981, 1 son, 1 daughter. (2)John Ritblat, 1986. *Education:* Completed Bar Exams, 1960-63; Called to Bar (Garys Inn), 1964; BA (Hons) History of Art, Westfield College, London University, 1980-83. *Appointments:* Pupillage to Robin Simpson (now QC), Victor Ovrand & Jeremy Hutchinson's Chambers, 1964-65; Alternate delegate for International Council of Jewish Women, United Nations, Geneva, 1978-79; Chairman Patrons of New Art, Tate Gallery. *Memberships:* Council of the Museum of Modern Art, Oxford; Jury of Painting in the Eighties, 1987; Turner Prize Jury, 1988; International Council Jerusalem Museum. *Hobbies:* Art; Opera; Travelling; Skiing; Food; People. *Address:* 10 Cornwall Terrace, London NW1, England.

RITCHIE Elisavietta Artamonoff, b. 29 June 1932, Kansas City, Missouri, USA. Writer; Poet; Translator; Teacher; Editor. m. Lyell Hale Ritchie, 11 July 1953, divorced, 2 sons, 1 daughter. *Education:* Cours de Civilisation Française, Sorbonne, PAris, 1951; BA, University of California, Berkeley, 1954; MA, French Literature, American University, 1976. *Publications:* Tightening the Circle Over Eel Country; Raking the Snow; The Problem with Eden; The Chattanooga Cycles; A Sheath of Dreams and Other Games; Moving to Larger Quarters; Timbot, 1970; Edited: The Dolphins Arc, 1989; Finding the Name, 1983; articles, poetry, short stories, reviews, translations & photographs in various journals and magazines including: New York Times; Washington Post; Poetrry, American Scholar; etc. *Memberships:* Numerous professional organisations. *Honours Include:* Washington Writers Publishing House Competition Winner, 1981; Armstrong State College Chapbook Competition, 1985; Empty Windows Review Chapbook Competition, 1985; 2 Annual Poetry Society of America Awards; 2 Individual Artist Grants, DC Commission in the Arts; Nominee, Pushcart Prize, several times; 3 times winner, PEN Syndicated Fiction Project. *Address:* 3207 Macomb Street NW, Washington, DC 20008, USA.

RITCHIE Margaret Claire, b. 18 Sept. 1937, Hebburn, England. Headmistress. *Education:* BSc, University of Leeds, 1955-59; Post graduate Certificate of education, University of London, 1959-60. *Appointments:* Assistant School Mistress, St Leonards School, St Andrews, 1960-64; Head of Science, Wycombe Abbey School, 1964-71; Head Mistress, Queenswood, Hatfield, 1971-81; Headmistress, Queen Mary School, Lytham, 1981-. *Memberships:* Secondary Heads Association; Girls' Schools Association. *Address:* Queen Mary School, Lytham, Lancs FY8 1DS, England.

RITENOUR Sharon Rebecca, b. 24 Mar. 1950, Winchester, Virginia, USA. Documentary Historian; Editor. m. Norman Scott Stevens, 25 June 1989. *Education:* BA, History & Political Science, Bridgewater (VA)College, 1972; MA, History, James Madison University, 1978. *Appointments:* History Teacher, Virginia Secondary Schools, 1973-77; Librarian 1978-79, Assistant and Associate Editor of The Papers of George Catlett Marshall, 1979-, George C Marshall Research Library. *Publications:* Coeditor, The Papers of George Catlett Marshall, vol 1, The Soldierly Spirit, 1981, vol 2, We Cannot Delay, 1986, 4 vols forthcoming; Coeditor, Proceedings of the Rockbridge (VA) Historical Society, vol 9, 1982. *Memberships:* Editor, Documentary Editing, Association for Documentary Editing, 1983-89; Organization of American Historians; American Historical Association; Phi Alpha Theta Honor Society; Lambda Honor Society. *Honours:* Award for academic achievement, History and Political Science, Bridgewater College, 1972; Philip M Hamer Award, Society of American Archivists, 1982; Distinguished Service Award, Association for Documentary Editing, 1986; Lyman H. Butterfield Award, Association for Documentary Editing, 1989. *Address:* George C Marshall Research Library, P O Box 1600, Lexington, Virginia 24450, USA.

RITSON Rouviere Denise, b. 23 Dec 1940, Durban,

South Africa. Headmistress. m. Colin R Ritson, 6 Jan. 1962, 1 daughter. *Education:* BA, 1960, University Education Diploma, 1966, University of Natal; BA, Honours, University of South Africa, 1970; MA, Concordia University, 1975. *Appointments:* Assistant Head, Trafalgar School for Girls, Montreal, Canada, 1975-82; Headmistress, York House School, Vancouver, 1984-. *Memberships:* National Association of Principals of Schools for Girls. *Hobbies:* Reading; Gardening; Tennis. *Address:* 5969 Athlone Street Vancouver, BC, V6M 3A3, Canada.

RITTER Ann L, b. 20 May New York City, USA. Lawyer. *Education:* BA, Hunter College, 1954; JD, New York Law School, 1970; Postgraduate, Law School, New York University, 1971-72; Bar, New York, 1971, US Court of Appeals (2nd circuit), 1975, US Supreme Court, 1975. *Appointments:* Writer, 1954-70, Editor, 1955-66; Teacher, 1966-70; Attorney, American Society Composers Authors and Publishers, New York City, 1971-72, Greater New York Insurance Co., 1973-74; Senior Partner, Brenhouse & Ritter, New York City, 1974-78; Sole Practice, New York City, 1978-. *Publications:* Editor, New York Immigration News, 1975-76. *Memberships:* ABA; American Immigration Lawyers Association, Treasurer 1983-84, Secretary 1984-85, Vice chair, 1985-86, Chair, 1986-87; New York Sate Bar Association; New York County Lawyers Association; Association of Trial Lawyers of America; New York State Trial Lawyers Association; New York City Bar Association. *Address:* 47 E 87th St., New York, NY 10128, USA.

RITTER Deborah Elizabeth, b. 16 May 1947, Philadelphia, Pennsylvania, USA. Anaesthesiologist. *Education:* BA, Susquehanna University, 1968; MS, University of Pennsylvania, 1969; MD, Medical College of Pennsylvania, 1973; Graduate training, Thomas Jefferson University Hospital & Philadelphia Children's Hospital, 1973-77. *Appointments:* Frankford Hospital, 1977-78; Medical College of Pennsylvania, 1977-78; Clinical Instructor 1978-80, Clinical Assistant Professor 1980-86, Vice Chair, Department of Anaesthesia 1985, Clinical Associate Professor of Anaesthesiology 1986-, Thomas Jefferson University Hospital. *Memberships:* American Medical Association; American Women's Medical Association; International Anaesthesia Research Society; American & Pennsylvania Societies of Anaesthesiologists; Society for Education in Anaesthesia; Save-the- Redwoods; Wilderness Society; Association on American Indian Affairs. *Hobbies:* Music; Gardening; Embroidery; Wilderness preservation; American Indians. *Address:* Department of Anaesthesia, 6275 NH, Thomas Jefferson University Hospital, 11th & Walnut Streets, Philadelphia, Pennsylvania 19107, USA.

RIVERA MONTALVO Mary E., b. 11 Oct. 1946, Santurce, Puerto Rico. Social Worker; Clinical Psychologist. 1 son, 1 daughter. *Education:* MSW, 1971; MS, 1979; PhD, 1986. *Appointment:* Clinica Ginecoquirurgica y Planificacion Familiar, Reparto Metropolitano. *Creative work includes:* Co-author, Initial Approach to Patients with Sexual Dysfunctions; Medical Sciences Campus Research Week, Department of Obstetrics & Gynaecology, UPR School of Medicine. *Memberships:* Junta Directores, Casa Julia de Burgos; Centro de Encuentro Paterno-Filial; Instituto de Preferencial Sexual de Puerto Rico; Fundacion SIDA de Puerto Rico. *Honour:* Dean's Honour List, 1980. *Hobbies:* Karate; Metaphysics; Swimming; Gardening; Dancing. *Address:* Calle Hortensia no. 1121, Mansiones de Rio Piedras, Puerto Rico 00926, USA.

RIVERO Y MENDEZ Isel Leonor, b. 18 May 1941, Havana, Cuba. Social Affairs Officer. *Education:* Sociology, University of Havana; New School of Social Research, New York University. *Education:* UN Industrial Development Organization, Vienna, Austria, 1968-82; UN New York, 1982-. *Publications:* Poetry: Fantasias De La NOche; La Marcha de los Hurones; Tundra; Night Rained Her; Songs: El Banqvete. *Memberships:* Board, Sisterhood is Global Institute; Vice President, Treasurer,

Federation of Internaitonal civil Servants Association. *Honours:* Recipient, Cintas Fellowship, 2 consecutive years, poetry. *Hobbies:* Music; Opera; Horse Riding; Feminist Politics. *Address:* United Nations, Dept. of International Social & Economic Affairs, Room DC 2 2342, New York, NY 10017, USA.

RIVERS Joan, b. Brooklyn, New York, USA. Comedienne; Writer; Actress; Talk Show Hostess. m. Edgar Rosenberg, 15 July 1966. 1 daughter. *Education:* BA, Barnard College. *Appointments:* Appearance on television with Johnny Carson in The Tonight Show, 1964; Featured opposite Burt Lancaster in United Artist's The Swimmer, 1969; Staff Writer for Candid Camera, 1969-71; Wrote and starred in syndicated talk show, That Show, 1969- 71; Co-writer of Fun City, starring in its Broadway production, 1971; Writer of ABC television film, The Girl Most Likely To, 1973; Columnist for Chicago Tribune, 1973-76; Made debut as film director with Rabbit Test, written with Jay Redak, 1978; Permanent guest hostess on The Tonight Show, 1983-86; Appeared as Sole guest on Audience With, 1984, on London Weekend Television, followed by a series of six 1 hour specials, Joan Rivers: Can We Talk?, BBC-TV, 1985; Currently appearing in The Late Show Starring Joan Rivers, premiered on Fox Broadcasting Network, 9 Oct. 1986. *Publications:* Having a Baby Can Be a Scream, 1974; What Becomes of Semi-Legend Most? (record album), 1983; The Life and Hard Times of Heidi Abromowitz, 1984; Joan Rivers and Friends Salute Heidi Abromowitz (TV comedy), 1985; Enter Talking, 1986. *Membership:* National Spokesperson, Cystic Fibrosis Foundation. *Honours:* Harvard Hasty Pudding Woman of the Year Award, 1984; Humanitarian Award, Gay & Lesbian Community Services Center, Los Angeles, 1985; Jimmy Award; Georgie Award as Best Comedienne, American Guild of Variety Artists; Nightclub Performer of the Year, New York Friars Club; Las Vegas Comedienne of the Year (twice); 2 Clio Awards for Best Performance in a Television Commercial. *Address:* c/o Bill Sammeth, 9200 Sunset Boulevard Suite 1001, Los Angeles, CA 90069, USA.

RIVERS Marie Georgine Bie, b. 12 July 1928, Tampa, Florida, USA. Author; Businesswoman; Radio Broadcaster. m. Eurith Dickinson Rivers, 3 May 1952, 2 sons, 3 daughter. *Appointments:* President 1969-87, Board Chairman 1983-, Radio Station: WEDR, Miami, WGUN, Atlanta, WWJD and WEAS, Savannah, KWAM and KR NB, Memphis, WSWN AM & FM, Palm Beach County, WXOS, Islamorada, Florida, WAAC and WGOV, Valdosta, Georgia, Stars, Inc., Miami Beach, Deesown Corporation, Miami Beach; Board Chairman, Suncoast Broadcasting Co., 1982-; Board Chairman, Creative Christian Concepts Corp., Ocala, Keystone - 9, Ocala, 1984-; Board Chairman, Laser Acceptance Corp. 1987-; Board Chairman, M. Bie Corp., Chicago, 1988-; Owner, Lazy Rivers Ranch, Ocala. *Publications:* A Woman Alone, under pen-name, Georgine Bie. *Memberships:* Florida Association of Broadcasters, Board 1984-88; Youth Director, Florida Appaloosa Horse Club, 1972-76. *Honours:* Honoraria: Tennessee Association Children with Learning Disabilities, Amyotropic Lateral Sclerosis Foundation. *Hobbies:* Sailing; Swimming; Horsemanship; Travel; Volunteer - Working with Handicapped Youth, and Elderly. *Address:* 13334 Polo Club Road No 342, Palm Beach Polo & Country Club, West Palm Beach, FL 33414, USA.

ROBBIE Sue, b. 5 July 1949, London, England. Television Presenter. *Education:* BA Joint Honours Degree in Psychology and English, Keele University, 1967-71; Postgraduate Certificate of Education in English and Drama, Crewe College of Education, 1972-73; Postgraduate Diploma in Management Studies, Manchester Polytechnic, 1980-82. *Appointments:* English Teacher, Hazel Grove High School, Stockport, 1973-77; Warden of Short-Stay Residential Unit, Abraham Moss Centre, Manchester, 1977; Stewardess, British Airways, 1978-82; Continuity Announcer, Presenter, Granada Television, 1982-86; Freelance Presenter, 1986-. *Hobbies:* Horseriding; Walking; Reading; Yoga; Swimming; Theatre; Cinema; Women's

Issues; Psychology-related topics such as self-help groups etc; Wildlife; Conservation. *Address:* c/o Arlington Enterprises Limited, 1-3 Charlotte Street, London W1P 1HD, England.

ROBBINS Martha Helen, b. 22 Sept. 1952, La Junta, Colorado, USA. Corporation Owner and Administrator. *Education:* BA 1972, Masters in Public Administration 1973, Drake University. *Appointments:* Health Planner 1973-75, Director Health Manpower Project 1975-77, Governor's Office for Planning & Programming, Des Moines, 1973-75; Instructor, Public Administration, Drake University, 1974; Director, Resources Development Western Co Health Systems Agency, Grand Junction, 1977-78; Planning Specialist, Colo Hospital Assoc, Denver, 1978-79; Admin, Davis Institute on Aging, Denver, 1979-80; Assistant Admin, The Childrens Hospital, Denver, 1980-84; Vice President/Co-owner, Medical Systems for Business and Industry, 1981-; Corp Staff Specialist, Rocky Mtn Child Health Services, Denver, 1984-86; Gen & Managing Partner, 5400 Investment Co, Denver, 1985-; Vice President and Co- owner, Work Rite of Cold, Inc, Denver, 1985-; Gen & Managing Partner, Work Rite, Ltd, Denver, 1986-. *Publications:* Iowa Health Manpower Plan, 1975; Iowa Health Manpower Plan, 1976-77; Numerous articles in the field. *Memberships:* American Society of Public Administration; Mountain Plains Meat Dealers; Denver Chamber of Commerce; Denver Athletic Club; Hospice of St John, Board Member, 1988-; Volunteer, Junior Achievement of Metro Denver, 1987-. *Honours:* Phi Beta Kappa, 1972; Pi Alpha Alpha, 1973. *Hobbies:* Swimming; Classical music; Reading; Art; Travel; Hiking. *Address:* Clinicare, 5400 N Washington St, Denver, CO 80216, USA.

ROBBINS Mary Susannah, b. 4 June 1946, Randolph, Vermont, USA. Writer; Painter. *Education:* BA, Radcliffe College, 1967; Ph.D., Boston College, 1973. *Appointments:* Copy Editor, Houghton Mifflin, 1968; Teaching Fellow, Boston College, Massachusetts, 1971-73; Assistant Professor of English, Vassar College, 1973-76; Writer, Painter, Editor, 1976-. *Creative works include:* AMELIE, book of poems and etchings, 1986; Numerous poems in national magazines; Art work in numerous shows, Boston and New York areas. *Memberships:* American Association of University Women; SANE; Sierra Club; ACLU; World Wildlife Federation. *Honours:* Ommation Press Book Prize for AMELIE, 1985. *Hobbies:* Politics, working for local, state and national Democratic candidates; Working for nuclear- free Cambridge; Organizing world's largest collection of anthropological and ethnological photographs at The Peabody Museum, Harvard; Singing; Playing the guitar. *Address:* 13 Shepard Street, Cambridge, MA 02138, USA.

ROBBINS Susan Paula, b. 15 Aug. 1948, Brooklyn, New York, USA. Associate Professor. *Education:* BA, Hamline University, 1974; MSW, University of Minnesota, 1976; DSW Tulane University, 1979. *Appointments:* Seminole Tribe of Florida, 1977-80; St Mary's Dominican College, 1978-80; University of Houston Graduate School of Social Work, 1980-. *Publications:* Articles in various journals. *Memberships:* Phi Kappa Phi; National Association of Social Workers; Council on Social Work Education; American Society of Criminology; Southern Sociological Association. *Honours:* Many honours including: Dean's Award, Liberal Arts Award, Manhattan Community College, 1972; Department Honours, Sociology, Hamline University, 1974; Outstanding Faculty, University of Houston, Graduate School of Social Work, 1988. *Hobbies:* Guitarist; Calligrapher; Photographer. *Address:* Univesity of Houston Graduate School of Social Work, Houston, TX 77004, USA.

ROBBINS WILF Marcia S, b. 22 Mar. 1949, Newark, New Jersey, USA. Assistant Adjunct Professor. m. Leonard A Wilf, 21 June 1970. 1 son. *Education:* BA, George Washington University, 1969-71; MA Educational Psychology, New York University, 1973-75; MS, Spec in Reading and Administration 1981, Dr of Education 1986, Yeshiva University. *Appointments:* Founding Board Member, Stern College for Women, New York City, 1987; Co-Chairperson, Jewish Book Festival, YM—YWHA, West Orange, New Jersey, 1987; Adjunct Professor, Middlesex County College, Middlesex, New Jersey, 1987; Visiting part-time Lecturer, Rutgers University, New Brunswick, 1988; Educational Consultant, Cranford High School, 1988; Assistant Adjunct Professor, Long Island University, 1988; Assistant Adjunct Professor, Pace University, New York City, 1988. *Creative works:* Presenter of Workshops; Article in professional journal. *Memberships:* Life Member, NY Acad of Sciences; NJ Council Teachers of English; Natl Council Teachers of English; American educationasl Research Assn; Life Member, College Reading Assn; Life Member, Phi Delta Kappa; NJ Orton Dyslexia Society. *Honours:* Professional Certificates of attendance, In-service Workshops for the Star Ledger's Newspaper in Education Program 1985 and 1986; Professional Improvement Awards (Seton-Essex Reading Council), 1985-86 and 1984-85; Co- Recipient, American Heritage Award, 1985. *Hobbies:* Reading; Theatre; Travelling; Volunteer work; Antiques. *Address:* 242 Hartshorn Drive, Short Hills, New Jersey 07078, USA.

ROBERSON Carolyn, b. 12 Jan. 1950, McComb, Mississippi, USA. Teacher. m. Sylvester Roberson, 17 June 1975. 1 daughter. *Education:* BS Business, Phy Ed, 1972; MS, Special Ed, 1978; MS, Guidance/Counseling, 1987; PhD, Loyola Chicago, 1985-continuing. *Appointments:* Teacher of MMI, 1978-79; Teacher of Severly Emotional Disturbed, 1980; Teacher of Physically Handicapped, 1980-83; Disciplinarian/Asst Prin, 1983-85; Teacher of Physically Handicapped, 1985-88. *Memberships:* PDK; AACD; ASCD. *Honours:* 2 year grant/scholarship, TEP program from the Institute for Psychoanalysis, 1982-84; Grant, University of Chicago, Teaching Science to the Handicapped, 1984-85; Departmental Scholarship, Chicago State University, Guidance and Counseling, 1986-87. *Hobbies:* Bowling; Golf; Reading. *Address:* 10216 S Lafayette, Chicago, ILL 60628, USA.

ROBERSON Paula Karen, b. 26 Nov. 1952, Memphis, USA. Biostatistician. *Education:* BS, Southern Methodist University, Dallas, 1974; PhD, Biomathematics, University of Washington, 1979. *Appointments:* Statistician, Chief Biostatistician & Data Processing Health Effects Research Lab, US Environmental Protection Agency, Cincinnati, 1979-81; St Jude Children's Research Hospital, 1982-. *Memberships:* American Statistical Association; Biometric Society; American Association for the Advancement of Science; American Society of Clinical Oncology; Society for Risk Analysis. *Hobbies Include:* Reading; Needlework. *Address:* Biostatistics & Information Systems, St Jude Children's Research Hospital, PO Box 318, Memphis, TN 38101, USA.

ROBERTS Barbara Jean Roberts, b. 28 Apr. 1934, Burley, Idaho, USA. Laboratory Material Supervisor, Biological Sciences. *Education:* BA 1969, Master of Teaching Science, Biological Sciences 1972, Idaho State University. *Appointments:* Senior Laboratory Assistant 1970-79; Laboratory Material Supervisor 1979-, Idaho State University, Pocatello. *Creative works:* Local Theatre: Annie Oakley; My Fair Lady; South Pacific; Where's Johnny? When the Showboat Came to Town; Barbershop and All that Jazz; Gallery Exhibit for National Women's History Month, 1987. *Memberships:* State of Idaho Women's Commn; National Association Sci Material Managers; Idaho Pub Employees Association (Chapter Vicepresident 1985); National Assn Female Executives; Idaho State University Professional Women; Sweet Adelines (Show and Pub Chair, 1979-80). *Honour:* Mortar Board National Academic Honor Society, 1969. *Hobbies:* Real estate investment; Travel; Barbershop music; Mediation; Theatre. *Address:* 344 No 15th, Pocatello Heights 8-B, Pocatello, Idaho 83201, USA.

ROBERTS Barbara, b. 21 Dec. 1936, Corvallis,

Oregon, USA. Secretary of State. m. Senator Frank L Roberts, 29 June 1974. 2 sons. *Appointments:* Office Manager, Accounting, 1965-75; County Commissioner, 1978; Campaign Consultant, 1979-80; State Representative, 1981- 85; House Majority Leader, 1983-85. *Publications:* Political articles: The Political Trustee; The Power and Politics of State Education Policy, ACCT Trustee, 1981-82. *Memberships:* Northwest Osteopathic Medical Foundation, Oregon Board of National Committee for Prevention of Child Abuse; Eastmoreland General Hospital Board; League of Women Voters; Oregon Fair Share; 1000 Friends of Oregon; Oregon Women's Political Caucus; National Society of Autistic Children; Oregon Environmental Council; Democratic Party National Policy Committee; Oregon YMCA Youth and Government Board of Directors. *Honours:* Civil Liberties Award for Handicapped Children, 1980, for Juvenile Rights, 1981; Community Colleges of Oregon Students' Association, 1981; President's Award, Oregon Speech & Hearing Association, 1982; Mary Rieke Award, Oregon Women's Political Caucus, 1983; Distinguished Service Award, Oregon Commission for the Handicapped, 1984. *Address:* Salem, OR 97310, USA.

ROBERTS Beverly Nance, b. 29 Apr. 1954, Newton, Massachusetts, USA. Physician. m. 16 Oct. 1976. *Education:* BA, 1976; DC, 1981; MD, 1983. *Appointments:* Washington Health Center, Washington, District of Columbia, 1983-. *Publications:* Article on Menieres disease, current treatment modalities, in Journal of Manipulative Medicine. *Memberships:* Vice-President, Mortar Board; National Women's Honour Society; Arthritis Foundation; American Holistic Health Association. *Honours:* Student Government Leadership Award, George Washington University. *Hobbies:* Tennis; Squash. *Address:* 1660 B Beekman Place NW, Washington, DC 20009, USA.

ROBERTS Beverly Randolph, b. 28 Jan. 1948, Alexandria, Louisiana, USA. Corporate Tax Manager. 1 son. *Education:* BA, Lawrence University, 1969; Accounting and Business courses, Drake University, 1972-75; Candidate, Master of Business Taxation, University of Minnesota, 1990. *Appointments:* Staff Accountant, McGladrey Hendrickson & Pullen, Des Moines, 1975-77; Audit Sr, Deloitte Haskins & Sells, Des Moines, 1977-79; Audit Manager, Coopers & Lybrand, 1979-84; Corporate Accounting Manager, Corporate Tax Manager, Tennant Company, Minneapolis, 1985-. *Memberships:* AICPA; Ruling elder and financial advisor, Faith Presbyterian Church of Minnetonka. *Honours:* Excellence in Accounting Award, Drake University, 1975; Recipient of endowed scholarship, Lawrence University; Lawrence University Honour Roll; Century Club. *Hobbies:* Stained glass; Downhill skiing; Jogging. *Address:* 3365 Shavers Lk Road, Deephaven, MN 55391, USA.

ROBERTS Elizabeth H, Podiatrist. m. Nathan Wasserheit, 22 Nov. 1951, deceased, 1 daughter. *Education:* DPM, Long Island University, College of Podiatry, 1943. *Publicaitons:* Manual of Practice Administration, 1951; On Your Feet, 1975; many articles. *Memberships:* various professional organisations. *Honours:* Fellow: American Society Podiatric Medicine, American Academy of Podiatry Administration, American Society of Podiatric Dermatology. *Hobbies:* Travel; Writing; Art. *Address:* 210 West 90th Street, New York, NY 10024, USA.

ROBERTS Irene Myrtle, b. 27 Sept. 1925, London, England. Author. m. Trevor Granville Leonard Roberts, 26 Dec. 1947, 2 sons, 1 daughter. *Appointments:* Womens Army (Land), World War II; Freelance Writer; Tutor, Creative Writing; Broadcaster. *Publications:* Author, over 100 novels including: (As Ivor Roberts): Jump into Hell, 1959; Green Hell, 1959; Trial by Water, 1960; Old Venturer, 1960; etc; (As Irene Roberts): Squirrel Walk, 1961; Shrine of Marigolds; The Lion and the Sun; Echo of Flutes; Fire Dragon; Historical Novels: The Throne of Pharaohs, 1970; Hatshepsut: Queen of the Nile, 1976; Kingdom of the Sun; Song of the Nile;

Moonpearl; Time of the Seventh Moon; Hour of the Tiger; Sea Jade; Crystal Lily. *Memberships:* Life Member, West Essex Writers; Life President, Kingsbridge Writers. *Hobbies:* Egyptology; Chinese History; Psychology; Oil Painting; Reading. *Address:* Alpha House, Higher Town, Marlborough, Nr Kingsbridge, South Devon TQ7 3RL, England.

ROBERTS Janine, b. 5 May 1947, Olympia, Washington, USA. Professor and Family Therapist. 1 daughter. *Education:* BA, University of WA, Seattle, 1970; MEd, Antioch Grad School, 1971; EdD, University of Massachusetts, Amherts, 1982. *Appointments:* Assoc Professor & Dir, Family Therapy Specialty Area, University of Massachusetts, 1982-; Consultant to various school districts & mental health clinics, 1982- . *Publications:* Editor with E Imber Black & R Whiting, Rituals in Families & Family Therapy, 1988; Published over 15 articles and chapters in various journals and books; Co-editor, Journal of Strategic & Systemic Therapies; Advisory Editor, Family Process. *Memberships:* American Family Therapy Association; American Association for Marriage & Family Therapy. *Honours:* Lilly Endowment Teaching Fellow Award, 1988-89; Junior Fellowship Award, Institute for the Advanced Study of the Humanities, 1987; American Association for Marriage & Family Therapy research award for doctoral research, 1981. *Hobbies:* Cross-cultural issues and psychotherapy; Violin; Writing poetry and fiction; All outdoor sports; Travel. *Address:* P O Box 277, 4 Maple Lane, Leverett, MA 01054, USA.

ROBERTS Joan I, b. 26 June 1935, Salt Lake City, USA. Professor; Psychologist. *Education:* BA, University of Utah, 1957; MA, 1960, EdD, 1970, Social Psychology, Columbia University. *Appointments:* Associate Professor, 1978-84, Professor, 1985-, Syracuse University. *Publications:* School Children in the Urban Slum, 1966; Group Behavior in Urban Classrooms, 1968; Scene of the Battle: Group Behavior in Urban Classrooms, 1970; Beyond Intellectual Sexism: A New Woman, A New Reality, 1976; Educational Patterns and Cultural Configurations: The Anthropology of Education, Volume 1, 1976; Schooling in the Cultural Context: Anthropological Studies of Education, Volume II, 1975; The Ethos of Learning: Culture and Education, 1989; articles in numerous journals. *Memberships Include:* American Anthropological Association; American Psychological Association; American Society for Psychical Research; Association for Women in Psychology; Association for Women in Sociology; etc. *Honours:* Recipient, honours & awards. *Address:* 235 Waring Road, Syracuse, NY 13224, USA.

ROBERTS Neva Elizabeth Brown, b. 5 Jan. 1937, Los Angeles, California, USA. City Council Member; Artist; Writer. m. 4 June 1955, div., 3 June 1986, 2 sons. *Education:* Art study, Pierce College; Religious Philosophy study, Lake Tahoe Community College. *Career includes:* Homemaking and raising family; Professional modelling; Painting; Commercial artist; Songwriter; Mayor, 1985-86, 2nd term Member, currently, City council. *Creative works include:* Paintings in LBJ Center, Austin, Texas, also in orphanages and medical institutions worldwide. *Memberships:* Board Member (or alternate): Cultural Arts Alliance; Commission on Aging; El Dorado CoTransportation Commission; Tahoe Regional Planning Agency; Chair (2nd term), Local Agency Formation Commission; CALAFCO Executive Board; Governor Deukmejian's Statewide Earthquake Task Force; Volunteer, International Book Project. *Honours:* Yearly awards for volunteerism, 1965-; Honoured for strong involvement in anti-litter and fire prevention programmes statewide, 1982-; Special Disaster training, 1985. *Hobbies:* Exploring ancient cities and sites worldwide; Flying small single-engined aircraft. *Address:* PO Box 8306, South Lake Tahoe, CA 95731, USA.

ROBERTS Priscilla S., b. 18 June 1949, Birmingham, Alabama, USA. Executive Administrator, Family Medicine. 1 son. *Education:* BS, Business Administration 1981, ABD, PhD candidate, Health

Services Administration in progress, University of Alabama; MA, Management, Birmingham Southern College, 1984. *Appointments:* Revenue Examiner, Finance Department, City of Birmingham, 1979-84; Assistant Director, Research & Grants Administration 1984-88, Executive Administrator Family Medicine 1988-, University of Alabama, Birmingham. *Memberships:* Society of Research Administrators; Medical Group Management Association. *Honours:* Scholarship, National Secretaries' Association, 1967; Biographical recognition. *Hobbies:* Piano music; Mystery & fiction novels. *Address:* 5035 LaPine Drive, Adamsville, AL 35005, USA.

ROBERTS Teri Lawless, b. 23 Jan. 1957, Marianna, Florida, USA. Computer Consultant. m. John Stanley Roberts, 12 Oct. 1985, 1 daughter. *Education:* BS, Accounting, Samford University, Alabama, 1978; MBA, University of North Florida, 1982. *Appointments:* Staff accountant 1978-79, Payroll Department Supervisor 1980, Assistant to Vice-President (Finance) 1981-83, Assistant Controller 1983-84, Florida Rock Industries; Controller, Anchor/Lith Kemko, 1984-88; Computer Consultant, Aries Software Corporation, 1988-. *Memberships:* Data Processing Management Association; Beta Gamma Sigma. *Honour:* Loren F. Fitch Scholarship, 1981. *Hobbies:* Antiques; Cooking; Pets; Public Service; Children. *Address:* PO Box 1394, Palmetto, Florida 34220, USA.

ROBERTS Willo Davis, b. 29 May 1928, Grand Rapids, Michigan, USA. Freelance Writer. m. David Roberts, 20 May 1949, 2 sons, 2 daughters. *Appointments include:* 5 years' work, hospital & doctor's surgeries; Freelance writer, 1955-. *Publications:* Over 80 books. Juvenile & Young Adult titles include: View from the Cherry Tree, 1975; Don't Hurt Laurie!, 1977; Minden Curse, 1978; Girl with Silver Eyes, 1980; Eddie & the Fairy God Puppy, 1984; Baby Sitting is a Dangerous Job, 1985; Magic Book, 1986; Nightmare, 1989. Adult titles include: Murder at Grand Bay, 1955; Return to Darkness, 1969; Shadow of Past Love, 1970; Ghosts of Harrel, 1971; Nurse Robin, 1973; White Jade, 1975; House of Imposters, 1977; Destiny's Women, 1980; Face at the Window, 1981; Sniper, 1984; My Rebel, My Love, 1986; To Share a Dream, 1986. *Memberships:* Science Fiction Writers of America; Founder NW Seattle Chapter, Past Regional Vice President, Mystery Writers of America; Society of Childrens Book Writers; Seattle Freelances; Pacific Northwest Writers Conference. *Honours:* Children's book awards including: Young Hoosier, Evansville, Georgia Children's, Young Readers of Western Australia, A Notable Children's Trade Book in the Field of Social Studies, Young Readers of California, Mark Twain, Children's Books of the Year (Library of Congress), 1980 and 1983, South Carolina Children's; Junior Literary Guild selection, 1984; Nevada Young Reader's Award; Weekly Reader Book Club, 1984; Runner-up, Texas Bluebonnet Award, 1985. Also: Achievement Award, Pacific Northwest Writers, 1986; Media award, best magazine article, American Diabetes Association, 1987; Junior Library Guild Edgar Allen Poe Award, 1988. *Hobbies:* Reading; Organ playing; Walking; Travel. *Address:* 12020 Engebretson Road, Granite Falls, Washington 98252, USA.

ROBERTS Winifred Laura, b. 16 June 1920, Dublin, Ireland. Retired Psychiatric Social Worker. *Education:* Teaching Diploma, 1946-47; Diploma in Social Sciences, 1954; Mental Health Certificate, 1959. *Appointments:* Army Welfare Woman, 1939-45; Teacher, London, England, 1947-52; Social work, University Settlement, Bristol, 1952-58; Psychiatric Social Worker: West Middlesex Hospital, 1958-65; Woodberry Down Clinic, 1965- 77; Marlborough Hospital, 1977-81; Staff Consultant, various agencies, 1981-. *Publications:* Contributor of articles to professional journals and chapters to books on Family and Group Therapy. *Memberships:* Group Analytic Society (Teacher therapist); Founder Member, Institute of Family Therapy (Teacher/Therapist); Group for Advancement in Psychotherapy in Social Work. *Hobbies:*

Gardening; Tapestry weaving and sewing; Reading. *Address:* 59 Normanby Road, Dollis Hill, London NW10 1BU, England.

ROBERTS-WRAY Mary Howard, b. 1 June 1913, Croydon, Surrey, England. m. (1)Sir Ernest Hillas Williams, 23 Feb. 1935, 1 daughter, (2)Sir Kenneth Owen Roberts-Wray, 3 Dec. 1965. *Education:* MCSP, St thomas' Hospital, London. *Address:* The Old Golf House, Forest Row, Sussex RH18 5BD, England.

ROBERTSON Barbara Anne, b. 20 July 1931, Toronto, Ontario, Canada. Writer. m. 16 May 1953, 3 daughters. *Education:* BA, Modern History, University of Toronto, 1953; MA, Canadian History, Queen's University, Kingston. *Appointments:* Tutor, Instructor, Queen's University, 1954-76; Research for Queen's University History, 1976-83. *Publications:* Compiler, with M. A. Downie, The Wind Has Wings 1968, The New Wind Has Wings 1983; Author, Wilfrid Laurier: The Great Conciliator, 1971; Co-author with M. A. Downie, The Well-Filled Cupboard, 1987. *Memberships:* Canadian Historical Association; Ontario Historical Society. *Honours:* Sir James Aikins Fellowship, Canadian history, 1954; Canada Council Explorations Award, 1972. *Hobbies:* Cooking; Gardening. *Address:* 52 Florence Street, Kingston, Ontario, Canada K7M 1Y6.

ROBERTSON Carmeta Fern Pierce Robertson, b. 22 Oct. 1926, Albany, Gentry County, Missouri, USA. Author; Genealogical Researcher; Accredited Record Technician. m. Olin E. Robertson, 17 Aug. 1946, 2 daughters. *Education:* Accredited Medical Record Technician, 1981; Licensed Emergency Medical Technician, 1981; Data Process Concept, Trenton Junior College, 1985. *Appointments:* Secretary to Prosecuting Attorney, Gentry County, Missouri, 1943-45; Supervisor, Old American Insurance Co, 1945-47; Clerk Stenographer, then Medical Record Technician II, Albany Regional Center, Missouri, 1967-82; Medical Record Consultant, Kansas City Regional Center, Missouri, 1982-83; Professional Genealogist, researching for families. *Publications:* Faith is Renewed, song, 1975; Compilation of Funeral Home Records, Gentry County, Missouri, vols I and II, 1984-85; Sturdy Pioners, poem, 1987; They Paved the Way, Gentry Country, Missouri 1800-1875, book, 1988; Currently researching for follow-up book on Gentry-Worth Counties. *Memberships:* American Medical Record Association; Missouri Historical Society; Board Member, Northwest Heritage Association; Mt Moriah Baptist Association (Clerk 1970-86); Northwest Baptist Mission Group (Committee Chair); Genealogical Chairman, Daughters of the American Revolution local chapter. *Honours:* Member, Masque and Gavel National Honour Society, 1943-44; Husband, children and self Missouri State Farm Family from Gentry County, Missouri, 1964; Member, Secretary, Committeeperson, Missouri Department of Mental Statewide Data Processing Analysis & Implementation Task Force, Albany Regional Center, 1979-81; Employee of the Year, Albany Regional Center, 1982; President, many organisations. *Hobbies:* People; Travel; Reading; Piano-playing; Choir member; Royals fan (Kansas City Baseball Club); Stimulating conversation; Church activities. *Address:* Route 5, Box 210, Ozark, MO 65721, USA.

ROBERTSON Lynne Nannen, b. 10 Sept. 1936, USA. Food Service Consultant. m. Theodore A. Robertson, 20 Dec. 1985, 2 sons. *Education:* BS, Iowa State University, 1958; MS 1966; PhD, 1978. *Appointments:* Dietitian, Stouffer Corp, Cleveland & Pittsburgh, 1958-60; Chief Dietitian, Methodist Hospital, Sioux City, 1960-64; Therapeutic Dietitian, Iowa Methodist Hospital, Des Moines, 1965-66; Dietitian, Friley Hall, Iowa State University, 1964-66; Dietary Consultant, Iowa Department of Health, 1966-70; Co-ordinator, Instruction, Nutrition & Dietics, University of Missouri Medical Centre, Columbia, 1970-71; Instructor, Food Service Programmes, Des Moines Area Community College, Ankeny, 1971-72, Director, Food Services, 1972-76; Supervisor, Business Enterprises, Iowa Community for Blind, 1976-78; Assistant Director,

Dietetics, Iowa Methodist Medical Centre, 1978- 79; President, Creative Concepts, Ankeney, 1979-. *Publications:* Home Study Course on Modified Diets, 1967; Home Study Course on Work Simplification, 1968; Home Study Course on Food Purchasing, 1969; Programme Instruction in Work Simplification, 1971; Food Service Equipment: Selection & Layout, 1973; Programmed Instruction in Work Simplification, Spanish, 1975; Metric Measurement in Food Preparation & Service, 1978; Food Service Equipment, 3rd edition 1988; Purchasing in Food Service:Individualised Instruction, 1984; contributor to numerous journals and magazines. *Memberships:* Many professional organisations. *Honours:* Recipient, various awards. *Address:* 814 SE Sherman Dr., Ankeney, IA 50021, USA.

ROBINETTE Sheree, b. 3 Dec. 1957, Tampa, Florida, USA. Commercial Building Contractor. *Education:* BA, University South Florida, 1980. *Appointments:* Manager, Fontaine Sujpply, 1977-80; Owner/Manager, Tampa Accessory Inc, 1980-. *Memberships:* Nat Assn Women in Constrn; Nat Society Professional Estimators; Construction Trade Assoc. *Hobbies:* Antiques; Ballet; Cycling; Gardening; Pets. *Address:* 4725 Traverline Drive, Tampa, FL 33615, USA.

ROBINS Deborah, b. 14 Nov. 1956, Miami, Florida, USA. Film Producer. *Education:* BA, Kenyon College, 1978. *Appointments:* Worked for Ladd Company, 1980-82; LeVine-Robins Productions (independent company formed Jan. 1982), 1982-83; Fries Entertainment, 1983-85; Dick Clark Productions, 1985-. *Creative Works include:* Samaritan-The Mitch Snyder Story, produced by LeVine-Robins Productions for CBS TV. *Address:* c/o Dick Clark Productions, 3003 W Olive Avenue, Burbank, CA 91505, USA.

ROBINSON Ann Elisabeth, b. 9 Apr. 1933, Essex, England. Public Servant; Former Toxicologist. m. (1) Dr Richard George Lingard, 1960. (2) Professor Francis Edward Camps, 1972, both deceased. *Education:* BPharm, Honours, 1955, PhD 1958, University of London. *Appointments:* Assistant Lecturer, Lecturer, Pharmaceutical Chemistry, Chelsea College, 1957-64; Lecturer, Senior Lecturer, Forensic Medicine, London Hospital Medical College, 1964-77; Chief Occupational Health Laboratory, Consultant in Toxicology, Ontario Ministry of Labour, Canada, 1978-80; Assistant Deputy Minister 1980-87, Science Policy Adviser, 1987-, Occupational & Environmental Health & Safety, Ontario Minsitry of Labour. *Creative Works:* Numerous publications in scientific journals; Co-editor, 3rd edition Gradwohl's Legal Medicine, 1976. *Memberships:* Chemical Institute of Canada; Royal Society of Chemistry, UK; Medicolegal Society of London; Royal Institution of Great Britain; Association of Chemical Profession of Ontario; British Academy of Forensic Science, Executive Council, 1971-77; American Academy of Forensic Sciences, Programme Chairman, 1979-80; Governor, Canadian Centre for Occupational Health & Safety, 1980-88; Royal Commonwealth Society, Toronto Section; Soroptimist International of Toronto, Director 1983-85, President, 1985-87. *Honours:* Adjunct Professor, University of Toronto, 1979-. *Address:* 80 Quebec Avenue, No 601,Toronto, Ontario, Canada M6P 4B7.

ROBINSON Ethel Luvenia Sands, b. 20 Aug. 1948, Chicago, Illinois, USA. Officer, US Air Force. m. Clarence J Robinson. *Education:* BA, Fine Arts 1970, MLS, Library Science 1971, MA, Counseling 1975, University of Maryland; Officer Training, Commission, 1982. *Appointments:* Arts Specialist, Natl Endowment for the Arts, 1979-81; Chief, Personnel Utilization 1982-83, Senior Instructional Analyst 1983-85, Career Field Manager 1985-, USAF. *Publication:* Glossary of Military Training Terms, 2nd Edition, Editor. *Memberships:* Natl Society for Perf & Instruction Toastmaster, Admin Vice Pres; National Council of Negro Women, Treasurer; National Assoc of Female Executives; Air Force Association; Kappa Delta Pi Educational Organization. *Honours:* Air Force Commendation Medal, 1986;

Company Grade Officer of the Quarter, 1985; Air Force Achievement Medal, 1982. *Hobbies:* Antiques and collectibles; Performing arts; Public speaking. *Address:* 3402 Meadow Head, Cibolo, Texas 78108, USA.

ROBINSON Geraldine Marlene Helwing, b. 5 Apr. 1947, Milwaukee, Wisconsin, USA. Psychologist; Psychoanalyst. m. Ian Robinson, 23 June 1969. 3 daughters. *Education:* BS Psychology 1965-70, MS School Psy 1970-75, University Wis-Stout, Menomonie; Interpersonal Sullivanian Psychoanalytic Preceptorship with J M Tobin, MD, 1970-78. *Appointments:* Northwest Psychiatric Clinic, Eau Claire, 1974-77; Adjunct Assistant Professor, St Mary's Graduate College, Department of Counseling and Psychological Services, Minneapolis, 1977-78; Private Practice, Psychology, 1978-80; Partner, Institute for Psychological Therapies, 1980-84; Owner, Psychol practice, Robinson & Association, 1984-88; Co-owner, VP, computer software manufaturing company, Interactive Analytic Node, 1985-87. *Publications:* Author of numerous papers to professional journals and presentations to conferences. *Memberships include:* GWAN, Group-Without-A-Name 1973-; International Association for Infant Mental Health, 1985-, Board of Directors, 1988-; Minnesota Psychological Association, 1985-87; Minnesota Women Psychologists; Midwest Association for Comatose Care, 1985-87; International Society for Human Ethology 1985-; Clan Gunn Society of N America. *Hobbies:* Tae Kwondo Karate (red belt); Painting; Music; Geneaology; Writing. *Address:* Bellevue, Washington, USA.

ROBINSON Jancis Mary, b. 22 Apr. 1950, Carlisle, England. Writer; Broadcaster. m. Nicholas Lander, 22 Oct. 1981. 1 son, 1 daughter. *Education:* MA, Maths and Philosophy, St Anne's College, Oxford, 1968-71. *Appointments:* Editor, Wine & Spirit; Haymarket Publishing, 1975-80; Wine Writer, Sunday Times, 1980-86; Wine Correspondent, Evening Standard, 1987-88. *Publications:* The Wine Book, 1979; Which? Wine Guide 1981, 1980; Which? Wine Guide 1982, 1981; The Great Wine Book, 1982; Masterglass - a practical course in testing wine, 1983; How to Choose and Enjoy Wine, 1984; Vines, Grapes and Wines, 1986; Jancis Robinson's Food and Wine Adventures, 1987; The Demon Drink, 1988. Television: Presenter/Writer of 3 series of The Wine Programme, 1983, 1985, 1987; Presenter, Jancis Robinson's Christmas Wine List, 1985; Commentary writing and narration for BBC2's 40 Minutes on nuclear dumps, 1986; Presenter of the BBC Design Awards, 1986-87; Narrator of Design Classics, BBC2, 1987; Presenter and writer of Jancis Robinson Meets..11 half-hour personal profile programmes for Thames Television, 1987. Contributor to professional journals and newspapers. *Membership:* Master of Wine (Member of the Institute of Masters of Wine). *Honours:* Winner, Wine and Spirit Education Trust's two-year Diploma exams, 1978; Second woman to be made a member of the medieval Jurade de St Emilion, France, 1983; Glenfiddich Award, 1983; Overall Glenfiddich Trophy winner, Wine and Food writer/broadcaster of the year, 1984; Winner, Marques de Caceres Award, 1985; Glenfiddich Wine Writer of the Year and Glenfiddich Food Writer of the Year, 1986; Winner of the Wine Guild of the United Kingdom Premier Award, 1986; Winner of the Andre Simon Memorial Award, 1987; Winner of the Wine Guild Award, 1987; Winner of Clicquot Book of the Year, USA, 1987. *Hobbies:* Wine; Food; Words. *Address:* 24 Belsize Lane, London NW3 5AB, England.

ROBINSON Joyce Lilieth, b. 2 July 1925, St Elizabeth, Jamaica. Managing Director, Human Employment and Resource Training (HEART) Trust. m. Professor Leslie Robinson, 15 Jan. 1957. 1 son, 1 daughter. *Education:* St Simon's College, Kingston, Jamaica, 1938-44; ALA 1954, FLA 1959, North Western Polytechnic, London, England; Doctor of Laws (Honorary) Dalhousie University, Nova Scotia, Canada, 1979. *Appointments:* Duirector, Jamaica Library Service, 1957-73; Director, JAMAL Foundation, 1973-81; General Manager, JBC, 1981-82; Managing

Director, HEART Trust, 1982-. *Publications:* Rural Library Development in Jamaica, UNESCO Bulletin for Libraries, 1967 and 1973; Libraries in Jamaica, Encyclopaedia of Library and Information Science; Co-Author, Jamaica Library Service: 21 years of Progress in Pictures, 1948-1969, 1972; Public Libraries with Special Reference to the Commonwealth Caribbean area, Libraries and the Challenge of Change; The Jamaican Situation, National and International Library Planning; The JAMAL Experience - Technology in Basic Adult Education, Report on Caribbean Sub- Regional Seminar; Continuing Education for New Literates - With Reference to the Jamaica Experience, paper presented at the Commonwealth Specialist Conference on Non-Formal Education in New Delhi, 1979; The Planning and Organization of Literacy Programmes. *Memberships:* Vice President, International Council on Adult Education; Honorary Vice President, The Library Association, (Great Britain). *Honours:* MBE 1959, Silver Musgrave Medal, Institute of Jamaica, 1970; Commander, Order of Distinction, 1975; Carl Milan Lecture Award (American Library Association), 1979; Woman of Distinction (Bureau of Women's Affairs, Jamaica), 1985; Odrer of Jamaica, equivalent to the English Dame, addressed as Dr. the Honourable, 1987. *Hobbies:* Gardenuing; Interior Decorating; Reading; Cooking; Education; Librarianship. *Address:* c/o The Human Employment and Resource Training (HEART) Trust, 4 Park Boulevard, Kingston 5, Jamaica.

ROBINSON June, b. 6 Dec. 1957, Syracuse, New York, USA. Communications Consultant. *Education:* BA magna cum laude, honours, University of Vermont, 1979; MPPM, Yale School of Organization and Management, 1986. *Appointments:* Public Affairs, Canadian Consulate General, Boston, Massachusetts, 1979-84; Marketing Research, Genesys Software Systems Inc, 1986-88; Communications Consultant, The Wyatt Company, 1988-. *Memberships:* Greater Boston OD Network; Human Resource Systems Professionals, Board Member 1987-89, National Editorial Board 1989-. *Honours:* Outstanding Senior of French Department, University of Vermont, 1978; Phi Beta Kappa, 1978; Member of the Year, Human Resource Systems Professionals, 1989. *Hobbies:* Calligraphy; Quilting; Amateur bassoonist; Contio dancing. *Address:* 12 Derby Street, Waltham, MA 02154, USA.

ROBINSON Linda Gosden, b. 10 Jan. 1953, Los Angeles, California, USA. Communications Company Executive. m. (1) Stephen M. Dart, div. June 1977, (2) James Dixson Robinson III, 27 July 1984. *Education:* University of California, Los Angeles, 1970-72; BA summa cum laude, Psychology, University of Southern California, Los Angeles, 1978. *Appointments:* Deputy Press Secretary, Reagan Presidential Campaign, Los Angeles, California, 1979; Press Secretary, Director of Public Relations, Republican National Committee, Washington DC, 1979-80; Director of Public Affairs, US Department of Transportation, Washington DC, 1981-83; Partner, Public and Government Affairs, Heron, Burchette, Ruckert & Rothwell, Washington DC, 1983; Senior Vice-President, Corporate Affairs, Warner Amex Cable Communications, New York City, 1983-86; Deputy to Special Envoy, Office of the President, New York City, 1985; President, Chief Executive Officer, Robinson, Lake, Lerer & Montgomery, New York City, 1986-; Board of Directors: SmithKline Beckman, Philadelphia, Pennsylvania; Coro Foundation, New York City; Bozell, Jacobs, Kenyon & Eckhardt, New York City; Andrews Group, New York City. *Memberships:* Women Achievers Academy; National Women's Economic Council; YWCA; Phi Beta Kappa; Delegate, Republican National Convention, 1985. *Hobbies:* Horse showing; Tennis; Golf. *Address:* Robinson, Lake, Lerer & Montgomery, 75 Rockefeller Plaza, New York, NY 10019, USA.

ROBINSON Margaret Ruth, b. 27 July 1918, Dunedin, New Zealand. Retired. m. (1)Reuben Alfred Lockett, 10 Aug. 1940. (2)William Eric Robinson, 27 Mar. 1986. *Creative works:* Spent working lifetime helping elderly in their own homes; Convenor, Meals-on-Wheels since its inception in Riverton in 1963; Secretary/Treasurer, Local Hospital Mobile Schop Committee since its inception, 1977-. *Memberships:* Womens' Division Federated Farmers, all offices at Branch Level, mostly Treasurer, now Life Member; Elder, Riverton Union Parish Church. *Honour:* Life Membership, WDFF, 1975. *Hobby:* Stamp collecting (very small way). *Address:* 27A James Street, Riverton, Southland, New Zealand.

ROBINSON Rob, b. 17 June 1955, Chicago, Illinois, USA. Publishing Executive; Regional Sales Manager. *Education:* BA, Northern Illinois University, 1977. *Appointments:* Account Executive, Meldrum and Fewsmith, 1978-81; Sales Representative, Jack O'Grady, Inc, 1981; Sales Representative, Leigh Comm, Inc, 1982; Midwest Sales Representative, Modern Metals Pub Co, 1982-83; Regional Sales Manager, Morgan-Grampian Pub Co, 1983- 86; Regional Sales Manager, Cahners Pub Co, 1986-. *Memberships:* Electronic Young Tigers; Officer, SMTA/Chicago, 1986; Board of Directors, Women in Electronics, 1985; American Advertising Fedeeration, Board of Directors, 1981, Executive Committee, 1981; Women's Ad Club of Chjicago, Co- chairman, 1982, ADDY Committee and Officer, Board of Directors, 1980; B/PAA, Chicago Chapter; Chicago Area Runners Association. *Hobbies:* Competitive long distance running; Tennis; Horseback riding; Cycling; Native American Indian art; Native American art; Photography; Painting; Drawing; Writing. *Address:* 200 North Arlington Heights Road, Arlington Heights, IL 60004, USA.

ROBINSON-MCAULEY Marygrace, b. 2 July 1935, Jersey City, New Jersey, USA. Psychotherapist; Psychoeducator. m. William Albert Robinson, 1 July 1972. 2 sons. *Education:* BS, Sociology, Spring Hill College, Mobile, Alabama, 1965; MSW, Catholic University of America, 1967; Graduate Studies, Dr Mary Bowen, 1967; Postgraduate studies with Virginia Satir, 1969- 88; PhD, Seton Hall Univ, South Orange, NJ, 1990. *Appointments:* Child & Family Service, Mobile, Alabama, 1969-72; Children's Psychiatric Center, New Jersey, 1972-73; Children's Services, Mount Carmel Guild, NJ, 1973; Psychotherapy/Psychoeducation, Director, Monarch Seminars & Family Training Institute, 1973-. *Publications:* Home therapy with Families, 1969-70; Alternative to Institutionalization of an Autistic Child, 1971. *Memberships:* American Association of Marriage & Family Therapy;. American Assoc of OrthoPsychiatry; Fellow, Internat Assoc of Social- Psychiatry; Fellow, National Association of Social Workers; American Psychological Association; Academy of Certified Social Workers. *Address:* P O Box 378, Maplewood, NJ 07040, USA.

ROBISON Barbara Jane, b. 17 Oct. 1924, Brooklyn, New York, USA. Tax manager. m. Morris M Robison, 30 Aug. 1945, 1 daughter. *Education:* BSc., Ohio State University, Columbus, 1945; MBA, Xavier University, 1976; CPA Certification, 1982. *Appointments:* Office Manager, Master Distr. Inc., 1951-56; Treasurer, Antlab Inc., 1956-69; Tax Accountant, 1969-76, Tax Manager, 1976-, AccuRay Corp. *Memberships:* American Institute CPA's; Ohio Society of CPA's; American Society Women Accountants, President 1978-79; Columbus Chapter, American Payroll Association. *Address:* 1888 Jewett Road, Powell, OH 43065, USA.

ROBISON Judy Kay, b. 26 Mar. 1947, Rosebud, Texas, USA. Nursing Home Administrator. m. (1) James Harold Cunningham, 19 Mar. 1971, divorced 1976, 1 daughter. (2) Donnie Ray Robison, 20 Dec. 1976, divorced 1982. *Education:* AAS, McLennan Community College, 1980. *Appointments:* Designer Green Flower Shop, Rosebud, 1961-65; Executive Secretary, Gary Job Corps Ctr, San Marcos, Texas, 1965-74; Assistant Administrator 1975-77, Administrator 1977-82, Rosebud Med Services; Community Administrator, Hosp Assn of Texas, Inc, Rosebud, 1982-; Adv Board, Foodservice Research Center, 1984, Temple Jr College Texas, 1982, 1985; TV Telethon Coordinator, Easter Seal

Soc, 1985; Advisory Board, R-L Independent School District, 1979-. *Membership:* American Coll Nursing Home Administrators. *Honour:* Friend to Education Award, Texas State Teacher's Association, Falls County. *Hobbies:* Music; Horticulture; Tennis; Skiing; Dancing. *Address:* 503 E Ave G, Rosebud, TX 76570, USA.

ROBLES Marisa, b. 4 May 1937, Madrid, Spain. Concert Harpist. m. (1) Clyde S. Harvey, 1960 (div. 1967), 1 son, (2) Christopher Hyde-Smith, 1968 (div. 1984), 1 son, 1 daughter, (3) David Bean, 1985. *Education:* Madrid National School; Honours, Royal Madrid Conservatoire, 1958; Honours, Royal College of Music, UK, 1973. *Appointments:* Concert harpist: Tours, Europe, UK, Australia, Japan, South America, USA, Canada, numerous solo appearances with orchestras & in recitals. Also: Professor of Harp, Royal Madrid Conservatoire 1958-60, Royal College of Music 1971-. *Creative works include:* Recordings: Rodrigo's Concerto de Aranjuez; Moreno Buendia's Suite Concertante; Harp Music of France; Harp Music of Spain; Clair de Lune, Music of Debussy; 18th Century Harp Concerti; Mozart's Flute & Harp Concerto (various labels). *Memberships:* UK Harp Association; Royal Overseas League; Vice Chair, International Harp Competition, Israel; Anglo-Spanish Club. *Honours include:* Fellow, Royal College of Music, 1983. *Hobbies:* Gardening; Theatre; Indoor plants; Family times in general. *Address:* 38 Luttrell Avenue, London SW15 6PE, England.

ROCHA Marilyn Eva, b. 23 Oct. 1928, San Bernardino, California, USA. Clinical Psychologist. m. hilario V Rocha, 25 Mar. 1948, deceased, 1 son, 3 daughters. *Educaiton:* AA, Criminal Justice, 1970; BA, Psychology, 1973; MA, Psychology, 1974; PhD, Clinical Psychology, 1981. *Appointments:* Home Teacher for Physically Ill Children, 1956-68; Police Dispatcher, Matron, 1968-75; Psychologist, United States Navy Drug Rehabilitation Centre, 1975-85; Clinical Psychologist, California Youth Authority Northern Reception Centre Clinic. *Publications:* Poetry; short story for reading-disabled juveniles. *Memberships:* American Psychological Association; California State Psychological Association; 4-H Leader; Cub Scout Den Mother. *Honours:* Life Member, California Scholarship Federation, 1946; Honorary Life Member, PTA, 1961. *Hobbies:* Gardening; Tennis; Reading; Creative Writing; 8 Grandchildren; Travel; New Learning. *Address:* 4919 Gastman Way, Fair Oaks, CA 95628, USA.

ROCK Patricia Jean, b. 19 Aug. 1947, London, England. Consultant; Trainer on Disability Issues. *Education:* Hillcroft College for Women, Surrey, 1970-71; BA (Hons) University of Keele, Staffs, 1976; PhD, University of London, pending. *Appointments:* Secretarial jobs, 1965-78; DIG Advisor on disability benefits, 1978; Director CAP, St Georges Hosp Medical School, 1981; Research & Information London Team on Disability, 1986; Adviser on discrimination and disability, BBC CPU, 1988; Self employed Consultant and Trainer on disability, 1989-. *Memberships:* Founder SAD, Sisters Against Disablement; Community Aide Programme; Joint Founder, Lesbian Housing Trust Rock October Women's Trust. *Honours:* Snowdon Award, 1987; Gold Medalist Swimming Commonwealth Games, Scotland, 1969. *Hobbies:* Disability activist; Lesbian organisations especially for women with disabilities; Dreams interpretation; Women's movement; Feminist writings; Old movies. *Address:* Welwyn Garden City, Herts AL7 1QW, England.

ROCKELMAN Georgia Fowler Benz, b. 7 June 1920, Jefferson City, USA. Retail Furniture Executive. m. Elvin J. Rockelman, 11 Nov. 1940, 1 daughter. *Education:* BSc., 1964, MA, 1977, Lincoln University. *Appointments:* Benz Enerprises; Benz Rent-A-Ford; Benz Furniture; Benz Wood Products; Partner, Benz Furniture, 1960-74; Vice President, Secretary, Benz-Rockelman Ltd., 1974-. *Memberships:* Lutheran PTA; PTA Council. *Hobbies:* Antiques; Organisatironal Civic Activities. *Address:* 121 W. Dunklin St., Jefferson City, MO 65101, USA.

ROCKWELL Sally Jean, b. 23 Feb. 1933, Astoria, Oregon, USA. Nutritionist; Author; Teacher. m. (1) Elliot Fallis, 16 Oct. 1952, div. 1962, (2) Donald Rockwell, 13 Oct. 1966, div. 1968. 2 sons, 1 daughter. *Education:* BSc, Nutrition, University of Washington, 1981; PhD studies, Union Graduate School, Cincinnati, Ohio, 1986-. *Appointments include:* Various employment, 1951-75; Teacher, University of Washington, City University, community events, J. B. Naturopathic College, 1981-; Consultant, Alaska Indians, Oregon State Mental Health, 1981-; Self-employed counsellor, 1981-; Owner/Manager, Diet Design. *Creative works:* Rotation Game; Coping with Candida, cookbook & audiotape; Allergy Free Recipe Book; Editor, Allergy Alert newsletter; Conquering Allergies, audiotape; Rotation Diets, videotape. *Memberships:* American Academy of Environmental Medicine; American Academy of Otolaryngic Allergy; Pan American Allergy Society; American Holistic Medical Association; International Academy of Preventive Medicine; National Health Federation. *Honours:* Scholarships: Soroptomists 1976, Valley General Hospital 1978, University of Washington 1980; Business Woman of Month, Women's Business Exchange, 1985; Nominee, Nellie Cashman Award, Women Entrepreneurs Network. *Hobbies:* Writing; Dance; Recipe development; Personal growth; Education; Outdoor recreation. *Address:* 4703 Stone Way North, Seattle, Washington 98103, USA.

RODANO Maria Lisa Cinciari, b. 21 Jan. 1921, Rome, Italy. Member, European Parliament. m. Franco Rodano, 13 Feb. 1943, died 1983, 3 sons, 2 daughters. *Appointments:* Town Counsellor, Rome, 1946-56; Member, Chamber of Deputies, Rome, 1948-68; Vice Chairman, Chamber of Deputies, 1963- 68; Senator, 1968-72; Provincial Counsellor, Rome, 1969-79; MEP, 1979-. *Memberships:* President, Union of Italian Women, 1955-59. *Address:* Via IV Novembre 149, Rome 00187, Italy.

RODDENBERRY Bonnie Lindquist, b. 26 June 1948, Lafayette, Indiana, USA. Attorney. m. Stephen K Roddenberry, 12 June 1971. 3 sons. *Education:* BA, Phi Beta Kappa, Wellesley College, 1970; Cum laude, Harvard Law School, 1973. *Appointments:* Cravath, Swaine & Moore, New York, 1973-78; Morgan, Lewis & Bockius, Miami, 1978-80; Sole practitioner, 1980-. *Publications:* Chapter on Corporate Dissolutions in Florida Corporations, 1985; New Florida Uniform Limited Partners Act, 1986. *Memberships:* Chairman Corporations Committee, Florida Bar, 1984-86; Secretary, Wellesley Club of Miami, 1989-90; Director, Harvard Club of Miami, 1981-85; President elect, Harvard Law School Association of Florida. *Hobbies:* Reading; Tennis; Water skiing; Interior design; Painting. *Address:* 14140 S W 69th Avenue, Miami, Florida 33158, USA.

RODGERS Catherine Anne, b. 26 Mar. 1955, Chicago, Illinois, USA. Corporation Manager; Hazard Management Specialist. m. Steven Edward Emick, 5 June 1982, 1 daughter. *Education:* BA, Physical Education, University of California State, Chico, 1976; MA, Hazard Management, University of California State, 1978; MBA, Management and Finance, Golden Gate University, 1984; Postgraduate studies, University of Santa Clara, 1987-; Certified Paramedic; Licensed Teacher, California. *Appointments:* Research Assistant in Neuroanatomy, National Institute of Health, Bethesda, Maryland, 1974; Paramedic, Butte County, Chico, California, 1977; Instructor, Butte (California) Junior College, 1978; Safety Engineer, 1978-80; Emergency Response Manager, 1980-82, 2nd Level Hazard Manager, 1982-84, Manager, Site Chemical Operations, 1984-85, IBM Corporation, San Jose, California; Programme Manager, Corporate Headquarters, IBM Corporation, Purchase, New York, 1985-86; Vice-President, Seecar Inc, Morgan Hill, California, 1986-. *Memberships:* Chairman, Government's Earthquake Preparedness Task Force Office of Emergency Services, Sacramento, 1976-87; Board of Director, ARC; Santa Clara County Disaster Preparedness for Business and Industry, 1985;

Instructor, American Red Cross and American heart Association, Los Altos, California, 1972-78; American Society for Industrial Security; Aircraft Owners and Pilots Association; National Association of Female Executives. *Honours:* Woman of the Year, Santa Clara County, 1983. *Hobbies:* Flying; Skiing; Riding; Softball. *Address:* 1010 East Street, Morgan Hill, CA 95037, USA.

RODMAN Cynthia W. (Cyndie), b. 21 Feb. 1960, Norfolk, Virginia, USA. Marketing Executive. *Education:* AB, Psychobiology, Mount Holyoke College, 1982. *Appointments:* Brand Assistant, 1982-83, Assistant Brand Manager, 1983-85, Procter & Gamble Co; Product Manager, 1985-87, Group Product Manager, 1987-89, Marketing Director, 1989-, Kellogg Co. *Memberships:* Mount Holyoke College Club of Cincinnati (Admissions Representative 1983- 85); Secretary, Mount Holyoke College Club of Western Michigan. *Hobbies:* Tennis; Crafts; Swimming; Skating; Reading; Volunteer work. *Address:* 3704 Tartan Circle, Portage, MI 49002, USA.

RODMAN Sue A., b. 1 Oct. 1951, Fort Collins, Colorado, USA. Arts & Crafts Company Executive. m. 13 Dec. 1970, 1 daughter. *Education:* Colorado State University, 1970-73. *Appointments:* Silversmith, Pinel Silver Shop, Loveland, Colorado, 1970-71; Assistant Manager, Travelling Traders, Phoenix, Arizona, 1974-75; Co-Owner, Co-Manager 1975-85, Executive Vice President 1985-, Deer Track Traders (wholesale American Indian arts & crafts). *Publication:* Book of Contemporary Indian Arts & Crafts. *Memberships:* Indian Arts & Crafts Association; National Association of Female Executives; Civil Air Patrol; International Platform Association. *Honours:* Scholarship, Beta Loveland Women's Club, 1969; Gordon M. Walker Aviation Memorial Flight Scholarship, Valley Airpark Inc, 1970. *Hobbies:* Museums; Recreational research; Fashion design; Reading; Flying (private pilot). *Address:* PO Box 448, Loveland, Colorado 80539, USA.

RODRIGUEZ Judith Catherine, b. 13 Feb. 1936, Perth, Western Australia. Writer; Lecturer. m. (1) Fabio Rodriguez, 1 July 1964, 1 son, 3 daughters, (2) Thomas Shapcott, 11 Oct. 1982. *Education:* BA Honours, University of Queensland, 1957; BA Honours 1962, MA, University of Cambridge, UK; Certificate of Education, University of London, 1968. *Appointments:* Lecturer in English, University of West Indies, Jamaica 1963-65, St Mary's College of Education, Twickenham, UK 1966-68; Lecturer, then Senior Lecturer, La Trobe University (Australia) 1969-85, Macquarie University 1985, West Australian Institute of Technology 1986, Macarthur Institute of Higher Education 1987; Royal Melbourne Institute of Technology, 1988; Lecturer in Writing, 1989-; Poetry Editor, Penguin Books Australia Limited, 1990-. *Publications:* Nu-Plastik Fanfare Red, 1973; Water Life 1976, Shadow on Glass 1978, Mudcrab at Gambaros 1980, with own linocuts; Witch Heart, 1982; Editor & introduction, Mrs Noah & the Minoan Queen, 1983; House by Water: New & Selected Poems, 1988. *Memberships:* Past Executive, Australian Society of Authors; South Pacific Association for Commonwealth Language & Literature Studies; Association for Study of Australian Literature; International P.E.N., Executive Committee 1984-85, President 1990. *Honours:* Travelling scholarship, 1962; South Australian Biennial Award, 1978; Shell/Artlook Award, 1980; Poetry prize, PEN, 1981; Writing fellowships, Australia Council Literature Board, 1974, 1978, 1983; Writer in Residence, USA 1986, Australia 1988. *Hobbies:* Print making; Chamber music. *Address:* Ormond College, Parkville, Victoria 3052, Australia.

ROE Marion Audrey, b. 15 July 1936. Parliamentary Under Secretary of State, Department of the Environment, 1987-88. m. James Kenneth Roe, 1958, 1 son, 2 daughters. *Appointments:* Member, Conservative, Bromley Borough Council, 1975-78, for Ilford N, GLC, 1977-86; Parliamentary Private Secretary to: Parliamentary Under-Secretary of State for Transport, 1985; Minister of State for Transport, 1986, Secretary of State for Transport, 1987. *Memberships:* President, Womens National Cancer Control Campaign,

1985- 87; Patron, UK National Committee for UN Development Fund for Women, 1985-88. *Address:* House of Commons, London SW1A 0AA, England.

ROEBLING Mary G., b. Collingswood, New Jersey, USA. Banker. m. Seigfreid Roebling, 1 son, 1 daughter. *Education:* University of Pennsylvania; New York University. *Appointments:* President, Trenton Trust Company, 1937, President and/or Chairman, 1937-72; Chairman, National State Bank (into which Trenton Trust Company was merged), 1972-84; Chairman Emeritus of National State Bank, 1984-; Chairman Emeritus, The Women's Bank, NA, Denver, Colorado, 1984. *Publications:* Contributor to Edgar Scott's How to Lay a Nest Egg, 1950, Michigan Business Review, 1972; Chemtech, Feb. 1974. *Memberships:* American, New Jersey and Mercer County Bankers Associations; Trustee, US Council, International Chamber Commerce; Founding President, US Army War College Foundation; Civilian Aide to the Secretary of the Army for First Army Area, Emeritus. *Honours:* International Boss of the Year, National Secretaries Association; Commendatore, Order of the Star of Solidarity, president of Italy; Royal Order of Vasa, HM The King of Sweden; Department of Defense Medal for Distinguished Public Service, Art and Antique Buttons. *Address:* 120 Sanhican Dr., Trenton, NJ 08618, USA.

ROEMBACH-CLARK Jeanine Louise, b. 24 June 1952, Wichita, Kansas, USA. Child Psychiatrist. m. Gregory Darwin Roembach-Clark, 4 Dec. 1976, 1 son, 2 daughters. *Education:* MD, University of Kansas School of Medicine, 1975; Candidate, Topeka Institute for Psychoanalysis; Diplomate in General and Child Psychiatry, American Board of Psychiatry and Neurology. *Appointments:* Staff Child Psychiatrist, Children's Division, Assistant Director of Preschool Day Treatment Center, Supervisor, Karl Menninger School of Psychiatry, Menninger Foundation, 1982-. *Hobbies:* Music; Needlework; Cooking; Poetry; Environmental conservation; Child welfare and education. *Address:* PO Box 829, Topeka, KS 66601, USA.

ROENISH Dana, b. 12 Dec. 1955, New Brunswick, New Jersey, USA. Office Manager; Real Estate Agent. *Education:* Graduate, Professional School of Business, Union, New Jersey, 1986; Studying currently, CPS Rating (Certified Professional Secretary), Current Licensed Real Estate Agent. *Appointments:* Various positions, Middlesex County Civil Service System, New Brunswick, 1974-76; COB & No Fault Claims Examiner, New Jersey Blue Cross & Blue Shield, 1976-81; Executive Secretary, Action Temps Inc, 1981-82; Northeastern/Southeastern Regional Sales Assistant, Osborne Computer Corp, 1982-83; Northcentral Regional Sales Assistant, Fujitsu Microsystems of America, 1984-86; Real Estate Agent, Sun Realty, 1986-88; Office Administrator, Rothe-Johnson Associates, 1986-88; Real Estate Agent, Century 21-Golden Post Realty, 1988-; Office Manager, Metropolitan Glass Co Inc, 1988-. *Memberships:* Ambassadors for Friendship, 1974; National Association for Female Executives; New Jersey Society of Architectural Administrators; National Society of Architectural Administrators; Middlesex & Somset County Boards of Realtors: Sweet Adelines/Harmony International. *Hobbies:* Professional singing; Guitar; Piano; Reading; Tutoring math. *Address:* 260 Grant Avenue, Piscataway, New Jersey 08854, USA.

ROETTGER Dorye, b. 22 Oct. 1932, Utica, New York, USA. Creative Analyst. *Education:* B.Mus., University Extension Conservatory, Chicago, 1955; PhD, University of Eastern Florida, 1972. *Appointments:* Founder, Executive Director, Festival Players of California, 1957-; Freelance Writer, 1962; Professional Speaker, 1971-; Creative Analyst, 1985-. *Publications:* Editor, Independent News Bureau, 1967-; articles in professional journals; Syndicated Column, Bridging the Culture Gap; Author, Beyond Performance in Royal Publishing anthology, Creative Innovators, 1988. *Memberships:* National Speakers Association; National Writers Club; Nonprofit Management Association; Public Interest Radio & TV Educational Society;

American Council for the Arts. *Honours:* Recipient, various honours and awards. *Hobbies:* Folk Dancing; Travel; Animals. *Address:* 3809 DeLongpre Avenue, Los Angeles, CA 90027, USA.

ROFHEART Eleanor Frances, b. 13 June 1928, New York City, USA. Educational Consultant; Law Student. m. Norman H Rofheart, 3 June 1931, divorced 1979, 1 son, 1 daughter. *Education:* BS, Fordham University, 1950; MS, 1965, EdD, 1984, Hofstra University. *Appointments:* Elementary School Principal, North Merrick, 1976-84; Superintendent of Schools, Woodbridge Ct., 1984-85; Educational Consultant, 1985-. *Publications:* The Role of Physical Attractiveness in Selection of White Femals for Elementary Secondary School Principalships in New York State, Dissertation. *Memberships:* American Bar Associatiron; Association of Trail Lawyers of America; Phi Delta Kappa; National Organization for Women; National Network of Hispanic Women; etc. *Honours:* Distinguished Service Award, Phi Delta Kappa; Hofstra University Fellowship; Harvard University, Summer Fellowhsip; etc. *Hobbies:* Balletomane; Jazz; Singer; Tennis; Reading. *Address:* 412 N. Kenwood No 204, Glendale, CA 91206, USA.

ROGERS Brenda Mary (Lady), m. Sir Philip James Rogers, CBE, 1939. *Career:* Joined British Red Cross, Somerset, England, 1936; General duties during the war in Great Britain and Nigeria, West Africa; Commandant First Lagos (Nigeria) Detatchment, Red Cross; President, Nairobi Division, Red Cross, 1953; Deputy President, Kenya Branch, 1956; Red Cross Representative, Mauritius Hurricane Disaster Relief Committee, 1960; Red Cross Organizer of Refugees from Belgian Congo, 1960; Member, National Executive Committee, British Red Cross Society, 1964-67 and 1969-73; Deputy President, Sussex Counties Branch, 1968-. *Membership:* Served on numerous Councils and Committees; Governor, Delamere Girls' School, Kenya, 1960-62. *Honours:* CBE; Specially struck medal, Belgian Government; Honorary Vice President, British Red Cross Society. *Address:* Church Close, Newick, Sussex, England.

ROGERS Diane Elizabeth, b. 24 Apr. 1948, Holyoke, Mass., USA. Psychotherapist. m. Joseph M. Long, 26 Oct. 1977, 1 son. *Education:* BA, Harvard University, 1970; MA, Eds,, 1973, PhD, 1982, University of Florida. *Appointments:* Faculty, University of Florida Medical School, 1983-86; Director, Private Counseling & Consulting Practice, 1987-. *Publications:* Numerous articles for professional journals. *Memberships:* Fellow, Diplomate, American Board of Medical Psychotherapy; American Association of Counseling & Development; American Public Health Association; Phi Beta Kappa; President, Citizens Addiction Advisory Group. *Honours:* Disseration of the Year Nomination, Phi Beta Kappa, 1982; Young Scientist of the Year, CIBA, London, 1988. *Address:* 4140 NW 27th Lane, Suite A, Gainesville, FL 32606, USA.

ROGERS Elyse Jeanne, b. 28 Sept. 1932, Kearny, New Jersey, USA. Author; President, MAC International Ltd. m. 18 July 1952. 3 daughters. *Education:* Registered Nurse (RN), Mountainside Hospital, New Jersey, 1953; BS Nursing, Indiana University, 1957; MA, English Literature, Purdue University, 1973. *Appointments:* Ex VP, Oak Assoc, Tokyo, Japan, 1981- 85; Columnist, Japan Times, 1981-; Columnist, Tokyo Weekender, 1981-; Columnist, Daily Yomiuri, 1981-88; President, MAC International Ltd, 1985-; Health Editor, Mature Health magazine, USA, 1988-. *Publications:* Books: Staying Healthy in Japan, 1985; Cross Cultural Textbook, 1984; Over 500 articles and fiction published in national magazines and newspapers in both USA and Japan, 1963-. *Memberships:* American Society of Journalists and Authors; American Medical Writer's Association; Board of Directors, American Chamber of Commerce, Japan, 1985-87; Vice Chair, Asian- Pacific Ch of Commerce, 1986-87; Rotary; Zonta; Northwood University Steering Board; Original President and Co-founder, FEW (Foreign Exec Women), Japan, 1981-84. *Honours:* Named Fellow, American Medical Writers

Assoc, 1980; Scholastic Award at Graduation, 1953. *Hobbies:* Speaking and reading/writing Japanese; Tennis; Jogging; General medical/scientific reading. *Address:* MAC International Ltd, P O Box 2409, Midland, MI 48641, USA.

ROGERS Janet Lynn Kulig, b. 27 Sept. 1950, Morris, Illinois, USA. Administrator. m. Jesse C Rogers 3 Sept. 1974, divorced 1981. 1 daughter. *Education:* BS 1973; Reg Social Workers, 1983; Continuing education in Gerontology. *Appointments:* Outreach Worker 1980-82, Fiscal Manager 1982-87, Assistant Director 1982-87, Administrator 1987-, Grundy County Senior Services. *Publication:* Pilot programme in Mazon, Illinois for Nutrition Site. *Memberships:* National Assoiacation of Nutrition and Aging Service Providers; Illinois Gerontology Consortium; Grundy County Inter Agency Council; Morris Jr Woman's Club. *Hobby:* Handicrafts. Interests: Counselling abused women and children; Geology. *Address:* 2427 Parklake Drive, Morris, IL 60450, USA.

ROGERS Judith W, Chief Judge. *Education:* AB, cum laude, Radcliffe College, 1961; LLB, Harvard Law School, 1964; LLM, University of Virginia, 1988. *Appointments:* Law Clerk, Juvenile Court 1964-65, Assistant US Attorney 1965-68, District of Columbia; Trial Attorney, San Francisco Neighborhood Legal Assistant Foundation, 1968-69; Attorney, US Department of Justice, 1969-71; General Counsel, Congressional Commission on Organization of District of Columbia Government, 1971-72; Legislative Program Coordinator, Office of Deputy Mayor, District of Columbia, 1972-74; Special Assistant to the Mayor for Legislation, District of Columbia, 1974-79; Assistant City Administrator for Intergovernmental Relations, District of Columbia, 1979; Corporation Counsel for the District of Columbia, 1979-82; Associate Judge, DC Court of Appeals, 1983-. *Memberships:* ABA, 1984-; DC Bar, 1965-; Bar Association of DC, 1965-68; Grievance Committee, US Dist Court for DC, 1982-83; Harvard Law School Visiting Committee, 1984-; Board of Trustees, Radcliffe College, 1984-; Board of Directors, Wider Opportunities for Women, 1972-74; Board of Directors, Friends of the DC Superior Court, 1972-74; DC Law Revision Commission, 1979-83; Mayor's Commission on Crime and Justice, 1982. *Honours:* Phi Beta Kappa, 1986; Distinguished Public Service Award, District of Columbia Government, 1983; Award for Outstanding Performance, District of Columbia, 1977-78. *Address:* District of Columbia Court of Appeals, 500 Indiana Avenue NW, Washington, DC 20001, USA.

ROGERS Vera Ann, b. 17 Dec. 1920, London, England. Retired. m. Wilfred Hugh Rogers, 23 Oct. 1948, 1 son, 1 daughter. *Education:* Teachers' Certificate, Hockerill College, 1941; Special Education Specialist, Ontario Ministry, 1969; BA, Waterloo Lutheran University, 1973; Principal's Certificate, Ontario Ministry, 1976; MEd, University of Toronto, 1977. *Appointments:* Teacher, London, 1941-46; Headmistress, Wiltshire, 1946-48, 1955-57; Teacher, Ontario, Canada, 1961-65; Special Education Consultant, 1965-74; Principal, Dufferin Co., 1974-80; Primary Supervisor, 1980-82; Lecturer, Consultant, 1982-83. *Publications:* Curriculum: Communications from Kindergarten to Grade 13; Early Childhood - Observation Techniques; Kindergarten programmes; etc. *Memberships:* Dufferin Association Women Teachers, President; Dufferin Association Mentally Retarded Director; Orangeville Big Brothers, Director, Secretary; Orangeville Day Care Centre, Committee; Dufferin Women's Institute; etc. *Honours:* School Trustee, Dufferin Co. Board of Education, 1983-87; Nominated, Fred L. Bartlett Memorial Award, 1983; Provincial Appointment, Governor of Georgian College, 1983-86. *Hobbies:* Gardening; Early Childhood Development; Music; Travel. *Address:* 7432 Leary Crescent, Sardis, British Columbia, V2R 1J5, Canada.

ROGOVIN Sheila Anne, b. 28 Feb. 1931, New York City, USA. Psychology. m. Mitchell Rogovin, 31 Jan. 1954. 1 son, 2 daughters. *Education:* BA, Queens

College, 1952; PhD, The American University, 1972. *Appointments:* NYC Public Schools, 1952-54; California Public Schools, 1954-60; Fairfax County Public Schools, 1966; Montgomery County Health Department, 1972-76; Private Practice, 1977-. *Publication:* Research: Battered Women in Violent Marriages. *Memberships:* American Psychological Association; Maryland Psychological Association; District of Columbia Psychological Association; American Group Psychotherapy Association. *Address:* 8720 Georgia Ave, Suite 206, Silver Spring, MD 20910, USA.

ROHRER Mary Anne Schober Harrison, b. 10 Apr. 1946, Milwaukee, Wisconsin, USA. Executive/President, SCR Inc. m. Dallas L Rohrer, 9 May 1984. 2 sons. *Education:* BSW Major, University of Wisconsin, Madison, 1964-67; BSW Major, University of California, Berkeley, 1970; University of California, Berkeley, 1970-71; Attended Graduate School, Psychiatric Social Work. *Appointments:* Management Training Program, Customer Service Representative, Blue Cross, Blue Shield, Oakland, California, 1967-68; Public Relations Director, Phipps Land Company, Atlanta, 1972-74; Secretary-Treasurer, Village Planter Inc, Atlanta, 1974-76; Executive Vice President, ID Inc, Atlanta and London, 1979-81; President, FSC Consulting Services Inc, Atlanta, 1981-82; President, SCR Inc, Atlanta, 1982-86; Vice President, Board of Directors, Aftermarket Specialities Inc, Atlanta, 1985; Board of Directors, Secretary, RCS Inc, 1988-. *Publications:* Hidden Assets or Liabilities, 1982. *Memberships:* American Society of Personnel Administrators, Sales and Marketing Executives; Alpha Chi Omega Sorority, 1964-67. Social Chairman; Internships and volunteer work: YWCA Milwaukee, Wisconsin working with under-privileged youth, 1966; Goodwill Industries, working with emotionally disturbed and mentally retarded adults, 1967; Berkeley Suicide Prevention Center, 1970-71; National Trust for Historic Preservation Society, 1985-86; Charter Member, National Museum of Women for the Arts, 1986; National Association of Female Executives, 1984-86; Volunteer Teacher for Atlanta Fulton Co, 1974-75. *Honours:* Participated in: Women's Changing Role in Business-Television Series, Channel 17, 1981. *Hobbies:* Piano; International travel; Golf; Indoor tropical plants; Dance Aerobics. *Address:* 1145 Edgewater Drive NW, Atlanta, GA 30328, USA.

ROLFE Belinda Ann, b. 6 Jan. 1960, Hartselle, USA. Pharmacist. *Education:* BS, Pharmacy, Samford University, 1984. *Appointments:* Pharmacy Extern, Reynolds Pharmacy, Birmingham, 1982-84; Weldon's Pharmacy, Hurytown, 1984; BMC Princeton, 1984; Pharmacy Intern, Big B Drugs Inc. Roebucck, 1984-85; Registered Pharmacist, Big B, Pelham, 1985-; Pharmacy Consultant, Pharmacy Preceptor. *Memberships:* American, Alabama Pharmaceutical Associations; Lambda Kappa Sigma; Alpha Omicron Pi. *Honours:* International Leader in Achievement, 1989. *Hobbies:* Reading; Crafts; Tennis; Water Sports. *Address:* 2075 Montreat Circle, Birmingham, AL 35216, USA.

ROMANES Constance Margaret, b. 9 Aug. 1920, Lowick, Northumberland, England. Justice of the Peace. m. Giles John Romanes, 29 June 1943. 1 son, 2 daughters. *Education:* Scholar, Girton College, Cambridge, 1938-41, First class Modern Languages Tripos, 1941, T Montefiore Prize Winner. *Appointments:* Member (Lord Chancellor's nominee) on Legal Aid Duty Solicitor Committee, 1986-89; Member, James Committee on Distribution of Criminal Business, 1973-76. *Publications:* Articles in Justice of the Peace and Papers for conferences and seminars on judicial subjects e.g. Drugs and the protection of the Citizen; Young Offenders and the Parole System. *Memberships:* Appointed Justice of the Peace, 1965-; Dep Chairman Magistrates Association, 1981-87; Chairman and now President, Dorset Branch Magistrates Association; Chairman, Dorset Care Trust, 1984-; Member and Chairman, Portland YCC Board of Visitors and Chairman of National Conference, 1979-81. *Honour:* Officer of the Order of the British Empire (OBE), 1981. *Hobbies:* Music, active performer in orchestras and chamber music;

Gardening; Sometime member of Deanery and Diocesan Synods and Bishops Selector for ACCM, 1976-85. *Address:* Portesham House, Nr Weymouth, Dorset, DT3 4HE, England.

ROMANOW Marina, b. 13 Mar. 1955, Ionia, Michigan, USA. Company President. m. Peter Bloom Veerhusen, 18 Sept. 1982, 1 son, 1 daughter. *Appointments:* Vice President, 1979-82, President, 1982-, Romanow Building Services. *Memberships:* Building Service Contractors Association, International Board of Directors; Chamber of Commerce. *Honours:* Top 50 Michigan Women Business Owners, 1987 and 1988. *Hobbies:* Computer Programming; Reading; Swimming; Travel. *Address:* 3900 Valley Drive, Midland, MI 48640, USA.

ROMULO Beth Day, b. 25 May 1924, Ft Wayne, Indiana, USA. Freelance writer; Journalist. m. General Carlos P Romulo, deceased. *Education:* BA, University of Oklahoma; LLD, Philppine Womens University and Baguio Colleges Foundation. *Appointments:* Freelance, 1948-86; Columnist, Bulletin Manila Philippines, 1986-. *Publications:* Little Professor of Piney Woods, 1955; Grizzlies in Their Back Yard, 1956; Glacier Pilot, 1957; No Hiding Place, 1958; A Shirttail To Hang To, 1960; This Was Hollywood, 1959; Hey, I'm Alive, 1964; Passage Perilous, 1962; Special Agent, 1961; Sexual Life Between Blacks and Whites, 1972; I'm Done Crying, 1970; All My Children, 1971; Modern Motherhood, 1968; My Name is Dr Rantzau, 1970; The Philippines, Shattered Showcase of Democracy in Asia, 1974; The Manila Hotel, 1979; Romulo, 40 years at the UN, 1986; Inside The Palace, 1987. Juvenile Books: Will Rogers, Boy Roxper, 1952; Joshua Slocum, 1953; Talk Like A Cowboy, 1955; Eugene Rhodes, Cowboy, 1955; Lucille Malhall, Cowgirl, 1956; Grizzlies, 1971; Secret World of the Baby, 1968; Life on a Lost Continent, 1969; Numerous articles to journals, magazines and newspapers. *Memberships:* American Society of Journalists and Authors; Authors League; Society of Women Geographers; Chaine Des Rotisserus; Les Disciples d'auguste Escoffier. *Hobbies:* Food/wine; Swimming; Badminton; Board member, Ballet Philippines; Friends of National Museum; President, Corregidor Foundation. *Address:* 2411 Bouganvilla, Dasmarinas Village, Makati, Metro Manila, Philippines.

RONCELLI Janet Maria, b. 16 Dec. 1948, Detroit, USA. Educator; Associate Professor; Management Consultant. m. Daniel Gorney, 6 July 1979 *Education:* Ma 1974, PhD, 1978, Rhetorical theory, Wayne State University. *Appointments Include:* Instructor, Graduate Assistant, Speech Communication, Theatre & Journalism, Wayne State University, 1975-78; Consultant, Communications Skills Seminary, General Motors, Michigan State University, 1978; Seminar Leader, Speaker, Indiana Purdue Continuing Education Programmes, YWCA, Kiwanis, Chartered Property and Casualty Underwriters, Fort Wayne, 1982-; General Manager, Bermar Associates Inc., Troy, 1985-. *Publications:* various articles in professional journals; Author, 13 competitive and/or invited research papers; Director 4, major readers theatre productions. *Memberships:* Various profesisonal organisations. *Honours:* Recipient, various awards including Grants, Indiana 1981, 1983; Citation, Womens Caucus, Central States Speech Association, 1983. *Hobbies:* Bicycling; Theatre; Travel. *Address:* 6743 White Pine Court, Birmingham, MI 48010, USA.

ROOKE Daphne Marie, b. 6 Mar. 1914, Boksburg, Transvaal, South Africa. Novelist. m. 1 June 1937, 1 daughter. *Publications:* Novels: A Grove of Fever Trees; Mittee; Ratoons; Wizards' Country; Beti; A Lover for Estelle; The Greyling; Diamond Jo; Boy on the Mountain; Margaretha De La Porte. *Honours:* 1st Prize, Afrikaans Pers BPK Novel Competition, 1946. *Hobbies:* Bush Walking; Golf; Bridge. *Address:* 34 Bent Street, Fingal Bay, NSW 2315, Australia.

ROOP Constance Betzer, b. 18 June 1951, Elkhorn,

Wisconsin, USA. Teacher; Author. m. Peter G. Roop, 4 Aug. 1973, 1 son, 1 daughter. *Education:* BA, Lawrence University, 1973; Master's degree, Science Teaching, Boston College, 1980. *Appointments:* Science Teacher, Appleton Area School District, 1973-; Fulbright Teachers' Exchange, Lady Hawkins Comprehensive School, Kington, Herefordshire, UK, 1976-77. *Publications:* Co-author, with P. Roop: Keep the Lights Burning, Abbie; Buttons for General Washington; Space Out!; Out to Lunch!; Let's Celebrate!; Going Buggy!; Go Hog Wild!; Stick Out Your Tongue!; Dinosaurs; Solar System; Poltergeists; Stonehenge; Seasons of the Cranes; Snips the Tinker; Harmony in America: We Sought Refuge Here. *Memberships:* Treasurer 1987-89, Wisconsin Society of Earth Science Teachers; Wisconsin Society of Science Teachers; Offices, American Association of University Women; Offices, American Field Service. *Honours:* Wisconsin Leader in Education, AAUW, 1988; Irma Simonton Black Honour Book, 1986; Reading Rainbow feature book, National Council of Teachers of English, 1986; Outstanding Trade Book in Social Studies and Science, Children's Book of Year, Children's Choice. *Hobbies:* Reading; Travel; Camping; Sewing; Skiing; Family activities. *Address:* 2601 North Union Street, Appleton, Wisconsin 54911, USA.

ROOSENBURG Anna Maria, b. 27 Aug. 1918, Indonesia. Retired. *Education:* Study of Medicine, State University, Utrecht, 1937-45; Registrar, Neurology and Psychiatry, 1946-49, State University Hospital, Utrecht. *Honours:* Hon. Fellow, Royal College of Psychiatry, 1976; Ridder Order Nederlandse Leeuw. *Hobbies:* Arts; Painting; Drawing; Handicrafts; Classical Music; Gardening; Travel. *Address:* Mauritsstraat 71, 3583 HK Utrecht, The Netherlands.

ROOSEVELT Frances Webb, b. 24 June 1917, Kansas City, Missouri, USA. Artist. m. Quentin Roosevelt, 12 Apr. 1944, 3 daughters. *Education:* BA, Smith College, 1938. *Appointments:* Painter, Lecturer, Ancient Art, Wm. R. Nelson Gallery of Art, 1938-43; American Red Cross Clubmobile, England & France, 1943-44; Studied Chinese Painting with Professor of Shanghai University, 1948; Freelance Court Artist for New York Times Post & Journal American, 1949-52; Professor, Technique of Painting, C W Post College, 1957-66. *Creative Works:* Paintings: Many exhibitions, commissions, portraits, landscapes; Paintings of Far East for Womens Home Companion. *Memberships:* National Arts Club; Womens National Republican Club. *Honours:* Many Ribbons, 1932-; *Hobbies:* Bridge; Friends; Swimming; Snorkeling; Cruises; Painting; Grandchildren. *Address:* 160 Cove Neck Road, Oyster Bay, NY 11771, USA.

ROOSEVELT Selwa S., b. 13 Jan. 1929, Kingsport, Tennessee, USA. Writer. m. Archibald B. Roosevelt Jr, 1 Sept. 1950, 1 stepson. *Education:* BA, Vassar College, 1950. *Appointments:* Reporter, columnist, Washington Star, 1954-58; Special assistant to Head, Kennedy Centre for Performing Arts, 1961; Feature writer, Washington Post, 1961; Contributing editor, Town & Country, 1976-82; Chief of Protocol, USA, 1982-89. *Creative work includes:* Book, in progress. *Memberships:* Folger Shakespeare Library; F Street Club, DC; Colony Club, NYC; Board, Duke University Comprehensive Cancer Centre; Board, Children's Hearing & Speech Centre, Washington DC Children's Hospital; Board, Spoleto Festival, USA; Board, Hariri Foundation. *Honours:* Medal, Outstanding Civilian Service, Department of Army, 1983; Betty Ford Award, Susan Komen Foundation, Dallas, Texas, 1985; Salute to Republican Women Award, Ripon Society 1987; Decoration, Grand Official of The Order of Merit of The Republic of Italy, 1989. *Address:* 3400 R Street NW, Washington DC 20007, USA.

ROOT Hilary Margaret, b. 7 July 1945, Hindhead, Surrey, England. Stockbroker. *Education:* BA, Trinity College, Dublin, 1968. *Appointments:* Fund Manager, Sheppards, Stockbrokers, 1969-. *Membership:* International Stock Exchange. *Hobbies:* Travel;

Archaeology; Entertaining. *Address:* 18 Bywater Street, London SW3 4XD, England.

ROSCHER Nina, b. 8 Dec. 1938, Uniontown, Pennsylvania, USA. Professor of Chemistry. m. David Roscher, 27 Dec. 1964. *Education:* BS, Chemistry, University of Delaware, 1960; PhD, Chemistry, 1964, Postdoctoral Fellow, 1964-65, Purdue University. *Appointments include:* Senior Staff Chemist, Coca-Cola Export Corporation, 1967-68; Assistant Professor, 1968-74, Assistant Dean, 1971-74, Douglass College, Rutgers, The State University; Director, Academic Administration, 1974-76, Associate Professor, 1974-79, Associate Dean, Graduate Affairs and Research, College of Arts and Sciences, 1976-79, Vice-Provost, Academic Services, 1979-82, Professor of Chemistry, 1979-, Dean, Faculty Affairs, 1981-85, Vice-Provost, Academic Affairs, 1982- 85, The American University, Washington DC; Programme Director, National Science Foundation, 1986-. *Publications:* The Dark Reaction of Alcohols with Silver Compounds and Bromine, 1971; Thin Layer Chromatographic Analysis of Oxo and Thio Compounds (with John H.Onley), 1977; Improving Information on College Services and Academic Programs, 1980; Women Chemists 1985, book, 1986; Issues for Chemistry Faculty in Re-Entry Programs, 1987; Other articles and book chapters. *Memberships:* American Chemical Society, numerous committees, Past Section Treasurer and Chair; Iota Sigma Pi, Past offices including Past National Vice-President; Fellow, American Institute of Chemists, committees and offices; Fellow, American Association for the Advancement of Science; New York Academy of Sciences; Sigma Xi; Phi Kappa Phi, Past Chapter President and Secretary-Treasurer; Association of Women in Science; Society for Applied Spectroscopy; Scientific Manpower Commission, Commission on Professionals in Science and Technology, Commission President 1981-82; Fellow, Washington Academy of Sciences; Council of Chemical Research; National Science Foundation. *Honours:* National Honorary Membership, Sigma Delta Epsilon, 1982; Senior Scholar, College of Arts and Science, The American University, 1985; Many awards, fellowships and grants. *Address:* Department of Chemistry, The American University, 4400 Massachusetts Avenue NW, Washington, DC 20016, USA.

ROSE Gail Elaine, b. 14 Sept. 1949, Chicago, Illinois, USA. Administrator. *Education:* AA, Applied Science, Morton College, Cicero, Illinois, 1969; BA, National College of Education, Evanston, 1984. *Appointments:* Dental assistant, 1968-71, 1971-73; Instructor, Dental Assisting, Morton College, 1969-71; Administrative assistant 1973-78, administrative manager 1978-87, director, Administrative Department 1987-, KYB Corporation of America, Lombard, Illinois. *Memberships:* American Management Association; National Association of Female Executives; Associate, Illinois Sheriff's Association; Republican National Committee; Secretary- treasurer, West Surburban Dental Assistants Association; Lodge, Women of the Moose; Japan-American Society, Chicago. *Hobbies:* Physical fitness; Cycling; Reading. *Address:* 2S531 Emerald Green Drive, Warrenville, Illinois 60555, USA.

ROSE Joyce Dora Hester, b. 14 Aug. 1929, London, England. Justice of the Peace for Hertfordshire. m. Cyril Rose, 6 Oct. 1953. 2 sons, 1 daughter. *Education:* King Alfred School, London; Queen's College, London. *Appointments:* Solicitors Clerk and Solicitors Articled Clerk, 1949-55; Director of a Retail Group with special responsibility for Personnel, 1975-79. *Memberships:* Co Dep Chairman, Magistrates Association; Dep Chairman Watford Adult, Juvenile and Domestic Courts; Chairman, Herts Branch Mag Association; President, Liberal Party, 1979-80; Chairman, Liberal Party, 1982-83; President and Chairman, Women's Liberal Federation, 1972 and 1973; President, S W Herts Constituency Social and Liberal Democrats, 1988-; Vice Chairman, National Executive UK Committee for UNICEF, 1968-70. *Honour:* CBE, 1981. *Hobbies:* Advancement of Women; Protection and development of children and young people; Animals; Family. *Address:* 38 Main Avenue, Moor Park, Northwood, Middx HA6 2LQ, England.

ROSE Judy Dale Sizemore, b. 28 Apr. 1939, Manchester, Kentucky, USA. Teacher. m. James L. Rose, 14 Apr. 1962, 2 sons, 1 daughter. *Education:* Cumberland College, 1958; Honorary DHL, Cumberland College. *Appointments:* Teacher, Clay County High School; Owner, Supermarket; Owner, Art Galleries; Vice President, Tri State Realty. *Memberships Include:* Vice President, Younger Womens Club; Board of Trustees, Cumberland College; American Heart Association, Board, Lexington Division; Kentucky Mountain Laurel Festival, Board; National Federation of Republican Women. *Hobbies:* Reading; Singing; Piano; Skiing; Swimming. *Address:* PO Box 756, London, KY 40741, USA.

ROSE Rosemary Catherine, b. 2 Jan. 1931, Antigo, Wisconsin, USA. Executive. 1 son. *Education:* Secretarial, Stratton College, 1955; Real Estate Brokers, Spencerian College, 1965; American Institute for Paralegal Studies, 1985. *Appointments:* Administrative Assistant, 1951-55; Owner, Motel, 1955-66; Owned, Restaurant, Garage, Dry Cleaning Store, 1960-65; Principal Owner, Alrose Realty Co., 1965-; Executive Secretary, 1967-70; Owner, Operator, Solid Waste Disposal Service, 1970-74; Owner, Operator, Supper Club, 1975-79; Vice President, Executive Secretary, Commercial Printing Firm, 1979-82; General Manager, Hotel, 1983-84; Executive Housekeeper, 1984-85; Office Manager, Cedar Disposal Inc., 1985-87; Administration Assistant/Office Manager, A-1 Service Co., Inc., 1985-87. *Memberships:* National Association for Female Executives Inc; National Rifle Association; National Board of Review; American Biographical Institute; National Museum for Women in the Arts. *Hobbies:* Reading; Gardening; Cooking; Theatre; Music. *Address:* N 105 W 15750, Hamilton Court, Germantown, WI 53022, USA.

ROSE, Helen Carlotta, b. 14 June 1920, New York, USA. Interior Designer; Community Planner. m. Cecil S. Rose, 1 son, 1 daughter. *Education:* BA, 1938, MA, 1955, LHD, 1978, Emerson College. *Appointments:* Interior Designer, 1941-; Community Planner, Speech and Hearing Handicapped, 1953-. *Memberships:* Trustee, Emerson College; Founder, Robbins Speech and Hearing Clinic, Emerson College; National Board, Womans Medical College, (Med. College of Pa.); Founder, Speech and Hearing Foundation, Massachusetts; Initiator, Adult Education for the Deaf in Massachusetts, 1962. *Hobbies:* Family; Food; Fashion. *Address:* 150 Bradley Place, Palm Beach, FL 33480, USA.

ROSE-ACKERMAN Susan, b. 23 Apr. 1942, Mineola, New York, USA. Ely Prof of Law and Political Economy, Yale University. m. Bruce A Ackerman, 29 May 1967. 1 son, 1 daughter. *Education:* BA, Wellesley, 1964; PhD, Yale, 1970. *Appointments:* Assistant Professor, University of Pennsylvania, 1970- 74; Assistant Professor, Economics 1975-78, Associate Professor, Economics, 1978-82, Yale; Professor, Columbia Law, 1982-87; Director, Center for Law and Economic Studies, Columbia University, 1983-87; Professor Law & Political Science, Yale, 1987-. *Publications:* The Uncertain Search for Environmental Quality, with B Ackerman, J Sawyer & D Henderson; Corruption: A Study in Political Economy; Editor, The Economics of Nonprofit Inst; The Nonprofit Enterprise in Market Economies, with E James. *Memberships:* American Econ Assoc; Assoc of Amer Law Schools; Assoc for Public Policy Analysis and Management; Am Polit Science Asso. *Honours:* Phi Beta Kappa, 1964; Winner Henderson Prize, Harvard Law School for Uncertain Search for Environmental Quality, 1982. *Address:* Box 401A, Yale Station, New Haven 06515, USA.

ROSENAU Anita H, b. 25 Aug. 1923, Philadelphia,

Pennsylvania, USA. Playwright. m. Gary Rosenau, 24 Apr. 1945. 1 son, 1 daughter. *Education:* University of Pennsylvania, LA, 1944; MA, Playwriting, Temple University, 1956. *Appointment:* Jr Economist, War Labor Board, 1944-45; Playwright. *Creative works:* Plays: Lancelot and Guinevere; Strangers Islands; Bridges; Future Murder; Mandate for Murder; Murder for Love (Screen play); Journey into Murder; Sylvia and Sylvia's Marriage (screen play, adaptation of books by Upton Sinclair); Paul, in progress. Opera: Guinevere. Productions: Poetry Reading. Published articles and poems in journals; Books for children in verse: Tell Me About the Ten Commandments; Tell Me About the Lord's Prayer; Tell Me About the Beatitudes; Tell Me About Angels; Tell Me About Miracles. *Memberships:* Poetry Society of America; Prof Member, Dramatists Guild. *Honours:* Honorable Mention, PEN Pikes Peak Branch for Along a Lonely Field; North American Mentor Magazine for Indian Arts Festival and En Route. *Hobbies:* Golf; Bridge; Skiing; Travel. *Address:* 424 Sinclair Road Box 5667, Snowmass Village, CO 81615, USA.

ROSENBAUM Belle Sara, b. 1 Apr. 1922, New York City, USA. Interior Designer; Personal Property Appraiser. m. Jack Rosenbaum, 12 Mar. 1939. 1 son, 3 daughters. *Education:* Certificate, NY School of Interior Design, 1945; Senior Member, Amer Soc of Appraisers, 1979. *Appointments:* Design Consultant, Marc Daniels, 1945; Design Consultant 1955, President 1959, Jarvis Designs Inc; Vice President, Lord & Lady Originals Inc, 1955-70; Vice President, Cardio-Bionic Scanning Inc, 1975-78; Vice President Treasurer, Rapitech Systems Inc, 1985; President, Design Assoc Bls, 1970-78. *Creative works:* Short stories, 1947-48; Articles on interior design in various professional journals; Teacher of Judaica, Yeshiva University; Director, Rosenbaum Museum of Contemporary Judaica. *Memberships:* Bd of Gov, Yesh Univ Museum, 1987; Bd of NY State Council of Arts, 1988; Hon Pres, Yeshiva of Hudson County, 1955; Pres, Amit Women, 1955-57; Treas, Ami Women, 1948-78; Treas, Brit Avrom, 1980; Bd of Dir, American Friends of Migdal Ohr, 1970; Editorial Bd, Light Foundation, 1987. *Honours:* Herald Tribune Short Story Prize, 1939; Woman of Valor Award, State of Israel, 1960; Economics Award 1939, Art Scholarship 1939, Roosevelt School; Founders Award, Migdal Ohr Schools of Israel, 1988. *Hobbies:* Collector of Judaica (completing a book on Judaica Upon Thy Doorposts); Collector of Art, antiques and people; Artist; Gardening; Communal and charity work.

ROSENBERG Jenifer Bernice, b. 1 Oct. 1942, London, England. Managing Director. m, Ian David Rosenberg, 8 Feb. 1982. *Appointments:* Various positions to Senior Buyer, Marks & Spencer PLC, 1960-74; Managing Director, J & J Fashions Ltd, London, 1974-; Lecturing to design colleges. *Memberships:* Design 2000 Committee, Clothing and Allied Products Training Board Design; Honorary Consultant, Bournemouth and Poole College of Art and Design; Various charity committees; Council for National Academic Awards; Advisory Committee on Women's Employment; Department of Trade and Industry Advisory Panel on Deregulation. *Honours:* Companion, British Institute of Management; 1st woman recipient of Twice Award for Industrial and Commercial Enterprises, Tyne and Wear Council; Winner, Veuve Clicquot Business Woman of the Year Award, 1986; OBE, New Years Honours, 1989; Governor of the London Institute. *Hobbies:* Theatre; Music; Travel; Photography; After-dinner speaking. *Address:* J & J Fashions Ltd, 260 York Way, London N7 9PQ, England.

ROSENBERG Priscilla Elliott, b. 17 Feb. 1952, Rochester, New York, USA. Attorney. m. Alan Mark Rosenberg, 7 May 1983, 2 daughters. *Education:* University of Rochester, 1973; Rochester Institute of Technology, 1973-74; BA, State University of New York, Stony Brook, 1975; JD, Brooklyn Law School, 1978. *Appointments:* Associate, Shearman & Sterling, New York City, 1978-84; Assistant counsel 1985-86, associate counsel 1986-, Siemens Corporation, NYC. *Publications:* Various articles, professional journals.

Memberships: American, & New York State Bar Associations. *Honours:* Moot Court Honour Society, Brooklyn Law School, 1976-78; Law Review, ibid, 1977-78; Various other awards, earlier education. *Hobbies:* Two young daughters, Anne Marian & Tracy Jean. *Address:* c/o Siemens Corporation, 767 Fifth Avenue, New York, NY 10153, USA.

ROSENBERG Shirley Sirota, Writer; Editor. m. Jerome D Rosenberg. 1 daughter. *Education:* BA, Brooklyn College. *Appointments:* Managing Editor, Brooklyn Jewish Examiner, 1946-48; Independent writer-editor, 1956-71; Chief Speechwriter, Children's Bureau, Department of Health, Eduation and Welfare, 1967-69; Washington correspondent, Parents' Magazine, 1968-79; Director of Publications, Interdisciplinary Communications Program, Smithsonian Institution, 1972-77; Instructor, The Compleat Editor, GWU Publications Specialist Program, George Washington University, 1979-; President, SRR, Incorporated, 1977-. *Memberships:* American Society of Journalists and Authors (former DC chair); Association of Editorial Businesses (founder, former vice president); American Medical Writers Association; Federal Design Council; International Association of Business Communicators; Board Member, Kennedy Institute; National Association of Government Communicators; National Book Publishers Association; National Press Club; Smithsonian Institution Womens' Network; Washington Independent Writers; Board Member, Washington Women in Public Relations; Womens National Book Publishers. *Honours:* First place, National Association of Government Communicators, 1981; International Association of Business Communicators, 1983; Society of Technical Communicators, 1983; Merit Award, Art Directors Club, 1984; Ed Press, 1984, 1986. *Addres:* 116 Fourth Street SE, Washington, DC 20003, USA.

ROSENFELD Rachel Ann, b. 15 Nov. 1948, Baltimore, Maryland, USA. Professor. *Education:* BA, Carleton College, 1970; MS, 1974, PhD, 1976, University of Wisconsin. *Appointments:* Assistant Professor, McGill University 1976-80; Senior Study Director, National Opinion Research Centre, 1978-81; Assistant Professor to Professor, Sociology, University of North Carolina, 1981-. *Publications:* Farm Women, 1985; numerous professional articles in: American Sociological Review, Social Forces, etc. *Memberships:* American Sociological Association; Southern Sociological Society; International Sociological Association; Population Association of America. *Address:* Dept. of Sociology, CB No 3210 Hamilton Hall, University of North Carolina, Chapel Hill, NC 27599, USA.

ROSENFIELD Patricia Lee, b. 18 Dec. 1948, New York City, USA. Foundation Officer; Economist. m. 27 Sept. 1978. 1 daughter. *Education:* AB, cum laude with Honours Geology, Bryn Mawr College, 1970; PhD (Geography and Environmental Engineering) Johns Hopkins University, Baltimore, 1975. *Appointments:* Research Associate, Resources for the Future, Washington, DC, 1975-78; Economist/Scientist and Secretary, Scientific Working Group and Steering Committee on Social and Economic Research in Tropical Diseases, World Health Organization, Geneva, Switzerland, 1978-87; Program Officer, Carnegie Corporation, New York, 1987-. *Publications:* Economics of Tropical Diseases, 1989 (co-editor Alex Herrin); The Management of Schistosomiasis, Resources for the Future, 1979; Schistosomiasis Transmission Model, 1975. *Memberships include:* Water Science and Technology Board, National Research Council (US); Board Member, Society for International Development, NYC Chapter; Editorial Board Memberships: Social Science and Medicine; Culture, Medicine and Psychiatry; Health Systems and Medical Care; International Journal of Health Education; Interphil; Women and Foundations/Corporate Philanthropy. *Honours include:* National Science Foundation Traineeship, Johns Hopkins University, 1970-74; Foreign Affairs Specialist (Intern program) US Agency

for International Development Award for PhD research, 1972-74; Term-Member, Council on Foreign Relations, 1972-77, Member, 1990-. *Hobbies:* Photography; Flower arranging; Gardening. *Address:* 1365 York Avenue, Apt. 3A, New York, NY 10021, USA.

ROSENZWEIG Daphne Lange, b. 7 July 1941, Evanston, Illinois, USA. Professor; Appraiser; Museum Consultant. m. Abraham Rosenzweig, 31 May 1969, 1 daughter. *Education:* AB, Mount Holyoke College, 1963; MA Asian Art & Archaeology 1967, PhD Far Eastern Languages & Literature 1973, Columbia University. *Appointments:* White House Fellow, Economic Analysis, Bureau of Mines, 1963; Instructor, Adelphi University, Summer 1967; Translator, Interpreter, National Palace Museum, 1967-69; Lecturer, University of New Mexico, 1969-73; Assistant Professor, Oberlin College, 1973-78; Associate Professor, University of South Florida, 1979-. Also: Organiser, Museum Exhibitions; Appraisals, Oriental Art; Co-owner (with husband), Rosenzweig Associates Consultant Service. *Creative work:* Publications: Numerous books & articles, Oriental art including Chinese & Japanese paintings, Japanese prints, Chinese jades, symbolism. Also: Stage Sets, Ringling Circus; Design Consultant, Busch Gardens, Tampa. *Memberships include:* American Oriental Society; Association for Asian Studies; College Art Association; International House of Japan; Japan-America Society, Central Florida; Society for Study of Chinese Religions; International Society of Appraisers (ISA). *Honours include:* Fulbright Fellowship, Taiwan, 1967-69; Lamp of Knowledge, ISA, 1988; Achievement Award, National Home Study Course Guide, 1988; Various Government Language Study Grants, University Travel Awards. *Hobbies:* Oriental art; Travel; English Mysteries; Stamps of Asia. *Address:* c/o PO Box 16187, Tampa, Florida 33687, USA.

ROSHONG Dee Daniels, b. 22 Nov. 1936, Kansas City, USA. Director of Counselling. *Education:* B.Mus.Ed., University of Kansas, 1958; MA, Counselling, Stanford University, 1960; D.Ed., University of San Francisco, 1980. *Appointments:* Director, Vocal Music, Antioch Schools, 1958-59; Counsellor, Psychometrist, Fresno City College, 1961-65; Counsellor, Psychometrist, Psychology Instructor, 1965-75, Director of Counselling, 1975-, Chabot College. *Publications:* Writer, Co-ordinator of Symposia: I, a Woman, 1974; Feeling Free to Be You and Me, 1975; All for the Family 1976; I Celebrate Myself, 1977; Person to Person In Love and Work, 1978; Sources of Strength, 1982; Love and Friendship, 1983; Self-Esteem, 1984; How to Live In the World and Still Be Happy, 1988; Sound Mind - Sound Body, Symposium, 1989; Healing, 1989. *Memberships:* Humanistic Psychologists Association; Western Psychological Association; California Association of Community Colleges Commission on Student Services; Task Force on Counselling. *Honours:* Chabot College Counselling Association, Distinguished Service Award, 1984; California Community Colleges Counsellors Association, Distinguished Service Awards, 1987, 1988; Author, Counseling Needs of Community College Students. *Hobbies:* Music; Writing. *Address:* 808 Comet Drive, Apt. 208, Foster City, CA 94409, USA.

ROSOFF Jeannie. President, Alan Guttmacher Institute. *Education:* BA, University of Paris Law School, 1946. *Appointments Include:* Research Assistant, Assistant and Community Organizer, 1951-60; Associate Director, New York Committee for Democratic Voters, 1960-64; Special Projects Co-ordinator, 1964-74, Associate Director, Centre for Family Planning Programme Development, 1968-74, Vice President, Governmental affairs, 1976-77, Director, Washington Office, 1976-81, Planned Parenthood Federation of America; Senior Vice President, 1974-78, President, 1978-, Alan Guttmacher Institute. *Memberships Include:* National Institutes of Child Health & Human Development; National Health Lawyers Association; Population Association of America; American Public Health Association; National Abortion Federation; etc.

Memberships: Recipient, various honours & awards. *Address:* The Alan Guttmacher Institute, 2010 Massachusetts Avenue NW, Washington, DC 20036, USA.

ROSOVSKY-KAMINER China, b. Russia. Actress; Art Gallery Manager. m. Leon Kaniner, 1 daughter. *Education:* Institute of Performing Arts, Leningrad; Theatre Studio, Israel. *Appointments:* Habina Theatre, many performances all over the country; Regular appearances on TV, Radio and Films. *Memberships:* Israeli Union of Performing Artists; Union of Musicians and Actors; Israel Council of International Theatre; Civil Defence Institute. *Honours:* Recipient, various honours and awards. *Hobbies:* Theatre; Music; Dancing; Palmistry. *Address:* 22 Mapll Str., 63434 Tel-Aviv, Israel.

ROSS Debra Benita, b. 1 May 1956, Carbondale, Illinois, USA. Director of Marketing. *Education:* BS, Business Administration, University of Illinois, Urbana-Champaign, 1978; MS, Business Administration, University of Wisconsin, Madison. *Appointments:* Director of Marketing, Ambion Development Inc, 1983-89; Director of Marketing, Fitness Quest International Inc, 1989-. *Memberships:* American Marketing Association; Chicago Advertising Club. *Address:* 1853 Mission Hills Lane, Northbrook, IL 60062, USA.

ROSS Diana, b. 26 Mar. 1944, Detroit, USA. Singer; Actress. m. (1) Robert Ellis Silberstein, 1971, divorced 1976. 3 daughters. (2) Arne Naess, 1985. *Career:* Former lead singer, Diana Ross and the Supremes; Solo Singer, 1970-. Numerous records with Supremes and solo. Television specials. *Creative Works:* Films include: Lady Sings the Blues, 1972; Mahogany, 1975; The Wiz, 1978. *Honours:* Citation from Vice President Humphrey for efforts on behalf of President Johnson's Youth Opprotunity Programme; from Mrs Martin Luther King and Rev. Abernathy for contribution to Southern Christian Leadership Conf. cause; Billboard, Cash Box and Record World magazine awards as world's outstanding female singer; Grammy Award, 1970; Female Entertainer of the Year, Nat. Asscn. for the Advancement of Colored People, 1970; Cue Award as Entertainer of the Year, 1972; Golden Apple Award, 1972; Golden Medal Award, Photoplay, 1972; Antoinette Perry Award, 1977; Golden Globe Award, 1972. *Address:* c/o RTC Management, P O Box 1683, New York, NY 10185, USA.

ROSS Dina Josephine, b. 26 Sept. 1958, London, England. Writer; Company Director. m. David Lawrence Scheel, 14 Dec. 1981. *Education:* BA, Honours, languagoo, King's College, London University, 1980; MA, Journalism, Polytechnic of Central London, 1981. *Appointments:* Assistant Editor, ADAM International Review, 1979-81; News Reporter, Scriptwriter, Producer, BBC Radio 4 World & External Services, 1981-84; Head, Broadcast Unit, Burson-Marsteller Public Relations, 1984-87; Managing Director, Intervox Media Services, 1987-; Guest Lecturer, Media Relations & Communications, Institute of Directors, Institute of Marketing, London Business School. *Creative Works:* Adaptation of Jean Giraudoux, Supplement au Voyage de Cook for National Theatre of Great Britain, 1983; Evirato, play, BBC Radio 3, 1984; Reference Books: Cambridge - a Guide for Scientists, 1986; PR Opportunities in the National Press, with Michael Bland, 1987; Surviving the Media Jungle, W.H. Allen Business Books, 1989. *Memberships:* Institute of Journalists; World Wildlife Fund; Institute of Public Relations. *Honours:* Sunday Telegraph Student Journalist of the Year Award, 1979; William Stebbing Prize for Literature, London University, 1980; British Association of Industrial Editors Award, Best Audio Programme 1989. *Hobbies:* Music; Theatre; Art; Wildlife Conservation. *Address:* Moonrakers, St Martin, Jersey, Channel Islands.

ROSS Dorothy Dickson, b. 13 Jan. 1928, Sydney, New South Wales, Australia. Retired farmer. *Education:* Diploma, Bedford Phs Training College, 1949; Diploma,

Phys Ed, London University, 1949. *Appointment:* Phys Ed, Frensham Mittagong, 1950-51. *Publications:* Co-author, Rural Communities for Habitat conference; Regular contributor to Land. *Memberships:* National President 1985-88, State President NSW 1971-74, Country Womens Association; Deputy Chairman, Australian Press Council, 1976-. *Honours:* Officer, Order of the British Enmpire, 1975; Queen's Silver Jubilee Medal, 1977; Justice of the Peace, 1974. *Hobbies:* Connemara Ponies; Australian Historical Society; Lawn bowls. *Address:* Tintagel, Holbrook, New South Wales 2644, Australia.

ROSS Mary Adelaide Eden, b. Apr 1896, Ealing, England. Writer. m. Nicholas Ross, 25 Aug, 1951, deceased. *Education:* Bedford College, London, 1921. *Appointments:* Worked for C Kogden on Cambridge Magazine, 1918; Hospital worker during World War II; Head Housewife, Women's Voluntary Service, 1940. *Publications:* In the name of Adelaide Phillpotts: Illyrion and Other Poems, 1916; Arachne, 1920; Man: A Fable, 1922; The Friend, 1923; Savitin the Faithful, 1923; Camillus and the Schoolmaster, 1923; Yellow Sands, with Eden Phillpotts, 1926; Akhnaton, 1926; Lodgers in London, 1926; A Tomak the Sculptor, 1927; A Marriage, 1928; The Atoning Years, 1929; Yellow Sands: Novel of Play, 1930; The Youth of Jacob Ackner, 1931; The Founder of Shandon, 1932; The Growing World, 1934; Onward Journey, 1936; Broken Allegiance, 1937; What's Happened to Rankin, 1938; The Gallant Heart, 1939; The Round of Life, 1940; Laugh with Me, 1941; Our Little Town, 1942; From Jane to John, 1942; The Adventurers, 1944; The Lodestar, 1945; The Fosterling, 1946; Stubborn Earth, 1951; Copies of Poetry Review with Poems, 1951. In the name of Adelaide Ross: A Song of Man, 1959; Panorama of the World, 1969; Letters from J C Powys to Nicholas Ross, 1971; Reverie, Autobiography, 1981; Letters from J C Powys to Nicholas Ross, edited by Arthur Uphill, 1988; Village Love (novel), 1988; The Beacon of Memory, to be published. *Honour:* Winner of Short Story Competition, West Country Writers Association, 1952. *Hobbies:* Art; Nature. *Address:* Cobblestones, Kilkhampton, Bude, Cornwall, EX 23 9QU, England.

ROSS Ruth Winifred, b. 3 May 1924, Thirroul, Australia. Physiotherapist. *Education:* Diploma, Physiotherapy, University of Sydney. *Appointments:* Private Practice, 1945-88. *Memberships:* President, Australian Federation BPW, 1974-76; Vice President, IFBPW, 1977-83; President, Illawarra Zonta, 1980-82; Australian Physiotherapy Association. *Honours:* Queen Elizabeth Silver Jubilee Medal, 1977; MBE, 1978; JP, 1979; Life Member, Royal Institute for Deaf & Blind Children, 1979. *Hobbies:* Travel; Reading; Music; Tapestry. *Address:* 28 Railway Avenue, Austinmer, 2515 NSW, Australia.

ROSS Susan Julia, b. 24 July 1943, Philadelphia, Pennsylvania, USA. Attorney. div. *Education:* BA magna cum laude, 1965, JD magna cum laude, 1969, University of Pennsylvania; BLitt programme, Somerville College, Oxford, England, 1969-70. *Appointments:* Associate, Dewey, Ballantyne, Bushby, Dalmer & Wood, New York City, 1969-76; Partner, Natelson & Ross, TAos, New Mexico, 1976-; Visiting Associate Professor of Law, University of Oregon, Eugene, autumn 1978. *Memberships:* Director, Beneficial Corporation, Wilmington, Delaware; Director, Harbour Island Inc, Tampa, Florida; Trustee, Millicent Rogers Museum, TAos, New Mexico. *Honours:* Phi Beta Kappa, University of Pennsylvania; Order of the Coif and Editor, Law Review, University of Pennsylvania Law School. *Hobbies:* Skiing; Tennis; Scuba diving; Windsurfing; Riding. *Address:* PO Box 2286, Taos, NM 87571, USA.

ROSS Susan Kohn, b. 10 Nov. 1945, Plymouth, England. Attorney-at- Law. m. James Wilson Ross, 24 July 1976. *Education:* BA, History, University of California, Los Angeles, USA, 1967; JD, Southwestern University School of Law, Los Angeles, 1977; Admitted to California State Bar. *Appointments:* Various positions in Custom House Brokerage, 1967-79, including

Partner, Yokeum/Ross & Associates; Law Clerk, Stein, Shostack, Shostack & O'Hara, and Mandel and Grunfeld; Sole Practitioner, Law, Huntington Beach and Manhatten Beach, 1978-80, San Francisco, 1980-81, Beverly Hills, 1982, Los Angeles, 1983-; Director of Civil Litigation, Senior Family Law Attorney, Yanello & Flippen, Oakland, California, 1981-82; Associate, Grayson Maxwell & Sugarman, Los Angeles, California, 1982-83; Partner, Herrick and Ross, Los Angeles, 1986-; Instructor, Transportation Training Institute, Los Angeles, Transportation Education Center, Oakland, formerly; Mediator, Van Nuys Superior Court, 1985, Santa Monica Superior Court, 1986. *Publications:* Discovery Options, 1986. *Memberships:* Judge Pro Tem Panel: Santa Monica Bar Association, Los Angeles County Bar Association; W&IC 317 Panel, Los Angeles Juvenile Court; American Bar Association; Los Angeles County Bar Association (committees); Harbor Transportation Club (Board of Directors 1985-87); National Customs Brokers and Freight Forwarders Association; American Association of Exporters and Importers; Women in International Trade. *Honours:* American Jurisprudence Book Award, 1973; Executive Editor of Commentator, Southwestern University School of Law, 1975- 76; Silver Key, Law Student Division, American Bar Association, 1976, 1977; 9th Circuit Citation Award, 1976; Outstanding Service Award, Student Bar Association, 1976-77. *Address:* 13101 Washington Boulevard, Suite 234, Los Angeles, CA 90066, USA.

ROSSANT Janet, b. 13 July 1950, Chatham, Kent, England. Research Scientist. m. Alex Bain, 18 June 1977. 1 son, 1 daughter. *Education:* BA (MA) Hons, Oxford, 1972; PhD, Cambridge, 1976. *Appointments:* Assistant Professor, Biological Sciences, Brock University, 1977-81; Associate Professor 1981-85, Senior Research Scientist, 1985-, Mount Sinai Hospital Research Institute Toronto, 1985-; Associate Professor, Professor, Department of Medical Genetics, University of Toronto, 1985-. *Publication:* Experimental approaches to mammalian embryonic development, 1986 (Eds J Rossant & R A Pedersen). *Memberships:* British Society for Developmental Biology; American and Canadian Societies for Cell Biology; Associate Editor, Developmental Biology. *Honours:* Beit Memorial Fellowship, 1977; EWR Steacie Fellowship, 1983. *Interests:* Research into early development in mammals, especially the genetic control of developmental processes. *Address:* Mount Sinai Hospital Research Institute, 600 University Avenue, Toronto, Ontario, Canada, M5G 1X5

ROSSI-MANARESI Raffaella, Director of Research. m. Professor Carlo Alfonso Rossi. *Education:* Dr in Chemistry, Bologna University; Postgraduate Scholarships: Institute of Physical Chemistry and Institute of Biochemistry, Bologna University; Scientific Department National Gallery, London; Institute of Mineralogy-Petrography, Siena University. *Appointments:* Director of Research, Centro Cesare Gnudi Bologna, 1981; Scientific Officer, Centro Conservazione Sculture all'aperto, Bologna, 1969. *Publications:* About 80 scientific-technical publications (papers and books) on conservation of works of art (stone, paintings, architectural finishes, polychromed stone and glass). *Memberships:* Member of Council, International Institute Conservation; Member of Commissions of: RILEM; ICOM; ICOMOS; Member of Restoration Commissions in Rome, Venice, Bologna. *Address:* Fondazione Cesare Gnudi-Centro di Ricerca, Via Belle Arti 56, 40126 Bologna, Italy.

ROSSINGTON Patricia Jane, b. Derby, England. Actress. m. David Harry Dunger, 16 June 1972. 1 son, 1 daughter. *Education:* Speech and Drama School. *Appointments:* Various Theatre and TV appearances including: Radio: The Archers. TV: Emergency Ward 10; Crossroads. *Hobbies:* Gardening; Tapestry. *Address:* Nr Lichfield, Staffordshire, England.

ROSSNER Marilyn Sylvia, b. Montreal, Canada. Professor; Ordained Minister. m. Dr John Rossner, 15 July 1974. *Education:* Teaching Diploma, 1957; BA, Geography, 963; MA, 1967, PhD, 1985, Special Education. *Appointments:* Behaviour Therapist, 1972-; Teacher, Protestant School Board; Professor, Special Education, Vanier College, 1972-. *Publications:* The Emotionally Disturbed Child; Yoga, Psycho Therapy and Children; Tapes: Meditation & Relaxation; Yoga for All Ages; Psychic and Spiritual Awareness. *Memberships:* Founder, Yoga Camps for Children with Special Needs; Quebec Association for Special Education; Quebec Association for Children with Learning Disabilities; Society for Emotionally Disturbed Children; Association for the Advancement of Science; Founder President, Spiritual Science Fellowship; Founder President, International College of Spiritual and Psychic Sciences. *Honours:* Maser Teacher, Protestant School Board, Montreal; Life Member, Quebec Association for Children with Learning Disabilities; Outstanding Canadian Educators, GEMS. *Hobbies:* Yoga Mediation Parapsychology; Stress Reducation Techniques; Creative Awarenss & Visualisation. *Address:* PO Box 1445 Stn. H, Montreal, Quebec, Canada H3G 2N3.

ROSSOW Rachel Lee Wheeler, b. 20 Mar. 1939, Long Beach, USA. Consultant/Psychiatric Mental Health Nursing. m. Carl Joseph Rossow, 27 Dec. 1964. *Education:* BS, Salve Regina College, 1960; MSN, Catholic University of America, 1973; DHL, Salve Regina, 1984. *Appointments:* Head Nurse, Medfield State Hospital, 1960-61; Novice, Discalced Carmelite Monastery, 1961-63; Nurse Clinical Specialist, Edgemeade Residential School, 1963-64; Nurse clinical Specialist, Kentucky, 1965-66; President, Alpha & Omega Inc., 1974-; Consultant, Children & Youth Services, State of Connecticut, 1987-. *Publications:* Booklet, A Child is a Child is a Child, 1983; articles in various journals. *Memberships Include:* Community Health Commission; Director, Secretary, Community Child Guidance Clinic, 1974-79; Co-Chair, Planning committee, Connecticut Developmental Disabilities Council, 1977-84. *Hobbies:* Nature; Photography; Painting. *Address:* 15 1/2 Lanz Lane, Ellington, CT 06029, USA.

ROTBERG Iris Comens, b. 16 Dec. 1932, Philadelphia, Pennsylvania, USA. Psychologist; Government Employee. m. Eugene Harvey Rotberg, 29 Aug. 1954, 2 daughters. *Education:* BA 1954, MA 1955, University of Pennsylvania; PhD, Experimental Psychology, Johns Hopkins Universty, 1958. *Appointments include:* Research psychologist Early Learning Task Force, Deputy Director Compensatory Education Study, Assistant Director, Senior Research Associate, National Institute of Education, 1973-84; Programme Director, Directorate for Science & Engineering Education, National Science Foundation, 1984-87, 1989-; Principal Investigator, Technology Policy Study, Committee on Science, Space & Technology, U.S. House of Representatives 1987-89. *Publications include:* Various articles, public policy issues, basic psychological research, journals including Harvard Education Review. *Memberships include:* American Psychological Association, Oversight Committee, Department of Educational Accountability, Montgomery County, (Maryland) Public Schools; American Association of University Professors; Association for Policy Analysis & Management. *Honours:* Academic scholarship, Johns Hopkins University, 1956-58; National Science Foundation Fellowships 1956-57, 1957-58; research grant, psychiolinguistics & learning, at Johns Hopkins 1963-66, National Science Foundation. *Hobbies:* Opera; Travel; Architecture; East Asian affairs; Politics; Sports. *Address:* 7211 Brickyard Road, Potomac, Maryland 20854, USA.

ROTCHFORD Patricia Kathleen, b. 17 Nov. 1945, Chicago, USA. Lawyer. m. Donald J Brayer, 1 son. *Education:* BA, Rosary College; JD, Northern Illinois University; MA, George Williams University. *Appointments:* Teacher, 1969-77; Private Legal Practice, 1977-79; Counsel for Shand Morahan Inc., 1979-82; Counsel for CNA Insurance Inc., 1983- 86;

General Counsel, UP Corp, 1986-87; General Counsel, UP Corp. Sec. for Inland Holdings Inc., 1987-. *Publications:* Womens Resource Guide; Womens Insurance & Finance Resource Guide & Workbook. *Memberships:* Womens Bar Association of Illinois; President, North Shore Chapter, National Association for Women in Careers; Business & Professional Women; National Association of Women Business Owners. *Honours:* Nominated for Woman of the Year Award. *Address:* 4105 Terrilyn Lane, Northbrook, IL 60062, USA.

ROTH June Doris Spiewak, b. 16 Feb. 1926, Haverstraw, New York, USA. Author; Syndicated columnist. m. Frederick Roth, 7 July 1945. 1 son, 1 daughter. *Education:* BA, Thomas Edison College, 1981; MS, University of Bridgeport, 1982. *Publications:* Author: The Freeze and Please Homefreezer Cookbook, 1963; The Rich and Delicious Low-Calorie Figure Slimming Cookbook, 1964; Thousand Calorie Cookbook, 1967; How to Use Sugar to Lose Weight, 1969; Fast and Fancy Cookbook, 1969; How to Cook like a Jewish Mother, 1969; The Take Good Care of My Son Cookbook for Brides, 1969; The Indoor/Outdoor Barbecue Book, 1970; The Pick of the Pantry Cookbook, 1970; Let's Have a Brunch Cookbook, 1971; Edith Bunkers' All in the Family Cookbook, 1972; The On-Your-Own Cookbook, 1972; Healthier Jewish Cookery: The Unsaturated Fat Way, 1972; Elegant Desserts, 1973; Old-Fashioned Candymaking, 1974; Salt-Free Cooking with Herbs and Spices, 1975; The Troubled Tummy Cookbook, 1976; Cooking for Your Hyperactive Child, 1977; The Galley Cookbook, 1977; The Food/Depression Connection, 1978; Aerobic Nutrition, 1981; The Allergic Gourmet, 1983; Living Better with a Special Diet, 1983; The Pasta Lover's Diet Book, 1984; The Executive Success Diet, 1986; Reversing Health Risks, 1988; Author national syndicated newspaper column Spl Diets, 1979; Recipe developer: The Pritikin program for Diet and Exercise, 1979. *Memberships:* Vice Pres evening group Teaneck (NJ) Br Nat Council Jewish Women, 1954, pres 1955, vp day group 1956; Authors League Am; Am Soc Journalists and Authors. *Honour:* RT French Tastemaker Award, 1975. *Address:* 1057 Oakland Court, Teaneck, NJ 07666, USA.

ROTH Marlen Deanne, b. 19 Nov. 1949, Havana, Cuba. State Government Professional; Translator. m. Karl Paul Roth, 19 Apr. 1980. *Education:* Graduate, Cosmopolitan Preparatory School, 1968; Italian, Business Law, Accounting, Business Administration, Insurance, Journalism, Political Science, Civics. *Appointments:* Freelance Translator, Writer, 1966-; Secretary, McMaster Carr Supply Co, Chicago, Illinois, 1966-70; Executive Actuarial Secretary, Iowers, Perrin, Forster & Crosby, Chicago, 1970-72; Administrative Assistant, Robert H. Hayes & Associates Inc, Chicago, 1972-73; Office Manager, Executive Assistant, Agencia Machado, Chicago, 1973; Executive Assistant, The Seidner-Malacara Agency, Guardian Life Insurance Co, Chicago, 1973-75; Office Manager, Executive Secretary, The Great-West Life Insurance Co, Chicago, 1975- 76; Executive Secretary, International Operations, Unitech Chemical Inc, Division of Esmark Inc, Chicago, 1976-77; Office Manager, Executive Secretary, 1977-78, Administrative Aide, 1977-84, Governor's Office, Illinois Office of Interagency Cooperation, Chicago; Deputy Director's Executive Assistant, Bureau of Marketing, Illinois Department of Commerce and Community Affairs, Chicago, 1984-87; Director's Executive Assistant, Illinois State Lottery, Chicago, 1987-; Associate Editor, Art Critic, Chicago Hispano Newspaper, 1973- 77; Art Critic/Interviewer/News Announcer/Show Host, WOPA Radio Station, 1978-83; TV/radio Translator (English/Spanish), Illinois Information Service, 1988- ; Notary Public. *Memberships:* Doris Day Animal League; Former member: International Visitors Center; American Society of Notaries; Sub-Committee on Minority Women, Illinois Commission on the Status of Women; Many past political activities include: Chair, Illinois Republican State Committee (1981-88); Deputy Committeeman, Hispanic Affairs, Proviso Township, 1984-86. *Honours:* Subject of Que Pasa

show on Hispanic women issues, Oakton Community College. *Hobbies:* Travel; Politics.

ROTH Melissa Jane, b. 15 Apr. 1949, Birmingham, Alabama, USA. President of two companies. m. Jeffrey L Roth, 22 July 1978. 1 daughter. *Education:* BSc, University of Montevallo, Alabama, 1967-72; Numerous postgraduate classes at various universities. *Appointments:* Recruiter/Sales, Burroughs-Wellcome Co, Research Traingel Park, North Carolina, 1973-77; Professional Recruiter, Abbott Laboratories, Chicago, 1977-78; Personnel Specialist, Vulcan Materials, Birmingham, Alabama, 1979-80; Senior Consultant, Robert Johnson Associates, Birmingham, Alabama, 1980-82; President, Career Advisors, Inc, Birmingham, Alabama, 1982-; President, 1st Impressions Printing. *Publications:* Author, Business trends/methods, 1983; Author, Career/Employment Trends, 1983; Lecturer to Human resources/accounting classes and professional associations, 1974-. *Memberships:* President, National Association of Accountants Magic City Chapter, 1987-88; Hoover Chamber of Commerce; Founding Member, Clark Co Young Republicans, Athens, Georgia, 1975-77; Past Treasurer, Alabama Association of Personal Consultants, 1983-84; Past Officer, National Association of Personal Consultants, 1983-84. *Honours:* Barnhardt Award, 1985-86; Nominated for Top 40 under 40 for Birmingham Business Journal. *Hobbies:* Horseback Riding; Snow skiing; White water rafting; Gardening; Travelling; Photography. *Address:* c/o Career Advisors, Inc, 2117 16th Avenue South, Birmingham, AL 35205, USA.

ROTH Nancy, b. Philadelphia, Pennsylvania, USA. Director, Religious Education. *Education:* Franklin College; Century University; Temple University; St Joseph's University; Gratz College; St Charles Seminary; University of San Francisco; Xavier University. BS, Business Administration; BA, Public Administration; Candidate, MS, Counselling. Numerous certificates, aspects of religious study. *Appointments:* Inspector, EEO Counsellor, Bureau of ATF, US Treasury, 1967-88; Board member, President, Lee H Are, 1967- 83; Director, EEO Counsellor, CLC Centre, 1988-; Director Religious Education & teacher, St James Church, 1962-; CRE & teacher, North Pennsylvania Regional Parish Religious Education School, 1985-. *Publications:* Inexpensive Craft Projects for Groups, 1972-; Your Adult Pray-er, 1976, 1983; Editor: Sacred Heart Devotion News 1966-, Interchange 1968-71, Retreat Directory 1976- , Marian News 1986-; Articles, various professional journals. *Memberships include:* Offices, past/present, various professional, religious & community organisations. *Honours:* Sullivan Zigler Lay Ministry Award, 1986; Jos. Colman Theology Award, 1965; 1972 National Young Adult; US Treasury Award, 1985; NFCLO Service Award, 1981; Annual award, Inter-Sodality Committee, 1974; Wigs 1988 Pennsylvania Woman of Year. *Address:* Box 202, Lansdale, Pennsylvania 19446, USA.

ROTHENBERG Saundra Hamm, b. 30 May 1943, New York City, USA. Regional Field Consultant for the State of Florida for AMIT Women. m. Max Rothenberg, 21 Feb. 1965, 1 son, 1 daughter. *Address:* 1320 NE 172 St., No. Miami Beach, FL 33162, USA.

ROTHROCK Jan Campbell, b. 24 Jan. 1935, Duncan, USA. CPA; Real Estate Broker; Lecturer. m. E. S. Rothrock, 6 Mar. 1972, 4 sons, 3 daughters. *Education:* Studies at various Universities including: Univeristy of Houston, 1972, University of St Thomas, 1975, 1977, Keele University, England, 1976. *Appointments:* Secretary, Treasurer, RES Leasing & Management, Houston, 1967-72, President 1972-; Jan Rothrock, Broker, Houston, 1976-; Jan Campbell, CPA, Houston, 1979-; Successor Trustee, Big State Grass Farms, 1979- ; Board of Directors, various Companies. *Memberships:* Lupus Foundation of America, Membership Chairman, Houston Chapter, 1986; Texas, National Associations of Realtors; Houston Board of Realtors; AICPA; TSCPA. *Honours:* Phi Eta Sigma; Alpha Lambda Delta. *Address:* 3257 Ella Lee Lane, Houston, TX 77019, USA.

ROTHSCHILD Miriam Louisa (Hon Mrs Miriam Lane), b. 5 Aug. 1908. Retired. m. Capt George Lane, MC, 1943 (dissolved 1957). 1 son, 3 daughters (1 deceased). *Education:* Six Honorary Doctorates (Science). *Publications:* 320 scientific papers and 12 books; Catalogue Rothschild Collection of Fleas (6 vols), British Museum); (with Theresa Clay) Fleas, Flukes and Cuckoos; Dear Lord Rothschild, Animals & Man. *Memberships:* Zoological and Entomological Research Council; Marine Biological Assoc; Royal Entomological Society; Systematics Assoc; Soc for Promotion of Nature Conservation, Ed, Novitates Zoologica, 1938-41; Publications Committee, Zoological Society; Foreign Office, 1940-42; Trustee, British Museum of Natural History, 1967-75; American Academy of Arts and Sciences. Romanes Lecturer; Visiting Professor in Biology, Royal Free Hospital. *Honours:* Hon Fellow, St Hugh's College, Oxford; Hon DSc, Oxford, Gotenburg, Hull, Leicester, North Western University (Chicago), Open University U.K; Defence Medal (1940-45); FRS; CBE; Wigglesworth Medal; Medal Soc. Chemical Oecology Floral Medal Lisin. Society, Gold Medals R.H.S; Fellow, The Royal Entomological Society; Foreign Member, The American Society of Parasitologists; Fellow, Institute of Biology. *Hobby:* Watching butterflies. *Address:* Ashton, Peterborough, England.

ROTHSTEIN Beverly Doris, b. 22 Feb. 1935, New York City, USA. Psychotherapist. m. Toby Frankel, 20 May 1965, 1 son, 1 daughter. *Education:* BA, 1953, MS, 1956, Hunter College; MA, Columbia University, 1954; PhD, New York University, 1959. *Appointments:* Teacher, Guidance Counsellor, 1955-58; Teacher, Emotionally Disturbed Children, 1958-59; Lecturer, Psychology, Westchester Community College; Private Practice, 1959-; Assistant Director, Student Activities, Queens College, 1961-64. *Publications:* Contributor to psychology journals. *Memberships:* American, Eastern Group Psychotherapy Associations; New York Society of Clinical Psychologists. *Hobbies:* Painting; Sketching; Ice Skating; Skiing; Theatre; Films; Gardening. *Address:* 65 Clover Drive, Great Neck, NY 11021, USA.

ROTHWEILER Therese M, b. 18 Feb. 1929, Iowa, USA. Nurse/CEO. m. George, 12 Sept. 1953, 3 sons, 2 daughters. *Education:* BS, Loretto Heights College, 1951; MS, 1972, PhD, 1980, University of Minnesota; MOA St. Thomas College, 1989. *Appointments:* President, Health Professional Nursing Service Inc.; Assistant Professor: Gustavus Adolphus College, 1975-80; University of Minnesota, 1980-87. *Publications:* Articles in: Nurse Educator; Nursing Management; RN. *Memberships:* Rotary International; Chamber of Commerce; Minnesota Nurses Association, District Board of Directors. *Honours:* Sigma Xi; Sigma Theta Tau; Nominee Athena Award. *Hobbies:* Travel; Cross-Country Skiing; Biking; Hiking; Reading. *Address:* 8707 Grospoint Av. S., Cottage Grove, MN 55016, USA.

ROTTER Doris, b. 13 June 1936, Stuttgart, Federal Republic of Germany. Psychologist. *Education:* Reck Language School, Heilbronn, Germany, 1959-61; BA, California State University, Los Angeles, USA, 1970; MA, 1971; PhD, 1974, Claremont Graduate School; Postdoctoral Fellow, Neuropsychiatric Institute, University of California, Los Angeles, 1974-75. *Appointments:* Translator, North Atlantic Treaty Organization, France, 1961-64; Senior Psychometrist, Neuropsychiatric Instutute, University of California, Los Angeles, 1974; Assistant Professor, Medical School, Psychology, University of Minnesota, 1975-77' Core Faculty, California School of Professional Psychology, 1977-78; Lecturer, Medicine, University of California, San Francisco, 1977-78; Affiliated professional staff, San Francisco General Hospital, 1978-; Faculty, Wright Institue, Berkeley, 1979-80; Private Practice, A Rotter Psychology Centre, Brekeley & San Francisco, 1978-. *Publications:* co-author, Theoretical Issues and Clinical Application in Sex Therapy; Workshops Presented, University of Mannheim and University of Köln, Germany, 1975; contributor of articles in professional journals. *Memberships Include:* American & California State Psychological Associations; Licensed Psychologist

State of California. *Honours:* Research Grant, University of Minnesota, 1976-77; NDEA Title IV, 2 years, National Science Foundation Traineeship, 1 year, Claremont Graduate School, etc. *Hobbies:* Skiing; Windsurfing; Tennis. *Address:* 555 Dwight Place, Berkeley, CA 94704, USA.

ROUDYBUSH Alexandra, b. 14 Mar. 1911, Hyres, France. Novelist. m. Franklin Roudybush, 1942. *Education:* Attended school at Broadstairs, England; St Paul's School for Girls, London; London School of Economics, London. *Appointments:* Washington Correspondent for the London Evening Standard, 1931; Time Magazine, 1933; Columbia Broadcasting System, Washington DC, USA, 1935; White House Correspondent for Mutual Broadcasting System, 1940. *Publications:* Before the Ball was Over, 1965; Death of a Moral Person, 1967; Capital Crime, 1969; House of the Cat, 1970; A Sybaritic Death, 1972; Suddenly in Paris, 1975; The Female of the Species, 1977; Blood Ties, 1981. 10 American and British Crime Writers. *Honour:* Poe Prize. *Hobby:* Turkish cooking. *Address:* Sauveterre de Rougergue, 12800 Aveynon, France.

ROUECHE Suanne Davis, b. 6 Aug. 1942, Dallas, Texas, USA. Educational Administrator. m. John Edward Roueche, 22 May 1976, 1 son, 2 daughters. *Education:* BA English 1964, MA 1967, North Texas State University; PhD, Educational Administration, University of Texas, Austin, 1976. *Career:* Teacher, English, Sam Houston High School, Arlington, Texas 1964-65, MacArthur High School, Irving 1966-67; Instructor, Developmental Writing, El Centro College, Dallas, 1967-74; Director, National Institute for Staff & Organisational Development, 1977-. *Publications:* Co-author: Awareness, 1972, revised 1977; Developmental Education: Primer for Program Development & Evaluation, 1977; Literacy in Development: Multidisciplinary Field Investigation of Literacy Development at Community Colleges (final report, NIE project), 1981; College Responses to Low-Achieving Students: Report on National Study, 1984. Co-editor, Proceedings, National Conference on Teaching Excellence, 1984-86. Numerous book chapters; Articles, professional journals. *Memberships:* American Association of Community & Junior Colleges; AACJC Council of Universities & Colleges; American Association of Women in Community & Junior Colleges; National Council for Staff, Program & Organisational Development. *Honours:* Numerous awards & recognitions, contributions to higher education. *Hobbies:* Needlepoint; Wildlife Rescue Inc; Reading. *Address:* 6804 Edgefield Drive, Austin, Texas 78731, USA.

ROURKE Kelli (Kali) Priestley, b. 21 Dec. 1958, Bellingham, Washington, USA. Businesswoman. m. Daniel Jeremiah Rourke III, 4 Oct. 1986, 1 son. *Education:* Graduate, Texas Savings & Loan School; Course I, Mortgage Bankers Association School; 'NTP' sales training, PMI Mortgages Insurance Company. *Appointments:* Closing Coordinator, Mason McDuffie Mortgage Company, 1979-80; Branch Manager, Escrow Officer, Austin Title Company Inc, 1980-83; Assistant Vice President, Escrow Officer, Travis Title Company, 1983; Account Executive, PMI Mortgage Insurance Company, 1983-87; Assistant Vice President, Closing Operations Manager, 1st Federal Savings division, Guaranty Federal Savings Bank, Austin, Texas. *Memberships:* Vice President, Austin Association of Professional Mortgage Women; National Association of Female Executives; Austin Circle of Theatres; Austin Women's Council of Realtors. *Honours:* Silver Circle Award (sales) 1985, President's Circle Award 1985, PMI Mortgage Insurance Company. *Hobbies:* Professional singer & actress, local theatre & theatre support groups. *Address:* First Federal Savings-Residential Lending, 200 East 10th Street, Austin, Texas 78701, USA.

ROVER Constance, b. 15 Dec. 1910, Cockermouth, Cumbria, England. Retired. m. Frederick Herbert Rover, 22 Apr. 1944, deceased. 1 daughter. *Education:* BSc (Econ) 1948, MSc (Econ) 1961, PhD 1966, University of London. *Appointments:* Freelance Lecturer, Worker's Educational Association and various local educational authorities, 1948-57; Lecturer, Principal Lecturer and Deputy Head of Department of Sociology and Law, 1957-72, Polytechnic of North London. *Publications:* The Punch Book of Women's Rights, 1967; Women's Suffrage & Party Politics in Britain 1867-1914, 1967; Love, Morals and the Feminists, 1970. Contributor to International Women's News and other feminist journals. *Memberships:* International Alliance of Women; Fawcett Society; Friends of the Fawcett Library; Former Member, Suffragette Fellowship; National Women's Citizens Association. *Hobbies:* The Women's Movement generally; Foreign Travel; Bridge; Education generally. *Address:* Flat 3, 42 Shorncliffe Road, Folkestone, Kent, CT20 2NB, England.

ROWBOTHAM Sheila, b. 27 Feb. 1943, Leeds, England. Freelance Writer; Teacher. 1 son. *Education:* St Hilda's College, Oxford, 1961- 64. *Appointments:* Part-time Teacher, Schools of Further Education, 1964-74; Part-time Teacher, Workers Education Association, 1968-78; Visiting Professor, Amsterdam University, Netherlands, 1981-83; Newspaper Editor, Greater London Council, 1982-86; Currently Teacher, Kent University, and Writer. *Publications:* Women's Resistance and Revolution; Woman's Consciousness, Man's World; Hidden from History; Stella Browne, A New World for Women; Dreams and Dilemmas; Friends of Alice Wheeldon; Socialism and the New Life (with Jeff Weeks); Edward Carpenter and Havelock Ellis; Dutiful Daughters (with Jean McCrindle); Beyond the Fragments (with Hilary Wainwright and Lynne Segal); Contributions to Fathers (edited Ursula Owen) and Truth Dare or Promise (edited Liz Heron); The Past is Before Us, Feminism in Action since the late 1960's; Pandora, 1989. *Honours:* Honorary Fellow, Womens Studies, North London Polytechnic. *Hobbies:* Swimming; Cooking; Dancing; Visiting places of historic interest especially old prehistoric settlements; Reading science fantasy; Children's films based on fantasy stories. *Address:* 97 Powerscroft Road, London E5 0PT, England.

ROWE Dorothy Isdell, b. 1 Sept. 1929, Springfield, MO, USA. Supervisor. m. Melvin E. Rowe, 25 Nov. 1950, 2 sons, 2 daughters. *Education:* Ferrum College 1947-48; American University , 1950; AS, Chaffey Collee, 1986. *Appointments:* Department of Defense, 1948-50; Clerk, Law Firm, 1965-67; Research, Department of Defense, 1967-69; Supervisor, San BDNO Co., 1971- . *Publication:* Co-Author, Isdell-Kidd Ireland & USA. *Memberships:* DAR; First Families of Ohio; Provincial Families of Maryland. *Honours:* Awards, Certificates, DAR, 1984, 1985, 1988. *Hobbies:* Travel; Genealogy; Music; Sponsor of Foreign Students. *Address:* 9095 Helena Ave., Montclair, CA 91763, USA.

ROWE Geneva L, b. 11 Aug. 1927, Atlanta, GA, USA. Psychotherapist. m. Fred. E. Rowe, 3 May 1958, 1 son, 2 daughters. *Education:* AB, 1968; MSW, University of Georgia, 1970; PhD, Florida State University, 1978. *Appointments:* Lecturer, Sociology, Oglethorpe University, 1978-81; Director, President, Northeast Counseling Center, 1978-; Allied Health Professional, CPC Parkwood Hospital; Consultant to business organizations regarding Stress Management. *Publications:* Articles in professional journals. *Memberships* Numerous professional organisations including: American Association for Marriage & Family Therapy; Georgia Association for Marriage & Family Therapy; International Council of Sex Education & Parenthood; National Council of Family Relations. *Address:* 2005 Woodsdale Road NE, Atlanta, GA 30324, USA.

ROWE Myra Owen, b. 4 Mar. 1927, Mt Holly, Arkansas, USA. Novelist. m. W C Rowe, 29 Dec. 1945. 1 son, 3 daughters. *Education:* BA, English, Southern Arkansas University, 1960; MA, English, Northeast Louisiana University, 1965; Postgraduate study, University of Southern Mississippi, 1971. *Appointments:* Teacher: English, History, Lee Jr High, Monroe, 1960-68; English Teacher, Jones Co Jr College,

Ellisville, 1968- 72; English Teacher, River Oaks High School, Monroe, 1972-73 and 1975-76. *Publications:* Wild Embrace, 1985; Louisiana Lady, 1986; Cajun Rose, 1987; River Temptress, 1987; Treasure's Golden Dream, 1988. Articles published in Romance Writers Report; Fiction Writers' Magazine; Romantic Times. Book to be published in 1988, A Splendid Yearning. *Memberships:* National League of American Pen Women; Romance Writers of America; Northeast Louisiana Chapter of Romance Writers of America; Sigma Tau Delta, National English Fraternity, Charter President, 1959-60. *Honours:* Reviewer's Choice Award from Romantic Times for Most Exotic Setting in Cajun Rose, 1987. *Hobbies:* Reading; Walking; Ballroom dancing; Travelling; Collecting demi-tasse cups; Collecting clown dolls. *Address:* 428 Eastlake, Rt No 4, Monroe, LA 71203, USA

ROWETT Helen Graham Quiller, b. 30 Dec. 1915, London, England. Retired Lecturer. *Education:* MA, Cambridge University, 1938; M.I.Biol., F.R.S.A. *Appointments:* Graduate Research Scholarship, Manchester University; Teacher: Melville College, Edinburgh, Berwick Grammar School; Lecturer, Zoology, Plymouth College of Technology, 1944-1967; Lecturer in Educational Technology, 1967-76. *Publications:* Guide to Dissection, Parts 1-5; Dissection Guide; Histology & Emryology; The Rat as a Small Mammal; Basic Anatomy & Physiology; Guide to the Two Moors Way. *Memberships:* Society of Authors; West Country Writers, Committee; Tavistock Group of Artists, Secretary, Chairman, now Exhibition Secretary. *Honours:* Gwendoline Crewdson Memorial Prize, 1938; Theresa Montifiore Prize, 1939; Yarrow Scholarship. *Hobbies:* Art; Theatre; Craftwork; Walking. *Address:* 3 Manor Park, Dousland, Yelverton, Devon PL20 6LH, England.

ROWLAND Diana Kathleen, b. 13 Oct. 1950, Hemet, California, USA. Consultant. m. Jeremy Giddings, 20 June 1971, div. 1974. *Appointments:* Gakken Publishing Co and International Horizons, Japan, 1974-77; Meadowlark Holistic Health Center, 1977-78; Classical Guitar Instructor, Mt. San Jacinto College, 1979-81; Liaison, Gosho International, 1982-85; Consultant, 1985-. *Publications:* Japanese Business Etiquette, 1985; Dances: Duality; 1 Ching. *Memberships:* United States Parachute Association; Society for Intercultural Education, Training and Research; World Trade Association; San Diego Chamber of Commerce. *Honours:* Member, 1st Place Skydiving Team, Pope Valley, California, 1978; Member, 1st Place Skydiving Team, Rumble Seat Meet, Perris Valley, California, 1070; Organiser, World Record Largest Nighttime Skydiving Formation, 1979; 24 Hours Freefall, 1980; Co-Organiser, World Record Largest Skydiving Formation, 1981; 1000 Parachute Jumps, 1981. *Hobbies:* Skydiving; Classical guitar; Hiking; Speaking Japanese; Eating sushi; Reading. *Address:* 3166 Midway Drive, Suite 124, San Diego, CA 92110, USA.

ROWLATT Penelope Anne, b. 1 May 1936, London, England. Economist. m. Charles Rowlatt, 12 may 1961, 1 son, 3 daughters. *Education:* BA Oxon, Natural Science, Physics, 1958; PhD, London, Mathematical Physics, 1963; MSc LSE, Econometrics & Mathematical Economics, 1973. *Appointments* include: Lecturer, Westfield College, 1961-63; Economic Models Ltd, 1975- 76; National Institute for Economic & Scientific Research, 1976-78; Government Economic Service, 1978-87; National Economic Research Association, 1987-. *Publications:* General Equivalence Theorem in Vector Field Theory, article, in Nuclear Physics, 1961; Book, Group Theory & Elementary Particles, 1966; Various academic papers on modelling wages & prices, 1976-88. *Hobbies:* Travel; Walking; Ocean sailing; Conversation; Thinking; Listening to Music. *Address:* 10 Hampstead Hill Gardens, London NW3 2PL, England.

ROWLES Alison H, b. 29 Oct. 1950, Connecticut, USA. Managing Director. m. David A Lawson, III, 2 July 1985. 2 sons. *Education:* BFA, Washington University, 1968-72; Business Management Seminars, University of Chicago, 1973. *Appointments:* Sales Representative, Hershey Video Systems, Inc, Chicago, USA, 1969-71; Director of Marketing, Perceptive Group Companies, Inc, Chicago, 1971-73; Owner/Manager, Rowles Woods (Aspen Design Studio), Aspen, 1974-76; Sales Representative then Marketing Manager, International, QWIP Systems (Division of Exxon), Orlando, Florida, 1977-81; Operations Manager, Exxon Office Systems, International, Geneva, Switzerland, 1981-83; Sales Manager, Otrona Advanced Systems, SA, Geneva, 1983-85; Managing Director, Boxmart, SA, Geneva, 1985-. *Address:* 1 Chemin Taponnet, CH 1291 Commugny, Switzerland.

ROZAR Beverly Lorraine Blalock, b. 30 Dec. 1950, Jacksonville, Florida, USA. Executive Director. m. 11 Dec. 1971, 1 daughter. *Education:* AA, Business; BA Communications; MPA. *Appointments:* Fund Raiser, Baptist Medical Centre; Director of Development, Miami Children's Hospital; Executive Director, Arthritis Foundation. *Publications:* Freelance Writer; articles in local papers, magazines, etc. *Memberships:* Pilot Club International; International Association of Business Communicators; National Society for Fund Raising Executives. *Honours:* One of America's Most Outstanding Young Women, 1986; Graduated, summa cum lade; Dean's List. *Hobbies:* Reading; Writing; Horse Riding; Skiing; Chess; Travel. *Address:* 2445 Jones Road, Jacksonville, FL 32220, USA.

ROZZELL Andrea Leslie, b. 20 Jan. 1959, Little Rock, Arkansas, USA. Architect. m. W. Scott Breeding, 26 Dec. 1987, 1 child. *Education:* BArch, cum laude, Arizona State University, 1982; Registered Architect, Arizona; Certified, National Council of Architectural Registration Boards. *Appointments:* Myron Riggs Brower, Architect Inc, 1982; Knight Sevey Design PC, 1985; Linthicum Constructors Inc, 1986; Clark & Van Voorhis, Architects Inc, 1986; Reid & Associates, Architects Inc, 1987; A. Leslie Rossell, Architect (own firm), 1987-. *Membership:* American Institute of Architects. *Honour:* Award, Construction Specifications Institute, 1982. *Address:* 2102 West Knox Road, Chandler, Arizona 85224, USA.

RUBENS Bernice Ruth, b. 26 July 1928, Cardiff, Wales. Novelist. m. Rudi Nassauer, 29 Dec. 1947. 2 daughters. *Education:* BA (Hons) English, University of Wales, Cardiff. *Appointments:* Followed teaching profession, 1950-55. *Publications:* Set on Edge, 1960; Madame Sousatzka, 1962; Mate in Three, 1965; The Elected Member, 1969; Sunday Best, 1971; Go Tell the Lemming, 1973; I Sent a Letter to my Love, 1975; The Ponsonby Post, 1977; A Five Year Sentence, 1978; Spring Sonata, 1979; Birds of Passage, 1981; Brothers, 1983; Mr Wakefield's Crusade, 1985; Our Father, 1987. *Memberships:* Society of Authors; PEN (Executive). *Honours:* Booker Prize, 1970; Welsh Arts Council, 1988; American Blue Ribbon award for documentary film, Stress, 1968. *Hobbies:* Playing the 'cello. *Address:* 16A Belsize Park Gardens, London NW3 4LD, England.

RUBIN Diana Kwiatkowski, b. 30 Dec. 1958, New York City, USA. Editor; Poet; Writer. m. Paul L. Rubin, 1 Apr. 1986. *Education:* BA, Marymount, Manhattan College, 1988. *Publications:* Panorama, 1979; The Poet Pope, 1980; View from this Side of Heaven, 1982. *Memberships:* Poets & Writers; Academy of American Poets; Writers Community Inc. *Honours:* various awards & prizes for poetry & fiction. *Hobbies:* Writing; Reading; Ceramics; Drawing; Needlepoint. *Address:* 12 Gales Road, Edison, NJ 08837, USA.

RUBIN Nancy Zimman, b. 25 Nov. 1944, Boston, USA. Journalist; Author. m. Peter Rubin, 9 July 1967, 2 daughters. *Education:* BA, Jackson College, Tufts University, 1966; MAT, Brown University Graduate School, 1967. *Appointment:* Freelance Journalist; Author. *Publications:* The New Suburban Woman: Beyond Myth and Motherhood, 1982; The Mother Mirror: How a Generation of Women is Changing Motherhood in America, 1984; Contributing Editor, Parents; contributor to: New York Times; McCall's;

Ladies Home Journal; Savvy; Travel & Leisure. *Memberships:* American Society of Journalists & Authors; Author's League of America. *Honours:* Time Inc. Scholar, 1979; Bread Loaf Writers' Conference; Fellow, McDowell Colony, 1981. *Hobbies:* Literature; Dance; Music; Horticulture; Skiing; Sailing. *Address:* c/o Agnes Birnbaum, Bleecker Street Associates, 88 Bleecker St, Suite 6P, New York, NY 10012, USA.

RUBINSTEIN Eva (Anna), b. 18 Aug. 1933, Buenos Aires, Argentina. Photographer; Teacher. m. The Rev. William Sloane Coffin Jr, 12 Dec. 1956, div. 1968, 2 sons (1 dec.), 1 daughter. *Education:* Scripps College, USA, 1950-51; Theatre Department, University of California, Los Angeles, 1952; Studied Photography with Sean Kernan, 1967, Lisette Model, 1969, Ken Heyman, 1970, Jim Hughes and Diane Arbus, 1971. *Career:* Dancer and Actor, On and Off Broadway and on tour, Europe; Played in The Diary of Anne Frank original production, New York, 1955-56; Photographer, 1967-; Numerous 1-person and group shows throughout USA, Netherlands, France, Belgium, Federal Republic of Germany, Italy, UK, Spain, Portugal, Poland, Sweden, Canada, Japan; Many workshop and teaching assignments including: Faculty, New School for Social Research, New York, 1980, 1981, 1982, 1983; State Higher School of Film, Theatre and Television, Lodz, Poland, spring 1986, autumn/winter, 1986-87; Seminars, symposia, conferences, slide shows. *Creative works include:* Photographs in collections at museums and universities, USA, France, Belgium, Jerusalem, Sweden, Poland, Federal Republic of Germany, Italy; Work in various books, major magazines and photographic publications, USA, Europe, South America, including; Eva Rubinstein-Portfolio I (12 photographs), 1975, Portfolio II (17 photographs), 1980-81; Persephone, 20 years of photographs by Eva Rubinstein, 1989. *Memberships:* American Society of Magazine Photographers; Polish Institute of Arts and Sciences in America. *Hobbies:* Passion for music and books. *Address:* 145 West 27th Street, New York, NY 10001, USA.

RUBINSTEIN Helge, b. 27 Aug. 1929, Nurnberg, Germany. Writer; Entrepreneur. m. Hilary Harold Rubinstein, 6 Aug. 1955, 3 sons, 1 daughter. *Education:* MA, Somerville College, Oxford, 1951. *Appointments:* Assistant to Director, World Federation for Mental Health, 1952-55; Marriage Counsellor, 1966-; Chairman, London Marriage Guidance Council, 1976-80. *Publications:* numerous cookery books, best known: Penguin Freezer Cookbook, 1973; The Chocolate Book, 1981; Regular contributor to Homes & Gardens, 1973-83; Agony Aunt, Parents Magazine, & Brides Magazine; Oxford Book of Marriage, anthology, 1989. Managing Director, Ben's Cookies - Shops in London, Oxford, Stratford-upon-Avon and Bath. *Address:* 61 Clarendon Road, London W11 4JE, England.

RUBINSTEIN Shirley Joy, b. 19 Nov. 1927, Toronto, Ontario, Canada. Chief Executive Corporate Officer. m. Philip Rubinstein, 17 Aug. 1947, deceased. 1 son, 2 daughters. *Appointments:* Jewish Agency for Palestine, 1945-48; Founded Nursing Services Inc, 1978; Founded Fantasy Factory Inc and Pegasus Limousine Services Inc. *Memberships:* DC Cancer Society; B'Nai Brith. *Hobbies:* Collect Antique furniture and Jewellery; Collect contemporary netsukes. *Address:* 410 Apple Grove Road, Silver Spring, Maryland 20904, USA.

RUBY Thelma, b. 23 Mar. 1925, Leeds, Yorkshire, England. Actress. m. Peter Frye, 23 Dec. 1970. *Education:* Finch College, New York, USA; Yale Drama School. *Appointments:* Played Golda Meir in Golda by William Gibson, South Africa, 1978; 13 programmes in English for Educational TV, 1970-79; Appearances in England: Cowardy Custard by Noel Coward; A Funny Thing Happened on the Way to the Forum; So Who Needs Men; Fallen Angels, by Noel Coward; The Rose and the Ring, by W M Thackeray; Me by C P Taylor; Momma Golda; Cinderella; Handy Dandy; Fiddler on the Roof at London's Apollo, Victoria; Numerous other starring roles, countless TV appearances, films and cabaret. *Address:* c/o Roger Carey, 64 Thornton Avenue, London W4 1QQ, England.

RUDDICK Bonnie Lou Kneebone, b. 29 Aug. 1946. Writer; Lecturer. m. Douglas Hampton Ruddick, 12 July 1980, 1 son, 1 daughter (by previous marriage), 1 stepson, 1 stepdaughter. *Education:* BA, East Stroudsburg University, 1977; MA, 1985. *Appointments:* Public Speaker to Sales & Civic Orgnisations, 1979-; Freelance Writer, 1966-; Owner, Markim Associates Public Relations & Writing Consultant, 1985-; Community Activist Teacher, appointed to Pennsylvania Council of Community Leaders, 1987; Candidate to Pennsylvania House of Representative, 1987. *Publications:* Writer, producer, Childrens programmes with religious themes; Writer, moderator religious book discussion groups, Inspiration Exchanges, 1980-. *Memberships:* Founder, Speakers Bureau, 1987, Parents for Students Against Drunk Drivers; Moravian League of Women Voters Historical Society; American Association of Unviersity Women; Phi Alpha Theta; Chemical Free Graduation Parties; Senior Citizens Information Day Expose. *Hobbies:* Designer, Needlepoint Canvasas; Oil Painting; Sewing *Address:* RD2 Box 443B, Saylorsburg, PA 18353, USA.

RUDNICK Lois Palken, b. 18 June 1944, Boston, Massachusetts, USA. Educator. m. Steven Rudnick, 27 June 1965, 1 daughter. *Education:* BA magna cum laude, English Literature, Jackson College, 1966; MA, Humanistic Studies, Tufts University, 1968; PhD, American Civilisation, Brown University, 1977. *Appointments:* Assistant Professor 1977-83, Associate Professor 1983, English Department, University of Massachusetts, Boston. *Publications:* Mabel Dodge Luhan: New Woman, New Worlds, 1984, 1987; Introduction to republication, M. D. Luhan's memoirs, Movers & Shakers & Edge of Taos Desert, 1985, 1987. Also: Co-editor, The Cultural Moment: 1915, volume of essays about Modernism in American Culture, Politics and Soceity, in progess; History of counter-culture, northern New Mexico, 20th century, in progress. *Memberships:* American Studies Association; Council, New England American Studies Association; Multi-Ethnic Literature of US. *Honours:* Phi Beta Kappa, 1966; President's Award, In Honour of Writer, University of Massachusetts, 1985; Grants, National Endowment for Humanities, 1986, 1989. *Interests:* American studies, women's studies, immigration & ethnicity, specialising in Progressive era (1890-1920). *Address:* American Studies Program, University of Massachusetts, Harbor Campus, Boston, MA 02125, USA.

RUFFIN Darlene Louise Marshall, b. 3 Dec. 1940, Dallas, Texas, USA. Health Care Administrator. m. (2) Lee M. Zachery, 17 Oct. 1984. 2 sons, 2 daughters. *Education:* Diploma, Palestine School of Nursing, 1962; AAS, El Centro College, 1968; BA, La Verne College, 1971; BS, College of St Francis, 1980; CNA, American Nurses Association, 1984; PhD, Union Graduate School, 1985. *Appointments include:* Assistant Administrator, Hubbard Hospital, Nashville 1980-84, Medical Arts Hospital, Houston, Texas 1983-85, St Elizabeth Hospital 1983-85; President, Chief Executive Officer, DMR International, Houston/Atlanta, 1986-. *Publication:* Nursing Shortage: A Black Nurse's Perspective, 1981. *Memberships include:* Numerous offices, various professional organisations. *Honours:* National Woman of Status, NWOA, 1989; Distinguishd Service Award 1986; Contractor of Year 1985, AMC; Member Award, ABNA, 1979; Sickle Cell Anaemia Achievement Award, 1975; Citizen of Year, DNC, 1971. *Hobbies:* Collecting matches; Working with young adults; Tennis; Church work, Brentwood Baptist Church, Houston, Texas. *Address:* 2156 Shancey Lane, College Park, Georgia 30349, USA.

RUFFLE Joan Madeline, b. 28 Dec. 1945, Rockville Center, New York, USA. Anesthesiologist. *Education:* AB, Chemistry, Brown University, 1969; MD, Hershey Medical Center, Pennsylvania State University, 1973; Intern and Resident in Surgery, Boston University, 1973-75; Resident in Surgery, 1975-76, Resident in Anaesthesia, 1977-79, Hartford Hospital; Assistant Professor of Anaesthesia, Hershey Medical Center, Pennsylvania State University, 1979-. *Publications:* Rapid Induction of Halothane Anesthesia in Man, 1985; Comparison of Rapid and Conventional Inhalation Inductions of Halothane Oxygen Anesthesia in Healthy Men and Women, 1987. *Memberships:* American Society of Anesthesiologists; Society for Pediatric Anesthesia; American Academy of Pediatrics; International Anesthesia Research Society; Pennsylvania Society of Anesthesiologists; American Medical Association; Pennsylvania Medical Society; Dauphin County Medical Society. *Hobbies:* Tennis; Walking; Reading; Cooking. *Address:* Hershey Medical Center, Department of Anesthesia, PO Box 850, Hershey, PA 17033, USA.

RUGGIERO Deborah Lee, b. 2 Apr. 1958, Providence, Rhode Island, USA. Director of Sales and Marketing; Media Trainer. *Education:* BA magna cum laude, English, Communications, Boston College, 1980. *Appointments:* Radio News Anchor, CBS, Boston, Massachusetts, 1979-83; Morning News Anchor, WMJX, Boston, 1984-88; Professor of Radio Performance, Emerson College, Boston, 1984-; Director of Sales and Marketing for Creative Communications, Media Consulting, East Providence, Rhode Island, 1988-. *Creative works:* American Cancer Society Multimedia presentation, 1982; Narrations: Giant Ocean Tank, New England Aquarium, Boston, 1982; Video Encyclopedia of 20th Century, 1989. *Memberships:* National Organization of Women; Italian-Americans in Communication. *Honours:* Voted Most Likely to Succeed and Most Outstanding, Lincoln Senior High School, 1980; Celebrity Presenter to Bell Ringer Awards, Boston, for Excellence in NE Public Relations, 1987. *Hobbies:* Gardening; Music; Billiards; Tennis. *Address:* 12 Farnum Pike, Smithfield, RI 02917, USA.

RUIVO Beatriz, b. 20 June 1940, Evora, Portugal. Senior Officer, Science Policy & Human Resources. *Education:* Chemist, University of Lisbon, 1963; Individual Study Fellow, Economic Development & Science Policy, Institute of Development Sudies, University of Sussex, England, 1979-80. *Appointments:* Senior Officer, Science Policy & Human Resources, JNICT, 1973-. *Publications:* Research on the representation of women in scientific research & higher education. *Memberships:* Founder, President, Executive Committee, Intervencao Feminina, 1987-89. *Hobby:* Womens Rights. *Address:* Rua Mem Rodrigues 4 1st Floor Apartment C, 1400 Lisbon, Portugal.

RUIZ Vicki L, b. 21 May 1955, Atlanta, Georgia, USA. Associate Professor. m. Jerry Ruiz, 1 Sept. 1979, 2 sons. *Education:* PhD, History, Stanford Universtiy, 1982. *Appointments:* Assistant Professor, 1985-87, Associate Professor, 1987-, History, University of California. *Publications:* Cannery Women, Cannery Lives; Women on the US Mexico Border, Co-Editor; Western Wome : Their Land, Their Lives, co-editor. *Memberships Include:* Organization of American HIstorians, Nominating Board; American Historical Association; American Studies Association; Oral History Association; National Association for Chicano Studies. *Honours:* American Council of Learned Societies Fellowship, 1985; David M. Potter Fellow; Stanforth Foundation Fellowship; Stanford Chicano Fellow. *Hobbies:* Needlework; Walking. *Address:* Dept. of History, University of California, Davis, CA 95616, USA.

RULEWICZ Wanda Maria, b. 27 Dec. 1947, Bielsko-Biala, Poland. Research Worker; Academic Teacher. Divorced. *Education:* MA, 1969, post-graduate studies, 1969-73, PhD, 1974, Warsaw University, Docent dissertation, 1986. *Appointments:* Assistant Professor, 1973-87, Associate Professor 1987-, Warsaw University. *Publications:* English Poetry of the Twentieth Century, 1979; A Semiotic Study of the Plays of Edward Bond, 1987; Poetry of T S Eliot, A Selection of poems, 1989; about 200 essays on literature and literary theory. *Memberships:* Polish Writers' Association. *Honours:* Prizes of the Chancellor of Warsaw University, 1976,

1979, 1984. *Hobbies:* Music; Drama and theatre. *Address:* Tolstoja 1-157, 01-910 Warsaw, Poland.

RUMBOLD Angela Claire Rosemary, b. 11 Aug. 1932. Member of Parliament. m. 15 Mar. 1958. 2 sons, 1 daughter. *Education:* London University, King's College. *Appointment:* Minister of State for Education. *Honour:* CBE. *Address:* House of Commons, Westminster, London, England.

RUMFOLO Marilu, b. 19 July 1953. Executive Director. *Education:* Arron's School of Real Estate, 1978; Student, University of Houston, 1979. *Appointments:* Junior Accountant, General Leasure Corp., 1973-75; Security Consultant, Burns International, 1975-77; Founder Director, Governmental Affairs, Time Energy Systems, 1977-83; Founder, Board Member, The Children's Drug Abuse Network. *Publications:* Know Your Drugs; Producer, Feeling Good Naturally; articles in professional journals. *Memberships:* Chairman, Board, Citizens United for Public Education; Officer, Order of the Eastern Star, 1986-87; Chairman, Board, Children's Drug Abuse Network; Team Captain, American Heart Association; Board, Eliza Johnston Home for the Aging. *Honours:* Drugbuster Award, 1985; Appreciation Breakfast County Commissioner for outstanding community work, 1986. *Hobbies:* Reading; Swimming; Writing Poetry; Walking; Genetic Engineering; Space Technology. *Address:* 1121 Walker Suite 1000, Houston, TX 77002, USA.

RUNOWICZ Carolyn Dilworth, b. 1 May 1951, Willimantic, Connecticut, USA. Physician; Gynaecologist; Gynaecologic Oncologist. m. Sheldon H. Cherry, 25 Apr. 1987. *Education:* BA Honours, summa cum laude, University of Connecticut, 1973; MD, Jefferson Medical College, 1977; Diploma 1984, Certificate (special competence) in Gynecologic Oncology, 1985, American Board of Obstetrics & Gynaecology. *Appointments:* Mount Sinai Hospital, New York City, 1977-83; Sloane-Kettering Memorial Hospital, NYC, 1980; Instructor, Mount Sinai, 1983-85; Assistant Professor, Director, Division of Gynaecolic Oncology, Albert Einstein College of Medicine, Montefiore Medical Centre, NY, 1985-. *Creative work includes:* Lecturer in field; Various articles, book chapters. *Memberships include:* Fellow, American College of Obstetrics & Gynaecology, American College of Obstetric Surgeons; American Medical Association; American Medical Womens Association; New York County Medical Association; Society of Gynaecologic Oncology; NY Obstetrical Society; NYC Metropolitan Club. *Honours include:* Phi Beta Kappa, 1972; Alpha Omega Alpha, various prizes, Jefferson College, 1976-77. *Hobby:* Sailing. *Address:* 1300 Morris Park Avenue, Belfer Building Room 501, Department of OBS-GYN, Bronx, New York 10461, USA.

RUNYON Mary Lucille, b. 17 Aug. 1927, Kentucky, USA. Company Vice President. m. Troy H. Runyon, 23 Feb. 1949, 3 daughters. *Education:* University of Kentucky, 1947. *Appointments:* First National Bank, Vice President 1963-85; Vice President, Bankers Trust, 1985-. *Memberships:* Vice President: Adopt-A-Family of PB, Volunteer Center, Good Samaritan Hospital Aux.; Governor, PB League of Charities; Board, Hope House; Auciton Board Chairman, American Heart Auction. *Honours:* Private Section Award, 1980; Jefferson Ward, 1980. *Hobbies:* Jogging; Art; Volunteer. *Address:* 12062 Basin Street South, West Palm Beach, FL 33414, USA.

RUPPE Loret Miller, b. 3 Jan. 1936, Milwaukee, USA. Director, US Peace Corp. m. Phillip E. Ruppe, 30 Nov. 1957, 5 daughters. *Education:* Marquette University, 1955-56. *Appointments:* George Bush Campaign Manager for the State of Michigan, 1979; Reagan-Bush Campaign Manager, State of Michigan, 1980; Director, Peace Corps, 1981-. *Memberships:* International Neighbors Club, 1972-; Past President, Michigan Right to Life; League of Women Voters. *Honours:* Honorary Doctorates: Northern Michigan University, 1981, Marymount College, 1981, Illinois College, 1982,

Wheeling College, 1982, St Ambrose College, 1983; etc. *Honours:* Tennis; Reading. *Address:* US Peace Corps, 1990 K Street NW, Washington, DC 20526, USA.

RUSH Jennifer, b. 19 Feb. 1937, Taihape, New Zealand. Company Principal. Divorced, 3 daughters. *Education:* BA Behavioral Sciences, MacQuarie University, Sydney. *Appointments:* Manager, Survey Research, Auckland, 1981-83; Project Director, Reark Research, Sydney, 1983-85; Principal, Axia, 1985-. *Publications:* Articles in various journals. *Memberships:* Social Research Association, Australia, Founding Member; Market Research Society of Australia, past President; etc. *Hobbies:* Reading; Writing; Development Education; South Pacific Womens Issues. *Address:* Suite 102, 247 Pacific Highway, North Sydney, NSW 2060, Australia.

RUSH Judith Lynn (Hansen), b. 20 Sept. 1948, Haywrd, California, USA. Teacher; Administrator. m. Kenneth Rush, 17 Dec. 1966, 2 sons. *Education:* BA Art, BA English (magna cum laude), California State University, Fresno, 1973; Graduate study, Fresno Pacific College, 1986-; Secondary teaching credential 1974, life credential 1977, administrative services 1986, California; Master's degree, Administration, in progress. *Appointments:* Teacher, various schools, Fresno Unified School District, 1973-; Supervisor, Work Experience programme, Duncan High School, 1985-. Also: Founder, President, School-Rite, 1978-. *Creative work:* Developer, Reading Laboratory, 1975; Inventor, Developer, Marketer, School-Rite Handwriting Instruction Guides, 1978-; Co-author, Developer of Pilot Programme, Communicative Arts, 1979; Editor, Nutshell Newsline, 1985-86; Co-sponsor, Speech Fest 1985, Career Day 1989. *Memberships include:* National School Supply Equipment Association; Toy Manufacturers of America; National Education Association; California & Fresno Teachers Associations; Offices, California Association of Work Experience Educators, Fresno County & City Chamber of Commerce. *Honours:* Dean's List, 1971, 1972; Numerous recognition awards, teaching; Paul Harris Fellow, Rotary International, 1986. *Hobbies:* Community Service; Travel; Water Sports. *Address:* School-Rite, PO Box 12547, Fresno, California 93778, USA.

RUSH Mary Ellen Rheutan, b. 14 Oct. 1947, Richmond, Virginia, USA. Medicla Technologist. m. Wayne Franklin Rush, 16 Apr. 1977. *Education:* AA, 1968; BS, Medical Technology, Commonwealth University, 1970. *Appointments:* Medical Technologist, Norwood Hospital, 1970-73; Cancer Research, Grady Memorial Hospital, 1973-75; Medical Technologist: Cherokee Atomedic Hospital, 1975-77; Medical Technologist, 1980-84, Director, Red Cell Products, 1984-, Serologicals Inc. *Memberships:* American Association of Blood Banks; Palmetto Blood Bankers Association, President Elect, 1988-89; North Carolina, South Eastern Associations of Blood Bankers. *Honour:* Henry Kupfer Award, 1970. *Hobbies:* Cooking; Sewing; Needlework; Tennis; Dogs. *Address:* 107 Edisto Avenue, Columbia, SC 29205, USA.

RUSSELL Beverly Anne, b. 9 Dec. 1934, London, England. Editor in Chief. m. Jon Naar. 1 son. *Appointments:* Fleet Street, 1954-66; Brides Magazine, USA, 1967-70; House Beautiful, USA, 1970; House & Garden, USA, 1970-79; Editor in Chief, Interiors Magazine, New York, USA, 1979-. *Publications:* House & Garden's Book of Remodeling, 1978; Designer's Workplaces, 1982; American Design, 1970-1990; Numerous articles in magazines and newspapers. *Memberships:* IBD, Women in Design; ASID, Decorators Club; Soc. Prof. Journalists; American Society of Magazine Editors; IFDA. *Honours:* Numerous awards for Excellence in Journalism; Proclamation of Beverly Russell Day in New York, 21 August 1986, by Mayor Edward Koch; Well known Lecturer at Design Schools worldwide. *Hobbies:* Gardening; Music; Painting. *Address:* 1 Coffey Lane, New Paltz, NY 12561, USA.

RUSSELL Bonnie Faye, b. 20 June 1939, Fort Edward, New York, USA. Laboratory Technician; Businesswoman. *Education:* Central College, 1957-59; BS, Chemistry, Ohio Northern University, 1961; Various other university courses, medical & business. *Appointments:* Glen Falls Hospital, 1961-63; Williams Ceramic Laboratory, 1963-75; Orlando Plasma Centre, 1976-78; Houston Plasma Centre, 1978-79; Lopapa Institute Inc, 1979-85; Researchers, 1985-88; Fashion Dynamics, 1984-86; Diamite, 1987-; Novo Immune Inc, 1987-88. *Creative work:* Inventor, plasma expressor. *Memberships:* Vice president, California Business Womens Network; Committee, Glen Falls Democratic Party; Vice president, Rebekaks; City-State Tentor Advisory Committee; National Association of Female Executives; American Management Association; New York Academy of Sciences; Womens Marathon Olympic Committee; Research Council, Scripps Clinic & Research Foundation; Citizens Advisory Council, American Institute for Cancer Research. *Honours:* Clinical Laboratory Technician's licence, State of Florida; General Laboratory Supervisor, Radiation Safety Officer, State of California; Biographical recognitions. *Hobbies:* Crossword puzzles; Sewing; Piano playing; Horseback riding; Skiing; Singing; Chess; Cards. *Address:* 722 South Ardmore 36, Los Angeles, California 90005, USA.

RUSSELL Carol Ann, b. 18 Sept. 1951, Fargo, North Dakota, USA. English Educator. m. Michael Schlemper, 19 July 1986. *Education:* BA, St Cloud State University, Minnesota, 1973; MA 1976, MFA 1979, University of Montana; PhD, University of Nebraska, 1988. *Appointments:* Assistant Professor, Tarkio College, Missouri, 1981-85; Teaching assistant, University of Nebraska, 1985-86; Assistant Professor, Southern Connecticut State University, 1986-88; Associate Professor, Bemidji State University, Minnesota, 1988-, *Publication:* Red Envelope, poetry collection, 1985. *Memberships:* Poetry Society of America; Associated Writing Programs; Modern Language Association; Delta Kappa Gamma International. *Honours:* Grants/awards from: National Endowment for Arts, 1987-88; English Department, SCSU, 1988; University of Utah, 1987; Midwest Poetry Society of America; University of Nebraska, 1985-86; Academy of American Poets, 1978; Pacific Northwest Writers Conference, 1977. *Address:* 1109 Lake Boulevard, Bemidji Minnesota 56601, USA.

RUSSELL Cheryl Anne, b. 19 Aug. 1952, Tooele, Utah, USA. Attorney. *Education:* BS in Pre-law, Utah State University, 1973; JD, Brigham Young University, 1976. *Appointments:* Public Defender, Rich, Cache and Box Elder Counties, 1977-83 Public Defender, Cache County, Utah, 1981-83; County Attorney, Rich County, Utah, 1083-00, Guardian Ad Litem, State of Utah, 1987-; General Practice, 1976-. *Memberships:* Logan Soroptimists; Alpha Lambda Delta; Phi Kappa Phi; Phi Sigma Alpha; J Rueben Honor Society; Law Fellow Bd of advocates at Brigham Young University; America Bar Assoc; Utah Bar Assoc; Cache County Bar Assoc; United States Supreme Court Bar Assoc; Statewide Assoc of Prosecutors of Utah; National Assoc of District Attorneys; United Way Selection Committee; Citizens Against Physical and Sexual Abuse; Teen Pregnancy Advisory Board. *Honours:* Magna cum laude, Utah State University, 1973; Humanities and Arts Certificate and Academic Achievement, Utah State University, 1970-73; Board of Advocates, Brigham Young University Law School, J Rueben Clark Honor Society, 1976-. *Hobbies:* Skiing; Scuba diving; Remodelling; Antiques; Arts and crafts. *Address:* 256 North First West, Logan, Utah 84321, USA.

RUSSELL Helen Ross, b. 21 Feb. 1915, USA. Free-lance Environmental Educator. m. Robert S Russell, 24 Sept. 1960. *Education:* BA, 1943; MA, 1947, PhD, 1949. *Appointments:* Elementary Teacher, 1934-45; Science Teacher, 1943-46; Professor, Biology, Fitchburg State college, 1949-66. *Publications:* 12 books including: 10 Minute Field Trips; using the School Grounds to Teach; City Critters; Foraging for Dinner; Winter Search Party; A Guide to Insects & other Invertebrates; over 300 articles in periodicals. *Memberships:* Pen & Brush;

Environmental educaiton Action; American Nature Study Society, President 1975; etc. *Honours:* Recipient, various honours and awards. *Hobbies:* Skiing. *Address:* 44 College Drive, Jersey City, NJ 07305, USA.

RUSSELL Laura Lee Wimberley, b. 17 Aug. 1949, Rapid City, South Dakota, USA. Artist. m. 21 Aug. 1971. *Education:* BA, College of Creative Studies, University of California, Santa Barbara, 1970; MA, San Jose State University, 1974. *Creative work includes:* 10 solo exhibitions, California, Texas, Oregon, New York, 1976-, including: William Sawyer Gallery, San Francisco, 1976; Contemporary Arts Museum, Houston, Texs, 1983; Southwest Texas University, San Marcos, 1985; Elizabeth Leach Gallery, Portland, Oregon, 1988; Butler Gallery, Santa Monica, 1989. Participant, numerous group exhibitions throughout USA, 1974-. Work reviewed, journals including: Texas Homes, Houston Home & Garden, Art in America, various catalogue essays. *Honours include:* Individual fellowship, National Endowment for Arts, 1981. *Address:* 110 Delacosta, Santa Cruz, California 95060, USA.

RUSSELL Sandra, b, 6 Nov. 1946, Pittsburgh, Pennsylvania, USA. Writer. m. Frank G. Little, 23 Oct. 1964 (div. 1968), 1 son, 1 daughter. *Education:* BA, English, Georgian Court College, 1977; Graduate studies in Creative Writing and Communication, University of Pittsburgh, 1978-79, 1980-81. *Appointments:* Mary Immaculate High School, 1984-86; Keys Advertising and Marketing, Florida, 1986-87; Executive Editor, Youth Scene, 1988. *Publications:* The Sister, 1979; Rivering, 1982; My Children Toward Winter, 1984; Grandma was a Hellcat, 1985; Father Sang Hank Williams, 1985; New Orleans, 1985, 1988; The Informer (opera libretto), sung Texas Opera Theater and Rutgers University Department of Music, 1985; Brooklyn College, New York Conservatory of Music, and Duke University, 1987; Sacrifice, 1987; The Women, 1988; Unraveling Riddles in the Eternal City, 1988; Eat the Shark, Become the Shark, 1988. *Honours:* Viola Hays Parsons Award for Poetry, 1979; 1st Prize, H J Heinz International Poetry Awards, 1982; Fellowship, Virginia Center for the Creative Arts, 1984; Distinguished Poem Award, Anhinga Press, University of Florida, 1985; 2nd Prize, 6th Annual Brooklyn College Chamber Opera Competition, 1987; Ravenswood Prize, 1988. *Address:* 508 Simonton, Key West, FL 33040, USA.

RUSSO Helen Teresa, b. 30 July 1939, Cincinnati, Ohio, USA. Psychologist; Lecturer; Teacher. *Education:* BA magna cum laude 1963, MEd 1965, Xavier University, Nationally Certified School Psychologist, Jan. 1989. *Appointments:* Teacher, St Francis Seraph School 1959-65, Reading Middle School 1965-68; Psychologist, Hamilton County Office of Education, 1968-; Travelled to Russia with Educational Consultants on Drug/Substance Abuse Seminar, July 1989. *Creative work includes:* Presenter, lectures, workshops seminars, study groups, courses, panel discussions. Subjects include child development, discipline, parenting, mental health, child abuse, handicapped children, effects of divorce & death on children. *Memberships:* Charter member, National Association for School Psychologists; Ohio & Southwestern Ohio Associations for School Psychologists; Forum on Death & Survival; Coalition for Prevention of Sexual Abuse; Numerous community bodies. *Honours:* Amaranth Award, Roger Bacon Alumni Board, 1986; Volunteer awards, Xavier University 1978, Mental Health Association 1986; Presidential citation, Xavier Board of Governors, 1975; Biographical listings. *Hobbies include:* Hiking; Writing (police column, monthly Northside Community News); Singing (leads congregation as cantor, weekly); Attending concerts; Travel. Professional interests involving children. *Address:* 4129 Kirby Avenue, Cincinnati, Ohio 45223, USA.

RUTAN Randi Lee, b. 6 Mar. 1957, Harlingen, Texas, USA. Research Nurse. m. Thomas Carl Rutan, 17 Sept. 1980. 1 son, 1 daughter. *Education:* 91B, Field Medic, 1978, 91C, Practical Nurse, 1980, US Army Ft Sam

Houston; BSc, Nursing, cum laude, 1984. *Appointments:* Staff Nurse, Institute of Surgical Research, Ft Sam Houston, 1980-82; Staff Nurse II/III, University of Texas Medical Branch, Galveston, 1984-86; Research Nurse, Shriners Burns Institute, Galveston, 1986-. *Publications:* Nursing Care of the Adult Burn Patient, book chapter, 1989; Growth Delay in a Postburn Pediatric Population, article, 1988; Longitudinal assessment of breast development in Adolescent female patients with burns involving the nipple-areolar complex, co-author, 1989. *Memberships:* American Association for the Advancement of Science; American Burn Association, Education Committee Member; International Society for Burn Injuries; New York Academy of ciences; Phoenix Society. *Honours:* Director's Award for Clinical Excellence, 1980; Letter of Commendation, US Army, 1980 and 1982. *Hobbies:* Gardening; Needlework; Reading, particularly science fiction. *Address:* Shriners Burns Institute, 610 Texas Ave, Galveston, TX 77550, USA.

RUTLEDGE Cheryl Juanita, b. 18 May 1946, Chattanooga, Tennessee, USA. Professor & Co-Chairman. *Education:* BM, magna cum laude, University of Chattanooga, 1968; MA, Jacksonville (Alabama) State University, 1973; PhD, Louisiana State University, 1983; Additional Doctoral study, University of Mississippi, summers 1978-80. *Appointments:* Instructor of Piano, Cadek Conservatory of Music, University of Tennessee at Chattanooga, 1968-69 and 1973-81; Director of Piano, Suzuki Institute for Musical Training, Little Rock, Arkansas, 1984-85; Professor & Co-Chairman, Department of Sacred Music, Sheng-te Christian College, Chungli, Taiwan, Republic of China, 1986-; Adjunct Associate Professor, Department of Music, Soochow University, Taipei, Taiwan, Republic of China, 1987-. *Publication:* Rote 'n' Read: A Piano Book for the Young Beginner, 1986. *Memberships:* The College Music Society; Suzuki Association of the Americas; Music Teachers National Association & Affiliates; Tennessee MTA and Chattanooga MTA; The MacDowell Club of Chattanooga. *Honours:* Teacher of the Year Award, Chattanooga Music Teachers Association, 1978; Professional Certificate in Piano, Music Teachers National Assoc, 1974, 1979, 1984; Certificate of Professional Advancement, Tennessee Music Teachers Assoc, 1978, 1983, 1985; Phi Kappa Phi, 1984; Pi Kappa Lambda National Music Honor Society, 1983; Alpha Society, 1968; Alpha Lambda Delta, 1965; Co-Valedictorian, Class of 1964, Red Bank High School, Chattanooga. *Hobbies:* Reading; Sewing; Travelling. *Address:* 5313 McCahill Road, Chattanooga, Tennessee 37415, USA.

RUTMAN Gisele-Francine, b. 12 Jan. 1932, Le Raincy, France. Executive President, Institut International de Promotion et de Prestige. m. Jacques Rutman, 21 Nov. 1959, divorced 19 Oct. 1982. 1 son, 1 daughter. *Education:* Baccalaureat, Institut Legay, 1950; Student in Graphology, Institut Francais de Culture Humaine. *Appointments:* Executive President, Institut International de Promotion et de Prestige, international organisation under Swiss Law awarding all those who endeavour to progress in the humanitarian, cultural, scientific and industrial fields, 1963-. *Creative works:* Painter-creator of new technique combining painting, sculpture and semi-precious stones; works have been sold in 42 countries in the world. *Membership:* The Societe de Graphologie. *Honour:* Silver Medal, City of Paris, 1983. *Hobby:* Gardening. *Address:* 1 rue de Monbel, 75017 Paris, France.

RUYS Christina, b. 18 July 1945, Chicago, Illinois, USA. President of Public Relations Firm. div. *Education:* BA, English, Illinois State University, 1971. *Appointments:* Vice-President, Martin. E.Janis and Co, Public Relations, 1972-77; Vice-President, Richardson and McElveen, Public Relations, 1977-83; President, Owner, Chris Ruys Communications, Chicago, Illinois, 1984-; Freelance Journalist. *Publications:* Contributor to Chicago Tribune, Chicago Sun-Times. *Memberships:* Publicity Club of Chicago; National Association of Women Business Owners. *Hobbies:* Writing; Watercolour painter; Tennis; Travel. *Address:* Chris Ruys Communications, Public Relations, 676 N. St. Clair, Suite 1900, Chicago, IL 60611, USA.

RYAN Eliz Ann, b. 10 Oct. 1947, Campbell County, Tennessee, USA. Airline Official. m. Patrick James Ryan, 6 June 1986, 1 daughter. *Education:* BSc Zoology & Philosophy, Teacher's Certificate, University of Tennessee, 1969; Postgraduate Zoology, University of Capetown, South Africa, 1972; Doctoral candidate, University of Cambridge, UK, 1976; MBA, University of Phoenix, Colorado, USA, 1986. *Appointments:* Research, Haardewijke, Cambridge, UK, 1974-76; Pilot's Licence, Bellas Aviation, Colorado, 1977-79; A&P School, General Aviation Company, 1979-82; Manager, MX Planning, Air US, 1982-83; Manager, A/C Records & Planning, FrHor/SB, 1983-86; Production Coordinator, Continental Airlines, 1986-88; Impacts Supervisor, UPS, 1988-. *Publications:* Book, How Hurty Put Humpty Back Together Again; Article, Women in Management; Illustrated HUD Objectives. *Memberships:* Coach, Olympics of Mind, 1985; Pride in Performance Award, California, 1988. *Hobbies include:* Horseback Riding, 3-day eventing; Swimming; Back-Packing; Snow & Water Skiing; Handcrafts; Community Improvement; Private Pilot. *Address:* 1554 St Paul Street, Denver, Colorado 80206, USA.

RYAN Madeleine Alice, b. Inverell, Australia. Principal, Ursula College. *Education:* BSc Hons, BA, Australian National University. *Appointments:* Teaching Secondary, 1957-66; Tertiary, 1973-83; Researcher, Immunology Department, John Curtis School of Medical Research, 1970-74; Dean Student, 1974-83, Principal, 1983-, Ursula College, Australian National University. *Publications:* Several scientific papers dealing with Immunology. *Memberships:* MACE; FIBA; MAIS. *Honour:* Prize for Biological Medics, Professional Business Award, 1969. *Hobbies:* Photography; Ornithology; Dressmaking; Ikebana. *Address:* Ursula College, Australian National University, Cnr of Daley & Dickson Road, Acton 2601, Australia.

RYAN Mary Gene Guzinski, b. 11 Sept. 1953, Corona, California, USA. Nurse; United States Air Force, Environmental Health Nurse. m. Robert E Ryan, III, 9 June 1979. 1 son, 1 daughter. *Education:* BSN, Southern Connecticut State College, 1975; MPH, University of Texas, 1980. *Appointments:* Staff Nurse, University of Connecticut, Maternal-Child, 1975-76; Staff Nurse, Williams Air Force Base, 1976-77; Flight Nurse, Rhein-Main, Germany, 1977-79; Environmental Health Nurse, Lackland, Texas, 1980-84; Environmental Health Nurse, Ewards Air Force Base, California, 1984-88. *Creative works:* Contributor to: Aviation, Space and Medicine, 1980; ASMA Scientific Pre-Prints, 1981, 1982. *Memberships include:* Flight Nurse Section, ASMA; Society of Environmental Health Professionals; Western Regional Association of Occupational Health Nurses; California Association of Occupational Health Nurses; American Association of Occupational Health Nurses; American Public Health Association; California Central Coast Association of Occupational Health Nurses. *Honours:* Leistungsabzeichen in Bronze (Zbxechen fur Leistiengen im Truppendienst), 1978; Meritorious Service Award, Rhein Main Chapel, 1979; Outstanding Unit Award, United States Air Force, 1980, 1984 and 1985. Meritorious Service Award, 1984; Certified Occupational Health Nurse, 1986. *Hobbies:* Choir member and soloist, Edwards Air Force Base Chapel, Edwards Air Force Base, California; Lay Eucharistic Minister, Edwards Air Force Base, California; Singing; Sewing; Embroidery; Skiing; Swimming; Teaching religion; Cooking. *Address:* 5415 Topa Topa Drive, Ventura, CA 93003, USA.

RYDER OF WARSAW Susan Margaret Ryder, Baroness, b. 3 July 1923, Leeds, England. Social Worker and Founder of The Sue Ryder Foundation. m. Group Captain Leonard Cheshire, VC, OM, DSO, DFC, 5 Apr. 1959. 1 son, 1 daughter. *Education:* Benenden School, Kent. *Appointments:* Served during the 1939-45 War with FANY and with Special Operations Executive; Social Worker and Founder, The Sue Ryder Foundation; Co-Founder, Ryder-Cheshire Mission for the relief of suffering; Trustee, The Leonard Cheshire Foundation. *Publications:* And the Morrow is Theirs; Child of my Love; Remembrance, annual magazine of The Sue Ryder Foundation. *Membership:* SOE Club. *Honours:* Officer's Cross, Order of Polonia Restituta, 1965; Medal of Yugoslav Flag with Gold Wreath and Diploma, 1971; Honorary LLD: Liverpool University, 1973; Golden Order of Merit (Poland), 1976; Exeter University, 1980; London University, 1981; Order of Smile (Poland), 1981; Honorary DLitt, Reading University, 1982; Leeds University, 1984; Honorary DCL, Kent University, 1986. *Hobbies:* Music; Architecture; Building. *Address:* Sue Ryder Home, Cavendish, Sudbury, Suffolk CO10 8AY, England.

RYERSON Alice Judson, b. 2 July 1922, Chicago, Illinois, USA. Writer. m. Edward Ryerson, 22 June 1941, 1 son, 3 daughters, (2) Albert M Hayes, 9 Sept. 1981. *Education:* BA, University of Chicago, 1950; Ed.D, Harvard University, 1960. *Appointments:* School Psychologist, 1960-75; Archaelogist, 1970-76; Founder, Director, Ragdale Foundation, 1976-. *Publications:* Poetry: Excavation, 1980; Marital Picnic, 1982 New & Selected Poems, 1987. *Memberships:* Board Member: Modern Poetry Association, Poetry Center, Educators for Social Responsibility, Chicago; Educational Council, Francis W Parker School; President, Board of Ragdale Foundation. *Honours:* Poetry Prize, 1983, Fiction Prize, 1988, Illinois Arts Council; Poetry Readings in New York, Boston, Chicago. *Hobbies:* Education; Archaeology; Water Colour Painting. *Address:* 1230 N Green Bay Road, Lake Forest, IL 60045, USA.

RYKIEL Sonia, b. 25 May 1930, Paris, France. Fashion Designer. m. Samuel Rykiel. 1 son, 1 daughter. *Education:* Cours Secondaire de Jeune Fille, Neuilly; Baccalaureat (B). *Appointments:* Fashion Designer, Sonia Rykiel, Paris, 1968-; Boutique Laura owned by husband. *Publications:* Et Je La Voudrais Nue, 1979. *Memberships:* Jury de l'Affiche; Club des Croqueurs de Chocolat; Vice President, Chambre Syndicale du Pre-a-Porter des Couturiers et des Createurs de Mode. *Honours:* Chevalier de l'Ordre des Arts et des Lettres, 1983; Chevalier de la Legion d'Honneur, 1985; Award 1st Fashion Oscar, Paris Opera House, Paris, 1985. *Hobbies:* Travel; Reading; Writing. *Address:* 6 rue de Grenelle, 75006 Paris, France.

RZEPINSKA Maria Krystyna, b. 14 Feb. 1918, Lwow, Poland. Art historian. m. Czeslaw Rzepinski, 1945, divorced 1979. *Education:* MA, University of Lwow, 1940; PhD, University of Warsaw, 1961; Assistant Professor, Jagellonian University, 1965; Full Professor, Art Academy, Cracow, 1965. *Appointments:* Secretary 1945-49, Translator 1949-56, Art Revue, Cracow; Lecturer 1956-61, Head and Chair of Art History 1961-85, Academy of Art. *Publications:* 14 books including: Studies on the theory and history of Colour, 1966; History of Colour, Volume I 1970, second edition 1973; Malarstwo Cinquecenta, 1976; La donna dell'ermellino, 1977; Siedem wiekow malarstwa europejskiego, 1979, 2nd edition 1986, 3rd edition 1988; History of Colour, Volume II, 1979; In the circle of Painting, Selected Studies, 1988; Leonardo's Trattato della Pittura, 1984; 100 articles in professional journals. *Memberships:* Art Historians Association; Phil Society in Poland; Commission of Art History and Comm of Architectur at Polish Academy of Sciences, Cracow; Committee of Art, Polish Aca, Warsaw; Editorial Board, Folia Historiae Artium and Studies of Aesthetics; PEN Club. *Honours:* Prize of Art Historian Association, 1961; Twice, Rector of Academy of Art; First degree, Ministry of Culture and Art, 1976; Polish Academy of Sciences in Warsaw, 1980; Prize, Miesiecznik Literacki (Literary Monthly), 1980; Prize, Town of Cracow, 1983; Knight's Cross Polonia Restituta, 1977. *Hobbies:* Literature; Travelling; Swimming; Classical music. *Address:* Ul 18 Stycznia 61/33, 30 081 Krakow, Poland.

S

SAARI Lise Margaret, b. 30 Dec. 1953, Oakridge, Tennessee, USA. Organisational Psychologist. m. Steven Bruce Young, Dec. 1980, 1 daughter. *Education:* BS cum laude 1977, MS 1979, Psychology, PhD Organisational Psychology 1982, University of Washington, Seattle. *Appointments:* Research Consultant, Weyerhaeuser Company, 1977-80; Human Resources Researcher, G. P. Latham Inc, 1980-82; Affiliate Professor, Business, University of Washington, 1982-; Research Scientist, Battelle Research Institute, 1982-86, 1988-; Professor, Business Division, Richmond College, London, UK, 1987-88; Principal Research Scientist, The Boeing Company, 1989-. *Publications:* Professional articles including: Goal Setting & Task Performance, 1981; Importance of Union Acceptance for Productivity Improvement, 1982; Employee Reactions to Reinforcement Schedules, 1982; Further Studies on the Situational Interview, 1984; Putting New Technical Knowledge to Work, 1985. *Memberships:* American Psychological Association; National Academy of Management. *Honours include:* Phi Beta Kappa, 1977-. *Hobbies:* Gardening; Skiing. *Address:* 2015 Condon Way West, Seattle, Washington 98199, USA.

SABAU Carmen Sybile, b. 24 Apr. 1933, Cluj, Rumania. Radiochemist; Chemist. m. Mircea Nicolae Sabau, 11 July 1956, 1 daughter. *Education:* Baccalaureat, Bucharest, 1951; MS, Inorganic and Analytical Chemistry, Faculty of Chemistry, C.I.Parhon University, Bucharest, 1955; PhD, Radiochemistry, Fredericiana University, Karlsruhe, Federal Republic of Germany, 1972. *Appointments:* Researcher, then Senior Researcher, Institute of Atomic Physics, Bucharest, 1956-74; Senior Scientist, Joint Institute of Nuclear Research, Dubna-Moscow, 1974-75; Visiting Scientist, Nuclear Research Center, Karlsruhe, Federal Republic of Germany, 1976; Chemist, Argonne National Laboratory, Argonne, Illinois, USA, 1976-. *Publications:* Book: Ion Exchange: Theory and Applications in Analytical Chemistry, 1967; 31 contributions to refereed journals; 5 support documents; 3 annual reports. *Memberships:* American Chemical Society; American Nuclear Society; Association for Women in Science; New York Academy of Science; Sigma Xi; American-Rumanian Academy of Arts and Science. *Honours:* Good Student Fellowships, Lycee, 1945-49, University, 1952-55; International Atomic Energy Agency Fellowship, Atomic Institute, Vienna, 1967-68; Humboldt Fellowship, Nuclear Research Center, Karlsruhe, 1970-72. *Hobbies:* Art (painting, sculpture); History of Art; Music (classical, folkloric, and Spanish, Italian and French songs); Travel, especially to visit museums, churches, castles; Foreign Languages; Literature (biographies, romantic novels, historical books, geography of exploration). *Address:* 6902 Martin Drive, Woodridge, IL 60517, USA.

SACINO Sherry Wheatley, b. 14 July 1959, Wilmington, Delaware, USA. President of Public Relations Firm. m. Ronald Sacino, 29 Dec. 1984. *Education:* BA Journalism, Arizona State University, 1980; Private Pilot License, 1986. *Appointments:* Public Relations, National Representative, McDonald's Restaurants, 1974-79; Press Secretary, National Rifle Association, Phoenix, Arizona, 1979; Promotions Director, KUPD/KUKQ Radio, Phoenix, 1980; Public Relations Director, Phoenix Pro Soccer, 1980; Owner, Sherry Wheatley Sacino Incorporated (Public Relations), 1981-; Founder, Chief Executive Officer, Tampa Bay Council for International Visitors Incorporated (Non-profit), 1984-; Publicist, Moscow International Peace Marathon, 1988; Marketing Agent, Citrus Industry of Costa Rica, 1988-. *Creative works:* Creator: Rugby Slippers Kit; Inflatable Business Cards. Thesis: Propaganda in Childrens Literature: A Case Study, Lincoln and Washington. *Memberships:* Board of Directors, March of Dimes; Super Task Force; Tampa Bay International Trade Council; Aircraft Owners and Pilots Association; North Aemrican Association for Ventroloquists. *Honours:* Selected to travel to Soviet Union for USA/CCCP Cultural Exchange, 1986; Selected national spokesperson, McDonalds Restaurants, 1979; Appointed to Governors Council on Health and Physical Fitness, Arizona, 1983. *Hobbies:* Flying; Travelling; Languages; Developing cultural awareness. *Address:* 2507 Pass-A-Grille Way, Pass-A-Grille, FL 33706, USA.

SACKHEIM Kathryn K, b. 27 Feb. 1945, Syracuse, New York, USA. Graphologist. m. Ronald A Sackheim, 19 Dec. 1965. 3 daughters. *Education:* BA, Northwestern University, 1967; General Course, Graphoanalysis Society, 1982; Master Course, IGAS, 1985. *Appointments:* XL Screw Corp, Wheeling, Illinois, 1977-82; President, KKS, Graphoconsultants, 1982-. *Publication:* Co-author with Dr Susan Taylor, article in Personnel Administrator, 1988. *Memberships:* Treasurer, Illinois Chapter, International Graphoanalysis Society; Life Member, International Graphoanalysis Society; World Association of Document Examiners; National Association Women Business Owners, 1983-; Trustee, North Shore Congregation Israel, Glencoe, Illinois, 1986-; Trustee, Centre for Psychoanalytiuc Study, Chicago, 1983-. *Honour:* President's Citation of Merit, International Graphoanalysis Society, 1985. *Address:* 429 Groveland Avenue, Highland Park, IL 60035, USA.

SADDLEMYER (Eleanor) Ann, b. 28 Nov. 1932, Prince Albert, Canada. Master, Massey College; Professor *Education:* BA, University of Saskatchewan, 1953; MA, Queen's University, 1956; PhD, London, England, 1961. *Appointments Include:* All ranks, University of Victoria, 1960-71; Professor, English, Victoria College, 1971-; Professor, Drama, 1971-, Master, Massey College, 1988-, University of Toronto. *Publications:* The World of W.B. Yeats, co-author, 1965; In Defence of Lady Gregory, Playwright, 1966; The Plays of J M Synge, Books 1 and 2, 1968; Synge and Modern Comedy, 1968; The Plays of Lady Gregory, 4 volumes, 1970; A Selection of Letters from J M Synge to W B Yeats & Lady Gregory, 1971; Letters to Molly, 1971; Theatre Business, the Correspondence of the First Abbey Theatre Directors, 1982; The Collected Letters of J M Synge, Volume 1, 1983, Volume 11, 1984; Lady Gregory Fifty Years After, co-author, 1987; numerous articles in professional journals. *Memberships Include:* International Association Study Anglo-Irish Literature, past Chairman; Association Canadian Theatre History, Founding President. *Honours:* Recipient, various honours and awards including various Fellowships, Grants and Scholarships, Honorary Degree. *Hobbies:* Acting; Book Collecting; Music; Theatre; Travel. *Address:* 100 Lakeshore Road East, No 803, Oakville, Ontario L6J 6M9, Canada.

SADLER Joan, b. 1 July 1927. Teacher. *Education:* BA, Honours, University of Bristol; Diploma in Education. *Appointments:* History Teacher, 1950-567, Head, History Department, 1956-58, Downe House, Cold Ash, Newbury; Head, History, 1958-68, Senior Mistress, 1966-68, Heriots Wood School, Stanmore, Middlesex; Headmistress, Howell's School, Denbigh, 1968-79; Principal, Cheltenham Ladies College, 1979-. *Memberships:* Chairman, Independent Schools Curriculum Committee; Institute of Directors; Common Entrance Board; Girls' Schools Association Executive; Board Member, Central Bureau for Educational Visits and Exchanges; Secondary Heads Association. *Honour:* Honorary Freewoman, Citizen & Draper of London, 1979. *Hobbies:* Music; Theatre; Reading. *Address:* The Cheltenham Ladies College, Bayshill Road, Cheltenham, Gloucestershire GL50 3EP, England.

SAFILIOU Anna, b. Apr. 1916, Preveza, Greece. Author. m. Constantine Safilios, July 1935, 1 daughter. *Education:* College in Preveza; Literary studies. *Career includes:* Worked for children's morning radio programme, Greek radio EPT, 1977-85; Writing novels and short stories. *Publications:* Children's books:

Marianna's Dream, 1973; Marianna in Africa, 1975, 1975; The Secret of Simos, 1977; My Dog and Mina, 1979; Our Own Stories, 1979; A Happy Man, 1980; Figures from the Space, 1981; A Good Idea, 1982; New and Unexpected, 1984; Adventure, 1986. *Memberships:* Greek Children's Book Circle; Societe nationale des gens de lettres Hellenes. *Hobbies:* Painting; Music (violin). *Address:* Anapiron polemou 4, 11521 Athens, Greece.

SAFIR Marilyn P(hyllis), b. 27 Mar. 1938, New York City, USA. Associate Professor. m. Efraim Mizrahi, 1969. *Education:* BA, CUNY, 1959; PhD, Syracuse University, 1968. *Appointments Include:* Various positions, Syracuse University, 1959-67; Supervising Psychologist, St Joseph's Hospital, Syracuse, 1967-68; Research Associate, Tel Aviv University, Israel, 1969-70; Exernal Teacher, 1969-72, Supervising Clinical Psychologist, 1972-77, Lecturer, 1972-78, Acting Director, 1975-76, Associate Professor, 1978-, University of Haifa; Private Practice, 1971-82; Lecturer, Tel Aviv University, 1979-80; Center for Sexual Therapy Counselling & Education, Rambam Hospital, 1980-81; Visiting Scholar, Stanford University, 1983. *Publications:* Sexual Equality, The Israeli Kibbutz Tests the Theories, 1983 co-editor; Women's Worlds: From the New Scholarship, co-editor, 1985; contributor to numerous journals & magazines. *Honours:* Recipient numerous honours & awards including: Elected Fellow, American Psychological Association, 1987; Award for Excellence, MENSA Education & Research Foundation, 1987; Elected Member, New York Academy of Science, 1987. *Hobbies:* Travel; Handicrafts; Reading; Walking. *Address:* Dept. of Psychology, University of Haifa, Mt. Carmel, Haifa 31999, Israel.

SAGGERS Cairistiona (Kirstie) Anne, Lady, b. 7 Jan. 1955, Harare, Zimbabwe. m. 8 May 1982, 2 daughters. *Education:* Edinburgh College of Commerce, Scotland; Ruskin School of Fine Art, Oxford, England. *Appointments:* Portrait Painter. *Creative Works:* Portraits in: Zimbabwe, Australia, Scotland, England, Germany. *Memberships:* Scottish Australian Heritage Council, Patron; Chieftan, Representative of Clan Graham in Australia. *Hobbies:* Painting; Drawing; Antique Furniture; Photography; Gemology; Gardening. *Address:* NSW, Australia.

SAKKA Galatia, b. 28 Sept. 1926, Athens, Greece. Housewife. m. (1) Dimitris Karabinis, 30 Mar. 1944, divorced 1948, 1 daughter. (2) Nikos Sakkas, 15 Aug. 1950, 1 son. *Education:* Graduated, Commercia School, 1945. *Appointment:* Women's Fashions, 1946-63. *Publication:* To Dachtylidi tou Pappou (Grandfather's Ring), 1975. *Memberships:* Greek Resistance, 1941-44; YWCA (Greece) 1969-; Founding Member, Study Group for Women's problems of KO.DH.SO (Greek Social-Democratic Party), Head of Group 1979-85; Candidate in 1981 General Election; President, Association Greek Housewife (3 times), 1984-86; Democratic Women's Movement (Vice President, Ambelokipi Section in Athens) 1975; Founding Member, Greek Family Planning Association, 1975 (Member of the Board, 1976-88). *Hobbies:* Farming; Handicraft. *Address:* Alexandrou Soutsou 5, GR 106 71 Athens, Greece.

SAKS Judith Ann, b. 20 Dec. 1943, Anniston, Alabama, USA. Artist. m. Haskell Irvin Rosenthal, 22 Dec. 1974, 1 son. *Education:* Texas Academy of Art, 1957-58; Houston Museum of Fine Art, 1962; Rice University, 1962; Sophie Newcomb College of Tulane University, BFA, 1966; University of Houston, 1967. *Appointments:* Curator, Student Art, University of Houston, 1968-72; Professional Artist, 1967-. *Publications:* Houston Chamber of Commerce, Christmas Card Design, 1970; Painting, Nichols Rice Cherry House, Harris County Heritage Society Museum; Etching, Johnson Manned Space Museum; 6 Historical Paintings, Port of Houston Authority's American Revolution Bicentennial Project Artist; Lithographs of this project were accepted by US President Jimmy Carter, Queen Elizabeth II, His Excellency Dvar Nordli, Prime Minister of Norway; reproductions of work on magazine covers and articles. *Memberships:* Houston

Museum of Fine Arts; Houston Art League; Curator, Lady Washington Chapter, DAR; Houston Museum of Natural Science. *Honours:* Archives of American Art, Smithsonian Institution, 1980; Print Selected for Year's Tour, Mississippi Art Association, 1970-71; Houston Art League, 1st Prize, Watercolour, 1969; 1st Prize, Graphics, 1969; 1st Prize, Sculpture, 1969; many other honours & awards. *Hobbies:* Horse Riding; Skating. *Address:* Post Office Box 1793, Bellaire, TX 77401, USA.

SALAMAN Maureen, b. 4 Apr. 1936, Glendale, California, USA. Author; Magazine Editor; Talk Show Hostess. 1 son, 1 daughter. *Education:* MSc Nutrition, University of Nevada. *Appointments:* Hostess, Totally Yours Talk Show, KEST Radio-SF, 8 years; Hostess, The Gift of Health, KFAX Radio-SF, 2 years; Currently TV Hostess, Maureen Salaman's Accent on Health, Channel 42 TV Conconrd, California. *Publications:* Nutrition, The Cancer Answer; Foods That Heal; Diet Bible; Editor of Public Scrutiny; Health Freedom News. *Memberships:* President, National Health Federation; Board Member, Arrive Alive. *Honours:* Awarded Honorary PhD, Institute of Drugless Therapy, Edinburgh, Scotland; Vice Presidential Candidate of Populist Party; Patrick Henry Liberty Award, 1978; Former Vice President of Project Freedom to rescue America's POW's. *Hobbies:* Flying (licensed pilot); Scuba diving (licensed); Tennis; Windsurfing; Sailing; Advanced aerobics. *Address:* 1259 El Camino Real Apt 1500, Menlo Park, CA 94025, USA.

SALEMME Martha Anna Caroline, b. 30 Aug. 1912, Geneva, Illinois, USA. Registered Nurse (retired); Artist (Painter). m. Antonio Salemme, 5 Aug. 1941. *Education:* RN, Augustana Hospital School of Nursing, 1934; Studied painting with Antonio Salemme. *Appointments:* Registered Nurse: Augustana Hospital, 1934; New York Hospital, New York City, 1934-36, 1944-57; Nurse-Secretary to Dr Mather Cleveland, New York City, 1936-43; Special duty, self-employed, 1957-72; Exhibited paintings: Van Diemen-Lilienfeld Gallery, 1948, Sagittarius Gallery, 1963; Galerie Mouffe, Paris, 1974; Community Center, Hyssna, 1975, 1976, 1980, Fahlnass Gallery, Gothenburg, 1975, 1976, Horred Library, Horred, 1980, Skene Hospital Gallery, Skene, 1983, Bjorketorp, 1987, Sweden; Participant in national exhibitions, Hudson River Museum, Yonkers, New York, 1958, Jersey City Museum, New Jersey, 1959, 1961, Artists Equity Triennial, Philadelphia, Pennsylvania, 1984, Philadelphia Art Show, 1986; Participant in international exhibitions, Centre International d'Art Contemporain, Paris, 1985, Art Contemporain Cabinet des Dessins, Espace Delpha, Paris, 1986. *Creative works include:* Poems in The Silver Treasury of Light Verse (edited Oscar Williams); Paintings in collections in USA, Italy, France and Sweden. *Hobbies:* Photography; Antiques; Theatre. *Address:* 189 Gaffney Hill Road, Easton, PA 18042, USA.

SALPETER Miriam, b. 8 Apr. 1929, Riga, Latvia. Professor. m. Edwin Salpeter, 11 June 1950, 2 daughters. *Education:* BA summa cum laude, Psychology, Hunger College; PhD, Psychobiology, Neuroanatomy, 1953; Postdoctoral Fellow in Neuroanatomy, Case Western University and Cornell University, New York, 1957-61. *Appointments:* Teaching Assistant, Research Assistant, 1956-57, Research Associate, 1961-63, Senior Research Associate, 1963-66, Associate Professor, 1966-72, Professor, 1972-, Chairman, 1982-88, Cornell University, Ithaca, New York. *Publications:* Various including research in areas of development and calibration of quantitative procedures for EM autoradiography, synaptogenesis and neural control of that process, molecular organisation of adult synapses and its physiological consequences (with vertebrate neuromuscular junction as the model synapse). *Memberships:* American Association for the Advancement of Science; American Society of Cell Biology; New York Academy of Science; Society for Neuroscience. *Honours:* Career Development Award, 1962-72; Elected Fellow, American Association for the Advancement of Science; Hunter College Graduate Prize; Phi Beta Kappa, Sigma Xi; Susan Linn Sage

Fellowship; Appointed to Executive Council, Society of Cell Biology and Editorial Boards, Journal of Morphology, Journal of Cell Biology, Journal of Electron Microscopy Technique; Member, Board of Scientific Counsellors, NINCDS. *Address:* Cornell University, Department of Neurobiology and Behavior, W113 Mudd Hall, Ithaca, NY 14853, USA.

SALTER Margaret Miller, b. 5 Jan. 1919, Pittsburgh, USA. Feature Writer and Editorial Assistant. m. John Matthew Salter, 3 Nov. 1946, 1 son. *Education:* BA, 1941, MA 1942, University of Tennessee; Certificate, Tower Operator, 1943; Certificate, Airway Weather Observations, 1943; Junior Rating, LaGuardia Tower, 1943; Qualified Observers Certificate, Sperry Observatory, 1974. *Appointments Include:* Various Teaching Positions, 1967-79; Communications Co-ordinator, Warwick Insurance Company, Morristown,1979-88; Editorial Assistant, Communications Department, Coporate Staff, Warwick Insurance Company, 1988-. *Publications:* Contributor To: Playbill, 1940, Poems by Poets of the IPA Academy of Poets, 1983, From to Sea to Sea in Verse, 1986. *Memberships:* International Platform Association; Amateur Astronomers Inc, Recording Secretary 1978-86, Life Member, 1986; International Biographical Association. *Honours:* Pauline Capell Walker Prize for Scholarship, University of Tennessee, 1941; Commemorative Medal of Honour, American Biographical Institute, 1986, USA.

SALTZ Elizabeth, b. 15 June 1925, Brooklyn, New York, USA. Freelance Writer. m. David Klinick, 23 Sept. 1963. 1 son, 1 daughter. *Education:* BA, Queens College; Masters, Philosophy, Flushing, Long Island; Psychology, New School for Social Research, New York. *Appointments:* Administrative Assistant, Federal Government, State City Government, New York, 1940-45; Social Worker, 1963-; Teacher, Freelance Writer, 1980-. *Publications:* Poetry, 1980-88. *Memberships:* Queens College Alumni Association; New School for Social Research Writers Club. *Honours:* 30 Award of Merit Certificates, American Poetry Association, Santa Cruz; Golden Poet Awards, 1985, 1986, 1987, World of Poetry Press, Sacramento. *Hobbies:* Photography; Painting; Music. *Address:* 88-10 178th Street, Jamaica, New York 11432, USA.

SALTZMAN Irene Cameron, b. 23 Mar. 1927, Cocoa, Florida, USA. Manufacturing Perfumer; Art Gallery Owner. m. Herman Saltzman, 23 Mar. 1946, 1 son, 1 daughter. *Education:* Perfume & Manufacturing Studies in Europe, Near & Far East. *Appointments:* Irene Gallery of Fine Arts; Irene Parfumes & Cosmetiques Laboratory. *Publications:* Oil Paintings. *Memberships:* Cummer Gallery of Art; National Museum of Women in the Arts; International Association of Fine Arts; American Society of Professional and Executive Women; International Platform Association; Air Force Association; Chamber of Commerce City of Jacksonville. *Hobbies:* Golf; Swimming; Art Collecting; Learning to Pilot a Plane. *Address:* 2701 Ocean Dr. So., Jacksonville Beach, FL 32250, USA.

SALVAS-BRONSARD Lise, b. 2 Apr. 1940, Montreal, Canada. Professor. m. Camille Bronsard, 10 Feb. 1962, 1 son, 1 daughter. *Education:* PhD, Economics, Louvain, 1972. *Appointments:* Professor, Economics, University of Montreal, 1970-. *Publications:* Articles in professional journals. *Address:* Department of Economics, Box 6128 Succ A, Montreal, H3C 3J7, Canada.

SALZER Linda Parsons, b. 13 June 1951, Middletown, USA. Clinical Social Worker; Author. m. Richad L. Salzer, 21 June 1980, 2 sons. *Education:* BA, Duke University, 1973; MSS, Bryn Mawr College, 1975; Ackerman Institute for Family Therapy, 1981-82. *Appointments:* Albert Einstein Mental Health Center, 1976-78; Insititute for Child Development, Hackensack, 1978-80; Community Mental Health Organization, Englewood, 1980-83; Private Practice, 1982-.

Publication: Infertility - How Couples Can Cope, 1986. *Memberships:* National Association of Social Workers; Resolve Inc., President 1985-88; Academy of Certified Social Workers; New Jersey State Marriage Counsellors. *Honour:* Phi Beta Kappa. *Hobbies:* Running; Gardening; Piano; Travel. *Address:* 163 Engle Street, Englewood, NJ 07631, USA.

SAMARA Patrice, b. 28 July 1947, Pennsylvania, USA. Film and Video Producer/Developer; Company President. m. Michael H Glyn, 30 May 1970. 1 daughter. *Education:* University of South Florida, 1966; The New School for Social Research, 1968. *Appointments:* Abramowitz Studio, 1970-72; Patrice Samara Productions Limited, 1973-; Board Member, Manhattan Community College. *Publications:* Contributor of numerous articles in national and international journals and newspapers. *Memberships:* Women in Film International; Women in Communications. *Honours:* CINE Golden Eagle, 1981, 1982, 1983, 1984, 1986, 1987, 1988; CINDY Gold Award, 1984; American Film Festival, 1983, 1985; Chicago International Film Festival, 1982; National Educational Film Festival, 1985. *Hobbies:* Photographer; Gourmet. *Address:* 356 West 58 Street 3rd Floor, New York, NY 10019, USA.

SAMINS Sally Jean, b. 24 June 1954, Australia. Photographer. m. Chris Todter, 14 May 1988, 1 son. *Education:* Degree, Visual Communications, 1976. *Appointments:* Photographer's assistant, David Levin, London 1977, Howard Jones, Greg Barrett, 1978-80; Photographer, ABC, 1980-83; Freelance photographer, 1983-. Only freelance at America's Cup, 1983; Official photo, 1987; Official Photographer Trans Australia Balloon Race. *Publications:* Books: Australia II, Official Record; Channel Nine Worldwide Sport; 12 Metre New Breed; Official Record, America's Cup. *Hobbies:* Sailing; Squash; Horse riding; Music. *Address:* 28 Smith Street, Rozelle, New South Wales 2039, Australia.

SAMPLE Karen Ann, b. 12 July 1949, Oklahoma, USA. Science Instructor; Administrator. m. Alan Sample, 7 Dec. 1970, 2 sons. *Education:* BS, University of Oklahoma, 1975; MEd., East Central University, 1978; Post Graduate, University of Oklahoma, 1987-88. *Appointments:* Science Instructor, Ada Senior High School, 1977-81; Science Instructor, Chairman, Science Dept., Noble Senior High School, 1981-; Special Consultant, Independent Study Dept., University of Oklahoma, 1983-. *Publications:* Author, 2 Correspondence Texts: Biology A and Biology B, 1983. *Memberships:* National Science Teachers Association; NEA; Oklahoma Education Association; Beta Sigma Phi. *Honours:* Teacher of the Month, Noble, 1981. *Hobbies:* Astronomy; Botany; Travel. *Address:* 212 Forest HIlls, Noble, OK 73068, USA.

SANCHEZ Mary Virginia, b. 28 May 1943, Meyersdale, Pennsylvania, USA. Director General, American School of Quito; Educator. m. Diego P Sanchez Orejuela, 26 Jan. 1968. 1 son, 3 daughters. *Education:* BS, Georgetown University, 1965; MA, University of Alabama, 1975. *Appointments:* Teacher, Marion County School Dis, 1965-67; Teacher 1967-68, Elementary Principal 1968-72, English Coordinator 1972-83, Director General 1983-, American School of Quito. *Publication:* Five year staff development plan, Colegio Americano de Quito. *Memberships:* Southern Association of Colleges and Schools; Association of American Schools of South America, Treasurer-Secretary; Treasurer, Association of American Schools of Colombia and Caribe; Association for Advancement of International Education. *Hobbies:* Bridge; Travelling. *Address:* c/o American School of Quito, P O Box No 157, Quito, Ecuador.

SANDERLIN Owenita Harrah, b. 2 June 1916, Los Angeles, California, USA. Writer. m. 30 May 1936, 2 sons, 2 daughters. *Education:* BA, summa cum laude, The American University, 1937; Postgraduate, University of Maine, University of California, San Diego State University; California State Teaching Credential,

1969. *Appointments:* Freelance Writer, Speaker, 1940-; Teacher, English, University of Maine, 1942, 1946; Head, Dept Speech and Drama, Acad of Our Lady of Peace, San Diego, 1961-68; Consultant, Gifted Programs, San Diego City Schools, 1971-73 and 1980-85. *Publications:* Jeanie O'Brien, 1965; Johnny, 1968 and 1978; Creative Teaching, 1971; Teaching Gifted Children, 1973; Tennis Rebel, 1978; Match Point, 1979; Gifted Children: How To Identify and Teach Them, Co-author with Ruthe Lundy, 1979; Numerous articles to magazines and journals. *Memberships:* American Association of University Women; Mortar Board; San Diego Natural History Museum; The Covey; Singing Hills Tennis Club. *Honours:* Most Outstanding Junior Girl, Radcliffe Award, 1932; Poetry Award, Alpha Chi Omega, 1936; National Forensics League, Double Ruby Award, 1965; Greater San Diego Reading Association Honoree, 1987; Tennis Trophies. *Hobbies:* Tennis; Bridge; Children. *Address:* 997 Vista Grande Road, El Cajon, California 92019, USA.

SANDERS Deidre (June), b. 9 June 1945, Bristol, England. Advice Columnist; Broadcaster. m. 12 Dec. 1969, 2 daughters. *Education:* BA, Honours. *Appointments:* Consumer Columnist, Woman's Own magazine, 1974-79; Advice Columnist, Daily Star 1979-80, The Sun 1980-. *Publications:* Kitchen Sink or Swim; Women and Depression; 101 Questions About Sex; The Woman Book of Love and Sex; The Woman Report on Men. *Memberships:* British Society for Research on Sex Education; British Association for Counselling; Lay Forum of Royal Society of Medicine; National Association of Young People's Counselling and Advisory Services. *Honours:* Consumer Journalist of the Year, 1977; Jubilee Medal, 1977. *Hobbies:* Holistic Therapies; Horse Riding. *Address:* PO Box 488, The Sun, Virginia Street, London E1 9BZ, England.

SANDERS Diane, b. 26 Oct. 1950, Kansas City, USA. Teaching Dietitian; Culinary Educator. *Education:* BS, 1973, MS, 1974, Kansas State University; Registered Member, American Dietetic Association, 1975; Certified as Culinary Educator, American Culinary Federation, 1984. *Appointments:* Graduate Teaching Assistant, Kansas State University, 1973-74; Clinical Dietitian, Saint Mary Hospital, 1974-75; Food Service Co-ordinator, Manhattan Area Vocational-Technical School, 1975-. *Publications:* various courses. *Memberships:* American, Kansas, Kaw Valley, Dietetic Associations; American Culinary Federation; Riley Chef Association; Kansas Nutrition Council; Society for Nutrition Education; etc. *Honours:* Martha S Pittman Scholarship, 1974; National Restaurant Association Award of Excellence, 1907. *Hobbies:* Water Sports; Crafts; Reading. *Address:* 5012 Vista Acres Drive, Manhattan, KS 66502, USA.

SANDERS Hannah-Reeve, b. 25 Aug. 1928, Cape Town, South Africa. Health Care Administrator. 1 son. *Education:* MB ChB, University of Cape Town, 1952. *Appointments:* Chief Medical Superintendent, Groote Schuur Hospital, 1976-86; Chief Director, Hospital and Health Services, Cape Provincial Administration, South Africa, 1986-; Hon Sen Lecturer Community Health, University of Cape Town. *Memberships:* Soroptimist International of Cape of Good Hope, 1978; Women's Bureau, 1980-; Associate Founder, College of Medicine of South Africa, 1976; Medical Women's International Assoication; Rhodes Scholarship Selection Committee, Chairman, 1986-. *Honours:* Merit Award for Outstanding Service to Medical Administration, Medical Association of South Africa, 1981; Women of Achievement Award, Women's Bureau, Cape, 1986. *Hobbies:* Classical music; Outdoor walking; Mountaineering. *Address:* 14 Florentia, 329a Beach Road, Bantry Bay, 8001 Cape Town, Republic of South Africa.

SANDERS Marlene, b. 10 Jan. 1931, Cleveland, Ohio, USA. News Correspondent. m. Jerome Toobin, 27 May 1958, deceased, 1984, 2 sons. *Education:* Ohio State University, 1948-49; The Sorbonne, Paris, France, summer 1950. *Appointments:* Production Assistant, Mike Wallace with the News; Associate Producer, Night Beat with Mike Wallace; Producer, various public affairs programmes, Dumont Broadcasting Corporation, New York City, 1955-60; Proder-Writer, PM East, Westinghouse Broadcasting corporation, New York City, 1960-62; Assistant Director, News & Public Affairs, WNEW Radio, New York City, 1962-64; Correspondent, Anchorwoman, 1964-72, Documentary Producer, 1972-76, Vice President, Director of Documentaries, 1976-78, ABC News, New York City; Correspondent, CBS News, New York City, 1978-. *Memberships:* Women in Communicatirons (Former President, New York City Chapter); American Women in Radio & TV; Woman's Forum; American Federation of TV and Radio arts; Writers Guild ofAmerica. *Honours Include:* Broadcast Woman of the Year Award American Women in Radio & TV, 1975; New York State Broadcasters Association Award, 1976; National Press Club Award, 1976; Silver Satellite Award, 1977; Ohio State, Front Page and Writers Guild of America Awards; Christpher Award, 1979; 2 Emmy Awards, 1980; Emmy Award, 1981. etc. *Hobbies:* Swimming; Gardening; Reading. *Address:* CBS News, 524 West 57th St., New York, NY 10019, USA.

SANDERSON Lillian Linda (Lil), b. 9 July 1960, La Ronge, Sasktchewan, Canada. Political Constituency Assistant; Administrator. *Education:* Certificate, Indian Social Work, Saskatchewan Indian Federated College, University of Regina, 1983. *Appointments include:* School Secretary & Librarian, 1978-80; Returning Officer, Northern Municipal Council, 1980; Secretary-Receptionist, Key Lake Mining Company, 1981; Student, 1981-83; Field Officer, Programme Counsellor, Gabriel Dumont Institute of Native Studies & Applied Research, Saskatoon, 1984-86; Research Officer, Prairie Justice Research, University of Regina, 1986; Instructor, Pre-Trades for Women 1987, Resident Supervisor (part-time) 1987-88, La Ronge Community College; Constituency Assistant to Keith N. Goulet (Member, Legislative Assembly), La Ronge, 1987-; Area Director, Northern Region 1, Metis Society of Saskatchewan, 1989-. *Memberships include:* Past President, Council, La Ronge Native Women's Organisation; Elected member-at-Large, Aboriginal Women's Council, Saskatchewan; Local Advisory Council, Canada Employment & Immigration Commission; La Ronge Local School Board; Representative, Native Women's Association of Canada, to Indigenous Survival International Organisation. *Honours:* Amok Scholarships, Northern Students Award, 1982, 1983. *Hobbies:* Reading; Writing; Organising; Visiting; Political discussions; Making things happen. *Address:* Box 1204, La Ronge, Saskatchewan, Canada 5OJ, 1LO.

SANDLES Faith Dale Meyer, b. 9 Apr. 1942, Albany, New York, USA. Freelance Interior Decorator; Coordiantor, Senior Companion Program. m. Albert Warren Sandles, 28 Oct. 1972. 1 daughter. *Education:* BA Psychology, Hartwick College, Oneonta, 1964; Certificate in Gerontology, University of Michigan, 1971. *Appointments:* Program Director, Troy-Cohoes YWCA, 1964-67; Executive Director, Cohoes Multi-Service Sr Citizens Center, 1967-77; Consultant, NYS, 1970-84; Freelance Interior Decorator; Coordinator, Senior Companion Program, OD Heck Development Center. *Creative works:* Co-Founder, Capital District Parkinsons Support Group, 1985; Developed Senior Citizens Centre to 2500 members, 1967-77; Innovative Programs; Assisted Diocese of Albany in Creating County Office for the Aging. *Memberships:* Board of Directors, Troy Cohoes YWCA, 1978-84, Exec Comm III Vice President; Hartwick College Alumni Association, Board of Directors, Class Agent, NYS Assoc Learning Disabled, Cap Dist Chap Bd of Directors, Secretary. *Honours:* New York State Legislative Resolution: Senate No 258, Assembly No 385, Commendation on work with the Elderly, 1977; White House Conference on Aging, Official Delegate NYS, 1971; HEW Fellowship, University of Michigan, Institute of Gerontology, 1971; Training Consultant, International YWCA, West Indies, 1965. *Hobbies:* Travel; Skiing; Sewing; Anthropology; Gerontology; Developmentally Disabled; Interior Design. *Address:* Albany, New York, USA.

SANFORD Gillian Yvonne, b. 19 Apr. 1934, Beckenham, Kent, England. Nurse. *Education:* Middlesex & Shenley Hospitals, Hertfordshire, 1953-57. *Appointments:* Ward Sister-Assistant Matron, Middlesex Hospital; Senior & Principal Nursing Officer, Northwick Park Hospital, Harrow; District Nursing Officer, South West Hertfordshire; Deputy General Secretary, Royal College of Nursing, 1981-. *Hobby:* Participation in Anglican Church activities. *Address:* Royal College of Nursing, 20 Cavendish Square, London W1M 0AB, England.

SANRAMA I FELIP Magdalena, b. 5 Nov. 1927, Barcelona, Spain. Musicologist. m. Isidro Parellada i Fortuny, 21 July 1951, 2 sons, 1 daughter. *Education:* Degree, Hispanic Archeology, 1977. *Appointments:* Technical Secetary, 1945-51; Photography Shop, 1950-85; Journalist, 1960-75; Musicologist, 1967-. *Publications:* Recortes de Prensa, 1960-75, 1975; Cases Natals de Catalunya, 1985; Casas Natales de Catalunya y Aragon, in press. *Memberships:* Founder, Creator, Maternity Art Museum, 1967; President, Centro de Estudios y Acti Vidades Maternas, 1985; Co-Founder, Consejo Nacional de Muje res de Espana, 1981; Co-Founder, Women Catalan Association. *Honours:* Recipient, many honours. *Hobbies:* Theatre; Research. *Address:* Barcelona Street No. 302, 08620 Sant Vicenc Deus Horts, Barcelona, Spain.

SANSON Barbara Elizabeth, b. 25 Jan. 1955, Wiesbaden, West Germany. Attorney. *Education:* AB, Bryn Mawr College (USA) & University of London (UK), 1977; JD, Dickinson School of Law, USA, 1980. *Appointments:* Judicial law clerk, 1980-82; Associate, Duane, Morris & Heckscher, 1982-84; Attorney, ICI Americas Inc, 1984-. *Publications:* Contributions, Dickinson Law Review, 1979, 1981. *Memberships:* American, Pennsylvania & Philadelphia Bar Associations. *Hobbies:* Ice skating; Collecting antiques. *Address:* 1510 Naudain Street, Philadelphia, Pennsylvania 19146, USA.

SARGENT Carolyn Nelson, b. 22 Aug. 1946. m. Joseph Sargent. *Career:* Acress: Red Skelton Show; Start Trek; It Takes a Thief; Marcus Nelson Murders; Passion Flower, etc. *Publications:* Articles in Los Angeles Times, Town and Country; Herald Examiner; Beverly Hills People; US Magazine; Womens Wear Daily, etc. *Memberships:* Founder, President, Free Arts Clinic for Abused Children; Member, Neighbour of Watts; Malibu Chamber of Commerce. *Honours:* Mayors Award for Los Angeles Street Scene; US Magazine Humanitarian Award; International Year of the Child Service Award; Board of Supervisors Award. *Hobbies:* Horse Riding; Reading; Charity events; Public speaking. *Address:* 33740 Pacific Coast Highway, Malibu, CA 90265, USA.

SASHA b. 21 Mar. 1957, Pennsylvania, USA. Fitness Business Owner; Consultant; Lecturer; Trainer; Author. m. Alexander R Jackson, 9 Oct. 1987. 1 son, 1 daughter. *Education:* BA Geology, 1979, MA Geophysics, 1983, University of California, Santa Barbara. *Creative works:* Sasha & Company Professional Fitness Instructor Training Course; Articles published in professional journals and magazines. *Memberships:* Aerobics and Fitness Association of America, Consultant, Continuing Education Provider; International Dance-Exercise Association, Accredited Trainer, Continuing Education Provider; Centennial Chamber of Commerce; Denver-Metro Convention & Visitors Bureau. *Honour:* 1988 Woman to Watch, Denver. *Address:* c/o Sasha & Company - The Workout Studio, 6979 South Holly Circle, Englewood, Colorado 80112, USA.

SASS Shelley Kay, b. 12 Jan. 1955, Fort Worth, Texas, USA. Architectural Conservator. *Education:* BFA, 1976, MA, 1983, University of Texas; Certificate in Conservation, New York University, 1985. *Appointments:* Heritage Canada, 1984-85; Senior Conservator, The Center for Preservation Research, Columbia University, New York, 1985-88; Currently in private practice. *Memberships:* Board of Directors, Zonta International, New York Club; American Institute for Conservation; Association for Preservation Technology; Representative, New York City Historic Districts Council. *Honours:* National Museum Act Grants, 1982, 1983. *Address:* 324 West 80th Street, New York, NY 10024, USA.

SASSO Maria Dolores, b. 21 Apr. 1949, Kingston, Jamaica, West Indies. International Marketing Executive. m. Michael Eugene Richardson, 12 June 1971. 1 son, 2 daughters. *Education:* BA, Mount Saint Mary College, Newburgh, New York, 1970; MA, University of Arkansas, Ramstein, West Germany, 1974. *Appointments:* Administrator (High School Principal)/ Teacher/Counsellor Army Education, Baumholder, West Germany, 1970-76; Director Operations, Bouton-Brady Corporation, 1979-80; International Sales, G A Knudson, Colorado, 1980-83; Partner, MMJV Enterprises, 1986-; President, M S International, SA, Guatemala, 1988-. *Memberships:* Board of Directors, Embassy Committee, International Trade Association of Northern Virginia, 1985-; President, Virginia Association of Female Executives, 1987-89; Suburban Maryland International Trade Association, 1984-. *Hobbies:* Reading; Horseback Riding; Painting. *Address:* 8512 Jeffersonian Court, Vienna, VA 22182, USA.

SATHOFF Karen Marie Ehrlich, b. 8 July 1958, Chicago, Illinois, USA. Architect. m. Rodney H. Sathoff, 8 May 1982, 2 sons. *Education:* University of Illinois, Urbana, 1976-79; University of Illinois, Versailles, France, 1979-80; BSc, Architectural Studies. *Appointments:* Skidmore, Owings & Merrill, summer 1978; Kessler, Merci & Associates, summer 1979; Skidmore, Owings & Merrill, 1980-85; Kes Development Corporation, 1987; Berners-Schober Associates Inc, 1988-. *Memberships:* American Institute of Architects; Wisconsin Society of Architects. *Honours:* Plym Prize, art, 1979; Earl Prize, design, 1980; Bronze Tablet, highest university honours, 1980. *Hobbies:* Music; Windsurfing; Cycling; Weight training; Photography; Downhill & Cross-country skiing. *Address:* 2712 Old Coach Road, Green Bay, Wisconsin 54302, USA.

SATO Eunice N., b. 8 June 1921, Livingston, California, USA. Retired Local Government Official. m. Thomas T. Sato, 9 Dec. 1950, 2 sons, 1 daughter. *Education:* AA, Modesto Senior College, California, 1941; BA, University of Northern Colorado, 1944; MA, Columbia University Teachers College, 1948. *Appointments:* Teacher, Michigan, 1944-47; Educational missionary, Yokohama, Japan, 1948-51; Member, City Council 1975-86, Mayor 1980-82, City of Long Beach, California. *Publications:* Monthly articles, neighbourhood papers, 1975-86. *Memberships include:* President: Local chapters, American Red Cross, National Conference of Christians & Jews, Industry Education Council, Lakewood-Long Beach Republican Women Feeration; Offices: National League of Cities, League of California Cities, Southern California Association of Governments, Independent Cities Association, Girl Scouts, Industry Education Council, United Way; California Council on Criminal Justice; State Advisory Group, Juvenile Justice & Delinquency Prevention; Board of Global Ministries, United Methodist Church; *Honours include:* 1st female Lion, 1987; Various honours & awards, State Chamber of Commerce Women's Council 1979, South Coast Ecumenical Council 1976, National & California Parent Teacher Associations 1974, 1963, Daughters of American Revolution 1982, Federal Managers Association 1982, Long Beach Coordinating Council 1969. *Hobbies:* Gardening; Reading; Classical Music; Art & craft work. *Address:* 551-101 Pittsfield Court, Long Beach, CA 90808, USA.

SATOW Aiko, b. 27 Jan. 1929, Hamamatsu-city, Japan. Professor of Behavioural Science. *Education:* BA, Japan Womens University, 1954; MA 1965, Graduate course, Psychology 1963-68, Kyoto University; DLitt,

1979. *Appointments:* School Teacher, Shizuoka, 1958-61; Prefectual High Schools; Staff, Department of Psychology, 1961-63, Instructor 1968-74, Nara Womens University; Associate Professor, Hamamatsu University School of Medicine, 1974-89; Professor, 1989-. *Publications:* What is Optimum? In sensory environment of urban area in Japan, 1982; Author of numerous scientific papers in national and international journals. *Memberships:* International Association for the Study of Pain (IASP); Japanese Psychological Association; Japanese Psychonomic Society; Illuminating and Engineering Institute of Japan; Japanese Ergonomics Society. *Honour:* 24th Award for Women Researchers in Science, Japanese Association of University Women, 1972. *Hobbies:* Batik; Calligraphy; Music; Touring architecture. *Address:* B408-3776 Handa-cho, Hamamatsu-city 431 31, Japan.

SATTERTHWAITE Helen, b. 8 July 1928, Pennsylvania, USA. State Representative. m. Cameron B. Satterthwaite, 1950, 4 sons, 1 daughter. *Education:* BS, Chemistry, Duquesne University, 1949. *Appointments:* Laboratory Technician: University of Pittsburgh; Gulf Research & Development; E.I. DuPont de Nemours; University of Illinois School of Life Science & College of Agriculture; Iowa State University College of Agriculture; US Department of Agriculture; Natural Science Laboratory Technician, University of Illinois College of Veterinary Medicine, 1971-74; Representative, 103rd District, State of Ilinois General Assembly, 1975-, (re-elected to serve until 1990). *Memberships Include:* State Assembly Committees: Executive Chair, Education; Chair, Higher Education Committee, Economic Development; various other State Committees; Delta Kappa Gamma. *Honours:* Numerous awards, certificates & recognitions. *Hobbies:* Community Activities. *Address:* 101 East Florida, Urbana, IL 61801, USA.

SAUCIER Karen Anite, b. 7 Oct. 1954, Hattiesburg, Mississippi, USA. Professor of Nursing; Administrator. m. Joel Christopher Lundy, 27 Dec. 1986. *Education:* BS, University of Southern Mississippi, 1976; MS 1978, MA 1987, PhD 1988, University of Colorado. *Appointments:* Nursing staff (RN), University of Mississippi Medical Centre; Clinical specialist, US Public Health Service, 1978-80; University of Mississippi Medical Centre, 1980-81; Faculties, University of Colorado 1982-85, Delta State University 1985- (Dean, School of Nursing, Professor). *Publications:* Healers & Heartbreakers: Images of Women & Men in Country Music, in Journal of Popular Culture, 1986; Community Health Nursing, workbook, 1988. *Memberships:* Offices, past/present: Mississippi Council of Deans & Directors, American Association of Colleges of Nursing, National League for Nursing, American Nurses Association, National Student Nurses Association. Member: Western Social Science Association; American, & Southern Sociological Associations; American Public Health Association. *Honours:* Merit scholarship, American College Test, 1972-75; Graduate fellowship, HEW/US Public Health Service, 1977; Various honour societies; Biographical listings. *Hobbies:* Tennis; Golf; Photography; Gardening; Reading for pleasure. *Address:* 202 North 3rd Avenue, Cleveland, Mississippi 38732, USA.

SAUER Mary Julia, b. 10 Oct. 1949, Pittsburgh, Pennsylvania, USA. Special Education Programme Specialist. 1 son. *Education:* BS, Art Education, Edinboro State College, 1971; Teaching Certificate, Elementary and Special Education, Genesco State College, 1973; MS, Special Education, Clarion State College, 1980; Doctoral class, University of Pittsburgh, 1988. *Appointments:* Teacher, Polk State School and Hospital, Polk, Pennsylvania, 1971-72; Vista Volunteer Worker, Bath, New York, 1972-73; Teacher, 1973-80, Programme Specialist, 1980-, Polk Center, State Institution for Mentally Retarded, Polk, Pennsylvania, 1980-; Cake Maker/Decorator; Landlord, 3 single-unit houses. *Creative works include:* Thesis and video on History of Polk Center, also numerous talks on same; Patent for beer-bottle-shaped cake pan, 1987.

Memberships: International Cake Exploration Society. *Honours:* Reader's Spotlight, Mailbox News magazine for cake decorators, 1984; Over 50 pictures of her cakes, 1984-, Cake of the Month, 1988, Mail Box News; Cakes shown in Needlepoint News, 1987, Dog Fancy, 1987, Country Decorating Ideas, 1988, 3 & 4 Wheel Action, 1988, Quilting Today, 1988, Klaxon, 1988, Quilting USA, 1988, Quilt World, 1989; OID Old Fashioned Patchwork, 1989; Horse and Horseman, 1990. *Hobbies:* Spending time with son Jason including attending Catholic Church; Reading non-fiction and novels about interesting people; Walking; Creative cake decorating; Selling cake decorating items; Maintaing her rental houses; Conversing with others. *Address:* PO Box 98, Stoneboro, PA 16153, USA.

SAUNDERS Ann Loreille Cox-Johnson, b. 23 May 1930, St Johns Wood, London, England. Historian. m. Bruce Kemp Saunders, 4 June 1960. 1 son, 1 daughter, deceased. *Education:* Henrietta Barnett School, 1934-46; Queen's College, Harley Street, 1946-48; BA Hons, History, University College, London, 1951; PhD, Leicester University, 1965. *Appointments:* Deputy Librarian, Lambeth Palace, 1952-55; Assistant Keeper, British Museum, 1955-56; Archivist, Marylebone Public Library, 1956-63. *Publications:* John Bacon, RA, 1961; Regent's Park, 1969, 2nd ed 1981; King's England vols on London rewritten; Art & Architecture of London 1984, 2nd ed 1988. *Memberships:* Fellow, Society of Antiquarians (Currently on Council); Editor, Costume Society, 1967-; Editor, London Topographical Society, 1975-; President, Camden History Society, 1984-89; President, St Marylebone Society, 1986-89; President, Regent's Park Branch of NADFAS, 1989-. *Honours:* Plumptre Scholar, Queen's College, 1946-48; London Tourist Board winner for specialist Guide Book of 1984. *Hobbies:* London; History; Cooking; Embroidery; Walking gently. *Address:* 3 Meadway Gate, London NW11 7LA, England.

SAUNDERS June Alison A. (Cuffley), b. 6 June 1949, St George, Grenada, West Indies. Religious Education Teacher. m. Clive Saunders, 18 Dec. 1985. *Education:* NA Honours, Theology, University of West Indies, 1974. *Appointments:* Library assistant, 1967-69; Part-time Diocesan youth worker, Anglican Church in Jamaica, 1969-70; Teacher, Religious Education, 1975-. *Creative work includes:* Occasional songs for youth programmes. *Memberships:* Ranger Guider, District Commissioner & Trainer, Deputy Chief Commissioner for Jamica, Western Hemisphere Trainers Pool, substitute member Western Hemisphere Committee, Girl Guides Association. *Honours:* Commendation Certificate, Merit Certificate, Medal of Merit & Bar, Gallantry Award, Girl Guides; National Award, Youth Leader of Year, Jaycees; Outstanding Teacher, Ministry of Education, 1989. *Hobbies:* Singing; Camping; Travel; Reading; Meeting & working with people. *Address:* 6 Halart Drive, Kingston 6, Jamaica, West Indies.

SAUNDERS Kay Elizabeth Bass, b. 19 Aug. 1947, Brisbane, Australia. Academic; Script Writer. m. Raymond Evans, 21 Dec. 1968 (divorced 1982), 1 daughter. *Education:* BA 1st Class Honours 1970, PhD 1975, University of Queensland. *Appointments:* Tutor 1975-79, Senior Tutor 1980-84, Senior Lecturer 1985-, University of Queensland. *Publications:* Books: Race Relations in Colonial Queensland; Indentured Labour in British Empire; Workers in Bondage: Origin & Bases of Unfree Labour in Queensland 1826-1916. *Memberships:* Australian Historical Association; Anti-Apartheid Group, Brisbane; Land Rights Support Group. *Honours:* Commonwealth Postgraduate Scholarship, 1970-73; Award, Australian University Grant Scheme, 1979-81; Research Council, Griffith University, 1987. *Hobbies:* Cinema; Reading; Travel. *Address:* History Department, University of Queensland, Queensland, Australia.

SAUNDERS Lonna Jeanne, b. 26 Nov. 1952, Cleveland, Ohio, USA. Lawyer; Broadcast Journalist. *Education:* AB, Political Science, Vassar College, 1974; JD, Northwestern University Law School, 1981.

Appoinments Include: News Anchor, WCIU TV, Chicago, 1982-85; News Anchor, WBMX FM Radio, Chicago, 1984-86; Talk Host WKQX Radio, Chicago, 1987; WMAQ Radio (NBC) Chicago, 1988-. *Publications:* Contributing Editor, Chicago Life Magazine, 1986-. *Memberships:* Womens and Chicago Bar Associations; National academy of TV Arts & Sciences; American Bar Association, Executive Committee; Lawyers for the Creative Arts. *Honours:* Recipient, various honours and awards. *Hobbies:* Theatre; Piano. *Address:* 24051 Ambour Drive, North Olmsted, OH 44070, USA.

SAUVÉ Jeanne, b. 26 Apr. 1922, Prud'Homme, Saskatchewan, Canada. Governor General of Canada. m. The Honourable Maurice Sauve, 1 son. *Education:* University of Ottawa; Diploma, French Civilization, Universite de Paris, 1952. *Appointments:* National President, Jeunesse Etudiante Catholique Movement, 1942-47; Founder, Federation des mouvements de jeunesse du Quebec, 1947; Studied, Economics, London, England, Teacher, French, London County Council, 1948-50; Assistant to Director, Youth Department of UNESCO, 1951; Freelance Broadcaster, Journalist, canadian Broadcasting Corporation, 1952-72; Liberal Member of Parliament, Ahuntsic, Montreal, 1972, re-elected for Laval-des-Rapides, 1979, Speaker of the House of Commons, 1980-84; Governor General & Commander in Chief of Canada, 1984-. *Memberships:* various professional organisations. *Honours:* Privy Councillor; Companion of the Order of Canada; Commander, Order of Military Merit; Canadian Forces Decoration; DHL; Honorary DSc.; Hon. LLD. *Address:* Government House, 1 Sussex Drive, Ottawa, Ontario, Canada K1A 0A1.

SAVAGE Carole A, b. 15 Aug. 1937, Texas, USA. Realtor Associate. m. Edward W Savage Jr, MD, 6 June 1959. 1 son, 2 daughters. *Education:* BS Tenn State University, 1959; Special Ed Cert 1966, Special Education Introduction 1967, Brooklyn College. *Appointments:* Public School Teacher: Chicago, Ill, 1959; Syracuse, NY, 1960; Fairfield, CA, 1961; Brooklyn, NY, 1966; Sub Los Angeles, 1976; Realtor Associate, Rolling Hills Realty, 1981. *Memberships:* Chicago Teachers Assoc; New York Teachers Assoc; Charles Drew Med Wives Aux; St Francis Med Wives Aux; National Med Assoc Aux; National Notary Assoc. Notary Public; National Assoc of Realtors. *Honours:* Real Estates Sales, Highest Value, 1985; Highest Classroom Achievement 1967, Most Accomplished 1968, Special Education, Brooklyn, NY. *Hobby:* Newspaper puzzles. *Address:* 710 Silver Spur Road Suite 260, Rolling Hills Ests, CA 90274, USA.

SAVAGE Gretchen Susan, b. 15 Jan. 1934, Seattle, Washington, USA. Company President; Information Management Consultant. m. Terry R. Savage, 26 Sept. 1964, 3 sons. *Education:* BA, Education, University of California, Los Angeles, 1955; Graduate work in Education, Art, Library and Computer Science, 1957-70; Life Credential, Librarianship, California. *Appointments:* Head Librarian, Douglas Missiles and Space Systems, Los Angeles, California, 1957-63; Division Director, NASA Scientific and Technical Information Facility, Bethesda, Maryland, 1963-64; Consultant, Library Automation, 1964-77; President, Savage Information Services, information management consulting company, 1977-. *Publications:* Numerous papers and presentations to professional organisations and conferences in information management, library automation, information entrepreneurship. *Memberships:* Information Technology Division Chair, Consultants Section Chair, Professional Development Committee Member, Special Libraries Association; Professional Development Committee, American Society for Information Science; Alpha Phi Sorority; Soroptimists; Association of Records Managers and Administrators. *Honours:* Phi Beta Kappa, Delta Phi Upsilon, Pi Lambda Theta, Mortarboard, 1955; Woman of the Year, Palos Verdes Women's Clubs, 1984. *Hobbies:* Active in community with support for community theatre, art center and library; Gardening;

Cooking. *Address:* 30000 Cachan Place, Rancho Palos Verdes, CA 90274, USA.

SAVAGE Wendy Diane, b. 12 Apr 1935, Thornton Heath, Surrey, England. Senior Lecturer; Honorary Consultant in Obstetrics & Gynaecology. m. Miguel Babatunde Richard Savage, July 1960. 2 sons, 2 daughters. *Education:* BA, Girton College, Cambridge, 1953-57; MB BCh Cantab, London Hospital Medical College, 1957-60; MRCS LRCP, 1959; MRCOG 1971; FRCOG 1985. *Appointments:* Preregistration posts, 1959-61; Research Fellow 1962-64, Harvard University, Camb., USA, Medical Officer; Awo-Omanma and Enugu General Hospitals, Nigeria, 1964-67; Registrar, Kenyatta National Hospital, Kenya, 1967-69; Registrar, Royal Free Hospital, London, England, 1970-71; Various Posts, 1971-73; Specialist in O&G, Venereology Family Planning, Cook Hospital, Gisborne, New Zealand, 1973-76; Lecturer in O&G London Hospital Medical College, 1976-77; Honorary Senior Registrar, Senior Lecturer, 1977-, The London Hospital & Medical College. *Publications:* Hysterectomy; Coping with Caesarian section and other difficult births, with Fran Reader; A Savage Enquiry: who controls childbirth, 1986. *Memberships:* Birth Control Campaign; Simon Population Trust; Institute of Psychosexual Medicine; Founding Member, Women in Medicine; Founding Member, Women in Gynaecology & Obstetrics; Chair Forum of Maternity & Newborn, Royal Society of Medicine. *Hobbies:* Playing the piano; Reading novels; Travel. *Address:* 19 Vincent Terrace, London N1, England.

SAVAKI Helen, b. 16 Sept. 1960, Greece. University Professor. m. Joseph Papamatheakis. *Education:* MD, University of Athens, 1975; Licensed Medical Practitioner, Greece; Dr.Sci, Doctorate Degree in Basic Medical Science, University of Athens, 1976. *Appointments:* Research Assistant, Biological Chemistry, Athens University School of Medicine, 1972-76; Research Fellow, Psychobiology, Medical School of Sao Paulo, Brazil, 1975; Research Fellow, Anesthesiology, Columbia University, New York, USA, 1976; Postdoctoral Research Fellow, National Institute of Mental Health, Bethesda, Maryland, USA, 1976-79; Postdoctoral Research Fellow, Wellcome Surgical Institute, University of Glasgow, UK, 1979-80; Postdoctoral Research Fellow, College de France, 1980-84; Associate Professor, Physiology, 1984-, Director, Basic Sciences Dept., 1987-88, University of Crete. *Publications:* Numerous articles in professional journals including: Nature; Journal of Physiology; Science; Brain Research; Journal of Neurochemistry; Circulation Research; Journal of Comparative Neurology; etc. *Memberships:* Society for Neuroscience, USA; New York Academy of Sciences; Society for Neuroscience, Greece. *Honours:* Recipient, numerous honours, awards and grants. *Address:* Laboratory of Physiology, Department of Basic Sciences, School of Medicine, University of Crete, 71409 Iraklion, Crete, Greece.

SAVARD Lorena Flora Berube, b. 30 Aug. 1942, Putnam, Connecticut, USA. Accounting & Bookkeeping Services. m. Roger D Savard. 1 son. *Education:* Associate in Science Degree, Accounting 1976, Management 1978, Quinebaug Valley Community College; Data Processing Courses, Thames Valley Technical College, 1979; Advanced Computer Awareness Certificate, Northeast CT Regional Community and Adult Education program, 1981; BS, Business administration, Nichols College, 1989. *Appointments:* Manager, DKH Credit Union, Inc, Putnam, CT, 1974-80; Office Manager, Waters Bros Oil Co, Inc, 1982-83; Head Administrative Clerk, Spectrum Information Systems Inc, 1984-85; Clerical Temporary, Danielson Federal Savings, Danielson, 1986-87; Accountant, Temporary, Putnam Redevelopment Agency, 1987; Personnel/Payroll Assistant, American Trim Products Inc, 1987-88; Temporary, Talent Tree Personnel Services, 1988-89. *Memberships include:* Volunteer, VITA, 1985; Board Member, Quinebaug Valley Youth Services Bureau, 1981-87; Life Patron, American Biographical Institute Research Association,

1981-; International Platform Association, 1981-. *Honours:* Dean's List, Delta Mu Delta, Zeta Alphi Phi, Nichols College, 1987-89; Dean's List, Quinebaug Valley Community College, 1974-78. *Address:* RFD No 1, Box 172, Putnam, CT 06260, USA.

SAVARY OGDEN Geraldine, b. 22 Sept. 1929, Brooksville, USA. Business Executive; Developer; Research; Writer. m. Robert T. Ogden, 12 Aug. 1950, 1 son, 1 daughter. *Education:* On the Job Training: Horticulture, Nursing, Advertising; diploma 12th. *Appointments:* President, Sign of the Times, Selden, New York, 1970-74; BG Micro Purchasing Inc., Scottsdale, Arizona, 1979; Owner, Ogden Nursery, Inverness, Florida, 1974-79, Dove Systems, Scottsdale, 1980; Vice President, Stock Holder, Computer Clinic Inc., Mesa Arizona, 1982-84; Law Insurance Co., Scottsdale, 1984; Owner, Dove Landscaping and Citrus Nursery, Floral City, Florida, 1989. *Publications:* Citrus County Guide Tax, 1978; A Touch of Soul, 1983; From a Liberal Mind, poetry, 1972; Favorite Rec. US Presidents, 1985; Designer, dove Symbol, Womens Liberation, 1970. *Memberships:* Association of Business & professional Women; National Association of Women; US Independent Computer Conultants Association; Phoenix IBM-PC Users Group. *Hobbies:* Research; Cooking; Fishing; Boating; Hunting. *Address:* PO Box 854, Floral City, FL 32636, USA.

SAVOURS Ann Margaret, b. 9 Nov. 1927, Stoke-on-Trent, England. Author; Housewife. m. 18 Nov. 1961. 2 sons. *Education:* BA (Hons) History, London University (Royal Holloway College), 1946-49; Sorbonne: Cours de Civilisation Francaise (Diplome), 1949-50. *Appointments:* King's College Library, Aberdeen University, 1951-54; Curator of MSS, Maps, Pictures, Scott Polar Research Institute, Cambridge, 1954-66; Assistant Keeper, National Maritime Museum, Greenwich, 1970-87. *Publications:* Edward Wilson's Discovery Diaries 1901-04, Editor, 1966; Scott's Last Voyage, 1973; Voyages of the Discovery, to be published; Numerous papers in professional journals. *Memberships:* Member of Council, Hakluyt Society; Hon Secretary, Society for Nautical Research; Former Council Member, Member of Library & Maps Committee, Royal Geographical Society. *Honours:* Johnston and Florence Stoney Studentship, British Federation of University Women to Australia & New Zealand, Australian National University, Canberra, 1960-61; British Council (Australia) lecture/travel award, 1989; Exhibition to Royal Holloway College, University of London, 1946. *Hobbies:* Countryside; Gardening; Conservation. *Address:* Little Bridge Place, Nr Canterbury, Kent CT4 5LG, England.

SAWYERR Judith Sara, b. 7 Mar. 1942, New York, USA. Principal. m. Professor Akilagpa Sawyerr, 24 Sept. 1967, 1 son, 1 daughter. *Education:* BS, Cornell University, 1963; Diploma Education, 1965. *Appointments:* Teacher, St Joseph's Secondary School, Dar es Salaam, 1968-70; Teacher, Lincoln Community School, Accra, 1970-73; Teacher, Ghana International School, 1974-79; Teacher, Port Moresby International School, 1979-84; Principal, Ghana International School, 1985-. *Memberships:* Various Parent-Teaher and Community Education Groups; Patron, Library Association of Ghana. *Hobbies:* Sports; Aerobics; Reading. *Address:* c/o Vice Chancellor's Office, University of Ghana, Legon, Ghana.

SAX Mary Randolph TePoorten, b. 13 July 1925, Pontiac, Michigan, USA. Speech and Language Pathologist, CCC. m. William Martin Sax, 7 Feb. 1948. *Education:* BA magna cum laude, Michigan State University, 1947; MA, University of Michigan, 1949; Postgraduate courses, above universities and Wayne State University, Detroit. *Appointments:* Supervisor, Speech Correction Department, Waterford Schools, Pontiac, Michigan, 1949-69; Lecturer, Marygrove College, Detroit, Michigan, 1971-72; Private Practice in Speech and Language Pathology, Wayne and Oakland Counties, Michigan, 1973-; Adjunct Speech Pathologist, Southfield and Farmington, Michigan, 1987-; Adjunct Faculty, SS Cyril and Methodius Seminary, Michigan, 1989-. *Publications:* Importance of Speech Correction Supervision in Public School Setting, 1967; Case Selection in a Growing Area, 1968; Language, Speech and Hearing Services in Schools; A Longitudinal Study of Articulation Change, 1972; Listing in Journal of Language and Language Behavior Abstracts, 1973. *Memberships:* Scientific Council on Stroke, American Heart Association; American Speech, Language, Hearing Association; Michigan Speech, Language, Hearing Association (Committee on Community and Hospital Services); American Heart Association, Michigan (Stroke Committee); International Association of Logopedics and Phoniatrics, Switzerland; American Association of University Women; Gamma Phi Beta; Founders Society of the Detroit Institute of Arts, Michigan; Michigan Humane Society. *Honours:* Tau Sigma, 1946; Kappa Delta Pi (Past President), 1946; Theta Alpha Phi (Past President), 1946; Phi Kappa Phi, 1946; State College Scholar, University of Michigan Award, 1947; Educational grants to Audiology Seminar, Michigan State University, 1963, Institute on Articulation and Learning, Oberlin College, 1969; Professional Service Recognition, College of Education, Michigan State University, 1964, 1968; Waterford Schools Commendation for Exemplary Service, 1969. *Hobbies:* Demography; Drama; Embroidery. *Address:* 31320 Woodside, Franklin, MI 48025, USA.

SAYER Kimberly Dawn Mary, b. 4 Apr. 1959, Bristol, England. Company President. *Education:* Various colleges. *Appointments:* Fashion Assistant, Model, Tony Chase Inc., New York City, 1979-80; Model, Barbizon Modelling Agency, New York City, 1979-80; Skin Care Manager & Make-up, Something Different Beauty Salon, 1980-81; President, Kimberly Sayer Beauty Care Inc., New York City, 1981-. *Publications:* Mime Work. *Memberships:* World Vision; Beauty Without Cruelty; People for the Humane Treatment of Animals; National Association Female Executives; Sigma Pi Epsilon. *Honours:* Recipient, several honours & awards. *Hobbies:* Riding; Mime & Theatre; Dance; Art; Scuba Diving; Travel. *Address:* 61 West 82nd St., Suite 5A, New York, NY 10024, USA.

SBAR Claire, b. 17 Jan. 1941, Philadelphia, Pennsylvania, USA. Executive. 3 sons, 1 daughter. *Education:* BA, Temple University, 1961; Advanced Studies, 1963. *Appointments:* President, Claire's Demo Company, 1968-72; Office Manager, Medical Associates, 1973; Manager, Single apartment complex, 1984; Assistant Territorial Manager, Nine apartment complexes, 1985-86; Territorial Manager, Kamson Corporation, Real Estate Management, 1987-; Consultant, US Housing & Urban Development, Bucks County Housing Authority, 1987-. *Publications:* Author of various technical manuals. *Memberships:* Parent Teachers Association; Chamber of Commerce; Red Cross; Police Benevolent Association; National Paralegal Association; Business and Professional Women. *Honour:* Award of Merit, Chamber of Commerce. *Address:* 3000 Ford Road, Bristol, PA 19007, USA.

SCARR Dee, b. 20 Feb. 1948, New York, USA. Writer; Photographer; Dive Guide; Speaker. m. C. David Batalsky, 30 Oct. 1985. *Education:* BA, English, 1969, MA, English, Speech, 1971, University of Florida. *Appointments:* Teacher, English, Public Speaking, North Miami Beach High School, Florida, 1972-77; Scuba Instructor, Dive Guide, 1975-82; President, Touch The Sea, Bonaire, Netherlands Antilles, 1982-. *Publications:* Books: Coral's Reef, 1985; Touch the Sea, 1987; The Gentle Sea, 1989; Slide shows: Touch the Sea; I Only Have Eyes for You; The Gentle Sea. *Memberships:* International Oceanographic Association; Divers Advisory Board, American Littoral Society; Advisory Board, Friends of the Sea; Divers Alert Network. *Address:* c/o Touch The Sea, Box 369, Bonaire, Netherlands Antilles.

SCHAEFER Susan Marie, b. 31 Jan. 1952, Minnesota, USA. Licensed Psychologist; Certified Chemical Dependency Practitioner. *Education:* BA,

Psychology 1974, Chemical Dependency Counselling Training Programme 1976, MA Psychology 1978, University of Minnesota; PhD, Clinical Psychology, Saybrook Institute, ongoing. *Appointments:* Instructor, Teaching Association, Teaching Assistant, University of Minnesota, 1975-78; Mental Health and Chemical Dependency Counselor, 1976-81; Program Manager, Chrysalis Outpatient Treatment Programme, 1978-80; Psychologist, Relate Counselling Center, 1981-83; Adjunct Assistant Professor, St Mary's Junior College, 1984-86; Consultant/Trainer, University of Minnesota Medical School, 1987-; Consultant/Trainer, The Model Women's Treatment Project, 1986-87; Private Practice, 1982-. *Publications:* Numerous articles to professional journals and magazines. *Memberships:* Minnesota Psychological Association; Minnesota Licensed Psychologist; Minnesota Women Psychologists; Institute for Chemical Dependency Professionals of Minnesota, Inc. *Honours:* APA Research Award, 1988; Allis Scholarship, University of Minnesota, 1973; Creighton University Scholarship 1970, 1971. *Hobbies:* Classical music; Raquetball; Guitar; Photography; Rubber rafting. *Address:* 2400 Blaisdell Ave South, Minneapolis, MN 55404, USA.

SCHAEFFER Barbara Hamilton, b. 26 Apr. 1926, Newton, Massachusetts, USA. Company President. m. John Schaeffer, 7 Sept. 1946, 2 sons, 1 daughter. *Education:* Skidmore College, 1943-46; AB, English, Bucknell University, 1948; Graduate School: Montclair State University, 1950- 51; Bank Street College of Education, 1959-61; Yeshiva University, 1961-62. *Appointments:* Director, Pompton Plains School, New Jersey, 1959-62; Advisor, Episcopal School, Towaco, New Jersey, 1968-70; President, Monroe Heavy Equipment Rentals Inc, Orange City, Florida, 1981-; Lecturer on children's art, 1959-70. *Publications:* Articles in various publications. *Memberships:* International Platform Association; President, Trolley Lines Travel Club; Charter Member, Small Business Development Regional Center, Stetson University Chapter; Delano Area Chamber of Commerce, Transportation Committee; Orange City Chamber of Commerce. *Hobbies:* Restoring old historical home in Massachusetts; Oil painting; Encouraging her children; Grandmothering Holly and Dena; Travel. *Address:* Monroe Heavy Equipment Rentals Inc, 2425 Enterprise Road, Orange City, FL 32763, USA.

SCHAEFFER Sara Sue, b. 6 Oct. 1947, Sturgis, Michigan, USA. Professional Counsellor & Consultant. m. 27 June 1986, 1 son, 1 daughter. *Education:* BA, 1969; MA, 1971; EdS, 1975; EdD, 1983. *Appointments:* Self-employed counsellor & consultant, & owner, agency, 1979-; Associate Chief of Staff, Education, UA Medical Centre, Battle Creek, Michigan, 1980-89. *Publications:* Effects of Cognitive Stress Management Programme on Perceptions of Stress Levels, doctoral dissertation, 1983; Articles, various professional journals. *Memberships:* Offices, numerous professional organisations. *Honours:* William D. Martinson Distinguished Alumni, 1989; George Hilliard Outstanding Counsellor, 1979; Professional Leadership Award, MACD, 1981; Distinguished Professional Contributions, MMHCA, 1984; Phi Beta Kappa, 1969; Alpha Lambda Delta, 1966. *Hobbies:* Sailing; Reading; Gourmet cooking. *Address:* 909 East Chicago Road, Sturgis, Michigan 49091, USA.

SCHAEFFER Susan Fromberg, b. 25 Mar. 1941, Brooklyn, USA. Writer; Professor. m. Neil J. Schaeffer, 11 Oct. 1970, 1 son, 1 daughter. *Education:* BA, 1961, MA Honours, 1963, PhD, Honours, 1966, University of Chicago. *Appointments:* Instructor, Wright Junior College, 1964-65; Instructor, 1965-66, Assistant Professor, 1966-67, Illinois Institute of Technology; Assistant Professor, 1967-70, Associate Professor, 1970-75, Professor, 1975-, Brooklundian Professor, 1984-, Brooklyn College. *Publications:* Novels: Falling, 1973; Anya, 1974; Time in Its Flight, 1988; Love, 1981; The Madness of a Seduced Woman; Mainland, 1985; The Injured Party, 1986; Buffalo Afternoon, 1989; Poetry: The Witch & the Weather Report, 1972; Granite

Lady, 1974; Rhymes & Runes of the Toads, 1976; Bible of the Beasts of the Little Field, 1980; short fiction: The Queen of Egypt, 1980; Childrens Books; The Dragons of North Chittendon, 1986; The Four Hoods and Great Dog, 1988. *Honours:* Edward Lewis Wallant Award, Friends of Literature Award, 1974; PEN Anthology of British Poetry, 1978; O Henry Best Short Stories Award, 1978; John Simon Guggenheim Foundation Fellowship, 1984-85; Prairie Schooner's Lawrence Award, 1985. *Address:* c/o Virginia Barber Literary Agency, 255 W. 21 St., New York, NY 10011, USA.

SCHANSCHIEFF Juliet Dymoke de, b. 28 June 1919, Enfield, Middlesex, England. Author. m. 9 May 1942. 1 daughter. *Appointments:* Bank of England, 1937-42; Canadian Medical Records, 1942-43; MacGraw-Hill Publishers, 1968-69. *Publications:* 4 books for children; 28 Historical novels, published under the name of Juliet Dymoke. *Hobbies:* The Countryside; Ancient Buildings; General history; Music; Swimming; Gardens. *Address:* Heronswood, Chapel Lane, Forest Row, East Sussex, RH18 5BS, England.

SCHANSTRA Carla Ross, b. 4 Sept. 1954, Berwyn, USA. Technical Writer. *Education:* BA, Western Illinois University, 1976. *Appointments:* Assciate Editor, Hitchock Pub., Wheaton, 1976-80; Associate Product Manager, Advanced Systems Inc., Elk Grove Village, 1980-81; Technical Writer, Professional Computer Resources, Oak Brook, 1982; Senior Technical Writer, AT&T Bell Labs., Naperville, 1982-; Freelance Writer. *Publications:* Stage Plays: A Little Bit of Both; The Reversible Play; Survivors; Snakes and Apple Pie; It Should be Obvious; contributor of articles to professional journals. *Memberships:* Dramatists Guild; Feminist Writers Western Suburbs, Founder; International Society of Dramatists; Feminist Writers Guild; Illinois Theatre Association. *Address:* 2 S 709 Winchester Cir., Warrenville, IL 60555, USA.

SCHAUB Danielle, b. 24 Aug. 1954, Kuala Belait, Borneo. Lecturer. m. Samuel Joseph Wajc, 11 Sept. 1982, 1 son, 1 daughter. *Education:* MA English and Dutch, 1st Class, English & Dutch Certificate of Education, 1976; MA Spanish, 1st Class, Spanish Certificate of Education, 1977, University of Brussels, Belgium; Postgraduate Research, Clare Hall, University of Cambridge, England, 1977-80. *Appointments:* Teacher, English & Dutch, Belgian Chamber of Commerce, Brussels, 1976-77; Supervisor, English Tripos, Downing College, Cambridge, 1979-80; Lecturer, Free University of Brussels, 1980-88; Visiting Lecturer, 1985-86, Lecturer, Oranim, 1988-, University of Haifa, Israel. *Publications:* Paintings; Lithographs. *Memberships:* Belgian Association of Anglicists in Higher Education. *Honours:* 2 Scholarships, Wiener Anspach Foundation, 1975, 1977; Scholarship, Rotary Foundation, 1975-80; various other scholarships and grants. *Hobbies:* Classical Music; Theatre; Art; Tennis; Volleyball. *Address:* University of Haifa, Dept. of English, Oranim, Tivon 36910, Israel.

SCHAUWECKER Liddie Margaret McKinster, b. 28 July 1934, Louisa, Kentucky, USA. Construction Executive. m. Norman Walter Schauwecker, 31 Aug. 1953 (divorced Oct. 1968), 1 son, 2 daughters. *Education:* Bliss College, Columbus, Ohio, 1952-54; El Segundo College, Los Angeles, 1957-59. *Appointments:* Secretary: North American Aviation, Columbus, Ohio 1952-55, Gilfillan Electronics, Los Angeles 1956-62; Columbus Wood Preserving Company 1970-78; Owner, Ohio State Tie & Timber Inc, Louisa, Kentucky, 1978- . *Memberships:* American Wood Preservers Association; Railway Tie Association; Business & Professional Women in Construction; Louisa Women's Club; Order of Eastern Star; Rebekah Lodge. *Honours:* Kentucky Colonel, 1984; Achievement awards, sales, Ohio Department of Economic Development, 1980, 1981, 1982; Top 100 Small Businesses in Ohio, Ohio House of Representatives. *Hobbies:* Genealogical research; Writing. *Address:* Route 1, Box 2360, Louisa, Kentucky 41230, USA.

SCHECHTER Ruth Lisa, b. Boston, Massachusetts, USA. Working poet; Instructor; Lecturer and Certified Poetry Therapist. *Appointments:* Certified Poetry Therapist, 7 years on national rehabilitation agency for the chemically addicted; Instructor and Lecturer in poetry, Poet-in-Residence, Chicago's Mundelein College, South Dakota State, UCLA, University of Maine, Exeter Pre (HN), and Syracuse University; Guest writer, Hofstra Writers Conference; Teacher, Creative Writing; Visiting Artist Program, State Arts Council of Oklahoma; Visiting Artists LIFT Program, Westchester County. *Publications:* Poetry includes: Near the Wall of Lion Shadows; Suddenly Thunder; Offshore; Clockworks; Speedway, 1983; Chords & Other Poems, 1986; Double Exposure; Many Rooms in a Winter Night; New and Selected Poems; Let's Speak. *Memberships:* PEN; Poetry Society of America; Founder and Executive editor Croton Review. *Honours:* Recipient of numerous grants; Fellowship, MacDowell Colony; Fellowship, Virginia Center for the Creative Arts, 1984; Cecil Hemley Award, Poetry Society of America. *Address:* 9 Van Cortlandt Place, Croton-on-Hudson, NY 10520, USA.

SCHECTER Mary Virginia, b. 15 Aug. 1909, Robards, USA. Retired. m. Jesse Jay Schecter, 5 Nov. 1944, died 1986, 1 son. *Education:* Diploma, Dale Carnegie, 1929. *Appointments:* Merchandising & Management, Schears Dept. Store, 1928-37; Universal Productions, 1937-41; Auditor, Supervisor, 1941-45; Publicity & Politics, 1945- ; Appointed by Governor of Texas to Hale-Aiken Committee, 1957; Appointed by Governor of Oregon, Listening Post Director, 1980-88; Appointed by Governor of Oregon to Conference on Senior Citizens and the Handicapped, 1988-. *Publications:* Sales Manuals: History of Republican Party, 1976; articles in Chicago Tribune, Dallas Morning News, Oregonian. *Memberships:* PTA, President, Dallas County Council of PTA's. *Honours:* Life Member, Texas Congress of PTA's' Outstanding Achievement Award, American Cancer Society, 1960, 1961, 1962; Member of the Electoral College, (Presidential Elector) 1976, 1984; Outstanding Award, Young Federation of Oregon Republicans, 1981; Outstanding Member, Young Oregon Federation of Republican Women, 1982; Outstanding County Chairman Award of Oregon Republican Party, 1986. *Hobbies:* Volunteer Work. *Address:* PO Box 304, 609 NW Inlet Ave., Lincoln City, OR 93767, USA.

SCHEMBRI ORLAND Lorraine Marie, b. 21 June 1959, St Julian's, Malta. Advocate. m. George Schembri Orland, 18 June 1983, 1 son. *Education:* LLD, University of Malta, 1982. *Appointments:* Parliamentary correspondent, The Times, Malta, 1970-87, Private practice, civil & commercial law, 1982-. *Publications:* Thesis, Liability of Multimodal Transport Operator, 1981; Various articles, civil & commercial law, status of women. *Memberships include:* 1st female committee member, Chamber of Advocates, 1986-87; President, Legal Consultant, National Council of Women, Malta; Founder member, Institute for Family Life Education; Committee, Presidential Fund for Overseas Relief; Vice Chair, National Commission on Advancement of Women. *Honours:* Salzburg Fellow, American Law & Legal Institutions, 1985; International Visitors' Programme to USA, Women & Minorities in Public Affairs, 1986. *Hobbies:* Extensive reading; Travel; Women's issues. *Address:* Nampara, Old Railway Track, Attard, Malta.

SCHENCK Susan Jane, b. 20 July 1949, Providence, Rhode Island, USA. Associate Professor of Special Education. *Education:* AA, Rhode Island Junior College, 1969; BS 1972, MEd 1975, RI College; CAGS 1977, PhD 1979, University of Connecticut. *Appointments include:* Special education teacher, 1972-76; Research assistant, University of Connecticut, 1976-78; Assistant Professor, Special Education, State University of New York, Plattsburgh, 1978-79; Assistant Professor (Special Education) 1979-85, Associate Professor 1985-, Coordinator, Learning Disability Services 1988-, College of Charleston. *Publications:* Books, monographs & reviews including: Co-author, State of the Art in

Connecticut, monograph, 1979; Chapters, Volumes I & II, 9th Mental Measurements Yearbook, 1985; Review, Styles of Training Index, Buros Institute Database; Numerous articles, various professional journals; Presentations. *Memberships:* American Educational Research Association; Council for Exceptional Children; Council for Learning Disabilities; Various other professional bodies, honour societies. *Honours:* Special Education Fellowship, Department of Educational Psychology, University of Connecticut, 1976-78; Outstanding Young Woman in America, 1980; Lilly Research Fellowship, College of Charleston, 1981. *Hobbies:* Reading; Photography; Cooking. *Address:* Education Department, College of Charleston, Charleston, South Carolina 29424, USA.

SCHIFFMAN Susan, b. 24 Aug. 1940, Chicago, USA. divorced 1976, 1 daughter. Professor of Medical Psychology. *Education:* BA cum laude, Syracuse University, 1965; PhD, Duke University, 1970. *Appointments:* Assistant Professor 1972-78; Associate Professor 1978-83, Full Professor 1983-, Duke University. *Publications:* Book, Introduction to Multidimensional Scaling: Theory, Methods & Applications, 1981; Numerous scientific publications on taste & smell. *Memberships:* European Chemoreception Research Organisation; Association of Chemosensory Sciences. *Honour:* Elected, Sigma Xi, 1965. *Hobbies:* Jazz; Travel; Theatre. *Address:* c/o Department of Psychology, Duke University, Durham, North Carolina 27706, USA.

SCHILD Joyce Anna, b. 26 May 1931, Chicago, USA. Otolaryngologist; Surgeon. m. John A. Hegber, 15 Dec. 1973. *Education:* BS, 1954, MD, 1956, University of Illinois, Chicago; Diplomate, American Board, Otolaryngology. *Appointments:* Intern, St Francis Hospital, 1956-57; Residency, University of Illinois, 1958-61; Fellow, Bronchoesophagology, 1961-62; Clinical Instructor to Associate Professor, 1958-82, Professor, 1982-, Otolaryngology, University of Illinois. *Publications:* Numerous presentations & lectures in the field. *Memberships:* AMA; Chicago Medical Society; Illinois State Medical Society; American Laryngological, Rhinological & Otolaryngological Society. *Honours:* Recipient, various honours and awards. *Address:* Dept. of Otolaryngology, University of Illinois, 1855 W. Taylor Suite 2.42, Chicago, IL 60612, USA.

SCHINBEIN Marilyn Ruth, b. 21 Aug. 1931, Toronto, Canada. Registered Insurance Broker. m. William Earl Schinbein, 28 Jan. 1952, 3 sons, 3 daughters. *Education:* Associate of Municipal Clerks & Insurance Brokers, 1981. *Appointments:* Commercial artist, 1952-77; Hanover Town Council, 1976-85; Registered Insurance Broker, 1981; Vice-Chairman, Board of Governors of Georgian College, 1983-88; Hanover Police commission, 1986-88; Hanover Library Board, 1988. *Memberships:* Insurance Brokers Association of Ontario, 1986; Insurance Brokers of Grey-Bruce; Catholic Womens League; Liberal Associations. *Hobbies:* Travel; Lawn Bowling; Photography. *Address:* 275 10th Street, Hanover, Ontario, Canada N4N 1P1.

SCHINDLER Barbara Ann Kleiner, b. 28 Jan. 1944, Fort Lauderdale, Florida, USA. Physician; Psychiatrist. m. 20 Aug. 1966, 2 sons, 1 daughter. *Education:* BA, Boston University, 1966; MD, Woman's Medical College, 1970; Psychiatric residency, Medical College of Pennsylvania, 1970-75. *Appointments include:* Current: Associate Professor of Psychiatry, & Chief, General Hospital Section, Medical College of Pennsylvania. *Memberships:* American Psychiatric Association; Academy of Psychosomatic Medicine; Psychosomatic Society. *Honour:* Alpha Omega Alpha, honorary medical society. *Address:* Department of Psychiatry, Medical College of Pennsylvania, 3300 Henry Avenue, Philadelphia, Pennsylvania 19129, USA.

SCHINDLER Judith Kay, b. 23 Nov. 1941, Chicago, Illinois, USA. Marketing Executive. m. Jack J. Schindler, 1 Nov. 1964, 1 son. *Education:* Michigan State

University, East Lansing, 1961-63; BS, Journalism, University of Illinois, Champaign-Urbana, 1963. *Appointments:* Associate Editor, Irving-Cloud Publishing, 1963-64; Assistant Director of Public Relations, State of Israel Bonds, 1965-69; Vice-President, Public Relations, Realty Co of America, 1969-70; Director of Public Relations, private Telecommunications Inc, 1970-78; Founder, President, Schindler Communications, Chicago, Illinois, 1978-. *Memberships:* National Association of Women Business Owners (Vice-President 1988-89, Founder, Past President, Chicago Chapter, Board of Directors 1980-81, 1984-85); Board of Directors, Friends of the Chicago Public Library (Membership Chair 1988); Board of Advisors, Entrepreneurship Institute, Chicago; University of Illinois Alumnae Association; Founder, Independent Business Association of Illinois; Home Builders Association of Greater Chicago; Forum for Real Estate Discussion and Analysis; Publicity Club of Chicago. *Honours:* Elected Delegate, White House Conference on Small Business, 1980, 1986; Women in Business Advocate, State of Illinois and USA, 1986; Chicago Women Business Owner of the Year, 1989; Appointed Small Business Committee, Illinois Development Board, 1988-89. *Address:* Schindler Communications Inc, 869 N Dearborn, Chicago, IL 60610, USA.

SCHLAFLY Phyllis Stewart, b. 15 Aug. 1924, St Louis, USA. Author; Lawyer. m. Fred Schlafly, 20 Oct. 1949. 4 sons, 2 daughters. *Education:* BA 1944, JD 1978, Washington University, St Louis; MA, Harvard University, 1947; LLD, Niagara University, 1976; Called to Bar of: Illinois 1979, District of Columbia, 1984, Missouri, 1985, US Supreme Court, 1987. *Appointments:* Syndicated columnist, Copley News Service, 1976-; President, Eagle Forum, 1975-. *Publications:* Phyllis Schlafly Report, 1967-; Broadcaster, Spectrum, CBS Radio Network, 1973-78; Commentator, Cable TV News Network, 1980-83; Matters of Opinion, Radio station WBBM, Chicago, 1973-75; Author: A Choice Not an Echo, 1964; The Gravediggers, 1964; Strike From Space, 1965; Safe Not Sorry, 1967; The Betrayers, 1968; Mindszenty The Man, 1972; Kissinger on the Couch, 1975; Ambush at Vladivostok, 1976; The Power of the Positive Woman, 1977; Child Abuse in the Classroom, 1984; Pornography's Victims, 1987. Editor: Equal Pay for Unequal Work, 1984. *Memberships:* Del. Republican National Convention, 1956, 1964, 1968, 1968, alt, 1960, 1980; President, Illinois Federation Republican Women, 1960-64; 1st Vice President, National Federation Republican Women, 1964-67; Illinois Commission on Status of Women, 1975-85; National Chairman Stop ERA, 1972-; Ronald Reagan's Defence Policy Advisory Group, 1980; Commission on Bicentennial of US Constatution, 1985-; Administrative Conf US, 1983-86; DAR (National chairman, American History 1965-68, National Chairman Bicentennial com 1967-70, National chairman, nat def 1977-80, 1983-); American III Bar Associations; Phi Beta Kappa; Pi Sigma Alpha. *Honours:* Recipient 10 Honour awards Freedoms Found; Brotherhood award NCCJ, 1975; Named Woman of Achievement in Pub Affairs St Louis Globe-Democrat, 1963, one of ten most admired woman in world Good Housekeeping poll, 1977. *Address:* 68 Fairmount, Alton, IL 62002, USA.

SCHLEGEL Ilse Nielsen, b. 7 Apr. 1945, Denmark. m. Christian Schlegel, 18 Aug. 1972. 1 daughter. *Education:* Teacher's Degree, 1968; Cand Paed Psych Degree, Copenhagen University, 1973; Study as Psychoanalyst, 1985-. *Appointments:* School Psychologist, 1973-76; Deputy Chief Psychologist, 1976-81; Chief Psychologist, 1981-. *Publications:* Contributor of numerous articles. *Memberships:* District Group Concerning Violence Toward Children; County Group for Crime Prevention Among Children, 1984-. *Hobbies:* Children's Development; Therapy; Psychoanalysis; Tennis; Cooking. *Address:* Johannevej 9, 2740 Skovlunde, Denmark.

SCHLEGEL Janet Catherine, b. 7 Dec. 1940,

Dubuque, Iowa, USA. College Professor. m. Robert H. Deans, 30 Apr. 1966, 1 son, 1 daughter. *Education:* BA magna cum laude, Economics, Clarke College, 1963; MA, Economics, George Washington University, 1967. *Appointments:* US Department of Labor, 1963-65; US Department of Defense, 1965-66; LaSalle College, 1971-72; Chestnut Hill College, 1978-. *Publications:* John Rae and Problems of Economic Development, 1972, cited in D.F.O'Brien's Classical Economics, 1977; Strengthening the Connection between Campus and Business, 1986; Nicholson as Imperialist, 1987. *Memberships:* American Economic Association; Association of Social Economics. *Honours:* Member, Editorial Board, Forum for Social Economics, 1984-; Leavey Award (national) for Excellence in Teaching Private Enterprise. *Hobbies:* Gardening; Tennis; Opera. *Address:* 9 Laurence Place, Plymouth Meeting, PA 19462, USA.

SCHLENKER Emily Catherine Diehl, b. 18 Feb. 1939, Moline, USA. Professional Nurse; Consultant. m. George John Schlanker, 28 Apr. 962, 1 son, 1 daughter *Education:* BA, 1962; RN, Lutheran Hospital School for Nurses; BSN, Marycrest College, 1977; MS, Northern Illinois University, 1979. *Appointments:* Assistant Professor, Marycrest College, 1977-84; Quality Assurance Director, Davenport Medicla Centre, 1984-86; Adjunct Faculty, Lutheran School, 1986-88; Owner, Principal Consultant, Health Management & Associates, 1986-. *Publications:* Articles in journals. *Memberships:* American Association for Advancement of Science; National Associaton of Female Executives; American Management Association; American Nurses Association; Illinois Nurses Association. *Honours:* Essay Award, American Journal of Nursing, 1979; Sigma Theta Tau; US Public Health Service Grantee, 1979; Nominee, Distinguished Alumni Award, Lutheran School, 1988. *Hobbies:* Target Rifle; Classical Music; Hiking; Travel; Language Study. *Address:* 3611 33rd Avenue, Rock Island, IL 61201, USA.

SCHLERT Mary Esther, b. 13 Aug. 1908, Easton, Pennsylvania, USA. Teacher and Freelance Writer. *Education:* BS, Georgian Court College, 1945; Fordham University, summer 1957; MA, US History, University of Notre Dame, 1969. *Appointments:* Teacher, History, Camden Catholic HS, New Jersey, 1962-68; Teacher, History, Notre Dame HS, Lawrenceville, NJ, 1968-69; Executive Secretary, Mount Carmel Guild, Trenton, NJ, 1969-78. *Publications:* Short stories, book reviews, professional articles, Little Theater plays; ghost-writer for speakers, being honored locally. *Appointments:* Former member, Advisory Board, NJ High school Historical Society; Numerous education associations; Chaplain, Soroptomist International, Trenton NJ Chapter. *Honour:* City of Trenton, NJ Outstanding Service Award, presented by Mayor Arthur J Holland, 1979. *Hobbies:* Classical music; Reading; Walking; Social issues of the day; Raising herbs in the kitchen. *Address:* Mercy Convent, 129 Roseberry Street, Phillipsburg, NJ 08865, USA.

SCHMIDL Mary Katherine, b. 11 Aug. 1951, Marysville, California, USA. Nutritionist. *Education:* BSc, University of California, Davis, 1973; MSc (Food Science) 1976, PhD (Food Chemistry) 1978, Cornell University. Numerous postgraduate courses. *Appointments:* Research assistant 1973-75, teaching assistant 1975-78, Cornell University; Research chemist 1978-80, Department Head 1980-82, Nutrition Research, Medical Products Division, Cutter Laboratories Inc; Group Leader, research & development Clinical Nutrition Division 1982-87, corporate research 1987-88, Sandoz Nutrition Corporation; Director, Clinical Product Division of Research, 1988-. *Publications:* Author, co-author, over 40 publications, patents & book chapters. Book reviewer, Journal of Food Processing & Preservation, 1983-; Editorial Board, book reviewer, Food Technology, 1984-; Contributing editor, Restaurant Business Magazine, 1986-. *Memberships include:* Numerous offices, local & national, including National Executive Committee 1987-90, Institute of Food Technology; Offices, American Oil Chemist

Society; Minnesota Nutrition Council; American Association of Cereal Chemists; American Dietetics Association; Society for Nutrition Education. *Honours include:* Miss Teenage Citizen scholarship, 1969; Life member, California Scholarship Federation, 1969; Omicron Nu, 1973; NY State assistantship, Cornell University, 1973-78; Outstanding graduate paper, annual meeting, IFT, 1978; Judge, National IFT College Bowl Competition, 1986-87; Biographical recognitions. *Address:* 1870 Stowe Avenue, St Paul, Minnesota 55112, USA.

SCHMIDT Diane J b. 10 Oct 1953, Lake Forest, Illinois, USA. Photojournalist. *Education:* BA, Prescott College, 1974; BFA, Rhode Island School of Design, 1976. *Appointments:* Independent Photojournalist 1977-. *Publications:* Books: The Chicago Exhibition, 1985; Where's Chimpy, 1988; Abstract Relations, 1980; I am a Jesse White Tumbler, 1990; Articles: cover stories for the Sunday Chicago Tribune Magazine, also published photographs worldwide. *Memberships:* American Society of Magazine Photographers. *Honour:* 1987 Arts Midwest/National Endowment for the Arts. *Address:* 2259 Sheridan Road, Highland Park, IL 60035, USA.

SCHMIDT Marlene Ruth, b. Chicago, Illinois, USA. Producer; Writer; Actress. m. Howard Avedis, 26 Dec. 1969, 3 step-daughters. *Education:* BA, Communications, University of Washington, 1956; 1970-, yearly took numerous courses on a continuing bases at both U.C.L.A. and University of Southern California in writing, entertainment and law. *Appointments:* Screen Gems, Columbia Pictures Television, 1955; Producer, Daily News & Talk Show, KIRO-TV (CBS-TV), Seattle, Washington, 1959-62; Lead Actress in foreign films, 1965-70; Associate Producer, Motion Pictures for Magic Eye Poductions, 1970-73; Motion Picture Film Producer & Writer, Hickmar Productions Incorporated, Hollywood, California, 1974-. *Publications:* Writer/Producer: The Stepmother, 1972; The Teacher, 1974; Scorchy, 1976; Texas Detour, 1977; The Fifth Floor, 1978; Separate Ways, 1979; Mortuary, 1982; They're Playing with Fire, 1984; Kidnapped, 1985; all co-written with Howard Avedis. *Memberships:* Screen Actors Guild; AFTRA; Writers Guild of America; Women in Film; Served as Judge for the past two years at the National Academy of Cable Programming, ACE Awards for outstanding programming; Participant in UCLA Film Seminar as Professor and Guest Lecturer. *Honours:* Academy Award Nomination, Best Song, The Stepmother, 1972; Miss Washington State Finalist. *Hobbies:* Writing; Traveled extensively around the world while living in Rome, Italy, for five years whilst making movies; Reading; Filmmaking; Viewing. *Address:* Hickmar Productions Incorporated, The Burbank Studios, 4000 Warner Boulevard, Burbank, CA 91505, USA.

SCHMIED Sylvia, b. 11 Nov. 1953, El Salvador. Businesswoman. m. 5 Dec. 1972, 3 sons, 2 daughters. *Education:* AS, Nursing, University of Bridgeport, USA, 1974; BA, Psychology, Fairleigh Dickinson University, 1979. *Appointments:* Staff Nurse, Senior Staff Nurse, 1974-77; Head Nurse, 1977-79; Nursing Coordinator, 1980-82; Owner-Officer, Bagelsmith Food Store & Delicatessen, 1983-; Owner, Corporation Financial Officer, Smith & Barrera Associates, 1982-; Vice President, Chief Executive Officer, Smith & Barrera Franchising Company Inc, 1987-. *Memberships:* Chamber of Commerce; Board, Acorn Montessori School. *Honour:* Entrepreneur Small Business Award, Hunterdon County Chmber of Commerce, 1985. *Address:* RD 1, Box 195, Hamden River Road, Annandale, New Jersey 08801, USA.

SCHMITT Rosina (Roselyn Josephine), b. 5 Jan. 1935, St Cloud, MN, USA. Professor. *Education:* BA, College of St Benedict, 1960; MA, 1966, PhD, 1977, St Louis University. *Appointments:* College of St Benedict, 1966-, Director of CORE Senior Seminar 1988-, Professor, Philosophy, 1988-. *Publications:* The End of Evolution in Peirce's Cosmology, 1978; Study Guide for Philosophy Competences, 1978; contributor to: ITEST; Horizons; Grapevine; Sisters Today. *Memberships:* Center for Process Studies; Process and Faith; Institute for Theological Encounter with Science and Technology; Alpha Sigma Nu; etc. *Address:* College of St Benedict, 37 South College Avenue, St Joseph, MN 56374, USA.

SCHMITZ Marcia Allen, b. 25 Dec. 1945, Alliance, Ohio, USA. Political Administrator. *Education:* BA, Kent State University, 1967. *Appointments include:* Legislative Director, Congressman Dante Fascell, US House of Representatives, Washington DC, 1971-. *Honours:* College honorary societies, Pi Gamma Mu, Pi Sigma Alpha. *Address:* 1301 South Arlington Ridge Road no. 605, Arlington, Virginia 22202, USA.

SCHNEIDER Claudine C, b. 25 Mar. 1947, Clairton, Pennsylvania, USA. US Congresswoman. *Education:* University of Barcelona, Spain; Rosemont College, USA; BA, Windham College, Vermont, 1969. *Appointments:* Executive Administrator, Concern Incorporated, 1969; Founder, Rhode Island Committee on Energy, 1973; Executive Director, Conservation Law Foundation, 1974; Federal Co-ordinator, Rhode Island Coastal Zone Management programme, 1978; Producer, Public Affairs programme WJAR-TV, Providence, Rhode Island, 1978-79. *Memberships:* Co-Chair, Congressional Competitiveness Caucus; Executive Board, Congressional Caucus on Women's Issues; Northeast-Midwest Coalition; Environmental & Energy Study Conference; World Women Parliamentarians for Peace; Congressional Committees; Science, Space & Technology; Merchant Marine & Fisheries; Select Aging. *Honours:* Woman of the Year, Rhode Island Women's Political Caucus, 1978; Outstanding Young Person of the Year, Southern County Jaycees, 1979, 1983; Consumer Hero, Consumer Federation of America, 1986; Conservation Advocate of the Year, Energy Conservation Coalition, 1986. *Hobbies:* Running; Designing & Sewing Clothes. *Address:* 1512 Longworth House Office Building, Washington, DC 20515, USA.

SCHNEIDER Jane Harris, b. 2 Jan. 1932, Trenton, New Jersey, USA. Sculptor. m. Alfred R. Schneider, 25 July 1953, 2 sons, 1 daughter. *Education:* BA, Welles;ey College, Wellesley, Massachusetts. *Creative Works:* Selected Solo Exhibitons: Walking Trees, Little Center Gallery, Clark University, 1982; Wood Sculpture, Alternative Museum, New York City, 1985; Sculpture in Place, BMCC, New York City, 1986; Selected Group Works: Alliance in the Park, 1987; In the Spirit of Wood, Kenkelaba Gallery, 1987; Chimeras: Chiseled and Sawn, Nassau County Museum of Fine Art, 1988; Mythical Menagé, Jane Kelly Gallery, New York City, 1988; etc. *Memberships:* Founder, Director, Art Career Management, 1980-85; Founder, Director, Larchmont Little Art School, 1963-68. *Hobbies:* American Indian Artifacts. *Address:* 1 Moog Road, RFD 2, Garrison, NY 10524, USA.

SCHNEIDER Jenny, b. 7 Dec. 1924, The Hague, Netherlands. Retired Director, Swiss National Museum. *Education:* PhD, Basle University, 1951. *Appointments:* Swiss Folk Art Museum, Basle, 1954-56; Assistant, 1956-61, Curator, Department of Stained glass, textiles and costumes, 1961-71, Vice Director, 1971-81, Director, 1982-86, Swiss National Museum, Zurich. *Publications:* Catalogues and many articles on stained glass, textiles, costumes and textile conservation, general museum problems. *Memberships:* Chairman, Int Committee for the Museums & Collections of Costume, 1974-80; Board member, Foundation of the Int. Council of Museums, 1977-86; Conseil de Direction, Centre Int d'Etude des Textiles Ancins, Lyon, France, 1976-86; International Federation of University Women; International Federation of Business and Professional Women. *Honour:* First Honorary Member, International Committee of the Museums & Collections of Costume, 1987. *Interests:* Holland; Research history of Indonesian batik. *Address:* Spiegelgasse 13, CH-8001 Zurich, Switzerland.

SCHNEIDERS Sandra Marie, b. 12 Oct. 1936, Evanston, USA. Associate Professor. *Education:* BA, Marygrove College, 1960; MA, University of Detroit, 1967; STL, Institut Catholique, Paris, 1971; STD, Pontifical Gregorian University, Rome, 1975. *Appointments:* Marygrove College, 1971-72; Professor, New Testament Studies & Spirituality, Jesuit School of Theology, 1976-. *Publications:* New Wineskins; Women and the Word; The Johannine Resurrection Narrative; Spiritual Direction; How to Read the Bible Prayerfully. *Memberships:* Catholic Theological Society of America; Catholic Biblical Association of America; Society of Biblical Literature, President, Western Region, 1988-89; American Academy of Religion; Pacific Coast Theological Society; etc. *Honours:* many honours including: Honoured Scholar, Delta Epsilon Sigma, 1986; Delta Epsilon Sigma, 1987; DD, hc, St Bernard's Institute, Rochester, 1988. *Hobbies:* Jogging; Swimming; Reading; Classical Music; Painting; Hiking; Travel. *Address:* Jesuit School of Theology at Berkeley, 1735 LeRoy Ave., Berkeley, CA 94709, USA.

SCHOEMAN Amy Johanna, b. 3 July 1941, Woking, England. Freelance Photographer/Writer. m. Johannes Louw Schoeman, 7 Mar. 1980, 2 sons, 4 step-sons, 1 step-daughter. *Education:* B.Com., University of Stellenbosch, 1963. *Appointments:* Teacher, Centaurus High School, 1975-76; Photographer, Journalist, Dept. of Nature Conservation, Namibia, 1977-82; Head, Public Relations, 1983-85. 18 one man photographic exhibitions throughout Namibia & South Africa; Acceptance Cape Town Triennial, 1988. *Publications:* Notes on Nature, 1984; Skeleton Coast, 1984; Tones & Textures, 1988; Notes on Nature II, 1988. *Membership:* Associate, South African Institute of Photographers. *Hobbies Include:* Photography; Writing; Art Conservation. *Address:* PO Box 20790, Windhoek 9000, SAW/Namibia.

SCHOEMAN Johanna Carolina Fransina, b. Windhoek, Namibia, South Africa. Businesswoman. m. Hendrik Petrus Schoeman, 17 Dec. 1943, 3 sons. *Education:* Diploma, Institute of Administration & Commerce. *Appointments:* Co-Founder, Managing Director: Schoemans Office Systems (Pty) Ltd., Fastkopi (Pty) Ltd., Henjo Properties (Pty) Ltd., 1960-; Director, South West Africa Building Society, 1978-; Director, Bank of SWA/Namibia, 1982-. *Memberships:* Executive Member, Past President, Windhoek Sakekamer; Administrator General's Economic Financial Advisory Committee; Member: Cabinet Committee for Finance and Economics; Founder, National President, SWA Federation of Business and Professional Women, 1962; Trustee: South Africa Foundation, 1968, University of South Africa, 1970; Patron, Private Sector Foundation; etc. *Honours:* Business Woman of the Year, SWA/Namibia, 1975; Nominee: Business Woman of the Year, 1981, 1982, Star Woman of the Year, 1984, Marketing Man of the Year, 1984; Awards of Merit: Rotary International Windhoek Club, 1985, Business and Professional Women, 1986. *Hobbies:* Finance & Economics. *Address:* 23 Berg Street, Windhoek, Namibia, South West Africa.

SCHOEN Barbara Carr, b. Minden, Louisiana, USA. CEO, Financial Consultant and Analyst. m. Irving Schoen, 2 Jan. 1960. 1 son. *Education:* BA, Fisk University; BS, Tennessee University; Psychology, Harvard University; MBA, University of Utah; Computer Sciences, Darwin College. *Appointments:* Administrative Director, City of New York; Certified Psychologist, Tennessee; Chief Executive Officer, Schoen Carr and Associates. *Publication:* Book: Local Differences in Interests, Hobbies and Avocations. *Memberships:* International Society of Business and Financial Consultants, 1968-; Phi Beta Kappa. *Honours:* Science Award, National Association, 1970; 25 year Service Award, City of New York, 1985; World Cup of Thoroughbred Racing and Handicapping, Summer 1988. *Hobbies:* Contract bridge; Tennis; Music. *Address:* 800 Grand Concourse, Bronx, NY 10451, USA.

SCHOEN Barbara T, b. 4 July 1924, New York City,

USA. College Professor. m. 9 Nov. 1946. 2 sons, 2 daughters. *Education:* BA cum laude, Bryn Mawr College, 1946; MA, Boston University, 1948. *Appointments:* Technician, Biophysics Lab, Harvard University, 1946-47; Faculty, State University College at Purchase, 1969-. *Publications:* Short stories to Seventeen Magazine, 1965-67; Novels: A Place and a Time, 1967; A Spark of Joy, 1969. *Memberships:* National Council of Teachers of English; The Authors Guild. *Hobbies:* Gardening; Snorkelling; Travel. *Address:* Humanities Division, SUNY College at Purchase, Purchase, NY 10577, USA.

SCHOENTAL Regina, b. 12 June 1906, Dzialoszyce, Poland. Researching the aetiology of cancer. *Education:* MChem 1929, PhD 1930, University of Cracow, Poland; DSc, University of Glasgow, Scotland, 1950. *Appointments:* Institute Forensic Medicine 1933-38, Laboratory of Cancer Research 1933-38, University of Cracow, Poland; School Pathology, University of Oxford, England, 1939-46; Dept Chemistry, University of Glasgow, Scotland, 1946-50; Labor. Cancer Research, 1950-54; MRC Toxicology Unit, Carshalton, 1954-71; Royal Veterinary College, London, 1971-. *Publications:* Numerous articles and papers in scientific journals and magazines. *Memberships:* Chemical Society, London; Biochemical Society, London; British Association Cancer Research; American Association Cancer Research; Royal Society Medicine, Oncology Section, Member of Council 1979-82. *Hobby:* Interpreting the Bible from a scientific point of view. *Address:* 15 Birdhurst Court, Woodcote Road, Wallington, Surrey SM6 0PG, England.

SCHOLFIELD Phoebe Jill Casson, b. 9 June 1958, Southend, England. Actress. *Education:* Special Honours, Drama Degree (11-1), Hull University, 1979. *Appointments:* Theatre Work includes: Lear, Threepenny Opera, And So To Bed, Bulbenkian Studio Theatre, 1976-79; Kes, Animal Farm, Snap Theatre Company, 1980-81; Conversations with a Golliwog, School for Clowns, Santa in Outer Space, Canterbury Tales, Omega Theatre Company, 1981-82; The Lesson, Exiles in Paradise, London Fringe Venues, 1983; Radio Work, The Lonely Sea, 1983; TV Work: Allo, Allo, (2 series) BBC, 1984, 1985; No Future for Robots, STC Documentary, 1984; Jenny's War, HTV, 1984. *Honours:* Scholarship, Strasbourg University to study French, German Literature, 1975. *Hobbies:* Squash; Swimming. *Address:* Colin, Stewart, Beret Associates, The Old Clubhouse, Cambridge Park, St Margarets, Twickenham, England.

SCHOLL Idamae, b. 2 Aug. 1933, St Paul, Minnesota, USA. Administrative officer, Norwest Corporation. m. Lloyd Leonard Scholl, 24 Apr. 1951. 3 sons. *Education:* BA, University of Missouri, Carthage, 1954; Postgraduate business management, Management Centre, 1970; Postgraduate management science, Mpls Tech Inst., 1971; Postgraduate telecommunications, Drake University, 1984. *Appointments:* Savs. supr. First National Bank, St Paul, 1963-69; Savs. supr, 1969-, Administrative Officer, 1982-, Norwest Corporation, St Paul; President, Board of Directors, Capitol Community Services, St Paul, 1983-; Board of Directors, National College Board, St Paul, 1982; Volunteer, Battered Women's Shelter, St Paul, 1983-86; Float Chairman, St Paul Winter Carnival Association, 1983, 1985; Solicitor St Paul United Way, 1985-86; ARC, 1983-86; American Cancer Soc., 1985-86. *Memberships:* International Women in Telecommunications (charter); 1st Vice President, 12987-88, President elect, 1988-89, National Fedceration of Business and Professional Women (Nat. task force, 1985-86, Minn. 2nd v.p. 1986-87, named Business Woman of Year, 1983; National Association Bank Women; American Institute of Banking; Minnesota Women's Consortium; Minnesota Economic Development Association; Female Executives, Minnesota; Minnesota Minority Purchasing Council. *Honours:* Recipient Theme Awards, St Paul Winter Carnival Association, 1983, 1986; YWCA Leadership award, Norwest Corp., 1984, 1986, 1987, 1988. *Hobbies:* Breeding and raising registered horses.

Address: 6301 Oak Knoll Plaza, Woodbury, MN 55125, USA.

SCHOLTE Suzanne, b. 13 June 1959, Norwalk, Connecticut, USA. Executive Director; President. m. Chadwick Rene Gore. 1 son. *Appointments:* Field Director, National Teenage Republicans; Projects Director, State Affiliates Liaison, American Conservative Union, 1981-82; Editor, Battleline, 1981-82; Projects Director, Citizens for Reagan, 1983-84; Political Director, Fund for a Conservative Majority, 1982-84; Chief of Staff, US Congressman Mac Sweeney, 1985-88; Executive Director, US Conservative PAC; President, CHG Associates, Inc. *Publications:* Editor: FCM Report; FCM Annual Report; Citizens for Reagan Newsletter. *Memberships:* Boardmember, Defense Forum Foundation; President, American Leadership Council; Administrative Assistants Association American Association of Political Consultants; Republican Party of Virginia; Precinct Chairman; National Director and State Chairman, Young Americans for Freedom; State Chairman, Youth for Reagan Committee; State Chairman, Virginia Teenage Republicans. *Honours:* Lecturer, Speaker, Campaign Management College, 1986; Lecturer, Speaker, National Republican Congressional Committee Campaign School, 1986; Outstanding Service Award, Young Conservative Movement, 1984; Outstanding Young Women of America, 1981, 1983, 1985, 1986, 1987; Best Black Captain Organization, Mason District, Fairfax County Republican Party, 1984; DAR Citizenship Award, Journalism Award, National Honor Society Award, Public Speaking Award, Balfour Key for leadership Award, English Award, 1977. *Hobbies:* Writing; Painting; Snow skiing. *Address:* 3014 Castle Road, Falls Church, VA 22044, USA.

SCHOR Lynda, b. 18 Apr. 1938, Brooklyn, New York, USA. Author; Professor. 2 sons, 1 daughter. *Education:* BFA, The Cooper Union, 1959. *Appointments:* Distinguished Writer-in-Residence, Western Washington University, 1980-81, Miami International University, 1983-84; Lang College, New School for Social Research, New York City, 1985-. *Publications:* Books: Appetites; True Love and Real Romance; Stories in Village Voice, Mademoiselle, Redbook, Playboy, Minnesota Review, anthologies. *Memberships:* PEN; The Authors League; Poets and Writers; The American Association of Art Therapists; Association of Poetry Therapists. *Honours:* Fellow, MacDowell Colony; Fellow, Blue Mountain Center; Fellow, Virginia Center for Creative Arts; Mellon Grant. *Hobbies:* Painting; Reading; Psychology; Films. *Address:* 463 West Street 610C, New York, NY 10014, USA.

SCHRAM-MCRAE Norma Cheryl, b. 4 May 1958, Houston, Texas, USA. Consultant. m. John R McRae, 5 Sept. 1988. *Education:* BSED, North Texas State University, 1980; MED, Texas Christian University. *Appointments:* Admissions Counsellor, Ols Co. Comm. Col. Dist., 1978- 80; Interim Youth Director, Assistant to Single Adult Minister, Park Cities Baptist Church, 1980-83; Admissions Counsellor, Acting Director, Director of Student Affairs, Dallas Baptist University, 1983; Training Specialist, Consultant, Norma Schram & Associates, Dallas, 1984-. *Memberships:* NAHRO; American Society of Training & Development; Association of Female Executives. *Hobbies:* Antiques; Racquetball. *Address:* 704 Versailles, Mesquite, TX 75149, USA.

SCHROEDER Mary Lou Williams, b. 6 Feb. 1937, Lackawanna County, Scranton, Pennsylvania. Community Education Specialist; Psychaitric Nurse. m. Stephen Gregory Schroeder, 20 May 1978. 1 son. *Education:* Nursing Diploma, Hospital of the University of Pennsylvania, 1958; BS, Syracuse University, 1963; MEd, Teacher's College, Columbia University, 1968. *Appointments:* Visiting Nurse Associate, Scranton, Pennsylvanian Public Health Nurse; Assistant Professor, University of Wisconsin; Continuing Education Lecturer, Milton College; Board for Alcohol and Drugs; Mental Health Services; Community Education Specialist, Rock County 51-42 Board. *Publication:* Meeting the Needs of the Alzheimer's Caregiver, 1984. *Memberships:* WI Prevention Network; Mental Health Association; Alliance for the Mentally Ill; American Mental Health Fund; Alzheimer's Disease and Related Disorders Association. *Honours:* Annual Award, Mental Health Association Board of Directors, 1982; Woman of Distinction Award in Education, Janesville YWCA, 1988; cum laude, Syracuse University, 1963. *Hobbies:* Biking; Knitting; Hiking; Gardening; Reading; Travelling; Attending concerts and theatre; Canoeing. *Address:* Rock County 51-42 Board, North Parker Drive, P O Box 351, Janesville, WI 53547, USA.

SCHUBERT Helen Celia, b. 30 May, Washington County, Wisconsin, USA. Public Relations Executive. *Education:* BS, University of Wisconsin-Madison. *Appointments:* Dir Cons Div, Philip Lesly Co, 1956-61; PR Dir, United Cerebal Palsy, 1961; Am Dir, National Design Center, 1962-67; Schubert Public Relations, 1967-. *Publication:* Contributing author to World Boook on Interior Design. *Memberships:* Art Institute of Chicago, Life Member; University of Wisconsin Alumni Association, Life Member; American Society of Interior Designers, Allied Member; Women's Ad Club of Chicago, Past President; Women in Communications Inc, Past President; Interior Furnishings & Design Association. *Honours:* Advertising Woman of the Year, 1987; Fellow, Interior Furnishings & Design Association, 1978; Communications Award, 1979, 1983, 1988, American Society of Interior Designers, IL Chapter; Headliner, Chicago, Women in Communications Inc, 1981; Dist Service, Publicity Club of Chicago, 1969. *Hobby:* Tennis. *Address:* 1360 Lake Shore Drive No 908, Chicago, IL 60610, USA.

SCHUERCH Margaret (Childs) Pratt, b. 9 Aug. 1923, New York City, New York, USA. Physician. m. Conrad Schuerch Jr, 26 June 1948, 3 sons, 1 daughter. *Education:* MD, University of Manitoba, Canada, 1945; LMCC, 1945; Diploma in Anaesthesia, McGill University, 1948; Diploma, American Board of Anesthesiology, 1959; Fellow, American College of Anesthetists, 1959; Interne, General Hospital and Children's Hospital, Winnipeg, 1944-45; Resident, 2 years, Fellow, McGill Diploma course in Anaesthesiology, 1 year, Associated Montreal Hospitals, 1946-49; Resident, Anaesthesiology, Crowse-Irving Hospital, Syracuse, New York, 1950, St Joseph's Hospital, Syracuse, 1956-57. *Appointments:* Captain, Canadian Army Medical Corps, 1946; Anaesthesiologist, 1957-59, Staff Member, Onondaga Community Hospital and 1959-, St Joseph's Hospital; Anaesthesiologist, Syracuse Veterans' Hospital, 1961-63; Anaesthesiologist, Benjamin Rush Center, 1961-81; Courtesy Staff Member, University Hospital, Syracuse, 1961-81; Courtesy Staff Member, Community General Hospital, Syracuse, 1963-85. *Memberships:* American Medical Association; Medical Society of State of New York; Onondaga County Medical Society; American Society of Anesthesiologists; New York State Society of Anesthesiologists; District V, New York State Society of Anesthesiologists. *Honours:* Several scholarships to and at University of Manitoba, 1939-44; Panhellenic Cup, University of Manitoba, 1941; NRC Fellowship in Anaesthesiology (USA), 1947. *Hobbies:* Reading; Sewing; Travel; Family activities. *Address:* 125 Concord Place, Syracuse, NY 13210, USA.

SCHULDT Karen, b. 14 Apr. 1957, Schnectady, New York, USA. President of Human Resource Consulting Firm. *Education:* BA, Dartmouth College, Hanover, New Hampshire, 1979. *Appointments:* Job Analyst, Dartmouth College, Hanover, 1979-80; Compensation Analyst, ITEK Corporation, 1981-82; President, Robert R Schuldt & Associates Ltd, 1983-. *Memberships:* American Compensation Association; American Management Association; American Society of Personnel Administrators; National Association of Women Business Owners. *Honour:* Member, White House Task Force on Small Business, 1985-86. *Hobbies:* Black and white photography, film development and printing; Travel; Weightlifting; Riding. *Address:* 1324 Skipwith Road, McLean, VA 22101, USA.

SCHULER Ruth May Wildes, b. 11 Feb. 1933, Salem, Massachusetts, USA. Writer; Editor. m. Charles Albert Schuler, 8 Sept. 1954, 1 son, 1 daughter. *Education:* BA 1957, MA 1971, San Francisco State University. *Publications include:* Author: Daughter from Other Side of Drawbridge, 1977; Born of Buffalo Bone, 1978; Portraits of a Poet Passing Through, 1978; February's Child, 1979; Dreaming in the Dawn, 1980; American in Age of Aquarius, 1980; Beware of Wolves, poetry, 1982; Beneath the Mushroom Cloud, 1984; Prophet's Return From Exile, poetry, 1984; Princess in Ivory Tower, 1985; Of Porcupines & Death, short stories, 1985; Shades of Salem, poetry & prose, 1987; Mistress of the Darkened Rooms, short stories, 1988. Editor: Dragon Fire, Dancing Dogs & Dangling Dreams, 1978; Calico Sphinx, 1977; Trends No. 8, Native American Poetry, 1983; Prophetic Voices, international literary magazine. *Honours:* Awards: Berkeley Poets; Ina Coolbrith Circle; Contra Costa County Fair; New York Poetry Forum. Biographical listings. *Hobbies:* Writing; Travel; Stamps; Books. *Address:* 94 Santa Maria Drive, Novato, California 94947, USA.

SCHULTZ Janice Lee, b. 23 July 1945, Cleveland, Ohio, USA. Professor. *Education:* BA, 1969; MA, 1972, PhD, 1978, Philosophy, State University of New York, Buffalo. *Appointments:* Instructor, Ryerson Polytechnical Institute, 1974-79; Assistant Professor, 1979-85, Associate Professor, 1985-89, Full Professor, 1989-, Philosophy, Canisius College. *Publications:* Articles in: The Thomist; Modern Schoolman; New Scholasticism; Polish Review. *Memberships:* American Catholic Philosophical Association; American Philosophical Association; Polish Institute of Arts & Sciences. *Honours:* Recipient, various honours and awards. *Hobbies:* Classical Music; Physical Culture. *Address:* Dept. of Philosophy, Canisius College, 2001 Main St., Buffalo, NY 14208, USA.

SCHULZE Hertha Joan, b. 10 Feb. 1935, Minneapolis, USA. Writer; Teacher. m. Howard Linsay Peterson, 1969, divorced 1972. *Education:* BA, 1956, PhD, 1967, University of Minnesota; MA, Harvard College, 1959; PhD, University of Toronto, 1982. *Appointments:* Junior Curator, Detroit Art Institute, 1957-58; Reference Assistant, Frick Art Library, 1959-60; Teacher, The Grammar School, Putney, 1960-61; Instructor, Michigan State University, 1963-66; Assistant Professor, 1967-69, University of Minnesota; Associate Professor, Rochester Institute of Technology, 1970-80; Associate Professor, Colorado College, 1980-81; Assistant Director, Department of Independent Study, University of Minnesota, 1986-. *Publications:* A Delicate Balance; Before and After; Solid Gold Prospect; Twice a Miracle; Edition: Ecclesia by Ravisius Textor. *Hobbies:* Printing; Weaving; Academic Specialities. *Address:* 2650 Irving Avenue N, Minneapolis, MN 55411, USA.

SCHUMACK Joan Maria, b. 4 Nov. 1953, Methoni, Greece. Poet; Journalist. *Education:* BA, Journalism, Marquette University, 1988. *Appointments:* Community Editor, Post Newspapers, West Allis, 1975-79; Freelance Journalist, 1979-81; Public Information Officer, Milwaukee Common Council, 1981-84; Founder, Editor, Publisher, Ethnos Magazine, 1985-88. *Memberships:* Phil-Hellenic Greek Professional Society; Hellenic Business Association; National Organization for Women; Women in Communication; Society of Professional Journalists; Wisconsin Regional Writers; etc. *Honours:* National Council of Teachers of English Award, 1972; Society of Professional Journalists Mark of Excellence Award, 1975; Election to Jesuit National Honour Society, 1975; Election to Kappa Tau Alpha, 1975, 1985. *Hobbies Include:* Piano; Foreign Languages; Kite Flying; Bicycling; Soap Carving. *Address:* Pencraters, PO Box 25805, Milwaukee, WI 53225, USA.

SCHUSTER-EAKIN Cynthia Anne, b. 15 Sep. 1952, Sharon, Pennsylvania, USA. Editor; Freelance Writer. m. Eric Judson Eakin, 26 May 1979, 1 son, 1 daughter. *Education:* BA, Journalism/News Editorial, Kent State University, Kent, Ohio, 1975. *Appointments:* Associate Editor, Modern Tire Dealer magazine, Akron, Ohio, 1977-80; Editor, Where magazine, Cleveland, Ohio, 1980-82; Contributing Editor, Ohio Restaurant News, Columbus, Ohio, 1982-; Associate Publisher, Athletic Administration magazine, 1982-88; Editor, This Week in Cleveland, 1982-. *Memberships:* Cleveland Press Club. *Hobbies:* Gourmet cooking; Gardening; Reading. *Address:* 440 Bradley Road, Bay Village, OH 44140, USA.

SCHUTTE Paula Marion, b. 29 Oct. 1941, St Paul, Minnesota, USA. Information Technologies Strategist; Planner; Consultant. *Education:* BA Chemistry, Rosary College, 1963; MBA, International Business, New York University, 1985. *Appointments:* Med. Research Chemist, Geigy Chemical Corporation, Ardsley, 1964-70; Group Leader, SCI Systems, 1970-77, Director, Med. Systems, 1977-80, Manager, Sci. Info. 1980-83, Director, Sci. Info. Systems, 1983-85, Director, End User Svcs, 1985-87, Director, Information Technologies, 1987-, Ciba-Geigy Corporation. *Creative Works:* Patentee in Medicinal Chemistry. *Memberships:* Prism Research Coordinator, 1985-; Pace University Information Technology Advisory Council; Chemical Process Industry Emerging Technology Subgroup. *Hobbies:* Ornithology; Geography; Golf; Boating; Ethology. *Address:* Ciba-Geigy Corporation, 444 Saw Mill River Road, Ardsley, NY 10502, USA.

SCHWARCZ Vera, Professor. *Education:* BA, Vassar College, 1969; MA, Yale University, East Asian Studies, 1971; PhD, Chinese History, Stanford University, 1977. *Appointments:* Instructor, History, Stanford University, 1973; Lecturer 1975-77, Assistant Professor 1975-83, Chair of East Asian Studies, 1985-88, Mansfield Freeman Professor of East Asian Studies 1988-, Professor of History 1988-, Wesleyan University; Visiting Scholar, Beijing University, China, 1983, 1986 and 1989; Visiting Scholar, Centre de Documentation sur la Chine Contemporaine, Paris, France, 1985. *Publications:* Historical Amnesia: The Life of Zhang Shenfu, in progress; Editor, Encounters Dictated By Fate; Zhongguo de qimeng yundong, 1989; The Chinese Enlightenment: The Legacy of the May Fourth Movement in Modern China, 1986; Long Road Home: A China Journal, 1984; China: Inside the People's Republic, 1972 (co-editor); Author of numerous articles to professional journals and magazines; papers presented to conferences; Reviews. *Memberships:* China Council, Association for Asian Studies, 1989-; President, New England Association for Asian Studies, 1988-89; American Historical Association; American Association of University Professors. *Honours:* Recipient of numerous honours and awards including Guggenheim Fellowship, 1989-90. *Address:* Center for East Asian Studies, Wesleyan University, 343 Washington Terrace, Middletown, CT 06457, USA.

SCHWARTZ Cheryl Ann, b. 4 Sept. 1949, Cincinnati, Ohio, USA. Producer; Writer; Actress; Women's Health Lecturer. *Education:* AsS Business Administration University of Cincinnati, 1967-72; Biology, West Los Angeles, 1977-79; Cell & Molecular Biology-Pre Med California State University, 1979-80; Media, Pierce College, 1981-83. *Appointments:* Owner, Casting Enterprises, 1972-76; Founder/Director, International Toxic-Shock Syndrome Network, 1980-; Director, Hawaii Express, 1982; President, Cheryl A Schwartz Productions, 1982-; Owner, C A Schwartz & Associates, 1982-. *Publications:* The Well Woman, Editor; In the Gutter Looking at Stars; Jaw Surgery: How to Have a Comfortable & Creative Recovery, Producer & Host, The Well Woman; Cheryl & Company, television shows. *Memberships include:* Inter-Agency Council on Child Abuse & Neglect; Screen Actors Guild; American Federation of Television & Radio Artists; American Society for Testing & Materials; American Film Institute; Writers Guild of America; Board of Directors, Womens Equal Rights Legal Defence & Education Fund;

Consultant, National Women's Health Network; National Association for Female Executives. *Honour:* Commendation, Mayor of Los Angeles, 1984. *Hobbies:* Polo; Private Pilot; Pistol shooting; Swimming; Backgammon; Horseback Riding; Films; Reading. *Address:* PO Box 1248, Beverly Hills, CA 90213, USA.

SCHWARTZ Eleanor, b. 1 Jan. 1937, Kite, Georgia, USA. Vice Chancellor, Academic Affairs. 1 son, 1 daughter. *Education:* BBA 1962, MBA 1963, DBA 1969, Georgia State University. *Appointments include:* Acting Chair, Associate Dean, Cleveland State University, Ohio; Dean, Henry W. Bloch School of Business & Public Administration, Interim Vice-Chancellor, Vice Chancellor for Academic Affairs (current), University of Missouri, Kansas City (UMKC). *Publications:* Books: Principles of Supervision (instruction manual); Contemporary Readings in Marketing; Sex Barrier in Business. Also: Chapter, Encyclopaedia of Professional Management; Numerous articles, economics & business journals. *Memberships:* Past Board, American Assembly of Collegiate Schools of Business; Past Governor, Beta Gamma Sigma; Alpha Iota Delta; American Institute for Decision Sciences; American Management Association. *Honours:* Faculty initiate, UMKC Circle, Omicron Delta Kappa, 1986; Phi Kappa Phi, 1986; Career recognition award, Zonta, 1984. *Hobbies:* Piano; Painting. *Address:* 221 Scofield Hall, University of Missouri, Kansas City, MO 64110, USA.

SCHWARTZ Lita Joan Linzer, b. 14 Jan. 1930, New York City, USA. Psychologist; College Professor. m. Melvin J Schwartz, 18 June 1950, divorced 1983, 3 sons. *Education:* AB, Vassar College, 1950; Ed.M, Temple University, 1956; PhD, Bryn Mawr College, 1964. *Appointments:* Psychologist, Psychological Service Centre, 1957-62; Lecturer, Temple University, 1959; Assistant Professor to Professor, Educational Psychology, Pennsylvania State University, 1962-. *Publications:* American Education: A Problem Centred Approach, 1969, 2nd edition 1974, 3rd edition 1978; Educational Psychology: Focus on the Learner, 1972, 2nd edition 1977; The Exceptional Child: A Primer, 1975, 2nd edition 1979; Resource Guide for Teaching Educational Psychology, with J K Davis, 1977; Life Span Development : A Reader, co-author, 1979; Exceptional Students in the Mainstream, 1984; The American School and the Melting Pot, with N Isser, 1985; The Dynamics of Divorce, with F W Kaslow, 1987; History of Conversion and Contemporary Cults, with N. Isser, 1988. *Honours:* Recipient, various honours and awards. *Hobbies:* Photography, Music. *Address:* Cedarbrook Hill Apts. C-PII-13, Wyncote, PA 19005, USA.

SCHWARTZ Sheila R., b. 15 Mar. 1936, New York City, New York, USA. Professor; Author; Lecturer. 1 son, 2 daughters (1 deceased). *Education:* BA, Adelphi University, 1956; MA, Teachers College, Columbia, 1958; EdD, New York University, 1964. *Appointments:* Hofstra University, 1958-60; Hunter College, 1962-63; State University College, New Paltz, New York, 1963-. *Publications:* Teaching the Humanities, 1973; Earth in Transit, 1977; Growing Up Guilty, 1978; Like Mother, Like Me, 1978; Teaching Adolescent Literature, 1979; Solid Gold Circle, 1980; Hollywood Writers' Wars, 1981; One Day You'll Go, 1982; Jealousy, 1983; The Most Popular Girl, 1988; Bigger is Better, 1988; Sorority, 1988. *Memberships:* President: New York State English Council; National Association for Humanities Education; New York State Conference of English Educators; President, Adolescent Literature Association; New Paltz UUP (union); SLATE (political arm), National Council of Teachers of English; International PEN; Authors Guild. *Honours:* New York State English Council Fellows Award, 1969; Fulbright Fellow, University College, Cork, Republic of Ireland, 1977; Excellence in Letters, Excellence in English Education, New York State, 1979; Annual Award for Contribution to the Field, 1980; Research Fellowship, State University of New York, 1983. *Hobbies:* Cross country skiing; Riding; Theatre; Fine food; Films; Reading; Piano. *Address:* State University College, New Paltz, NY 12561, USA.

SCHWARZENBACH Sibyl Ann, b. 12Dec. 1951, Stamford, USA. Assistant Professor. *Education:* BA, Philosophy, Cornell University, 1975; Fulbright Scholar, Heidelberg University, 1975-76; PhD, Harvard University, 1985. *Appointments:* Teaching Fellow, Harvard University, 1979-84; Assistant Professor, Baruch College, CUNY, 1985-; Visiting Assistant Profesor, Princeton University, Spring 1988. *Creative Works:* Towards a New Conception of Ownership, 1985; contributor to: Canadian Journal of Philosophy; Metaphilosophy; Social Theory & Practice; Ethics. *Memberships:* American Philosophical Association; New York University Law & Philosophy Colloquium; New York Society for Philosophy & Public Affairs. *Honours:* Phi Beta Kappa; Deutsch Akademische Austausch Dienst Scholarship, 1975; Fulbright Scholarship, 1975-76; PSC CUNY Summer Research Awards 1987, 1988; CUNY Scholar Incentive Award, 1989. *Address:* Baruch College, City University of New York, 17 Lexington Ave., New York, NY 10010, USA.

SCHWOERER Lois G., b. 4 June 1927, Roanoke, Virginia, USA. Professor of History. m. Frank Schwoerer, 25 June 1949, 1 son. *Education:* BA summa cum laude, Smith College, 1949; MA, 1952, PhD, 1956, Bryn Mawr College. *Appointments:* Social Studies Teacher, Shipley School, Bryn Mawr, Pennsylvania, 1949-51; Instructor, Bryn Mawr College, 1954-55; Lecturer, University of Pittsburgh, 1962-63; Associate Professorial Lecturer, 1964-65, Assistant Professor, 1965-68, Associate Professor, 1968-75, Professor, 1976-, Chairman, 1979-81, History Department, George Washington University, Washington DC. *Publications:* No Standing Armies! The Anti-Standing Army Ideology in Seventeenth-Century England, 1974; The Declaration of Rights, 1981; Lady Rachel Russell (1637-1723): One of the Best of Women, 1988; Articles, book-chapters, reviews. *Memberships:* American Historical Association (Robert Livingston Schulyer Prize Committee 1980-81); President, North American Conference on British Studies (other former offices); Phi Beta Kappa; Renaissance Society of America; Fellow, Center for History of Freedom, Washington University, St Louis; Steering Committee, Center for Study of British Political Thought, Folger Institute for Renaissance & 18th-Century Studies, 1982-, Steering Committee, Renaissance Colloquium, 1976, Award Committee, 1969-70, Chairman, Seminar in 17th-Century English History, 1968-69, Folger Shakespeare Library; American Associate Committee, Parliamentary History; Anglo-American Historical Committee, Institute of Historical Research, London University, 1984-86, 1989-91; Cosmos Club, Washington. *Honours include:* Best Book, Berkshire Conference of Women Historians, 1975; Walter D. Love Prize for Best Article in British Studies, 1985; Best Paper, Carolinas Symposium on British Studies, 1987; 2 honourable mentions for book, 1981, 1983; Senior Fellow: National Endowment for the Humanities, 1975; Research Conference Grant, National Endowment for The Humanities, 1989; Folger Shakespeare Library, 1978; Fellow, Royal Historical Society, 1980; George Washington Award for Outstanding Contribution to the University, 1988. *Address:* Department of History, George Washington University, Washington, DC 20052, USA.

SCIBERRAS Mary, b. 9 Mar. 1940, Mdina, Malta. Medical Practitioner. m. Raymond Sciberras, 2 Feb. 1964, 1 son, 1 daughter. *Education:* Graduate, Medicine & Surgery, Royal University, Malta, 1961. *Appointments:* House officer, St Luke's Hospital, 1961-64; Medical officer, Mount Carmel Psychiatric Hospital, 1966-76; General practitioner, 1964-; Medical officer, Detoxification Unit, St Luke's Hospital, 1987-. *Publications:* Id-Droga, book on drugs for parents & teachers, 1987; Various articles & leaflets, drugs, health, family life. *Memberships:* Co-founder, CARITAS, Core Group for Drug Prevention & Action; Interdepartmental Commission Against Drug Abuse; Prisoners Board of Visitors; Medical Council, Malta; Council of Women; Diocesan Pastoral Council; Diocesan Secretariat for Parishes. *Hobbies:* Horticulture; Flower arranging (member, Floral Club). *Address:* Galenica, P. P. Saydon Street, Zurricq, Malta.

SCIOSCIOLI Valeria Bianca Maria, b. 19 Dec. 1937, Rome, Italy. Economic Market Analyst. m. Csaba Horvath, 24 July 1963, divorced 1986, 2 daughters. *Education:* JD, University of Rome, 1960; MS, South Connecticut State University, 1970; MA, New York University, 1980. *Appointments:* Asssociate Director, Research, International Ladies Garment Workers Union, 1980; Project Analyst, 1980-, Chief Economist, 1981-86, Business Communications Co., Inc. *Publications:* The Economics of Aging, 1988; The Changing Dairy Industry, 1985; Protein Supply/Demand : Changing Styles, 1982. *Memberships:* National Association of Business Economists; Economic Forecasting Panel; International Association of Economic Forecast; New York Academy of Science; American Association for the Advancement of Science. *Honour:* Ford Svimez Award, 1960. *Hobbies:* Renaissance Music and Art; various Voluntary Work. *Address:* 94 Livingston Street No 35, New Haven, CT 06511, USA.

SCITOVSKY Anne A, b. 17 Apr. 1915, Ludwigshafen, West Germany. Health Economist. m. Tibor Scitovsky, 5 Sept. 1942, divorced, 1 daughter. *Education:* BA, Barnard College, 1937; MA, Economics, Columbia University, 1941. *Appointments:* Economist, 1944-46; Senior Research Associate, 1963-73, Chief, Health Economics, Research Institute, Palo Alto Medical Foundation, 1973-; Lecturer, Institute for Health Policy Studies, School of Medicine, University of California, San Francisco, 1975-. *Publications:* numerous articles. *Memberships:* American Public Health Association; American Economic Association; President's Commission on Medical Ethics, 1979-82. *Honours:* Institute of Medicine; National Academy of Sciences. *Hobbies:* Photography; Swimming. *Address:* Palo Alto Medical Foundation/Research Institute, 860 Bryant Street, Palo Alto, CA 95025, USA.

SCOGLAND Victoria L., b. 4 Jan. 1950, Geneseo, illinois, USA. Art Appraiser; Lecturer. m. 9 Oct. 1976, 1 son. *Education:* BA, Western Illinois University, 1976; MA, University of Wisconsin, Milwaukee, pending. *Appointments:* Principal, VS Valuations Ltd fine art appraisal firm, 1981-. *Memberships:* American Society of Appraisers; Art Institute Prints and Drawings Club; New Group, Museum of Contemporary Art; Terra Museum; Arts Club of Chicago. *Honours:* Board Member, Chicago Chapter, American Society of Appraisers. *Hobby:* Riding. *Address:* 222 Wisconsin Avenue, Suite 102, Lake Forest, IL 60045, USA.

SCOTT Bonnie Kime, b. 28 Dec. 1944, Philadelphia, Pennsylvnia, USA. Professor of English. m. Thomas R. Scott, 17 June 1967, 1 son, 2 daughters. *Education:* BA, Wellesley College, 1967; MA 1969, PhD 1973, University of North Carolina. *Appointments:* Assistant Professor 1975- 80, Associate Professor 1980-86, Profesor of English 1986-, Acting Coordinator of Women's Studies 1980-81, Acting Director, Centre for Teaching Effectiveness 1987-88, University of Delaware. *Publications:* Books: Joyce & Feminism, 1984; James Joyce, Feminist Readings, 1987. Editor, New Alliances in Joyce Studies, 1988; The Gender of Modernism, 1990. Numerous articles, Irish Literature, Women Writers. *Memberships:* Modern Language Association; American Conference for Irish Studies; Delaware Humanities Forum; James Joyce Foundation; Virginia Woolf Society. *Honours:* Delaware Outstanding Young Woman, 1970; Mortar Board Outstanding Faculty Award, 1984; Phi Beta Kappa, 1967. *Hobbies:* Ecology; Astronomy; Gardening; Birds; Travel; Race Gender & Politics. *Address:* Department of English, University of Delaware, Newark, DE 19716, USA.

SCOTT Eleanor Meyer, b. 10 Mar. 1933, Houston, Texas, USA. Teacher of the Gifted, Kindergarten-3rd Grade. m. Henry Lee Scott, 2 June 1956, 2 sons. *Education:* BS, University of Texas, Austin, 1956; MEd, University of Houston, Park, 1976; Certification in Gifted, University of St Thomas, Houston, 1989. *Appointments:* Elementary Teacher, Clear Creek Schools: League City Elementary, 1958-64, Stewart Elementary, 1964-66, White Elementary, 1969-72, Clear Lake City Elementary, 1976-85; Teacher of Gifted, Clear Creek Schools, 1985-. *Publications:* Book: Math Manipulatives for the Primary Child, 1986; Article: Gifted Education at the Preschool and Primary Level: Modifying the Strategies, 1989. *Memberships:* Delta Kappa Gamma Society International, Computer, Programme and Personal Growth and Services state committees, local Parliamentarian and President; Charter Member, Yearbook Chairman, Delta Gamma Alumni Group Bay Area; Yearbook Chair, Bay Area Panhellenic. *Honours:* Golden Egg Awards, 1972, 1973, 1974, Citation Award for Most Outstanding Member, 1975-76, Bay Area Panhellenic; Chapter Achievement Award for Most Outstanding Member, Delta Kappa Gamma Society International, 1988; Scholarships: Delta Kappa Gamma, State of Texas, 1986; Clear Creek Educators Association, 1987; Delta Kappa Gamma Chapter, 1989; President: Homeowners Association; Civic Club of Seabrook; Delta Kappa Gamma Chapter. *Hobbies:* Travel; Cooking; Decorating her home; Enjoying her family; Going to school. *Address:* 625 Bay Club Drive, Seabrook, TX 77586, USA.

SCOTT Judith Johnson, b. 30 Aug. 1945, Washington, USA. Corporate Vice President; General Counsel. m. Robert C. Scott, 2 Jan. 1988, 2 daughters. *Education:* BS, Virginia State University, 1966; PB, Swarthmore College, 1967; JD, Catholic University, 1975. *Appointments:* Alexandria Economic Opportunities Comm., 1969-71; Attorney General Office, 1975; Virginia Housing Development Authority, 1975-82; Office of the Governor, 1982-85; Systems Management, American Corp., 1985-. *Memberships:* American, Norfolk & Portsmouth, Old Dominion, Virginia State Bar Associations. *Honours:* Recipient, many honours & awards. *Hobbies:* Politics; Municipal Bond Financing; Real Estate Development. *Address:* 254 Monticello Avenue, Norfolk, VA 23510, USA.

SCOTT Margaretta, b. 13 Feb. 1912, London, England. Actress. m. John de Lacy Wooldridge, 14 Sept. 1948, deceased, 1 son, 1 daughter. *Education:* Royal Academy of Dramatic Art, London; & with Rosina Filippi. *Performances Include:* Numerous stage roles, 1926-; Films, 1934-; Television, radio and theatre parts include: Beatrice, Much Ado About Nothing, Oxford, 1931; Mary, The Traveller in the Dark, Aldwych, 1932; Alithea, The Country Wife, 1934; various Shakespearian Roles, Open Air Theatre, 1934, Old Vic 1936; Elsa Brandt, Alien Corn, 1939; Juliet, Viola, Portia, 1941, Lady Macbeth, Rosalind, 1942, Stratford on Avon Memorial Theatre; ENSA Tour, North Africa, Italy, 1944; Connie, Written for a Lady, 1948; Lady Macbeth, 1949; Way of the World, Saville, 1956; Queen, Hamlet, Bristol Old Vic, 1958; Mrs Rossiter, The Right Honourable Gentleman, Her Majesty's, 1965; Toured South Africa, 1971; Birmingham Repertory, 1972; Lady Bracknell, Importance of Being Earnest, Sheffield Crucible, 1974; Toured SE Asia, British Council, 1976; Toured England & Canada, 1977; Chichester Festival, 1978, etc; TV appearances include: The Duchess of Duke Street; What Every Woman Knows; All Creatures Great & Small, etc. *Memberships:* Council/Committees of: King George's Pension Fund for Actors & Actresses; Actors Charitable Trust; Theatrical Ladies Guild; Stars Organisation for Spastics; London Academy of Music & Dramatic Art. *Hobbies:* Family. *Address:* 30 Molyneux Street, London W1, England.

SCOTT Marian Dale, b. 26 June 1906,, Montreal, Quebec, Canada. Painter. m. F R Scott, 28 Feb. 1928. 1 son. *Education:* Studied at: Montreal Arts Association; Monument National; Ecole des Beaux Arts Montreal and Slade School of Art, England. *Appointments:* Art Teacher, St George's School, Montreal, 1938-39; Art Teacher, Montreal Museum of Fine Arts. *Creative Works:* Numerous Exhibitions including: McGill University, Faculty of Art Education, 1977; Montreal Museum of Fine Arts, 1949 and 1960; London Regional Art Gallery, 1983; Edmonton Art Gallery, 1984; Cultural Centre, Paris, France, 1985; Salon International des Galeries d'Art Palais du Concres de Montreal, 1986; Art Gallery of Hamilton, Ontario, 1987, etc. Represented in Numerous Galleries. *Memberships:* Contemporary Art Society; Canadian Group of Painters; Royal Canadian Academy of Arts; Conseil des Artistes Paintres du Quebec. *Honours:* Canadian Group of Painters Exhibition (prize), 1966; Purchase Award, Thomas More Institute, Montreal, 1967; Centennial Medal, 1967; Baxter Purchase Award, The Ontario Society of Artists, 1969. *Hobby:* The Peace Movement. *Address:* 451 Clarke Avenue, Montreal, Quebec, Canada, K3Y 3L5.

SCOTT Martha Fitts, b. 11 Nov. 1916, Washington, District of Columbia, USA. Artist; Teacher. m. 10 Aug. 1940, 2 sons, 1 daughter. *Education:* Johns Hopkins Teachers College, 1935; Diploma, Maryland Institute College of Art, Baltimore, 1936; Cane School of Art, New York, 1937; Cleveland Institute of Art, 1960-64. *Appointments:* Designer, Norcross, New York, 1937-43; Book Illustrator, Wilcox & Follett, 1940s; Freelance Advertising Designer, 1945; Public Relations, Teaching, Arts Director, Village of Cross Keys, Baltimore, Maryland, 1965-88; Teacher of Sculpture, Jemicy School for Dyslexic Children, Baltimore, 1988. *Creative works include:* Pat'N Penny (children's book), 1944; 50 original etchings exhibited nationally and internationally, 1963-78; 35 to 40 small alabaster sculptures exhibited in Maryland, 1970s-88. *Memberships:* Board of Trustees, Cleveland Institute of Art, Ohio, 1950's; Buyer, Cleveland Art Association, 1950's; Baltimore Museum of Art (Maryland Artists Committee 1967). *Honours:* Full Scholarship, Maryland Institute College of Art, 1933; 1st Prize Award on graduation, 1936; Purchase Prize for etching, Jewish Community Center, Cleveland, Ohio, 1962; Purchase Prize for etching, Cooperstown Art Association, Cooperstown, New York, 1968; Honourable Mentions for etchings, Loyola College, Baltimore and International Platform Association, Washington DC. *Hobbies:* Astronomy; Gardening; All arts and crafts. *Address:* 6013 Hunt Ridge Road, Baltimore, MD 21210, USA.

SCOTT Mildred Hope, b. 5 July 1926, Miami, Florida, USA. Nurse. m. Thomas W Scott, 19 Dec. 1958. 1 son, 1 daughter. *Education:* Bachelor of Bible Theology, International Bible Institute and Seminary, 1982. *Appointments:* Licensed Practical Nurse various hopsitals and nursing homes in Florida and Missouri, 1968-86; School Nurse, Orlando, 1974-78; Private Duty Nurse, Florida and Missouri, 1974-88; Allergy Nurse, Aggarwal Allergy Clinic, Raytown, Missouri, 1987-88. *Publications:* Poems: My Ministry; Love Is; A Better Way; Little Janelle; Lover's Thoughts; Let God; Earnest Christian; The Robin. Songs: Lover's Plea; TV Preachers; I Hate Later; The Man; I Have to Be Me. *Memberships:* DeSoto Church of the Nazarene; Disciples Fellowship International; Association of International Gospel Assemblies. *Honours:* Medal, Greater Miami Women's Club for the poem, The Robin, 1941; Damenstein Medal, Andrew Jackson Junior High School, Miami, 1941; Valedictorian, Eastern Nazarene Academy, 1954; Honorary Staff Writer, Majestic Records, Countrywine Publishing, 1988. *Hobbies:* Writing poems and songs under the pen name of Hope Scott; Listening to gospel music. *Address:* 111A Sunny Drive, Belton, Missouri 64012, USA.

SCOTT Patricia Alice, b. 5 Sept. 1930, Denver, Colorado, USA. Individual, Marital & Family Therapist; Workshop Facilitator. m. James N Franz, 5 Aug. 1955, divorced. 2 sons. *Education:* BA, The Colorado College, 1952; MA, Stanford University, 1954; PhD, Columbia University, 1986. *Appointments:* Counsellor, Therapist, Jefferson County Schools R-1, 1965-86; Private Practice, 1982-89; Mind-Body Self-Help Workshops for Chronically Ill, 1988-89. *Publications:* Articles: The Isle of Man; Family Therapy and Loss; Separation and Loss. *Memberships:* Amer Assoc for Marriage & Family Therapy (Clinical Member); Colorado Assoc for Marriage & Family Therapy; Institute for Child abuse and Neglect (I-CAN); American Assoc for Counselling & Development; American Orthopsychiatric Association. *Honours:* Phi Beta Kappa, 1952; Mensa International 1984. *Hobbies:* Travel; Reading; Classical music; Opera; Knitting; Remodelling houses; Interior decorating;

People. *Address:* 333 Fairfax Street, Denver, Colorado 80220, USA.

SCOTT Suzanne Marie, b. 23 Jan. 1961, Burlingame, USA. Interior Designer. m. Randall Abell Scott, 26 July 1986. *Education:* AA, 1981; National Council for Interior Design Qualification, 1985. *Appointments:* Assistant Designer, Space Planning & Interior Design, 1981-83; Interior Designer, Business Invirons Inc., 1983-85; Senior Designer, Office Furniture Inc., 1985; Senior Designer, Williams Contract Furniture, 1985-88; Architectural & Design Representative, Williams Contract Furniture, 1988-. *Publications:* Contributor to various journals & magazines. *Memberships:* Institute of Business Designers, Board of Directors. *Hobbies:* Travel; Art Collecting; Golf. *Address:* Williams Contract Furniture, 201 West Broad Street, Richmond, VA 23220, USA.

SCRANTON Mary Isabelle, b. 28 Feb. 1950, Atlanta, Georgia, USA. Associate Professor; Oceanographer. m. Roger D. Flood, 3 Jan. 1981, 1 son. *Education:* BA, Mount Holyoke College, 1972; PhD, Woods Hole Oceanographic Institution MIT, 1977. *Appointments:* National Research Council Resident Research Associate, Naval Research Laboratory, 1977-79; Marine Sciences Research Centre, State University of New York, Stony Brook, 1979-. *Publications:* 22 scientific publications. *Memberships:* American Geophysical Union; American Society of Limnology and Oceanography, Editorial Board; AAAS. *Honours:* Phi Beta Kappa, 1971; Sigma Xi, 1972; NAS/NRC Postdoctoral Associate, 1977-79; Naval Research Laboratory Publication Award, 1981. *Hobbies:* Gardening; Sewing; Boating. *Address:* Marine Sciences Research Center, State University of New York, Stony Brook, NY 11794, USA.

SCUTT Jocelynne Annette, b. 8 June 1947, Perth, Western Australia. Barrister-at-Law; Author. *Education:* LLB, University of Western Australia, 1969; LLM 1972, Diploma of Jurisprudence 1973, University of Sydney; Diploma of Legal Studies, University of Cambridge, England, 1976; LLM 1974, SJD 1979, University of Michigan, USA; MA, University of New South Wales, 1985; Admitted Barrister and Solicitor, High Court of Australia, 1980, Supreme Court of Victoria, 1981, Barrister-at-Law, Supreme Court of New South Wales, 1981; Barrister, Solicitor, Supreme Court, ACT 1981. *Appointments:* Senior Research Assistant, Faculty of Law, University of Sydney, 1969-73; Research Scholar, University of Michigan, 1973-74; Girton College, University of Cambridge 1974-76. Max-Planck-Institut for Foreign & International Criminal Law, Freibug/ Breisgau, Federal Republic of Germany, 1975-76; Senior Law Reform Officer, Australian Law Reform Commission, 1976-77; Research Criminologist, Australian Institute of Criminology, Canberra, 1978-81; Barrister-at-Law, Sydney Bar, 1981-82; Associate to the Hon Justice Murphy, High Court of Australia, 1982-83; Director of Research, Legal & Constitutional Committee, 1983-84; Deputy Chairperson, Law Reform Commission, Victoria, 1984-86; Deputy Chairman, Advisory Council to the Australian Archives; Legal Member/Chairperson, Social Security Appeals Tribunal, 1984-87; Various teaching, lecturing & administrative posts. *Publications:* Author of various Victoria Government Reports; Substantial contributor to reports of the Australian Law Reform Commission; 18 monographs and papers; More than 150 articles, reviews and magazine contributions. *bb3Memberships:* Industrial Relations Society; Feminist Legal Action Group; Institute of Public Administration; Director, later Deputy Chairperson, Australian Institute of Political Science, 1979-84; Australian & New Zealand Society of Criminology; University of Sydney Law Graduates Association; New South Wales Bar Association; NSW Womens Lawyers Organisation; Victoria Women Lawyers Association; Australian Archives Society; Womens Electoral Lobby; Committee Member, Premier's Literary Awards, 1987; The Age Book of the Year Award, 1988; Judy Chicago-Dinner Party Committee. *Honours:* Numerous awards, grants &

Fellowships in Australia, USA, England, Germany. *Hobbies:* Reading; Writing; Feminism; Politics. *Address:* Owen Dixon Chambers West, 205 William Street, Melbourne, Victoria 3000, Australia.

SEARS Ruth Ann, b. 15 June 1954, Kansas City, Missouri, USA. Attorney. m. Irwin Curtis Sears Jr, 6 Aug. 1977, 1 son. *Education:* BA, English, Business, Central Methodist College, 1976; JD, University of Missouri, Columbia, 1979. *Appointments:* Law Clerk, Hon Robert Donnelly, Supreme Court of Missouri, 1979-80; Attorney, Southwestern Bell Telephone Co, Topeka, Kansas, 1980-88. *Publications:* Grand Jury May Not Report on Misconduct of Public Official Without Indictment, 1978. *Memberships:* Topeka Bar Association; Kansas Bar Association; Missouri Bar Association; Topeka Women's Association (Vice-President 1987); Vice- President, Board of Directors, Cerebral Palsy of Topeka, 1987. *Honours:* Scholarship, Clinton County Democratic Association, 1970-71; Valedictorian, Lathrop High School, 1972; Valedictorian, Central Methodist College Class, 1976; Outstanding Senior, Central Methodist College, 1976; Note and Comment Editor, Missouri Law Review, 1978-79; Omicron Delta Kappa; American Jurisprudence Award; Dean's List, all semesters. *Hobbies:* Reading; Cycling; Sewing; Crafts. *Address:* 2303 Wayne, Topeka, KS 66611, USA.

SEBASTIAN Fay Dolores, b. 27 Oct. 1941, Detroit, Michigan, USA. Child Welfare Worker. 2 sons, 1 daughter. *Education:* Numerous courses, business, English, writing, self-esteem, parent training. *Appointments include:* Various jobs, 1959-64; Assistant, local Presidential campaign, human rights movements, 1964-74; Volunteer coordinator, Portland Oregon branch, Parents Anonymous, self-help, parents who abuse children physically or emotionally, 1974-76; Volunteer, crisis line & counselling, Women's Emergency House, Vancouver, Washington, 1976-78; State Coordinator, Washington State Parents Anonymous, 1977-82; Facilitator, Parents Anonymous groups, & co- planner, numerous conferences on child abuse, foster care, 1978-79; Trainer, consultant, child abuse problems, & Director, Crossroads Motivational Service, 1980-. Greatest achievement: Once an abusing parent herself, now able to counsel others. *Creative works:* Currently writing books, numerology & tarot cards, & combination of humour & anger. *Memberships include:* Greenfair; Past Vice President, Washington State Foster Care Association; Tacoma Runaway Advocate, Clark & Pierce Counties; Boards, Council for Prevention of Child Abuse & Neglect; Homeowners Association; Numerous other community welfare associations. *Honour:* Woman of Year, Tacoma, 1981. *Hobbies:* Tarot; Numerology; Psychic development. *Address:* 265 Fairgrounds Drive, Sacramento, California 95817, USA.

SECCOMBE Joan Anna Dalziel, Dame, b. 3 May 1930, Birmingham, England. Vice Chairman, Conservative Party. m. Henry Lawrence Seccombe, 15 July 1950. 2 sons. *Education:* St Martins, Solihull, 1942-48. *Memberships:* Governor, Muffield Hospitals; Governor, St Martins, Solihull; Chairman, Conservative Womens National Comm, 1981-84; Ch, National Union, 1987-88; Magistrate, 1968-; Chair Bench, 1981-84; Heart of England Tourist Bd, 1977-81 (Chm Marketing Sub-Cottee, 1979-81); Chairman, W Midlands Area Cons Womens Cttee, 1975-78; Cons Party Social Affairs Forum, 1985-; Dep Chm, W Midlands Area Cons Council, 1979-81; W Midlands CC, 1979-81 (Chm Trading Standards Cttee, 1979-81). *Honour:* Dame of the British Empire, 1984. *Hobbies:* Golf; Skiing; Embroidery. *Address:* Tythe Barn, Walsal End Lane, Hampton in Arden, Solihull, West Midlands B92 0HX, England.

SEDACCA Rosalind P., b. 7 Mar. 1947, New York City, USA. Advertising & Public Relations Writer & Consultant. m. Michael Sedacca, 4 July 1966, 1 son. *Education:* BFA, Pratt Institute, 1967; Continuing professional studies, New York University.

Appointments: Creative Director, circulation promotion, Conde Nast Publications, NY, 1967-70; Freelance writer, advertising agencies, Nashville, St Louis, 1970-80; Copy Director, MBI Advertising, Florida, 1980-84; Rosalind Sedacca & Associates, advertising & marketing services, 1984-. Speaking engagements include: Annual State Conference, Florida Freelance Writers Association, 1987; Advertising & Marketing seminars, Palm Beach Junior College, 1987-88; Marketing seminars, Small Business Development Centre, 1987-88. *Memberships:* Florida Freelance Writers Association; Florida Public Relations Association; American Marketing Association; Women in Communication. *Honours:* 4 Addy Awards, Advertising Federtion of Florida, 1982-; 7 advertising awards, Post & Evening Times, 1983; Judge, Direct Mail Advertising Association Annual Awards Competition, 1986; Guest speaker, various professional bodies. *Hobbies include:* Health; Nutrition; Ecology; Animals; Swimming; Outdoor sports; Writer, feature articles in publications, broad range of topics especially women's interests. *Address:* 4594 Centurian Circle, Lake Worth, Florida 33463, USA.

SEDEI-GODLEY Cheryl Ann, b. 25 Sept. 1959, Warren, Ohio, USA. Registered Music Therapist, Board Certified, Private Practice. m. Gary MacGodley, 30 Aug. 1986. *Education:* BA, Music Therapy, 1981; Certification, Elementary Education, 1983; MM, Music Therapy, 1986; Certification (Board Certified) Music Therapy, 1988. *Appointments:* Music Therapist, 1979-80; Music Specialist 1980, Preschool Teacher 1982, Widefield School District; Biofeedback and Music Therapist, Omega Pain Clinic, 1983-84; Graduate Teaching Assistant, Music Therapy, University of Miami, Coral Gables, 1984-86; Music Therapist, Private Practice, Biofeedback & Music Therapy Services, Sheridan, 1987-; Editorial Staff, Music Therapy Perspectives 1987-, Examination Committee, Certification Board for Music Therapist 1988-, National association for Music Therapy. *Publications:* Author of articles to professional journals and papers to conferences. *Memberships:* National Federation of the Blind; Phi Kappa Phi; Delta Omicron; National Association for Music Therapy; American Association for the Advancement of Science; National Federation of Business and Professional Women's Clubs; American Federation for the Blind. *Honours:* Colorado State University, Delta Omicron, Outstanding Academic Achievement Award, 1981; Certificate of Merit for Outstanding Scholastic Achievement and Award, Recordings for the Blind, Inc, 1981; Floyd Qualls Memorial scholarship for Outstanding Blind Graduate Student in the Nation, American Council for the Blind, 1985; Certificate for BPW Young Career Woman of the Year, Sheridan Chapter, Business and Professional Women's Clubs, 1987. *Hobbies:* Swimming; Walking; Playing piano; Music; Knitting; Crocheting; Literature; Raising calves. *Address:* 826 US Highway 14, Sheridan, Wyoming 82801, USA.

SEDGWICK Rhonda Coy, b. 20 Oct. 1945, Missoula, Montana, USA. Freelance Writer/Photographer; Musician; Horsewoman; Cowboy Poet; Rodeo Historian; Christian Evangelist. *Education:* High School. *Career:* Self- employed Rancher, until 1979; Horsewoman and Equitation Instructor; Organist at Pro Rodeos in 15 states, 1966-; Freelance Writer, 1977-. *Publications:* Some 300 articles in The Western Horseman, Horse and Horseman, Hoof and Horn, The World of Rodeo, Pro Rodeo Sports News, Quarter Horse Journal, Paint Horse Journal, Appaloosa News; Sky Trails, book, 1988, 2nd Printing 1989. *Memberships:* Western Writers of America; National Writers Club; Prorodeo Historical Society; Cowboy Chapter, Fellowship of Christian Athletes; United Methodist Church; PEO Sisterhood. *Honours:* National High School Rodeo Queen, 1960; National High School Rodeo Pole Bending Champion, 1961, 1962; Miss Rodeo Wyoming and Horsemanship Winner, Miss Rodeo America Contest, 1963; Wyoming Barrel Racing Champion, 1964, 1965; Inducted into National Cowgirl Hall of Fame, 1977; Named Outstanding Young Woman of Wyoming, Outstanding Young Women of America Foundation; Outstanding Young Religious Leader, 1981; Best Published Work,

Wyoming Writers, 1981; Historical Award, Wyoming Historical Society, 1983; Friends of 4-H; FFA Honorary Chapter Farmer. *Hobbies:* Big game hunting and fishing; Training dogs; Cooking and cake decorating; Travel; History of the American West; Horses (all breeds); Christian evangelism especially to ranchers and cowboys of Western America; Children; Senior citizens. *Address:* 1159 State Highway 450, Newcastle, WY 82701, USA.

SEDLAK Valerie Frances, b. 11 Mar. 1934, Baltimore, Maryland, USA. University Professor. *Education:* AB English, College of Notre Dame of Maryland, 1955; MA English, University of Hawaii, 1962; ABD English, University of Pennsylvania, 1982. *Appointments:* Graduate Teaching Fellow, University of Hawaii, East-West Cultural Center, 1959-60; Administrative Assistant, Korean Consul General, Honolulu, 1959-60; Teacher, Boyertown Senior High School, Pennsylvania, 1961-63; Assistant Professor of English, University of Baltimore, 1963-69; Assistant Professor of English, Morgan State University, Baltimore, 1970-. *Publications:* Poetry: Christmas Away; February Ocean; Black Crow Time; Moving Green, 1981; January Waterford; Heritage, 1982; Archibald MacLeish: The End of May; Twilight in Overture; Tonight the Frost; At Mid-Point; The Time Between, 1985; Amaryllis; September Passage; Journey for Lisa, 1986; Waiting, 1986; And Holding, 1987; A SW-Step Program in Writing, Literature and the Humanities: A Two-way Contract, 1988; And Gladly Would They Run, 1988; Articles: Alice Meynell's A Thrush Before Dawn: A Response to Sound, 1984. *Memberships:* MLA; CEA; College Language Association; Literary Society; Maryland Council for English Education; Middle Atlantic Writers Association, Founding Member, 1982-; College English Association/Middle-Atlantic Group, Vice-President 1986-; Womens Council for the Modern Languages; The University Club at Auburn; The Maryland Poetry and Literary Society; South Atlantic Modern Language Association; American Association of University Women. *Honours:* Outstanding Teaching Professor, College of Liberal Arts, University of Baltimore, 1965-66; Morgan-Penn Faculty Fellow in English, 1977-79; Secretary to the Faculty, 1981-83; Faculty Research Scholar, Morgan State University, 1983; National Endowment for the Humanities Fellow, 1984; Outstanding Teaching Professor in English, Morgan State University, 1986-87; Delta Epsilon Sigma, National Scholastic Honor Society, 1988. *Hobbies:* Golf; Performing Arts. *Address:* 102 Gorsuch Road, Lutherville-Timonium, MD 21093, USA.

SEEAR Beatrice Nancy (Baroness), b. 7 Aug 1913, Epsom, England. Leader, Liberal Peers, House of Lords; Freelnce Lecturer & Writer. *Education:* BA, Cambridge Historical Tripos, Newnham College, 1935; Social Sciences Certificate, LSE, 1936. *Appointments:* Personnel Manager, C & J Clark Ltd., Street Somerset, 1936-46; Lecturer, reader, Personnel Management, LSE. *Publications:* Married Women Working (co- author), 1962; A Career for Women in Industry (co-author), 1964; The Re-entry oWomen into Employment, report for OBCD, 1971. *Memberships:* Honorary Visiting Professor, Personnel Management, City University, London; Chairman, Apex Trust; Chairman, Charta Mede Limited; President, Council, Tavistock Institute for Human Relations; Chairman, National Council for Carers and Their Elderly Dependants; Chairman, Manpower Services Commission, Area Manpower Board for Buckinghamshire. *Honours:* Libeal Life Peer, 1971; Honorary Doctorate, Leeds, 1979; Honorary Doctorte, Bath, 1982; Leader, Liberal Peers, House of Lords, 1984; Privy Counsel, 1985. *Address:* The Garden Flat, 44 Blomfield Road, London W9 2PF, England.

SEED Cecile Eugenie, b. 18 May 1930, Cape Town, South Africa. Writer. m. Edward Robert Seed, 31 Oct. 1953, 3 sons, 1 daughter. *Publications:* 50 books for children, many of which are historical novels. *Honours:* MER Literary Award, 1987. *Hobbies:* Tennis; Reading. *Address:* 10 Pioneer Crescent, Northdene, Natal 4093, South Africa.

SEELIG Sharon Cadman, b. 1 Aug. 1941, Mountain Lake, Minnesota, USA. Associate Professor of English. m. 30 Dec. 1967. 1 son, 1 daughter. *Education:* BA, Carleton College, 1962; MA 1964, PhD 1969, Columbia University. *Appointments:* Instructor in English, Wellesley College, 1967-69; Northfield School, 1969-70; Lecturer then Assoc Prof of English, Mount Holyoke College, 1970-80; Lecturer then Assoc Professor of English, Smith College, 1980-. *Publications:* The Shadow of Eternity: Belief and Structure in Herbert Vaughan & Traherne, 1981; Published articles on Milton, Traherne, Browne. *Memberships:* Modern Language Association; American Association of University Professors; Milton Society; John Donne Society. *Honours:* BA, summa cum laude, 1962; Phi Beta Kappa, Woodrow Wilson Fellow, 1962-634; Fulbright Fellow, 1963-64; President's Fellow and Lizette Fisher Fellow, Columbia University, 1964-66; Newberry Library Junior Fellow, 1966-67. *Hobbies:* Photography; Hiking; Camping. *Address:* Amherst, Massachusetts, USA.

SEEWALD Elsbeth M., b. 24 Aug. 1927, Hamburg, West Germany. Manager, Real Estate Division, Legal Firm. m. George Seewald, 4 Feb. 1978, 1 stepson. *Education:* High school & commercial college, Germany; Additional studies including continued legal education, Wisconsin, USA. *Appointments:* Modine Manufacturing Company, Racine, Wisconsin, USA, 1957-60; Brach & Wheeler, Attorneys, Racine, 1960-63; Heide, Hartley, Thom, Wilk & Guttormsen, Attorneys, Kenosha, 1963-. *Publications:* Editor, occasional contributor, Der Deutsch-Amerikaner, official newspaper, German-American National Congress. *Membership:* National President, German- American National Congress, Chicago. *Honours:* 'Honoured American' awarded by 'American by Choice' 1986; Ellis Island Medal of Honour, US Congress, 1986; Recipient, Officers Cross of the Order of Merit, Federal Republic of Germany, 1988. *Address:* 9804 8th Avenue, Kenosha, Wisconsin 53140, USA.

SEGAL Harriet N, b. 8 Oct. 1944, Atlantic City, USA. Businesswoman; Author; Lecturer; Judge. m. 26 June 1966, 1 son, 1 daughter. *Education:* BA, Douglass College, 1966; Elsa williams School of Needle Art, 1979. *Appointments;* Lecturer, Designer, Teacher, 1974-; Embroidery Shop Owner, 1975-; Needlework Author, 1976-; Needlework Judge, 1981-; Owner, Embroidery Mail Order Business, 1987-. *Publications:* Contributor to: Needle Arts Magazine; Needlepoint News Magazine; Jewish Yellow Pages; Needlejoy: A Guide to Teaching Embroidery to Children,, 1981; Teach Me, National Slido Programme & Booklet on how to teach children, 1987. *Memberships:* Embroiderer's Guild of America; National Education Committee; National Embroidery Teacher's Association, East Coast Representative, 1985-; Founder, Shalom Wagon. *Honours Include:* Master Craftsman Award, Canvas Embroidery, Embroiderer's Guild of America, 1980; Recipient, many 1st prizes. *Hobbies:* Needlework; Designing; Reading. *Address:* 1042 Victory Drive, Yardley, PA 19067, USA.

SEGAL Lore, b. 8 Mar. 1928, Vienna, Austria. Writer; Teacher. m. David I. Segal, 3 Nov. 1960, dec., 1 son, 1 daughter. *Education:* BA, English, Bedford College, University of London, England, 1948. *Appointments:* Professor, Writing Division, School of Arts, Columbia University, New York City, USA, also Princeton University, Sarah Lawrence College, Bennington College; Professor of English, University of Illinois, Chicago. *Publications:* Other People's Houses, 1964; Novels: Lucinella, 1976; Her First American, 1985; Children's books: Tell Me A Mitzi, 1970; All the Way Home, 1973; Tell Me a Trudy, 1977; The Story of Mrs Brubeck and How She Looked for Trouble and Where She Found Him, 1981; The Story of Mrs Lovewright and Purrless Her Cat, 1985; Translator (with W D Snodgrass): Gallows Songs, 1968; The Juniper Tree and Other Tales from Grimm, 1973; The Book of Adam to Moses; Short stories and articles in New York Times Book Review, Partisan Review, New Republic, The New Yorker. *Honours:* Guggenheim Fellow, 1965-66; Council of Arts and Humanities Grantee, 1968-69; Artists Public Service Grantee, 1970-71; CAPS Grantee, 1975; National Endowment for the Arts Grantee, 1982, 1987; NEH Grantee, 1983; Academy of Arts and Letters Award, 1986. *Address:* 280 Riverside Drive, New York NY 10025, USA.

SEGAL Svetlana Gersh, b. 8 July 1941, Kiev, USSR. Medical Doctor. 1 son. *Education:* MD, Kiev Medical Institute, USSR, 1964; PhD, Institute for Advanced Medical Training, 1970. *Appointments:* Associate Professor, Kiev Cardiology Centre, USSR, 1971-79; Private practice, Cardiology, Los Angeles, USA, 1982- . *Publications:* 29 publications in Cardiology and Internal Medicine. *Memberships:* California Medical Association; Los Angeles County Medical Association; American-Russian Medical and Dental Association, Past President 1986-87. *Hobbies:* Travelling; Art; Music. *Address:* 6221 Wilshire Blvd No 607, Los Angeles, CA 90048, USA.

SEGER Linda Sue, b. 27 Aug. 1945, Marinette, Wisconsin, USA. Script Consultant. *Education:* BA, Colorado College, Colorado Springs, 1967; MA, Northwestern University, Illinois, 1968; MA, Pacific School of Religion, Berkeley, California, 1973; ThD, Religion & Arts, Graduate Theological Union, Berkeley, 1976. *Appointments:* Assistant Professor, McPherson College (Kansas), LaVerne University (California), 1977-79; Administrator, Provisional Theatre, 1979-80; Freelance story analyst & researcher, 1981-83; Script consultant, 1983-. *Publication:* Making the Good Script Great, 1987. *Memberships:* Luminas Awards Committee Chair, creator & moderator, producer's workshop, Women in Film; Independent Feature Project-West; Academy of Television Arts & Sciences. *Hobbies:* Playing piano; Singing; Travel; Tennis; Horseback riding. *Address:* 3920 Huron Avenue no. 4, Culver City, California 90230, USA.

SEGGIE Jo Ann, b. 26 Dec. 1944, Toronto, Ontario, Canada. Scientist; Professor. m. Alexander Caryl Seggie, 9 July 1966. 3 sons, 3 daughters. *Education:* BSc, 1965; MA, 1967; PhD, 1970. *Appointments:* Clarke Institute of Psychiatry, 1969-77; Faculty of Health Sciences, McMaster University, 1977-. *Publications:* Melatonin, the Retinal-Hypothalamic-Pineal Axis and Circadian Rhythm Regulation. Lithium Therapy Monographs, Volume 2, F N Johnson (Ed), 1988. *Memberships:* Canadian College of Neuropsychopharmacology, Memberships Committee; Society for Neuroscience; Association for Research in Vision and Ophthalmology; Intenrational Society of Psychoneuro-endocrinology. *Honours:* Ontario Mental Health Foundation Research Associateship, 1978-; John Dewan Award for Research in Mental Health, 1976. *Hobbies:* Sheep farming; Raising border collies. *Address:* Seggie's Shire Farm, RR No 3 Puslinch, Ontario, Canada, N0B 2J0.

SEGRAVES Kathleen Blindt, b. 25 Aug. 1947, Chicago, Illinois, USA. Assistant Professor of Psychiatry (Research, Psychotherapy). m. R. Taylor Segraves, 5 July 1983, 2 stepsons. *Education:* BA summa cum laude, Psychology, Illinois Benedictine College, 1977; MA, 1980, PhD, 1984, School of Social Service Administration, University of Chicago; Fellow, Diplomate, American Board of Medical Psychotherapists; Certified Clinical Social Worker; Diplomate, Clinical Social Work, National Association of Social Workers. *Appointments:* Co-Director, Biofeedback Lab/Clinic, College of DuPage, Glen Ellyn, Illinois, 1977-79; Lutheran Family Services of Illinois, Chicago, 1978-79; Clinician, Michael Reese Hospital, Wexler Clinic, Chicago, 1979-80; Assistant Professor, School of Social Service Administration, Co-Director, Biofeedback Clinic, Department of Psychiatry, School of Medicine, University of Chicago, 1982-85; Assistant Professor, Department of Psychiatry & Neurology, Assistant Director, Adult Psychiatry Ambulatory Services, Tulane University Medical Center, New Orleans, Louisiana, 1985-87; Assistant Professor, Case Western Reserve University School of Medicine and Cleveland Metropolitan Hospital, Cleveland, Ohio, 1987-

; Researcher, sexual functions of males and females, women's issues (behavioural medicine, chronic pain, hypnosis, biofeedback training). *Publications include:* Psychiatric screening of candidates for penile prosthetic surgery (with R T Segraves), 1985; Differentiation of Biogenic & Psychogenic Impotence with the Eysenck Personality Inventory and the Sexual Attitudes Survey (with R T Segraves), 1986; Use of Sexual History to Differentiate Organic from Psychogenic Impotence (with R T Segraves and H W Schoenbert), 1987. *Memberships:* Phi Theta Kappa; Psi Chi. *Hobbies:* Travel; Fishing. *Address:* Case Western Reserve University, Cleveland Metropolitan General Hospital, Department of Psychiatry, 3395 Scranton Road, Cleveland, OH 44109, USA.

SEIFERT Betty Lynn, b. 13 Aug. 1940, Dallas, Texas, USA. Conservator. m. Walter Seifert, 31 May 1970, 1 son, 1 daughter. *Education:* BA Library Science, BS Chemistry, Texas Woman's University, 1962; MS, Library Science, Rutgers University, 1964. *Appointments:* Conservator, Ronson Ship-Soil Systems, 1976-82; Consultant, various wet archaeological sites, 1982-; Conservator, director, Archaeological Conservation Lab Inc., 1982-84; Conservator, Spring Point Museum, Snow Squall Project, 1984-88; Conservator State of Maryland, 1989. *Publications:* Articles in: Forest Products Journal; JAIC; Proceedings of the CUA. *Memberships:* American Institute of Conservation; New England Conservation Association. *Honours:* Alpha Lambda Delta, 1959; New York Public Library Scholarship, 1962; Governor's Distinguished Service Award, Maine, 1978. *Hobbies:* Weaving; Spinning; Data Base Management. *Address:* 582 North Main Street, Groton, MA 01450, USA.

SEITAMO Leila Kaarina, b. 13 Dec. 1930, Rovaniemi, Finland. Chief Psychologist. *Education:* Teacher Training Primary School, 1951, Candidate of Educational Sc, 1960, PhLic, 1982, University of Jyvaskyla; Diploma, Training in Behaviour Therapy, 1985; Qualifiacation, Associate Professor in Psychology, 1988. *Appointments:* Primary School Teacher, Oulu, 1951-54, Sipoo, 1954-60; Psychologist, Child Guidance Clinic, Oulu, 1960-66; Chief Psychologist, Paediatrics, 1966-, University of Oulu, (on leave from 1987 and serving as an Associate Professor in Psychology, Social Sciences, University of Lapland, Rovaniemi, Finland, 1987-); Researcher of National Board of Education, 1972-74 and the Finnish Academy, 1985-88. *Publications:* Contributor, numerous articles in professional & scientific journals. *Memberships:* International Biological Programme/Human Adaptability Expedition in Finland's Lapland, 1968-70; Committee Member, Development of Education among the Lapps; Member, Working Groups, Planning the Curriculum of Lappish School System; Chairman, Section in Culture & Education, Association for Developing Skolt Culture; General Council of Union of Finnish Psychologists; President, Local Union of Finnish Psychologists in Oulu; Executive Committee, International Society of Psychosomatic Obstetrics and Gynaecology. *Hobbies:* Research Work; Travel; Reading. *Address:* Dept. of Paediatrics, University of Oulu, 90220 Oulu, Finland.

SEKICH Karen Sue, b. 12 June 1939, Longmont, Colorado, USA. Management. m. Nick Sekich Jr, 7 July 1962, 2 sons, 1 daughter. *Education:* AA honours, Aims Community College, Greeley, Colorado, 1986; BS magna cum laude, Business Administration, Regis College, Denver, 1988; Numerous courses and seminars. *Appointments:* Writer for Phillips Marketing, 1974-77; Co-Owner, Sekich Business Park, 1974-; Accounts Receivable/Collection Specialist, Sekich Equipment Co, 1977-82; Full-time Board Member, Vice-Chair, Secretary, St Varin Valley School District, 1977-80; Manager, Furrow Restaurant, 1980-86; Republic Candidate, Campaign Manager, State of Colorado House of Representatives Seat, 1980; Owner/Manager, Quest R & I Ltd collection agency, 1981-; Weld County Republican Campaign Coordinator, 1982; Credit & Collection Seminar Leader, Sklar Financial Control Corporation, 1987-; Franchisee Owner, Partner,

Collectemps, Northern Colorado, 1988-. *Memberships:* Healthcare Client Services Programme, Legislative Committee, Colorado/Wyoming Unit Board of Directors, American Collectors Association; American Commercial and Western States Collectors Association; SouthWest Weld Economic Development Council, Chair 1988, Executive Committee 1989; Board of Directors, Longmont Area Chamber of Commerce, 1989; Advisory Board, Economic Development Association Partnership of Greely/Weld; The Chamber, Greeley, Colorado; Fort Lupton, Platteville and Carbon Valley Chambers of Commerce; National Federation of Independent Business; Past Advisor, Phi Beta Lambda, University of Northern Colorado, Greeley; Executive Board, Northern Colorado Consortium; Steering Committee, E-470 Northern Colorado; Consumer Resource Committee, Union Rural Electric Association Inc; Past Member: Alternatives For Youth Board; Olde Columbine Youth Advisory Board. *Honour:* Winner, State Businessperson of the Year Award, 1984. *Hobbies:* Reading; Hiking in the Rockies. *Address:* 6769 WCR 32, Longmont, CO 80501, USA.

SELBE Jane Williams, b. 16 Mar. 1926, Rocky Ford, USA. Dentist. m. 5 Sept. 1948, divorced 1971, 1 son, 2 daughters. *Education:* DDS, Northwestern University, 1951. *Appointments:* Pedodontist, Dr Corvin Stine, 1952-54; Private Practice: Skokie, 1954-60, Glenview, 1960-70; General Practice, Dentistry, Glenview, 1970-. *Publications:* Articles in: Illinois Dental Journal; Dental Students Journal; Dental Survey. *Memberships:* American Association of Women Dentists, President 1976; American Dental Association; Illinois State Dental Society, Executive Council; Chicago Dental Society; Illinois Society of Dentistry for Children, President 1960-61. *Honours:* Recipient, many honours and awards. *Hobbies:* Music; Gardening; Travel; Nutrition. *Address:* 938 Kenilworth Lane, Glenview, IL 60025, USA.

SELDES Marian, b. New York City, USA. Actress. m. Julian Claman, 3 Nov. 1953, divorced, 1 daughter. *Education:* Graduate, Neighborhood Playhouse, New York City, 1947; DHL, Emerson College, 1979. *Appointments:* Faculty Member, Theatre Division, Juilliard School, Lincoln Center, New York City, 1969-; Appeared with Cambridge Massachusetts Summer Theatre, 1945; Boston Summer Theatre, 1946; St Michael's Playhouse, Winooski, Vermont, 1947-48; Bermudia Theatre, Hamilton, 1951; Elitch Gardens Theatre, Denver, 1953; Broadway Appearances Include: Medea, 1947; Crime & Punishment, 1948; That Lady, 1949; Tower Beyond Tragedy, 1950; The High Ground, 1951; Come of Age, 1952; Ondine, 1954; The Chalk Garden, 1955; The Wall, 1960; A Gift of Time, 1962; Tiny Alice, 1965; A Delicate Balance, 1967; Before You Go, 1968; Father's Day, 1971; Equus, 1974-77; The Merchant, 1977; Deathtrap, 1978-82; Off-Broadway appearances in many plays; Films include: The Greatest Story Ever Told. *Publications:* The Bright Lights, 1978; Time Together, 1981. *Memberships:* Board of Directors, neighborhood Playhouse; The Acting Company. *Honours:* TONY Award, Best Supporting Actress, 1967; Drama Desk Award, 1971; Obie Award, 1973, 1976; Outer Circle Critics Award, 1983. *Address:* 17 West 71st Street, New York, NY 10023, USA.

SELIGMAN Roslyn, b. Augusta, Georgia, USA. Psychiatrist/Child & Adolescent Psychiatry. *Education:* BS, University of Georgia, 1957; MD, Medical College of Georgia, 1961. *Appointment:* Associate Professor of Psychiatry, University of Cincinnati College of Medicine, 1974. *Publications:* Book Chapters: Current Pediatric Therapy, Vol 7, Chapter 3; Modern Perspectives in Psychiatric Aspects of Surgery; The Experience of Dying; Burn Nursing: A Comprehensive Approach, in press. *Memberships:* Fellow 1972, American Psychiatric Association; President 1981-82, Ohio Psychiatric Association; President 1982-83, Education Research Foundation; President 1975, Cincinnati Psychiatric Society; Fellow 1976, American Academy of Child & Adolescent Psychiatry. *Honours:* The American Board of Psychiatry & Nerology, Child Psychiatry No 851, 1975; American Board of Psychiatry & Nerology, General

Psychiatry, 1973. *Address:* 2401 Ingleside, Cincinnati, Ohio 45206, USA.

SELLARS Elizabeth, b. 6 May 1921, Glasgow, Scotland. Actress. m. Francis Austin Henley, 8 Sept. 1960, 1 stepson. *Education:* RADA, 1938- 39. *Career:* Repertory, Wilson Barrett Company, 1940; Many Films: Tea & Sympathy, Desire, The Italian Girl, Last Love, Winter Sunlight; TV Includes: Voyage Round My Father. *Hobbies:* Golf; Gardening. *Address:* Herefordshire, England.

SELLERS Georgeanna, b. 23 Dec. 1955, Lexington, USA. Instructor, Visiting Lecturer. *Education:* AA, 1976; BA, honours, 1981, MA, 1984, University of North Carolina. *Appointments:* Vice President, Piedmont Freight System Inc., 1979-84; Visiting Tutor, Davidson County Community College, 1980- 82; Lecturer, English, High Point College, 1984-. *Memberships:* Phi Theta Kappa; University of North Carolina Alumni Association; VFW Auxiliary; National Council of Teachers of English; National League of Families of POW's & MIA's. *Hobbies:* Human & Animal Rights; Woodworking; Writing; Reading; Pets. *Address:* Rt. 17, Box 2923, Lexington, NC 27292, USA.

SELTZER Joanne, b. 21 Nov. 1929, Detroit, Michigan, USA. Poet; Writer. m. Stanley Seltzer, 10 Feb. 1951, 1 son, 3 daughters. *Education:* BA, University of Michigan, 1951; MA, College of Saint Rose, 1978. *Appointments:* Freelance Writer, 1973-. *Publications:* Airondack Lake Poems, 1985; Suburban Landscape, 1988; Inside Invisible Walls, 1988; numerous poems, articles, essays, short fiction and translations of French Poetry in many journals & anthologies. *Memberships:* Poets & Writers; Poetry Society of America; Associated Writing Programs. *Honours:* Scholarship, Wesleyan/Suffield Writers Conference, 1977; Medallion Winner, Triton College All Nations Poetry Contest, 1978; Award Finalist, Willow Bee Publishing House, 1985; Residency, Ragdale Foundation, 1988. *Hobbies:* Vegetarianism and Macrobiotics; Oriental Philosophy; T'ai Chi. *Address:* 2481 McGovern Drive, Schenectady, NY 12309, USA.

SELTZER Ronni Lee, b. 24 Apr. 1952, New York, USA. Physician; Psychiatrist. m. Gary Broder, 20 Jan. 1980. *Education:* BA, Syracuse University, 1973; MD, Chicago Medical School, 1977; Internships, Residencies,New York University Medical Center, 1977-81. *Appointments:* Teaching Assistant, Psychiatry, New York University Medical Center, 1980-; Medical Staff, Englewood Hospital, 1981-; Medical Staff, Holy Name Hospital, 1984-; Medical World News Physician's Advisory Panel, 1984-. *Publications:* Articles in American Journal of Psychiatry; Lectures. *Memberships Include:* American, New Jersey, Eastern Psychiatric Associations; American, Bergen County Medical Associations. *Address:* 200 Engle Street, Englewood, NJ 07631, USA.

SEMAS Judith Ann, b. 11 June 1942, Taunton, Massachusetts, USA. Nonprofit executive. *Education:* BS, Business Administration, University of California at San Jose, 1980. *Appointments:* Corporate Personnel Officer, Union Bank, San Francisco and Palo Alto, 1966-73; Personnel Director, City of Santa Clara, 1973-80; Executive Director, The Foundation for HOPE 1981-84; Development Director, HOPE Rehabilitation Services, 1981-82; President, CEO, HOPE Rehabilitation Services, 1982-. *Memberships:* Rotary Club, San Jose; Governor's Committee for Employment of the Disabled; Speakers' Bureau, Rotary Clubs; International Platform Association; Career Information Bureau, Unviersity of California at San Jose; Board of Directors, Grantsmanship Resource Center; Board of Trustees, The Foundation for HOPE; Adivsory Board, Mission City Community Fund; Advisory Board, Twin Creeks Foundation; California Association of Rehabilitation Facilities; National Association of Rehabilitation Facilities; Commission on Accreditation of Rehabilitation Facilities. *Honours:* Outstanding Business Woman Award, Bay Area Council, Northern California American

Business Womens Association, 1987; Woman of Achievement in Business nominee, The Womens Fund, 1985; Outstanding Small Business Person nominee, Small Business administration, San Francisco; Life Member, California Scholastic Federation; Dean's List, California State University at San Jose and Santa Clara University. *Hobbies:* Jogging; Gardening; Playing piano; Reading; Bicycling; Poetry; Ancient history; Music. *Address:* Hope Rehabilitation Services, 1539 Parkmoor Plaza, San Jose, CA 95128, USA.

SENIOR Elinor Laurie Kyte, b. 30 Dec. 1926, Sydney, Nova Scotia, Canada. Historian; Professor. m. Hereward Senior, 22 Sept. 1954, 3 sons, 1 daughter. *Education:* BA 1952, PhD 1976, McGill University, Montreal; MA, Memorial University, Newfoundland, 1959. *Appointments include:* Bishops's University, Lennoxville, 1956-57; University of Victoria, British Columbia, 1960-61; University of Toronto, 1962-63; McGill Centre for Continuing Education, 1973-78; St Francis Xavier University, Nova Scotia; Assistant Professor: McGill University 1984-85, Acadia University 1986-87, St Francis Xavier 1987-88; Associate Professor, Acadia, 1988-. *Publications include:* Books: British Regulars in Montreal: Imperial Garrison 1832-54, 1981; Roots of Canadian Army in Montreal District 1846-70, 1981; From Royal Township to Industrial City: Cornwall 1784-1984, 1983; Redcoats & Patriots: Rebellions in Lower Canada 1837-38, 1985. Also: Numerous articles, biographies, entries in encyclopaedias & dictionaries; Editor, Cannon's Mouth. *Memberships:* Council, Society for Army Historical Research, London, UK; Commissioner, Canadian Commission of Military History; Military History Society of Ireland; Canadian Military History Group. *Honours:* Doctoral Fellowship, Canada Council, 1970-72; Summer Research Grant, Montreal Military & Maritime Museum, 1975; Postdoctoral Fellowship, Department of National Defence, 1979-80. *Hobbies:* Fencing; Music. *Address:* 2043 Vendome Avenue, Montreal, Canada H4A 3M4.

SENSABAUGH Mary Elizabeth, b. 15 Aug. 1939, Eastland, Texas, USA. Secretary; Treasurer; Financal Consultant. m. Dwight L. Sensabaugh, 22 Dec. 1956, 2 sons. *Education:* North Texas State University, 1963-67. *Appointments:* Senior Acocuntant, Braniff International Airlines, 1967- 68; Accountant, Computer Business Service, 1968-72; Secretary Treasurer, Robert D. Carpenter, Inc., 1972-76; Controller, Broadway Warehouse, 1976-78; Assistant Controller, Southwest Offset, 1978-79; Secretary Treasurer, Carpenter Carruth & Hover, 1979-. *Memberships:* National Association of Women in Construction, Board, Dallas Chapter, 1973-74; Beta Sigma Phi, President, Irving, Chapter, 1973-74. *Hobbies:* Reading; Handcrafts; Organ; Doll Collecting. *Address:* 702 Hughes, Irving, TX 75062, USA.

SENSOR Mary Delores, b. 20 July 1930, Erie, Pennsylvania, USA. Hospital Official; Consultant. m. Robert Louis Charles Sensor, 21 Apr. 1945, 2 sons, 2 daughters. *Education:* BS, Hospital Administration, 1972; MS, Health Care Administration, 1986. *Appointments:* Intern, Hospital Administration, Harvard University, 1972; Director, Medical Records, St Mary Hospital, Langhorne, 1972-74; Moses Taylor Hospital, Scranton, 1975-77; Erie County Geriatric Centre, Fairview, 1977-82; Director, Utilization Rev., Millcreek Community Hospital, Erie, 1983; Board of Directors, Christian Health Care Centre, Erie, 1983-84; Consultant Professor, hospital administration. *Memberships:* Board of Directors, St John Kanty Prep. School, Erie, 1970-71; President, Ladies Auxiliary, 1970-71; American Medical Record Association; Pennsylvania Medical Record Association; NW Pennsylvania Medical Record Association, Secretary Treasurer, 1982-84; National Association Quality Assurance profiles; Pennsylvania Association Quality Assurance Profiles. *Hobbies:* Gourmet Cooking; Collecting Jazz. *Address:* 3203 Regis Dr., Erie, PA 16510, USA.

SEPPALA Mirja Inkeri, b. 18 Aug. 1923, Orimattila,

Finland. Librarian. m. Arvo Seppala, 15 Sept. 1972. *Education:* MA, University of Helsinki, 1952; Examination in Librarianship, School of Social Sciences, 1954. *Appointments:* Assistant Librarian, 1955-59, Acting Librarian, 1959-60, Sub-Librarian, 1959-70, Librarian, 1970-86, University of Tampere. *Publications:* Luettelo suomalaisen kirkjallisuuden edistamisvaroin avustetusta kaunokirjallisuudesta, Bibliophilos 15, 1956; Hakemisto suomalaisten kirjailijain elamakerta ja muistelmakokoelmiin, Bibliophilos 16, 1957; Tampereen ja lahiympariston kirjastojen kurssikirjallisuus, Tampere, 1969. *Memberships:* Tampere Club of the Zonta International; Staff Association, University of Tampere, Secretary 1957-64; Finnish Library Association; Finnish Research Library Association; Staff Association, Research Libraries; International Biographical Association. *Honours:* Order of the Lion of Finland, 1971; Grants: University of Tampere, 1969, 1970 and 1977. *Interests:* Literature. *Address:* Vallerinkatu 23 as. 10, 33270 Tampere, Finland.

SEQUOIA Anna, b. 3 June 1945, New York City, New York, USA. Author. *Education:* Attended Bard College, 1962-63; Washington Square College, New York University, 1965-67; Faculty for Foreigners, University of Florence, Italy, summer 1966; BA, Goddard College, Adult Degree Program, Plainfield, Vermont, 1978. *Appointments:* Copywriter, Rapp & Collins, Advertising, 1970-71; Assistant to Editor-in-Chief, Atheneum Publishers, 1971- 73; Associate Editor, Special Contributor and Book Reviewer, New Times, 1973- 74; Co-founder, Vice-President, North Country Mountaineering, 1974-76; Creative Group Supervisor, American Management Association, 1976-82; President, Sequoia Direct Response, Advertising and Sequoia Book Purchasing Company, 1982-86; Senior Copywriter, The Franklin Mint, 1986-87; Editor, Almanac Magazine, 1987-89; Director, Incremental Sales, The Franklin Library, 1988-89, Director, Continuity Marketing, The Franklin Mint, 1989-. *Publications:* The Climbers Sourcebook (with Steve H Schneider), 1976; Backpacking on a Budget (with Steven H Schneider), 1979; The Complete Catalog of Mail Order Kits, 1980; The Official JAP Handbook, 1982; The Official JAP Paper Doll Cut-Out Book (with Patty Brown), 1982; No Bad Men (with Sarah Gallick), 1984; Chunks (with Patty Brown), 1984; Articles and reviews published in New York, New Times, Climbing, Viva, Publishers Weekly; Almanac. *Memberships:* Charter Member, National Book Critics Circle; Co-Founder, Coalition of New York Women Artists. *Address:* 210 Locust Street, Philadelphia, PA 19091, USA.

SEREX-DOUGAN Diane Ruth, b. 13 Sept. 1955, Baltimore, USA. Optometrist. m. Richard J Dougan, 1 July 1978. *Education:* BA, Biology, Alfred University, 1977; OD, Southern College of Optometry, 1981; Residency, Pediatric Optometry & Vision Therapy, Southern College of Optometry, 1982; Fellow, College of Optometrists, Vision Development, 1986. *Appointments:* Associate Professor, 1982-, Director, Residency Programmes, 1987-, Southern College of Optometry; Private practice, Memphis Family Vision, 1986-. *Memberships:* Optometric Extension Programme Foundation, Clinical Associate; American, Tennessee Optometric Associations; American Public Health Association. *Honours:* Beta Sigma Kappa; Sigma Alpha Sigma; Optometric Recognition Award, American Optometric Association, 1987. *Hobbies:* Antiques; Cats; Travel; Needlework. *Address:* 2246 Easton Drive, Cordova, TN 38018, USA.

SERFER Marsha, b. 13 Nov. 1948, New York City, New York, USA. Retirement Hotel Administrator. m. Henry Serfer, 17 May 1969. 1 son, 2 daughters. *Education:* University of Miami, 1966-69. *Appointments:* Interior Designer, Self employed, 1969-79; Owner, Administrator Midtown Manor Retirement Hotel, 1979-. *Memberships:* Broward County Adult Care Assoc. National Association of Retirement Care Facilities; Gold Coast South Home Health Agency Advisory Board; Florida Tennis Association; National

Association of Women Business Owners; Jewish Federation of South Broward. *Honours:* Hollywood Chamber of Commerce Nominee for Small Business of the Year; Placement and Directory Award for Best Value in Broward County, Retirement Homes; Nominee Best Landscaping Design in City of Hollywood. *Hobbies:* Interior design; Construction, development and restoration of 50 year old building; Junior tennis, daughter player in national tournaments. *Address:* 9801 SW 2nd Street, Plantation, Florida 33324, USA.

SEROKE Notemba Joyce, b. 11 July 1933, Johannesburg. Social Worker. m. Theodore Seroke, 11 July 1969, 1 daughter. *Education:* BA, 1958; University Education Diploma, 1959. *Appointments:* Teacher, High School, 1960-62; Market Research Officer, 1963-64; General Secretary, YWCA, Durban, 1964; National General Secretary, World Affiliated YWCA of South Africa. *Publications:* Co-producer, Mama I'm Crying, documentary. *Memberships:* Vice President, World YWCA; Vice President, Black Consumer Union; Women under Apartheid; Board, Transvaal Board of Urban Foundation. *Hobbies:* Opera; Jazz; Womens Issues; Reading. *Address:* 1147 Machaba Drive, Mofolo Central, Soweto, Johannesburg, South Africa.

SERVADIO Gaia Cecilia, b. 13 Sept. 1938, Padoua, Italy. Writer; Journalist; Lecturer; Broadcaster. m. 28 Sept. 1960, 2 sons, 1 daughter. *Education:* NDD, 1960. *Appointments:* Staff, Daily Telegraph Magazine, 1967; Arts Correspondent, La Stampa, 1975-; Contributing Editor, Business, 1986-. *Publications:* Melinda; Don Juan; Il Metodo; A Siberian Encounter; A Profile of a Mafia Boss; Mafioso; Insider Outsider; Women in the Renaissance; Luchino Visconti, a Biography; To a Different World; Il Lamento di Arianna; A Different Childhood; Contributor to various magazines including: Partisan Review; Espresso; Il Mondo, Capital, Cosmopolitan, etc. *Memberships:* Vice President, Foreign Press Association, 1970-72; President, Emigrazione e Cultura, 1978; Executive Member, London Symphony Orchestra, 1979-86; General Secretary, Mahler Festival, 1984-85. *Honours:* Cavaliere Ufficiale della Repubblica Italiana, 1970; NUJ; Society of Authors. *Hobbies:* Opera; History; Music; Gastronomy; Skiing. *Address:* 31 Bloomfield Terrace, London SW1W 8PQ, England.

SERVAIS Donna Jean, b. 20 Oct. 1946, Marinette, Wisconsin, USA. English Instructor. m. John Servais, 5 July 1972. 1 son, 1 daughter. *Education:* BA, English, Macalester College; MA, English, University of Wisconsin, Madison; Master of Professional Development, University of Wisconsin, La Crosse. *Appointments:* Business Communications Instructor, University of Wisconsin, 1984-85; English Instructor, Winona State University, 1985-. *Publications:* Songs Along the Highway; Life to Life: A Women's Portrait Album; City House/Country House. *Memberships:* Phi Delta Kappa; Lanbach Literacy International. *Hobbies:* Design quilting; Nature photography. *Address:* English Department, 102 Minne Hall, Winona State University, Winona, Minnesota, USA.

SERVICE Louisa Anne, b. 13 Dec. 1931, Paris, France. Publisher. m. Alastair Stanley Douglas Service, 28 Feb. 1959, divorced 1984, 1 son, 1 daughter. *Appointments:* Export Director, Ladybird Appliances, 1955-59; Municipal Group, 1959-, PA to Chairman 1959, Financial Director, 1960, Deputy Chairman, 1974, Joint Chairman, 1976-; Chairman of Glass's Guide Services Ltd, 1982. *Publications:* Articles in various journals & newspapers. *Memberships Include:* Chairman, Mayer-Lismann Opera Workshop; Chairman, Hackney Juvenile Court, 1975-82; Chairman, Westminster Juvenile Court, 1982-88; Chairman, Hammersmith Juvenile Court, 1988-; Chairman, Rota Goup 3 Area of Inner London Juvenile Courts; Council Member, Youth and Music; Member of the Management Committee of the Friends of Covent Garden, (since 1983). *Hobbies:* Travel; Music. *Address:* c/o Hemming Publishing Ltd., 178/202 Great Portland Street, London W1N 6NH, England.

SETH Mira, b. 5 Mar. 1936, Lahore, West Pakistan. Government Servant. *Education:* BA Honours 1955, MA 1957, History, University of Delhi; MSc Economics Public Administration Group, London, UK; PhD, Fine Arts, Calcutta University, India. *Appointments:* Joined Indian Administrative Services, 1958, positions include: Sub-Divisional Magistrate, 1961-62; Deputy Commissioner & District Magistrate, Gurgaon, 1965-67; Deputy Secretary & Director, Ministry of Industrial Development, Government of India, 1968-74; Secretary, Industrial Development, Public Works, Health, Labour, Irrigation & Power, 1974-78, Government of Haryana; Joint Secretary, Ministry of Labour, India, 1978-83; Secretary, Health & Labour, Haryana, 1983-85; Family Planning Commissioner & Additional Secretary, Ministry of Health, India, 1985-88; Secretary, Department of Civil Supplies, India, 1988-. *Publications:* Various Writings, History of Art, including: Wall Paintings of Western Himalayas; Dogra Wall Paintings in Jammu & Kashmir. *Membership:* Indian Administrative Services Association. *Honours:* Various student awards. *Hobbies:* Western & Indian Classical Music; Theatre. *Address:* D-149, Defence Colony, New Delhi 110 024, India.

SEVERIN Dorothy Sherman, b. 24 Mar. 1942, Los Angeles, USA. Spanish Language & Hispanic Studies Educator. m. Giles Timothy Severin, 24 Mar. 1966, divorced 1979, 1 daughter. *Education:* AB, summa cum laude, Harvard University, 1963; AM, 1964; Phd 1967. *Appointments:* Tutor, Harvard University, 1964-66; Visiting Lecturer, UWI, 1967-68; Assistant Professor, Vassar College, 1968-69; Lecturer, Westfield College, London, 1969-82; Visiting Associate Professor: Harvard University, 1982, Columbia University, 1982, New York City, 1985, Yale University, 1985; Professor, Spanish, Head Hispanic Studies, Liverpool University, England, 1982-; Editor, Bulletin of Hispanic Studies, 1982-. *Publications:* Editor various publications. *Honours:* Ann Radcliffe Scholar, 1959-60; Woodrow Wilson Fellow, 1963-64, 1966-67; Fellow of the Society of Antiquaries, 1988-. *Address:* Dept. of Hispanic Studies, Modern Languages Building, University of Liverpool, PO Box 147, Liverpool, L69 3BX, England.

SEVERINO Elizabeth Forrest, b. 29 Dec. 1945, Bryn Mawr, USA. Consulting Company Executive. m. Joseph D. Severino, 20 Oct. 1973, 1 daughter. *Education:* AB, Vassar College, 1967; MS, Syraacuse University, 1969. *Appointments:* Systems Programmer, IBM, 1967-71; Systems Analyst, Fidelity Bank, 1971-72; Managing Editor, Auerbach Pubishers, 1972-77; Competitivve Analyst IBM, 1977-79; Vice President, Datapro, 1979-81; VP, Symcro Systems, 1981-82; President, The Pc Group Inc., 1982-. *Publications:* Over 125 articles on computers; over 400 speeches; editor, 6 books. *Memberships:* Association of Personal Computor Consultants. *Honours:* IBM, Outstanding Employee, 1969; Outstanding Employee, Auerbach, 1973, 1974, 1975; Regional Manager's Award, iBM, 1978; Headquarters Competitive Analysis Award, IBM, 1979. *Hobbies:* Ballroom Dancing; Skiing; Golf. *Address:* The PC Group Inc., 1050 N Kings Highway Suit 105, Cherry Hill, NJ 08034, USA.

SEWITCH Deborah E, b. 21 Nov. 1954, Perth Amboy, New Jersey, USA. Specialist in Sleep Disorders Medicine/Sleep Researcher. *Education:* BA, Duke University, 1976; MA 1980, MPhil 1982, PhD 1982, City University of New York. *Appointments:* Associate Director, Sleep Disorder Center, Columbia-Presbyterian Medical Center, New York, 1980-81; Senior Clinician, 1982-84, Associate Director, 1985-86, Sleep Evaluation Center, Western Psychiatric Institute & Clinic, Pittsburgh; Director, Sleep Disorders Center, Griffin Hospital, 1986-; Assistant Clinical Professor, Department of Psychiatry, Yale University School of Medicine, 1987-. *Publications:* Numerous papers in journals; NREM Sleep Continuity and the Sense of Having Slept in Normal Sleepers, 1984; The Perceptual Uncertainty of Having Slept, 1984; Slow Wave Sleep Deficiency Insomnia: a Problem in Thermodownregulation at Sleep Onset, 1987.

Memberships: Sleep Research Society; Society for Psychophysiological Research; New York Academy of Sciences; Society for Neuroscience; Clinical Sleep Society. *Honour:* Semi-Finalist, James- McKeen-Cattell Award in Psychology, New York Academy of Sciences. *Hobbies:* Singing; Horseback Riding; World Religions and Mythology; Writing; Astrology. *Address:* The Griffin Hospital, Sleep Disorders Center, 130 Division Street, Derby, CT 06418, USA.

SEXTON Virginia, b. 30 Aug. 1916, New York City, New York, USA. College Professor. m. Richard J. Sexton, 21 Jan. 1961. *Education:* BA cum laude, Classics, Hunter College, 1936; MA, 1941, PhD, 1946, Post-doctoral training, 1949-51, Psychology, Fordham University; Post-doctoral training, Psychology, Neuroanatomy, Columbia University, 1952-53. *Appointments include:* Lecturer to Associate Professor, Chairman of Department of Psychology, Guidance Director, Notre Dame College, Staten Island, 1944-52; Lecturer, School of General Studies, 1945-1949, Instructor, 1953-56, Assistant Professor, 1957-60, Associate Professor, 1961-66, Professor, Psychology, 1967- 68, Hunter College, City University of New York; Professor, 1968-79, currently Professor Emerita, Herbert H. Lehman College, City University of New York, 1968-79; Distinguished Professor of Psychology, St John's University, Jamaica, New York, currently. *Publications:* Clinical Psychology: An Historical Survey, 1965; With H.Misiak: Catholics in Psychology: A Historical Survey, 1954, Spanish translation, 1955; History of Psychology: An Overview, 1966; Historical Perspectives in Psychology: Readings, 1971; Phenomenological, Existential & Humanistic Psychologies: A Historical Survey, 1973; Psychology Around the World, 1976; Editor: History & Philosophy of Science: Selected Papers (with J.Dauben), 1983; Numerous articles, papers, & biographical contributions to encyclopedias; Abstractor, Psychological Abstracts, 1947-72; Various editorial assignments. *Memberships include:* Phi Beta Kappa; Eta Sigma Phi; Sigma Xi; Delta Kappa Gamma; Past President, Psi Chi; Fellow, American Psychological Association; Fellow, American Association for the Advancement of Science; Fellow, New York Academy of Sciences; New York State, Nassau County, Queens, Eastern Psychological Associations; International Council of Psychologists; American Association of University Professors; American Association of University Women; Many others; Numerous offices. *Honours:* Hon LHD, Cedar Crest College, 1980; Wilhelm Wundt Award, New York State Psychological Association, 1987; Many more. *Address:* 188 Ascan Avenue, Forest Hills, NY 11375, USA.

SEYFRIT Carole L, b. 12 July 1951, Pasco Washington, USA. Assistant Profssor. *Education:* BA, summa cum laude, Sociology, Indiana Institute of Technology, 1975; MS, Utah State University, 1978; PhD, Sociology, University of Maryland, 1984. *Appointments:* Instructor, Sociology, Augusta College, 1981-83; Research Associate, University of Arkansas, 1983-84; Instructor, Sociology, West Georgia College, 1984-85; Assistant Professor, Sociology, Eastern New Mexico University, 1985-86; Assistant Professor, University of Wisconsin, 1986-89; Assistant Professor, Mississippi State University, 1989-. *Publications:* Articles in journals & magazines. *Memberships:* American, Rural Sociological Associations; Southern Sociological Society; Pacific Sociological Society. *Honours:* German Marshall Fund of US Research Fellowship,National Science Foundation Research Traineeship, 1975-77; Phi Kappa Phi, 1978; Alpha Kappa Delta 1975. *Address:* Dept. of Sociology, Mississippi State Univerity, Mississippi State, MS 39762, USA.

SEYLER Athene, b. 31 May, 1889, London, England. Actress. m. (1) J B Sterndale-Bennett, 1914. deceased 1918, 1 daughter. (2) Nicholas James Hannen. *Education:* Academy of Dramatic Art. *Career:* Debut, Kingsway Theatre, 1909 as Pamela Grey in The Truants. *Creative Works:* Appearances in over 100 plays from 1909, including: The Gentleman Dancing Master, 1961; The Chances, 1962; The Dark Stranger, 1964; The Reluctant Peer, 1964; Too True to be Good, 1965; Arsenic and Old Lace, 1966. Numerous film appearances since 1932 including The Perfect Lady. Directed: The Tragic Muse, 1928; Dandy Dick, 1948. Author, with Stephen Haggard, The Craft of Comedy, 1944. *Honours:* President, Council of the Royal Academy of Dramatic Art, 1950; CBE, 1959. *Hobbies:* Music; Walking in the country; Going to the theatre. *Address:* Coach House, 26 Upper Mall, London W6, England.

SEYMOUR Charlena Moten, b. 12 Mar. 1943, Washington DC, USA. Professor. m. Harry Seymour, 2 Sept. 1966, 1 son, 1 daughter. *Education:* BFA, Howard University, 1965; MA 1967, PhD 1971, Ohio State University. *Appointments:* Assistant Professor 1971-78, Associate Professor 1978- 79, Professor 1989-, University of Massachusetts, Amherst; Visiting Professor, University of Linkoping, Sweden, 1986. *Membership:* Vice President for Standard & Ethics 1990-92, American Speech Language Hearing Association. *Honours:* Danforth Associate, 1975; Fellow, ASLHA, 1987. *Hobbies:* Tennis; Jogging; Acting; Piano. *Address:* Department of Communication Disorders, University of Massachusetts, Amherst, MA 01003, USA.

SEYMOUR Jane, (Joyce Frankenberg), b. 15 Feb. 1951, England. Actress. *Career:* Dancer with London Festival Ballet at 13. Theatrical film debut, Live and Let Die, 1973. On Broadway in Amadeus. *Creative Works:* Films: Sinbad and the Eye of the Tiger; Battlestar Galactica; Oh, Heavenly Dog; Somewhere in Time; Lassiter. Television Movies: Frankenstein; The True Story; Captains and the Kings; Benny and Barney; Las Vegas Undercover; Seventh Avenue; Killer on Board; The Four Feathers; The Awakening Land; Love's Dark Ride; Dallas Cowboys; Cheerleaders; East of Eden; The Haunting Passion; Dark Mirror; The Sun Also Rises; Obsessed with a Married Woman; Crossings. *Address:* c/o James Sharkey Ass. Ltd, 3rd Floor Suite, 15 Golden Square, London W1R 3AG, England.

SEYMOUR Lynn, b. 8 Mar. 1939, Wainwright, Canada. Ballet Dancer; Choreographer. 3 children. *Education:* British Columbia & Vancouver, Canada; Sadler's Wells Ballet School, UK. *Appointments include:* Member or guest dancer, leading ballet companies, UK, Germany, France, USA, Yugoslavia, Netherlands, Austria, Canada; Numerous film & television appearances; Teacher, Royal Ballet School, Ballet Rambert, American Ballet Theatre, Paris Opera Ballet, Yorkshire Ballet seminars, Janet Smith & Dancers, Balletto di Toscano, Pacific Ballet Vancouver; Director & Principal Dancer, Bavarian State Opera, Munich, Germany, 1978-. *Creative works:* Repertoire, over 60 ballets including: Coppelia; Swan Lake; Pineapple Poll; Giselle; Solitaire; Sleeping Beauty; Les Sylphides; Boutique Fantasque; Spectre de la Rose; Rituals; Month in the Country; Aureole; Taming of the Shrew; Salome; etc. Publications: Autobiography, Lynn, with Paul Gardner; Subject, authorised biography, photographic study. Choreography, 14 ballets, stage & television, various countries, titles include: Night Ride, Breakthrough, Rashomon, Court of Love, Leda & the Swan, Tattoo, Love is in the Air. *Honours include:* Commander, Order of British Empire (CBE), 1976; Dancer of Year, Dance & Dancers magazine, 1960; Evening Standard Award for Ballet, 1976. *Address:* c/o Artistes in Action, 16 Balderton Street, London W1Y 1TF, England.

SEYMOUR Rosemary, b. 28 Oct. 1922, London, England. Running Grade I Historic House, open to the public. m. George Fitzroy Seymour, 1 June 1946. 1 son, 1 daughter. *Education:* 1st Class Diploma, Dairy Farming, Downham, Queens College, Reaneheath Agricultural College. *Memberships:* Children's Society (Nottinghamshire Branch) President; Linen Guild and League of Friends, Nottingham General Hospital, President. *Hobbies:* Gardening; Care of antiques; Reading; Needlework. *Address:* Thrumpton Hall, Nottingham, NG11 0AX, England.

SHACKLOCK Constance, b. 16 Apr. 1913, Sherwood, Nottingham, England. Opera & Concert Singer. m. Eric Mitchell, 23 July 1947, (dec. 1965). *Education:* Royal Academy of Music, 1939-43; LRAM, FRAM. *Performances Include:* International Ballet, Goddess Sabrina in Milton's Comus, 1946; Covent Garden, 1946-56; Berlin State Opera, 1952; Teatro Colon, Buenos Aires, 1956; Elizabethan Opera, Australia, 1957; Bolshoi, Moscow, USSR, 1958; Kirov, Leningrad, USSR, 1958; Palace Theatre, London, UK, 1961; Sung with many famous conductors including: Beecham, Kleiber, Kempe, Krauss, De Sabata, Barbirolli, Kubelik, Rank, Sargent. *Memberships:* President, RAM Club; President, English Singers & Speakers; President, Nottingham Operatic Society; Adjudicator, National Federation of Music Festivals. *Honours:* Member, Order of the British Empire, 1970; Fellow, Royal Academy of Music, 1953. *Hobbies:* Tapestry; Nature; Animals. *Address:* East Dorincourt, Kingston Vale, London SW15 3RN, England.

SHAEFFER Claire Brightwell, b. 2 Dec. 1939, Weston, USA. Sewing Specialist; Lecturer; Author. m. Charlie Willard Shaeffer, Jr., 24 Feb. 1959, 2 sons. *Education:* AA, Peralta College, 1968. *Appointments:* Teacher, Adult Education, Montgomery County MD, 1969-70; Designer, Consultant, Portsmouth Public Schools, 1972-73; Teacher, College of the Desert, 1975- . *Publications:* 101 Sewing Shortcuts, 1978; The Complete Book of Sewing Short Cuts, 1981; Sew Successful, 1984; Sew A Beautiful Gift, 1986; Claire Shaeffer's Sewing SOS, 1988; Claire Shaeffer's Fabric Sewing Guide; articles in: Woman's Day; Threads; Sew News; Sewing Update; Handwoven; etc. *Memberships:* Costume Society, England; Friends of Fashion, London Museum; Costume Society of America; Costume Council, LA County Museum; Association of Professors of Textile & Clothing; Textile Study Centre de Young Museum. *Hobbies:* Reading; Sewing; Travel. *Address:* PO Box 157, Palm Springs, CA 92263, USA.

SHAFER Diane Elain, b. 30 Apr. 1952, Oil City, Pennsylvania, USA. Orthopaedic Surgeon. 1 daughter. *Education:* BS, Pennsylvania State University, 1972; MD, Temple University, 1975; Intern, Hamot Medical Center, Erie, Pennsylvania, 1975-76; Resident in Orthopaedic Surgery, 1976-78. *Appointments:* Resident Orthopaedic Surgery, Pennsylvania State Hersey Medical Center, 1978-80; Private Practice Medicine, specializing in Orthopaedic Surgery, Williamson, West Virginia, 1980-; Medical Director, Dept Phys Medicine, Williamson Appalachian Regional Hospital, 1980-; Attending physician, Orthopaedic surgery, Williamson Memorial Hospital, 1980-; Paul B Hall Medical Center, Highlands Regional Medical Center, Prestonsburg, Kentucky; Partner, Lock, Stock and Barrel Restaurant. *Memberships:* Chairperson Advisory Board, Salvation Army, 1982-; President, Board of Directors, Tug Valley Recovery Shelter, 1980-; Founder, Domestic Violence Center; AMA; West Virginia Medical Association (Counselor, del, 1980-); Kentucky Medical Association; Pike County Medical Association; Mingo County Medical Society (Secretary- Treasurer); American Back Society (Board of Directors); American Academy Neurologic and Orthopaedic Surgery (diplomate); Certificate, American Board of Thermology. *Address:* Box 749, Williamson, WV 25661, USA.

SHAFER Ingrid H, b. 3 Aug. 1939, Innsbruck, Austria. University Teacher. m. (1) W Thomas Poole, 30 Apr. 1961, divorced, 1974, 1 son, 1 daughter. (2) R W Shafer, 1 May 1977, deceased 1986. *Education:* Studied at Universitat Wien, Austria, 1958-59; PhD Candidate, Universitat Innsbruck, 1960; MA German Literature, 1967; MA Human Relations, 1975; PhD Philosophy, 1984, University of Oklahoma, USA. *Appointments:* Special Instructor, German, University of Oklahoma, 1967-68; Assistant Professor 1968-84, Associate Professor 1984-88, Professor of Philosophy and Religion 1988-, University of Science and Arts of Oklahoma. *Publications:* Andrew Greeley's World: an Anthology of Critical Essays, 1989; The Incarnate Imagination: Essay in Theology, the Arts and Social Sciences in Honor of

Andrew Greeley. A Festschrift, 1988; Eros and the Womanliness of God: Andrew Greeley's Romances of Renewal, 1986. Articles in numerous professional journals. Television: Participant and panelist in The Woman's Place, 9-part education series, 1977. *Memberships:* American Academy of Religion; American Institute for the Study of Religious Cooperation; Hegel Society of America; Institute for Evolutionary Psychology; NEH Berkeley/Chicago/Harvard Summer Institutes: The Study of Religion in the Liberal Arts: Towards a Global Perspective; North East Modern Language Association; Oklahoma Academy of Science; Popular Culture Association (Area Chair for Andrew Greeley's Fiction); State of Humanities in Oklahoma Higher Education Commission, 1988. *Honours:* Regents Superior Teaching Award, 1981; Matura "mit Auszeichnung" 1958; Award for Academic Excellence, Republic of Austria, 1958. *bb3Hobbies:* Painting; Computers; Writing poetry and fiction. *Address:* P O Box 2628, University of Science and Arts of Oklahoma, Chickasha, OK 73018, USA.

SHAH Fatima, b. 11 Feb. 1914, Bhera, Punjab, Pakistan. Social Worker; Medical Doctor. m. Syed Jawad Ali Shah, 31 Oct. 1937, dec. 1981, 2 daughters. *Education:* Gold Medal, High School, 1928; MB,BS, 1936; Postgraduate, Obstetrics & Gynaecology, Hammersmith Medical School, London, UK, 1948. *Appointments include:* Dufferin Medical Service WMS, India, 1936-37; Self-employed, maternity home & clinic, Karachi, Pakistan, 1947-56; Retired from medical work due to loss of sight, 1956-. *Creative work includes:* Motivation & development of self-help amongst the blind & disabled nationally & internationally; Publications, various papers presented, aspects of disability, international conferences & seminars. *Memberships include:* Founder member, offices, Central Cabinet, All-Pakistan Women's Association, 1948-57; Founder, Life Member, President 1960-84, Pakistan Association of the Blind; Founder member, offices, President 1974-79, International Federation of the Blind; Executive 1974-79, International Agency for Prevention of Blindness; Convenor & Chair 1982-87, Disabled People's Federation, Pakistan; Pakistan Parliament, 1981-85; World Council of Disabled People's International, representing South Asia, 1981-. *Honours:* Numerous awards & recognitions including: Member, Order of British Empire 1952; Testimonial, United Nations Secretary-General, 1987. *Address:* No. 54, 12th Street, off B-4 Street, Phase V, Defence Housing Society, Karachi-46, Pakistan.

SHAHAN Janet Lynn, b. 20 Nov 1954, Froono, California, USA. Certified Public Accountant. *Education:* BA Economics, Uniersity of California, Davis, 1977; MBA Finance, University of California, Berkeley, 1980. *Appointments:* Cost Accountant, Accata National, San Francisco, 1976-78; Staff Auditor, Holiday Clubs International Sausalito, 1979; CPA, Seiler & Co, San Francisco, 1980-83; CPA, Sole proprietor, San Francisco, 1983-. *Membership:* AICPA, 1984-. *Hobby:* Volunteer for improvement of San Francisco Residential Parking. *Address:* 1952 Leavenworth, San Francisco, CA 94133, USA.

SHAKERLEY Elizabeth Georgiana (Lady Elizabeth Anson), b. 7 June 1941, Windsor, England. Proprietress, Party Planners. m. Sir Geoffrey Adam Shakerley, 6 Bt, 1972, 1 daughter. *Education:* Privately educated in England and France. *Appointments:* Proprietress of Party Planners, 1961-. *Publication:* Lady Elizabeth Anson's Party Planners Book, 1986. *Memberships:* Director of Kanga; Director of Mosimann's. *Honour:* Courvoisier Book of the Best Awarded a plaque for Best Caterers, 1988. *Hobbies:* Theatre; Gardening; Music; Travelling. *Address:* 56 Ladbroke Grove, London W11 2PB, England.

SHALVI Alice, b. 1926, Germany. m. Moshe Shalvi, 6 children. *Education:* BA, English Literature, 1947, MA, 1950, Newnham College, University of Cambridge, England. *Appointments:* Faculty Member, English, Hebrew University, Jerusalem, 1950-, Senior Lecturer,

1967, Associate Professor, 1971; Founding Chair, English, Ben Gurion University of the Negev, 1969-73; Head, Institute of Languages & Literature, Hebrew University, 1973- 76; Principal, PELECH Religious Experimental High School for Girls, Jeruselem, 1975-. *Memberships:* Founding Chair, Israel Womens Network; Chair, Ohel Joseph; Israel Council for the Arts & Culture; National Council for Advancement of the Status of Women. *Address:* POB 3828, 91037 Jerusalem, Israel.

SHAMI Janset Berkok, b. 7 Apr. 1927, Istanbul, Turkey. Music Centre Proprietor. m. Khalid Shami, 21 Sep. 1951, 1 son, 1 daughter. *Education:* BA, English Literature, 1948; External student, Queen Mary College, London University, England, 1954-55. *Appointments:* BBC Turkish Section, London, England, 1954-55; Programme Presenter, Magazine, Jordan TV, 1968-74; Art Teacher, CMS High School, Amman; Owner, Twang musical instruments shop, Amman, currently. *Creative works include:* Short stories in The Cornhill Magazine; Writer and Producer, TV work with marionettes, 1968-74; Exhibitions of paintings, London, Baghdad, Amman, Beirut. *Memberships:* Founding Member, Royal Fine Arts Society, Amman; Founding Member, Jordan Heritage Society; Founding President, Jordan Crafts Society, affiliated to World Crafts Society. *Hobbies:* Painting; Printing; Writing; Swimming; Skiing; Music; Marionettes; Shadow puppets. *Address:* PO Box 35034, Amman, Jordan.

SHANK Brenda Mae, b. 25 Sept. 1939, Cleveland, Ohio, USA. Radiation Oncologist. m. Charles Vernon Shank, 16 June 1969. *Education:* BA, Chemistry, 1961, PhD, Biophysics, 1966, Case Western Reserve University; MD, Rutgers Medical School, 1976. *Appointments:* Research Biophysicist, 1966-68; Assistant Professor, Radiology, Case Western Reserve University, 1969; Instructor, Assistant Professor, CMDNJ, 1970-75; Instructor to Associate Professor, Radiology & Radiation Oncology in Medicine, Cornell University Medical College, 1980-89; Clinical Assistant to Associate Attending Radiation Oncologist, Radiation Therapy, Memorial Sloan-Kettering Cancer Centre, 1980-89; Assistant Attending Radiologist to Associate Attending Physician, New York Hospital, 1980-89; Chairman and Professor, Director, Radiation Oncology, Mount Sinai School of Medicine, 1989-. *Publications:* many journal articles & book chapters. *Memberships:* New York Cancer Society; New York Roentgen Society; Radiation Research Society; American Endocurietherapy Society; American Society Therapeutic Radiology Oncology. *Honours:* Merck Index Award, 1960; NASA AIBS Fellowship, 1964; American Cancer Society Junior Faculty Clinical Fellowships, 1981-83; Editor's Recognition award, Distinction, Radiology Journal, 1987; Distinguished Alumna Award, Case Western Reserve University, 1988. *Hobbies:* Flying - Private Pilot's License; Reading; Photography. *Address:* Radiation Oncology Dept., Mount Sinai Medical Center, One Gustave Lane, Levy Place, New York, NY 10029, USA.

SHANKS Ann Zane, b. New York City, New York, USA. Filmmaker; Photographer; Writer. m. (1) Ira Zane, deceased, 1 son, 1 daughter. (2) Robert Horton Shanks, 25 Sept. 1959. 1 son. *Education:* Carnegie Mellon University; Columbia University. *Appointments:* Photographer, filmmaker, writer for numerous magazines, newspapers, including: Life; Time; Esquire; Fortune; NY Times; Redbook; Cosmopolitan. Producer, Women on the Move, NBC-TV; Script editor, CBS, also dir. nat. TV script competition for college students; Asso. producer World Video Inc. *Creative Works:* Producer director, Central Park; Denmark. A Loving Embrace; Tivoli; TV series American Life Style, 1972; Exhibited photographs: Mus Modern Art; Mus City New York; Met Mus Art; Caravan Gallery; Parents Mag. *Publications:* The Name's the Game (photographs and text), 1961; New Jewish Ency (photographs), 1966; Adolescent Development (photographs), 1967; Old Is What You Get (photographs and text), 1976. *Memberships:* American Soc Mag Photographers (board of Governors); Overseas Press Club Am (Chairman 1970 photog awards). *Honours:* Recipient 4 awards, internat. competitions; Named one of 6 young talents in Am Photography Mag. Award US Cameras Ann; 3 awards for photography Nat Housing Yearbook; Cine Golden Eagle, Cambodia Film Festival Award; Cine Golden Eagle, 1973; San Francisco Film Festival Award; American Film Festival Award; 1 silver and 4 gold medal awards, Internat. TV and Film Festival, New York; 2 Golden Eagle awards. *Address:* 201B E 82nd Street, New York City, NY 10028, USA.

SHANLEY Barbara, b. 3 Oct. 1935, San Francisco, California, USA. Antique & Fine Arts Appraiser; Antique Furniture Conservator. m. (1)Larry Shanley, Apr 1965, deceased 1972, 1 daughter. (2)Raymond Diebold, Dec 1976, divorced 1986. *Education:* BA, University of California, Berkeley, 1956; New York School of Interior Design, 1959; Intern Soc of Appraisers Core Courses, Indiana Univ, 1985. *Appointments:* Self employed with husband, Shanley Furniture Finishing, antique restoration, 1963-; Purchased E Holmer, Furniture Refinishing, 1976; Appraisal business, 1979-; Antique restorer and conservator, under my own name, New York and San Francisco, 1967-; Appraiser of antique furniture, Fine Arts, specializing in furniture and Oriental arts, 1978-. *Publication:* Author: The Appraisal of Antique Furniture. *Memberships:* Senior member, American Society of Appraisers; Designated member, International Society of Appraisers; Fellow, Bay Area Art Conservation Guild; Instructor, Indiana University Teaching credential, California; Netsuke Kenkyukai; San Francisco Soceity for Asian Art; American Decorative Arts Forum; Charter Member, National Museum for Women in the Arts. *Honour:* Distinguished Service Award, International Soc of Appraisers, 1986. *Hobbies:* Lecturer on appraising and identifying antique furniture; Travel. *Address:* 644 Clarendon Avenue, San Francisco, CA 94131, USA.

SHANNON Mary Louise, b. 13 May 1923, New York, New York, USA. College Professor. m. James Anthony Shannon, 6 Sept. 1947. 1 son, 1 daughter. *Education:* BS in Secondary Education, University of Florida, 1960; MS in Education, College of William & Mary, Willimasburg, Virginia; EdD, Nova University, 1978. *Appointments:* English Instructor, 1945-47; Department Store Buyer, 1948-51; TV Instructor and Administrator in English, 1960-63; Dean of Women in High School; Speech, Humanities Professor, Florida Community College at Jacksonville, 1974-; Communication Consultant. *Publications:* An Excperimental Study of Evaluation Criteria for Speaking, Listening and Cognitive Knowledge Activities at Florida Junior College, 1985; The Development of the Downtown Campus of Florida Junior College at Jacksonville, 1979; Part Time Instructional Personell in College Governance; Supplying Community College Needs in Basic Speech Courses at Florida Junior College, 1982; Manual for TV Classroom Teachers of English 10, 1963. *Memberships include:* Kappa Delta Pi, 1976; Phi Kappa Phi, 1960; Delta Kappa Gamma; William & Mary Society Career Representative; International Listening Association; National Association of Parliamentarians; Speech Communication Association at National state & Local Levels; Florida Association of Community Colleges; Delta Zeta Sorority, etc. *Honours:* Merit Teacher Award; Outstanding Speech Teacher Award, 1980; Licensed Real Estate Sales; Speaker's Bureau Director for FCCJ; Jacksonville Chamber of Commerce; Member of Notary Public Association. *Address:* 66 Harmony Hall Road, Doctor's Inlet, Florida 32030, USA.

SHAPIRO Betty K, b. 26 Sept. 1907, Washington, USA. Retired. m. Michael, 5 Jly 1936, deceased. *Appointments:* Secretary: Langley Junior High, Washington, 1924-28; South Pasadena Junior High, 1928; Secretary, Office Manager, Hebrew Immigrant Aid Society, Washington, 1929-43. *Memberships:* International President, B'nai B'rith Women, 1968-71; Chair, Jewish Womens Caucus, 1977-; Board Member, National Woman's Party; National Women's Conference Committee, etc. *Honours:* Many honours and awards.

Address: 3001 Veazey Terrace NW, No 1604, Washington, DC 20008, USA.

SHAPIRO Erin Patria Margaret (Pizzey), b. 19 Feb. 1939, Tsingtao, China. Author; Founder, Chiswick Womens Aid, World's first refuge for the victims of domestic violence. m. Jeffrey Scott Shapiro, 19 Dec. 1980. 1 son, 1 daughter. *Appointments:* Journalist, Author, Social Reformer; Founder of Refuge movement for battered men, women and children, 1971; Contributor to Cosmopolitan Magazine. *Publications:* Books: Scream Quietly or the Neighbours will Hear; Infernal Child; The Slut's Cookbook; Erin Pizzey Collects; Prone to Violence. Viction: The Watershed; In the Shadow of the Castle; First Lady; The Consul General's Daughter; The Snow Leopard of Shanghai. *Membership:* The Soceity of Authors. *Honours:* Nancy Astor Award for Journalism, 1983; International Order of Volunteers for Peace Diploma of Honour, 1981; World Congress of Victimology, Distinguished Leadership Award, 1987. *Hobbies:* Books; Travel; Wine; Gardening; Violin. *Address:* c/o Christopher Little Literary Agent, 49 Queen Victoria Street, London EC4N 4SA, England.

SHAPIRO Johanna Freedman, b. 26 May 1949, USA. Associate Professor; Psychologist. m. Deane Shapiro, 26 Apr. 1970, 1 son, 2 daughters. *Education:* BA, 1971, MA, 1973, PhD, 1975, Stanford University. *Appointments:* Social Scientist, Stanford Medical School, 1976-77; Staff Psychologist, Mental Research Institute, 1976; Associate Professor, Family Medicine, University of California, 1978-. *Publications:* over 40 articles. *Memberships:* American Psychological Association; Society of Teachers of Family Medicine; Diplomate, Behavioral Medicine, International Academy of Behavioral Medicine; American Association of Marriage & Child Counsellors. *Honours:* Phi Beta Kappa; Manga Cum Laude, 1971. *Hobbies:* Singing; Jewish Studies. *Address:* Dept. of Family Medicine, University of California Medical Centre, 101 City Dr. South, Orange, CA 92668, USA.

SHARMA Archana, b. 16 Feb. 1932, Poona, India. Professor of Genetics. m. Arun Kumar Sharma, 8 May 1959. *Education:* BSc,1949; MSc, 1951; PhD, Science, 1955; DSc, 1960. *Appointments:* Research Officer, pre-1971; Professor of Genetics, Centre for Advanced Study in Cell and Chromosome Research, Department of Botany, University of Calcutta, 1971-. *Publications:* Author, 7 books; Editor, 11 books; Nearly 300 research papers on genetics in international journals. *Memberships:* Indian Science Congress Association (General President 1986-87, Secretary-General 1983-85); Fellow, Council Member, National Academy of Sciences, India, Allahabad (President, Biological Sciences, 1985); Fellow, Council Member, Indian National Science Academy, New Delhi; Fellow, Council Member, Indian Academy of Sciences, Bangalore; University Grants Commission, 1986-92; National Committee on Women, 1988-89. *Honours:* 1st J.C.Bose Award in Life Sciences, University Grants Commission, 1974; S.S.Bhatnagar Award, Council of Scientific and Industrial Research, 1976; National Lectureship, University Grants Commission, 1980; Padma Bhushan, President of Government of India, 1984; Birbal Sahni Medal, Indian Botanical Society, 1984; FICCI Award in Life Sciences, 1984; President, Indian Botanical Society, 1989. *Hobbies:* Handicrafts. *Address:* Centre for Advanced Study in Cell and Chromosome Research, Department of Botany, University of Calcutta, 35 Ballygunj Circular Road, Calcutta 700010, India.

SHARP Roxanne Wehrmann, b. 29 July 1956, La Grange, USA. Company President. m. 29 Sept. 1985. *Education:* BA, Graphic Design, University of Tulsa, 1978; Currently studying for MA, California State University. *Appointments:* Multi Media Art, 1978-79, Adjunct Faculty, 1979-, Triton College; Advertising Artist, 3 Newspapers, 1980-; Art Director, Waterfront Magazine, Newport Beach, 1981-83; Creative Director, National Marketing Sales Promotion, 1984-85; President, Sharp Design Group, 1985-. *Memberships:* Advertising Club of Orange County; Costa Mesa

Chamber of Commerce; So Cal Women in Advertising; Greenpeace. *Honours:* Award of Excellence, Consolidated Papers Inc. *Hobbies:* Painting; Sculpture; Ceramics; Travel. *Address:* 170 E. 17th Street, Suite 200C, Costa Mesa, CA 92663, USA.

SHAUGHNESSY Marie Kaneko, b. 14 Sept. 1924, Detroit, Michigan, USA. Retired Executive; Practising artist. m. John Thomas Shaughnessy, 23 Sept. 1959. *Education:* Keisen Women's College, Tokyo, Japan, 1941-44; AA, Liberal Arts, University of Alaska, USA, 1976; George Mason University, Fairfax, 1988-89. *Appointments:* Operations Manager, Webco Alaska, Anchorage, 1970-87; Partner, Webco Partnership, 1983-; Watercolour Instructor, Alaska State Council on the Arts, 1973-81. *Creative works:* Watercolours: Water Wheel at Rock Springs, 1987; The Fence, 1986; Blooms, 1985; Lilacs; Birch in Alizarin. *Memberships:* Board of Directors, Potomac Valley Watercolorists; Board of Directors, National Capitol Area Chapter, Sumi-e Society of America; Charter Member, Alaska Watercolour Society; Board of Directors, (President and Grants Officer), Alaska Artists Guild; San Diego Watercolour Society; Associate Member, American Watercolour Society; Organizing Committee, Japanese Society of Alaksa; The Art League; Commissioner, Fine Arts Commission, Municipality of Anchorage. *Honours:* Arts Affiliates Award, Anchorage Community College, 1975, 1978, 1984; Watercolour Award, All Alaska Watercolour Juried Exhibit, 1980; Purchase Award, All Alaska Watercolour Juried Exhibit, 1986; Awarded Title, University Artists, Alaska Pacific University, 1986. *Interests:* Japanese Culture and language; Music; Performing arts. *Address:* 1200 Allendale Road, McLean, Virginia 22101, USA.

SHAW Mary Magdalene (Dovie Loreana Loree), b. 11 Feb. 1921, Alabama, USA. m. Lew Cline, 31 Dec. 1940, 2 daughter. *Memberships:* Mary Magdalene Foundation: Grace Church Universe, Mary Magdalene Rural Home Missionary College; Saint Nicholas Chapter; Alabama Homesteads. *Address:* 1336-A Casler Avenue, Gadsden, AL 35901, USA.

SHAW Tessa Frances Valerie, b. 2 Apr. 1936, London, England. Actress. m. George Fathers, 17 Aug. 1963, divorced 1980, 2 sons, 1 daughter. *Education:* Thronton College, Bletchley, 1946-47; Ursuline Convent, Greenwich, 1947-53; Teachers: Speech and Drama Diploma, Guildhall School of Music & Drama, 1956; BA, Honours, Psychology, University of London, 1965. *Appointments:* Salford Repertory Company, 1957; appearances on tours in various theatres, 1958-60; Visiting Teacher, Speech & Drama, ILEA, 1960-64; various TV appearances including: Dr Who, Doomwatch, Adela Quested in Howards End, 1961-71; Suddenly at Home, Fortune Theatre, 19710-72; Sister Rochford in General Hospital, ATV, 1972-73; Amy Johnson in Amy, Wonderful Amy, Armchair Theatre, Thames TV, 1973; Miss Watts in Jane Eyre, BBC TV, 1983; Sister Smith in Murphy's Mob, Central TV, 1984; Feature Film, Hitler SS, 1984; Mrs Gordon in Tucker's Luck, BBC TV, 1985. *Memberships:* Equity; NUT; Former Ward Chairman, & Treasurer, Liberal Party; Roehampton Club. *Honours:* Principal's Prize for Acting, Guildhall School of Music & Drama, 1955. *Hobbies:* Attending Antique Sales, particularly of Georgian Glass; Reading the Newspaper. *Address:* PTA, 10 Sutherland Avenue, London W9 2HG, England.

SHEAHAN Patricia Ann, b. 14 June 1938, Ottawa, Ontario, Canada. Consulting Geoscience Information Geologist. m. Garry Sheahan, 30 Dec. 1961. 2 daughters. *Education:* Bachelors degree in Geology. *Appointment:* President, Konsult Int. Inc, 1965-. *Publications:* Microform No 15 Bibliography on the mid continent, 1984; Bibliography of igneous rocks of Arkansas, 1987; Bibliography of Geostatistics, 1988; Ore deposit models, 2, 1988. *Honours:* Director, Continental Precious Minerals; Chairman, Geological Association of Canada, Mineral Deposits Publications; Advisory Committee to American Geological Institute Thesaurus; Fellow, Geological Association of Canada;

Society of Economic Geologist. *Hobbies:* Travelling; Reading; Tennis; Active in Conference organizations specific to exploration i.e. Gold 86 Conference. *Address:* Konsult Int. Inc, 44 Gemini Road, Willowdale, Ontario, M2K 2G6, Canada.

SHEETZ Christine Ninfa, b. 10 Nov. 1940, Hilongos, Leyte, Philippines. Food Service Director. m. Donald L. Sheetz, 9 May 1981. *Education:* BS, Home Economics, 1962; MA, Education, 1974. *Appointments:* Teacher, Philippine Public School, 1962-65; High School Teacher, 1965-70, Instructor, 1970-73, Franciscan College; Secondary Principal: St Nino Academy, 1973-76, St Christopher Academy 1976-79, Resident Advisor, Threshold Rehabilitation Services, 1981-82; Food Service Supervisor, 1983-86; Food Service Director, Exeter Township School District, 1986-. *Memberships:* PTA. *Honours:* BS, Magna cum laude. *Hobbies:* Reading; Sewing; Cooking. *Address:* RD 4 Box 4355A, Fleetwood, PA 19522, USA.

SHEFELMAN Janice Jordan, b. 12 Apr. 1930, Baytown, Texas, USA. Author. m. Thomas Whitehead Shefelman, 18 Sept. 1954. 2 sons. *Education:* BA 1951, MEd 1952, Southern Methodist University; Library Certification, University of Texas, 1980. *Appointments:* Elementary School Teacher, Dallas Independent School District, 1952-54; St Andrews Episcopal School, 1955-57; Librarian, Lake Travis Independent School District, 1980-84. *Publications:* Books: A Paradise Called Texas; Willow Creek Home; Spirit of Iron; Victoria House. *Memberships:* Society of Children's Book Writers; Austin Writers League. *Honour:* Texas Bluebonnet Award Master List, 1985-86. *Hobbies:* Skiing (snow); Reading; Sailing. *Address:* 1405 West 32nd Street, Austin, Texas, USA.

SHEFF Sylvia Claire (Glickman), b. 9 Nov. 1935, Manchester, England. Director. m. Alan Frederick Sheff, 28 Dec. 1958 (dec), 1 son, 1 daughter. *Education:* BA, University of Manchester, 1957. *Appointments:* Teacher, 1957-77; Magistrate, 1976; National projects director 1974-85, assistant national director 1985-, Conservative Friends of Israel (UK); Founder, director, Friendship with Israel group, European Parliament, 1979-; Founder chairman 1972-80, president 1980-, Manchester 35 Group, Womens Campaign for Soviet Jewry; Management committee, Bury Family Conciliation Service, 1985-87; Council 1975-, Hon secretary 1986-, National Council for Soviet Jewry, UK & Ireland. *Memberships:* Past chair, Whitefield Hebrew Congregation Ladies Guild; Public Relations Council, Greater Manchester & Region, 1972-76; Executive, Jewish Representative Council, Greater Manchester & Region, 1974-81; Lecturer, Jewish Representative Council, 1980-. *Honours:* Governor's prize, English literature, Stand Grammar School for Girls, Whitefield, 1952; Justice of the Peace, 1976. *Hobbies:* Bridge; Travel; Antiques; Theatre. *Address:* 6 The Meadows, Old Hall Lane, Whitefield, Manchester, M25 7RZ, England.

SHEININ Rose, b. 18 May 1930, Canada. Biochemist. m. Joseph Sheinin, 1 son, 2 daughters. *Education:* BA, Physiology & Biochemistry, 1951, MA 1953, PhD 1956, Biochemistry, University of Toronto. *Appointments include:* University of Toronto, 1951-53; University of Cambridge, UK, 1956-57; National Institute of Medical Research, London, UK, 1957-58; Ontario Cancer Institute, 1958-67; Assistant Professor, Microbiology, 1964-75, Assistant Professor 1967-72, Associate Professor 1972-78, Graduate Secretary 1973-75, Professor 1978-, Medical Biophysics, Chair 1975-82, Professor 1975- 82, Microbiology & Parasitology, Professor, Microbiology 1982-, Senior Fellow, Massey College 1983-, Vice Dean, Graduate Studies 1984-89, University of Toronto; Various consultancies, visiting professorships. *Publications:* Associate editor, board, various professional journals; Author, co-author, over 100 scientific articles. *Memberships include:* Offices, past/present: Toronto Biochemical & Biophysical Society; Canadian Biochemical Society; Canadian Society for Cell Biology; Science for Peace; Canadian

Federation of Biological Societies. Numerous other professional memberships. *Honours include:* Scholarships, bursaries, fellowships, including: National Cancer Institute of Canada 1953-56, 1958-61, British Empire Cancer Campaign 1956-58; Visiting Professor, University of Alberta, 1971; Member, Government of Canada Ministerial Scientific Delegation to China, 1973; Queen's Silver Jubilee Medal, 1978; Member, Science Council of Canada, 1984; Honorary doctorates. *Address:* 7141 Sherbrooke Street West, Montreal, Quebec, Canada H4B 1R6.

SHELLENBERGER Verna S, b. 4 Jan. 1915, Meyersdale, Pennsylvania, USA. Retired. m. (1)Almer Phillippi, 10 Sept 1943, deceased 4 Dec. 1944. (2)Philbest Shellenberger, 12 Jan. 1957, divorced 20 Feb. 1975. *Education:* Graduate, Lincoln Prep; Philadelphia Bible College; Philadelphia Academy of Music; Philadelphia Academy of Fine Arts; Studied writing, by mail. *Appointments:* Retired from main office, Acme Markets. *Publications:* In Readings for Little People: False Pride; The Neurotic Dog; Numerous poems published. *Membership:* Grace Brethern Church and Baptist Mission work. *Honours:* 3 Gold Medal Awards, Poetry; Hall of Fame, Nashville, Tennessee, 1978. *Hobbies:* ssa 00Painting in oil; Sewing, creating different items; Music, piano, guitar and violin; Writing songs. *Address:* 123 S Oak Ave Apt 1, Mt Ephram, NJ 08059, USA.

SHELNUTT Eve, b. 29 Aug. 1941, Spartansburg, South Carolina, USA. Professor of English. m. May 1982, 1 son. *Education:* English, University of Cincinnati, 1972; BA, English, 1973, MFA, Creative Writing, University of North Carolina. *Appointments:* Western Michigan University, 1974-80; University of Pittsburgh, Pennsylvania, 1980-88; Ohio University, Athens, 1988-. *Publications:* Story collections: The Love Child; The Formal Voice; The Musician; Poetry collections: Air and Salt; Recital in a Private Home; Texts on writing: The Writing Room; The Magic Pencil. *Memberships:* Modern Languages Association; PEN; Associate Writing Program. *Honours:* O Henry Prize for story; Pushcart Prize for story; Great Lakes Fiction Award. *Address:* Department of English, Ellis Hall, Ohio University, Athens, OH 45701, USA.

SHELTON Shirley Megan, b. 8 Mar. 1934, Kent, England. Magazine Editor. m. William Timothy Shelton, 1960, 1 son, 2 daughters. *Appointments:* Home Editor, Assistant Editor, Woman & Home, 1963-82; Freelance Editor, 1983-87; Editor, Home & Freezer Digest, 1988-. *Hobbies:* Travel; Music; Studying with Open University. *Address:* 59 Croftdown Road, London NW5 1EL, England.

SHELTON-COLBY Sally, b. 29 Aug. 1944, San Antonio, Texas, USA. Diplomat; Consultant. m. William E Colby, 20 Nov. 1984. *Education:* MA, International Relations, Johns Hopkins School of Advanced International Studies, Bologna, Italy & Washington DC, 1968; Fulbright Scholar, Institut des Sciences Politiques, Paris, France, 1968; BA, Hons., French, University of Missouri, 1966. *Appointments:* Deputy Assistant Secretary of State for Inter-American Affairs, 1977-79; US Ambassador to Grenada, Barbados & Eastern Caribbean, 1979-81; Fellow, Harvard University, 1981-82; Director, Political Analysis, Vice President, International Business Government Counsellors Inc., Washington DC, 1982-84; Vice President, Bankers Trust Co., 1984-86; Consultant to Multinational Corporations, 1986-; Adjunct Professor at Georgetown University, Washington DC. *Memberships:* Phi Beta Kappa; Board of Directors: National Endowment for Democracy, Council of American Ambassadors; US Committee of UN Fund for Women; Public Interest Video Network; Member of the Council fro Overseas Development Council; Natl. Women's Political Council. *Honours:* Phi Beta Kappa, 1966; Elected to: Council on Foreign Relations, Washington Institute of Foreign Affairs; Awarded Honorary Doctorate of Humane Letters, Honoris Causa by Mt. St. Mary's College, 1986. *Hobbies:*

Sailing; Ballet; Languages. *Address:* 3028 Dent Place NW, Washington DC 20007, USA.

SHEMONSKY Natalie K., b. 5 June 1934, Bridgeport, Connecticut, USA. Physician; Attorney. m. Sidney Shemonsky, 26 Aug. 1950, 3 daughters. *Education:* BA, Western Connecticut State College, 1967; MD, Woman's Medical College, 1971; JD, University of South Dakota School of Law, 1984. *Appointments include:* Clinical director, US Public Health Service Hospital, Rosebud, South Dakota, 1975-77; Managing partner, Internal Medicine Practice, Vermillion, SD, 1977-81; Medical-legal consultant, Armed Forces Institute of Pathology, 1984-. *Publications include:* Articles & Papers, infectious diseases, internal medicine & legal medicine; Co-author, chapter, New Textbook of Legal Medicine. *Memberships:* Fellow: American College of Physicians, American College of Legal Medicine; Member: District of Columbia, Pennsylvania, South Dakota & American Bar Associations. *Honour:* Joint Services Commendation Medal, 1986. *Hobbies:* Music; Jogging. *Address:* 7301 Miller Fall Road, Derwood, Maryland 20855, USA.

SHEPARD Lois Burke, b. 1 Feb. 1938, Hartford, Connecticut, USA. Director, Institute of Museum Services. m. Dr William SEtH Shepard, 25 June 1960. 1 son, deceased, 2 daughters. *Education:* BA, History, Vassar College, 1959; University of Vienna, Austria; Foreign Service Institute of the State Department; Senior Government Managers Program, Harvard University, 1987. *Appointments:* Educator, 1960-76; Co-Director, Overseas Americans for Reagan/Bush, 1980; Chairman, Americans Abroad for Reagan/Bush, 1984; Chairman, Republicans Abroad International, 1980-85; Director, Institute of Museum Services, 1986-. *Creative works:* Publications include: Taking the Long View: The Impact of a Decade of IMS Programs, 1988; The Nature and Level of Federal Funding for Museums, 1987; The Collaborative Spirit: Partners in America, 1987; Building Grassroots Political Organizations Among Americans Abroad, 1983. Speeches: Caring for Our Heritage: A Public Private Joint Venture, 1988; Conservation, The Critical Need: Perspective, Purpose and Plan, 1987. Numerous articles, editorials and essays in professional journals and magazines. *Memberships:* President's, Committee on the Arts and the Humanities; Federal Council on the Arts and the Humanities; Surrogate Speaker, George Bush for President; Executive Women in Government; Maryland Steering Committee, George Bush for President; US Department of State Overseas Schools Advisory Committee; Potomac Republican Women's Club; Task Force on Arts and Humanities, Coalition for Women's Appointments. *Honours:* Friond of Conservation Award, American Institute of Conservators, 1988; Trustee's Award, American Association of Museum Trustees, 1987; Leadership Commendation, American Association of Museums, 1987; Outstanding Republican Woman's Award, 1984. *Hobbies:* Travel; Gourmet Cooking; Siamese Cats; Collage. Interests: Voter reform; Oriental artifacts; American cultural history; Real estate. *Address:* 8602 Hidden Hill Lane, Potomac, Maryland 20854, USA.

SHEPHERD Antoinette, b. 19 Oct. 1943, Galveston, Texas, USA. Librarian. *Education:* BA, Our Lady of the Lake University, San Antonio, Texas, 1965. *Appointments:* University of Texas Medical Branch, 1965-69; Rosenberg Library, 1970-89; Helen Hall Library, League City, Texas, 1989-. *Memberships:* American Library Association; Texas Library Association; Beta Sigma Phi Sorority; Texas Notary Association; National Notary Association; American Association of University Women. *Hobbies:* Reading; Working with elderly; Crafts. *Address:* 1912-54th Street, Galveston, TX 77551, USA.

SHEPHERD Carol Nelson, b. 2 July 1952, West Point, New York, USA. Lawyer. m. William J. Henwood, 5 June 1982, 2 sons, 2 daughters. *Education:* Wells College, Aurora, New York, 1970-72; BA, Sociology, Arizona State University, 1975; JD, Syracuse University College of Law, 1978. *Appointments:* Attorney, Shrager, McDaid & Loftus PC, Philadelphia, 1978-87; Partner, Feldman, Shepherd & Wohlgelernter, 1987-. *Publications:* Articles, professional journals. Also: Frequent lecturer, professional seminars. *Memberships include:* Board of Governors, Association of Trial Lawyers of America; Governing board, Pennsylvania Trial Lawyers Association; President, Philadelphia Trial Lawyers Association; Board of Governors Pennsylvania & Philadelphia Bar Associations. *Honours include:* Merit award, Pennsylvania Trial Lawyers Association, 1981; Biographical recognitions. *Address:* Atlantic Building, Suite 640, 260 South Broad Street, Philadelphia, Pennsylvania 19102, USA.

SHEPHERD Sylvia-Lou Newton, b. 23 May 1927, Tacoma, Washington, USA. Music Consultant; Pianist; Lecturer. m. R Ernest Shepherd, 25 June 1955. 1 daughter. *Education:* MA, Music 1949, BEd 1950, MA, Music Education 1954, Washington State University; EdD, United States International University at San Diego, California, 1983. *Appointments:* Pianist, 1943-; Private Piano Teacher, 1943-85; Public School Teacher, 1962-83 (Curriculum Resource Teacher, 1980-82, for San Diego City Schools); Owner, Shepherd Consultants, Del Mar, California. *Contributions to:* Saturday Evening Post; Triangle. Composition, Little Prince Dance Drama. *Memberships:* Mu Phi Epsilon, Riverside Chapter, Charter President; California Association of Professional Music Teachers, Charter State Chair of Certification, Past Vice President, Conventions; San Diego City/Co Music Educators Association, Past President; Mu Phi Epsilon, San Diego Chapter, Past President, currently Treasurer; Honour Seminars of San Diego, Board Member San Diego Chamber Orchestra Guild; MTAC; MTNA; CMEA; MENC; NAPE; CA Association of Gifted; Charter Member, Beta Omega Chapter, Delta Gamma Fraternity, (WSU), 1950-; Organist, Church of Latter-Day Saints (Mormon); Co-originator, Contemporary Music Festival of Riverside (California); Charter Member of San Diego Chamber Orchestra Guild; Charter Member of Fairbanks Ranch Country Club. *Honours:* Superior w/honours rating, Washington State Music Teachers Festivals, Spokane, 1941-45; Valedictorian John R Rogers High School, Spokane, 1945; Phi Beta Alpha, 1949; Pi Lambda Theta, 1949; Thespian award, Poway High School, 1983. *Hobbies:* Travel; Pianist for Musicals, in San Diego County, most recently: Barnum; Dracula; Once Upon a Mattress; Pajama Game; Music Man; Reading; Bridge; Tennis; Concerts; Plays. *Address:* 4657 Vista de la Tierra, Del Mar, CA 92014, USA.

SHEPPARD Naomi Kate, Associate Professor. *Education:* AA, Temple Junior College, 1955; BA, University of Mary Hardin-Baylor, 1966; MSN, University of Texas, 1973. *Appointments:* Staff Nurse, 1960-63, Head Nurse, 1963-64, Scott & White Hospital, Temple; Inservice Education Co- Ordinator, 1966-71, Clinical Relief Nurse, 1966-71, Scott & White Hospital; Associate Professor, Univesity of Mary Hardin-Baylor, 1972-87. *Publications:* Articles in various journals. *Memberships:* American, Texas Nurses Association; American Cancer Fund Drive; Leukemia Fund Drive. *Address:* Box 440 UMHB Station, University of Mary Hardin Baylor, Belton, TX 76502, USA.

SHER Patricia Ruth, b. 19 June 1931, Washington, DC, USA. Legislator. m. William Sher, 13 Mar. 1955, 3 sons, 1 daughter. *Education:* Montgomery Community College, 1967-71; BS, Housing & applied Design, University of Maryland, College of Human Ecology, 1983. *Appointments:* Elected to Maryland House of Delegates, 1978, 1982, 1986. *Memberships:* Charter Member, Montgomery County Women's Political Caucus; Foreman, UP New Hampshire Estates Civic Association & Tifereth Israel Sisterhood. *Honours:* Hornbook Award, Maryland Psychological Association, 1984. *Hobbies:* Drawing; Painting; Fibre & Metal Art. *Address:* 1916 Rookwood Road, Silver Spring, MD 20910, USA.

SHERBECK Carmen Anderson, b. 25 May 1920,

Seattle, Washington, USA. Artist. m. Adair Sherbeck, 14 Feb. 1943, 1 son, 2 daughters. *Education:* Bethel College, St Paul, Minnesota, 1938-39; Banff School of Art, & University of Alberta, Canada, 1945; Studies with Maxwell Starr 1960, Hartwell Priest 1965, I. Hsiung Ju 1970, Ed Whitney 1982. *Creative works:* Solo exhibitions include: Museum of Art, Edmonton, Canada, 1946; Collectors Gallery, Washington DC, 1961; Staunton Fine Art Centre, Virginia, 1964, 1971; Raymond Duncan Galleries, Paris, France, 1963, 65, 66, 68; Ligoa Duncan Galleries, New York City, 1964, 65, 67, 68, 69; Bohmans Kunst Gallerie, Stockholm, Sweden, 1968; Lafayette Art Centre, Indiana, 1965; Rosequist Gallery, Tucson, Arizona, 1969; Parthenon, Nashville, Tennessee, 1972; Fine Art Centre, Warren, Pennsylvania, 1974; Charlottesville Airport, Virginia, 1976, 78, 84; Veerhoff Gallery, Washington DC, 1982, 1985-88. Exhibits at: Canadian Women, Riverside Museum, NYC, 1947; Annual exhibit, Royal Canadian Academy, 1947; National Exhibit, Tyler, Texas, 1962; Allied Artists of America, NYC, 1963; Salon d'Autumne, Paris, France, 1968; Southern Contemporary Art, 1964; Virginia Museum Biennale, 1969; Virginia Watercolur Society, 1983-85. *Memberships:* Past President (Waynesboro) Virginia Museum of Fine Arts; Art League, Alexandria, VA; VA Watercolour Society; Shenandoah Valley Art Centre; Albemarle Art Association; Paletteers, Waynesboro. *Honours include:* 8 awards, Albemarle Art Association, 1951-; 4 awards, Shenandoah Valley, 1962-; 4 awards, Staunton Outdoor Show, 1970-; Elmwood Park Show, 1970; 3 awards, Barracks Road Show, Charlottesville, 1971-; Best in Show, Southern Contemporary Exhibit, 1962. *Hobbies:* Music, Violin & Choir; Travel; Sailing; Gardening. *Address:* 1826 Cherokee Road, Waynesboro, Virginia 22980, USA.

SHERIDAN Dinah Nadyejda, b. 17 Sept. 1920, Hampstead, England. Actress. m. (1) Jimmy Hanley, 8 May 1942, 1 son, 1 daughter. (2) John Davis, March 1954. (3) John Merivale, May 1986. *Education:* Sherardswood School, Welwyn Garden City; Italia Conti Stage School, 1932-38. *Appointments:* Where the Rainbow Ends, 1932-33; Peter Pan, 1934, 1935, 1936; First Leading part in films, 1936; First appearance on TV, Picture Page, 1936; has appeared in all 3 mediums including the films: Genevieve, 1953, The Railway Children, 1970. *Memberships:* Officer Sister, St John Ambulance Brigade. *Hobbies:* Cooking; Gardening; Tapestry; Knitting. *Address:* c/o John Mahoney, 94 Gloucester Place, London W1H 3DA, England.

SHERMAN Julia Ann, b. 25 Mar. 1934, Akron, Ohio, USA. Clinical Psychologist. m. Stanley Payne, 16 June 1961, 1 son. *Education:* BA, Case Western Reserve University, 1954; PhD, State University, Iowa, 1957. *Appointments:* Hospital & private practice, 1958-62; Consulting, writing, 1962-71; Teaching & research, University of Wisconsin, Madison, 1971-74; Director, Women's Research Institute, 1974-80; Madison Psychiatric Association, 1980-87; Mental Health Association, 1987-. *Publications:* Author: On the Psychology of Women: Survey of Empirical Studies; Sex-Related Cognitive Differences. Editor, Prism of Sex & Psychology of Women: Future Directions of Research. *Memberships:* Office, American Psychological Association; President, Wisconsin Women in Psychology; American Women in Psychology; Wisconsin Psychological Association. *Honours:* Psi Chi; Phi Beta Kappa; Sigma Xi; Award, Psi Chi, 1974; Fellow, American Psychological Association. *Hobby:* Nature. *Address:* 3917 Plymouth Circle, Madison, Wisconsin 53705, USA.

SHERMAN Susan Carol, b. 21 Oct. 1949, Michigan, USA. Professional Genealogist. m. Neil Sherman, MD, 1977. 2 sons. *Education:* Santa Monica College, 1969-71; Calif State Univ, Los Angeles, 1971-72; CG (Certified Genealogist), Board for Certification of Genealogists, Washington, DC, 1989. *Appointments:* Genealogist, 1980-, specializing in Jewish records in USA, Eastern Europe and Sefardic Migrations; Adoption Research; Historical research for Jewish Cemetery Assoc of Massachusetts, 1986-88; Lecturer on genealogy for various groups, 1986-. *Creative works:* Hard Facts From Old Stones, lecture presented at 8th Summer Seminar on Jewish Genealogy, Philadelphia, 1989; History of Boston Jewish Community, 1989; Jewish Sources in Houston (author), 1989, Houston General Record, 1989; Lecture: Sources for Study of Bostons Jewish Community, 1990; Papers: Hard Facts from Old Stones, 1990; Sephardic Migration into Poland, Russia and Lithuania, 1990. *Memberships:* Houston Jewish Genealogical Society; New England Historic Gen'l Society; Century Member, American Jewish Historical Society; Jewish Gen'l Socs of New York, Philadelphia, Washington DC; Founding member, Committee of Professional Jewish Genealogists; Association of Professional Genealogists. *Hobby:* Gourmet cooking. *Address:* Houston, Texas, USA.

SHERREN Anne Ayres Terry, b. 1 July 1936, Atlanta, USA. Professor. m. William S. Sherren, 13 Aug. 1966. *Education:* BA, 1957; PhD, University of Florida, Gainesville, 1961. *Appointments:* Graduate Assistant, University of Florida, 1957-61; Instructor, 1961-63, Assistant Professor, 1963-66 Texas Woman's University, Associate Professor, 1966-76, Professor, 1976-, North Central College; Chairman, Science, North Central College, 1983-87. *Publications:* Contributor to: Analytical Chemistry; Texas Journal of Science, Inorganic Chemistry, Applied Spectroscopy. *Memberships:* American Chemical Society; American Institute of Chemists; Iota Sigma Pi; American Association for the Advancement of Science; Sigma Xi; Midwestern Association of Chemistry Teachers in Liberal Arts. *Honours:* Illinois Institute of Chemists Honour Scroll Award, 1984. *Hobbies:* Gardening; Travel; Cooking; Sewing; Reading; Bible Study Teacher; Church Officer. *Address:* Dept. of Chemistry, North Central College, Naperville, IL 60566, USA.

SHERRICK Anna Pearl, b. 26 Nov. 1899, Illinois, USA. Retired Nurse; Educator. *Education:* BS, Illinois Womens College, 1924; MS, Univerity of Michigan School of Nursing, 1934; Ed.D., University of Washington, 1954. *Appointments:* Private Duty Nurse, 1927-29; Instructor, St Lukes, Chicago, 2 years; Parkview Hospital, Pueblo, 2 years; Montana State University, 1935-70. *Publications:* The Montana State University School of Nursing, 1976; Nursing in Montana, 1960; etc. *Memberships:* American Nurses Association; Business & Professional Women; American Association of University Women; etc. *Honours:* Recipient, various honours & awards. *Hobbies:* Bird Watching; Gardening. *Address:* 1106 South Willson, Bozeman, MT 59715, USA.

SHERWOOD Midge, b. Ironton, Ohio, USA. Author. m. Jack E Sherwood, 2 daughters. *Education:* BJ, University of Missouri, 1938. *Appointments:* Author, Lecturer, Editorial Staff, Ironton O Daily Tribune; Editorial Staff, City Editor, Ironton Daily News; Assistant Manager, west Coast News Bureau Transworld Airlines; Public Relations Director, Western Air Lines, Los Angeles; Aviation Writer, Correspondent, Skyways Magazine, Aviation Columnist, Southern Flight Magazine; Owner Manager, Midge Winters News Bureau, Los Angeles; Associate Editor, Matrix Magazine; Former Book REviewer, Los Angeles Times; Historical Journalist. *Memberships:* Founder, San Marino Historical Society, 1973; Bicentennial Chairman, City of San Marino, 1973-76; Founder, Huntington Coral of Westerners International; Director, Westerns International Ind; Founder, Docents of the Old Mill; Founding Member, Friends of The Old Mill; Founder, San Marino Poets & Friends; Western Writers of America; Society of Fellows, Huntington Library, 1986; Chairman, for the establishment of Hertrich memorial at Huntington Library; Former Member, City Beautification Committee, San Marino. *Honours:* Bi-Centennial Award, Conference of California Historical Societies, 1976. *Hobbies:* Art-Watercolourist; Sculptor; Stained Glass. *Address:* Box 80241, San Marino, CA 91108, USA.

SHETTEL Patricia Frances, b. 11 Nov. 1934, McKees

Rocks, Pennsylvania, USA. Research Executive. m. (1) Anthony Vitale, 16 Feb. 1954, 1 son, 1 daughter, (2) Harris H. Shettel, 20 Mar. 1984, 1 stepson, 1 stepdaughter. *Education:* University of Pittsburgh, 1964-65; Montgomery College, 1975-82; George Washington University, 1987. *Appointments:* Office work: Alcoa Company (Pittsburgh) 1952-54, Equitable Life Assurance Society (Denver, Colorado) 1954-55, W. Craig Chambers Advertising (Pittsburgh) 1958-60, WQED-TV 1961-64, University of Pittsburgh 1964-65; Executive Secretary & Office Administrator, Miller-Thomas-Gyekis Inc, 1965-71; Administrative Associate 1971-80, Administrative Officer 1980-88, Director Research Support Services 1988-, American Institutes for Research, Washington DC. *Publications:* Serialised Bibliography, 2 volumes 1979, 3 volumes 1987; Sponsor Index, 5 editions, 1978-88; Staff Reference Book, 4 editions, 1980-84. *Memberships:* National Museum, Women in the Arts; Rockville Little Theatre; National Association for Female Executives; Board, Exhibit Communications Research Inc. *Hobbies:* Museums & art galleries; Travel; Ceramics; Knitting; Crochet; Sewing; Cooking international recipes; Reading; Antiques. *Address:* American Institutes for Research, 3333 K Street NW, Washington DC 20007, USA.

SHIELDS Carol Ann Warner, b. 2 June 1935, Oak Park, Illinois, USA. Writer; Professor. m. Donald Hugh Shields, 20 July 1957. 1 son, 4 daughters. *Education:* BA, Hanover College, USA, 1957; MA, University of Ottawa, Canada, 1975. *Appointments:* Editorial Assistant, Canadian Slavonic Papers, 1973-74; Lecturer, University of Ottawa, 1977-78; Lecturer, University of British Columbia, 1978-79; Assistant Professor, University of Manitoba, 1980-. *Publications:* 2 books poetry: Others; Intersect. 1 book criticism: Susanna Moodie. 1 book short stories: Various Miracles. 5 novels: Small Ceremonies; The Box Garden; Happenstance; A Fairly Conventional Woman; Swann. *Memberships:* Writers Union of Canada; Manitoba Writers Guild; Manitoba Association of Playwrights. *Honours:* CBC Young Writers Competition, 1965; Canadian Authors Association Award, 1976; National Magazine Award, 1984-85; CBC Drama Award, 1983; Nominated, Governor General's Award, 1988; Canada Council Senior Award, 1986. *Hobbies:* Reading; Book reviewing; Theatre; Walking. *Address:* 701-237 Wellington Cr, Winnipeg, Manitoba, Canada R3M 0A1.

SHIELDS Karen Louise Bethea-, b. 29 Apr. 1949, Raleigh, North Carolina, USA. Former District Court Judge; Attorney at Law. m. (2)Linwood Bailey Shields, 31 Dec. 1984. *Education:* JD, Duke University, 1974. *Appointments:* Co-Counsel, Joan Little Defense Team, 1974-75; Paul Rowan Keenan and Galloway, 1974-77; Loflin Loflin Galloway, Leary & Acker, 1979-80; District Court Judge, 14th Judicial District, 1980-85; Founder, Durham Co. Probation Challenge Programme, 1981-85; Sole Practitioner, 1986-88. *Memberships:* National Institute of Trial Advocacy; American Judicature Society; National Association of Black Women Attorneys; National College of Criminal Defence Lawyers, Trial Practice Instructor; NAACP. *Honours Include:* Lawyer of the Year, National Conference of Black Lawyers, 1977; NAACP Distinguished Achievement Award, 1981; Outstanding Young Woman of the Year, 1984, 1985, 1986. *Hobbies:* Reading; Civic Organizing; Church Participation; Politics. *Address:* 3525 Mayfair St., No 205, Durham, NC 27707, USA.

SHIELDS Margaret Kerslake, b. 18 Dec. 1941. New Zealand Politician. m. Patrick Shields, 25 Nov. 1960, 2 daughters. *Education:* Graduate, Sociology, Victoria University, 1973. *Appointments:* Researcher, Consumer Institute & Department Statistics; Member of Parliament for Kapiti, 1981; Minister, Customs and Consumer Affairs, 1984. *Hobbies:* Tennis; Hiking; Skiing; Music; Drama. *Address:* Parliament Buildings, Wellington, New Zealand.

SHIH Joan Fai, b. 4 Sept. 1932, Swatow, China. Painter; Educator. *Education:* Studied, Chinese Painting & Calligraphy, Hong Kong, 1949- 52; BFA, 1956, MFA,

1961, Kansas City Art Institute, USA. *Appointments:* Instructor, Kansas City Arts Institute, 1959-61, Converse College, Spartanburg, 1966-67; Lecturer, Studio Art, Rosemont College, 1969-. *Creative Works:* Solo Exhibitions: Danville Museum of Fine Arts, Virginia; British Council, Hong Kong, others; Group Exhibitions Include: Huntington Museum, New York; National Academy Galleries, New York; Bergen Museum, Paramus; Philadelphia Civic Centre Museum; Nelson & Atkins Museum, Kansas City; including 94 other exhibitions. *Honours:* Recipient, various honours and awards; Marion Cohee Memorial Award (First Prize), Plastic Club Open Juried Annual Art Exhibition, Philadelphia, 1989. *Hobby:* Music. *Address:* 2013 Locust Street, Philadlephia, PA 19103, USA.

SHIN Tong-choon, b. 18 May 1931, near Yalu River, Korea. University Professor. m. Jong-mo Ha, 22 Feb,. 1955, 3 sons, 1 daughter. *Education:* BA, English Language and Literature, Ewha Women's University, Seoul, Korea, 1953; Research, Graduate School, Seoul National University, 1953-56; MA, Hanyang University, Seoul, 1977. *Career:* English Teacher, Ewha Girls' High School, Seoul, 1953-56; Lecturer, Internal School of Sacred Heart, 1957-60; Full-time Lecturer, Women's College of Sacred Heart, 1964-68; Professor, Hanyang University, Seoul, 1968-; Academic research abroad: Contemporary English Literature, Warwick University, England, 1976; 19th Century English Literature, University of Edinburgh, Scotland, 1980; Zen Buddhism, University of California, Berkeley, USA, 1981; International literary activity: Speech at World Poets Conferences, 3rd, Baltimore, 1976, 4th, Seoul, 1979, 5th, San Francisco, 1981, 6th, Madrid, 1982, 7th, Marrakech, 1984, 8th, Corfu, Greece, 1985, 9th Taipei, Taiwan, 1986. *Creative works:* A Certain Day, poetry, 1970; Selection of Alfred Tennyson's Poetical Works, translation, 1974; Tenacity and Thereafter, poetry, 1976; Without End, poetry in English, 1979; Hypothesis and Distance, poetry, 1980; Preface to Love, essay, 1980; Mandala Blooming Sky, poetry, 1985; Metamorphose, poetry translated into French, 1985; For Solitude: Essays on Poetry and Buddhism, 1986; Selected Works of W.B.Yeats, translation, 1987. *Memberships:* Member, Board of Directors, The International PEN Club, Korean Centre; Member, Board of Directors, The Korean Modern Poetry Association; The English Literary Society of Korea; International Comparative Literary Institute; The Korean Literary Association; The Arthurian Studies Society, British Branch; Nominated Vice President, The Korean Buddhist Professors Association, 1990. *Honours:* 6th Poetic Literature Prize, 1981; Publishing Prize, Hanyang University, 1985. *Hobby:* Calligraphy. *Address:* Department of English, Hanyang University, Seoul, Korea.

SHINE Frances Louise, b. 8 Jan. 1927, Worcester, Massachusetts, USA. Author; Educator (retired). *Education:* BA, English Literature, Radcliffe College, Cambridge, Massachusetts, 1948; MA, Creative Writing, Cornell University, Ithaca, New York, 1952. *Appointments:* Secretary, Trustees Office, Boston Public Library, Boston, Massachusetts, 1948-50; Secretary, Inter-Departmental Committee on Literature, Cornell University, 1951-52; Secretary, Hardy, Hall, Iddings & Grimes law firm, 1952-53; Teacher, St Monica's School, Montreal, Canada, 1953-54; Teacher, Gloucester Public Schools, USA, 1954-56; Teacher, Framingham Public Schools, Framingham, Massachusetts, 1957-81. *Publications:* Novels: The Life-Adjustment of Harry Blake, 1968; Johnny Noon, 1973; Conjuror's Journal, 1978. *Memberships:* National Retired Teachers Association; Authors Guild; New England Historical and Genealogical Society; New England Audubon Society; Mystic Valley Railway Society; Radcliffe Club of Bsoton; New England Nature Conservancy. *Honours include:* Alternate Selection for Conjuror's Journal, Book of the Month Club, 1978. *Hobbies:* Golf; Hiking; Swimming; Body-surfing; Genealogical research; Gardening. *Address:* 17 Clark Street, Framingham, MA 01701, USA.

SHIPE Jamesetta Denise Holmes, b. 30 May 1956, Knoxville, Tennessee, USA. Public Relations Assistant;

Journalist. m. Able Shipely Jr, 10 Oct. 1987. 4 stepsons, 2 stepdaughters. *Education:* BS, Communications, Journalism, University of Tennessee, 1980; AS, Business, Cum laude, Cooper Institute, 1982; Currently studying, AS, Electrical Engineering Technology. *Appointments:* Public Relations Assistant, Federal Bureau of Investigation, Office of Public and Congressional Affairs, Washington, 1982- 83; Public Relations Assistant, Martin Marietta Energy Systems, Inc, Oak Ridge, 1983-. *Publications:* Editor, Knoxville Women's Center Magazine, 1978; Public Relations Coordinator, Wesley House Community Center and composed newsletter; Editor, FBI Today, radio show. *Memberships:* Sigma Delta Chi, Society of Professional Journalists; Smithsonian Institute; Associate Member, NAACP, Knoxville YWCA; University of Tennessee Alumni Association. *Honours:* Minority Newspaper National Scholarship, 1974-77; Knoxville PTA Scholarship, 1974. *Hobbies:* Aerobics; Physical fitness; Reading; Sports; Sewing; Writing; Old films; Theatre; Opera; Ballet; Symphony Orchestra. *Address:* 821 W Vanderbilt Drive, Oak Ridge, Tennessee, 37830, USA.

SHIPLEY V. Fern Wilson, b. 29 Sept. 1921, Manchester, Oklahoma, USA. Executive Recruiting President. m. 21 Jan. 1943, divorced 1968, 1 son, 1 daughter. *Education:* University of Colorado, 1961-62. *Appointments:* Cartwright Employment Agency, Consultant, 1969-71, Head Consultant, 1973-77; Manager, Consultant, Western Permanent Services, Boulder, 1972; President, Owner, Manager, Shipley Personnel Recruiting, Boulder, 1978- *Publications:* Research on Book: Executive Recruitment, 1987; Avid Oil Painter; Interior Design. *Memberships:* National Association of Personnel Consultants; Boulder Chamber of Commerce; Executive Female; Charter Member, Mountain View Methodist Church. *Honours:* Recipient, University of Ccolorado Wardenburg Student Health Centre for Volunteer Contribution, 1965; University of Colorado Honorary Degree, PHT, 1949. *Hobbies Include:* Reading; Travel; Oil Painting; Sewing; Swimming. *Address:* 7205 Ballygar Way, Elk Grove, CA 95758, USA.

SHIPPE Mary Lou, b. 25 Nov. 1942, Kansas City, Missouri, USA. Training Representative. m. Donald Louis Shippe, 13 Aug. 1966, 1 son, 1 daughter. *Education:* BA, Kansas University, 1964; Management teaching certificate, Los Angeles Community College Overseas, 1978; MPA, Oklahoma University, 1979; Doctoral candidate, Nova University. *Appointments:* Analyst, NSA, 1964-66, 1970-71; Instructor, Misawa English School, Tohuku Language School, Misawa, Japan, 1976-79; Manager, Town Centre, Columbia, Maryland, 1980-83; Training representative, Ford Aerospce Corporation, 1983-. *Memberships include:* Past president, various offices, ABWA; Citizen Ambassador, technology delegation, People to People, Australia & New Zealand, 1988; Board, vice president, President, Zonta Club, Baltimore; Past President, LWV; Board, Voluntary Action Centre; Chairman, thrift shop, Officers' Wives' Club; *Hobbies:* Travel; Cooking; Reading; Boating; Swimming. *Address:* 9573 Long Look Lane, Columbia, Maryland 21045, USA.

SHIRK Cynthia Marie(Mazurkiewicz), b. 16 Sept. 1954, St Paul, Minnesota, USA. Instructor of Music/ Voice. m. Craig Roger Shirk, 25 Oct. 1975. 1 son, 1 daughter. *Education:* BSc, St Cloud State University, St Cloud, 1977; Master of Music, Mankato State University, Mankato, 1984. *Appointments:* Instructor of Voice, Mankato State University, 1983-84; Instructor of voice and music theory, Bethany College, Mankato, 1986-87; Instructor of music and High Potential music, Mankato Public Schools, 1985-. *Publication:* Thesis: The Effects of Selected Vocalises on the Upper Voice Ranges of Primary Level Elementary School Children. *Memberships:* Treasurer, 1985-, Board of Directors of Minnesota Valley Chorale; District Representative, Minnesota Elementary Music Educators; Music Educators, National Conference, Minnesota Education Association; National Education Association; Choral Directors Association. *Honour:* Choral Scholarship, St Cloud State University, 1975 and 1976. *Hobbies:*

Composing; Writing; Drawing; Gardening and landscaping; Soprano soloist for Minnesota Valley Chorale. *Address:* 150 Stoney Creek Road, Mankato, Minnesota 56001, USA.

SHIRLEY Vera Stephanie (Steve), b. 16 Sept. 1933, Germany. Founder Director. m. Derek George Millington Shirley, 14 Nov. 1959. 1 son. *Education:* BSc Spec, Sir John Cass College, London. *Appointments:* Post Office Research Station, Dollis Hill, 1951-59; CDL, 1959-62; Founder Director, F I Group PLC, 1962-. *Publications:* Articles in professional journals, reviews. *Memberships:* FBCS, 1971; President, British Computer Society, 1989; CBIM, 1984; Trustee, Help the Aged; Patron, Disablement Income Group; National Council for Vocational Qualifications, 1986-89; Council, Industrial Society; Court of Assistants; Company of Information Technologists. *Honours:* OBE, 1987; Freeman, City of London, 1987; FRSA, 1985; Hon CGIA, 1989; Hon Fellow Manchester Polytechnic, 1989. *Hobby:* Sleep. *Address:* F I Group PLC, 300 The Campus, Maylands Avenue, Hemel Hempstead, Hertfordshire, England.

SHOOK Brenda Lee, b. 30 Nov. 1952, Newport Beach, California, USA. Research Anatomist, Experimental Neuroanatomy. *Education:* BA 1975, MA 1976, California State University, Stanislaus; PhD, Brandeis University, 1982; Postdoctoral Fellow of Developmental Neurobiology, UC Davis, 1982-85. *Appointments:* Visiting Lecturer and Scholar, University of California, Davis, 1982-85; UCLA School of Medicine, Department of Anatomy, 1985-. *Publications:* Scientific publications in: Developmental Brain Research; Proceedings of the National Academy of Science; Experimental Brain Research; Journal of Neuroscience Methods; Society for Neuroscience. *Memberships:* Society for Neuroscience; International Brain Research Organization; American Assoc. for the Advancement of Science; New York Academy of Science. *Honours:* Outstanding Junior in Psychology, 1974; Scholarship, Fellowship, Brandeis University, 1976-82; National Institute of Health Research Fellow, 1982-85; Biomedical Research Grant, 1987. *Hobbies:* Ink drawing; Graphic art; Music; Badminton. *Address:* 4810 Hollow Corner Rd., No 245, Culver City, CA 90230, USA.

SHORE Elizabeth Catherine, b. 19 Aug. 1927, Oxford, England. Medical Practitioner; Postgraduate Medical Dean. m. Rt. Hon. P D Shore, 27 Sept. 1951, 2 sons (1 deceased), 2 daughters. *Education:* St Bartholomews Hospital, London, 1948-51; MB, 1951; LRCP MRCS, 1951; FFCM, 1972; FRCP, 1985. *Appointments:* Assistant County Medical Officer: Hertfordshire 1954-55, London County Council, 1955-62; Medical Civil Service, 1962-84; Postgraduate Medical Dean, North West Thames Region, 1985-. *Publications:* numerous articles in professional journals. *Memberships:* BMA; Medical Womens Federation, Council Member, 1988; Child Accident Prevention Trust, Chairman of Council, 1985-. *Honour:* CB 1979. *Hobbies:* Swimming; Tennis; Cooking; Gardening; Opera; Modern Novel. *Address:* British Postgraduate Medical Federation, 33 Millman St., London W1N 3EJ, England.

SHORE Susan Ellen, b. 27 Aug. 1950, South Africa. Physiologist. m. Dennis Leslie Shore, 1970, divorced 1973, (2) Jun A Yates, 1980, divorced 1988, 1 son. *Education:* BA, 1972; MA, 1975; PhD, 1980. *Appointments:* Speech & Hearing Therapist, 1972-74; Teaching Assistant, Physiology, 1975-80; Postdoctoral Scholar, 1981-84; Faculty Research Position, 1985-88. *Publications:* Articles in: Science; Journal Acoustic Society of America; American Journal Otolaryngology. *Memberships:* Association for Research in Otolaryngology; Acoustical Society of America; American Association of Scientists; Sigma Xi. *Honours:* Recipient, various honours and awards. *Hobbies:* Running; Dance; Music; Child Rearing; Psychology. *Address:* 828 E 5 Mile Rd, Whitmore Lake, MI 48189, USA.

SHORT Clare, b. 15 Feb. 1946, Birmingham,

England. Member of Parliament. m. Alex Lyon, 19 Feb. 1981. *Education:* BA, Honours, Political Science, Leeds University. *Appointments:* Home Office, 1970- 75; Director, Affor (Community Organisation in Birmingham), 1976-77; Director, Youth-Aid, 1978-83; Member of Parliament, 1983-. Front Bench spokesperson on Employment 1984-. Member of the Labour Party National Executive Committee since 1988 *Publications:* Talking Blues - Study of the Relationship Between the Police and Young Blacks in Handsworth, 1978; Handbook of Immigration Law, 1980. *Membership:* National Union of Public Employees. *Hobbies:* Family; Dog; Swimming. *Address:* House of Commons, London SW1A 0AA, England.

SHOSHANA Shrira, b. 10 Mar. 1917, Poland. Writer; Journalist. m. Ariel Kohn, 1 son. *Education:* London University, 1925-38. *Appointments:* Journalist, Writer, 1939-. *Publications:* The Green River, stories, 1942; Bread of the Beloved, novel, 1950; The Gates of Gaza, novel, 1960; Thanks to the Fig Trees, stories, 1972; For Whom for Whom For Whom, childrens book, 1972; The Yellow Grass Widowers, stories, 1979. *Memberships Include:* Journalist Association of Israel; Hebrew Writers Association, Council Member, 1970-; PEN; Acum; etc. *Honours Include:* The Kessel Literary Prize, Mexican Jewery, 1950; The Usishkin Literary Prize, Jerusalem, 1960; The Tel-Aviv Municipality Award of literature, 1972; etc. *Hobbies:* Music; Painting. *Address:* 9 Bezalel St., Tel- Aviv, Israel.

SHOWALTER Gloria Hale, b. 28 Dec. 1949, Rehobeth, New Mexico, USA. Elementary School Assistant Principal. divorced, 2 sons, 1 daughter. *Education:* BA, 1975; MA, 1981. *Appointments:* Teacher, Kemper Elementary School, 1975-76; Teacher, 3rd Grade, Window Rock Elementary School, 1976-82; Assistant Principal, Fort Defiaance Elementary School, 1982-. *Publications:* Community Safety Profile Analysis, Indian Youth Safety, 1980. *Memberships:* Alpha Delta Kappa; Navajo Nation Association for the Education of Young Children, Past President, Board of Directors; American Indian Safety Council, Board; Arizona & American Association of School Administrators. *Honours:* National Indian Honour Society, 1982; Child Development Specialist Employee of the Year Award, 1974; Navajo Nation Scholarships, 1976, 1979-81. *Hobbies:* Music, Camping and Hiking, Reading, Traveling, Bowling and Jogging. *Address* PO Box 144, Window Rock, AZ 86515, USA.

SHULMAN Carole Karen, b. 25 Nov. 1940, Minneapolis, Minnesota, USA. Executive Director, Professional Skaters Guild. m. David Arthur Shulman, 26 Mar. 1962, 1 son, 3 daughters. *Education:* Colorado College, 1958-60; California Coast University, 1987-. *Appointments:* Professional Instructor, 1962-64; Skating Director, 1964-79, Consultant, 1979-, Rochester Figure Skating Club, Rochester, Minnesota; Executive Director, Professional Skaters Guild of America, 1984-. *Publications:* Editor, Professional Skater Magazine, 1984-. *Memberships:* Gamma Phi Beta; Professional Skaters Guild of America; Executive Producer, US Open Professional Figure Skating Championships; Past President, Rochester Area Council for the Arts; American Harp Society; Rochester Amateur Sports Commission. *Honours:* Master-rated in Figures, Freestyle, Pairs, Group, Choreography and Style, and Programme Administration, Senior-rated in Dance, Professional Skaters Guild of America; Triple Gold Medallist, United States Figure Skating Association; Outstanding Arts Volunteer in Rochester, 1986. *Hobbies:* Harpist; Skier. *Address:* PO Box 5904, Rochester, MN 55903, USA.

SHUTTLE Penelope Diane, b. 12 May 1947, Staines, Middlesex, England. Poet. m. Peter Redgrove, 1 daughter. *Publications:* 4 volumes poetry, 5 novels, 2 radio plays, numerous poems in magazines. Novels include: Excusable Vengeance, 1967; All the Usual Hours of Sleeping, 1969; Wailing Monkey Embracing a Tree, 1974; Rainsplitter in Zodiac Garden, 1977 (USA 1980, France 1981); Mirror of the Giant, 1980 (France

1989). Poetry collections include: Orchard Upstairs, 1980; Child-Stealer, 1983; Lion from Rio, 1986; Adventures with My Horse, 1988. Radio drama: Girl Who Lost her Glove, 1974; Dauntless Girl, 1978. Numerous contributions to anthologies, radio recordings, public readings. Also co- author with Peter Redgrove, various titles including The Wise Wound: Menstruation & Everywoman, 1978, 1980, updated 1986 (USA, Germany, Holland). *Honours:* Joint 3rd prize, Radio Times Drama Bursaries Competition, 1974; Arts Council awards, 1969, 1972, 1985; Greenwood Poetry Prize, 1972; E. C. Gregory Award, poetry, 1974. *Hobbies:* Walking; Playing piano; Cinema. *Address:* c/o David Highams Associates Ltd, 5-8 Lower John Street, Golden Square, London, England.

SIBLESZ Isabel Maria, b. 17 May 1962, Miami, USA. Business Education Instructor. *Education:* AA, 1981; BSc., 1983, MSc., 1986, Business Education, Florida International University. *Appointments:* Instructor, Miami-Dade Community College, 1982, 1983-85; Word Processing Supervisor, Miami Herald Publishing Co., 1983-88; Instructor, Miami Edison Middle School, 1988-. *Publication:* Article in Business Education Forum. *Memberships:* Dade County Business Education Association; Dade Association Adult & Community Education; Florida Vocational Association; Florida Association Supervisory & Curriculum Development; American Society of Notaries; NAFE. *Honours:* Recipient, many honours & awards. *Hobbies Include:* Reading; Writing; Racquetball; Photography. *Address:* 11880 SW 19 Lane No 173, Miami, FL 33175, USA.

SIBLEY Antoinette, b. 27 Feb. 1939. Prima Ballerina. m. (1) M G Somes, divorced 1973, (2) Panton Corbett, 1974, 1 son, 1 daughter. *Education:* Royal Ballet School. *Appointments:* First Performance on Stage as Student with Royal Ballet at Covent Garden, a swan, 1956; joined company, 1956; appeared with company or as guest artist in many countries; Leading Role in: Swan Lake; Sleeping Beauty; Giselle; Coppelia; Cinderella; The Nutcracker; La Fille Mal Gardee; Romeo and Juliet; Harlequinn in April; Les Rendevous; Jabez and the Devel (created role of Mary); Hamlet; Ballet Imperial; Two Pigeons; etc. *Publications:* Sibley and Dowell, by Nicholas Dromgoole and Leslie Spatt, 1976; Antoinette Sibley, 1981; Reflections of a Ballerina, by Barbara Newman, 1986. *Hobbies:* Doing Nothing; Opera; Books. *Address:* Royal Opera House, Covent Garden, London WC2, England.

SICHOL Marcia Winifred, b. 17 Oct. 1940, Lewiston, Maine, USA. Planning Director; Lecturor. *Education:* BA magna cum laude, Humanities, Villanova University, 1969; MA 1977, PhD 1984, Philosophy, Georgetown University. *Appointments:* Teacher, Assistant Principal, St Leonard's Academy, Rosemont School, 1961-70; Headmistress, Rosemont School, School of Holy Child, Drexel Hill, Pennsylvania, 1970-79; Assistant Dean, Rosemont College, 1979-80; Assistant Professor, Xavier University 1984-85; Neumann College 1985-88; Area Superior, Planning Director, American Province, Society of Holy Child Jesus, 1988-. *Publication:* Book, The Making of a Nuclear Peace: The Task of Todays Just War Theorists, 1989. *Memberships:* Society of Holy Child Jesus (SHCJ); Trustee, Rosemont College; Society of Christian Ethics. *Honours include:* Hubert Humphrey Fellowship, arms control & disarmament, 1983-84. *Hobbies:* Geology; Astronomy; Music; SKilng; Snorkeling. *Address:* 460 Shadeland Avenue, Drexel Hill, Pennsylvania 19026, USA.

SIDDELLEY Barbara, b. Dukinfield, Cheshire. Professor of Singing; Adjudicator; Singer; Music critic; Writer; Journalist. *Education:* Associate, Royal Manchester College of Music. *Appointments:* Adjudicator, Professor of Signing, Specialist Voice Coach, Number of performances in Opera, Oratorio and on stage in broadcasts and television; Many years work with Arts Council of Great Britain and BBC; Distinguished performances with World's leading singers and orchestras. Concert Director; Songs specially written for and dedicated to Barbara Siddelley by Michael Head and Gerald Gover. *Memberships:* British Federation of Music Festivals Adjudicator; Halle Society; Advisory Panel, American Biographical Institute. *Honours:* ARMCM (Honours), Royal Manchester College of Music; Hilary Haworth Memorial Prize for Lieder Singing. *Hobbies:* Walking; Motoring; Fashion; Horse Racing. *Address:* Linden Lea, 8A Old Road, Mottram-in- Longdendale, Cheshire, SK14 6LG, England.

SIEGEL Mary-Ellen, b. 12 Feb. 1932, New York City, USA. Writer; Social Worker. m. (1) Edgar Kulkin, 1951, 1 son, 2 daughters, (2) Walter Siegel, 24 Aug. 1980. *Education:* BA, City University, New York, 1974; MSW, Columbia University School of Social Work, 1976. Diplomate, National Association of Social Workers. *Appointments:* Department of Social Work, Mount Sinai Hospital, 1976-82; Senior Teaching Associate, Department of Community Medicine (social work), Mount Sinai School of Medicine, New York, 1982-. *Publications:* Author: Her Way: Guide to Biographies of Women for Young People, 1984, 1986; Reversing Hair Loss, 1985; Cancer Patient's Handbook, 1986. Co-author: What Every Man Should Know About His Prostate, 1983, revised 1988; More Than A Friend: Dogs With A Purpose, 1984; Suffering: Psychological & Social Aspects in Loss, Grief & Care, 1986; The Nanny Connection, 1987. *Memberships:* National Association of Social Workers; American Society of Journalists & Authors; Authors Guild; American Medical Writers Association; University Seminar Associate, Columbia University. *Hobbies:* Cooking; Swimming; Travel; Tennis. *Address:* 75-68 195th Street, Fresh Meadows, New York 11366, USA.

SIEGERT Barbara Marie, b. 22 May 1935, Boston, USA. Community Mental Health Director. m. Herbert Christian Siegert, 1958, 1 son, 1 daughter. *Education:* Diploma, Newton Wellesley Hospial School of Nursing, 1956; MEd., Antioch University, 1980. *Appointments Include:* Various Nursing Positions, 1956-59; Crisis Screening, 1959-73; Nursing Supervisor, Hogan Regional Centre, Hathorne, 1974-78; Community Mental Health Nursing Advisor, Cape Ann Area, Beverly, 1978-79; Director of Case Management, Dept. of Mental Health, Cape Ann Area Office, Beverly, 1979-88, Greater North Shore Area Office, Beverly, 1988-. *Memberships:* Fellow, American Board of Medical Psychotherapists, Massachusetts Nurses Association; Association for Research and Enlightenment. *Honours Include:* Special Recognition Award, 1973; Peter Torci Award, 1974; Citation for Outstanding Performance, State of Massachusetts Performance Recognition Programme, 1984; Vanguard Award Nominee, 1988. *Hobbies:* Travel; Metaphysics; Reading; Cultural Activities. *Address:* Greater North Shore Area, Dept. of Mental Health, 180 Cabot Street, Beverly, MA 01915, USA.

SIEMENS Barbara Anne Wolfe, b. 20 June 1922, Fremont, Ohio, USA. Architect. m. Miros Siemens, 26 Oct. 1946, 3 sons, 5 daughters. *Education:* BArch, Ohio State University, 1945; Registered Architect, Indiana, Ohio, New York. *Appointments:* Huszgath & Demuth, Architects, Chicago, Illinois, 1945-48, 1949-50; Herman C. Light, Architect, Los Angeles, 1948-49; Private practice, West Lafayette, Indiana, 1952-70; Chief Architect, H. Stewart Kline & Associates, Lafayette, 1970-. *Memberships:* Past President, offices, Central Southern Indiana chapter, American Institute of Architects; Past Board, Indiana Society of Architects, AIA; Offices, Wabash Centre Inc; Past Chapter President, National Association of Women in Construction; United Way of Lafayette. *Hobbies:* Travel; Skiing; Reading; Gardening. *Address:* H. Stewart Kline & Associates Inc, PO Box 1684, Lafayette, Indiana 47902, USA.

SIEMER Deanne C, b. 25 Dec. 1940, Buffalo, New York, USA. Lawyer. m. Howard P Willens, 21 Dec. 1977. 1 son. *Education:* BA, George Washington University, 1962; LLB, Harvard Law School, 1968. *Appointments:* Wilmer, Cutler & Pickering, 1968-77 and 1980-; General Counsel, US Department of Defense, 1977-80. *Publications:* Tangible Evidence; Manual on Litigation Support Databases. *Memberships:* American Bar Association; Board of Trustees, National Institute for Trial Advocacy; District of Columbia Bar Association. *Honours:* Commendation, The President of the United States; Defense Distinguished Service Medal. *Address:* Wilmer Cutler & Pickering, 2445 M St NW, Washington, DC 20037, USA.

SIKES Mary Montague Hudson, b. 1 Oct. 1939, Virginia, USA. Artist; Writer; Teacher. m. Olen H Sikes, 3 Aug. 1957, 3 daughters. *Education:* BA, Mary Washington College; Studio Courses, College of William and Mary; MFA, Painting, Virginia Commonwealth University. *Appointments:* Elementary School Teacher, 1957-60, 1966-67; Richmond News Leader-Writer, 1963-73; High School Teacher, French Art, 1967-81; Studio Artist, 1980-; Freelance Writer, 1984-. *Publications:* Numerous paintings in public & private collections in USA & Canada. *Memberships:* Richmond Artists Association, President 1986-88; Chesapeake Bay Pen Women, Vice President 1986-88; Romance Writers of America; Virginia Romance Writers, Treasurer, 1986-89; Maryland Pastel Society; Women's Caucus for Art. *Honours Include:* Guild Award, Peninsula Fine Arts Centre, 1980; Flambeau Award, Maryland Pastel Society, 1987; American Drawing Biennial, 1988. *Hobbies:* Tennis; Travel. *Address:* PO Box 182, West Point, VA 23181, USA.

SILBER Evelyn Ann, b. 22 May 1949, Welwyn Garden City, England. Museum Curator; Art Historian. *Education:* MA, 1972, PhD, 1982, Cantab; MA, University of Pennsylvania, USA, 1973. *Appointments:* Copywriter, Publicity Manager, A B Publishers Ltd., 1973-74; Addison Wesley Publishers Ltd., 1974-75; Lecturer, Art History, Glasgow Univesity, 1978; Curator, Fine Art, 1979-85, Assistant Director, 1985-, Birmingham Museums and Art Gallery. *Publications:* The Sculpture of Epstein, 1986; Jacob Epstein Sculpture and Drawings, 1987; articles in journals; author of catalogues. *Memberships:* Museums Association; Art Galleries Association; Association of Art Historians, Secretary 1972-73; Leverhulme Research Fellow, History of Art, Cambridge University, 1975-76. *Honours:* Thouron US/UK Fellowship, 1972-73. *Address:* Birmingham Museum and Art Gallery, Chamberlain Square, Birmingham B3 3DH, England.

SILBER Joan Karen, b. 14 June 1945, Millburn, New Jersey, USA. Writer. *Education:* BA, Sarah Lawrence College, 1967; MA, New York University, 1979. *Appointments:* Faculty, Sarah Lawrence College, 1985-; Warren Wilson College MFA Program for Writers, 1986-; University of Utah 1988. *Publications:* Novels: Household Words, Viking 1980, Penguin 1985; In The City, Viking 1987, Penguin 1988. *Memberships:* PEN; Authors League; Poets and Writers; Amnesty International; Sierra Club. *Honours:* NEA 1986; New York Foundation for the Arts, 1986; Guggenheim 1984-85; Ernest Hemingway Foundation Award, 1981. *Address:* 43 Bond Street, New York, NY 10012, USA.

SILBERT Mimi Halper, b. 29 Mar. 1942, Boston, USA. Company President. 2 sons. *Education:* BA, English, University of Massachusetts, 1963; MA, Counselling Psychology, 1965; PhD, Criminology & Psychology, 1968, University of California, Berkeley. *Appoinments Include:* Principal Investigator, NIMH Study, Sexual Assault of Prostitutes, 1979-82; President, CEO, Delancey Street Foundation, San Francisco, Los Angeles, New York, New Mexico, North Carolina, 1973-. *Publications:* Book Chapters; articles in professional journals. *Honours:* San Francisco Board of Supervisors, 1980, 1987; California State Legislature Award, 1987; San Francisco Suicide Prevention, Life Preservbation Award, 1987. *Address:* Delancey Street Foundation, 2563 Divisadero Street, San Francisco, CA 94115, USA.

SILK Susan, b. 20 Sept. 1945, Detroit, Michigan,

USA. Media Strategist; Trainer; Lecturer; Writer. *Education:* BEd, Michigan State University, East Lansing, 1967; MEd, Wayne State University, Detroit, 1971; Postgraduate studies, De Paul University, Chicago, 1980. *Appointments:* The Detroit News, Detroit, Michigan, 1971-84; WXYZ-TV (ABC), Detroit, 1975-76; WJBK-TV, CBS, Detroit, 1976-77; WNAC-TV, CBS, Boston, Massachusetts, 1977-78; WBBM-TV, CBS, Chicago, Illinois, 1978-85; President, Media Strategy Inc, Chicago, 1985-. *Memberships:* National Academy of Television Arts and Sciences; National Association of Women Business Owners; International Association of Business Communicators; American Society of Training and Development; Women in Communication Inc; Publicity Club of Chicago. *Honours:* Best Documentary Award for Spirit of Detroit, Michigan Associated Press, 1976; Best Documentary Award for Methadone-Licensed Excuses, and Best Community Service Award for documentary Sirens, New England Associated Press, 1977; Clarion Award for Sirens, National Women in Communication, 1978; Silver Medal for Beauty and the Bucks, International Film and Television Festival, 1984; Chicago EMMY for WBBM-TV documentary Notario Publico, 1984; Silver Gavel for Notario Publico, American Bar Association, 1984. *Hobbies:* Theatre; Cycling; Swimming; Bridge; Girl Scouts of America volunteer; Community volunteer work; Reading; Bowling; Cinema; Local satirist; Gardening. *Address:* Media Strategy Inc, 343 West Erie, Suite 220, Chicago, IL 60610, USA.

SILLUP Mary M, b. 25 Jan 1951, Long Island City, New York, USA. Marriage and Family Therapist. m. 26 Dec 1971, 1 son, 1 daughter. *Education:* BA, Education, William Paterson College, New Jersey, 1972; MS, Counselling, Psychology, Mental Health, Wright State University, Ohio, 1977; EdS, Counselling, Psychology, Seton Hall University, New Jersey, 1985. *Appointments:* Director, Family Counselling Programme, South Amboy Hospital, 1979-85; Director, Quality Assurance, CPC Mental Health Services, Adjunct Professor, Middlesex County College, New Jersey, 1987-; Private practice, Marlboro, New Jersey, 1986 -. *Publications:* Editorial Board, New Jersey Professional Counsellors Journal, 1985; Article: Family Therapy of Schizophrenics: An Article Review. *Memberships:* Past President, New Jersey Mental Health Counsellors Association; Clinical Member, American Association for Marriage and Family Therapy; Member, New Jersey Professional Counsellors Association. *Address:* 170 RT 9, Marlboro-Englishtown, NJ 07726, USA.

SILVER Ivy Ellen, b. 15 July 1955, New York, USA. Employee Benefits broker and Consultant. m. Steven Leshner, 30 Sept. 1982. 1 son, 1 daughter. *Education:* AA, Bucks County Community College, Newtown, Pennsylvania, 1976; Certificate Management, Harvard University, Cambridge, 1977; Certificate Management, Columbia University School of Business, New York, 1980; BBA Wharton University of Pennsylvania, Philadelphia, 1981. *Appointments:* Principal, Leshner, Silver & Associates, Philadelphia; Executive Director, The Children's Museum of North Eastern, Pennsylvania; Executive Director, Artmobile, Newtown, Pennsylvania. *Memberships:* Vice President and Director, Business Women's Network; Community Leadership Seminar Alumni Group Advisor; Pennsylvania Horticulture Society; Board of Advisor, University City Science Center Entreprenurial Management Resource Group. *Honours:* Outstanding Graduate Senior, Wharton Evening School, University of Pennsylvania, 1981. *Hobbies:* Art; Architecture; President, Beth Zion-Beth Isreal Playschool, 1987-89; President, The Photo Review, 1987-88; Director, The Bucks County Art Alliance, 1976-78; Board of Directors, The Greentowne School, 1988. *Address:* 1510 Walnut Street, Philadelphia, Pennsylvania 19102, USA.

SILVERMAN Catherine Sclater Parker, b. 9 Apr. 1921, Portland, Maine, USA. Historian. m. Joseph Silverman, 26 June 1953, 2 daughters. *Education:* BA, Sweet Briar College, Sweet Briar, Virginia, 1943; MA, History, City College of New York, 1964; PhD, History, City University of New York, 1972. *Appointments:* Lecturer, Instructor, US History, City College of New York, 1964-71; Visiting Assistant Professor, Hunter College, City University of New York, 1972; Assistant Professor, US History, State University of New York, Stony Brook, 1972-73; Investigator, 1972-77, Administrator, 1977-81, Director, Field Operations, 1981-83, Director, Federal Contracts, 1983-87, New York State Division of Human Rights; Associate Professor, New Jersey Community College, Mercer County, summers 1984, 1985; Adjunct Associate Professor, American History, City College, City University of New York, 1986-88. *Publications:* Dissertation: Of Wealth, Virtue, & Intelligence: The Triumph of the Redeemers of Virginia & North Carolina; Articles on Henry St George Tucker, Chas T.O'Ferrall, John E.(Parson) Massey, Henry DeleWarr Flood, in The Encyclopedia of Southern History, 1979; The South in the 19th Century; Trends in Black Reconstruction History, 1983; Review, Horace W.Raper's William W.Holden: North Carolina's Political Enigma, 1986. *Memberships:* American and Southern Historical Associations; Institute for Research In History; Organization of American Historians; Southern Association for Women Historians; Editorial Associate, Women's Foreign Policy Council. *Honours:* Graduate Research Fellow, History Department, City College of New York, 1963-64; Fellowships, 1966-67 (declined), 1967-68, American Association of University Women; NDEA Fellowship, 1966-68; Fellow, Center for the Study of Human Rights, Columbia University, 1985-86. *Hobbies:* Music; Sewing; Reading; Writing; The environment; Human rights. *Address:* 276-C Milford Lane, Jamesburg, NJ 08831, USA.

SILVERMAN Donna Lee, b. 20 June 1960, Lynn, Massachusetts, USA. Director of Personnel. *Education:* BA, Management & Psychology, Eckerd College, 1982; MS, Human Resource Management, Nova University, 1986; PHR (Professional in Human Resources) designation, Personnel Accreditation Institute, 1987. *Appointments:* Director of Personnel, Mass Mutual Life Insurance Co, 1984-; Adjunct Professor, Nova University, 1987-89; Part-time HRD Consultant, 1988-. *Memberships:* Board Member, Broward County National Multiple Sclerosis Society; Board of Directors, Plantation Chamber of Commerce; Chairman, Expo Task Force, 1988-89; Chairman, Speakers Bureau, 1987-88; Florida Speakers' Association, 1988-; American Society of Personnel Administrators, 1986-; Board of Governors, Personnel of Broward County, 1990-93, Personnel Association of Broward County, 1986-; Chairman, Student Chapter Liaison Committee, 1990-91. *Honours:* Thomas Presidential Scholarship, Eckerd College, 1978-82; National Register of Outstanding College Graduates, 1982; Plantation Business & Professional Women's Graduate Scholarship, 1985; Plantation Women's Club Graduate Scholarship, 1985-86; National Dean's List, 1986. *Hobbies:* Singing; Theatre; Reading; Travel. *Address:* 7027 West Sunrise Blvd, Plantation, FL 33313, USA.

SILVESTRIS Elaine Joy Gustafson, b. 8 Jan. 1943, Worcester, MA, USA. Manager. m. Maurice Richard Silvestris, 6 Nov. 1965. *Education:* Allentown College of St. Francis de Sales, Center Valley, PA, Courses of Study, BS Marketing, BA Business, 1988-89; Certificate, Human Resources, Moravian College. *Appointments:* Legal Secretary: 1961-77; Senior Stenographer, 1978-82, Workers' Compensation Supervisor, 1982-84, Manager, Employee Relations, US Postal Service. *Membershps:* National Association of Professional Saleswomen, Fund Raising Committee, 1987-; National Association for Female Executives; PA Society of Professional Engineers; National Society of Professional Engineers Auxiliary, President, Vice President, Secretary and PA State Delegate, 1978-84; Notary Public, Lehigh County PA, 1973-89. *Honours:* Certificate of Appreciation, Commonwealth of Pennsylvania Blindness & Visual Services, 1987. *Hobbies:* Gardening; Reading; Walking; Swimming. *Address:* 703 N. 21st Street, Allentown, PA 18104, USA.

SIME (Emmy Josephine) Mary, b. 28 Mar. 1911, Tollesbury, Essex, England. Educator of Teachers (formerly Principal Lecturer in Education, Choley College, Lancashire); Freelance Lecturer. *Education:* BA, University of London; Postgraduate Diploma of Education, Oxford University. *Publications:* A Child's Eye View, 1973; translated into Dutch, Swedish, Italian, German, Danish, Norwegian, Japanese, & Korean; Read Your Child's Thoughts, 1980, translated into Italian & Japanese; contributor to Developments in Mathematical Education, Editor, Howson (Proceedings of 2nd Int. Congress on Math. Edu., Exeter, 1972); various Quaker Journals, UK & USA & to professional journals including: Times Educational Supplement; Forebel Journal; Oxford Times; Primary Maths, Editorial Board. *Memberships:* London Yearly Meeting of the Society of Friends; British Comparative and International Education Society (GB BR., Founder Member); The British Society for Research into Learning Mathematics (Founder member) *Address:* 105 Mell Road, Tollesbury, Essex, England.

SIMMONS Adele Smith, b. 21 June 1941, Lake Forest, Illinois, USA. President, John D and Catherine T MacArthur Foundation. m. John Leroy Simmons, 18 Sept. 1966, 2 sons, 1 daughter. *Education:* BA, Radcliffe College, 1963; DPhil, Oxford University, UK, 1969. *Appointments include:* Dean, Jackson College, Tufts University, 1970-72; Assistant Professor of History, Dean of Student Affairs, Princeton University, 1972-77; President, Hampshire College, Amherst, Massachusetts, 1977-8. *Publications:* Maudern Mauritius, 1980; Articles, professional journals. *Honours:* Honorary LHD degrees: Lake Forest College, 1976; Amherst College, 1977; Franklin Pierce College, 1978; University of Massachusetts, 1982; Alverno College, 1986; Marlboro College, 1987; Mount Holyoke College, 1989; Smith College, 1989. *Address:* The John D. & Catherine T. MacArthur Foundation, 140 South Dearborn Street, Chicago, Illinois 60603, USA.

SIMMONS Belinda Mitchell, b. 30 June 1952, Albany, Georgia, USA. Technical Support. 1 son. *Education:* BA, Bus Educ, 1973; BS, Bus Adm, 1988. *Appointments:* Presentation Support Administrator, Georgia Power Company, 1974-. *Memberships:* Asst Secretary, American Association of Black in Energy; Past President, Women of Georgia Power; Electrical Women's Rioundtable; Natl Council of Negro Women. *Hobby:* Working with charities. *Address:* Georgia Power Co, 45 Technology Park, Norcross, GA 30092, USA.

SIMMONS Marie, b. 28 Oct. 1941, Montrose, Scotland. Headmistress. m. Bertram John Simmons, 16 July 1970, 1 son, 1 daughter. *Education:* BSc., Honours, 1963, Dip.Ed., 1965, Edinburgh University; ALAM; LRAM. *Appointments:* Research Chemist, Ferranti, 1963-64; Teacher, Housemistress, St George's School Edinburgh, 1965-72; Teacher, Housemistress, Fettes College, 1972-77; Headmistress, Cranborne Chase School, Wiltshire, 1982-. *Memberships:* Women in Management; Girls Schools Association, Secretary for SW England & Wales. *Hobbies:* Theatre; Opera; Reading; Gardening; Director, Somerset Opera Group, 1977-83. *Address:* Cranborne Chase School, Wardour Castle, Tisbury, Wiltshire, England.

SIMON Brona G., b. 14 Nov. 1951, Boston, Massachusetts, USA. Archaeologist. *Education:* BA magna cum laude, Anthropology, University of Massachusetts, Amherst, 1973; MA, Anthropology, University of New Mexico, 1976. *Appointments:* Principal Investigator/Resesarch Archaeologist, Public Archaeology Laboratory, Department of Anthropology, Brown University, 1977-82; Preservation Planner, 1982-84, State Archaeologist, 1984-, Director, Technical Services, 1986-, Massachusetts Historical Commission, Boston. *Publications include:* Prehistoric Settlement Processes in Southern New England: A Unified Approach to Cultural Resource Management and Archaeological Research (with P.Thorbahn, L.W.Loparto and D.C.Cox), 1980; Planning vs Crisis Management (with V.A.Talmage), 1986; Conservation and the Practicalities of the Real World. Planning for the Future of the Archaeological Resource Base, 1988; Various reports on archaeological sites and surveys; Presentations including: Contract Archaeology and Research Archaeology: Is there a Conflict?, 1984; The Double P Site, Bridgewater, Massachusetts, 1984; Promoting the Past into the Future: Practical Approaches to Site Protection, 1986; The States' Role in Archaeological Heritage Management in the United States, 1987; An Evaluation of the Results and Archaeological Benefits of the Implementation of the Unmarked Burial Law in Massachusetts, 1988. *Memberships:* National Assocaition of State Archaeologists (President 1986-88); Society for American Archaeology (Northeast Regional Conference Task Group 1984); Conference on New England Archaeology (Steering Committee 1987- 89); Massachusetts Archaeological Society Inc; Historic Massachusetts Inc. *Honours:* Phi Beta Kappa, 1973; Phi Kappa Phi, 1973. *Hobbies:* Mountain climbing; Swimming; Travel. *Address:* Massachusetts Historical Commission, 80 Boylston STreet, Boston, MA 02116, USA.

SIMON Doris Marie Tyler, b. 24 Jan. 1932, Akron, Ohio, USA. Registered Nurse; Nurse Manager; Transplant Coordinator. m. Matthew H Simon, CLU, LtCol retired Army, 20 Apr. 1952. 1 son, 3 daughters. *Education:* Assoc Degree Nursing, 1976; BSPA, Student. *Appointments:* Pharmacist Assistant, 1948-50; Medical Assistant, 1950-52, 1960-61 and 1967-70; Medical Assistant, Instructor, 1970-72; Music Teacher, Elem School, 1963-67; Choirs Dir, 1963-67 and 1970-73; Dialysis Instructor, 1977-87; Transplant Nurse Manager, 1977-. *Publications:* Home hemodialysis training book and manual; Patient teaching for transplants. *Memberships:* American Medical Assistants Assoc, President; Girl Scouts of America, Leader; American Nurses Assoc; Texas Nurses Assoc; American Nephrology Nurses Assoc; El Paso Chapter, American Nephrology Nurses Assoc, President; Links, Inc, Community Service. *Honours:* Delegation Member, Nephrology Nurse Ambassador People to People group to republic of China, 1988; Recipient of Molly Pitcher Award, US Army, 1966-67. *Hobbies:* Sewing; Singing; Pianist; Bicycling; Community service to youth rough fund raising for scholarships. *Address:* Transplant Coordinator, Providence Memorial Hospital, 2001 N Oregon St, El Paso, Texas 79902, USA.

SIMON Esther Borowski, b. 16 Aug. 1952, Israel. Architect. m. Roy Allan Simon, 8 Apr. 1979, 1 son, 1 daughter. *Education:* BArch cum laude, Israel Institute of Technology, 1976; MArch, full scholarship, Carnegie Mellon University, USA, 1978. *Appointments:* Moshe Safdie Architects Ltd, 1977; VVKR Partnership, Alexndria, Virginia, USA, 1978-79; Wilkes & Faulkner Associates, Washington DC, 1979-81; Weihe Partnership, Washington DC, 1981-. *Creative work includes:* Project Manager: Crystal Plaza Retail Renovation; Crystal Park Office Building no. 3; Chevy Chase Plaza; Portals Office Building B. *Membership:* American Institute of Architects. *Honour:* 1st female promoted associate, Weihe Partnership. *Hobbies:* Drawing & painting; International education; Assisting homeless. *Address:* The Weihe Partnership, Architects & Planners, 1666 K Street NW, Suite 1000, Washington DC 20006, USA.

SIMON Linda Ann, b. 13 July 1948, Lubbock, Texas, USA. Commercial Pilot (Captain). m. Col. Paul N. Simon, 25 May 1975, 2 sons, 1 daughter. *Education:* BS, Physical Educaitron, 1970, MEd., Supervision, 1972, Texas Christian University; PhD, Aviation management, Pacific Western University, 1985. *Appoiintments:* Teacher, Coach, Dept. of Def Overseas School System, Goose Bay, Labrador, Zama Japan, Machinato, Okinawa, 1972-75; Graduate Studies Co-ordinator, Pepperdine University, 1976-78; Flight Instructor, Charter Pilot, Augusta Avn., 1980-83; Chief Pilot, R W Allen Corp, 1983-84; Airline Pilot, Atlantic Southeast Airlines, 1984-88; Captain, Epps Air Service, 1989-. *Memberships:* National Association of Flight Instructors;

Airplane Owners & Pilots Asociation; Safety Officer, Civil Air Patrol, Airline Pilots Association. *Honours:* Texas State Water Skiing (Slalom) Champion, 1966-67. *Hobbies:* Sailing; Water Skiing; Tennis. *Address:* 3303 Cockatoo Road, Augusta, GA 30907, USA.

SIMON Maurya, b. 7 Dec. 1950, New York City, New York, USA. Adjunct Professor in Creative Writing. m. Robert Falk, 17 June 1973, 2 daughters. *Education:* University of California, Berkeley, 1968-71; BA, Pitzer College, 1980; MFA, University of California, Irvine, 1984. *Appointments:* University of California, Irvine, 1982-84; Pitzer College, 1983-84, 1985-86; Adjunct Professor, Creative Writing, University of California, Riverside, 1984-; Scripps College, 1986-87; University of Redlands, 1988. *Publications:* The Enchanted Room, poetry, 1986; Days of Awe, volume of poetry, 1989. *Memberships:* Modern Languages Association; Poetry Society of America; The Academy of American Poets; Vice- Moderator, Town Hall, Mt Baldy, California. *Honours:* University Award, Academy of American Poets, 1983; 1st Prize, National Federation of State Poetry Societies, 1984; 1st Prize, SCCA International Poetry Competition, 1987; 1st Prize, Georgia State Poetry Award, 1988; Appointed Judge, The Los Angeles Times Book Award in Poetry, 1988-90. *Hobbies:* Etymology; Entomology. *Address:* 28 San Antonio Falls, PO Box 0203, Mt Baldy, CA 91759, USA.

SIMON Wendy Lorraine, b. 14 July 1946, Kingswood, Bristol, England. Fine Arts Professor; Artist. nm. Jean-Pierre Simon, 3 Feb. 1972. *Education:* BSc, University of London, England, 1971; BFA, Concordia University, Montreal, Canada, 1980. *Appointments:* Research, Guy's Hospital Medical School, Pediatric Research Unit, 1966-71; Prof, School of Biophysics & Biochemistry, Unviersity of Havana, 1971-73; Studio Manager, La Guilde Graphique, Montreal, Canada, 1980-83; Professor, Fine Arts, Concordia University, Montreal, 1983-. *Creative works:* Numerous prints shown in solo and group exhibitions in Quebec, Canada and Europe, 1980-. *Memberships:* Vice President, Montreal Print Collectors Society; Vice President, Conseil Quebecois de L'Estampe. *Honours:* Purchase Award, Liberal Arts College, Concordia University, 1980; Govt Grant to Visit Viennale of Prints in Ljuljbiana Yugoslavia, 1987. *Hobbies:* Swimming; Walking; Natural history; Kendo; Music; Philosophy. *Address:* Dept of Printmaking & Photography, Faculty of Fine Arts, Concordia University, 1455 de Maisonneuve Blvd Qouest, Montreal, Canada.

SIMONE Debra Dannielle, h 29 Apr. 1955, New Haven, Connecticut, USA. Assistant Academic Dean; Professor of Art History. m. S P Rodgers. 2 sons, 1 daughter. *Education:* BA, Wheaton College, 1977; MAH, University of New Haven, 1984. *Appointments:* Instructor, University of New Haven, 1984-89; Professor of Art History 1986-; Assistant to Academic Dean for Admissions and Academics 1989-, Paier College of Art; Artist/Copiest, 1978-; Art Restoration, 1978-. *Creative works:* Original paintings; Copiest paintings; Published short story and poetry in The Noiseless Spider Literary Magazine; Art Critic for New Haven Register (Newspaper). *Memberships:* US Marine Corps, Officer Candidate School, Honorable Discharge; Association of Volunteers in Administration. *Hobbies:* Computers; Sculpture; Furniture resotration; Pottery; Automobile repair; Historical research; Farming (organic); Theatre set design; Carpentry. *Address:* Paier College of Art, 6 Prospect Court, Hamden, CT 06514, USA.

SIMONE Peggy, b. 1 Sept. 1935, Champaign, Illinois, USA. State Representative. m. Jack Simone, 6 June 1961. *Education:* BA, Rosary College, 1956. *Appointments:* Self-employed until 1975; Senior Editor, Better Homes & Gardens Magazine; Member, Florida House of Representatives. *Memberships:* Manatee County Republican Club; League of Women Voters. *Hobbies:* Duplicate Bridge; Cooking. *Address:* 4301-345th Street West, Suite C-14, Bradenton, FL 33505, USA.

SIMONS Frances Estelle Reed, b. 26 Apr. 1945, Vancouver, British Columbia, Canada. Paediatrician; Allergist; Clinical Immunologist. m. Keith John Simons, 21 Dec. 1968, 1 son, 1 daughter. *Education:* BSc, 1965, MD honours, 1969, University of Manitoba; Rotating Intern, Vancouver General Hospital, 1969-70; Paediatric Pathology Resident, 1970-71, Paediatric Resident, 1971-73, University of Washington and affiliated hospital, USA; Fellow in Allergy and Clinical Immunology. *Appointments:* Associate Professor, 1980-85, Professor, Head, Section of Allergy and Clinical Immunology, Deputy Chairman, 1985-, Department of Paediatrics and Child Health, University of Manitoba, Winnipeg, Canada. *Publications:* Over 100 including reports of original research, review articles and books. *Memberships:* Fellow, Member, Accreditation Committee and Committee on Drugs, American Academy of Allergy; Chairman, Allergy Section, Canadian Pediatric Society; Chairman, Royal College of Physicians, Committee on Clinical Immunology and Allergy Past President, Canadian Society of Allergy and Clinical Immunology; Founder, Past President, Manitoba Allergy Society. *Honours:* Centennial Prize in Medicine, University of Manitoba, 1969; Queen Elizabeth II Scientist Award, 1975-81; Rh Award for Outstanding Contributions to Medical Science, University of Manitoba, 1988; Chown Professorship, 1990. *Hobbies:* Travel; Music; Photography. *Address:* Section of Allergy and Clinical Immunology, Department of Pediatrics and Child Health, Room AE101, Children's Hospital of Winnipeg, 840 Sherbrook Street, Winnipeg, Manitoba, Canada R3A 1S1.

SIMONS Mary E, b. McIntosh, Alabama, USA. Librarian. m. (2)Paul A. Simons, 27 Aug. 1988, 1 son, 3 daughters by previous marriage. *Education:* BS, Alabama State University; MA, Xavier University. *Appointments:* Teacher, Cincinnati Public Schools, 1968-77; Librarian, Cincinnati Public Schools, 1977-. *Publications:* Module I, Future Leaders programme, 1987; Poetry: The National Library of Poetry; The World of Poetry; Tribute to Dr Martin Luther King, Junior. *Memberships:* Founder, President, Co-Ordinator of Program;me, Future Leaders Programme; Delta Sigma Theta; NAACP; Urban League of Cincinnati; National Council of Negro Women; Ohio Parent Teachers Association; Alabama State Alumni; Secretary, Sickle Cell Awareness Group. *Honours Include:* Cum Laude National Honour Society for Teachers, 1973; Teacher Appreciation Award, 1987; Delta Kappa Gamma Society International, 1988; Editor's Choice Award National Library of Poetry, 1988; Hon. mention, Merit-World of Poetry, 1988; Volunteer Service Award, Cincinnati Union Rethel, 1988; Phi Delta Kappa, 1989. *Hobbies:* Writing; Reading; Sewing; Working with Inner City Youth. *Address:* 1420 Kingsbury Drive, Cincinnati, OH 45240, USA.

SIMONS-NEWALL Joy, b. 5 Mar. 1929, Australia. Writer; producer; Lecturer. m. (1) Bernard Simons, 4 May 1957, 1 son, 2 daughters. (2) John Robert Newall, 8 Aug. 1987. *Education:* Sydney Kindergarten Training College. *Appointments:* Teacher, 1948-50; Education Director, 1950-54; Freelance Writer. *Publications Include:* Mr Dressup; Sesame Street; Nursery School Time; I Wish You Peace; Take-Off to USSR; Junk for Joy; Butternut Square; The Parks People. *Memberships:* Member, Composers Authors and Publishers of Canada Ltd.; Association Canadian Cinema Radio TV Artists; Children's Broadcast Institute. *Honours:* Best Children's TV Programme, 1978; CBI Award, 1978. *Hobbies:* Reading; Gardening; Cooking; Entertaining; Theatre. *Address:* 11920 Pilon Rd, RR1, Ladysmith, BC, Canada VOR 2EO.

SIMONSUURI Kirsti Katariina, b. 26 Dec. 1945, Helsinki, Finland. Professor; Writer. *Education:* PG Diploma, University of Edinburgh, Scotland, 1969; MA Honors, University of Helsinki, Finland, 1971; PhD, Cambridge University, England, 1977; Postgraduate studies, University of Strasbourg, France, 1975-76. *Appointments:* Professor of Comparative Literature, University of Oulu, Finalnd, 1978-81; Senior Research

Fellow, Academy of Finland, 1981-; British Academy Wolfson Research Fellow, 1981-82; Fulbright Visiting Scholar, Harvard University, USA, 1984-86; Visiting Scholar, Columbia University, USA, 1986-88. *Publications:* Numerous collections of poetry including: The Ivy Balustrade 1980; The Abduction of Europa, 1984. Fiction: The Northern Nightbook, 1981; The Devil Boy, 1986. Scholarship Essay: Homer's Original Genius, 1979. Numerous essays, critics *Memberships:* International PEN; Finland's Writers' Association; MLA. *Honours:* J H Erkko Prize, Best First Book in Finland, 1980; British Academy Wolfson Fellowship Award, 1981; Osk Huttunen Centenary Fellowship Award (Finland's Rhodes), 1971; Fulbright Postdoctoral Fellowship, 1984. *Hobbies:* Visual Arts; Wilderness. *Address:* c/o Academy of Finland, Ratamestarinkatu 12, 00520 Helsinki, Finland.

SIMPSON Diana, b. 26 Sept. 1929, England. Principal Consultant. m. W. Gordon Simpson, 2 Apr. 1960. *Education:* MRSH, 1961; FRSH, 1966; MPhil, 1970; PhD, 1974; C.Chem.FRSC, 1975; FPRI, 1979. *Appointments:* Imperial Chemical Industries Ltd., 1945-53; Pfizer Ltd., 1953-60; Part-time Teaching & Lecturing, 1960-64; Bakelite Xylonite Ltd., 1964-75; Principal Consultant, Analysis For Industry, 1975-. *Publications:* Chromatography of Ester Plasticizers; Antioxidants, U V Absorbers, Stabilizers, in The Analyst; contributions to various journals and magazines. *Memberships:* Royal Society of Chemistry, Council Member, Professional Affairs Board, Committees of Education, Analytical and Industrial Division, etc; UK Delegate to International Standards Organization; Fellow, Royal Microscopical Society. *Honours:* Distinguished Service Award, Analytical Division, Royal Society of Chemistry, 1984. *Hobbies:* Reading; Watching Cricket; Swimming; Compiling & Solving Crosswords. *Address:* Analysis For Industry, Factories 2/3, Bosworth House, High St., Thorpe Le Soken, Clacton-on- Sea, Essex CO16 0EA, England.

SIMPSON Jacqueline Mary, b. 25 Nov. 1930, Worthing, Sussex, England. Author. *Education:* BA, Honours, London, 1952; MA, London, 1955; DLit, London, 1980. *Appointments:* Honorary Editor, Folklore, the journal of the Folklore Society, London, 1979-. *Publications:* Penguin English Dictionary, (with G N Garmonsway), 1964; The Northmen Talk, 1964; Beowulf and its Analogues, (with G N Garmonsway), 1968; Everyday Life in the Viking Age, 1967; Icelandic Legends and Folktales, 1971; The Folklore of Sussex, 1973; The Folklore of the Welsh Border, 1976; The Viking World, 1980; British Dragons, 1980; European Mythology, 1987; Scandinavian Folktales, 1988. *Memberships Include:* Folklore Society, Committee Member, 1966-; Viking Society for Northern Research. *Address:* 9 Christchurch Road, Worthing, West Sussex, BN11 1JH, England.

SIMPSON Mary Michael, b. Evansville, Indiana, USA. Priest; Psychoanalyst. *Education:* BA, BS, Journalism, Texas Woman's University, 1946; Diploma, New York Training School for Deaconesses, 1949; Certificate, Westchester Institute for Training in Psychoanalysis & Psychotherapy, 1976; Certified Psychotherapist, 1980; STM, General Theological Seminary, 1982. *Appointments:* College Worker, Parish Assistant, St Barnabas Church, Denton, 1948-50; Misisonary, Holy Cross Mission, Liberia, 1950-52; Entered Order of St Helena, Vails Gate, New York, 1952-61; Ordained Deacon, 1974-77; Ordained Priest, Canon Residentiary, Cathedral of St John the Divine, 1977-; Priest in Charge, St John's Church, Wilmot, 1987-. *Publications:* Contributor to professional journals. *Memberships Include:* National Association for the Advancement of Psychoanalysis & the American Board for Accreditation & Certification; New York State Association of Practicing Psychotherapists. *Honours:* 1st Woman Religious to be Ordained to the Priesthood in Modern Times; First Woman Canon Residentiary of a Cathedral in Modern Times; First Ordained Woman to preach in Westminster Abbey, 1978; First Woman Candidate for the Episcopacy in Modern Times, 1979.

Address: 225 East 95th Street No. 3B, New York, NY 10128, USA.

SIMPSON Myrtle Lillias, b. 5 July 1931, Aldershot, England. m. Hugh Simpson, 21 Mar. 1959, 3 sons, 1 daughter. *Appointments:* Lecturer, Extra Mural Department, Aberdeen University, Scotland, 1970-; Lecturer, Writer at Large Scheme, Scottish Arts Council. *Publications:* 5 Travel Books; 2 biography; 7 Childrens books, numerous articles; Broadcaster & Lecturer, 1950-; First Woman to Ski across Greenland Ice Cap, 1965- various 1st ascents in Peru & Himalayas, 1950-88; Attempted to Ski to North Pole, 1969. *Memberships:* PEN, Former Committee Member; Scottish Ski Club; Scottish National Ski Council, ex Chairman; etc. *Honours:* Munro Park Medal for Exploration in Artic Regions. *Hobbies:* Skiing; Climbing; Canoeing. *Address:* Farletter, Kincraig, Inverness-shire, Scotland.

SIMS Joan, b. 1930, London, England. Actress. *Creative Works:* Films Include: Dry Rot; Off the Record; No Time for Tears; Just My Luck; The Naked Truth; The Captain's Table; Passport to Shame; Emergency Ward 10; Most of the Carry On films; Doctor in Love; Watch Your Stern; Twice Round the Daffodils; The Iron Maiden; Nurse on Wheels; Doctor in Clover; Doctor in Trouble; The Garnett Saga; Not Now Darling; Don't Just Lie There Say Something; Love Among the Ruins; One of Our Dinosaurs Is Missing; Till Death Us Do Part;' The Way of the World; Deceptions. Television: Born and Bred; Worzel Gummidgel; Ladykillers; Crown Court; Cockles; Fairly Secret Army; Tickle on the Tum; Miss Marple; A Murder is Announced; Hay Fever; In Loving Memory; Drummonds; Farrinton of the F.O.; Dr Who. *Address:* c/o John Mahoney, 30 Chalfont Court, Baker Street, London, England.

SIMS Margarita Maria, b. 16 Sept. 1964, New Orleans, USA. Music Therapist. *Education:* BMT, Loyola University of the South, 1986. *Appointments:* Music Therapist: Willow Wood Home for the Jewish Aged, 1986-87, Therapy Associates of Louisiana, 1988, June Collins Pulliam and Associates, 1988; Music Therapist, University of Texas Medical Branch, 1988-. *Memberships:* National Association for Music Therapy Inc; Former Member, National Association for Music Therapy Students. *Honours:* Alpha Sigma Nu; Blue Key; Mu Alpha theta; Tri-M National Music Honour Society; Freedom's Foundation Award, 1980. *Hobbies:* Faith Development; Theatre. *Address:* 3401 Nashville Avenue, New Orleans, LA 70125, USA.

SIMSON-VALENTINE Jo Anne, b. 19 Nov. 1936, Chicago, Illinois, USA. Professor of Anatomy. m. (1) Arnold Simson, 11 June 1960, (2) Michael Smith, 10 Nov. 1971. 3 daughters. *Education:* BA, Kalamazoo College, 1959; MS, University of Michigan, 1961; PhD, State University of New York (SUNY), Syracuse, 1969. *Appointments:* Instructor, Anatomy, SUNY, 1967-68; Postdoctoral Fellow, Temple University Health Science Centre, 1968-70; Assistant Professor, Pathology 1970-75, Associate Professor, Anatomy 1976-82, Professor 1982-, Medical University of South Carolina. *Publications:* 52 scientific papers in refereed journals; 5 short stories, 4 poems, literary magazines; Editorial board, Anat Rec, 1974-84. *Memberships:* Past Secretary, Histochemical Society; Council 1985-89, American Association of Anatomists. *Honours:* Phi Beta Kappa, 1959; Predoctoral fellowships, National Science Foundation 1959, National Institutes of Health 1966-67; Fogarty Senior International Fellowship, 1987-88; Science fiction project award, 1985. *Hobbies:* Writing; Camping; Hiking. *Address:* 1760 Pittsford Circle, Charleston, South Carolina 29412, USA.

SINCLAIR Olga Ellen, b. 23 Jan. 1923, Watton, Norfolk, England. Writer. m. Stanley George Sinclair, 1 Apr. 1945. 3 sons. *Appointments:* ATS, War Service, 1942-45; Housewife; Writer. *Publications:* Man at the Manor, 1966; Man of the River, 1967; Hearts by the Tower, 1968; Bitter Sweet Summer, 1969; Wild Dreams, 1971; My Dear Fugitive, 1975; Never Fall in

Love, 1976; Master of Melthorpe, 1978; Tenant of Binningham Hall, 1975; Where the Cigale Sings, 1976; Gypsy Julie, 1979; Orchids from the Orient, 1986; When Wherries Sailed By, 1987; Gretna Green, 1989. Childrens' Books: Gypsies, 1967; Dancing in Britain, 1970; Children's Games, 1972; Toys and Toymakers, 1974; Gypsy Girl, 1981. As Ellen Clare: Ripening Vine, 1981. As Olga Daniels: Lord of Leet Castle, 1984; The Gretna Bride, 1986; The Bride from Faraway, 1987; The Untamed Bride, 1988. *Memberships:* Society of Authors; Society of Women Writers & Journalists; Romantic Novelists Association. *Hobbies:* Folk dance; Gardening; Walking; Reading; Family. *Address:* Dove House Farm, Potter Heigham, Norfolk, NR29 5LJ, England.

SINDHU Avinash, b. 6 Nov. 1947, Jalandhar, India. Teaching. *Education:* BA, 1965; MA, Political Science, 1967; MA, Physuical Education, 1967; PhD, German College of Physical Culture, Leipzig, German Democratic Republic, 1983. *Appointments:* Director of Physical Education, College of Education, 1970-72; Lecturer 1972-84, Reader in Sport Psychology 1984-, Lakshmibai National College of Physuical Education. *Publications:* Contributor to professional journals and magazines on sports and physical education. *Memberships:* Selector, Indian Universities Women Hockey Team and Indian Women Hockey Team; Executive Member, Sport Psychology Association of India. *Honours:* Gold Medal, Physical Education; Recipient of numerous awards and scholarship for outstanding performance in sport at University, State and National level. Captain ed Hockey Team, 1968 & 1970, and Volleyball, 1970; Represented India 8 times for Hockey and twice for Volleyball. *Hobbies:* Reading; Gardening; Interior Decoration; Sewing. *Address:* Lakshmibai National College of Physical Education, Shaktinagar, Gwalior - 474 002 (MP), India.

SINGER Sarah Beth, b. 4 July 1915, New York City, USA. Poet. m. Leon E. Singer, 23 Nov. 1938, 1 son, 1 daughter. *Education:* BA, 1934; Graduate studies, 1963-66. *Appointments:* Private tutor, poetry techniques, 1934-; Consulting Editor, Poet Lore, 1976-81; Executive Director, Poetry Society of America, Long Island, 1979-83; Teacher, poetry seminars & workshops, YMCA, YWCA, Queens, New York, 1981-83. *Publications:* Books of Verse: After the Beginning, 1975; Of Love & Shoes, 1987. *Memberships include:* Past Vice president, Poetry Society of America, 1960-; Member 1957-, Poetry Chair, Long Island branch 1957-87, National League of American Penwomen; Poets & Writers, 1979-. *Honours:* Numerous poetry awards, 1968-. Most recent include: Pasadena branch, NLAP, 1984; Lyric Poetry Magazine, 1085; Alexandria branch, NLAP, 1985; Biennial Owl Award, Seattle branch, NLAP, 1988. Numerous biographical recognitions. *Hobbies:* Music; Reading; Travel. *Address:* 2360 43rd Avenue East, Unit 415, Seattle, Washington 98112, USA.

SINGH Nikky Guninder Kaur, b. 10 Oct. 1956, Ferozepur, India. Assistaant Professor, Philosophy/Religion. *Education:* BA, Wellesley College, 1978; MA, University of Pennsylvania, 1982; PhD, Temple University, 1986. *Appointments:* University of Northern Arizona, Flagstaff, 1985- 86; Assistant Professor, Colby College, 1986-. *Publications:* Book: The Guru Granth Sahib: Its Physics and Metaphysics; Papers: Nur and Jyotio: A Comparative Analysis; Otherworld in This World: An Indian Interpretation of The Yamamba. *Memberships:* American Academy of Religion; Phi Beta Kappa, Membership Committee; Women's Studies. *Honours:* PhD with distinction, 1986; Outstanding Young Women of America Award, 1985; Phi Beta Kappa, 1978; Durant Scholar, 1978; Meiling Soong Award for best research paper, 1976; Daughters of the American Revolution Award, 1974. *Hobbies:* Writing; Travelling; Aerobics; Music. *Address:* Taylor Hall, Colby College, Waterville, ME 04901, USA.

SINGLETARY Eloise, b. 21 Aug. 1942, Lake City, USA. Business Education Teacher. *Education:* BS, Fayetteville State University, 1973; M.Ed., 1978; MEd., School Administration, 1982. *Appoiintments:* Lake View

High School, Business Teacher, 1969-76; Hemingway High School, Business Teacher, 1976-83; Business Teacher, Florence Area Vocational Centre, 1983-. *Memberships:* NAACP; National Business Educators Association; National Education Association; NAFE; Association for Supervision & Curriculum. *Honours:* Recipient, many honours & awards. *Hobbies:* Reading; Spectator Sports; Tennis; Sewing; Collecting Patterns. *Address:* Route 3, Box 202A, Lake City, SC 29560, USA.

SISK Rebecca Benefield, b. 22 Aug. 1936, Randloph County, Alabama, USA. College Professor. m. Rodney R. Sisk, 15 Mar. 1957, 1 son, 1 daughter. *Education:* BSc., 1957; MHE, 1961. *Appointments:* Teacher, Home Economics,, 1960-67; Teacher, Woodham High School, 1967-68; Professor, Pensacola Junior College, 1968-. *Publications:* Textiles Lab Manual and Study Guide; Fashion Internship Workbook; Programmed Independent Study in Clothing Design; Design & Patternmaking Workshop; Pride of Pensacola Cookbook Chairman. *Memberships:* American, Florida Home Economics Associations; American Vocational Association; Florida Vocational Association; *Honours:* Omicron Nu; Phi Delta Kappa; Delta Kappa Gamma. *Hobbies:* Tailoring; Interior Design; Reading; Writing. *Address:* Dept. of Home Economics, Pensacola Junior College, 1000 College Blvd., Pensacola, FL 32504, USA.

SISSON Verda M, b. 16 Dec. 1945, Ann Arbor, USA. Classification Director. 1 son, 1 daughter. *Education:* AS, 1971; BS, Eastern Michigan University, 1978. *Appointments:* Head Counsellor, STOP, Lansing Programme, 1981; Co-ordinator, Ingham Inter School District, Dept. of Correction, Mason, 1983-. *Memberships:* American Correction Organisation; Michigan Correction Organisation; National Association Negro Women; NAACP. *Hobbies:* Camping; Sewing. *Address:* 36 South Hewitt Rd, No 103, Ypsilanti, MI 48197, USA.

SITARZ Paula Gaj, b. 25 May 1955, New Bedford, MA, USA. Freelance Writer. m. Michael James Sitarz, 26 Aug. 1978, 1 son, 1 daughter. *Education:* BA, Smith College, 1977; MLS, Simmons College, 1978; Diploma, Institute of Childrens Literature, 1983. *Appointments:* Children's Librarian, Thomas Crane Public Library, 1978-84; Director, Readers Theatre Workshop, 1985. *Publications:* Picture Book Story Hours : From Birthdays to Bears, 1986. *Memberships:* New England, Massachusetts Library Associations; Beta Phi Mu. *Honours:* Appointed to Mayor's Advisory Board, Office of Tourism and Cultural Affairs, City of New Bedford, 1087. *Hobbies:* Singing, Theatre, Volunteer. *Address:* 26 Swanson Drive, So. Dartmouth, MA 02748, USA.

SIBA Noreen Edith, b. 9 Sept. 1949, Birmingham, England. Charity Director. *Education:* BSc, Sociology, Aston University, 1970; Postgraduate Certificate, Community Work, Leicester University, 1971. *Appointments:* Research & Development Officer 1970-71, Director, Young Volunteers 1971-73, Birmingham Council of Social Services; Community Development Officer, Lewisham Social Services Department, London, 1973-75; Specialist Community Worker, mentally & physically handicapped children & their families, London Borough of Wandsworth, 1975-79; Director, Contact a Family, national charity for handicapped children & their families, 1979-88; Director ADS, 1988-; Chair, NSHSC, 1987-90. *Hobbies include:* League, tournament & social tennis & squash; Badminton; Cycling; Walking; Camping; Home & garden; Local village involvement, including Treasurer, Woodmansterne Village Hall, representative, Woodmansterne Festival & Sports Club committees. *Address:* The Seven Hurdles, Tonbridge Close, Woodmansterne, Surrey SM7 3JD, England.

SKALSKY Cheryl Colleen, b. 4 Jan. 1944, Kenmare, N Dakota, USA. Social/Business Administrator; Executive Director. m. Duane, 24 Aug. 1963. 2 sons. *Education:* University of ND, 1963, 1981; N VA Community College, 1976; Minot State College, 1977, 1982; Pima Community College, 1986-88; University of Phoenix, 1987-89; Licensed Social Worker, 1984; Bachelor of Science, Business admin, 1989. *Appointments:* Reporter/Columnist, Beulah Beacon, 1977-79; Executive Director, Mercer County Women's Action and Resource Center, 1979-86l; Executive Director, Pima Council on Developmental Disabilities, 1986-. *Memberships:* Resources for Women, Group Leader; Eagles Auxiliary No 3728 President; Business and Prof Women, Treasurer; ND Council on Abused Women, vice president; ND Governor's Council on DUI, Ex officer; Council Woman, Oro Valley; Tucson Commission on Handicapped, Chair, Human Rights and Ethics Committee. *Hobbies:* Politics; Equestrian; Human rights; Bridge; Singing; Painting; Writing. *Address:* 9110 N Shadow Mountain Drive, Oro Valley, AZ 85737, USA.

SKARD Torild, b. 29 Nov. 1936, Oslo, Norway. Director General. m. Kare O Hansen, 20 July 1977. *Education:* Teachers' College, Oslo, 1958; BA 1962, MA 1965, Oslo University; Certificate as Psychologist, 1975. *Appointments:* Teacher, Oslo, 1954-61; Psychologist, 1965-67; Lecturer, Norwegian Post Graduate Teachers' College for Special Education, 1965-72; First lecturer, Institute for Social Sciences, University of Tromso, 1972-73; Member of Parliament, President of the Lagting (Senate) and vicepresident, judiciary committee, Norway, 1973-77; Senior researcher, Work Research Institutes, Oslo and leader, Norwegian National Commission for UNESCO, 1978- 84; Director, UNESCO, Paris, France, 1984-86; Director General, Multilateral Department, The Royal Norwegian Ministry of Development Cooperation. *Publications:* Books include: New Radicalism in Norway, editor, 1967; Youth in Youth Clubs, 1970; What Happens in Primary School? 1971; Workshop for Self-confidence, about Youth in Youth Clubs, 1973; It is Oslo that is Remote, 1974; Half of the Earth, Introduction to Women's Politics, 1977; Women's Coup, editor, 1979; Cnosen for Parliament - A Study of Women's Progress and Men's Power, 1980; Everyday Life in Parliament - Personal Experiences, 1981; The Unfinished Democracy-Women in Nordic Politics, co-editor and author, 1983; From Harem to Equality, about Women in Other Cultures, co-editor, 1984; You Pay a Price to be a Tough Guy-Especially if You are a Woman: Women Journalists in Norway, 1984; Norwegian Local Councils-a Place for Women? co-author, 1985. *Memberships:* Norwegian Sociological Association; Norwegian Civil Servant Organization; The Norwegian Women's Rights Organization; Forum for Women Writers; Norwegian University Women; Amnesty International; Humanist Society; The Norwegian Association for Conservation of the Environment; The Socialist Left Party. *Address:* Multilateral Department, The Royal Norwegian Ministry of Development Co-operation, P O Box 8142 Dep, 0033 Oslo 1, Norway.

SKELLEY Eva, b. Oct. 1932, Prague, Czechoslovakia. Managing Director. m. Francis Jeffrey Skelley, 26 July 1957, 1 daughter. *Education:* MA (English & Russian), 1956; PhD (English Literature), 1968; Charles University, Prague. *Appointments:* Journalist, English Section, Czechoslovak Radio, Prague, 1956-57; Managing Director, Collets International Bookseller's Publishers, Subscription Agents, Denington Estate, Wellingborough, Northants. *Creative Works:* PhD Thesis: Women Characters in the Novels of Sir Walter Scott. *Hobbies:* Music; Gardening; Skiing. *Address:* 19 Baskerville Road, London SW18 3RW, England.

SKOMPSKA Lucyna Krystyna, b. 6 Jan. 1949, Lodz, Poland. Writer. m. Jan Czerny, 3 Nov. 1984, deceased 1985. *Education:* MA, University of Lodz, 1974. *Publications:* Poetry: Milosc smierc totalizator sportowy, 1974; Dopoki plonie, 1981; Bez powodu, 1986. Books for Children: Wakacje na Guziku, 1986; Przygody kota Kacpra i myszki Lulu, 1987. *Memberships:* ZLP; Society of Polish Writers. *Honour:* Literary scholarship, Andrzej Bursa, 1975. *Hobbies:* Classical music; Painting; Plants. *Address:* ul. Zgierska 110/120 m.15, 91-303 Lodz, Poland.

SKULAS Irene Michelle, b. 21 July 1951, Toledo,

Ohio, USA. Instructor; Researcher. *Education:* BEd, Intensive Sciences, 1973; MA, MEd, Physical Anthropology, Education, 1975; PhD, Health, 1982. *Appointments:* Instructor 1973-, Chair, Science Department 1978-, Bedford Public Schools; Summer instructor, home-bound instructor (intermittent), Washington Local Schools, 1978-; Consultant, 1982- . *Publications:* Experimental Communications Between Homo Sapiens & Tursiops Truncatus, 1975; Health Risks Associated With Asbestos, dissertation, 1982; Science Curriculum, Bedford Public Schools, 1985; Pamphlet, Some Facts About Steroids, 1986. *Memberships:* Past office, American Chemical Society; National, Michigan & Bedford Education Associations; American Public Health Association; National Science Teachers Association. *Honours include:* 3 Grants, National Science Foundation, 1978-; Various recognition awards, scholastic honours. *Hobbies:* Cooking, vegetarian & macrobiotic; Athletic training; Lobbyist, consumer health issues; Preservation of marine mammals; International travel, especially for comparative education observations; Health & safety in public schools. *Address:* Bedford Senior High School, Temperance, Michigan 48182, USA.

SLAPPEY Mary McGowan, b. 22 Nov. 1914, Kitrell, North Carolina, USA. Writer; Artist; Publisher. *Education:* AB, George Washington University, 1947; JD, 1987; Honorary Certificate (10 years study Fine Arts), Corcoran Gallery School. *Appointments:* American Red Cross, 1930's; US Navy, 1943-46; Teacher, Business College, 1950'2; Editor, National Neuman Apostolate, USCC, 1960's; Freelance Writer; Artist. *Creative Works:* Oil painting: Compositions and illustrations. Books: Exploring opportunities of Women in Military Service, 3rd edition; Glory Wooden Walls; Muscle of Believing, Poetry; Plum Blossom; Plays: Amethyst Remembrance, etc. *Memberships:* Federal Poets Aff. Natl. Association State Poetry Societies Chapter Pres, 1981-83; George Washington University Columbian Women, Historian, 1981-83; National League American Pen Women; Retired Officers Association, etc. *Honours:* US Navy Commendation, 1945; Honorary Cultural Doctorate Literature, World University, 1981; Alumni Certificate of Distinction, Central High School, 1981; Diplomas, Gold Medals, Victory Accademia Italia del Arts and La Da Vinci Society, 1980; Laurel Wreath, World Poetry Association, 1978. *Hobbies:* Flowers and garden; Gourmet cooking; Reading; Writing; Art. *Address:* 4500 Chesapeake St, NW, Washington, DC 20016, USA.

SLATER Andrea Theresa, b. 10 Nov. 1958, Troy, New York, USA. Engineering Section Head, New Product Development. m. Jeffrey Clark Slater 26 Sept. 1982, divorced 1989. 1 son. *Education:* BSc, Mechanical Engineering, 1981, BSc, Biology 1981, Union College, New York. *Appointments:* Mechanical Engineer I, Instrumentation Laboratory, Lexington, MA, 1981-82; Product Development Engineer 1982-83, Project Engineer 1983-85, Senior Project Engineer 1985-87, Engineering Section Head 1987-, New Product Development, USCI Division, C R Bard Inc, Billerica, MA. *Memberships:* American Association for the Advancement of Science; National Association of Female Executives; Society of Plastics Engineers; American Society of Mechanical Engineers; Society of Women Engineers; International Platform Association. *Hobbies:* Nautilus; Aerobics; Volleyball; Travel; Calligraphy. *Address:* USCI Division, C R Bard Inc, 129 Concord Road, Billerica, Massachusetts 01821, USA.

SLATER Kay Frances Ross, b. 20 Sept. 1942, Iowa City, Iowa, USA. Business Woman. m. Richard Edward Slater, 10 May 1986. 1 son, 1 daughter. *Education:* CSU, San Diego, 1965; MBA, Nat Univ, 1984; Postgraduate courses, UCSD and CSUSD; Business and Industrial Managment, Marketing and Sales, Community College, 1984. *Appointments:* Career Teacher, San Diego City Unif School District, 1965-74; Senior Sales positions, BF Ascher, GD Searle and Stuart Inc, 1974-81; Director of Marketing and Medical Seminar Presentations, San Diego Foundation for

Medical Care, 1982-84; Director of Site Operations, Western Health Medical Clinics, Inc, 1985-86; Administrator, Harbor Medical Center, 1988-; Internal Medical Specialty Group; Instructor, Medical Management Courses, Moorpark College, 1986-89; Instructor, English as a Second Language, Simi Valley Adult School, 1988-89; President/Owner, Ross Resources & Associates, 1984-. *Memberships:* Association of Adult Cal Educators; Medical Group Management Association; California Medical Group Managers Association, National Medical Group Managers; Society for Health Care Executives; Women in Health Administration; Simi Valley Chamber of Commerce, 1987-; American Marketing Association; Simi Valley Employers Advisory Council, 1990-. *Honours:* Noel Bouley Scholar, 1960-64; Lane Bryant Scholar, 1962. *Address:* 469 Quiet Ct, Simi Valley, CA 93065, USA.

SLAYDON Jeanne Miller, b. Kansas City, USA. Educator. m. Glynn Slaydon, 2 daughters. *Education:* BA, Texas Christian University; MEd., University of Houston. *Appointments:* Private Tutor, Midland, Texas; Teacher, Elementary School; Teacher, Secondary Social Studies, Spring Branch Independent School District; District Social Studies Co-ordinator, 1977-. *Publications:* Economics Curriculum: Confluent Economic Education; Consultant on textbooks in US History and World History. *Memberships:* National Council for the Social Studies, House of Delegates, Resolutions Committee; Texas Council for Social Studies, President, 1988-89; President, Treasurer, Spring Branch Council for Social Studies; Texas Association for Advancement of History. *Hobbies:* Drawing; Painting; Reading; Hiking; Music. *Address:* Spring Branch ISD, 955 Campbell, Houston, TX 77024, USA.

SLEIGH Sylvia, b. Llandudno, Wales. Painter. m. Lawrence Alloway, 29 June 1954. *Appointments:* Visiting Assistant Professor, SUNY, Stony Brook, 1973; Instructor, New School Social Research, 1974-77 and 1978-80; Edith Kreeger Wolf Dist Professor, NWU, Illinois, 1977; Visiting Artist, Baldwin Seminar, Oberlin College, 1982. *Creative works:* Numerous one-artist and group exhibitions including: Bennington College, Vermont, 1963; Hemingway Galleries, New York, 1968, 1969, 1971; AIR Gallery, 1974, 1976, 1978; G W Einstein Co, Inc, 1980, 1983, 1985; Sonya Zaks, Chicago, 1985, 1987. *Memberships:* College Art Association; Women's Caucus for Art, Vice president, New York Chapter, 1986. *Honours:* National Endowment for the Arts, Visual Fellowship Grant, 1982-83; Pollock-Krasner Foundation, 1985. *Hobbies:* Gardening; Art History. *Address:* 330 West 20 Street, New York, NY 10011, USA.

SLIGHT Peggie (Marjorie Jessica), Journalist. m. Dudley Slight, 7 Sept. 1932. 3 sons, 1 daughter. *Education:* Diploma with honours, Academy of Beauty Culture, 1948; Teacher's Diploma, Association of Beauty Therapists, 1969; Fellow, Faculty of Physiatrics, 1971; Diplome de Cathiodermiste, Laboratoire de Cosmetologie Rene Guinot, Paris, France, 1972. *Appointments:* Principal, College of Beauty Therapy, 1952; Beauty Editor, ICM Group, Radcliffe Press, 1957; Beauty Editor, Tatler magazine, 1970; Resident Therapist, Post-operative Treatments, Sherwood Court Cosmetic Surgery, 1975; UK Representative, Les Nouvelles Esthetiques, 1979-. *Creative Works:* Oil paintings. *Memberships:* Society of Applied Cosmetology; Council Member, Association of Beauty Therapists; Faculty of Physiatrics. *Honour:* Award for portrait in opils, Nottingham College of Art, 1954. *Hobbies:* Painting; Poetry; Music; TV series (beauty advice for women). *Address:* 55 Lucknow Avenue, Mapperley Park, Nottingham NG3 5AZ, England.

SLOANE Doreen, b. 24 Feb. 1934, Birkenhead, Cheshire, England. Actress. m. (1) 30 Nov. 1957, (divorced 1966), 2 sons, 2 daughters, (2) Len Mordaunt, 1979. *Education:* Birkenhead High School; GPDST, Wirral; Elliott Clarke School of Dance & Drama, Liverpool. *Appointments:* Student, Liverpool Playhouse & various Repertory Companies throughout Britain; TV appearances include: 2 parts in Emmerdale Farm, 4 parts in Coronation Street, various other series including: How We Used to Live, Last of the Summer Wine, Victorian Scandals, Life for Christine, All for Love, Crown Court; Film Appearances: Yanks; Chariots of Fire; local radio serial, various plays for BBC North; presently, Annabelle Collins in Brookside in Channel 4. *Memberships:* Chairman, Wirral Branch, Cheshire Wildlife Appeal; Cheshire Wild-Life Appeal Council. *Hobbies:* Horse Riding; Daily Telegraph Crossword Puzzles; Reading; Walking; Listening to Brass Bands. *Address:* c/o Leading Players Management Ltd., 31 Kings Road, London SW3, England.

SLOANE Marilyn Austern, b. 29 June 1944, New York, USA. Attorney. m. Judd Sloane, 8 May 1966, divorced 1981, 1 son. *Education:* BA, University of Vermont, 1965; JD, Columbia Law School, 1968. *Appointments:* Long Island Lighting, 1968-70; Nassau County EO, 1970-72; Hofstra Law School, 1972-74; Mutual of America, 1974-, Vice President 1977, Senior Vice President 1985-. *Memberships:* Chartered Life Underwriters. *Hobbies:* Skiing; Aerobics; Tennis; Reading; Knitting. *Address:* 8 Shawnee Trail, Harrison, NY 10528, USA.

SLOAT Linda Mary, b. 4 June 1954, Barrie, Ontario, Canada. Nurse's Aide. *Education:* BA, Anthropology and Russian, Laurentian University, 1976. *Appointments:* Archaeological Laborer, Whitefish II, 1974; Labourer, Site Assistant, Ft. St Joseph, 1975, 1977-78; Labourer, Renard Site, 1975, Benson Site, 1976, Pickering Airport, 1976, Butler's Barracks, 1981. *Membership:* Ontario Archaeological Society. *Hobbies:* Gardening; Crafts. *Address:* 9 Jacwin Dr., Ajax, Ontario, Canada L1S 6H6.

SLOBODA Stephanie S, b. 9 Feb. 1952, Philadelphia, Pennsylvania, USA. Chiropractic Physician. *Education:* BA, Sociology, Anthropology, English, Education, Livingson College, Rutgers University, New Jersey, 1973; DC, New York Chiropractic College, 1978; MS, Biology, Nutrition, University of Bridgeport, Connecticut, 1981. *Appointments:* Private Chiropractic Practice, 1979-; Postgraduate Faculty Member, New York Chiropractic College. *Publications:* Women Doctors - Women Patients, American Chiropractic Association Journal, 1987. *Memberships:* American Chiropractic Association; Board of Directors, Past President, Southern New Jersey Chiropractic Society; Board of Directors, New Jersey Chiropractic Society; Board of Directors, Young Women's Christian Association, Trenton, Career Options Programm Chairwoman for Tribute to Women in Industry & Government of YWCA, Trenton. *Honours:* New Jersey Chiropractic Society Meritorious Service Award, 1985, Distinguished Service Award, 1986, 1987, 1988; Lycoming Scholar, Lycoming College, 1969. *Hobbies:* Scuba Diving; Tennis; Volleyball; Raising Golden Retrievers. *Address:* Titusville, New Jersey, USA.

SLOVER Gail Penniman Turner, b. 14 Mar. 1938, Bradford, Pennsylvania, USA. Chronobiologist; Researcher; Lecturer. m. William Pyle Slover Jr, MD, 18 June 1960, divorced 19 July 1984. 2 sons, 1 daughter. *Education:* BA, Zoology, Connecticut College, 1960; Master Education, University of Hartford, 1978; Chautaqua Course in Chronobiology, National Science Foundation, 1979-80. *Appointments:* Medical Technologist Trainee, Harbor General Hospital, Torrance, California, 1960-61; Biochemistry Research Assistant, Institute of Living, Hartford, 1961-64; Independent Instructor, Parent and Teacher Effectiveness Training, 1978-80; Substitute teacher grades 6-12, Glastonbury and Manchester Public School System, 1984-87; Chronobiologist, Teacher, Researcher, Talcott Mountain Science Center for Student Involvement, Avon, 1983-87; Chronobiologist, Independenty Researcher and Lecturer, 1986-. *Publications:* Author of numerous articles to professional journals and to conferences. *Memberships:* International Society for Chronobiology; European

Society for Chronobiology; Toastmasters International, Nathan Hale Club No 1484; and others. *Hobbies:* Bible study; Dancing; Walking; Weaving; Gardening; Singing. *Address:* 20-C Esquire Drive, Manchester, Connecticut 06040-2450, USA.

SLUSSER Mary Catherine, b. 16 June 1949, Huntington, West Virginia, USA. Archaeologist; Anthropologist. *Education:* BA, College of William & Mary, 1971; MA, Eastern New Mexico University, 1973; PhD, State University of New York, Binghamton, 1982. *Appointments:* Instructor, Research Assistant, State University of New York, 1974-80; Adjunct professor, Wilkes College, 1980; Cultural Resource Specialist, EDAW Inc., San Francisco, 1981; Visiting Assistant Professor, Northwestern University, 1981-82; Adjunct Assistant Professor, Virginia Commonwealth University, 1983; Senior Archaeologist, Dept. of Consumer & Regulatory Affairs, Washington, 1983-87; Adjunct Professor, University of the District of Columbia, Washington, 1984; Virginia State Archaeologist, 1987-. *Publications:* Mayan Spatial Cognition: Verbal and Non Verbal Models of Space in a Yucatecan Community, PhD Dissertation, 1982. *Memberships Include:* President, 1984-86, Executive Board Member, 1986-87, Washington Archaeological Sociey; American Anthropological Association; Society for American Archaeology; etc. *Honours:* Phi Kappa Phi; Outstanding Graduate Student Award, 1972; Dissertation Year Fellowship, 1977. *Hobbies:* Travel; Reading; Traditional Decorative Arts. *Address:* 221 Governor Street, Richmond, VA 23219, USA.

SMALL Barbara Ann Finnerin, b. 1 June 1935, Fairmont, West Virginia, USA. Healthcare Executive. m. Edward S. Small, 11 July 1974. *Education:* RN, St Mary's Hospital School of Nursing, Charleston, 1959; BSN, Catholic University of America, 1964; MHA, St Louis University, Missouri, 1966. *Appointments:* Chief Executive Officer, St Mary's Hospital, Clarksburg, WV, 1967-69; Associate Director, Veterans Administration Medical Centres, Florida, Pennsylvania, California, Washington DC, 1974-81; Chief Executive Officer, VAMCs, Boston, Maryland 1981-85, San Diego, California 1985-87, Durham, North Carolina 1987-. Associate Clinical Professor of Medicine, University of California San Diego School of Medicine; Clinical Assistant Professor, Smith College. *Publications:* Various articles, medical management information systems, developing clinical patterns of care for reimbursement purposes, planning for modernisation, strategic planning, Editorial Board, Hospital & Health Services Administration. *Memberships include:* Fellow, American College of Healthcare Executives; Board, Council of Teaching Hospitals. *Honour:* Presidential Rank Award, Meritorious Executives, 1988. *Address:* 13 Gatlin Court, Durham, North Carolina 27707, USA.

SMALL Rebecca Elaine, b. 5 Apr. 1946, Meridian, Texas, USA. Certified Public Accountant. 1 son, 1 daughter. *Education:* Tested Out 3 years, Calsbad NM High School, 1968; Business Degree, OK School of Banking and Business, 1972; BS, Accounting, Honorary Degree, Central State University; MA Degree, in progress. *Appointments:* Staff Accountant, Robert Mosley CPA 1972-74, Robert, Stewart CPA 1974-75, Lowder and Co, 1975-81; Founder, President, Rebecca E Small CPA Inc., 1981-. *Publications:* Poems: Reach for the Stars, 1983; Model, 1983; Deep Feelings, 1983; Best Friends, 1985; Published Works: I Am, 1985, Poem Song. *Memberships:* AICPA, 1978-87; OKLA Society of CPA's, 1978-87; American Women's Society of CPA's 1978-87; Oklahoma Women's Business Owners, Chairman, 1982. *Honours:* Alpha Lambda Delta, 1974; Alpha Chi, 1975; Scholarship, 1975; Central State University, School of Business, Edmond, 1975; Scholarship, Business and Professional Womens Club, Edmond, 1976; Honorary Membership, National Association of Accountants, Arthur Young & Co National Firm, Oklahoma City, 1976; Bronze Key, 1977. *Hobbies:* Writing Poetry; Psychology; Horticulture; Interior Decorating. *Address:* 6488 Avondale Dr 309, Oklahoma City, OK 73116, USA.

SMEDSTAD Kari Gunhild, b. 18 Apr. 1942, Oslo, Norway. Physician. m. Brian James Sealey, 6 June 1969, divorced 1980, 1 son, 2 daughters. *Education:* MB.ChB, Birmingham, England, 1967; Cand.Med, Oslo, Norway, 1967; LMCC, 1972; FRCP(C), 1980. *Appointments:* Internship, 1967-68; District Physician, Norway, 1968-69; General Practitioner, Kirkland Lake, Ontario, 1970-71; Research Fellow, Part-time, 1972-73; General Practice, Hamilton, 1973-77; Residency, Anaesthesis, McMaster University, 1977-80; Assistant Professor, McMaster University, 1981-. *Memberships:* Federation of Medical Women of Canada, President 1985-86; Ontario Medical Association; Medical Womens International Association, National Corresponding Secretary, Canada. *Honours:* Joseph Sanley Prize, 1967. *Hobbies:* Womens Issues. *Address:* Dept. Anaesthesia, McMaster University, 1200 Main St. W, Hamilton, Ontario L8N 3Z5, Canada.

SMELTZER Carolyn Hope, b. 26 Feb. 1951, Oak Park, Illinoiis, USA. Nurse; Administrator. *Education:* Nursing Diploma, 1972; BSN, 1974; MSN, Medical & Surgical Nursing, 1977; EdD, Educational Psychology, 1983. *Appointments include:* Senior Associate Hospital Director, Tucson, 1986-88; Assistant Dean & Clinical Professor, University of Illinois, 1988-; Associate Professor, Rush, 1988-; Clinical Professor, Loyola, 1988-; Vice President, Nursing, University of Chicago Hospitals, 1988-. *Publications:* Various papers & articles, professional subjects. *Memberships:* Illinois Hospital Association; Illinois Nurses Association; Illinois Organisation of Nurse Executives; American Academy of Nursing; Fellow, American Organisation of Nurse Executives; National & Illinois Leagues for Nursing; American College for Healthcare Executives. *Honours:* 1st place, Nursing Medical Electronics for Videotape, Sigma Theta Tau, 1987; Award, Distinguished Scholar (presented once in 50 years), Loyola University, 1985; Outstanding Young Women of America, 1981; Sigma Theta Tau, 1976. *Hobbies:* Skiing; Tennis. *Address:* Department of Nursing, Hospital Box 416, University of Chicago Hospitals, 5841 South Maryland, Chicago, Illinois 60637, USA.

SMITH Alice Marie (Vaughn), b. 22 July 1921, Water Valley, Mississippi, USA. Retired. m. Hugh Alton Smith, 9 Feb. 1941, 1 son, 2 daughters. *Education:* Teaching Certificate, DeShazo College of Music, 1940; Los Angeles Conservatory of Music, 1941. *Appointments:* Piano Teacher, Memphis, Tennessee, 1950-54; Piano Teacher, Huntsville, Alabama, 1955-68; Kindergarten Music Teacher, Huntsville, 1956-60; Certified Flower Judge, State of Tennessee, 1951-53. *Memberships:* Beethoven Club, Memphis, 1936-39; Associate Advisor, Rainbow Girls, Memphis, 1935-39; Associate Worthy Matron, Eastern Star, Corpus Christi, Texas, 1941-45; Past President, Highland Heights Garden Club, Memphis; Choir Member, Highland Heights Methodist Church, 1947-49; Charter Member, Sunday School Teacher, Westminster Presbyterian Church, Huntsville; Sponsor, National Federation of Music Clubs, Huntsville; Past President, former Southeast Area Representative, former Bible Teacher, Christian Women's Club, Huntsville; Organizing Chairman, Tennessee Valley Women's Retreat, 1973; Travelling Ambassador to Southeast Asia, World Vision, 1968; Trainer, Evangelism, Coral Ridge Presbyterian Church, Ft Lauderdale, Florida, 1979-81. *Hobbies:* Music; Travel; Decorating; Reading. *Address:* PO Box 3190, Huntsville, AL 35810, USA.

SMITH Ancelyn Greene, b. 25 Oct. 1936, Waco, Texas, USA. Manager. m. Donald Joseph Smith, 7 July 1956, 4 sons. *Education:* AA, Richland College, 1973. *Appointments:* Promotional Director, Treehouse Shopping Centre, Dallas, 1975-77; Office Manager, GSA Agency, Garland, 1977-81; Manager, Keep Garland Beautiful, 1981-84; EUP Garland Chamber of Commerce, Garland, 1984-88; Manager, Garland Convention & Visitors Bureau, 1988-. *Memberships:* Board, Womens Activities Building Council; Garland Park & Recreation Board, Chairman; North Central Texas Council of Governments, Resource Committee, Vice

Chairman; Garland Executive Women; Garland Federation of Womens Clubs, President. *Honours:* M Award, SMU, 1955; Outstanding Club Women, GFWC, 1977; Outstanding Secretary, Exchange Clubs of America, 1987. *Hobbies:* Reading; Writing; Tennis; Sailing; Fishing. *Address:* 3416 Lakeside Drive, Rockwall, TX 75087, USA.

SMITH Barbara Herrnstein, b. 6 Aug. 1932, New York, USA. Educator. m. (1) Rich J Hernstein, 28 May 1951, divorced 1961. (2) Thomas H Smith, 21 Feb 1964, divorced 1974. 2 daughters. *Education:* BA, 1954; MA, Eng & American Lit 1955, PhD, Eng & American Lit 1965, Brandeis University. *Appointments:* Member of Faculty, Division of Literature and Language, Bennington College, 1961-73; Visiting Lecturer in Communications, Annenberg School 1973-74, Professor of English and Communications 1974-80, University Professor of English and Communications 1980-87, Member, Graduate Group in Comparative Literature and Literary Theory 1979-87, University of Pennsylvania; Braxton Craven Professor of Comparative Literature and English, Duke University, 1987-. *Publications:* Discussions of Shakespeare's Sonnets, Ed, 1964; Poetic Closure: A Study of How Poems End, 1968; Shakespeare's Sonnets, Ed and Intro, 1969; On the Margins of Discourse: The Relation of Literature to Language, 1978; Contingencies of Value, 1988. *Memberships include:* President, Modern Language Association of America, 1988; President, Academy of Literary Studies, 1983-84; Superv Comm, 1978-80, Trustee 1986-93, The English Institute; President, Society for Critical Exchange, 1986-89. *Honours include:* Recipient of numerous awards and fellowships. *Address:* 325 Allen Building, Duke University, Durham, NC 27706, USA.

SMITH Barbara Mary Moore, b. 22 Apr. 1944, Nottingham, England. Lecturer; Public Accountant. m. Michael John Smith, 20 July 1963, 2 sons. *Education:* BA, Business, VIC, 1979; Diploma of Education, 1982; BA, Education, Latrobe University, 1984. *Appointments:* Personal Assistant, John Palemo Pty Ltd., 1972-77; Accountant, Melbourne Moomba Festival, 1977-82; Public Accountant, Own Accounting Practice, 1981-; Lecturer, Accounting, School of Business, Phillip Institute of Technology, Coburg, 1983. *Publications:* FCA Taxation Guide, Journal of Advanced Education, 1987; Introducing Computer Programming, Compac, 1983. *Memberships:* Associate, Australian Society of Accountants; Fellow, Taxation Institute of Australia; Registered Tax Agent; International Financial Planners Association; Thailand Business Management Study Iour, etc. *Honours:* Elected Councillor to the Shire of Diamond Valley, August 1987; Hon. Secretary Treasurer, Jigsaw Adoption Informatiron Service of Victoria Ltd, 1978-80; Founder, Chairperson, Women Accountants Discussion Group, Victoria, 1985-; etc. *Hobbies Include:* Sutherland Homes for Children Management Group; Greensborough Festival Committee; etc. *Address:* 153-161 River Avenue, Plenty, VIC 3090, Australia.

SMITH Bert (ha Mae) Kruger, b. 18 Nov. 1915, Wichita Falls, Texas, USA. Consultant. m. Sidney S Smith, 19 Jan. 1936, 2 sons, (1 deceased), 1 daughter. *Education:* BJ, 1936, DHL, Hon., 1985, University of Missouri; MA, University of Texas, 1949. *Appointments:* Wichita Falls Post, 1936-37; Daily Alaska Empire, 1937; Coleman Daily Democrate-Voice, Associate Publisher, 1951-52; Junior College Journal, Editor, 1952-55; Hogg Foundation for Mental Health, 1952-. *Publications:* Host, The Human Condition, half hour radio show, 10 years; Looking Forward, 1983; The Pursuit of Dignity, 1977; Aging in America, 1973; Insights for Uptights, 1973; A Teaspoon of Honey, fiction, 1970; Your Non-Learning Child, 1968; No Language but a Cry, 1964; articles in numerous journals. *Memberships:* Authors Guild; Women in Communication; National Association of Science Writers; Delta Kappa Gamma; many others. *Honours:* Recipient, numerous honours and awards most recent: Texas Women's Hall of Fame, 1989; Governor's Commendation for Public Service, 1986;

Texas Long Term Care Volunteer Award, 1988. *Hobbies:* Family; Writing; Walking. *Address:* 5818 Westslope Drive, Austin, TX 78731, USA.

SMITH Carol Jean, b. 12 Oct. 1947, Anniston, Alabama, USA. Attorney. *Education:* BS, Education, Jacksonville State University, Jacksonville, Alabama; JD, University of Alabama School of Law, Tuscaloosa. *Appointments:* Law Clerk, Lybrand, Sides & Hamner, 1971-73; Law Clerk, Supreme Court of Alabama, 1973-74; Assistant Attorney General, State of Alabama, 1974-. *Memberships:* Farvah Law Society; American, Alabama and Montgomery County Bar Associations; University of Alabama Alumni Association; Jacksonville State University Alumni Association; National Women's Political Caucus; National Alumnae Vice-President, National Financial Vice-President, Alpha Delta Xi; 1st Vice-President, Recording Secretary, Board Member, Montgomery Club, Zonta International; Montgomery Board Member, League of Women Voters; Board Member, American Association of University Women. *Honours:* Kappa Delta Epsilon, 1968; Pi Gamma Mu, 1968; Bench Bar Legal Honour Society, 1973; Dean's Award, University of Alabama Law School, 1973; Outstanding Alumnae, Jacksonville State University, 1985. *Hobbies:* Collector of elephants; University of Alabama; Football and Basketball fan. *Address:* 2014 Rexford Road, Montgomery, AL 36116, USA.

SMITH Cerita M., b. 18 Dec. 1954, Lawton, Oklahoma, USA. Graphic Designer. *Education:* BS with academic distinction, Advertising Art, East Texas State University, 1978. *Appointments:* Designer & Art Director, A Pretty Good Shop 1979, Cap Pannell & Company 1979-83, Dallas, Texas; Sole proprietor, Cerita Smith Design, Dallas, 1983-85; Partner/Inc, Smith & Mann Design, Dallas, 1985-87; Partner, Smith Taylor Design, 1988-. *Memberships:* National chapter, founding member Texas chapter, American Institute of Graphic Arts; Dallas Society of Visual Communications; US & North Dallas, Chambers of Commerce; Dallas Museum of Fine Arts. *Honours:* Professional awards from: Print Magazine; AIGA; Houston Art Directors Club; New York Art Directors Club; Dallas Society of Visual Communications; Dallas Ad League. *Address:* 2123 St Francis, Dallas, Texas 75228, USA.

SMITH Corinne Roth, b. 22 May 1945, USA. Psychoeducator. m. Lynn Helden Smith, 2 daughters. *Education:* BA 1967, PhD 1973, Syracuse University; MA, Temple University, 1969. *Appointments:* Founder, Director, Associate Professor, Psychoeducation Teaching Laboratory, 1972-; Founder, Director, Comprehensive Assessment Centre, Syracuse University & Public School District, 1981-83. *Publications:* Books: Learning Disabilities: Interaction of Learner, Task & Setting; Drugs, Decisions & You: Teacher's Resource; Drugs, Decisions & You. *Memberships:* American & Central New York Psychological Associations; Council for Exceptional Children; National Association for Children & Adults with Learning Disabilities; National Association of School Psychologists. *Honours:* Distinguished Service Award, Syracuse Jewish Community Centre, 1976; New York State Council for Youth, 1984-88; Community Leadership Award, Syracuse Jewish Federation, 1986; Various biographical recognitions. *Hobbies:* Voluntary work; Tennis; Gardening; Cycling; Jewiish community fund raising. *Address:* 14 Bovington Lane, Fayetteville, New York 13066, USA.

SMITH Donna, b. 22 May, 1947, Moab, Utah, USA. US Army officer, Major. 1 daughter. *Education:* BS 1970, MS 1973, Master of Engineering Administration 1987, University of Utah; Military Education, 1977-83. *Appointments:* Teacher, Mexican Hat Elementary School, Utah, summer 1971; Teacher, Monticello High School, Utah, 1970-71; Chief, Active Market Analyst Branch for Army Recruiting, Ft Sheridan, Operation Research Systems Analyst Officer, Ft Monmouth, Area Commander of Army Recruiting, Salt Lake City, Movement Control Officer for Cubian Refugee Crisis, Federal Emergency Management Agency, Key West,

Florida, Material Systems Analyst, Logistics Center, Ft Hood, Commander, Truck Company, Ft Hood, Chief of Transportation/Services Branch, Military Community, Heidelberg, Germany, Platoon Leader, Transportation Car Company, Heidelberg, Executive Officer, Women's Army Corps Company, Heidelberg, United States Army, 1973-. *Publications:* Motivation-Hygiene Theory profile of United States Army Recruiters, 1987. *Memberships:* The American Legion; Spa Fitness Center; Coast to Coast Resorts Travel Club; Women's Army Corps Veterans Association; Operations Research Society of America/ Military Operations Research Society. *Honours include:* Meritorious Service Medal, 1982; Army Commendation Medal with 2nd Oak Leaf Cluster, 1978, 1980 and 1985; Humanitarian Service Medal, 1980; Armed Forces Reserve Medal, 1984; Certificate of Achievement (Physical Fitness), 1985; First Female Officer to successfully complete command with US Army Recruiting, 1988. *Hobbies:* Camping; Reading; Physical Fitness; Travelling. *Address:* P O Box 276, Ft Sheridan, IL 60037, USA.

SMITH Dorothy Louise, b. 29 Apr. 1946, Regina, Canada. Pharmacy Consultant; Author. *Education:* BSc., 1968; Residency in Hospital Pharmacy, 1969; Pharm.D., 1972. *Appointments:* Assistant Professor, Pharmacy, UBC, Vancouver, 1972-74; Co-ordinator, Ambulatory Pharmacy, Sunnybrook Medical Center, Toronto, 1974-80; Director, Clinical Affairs, American Pharmaceutical Association, 1980-83; President, Consumer Health Information Corp, 1983-. *Publications:* Medication Guide for Patient Counseling, 1977; Patient Advisory Leaflets, 1979; Family Guide to Prescription Drugs, 1980; Patient Guide to Prescription Information, 1979; Understanding Drugs, 1986; Pharmacists Therapeutic Reference, 1987; Understanding Canadian Prescription Drugs, 1989. *Memberships:* many professional organisations. *Honours:* Recipient, various honours and awards. *Hobbies:* Athletics; China Painting; Organist; Sewing; Cooking. *Address:* Consumer Health Information Corp, 8350 Greensboro Drive, Suite 521, McLean, VA 22102, USA.

SMITH Elaine Cecile Thompson, b. 20 Mar. 1947, New Orleans, Louisiana, USA. Dance Teacher; Choreographer. m. Frank Bernard Smith, III, 20 July 1969. 2 sons. *Education:* BA, Dillard University, 1969; Health Educ Cert, Hunter College, NYC, 1973; MA, Columbia University, NYC, 1977; Cosmetology Degree, Wilfred Academy, Bronx, 1987. *Appointments:* Aerobics Instructor, YMCA, New Orleans, 1968-69; Phy Ed/ Dance Teacher, IS271K, 1969-70; Dance Teacher, IS136M, 1970-85; Dance Instructor, YMCA, Harlem, 1979-80; Dance Instructor, Barnes Center Day Camp, NY, 1978-82; Dance Teacher, ISIOM, NY, 1985-; Dance Teacher Liaison, DITH, NY, 1970-. *Creative works:* Staged, choreographed, costumed, dance concerts for numerous organisations. *Memberships:* UFT; Committee for Positive Youth; NYSUT; Phi Delta Kappa Sorority, Beta Epsilon Chapter; NAUW, Honorary Member; NAAPHERD; NEA; NDA; Dance Educators of America. *Honours:* Plaque, Committee for Positive Youth, 1988; Plaque, Hal Jackson Talented TEen International, 1989. *Hobbies:* Sewing and designing women, mens, childrens clothing and costumes; Attending dance theatre; Listening to all kinds of music; Hair sculpting and make-up; Entertaining the elderly and handicapped; Keeping children away from drugs through dance/arts. *Address:* 100-24 Darrow Place No 24G, Bronx, NY 10475, USA.

SMITH Elizabeth Joy, b. 6 July 1928, Hobart, Tasmania, Australia. Education Research & Administration (retired). *Education:* BA Hons, 1949, Diploma of Education 1950, MA Classics 1957, Diploma of Public administration 1960, University of Tasmania; Tasmanian Teacher's Certificate, 1955. *Appointments:* Teacher, Hobart High School, 1950-51; Commonwealth Office of Education, 1951; Supervisor of Commonwealth Scholarship Scheme, 1952-67; Senior Research Officer 1968-70, Senior Education officer, 1971-85, including Chairman, Migrant Education Committee, 1975-84, Foundation Chairman, State Multicultural Education Coordinating Committee, 1979-85, Tasmanian Education Department. *Publications:* Several research publications and conference papers and resolutions. *Memberships:* President, Hobart Business & Professional Womens' Club, 1961-62; Australian College of Education, 1963-; Teachers & Schools Registration Board, Representative, Education Department, 1974-84; United World Colleges, Tasmanian Committee, 1977-; State Honorary Secretary & a Director of UWC (Australia) Trust, 1977-85; Australian Institute of Multicultural Affairs, 1981-84; Friends of Tasmanian Museum & Art Gallery; Tasmanian Orchestral Subscribers' Association & Musica Viva Society. *Honours:* Various scholarships and prizes at University. *Hobbies:* United World Colleges; Multiculturalism, including ethnic radio & television; Music; Art; Poetry; Photography; Reading; Gardening; Relaxing at seaside holiday cottage; Helping the elderly, meals on wheels. *Address:* 62 Doyle Ave, Lenah Valley, Tasmania, Australia.

SMITH Ella, b. 28 Sep. 1933, Danbury, Connecticut, USA. Author; Theatrical Director; Actress. *Education:* BS, Danbury State College, 1955; MFA, School of Drama, Yale University, 1961. *Appointments:* Assistant Professor of Theatre and Film, Immaculate Heart College, 1975-76; Acting Coach, Star Search TV series, 1984-86; Director, Acting Coach, Tracy Roberts Acting Studio, 1984-88. *Publications:* Author of introduction to Richard Lawton's A World of Movies, 1974; The Transference (novel), 1981; Starring Miss Barbara Stanwyck (author, designer), enlarged edition, 1985. *Address:* Box 366, Beverly Hills, CA 90213, USA.

SMITH Elouise Beard, b. 8 Jan. 1920, Richmond, Texas, USA. Businesswoman. m. Omar Smith, 27 Nov. 1940, 2 sons, 1 daughter. *Education:* Texas Womens University, 1937-39. *Appointments:* Secretary, First National Bank, Rosenberg, Texas, 1939-41; Owner, Smith Dairy Queens, 1947-. *Publications:* The Haunted House; Editor, The College Widow, 1986. *Memberships:* American Association of University Women, Charter Member; Texas Dairy Queen, American Dairy Queen, International Dairy Queen Associations. *Honours:* Omar and Elouise Beard Smith Education Chair named in their honour, Texas A&M University, 1983; Elouise Beard Smith Human performance Laboratories named in her honour, Texas A&M University, 1984. *Hobbies:* Exploring England; Restoring Old Cemeteries; Genealogy. *Address:* 411 Crescent Drive, Bryan, TX 77801, USA.

SMITH Emma, b. 21 Aug. 1923, Newquay, Cornwall, England. Writer. m. Richard Llewellyn Stewart-Jones (d. 1957), 31 Jan. 1951, 1 son, 1 daughter. *Publications:* Maiden's Trip, 1948; The Far Cry, 1949; Emily, 1959; Out of Hand, 1963; Emily's Voyage, 1966; No Way of Telling, 1972; The Opportunity of a Lifetime, 1978; Contributor to various magazines. *Honours:* Atlantic Award, short stories, 1948; John Llewellyn Rhys Memorial Prize, 1948; James Tait Black Memorial Prize, 1949. *Address:* c/o Curtis Brown, 162-168 Regent Street, London W1R 5TB, England.

SMITH Holly Martin, b. 15 Nov. 1944, Evanston, Illinois, USA. University Professor. m. Alvin J. Goldman, 15 June 1969, 1 son, 1 daughter. *Education:* BA, Wellesley College, 1966; MA, 1970, PhD, 1972, University of Michigan. *Appointments:* Tufts University, 1970-71; University of Michigan Flint, 1971-72; University of Pittsburgh, 1972-73; University of Michigan Ann Arbor, 1973-80; University of Illinois, Chicago, 1980-83; Professor, Head, Philosophy, University of Arizona, 1983-. *Publications:* Articles in: Philosophical Review; Nous. *Membership:* American Philosophical Association. *Honours Include:* National Merit Scholar, 1962-63; Phi Beta Kappa, 1966; Wellesley College Special Honours & First Trustee Fellow, 1966; Danforth Graduate Fellowship, 1966-70; University of Arizona Social & Behavioral Sciences Research Professorship, 1987. *Address:* Philosophy Dept., 213 Social Sciences Building, University of Arizona, Tucson, AZ 85721, USA.

SMITH Iris, b. 6 July 1945, Manhatten, New York, USA. Director IPA Operations. *Education:* BS, University of Bridgeport, 1967; Teaching Credential, San Francisco State University, 1976. *Appointments:* Mathematics Teacher, Long Beach Junior High School, 1967-70; Computer Room Supervisor, Pacific Telephone Co, San Francisco, 1970-71; Intake Social Worker, Personnel Administrator, City & County of San Francisco, 1971-73; Supervisor Admitting Department, Financial Coordinator, Presbyterian Hospital of Pacific Medical Center, 1973-77; Regional Quality Assurance Director, Quality Care Nursing Services, 1977-80; Marketing Representative, Heals Health Plan, Emeryville, 1981-83; Director Provider Relations, Regional Sales Manager, The Health Plan of America, 1983-88; Director IPA Operations, St Jude Hospital and Rehabilitation Center, Fullerton, 1988-. *Memberships:* National Association of Female Executives; Active 20/30 Club of Orange, 1st VP 1986-88; American Friends of the Hebrew University. *Hobbies:* Scuba Diving; Snow Skiing; Tennis. *Address:* 57 Laurel Creek Lane, Laguna Hills, California 92653, USA.

SMITH Juanita Rose Rankin, b. 1 Nov. 1949, Bridgeton, New Jersey, USA. Teacher; Accountant. m. Ronald D. Smith, 23 Mar. 1968, div. Nov. 1978, 1 daughter. *Education:* AS, Cumberland County College, 1980; BS, Glassboro State College, 1982. *Appointments:* Substitute Teacher, Bridgeton Board of Education, New Jersey, 1982-84; Accountant, US Army, 1984-; Teacher (part-time), Union Technical Institute, 1989. *Memberships:* National Association of Negro Business and Professional Women; Financial Secretary, Central Jersey Club; Association of Government Accountants, Central New Jersey Chapter; President, Bridgeton Parent-Teachers Association, 1982; Director of Education, Macedonia Baptist Church, Trustee 1985; Board of Directors, Bridgeton Housing Corporation, 1984; National Association of Negro Business and Professional Women, 1986-, Financial Secretary, Central Jersey Club, 1988-90; Association of Government Accountants, 1988-; Director of Education, Central New Jersey Chapter, 1988-. *Hobbies:* Theatre; Religious and devotional readings; Tennis; Writing short stories and essays. *Address:* 2130 Aldrin Road, Aprtment 6A, Ocean, NJ 07712, USA.

SMITH Katherine (Kay) Bailey, b. 26 June 1931, Egypt, Mississippi, USA. Director/Organizer. m. James E Smith, 7 July 1966. 3 sons. *Education:* Undertook courses at: University of Cincinnati; University of Xavier; Xavier University of Ohio. *Appointments:* Section/Department Supervisor (Uniform Factory), 1956-86; Director/Organizer, 1986-. *Publications:* Wrote Practicum Paper/Social Justice; Composition/Development of Self-Esteem through Social Justice in Low Income Areas; Wrote Project Book/Organized Program for Low-Income Housing through a Cooperative Organization. *Memberships:* Alumni-Lay Pastoral Minister Prog, Co-chairperson, Human Resources, St John's Social Service Center; Treasurer Neighbourhood Devel Communts; Director, Community Land Cooperative of Cincinnati, Ohio; Conslt/teacher religion programs, Archdiocese of Cincinnati, Ohio; Vice President/JKS Associates Real Estate Consultants/Managers. *Honours:* 30 year Service Award, Employment/Supervisor, 1986; Commissioned as Lay Pastoral Minister, Roman Catholic Church, 1985; Honoured as Volunteer worker for St Joseph Church, 1982-86; St John Social Service Center, 1984-87; American Cancer Society, 1986-88; Archibishop Fund Drive, 1980-82; Commissioned as Liturgical Minister, 1978; Cited in local paper (Cincinnati Enquirer) Land Coop Director Gets Things Moving; Honoured 20 years in St Agnes Parish/Service in various positions. *Hobbies:* Reading; Environment; Travelling; Nature. *Address:* 1600 Pelham Place, No 2, Cincinnati, Ohio 45237, USA.

SMITH Kathleen Joan, b. 25 June 1929, Luton, England. Writer; Director. *Education:* University College, North Wales. *Appointments:* Farm Worker, 1942-50; Actress, 1950-56; Assistant Governor, Holloway Prison, London, 1956-60; Writer, 1960-; Director, Museum of Old Welsh Country Life, 1980-. *Publications:* Twelve Months, Mrs Brown; A Cure for Crime; The Young and the Pity; Devils Delight; Help for the Bereaved; Old Welsh Country Life; The Company of God; Meditations for Eagles; TV Plays: The Slap; The Prison Cat; A Regular Friend; New Girls; Love and the Chaplain; Stage Plays: Back to Nature; The Bronte Story; Women Without Men. *Memberships:* Transport Users Consultative Committee; Writers Guild of Great Britain; Deputy Chairman, The Electricity Consultative Council, Merseyside & North Wales Area. *Hobby:* Being. *Address:* Felin Faesog, Clynnogfawr, Caernarvon, Gwynedd LL54 5DD, Wales.

SMITH Kay Nolte, b. 4 July 1932, Eveleth, Minnesota, USA. Novelist. m. Phillip J. Smith, 30 May 1958. *Education:* BA, summa cum laude, University of Minnesota, 1952; MA, University of Utah, 1955. *Appointments:* Advertising copywriter, Stern Brothers 1957-59, Fletcher Richards Inc 1959-62, New York; Professional actress (as Kay Gillian), 1962-75; Instructor & adjunct, various colleges, New Jersey, 1975-82; Writing consultant, AT&T Bell Laboratories, 1978-. *Publications:* Novels: The Watcher, 1980; Catching Fire, 1982; Mindspell, 1983; Elegy for a Soprano, 1985; Country of the Heart, 1988. Translation: Edmond Rostand's Chantecler, 1987. Numerous stories, widely anthologised. *Memberships:* Authors Guild; Board of Directors, Mystery Writers of America. *Honours:* Phi Beta Kappa, 1951; Edgar Allan Poe Award, best 1st novel, Mystery Writers of America, 1981. *Hobbies:* Classical music; Psychology; French Literature. *Address:* 73 Hope Road, Tinton Falls, New Jersey 07724, USA.

SMITH Louise Hamilton, b. 12 Sept. 1926, Columbus, Lowndes County, Mississippi, USA. Freelance Writer. m. Felton Lomax Smith, 11 June 1948, 1 son, 3 daughters. *Education:* GED Certificate, 1955; Mississippi University for Women, Columbus, 1955. *Appointments:* Operator, South Central Bell Telephone Company, 1947-78; Currently Freelance Writer. *Publications:* Articles and filler in Woman's Day, Yankee, Christian Science Monitor, National Features Syndicate, Grit, True Story, True Romance, The Commercial Dispatch. *Membership:* Telephone Pioneers of America. *Hobbies:* Genealogy; Reading; Sewing. *Address:* 1524 Bell Avenue, Columbus, MS 39701, USA.

SMITH M. Sharon, b. 30 Jan. 1943, Pensacola, Florida, USA. Counsellor; Hospice Director. *Education:* BA, 1964; MS, 1966; EdS, 1984; EdD, 1986; Diploma, Institute of Children's Literature; Licensed Professional Counsellor, State of Georgia; Certified Medical Therapist. *Appointments:* Educator, Pinellas County Schools, Florida, 1964-65; Head Resident, Florida State University, Tallahassee, Florida, 1965-66; Counsellor, Palm Beach County Schools, Florida, 1966-68; Chairperson, Counselling Department, Counsellor, Developmental Research School, Florida State University, Tallahassee, 1968-77; Counsellor, Gwinnett County Schools, Georgia, 1977-85; Director, Kennestone Regional Hospice, Marietta, Georgia, 1985-. *Publications:* A Time to Grieve; Happy Rainbow Days!; The Challenge of Change; The Gift of Yourself; Listen With Your Heart; Look to This Day; A Step Ahead; Ideas for Parents, vols I, II, III (editor); Resource Book for Parents, vols I, II (editor); Development of an Oncology Counseling Model Within an Outpatient Treatment Center (dissertation). *Memberships:* American Association of Counseling and Development; Phi Kappa Phi; President, Georgia Hospice Organization; Governing Board, American School Counselor Association; Secretary, Florida Personnel and Guidance Association. *Honours:* Writer of the Year, Gwinnett County Counselors, 1982; Writer of the Year, 9th District, Georgia School Counselors Association, 1983; Writer of the Year, Georgia School Counselors Association, 1983; Writer of the Year (honourable mention), American School Counselors Association, 1984. *Hobbies:* Reading; Writing; Attending theatre and symphony; Hiking; Gardening. *Address:* 6804 Park Avenue NE, Atlanta, GA 30342, USA.

SMITH Marie Evans, b. 21 Jan,. 1928, Philadelphia, Pennsylvania, USA. Director; Clinical Psychologist. m. Charles N Smith, 14 Sept. 1943. 3 daughters. *Education:* BS, Temple University, 1972; MED, Antioch University, 1974; PhD, Kensington University, 1985. *Appointments:* Educator, Parkway Day School, 1970; Administrator, Early Education, 1972; Psychologist 1973, Faculty 1974, Hahneman Medical College; Consultant, Phildaelphia School Dist, 1974-; Director, John F Kennedy Mental Health Clinic, 1988-. *Memberships:* Zeta Phi Sorority Inc, Life Member; Philadelphia Counseling Association; American Legion, Auxiliary, President; American Women's Heritage Society, Board Member; Germantown Historical Society; Consultant, Developmental Learning Center; President, Wellesley Civic Association. *Honours:* American Legion Service Award, 1960; Legion of Honor Award, Chapel of Four Chaplins, 1965; Parkway Day school Achievement Award, 1969; School District of Philadelphia Certirficate of Service Award, 1988; Distinguished Service Award, Mental Health Association, 1988; John F Kennedy Mental Health and Mental Retardation Special Service Award, 1988. *Interests:* Lecturing; Conducting mental health education workshops; Supervising students in Clinical Psychology; Mental health consulting; Travelling; Public speaking. *Address:* 518 Wellesley Road, Philadelphia, Pennsylvania 19119, USA.

SMITH Martha A., b. 2 May 1938, Texas, USA. Teacher. m. Homer A. Smith Jr, 26 Aug. 1959, 1 son, 1 daughter. *Education:* BA, Speech & Dramatics Education, Oklahoma State University, 1961; MS, Special Education, Indiana University, 1978. State Teacher Certifications: Preschool Handicapped, Learning Disabilities, Dramatics & Costume Design, Speech & Public Spaeking, Early Childhood Special Education. *Appointments:* Substitute teacher, Farmville, Virginia, 1969-75; Teacher, pre-school handicapped, Buckingham County Public Schools, Virginia, 1979-85; Teacher, learning disabilities, Macon-Piatt Special Education Division, 1985-86; Teacher, early childhood special education, Tuscola, Illinois, 1986-87; Substitute teacher, Decatur & Morrisonville, 1987-88. *Creative work includes:* Author, 4 proposals for pre-school equipment (resulting in mini-grants), for Virginia Department of Education, 1981-85. *Memberships include:* Regional representative (voluntary), Developmental Disabilities Protection & Advocacy Office, Virginia, 1978-80; Monroe County Parent Advisory Board for Exceptional Children, Indiana, 1977-78; Deacon, numerous offices, College Presbyterian Church, Hampden-Sydney, VA. *Hobbies include:* Quilting; Reading; Travel. *Address:* 346 South Wooddale, Decatur, Illinois 62522, USA.

SMITH Martha Evans Lewis, b. 27 Nov. 1923, Washington, USA. Consultant, Nursing Education; Captain U.S.P.H.S. m. (1) Marshall Lewis, 27 Nov. 1955, 1 son, 1 daughter, (2) Walter J. Smith, 21 July 1985. *Education:* BSc., Nursing Education, 1950; MSc., Nursing, 1963; EdD, 1980. *Appointments:* Co-ordinator, Nursing, Washington Technical Institute, 1968-76; Assistant Director, Chairperson, Professor, Nursing Education, 1976-83; Director, Nursing Education, 1983-87, University of District of Columbia. *Memberships:* American Association of University Women; DCNA; ANA; DCLN; NLN; Phi Delta Gamma; Chi Eta Phi; CUA; American University Alumna Association; many other professional organisations. *Honours:* Soror of the Year, Chi Eta Phi, 1983-84; Special Achievement & Public Service Placques, Awards & Certificates, University of District of Columbia, 1976-88. *Hobbies:* Deep Sea Fishing; Creating Cork Bottle Top Faces; Bibliomancy. *Address:* 1444 Juniper Street, NW, Washington, DC 20012, USA.

SMITH Mary Louise, b. 6 Oct. 1914, Eddyville, Iowa, USA. Politics; Public Affairs. m. Elmer M. Smith, 7 Oct. 1934, deceased, 2 sons, 1 daughter. *Education:* BA, University of Iowa, 1935. *Appointments:* Republican National Chairman, 1974-77; Vice Chair, US Commission on Civil Rights, 1982-83. *Memberships:* Iowa Peace Institute, Board Member; Planned Parenthood, Board Member; YWCA; University of Iowa Foundation, Board; Hoover Presidential Library Association, Board; National Women's Political Caucus, Advisory Board. *Honours:* Various honours & awards including: Honorary LLD, Grinnel College, 1984; Cristine Wilson Medal, Iowa Commission on Status of Women, 1984. *Hobbies:* Reading; Writing; Gradening. *Address:* 654 59th Street, Des Moines, IA 50312, USA.

SMITH Nancy Hohendorf, b. 30 Jan. 1943, Detroit, Michigan, USA. Marketing Executive. m. Richard Harold Smith, 21 Aug. 1978, divorced 1984. *Education:* BA, Wayne State University, 1969. *Appointments:* Customer Rep., Detorit, 1965-67, Marketing Rep., University Microfilms Subs., Ann Arbor, 1967-73; Major Account Marketing Executive, Hartford, 1978-79, New Haven, 1979-80, State of New York Account Executive, 1981, New York Regional Manager, Customer Support, 1982, New York Region Sales Operations Manager, Greenwich, 1982, State of Ohio Account Executive, Columbus, 1983, New Business Sales Manager, Dayton, 1983, Major Account Sales Manager, Dayton, 1984, Information Systems Sales & Support Manager, Quality Specialist, Southfield, 1985-87, Operations New Product Launch Manager, Operations Quality Manager, Southfield, 1988, District Marketing Manager, District Quality Manager, Southfield, 1989-, Xerox Corp. *Memberships:* National Association Female Executives; Women's Economic Club; Detroit Institute of Arts, Founders Society. *Honours:* Recipient, various honours and awards. *Address:* 23308 Reynard Dr., Southfield, MI 48034, USA.

SMITH Patricia E, b. 15 Sept. 1943, USA. Director of Graduate Admissions. m. Richard R. Kuntz, 26 Nov. 1966, 1 daughter. *Education:* BA, Univerity of South Carolina, 1966; MA, Georgia State University, 1970. *Appointments:* Director, Graduate Admissions, Savannannah College of Art & Design, 1987-. *Creative Works:* Fiber Sculptures/Works Displayed at: Arnot Art Museum, New York; Rockwell Musem, New York; Thousand Islands Museum, Canada; State University of New York; Eversons Museum of Art, New York. *Hobbies:* Sailing; Off Shore Racing. *Address:* PO Box 775, Tybee Island, GA 31328, USA.

SMITH Rhea Dawn Wilcox, b. 21 Oct. 1951, Bedford, Indiana, USA. Association Executive. m. Rick A Smith, 15 Dec. 1973. *Education:* BS, Restaurant, Hotel, Institution Management 1973, MS, Technology/Supervision 1976, Purdue University. *Appointments:* Food Services Assistant Manager, Nthn Illinois University, 1973-77; Residence Hall Assistant Manager, Purdue University, 1977-83; Manager, Association of College & University Housing Officers International, 1984-. *Creative works:* Paintings: Winter in the Meadow; A Typical Fall. Photographs: Hard at Work; Winter's Work; Kentucky Spring; 7.45 PM. *Memberships:* Membership and Education Committees; Women in Communication, Columbus Chapter; Naational Association for Female Executives; American Society of Assn Executives, International Group. Ohio Society of Assn Executives, Fall Conference Social Committee; Ohio Photographic Society; MENSA International & Central Ohio; Faculty & Professional Women's Society; Faculty & Staff Fitness Program (OSU). *Honours:* Conference presenter, International Conference, 1980; Council for Management Development, Purdue University, 1981-82. *Hobbies:* Photography; Landscaping; Reading; Running; Raquetball; Organization Psychology; Creativity. *Address:* 101 Curl Dr Suite 140, Columbus, OH 43210, USA.

SMITH Riette T, b. 4 June 1936, Canton, Ohio, USA. Marriage & Family Therapist. m. Sidney R. Smith, 6 Apr. 1958, 1 son, 1 daughter. *Education:* AA, Stephens College, 1956; BS, 1958, MS 1967, Indiana University. *Appoinments:* Private practice, 1974-. *Memberships:* American Association of Sex Educators, Counsellors and Therapists; Academy of Family Mediators; AAMFT. *Address:* PO Box 1965, Bloomington, IN 47402, USA.

SMITH Rose Meisner, b. 7 July 1947, Deggendorf, Germany. Public Relations Professional. m. Carl M Smith, 13 Apr. 1969. 1 son. *Education:* BS Communications 1969, MA Sociology 1972, Temple University; MBA Finance, Manhattan College, 1983. *Appointments:* Public Information Trainee 1969-70, Public Information Assistant 1970-72, Principal Pub Inform Assistant 1972-75, New Jersey Department of Community Affairs; Public Affairs Officer, NJ Housing Finance Agency, 1975-82; Public Affairs Administrator, NJ Economic Development Authority, 1982-89. *Memberships:* International Association of Business Communicators; New Jersey Council for Urban Economic Development, Chairman, Public Relations Committee. *Honours:* Award of Excellence, District I, International Association of Business Communicators for 1984 Annual Report of the NJ Economic Development Authority; Communications Award, Temple University, 1969; Partial Scholarship, 1965-69 awarded by Philadelphia Board of Education for academic standing. *Hobbies:* Physical Fitness Training; Dance Roller Skating. *Address:* 1106 Tannerie Run Road, Ambler, Pennsylvania, USA 19002.

SMITH Selma Moidel, b. 3 Apr. 1919, Ohio, USA. Lawyer; Composer. 1 son. *Education:* JD, Pacific Coast University, 1942. *Appointments:* General Practice Law; Member, Moidel, Moidel, Moidel & Smith; Field Director, Civilian Advisory Committee, WAC 1943. *Memberships Include:* American, California, Los Angeles Bar Associations; National Association Women Lawyers; Inter-American Bar Association. *Honours:* Order del Merito Juan Pablo Duarte, Dominican Republic. *Address:* 5272 Lindley Ave., Encino, CA 91316, USA.

SMITH Shelley Owen, b. 9 Feb. 1955, Napa, California, USA. Nautical Archaeologist. m. Warren Curtis Riess, 28 Nov. 1980, divorced 1988. 1 daughter. *Education:* BA, Anthropology, University of Arizona, 1976; MS, Nautical Archaeology, Texas A & M University, 1979; MA 1983, PhD 1986, Historical Archaeology, University of Pennsylvania. *Appointments:* Shipwreck Investigations include: Defence, Stockton Springs, 1978-81; Ronson ship, New York, 1982; Snow Squall, Falkland Islands, 1983; Isle aux Morts shipwreck, Isle aux Morts, Newfoundland, 1983; Yorktown shipwreck, 1985; Hart's Cove Wreck, New Castle, 1986-87; La Grange, Sacramento, 1987. *Creative works:* Archaeology in Solution, co-author J W Foster, 1988; La Grange: A Gold Rush Legacy, co-author S James, 1988; Life at Sea, The Sea Remembers, editor Peter Throckmorton, 1987; The Defence; Life at Sea as Reflected in an Archaeological Assemblage from an Eighteenth Century Privateer, 1986; The Ship Beneath the City, co-author W C Riess, 1982. *Memberships:* Maritime Archaeological and Hisotircal Research Institute, chair; Society of Historical Archaeology, publications committee; Institute of Nautical Archaeology. *Honour:* Municipal Art Society of New York City, Merit Award for Excavation of the Ronson ship, 1982. *Hobbies:* Scientific illustration; Flying; Photography; Exploring Exotic Places. *Address:* 4041 Encina Dr, Napa, CA 94558, USA.

SMITH Sheryl (Sherry) Sue, b. 28 Apr. 1952, Norfolk, Virginia, USA. Assistant Professor. *Education:* BS Biology, College of William & Mary, Williamsburg, VA, 1974; PhD Physiology, University of Texas Health Science Center at Dallas, Texas, 1983. *Appointments:* Post-doctoral Fellow, Dept of Cell Biology, Southwestern School of Biomedical Science, Dallas, Texas, 1983-87; Assistant Professor, Dept of Anatomy, Hahnemann University, Philadelphia, 1987-; NIH funded research: Hormonal Control of Synaptic Efficacy In The CNS. *Publications:* 18 first author scientific publications in neuroscience or endocrine basic research journals; 5 scientific reviews/chapters; 15 presentations at scientific meetings. *Memberships:* Phi Beta Kappa; Society for Neuroscience; Endocrine Society; NY Academy of Science. *Honours:* Phi Beta Kappa, National Honorary Society; Alpha Lambda Delta, Freshman Honorary Society; Phi Sigma and Sigma Xi, Scientific Honorary Societies; William & Mary Merit Scholarship,

1971; Nominata Award, 1983 (Southwestern Medical & Graduate School): scholarship and research excellence as a graduate student; National Research Training Award, 1983-85. *Hobbies:* Modern dance; Ballet; Photography; Ancient mythology. *Address:* 208 Carriage House Lane, Riverton, New Jersey 08077, USA.

SMITH Tracy Michelle, b. 28 Dec. 1968, Union County, South Carolina, USA. Dispatcher. *Education:* AA, Marketing, Sparrtanburg Technical College, 1989. *Appointment:* Dispatcher, Whitmire Police Department. *Honours:* National Honour Roll, 1984-85; Academic All-American, 1984, 1986. *Hobbies:* Skating; Dancing; Bowling; Swimming; Walking; Biking; Working. *Address:* Rt. 1, Box 430, Whitmire, SC 29178, USA.

SMITH Vangy Edith, b. 17 Dec. 1937, Saskatoon, Saskatchewan, canada. Accountant; Consultant; Writer; Artist. m. (1) Clifford Wilson, 12 May 1958, deceased 1978. 5 children. (2) Terrance Raymond Smith, 14 Dec. 1979. *Education:* Student, Saskatoon Techn Collegiate Inst, 1956, BBA 1958, MBA 1967, PhD in English with honours 1988. *Appointments:* Accounts Payable Clerk, Maxwell Labs Inc, San Diego, 1978; Invoice Clerk, Davies Electric, Saskatoon, 1980-81; Office Manager, Ladee Bug Ceramics, Saskatoon, 1981-87; Lazars Investments Corp, Eugene, Oregon, 1987; Bookkeeper Accounts Payable, Pop Geer, Eugene, Oregon, 1987; Office Manager, Bookkeeper, Willamette Sports Ctr, Inc, Eugene, 1987-. *Publications:* Contributor of articles to scholarly journals. *Memberships:* Women's Christian Temperance Union, 30 years (President-State Director); Board of Trustees, Childrens Farm Home, Govt/Community Relations; Foundation for Christian Living; American Society of Writers; Beta Sigma Phi. *Honours:* Recipient 3rd and 4th place Artists' Awards, Lane County Fair, 1987; 1st and 2nd place awards, nat Writing, 1987, 1988. *Hobbies:* Needlework; Rug Hooking; Reading; Writing; Oil painting. *Address:* 1199 North Terry Street Sp 371, Eugene, OR 97402-1456, USA.

SMITH Virginia Dood, b. 30 June 1911, Randolph, Iowa, USA. Congresswoman. m. Haven N Smith, 1931. *Education:* Iowa Public Schools; BA, University of Nebraska, 1934. *Appointments:* National Chairman, American Farm Bureau Women, 1955-74; Member, Nebraska State Normal Schools Board Education, 1950-60; Governor's Commission on Status of Women, 1964-68; Member, House of Appropriations Committee, Sub-Committees on Agriculture and Energy & Water Development, 1974-, Vioo Chairman Agriculture Appropriations Sub-committee. *Memberships:* Delegate, White House Conference on Children & Youth, 1960; Chairman, Presidential Task Force, Rural Development, 1971-72. *Honours:* Recipient, Freedom Foundatiron Top Public Address Award, 1966; Deputy President, Associated Country Women of the World, 1962-68; President American Country Life Association, 1951-53; Board of Directors, Agricultural Hall of Fame; Vice President, Farm Film Foundation; Delegate, Republican National Conventions, 1956, 1960; Distinguished Service Award University of Nebraska, 1956; Many other honours and awards. *Address:* 2202 Rayburn House Office Building, Washington, DC 22215, USA.

SMITH BURKE Ellen Marie, b. 23 Apr. 1952, Mt Kisco, New York, USA. Director of Human Resources. m. Edward Burke, 24 Mar. 1979, widowed 1989. 1 daughter. *Education:* BA, Writing Arts/English, Oswego University, 1974; MBA, Industrial Relations, Pace University, 1979. *Appointments:* Service Representative, New York Telephone Co, 1974-76; Wage and Salary Asst, Albert Einstein College of Medicine, Bronx, 1977-78; Asst Director of Personnel 1978-84, Director of Human Resources 1984-, Beth Abraham Hospital, Bronx. *Publications:* Author, Wage and Salary Training/Desk Reference Manual; The Dunes; The Chess Game; Combination of Two; The Marriage; Second Attempt and other published poems. *Memberships:* American Society of Hospital Human

Resource Administrators; Association of Human Resource Systems Professionals; Society for Human Resources MGT; American Mensa Society; Daughters of the American Revolution; American Arbitration Association; New York Association of Hospital Human Resource Administrators, editor, newsletter, 1989/90; Chairperson for Program Planning, 1990/91; International Foundation of Benefits Administrators; National Association of Female Executives. *Honours:* Scholarship, US National Merit Society, New York, 1970; NY State Board of Regents Scholarship, 1970-74; Scholarship, Mellon Foundation, 1976-79. *Hobbies:* Squash; Skiing and other sports; Needlework; Fishing; Writing. *Address:* Raymond Road, North Salem, NY 10560, USA.

SMITH-KINNARD Janet Elizabeth, b. 12 Nov. 1937, Lake County, USA. Company President; Tour Operator. m. James Cannon Kinnard, 13 Dec. 1956, 1 daughter. *Education:* AAB, Clayton Junior College, 1973; AB, 1976, MA, 1978, Georgia State University. *Appointments:* Accounting Positions, various firms, 1956-71; Contact Atlanta, 1976-80; Director, Training, Crisis Board Member, Stockholder, Tour Director, Carefree Motorcoach Tours Inc., 1980-84; President, Renaissance Tours, 1984-. *Memberships:* Mu Rho Sigma; Southern Sociological Society; Kentucky Colonels; Business & Professional Womens Association; American Business Association; National Tour Association. *Honours:* Mortar Board Hoor Society, GSU, 1976; various other honours and awards. *Hobbies:* Travel; Reading; Music; Painting; Horse Riding. *Address:* PO Box 131, Decherd, TN 37324, USA.

SMITH-YOUNG Anne Victoria, b. 25 Aug 1947, Long Beach, California, USA. Technician/Administrator; Co-Director; Administrative Secretary. m. (1) Lynn Walker Smith, II Aug 1968, divorced Feb 1980, twin daughters; (2) Stephen Nicholas Young, 29 May 1982. *Education:* AS, Long Beach City College, 1967; BS, Marymount College, 1984; Diplomate, American Board of Urologic Allied Professionals. *Appointments:* Manager, office of Williams-Brinton Medical Corporation, Huntington Beach, California 1975-80; Administrator, Westchester Urological Associates, White Plains, New York, 1980-82; Administrator, Pediatric Urology Associates, Westchester County Medical Center, Valhalla, New York, 1982-86, Clinical Co-ordinator Urodynamics Laboratory, Department of Urology, 1986-, Chairperson Executive Committee Employee Advisory Council, 1987-; Consultant. Office Career Services, Marymount (New York) College, 1984-; Administrative Secretary, American Board of Urologic Allied Health Professionals 1987- (Consultant 1984-89; Co-founder, Co-director, President, Continence Restored, Inc, New York City, 1985-; Participant, People to People Medical Delegation to China, 1986, Hearings for National Kidney & Urologic Diseases Advisory Boardr, HHS, 1988; Lecturer in field; Board of Directors, Help for Incontinent People, Spartanburg, S C, 1985-89; Participant IAET Incontinence Task Force for HCFA, 1987. National Agenda to Promote Urinary Continence, 1984. *Publications:* Contributor to professional journals. *Memberships:* American Urologic Association Allied (national fundraiser 1980-86, Board of Directors, New York Chapter 1988-; Board of Directors, Association of Urinary Continence Control; Board of Directors, Lions Club of White Plains; American Association of Medical Assistants; National Association of Female Executives; International Platform Association; National History Preservation Trust. *Address:* 407 Strawberry Hill Ave, Stamford, CT 06902, USA.

SMITHFIELD Mary, b. 6 Aug. 1934, West Morden, England. Company Manager. *Education:* BA, honours, University of Essex, 1956. *Appointments:* Freelance Advertising Consultant, 1966-75; Manager, Interfridge Products, 1975-. *Hobbies:* Golf; Reading. *Address:* Interfridge Products, 26 Link Lane, Sutton, Cambridgeshire, CB6 2NF, England.

SMITHSON Alison Margaret, b. 22 June 1928, Sheffield, England. Architect. m. Peter Denham Smithson, 18 Aug. 1949. 1 son, 2 daughters. *Education:* Dip (Dist), Dunelm. *Appointments:* Private Practice, Architect, 1950-. *Creative works:* Buildings; Books; Essays; Paintings; Sculpture; Graphics; Clothes; Furniture. *Address:* Cato Lodge, 24 Gilston Road, London SW10 9SR, England.

SMOIRA-COHN Michal, b. 13 Feb. 1926, Tel-Aviv, Israel. Musicologist; Head of Music Broadcasting. m. Justice Haim Cohn, 1 son, 1 daughter. *Education:* Diploma, Palestine Academy of Music, Jerusalem, 1946; Phil.kand, Department of Musicology, University of Uppsala, Uppsala, Sweden, 1958. *Appointments:* Lecturer, Aesthetics of Music, Tel-Aviv University, 1959-66; Music Critic, Ha'a Metz Hebrew Daily, 1966; Head of Music, Broadcasting Authority, 1968-; Head of Rubin Academy of Music, 1979-84. *Publications:* Books: Introduction to Music History (in Hebrew); Israeli Folk Songs (in English); Meaning in Music (in Hebrew); Dictionary of Music (in Hebrew). *Memberships:* President, Council of Women's Organisations in Israel; Chairman, Tolerance, movement for non-violence; International Convener, Mass-Media ICW. *Address:* Jerusalem, Israel.

SMUCKER Barbara Claassen, b. 1 Sept. 1915, Newton, Kansas, USA. Writer; Lecturer. m. Donovan Ebersole Smucker, 21 Jan. 1938, 2 sons, 1 daughter. *Education:* BS, Kansas State University, 1936; Library Science, Rosary College, Illinois, 1960-64. *Appointments:* High School English Teacher, Kansas, 1937-38; Newspaper Reporter, 1939-41; Children's Librarian, Ontario, Canada, 1969-77; Head Librarian, Renison College, Waterloo, Ontario, 1977-84. *Publications:* Children's books: Henry's Red Sea, 1955; Cherokee Run, 1957; Wigwam in the City, 1966; Underground to Canada, 1977; Days of Terror, 1979; Amish Adventure, 1983; White Mist, 1985; Jacob's Little Giant, 1987. Translations, 8 languages, sales 16 countries. *Memberships:* Canadian Association of University Women; Canadian Association of Authors & Illustrators; Children's Reading Round Table, Chicago; Canadian Writers Union; Children's Book Centre, Canada; Board, Lion & Lamb Peace Centre for Children, USA. *Honours include:* Brotherhood Award, National Conference of Christians & Jews, 1980; Distinguished Service Award, Kansas State University, 1980; Honorary DLitt, University of Waterloo, 1986; Childrens Literary Award, best book of year, Canada Council, 1979; Award, best book selected by high school students, Ruth Schwartz Foundation, 1979; Vicki Metcalf Award, best total contribution to children's books, Canadian Authors Association, 1988. *Hobbies:* Hiking, Cycling & Swimming; Theatre, Music & Lectures; Children & Grandchildren. *Address:* c/o Penguin of Canada, 2801 John Street, Markham, Ontario, Canada L3B 1B4.

SMUTNY Joan Franklin, b. Chicago, USA. Educator. m. Herbert Paul Smutny, 1 daughter. *Education:* BS, MA, Northwestern Univesity. *Appointments:* Teacher, New Trier High School; Faculty Member, Founder, Director, National High School Institute, Northwestern University School of Education; Faculty, Founder Director, High School Workshop in Critical Thinking & Education, Chairman Dept., Communications, National College Education, Evanston, 1967-; Executive Director, High School Workshops, 1970-75; Director of the Center for Gifted National College of Education, 1985-. *Publications Include:* A Thoughtful Overview of Gifted Education, 1989; Your Gifted Child, 1989; Introduction to Gifted Education: programmes & perspectives, 1989; Education of the Gifted, 1981; Individualizing Career Education Programme, 1980; Thinking for Action in Career Education, 1981-82. *Memberships:* Various professional organisations. *Honours:* Pi Lambda Theta; Phi Delta Kappa. *Address:* 633 Forest Ave., Wilmette, IL 60091, USA.

SMYTH Anne Elizabeth, b. 10 June 1953, Birmingham, England. Headmistress. m. Michael Andrew Smyth, 22 Mar. 1980, 1 son. *Education:* Certificate of Education, 1975. *Appointments:* Primary School Teacher, Smethwick, 1975-77; various clerical positions, 1977-80; Primary School Teacher, Swans School, Spain, 1980-81; Civil Service & Swimming Teacher, 1981-82; Primary Teacher, 1982-85; Headmistress, 1985-, Swans School, Spain. *Memberships:* International Swimming Teachers Association; Swimming Teachers Association. *Honours:* 2nd Dan Black Belt, Karate, 1988. *Hobbies:* Swimming; Karate. *Address:* Swans School, Capricho 2, Marbella, Spain.

SMYTH Rosaleen, b. 16 Nov. 1939, Sydney, Australia. Principal Research Officer, Royal Commission into Aboriginal Deaths in Custody, Australia. *Education:* BA, Sydney University, 1960; MA 1976, PhD 1983, University of London, England. *Appointments:* Teacher, Western Samoa, 1964-65; Actress, England, 1966-70; Teacher, Zambia; Sudan, 1971-74 and 1979; Lecturer, History Methods, University of Zambia, 1979-83; Communications Research, Aboriginal Affairs, Canberra, 1983-85; Senior Legislative Research Specialist, Parliamentary Library, Canberra, 1985-88. *Publications:* Historical Articles on Mass Media in Africa in: Journal of African History; African Affairs; Historical Journal of Film, Radio and Television; Journal of Commonwealth History, et al. Appeared in the play, The Mousetrap, Ambassadors Theatre, London, England, 1969. *Memberships:* International Institute of Communications; Amnesty International. *Honours:* Commonwealth Scholarship, Sydney University, 1956; Best Actress Award, Lusaka, Zambia, 1983. *Hobbies:* Theatre; Swimming; Aerobics. *Address:* 3/4 Mowatt Street, Queanbeyan, New South Wales, Australia.

SMYTHE Patricia Rosemary Koechlin, b. 22 Nov. 1928, East Sheen, England. m. Samuel Koechlin, 10 Sept. 1963. 2 daughters. *Education:* Pates GS Cheltenham; St Michael's Cirencester. *Career:* Equestrian; British Show Jumping Team, 1947-64. *Publications:* Books (as Pat Smythe), Jump for Joy: Pat Smythe's Story, 1954; Pat Smythe's Book of Horses, 1955; One Jump Ahead, 1956; Jacqueline Rides for a Fall, 1957; Three Jays Against the Clock, 1957; Three Jays on Holiday, 1958; Three Jays Go To Town, 1959; Three Jays Over the Border, 1960; Three Jays Go To Rome, 1960; Three Jays Lend a Hand, 1961; Horses and Places, 1959; Jumping Round the World, 1962; Florian's Farmyard, 1962; Flanagan My Friend, 1963; Bred to Jump, 1965; Show Jumping, 1967; A Pony for Pleasure (with Fiona Hughes), 1969; A Swiss Adventure, 1970; Pony Problems (with Fiona Hughes), 1971; A Spanish Adventure, 1971; Cotswold Adventure, 1972. *Memberships:* World Wild Fund for Nature Int Cncl and UK Cncl; President, British Show Jumping Association, 1982-86; Freeman, Worshipful Co of Farriers 1955; City of London 1956; Worshipful Co of Loriners 1961, Worshipful Co of Saddlers 1963. *Honours:* Winner of numerous prizes including: Leading Show Jumper of the Year 1949, 1958 and 1962; Set Ladies' record for high jump Brussels 1954; Won Show Jumping Team Bronze Medal, 10th Individual, 1956; 10 Individual, 1960. *Hobbies:* Sport; Music. *Address:* Sudgrove Ho, Miserden, Nr Stroud, Glos, GL6 7JD, England.

SNEAD Stella, b. 2 Apr. 1910, London, England. Photographer; Painter. *Education:* Studied painting, Ozenfant Academy of Fine Arts, London, 1936-41. *Creative works:* 11 exhibitions of painting in London, New York, New Mexico and California, 1941-50; 40 exhibitions of photography in India, England, America, Australia, 1965-87; 6 books, 1 to be published 1989; Numerous photo-essays in magazines. *Honour:* In permanent collection of Victoria & Albert Museum, London, England. *Hobbies:* Extensive travelling; Cycling; Trying to understand Cosmology and Chaos. *Address:* 160 West End Avenue, Apt 21B, New York, NY 10023, USA.

SNODGRASS Faye B, b. 3 Apr. 1941, Nashville, USA. Company President. m. William Ramsey Snodgrass, 28 Dec. 1968, 1 son, 2 daughters. *Education:* Certified Teacher. *Appointments:* Teacher, Indianapolis Public Schools, 1962-65; Organizer, Director, Gallatin (Tenn.) Day Care Centre, 1965-66; Assistant to Vice President, Alumni-Development, Vanderbilt University, 1966-68; Assistant Account Executive, Holder Kennedy Public Relations, Nashville, 1980-82; Account Executive, Burson Marstellar, Cohn & Wolf Public Relations, 1982-84; President, Chairman, Communications Network Inc., 1984-. *Memberships:* Numerous civic and professional organisations. *Hobbies:* Travel; Entertaining; Reading. *Address:* The Communications Network Inc., 1812 Broadway, Nashville, TN 37203, USA.

SNOW Helen Foster, b. 21 Sept. 1907, Utah, USA. Author; Researcher; Genealogist. m. Edgar Snow, 25 Dec. 1932 (divorced 1949). *Education:* University of Utah, 1925-27; Yenching University, Peking, China, 1934-35. *Appointments:* China correspondent, Scripps Canfield Newspapers 1931-32, China Weekly Review (Shanghai) 1935-37; Book reviewer, Saturday Review of Literature, New York, 1941-46; Freelance journalist. *Publications:* 8 trade books, various others of historical research. Titles include: Inside Red China, 1939, 1974; China Builds for Democracy, (1st history of Gung Ho industrial co-ops), 1941; Chinese Communists, 1952, 1972; Saybrook Story (England 1619-), 1978; Land Beyond Kuttawoo: Madison Story, 1974; Totemism, Tao-Tieh & Chinese Ritual Bronzes, 1978; History of Damariscove Island in Maine from 1614, 1979; My China Years, 1984 (translations to Chinese & Japanese, film planned); Gung Ho Papers (industrial co-ops), 1985. *Memberships:* Honorary member, US-China Friendship Association; Chair, American Committee for Industrial Cooperatives. *Honours include:* Nominated, Nobel Peace Prize (work for East-West understanding, including work as prime mover (China 1938, India 1942) for establishment of industrical co-ops), 1981; Honorary DLitt, St Mary's of the Woods, Indiana, 1981. *Hobbies include:* Wildlife preservation, conservation; Promotion of workers industrial cooperatives in 3rd world, for refugee relief, unemployment, status of women, 1938-. *Address:* 148 Mungertown Road, Madison, Connecticut 06443, USA.

SNOWDON Jane Louise, b. 17 July 1959, Ann Arbor, Michigan, USA. Industrial Engineer. *Education:* BS, Industrial & Management Systems Engineering, Pennsylvania State University, 1981; MS, Industrial Engineering, University of Michigan, 1982. *Appointment:* E I Dupont, 1981; Graduate Teaching/Research Assistant, University of Michigan, 1981-82; Semiconductor Cost Engineering co-ordinator, 1982-, IBM. *Publications:* Manufacturing Review. *Memberships:* Institute of Industrial Engineers; Operations Research Society of America; Phi Mu; Society of Manufacturing Engineers. *Honours:* Recipient, several scholarships. *Hobbies:* Racquet Sports; Swimming; Travel. *Address:* 1185 Collier Road NW No 18F, Atlanta, GA 30318, USA.

SNUGGS-MCGUIRE Joan Frances, b. 8 July 1934, Washington, USA. Claims Representative. m. William Henry McGuire, 2 Mar. 1956, divorced 1966, 1 son. *Education:* BS, Bethune-Cooeman College, 1976. *Appointments:* Recreation Specialist, 1976-78; Special Assistant to Director, 1979-81; Computer Specialist, SSA, 1981-87; Claims Rep., Social Security Administration, 1987-. *Memberships:* American Association of Public Administration; EDGE; Gov.EDGE; Mid Atlantic Xerox Users Group. *Honours:* Academic Achievement, 1952; Phi Theta Kappa, 1973; UNCF Freedman Scholar, 1975; Alpha Kappa Mu, 1976; Hew Title XX Public Service Fellow, 1976; Presidential Management Intern, 1978-80. *Hobbies Include:* Painting; Sculpting; Writing; Organic Gardening; Sailing; Music. *Address:* 717 West University Road, Mesa, AZ 85201, USA.

SNYDER Jane Lois, b. 19 Dec. 1916, Greensburg, Pennsylvania, USA. Speech and Language Therapist (retired). *Education:* BEd 1937, MEd 1948, University of Pittsburgh; Post-graduate, Pennsylvania State College, 1957-58; several summer courses. *Appointments:* Elementary Teacher, Avonworth, Pennsylvania, 1937-47; Specialist in Speech and

Language Therapy, Pittsburgh Schools, 1947-79; Certified Supervisor, Special Education. *Publications:* 2 poems in National Poetry Anthology, 1st Survey of Non-English Speaking Students in Pittsburgh, grant from AAUW, 1969; Writer and participant in Education TV Speech Programmes for 5 years; Speaker, County Institute for Kindergarten Teachers, 1964; Project on Teaching Non-Verbal Children in Pittsburgh Schools, 1968. *Memberships include:* Life Member, Co-founder, Pennsylvania Speech and Hearing Association; Secretary 1963-64, Chairman, Educational Funding, 1979-80; American Association of University Women, Secretary 1963-64; Smithsonian Institution; Carnegie Institute; Frick Scholarship Alumnae Assocation, Board Member, 1970; American Association of Retired Persons, President, Swissvale Ch. 1983-84; Allegheny County League of Women Voters, 2nd Vice President, 1981-86; Program Director, Veterans Hospital Radio & Television Guild, 1964-86; Founding Member, Fort Pitt Museum Associates, Secretary 1984; Chairman, Programs for Better Films & TV Guild; Co-Chairman, Pet Therapy for 18 hospitals, rest homes & senior citizens, 1984-86. *Honours:* Grant for survey of Students in High School Non-Drop-Outs, 1978; Accepted member, Pittsburgh Poetry Society, 1986 and elected 2nd Vice President. *Hobbies:* Little Theatre Productions; Poetry; Collecting unusual music boxes. *Address:* Apt 3 1713 Tonette Street, Pittsburgh, PA 15218, USA.

SODEINDE Esther Olufunso, b. 30 July 1941, Abeokuta, Nigeria. Principal of Federal Government Girls' College; College Administration. 2 sons. *Education:* NCE (Nigerian Certificate in Education), 1962; BSc (Hons) Botany, 1966; Diploma in Science Education, 1977; Certificate in College Administration, 1980; MEd (Administration & Planning), 1982. *Appointments:* Science Teacher, Abeokuta Girls' Grammar School, 1963; Head of Department and Science & Biology Teacher, Okeona Grammar School, 1966-73; Head of Department of Biology and Biology Teacher, King's College, Lagos, 1973-77; Principal, Federal Government Girls; College, Bida, Niger State, 1978-84; Principal, Federal Government Girls; College, Akure, 1985-; Assistant Director of Education, 1986- . *Publications:* Cultivation of Oil Palm Mushroom, 1966. *Memberships:* Science Teachers' Association of Nigeria; Association of Science Education, Britain; Zonta International; Motherite Club; University of Ife, Alumni Association; Abeokuta Grammar School Old Boys Association. *Honours:* Academic Merit Scholarship Award, 1955, 1958; Books Prizes in Academics, 1953-56; Deputy College Prefect, 1958; Assistant Secretary, Literary & Debating Society, 1955; Deputy Leader (Music), 1955. *Hobbies:* Gardening; Sewing; Reading Novels; Music. *Address:* Federal Government Girls' College, PMB 759, Akure, Ondo State, Nigeria.

SOFTLY Barbara Charmian, b. 12 Mar. 1924, Ewell, Surrey, England. Retired. m. Alan J R Softly, 24 Mar. 1951. *Education:* Nonsuch High School, Cheam, Surrey, England, 1938-43. *Appointments:* Teacher of English and History, 1945-57. *Creative Works:* Publications: Plain Jane; Place Hill; A Stone in a Pool; Magic People; More Magic People; Ponder & William Series, 4 books; Geranium; Queens of England; A Lemon Yellow Elephant; Hippo Potta & Muss. Appearances on: Radio - BBC Woman's Hour; TV - Channel Four Gardening Programme. Contributor to short story anthologies and gardening magazines. *Memberships:* Council Member, Surrey Wildlife Trust; Life Member, Devon Gardens Trusts; Life Member, National Trust; RSPB; RSPCA; Cats Protection League. *Hobbies:* Gardening; Historical Research; Wildlife Conservation. *Address:* Bundels, Ridgway, Sidbury, Devon EX10 0SF, England.

SOLANTAUS Tytti, b. 3 Sept. 1946, Turku, Finland. Child Psychiatrist; Researcher. m. Juhani Solantaus, 21 May 1976, 2 sons, 1 daughter. *Education:* MD 1974; Specialist, Child Psychiatry, 1981. *Appointments:* General Practice, 1974-75; Child Psychiatry, 1975-83; Researcher, Finnish Academy, 1983-. *Memberships:* Finnish Child Psychiatric Association; Helsinki Women Researchers; Physicians for Social Responsibility;

Africa, Committee. *Honours:* Member, IPPNW, Nobel Peace Prize, 1985. *Hobbies:* Books; Theatre; Films; Writing Letters. *Address:* Juholankatu 23, 04400 Jarvenpaa, Finland.

SOLBRIG Ingeborg, b. 31 July 1923, Weissenfels, Germany. Professor of German. *Education:* Halle/Saale, Germany: State-lic. chemist; BA summa cum laude, San Francisco State University, 1964; Graduate student, University of California, Berkeley, 1964-65; MA 1966, PhD Humanities and German, 1969, Stanford University. *Appointments:* Chemist with Schoeller Co, Osnabruck, Germany, 1950-58; Naples, Italy, 1958-61; Assistant Professor, University of Rhode Island, USA, 1969-70; Assistant Professor, University of Tennessee, Chattanooga, 1970-72; Assistant Professor, University of Kentucky, Lexington, 1972-75; Associate Professor 1975-81, Professor 1981-, University of Iowa. *Publications:* Hammer-Purgstall University of Goethe, 1973; Rilke-heute, 1975; Goering, Seabattle, 1977; Numerous contributions to books and refereed scholarly journals (international). *Memberships:* MLA; AATG; American Society Eighteenth Century Studies; Canadian Society Eighteenth Century Studies; Founding Member, Goethe Society of North America; Goethe Gesellschaft, Weimar; Deutsche Schiller Gesellschaft. *Honours:* Recipient of numerous honours and awards including: Gold Medal, pro orientalibus, Austria, 1974; Old Gold Fellow, Iowa, 1977; Germany Acad Exch Serv grant, 1980; Senior Faculty Research Fellow in the Humanities, Iowa, 1983; National Endowment for the Humanities grant-in-aid, 1985; May Brodbeck Research Fellow in the Humanities, Iowa, 1989. *Hobbies:* Horseback riding; Photography; Reading; Gardening; Writing. *Address:* Department of German, University of Iowa, Iowa City, IA 52242, USA.

SOLER Dona Katherine, b. 7 Mar. 1921, Grand Rapids, USA. Civic Worker. *Education:* Graduate, Catholic Central. *Appointments:* Artist; Instructor; Metaphysical Councelor; Researcher; Editor. *Publications:* Publisher, Psychic Exchange, 1979-; What God Hath Put Together; Our Heritage from the Angels; Expose the Dirty Devil; For Love of Henry; Greyball; House of Evil Secrets. *Memberships:* Founder, 1st President, South Coast Art Association, 1963-65, Orange Coast Catholic Singles, 1970-73, Lake Riverside Estates Communicators, 1974-79, Psychic Exchange, 1979-; Member: Platform Association; Republican National Committee; National Tax Limitation and Balanced Budget Committee; California Tax Reduction Movement; Halt Legal Reform and many Animal Protection groups. *Address:* 2604 Willo Lane, Costa Mesa, CA 92627, USA.

SOLODAR Edna, b. 15 Mar. 1930, Kibbutz Gesher, Ashdot-Yacov, Israel. Member of Knesset, 1982-. m. Raziel Solodar, 1951, 1 daughter (deceased). *Education:* Music Academy, Tel Aviv; Liberal Arts, Kibbutz Seminary, Efal. *Appointments:* Musician; Secretary, Kibbutz Gesher, 1967-71, 1978-80; Secretary, Hakibbutz Homewhat Movement, 1972-76. *Hobby:* Music. *Address:* Kibbutz Gesher, 10880, Israel.

SOLOMON Ilene Sinsky, b. Washington DC, USA. Teacher. m. Marvin M. Solomon, 11 Sept. 1966, 2 sons. *Education:* BA, University of Maryland, 1966; MA, George Washington University, 1969; MA, American University, 1975. *Appointments:* Teacher, Montgomery County Public Schools, 1966-69, 1980-88; Director, Day Camp, Montgomery County Recreation Department. *Creative work includes:* Acting, directing. *Memberships:* Council for Exceptional Children; Past President, Columbian Women of George Washington University; Alumni Association, University of Maryland; American University School of Intal Service; Friends of Corcoran Gallery; *Honours:* Leadership award, Business & Professional Women, Washington DC, 1981; Delegate, General Alumni Association, George Washington University, 1981-83; Member, Pi Sigma Alpha, political science honour society. *Hobbies:* Acting; Painting; Directing; Candidate, Montgomery County Council,

Maryland, 1986; Radio announcer. *Address:* 8009 Westover Road, Bethesda, Maryland 20814, USA.

SOLT Mary Ellen, b. 8 July 1920, Gilmore City, Iowa, USA. Poet; Critic; University Professor. m. Leo F Solt, 22 Dec. 1946, 2 daughters. *Education:* BA, Iowa State Teachers College, 1941; MA, University of Iowa, 1948. *Appointments:* Iowa High Schools, 1941-45; University High School, Iowa City, 1945-48; Bentley School, New York, 1949-52; Indiana University, Boomington, 1970- . *Publications:* Flowers in Concrete, 1966; The Peoplemover 1968, 1978; A Trilogy of Rain, 1970; Marriage: A Code Poem,1976; Concrete Poetry: A World View, 1968, Editor; Dear Ez: Letters from William Carlos Williams to Ezra Pound, 1985, Editor. *Memberships:* Modern Language Association of America; Academy of American Poets; National Society of Arts and Letters; William Carlos Williams Society, President 1983-85. *Honours:* Fellowship, University Teachers, NEH, 1987-88. *Address:* 836 Sheridan Road, Bloomington, IN 47401, USA.

SOLTER Aletha Lucia Jauch, b. 21 Dec. 1945, Princeton, New Jersey, USA. Author; Publisher; Developmental Psychologist. m. Kenneth Solter, 10 July 1971, 1 son, 1 daughter. *Education:* Graduated, Swiss High School, Geneva, Switzerland, 1964; Master's degree in Human Biology, University of Geneva, 1969; PhD, Psychology, University of California, Santa Barbara, USA, 1975. *Appointments:* Lecturer, Department of Psychology, 1975-76; Postdoctoral Research Assistant, Department of Education, 1980-81, University of California, Santa Barbara; Instructor of Parenting Classes and Workshops, Continuing Education Division, Santa Barbara City College, 1985- . *Publications:* Books: The Aware Baby: A New Approach to Parenting, 1984; Helping Young Children Flourish, 1989. *Membership:* National Association for the Education of Young Children. *Honours:* National Science Foundation Predoctoral Traineeship, 1972-74; National Institute of Mental Health Predoctoral Fellowship, 1974-75. *Address:* PO Box 206, Goleta, CA 93116, USA.

SOLTI Anne Valerie Lady, b. 19 Aug. 1937, Horsforth, Yorkshire, England. Actress; Writer; Broadcaster. m. Sir Georg Solti, 11 Nov. 1967, 2 daughters. *Education:* Leeds Girls' High School; Leeds College of Music; Royal Academy of Dramatic Art, Diploma. *Appointments:* Reading Repertory, Cambridge Arts Theatre 1958; Roseland Variation on a Theme, West End, 1959; Granada TV, People's Places, 1959; Tyne Tees TV, 1959-60; Announcer, BBC TV, 1960-65; Freelance, BBC TV, 1965-70; Playschool BBC, 1968-70; Face the Music, BBC, 1971-83; Consultant, YTV, 1978-83. *Memberships Include:* Trustee, London Philharmonic Orchestra; Director, Opera 80; member, Development Committee, Royal College of Music; Patron, International Liszt Centre; member, BBC S. East Advisory Council; Committee of Management - Hampstead Old Peoples' Housing Trust. *Honour:* RCM (Hon), 1987; Patron: New World Symphony Orchestra. *Hobbies:* Painting; Architecture Design; Music; Theatre; Gardening; Walking; Swimming. *Address:* Chalet Le Haut Pre, Villars Sur Ollon, Vaud, Switzerland.

SOMAN Jean Powers, b. 17 Feb. 1949, New York City, New York, USA. Writer. m. William David Soman, 15 June 1969. 2 daughters. *Education:* University of Wisconsin, 1967-70; BA History, University of Miami, 1970-71. *Appointments:* Para-legal Assistant, Law Office of William Soman, 1980-88. *Publications:* Your True Marcus, The Civil War Letters of a Jewish Colonel, with Frank Byrne, 1985; numerous articles to magazines. *Memberships:* Fellow, Historical Museum of Southern Florida; Life Member, National Council of Jewish Women. *Honours:* Alternate choice of B'nai B'rith Jewish Book Club, 1986 for Your True Marcus. *Hobbies:* Tennis; Swimming; Reading; Oral Histories; Travel. *Address:* 9000 Arvida Drive, Coral Gables, Florida 33156, USA.

SOMERS Suzanne, b. San Bruno, California, USA.

Actress. m. Alan Hamel. *Education:* Attended, Lone Mountain School; San Francisco College for Women; Acting Tuition with Charles Conrad. *Appointments:* Nurses Aide; Model; Regular appearances on: Man Trap, a talk show; Roles in Films: Bullitt; Daddy's Gon-a-Hunting; Fools; Magnum Force; American Graffiti; 3 seasons in shows, Guy's & Dolls' Annie Get Your Gun, The Sound of Music and The Boyfriend; Guest-star role, in Dom Deluise TV series, Lotsa Luck; many appearances on Johnny Carson's Tonight Show; appearances on, Three's Company; High Rollers; One Day at a Time; The Rockford Files; Starsky & Hutch; appeared in films; Yesterday's Hero; co-starred in, Nothing Personal; Enlisted for Military Tours appearing in Korea, 1980, USS Ranger Aircraft Carrier, 1981, and Ramstein Air Force Base, and others, Germany, 1982; ABC TV appearances in mini-series, Hollywood Wives' and Goodbye Charlie, 1985. *Publication:* Book of Poetry, Touch Me. *Hobbies:* Gourmet Cooking; Entertaining; Decorating & Furnishing Home; Writing Cookery Book. *Address:* c/o Michael Levine Public Relations Co, 9123 Sunset Blvd., Los Angeles, CA 90069, USA.

SOMMER Elke, b. 1941 Germany. Actress. *Career:* Entered films in Germany, 1958. Made debut in British films, 1960. *Creative works:* Films include: Friend of the Jaguar; Travelling Luxury; Heaven and Cupid; Ship of the Dead; Don't Bother to Knock; The Victors; The Money Trap; Love the Italian Way; A Shot in the Dark; The Venetian Affair; Deadlier than the Male; Frontier Hellcat; The Corrupt Ones; The Wicked Dreams of Paula Schults; They Came to Rob Las Vegas; The Wrecking Crew; Baron Blood; Percy; Zeppelin; Ten Little Indians; Lisa and the Devil; The Prisoner of Zenda; The Astral Factory; Lily in Love. Television: Jenny's War; Peter the Great. *Address:* c/o 540 N Beverly Glen, Los Angeles, CA 90024, USA.

SOMMERS Estelle Joan, b. Baltimore, Maryland, USA. Retail Executive. m. Ben Sommers, 2 Dec. 1962, 3 daughters. *Education:* High School Graduate. *Appointments:* Stylist, owner, Loshins, Cincinnati, 1948-62; Manager, owner, Capazio Fashion Shop, New York City, 1964-79; Owner, Estar Ltd, NYC, 1969-79; Head Administrator, Joint Owner, Capezio Dance-Theatre Shops, NYC, Boston, Chicago, Hollywood (California), 1970-. *Memberships:* US Chair, Dance Library of Israel; Board, Dance Notation Bureau; American-Israel Cultural Foundation 1979-82; Centre for Dance Medicine; Co-chair, National Advisory Committee, International Ballet Competition, USA; Acting President, International Dance Alliance; Board, The Yard: Artistic Advicory Committee, International Conference, Jews & Judaism in Dance, 1986; Board, Joffrey School of Ballet. *Honour:* Peridance Award, Peridance Dance Centre, Lifetime's Service to Dance, 1987. *Hobbies:* Dance in all Manifestations; Theatre; Travel. *Address:* Capezio Dance-Theatre Shop, 755 7th Avenue, New York, NY 10019, USA.

SONCHIK Susan Maria, b. 10 Mar. 1954, Maple Heights, Ohio, USA. Analytical Chemist. *Education:* BS, John Carroll University, 1975; MS, Analytical Chemistry, 1978; PhD, Physical Chemistry, Case Western Reserve University, 1980. *Appointments:* Assistant Chemist, Horizons Research Inc., Beechwood, Ohio, 1974-75; Chemist Specialist, Standard Oil of Ohio Research Centre, 1975-79; Organic Chemistry Branch Manager, Versar Inc. Springfield, 1980-83; Advisory Engineer, Radiation Safety Officer, Gas Chromatography Programme Manager, IBM Instruments Inc., Danbury, 1983-87; Advisory Engineer, Lithography, IBM Corp, Burlington, 1987-. *Publications:* Articles in numerous journals and magazines; Speaker for 27 Technical Presentations; Book: African Walking Safari, 1985. *Memberships Include:* American Society for Testing and Maerials; American Chemical Society; National Association for Female Executives. *Honours:* Award, Technical Contribution to 10th International Congress of Essential Oils, Flavors and Fragrances, 1986; Distinguished Leadership Award, American Biographical Institute, others. *Address:* 14 Forest Road, Essex Junction, VT 05452, USA.

SONDEY Linda Marie, b. 24 Mar. 1953, Passaic, New Jersey, USA. Credit Manager. *Education:* BA, William Paterson College, New Jersey, 1976; NJ National Exchange Programme, semester abroad, Eastbourne College of Education, UK, 1973. *Appointments:* Teacher, Garfield Day Nursery, 1976-78; Administrator, Gannett Outdoor Advertising, 1978-80; Credit Collector, Manager, Personnel Manager, SIPCA Industries of America, 1980-87; Credit Analyst, PMC Inc, 1987-88; Credit Manager, Mid-Atlantic Region, Fuji Photo Film USA, 1988-. *Memberships:* National Association of Female Executives; American Society of Professional & Executive Women; National Committee to Preserve Social Security & Medicare; National Association of Credit Management; Mass Merchandise & Audio Credit Groups, Riemer Reporting Service. *Honours:* 1st Homecoming Queen, & National Honour Society, high school, 1971; Achievement Certificate, ASPEW, 1987-90; NJ State Scholarship, 1971-75; NJ International Exchange Programme, 1973. *Hobbies:* Tennis; Swimming; Crossword puzzles; Travel. *Address:* 345 4th Street, Saddle Brook, New Jersey 07662, USA.

SONDOCK Ruby Kless, b. 26 Apr. 1926, Houston, USA. Judge. m. Melvin Sondock. *Education:* BS, University of Houston, 1959; LLB, University of Houston College of Law, 1962. *Appointments:* General Law practice, Houston, 1961-73; Judge, Harris County Court of Domestic Relations, 1973-77; Judge, 234th Judicial District Court, 1977-82, 1983-89, Justice, Supreme Court of Texas, Austin, 1982; Of Counsel, Weil, Gotshal & Manges. *Memberships:* American, Texas & Houston Bar Associations; Kappa Beta Pi; Houston Association of Women Attorneys. *Address:* 700 Louisiana, Suite 1600, Houston, Texas 77002, USA.

SONENBERG Maya, b. 24 Feb. 1960, New York City, New York, USA. Fiction Writer. *Education:* BA, Wesleyan University, Middletown, Connecticut, 1982; AM, Brown University, Providence, Rhode Island, 1984. *Appointments:* Teaching Assistant, Choate Rosemary Hall, 1983; Teaching Fellow, Brown University, Providence, 1984; Lecturer, Sonoma State University, 1987. *Publications:* Stories: Nature Morte, 1982; Cartographies, 1984; Afterimage, 1985; June 4, 1469, 1988; Book: Cartographies, 1989. *Memberships:* Listed Author, Poets and Writers Inc; Associated Writing Programs. *Honours:* Phi Beta Kappa, 1982; Winchester Fellowship, Wesleyan University, 1982; University Fellowship, Brown University, 1982-83; MacDowell Colony Fellow, 1987; Drue Heinz Literature Prize, 1989. *Address:* 217 East 23rd Street, New York, NY 10010, USA.

SONG Agnes Young-Ok, b. 28 July 1937, Korea. Chief Psychologist. m. Ralph Song, 28 July 1968, 1 son, 2 daughters. *Education:* BA, College of St. Francis Joliet; MA, PhD, Catholic University of America. *Appointments:* Maryland State Dept. of Mental Hygiene, 1964-68; Lecturer, Johns Hopkins University, 1968; School Psychologist, 1968-71; Staff Clinical Psychologist, Southern Wisconsin Centre, 1971-75; Director, Psychological Services, Central Wisconsin Centre, Madison, 1976-. *Publications:* 13 journal articles; Author, Child Developmental Test. *Memberships:* American, Wisconsin Psychological Associations; Society of Clinical and Consulting Psychology; Vice President, Psychology, AAMD Wisconsin Chapter, 1978-80. *Honours:* Soroptimist Foundation Fellowship Award, 1964; NIMH Research Grant, 1968. *Hobbies:* Listening to good Music, Camping, Hiking, Cross-Country Skiing. *Address:* Psychological Services, Central Wisconsin Centre, 317 Knutson Drive, Madison, Wisconsin 53704, USA.

SONG Jeong-Sook, b. 28 Oct. 1936, Ockchun, Chungcheong-Nam-Do, Korea. Novelist; Journalist. m. Byung-Sung Oh, 25 June 1964, 1 son. *Education:* BA, Kunkuk University, 1962; MA studies, Sungkyun-Kwan University, 1962-63. *Appointments:* Reporter, Culture Department, Ilil Shinman newspaper 1961, Weekly Magazine, Hankook Ilbo newspaper 1962; Reporter 1970, Editor 1972, Department of Culture, Editorial Writer 1980-, Seoul Shunmun newspaper. *Publications include:* Non-fiction book: Only Mothers Can Make Children Wise; Novels: I'm Mr Lee's Wife, On My Wife, A Bastard, 2 Hours & 25 Minutes. Also: Seoul Column, Seoul Shinmun newspaper, 1988-; Numerous writings, articles, essays, various priodicals. *Memberships:* PEN Club, Korea; UNIMA, Korea; Korean Broadcasting Deliberations Committee; President 1980, Kwanhun Journalists Club; Trustee, Shinyong Journalism Fund, Kwanhun Club Board. *Hobbies:* Physical exercises; Jogging; Swimming. *Address:* c/o Seoul Shinmun Newspaper, 25, 1-Ga Taepyongno, Choong-Gu, Seoul, Republic of Korea.

SOPER Gay, b. 12 Sept. 1945, Surrey, England. Actress; Singer. m. Barry Stokes, 6 Dec. 1975, divorced 1985, 1 son. *Education:* St Anne's College, Sanderstead, Surrey; London Academy of Music & Dramatic Art, 1963-65. *Appointments:* Leading Roles in West End Productions including: Canterbury Tales, Godspell, Billy (Drury Lane), The Mitford Girls, Les Misèrables (current), all musicals; Opera, The Ratepayers, Iolanthe; Plays: Good, (Royal Shakespeare Company), and The Licentious Fly, (Mermaid Theatre); Leading Roles in TV productions include: Romany Jones, London Weekend TV; The History of Mr Polly, BBC; Father, Dear Father, Bless this House; Rude Health; appeared in Betjemania, in New York & London, 1980. *Hobbies:* Family Life; Entertaining; Cooking; Travel especially to Far East; Religion; Music. *Address:* c/o April Young Ltd., 2 Lowndes Street, London SW1X 9ET, England.

SORENSEN Elizabeth (Betty) Julia, b. 24 Nov 1934, Kenora, Ontario, Canada. Cultural Program Co-ordinator. m. Oliver Leo Paul Sorensen, 7 July 1956, divorced 1963, 1 daughter. *Education:* Secretarial Certificate, Success Business College, Winnipeg, Manitoba, Comm-Voc, Teaching Certificate, Ontario 1963-65; BA, Lakehead University, 1970; MA (BYU) 1972; ARCT, University of Toronto, 1977; AMRC, Mount Royal College, Calgary, 1977. *Appointments:* Legal Secretary, Winnipeg 1954-63; Teacher, Fort Frances, Ontario 1963-70; Instructor of Drama, Speech and English, Lethbridge, Alberta, Community College, 1972-77; Teacher, Business Education, Henderson College of Business, Lethbridge, 1978-80; Co-ordinator, Cultural Program, City of Medicine Hat, 1980-. *Memberships:* Canadian Conference of the Arts; Alberta Municipal Association for Culture, Treasurer; Alberta Recreation and Parks, Programming Seminar Committee 1987-89, Chairman 1989; Southern Alberta Touring Council, Vice-Chairman 1985-89; Allied Arts Council; MH Historical Society; MH Royal Scottish Country Dance Association; Firehall, Hatterland and Musical Theatres. *Honours:* Received 7 silver medals for Speech Arts at Mount Royal College and Royal Conservatory of Music. *Hobbies:* Directing plays; Writing; Puppetry; Sewing; Crafts. *Address:* 580-1 Street SE, Medicine Hat, Alberta, Canada T1A 8E6.

SORLEY WALKER Kathrine, b. Aberdeen, Scotland. Freelance Writer. *Education:* Crouch End College, London; King's College, University of London; Besancon University, France; Trinity College of Music, London. *Appointments:* Editorial Assistant, The Geographical Magazine, London, 1951-57; Freelance Writer, 1957-; Ballet and Dance Critic, The Daily Telegraph, London, 1968-. *Publications:* Robert Helpmann, 1958; The Heart's Variety, 1960; Raymond Chandler Speaking, 1962; Eyes on the Ballet, 1963, Revised Edition, 1965; Eyes on Mime, 1969; Saladin - Sultan of the Holy Sword, 1971; Dance and its Creators, 1972; Joan of Arc, 1972; Writings on Dance 1938-68 by A.V.Coton, 1975; Ballet for Boys and Girls, 1979; Emotion and Atmosphere, 1979; The Royal Ballet: a Picture History, 1981, Updated Edition, 1986; De Basil's Ballets Russes, 1982; Ninette de Valois: Idealist without Illusions, 1987; Contributor to: The Dancing Times, London; Dance Chronicle, New York; Dance Gazette, London; Vandance, Vancouver; The World and I, Washington DC; Dance and Dancers, London; other magazines; International Encyclopedia of Dance, USA; Encyclopedia Britannica; Enciclopedio dello Spettacolo, Rome; Encyclopaedia of the Dance and Ballet; Dance Encyclopedia, USA; Pipers Enzyklopädie, Munich; Programme Notes for the Royal Ballet, Australian Ballet and London Festival Ballet. *Memberships:* Critics Circle, London. *Hobbies and Interests:* Painting; Sculpture; History; Archaeology; Flora and Fauna. *Address:* 60 Eaton Mews West, London SW1W 9ET, England.

SOROKIN Ethel S., b. USA. Attorney. *Education:* BA, Vassar College, 1950; LLB with honours, University of Connecticut, 1953. *Appointments:* Faculty Advisor to Law Review, Lecturer in Law, University of Connecticut, 1955-58, 1961-66; Member, Connecticut Judicial Review Council, Attorney Representative, Term 1978-83, 1983-89; Currently Attorney, Sorokin & Sorokin PC, Hartford, Connecticut; Lecturer, Speaker on legal aspects of taxation and women's needs/rights, various bodies. *Publications:* Family Relations Jurisdiction, Connecticut (editor); Duty of Father to Support Minor Child - Effect of Wrongful Deprivation of Custody (author). *Memberships:* Trustee, Past President, University of Connecticut Law School Foundation; Hartford County, Connecticut, Bar Association, Member of Sections on Estates and Probate, Family Law, Antitrust and Trade Regulation, Chair of Family Law Legislation Committee, Chair of Uniform Marital Property Act Study Committee 1986; American Bar Association, Committee on Business Torts, Litigation, Family, Probate and Trust Sections, Judicial Administration Division Sanctions Committee and First Amendment Committee; The Association of Trial Lawyers of America; Board of Editors, Connecticut Bar Journal, 1951-55; University of Connecticut Law School Student Board of Editors, Editor-in-Chief 1953. *Address:* Sorokin & Sorokin PC, One Corporate Center, Hartford, CT 06103, USA.

SOUDERS Barbara Jean, b. 27 Feb. 1932, Chicago, Illinois, USA. Radio Hostess; Writer. m. John Edward Souders, 7 May 1955, 2 sons, 3 daughters. *Education:* AA cum laude, Manatee Community College, 1986; BA, Literature major, University of Southern Florida, 1988. *Appointments:* Writer, Editor, New Direction church testimonial magazine; Total responsibility for Over the Coffee Cup weekly radio programme; Freelance Writer for Nursery Business and Sarasota Town and County, 5 years; Religion and Feature Writer, Business Editor, Sarasota Journal, Sarasota, Florida, 1973-79; Staff Writer, Florida Tourist News, 1981; Religion Correspondent, Sarasota Herald-Tribune, 1983-88; Reviewer for Christian Film & Video, 1984-; Hostess, WJIS daily call-in radio show, Sarasota, 1986-; Sunday School Teacher. *Publications:* Magazine articles for several publications; Newspaper features. *Memberships:* Past President, International Training in Communications; The National Writers Club. *Honours:* College Award for Personal Contribution; College Award for Outstanding Achievement; Phi Theta Kappa National Honor Fraternity; Golden Key National Honor Society; School Bell Award for Teachers Speak Up in Sarasota Town and County Magazine, Florida National Education Association. *Hobbies:* Gardening; Photography; Writing; Reading. *Address:* Sarasota, FL 34243, USA.

SOULIOTI Stella, b. 13 Feb. 1920, Limassol, Cyprus. Advocate; Barrister at Law; Former Attorney-General, Republic of Cyprus. m. Dr Demitris Souliotis, 20 Aug. 1949, 1 daughter. *Education:* Diploma & Shield, St James' Secretarial College, London, England, 1937; Barrister-at-Law, Gray's Inn, London, 1948-51; Honorary LLD, University of Nottingham, 1972; Visiting Fellow, Wolfson College, Cambridge University, 1982-83. *Appointments:* Public Information Office, Cyprus Government, 1939-42; Served, WAAF, 1943-46; Law Practice, Limasol, Cyprus, 1951-60; Minister of Justice, Government of Cyprus, 1960-70; Minister of Health, 1964-66; Law Commissioner in Charge of Service for the Revision and Consolidation of the Cyprus Legislation, 1971-84; Attorney General, Republic of Cyprus, 1984-88; Member of Executive Board of UNESCO, 1988-. *Publications:* Contributor, numerous papers and talks on professional subjects. *Memberships*

Include: President, 1961-, Cyprus Red Cross Society; Chairman, 1962-, Cyprus Scholarship Board; Chairman, Cyprus Town & Country Planning Committee, 1967-70; Vice President, Cyrpus Anti Cancer Society, 1971-; Co-ordinator, Foreign Aid to Refugees, 1974-; Adviser, Cyprus Intercommunal Talks, 1976-; Chairman, Cyprus Overseas Relief Fund, 1977-82; Trustee, Cambridge Commonwealth Scholarship Trust for Cyprus, 1983-. *Honours:* Certficate of Good Service, RAF, 1947; Medal, Order of the Knights of St Katherine, Sina Oros, 1967; Gold Medal, International Association of Lions Clubs for Outstanding Humanitarian Work, 1975; Officer, Cedars of Lebanon, 1975; Paul Harris Fellow, Rotary International, 1988. *Hobbies:* Reading; Writing; Theatre. *Address:* PO Box 4102, Nicosia, Cyprus.

SOUTHCOTT Heather Joyce, b. 15 Nov. 1928, Adelaide, Australia. Part-time Pharmacist; Volunteer. m. Ronald Vernon Southcott, 5 Apr. 1952. 2 daughters. *Education:* AUA, Pharmacy, University of Adelaide, 1948. *Appointments:* Worked in Pharmacy in Hospital and retail areas; Member of State Parliament, 1982; Voluntary work. *Memberships:* United Nations Association of Australia (Fed President, 1987-88; State President, 1986-88); Australian Democrats (Federal President, 1984-87); National Council of Women of Australia (Int Secretary, 1976-79); Member of many other community groups. *Hobbies:* Music; Reading; Theatre; Opera; Ballet. *Address:* 2 Taylors Road, Mitcham 5062, South Australia, Australia.

SOVIK Ruth, b. 21 Dec. 1928, St Paul, Minnesota, USA. Deputy General Secretary, World Council of Churches. m. Arne Sovik, 31 Dec. 1949, 2 sons, 2 daughters. *Education:* BA, St Olaf College, Minnesota, 1950; MA and Secondary Teaching Certificate, Montclair State University, New Jersey, 1970. *Appointments:* Teacher of English, Ecole Internationale, Geneva, Switzerland, 1963-65, 1972-73; Assistant Editor, 1965-67, Managing Editor, 1973-77, International Review of Mission; Teacher of English, East Orange High School, East Orange, New Jersey, USA, 1969-71; General Secretary, World YWCA, 1980-85; Deputy General Secretary, World Council of Churches, 1986-. *Publications:* Numerous reports, articles in religious publications; Editor, various books. *Honours:* Phi Beta Kappa, 1950; Distinguished Alumna Award, St Olaf College, 1985. *Hobby:* Interior decoration. *Address:* 3 chemin de la Flechere, 1255 Veyrier, Switzerland.

SOWELL Betty Ann, b. 2 Sep. 1949, Ruston, Louisiana, USA. Director of Financial Aid. m. Oswald Henry Sowell, 2 June 1972, 1 daughter. *Education:* BA, Louisiana State University, Shreveport, 1977; BS, Law, 1982, JD, 1984, Glendale College of Law. *Appointments:* Bookkeeper, Powerline Supply Co, Bossier City, Louisiana, 1974-76; Financial Aid Counsellor, University of Arizona, Tucson, Arizona, 1976-78; Director of Financial Aid, Pacific Oaks College, Pasadena, California, 1978-. *Memberships:* California Association of Student Financial Aid Administrators; National Association of Student Financial Aid Administrators; National Association of Female Executives. *Honours:* Alpha Lambda Delta, 1967. *Hobbies:* Oil and tole painting; Camping; American Indian art; History (Civil War, World War II and California Gold Rush era; Genealogy. *Address:* Palmdale, CA 93550, USA.

SPADY Callie Jeanetta, b. 24 Aug. 1938, Townsend, Virginia, USA. Human Resource Administrator/ Investigator. *Education:* BA Mus.Ed., Allen University, 1961. *Appointments:* Teacher, English, Marion County School Board, 1961-62; Children's Counselor, New York City Human Resources Administration/Bureau of Child Welfare, 1962-76; Human Resource Administrator/ Investigator, New York City, 1976-. *Memberships Include:* Charter, Founding, Patron, The National Museum of Women in the Arts; International Federation Business & Professional Women; American Association of Retired Persons; National Trust for Historic Preservation; numerous other professional organisations. *Honours Include:* Recipient, Twenty years Dedicated Service Award, New York City, 1984, Twenty Five Years Award, 1987. *Hobbies:* Reading; Religious Activities; Politics; Arts; etc. *Address:* Washbridge Station, Post Office Box 211, New York, NY 10033, USA.

SPALDING Elaine, b. 26 June 1940, New York City, USA. Administrative Aide. m. Larry Spalding, 24 Dec. 1966. 1 son, 1 daughter. *Education:* College, Wooster, 1958-60. *Appointments:* Medical Secretary, Duke University Medical Centre, Durham, 1967-70; Administrative Secretary, Tampa Heights Hospital, 1973-74; Lead Distributor, Seyforth Labs Inc, Dallas, 1975-79, Futuron Industries Inc, Dallas, 1979-83; Director, Futuron Distribution Organisation, 1979-; Lead Distributor, Slendernow International, 1984-; Aide to Pinellas County Commissioner, Barbara Sheen Todd, 1980-. *Memberships:* Vice President, Peninsula Republican Club, 1982-; Women in Management. *Honours:* Distributor of The Year Award, 1980; Spirit of Futuron Award, 1981. *Address:* 1211 Brookside Drive, Clearwater, FL 34624, USA.

SPARKS Mary Belle, b. 14 Feb. 1936, Bedford County, Tennessee, USA. Chapter I Reading Teacher. m. Herbert Blackman Sparks, 18 Apr. 1958, 2 sons. *Education:* BSc, George Peabody College for Teachers, 1957; MEd summa cum laude, Middle Tennessee State University, 1971. *Appointments:* 6th Grade Teacher, Bedford County Schools, 1957-58, 1959-60; 4th, 3rd grades, Chapter I Teacher, Tullahoma City Schools, 1964-73; Chapter I Teacher, Bedford County Schools, 1973-. *Memberships:* National, Tennessee & Bedford County Education Associations; President, Tullahoma Education Association; Delta Kappa Gamma; Recording Secretary, Mary Tom Berry Council; International Reading Association; National Geographic Society; Smithsonian Associates. *Honours:* Treasurer & Assistant Chairperson, Administrative Board, Normandy United Methodist Church; Career Level III, State Department of Education, Nashville; Member, Steering Committee, Harris Middle School, Shelbyville. *Hobbies:* Painting; Sewing; Reading; Needlework. *Address:* 410 Cortner Road, Normandy, Tennessee 37360, USA.

SPARROW Janet Cruz, b. 4 May 1934, Los Angeles, USA. Aerospace Manager. m. Edward Akers Sparrow, 23 July 1957, divorced, 2 sons, 1 daughter. *Education:* AA, Los Angeles City College, 1961; BA, California State University, Los Angeles, 1963; MEd., Loyola Marymount University, 1973; JD, University of West Los Angeles, 1979. *Appointments:* Principal, Inglewood School District, 1974-76; Seniorubcontract Administrator, 1981-85, Subcontract Specialist, 1986-87, Manage,r 1987-, Hughes Aircraft Company. *Memberships:* Hughes Aircraft Company Federal Credit Union, Supervisory Committee, Board of Directors. *Honours:* Outstanding Achievement Award, YMCA, 1985; Superior Performance Award, Hughes Aircraft Company, 1985; Superior Team Award, Hughes Aircraft Company, 1985. *Hobbies:* Films; Reading; Travel; Gardening. *Address:* 5420 Holt Avenue, Los Angeles, CA 90056, USA.

SPEAR Laurinda Hope, b. 23 Aug. 1950, Rochester, Minnesota, USA. Architect. m. 4 Sept. 1976. 3 sons, 1 daughter. *Education:* BA, Brown University, 1972; MArchitecture, Columbia University, 1975. *Appointment:* Principal, Arquitectonica International Corporation, 1977-. *Creative works:* Atlantis, 20-storey, 96-unit apartment condominium, Biscayne Bay; Interior design and space planning for: Banco de Credito del Peru; North Dade Justice Center, North Miami, Florida; Center for Innovative Technology, Washington, DC; Colson, Hick & Eidson, PA, Miami; The Fur Vault; Interior design: Kushner House, Northbrook, Illinois; Walner House, Glencoe, Illinois; Mulder House (Casa Los Andes), Lima, Peru; Moosart Gallery, Miami Design District; Romann & Tannenholtz, Miami; Interior design and renovation of two buildings, Kitsos Medical Building, Miami. *Membership:* American Institute of Architects. *Honours:* Progressive Architecture Design Awards, 1978, 1980, 1982; AIA Honor Awards, 1980, 1982,

1988; Rome Prize, American Academy in Rome, 1978. *Hobby:* Painting. *Address:* c/o Arquitectonica International Corporation, 2151 Le Jeune Road Suite 300, Coral Gables, FL 33134, USA.

SPEARS Jae, b. Latonia, Kentucky, USA. State Senator. m. Lawrence E. Spears, 2 sons, 2 daughters. *Education:* University of Kentucky. *Appointments:* Reporter, Cincinnati Post, Enquirer; Research stations WLW-WSAI; Teacher, Jiya Gakuen School, Japan; Lecturer, US military installations, East Anglia, England; Delegate, West Virginia Legislature, 1974-80; State Senator, 1980-. *Memberships:* Advisory Board, West Virginia Womens Commission; State Visitors Committee, WV University College of Extension; Council, WV Autism Task Force; WV Executive, Literacy Volunteers of America; Board, Foundation of Independent Colleges of WV. *Honours:* Various Awards: NOW, 1982; Military Order Purple Heart, 1984; Professional Educators Association, 1986; WV State Veterans Commission; US Department of Labour, 1984; WV Veterans Council, 1984; Admiral, North Carolina Navy, 1982; Honorary Brigadier General, WV National Guard, 1984. *Address:* PO Box 2088, Elkins, West Virginia 26241, USA.

SPECK Hilda, b. 2 March 1916, Staylbridge, England. Retired. m. Willmot Hilton Speck, 4 Sept. 1937, (deceased), 2 Foster Daughters. *Appointments:* Director, Salvation Army Family Service Department, Flint, Michigan, USA, 1945-86; Licensed Social Worker. *Memberships:* Zonta International, Flint; Salvation Army of Flint Advisory Board; Board, Red Feather Million Dollar Disaster Fund, 1953. *Honours:* Woman of the Week, Radio Station WFDF, 1952; Life Member, Flint Salvation Army Advisory Board, 1984; 20 year Service Award, Big Brothers of Flint, 1981. *Hobbies:* Reading; Sewing; Volunteer Work; Church Work; Visiting Shut-Ins. *Address;* 2015 Stoney Brook Ct., Flint, MI 48507, USA.

SPECTOR Bettie Ann, b. 25 Nov. 1929, Denver, Colorado, USA. Family Therapist; Lecturer. m. Dr Sydney Spector, 20 June 1948. 1 son, 1 daughter. *Education:* BA, University of Denver, 1951; MEd, University of Maryland, 1964; EDS, Seton Hall University, 1982. *Appointments:* Counselor & Lecturer, St Louis, 1951; Research in Community Problems, St Louis Social Planning Council, 1952-53; Private Practice & Lecturer, 1956-66; US Atomic Energy Commission, 1966-68; Psychology, Livingston High School, 1971-80; Family Therapist, Women's Haven, 1980-83; Private Practice, Family Therapy, 1983-. *Publications:* Understanding Children; Articles on Family Violence, Battered Women. *Memberships:* Clinical Member, Amer Assoc Marriage & Family Therapists; Board of Directors, City of Hope (Wash DC Area); Pi Gamma Mu, Natl Soc Science Honor Society; Pi Delta Kappa, Ntl Honor Education Society. *Honours:* Estelle Hunter Memorial Scholarship, University of Denver, 1947; National Assoc Christians & Jews Grad Fellowship, Columbia University, 1952. *Hobbies:* Travelling; Studying family and cultural life in countries around the world. *Address:* 600 Green Park, Nashville, TN 37215,

SPECTOR Eleanor Ruth, b. 2 Dec 1943, New York, USA. Deputy Assistant Secretary. m. Mel A. Spector, 10 Dec. 1966, 1 son, 1 daughter. *Education:* BA, Barnard College, 1964. *Appointments:* Contracting Officer, Navy, 1965-82; Division Direcor, Cost Analysis, 1982- 84; DASD (P), 1984-. *Memberships:* Advisor, National Contract Management Association; Advisor, Defense Systems Management College. *Honours:* Navy Distinguished Civilian Service Award, 1984; DOD Meritorious Civilian Service Award, 1986. *Address:* The Pentagon, Room 3E 144, Washington, DC 20301-8000, USA.

SPEDDING Linda Susan, b. 9 Jan. 1952, Newcastle upon Tyne, England. Lawyer; Author. *Education:* LL.B., London University, 1972; LL.M., London University, 1977; PhD, London University, 1984; Admitted to New

York Bar, USA, 1985. *Appointments:* Articled Clerk, 1973-75; Admitted as Solicitor to Supreme Court of England & Wales, and Lawyer of the European Court of Justice, Luxembourg, 1975; Legal Advisor, Solicitor, Pitt House Schools Limited & Associated Companies, 1975-84; Private Practice, 1975-85; Associate, Messers Clifford Turner, 1977-78; International Associate, Akermann Senterfitt & Eidson, Orlando, 1983; Solicitor, Professional Purposes, Law Society, London, 1985-; Private Practice, 1985-. *Publication:* Transnational Legal Practice in the EEC and the United States. *Memberships:* various professional organisations. *Honours:* Recipient, honours & awards. *Hobbies:* Environment; Philosophy; Music; Yoga; Travel. *Address:* Suite 26, 17 Clarges Street, Mayfair, London W1Y 7PG, England.

SPEED Shirley Anne Adams, b. 9 June 1937, Spokane, Washington, USA. Principal Software Specialist; Data Processing Management. m. Marvin Ernest Speed, 9 July 1958. 1 son, 1 daughter. *Education:* BS Maths, University of Washington, 1958; BS, Business Admin 1985, MBA, CCU, California; Postgraduate, Hardin Simmons University; American management Assoc; IBM, Digital Tech Study. *Appointments:* Teacher of Mathematics; DP Professional, ATNA Life & Casualty, Hartford, 1976-85; Independent DP Consultant, 1985-86; Digital Equipment Corporation, West Hartford, 1986-. *Publications:* Speedy Writing Tips, 19?8; Development of Management Training Program for Data Processing, 1985; Systems Testing Methodology, 1988. *b3Memberships:* Data Processing Management Association; Association of Systems Managers; Association of Women in Computing; Urban League; national Association for Advancement of Coloured People. *Honours:* Keynote Speaker, United Nations International Woman's Conference, Upper Heyford AFB, England, 1975; Speaker for National Conference Women in Computing, Chicago, Illinois, 1985; Speaker, Executive, Forum Young Executives of Hartford, CT, 1983-84; DP Lectures, New York University, University of Hartford, Atlanta University Consortium, 1980-84. *Interests:* People to people communication to create understanding among diverse cultures; Extensive world travel; Human factors and technology research. *Address:* 55 Windbrook Drive, Windsor, CT 06095, USA.

SPENCE Janet Blake Conley, b. 17 Aug. 1915, Upper Montclair, New Jersey, USA. m. Alexander Pyott Spence, 10 June 1939. 2 sons, 1 daughter. *Education:* Diploma with honours, The Masters School, 1933; Vassar College, 1933-35; Certified (diploma) Katharine Gibbs Secretarial School, 1936. *Memberships:* Volunteer, Junior League; American Red Cross; Girl and Boy Scouts, USA; Darien Royle School Board; Secretary and Chairman, Darien Assembly; Secretary and Chairman, Wilton Junior Assembly; Wilton Public Health Nursing Association; Secretary, Treasurer, New Jersey Symphony Orchestra; Morris County League President, 1985-89; Membership Chairman, 1987-89, Home Economics Club, Washington Valley; Dobbs Alumnae Association; Vassar Club, New Jersey Hills; Program co-chairman, Washington Valley Community Association; Council Representative, Vassar College, 1973-78, a fund raiser for 50th reunion class '37; Morris County Art Association. *Hobbies:* Painting; Travel; Music; Enjoying my animals, children and grandchildren; Gardening. *Address:* Hilltop, Washington Valley Road, Morristown, NJ 07760, USA.

SPENCER Cherrill Melanie, b. 17 Feb. 1948, Derbyshire, England. Experimental Physicist. *Education:* BSc., Honours, Physics, London University, 1969; D.Phil., Oxford University, 1972. *Appointments:* Italian National Lab., Italy, 1972-74; University of Wisconsin, Madison, USA, 1974-77; Florida State University, 1977-79; Staff Scientist, Science Applications Inc., Sunnyvale, 1979-84; Physicist, Resonex Inc., 1984-88; Magnet Physicist, Stanford Linear Accelerator Center, 1988-. *Publications:* Numerous articles in professional journals; Designer, World's Most Uniform Magnetic Fields. *Memberships:* Math/Science Network, President, 1985-88; Forward Looking Strategies Comm., UN Association, USA; Association for Women in Science; AAAS; Institute of Physics. *Honours:* Holloway Prize, Royal Holloway College, University London, 1969; Royal Society European Fellowship, 1972-74. *Interests:* Increasing participation of women in science; Preserving natural diversity through land conservation. *Address:* B1N 12W, SLAC, PO Box 4349, Stanford, CA 94309, USA.

SPENCER Jean W, b. Philadelphia, Pennsylvania, USA. Author; Writer; Public Information/Public Relations; Photographer. m. John M Spencer, 1953. 2 daughters. *Education:* Ventura College, California; Upper Darby High School, Pennsylvania. *Appointments:* Public Information Officer, Oxnard College, 1975-; Freelance Writer. *Publications:* Images: Women in Transition Exploring Careers as a Computer Technician; Exploring Careers in the Electyronic Office; Exploring Careers in Word Processing & Desktop Publishing; Numerous articles, poems, photographs. *Memberships:* Presbyterian Church of the USA, Ordained Elder, Ordained Deacon; Faith at Work; PUCA, Public Information Communicators, A Founder and Life Member; California Assn of Community Colleges; Commission on Society of Children's Book Writers; Public Information California Writers Club; Conejo Ventura Macintosh Users Group. *Honours:* Women Helping Women, Soroptimist International, 1989; Awarded Life Members in PICA, 1987. *Interests:* Writing; Photography; Spiritual; Eclectic. *Address:* 1534 Loma Drive, Camarillo, CA 93010, USA.

SPENCER Margaret Roan, b. 13 Feb. 1927, Larksville, Pennsylvania, USA. Executive Director. m. L Robert Spencer, 21 Apr. 1956. 1 daughter. *Education:* BA, Economics, University of Pennsylvania, 1948. *Appointments:* Director, Valley Crest Day Care Center, 1964-68; Exeuctive Director, Luzerne County Bureau for the Aging, 1968-74; Executive Director, Pennsylvania Association of Older Persons, 1974-77; Executive Director, Heritage House, 1977-. *Publications:* Articles in professional journals and papers given to conferences. *Memberships:* President, PANPHA; NOR-PANPHA; President, Pennsylvania Council on Aging; Northeast Regional Council on Aging; American Association of Homes for the Aging; Gerontological Society; American College of Health Care Administrators. *Honours:* Women of the Year in the Professions Award, West Side Business and Professional Women Award, 1974; Outstanding Service Award, Foster Grandparents Program, 1974; Distinguished Service Award, PANPHA, 1983; Meritorious Service Award, American Association of Homes for the Aging, 1983; Community Service Award, Luzerne/Wyoming Counties Bureau for the Aging, 1983; Public Relations Award, PANPHA, 1985. *Hobbies:* Golf; Travelling; Reading. *Address:* 407 Orchard West, Dallas, Pennsylvania 18612, USA.

SPENCER Susan S, b. 9 July 1948, Budapest, Hungary. Associate Professor of Neurology (Neurologist; Epileptologist; Electroencephalographer). m. Dennis D Spencer, 14 Feb. 1980. 2 daughters. *Education:* BS, magna cum laude, Chemistry, 1970; MD 1974, University of Rochester, Rochester, New York. *Appointments:* Intern in Medicine, Dartmouth Medical School, 1974-75; Resident in Neurology, 1975-78; Assistant Professor of Neurology, 1980-83, Associate Professor of Neurology, 1983-, Yale University School of Medicine. *Publications:* Over 40 articles addressing the treatment of epilepsy and new approaches to treatment and diagnosis. *Memberships:* Phi Beta Kappa; American Epilepsy Society; American EEG Society; American Academy of Neurology; Society for Neuroscience. *Honours:* Visiting Professor in Taipei, Taiwan under auspices of Epilepsy Foundation of America; Multiple invited lectures. *Hobbies:* Pianist; Oboist; Collect marbles. *Address:* 333 Cedar Street, New Haven, CT 06510, USA.

SPENCER The Countess, m. (1)The Earl of Dartmouth, 3 sons, 1 daughter, (2)The Earl Spencer, 1976. *Appointments:* Voluntary Care Committee

Worker, Wandsworth & Vauxhall, London County Council, England; Membe, Citizen's Advice Bureau Committee for Central London, 2 years; Member, Richmond on Thames on the Greater London Council; Chairman, Covent Garden Joint Development Committee until 1972; Chairman, GLC Historic Buildings Board, 3 years; Westminster City Councillor, 1954-65; Represented Lewisham West on London County Council, 1958-65; Served on Town Planning Parks and Staff Appeals Committee, London County Council; actively interested in the welfare of the elderly, visiting homes and clubs for old people throughout the country. *Publications:* Do You Care About Historic Buildings?; co- author with The Earl Spencer, The Spencers on Spas. *Memberships:* Board Member, British Tourist Authority; Chairman, Spas Committee; Chairman, BTA Hotels & Restaurants Committee; Chairman, Commended Hotels Panel; Infrastructure Committee; Minister of Arts committee for Business Sponsorship of the Arts; etc. *Honours:* Gold Medal, Public Speaking; Hon. LL.D., Dartmouth College, USA. *Address:* Althorp, Northamptonshire NN7 4HG, England.

SPICAK Doris Elizabeth Fletcher, b. 6 Sept. 1943, Baltimore, Maryland, USA. Registered Nurse; Administrator. m. Marvin Ray Spicak, 18 May 1968, 1 son, 1 daughter. *Education:* Registered Nurse Diploma, Sinai Hospital Nursing School, 1965; ASc, Bee County College, 1976. *Appointments:* US Army Nursing Corps, 1964-68; Director, Inservice Education, Beeville Memorial Hospital, 1976; Director of Nursing, Hillside Lodge 1978-80; Beeville Hospital 1980-81; Director, Home Health Agencies, Coastal Bend 1981-85, Crossroads 1985-. *Memberships:* Past Treasurer, Coastal Plains Continuity of Care; National Home Health Association; Texas Association of Home Health Agencies; Chair, Medical Committee, Victoria Chamber of Commerce. *Hobbies:* Reading; Travel; Genealogy. *Address:* 205 Kelly Crick, Victoria, Texas 77904, USA.

SPIELMAN de PATRAS Patricia Conseula O'Connor (Countess), b. 19 Sept. 1917, St Paul, Minnesota, USA. Board Chairman (retired). widow. 1 son, 2 daughters. *Education:* University of Minnesota, 3 years. *Appointments:* Chairman of the Board (retired), RHS Carpet Mills. *Memberships:* National Board of Directors, Child Help; Life Member, National Arthritis Foundation; Life Member, Cancer Institute. *Honours:* Countess de Patras, 1985; Dame Grand Cross of Justice, Knights of Malta, 1985; Dame of Justice, Order of St George, 1985; Dame grand Cross Sovereign Order of the Oak. *Hobbies:* Bridge; Numismatics. *Address:* Penthouse 510, Balboa Bay Club, 1221 West Pacific Coast Highway, New Port Beach, CA 92663, USA.

SPIERING Nancy Jean, b. 15 Apr. 1958, Park Ridge, USA. Accounting Manager; CPA. *Education:* BS, Accounting, DePaul University, 1982; CPA, 1985; MBA Candidate, 1989-. *Appointments:* Cargill Inc., 1984-. *Memberships:* American Society of CPA's; Chicago Society of Women CPA's; Illinois CPA Society. *Honours:* Recipient, several honours & awards. *Hobbies:* Reading; English Darts; Training Dogs; Running. *Address:* 875 Mohawk Drive, Eglin, IL 60120, USA.

SPIRA Patricia Goodsitt, b. Milwaukee, Wisconsin, USA. Association Executive. m. Marvin Spira, 12 July 1952, 2 sons, 2 daughters. *Education:* BA, History, University of Wisconsin, 1967. *Appointments:* Creative Dramatics Teacher, 1962-67; Box Office Manager, Performing Arts Center, Milwaukee, Wisconsin, 1969-80; Director of Development, St Louis Conservatory and Schools for the Arts, St Louis, Missouri, 1980-81; Executive Director, President, Board of Directors, Box Office Management International, 1981-; Editor, Box Office Management International Newsletter; Board of Directors, President, Box Office Management Educational Corporation; Lecturer on Box Office Management. *Memberships:* Board Chairman, Great American Children's Theatre, 1976-80; Board of Directors, Milwaukee Chamber Music Society, 1974-80; Advisory Council, Town Hall Foundation; Board of Directors, TADA! Theatre and Dance Alliance of New

York, 1987-89; New York Society of Association Executives; American Society of Association Executives; Life Member, University of Wisconsin Milwaukee Alumni. *Hobbies:* Theatre; Opera; Books; Travel. *Address:* 333 East 46th Street 1B, New York, NY 10017, USA.

SPITZ Sheryl, Analyst; Writer. *Education:* BA, Barnard College, Columbia University, USA; MA, Columbia University; Certificate (MA), Harriman Institute, Columbia University; PhD, Stanford University. *Appointments:* Analyst/Writer-Consultant; International Trade Specialist, US Department of Commerce; Research Analyst, Library of Congress; Teaching Staff, Stanford University. *Memberships:* Phi Beta Kappa Association; President, Chevy Chase Chess Club; Stanford Alumni Association. *Honours:* Teaching Award, Parent-Teachers Association; New York State Regents Scholarship; Phi Beta Kappa; National Defense Foreign Language Fellowship; President's Scholarship, Columbia University; Graduate Fellowship, Harvard University; Graduate Fellowship; Yale University; Fellowship, Stanford University; Scholarship and Honorary Membership, World Affairs Council of North California; International Research and Exchanges Fellowship. *Hobbies:* Classical piano; Chess; Folklore. *Address:* 4450 South Park Avenue, No. 916, Chevy Chase, MD 20815, USA.

SPIVACK Charlotte, b. 23 July 1926, Schoharie, New York, USA. University Professor. m. Bernard Spivack, 17 Oct. 1956, 1 son, 1 daughter. *Education:* BA, State University of New York, 1947; MA, Cornell University, 1948; PhD, University of Missouri, 1954. *Appointments:* College of William & Mary, Richmond, Virginia, 1954-56; Fisk University, Nashville, Tennessee, 1956-64; University of Massachusetts, Amherst, 1964-. *Publications:* Books: Early English Drama, 1966; George Chapman, 1967; Comedy of Evil on Shakespeare's Stage, 1978; Ursula K. L. Guin, 1984; Merlin's Daughters, 1987. *Memberships:* Modern Language Association, US & Northeast; Dante Society; International Association of the Fantastic in Arts; Southeastern Renaissance Society; Science Fiction Research Association. *Honours:* Fellowship, American Association of University Women, 1959- 60; Distinguished Teaching Award 1985-86, Chancellor's Medal 1987, Distinguished Faculty Lectureship 1987, University of Massachusetts. *Address:* English Department, University of Massachusetts, MA 01003, USA.

SPIVACK Edith I, b. 19 Apr. 1910. m. Bernard H. Goldstein, 2 daughters. *Education:* Barnard College, 1925-29; Columbia Law School, 1929-32. *Appointmnt:* Clerk, 1932-33; Volunteer Worker, Corportion Counsel's Office Workmens Compensaiton Division, 1934; Assistant Corporation Counsel, 1934, 1935; Real Estate Tax Division, 1944; Executive Assistant Corporation Counsel, 1976-. *Memberships:* New York State Bar Association; Association of the Bar; New York County Lawyers Association. *Honours Include:* William Nelson Cromwell Medal, New York County Lawyer's; Alumni Association Medal, Columbia University; Fellow, New York Bar Foundation. *Address:* 21 Colonial Road, Port Washington, NY 11050, USA.

SPIVACK Ellen Sue, b. 2 Dec. 1937, Trenton, USA. Businesswoman. m. Roger Spivack, 15 May 1960, 1 son, 2 daughters. *Appointments:* Teacher, 1960-63; Sub-Teacher, 1963-73; Owner, Deep Roots, 1976-. *Publications:* Johnny Alfalfa Sprout Handbook; Whole Foods Experience; Soup to Nuts Coloring Book; Beginner's Guide to Meatless Casseroles; Fresh Whole Foods from A to Z. *Memberships:* Lyco Co Peace Campaign; International Womens Writing Guild; Douglass Alumnae Association. *Honours:* Director Johnny Alfalfa Sprout. *Hobbies:* Writing; Reading; Swimming. *Address:* 2300 E 3rd St., Williamsport, PA 17701, USA.

SPIZIZEN Louise Fleur Myers, b. 24 Aug 1928, Lynn,

USA. Musician; Writer. m. (1)Eugene Schlesinger, 19 June 1948, 3 sons, 1 daughter, divorced 1966, (2)John Spizizen, 26 Apr. 1968. *Education:* AB, Vassar College, 1949; MA, University of California, San Diego, 1972; Postgraduate Study in Music Composition, Harpsichord Performance, Chinese Language. *Appointments:* Staff Music Critic, La Jolla Light, 1973-79, Tucson Weekly, 1984-; Freelance Music Writer; Lecturer, Music History, Literature, Baroque Performance, San Diego Community College, 1974-79; University of California, 1977-79; Guest Lecturer, Conservatories of Music, Beijing & Shanghai, China, 1985; Lecturer, University of Arizona, 1985-. *Creative Works:* Compositions: Weary with Toil, 1969; Musical Director, Composer, The Invisible Theatre, Tucson, 1980-. *Memberships:* various professional organisations including: Founder/Artistic Director, Arizona Mini- Concerts Inc; Former President, Arizona State Music Teachers Association. *Honours:* Recipient, various honours & awards. *Address:* 2540 Camino La Zorrela, Tucson, AZ 85718, USA.

SPOKES SYMONDS Ann (Hazel), b. 10 Nov. 1925, Edgbaston, Birmingham, England. m. Richard Symonds, 30 Dec. 1980. *Education:* BA, St Anne's College, Oxford, 1947; Conservative Agent's Certificate, 1954. *Appointments:* Organiser, Conservative Party, 1949-56; Organising Secretary, Oxford Council for Voluntary Service, 1959-74, Age Concern, Oxford, 1958-80; Parliamentary candidate (Con) for NE Leicester (1959) and Brigg (1966 and 1970); Non Executive Director, ATV, 1978-81; Non-Executive Member, West Midlands Board, Central Independent TV, 1981-. *Publication:* Celebrating Age : An Anthology, 1987. *Memberships:* Chairman, Age Concern, England, 1983-86, Vice President 1986-; Prince of Wales Advisory Group on Disability; Hearing Aid Council; Charities Effectiveness Review Trust; Oftel Advisory Committee for Disabled & Elderly People; Board of Anchor Housing Association; Oxford City Council, 1957-, Lord Mayor 1976-77; Oxfordshire County Council, 1974-85, Chairman 1981-83. *Honours:* R.F. Butler Prize, 1946; County Colours, Oxfordshire Womens Hockey Team, 1960. *Hobbies:* Lawn Tennis; Photography; Travel; Writing; Drawing. *Address:* 43 Davenant Road, Oxford OX2 8BU, England.

SPREITZER Cynthia Ann, b. 16 July 1953, Chicago, Illinois, USA. Lead Analyst/Computer Programming Professional. *Education:* BS, Mathematics, Loyola University, Chicago, 1975. *Appointments:* Senior, Arthur Andersen and Co, Chicago, 1975-80; Lead Analyst, Larimer County, Ft Collins, 1980-. *Memberships:* Assn Inst Cert Computer Professionals; Computer Security Institute; Data Processing Management Assoc; National Assoc Female Execs *Honour.* Certified Data Processor (CDP), 1986. *Hobbies:* Reading; Music; Hiking; Skiing; Travelling. *Address:* 610 Grove Ct, Loveland, CO 80537, USA.

SPRINGER Adele I, b. 30 Dec. 1907, New York City, USA. Lawyer; Journalist. *Education:* LLB, 1930, LLM, 1931, St John's University; Geneva School of International Studies, Switzeralnd, 1932; Univesity of Geneva, 1933; Academy of International Law, The Hague, Holland, 1934. *Appointments:* Attorney at Law, 1931-38; Private Practice, New York, 1938-50, Los Angeles, 1950-. *Publicatirons:* Drafted the Safety at Sea Laws enacted by Congress, 1936; Publisher, The Women Lawyers JOurnal, 1947. *Memberships:* President, National Association of Women Lawyers; Delegate, House of Delgates, American Bar Association; Founding Member, World Association of Lawyers; etc. *Honours:* Certificate of Merit, American Bar Association; Pax Orbis Jure Award, 1971; Wilshire Bar Association Award; many other honours and awards. *Hobbies:* Travel. *Address:* 3278 Wilshire Boulevard, Los Angeles, CA 90010, USA.

SPRINGER Elaine S, b. 24 July 1932, Ogden, Utah, USA. m. (1)Edward L Robins, 24 Apr. 1951, divorced 17 Aug. 1969, 2 sons, 1 daughter. (2)Walton J Springer, 17 Mar. 1984, divorced June 1986. *Education:* Weber State College, Ogden, Utah, 1950; University of Nevada, Las Vegas; Clark County Community College, Las Vegas;

Joseph Bernard School of Acting; Graduated, certified teacher for Duncan Ceramic Products, 1975. *Appointments:* Federal Reserve Bank of San Francisco, 1952-53; Air Force Logistics Command, Hill Air Force Base, Utah, 1961-73; Receptionist, Public Defender's Office, 1979-80, Legal Secretary District Attorny 1980-82, Clark County Nevada; Research on paper for part of scholarship application to attend Oxford University, Oxford, England. *Publications:* Author of numerous compositions and a collection of poetry; Teach ceramics, specialising in creating porcelain pieces and porcelain dolls. *Memberships:* President, Cosmopolitan Club, Weber County, 1989-90; Ladies Auxiliary Roy Aerie No 3355, Fraternal order of Eagles; Utah Scottish Association; International Association Certified Duncan Teachers. *Honours:* General Scholarship, Utah State University, 1950; invited to join Honours Program, Weber State College, Ogden, 1975; Honor Roll, Ogden High School, 1950. *Hobbies:* Preparatory work on book to be titled Scotland Forever-My Home; Ceramics; Needlework; Fishing. *Address:* 3750 So. Midland Dr., Sp. 78, Roy, UT 84067, USA.

SPRINGER Marlene Ann, b. 16 Nov. 1937, Murfreesboro, Tennessee, USA. Associate Vice Chancellor; Professor of English. 2 daughters. *Education:* BA, Centre College, Danville, Kentucky, 1959; MA 1963, PhD 1969, Indiana University, Bloomington. *Appointments:* Teaching Associate, Indiana University, 1961-63 and 1964-66; Instructor, University of Southwestern Louisiana, 1963-64; Lecturer, University of Kansas, 1968-69; Assistant Professor 1970-75,I Associate Professor 1975-80, Professor 1980-, University of Missouri-Kansas City; Visiting Professor, Universidade Federal Fluminense, Rio de Janeiro, Brazil, 1975-76. Administrative Appointments: Department Chair, English, 1980; Acting Associate Dean, Graduate School, 1982; American Council on Education Administrative Fellow, University of Kansas, 1982-83; Dean of the Graduate School, 1983-84; Associate Vice Chancellor for Academic Affairs and Graduate Studies, 1985-. *Publications include:* Books: Edith Wharton and Kate Chopin: A Reference Guide, 1976; What Manner of Woman: Essays on English and American Life and Literature, 1977; Thomas Hardy's Use of Allusion, 1983; The Diary of Martha Farnsworth, 1986; Numerous articles in professional journals and books. *Membership:* Modern Language Association. *Honours:* Rotary Foundation Fellowship, University of Calcutta, Calcutta, India, 1959-60; University Graduate Fellowship, Indiana University, 1966-67; Mortar Board Award for Outstanding Teacher, 1974; Faculty Research Grants, University of Missouri-Kansas City, 1975, 1978, 1982; Phi Kappa Phi, 1081; Mid-America State Universities Association, Honor Lecturer, 1980-81; Huntington Library Fellow, 1988. *Address:* Academic Affairs, 224 Scofield Hall, University of Missouri-Kansas City, Kansas City, Missouri 64110, USA.

SPRINGER Wilma Marie, b. 13 Jan. 1933, Goshen, Indiana, USA. Educator; Teacher. m. W Frederick Springer, 25 May 1957. 2 sons, 1 daughter. *Education:* BA, Goshen College, 1956; MS, Bradley University, 1960. *Appointments:* Teacher, Topeka Elementary School, 1956-57; Teacher, Metamora Grade School, 1957-59; Teacher, Bellflower Unified School District, 1960-61 and 1968-. *Publications:* Author, article, Youth Companion, 1954; Member District Writing Study guides, State Core Literature, 1988. *Memberships:* Bellflower Education Association, Elementary Director, 1986-88, Treasurer, 1988-89; California Teachers Association, Service Center Council Delegate, 1986-87, Publicity & WHO Committees, 1988-89; National Education Association, Delegate NEA Convention 1986 and 1987; Chairperson, Gifted & Talented Education, Lindstrom Elem School, 1986-89; CA State Program Quality Review Team, 1989; Women's Ministries of Crystal Cathedral, Board of Directors, 1978-88, Co-chairperson, 1986-88; Stage Manager, Hour of Power International Television, Crystal Cathedral, 1983-; Bellflower Education Association, Vice-President, 1989-; Service Center Council Delegate, 1989-; Delegate NEA Convention, 1990; Chairperson, Gifted & Talented

Education, Jefferson Elementary School, 1989-. *Honours:* Grant, Classroom Teachers Instructional Improvement Program, 1986-87; Regional Educational Television Advisory Council Teacher Recognition Award, RETAC, 1986; Cathedral Star, Crystal Cathedral, 1985; Blue Ribbon, Los Angeles County Fair, Quilt Comforter, 1986; Weekly Reader Teachers Advisory Board, 1989-. *Hobbies:* Reading biographies; Quilting; Water colour painting. *Address:* 3180 Marna Avenue, Long Beach, CA 90808, USA.

SPURLING Teresa Phillips, b. 2 May 1946, Campbellsville, Kentucky, USA. Teacher. m. 18 Jan. 1963, 4 sons. *Education:* BS, Campbellsville College, 1970; MA 1973, Rank 1 (MA 30 hours) 1979, Western Kentucky University; Professional Certificate, School Administration & Supervision; Kentucky Certificate, Teacher, Kindergarten to 8 years. *Appointments:* Sales Clerk, 1962-63; Teacher, Taylor County Board of Education, Campbellsville, 1971-; Resource Teacher, Kentucky Intern Teacher Programme, 1986-. *Creative work includes:* Historical Research, Railroad & Growth of Spurlington Community, found in Folklife Archives, Western Kentucky University, 1969. *Memberships:* Past President, offices, Taylor County Education Association; Kentucky & National Education Associations; Kentucky Teachers of Mathematics; Taylor County Extension Council; Executive, Spurlington United Methodist Church. *Honours:* Representative, National Mathematics & Science Convention 1986, American Interdependence Institute 1986-87; NEA Delegate, Mid-Atlantic Regional Educational Convention, 1988; KEA Delegate, Convention, 1988; Chosen by Farm Bureau to pilot 'Farm & Food Bytes' software, & present research, Kentucky Farm Bureau Women's Leadership Conference. *Hobbies:* Genealogical Research; Reading; Sewing; Quilt Making; Gardening; Public speaking; 4-H leader; Church work; Kentucky-Ecuador Partner in Education. *Address:* 129 Pearl Avenue, Campbellsville, Kentucky 42718, USA.

SPURR Margaret Anne, b. 7 Oct. 1933, Sheffield, England. Headmistress. m. John Spurr, 7 Nov. 1953, 1 son, 1 daughter. *Education:* BA, Honours, PGCE, University of Keele. *Appointments:* Lecturer in English University of Glasgow, Deputy Head, Fair Oak School, Rugeley; Headmistress, Bolton School Girls' Division, Lancashire, 1979-. *Memberships:* President, Girls Schools Association, 1985-86; Chairman, Independent Schools Information Service, 1986-. *Hobbies:* Reading; Sailing; Gardening. *Address:* The Old Vicarage, Croxden, Uttoxeter ST14 5JQ, England.

SQUILLANTE Judith Ann, b. 29 Jan. 1942, Providence, Rhode Island. Vice President. Divorced, 2 sons. *Education:* BS, Bryant College, 1960; Management Certification Programme, URI, 1965. *Appointments:* Assistant to Town Treasurer, Bristol, 1960-64; Operations Co-ordinator, Speidel, Providence, 1964-71; Assistant Vice President, CE Maguire, 1971-78; Manager, Customer Affairs, Deltona, 1978-79; Vice President, Director, Human Resources, 1979-. *Memberships:* Various professional organisations. *Honours:* Outstanding Woman in Business & Industry, YWCA, 1983; Outstanding Company Achievement in Human Resources, Personnel Associatiron of Greater Miami, 1987. *Hobbies:* Card Player; Table Tennis; Dancing; Photography; Theatre. *Address:* 9725 SW 64th St., Miami, FL 33173, USA.

SQUIRE Laurie, b. 30 Jan. 1953, Forest Hills, New York, USA. Radio Producer/Writer. m. Herbert E. Squire Jr, 6 Aug. 1975, 2 daughters. *Education:* BA cum laude, English, Theatre Arts, Finch College, 1974; MA, Media Ecology, New York University, 1976; Doctoral study, Mass Communication, Columbia University, 1980-; Certificate, Public Access TV Workshop, 1985. *Appointments:* Foundation Office Aide, American Ballet Theatre, New York City, 1972-74; WBAI Radio, New York, spring 1973; WNET-TV (including Music Production Coordinator, American Ballet Theatre TV special), New York, autumn 1973; Assistant to Director of Public Affairs, New York Cultural Center, spring 1974;

Assistant Merchandising Director, RKO General, New York, 1974-76; Producer, Jean Shepherd Show, Executive Producer, Bernard Meltzer Show, other production responsibilities, WOR Radio, New York, 1974-80; Radio Production/Public Relations/Copy Consultant, 1980-: Ongoing assignments: Broadcast Stage Manager, Texaco-Metropolitan Opera Radio Network; Press Representative, Publications Editor, Village of Great Neck Plaza; Press Representative, Publications Editor, Chanry Communications; Other clients include Long Island Playhouse, Cablevision, ABC-TV, Show Business trade journal, Nassau County Museum of Fine Art, Nassau Lyric Opera, United Community Fund. *Memberships:* International Radio and Television Society; Career Advisory Board, Mademoiselle magazine; Board Member, United Community Fund, Great Neck-Manhassett. *Honour:* Peabody Citation for Metropolitan Opera broadcast work. *Address:* 892 Middle Neck Road, Great Neck, NY 11024, USA.

SQUIRES Norma Jean, b. 15 Feb. 1943, Toronto, Canada. Artist; Consultant; Curator. m. Gerald Hopman, 1 daughter. *Education:* Apprentice, Jas Rosati, New York, 1964; BFA, The Cooper Union, New York, 1979; MA, California State University, Northridge, 1983. *Career:* Commercial Artist, Videocrafts, 1965-67; Instructor, Lucinda Art School, Tenefly, New Jersey, USA, 1967-68; Artists' Agent/Curator, 1986-; Numerous, group exhibitions including: Affect-Effect, La Jolla Museum of Art, 1969, 4x4 4x8, Newport Harbour Museum, 1975, The Many Arts of Science, California Institute of Technology, 1976, Woman & Energy, Angels Gate Cultural Center, 1988; Solo exhibitions include: Hudson River Museum, Yonkers, New York, 1968, California Polytechnic University, Pomona, 1987, New Salon, Venice, California, 1988. *Creative works:* Numerous kinetic sculptures; Numerous acrylic paintings; Works in public collections, New York, Los Angeles, Burbank, Santa Monica, Simi Valley and Redwood City Public Library, California, and Madrid, Spain, also private collections, New York and California; 3 children's books: I am a Picture Book; The Mouse in the Magic Forest; The Witch Who Whistled. *Memberships:* Museum of Contemporary Art; Los Angeles County Museum of Art; Los Angeles Contemporary Exhibitions; Women's Caucus for Art; Artists Equity; Public Corporation for the Arts. *Honours:* F.J.Friedrichs Award for Sculpture, Hudson River Museum, 1968; Sarah Cooper Hewitt Award, Cooper Union, 1979; Recognition Award for Creative Work, California State University, Northridge, 1983; Phi Kappa Phi, 1983; Thousand Oaks Art Association Award for Sculpture, 1984; Purchase Award, Redwood City Public Library, 1988. *Hobbies:* Cosmology; Particle Physics; Brazilian dancing; Flamenco dancing; Guitar. *Address:* 2764 Woodwardia Drive, Los Angeles, CA 90077, USA.

S-ROZSA Katalin, b. 29 Nov. 1930, Jaszszentandras, Hungary. Scientific Adviser; Biologist. m. Janos Salanki, 29 Dec. 1960. 2 daughters. *Education:* PhD, Moscow State University, Lomonosow, USSR, 1958-61; DSc, biology, Hungarian Academy of Sciences, Budapest, Hungary, 1974. *Appointments:* Kossuth University Debrecen, Hungary, 1961-63; Biological Research Institute of the Hungarian Academy of Sciences, Tihany, 1963- (present name: Balaton Limnological Research Institute of the Hungarian Academy of Sciences). *Publications:* More than 130 scientific articles in international scientific journals; Editor of the Proceedings of scientific Symposia; Neurotransmitters of Invertebrates, 1980; Neurobiology of Invertebrates, 1987; Editor of Annal Biol Tihany, 1967-77. *Memberships:* Hungarian Physiological Society; Hungarian Biological Society; Hungarian Pharmacological Society; Hungarian Biophysiol Society; Int Society for Invertebrate Neurobiology. *Honours:* Prizes of the Hungarian Academy of Sciences, 1972, 1977, 1980; Honorary Professor of Eotvos University, Budapest, 1982. *Hobby:* Shell collector. *Address:* Balaton Limnological Research Institute of the Hungarian Academy of Sciences, P O B 35, H-8237 Tihany, Hungary.

ST CLAIR Annetta Elaine, b. 6 Feb. 1938, Clarksburg, Indiana, USA. Professor. m. 21 Dec. 1965, 1 daughter. *Education:* BA, Kansas State College, 1960; MA, History, 1964, MS, Political Science, 1969, Pittsburgh State University. *Appointments:* Joplin Public Schools, 1960-63; Missouri Southern State College, 1964-. *Memberships:* National Education Association; Missouri NEA; MSSC/NEA, Secretary, Treasurer; Midwest PreLaw Advisers Association; Missouri Political Science Association. *Hobbies:* Water Skiing; Swimming. *Address:* Missouri Southern State College, Joplin, MO 64801, USA.

ST JEAN Catherine Avery, b. 10 Oct. 1950, Dubuque, Iowa, USA. Advertising Executive. m. 7 Mar. 1987. *Education:* BA, Communications, Loyola University, Chicago, 1977. *Appointments:* Audio-Visual Coordinator, 1977, Editor, Camera Person, Test Commercials, 1977-79, Assistant Manager, Creative Department, 1979-80, Manager, Presentations Services, 1980- 81, Director, Presentations Services, 1981-82, Needham Harper & Steers, Chicago, Illinois; Director, Communication Services, 1982-86, Vice-President, 1983-88, Director, Creative Services, 1986-, Senior Vice-President, 1988-, Corporate Headquarters, DDB Needham Worldwide, New York City. *Memberships:* Former Editor and Newsletter Chair, Board of Directors, Annual Fundraiser, 2nd Vice-President, Advertising Women of New York; Advisor AWNY Ad Agency and Cannes Gala Benefit. *Honours:* Bronze Medal, New York International Film and TV Festival, 1984; Crystal Prism AWard, American Advertising Federation, 1986. *Address:* DDB Needham Worldwide, 437 Madison Avenue, New York, NY 10022, USA.

STABENOW Deborah Ann, b. 29 Apr. 1950, Gladwin, Michigan, USA. State Representative. 1 son, 1 daughter. *Education:* BA, Magna cum laude 1972, MSW 1974, Michigan State University; Women in Leadership Program, State Legislative Leadership Foundation and Institute of Politics, John F Kennedy School of Government, Harvard University, 1988. *Appointments:* Ingham County Commissioner (Chairperson 1977-78), 1975-78; Michigan House of Representatives, 1979-; Assistant Associate Speaker Pro-Tem, House of Representatives, 1987-90, Committee Assignments: Mental Health, Judiciary, Agriculture, House Oversight, Public Health, Economic Development and Energy. *Memberships:* Founder, Ingham County Women's Commission; Co-Founder, Council Against Domestic Assault; Democratic Business and Professional Club; Honorary Life- time Member, Lansing Boys' Club; Michigan Democratic Women's Political Caucus; Grace United Methodist Church. *Honours:* Recipient of numerous honours and awards including: One of the Ten Outstanding Young Americans for 1986 presented by the United States Jaycees; Named one of the women most admired by Michigan Women in the Detroit Free Press Magazine, 1988; Distinguished Citizen Award, Michigan McDonald's Operators Association, 1988; Distinguished Alumni Award, Michigan State University, 1987; Friend of Nursing Award, Michigan Nurses Association, 1987. *Address:* 2709 S Deerfield, Lansing, MI 48911, USA.

STABLEIN Marilyn E, b. 22 Aug. 1946, Los Angeles, California, USA. Freelance writer; Editor; Publisher. m. William Stablein, 22 Jan. 1971. 1 son, 1 daughter. *Education:* BA, Creative Writing, University of Washington, Seattle; MA, Creative Writing, University of Houston, Texas. *Appointments:* Teaching Assistant, Dept of Eng, University of Houston, 1982-84; Literary Coordinator, Bumbershoot Arts Festival, Seattle, 1981, 1982; Director, The Literary Center, 1985-89. *Publications:* Ticketless Traveler, 1982; The Census Taker: Tales of a Traveler in India & Nepal, 1985; Intrusions in Ice, 1988. *Memberships:* Phi Beta Kappa, 1981; Omicron Delta Kappa, 1983; Pres Graduate English Society; Seattle Free Lances; Board of Directors, Seattle Arts & Lectures, 1988-. *Honours:* Cullen Graduate Fellowship, Univ of Houston, 1982-83; King County Arts Commission Publication Award, 1984; Brazos Fiction Award, Univ of Houston, 1984; Seattle Arts Commission Individual Artist Award, 1987; Finalist, Nat League of Am Pen Women, Letters Award, 1988. *Hobbies:* Founding publisher, The Literary Center Quarterly; Mixed media performance artist; Video production and TV broadcasts of literary readings. *Address:* 5210 16th NE, Seattle, WA 98105, USA.

STABLER Nancy Rae Redmer, b. 15 June 1946, Elgin, Illinois, USA. Head of Human Resources Telecommunications. m. Jay A Stabler, 28 Mar. 1970. 1 daughter. *Education:* AAS, Electronic Data Processing Programmer, (Hons), 1982; AA (Hons), 1985. *Appointments:* Programmer Analyst, Houghton-Mifflin Publishing Co, Geneva, Illinois, 1966-77; Project Leader, Kane County, Geneva, Illinois, 1978-83; Systems Designer, Burgess Norton Mfg Co, Geneva, 1983-86; Head of Human Resources Telecommunications, Recon Optical, Barrington, 1987-; Tutor, Elgin Comm College, 1983-. *Hobbies:* Reading; Education; Law; Family. *Address:* 775 South Street, Elgin, Illinois 60123, USA.

STACEY Shari Lynn, b. 22 Aug. 1954, Rockford, Illinois, USA. Trainer; Consultant; Speaker; Writer. m. Wayne Eugene Nichols, 4 Oct. 1986. *Education:* BA, Mathematics, 1976; MBA, Management/Finance, 1981. *Appointments:* Product Supply Representative, Director of Budgets & Forecasting, Senior Analyst, Warren Petroleum, Division of Chevron Oil USA, 1976-85; President and Founder, Leadership Management Dynamics, 1985-. *Publication:* Newsletter, The Leadership Edge. *Memberships:* The Greater Houston Partnership (Chairman - Small Business Issues Committee); Houston Business Alliance (Board Member); American Society of Training & Development; Unity Church (Board Member); American ManageMeNt Association. *Hobbies:* Flying; Cross country skiing; Waterskiing; Back packing; Hiking; Horseback riding; Sailing; Raquetball; Reading; Jogging. *Address:* 1942 Shadow Rock, Kingwood, TX 77339, USA.

STACK Joanne Tunney, b. 8 Aug. 1952, New York City, USA. Attorney; Writer. m. William Michael Stack, 1 Feb. 1975, 1 son, 1 daughter. *Education:* BA, Manhattanville College, 1974; JD, Fordham University School of Law, 1977. *Appointments:* Attorney, Writer, West Publishing Company, 1977-85; Senior Editor, Research Institute of America, 1985-86; Manager, Editor, US Firm Tax Newsletter, Price Waterhouse, 1986-. *Creative Works:* Contributor To: Family Legal Guide; Guide to American Law; How To Do Just About Anything; You and the Law; Tax Recommendations; US Taxes; Viowo & Reviews, Shortcuts and Substitutes (book); Price Waterhouse Personal Tax Advisor; Price Waterhouse Guide to Your Children's Taxes. *Memberships:* American Bar Association; New York State Bar Association. *Honours:* Various academic scholarships. *Hobbies:* Travel; Writing; Gardening. *Address:* 193 Hoyt Farm Rd., New Canaan, CT 06840, USA.

STAFFORD Rebecca, b. 9 July 1936, Topeka, Kansas, USA. College President; Sociologist. m. Willard VanHazel, 12 Apr. 1973. *Education:* AB magna cum laude 1958, MA 1961, Radcliffe College; PhD, Harvard University, 1964. *Appointments include:* Lecturer, Department of Sociology, Harvard University, 1964-70; Associate Professor 1970-73, Professor 1973-80, Chair, Department of Sociology 1974-77, University of Nevada; Dean, College of Arts & Sciences, 1977-80; President, Bemidji State University, Minnesota, 1980-82; Executive Vice President, Colorado State University, Fort Collins, 1982-83; President, Chatham College, Pittsburgh, 1983-. Member, various boards & committees. *Publications:* Various research papers, sociology. *Memberships include:* Board of Directors 1985-87, Harvard University Alumni Association; Phi Beta Kappa; Phi Kappa Phi. *Honours:* McCurdy-Rinkle Prize, research, Eastern Psychiatric Association, 1970; Various grants. *Address:* Chatham College, Woodland Road, Pittsburgh, PA 15232, USA.

STAHL Donna Laura, b. 17 Apr. 1945, Davenport, Iowa, USA. General Surgeon. *Education:* BA, Augustana College, Rock Island, Illinois, 1967; MD, University of Iowa, Iowa City, Iowa, 1971; Internship 1971-72, Residency 1972-77, Chief Residency 1977-78, University of Cincinnati, Ohio; Licensure, State of Iowa, 1971, State of Ohio, 1973; Certification, American Board of Surgery, 1980. *Appointments:* Assistant Professor of Surgery, 1978-82; Associate Professor of Surgery, 1982-, University of Cincinnati Medical Centre; Attending Surgeon, VA Hospital and Children's Hospital, Cincinnati; Consultant, Shriners Burns Institute, Cincinnati, Ohio. *Memberships:* Local Unit, Past Secretary and Board Member, American Cancer Society; Cancer Commission Surveyor, American College of Surgeons; Cancer Commission Member, Chair-elect, Committee of Approvals; American Medical Association; Association of Academic Surgeons; Ohio State Medical Association; Phi Beta Kappa. *Interests:* Benign and malignant breast disease. *Address:* Department of Surgery, University of Cincinnati Medical Centre, Cincinnati, OH 45267, USA.

STAHL Dulcelina Albano, b. 10 Aug. 1943, Philippines. Administrator, Health Care Services & Program Development. m. Wendelin Walter Stahl, 1968. 1 son, 2 daughters. *Education:* Diploma in Nursing, 1966; BA, summa cum laude, 1969; MA 1970; MS 1973; PhD 1976. *Appointments:* Assistant Director of Nursing, University of Illinois Hospital, 1971-72; Faculty School of Nursing, South Chicago Community Hospital, 1972-75; Director of Nursing, Bethany Hospital, 1975-80; Senior Associate Administrator, Olympia Fields Osteopathic Medical Center, 1980-85; Corp. Admin. COMCs, 1980-. *Publications:* Co-Author: Cancer Nursing, 1982; Alternative Scheduling for Intensive Care Unit, 1982; Author: Developing and Marketing Ambulatory Care Programs, 1984. *Contributions to:* Schaefer's Textbook of Medical Surgical Nursing, 1971. *Memberships:* Affiliate-American College of Healthcare Executives; Advisory Board Member, South Suburban Hospice; ANA; McCOA; MACA; ILN; Hastings Center; PNAC; AMA. *Honours:* Captain Gold Trophy Winner, Australian Ford Debate Tournament, 1965; Best Athlete of the Year, Geelong, Australia, 1965; Arthur J Schmidt Foundation for Superior Scholarship and Academic Excellence, 1969; Most Oustanding Filipino Nurse in the Midwest, USA, 1979; DePaul University Distinguished Alumni Award, 1985. *Hobbies:* Singing; Dancing; Fishing; Reading; Writing Poetry, Programs and Articles; Swimming; Collecting coins and stamps. *Address:* 2269 Post Road, Northbrook, Illinois 60062, USA.

STAINES Laura Catherine, b. 25 Nov. 1953, Brooklyn, New York, USA. Architect and Professional Planner. m. Michael Laurence Staines, 11 May 1974, 2 daughters. *Education:* BA, University of Pennsylvania, 1975; Postgraduate, Drexel University, 1980. *Appointments:* Architects Workshop, 1976-77; Schnadelbach & Braun, 1977-78; Hugh Zimmers Associates, 1978; Martin Organization, 1978-80; Wallace Roberts & Todd, 1980-81; Principal, Martin Organisation, 1981-. *Memberships:* American Institute of Architects; Commercial Real Estate Women; Philadelphia Art Alliance; National Association of Home Builders; International Council of Shopping Centers; Candidate, Industry of Residential Marketing. *Hobbies:* Sailing; Gardening; Painting; Member, 1976 Olympic rowing team. *Address:* c/o Martin Organisation, 242 North 22nd Street, Philadelphia, Pennsylvania 19103, USA.

STALKER Jacqueline Ann D'Aoust, b. 16 Oct. 1933, Penetang, Canada. Educator; Administrator. m. Robert Stalker, 3 daughters. *Education:* B.Ed., Honours, 1977, MEd., 1979, University of Manitoba; DEd., Nova University, Florida, USA, 1985. *Appointments:* Administrator, Teacher, Schools, 1952-65; Area Commissioner, Girl Guides of Canada in Europe, 1965-69; Administrator, Master Teacher, Algonquin Community College, Ottawa, 1970-74; Programme Developer, Teacher, Frontenanc County Board of Education, Kingston, Ontario, 1974-75; Lecturer, Education, University of Manitoba, 1977-79; Consultant, Manitoba Community Colleges, 1980-81; Senior Consultant: Community College Programming, Manitoba Dept. of Education, 1981-84, Adult & Continuing Education, Manitoba, 1985-89. *Publications:* Articles in professional journals. *Memberships:* Chairperson: Accreditation Committee, Teacher Training Programme, Task Forces; University Senate; numerous International, National, Provincial & Professional committees. *Honours:* Dean's Honour List, University of Manitoba, 1977; University of Manitoba Graduate Fellowship, 1978; YWCA Woman of the Year Nominee, Professional Category, 1982. *Hobbies:* Travel; Arts. *Address:* 261 Baltimore Road, Winnipeg, Manitoba Canada R3L 1H7.

STALKER Suzy Wooster, b. 12 Oct. 1948, Atlanta, Georgia, USA. Vice President Personnel, Gulf States Mortgage Co, Inc. m. James Marion Stalker, 11 Nov. 1966. 1 son, 1 daughter. *Education:* Studying Urban Studies, Georgia State University, Atlanta, 1981-. *Appointments:* Training Rep 1980-81, Training Supv 1981-82, Regional Training Coor 1982- 83, Employee Communications Specialists 1983-84, Rich's, Atlanta; Director of Human Resources, Home Federal S & L of Atlanta, 1984-88; Vice President Personnel, Gulf States Mortgage Co, Inc, 1988-. *Publications:* Editor of Richbits, Rich's Atlanta, 1983-84; Watercolours. *Memberships:* Leader, Girl Scouts, USA 1972-74; President, Clarkdale PTA, 1975-76; National Assn for Female Executives, Inc; Georgia Executive Women's Network, Atlanta. *Hobbies:* Sailing; Watercolours; Cross stitching; Interior design/antiques. *Address:* 4820 Glore Road, Mableton, Georgia 30059, USA.

STALLARD Maryann Magdalen, b. 13 Dec. 1949, Chicago, Illinois, USA. Chairperson, Dept of Philosophy/ Theology. *Education:* AA, Felician College of Chicago, 1981; BA (Theology) 1986, MA (Theology) 1988, Loyola Univeristy of Chicago; Candidate DMin, University of St Mary of the Lake. *Appointment:* Chairperson of Philosophy/Theology, Montay College, 1985- *Memberships:* Theta Alpha Kappa; Alpha Sigma Nu; Chicago Center for Peace (Steering Committee). *Honours:* Dean's Key Award, Loyola University, 1986; Graduation Summa cum laude, Felician College; Graduation Summa cum laude, Loyola University. *Hobbies:* Greek, Roman & Celtic mythology; Romantic poets; Music; Signing (American sign language); Ancient Greek philosophy & culture; Reading. *Address:* 6687 Ionia, Chicago, Illinois 60646, USA.

STALLS Madlyn, b. 22 Oct. 1947, Metropolis, USA. Developmental Skills Specialist; Educationist. 1 son. *Education:* BA 1970, MS 1976, PhD forthcoming, Southern Illinois University. *Appointments:* Social Worker, Illinois Department of Children & Family Services, 1970-75; Manpower Services Rep, Illinois Farmers Union, 1976-77; Vocational Counselor, 1977-78, Developmental Skills Specialist, 1980-, Southern Illinois University- C. *Memberships:* American Assoc of Counselling & Development; Illinois Comm on Black Concerns in Higher Education; Assoc of Multicultural Counselling & Development. *Honours:* Iota Phi Theta Quintessence Award, 1984; SIU-C Black Affairs Council Academic Excellence Award, 1987; Service to Hayes Child Care Parent Advisory Committee, 1977; Initiated into Kappa Delta Pi, scholastic honorary, 1987; Fellow, Illinois Comm on Black Concerns in Higher Education, 1985; Black Affairs Council Outstanding Faculty/Staff Award, 1988. *Hobbies:* Writing; Reading; Playing and listening to music; Dancing; Aerobics; Cooking; Creative design; Construction; Travelling; Photography; Cooking; The Arts; Public Speaking. *Interests:* Community Development, community education, youth and activities which encourage their development. *Address:* 407 N Barnes Street, Carbondale, IL 62901, USA.

STAMBAUGH Harriett Wynn McCardell, b. 10 May 1922, Philipsburg, Pennsylvania, USA. Clinical Social Worker. m. James Arthur Stambaugh, 1 May 1954, 3 sons. *Education:* BA, Juniata College, Pennsylvania,

1942; MS in S.S., School of Social Work, Boston University, 1947. *Appointments include:* Secondary school teacher, 1942-44; American Red Cross, Lancaster, Pennsylvania 1944-45; American Red Cross, Cincinnati, Ohio, 1947-54; Department of Public Welfare, Virginia, 1958-61; State Department of Child Welfare, Kentucky, 1962; Hope Cottage Children's Bureau, Dallas, Texas, 1963; Coordinator, Mental Health & Mental Retardation Services, Dallas, Texas, 1963-66; Instructor 1966-67, Assistant Professor 1968-80, Paediatrics, University of Texas Health Science Centre, 1966-80; Director, Clinical Social Work, Children's Medical Centre, Dallas, Texas, 1967-80; Adjunct Professor, Sociology & Social Work, Texas Women's University, 1977-80; Director, Clinical Social Work, University of New Mexico Hospital, 1981-84; Supervisor 1985-87, part-time Clinical Social Worker 1988-, Chaparral Maternity & Adoption Division of Family & Children's Services. *Publications:* Various articles, professional journals; Papers, various conferences. *Memberships include:* New Mexico Board, American Association of Marriage & Family Therapists; Academy of Certified Social Workers; Many local offices, National Association of Social Workers. *Honours:* Awards & recognitions: Dallas, Texas, Chapter, NASW; Titches Inc, Dallas, Texas; Dallas, Texas, Association for Education of Young Children; Texas House of Representatives; Commissioner's Court, Dallas County, Texas; Dallas, Texas, City Council; New Mexico Society of Hospital Social Work Directors. *Address:* 5023 Calle de Luna NE, Albuquerque, New Mexico 87111, USA.

STAMBAUGH Joan, b. 10 June 1932, Pittsburgh, USA. Professor. *Education:* BA, Vassar College, 1953; MA, Columbia University, 1955; PhD, University of Freiburg, Germany, 1958. *Appointments:* Vassar College, 1964-69; Hunter College, City University of New York, 1969-. *Publications:* Nietzsche's Thought of Eternal Return; The Problem of Time in Nietzsche; The Real is not the Rational; Impermanence is Buddha-nature. *Memberships:* American Philosophical Association; Society for Phenomenology & Existential Philosophy; Society for Asian & Comparative Philosophy; North American Nietzsche Society; Heidgger Conference. *Address:* Dept. of Philosophy, Hunter College, 695 Park, New York, NY 10021, USA.

STAMERS-SMITH Eileen, b. 17 Apr. 1929, Castleford, Yorkshire, England. Lecturer/Tutor. m. Henry Arthur Stamers-Smith, 19 Dec. 1970, (died 1982). *Education:* BA, Honours, 1951, MA, 1956, Lady Magaret Hall, Oxford. *Appointments:* Abbeydale Girls' Grammar School, Sheffield, 1952-57; Cheltenham Ladies' College, 1957-67; Headmistress. Bermuda Girls' High School, 1967-71; Headmistress, Malvern Girls' College, 1984-85; Lecturer/Tutor in English, Garden History and Art History for Oxford University Dept. of External Studies, W.I. (Denham College and Branches), WEA (Oxford Branch), National Gardens Scheme, Venice in Peril, etc. *Publications:* Articles in professional journals. *Memberships:* Hon. Editor, Garden History Society Newsletter, 1986-. *Hobbies:* Music; Garden History; Photography; Calligraphy; Writing Poetry; Venice. *Address:* 8 Mavor Close, Old Woodstock, Oxfordshire OX7 1YL, England.

STAMEY Sara Lucinda, b. 23 Jan. 1953, Bellingham, USA. Writer. *Education:* BA, English Literature, Writing, Western Washington University, 1981; MA, English, Western Washington University, 1989. *Appointments:* Nuclear Reactor Control Operator, 1974-78; Scuba Diving Instructor, 1981-85; Writer, 1986-. *Publications:* Assorted Flavors, 1978; Wild Card Run, 1987; Win, Lose, Draw, 1988; Double Blind, 1990. *Memberships:* Science Fiction Writers of America; Professional Association of Dive Instructors. *Hobbies:* Outdoor Sports; Playing Classical Piano. *Address:* 324 N. State St., No 1, Bellingham, WA 98225, USA.

STANCZYK Anna Maria, b. 12 Sept. 1948, Opoczno. Concert Pianist. m. Antoni Grudzinski, 10 Sept. 1972, 1 daughter. *Education:* MA, Warsaw Academy of Music, 1975; Postgraduate Scholarship, Budapest, 1976-77;

Master in Stage Performance, with Louis Kentner, London, 1978-81. *Appointments:* Concert Pianist, over 700 performances Worldwide, 1975-. *Publications:* Recordings: Szymanowski, Lessel, Chopin; Anna Maria Stanczyk plays Liszt. *Memberships:* Association of Polish Musicians; Incorporated Society of Musicians in England; Committee Member, Chopin Society, London; President, Friends of English Heritage Orchestra. *Honours:* Slupsk Piano Festival Award, Poland, 1975; Franz Liszt Medal, Hungarian Ministry of Culture, 1986; Medal, Polish Artists Association, 1987; Order of Honour, Ministry of Culture, Poland, 1987. *Hobbies:* Books; Literature; Sport; Theatre. *Address:* 77 Colwith Road, London W6 9EZ, England.

STANFIELD Elizabeth Poplin, b. 9 Aug. 1930, Jacksonville, Florida, USA. Assistant Professor. m. William Thomas Stanfield, 30 June 1956, 2 sons. *Education:* BA, University of North Carolina, 1952; MA, Emory University, 1966. *Appointments:* Faculty Member, Georgia State University, Atlanta, 1967-; Contributing Editor, Southeern Homes Magazine. *Publications:* From Plantation to Peachtree : A Century and a Half of Classic Atlanta Homes, 1987. *Memberships:* Phi Beta Kappa; Sigma Delta Pi; Phi Sigma Iota; Omicron Delta Kappa; American Association Teachers of Spanish; MLA; Atlanta Association of Interpreters & Translators, Board of Directors; Academic Alliances in Georgia. *Honours:* Rockefeller Foundation Grant, American Association University Women, 1964. *Hobbies:* Calligraphy; Geneaology; etc. *Address:* Po Box 71, Georgia State University, University Plaza, Atlanta, GA 30303, USA.

STANG Sondra Judith, b. 26 Apr. 1928, New York City, New York, USA. Adjunct Professor. m. Richard Stang, 17 June 1946, 2 sons, 1 daughter. *Education:* BA, Hunter College; MA, Columbia University. *Appointments:* Lecturer and Adjunct Professor, Department of English, Washington University, St Louis, Missouri, 1962-. *Publications:* Ford Madox Ford, 1977; The Presence of Ford Madox Ford, 1981; Ford Issue of Antaeus Magazine (editor), 1986; The Ford Madox Ford Reader, 1986; Ford's A History of Our Own Times (co-editor), 1988; Collective Wisdom (co-editor), 1988; The Three-Ingredient Cookbook. *Honours:* Honorary LittD, Washington University, 1989; Hall of Fame, Hunter College, 1989; Phi Beta Kappa. *Hobbies:* Music; Cooking. *Address:* c/o Department of English, Washington University, St Louis, MO 63130, USA.

STANLEY Jean Agatha Fuller, b. 17 Sept. 1951, Jamaica. Educator. m. Ernie Stanley, 2 Oct. 1970, 2 daughter. *Education:* BSc., honours, University of London, 1976; MS, Chemistry, 1980, PhD, Chemistry, 1984, University of Nebraska, USA. *Appointments:* Teaching Assistant, University of Nebraska, 1978-84; Assistant Professor, Chemistry, Wellesley College, Massachusetts, 1984-. *Publications:* Articles in professional journals including: Organic Mass Spectrometry; Journal of Organic Chemistry. *Memberships:* Royal Society of Chemistry; American Chemical Society; Phi Lambda Epsilon; Sigma Xi. *Hobbies:* Sports; Music; Dancing; Reading; Sewing. *Address:* Chemistry Dept., Wellesley College, Wellesley, MA 02181, USA.

STANLEY Marjorie Jean Thines, b. 20 Feb. 1928, Ashland, Wisconsin, USA. Professor. m. John Deane Stanley, 17 Feb. 1951, divorced 1976, 2 sons. *Education:* BA, University of Wisconsin, 1949; MA, 1950, PhD, 1953, Indiana University; M.Div., Seabury-Western, 1988. *Appointments:* Instructor, 1953- 54, Assistant Professor, 1954-55, University of Arkansas; Adjunct Professor Economics, 1964, 1965-66, Finance, 1966-72, Associate Professor, 1972-82, Chairman, Finance & Decision Sciences, 1983-86, Professor, Finance, M J Neeley School of Business, 1982-, Texas Christian University. *Publications:* Articles in: Journal of International Business Studies; Financial Management; CFA Digest; The Financial Review. *Memberships:* Academy of International Business, Southwest Regional Chair; American Economics Association; American

Finance Association. *Honours:* Recipient, various honours and awards. *Hobbies:* Music; Tennis; Swimming. *Address:* Texas Christian Univesity, Box 32868, Fort Worth, TX 76129, USA.

STANTON Elizabeth McCool, b. 12 Apr. 1947, Lansdale, USA. Attorney. m. 13 June 1970, 2 sons. *Education:* BS, Drexel University, 1969; JD, University of Houston, 1979. *Appointments:* Senior Computer Programmer, 1969-70; Research Computer Programmer, Cornell University, 1970- 74; Law Clerk, Albert C. Barclay Esq., 1977-78; Attorney, Friedman & Chaffin, 1979-80; Attorney, Law Offices of Elaine Brady, 1980-81; Attorney, Moots Cope & Weinberger, 1982-86; Attorney, Moots Cope & Kizer Co., 1986-. *Memberships:* Thomas Moore Society; Women Lawyers of Franklin County; National Association of Women Lawyers; Plaintiff Employment Lawyers Association; Columbus, Ohio, American, Texas Bar Associations. *Address:* 3600 Olentangy River Road, Columbus, OH 43214, USA.

STANTON Jeanne Frances, b. 22 Jan. 1920, Vicksburg, Mississippi, USA. Lawyer. *Education:* Student, George Washington University, 1938-39; BA, University of Cincinnati, 1940; JD, Salmon P. Chase College of Law, 1954; Admitted to Ohio Bar, 1954. *Appointments:* Chief Clerk, Selective Service Board, Cincinnati, 1940-43; Instructor, USAAF Technical School, Biloxi, Mississippi, 1943-44; Procter & Gamble, Cincinnati, 1945; Legal Assistant, 1952-54; Manager Advertising Services, 1973-84 (retired). *Publications:* Cincinnati Lawyers in Business in the Law in South Western Ohio (Centennial Publication of Cincinnati Bar Association). *Memberships:* Lawyers Club of Cincinnati, President, 1983, 1st Vice President, Executive Committee, 1982, Secretary, 1980, Treasurer, 1979; Executive Committee of Lawyers Central Cincinnati, 1979-; Cincinnati, Ohio State and American Bar Associations; Cincinnati Club; Vicksburg & Warren County Historical Societies; Cincinnati Historical Society; Otago Early Settlers Associaiton (Associate); Chairman, Subcommittee 4, Committee 307 of Rights of Authors of American Bar Association Section on Patent Trademark and Copyright Law. *Honours:* Official Commentator, Australasia Business & Law Symposium, Auckland University, New Zealand, 1968. *Hobbies:* Reading; Golf; Archaeology; Genealogy. *Address:* 2302 Easthill Avenue, Cincinnati, OH 45208, USA.

STANTON Sandra Margot, b. 9 Dec. 1948, New York, USA. Painter. *Education:* BA, Pace University, 1969; Art Students League, 1967-74. *Creative Works:* Numerous paintings of visionary genre; solo exhibitions held at: Clovelly Lane Gallery, New York City; New York University Contemporary Arts Gallery; Westbroadway Gallery; National Art Centre, New York City; Mussavi Arts Centre, New York City; Group Exhibitions include: Pace University; International Women Artists' Slide Exhibition; Museum of the City of New York; Hunter College; Stadtische Galerie, West Germany; Salon des Artistes, New York City, etc. *Memberships:* Foundation for the Community of Artists; Artists Equity; Life Member, Art Students League. *Address:* 345 East 93rd Street, New York, NY 10128, USA.

STANWYCK Barbara, (Ruby Stevens), b. 16 July, 1907, Brooklyn, New York, USA. Actress. m. (1) Frank Fay, 1928 divorced 1935. 1 son. (2) Robert Taylor, 1939 divorced 1951. *Career:* Appeared in several Ziegfeld Follies and George White Scandals; Appeared on Broadway in Burlesque 1927; Tattle Tales, 1933; Film debut in The Locked Door, 1929. *Creative Works:* Films include: Ladies of Leisure, 1930; Miracle Woman, 1931; Night Nurse, 1931; Forbidden, 1932; The Bitter Tea of General Yen, 1933; Baby Face, 1933; The Secret Bride, 1935; Annie Oakley, 1935; His Brother's Wife, 1936; Stella Dalls, 1937; Always Goodbye, 1938; Golden Boy, 1939; The Lady Eve, 1941; Meet John Doe, 1941; Ball of Fire, 1941; Flesh and Fantasy, 1943; Double Indemnity, 1944; My Reputation, 1945; The Strange Love of Martha Ivers, 1946; Two Mrs Carrolls, 1947; Sorry Wrong Number, 1948; The Furies, 1949; Clash

by Night, 1953; Titanic, 1953; Executive Suite, 1954; Witness to Murder, 1954; Escape to Burma, 1955; Crime of Passion, 1957; Forty Guns, 1957; Roustabout, 1964; The Night Walker, 1965. Television appearances include: Jack Benny; Ford Theater; Zane Grey; Alcoa Goodyear; Barbara Stanwyck Show (series), 1960-61; The Big Valley (series), 1965-69; The House That Would Not Die, 1970; A Taste of Evil, 1971; The Letters, 1973; The Thornbirds, 1983; The Colbys, 1985. *Honours:* Special Academy Award, 1982; Emmy Award for Best Actress, 1983; Lifetime Achievement Award, American Film Institute, 1987. *Address:* c/o A Morgan Maree & Associates Ltd, 6363 Wilshire Boulevard, Suite 600, Los Angeles, CA 90048, USA.

STARA Jana, b. 21 Apr. 1942, Pisek, Czechoslovakia. Mathematician. m, Vladimir Stary, 17 Aug. 1963, 2 sons, 1 daughter. *Education:* Graduated, 1964, Candidate of Sciences, 1971, Faculty of Mathematics and Physics, Charles University, Prague. *Appointments:* Assistant, Lecturer, Senior Lecturer, Faculty of Mathematics and Physics, Charles University, Prague. *Publications:* Mathematical papers on partial differential equations; Lecture notes on functional analysis. *Hobbies:* Music; Gardening. *Address:* Na Lise 1231, 14100 Prague 4, Czechoslovakia.

STARFIELD Barbara Helen, b. 18 Dec. 1932, Brooklyn, New York, USA. Physician; Educator. m. Neil A Holtzman, 12 June 1955. 3 sons, 1 daughter. *Education:* AB, Biology, Swarthmore College, 1954; MD, State University of New York, 1959; MPH, Johns Hopkins University, 1963. *Appointments:* Asst Prof, Assoc Prof, Professor of Hlth Policy & Pediatrics 1967-, Director, Pediatric Clinical Scholars Program 1971-76, Professor & Div Head Health Policy 1976-, Johns Hopkins University School of Hygiene & Public Health. *Publications:* Over 100 original contributions regarding health services and health policy, also health of children. Book: Effectiveness of Medical Care: Validating Clinical Wisdom, 1985. *Memberships:* Institute of Medicine, National Academy of Sciences, Council 1980-83; Ambulatory Pediatric Assn, President, 1980. *Honours:* Dave Luckman Memorial Award, 1958; Career Development Award, 1970-75; Armstrong Award (Ambulatory Ped Assn), 1983; Member, Institute of Medicine, National Academy of Sciences. *Address:* 624 North Broadway Room 452, Baltimore, Maryland 21205, USA.

STARKES Janet Lynn, b. 7 Apr. 1952, Calgary, Canada. Professor. *Education:* BA Physical Education, University of Western Ontario, 1974; MSc Kinesiology, 1976, PhD 1980, University of Waterloo; Postdoctoral Fellowship, Clin. Neuropsych, Mt Sinai Hospital, 1986. *Appointment:* Faculty Member, McMaster University, Hamilton, Ontario, 1979-. *Publications:* Thirteen research articles in professional journals; Three book chapters on expert-novice differences in perception; Thirty published research abstracts and Presentations at conferences. *Memberships:* Society for Neuroscience; Canadian Society for Psychomotor Learning & Sport Psych; North American Society for the Psychology of Sport and Physical Activity; Coaching Association of Canada, Research Chair; Canadian Association for the Advancement of Women in Sport. *Address:* School of Physical Education, McMaster University, 1280 Main Street W, Hamilton, Ontario, Canada L8S 4K1.

STARMER Alice Strickland, b. 12 Sept. 1921, Yazoo City, Mississippi, USA. Hospital Administration; Assistant Admin. for Community Affairs and Development. m. Garrett L Starmer, 2 Apr. 1946. 2 sons, 2 daughters. *Education:* Louisiana State University, Baton Rouge, Louisiana, 1941-43; BA, Sociology, Psychology and English, University of Alabama, 1943-45; MA, Personnel and Counseling, Columbia University, New York City, 1945-46. *Appointments:* Camp Counselor, Ridgecrest, 1940 and 1943; Counselor to Freshman Women, University of Alabama, 1944-45; Dean of Students, Central College, Conway, Arkansas, 1945-46; Assistant Dean of Women, University of California, Santa Barbara, 1946-47; Executive Director of Girl Scouts of Memphis and Shelby Counties, 1947-48; Executive Director of Girl Scout Camp, Memphis, Tennessee, 1948; Community Service Director, 1969-73; Assistant Administrator for Community Affairs & Development, 1973-83, 1985-, Enloe Memorial Hospital; Rotary District Wife, 1983-84. *Publications include:* Editor, Hospital Monthly Newsletter for 13 years; Patient Handbook; other hospital publications, brochures and public information material. *Memberships include:* Steering Committee and founding member, Hospital Public Relations Association of Northern California, Area Council Representative, Executive Board, 1971-83; National Society of Fund Raising Executives, 1971-84; National Association of Hospital Development, 1971-; Chairman of Accreditation for NAHD, Northern California, 1976-83 and 1985-86; Member, National Accreditation Committee for NAHD, 1976-83 and 1985-86; National Parity Committee for NAHD; Membership Committee for NAHD, Northern California; Soroptimist International of Chico, Past Oficer, Committee Chairman, etc; North Valley Estate Planning Council; Chairman Ambassadors Chamber of Commerce; Reach to Recovery Volunteer; Creative Arts Board; Salvation Army Board; Chairman, Nominating Committee, Region II, 1987-88; Editorial staff, NAHD Journal, 1980-81; Advisory Committee, Speech and Hearing, Chico State University, etc. *Honours:* President and Supervisor, Calif. Girl Scout Council and Sierra Calif. Girl Scout Council, 1951-58; 1st Girl Scout Thank You Award, Northern California, 1956; Executive Board of Boy Scouts in America, 1974; Kiwanis Club, Ohio, 1975, 1976, 1982; Certificate of Appreciation: American Cancer Society, 1978; Fellow, National Association of Hospital Development, 1980; Durham Rotary Club, 1981; Venture Club, 1981; Resolution of Appreciation & Commendation, California Assembly Members, 1983; Rotary Fellow, 1983; Secretary, Board of Trustees, Enloe Memorial Hospital, 1984; Board of Directors, Enloe Hospital Foundation. *Hobbies:* Bridge; Gardening; Reading; Spectator Sports; Sewing; People. *Address:* 14 Lindo Park Drive, Chico, CA 95926, USA.

STARR Joan Elizabeth, b. 1 Apr. 1927, Tenterfield, New South Wales, Australia. Journalist; Grazier; Public Relations Consultant. m. David Shearston Thompson, 11 Sept. 1948, dissolved 1965, 1 son, 1 daughter. *Education:* Advanced English, 1950-52, Italian, 1970-74, University Extension Service; Diploma of Journalism, RMIT, 1974-77. *Appointments:* Show and Rodeo Reporter, Hoofs and Horns, 1947-57; Editor, Tenterfield Star, 1963-64; Journalist, Sub-Editor, Cairns Post, 1965-70; Cable Sub-Editor, Queensland Times; Senior Editorial Officer, Queensland Health Education Council, 1972-76; Journalist, then Assistant Manager of Public Relations, Australia Post, Queensland, then Victoria, 1976-83; Freelance Journalist and Public Relations Consultant, 1983-; Grazier, Tenterfield. *Publications:* Numerous feature stories; 1 novel; 6 regional histories: Pioneering New England (with artist Mike Nicholas), 1978; Settlers on the Marthaquy (with Marion Dormer); Wines and Wineries of the Granite Belt; The Wellington Caves...a Treasure Trove of Fossils; Melton...Plains of Promise; Moreton Shire...Discovery and Settlement, 1988; Writer/editor, numerous smaller histories of various places; Numerous poems including 1 in anthology of Australian poems; Short stories; Brochures, booklets, trade journals. *Memberships:* Royal Historical Society, Queensland; Society of Australian Genealogists; Australian Light Horse Association, Queensland; Fellow, World Literary Academy; Public Relations Institute of Australia. *Hobbies:* Breeding Arabian horses, Merino sheep, Angora goats; History; Bushwalking; Music; Ballet; Skating. *Address:* Arakoon, via Tenterfield, New South Wales 2372, Australia.

STARR Joyce R, b. 1945, Philadelphia, USA. Director. *Education:* BA, University of Michigan, 1967; MA, 1977, PhD, Sociology, 1973, Northwestern University. *Appointmeents:* various posts & activities, 1971-76; Member, Atlanta Staff, Carter-Mondale Campaign, 1976-77; Associate Special Assistant to President Carter, The White House, 1977-79; Director,

Near East Studies Programme, Overseas Representative, Near East, Centre for Strategic & International Studies, Washington, 1979-. *Publications:* Intersevice Rivalries Among Western Allies, 1987; Banks, Petrodollars and Sovereign Debtors: Blood from Sone, 1985, contributing author; articles in journals and magazines. *Address:* Center for Strategic & International Studies, 1800 K Street Northwest, Suite 400, Washington, DC 20006, USA.

STARR Miriam Carolyn, b. 13 Apr. 1951, Pittsburgh, Pennsylvania, USA. Financial Manager. *Education:* BS, Mathematics, Bucknell University, 1973; MBA, Finance, Drexel University, 1984. *Appointments:* Management Trainee 1973-75, Assistant Equipment Engineer 1976-77, Short Range Planning, 1976-77, Switching System Supervisor 1977-78, Long Range Planner, 1978-80, Cost Analyst 1980-81, Price/Demand Analyst 1981-83, Bell Telephone Co of Pennsylvania, Inc; Inventory Analyst 1983-85, Budget Analyst 1985-87, Expense Analyst 1987-88, Assistant Controller, General Business Systems Unit 1988-, American Telephone and Telegraph Co Inc. *Memberships:* National Association of Female Executives; American Society of Professional and Executive Women; Delta Zeta Sorority; Stone Run II Neighborhood Assoc, Treasurer 1987-, Covenants Committee 1986-87. *Hobbies:* Mystery stories; Golf. *Address:* 16 Cambridge Road, Bedminster, New Jersey 07921, USA.

STARR Nina Kennedy, b. 2 Feb. 1942, Greensboro, North Carolina, USA. University Administrator; Lecturer. m. William B Starr, 22 Aug. 1964, divorced 1985. 1 son, 1 daughter. *Education:* BA, Sociology 1964, MEd, Counseling 1966, EdS, Stud Personnel 1980, EdD, Ed Admin-Hi Ed 1987, UNC Greensboro. *Appointments:* Research Assoc, 1980-83, Assoc Dir, Center Ed Studies & Dev and Lecturer, Dept of Counselor Ed 1983-87, Acting Dir Center Ed Stud & Dev Admin Coord, Collegium for Advance of School, Schooling & Ed, Lecturer, Dept Ed Administration, 1987-89, Director, Center Ed Stud & Dev, Admin Coord, Collegium for Advance of School, Schooling & Ed, Lecturer, School of Educ 1989-, UNC Greensboro. *Publications:* Increased Effectiveness of Teacher Ed, Journal of Instructional Psych, 1989; Promotion & Tenure: Faculty Perception of the Nexus with Univ Teaching, 14th Internation Conf on Imp Univ Teach, Umea, Sweden, 1988; Reported Import of Teaching 13th Intern Conf on Imp Univ Teaching, Israel, 1987. *Memberships:* Bd of Trustees, Guilford Tech Commun College, 1983-; Bd Directors, No Carolina Art Council, 1981-84; Observ Delegate, White House Conf on Aging, 1981. *Honours:* Chi Sigma Iota Counseling Academic & Prof Honor Society; National Board Certified Counselor; Fellow, American Orthopsychiatric Assoc; Service Certificate of Appreciation, James B Hunt, Jr Governor of North Carolina, 1984. *Hobbies:* Tennis; Reading; Needlepoint; Bridge; Collection of Japanese Netsuke. *Address:* School of Education, Curry Building, UNC Greensboro, Greensboro, NC 27412, USA.

STAUFFER Helen Winter, b. 4 Jan. 1922, Mitchell, South Dakota, USA. Professor of English. m. Mitchell (Mike) Stauffer, 30 Mar. 1944, 1 son, 3 daughters. *Education:* BA 1964, MS 1968, Kearney State College, Nebraska; PhD, University of Nebraska, Lincoln, 1974. *Appointments:* Grand Island High School, 1964-67; Faculty 1967-, Professor 1976-, Kearney State College. *Publications:* Co-Editor, Women in Western American Literature, 1982; Author, Mari Sandoz, Story Catcher of the Plains, 1982; Editor, Welded Women, poetry, 1983; Various articles, book reviews; Scholar for Great Plains Chautauqua (portrayed Mari Sandoz, Elizabeth Custer), 1985- 87. *Memberships include:* National Education Association; Modern Language Association; Past President, Western Literature Association; Executive, Sandoz Heritage; Board, Great Plains Chautauqua. *Honours:* Alumni Roll of Honour, Grand Island School, 1983; Dean's Award, KSC, 1984; Fellowship, University of Nebraska; Pratt-Heins Award, 1985; Nebraska Regents Fellowships, 1970-73; Summer Research Grant, 1976; Mary Major Crawford

Award, English Department, 1982. *Hobbies:* Travel; Western American history; Indian Wars history; Reading; Research; Grandchildren; Performing for Chautauqua. *Address:* 808 West 24th Street, Kearney, Nebraska 68847, USA.

STAUFFER LeeAnn, b. 22 Jan. 1962, Manchester, USA. Journalist. *Education:* BSFS, Georgetown University, 1984; MS, Journalism, Columbia University, 1986. *Appointments:* Freelance Foreign Correspondent, Nairobi, Kenya, 1986-; Resident Correspondent, ABC Radio News, Christian Science Monitor Radio, Voice of Germany. *Membership:* American Women in Radio & TV. *Hobbies:* Horse Riding; Swimming; Psychology. *Address:* PO Box 47405, Nairobi, Kenya, Africa.

STAVRAKAKI Chrissoula, b. 20 Nov. 1945, Athens, Greece. Director, Child Psychiatry. 1 daughter. *Education:* Doctorate of Medicine, 1970; Diploma of Psychological Medicine (London conjoint), 1977; Doctorate of Philosophy, 1978; Member of Royal College of Psychiatrists, London, England, 1978; Fellow, Royal College of Physicians & Surgeons of Canada (Psychiatry), 1981. *Appointments:* Lecturer, Child Psychiatry/Mental Deficiency, 1977, Senior Lecturer, Child Psychiatry/Mental Deficiencey, 1978 St George's Hospital Medical School; Assistant Professor of Psychiatry, University of Ottawa, School of Medicine, 1979-; Director, Child Psychiatry, Regional Children's Centre, Royal Ottawa Hospital, 1982-; Vice-Chairperson, Division of Child & Adolescent Psychiatry, University of Ottawa, 1984-. *Publications:* Books: Psychiatric Perspectives on Mental Retardation, 1986; Affective Disorders & Anxiety in the Child & Adolescent, 1988. Chapters: Developmental Disabilities: Recent Trends in Prevention and Treatment, 1985; 1986 & Beyond: A Look into the Future in Psychiatric Perspectives on MR, 1986; Psychotherapies with the Mentally Retarded, 1986; Mental Retardation, 1987; Articles to professional journals. *Memberships:* Royal Society of Medicine, England; Society of Clinical Psychiatrists, England; Royal College of Physicians and Surgeons, Canada; Canadian Psychiatric Association; Canadian Public Health Association; Ontario Health Association; Canadian Academy of Child Psychiatry; American Academy of Child Psychiatry. *Honours:* Honors Medical School & Scholarship, 1975; Elected Fellow, Royal Society of Medicine, 1975; Elected Founding Member 1980 and Secretary/Treasurer 1985-87, Canadian Academy of Child Psychiatry; Elected Affiliate Member, American Academy of Child Psychiatry, 1983. *Hobbies:* Writing; Poetry; Music; Painting; Opera. *Address:* 10 Burrows Road, Gloucester, Ontario, K1J 6E6, Canada.

STEAFEL Sheila, b. 26 May 1935, Republic of South Africa. Actress. m. Harry H Corbett, 20 Oct. 1958, divorced 1964. *Education:* BA, Fine Arts, University of Witwatersrand; Webber Douglas School of Drama. *Appointments:* Appearances in West End Plays: Billy Liar, 1960; How the Other Half Loves, 1972; Harpo in A Day in Hollywood A Night in the Ukraine, 1979; Revival of, Salad Days, 1976; Twelfth Night, 1983; The Duenna, 1983; Played the Witch in Humperdinck's Opera, Hansel and Gretel, 1983; Royal Shakespeare Company, 1985; Facade, 1986; Appearances in TV Series include: The Frost Report, 1966; Beachcomber, 1969; Howe's Your Father, 1974; Ghosts of Motley Hall, 1975; Diary of a Nobody, 1978; Sheila, One Woman Show, 1982; You Must Be The Husband, BBC, 1986, 1987; Appearances in: One Woman Shows: The Late Sheila Steafel, 1981; Steafel Solo, 1981-82; Steafel Revisited, 1982; Steafel Variations, 1982; Steafel Lately, 1983; Steafel Express, 1985; Her film appearances include: Baby Love, 1969; Some Will Some Won't, 1969; Tropic of Cancer, 1970; Percy, 1971; SWALK, 1971; The Waiting Room, 1976; Towers of Babel, 1981; Bloodbath in the House of Death, 1983; Appearances on Radio, Week Ending, 1977; Jason Explanation, 1978; Steafel Plus, 1982; Steafel with a S, 1984; Voices for the Perishers, 1978, Super Ted, 1986-1987, Stretch and Slim, 1988. *Honours:* Comedy Award, Webber Douglas School, 1954.

Hobbies: Painting; Dogs. *Address:* c/o Ken McReddie 91 Regent Street, London W1, England.

STEBER Eleanor, b. 17 July 1916, Wheeling, West Virginia, USA. Soprano. *Education:* MusB, New England Conservatory of Music, 1938. *Career:* Singer, 1930-; Won Metropolitan Auditions of Air, 1940; Sang with Metropolitan Opera Co, 1940-66, San Francisco Opera Co, 1945, Central City Opera Festival, 1946, 1951, Cincinnati Summer Opera, 5 summers, Lyric Opera, Chicago, 1954-57; Appeared with all major American opera companies and all major European Festivals including: Glyndebourne, Edinburgh, 1948; Vienna Festival and opened Bayreuth, 1953; Florence and Brussels Worlds Fair, 1954; Salzburg, 1959; Sang with 7 opera companies, Yugoslavia, 1955, Vienna Staats Oper, 1956; Appointed Ambassador to Music by President Eisenhower, gave 33 concerts in 3.1/2 months, 17 Near and Far East countries, 1956; Soloist with New York Philharmonic, NBC, Boston, Minneapolis, Chicago, Cincinnati, Kansas City, Denver, Montreal, Philadelphia Symphony Orchestras, conductors Bruno Walter, Arturo Toscanini, George Szell, Sir George Solti, Dimitri Mitropoulos, Eric Leinsdorf, Sir Thomas Beecham, Fritz Reiner; Radio and TV appearances; Star, TV's Voice of Firestone, 10 years; Concert tours throughout USA, Canada, Europe, Orient; Head, Vocal Department, Cleveland Institute of Music, 1963-73; Voice Faculty: Juilliard School of Music, New England Conservatory of Music, 1971-; College-Conservatory of Music, University of Cincinnati, 1974; Philadelphia Music Academy, 1975; University of Missouri, Columbia, 1978; American Institute of Musical Studies, Graz, Austria, 1978-; Pepperdine University, Malibu, California, 1979; University of Oklahoma, Norman, 1982. *Memberships:* Board of Directors, Brooklyn Company; Opera Society, Washington; New Music for Young Ensembles; Bruno Walter Society; Honorary Member: Delta Omicron; Beta Sigma Phi; Pi Kappa Lambda; President, Eleanor Steber Music Foubndation. *Honours:* Several honorary doctorates. *Address:* Port Jefferson, NY 11777, USA.

STECKEL Julie Raskin, b. 3 Jan. 1940, Los Angeles, USA. Psychotherapist; Lecturer; Consultant. m. Richard Jay Steckel, 16 June 1960, 1 son, 1 daughter. *Education:* BA, UCLA, 1960; MSW, 1975; MA, teaching, Harvard University, 1961. *Appointments:* Psychological Consultant, BMA Dialysis Units, Torrance, California, 1976-83; Private Practice Psychotherapy, 1976-; Affiliate Staff, Del Amo Hospital, Torrance, 1983-; Lecturer, Consultant, UCLA Dental School, 1984; Lecturer, Social Welfare, UCLA Graduate School, 1985-. *Publications:* Contributor of articles to professional journals. *Memberships:* National Association Social Workers; Fellow, Society Clinical Social Workers. *Address:* 12301 Wilshire Blvd Suite 413, Los Angeles, CA 90025, USA.

STEELE Linda Hopkins, b. 18 June 1947, Kansas City, Missouri, USA. Attorney. m. Gerald R Steele, 7 July 1967. *Education:* Honour student, Centre College of Kentucky, 1965-67; JD magna cum laude, Woodrow Wilson College of Law, Atlanta, Georgia, 1979. *Appointments:* US Civil Service, 1969-72; Self employed, music business, 1973-79; Sole practice, attorney, 1979-. *Publication:* Article, Kentucky Coal Journal, 1986. *Memberships:* American & Georgia Bar Associations; National & Georgia Associations of Women Lawyers; Belvedere Civic Club. *Honour:* American Jurisprudence Constitutional Law Award, 1979. *Hobbies:* Music; Nature. *Address:* 2909 Santa Barbara Drive, Decatur, Georgia 30032, USA.

STEFANICK Patti Ann, b. 25 Sept. 1957, Elizabeth, New Jersey, USA. Surgeon. *Education:* BA, Biol Science, Rutgers College, Rutgers University, 1979; DO, University of New England College of Osteopathic Medicine, 1983. *Appointments:* Internship, Kennedy Mem Hospital, Stratford, NJ, 1983-84; Gen Surg Residency, Metropolitan Hosp, Philadelphia, 1984-88; Breast Cancer Fellow, Memorial Sloan-Kettering Cancer Center, NY, 1988-. *Memberships:* AMA; AOA; NJ Assoc of Osteopathic Phys & Surg, Alumni Board; Penn Osteopathic Medical Assoc; Rutgers Alumni Assoc. *Honours:* Chief Resident, Gen Surgery, 1986-88; Co Chief Resident, Metropolitan Hospital, 1987-88. *Hobbies:* Music, piano, organ, French horn; Photography. *Address:* 1708 Linden Hill Apts, Lindenwold, NJ 08021, USA.

STEFANICS Charlotte Louise, b. 30 Dec. 1927, USA. Psychiatric Mental Health Clinical Nurse Specialist. *Education:* Bsc., Nursing, Seton Hall University, 1968; MSc., Nursing, Ohio State University, Columbus, 1971; DEd, University of Sarasota, 1982. *Appointments:* Charge Nurse, 1948; Medical, Surgical, Psychiatric Nurse, Toledo State Hospital, 1948-49; Pediatric Nursing, St Elisabeth Hospital, Dayton,1949-52; VA Hospital, Dayton, 1949-51; entered Bendictine Convent, Nursing, 1952-69; Orthopedics, New York University Medical Centre, 1969-70; Private Pracice, 1971-73; Community Hospital, Springfield, 1971-74; Duke University School of Nursing, Durham, 1974-77; VA Medical Centre, Bay Pines, 1977-. *Publications:* Articles in: Nursing Families in Crisis; many other journals; Special invitation to China, 1984. *Memberships Include:* New York, Ohio, North Carolina, Florida, Nurses Associations. *Honours:* Guest Speaker for Graduation Class of 1973, Community Hospital School of Nursing; Service Award, Mental Health Association of Pinellas Co., 1981; Nominated, Nurse of the Year, 1985; *Hobbies:* Travel; Reading; Classical Music. *Address:* 11511, 113th Street N, No 22A, Seminole, FL 34648, USA.

STEFFLER Christel D E, b. 30 July 1930, Neustettin, Germany. Diplomat. *Education:* Interpreter's Diploma in Modern Languages, Mayence University, 1954; Licence es Sciences Poliques, Graduate Institute of International Studies, Geneva, Switzerland, 1956. *Appointments:* Staff 1957-, 2nd Secretary 1960-, Foreign Ministry 1965-70, 1973-77 and 1981-84, Foreign Service, Bonn, Federal Republic of Germany; Consulate General, 1961-65,Deputy Consul-General, 1963-65, Calcutta, India; Counsellor, Embassy, Paris, France, 1970-73; Deputy Head of Mission, Embassy, Tel Aviv, Israel, 1977-80; Ambassador of the Federal Republic of Germany to the United Republic of Tanzania, 1984-. *Membership:* Former Member, North Atlantic Treaty Organisation Defense College, Rome. *Hobbies:* Hiking; Music; Horseriding; Theatre. *Address:* Spechtweg 10, 2150 Buxtehude, Federal Republic of Germany.

STEGEMAN Beatrice Ann Carlson, b. 7 Feb. 1936, Evanston, USA. Philosophy Teacher; Activist. m. Richard Stegeman, 7 June 1958, 1 daughter. *Education:* BS, 1958; MA, 1960, PhD, Philosophy, Southern Illinois University, 1967. *Appointments:* Southern Illinois University, 1958-65; American University, Cairo, 1965-68; Central Connecticut State University, 1969; State Community College, 1970-. *Publications:* Yesterdays, 1988; Black Background, 1988; Five Copyrights; Scholarly articles. *Memberships:* SAFER; SCC AAUP; SCC, Faculy Senate, President 1973-75. *Honours:* Fulbright Summer Study: to Turkey 1988, Pakistan, 1984; Alice Paul Award, 1980. *Hobbies:* Reading; Hiking; Travel. *Address:* 306 Dana, Collinsville, IL 62234, USA.

STEHR Carla, b. 7 Oct. 1953, Olympia, Washington, USA. Fisheries Biologist. m. Michael Bailey, 25 Feb. 1989. *Education:* BA, The Evergreen State College, Olympia, Washington, 1975; MS, University of Washington, Seattle, 1982. *Appointments:* Fisheries Biologist 1976-84, Fisheries Biologist (Research), Head Electron Microscopy laboratory, 1984-, National Marine Fisheries Service, Seattle, Washington. *Publications:* Several scientific papers published in professional journals. *Memberships:* American Fisheries Society; Electron Microscopy Society of America; American Society of Zoologists. *Honours:* Sustained Superior Performance Award, 1979, 1982, and 1987, US Department of Commerce; Diatome US Award of Honourable Mention for Photomicrographic Excellence, 1986, Annual Meeting of the Electron Microscopy Society of America. *Hobbies:* Photography; Sea kayaking. *Address:* National Marine Fisheries Service, 2725 Montlake Blvd E, Seattle, Washington 98112, USA.

STEIN Elizabeth Ann, b. 27 May 1931, Burlington, Kansas, USA. Research Immunologist. m. Joseph Stein, 1 Sept. 1956, divorced 1986, 1 son, 1 daughter. *Education:* BA, BS, Education, Kansas State Teachers College, 1952; MA, 1954, PhD, 1960, University of California, Los Angeles. *Appointments:* Teaching Assistant, KSTC, 1950-52; High School Biology Teacher, 1952-53; Teaching Assistant, 1953-56, Assistant Research Anatomist, 1975-86, Research Immunologist, 1986-, University of California, Los Angeles; NSF Fellow, 1956-58. *Publications:* 40 in comparative immunology and the immunology of diabetes. *Memberships:* American Association for the Advancement of Science; International Society for Developmental & Comparative Immunology; Western Society of Naturalists; Research Society of Sigma Xi. *Honours:* National Science Foundation Fellowship, 1956-58. *Hobbies:* Hiking; Camping; Horse Riding; Gardening. *Address:* Division of Endocrinology, Dept. of Medicine, School of Medicine, University of California, Los Angeles, CA 90024, USA.

STEIN Linda J., b. 1 June 1958, Ridgewood, New Jersey, USA. Commercial Lending Officer; Financial Planner. *Education:* BSBA, Bucknell University, Pennsylvania, 1980; MBA, Pace University, New York, 1984; Licences, life insurance, health insurance, securities brokerage, 1985; School for Continuing Studies, Johns Hopkins Universty, 1988. *Appointments:* Telecommunications Service Manager, 1980-82; Departmental Controller, International Operations, Chemical Bank, 1982-84; Financial Planner, Lebowitz & Associates Inc, 1985-87; Divisional Controller 1984-86, Commercial Lender 1986-, 1st National Bank, Maryland. *Publications:* Various articles, local newspapers. *Memberships:* Secretary, Women's International Bowling Association; Bucknell University Alumni Association; Pi Beta Phi; Montgomery County Chamber of Commerce; Sierra Villas Condominium Association. *Honours:* Award, suggestion for electronic funds transfer system, Chemical Bank, 1983; Appointed leadership trainer, New Jersey State Student Government, 1978-82. *Hobbies:* Tennis; Boating; Soccer; Bowling; Sewing; Reading; Piano; Coin collecting. *Address:* 11239 Slalom Lane, Columbia, Maryland 21044, USA.

STEIN Seena Deborah, b. 20 Apr. 1941, Bronx, New York, USA. Real Estate Executive. m. Sanford Stein, 2 Nov. 1974, 1 son, 4 daughters. *Education:* B3, Purdue University, 1963; MLS 1970, MBA 1978 Rutgers University. *Appointments:* Director of Information, Englehard 1967-73, CMD-NJ 1973-77; Arbitrage researcher, Ivan Boesky, 1978; Salesperson 1979-80, Vice President 1980-82, Archie Schwartz Company; President, Seena Stein Inc, 1982-83; Director, Sales, Helmsley-Spear, 1983-85; Senior Vice President & Director, Sales & Leasing, Jacobson, Goldfarb & Tanzman Associates, 1985-. *Memberships:* Industrial & Commercial Real Estate Women; Industrial & Office Real Estate Brokers Association; National Association of Corporate Real Estate Executives; National Association of Executive Women; International Association of Women in Real Estate. *Honour:* Featured, Successful Woman magazine, American Society of Professional & Executive Women, 1986. *Hobbies:* Sailing; Reading. *Address:* c/o Jacobson, Goldfarb & Tanzman Associates, 10 Woodbridge Center Drive, PO Box 1408, Woodbridge, New Jersey 07095, USA.

STEINBERG Hannah, Professor of Psychopharmacology/Head of Psychopharmacology Group & Dept. UCL. *Education:* Cert. Comm, University of Reading; Denton Sec. College, London; BA 1st Class Honours Psychology, PhD, University College London. *Appointments:* Secretary to Managing Director, Omes Ltd; Assistant Lecturer in Pharmacology, Lecturer in Pharmacology; Reader in Psychopharmacology, 1954-70; Professor of Psychopharmacology, 1970-, University College London; Honorary Consulting Clinical

Psychologist, Department of Psychological Medicine, Royal Free Hospital, 1970; Visiting Professor in Psychiatry, McMaster University, Hamilton, Ontario, Canada, 1971. *Publications:* Trans/Ed. jointly: Animals and Men by David Katz, 1951; Editor of symposia: Animal Behaviour & Drug Action, 1963; Scientific Basis of Drug Dependence, 1968; Psychopharmacology, Sexual Disorders and Drug Abuse, 1972; Physical Exercise and Mental Health (forthcoming); Articles and reviews in professional journals and books. *Memberships:* President, University of London (Students') Union, 1947-48; Fellow, British Psychological Society; Scientific Fellow, Zoological Society of London; Vice President, Collegium Internationale Neuro-Psychopharmacologicum (CINP), 1968-74; Vice President, Brit. Assoc. Psychopharmacology, 1974-76; Convener, Academic Women's Achievement Group, 1979-; Special Trustee, Middlesex Hospital, 1988-; Member, Editorial Board, Psychopharmacologia, 1965-80; Founder member, European Behavioural Pharmacology Society; Bulletin of British Pharmacological Society; Member, Editorial Board, 1965-72; Founder member, European College of Neuro- Psychopharmacology, etc. *Honours:* Postgraduate Studentship, University of London, Troughton Scholarship, University College London, 1948- 50; Distinguished Affiliate, American Psychological Association, Psychopharmacology Div. 1978; Honorary Member, British Association of Psychopharmacology, 1988. *Address:* University College London, Kathleen Lonsdale Building, Gower Street, London WC1E 6BT, England.

STEINMAN Joan, b. 19 June 1947, Brooklyn, New York, USA. Law Professor. m. Douglass W. Cassel Jr, 1 June 1974 (div. 1986), 2 daughters. *Education:* AB, High Distinction, University of Rochester, 1969; Philosophy (non-degree), University of Birmingham, UK, 1968; JD, Harvard Law School, 1973. *Appointments:* Associate attorney, Schiff, Hardin & Waite, 1973-77; Associate Professor (with tenure) 1982-86, Professor of Law 1986-, Kent College of Law, Illinois Institute of Technology (IIT). *Publications include:* Contributions, various legal journals. *Memberships:* Society of American Law Teachers, 1986-88; Chicago Council of Lawyers, 1973-88; American Bar Association, 1973-83, 1987-90; State of Illinois Bar, 1973-. *Honours:* Norma and Edna Freehling Scholar (1989-); Order of the Coif (1989); Invited participant, Liberty Fund & Institute of Human Studies colloquium, Concept of Freedom of Association: Historical, Philosophic & Legal Exploration, 1984; Phi Beta Kappa, 1968; Honorary Scholarship, University of Rochester, 1965. *Hobby:* Tennis. *Address:* Illinois Institute of Technology, Chicago-Kent College of Law, 77 South Wacker, Chicago, Illinois 60606, USA.

STELLMAN Jeanne M, b. 27 May 1947, Bensheim, Germany. US Citizen. m. Steven D. Stellman, 1 son, 1 daughter. *Education:* BS, Chemistry, 1968, PhD, Physical Chemistry, 1972, City University of New York. *Appointments Include:* Instructor, Chemistry, 1969-72, Adjunct Professor, 1971-74, Rutgers Labor Education Centre; Chief, American Health Foundation, New York, 1977-81; Associate Professor, School of Public Health, Columbia, University, 1980-; Editor, Women & Health, 1985-; Founder, President, Foundation for Worker, Veteran & Environmental Health Inc., 1986-; Visiting Associate Professor, University of Medicine & Dentistry of New Jersey, 1986-. *Publications:* Co-author: Office Work Can be Dangerous to Your Health, 1984, 1989; Work is Dangerous to Your Health: A handbook of Health Hazards in the Workplace & What You Can Do About Them, 1973; Author: Womens Work, Womens Health: Myths and Realities, 1978; book chapters, monographs and articles in professional journals. *Memberships Include:* American Chemical Society. *Honours:* Recipient, various honours & awards. *Address;* Foundation for Worker, Veteran & Environmental Health Inc., 117 St Johns Place, Brooklyn, NY 11217, USA.

STELTZLEN Janelle Hicks, b. 18 Sept. 1937, Atlanta, Georgia, USA. Attorney at Law. div. 1987. 1 son, 1 daughter. *Education:* BSc 1958; MSc 1961; Juris Doctor, 1981. *Appointments:* Registered Dietitian, 1959-; Attorney at Law, Head of Janelle H Steltzlen & Associates, 1981-. *Contributions to:* University of Tulsa Law Journal, 1980. *Memberships:* First United Methodist Church; Tulsa Title & Probate Lawyers; Executive Committee Family Law Division; Volunteer Lawyers Association; Delta Zeta Sorority; Legal Counseling Ministry. *Honours:* Dubois Scholarship, 1959; Phi Sigma, Outstanding Member, 1958; Tulsa University College of Law, Academic Scholarship, 1979-81. *Hobbies:* Sewing; Swimming; Jogging; Cycling; Reading; Painting; Languages; Serving in the First United Methodist Church. *Address:* 1150 E 61st Street, Tulsa, Oklahoma 74136, USA.

STEPHENS Barbara D, b. 14 May 1940, Jamaica, New York, USA. Psychologist. 1 daughter. *Education:* BA, Marquette University, 1961; MS, Counselling, 1971, MSSW, 1972, PhD, 1974, University of Wisconsin. *Appointments:* Staff Writer: Forbes Magazine, 1963-68; Associate Professor, University of Wisconsin, 1973-80; Associate Professor, University of California, Los Angeles, 1980-83; Associate Professor, University of Southern California, 1983-. *Publications:* Articles in numerous journals & magazines; Editor: Family Medicine, 1979-81; The Preceptor, 1982-84; etc. *Memberships:* American Psychological Association; California State, Los Angeles Psychological Associations; Association for Women in Psychology; Women in Psychoanalysis; etc. *Honours:* Pi Gamma Mu, 1960; Distinguished Teaching Award Nominee, University of Southern California, 1988 & University of Wisconsin, 1977; Outstanding Symposium Presentor, Society of Teachers of Family Medicine, 1978; UCLA Chanellor's Advisory Commission on the Status of Women, 1980, 1981; etc. *Address:* 1355 Silvius Avenue, San Pedro, CA 90731, UsA.

STEPHENS Elizabeth Shirley Eileen, b. 30 Nov. 1941, Hampstead, London, England. Actress. *Education:* Gold Medals, Speech & Acting, Lambda Gold Medal & Diploma, Acting, New Era Bronze Medal, Poetry Society, Silver Medal, New Era Academy of Drama & Music, London. *Appointments:* Arts Theatre, Belfast, 1967-71; Metropole Theatre, Glasgow, 1968; Playhouse Theatre, Bary, 1973, 1979; Playhouse Theatre, Skegness, 1975; Civic Theatre, Ayr, 1981, 1982, 1983; Leas Pavilion Theatre, Folkstone, 1982, 1984; Pantomimes & Tours, The Mating Season, Cinderella, Puss in Boots, Christmas Carol, A Kiss for Cinderella, 1976-84. *Honours:* Gold Medals, Speech & Acting, Lambda; Gold Medal & Diploma, Acting, New Era Academy of Drama & Music, London; Bronze & Silver Medals, Poetry Society. *Hobbies:* History; Latin; Shakespeare. *Address:* 89 Chandos Road, Stratford, London E14 1TT, England.

STEPHENS Lisa Ann, b. 21 Aug. 1959, Brady, USA. Real Estate Appraiser. *Education:* BS, Agricultural Economics, Texas A & M University, 1982. *Appointments:* Manager, The Stephens Company, San Angelo, Texas, 1982-84; Manager, Stephens Real Estate, San Angelo, Texas, 1984-86; Staff Appraiser, Robert A. Elliott Real Estate, San Angelo, Texas, 1987; Property Manager, City of San Angelo, 1987; Manager, Salesperson, Stephens Real Estate, Brady, 1988-. *Memberships:* American Institute of Real Estate Appraisers; National Board of Realtors, Texas Board of Realtors; Assistant Division Superintendent, San Angelo Stock Show & Rodeo Association, 1985-87. *Honours:* Various honours & awards. *Hobbies:* Travel; Reading; Dancing. *Address:* 1017 W. 12th Brady, TX 76825, USA.

STEPHENSON Kathryn Lyle, b. 30 July 1912, Kansas City, MO, USA. m. Jack M Mosely, MD, divorced 1972. 1 son, 1 daughter. *Education:* BA, University of Arizona, 1934; MD, University of Kansas, 1941. *Appointments:* Associate, Dr Earl C Padgett; Staff, Los Angeles Children's Hosp, 1950-54; Private practice, Santa Barbara 1919-78. *Publications:* Editor, Jnl of Plastic and Reconstructive Surgery, 1965-67; Year Book of Plastic Surgery, 1976-77; Contrbt chapters to Symposium on Medical Writing, Everywoman's Health, 1980-82, 1985; Author: Plastic and Reconstructive Surgery (with E C Padgett), 1948. *Memberships:* American Association Plastic Reconstructive Surgery; President, California Society of Plastic Surgery; Am College of Surgeons. *Honours:* Research Certificate of Merit; Award, Plastic Reconstructive Surgery, 1977; Distinguished graduate, Pembroke Hill School, 1985. *Hobbies:* Golf; Painting; Home. *Address:* 780 Rockbridge Road, Santa Barbara, CA 93108, USA.

STEPHENSON Linda Sue Koehlinger, b. 30 June 1939, Monroeville, Indiana, USA. Businesswoman. m. Jack L. Stephenson, 31 Dec. 1961. *Education:* Professional model training, 1959; Personal development institute training, 1961; Esthetician Certificate, 1981; Image projection teacher training, 1982. *Appointments:* Professional model, 1960-76; Director, model talent agency, 1960-64; Co-owner, instructor, finishing school, 1964-65; Director, trainer, cosmetic company, 1969-81; Founder, owner, cosmetic & fashion accessory company, 1981-. *Publications:* Articles; New Dimensions; Eyes on Fort Wayne; National Beauty School journal. *Memberships:* Fort Wayne Women's Bureau, Civic Theatre Guild, & Chamber of Commerce; Women Business Owners Association; National Association of Female Executives; National Hairdresses Association. *Honours:* National Farmers Equity Queen, 1960; Car winner, Fashion Two Twenty, 1969-71; Top Director, national cosmetic company, 1979, 1980, 1981. *Hobbies:* Physical fitness; Flower gardening; Bird watching. *Address:* 5821 Decatur Road, Fort Wayne, Indiana 46816, USA.

STERLING Dorothy, b. 23 Nov. 1913, New York City, New York, USA. Author. m. Philip Sterling, 14 May 1937, 1 son, 1 daughter. *Education:* Wellesley College; Barnard College, BA, 1934. *Appointments:* Secretary, Architectural Forum, New York City, 1936-41; Researcher, Life, New York City, 1941-49; Freelance Writer; Consulting Editor, Firebird Books, Scholastic Book Services; Editorial Consultant on black history, Beacon Press. *Publications:* For children: Sophie and Her Puppies, 1951; The Cub Scout Mystery, 1952; Billy Goes Exploring, 1953; Trees and Their Story, 1953; Insects and the Homes They Build, 1954; Polio Pioneers: The Story of the Fight against Polio (with Philip Sterling), 1955; The Story of Mosses, Ferns, and Mushrooms, 1955; Wall Street: The Story of the Stock Exchange, 1955; The Brownie Scout Mystery, 1955; The Story of Caves, 1956; The Silver Spoon Mystery, 1958; Secret of the Old Post-Box, 1960; Creatures of the Night, 1960; Caterpillars, 1961; Ellen's Blue Jays, 1961; Forever Free; The Story of the Emancipation Proclamation, 1963; Spring Is Here!, 1964; Fall Is Here!, 1966; It Started in Montgomery: a Picture History of the Civil Rights Movement, 1972; For young adults: United Nations, N.Y., 1953, Revised Edition, 1961; Freedom Train: The Story of Harriet Tubman, 1954; Captain of the Planter: The Story of Robert Smalls, 1958; Tender Warriors (with Donald Gross), 1958; Mary Jane (novel), 1959; Lucretia Mott: Gentle Warrior, 1964; Lift Every Voice: The Lives of Booker T.Washington, W.E.B.Du Bois, Mary Church Terrell, and James Weldon Johnson (with Benjamin Quarles), 1965; The Outer Lands: A Natural History Guide to Cape Cod, Martha's Vineyard, Block Island, and Long Island, 1967, Revised Edition, 1978; Tear down the Walls!: A History of the American Civil Rights Movement, 1968; The Making of an Afro-American: Martin Robison Delany, 1812-1885; Black Foremothers: Three Lives, 1979, 2nd Edition, 1988; Contributor: Notable American Women, 1980; Dictionary of American Negro Biography, 1982; Editor: We Are Your Sisters: Black Women in the Nineteenth Century, 1984; Speak Out in Thunder Tones: Letters and Other Writings by Black Northerners, 1973; The Trouble They Seen: Black People Tell the Story of Reconstruction, 1976; I Have Seen War: Twenty-Five Stories from World War II, 1960; Turning the World Upside Down: Proceedings of the Anti-Slavery Convention of American Women, 1987. *Memberships:* Authors Guild; Authors League of America; National Association for the Advancement of Colored People. *Honours:* Nancy Block Award, 1958,

1959; Carter G.Woodson Award, National Council for the Social Studies, 1977. *Address:* Box 755, Wellfleet, MA 02667, USA.

STERN Barbara B., b. 12 Mar. 1939, New York City, USA. College Professor. m. Harry Stern, 28 June 1959, 2 daughters. *Education:* BA, Cornell University, 1959; MA, Hunter College, 1961; PhD, English, City University, New York (CUNY), 1965; MBA, Fordham University, 1981. *Appointments include:* Hunter College & NY City Community College, CUNY, 1961-75; St Peter's College, 1975-79; Montclair State College, 1981; Associate Professor, Marketing (tenure, 1986), & Assistant Chair, Management Science, Kean College, New Jersey, 1982-86; Associate Professor, Marketing, Rutgers, State University of New Jersey, Newark Campus, 1986-. *Publications include:* Books: Entrapment & Liberation in James Joyce's Daedalus Fiction, dissertation, 1965; Is Networking for You? Working Woman's Guide to the Old Boy System, 1981. Numerous articles, refereed journals; Refereed proceedings; Book chapters; Trade articles. *Memberships include:* Founder, New Jersey Network of Professional Women, Fordham MBA Womens Network; Executive, NY Chapter, American Association of Individual Investors; American Marketing Association; Academy of Marketing Sience. *Honours include:* 3 grants, Rutgers University, 1986-87; Leavey Award 1984, JCEE Award 1985, Kean College; Teaching awards, 1984, 1985; CUNY Doctoral Fellowship, 1963-64; NY State Regents Fellowship, 1964-65; Womens Press Institute Prize, 1978; Fordham University Fellowship, 1979-81; Various honour societies. *Address:* 160 East 84th Street, 16C, New York, NY 10028, USA.

STERN Cindy Debra, b. 15 June 1952, Amityville, New York, USA. Professor of Philosophy. *Education:* BA, College of William & Mary, 1974; MLS 1975, PhD 1980, Syracuse University. *Appointments:* Assistant Professor, Philosophy, University of North Carolina 1980-81, University of Notre Dame 1981-84, University of Oklahoma 1984-. *Creative works:* Dissertation: Causation, Necessity & Logic of Causal Statement. Articles: Paraphrase & Parsimony; Prospects for Elimination of Event Talk; Logical Features of Reference to Facts in Causal Statements; Lewis's Counterfactual Analysis of Causation; Hume & the Self at a Moment; Natural Kind Terms & Standards of Membership. *Membership:* American Philosophical Association. *Honours:* Chancellor's Citation 1980, University Fellowship 1977-80, Syracuse University; Junior Faculty Summer Fellowship 1985, Associate Distinguished Lectureship 1985-86, University of Oklahoma. *Hobbies:* Playing piano; Swimming; Knitting. *Address:* Department of Philosophy, University of Oklahoma, 455 West Lindsey, Suite 605, Norman, Oklahoma 73019, USA.

STERN Rosella L. Felsenfeld, b. 6 June 1941, USA. Poet; Teacher. div, 1 daughter. *Education:* BA, Roosevelt University, Chicago, 1962; MA, English, Northwestern University, 1967; PhD studies, Contemporary Poetics, University of Wisconsin, 1970-75. *Appointments include:* Instructor; University of Wisconsin, Lone Mountain College, Dominican College of San Raphael, San Francisco Art Institute, North Seattle Community College; Writer, freelance & for various corporations, arts organisations & publications including Chevron USA, Weyerhaueser, Forbes, American Photographer, San Diego Opera, Museum of Photographic Arts, Seattle Times Pacific Magazine, Seattle Weekly; Readings, Midwest & West Coast, 1970's & 80's. *Publications:* Small press books including: Saying Yes; People's Lives. Inclusion, Poetry From Violence. Contributor to: Seattle Image; Kaleidoscope; Bugle American; Amazon; Offstage Voice; Street Sheet; Wisconsin Poets in the Schools. *Honours:* Grants: California Arts Council, 1976; National Endowment for Arts, 1979. *Address:* 329 25th Avenue East, Seattle, Washington 98112, USA.

STERNBERG Francesca Nicola, b. 21 Aug. 1962, London, England. Equestrienne. *Memberships:* British Horse Society; Side Saddle Association; BSJA;

American Quarter Horse Association; National Reining Horse Association. *Honours:* 1988: 1st European to Qualify & Compete at World Quarter Horse Championships in Oklahoma City; Leading International Rider, European Championships for Western Riding; Winnder, National Swiss Cup for Reining for the Second Year. *Hobbies:* Travel; Skiing; Reading. *Address:* Plurenden Manor, High Halden, Nr. Ashford, Kent TN26 3JW, England.

STERNHAGEN Frances, b. 13 Jan. 1930, Washington, DC, USA. Actress. m. Thomas A Carlin, 13 Feb. 1956, 4 sons, 2 daughters. *Education:* BA, Vassar College, 1951. *Appointments:* Arena Stage, Washington DC, 1952-54; Plays on Broadway: Equus; The Good Doctor; On Golden Pond; Angel; Home Front/ The War at Home; Off Broadway: The Admirable Bashville; The Country Wife; Misalliance; The Red Eye of Love; The Pinter Plays; Laughing Stock; Films: The Hospital; Starting Over; Outland; Independence Day; Romantic Comedy. *Honours:* Clarence Derwent Award, 1956; Obie Award, 1956, 1965; Tony Nominations, 1971, 1974, 1975, 1978, 1979; Tony Award, 1974; Drama Desk Award, 1975; Delia Austrian Medal, 1979. *Hobbies:* Group Singing; Painting; Reading; Dancing; Sailing; Swimming; Walking. *Address:* c/o Triad Artists Inc., 888 7th Avenue, New York, NY 10019, USA.

STETTLER Katherine Anne Hagen, b. 10 Nov. 1944, Evanston, Illinois, USA. Children's Services Worker, Volunteer Coordinator, Social Work. m. Jerry Stettler, 11 June 1966, divorced. 1 son. *Education:* AB, Sociology, College of William and Mary, Williamsburg, 1966; MA, Clinical & Community Psychology, California State University, Dominguez Hills, 1986; Organisational and Managerial Development, The Adizes Institute, Santa Monica, 1987. *Appointments:* Children's Treatment Worker, Los Angeles County DPSS, Child abuse section, 1972-79; Consultant, Group Home Evaluation Unit, 1979-81; Children's Services Worker III, 1974-; Volunteer Coordinator, 1981-88; Organizational Development Staff, 1988-, Los Angeles County Department of Children's Services; Supervising Children's Social Worker, Los Angeles County Department of Children's Services, Organizational Development Program, 1989-. *Memberships:* Directors of Volunteers in Agencies, 1981-; Children's Services Advisory Committee (DCS/DPSS), 1979-88 (former co-chairperson for 2 terms). *Honours:* Outstanding Services for Children, LA County Department of Children's Services, 1987; Psi Chi, National Honor Society Branch of the American Psychological Association, 1986; Kappa Delta Pi, Honorary Education Society, 1966. *Hobbies:* Travel, especially cruises; Family and social gatherings; Photography; Dancing. *Address:* Department of Children's Services, 10355 Slusher Avenue, Santa Fe Springs, CA 90670, USA.

STEVENS Barbara, b. 7 July 1924, Cheshire, England. Editor. m. Murry B Stevens, 15 Aug. 1948. 1 son, 4 daughters. *Appointments:* Teacher, Teen Theatre, 1965-72; Columnist for Gloucester Journal, England, 1949-67; Editor, Pasque Petals, State Poetry Magazine. *Publications:* Poetry Books: Crooked Paths; Cats Who Have Owned Me. *Memberships:* President, Community Playhouse, 1975-78; President, S D State Poetry Society, 1975-80; President, National Federation of State Poetry Societies, Inc, 1985-87. *Honours:* Best Actress Awards, Community Playhouse, 1968 and 1971; Volunteer of the Year, 1979; Several certificates for Volunteer Hours of Narration for the Blind, 1982 and 1984. *Hobbies:* ssa OOPainting; Sketching; Silversmithing; Gardening; Skiing; Golf. *Address:* 909 E 34th Street, Sioux Falls, SD 57105, USA.

STEVENS Mary Louise Tucker, b. 15 Aug. 1945, Duluth, Minnesota, USA. Licensed Consulting Psychologist. m. Larry Stevens, 11 Feb. 1967. 1 son. *Education:* BA, Psych, University of Minn, 1964-66; MA, Psych, Indiana University, 1969-70; PhD, Psych, West Mich University, 1977-80. *Appointments:* Psych, Central State Hops, 1970-72; School Psychologist, Burnsville PS 1973-77 and 1980-81; Private practice,

Psychologist, 1981-90. *Memberships:* Chair of Membership Committee, Minn Psych Assoc; International Assoc of Behaviour Analysts; Minnesota Assoc of Behaviour Analysts; Minnesota National Speakers Assoc. *Honours:* Phi Kappa Phi, Honor Society, 1975; Member, MENSA International IQ Society, 1976. *Hobbies:* Downhill and crosscountry skiing; Fitness, aerobics, swimming, running, triathelon events; Dancing, ballroom and swing; Sports cars; Comedy; Theatre; Sailing and boating. *Address:* 7101 York Avenue South, Edina, MN 55435, USA.

STEVENS Priscilla Jane d'Eresby, b. 16 Apr. 1940, Plymouth, England. Stoma Care Nursing Sister. m. Dr John Edward Stevens, 3 Oct. 1964. *Education:* SRN, St Bartholomew's Hospital, London, 1958-62. *Appointments:* Sister, St Bartholomew's Hospital, London, 1966-71; Sister, Cardio-Thoracic Unit 1971-72, Sister, Accident Trauma Unit 1973-74, Chief Professional Nurse, Stoma Care Unit 1974-89, Groote Schuur Hospital, Cape Town, South Africa. *Publications:* Book: Atlas of Stomal Pathology, with A Francini and B Cola, 1983; Numerous articles to professional journals and magazines; Chapter in book; Papers in International Proceedings. *Memberships:* South African Nursing Association; Southern African Stomatherapy Association, Founder, President 1978-88, Education Chair, 1988; World Council Enterostomal Therapists (Second) President, 1980-84, Chairman Education 1984-90. *Honours:* World Council of Enterostomal Therapists Presentation, Munich, 1982; South African Nursing Association, Certificate Appreciation, 1987. *Hobbies:* Golf; Tennis; Cycling; Swimming; Represented Western Province, Cape Town Squash, 1986; Travelling internationally; Wildlife viewing; People; Nursing practice worldwide. *Address:* Stomatherapy Unit, E22S Groote Schuur Hospital, Observatory, Cape, South Africa.

STEVENS Rebecca Louise, b. 26 Jan. 1956, Sandusky, Ohio, USA. Registered Architect. *Education:* BArch, University of Cincinnati, 1980. *Appointments:* Apprentice architect, Bay Construction Corporation 1976, Goetzman Associates 1977; Construction Supervisor, Golden Gate National Recreational Area 1978, Channel Islands National Park 1980-82, Architect, Denver Service Centre 1982-84, San Francisco Regional Office 1984-88, National Park Service; Regional Historical Architect, Washington DC, 1988-. *Creative work includes:* Private residence designs, California, Idaho, West Virginia, Maryland. *Memberships:* American Institute of Architects; Past Chapter President, Association for Preservation Technology; National Trust for Historic Preservation; American Association of University Women; Greenpeace; Natural Defence Council. *Honour:* Design award, architectural thesis, AIA, 1980. *Hobbies:* Bird watching; Painting; Gardening; Hiking; Travel; Collecting antique quilts; Environmental issues. *Address:* 7517 Planter Lane, Gaithersburg, Maryland 20882, USA.

STEVENS Serita Deborah Mendelson, b. 20 Jan. 1949, Chicago, USA. Writer. m. 29 Aug. 1971, divorced 1 July 1980. *Education:* BN, University of Illinois, 1971; MLitt (honours), Antioch, London, England, 1977. *Appointments:* Self-employed writer. *Publications:* This Bitter Ecstasy, 1981; The Importance of Being Vashti, 1981; The Honorable Way, 1981; Tame The Wild Heart, 1983; Shrieking Shadows of Penporth Island, 1983; A Price to Pay, 1983; Sir Christopher Wren; William Harvey; A Dream Forever, 1984; Spanish Heartland; Home Fires; Cagney and Lacey, 1985; Son of A Star; the Kaddish; Bloodstone Inheritance, 1985; Secrets at Seventeen, 1986; A Gathering Storm; Days of Our Lives; Lighting And Fire, 1987; Deceptive Desires, 1987; Daughters of Desire, 1987; Unholy Alliance No 1, 1988; Heathen Heart, 1988; Nighthawk; Beyond the Shadows; Wild is the Heart; Beyond All Time; Mystery Writer's Handbook of Poison. Videos: Lilac Dreams; Moonlight Flight; Champagne For Two; Video Calendar 1986; numerous articles in magazines. *Memberships:* Board Member, Socal Mystery Writers of America; Midwest Regional Director, Romance Writers of America;

Contributing Writer, Society of Children's Bookwriters, Bulletin. *Honours:* Dell, Best Synopsis; Scholarship, Cape Cod Writers Conf. *Hobbies:* Cats; Dog; Horseback riding; Flying; Cooking; Television; Dancing; Travel; History. *Address:* 2265 Westwood No 271, Los Angeles, CA 90064, USA.

STEVENSON Anne Katharine, b. 3 Jan. 1933, Cambridge, England. Freelance Writer; Affiliated to University of Edinburgh. m. (4)Peter David Lucas, 3 Sept. 1987, 2 sons, 1 daughter by previous marriages. *Education:* BA, 1954, MA, 1961, University of Michigan, USA; Fellow, Bungint Institute, Harvard, 1969-70; Fellow, Lady Margaret Hall, Oxford, 1975-77. *Appointments:* Publisher, A.C. Black, London, 1956-58; Teacher, Cambridge School of Weston, Massachusetts, 1962-64; Bookseller, Wales, 1978-81; Northern Arts Literary Fellow, 1981-82, 1985-86; University of Edinburgh, 1987-89. *Publications:* Elizabeth Bishop, 1966; Reversals, 1969; Corespondences, 1974; Travelling Behind Glass, 1974; Enough of Green, 1977; Minute by Glass Minute, 1982; The Fiction Makers, 1985; Selected Poems, 1987. *Memberships:* Fellow, Royal Society Literature; Society of Authors; Poetry Book Society, Board, 1983-87; Poetry Society, London. *Honours:* Hopwood Awards, University of Michigan, Minor, 1951, 1952, Major 1954; Scottish Book Award, 1974; Poetry Book Society Choice, 1985, Recommendation, 1987. *Hobbies:* Travel; Music; Languages. *Address:* 30 Logan Street, Langley Park, Durham, DH7 9YN, England.

STEVENSON Juliet, b. 30 Oct. 1956, Kelvedon, Essex, England. Actress. *Education:* Honours Diploma, Royal Academy of Dramatic Arts, London, 1977. *Appointments:* With Royal Shakespeare Company, 1978-80, 1981-82, Royal Court Theatre, London, 1983, Royal Shakespeare Company, 1983-; TV Appearances include: The Mallens, series, Granada TV, 1980; Maybury, series, BBC, 1981; Bazaar & Rummage, play, 1983; Freud, series, 1983; Pericles, Shakespeare Series, 1983; Antigone, Play of the Month, in title role, 1984, BBC; various radio plays and in the Lotus and the Wind Series, 1984. *Memberships:* Made Associate Artist of the Royal Shakespeare Company in 1986; British Actors Equity Association; Women in Entertainment; Arts for Labour; The Labour Party; Campaign for Nuclear Disarmament; Greenpeace. *Honours:* Bancroft Gold Medal, Royal Academy of Dramatic Art, 1977; Voted Best Actress, Drama Awards, 1984; Nominee for Best Actress in a Revival, Society of West End Theatres, 1984, 1986 and 1987. *Hobbies:* Piano; Singing; Cinema; Theatre; Travel; Political Activism; Reading. *Address:* c/o Plant and Froggatt Ltd, 4 Windmill Street, London W1, England.

STEVENSON Nora Carroll, b. 18 Nov. 1924, Beaumont, Texas, USA. Research Associate. m. (1) Edward A. Cary, 17 Aug. 1946, (2) Charles Stevenson, 16 Dec. 1965, 2 sons, 3 daughters. *Education:* BA, University of Texas, 1944; MS, University of Michigan, 1950; MM, Music History & Musicology, 1972. *Appointments:* Biostatistics Section, Parke Davis & Co., 1959-61; Research Associate, Darwin Correspondence, 1980-; Violist, Divertimento Chamber Ensemble, 1986-. *Publications:* Calendar of the Correspondence of Charles Darwin, 1984; Correspondence of Charles Darwin, 1985-. *Honours:* Mortar Board, University of Texas, 1944. *Hobbies:* Chamber Music; Gardening. *Address:* 34 Monument Ave., Bennington, VT 05201, USA.

STEWART Ann Harleman, b. 28 Oct. 1945, Youngstown, Ohio, USA. Writer; Educator. m. Bruce A. Rosenberg, 20 June 1981, 1 daughter. *Education:* BA, English, Russian, Rutgers University, 1967; PhD, Linguistice, Princeton University, 1972; MFA, Creative Writing, Brown University, 1988. *Appointments:* Assistant Professor, English, Rutgers University, 1973-74; Assistant Professor, 1974-79, Associate Professor, 1979-84; Visiting Associate Professor, Research Affiliate, Massachusetts Institute of Technology, 1984-86; Visiting Professor, English, Dartmouth College,

1982-83; Visiting Scholar, American Civilization, Brown University, 1986-. *Publications:* Books: Graphic Representation of Models in Linguistic Theory, 1976; Ian Fleming: A Critical Biography (with Bruce A. Rosenberg), forthcoming; Women's Stories (translation with Sam Driver of Zernova's Zhenskije Rasskazy); Articles in Journal in English Linguistics, Papers on Language and Literature, Papers in Linguistics, Old English Newsletter; Short fiction: The Cost of Anything (collection); It Was Humdrum, 1986; Urban Fishing, 1986; Someone Else, 1987; The White Hope of Cleveland, 1987; Limbo, 1987; Poems in Pivot, The Greensboro Review, High Plains Literary Review, The Southern Review, Ascent, Bellingham Review, Kansas Quarterly. *Memberships:* Linguistic Society of America; Modern Language Association (Chair, Executive Committee on General Linguistics, 1981-86); Poets and Writers. *Honours include:* Winner, Raymond Carver Short Story Contest, 1986; Various fellowships including: Guggenheim Fellow, 1976-77; Huntington Library Fellow, 1979, 1980; Fulbright Fellow (Poland), 1980-81; NEH Fellow, Institute for Literary Translation, 1988; ACLS/IREX Senior Scholar (USSR), 1976-77. *Hobbies:* Painting; Counselling work with women's groups. *Address:* 55 Summit Avenue, Providence, RI 02906, USA.

STEWART Barbara Dean, b. 17 Sept. 1941, Rochester, New York, USA. Company President, 2 daughters. *Education:* BA, Cornell University, 1962; MS, Library Science, Simmons College, 1964; Eastman School of Music, part-time study. *Appointments:* Partner, Stewart Lofstrom associates, 1979-85; President, Smart Writers Inc., 1985-. *Publications:* Virtual Machine Class, transcription rewriting & final editing & production for Xerox Corporation, 1987; Software Development & Delivery Process, Xerox Corporation, 1987; Software Development and Management for Microprocessor-Based Systems, final editing of Omlinson Rauscher/Linda Ott Manuscript, 1987; How to Kazoo, 1983; Squash Racquets: Pro and Khan, with Hashim Khan, 1987. *Memberships Include:* ASCAP; American Federation of Musicians. *Honours:* US Squash Racquets Association Achievement Bowl, 1981; New York Metropolitan Athletics Congress, Outstanding Masters Achievement Award, 1987; Track & Field Competitor: 15 National Masters Championships, 9 Empire State Games Gold Medals (7 ESG Records); 11 Regional Championships, 1 World Record (pending), 1 American Record, 6 Canadian Records. *Address:* 292 Wintergreen Way, Rochester, NY 14618, USA.

STEWART Barbara Rusciolelli, b. 21 Jan. 1942, Detroit, Michigan, USA. Accountant; Educator. m. Richard W. Stewart, 26 June 1964, 1 son, 1 daughter. *Education:* AB, Barnard College, 1964; PhD, Columbia University, 1969; Certified Public Accountant (CPA), Maryland, 1984. *Appointments:* Lecturer, Barnard College, 1969-77; Instructor, Columbia University, 1969-70; Assistant Professor, Brooklyn Polytechnic Institute 1970, University of Baltimore 1985-88; Accountant, Assistant Controller, AMAF Industries, Columbia, Maryland, 1981-85; Towson State University, 1988-. *Memberships:* American & Maryland Institutes of CPAs; American Woman's Society of CPAs; American Accounting Association; Sigma Xi. *Honours:* National Merit Scholar, 1960; Fellowship, National Science Foundation, 1964; Elijah Watt Sells Silver Medal (AICPA), 1984. *Address:* 5783 Yellowrose Court, Columbia, Maryland 21045, USA.

STEWART Connie Ward, b. 19 Nov. 1938, Athens, Georgia, USA. Higher Education Administration; Public Relations; Lecturer. m. (1) Donald G Stewart, 28 Feb. 1960. 1 daughter. (2) Nicholas Vista, 16 Apr. 1982. *Education:* ABJ 1959, MA 1968, University of Georgia; Postgraduate study: George Washington University, 1979 and Harvard University, 1985. *Appointments:* WSB-TV, Atlanta, Georgia, 1959-61; Teacher, DeKalb County (GA) Schools, 1961-62; Associate Director, GA State Scholarship Commission, 1966-67; Faculty of Journalism, University of Georgia, 1967-71; HEW 1977-

78, US Dept of Ed 1979, Jimmy Carter Administration, White House; 1st Woman Vice-Pres, Michigan State University, 1980-87; Associate Vice-President, Emory University, 1987-. *Publications:* Editor and columnist, Oconee Enterprise Newspaper (GA); Contributor to North Georgia Life Magazine; Contributor, Greater Communications Effectiveness (book), 1966, John E Drewry Editor. *Memberships:* Vice Pres and President, Michigan State University Phi Beta Kappa; Phi Kappa Phi; National Press Club, Washington DC; Society for Professional Journalists; Di Gamma Kappa; Zeta Phi Eta; Kappa Tau Alpha; Zeta Tau Alpha Sorority. *Honours:* Michigan Film-TV Council appointed by Governor James Blanchard, 1984-86; Georgia Motion Picture and Television Board, Governor Jimmy Carter, 1972-76; Georgia State Scholarship Commission, by Governor Carl Sanders, 1965-67; Governor's Commission on Education by Governor Carl Sanders, 1965-67; Military Academies Screening Committees, by US Senator Donald Riegle, 1984-86; Awarded Honorary Alumnus and Lifelong Member, Michigan State University Alumni Association, 1987. *Hobbies:* Reading; Writing; Travel; Theatre. *Address:* 3229 Bolero Dr NE, Atlanta, Georgia 30341, USA.

STEWART Dena, b. 1 Oct. 1948, New York City, USA. Artist. m. Stewart Stewart, 25 Oct. 1973. *Education:* BBA, Pace University, 1974. *Appointments:* Fund Raiser/Administrator, Polytechnic Institute of Brooklyn, 1969-74; Teacher, Cathedral High School, 1974-75; Editor, Harcourt Brace Jovanovich, 1975-77; Employment Manager, Korvettes Department Stores Inc., 1977-79; Teacher, Miami Dade Community College, 1979-89; Artist, 1987-. *Publications:* A Christmas Tree in the City, UNICEF Xmas Card, 1982, 1983, 1984, 1989. *Memberships:* Deco Echo Artists Delegation; South Florida Art Centre; Artists Equity. *Honours:* Numerous honours & awards including: owner, Why Not, Gallery 1988. *Hobbies:* Writing & Illustrating Short Stories. *Address:* 841 Lincoln Road, Miami Beach, FL 33139, USA.

STEWART Ida Barksdale Crawford, b. 13 Dec. 1922, Clinton, South Carolina, USA. Advertising Promoter. m. Robert Murray Stewart, 18 Dec. 1954. *Education:* AB, Winthrop College, 1943; MA University of Maryland, 1951. *Appointments:* Grammar School Teacher, 1943-46; Winthrop College, 1946-49; University of Maryland, 1949-50; Bristol Myers, 1950-61; Coty Cosmetics, 1960-61; Estee Lauder Cosmetics, 1961-. *Creative works:* Camp Counselling Textbook; Many Oil Paintings. *Memberships:* American Association of University Women; Fashion Group. *Honours:* Keys To Cities in USA; Mary Mildred Sullivan Award. *Hobbies:* Swimming; Walking; Gardening; Museuming; Theatre. *Address:* 45 Sutton Place S, New York City, NY 10022, USA.

STEWART Jeannie, C. b. 29 Nov. 1913, Aberdeen, Scotland. Psychologist. *Education:* AB magna cum laude, Brown University, USA, 1945; AM, University of California, Berkeley (UCB), 1945; Graduate study, Stanford University. *Appointments:* Various jobs before university; Teaching assistant, UCB, 1944-45; Research assistant, Instructor, Vassar College, 1946-48, 1949-50; Student House Director, Pembroke College, Brown University, 1954-61; Secretary, physicians' office, 1961-64; Adviser: Garland Junior College (Boston) 1965-66, 1970-71; Boston University Residence Programme 1967-70; House Director, House in the Pines School, 1971-72; Stone & Webster Engineering Corporation, Boston, 1973-84; Skill Bureau, Boston, 1984-86; Junior League, Boston, 1986-. *Publications:* Co-author, article, Journal of Comparative & Physiological Psychology, 1947; Co-author, abstract, American Psychologist, 1948; Author, books: Ancient & Cherished Treasures of Scotland 1982, Ancient Castles of Scotland, in progress. *Memberships:* Life, American & Eastern Psychological Associations; Emeritus, American Association for Advancement of Science; Board, English Speaking Union, Boston; Various other community & historical organisations, USA & UK. *Honours:* Fellowships, Brown University 1948, Vassar College 1950; Honour societies, 1945,

1950; Delegate, psychology conferences, England, USA; IBC and ESU World Conferences England, USA, Holland, Scotland, 1969-88. *Hobbies & interests:* Reading; Walking; Swimming; Theatre; Music; Art; Travel. *Address:* 3 Concord Avenue, Apt. B/3, Cambridge, Massachusetts 02138, USA.

STEWART Marian Louise Vail, b. 1 Jan. 1921, Lansing, Michigan, USA. Secretary, John A Stewart, MD, Inc. m. 23 June 1945. 2 sons, 1 daughter. *Education:* Graduate, Gradwohl School of Medical Technology, 1940-41. *Appointments:* Shoemaker Clinic, 1941-42; Longview State Hospital, 1942-43; University Hospital, Pathology Laboratory, 1943-45; Harper Hospital, Haematology, 1945-46; Parke Davis Laboratory, 1948-49; Technician/Office Manager, 1951-87. *Creative Work:* Since 1974 Nursing Scholarship - Barbara Vail Stewart Nursing Scholarship. *Memberships:* Fort Hamilton-Hughes Hospital Board of Trustees, helped co-ordinate Meals-on-Wheels; Chairman Scholarship Committee, 1961; Medical Auxiliary; Hamilton Garden Club; Secretary, PEO Sisterhood; Secretary, Historic Hamilton; Secretary, Southwest Ohio District Hospital Volunteers; Life Member, Fort Hamilton-Hughes Hospital Auxiliary; Life Member, Butler County Historical Society; YWCA; Ohio Genealogy Society. *Honours:* Ordained Deacon, Presbyterian Church. *Hobbies:* Volunteer in hospital and Sharonwoods Museum; Needlepoint; Cooking; Counted Crosstitch; Rug Making; Collecting Odds and ends; Home-maker; Quilt making. *Address:* 701 Oakwood Drive, Hamilton, OH 45013, USA.

STEWART Mary Florence Elinor, b. 17 Sept. 1916, Sunderland, Co Durham, England. Author. m. Frederick H Stewart, 24 Sept. 1945. *Education:* BA 1939, MA 1941, Durham University. *Appointments:* Lecturer in English 1941-45, part-time Lecturer, English 1948-58, Durham University. *Publications:* Madam Will You Talk? 1954; Wilfire at Midnight, 1956; Thunder on the Right, 1957; Nine Coaches Waiting, 1958; My Brother Michael, 1959; The Ivy Tree, 1961; The Moonspinners, 1962; This Rough Magic, 1964; Airs Above the Ground, 1965; The Gabriel Hounds, 1967; The Wind off the Small Isles, 1968; The Crystal Cave, 1970; The Little Broomstick, 1971; The Hollow Hills, 1973; Ludo and the Star Horse, 1974; Touch Not the Cat, 1976; The Last Enchantment, 1979; A Walk in Wolf Wood, 1980; The Wicked Day, 1983; Thornyhold, 1988; Also poems, articles. *Membership:* PEN. *Address:* c/o Hodder & Stoughton, 47 Bedford Square, London W1B 3DP, England.

STEWART Rosemary Gordon, b. 26 Dec. 1924, London, England. University Teacher & Administrator; Author. m. Ioan M. James, 1 July 1961. *Education:* BA, 1945; MSc, 1949; PhD, 1967. *Career includes:* Research worker 1950-52, 1954-56, Director 1956-61, Acton Society Trust; Fellow (Management Studies), London School of Economics, 1964-66; Fellow (Organisation Behaviour) 1966-, Dean 1983-85, Templeton College, Oxford University. *Publications include:* The Boss, with Roy Lewis; Reality of Management; Reality of Organisations; How Computers Affect Management; Managers & Their Jobs; Contrasts in Management (award); Choices for the Manager; Leading in National Health Service, 1989. *Memberships:* Fellow, Royal Economics Society; Authors Society; Asociation for Management Education & Development. *Honour:* John Player Award, best UK management book, 1976. *Hobbies:* Golf; Gardening; Travel; Old paintings. *Address:* Templeton College, Oxford Centre for Management Studies, Kennington, Oxford OX1 5BJ, England.

STEWART Sally, b. 16 May 1933, Chicago, Illinois, USA. Poet; Playwright. m. 10 Feb. 1951. 1 son, 1 daughter. *Education:* BA, Anthropology, California State, Dominquez Hill; AA, Humanities, West Los Angeles, Culver City, California. *Publications:* Publisher and author of: Dismal Blues Book of Poetry; Great Treasury of World Poems by Eddie Loucole and The Poetic Village; The Fly in the Buttermilk. Author: Small Scope; Cadence and My father's House. *Memberships:* Ex Cathedra Parliamentary Vice President League of Women Voters; Co Chairman Los Angeles Theatre Usher Captain International Training Communication; Vice President of Parliers Club; Advisory Board, Los Angeles City Women of Color. *Honours:* Honorary Award, AppleOne Temporary Services, 1982; Certificate of Appreciation, Council One, Golden West Region, International training in Communication, 1988; Golden Poet Award 1988, Award of Merit Certificate 1987 and 1988, World of Poetry; Certificate of Appreciation, Captain's Captain, The Los Angeles Theatre Cntr also for Press Department at Los Angeles Theatre Center, 1984-85. *Hobbies:* Reading; Jogging; Travelling. *Address:* 5762 Clemson Street, Los Angeles, California 90016, USA.

STEWART-WALLACE (Helen) Mary, b. 7 Mar. 1914, Sutton, Surrey, England. m. Dr A M Stewart-Wallace, MD, FRCP, Consultant Neurologist, 4 Nov. 1939. 1 son, 2 daughters. *Education:* Central School of Speech Training & Dramatic Art; Diploma in Dramatic Art, London University. *Appointment:* Private teacher of Speech and Drama. *Publications:* Author of published research into Secondary Education in Comparable Western Democracies, 1978. *Memberships:* Society of Genealogists; Conservative Womens' Constituency Committee; South East Panel of Conservative Speakers; Former Associate Member Education Commission of European Union of Women; Former Vice-Chairman, Ditchling Parish Council. *Interests:* Writer of Genealogical articles and occasional reviewer; Frequently published letter writter to The Times, Telegraph, Financial Times, Frequent speaker at Conservative National Womens' Conference. *Address:* The Moot House, Ditchling, Sussex, BN6 8SR, England.

STICKLES Frances Copeland, b. 3 Mar. 1929, Portland, Oregon, USA. Writer; Conservator Picture framer; Librarian. m. Milton J Stickles, Jr, 26 Dec. 1957. 1 son, 1 daughter. *Education:* BA, Whitman College, 1950; MA, University of Washington, 1954. *Appointments:* Librarian, Bellevue, Washington, USA and Beirut, Lebanon, 1950-58; Exhibit Designer for Middle East Exhibits & Training, 1967-71; Library Consultant, 1970-; Conservator picture framer as The Green Mermaid, 1980-. *Publications:* Land Between, 1958; Land and People of Jordan, 1972; The Flag Balloon, 1988; A Crown for Henrietta Maria, 1988. *Memberships:* YWCA, District of Columbia, President 1974-76; Friends of Rockwood, Girl Scout Room Archivist, 1981-87; Westmoreland United Church of Christ, Moderator, 1978-79; Middle East Exhibits & Training, President, 1970-73; Musa Alami Foundation, Secretary, vice-president, 1970-; American Institute for Conservation. *Honour:* Whitman College centennial play competition prize for one-act Turning Point, 1959. *Hobbies:* Painting; Gardening; Travel; Needlepoint. Interests: British, Middle East & American history; Palestinian rights. *Address:* 3914 Blackthorn Street, Chevy Chase, Maryland 20815, USA.

STIEREN Patricia Magdalena, b. 4 Dec. 1957, Springfield, Illinois, USA. International Advertising Account Executive. *Education:* BA, French Language and Literature, University of Illinois, Chamcpaign, 1980; Master of International Management, American Graduate School of International Management, Glendale, Arizona, 1982. *Appointments:* Assistant Manager, Zorba's Restaurant, Champaign, Illinois, 1977-81; Account Representative, M & T Publishing Company, Palo Alto, California, 1983-84; Account Coordinator, Grey Advertising, San Francisco, California, 1984; Assistant Account Executive, Grey Direct Marketing Group, San Francisco, 1985-86; Account Executive, Grey Direct International, Frankfurt-am-Main, Federal Republic of Germany, 1986-87; Account Executive, D & H Agentur fur Direkt-Marketing, Hamburg, Federal Republic of Germany, 1987-88; Freelance International Advertising Consultant, 1988-. *Membership:* MENSA. *Honour:* International Advertising Award, Arizona Republic, 1982. *Hobbies:* Skiing; Squash; Travel; Creative writing; Biking.

Address: Waldstrasse 53, 6082 Walldorf, Federal Republic of Germany.

STILES Linda Rose, b. 8 July 1951, New York, USA. Medical Psychotherapy. m. Nelson Edgar Stiles, 28 Apr. 1973, 1 son, 1 daughter. *Education:* BA, 1973, MA, 1983, University of Central Florida. *Appointments:* Counsellor, The Door of Central Florida, Apopka, 1975-78; Primary Therapist, Drug Abuse Comprehensive Co-ordinating Office, 1978-79; Programme Director, The Door of Central Florida, 1979-81; Watson Deutsch & Associates Inc., Orlando, 1981-82; Vocational Consultant, Crawford Rehabilitation, 1982-85; Private Practice, Theracise, 1985-. *Memberships Include:* Founder/Chairperson, Reflect Sympathetic Dystrophy Association of Florida Inc.; President, Florida Association Rehabilitation; Professionals Private Sector. *Hobbies:* Theracise; Dance; Singing. *Address:* 14006 Lake Price Dr., Orlando, FL 32826, USA.

STILES Mary Ann, b. 16 Nov. 1944, Tampa, USA. Attorney; Author; Legislative Consultant. *Education:* AA, 1973; BS, Florida State University, 1975; JD, Antioch School of Law, 1978. *Appointments:* Analyst, Florida Legislature, 1971-73; Intern, US Senate, 1977; General Counsel, Associated Industries of Florida, 1978-81; Senior and Founding Partner, Stiles, Allen & Taylor, 1981-; Governor's Oversight Board on Workers' Compensation, 1989. *Publications:* Florida Handbook for Employer Workers Compensation, 1979, 6th edition 1989. *Memberships:* Florida, American Hillsborough County Bar Associations; Hillsborough County, Florida, Association od Women Lawyers; Athena Society; Florida Women's Network; Tiger Bay Club, President. *Honours:* Presidential Scholarship to Florida State University. *Hobbies:* Thoroughbred Breeding & Racing; Reading. *Address:* 315 Plant Ave., Tampa, FL 33606, USA.

STIRBA Anne Melinda Morr, b. 12 July 1951, Orrville, Ohio, USA. Attorney. m. Peter Stirba, 19 June 1973, 2 daughters. *Education:* BA, College of Wooster, 1973; JD, University of Utah College of Law, 1978. *Appointments:* Senior Research Attorney, Utah Supreme Court, 1978-80; Assistant Attorney General, State of Utah, 1980-86; Administrative Law Judge, Utah Public Service Committee, 1986-87; Assistant US Attorney, DOJ, District of Utah, 1987-. *Publications:* Articles in Journal of Energy Law and Policy. *Memberships:* Utah State Bar; Women Lawyers of Utah Inc; Salt Lake Couny Bar; American Cancer Society. *Honours:* Recipient, many honours and awards including: First Woman Elected to Bar Commission, 1984; Outstanding Young Lawyer of the Year, Utah State Bar, 1987. *Hobbies:* Skiing; Tennis; Horse Riding. *Address:* 476 US Courthouse Bldg., 350 So. Main St., SLC, UT 84101, USA.

STOCK Peggy A., b. 30 Jan. 1936, USA. College President. m. Robert J. Stock, 2 sons, 3 daughters. *Education:* BS, Psychology, St Lawrence University, 1957; MA, Counselling, Teaching Certificate, 1963, EdD, Counselling Psychology, 1969, University of Kentucky. *Appointments:* President, Midwest Institute for Training and Education, Cincinnati, Ohio, 1971-79; Staff, 1979-86, Vice-President, Administration, 1981-86, University of Hartford, Hartford, Connecticut; President, Colby-Sawyer College, New London, New Hampshire, 1986-. *Publications:* Attitudinal & Behavioural Change of Advisors & Students: Sex Role Stereotyping in Vocational Choice; Reduction of Sexual Stereotyping & Bias with Regard to Career Choice. A Land Grant Institution of Higher Education. *Memberships:* American Council on Education (Chair, Council of Fellows 1985); Commission on Women in Higher Education (ACE), 1988-; Leadership Development Committee (ACE) 1986; New London Business Advisory Board. *Honours:* Mental Health Award, Lexington, Kentucky, 1966; Mental Health Fellowship, University of Kentucky, 1966-68; Distinguished Alumna, St Lawrence University, 1989; Fellow, American Council on Education, 1979-80; United Jewish Committee Fellowship, 1981; State Coordinator, Connecticut Identification Programme for

Advancement of Women in Higher Education, 1985. *Hobbies:* Breeding Arabian horses; Fishing. *Address:* Colby-Sawyer College, New London, NH 03257, USA.

STOCKHAUSEN Sharron Renee, b. 19 Aug. 1948, Rochester, Minnesota, USA. Civil Servant. m. Harry Stockhausen, 4 May 1968, 1 son, 1 daughter. *Education:* University of Minnesota, 1966; Cameron University, 1979; Anoka-Ramsey College, 1980-87; BA, Business, Metro State Universty, 1989. *Appointments:* Purchasing Agent 1976-80, Procurement Assistant 1980-84, Government Contract Administrator 1984-, EEO Manager 1984-88, EEO Counsellor, 1988-, Department of Defence, US Government. Also: Instructor, Anoka-Hennepin Schools, 1980-. *Publications:* Newspaper columnist, Cache, Oklahoma, 1979-80; Editor, Comanche County Cookbook, Lawton, Oklahoma, 1978. *Memberships:* National Association of Female Executives; Offices, National Contract Management Association; Founder, President, Homemakers Plus Extension Group. *Honours:* Professional designation, contract management, 1987; Educator of Year, 1984; Speech Award, Oklahoma Jaycettes, 1979. *Hobbies:* Reading; Writing; Needle Arts; Bowling; Golf; Assistant Coach, Men's Softball. *Address:* 14314 Thrush Drive NW, Andover, Minnesota 55304, USA.

STOCKTON Fay, b. 12 Nov. 1953, Cheshire, England. Barrister. m. Lawrence Millett, 25 Jan. 1984. 1 son. *Education:* LLB Hons, Manchester University, 1972-75; Bar Finals, College of Law, 1975-76. *Appointments:* Called to The Bar, The Honourable Society of Lincoln's Inn, 1976; Practised at The Bar, Manchester, 1977- and London, 1988-. *Honours:* Awarded Hardwicke Scholarship, 1975; Mansfield Scholarship, 1976, Lincoln's Inn. *Hobbies:* Computers and information technology; Tropical and marine fish; Alternative medicine. *Address:* Didsbury, Manchester, England.

STOFFLE Carla J, b. 19 June 1943, Pueblo, Colorado, USA. Deputy Director & Associate Director for Public Serv; Librarian. m. Richard W, 12 June 1964. 1 son, 1 daughter. *Education:* AA, Southern Colorado St College, Pueblo, 1963; BA, University of Colorado, 1965; MSLS, University of Kentucky, 1969; PhD Candidate, University of Wisconsin, Madison, 1980-. *Appointments:* Hd, Govt Public E Ky University, 1969-72; Hd, Publ Serv, 1972-76, Executive Assistant to Chancellor 1978, Assistant Chancellor Ed Serv 1979-85, University of Wisconsin, Parkside; Associate Director 1985-, Deputy Director 1986-, University of Michigan. *Publications:* Admin of Gov Doc Coll (with Harleston), 1974; Materials & Methods for History Research (with Karter), 1979; Materials & Methods for Political Sci Res (with Karter & Pernacciaro), 1979. *Memberships:* American Library Association, Treasurer, Executive Board, Councillor at Large, COPES, Pres Program Com, Chair of Vol Sec; Association of College & Resident Libraries, President, Exec Committee; Bd of Directors; Strategic Plan Task Force; Comm to draft an activity model for 1990; Library Admin and Management Association; Reference and Adult Services Association; Library Instruction Round Table; Social Responsibilities Round Table; Michigan Library Association; Wisconsin Library Association, Library Education Committee, Public Relations Committee. *Honours:* Library Intern, University of Kentucky Library, Lexington, 1967; The J Morris Jones Award, ALA Divisional Leadership Enhancement Program, Div of ALA, 1983-85; Reference Service Press Award, Authors of most Outstanding Article in RQ, 1986; Outstanding Alumnus College of Library and Information Science, University of Kentucky, 1989. *Hobbies:* Jogging; Sports fan; Reading mysteries/thrillers. *Address:* Library Administration, 818 Hatcher Graduate Library, University of Michigan, Ann Arbor, Michigan 48109, USA.

STOKELY Edith Margaret, b. 23 Jan. 1922, Manhattan, Kansas, USA. Medical Technologist. m. Raymond Elmer Stokely, 6 Dec. 1942, 2 daughters. *Education:* BMed.Tech., Manhattan Kansas, 1943. *Appointments:* Research Technologist, Kansas State University, 1942-44; Medical Technologist, Kecoughtan

Station Hospital, 1944-45; Cleveland Clinic Blood Bank, 1945-47; Medical Technologist, various Doctors, 1969-72, 1972-78, 1978-79; Laboratory Supervisor, University of Illinois College of Medicine, 1979-88. *Memberships:* various professional organisations including: Alpha Xi Delta; Rockford Area Council of Churches. *Honours:* Omicron Nu; Phi Kappa Phi. *Hobbies:* Astronomy; Bird Watching; Snorkelling; Swimming; *Address:* 5427 Brookview Road, Rockford, IL 61107, USA.

STOKES Theresa E. (Teri), b. 9 Apr. 1943, Boston, USA. Sales/Marketing Executive. m. (1) Ivan L. Stokes, 12 June 1965, divorced 1977, 1 son, 1 daughter, (2) Peter R. Yensen, 30 Apr. 1982. *Education:* BA, Biology, 1965; MT (ASCP), Medical Technology, 1966; NSF Certificate, Chemistry and Maths, Wellesley College, 1970; MS, Applied Management, 1987. *Appointments Include:* Medical Technologist, Hospitals & University Research, 1964-73; Sales Manager, Shaklee Products, 1972-76; Laboratory Supervisor, Bioran Medical Labs, Somerville Hospital, 1976-77; Director, Processing & Communications, Bioran Medical Labs, 1977-79; Marketing Communications, Digital Equipment Corp. Large Systems Group, 1979-82; IR&D Operations Specialist, 1982-83, Pharmaceutical Market Manager, 1983-86, Laboratory Data Products; Strategic Account Manager, Kodak Corporate Account, 1986-. *Publications:* Presentations at Seminars; articles in professional journals. *Memberships:* DIA; AOAC; New York Academy of Sciences; Tridelta Fraternity. *Honours:* National Science Foundation Scholarship, Wellesley College, 1970. *Hobbies:* Reading; Piano; Organ; Walking; Swimming. *Address:* Digital Equipment Corp, 1250 Pittsford Victor Road, PO Box 23227, Rochester, NY 14692, USA.

STOKLOSA Evelynne Bates, b. 13 Mar. 1946, Camden, New Jersey, USA. Home Economics Teacher; Freelance designer and consultant. m. Leslie Edward Stoklosa, 15 Apr. 1968. 1 son, 1 daughter. *Education:* BS 1968, MS 1971, Buffalo State University College, Buffalo, New York. *Appointments:* Teaching in Areas, Elementary HEC, 1968; Middle School HEC, 1980-89; Jr HS, HEC, 1977-80; HS, HEC, 1968-75; Continuing Education, 1979-88; Kenmore Town of Tonowanda Schools, Kenmore, 1968-; Owner, Interior Design and Consulting Firm, EBS Decors. *Publications:* Numerous essays about Believing in Buffalo, USA; Educational (10 Year) Package for Villa Maria College (Int Des Dept), Buffalo; Career Educational Manual K-12, 1984; 4-Mat Interdisciplinary Lesson Pkg., 1987; Participated in Arts and Crafts Festivals, 1984-88. *Memberships:* American Association of University Women; Phi Upsilon Omicron Honor Society; American Federation of Teachers; New York State United Teachers; New York State Home Economics Teachers Association; Kenmore Teachers Association; KMS/PTA; Sweethome PTA; Tonawanda-Sweet Home Schools Tax Payers Association. *Honours include:* Outstanding Creativity and Leadership in Home Economics Education Award, NYSHETA, 1987; Recognized by Villa Maria College for 5 Year Service, 1984, 10 Year Service, 1989; Recognized by Ken-Ton Board of Education and Ken-Ton PTSA Council for work in Home Economics Education and Home and Career Programs; Recognized by Ken-Ton Board of Education for work in the school district for: School Planning, School Design Teams, 4-Mat Lesson Plan Manual, Guidance Workshop, Clinical Supervision program, School-wide Staff Development Workshops, Planning and Facilitating, 1984-89. *Hobbies:* Travel; Designing especially with Fabric, Food or Interior environments; Creative writing; Patron of all art forms; Interested in promoting Buffalo, USA as an Educator, Businessperson and Resident of the area. *Address:* 165 Greentree Road, Buffalo, NY 14150, USA.

STOLLENWERK Katherine Lubner, b. 19 Jan. 1949, Milwaukee, Wisconsin, USA. Petroleum Geologist. m. Kenneth G. Stollenwerk, 21 Sept. 1974. *Education:* BS, Geology, University of Wisconsin, Milwaukee, 1972; MS, Geology, Wright State University, 1974. *Appointments:* Uranium Exploration Geologist,

Wyoming Mineral Corporation, 1974-78; Uranium Production Geologist, Mobil Energy Minerals/Nufuels Corporation, 1978-81; Senior, Staff Production Geologist, Mobil Exploration and Production US, 1981-. *Publications:* Neutralization of Acid Mine Drainage Using Rock Phosphate (with P G Malone and M J Smith), 1974; Trace Element Content of Bacterial Iron Oxide (with P G Malone), 1974; Trace Element Content of Iron Hydroxide Produced by Iron Oxidizing Bacteria, MS thesis, 1974. *Memberships:* Association for Women Geoscientists, Secretary 1987-88; Rocky Mountain Association of Geologists, Membership Chairman 1986-87; American Association of Petroleum Geologists; Colorado Scientific Society. *Hobbies:* Golf; Yoga; Nutrition. *Address:* 483 South Race Street, Denver, CO 80209, USA.

STONE Carla Sydney, b. 7 Sept. 1950, Pittsburgh, Pennsylvania, USA. President, Business & Policy Associates, Inc, International Trade Firm; Author; Lecturer; Professor. m. John Bone Bassett. 1 son, deceased, 1 daughter. *Education:* BS Mining Engineering 1973, MS Mining Engineering and Mineral Economics 1974, Henry Krumb School of Mines, Columbia University. *Appointments:* Bethlehem Steel, Asarco Inc; Morgan Guaranty Trust Co; Conoco, Inc; Consolidation Coal Co; Conoco Coal Development Co; Industrial Publications, Inc; University of Delaware College of Business & Economics; American Management Association; All-Union Foreign Trade Academy of the USSR. *Publications:* Articles: Anticipating 1997. The Effect of the Chinese Takeover of Hong Kong on the Investment Plans of American Corporations, 1988; And They're Off! Foreign Law Firms Race to Tokyo?, 1988; The Great Globe Itself, 1988; China's Energy Situation and the Implications for Foreign Investment, 1985; Preparing for a China Delegation, 1985; A Political/Economic Overview of the Chinese Coal Industry with an Assessment of Constraints to Production, 1982; Is Environmentalism A Luxury?, 1982; Surface Mining Issues in Perspective, 1974; Women in the Earth Science, 1972. Books: Assoc Ed, Economics of the Minerals Industry, 1985; Ed, Economics in Transition, AIME Economics Transactions, 1982; Ed, Conflicts and Resolution, Proceedings, Council of Economics of AIME, 1979. *Memberships:* 1st Woman Officer, American Institute of Mining, Metallurgical and Petroleum Engineers; Chairman, AIME Economics Committee; Governor's International Trade Council; National Council for US-China Trade; Japan Society; Society of Women Engineers; Delaware State Chamber of Commerce; World Affairs Council; Wilmington Women in Business; Junior League of Wilmington. *Honours:* US Small Business Administration Exporter of the Year Award for Delaware, 1987; Delegate, White House Conference on Small Business, 1985-86; Senior Member, Society of Women Engineers, 1988; Finalist, White House Fellowship Program, 1979-80; Fellowship, ASARCO, Inc, 1973-74; Henry Krumb Scholarship Award, 1973; Speakers Awards, Conoco, Inc, 1977-82. *Address:* Business & Policy Associates, Inc, P O Box 3706, Greenville, DE 19807, USA.

STONE Doris Mary, b. 1 May 1918, Waterford, Republic of Ireland. Author; Teacher. m. 3 Apr. 1951. 1 son, 1 daughter. *Education:* BA, Somerville College, 1940, Diploma in education, 1941, MA 1944, University of Oxford, England. *Appointments:* Biology Teacher, English Girls' Schools, 1941-51; Cheltenham Ladies' College, 1949-51; British Exchange Teacher, Lansing, Michigan, USA, 1947-48; Biology Instructor, Wheelock College, Boston, 1951-53; Plant-breeder, Brooklyn Botanic Garden, New York, 1957-67; Biology Instructor, Rye County Day School, New York, 1969-73; Education Coordinator, New York Botanical Garden, 1973-79; Director of Education, Brooklyn Botanic Garden, 1982-84. *Publications:* Projects: Botany, 1964; Great Public Gardens of the Eastern United States, 1982; The Lives of Plants, 1983. Contributor of numerous articles in magazines. *Memberships:* Association of Garden Writers of America; Association of American Botanical Gardens and Arboreta; Torrey Botanical Club. *Honours:* Quill and Trowel Award-Plaque, (Books), 1st Place for

Great Public Gardens of Eastern United States, 1983; Quill and Trowel Award-Plaque (Books of General Interest), 1st Place for The Lives of Plants, 1984, Garden Writers of America. *Hobbies:* Travel; Nature photography; Vegetable gardening; Culinary arts. *Address:* 2 Tudor City Place, Apt 4FN, New York, NY 10017, USA.

STONE Julie Lynn, b. 9 Nov. 1959, Manistee, Michigan, USA. Writer. *Education:* AA, 1985. *Creative works:* Screen play. *Memberships:* Poets and Writers Inc; Poetry Society of America; The Feminist Writers Guild. *Hobbies:* Writing; Reading; Auto Mechanics. *Address:* 3755 Henry Street, Muskegon, MI 49441, USA.

STONE Lucy Frances, b. 9 Aug. 1914, Sydney, Australia. Company Managing Director. m. Herbert Stone, 29 Oct. 1938. 1 son, 1 daughter. *Appointments:* Secretarial, Motor Industry, 1932-38; Office Manager, 1940-69, Managing Director, Herbert Stone Pty Ltd, 1969-88. *Memberships:* Girl Guides Association Australia; Uniting Church of Australia; Acting State Commissioner of Girl Guides Association; Trainer, Religious Policy Adviser; Development Adviser; Life Member, Torch Bearers for Legacy; Strathfield Lantern Club. *Honours:* Queen's Jubilee Medal, 1977; Award of Red Kangaroo, 1978; Member of the Order of Australia, 1979. *Hobbies:* Historical Records; Church Mission; Gardening; Fund raising. *Address:* 20 Birnam Grove, Strathfield, NSW 2135, Australia.

STONE Vivian Rene, b. 21 Dec. 1954, Indianapolis, USA. Executive. *Appointments:* Assistant Manager, Hilton Hotel, San Francisco, 1978-83; Director, Front Office, Meridien Hotel, San Francisco, 1983-84; Operations Manager, Sterns & Walker, 1985-86; Executive, Staff & Building Services, State Bar of California, San Francisco, 1986-. *Memberships:* American Heart Association; Association of Legal Administrators; Association of Records Manages & Administrators; Commonwealth Club of California. *Hobbies:* Teaching CPR/ Emergency Preparedness Classes; Cooking; Dancing; Reading; Travel. *Address:* State Bar of California, 555 Franklin St., San Francisco, CA 94102, USA.

STOPPARD Miriam, b. 12 May 1937, Newcastle, England. Physician; Writer; Broadcaster. m. Tom Stoppard, 11 Feb. 1972. 4 sons. *Education:* MB, BS, 1961l; MD 1966; MRCP 1964. *Appointments:* Senior Registrar in Dermatology, Research Director, Managing Director, Syntex; Managing Director, David Linley Furniture; Independent TV Producer. *Publications:* Baby Car; Your Baby; Healthcare; Everywoman's Lifeguide; 50 Life Guide; Pregnancy & Birth Book; A-Z Baby & Child Medical; Talking Sex; Family Food Book; First Food Book; Everygirl's Lifeguide; Health & Beauty Book. *Memberships:* Royal College of Physicians; Royal Society of Medicine. *Interests:* Sons. *Address:* Iver Grove, Iver, Bucks SL0 0LB, England.

STORFJELL Judith Irene, b. 5 Oct. 1943, Vancouver, Washington, USA. Nursing Educator. m. J. Bjornar Storfjell, 14 July 1963, 2 sons. *Education:* BS cum laude, Nursing, Walla Walla College, College Place, Washington, 1966; MS, Community Health Nursing, 1980, PhD, Nursing, 1987, University of Michigan. *Appointments:* President, Health Care at Home, St Joseph, Michigan, 1979-86; Assistant Professor, University of Michigan, 1987; Consultant, Storfjell Associates, 1987-; Assistant Professor, University of Illinois, 1988-. *Publications:* A Quantification Model for Home Health Care Nursing Visits, 1987; Easley-Storfjell Instruments for Caseload-Workload Analysis, 1988. *Memberships:* American Public Health Association; National League for Nursing; American College for Healthcare Executives; National Association for Home Care. *Honours:* Fellowship, Michigan Department of Public Health, 1978; Inducted, Sigma Theta Tau, 1980; Emilie Gleason Sargent Award, University of Michigan,

1980. *Hobbies:* Sailing; Canoeing. *Address:* 4720-1 E Hillcrest Drive, Berrien Springs, MI 49103, USA.

STORM Jackie, b. 20 Sept. 1943, Halifax, Nova Scotia, Canada. Nutrition Educator. m. Gerald Miller, 10 Nov. 1985. *Education:* BA 1979, MA 1982, PhD Candidate, New York University. *Appointments:* Nutrition Counseling, The New York Health Racquet Club, 1973-; Faculty Member, New School for Social Research, 1980-87; Consultant, Eating Disorders Center, Masnhattan, 1983-; Adjunct Professor, Allied Health Dept, St Francis College, Brooklyn, 1987-; Adjunct Professor, Dept of Health, Physical Education & Recreation, Kingsborough Community College, Brooklyn, 1987-. *Publications:* Workbook: There's No Such Thing As A Fattening Food!; Articles: Should You Worry About Sulfites?; The Truth about Candida!; Second Thoughts on New Year's Resolutions; The New Diets: Fact or Fad? *Memberships:* Society for Nutrition Education; Society for Public Health Education; Association for advancement of Health Education; American Public Health Association. *Honour:* Founders Day Award for Outstanding Scholarship, 1979. *Hobbies:* Carpentry; Gardening. *Address:* 26 E 13 Street No 3C, New York, NY 10003, USA.

STOTT (Charlotte) Mary, b. 18 July 1907, Leicester, England. Journalist; Author. m. Kenneth Stott, 18 Feb. 1937, 1 daughter. *Appointments:* Leicester Mail, 1925-31; Bolton Evening News, 1931-33; Co-operative Press, Manchester, 1937-45; Manchester Evening News, 1945-50; Manchester Guardian, 1957; The Guardian, 1972-. *Publications:* Forgetting's No Excuse, 1973; Organisation Woman, 1978; Ageing for Beginners, 1980; Before I Go, 1985; Women Talking, 1987. *Memberships:* First Woman Chairman, Manchester Branch, NUJ; Last President, Womens Press Club; Chairman, Fawcett Society, 1980-82; University Womens Club. *Honours:* OBE, 1975; Honorary Fellow, Manchester Polytechnic. *Hobbies Include:* Music; Painting; Gardening. *Address:* Flat 4, 11 Morden Road, Blackheath, London SE3 0AA, England.

STOUT Juanita Kidd, b. 7 Mar. 1919, Wewoka, Oklahoma, USA. Justice, Supreme Court. m. Charles O. Stout, 23 June 1942. *Education:* BA, 1939; JD, 1948; LLM, 1954. *Appointments:* Teacher, grade and high school, 1939-42; Secretary to Charles H. Houston Esq, 1942-44; Professor, Florida A & M and Texas Southern Universities, 1949-50; Administrative Secretary, US Court of Appeals, 1950-54; Private Practice of Law, 1954-56; District Attorney's Office, 1956-59; Judge, Municipal Court, 1959-69; Judge, Court of Common Pleas, 1969-88, Justice, Supreme Court of Pennsylvania, 1988-. *Memberships:* American Bar Association; Pennsylvania Bar Association; National Bar Association; Philadelphia Bar Association. *Honours:* Recipient of over 250 including: Jane Addam's Medal, Rockford College, Rockford, Illinois, 1966; National 4-H Alumni Recognition Award, 1968; Distinguished Service Award, University of Iowa, Iowa City, 1974; Henry G. Bennett Distinguished Service Award, Oklahoma State University, 1980; Inducted into Oklahoma Hall of Fame, 1981; MCP/Gimbel Award for Humanitarianism, 1988; Distinguished Daughter of Pennsylvania, 1988; Outstanding Woman Justice of the Year, 1988. *Hobbies:* Music; Travel; Bridge; Cooking; Reading. *Address:* 1919 Chestnut Street, Apt 2805, Philadelphia, PA 19103, USA.

STRACHER Dorothy Altman, b. 11 May 1934, New York, USA. Associate Professor; Writer. m. Alfred Stracher, 4 July 1954, 2 sons, 1 daughter. *Education:* BA, Brooklyn College, 1955; MA, Teachers College, Columbia University, 1957; Reading Cert., Adelphi University, 1970; PhD, Hofstra University, 1979. *Appointments:* New York City School Teacher, 1956-62; Consultant Reading Teacher, 1962-79; Professor, St John's University, 1979-86; Associate Professor, Education, Dowling College, 1986-. *Publications:* Literature: Reading Writing & Reasoning, 1989; Developing Differentiated Curricula, 1986; Integrating Reading & Writing Assessment & Instruction for the

Language Disabled, 1982; First the Fundamentals: Reading & Writing for the Gifted, 1980; What Do You Call a Well-Behaved Martian? A Manual for Thinkers' Parents, 1980; Articles in various journals, book chapters. *Memberships:* Many professional organisations including: Orton Society; International Reading Association, President, Reading Reform Foundation. *Honours:* Recipient, many honours including: Kappa Delta Pi; Academic Visitor, Oxford University, 1973-74. *Hobbies:* Reading; Writing; Travel. *Address:* 47 The Oaks, Roslyn, NY 11576, USA.

STRAHLENDORF Jean Carol Roberts, b. 29 Jan. 1949, Houston, Texas, USA. Associate Professor. m. Howard Kurt Strahlendorf, 9 June 1973. *Education:* BS, Pharmacy, University of Houston, 1972; MS, Pharmacology, 1974, PhD, Pharmacology, 1978, Philadelphia College of Pharmacy and Science. *Appointments:* Teaching Assistant, Pharmacology, Philadelphia College, 1972-76; NIH Postdoctoral Fellow, Physiology, Texas Technical Health Science Centre, 1977-80; Assistant Professor, Physiology, Texas Tech University Health Science Centre, 1980-86, Associate Professor, 1986-. *Publications:* Brainstem and Cerebellar Mechanism of Cardiovascular Control, in Neural Control of Circulation, 1980; Electrophsyiology of Serotonin on Cerebellar Purkinje Cells, in New Concepts in Cerebellar Neurobiology; etc. *Memberships:* American Heart Association; FASEB; Society for Neuroscience; AWIS; American Physiological Society; International Brain Research Organization; American Association for the Advancement of Science. *Honours:* Recipient, various honours and awards. *Hobbies:* Gardening; Skiing; Outdoor Sports. *Address:* Dept. of Physiology, Texas Tech University Health Sciences Centre, 3601 4th Street, Lubbock, TX 79430, USA.

STRAHS Gail R., b. 22 June 1950, New York City, New York, USA. Oral and Maxillofacial Surgeon. m., 1 son, 1 daughter. *Education:* BS, Microbiology, Cornell University, Ithaca, New York, 1972; DDS, School of Dentistry, University of California, Los Angeles, 1976; Residency, Oral and Maxillofacial Surgery, Los Angeles County-University of Southern California Medical Center, 1976-79; Independent study, Department of Oral Surgery, Middlesex Hospital, London, England, 1981; Licensed, National and California State Boards of Dental Examiners, 1976; General Anaesthesia Permit, Board of Dental Examiners, 1980-; Diplomate, American Board of Oral and Maxillofacial Surgery, 1981; Advanced Cardiac Life Support, 1987. *Appointments:* Private Practice in Oral Maxillofacial Surgery, Los Angeles, California; Lecturer, Clinical Instructor, Department of Oral Surgery, 1976-79, Clinical Instructor, Department of Continuing Education, 1977, University of Southern California; Clinical Faculty, Department of Oral and Maxillofacial Surgery, University of California, Los Angeles, 1981-; State Board Examiner for General Anaesthesia Permit, 1987-. *Publications:* Panoral Verrucous Dysplasia: Report of a Case Treated with Split Thickness Skin Graft, 1980; Malignant Fibrous Histiocytoma, Myxoid Variant Metastatic to the Oral Cavity, 1980. *Memberships:* American Association of Oral and Maxillofacial Surgery; American and California Dental Associations; Legislative Committee, Western Dental Society; Marsh Robinson Academy of Oral Surgery; Fellow, Southern California Academy of Oral Pathology; American Association of Women Dentists (President, Los Angeles Chapter, 1985); Cornell Alumni Association of Southern California; National Association of Female Executives.

STRATTON Evelyn J, b. 25 Feb. 1953, Bangkok, Thailand. Attorney. m. R Stephen Stratton, 16 June 1973, 1 son, 2 daughters. *Education:* AA, University of Florida, USA, 1973; BA, History, University of Akron, 1976; JD, Ohio State University College of Law, 1978. *Appointments:* Law Clerk, Knepper White Arter & Hadden, 1977-78; Senior Law Clerk, Crabbe Brown Jones Potts & Schmidt, 1978-79; Hamilton Kramer Myers & Cheek, 1979-85; Principal, Wesp Osterkamp & Stratton, 1985-. *Memberships:* Supreme Court of Ohio; US District Court, Southern District of Ohio; US

Court of Appeals; American, Ohio, Columbus Bar Associations; Women Lawyers of Franklin County; Linc Resources Inc; Columbus Countrywide Development Corporation; etc. *Honours:* Ohio House of Representatives, Commendation for Service, 1984; Outstanding Young Women of America, 1983, 1985. *Address:* Wesp, Osterkamp & Stratton, Suite 812, 42 East Gay Street, Columbus, OH 43215, USA.

STRATTON Pauline Ann, b. 18 Feb. 1946, Chicago, Illinois, USA. Politican; School Board Member; Substitute Teacher. m. George W Stratton, 25 June 1967. 1 son, 1 daughter. *Education:* BEd, National College of Education, 1967. *Appointments:* Elementary Teacher 1967-70, Substitute Teacher 1971-87, Worth School District No 127; Substitute Teacher, North Palos Elementary School District No 117, 1987-. *Memberships:* St Helen Women's Philptochos; Board of Directors, Agia Paraskevi; Medea Chapter, No 128; Sts Constantine & Helen Church; Grand President, USA and Canada, American Hellenic Educational Progressive Association; Volunteer, American Cancer Society; Amos Alonzo Stagg Athletic Boosters; Eastern Illinois University Parent Organization. *Honours:* Board of Directors, American Cancer Society, 1987-88; Certificate of Honorary Life Membership, Illinois Congress of Parents & Teachers, 1984; Elected to North Palos Board of Education No 117, 1983-87, 1987-; Elected Second Ward Alderman, City of Palos Hills, first time female elected to two taxing bodies at the same time in the history of the City of Palos Hills, 1987. *Hobbies:* School Board Member, North Palos School District No 117; City of Palos Hills Alderman. *Address:* 10315 Alta Drive, Palos Hills, IL 60465, USA.

STRAUCH-SINDEMANN Elke, b. 16 Dec. 1942, Konigsberg, Prussia, Germany. Lawyer. m. Dieter Strauch, 20 Dec. 1968. *Education:* University law exams, Frankfurt/Main, 1968; Bar exams, Hamburg, 1971; Psychology studies, Regensburg, 1985-. *Appointments:* Self-employed, small law office, Regensburg, 1972-. *Creative work includes:* Ceramics, 1976-; Actress, Scenes from Goethe's Faust, Regensburg, 1987, 1988. *Memberships:* Deutscher Juristentag; Bund Naturschutz. *Hobbies:* Ceramics; Playing Recorder; Theatre, Acting & Watching; Psychology; Nature. *Address:* Erlenstrasse 18, 8401 Pentling, Federal Republic of Germany.

STRAUSS Annette, b. 26 Jan. 1924, Houston, USA. Mayor, City of Dallas. m. Theodore Strauss, 2 daughters. *Education:* BA, Sociology, University of Texas, Austin, 1944; MA, Columbia University, 1945. *Past Appointments:* Public Relations Consultant. *Memberships Include:* John F. Kennedy Center for the Performing Arts, Board of Trustees; National Council, Friends of the Kenendy Center; Board of Trustees or Advisory Board: St Paul's Hospital Foundation; National Jewish Hospital; Childrens Medical Center Foundation; National Council of American Jewish Committee; Dallas Volunteer Center; Junior Black Academy; etc. *Honours:* Numerous including: Zonta Award, 1968; Linz Award, 1975; Dallas County Fundraiser of the Year Award, 1982; Dallas Press Club Headliner's Award, 1987; John F Kennedy Commitment to Excellence Award, 1987; Jewish National Fund, Person of Valor Award, 1987; Women's Centre of Dallas, Women Helping Women Award, 1988. *Address:* Dallas City Hall, 1500 Marillo, Dallas, TX 75201, USA.

STRAUSS DAVIS Jane Lynn, b. 3 July 1944, Chicago, Illinois, USA. Vice President, Bankers Trust Co. m. Muller Davis, 28 Dec. 1963. 2 sons, 1 daughter. *Education:* BA Honours, American Culture, Northwestern University, 1980. *Appointments:* Residential Real Estate, Chicago's North Shore, 1970-77; Personal Trust Department, Harris Trust & Savings Bank, 1983-89; Vice President, Bankers Trust Company, 1989-. *Memberships:* Director, United Charities of Chicago; The Woman's Board of Rush-Presbyterian St Lukes Medical Center; Northwestern University Campaign for Great Teachers; Costume Committee Chicago Historical Society; Chicago Estate Planning

Council. *Hobbies:* Bicycling; Study of Rural America; Reading. *Address:* 1020 East Westleigh Road, Lake Forest, Illinois 60045, USA.

STREEP Meryl (Mary Louise), b. 22 June 1949, Basking Ridge, New Jersey, USA. Actress. m. Donald Gummer, 1978. 1 son, 2 daughters. *Education:* Singing studies with Estelle Liebling; Studied drama at Vassar, Yale School of Drama. *Career:* Stage debut in New York in Trelawny of the Wells, 27 Wagons Full of Cotton; New York Shakespeare Festival 1976 in Henry V, Measure for Measure; also acted in Happy End (musical); The Taming of the Shrew; Wonderland (musical); Taken in Marriage and numerous other plays. *Creative Works:* Films include: Julia, 1976; The Deer Hunter, 1978; Manhattan, 1979; The Seduction of Joe Tynan, 1979; The Senator, 1979; Kramer vs. Kramer, 1979; The French Lieutenant's Woman, 1980; Sophie's Choice, 1982; Still of the Night, 1982; Silkwood, 1983; Plenty, 1984; Falling in Love, 1984; Out of Africa, 1985; Heartburn, 1985. Television appearances include: The Deadliest Season; Uncommon Women; Holocaust. *Honours:* Academy Award for Best Supporting Actress for Kramer vs. Kramer, 1980; Best Supporting Actress awards from National Society of Film Critics for The Deer Hunter; New York Film Critics Circle for Kramer vs. Kramer, The Seduction of Joe Tynan and Sophie's Choice; Emmy Award for Holocaust, British Academy Award, 1982, Academy Award for Best Actress, 1982; Honorary Doctorate (Yale), 1983. *Hobbies:* Visiting art galleries and museums. *Address:* c/o International Creative Management, 40 West 57th Street, New York, NY 10019, USA.

STREETER Minette Cline, b. 13 June 1942, Birmingham, Alabama, USA. Consultant. *Education:* University of Alabama; Pensacola Junior College. *Appointments:* Myrtle Grove Business & Tax Service; The Friends Programme International; ABC News World News Tongith, with Peter Jennings; Soviet Life Magazine, Special Consultant. *Publications:* Articles in various journals & magazines. *Memberships Include:* National Association of Accountants; Women of the Moose; Divorced Catholics; Mental Health Association. *Honours:* Apostle of the Word, Catholic Press Association, 1959; Commendation, President Ronald Reagan, 1981; *Address:* The House of Romanov, 6880 West Fairfield Dr. Apt. 40, Pensacola, FL 32506, USA.

STREISAND Barbra, b. 24 Apr. 1942, Brooklyn, New York, USA. Actress; Singer. m. Elliot Gould, 1963, divorced 1971. 1 son. *Education:* Erasmus Hall High School. *Career:* Nightclub debut at Bon Soir, 1961; Appeared in off-Broadway revue, Another Evening with Harry Stoones, 1961; Appeared at Caucus Club, Detroit and Blue Angel, New York, 1961; Played in musical comedy, I Can Get It for You Wholesale, 1962; Began recording career with Columbia records, 1963; Appeared in musical play, Funny Girl, New York 1964, London 1966; Television programme, My Name is Barbra shown in England, Holland, Australia, Sweden, Bermuda and the Phillipines; second programme, Color Me Barbra, also shown abroad; numerous concert and nightclub appearances. *Creative Works:* Films: Funny Girl, 1968; Hello Dolly, 1969; On a Clear Day You Can See Forever, 1969; The Owl and the Pussycat, 1971; What's Up Doc? 1972; Up the Sandbox, 1973; The Way We Were, 1973; For Pete's Sake, 1974; Funny Lady, 1975; A Star is Born, 1977; Yentl, 1983 (also directed and produced). *Honours:* Critics Best Supporting Actress Award, New York, 1962; Grammy recording awards; London Critics' Musical Award, 1966; Academy Award (Oscar) for film Funny Girl, 1968; American Guild of Variety Artists' Entertainer of the Year Award, 1970; Commdr. des Arts et Lettres, 1984. 5 Emmy awards for My Name is Barbra. *Address:* c/o Stan Kamen, William Morris Agency, 151 El Camino, Beverly Hills, CA 90212, USA.

STRETTON Virginia Valda, b. 14 Feb. 1947, Melbourne, Australia. Civil Servant. m. Colin Teese, 16 July 1977, divorced 1983. *Education:* BA, 1972. *Appointments:* Various positions, Australian Public

Service, 1964-86; Executive Director, Industry Research & Development, Department of Industry, Technology & Commerce, 1986-88; National Manager, Industry Assistance, Australian Customs Service, 1989-. *Hobbies:* Skiing; Reading; Music; Tennis; Golf; Windsurfing; Backgammon. *Address:* 65 Flinders Way, Manuka, ACT 2603, Australia.

STRICKER Ruth Ann, b. 12 Mar. 1935, Mitchell, South Dakota, USA. Health & Fitness Executive. m. Bruce Dayton, 26 Dec. 1958, div. 1985, 1 son, 1 daughter. *Education:* BS, Macalester College, St Paul, Minnesota; Dance studies, University of Hawaii. *Appointments include:* Professional dancer, Hawaii; Camp Director, YWCA Chicago, & private girls' camp, Brainerd, Minnesota; Health Education Director, YWCA, Chicago; Owner, Ruth Stricker's Fitness Unlimited, 1970-84; Owner/Director, Ruth Stricker's The Marsh, A Wellness Centre, 1984-. *Creative work:* Registered excercise method, Fitness Unlimited, 1975. *Memberships include:* Trustee, Macalester College; Board, Minneapolis YWCA; Minneapolis Urban & Junior Leagues; Elder, St Luke's Church; Minnesota Women's Consortium; American Society of Professional & Executive Women; Association of Female Executives; American College of Sports Medicine. *Honours:* Distinguished Citizen, Macalester College, 1987; Finalist, Entrepreneur of Year 1986, Nominee/Honoree, Women of Achievement 1979/81, Twin West Chamber of Commerce; Nominee, Woman of Year 1986, Recognition Award 1985, YWCA. *Hobbies:* Sports; Flowers; Music; Eastern philosophy. *Address:* 18125 Shavers Lane, Wayzata, Minnesota 55391, USA.

STRIEGEL Peggy S, b. 12 July. 1941, USA. Advertising Agency President. m. (1) James P. Simsarian, 4 Sept. 1965, 2 daughters, (2) Louis E. Striegel, 14 Sept. 1976. *Education:* BA, Sarah Lawrence College, 1963. *Appointments:* Assistant Editor, Oxford University Press, 1963-64; Picture Editor, Western Publishing, 1964-66; Art Editor, Houghton Mifflin, 1966-68; President, Peggy's Graphics, 1968-78; President, Striegel Advertising Inc., 1978-. *Memberships include:* Board of Directors, Gateway Foundation, Broken Arrow; Board Member, Planned Parenthood, 1987; Treasurer, Women in Communication, Tulsa, 1987. *Honours Include:* Award of Excellence, World's Fair, 1982; Gold Quill, 1983; AIGA Award of Excellence, 1983. *Address:* Striegel Advertising Inc., 716 S Main, Broken Arrow, OK 74012, USA.

STROBEL Kate, b. 23 July 1907, Nurnberg, Federal Republic of Germany. German Politican. m. 22 Nov. 1928, 2 daughters. *Education:* Technology School. *Appointments:* Clerk, 1923-1938, 1945-46. *Memberships:* Member, SDP 1925-; State Chairman, Youth Organization, 1933; West German Politician, 1949-72; Member, European Parliament, 1958-66, EEC 1974-86. *Address:* Erlachweiherstrasse 3, 8500 Nurnberg 60, Federal Republic of Germany.

STRONG Ann L., b. 26 Apr. 1930, Amsterdam, New York, USA. Associate Dean; Professor. m. Michael L. Strong, 24 July 1954, 2 sons. *Education:* BA, Vassar, 1951; JD, Yale, 1954. *Appointments:* Law Practice, 1954-58; Successive ranks to Professor, Departmental Chairman, Associate Dean of Graduate School of Fine Arts, University of Pennsylvania, Philadelphia, 1959-. *Publications:* Open Space for Urban America; The Plan and Program for the Brandy-wine; Planned Urban Environments; Private Property and the Public Interest; Land Banking; The Book of the School, 1990; A Century of the Graduate School of Fine Arts, co-author George E Thomas; Many articles. *Memberships:* New York, Florida and Pennsylvania Bar Associations; American Planning Association; American Institute of Certified Planners; Pennsylvania Planning Association. *Honours:* Professor, Salzburg Seminar in American Studies, 1968; Senior Fellow, National Endowment for the Humanities, 1972-73; Visiting Professor, Yale School of Forestry, 1979; MA(hon), University of Pennsylvania. *Hobbies:* Cooking; Piano; Gardening. *Address:* 127 Meyerson Hall, University of Pennsylvania, Philadelphia, PA 19104, USA.

STROUD Sharron Patricia, b. 29 July 1944, Okemah, Oklahoma, USA. Minister. m. Neil Stroud, deceased. 1 daughter. *Education:* CSU Northridge, 1963-64; Pierce City Coll, 1964-65; Ministerial Degree, United Ch of Religious Science Sch of Min, 1973-75; Masters Degree, Motivational Science Humanetic Inst, 1976; PhD cand in Behavor Psych, La Jolla University. *Appointments:* Religious Science Minister and Motiv Instructor, Self Image Inst, Santa Ana College of Para medical arts & Sic, 1972-73; Num self image seminars, 1972; Founding Minister, Sci of Mind Church of Positive Thinking, 1975-78; Minister Rel Sci Church Ctr, San Diego, 1978; Minister, San Diego Community Church of Religious Science, 1978; Founder, Center for the Celebration of Life, 1989. *Creative works:* Numerous TV & Radio appearances, prod radio show, The Choice is Yours; Host local TV ministry, Passport to Life; Torch Carrier, First Earth Run, 1986; Participant Human Unity Conf and March for Peace & Hands Across Am; Lecturer UN University for Peace, Costa Rica, chaired Planetary Commission, World Peace Event (SD). *Memberships:* United Clergy of Religious Science, VP, 1986-87; Rel Advy Council, US 42nd Congl Dist. *Honours include:* Recipient speaking awards, Nat Forensic League, 1961; United Ch Rel Sci Sch of Ministry Resolution San Diego City Council, 1975; Woman of Religion award, Soroptimists Intern; First woman president, Sch of Ministry, 1974-75. *Hobbies:* Bicycling; Yoga; Swimming. *Address:* Center for the Celebration of Life, 2831 Camino del Rio South, Ste 215, San Diego, CA 92108, USA.

STRUNECKA Anna, b. 24 Jan. 1944, Prague, Czechoslovakia. Professor of Physiology and Head of Department. m. Otakar Strunecky, 11 Mar. 1965. 1 son, 1 daughter. *Education:* Biology and Chemistry 1966, PhD Physiology 1970, Dr Sc, 1987, Faculty of Science, Charles University. *Appointments:* Postgraduate study, 1966-70; Assistant, Department of Physiology 1970-80, Assistant, Habilitation, 1980, Head of Department of Physiology, 1981-, Professor, 1988-, Charles University. *Publications:* Exercise book: Biology for Biochemists and Biophysics. numerous articles in professional journals. *Memberships:* IUBS-Biochemical Society; IUPS-Purkyne Medical Society. *Hobbies:* Gardening. Interests: Cell physiology; Phospholipids, my work. *Address:* Department of Physiology and Developmental Biology, Faculty of Science, Charles University, Vinicna 7, 128 00 Prague 2, Czechoslovakia.

STUART Ann, b. 22 Dec. 1935, Madisonville, USA. Dean; Professor; Author. m. Raymond R. Poliakoff, 22 Aug. 1980. *Education:* BA, University of Florida, 1958; MA, English, University of Kentucky, 1962; PhD, English, Southern Illinois University. *Appointments:* Professor, 1962-88, Assistant Dean, 1979-81, 1986-87, University of Evansville; Visiting Professor, Purdue University, 1987-88; Dean, School of Arts and Sciences, East Stroudsburg University, 1989-90. *Publications:* Writing & Analyzing Effective Computer System Documentation, 1984; The Technical Writer, 1988; Corresponding with Customers, 1986. *Memberships:* Alpha Sigma Lambda; Indiana Teachers of Writing; Phi Kappa Phi; National Council of Teachers of English. *Honours:* NEH, 1976; Alumni Certificate of Excellence for Professional Achievment as Faculty, 1987. *Hobbies:* Theatre; Museums; Gardens; Concerto. *Address:* 608 Fulmer Avenue, Stroudsburg, PA 18360, USA.

STUART Michelle, b. USA. Painter; Sculptor. Creative work: Exhibitions, Europe, Asia, USA. Work in public collections: New York; Minneapolis; Brooklyn; Buffalo; Chicago; Philadelphia; Stockholm, Sweden; Munchen Gladbach, Krefeld, West Germany; Hague, Holland; National Collection, Australia. Numerous commissions, public & private collections. Sculpture commissions include: Stone-Alignments-Solstice-Cairns, Rowena Plateau, Columbia River, Oregon, 1979; Polychromed bronze relief sculpture, Four Seasons, College of Wooster, Ohio, 1987. Painting commissions include: Cueva Pintada, Baldwin House, Emerald Bay, California;

Desert Sunset, Security Pacific National Bank, Los Angeles; Minnesota Time Contour, State Building, St Paul, Minnesota. Institution exhibits include: Primitivism in 20th Century Art: Affinities of Tribal & Modern, Museum of Modern Art, New York, 1984; Inaugural Exhibition: Permanent Collection, Australian National Gallery, Canberra, 1984; Sacred Precincts: From Dreamtime to South China Sea, Neuberger Museum, Purchase, 1984; Paradisi: Garden Mural, Brooklyn Museum, 1986; Silent Gardens: American Landscape, Michelle Stuart, Rose Art Museum, Hartford, Connecticut, 1988. Over 30 solo exhibitions, New York, Sweden, West Germany, 1980-. *Honours include:* 10 Grants & Fellowships, National Endowment for Arts, New York Foundation for Arts, John S. Guggenheim Foundation. 1974-. *Address:* 152 Wooster Street, New York, NY 10012, USA.

STUBBS Jean, b. 23 Oct. 1926, Denton, Lancashire, England. Author. m. (1) 1948 (divorced 1962), 1 son, 1 daughter, (2) Roy Oiver, 5 Aug. 1980. *Education:* Manchester Art School, 1944-47. *Appointments:* Copywriter, Henry Melland, 1965-66; Otherwise freelance. *Publications include:* Rosegrower; Travellers; Hanrahan's Colony; Straw Crown; My Grand Enemy; Passing Star; Case of Kitty Ogilvie; An Unknown Welshman; Dear Laura; Painted Face; Golden Crucible; Kit's Hill; Ironmaster; Vivian Inheritance; Northern Correspondent; A Lasting Spring; Like We Used to Be; 100 Years Around the Lizard; Great Houses of Cornwall. *Memberships:* PEN; Past committee member, Crime Writers Association; Detection Club; Society of Women Writers & Journalists; Lancashire Authors Association; West Country Writers Association. *Honours:* Tom Gallon Award, 1966; Book of Month Club, 1973, 1979, 1987; Daughter of Mark Twain, 1973; Writer in Residence, Avon, 1984. *Hobbies:* Cookery; Yoga; Music; Theatre; Cinema; Art; Buddhism. *Address:* Trewin, Nancegollan, Helston, Cornwall TR13 0RJ, England.

STUBER Margaret Lois, b. 26 Mar. 1953, New York, USA. Medical Doctor; Educator. m. Lawrence Ross Gail, 31 Jan. 1987. *Education:* BS, Denison University, 1975; MD, University of Michigan Medical School, 1979. *Appointment:* Assistant Professor in Residence, Department of Psychiatry & Biobehavioural Sciences, Neuropsychiatric Institute & Hospital, University of California, Los Angeles, 1987-. *Publications:* Group Therapy in Treatment of Adolescents with Bulimia: Some Preliminary Observations; Group Therapy for Chronic Mental Illness: Multi-Diagnosis Group. *Memberships:* Group for Advancement of Psychiatry, American Academy of Child & Adolescent Psychiatry; American Psychiatric Association; International Psyoho Oncology Society; Southern California Psychiatric Society; Chair, Task Force on Children of Parents with Cancer, American Cancer Society (California Division). *Honours:* Phi Beta Kappa, 1975; CIBA award, community service, 1977; Resident award, Southern California Psychiatric Society, 1984. *Hobbies include:* Research with children & families dealing with Cancer, AIDS, Transplantation, Bereavement; Singing. *Address:* UCLA Neuropsychiatric Institute, 760 Westwood Plaza, Room 68-237, Los Angeles, California 90024, USA.

STUERMER Claudia A O, b. 14 Aug. 1950, Essen, Germany. Scientist; Neurobiology; Lecturer. *Education:* Diploma in Biology, 1975; Doctor rer nat, 1978; Habilitation and Privat Dozent, 1986. *Appointments:* Unit of Morphological Brain Research, University of Freiburg, Federal Republic of Germany, 1978-81; DFG Fellow, Division of Biology, University of Michigan, USA, 1981-83; Max-Planck-Institute of Dev Biol, Tubingen, Federal Republic of Germany, 1983-86; Friedrich-Miescher-Laboratory, Max Planck Society, Tubingen, 1986-. *Publications:* Contributions to: Lesion Induced Neuronal Plasticity of Sensorimotor Connections, 1981; Making of the Nervous System, 1988; Post-Lesion Neural Plasticity, 1988. *Memberships:* American Neuroscience Association; Deutscher Hochschulverband. *Hobbies:* Country skiing; Jogging; Row-boating; Swimming; Music; Psychology, especially psychoanalysis. *Address:* Friederich-Miescher-Laboratorium der Max-Planck-Gesellschaft, Spemannstr 37-39, 7400 Tubingen, Federal Republic of Germany.

STULMAN Janis Eleanore Dremann (professional name, Carter), b. 10 Oct. 1917, Cleveland, Ohio, USA. Actress; Theatre Administrator. m. (1) Carl Prager, (2) Julius Stulman, 26 Dec. 1956. *Education:* BA, Case Western Reserve University; Musical graduate work, New York City. *Appointments:* Various appearances, stage & screen including: I Married an Angel, Broadway, 1938; DuBarry Was A Lady, 1939; Panama Hattie, 1940; Contracts, 20th Century Fox, Columbia Pictures, RKO, Hollywood; Numerous television dramas, 1952-57; Summer stock in Man Bites Dog, US East Coast, with Fay Bainter, William Prince, Kay Medford; Researcher & writer, Philip Lord's radio show, We The People. *Honours:* Louella Parsons' Best performance, in Woman on Pier 13; Most travelled actress, Eleanor Roosevelt Show; Several awards, painting, New York City & Longboat Key Art Centre, Florida; Sweater Girl award; Most Beautiful Eyes, 1948. *Hobbies include:* Theatre, active all aspects including 4 executive boards, Florida State Theatres, especially Asolo Centre for Performing Arts, Sarasota; Music; World travel. *Address:* 603 Longboat Key Club Road N-801, Longboat Key, Florida 34228, USA.

STUMP Sandra Sue, b. 11 Feb. 1936, Fort Wayne, Indiana, USA. Programme Director. *Education:* BA, DePauw University, 1958; MT Education, Borgess Hospital, 1958-59; MI (ASCP) Certification, 1959. *Appointments:* Chief Medical Technologist, 1964-65, Microbiology Supervisor, 1965-77, Chemistry Technologist, 1976-77, Programme Director, School of Medical Technology, 1977-, The Lutheran Hospital of Fort Wayne Inc. *Memberships:* American Society for Microbiology; American Society for Clinical Pathologists; South Central Association for Clinical Microbiology; Consortium of Indiana Medical Laboratory Educators, various offices including: President, 1984-85. *Honour:* Phi Epsilon Phi. *Hobbies:* Watersports; Reading; Travel; Work. *Address:* 3024 Fairfield Avenue, Fort Wayne, IN 46087, USA.

STUPICA Marija Lucija, b. 13 Dec. 1950, Ljubljana, Yugoslavia. Painter; Illustrator. m. Jeff Husref Pivac, 13 Dec. 1985. 1 daughter. *Education:* School of Art and Design 1971; Academy of Fine Arts, 1976; Master's Degree of Arts, 1978, Ljubljana. *Appointments:* Freelance illustrator (for Childrens books), 1976-; Costume and set designer, 1977-. *Creative works:* Illustrated books include: Locomotivo, Locomutive, 1981; Medicine for Mischief, 1982; 12 Months, 1983; The Flying Suitcase, 1983; Croaking Kate and Jumping Jill, 1983; The Shepherdess and the Chimney-Sweep, 1984; A Tale of a Cloud, 1984; Poems for Girls and Boys, 1984; The Little Mermaid, 1986; The Little One and Cathy, The Impish Playmate, 1987; The Little One, 1987; The Swineherd, 1988; The Little One in the Four Seasons, 1988. Exhibitions include: Independent Exhibition of Illustrations, Yugoslav Cultural Centre, Paris and Central Child and Youth Library, Frankfurt, 1988; Exhibition at the 6 and 7 International Childrens Book Illustration in Sarmede, Italy, 1988, 1989; Independent Exhibitions in Prague and Bratislava, 1990. *Memberships:* DOS, Slovene Association of Designers; DSLU, Slovene Association of Artists; SULUJ, Yugoslav Association of Artists; ICOGRADA, International Council of Design; AIAP, Association Internationale des Arts Plastiques; OISTT, Organisationes Internationales des Scenographes et des Techniciens de Theatre. *Honours include:* The Golden Apple-BIB, 1985; Levstik Award, 1986; Kajuh Award, 1987. *Hobby:* Literature. *Address:* Svetceva 1, 61000 Ljubljana, Yugoslavia.

SU Helen Chien-Fan, b. 26 Dec. 1922, Nanping, Fujian, China. Research Chemist. *Education:* BA, Hwa Nan College, Fujian, 1944; MS, 1951, PhD, 1953, University of Nebraska, USA. *Appointments:* Assistant Instructor, Chemistry, Hwa Nan College China, 1944-49; Professor, chemistry, Lambuth College, Jackson, USA, 1953-55; Research Assistant, Auburn Research

Boundation, Auburn, AL, 1955-57; Senior Chemist, Project Leader, Borden Chemical Company, Philadelphia, PA 1957-63; Scientist, Lockheed-Georgia Research Laboratory, Marietta, GA 1963-67; Research Chemist, Agricultural Research Service, US Dept. of Agriculture, Savannah, Georgia, 1968-. *Publications:* Author, Co-Author, 44 technical publications in professional journals including: Journal of American Chemical Society; Journal of Organic Chemistry; Journal of Medicinal Chemistry; Analytical Biochemistry; Journal of Agricultural and Food Chemistry, etc. *Memberships:* American Chemical Society; American Association for the Advancement of Science; New York Academy of Science; Fellow, American Institute of Chemists; Fellow, Georgia Institute of Chemists; Entomological Society of America; Georgia Entomological Society; Sigma Xi; Sigma Delta Epsilon. *Honours:* 3 Patents on Hydrophobic Coatings from France, Italy and New Zealand, 1968; Recipient, IR-100 Award, Industrial Research Magazine 1966. *Hobbies:* Reading; Gardening. *Address:* 610 Highland Drive, Savannah, GA 31406, USA.

SUAREZ Mary Ann Rita, b. 20 July 1953, Philadelphia, Pennsylvania, USA. Municipal Official. *Education:* AS, Harcum Junior College, Bryn Mawr, 1973; BS, Cabrini College, Radnor, 1987. *Appointments:* Substitute teacher, Radnor Schools, 1980-83; Administrative assistant, Sears Roebuck & Company, 1983-86; Township Secretary, Thornbury Township, Chester County, 1986-. *Publications:* Contributions, American Poetry Anthology, 1982-83. *Memberships:* Local Government Secretaries' Association; Business & Professional Women's Association; Alumni Admissions Board, Cabrini College. *Hobbies:* Reading; Writing poetry; Camping; Travel; Stamp collecting; Music. *Address:* 223 Matthew Road, Merion Station, Pennsylvania 19066, USA.

SUBICH Linda Mezydlo, b. 27 Jan. 1956, USA. Associate Professor. m. 23 Aug. 1980. *Education:* BS, University of Wisconsin, 1977; MA, 1979, PhD, 1981, Psychology, Ohio State University. *Appointments:* Associate Professor, University of Akron, 1981-. *Publications:* Articles in: Journal of Counselling Psychology; Journal of Vocational Behaviour; Career Development Quarterly; Sex Roles. *Memberships:* American Psychological Association; Association of Women in Psychology; American Psychological Society; American Association for Counseling and Development. *Honours:* Phi Beta Kappa; Research Award, Association for Specialists in Group Work, 1985; National Academy of Science Research Grant, 1986. *Hobbies:* Reading; Cooking; Hiking; Travel. *Address:* Dept. of Psychology, University of Akron, Akron, OH 44325, USA.

SUCHY-PILALIS Jessica Ray, b. 6 July 1954, Milwaukee, USA. Faculty Member; Harpist. m. Labros E. Pilalis, 27 July 1985. *Education:* BFA, University of Wisconsin, 1976; MM, Harp, 1979, MA, Theory, 1982, Eastman School of Music; D.Mus., in progress, Indiana University. *Appointments:* Harpist, solo tours & appearances, 1984-; Principal Psalti (Cantor), Holy Tinity Greek Orthodox Church, 1984, 1986-; Faculty Member, University of Wisconsin, 1986-88; Butler University, 1989-; Recording: Two Hymns of Kassia on Historical Anthology of Music by Women. *Publications:* Jacket Notes: Arnold Bax : Fantasy Sonata and Sonata for Viola and Piano, 1983. *Memberships:* American Harp Society, Vice President Milwaukee Chapter, 1975-76; Delta Omicron; Pi Kappa Lambda; Society for Music Theory; College Music Society; American String Teachers Association; Modern Greek Studies Association. *Honours Include:* Deans Honour Award, 1976; Eastman Educational Opportunity Grant, 1978; Taylor Foundation Grant, 1984-85; Indiana Arts Commission/NEA Master Fellowship, 1988. *Hobby:* Tennis. *Address:* 2601 E. Newton Ave., Milwaukee, WI 53211, USA.

SUESSMUTH Rita, b. 17 Feb. 1937, Wuppertal, Germany. President of the German Bundestag. m. Hans Suessmuth, 1964. 1 daughter. *Education:* First state examination in French and History, 1956-61; Postgraduate studies, Education, Sociology and Psychology, 1961-64; Dr Phil degree, 1964. *Appointments:* Lecturer, International Comparative Education, 1969; Professor of Education, Dortmund University, 1980; Director, Frau und Gesellschaft (Women and Society) Institute, Hannover, 1982; Federal Minister of Youth, Family Affairs, Women and Health, 1985; President of the German Bundestag, 1988. *Publications:* Studien zur Anthropologie des Kindes (Studies on the subject of child anthropology), 1968; 3.Familienbericht 1979 (3rd Report on Family Affairs, 1979; Frauen-der Resignation keine Change (Women-Do not give resignation a chance), 1985; AIDS-Wege aus der Angst (AIDS-Ways of overcoming fear), 1987; Kämpfen und Bewegen-Frauenreden (To struggle and to change - Speeches on Women's Situation). *Memberships:* Vice-President, Family Union of German Catholics, 1980; Central Committee Member of German Catholics, 1982; Chairwoman, Women's Union of the CDU of Germany, 1986; Deputy Chairwoman, CDU of Germany, 1987; Member of the German Bundestag, 1987; President of the German Association of Adult Education Centres, 1987. *Honour:* Honorary doctorates from Hildesheim, 1988 and Bochum 1990. *Address:* Deutscher Bundestag, Prasidialburo, Bundeshaus, D-5300 Bonn 1, West Germany.

SUGARMAN Bahira Hannah, b. 8 Apr. 1945, Fall River, Massachusetts, USA. Clinical Social Worker. m. Sheldon Robert Isenberg, 6 Apr. 1986. *Education:* AB, Connecticut College, 1967; MSSW, Columbia University School of Social Work, 1972; LMT, Florida Institute of Health, 1980. *Appointments:* Psychiatric Social Worker, Clifford Beers Child Guidance Centre, 1972-73; Instructor of Social Work in Psychiatry, University of Florida, 1973-79; Clinical Social Worker, Marriage & Family Therapist, Private psychotherapy practice, 1979-; Faculty & Co-founder, Institute of Traditional Healing Arts, 1984-; Partner, Living Tree Associates, 1987-. *Publications:* Toward a Jewish Tantra: Generating Spirituality in Our Relationship, 1986; Atypical Children; Perspectives on Parent-Professional Interaction, 1979. *Memberships:* Fellow, American Orthopsychiatric Association; Clinical Member, Association of Marriage & Family Therapists; Florida Association for Clinical Social Workers; Academy of Certified Social Workers; National Association of Social Workers, Treasurer, Gainesville Chapter; Council on Social Work Education; Association for Transpersonal Psychology. *Interest:* Apprentice instructor, School of Tai Chi Chuan; Research issues re death & dying. *Address:* 115 North East Seventh Avenue, Gainesville, Florida 32601, USA.

SUISALA Emoni Tesese, b. 16 Mar. 1948, Mototua, Apia, Western Samoa. Businesswoman; Administrator. m. Tuipoloa Suisala, 26 Jan. 1978. *Education:* Fulton College, Fiji, 1961-65. *Appointments:* Principal, Tesese Secretarial School, 1971-; Manager Administration, Electric Power Corporation, 1979-. *Membership:* Commercial Education Society of Australia (CESA). *Honour:* Special Proficiency Prize for Pacific, CESA, 1965. *Hobby:* Reading. *Address:* PO Box 2011, Apia, Western Samoa.

SULLIVAN Claire Jean Potter Ferguson, b. 28 Sept. 1937, Pittsburg, Texas, USA. Professor. m. David E. Sullivan, 2 Nov. 1984, 1 son. *Education:* BBA, 1958, MBA, 1961, University of Texas, Austin; PhD, North Texas State University, 1973. *Appointments:* Instructor of Marketing, Southern Methodist University, 1965-70; Assistant Professor, Marketing, University of Utah, 1972-74; Associate Professor, Marketing, University of Arkansas, 1974-77; Associate Professor, Marketing, University of Texas, Arlington, 1977-79; Associate Professor, Marketing, Illinois State University, 1980-84; Professor, Chair, Marketing, Bentley College, 1984-. *Publications:* Marketing Articles, 1973-87; Monograph: Pre-adolescent Children's Attitudes Toward Television Commercials, 1975. *Memberships:* American, Southern & Southwestern Marketing Associations; Sales & Marketing Executives of Boston. *Honours Include:* Outstanding Professor, Southern Methodist University, 1970; Beta Gamma Sigma, 1973; Outstanding

Performance in Teaching, Illinois State University, 1981; Fellowship, American Marketing Association, 1985; etc. *Hobbies:* Music; Tennis; Theatre. *Address:* Marketing Dept., Bentley College, Waltham, MA 02254, USA.

SULLIVAN Clara K., b. 4 Apr. 1915, Brooklyn, New York, USA. Consultant, Public Finance. m. 7 Feb. 1948. *Education:* AB, Mount Holyoke College, 1936; MA 1943, PhD 1959, Columbia University. *Appointments:* Research assistant, Chase Manhattan Bank, 1943-48; Economist, International Programme in Taxation, Harvard Law School, 1958-62; Senior Economist, International Economic Integration Programme, Columbia University, 1963-64; Massachusetts Higher Education Programme, 1965-66; Economics Editor, Houghton Mifflin Company, 1967-69; Tax Consultant, 1969-. *Publications:* Tax on Value Added, 1965, translated Spanish; Search for Tax Principles in European Economic Community, 1963; 3 chapters, indirect taxation, in Fiscal Harmonization in Common Markets, Volume II, ed. Carl Shoup, 1967; Critique of Draft of a Model Value Added Tax Statute & Commentary, for Committee on Value Added Tax, American Bar Association, 1988. *Memberships:* American Economic Association; Advisory Board, Tax Analysts, Washington DC; National Tax Association; Tax Institute of America. *Honour:* Speaker, 16th Annual Tax Conference, Canadian Tax Foundation. *Hobbies:* Gardening; Boating. *Address:* 336 Pensacola Road, Venice, Florida 34285, USA.

SULLIVAN Connie Castleberry, b. 8 Jan. 1934, Cincinnati, Ohio, USA. Artist-Photographer. m. John J. Sullivan, 6 June 1959, 2 daughters. *Education:* BA, Manhattanville College, 1957. *Appointment:* Freelance photographer; Solo exhibits, many US cities, also London & Paris; Work in many museum collections, US & France. *Publication:* Petroglyphs of the Heart, Photographs by Connie Sullivan, 1983. *Memberships:* Graphic Arts Forum; MacDowell Society; Trustee 1987-, Images, Centre for Fine Photography. *Honours:* Nomination, Post-Corbett Award for Arts, Cincinnati, 1986; Best of Show, Images Gallery, Cincinnati 1987, Toledo Friends of Photography 1988; Grant, Aid to Individual Artists, Summerfair Inc, 1987; Fellowship, Arts/Midwest National Endowment for Arts, 1989. *Hobbies:* Travel; Reading; Gardening; Music. *Address:* 9 Garden Place, Cincinnati, Ohio 45208, USA.

SULLIVAN Eleanor J, b. 20 Sept. 1938, Indianapolis, USA. Associate Dean; Associate Professor. m. David Sullivan, 15 June 1956, deceased, 3 sons, 2 daughters. *Education:* BS, Nursing, 1975, PhD, Education, 1981, St Louis University, MS, Nursing, Southern Illinois University, 1977. *Appointments:* Visiting Nurses Association, St Louis, 1976-77; Assistant Professor, Southern Illinois University, 1977-78; Assistant Professor, Maryville College, 1978-81; Associate Dean, Associate Professor, Nursing, University of Missouri, 1981-85; Associate Professor, University of Minnesota, 1985-. *Publications:* Co-author, Effective Management in Nursing, 2nd edition, 1988; articles in professional journals. *Memberships:* American, Missouri, Minnesota Nurses Association; Sigma Theta Tau; Phi Kappa Phi. *Honours:* American Journal of Nursing, Book of the Year, 1985. *Hobbies:* Theatre; Symphony. *Address:* University of Kansas School of Nursing, 1038 Eleanor Taylor Building, 39th & Rainbow, Kansas City, KS 66103, USA.

SULLIVAN Mary Jane Noreen, b. 3 Nov. 1939, Brooklyn, New York, USA. University Administrator. m. 26 Dec. 1959. 1 son, 2 daughters. *Education:* BA, Hunter College, 1960; MA 1976, EdD 1980, Ball State University. *Appointments:* Freelance Writer, NY Daily News, 1959-69; Teacher, Westfield, New Jersey Public Schools, 1973-75; University Administrator, Southern Illinoise University and University of Wisconsin-Superior, 1978-. *Publications:* Numerous articles in professional journals. *Memberships:* Research Committee, National University Continuing Education Association, 1988-91; Professional development Committee, NUCEA Region IV, 1985-88. *Honours:* NUCEA Award for Scholarly Publications, 1984; 3

Grants, National Science Foundation. *Hobbies:* Cross country skiing; Reading; Needlepoint. *Address:* University of Wisconsin-Superior, 1800 Grand Avenue, Superior, WI 54880, USA.

SULLIVAN Susan, b. 20 Aug. 1958, Teaneck, New Jersey, USA. Graduate Student. m. 23 Feb. 1974, divorced 1979, 2 daughters. *Education:* AAS, Bergin Community College; BS, Chemistry, Ramago College of NJ; MS, University of Rochester, 1988; Studying for PhD in Neurobiology & Anatomy, University of Rochester. *Appointments:* Research Assistant, Technologist, various Hospitals, 1982-85; Course Co-ordinator, Head & Neck Gross Anat Review, 1986-; Teach Associate, University of Rochester School of Medicine, 1986-. *Publications:* Editor, several chapters of The Histology Lab Manual. *Memberships:* American Society of Clinical Pathologists; Society for Neuroscience, Student Representative; Iota Sigma Pi; Past Vice President, Ramapo Chemistry Club; Student Rep Assoc of Grad Students, University of Roch. *Honours:* Academic Honours, Bergen Community College, 1982; Ollie Otten Academic Achievement Award, 1984, Merck Award, 1985, Ramapo College; etc. *Hobbies:* Volunteer Worker for Girl Scouts of America, & the Juvenile Diabetes Foundation; Reading; Biking; Boating; Hiking. *Address:* University of Rochester, School of Medicine, Dept. of Neurobiology & Anatomy, 601 Elmwood Ave., Rochester, NY 14642, USA.

SULLIVAN Zola Tiles, b. 5 Nov. 1921, Tallahassee, Florida, USA. Educator. m. William David Sullivan, 1 Apr. 1956, 1 son, 1 daughter. *Education:* BS 1942, MS 1950, Florida A&M University; Graduate study, USA & England; PhD, University of Illinois, 1970. *Appointments:* Principal Teacher, Florida schools, 1942-53, 1953-71; Assistant Professor, Florida A&M University, 1950-53; Associate Professor of Education, Florida International University, 1971-. *Creative work:* Research dissertation, Factors That Affect the Teaching Learning Process of Cuturally Different Students in Sixth Grade; Programme To Meet Educational Needs of Migrants; Sullivan's Inventory of Cross Cultural Poetry, in press. *Memberships:* National Education Association; Phi Delta Kappa; Board, Black Heritage Museum, Dade County; National Council of Teachers of English; American Association of University Women. *Honours:* National Defence Education Scholarship, University of Miami, 1962-63; James Scholar 1968-70, NDEA Fellowship 1967-68, University of Illinois; Triple T Programme, University of Miami, 1963; 1st black female, Greater Miami, to receive PhD; 1st faculty member hired, Florida International University; Governor's Certificate, Outstanding Florida Educators. *Hobbies:* Doll collecting; Travel; Sewing & craft work; Art & antique collecting. *Address:* c/o School of Education, Florida International University, Miami, FL 33199, USA.

SULZBY Elizabeth, b. 25 Feb. 1942, Walker County, Alabama, USA. Associate Professor. m. Mitchell Frank Rouzie, 8 July 1980, 1 daughter. *Education:* BA, Birmingham-Southern College, 1963; Postgraduate, Divinity School, Harvard University, 1963-64; MEd, College of William & Mary, 1969; PhD, University of Virginia, 1977. *Appointments Include:* Public School Teacher, 1966-75; Instructor, School of Education, Jacksonville University, 1970-71; Instructor, Graduate School of Education, Rhode Island College, 1973-74; Instructor, School of Education, University of Virginia, 1975-77; Assistant Professor, 1977-83, Associate Professor, 1986-, Northwestern University; Associate Professor, University of Michigan, 1986-. *Publications Include:* Text, as an Object of Metalinguistic Knowledge, 1982; Oral and Written Mode Adaptations, 1982; Children's Use of Reference, 1984; Children's Emergent Reading of Favourite Storybooks, 1985; Kindergarteners as Writers and Readers' in Advances in Writing Research Volume 1, (editor Farr); Emergent Literacy: Writing & Reading, with William Teale, 1986; Emergent Reading and Writing in 5-6 Year Olds: A Longitudinal Study, in press. *Memberships:* various professional organisations. *Honours:* National Merit Scholarship, 1959-63; Woodrow Wilson Fellowship, 1963-64; Harvard Honour Scholarship, 1963-64; Grants include: NIE, 1980-82; Spencer Foundation, 1981-83, 1984-86. *Hobbies:* Reading; Knitting; Gardening; Running. *Address:* School of Education, University of Michigan, 610 East University, Ann Arbor, MI 48109, USA.

SUMMERFIELD Joanne, b. 30 June 1940, Brookline, USA. m. Abraham Karlikow, 1988, 3 daughters from previous marriage. *Appointments:* President, Today's World, a professional consulting company specialising in marketing communications, public affairs and publishing activites; Consultant, Government of Canada and to Price Waterhouse; Has 15 years experience in presenting seminars on topics including: Marketing Yourself in a Career; For Women Only; Interviewing Techniques for the Successful Manager; Communicating at the Top; The Psychology of Starting Your Own Business; How to Develop and Manage a Profitable Practice; 101 Ways to Protect Your Job; Selling Professional Services; Working with People; Frequently conducts in-house training programmes for small, medium and large companies. *Publications:* Corporate Lives; Listening-It Can Change Your Life; 101 Ways to Protect Your Job; Legacy of Love, poetry; Contributor of nuemrous articles in business journals; Has co-authored several books. *Honours:* University of Wyoming Archive of Contemporary History lodged poetry, papers and taped celebrity interviews; Lehigh University Rausch Center for Business Communications Executive-in-Residence.*Address:* 315 West 57th Street, New York, NY 10019, USA.

SUMMERFORD Sherry R, b. 21 Jan. 1948, Hartselle, USA. Brokerage Company Executive; Representative. m. Robert Copeland Summerford, 6 Mar. 1965, 3 daughters. *Appointments:*Collector, Credit Bureau of Decatur, 1976- 78; Timekeeper, Albert G. SmithConst. Co., 1978-79; Bookkeeper, Assistant Manager, Hogan's Ready Mix, Hartselle, 1979-82; Representative, Dewline inc., 1982-; President, Summerford & Summerford Enterprises Inc., President SCT Warehouse Inc., 1989-. *Memberships:* National Association Female Executives; Decatur Chamber of Commerce; National Federation Industry Business; American Legion Ladies Auxiliary. *Honours:* Various Honours & Awards. *Hobbies:* Reading; Gardening. *Address:* Summerford & Summerford Enterprises & SCL Warehouse Inc., 9324 Hwy 20 W, Suites 19-20, Madison, AL 35758, USA.

SUMMERTON Pia Marie, b. 24 July 1964, Kingston, Jamaica. Analytical Engineer. m. James Alan Summerton, 27 Aug. 1988. *Education:* BSc., 1985. *Appointments:* Pratt & Whitney, 1985-. *Memberships:* Auxilliary Chairman, American Society of Mechanical Engineering, Regional Conference, Boca Raton, 1988; ASME; Maplecrest Homeowner's Association. *Honours:* National Deans List, 1985; Outstanding Service Award, Pratt & Whitney, 1987. *Hobbies:* Travel; Dancing; Reading. *Address:* 193 Maplecrest Circle, Jupiter, FL 33458, USA.

SUN Fengcheng, b. 7 Sept. 1934, Suzhou City, people's Republic of China. University Professor. m. Xingjun Yan, 1 May 1961. 1 son. *Education:* Diploma, German Language & Literature, 1956, Diploma for Graduate Studies, German Lit, Dept of Western Languages, Peking University. *Appointments:* Instructor 1961-78, Lecturer 1979-82, Associate Professor 1983- , of German, Department of Western Languages, Peking University, Beijing. *Publications:* Co-author: A Brief History of German Literature, 1958; The History of European Literature, vol 1, 1964, vol 2, 1972; Contemporary Literature in Europe and America, 1982; Chinese Encyclopedia, part of the entries on German Literature, 1982; History of Foreign Literature, 1984; Concise Edition of Foreign Literature, 1985. Articles: On The Red and The Black by Stendhal, 1981; Brecht in China, 1985; The Influences of German Literature in China, 1986; Remarks on Modernistic Literature in the West, 1987; Heine in China, 1988. Translations:

Mutter Courage und Ihre Kinder, 1959; Die Verlorene Ehre der Katharina Blum, 1980. *Memberships:* IVG (Internationale Vereinigung fur Germanistische Sprache und Literatur Wissenschaft); All China Writers Association; China Association of Comparative Lit. *Honours include:* Co-Winner, 1st Prize awarded by State Education Commission for Excellent University Textbooks of Foreign Literature, 1987. *Hobbies:* Music; Art; Popular science. *Address:* Department of Western Languages, Peking University, Beijing 10087, China.

SUNDE Karen, b. 18 July 1942, Wausau, Wisconsin, USA. Actor; Playwright. 2 sons. *Education:* BS, Iowa State University, 1963; MA, Kansas State University, 1965. *Appointments:* Associate Director, Actor, City Stage/CSC Repertory, 1971-85; 60 roles performed including: Clytemnestra, The Orestia; Alice, Dance of Death; Hedda Gabler; Ruth, The Homecoming; Portia, The Merchant of Venice; Ase, Peer Gynt; Jocasta and Antigone, The Oedipus Cycle; Lotte, Big and Little, (Strauss). *Publications:* Produced To Moscow, Minneapolis, 1986; Kabuki Othello, Philadelphia & Chicago, 1986; Balloon, Radio France, Paris, 1987; Dark Lady, California & Denmark, 1986; produced & published, Balloon, 1983; Produced, The Running of the Deer, New York, 1978; Quasimodo, Concert Version, Ohio, 1986; Day Before Noon, The Sound of Sand, Produced 1963; etc. *Honours:* Bob Hope Award, 1963; Production Grant, Finnish Literature Centre, 1983; Best Direction, Villager Award, 1983; Best Play, Village Award, 1983; McKnight Fellowship, Playwrights, 1986-87; Theatre Panel, New Jersey State Council on the Arts, 1986. *Address:* Manhattan, NY 10014, USA.

SUNDERRAJ Mary, b. 15 May 1944, India. Dentist. m. Sunderraj, 12 May 1975, 1 son, 2 daughters. *Education:* SSLC, 1962; DDS, 1984. *Appointments:* Dental Surgeon India, 1970-76; Instructor, Dentistry, New York University, 1980-; Co-ordinator, Dental School, 1981-85. *Publications:* Articles in: New York State Jurnal of Medicine; Journal of Oral Medicine; Cancer. *Memberships:* American Dental Association; American Oral Pathology; Indian Dental Association. *Honours:* Recipient, many honours & awards. *Hobbies:* Music; Nature *Address:* 4317 Marathon Parkway, Little Neck, NY 11363, USA.

SUPPLEE Patricia Elizabeth, b. 26 Apr. 1956, West Chester, Pennsylvania, USA. Practising Architect; Professor of Architecture. *Education:* BS, University of Virginia, 1973; MArch, Columbia University, 1982. *Appointments:* Designer, Martin E.Rich, Architect, 1982-84; Designer, Frank Williams & Associates, 1985-86; Architect, Fox & Fowle Architects, 1987-88; Sole Owner, Pat Supplee Architer, 1988-; Professor of Architecture, New York University of Technology, 1988- . *Publications:* Exibitor, in Washington Women in Architecture, 1979; Designs published in Precis, 1981. *Memberships:* American Institute of Architects; Museum of Modern Art. *Honours:* Graduating Class Faculty Award in Design Excellence, University of Virginia, 1978; Team member of winning entry, South Ferry Competition, 1986. *Hobbies:* Skiing; Scuba diving; Photography; Painting. *Address:* Kew Gardens, NY 11918, USA.

SURGALLA Lynn Ann, b. 12 Dec. 1951, Chicago, Illinois, USA. Biophysicist; Electronics Executive; Author; Lecturer. m. Thomas Francis Valone, 17 Aug. 1986. *Education:* BA, English 1974, BS Physics 1979, Florida Atlantic University; BA, Social Sciences 1982, MS Natural Sciences 1985, PhD Candidate, Biophysics 1985-, SUNYAB; MS, Student Personnel Administration, SUCB, 1984. *Appointments:* Technical Writer, Roswell Park Memorial Institute, 1975-76; Laboratory Assistant, Department of Physics, Florida Atlantic University, 1978-79; Satellite Operations Engineer, Lockheed Missiles & Space Company, 1979-81; Vice President, Integrity Electronics & Research, Inc, Buffalo, NY, 1983-; Supervisor of Women's Health Club, Northeast YMCA, 1975-77; Erie County Coordinator for Election News Coverage, NBC Television Network, 1976-77; Academic Assessor, Allentown Youth

Services Consortium, 1983-84; Teacher/Activities Coordinator, Frederick Academy of the Visitation, 1970-73; Special Tutor/Academic Counselor, New York State Education Department, Office of Vocational Rehabilitation, 1982-84; Editorial Staff (Reporter/Announcer), WMSM Radio Station, 1969-70; Freelance Journalism, 1970-. *Publications:* Book: The Nonsmoker's Companion, 1988; Numerous articles to professional journals; Conference presentations (videos). *Memberships include:* American Institute of Aeronautics and Astronautics; New York Academy of Science; American Association for the Advancement of Science; and many others. *Honours:* Kodak Fellowship Research grant, 1986-88; Maryland State Senatorial Scholarship, 1969; National Honor Society, 1969; National Merit Association, 1969. *Hobbies:* Yoga; Dance; Tai Chi; Poetry; Mathematics. *Address:* Integrity Electronics & Research, Inc, 558 Breckenridge Street, Buffalo, NY 14222, USA.

SURLES Georgina, b. 16 Aug. 1957, Chicago, Illinois, USA. Dance Instructor (Ballet, Modern, Jazz). m. John Landovsky, 23 Aug. 1986. *Education:* BA, Dance, University of Illinois, Urbana-Champaign, 1979. *Appointments:* Larry Richardson Dance Company, 1980; Duluth Ballet Company, 1980-82; Ballet Hawaii, 1982-83; Member, Assistant Director, Hawaii State Ballet, 1983-. *Creative works include:* Choreography: Zobo, Duluth Ballet; Time Cycles, Ballet Hawaii; Prayer, Grecian Winds, Winter Afternoon, Hawaii State Ballet. *Memberships:* University of Illinois Alumni Association. *Hobbies:* Painting; Music; Theatre; Film & Film Making. *Address:* 501 Hahaione Street 1-1C, Honolulu, Hawaii 96825, USA.

SURTEES Virginia, b. London, England. Author. m. (1) Sir Ashley Clarke, GCMG (divorced), (2) David Craig, OBE (divorced). *Publications:* D G Rossetti, A Catalogue Raisonne, 1971; Sublime & Instructive, 1972; Charlotte Canning, 1975; The Beckford Inheritance, 1977; Reflections of a Friendship, 1979; The Diary of Ford Madox Brown, 1981; The Ludovisi Goddess, 1984; Jane Welsh Carlyle, 1986; The Artist and the Autocrat, 1988; Contributor To: Burlington Magazine; Apollo; Princeton University Library Chronicle. *Membership:* Fellow, Royal Society of Literature. *Address:* c/o Royal Bank of Scotland, 43 Curzon Street, London W1, England.

SUTER Carol J., b. 5 Mar. 1949, Highland Park, Michigan, USA. Attorney; Administrator. m. Eugene W. Suter, 21 Mar. 1970, 2 daughters. *Education:* BSc, Education, Bowling Green State University, Ohio, 1971; JD, Ohio Northern University, 1981. *Appointments:* High School Teacher, English & Speech, 1971-78; Attorney, Schroeder, Schroeder & O'Malley, Ottawa, Ohio, 1979-84; Development Director, General Conference, Mennonite Church, Newton, Kansas, 1984-88; Director, External Affairs, Pettit College of Law, Ohio Northern University, 1988-. *Publication:* Managing a Law Practice, in Ohio State Bar Association Desk Manual, 1984. *Memberships:* Bar Associations: Ohio State, NW Ohio, Putnam County (past president), American (past board, Law Student Division); Ohio Supreme Court Committee on Judicial Qualification, 1983-84; Trustee, General Conference, Mennonite Church, 1980-83. *Honour:* Gold Key, American Bar Association, Chicago, 1981. *Hobbies:* Politics; Religion. *Address:* Pettit College of Law, Ohio Northern University, Ada, Ohio 45810, USA.

SUTHERLAND Jeanne Edith, b. 9 Dec. 1927, Hay on Wye, Hereford, England. m. Iain Johnstone Macbeth Sutherland, 15 Oct. 1955, 1 son, 2 daughters. *Education:* BA, London, 1948; MA, London, 1977; RSA Diploma, Teaching of English as Foreign Language, 1979. *Appointments:* Barclays Bank, 1948-49; Air Ministry, 1949-51; Diplomatic Service, 1951-56; Part-time Lecturer, Polytechnic of North London, 1966-78. *Publications:* Articles on Soviet Education, in Soviet Education Study Bulletin, 1985, 1986. *Memberships:* UK Study Group on Soviet Education, Treasurer; Greek Animal Welfare Fund, Chairman. *Hobbies:* Literature;

Theatre; Art; Travel; Languages; Tennis. *Address:* 24 Cholmeley Park, London N6 5EU, England.

SUTHERLAND June Conran, b. 23 June 1934, Melbourne, Australia. Midwife. m. Bruce Sutherland, 11 Mar. 1958, 4 sons. *Education:* SRN,Royal Childrens' Hospital, 1955; SCM, Queen Victoria Hospital, 1956; IWC, Berry St Foundling Home, 1957. *Appointments:* Victorian Health dept., 1957-59 Sister in Charge, Consultant's Rooms, 1980-83; Director, Nursing, Hawthorn Birth & Development Centre, 1984-. *Hobbies:* Tapestry; China Painting; Reading; Travel. *Address:* 29 Swinburne Avenue, Hawthorn, VIC 3122, Australia.

SUTHERLAND Sheena, b. 4 Dec. 1938, Fraserburgh, Scotland. Clinical Virologist. m. Stewart R. Sutherland, 1 Aug. 1964, 1 son, 2 daughters. *Education:* MB,ChB, 1963; MRCPath, 1982. *Appointments:* Registrar, Institute of Virology, Glasgow, 1975-77; Lecturer, Virology Department, Middlesex Hospital Medical School, London, 1978-84; Consultant Virologist, Dulwich Public Health Laboratory, & Honorary Senior Lecturer, King's College School of Medicine & Dentistry, London University, 1985-. *Publications:* Articles, viral topics, various scientific journals. *Memberships:* Royal Society of Medicine; Society for General Microbiology. *Hobbies:* Gardening; Weaving; Visual Arts.

SUTHERLAND Veronica Evelyn, b. 25 Apr. 1939. H.M. Ambassador. m. Alex James Sutherland, 29 Dec. 1981. *Education:* BA, German, London University, 1961; MA, German, Southampton University, 1965. *Appointments:* Third, later Second Secretary, Foreign Office, 1965; Second later First Secretary, Copenhagen, 1967; FCO, 1970; First Secretary, New Delhi, 1975; FCO, 1978; Counsellor, Permanent UK Delegate to UNESCO, 1981; FCO, 1984; HM Ambassador, Abidjan, 1987-. *Honours:* CMG, Birthday Honours, 1988. *Address:* c/o FCO, London SW1A 2AH, England.

SUTHERLAND SMITH Beverley Margaret, b. 1 July 1935, Melbourne, Australia. Food Writer; Author; Teacher. m. 10 May 1959, divorced 1982, 2 sons, 2 daughters. *Appointments:* Own Cooking School, 1967; Food Writer, The Age, Melbourne, 1978; Restaurant Critic, 1980; ABC Radio, 1987. *Publications:* A Taste for All Seasons; A Taste of Class; A Taste in Time; The Best of Beverley; A Taste of Summer; Bread & Beyond; Gourmet Gifts; Chocolates & Petit Fours; The Complete Beverley Sutherland Cookbook; The Beverley Sutherland Smith Collectors Edition; A Taste of Indpendence; Contributor to journals and magazines including: Gourmet & Epicurean. *Memberships:* Wine Press Club; Chaine Des Rotisseurs, Grand Dame; International Association of Cooking Professionals; Ladies Wine & Food Society, Foundation Member, Food Master. *Honours:* Gold Book Award, for a Taste in Time. *Hobbies:* Painting; Tennis. *Address:* 29 Regent St., Mt. Waverley, 3149 VIC, Australia.

SUTLIFF Joyce Elaine, b. 9 Oct. 1939, Moran, Kansas, USA. Attorney; Hearing Officer. m. Gerald M. Sutliff, 26 July 1966, 1 son, 2 daughters. *Education:* Long Beach City College, 1963; JD, John F. Kennedy University School of Law, 1985. *Appointments:* Lecturer, self- representation, various public employment positions, 1974-78; Self-employed Advocate, Labour Relations & Administrative Hearings, 1974-85; Arbitrator & Mediator, 1981-; Hearing Officer, Mental Health Hearings, 1982-; Attorney, Family & Criminal Law, 1985-. *Publications:* Training material: Mental Health Hearing Officers & Physicians; Labour Representation in Public Schools. *Memberships include:* Public member, Processing Strawberry Advisory Board of California; Past member, California Apple Advisory Board; Consumer Advisory Committee, Department of Food & Agriculture; Co-Chair, Volunteer Liaison Committee, California Community Dispute Services; National Association of Women Executives; California Women Lawyers; Commonwealth Club of California. *Honours:* Special award, Lindsay Junior Museum, 1973; Biographical recognitions. *Hobbies:* International relations; Studying other languages & cultures (speaks some Spanish, Japanese, Russian); Hand stitchery; Gourmet cooking; Computer games; Gardening. *Address:* 1735 North Broadway, Walnut Creek, California 94596, USA.

SUTTLE Helen Jayson, b. 13 Dec. 1925, Plattsburgh, NY, Clinton County, USA. Classroom Teacher. 1 daughter. *Education:* BA, Limestone College, 1957-61; MAT, WinthroP College, 1973; Psychology, University of LaVerne, 1980; University of South Carolina, 1985. *Appointments:* Teacher, ZL Madden Elementary, Spartanburg District No 7, 1961-71; Teacher, West Junior High School, Cherokee County District No 1, 1971-80; Teacher, L L Vaughan Elementary School, Cherokee County District No 1, 1980-88. *Publications:* The Twilight Hour, 1959-60; The Shower, 1960-61. *Memberships:* President, Limestone College Alumni Association, 1978-80; President Cherokee Chapter, Limestone College Alumni Association, 1970-74; AAUW, 1982-83 and 1983-84; Charter Member, Limestone College Fountain Club, 1972; Chairman Cherokee County Republican Party, 1978-; President Sacred Heart Women's Guild, 1970 and 1974; President, Sacred Heart Seniors Club, 1987-; Cherokee County Education Association, 1971-88; President, Cherokee Chapter, International Reading Association, 1988; Tutor, Laubach Literacy Association, 1988-. *Honours:* Kalosophia, Limestone College, 1961; Kappa Delta Epsilon, Limestone College, 1959; Teacher of the Year, L L Vaughan Elementary School, 1988; Service to Church & Community, Dunton United Methodist Church, 1986; Presidential Achievement Award, President Ronald Reagan, 1982; Medal of Merit, Presidential Task Force, President Ronald Reagan, 1980; Certificate of Appreciation, SC Education Association, 1978 and 1979; Plaque of Sincere Appreciation, Limestone College Alumni Association, 1980. *Hobbies:* Gardening; Painting, sketching; Writing. *Address:* 201 Trenton Road, York Hills, Gaffney, South Carolina 29340, USA.

SUTTON Beverly Jewell, b. 27 May 1932, Rockford, USA. Physician. m. H. Eldon Sutton, 7 July 1962, 2 daughters. *Education:* MD, University of Michigan Medical School, 1957; Postdoctoral Study. *Appointments:* Director, Child and Adolescent Psychiatric Service, Austin State Hospital, 1962-. *Memberships:* Fellow: American Academy of Child and Adolescent Psychiatry, American Academy of Pediatrics, American Psychiatric Association; Member, American Medical Association; Texas Medical Association; ASHG; Texas Society of Child and Adolescent Psychiatry, President, 1979. *Address:* 1103 Gaston, Austin, TX 78703, USA.

SUTTON Norma Sams, b. 11 June 1952, Chicago, USA. Attorney. 1 son. *Education:* BA, 1974; MA 1976; JD 1980. *Appointments:* Leagal Assistant, North American Co., 1977-80; Judicial Clerk, Appellate Court, 1980-82; Corporate Counsel, Soft Sheen Products, 1982-85; Managing Attorney, Digital Equipment Coporation, 1985- *Publications:* Confessions of the Unserious, Management Strategy Newsletter, 1985; We Can Have It All - or Can We?, Illinois State Bar Association Young Lawyers Newsletter. *Memberships:* Illinois State Bar Association, Young Lawyers Division, Vice Chair, 1987-88, Secretary, 1986-87; American Bar Association, Young Lawyers Division; etc. *Honours:* Regional Finalist, President's commission, White House Fellowships, 1983; etc. *Hobbies:* Theatre; Piano; Foreign Languages. *Address:* 1227 W. Lunt, Chicago, IL 60626, USA.

SUTTON Sharon Egretta, b. 18 Feb. 1941, Cinti, Ohio, USA. Architectural Educator; Graphic Artist. *Education:* B.Mus., University of Hartford, 1963; M.ARch., Columbia University, 1973; MA, PhD, psychology, M.Phil., City University of New York. *Appointments:* Professional Musician, 1963-68; Apprentice Architect, 1973-76; Practicing Architect, 1976- 84; Architectural Educator: Pratt Institute, Columbia University, University of Cincinnati, University

of Michigan, 1975-. *Publications:* Learning Through the Built Environment, 1985; articles in various journals. *Memberships:* American Institute of Architects; American Psychological Association. *Honours:* Project Director, NEA Design Arts Grant, 1989-90; W K Kellog Foundation; NEA Design Research Recognition Award, 1983; Danforth Graduate Fellowship; Metropolitan Applied Research Centre Research Fellow; American Institute of Architects Travel Award. *Hobbies:* Opera; Plants; Small Animals. *Address:* College of Architecture & Urban Planning, University of Michigan, Ann Arbor, MI 48109, USA.

SUTTON-SALLEY Virginia Belmont, Corporation Executive. *Education:* Rollins College (as special student in drama), Florida. *Appointments:* Junior Partner, Sutton Jewelry Compania, Miami, 1948-50; Professional singer, Gloria Manning (professional name), featured singer in Vincent Lopez Orchestra and Ben Ribble Orchestra, Statler Hotel Chain and Club engagements USA & Canada, Radio New York City & Miami, 1951-60; Guest on Joe Franklin Show, WOR TV, New York City, 1984; various engagements, 1971-; Owner, Wiscasset Antiques, Maine, 1965-; Historian, The Good News Publication, Dade County, Florida, 1986-. *Publications:* Royal Bayreuth China, 1969, summplement 1980 (co-author); Articles to professional journals. *Memberships:* National Society of Arts & Letters; Former Member, Board of AGVA; Former Member, Vice Chairman, Metro Zoning Appeals Board, Dade County, Florida; Founder, twice President, Theatre Arts League of Greater Miami, (Life Membe); Founder, President, Junior Theatre Guild, Miami; Young Patronesses of the Opera, Admissions Committee (Life Member); League of American Pen Women. *Hobbies:* Swimming; Croquet; Flying. *Address:* Sutton-Manning Corporation, Suite 700, 100 N Biscayne Boulevard, Miami, FL 33132, USA.

SVETLOVA Marina, b. 3 May 1922, France. Ballerina; Educator; Choreographer. *Education:* Student, Vera Trefilova, Paris, 1930-36; L Egorova & M Kschessinska, Paris, 1936-39; A Vilzak, New York City, 1940-57. *Appointments:* Debut, Paris Opera, 1932; Baby Ballerina, Original Ballet, Rousse de Monte Carlo, 1939-41; Guest Ballerina, Ballet Theatre, Metropolitan Opera Tour, 1942; Prima Ballerina, Metropolitan Opera Company, New York, USA, 1943-50; New York City Opera, 1950; New York City Opera, 1950-52; appeared, Jacob's Pillow Summer Festival, 1949; Own Concert Group under management, Columbia Artists Management, 1944-58; National Artists Corporation, 1958-69; Ballet Tours in USA 1944-; Guest Ballerina: London's Festival Ballet, England, 1953; Teatro dell Opera, Rome, Italy, 1953; National Opera, Stockholm, Sweden, 1955; Suomi Opera Helsinki, Finland, 1956; Het Nederland Ballet, Holland, 1954; Cork Irish Ballet, 1955; Paris Opera Comique France, 1958; London Palladium England 1959-60; Appeared in: Les Sylphides, 1943; Bluebeard, 1943; Balustrade; Giselle, 1953; Pas de Quatre; Swan Lake; appearances in various classical ballets; Choreographer: Seattle Opera, 1961-62; Dallas Civic Opera, 1964-67; Kansas City Performing Arts Foundation, 1965-67; Founder and Director Svetlova Dance Center, Dorset, Vermont, 1965-; Fort Worth Opera, 1967-; Chairman, Full Professor of Ballet at Indiana University School of Music, Bloomington, Indiana 1970-. *Publications:* Contributor, numerous articles in professional journals. *Memberships:* many professional organisations. *Honours:* Doctor Honorous Causa, 1988 from Federation Française de Danse Minister of Culture. *Address:* 2100 Maxwell Lane, Bloomington, IN 47401, USA.

SVOBODA Margaret Ann, b. 31 Mar. 1952, Cleveland, Ohio, USA. Assistant Treasurer. *Education:* BS summa cum laude, Education, Cleveland State University, 1973. *Appointments:* Assistant Analyst, 1973-78, Manager, Information Systems, 1978-84, District Manager, Regulatory Accounting, 1986-87, Assistant Treasurer, 1987-, Ohio Bell Telephone Company, Cleveland, Ohio; Director, Systems Development, Ameritech Billing Systems, 1984-86.

Memberships: Cleveland Treasurers Club; National Society of Rate of Return Analysts; Cleveland Society of Security Analysts. *Honours:* Pentilicus Honorary Society, 1973. *Hobby:* Pianist. *Address:* 45 Erieview Plaza, Cleveland, OH 44114, USA.

SWABY Pamela Larserila (Lady), b. 8 Nov. 1929, Kingstown, St Vincent, West Indies. Managing Director. m. Lure Alva Michael Ashton Swaby, 14 Nov. 1948. 2 daughters. *Appointments:* North American Sales Manager, Jamaica Association of Villas & Apartments, New York, USA, 1969-75; Director of Sales, Ocho Rios Intercontinental Hotel, Jamaica, 1975-76; Reservations Manager, Calypso Holidays, Toronto, Canada, 1976-77; General Manager, Trident Hotel & Villas, Port Antonio, Jamaica, 1978-79; Sales Manager, Dream Inn, Santa Cruz, California, 1982-83; Managing Director, Beach Club Colony, Grand Cayman, 1986-. *Memberships:* Past President/First Woman President, Cayman Island Hotel & Condominium Association; Pat Marketing Chairman, Tourism Advisory Board, Grand Cayman, Board Member, 1984-. *Honours:* Marketing Award, Cayman Islands Hotel & Condo Ass, 1986; Award for Outstanding Contribution to development of tourism in Cayman and Little Cayman, 1989; Dame of Grace, Grand Sovereign Dynastic Hospitaller, 1988; Order of St John, Knights of Maga, Dame of Grace, Sovereign Order of the Oak, 1989. *Hobbies:* Public speaking; Swimming; Sewing; Stamps and coin collecting; Cooking. *Address:* 3601 Upperdale Park, Mississaugh, Ontario, L5L 3A6, Canada.

SWAN Rita Marie, b. 27 June 1943, Ogden, Utah, USA. Child Protection Promoter. m. Douglas A. Swan, 25 Aug. 1963, 1 son (deceased), 2 daughters. *Education:* BA, English, Kansas State Teachers College, 1963; MA, English, University of Wisconsin, 1965; PhD, English, Vanderbilt University, 1975. *Appointments:* Editor, Environmental Programme, University of Vermont, Burlington, 1973-75; Assistant Professor of English, Jamestown College, Jamestown, North Dakota, 1979-82; President, CHILD Inc, (Children's Healthcare Is a Legal Duty), Sioux City, Iowa; TV appearances; Radio interviews. *Publications:* Christian Science: Threat to Children?, 1980; Faith Healing, Christian Science, and the Medical Care of Children, 1983; Laws Protect Parents Who Let Children Die, 1983; Christian Science, Faith Healing and the Law, 1984; The Law Should Protect All Children, 1987; Spiritual Healing Claims Wither on the Vine of Investigation, 1988; Faith Healing Sects and Children's Rights to Medical Care, workshop synopsis; Barriers to the Medical Care of Children: How You Can Help, 1989; Fragile Life: Religious Beliefs that Kill Children, 1989; The Laws Response when Religious Beliefs against Medical Care Impact on Children, in press. *Memberships:* Affiliate, National Council against Fraud; American Family Foundation; Cult Awareness Network; National Association of Counsel for Children; Justice for Children Inc; Siouxland Council on Child Abuse and Neglect. *Honours:* Various college scholarships, 1961-64, 1967-68; Award for Excellent Teaching, 1982; Research Grant, National Council against Health Fraud; 6 live and 5 filmed appearances on national TV. *Hobbies:* Riding; Camping. *Address:* CHILD Inc, Box 2604, Sioux City, IA 51106, USA.

SWANBERG Carol Jean, b. 28 Oct. 1961, New York City, USA. Assistant Director of Admissions. *Education:* BA, 1983, MBA Candidate, University of Pittsburgh. *Appointments:* Administrative Specialist, Office of Admissions & Student Aid, 1984-85; System Administrator, Katz Graduate School of Business, 1985-89, University of Pittsburgh; Assistant Director of Admissions, Katz Graduate School of Business, 1989-. *Memberships:* National Association of Female Executives; American Management Association; International Platform Association. *Hobbies:* Tailoring; Consulting; Part-time Teaching. *Address:* Joseph M. Katz Graduate School of Business, University of Pittsburgh, 315 Mervis Hall, Pittsburgh, PA 15260, USA.

SWANTON H Rae, b. 9 Oct. 1918, Fibre, Michigan, USA. Housewife. m. Bradford Y Swanton, 5 Aug. 1939.

1 son, 2 daughters. *Education:* Attended courses at Michigan State University, Michigan Technical University and Office of Civil Defense Staff College, 1965-69. *Appointments:* Post Clerk 1936-37, Receptionist & Private Secretary 1937-38, Associates Investment Co, Detroit; Switchboard Operator/Receptionist/Secretary, 1937-38, General Disc Corporation, Detroit; Secretary, Burns Chiropractic Clinic; Private Secretary, Bureau of Social Aid, Bay City, 1952-54; Financial Secretary, 1st Presbyterian Church, Bay City, 1956-58; Part-time, Mary Kay Beauty Consultant, 1979-87. *Creative works:* Founder and Editor, Quantor, 1st Presbyterian Church Newspaper, 1957-58; Youth for Understanding Script, Channel 5 TV, Bay City. Paintings: City on the Horizon; The Fishing Wharf; Weeping Dove; Evangeline. *Memberships:* Michigan State Federation of Womens Clubs, State Communications Chairman, 1958-60; Civil Defense USA, 1969; Bay Co Shelter Instructor for Civil Defense, 1965-66; Shelter Coordinator, Bay City, 1969-70; Charter Member, Repbulican Presidential Task force, 1982-; Rudyard Twp Senior Citizens Services Inc, Founder and Coordinator, 1984-88. *Honours:* Thyra Bixby Radio & TV Award, Michigan State Federation of Womens Clubs, 1959; Certificate of Appreciation, Michigan 74th District Court, 1974; American Security Council Education Foundation, Special Recognition Award of Center for International Security Studies, 1979; Honored by Special Invitation to attend 1988 Republican National Convention from Chairman Fahrenkopf; Name entered on the United States Postal Register for Clerks on July 1, 1988-90; Chippewa County Republican Committee Chair Person, 1989-90. *Hobbies:* Music; Gardening; Painting; Fishing; Hunting; Bowling; Playing cards; Family. *Address:* R2, Box 848, Biscuit Road, Rudyard, MI 49780, USA.

SWEANEY Anne Landoy, b. 18 June 1943, Darjeeling, India. Home Economist; Professor. m. David R. Sweaney, 7 Sept. 1970, 2 sons, 2 daughters. *Education:* BA, Home Economics Education, University of Northern Iowa, USA, 1965; MA, Home Economics Education, 1970, PhD, Business Administration, 1977, University of Alabama. *Appointments:* Home Economics Teacher, Mason City, Iowa, USA, 1965-69; Instructor, University of Alabama, 1970-74; Assistant Professor, Housing Specialist, North Carolina State University, Raleigh, 1977-78; Home Economics Consultant, Thermador Waste King, Salinas, California, 1980; Associate Professor, Housing and Consumer Economics Department, College of Home Economics, University of Georgia, Athens, 1981-. *Publications:* Refereed proceedings including: Including preschool children in family work (with C Wallings), 1983; Preschool Children's Perceptions of their Residential Environment: Does Crowding Affect Quality of Life (with C R Wallinga and M Inman), 1985; Studying Planned Communities Through Site Visits (with C B Meeks), 1986; The Relationship of Housing Condition and Satisfaction to Widowhood, 1988; Articles in refereed and other journals; Reports. *Memberships:* Board of Directors, Research Chair, National and State Membership Chair, American Association of Housing Educators; American Home Economics Association, Building Committee 1988; American Council on Consumer Interests, Local Arrangements Committee 1984; Phi Upsilon Omicron Alumni; Georgia Home Economics Association; College Educators of Household Equipment; International Association of Housing Science; Electrical Women's Roundtable. *Honours:* Creswell Award, College of Home Economics Alumni Association, 1986; Outstanding Home Economist, Georgia Home Economics Association, 1987; Gamma Sigma Delta; Beta Gamma Sigma; Julia Kiene Fellowship, Electrical Women's Roundtable 25th Anniversary. *Hobbies:* Collecting Flow Blue-China; Reading self-help books. *Address:* College of Home Economics, Department of Housing and Consumer Economics, Room 252 Dawson Hall, University of Georgia, Athens, GA 30602, USA.

SWEDIN Donna Jean, b. 4 Apr. 1955, Groton, Connecticut, USA. Management Consultant/Retained Search. *Education:* BS, University of Connecticut, 1977. *Appointments:* Counsellor, Info Line of S.E.Connecticut,

1977-78; Coordinator, Literacy Volunteers of S.E.Connecticut, 1978-79; Director, Info Line of N.E.Connecticut, 1979-82; Human Resource Generalist, Motts Supermarkets Inc, 1982-84; Director of Human Resources, Actmedia Inc, 1984-86; President, QVS International, 1986-. *Memberships:* Board of Directors, Executive Committee, Academy Theatre; Executive Committee, Business Volunteers for the Arts; Executive Committee, N.W. Branch, Atlanta Chamber of Commerce; Cobb Chamber of Commerce; Arts Alive Steering Committee; Kappa Kappa Gamma Alumni Association. *Hobbies:* Walking; Theatre; Reading. *Address:* 1640-21 Powers Ferry Road, Atlanta, GA 30067, USA.

SWEENEY Beatrice Marcy, b. 11 Aug. 1914, Boston, USA. Biologist. m. 3 Nov. 1961, 2 sons, 2 daughters. *Education:* Smith College, 1936; PhD, Radcliffe College, 1942. *Appointments:* Postdoctoral Fellow, Mayo Foundation, 1942-43; Research Biologist, Scrupps Institution of Oceanography, 1948-61; Lecturer, Yale University, 1962-67; Professor, University of California, 1968-. *Publications:* Rhythmic Phenomena in Plants, 2 editions; 145 research papers in scientific journals. *Memberships:* American Institute of Biologicla Sciences, President 1979-80; American Association for the Advancement of Science, Fellow, 1965, Pacific Section President 1979-80; American Society for Photobiology, President, 1979-80. *Honours:* Phi Beta Kappa; Sigma Xi; Honorary Doctorates: Umea University, Sweden, 1985, Knox College, 1986. *Hobbies:* Photography; Skiing; Flying. *Address:* Dept. of Biological Sciences, University of California, Santa Barbara, CA 93106, USA.

SWEENEY Ermengarde Collins, b. 3 Nov. 1922, Texas, USA. Financier. m. William Wallace Walton, 8 Nov. 1940, 1 son, 2 daughters. *Education:* Texas School of Fine Arts. *Appointments:* Independent Invester. *Publications:* Produced an exceptional line of Arabian horses through selective breeding on careful genetic study. *Memberships:* Arabian Horse Club of Texas, Publicity Chairman; Texas Humane Information Network, Region 5 Director, Board of Directors; Corpus Christi Kennel Club, Secretary; Paws, Gulf Coast Humane Society, President; Advisory Board to City Council on Animal Control. *Honours:* Recipient, numerous honours, awards, ribbons and trophies. *Hobbies:* Gardening; Animal Welfare; Art; Antiques. *Address:* 3461 Floyd, Corpus Christi, TX 78411, USA.

SWEENEY Ernestine Kay, b. 26 Oct. 1959, Savannah, Georgia, USA. Registered Nurse. Divorced. *Educaiton:* AA, Nursing Science, Northwestern State University. *Appointments:* Bossier Medical Centre, 1982-, Orthopedic Surgery, 1982-86, General Medical 1986-87, Cardiac Care, Night Charge Nurse, 1987-. *Publications:* Contributor to professional journals. *Memberships:* National Associaitron of Orthopedic Nurses; American Association Critical Care Nurses; International Order of the Eastern Star; National Organisaiton for Women. *Honours:* Vice Chairman, Clinical Services Council Nursing Service Department, Bossier Medical Centre, 1988-. *Hobbies:* Reading; Body Building; Travel. *Address:* 3314 Schuler Drive, Bossier City, LA 71112, USA.

SWEETLAND Loraine Fern Bloomfield, b. 13 Aug. 1933, Morristown Corners, Vermont, USA. Director of Library Services. m. 1 July 1950, 1 son (deceased), 1 daughter (1 deceased). *Education:* BS, Elementary Education, Columbia Union College, 1968; MSLS (Library Science), Syracuse University, 1973. *Appointments:* Teacher, 1st and 2nd grade, Bettsville SDA School, Bettsville, Maryland, 1960-67; Assistant Librarian, Cataloguer, Vermont Technical College, Randolph Center, Vermont, 1968-70; Middle School Librarian, city schools, Barre, Vermont, 1970-74; Teacher, Principal, Central Vermont SDA School, Barre, Vermont, 1974-76; Teacher, Principal, Brookland SDA School, Bridgeport, Connecticut, 1976-81; Medical Librarian, Washington Adventist Hospital, Tahoma Park, Maryland, 1981-85; Director of Library Services, SDA

World Headquarters, Takoma Park, 1985-. *Memberships:* American Library Association; Trustee, Randolph, Vermont, Public Library, 1970-71; Secretary, National Metropolitan Area Hospital Council, Librarians Section, DC, 1985; Seventh Day Adventist Library, ASDAL; Medical Library Consultant, Baltimore, 1983-85. *Hobbies:* Reading; Sewing; Gardening; Photography; Computing and computers; Church work; Nutrition seminars. *Address:* 10182 High Ridge Road, Laurel, MD 20723, USA.

SWEGER Glenda Lee, b. 26 July 1946, Harrisburg, Pennsylvania, USA. Teacher. *Education:* BS, Indiana University, 1968; MA, California State University, Fullerton, 1981. *Appointments:* Teacher, Greensburg-Salem Unified School District, Pennsylvania, 1968-69; English teacher, Covina Valley Unified School District, California, 1969-; Publications adviser, Covina, 1970-. *Publication:* Male & Female Reporters: Differences in Readers' Perceptions. *Memberships include:* Parent Teacher Organisation; Orange County AIDS Foundation; Statue of Liberty Foundation; Ellis Island Foundation; National Education Association; California Teachers' Association; Southland Council Teachers of English; National Council Teachers of English; Columbia Scholastic Press Advisors Association; Journalism Education Association; National Wildlife Federation; Covina-Valley Unified Education Association. *Honours:* Chair, Accreditation Committee, 1988-; Mentor Teacher, 1988-; Member, Curriculum Development Advisory Board, 1988; Recipient, SGV Educators' Grant, 1986; Board of Directors, California Scholastic Publications Associations, 1972-82. *Hobbies:* Golf; Writing poetry; Cycling; Reading. *Address:* 3372 Rowena Drive, Rossmoor, California 90720, USA.

SWENSON Karen, b. 29 July 1936, New York City, USA. Professor; Writer. m. 23 Nov. 1957, 1 son. *Education:* BA, Barnard College, 1959; MA, 1971, ABD, New York University. *Appointments:* Lecturer, Instructor, City College of New York, 1968-76; Poet in Residence: Clark University, 1976, Skidmore College, 1977-78, University of Idaho, 1979-80, University of Denver, 1979-80; Assistant Professor, Scripps College, 1980-82; City College, City of New York, 1982-. *Publications:* An Attic of Ideals, 1974; East-West, 1980; A Sense of Direction, in press. *Memberships:* Associated Writing Programres; Modern Lanuage Association; PEN; Writer's Union; Poetry Society of America. *Honours:* Trans Atlantic Fellowship, 1974; Nominated for Pushcart Prize, 1986, 1987; Runner Up, Arvan Award, & Ann Stanford Award, 1988; Honorable Mention, Pushcart Prize, 1988. *Hobbies:* Travel; Gardening. *Address:* 430 State St., Brooklyn, NY 11217, USA.

SWIETLICZKO Irena, b. 29 Feb. 1923, Aleksandrow, Poland. Physician. m. 30 Aug. 1949. *Education:* Physician's Diploma, Medical Academy, Lodz, 1951; Doctorate, 1960; Assistant Professor, 1964; Full Professor, 1977. *Appointments include:* Research fellow, Fight for Sight programme, Bascom Palmer Eye Institute, University of Miami School of Medicine, USA, 1966-67; Head, Ophthalmological Department, Medical Academy, Lodz, 1972-. *Creative work:* Research, 150 scientific papers in national & international periodicals, neuro-ophthalmology. *Memberships:* Chairman, Lodz branch, & vice president, Central Board, Polish Society of Ophthalmologists; Polish Medical Society; Committee of Ophthalmological Sciences, Polish Academy of Sciences. *Honours:* Gold Cross of Merit, 1974; Cavalier's Cross, Polonia Restituta, 1978. *Hobbies:* Operatic music; Touring. *Address:* Szpital Barlickiego, Klinika Okulistyczna AM, 90-153 Lodz, Kopcinszkiego 22, Poland.

SWIFT Carolyn, b. 21 Sept. 1923, London, England. Writer; Former Actress & Theatre Director. m. Alan P. Simpson, 1947 (deceased), 3 daughters (1 deceased). *Education:* Kerr-Sanders Secretarial College. *Appointments include:* Secretary, British Council, 1941-46; Member, Company, Gate Theatre, Dublin, Ireland, 1947; Theatres, London & Limerick, 1948; Co-founder with husband, Pike Theatre Producations, Dublin 1953-

61; Director, Writers Seminars 1967, Script Reader 1967-68, 1972-79, Abbey Theatre, Dublin; Script Reader, Gate Theatre, Dublin, 1969-71; Script Editor, Radio-Telefis Eireann (Irish TV), 1961-64, 1967-70; Director, Muserights Ltd (theatrical scripts 1964-71. *Creative work includes:* Stage: Plays: The Millstone 1951, Resistance 1977, Lady G 1987; Revues, Dublin & London, 1953-76; Puppet plays, Ballad Shows, Pantomime. Ballet Critic, Sunday Independent, 1953-56; Dance correspondent, Irish Times, 1979-; 5 radio plays, 1979-; Numerous Educational Radio Dramas, Drama Series, Serials, 1978-; Short Story, Commercials, Radio talks, Films, song Lyrics. Series, Children's Adventure Books, 1981-; Various Children's Stories; Features, Fiction, Book Reviews, various papers & journals; Autobiography, Stage by Stage, 1985. *Honours:* Awards for Lyrics, Castlebar, 1967; Almeria, 1971. *Hobbies:* Archaeology; Hill Walking. *Address:* 121 Upper Leeson Street, Dublin 4, Republic of Ireland.

SWIFT Mary Grace, b. 3 Aug. 1927, Bartlesville, Oklahoma, USA. History Professor. *Education:* BS 1956, MA 1960, Creighton University; PhD, Notre Dame University, 1967. *Appointments:* History Department, Loyola University, New Orleans, 1966-. *Publications:* The Art of The Dance in the USSR, 1968; A Loftier Flight, 1974; With Bright Wings, 1976; Belles and Beaux on their Toes, 1980. *Honour:* De la Torre Bueno Prize for best manuscript on dance, 1973. *Address:* Box 192, Loyola University, New Orleans, LA 70118, USA.

SWIT Loretta, b. 4 Nov. 1939, Passaic, New Jersey, USA. Actress. *Education:* American Academy of Dramatic Arts; Gene Frankel Repertoire Theatre, New York. *Creative Works:* Stage appearances include: A Do, A Do; The Mystery of Edwin Drood; Any Wednesday; The Odd Couple; Mame; The Apple Tree; Same Time Next Year. Films include: Stand Up and Be Counted, 1972; Freebie and the Bean, 1974; Race with the Devil, 1975; S.O.B., 1980; Beer, 1984; Whoops Apocalypse, 1985. Television: MASH, 1972-83; Shirts/Skins; Hostage Heart; Coffeeville; Superman; The Loveboat Movie; Mirror, Mirror; Valentine; Friendships, Secrets and Ties; The Love Tapes; The Kid From Nowhere; Cagney and Lacey (played Cagney in the TV movie); Games Mother Never Taught You; First Affair; The Election; Dreams of Gold; The Best Christmas Pageant Ever; Miracles of Moreaux; Gunsmoke; Hawaii Five-O; Mission Impossible; The Doctors; Cade's County; Love, American Style; Bonanza; Mannix; The Perry Como Show; Tony Orlando and Dawn; Sonny and Cher; The Dolly Parton Show; The Muppet Show; Bob Hope Christmas Special. *Memberships:* AFTRA; Screen Actors Guild; Actors Equity. *Address:* c/o William Morris Agency, 151 El Camino Avenue, Beverly Hills, CA 90212, USA.

SYLVESTER Doreen R, b. 21 Jan. 1947, Brigg, Lincolnshire, England. Freelance Artist. m. 10 July 1983. *Education:* Diploma, London Art College, 1968. *Appointments:* Freelance Illustrator, 1970-. *Publications:* Loveliness of Earth & Trees, 1969; Over 1000 paintings, drawings, prints. *Memberships:* Founder Member, International Poetry Society; Associate, South Humberside & Lincolnshire Artist Society; Poetry Foundation. *Honours:* 2nd Prize, Poetry Day, London School of Economics, 1967; Runner Up, Vincent Bowen Poetry Award. *Hobbies:* Classical Music; Philately; Photography; Reading; Walking; Visiting Museums. *Address:* 32 St Paul's Road, Ashby, Scunthorpe, South Humberside, DN16 3DJ, England.

SYMS Sylvia, b. 1934, London, England. Actress. *Education:* Convent and Grammar School. *Career:* Film debut, 1955 in My Teenage Daughter. *Creative Works:* Films include: No Time for Tears; Birthday Present; Woman In A Dressing Gown; Ice Cold in Alex; The Devil's Disciple; Moonraker; Bachelor of Hearts; No Trees in the Street; Ferry to Hong Kong; Expresso Bongo; Conspiracy of Hearts; The World of Suzie Wong; Flame in the Streets; Victim; Quare Fellow; Punch & Judy Man; The World Ten Times Over; East of Sudan; The Eliminator; Operation Crossbow; The Big Job; Hostile

Witness; The Marauders; The White Colt; Danger Route; Run Wild, Run Free; The Desperados; The Tamarind Seed; Give Us This Day; There Goes the Bride; Absolute Beginners; A Chorus of Disapproval; Shirely Valentine. Television appearances include: The Human Jungle (series); Something to Declare; The Saint (series); The Baron (series); Bat Out of Hell; Department in Terror; Friends and Romans; Strange Report; Half-hour Story; The Root of All Evil; The Bridesmaid; Clutterbuck; Movie Quiz; My Good Woman; Looks Familiar; Love and Marriage; The Truth About Verity; I'm Bob, He's Dickie; Blankety Blank; The Story of Nancy Astor; Give Us a Clue; Sykes; Crown Court; A Murder is Announced; Murder at Lynch Cross; Intimate Contact; Rockcliffs Follies; Countdown. *Address:* c/o Barry Brown, 47 West Square, London, SE11, England.

SYROKOMLA Irena Ewa, b. 17 May 1947, Lodz, Poland. Finance Manager. divorced. 1 daughter. *Education:* English Department, University of Warsaw, Poland 1965-70, Western Ontario, Canada 1971-72; BA Honours, Sociology, University of Toronto, 1975; Certified General Accountant, 1989. *Appointments:* Office Manager 1983-85, Finance Manager 1985-, Reinforced Earth Company Ltd. *Publications:* Various articles, ageing, poverty, childlessness, in Alliancer, & Outcry, 1974-76; Poetry. *Memberships:* Certified General Accountants Association; Tax Foundation of Canada; Mensa. *Hobbies:* Gardening; Travel; Classical Music; People; Theatre. *Address:* 39 Glenora Crescent, Brampton, Ontario, Canada L6S 1E1.

SZABLYA Helen Mary (Bartha-Kovacs), b. 6 Sept. 1934, Budapest, Hungary. Writer; Columnist; Translator; Lecturer. m. John Francis Szablya, 12 June 1951, 3 sons, 4 daughters. *Education:* BA, Foreign Languages & Literature, Washington State University, USA, 1976; Diploma, Sales & Marketing Management, University of British Columbia, Canada, 1962. *Appointments:* Writer, translator, 1967-; Columnist, Catholic News, Caribbean; Inquiring Mind Lecturer, Washington Commission for Humanities, 1987-89; Faculties, Christian Writers Conference 1983-, Bellevue Community College 1987-. *Cretive work includes:* Co-author, co-producer, oral history drama, Hungary Remembered, English & Hungarian (major grant); Book, 56-os Cserkeszcsapat, 1986; Translation, Tottosy's Mind Twisters, 1987; Over 500 articles, various journals. *Memberships include:* President, Washington Press Association; American Translators Association; Authors Guild; National Writers Club; Arpad Academy; Society for Professional Journalists; Committee member, National Federation of Press Women. *Honours include:* George Washington Medal, Freedoms Foundation, 1988; Arpad Gold Medal, & Special Medal, Guardian of Liberty publisher, 1987; Various awards, National Federation of Press Women, Washington Press Association, 1983-; Senator Tom Martin Award, social or political commentary, 1979; Various grants. *Hobbies:* Children; Reading; Dancing; Swimming; Travel; Languages. *Address:* 4416 134th Place SE, Bellevue, Washington 98006, USA.

SZALAY Marianne E, b. Hungary. President, Significant Management Systems, Inc. 1 son. *Education:* BS Physical Education; BA Mathematics. *Appointments:* Regional Manager, National Medical Care Inc. In charge of Dialysis Facilities in the State of Florida and Puerto Rico. *Honours:* Player for US Table Tennis Association, 1967-72; Ranked No1 player in the Southwest in Table Tennis; Texas State Champion several times; Florida State Champion; Member of International Team Squad and ranked No 9 in the US in 1968. Recipient of the 1972 Table Tennis Barna Award. *Hobbies:* Arts; Music; Table tennis; Dancing. *Address:* 14517 Clifty Court, Tampa, Florida 33624, USA.

SZEKELY Deborah, b. 3 May 1922, Brooklyn, New York, USA. Management Consultant; Author; Voluntary Worker. m. (1) Edmond Szekely, 1939 (divorced 1969), 1 son, 1 daughter, (2) Vincent Mazzanti, 1972 (divorced 1978). *Education:* USA, Tahiti, Mexico, UK. *Appointments include:* Management Consultant: Ritz,

Paris, France; Hartford Holdings Group, Hawaii; Cunard Line; Menninger Foundation; Various multinational corporations; National Boards (past/present): National Centre, & Partners for Livable Places, Washington DC; Menninger Foundation, Kansas; Trustee, California School of Professional Psychology. Boards & Special Memberships (past/present): Founder, Combined Arts & Education Council, San Diego County, 1964; Founder, Member, University of California San Diego School of Medicine Associates; Trustee, San Diego Centre for Children; President's Circle, San Diego Museum of Art; Advisory Board, University of San Diego School of Business; Womens Athletic Adviser, San Diego State University; Numerous other appointments or affiliations, educational, community, cultural. Public Service: President's Councils, Physical Fitness & Sports, Nixon 1970-74, Ford 1975-78; Advisory Council, Small Business Administration, 1982-84; Initiator, Bipartisan Congressional Management Project, American Volunteers & American University, Washington DC, 1984-. *Publications include:* Fitness section, Ann Landers Encyclopaedia; Secrets of Golden Door, 1977, 1979-80; Golden Door Cookbook, 1983; Numerous contributions, various periodicals; Convention speaker, volunteerism, management, fitness, nutrition. *Honour:* Numerous awards & recognitions, 1976-. *Address:* Golden Door, 3085 Reynard Way, San Diego, California 92103, USA.

SZILAGYI Elizabeth Maria. b. 28 Dec. 1949, Chicago, Illinois, USA. Social Services Administrator. *Education:* BS, Social Welfare, Olivet Nazarene University, 1973. *Appointments:* Social Worker, 1980- 84, Director of Senior Services, 1984-, Proviso Council on Aging. *Memberships:* Older Adults Job Fair Comm. Operation Able, 1986-87; Proviso Coordinating Council, Sr Comm Pres. 1986-87; Vice President, 1985-86, President, 1986, Family Care Sr Companion Advisory Council. *Honour:* Registered Social Worker, Illinois, 1983-. *Hobbies:* Bicycling, Swimming, Sewing. *Address:* Illinois, USA.

SZLAGA Krystyna, b. 6 Mar. 1938, Krakow, Poland. Writer; Journalist. *Education:* Magister, Russian, Uniwersytet Jagiellonski, Krakow, 1966. *Appointment:* Journalist, Polskie Radio, 1968-. *Publications:* Poems: Korzeniami w ziemie, 1967; Dialog, 1970; Arena, 1978; Slowo Wilka, 1982; Ziemia, 1986. Plays: Utwory sceniczne, 1988; Radio plays. *Memberships:* Zwiazek Literatow Polskich; Stowarzyszenie Dziennikarzy Polskich. *Honours:* Prize for play Mielizna, Lodz, 1977; Prize m.Krakow, 1985. *Hobbies:* Theatre; Mountaineering; Skiing. *Address:* ul Ulanow 48, 60m, 31-455 Krakow, Poland.

SZPAKOWSKA Maria Matgorzata, b. 18 May 1940, Warsaw, Poland. Literary and Drama Critic; Editor; Professor. *Education:* Graduated, Polish Philology 1964, Philosophy 1966, Warsaw University; Doctor of Philosophy, 1975. *Appointments:* Assistant, Warsaw University, 1966-69; National Library in Warsaw, 1970-72; Editor of Dialog, Monthly of Theatre and Drama, 1972-; Professor, Warsaw Drama Academy, 1985-. *Publications:* Books: Swiatopoglad Stanislawa Ignacego Witkiewicza (The Outlook of Witkiewicza), 1973; O Kulturze I Znaghorach (about Culture and Medicine-Men), essays about culture theories, 1983; Current Drama and Literary Criticism in Tworczosc and Dialog. *Memberships:* PEN; ZAiKS (Society of Authors). *Honour:* Prize of Koscielscy Foundation, Geneva, Switzerland, 1976. *Hobbies:* Books; Gardening. *Address:* Aleje Ujazdowskie 47 M.14, 00536 Warsaw, Poland.

SZUBINSKI (Sally) Gale Maryanne, b. 8 Oct. 1954, Augusta, Georgia, USA. Educator. m. 11 Oct. 1975, 2 sons, 1 daughter. *Education:* BS, George Peabody College for Teachers, Nashville, Tennessee, 1975; MEd 1979, graduate study 1985, University of New Orleans. *Appointments:* Area Consultant, Special Education Services Corporation, 1982-86; Principal, St Charles Borromeo Elementary School, 1986-89; Special Educational Regional Coordinator, Louisiana State Department of Education, 1989-. *Memberships:* Vice-President, Council for Educational Diagnostic Services, Division CEC; Louisiana Association of Principals; National Association of Elementary Principals; Association for Curriculum & Development; Phi Kappa Delta; International Reading Association; National Catholic Educators Association. *Hobbies:* Reading; Dance; Tennis. *Address:* 16 Belle Helene, Destrehan, Louisiana 70047, USA.

SZUMIEL Irena, b. 10 Feb. 1936, Warsaw, Poland. Radiation Biologist. *Education:* MSc Biology 1960, PhD Biochemistry 1965, DSc 1979, Warsaw University. *Appointments:* Assistant, Biochemistry Department, Warsaw University, 1960-68; Adjunct 1968-80, Docent (Associate Professor) 1980-, Institute of Nuclear Research. *Publications:* Over 100 papers on biochemical and radiobiological topics (mostly cellular radiation biology). *Memberships:* European Society for Radiation Biology (Member of the Council); Polish Association for Radiation Research; Polish Biochemical Society; Radiological Health and Radiation Biology; Committee, Polish Academy of Sciences (President 1987-89); Editorial Board, International Journal of Radiation Biology. *Honours:* Two Awards, 1973, 1979, State Council for Atomic Energy Utilization; Three Awards, Polish Association for Radiation Research, 1976, 1982, 1986. *Hobbies:* Classic music; Books; Walks in the forest; Picking mushrooms; Dry plant bouquets. *Address:* Lotewska 14-2, PL-03-918 Warsaw, Poland.

T

TABACARU Roxandra, b. 27 Feb. 1962, Iasi, Rumania. Stage Director. *Education:* O Bancila School of Art, 1980; G Enescu Conservatory, Iasi, 1986. *Appointments:* Stage Director, N Leonard Musical Theatre, Galati, 1987-. *Creative works:* Performances: Mariana Pineda (Garcia Lorca); Il Barbiere di Sevilla (Rossini); Rose Marie (R Friml); Les Precieuses Ridicules (Moliere); Gianni Schicchi (Puccini). *Honours:* 3rd Prize, 7th Scientific National Session, Bucharest, 1984; 2nd Prize for Opera (Les precieuses ridicules), Festival of Student Art, Bucharest, 1985; 2nd Prize, 8th Scientific National Session, Cluj, 1986; 1st Prize, Festival of Student Art, Iasi, 1987. *Hobbies:* Painting; Swimming; Badminton. *Address:* Str Pacurari nr 18, bl 3, sc A, et I, ap 5, cod 6600, Iasi, Rumania.

TABER Carol, b. 29 Mar. 1945, New Jersey, USA. Publisher. *Education:* AA, Green Mountain College; American Advertising Federation's Marketing Management & Advertising Course, Harvard Business School. *Appointments:* Systems Programmer, Scudder Reliance Systems; Network Manager, Media Networks Inc; Pime Showcase Manager, Ladies Home Journal; New York Manager, Ladies Home Journal; Advertising Director, Vice-President, Publisher, Vice President, Working Woman Magazine. *Memberships:* Academy of Woman Achievers; Sales Executive Club; Women in Communications; Advertising Women of New York; Liberty Club. *Hobbies:* Skiing; Whitewater Rafting. *Address:* 342 Madison Avenue, New York, NY 10173, USA.

TABER Patricia Elizabeth Blair, b. 22 Feb. 1926, Sydney, Australia. Retired. m. Alan James Taber, 14 Dec. 1946. 2 sons, 1 daughter. *Education:* Staff Teacher Childrens Art, Gunnedah NSW Technical College, 1957-59. *Appointment:* Office duties, Sydney, 1940. *Creative Works:* Numerous paintings in private collections in Australia and overseas. *Memberships:* Royal Art Society, Sydney, NSW Exhibiting Member now Branch Gold Coast; Queensland Australia, Exhibiting Member. *Honours:* 1st Fairfield Council, 1968; Bullen Bros Award, Fairfield Council, 1974; 1st Merrylands, Australiana, 1976; Art Award, 1978, 1979; Numerous exhibitions awards including: Padramatta Art Soc, 1982; Macquarie Towns Art Award, 1st. *Hobbies:* Painting; Teaching art to a few selective pupils of childrens art; Faceting; silversmithing; All forms of art; Coins; Lapidary; Historical data: Pioneer on Early Australiana. *Address:* c/o Post Office, Nerang, Queensland 4211, Australia.

TACIER Louise Arlene, b. 4 Nov. 1935, Johannesburg, South Africa. Professor of Law. m. Harris Tacier, 5 July 1955, 1 son, 2 daughters. *Education:* BA, 1967, LLB cum laude, 1970, Higher Diploma in Tax Law cum laude, 1975, University of Witwatersrand; LLM, Harvard University, USA, 1978. *Appointments:* Tutor in Law, 1969, Senior Bursar, 1970, Lecturer in Law, 1971-74, Professor of Law, 1978-, Dean, Faculty of Law, 1981-85, University of Witwatersrand; Executive Officer, Law Review Project, 1985-. *Publications:* Law of Negotiable Instruments Title in Law of South Africa; Law of Negotiable Instruments - Student Tax; Chapters in Annual Survey of South African Law: Law of Sale; General Principles of Contract; Law of Taxation; Articles on delict, tax, contract, negotiable instruments, in South African Law Journal. *Memberships:* Editorial Board, Annual Survey; Editorial Board, South Africa Tax Journal; Co-opted Member, Margo Commission of Inquiry into the Tax Structure of South Africa; Competition Board, Deregulation Committee; Johannesburg Standing Committee, Small Claims Court. *Honours:* Intermediate Moot Winner, Annual Survey Moot Prize, 1969; Final Year Moot Winner, Society of Advocates Prize, 1970; Prize for the Most Outstanding Graduate in final LLB year, Society of Advocates, 1970; Joint Winner, Claude Franks Memorial Prize for the Best Student in Jurisprudence and Conflict of Laws, 1970. *Hobbies:* Aerobics; Gardening; Tennis. *Address:* 48-8th Avenue, Lower Houghton, Johannesburg 2198, South Africa.

TAFOLLA Carmen, b. 29 July 1951, San Antonio, Texas, USA. Poet; Writer; Educator. m. Ernesto M. Bernal, 29 June 1979, 1 son, 3 daughters (1 dec.). *Education:* BA 1972,, MA 1973, Austin College; PhD, Foreign Language & Bilingual Education, University of Texas, 1981. *Appointments:* Director, Mexican-American Studies, Texas Lutheran College, 1973-76; Coordinator, multi-media parent training, Southwest Educational Development Laboratory, 1976-77; Head writer, Sonrisas, bilingual TV series, 1978-79; Vice-President, Operations, Creative Educational Enterprises, 1980-84; Associate Professor, Women's Studies, California State University, Fresno, 1984-85; Visiting Associate Professor and Special Assistant to the President, Northern Arizona University, 1988-. *Publications:* Get Your Tortillas Together, poetry, 1976; La Isabela de Guadalupe, poetry, 1983; Curandera, 1983; To Split A Human: Mitos, Machos y la Mujer Chicana, 1984; Patchwork Colcha, 1987. *Memberships:* National Association for Bilingual Education; Advisory Board, Arizona Arts Association; Multi-Ethnic Literature in USA; Academy of American Poets; Coordinating Council, Mexican-American Affairs. *Honours:* Woman of Year, Mexican-American Business & Professional Women's Association, 1983; 1st place, poetry, UCI National Chicano Literary Competition, 1987. *Hobbies:* Photography; Dance; Southwestern Arts & Pottery; Biculturalism. *Address:* 6220 North Mountaineer Road, Flagstaff, Arizona 86004, USA.

TAJON Encarnacion (Connie) Fontecha, b. 25 Mar. 1920, Philippines. Retired Educator; Businesswoman. m. Felix Tajon, 17 Nov. 1948, 1 son, 1 daughter. *Education:* BA, Education, Far Eastern Univerity, manila, 1947; MEd., Seattle Pacific Univerity, USA, 1976. *Appointments:* Home Economics Teacher: San Narciso, 1941-42, Manila City Schools, 1944- 48; Teacher, Union College, Manila, 1947-48; Substitute Teacher, Auburn School District, 1956-58; Sunday School Teacher, Auburn First United Methodist Church, 1956-58; Elementary School Teacher, Renton School District, 1958-78; Founder, Tajon-Fontecha Inc., 1980-. *Memberships:* Allied Arts of Renton; University of Washington Alumni Association; Board, Renton Area Youth Services; Life Member, Renton Historical Museum; Delta Kappa Gamma International Kappa Chapter; United Nations USA Seattle chapter; National Education Association; Washington Education Association Retired; Charter Member, Better World Society; Board Member, Girl's Club of Puget Sound, 1989-1991; Board Member, Ethnic Heritage Council of the Pacific Northwest; Appointed Board of Governors of the American Biographical Institute Research Association; Awarded Certificate of Award, 2000 Notable American Women. *Hobbies:* Volunteer Work - Fundraising; Reading; Cooking; Gardening; Walking; Crochet. *Address:* 2033 Harrington PL. NE., Renton, WA 98056, USA.

TAKASE Fumiko, b. 23 Mar. 1927, Nishinomiya, Japan. Professor of English. *Education:* Kobe College, 1946; BA, Berea College, 1962-64; MA, Mount Holyoke College, USA, 1964-66; Tulane University, 1972-75. *Appointments:* Instructor of English, Mukogawa Girls High School, 1949- 50; Instructor of English, Yamate Girls' High School, 1950-52; Assistant to the Dean of Women, 1957-61, Instructor of English, 1966-70, Assistant Professor of English, 1970-77, Professor of English, 1977-, Chairman of the English Department, 1981-85, Director of the Women's Studies Center, 1985-, Kobe College. *Creative Works:* How I Feel About America, translation of Pearl S Buck, 1971; The Houhynhnms and the Eighteenth Century Gout Chinois, 1980; The Function of Disguise in Ben Jonson's Comedies, 1984; Some Considerations of the Man of the Hill in Tom Jones; English Studies: A Journal of English Language and Literature, 1988. *Memberships:* Renaissance Society of America; Sixteenth Century Studies (National Editor of the Sixteenth Century

Studies (National Editor of the Sixteenth Century Journal); Modern Language Association of America; English Literary Society of Japan; Emily Dickinson Society of Japan; Trustee, Kobe College Alumnae Association, 1967-72; Official of Kobe branch, Japan University Women's Association, 1967-69; Examiner of English Proficiency, English Proficiency Examining Committee of Japan, 1971-72. *Honours:* Danforth Fellowship 1964-65; PEO International Peace Scholarship, 1974-75. *Hobbies:* Gardening; Listening to music. *Address:* 2-2-7 Kotoen, Nishinomiya, Hyogo 662, Japan.

TAKATA Susan Reiko, b. 18 Aug. 1953, Gardena, California, USA. Sociologist. m. Richard G. Zevitz, 26 Jan. 1980. *Education:* BA, California State University, Dominguez Hills, 1974; MA, PhD 1983, University of California, Berkeley. *Appointments:* Project Director, Institute for Study of Social Change, UC Berkeley, 1980-82; Lecturer (Milwaukee campus) 1984, Assistant Professor (Parkside campus) 1984-, Departments of Sociology, University of Wisconsin. *Publication:* Co-author, Controlling the Ascent Through Sociology, 1986. *Memberships:* Chair 1987-89, Section on Asia & Asian America, American Sociological Association; President-Elect 1988, Wisconsin Sociological Association; Office, Society for Study of Social Problems. *Honours:* Spivack Dissertation Award, ASA, 1979-80; Graduate Minority Fellowship, UC Berkeley, 1979-80; Minority Fellowship, American Sociology Association, 1976-79; Great Distinction in General Scholarship, California State University, 1974. *Hobbies:* Travel; Running. *Address: (F)Department of Sociology, University of Wisconsin, Parkside, Box 2000, Kenosha, Wisconsin 53141, USA.*

TAKESHITA Yukiko, b. 16 Mar. 1932, Osaka, Japan. Professor of Psychology. *Education:* BA 1954, MA 1956, University of Tokyo. *Appointments:* Research Institute of Student's Affairs, 1958-62; Professor of Psychology, Niigata University, 1962-. *Publications:* Psychology of Teacher; Development of Educational Psychology; Psychology of Teacher-Student Relationships. *Memberships:* Japanese Association of Educational Psychology; Japanese Society of Social Psychology. *Hobbies:* Drawing; Poetry. *Address:* 807 Ekinan Heights, 3-23 3 Chome, Yoneyama, Niigata City, Japan.

TALAMO Barbara R Lisann, b. 30 May 1939, Washington, District of Columbia, USA. Professor. m. (1) Richard C Talamo, 22 June 1958, deceased 1982, 2 sons, 1 daughter. (2) John S Kauer, 2 Feb. 1985. *Education:* AB, Radcliffe College, 1960; PhD, Harvard University, 1972. *Appointments:* Tutor, Biochemical Sciences, Harvard College, 1971-74; Asst Prof Neurol; Physicological Chemistry, Johns Hopkins Med School, 1974-80; Asst Prof. Neurol/Physiology 1980-83, Associate Professor, 1983-, Director, Graduate Program in Neurosciences, 1983-, Tufts University School of Medicine. *Memberships:* Soc Neuroscience; American Soc Neurochemistry; International Soc Neurochemistry; Association for Chemoreception Sciences. *Interests:* Developmental regulation of neurotransmission and second messenger systems; Secretion; Olfaction; Alzheimer's disease. *Address:* Neurosciences Labs, Tufts University School of Medicine, 136 Harrison Ave, Boston, MA 02111, USA.

TALBOT Mary Lee, b. 18 Apr. 1953, Cleveland, Ohio, USA. Clergywoman. *Education:* BA, College of Wooster, 1975; M.Div., Andover-Newton Theological Coalition, 1979. *Appointments:* Associate Editor, 1979-80; Co-Director, Youth and Young Adult Ministry, Program Agency, Presbyterian Church, USA, 1981-88. *Publications:* Editor, Guidebook for Youth Ministry; Writer, Editor, Suicide and Youth, International Youth Year; Editor, One Fantastic Book. *Memberships:* Kappa Delta Pi; Treasurer, Religious Education Association; Association of Presbyterian Church Educators. *Hobbies:* Travel; Sailing; Swimming; Theatre. *Address:* 501 West 123rd Street, 14G, New York, NY 10027, USA.

TALLEY-MORRIS Neva Bennett, b. 12 Aug. 1909, Judsonia, Arkansas, USA. Lawyer; Author; Lecturer. m. (1)James L Woodfin, 26 Sept. 1931, div. 17 Nov. 1945; (2)Cecil C Talley, 1 Jan. 1946, dec. Oct. 1948; (3)Joseph H Morris, 22 Mar. 1952, dec. 5 Dec. 1974. *Education:* BA, magna cum laude, Ouachita Baptist University, 1930; MEd, University of Texas, Austin, 1938; PhD Law, World University, 1984; DDL (Hon) International University, 1987. *Appointments:* Classroom Teacher, Arkansas, 1930-37; High School Principal, McRae, Arizona, 1937-42; Ordnance Inspector, US Civil Service, 1942-46; Law Office Assistant, Little Rock, 1946-47; Lawyer, General Civil Practice, 1947-80; Author, Law Textbooks and Skills, 1974-88. *Publications:* Family Law Practice & Procedure, 1974; Civil Appealate Practice & procedure, 1976; World Peace through Law pamphlets: Family Lawyer - Problem Solver and Peace Maker, 1985; Alternative Dispute Resolutions, 1986; Elevating Image of Family Lawyers, 1987. *Memberships:* Goals Committee, World Peace Through Law Center; Founder, World Association of Lawyers, 1975; Family Law Chair, 1970, American Bar Association; President, 1956, National Association of Women Lawyers; President, 1950, Arkansas Association, Women Lawyers; Chairman, 1952-54, Arklansas Council, Children & Youth; Life Member, 1948-, American Association University Women. *Honours:* Board of Governors, American Biographical Institute, 1984; Executive Life President, World Institute of Achievement, 1984; First Woman Chairman, American Bar Section, 1970; First woman elected member, Phi Alpha Delta International Legal Fraternity; Board of Governors, First Woman American Academy of Matrimonial Law, 1974-80. *Hobbies:* World travel for peace; Writing; Sewing; National preservation of Historical buildings. *Address:* 1013 West Markham Street, Little Rock, Arkansas 72201, USA.

TALMADGE Sharon S, b. 5 Jan. 1950, Ft Belvoir, Virginia, USA. Latent Print Examiner Supervisor. m. 22 Apr. 1972, (divorced). 1 daughter. *Education:* Studying for AA Degree. *Appointments:* Fingerprint Technician, Federal Bureau of Investigation, 1970-71; Latent Print Examiner Supervisor, Baltimore Police Department, 1971-. *Memberships:* International Association for Identification; Chesapeake Bay Division of the International Association for Identification, Past President 1984-85, Board of Directors, Historian, Certification Committee; Associate, International Police Association. *Honours:* Sar Law Enforcement Medal, Maryland Society of The Sons of the American Rev, 1981; Bronze Star, Baltimore Police Dept, 1981; Certificate of Appreciation, Baltimore County Police Dept, 1981; Distinguished Service Award, Baltimore Police Dept, 1984; Certificate of Appreciation, Baltimore Police Dept, 1984. *Hobbies:* Running; Camping; Skiing; Reading. *Address:* Baltimore Police Dept, 601 E Fayette St, Baltimore, Maryland 21202, USA.

TANA Alice Mcfadden, b. 17 Oct. 1935, Freeland, Pennsylvania, USA. Business services firm executive. m. Yasuto Tana, 13 Oct. 1973. *Education:* Georgetown University, 1968-70; Catholic University, 1967- 69; University of Michigan, 1963-67; Eastern Michigan University, 1963-67; University of California, San Diego, 1977-79; also numerous workshops, symposia. *Appointments:* Supr order dept, Gallant Inc, Washington, 1954-58; Teacher, Mary Anne Baldwin School, Pittsburgh, 1958-60; Dir Sr citizen and women, City of Ypsilanti, Michigan, 1961-67; Regional dir, Nat Council on Aging, Washington, 1967-70; Liaison officer congl/pvt sector Exec Office of President, Washington, 1971-72; Dir Presidents Task Force on Aging, Washington, 1972-73; Teaching specialist Japanese Self Def Force/Sumitomo Corp, Taura, Japan, 1973-76; Econ devel specialist, County San Diego, California, 1977-80, project dir transp research and mktg study, 1980, budget analyst 1981-82; Founder, Ask Alice, San Diego, 1982-; Asst dir pub info County of San Diego, 1984-85; Founded Tana & Associates, public relations and marketing, La Jolla, 1987-. *Memberships:* Advisory Board Women and Management, Georgetown University; Women in politics and governtment, Rutgers University, 1980-81; Founder, president, Diversified Business Women, ednl orgn, San Diego; Trustee, World

Family Living, San Diego, Internat Student Exchange Program TZ Assocs, San Diego; Calif Women in Govt (president 1980-81); San Diego C of C (Econ Research Council; Am Soc Public Administrators; Nat Assn Female Execs; San Diego Women Execs; Network GROW (dir); Business and Professional Women; Eastern Michigan University Alumni Association; Econ Research Bur. *Honours:* B-MAC Award, Michigan Recreation and Parks Assiation, 1967; Distinguished Service in Disaster Operations award Pres US 1972; Certicate appreciation Japanese Self-Defence Force, 1975; Public Relations Society of America Outstanding Award, 1987; Outstanding award, Exchange, 1967; Outstanding award, Optimists, 1963. *Address:* Tana & Associates, 4275 Executive Square, Suite 800, La Jolla, CA 92037, USA.

TANCK Catherine Ann, b. 28 Aug. 1957, Canton, South Dakota, USA. Law Clerk. *Education:* BA, Augustana College, 1979; JD, University of South Dakota, 1987. *Appointments:* Internal Revenue Service, 1977- 79; McGladrey & Pullen, 1979-85; Hagen & Wilka, 1985; Davenport, Evans Hurwitz & Smith, 1986; 8th Circuit Court of Appeals, 1987-. *Publications:* Depreciation of the Core Deposit Intangible: A Tax Incentive to Acquire a Failed Bank; Investment Tax Credit: A New Test for "Inherently Permanent"; Impact of Reagan's Tax Proposal on Agriculture. *Memberships:* American Bar Association; American Institute of Certified Public Accountants; South Dakota Society of Certified Public Accountants. *Honours:* Thomas Sterling Honor Society; West Publishing Co. Awards. *Hobbies:* Tennis; Volleyball. *Address:* 1701 S West Ave., Sioux Falls, SD 57105, USA.

TANG Suren, b. 18 Feb. 1937, Hunan Province, China. Associate Professor. m. 4 Aug. 1963. 1 son, 2 daughters. *Education:* Central South Institute of Mining and Metallurgy, 1956-61. *Appointments:* Daye Nonferrous Metal Co, 1961-71; Wuhan University of Technology, 1972-. *Memberships:* Geological Association of China; Chinese Silicate Society. *Hobbies:* Music; Drama. *Address:* Dept of Resources Engineering, Wuhan University of Technology, 14 Luoshi Road, Wuhan, Hubei, China.

TANN Jennifer, b. 25 Feb. 1939, Bedford, England. University Educator. m. 12 Oct. 1963, 2 sons. *Education:* BA, 1961; PhD, 1964. *Appointments:* Research Assistant, Historic Towns Project, 1964-66; Lecturer, 1969-73, Reader, 1973-86, Aston University; Visiting Professor, University of Queensland, Australia, 1985; Director of Continuing Education, University of Newcastle-upon-Tyne, 1986-; Professor of Innovation Studies, Head of School of Continuing studies, University of Birmingham, 1989-; Visiting Professor of Management, University of Newcastle-upon-Tyne, 1989-. *Publications:* The Development of the Factory, 1971; Children at Work, 1981; Selected Papers of Boulton and Watt, 1981; Papers and special reports for conferences; Journal contributions. *Hobbies:* Reading; Music; The Countryside; Family. *Address:* School of Continuing Studies, University of Birmingham, Birmingham B1S 2TT, England.

TANNEN Deborah F., b. 7 June 1945, New York City, New York, USA. Professor of Linguistics. *Education:* BA, English Literature, Harpur College, State University of New York, 1966; MA, English Literature, Wayne State University, 1970; MA, Linguistics, 1976, PhD, Linguistics, 1979, University of California, Berkeley. *Appointments:* Instructor, Detroit Institute of Technology, Detroit, Michigan, 1969; Instructor, Mercer County Community College, Trenton, New Jersey, 1970-71; Lecturer, Department of Academic Skills, Herbert H.Lehmann College, City University of New York, 1971-74; Assistant Professor, 1979-85, Associate Professor, 1985-89, Professor, 1989-, Linguistics, Georgetown University, Washington DC; Research Associate, Joint Programme in Applied Anthropology, Teachers College, Columbia University, 1986-87. *Publications:* Lilika Nakos, 1983; Conversational Style: Analyzing Talk Among Friends, 1984; That's Not What I Meant!: How Conversational Style Makes or Breaks Your Relations with Others, 1986, Paperback, 1987, UK Edition, 1987, Japanese Edition, 1989, Danish & Swedish editions 1990About 60 articles and papers in field of linguistics; Editor, 6 books; Roses for Remembrance, Pansies for Thought (short story), 1975; Poems; Talking Voices: Repetition Dialogue and Imagery in Conversational Discourse, 1989; You Just Don't Understand: Women and Men in Conversation, 1990. *Memberships:* Linguistic Society of America (committees); American Association for Applied Linguistics (committees); Consultation Board, International Pragmatics Association; Authors Guild; American Anthropological Association; American Dialect Society, Modern Language Association; Modern Greek Studies Association; Washington Linguistics Society; Editorial Boards: Language in Society, Text, Journal of Pragmatics, American Speech, Oral Tradition, Research on Language and Social Interaction. *Honours:* Elizabeth Mills Crothers Prize, Literary Compositiion, 1976; Dorothy Rosenberg Memorial Prize, Lyric Poetry, 1977; Joan Lee Yang Memorial Poetry Prize, 1977; Shrout Short Story Prize, 1978; Emily Chamberlain Cook Prize, Poetry, 1978; Danforth Fellow, 1977-79; Rockefeller Fellow, 1982-83; Grants: National Endowment for the Humanities; Others. *Address:* Department of Linguistics, Georgetown University, Washington, DC 20057, USA.

TANSEK Karin Marye, b. 13 Jan. 1948, Columbus, Ohio, USA. Surgeon. m. 14 July 1984. *Education:* BS 1970, MS 1972, Wayne State University; MD, Michigan State University, 1976; Intern & resident, general Surgery & Otolaryngology, University Hospitals of California, Yale, Northwestern, 1976-84; Affiliated Otolaryngologists, Robbinsdale, Minnesota, 1984-85; ENT Professional Associates, Minneapolis, 1985-. *Publications:* Articles, professional journals, 1983, 1985. *Memberships:* American & Minnesota Academies of Otolaryngology; American Medical Association; President, Minnesota Women Physicians; Minnesota & Hennepin County Medical Associations. *Hobbies:* Cycling; Cross-country skiing; Swimming; Photography. *Address:* 322 Medical Arts, Minneapolis, Minnesota 55402, USA.

TANSEY (Iva Lee) Marie, b. 6 Jan. 1930, Elyria, Ohio, USA. State Representative, Ohio Legislature. m. Charles J Tansey, 7 Sept. 1948. 3 sons. *Education:* Lorain Business College, 1965. *Appointments:* Vermilion High School Secretary, 1959-64; Executive Secretary, Vermilion Chamber of Commerce, 1964-67; Branch Secretary and Assistant Manager Cardinal Federal Savings and Loan Association, 1967-76; Elected State Representative of Ohio, 72nd House District, 1976-89; Vermilion City Council, 1969-75. *Memberships:* Congregational Church, president SS Class; Vermilion Chamber of Commerce; Federation of Republican Women's Clubs; President, Vermilion Women's League; Ohio Federation of Woemn's Clubs; National Order of Women Legislators; USA Business and Professional Women; Charter Member, Vermilion Lioness Club; national Council of State Legislators; American Legislative Exchange Council. *Honours:* Lorain County, 1st Runner Up Mrs America, 1959; Lorain County Woman of Achievement, 1982; Vermilion Outstanding Woman of the Year, 1974; Ohio House of Representatives Recognition Community Service, 1974; Cuyahoga County Spotlight Salute to Ohio Women, 1982; National Winner, Harper's Bazaar-DeBeers Superwoman, 1980. *Hobbies:* Writing poetry; Camping; Swimming; Fishing; Travel in USA and abroad. *Address:* 5503 Hartford Av, Vermilion, OH 44089, USA.

TAPERELL Kathleen Joan, b. 15 Feb. 1939, Sydney, Australia. Public Servant. m. John Tucker, 9 Jan. 1960, 1 son. *Education:* BA, Sydney University, 1959; Dip.Ed, University of New England, 1969. *Appointments:* Librarian, 1959; Teacher, 1967-72; Electorate Secretary, 1973; Senior Research Officer, Royal Commission on Australian Government Administration, 1974-76; Assistant Director, Equal Opportunities Office, Public Service Board, 1976-77; Senior Adviser, 1977,

Director, 1978-83, Office of Women's Affairs; Assistant Secretary, Foreign Affairs, 1984-86; Assistant Secretary, Department of the Prime Minister & Cabinet, 1986-. *Publications:* Sexism in Public Service: The Employment of Women in Australian Government Administration, (with Fox & Roberts), 1975. *Memberships:* Numerous societies. *Hobbies:* Films; Novels; Theatre; Music; Travel; Current Affairs; International Affairs. *Address:* 113 Schlich Street, Yarralumla, ACT 2600, Australia.

TARLTON Shirley M, b. 8 Aug. 1937, Raleigh, North Carolina, USA. Dean of Library Services. *Education:* BA, French, Queens College, 1960; MS, University of North Carolina, Chapel Hill, 1966. *Appointments:* Head, Technical Services, University of North Carolina, Charlotte, 1961- 68; Associate College Librarian, Technical Services, 1968-73, Acting College Librarian, 1971, 1973-74, Dean, Library Services, 1974-, Winthrop College Library. *Publications:* Articles in: The SC Librarian; Wilson Library Bulletin; others. *Memberships:* American, Southeastern, North Carolina, South Carolina and Metrolina Library Associations; Charlotte Area Educational Consortium. *Honours:* Sigma Pi Alpha; Phi Theta Kappa Scholarship; Beta Phi Mu; Phi Kappa Phi Scholarship; etc. *Hobbies:* Reading; Walking; Boating; Tennis. *Address:* 7406 Windyrush Road, Matthews, NC 28105, USA.

TARNOPOL, Muriel, b. 30 Apr. 1928, Port Washington, New York, USA. Professor; Lecturer; Author; Musician. m. Lester Tarnopol, 1 June, 1955. 2 sons. *Education:* BMus, University of Miami; MA, San Francisco State University, 1957; Postgraduate studies, University of the Pacific, Stockton, California. *Appointments:* Teacher in California elementary and secondary schools, 1950-59; Consultant in special education, 1959-; Professor of Counseling and Special Education, San Francisco State University, 1972-. *Publications:* Reading Disabilities - an International Perspective, with Lester Tarnopol, 1976; Brain Function and Reading Disabilities, 1977; Comparative Reading and Learning Difficulties, 1981; Disturbios de Leitura - uma Perspectiva International, 1976. Articles in professional journals: Skolepsykologi; Academic Therapy; Focus on Learning Problems in Mathematics; Bulletin of the Orton Society; Journal of Learning Disabilites. Chapter in book: Handwriting: Research and Implications for Practice, with Nusia de Feldman, 1987. *Memberships:* California Association for Neurologically Handicapped Children and Adults: Program Chairman, Symposium Chairman, Grant Chairman (San Francisco Chapter); San Mateo Chapter CANHC Member of the Board, Program Director, Advisor at large; Member of Advisory Board, the Charles Armstrong School Menlo Park; Orton Dyslexia Society; International Reading Assocation. *Honours:* Rotary Club Scholarship, 1946; University of Miami Scholarship, 1949, 1950; Denton Scholarship, 1952; Sigma Alpha Iota Award, 1957; Pi Kappa Lambda Award, 1967. *Hobbies:* Trained as a professional bassoonist, studied with Manual Zegler, first bassonist of the New York Philharmonic; Bassoonist with Miami Symphony, Sacramento Symphony; International Travel; International research in reading and learning disabilities. *Address:* 769 Edgewood Road, San Mateo, California 94402, USA.

TARR Judith Ellen, b. 30 Jan. 1955, Augusta, Maine, USA. Writer (Author); Lecturer. *Education:* AB, magna cum laude, Mt Holyoke College, 1976; BA Classics 1978, MA 1983, Cambridge University; MA 1979, PhD Medieval Studies, 1988, Yale University. *Appointments:* Teacher of Latin, Edward Little High School, Auburn, ME, USA, 1979-81; Student/Author, 1984-88; Full-time Author, 1988-. *Publications:* Novels: The Isle of Glass; The Golden Horn; The Hounds of God; The Hall of the Mtn King; The Lady of Han- Gilen; A Fall of Princes; A Wind in Cairo; Pontifex Magicus; Alamut. Contributor to Isaac Asimov's Science Fiction Magazine, Amazing Stories. *Memberships:* Science Fiction Writers of America; Modern Language Association; International Association for the Fantastic in the Arts. *Honours:* William Crawford Memorial Award, International Association for the Fantastic in the Arts, 1987; Mary Lyon Award, Mt Holyoke College, 1989. *Hobbies:* Equestrian, classical dressage; Arabian horses, riding, training, history; Historical research especially Middle Ages; Travel. *Address:* c/o Jane Butler, Literary Agent, PO Box 278, Milford, PA 18337, USA.

TASKA Eileen Ruth Johnson, b. 22 May 1932, Brooklyn, New York, USA. Psycho-Educational Therapist; Sculptor; Designer; Inventor. m. Frederick A. Taska, 27 May 1956, 1 son, 3 daughters. *Education:* Cooper Union, New York City, 1954-55; Private study, sculpture, 1969-72; Anatomy, Yale Medical School, 1972-74; BA, Goddard College, Vermont, 1973; MS, College of New Rochelle, 1974; Interdisciplinary PhD, Inventive Approach to Therapeutic Education, Gross Anatomy, & Sculpture, The Union Institute, 1975. *Appointments:* Freelance graphic artist, 1956-68; Stone sculptor, 1970- ; Designer, educational tools, games, devices & puzzles, 1973-; Psycho- educational therapist, 1975-; Lectures, workshops in field. *Creative work includes:* Creator, E. Taska Originals; Exhibitions, stone sculptures, wood carvings, various states; Work in numerous private collections; 4 stone pieces completed in series, endangered species; Conceived & executed numerous small children's books, including calligraphy, illustration & hand-binding. *Honours:* Awarded patents: Segmented Inclined Plane, & Learning Kit for Children with Learning Disabilities 1975. *Hobbies include:* Landscape & house design, projects include wildlife sanctuary, 19-room house with pool, floating marina, commercial kitchen; Historic restoration; Playing cello; Cooking. *Address:* 1035 North Street, Greenwich, Connecticut 06831, USA.

TASSANI Sally Marie, b. 30 Dec. 1948, Teaneck, USA. Company President. *Education:* BA, American University, 1970; Studies, various other Universities. *Appointments:* Elementary School Teacher, Washington, 1970-72; Assistant Promotion & Production Manager, First National Bank, Chicago, 1973-74; Executive Vice President, Managing Director, Jack O'Grady Graphics Inc., Chicago, 1974-76; Creative Director, Dimensional Marketing Inc., 1976-78; President, Founder, Nexus, Chicago, 1978-86; President, Founder, Tassani Communications Inc, 1986-. *Memberships:* American Management Association; Women in Design; Women in Healthcare; Women's Advertising Club of Chicago; World Organization on Foreign & Domestic Affairs. *Honours:* Recipient, various honours including: Spectra Award, International Association of Business Communications. *Hobbies:* Graphic Design; Arts; American Crafts; Photography; Sailing; Race Walking. *Address:* Tassani Communications Inc., 625 North Michigan Avenue, Suite 1600, Chicago, IL 60611, USA.

TATELBAUM Judith Ann, b. 22 Sept. 1938, Rochester, New York, USA. Author; Lecturer; Psychotherapist. m. (1) David Allan Gross, 1965, divorced 1966, (2)Allan G. Marcus, 18 June 1988. *Education:* BS, Syracuse University, 1959; MSW, Simmons College School of Social Work, 1961; Certified, Gestat Therapy, 1972. *Appointments:* Caseworker, Massachusetts Mental Health Centre, 1961-63; Caseworker, Adult Outpatient Clinic, Payne Whitney Clinic, New York Hospital, 1963-71; Field Supervisor, Columbia University School of Socialwork, 1968-71; Private Practice, 1972-. *Publications:* The Courage to Grieve, 1980; You Don't Have to Suffer, 1989. *Memberships:* National Association of Social Workers; American Group Psychotherapy Association; Association for Humanistic Psychology; Association for Transpersonal Psychology; American Academy of Psychotherapists; National Organization of Women, National Speakers Association. *Honours:* Alumni Recognition, Simmons College, 1981. *Address:* 60 Middle Canyon Road, Carmel Valley, CA 93924, USA.

TAVARES Salette, b. 31 Mar. 1922, Lourenco Marques, Portugal. Writer. m. Jose Francisco Aranda, 21 June 1950, 1 son, 2 daughters. *Education:* Faculty of Letters, Lisbon Univesity, 1948. *Publications:*

Philosophy Aproximacao Do Pensamento Concreto De Gabriel Marcel, 1948; Poetry: Espelho Cego, 1957; Conserto Em Mimaior Para Clarinete e Bateria, 1959; Quadrada, 1967; 14563 Letras de Pedro Sete, 1965; Lex-Icon, 1971; Poesia Espacial, 1948-. *Memberships:* International Association of Art Critics; International Committee of Museums; PEN; Portugese Association of Writers; Portuguese Society of Authors. *Honours:* Poetry published in: Italy, Germany, USA, England, Norway & Sweden; etc. *Hobbies:* Writing; Art; Gardening. *Address:* Costa Do Castelo 44 1 DTO, 1100 Lisbon, Portugal.

TAYLOR Ann, b. 23 Mar. 1941. Artist. m. Paul Wendall Brown, 1 Jan. 1988, 1 daughter. *Education:* BA, New School for Social Research, 1962. *Creative Works:* Solo Exhibitions Include: Marilyn Butler Fine Art, Scottsdale Oxford Gallery; Kaurffman Galleries; Gallery Vander Woude, Palm Springs; Beaumont Art Museum; C.G. Rein Galleries, Scottsdale; Yuma Art Centre; Miller Gallery; York Gallery, New York, etc; Museum & Corporate collections include: Palm Springs Desert Museum; Scottsdale Center for the Arts; Memorial Art Gallery, University of Rochester; Arizona State University, Tempe; Yuma Art Centre; Bank of America, Houston; A.C. Neilsen Corporation, Chicago; American Express, Phoenix. *Address:* 7209 E. McDonald Drive No 31, Scottsdale, AZ 85253, USA.

TAYLOR Anna, b. 14 July 1943, Preston, Lancashire, England. Writer; Lecturer. m. J. E. D. Coombes, 22 Dec. 1967, div. 1982, 1 son. *Education:* BA Hons, German and English, Bristol University, 1965; Certificate of Education, York University, 1967; MA, Modern Aesthetics, Essex University, 1980. *Appointments include:* Lecturer in English as a Foreign Language and German, De Havilland College, Welwyn Garden City, 1973-74; Lecturer (part-time) in Modern British Poetry, Bretton Hall College, West Bretton, West Yorkshire, currently; Artistic Collaborator and Model for French sculptor Serraz, 1969-. *Publications:* Fausta, 1984; Pro Patria: A Private Suit, 1987; Cut Some Cards, 1988; Poetry in magazines and anthologies including Purple and Green, 1985, and Transformation, 1988; Fiction and drama. *Memberships:* Theatre Writers Union; Yorkshire Playwrights; Labour Party; Northern Association of Writers in Education; New Playwrights Trust. *Honours:* Poems short-listed in 3 competitions: New Poetry, 1980; Wetherby, 1984; York, 1985. *Hobbies:* Reading own and other poetry at various venues including Cheltenham Festival and Leeds Cabaret; All past and present art forms; Politics; Walking; Swimming; Cycling. *Address:* c/o Rivelin Grapheme Press, The Annexe, Kennet House, 19 High Street, Hungerford Berkshire, England.

TAYLOR Conciere Marlana, b. 30 Oct. 1950, New York City, New York, USA. Writer; Editor. *Education:* AA, Queensborough Community College; BFA (correspondence), Literary Institute University. *Appointments:* Editor, 1976-80, Editor-in-Chief, 1982, Source Literary Magazine, 1976-80; Coordinator, Literary Arts Division, Queens Council on the Arts. *Publications:* Ceasefire, chapbook; Poetry in Modus Operandi, Whetstone, Source, New York Times; Short stories: Scapes; Shock Treatment; Edges. *Memberships:* New York Film and Video Council; Lincoln Center Film Society; Poets and Writers; Poetry Society of America; Academy of American Poets. *Hobbies:* Collecting stamps, books, plates. *Address:* 67-08 Parsons Boulevard 6B, Flushing, NY 11365, USA.

TAYLOR Dorothy Lee, b. 10 Apr. 1938, Detroit, Michigan, USA. Criminologist and Therapist. m. Amos Taylor III, MD, 26 May 1973. 2 daughters. *Education:* Associate Degree, Mental Health, 1979; BSW, 1981; MSW, 1982; PhD, Criminology, 1989. *Appointments:* Developed and staffed, Resource Center for Jobfare Program, 1984; Sickle Cell Counselor, 1983-84; Private practice, Dorothy L Taylor & Associates, individual family/substance abuse counseling and presentence investigating, 1982-. *Publications:* Dissertation: An Assessment of Factors Related to Female-Headed

Households and Their Effect Upon Juvenile Chronic Maladaptive Behaviour in African- American Families. *Memberships:* Association of Black Social Workers; National Association of Social Workers; Wayne State University Alumni Assoc; Golden Key National Honor Society; American Society of Criminology; Academy of Criminal Justice Science; NAACP; Urban League; SCLC. *Honour:* Association of Black Social Workers, Student Chapter, Wayne State University Annual Recognition Award for Distinctive Professional Services, 1984. *Hobbies:* Reading; Jumping rope; Walking; Golfing; Fishing; Communing with nature; Meditating; Travelling. *Address:* 23777 Greenfield Ste 165, Southfield, MI 48075, USA.

TAYLOR Elizabeth Jane Lucas, b. 27 Oct. 1941, Tiffin, Ohio, USA. Business Development Consultant. m. Gaylen Lloyd Taylor, 11 July 1977. *Education:* Attended: Heidelberg College, Tiffin, Ohio; Austin Community College, Austin, Texas; The Real Estate Education Center, Austin; Institute of Real Estate, Austin. *Appointments:* Corp. Director, Unitron, Inc, 1979-82; Corp. Director, Sibrow & Assoc. 1981-83; Journalist, Austin Woman Magazine, 1984-86; President, Business Connection, 1981-86; International Sales Associate, Alliance Sales & Property Mgmt, 1985-; Partner, Hahn-Taylor International Finds, 1981-; Chief Executive Officer, Taylor & Associates, 1986-. *Publications:* Letters From Home, 1985; Monthly Column, Austin Woman Magazines, 1984-86; Best New Poets of 1986; American Peotry Anthology, 1986; The Silva Method for Business Managers, contributed 1983; The Spy Bazaar, 1986. *Memberships:* Vice President, 1982-83, American Congress on Real Estate; Int. Sec. 1981, Toastmasters; Vice President, Board of Directors, 1984-, Austin World Affairs Council; Advisory Panel, 1984-86, Austin Womans Magazine; Advisory Panel, 1984-86, Austin Womens Extra; NAFE Director, 1979-87; Speakers Bureau, 1981-, International Platform Association. *Honours:* Distinguished Leadership Award, Outstanding Achievement in Business and Finance, 1986; Texas Women's Hall of Fame Nominee, 1984; Commemorative Gold Medal of Honour for Lifelong Achievement, ABI, 1987; 2000 Notable American Women, 2nd Edition. *Hobbies:* Writing; Hypnosis & behaviour modification; Horses; Travel; Old Books; History. *Address:* 3406 Danville Drive, Cedar Park, TX 78613, USA.

TAYLOR Jennifer Evelyn, b. 12 Apr. 1935, Sydney, New South Wales, Australia. Architect. m. Thomas Kinman Taylor, 9 Aug. 1957, 1 son, 1 daughter. *Education:* School of Architecture, Oxford Institute of Technology, England, 1962-63; BArch, 1967, MArch, 1969, University of Washington, Seattle, USA. *Appointments:* Tutor, 1970, Lecturer, 1971-75, Senior Lecturer, 1980-82, Associate Professor, 1983-, Department of Architecture, University of Sydney, Sydney, New South Wales. *Publications:* An Australian Identity: Houses for Sydney 1953-63, 1972, 2nd Edition, 1984; Developments in Australian Architecture since 1940, in The International Handbook of Contemporary Developments in Architecture, 1981; Architecture a Performing Art, 1982; Since the Nineteen Fifties, in The History and Design of the Australian House, 1985; Australian Architecture Since 1960, 1986, 2nd Edition, 1990; Oceania: Australia, New Zealand, Papua New Guinea and the Smaller Islands of the South Pacific, in History of Architecture, 19th Edition, 1987. *Memberships:* Australian Society of Authors; Associate, Royal Australian Institute of Architects; Art Association of Australia; International Council on Monuments and Sites; International Committee of Architectural Critics; Society of Architectural Historians, Australian and New Zealand; Fellow, Research Institute for Asia and the Pacific; Architectural Design Teaching and Research Association of Australia and New Zealand. *Honours:* Japan Foundation Professional Fellowship, 1975. *Address:* 712 Billyard Avenue, Elizabeth Bay, New South Wales 2011, Australia.

TAYLOR Joyce, b. 14 Mar. 1948, Glasgow, Scotland. Director of programmes. m. John Huw Lloyd Richards,

13 Apr. 1982, 1 son, 1 daughter. *Education:* BA, University of Strathclyde, 1968; BA, Honours, Administration, University of Strathclyde, 1975. *Appointments:* BBC TV, 1968-69; Researcher, University of Strathclyde, 1975-77; Producer, Director, Educational Films, University of Glasgow, 1978-85; Director, Programmes, Clyde Cablevision, 1985-. *Publications:* numerous educational films & videos including: 1983 Scottish Royal Television Society Educational Film Award for Brachiopods. *Memberships:* Royal Television Society; John Logie Baird Advisory Board; Educational Television Association; etc. *Honours:* Premier Award, Royal TV Society, 1983; British Medical Association Video Competition Silver Award, 1988. *Hobbies:* Reading; Film; TV; Theatre; Squash. *Address:* 19 Kessington Drive, Bearsden, Glasgow G61 2HG, England.

TAYLOR June Marie, b. 11 July 1954, Duluth, Minnesota, USA. Logistics Management Specialist. m. William R Taylor, Jr, 8 June 1978. *Education:* BS, Business Management, 1976; MS, Logistics Management, 1988, Wright State University, Fairborn. *Appointments:* Secretary/Receptionist, 1972-79; Logistics Management Specialist Trainee, 1979-82; Installation Mobility Officer, 1982-84; Deputy Program Manager for Logistics, 1984-. *Memberships:* Society of Logistics Engineers; National Association for Female Executives; Masters Business Administration Association, Wright State University. *Honours:* Military Airlift Command Outstanding Logistics Plans Civilian for Fiscal Year, 1983; Outstanding Young Women of America, 1984; Various work-related performance awards, 1972-87. *Hobbies:* Walking; Bowling; Reading. *Address:* 398 Big Stone Drive, Xenia, Ohio 45385, USA.

TAYLOR Lisa Suter, b. 8 Jan. 1933, New York City, USA. Museum Director. m. Bertrand L. Taylor III, 30 Oct. 1968, 1 son, 1 daughter. *Education:* Corcoran School of Art, 1958-65; Georgetown University, 1958-62; Johns Hopkins University, 1956-58. *Appointments:* Administrative Assistant, President's Fine Art Committee, 1958-62; Membership Director, Corcoran Gallery Art, 1962-66; Programme Director 1966-69, Director, Smithsonian Institution; Director, Cooper-Hewitt Museum of Decorative Arts & Design 1969-88, Smithsonian Institution (now Director Emeritus). Also: Advisory Boards. *Creative work includes:* Urban Open Spaces, 1979; Cities, 1981; Phenomenon of Change, 1984; Housing: Symbol, Structure, Size, 1989; Co-director, film, Living Museum, 1968. *Memberships:* Smithsonian Institution (Honorary Life); Advisory Boards: New York Historical Society; Katonech Gallery; Center for Childhood; Arthur Ross Gallery, University of Pennsylvania; Design Museum, London. *Honours include:* Joseph Henry Medal, Thomas Jefferson Award, 1976; Bronze Plaque, Johns Hopkins YMCA, 1958; Medal of Honour, American Legion, 1951; Bronze Apple Award, American Society of Industrial Designers, 1977; Trailblazer of Year, National Home Fashion League, 1981; Dame of Honour, Order of St John of Jerusalem; Honorary Member, American Society of Interior Designers, American Institute of Architects; Honorary DFA degrees, Parsons School of Design 1977, Cooper Union 1984. *Address:* Seven Gates Farm, Vineyard Haven, MA 02568, USA.

TAYLOR Pauline Elizabeth, b. 15 Dec. 1948, Kew, Australia. Economist Investment Analyst. m. Mark Hedley Taylor, 6 Aug. 1971, 3 sons. *Education:* BCom., University of Melbourne, 1969; Diploma, Securities Institute of Australia, 1981. *Appointments:* Research Officer, Federal Department of Employment, 1969-71; Consultant, Economist Intelligence Unit, 1971-73; Economist, Commercial Bank of Australia Ltd., 1973-78; Economist, Potter Partners, 1978-81; Secretary, Economic Society of Australia, 1982-88; Investment Analyst, Investment & Business Research Ltd., 1987-88; Senior Analyst, Australian Ratings Pty. Ltd., 1989-. *Memberships:* Economic Society of Australia; Associate, Securities Institute of Australia. *Hobbies:* Handcrafts. *Address:* 4 Tara Ave., Kew, Victoria, Australia.

TAYLOR Vivian Lorraine, b. 28 June 1948, Philadelphia, Pennsylvania, USA. Occupational Work adjustment Teacher, Coordinator. m. Rev. Sinthy Eugene Taylor, 27 June 1970. *Education:* BA, Elementary Education, 1970, MA, Teaching 1971, Antioch College. *Appointments:* English and History Teacher, Dayton Board of Educat, 1970-72; Director Youth Girls Program, National Boys Clubs of America, 1970-72; Director, Tutorial Aide Program, 1972-77; College Recruiter for High School Students into Wright, 1974-76; Occupational Work Adjustment Teacher Coordinator, Dayton Public Schools, 1972-; Business Manager, MacFarlane Middle School, Dayton City Schools, 1986-; Co-owner and Business Manager, Midas Landscaping & Development Co Inc, 1986-. *Memberships:* National Education Association; Ohio Education Association; Dayton Education Association; Southwest Dayton Priority Board, Recording Secretary, 1974-76; Order of the Eastern Star, Chapter PHA, Financial Secretary, 1982-; Miami Assembly No 22, Order of Golden Circle; Montgomery County Republican Party, 3rd Vice Chairman, 1982; Burning Bush Court No 3 Heroines of Jericho, 1983; American Court No 65, Daughters of Isis, 1983-; Truth Guild No 2 Heroines of the Templars Crusade, 1984-. *Honours:* Rockefeller Foundation Full Scholarship to Antioch College, 1965; Voted Most Likley to Succeed, Rockefeller Program, Antioch College, 1969; Dayton Public Schools, Academic Achievement Award, 1973-79; Reconigition of Service Award, Mayor, City of Dayton, 1975; Southwest Priority Board Outstanding Service Award, 1976; Selected Outstanding Young Woman of America, 1977; Received National Kizzy Award, Kizzy Scholarship Fund, 1983; Selected Vocational Teacher of the Year, Dayton Public Schools, 1984; Received Frank Aldora Excellence in Vocational Education Award, Dayton Public Schools, 1988. *Hobbies:* Cooking; Astrology; Backgammon. Interests: Involvement in civic, political and religious organizations; Volunteer work, Hickory Creek Nursing Home. *Address:* 4526 Alfred Drive, Dayton, OH 45417, USA.

TEETERS Linda Marie, b. 22 Aug. 1945, Cincinnati, Ohio, USA. Teacher; Education. *Education:* University of Cincinnati, College of Pharmacy, 1963-66; Certificate, Qualified Dental Assistant, Cincinnati College of Dental Medical Assistants, 1967; Dental Assisting Certification, University of North Carolina, 1970-73. *Appointments:* Pharmacy Intern, Edward W Wolff Pharmacy, 1963-67; Dental Assistant, Jacque Cain, DDS, 1967-72; Dental Assistant, David Ventker, DDS, 1972-73; Dental Assistant, Cincinnati Dental Services, 1973; Dental Assistant/Manager of Clinics, Hamilton County Board of Health Dental Clinics, 1973-76; Dental Assisting Instructor, Cincinnati Board of Education, 1976-. *Memberships include:* President, 1971-72 and 1977-78, Cincinnati Dental Assistant Society; President, 1982-83, Ohio Dental Assistant Association, Inc; Third District Trustee, 1984-85, 1985-86, 1986-87, American Dental Assistant Association; President Queen City Club of Internationally Yours, Inc, 1985-89 and International President, 1989-; Delhi Civic Club; Delhi Democratic Club; Attended numerous conferences, etc. *Honours:* Achievement Award, Cincinnati Dental Assistant Society, 1982; Cincinnati Dental Society Citation for work during Children's Dental Health Month, 1982; Proclamation from the Ohio State House of Representatives for Professional Achievements, 1982; United Appeal and Community Chest Agency Volunteer Award, Honoured Nominee for work with Public Dental Service Society, 1986; Teacher of the Year Award, Ohio Vocational Association, Health Occupations, Dental Assistant Division, 1987. *Hobbies:* Arts and crafts; Cake decorating; Reading; Travelling. *Address:* 5260 Old Oak Trail, Apt 66, Cincinnati, Ohio 45238, USA.

TEIUS Sabina, b. 3 May 1937, Romania. Professor. m. Teius Vasile, 9 Aug. 1958, 2 daughters. *Education:* Doctor, Romanian Philology, 1976. *Appointments:* Researcher, Institute of linguistics, Academy Cluj-Napoca, 1958-81; Visiting Teacher, Romanian Language & Literature, L'Universita degli Studi di Roma, Italy, 1981-85; Researcher, Institutà of Linguistics, Cluj Napoca, 1985-. *Publications:* Co-ordination in Daco-

Romanian subdialects, Bucuresti, 1980; many studies and articles on linguistics field, prose and poetry translations; collaborations: Romanian Language Dictionary: Dictionarul limbü române, Litera O, Bucuresti, 1969, Litera R, 1975, Litera T, 1982 and 1983; Correct Romania, Bucuresti, 1973. *Memberships:* Societatea Româna de linguistica romanica; Grupul român de linguistica aplicata; Associazione l'Espressione Latina, Roma. *Honours:* Recipient, various honours and awards; Academy Prize, 1981, for co-ordination in Daco-Romanian subdialects. *Hobbies:* Poetry Translations; Music; Theatre; Arts; Nature; Dressmaking. *Address:* Str. Hateg., Bl.G, Sc.A, Ap 2, 3400 Cluj-Napoca, Romania.

TELEKI Margot, b. 24 May 1935, Cleveland, Ohio, USA. President, Chief Executive Officer, TAL International Marketing Inc. m. 29 Oct. 1952, divorced 1961. *Education:* BM, New England Conservatory of Music, 1952; Harvard University, 1950-51; Hunter College, National Academy of Dramatic Arts. *Appointments:* Media Exec. J Walter Thompson Co., New York City, 1958-60; Head Broadcast Buyer, Reach McClinton & Co, Inc, New York City, 1960-62; Media Research Manager, 1962, Research Director, Station WNEW, New York City, 1963-64; Snr Research Analyst, Young & Rubicam, New York City, 1964-65; Media Exec. N W Ayer & Son, Inc, Philadelphia, 1965-68; Senior Editor, Media-Scope Magazine, New York City, 1968-70, also Columnist, 1969-; President, Teleki Associates Ltd, New York City, 1970-82; President, TAL Communications, Inc, Morristown, New Jersey, 1982-. *Publications:* Contributor of articles to various publications on numerous subjects; Writer for Vierteljahreshefte, published in Hamburg, Germany, for 2 years. *Hobbies:* Music; Drama; Enjoying my Gardens; Travel; Writing; Animal Protection and Nature Conservancy Causes. *Address:* PO Box 9179, Morristown, NJ 07960, USA.

TELFER Nancy Ellen, b. 8 May 1950, Canada. Music Composer, Conductor & Speaker. m. Stuart Beaudoin, 20 Mar. 1981, 2 sons. *Education:* BA, 1971; BMus, 1979. *Appointments:* Teacher, 1972-76; Composer (freelance), 1980-. *Creative works:* Numerous published vocal works including: SATB secular & sacred; 2-part SSA; Unison; Folk song arrangements for choral groups; Vocal solos; Piano & organ pieces. *Memberships:* Canadian Music Educators Association; Association of Canadian Choral Conductors; Percussive Arts Society; Canadian Music Centre; Royal Canadian College of Organists. *Address:* 629 Queen Street, Newmarket, Ontario, Canada L3Y 2J1.

TEMKO Florence, b. 20 Oct. 1921. Author. *Education:* London University; New School for Social Research. *Appointments:* Workshop Instructor: UCSD, Metropolitan Museum of Art, San Diego Museum of Art, Smithsonian Institution, University of Massachusetts, Chicago Cultural Center. *Publications:* 24 books and many articles on folkcrafts and paper arts. *Memberships:* Authors Guild; ASJA; International Pen. *Address:* 5050 La Jolla Boulevard, Suite P-C, San Diego, CA 92109, USA.

TEMPLETON Edith. b. 7 Apr. 1916, Prague. Writer. m. Edmund Ronald, 24 Sept. 1955, 1 son. *Education:* Medical University, Prague, 3 years. *Appointments:* Medical Coding, US Forces, Cheltenham and London, 1945-46; Conference and Law Court Interpreter for British Army, Federal Republic of Germany; Captain's rank. *Publications:* Novels: Summer in the Country; Living on Yesterday; This Charming Pastime; Gordon; Island of Desire; Travel: Surprise of Cremona; Fiction and travel in The New Yorker, Harpers, Vogue, Transatlantic, Holiday, Housewife, Woman and Beauty; Anthologies: New Yorker Short Stories; Abroad, Gourmets Companion, Compleate Imbiber. *Honour:* Book Society Choice, 1954. *Hobby:* Travel in greatest possible comfort. *Address:* 55 Compayne Gardens, London NW6 3DB, England.

TEMPLETON Fiona Anne, b. 23 Dec. 1951, Scotland. Theatre Writer; Director; Performer. *Education:* MA Honours French, Edinburgh University, Scotland, 1973; MA Poetics, New York University, USA, 1985. *Creative Works:* As founding member of The Theatre of Mistakes, London, England: The Street, 1975; 5 Concert Pieces and a Free Session, 1975; The Ascent of the Stedelijk, 1976; A Waterfall, 1977; Going, 1977; 2 Freedoms, 1979. Thought/Death, 1980; Cupid and Psyche, 1981; There Was Absent Achilles, 1982; The Seven Deadly Jealousies, 1982; Under Paper Spells, 1982; Defense, 1982; Against Agreement, 1982; Experiments in the Destruction of Time, 1983; Five Hard Pieces, including The New Three Act Piece, 1983; Out of the Mouths, 1984; A/Version, 1985; Only You, 1986; The Future, 1987; Showing it Again, 1987; The Hypothetical Third Person, 1988; You - The City, 1988. *Publications:* Elements of Performance Art, 1976; London, poem, 1984; Numerous reviews, articles and interviews to magazines. *Honours:* Foundation for Contemporary Performance Arts Grant, 1987; New York State Council on the Arts Sponsored Project Grant, 1987-88; National Endowment for the Arts Interarts Project Grant, 1987-88; Pen Writers' Fund Grant, 1986; New York Foundation for the Arts Interarts Fellowship, 1985; Jerome Fund for Performance Art Award, 1985; National Endowment for the Arts New Genres Fellowship, 1983; funding from The Arts Council of Great Britain and British Council, 1975-78. *Interests:* The Arts; Human Rights. *Address:* 100 St Mark's Place, No 7, New York, NY 10009, USA.

TENGUM Phyllis Zybl Ruth, b. 2 Aug. 1922, Swift Current, Saskatchewan, Canada. General Manager, The Inventors Association. m. Albert Leroy Tengum, 5 July 1967. 1 stepdaughter. *Education:* Secretarial Course, Swift Current Collegiate, 1943. *Appointment:* Secretary 1955, Secretary-Treasurer, General Manager, The Inventors Association. *Memberships:* American Pyramid research Society; Director, Ways and Means Committee, Society for the Prevention of Cruelty to Animals; Associate Director, Swift Current Agricultural and Exhibition Association; Wildlife Federation of Saskatchewan; St Georges Society; International Order of Volunteers for Peace; Sakharov International Committee, Inc, Washington DC; National Geographic Society, 1986. *Honour:* Donor Certificate, Western Development Museum. *Address:* 54 - 3rd Ave NE, Swift Current, Saskatchewan, Canada S9H 2G2.

TENNANT Carolyn G, b. 19 June 1947, Janesville, USA. College Administrator. m. 28 Dec. 1968. *Education:* BA, 1969, MA 1973, PhD, 1979, University of Colorado. *Appointments:* Teacher, 1969-73, Special Programmes Co-ordinator, 1969-73, Adams Co. School District 12; Director, Gifted & Talented, Instructor, Staff Development, Denver, 1978-79; Director Instructor, Cognitive Development, Denver, 1978-81; Dayton, 1981-83; Vice President, Sudent Life, North Central Bible College, Minneapolis, 1983-. *Publications:* Elementary & Secondary Level Programmes for the Gifted & Talented, 1980; numerous articles, booklets & curriculums. *Memberships:* Ordained to Ministry, Assemblies of God Church, 1985; Association Supervision & Curriculum Development; Association Christians in Student Development; National Association Gifted Children; Colorado Language Arts Society, Treasurer, 1973-74; National Council Teachers English; International Reading Association. *Hobbies:* Reading; Writing; Knitting; Cross Stitch. *Address:* North Central Bible College, 910 Elliot Avenue South, Minneapolis, MN 55404, USA.

TENUTA Jean Louise, b. 12 Apr. 1958, Kenosha, Wisconsin, USA. Sports Writer; Medical Technologist. *Education:* BS, Life Science, University of Wisconsin, 1979; BA, News Editorial Journalism, Marquette University, 1983; Clinical Internship, Veterans Administration Medical Centre, Milwaukee, Wisconsin, 1979-80; Washington Journalism Semester, American University, 1984; MS, Journalism, Northwestern University, Evanston, Illinois, 1989. *Appointments:* Sports Writer, Racine Journal & Times, Racine,

Wisconsin, 1988-; Night Shift Technologist, St Therese Medical Centre, Waukegan, Illinois, 1986-87; Clinical Laboratory Supervisor, Group Health Association, Washington DC, 1985-86; Sports Writer, The Journal Messenger, Manassas, Virginia, 1986; Sports Writer, The Washington Post, Washington DC, 1984-86; Sports Writer, Kenosha News, 1978-84. *Publications:* Contributor of sports articles in newspapers. *Memberships:* National Federation of Press Women Inc, Capital Area Treasurer, 1985-87; Society of Professional Journalists Sigma Delta Chi; Women in Communications Inc; American Association of University Women; Daughters of the American Revolution; Marquette University Alumni; University of Wisconsin Alumni; American Society of Clinical Pathologists, Associate Member; National Writers Club; Association of Women in Sports Media. *Honours:* 1st place Writing Award, Sports Features, National Federation of Press Women, 1986; Capital Press Women 1st Place, Sports Features, 1986; 3rd Place, General Features, 1986; Wisconsin Newspaper Association Scholarship, 1983; University of Wisconsin Alumni Scholarship, 1975; George Nelson Tremper Fund Scholarship. *Hobbies:* Basketball; Softball; Health, diet and exercise; Travel. *Address:* 9023-17th Avenue, Kenosha, WI 53140, USA.

TEREGEYO Ana Sablan, b. 9 Feb. 1948, Saipan, Mariana Islands. Executive Director, Arts and Culture Council. m. Joaquin Teregeyo, 2 July 1964, 3 sons, 3 daughters. *Education:* Management Development Programme, University of Nebraska, Lincoln, USA, 1972-76. *(Appointments:* Personnel Management Intern, 1974-75, Employees Development and Training Specialist, 1976-79, CETA Administrator, 1979-80, TTPI; Executive Director, Commonwealth Council for Arts and Culture, Saipan, Mariana Islands, 1980-; Associate Professor, Institute of Culture and Communication, East-West Center, Hawaii. *Creative works:* Basis skills in basket weaving; Macrame. *b3Memberships:* Vice-Chairman/Chairman, Pacific Arts Regional Organization; Vice-Chairman, Northern Mariana Islands UN Day Celebration, 1981; Chairman, Flame Tree and Liberation Day Festivities, 1983; Past President, Saipan Women's Bowling Association; President, Marianas High School PTA; Chairman, Community Health Center Board of Directors; Secretary, Founder, Director, Northern Mariana Islands Cultural and Performing Arts Center Foundation. *Honours:* Recognition for Merit/Quality Increases for exceptional performances by NMI State Arts Agency Board of Directors, 1981-; Candidate, Employee of the Year Award, Government of the Northern Marianas, 1982; Governor's Service Award for 22 years of dedicated public services, 1988; Letters of Commendation for Exceptional Performance, national, regional and international arts and culture organisations. *Hobbies:* Bowling; Computer programming and games; Reading novels; Listening to soft music. *Address:* PO Box 51, CHRB, Saipan, MP 96950.

TERPENING Virginia Ann Shoup, b. 17 July 1917, Lewistown, Missouri, USA. Artist. m. (1)Jack Baltzelle, 26 Dec. 1940, divorced 1949, 1 daughter, (2)C W Terpening, 5 July 1951, died, 5 Marr. 1988. *Education:* Washington University School of Fine Art, 1937-40. *Publications:* Paintings: Carnival in the Park; To the Days That Were; Mums, Mississippi River Boat; Signs of Spring; Geranium in a Bucket; That Third Dimension; The Homestead Circca 1896; Country Auction. *Memberships:* Artists Equity Association Inc; National Museum of Women in Art, Charter Member; International Platform Association. *Honours:* Certificate of Merit, Latham Foundation, 1960-63; Gold Medallion Awards, Two Flags Festival of Art, 1975-78; Purchase Award, 1977; etc. *Hobbies:* Miniature Collection; Horticulture; Animal Rights. *Address:* PO Box 117 1055 Vine St., Lewistown, MO 63452, USA.

TERPSTRA Margery S. De La More Williams, b. 20 Mar. 1925, Portland, USA. Psychologist; Holistic Educator. m. Chester Terpstra, 10 Aug. 1945, 3 sons. *Education:* BA, 1953, MEd., 1967, PhD, 1972, University

of Hawaii. *Appointments:* War Production Training Materials production, 1942-43; Honolulu Council of Churches, 1945-46; Missionary Teacher, Church Worke, 1940-61; Foreign Contracts, University of Hawaii, 1967-71; Self employed, 1975-. *Publications:* Articles in professional journals. *Memberships:* PTA; President, Hawaii Div., American Association for Marriage & Family Therapy; CAPS; Hawaii Psychological Association. *Honour:* Hawaii State Mother of the Year, 1986. *Hobbies:* Travel; Reading; Walking; Swimming. *Address:* 1750 Kalakaua Ave., Suite 2110, Honolulu, HI 96826, USA.

TERR Lenore Frances Cagen, b. 27 Mar. 1936, New York, USA. Child Psychiatrist; Author; Lecturer. m. Abba Terr, 23 June 1957, 1 son, 1 daughter. *Education:* AB, Western Reserve University, 1957; MD, University of Michigan, 1961. *Appointments:* Western Reserve University School of Medicine, 1966-71; Univerity of California, San Francisco, 1971-; University of California, Berkley & Davis, Law Schools, Visiting Faculty, 1974-. *Publications:* Too Scared to Cry, 1990; articles in journals. *Memberships:* American Board of Psychiatry & Neurology, Director, 1988- ; American Academy of Child & Adolescent Psychiatry, Fellow, Councillor, 1985- 87; American Psychiatric Association, Fellow; Group for the Advancement of Psychiatry, Board, 1986-88; etc. *Honours:* NIMH Career Teacher, 1968-70; Rockefeller Foundation, Scholar in Residence, 1981, 1988. *Hobby:* Music (Piano). *Address:* 450 Sutter Street, San Francisco, CA 94108, USA.

TERRIS Susan, b. 6 May 1937, St Louis, Missouri, USA. Author. m. David Warren Terris, 31 Aug. 1958, 2 sons, 1 daughter. *Education:* AB, Wellesley College, 1959; MA, San Francisco State College (now San Francisco State University), 1966. *Career:* Teacher, Writing for Children course and writing workshops, University of California Extension, San Francisco; Tutoring; Library work; Researcher; Lecturer on children's books to schools and libraries. *Publications:* The Upstairs Witch and the Downstairs Witch, 1970; The Backwards Boots, 1971; On Fire, 1972; The Drowning Boy, 1972; Plague of Frogs, 1973; Pickle, 1973; Whirling Rainbow, 1974; Amanda, the Panda and the Redhead, 1975; The Pencil Families, 1975; No Boys Allowed, 1976; The Chicken Pox Papers, 1976; Two Ps in a Pod, 1977; Tucker and the Horse Thief, 1979; Stage Brat, 1980; No Scarlet Ribbons, 1981; Wings and Roots, 1982; Octopus Pie, 1983; Baby-Snatcher, 1984; The Latchkey Kids, 1986; Nell's Quilt, 1987; Contributor to a series of elementary school texts; Stories and articles in magazines; Book reviews in New York Times. *Hobbies:* Sewing; Knitting; Needlepoint work; Fancy cooking; Hiking. *Address:* 11 Jordan Avenue, San Francisco, CA 94118, USA.

TERRY Megan, b. 22 July 1932, Seattle, Washington, USA. Playwright. *Education:* BEd, University of Washington; Graduate studies, University of Alberta & Banff School of Fine Arts, Canada; Fellowship, Yale University; Theatre studies, Seattle Repertory Playhouse. *Appointments include:* Reorganiser, Cornish Players, Seattle; Tour, northwest, 2 years; Founding member, Open Theatre, New York Theatre Strategy, Women's Theatre Council, New York; Playwright-in residence, Omaha Magic Theatre, Nebraska, current; Appointed member, Nebraska Committee for Humanities, 1983-; Lecturer, numerous colleges, writing conferences; Adjudicator, various play writing competitions. *Creative work:* Over 50 plays, various types including serious musicals, performance art, transformation plays, radio & TV, produced worldwide, translated every major language, numerous commissions. Titles include: Approaching Simone; American Wedding Ritual; Sanibel & Captiva; Fireworks; Future Soap; One More Little Drinkie; Nightwalk; Comings & Goings; Magic Realists; Eat At Joe's; Babes in the Bighouse; American King's English for Queen's; Dinner's in the Blender; *Honours include:* Obie Award, Best Play, 1970; Winner, national radio play contests; Dramatists Guild Annual Award, 1983; Rockefeller fellowship, 1987-88; Guggenheim fellowship;

Nomination, Nebraska Poet Laureate; Stanley Drama Award; 2 grants, Office of Advanced Drama Research, University of Minnesota; Various other grants, fellowships. *Address:* c/o Elisabeth Marton, 96 Fifth Avenue, New York, NY 10011, USA.

TETERYCZ Barbara Ann, b. 23 Jan. 1952, Chicago, Illinois, USA. Entrepreneur. m. Robert Nathan Estes, 13 Oct. 1984. *Education:* BA University of Illinois, 1970-74 and 1976-77; Postgraduate, Parkland College, 1975-76. *Appointments:* Teller, First Federal of Champaign, 1974-75; Cashier, Kroger Co, 1975-77; Merch Rep, Rustcraft Greeting Cards, 1977-78; Sales Rep, Hockenberg-Rubin, Champaign, 1978; Sales Rep, John Morrell & Co, Champaign, 1978-80; Account Executive, WKO TV, Champaign, 1981-86; Owner, Left-Handed Compliments, Champaign, 1985-. *Creative works:* Left-handed Calendar; Left-behind Shorts and Sweatpants; Contributing editor, Champaign County Business Reports Magazine, 1986. *b3Memberships:* International Platform Association; American Cancer Society; Committee to Elect & Re-Elect Beth Beauchamp to City Council, 1984 & 1987; Women's Business Council of Urbana; Champaign Chamber of Commerce; Founding member, Entrepreneurs Roundtable; University of Illinois Alumni Association; National Association of Female Executives; AD Club of Champaign-Urbana. *Honours:* Illinois State Scholar, 1970-74; Alpha Omega Society Honorary Scholastic Society, Parkland College, 1975-76; Finalist, AD Club Creative Copywriting, 1975-76; National/Regional Consumer Magazine; Local Radio 60 second commercial, 1987. *Hobbies:* Reading; Writing; Bicycling; Weightlifting. *Address:* Left-handed Compliments, 723 S Neil St, Champaign, IL 61820, USA.

THAPAR Romila, b. 30 Nov. 1931, Lucknow, India. Professor of History. *Education:* BA Honours, Pubjab University; BA Honours, PhD, London University, England. *Appointments:* London University, 1959-60; Kurukshetra University, 1961-62; Delhi University, 1963-70; Jawaharlal Nehru University, New Delhi, 1970-. *Publications:* Asoka & Decline of the Mauryas; History of India; Ancient Indian Social History; From Lineage to State; Mauryas Revisited. *Memberships:* Fellow, Royal Asiatic Society; Corresponding Fellow, Royal Historical Society; Honorary Fellow, Lady Margaret Hall, Oxford University. *Honours:* Professor-at-Large, Cornell University, USA, 1980; General President, Indian History Congress, 1983; Nehru Fellow, 1976, 1977; National Fellow, ICSSR, India, 1988, 1989. *Address:* 23 B Road, Maharani Bagh, New Delhi 110065, India.

THARP Marye Charlese, b. 10 Apr. 1947, Knoxville, Tennessee, USA. professor. *Education:* BA 1967, BBA 1970, MBA 1973, PhD 1976, The University of Texas at Austin. *Appointments:* University of Texas at Austin, 1970-75 and 1987-; University de Las Americas, 1972-73; University of Texas at San Antonio, 1975-87; University del Pacifico, 1980; University of Kent, 1986. *Publication:* Marketing in the International Environment, with Edward W Cundiff, 2nd edition, 1988. *Memberships:* American Academy of Advertising (Chair, Membership Committee); American Marketing Association. *Honours:* Fulbright Scholar, 1980; Governor's Club Award, Oustanding Community Service, 1982; Visiting Professor Program, American Academy of Advertising, 1982; Faculty Member, London Semester Program, UT System Consortium, 1986; Latin American Teaching Fellow, Tufts University, 1972. *Address:* Department of Advertising, CMA 7.142, The University of Texas at Austin, Austin, TX 78712, USA.

THATCHER Margaret (Hilda), Rt. Hon. Mrs. b. 13 Oct. 1925, England. Prime Minister & First lord of the Treasury. m. Denis Thatcher, 1 son, 1 daughter (twins). *Education:* BSc., MA, Somerville College, Oxford. *Appointments:* Research Chemist, 1947-51; Called to the Bar, Lincoln's Inn, 1954; MP, Conservative, Finchley 1959-; Hon. Bencher, 1975; Leader of the Opposition, 1975-79; Prime Minister, First Lord of the Treasury, 1979-. *Publication:* In Defence of Freedom, 1986. *Honours:* Hon. Fellow, Somerville College, 1970;

Freedom of Borough of Barnet, 1980; Donovan Award, USA, 1981; FRS, 1983. *Hobbies:* Music; Reading. *Address:* House of Commons, Westminster, London SW1, England.

THELEN Christine, b. 15 May 1913, Madison, Wisconsin, USA. Retired MD. *Education:* BS, Medical Science, Univesity of Wisconsin, 1934; MD, Medical College of Virginia, 1937; Internship & Residency, various hospitals. *Appointments:* College Physician, Greensboro College, 1939-41; Jackson Clinic Staff, Madison, 1945-50; Private Practice, Wichita, 1951-80. *Memberships Include:* Board: YWCA; Big Brothers; Big Sisters; Family Consultation Service; County State & American Medical Associations; Life Member, American College Obstetricians & Gynaecologists; Zonta. *Honours:* Woman of Achievement, Matrix Table of Women in Communication, 1975. *Hobbies:* Travel; Photography; Spectator Sports. *Address:* Larksfield Place Apt. 1123, 7373 E. 29th St. No., Wichita, KS 67226, USA.

THEODORAS Mary Louise, b. 27 Feb. 1932, Dayton, Ohio, USA. Osteopath; College Dean. m. George A. Saul, 13 May 1960, 1 son, 1 daughter. *Education:* BS, University of Dayton, 1952; DO, Kirksville College of Osteopathic Medicine, 1956; Intern, Grandview Hospital, 1957; General Practice Certification, 1973. *Appointments:* Volunteer Laboratory Technician, summers 1948-49, Surgical Assistant, 1949-53, Miami Valley Hospital, Dayton, Ohio; Surgical Assistant, Grandview Hospital, Dayton, summers 1953-55; Self-employed, Family Practice, Huber Heights, Ohio, 1957-58, 1986; Regional Assistant Dean, Southwest Ohio Region, Ohio University College of Osteopathic Medicine, Dayton, 1978-. *Memberships:* 2nd Vice-President, American Osteopathic Association; Past President: Ohio Osteopathic Association; Dayton District Academy of Osteopathic Medicine; Ohio Society of American College of General Practice in Osteopathic Medicine; Kirksville College Alumni Board; Past Chief of Staff, Grandview Hospital and Medical Center; American College of General Practice in Osteopathic Medicine; Past Secretary, Kirksville College Board of Trustees; Drug Education Committee, Health-O-Rama Committee, Medical Advisory Committee, United Way; Academy of Osteopathic Directors of Medical Education. *Honours:* Fellowship, American College of General Practitioners in Osteopathic Medicine and Surgery, 1974; United Health Services for Outstanding Community Service, 1981; Certificate of Merit, Dayton YMCA, 1985; Honoured Patron Award for outstanding service to the Kirksville College of Osteopathic Medicine and philanthropic support of its programmes, 1986; Boss of the Year, Ohio Osteopathic Medical Assistants Association, 1987. *Hobbies:* Piano, Scuba diving; Fishing; Travel. *Address:* Ohio University College of Osteopathic Medicine, Grandview Hospital and Medical Center, 405 Grand Avenue, Dayton, OH 45405, USA.

THEODORE Crystal, b. 27 July 1917, Greenville, South Carolina, USA. Author; Painter; Retired University Professor of Art. *Education:* AB, magna cum laude, 1938; MA 1942, EdD 1953, Columbia University. *Appointments:* Instr of Art, Winthrop College, 1938-42; Engineering Draftsman, Tenn Valley Authority, 1943; US Marine Corps Reserve, G-2, 1944-46; Professor of Art and Head of Dept, Huntingdon College, 1947-52; Professor of Art and Head of Department, East Tennessee State University, 1953-57; Professor of Art and Head of Dept, James Madison University, 1957-83. *Creative works:* Articles: The Idea of Catharsis in the Arts; Art X+1 Again; Women As Artists. Paintings included in: Hunter Gallery Annual; Sixth Annual Painting of the Year; Third South Coast Annual; 227 Annual; Butler Gallery. *Memberships:* American Association of University Women (Board of Directors, national, State & Local); Delta Kappa Gamma Society International (branch president); American Mensa Ltd; Virginia Museum (Board of Directors, local chapter). *Honours:* Carnegie Foundation for the Advancement of Teaching Awards, 1948, 1949, 1950, 1951; Fellowship, Rockefeller Educational Foundation, 1952-53; Grant,

Ed TV and Radio Ctr, 1956; Grant, American Association of University Women, 1981-82; Numerous awards for paintings; most recent: Honorable Mention, 1987 National Greek Art Exhibition (Massachusetts). *Hobbies:* Gardening; Reading; Painting; Writing; Travel. *Address:* Rt 5 Box 202, Harrisonburg, VA 22801, USA.

THIRSK (Irene) Joan, b. 19 June 1922, London, England. Historian. m. James Wood Thirsk, 12 Sept. 1945. 1 son, 1 daughter. *Education:* Westfield College, London University, 1941-42 and 1945-47; BA Honours, History; PhD, 1950. *Appointments:* Assistant Lecturer, Sociology, London School of Economics, 1950-51; Senior Research Fellow, Agrarian History, Department of English Local History, Leicester University, 1951-65; Reader in Economic History, Oxford University, 1965-83. *Publications:* English Peasant Farming, 1957; editor and part author of The Agrarian History of England and Wales IV, 1500-1640, 1967; V, 1640-1750, 1984-85; The Restoration, 1976; Economic Policy and Projects, 1978; England's Agricultural Regions and Agrarian History 1500-1750, 1987. *Memberships:* President, British Agricultural History Society, 1983-86; President, British Association for Local History, 1986-; Member of Council, Economic History Society, 1955-83; Member of Council, Kent Archaeological Society, 1987-; Foreign Member, American Philos Soc, 1982-; Corresp Member, Colonial Soc Massachusetts, 1983-. *Honour:* Honorary DLitt, University of Leicester, 1985. *Hobbies:* Sewing; Machine Knitting; Gardening. *Address:* 1 Hadlow Castle, Hadlow, Tonbridge, Kent, TN11 0EG.

THOEN Doris Rae, b. 1 Feb. 1925, Corvallis, Oregon, USA. Trucking Partner; Office Manager. m. Monte L Thoen, 22 Oct. 1950. 2 sons. *Education:* BA Business Adm, Oregon State University, Corvallis, 1947. *Appointments:* St Treas Office, St Of Oregon, Salem, 1947-48; Pac N W Bell Tel, Corvallis, Oregon, 1948-49; Loan Closer, Far West Sav. Bk, 1949-50; US Govt Personnel Dir, Klamath Falls, 1950-52; Manage Trucking Company, 1954-. *Memberships:* Oregon Parents & Teachers Association, St Brd; American Assoc of University Women; Portland Alum of Delta Zeta, national Collegiate Sorority; Regional Pub Relations Dir, Oregon Republic Party; Oregon Fed of Republican Women; Beaverton-West Slope Republican Women; American Cancer Society, full time volunteer for 29 years; Sunset Valley Home Extension. *Honours:* Oregon Woman of Year, Delta Zeta National Sorority, 1961; Grant, American Association of University Women, 1974; Order of Red Sword, American Cancer Soc, Multnomah Unit, 1968; St George Award, National Divisional Award, Am Can Soc, 1987; Oregon St Extension Service, Certificate of Appreciation for volunteering, 1983; Presidential Citation for Volunteer Services, President Nixon, 1974. *Hobbies:* Volunteering for numerous organizations, and St Vincents Cancer Information Center; Reading; Flying with husband; Genology. *Address:* 13124 N W Sue Street, Portland, Oregon 97229, USA.

THOMAE Betty Kennedy, b. 9 Sept. 1920, Columbus, Ohio, USA. Legal secretary; Writer; Poet; Songwriter. 1 son, 1 daughter. *Education:* Franklin University, 1960-65; Certified Professional Secretary, 1964; Professional Legal Secretary, 1970. *Appointment:* Delligatti, Hollenbaugh, Briscoe & Milless, Columbus, Ohio. *Creative works:* Peoms: Roses and Thorns, 1970; Stand Still, Summer, 1987; 150 poems in anthologies, magazines, newspapers and read over radio programmes; Published approximately 35 articles in secretarial field in magazines; Legal Secretary's Desk Book-With Forms, 1973; Legal Secretary's Encyclopedic Dictionary, 1977, edited and revised second edition; Author of numerous songs. *Memberships:* National Association of Legal Secretaries; World of Poetry; Verse Writers Guild of Ohio; World Literary Academy; Broadcast Music, Inc. *Honours:* Selected a Danae, International Clover Poetry Association; Diploma of Merit and Medal of Honour, Centro Studi a Scambi of Rome, Italy; Citation of honour, World Poetry Society; Golden Poet Award 1985-89; World of Poetry; 2 citations, International Clover Poetry Association;

Advisory Member, Marquis Biographical Library Society; 1st place, Freelance Writer's Contest; Legal Secretary of the Year, Columbus Chapter, National Association of Legal Secretaries, 1970; Many certificates of achievement and honourable mention certificates for poetry. *Address:* 1008 Hardesty Place West, Columbus, Ohio 43204, USA.

THOMAS Ellidee Dotson, b. 20 July 1926, Huntsville, USA. m. Ulysses Gordon Thomas, 9 Jan. 1960, 1 daughter. *Education:* BA, 1947, MS, MD, 1958, University of Arkansas. *Appointments:* Arkansas Association for Crippled Children, 1949-50; Moody State School for C.P, Texas, 1951-52; Air Force of USA, 1952-54; Univesity of Oklahoma for Health Sciences, 1965-69, 1969-85; Children's Medical Centre, 1968-69; University of Arkansas for Medicla Sciences, 1986-. *Memberships:* International Child Neurology Association; Child Neurology Society; American Academy for Cerebral Palsy and Developmental Medicine; American Academy of Neurology; Oklahoma Medical Womens Association, President, 1983-84. *Honours:* Special Award, Oklahoma Association for Children with Learning Disabilities, 1974. *Hobbies:* Reading; Music; Public Affairs; Spectator Sports; Ceramics; Cooking. *Address:* Dept. of Peaediatrics, University of Arkansas Medical Sciences, Northwest Arkansas Neurodevelopment Centre, 1101 N. Woolsey St., Fayetteville, AR 72703, USA.

THOMAS Esther Merlene, b. 16 Oct. 1945, San Diego, USA. Teacher. *Education:* AA, 1966; BA, San Diego State University, 1969; MA, University of Redlands, 1977. *Appointments:* San Diego State University Lab School, 1968-69; Cajon Valley Union School District, 1969-. *Publications:* Lakeside Portraits, Newspaper Column, 1964; Individualized Curriculum In the Affective Domain for Individual and Social Attitudes In Levels K-6, 1977; articles in journals. *Memberships Include:* Charter Member, Presidential Task Force; International Christian Business & Professional Women; Business & Professional Women; National, California, Cajon Valley, Teachers Associations; Lakeside Historical Society; Life Member, San Diego Aerospace Museum; Marine Corps Association; Smithsonian Institution; *Honours Include:* Christian Ambassador to Madame Chiang Kai-Sek, with President Okja Choi Choo of Soodoo Teachers College, Seoul, Korea, International Christian Womens Club, 1974; Certificate of Merit, Presidential Task Force, 1986; Medal of Merit, President Ronald Reagan, Task Force, 1986. *Hobbies:* Piano & Guitar; Signing; Horseriding; Gardening; Travel; Hiking. *Address:* 1251 Finch Street, El Cajon, CA 92020, USA.

THOMAS Gayle, b. 28 Jan. 1944, Montreal, Canada. Filmmaker. 1 daughter. *Education:* Montreal Institute of Technology, 1961-63; Ecole Des Beaux Arts, Montreal, 1964; BFA, Concordia University, Montreal, 1968. *Appointments:* Drafting, Bell Canada, 1961-63; Potterton Production Film Co., 1969-70; Filmmaker, Scriptwriter, Animator, Director, Producer, National Film Board of Canada. *Memberships:* ASIFA. *Honours:* Recipient, many honours and awards. *Hobbies:* Reading; Creative Writing; Cycling; Skiing. *Address:* National Film Board of Canada, Box 6100, Station A, Montreal, PQ, Canada.

THOMAS Gwyneth Anne, b. 9 Feb. 1916, Melbourne, Australia. Medical Records Administrator. *Education:* Registered Medical Record Administrator. *Appointments:* VAD and Australian Army Medical Womens Service, 1941-46; Repatriation Department, Australian Public Service, 1946-70; Australian Bureau of Statistics, 1970-77; Part-time Research Work, Royal Children's Hospital, Melbourne, Royal Womens Hospital, Melbourne, Australian Veterans Herbicidal Study. *Publications:* Thoracoplasty for Pulmonary Tuberculosis in the Repatriation Department, Victoria Branch, co-author, 1943-64; contributor of numerous other articles. *Membership:* Foundation Member, 1st Vice President, President Secretary, Committee Member, Victorian Association of Medical Record

Administrators, 1948-78; President, Secretary, Australian Federation of Medical Record Administrators; Life Member, Medical Record Associationa of Australia, 1988. *Honours:* Honorary Life Member, Royal Prince Alfred Hospital, Sydney, New South Wales. *Hobbies:* Entertaining; Dressmaking; Gardening. *Address:* 7/7 Ferncroft Avenue, East Malvern, 3145 Victoria, Australia.

THOMAS Hilary Joan, b. 27 May 1935, London, England. Historical Researcher; Genealogist. m. Rowland Humphrey Thomas, 15 June 1963, 1 son, 1 daughter. *Education:* SRN, St Thomas' Hospital, 1959. *Appointments:* Nursing, 1955-66; Journalist, Researcher, 1972-. *Publications:* Travel books especially on London; Biographies; Genealogies. *Memberships:* Association of Genealogists & Record Agents; Society of Genealogists. *Hobbies:* Travel; Theatre; Books; Music; Country Walking. *Address:* 27 Grasvenor Avenue, Barnet, Herts EN5 2BY, England.

THOMAS Linda Irene, b. 14 Mar. 1944, Seattle, USA. Finance Director. m. (1)Robert Keith Reed, 8 Jan. 1968, (2)Alfred Richard Thomas, 16 Feb. 1972, 2 daughters. *Education:* BA, Evergreen State College, 1988. *Appointments:* Office Manager, Tacoma Moving & Storage Co., 1969-72; District Account Fife School District, 1972-76; Staff Accountant, Nelson Johnson & Barlow, 1976-78; President, Thomas Accounting, Tacoma, 1978-82; Washington State Representative, 26th District, 1984-86; Project Director, Pacific Institute, 1987; Field Representative, NFIB Business Activation Programme, 1988; Finance Director, Washington State Republican Party, 1988-. *Publications:* Payroll Taxes Without Tears, 1981; Producer, Cassette Tape, Business Recordkeeping Success, 1983. *Memberships:* Various professional organisations. *Honours:* SBA Women in Business Advocate Award, 1986. *Address:* PO Box 708, Gig Harbor, WA 98335, USA.

THOMAS Lucille Cole, b. 1 Oct. 1921, Dunn, North Carolina, USA. Library Consultant; Researcher. m. George B Thomas, 24 May 1943, 1 son, 1 daughter. *Education:* BA, Bennett College, 1941; MA, New York University, 1955; MS Columbia University, 1957. *Appointments:* Young Adult Librarian, Brooklyn Public Library, 1955-56; School Librarian, New York City Schools, 1956-68; Supervisor, School Library Service, New York City, 1968-77; Assistant Director, School Library Services, New York City Public Schools, 1977-83; Adjunct Professor, Queens College, City University of New York, 1987-. *Publications:* Articles in professional journals. *Memberships:* American Library Association, Executive Board; International Association of School Librarianship; International Federation of Library Associations; New York Library Association, President 1977-78; New York Library Club; etc. *Honours:* Recipient, several awards including: Programs of Service Award, Eta Omega Chaptr, Alpha Kappa Alpha, 1986; Achievement Award, Columbia University, School of Library Services, 1987; Grolier Foundation Award, 1988. *Hobbies:* Theatre; Reading; Sewing. *Address:* 1184 Union Street, Brooklyn, NY 11225, USA.

THOMAS Lucinda Ellen b. 21 May 1932, Fort Collins, Colorado, USA. University Administrator. 2 sons. *Education:* BS 1953, MEd 1968, Colorado State University. *Appointments:* Teacher, Agana Junior High School, Guam, Marianas Islands, 1953-54; Director, Guidance Services, American Community School, Buenos Aires, Argentina, 1962-65; Director, University Testing Service, & staff psychologist, University Counselling Centre, Colorado State University, Fort Collins, 1968-. *Publications:* Numerous articles, professional journals. *Memberships:* American Psychological Association; American Association of Counselling & Development; American College Personnel Association. *Honours:* Phi Delta Kappa, 1980-; National Certified Career Counsellor, 1985; National Certified Counsellor, 1985. *Hobbies:* Travel; Reading. *Address:* University Testing Service, Colorado State University, Fort Collins, Colorado 80523, USA.

THOMAS Mable, b. 8 Nov. 1957, Atlanta, Georgia, USA. State Representative. *Education:* BS, Public Administration, Georgia State University, 1982; Studying for a Masters Degree in Public Admin, currently. *Appointments:* Personnel Assistant, Georgia Department of Natural Resources, 1978-79; Recreation Supervisor, City of Atlanta Parks and Recreation, 1980-81; Research Assistant Educational Talent Search 1981-82, Chairperson, Black Life & Culture Committee 1982-83, Georgia State University; Worksite Monitor, City of Atlanta Community Development, 1983; Senate Intern (Senator Julian Bond), 1984; State Representative 1984-, Georgia General Assembly, District 31. *Creative works:* Lectured at workshops, seminars, forums, conferences and assemblies. *Memberships:* National Association for the Advancement of Coloured People; Founder, Vine City Community Improvement Association; Consultant, Georgia Democratic Party; Board of Directors: Georgia Legislative Black Caucus; National Political Congress of Black Women; American Cancer Society; West End Medical Center. *Honours:* Recipient of numerous honours and awards including: Dedicated Service to the Community Award, Zion Grove Baptist Church, Youth Day, 1988; Community Service Award, The Disabled in Action Volunteer Organization, 1988; Top Female Vote Getter Jesse Jackson Delegate, Democratic National Convention, 1988; Fulton County Board of Education, Certificate of Recognition, 1988; Georgia Association of Black Elected Officials "Speakers" Award, 1989. *Address:* Legislative Office Bdg Rm 512-D, Atlanta, Georgia 30334, USA.

THOMAS Mable, b. 8 Nov. 1957, Atlanta, Georgia, USA. Local Politician; Realtor. *Education:* BS (Public Administration) 1982, MS in progress, Georgia State University. *Appointments include:* Assistant, Georgia Department of Natural Resources, 1978-79; Recreation Supervisor, City of Atlanta Parks & Recreation, 1980-81; Research assistant, Georgia State University Education Talent Search, 1981-82; Worksite Monitor, City of Atlanta Community Development, 1983; State Chair, University of Georgia Black Life & Culture Committee, 1982-83; Senate Intern 1984, State Representative 3 terms (current), House Education, Special Judiciary & Industrial Relations Committees, Georgia General Assembly; Various other civic or community positions. *Memberships include:* Board, Georgia Legislature Black Caucus, 1985-88; Various offices, Black Women's Health Project, National Association for Advancement of Coloured Peoples; Southern Christian Leadership Conference, Martin Luther King Centre for Non-Violent Social Change. *Honours:* Numerous awards (community service, leadership, academic excellence) including: Woman of Excellence, Georgia State University, 1983; Top Jesse Jackson delegate, Democratic National Convention, 1984; 30 Leaders of the Future, Ebony magazine, 1985; Humanities award, National Association of Black Social Workers, 1986. *Address:* 765 Jones Avenue NW, Atlanta, Georgia 30314, USA.

THOMAS Margaret Ann (Peg), b. 2 June 1945, Cleveland, Ohio, USA. Psychologist. m. James Blake Thomas, 14 Sept. 1978, 2 stepsons, 1 daughter. *Education:* BA, Albion College, Albion, Michigan, 1967; MA, 1969, Psychology Intern, 1977-79, PhD, 1981, Michigan State University, East Lansing. *Appointments:* Head Advisor, 1970-72, Associate Director, Holmes Hall/Lyman Briggs College, 1972-74; Graduate Assistant, Department of Psychiatry, 1974-79, Michigan State University, East Lansing; Consultant, Stress Management Inc, Okemos, Michigan, 1979-80; Psychologist, James Blake Thomas MD PC, Okemos, 1980-89; Psychologist, Psychological Health Systems, P.C., Lansing, 1989-90. *Publication:* Co-author, article in Journal of Behavior Therapy and Experimental Psychiatry, 1984. *Memberships:* Member, President, Parent Advisory Committee, Michigan State University Day Care Center, East Lansing, 1975-77; Friends of Bob Carr (US House of Representatives), East Lansing, 1982; Parent Advisory Committee, Mason Middle School, Mason, Michigan, 1985-86; Founding Member, Greater Lansing Area Women Therapists, Chairperson 1983-

84; Michigan Psychological Association; American Psychological Association; National Association of Career Women, Lansing Founding Chapter, Secretary 1985-87. *Hobbies:* Genealogy; Gardening. *Address:* Box 66, Penobscot, ME 04476, USA.

THOMAS Margaret Ann, b 19 June 1951, Waukesha, USA. Art Educator. 1 child. *Education:* BA, Beloit College, 1974; MA, University of Wisconsin, 1981. *Appointments:* Teacher, Beloit Public Schools, 1974- 87; Muralist, 1985-87, Art Specialist, Gifted & Talented Students, 1987-; Teacher, Beloit College; Director, Founder, Summer Explorers, Saturday Explorers, Beloit College, 1986-87; Director, Rock Prairie Showcase FEstival, 1986. *Publications:* Co-author: Effective Schools and Effective Teachers, 1988. *Memberships:* Chairman, Rock County Violence Council; President, YWCA; President, WCGT. *Address:* 3211Canterbury Lane, Janesville, WI 53545, USA.

THOMAS Patricia Anne, b. 21 Aug. 1927, Cleveland, Ohio, USA. Library Director, US Courts. *Education:* AB, 1949, JD, 1951, Case Western Reserve University. *Appointments:* Librarian, Arter & Hadden, Cleveland, 1951-62; Librarian, Internal Revenue Service, Washington DC, 1962- 78; Library Director, Administrative Office of the US Courts, 1978-. *Publications:* Editor, United States Courts' Library Management Manual. *Memberships:* American Association of Law Libraries; Law Librarians Society of Washington DC, President 1967-69; Bar of Ohio; Bar of the Supreme Court of the USA, 1980-. *Hobbies:* Travel; Painting; Gardening; Photography. *Address:* Administrative Office of the US Courts, Washington, DC 20544, USA.

THOMASON Jessica Love, b. 16 Apr. 1955, Gaffney, South Carolina, USA. Physician. *Education:* MD, University of North Carolina, Chapel Hill, 1974; Intern, University of California, San Diego, 1975; Resident: University of Florida, Jacksonville, 1978; University of Florida, Gainesville, 1979; Fellowship, Maternal Foetal Medicine, University of Illinois, 1980-82. *Appointments:* Faculty, University of Illinois Medical School, 1980-84; Faculty, 1984-, Director, Division of Gynaecology, Head, Section for Information Dissemination, Department OB/GYN, currently, University of Wisconsin, Milwaukee. *Publications:* Articles, book chapters, seminars and presentations. *Memberships include:* American Board of Obstetrics and Gyncaelogy, 1980; Division of Maternal-Foetal Medicine, 1984; Fellow, American College of Obstetrics and Gynecology, 1980; Society for Gynecological Invest; Information Dissemination Society for Obstetrics and Gynecology; Information Dissemination Society of America; Society for Perinatal Obstetrics; American Association for the Advancement of Science; American Association for Gynecological Laparotomy. *Honours:* Outstanding Faculty Award, University of Wisconsin, Milwaukee, 1984; Medical Alumni Award for Distinguished Teaching, University of Wisconsin, 1987; Appointed Oral Examiner, American Board of Obstetrics and Gynecology, 1987. *Address:* Division of Gynecology, Department of Obstetrics & Gynecology, University of Wisconsin, Milwuakee Clinical Campus, Sinai Samaritan Medical Center, PO Box 342, Milwaukee, WI 53201, USA.

THOME Diane, b. 25 Jan. 1942, Pearl River, New York, USA. Composer; Pianist; College Professor; Lecturer. *Education:* Performer's Certificate, Piano, BMus with distinction, Composition, Eastman School of Music, 1963; MA, Theory, Composition, University of Pennsylvania, 1965; MFA, 1970, PhD, 1973, Princeton University; Piano studies with Dorothy Taubman, New York City; Composition studies with Robert Strassburg, Darius Milhaud, Aspen, Colorado, Roy Harris, Inter-American University, Puerto Rico, A.U.Boscovich, Israel, Milton Babbitt, Princeton University. *Appointments:* Taught Piano, Princeton University, New Jersey, 1973-74; Theory, 20th Century Music, State University of New York, Binghamton, 1974-77; Associate Professor of Theory and Composition, University of Washington School of Music, Seattle,

currently. *Creative works:* Chamber, orchestral, piano and vocal works; Electronic music; Multimedia compositions; Recent works include: Three Psalms, 1979; Three Sonnets by Sri Aurobindo: Settings for Soprano and Orchestra, 1984; The Golden Messengers, orchestra, 1985; Levadi (Alone), soprano and tape, 1986; Ringing, Stillness, Pearl Light, piano and tape, 1987; Stepping Inward, chamber music, 1987; Veils, solo tape, 1988; Cassia Blossoms, chamber music, 1988; Summer Serenade, chamber music, 1988; Several recordings. *Honours:* Fellowships: Woodrow Wilson Foundation; University of Pennsylvania; Princeton University; Tanglewood; Inter-American University, Puerto Rico; Honorary Fellowship, Columbia University; Numerous grants including: National Endowment for the Arts; National Society of Arts and Letters; Martha Baird Rockefeller Foundation; Jerome Foundation; American Music Center; National Federation of Music Clubs; University of Washington Graduate School Research Foundation; National League of American Pen Women. *Address:* University of Washington, School of Music DN-10, Seattle, WA 98195, USA.

THOMPSON Charlcie W Casey, b. 3 July 1932, Buffalo, Leon County, Texas, USA. General Construction Contractor (WOB). m. (1)1 son; (2)Joe B Thompson, 26 Sept. 1972. *Education:* BS 1955, Graduate Work 1968-72, Sam Houston State University, Huntsville; Real Estate Course & Insurance School, 1972-85. *Appointments:* Cashier, Citizens State Bk Ysleta, Texas, 1950-55; Bookkeeper, 1955-57; Gen Bookkeeping, 1959-62; Management & Operation of Concrete Plant, 1962-74; Partner, General Construction Contractor, 1974-. *Memberships:* Daughter's of Republic of Texas; United Daughters of Confedercy; Order of the Eastern Star; General Federation Women's Club, Texas' County Chairperson, Republican Party, Leon County, Texas; School Trustee, Buffalo Independent School, Buffalo, Texas; State of Texas, Appointment to Long Term Coordinating Health Care for the Elderly. *Interests:* Charity, elderly; Special education work, Head start Programs, Children; Work for Republican Party of Texas; Church work, Protestant Churches. *Address:* P O Box 866, Buffalo, Texas 75831, USA.

THOMPSON Elizabeth Heisler, b. 2 June 1951, Philadelphia, Pennsylvania, USA. Architect. *Education:* BA 1973, BArch 1973, MArch 1974, Syracuse University, Syracuse, NY; Land Arch Cert, G Washington University, Washington DC, 1981. *Appointments:* Blake Constr Co, Washington DC, 1975-76; Chloethiel Woodard Smith & Assoc Arch, 1977; Partner, Heisler-Donald Assoc, 1978-81; Job Captain, Skidmore, Owings & Merrill, 1982- 83; Associate, Butler, Rogers, Baskett, New York City, 1984-85; Associate, Robt A M Stern Architects, 1986-89; Elizabeth Thompson Architect, 1989-. *Creative work:* Tee shirt design (Copyright H-67300) with Linda Donald, 1976. *Membership:* American Institute of Architects. *Honour:* Exhibitor, AIA Women in Architecture, Design Exhibit, 1988. *Hobbies:* Acoustic drumset player, rock, blues, jazz; Landscape gardening; Sports, squash, swimming. *Address:* 316 Mott Street Apt 3B, New York, NY 10012, USA.

THOMPSON Gale J, b. 4 Aug. 1948, Provo, Utah, USA. Employment and Career Consultant; Computer Software Management Analyst. *Education:* University of Utah, Business Administration, 1972. *Appointments:* Salt Lake City Police Department, 1972-80; West Valley City Police Department, 1980-81; Jet Propulsion Laboratory, Pasadena, California, 1981-; Employment and Career Consultant, 1984-. *Creative works:* Lecturer; Seminars; Workshops; Training. *Memberships:* Hostess, California-Utah Women Association; The Right Connection Womens Network. *Hobbies:* Interior decoration; Resume composition; Volunteer organizations; Teaching; VAX Mainframe computers; Personal computer software. *Address:* 4289 Williams Ave., La Verne, CA 91750, USA.

THOMPSON Helen Virginia, b. 14 May 1941, Frederick, Maryland, USA. Certified Registered Nurse Anesthetist. *Education:* BS, Education, 1963; Diploma,

Frederick Memorial Hospital School of Nursing, 1968. *Appointments:* Staff RN, Frederick Memorial Hospital, 1968-69; Instructor 1973-79, Assistant Director 1975-79, Charleston Area Medical Center School of Anesthesia; Staff Anesthetist, Herbert J. Thomas Memorial Hospital, 1979-. *Publications:* Editor, Student Nurse News, 1969; Editor, co-Founder, Pantisocracy. *Memberships:* AANA; WVANA; National Air National guard Association. *Honours:* Politically Active Nurse of the Year Award, 1985. *Hobbies:* Farming; Poetry; Music. *Address:* Route 1, Box 166, Walton, WV 25286, USA.

THOMPSON Jacqueline Anne, b. 4 Dec. 1945, Morristown, New Jersey, USA. Writer. m. Panos Foscolos, 20 Feb. 1987. *Education:* Graduate, Barnard College, Columbia University. *Appointment:* Self-employed public relations writer & consultant, various business & industrial clients. *Publications:* Books: The Very Rich Book: America's Supermillionaires & Their Money, 1981, 1982; Future Rich: Creating America's New Fortunes, 1985; Editor, Image Impact: Aspiring Woman's Personal Packaging Programme 1981, Image Impact for Men 1985; New Aerobics for Women (ghosted for Cooper), 1988; Color Wonderful (ghosted for Nicholson & Lewis-Crum), 1986; Upward Mobility, 1982; Directory of Personal Image Consultants, 8 editions, 1978-. Also: Research, various instructional books; Numerous articles, nationally circulated magazines, career planning, management practices, employment discrimination, executive recruiting, wealth, fashion, profiles. *Memberships:* American Society of Journalists & Authors; Authors Guild. *Address:* 10 Bay Street Landing 7K, Staten Island, New York 10301, USA.

THOMPSON Kay Ellen, b. 24 Aug. 1942, Berkley, California, USA. Executive Director. 3 sons. *Education:* University Pacific, 1960-61; College San Mateo, 1961-62; West Valley College, San Jose, California, 1962-64; No Nevada Comm College, 1973. *Appointments:* Salesperson, Lillians Inc, Elko, 1957-62; Secretary, Western Electric Sunnyvale, California 1963-66; Salesperson, Avon, San Jose, 1969-72; Ceramics Designer, Elko & San Jose, 1971-72; Advisor, Summer Playscheme, Edinburgh, Scotland, 1973; Gen Supr, Elko Co Fair Exhibits, 1977-79; Columnist, Elko Daily Free Press, 1977-84; Owner, Stockmens Beauty Salon, Elko, 1981-83; Legal Secretary, Woodbury & Torvinen Elko, NV, 1982-84; Secretary, Executive secretary 1984-85, Admin Asst 1985, Acting Director 1986, Executive Director 1986-, Elko Convention & Visitors Authority. *Publications:* Author, Heartstrings (Poems); Editor, Rotary Barbwire, 1978-80; Designer needlework, Pre-Deiu for St Pauls Episcopal Church, Elko *Memberships:* International Assn Auditorium Mgrs; National Assn Female Executives; American Soc Assn Executive; Nevada Assn Executives; Manager, Nev Assembly Candidate Campaigning, 1980; Co-chairman, Jr Golf Program 1981-82; Trustee Elko Co Library. *Honours:* Nominee Women of the Year, 1980; Rotary Ann, 1979; Silver Thimble Award, 1980. *Hobbies:* Needlepoint; Writing; Poetry; Needlework. *Address:* 649 1st Street, Elko, NV 89801, USA.

THOMPSON LaVerne Elizabeth Thomas, b. 17 July 1945, Brooklyn, New York, USA. Educator. m. Robert Louis Thompson, 28 Sep. 1968. *Education:* BA, English, Bluffton College, 1967; MS, Educational Administration/Supervision, University of Dayton, 1977; Certifications, Ohio: School Principal, Secondary School Supervisor, Notary Public, Realtor. *Appointments:* Instructor, English, Speech, Piqua Central High School, Ohio, 1967-68; Instructor, English, Lima Senior High School, 1968-77; Instructor, English, Shawnee High School, Lima, 1977-86; Real Estate Sales Agent: Alberta Lee Realty, Lima, 1978-82; Slonaker Realty, Lima, 1982-84; The Gooding Company, Lima, 1985-; Doctoral Graduate Assistant, Higher Education, University of Toledo, Toledo, Ohio 1986-; interim counselor/administrator, Student Support Services, The University of Toledo, spring-summer, 1989. *Memberships:* New Homemakers of America (National President 1963, State President of Virginia

Association 1962); Participant, 17th Annual National Conference on Citizenship, Washington DC, 1962; American Association of University Women (Piqua 1967-68, Lima 1968- 74); Board of Directors, YWCA, Lima, 1971; Co-Chair, Brotherhood Dinner, Lima, 1976; Phi Delta Kappa, Bowling Green, Ohio, State University Chapter, 1978-80; Charter Member, West Central Ohio Chapter, Phi Delta Kappa; Blackwell Family Association, USA; National Association for Female Executives; Charter Member, Club Anri, G. Armani Society, Gartland USA Collectors' League, Lladro Collectors Society and Lalique Society of America; Belleek Collectors Society; M.I. Hummel; Royal Doulton International Collectors Club. *Honours:* May Queen, Arlington Elementary School, Hopewell, Virginia, 1957; Miss Hopewell, Virginia Improvement Association, 1960; Elected Best Female Teacher, 1984, 1985, 1st runner-up, 1986, Shawnee High School graduating seniors. *Hobbies:* Collecting Lladro, Belleek, Hummel, Waterford, Club Anri, Bing and Grondahl, Capodimonte, Royal Doulton, Lalique and sports items; Reading periodicals; Dancing; Light jogging; Attending cultural events; Studying and writing about issues related to business, higher education, social dynamics and dysfunction. *Address:* 24501 West River Road, Perrysburg, OH 43551, USA.

THOMPSON Marie Therese Oliver Jackson, b. 14 Aug. 1947, Pittsburgh, Pennsylvania, USA. Judge. m. (1)Peter Jackson, 8 June 1971, 2 sons. (2)Henry Quentin Thompson Jr, 14 Feb. 1987, 1 stepson. *Education:* BA, Mount Holyoke College, 1969; JD, Harvard Law, 1972; MJS, University of Reno, ongoing. *Appointments:* General trial work, Cambridge and Somerville Legal Services, 1972-74; Visiting Lecturer, Tufts University Experimental College (Part-time), 1973-74; Investigator, Massachusetts Commission Against Discrimination, 1974-76; Administrative Justice, Division of Hearing Officers, 1976-77; General Counsel, Executive Office of Administration and Finance, 1977-80; Justice, 1980-. *Memberships:* Board of Directors, National Conference of Christians and Jews; Massachusetts Juvenile Justice Advisory Committee; Middlesex County District Attorney's Child Sexual Abuse Task Force; District Court Standards Committee for Care & Protection; CHINS. *Honours:* Sesquicentennial Award, Mount Holyoke Alumnae, 1988; Community Justice Award, Massachusetts Justice Resource Institute, 1985; Sojourner Truth National Award, National Association of Negro Business and Professional Women Inc, Boston & Vicinity Chapter, 1985; 2nd place Programming Award, American bar Association Law Day USA; Public Service Award Competition, 1985; Tribute to Women 1985 Leadership Award, Cambridge YWCA. *Hobbies:* Writing; Freshwater aquariums, Photography; Public speaking. *Address:* 40 Thorndike Street, Cambridge, MA 02141, USA.

THOMPSON Marion Elizabeth, b. 4 June 1921, Madison, Wisconsin, USA. Professor. m. 30 May 1942, 2 sons, 1 daughter. *Education:* BA, 1943, MA 1960, PhD, 1971, University of Wisconsin. *Appointments:* Assistant Professor, William Patterson College, 1972-74; Associate Professor, Emerson College, 1976-81; Visiting Professor, Comparative Broadcast System, Boston University, 1977; Director, Graduate Studies, Emerson College, 1980. *Publications:* Dissertation: A Study of International Television Programming within the Structure of Global Communications. *Memberships:* World Communication Association; International Communicators Association; National Academy of TV Arts & Sciences; American Association of University Professors; Speech Communicators Association; Phi Beta; American Association of University Women; etc. *Hobbies:* Music; Horticulture; Environmental Preservation. *Address:* 1127 Vernon Court, Marco, FL 33937, USA.

THOMPSON Mary Anne, White House Assistant General Counsel. *Education:* BA, Auburn University, 1977; JD, Cumberland School of Law, 1981. *Appointments:* Campaign Manager, Elliott for Congress Committee, 1981-82; Special Assistant to the Director, US Dept. of Transportation, 1983- 84; Group Director,

Personnel & Volunteer Operations, Presidential Inaugural Committee, 1984-85; Special Assistant to Administrator, 1984-85, Attorney/Advisor, 1985, US Dept. of Transportation, Assistant General Counsel, Thee White House, 1986-. *Memberships:* Various professional organisations *Address:* 1300 Belle View Boulevard No A-2, Alexandria, VA 22307, USA.

THOMPSON Vivian L., b. 7 Jan. 1911, Jersey City, New Jersey, USA. Writer; Playwright. m. 17 Mar. 1951. *Education:* BS 1939, MA 1943, Columbia University; Maren Elwood School of Professional Writing, 1948; Private student, juvenile fiction, Odessa Davenport, 1948-49. *Appointments:* Teacher, Kindergarten-Grade III, New Jersey, New York, California, Hawaii, 1930-51; Various workshops, readings, writing courses, Hawaii, 1979-. *Publications:* 16 children's books, 5 children's plays (further 3 produced). Titles include: Books: Camp-in-the-Yard, 1961; Sad Day, Glad Day, 1962; Horse That Liked Sandwiches, 1962; Kimo Makes Music, 1962; Ah See & the Spooky House, 1963; Faraway Friends, 1963; George Washington, 1964; Hawaiian Myths of Earth, Sea and Sky, 1966, 1988; Keola's Harraisan Donkey, 1966; Hawaiian Legends of Tricksters & Riddlers, 1969; Maui-Full-of-Tricks, 1970; Hawaiian Tales of Heroes & Champions, 1971, 1987. Plays: Keola's Hawaiian Donkey, 1982; Neat! Said Jeremy, 1982; Scary Thing-Snatcher, 1982. *Memberships:* Society of Childrens Book Writers; Literacy Volunteers of America. *Honours:* Award, literature, Hilo YWCA, 1984; 14 publications in de Grummond Children's Collection, University of Southern Mississippi, 1966-88; Citation, New Jersey Association of Teachers of English, 1963; Selection, Junior Literary Guild, 1961; Community service award, Hamakua Mill Company, Hawaii, 1961. *Hobbies:* Teaching adults to read; Needlecrafts; Piano. *Address:* 936 Kumukoa Street, Hilo, Hawaii 96720, USA.

THOMPSON-SCOTT Sherry Lynn, b. 20 Jan. 1955, Cincinnati, USA. Regional Sales Consultant. divorced, 1 daughter. *Education:* BA, Business Administration, Union for Experimenting Colleges & Universities, 1984. *Appointments:* Major Account Representative, The Gillette Co., 1978-80; Territory Representative, The Wrigley Co., 1980-84; Account Manager, Frito Lay Inc., 1984-86; Regional Sales Consultant, Nurre-Caxton, 1986-. *Memberships:* Women in Communications; American Marketing Association; Garden Civic Club; Black Career Women, Board Member; Bond-Hill Chiild Development, Board Member, President. *Honours:* Outstanding Young Women of America Award, 1984. *Hobbies:* Reading; Gardening; Golf; Horse Riding; Fine Art; Music; Travel; Spectator Sports. *Address:* 6529 Stoll Lane, Cincinnati, OH 45236, USA.

THOMSON Daisy Hicks, b. 14 June 1918, Rothesay, Bute, Scotland. Novelist. m. William Hugh Thomson, 1 Mar. 1945. 1 son, 1 daughter. *Education:* Privately in France, Switzerland and Algiers; Lycee of Nice; Rothesay Academy; MA, Edinburgh University. *Appointments:* Assistant Welfare Officer, Bute County, 1939-45; Assistant Registrar Births, Marriages and Deaths, Rothesay, 1941-45; Freelance Writer, 1945-. *Publications:* Short stories, articles and novels including: Prelude to Love; To Love and Honour; Jealous Love; Portrait of My Love; Love for a Stranger; A Truce for Love; By Love Betrayed; Journey to Love; Be My Love; My Only Love; Five Days to Love; The Italian For Love; Summons To Love; Hello My Love; Woman In Love; The Beginning of Love; The Summer of Love; My One and Only Love; The Magic Island; From Solitude With Love; The Voice of Love; Myrtle for My Love; A Time for Love; In Love, In Vienna; Suddenly It Was Love; A Nightingale for Love. *Memberships:* National Trust for Scotland; Romantic Novelists Association. *Hobbies:* Oil painting; Travel; Gardening. *Address:* 28 Clover Court, Church Road, Haywards Heath, West Sussex RH16 3UP, England.

THOMSON June Valerie, b. 24 June 1930, Kent, England. Author; Former Teacher. div, 2 sons. *Education:* BA Honours, English, Bedford College,

University of London. *Appointments:* Teacher, various state schools, 1958-85. *Publications:* 15 detective novels including: Not One Of Us; Death Cap; Shadow of a Doubt; A Dying Fall; Sound Evidence; No Flowers by Request; Rosemary for Rememberance. *Memberships:* Former committee member, Crime Writers Association; Detection Club. *Honour:* Prix du Roman d'Aventures, 1983. *Hobbies:* Gardening; Cooking; Theatre. *Address:* 177 Verulam Road, St Albans, Hertfordshire AL3 4DW, England.

THOMSON Susan Mary, b. 6 Aug. 1938, London, England. Publisher. m. Andre R Davis, 14 Feb. 1978, 1 daughter. *Education:* Christ's Hospital, Hertford, 1947-56. *Appointments:* Thames & Hudson Limited, 1959-63; Conde Nast Publications Limited, 1963-65; The Law Society, 1965-67; The Hamly Publishing Group Limited, 1967-71; Managing Director, 1971-77, Executive Director, 1977-86, Octopus Books Limited/Octopus Publishing Group Plc; Sue Thomson Ltd., 1986-. *Memberships:* Network; 300 Group; University Women's Club. *Hobbies:* Children & Family Affairs; Book Publishing; Travel; Medieval Domestic Architecture.

THORBERGS Ingibjorg, b. 25 Oct. 1927, Reykjavik, Iceland. Radio Programme Director, Retired. m. Gudmundur Jonsson, 12 Aug. 1976. *Education:* Music Teachers Diploma, 1957; Courses in Italy, 1962. *Appointments:* Various Radio Programmes, Icelandic State Broadcasting System, 1952-85; Singer, Popular Music, Gramophone Records, 1953-; Singer, many choruses, National Theatre Chorus, 1953-76. *Publications:* Classical and Popular Songs; Childrens Musical; Radio Plays; 10 Christmas Songs; etc. *Memberships:* Writers Union of Iceland; Songwriters Association; Music Teachers Association. *Honours:* 1st Prize, Iceland, English Poem, Childrens Year, 1979; 1st Prize, International Contest for New Children's Song, UNICEF, 1982; etc. *Hobbies:* Travel; Swimming. *Address:* Langabrekka 41, 200 Kopavogur, Iceland.

THORNTON Sigrid Madeline, b. 12 Feb. 1959, Canberra, Australia. Actress. 1 son. *Education:* Matriculated, St Peters Lutheran College, Brisbane; Drama Studies, Queensland University. *Appointments:* numerous appearances professional since age 13; played guest role in Hoicide-Division 4, Matlock Police; Guest Lead, Logie series, 1975; Feature films include: The F J Holden, 1975; The Getting of Wisdom, 1976; Leading Role in Snapshot, 1979; played in features: Duet for Four, The Man from Snowy River, Street Hero, Niel Lynne; The Lighthorsemen played in internationally shown TV series, 1915, and All the Rivers Run; most recent mini-series, The Far Country; Great Expectations The Untold Story; (Played & Associate Producer); (Slate and Wyn, feature and Blanche McBride); Lead role in American TV series, Paradise, for Lorimar/CBS, 1988-89. *Memberships:* Actors Equity of Australia; Australian Film Institute; Deputy Member, Board, Victorian film Corporation. *Honours:* Sammy award for best Performance by a Juvenile, 1976; Logie Award Best Performance by a Lead Actress. *Address:* c/o International Casting Service, 147A King Street, Sydney, NSW 2000, Australia.

THORNTON Valerie Genestra Marion, b. 13 Apr. 1931, London, England. Painter; Etcher. m. Michael Chase, 29 Oct. 1966. *Education:* Byam Shaw School of Drawing & Painting, 1949-50; Regent St. Polytechnic, 1950-53; Atelier 17, Paris, 1954. *Creative Works:* Solo Exhibitions Include: Zwemmer Gallery, London, 1965; Oxford Gallery, Oxford, 1975/81; Bruton Gallery, Bruton, 1976/83; Touring Exhibition, Faces of Stone, Anthony dawson, 1977; Touring Exhibition, Faces of Stone II, Anthony Dawson, 1982; Touring Exhibition Two Journeys with Michael Chase (Anthony Dawson), 1985-86; Group Exhibitions Include: Royal Academy; Royal Society of Painter-Etchers 7 Engravers; Work in Public Collections: British Museum; Department of Environment; Tate Gallery; Victoria & Albert Museum; Ashmolean Museum, Oxford; Glasgow Museum & Art Gallery; Works in Belgium, Canada, France, Germany, Holland & USA. *Memberships:* Fellow, Royal Society of Painter Etchers & Engravers. *Hobbies:* Looking at Works of Art; Classical Music. *Address:* Lower Common Farmhouse, Chelsworth, Ipswich, Suffolk IP7 7AY, England.

THORNTON-LOCKWOOD Barbara Rae, b. 30 June 1931, Minneapolis, Minnesota, USA. Food Marketing Consultant. m. James Franklin Lockwood, 4 May 1974. *Education:* BS, Foods in Business, University of Minnesota, Minneapolis, 1953. *Appointments:* Consumer Correspondent, 1953-55, Manager, Consumer Correspondence, 1955-57, Product Group Head, Variety Mixes, 1957-61, Product Group Head, Grocery Mixes, 1961-63, Home Service Center, Pillsbury; Associate Director, Grocery Mixes, New and Existing Products, Ann Pillsbury Consumer Service, Pillsbury, 1963-67, Director of Consumer Service, Ann Pillsbury Consumer Service Kitchens, Pillsbury, 1967-70; President, Barbara Thornton Associates, Food Marketing Consultants, Minneapolis, Minnesota, 1970-. *Publications:* Red Star Centennial Bread Sampler Cookbook, 1982; Cooking For One Cookbook, 1987. *Memberships:* American Home Economics Association; Minnesota Home Economics Association; Twin Cities Home Economics in Business; Institute of Food Technologists; University of Minnesota Alumni Association; Life Associate, Institute of Agriculture, Forestry and Home Economics Advisory Council, University of Minnesota. *Honours:* Honorary Member, Phi Upsilon Omicron National Home Economics Fraternity, 1970; Board Member, National Alumnae Board, University of Minnesota, 1977-81; Contributing Editor, Better Homes and Gardens; Distinguished Leadership Award, International Directory of Distinguished Leadership. *Hobbies:* Churchwork for Evangelical Lutheran Church in America, 24 years; Flowers and Gardening; Interior design; Birdwatching; Gourmet cooking/entertaining. *Address:* Barbara Thornton Associates, 8001 Pennsylvania Road, Minneapolis, MN 55438, USA.

THOROGOOD Alfreda, b. 17 Aug. 1942, England. Deputy Ballet Principal/Director. m. David Wall, CBE, 1 Aug. 1967, 1 son, 1 daughter. *Education:* Lady Eden's School; Royal Ballet School (Junior and Senior School). *Appointments:* Joined Sadlers Wells Royal Ballet Company, 1960; Soloist, Principal Dancer, 1963-80, transferred to resident Royal Ballet Co. in 1970 and left in 1980; Senior Teacher, Bush Davies School, 1982; Advisory Panel for Dance Arts Council of Great Britain, 1982; Board of Management, Deputy Ballet Principal, 1984, Director, 1988-, Bush Davies School. *Memberships:* British Actors Equity Association; Honorary Member, Royal Academy of Dancing; ARAD; Dip.PDTC. *Hobbies:* Music; Interior Design; Cookery. *Address:* 34 Croham Manor Road, South Croydon, Surrey CR2 7BE, England.

THORSSON Inga, b. 3 July 1915, Malmo, Sweden. Ambassador; Politician. m., 1944, widowed, 1979, 2 sons. *Education:* 2 degrees in Education. *Appointments:* Chairman, Swedish Social Democratic Women, 1952-64; Member of Swedish Parliament, 1956-58, 1970-79; Swedish Ambassador to Israel, 1964-66; Director, UN Secretariat, New York City, 1967-70; Under-Secretary of State, Chairman, Swedish Disarmament Delegation, 1973-82; Delegate and Chairman, various UN bodies, 1970-82; Chairman, Great Peace Journey, 1984-89; Chairman, Stockholm International Peace Research Institute, 1988-. *Honour:* DrPh h.c., University of Gothenburg, 1987. *Hobbies:* English literature; Music. *Address:* Malmgardsvagen 59C, S-11638 Stockholm, Sweden.

THORSTAD Linda, b. 21 Apr. 1954, Vancouver, Canada. Businesswoman; Geologist. *Education:* BSc., Honours, 1976; MSc., 1978, 1983. *Appointments:* Geological Survey of Canada, 1974-78; Ventures West Minerals, 1979-81; Thorstad Consulting, 1982-83; President, Questore Consultants, Geological and Engineering Consultants, 1983-86; Vice President, International Resource Ltd., 1986; President, Interaction Resources Ltd., 1986-*Publications:* Contributor of numerous articles in professional journals and magazines. *Memberships:* Canadian Institute of Mining & Metallurgy; Geological Association of Canada; Nevada Mining Association; Northwest Mining Association; Prospectors & Developer Association. *Hobbies:* Skiing; Cycling; Tennis; Antique Collection; Investment. *Address:* 720-800 West Pender Street, Vancouver, BC, Canada V6C 2V6,

THULIN Ingrid, b. 27 Jan. 1929, Solleftea, Sweden. Actress; Director. m. Harry Schein. *Education:* Royal Dramatic Theatre School, Stockholm, 1950. *Appointments:* Royal Dramatic Theatre, Stockholm, 1950-52; Malmo Municipal Theatre, Malmo, 1956-60; Stockholm Municipal Theatre, 1960-63. *Publications:* Writer, Director, Film, Devotion & Broken Skies. *Honours:* Recipient, numerous awards for best actress in Festivals. *Address:* Kevinge Strand 7b, 18231 Danderyd, Sweden.

THURMAIER Mary Jean Pech, b.14 Dec. 1931, Delavan, Illinois, USA. Convention Consultant. m. Roland J. Thurmaier, 22 Oct. 1955, 3 sons, 1 daughter. *Education:* Illinois State Normal University, 1951; BA, University of Iowa, 1960; MST, University of Wisconsin, Stevens Point, 1971. *Appointments:* Elementary Teacher, Green Valley, Illinois, 1952-55; Manager, City Transit System, PABCO, 1974-78; Executive Director, Democratic Party, 1979; Office Manager, Political Campaign, 1979-80; Executive Director, Stevens Point Area Convention and Visitors Bureau, 1986-89; Coalition of Wisconsin Aging Groups, Convention Consultant and Coordinator, 1990. *Memberships:* Treasurer, Clerk, Stevens Point Area Board of Education; Trustee, St Paul's United Methodist Church; Administrative Committee, 7th District Chairperson, National Committeewoman-DNC, Democratic Party of Wisconsin. *Honours:* Business & Professional Woman of the Year. *Hobbies:* Travel; Bridge; Reading; Cooking and baking. *Address:* 1926 Center Street, Stevens Point, WI 54481, USA.

THURMAN Marjorie Ellen, b. Whiteville, North Carolina, USA. Business Education Teacher. *Education:* BS, Fayetteville State Universiy, 1969; MA, Seton Hall University, 1977. *Appointments:* Teaccher, Newark Board of Education, 1969-; Essex College of Business, 1975-85; Sawyer Business School, Evening Dean, 1979-80; SCS Business & Technical Institute, 1986-. *Publications:* Programme in Newark, Newark Business Skills Olympics. *Memberships:* National Business Education Association; New Jersey Business Education Association; Newark Teachers Union; American Federation of Teachers; Minority Business Organization; Alpha Kappa Alpha. *Honours:* Outstanding Teacher of the Year, 1983; Teacher of the Month, 1987, 1988, SCS Business & Technical Institute. *Hobbies:* Reading; Travel; Jogging; Exercising. *Address:* 222 D Davey Street, Bloomfield, NJ 07003, USA.

THURMAN Mary J Rutherford, b. 22 Feb. 1942, Indianapolis, Indiana, USA. Marketing. m. B L Thurman, 3 Apr. 1960. 1 son, 1 daughter. *Education:* ABS, University of Indianapolis, 1984. *Appointments:* Public Relations Assistant, Indianapolis Public Schools, 1972-78; Executive Secretary, 1978-85, Marketing Planner & Special Events Coordinator, 1985-88, Marketing Representative, 1988-, Indianapolis Power & Light Company, Indianapolis. *Membership:* Delta Psi; Meeting Planners International; Indianapolis Chamber of Commerce; Membership Chair, Electrical Womens Round Table; Builders Association of Greater Indianapolis; Emmerich Manual Alumni Association. *Honours:* Delta Psi, 1988. *Hobbies:* Reading; Travel; Spectator Sports; Dancing. *Address:* 7018 Chimney Rock Court, Indianapolis, Indiana 46217, USA.

THWAITE Ann, b. 4 Oct. 1932, London, England. Writer. m. Anthony Thwaite, 4 Aug. 1955, 4 daughters. *Education:* St Hilda's College, Oxford; MA(Oxon). *Appointments:* Member, Editorial Board, American childlren's magazine Cricket, 1979-; Visiting Professor,

Tokyo Women's University, Tokyo, Japan, 1985-86. *Publications:* Many children's books including The Camelthorn Papers, 1969. Biographies: Waiting for the Party: the life of Frances Hodgson Burnett, 1974; Edmund Gosse: A Literary Landscape, 1984; A.A.Milne his life, 1990. *Memberships:* Fellow, Royal Society of Literature; Society of Authors. *Honours:* Duff Cooper Memorial Prize for Edmund Gosse, 1985. *Address:* The Mill House, Low Tharston, Norwich NR15 2YN, England.

TICKETT Deborah Diane Laney, b. 18 May 1951, Jacksonville, Florida, USA. Insurance Agent. m. 15 Mar. 1969, 2 sons. *Education:* Pinellas Vocational Technical Institute; Tampa University. *Appointments:* Secretary, 1974-75; Bookkeeper, 1975-77; Assistant Manager, 1976-77, Vice President, Manager, 1979-85, President, Owner, 1986-, Laney and Associates Inc; Manager, 1985-, Secretary/Treasurer, 1986-, Debco Electric Inc.. *Creative Works:* Drafted and designed own home. *Memberships:* Independent Insurance Agents of America; Insurance Women of St Petersburg, Florida, USA; National Association of Insurance Women. *Honours:* Woman of the Year Award, 2 years, Beta Sigma Phi. *Hobbies:* Design; Travel; Decorating; Gardening. *Address:* c/o Laney and Associates Inc., 516N. Ft. Harrison Avenue, Clearwater, FL 34615, USA.

TICKNER Ellen Mindy, b. 3 May 1951, Philadelphia, Pennsylvania. Attorney. *Education:* BA, Northwestern University, Evanston, Illinois, 1973; University of Miami Law School, Coral Gables, Florida, 1973-74; JD, DePaul University Law School, Chicago, 1976; Bar admissions: Illinois, Michigan; US District Court, Eastern District, Michigan; US Court of Appeals, 6th Circuit. *Appointments:* Instructor, University of Detroit School of Law, Michigan, 1976-77; Staff Attorney, Juvenile Defender Office, Detroit, 1977-79; Litigation Attorney, Institute of Gerontology, 1980, Clinical Assistant Professor of Law, University of Michigan Law School, 1980-82; Clinical Assistant Professor of Law, 1982-83; Associate, Raymond, Rupp, Wienberg, Stone & Zuckerman PC, Troy, Michigan, 1984-87; Associate, Miller, Canfield, Paddock and Stone, Detroit, 1987-. *Publications:* Voir Dire: Observations of a Student, 1974; Introduction to the Legal System, 1980; Legal Strategies When No Trial of Treatment is Indicated, 1982; Legal Limitations of Protective Services Investigation, 1982; Interdisciplinary Management of Child Sexual Abuse, 1982; Representing the State in Child Abuse and Neglect Proceedings (videotape), 1982. *Memberships:* American Bar Association, Section on Litigation; Detroit Bar Association; Federal Bar Association; Oakland County Bar Association, Vice-Chair of Continuing Legal Education Committee; Association of Trial Lawyers of America; Michigan Trial Lawyers Association; Women Lawyers Association of Michigan, Wayne Region (Director 1981-82); ACLU; Amnesty International; The Ark; Greenpeace; National Organization for Women; National Women and the Law Association; WDET FM 102 Club; Women's Economic Club. *Honours:* Editorial Associate, DePaul Law Review, 1975-76. *Hobbies:* Music; Photography; Reading. *Address:* Miller, Canfield, Paddock and Stone, 150 West & Jefferson, Suite 2500, Detroit, MI 48226, USA.

TIEMEYER Hope Elizabeth Johnson, b. 20 May 1908, Fort Wayne, Indiana, USA. Advertising Company Executive. m. Edwin Herman Tiemeyer, 30 Oct. 1929, Dec., 1 son (dec.), 1 daughter. *Education:* BA, University of Cincinnati, 1932. *Appointments:* President, Owner, Mail-Way Advertising Company (Printing), Cincinnati, Ohio, 1955-. *Memberships:* Regent, Cincinnati Chapter, Daughters of the American Revolution, 1956-58; Chair, National School Survey Commission, 1961-62; National Vice-Chair, Americanism Manual for Citizenship, 1962-65; Continental Congress Programme Commission, 1962-65; Congress Marshall Commission, 1966-68; Congress Hostess Commission; President, Officers Club, 1974-77; Recording Secretary, National Chairman's Association, 1969-71; Children of the American Revolution, Senior National Membership Chair 1985-60, Senior National Recording Secretary 1960-62; Honorary National Life President, Mountain School,

several other offices; National Officers Club, 1st Vice-President 1965-69, President 1970-73; Honorary Senior Life President, Ohio Society; Honorary Life Member, Ohio Congress PTA, Treasurer 1957-62, Vice-President, Director of Department of Health, 1962-63; Honorary Life Member, National Congress PTA; Life Member, Past President, Kappa Alpha Theta Mothers Club; Director, American Association of University Women, 1963-64; Area Chair, State House Conference on Education, 1953; President, Singleton's of Cincinnati Club; Life Member, Craftshops for Handicapped; Music and Tea Room Committees, Cincinnati Woman's Club; Numerous other societies and committees. *Honours:* Jonathon Moore Citation and Award, Indiana Society, SAR, 1967; Good Citizenship Medal, National Society, 1967; Member: National Platform Association, English Speaking Union, Order of Kentucky Colonels, and National Gavel Association. *Hobbies:* Travel; Music; Art. *Address:* 2786 Little Dry Run Road, Cincinnati, OH 45244, USA.

TIERNEY Ann Jane, b. 16 Dec. 1955, Washington, District of Columbia, USA. Neurobiologist. *Education:* BA, Cornell University, 1978; PhD, University of Toronto, 1985. *Appointments:* Graduate teaching assistant, Graduate research assistant, University of Toronto; Postdoctoral research associate, Boston University. *Publications:* Numerous articles to professional journals. *Memberships:* Society for Neuroscience; Animal Behaviour Society; Crustacean Society; American Society of Zoologists. *Honours:* BA Summa cum laude, 1978; Open Fellowship, University of Toronto, 1980; Ontario Graduate Scholarship, 1983; Ramsey Wright Scholarship, 1984; US Environmental Protection Agency Postdoctoral Grant, 1985; Individual National Research Service Award, 1987. *Address:* Section of Neurobiology and Behaviour, Seeley G Mudd Hall, Cornell University, Ithaca, NY 14853, USA.

TILDEN Lorraine Henrietta Frederick, b. 16 May 1912, Peoria, Illinois, USA. Writer; College Professor, Lecturer (retired). m. Wesley R. Tilden, 20 June 1948. *Education:* AA, Illinois State University, 1931; BA, University of California, Los Angeles (UCLA), 1948; MA, Claremont Graduate School (CGS), 1954; PhD studies, University of Madrid, Spain, 1955; UCLA, 1956-57; University of Redlands, 1961; University of Guanajuato, Mexico, 1964; University of California, Riverside, 1967; California State University, San Francisco, 1971. *Appointments include:* Lecturer, Scripps College, Claremont Men's College & UCLA 1950-62, Mount San Antonio College 1954-61; Associate Professor, Humanities, Upland College, 1962-65; Teacher, World Mythology & Spanish, Glendora High School, 1967-77; Director, Alumni Records Project, CGS, 1978-84; Writer, CGS News, 1983-84. *Publications include:* Contributor, various professional journals & newspapers, 1929-; Modernism in the Poetry of José Asunción Silva, 1954; Editor: Ambiciones, El Porvenir, El Futuro (Spanish dialogues), 1971; Books of light verse. *Memberships:* American Association of University Women; Modern Language Association, Southern California; Vachel Lindsay Association; Asociación Panamericana de Escritores y Artistas; CGS Alumni Association; Honour societies. *Honours include:* Honorary Citizen, Guanajuoto, 1963; Citations, Claremont City Council, 1964, 1966; Awards, Town Affiliation, 1965, 1966; Distinguished Service, CGS Alumni, 1975. *Hobbies:* Travel, & making colour travelogues; Foreign languages; Swimming. *Address:* 351 Oakdale Drive, Claremont, California 91711, USA.

TILLY Anne Lindberry Peterson, b. 18 Nov. 1915, USA. m. (1)William Marcus Peterson, 30 Aug. 1936, died 1968, 2 sons, 1 daughter, (2)E V Tilly, 1970. *Creative Works:* Oil Painting; Water Colours; Japanese Embroider; Book: 20 Years Published Lessons. *Memberships:* Soroptimist International; Daughters of the Nile; President, International PM and PP. *Honours:* Recipient, Best of Show, Embroidery, many times. *Hobbies:* Swimming; Hiking; Oil Painting; Travel. *Address:* 324 N Emerson, Wenatchee, WA 98801, USA.

TILLY Louise A., b. 13 Dec. 1930, Orange, New Jersey, USA. Professor of History and Sociology. m. Charles Tilly, 15 Aug. 1953, 1 son, 3 daughters. *Education:* AB. Rutgers University, 1952; MA, Boston University, 1955; PhD, University of Toronto, Canada, 1974. *Appointments:* Assistant Professor of History, Michigan State University, 1972-75; Assistant Professor to full Professor, University of Michigan, 1975-84; Professor, Graduate Faculty, New School for Social Research, New York City, New York, 1984-. *Publications:* The Rebellious Century (with Charles and Richard Tilly), 1975; Women, Work and Family (with Joan W.Scott), 1978, 2nd Edition, 1987, French translation, 1988; Class Conflict and Collective Action (edited with Charles Tilly), 1982. *Memberships:* American Historical Association (Council Member 1985-87); Social Science History Association (President 1981-82); Berkshire Conference of Women Historians; Phi Beta Kappa. *Honours:* Elected to Phi Beta Kappa, 1952; Prize for best Book by Women Historians for Women, Work and Family (Tilly and Scott), Berkshire Conference of Women Historians, 1979. *Hobby:* Travel. *Address:* Committee on Historical Studies, New School for Social Research, 64 University Place, New York, NY 10003, USA.

TIMMERMAN Joan Hyacinth, b. 14 Nov. 1938, Dickeyville, Wisconsin, USA. College Professor. *Education:* BA 1961, MA 1968, PhD 1974, Marquette University. *Appointments:* Faculty, Department of Theology, College of St Catherine, St Paul, Minnesota, 1968-. *Publications:* Books: Not Yet My Season, 1969; The Mardi Gras Syndrome; Rethinking Christian Sexuality, 1984. Tape Program: Thank God It's Tuesday. *Memberships:* AAR; CTS (Regional President); CTSA; AASECT. *Honours:* Schmitt Fellowship, Marquette University, 1972-73; Akademischer Austauschdienst, Munich, Germany, 1974. *Hobbies:* Horses; Reading; Computers; Travel. *Address:* College of St Catherine, St Paul, MN 55105, USA.

TINGEY Carol, b. 24 Sept. 1933, St James, Missouri, USA. Psychologist. 4 sons, 1 daughter. *Education:* BS magna cum laude, Elementary Education, 1970, MEd, Special Education, Mental Retardation Fellowship, 1971, PhD, Psychology, 1976, University of Utah. *Appointments:* Public School Teacher, 1969-72; Clinical Instructor, University of Utah, 1972-75; Assistant Professor, University of North Iowa, 1975-77; Assistant Professor, Trinity College, 1977-78; Assistant Professor, George Mason University, 1978-79; Associate Professor, Northwestern University, Louisiana, 1979-81; Associate Professor, Illinois State University, 1981-83; Associate Professor, Utah State University, Logan, 1983-88; Clinical Psychologist, Bear River Mental Health, 1988-90; Clinical Psychologist, Psychological Associates, 1990-. *Publications:* Books: Home School Partnerships in Education, 1980; Handicapped Infants and Children, 1983; New Perspectives in Down Syndrome, 1987; Down Syndrome: A Resource Handbook, 1988; Implementing Early Intervention, 1989; 4 record albums for teaching, 1979-81. *Memberships:* America Association on Mental Retardation; Professional Advisory Board Member, National Down Syndrome Congress; Council for Exceptional Children. *Honours:* Honour Graduate, Girls State, 1950; Student Body Vice-President, 1951; State Championship Debator, High School, 1951; Master's Fellowship, University of Utah, 1970; Phi Kappa Phi, 1970; Fellow, American Association on Mental Deficiency (now American Association on Mental Retardation), 1983; Editorial Advisory Board: The Exceptional Parent; Infants and Young Children. *Hobbies:* Writing; Sewing; Lecturing; Making personal gifts for her grandchildren. *Address:* Psychological Associates, Salt Lake City, UT 84102, USA.

TINKER Debra Ann, b. 27 June 1951, Cleveland, Ohio, USA. m. Charles Earl Enos, 6 Aug. 1983. 2 sons. *Education:* BS, cum laude, Ohio University, 1973; MA, Clinical/Community Psychology, Chapman College, 1988. *Appointments:* Teacher, English, remedial reading, Northmont Jr High School, Clayton, Ohio, 1973-76; Dance instructor, Schehera's Studio, Dayton, 1974-76; Substitute Teacher, Knox County Schools, Mt Vernon, 1976; Teacher, English, remedial reading, Ohio Youth Commn, Massillon, 1977; Coordinator special needs program, Knox County Joint Vocat School, Mt Vernon, 1977-82; Life Insurance Sales, Belding and Assocs, Mt Vernon, 1980-82; Student control officer, Naval Air Training Unit, Sacramento, 1982-85; Director, Navy Counseling and Assistance Centre, Charleston, 1985-88; Chief, Counselling Services, Navy Family Service Centre, Charleston, 1988-. *Publications:* Article: Teaching English in Junior High School; Executive Producer 1977- 81, Mt Vernon AWARE (public service TV programme). *Memberships:* National Council of Teachers of English, 1973-76; US Naval Institute, 1983-85; Leader Girl Scouts Am, Dayton, Ohio counsel, 1975-76; Cons North Charleston, SC, 1987-; Navy Family Advocacy Support Team, 1985-; Navy Alcohol and Drug Advisory Council, 1985-88; Board of Directors, Exchange Club Center for the Prevention of Child Abuse, Charleston, 1987-88; Served to Lieutenant, USNR, 1982-; Charleston Women Officers' Association; SC Mental Health Counselors' Association; Society Mayflower Descendants; Mensa; Associate member of American Psychological Association, 1989-; member of Charleston Area DUI Prevention Council, 1988-; served on South Carolina Department of Social Services Committee on Defining Child Abuse and Neglect, 1989. *Honours:* President's Honor Award, Ohio University, 1969-73; Kappa Delta Pi, Honorary Education Society. *Hobbies:* Piano; Reading; Needlework; Dance; Model Trains. *Address:* 202 Brailsford Road, Summerville, SC 29485, USA.

TINSLEY Eleanor, b. 31 Oct. 1926, Dallas, Texas, USA. Council Member, City of Houston. m. James A Tinsley, 20 Mar. 1948. 1 son, 2 daughters. *Education:* BA, Baylor, 1946; *Appointments:* Elected At-Large Member, Houston School Board, 1969-73; Elected At-Large Member, Houston City Council, 1979, 1981, 1983, 1985, 1987. *Memberships include:* Texas Council of Child Welfare Boards (president); Vocational Guidance Service; Houston Council on Human Relations; Board, Houston World Trade Association; Advisory Boards: Alley Theater; Stages Repertory Theater; The Volunteer Center; CASA Child Advocates, Inc. *Honours:* Alpha Omega Dental Fraternity Award, 1980; Certificate of Notable Accomplishment, Julia C Hester House, 1980; Appointed to Serve on White House Conference for Children and Youth Committee, 1980; Susan B Anthony Woman of the Year Award, Harris County Women's Political Caucus, 1980; Distinguished Service Award, Citizens Chamber of Commerce, 1981; Woman of Valor, Jewish National Fund, 1982; Outstanding Crime Prevention Citizen Award, Texas Crime Prevention Association, 1982; Honorary Member, Texas Society of Architects, 1983; Honoree, Organization for Rehabilitation through Training, 1984; Community Service Award, Houston Area Women's Center, 1984; Appointed to National League of Cities Transportation and Communications Steering Committee, 1985; Wonder Woman, Ultra Magazine, 1985; Feminist of the Year Award, Texas NOW, 1985; Leadership Award, Park People, 1985; Best Public Official, Houston City Magazine, 1985; Liberty Bell Award, Houston Young Lawyers Association, 1986; Appreciation Award, The Gulf Coast Coalition of Texans with Disabilities, 1986; First Merit Award, Council of Texas Archeologists, 1986; Environmental Stewardship Award, Texas Chapter, American Society of Landscape Architects, 1987; Texas Chapter Award, Texas Chapter, American Planning Association, 1987; Institute of Rehabilitation and Research President's Award, 1987; Public Advocacy Award, American Lung Association of Texas, 1988; Highway Beautification Award, Coalition for Scenic Beauty, 1988; Named to the Order of the Silver Thistle, Scottish Heritage Foundation, Inc., 1988; Outstanding Houston Professional Women Award, The Federation of Houston Professional Women, 1988; Named to the Texas Women's Hall of Fame, Governor's Commission for Women, 1989; Distinguished Citizen Award, The Institute of Religion, 1989; Outstanding Women's Award, YWCA, 1989. *Address:* 15 Greenway Plaza 19E, Houston, Texas 77046, USA.

TIRELLA Julia, b. 16 Mar. 1940, Italy. Real Estate Broker; Teacher; Civic Leader. m. Alfred Tirella, 24 Nov. 1956, 4 sons, 1 daughter. *Education:* Teacher, Liberal Arts, Scuola Magisrale, 1956; Licensed Real Estate Broker, 1970. *Appointments:* Real Estate Sales Lady, 1968- 70; Voluntary Teacher, Italian, 1972-73; Voluntary Teacher, English Bible, 1977-88; Real Estate Appraising, 1979-88; Real Estate Education 1979-88; Continuing Real Estate Education,Miami Board of Realtors, 1979-88. *Memberships:* Various professional organisations. *Hobbies:* Aerobic Exercises; Swimming; Bicycling; Dancing; Reading. *Address:* 2240 Magnolia Drive, North Miami, Keystone Point, FL 33181, USA.

TISHEFF-SVEZIA Vera, b. 5 Sept. 1935, Ohio, USA. Concert Pianist; Music Producer. m. Rudolph Svezia, 14 Mar. 1970. 1 son, 1 daughter. *Education:* Yale University, New Haven; The Eastman School of Music, Rochester; Michigan State University; Julliard School of Music, New York City studied with Rosina Lhevinne. *Creative Works:* Public performing debut at the age of 9, New York City; Concerts with leading orchestras in the USA, Europe, South America and Mexico; Performed the American premier of piano works by composer Charles Whittenberg; Performances include television and radio and commercial recordings in the USA; Lectured in major European cities. Publications include: The Bella Bartok Sonate - A Study. *Memberships:* United State congressional advisory board. *Honours:* Cited for outstanding achievements in music by the board or governor and membership committees of: International Platform Association; The American Association of University Women; The Martha Baird Rockefeller Foundation of the Arts; The MacDowell Music Colony; The Society of Distinguished Americans; Delta Omnicron (Life Member). *Address:* 130 East Hamilton Avenue, Englewood, NJ 07631, USA.

TOAL Jean Hoefer, b. 11 Aug. 1943, Columbia, South Carolina, USA. Lawyer; Associate Justice. m. William Thomas Toal, 24 Aug. 1967, 2 daughters. *Education:* BA, Agnes Scott College, 1965; JD, University of South Carolina Law School, 1968. *Appointments:* Lawyer: Haynsworth, Perry, Bryant, Marion & Johnstone, 1968-70; Belser, Baker, Barwick, Ravenel, Toal & Bender, 1970-88. Associate Justice, South Carolina Supreme Court, 1988-. *Publications:* Managing Editor, SC Law Review, 1967-68. *Memberships:* South Carolina House of Representatives, 1975-88; Chairman, House Rules Committee, 1980-88; Subcommittee Chairman, House Judiciary Committee, 1977-88; Lector, St Joseph's Catholic Church; Member, South Carolina, Richland County & American Bar Associations. *Hobbies:* Golf; Gardening. *Address:* South Carolina Supreme Court, 1231 Gervais Street, Columbia, SC 29201, USA.

TOBIAS Cynthia Lee, b. 6 July 1945, Dayton, Ohio, USA. Computing Manager and Consultant. m. Riaz A Gondal, 4 July 1981. *Education:* BS Spanish, 1967; MA Sociology, 1969; MS Industrial Engineering, 1986; PhD Sociology, 1977. *Appointments:* Lecturer, Kano, Nigeria, 1977-78; Research Associate, University of Arizona, 1984-87; International Development Consultant, 1979-; Computing Manager, University of Arizona, College of Medicine, 1987-. *Publications:* The Health & Sympton Care of Widows, 1988; Technology Transfer to developing Countries: The Case of the Burundi Peat Stove, 1988; Computers and the Elderly, 1987, and numerous others. *Memberships:* Human Factors Society, Treasurer, Arizona Chapter, 1988- 89; Institute of Electrical and Electronics Engineers; American Sociological Association; Washington Association of Professional Anthropologists; Society of Women Engineers, Vice President, Tucson, 1987-88. *Honours:* Organization of American States Fellow, Argentina, 1975-76; National Institute of Health, graduate fellowship, 1969-72; BSL cum laude, 1967. *Hobbies:* Travel; Reading; Swimming. *Address:* PO Box 42064, Tucson, Arizona 85733, USA.

TODARO Laura Jean, b. 8 June 1956, Neligh, Nebraska, USA. Attorney. *Education:* BA, Political Science, University of Illinois, 1978; JD, Loyola University, 1981. *Appointments:* Associate, Dutel & Dutel, 1979-85; Partner, Todaro & Todaro, 1985-; City Attorney of Kenner, 1985-87; City Prosecutor & Executive Counsel to the Mayor of Kenner, 1987-. *Memberships:* American & Louisiana State Bar Associations; Kenner YMCA, Secretary, Board of Managers; Metropolitan New Orleans YMCA, Board of Directors, 1987-; Advisory Board Member, Institute for Legal Studies; Board of Directors, Metropolitan Battered Women's Association; Louisiana City Attorney's Association; Phi Delta Phi. *Hobbies:* Sailing; Skiing. *Address:* 720 Vanderbilt Lane, Kenner, LA 70065, USA.

TODD Barbara Sheen, b. 10 Mar. 1942, Pennsylvania, USA. Pinellas County Commissioner, Florida. m. Tom Todd. 3 daughters. *Education:* BA, Spanish, Sociology, 1963, MA, Foreign Language Education 1964, Florida State University; Instituto Tecnologico, Monterrey, Mexico, Summer 1962. *Appointments:* Personnel Management, State of Florida and private industry; State Administrator for special programs, Florida Board of Regents; State of South Dakota, Acting assistant Secretary for Administration, office of Secretary of Education and Cultural Affairs; Own consultant firm which provided administrative, efficiency, managamement and planning studies and services; Member and Officer of numerous local Councils. *Memberships include:* State Legislative Chairperson, South Dakota Parent-Teacher Association; Board of Directors, Florida State University, University School; American Society for Public Administration; Capitol Business and Professional Women's Club (several offices); Pilot Club; Beta Sigma Phi; National University Extension Association; American Association of School Administrators. *Honours include:* Leadership Award, Florida School Boards Association, 1974; Pinellas County Extension Horticultural Advisory Committee, Award for Outstanding Service; Award for Patriotic Services to Community, Veterans of Foreign Wards; Nominated by Leon High School Students for Jaycees Distinguished Service Award, 1972. *Address:* Pinellas County Courthouse, 315 Court Street, Clearwater, FL 34616, USA.

TODD Shirley Ann, b. 23 May 1935, Virginia, USA. Director of Guidance. m. Thomas Byron Todd, 7 July 1962, deceased. *Education:* BSc., Education, Madison College, 1956; M.Ed., University of Virginia, 1971. *Appointments:* Elementary Teacher: 1956-66; 8th Grade HIstory Teacher, 1966-71, Guidence Counsellor, 1988-, Director of Guidance, 1988-, James Finimore Cooper International School. *Memberships Include:* Northern Virginia Counsellors Association, Chairman, Hospitality/Social, Executive Board; Virginia Counsellors Association; Virginia School Counsellors Association; Ameican Association for Counselling and Development; Fairvax Education Association; etc. *Hobbies:* Tennis; Golf. *Address:* 6543 Bay Tree Court, Falls Church, VA 22041, USA.

TOKAR Bette Lewis, b. 26 Mar 1935, Philadelphia, Pennsylvania, USA. College Professor. m. Jacob John Tokar, 1 Oct 1955, 2 sons, 2 daughters. *Education:* Studies, Ursinus College, 1953-55; BA, Holy Family College, 1967; MA Temple University, 1973; Doctoral Candidate, Economics and Business Education, Temple University, 1980-. *Appointments:* Lecturer 1972-75, Instructor, Business Administration, 1975-78, Assistant Professor 1978-82, Associate Professor 1982-, Chairman, Department of Business Administration and Computer Science, 1977-85, Holy Family College, Philadelphia, Pennsylvania; Lecturer, Community College of Philadelphia, 1985-; Lecturer, La Salle College, 1978; Assessor CLEO, 1979-. *Publications:* The Role of the US Dollar as a Key Currency, Masters thesis; The Social Cost of Poor Pre-Natal Care. *Memberships:* Academy of International Business; American Accounting Association; American Economics Association; American Management Association; Mensa; Delta Pi Epsilon; Pi Gamma Mu; Association for Social Economics; Past Committeewoman, Treasurer and Candidate for Township Auditor, Lower Southampton Democrats; Past Board of Directors, Pine

Tree Farms Association. *Honours:* Manpower Scholarship, 1972; Mensa; Delta Pi Epsilon; Pi Gamma Mu, 1955; Journalism Prize, Abraham Lincoln High School, 1953. *Hobbies:* Reading; Doll-house miniatures; Design; Choral singing. *Address:* 153 Pine Hill Road, Feasterville, PA 19047, USA.

TOKAR Joyce Lynn, b. 27 Jan. 1958, Pittsburgh, USA. Visiting Scholar. *Education:* BSc., 1979, MSc., 1981, Computer Science; PhD, Computer Engineering, 1988. *Appointments:* System Architect, Gensoft Corp, 1982-84; Software Engineer, 1986-87, Consultant, 1987-88, AT & T Bell Labs; Visiting Scholar, University of Natal, South Africa, 1988-. *Publications:* A New Task Paradigm for Reusability, PhD Dissertation, 1988. *Memberships:* Association of Computing Machinery; IEEE. *Honour:* AT & T Bell Laboratories Research Fellowship, 1985-86. *Hobbies:* Hiking; Skiing; Reading. *Address:* 424 Longview Dr., Monroeville, PA 15146, USA.

TOLBERT Alice Morrow, Cisi, b. 31 Dec. 1941, Sumter, South Carolina, USA. Freelance Writer; Editor, Ghostwriter. m. 16 Sept. 1964. 3 sons, 2 daughters. *Education:* Certificate, University of GA, 1969; Diploma, Institute Children's Literature, 1982; BA, Journalism (Creative Writing), Georgia State University, 1985. *Appointments:* Freelance writer, 1975-88; General Office, Tolbert and Associates, 1981-82; part time, Sun Finance Co, 1972. *Publications:* Life Matters, newsletter, 1982-88, editor, writer. *Memberships:* Georgia-Gwinnett Right to Life, Vice President, Co-Director, Public Relations 1988-; Society of Professional Journalists, Delta Sigam Chi; Gwinnett Council for the Arts, Golden Key Honor Society; Scribe Tribe Writers of Atlanta, 1975-82. *Honours:* Golden Key Honor Society, GA State Univ, 1984-85; Mortar Board's Outstanding Scholarship Award, 1985; Georgia-Gwinnett Right to Life certificate of merit, 1987. *HoBBIes:* Arts and crafts; Aerobic exercising; Gourmet cooking; Swimming; Reading. *Address:* 5763 Renee Court, Lilburn, GA 30247, USA.

TOLIVAR Carmen R. (Menendez Nunez), b. 22 Jan. 1939, Puerto Rico. Independent Consultant, Public Affairs. m. A. Fernando Tolivar, 1 son, 1 daughter. *Education:* BA 1950, postgraduate 1959-60, University of Puerto Rico; Postgraduate, University of Colorado, 1960-62; MA, Spanish Literature, University of California Los Angeles, 1965; Coro Foundation Fellows Programme, 1985. *Appointments:* Instructor, California State University, 1968-72; Teacher & Chair, Spanish Department, Westlake School, 1972-81; Assistant to Director of Programmes Los Angeles Education Department, 1985; Director, Special Programmes, Coro Foundation, 1985-87; Independent Consultant, public affairs, 1987-. *Creative works:* Essays, poems. *Memberships:* Board President, Southern California Advocates for Nursing Home Reform; National Association for Women; Los Angeles County Latino Assessment Project; Executive, offices, Comision Femenil Mexicana Nacional. *Honours:* Award, Comision Femenil; Faculty scholarship, study in Spain; Hispanic leaders' trip, Israel. *Hobbies:* Gardening; Piano playing; Writing; Reading. *Address:* 14655 Weddington Street, Van Nuys, California 91411, USA.

TOMALIN Ruth, b. Bessborough Gardens, County Kilkenny, Republic of Ireland. Writer. m. (1) V. R. F. Leaver, 25 July 1942, 1 son, (2) W. N. Ross, 4 November 1971. *Education:* Chichester High School, Sussex, England, 1931-38. *Appointments:* Women's Land Army, 1941-42; Staff Reporter, The Evening News, Portsmouth, and various other newspapers, 1942-65; Press Reporter, London law courts, 1965-75. *Publications:* Over 20 books including: Threnody for Dormice (verse), 1947; Deer's Cry (verse), 1952; All Souls (novel), 1952; The Sea Mice (for younger readers), 1962; The Garden House (novel), 1964; W. H. Hudson (biography), 1982; Long Since (for younger readers), 1989. *Hobbies:* Natural history; English country life. *Address:* c/o Barclay's Bank, 15 Langham Place, London W1A 4NX, England.

TOMASEK Hana, b. 4 Apr. 1935, Prague, Czechoslovakia. Organization Development Professional; Educator. m. Jaroslav Tomasek, 6 Nov. 1959. *Education:* MSEE 1958, PhD, 1967, Technical University of Prague, Czechoslovakia; Professional Certificate, Training and Development in Industry and Business, University of Minnesota, 1984. *Appointments:* Des Eng, Barrandov Movie Studio, Prague, Czechoslovakia, 1959-60; Assoc Professor, Charles University of Prague, 1960-72; Research Instructor, University of Minnesota, 1973-76; Staff Dev Coordin, Technical Institute, St Paul, Minnesota, 1976-83; President, Innovative Consulting Services (INCOS), Minneapolis, 1983-. *Creative works:* Author and co-author of textbooks including: Basic Electronics for Educators; articles in teacher education and organization development. Presentations in USA, Norway, Germany, Yugoslavia, Canada. *Memberships:* Organization Development Institute; American Soc for Training & Development; Board member, Nat Society for Performance & Instruction; Board member, Minnesota Software Assoc. *Honour:* Professional Excellence Award, Trainer of Trainers, ASTD, 1985. *Hobbies:* Travel; Sports. *Address:* 10024 South Shore Drive, Minneapolis, MN 55441, USA.

TOMASSINI-PATERNO TOMASI LEOPARDI OF CONSTANTINOPLE Margherita Andreana (Princess), b. London, England. Artist; Businesswoman. m. Prince Hugo-Jose, Head of the Imperial House of Constantinople, 28 Feb. 1956. *Education:* Doctor of Languages, Italian, Spanish, Portuguese, French, German, English, 1950; MFA, 1960; Professor of Fine Art, 1961; Master of Administration in Real Estate, Georgia, USA. *Appointments:* Artist, Oil Painting & imaginative impressionism, signing herself as Ritandreana; Businesswoman, Real Estate. *Publications:* Contributor, numerous articles to professional journals. *Memberships:* Numerous cultural institutions worldwide. *Honours:* Recipient, numerous honours, prizes & awards for art, merit & sports, 1946-; Recipient, many honorary degrees, decorations including Ranks in Orders of Chivalry in various countries. *Hobby:* Marathon Running.

TOMBLESON Esme Irene, b. 1 Aug. 1917, Sydney, Australia. Retired. m. Thomas William John Tombleson, MM, JP, 22 Feb. 1957. *Education:* UE SCEGG, Sydney; Imperial Soc Teachers Dancing, London. *Appointments:* Italian Grand Opera Co (Ballet), 1932; Fullers British Grand Opera Co (Ballet), 1934; Cander, Montague Show 1937-38; Dancer, Marcus Show, 1938; Dancer, De Basil Ballet, 1938-39; Signaller Womens Emergency Signalling Corps, 1940-42; Secretary, NSW State Committee Advice, 1942-45; Sec, Printing, Timber Industry, Building Trades, Ships Painters & Dockers, Ships Iron Workers, Ships Tally Clerks, Ships Carpenters, Manpower Committees, 1942-46; OC Female employment, Willougby-Hornsby, New South Wales, 1946-48; OC Feamle Employment domestic/farm section, Commonwealth Employment Service, 1948-51; Choreography, Bjelke-Petersens Dance Group, 1942-57; Member of Parliament, Gisborne, New Zealand, 1960-72; Ch Maori Affairs Select Committee (Parliament), 1969-72; Ch NZ Island Territories Select Committee, 1969-72; NZ Parliamentary Select Fishing Com, 1960-72; Leader Parliamentary Delegation, 1965-; Womens' Rep NZ Road Safety Council, 1963-66; Trustee, Winston Churchill Trust Board, 1966-75; Councillor NZ Advisory Com for Disabled, 1975-87; Co-founder, NZ Nat Multiple Sclerosis Soc, 1961-, Vice President, Nat MS Society, 1968-75, NZ Nat Pres MS Soc, 1975-82; Int Patient Services Com, 1975-; Executive International Federation MS Soc, 1979-; Executive NZ Neurological Foundation, 1975-; Management Committee, NZ MS Soc, 1968-; Sec Disabled Persons Assembly Gisborne, 1984-; President Gisborne East Coast MS Soc, 1988-; Community Service Committee, Gisborne Area Health Board, 1988-. *Publications:* Various articles on Womens affairs in NZ Farmer and NZ Womens Magazines. *Memberships:* Assoc Member, Federated Farmers, NZ; NZ Post-Grad Med Assoc, Gisborne; Commonwealth Parliamentary Assoc; NZ Parliamentary Assoc; V President, Watties

Cycling Club; Vice President, Gisborne Athletic Club; Gisborne Music Society. *Honours:* Commander, QSO, 1977; Life Member, NZ Nat MS Soc, 1983; Com Medal Honour IBM, 1988; Life Vice President, NZ Nat MS Soc, 1983; Member, IBC, 1988; Leader Parliamentary Delegations, 1965; Int Fed MS Soc Rep Social Welfare, 1980. *Hobbies:* Music; Reading; Gardening; Travel; Charitable work. *Address:* Burnage Station, R D Matahwai, Gisborne, New Zealand.

TOMKIEL Judith Irene, b. 4 Nov. 1949, St Louis, Missouri, USA. m. William George Tomkiel, 15 Dec. 1972. 3 sons, 2 daughters. *Education:* Graduate for Computer op Small Business, International Correspondence School; Institute of Children's Literature, graduated 1982, 1985. *Appointments:* Foster Parent for Orange County, 1979-86; Founder/Owner, The Idea Shoppe, 1985-; Publisher, Shoppe Talk, 1986-; Crafts person for Clothworld, 1988-. *Publications:* Poems: Sonny Boy; Christopher; Life's Circle; Snack Time; My Son; Writer's Rights; Whose Son?; The Lesson; One Family; The Second Birthday Gone; To Daddy with Love; Mail Order; Mother's Thoughts; Shoppe Talk (Newsletter). *Memberships:* National Writer's Club; National Association of Female Executives; Mail Order Business Board; Fellow, The World Literary Academy; Society of Scholarly Publishing; Amnesty International. *Honours:* Third place poetry contest, 1985; Honourable mention for poem, 1987; Golden Poet Award, 1987; Cover of New Writer's Magazine, July/August 1988. *Hobbies:* Playing flute, piano and organ; Writing poetry; Printing; Sewing; Crafts. *Address:* 13351 Hale Avenue, Garden Grove, CA 92644, USA.

TOMLINSON Elvira Mary, b. 13 Sept. 1922, Willaston, England. Chairman, various Private Companies. m. John Michael Tomlinson, 31 May 1947. *Memberships:* Institute of Directors; Conservative West Africa Committee. *Address:* Moel-y-Don, Llanedwen, Llanfairpwll, Anglesey, Gwynedd, Wales LL61 6EZ.

TOMPKINS Susie, b. San Francisco, USA. Design Director. m. Doug Tompkins, 1964, 2 daughters. *Education:* San Francisco Art Institute. *Appointments:* Co-Founder, Plain Jane Dress Company, 1968 (remaned Esprit De Corp 1978). *Memberships:* many National and Bay Area Organizations. *Hobby:* Travel. *Address:* 900 Minnesota Street, San Francisco, California 94107, USA.

TOMSIC Vida, b. 26 June 1913, Ljubljana, Yugoslavia. Honorary Professor (Family Law). m. Professor Dr F Novak, 31 Aug. 1946. 2 sons, 1 daughter. *Education:* Graduate, Faculty of Law, 1941; Honorary PhD 1979, University of Ljubljana. *Appointments:* Minister, Government of Socialist Republic of Slovenia (SRS), Socialist Federative Republic of Yugoslavia (SFRY), 1945-46; President, Antifascist Fron of Women of SFRY, 1948-52; President, Parliament of SRS, 1962-63; President, House of Nations, Parliament of SFRY, 1967-68; Member, Presidency of SRS, 1974-84; Member, Council of Federation, 1984-. *Publications:* Books: A Selection of Articles and Speeches on the Status of Women and Family Planning in Yugoslavia, 1975; Woman, Labour, Family, Society, 1978; Woman in the Development of Socialist Self-managing Yugoslavia, 1980; Policy of Non- Alignment, Struggle for the New International Economic Order and the Role of Women in Development, 1983; Facing Change with Women, 1986; Self-Management & Participation of Women in Development, 1986; South-South Cooperation and The Role of Women in Development, 1987. *Memberships:* President, Federal Council for Family Planning, 1971-76; President, Socialist Alliance of Working People of SRS, 1963-67; Yugoslav Rep, Social Development Commission, ECOSOC, New York, 1960-63 and 1971-74; Board Member, International Research & Training Institute for the Advancement of Women, 1979-85; Council Member, Yugoslav Center for Theory & Practice of Self-Management, 1980-. *Honours:* Order of Partisan Combatan Since 1941; Order of National Hero, 1953; Order of Hero of Socialist Work, 1973; El grado de banda de primera clase, Mexico, 1963;

Das Grosse Silberne Ehrzeichen am Bande fur Verdienste um die Republik Osterreich, Austria, 1982; Ordre national du merite, France, 1983. *Interests:* Role of women in society and development; Family planning; International relations; Countryside excursions. *Address:* Valvazorjeva 7, 61000 Ljubljana, Yugoslavia.

TONGUE Carole, b. 14 Oct. 1955, Lausanne, Switzerland. Member of European Parliament. *Education:* BA, Honours, Loughborough University, 1977. *Appointments:* Assistant Editor, Laboratory Practice, 1977-79; Courier, Sunsites Ltd., France, 1978-79; Scholarship to European Parliament for Research in Social Affairs, 1979-80; Administraation Assistant, Socialist Group, European Parliament Secretariat, 1980-84; Member, European Parliament, London East, 1984-. *Memberships:* UK Labour Party; UK Co-Op Party; Campaign for Nuclear Disarmament; Quaker Council for European Affairs; Vice President, SERA; Council Member, ISDD; Trade Union: MSF/APEX. *Honour:* School Prize for All Round Achievement, 1974. *Hobbies:* Piano; Cello; Tennis; Squash; Horse Riding; Skiing; Cinema; Theatre; Opera. *Address:* 84 Endsleigh Gardens, Ilord, Essex IG1 3EG, England.

TONSETH Margot Lilian, b. 29 Dec. 1935, West Wyalong, New South Wales, Australia. Educator. m. Kare Kjeldsberg Tonseth, 26 July 1960, 1 son, 2 daughters. *Education:* Primary Teacher's Certificate, Toorak Teachers' College, Melbourne, Victoria, 1956. *Appointments:* Teacher, Portland, England, Scotland, 1956-60; Adult Education Teacher, English as a Second Language, Norway, 1960-75; Founder, Teacher, Principal, Birralee International School, Trondheim, 1973-89. *Memberships:* Area Director, Zonta International, Norway; Chairman, Anglo Norse Society; Amnesty International. *Honours:* Honorary Doctor of Education, 1988. *Hobbies:* Art; Music; Theatre; Travel; Family; Conditions and rights for children and women. *Address:* Birralee International School, Bispegate 9 c, 7013 Trondheim, Norway.

TONSING Cecilia Ann Degnan, b. 20 Apr. 1943, Washington DC, USA. Voluntary Organisation Executive. m. Michael John Tonsing, 29 Jan. 1966, 1 son, 1 daughter. *Education:* BA, Holy Names College, Oakland, California, 1965; MPA magna cum laude, California State University, Hayward, 1976; Certificates, volunteer work. *Appointments include:* Executive Director, California State Parks Foundation, 1981-84; President & Chief Executive Officer: Providence Hospital Foundation, Oakland 1984-87; St Luke's Hospital Foundation, San Francisco 1987-. *Memberships:* Past President, Law League of East Bay; Board, California Archives Foundation; Chair, State Commission on Heritage Preservation; Society of California Pioneers; California Heritage Club; National volunteer, Girl Scouts of USA; SF Bay Girl Scout Council; American Association of University Women; League of Women Voters; Various clubs. *Hobbies:* Historic touring & restoration; Gardening; Gourmet cooking. *Address:* 911 Longridge Road, Oakland, California 94610, USA.

TOONA Elin-Kai, b. 12 July 1937, Tallinn, Estonia. Writer. m. Donald Frederick Gottschalk, 9 Oct. 1967, deceased, 1 son. *Appointments:* Actress, 1960-64; Writer, 1964-. *Publications:* Novels in English: In Search of Coffee Mountains, UK 1979, USA 1977; Lady Cavaliers, 1977; Novels in Estonian published in Sweden: Puuingel, 1965; Lotukata, 1969; Sipelgas Sinise Kausi All, 1973; Kalevikula Viimne Tutar, 1988. *Memberships:* International PEN; American Pen Women; Estonians in Exile Literary Associations. *Honours:* Storyteller, 1962; National League of American Pen Women, 1985. *Hobbies:* Music; Painting; Travel; Photography. *Address:* 1805 Cathedral Road, Huntingdon Valley, PA 19006, USA.

TOPAZ Muriel, b. 7 May 1932, Philadelphia, Pennsylvania, USA. Director of Dance Division, The Juilliard School. m. Jacob Druckman, 5 June 1954, 1 son, 1 daughter. *Education:* New York University, 1950-

51; Juilliard School, 1951-54; Dance Studies with Martha Graham & Antony Tudor; Dance Notation Bureau, Certified Labanotation Teacher, 1958, Certified Professional Notator, 1961. *Appointments:* Faculty, The Juilliard School, 1959-70; Dance Notation Bureau, 1970-78; Executive Director, Dance Notation Bureau, 1978-85; Organiser, Co-Chairman, First International Congress on Movement Noation, Tel-Aviv, Israel, 1984. *Publications:* Changes and New Developments in Labanotation, 1966; Elementary Study Guide, with Hackney and Manno, 1970; Elementary Reading Studies, with Hackney and Manno, 1970; Intermediate Reading Studies, 1972; Readings in Modern dance, with Edelson, 1972; Intermediate Study Guide, 1972; Notator, Ballets by Tudor Robbins Humphrey Taylor Graham and Jooss; Editor: Choreography and Dance: The Notation Issue, 1988. *Memberships:* Dance Notation Bureau, Board of Directors; Board Member, 1983-85, Committee on Research in the Dance; Board Member, 1981-85, National Association of Schools of Dance. *Honours:* National Association of Regional Ballet, Adjudicator, 1979, 1980, 1981, 1983; Fellow, International Council of Kinetography; Dance Panel: New York State Council on the Arts, 1980-82, Panel Chair, 1982-83. *Hobbies:* Tennis; Swimming. *Address:* Dance Division, The Juilliard School, Lincoln Centre, New York, NY 10023, USA.

TORBERG Virginia June Hubbard, b. 8 May 1922, Minneapolis, Minnesota, USA. Soap Manufacturer. m. Bernie Richard Torberg, 18 Sept. 1948. 4 sons, 1 daughter. *Education:* University of Minnesota, night school, 1943; National Honor Society, 1940. *Appointments:* Exec Secretary, Marsh & McLennan to 1947; Manufacture and sales of North Country Glycerine Soap and Mother Hubbard Glycerine Soap, currently. *Creative works:* Wood Carver, displayed carvings at: Sons of Norway; MN State Fair; Greater Mississippi Valey Show, Davenport, IA; Lutheran Brotherhood Art Museum. Books: Why Carve Just One; Country Pattern Book; Something About Soap; Frontier Journal; 1-2-3 Ways to Make Money at Home. Article: What Do You Mean--Work?. *Memberships:* Museum Store Association; LWV; International Platform Association; National Carvers Association; Weaver's Guild; Professional Association of Innkeepers, International. *Honours:* Ribbons on Carvings, 1973, 1974; Ribbon on Soap; Four Registered Trade-Marks and five copyrights. *Hobbies:* Woodcarfing; Writing; Herbs; Pot pourri. *Address:* 7888 County Road No 6, Maple Plain, MN 55359, USA.

TORNABENI Jolene, b. 2 Dec. 1947, Clarion, USA Company Vioo President. m. Joël Tornabeni, 10 Dec. 1975, 1 son, 1 daughter. *Education:* BS, Health Services, 1981; MA, University of Phoenix, 1983. *Appointments:* Head Nurse, L.A. Weiss Hospital, Chicago, 1969-75; Head Nurse, Hermann Hospital, Houston, 1976-78; Vice President, Phoenix Memorial Hospital, 1979-85; Administrator, Phoenix Children's Hospital, 1986-; Vice President, Mercy Hospital & Medical Centre, San Diego, 1987-. *Memberships:* American College of Healthcare Executives; American Organisation of Nurisng Executives; California Society for Nursing Service Administrators; Director, Health Care Executive, San Diego. *Honours:* Certified NursingAdministrator, Advanced, 1985; Tribute to Women in Industry, Honoree, 1988. *Hobbies:* Walking; Reading. *Address:* 4077 Fifth Avenue, San Diego, CA 92013, USA.

TORNATORE-MORSE Kathleen Mary, b. 25 Feb. 1955, New York, USA. Assistant Professor. m. Gene D. Morse, 13 Oct. 1984, 1 daughter. *Education:* BS, Pharmacy, Albany College of Pharmacy, 1978; Doctor of Pharmacy, SUNY, Buffalo, 1981. *Appointments:* ASHP Hospital Pharmacy Resident, 1978-79; Clinical Pharmacy Co-ordinator, Buffalo General Corporation, 1981-83; Assistant Professor, Pharmacy, SUNY, Buffalo, 1983-. *Publications:* Articles in: Clinical Pharmacology; British Journal Clinical Pharmacology. *Memberships:* American Society of Hospital Pharmacists; American Association of Colleges of Pharmacy; American College of Clinical Pharmacists;

American Association for the Advancement of Sciences. *Honours:* Outstanding Young Woman of America, 1984; Achievement Award, Albany College of Pharmacy, 1984; Rho Chi. *Hobbies:* Sewing; Weightlifting; Tennis. *Address:* 813 Cooke Hall, School of Pharmacy, State University of New York, Buffalo, NY 14260, USA.

TORRE-RECK Elizabeth, b. 17 June 1931, Winston-Salem, North Carolina, USA. Social Work Educator. m. (1) Mottram Torre, 13 Apr. 1947, dec. 1981, (2) Andrew Joseph Reck, 17 June 1987. *Education:* BA, Duke University, 1952; MRE, Union Theological Seminary, New York, 1957; MSW, 1966, PhD, 1972, Tulane University. *Appointments:* NGO, World Federation for Mental Health, 1957-61; Family Outreach Programme, Riverside Church, New York City, 1958-60; Faculty, School of Social Work, Tulane University, 1966-. *Publications include:* Adaptation of the Group Psychotherapy Approach for Use in Poverty Area Elementary Schools (with Mottram Torre), 1971; Classroom Teaching of Community Mental Health in a MSW Program, 1975; Prevention Strategies of a Self-empowered Group of Professional Women, 1987. *Memberships:* New York Junior League, Treasurer and Vice-President 1960-63; National Association of Social Workers, Board Member, Louisiana Chapter, 1987-89; Council on Social Work Education; Fellow, American Orthopsychiatric Association; American Association of University Professors; American Association of University Women. *Honours:* Phi Beta Kappa, Duke University, 1952; Several listings. *Hobbies:* Mental health prevention; Work and family; Music; Travel; Fiction particularly by women. *Address:* 6125 Patton Street, New Orleans, LA 70118, USA.

TOTH Erzsebet Margit, b. 26 June 1920, Romania. Actress. m. Medard Francis Kerkes, 14 June 1958, 1 son, 1 daughter. *Education:* State Academy of Dramatic Art. *Appointments:* Hungarian Theatre of Marosvasorhely, Actress, 1954-57; Soloist, State Hungarian Folk Ensemble of Marosvosarhely, Romania, 1957-. *Publications:* Many performances in plays, over 20 records with folk songs & light music; numerous TV & Radio appearances. *Address:* Str. C. Romanu-Vivu D/4, 4300 Tirgu Mures, Romania.

TOTH Judith Coggeshall, b. 21 Oct. 1937, Rochelle, Illinois, USA. Politician. 2 daughters. *Education:* BA, Northwestern University, 1955- 59; Graduate studies in Latin American Studies, Georgetown University, 1960- 61; Economics, University of Andes, Bogota, Colombia, 1965-66; Montgomery College, Rockville, Maryland, 1980-81; University of Maryland, 1981-83; MPH, Johns Hopkins University, School of Hygiene and Public Health, 1985. *Appointments include:* Delegate to the Maryland General Assembly, 1975-; Maryland Ethnic Heritage Commission, 1986-; Apointee, Washington Metropolitan Council of Governments, 1975-; Appointee, National Conference of State Legislatures, 1982-; Women's Legislative Caucus, 1975-; National Organization of Women Legislators, 1975-; Owner, Judy Toth Ltd, 1985-; Consultant to a variety of federal agencies and private organizations, 1975-. *Memberships include:* American Public Health Association; League of Women Voters, Potomac Valley League, PTA; Founding editor, Cabin John Village News; Kappa Kappa Gamma Sorority, etc. *Honours:* Washington Star Cup for Civic Activity, 1974; Numerous awards including: Mary Pirg; Hispanic Federation of Maryland; Maryland State Podiatry Association; Maryland Dental Hygienists Association; Veterans of Foreign Wars; Montgomery County Farm Bureau; Montgomery County Education Association; Humane Society of Montgomery County. *Hobbies:* Piano; Swimming; Hiking; Sewing; Gourmet cooking. *Address:* Lowe House Office Building, Annapolis, Maryland 21401, USA.

TOUTLOFF Betty Jane, b. 9 Jan. 1940, Sheboygan, Wisconsin, USA. Social Worker. m. John L Toutloff, 7 Sept. 1963. 2 daughters. *Education:* BA, Lakeland College, 1963; MA, No Michigan University, 1977. *Appointments:* Wisconsin Dept of Social Services, 1963-

67; Delta- Schoolcraft Intermediate School District, Michigan, 1974-76; Child & Family Services, 1978-79; Escanaba Area Public Schools, 1979; Juvenile Diversion, Probate Court, 1980-. *Hobbies:* Travel; Sewing and needlework; Reading. *Address:* 920 5th Avenue South, Escanaba, Michigan 49829, USA.

TOWNER Naomi Whiting, b. 8 May 1940, Providence, Rhode Island, USA. University Professor; Artist; Author; Lecturer. *Education:* BFA, Textile Design, Rhode Island School of Design, 1962; Foreningen Handarbetets Vanner, Stockholm, Sweden, 1962-63; Independent Graduate Study and Research in Textile Design, 13 European countries and Morocco, 1963; MFA, Textile Design, School for American Craftsmen, Rochester Institute of Technology, NY, USA, 1965; International Studies, Illinois State University College of Fine Arts Faculty Exchange. *Appointments:* Teaching Graduate Assistantship 1964-65, Instructor in Textile Design 1964, School for American Craftsmen, Rochester Institute of Technology, Instructor 1965-68, Assistant Professor 1968-72, Member, Graduate Faculty 1969-, Associate Professor 1972-76, Professor 1976-, Illinois State University. *Creative works:* Work shown in Museums, in Collections, Exhibitions/Competitions/Fairs, National and International. Commissions. *Memberships:* American Craft Council; Sawtooth Center for Visual Design; Fiberarts Slide Library. *Honours:* Textron Fellowship, 1962-63; Award for Service 1985, Award of Superior Achievement: Textile Conservation Project 1985, McLean County Historical Society; Teacher of the Year Award, 1986. *Hobbies:* Life; Photography; Cooking; Gardening; Travel. *Address:* 610 East Taylor Street, Bloomington, Illinois 61701, USA.

TOWNS Kathryn Louise, b. 24 May 1923, Jamestown, New York, USA. Associate Professor, Community Psychology and Womens Studies. divorced. 1 son, 3 daughters. *Education:* BS ED, 1944; MEd, 1965; PhD 1970; Licensed Psychologist Pennsylvania. *Appointments:* Pennsylvania State University, 1965-; PA and Ohio School Teacher, 1952-64; Cost Accountant, Standard Brands, 1945-46; USN Waves, 1944-45; Mathematician, Linde Air, 1944; Research Statistician, Scripps Howards, 1943-44. *Publications:* 18 articles; 26 reports to government/agencies; over 2 million in grants to assist displaced homemakers enter or re-enter the labor force. *Memberships:* Amer Ed Research Assoc; Ameri Psychological Assoc; Eastern Psychological Assoc; Assoc for Women in Psychology; National Women's Studies Association; Amer Assoc University Women; Phi Delta Kappa. *Honours:* National Science Foundation Fellowship, 1964-65; First Service to Women Award, PA Commission for Women, 1986; Jordan Award for Excellence in teaching, 1989. *Hobbies:* Travel; Knitting; Hooking rugs. *Address:* Pennsylvania State University, Harrisburg, Middletown, PA 17057, USA.

TOWNSEND Cheryl Ann, b. 21 May 1957, Rochester, New York, USA. Editor; Publisher; Store Detective. m. Jerry Grimm, 24 June 1982. 3 sons, 1 daughter. *Education:* High School Graduate, 1975; Broadcasting Arts Graduate, 1975. *Appointments:* Publisher, Editor, Impetus/Implosion Press, 1984-; Model, 1985-87; Store Detective, 1986-88. *Publications:* Poetry: An Ordinary Girl, 1984; Special Orders To Go, 1985; Dancin' On Your Fingers, 1987. *Memberships:* Secretary, Automotive Service Councils of Ohio; Women's Network; Akron Rape Crisis Center. *Honours:* Rookie Magazine of the Year for Impetus, 1985; Outstanding Volunteer, Rape Crisis Center, 1986; Outstanding Ascette, Automotive Service Councils of Ohio, 1985. *Hobbies:* Photography; Art; Poetry; Raquetball; Tennis; Volunteer work; Body building; Running. *Address:* 4975 Comanche Trail, Stow, Ohio 44224, USA.

TOWNSEND Jane C Kaltenbach, b. 21 Dec 1922, Chicago, Illinois, USA. Educator; Biologist. m. Robert L Townsend, 28 Aug. 1966. *Education:* BS, Beloit College, 1944; MA, University of Wisconsin, 1946; PhD, University of Iowa, 1950. *Appointments:* Graduate Teaching, Research Assistant, Zoology, 1944-50, Project Associate, Pathology, 1950-53, University of Wisconsin; Fellow, American Cancer Society, Wenner Grens Institute, Stockholm, Sweden, 1953-56; Assistant Professor, Biology, Northwestern University, 1956-58; Assistant Professor, Associate Professor, Professor & Chairman, Zoology, Biology, Mt. Holyoke College, 1958-. *Publications:* 50 research papers in biological journals (as Jane C Kaltenbach). *Memberships:* American Association for the Advancement of Science, Secretary, Biology, 1974-78; American Society of Zoologists, Executive Committee, 1976-79; American Institute of Biological Sciences; American Association of Anatomists; etc. *Address:* Dept. of Biological Sciences, Mount Holyoke College, South Hadley, MA 01075, USA.

TOYE Wendy, b. 1 May 1917, London, England. Director/Dancer. m. Edward S Sharp, dis. *Education:* Private Education. *Appointments Include:* Produced first ballet at Palladium at 10 years of age; First appearance on stage, Old Vic, 1929; Danced in various productions including: Hiawatha, Savoy, 1931; played Phoebe and the White Rabbit in Toad of Toad Hall, Lyceum, 1932; played Masked Dancer in Ballerina, Coliseum, 1934; Principal Dancer, The Golden Toy; toured with Anton Dolin, 1934-35; produced, Mother Earth, 1929, Th Legend of the Willow Pattern, 1930; Choreographed, Frank Bridges, There is a Willow That Grows Aslant the Brook, 1931; arranged dances for all George Blacks Productions, 1938-45; Directed, The Shepherd Show, Birmingham, 1946; sent her company, Ballet-Hoo de Wendy Toye to Paris, 1948 for the season; Directed, Peter Pan, with John Burrell, 1950; arranged dances for Joyce Grenfell's Request the Pleasure, 1954; Directed, Wild Thyme, 1955; Lady at the Wheel, 1958; Choreography for Concerto for Dancer, and also danced it, Edinburgh Festival,1 598; directed, As You Like It, 1960; Choreographed, Directed, Robert and Elizabeth, 1964; Jack and the Beanstalk, Guildford, 1967; Boots with Strawberry Jam, Nottingham Playhouse, 1967; Showboat, 1971; Once More with Music, 1976; This Thing Called Love, 1982; Associate Producer: Singing in the Rain, 1983; Barnum; Tribute to Joyce Grenfell, 1985; Associate Producer, Torvill and Dean Ice Show World Tour; numerous other productions. *Memberships:* Many professional organisations. *Honours:* Silver Jubilee Medal, 1977; Hon. Lieutenant, 8th Army Air Force, USA. *Address:* c/o Jay Benning & Co., Canberra House, 315 Regent Street, London W1R 7YB, England.

TRACHTENBERG Gloria Pearl, b. 25 June 1935, New York City, USA. Artist and Designer. m. Norman Trachtenberg, 10 Oct. 1954. 1 son, 1 daughter. *Education:* Art courses: Pratt Institute, Art Students League, Fashion Institute of Technology, Brooklyn Museum Art School, School of Visual Arts, Provincetown Workshops; AA, New York State Institute of Applied Arts & Sciences, 1956; BA, cum laude, Brooklyn College, 1971; MFA, New York University, 1973. *Appointments:* Assistant Art Designer, Children's Digest magazine, 1959; Art Editor, Silver Burdett Book Publishers, 1955; Art Director, Gajon Press, 1956; Art Instructor, School of Visual Arts, 1979-80; Kingsborough Community College, 1980-82; Freelance Illustrator and Designer, 1970. *Creative works:* Art exhibitions: Metropolitan Museum of Art; Brooklyn Museum; Long Beach Museum of Art; Salmagundi Club; New York Unviersity; Brooklyn College; Lincoln Centre; Purdue University; Westenyhook Gallery (New England invitational); Fordham University; Alfred University; National Arts Club. Children's books published: If I Were You; Fun at the Beach. *Memberships:* Artists Equity; National League of American Pen Women; American Society of Contemporary Artists; Women Business Owners of New York. *Honours:* Numerous commissions, paintings reproduced and internationally distributed by Arthur S Kaplan, 1961, 70, 72; BLD Ltd 1973, Graphic Arts Unlimited 1979; Serigraphs featured in Decor magazine, 1980; Paintings in permanent collections: New York University Medical Centre; Brooklyn College; Mount Sinai Hospital; Mishkon Children's Home, etc. American Artist Magazine Drawing Award, 1970; 1st prize, oil painting, Long Beach Art Association, 1972; Prints in collections, USA, Europe, Australia, Mexico, Japan; Andrew Nelson Whitehead Award, for drawing, Greenwich Art, 1980; Central Federal Graphics Award, 1983. *Hobbies:* Art history, consultant and artist to project for Leon Pomerance of Archaeological Society of New York. *Address:* 1768 Ocean Avenue, Brooklyn, NY 11230, USA.

TRACY Sheila, b. 10 Jan. 1934, Helston, Cornwall, England. Broadcaster. m. John Arnatt, 26 Oct. 1962, 1 son. *Education:* LRAM, Royal Academy of Music, 1952-56. *Appointments:* Trombonist with Ivy Benson's All Girls Band, 1956-58; Tracy Sisters, singing & trombone duo, 1959- 61; BBC TV Announcer, 1961-63; Freelance TV & Radio Presenter, 1963-73; BBC Radio 4 Newsreader, 1973-77' BBC Radio 2 Staff Announcer, 1977-81; Freelance Broadcaster, 1981-. *Publications:* Around Helston & Lizard with Sheila Tracy, 1980; Who's Who on Radio, 1983; Who's Who in Popular Music, 1984. *Memberships:* Equity. *Honours:* First Woman to Read News on Radio 4, 1974; Devised and Presented the Truckers Hour for Radio 2, 1980-82; Sony Radio Awards, Nomination Female UK Radio Personality of the Year, 1984. *Hobbies:* Playing Bass Trombone; Golf; Driving; Crochet; Travel. *Address:* 3 Warren Cottages, Woodland Way, Kingswood, Surrey KT20 6NN, England.

TRAN Fanny, b. 25 June 1949, Brussels, Belgium. Music Teacher; Pianist; Composer. *Education:* Licence, History of Art, Musicology, Brussels Free University, 1973; Various diplomas, Brussels and Liege Conservatoires; Warsaw Academy of Music, Poland, 1980-83; Goldsmith's College, London, England, summer 1983; MA, Music Composition, SUNYAB, USA, 1986. *Appointments:* Music Professor, music schools, Brussels; Teaching Assistant, SUNYAB, USA, 1985-86. *Compositions:* Warszawian Echoes; Repercussions; Majavka; Space Music; Tuba Mi-Rak-ul-um; Omaggio a Jo; Ties between present-future Constellations; Five rounds of the star of the prophet; Crossing Masses; The more they starve, the more they sing; Chopaderzewski. *Membership:* American Biographical Institute. *Honours:* Belgian Government Scholarship, 1980-83; British Council Scholarship, summer 1983; Woodburn Scholarship, SUNYAB, 1984-86. *Hobbies:* Swimming; Caravanning; Philosophy; Tarots; Natural medicines. *Address:* 157 J. Besme str, 1080 Brussels, Belgium.

TRASK Betty May, b. 28 Jan. 1928, Laconia, New Hampshire, USA. Journalist. m. Allison K. Trask, 28 June 1947, 4 sons. *Appointments:* Woman's Editor, Reporter, Photograher, Laconia Evening Citizen, 1966-70; County Editor, Travel Columnist, Laconia Evening Citizen, 1970-; Secretary, N.H. Vocational-Technical College at Laconia, advisory Board, 1972-78; Treasurer, N.H. Commission on Status of Women, 1974-76; State Advisory Committee to N.H. Vocational-Technical Colleges & Institute, 1981-84. *Memberships:* Atrusa Club of Laconia, President, 1977-78; District Director, Laconia Business & Professional Womens Club, 1978-79, President, 1968; Salvation Army Advisory Board, 1973-; Belknap County Easter Seal Board, 1980; etc. *Honours:* Lakes Region Citizenship Award, presented by New Hampshire Vocational Technical College, 1978; Lions Club Recognition Award, 1977. *Hobbies:* Travel; Photography; Family (including 9 Grandchildren). *Address:* Gilford, NH 03246, USA.

TRAU Jane Mary, b. 3 Feb. 1951, Florida, USA. Assistant Professor of Philosophy. m. David Trau. *Education:* BA 1980, MA 1984, PhD 1986, University of Miami, Florida. *Appointments:* Department of Philosophy 1982-86, School of Continuing Studies 1986-87, University of Miami; Department of Religious Studies & Philosophy, Barry University, 1986-90. *Creative works:* Publications: Distinguishing Rights: Feminism's Misconceptions on Abortion, in Catholicism in Crisis, 1985; Fallacies in the Argument from Gratuitous Suffering, in New Scholasticism, 1986. Dissertation: Co-Existence of God & Evil. Numerous papers presented, various scholarly gatherings.

Memberships: American & Florida Philosophical Associations; American Catholic Philosophical Association; Society of Christian Philosophers. *Honours:* Graduate Assistant 1981-86, Outstanding Teaching Assistant Fellowship 1984-85, University of Miami; Award, Professional Achievement, Barry University, 1986-87, 1987-88, 1988-89. *Interests:* Ethics; Philosophy of religion; Biomedical Ethics. *Address:* Barry University, 11300 NE Second Avenue, Miami Shores, FL 33161, USA.

TRAUGOTT Elizabeth Closs, b. 9 Apr. 1939, Bristol, England. Professor. m. Sept. 1967, 1 daughter. *Education:* BA, English Language, Oxford University, 1960; PhD, University of California, Berkeley (UCB), USA, 1964. *Appointments:* Assistant Professor, UCB, 1964-68; Faculty 1968-, Professor 1977-, Vice Provost & Dean of Graduate Studies 1985-, Stanford University. *Publications:* History of English Syntax, 1972; Co-author with Mary Pratt, Linguistics for Students of Literature, 1980; Numerous articles, professional journals; Editor, several books. *Memberships:* Past President: International Society of Historical Linguistics, & Linguistic Society of America; Modern Language Association; American Association of University Professors. *Honours:* Fellow, ACLS, 1976-77; Guggenheim Fellow, 1983-84; Fellow, Centre for Advanced Study in Behavioural Sciences, 1983-84. *Hobbies:* Hiking; Music. *Address:* Department of Linguistics, Stanford University, Stanford, California 94305, USA.

TRAVELL Janet Graeme, b. 17 Dec. 1901, New York City, USA. Physician. m. John W G Powell, 6 June 1929, deceased 10 July 1973. 2 daughters. *Education:* Intern and House Physician 1927-29, Physician to Out-Patients 1941-66, The New York Hospital; Fellow, Digitalis-Pneumonia Study, Bellevue Hospital, 1929-30; Fellow, Arterial Disease Study, Josiah Macy Jr Foundation, Beth Israel Hospital, 1939-41; Assistant then Associate Visiting Physician, Cardiology, Sea View Hospital, 1936-45; Instructor in Pharmacology 1930-47, Assistant Professor of Clinical Pharmacology 1947-51, Associate Professor of Clinical Pharmacology 1951-63, Cornell University Medical College; Associate Physician, Cardiovascular Research Unit 1941-63, Associate Physician, Department of Medicine (Cardiovascular Diseases), 1964-89, Honorary, Beth Israel Hospital; Associate Clinical Professor of Medicine 1961-70, Emeritus Clinical Professor of Medicine 1970-, The George Washington University School of Medicine and University Hospital, Washington, 1964-89, Honorary; Active Staff 1973-77, Emeritus 1977-79, Department of Medicine, Division of Rheumatic Diseases, Doctors Hospital; Member, Scientific Advisory Board, Joseph P Kennedy Jr Foundation, 1959-61; Special Consultant, USAF, 1962-64; Physician to the President of the United States, 1961-63 and 1963-65; Chairman, Medical Care and Public Health Committee of the 1965 Inaugural Committee for President Johnson; Consultant, Rehabilitation Medicine Service, Long Beach Veterans Administration Hospital, 1974-86. *Publications:* Office Hours: Day and Night, the Autobiography of Janet Travell, MD, 1968; Myofascial Pain and Dysfunction: The Trigger Point Manual, with David G Simons, 1983; Numerous articles to professional journals. *Memberships:* Medical Society of the District of Columbia; Medical Society of the County of New York, Associate, 1989 Life Member; American Medical Association; American Medical Women's Association; Fellow, The New York Academy of Medicine; Rheumatism Society of the District of Columbia; American Society for Pharmacology and Experimental Therapeutics; Pan American Medical Association (Honorary); North American Academy of Manipulative Musculoskeletal Medicine; National Board, The Medical College of Pennsylvania; Fellow, Royal Society of Medicine; International Association for the Study of Pain, Founding Member, Honorary; American Academy of Craniomandibular Disorders, Honorary. *Honours:* Wellesley Colelge Durant Scholar, 1921, 1922; John Metcalf Polk Memorial Prize, 1926; Phi Beta Kappa; Alpha Omega Alpha; Spirit of Achievement Award, 1961; Society of Oral Physiology and Occlusion, Steven W Brown Medal, 1971; Honorary Degrees: The Medical College of Pennsylvania, 1961; Wilson College, 1962; Hahnemann University, 1983. Honorary portrait unveilled, Cornell University Medical College, Women in Medicine, 1988. *Hobbies:* Reading; Writing letters; Gardening; Summer vacation with family. *Address:* 4525 Cathedral Avenue NW, Washington, DC 20016, USA.

TRAVER Leanne Everett, b. 25 Oct. 1962, Cortland, New York, USA. Corporate Treasurer; Financial Analyst. m. Edgar H. Traver, Jr., 23 May 1981. *Education:* AA, 1983, BS, Business Administration, 1984, University of Central Florida. *Appointments:* Director, Co-Founder, 1980-, Corporate Treasurer, 1980-82, Research Assistant, 1982-84, Corporate Treasurer, 1985-, SSC, a woman controlled business; Publisher, Computers in Education (Co-Ed), Journal, 1986. *Publications:* The Formation of a Woman-Controlled Small Business; Computers in Education Journal. *Memberships:* Computers in Education Division, ASEE. *Hobbies:* Tennis; Water-skiing; Cooking; Horse Riding; Computers; Needlework; Crafts. *Address:* SCEEE Services Corporation, Box 68, Port Royal Square, Port Royal, VA 22535, USA.

TRAVIS Susan Topper, b. 10 Sept. 1951, Peckskill, New York, USA. Attorney; Lecturer. m. Donald Travis, 30 May 1982, 1 daughter. *Education:* BS, cum laude, Pennsylvania State University, 1972; JD, Syracuse University, 1975. *Appointments:* Assistant Counsel, NYS United Teachers, 1976-79; Operations Counsel, Xerox Corp., 1979-83; Region Counsel, Xerox Corp., 1984-86; Special Litigation Counsel, Xerox Corp. 1987-88; Lecturer, Pace University School of Law, 1987-; Attorney, Keane & Beane, 1988-. *Publications:* Book Chapter: Allegations in Toxic Torts, 1983; articles in professional journals. *Memberships:* American, New York State, Westchester County Bar Associations. *Honours:* President, Pennsylvania State University Alumni Society, 1982-84; many other honours & awards. *Hobbies:* Sports; Flying - Private Pilot, 1981. *Address:* Keane & Beane, PC, 14 Mamaroneck Ave., White Plains, NY 10601, USA.

TREADGOLD Mary, b. 16 Apr. 1910, London, England. *Education:* BA Hons (Eng Lit), MA, Bedford Coll, London, 1930-36. *Appointments:* Children's Editor, Heinemann, 1938-40; Mechanised Transport Corps, 1940- 41; Producer/Literary Editor, BBC World Service, 1941-60. *Publications:* Books: 14 children's books including: We Couldn't Leave Dinah; Novel: The Running Child; Short stories included in Cynthia Asquith's 3rd Ghost Book and Raoul Dahl's. *Memberships:* PEN English Centre, 1954-89; Served Executive Committee, variously 1956-73, Chairman Programme Committee 1957-63. *Honours:* Carnegie Medal for Best Children's Book of the Year, We Couldn't Leave Dinah, 1942; Book Society Recommendation for The Running Child, 1951. *Hobbies:* Cookery; Embroidery; Drama; Travel; Reading.

TREBILCOT Joyce, b. 15 Feb. 1933, San Diego, California, USA. Feminist Lesbian Philosopher. *Education:* BA 1957, MA 1966, PhD 1970, University of California. *Appointments:* Teacher, Res. Bryn Mawr College, 1967-69; Lecturer, University of Wisconsin, Milwaukee, 1969-70; School/Teacher Women's Studies, University of New Mexico, 1977-78; Visiting Professor Feminist Thought, Wheaton College, Massachusetts, 1969-70; Assistant Professor 1970-77, Associate Professor, Philosophy 1977-, Coordinator Women's Studies 1980-, Washington University, St Louis. *Publications:* Taking Responsibility for Sexuality (pamphlet), 1983; Mothering: Essays in Feminist Theory (edited), 1984; In Process: Radical Lesbian Essays; Numerous articles. *Memberships:* Society for Women in Philosophy; National Women's Studies Association; American Philosophical Association. *Honours:* Achievement in Philosophy Award, University of California, Berkeley, 1957; NEH Teaching Residency, Bryn Mawr College, 1967-69; NEH Younger Humanist Fellowship, 1974- 75; Faculty Research Grants, Washington University, several years. *Address:*

Women's Studies Program, Washington University, One Brookings Drive, St Louis, MO 63130, USA.

TREES Candice D, b. 18 July 1953, Springfield, USA. Clerk. m. 3 daughters. *Education:* BA, Sangamon State University, 1981. *Appointments:* Executive Correspondent, State of illinois Governors Office, 1977-79; City Clerk, City of Springfield, 1979-86; Clerk, Circuit Court, Sangamon County, 1986-. *Memberships:* International Institute of Municipal Clerks; Municipal Clerks of Illinois; Illinoise Association of Court Clerks; National Association of Court Managers. *Honours:* Registered Municipal Clerk; Outstanding Young Woman of America, 1981, 1987; Copley First Citizen Award, Juding Panel, 1986. *Hobbies:* The Arts; Music; Singing; Cooking. *Address:* Clerk of the Circuit Court, Sangamon County, 800 East Monroe St., Room 412, Springfield, IL 62701, USA.

TREPPLER Irene, b. 13 Oct. 1926, St Louis, USA. State Senator. m. Walter J. Treppler, 3 sons, 1 daughter. *Education:* Meramec Community College. *Appointments:* Elected to Senate, 1984 after serving 12 years in the Missouri House of Representatives. *Memberships:* National Order of Women Legislators; Missouri Council on Womens Economic Development & Training; Task Force on Unwed Adolescent Sexual Activity & Pregnancy; etc. *Honours:* Recipient, various honours and awards. *Address:* 4579 Telegraph Rd, Chestnut Park Plaza, Oakville, MO 63129, USA.

TRIBE Anne Marie Rahou Gilbert, b. 31 Oct. 1921, Joinville le Pont, France. Homemaker; Writer. m. Harry Edwin Gilbert, 5 May 1945, 1 son, 3 daughters. *Education:* College Maintenon Fontainebleau; Conservatoire de Paris, Teacher Lousi Jouvet (Paris Conservatory). *Appointment:* Writer. *Publications:* (Films) La Duchesse de Langeais; Les Anges de la Nuit; La Marseillaise; Book, Men, My Love, (in progress). *Memberships:* Everglades Club, Palm Beach; Palm Beach Polo and Country Club. *Hobbies:* Writing; Swimming; Bicycling; Cooking. *Address:* 13334 Polo Club Road, Bagatelle 334, West Palm Beach, FL 33414, USA.

TRICKETT (Mabel) Rachel, b. 20 Dec. 1923. Principal, St Hugh's College, Oxford. *Education:* BA Honours 1st Class, English, MA 1947, Lady Margaret Hall, Oxford. *Appointments:* Assistant to Curator, Manchester City Art Galleries, 1945-46; Assistant Lecturer, English, Hull University 1950-54; Fellow and Tutor, English, St Hugh's College, Oxford, 1954-73. *Publications:* The Honest Muse (a study in Augustan verse), 1967; Novels: The Reurn Home, 1952; The Course of Love, 1954; Point of Honour, 1958; A Changing Place, 1962; The Elders, 1966; A Visit to Timon, 1970. *Address:* St Hugh's College, Oxford OX2 6LE, England.

TRILLING Diana, b.21 July 1905, New York City, New York, USA. Writer. m. Lionel Trilling, 12 June 1929, 1 son. *Education:* AB, Radcliffe College, 1925. *Appointments:* Fiction Critic, The Nation, 1941-49; Freelance Writer on literary, social and political subjects, 1949-. *Publications:* Claremont Essays, 1964; We Must March My Darlings, 1977; Reviewing the Forties, 1978; Mrs Harris: The Death of the Scarsdale Diet Doctor, 1981; Numerous magazine articles; Editor, Viking Portable (D. H. Lawrence), 1947; Editor, Uniform Edition of the works of Lionel Trilling, 1978-80. *Memberships:* American Academy of Arts and Sciences. *Honours:* Guggenheim Fellow, 1950-51; Rockefeller-National Endowment for the Humanities Grantee, 1977-79. *Address:* 35 Claremont Avenue, New York, NY 10027, USA.

TRISTRAM-NAGLE Stephanie Ann, b. 21 Nov. 1948, New York City, New York, USA. Research Biologist. m. John F. Nagle, 31 Dec. 1980, 2 daughters. *Education:* BA, French, Douglass College, New Brunswick, New Jersey, 1970; PhD, Comparative

Biochemistry,, University of California, Berkeley, 1981. *Appointments:* Clinical and Research Radioimmunoassay Technician, Clinical Assays, Cambridge, Massachusetts, 1972-75; Teaching Assistant and Reader, Biomembrane Course, University of California, Berkeley, 1976-78; Postdoctoral Research Biologist, 1982-86, Research Biologist in Membrane Structure and Thermodynamics, 1986-, Carnegie Mellon University, Pittsburgh, Pennsylvania. *Publications:* Contributions to: Biochemistry International, 1981; Journal of Membrane Biology, 1983; Information and Energy Transduction of Biological Membranes, 1984; Biochimica-Biophysica Acta, 1986, 1988; Biochemistry, 1987; Biophysics Journal, 1989. *Memberships:* Biophysical Society; Association for Women in Science. *Honours:* Honour Students Society, University of California, Berkeley, 1978; Sigma Xi, Carnegie Mellon University Chapter, 1982; Samuel and Emma Winters Grant, Pittsburgh, 1985-88. *Hobbies:* Tennis; Music; Gardening. *Address:* Department of Biological Sciences, Carnegie Mellon University, 4400 Fifth Avenue, Pittsburgh, PA 15213, USA.

TROLLOPE Joanna, b. 9 Dec. 1943, Gloucestershire, England. Novelist; Feature Writer. m. Ian Curteis, 12 Apr. 1985. 2 daughters. *Education:* BA 1965, MA 1972, St Hughs College, Oxford. *Appointments:* Research Assistant, African and Far Eastern Affairs, Foreign Office, London, 1965-67; Teacher, 1968-80; Writer, 1978-. *Publications:* Eliza Stanhope, 1978; Parson Hardings Daughter, 1979; Leaves From The Valley, 1980; The City of Gems, 1981; The Steps of the Sun, 1983; The Taverners Place, 1986; Britannias Daughters, 1983; The Choir, 1988; A Village Affair, to be published. Numerous articles to magazines. *Memberships:* Society of Authors; PEN; Trollope Society. *Honour:* Romantic Historical Novelist of the Year, 1979. *Hobbies:* Reading; Theatre; Looking at Paintings and Buildings; Talk. *Address:* The Mill House, Coln St Aldwyns, Cirencester, Gloucestershire, England.

TROTMAN-DICKENSON Danusia Irena, b. 25 Feb. 1929, Warsaw, Poland. Author; Lecturer. m. Aubrey Fiennes Trotman-Dickenson, 11 July 1953. 2 sons, 1 daughter. *Education:* BCom 1948, PhD 1955, University of Edinburgh; MSc, Econ, London School of Economics, 1951. *Appointments:* Lecturer/Tutor: University of Manchester, 1951-52; University of Edinburgh, 1952-54; University College of Wales, Aberystwyth, 1960-68; Llandaff College of Education, 1969-75; The Open University, 1970-75; Polytechnic of Wales, 1975-; Examiner, University of London, 1955-; Consultant to publishers, 1969. *Publications:* Six books on public finance, economics and education; Contributor of articles in learned and professional journals. *Memberships:* Institute of Welsh Affairs, Member Committee on Arts; Chairperson, Welsh Heritage Youth Initiative, Committee, Member of the Council of the Institute. *Hobbies:* Going to theatre; Gardening. *Address:* Radyr Chain, Llanaff, Cardiff CF5 2PW, Wales. 188.

TROUT Deborah Lee, b. 8 May 1953, Manistee, Michigan, USA. Clinical Psychologist. m. Curtis L. Harris, 5 June 1982, 1 daughter. *Education:* AB cum laude, Psychology, Art, Bucknell University, 1975; MA, Clinical Psychology, 1978, PhD, Clinical Psychology, 1980, University of Kansas; Internship, University of Minnesota, 1979-80; State Licensed Consulting Psychologist, 1983. *Appointments:* Psychology Section, 1980-82, Director of Prepaid Psychiatry, 1986-88, Director of Managed Care and Off Campus Operations, 1988-, Department of Psychiatry, Ramsey Clinic, St Paul, Minnesota; Psychotherapist, HSI, Washington County, 1981-83; Psychologist, Maplewood Clinic, 1983-86. *Creative works:* Articles: The Role of Social Isolation in Suicide; The Effect of Postural Lean and Body Congruence on the Judgment of Psychotherapeutic Rapport, 1980; Special interest in managed health care, behavioural medicine, gerontology. *Memberships:* American Psychological Association; Minnesota Psychological Association, Chair, Prepaid/Managed Care Subcommittee of Insurance Committee, 1988-1990; National Register for Health Service Providers in Psychology; Minnesota Women's Consortium; National Women's Political Caucus; Group Health Association of America; National Association of Female Executives; National Association of Women Business Owners; Women's Health Leadership Trust. *Honours:* Inducted into Alpha Lambda Delta, Phi Beta Kappa and Psi Chi, 1971-75. *Hobbies:* Drawing; Sculpture; Travel; Skiing. *Address:* Department of Psychiatry, Ramsey Clinic, Jackson at University, St Paul, MN 55101, USA.

TRUMPINGTON Jean Alys Barker, (Baroness, cr 1980 of Sandwich in the County of Kent) b. 23 Oct. 1922, London, England. Peer of the Realm. m. William Alan Barker, 18 Mar. 1954, 1 son. *Education:* Privately Educated. *Appointments:* Landgirl to the Rt. Hon. Lloyd George, MP, 1939-40, Bletchley Park, 1941-46 European Central Inland Transport Organisation, 1946-49; Mayor of Cambridge, 1946-72, Deputy Mayor, 1972-73; City Councillor, Cambridge, 1963-73; UK Delegate, UN Status of Women commission, 1979-81; Baroness in Waiting, 1983-. *Memberships:* Member/Chairman, Air Transport Users Committee, 1973-80; Mental Health Review Tribunal, 1976-81; Board of Visitors, HM Prison, Pentonville, 1976-81; Honorary Councillor, City of Cambridge, 1976-; Honorary Fellow, Lucy Cavendish College, Cambridge, 1980-; JP, Cambridge, 1972-75, South Westminster, 1976-82. *Honour:* Created Life Peer, 1980. *Hobbies:* Racing; Golf; Needlepoint; Antiques. *Address:* Luckboat House, King Street, Sandwich, Kent, England.

TRUSZKOWSKA Teresa, b. 21 Apr. 1925, Milanowek, Poland. Poet; Essayist; Translator. m. Wojciech Truszkowski, 15 Aug. 1948. 1 daughter. *Education:* MA 1948, PhD 1968, English Philology, Jagellonian University. *Appointment:* Lecturer, Jagellonian University, 2 years. *Publications:* 8 volumes of poetry including: Krag ciszy (The Circle of Silence), 1963; Strumien swiatla (A Stream of Light), 1965; Ku zrodlom (Toward the Springs), 1972; Amfiteatr wyobrazni (The Amphitheatre of Imagination), 1977; Translations of American and Egnlish poetry and prose. *Membership:* Association of Authors ZAIKS. *Honours:* Two prizes in American Poetry Association's Annual Contest. *Hobbies:* History of art; Mythology; Cinema; Theatre. *Address:* Smolki 12 b/5, 30-513 Krakow, Poland.

TRUTA Marianne Patricia, b. 28 Apr. 1951, New York City, USA. Maxillofacial Surgeon. m. Dr William C Donlon, 28 May 1983. *Education:* BS, St John's University, 1974; DMD, State University of New York at Stony Brook, 1977; Intern 1977-78, Resident 1978-80, Chief Resident 1980-81, The Mt Sinai Medical Center. *Appointments:* Clinical Assistant Professor, Dept of Oral Surgery 1982-86, Asst Dir Facial Pain Research Center, Dept of Diagnostic Sciences 1986-, University of the Pacific; Peninsula Maxillofacial Surgery, 1985-. *Publications:* Author of several scientific papers; Chapter co-author in Headache and Facial Pain, 1990. *Memberships:* Amer Assoc Oral & Maxillofacial Surgeons; Amer College Oral & Maxillofacial Surgeons; Amer Dental Soc Anesthesiology; Amer Assoc Women Dentists; Amer Dental Assoc; Amer Acad Cosmetic Surgery. *Hobbies:* Popular music; Theatre; Dog breeding. *Address:* Peninsula Maxillofacial Surgery, 1860 El Camino Real Suite 300, Burlingame, California 94010, USA.

TRZEBINSKI Errol Georgia Jones, b. 24 June 1936, Gloucester, England. Writer. m. Zbigniew Waclaw Trzebinski, 8 May 1959, 2 sons, 1 daughter. *Appointments:* Student Nurse; Telephonist; Receptionist; Advertising Media; Sales Assistant; Interior Decorator; Cookery Columnist; Biographer. *Publications:* Cookery Columnist, Sunday Nation, 3 years; 10 Small Cookery Books for Rigby Ltd; Silence Will Speak, Biography of Denys Finch Hatton; Source for, Out of Africa, 1985; The Kenya Pioneers, 1986; The Lives of Beryl Markham, 1989. *Membership:* Fellow, Royal Geographical Society. *Hobby:* Life. *Address:* Mombasa, Kenya.

TSUI Pauline Woo, b. 2 Oct. 1920, China. Executive Director, Organization of Chinese American Women. m. Tswen-Ling Tsui, 26 July 1947. 1 son, 1 daughter. *Education:* BA Education, St John's University, China, 1943; MA Education, Columbia University, New York City, USA, 1947. *Appointments:* Federal Women's Program Manager, Defense Mapping Agency, Hydrographic Topographic Center, 1976-80; Project Director, 1978-; Executive Director, Organization of Chinese American Women, 1981-; Chair 1988-; Member 1987-89, DC Commission for Asian and Pacific Islander Affairs. *Memberships:* Independent Sector, Member representing Organization of Chinese American Women; Organization of Chinese American Women, Founding President; Organization of Chinese Americans incorporated, Past National Vice- President; Federally Employed Women, Founding Member of Potomac Palisade Chapter; Sin-American Cultural Society, Board Member; Vice President, Coalition of Minority Women in Business, 1985-; Advisory Board, National Association of Professional Asian American Women, 1988. *Honours:* National Volunteer Award, 1974; Honorary Member Award, Organization of Chinese Americans, 1982; Outstanding Award, Federally Employed Women, Potomac Palisade Chapter, 1984; Appreciation Award, Organization of Chinese American Women, Houston Chapter, 1985. *Hobbies:* Organizing Community Projects; Music. *Address:* 1525 O Street NW, Washington, DC 20005, USA.

TUCKER Marcia, b. 11 Apr. 1940, New York City, USA. Museum Director. *Education:* BA, Connecticut College, 1961; Ecole du Louvre, Paris, France; MA, Institute of Fine Arts, New York University, 1965. *Appointments:* Museum of Modern Art, 1961-62; Editorial Associate, Art News, 1965-69; Curator, Painting & Sculpture, Whitney Museum of American Art, 1969-77; Founder, Director, New Museum of Contemporary Art, 1977-. *Publications:* Aricles in professional journals including: New York Times; Arts Quarterly; Art Journal; Art in America; Vogue Magazine; etc. *Memberships:* American Association of Museums; American Federation of Arts; Art Museum Association; Association of Museum Directors; International Art Critics Association; New York State Council on the Arts, Visual Arts Panel. *Honours:* Phi Beta Kappa; DFA, hc, San Francisco Art Institute, 1983. *Address:* The New Museum of Contemporary Art, 583 Broadway, New York, NY 10012, USA.

TUCKER Wanda Hall, b. 6 Feb. 1921, Los Angeles, California, USA. Writer; Communications Consultant. m. Frank Robert Tucker, 16 Apr. 1943, 1 son, 1 daughter. *Education:* AA, Citrus College, Azusa, California, 1939. *Appointments:* Society Editor, City Editor, Editor, Azusa Herald, Azusa, California, 1939-43; City Editor, San Marino Tribune, San Marino, California, 1943-45; Editor, Canyon City News, Azusa, 1950-52; Reporter, City Editor, Managing Editor, Senior Managing Editor, Pasadena Star-News, Pasadena, California, 1953-84; Editor and Associate Publisher, Foothill Intercity Newspapers, 1984-86; Communications Consultant, 1986-. *Publications:* Newspaper columns, Azusa Herald, San Marino Tribune, Pasadena Star-News, Foothill Intercity Newspapers. *Memberships:* Current: Greater Los Angeles Press Club; The Desert Press Club; Society of Professional Journalists; Sigma Delta Chi; National Association for Female Executives; Commissioner, City of Palm Desert Rent Review Commission; Former Director, Silver Spur Ranchers Association. *Honours:* Honoured by resolutions: Cities of Azusa, Duarte and Glendora, 1964; City of Los Pasadena and County of Los Angeles, 1968; Writing awards: California Newspaper Publishers Association, 1965; Greater Los Angeles Press Club, 1971-72; Named Woman of the Year: Pasadena Women's Civic League, 1974; Pasadena Chapter, National Association for the Advancement of Colored People, 1977; Woman of Achievement, Pasadena Community College, 1984. *Hobbies:* Travel; Gardening; Reading; People. *Address:* 45375 San Luis Rey, Palm Desert, CA 92260, USA.

TUDRYN FRIBERGER Joyce Marie, b. 27 July 1959, Chicopee, Massachusetts, USA. Association Executive. m. William W. Friberger III, 18 Sept. 1982. *Education:* BS, Public Communications, Syracuse University, Syracuse, New York. *Appointments:* Assistant Editor, National Association of Broadcasters, Washington DC, 1981-82; Director of Programmes, 1982-88, Associate Executive Director, 1988-, International Radio and Television Society, New York City; Associate Producer of Images; Producer/Writer of Your Department of Defense; Actress, roles in Antigone, The Crucible, Company. *Publications:* Columnist, TV Facts, Figures and Film magazine; Editor, International Radio and Television Society News. *Memberships:* Vice-President, Corporation for Educational Radio and Television; National Advisory Council, Alpha Epsilon Rho Broadcasting Society; National Academy of Television Arts and Sciences; Women in Communications; Intercorporate Communications Group; Council on Education in Electronic Media. *Honours:* Chicopees Junior Miss, 1977; S.I.Newhouse Scholar; Federal Intern, Office of the Secretary of Defense/Public Affairs, Pentagon, Washington DC, 1980; 2nd Place New Jersey Festival on the Green Photography Competition; Judge, New York Television Festival, 1988; Keynote Speaker, Alpha Epsilon Rho East and East Central Region Conventions, 1988. *Hobbies:* Photography; Tap dancing; Antiques; International correspondence. *Address:* International Radio and Television Society, Suite 531, 420 Lexington Avenue, New York, NY 10170, USA.

TUFTY Barbara Jean, b. 28 Dec. 1923, Iowa City, Iowa, USA. Conservation Writer; Editor. m. Harold Guilford Tufty, 29 Dec. 1948, 2 sons, 1 daughter. *Education:* BA, Botany, Duke University, 1945; Postgraduate courses, New School for Social Research 1946, Sorbonne 1948, University of Colorado 1949-51. *Appointments:* Editor, Union Carbide & Carbon, 1945-47; Information writer, University of Colorado, 1947-51; Science writer (staff, freelance), Science Service, 1948-72; News writer, National Academy of Sciences, 1970-72; Editor, writer, National Science Foundation, 1972-84; Writer, Editor, Audubon Naturalist Society, 1986-. *Publications include:* Books: 1001 Questions Answered About Storms; 1001 Questions Answered About Land Disasters; Cells, Units of Life. Also: Translation, book, Crafts of the Ivory Coast; Numerous articles, magazines & newspapers. *Memberships include:* National Association of Science Writers; American Association for Advancement of Science; New York Academy of Science; Nature Conservancy; Friends of Earth. *Honours:* Chi Deta Phi, 1945; Honorary Life Member, Bombay Natural History Society, 1960; Honorary mention, writing awards, Thomas Stokes, Catherine O'Brien, 1970's. *Hobbies:* Reading; Painting; Walking. *Address:* 3812 Livingston Street NW, Washington DC 20015, USA.

TULLY Susan Lorna, b. 20 Oct. 1967, London, England. Actress. *Appointments:* Appearances In: Our Show, LTW TV, 1977-78; The Saturday Banana, Scottish TV, 1978; Why Can't I Go Home?, Associated TV, 1979; Second Star to the Right, film, 1980; Grange Hill, BBC TV Series, 1981-84; A Little Like Drowning, Hampstead Theatre, 1984-; Eastenders, BBC TV Series, 1984-. *Memberships:* Equity; Anna Scher Theatre. *Honour:* Best Actress Anna Scher Theatre, 1984. *Hobbies:* Drama; Reading; Cinema. *Address:* Islington, London, England.

TURDIU Jelena Simunec-Muhek, b. 21 Nov. 1915, Marija Bistrica, Croatia, Yugoslavia. Clinical Psychologist; Neuropsychologist. m. Faik Turdiu, 19 June 1957, dec. 1982. *Education:* Graduated, Faculty of Arts, Department of Psychology, University of Zagreb, 1946; Specialist Degree in Clinical Psychology, Zagreb, 1963; PhD, University of Skoplje, Macedonia, 1975; Specialisation course in Neuropsychology, Paris, France, 1976. *Appointments:* Psychologist, Department of Neuropsychiatry, General Hospital, Zagreb, 1946; Founder, 1st Clinical Psychological Service at General Hospital, Zagreb (also 1st in all Yugoslavia); Department of Neurology and Psychiatry, School of Medicine, University of Zagreb, 1963; Chief Psychologist, 1st

Neuropsychological Laboratory in Yugoslavia, 1973-81; Participant, 7 scientific research projects on cerebrovascular disease and cerebral trauma, also in pesticides programme supported by NIOSH, USA, 1972-76. *Publications:* 45 papers on clinical and neuropsychology in Yugoslavian professional journals; 54 public lectures, Yugoslavia; Contributor to books: Interna medicina u praksi 1984 and 1987, Medicinska enciklopedija, 1986, Neurologija, 1989. Author: Klinicka neuropsihologija (textbook), 1989. *Memberships:* Croatian Society of Psychologists; Yugoslav Association of Psychologists; IAAP; International Neuropsychological Society (INS). *Hobbies:* Translating psychological literature from English, French and German into Croatian; Horticulture (cultivation of flowers especially roses). *Address:* 88 Borongajska, 41000 Zagreb, Yugoslavia.

TURK Frances Mary, b. 14 Apr. 1915, Huntingdon, England. Novelist. *Appointments:* Confidential Secretary, Farmers Glory Limited, 1936-1940; Assistant Company Secretary, Huns Cambs and Ely Womens Land Army, 1940-48; Secretary, Huntingdonshire Womens Voluntary Service, 1950-62. *Publications Include:* Paddy O'Shea, 1937; The Precious Hours, 1938; Paradise Sreet, 1939; Green Garnet, 1940; Lovable Clown, 1941; Angle Hill, 1942; Candle Corner, 1943; Wideawake, 1944; The House of Heron, 1946; Ancestors, 1947; Jerninghams, 1948; Salutation, 1949; Time and Tranquility, 1950; The Small House at Ickley, 1951; The Gentle Flowers, 1952; The Laughing Fox, 1953; The Dark Wood, 1945; Dinny Lightfoot, 1956; A Vain Shadow, 1957; The White Swan, 1958; The Temple of Fancy, 1959; A Time to Know, 1960; The Golden Leaves, 1961; A Flush of Scarlet, 1963; The Guarded Heart, 1964; The Summer Term, 1965; The Recory at Hay, 1966; Legacy of Love, 1967; The Lesley Affair, 1968; For Pity, for Anger, 1970; The Absent Young Man, 971; Whispers, 1972; Goddess of Threads, 1975; No Through Road, 1976; A Visit to Marchmont, 1977; The Five Grey Geese, 1980; Fair Recompense, 1983; The Living Fountains, 1985; etc; Contributor To: various journals and magazines. *Membershps:* Numerous professional organisations. *Hobbies:* Reading; Gardening; Painting; Crafts. *Address:* Hillrise, Brampton Road, Buckden, Huntingdon PE18 9JH, England.

TURKI Douja, b. 12 Sept. 1945, Menzel-Jemil, Tunisia. Professor, Faculty of Human and Social Sciences. *Education:* DEA, Political Sociology and International Relations, EHESS, Paris, 1980; DESS, Political, Administrative and Social Organisation, Sorbonne, Paris, 1980; DEA, Social and Cultural Anthropology, Sorbonne, 1980; Doctorate in Political Sociology, Sorbonne, 1982. *Appointments:* Teacher, Socio-cultural animation, Ministry of National Education, 1968-83; Counsellor, General Direction, National School of Public Administration (ENA), 1983-85; Professor, Faculty of Human and Social Sciences, Ministry of High Education and Scientific Research (Universities), 1984-; In France: International Diplomatic Academy, Paris. *Publications:* Woman and Political Power: The French Woman in Political Parties and Pressure Groups; Socio-Political Portrait: Bourguiba in Three Stages: Student, Militant, President; The Settlements of International Reconciliation: The International Diplomatic Academy; International Political Elite: The Heads of State; The Foundations of the Evolution toward a Universal Global Society; The Sacred and the Power; Toward an International Civilisation: Politics and Values; Public and Semi-public Sector Responsibilities in Economic Unsticking of African Countries: The Trilogy: Politics, Administration and Underdevelopment. *Memberships:* Trade Union Representative; CGTFO Paris Centre; Political Party, Tunisia, PSD; International Fellows for Social and Economic Development Inc, Australia; American Political Science Association, USA; International Political Science Association, Canada; International Studies Association, Tunisia. *Honours:* Prize of Excellency, 1961, 1962, 1963, 1964, Bizerte. *Hobbies:* Gardening; Skating; Tennis. *Address:* Faculte des Sciences Humanies et Sociales, Boîte Postale No 277, Tunis-Belvedere 1002, Tunisia.

TURNER Anna Winifred Samson, b. 6 May 1918, Rio De Janeiro, Brazil. Actress; Nurse. *Appointments:* West End Plays, 1944- including, Stage Door, 1946; We Proudly Present; Indifferent Shepherd; Daphne Laureold; Waiting for Gillian; Bride and the Bachelor; TV work includes: Champion Road; Emergency Ward 10; reurned to nursing, Charing Cross Hospital, 1970-81; Returned to TV including: All Creatures Great & Small, 1987; Empire of the Sun. *Honours:* Qualified as SEN, Charing Cross. *Hobbies:* Sewing; Painting. *Address:* 27 Bronsart Road, London SW6, England.

TURNER Bridget, b. 22 Feb. 1939, Cleethorpes, Lincolnshire, England. Actress. *Education:* Wintringham Grammar School, Grimsby. *Career:* RADA trained. Repertory theatre work at: Coventry, Hornchurch, Ipswich, Leatherhead. Appeared in: Romeo and Juliet, Othello, The Cherry Orchard, Nottingham; All My Sons, Liverpool Playhouse. RSC tour: Twelfth Night, The Three Sisters. Hampstead Theatre, The Seagull, 1962, The Square 1963, Curtains, 1987; London Theatre: Royal Court: Roots, 1967, The Fool, 1975; ERB, Strand, 1970; Time and Time Again, Comedy, 1972; Criterion: Absurd Person Singular, 1973, Last of the Red Hot Lovers, 1979; The Norman Conquests, Globe, 1974; Season's Greetings, Apollo, 1982; The Nerd, Aldwych, 1984; The Corn is Green, Old Vic, 1985; Soho Poly (Fringe): Leaving Home, 1986; National Theatre: A Small Family Business 1987-88, 'Tis Pity She's A Whore, 1988; Hedda Gabler, The Shaughraun, 1989. Television includes: Resurrection (BBC classic serial); Series: Sutherland's Law, Target, Two's Company, Get Lost, Two People, The Brief, Driving Ambition. Plays: Slattery's Mounted Foot, Love Lies Bleeding, Home is the Sailor, Time and Time Again, Season's Greetings. Films: Under Mild Wood, The Walking Stick, Runners. *Honours:* Gilbert Prize for Comedy; Clarence Derwent Award, 1972. *Address:* c/o Marmont Management, 302/308 Regent Street, London W1R 5AL, England.

TURNER Janet Marguerite, b. 27 Mar. 1944, Barrie, Ontario, Canada. Teacher. m. Ross John Turner. 2 sons, 1 daughter. *Education:* Honours BA, Latin & Greek, Victoria College, 1965, MA Classics, 1966, University of Toronto; High School Specialists Teacher Certificate in Latin, 1969; High School Specialists Teaching Certificate in Special Education Gifted 1989. *Appointments:* Teacher of Latin, Clarke High School, Northumberland/Durham Board of Education, Ontario, 1966-68; Minor Head of Classics, Earl Haig School, North York Board of Education, 1968-74; Teacher of Latin, History & English, Base Borden College, Canadian Forces Base/Borden Board of Education, 1974-76; Teacher of Latin, Gifted Education, Barrie Central College, Simcoe County Board of Education, 1976-88. *Publications:* Curriculum Writer for SCBE: Social & Environmental Science Studies K-12, 1980; Multiculturalism Course, 1981; Impact of the Environment upon a People - The Hurons, 1983; Mythology, 1983; Teaching Archaeology in Schools, 1985; Partner and Author of EDUCOM (Ed Computer programmes in Latin). *Memberships:* Life Member, Ontario Archaeological Society; Board of Directors, Simcoe Centre Prov Liberal Association; Board of Directors, Simcoe South, Simcoe Centre Federal Lib Assoc. 1988; Board of Directors, South Lake Simcoe Conservation Authority, 1987-90. *Honours:* Head Girl 1961, Valedictorian, 1961, Barrie Central Collegiate; Guest Speaker at OHASSTA on Teaching Archaeology in Schools, 1983; Co-Keynote Speaker, Classics Conference for Ontario Teachers, 1984; President's Outstanding Volunteer Award, Liberal Party of Canada in the South Simcoe Riding, 1988. *Hobbies:* Archaeology; Politics; Travel. *Address:* RR No 1 Thornton, Ontario, Canada, LOL 2NO.

TURNER Lisa Phillips, b. 10 Apr. 1951, Waltham, Massachusetts, USA. Human Resource Management Professional. m. Randolph Herbert Petren, 28 May 1988. *Education:* BA, Education & Philosophy, 1974; AS, Electronics Techology, 1982; MBA, 1986; D.Sc., Human Resource Management, 1989. *Appointments:* Founder,

Owner, Turner's Bicycle Service Inc., 975-80; Qualiy Assurance Engineer, Audio Engineering & Video Arts, 1980-81; Technical Writing Instructor, Palm Beach Junior College, 1982; Training & Development Admin. Mitel Inc., 1982-88; Communicatirons & Employee Relations Manager, Modular Computer Systems Inc., 1988-. *Publications:* Quality Circle Steps Guide, 1982; articles in various journals & magazines. *Memberships:* American Society for Training & Development; American Society for Quality Control; Academy of Management; American Society for Personnel Administration; Association for Quality & participation. *Honours:* Senior Womens Honour Society, 1973; Distinguished Academic Achievement Award, Nova University, 1986. *Hobbies:* Carpentry; Landscaping; Reading; Mechanics; Electronics. *Address:* 2027 SW 12th Court, Delray Beach, FL 33445, USA.

TURNER Mary Louise, b. 24 June 1954, Glens Falls, New York, USA. Banker; Computer Operator. *Education:* AAS, Business Administration, Adirondack Community College. *Appointments:* Bookeeping 1974-77, Data Processing 1977-, Glens Falls National Bank and Trust Company. *Publications:* Novel: Today Begins Tomorrow; Poetry: Why Me; Auf Wiedersehen; Jealousy; What If Time Stood Still; You've Got To Be Kidding. *Membership:* Secretary, High school Business Club, 1972. *Honours:* Poet of Merit, American Poetry Association, 1989; Editor's Choice, A Selection of John Frost's Favorite, 1988; Best New Poets of 1987 and 1988. *Hobbies:* Counted cross stitch, needlework; Writing; Sports; Reading; Travel. *Address:* 372A Circuit Lane, Newport News, VA 23602, USA.

TURNER Naomi Cocke b. 19 Dec. 1903, Austin, Texas, USA. Retired. m. Professor Clair Elsmere Turner, 24 Dec. 1924, 1 son, 1 daughter. *Education:* BA, University of Texas, Austin, Texas, 1926; Ed.M, Harvard University, Cambridge, Massachusetts, 1930. *Appointments:* Research Associate, Forsyth Dental Infirmary for Children, Boston, Massachusetts, 1944-57; Research Associate, Harvard School of Public Health, Boston, Massachusetts, 1954-60. *Publications:* Author of over 33 research papers published in professional Dental journal.s. *Memberships:* Sigma Xi, Radcliffe Chapter; Fellow, American Association Advancement of Science; International Association for Dental Research; American Public Health Association; Royal Society of Health. *Hobbies:* Gardening; Needlepoint. *Address:* 19 Village Lane, Arlington, MA 02174, USA.

TUROCK Betty Jane, b. 12 June, Scranton, Pennsylvania, USA. University Professor, Consultant. m. Frank M Turock, 16 June 1956. 2 sons. *Education:* BA, magna cum laude, Syracuse University, 1955; Post graduate scholar, University of Pennsylvania, 1956; MLS 1970, PhD 1981, Rutgers University. *Appointments:* Library Coordinator, Holmdel (NJ) Public Schools, 1963-65; Story-teller, Wheaton (IL) Public Library, 1965-67; Educational medica specialist, Alhambra Public School, Phoenix, 1967-70; Branch Librarian, Area Librarian, Head extension service, Forsyth County Public Library System, Winston-Salem, 1970-73; Assistant director, 1973-75, Director 1975-77, Montclair (NJ) Public Library; Assistant Director, Monroe County Library System, Rochester, 1978-81; Assistant Professor, 1981-87, Associate Professor, 1987-Rutgers University Graduate School, Communications, Info and Library Studies; Senior Advisor, US Department of Education, Office of Library Programs, 1988-89. *Publications:* Author: Serving Older Adults, 1983. Editor: The Bottom Line, 1984-. Contributed over 40 articles to professional journals. *Memberships:* National Director, member Executive Board, 1985-, Beta Phi Mu; American Libr. Association, Council, 1984; President, LAMA Statustics Sect., 1981-83; Treasurer Social Resp. Round Table, 1978-82; Coordinator Task Force on Women, 1978-80; President, 1977-78, Rutgers GSLIS Alumni Association; American Society for Information Science, 1970-; American Association of University Professors, 1980. *Honours:* Phi Theta Kappa 1953; Phi Chi 1955; Beta Phi Mu 1971,

National Honorary Societies; Charles Weston Scholar, 1956; Woman of the Year, Raritan-Holmdel Women's Club, 1965. *Hobby:* Furniture refinishing. *Address:* 11 Undercliff Road, Montclair, New Jersey 07042, USA.

TUSHINGHAM Rita, b. 14 Mar. 1942, Liverpool, England. Actress. m. (1) Terence William Bicknell, dissolved 1976, 1 daughters. (2) Ousama Rawi, 1981. *Education:* La Sagesse Convent, Liverpool; Student, Liverpool Playhouse, 1958-60. *Creative Works:* Stage appearances: Royal Court Theatre: The Changeling, 1960; The Kitchen, 1961; A Midsummer Night's Dream, 1962; Twelfth Night, 1962; The Knack, 1962. Other London theatres: The Giveaway, 1969; Lorna and Ted, 1970; Mistress of Novices, 1973; My Fat Friend, 1981; Children, Children, 1984. Films: A Taste of Honey, 1962; The Leather Boys, 1962; A Place to Go, 1963; Girl with Green Eyes, 1963; The Knack, 1964; Dr Zhivago, 1965; The Trap, 1966; Smashing Time, 1967; Diamonds For Breakfast, 1967; The Guru, 1968; The Bed-Sitting Room, 1970; Straight on till Morning, 1972; Situation, 1972; Instant Coffee, 1973; Rachel's Man, 1974; The Human Factor, 1976; Pot Luck, 1977; State of Shock, 1977; Mysteries, 1978; Incredible Mrs Chadwick, 1979; The Spaghetti House Siege, 1982; Flying, 1984; A Judgement in Stone, 1986; Single Room, 1986. Television appearances include: Red Riding Hood (play), 1973l; No Strings (own series), 1974; Don't Let Them Kill Me on Wednesday, 1980; Confessions of Felix Krull, 1980; Seeing Red, 1983; Pippi Longstocking, 1984; The White Whale-The Life of Ernest Hemingway (film), 1987. *Honours:* Variety Club award; Silver Goddess award, Mexican Association of Film Correspondents; British Film Academy; Variety Club Award for Most Promising Newcomer; New York Critics, Cannes Film Festival Award; Hollywood Foreign Press Association Award. *Hobbies:* Interior decorating; Cooking. *Address:* c/o Jonathan Altaraz, Duncan Heath Associates, 162 Wardour Street, London W1V 3AT, England.

TUTEN-PUCKETT Katharyn Elizabeth, b. 21 Apr. 1943, Denver, USA. Doctoral Student. m. James Carl Puckett, 13 Oct. 1962, divorced 1979, 1 son, 1 daughter. *Education:* BA, English, 1969, MA, Library Science, 1973, California State University; MA, Reading Education, Boise State University, 1987. *Appointments:* Idaho Office of Energy, 1976-79; Curriculum Specialist, Boise State University, 1983-84; Lobbyist, ladho NOW, 1986; Adjunct Faculty, Boise State University, 1987; Early Literacy Skills Specialist, Monroe County Library, 1987-88. *Publications:* 24 articles in professional journals. *Memberships:* Many professional Organisations. *Honours:* Research Board of Advisors, American Biographical Institute Inc., 1988. *Hobbies:* Reading; Politics; Spiritual Development. *Address:* c/o Betty Hubbard, 508 North Marcella, Rialto, CA 92376, USA.

TUTIN Dorothy, b. 8 Apr. 1930, London, England. Actress. m. Derek Waring, 1 son, 1 daughter. *Education:* Diploma, Royal academy of Dramatic Art. *Career Includes:* First starring roles as Rose in The Living Room; Sally Bowles, I Am a Camera; St Joan, The Lark; Dolly, Once More with Feeling; appearances as Viola, Ophelia, Juliet, Portia, Desdamona and Cressida with the Royal Shakespeare Company; Queen Victoria, Portrait of a Queen, Vaudeville Theatre & on Broadway, USA; Peter Pan, Colosseum; What Every Woman Knows, The Albery; Leading Player, National Theatre, Roles included: Madame Ranevskya, The Cherry Orchard, Lady Macbeth, Lady Plyant in The Double Dealer, Genia Hofreiter, Undiscovered Country and Lady Fancyful, Provoke'd Wife; Heste Collyer, The Deep Blue Sea, Greenwich Theatre; The Chalk Garden, Chichester; Brighton Beach Memoir, Aldwych Theatre; Thursdays Ladies, Apollo Theatre. Films Include: The Importance of Being Ernest; The Beggars Opera; Tale of Two Cities; Cromwell and Savage Messiah; TV appearances include; South Riding; Willow Cabin; The Eavesdropper; The Combination; Life After Death; Margot Asquith, Number 10; Beth, Landscape; Deborah, Kind of Alaska; Most Recent TV work for Granada TV as Goneril in King Lear with Sir Laurence Olivier; Laura in

Strindberg's The Father. *Honours Include:* Actress of the Year in a Revival, Society of West End Managers; Film Actress Award, Variety Club of Great Britain, 1972; CBE. *Address:* c/o Barry Burnett, Suite 42-43, Grafton House, 2-3 Golden Square, London W1.

TUTOLI Michele A., b. 18 May 1951, Teaneck, New Jersey, USA. Attorney. m. Stephen M. Lord, 27 Jan. 1979, 3 sons, 2 daughters. *Education:* George Washington University, 1970; AA, American College in Paris, France, 1971; AB, Georgetown University, 1973; JD, Brooklyn Law School, 1978. *Appointments:* Investment officer, Morgan Guaranty Trust 1973-80, American Bankers Association 1980-82; Vice President, Home Federal, San Diego, California, 1982-86; Regional Tax Director, IDS/American Express, 1986-87; Private Practice, 1987-. *Memberships include:* Chairman, Community Advisory Board, Olivenhain; Presdent, Olivenhain Town Council; American Bar Association; Women's Economic Round Table; Society of Financial Analysts; Bars of New York, New Jersey, California. *Hobbies:* Family; Land use; Drama. *Address:* 157 Rancho Santa Fe Road, Olivenhain, California 92024, USA.

TUTT Gloria J. Rutherford, b. 9 Jan. 1945, Texarkana, USA. Insurance Marketing. m. F. David Tutt, 27 Nov. 1964, 3 sons. *Appointments:* Agency Administrator, National Foundation Life, 1973-77; Corporate Secretary, Administrative Office Manager, Southern Capitol Enterprises, 1980-; Corporate Secretary, Insurance Management and Associates of Louisiana, 1989. *Memberships:* PTA/PTF, Vice President, 1972-88; Committee Member, Boy Scouts of America, Cub Master; American Red Cross Volunteer, 1963-64. *Honours:* Sales Achievement Awards, local level; 2000 Notable American Women, 1988. *Hobbies:* Boating; Fishing; Reading; Craftwork. *Address:* 19312 Creekround Ave., Baton Rouge, LA 70817, USA.

TUTWILER Margaret De-Bardeleben, b. 28 Dec. 1950, Birmingham, Alabama, USA. Assistant Secretary, US Department of Treasury. *Education:* BA, University of Alabama, 1973. *Appointments:* Special Assistant to the President, Executive Assistant to Chief of Staff, The White House, Washington, 1980-84; Deputy Assistant to the President for Political Affairs, The White House, 1984-85; Director, Public Liaison, 50th American Presidential Inaugural, 1984-85; Assistant Secretary, Public Affairs, Public Liaison, Department of Treasury, Washington, 1985-. *Memberships:* American Council of Young Political Leaders Delegation to Peoples Republic of China, 1982; Delegate to UN Decade for Women, Nairobi, Kenya, 1985; American Centre for International Leadership's Delegation from USA to Soviet Union, 1986. *Hobbies:* Aerobics Classes; Cooking; Needlepoint; Skiing. *Address:* Department of Treasury, Washington, DC 20220, USA.

TY-CASPER Linda, b. 1931, Philippines. Author; Lecturer. *Education:* Degrees, University of the Philippines, Harvard University. *Appointments:* Lecturer, Creative Writing, Ateneo de Manila University, summers 1978, 1980; Writer-in-residence, University of Philippines Creative Writing Centre, 1980, 1982. *Publications:* 11 books including: Transparent Sun, short stories, 1963; Peninsulars, historical novel, 1964; Three-Cornered Sun, historical novel, 1979; Hazards of Distance, novella, 1981; Awaiting Trespass, novella, 1985 (awards); Wings of Stone, novella, 1986; Ten Thousand Seeds, novel, 1987; A Small Party in a Garden, 1988. Also numerous short stories. *Honours include:* Grants, Harvard 1956-57, Silliman University 1963, Radcliffe 1974-75, Djerassi 1984, Massachusetts Artists Foundation 1988; Award (literature), Filipino-American Womens Network, 1985; Top 5 Womens Fiction Choice, UK Feminist Book Fortnight, 1986. *Address:* 54 Simpson Drive, Saxonville, Massachusetts 01701, USA.

TYCE Gertrude Mary, b. Wark, Northumberland, England. Professor of Physiology. m. F A Tyce, 26 June 1952. 1 son. *Education:* BSc, 1st class Honours, 1948; PhD, University of Durham, England, 1952. *Appointments:* Research Assistant, 1958-63; Research Associate, 1963- 71; Associate Consultant Biochemistry, 1971-75; Consultant Physiology, 1976; Professor of Physiologyl, 1981-, Mayo Medical School. *Publications:* 131 Scientific papers published. *Memberships:* American Society Neurochemistry; AAAS; American Chemical Society; American Society Experimental Pathology; Society Neuroscience; Society Experimental Biology and Medicine; New York Academy of Sciences; International Society for Neurochem; Sigma Xi. *Hobbies:* Antiquarian; Naturalist. *Address:* Physiololgy Department, Mayo Clinic and Foundation, 200 First Street, SW, Rochester, MN 55905, USA.

TYGER-ODOM Juie A., b. 29 Dec. 1958, USA. Senior Product Marketing Engineer. m. Jay Alan Odom, 1 Sept. 1985. *Education:* BSc., Industrial Engineering, Pennsylvania State University, 1980; MBA, Finance, Tulane University, 1984. *Appointments:* Wire Line Engineer, Schlumberger, 1981-82; Consultant, Graduate Assistant, Assistant to Dean, Tulane University, 1982-84; Senior Product Marketing Engineer, AMO, 1984-. *Memberships:* Pennsylvania & Tulane Alumni Associations. *Honours:* Cornelius Award, Merit Scholarship, 1984. *Hobbies:* Running; Aerobics; Bicycling; Swimming; Antiques. *Address:* Austin, Texas, USA.

TYSER Patricia Ellen, b. 1 July 1952, Rochester, New York, USA. Architectural Design Executive. *Education:* BA, Philosophy, St John Fisher College, Rochester, 1974; Studies with Barry Merritt, Rochester, 1982, Kathie Bunnell and Dan Fenton, Oakland, California, 1983, Johannes Schreiter and Lutz Haufschild, Toronto, Canada, 1984. *Career:* Manager, Stained Glass Works, Rochester, New York, 1974-78; Principal, Patricia Tyser Glass Studio, Rochester, 1978-85; Director, Architectural Glass Designs, Rochester, 1985-87; Instructor: State University of New York, 1987-88; Norman Howard School, Rochester, 1988-; 1-woman shows include Rochester, 1977-79, 1983, 1984, 1985, Honeoye Falls, New York, 1978-80, Ithaca, New York, 1984, Philadelphia Art Show, 1985, Huntington Galleries, West Virginia, 1986, Philadelphia Port of History Museum, 1987; Group shows include Rooney's, Rochester, 1982; Juried shows include Sibley's Artworks, Rochester, 1980-83, Interior Design Society, 1981, 1982. *Creative works include:* Glass and photography exhibits; Works in permanent collections. Louisiana State University Glass Department and Rochester Lead Works, also in private collections; Contributor, articles, slides and photographs to professional publications. *Memberships:* Volunteer, Rochester Radio Reading Service; Mediator, Center for Dispute Settlement. *Honours:* New York State's Award, Southern Tier Arts Association, 1981-82; Award for Excellence, Lake Country Craftsmen, 1983; Certificate of Excellence in Glass Metro Art, 1986; Honourable Mention, The Best Glass, 1986. *Address:* 7 Faraday Street, Rochester, NY 14610, USA.

TYSON Helen Flynn, b. North Carolina, USA. Retired Budget Analyst. m. James F Tyson, 25 Dec. 1940, deceased. *Education:* Guilford College of North Carolina; American University, Washington DC; Numerous seminars and specialist courses in financial management and related fields. *Appointments:* Budget Analyst, Headquarters, USAF, Washington DC, 1957-74, retired; Supervisory Budget Officer, Headquarters, MAC, 1955-57; Assistant Budget and Accounting Officer, 1949-55, Chief Clerical Assistant to Disbursing Officer, 1941-49, Pope AFB, North Carolina; Auditor, AUS Disbursing Office, Fort Bragg, North Carolina, 1935-41. *Memberships:* American Society of Military Controllers; Military District of Washington officers Club; American Institute of Parliamentarians; National Federation of Business and Professional Women; National Federation of Retired Federal Employees; The Salvation Army Women's Auxiliary; The Arlington Hospital Foundation; Arlington Committee of 100; Inter Service Club Council of Arlington; North Carolina Society of Washington; Life Fellow, American

Biographical Research Institute; National Association for Female Executives, Inc. *Honours:* Honorary Fellow, American Biographical Institute; Honorary Fellow, Anglo American Academy; Contribution to the War Bond Effort, US Treasury, 1945 and 1946; US State Department, 1970; Operation Friendship, First US Army, 1972; Congress of Women's organisations in Virginia; Woman of the Year, Arlington County, 1971; American Red Cross, 1977; Good Neighbour Award, Fort Belvoir Civilian-Military Advisory Council, 1978; Volunteer Activist Award of Washington Metropolitan Area, 1981; Outstanding Member, Washington Chapter American Society of Military Comptrollers, 1988. *Hobbies:* Motoring; Photography. *Address:* 4900 North Old Dominion Drive, Arlington, VA 22207, USA.

TYTLER Linda Jean, b. 31 Aug. 1947, Rochester, New York, USA. Marketing Communications Executive; State Representative. m. George Stephen Dragnich, 2 May 1970 (div. 1976). *Education:* ASc, Southern Seminary, Buena Vista, 1967; University of Virginia Northern Extension, 1973; Public Administration, University of Mexico Graduate School, 1981-82. *Appointments:* Xerox Corporation, Rochester (New York) & Arlington (Virginia), 1967-69; Congress, Mario Biaggi, 1969-71; Special Assistant, Congressman John H. Buchanan Jr, 1971-75; Legislative Analyst, US Senator Robert P. Griffin, 1975-77; Operations Supervisor, President Ford Committee, 1976; Office Manager, US Senator Pete V. Domenici Re-Election Committee, 1977; Public Information Officer, Southwest Community Health Services, 1977-83; Consultant, 1983-84; Account Executive, St Joseph Healthcare Corporation, 1984-; Elected member, New Mexico State House of Representatives, 1982-; Republican Caucus Chair, 1985-; Vice-Chair, House Appropriations & Finance Committee, 1985-86. *Memberships:* American Marketing Association; National Advertising Federation; Society for Hospital Planning & Marketing. *Honours:* Various awards: NM Advertising Federation, Regional Advertising Federation, Health Care Marketing Report, NM Cancer Society, NM Wildlife Federation. *Hobbies:* Photography; World travel; Reading; Music; Writing poetry. *Address:* 6031 McKinney Boulevard NE, Albuquerque, New Mexico 87109, USA.

U

UHLEIN Gabriele Anna, b. 25 Apr. 1952, West Germany. Teacher; Lecturer; Author; Artist. *Education:* BS, Clinical Psychology; MA, Religious Studies/ Spirituality, 1982. *Appointments:* Preaching Staff, Mt. St. Francis Retreat Center, Indiana, 1976-78; Staff, Mental Health, Health Dept., DuPage, 1979-80; Regional Social Service Co-ordinator, Catholic Charities, 1982-83; Education/Mission Services, Wheaton Franciscan Services, Inc., 1983-88. *Publications:* Meditations with Hildegard of Bingen, 1983; Zen and the Art of Canticle Singing: A Challenge for Contemporary Franciscans, 1987; Contributor to: hospice, 1982; Illustrator: Along the Water's Edge, 1980. *Memberships:* Hospice of Dupage, Trustee, Training Coordinator; Francis Heights/Clare Gardens Trustee; Academy for Catholic Health Care Leadership; West Chicago Prairie Stewardship Group; Institute for Creation Centered Spirituality; Franciscan Sisters. *Honours:* Tempo Woman, Chicago Tribune, 1987. *Hobbies Include:* Weekly Meditation Practice Sessions. *Address:* Franciscan Sisters, PO Box 667, Wheaton, IL 60189, USA.

UHRMAN Celia, b. 14 May 1927, New London, USA. *Education:* BA, Brooklyn College, 1948; MA, 1953; PhD, University of Danzig, 1977. *Appointments:* Writer, Artist, Poet Teacher, New York City School System, 1948-82; Partner, Uhrman Studio, 1973-83. *Publications:* Love Fancies, 1987 The Chimps are Coming, 1975, educational novel; A Pause for Poetry for Children, 1973; Poetic love Fancies, 1970; A Pause for Poetry, 1970; Poetic Ponderances, 1969; Impressionistic Oils and Free Style and Realist Water Colours. *Memberships:* Founding Fellow, World Literay Academy; Intenational Academy of Poets; Commandeur Member, International Arts Guild Monaco; etc. *Hobbies:* Dancing; Hiking; Swimming; Theatre; Reading. *Address:* 1655 Flatbush Ave., Apt C106, Brooklyn, NY 11210, USA.

UHRMAN Esther, b. 7 July 1921, New London, Connecticut, USA. Writer; Artist; Philosopher. *Education:* Traphagen School of Fashion, 1955; AA, NYC Technical College, 1974; Labor Relations Degree, Cornell University, 1976; PhD, University of Danzig, Poland, 1977; Cornell University, 1984; UI Avocate Cert, 1976; Postgraduate, University of New Rochelle. *Appointments:* Self-employed Artist-Writer, 1954-; Staff, Trade Publications and Off-Beat Advertising Agencies, 1954 50; Partner, Uhrman Studio, 1973-83; Asst Editor, Inside Detective, 1977; Social Worker, 1959-76, retired, New York City. *Creative works:* Internationally known for Gypsy Paintings and Water Colours. Books: Gypsy Logic, poetry, 1970; From Canarsie to Masada, 1978; Mitras II, 1988. *Memberships:* Founding Fellow, World Literary Academy and International Academy of Poets; Commandeur Member, International Arts, Monaco; WPSI; New York Artists Equity. *Honours:* HYS Podiker Brotherhood Award, 1968; Golden Windmill Radio Drama Contest Award, 1971; Verso Meako Olympic Silver Medal for Olympic designs plus certificate for stamp designs, 1968; Diploma D'Honneur des Beaux Arts, Cultural Exchanges Between nations, International Arts Guild, Monaco, 1976; Honorary PhD Translator Poet Laureate, World Academy of Languages and Literature, 1977; Finalist, Dentsu Competition Tokyo, Japan, 1986. *Hobbies:* Walking; Reading; Theatre; Television; Anthropology. *Address:* 1655 Flatbush Ave Apt C106, Brooklyn, NY 11210, USA.

ULRICH Elise Vons, b. York, Pennsylvania, USA. Journalist. *Education:* AA, Cazenovia College, Cazenovia, New York; Certificate, Alliance Francaise, Paris, France. *Publications:* Articles in: Business Week Careers; Company; Cleo; Frequent Flyer; Redbook; L'Officiel; Rotarian; Health; McCall's; North America Times of London Syndicate; USA Today; Sunday Woman Plus. *Membership:* American Society of Journalists and Authors. *Hobbies:* Reading; Research; Swimming; Hiking; Sailing; Ice skating; Travel; Knitting. *Address:* 330 East 49th Street, New York, NY 10017, USA.

UMIKER-SEBEOK Jean, b. 1 Oct. 1946, Norfolk, Virginia, USA. Researcher; Editor. m. Thomas A. Sebeok, 31 Oct. 1972, 2 daughters. *Education:* BA, French Language & Culture, 1968; PhD, Anthropology, Indiana University, 1976. *Appointments:* Research Scholar, 1986-, Associate Chair 1985-, Semiotic Studies, Indiana University. *Publications:* Author or co-author, numerous papers, article, translations. Most recent include: Towards a Semiotics of Trademarks, case study; Semiotics of Advertisements; Semiotics & Marketing; Semiotics & Business. *Memberships:* Executive, Semiotic Society of America; International Association for Semiotic Studies; Fellow, American Anthropological Association; Society for Consumer Research. *Address:* PO Box 10, Bloomington, IN 47402, USA.

UNDERWOOD Joanna DeHaven, b. 25 May 1940, New York City, New York, USA. Company President. m. Saul Lambert, 31 July 1982, 1 stepdaughter, 1 stepson. *Education:* BA, Bryn Mawr, 1962; Diplome d'etudes de Civilisation francaise, with honours, Sorbonne University, Paris, 1965. *Appointments:* Researcher, Reporter, Time Inc, New York City, 1964-68; Audio-Visual Director, Planned Parenthood, New York City, 1968-70; Co-Director, Council on Economic Priorities, New York City, 1970-73; Founder, President, INFORM Inc, New York City, 1973-. *Publications:* Manufacturers of Anti-Personnel Weapons (editor), 1970; Paper Profits (co-author), 1971; The Price of Power (editor), 1972. *Memberships:* Fellow, Scientists Institute for Public Information; Advisory Panel, Congressional Office of Technology Assessment; Board of Directors: New York State Energy Research and Development Authority; Planned Parenthood; Hampshire Research Institute. *Honour:* Recipient of US EPA Environmental Achievement Award, 1987. *Address:* 381 Park Avenue South, New York, NY 10016, USA.

UNDERWOOD Nancy Espie, b. 29 Dec. 1945, Vancouver, Washington, USA. Environmental and Occupational Health and Safety Engineer. 1 daughter. *Education:* BA, Occupational Health and Safety Studies, 1974, Teaching Credential 1975, California State University; Engineering Certificate, Hartford, 1975; Environmental and Occupational Toxicology, University of San Francisco, 1978; Certification in Asbestos Abatement, US Environmental Protection Agency, Los Angeles, 1986. *Appointments:* Founder and President, Underwood Loss Control, Inc, Lynwood, California, 1982-. *Publications:* Supervisor Management Occupational Health and Safety Manual for General Industry Use, 1978; The Importance of Accident Prevention, 1980. *Memberships:* American Society of Safety Engineers; American Society of Industrial Hygiene; National Safety Council; American Society for Professional and Executive Women; Intersafe Association of Safety Professionals; US Congressional Advisory Board/American Security Council; American Management Association; Order of the Eastern Star. *Honours:* Numerous citations. *Address:* Underwood Loss Control, Inc, 3516 E Century Blvd, No 10, Lynwood, California 90262, USA.

UNGER Barbara, b. 2 Oct. 1932, New York City, USA. Professor; Author. m. Dr Theodore Sakano, 31 July 1987, 2 daughters. *Education:* BA, 1954, MA, 1957, City College of New York. *Appointments:* Rockland Community College, 1969-. *Publications:* Inside the Wind; The Man Who Burned Money; Basement Poems 1959-63. *Memberships:* PSA; CCCC. *Honours:* Squaw Valley Community of Writers Fellowship, 1980; Fellowship, State University of New York, 1981; Edna St Vincent Millay Colony Fellow, 1984; Ragdale Foundaiton Fellow, 1985; New York State Council for the Arts Writer in Residence, 1986. *Address:* 101 Parkside Drive, Suffern, NY 10901, USA.

UNGER Pamela Gale, b. 7 Mar. 1954, Allentown, USA. Physical Therapist. m. Jeffrey Michael Unger, 23 Apr. 1977, 1 son, 1 daughter. *Education:* Physical Therapy, University of Pennsylvania, 1976. *Appointments:* Physical Therapist, Clinical Co-ordinator, St Joseph Hospital, Reading, 1976-78; Physical Therapist, Berks Visiting Nurse, Home Health Agency, REading, 1978-81; Director, Physical therapy, Leadr Nursing & Rehabilitation Centre, Laureldale, 1981-84; Director, Physical Therapy, Berks Helm Reading, 1984-85; Director, Eastern Region, Martin McGough & Eddy Pt Services, 1987-. *Publications:* Wound Healing Using HVGS, Stimulus, 1985; articles in professionaljournals. *Memberships:* American, Pennsylvania Physical Therapy Associations. *Hobbies:* Coach, Kutztown Area High School Cheerleaders, Kutztown Borough Summer Swim Team; Skiing; Jogging. *Address:* 443 Wentz Street, Kutztown, PA 19530, USA.

UPDIKE Lynda Lee Thorpe, b. 27 Oct. 1945, Franklin, USA. Farmer. m. Glenn Hartwell Updike, 13 Apr. 1968, 1 son, 2 daughters. *Education:* BS, Home Economics, 1967; MS, Vocational-Technical Education, Virginia Technical College, 1979. *Appointments:* Home Economics Teacher, Franklin High School, 1967-68. *Memberships:* American, Virginia, Tidewater Home Economics Associations; President, Southampton County Historical Society; Franklin Southampton Drug Focus Commission; Local Human Rights Commission of Virginia. *Hobbies:* Sewing; Crafts; Local History. *Address:* Myrtle Acres Farm, Route 1, Box 80A, Newsoms, VA 23874, USA.

URBACH Phyllis Ann Rose, b. 29 June 1936, Minneapolis, Minnesota. Women's Fashion Designer; Manufacturer. m. (1) Thomas A Andersen, 14 Sept. 1953, div. 1970; (2) Robert D Urbach, 6 Nov. 1977, deceased 21 Nov. 1978. 4 sons, 2 daughters. *Education:* Minneapolis School of Art & Design, 1969; Normandale Jr College, 1969 and 1978; Private Tutoring, Art/Sculpture/Caligraphy, 1963-69; Business Classes, Sperry Unic, 1976. *Appointments:* Substitute Special Education & Art Instructor for Public & Private Grade Schools, 1961-75; Developed & Operated Andersen Originals Fine Arts School, 1963-83; Technician, Surface Navy Dept, Sperry Univac, 1975-76; Human Services, Director of Activities, Handicapped & Geriatrics, 1977-79; Self employed, Lady Huntress Fashions, creating & designing Womens hunting, safari & casual sports wear, 1983-. *Creative Works:* Commissioned works: Clay, oils, acrylic; Ceramic tile murals; caligraphy 1963-83; Women's Editor, Weekly Sports Paper, 1984-88; Contributor of articles and poetry for speciality publications, 1978-88. *Memberships:* Ladies Auxiliary, 1979- 88, Veterans of Foreign Wars; President & Therapy Director, Minnesota Ceramic Association, 1964-66; Secretary, St Paul Minneapolis English Bulldog Association, 1967-69; Outdoor Writers Association, 1984; Girl Scouts of America-Cub Scouts of America, 1963-66; Leader 4-H Club of America-Activities Director, 1965-68; Minnesota Colleagues of Calligraphy, 1973-75; Publicity & Programme Chairman, 1984-88, Minnesota Valley Womens Ducks Unlimited (National). *Honours:* Meritorious Award, Minnesota Aquatennial Association, 1975-76; Best in category awards: Sculpture in clay, special design in ceramic glazes, air brushing & incising techniques, 1964-69; Honours in display and competition, 1964-69. *Hobbies:* Dancing; Reading; Writing; Sculpture; Painting & design; Story Telling; Community Affairs and causes; Developing and implimention of Art Therpy Programmes; Specialized clothing for handicapped and geriatrics; Promotion of outdoor activities; Sports for women over age 30; Volunteer Council, Spiritual, Physical and Emotional development. *Address:* 4050 Grainwood Trail, Prior Lake, Minnesota 55372, USA.

URCH Elizabeth, b. 10 Sept. 1921, Larne, Northern Ireland. Retired Head Teacher. m. Walter Henry Urch, 24 Apr. 1943, deceased 5 Feb. 1959. 1 son, 2 daughters. *Education:* Diploma of Education, Stranmillis Training College, Northern Ireland, 1941. *Appointments:* Moyle School, Larne, Northern Ireland, 1959-66; Larne Grammar School, 1966-69; Newbigging School, Perth, Scotland, 1969-72; Logierait School, Perth, 1972-86. *Publications:* Queen of the Manse (pen name Elise Brogan); Be Still my Soul; For God's Sake Watch your Language; Ladders Up to Heaven; Christmas; Friendship; Sorrow; Worship. *Honours:* Ministry of Education Prize for Senior Certificate Exam, Northern Ireland, 1939; McMahon Prize for Best Student, Stranmillis Teacher Training College, 1941. *Hobbies:* Walking; Gardening; Music; Reading. *Address:* 11 Tomna-Moan Road, Pitlochry, PH16 5HL, Scotland.

URQUHART Judith Elliott, b. 30 Aug. 1942, Newton Abbot, Devon, England. Author. m. Brendan Lehane, 5 Aug. 1968, divorced 1976. *Publications:* Living off Nature, 1980; Food from the Wild, 1978; Keeping Honeybees, 1978; Animals on the Farm, 1983; Eigg - The Story of a Hebridean Island, 1987. *Memberships:* Rare Breeds Survival Trust; PEN. *Hobbies:* Films; Music; Pictures; Reading; Walking; Swimming. *Address:* Bigram, Port of Menteith, Perthshire, Scotland.

USCHAK Ann Maria, b. 24 Dec. 1955, Latrobe, USA. Senior Management Staff. m. David George Cress, 31 July 1983. *Education:* BA, University of Pittsburgh, 1977; MA, Communication, Pennsylvania State University, 1982; MA, Theatre, Film, Pennsylvania State University, 1989. *Appointments:* Information Co-ordinator, TIPs Information, 1980-82; Senior English Teacher, Kingsway Regional High School, 1982-85; Technical Writer, 1986-87; Contracted Consultant, Account Representative, DuPont, 1986- 87; Senior Account Management, External Affairs, E.I. Du Pont, 1987-. *Publications:* Thesis; Plato is the Rhetoricians, 1981. *Memberships:* President, Altar Rosary Society; Delta Zeta; Chi Delphia; American Cancer Association. *Honours:* Recipient, numerous honours including: Most Outstanding Student of the University, 1977; Stanton Chapman, 1977; URTA Awards, 1976. *Hobbies:* Singing; Dancing; Speaker for American Cancer Society; Acting; Reading. *Address:* 263 Harding Highway, Carneys Point, NJ 08069, USA.

USCHUK Pamela Marie, b. 10 Jun 1948, Lansing, Michigan, USA. Poet/Writer in Residence. m. William Pitt Root, 6 Nov l987. *Education.* BA, English cum laude, Central Michigan University, 1970; MFA, Fiction and Poetry, University of Montana, 1986. *Appointments:* Poet in Schools (Montana) 1983-87; Instructor, Marist College, New York, 1987-; Poet in Public Service, New York City, 1988-; Writer in Residence, Pacific Lutheran University, Washington, 1990; Editor in Chief (CUTBANK) 1984-86. *Creative Works:* Over 80 poems in magazines, journals and anthologies in USA, Scotland, Great Britain and France; Light From Dead Stars (poems) 1981; Loving The Outlaw, (pamphlet of poems) 1984. *Memberships:* Associated Writing Programs; Poets and Writers; Academy of American Poets; Native American Languages Institute (past member); Rocky Mountain Modern Languages Association (past member); Amnesty International; Greenpeace. *Honour:* ASCENT Poetry Prize, 1st place, University of Illinois, 1989; White Rabbit Poetry Award, University of Southern Alabama, 1989; Amnesty International Poerty Award, Special Honorable Mention, 1989; Stone Ridge Poetry Award, 1988; Bertha Morton Scholar, University of Montana, 1985-86. *Hobbies:* Photography; Travel; Russian literature; Poetry translation; Swimming; Wilderness preservation and environmental protection. *Address:* One Arden Lane, New Paltz, NY 12561, USA.

UVAROV Olga, (Dame), b. Ouralsk, USSR. Veterinary Surgeon. *Education:* MRCVS, Royal Veterinary College, London, England, 1934; Diploma, Sociology, Ealing College of Higher Educaiton, 1980. *Appointments:* Private Practice, Veterinarian, 1934-53; Head, Pharmaceutical Research, Pharmaceutical Industry, 1953-71; Head, Veterinary Advisory Department, 1967-70; Technical Information Officer, British Veterinary Association, 1972-78; Honorary Secretary, Research Defence Society, London, 1978-

82. *Publications:* Numerous articles in professional journals. *Memberships Include:* Former Council & Committee Member, Life Member, British Veterinary Association; Past President, Society of Women Veterinary Surgeons; The Central Veterinary Society; Association of Veterinary Teachers & Research Writers; Royal Society of Medicine, Section of Comparative Medicine; Past President, Royal College of Veterinary Surgeons; President, Laboratory Animals Science Association, 1984-85. *Honours:* Fellowship, Royal College of Veterinary Surgeons, 1973; DSc, HC, University of Guelph, Canada, 1976; Fellow, Royal Veterinary College, 1979; Hon. Fellow, Royal Society of Medicine, 1982; CBE, 1978; DBE, 1983; Vice President, Universities Federation Animal Welfare (UFAW), 1987-. *Hobbies:* Work; Poetry; Flowers; Travel. *Address:* 76 Elm Park Court, Elm Park Road, Pinner, Middlesex, HA5 3LL, England.

UZENDA Jara Carlow, b. 24 May 1946, Brookline, USA. Senior Technical Writer/Editor. m. BSc., 1975, MSc., 1978, University of Colorado, Boulder. *Appointments:* Research Writer, Arthur D. Little Inc., 1977- 79; Director, Research, Telecommunications Magazine, Boston, 1979-81; Documentation Specialist, Allied Information Systems, 1981-83; Senior Technical Writer, Paradyne Corp., 1983-86; Consultant, Data Communications Security, 1986-89. *Publications:* Articles in professional journals. *Memberships:* CIRUNA; Optimist International Mortar Board; SWE. *Honours:* Visiting Professor, Prescott College, 1972; Featured Artist, Denver Post Newspaper, 1973; Citation of Excellence from the Ninth International Animated Film Festival, 1975. *Hobbies:* Golf; Computer; Flying. *Address:* PO Box 603 Little River, SC 29566, USA.

UZUNER Buket, b. 3 Oct. 1955, Ankara, Turkey. Writer; Environmental Scientist. *Education:* BS, Biology, MSc, Biology, 1979, University of Hacettepe Hele, Turkey; Graduate studies, Biology, University of Bergen, Norway, 1981; Graduate studies, Public Health, University of Michigan, USA, 1983. *Appointments:* Columnist and Art Essayist, 1979-; Ecologist, Lecturer, Middle East Technical University, Turkey, 1985; Environmental Scientist, University of Tampere, Tampere, Finland, 1986; Public Relations Manager, 5-star ART Hotel, Turkey, 1988. *Publications:* Benim Adim Mayis, short story collection, 1986; The Most Naked Day of the Month short story collection, 1988; The Sun Eating Gypsy (fiction), 1989 - short stories; Travel Notes of a Dark Haired Women (Travel Memoirs), 1989; My Father's Girl Friend (fiction) in process, 1990. Fine Art articles and interviews in various magazines. *Memberships:* Continuing Education for Women Group, Ann Arbor, Michigan, USA, 1983; Immigrant Women Group, Bergen, Norway, 1979-81; Turkish Writers Syndicate, 1989-; The Society for the Protection of Nature, 1989-. *Awards:* Short-story Award (fiction), Yunus-Nadi 1989 June-Istanbul with Ultra-violet story under the title of Women Issues in Literature. *Hobbies:* Literature especially black humour and irony; Cinema; Painting especially expressionism and surrealism; Music (baroque, jazz, pop); Sociology and humanities. *Address:* Bogaz Sok 6/3, Doruk Apt, GOP, TR 06700, Turkey.

V

VADUS Gloria A, b. Forrestville, Pennsylvania, USA. Graphologist; Handwriting Expert. *Education:* MA Psychology 1983, BA Psychology-Counselling, Business Administration, 1982, Columbia Pacific University, California; Certified by - to: teacher, American Academy of Graphology, Washington, 1978; HAWU, Cole School Graphology, California, 1978; American Handwriting Analysis Foundation, California, 1979; Council of Graphological Societies 1980. *Appointments:* President-Owner, Graphinc Incorporated, 1976-; Accepted Instructor, Graphology, Montgomery Community College, Maryland, 1978; Psychogram Centre, all courses, 1978-; Private study, Thea Stein Lewinson, Maryland, 1987-. *Publications:* Monograph: Suicide - A Longitudinal Evaluation of the Ultimate Self-Aggression, 1985; Paper: Catch 22 Graphic Indicies involved in Depression, 1985; Co-author, research study: An Evaluation of the Graphological Implications of Printing/Cursive Handwriting, AHAF Research Committee, 1983; Resume: Project a long term pour le development de la grapholoy en Amerique, 1981; Paper: A Long Range Planning Assessment for American Graphology, 1980; numerous articles and, after articles professional papers. *Memberships include:* President, 1982- 84, American Handwriting Analysis Foundation; Chairman, 1981-86, Reseearch Committee-Advisory Board, Research (ABR); Chairman, Nominations Committee, 1985-86; Officiator, Installation-Officers, 1986; Policy/Planning and Ethics, 1986-, National Association Document Examiners, member Ethics Hearing Board, 1986, Chairman, Nominations Committee 1987-88; Chairman Elections, 1988, Parliamentarian, 1988-90; International Chairman, 1983, vice-President, 1987-88, Soroptimist International; COGS Board of Directors, 1983-85; National Forensic Center; National Writer's Club; The Menninger Foundation; The International Platform Association; Judge, 1976-, National Capital Jaguars Club of America; Chairman, Judge, flower shows, Henry Hicks Garden Club of the Westburys; International Conference Chairman, 1969-72, Institute of Electrical and Electronic Engineers, etc. *Honours include:* Gold Nibs Analyst Year, 1982; Honorary appointment, Research Board of Advisors, ABI; Listed in numerous world-wide biographies. *Address:* 8500 Timber Hill Lane, Potomac, MD 20854.

VAETH Agatha Min-Chun Fang, b. 19 Feb. 1935, China. Registered Nurse; Dance Instructor. m. Randy H. Vaeth, 20 July 1971, 2 sons, 1 daughter. *Education:* BS, St Joseph's College, 1986. *Appointments:* Staff Nurse, 1970-73, Charge Nurse, 1973-74, Stillwater Municipal Hospital; Clinical Nurse, USINH Hospital, 1974-75; Clinical Nurse, Relief Supervisor, National Hansens' Disease Centre, 1975-. *Publications:* Biological Illustration, Herpetology Lab. Manual, 1979; Translated English to Chinese, Video Tape on Hansen's Disease, 6 programmes, 1978, 1981; Exhibited Paintings. *Memberships:* Baton Rouge District Nurses' Association; Louisiana State Nurses Association; American Nurses Association; American Red Cross Association; Louisiana Art and Artists Guild; Arts and Humanities Council of Greater Baton Rouge. *Honours:* Recipient, various honours and awards. *Hobbies:* Ballroom Dancing; International Folk Dance; Painting; Travel; Reading; Writing. *Address:* PO Box 45292, Broadview Station, Baton Rouge, LA 70895, USA.

VAIL Iris Jennings, b. 2 July 1928, New York, USA. Civic Worker. m. Thomas van Husen Vail, 15 Sept. 1951. 2 sons, 1 daughter. *Education:* Graduate, Miss Porters Schoo, Farmington, Connecticut. *Appointments:* Interior Decorator with the late Isabel Thornley Interiors, New York, 1948-51. *Memberships:* Executive committee, Garden Club Cleveland, 1962-; Women's Council, Western Res. Hist. Soc. 1960-; Women's Council Clevel. Mus. Art, 1953-; Chairman, Childrens Garden Fair, 1966-75; Public Square Dinner, 1975; Board of Directors, Garden Center Greater Cleveland, 1963-77; Trustee, Cleve. Zool. Soc. 1971-; Ohio Arts Council, 1974-76; Endangered Species Committee, Cleve. ZOO Soc.; Board Member of the Public square Preservation and Maintenance Fund of The Cleveland Foundation, 1988. *Honours:* Recipient Amy Angell Collier Montague medal, Garden Club Am. 1976; Ohio Governor's Award, 1977; Magaret A. Ireland Award of Women's City Club of Cleveland, 1984. *Hobbies:* Dogs, English Springer Spaniels; Golf; Bird shooting; Skiing; Gardening; Antique collecting. *Address:* Hunting Valley, Chagrin Falls, OH 44022, USA.

VAIZEY Marina Valzey, Lady, b. 16 Jan. 1938. Art Critic. m. Lord Vaizey 1961 (d 1984), 2 sons, 1 daughter. *Eucation:* BA Medieval History and Lit, Radcliffe Coll, Harvard University; BA, MA, Girton College, Cambridge. *Appointments:* Art Critic, Financial Times, 1970-74; Dance Critic, Nowl, 1979-81; Member Arts Council, 1976-78 (Mem Art Panel, 1973-78, Dep Chm 1976-78). Member: Advisory Cttee, DoE, 1975-81; Paintings for Hospitals, 1974-; Cttee, Contemporary Art Soc, 1975-79, 1980-; Hist of Art and Complementary Studies Bd 1978-82, Photography Bd 1979-81, Fine Art Bd 1980-83, CNAA; Passenger Services Sub-Cttee, Heathrow Airport, 1979-83; Member, Fine Arts Adv Cttee, British Council, 1987-; Trustee, Nat Museums and Galleries on Merseyside, 1986-; Exec Dir, Mitchell Prize for the Hist of Art, 1976-87; Crafts Council, 1988-; Governor: Camberwell Coll of Arts and Crafts, 1971-82; Bath Acad of Art, Corsham, 1978-81. *Creative works:* Broadcaster, occasional exhibition organiser and lecturer; Organised Critic's Choice, Tooth's, 1974; Painter as Photographer, touring exhibn, UK, 1982-85; Co-Sec, Radcliffe Club of London, 1968-74; 100 Masterpieces of Art, 1979; Andrew Wyeth, 1980; The Artist as Photographer, 1982; Peter Blake, 1985; articles in various periodicals, anthologies, exhibition catalogues. *Hobbies:* Arts; Travel. *Address:* 24 Heathfield Terrace, London W4 4JE, England.

VALAD Paula Toltesy, b. 17 Sept. 1938, Brooklyn, New York, USA. World Bank Executive. div., 1 son. *Education:* BA, Goucher College, 1960; Editorial Practices, US Department of Agriculture Graduate School, 1972; Postgraduate study: George Washington University, American University. *Appointments:* Technical Editor, then Evaluation Officer, Loan Officer, Operations Officer, currently Projects Officer, World Bank. *Memberships:* Founding Member, Board Member, Association for Women in Development, 1982- 85; Society for International Development; Toastmasters. *Honours:* Vice-Chairperson, World Bank Staff Association, 1975; Appointed to Personnel Classification Review Panel, World Bank, 1980; Alternate Chairperson, Job Grading Review Panel, 1986-88. *Hobbies:* World travel for work and pleasure; Gardening; Reading; Writing. *Address:* 5221 Marlyn Drive, Bethesda, MD 20816, USA.

VALDEZ Linda A, Advertising Executive. *Education:* BS 1968, Graduate Study, 1970-75, University of Colorado, Boulder; Education Life Certificate, University of California, Berkely; Marketing Management Certificate, University of Southern California, 1978; Management Certificate, Northeastern University, 1980. *Appointments Include:* Supervisor, Market Information, Regional Transportation District, Denver, 1975-78; Manager, Marketing, VIA Metropolitan Transit San Antonio, 1978-80; Assistant Executive Director, San Antonio Convention & Visitors Bureau, 1980-82; Executive Vice President, Owner, Regnier, Valdez & Associate, 1982-. *Memberships Include:* Offices, American Marketing Association (San Antonio Branch), 1975-88; Women in Communications, 1978-86; American Alumni Council, 1978-79; American Public Transit Association, numerous offices. *Honours Include:* Biographical Listings, marketing awards; 8 awards, American Advertising Association, Colorado, 1975-78; Marketing Person of the Year, 1980, Marketing Firm of the Year 1980, AMA. *Address:* Regnier, Valdez & Associates, 5152 Fredericksburg Road, No 205, San Antonio, TX 78229, USA.

VALENZUELA Debra Guadalupe, b. 7 Mar. 1957, San Antonio, Texas, USA. Personnel & Safety Specialist. *Education:* BBA, 1979. *Appointments:* Personnel Assistant, Union Camp Corp., San Antonio, 1979-82; Benefits Administrator, 1982-85, Personnel & Safety Specialist, 1985-, City Water Board, San Antonio. *Memberships:* Board Member, San Antonio Water Board Federal Credit Union; American Water Works Association; National Association of Female Executives; National Notary Association. Hobbies: Sewing; Floral Arrangement; Swimming. *Address:* 144 Oelkers St., San Antonio, TX 78204, USA.

VALESCO Frances K., b. 3 Aug. 1941, Los Angeles, California, USA. Artist; Teacher. *Education:* BA, University of California, Los Angeles, 1963; MA, California State University, Long Beach, 1972. *Appointments:* Owner, Big Ink studio, 1969-; Instructor: University of California Extension, 1968-72; University of California, Berkeley, 1975-76, 1978; Sonoma State University, California, 1978-80, 1986, Academy of Art, San Francisco, California, 1982-; San Francisco State University, 1985-86; Artist, San Francisco Neighborhood Arts Programme, 1975-80; Artist in Residence in the Community, San Francisco, 1980-85; Over 150 group and solo exhibitions in museums, galleries, cultural centers. *Creative works:* 27 murals, San Francisco Bay area, 1975-89; Consigned work on 35 galleries, national and international; Media: Painting, drawing, printmaking,, currently mixed media on paper and canvas, computer generated images. *Memberships:* Los Angeles Society of Printmakers, 1966-72; Editorial Board, Community Murals Magazine, 1975-82; Women's Caucus for Art, 1980-88; World Print Council; California Society of Printmakers, Council Member and Historian 1978-80; San Francisco Mural Advisory Board; YLEM; Graphic Arts Council; Achenbach Foundation; Fine Arts Museum, San Francisco. *Honours:* UCLA Art Council Award, 1962; 3rd Prize for Graphics, Kingsley Annual, Sacramento, California, 1964; Purchase Prize, 2nd Small Print and Sculpture, Fremont, California, 1972; USIA Print Purchase for Embassies, 1968; California Art Council Grants, 1980-85; NIIP Grants to paint murals, 1981, 1982, 1986; Certificate of Honour, City and County of San Francisco, 1987; Oakland City Assets Award Nomination, 1988. *Address:* 135 Jersey Street, San Francisco, CA 94114, USA.

VALLANCE Elizabeth Mary, b. 8 Apr. 1945, Glasgow, Scotland. University Teacher. m. Iain Vallance, 5 Aug. 1967. 1 son, 1 daughter. *Education:* MA (1st Class Hons), St Andrews University, Scotland, 1967; MSc (with distinction), London School of Economics, England, 1968; PhD, University of London, 1978. *Appointments:* Lecturer in Politics 1968- 78, Senior Lecturer 1978, Reader in Politics 1986, Head of Department of Politics 1985-, Queen Mary College, University of London. *Publications:* Women in the House, 1979; Women of Europe, 1986; Biographical Dictionary of Women (Ed), 1983; MP: the job of a backbencher, 1987. *Memberships:* Association of University of Teachers; Political Studies Association. *Honours:* Davidson Bursary, 1965-66 and 1966-67; Queen's Philosophy Medal, 1965, 1966, 1967; Leverhulme Research Fellowship, 1976-77; EEC Research Fellowship, 1983-84. *Address:* Department of Political Studies, Queen Mary College, Mile End Road, London E1 4NS, England.

VALLBONA Rima-Gretel Rothe de, b. 15 Mar. 1931, San Jose, Costa Rica. Professor of Hispanic Literature; Writer. m. Carlos Vallbona, 26 Dec. 1956, 1 son, 3 daughters. *Education:* BA/BS, Colegio Superior de Senoritas, San Jose, 1948; Diploma, University of Paris, France, 1953; Diploma, University of Salamanca, Spain, 1954; MA, University of Costa Rica, 1962; DML, Middlebury College, USA, 1981. *Appointments:* School teacher, Costa Rica, 1955-56; Faculty 1964-, Department Head 1966-71, Chair, Modern Language Department 1978-80, Professor of Spanish 1978-, University of St Thomas, Houston, Texas, USA; Visiting Professor, various establishments. *Publications:* Novels:

Noche en Vela, 1968; Sombras que Perseguimos, 1983. Short story collections: Polvo del Camino, 1971; Salamandra Rosada, 1979; Mujeres y Agonias, 1982; Baraja de Soledades, 1983; Cosecha De Pecadores (short stories). Literary essays: Yolanda Oreamuno, 1972; Obra en Prosa de Eunice Odio, 1981. Editorial boards, various journals. *Memberships include:* Offices, past/present: American Association of Teachers of Spanish & Portuguese; Institute of Hispanic Culture, Houston; Casa Argentina de Houston; Houston Public Library. *Honours:* Aquileo J. Echeverria novel prize, Costa Rica, 1968; Agripina Montes del Valle novel prize, Columbia, 1978; Jorge Luis Borges short story prize, 1977; Literary award, Southwest Conference of Latin American Studies, USA, 1982; Research grant, Constantin Foundation, 1981; Ancora Award, best book, Costa Rica, 1983-84; Cullen Foundation Professor of Spanish, 1989; Condecorated with El Lazo De La Dama De La Orden Del Merito Civil by His Royal Majesty King Juan Carlos I of Spain, 1988. *Hobbies:* Drawing; Collecting pre-Hispanic artefacts. *Address:* 3002 Ann Arbor, Houston, Texas 77063, USA.

VALLENTINE Jo, b. 30 May 1946, Perth, Australia. Senator. m. Peter Fry, 16 Dec. 1972, 2 daughters. *Education:* BA, Dip.Ed., University of Western Australia. *Appointments:* Teacher; Parliamentarian; Senator, Nuclear Disarmament; Senator, Australian Federal Parliament. *Memberhips:* Parliament on the Single Issue; Disarmament Platform. *Address:* PO Box 137, West Perth Western Australia 6005, Australia.

VALVANNE Leena Ida Mathilda, b. 28 Jan. 1920, Helsinki, Finland. Counsellor, Public Health Care. m. Niilo Valvanne, 5 Sept. 1948. 2 sons, 1 daughter. *Education:* Qualified Nurse, 1943; Qualified Midwife, 1944; Qualified Public Health Nurse, 1948; Qualified Medical Social Worker, 1952; MSc, Helsinki University, 1962. *Appointments:* Nurse, Ward Sister, Helsinki University Central Hospital, Obstetr Clinic, 1945-47; Supervisor of Midwifery, College of Midwives, 1947-49; Chief Medical Social Worker, Finnish Population and Family Welfare League, 1949-53; Educational Coordinator of Midwifery and PHN, Uusimaa PH Teaching Area, 1954-55; District Midwife 1956- 58, Assistant Head Midwife 1959-61, Helsinki City; Provincial Supervisor of Midwifery, Uusimaa Province, 1962-83; Counsellor, Public Health Care. *Publications:* Books: Maija's and Matti's Birth School, 1968; Your Child is Growing Up, 1969; The First Moments of Life, 1984; Love Without Asking, Midwife of the State is Recalling Past Memories, 1986; Numerous articles, studies, guide books, to professional journals; Editor-in-Chief of The Finnish Midwives' Journal, 1957-85. *Memberships:* President, The Federation of Finnish Midwives 1969-83; Member of the Executive Committee of the International Confederation of Midwives 1971-81; Member of the Study Group in Co-ordinated Medical Research Programme, European Health Committee, Council of Europe, 1974; Member of the Perinatal Study Group, WHO, Europe 1979-83. *Honours:* Councellor of Public Health Care, 1980; Dame de Merite, ordre International de Saint Constantin le Grand, 1981; Honorary President, Federation of Finnish Midwives, 1986; Member, Knightly Association of Saint George The Martyr, USA, 1985. *Hobbies:* Music; Literary work. *Address:* Puistokaari 1 G 25, 00200 Helsinki, Finland.

VAN APPLEDORN Mary Jeanne, b. 2 Oct. 1927, Holland, Michigan, USA. Professor of Music; Composer; Pianist; Educator; Conductor. *Education:* B.Mus., 1948; M.Mus., 1950; PhD, Music, 1966, Eastman School of Music. *Appointments:* Teaching Fellow, Eastman School of Music, 1948-50, 1961-62; Professor, Music & Chairman of Music Composition & Theory, 1950-. *Publications:* Compositions: Lux, Legend of Santa Lucia; Cacophony, Concerto for Trumpet & Band; Concerto for Trumpet & Orchestra; Concerto Brevis for Piano and Orchestra; Cantata, Rising Night After Night; Passacaglia and Chorale, orchestra; Liquid Gold, Matrices, Alto Saxophone and Piano; Set of Five, Piano; Sonnet for Organ, 4 duos for alto saxophone; 4 duos for viola and violoncello; Suite for Carillon; A Celestial Clockwork for Carillon. *Memberships Include:* College Music Society; ASCAP; Mu Phi Epsilon; Kappa Kappa Psi; Tau Beta Sigma. *Honours:* Delta Kappa Gamma International Scholar, 1959-60; American Society of Composers, Authors & Publishers Standard Awards, 1980-87. *Hobbies:* Travel. *Address:* School of Music, PO 4239, Texas Tech University, Lubbock, TX 79409, USA.

VANCE Carrie Temple, b. 20 Nov. 1944, Jackson, Mississippi, USA. Registered Nurse. *Education:* AA, Nursing, San Joaquin Delta College, Stockton, California, 1974; BA, Health Services Admin, St Mary's College, Moraga, 1978; MS, Nursing Admin and Music 1985, PhD, Music Performance 1985, Columbia Pacific University, San Rafael. *Appointments:* Licensed Nurse, California Registered Nurse, Staff Nurse 1976-77, Charge Nurse 1977-80, Nursery Supervisor, Neonatal Admin Coordinator 1980-, Dameron Hospital. *Memberships:* San Joaquin General Hospital Delta College Nurse Alumni Association; St Mary's College Alumni Association; Society Nursing Service Admin; National Assoc Female Executives; Columbia Pacific University Alumni Association; National Association Neonatal Nurses; National Assoc of Unknown Players (for film and television). *Hobbies:* Photography; Music (piano, organ, marimba, vibrahapr, electrical keyboard); Travelling (foreign and domestic). *Address:* Stockton, California, USA.

VAN DAN Carla Helene, b. 28 May 1950, Eindhoven, Netherlands. Psychologist. m. Charles E. Bates, 29 Dec. 1972, 2 sons, 1 daughter. *Education:* BA, Psychology, 1971; MEd, Counselling, 1973; Diplomate, American Board of Medical Psychotherapists. *Appointments:* Instructor, Navajo Community College, USA, 1973-75; Instructor, University of Victoria, British Columbia, Canada, 1975-65; Communications Director, British Columbia Central Credit Union, 1976-77; Instructor, North Island College, 1977-85; Psychologist in Private Practice, 1985-88. *Publications:* The Path of Least Resistance: Isolation & the Paradox of Burnout Management, 1983; Low Incidence of Schizophrenia Among B.C. Coastal Indians, 1984; Abnormal Fatty Acid Metabolism in Indians on and off a Diet Exceptionally Rich in Salmon, 1985; Do Eskimos & Salmon Eating Canadian Indians Have a Pattern of Essential Fatty Acid Metabolism Different From Europeans, 1985; The Occurrence of Sexual Abuse in a Small Community; An Update on the Occurrence of Sexual Abuse, 1986; Sexual Abuse: Fact and Fantasy, 1986; A Safety and First Aid Manual for the Prevention and Treatment of Child Abuse, 1987. *Memberships:* Registered Psychologist, British Columbia Psychological Association, 1979; Canadian Psychological Association; American Psychological Association; Canadian Society of Clinical Hypnosis; Canadian Register of Health Service Providers in Psychology. *Honours:* Medal of Bravery, 1986. *Address:* 7112 Alderwood Court, Lacey, WA 98503, USA.

VANDE KEMP Hendrika, b. 13 Dec. 1948, The Netherlands. Clinical Psychologist; Educator. *Education:* BA, 1971; MS, 1974, PhD, 1977, Massachusetts. *Appointments:* Instructor, 1976-77, Assistant Professor, 1977-81, Associate Professor, 1981-, Graduate School of Psychology, Fuller Theological Seminary. *Publications:* Psychology and Theology in Western Thought, 1984; articles in: Teaching of Psychology; Journal of Psychology and Theology; Family Process; etc. *Memberships:* President, Psychologists Interested in Religious Issues, 1988-89; American Psychological Association; American Family Therapy Association; American Academy of Religion; Southern California C S Lewis Society. *Honours:* Eta Sigma Phi; Psi Chi; Pi Sigma Alpha; Phi Beta Kappa. *Hobbies:* Classical Music; British Detective Fiction; History of Psychology; Cats. *Address:* Graduate School of Psychology, Fuller Theological Seminary, 180 N. Oakland, Pasadena, CA 91182, USA.

VANDEN DRIESSCHE-OEDENKOVEN Therese, b.

16 July 1925, Brussels, Belgium. Professor at the University. m. Louis Vanden Driessche, 29 Dec. 1949. 2 daughters. *Education:* BSc 1946, MSc (Botany), 1948, PhD (Dr in Science) (Plant Physiology) 1963, University Libre Bruxelles; Agrege d'Universite (Molecular Cytology), Univ Libre Bruxelles. *Appointments:* Scientific Collaborator, Aquiculture Research Centre, 1948-50; Assistant Professor, Plant Physiology 1958-64, Assistant Professor, Animal Morphol 1964- 72, Professor, Molecular Biology 1972-, Universite Libre de Bruxelles. *Publications:* Scientific papers in international Journals on: The role of RNAs in circadian rhythmicity; The temporal organization of a unicellular alga; On the photosynthesis rhythm; On the pathways involved in morphogenetic signal transduction in the unicellular alga and its receptor; On the relation rhythms/morphogenesis. *Memberships:* Groupe d'Etudes des rythmes biologiques; Internat. Soc Chronobiology; Internat Soc Plant Molecular Biology; Soc Belge de Biologie cellulaire; Soc Belge de Biochime; Soc Physiologie vegetale francophone; Soc Belge de Biophysique; British Plant Growth regulators Group. *Honours:* Prix Leo Errera de l'Academie royale des Sciences, des Lettres et des Beaux-Arts, 1964; Inaugurated the Brachet Institute of Cell and Molecular Biology, Chronobiology Research Center, SB College, Changancherry, South India, 1986; Since 1979, invited Professor in the course of Chronobiology organized in Paris, France. *Hobbies:* Travel; Gardening. *Address:* Departement de Biologie moleculaire, Universite Libre de Bruxelles, 67 rue des Chevaux, 1640 Rhode St Genese, Belgium.

VANDENDORPE Mary Moore, b. 2 June 1947, Chicago, USA. Associate Professor. m. James Edward Vandendorpe, 16 Aug. 1969, 1 daughter. *Education:* AB, St Louis University, 1969; MS, 1975, PhD, 1980, Illinois Institute of Technology. *Appointments:* Copywriter, Spiegel Inc., 1969-73; Resident Head, 1973-74, Adjunct Instructor, 1975, IIT; Adjunct Instructor, 1975-79, Assistant Professor, 1980-85, Associate Professor, 1985-, Lewis University. *Publications:* 5 publications, 20 professional presentations including: The K-d Tree - A Hierarchial Model for Human Cognition. *Memberships:* American, Midwestern & Chicago Psychological Associations; Gerontological Society. *Honours:* 1st Prize, Creative Writing, St Louis University. *Hobbies:* Naperville Heritage Society; Sailing; Tennis; Skiing. *Address:* Dept. of Psychology, Lewis University, Romesville, IL 60441, USA.

VANDERBILT Caroline Grace, b. 11 Sept. 1946, California, USA. Director, International Ocean Institute. *Education:* BA, Ancient Theology, BA, Anthropology, University of Hawaii; PhD, Marine Biology (Mathematics), ABT. *Appointments:* Researcher in Fisheries, Fisheries Division, Food and Agricultural Organisation, United Nations, 1970-72; Executive Director, International Ocean Institute, Valletta, Malta, 1972-; Consultant: Forum Fisheries Agency, 1984-87; Indian Ocean Marine Affairs Coop Secretariat, 1985- . *Memberships:* 101 Planning Council; Secretary, 101 Board of Trustees; Editor, Across the Oceans; Editor, IO News; International Advisory Board, China Ocean Press; Council on Ocean Law; Planning Council, Foundation for International Studies. *Hobbies:* Photography; Cooking; Scuba diving. *Address:* International Ocean Institute, PO Box 524, Valletta, Malta.

VANDERHOST Leonette, b. 11 June 1924, Philadelphia, Pennsylvania. Psychologist. *Education:* BA, Hunter College, 1945; MA, 1949, PhD, 1961, New York University. *Appointments:* Private practice in Psychology, New York City, 1959-; Psychologist, West Nassau Mental Health Center, Franklin Square, New York, 1959-63; Psychotherapist, Hempstead Consultant Service, New York City, 1963-66. *Memberships:* American Psychological Association; New York State Psychological Association. *Address:* 250 East 87th Street, New York, NY 10128, USA.

VANDERLINDEN Camilla Denice Dunn, b. 21 July

1950, Dayton, Ohio, USA. Manager. m. David Henry Vander Linden, 10 Oct. 1980, 1 son. *Education:* BA, Spanish & Education, 1972, MS, Human Resource Economics, 1985, University of Utah. *Appointments:* Assistant Director, Davis County Community Action Programme, 1973-76; Director, South County Community Council, 1976-78; Customer Service Manager, Misc. Insurance Companies, 1978-82; Quality Assurance, Human Resource Management, American Express Co., 1982-. *Memberships:* ASQC; Adjunct Faculty, Westminster College, Salt Lake City, 1987-88. *Hobbies:* Swimming; Volunteer Translator for Latin Americans; American Red Cross. *Address:* c/o American Express Co., 1818 Inverness Dr. West, Englewood, CO 80112, USA.

VAN DER WAL Jeanne Huber, b. 7 Feb. 1954, Flushing, New York, USA. Stockbroker. m. Peter van der Wal, 8 May 1982. *Education:* AB magna cum laude, Colgate University, 1975; JD, Suffolk University, 1978. Bars: DC, 1979; US District Court, DC, 1979; US Court of Appeals, 1979; US Supreme Court, 1983. *Appointments:* Regulatory attorney, Washington 1978-83, corporate counsel, Roswell, Georgia 1983-86, Kimberley-Clark Corporation; Private practice, consultant, Northridge, California, 1986-87; Account executive, Drexel Burnham Lambert, Beverley Hills, 1987-. *Memberships include:* Offices, Century City Chamber of Commerce, British American Chamber of Commerce; US Mexico Chamber of Commerce; Australian-American Chamber of Commerce; Republican Presidential Task Force, Washington, 1985-87. *Honours include:* New York Regents scholar, 1971-75. *Hobbies:* Real estate; Sailing; Golf; Skiing. *Address:* PO Box 549, Southport, CT 06490, USA.

VANDERWOUDE Mary Elizabeth, b. 1 Dec. 1939, Grand Rapids, Michigan, USA. Writer; Teacher. *Education:* Saint Xavier College, Chicago; Chicago Teacher's College; Chicago City College; American Conservatory of Music, Chicago; Studied with Philip Farkas, Chicago, 1957-62, Lorenzo Sansone, New York City, 1963-66, Lela Hanmer, Chicago, (Piano), 1975-76, Helen Kotas Hirsch, Chicago, 1983-84. *Appointments:* Grand Rapids Symphony Orchestra, 1955-57; Chicago Chamber Orchestra, 1959-64; Freelance, Chicago, 1958-68; Freelance, St Louis, Missouri, 1970-71; Freelance, Phoenix, Arizona, 1977-80; Writer/Composer, Chicago, 1980-; Writer, Faculty, The University of Illinois at Chicago. *Publications:* French Horn Studies, 1962; Virtuoso Series (12 volumes), 1961-65; Atonalism for Horn, 1975; Numerous works for competition, solo, ensemble and orch arrang; Technical articles for professional journals. *Interests:* Continuing study in Moral Philosophy; Political activism; Piano study. *Address:* 1130 South Michigan Avenue, Chicago, Illinois 60605, USA.

VAN DE VATE Nancy Hayes, b. 30 Dec. 1930, Plainfield, New Jersey, USA. Composer. m. (1) Dwight Van de Vate, Jr, 9 June 1952, 1 son, 2 daughters. (2) Clyde Arnold Smith, 23 June 1979. *Education:* AB, Wellesley College, 1952; MM, University of Mississippi, 1958; DMus, Florida State University, 1968. *Appointments:* Assistant Professor of Music, Memphis State University, 1964-66; Associate Professor of Music, Knoxville College, 1968-69; Visiting Associate Professor of Music, University of Hawaii, 1975-76; Associate Professor of Music, 1978-80, Dean of Academic Affairs, 1979, Hawaii Loa College. *Creative Works:* Music compositions: Chernobyl; Concerto for Percussion and Orchestra; Concerto for Violin and Orchestra; Distant Worlds; Dark Nebulae; Journeys; Pura Besakih; Concerto for Piano and Orchestra; Adagio; Concertpiece for Cello and small orchestra; Variations for Chamber Orchestra. *Memberships:* Founder and Chairperson, 1975-82, International League of Women Composers; President 1973-75, Secretary, 1970- 73, Southeastern Composers' League; International Congress on Women in Music; American Association of University Women; Broadcast Music, Inc; National Association of Composers, USA; International Gesellschaft fur Neue Musik, Sektion Osterreich.

Honours: National Endowment for the Arts Composer's Fellowship, 1987-89; Maryland State Arts Council Artists Award, 1988; Resident Fellow, MacDowell Colony, 1987; Yaddo, 1974; The Tyrone Guthrie Centre at Annaghmakerrig, Ireland, 1988; Ossabaw Island, 1974; 6 Meet the Composer Awards, 1976, 1979, 1980, 1982, 1987, 1988. 1st Prize, Los Alamos Chamber Music Competition, 1979; Research & Project Award, American Association of University Women, 1988; Individual Award, Money for Women Fund, 1988; ASCAP Standard Awards, 1973-81; BMI awards, 1982-89. *Hobbies:* Travel; Photography; Languages. *Address:* Margaretenstrasse 125/15, A-1050 Vienna, Austria.

VAN DE WERVE DE SCHILDE Marie-Isabelle, b. 29 June 1961, Usumbura, Burundi. Paper Conservator. m. Yves Speeckaert, 24 July 1989. *Education:* Paper Conservation, Book Binding, National Institute of Arts and Crafts, Brussels, Belgium, 1981-85; Painting Restoration, L'Atelier, Art School of Marcel Hastir, Brussels. *Career:* Co-Founder, L'Atelier de Pascale (paper conservation and stucco), 1984; Founder, Princeton Studio (paper conservation), New Jersey, USA, 1988-; Exhibited paper conservation and watercolours in major multi-media Art Fair, Tourinnes-La Grosse, Belgium, 1987. *Memberships:* American Institute for Conservation of Historic and Artistic Work; Friends of the Princeton University Library, USA; Institut de Restauration et de Recherche Archeologiques et Paleometallurgique de Compiegne. *Hobbies:* Art; Travel; History; Philosophy; Religion; Nature. *Address:* 497 Cherry Valley Road, Princeton, NJ 08540, USA.

VANG Betty, b. 2 Apr. 1942, Aarhus, Denmark. Research worker; Architect. 1 stepson, 3 stepdaughters. *Education:* Dipl, Interior Design, 1965; Dipl, Community Development, 1974; Studies in Urban and Regional Planning, candidate for doctorate. *Appointments:* Private and public architect and planning offices in Denmark and Kenya, 1965-73 and 1975-81; Research Worker, Aarhus School of Architecture, 1982-83; Research worker, Women's Research-Center, Aarhus, 1986-. *Publications:* Books: Boligrammer-Menneskevaerd, 1978; Farvel til byen?, 1985; Det aristoteliske efterslaeb, 1987; Om kvinders levevilkar og fysisk planlaegning, 1988. *Memberships:* Danske Arkitekters Landsforbund/ Akademisk Arkitektforening (The Federation of Danish Architects); Foreningen af Byplanlaeggere (The Union of Town Planners). *Hobbies:* Gardening; Country walks; Reading. *Address:* Dr Margrethesvej 53, DK-8200 Arhus N, Denmark.

VAN GINKEL Blanche Lemco, b. London, England. Architect; Urbanist; Professor. m. H.P. Daniel Van Ginkel, 1 son, 1 daughter. *Education:* B.ARch, McGill University, Montreal; MCP, Harvard University, USA. *Appointments:* Partner, Van Ginkel Associates, 1957-; Dean, Architecture, University of Toronto, 1977-82; Adjunct Professor, McGill University, 1973-77; Visiting Professor, various Universities. *Publications:* Film: It Can Be Done; Atlas & Book: Communities of the Mackenzie; Guest Editor, Canadian Art, Environments; Contributor to: Architectural Design; Canadian Architect. *Memberships:* Canadian Institute of Planners; Royal Architectural Institute of Canada, Secretary, Treasurer; Founder, Vice President, Corporation of Urbanists of Quebec; President, Association of Collegiate Schools of Architecture, 1986. *Honours:* Mademoiselle Woman of the Year Award, 1957; Mersey medal, 1962; Montreal YWCA Award; Grand Prix for Film of IFHP, Vienna, 1956; Queen's Silver Jubilee Medal, 1977; ACSA Distinguished Professor 1989. *Address:* Faculty of Architecture, University of Toronto, 230 College St., Toronto, Ontario M5S 1A1, Canada.

VANHOOZER Jean McCarley, b. 4 May 1932, Marlow, Oklahoma. Manager, Lawton Teachers Federal Credit Union. m. 2 Sept. 1952. 2 sons, 1 daughter. *Education:* Public Accountant Cert. No 617, Midwestern University, Wichita Falls, 1967; BS Business Adm, Cameron University, Lawton, 1978. *Appointments:* Deputy Clerk/Deputy Custodian of Activity Funds/ Business Office Manager, Lawton Public Schools, 1952-

69; Manager, Lawton Teachers Federal Credit Union, 1969-. *Publications:* Credit Union's Small Computer System, 1978; Do it Yourself, or Hire The Help. *Memberships:* Oklahoma Society of Public Accountants; District Chapter of Public Accountants; Data Processing Association; Credit Union Executive Society; PTA & Booster Club; Chamber of Commerce, Education Committee. *Hobbies:* Sports; Coach "Little League" Basketball; Gardening; Sewing. *Address:* Rt1 Box 252, Lawton, Oklahoma 73501, USA.

VANLEEUWEN Liz (Elizabeth Susan Nelson), b. 5 Nov. 1925, Lakeview, Oregon, USA. State Legislator; Farmer. m. Geo VanLeeuwen, 15 June 1947, 3 sons, 1 daughter. *Education:* BS, Oregon State University, 1947. *Appointments:* Secondary School & Adult Teacher, 1947-70; Reporter, The Times, Brownsville, 1949-; Co-Manager, VanLeeuwen Farm, 1956-; State Representative, 1981-. *Memberships:* Linn CASA, Founder, Vice Chairman of Board; Oregon Women for Agriculture, President; Oregon Women for Timber; etc. *Honours:* Oregon Farm Family of Year Award, 1983; Outstanding Contribution, Republican House Caucus, 1987; etc. *Hobbies:* Gardening; Grandchildren. *Address:* 27070 Irish Bend Loop, Halsey, OR 97348, USA.

VAN LEEUWEN Patricia Ann Szczepanik, b. 27 May 1939, Chicago, USA. Research Specialist. m. G. Dale Van Leeuwen, 27 May 1978. *Appointments:* BS, Chemistry, 1961, MPH, 1987, University of Illinois; Doctorial Candidate. *Appointments:* Research Assistant, BIM Division, Argonne National Lab, 1961-76; Biochemist, 1976-80; Biochemist, Rer Div, 1980-82; Research Associate, University of Illinois, 1982-87; University of Illinois, Chicago, 1987-. *Publications:* 48 articles to scientific journals. *Memberships:* American Association Study of Liver Diseases; American Society Mass Spectrometry; National Environmental Health Association; American Public Health Association; Air Pollution Control Association; American Chemical Society. *Honours:* Phi Kappa Phi. *Hobby:* Genalogy. *Address:* University of Illinois, School of Public Health, Environ and Occupational Health Sciences Dept., PO Box 6998, Chicago, IL 60680, USA.

VAN LENGEN Karen, b. 9 Apr. 1951, Syracuse, New York, USA. Architect. *Education:* BA, Vassar College, 1973; MArch, Columbia University, 1976. *Appointments:* Associate, I. M. Pe & Partners, 1976-82; Own firm, Karen Van Lengen, Architects, 1985-. *Creative work includes:* Drawings exhibited, New York City: Women in Architecture, Columbia University, 1978; Home for Theatre, 1988; Works on Paper, 1988. *Memberships:* American Institute of Architects; National Historical Trust Association; National Council of Accreditation Registration Board. *Honours:* Fellowship, American Association of University Women, 1975- 76; Honourable Mention, Steedman Fellowship Competition, 1981; Fulbright Fellowship, Rome, Italy, 1982-83; 3rd prize, Formica Competition, 1988; 1st prize, AGB Public Library Competition, Berlin, West Germany, 1988. *Hobbies:* Drawing; Painting; Swimming; Skiing. *Address:* 424 Broome Street, Floor 5, New York, NY 10013, USA.

VAN METER Harriet Drury, b. 27 Dec. 1910, Fulton, Illinois, USA. Administrator. m. James F. Van Meter, 27 June 1931, 2 sons, 1 daughter. *Education:* AB magna cum laude Family Studies 1957, MA Sociology 1961, University of Kentucky. *Appointments:* Director, Sayre School, 1946-48; Assistant Foreign Student Adviser, University of Kentucky, 1955-65; Founder, Executive Director, International Book Project Inc 1965-85, Send a Book Abroad 1988-. *Publications:* Hands, Hands, Hands, children's book, poems & Music; Numerous Articles, Family Development; Poetry. *Memberships include:* Kappa Kappa Gamma; Junior League; Medical Auxiliary; Blue Book Social Registry; Presbyterian Church; Phi Beta Kappa. *Honours include:* AHEPA; 2 awards, Woman of Year, Kentucky; Veterans Medal, Community Service, World War II; Kentucky Colonel; Award, National Council of Christians & Jews; David A. Sayre Medallion; Kiwanis Community Award, 1977;

Various Awards, L.H.D. degree Transylvania, 2 University Libraries name for Philippines; Harriet Van Meter Library named at Baguio University; nomination, Nobel Peace Prize, 1985; International Kivonis Service Award, 1989; Algernon Sydney Sullivan Medallion from University of Kentucky. *Hobbies:* Reading; Travel. *Address:* 17 Mentelle Park, Lexington, Kentucky 40502, USA.

VAN NESS Patricia Catheline, b. 25 June 1951, Seattle, Washington, USA. Composer; Musician. m. Adam Sherman, 26 June 1983. *Education:* Wheaton College Conservatory of Music, 1969-70. *Appointments:* Electric violinist with rock band Private Lightning; Composer of music. *Creative works:* Compositions: The Goddess Inanna, 1985; Memoir, 1985; Place of Ambush, 1986-87; for Monica Levy's commissions with the Dance Company of Lisbon, Portugal and Transitions Company, London, England, 1988; Composed and orchestrated music for Boston Ballet's world premiere, 1988 Spoleto Festival USA, 1987-88; Composing and orchestrating full score of Hans Christian Andersen's The Wild Swans for Boston Ballet; Reaping; An Untitled Work for Guitars and Strings; Song of Twilight; Study of Strings; Character Sketch; The Red Skirt; The Gulf; Lake Desire; Spiritual; Untitled No 2, 3 and 4; In the Forest; Study for Violin; Study for Piano. *Membership:* American Women Composers. *Honours:* Recipient Massachusetts Arts Council Grant, City of Somerville, 1988; Recipient, New England Biolabs Foundation Grant, 1989. *Hobbies:* Reading; Major league baseball; Walking; Dogs. *Address:* Pierce Hall Room 126, 29 Oxford Street, Cambridge, MA 02138, USA.

VAN PRAAGH Peggy, (Dame) b. 1 Sept. 1910, London, England. Ballet Dancer; Teacher; Director. *Education:* Trained as classical dancer with Margaret Craske, Vera Volkova, Karasavina; Trained as Modern Dancer with Agnes de Mille; Fellow, examiner, Cecchetti Branch, Imperial Society of Teachers of Dancing, London, 1935-. *Appointments:* Opened private dance school, 1930; joined Ballet Rambert, 1933; Principal Dancer, Antony Tudo's London Ballet, 1938; Director, London Ballet, 1939; Initiated Lunch Hour Ballet, Arts Theatre, 1940; Dancer, teacher, performances in Coppelia and Patineurs, Sadler's Wells Ballet, 1941; Ballet Mistress, Sadler's Wells Theatre Ballet, 1946; Assistant Director to Ninette de Valois, 1951; Freelance Teacher & Producer, 1956; Dance Director, Edinburgh Festival Ballet & toured Europe with them, 1968; Teacher, Ted Shawn's Jacobs Pillow, USA 1959; The Royal Ballet School, 1959; Invited to Australia. *Publications:* How I Became a Ballet Dancer; The Choreographic Art, with Peter Brinson, 1963; The Arts in Australia-Ballet, 1966. *Memberships:* various professional organisations. *Honours:* DBE, 1970; Honorary DLitt, University of New England Australia, 1974; Honorary LLD Melbourne University; Queen Elizabeth Award Royal Academy of Dancing, London. *Address:* Flat 5, 248 The Avenue, Parkville, VIC 3052, Australia.

VAN SPANCKEREN Kathryn, b. 14 Dec. 1945, Kansas City, Missouri, USA. Associate Professor of English. m. Stephen Breslow, 26 June 1973, 1 son. *Education:* BA, Berkeley, 1967; MA, Brandeis University, 1968; MA 1969, PhD 1976, Harvard University. *Appointments:* Programme Officer & Acting Director, Coordinating Council of Literary Magazines, 1979-80; Fulbright Professor, Indonesia, 1982-83; Assistant, then Associate Professor of English, University of Tampa, Florida, 1983-. *Publications:* Editor, books: John Gardner, 1982; Margaret Atwood, 1988; Outline History of American Literature, forthcoming. *Memberships:* US & South Atantic Modern Language Associations; President, International Margaret Atwood Society, & International Committee for Promotion of East-West Cultural Relations. *Honours:* Phi Beta Kappa, 1967; Woodrow Wilson Fellowship, 1967; Ford Foundation Prize, 1967; Elector, National Medal for Literature, 1979; Fulbright to Indonesia 1982-83, China 1987; Grant, East-West Centre, 1985. *Hobbies:* Hiking; Natural history; Scuba diving. *Address:* 93 Martinique Avenue, Tampa, Florida 33606, USA.

VAN STOCKUM Hilda Gerarda Marlin, b. 9 Feb. 1908, Rotterdam, Holland. Still life painter; Children's book writer and illustrator. m. Ervin Ross Marlin, 27 June 1932. 2 sons, 4 daughters. *Education:* School of Art, Dublin, 1923-26; Rijks academie, Amsterdam, Holland, 1926-31; Corcasan Art School, Washington DC, USA, 1935-36; 1 year study in Paris, France, 1954-55. *Appointments:* Teacher, Child Ed Foundation, NY, 1934-35; Teacher (art and writing), Adult Education Centre, Washington DC, 1965-75; Teaching writing, Dacorum College, Berkhamsted, 1970-88. *Publications:* Numerous books, major works include: Harper, a day on skates, 1935; Viking, The cottage at Bantry Bay, 1938; Francie on the Run, 1939; Kersti and St Nicholas, 1940; Pegeen, 1941; Andries, 1942; Gerrit and the Organ, 1943; The Mitchells, 1945; Angels Alphabet, 1946; Canadian Summer, 1948; Patsy and the Pup, 1950; King Oberon's Forest, 1957; Friendly Gables, 1960; Winged Watchman, 1962; Little Old Bear, 1962; Mogo's Flute, 1966; Penengro, 1972; Borrowed House, 1975; Rufus Round and Round, 1976; Numerous paintings shown in Holland, Ireland, England, Switzerland, Canada, Kenya and USA. *Honours:* Honorary Member, Royal Hibernian Academy, Dublin, 1985; Nominated, Confraternity of Christians and Jews as having written a Friendship Book to promote friendship between Jews and Christians. *Hobbies:* Reading; Poetry; Walking; Health; Ecology; Education; Psychology; Religion; Philosophy; People; Animals; Scrabble. *Address:* 8 Castle Hill, Berkhamsted, Hertfordshire, England.

VANSTONE Amanda Eloise, b. 7 Dec. 1952, Adelaide, Australia. Senator. m. Anthony Vanstone. *Education:* Marketing Studies Certificate 1972, Graduate Diploma in Legal Practice 1983, South Australia Institute of Technology; BA 1981, LLB 1983, University of Adelaide. *Appointments:* Retailing; Wholesaling; Solicitor. *Membership:* Law Society of South Australia. *Address:* 150 Hindley Street, Adelaide, South Austrtalia 5000, Australia.

VAN VEEN Marcella, b. 28 Mar. 1943, Amsterdam, Holland. Managing Director. m. Peter Vincent Van Veen, 4 Sept. 1963, 1 son, 1 daughter. *Appointments:* Housewife, Far East until 1981; Founder, Dial A Char, 1981-; Founder, Frobishers Limousine Service, 1981-. *Membership:* Institute of Directors. *Hobbies:* Theatre; Opera; Travel. *Address:* 77 London Road, East Grinstead, West Sussex, England.

VAN VELZER Verna Jean, b. 22 Jan. 1929, State College, Pennsylvania, USA. Research Librarian. *Education:* BS, University of Illinois, 1950; MLS, Syracuse University, 1957. *Appointments:* Head Librarian, Fairchild Semiconductor R & D Lab, Palo Alto, 1964-65; Intelligence Librarian, Sylvania Elecric Products, Mountain View, 1965-66; Research Librarian, ESL Inc, Sunnyvale, 1966-. *Publications:* Various poems published in anthologies over the past 40 years. *Memberships:* Special Libraries Association; Institute of Electrical & Electronics Engineers; American Institute of Aeronautics & Astronautics; Association of Old Crows; Association for Computing Machinery; US Naval Institute; Armed Forces Communications & Electronics Association. *Honours:* National High School Honor Society, 1946; Beta Phi Mu, National Library Honor Society, 1957; Paul Reviere Bowl awarded at Santa Clara Camellia Society, 1968; Numerous blue ribbons awarded at various California camellia shows; Commemorative Medal of Honor, American Biographical Institute; International Cultural Diploma of Honor; 2nd prize, Essay for Dayton District Contest, 1946. *Hobbies:* Animal rescue; Wildlife rescue; International ecological conservation; Animal and human nutrition; Koi; Camellias; Azaleas; Gardening; Greenhouse management; Cats; Dogs; History; Holistic living; Ethics. *Address:* 4048 Laguna Way, Palo Alto, California 94306, USA.

VAN VLEDDER Lorraine May, b. 21 May 1949, Johannesburg, South Africa. m. Andre Van Vledder, 17 Feb. 1971, divorced, 30 May 1978. *Education:* Home Economics Diploma, 1969; La Varenne Cookery School Paris, 1980; Cape Wine Academy Certificate Course. *Appointments:* Food Editor, The Star Newspaper, 1970-81; Editor, Professional Caterer, 1981; Group PRO, Fedfood Group, 1981-83; Director, Elite Communications, 1983; Owner, On-Line PR, 1984-88; Consumer Promotions Manager, Home Economist, SA Sugar Association, 1988-. *Publications:* Co-Author: Cooking with Angela Day, Entertaining with Angela Day, Angela Day Fondue Book, Recipes from Ruto Mills. *Memberships:* Public Relations Institute of South Africa; South Africa Chefs Association; Bakers Dozen; Cape Wine Academy; Professional Culinary Circle. *Hobbies:* Cooking; Tennis; Wine; Music; Outdoor Life; Wildlife. *Address:* Durban, South Africa.

VAN VLIET Claire, b. 9 Aug. 1933, Ottawa, Canada. Printmaker. m. (1) W. R. Johnson, 31 May 1954 (div. 1960), (2) Michael Boylen, 29 Apr. 1968 (div. 1980). *Education:* AB, San Diego State University, California, USA, 1952; MFA, Claremont Graduate School, Claremont, California, 1954. *Career:* Founded Janus Press, West Burke, Vermont, USA, 1955; Various positions: Pickering Press, 1958-60; Philadelphia College of Art, Pennsylvania, 1959-65; University of Wisconsin, 1965-66; Self-employed, 1966-; Exhibitions: 25 year retrospective, Boston Public Library, 1977; Retrospective, Rutgers University Gallery, 1978; The Print Club, Philadelphia, 1979; Fleming Museum, University of Vermont, 1982; Dolan/Maxwell Gallery, Philadelphia, 1984; Mary Ryan Gallery, New York City, 1986. *Creative works include:* Sun, Sky & Earth, 1964; Satellite, 1972; Works in collections: National Gallery of Art, Washington DC; Montreal Museum of Fine Art; Cleveland Museum of Art; Philadelphia Museum of Art; Victoria and Albert Museum, London. *Memberships:* Society of Printers, Boston. *Honours:* Grantee, National Endowment for the Arts, 1976, 1979; Grantee, Ingram-Merrill Foundation, 1989; recipient MacArthur Prize Fellowship, 1989-94. *Address:* The Janus Press; RD 1, Box 53AA, West Burke, VT 05871, USA.

VAN WAGNER Judy Kay Collischan, b. 19 Oct. 1940, Red Wing, Minnesota, USA. University Art Gallery Director. 1 son. *Education:* BA, Hamline University, 1962; Graduate credit, National University of Mexico seminar, 1963; MFA, Ohio University, 1964; PhD, University of Iowa, 1972. *Appointments:* Instructor Kansas State University, 1964-66; Assistant Professor, University of Northern Iowa, 1970-71; Assistant Professor, University of Nebraska, 1972-75; Associate Professor, State University of New York, 1975-82; Museum Director, Long Island University, 1982-; Freelance Critic, 1982-. *Publications:* Women Shaping Art, book, 1983; Lines of Vision, Drawings by Contemporary Women, book, 1989; Barbara Zucker's Activated Objects, 1985; Grace Knowlton's Secret Spaces, 1986; Harmony Hammond's Painted Spirits, 1986; Judith Shea: A Personal Balance, 1987; Max Coyer's Painted Life of the Mind, 1987. *Memberships:* Art Table, 1987-90; International Association of Art Critics, American Section, 1987-90; American Association of Museums. *Honours:* Tozer Undergraduate and Graduate Scholarships, 1961-63; Kress Foundation Award, 1970; University Award, State University of New York, 1981. *Hobbies:* Reading; Travel; Sports. *Address:* 141 West 21 Street, Huntington Station, NY 11746, USA.

VARGAS Marsha Lynn, b. 26 Oct. 1943, New Orleans, Louisiana, USA. Oriental Art Appraiser/Valuer. m. Robert Louis Vargas, 23 Nov. 1970. *Education:* AA, Foothill College, Los Altos, California, 1973; University of Maryland, 1963-65; Numerous seminars and courses in Oriental Art. *Appointments:* Administrative Assistant, Lockheed Corporation, Sunnyvale, California, 1965-70; Exporter/Importer, Oriental Art from Far East, 1970-73; President, The Oriental Corner, Los Altos, 1973-. *Appointments:* Senior Member, American Society of Appraisers, San Jose

Chapter President 1982-83; Vice-President, International Netsuke Dealers Association; International Society of Appraisers, Regional Director 1979-82. *Hobbies:* Collector and student of Oriental ceramics and works of art. *Address:* c/o The Oriental Corner, 280 Main Street, Los Altos, CA 94022, USA.

VASILE Laura Lee, b. 9 Aug. 1960, New Britain, Connecticut, USA. Registered Sanitarian. *Education:* BS, Health Education, Western Connecticut University. *Appointments:* Office Administrator, Associated Neurologists, 1984; Health Inspector, Brookfield Health Department, 1985; Sanitarian, Oxford Health Department, Oxford, 1986; Registered Sanitarian, Bethel Health Department, Bethel, Connecticut, 1988- . *Memberships:* Connecticut Public Health Association; Connecticut Environmental Health Association; National Conference of Local Environmental Health Administrators; National Federation of Business and Professional Women's Club Inc, Washington DC; National Environmental Health Association. *Hobbies:* Reading; Teaching; Short sightseeing trips; Theatre; Fairs; Hiking; Swimming. *Address:* 27 Vail Road, Bethel, CT 06801, USA.

VAUGHAN Janet Maria, b. 18 Oct. 1899, Clifton, Bristol. Retired Physician. m. David Gourcay, 1930, 2 daughters. *Education:* Somerville College; Oxford University College Hospital (Goldsmith Entrance Scholar), Rodfeller Fellowship, 1929-30. *Appointments:* Principal, Somerville College, Oxford, 1943-57; Nuffield Trustee, 1943; Chairman, Oxford Regional Hospital Board, 1950; Officer in Charge, NW London Blood Safety Dept., MRC, Director, MRC Bone Seeking Safety Unit. *Publications:* The Physiology of Bone; one other book; papers and articles in scientific journals. *Honours:* OBE, 1944; DBE, 1957; Fellow, Royal Society, 1979; etc. *Hobbies:* Gardening; Travel. *Address:* 5 Fairlawn Flats, First Turn, Wolvercote, Oxford OX2 8AP, England.

VAUGHAN Judy, National Coordinator. *Education:* Master's degree, Sociology, San Diego State University, 1972; Doctorate, Religious Social Ethics, University of Chicago, 1982. *Appointments:* Teacher, Anthropology and Sociology, Mount St Mary's College, Los Angeles, 4 years; Coordinator, Los Angeles House of Ruth, 4 years; National Coordinator, Women's Coalition to Stop US Intervention in Central America and the Caribbean; National Coordinator, National Assembly of Religious Women, Chicago. *Publications:* Sociality, Ethics and Social Change, 1983; Numerous articles and presentations on feminist theology, social analysis, social ethics and social justice. *Memberships:* Pledge of Resistance; Advisory board, Witness for Peace, Voices on the Border: Campaign to Support Salvadoran Refugees in Colomoncagua; Weavers Project of Women for Guatemala; Sisters of St Joseph of Carondelet, Los Angeles Province. *Address:* 1307 South Wabash, Chicago, Illinois 60605, USA

VAUGHAN Mary Kathleen, b. 7 Sep. 1943, Houston, Texas, USA. Associate Professor. m. George Martin Vaughan, 2 July 1966, 3 sons. *Education:* BA, Biology, University of St Thomas, Houston, 1965; PhD, Anatomy, University of Texas Medical Branch, Galveston, 1970; Postdoctoral Fellow: University of Rochester, Rochester, New York, 1970-71; University of Texas Health Science Center, San Antonio, 1974; Guest Worker, National Institute of Health, Bethesda, Maryland, 1971-73. *Appointments:* Lecturer in Biology, University of Rochester, Rochester, New York, 1970-71; Assistant Professor of Anatomy, 1975-80, Associate Professor of Cellular and Structural Biology, 1980-, University of Texas Health Science Center, San Antonio. *Publications:* 22 scientific book chapters; 154 scientific articles in various journals; 121 abstracts presented at national and international meetings. *Memberships:* Sigma Xi; American Association of Anatomists; American Zoological Society; Endocrine Society; American Association for the Advancement of Science; International Society for Chronobiology; Foundation for Advanced Education in Science; Society for Experimental Biology and Medicine; Neuroscience Society; American Physiological Society; European Pineal Study Group; International Society for Neuroendocrinology. *Honours:* Mary Gibbs Jones Scholarship, 1961-65; USPHS Special Research Fellowship, 1974-75; American Men and Women in Science, 1986; UTHSCSA Presidential Teaching Award, 1989. *Hobbies:* Stamp collecting; Computers; Classical music. *Address:* Department of Cellular and Structural Biology, University of Texas Health Science Center at San Antonio, 7703 Floyd Curl Drive, San Antonio, TX 78284, USA.

VAUGHAN WILLIAMS Ursula, b. 15 Mar. 1911, Valletta, Malta. Writer. m. (1) Captain J M J Forrester Wood, 24 May 1933. (2) Dr Ralph Vaughan Williams, 7 Feb. 1953. *Creative works:* Opera Libretti: The Sofa, Maconchy; Melita, Camillieri; The Brilliant & The Dark, Williamson; David & Bathsheba, Barlow; Stars & Shadows, Hughes; King of Macedon, Steptoe; Echoes, Senator; Insect Play, Senator; Canterbury Tale, Roe. Cantatas: The Sons of Light, Vaughan Williams; Break to be Built, Milnes; The Icy Minor, Williamson; Man's Music is the Music of the Seasons, Teed; For Music, Williamson; Compassion, Tate; Song Cycles: Four Last Songs, Vaughan Williams; Aspects, Steptoe; The Looking Glass, Steptoe; The Inheritor, Steptoe; Lady & Unicorn, Hodclinott; The Silver Hound, Hodclinott. Songs to music by: Gerald Finzi; Herbert Howells; Byron Adams; Alan Ridout and Lutyens. 6 Books of poems latest, Aspects, 1984; Biography: RVW, a biography of R Vaughan Williams, 1964; Pictorial Biography of R Vaughan Williams, 1971. Novels: Metamorphoses, 1966; Set to Partners, 1968; The Yellow Dress, 1984. *Honours:* Fellow, Royal College of Music; Honorary Fellow, Royal Academy of Music; Member, Royal Northern College of Music. *Hobbies:* Theatre, concert and opera going; Reading; Travel; Gardening. *Address:* 66 Gloucester Crescent, London NW1 7EG, England.

VAUGHN Justine Katherine, b. 3 Sept. 1950, Chicago, USA. Fiberartist, Designer. m. John R. Vaughn, 13 Oct. 1973, 1 son. *Education:* Harper College; Northeastern Illinois State University. *Appointments:* Central Telephone Co., 1967-79; Self employed Fiberartist, 1979-. *Publications:* Line of Handpainted Clothing Justine. *Memberships:* Surface Design Association; DuPage Textile Arts Guild; American Craft Council; F.A.C.E.T.S. *Honours:* Recipient, various honours and awards. *Hobbies:* Reading; Needle Artist. *Address:* 302 Ardmore Ct., Vernon Hills, IL 60061, USA.

VAUPEL Bodil Gobel Larsen, b. 25 Sept. 1946, Roskilde, Denmark. Architect; Professor. m. James Walton Vaupel, 24 June 1967, 2 daughters. *Education:* BS, Architecture, Massachusetts Institute of Technology, 1972; MArch, North Carolina State University, 1974; Registered Architect: North Carolina, 1980; Minnesota, 1986; Certificate, National Council of Architectural Registration Board. *Appointments:* BRW, Minneapolis, Minnesota, USA, 1985-86; Principal, Architects Henning Larsen and Bodil Vaupel Inc, 1986-; Professor, Minneapolis College of Art and Design, 1987-. *Creative works:* Aviary, North Carolina (co-deisgner), 1980; Head House Greenhouse, North Carolina State University (co-designer), 1980; Addition, Pillsbury Research Center (co-designer), 1986. *Memberships:* American Institute of Architects; Minnesota Society, American Institute of Architects; Chair, Scandinavian Architecture Commission, Scandianvian Center, Augsburg College, Board Member, Programme Committee; Winter Cities. *Hobbies:* Drawing; Painting; Piano, organ and harpsichord; Skiing; Canoeing. *Address:* 917 Dartmouth Avenue S E, Minneapolis, MN 55414, USA.

VEASEY Josephine, b. 10 July 1930, London, England. Vocal Consultant. 1 son, 1 daughter. *Appointments:* Opera singer, 1949-83; Teaching privately and Vocal Consultant for English National Opera. *Creative Works:* Has sung every major mezzo-soprano role in repertory; many foreign engagements have included: Salzburg Festival, La Scala Milan, Metropolitan Opera House New York and Paris Opera;

Recordings with Karajan, Solti, Bernstein and Colin Davis. *Honours:* CBE, 1970; Honorary RAM, 1972. *Address:* 2 Pound Cottage, St Mary Bourne, Andover, Hants, England.

VELASQUEZ Ana Maria, b. 18 Nov. 1947, Callao, Lima, Peru. Language Teacher. m. Scott Mathew Nakada, 19 Mar. 1981. *Education:* BA, San Marcos University, Lima, 1969; Science courses, Federico Villareal University, Lima, 1970; Postgraduate, Paris VI University, France, 1971-72; Computer courses, Prince George College, Maryland, USA, 1983-84; Proficiency certificate, Quechua language, Yachay Wasi College, Lima, 1986. *Appointments:* Teacher, San Jose de Cluny, Lima, 1968-71; Translator, Aubert & Duval, Paris, 1972-76; Linguistic coordinator, Servicio de Maguinaria, Lima, 1977-80; Education consultant, Inlingua, Washington DC, USA 1981-83, CACI Inc, Arlington, Virginia 1982-84; Director, AKTA International, Silver Spring, Maryland, 1984-. *Publications:* Pronunciacion Basica Universal, 1974; South American Dialects, 1977; Abbreviated Telephone Communications System, 1984; Teaching Languages to Adults, 1985; Languages: 365 Days, 1986; Teaching Languages to Children, 1987. *Memberships:* Teacher Association, Washington DC; Past president, Chosica Chess Club, Peru; Various offices, Literacy Campaign, Chosica. *Honour:* Paula Scott Merit Award, Maryland, 1986. *Address:* 12404 Lima Drive, Silver Spring, Maryland 20904, USA.

VELLA Ruth Ann, b. 18 Aug. 1942, West Chester, USA. Realtor; Lecturer. m. Frank Vella, 8 Aug. 1961, 2 daughters. *Education:* Graduate, Realtor's Institute. *Appointments:* Realtor: Reeve Realty 1968-73, Heritage Realty 1973-; Instructor: Wilmington College 1974-85, Delaware State College 1975-, University of Delaware 1976-85; Speaker, numerous conventions & seminars throughout USA, Realtors National Marketing Institute, 1987-. *Memberships:* Instructor, National Association of Realtors (NAR); Dean, Assistant Dean, Instructor, Realtor's National Institute. *Honours:* Omega Tau Rou award, NAR, 1986; GRI designation, Realtor's Institute; CRB designation, Realtor's National Marketing Institute. *Hobbies:* Aerobics; Tennis; Racquetball; Dancing; Nutrition; Investing in real estate. *Address:* 23 Tenby Chase Drive, Newark, Delaware 19711, USA.

VELLACOTT Jo, b. 20 Apr. 1922, Plymouth, England. Writer. m. Peter Newberry, 7 Jan. 1949, div. 1976, 1 son, 2 daughters. *Education:* BA Honours History 1943, MA 1947, Oxford University; MA, Toronto University, Canada, 1964; PhD, History, McMaster University, 1975. *Appointments:* WRNS, 1944-46; Teacher, South Africa, 1947-49; Instructor, part-time, various Canadian universities, 1963-80; Assistant Professor, (History) Acadia University 1980-81, (Women's Studies) Simone de Beauvoir Institute, Concordia University, Montreal 1982-87; Adjunct Fellow, Simone de Beauvoir Institute, 1987-89. *Publications include:* Books: Bertrand Russell & Pacifists in 1st World War, 1980; Co-Editor, Militarism v. Feminism, 1987. Contributions to: Reweaving the Web of Life, ed. Pam McAllister, 1982; Peace Movements & Political Cultures, ed. Chatfield & Van Den Dungen, 1988; Various journals. Also Poetry, reviews. *Memberships:* Council of Peace Research in History; American Historical Association; Voice of Women. *Honours:* Fellow, Institute for Advanced Studies in Humanities, Edinburgh University, 1976; Calouste Gulbenkian Fellow, Lucy Cavendish College, Cambridge, 1976-78; Grants, Social Science & Humanities Research Council, Canada, 1969-70, 1987-88; Friend in Residence, Woodbrooke College (Quaker), UK, 1987-88; Honorary Life Fellow, Simone de Beauvoir Institute. *Hobbies:* Active, various capacities, Religious Society of Friends (Quaker); Study & practice of non-violence, & non-separatist feminist pacifism. Also: Tennis, photography, drawing, painting, hill walking. *Address:* Kingston, Ontario, Canada.

VELLENGA Kathleen, b. 5 Aug. 1938, Nebraska, USA. m. James Vellenga, 9 Aug. 1959, 1 son, 2 daughters. *Education:* BA, Macalester College, 1959. *Appointments:* St Paul Public Schools, 1959-60;

Minesota Montessori Foundation, 1972-73; Children's House Montessori, 1973-78; Minesota House of Representatives, 1981-. *Memberships:* Chair, Health Start, 1986-88; UC League of Women Voters; etc. *Honours:* Recipient, various honours and awards. *Hobbies:* Children; Music; Hiking. *Address:* 2224 Goodrich, St Paul, MN 55105, USA.

VELS Verna Barbara Robertson, b. 13 June 1933, Reitz, South Africa. Television Executive. *Education:* BA, University of Pretoria. *Appointments:* Staff, South African Broadcasting Corporation, 1954-; Radio announcer, arranger, presenter, children's, women's & arts programmes, 1954-74; Organiser, magazine & children's television programmes, 1974-83; Programme Director, African TV 1983-85,; Co-Productions & Sponsorships 1985-87; Coordinator, TV Children's & Educational Programmes, 1987-89; Director, Programme Services, Television, 1989-. *Creative work includes:* Author, various radio serials & plays, adults & children, 1956-73; Creator, children's character Liewe Heksie, (Dear Little Witch), stories originally for radio, book series published 1965-, also record series with self-narration; 2 Liewe Heksie series adapted for TV, 1978, 1982. *Memberships:* Afrikaans Writers Guild; Federation of Afrikaans Cultural Organisations; Wine Tasters Guild, Johannesburg. *Honours:* Federasie van Rapportryerskorpse (cultural organisation); Prize for Liewe Heksie, as contribution to South African children's literature. *Hobbies:* Travel; Music; Books; Wine; Cooking; Animals; Writing; Doing various voices for children's fantasy characters, radio & television. *Address:* South African Broadcasting Corporation, Private Bag X41, Auckland Park, Johannesburg 2006, South Africa.

VENZON Flordelinda, b. 1 Aug. 1941, Masbate, Masbate, Philippines. Teacher. m. Ricardo S Venzon, 6 Feb. 1960. 3 sons, 1 daughter. *Education:* BS, E.Ed, University of Manila, 1966; MA 1981, EdD 1987, Ortanez University. *Appointments:* Teacher, Quirino Elementary School, 1967-; Professor, Ortanez University, 1987-. *Memberships:* Quirino Elementary Teachers' Club; Boy Scout of the Philippines; Girl Scout of the Philippines; Legion of Mary; Association of the Philippine Colleges of Arts & Sciences; Women's Club; Pilipino Club, Adviser; Parents Teachers Association. *Honours:* College Scholar, 1963-66; Constant honour pupil in the Elementary Grades, 1948-54. *Hobbies:* b3Reading books; Gardening; Crocheting; Watching betamax; Going to the movies. *Address:* 109 K-7th Street, Kamias, Quezon City, Philippines 110?

VERBY Jane Crawford, b. 3 Oct. 1923, La Crosse, Wisconsin, USA. Writer. m. John Edward Verby, 15 June 1946, 3 sons, 1 daughter. *Education:* BA cum laude, Carleton College, Northfield, Minnesota, 1945; Various extension courses, writing. *Appointments:* Publication Department, Mayo Clinic, 1945-46; Minnesota Poll, Minneapolis Star, 1946-47; Tutor, Onondaga College, 1988. *Publications:* Books: How to Talk to Doctors, 1977; Patterns, novel, 1986. *Memberships:* President, County Medical Auxiliary; Historian, Pen Women; Newsletter Chair, Hennepin County Auxiliary. *Honours:* Valedictorian, high school, 1941; 2nd prize, article writing, Cardiff, Wales, UK, 1978. *Hobbies:* Swimming; Walking; Skiing. *Address:* 9609 Washburn Avenue South, Minneapolis, Minnesota 55431, USA.

VERDON-ROE Vivienne Marion, b. 15 July 1949, Winchester, Hampshire, USA. Film maker. m. Michael Porter, 6 Sept. 1987. *Education:* Montessori Kindergarten Teaching Diploma, 1968; Secondary School Teacher's Certificate (with distinction), 1974. *Appointments:* Kindergarten Teacher, London, 1969-70; Editor and Publisher of newsletter Spirals, USA, 1976-82; Independent film-maker, 1982-; President, Education Film & Video Prohject, 1983-. *Creative works:* Slide-tape show: The Desecration of a Sacred Lane; 5 films/videos: In the Nuclear Shadow: What can the Children tell Us?, 1983; What About the Russians? 1983; The Edge of History, 1984; Women for America, For the World, 1986; Go For It! 1987. *Memberships:* Academy of Motion Picture Arts and Sciences; International Documentary Assoc; Women in Film; Film Arts Foundation; National Council of Women of the US; Board of Directors, Rainforest Action Network; Board of Advisors, Women's Action for Nuclear Disarmament (WAND). *Honours:* Between 1983 and 1988 recipient of 25 film festival awards including 2 Academy Award nominations and one Oscar; Mt Diablo Peace Center, Certificate of Esteem and Appreciation, 1989; The Helen Caldicott Leadership Award, 1989. *Hobbies:* Photography; my dog, Oscar; Political activism; Women's issues; Interviewing interesting people. *Address:* P O Box 13157, Oakland, CA 94611, USA.

VERGERONT Susan B, b. 30 Nov. 1945, Milwaukee, Wisconsin, USA. State Representative, Wisconsin Assembly. m. 1 Apr. 1967, 2 sons, 1 daughter. *Education:* BS, Political Science, University of Wisconsin, Madison, 1967. *Appointments:* Research Associate, Wisconsin Legislative Council, 1968-70; Executive Director, Grafton Chamber of Commerce, 1978-80; Account Executive, Public Relations Firm, Vollrath Associates Inc., 1981-. *Memberships:* Grafton Jaycees, former regional, State Director, Vice President; Grafton Chamber of Commerce, Vice President, Grafton School Board; Ozaukee Council on Alcohol, Director on Board; Manitou Girl Scout Council, Director on Board; Assembly Committees on Labour, Ways & Means and Industry Trade & Small Business; Chair, Wisconsin Women's Council; Member, Wisconsin Coastal Management Council. *Honours:* Outstanding Young Woman, Grafton, 1980; Outstanding Young Wisconsinite, 1981; US Jaycee Women's Congress, 1983. *Hobbies:* Reading; Camping; Skiing. *Address:* 390 Vista View Drive, Cedarburg, WI 53012, USA.

VERNICK Andrea Merrill, b. 18 Nov. 1949, Newark, New Jersey, USA Executive. *Education:* BA, American University, 1971. *Appointments:* Clerical Promotion Department, 1972, Manager, Promotions USA, 1975, Director, Promotions USA, 1977, Estee Lauder Inc; Executive Director, Promotions & Co-Op Advertising, 1982; Vice President, Promotions & Co-Op Print Advertising, 1988. *Memberships:* National Association Female Executives; Fashion Group, Advertising Women of New York; American University Alumnae Association. *Hobby:* Reading. *Address:* c/o Estee Lauder Inc., 767 Fifth Avenue, New York, NY 10153, USA.

VICKLAND Saibra Selene, b. 18 Feb 1943, New York City, USA. Artist; Writer. m. Gary Heligman, 14 Jan. 1984. *Education:* AA, Dean's Honours, Santa Monica College, California, 1968; BA magna cum laude, University of California, Los Angeles (UCLA), 1970; MFA, Otis Art Institute, Parsons School of Design, Los Angeles, 1980. *Appointments include:* Contracts Administrator, technical illustrator, commercial artist, 1961-71; Art teacher, 1972-76; Art Library Assistant, Otis Art Institute, 1979-80; Administrative assistant to Suzanne Lacy 1981-82, and Rachel Rosenthal 1984-86, performance artists; Architectural model maker, 1982-83; Independent artist 1980-; Freelance writer, art critic, 1981-. *Creative works include:* Installations, sculpture, proposals, drawings, paintings; Contributions, various art publications; Book on performance art in preparation. 10 solo exhibitions, various locations, California, Pompeii (Italy), Dorset & Edinburgh (UK), 1971- ; Group exhibitions, California, 1970-; Work in various private collections. *Memberships:* Numerous professional bodies including: Artists Equity; California Confederation of Arts; College Art Association; International Platform Association; UCLA Arts Council. *Honours:* Woman of Year & scholarship, Bank of America, 1968; Leadership award & scholarship, Santa Monica College, 1968; Nominee, Fulbright-Hayes scholarship, Otis Arts Institute, 1979; Biographical recognition. *Hobbies include:* Environmental Conservation; Arts administration. *Address:* 12600 Indianapolis Street, Los Angeles, California 90066, USA.

VICZAY Marika von, b. Hungary. Psychologist;

Naturopath. divorced. *Education:* BBA, University of Budapest, 1954; MSD, Philosophy, University of New York, USA, 1962; PhD, Psychology, 1973. *Appointments:* St John Hospital, Budapest, 1954-56; Ancora State Hospital, New Jersey, USA, 1958-60; Founder, President, In Search of Inner Serenity Inc., 1972-. *Memberships:* American Holistic Medical Association; New York Academy of Sciences; National Federation of Business & Professional Womens Club; National Female Executive Association; Holos Institute of Health. *Honours:* Certificate, Superior Achievement to Cancer Research, Life Force co., 1986. *Hobbies:* Research; Education; Travel; Sun, Sand & Sea. *Address:* 16 Arlington Street, Asheville, NC 28801, USA.

VIEHMYER Laura Lacy, b. 3 Oct. 1955, Baltimore, Maryland, USA. Manager, Human Resources/Administration. m. James E Vaughn, 3 July 1982. 1 son. *Education:* BA, Psychology and Education, University of Maryland, 1986; Graduate coursework, Rollins College. *Appointments:* Senior Personnel Analyst, Seminole County Government, 1978-81; Director of Personnel, Piezo Technology, 1981-84; Manager, Human Resources/Administration, EBS, 1984- *Memberships:* American Society for Personnel Administration, State Director for Florida 1989, Professional Accreditation Coordinator 1988, District Director State Conference Chair 1987, Chapter President, Orlando 1985-86; Florida Public Personnel Association, East Central Florida Area Coordinator, 1981. *Honours:* Phi Kappa Phi, 1976; Psi Chi, 1976; University of Maryland State Scholarship, 1974; Personnel Executive of the Year (Central Florida), 1986; Earned SPHR (Senior Professional in Human Resources) designation, 1986; Outstanding Young Women of America, 1983; Federal Incentive Scholarship, 1974; University Student Scholarship, 1974. *Hobbies:* Aerobics; Cooking. *Address:* c/o Travelers/EBS, Inc, 2701 Maitland Center Parkway, Maitland, FL 32751, USA.

VIEIRA DA SILVA Marie-Helene, b. 13 June 1908, Lisbon, Portugal. Naturalizee 1956. m. Arpad Szenes. *Education:* Ecole de B.A. Portugal Eu France (1928); Acad de la Grande Chaumiere under Bourdelle and Despiau; Sculptor, studied painting under Dufresne, Friesz, Fernand Leger and Bissiere, also engraving under Hayter, L'Atelier 17. *Creative works:* First one-man exhibition 1932; in Portugal 1935, 1936; Brazil, 1940-47; settled in Paris 1947; One-man exhibitions at Galerie Pierre 1948, 1951, 1955; Galerie Jeanne Bucher (eleven between 1932 and 1986); Galerie Knoedler, New York 1961, 1963, 1966; Retrospective exhibitions at Kestner-Gesellschaft 1958, Musee de Grenoble, Galleria Civica d'Arte Moderna, Turin 1961, Museum of Modern Art, Paris, Boymans-van Beuningen, Rotterdam, Kunsternes Hus, Oslo, Kunsthalle Basel, Foundation Calouste Gulbenkian, Lisbon 1969-70; Galeries Nationales Gzaud Palais, Paris, 1988; Works in the major galleries of the world. *Honours:* 1st Int Prize Sao Paulo Biennal 1961; Prix Nat des Arts, Paris 1966; 1st Grand Prix Florence Gould 1986; Chevalier, Legion d'honneur, Commdr des Arts et Lettres, Grand Croix Saint Jacques a l'epee 1977; Nominee, honorary life membership, The Art Gallery of Ontario, Toronto, Canada; Honorary Member, The Royal Academy, London, England, 1988. *Address:* c/o Guy Weelen, 8 avenue Frochot, Paris 9e, France.

VIERLING Barbara Mathilde, b. 8 Aug. 1939, Weiden/OPF, Bavaria, Germany. Clinical Psychologist. *Education:* Abitur, Weiden/OPF, 1958; Studies in Psychology and Law, 1958-61; Pre-Diploma, University of Munich, 1961; Merrill-Palmer Institute for Human Development and Family Life, Detroit, USA, 1961-62; Psychology studies, Munich, 1962-64; Diploma in Psychology, Ludwig Maximilian University, Munich, 1964; Training in Psychoanalysis, Freud Institute, Frankfurt am Main, 1971-76. *Appointments:* Psychologist, Binghamton State Hospital, New York, USA, 1962; State Hospital, Haar, Munich, Federal Republic of Germany, 1965; Heckscher Hospital for Children, Munich, 1965; School Guidance Char.

Zillmann, Munich, 1966; Foundation for Child Guidance, Weiden/OPF, 1966-67; Child Guidance, Carites, Frankfurt am Main, 1971-80; Private Practice, Frankfurt am Main, 1980-. *Publications:* Contributor to professional journals. *Memberships:* Berufsverband Deutscher Psychologen e V. *Honours:* Fulbright Scholarship for 1 year at Merrill Palmer Institute, 1961-62; Victor Gollancz Scholarship for 1 year in 2 psychiatric hospitals, 1965-66. *Interests:* Divine Healing; Zen. *Hobbies:* Swimming; Skiing; TV; Reading. *Address:* Neuhofstrasse 36/II, 6 Frankfurt am Main 1, Federal Republic of Germany.

VIGLIANTE SZYDLOWSKI Mary Frances, b. 8 Sep. 1946, Albany, New York, USA. Writer. m. Frank Joseph Szydlowski, 17 Apr. 1971, 1 daughter. *Education:* BA, Anthropology major, Sociology minor, State University of New York, Albany, 1971. *Appointments:* Correspondent, The Record, Troy, New York, 1988-. *Publications:* Go Away Julie May (children's book); Novels: Worship the Night; Silent Song; The Colony; The Land; Source of Evil; The Ark. *Memberships:* Authors Guild; Authors League; Science Fiction Writers of America; Hudson Valley Writers Guild. *Hobbies:* Camping; Hiking; Fishing; Handicrafts. *Address:* 92 B Columbia Turnpike, Rensselaer, NY 12144, USA.

VILLARD Katharine Neilley, b. 29 Mar. 1938, New York City, USA. University Administrator; Graphic Artist; Editor. *Education:* BA, English, California State University, Los Angeles, 1979; MA Humanities 1981, MA History 1981, PhD History 1988, University of Arkansas. *Appointments:* University of Arkansas: Teaching assistant, Department of History, 1983- 84; Administrative assistant, summer, 1984; Senior Editor, UA Press, 1984-86; Graphic artist, Printing Services Office, 1987-88; Assistant Director, Admissions, 1988-. *Publications:* Articles: Semantics & Future Audiences, 1977; Scenes from an English Netherland, 1982; Great Railroad Celebration, 1983. Also: Villard: Years of Fortune, biographical study of Henry Villard 1835-, unpublished disserttion, 1988. *Memberships:* Women in Scholarly Publishing; Alumnae, Stanford University Publishing Institute. *Honours:* Honourable Mention, Poetry Centre, 1988; Outstanding Graduate Student, University of Arkansas, 1983; Phi Alpha Theta; National Dean's List; Dean's List, California State University. *Hobbies:* Editing scholarly non-fiction; Graphic design. *Address:* PO Box 441, Farmington, Arkansas 72730, USA.

VILLAROSA Celia Jessica L., b. 28 June 1953, Manila, Philippines. Clinical Psychologist; Airline Executive; Management Consultant. m. Leovigildo Villarosa, 3 May 1980, 1 daughter. *Education:* BS, Education; MA, Industrial Psychology; PhD, Counselling Psychology. *Appointments:* Manager, Personnel, Administration & Purchasing, Manila Gas Group of Companies, 1980-83; Managing Consultant, United Human Resources Management Inc, 1983-86; Managing Director, International Management Consultants Inc, 1986; Training Director, Century Park Sheraton-Manila, 1987; Manager for Personnel, Telefunken Semiconductors, 1988; Director, Personnel & Administration, Air Pacific Crake, 1988-. *Memberships:* Past President, Premiere Toastmasters Club; Personnel Management Association, Philippines; Philippine Society for Training & Development; Philippine Marketing Association; Philippines Psychological Association. *Honours:* Outstanding Dissertation Award; Outstanding Educator & Civic Leader, Friendly Christian Brotherhood Association, Philippines, 1988. *Hobbies:* Writing; Jogging; Aerobics. *Address:* 12 Talisay Road, Mahogany Homes, Bagumbayan, Taguig, Metro Manila, Philippines.

VILLENEUVE Gisele, b. 4 June 1950, Montreal, Canada. Writer. *Education:* BA, Communications, University of Quebec, 1972. *Appointments:* Writer-Producer, BBC, London, UK, 1975-76; Freelance Writer, translator, Ottawa & Calgary, 1976-; Journalist, Radio Canada, Calgary, 1983-84; Scriptwriter, Access, Alberta, 1979-. *Creative work includes:* Novel, Rumeurs

de la Haute Maison, 1987; 4 Radio dramas; 3 short stories. *Memberships:* ACTRA; Union des ecrivains quebecois. *Hobbies:* Reading Fiction & Non-Fiction; Gastronomy; Travel; Mountaineering. *Address:* c/o ACTRA, 260 Mount-Royal Place, 1414 8th Street SW, Calgary, Alberta, Canada T2R 1J6.

VINCENT Clare, b. 20 Aug. 1935, Jersey City, USA. Museum Curator. *Education:* AB, College of William & Mary, 1958; MA, Institute of Fine Arts, New York University, 1963; Certificate of Museum Training, Institute of Fine Arts and Metropolitan Museum of Art, 1963. *Appointments:* Assistant to Curator, Cooper Union Museum for the Arts of Decoration, 1961; Curatorial Assistant, Western European Arts, Metropolitan Museum of Art, 1962-67; Assistant Curator, 1967-72, Associate Curator, European Sculpture and Decorative Arts, 1972-; Consultant, Adler Plaentarium, Chicago, 1985-. *Publications:* Contributor To: Liechtenstein The Princely Collections, 1985; Author, Rodin at the Metropolitan Museum of Art, 1981; Co-author, To Finance a Clock, The Clockwork Universe, 1980. *Memberships:* American Section, Antiquarian Horological Society, Vice President 1977-; International Union of the History & Philosophy of Science; Scientific Instrument Commission, Corresponding Member, 1981-; New York Academy of Science, History of Science Section, Vice Chairman, 1988-; College Art Association, etc. *Honours:* Phi Beta Kappa, 1957; Lor Botetourt Medal, College of William & Mary, 1958. *Hobbies:* Ballet & Concert Going; Gardening. *Address:* European Sculpture and Decorative Arts, Metropolitan Museum of Art, Fifth Ave., & 82nd St., New York, NY 10028, USA.

VINCENT Morwenna Anne, b. 13 Dec. 1932, Perth, Western Australia. Academic. *Education:* Registration Certificate, Library Association of Australia, 1961; BA, Australian National University, 1968. *Appointments:* Librarian: Swinburne Institute of Technology, Melbourne, Victoria; Australian Forestry School, Canberra, Australian Capital Territory; CSIRO Research Laboratories, Canberra; Australian National University, Canberra; Canberra Public Library Service; Australian Parliamentary Library, Canberra, 1957-74; Lecturer in Library and Information Studies, Canberra College of Advanced Education, 1970-. *Publications:* Bibliographies and directories published by professional associations; Contributor of articles and reviews in professional journals; Several conference papers presented. *Memberships:* Australian Federation of University Women; Australian Federation of Academic Staff Associations; Federation of College Academics; Australian National University Convocation. *Hobbies:* People; Ideas. *Address:* Centre for Library and Information Studies, School of Liberal Studies, Canberra College of Advanced Education, PO Box 1, Belconnen, ACT 2616, Australia.

VINGE Joan (Carol) Dennison, b. 2 Apr. 1948, Baltimore, Maryland, USA. Writer. m. James Raymond Frenkel, 8 June 1980, 1 son, 1 daughter. *Education:* BA, Anthropology major, German minor, San Diego State University. *Appointments:* Salvage Archaeologist, 1971; Writer, 1972-. *Publications:* Catspaw; The Snow Queen; World's End; Psion; Phoenix in the Ashes; Other novels and stories. *Memberships:* Science Fiction Writers of America (Recent Member, Nebula Awards Jury). *Honours:* Hugo Award for Best Novelette, Eyes of Amber, 1977; Hugo Award for Best Novel, The Snow Queen, 1981; Nominated for several other Hugo and Nebula awards; Best Book for Young Adults, Psion, American Library Association. *Hobbies:* Needlework and sewing; Riding; Anthropology and mythology; Science and technology. *Address:* c/o Merrilee Heifetz, Writers House, 21 W 26th Street, New York, NY 10010, USA.

VIOLET Arlene M., b. 19 Aug. 1943, Providence, Rhode Island, USA. Lawyer. *Education:* AB, Salve Regina College, 1966; JD, Boston College Law School, 1974. *Appointments:* Public Interest Attorney, Civil Rights, Poverty Law, Criminal & Juvenile Justice Law Reform, Handicapped Law, Environmental Law, 1976-84;

Attorney General, Rhode Island, 1984-87; Partner, Pearlman, Vogel & Violet Law Firm, 1987-. *Publications:* Convictions, autobiography, 1988; It's Alright If You Leave Us, article, 1988. Also: Radio talk show hostess, WKRI-AM. *Memberships:* National Association of Attorneys General, 1984-87; National District Attorneys Association; Business & Professional Womens Association; Executive Women in Government. *Honours:* Adjunct Professor, RI School of Desgn, 1979-80; Visiting Lecturer, Carlow College 1983, University of Maine 1988; Scholar-in-residence, Wheaton College, 1983; Brainerd Currie Scholar, University of Macon Law School, 1985; Costello Scholar, Loyola College, 1986; Price Scholar, University of Houston, 1986; Honorary Doctorate, New England School of Law, 1986. *Hobbies:* Lecturing; Writing. *Address:* 750 East Avenue, Pawtucket, Rhode Island 02860, USA.

VIORST Judith, b. 2 Feb. 1931, Newark, New Jersey, USA. Writer. m. Milton Viorst, 30 Jan. 1960. 3 sons. *Education:* BA Rutgers, 1952; Research Affiliate, Washington Psychoanalytic Institute, 1981. *Publications:* Projects: Space, 1962; 150 Science Experiments Step by Step, 1963; The Natural World, 1965; The Changing Earth, 1967; Sunday Morning, 1968; I'll Fix Anthony, 1969; Try it Again Sam, 1970; The Tenth Good Thing About Barney, 1971; Alexander and the Terrible Horrible No Good Very Bad Day, 1972; My Mama Says There Aren't Any Zombies, Ghosts, Vampires, Creatures, Demons, Monsters, Fiends, Goblins, or Things, 1973; Rosie and Michael, 1974; Alexander, Who Used To Be Rich Last Sunday, 1978; The Good-bye Book, 1988. Poems: The Village Square, 1965-66; It's Hard to be Hip over Thirty and other Tragedies of Married Life, 1968; People and other Aggravations, 1971; How did I get to be Forty and other Atrocities, 1976; When Did I stop being Twenty and other Injustices, 1987. If I were in Charge of the World and other Worries, 1981. Psychoanalytic Publications: Creative Writing and Ego Development, 1980; Experiences of Loss at the End of Analysis: The Analyst's Response to Termination, 1982. Non-Fiction: The Washington Underground Gourmet, with Milton Viorst, 1970; Yes Married, 1972; A Visit from St Nicholas (To a Liberated Household), 1974; Love & Guilt & The Meaning of Life, Etc. 1979; Necessary Losses, 1986. *Memberships:* Washington Psychoanalytic Society; Board member, National Center for Clinical Infant Programs. *Honours:* Emmy Award, 1970; Silver Pencil Award, 1973; Penney-Missouri Magazine Award, 1974; Spirit of Achievement Award, Albert Einstein College of Medicine, 1975; Georgia Children's Picture Storybook Award, 1977; American Academy of Pediatrics Award, 1977; American Association of University Women Award, 1980. *Hobbies:* Reading; Movies.

VIRE-TUOMINEN Mirjam, b. 15 Aug. 1919, Kuhmoinen, Finland. Translator. *Education:* BA, Helsinki University, 1946. *Appointments:* Translator, Ministry of Social Affairs, 1947-49; Participant, Founding Congress, International Movement of the Defenders of Peace, Paris, 1949. *Memberships:* Presidential Committee, World Peace Council; Co-Founder, Finnish Movement, Defence of Peace, General Secretary, Finnish Peace Movement, 1949-; Councillor, Helsinki City Council, 1968-76; MP, 1970-79; General Secretary, WIDF, 1978-. *Honours:* International Lenin Prize. *Address:* Women's International Democratic Federation, Unter den Linden 13, Berlin 1080, German Democratic Republic.

VIRGO Julie Anne Carroll, b. 14 June 1944, Adelaide, South Australia. Management Consultant. m. Daniel Thuering Carroll, 20 Aug. 1977. *Education:* MA Librarianship 1968, PHD 1974, Executive MBA 1983, University of Chicago, USA. *Appointments:* Repatriation Department, South Australia, 1962-66; Senior Lecturer, University of Chicago, USA, 1968-; Director of Education, Medical Library Association, 1972-77; Executive Director, Association of College Research Libraries, American Library Association, 1977-84; Executive Vice President & Chief Operating Officer, Carroll Group Inc, 1984-. *Publications:* Costing & Pricing

Information Services, 1985; Marketing for Libraries, 1986; Strategic Planning for Not-for-Profit Institutions, 1986. *Memberships:* Past President, American Society for Information Science; American Library Association; Institute for Management Consultants; American Management Association. *Honours:* Fellow, University of Chicago, 1967-68; Grant, National Library of Medicine, 1967-69; HEA Title IIB Fellowship, 1969-72; Doctoral Award, ASIS; Outstanding Young US Leader, Council on US & Italy, 1985. *Hobbies:* Skiing; Tennis; Sailing; Reading; Theatre. *Address:* The Carroll Group Inc, 875 North Michigan Avenue, Suite 3311, Chicago, Illinois 60611, USA.

VISHER Emily B, b. 21 May 1918, Norwich, Connecticut, USA. Clinical Psychologist. m. John S. Visher, 31 Dec. 1959, 2 sons, 2 daughters, 2 stepsons, 1 stepdaughter. *Education:* BA, Wellesley College, 1940; PhD, Psychology, University of California, Berkeley, 1958. *Appointments Include:* Pannelist, Speaker, 1978-; Course leader, 1978-; Stepfamily Workshop Leader, 1979-; Instructor, University of California, 1983-. *Publications:* Articles in: Journal of Divorce; Conciliation Courts Review; Journal of Family Therapy; Families in Trouble, etc. *Memberships:* Co-Founder, Stepfamily Association of America Inc., President 1979-83, Director, 1984; American Orthopsychiatric Association; Wellesley College Alumnae Association; Founding Member, Stepfamily Association of California Inc.; American Association of University Women; etc. *Honours:* Phi Beta Kappa, 1940; Sigma Xi, 1940; Anne Louise Barrett Fellowship, 1953-54; National Fellowship, AAUW, 1956-57; Alumnae Achievement Award, Wellesley College, 1986. *Address:* 599 Sky Hy Circle, California 994549, USA.

VISSER Audrae Eugenie, b. 3 June 1919, Hurley, South Dakota, USA. Teacher; Poet. *Education:* BSc., South Dakota State University, 1948; MA, University of Denver, 1954. *Appointments:* Moody Co. Country Schools, 1939-43; Hot Springs Public School, Pierre Indian School, American Village School (Japan), 1943-55; HS English & Science in Elkton, Flandreau, DeSmet, Pierre, Windom & Verdi, 1955-88. *Publications:* Poetry: Rustic Roads, 1961; Poems for Brother Donald, 1974; Meter for Momma, 1974; Poems for Pop, 1976; South Dakota, 1980; Honyocker Stories, 1981; Country Cousin, 1986. *Memberships:* Delta Kappa Gamma; American Association of University Women; National League of American Pen Women; Western Women in the Arts; Business & Professional Womens club; National Federation of Womens Clubs; etc. *Honours:* Poet Laureate, South Dakota, Former Governor Richard Kneip, 1974; etc. *Hobbies:* Writing; Art; Photography; Science; Scrapbooks. *Address:* 710 Elk Street, Elkton, SD 57026, USA.

VISSER Maretha Johanna, b. 11 Jan. 1960, Bellville, South Africa. Psychologist; Researcher. m. Johan Neethling, 28 May 1988. *Education:* BA, cum laude, 1980; BA (Honours), cum laude, 1981; Master's degree, Counselling Psychology, cum laude, 1983; Teacher's Diploma, cum laude, 1987. *Appointment:* Psychologist, Centre for Child and Adult Guidance, Human Sciences Research Council, 1984-. *Publications:* Author of two academic publications. *Memberships:* Institute for Clinical Hypnosis; Secretary of Executive Committee, Institute for Counselling Psychology; Deputy chairman local branch, Institute for Counselling Psychology. *Honour:* Honoured as best student in Faculty, Rand Afrikaans University, 1980. *Hobbies:* Music; Pottery; Reading; Literature. *Address:* P O Box 914-1059, Elarduspark 0047, South Africa.

VITALE Emily R Murphy, b. 22 Sept. 1929, Philadelphia, USA. Sales. m. 8 Feb. 1952. *Education:* Diplomas, Certificates, various Colleges. *Appointments:* John McHugh, 1986-88; Central RE, 1986. *Publications:* 5 Paintings. *Memberships:* Various professional organisations. *Honours:* Senate Award, Standard Evening High School. *Hobbies:* Reading; Knitting; Politics. *Address:* 6730 Mongomery Ave., Upper Darby, PA 19082, USA.

VOGEL Mary, b. New York City, USA. Traffic Engineer. m. Frederick G Vogel. *Education:* BA, Sociology, Lake Erie College, 1964; MRPI, Urban and Regional Planning, Pennsylvania State University, 1984; MS, Traffic Engineering, Polytechnic University of New York, 1985. *Appointments:* URS Consultants, currently; Jacquemart Assoc; City of New York. *Memberships:* Institute of Traffic Engineers; Transportation Research Board; Enno Foundation for Transportation; Womens' Transportation Seminar; American Planning Association. *Hobby:* Computers.

VOGEL Willa Hope, b. 14 Jan. 1929, Valley Falls, Kansas, USA. Restaurateur. m. David Laverl Vogel, 25 Dec. 1943, 2 sons, 1 daughter. *Education:* High school. *Appointments:* Owner, manager, draper's shop, Topeka, 1956-68; Owner, Plantation Steak House 1962-, North Star Supper Club 1972-, Topeka. *Memberships:* Kansas & Topeka Restaurant Associations, (3rd V.P.); Greater Topeka Chamber of Commerce. *Honours:* Plantation Steak House included in book, Day Trips from Kansas City, 1984; North Star Supper Club featured, Midwest Living magazine, 1988; Kansas Steak House of Year. *Address:* Plantation Steak House, 6646 NW Topeka Boulevard, Topeka, Kansas 66617, USA.

VOGT Esther, b. 19 Nov. 1915, Collinsville, USA. Freelance Writer. m. Curt Vogt, 24 May 1942, deceased 1975, 1 son, 2 daughters. *Education:* AA, Tabor College. *Appointments:* Instructor, Christian Writers Institute, 1970-. *Publications:* Cry to the Wind, 1965; The Sky is Falling, 1968; High Ground, 1970; Ann, 1971; 14 books published. *Memberships:* Kansas Authors Club, 4th District President, 1965-; Delta Kappa Gamma, 1972-. *Honours:* Recipient, various honours & awards. *Hobbies:* Piano; Reading. *Address:* 113 South Ash, Hillsboro, KS 67063, USA.

VOIGT Leigh, b. 4 July 1943, Johannesburg, South Africa. Artist. m. Harold F Voigt, 25 Aug. 1966. 2 sons. *Education:* Johannesburg School of Art, 1961-63. *Appointment:* Worked in the studios of two Advertising Agencies, 1963-70. *Publications:* Illustrations in the following books: Mantis & The Moon, by Marguerite Poland; Once at Kwafubesi, by Marguerite Poland; Shadow of The Wild Hare, by Marguerite Poland; Foxtails by Ted Townsend; In The Wild, by Sue Hart; Nature's ABC, by Sue Hart; Back in the Wild, by Sue Hart; Eleven solo exhibitions and participation in many group shows both in South Africa and in North America. *Hobbies:* Nature and the preservation of our planet; Archaeology; Psychology; Reading; Music. *Address:* PO Box 81, Sohagen, 1207, South Africa.

VOIVODAS Gita Kedar, b. 2 May 1942, Baroda, India. Company President. m. Constantin Voivodas, 12 May 1972, deceased 1973. *Education:* BS, Maharaja Sayajirav University, Baroda, 1960; MA, Stanford University, USA, 1963; PhD, Columbia University, 1977. *Appointments:* Research Assistant, Cornell University, 1962; Teachers College, Columbia University, 1972-76; Assistant Professor, Fordham University, 1977-84; Research Director, Louis Harris & Associates, New York City, 1986-87; President, Professional Papers Associates, 1984-. *Publications:* Articles in: Journal of Education Psychology; RER. *Memberships:* Executive Board, Early Childhood Education; American Education Research Association; Society for Research on Child Development; National Society for the Study of Education; National Association of Female Executives. *Honours Include:* Valedictorian Gold Medal, 1960; PEO International Peace Scholarship, 1962-63; John Switzer Award, Stanford University, 1962-63; Grantee, Fordham University, 1981; Guest Editor, Journal of Educational Psychology, 1984. *Hobbies:* Travel; Cooking; Crosswords; Reading. *Address:* 390 Riverside Drive, New York, NY 10025, USA.

VOLID Ruth, b. Chicago, Illinois, USA. President, Owner, Ruth Volid Gallery Ltd. m. Paul Firedland, 9 Mar. 1941. 2 daughters. *Education:* Chicago Art Inst; Univ of Chicago; Chouinard Art School; Otis Art Inst; Am Acad of Art. *Appointments include:* Art Teacher; Owner, designer, fashion (hat) business; Owner, designer, dude ranch; Interior designer; Creative Dir, King Korn Stamp Co, 1962-70; PR, The Merchandising Grp, NY, 1970-72; Collectors' Showroom Inc, Chiago (Art cons to interior designers, archts, corp collectors), 1970-; Curator of fibre artists, scuptors & printmakers and painters one-person shows; President, Owner, Ruth Volid Gallery Ltd. *Publications:* articles to numerous professional publications. *Memberships include:* Mus of Contemporary Art Affiliate Bd; Archives of Am Art, Smithsonian Instn; Presidents Club; Arts Club of Chicago; Art Inst of Chicago; Life Member: Am Soc Interior Designers, Ind; Fndn Mbr. *Honours:* Distinguished Service Award 1984, Industry Award 1984, Industry Foundation Award 1985, ASID. *Hobbies:* Reading; Art Museums; Theatre; Tennis; Music. *Address:* Ruth Volid Gallery, 225 W Illinois, Chicago, IL 60610, USA.

VON DASSANOWSKY Elfriede Maria, b. 2 Feb. 1924, Vienna, Austria. Opera singer; Pianist; Educator; Businesswoman. divorced. 1 son, 1 daughter. *Education:* Hochschule für Musik und darstellende Kunst, Vienna; Piano studies with Emil von Sauer and Eugenie (Wild-Volek); Voice studies with Paula Mark-Neusser; Drama studies with Eduard Volters. *Appointments:* As singer (Soprano/Mezzo), Debut: Susanna in Le nozze di Figaro, St Pölten; Principal roles and concert appearances in Vienna, St Polten, Hamburg, Flensburg, 1940s-50s, including: Agathe, Freischütz; Inez and Azucena, Il Trovatore; Mimi, Boheme; Hansel, Gretel, Hansel und Gretel; Hannerl and Heiderl, Das Dreimaderlhaus; Title role, Carmen; Baroness Adelaide, Der Vogelhändler; Lola, Cavalleria Rusticana; Komtesse Lizzi, Das Sperrsechserl; Queen's Lady, Zauberflöte; Prince Orlofsky, Fledermaus; Principal roles in operettas by Lehar, Stolz, Kalman, Benatzky, Heuberger, Zeller. Numerous Lieder recitals; Concert and radio recitals as Pianist, Vienna and Hamburg; Lecturer in Piano, Hochschule für Musik, Vienna; Broadcaster, Forces Broadcasting, BBC, Vienna, 1948-49; Actress in theatre and film, Vienna, St Pölten, 1946-53; Private vocal coach and piano instructor; Businesswoman. *Memberships:* AKM, Vienna; Auslandsösterreicherwerk, USA. *Honours:* Numerous academic awards, Vienna. *Hobbies:* Nature and animals; Travel. *Address:* 4346 Matilija Avenue, Sherman Oaks, California 91423, USA.

VON FRIEDERICHS-FITZWATER Marlene Marie, b. 14 July 1939, Beatrice, Nebraska, USA. Professor; Researcher. m. Robert De Saeger, 18 June 1983. 4 sons from previous marriages. *Education:* BS, Communication/English, Westminster College; MA, Communication, University of Nebraska; PhD, University of Utah; Certificate, Death Education and Counseling, Temple University, Philadelphia. *Appointments:* Reporter, LA Times, 1957-78; Teaching Assistant, University of Nebraska and University of Utah, 1978-83; Assistant Professor, Mass Communications, University of So Colorado, 1983-85; Associate Professor, Communication Studies, California State University, 1985-; Developed and conducted workshops on Communications Skills: Bergan Mercy Hospital and Mercy Care Center, Omaha, 1980-81; American Cancer Society and Hospice of Salt Lake, 1981-82; Conduct workshops, seminars and courses in health communication, Utah, Colorado and California, 1983-; Assistant Clinical Professor, Family Practice, School of Medicine, UC, Davis, 1987-. *Memberships include:* Health Communication Association; Speech Communication Association; Association for the Behavorial Sciences and Medical Education; Association for Woemn in Science; American Association of University Professors; Health Care Public Relations & Marketing, Northern California; Public Relations Society of America, Health Division. *Honours:* Teaching Fellowships: University of Nebraska and University of Utah, 1979-83; Over 30 state, regional and national awards for excellence in writing, editing, publications design and photography; Faculty Merit recipient, Mass Communications Department, University of Southern Colorado, 1983-84. *Hobbies:* Volunteer work; President, Board of Directors, Hospice

Care of Sacramento, Inc, 1986-87. *Address:* 5020 Hackberry Lane, Sacramento, CA 95841, USA.

VON RAFFLER-ENGEL Walburga, b. 25 Sept. 1920, Munich, Germany. Company President; Professor Emerita. m. A. Ferdinand Engel, 1 son, 1 daughter. *Education:* Litt.D., University of Turin, Italy, 1947; MS, Columbia University, USA, 1951; PhD, Indiana University, USA, 1953. *Appointments:* Freelance Journalist, 1945-; Professor, Linguistics, Vanderbilt University, 1965-85, Emerita 1985; Senior Research Associate, Institute for Public Policy Studies, 1985-; President, Kinescis International Inc. *Publications:* 2 books, co-author 1 book; Editor, 10 books; 300 articles; Invited lectures: Americas, Europe, Asia. *Memberships:* various scholarly associations. *Honours:* Grants, many scholarly organizations in USA, and from NATO and UNESCO; First Woman Professor to Sue Vanderbilt University for Sex Discrimination, 1969. *Address:* 372 Elmington Ave., Nashville, TN 37205, USA.

VON SELDENECK Judith Carol Metcalfe, b. 6 June 1940, High Point, North Carolina, USA. President; Executive, Search firm. m. George Clay Von Seldeneck, 15 Apr 1972. 2 sons. *Education:* BA University of North Carolina, 1962. *Appointments:* Executive Assistant to Senator Walter Mondale, 1962-672; President, Diversified Search, Inc, 1972-; Chief Executive officer, Diversified Health Search, 1986-. *Memberships:* Board of Directors, Meridian Bank Corp; Keystone Insurance Co; Private Industry Council; Boy Scouts of Philadelphia; Fellowship Commission; Greater Philadelphia Chamber of Commerce; Zoological Society; Committee of 200 (top 200 women in business in USA). *Honours:* Industry Week Magazine, 1988. *Hobbies:* Golf; Reading; Jogging. *Address:* Diversified Search, Inc, Two Mellon Bank Center, Philadelphia, PA 19102, USA.

VOS SAVANT Marilyn, b. 11 Aug. 1946, Missouri, USA. Writer. m. Robert Jarvik, MD, 23 Aug. 1987. *Appointments:* Family Investment Business, 5 years; Full-time writer. *Publications:* Published short stories, essays and political satire in magazines and newspapers under pseudonym; Book in conjunction with Omni Magazine; Ask Marilyn, question-and- answer column, Parade Magazine; Brain Building, forthcoming book. Stage play: It Was Poppa's Will, recently produced; The New Patriot, in progress; Short Shorts, collection of humorous short stories, in progress. *Memberships:* MENSA; International Legion of Intelligence; Triple Nine Society; International Society for Philosophical Enquiry; Prometheus Society; Mega Society, Head, 1985-. *Honours:* Highest IQ for childhood and adult scores listed in Guinness Book of World Records. *Hobby:* Writing letters. *Address:* Parade Publications, Inc, 750 Third Avenue, New York, NY 10017, USA.

VOTAW Carmen Delgado, b. 29 Sept. 1935, Humacao, Puerto Rico, USA. Administrator. m. 10 Oct. 1960, 2 sons, 1 daughter. *Education:* Diploma, secretarial sciences, magna cum laude, University of Puerto Rico School of Business Administration; BA, International Studies, American University School of International Service, Washington DC.; Doctorate in the Humanities (Honorary) Hood College, MD. *Appointments include:* Participant, over 40 international & regional meetings, official United Nations & OAS-system bodies, 1964-; Vice president, director, Overseas Education Fund, League of Women Voters, 1964-81; National president 1976-78, President DC chapter 1975, National Board Member 1975-80, National Conference of Puerto Rican Women; Federal Programmes Specialist, Office of Commonwealth of Puerto Rico, Washington DC, 1972-76; Co-chair, National Advisory Committee on Women, 1977-79; US representative, executive committee 1977-81, president 1978-80, Inter-American Commission of Women, Organization of American States, Washington DC; Vice president, Information & Services for Latin America (ISLA), 1981-84; Administrative assistant (chief of staff), Congressman Jaime B. Fuster, US House of Representatives, 1985-. Numerous conferenes, committees, Women's Issues. *Publications:* Book,

Puerto Rican Women, some Biographical Profiles; Contributor, Notable American Women. *Memberships include:* Offices: Inter-American Institute of Human Rights, Girl Scouts USA, Western Hemisphere Committee; World Girl Guides and Girl Scouts Association (WAGGS); National Women's Conference, Pan American Development Foundation. Member, various other bodies. *Honours:* Numerous awards, certificates of appreciation & other recognitions, various organisations. *Hobbies:* Music; Reding; Tennis; Collecting Masks. *Address:* 6717 Loring Court, Bethesda, Maryland 20817, USA.

VOUKOVITCH DE AGUIRRE LUGO Stevane, b. 16 Oct. 1933, Brussels, Belgium. Essayist; Journalist. m. (1)P. B. Corbett, 2 sons, (2) Carlos de Aguirre Lugo. *Education:* Licence, Philosphie et Lettres, University of Louvain, Belgium, 1955; Diploma, English Studies, University of Cambridge, UK, 1964; Licenciatura en Letras Espanolas, Universidad Autonoma de Mexico, 1966. *Appointments:* Chief Editor, Journal du Petrole, World Congress, Mexico, 1967; Mexican correspondent 1967-78, 1982-86, special correspondent Central & South America 1967-78, various Belgian journals; Head, French Section, Linguistic Services, Olympic Games, Mexico, 1968; Professor, French Literature & Linguistics, Universidad Autonoma de Guadalajara, Mexico, 1971- 78; Assistant, Georges Sion, Secretaire Perpetuel, Academie Royale de Langue et de Litterature, Belgium, 1978-82. *Publications include:* Numerous articles, essays, French, English, Spanish, various countries. *Memberships:* Academie des Sciences, Arts et Belles-Lettres de Dijon; Founder member, Asociacion Mundial de Mujeres Periodistas y Escritoras Mexico; Institute of Linguists, UK. *Honours:* Francisco Zarco international trophy, journalism, Mexico, 1968; Bronze Medal, journalism, Olympic Games, 1968; Vice President, AMMPE, 1988. *Hobbies:* Piano playing; Watercolour painting; Gardening. *Address:* Chateau du Puits, Faverelles, 45420 Bonny-sur-Loire, France.

VRANA Muffy Stewart Fisher, b. 11 Mar. 1933, Omaha, Nebraska, USA. Author; Lecturer; Business & Manners Consultant. m. (1) Laird Fisher, 7 Aug. 1958 (dec. 1980), 2 sons, 1 daughter, (2) Theodore W. Vrana, 27 Nov. 1982. *Education:* BSc, Education, University of Nebraska, 1954. *Appointments:* Teacher, Omaha Public Schools, 1954-59; TV Editor, Sun Newspaper, 1963-65; Editor, Executive Magazine, 1972-75; Communications Director, Century 21 RE of Midwest, 1976-79; Public Relations & Promotions Director, Easter Seal Telethon, 1979-81; Muffy Fisher Associates, 1978-; Mass Media, 1978-; Seminars, 1978-; Manners Consultant, 1987-. *Publications:* Books: Cash from your Closet, 1984; Synergists, 1985; Alive & Writing in Nebraska, 1986; Picture Perfect, 1990. *Memberships:* Public Relations Society of America; American Society for Training & Development; National Speakers Association; Local & State President, National League of American Pen Women; Offices, various community organisations. *Honours:* Merit Mother, NMA, 1984; Essay award, 1985; Non-fiction book award, Non-Fiction Writers 1986; Commendation, Nebraska Writers Guild, 1987; President's Award, NLAPW, 1988. *Hobbies:* Reading; Teaching; Volunteer work. *Address:* 3260 Van Dorn, Lincoln, Nebraska 68502, USA.

VROMAN Barbara Fitz, b. Chicago, Illinois, USA. Author; Publisher; Speaker; Teacher. 2 sons, 1 daughter. *Appointments:* Editor & Columnist, Waushara Argus, 1968-72; Summer Instructor, University of Wisconsin, School of Arts at Rhinelander, 1977-89. *Publications:* Novels: Tomorrow Is A River; Sons of Thunder. Published: A Glory from the Earth; My Unicorn Thinks He is Real; Gift of the Strangers. *Memberships:* Wis Regional Writers Assoc; Board Member, Wis Author & Publisher Assoc. *Honours:* Milwaukee Journal Leslie Cross Award, 1977 and 1981; National Newspaper Assoc First Amendment Award, 1979. *Address:* Box 300 Rt 1, Hancock, Wisconsin 54943, USA.

VYAS Reeta, b. 25 May 1953, Morbi, Gujarat, India. Physicist. m. Dr Surendra P Singh, 19 May 1982. 1

son. *Education:* BSc (Hons) 1973, MSc Physics 1975, Banaras Hindu University, (BHU) India; PhD Physics, SUNY at Buffalo, USA, 1984. *Appointments:* Honorary Lecturer, BHU, Women's College, India, 1976; Visiting Assistant Professor 1984-88, Research Assistant Professor and Assistant Chairperson, 1988-, University of Arkansas, Fayetteville, USA. *Publications:* Over 20 articles to professional journals; Numerous papers presented at meetings. *Membership:* American Physical Society. *Honours:* CSIR (India) Junior Research Fellowship, 1976-78; Merit Scholarship, BHU, India, 1970-73; Merit Scholarship, Bihar Government, India, 1970-73. *Hobbies:* Dancing, learned Indian Classical Dance, Kathak; Performed and choreographed many classical dances, folk dances and dance dramas. *Address:* Physics Department, University of Arkansas, Fayetteville, AR 72701, USA.

W

WACHS Barbara Ruth Eidelman, b. 15 June 1936, Brooklyn, New York, USA. Coordinator of Social Action Activities; Educator. m. Saul P Wachs, 27 Jan. 1957. 1 son, 3 daughters. *Education:* Bachelor of Hebrew Literature, Jewish Theological Seminary, 1956; BS Education, City College of New York, 1957; MA Education, Ohio State University, 1969; Doctoral candidate, pending, Jewish Theological Seminary. *Appointments:* Tifereth Israel Religious School, 1966-70; Torah Academy, Columbus, Ohio, 1967-60; Cleveland College of Jewish Studies, 1968-69; Ramaz School, New York City, 1970-72; Solomon Schecter Day School, Newton, 1972-75; Akiba Hebrew Academy, 1975-; Gratz College, 1979-80. *Publication:* Article: Annotated Bibliography on Jewish family, 1987. *Memberships:* Life Member, Hadassah Women; Amit Women; Soviet Jewry Committee, Jewish Community Relations Council, Philadelphia; National Conference for Soviet Jewry; Conference for Alternative in Jewish Education; School Committee Akiba Hebrew Academy; Temple Beth Hillel; Family Educators Network; Interfaith Womens Committee; Founding Member, Action for Soviet Jewry, Boston. *Honours:* Hayim Greenberg Fellowship, Jewish Agency for Israel Jewish Theological Seminary, 1955; Chipkin Talmud Award, Jewish Theological Seminary, 1956; Saul & Barbara Wachs Endowment Fund, established, 1976; Jewish Agency Summer Fellowship, 1983; Louis A Pincus Senior Educators Fellowship, 1984-85. *Interests:* Communal service at geriatric facilities; Service to Homeless; Outreach Program of Philadelphia Committee for the Homeless; Active on behalf of Soviet Jewry. *Address:* 107 Maple Ave, Bala Cynwyd, PA 19004, USA.

WACHSNICHT Gale Annette, b. 10 Oct. 1946, Tampa, Florida. Advertising Executive. *Education:* Chelsea Art Institute, London, England, 1967-69; St Louis Community College, 1972, 1980; Washington University, St Louis. *Appointments:* Account Exec, food broker, Halls- Fanger-Leeker, St Louis, 1979-82; Account Exec, wine cons, Allied Wine and Spirits, St Louis, 1982-84; Account exec, nat advt, St Louis Globe Dem, 1984- 86; Nat advt manager 1986, Vice President, partner, Bates Advt & Assocs, St Louis, 1987-. President, Focus Advertising, 1987-. *Publications:* Contributor of articles to professional journals. *Memberships:* Board of directors, Soulard Restoration Group, St Louis, 1977-84; Press Club; Sierra Club; Landmarks Association; Allied Food Club. *Hobbies:* Renovating houses; Community activites; Antiques. *Address:* Focus Advertising and Assocs, 2351 S 13th St, Saint Louis, MO 63104, USA.

WADDINGTON Miriam, b. 23 Dec. 1917, Winnipeg, Canada. Writer; Professor Emeritus. m. Patric Waddington, 5 July 1939, 2 sons, 2 daughters. *Education:* BA, 1939; Diploma, Social Work, 1942; MA, 1968; MSW, University of Pennsylvania, 1945. *Appointments:* Various social agencies, 1942-63; McGill University, 1948-51; Professor, Literature, York University, Canada, 1964-. *Publications:* Green World, 1945; The Second Silence, 1955; The Season's Lovers, 1958; The Glass Trumpet, 1966; Call Them Canadians, 1968; Say Yes, 1969; The Dream Telescope, 1972; A M Klein, 1970; The Price of Gold, 976; Mister Never, 1978; The Visitants, 1981; Summer at Lonely Beach, stories; Collected Poems, 1986. *Honours:* J I Segal Prize, 1975, 1987. *Hobbies:* World Literature; Mountains; People. *Address:* 32 Yewfield Crescent, Don Mills, Ontario, Canada M3B 2Y6.

WADDS Jean Emeline, b. 16 Sept. 1920, Ontario, Canada. Corporate Director. m. (1) Clair Casselman, 24 May 1946, 1 son, 1 daughter, (2) Robert Wadds, 4 Aug. 1964. *Education:* BA, University of Toronto, 1940. *Appointments:* Member of Parliament, 1958-68; Ontario Municipal Board, 1975-79; Canadian High Commission, London, 1979-83; Royal Commission on Economic Union & Development Prospects for Canada, 1983-85. *Memberships:* Empire Club of Canada; Rideau Club, Ontario; Albany Club, Toronto. *Hours:* Honorary Doctorates, University of Toronto, Acadia University, Dalhousie University, St Thomas University; Freeman, City of London. *Hobbies:* Walking; Swimming; Travel. *Address:* PO Box 579 Prescott, Ontario, Canada KOE 1TO.

WADE Julia Howard, b. 2 Dec. 1928, Alexandria, Louisiana, USA. Owner, Furniture Store; Decorator. m. Nelson Ernest Brooks Wade, 29 June 1948, 2 sons, 2 daughters. *Education:* BA, Baylor University, 1948; Graduate study, Paris, France, 1952; Certified Home Furnishings Counsellor, SWHFA, 1979. *Appointments:* Organiser, Director, Children's Theatre, San Augustine, Texas, 1948-52; High school teacher, English 1948, Bible study 1956; Part owner, Augus Theatre, 1948-58; Partner, Decorator, Advertising Manager, Buyer, Nelsyn's Furniture Store, 1958-; Lecturer in field. *Creative work includes:* Writer, director, 250th anniversary historical pageant (cast of 350), San Augustine, 1967-68; Historical articles, East Texas Historical Quarterly, various newspapers; Design classes & articles; Director, Texas Sesquicentennial Pageant, San Augustine County, 1986. *Memberships:* Numerous professional & community organisations including: National Association of Decorating Products; National Association of Executive Females; International Platform Association; Vice President, San Augustine Chamber of Commerce; Development Board, East Texas Baptist University; Nelsyn's Store Outstanding Small Retailer in Southwest, 1979; Chairman Board Directors, San Augustine Public Library, 1984-85; Charter Member Window Coverings Association of America, 1986; Allied Member (Practitioner) American Society of Interior Designers (A.S.I.D.), 1990. *Honours:* Numerous community awards including: President's Award 1973, Citizen of Year 1987, SA Chamber of Commerce; Leadership award, Kirsch Drapery Hardware, 1984; Public service award, Rotary Club, 1980; Honorary 25-year membership, SA Historical Society; George Washington medal of Honor, Freedoms Foundation at Valley Forge, 1988. *Hobbies:* Interior decorating; Painting; Reading; Skiing; Travel; Collecting; Historical research; Family. *Address:* 128 East Columbia Street, San Augustine; Texas 75972, USA.

WADSTEIN Margareta, b. 14 Feb. 1945, Vasteras, Sweden. Judge, Stockholm City District Court. *Education:* Law degree 1970, Degree in Russian 1970, University of Uppsala; Degree in French, University of Stockholm, 1980. *Appointments:* Entered the judiciary, 1970; Stockholm Court of Appeal, 1973; The Rents and Tenancies Court of Appeal, 1975; Legal Adviser at the Ministry of Labour, 1981; Deputy Equal Opportunities Ombudsman, 1983; District Judge at the Stockholm City District Court, 1988. *Publications:* Articles on Women's issues in Swedish and international papers. *Memberships:* Fulltime trade union representative for the Swedish Judges Members of SACO/SR, 1978-79; Member of Legal Committee on Sex Discrimination of the Council of Europe, 1982-83; Member of UN Committee on the Elimination of Discrimination against Women (CEDAW), 1984-88; Rapporteur, 1987-88; Consultant to the UN, ILO on women's issues, 1989. *Address:* Alphyddevagen 53, S-131 35 Nacka, Sweden.

WAELTI-WALTERS Jennifer Rose, b. 13 Mar. 1942, Wolverhampton, England. University Professor; Author. m. 30 Dec. 1972. *Education:* BA, Honours, 1964, PhD, 1968, London; L-es-L (Lille), 1966. *Appointment:* University of Victoria, Canada, 1966-. *Publications:* Alchimie et litterature, 1975; J.M.G Le Clezio, 1977; Michel Butor, 1977; Fairytales and the Female Imagination, 1982; Icare ou l'evasion impossible: etude psycho- mythique de J.M.G. Le Clezio, 1981; Jeanne Hyvrard, 1988; Love as a Lifestyle: Feminist Novelists of the Belle Epogue, 1989. *Memberships:* Canadian Federation of the Humaniies, Board & Executive 1980-85; Association of Professors of French, Executive & Committees, 1980-85; Humanities Association, Executive 1981-86. *Hobbies:* Reading; Music; Travel;

Swimming; Photography. *Address:* 1934 Crescent Road, Victoria, Canada BC V8S 2H1.

WAGNER Judith Buck, b. 25 Sept. 1943, Altoona, Pennsylvania, USA. Investment Manager. m. 15 Mar. 1980. 1 daughter. *Education:* BA, History, University of Washington, 1965; Graduate, New York Institute of Finance, New York, 1968; Chartered Financial Analyst I, Professional Designation, Institute of Chartered Financial Analysts, University of Virginia, 1972. *Appointments:* Security Analyst, Morgan, Olmstead, Kennedy & Gardner, Los Angeles, California, 1968-71; Research Consultant, St Louis, Missouri, 1971-72; Security Analyst, Boettcher & Co, Denver, 1972-75; President, Wagner Investment Counsel, 1975-84; Chair, Wagner & Hamil, Inc, 1983-. *Memberships include:* Registered Investment Advisor, Securities and Exchange Commission, 1975-; Chair & Director, The Women's Bank, 1977-; Chair, Equitable Bankshares of Colorado, Inc, 1980-; Board of Directors, Denver Society of Security Analysts, 1976-83; Financial Analysts Federation, 1972-; Director, Equitable Bank of Littleton, 1983-; Board of Directors, Junior League Community Advisory Committee, 1979-. *Honours:* Cosmopolitan, Making It; Savvy, Women on the Go; Outstanding Young Women of America; Leadership Denver Outstanding Alumna, 1986; Salute Special Honoree Award, Big Sisters, 1987; Minora Yasui Community Volunteer Award, 1986. *Address:* 410 17th Street, Suite 840, Denver, Colorado 80202, USA.

WAHDAN Josephine Barrios, b. 11 Jan. 1937, Firebaugh, California, USA. Librarian. m. Khalid Wahdan, 28 Aug. 1973, divorced 1985. 1 son, 2 daughters. *Education:* BA, foreign languages with distinction, San Diego State Univ, 1970; MLS, University of Wisconsin-Milwaukee, 1975. *Appointments:* Community Librarian Intern, Milwaukee Public Library, 1972-74; Community Librarian, 1975-78, Acting County Librarion 1979, County Librarian 1980-, San Benito County Library. *Publications:* Poems: The American Poetry Anthology, Vol VI, 1986; Hearts on Fire: A Treasury of Poems on Love, Fol III, 1986. *Memberships:* Founder, Friends of San Benito County Library, 1979; Libraries Plus, 1983-84; South Bay Cooperative Library System, 1984-85; California Library Association; County Librarians Association; Reforma: Hispanic Chamber of Commerce; World Congress of Poets. *Honours:* Certificate of Appreciation, United Community Center and Milwaukee Library Board of Trustees, 1978; Library Bookfellow of the Year, Friends Milwaukee Public Library, 1974; Citizen of the Year, Mexican American Committee on Education, 1987. *Hobbies:* Tennis; Camping. *Address:* San Benito County Library, 470 Fifth Street, Hollister, CA 95023, USA.

WAHL Anna Maria, b. 25 Oct. 1956, Stockholm, Sweden. Researcher, Women's Studies. m. Hans P. C. Peterson, 1981, 1 son, 1 daughter. *Education:* MBA 1980, doctoral studies current, Stockholm School of Economics. *Creative work includes:* Currently preparing thesis, Female Economists & Engineers in Sweden. *Memberships:* Board, Association of Women's Studies, Stockholm; Forum for Kvinnliga Forskare och Kvinno Forskning. *Address:* Handelshögskolan, Box 650, 1383 Stockholm, Sweden.

WAIDLEY Ericka Kristine, b. 18 May 1949, Los Angeles, California, USA. Healthcare Administrator/ Nurse. m. R.E. Waidley, 13 June 1970, 2 sons. *Education:* BS, Nursing, San Diego State University, 1972; MS, Family Health Care Nursing, 1976, University of California. *Appointments Include:* Various Nursing positions in hospitals and schools of nursing, 1972-79; Assistant Director, Nursing/Coordinator Patient Care Planning, University of California, San Francisco, 1979-80; Clinical Instructor, General Pediatrics, 1980-83, Administrative Nursing Supervisor, 1983-86, Acting Director of Nursing, 1986, Miller Childrens Hospital; Assistant Professor, Maternal-Child Dept., University of California, Los Angeles, 1980-; Assistant Professor, Nursing, California State University, 1980-; Vice President, Patient Care Services, AMI/Irvine Medical

Centre, 1986-. *Publications:* Articles in: AJN; Pediatric Nursing; RN. *Memberships Include:* various professional organisations. *Address:* 9 Fallbrook, Irvine, CA 92714, USA.

WAINWRIGHT Hilda Alexander, b. 18 June, Teheran, Iran. Service Executive; Small Business Owner. m. (1) Boris Alexander, 27 May 1945, dec Aug 1961. 2 sons. (2) Richard A Wainwright, 18 Feb. 1977. *Education:* Ecole Jean D'Arc, Teheran, 1945; Brown Bus Sch, 1947; Gemological Inst Am, 1963; Banford Acad Styling, 1950. *Appointments:* Design Stylist, Elizabeth Arden, NYC, 1949-51; Owner, manager, Randough, NYC, 1960; Sales Rep, Roux Labs, Jacksonville, Florida also NYC, 1968-71; Mackey Internat Airline, Ft Lauderdale, Florida, 1971-73; Owner, Manager, CIR-Q-TEL Inc, Kensington, MD, 1980-; Exec vp, pres, 1982-84, Treas 1984-; Owner franchises Hairperformers Hair Salons; pres, HAW Enterprises; Pres, Armenian Gen Benevolant Union, NYC and Florida, 1945-. *Hobbies:* Tennis; Gardening; Painting in oil and acrylic; Bridge; Languages. *Address:* CQT Electronics Inc, 6600 Virginia Manor Road, Beltsville, MD 20705, USA.

WAITE Ellen Jane, b. 17 Feb. 1951, Oshkosh, Wisconsin, USA. Director of Unviersity Libraries. m. Thomas H Dollar, 19 Aug. 1977, divorced 1984. *Education:* BA, University of Wisconsin, Oshkosh, 1973; MLS, University of Wisconsin, Milwaukee, 1977. *Appointments:* Head of Cataloging, Marquette University, Milwaukee, 1977-82; Head Catalog Librarian, University of Arizona, Tuscon, 1977-82; Associate Director of Libraries 1983- 85, Acting Director Libraries 1985-87, Director of Libraries 1987-, Loyola University of Chicago. *Publications:* Contributing author: Research Libraries and Their Implementation of AACR2, 1985; Co-author, Women in LC's Terms, 1988. *Membership:* ALA. *Hobby:* Photography. *Address:* Loyola University of Chicago, Cudahy Library, 6525 N Sheridan Road, Chicago, IL 60626, USA.

WAKE Joanna Margaret (West), b. 8 May 1940, Crowborough, Sussex, England. Actress. m. Robert Peter West, 9 Feb. 1969, 1 son, 1 daughter. *Education:* Royal Academy of Dramatic Art, 1957-59. *Appointments:* Repertory, Prospect Theatre Company; Pop Theatre; many seasons with Young Vic Company touring; many shows abroad; West End Shows include: The Shot in Question, Getting Married, Joseph's Technicolour Dreamcoat, Dangerous Corner; TV Shows include: Series Sactuary, Compact, Lillie; worked extensively in radio. *Hobbies:* Collecting Ancient Bottles & Pots; Reading. *Address:* 4 Sibella Road, London SW4, England.

WAKE, Marvalee H, b. 31 July 1939, Orange, California, USA. Professor. m. David B Wake, 23 June 1962, 1 son. *Education:* BA, 1961, MS, 1964, PhD, 1968, University of Southern California. *Appointments:* Teaching Assistant, University of Southern California, 1961-64; Teaching Assistant, 1964-65, Instructor, 1966-68, Assistant Professor, 1969-73, University of Illinois; Lecturer, 1969-73, Assistant Dean, College of Letters & Science, 1972-73, Assistant Professor, 1973-76, Associate Professor, 1976- 80, Biology & Zoology, Associate Dean, College of Letters & Science, 1975-78, Vice Chairman, 1978-81, Professor, 1980-, Chairman, 1985-, Zoology, University of California, Berkeley; Guest Professor, various Universities. *Publications:* numerous articles in various journals including: Journal of Morphology; Herpetologica; Nature; Journal of Herpetology; Zoomorphologie; Experientia; American Zoologist; American Sciencist; etc. *Memberships Include:* AAAS; American Society of Ichthyologists & Herpetologists, President, 1984; American Society of Zoologists, Programme Officer, Vertebrate Morphology, 1986-88, Chair-Elect, 1988; Society for the Study of Evolution; etc. *Honours:* Recipient, John Simon Guggenheim Foundation Fellowship, 1988; numerous honours and awards. *Hobbies:* Art; Music; Archaeology. *Address:* Dept. of Zoology, University of California, Berkeley, CA 94720, USA.

WAKE-WALKER Anne (Lady), b. 4 Aug. 1920, London, England. Housewife; Voluntary Worker (charitable/community). m. Captain Christopher Wake-Walker, RN Retd., D.L. 10 Feb. 1944, 3 sons, 2 daughters. *Education:* Private, England, Paris, Vienna. *Appointments include:* WRNS officer, World War II. Current voluntary work: County President, Soldiers, Sailors & Air Force Association, Suffolk; President, National Society for Prevention of Cruelty to Children, East Suffolk; President, Olive Quantrill Singers; President, Stour Valley Arts & Music Society; President, East Bergholt Drama Group; Chairman, East Bergholt Committee, local Cheshire Home for Disabled. *Hobbies:* Classical Music; Gardens; Sewing & Patchwork; Antiques. *Address:* East Bergholt Lodge, Suffolk CO7 6QU, via Colchester, England.

WAKEFIELD Carolyn Denis Kampen, b. 2 Apr. 1955, St Louis, Missouri, USA. Missionary; Teacher. m. Dara Vernon Wakefield, 30 May 1975, 1 son, 2 daughters. *Education:* BA, Education, Lincoln University; MA, Korean Language, LTRC, Seoul, Korea; PhD, Korean History & Culture, Ko Chin Mal Univesity, Kwangju, Kore. *Appointments:* Elementary Teacher, Missouri, 1977-78; E. Song Hok School, Seoul, Korea 1985-87; Dean, Language Institute, Chook Um University, Kwangji, 1987-. *Publications:* Korean Language Acquisition for English Native Language Speakers, 1986; Article, Idiomatic Korean Language Patterns, 1987. *Memberships:* MSTA: F MB; KBM; Past President, Association of Korean Language Learners. *Honours:* Chestnut Queen, 1968; Honour Student, 1968-77; NHS Achievement Award; Kong Charome Award, Korea. *Hobbies:* Mountain Climbing; Hiking; Embroidery; Chinese character translation; Korean cooking; Education. *Address:* Korea Baptist Mission, PO Box 165, Seoul, South Korea 150.

WALDRON Sharon Elaine Cushman, b. 8 Nov. 1941, Boston, Massachusetts, USA. Real Estate Broker; Student Activities Worker. m. James E. Waldron, 15 Oct. 1961 (div. 1987), 1 son, 1 daughter. *Education:* AA, Massasoit Community College, 1984; Graduate, Realtors Institute, 1988. *Appointments:* Staff assistant, student activities, Massasoit Community College, 1983-; Anderson Real Estate Inc, 1984-. *Memberships:* Life member, American Society of Notaries; Brockton Board of Realtors; National Association of Realtors. *Honours:* Green Key Society, Massacoit Community College, 1983; Corrigan Award, BSA, 1975; Biographical listings. *Hobbies:* Reading; Travel. *Address:* 1725 Washington Street, East Bridge, Massachusetts 02333, USA.

WALDROP Rosmarie, b.24 Aug 1935, Kitzingen, Main, Germany. Writer/Translator. m. Bernard Keith Waldrop, 21 Jan 1959. *Education:* MA, 1960, PhD 1966, University of Michigan. *Appointments:* Wesleyan University 1964-70; SMU 1977; Brown University 1977-78; Tufts University 1979- 81; Brown University, 1983; Burning Deck Press 1963-. *Publications:* The Reproduction of Profiles, New Directions, 1987 (poems); The Hanky of Pippin's Daughter, Station Hill, 1987 (novel); Streets Enough to Welcome Snow, Station Hill, 1986 (poems). *Membership:* PEN. *Honours:* RI Governor's Arts Award, 1988; NEA Fellowship in Poetry 1980; Columbia Translation Center Award, 1978; Howard Fellowship 1974-75; Humboldt Fellowship 1970-71; Major Hopwood Award in Poetry, 1963. *Address:* 71 Elmgrove Avenue, Providence, RI 02906, USA.

WALFORD Diana Marion, b. 26 Feb. 1944, Southport, England. Doctor in Civil Service. m. Arthur David Walford, 9 Dec. 1970. 1 son, 1 daughter. *Education:* BSc (1st class) Physiology, 1965; MBChB 1968, MD, 1976, Liverpool University; MSc Epidemiol, London University, 1987; MRCP (UK), 1972; MRCPath, 1974; FRCPath, 1986. *Appointments:* Senior Registrar (Haematology) and other hospital posts, 1968-75; Medical Research Council Fellow, 1975-76; Senior Medical Officer, 1976-79; Principal Medical Officer, 1979-83; Senior Principal Medical Officer (Under-Secretary), Department of Health and Social Security,

1983-. *Publications:* Chapters in books on haematological side effects of drugs and use of blood and blood products; Scientific papers on alpha thalassaemia. *Memberships:* British Society for Haematology; Fellow, Royal Society of Medicine; Founder Member, British Blood Transfusion Society. *Honours:* George Holt Medal (Physiology), Liverpool University; J H Abram Prize (Pharmacology), Liverpool University; NLB and S Devi Prize (Epidemiology), London University. *Hobbies:* Theatre; Painting; Travel. *Address:* Department of Health and Social Security, Richmond House, Whitehall, London, England.

WALKER Annita Louise Curry, b. 28 Mar. 1941, Tallahassee, USA. Assistant Director. m. Leroy W. Walker, 15 Apr. 1965, 2 daughters. *Education:* BS, Chemistry, 1963; MS, Howard University, 1965; Diploma, Real Estate, 1974. *Appointments:* Research Chemist, US Treasury Dept. 1964-65, US Dept. of HEW, 1966-70, US Dept. Environmental Protection, 1970-72, University of Miami, 1974-76; Realtor, Universal Realty, 1976-79; Assistant Director, Information Services. *Publications:* A Diary of a Day; 15 research papers. *Memberships:* American Chemical Society, Speaker; Association of Official Analytical Chemists; Delta Sigma Theta; American Association for the Advancement of Science. *Honours:* Recipient, many honours and awards. *Hobbies:* Writing; Music; Needlepoint; Painting. *Address:* 2920 Harwood Street, Tallahassee, FL 32301, USA.

WALKER Candace Lea, b. 1 Aug. 1953, Middlesboro, USA. Forensic Psychiatrisst. m. Jerry East, 25 June 1983. *Education:* BS, 1974, MS, MD, 1978, University of Louisville; Residency Psychiatry, University of Louisville; Fellowship, Forensic Psychiatry, Medicaa College of Georgia. *Appointments:* Medical College of Georgia, Assistant Professor, 1985- 86; VA Medical Centre, Augusta, 1985-86; Kentucky Correctional Psychiatric Centre, Lagrange, 1986-. *Publications:* Articles in professional journals. *Memberships:* American Psychiatric Association; American Academy of Psychiatry and Law; American College of Forensic Psychiatry; Amerian Academy of Forensic Sciences. *Hobbies:* Teacher, Adult Sunday School; Adult Choir Member. *Address:* Kentucky Correctional Psychaitric Center, Lagrange, KY 40031, USA.

WALKER Carolyn Peyton, b. 15 Sept. 1942, Virginia, USA. Professor of English. m. Stuart Carter Walker, 26 Aug. 1967, divorced 1980. *Education:* BA, American Studies, Sweet Briar College, 1965; PhD Candidate Brown University, 1965-67; Certificate, French, Alliance Francaise, Paris, 1966; EdM, Education, Reading Tufts University, 1970; MA, English & American Literature 1974; PhD, English Education, College Reading & Composition, 1977, Stanford University. *Appointments:* Teaching Posts; Jamaica Plain, Massachusetts, 1966-67, Chesieres Switzerland, 1967-69, Boston, 1969-70, Newark, California, 1970-72; Instructor, School of Business, University of San Francisco, 1973-74; Evaluation Consultant, Institute for Professional Development, San Jose, 1975-76; Assistant Director, 1972-77, Director, 1977-84, Learning Assistant Centre, Stanford University; Associate Professor, English, San Jose State University, 1984-; President, Waverly Associates Educational Consulting, 1983-. *Publications:* Numerous papers, articles in professional journals. *Memberships Include:* National Council of Teachers of English; Northern Calfornia College Reading Association; National Reading Conference; Resource Centre for Women, Palo Alto; California Professors of Reading; International Reading Association; MLA. *Honours:* various awards in educational field. *Address:* 2350 Waverley Street, Palo Alto, CA94301, USA.

WALKER Gladys Lorraine, b. 11 Dec. 1927, Bridgeport, USA. Author; Journalist. m. Daniel R. Walker, 14 Apr. 1950, 3 children. *Education:* BA, College of Arts & Sciences, BA, School of Journalism, Syracuse University, 1949. *Appointments:* Freelance Writer. *Publications:* I Don't Do Portholes; contributor to textbooks; author, hundreds of magazine articles.

Honours: Non-Fiction Awards, National League of American Pen Women, 1962, 1970, 1972, 1974, 1987; Connecticut Press Club 2nd Prize, 1986, 3rd prize, 1988; National League of American Pen Women, Journalism Award, 1988. *Hobbies:* Music; Travel; Photography. *Address:* 21 Thorburn Ave., Trumbull, CTT 06611, USA.

WALKER Jeanne Murray, b. 27 May 1944, Parkers Prairie, Minnesota, USA. Professor of English. m. 16 July 1983. 1 son, 1 daughter. *Education:* BA, English, Wheaton College, 1966; MA, English, Loyola University, Chicago, 1969; PhD, English, University of Pennsylvania, 1974. *Appointments:* Haverford College, 1974-80; University of Delaware, 1975-88. *Publications:* Nailing Up The Home Sweet Home, 1980; Coming Into History, 1980; Fugitive Angels, 1985; Contributions to numerous journals and magazines. *Memberships:* MLA; Poets and Writers; PEN; Spenser Society of America. *Honours:* Atlantic Monthly Fellow, Bread Loaf School of English, 1965; English Fellow, University of Pennsylvania, 1972-73; Individual Artist Fellowship, Delaware State Arts Council, 1981; Individual Artist Fellowship, Pennsylvania State Council on The Arts, 1984, 1987, 1989; NEA Grant, 1984; Delaware Humanities Forum Fellowship, 1985; Award for Best Essay, Children's Literature Association, 1981. *Address:* 311 North 34th Street, Philadelphia, PA 19104, USA.

WALKER Lilly Julia Schubert, b. 2 May 1945, Jamestown, North Dakota, USA. Clinical Psychologist; Director Counselling Centre. m. James Walker, 24 Aug. 1969. 1 son. *Education:* BA, Jamestown College, Jamestown, 1967; MA 1969, PhD 1972, University of North Dakota; Internship, University of North Carolina Medical School, Chapel Hill, 1971-72. *Appointments:* Assistant and Associate Professor of Psychology 1972-87, Director of Counselling 1975-87, Brandon University, 1972-87; Counsellor 1987- 88, Director of Counselling 1988-, University of Manitoba, Canada. *Publication:* The Human Harvest: Changing Farm Stress to Family Success, 1987. *Memberships:* APA; CPA (Canadian Psychological Association); PAM (Psy Association of Manitoba); MPS (Manitoba Psychological Society); CMHA, Canadian Mental Health Association, President, Westman Branch. *Honours:* Westman Volunteer of the Year, CMHWA, 1986; Professional Woman of Distinction, YWCA, 1985; Founding Chairperson, Brandon University Daycare Centre, 1975; First Female Clinical Psychologist to graduate from University of North Dakota, 1972; Youngest Board Member appointed to Jamestown College Board of Trustees, 1972. *Hobbies:* Aerobics; Swimming; Biking; Tennis; Creative crewel; Writing (Poetry). *Address:* Counselling Centre, 474 University Centre, University of Manitoba, Winnipeg, Manitoba R3T 2N2, Canada.

WALKER Marjorie Ruth, b. 24 Aug. 1918, Kew, Victoria, Australia. Medical Practitioner. *Education:* Methodist Ladies College, Kew, Victoria; MB, BS 1944, Melbourne University; MRCOG 1950; FRCOG 1962; FRACOG 1980. *Appointments:* Alfred Hospital, 1944; Queen Victoria Hospial, 1945-47, 1949; Royal Children's Hospital, 1948; Mayday Hospital, Croydon, Surrey, England, 1951; Royal Melbourne Hospital, Australia, 1950; Honorary Obstetrician, 1956-68, Honorary Gynaecologist, 1956-83, Queen Victoria Hospital; Honorary Obstetrician, Queen Elizabeth Hospital for Mothers and Babies, 1956-80. *Publications:* Contributor of articles to medical journals. *Memberships:* Australian Medical Association; Victorian Medical Womens Association; Past President, Victorian Medical Womens Association; Melbourne Society of Women Painters and Sculptors. *Honour:* Member of the Order of Australia for Contribution to Medicine especially obstetrics and gynaecology, 1983. *Hobbies:* Wood sculpture; Needlework; Gardening; Cooking. *Address:* Flat 3, 9 Fordholm Road, Hawthorn, 3122 Victoria, Australia.

WALKER Moira Kaye Porter, b. 2 Aug. 1940, Riverside, California, USA. Company Vice President. m. Timothy Peter Walker, 30 Aug. 1958, divorced 1964,

3 sons, 1 daughter. *Education:* Riverside City College, 1973. *Appointments:* Bank of America, 1965-68; Abitibi Corp., 1968-70; Lily Division, Owens-Illinois, Riverside, California and Houston, Texas, 1970-77; Kent H. Landsberg Division, Sunclipse, 1977-. *Memberships:* National Association of Female Executives; Women in Paper, Treasurer, 1978-84. *Hobbies:* Reading; Gardening; Handicrafts. *Address:* Kent H. Landsberg div. Sunclipse, 1180 Spring St., Riverside, CA 92506, USA.

WALKER Sally Warden, b. 5 Feb. 1929, Wilmette, USA. Washington State Representative. m. O.B. Walker, 28 Dec. 1948, 1 son, 4 daughters. *Appointments:* Board Member, 1st Chairman, University Place Parks & Recreation Board, Tacoma, 1969-1975; Elected to Washington State House of Representatives, 1984-. *Memberships:* Tacoma/Pierce Co. Chamber of Commerce; Lakewood Chamber in Tacoma; etc. *Honours:* Recipient, various honours and awards. *Address:* 4617 Bellview Street West, Tacoma, WA 98466, USA.

WALKER Stella Archer, b. 29 Mar. 1907, Leicester, England. Writer. m. 23 Jan. 1942. *Education:* Stoneygate College, Leicester, 1918-24; Neuilly, Paris, France, 1924-25. *Appointments:* Wilson Barrett Company (Theatre), 1938-41; Art Correspondent, Horse & Hound, 1962-88. *Publications:* 4 anthologies; Horses of Renown; The Controversial Horse (with R.S.Summerhays); Sporting Art England 1700-1900; British Sporting Art in the 20th Century. *Memberships:* Founder, Trustee, British Sporting Art Trust; President, Donkey Breed Society; Governor, Arab Horse Society; Honorary Life Member, Society of Equestrian Artists. *Hobbies:* All country pursuits; Equestrian history; Reading; Art. *Address:* Watermill Farm, Rushlake Green, Heathfield, East Sussex TN21 9PX, England.

WALKER Wendy-Louise, b. 14 July 1935, Port MacQuarie, Australia. Psychologist. m. Geoffrey Shepherd Walker, 4 May 1956, 2 sons, 2 daughters. *Education:* BA Honours I 1959, PhD 1970, University of Sydney. *Appointments:* Lecturer, Senior Lecturer, Clinical Psychology, Department of Psychiatry 1964-73, Senior Lecturer & Acting Head 1974, Associate Professor & Head 1975-86, Associate Professor 1987-, Department of Behavioural Sciences in Medicine, University of Sydney. *Publications include:* Over 40 articles, professional journals; Co-author with S. Ballinger, Not the Change of Life: Breaking the Menopause Taboo, 1987. *Memberships:* Foundation Member & Board of Clinical Psychologists, Australian Psychological Society; International Society of Hypnosis; Offices, Australian Society of Hypnosis. *Honour:* Sydney University Medal, 1959. *Hobbies:* Painting; Reading; Genealogy, early Irish immigration to Australia; Keeping Whippets. *Address:* 14 Hammond Avenue, Croydon 2132, Sydney, Australia.

WALKER-SMITH Angelique Keturah, b. 18 Aug. 1958, Cleveland, Ohio, USA. Minister of Religion; Executive. m. R. Drew Smith, 16 Aug. 1980. *Education:* BA, Kent State University, 1980; MDiv, Yale University Divinity School, 1983. *Appointments:* Media associate, Urban League, 1979-80; Production associate, CBS-WFSB Radio, Hartland, Connecticut, 1981-82; Associate Minister, Convent Avenue Baptist Church, 1981-83; Associate Pastor, Central Baptist Church, 1983-86; Leader, Operation Crossroads Africa, 1983-85; Executive Director, Trenton Ecumenical Area Ministry, 1986-. *Publications:* Articles, American Baptist Magazine, National Baptist Voice; Response, Christianity's Crisis. *Memberships include:* Secretary, National Association of Ecumenical Staff; International Affairs Officer, Partners in Ecumenism; Wommen in Communications; Ecumenical Liaison, US National Baptist Convention; American Baptist Churches; Founder, Black Women in Ministry; National Association for Advancement of Coloured Peoples; US Black Churches Liaison Committee. *Honours:* Blue Key, 1979; Recognition award, Mercer County, 1987; Honoree, Operation Crosroads Africa, 1989; 1st runner-up, Miss America preliminary; Student award, Kent State, 1980;

2,000 Notable American Women, 1989. *Hobbies:* Tennis; Reading; Walking. *Address:* Trenton Ecumenical Area Ministry, 2 Prospect Street, Trenton, New Jersey 08618, USA.

WALL Susan Lee, b. 18 Feb. 1950, Cleveland, Ohio, USA. Artist. *Education:* BFA 1972, MFA 1974, Ohio University. *Creative Works:* One Woman Shows: Gallery 90, New York, 1974, 1976, 1978, 1980, 1982, 1984, 1986, 1988; Zanesville Art Center, 1975, 1986; Bonfoey On The Square (Strong Gallery), Cleveland, 1975, 1977, 1979, 1981, 1983, 1985, 1987; Gallery 200, Columbus, 1975, 1977, 1984, 1986; Canton Art Institute, 1976; Piccolo Mondo, Palm Beach, 1976, 1978; Sandusky Area Cultural Center, 1978; Foster Harmon Gallery, Sarasota, 1982, 1984, 1986; Classics, Kansas City, 1984. Also in Museums and Permanent Collections. *Memberships:* Catharine Lorillard Wolfe Art Club; Allied Artists of America, Inc; Nova-New Organization of Visual Arts; National Society of Painters in Casein & Acrylic; Victorian Society of America; National Historic Presentation. *Honours include:* 1st place award, Representational category and City of Atlanta Recognition Award, International Small Fine Art Exhibition, Phoenix Art Gallery, 1984; Special Mention, Artist Views the City, Gallery at the Old Post Office, Dayton, 1984; Honorable Mention, 9th Annual American National Miniature Show, Laramie Art guild, 1984; 2nd prize, 10th Annual American national Miniature Show, Laramie Art Guild, 1985; 2nd prize, 4th Annual International Small Painting Show, Cuyahoga Valley Art Center, 1986; Dr Maury Leibovitz Art Award, 1986, etc. *Address:* c/o Sue Wall Studio, 170 West End Avenue, Apt 30K, New York City, NY 10023, USA.

WALLACE Dora Eileen (Mrs Rash), b. 18 June 1897, Lorton, Cumberland. m. R H Rash, 4 Oct. 1922. 1 son, 2 daughters. *Education:* Malvern Girls' College; MA, Somerville College, Oxford. *Appointments:* 3 years Teaching in State Grammar Schools. *Publications:* 38 novels including: Barnham Rectory, 1934; Going to Sea, 1936; The Time of Wild Roses, 1938; Green Acres, 1941; the Noble Savage, 18945; Willow Farm, 1948; How Little We Know, 1949; The Younger Son, 1954; The Money Field, 1957; Richard & Lucy, 1959; Woman with a Mirror, 1963; The Turtle, 1969; Elegy, 1970; An Earthly Paradise, 1971; A Thinking Reed, 1973. *Memberships:* Numerous including PEN. *Honour:* Book Society Choice, 1934. *Hobby:* Painting. *Address:* 2 Manor Gardens, Diss, Norfolk, England.

WALLACE Elaine Maria, b. 15 May 1954, Newark, USA. Osteopathic Physician. *Education:* BS, Biology, University of Mississippi, 1976; DO, University Health Sciences, 1980. *Appointments:* Osteopathic Physician, Dept. Chairman, University of Health Sciences. *Publications:* Hospital Manual for Rape Crisis Intervention, 1982. *Memberships Include:* American Osteopathic Association; American Medical Association; American Women's Medical Association; Missouri, Jackson County Osteopathic Associations. *Honours:* DAR Good Citizen of the Year, 1976; Sigma Sigma Phi, 1979-80; Delta Omega Scholarship Recipient, 1980. *Address:* 5940 Kenwood, Kansas City, MO 64110, USA.

WALLACE Joan Scott, b. 8 Nov. 1930, Chicago, Illinois, USA. Civil Service, Administrator (Public Administration). m. Maurice Dawkins, 14 Oct. 1979. 3 sons. *Education:* AB, Bradley University, 1952; MSW, Columbia University, 1954; PhD, Northwestern University, 1973; Certificate for Educational Management, Harvard University, 1977; Certificate, Agribusiness Seminar. *Appointments:* Associate Professor, University of Illinois, 1967-73; Associate Dean and Professor, Howard University, 1973-76; Vice President, National Urban League, 1975-76; Vice President, Morgan State University, 1976-77; Assistant Secretary, US Department of Agriculture (USDA), 1977-81; Administrator, USDA Office of International Cooperation and Development, 1981-. *Memberships:* American Psychological Association; American Consortium for International Public Administration; Society for International Development; White House Committee on International Science, Engineering and Technology; National Association of Social Workers. *Honours include:* Outstanding Educator Award, University of Illinois, 1971; Distinguished Alumni Award, Bradley University, 1978; Honorary Doctorates: University of Maryland, 1979; Bowie State College, 1981; Presidential Rank of Meritorious Service, 1980; Senior Executive Service Superior Performance Bonus, USDA 1983, 1984, 1986; International Federation of Women in Agriculture, 1989. *Hobbies:* Collecting international art; Antiques. *Address:* USDA/OICD/OA, 14th and Independence Avenue, Washington, DC 20250, USA.

WALLACE Kathleen, b. 1 July 1950, Bronxville, New York, USA. Writer; University Professor; Philosopher. *Education:* BA cum laude, Rosemont College, 1972; PhD, State University of New York (SUNY), Stony Brook, 1983. *Appointments include:* Assistant Professor, Philosophy, Hunter College 1984, Hofstra University 1985-. *Publications:* Articles, professional journals: General Education & the Modern University, 1983; Philosophical Sanity, 1986; Substance, Ground & Totality, 1986; Nature, Power & Prospect: Justus Buchler's System of Philosophy, with Sidney Gelber, 1986; Making Worlds or Making Categories, 1987. Co-editor, introduction, Justus Buchler's Metaphysics of Natural Complexes, 2nd (expanded) edition. *Memberships:* American Philosophical Association; Metaphysical Society of America; Society for Advancement of American Philosophy; National Association for Female Executives. *Honours:* DAAD Direktstipendium (SUNY German academic exchange scholarship), University of Tubingen, 1977-78; Douglas Greenlee Award, best paper by new scholar, Society for Advancement of American Philosophy, 1984; Participant, Summer Institute, National Endowment for Humanities, 1986. *Hobbies:* Music; Opera; Travel; Swimming; Jogging. *Address:* Department of Philosophy, Hofstra University, Hempstead, New York 11550, USA.

WALLACE Sylvia, b. New York City, USA. Author. m. 3 June 1941, 1 son, 1 daughter. *Appointments:* West Coast Editor, Dell Publishing Company 1941-46, Photoplay Magazine 1951-56. *Publications:* Books: Fountains, 1976; Empress, 1980; Book of Lists 2, 1980; Intimate Sex Lives of Famous People, 1981. *Address:* PO Box 49328, Los Angeles, California 90049, USA.

WALLACH Leah, b. 26 Nov. 1947, New York City, USA. *Education:* BA, New School for Social Research, 1968. *Appointments:* Freelance Writer. *Publications:* Food Values: Cholesterol and Fats, 1989; Food Values: Calcium, 1989; Food Values: Carbohydrates, 1989; The Ordinary is Extraordinary, co-author, 1988; The Isle of Gladness, 1969; articles in: Washington Post; Metropolitan Home; Omni; Working Woman; Working Mother; Video. *Memberships:* Authors Guild; American Society of Journalists & Authors; Foundation for the Community of Artists. *Honours:* Yaddo Fellow, 1974; MacDowell Colony Fellow, 1974; New York Foundation for the Arts Grant, 1980; Rhode Island Creative Arts Centre, Fellow, 1983; Mercantile Library Writers Room, Fellow, 1984-85; Fellow, Blue Mountain Centre, 1986. *Address:* 153 Ridge St., New York, NY 10002, USA.

WALLER, Irene Ellen, b. 8 May 1928, Birmingham, England. Artist; Writer; Lecturer. m. Geoffrey Waller, 15 July 1955, 1 son, 2 daughter. *Education:* Birmingham College of Art, 1943-49; Studied in Sweden & Europe, 1948, 1969. *Publications:* Thread an Art Form, 1973; Tatting a Contemporary Art Form, 1974; Knots and Netting, 1976; The Craft of Weaving, 1976; Textile Sculptures, 1977; Fine Art Weaving, 1978; Design Sources for the Fibre Artist, 1978; TV Programmes: Serendipity, BBC, London, 1973; '60,'70,'80 Show, 1974, BBC London; Mastercraftsmen, 1974; Wool, ATV Midlands, 1975; Exhibitions throughout England and USA including: Cannon Hill Arts Centre, Birmingham; Malvern Festival Theatre; Foyles Gallery, London, etc;

Travels and lectures extensively in the USA and Canada. *Hobbies:* Family; Travel; Music; Reading. *Address:* 13 Portland Road, Edgbaston, Birmingham, England.

WALLERSTEDT-WEHRLE JoAnna, b. 14 Sept. 1944, Columbus, Indiana, USA. Freelance Writer. m. Jason William Wehrle, 24 June 1979. 3 daughters. *Education:* Graduated, Charlottesville High School, 1963; Indiana University, 1967-69. *Appointments:* Bookkeeper, State of Indiana, 1963- 65; Medical Aid, Riley Nursing Home, Greenfield Indiana, 1974; President, Day Care Center, Indianapolis, 1978-88; Pre School Teacher. *Publications:* Author of over 127 articles, poetry, and various songs. *Memberships:* American Association of Entrepreneurs, 1987-89; Associate member, Smithsonian Institute, 1987-89; National Poets Registry, 1986-89; Freelance Writers Association, 1988-89; Writers Data, 1988-89; Song Writers Assoc, 1986- 89. *Interests:* Family; Helping others; Writing. Hobby: Gardening. *Address:* Rt 3, Box 191, Nasdhville, IN 47448, USA.

WALLISON Frieda K., b. 15 Jan. 1943, New York City, USA. Lawyer. m. Peter J. Wallison, 24 Nov. 1966, 2 sons, 1 daughter. *Education:* AB, Smith College, 1963; LLB, Harvard University, 1966; Admission, New York Bar 1967, DC Bar 1982. *Appointments:* Associate, Carter, Ledyard & Milburn, NYC, 1966-75; Special Counsel, Division of Market Regulation, Securities & Exchange Commission, Washington DC, 1975; Executive Director, General Counsel, Municipal Securities Rulemaking Board, 1975-78; Partner, Rogers & Wells (NYC & Washington) 1978-83, Jones, Day, Reavis & Pogue 1983-. *Memberships:* Governmental Accounting Standards Advisory Council; National Council on Public Works Improvement; National Council for Governmental Accounting; National Association of Bond Lawyers; American, Federal, NYC Bar Associations. *Address:* 8325 Persimmon Tree Road, Bethesda, Maryland 20817, USA.

WALMAN Barbara Rosalynd, b. 27 Aug. 1956, Enfield, England. Research Director. m. James Reid, 20 May 1981, 1 daughter. *Education:* BA, Honours, Business Studies, 1978. *Appointments:* Researcher, 1978-84, Editor, 1980-86, Research Director, 1984-, Executive Editor, 1986-, RMDP. *Publications:* Editor, Retail Automation Magazine; Contributor, various journals and magazines; Co-Author, Guide to EPoS Systems, RMDP Handbooks, 1982, 1983, 1984; Regular Speaker, International Conferences. *Memberships:* Market Research Society; National Childbirth Trust, Editor, Local Branch Committee. *Address:* 61-63 Ship Street, Brighton, East Sussex, DN1 1AE, England.

WALSH Gwendolyn Elroy, b. 19 Mar. 1925, Cambridge, USA. Associate Professor. m. Douglas F. Walsh, 24 Sept. 1950, 1 son, 1 daughter. *Education:* BS, Education, Tufts University, 1946; M.Ed., University of Virginia, 1967. *Appointments:* Teacher, Abbot Academy, Andover, 1946- 50; Teacher, Katherine Delmar Bucke School, San Francisco, 1961-62; Assistant Professor, Physical Education, 1962-88. *Publications:* Articles in professional journals. *Memberships:* American Association of University Professors; American Association of University Women; American Dance Guild; US Fencing Association. *Honours:* Nominated, First Governor's Award for Arts in Virginia, 1979. *Hobbies Include:* Painting; Silk Screening; Sports; Gardening. *Address:* 340 East Beverley Street, Staunton, VA 24401, USA.

WALSH Mary D Fleming, b. 29 Oct. 1913, Whitewright, Texas, USA. Housewife. m. F Howard Walsh, 13 Mar. 1937. 3 sons, 2 daughters. *Education:* BA, Southern Methodist University, 1934. *Appointments:* President, Fleming Foundation; Vice President, Walsh Foundation; Partner, The Walsh Company. *Memberships include:* Big Brothers of Tarrant County; Broadway Baptist Church; Fort Worth Opera Guild; Honorary, Fort Worth Opera Board; Fort Worth Woman's Club; Director and Life Member, Fort Worth Boys' Club Council; Chi Omega Mothers Club, 1965-87; Organizer, 1935-, President, 1935, 1936, 1937, Outstanding Alumna Award, 1969, Chi Omega Alumnae; Honorary Chairman, 1986 Chi Omega Carousel; Financial Advisor, Tho Epsilon Chapter, Chi Omega at TCU, 1955-69; Charter Member, Jewel Charity Board; Sustaining Member, 1977-86, Associate Member, 1987, Woman's Board, Forth Worth Children's Hospital; TCU Woman's Club; Child Study Center Guild; American Guild of Organists, Fort Worth Chapter; President, 1940, Fort Worth Pan Hellenic; American Field Service; Honorary Board Member, Van Cliburn International Piano Competition; Texas Boys Choir Auxiliary; Honorary Life Member, Girls Service League; Fine Arts Foundation Guild, TCU; Round Table; AAUW, 1935-86; Ladies Auxiliary of Goodwill Industries; Tarrant County Auxiliary, The Edna Gladney Home; Fort Worth Art Association; Life Member, YWCA; President, 1968, Rae Reimers Bible Study Class; Commissioner, 1968-72, Advisory Council, 1972-84, Texas Commission on the Arts and Humanities; Honorary Life Membe Worth, 1968; Through the Walsh Foundation, The Texas Boys Choir and The Dorothy Shaw Bell Choir present The Littlest Wiseman as a Christmas gift to the City of Fort Worth each Christmas; Patron of the Arts, Fort Worth, 1970; Distinguished Service Award, Southern Baptist Radio and Television Commission, 1972; Edna Gladney International Grandparents, 1972; Opera award, Girl Scouts, 1977, 1978, 1979; Award, Streams & Valleys, 1976-77, 1978-79, 1980; Brotherhood Citation, National Conference of Christians and Jews, Tarrant County Chapter, 1978; Royal Purple Award, Texas Christian University, 1979; Honorary Degree, Dr of Laws, Texas Christian University, 1979; The Friends of the Texas Boys Choir Award, 1981; Appreciation award, Southwestern Baptist Theological Seminary, 1981; Citation, Southwestern Baptist Theological Seminary, 1981; BH Carroll Founders Award, 1982; The Senior Citizen Award, 1985. *Address:* 2425 Stadium Drive, Fort Worth, Texas 76109, USA.

WALTER Beverly Toney, b. 27 Mar. 1946, Comfort, USA. Self- employed. 1 son, 1 daughter. *Appointments:* Senior Regional Director, 1978-82, Director, recruitment, 1982-83, Corporate Sales Manager, 1983-84, National Sales Manager, 1984-85, Vice President, Sales & Marketing, Cosmetics, 1985-87, Executive Vice President, CEO, 1987-88, Nutri-Metrics International Inc.; President, Founder, Walter and Wouthworth Associates, 1988-. *Memberships:* Business & Professional Women; Sales and Marketing Executives of LA. *Honours:* Recipient, various honours & awards. *Hobbies:* Piano; Art; Physical Fitness. *Address:* 23 Los Coyotes Dr., Pomona, CA 91766, USA.

WALTER Nola Janice, b. 29 Mar. 1934, Eau Claire, USA. Artist. Divorced, 1 daughter. *Education:* Chippewa Valley Technical Institute. *Appointments:* Irwin Co., CPA, 1954-61; Robert Werhbach Attorney at Law & CPA, 1963-65; Office Manager, Bearson Steinmetz, 1974-85; Artist, Owner, Pablo's Gallery, 1985-. *Creative Works:* Oil Paintings: The Orange Nude; Baby; Kaleidoscope; Midnight; Midnight Rose. *Memberships:* American Biographical Institute; Research Board of Advisors, Smithsonian Institute. *Honours:* 2 First Awards, Home Economics, 1950; 3 First Awards & 1 Second Award, Music, 1952; many other honours. *Hobby:* Dancing. *Address:* 825 Barland St., Eau Claire, WI 54701, USA.

WALTERS Barbara R (Altizer), b. 21 Sept. 1948, Vincennes, Indiana, USA. Sociologist; Consultant. m. Thomas J J Altizer, 10 June 1987. *Education:* BA Psychology, Vanderbilt University, 1970; MA Sociology 1978, PhD 1978, SUNY, Stony Brook. *Appointments:* Visiting Assistant Professor, Sociology, William and Mary, 1974-75; Visiting Instructor, Vanderbilt University, 1975-76; Research Associate, Psychiatry, SUNY, Stony Brook, 1976-77; Director of Personnel, Vice President Human Resources; Vice President Administration; Vice President Strategic Planning, Farm Fresh Supermarkets, 1977-83; Interim General Manager, Virginia Opera, 1983-84. *Memberships:*

Board of Trustees, City of Norfolk Employees Retirement System, 1983-; Board of Directors, Virginia Opera, 1983-; American Sociological Association, Chair, Ethics Committee; Southern Sociological Society Commonwealth of Virginia, Board of Health Professions, Chair Scope and Standards of Practice Committee, 1984-; Governor's Task Force to study the definition of Nursing, 1986; Secretary's Task Force to study the Regulation of Psychology (Virginia), 1988. *Honours:* Vanderbilt University Summer Fellowship, 1968; SUNY, Stony Brook Summer Fellowship, 1971; SUNY Stony Brook, Teaching Assistanceship, 1971; NIMH Methodology Traineeship, 1971-74; Fellow, Center for Literature & Culture, Paris, 1972-73; SUNY, Stony Brook, Dissertation Grant-in-Aid, 1974: NIH Research in Service Award, 1977-78. *Address:* 1848 Fendall Avenue, Charlottesville, VA 22903, USA.

WALTERS Bette Jean, b. 5 Sept. 1946, Norristown, Pennsylvania, USA. Lawyer; Business Executive. *Education:* BA, University of Pittsburgh, 1967; JD 1970, LLM (Taxation) 1974, Temple Universty School of Law. *Appointments:* Attorney, private practice, 1970-73; Associate counsel, 1973-79, group counsel (manufacturing) 1979-83, Alco Standard Corporation; Vice president, secretary & general counsel, Alco Industries Inc. *Memberships:* American, Pennsylvania & Montgomery County Bar Associations; American Society of Corporation Secretaries; American Corporation Counsel Association; Daughters of American Revolution. *Address:* Alco Industries Inc, PO Box 937, Valley Forge, Pennsylvania 19482, USA.

WALTERS Teresa Hietbrink, b. Lincoln, Nebraska, USA. m. 2 Aug. 1974. *Education:* Doctorate, Peabody Conservatory, Johns Hopkins University; Ecole Normale de Musique, Paris. *Appointments:* Concert Pianist; Chairman, Music, College of St Elizabeth, 1985; Faculty Member: Pennsylvania State University, Elizabethtown College; Assistantships: Peabody Conservatory, University of Nebraska. *Publications:* Nadia Boulanger, Musician and Teacher; Compositions: 3 Cantatas; Mass for Bell Choir; Sonata for Prepared Piano; Songs for Women's Voices; Lullabye for Jonathan; Recordings: Teresa Walters in Recital; Teresa Walters, Album I, Album II. *Memberships:* Phi Beta Kappa; Mortar Board; Sigma Alpha Iota; Pi Kappa Lambda. *Honours Include:* Recital Debut: Carnegie Hall, New York; European Debut: Conservatorio Monteverdi, Italy; 3 Pi Kappa Lambda Awards for Composition; Boucher Medal. *Hobbies:* Art; Antiques; Animals; Travel; Fashion. *Address:* 138 Maple Street, Rutherford, NJ 07070, USA.

WALTON Amanda, b. 16 Sept. 1941, Georgia, USA. Elementary Education Teacher. m. Van L. Walton, 3 July 1966, 1 son, 1 daughter. *Education:* AA, Liberal Arts, 1975; BA, Political Science, 1980; MS, Education, City College, 1983. *Appointments:* Auxillary Trainer, 1974-81; Teacher, 1981-. *Publications:* Established The Read to Reading Club; The John Paul Roges Meorial Award. *Memberships:* International Reading Association; Manhattan Reading Council; National Notary Association. *Honours:* Recognition of Accomplishment, Millan News, 1988. *Hobbies:* Public Speaking; Reading; Bowling. *Address:* 221-39 112th Avenue, Queens Village, NY 11429, USA.

WAMPLER Barbara Bedford, b. 23 July 1932, New Bedford, USA. Entrepreneur. m. John Harley Wampler, 21 Oct. 1950, 4 sons. *Apointments:* Family Counsellor, serenity HIll, 1975-78; Counselling Service, Wampler Rehab., 1976-84; President, earth I & II Campg;ounds, 1984-; Real Estate President, Earth Enterprises, 1985-. *Publications:* articles in journals & magazines. *Memberships:* NAFE; National Association of Business Managers; National Association of Campground Owners; Massachusetts Association of Campground Owners. *Honours:* Scholarship, University of Hartford, 1976. *Hobbies:* Writing; Playing; Singing. *Address:* DBA Earth Enterprises Inc., PO Box 690 Route 8, Otis, MA 91253, USA.

WANDER Hilde, b. 1 Mar. 1915, Kiel, West Germany. Wissenschaftlich Direktorin, retired. Lecturer. *Education:* Studies in Economics, 1941-44; Diplom-Volkswirt, 1944; Dr Sc Pol, 1949; Research in population economics, Kiel Institute of World Econopmics, 1944-80; Wissenschaftliche Direktorin, *Appointments:* UN Demographer: Indonesia 1958-60; Jordan, 1966; Western Samoa, 1970. UNESCO Educational Economist: British Guyana, 1962-63. *Publications:* Numerous books and articles on demographic-economic subjects in national and international context. *Memberships:* Deutsche Gesellschaft fur Bevolkerungswissenschaft; IUSSP; European Association for Pop Studies; European Society for Pop. Economics; German Federation of University Women. *Honours:* Publication in honour of her 70th birthday, Zeitschrift für Bevolkerungswissenschaft, No 2, 1985; Fulbright grant, University of Pennsylvania in Philadelphia, 1953-54. *Hobbies:* Photography; Ancient history; Classical music. *Address:* Herderstr. 4, D-2300 Kiel 1, West Germany.

WANDOR Michelene Dinah, b. 20 Apr. 1940, London, England. Writer. m. Ed Victor, 1963, divorced 1975. 2 sons. *Education:* BA Hons, English, Newnham College, Cambridge, 1959-62; MA Sociology of Literature, University of Essex, 1975-76. *Appointments:* Poetry Editor, Time Out Magazine, 1971-82. *Publications include:* Poetry: Cutlasses & Earrings, 1977; Upbeat, 1981; Touch Papers, with Judith Karantzis and Michele Roberts, 1982; Gardens of Eden, 1984. Plays: Sink Songs, 1975; Strike While the Iron is Hot, 1980; Play Nine, 1981; Five Plays, 1984; Editor, Plays by Women, Volumes 1-4; The Wandering Jew with Mike Alfreds, 1987; Wanted, 1988. Prose Fiction: Tales I Tell My Mother, 1978; Guests in the Body, 1986; More Tales I Tell My Mother, 1987; Arky Types, 1987; Passion Fruit, 1986; Stepping Out, 1986; Close Company, 1987; Storia, 1988; Theatre: You Two Can be Ticklish, 1970; The Day After Yesterday, 1972; Spilt Milk and Mal de Mere, 1972; To Die Among Friends, 1974; Penthesilea, 1977; The Old Wives' Tale, 1977; Care and Control, 1977; Floorshow, 1977; Whores D'Oeuvres, 1978; Scissors, 1978; AID Thy Neighbour, 1978; Correspondence, 1979; Rutherford and Son, 1980; Aurora Leigh, 1981; The Blind Goddess, 1981; Future Perfect, 1981. Non-fiction: The Body Politic, 1972; The Great Divide, 1976; Precious Bane, 1978; Why Children?, 1980; Dreams and Deconstructions, 1980; British Alternative Theatre Directory, 1982; On Gender and Writing, 1983; Walking on the Water, 1983; Women's Writing: A Challenge to Theory, 1986; Carry On, Understudies, 1986; Look Back in Gender, 1987; Ruskin: Feminist Beginnings, 1990. Numerous articles in magazines, Radio and Television. *Membership:* Writers Guild of Great Britain. *Honour:* International Emmy 1987 for film The Belle of Amherts for Thames Television. *Hobbies:* Rennaissance and Baroque Music. *Address:* 71 Belsize Lane, London NW3 5AU, England.

WANG Ying, b. 24 Feb. 1935, Henan Province, China. Professor, Director, Chairman, Geo and Ocean Sciences, Centre of Marine Sciences. m. Da Kui Zhu, 1 Jan. 1934, 2 daughters. *Education:* Nanjing University; Beijing University. *Appointments:* Teaching Assistant 1961- 62, Lecturer, 1963-79, Research Fellow, 1979-82, Geology, Dalhousie University, Canada; and Visiting Scientist, Atlantic Geoscience Centre, Canada, 1980-82; Associate Professor, 1983-84, Professor, 1984-, Geo and Ocean Sciences, Nanjing University. *Publications:* The Coast of China, 1976; Marine Geography, co-author, 1978; Modal Atlas of Surface Textures of Quartz Sand, 1985; articles in professional journals. *Memberships Include:* Fellow, Geological Association of Canada; International Association of Sedimentologists; National Geographic Society, USA; Chinese Society of Oceanography; Chinese Society of Marine Geology; Chinese Society of Ocean Engineering; Geographical Society of China; Geological Society of China. *Honours:* 1st National Science Congress Award, 1978; Many other honours and awards; First Submarine geologist of China. *Hobbies:* Photography; Music; Films; Reading. *Address:* Dept. of Geo and Ocean Sciences, Nanjing

University, Nanjing, Jiangsu Province, Peoples Republic of China.

WANIEK Marilyn Nelson, b. 26 Apr. 1946, Cleveland, Ohio, USA. University Professor. m. (1) E F Waniek, 1970, divorced 1980; (2) Roger B Wilkenfeld, Nov. 1980. 1 son, 1 daughter. *Education:* BA, University of California, Davis, 1968; MA, University of Pennsylvania, 1970; PhD, University of Minnesota, 1978. *Appointments:* Lane Community College, 1970-72; Reed College, 1971-72; St Olaf College, 1973-78; University of Connecticut, 1978-. *Publications:* For The Body; Mama's Promises; The Homeplace. *Memberships:* MELUS; Society for Values in Higher Education; AWP; AAUP. *Honours:* Kent Fellowship, 1976-78; NEA Creative Writing Fellowship, 1982; NEA Creative Writing Fellowship, 1990. *Address:* c/o Department of English, Box U-25, Room 332, 337 Mansfield Road, University of Connecticut, Storrs, CT 06268, USA.

WARD Maureen A., b. 1 Aug. 1960, Rochester, New York, USA. Architect. m. Elie Antoine Atallah, 3 Sept. 1988. *Education:* Department of International Programmes Abroad (Florence, Italy) 1981-82, BArch 1983, Syracuse University. *Appointments:* Moshe Safdie & Associates, Boston, & Faculty, Boston Architectural Centre, 1985-86; Michael Dennis, Jeffrey Clark & Associates, Boston, 1988-89; Burwell & Boutel Architects, Rochester, 1983-85; Geddes, Brecher, Quaus & Cunningham, Philadelphia, 1989-. *Memberships:* American & Philadelphia Institute of Architects; Alliance Francaise, Philadelphia. *Hobbies:* Painting; Photography; French language & history; Classic English literature. *Address:* 250 South 13th Street, Box 39, Philadelphia, Pennsylvania 19107, USA.

WARD Roma Esther, b. 22 Dec. 1918, Melbourne, Victoria, Australia. Artist. m. William O'Neill, 17 Aug. 1971. 1 son. *Education:* Lauriston Girls School, Melbourne, 1925-35. *Creative works:* Paintings in oils and water colours; Hand painted articles for sale in shops. *Memberships:* Melbourne Society of Women Painters and Sculptors; Exhibiting Member, Royal Art Society of New South Wales. *Hobbies:* Music; Reading. *Address:* P O Box 234, Manly 2095, New South Wales, Australia.

WARD Tracy Louise, b. 22 Dec. 1958, London, England. Actress. *Education:* Diploma in Art History. *Appointments:* Model; Art Historian; Actress; Numerous appearances including: Theatre, Nottingham Playhouse; Solo Cabaret; Film: Dance with a Stranger. Television appearances: Mussolini, with George C Scott; If Tomorrow Comes; Dr Who; Cats Eyes. *Address:* London, England.

WARE Barbara, b. 26 July 1947, Cincinnati, Ohio, USA. Real Estate Broker. m. Billy James Ware, 12 June 1964, 1 son, 1 daughter. *Education:* GRI, Florida Association of Realtors; Graduate, Realtors Institute. *Honours:* Diamond Pin Club; Florida Association of Realtors. *Hobbies:* Swimming; Camping; Horse Riding; Antique Cars; Helping People. *Address:* 4841 Palm Beach Boulevard, Fort Myers, FL 33905, USA.

WARE Caroline F, b. 14 Aug. 1899, Brookline, Massachusetts, USA. Professor. m. Gardiner C Means, 2 June 1927. *Education:* BA, Vassar College, 1920; Oxford University, England, 1922-23; MA 1924, PhD 1925, Harvard University, USA. *Appointments:* Academic: Teacher, Baldwin School, 1920-22; Professor of History, Vassar College, 1925- 34; Professor of Social Sciences, American University Graduate School 1935-44 and Sarah Lawrence College, 1936-37; Professor of History 1942-44, Social Work 1945-61, Howard University; Visiting Professor, University of Puerto Rico, 1945-48, Schools of Social Work, Columbia 1953, El Salvador 1955, Chile 1962; Government: Special Assistant, National Recovery Administration, 1934-35; Deputy to Consumer Commissioner, National Defense Advisory Commission

and Office of Price Administration, 1940-42. *Publications:* The Early New England Cotton Manufacture, 1931; Greenwich Village 1920-30, 1935; The Modern Economy in Action, 1936; The Cultural Approach to History (editor), 1940; Consumer Goes to War, 1942; Labor Education in Universities, 1946; Estudio de la Comunidad, 1947; Organizacion de la Comunidad, 1954; History of Mankind (UNESCO) (author/editor volume on 20th century), 1966; Consumer Activists: They Made A Difference (co-author, editor), 1983; El Devarrollo de la Comunidad y el Trabajo Social en America Latina, 1988. *Memberships include:* American Historical Association; National Association of Social Workers; Consumer Advisory Committees to OPA and to Presidents Council of Economic Advisers; President's Commission on Status of Women and Citizens Advisory Council on Status of Women; Adviser, Latin American Assocaition of Schools of Social Work; Adviser, InterAmerican Commission of Women; Board InterAmerican Assocaition of Social Welfare; Washington Urban League; National Consumers League. *Honours include:* Hart, Schaffner and Marx Economics Prize, 1929; Honorary Professorship, University of San Marcos, Peru, 1965; Radcliffe Graduate Society Achievement Award, 1967; Whitney Young Award for Community Service, Washington Urban League, 1974; Trumpeter Award, National Consumers League, 1978. *Hobbies include:* Hiking; Canoeing; Camping; Gardening; Dog breeding; Reading; Travel. *Address:* 1600 Beulah Road, Vienna, VA 22180, USA.

WARE Susanna Kirkwood, b. 21 Nov. 1929, Beaumont, Texas, USA. Retired Music Teacher. m. Henry Ware, 31 July 1954. 2 daughters. *Education:* BA, Mary Allen College, Crockett, Texas, 1954; MMEd, Texas Southern University, Houston, 1976. *Appointments:* Music Teacher, Crosby Independent School District, Crosby, Texas; Music Directress: Bethlehem Missionary Baptist Church, South Texas District Association and Congress, Houston. *Creative works:* Music Compolsitions: Crosby's The Town; Zion Jubilee; Pleasing To Thee. *Memberships:* Texas State Teachers Assoc, Life Member; Matron, Luella Williams Court Heroines of Jericho; State Youth District Deputy Heroines of Jericho; Delta Sigma Theta Sorority Inc. *Honours:* This Is Your Life, 1968; 20 year Appreciation Plaque 1979, 30 year Appreciation Plaque 1989, Bethlehem Missionary Baptist Church; Retirement Luncheon and Plaque, Texas State Teachers Association, 1989; Retirement Banquet and Plaque, Drew Intermediate School, 1989; Reception and Plaque, Crosby Middle School, 1989; Music Tribute Ex Students (Plaque), 1989. *Hobbies:* Playing piano; Cooking; Travelling. *Address:* 4102 Hoffman Street, Houston, Texas 77026, USA.

WARFIELD Carol Anastasia, b. 26 Dec. 1951, Boston, Massachusetts, USA. Physician. m. G. Richard Warfield III, 10 Oct. 1976 (dec.), 1 son, 2 daughters. *Education:* BA, Jackson College, 1973; BSME, Tufts College of Engineering, 1973; MD, Tufts Medical School, 1976. *Appointments:* Director, Pain Management Center, Beth Israel Hospital, Boston, Massachusetts, 1980-; Assistant Professor of Anesthesia, Harvard Medical School, 1986-. *Publications:* Over 75 publications on pain management. *Memberships:* American Society of Anesthesiologists; American Pain Society; International Association for Study of Pain. *Address:* Pain Management Center, Beth Israel Hospital, 330 Brookline Avenue, Boston, MA 02215, USA.

WARING Virginia Clotfelter, b. 18 Oct. 1915, Dinuba, California, USA. Music Publisher; Pianist; Artistic Director. m. (1)Livingston Gearhart, 28 Feb. 1940, div. 1953, (2)Fred Waring, 2 Dec. 1954, 2 sons. *Education:* BA, BMus, graduating with honours, Mills College, 1937; Studied Piano with Robert Casadesus, Fontainebleau and Paris, France, 1937, 1938, 1939. *Career:* Member of 2-piano team Morley & Gearhart, touring under Columbia Artists Management, 1940-53; Owner, Interior Design Associates, East Stroudsburg, Pennsylvania, 1969-83; Assistant Conductor and

EmCee of Fred Waring's Pennsylvanians, 1980-83; Chairman, Board of Fred Waring Ent., Delaware Water Gap, Pennsylvania, 1983-; Artistic Director, Fred Waring Workshop, Pennsylvania State University; Owner, President, Shawnee Press Inc, Music Publishers, currently. *Recordings:* 4 2-piano record albums, Columbia Artists, 1945, 1948; 2 record albums, Omnisound, 1976-79. *Memberships:* Founding Board of Directors: Child Help USA, 1965; Pocono Art Center, Stroudsburg, Pennsylvania, 1965-75; Board of Directors, Palm Valley School, Palm Springs, California, 1967, 1968, 1969; President, Board of Trustees, Joanna Hodges Piano Competition, Palm Desert, California, 1983, 1984, 1985. *Honours:* Salutatorial, High School, 1934; Mills College Scholarship, 1934, 1935, 1936, 1937; Fleischman Trustee Fund Scholarship for study in France, 1937, 1938, 1939. *Hobbies:* Reading; Needlework; Tennis; Golf. *Address:* The Gatehouse, Shawnee-on-Delaware, PA 18356, USA.

WARNECK Janet Emily, b. 24 Apr. 1945, Cleveland, Ohio, USA. Psychotherapist; Consultant. m. Walter John Warneck Jr, 31 May 1969, 2 sons. *Education:* BA, Case Western Reserve University, 1967; MA, University of Missouri, 1970; Post-master's study, University of Connecticut, 1979; Certified Marital and Family Therapist, Connecticut. *Appointments:* Private Practice, Ridgefield, Connecticut, 1973-88; Private Practice and Vice-President, Walter J. Warneck Ltd, Savannah, Georgia, 1988-. *Memberships:* Clinical Member, American Association for Marriage and Family Therapy. *Honours:* Honour Scholarship, Flora Stone Mather College for Women, Case Western Reserve University, 1963; Membership, Sundial, Sophomore Women's Scholarship and Leadership Society, Case Western Reserve University, 1964; Membership, Pi Sigma Alpha, 1967. *Hobbies:* Ballet; Art; Michelangelo's drawings. *Address:* Walter J. Warneck Ltd, 1302 Central Park, 340 Eisenhower Drive, Savannah, GA 31406, USA.

WARNENSKA-JELONKIEWICZ Monika, b. 4 Mar. 1922, Mysezkow, Poland. Writer; Journalist. m. Czeslaw Jelonkiewicz, 28 Aug. 1945, 2 daughters. *Education:* Studies, Warsaw University, 1945-50. *Appointments:* Journalist, various magazines & journals. *Publications:* Many books in Polish, translated into Russian, German, Bulgarian, and Yugoslav. *Memberships:* Polish Writers Union; Polish Journalists Union. *Honours:* Recipient, various honours and awards including: Prize, Minister of Culture, 1967; Prize, Minister of Defence, 1974; Prize, Premier Minister, 1982. *Hobbies:* Literature; Art; Archaeology. *Address:* 15 Pod Skocznia Street, Warsaw 02-709, Poland.

WARNER Laverne, b. 14 Aug. 1941, Huntsville, Texas, USA. University Professor. *Education:* BS, 1962, MEd., 1969, Sam Houston State University; PhD, East Texas State University, 1977. *Appointments:* Port Arthurs ISD, Texas, 1962-64; Burlington Public Schools, Vermont, 1964-66; Aldine ISD, Texas, 1966-67; Spring Branch ISD, Texas, 1967-68; Crawfordsville Community Schools, Indiana, 1968-71; Sam Houston State University, 1975-. *Publications:* Co-Author: Tunes for Tots, 1982; Fun with Familiar Tunes, 1987; contributor to journals and magazines. *Memberships:* Area Coordinator, Phi Delta Kappa; Texas Association for the Education of Young Children, Vice President; Texas Elementary Kindergarten Nursery Educators, Past President; Association for Childhood Education; Port Arthur ISD Education of Young Children. *Honours:* Recipient, various honours & awards. *Hobbies:* Playing Piano & Guitar; Needlework; Reading. *Address:* Division of Teacher Education, Teacher Education Centre, Sam Houston State University, Huntsville, TX 77341, USA.

WARREN Barbara Leonard, b. 3 Nov. 1943, Fall River, Massachusetts, USA. Writer; Educator; Chief Executive Officer. m. B.W.Warren Jr, 8 Sep. 1972. *Education:* BA, English, Education, Bridgewater State College, Massachusetts, 1966; Graduate work, University of Massachusetts, University of Oregon, Northern Arizona University; MA, English, Education, Arizona State University, Tempe, 1976. *Appointments:*

Freelance Writer, 1966-; Teacher, Journalism, Gifted, English, Massachusetts and Arizona, 16 years; Publications Adviser, high school yearbooks and newspapers, 16 years; Women's Editor, Prescott (AZ) Courier, 1972; Part-time Instructor, Central Arizona College, 1980-; Reviewer, Gifted Child Today, 1987-, Gentle Strength Times, 1988-; Columnist, Write Right, Writer's Guidelines, 1987-, On the Brighter Side, Challenge, 1988-; Speaker, Mensa's Gifted Children's Speakers Bureau, 1987-; President, Chief Executive Officer, Imagine Rainbows Inc, 1988- *Publications include:* Capture Creativity: Photographs To Inspire Young Writers, 1982; Contributions to magazines and newspapers including Sunset, Splash, Arts and Contemporary Culture, Arizona, Righting Words, Indian Trader, Arizona Republic, Prescott (AZ) Courier, Providence (RI)Journal, Casa Grande (AZ)Dispatch, Women's Enterprise, Lady's Circle. *Memberships:* Communications Chairman, Delta Kappa Gamma; National Writers Club; COSMEP; National Association for Female Executives; National Association for Gifted Children. *Honours:* Scholarships: Aspen Writer's Workshop, Aspen, Colorado, 1966; Georgetown Writer's Workshop, Washington DC, 1967; Delta Kappa Gamma, 1986; Fellowship, Newspaper Fund Inc, University of Oregon, Eugene, 1968. *Hobbies:* Collecting rainbows; Walking. *Address:* PO Box P, Arizona City, AZ 85223, USA.

WARREN Nagueyalti, b. 1 Oct. 1947, Atlanta, Georgia, USA. Assistant Dean & Associate Professor, Emory University. m. Rueben, 14 June 1980. 1 son, 2 daughters. *Education:* BA, Fisk University, 1973; MA, Simmons College, 1974; MA, Boston University, 1974; PhD, University of Mississippi, 1985. *Appointments:* Instructor, Northeastern Unviersity, Boston, 1977-78; Lecturer, University of Calabar, Nigeria, 1979-80; Assistant Professor 1984-88, Chaired English Department, 1986-88, Fisk University; Assistant Dean, Emory University, 1988-. *Publications:* Poetry: Soft Black Impressions, 1972; To the Smoke Queens, 1982; Southern Comfort; Mississippi Woods; many other poems published. *Memberships:* Modern Language Association; College Language Association; South Atlantic Modern Language Association, Chair Special Session; American Association of University Women; National Council of Black Studies; Southern Association of Afro-American Studies, Advisory Board Member; WEB Du Bois Foundation, Board Member. *Honours:* Golden Poet Award, 1985; Award for contributions made during Black History Month, 1984; Gold Key Honor Society of Mortar Board, 1971; First Place Creative Writing Contest, 1973; United Church of Christ Faculty Development Grant, 1986; Fulbright Summer Seminar recipient, The American University in Cairo, 1988. *Hobbies:* Reading; Creative writing; Travel; Scholarly research on Black literature and culture. *Address:* 7469 Asbury Drive, Lithonia, Georgia 30058, USA.

WARSHAUER Irene Conrad, b. 4 May 1942, New York City, New York, USA. Attorney. m. Alan M. Warshauer, 27 Nov. 1966, 1 daughter. *Education:* BA with distinction, University of Michigan, 1963; LLB cum laude, Columbia University, 1966; Admitted: New York State Bar, 1966; US District Court, New York Southern District, 1969, Eastern District, 1969, Northern District, 1980; US Court of Appeals, 2nd Circuit, 1969; US Supreme Court, 1972. *Appointments:* New York State Mental Health Information Service, 1966-68; Associate, Chadbourne Parke Whiteside & Wolff, 1968-75; Member, Anderson Russell Kill & Olick PC, New York City, 1975-. *Publications:* The Asbestos Health Hazards Compensation Act: A Legislative Solution to a Litigation Crisis; Commentary: Medical Cost Containment Program Successful; Limiting Product Liability Verdicts; Analyzing the Relationship between the Civil, Governmental, and Criminal Obligations and Liabilities for Hazardous Waste (with Lynn Ann Stansel), 1986; Litigation Management Techniques: One Company, Repetitive Lawsuits; Strategies for Managing Multiple Defendant Litigation; 3 coursebooks. *Memberships:* New York Academy of Sciences; Bar Association of the City of New York (Judiciary Committee 1982-86); New York State Bar Association (Mental Hygiene Committee

1978-84, Chair, Mentally Disabled & the Community Subcommittee 1978-82; American Bar Association (Torts Committee, Vice-Chair, Toxic & Hazardous Substances & Environmental Law Committee 1986-87); Chair, Industrywide Litigation Committee, Defense Research Institute; Panel of Arbitrators, American Arbitration Association; Women's City Club of New York; American Management Association, 1982-83. *Honours:* Kentucky Colonel; CPR Legal Programme Significant Practical Achievement Award. *Hobbies:* Gardening; Cooking. *Address:* 505 East, 79th Street, New York, NY 10021, USA.

WARSHAVSKY Suzanne May, b. 22 July 1944, New York City, New York, USA. Attorney. m. Mordechai S. Warshavsky, 7 June 1964, 2 sons, 1 daughter. *Education:* AB, Vassar College, 1965; JD cum laude, New York University, 1968. *Appointments:* Associate, Dewey Ballantine Bushby Palmer & Wood, New York City, 1968-73; Associate, Milgrim Thomajan Jacobs & Lee, New York City, 1973-76; Partner, Warshavsky, Hoffman & Cohen PC, New York City, 1976-; Arbitrator, Civil Court, City of New York, 1975-86. *Memberships:* New York Women's Bar Association, Committee on Business and Taxation, Committee on Judiciary, Chair of Committee on Professional Ethics and Discipline, 1986-87; Magazine Publisher's Association, Legal Affairs Committee, 1985-87; American Arbitration Association, Panel of Commercial Arbitrators 1976-77; Association of Bar of City of New York, Committee on Professional and Judicial Ethics 1976-79; New York State Bar Association, Committee of Public Health 1972-77. *Address:* Warshavsky, Hoffman & Cohen PC, 500 Fifth Avenue, New York, NY 10110, USA.

WASHINGTON Loise, b. 1 NOv. 1944, Ft. Lauderdale, USA. Lecturer; MIS Analyst. m. Kenneth R. Washington, 9 May 1964, divorced 1984, 1 son 1 daughter. *Education:* BS, 1978, MS, 1981, City College of New York. *Appointments:* MIS Analyst Manager, Dr. MLK, J. Health Center, 1969-89; Science Tutor, 1977-81; Teacher, Special Education Co-ordinator, 1981-. *Memberships:* NAACP; NYC School Board District 9; Bronx Youth in Action, President. *Honours:* Recipient various honours and awards. *Hobbies:* Photography; Education; Travel. *Address:* 540 East 169th Street, Apt. 15C, Bronx, NY 10456, USA.

WASNIOWSKA Emilia Teresa, b. 20 Sept. 1954, Poznan, Poland. Writer. m. Jerzy Wasniowski, 25 June 1977. 1 son, 2 daughters. *Education:* MA, Polish philology, A Mickiewicz University, Poznan, 1973-77. *Appointments:* Specialist, Literary section, Palace of Culture, Poznan, 1977-79; Teacher of Polish, Grammar School, Poznan, 1979-85; Teacher of Polish, Saint Ursula Private Secondary School, Poznan, 1985-86; Speciliast, Polish Centre of Art for Children and Youth, Poznan, 1987-. *Publications:* Przychylic ziemi, 1983, Lyrical poems; Kajtek, 1985, Story for children; Mililililaw, 1988, poems for children; Czy pan widzial rudego chlopca, story in anthology for children, 1988; Przychodze do Ciebie, religious poems for children, in press. *Membership:* Towarzystwo Literackie im Adama Mickiewicza (Adam Mickiewicz Literary Society). *Honour:* Prize, literary competition, Ascending Generation, 1981. *Hobbies:* Literature for children and youth; Collection of postcards edited before 1945. *Address:* 60-682 Poznan, os.Boleslawa Smialego 2/126, Poland.

WASS Hannelore, b. 12 Sept. 1926, Heidelberg, West Germany. Professor. m. Harry H Sister, 1978, 1 son. *Education:* MA, 1960, PhD, 1968, University of Michigan. *Appointments:* University of Michigan Schools, University of Chicago Lab. School, 1958-63; Eastern Michigan University, 1963-69; University of Florida, 1969-. *Publications:* Professional Education of Teachers, 1974; Dying - Facing the Facts, 1979; Dying - Facing the Facts, 2nd edition 1988; Death Education : Annotated Resource Guide, 1980, volume 2 1985; Childhood & Death, 1984; help, Children Cope with Death, editor; etc. *Memberships:* American Psychological Association; Association for Death

Education & Counselling. *Honours:* Recipient, various honours & awards. *Hobbies:* Reading; Music; Swimming. *Address:* 6014 NW 54th Way, Gainesville, FL 32606, USA.

WASSERFALL (Adel Pryor) Adel, b. 2 Dec. 1918, Haugesund, Norway. Housewife. m. Aubrey Lionel Wasserfall, 30 June 1966, 1 stepson. *Appointments:* English Governess, Copenhagen, Denmark, 1936; Secreary to Danish Counsul in Cape Town, South Africa, 1938. *Publications:* Tangled Paths, 1959; Clouded Glass, 1961; Hidden Fire, 1962; Out of the Night, 1963; Hearts in Conflict, 1965; Forgotten Yesterday, 1966; Valley of Desire, 1967; Sound of the Sea, 1968; Free of a Dream, 1969; Her Secret Fear, 1971; A Norwegian Romance, 1976; All is Not Gold, 1979. *Membership:* Chairwoman, Cape Town Children's Service, Mission Branch, Maitland Cottage Homes. *Honours:* English Composition, 1934; Sir William thorne Award, 1937; Short Story Contest Award, 1946. *Hobbies:* Writing; Reading; Listening to Music. *Address:* 8 Iona Street, Tygerhof 7405, Cape, South Africa.

WASTON-BRODNAX Shirley, Microbiologist. m. Jack Brodnax, 31 July 1976. 3 daughters. *Education:* Associate of Arts in Education, 1978; BSc, Cell and Molecular Biology. *Appointments:* Secretarial Supervisor, US Government, Philadelphia and San Francisco, 1970-76; Research Assistant and Microbiologist, Kelly Technical Service, Oakland, California, 1986; Microbiologist, RJR Nabisco Brands, Inc, Oakland, 1986-. *Membership:* International Platform Association. *Honour:* Kennedy King Scholarship, 1978. *Hobbies:* Tennis; Reading; Horseback riding. *Address:* 1537 Hellings Avenue, Richmond, CA 94801, USA.

WATAI Madge Shinoe, b. 17 Dec. 1927, Honolulu, Hawaii. Judge, Superior Court. m. George Watai, 7 July 1952. 1 son, 1 daughter. *Education:* Bachelor of Music 1949, Master of Music 1950, Juris Doctor 1967. *Appointments:* Teacher & Performer, 1952-59; Legal Secretary, 1960-63; Attorney, 1968-78; Judge, Municipal Court, 1978-81; Judge, Superior Court, 1981-. *Memberships:* Charter Member, National Association of Women Judges; Board, Women Lawyuers Association of Los Angeles; Board, California Women Lawyers; American Bar Association; Los Angeles County Bar Association; Japanese American Bar Association; Criminal Courts Bar Association. *Honours:* TELACU, Women's Achievement Award, 1977; Women's Achievement Award, Soroptimist Infl of Gardona, 1980; Outstanding Achievement & Service Award, APWM, 1981; For Dedication, Involvement & Service to Community, Evenging Optimist Club, 1984; For Outstanding Personal Involvement in Community, El Camino Lions Club, 1985. *Hobbies:* Skeet shooting; Hiking; Fishing; Baking. *Address:* Superior Court, Los Angeles County, 111 N Hill Street, Los Angeles, California 90012, USA.

WATERHOUSE Elaine Ardyce Eddy, b. 4 Mar. 1928, Evanston, Illinois, USA. Freelance Writer. m. (1) Glenn F Blinzler, 1 son, 1 daughter, (2) Hugh H Waterhouse, 5 June 1976. *Education:* BJ, University of Missouri, 1950. *Appointments:* Copywriter, Marshall Field and Company, Chicago, 1950-52; Managing Editor, Phillips Petroleum, Texas, 1952-53; Freelance Writer Menninger Foundation, Topeka, 1969-71; Public Relations Director, Johnson County Mental Health Centres, Mission, Kansas, 1973-74; Freelance Writer, Assistant Editor, Box Office Magazine, Kansas City, MO., 1974-76; Copywriter, Alco-Duckwall Stores, Abilene, KS, 1977; Copy Supervisor, Sheplers Inc., Wichita, KS, 1977-79; Copywriter, Sullivan Higdon & Sink, Wichita, 1979-80; Freelance Copywriter, Sheplers Retail and Direct Mail, 1980-81; Freelance Editor, Institute of Logopedics, Wichita; Freelance Copywriter, Jones Stores and Macy's Midwest, Kansas City, MO; Copywriter, Cherokee Advertising, Lenexa, KS, 1982; Acting Manager, Advertising, Forest Jones & Co-Kansas City; Freelance Writer, Hallmark Cards, Kansas City, 1982-83; Manager, Direct Response Division, Hickey

Mitchell Company, St Louis, MO, 1983-87; Freelance Writer, 1988-. *Memberships Include:* Committee Member, Kansas City Professional Chapter, Women in Communications Inc.; Programme & Registrations Chairman, Womens Day, St Louis, Missouri. *Honours:* 1st Place, Direct Mail Category, Kansas Press Women, 1979; 1st Place Award, 1982, Honorable Mention 1983, 1984, Marketing Methods Competition, Professional Insurance Mass Marketing Association. *Hobbies:* Classical Music; Bridge; Swimming; Needlework; Sewing. *Address:* Lake Ozark, Missouri, USA.

WATERLOW Diana Suzanne, Lady, b. 21 Mar. 1943. Justice of the Peace; Director, The Securities Association; Governor, Cricklade College; Board, Holloway Prison. m. Sir Gerald Waterlow Bt, 10 July 1965. 1 son, 1 daughter. *Appointments:* Justice of the Peace, Westminster now West Berkshire, 1972-; Director, Interior Design Company, 1986-. *Hobbies:* Tennis; Bridge. *Address:* Windmills House, Hurstbourne Tarrant, Andover, Hants, England.

WATKINS Joan Marie, b. 9 Mar. 1943, Anderson, Indiana, USA. Osteopath; Physician. m. Stanley Watkins, 25 Dec. 1969 (div. 1974). *Education:* Certificate, Physical Therapy, Ohio State University, 1966; Doctor of Osteopathy, Philadelphia College of Osteopathic Medicine, 1972; MA, Health Professions Education, Centre for Educational Development, University of Illinois, 1986. *Appointments:* Cooper Medical Centre, Camden, New Jersey, 1974-79; Shore Memorial Hospital, Somers Point, NJ, 1979-81; St Francis Hospital, Blue Island, Illinois, 1981-82; Mercy Hospital, Chicago, 1982-; Resident in Occupational Medicine, The University of Illinois. *Memberships:* American College of Emergency Physicians; Society of Teachers in Emergency Medicine; American Occupational Medical Association; Jung Institute, Chicago. *Honour:* Fellow, American College of Emergency Physicians. *Hobbies:* Sailing; Needlepoint; Jung; Shakespeare. *Address:* 505 North Lake Shore Drive, no. 1509, Chicago, Illiniois 60611, USA.

WATKINS Judith Goodwyn, b. 2 Jan. 1949, Washington DC, USA. Painting Conservator. *Education:* BA, Art History, George Washington University; MA, Conservation, International University of Art, Florence, Italy. *Appointments:* Conservation for: US Department of State, 1980- 84; Art in Embassies Programme, & Hong Kong Museum of Art, 1983-84; US Department of Treasury, 1984-. *Creative works include:* Various paintings. *Memberships:* International & American Institutes of Conservation; Washington Conservation Guild. *Hobby:* Horseback riding. *Address:* 2627 Connecticut Avenue NW, Washington DC 20008, USA.

WATKINS Kay, b. 7 Feb. 1951, Atlanta, Georgia, USA. Cultural Arts Supervisor. m. Michael Hughes, 22 Apr. 1978, 1 son, 1 daughter. *Education:* BA, English, Speech & Dramatic Arts, Mercer University, 1973; MSc, Recreation, Oklahoma State University, 1983; Master, Certified, Therapeutic Recreation Specialist. *Appointments:* Coordinator, Project SHARE, Central Georgia Medical Centre, 1983-86; Supervisor, activity therapy, Emory University Hospital, 1986-88; Supervisor, cultural arts, Department of Parks & Recreation, Gwinnett County, Georgia, 1988-. *Publications:* Articles: I Can Do It! (Journal, Special Education for Mentally Retarded); Creative Dramatics Project (Journal, Visual Impairment & Blindness), 1981; How To Start A New Therapeutic Recreation Program (Georgia Recreator), 1988. Contributing writer, Leisure Knows No Handicap (dramatic games for handicapped). *Memberships:* Phi Kappa Phi; Past Vice President, Alpha Psi Omega; Office, Mary Lin Parent-Teacher Association. *Honours:* Scholar, leadership enrichment, Oklahoma University, 1983; National Education grant, 1981-83; Quoted, US News & World Reports, 1981. *Hobbies:* Acting; Story telling; Local neighbourhood column, community newspaper; Writing short stories. *Address:* 571 Terrace Avenue NE, Atlanta, Georgia 30307, USA.

WATSKY Donna Louise Kubiak, b. 4 Aug. 1944, 1 son, 1 daughter. Microbiologist. *Education:* BS, Medical Technology, State University of New York, Buffalo, 1966; MS, Virginia Commonwealth University, 1971. *Appointments:* Medical Technologist, Blood Bank, St Joseph Mercy Hospital, Ann Arbor, 1966-69; Medical Technologist, St Mary's Hospital, 1969-71; Microbiology Supervisor, Anne & Arundel Gen Hospital, 1971-. *Publications:* articles in various journals and magazines. *Memberships:* American Society for Medical Technology, 1966-; Maryland Society for Medical Technology, Board of Directors, 1981-84; American Society for Microbiology; New York Academy of Sciences. *Honours:* New York State Regents Scholarship, 1962-66; Allied Health Professions Grant, 1969-71; Omicron Sigma, 1981-82. *Hobbies:* Sponsors Programme, USNA, 1980-; Salvation Army Volunteer; Needlepoint; Quilting; Sewing. *Address:* Microbiology Dept., Anne Arundel Gen Hospital, Franklin & Cathedral Sts., Annapolis, MD 21401, USA.

WATSON Betty Rush Collier, b. 26 Aug. 1946, Thomasville, Georgia, USA. Senior Research Economist. m. Maxie Collier, 10 Apr. 1965. 3 sons, 3 daughters. *Eucation:* BA, History & English, Fisk, 1966-67; MA equivalent, Cornell, 1967-68; PhD, Economics, 1984. *Appointments:* Assistant Professor of Marketing, Sonoma State University, 1981-83; Associate Professor of Economics and Management, College of Notre Dame, 1986-; Senior Research Economist, National Urban League Inc. *Publications:* An Introduction to Regression Analysis; Business Mathematics and the Textbook Constraint; The Use of Systematic Instruction in Addressing Issues of Oppression; On Social Aspects of Consumer Behavior; Editorial Board, Renaissance Universal Journal. *Memberships:* Eastern Economic Association; Association of Social and Behavioural Scientists; American Evaluation Association. *Honours:* Freedom Foundation Award, Excellence in Economic Education, 1986; Outstanding Young Women in America, 1982; Woodrow Wilson Fellowship, 1967. *Hobbies:* Designing; Sewing; Reading; Writing; Music. *Address:* 6012 Jamina Downs, Columbia, MD 21045, USA.

WATSON Carol, b. 10 Apr. 1957, Nagoya, Japan. Staff Accountant. *Education:* University of MD/Eastern Shore, 1975-77; Bowie State College, 1978-80; BS, Accounting/Business Admin, Community College of the Airforce, 1986. *Appointments:* Maritime Administration, 1980-85; US Dept of Transportation, 1985-87; United States Airforce Reserves, 1985-; US Mint, 1987-88; Benchmark Communications Management, 1989-. *Memberships:* National Association of Female Executives; Association for Professional and Executive Women. *Honours:* Citizen Ambassador for the Professional Women in the People's Republic of China, 1987; Outstanding Airman of the Year 459th MAW, 1987; 2,000 Notable Women, 1988; 5,000 Notable Personalities of the US, 1988. *Hobbies:* Taxes; Riding bike; Running. *Address:* 117 Panorama Drive, Oxon Hill, Maryland 20745, USA.

WATSON Claire, b. 21 Aug. 1936, Selma, USA. Company President. m. 23 June 1956, divorced, 1 son, 1 daughter. *Education:* University of Alabama. *Appointments:* Office Manager, 1955-59, Key Account Sales,1958-63, Dr Pepper Bottling Co/Watson Sales; Secretary-Treasurer, 1963- 80, President, 1980-, Watson Sales; Vice President, S & C Associates, 1984-. *Publications:* A Collection of Short Stories. *Memberships:* 1st Woman President: Florida & Alabama Soft Drink Suppliers; President, Chi Omega; President, English Estates Civic Association. *Honours:* Outstanding Woman of the Year, Junior League, 1968; Outstanding Young Women of America, 1970. *Hobbies:* Travel; Reading; Writing; Football; Modelling; Swimming. *Address:* 108 Camphor Tree Lane, Altamonte Springs, FL 32714, USA.

WATSON Diane Edith, b. 23 Nov. 1933, Los Angeles, USA. California State Senator. *Education:* BA Education, University of California, Los Angeles, 1956; MS School

Psychology, California State University, Los Angeles, 1967; PhD Educational Admin. Claremont Graduate School, 1987. *Appointments:* Teacher, 1956-76; Psychologist, Los Angeles Public Schools, 1975-76; Associate Professor, California State University, Los Angeles, 1976; Member, Los Angeles County Board of Education, 1975-78; California State Senator, 1978-, involving membership of: Senate Standing Committees: Health and Human Services, Chairperson; Budget and Fiscal Review Committee; Education; Judiciary; Public Employment and Retirement; Senate Select Committees on AIDS; Border Issues, Drug Trafficking and Contraband; Children and Youth; Citizen Participation in Government; Substance Abuse and Join Committees: Oversight Committee on GAIN Implementation; Select Task Force on the Changing Family. *Publications:* Health Occupation Instructional Units, Secondary Schools Planning Guide for Health Occupations; Introduction to Health Care; Your Career in Health Care. *Memberships:* Chairperson, California Black Legislative Caucus; President, National Organization of Black Elected Legislators (NOBEL/WOMEN); National Conference of State Legislators (NCSL); California Commission on the Status of Women; NAACP; Urban League; California Business and Professional Women; National Education Association; Black Agenda, Inc; Friend of Golden State Minority Foundation; Alpha Kappa Alpha Sorority; Association of School Psychologists. *Honours:* Legislator of the Year, State Council on Developmental Disabilities, 1987; Legislator of the Year, California Association for Health Services, 1986; Senator of the Year, CSU, Los Angeles, 1983; Legislator of the Year, CA Trial Lawyers Association, 1982. *Hobbies:* Cooking; Travelling. *Address:* 4401 Crenshaw Blvd, Suite 300, Los Angeles, CA 90043, USA.

WATSON Marilyn Fern, b. 30 July 1934, Oklahoma City, Oklahoma, USA. Artist; Writer. m. Donald Wayne Watson, 14 Aug. 1954. 1 son. *Education:* University of Texas at El Paso, 1952-54; BS, magna cum laude, Eastern New Mexico University, 1973; Graduate study, Psychology, 1979-80; Additional study, University of Oklahoma, National Writer's Club, American Film Institute Workshops; Apprentice Technician in Creative Design, Santa Fe Opera, 1982. *Appointments:* Geological Draftsman, Lion Oil Company, 1955-56; Malco Oil Co, 1956; Private tutor, 1970's; Freelance Writer/Artist since, 1959-. *Creative Works:* Painting series, Spring River Corridor; in progress; Numerous articles published in magazines and journals. *Memberships:* Professional Member, National Writers Club; Phi Kappa Phi; Psi Chi; Historical Society of New Mexico; Writer/Historian, United New Mexico Bank at Roswell; Centennial Committee, 1989-90; Chaves County Historical Society. *Honours:* Recipient award, Writers Digest Magazine, 1959; Cotton Memorial Art Scholarship, 1952-54; Recipient, Guideposts Foundation Study Grant, 1978. *Hobbies:* Dress design; Bird watching; Opera; Hiking; Quilting; Gardening/ horticulture; History; Philosophy; Consdervation issues; Wildlife preservation; Psychology. *Address:* 15 Cedar Drive, Roswell, New Mexico 88201, USA.

WATSON Marsha Jean, b. 18 July 1957, Kansas City, Kansas, USA. Journalist; Businesswoman. *Education:* Journalism, English Literature, University of Missouri, Columbia & Kansas City. *Appointments:* President, Watson Writing Services, Kansas City, 1982- ; Secretary-Editor, Landauer Associates, Houston, Texas, 1985; Analyst, Aldrich, Eastman & Waltch Inc, Boston, Massachusetts, 1986-88; News Editor, Droves Journal, Kansas City part-time, 1989-. *Publications include:* Big & Beautiful, in Family Circle, 1985; Magic Diet Ingredient: Self Esteem, Woman's World, 1988; How to Perform Major Surgery, On Your Manuscript, Byline, 1988; Untitled poem, American Poetry Anthology, 1982. *Memberships:* National Association for Female Executives; National Writers Club; Manuscript Critic. *Honours:* Honourable Mentions: Writer's Digest short story contest 1984, 1985, article 1987, Byline romantic story 1986, essay 1987, article 1988, National Writers Club short story/article 1988; 2nd Place, Byline essay contest, 1985. *Hobbies:* Coin

collecting; Needlecrafts. *Address:* 231 Sheidley Avenue, Bonner Springs, Kansas 66012, USA.

WATTERSON Kathryn (Kitsi), b. 4 Feb. 1942, Iowa City, Iowa, USA. Author; Journalist. m. (1) Ford Burkhart, div. 1971, (2) Jack David, 1975, div. 1985. 1 son. *Education:* BA, University of Arizona, 1965. *Appointments:* Feature Writer, The Boca Raton News, 1964; Feature Writer, Reporter, The Fort Lauderdale News, 1964-66; Editor, The Pittsburgh Press, 1966; Teaching English as 2nd Language, Technical Teachers Training College, Kuala Lumpur, Malaysia, 1966-69; Reporter, Urban Affairs Feature Writer, The Philadelphia Evening Bulletin, USA, 1969-73; Teaching: Volunteer, Writers Workshop, Holmesburg Prison, 1970-73; Writers Workshop, New York University, 1977-78; Jorunalism and Writers Workshop, Fordham University, 1984-86, autumn 1988; Lecturer, Craft of Writing, Princeton University, New Jersey, 1988-. *Publications:* Under Kathryn Watterson Burkhart: Women In Prison, Doubleday, 1973, Popular Library, 1981; Growing Into Love: Teenagers Talk Candidly About Sex in the 1980's, 1981; The Birthday Party Book (co-author), 1987; Under Kathryn Watterson: The Safe Medicine Book, 1988; The Duke University Medical Center Book of Diet and Fitness Book (co-author), 1991. *Memberships:* Freedom-to-Write Committee Member, PEN American Center; Authors League; Authors Guild. *Honours:* American Political Science Association, for distinguished reporting, 1971; Certificate of Merit, The Gavel Awards, American Bar Association, 1971, 1974; Scales of Justice Award, Philadelphia Bar Association, 1971, 1973; Sigma Delta Chi, for outstanding reporting, 1971; Runner-up, Paul G Tobenkin Award, Columbia University Graduate School of Journalism, 1973; Mlle Award for Outstanding Achievement, Mademoiselle Magazine, 1974; Named 1 of tomorrow's literary luminaries, Saturday Review, 1974. *Address:* 122 Patton Avenue, Princeton, NJ 08540, USA.

WATTS Janet Hawkins, b. 23 Feb. 1951, Richmond, VA, USA. Associate Professor. m. Robert Allen Watts, 2 July 1977, 1 son, 1 daughter. *Education:* BA, College of William & Mary, 1973; MSc., Virginia Commonwealth University, 1977, Certificate in Aging Studies, VCU, 1986. *Appointments:* Richmond Day Treatment Center, 1977-78; Chesterfield County Department of Mental Health, 1978-80; Virginia Commonwealth University, 1980-. *Publications:* Articles in professional journals; Psychosocial Occupational Therapy, co-author, 1983-88; Bodies of Knowledge in Psychosocial Practice, co-author, 1988-; Occupational Therapy in Psychosocial Pratioo, co-author, 1988-. *Memberships:* American Occupational Therapy Association, 1977-; Virginia Occupational Therapy Association, 1977-1980, 1981- . *Hobbies:* Gardening; Organ Playing. *Address:* Virginia Commonwealth University, Dept. of Occupational Therapy, MCV Box 8, Richmond, VA 23298, USA.

WATTS Marian Joy, b. 22 Mar. 1948, London, England. Chartered Accountant; Business Consultant. *Education:* BA, Modern Languages, Univesity of Leeds, 1970; Institute of Chartered Accountants in England & Wales, 1973, Fellow, 1978. *Appointments:* Lovewell Blake & Co., Norwich, 1970-73; Coopers & Lybrand, Paris, 1973-76; Donnelley Marketing, France, 1976-80; Bendix, Europe, 1980-84; Frinault Fiduciaire, 1985; Self- employed Chief Executive, European Business Development Services, 1985-. *Memberships:* International Federation of Business and Professional Women, European Co-ordinator, 1985-87; Mensa France; Association of British Accountants in France; Franco British Chamber of Commerce & Industry. *Honours:* University of Leeds Senior Scholarship, Emsley Fund for Academic Distinction, 1968. *Hobbies:* Europe; Equal Opportunities for Women; Yoga. *Address:* 9 Rue de L'Arc de Triomphe, 75017, Paris, France.

WATTS Vivian Edna, b. 7 June 1940, Michigan, USA. Transportation & Public Safety. m. David Watts, 30 Jan. 1960, 1 son, 1 daughter. *Education:* BA, University of Michigan, 1962. *Appointments:* Fairfax Chamber of Commerce, 1977-79; State Legislative Aide, 1979-81;

Congressional Legal Assistant, 1980; Researcher, Arthur Young & Co., 1984-85; Member, VA House of Delegates, 1982-86; Secretary, Transportation & Public Safety, 1986-. *Publications:* Fairfax County Fiscal Comm. Report; Efficient Use of School Facilities; Fairfax County's Business Tax Base; Alternatives to Real Estate Tax. *Memberships:* Fairfax Area League of Women Voters, President, 1975-77; Executive Board, United Way, 1975-; Women Executives in State Government, National Board, 1986-87; Founding Member, Fairfax County Committee of 100. *Honours:* Washington StarCitizen of the Year, 1977; Network Business & Professional Women of the Year, 1986; Annandale Chamber of Commerce Citizen of the Year, 1986; International Rotary Paul Harris Fellow, 1987. *Hobby:* Downhill Skiing. *Address:* Office of the Secretary of Transportation & Public Safety, PO Box 1475, Richmond, VA 23212, USA.

WAUGH Dorothy, b. 23 Sept. 1896, Burlington, Vermont, USA. Retired. *Education:* Massachusetts School of Art; University of Massachusetts; Cleveland Museum School of Art; Graduate, Chicago Art Institute. *Publications:* Among the Leaves & Grasses, 1931; Warm Earth, 1943; Muriel Saves String, 1956; A Handbook of Christmas Decoration, 1958; Festive Decoration the Year Round, 1962; Emily Dickinson's Beloved, A Surmise, 1976; Illustrations for numerous other books; Contributions to Christian Science Monitor; Yankee; The Rotarian; American Mercury; Horticulture, etc. *Honours:* Books of design included among: Fifty Books of the Year, American Institute of Graphic Arts; Conducted a commentary and interview radio programme for 7 years for WVNJ; Planned TV programmes for Channel 13 and others. *Hobby:* 40 years research on the life and poetry of Emily Dickinson. *Address:* 38 East 38 Street, New York, NY 10016, USA.

WAYMAN Vivienne, b. 19 June 1926, London, England. m. Cecil John Wayman, 28 Dec. 1951. 1 daughter. *Education:* Diploma of Design, St Martin's School of Art, 1944; Art Teachers Diploma, Institute of Education, London, 1945. *Appointment:* Art Teacher, Barnhurst Kent, 1946-51. *Creative works:* Children's Stories read on BBC (RAdio): The Rose at Penny Spring, 1968; Emma of Larkwater Hall, 1969; The Alabaster Princess, 1970; The Cage in The Apple Orchard, 1972; The Seventh Bull Maiden, 1974; Panchit's Secret, 1975; Crime Fiction, The Golden Duck, 1990. *Hobbies:* Music; Ornithology. *Address:* 42 Old Church Lane, Stanmore, Middlesex, England. 3.

WEATHERBEE Linda, b. 20 July 1956, Decatur, Illinois, USA. Assistant Life Superintendent, State Farm Insurance. *Education:* BA, James Millikin University, 1974-77; Illinois State University, 1981-82; FLMI, 1982; CLU, 1987; ChFC, 1988. *Appointments:* Financial Analyst 1979-82, Bloomington, Supervisor 1982-86, Austin, Assistant Life Superintendent 1986-, Salem, State Farm Insurance; Teacher, LDS Church Education System, 1987-. *Memberships:* Willamette Ch of Am Society of CLU/ChFC (Bd of Directors, 1987-); Administrative Management Society, 1987-; Life Office Management Assoc 1981-86; Am Bus Women's Assoc, 1982-86; National Assoc of Female Executives, 1984-86; Am Horse Show Assoc, 1988-; Northwest Horse Council, 1988-; Phi Kappa Phi Honor Fraternity. *Honours:* Valedictorian, Douglas MacArthur High School, 1974; National Honor Society Gold Delta recipient, 1974; Phi Kappa Phi Honor Fraternity member; Magna Cum Laude Graduate, Millikin University, 1977. *Hobbies:* Adult basic education volunteer tutor; Hunter/jumper horse showing; Reading; Dancing; Cake decorating; Music/theatre; Cello. *Address:* State Farm Life Insurance, 4600 25th Avenue NE, Salen, Oregon 47313, USA.

WEAVER Donna Rae, b. 15 Oct. 1945, Chicago, Illinois, USA. College Administrator. m. Clifford L Weaver, 20 Aug. 1966. 1 daughter. *Education:* BSEd 1966, EdD 1977, National Illinois University; MEd, DePaul University, 1974. *Appointments:* Teacher, Harold L Richards High School, 1966-71; Teacher,

Sawyer College of Business, 1971-72; Assistant Professor, Oakton Community College, 1972-75; Visiting Lecturer, University of Illinois at Chicago, 1977-78; Director of Development, 1978-80, Dean, 1980-83, Mallinckrodt College; National College of Education, 1983-; Director, 1983-86, Associate Vice President and Director, 1986-, Chicago Campus; Dean, Division of Applied Behavioural Sciences, 1985-, National College of Education. *Memberships:* Past President, Corresponding Secretary, Historian, Delta Pi Epsilon, Lambda Chapter; Illinois Quality of Work Life Council. *Honours:* Elected Charter Distinguished Fellow, American Board of Master Educators, 1986; Recipient, Women in Management's Woman of Achievement Award, 1981; Holmes Prize Scholarship for Doctoral work, Northern Illinois University, 1976. *Hobby:* Travel. *Address:* National College of Education, 18 So Michigan Ave, Chicago, IL 60603, USA.

WEBB Bernice Larson, b. Ludell, Kansas, USA. Writer; Educator. m. (2) Robert M. Webb, 14 July 1961. 1 son, 1 daughter, previous marriage. *Education:* AB 1956, MA 1957, PhD 1961, Universty of Kansas; Doctoral research, University of Aberdeen, Scotland, UK, 1959-60. *Appointments:* Assistant Instructor, Department of English, University of Kansas, 1958-59, 1960-61; Assistant Professor 1961-67, Associate Professor 1967-80, Professor of English 1980-87, University of Southwestern Louisiana; Visiting Professor, World Campus Afloat. *Publications:* Basketball Man, 1973, translated Japanese 1981; Beware of Ostriches, 1978; Poetry on the Stage, 1979; Lady Doctor on a Homestead, 1987. Past Editor: State periodical, American Association of University Women; Editor, Louisiana State Poetry Society journal. *Memberships include:* Past President: Louisiana State Poetry Society, Phi Beta Kappa local branch, South Central College English Association. *Honours:* Coolidge Research Colloquium, 1985; Phi Beta Kappa, 1955; Fulbright scholarship alternate, France, 1959; Foreign exchange scholar, Scotland, 1959-60; 9 Carruth poetry prizes, 1946-61; Seaton award, 1980; 3 research grants, 1978-86. *Hobbies:* Acting; Travel. *Address:* 159 Whittington Drive, Lafayette, Louisiana 70503, USA.

WEBB Leslie Darlene, b. 8 Feb. 1949, Toronto, Canada. Actress; Poet. m. Gordon H. Webb, 28 June 1969, 1 son. *Appointments:* Special Events Co-ordinator, Centrestage Company, 1984-85. *Publications:* Chapbook, Original Innocence, 1988. *Memberships:* Arts Scarborough, Board of Directors, 1985-86; Scarborough Theatre Guild, Vice President, 1980- 85; Centrestage Co., Associate, Board of Directors; Theatre Ontario. *Honours:* Association of Community Theatre President's Award, 1984; *Address:* 8 Brenda Court, Lindsay, Ontario, Canada K9V 5W1.

WEBB Sharon Lynn, b. 29 Feb. 1936, Tampa, Florida, USA. Registered Nurse. Writer. m. W. Bryan Webb, 6 Feb. 1956, 3 daughters. *Education:* Florida Southern College, 1953-56; University of Miami, 1962; ADN, Miami-Dade School of Nursing, 1972. *Appointments:* Freelance Writer, 1960-66; Registered Nurse, South Miami Hospital, 1972-73; Registered Nurse, Union General Hospital, Towns County Hospital, Blairsville, Georgia, 1973-81. *Publications:* RN, 1981; Earthchild, 1982; Earth Song, 1983; Ram Song, 1984; Adventures of Terra Tarkington, 1985; Pestis 18, 1987; The Halflife, 1989; Over 40 short stories. *Memberships:* Authors Guild; Authors League; Science Fiction Writers of America, South/Central Director, Board of Directors. *Address:* Route 2, Box 2600, Blairsville, GA 30512, USA.

WEBB Susan Howard, b. 18 Aug. 1908, Burlington, Vermont, USA. Retired Administrator and Legislator, State of Vermont. m. 12 Sept. 1932. 1 son, 2 daughters. *Education:* AB, University of Vermont, 1930; AM, Radcliffe College (now Radcliffe-Harvard University), 1931. *Appointments:* Teacher, Classics, 1931-32; Co-Founder and Administrator, Farm & Wilderness Foundation, 1947-49; Elected Member, Vermont State Legislature in House of Representatives, 1939-; Appointed Member, Vermont State Committee, US Civil

Rights Commission, 1975-80. *Publications:* Summer Magic; Round the World Letters for Children; Articles in numerous magazines and journals. *Memberships:* Board of Directors, Vermont Childrens Forum; President and Member, Board of Directors, Calvin Coolidge Memorial Foundation Inc; Board Member and Member Advisory Committee, Vermont YWCA; Legislative Chairman, VT Churchwomen Limited; VT Council Social Concerns. *Honours:* Phi Beta Kappa, 1930; Legislator of the Year Award, Vermont Association of Pediatricians, 1977. *Interests:* Good laws for children; Education; Environment; Politics. *Address:* Brooksend, HCR70 Box 19, Plymouth, VT 05056, USA.

WEBB-WILLIAMS Dorothea, b. 6 July 1948, Nashville, USA. Dean, Professor. 1 daughter. *Educaiton:* BSN, Vanderbilt University, 1971; MSN, 1974, PhD, 1976, University of Michigan. *Appointments:* Dean/ Professor, Coppin State college, 1979-81; Director, Nursing, Brook Lane Psychiatric Centre, 1981-82; Professor, The William Patterson College of New Jersey, 1982-83; Faculty of Medicine, Columbia University, 1985-86; Dean, Professor, College of Nursing, Prairie View A&M University, 1986-. *Publications:* Articles in professional journals. *Memberships:* American Associate, Colleges of Nursing; American, National Black Nurses Associations; National League for Nursing; Southern Regional Education Board. *Honours:* Scholarships: Vanderbilt University, 1969-71; Alpha Kappa Alpha; Sigma Theta Tau; etc. *Hobbies:* Reading; Writing. *Address:* 2213 S. Braeswood Blvd., Suite 13H, Houston, TX 77030, USA.

WEBBER Christine Campbell, TV Broadcaster; Producer; Novelist. *Education:* Guildhall School of Music and drama. *Appointments:* Lead Singer, Black & White Minstrels; Presenter, Southern TV; Presenter, Anglia TV. *Publications:* Numerous TV Programmes and Videos; Novel: In Honour Bound, 1987, 1988. *Honours:* CEC Media Award, 1982; CEC Award for Distinguished Community Service, 1985. *Address:* c/o Anglia TV, Anglia House, Norwich, NR1 3JG, England.

WEBER Anne Elizabeth, b. 16 Jan. 1957, Passaic, New Jersey, USA. Architect. m. David Schure, 26 Oct. 1985. *Education:* BS, Engineering & Applied Science, Yale University, 1978; MArch, MS Historic Preservation, Columbia University, 1982. *Appointments:* David Peabody Architects, 1983-86; Colonial Williamsburg Federation, 1986-87; Magoon & Guernsey Architects, 1987-88; Short & Ford, Architects, 1988-. *Memberships:* Central New Jersey Chapter, American Institute of Architects; American Friends of Attingham Summer School. *Honours:* Charles E. Peterson Prize, 1983; Honour citation, Mississippi Chapter AIA, 1984; Donald Warren McCroskey Prize, 1978. *Hobbies:* Bagpipes; Photography; Decorative arts. *Address:* Box 864, Mapleton Road, Princeton, New Jersey 08540, USA.

WEBER Linda Ficklin, b. 11 Mar. 1926, Columbia, Missouri, USA. Psychotherapist; Educational Consultant. m. Joseph R. Weber, 29 Sept. 1946, 1 son, 3 daughters. *Honours:* BA cum laude, Elmhurst College, Elmhurst, Illinois, 1968; MS, Northern Illinois University, 1975; Graduated from master class, Gestalt Institute of Chicago, 1983. *Appointments:* Teacher, 1968-74, Counsellor, 1974-84, District 45 Schools, Villa Park, Illinois; Counsellor, Psychotherapist, Linda Weber and Associates, 1982-85; Administrative Secretary, Church of the Brethren, Washington Office, Washington DC, 1985-88; Pastoral Counsellor, Washington Pastoral Counselling Service, 1988-. *Memberships:* American Association for Counselling Development; American Association; American Association of Pastoral Counselors; Alpha Xi Delta; YWCA, Washington, Legislative Core Group. *Hobbies:* Travel; Learning; People; Reading. Executive Committee, National Board of Women for a Meaningful Summitt. *Address:* 2130 P St NW 524, Washington, DC 20037, USA.

WEBSTER (Jan) Janet Watson, b. 10 Aug. 1924,

Blantyre, Scotland. Writer. m. Andrew Webster, 10 Aug. 1946. 1 son, 1 daughter. *Education:* Hamilton Academy, Scotland. *Appointments:* Journalist, Kemsley Newspapers, 1941-48; Freelance Journalist. *Publications:* Colliers Row; Saturday City; Beggarman's Country; Due South; Muckle Annie; One Little Room; The Rags of Time; A Different Woman; Also short stories. *Hobbies:* Gardening; Reading; Scottish history. *Address:* c/o Robert Hale Ltd, 45-47 Clerkenwell Green, London EC1R OHT, England.

WECHTER Marilyn, b. 25 Aug. 1952, New York, USA. Psychotherapist. *Education:* BA, 1973, MSW, 1975, Washington University; ACSW, 1980; Clinical Register, 1982. *Appointments:* Psychotherapist, Quad City Mental Health Clinic, 1975-76; Psychotherapist, Growth Center, 1976-80; Private practice, 1980-; Adjunct Faculty, Washington University, 1984-85; Adjunct Faculty, Webster University, 1988-. *Memberships:* Diplomat, NASW; Society of Clinical Social Workers; Missouri Psychological Association; Society Advancement of Self Psychology; *Hobbies:* Music; Opera; Theatre; Art; Reading; Sailing. *Address:* 141 N. Meramec, Suite 205, Clayton, MO 63105, USA.

WECK Kristin Willa, b. 5 Nov. 1959, Elgin, USA. Savings & Loan Association Examiner. *Education:* BA, Augustana College, 1981. *Appointments:* Intern, Investment Banking Group, First Chicago Bank, London, 1980; Intern, Prudential Bache Co., Ft. Lauderdale, 1981; Residential Appraiser, Fox Valley Appraisal Counselors Ltd., 1982-84; Assistant Real Estate Loan Officer, Barrington, 1982-84, Savings & Loan Field Examiner, Illinois, Illinois Fedeal Home Loan Bank, Chicago, 1984-. *Memberships:* Society of Real Estate Appraisers; Brandywine Condominium Association, Vice President, 1983; National Association of Accountants, 1978; Licensed Real Estate Sales Broker, 1989-. *Hobbies:* Scuba Diving; Water Skiing; Bicycling; Reading. *Address:* 435A Brandy Drive, Crystal Lake, IL 60014, USA.

WEDDERBURN Dorothy Enid Cole, b. 18 Sept. 1925, London, England. Principal of Royal Holloway & Bedford New College, University of London. *Education:* BA Cantab, Economics Tripost Parts I & II, 1946; MA Cantab, 1950. *Appointments:* Research Officer, Senior Research Officer, Department Applied Economics, Cambridge University, 1950-65; Lecturer, Senior Lecturer, Professor of Industrial Sociology, Imperial College of Science & Technology, 1965-81; Principal of Royal Holloway & Bedford New College, University of London, 1001-. *Publications:* White Collar Redundancy, 1964; Redundancy and the Railwayman, 1964; Enterprise Planning for Change, 1968; The Economic Circumstances of Old People, with J Utting, 1962; The Aged in the Welfare State, with P Townsend, 1965; Old Age in Three Industrial Societies, 1968. *Memberships:* Fellow, Royal Statistical Society; British Industrial Relations Association; Executive Committee, International Industrial Relations Association; Honorary President, The Fawcett Society; The Court of London University; Pro-Vice-Chancellor, London University. *Honours:* Honorary Fellow, Imperial College of Science and Technology, 1986; Honorary Fellow, Ealing College of Higher Education, 1985; Honorary DLitt, Warwick University, 1984; Senior Research Fellow, Imperial College of Science and Technology, 1981. *Hobbies:* Politics; Walking; Cooking; Gardening. *Address:* Royal Holloway and Bedford New College, Egham, Surrey, TW20 0EX, England.

WEDDINGTON Sarah Catherine, b. 5 Feb. 1945, Abilene, Texas, USA Attorney at Law. *Education:* BD, McMurry College, Abilene, 1965; JD, University of Texas, 1967. *Appointments:* Member, Texas House of Representatives, 1973-77; General Counsel, US Department of Agriculture, 1977- 78; Assistant to President of the United States, 1978-81; Carl Hatch Professor, Law & Public Administration, University of New Mexico School of Law, 1981; Visiting Professor, Government, Wheaton College, Massachusetts, 1981-83; Director, Texas Office, State-Federal Relations,

1983-85; Private Law practice, 1985-; Senior Lecturer, University of Texas, Austin, 1986-. *Memberships Include:* Board, Population Council 1971-85; Director, Bottwinick-Wolfensohn Foundaiton, New York, 1981-83; American Bar Association, Standing Committee on Association Communications, 1979-; etc. *Honours:* Honorary LLD's, Hamilton College, McMurry College, 1979; Awards, Time Magazine, 1979, Ladies Home Journal, 1980, Esquire 1984. *Address:* 709 West 14th Street, Austin, TX 78701, USA

WEDELL PAPE Lis, b. 20 Feb. 1949, Aarhus, Denmark. Assistant Professor/Lecturer. 1 daughter. *Education:* MA, Scandinavian Language & Literature, 1975; BA, English Literature, 1977. *Appointments:* School Master, 1978-86; Assistant Professor, 1975-88; Assistant Professor/Lecturer, 1988-. *Publications:* Det Besatte Kon (The Possessed Sex), Treatise, 1986; Mellem Graes & Skrift (Between Grass & Ecriture), Essay on the Danish Author, Inger Christensen, 1988; Tekstens Galskab (The Insanity of Writing), Essay on E A Poe, 1988. *Memberships:* Master of Arts Association; Association of Teachers of Danish Literature & Language; Association of Danish Philosophers. *Hobbies:* Editing books (Women's research yearbooks) and periodicals; Gardening. *Address:* Svejstrupvej 18, Svejstrup, 8370 Hadsten, Denmark.

WEED Mary Theophilos, b. 11 Nov. 1928, Miami, Florida, USA. College Professor. m. Perry L Weed, 29 Mar. 1963, divorced. 1 daughter. *Education:* BA, University of Miami, Florida, 1953; MA, University of Chicago, 1960. *Appointments:* School Psychologist, Chicago Board of Education, 1960-62; Assistant Professor of Psychology, Chicago City Colleges, 1962-; Consultant to Social Security Disability Program, 1962-85. *Publications:* Numerous works in progress. *Memberships:* American Psychology Association; Illinois Phsychology Association. *Honours:* Licensed Psychologist, State of Illinois; Listed in national Register of Health Services Providers in Psychology. *Hobbies:* Creative writing; Theoretical issues in Psychology (innovative). *Address:* 5534 S Harper, Chicago, Illinois 60637, USA.

WEED Pamela Lee Bowlin, b. 31 July 1949, Alabama, USA. Assistant Principal; Fitness Instructor. m. Norman M. Weed, 12 Sept. 1970, 2 daughters. *Education:* BA, Auburn University, 1970; MA, University of Alabama, 1976; MA, University of Alabama, 1978. *Appointments:* Physical Education Instructor, Varsity Gymnastics Coach, Erwin High School, 1971-80; Assistant Principal, Hewitt Elementary School, 1980-84; Assistant Principal, erwin High School, 1984-. *Publications:* Dynamic Directions, 1981; Presentor: IDEA Educational Conference, Washington, 1987. *Memberships:* Birmingham BPW; International Dance Exercise Association; Aerobics & Fitness Association of America; National Education Association. *Honours:* IDEA Gold Certificate, 1986. *Hobbies:* Swimming; Boating; American Saddlebred Horses. *Address:* 3108 Bradford Place, Birmingham, AL 35243, USA.

WEEKS Brigitte, b. 28 Aug. 1943, England. Editor-in-Chief. m. Edward A. Herscher, 6 Sept. 1969, 2 sons, 1 daughter. *Education:* BA, University College of North Wales, Bangor, 1965. *Appointments:* Assistant Editor, Boston Magazine, USA, 1967-70; Editor, Kodansha International, Tokyo, Japan, 1970-72; Editor, Praeger Special Studies, 1973; Writer, United Mineworkers Union, 1973-74; Editor, Resources for the Future, 1974; Assistant Editor 1974-76, Managing Editor 1976-78, Editor 1978-88, Editor-in-Chief Book-of-the-Month Club 1988-, Wshington Post Book World. *Publications include:* Articles & reviews: New Republic; Ms magazine; Washington Journalism Review; American Film; Philadelphia Inquirer; Newsday; Nation; Writer; Publishers Weekly; National Geographic Traveler; Japan Times; Asia Magazine. Also: Editor, Book World Literary Quiz Book. *Memberships:* Board 1978-87, President 1984-86, National Book Critics Circle. *Address:* Book-of-the-Month Club, 485 Lexington Avenue, New York, NY 10017, USA.

WEEKS Jane Sutherland, b. 22 Feb. 1924, Birmingham, Alabama, USA. Consultant; Lecturer; Writer. m. Robert Andrew Weeks, 20 Mar. 1948, 3 sons, 1 daughter. *Education:* BA, 1948; MA, 1964. *Appoinments Include:* Specialist (S), US Navy, 1944-46; Researcch Assistant, Oak Ridge Naitonal Laboratory, 1950-53; Instructor, Sociology, 1956-69, Assistant Professor Sociology, 1972-80 Carson-Newman College, Visiting Professor, Religious Studies, 1980-81, Lecurer, Womens Studies, 1987, University of Tennessee; Senior Fellow, American University, Cairo, Egypt, 1970-71; Public Speaker, Consultant, Writer, Project Co-ordinator, Mothers and Children, Recovery Home for Susbstance Abuse Women. *Publications:* Contributor To: Cities; Appalachian Woman; Social Forces; Journal of Rehabilitation; numerous other magazines, journals, book reviews. *Memberships Include:* Agape, Board 1982-86; Matrix, Incorporator 1st President (Small Business Organization For Women and Minorities); Knoxville Womens Centre, Founder, 1st President 1974-76, Board of Directors 1984-86; many other professional organisations. *Honours Include:* Appalachian Studies Grant, TVA, 1977; NEH Scholar, 1979; Mayor's Award, City of Knoxville, 1982; Annie Selwyn Award, Knoxville Womens Centre, 1986. *Hobbies:* Writing; Travel; Gardening. *Address:* 2104 Tooles Bend Road, Knoxville, TN 37922, USA.

WEEMS Katharine Lane, b. 22 Feb. 1899, Boston, Massachusetts, USA. Sculptor. m. F. Carrington Weems, 15 Nov. 1947. *Education:* School of Museum of Fine Arts, Boston; Pupil of Charles Grafly, Anna Hyatt Huntington, George Demetrios and Brenda Putman. *Creative works include:* Dog Narcisse Noir; Kangaroo; 12-ft bronze group Dolphins of the Sea Water Plaza; Works in permanent collections: Greek Horse, Baltimore Museum of Art; Bear, Spee Club, Harvard; Whippet, Glenbow Foundation Musuem; Whippet and Fox, Colby College Art Museum, Waterville, Maine; Brick carvings, entrance doors, 2 bronze rhinoceri, Institute of Biology, Harvard; Sculpture on Lotta Fountain, Boston; Small bronzes in private collections; Permanent exhibition, Weems Gallery of Animal Sculpture, Museum of Science, Boston; Sculpted Goodwin Medal, Massachusetts Institute of Technology, US Legion of Merit Medal and Medal for Merit, Fincke Memorial Medal, Groton School Memorial, Massachusetts Art Commission, 1941-47. *Memberships:* NA Fellow, National Sculpture Society (Council 1949); Guild of Boston Artists; National Association of Women Artists; National Institute of Arts and Letters; Grand Central Art Galleries; Architectural League; American Artists Professional League; North Shore Arts Association; Huguenot Society; Lords of Colonial Manors; Massachusetts Society of Colonial Dames of America; Allied Artists of America. *Honours:* Chevalier, National Order of Merit, France; Bronze Medal, Sesqui-Centennial Exposition, Philadelphia, 1926; Widener Memorial Gold Medal, Pennsylvania Academy of Fine Arts, 1927; Joan of Arc Gold Medal, National Association of Women Painters and Sculptors, 1928; Saltus Gold Medal for Merit, National Academy of Design, 1960; Gold Medal, National Arts Club, New York City, 1961; Kalos Kagathos Foundation Sculpture Prize, 1981; Numerous other prizes and medals for her works. *Address:* PO Box 126, Manchester, MA 01944, USA.

WEGNER Mary Sue, b. 27 Feb. 1941, Centralia, Illinois, USA. Nuclear Engineer. m. Lloyd Arthur Wegner, 7 May 1961, divorced. 1 son, 2 daughters. *Education:* AA, Physics, McLennan Community College, 1972; BS, Nuclear Engineering, Texas A&M University, 1974; Postgraduate, Georgia Inst Tech, 1980-81. *Appointments:* Draftsman, USAF, Keesler AFB, Mississippi, 1959-60; Clerk, Mid-State Electric Co, Alexandria, Louisiana, 1963-66; Draftsman, Dresser Indsl Vale and Instrument div, Alexandria, 1966- 67; Aircraft Insp, Gen Dynamics, Waco, Texas, 1968-70; Draftsman, Lone Star Gas, Waco, 1971-72; Nuclear Field Engr, Gen Electric Co, Atlanta, 1974-81; Reactor

Systems Engr, Nuclear Regulatory Commn, Bethesda, MD, 1981-. *Membership:* Am Nuclear Soc, Chairman 1977. *Honours:* Cert governance Am Nuclear Soc; Engineering Excellence, 1983; High Quality Certificate, USNRC, 1982, 1986. *Hobbies:* Crafts, particularly lace crochet; Reading. *Address:* Nuclear Regulatory Commn Office Analysis and Evaluation of Operational Data, Washington, DC 20555, USA.

WEIDENFELLER Geraldine Marie Carney, b. 12 Oct. 1933, Kearny, New Jersey, USA. Speech Language Pathologist. m. 4 Apr. 1964. *Education:* BS, Newark State,1954; MA, New York University, 1963; Northwestern Univesity; University of Wisconsin. *Appointments:* Speech Therpist, Kearny, New Jersey, 1954-60, North Brunwick, 1960-65, Bridgewater, New Jersey, 1969-71; Speech Pathologist, Somerset County Education Services, 1983-87. *Memberships:* Toastmasters, Secretary 1984-85; Rosary, Vice President 1986-87; AAUW Executive Board, 1976-80; County Committee Women, 1981-86; Social Chairman, Kearny Education Association; Brownie Leader 1973; Vice President, Home & School Association. *Hobbies:* Painting Calligraphy; Reading. *Address:* 3 Banor Drive, Somerville, NJ 08876, USA.

WEIGEL Elsie Mae Diven, b5. 31 May 1948, Darby, Pennsylvania, USA. Writer; Editor. m. 19 Dec. 1970, divorced 1979. 1 daughter. *Education:* Academic Linguistic American University, Washington DC, 1964; Broadcast Journalism, 1966-70. *Appointments:* Editorial Asst, Water Pollution Control Federation, 1970-72; Asst Pub Dir, Amer Speech, Hearing & Lang Assn, 1972-78; Editor, Potato Chip Snack Food Assn, 1978-79; Dir of Pubs, Natl Soc of Public Accountants, 1979-80; Editorial Proj Dir, Energy Information Admin, US Dept of Energy, 1980-. *Publications:* Editor, Rittenhouse Family Newsletter; numerous articles for magazines of past associations; Astrological Tapes (audio). *Memberships:* Sigma Delta Chi, Honorary Journalism Society; Natl Assn for Female Execs; Board of Directors, Life Skills Center, Washington DC. *Honour:* Cash Award for Superior Job Performance, 1982. *Hobbies:* Astrology; Metaphysics; Gardening; Boating. *Address:* 8303 Pondside Terrace, Alexandria, VA 22309, USA.

WEIMER Rita J, b. 25 Aug. 1933, Boricourt, Kansas USA. Professor. m. Robert 2 Dec. 1977, 1 son, 1 daughter. *Education:* BS, 1956; MS, 1964, Ed.D., 1974, University of Kansas. *Appointments:* Business Teacher, Army Education Centre, Germany, 1956-58; Public Schools, 1958-66; Instructor, 1966-74, Professor, 1974, Kansas State University. *Memberships:* International Reading Association; Kansas Reading Association; National Council of Teachers of English; NOW; Association of University Professors; Phi Delta Kappa. *Hobbies:* Swimming; Reading; Walking. *Address:* 211 Bluemont Hall, College of Education, Kansas State University, Manhattan, KS 66506, USA.

WEIN Cynthia E, b. 24 Dec. 1957, Maryland, USA. President, Creative Planning International; Director, Great Inns of America. *Education:* BS Restaurant, Hotel, Institutional Management, Purdue University; MLS, Antioch School of Law, 1982. *Appointments:* Sales Manager, Sea Pines Plantation Resort, 1980-82; Sales/ Marketing Director, Sheraton Potomac Hotel, 1982-83; Sales Director, Ritz Carlton Hotel, Washington DC, 1983-84; President/Owner, Creative Planning International, 1983-; Assn Director, Great Inns of America, 1987-89. *Publication:* Great Inns of America, Guidebook, 1988-89. *Memberships:* Purdue Univ Alumni Club, President 1984-; Indiana State Society, 1986-; Meeting Planners Intl, 1980-; Greater Washington Society of Assn Execs, 1988-; American Society of Assn Execs, 1988-; Foundation for International Mtgs, Former Board member. *Honours:* Outstanding Alumna Nominee, Purdue University, 1989; Featured in Successful Meetings Magazine, 1986 and 1988; Appointed to Women in Transportation Committee, Sec Eliz Dole, 1986. *Hobbies:* Music; Country inn-hopping; International travel; Cullinary arts;

Interior decorating; Amateur photography. *Address:* 7627 Heatherton Lane, Potomac, MD 20854, USA.

WEINBERG Amy Sara, b.3 June 1955, Boston, Massachusetts, USA. Professor. m. Norbert Hornstein, 24 June 1979. *Education:* BA, 1st class honours, Linguistics/Philosophy, McGill University, 1976; PhD, Linguistics/Philosophy, Massachusetts Institute of Technology, 1988. *Appointments:* University of Maryland Linguistics Department, 1984-; University of Maryland, Institute for Advanced Computer Studies, 1986-. *Publications:* The Grammatical Basis of Linguistic Performance, MIT Press, with R Berwick; numerous articles. *Memberships:* Linguistic Society of America; Creative Linguistics of the Old World. *Hobbies:* Tennis; Gardening; Political activity. *Address:* Department of Linguistics, University of Maryland, College Park, MD 20742, USA.

WEINER Annette Barbara, b. 14 Feb. 1933, Philadelphia, USA. Profesor. m. (1) Martin Weiner, 1953, divorcd 1973, 1 son, 1 daughter, (2) Robert Palter, 1979, divorced 1981, (3) William E Mitchell, 1987. *Education:* BA, University of Pennsylvania, 1968; PhD, Bryn Mawr College, 1974. *Appointments:* Assistant Professor, 1974-80, Associate Professor, 1980-81, University of Texas, Austin; David B Kirser Professor and Chair, Anthropology, New York University, 1981-. *Publications:* Women of Value, Men of Renown: New Perspectives in Trobriand Exchange, 1976; The Trobrianders of Papua New Guinea, 1988; Cloth and Human Experience, co-editor, 1989; contributor to professional journals. *Memberships:* Society for Cultural Anthropology, Board 1983-88, President 1988-90; American Anthropological Association, Fellow; Royal Anthropological Institute, Fellow; Association of Social Anthropology in Oceania, Fellow. *Honours Include:* Guggenheim Fellow, 1980; Member, Institute for Advanced Study, Princeton, 1981; NEH Fellowship, 1985; Fellow, Institute for the Humanities, New York Univesity, 1987. *Address:* Dept. of Anthropology, New York University, 25 Waverly Place, New YOrk, NY 10003, USA.

WEINER Marcella Bakur, b. 13 Sept. 1925, New York City, New York, USA. Psychologist; Author. m. (2) William Weiner, 11 Oct. 1964. 2 sons. *Education:* BA 1963, MA 1967, City University; MEd 1971, EdD, 1972, Columbia University. *Appointments:* Psychotherapist, Private Practice, 1967-88; Senior Research Scientist, NYS Dept of Mental Hygiene, 1972-83; Adj Professor, Department of Psychology, CUNY, 1984-88. *Publications:* Over 50 publications including: The Theory and Practise of Self Psychology; Working with the Aged; The Starr/Weiner Report on Sex and Sexuality in the Mature Years, etc. *Memberships:* Fellow, American Psychological Association; Past President, Brooklyn Psychological Association; Task Force, NYS Psychological Association; Fellow, Gerontological Society; Task Force, American Group Psychotherapy Association; NY Academy of Sciences; Psychologists for Social Responsibility. *Honours:* Psi Chi National Honorary Society in Psychology, 1961; Research Fellowship, Administration on Aging, 1968; Certificate of Award, Community Leaders and Noteworthy Americans, 1978; Award, An Outstanding Cable TV Show on Aging, 1980. *Hobbies:* Belly dancing; Reading; Writing books, poems and articles; Theatre viewing; Contemplating life; Cooking. *Address:* 23 East 93rd Street, New York, NY 10128, USA.

WEINER-MCCULLOCH Beth Marilyn, b. 25 May 1930, Madison, Wisconsin, USA. Clinical Psychologist; Gerontologist. m. (1)Eugene L Winer, 13 June 1954, divorced 1969, 1 son, 1 daughter. (2)Garland James McCulloch, 10 June 1979, deceased 1987. *Education:* BS, Occupational Therapy, University of Illinois, College of Medicine, 1954; MA, Gerontology, University of South Florida, Tampa, 1969; PsyD, Massachusetts School of Professional Psychology, Newton, 1984. *Appointments:* Staff Occupational Therapist, St Louis State Hospital, 1954; Department Head/Consultant 1954-58, Director-Rehabilitation Services/Occupational Therapist 1954-56, Greenville General Hospital; Director-Rehabilitation

Services/Occupational Therapist, Roger Huntington Nursing Center 1962-66; Rehabilitation Counselor II, Division of Vocational Rehabilitation, Tampa, 1970-73; Chief-Rehabilitative Services, Hillsborough County Comprehensive Community Mental Health Center, 1973; Faculty, DWI, 1971-78; Associate Professor/ Assistant Professor 1973-79, Chairperson 1977-79, Florida International University; Faculty, University of Miami, 1975-79; Staff Clinical Psychologist/Post-Doctoral Intern, Trinity Mental Health Care Center, 1984-86; Staff Clinical Psychologist, Human Resource Institute, Brookline, Massachusetts, 1984-86; Private Practice, 1986- 87; Clinical Psychologist, New England Neurological Associates at Northeast Rehabilitation Hospital, Salem, 1986-87; Clinical Psychologist, Neuropsychiatric Institute, Tampa, 1987-. *Creative works:* Author of numerous papers and presentations to professional journals and conferences; Designed and taught courses, Florida International University. *Memberships include:* Commonwealth of Massachusetts Board of Registration of Psychologists; Florida Department of Professional Regulation Board of Psychological Examiners; Council for the National Register of Health Service Providers in Psychology; American Psychological Association; Florida Psychological Association. *Address:* 92 Huron Avenue, Tampa, FL 33606, USA.

WEINGARTEN Kathy, b. 13 Jan 1947, Brooklyn, New York, USA. Clinical Psychologist/Family Therapist. m. Hilary Goddard Worthen MD, 1 son, 1 daughter. *Education:* BA, Smith College, 1969; PhD, Harvard University, 1974. *Appointments:* Research Associate, Wellesley College Centre for Research on Women, 1975-79; Assistant Professor, Wellesley College, 1975-78; Director, Family Therapy Training, Department of Psychiatry, Children's Hospital and Judge Baker Children's Center, 1979-88; Faculty, Family Institute of Cambridge, 1982 -. *Publications:* With Pamela Daniels, Sooner or Later: The Timing of Parenthood in Adult Lives, 1982. *Memberships:* American Psychological Association; Society for Family Therapy and Research; Association of Women Psychologists; Massachusetts Psychological Association. *Honours:* Phi Beta Kappa 1968; Sigma Xi 1969; Undergraduate Fellow of the New England Psychological Asociation, 1969; NIMH Fellowship, 1971-73; Co-recipient with Dr James C Beck of the McCurdy- Rinkel Research Prize of the New England Psychological Association, 1972. *Hobbies:* Singing; Sailing; Baking. *Address:* 82, Homer Street, Newton Centre, MA 02159, USA.

WEINRICH Hildegard Anna Katharine, b. 4 Nov. 1933, Wuppental, Germany. Analytical Psychologist. *Education:* BA, London 1959; MA 1962, PhD 1965, Manchester; Diploma in Analytical Psychology, Zurich, 1986. *Appointments:* School of Social Work, Zimbabwe, 1965-66; University of Zimbabwe, 1966-75; University of Dar es Salaam, 1977-80; Government of Zimbabwe, 1980-82; Self employed Analyst, London, England, 1986-. *Publications:* Chiefs and Councils in Rhodesia, 1971; Black & White Elites in Rural Rhodesia, 1973; African Farmers in Rhodesia, 1975; The Tonga People, 1977; African Marriage in Zimbabwe, 1982; African Women in Zimbabwe, 1979; Die Kelch und die Schlange, 1989; 4 other books and 50 scientific articles. *Memberships:* Dominican Order; Formerly British Association of Social Anthropologists; International Association of Analytical Psychologists; Independent Group of Analytical Psychologists; Guild of Pastoral Psychology. *Hobbies:* Travel; Art; Other culture; Religion. *Address:* 38 Cranhurst Road, London NW2 4PL, England.

WEINSTEIN Grace W., b. New York City, USA. Financial Writer; Columnist; Author. m. Stephen D. Weinstein. *Education:* BA, Cornell University, 1957. *Appointments:* Columnist, Elks Magazine 1975-87, Good Housekeeping 1979-87; Syndicated columnist, Universal Press Syndicate, 'On Your Money' 1987-88; Columnist, contributing editor, Ms magazine, 1988-. *Publications include:* Books: The Lifetime Book of Money Management; Children & Money: A Parent's Guide;

Men, Women & Money: New Roles, New Rules; The Bottom Line, Inside Accounting Today; Money of Your Own; A Teacher's World; People Study People; Life Plans: Looking Forward to Retirement. *Memberships:* Past President, American Society of Journalists & Authors, Council of Writers Organisations; Member, Authors Guild. *Honours:* National Media Award, American Psychological Foundation, 1975; Science Writers Award, American Dental Association, 1979. *Hobby:* Travel. *Address:* c/o Harold Ober Associates, 40 East 49th Street, New York, NY 10017, USA.

WEINSTEIN Joyce, b. 7 June 1931, New York City, USA. Painter. m. Stanley Boxer, 28 Nov. 1952. *Education:* City College, New York City; Art Student's League, New York City. *Appointments:* Self-employed Artist. *Creative Works:* One Man Shows include: Perdalma Gallery, New York City, 1953, 1954, 1955, 1956; Dorsky Gallery, New York City, 1972, 1974; Meredith Long Contemporary Gallery, New York City, 1978-1979, and Meredith Long Gallery, Houston, Texas, 1988; Martin Gerard Gallery, Edmonton, Canada, 1979, 1981, 1982; Galerie Wentzel, Cologne, West Germany, 1982, 1988; Haber Theodore Gallery, New York City, 1983, 1985; etc; Group Shows include: Museum of Modern Art, New York City, NY 1981; Edmonton Art Gallery Museum, 1985; Richard Green Gallery, New York City, 1986; Centre de Creacio Contemporania, 1987; etc. *Memberships:* Women in the Arts Foundation Inc, Founding Member, Executive co-ordination, Board Member. *Honours:* various honours and awards. *Hobbies:* Reading; Sewing. *Address:* 37 East 18th St., New York, NY 10003, USA.

WEINSTEIN Rosemary Isabel, b. 23 Jan. 1944, Milford Haven, Dyfed, Wales. Museum Curator. m. Donald I. Weinstein, 17 June 1972. *Education:* BA, Honours, English, Manchester University, 1967; PhD History Candidate, London University (currently). *Appointments:* Research Assistant, National Museum of Scotland, 1968-70; Special Assistant, Medieval & Later Dept., British Museum, 1970-71; Research Assistant, then Senior Assistant Keeper, currently Keeper, Tudor and Stuart Department, Museum of London. *Publications:* Published extensively in Transactions of the London and Middlesex Archaeological Society, London Topographical Society, Proceeedings of the Huguenot Society of London. *Memberships:* FSA; FSA (Scotland); Hon. Secretary, Society for Post Medieval Archaeology; Editor, London Federation of Museums and Art Galleries. *Honours:* Shakespeare Prize, 1966; Freeman of the City of London. *Hobbies:* Travel; Theatre; Opera; Ballet; Natural History. *Address:* Museum of London, London Wall, London EC2 5HN, England.

WEINTRAUB Deborah Jane, b. 31 July 1953, Mexico City, Mexico. Architect. m. David Chilewich, 10 May 1986, 1 daughter. *Education:* AB magna cum laude, Princeton University, USA, 1975; MArch, Honours, University of California, Berkeley, 1978. *Appointments:* Giorgio Cavaglieri FAIA, 1979-82; Design Instructor, New Jersey Institute of Architecture, 1982-84; Samuel DeSanto & Associates, 1985; Private practice, 1985- . *Creative work includes:* Dancer & choreographer, modern dance, 1975-80; Over 200 private architectural projects, furniture design, graphics, drawings, paintings. *Membership:* American Institute of Architects. *Honour:* Graduated 1st, School of Architecture, Princeton, 1975. *Hobbies include:* Watercolour drawings. *Address:* 300 Elizabeth Street, New York, NY 10012, USA.

WEINTRAUB Jane A., b. 17 Nov. 1954, New York City, New York, USA. Dentist; Educator. *Education:* BS, University of Rochester, 1975; DDS, State University of New York, Stony Brook, 1979; MPH, Harvard School of Public Health, 1980; Research Fellow, 1979-82, Postdoctoral Certificate, Dental Care Administration, 1982, Harvard School of Dental Medicine; Dental Public Health Resident, New York State Department of Health, 1980-81; Diplomate, American Board of Dental Public Health, 1985. *Appointments include:* Instructor, Department of Dental Care Administration, Harvard

School of Dental Medicine, Boston, Massachusetts, 1982-84; Programme Analyst, Division of Dental Health, Massachusetts Department of Public Health, Boston, 1982-84; Supervising Dentist, Pit-and-Fissure Sealant Demonstration Programme, Massachusetts Department of Public Health and Massachusetts Health Research Institute Inc, 1983-84; Assistant Professor, School of Public Health, School of Dentistry, University of Michigan, Ann Arbor, 1984-88; Assistant Professor, School of Dentistry, School of Public Health, University of North Carolina, Chapel Hill, 1988-. *Publications:* Long term evaluation of a pit and fissure sealant, thesis, 1982; Biostats: Data analysis for dental health care professionals (with C.W.Douglas and D.B.Gillings), 1984, 2nd Edition, 1985; Various articles in the field. *Memberships:* American Association of Dental Schools; American Association of Public Health Dentistry, District Memberships Chair; American Association of Women Dentists, Colgate Palmolive Research Committee 1983-86, Mercury Exposure Committee Chair; American and North Carolina Dental Associations; American Public Health Association, Dental Health Section Council and Programme Committee; International Association for Dental Research; SUNY at Stony Brook School of Dental Medicine Alumni Association, Past President; Board of Directors, Behavioural Science Group, American Association for Dental Research. *Honours:* Preventive Dentistry Award, American Student Dental Association, 1978; Stony Brook Foundation Award, 1979; International College of Dentists Award, 1979; John Oppie McCall Award, 1979. *Address:* The University of North Carolina, School of Dentistry, Campus Box 7450, Chapel Hill, NC 27599-7450, USA.

WEINTRAUB Mary K. O'Brien, b. 28 Nov. 1952, Elgin, Illinois, USA. Educator; Historian; Bookseller. m. Karl Joachim Weintraub, 23 Apr. 1983. *Education:* BA 1975, MA 1976, PhD (European History) 1987, University of Chicago. *Appointments:* Assistant Manager, Seminary Cooperative Bookstore, 1975-; Lecturer, University of Chicago, 1988-. *Memberships:* Charter member, Erasmus of Rotterdam Society; American Historical Association; American Academy of Religion; History of Science Society. *Honour:* Howell-Murray Award, 1975. *Address:* 5844 South Stony Island, No. 5H, Chicago, Illinois 60637, USA.

WEIR Diana Dominguez, b. 9 Oct. 1943, New York, NY, USA. Director & Treasurer, American Legal Services, Inc. m. Robert David Weir, Sr. 8 Sept. 1962. 1 son, 1 daughter. *Education:* Data Processing, IBM Education Center, 1976; Burrough's Education Program, 1981; American Institute of Banking, 1982; Management Certificate, St Joseph's College, 1984-88. *Appointments:* Vice-President, Data Processing, 1074-83; Senior Vice-President, Director of Human Resources in charge of bank Operations & Data Processing, 1983-88. *Memberships:* National Association of Bank Women, Suffolk Chapter, President, 1986-87; Town of Smithtown Industrial Advisory Board, Treasurer; Smithtown School District Industrial Occupational Council, Chairman; Smithtown St John's Hospital Community Advisory Board; Adelante of Suffolk County, Hispanic Society, bi-lingual; Suffolk County Executive's Task Force on Child Care, Business Needs Committee; American Society of Personnel Administrators; Smithtown Business and Professional Women's Network; Smithtown Chamber of Commerce. *Honours:* NYS Regents' Scholarship, 1961. *Hobbies:* Politics; Walking; Knitting; Cooking. *Address:* 54 Crescent Place, Smithtown, NY 11787, USA,.

WEIR Gillian Constance, b. 17 Jan. 1941, New Zealand. Concert Organist. *Education:* Royal College of Music, London, England, 1962-65. *Appointments:* World-wide career as Concert Organist, 1965- including concerto appearances with all leading British Orchestras plus Boston SO, Seattle SO, Australian ABC orchestras, Wurttemberg Chamber; Regular appearances at all major international Festivals including: Edinburgh, Flanders, Aldeburgh, Bath, Proms, Europalia, Frequest radio and TV appearances; Adjudicator, international competitions; Artist-in-

residence major Universities; Lectures and master-classes internationally; Presenter and performer for own 6-part TV series BBC.2 (shown 1989 UK & Europe). *Creative works:* Contributor to: Grove's Dictionary of Music and Musicians; Fabbri's The Great Musicians; Various professional musical journals; Frequent talks on BBC Radio 3; Numerous recordings. *Memberships:* Incorporated Society of Musicians; Incorporated Association of Organists (1st woman president 1981-83); Council of Royal College of Organists, 1977- (1st woman member). *Honours include:* Winner, St Alban's International Organ Competition, 1964; Countess of Munster Award, 1965; Honorary Fellow, Royal College of Organists, 1976; International Performer of the Year, American Guild of Organists, 1981; Honorary Member, International Music Fraternity Sigma Alpha Iota, 1982; International Music Guide, A Musician of the Year, 1982; Honorary Fellow, Royal Canadian College of Organists, 1983; Honorary Doctorate, University of Victoria, Wellington, New Zealand, 1983; Turnovsky award for Outstanding Contribution to the Arts, 1985; CBE, Queen's Birthday Honours List, 1989. *Hobbies:* Books; Theatre; Eliminating Musak from the world! *Address:* 78 robin Way, Tilehurst, Berks RG3 5SW, England.

WEIR Molly, b. 17 Mar. 1920, Glasgow, Scotland. Actress; Writer. m. Alexander Hamilton, 13 Oct. 1938. *Education:* Skerry's College, Glasgow; Glasgow University; Bronze Medallist, Rapid Shorthand Writing; Highest Speed Writer in Britain in 1936 onwards. *Appointments:* Career: Radio Actress working for drama, Children's Hour and light entertainment, notably Tattie McIntosh in Itma, Aggie in Life with the Lyons, Rebecca in Rebecca of Sunnybrook Farm, and Susannah in Susannah of the Mounties; Ivy McTweed in The McFlannels; Regular contributor to Woman's Hour, 1947-85; TV, 11 years as Aggie with Life with the Lyons, 1949-60; other series include, Dixon of Dock Green, Ghost Squad, Within These Walls, Mogul, All creatures Great and Small, Huggy Bear, A Dickens of a Christmas, The Hogmanay Programme, The Andy Stewart Show, 1980-, Hazel, The McWitch in Children's TV Series, Rentaghost, now in its 8th year; many films & TV guest appearances, Highway, Wogan, etc. *Publications:* Molly Weir's Recipes, re-issued 1983; Autobiographical Writings, 1970-88, Shoes were for Sunday, Best Foot Forward, A Toe on the Ladder, Stepping into the Spotlight, Walking into the Lyons Den, One Small Footprint, Spinning Like a Peerie; Molly Weir's Triology of Scottish Childhood; Short Stories, articles, regular column in The People's Journal, Dundee, also in The Scottish Banner, Toronto, Canada. *Memberships:* Appeal's Committee, Equity; Associated London Speakers. *Honours:* This is Your Life, 1977; Included in The Guinness Book of Records, 1984, for writing longest autobiography by a female (642,350 words). *Hobbies:* Cooking; Walking; Gardening; Reading; Knitting; Talking. *Address:* c/o April Young Limited, 31 Kings Road, London SW3 4RP, England.

WEISS Debra S, b. 4 Dec. 1953, Three Rivers, USA. Construction Executive. *Education:* Albion College, 1972-73; Lake Superior State College, 1974-76; Industrialised Housing Institute Certificate, 1976; Falls Management Institute, 1984; Michigan State University Graduate School of Business, Course Certificate, 1985. *Appointments:* Weiss Construction Inc., Sales Manager, 1976-79; Board Chairman, Commercial Construction, Weiss Construction, 1980-; Corporate Officer, Weiss Corporation. *Memberships:* Eastern Upper Peninsula Private Industry Council, President, Board; Zoning Board of Appeals, City of St Ignace; City Council Member, City of St Ignace; Upper Peninsular Tourist & Recreation Association; National Organisation for Women; National Federation of Business & Professional Women; National Association of Female Executives. *Honours:* Ruth Huston Whipple Award, 1986; Garden City Award for Voluntary Services to Youth, 1986; Anna Howard Shaw Award for Outstanding Women's Programming, 1981, 1982; Outstanding Young Career Woman of Michigan, 1982; Woman of the Year, St Ignace BPW, 1981. *Hobbies:* Nordic & Alpine Skiing; Rock Repelling;

Reading; Water Sports. *Address:* 99 Bertrand Street, PO Box 465, St Ignace, MI 49781, USA

WEISS Elaine Landsberg, b. 4 May, New York City, USA. Housing & Community Development Official. *Education:* BA, Philosophy & Political Science, Brooklyn College, 1960; MA, Sociology, Hunter College, 1969. *Appointments:* NYC Dept Social Services, 1963-64; Asst. dir. housing and Operation Equality Nat. Urban League, 1965-67; Programme Asso. American Baptist Convention Div. Ch. Missions, 1967-70; President, E L Weiss Associates cons., 1970-76; Executive Director, Suffolk Community Devel. Corporation, Coram, New York, 1976-. *Publications:* Author of Porposals; brochures and booklets. *Memberships:* Fellowship Eleaner Roosevelt Found, 1964- 65; Nat. Association Housing Officials; NY State Housing & Redevl. Officials; LI Community Development Association (exec. com. 1978, 2nd vice president, 1977) Suffolk Human Rights Comm. *Honour:* Certificate of Commendation LI Council of Churches, 1981. *Hobby:* American Contract Bridge League- Life Master. *Address:* Walnut Avenue, E Quogue, New York, 11959, USA.

WEISS Jacqueline Betty, b. 26 July 1927, London, England. University Reader; Research Scientist. *Education:* DCC, Chelsea College, London, 1966; MSc., 1966, DSc., 1981, Manchester University. *Appoinments:* Senior Research Biochemist, Middlesex Hospital, London, 1960-64; Research Fellow, Biochemistry, Manchester, 1964-66; Lecturer, Biochemistry, 1966-71, Senior Lecturer, Biochemistry, 1971, Reader, Medical Biochemistry, 1978, Deputy Director, University Centre for the Study of Chronic Rheumatic Diseases, 1983-, University of Manchester; Honorary Lecturer, Chemistry, University of Wales; Honorary Consultant, Biochemist, Salford Health Authority; Director, Wolfson Angiogenesis Unit, University of Manchester, Hope Hospital. *Publications:* Co-Editor, Collagen in Health and Disease, 1982; chapters in books; articles in professional journals. *Memberships:* Biochemical Society; British Microcirculation Society; Editorial Board, Annals of Rheumatic Diseases. *Hobbies:* 20th Century Literature; Theatre; Cinema; Opera; Jazz. *Address:* Wolfson Angiogenesis Unit, Rheumatic Diseases Centre, University of Manchester Clinical Sciences Building, Hope Hospital, Salford M6 8HD, England.

WEISS Ruth, b. 24 June 1928, Berlin, Germany (came to USA 1939, naturalised citizen 1944). Poet; Performer; Playwright; Artist. m. Paul Blake, 1967. *Education:* College, Neuchatel, Switzerland, 1946-48. *Appointments:* Various jobs including artist's model, waitress; Innovator, poetry with jazz, 1950's; Readings, light-shows, slide-shows; Performances, various locations; Founder, weekly poetry theatre, 1973; Film, TV & radio appearances. *Creative works include:* Poems exhibited, various art shows, San Francisco, 1950's, 1960's; Paintings exhibited, group show 1965, solo 1980. Books of poems: Steps, 1958; Gallery of Women, 1959; South Pacific, 1959; Blue in Green, 1960; Light & Other Poems, 1976; Desert Journal, 1977; 13 Haiku, 1986. Plays include: B-Natural, 1961; 61st Year to Heaven, 1961; Figs, 1965; M & M, 1965; No Dancing Aloud, 1972; 13th Witch, 1983. Numerous contributions, various anthologies & journals; 16mm film, 1961; Video cassette, 1985. (Described as Beat Scene's Matriarch, Wilbur Wood in San Francisco Bay Guardian.) *Address:* Box 509, Albion, California 95410, USA.

WEISSMAN Ronee Freeman, b. 16 Apr. 1951, New York City, USA. Company Owner, Director. m. Eugene Weissman, 28 Jan. 1973, 1 son, 1 daughter. *Education:* BA, 1973, MA, 1978, Queen's College. *Appointments:* Owner, Director, Vice President, Weissman Teen Tours, 1974-; Youth Director, Sunday School Teacher, Temple Israel New Rochelle, 1979-81; Speech Pathologist, East Romepo School District, 1981. *Memberships:* Phi Beta Kappa; American Speech Language & Hearing Association; American Camping Association; New York City Speech Language & Hearing Association; etc.

Honours: Recipient, various honours & awards. *Hobbies:* Travel; Exercise; Dance; Modelling; Reading. *Address:* 517 Almena Ave, Ardsley, NY 10502, USA.

WEISSMAN Susan, b. 11 Feb. 1938, New York City, USA. Psychotherapist; Social Worker. m. Irwin Weissman, 2 June 1957, 2 daughters. *Education:* BA, Queens College, New York City, 1976; MSW, Columbia University; Doctoral candidate, City University of New York Graduate Centre, Hunter College School of Social Work. *Appointments:* Social worker & Psychoeducational Therapist, Long Island Jewish Hospital, 1978-81; Private practice, Psychotherapy, 1978-81; Founder & Executive Director, Park Centre Preschools (4 schools, 300 children, NYC), 1981-; President, Child Care Consultants Corporation, 1983-; Instructor, How to Open a Daycare Centre, Learning Annexe, NYC, 1985-. *Publications:* Book, Parents' Guide to Day Care; Numerous articles, journals including Parents' Magazine, Working Woman, Working Mother, Child Care Centre Magazine. *Memberships:* Women in Human Services; Board, Child Care Inc; Child Care Information Exchange Network. *Hobbies:* Cooking & entertaining; Exercise. *Address:* 36 Old Pond Road, Great Neck, New York 11023, USA.

WEIZMAN Savine Ruth Gross, b. 28 Oct. 1929, Cleveland, Ohio, USA. Psychologist. m. Alvin A. Weizman, 11 Feb. 1951, deceased, 2 sons, 1 daughter. *Education:* BS, Flora Stone Mathers, 1951; MS, 1968, PhD, 1975, Case Western Reserve. *Appointment:* Private Practice. *Publications:* About Mourning: Support & Guidance for the Bereaved, 1984; Pamphlet, Understanding the Mourning Process: When Your Mate Dies, 1977; Delayed & Complicated Grief: Psychotherapeutic Methods of Intervention, Chapter in Counseling and Therapy for Bereaved Persons. *Memberships:* American, Ohio, Cleveland Psychological Associations. *Address:* 3659 Green Road Suite No 325, Beachwood, OH 44122, USA.

WELDON Sybil Hudson, b. 11 Sept. 1951, Atlanta, Georgia, USA. Banker. m. Thomas B. Weldon, 20 Oct. 1973. *Education:* BA, Vanderbilt Universty, 1973. *Appointments:* Regional International Officer, Southeast Bank NA, 1974-82; Vice President & Manager, Tampa (Florida) Branch, Lloyds Bank PLC, 1982-. *Memberships:* Tampa Bay International Super Task Force; British-American Chamber of Commerce; Past Treasurer, Tampa Bay International Trade Council; Greater Tampa Chamber of Commerce; Tampa Club. *Address:* Lloyds Bank PLC, 100 South Ashley Drive, Suite 1780, Tampa, Florida 33602, USA.

WELLER Elizabeth Boghossian, b. 7 Aug. 1949, Beirut, Lebanon. Professor. m. Ronald A. Weller, 1 son, 1 daughter. *Education:* BS, 1971, MD, 1975, American University of Beirut. *Appointments:* Assistant Instructor, Psychiatry, Washington University School of Medicine, 1975-78; Assistant Professor, Psychiatry, 1979-84, Associate Professor, 1984-85, University of Kansas Medical Centre; Associate Professor, Paediatrics, University of Kansas, 1984-85; Professor, Psychiatry & Paediatrics, Ohio State University, 1985-. *Publications:* Co-Editor: Current Perspectives on Major Depressive Disorders in Children 1984, The Medical Basis of Child & Adolescent Psychiatry, 1989; Book Chapters, articles & papers. *Memberships:* American Medical Association; American Psychiatric Association; American Academy of Child Psychiatry; Childhood Affective Disorders Consortium; American Academy of Clinical Pharmacology & Therapeutics. *Honours:* Recipient, many honours & awards. *Hobbies:* Reading; Antiques; Gourmet Cooking. *Address:* The Ohio State University, 473 W. 12th Avenue, Room 245 Upham Hall, Columbus, OH 43210, USA.

WELLINGHAM-JONES Patricia Ann Clunn, b. 1 Feb. 1939, New Jersey, USA. Graphologist; Editor; Researcher; Author; Lecturer. m. Roy L Jones, 19 Apr. 1979, 1 son by previous marriage. *Education:* RN, PA School of Nursing, 1959; BA, 1980, MA, 1982, PhD,

1986, Columbia Pacific University. *Appointments:* RN, MA Memorial Hospital, 1961; Langley Porter Neuropsych. Institute, 1962-64; Self-employed, 1977-. *Publications:* Adolescence & Self-Esteem, 1984; Effects of Stress & Hypoglycemia in Handwriting, 1986; Mind/Body Connection, 1986; Evaluation of Adolescent S-E through Coopersmith S-E Inventory & Handwriting, 1986; Multiple Sclerosis, 1987; China Anthology, 1988. *Memberships:* President, American Handwriting Analysis Foundation; Board Member, Former Editor, American Ivy Society; Founding Member, American Association for Therapeutic Humor; Council of Graphological Societies; American Association of Handwriting Analysts; British Institute of Graphologists. *Honours:* Recipient, numerous honours and awards. *Hobbies:* Travel; Art; Reading; Writing. *Address:* PO Box 238, Tehama, CA 96090, USA.

WELLMAN Mary M, b. 20 May 1946, Brooklyn, USA. Psychologist; College Professor. *Education:* BS, 1967, MA, 1970, State University of New York; CAGS, 1974; PhD, University of Connecticut, 1980. *Appointments:* Teacher, Kings Park School, 1967-74; Reading Consultant, Thompson Public Schools, 1974-81; Reading & Learning Disabilities Clinician, Private practice, 1974-82; Adjunct Instructor, Counselling Psychology, Anna Maria College, 1980- 82; Adjunct Instructor, Worcester State College, 1982-84; Psychologist, Private Practice, 1985- ; Consulting Psychologist, Comprehensive Mental Health Services, Waban, 1983-85; Assistant Attending Child Psychologist, McLean Hospital, Belmont, 1986-88. *Publications:* Articles in numerous journals including: School Counselor; Brain & Language; Reading Improvement; Developmental Neuropsychology; Test Critiques. *Memberships Include:* American, Rhode Island Psychological Associations; Rhode Island Association for Women in Psychology; National Association of School Psychologists; Rhode Island School Psychologists Association. *Address:* Dept. of Counseling and Educational Psychology, Rhode Island College, Providence, RI 02908, USA.

WELLNER Julie Black, b. 3 Feb. 1959, Columbus, Ohio, USA. Architect. m. Dennis Wellner, 29 Sept. 1984. *Education:* Bachelor Environmental Design, 1982; BS, Architectural Engineering 1982, University of Kansas. *Appointments:* Intern Architect, Project Architect, HNTB, Kansas City, Missouri, 1982-87; Owner and Principal, Wellner, Moore Architects, 1987-. *Creative works:* Architectural design of Wheatley Elementary School Addition; KC Tech School Addition; Architectural renovation of several office and educational facilities; Tennant finish of several retail shops and restaurants. *Memberships* American Institute of Architects, Kansas City, Treasurer, 1989; Collaboration of Women in Architecture; The Great Kansas City Women's Political Caucus; The Greater Kansas City Chamber of Commerce. *Hobbies:* Tennis; Softball. *Address:* 712 Broadway, Suite 203, Kansas City, Missouri 64105, USA.

WELLS Donna Frances, b. 19 Dec. 1948, Lima, Ohio, USA. Purchasing Manager. m. Darrell Erickson, 26 Nov. 1980. *Appointments:* Fairmont Supply, 1973-. *Memberships:* National Association of Female Executives; VFW Auxillary; Americna Legion Auxillary. *Hobby:* Car Racing. *Address:* 105 Sequoia, Gillette, WY 82716, USA.

WELLS Judith Kay, b. 24 Dec. 1944, Valparaiso, Indiana, USA. Medical Psychologist. 2 sons. *Education:* BA Psychology, Indiana University, 1979; MA Psychology, 1983, PhD Psychology, 1985, University of Notre Dame. *Appointments:* Counseling Associates, Medical Psychology, Private Practice, 1982-; Vice President, Quality Assurance, Caresystems Rehabilitation, 1985-; Assistant Professor, Department of Psychology, Valparaiso University, 1987-. *Memberships:* American Psychological Association; American Academy of Medical Psychotherapists; National Association of Female Executives. *Honours:* National Distinguished Service Registry in Medicine and

Rehabilitation, 1987; National Social Register of Prominent College Graduates, 1980; Psi Chi, National Honor Society in Psychology, Charter President, Life Member; Magna cum laude, Indiana University, 1979. *Hobbies:* Running; Yoga; Tai Chi; Reading. *Address:* PO Box 645, Beverly Shores, IN 46301, USA.

WELLS Katharine Abbot Wells, b. 17 July 1906, South Dartmouth, USA. Community Organisation. m. Elwood Leffler, 12 June 1962. *Education:* AB, Mount Holyoke College, 1928; EDM, Harvard University, 1932; MS, Boston University, 1949. *Appointments:* Associate, Acting National Director, Episcopalian Agency for the US, Africa & Asia, 1937-40; War Related Programmes, USO, 1940-46; International Institutes of Boston, Jersey City, 1947-50; various organiszations of vocational educational & social rehabilitation programmes for psychiatric patients, 1951-72. *Membership:* American Association of University Women. *Hobbies:* Girl Scout Golden Eaglet; Professional Girl Scout Worker; Preservation. *Address:* 38 Plummer Avenue, Newburyport, MA 01950, USA.

WELLS Marrion, Dance/Music recitalist. *Education:* Sheffield University; Private study in music, dance and stage technique; BSc; LGSM; ANEA (Hons). *Appointments:* Varied theatrical experience, mainly in the musical and dance fields. Founded Arion Presentations, 1957-, mainly in educational theatre. *Publications:* Co-author, Drama in Therapy, 1981. Novel: Finale for a Piano Player, 1987; Theatrical memorabilia work, Get Out the Angels, 1988. *Memberships:* Theatrical Management Association; Equity; National Canine Defence League. *Honour:* TV South Charitable Award for pioneer work in jazz dance/exercise for the handicapped, 1983. *Hobbies:* Animal welfare conservation; Photography; Fitness-exercise/swimming . *Address:* Arion Presentations, 27 Middle Road, Hastings, East Sussex, TN35 5DL, England.

WELLS Melissa, b. 18 Nov. 1932, Tallinn, Estonia. US Ambarsador to Mozambique. m. 2 children. *Education:* BSFS, Georgetown University, 1956. *Appointments Include:* Foreign Service Officer, 1958-60, Personnel Officer, 1971-72, State Department, Washington; Political and Consular Office, US Embassy, Port of Spain, Trinidad & Tobago, 1961-64; Member, US Mission, Organization for Economic Co-operation & Development, Paris, France, 1964-66; Economic Officer, US Embassy, London, England, 1966- 70; International Economist, Bureau of Economic & Business Affairs, Washington, 1972-73, Deputy Director, Major Export Projects Division, Department of Commerce, 1973-75; Commecial Counsellor, US Embassy in Brasillia, 1975-76; US Ambassador to Cape Verde and Guinea Bissau, 1976-77; US Representative, to the UN Economic & Social Council, 1977-79; Ambassador to the Peoples Republic of Mozambique, 1986-. *Address:* Embassy of USA, CP 783, Maputo, Mozambique.

WELLS Rona Lee, b. 23 Aug. 1950, Beaumont, Texas, USA. Consumer Products Executive. m. Harry H. Wells, 22 Mar. 1975. *Education:* BS, Southern Methodist University, 1972. *Appointments:* Initial Management Dev. Programme, 1972-73, Engineer, 1973-74, Senior Engineering Supervisor, 1974-75, Engineering Project Supervisor, 1975-77, District Supervisor, Major Projects, 1977-79, District Supervisor, Materials, 1979, Southwestern Bell; Field Services Manager, 1979-80, Manager-Assistant to Vice President, 1980, Area Manager, Support Services 1980-82, Accounting Services, 1982, CNA Financial; Director, Building & Office Management, 1982-85, Operations Specialist, 1985-86, Acting Superintendent, 1985, Project Leader, 1986-88, Operations Manager, 1988-89, Mill Manager, 1990-, Kimberly Clark. *Memberships:* Board, United Way; Institute of Industrial Engineers; Society of Women Engineers; National Society of Professional Engineers. *Honours:* Recipient, many honours include: National Defense Executive Reserve, 1979; Sigma Tau. *Hobbies:* Antique & Art Collecting; Swimming; Music. *Address:* 3521 N. Rankin, Appleton, WI 54915, USA.

WELSH-ASANTE Kariamu, b. 22 Sept. 1949, Tomasville, North Carolina, USA. Professor; Choreographer; Dance Historian. m. 8 Jan. 1981, 2 sons. *Education:* BA, 1972, MA, 1975, State University of New York, Buffalo. *Appointments:* Kariamu and Company, School of Movement Drama & Music, Artistic Director, Resident Choreographer, 1971-81; Fulbright Professor, University of Zimbabwe, 1981-82; Artistic Director, National Dance Company of Zimbabwe, 1981-82; Director, Zora Neal Hurston Centre for African Culture, 1985, Assistant Professor, 1987-, Temple University. *Publications:* African Culture: Rhythms of Unity, Co-editor, 1985; Guide to African and African American Art: A Manual of African Art, with M. Asante, 1980; Textured Women, Cowrie Shells and Beetle Sticks, 1987. *Memberships:* African Choreographers; African American Museum Association; American Heritage Studies Association; many other professional organisations. *Honours:* NEA Choreography Fellowship, 1973; Various other Fellowships and Grants. *Hobbies:* Travel; Writing. *Address:* Temple University, Gladfelter Hall 025-26, Room 827, 12th Berks Mall, Philadelphia, PA 19122, USA.

WEND Joanne, b. 26 Nov. 1960, Detroit, Michigan, USA. Controller. m. Dennis J. Wend, 10 Oct. 1982. *Education:* BBA, Accounting, Detroit Institute of Technology, 1981. *Appointments:* Bookkeeper, Swick Business Associates, 1978-80; Revenue Agent, Internal Revenue Service, 1980; Junior Accountant, St Joseph's Hospital, 1981-83; Owner, Automated Financial Services, 1983-; Accountant, Detroit Macomb Hospital, 1983-85; Senior Budget Analyst, Portlac Osteopathic Hospital, 1986-88; Controller, Management Recruiters 1988, Annie's House Inc 1989-. *Memberships:* National Association of Female Executives; Healthcare Financial Management Association. *Hobbies:* Cross stitch; Cross country skiing; Cycling; Cake decorating; Calligraphy; Making silk wedding bouquets; Computers. *Address:* 1546 S. Bartlett Road, St. Claire, MI 48079, USA.

WENDELBERGER Joanne Roth, b. 22 June 1959, Milwaukee, Wisconsin, USA. Statistician. m. James George Wendelberger, 21 Jan. 1984. *Education:* AB, Mathematics, Economics, Oberlin College, 1981; MS, Statistics, University of Wisconsin, Madison, 1983. *Appointments:* Statistical Consultant, University of Wisconsin, Madison College of Agriculture & Life Sciences, 1983; Statistical Consultant, General Motors Research Laboratories, 1984-87; Research Assistant, Center for Quality and Productivity Improvement, University of Wisconsin, Madison, 1987-. *Publications:* Using SAS software in the Design and Analysis of Two-Level Fractional Factorial Experiments, 1986. *Memberships:* American Statistical Association; Institute of Mathematical Statistics; Society for Industrial and Applied Mathematics; Mathematical Association of America; Phi Beta Kappa. *Honours:* Wisconsin Alumnae Research Foundation Fellowship, 1981; National Merit Finalist, 1977. *Hobbies:* Wetlands preservation; International travel; Adventure travel; Swimming. *Address:* 5000 West Utica Road, Utica, Michigan 48087, USA.

WENDELBURG Norma Ruth, b. 26 Mar. 1918, Stafford, Kansas, USA. Musician: Composer & Performer. *Education:* BM, Bethany College, Kansas, 1943; MM, University of Michigan, 1947; MM 1951, PhD 1969; Eastman School of Music, Rochester, New York; 2 Fulbright grants, Mozarteum, Salzburg, & Academy of Music, Vienna, Austria, 1953-55. *Appointments:* Wayne State College, Nebraska, 1947-50; Northern Iowa University, 1956-58; Hardin-Simmons University, Texas, 1958-63; Southwest Texas State University, 1969-72; Dallas Baptist College, Texas, 1973-75; Friends' College, Haviland, Kansas, 1977-80. *Creative works:* Over 100 symphonic, chamber, choral, solo works including: String quartet No II, 1956; Suite No. II for Violin & Piano, 1964 (recorded 1988); Symphony, 1967; Affirmation (trombone-piano), 1980; Interlacings (organ), 1983; Land of Sky & Water (flute-piano), 1987. *Memberships:* American Society of Composers, Authors & Publishers; Sigma Alpha Iota;

American Music Centre; Minnesota Composers Forum; MacDowell Colonists; Music Teachers National Association; Piano League; Federated Music Clubs. *Honours:* Grants & fellowships including: Huntingdon Hartford Foundation 1958, 1961; MacDowell Colony 1960, 1970; NYC Meet the Composer 1980. Numerous awards, various establishments, music festivals, USA & Europe. *Hobbies:* Photography; Travel; Gardening. *Address:* 2206 North Van Buren, Hutchinson, Kansas 67502, USA.

WENNER Elizabeth Lewis, b. 17 Jan. 1950, Newport News, Virginia, USA. Marine Scientist. m. Charles Anthony Wenner, 26 Nov. 1976. *Education:* BS, Mary Washington College, 1972; MS 1975, PhD 1979, College of William & Mary. *Appointment:* South Carolina Marine Resources Research Institute, 1979-. *Publications:* 28 papers & reports, marine science. *Memberships:* Board of Governors, Secretary, The Crustacean Society; Estuarine Research Federation; National Shellfish Society. *Honour:* Phi Beta Kappa, 1972. *Hobbies:* Antiques; Cycling; Volunteer work, shelter for homeless. *Address:* 2027 Leadenwah Drive, Wadmalaw Island, South Carolina 29487, USA.

WENSLEY Penelope Anne, b. 18 Oct. 1946, Australia. Diplomat. m. Thomas Stuart McCosker, 31 Aug. 1974. 2 daughters. *Education:* BA 1st class honours, University of Queensland, 1967. *Appointments:* Foreign Affairs Trainee, 1968; Posting to Australian Embassy, Paris, France, 1969-73; Posting to Australian Mission to the United Nations, New York, USA, 1974-75; Deputy Head of Mission, Australian Embassy, Mexico, 1975-77; Deputy High Commissioner, Australian High Commission, Wellington, New Zealand, 1983-85; Australian Consul General, Hong Kong, 1986-88. *Honours:* Margaret Piddington Prize, 1964, Lizzie Heal-Warry Prize, 1964, University of Queensland. *Hobbies:* Reading; Music; Tennis. *Address:* c/o Department of Foreign Affairs and Trade, Canberra, ACT 2600, Australia.

WENTWORTH Winifred Lane, b. 15 May 1927, Miami, Florida, USA. Judge of Court of Appeal. m. Dean Wentworth, 11 June, 1947. 3 sons, 1 daughter. *Education:* AB Journalist, Florida State University, 1948; Juris Doctor, University of Florida, College of Law, 1951, High honours; Graduate work, Tax and Constitutional Law, University of Florida, 1976. *Appointments:* Law Clerk, Florida Supreme Court, 1952-68; Tax Division Chief, Florida Attorney General, 1968-76; General Counsel, Florida Board of Education, 1977-79; Appointment Commissioner of Industrial Relations, State of Florida, 1978-79; Elected appellate judge, 1980, 1986. *Publications:* Over 1000 judicial opinions published; chapters in 3 books for Florida Bar, 1958, 1984; Contrib. to Essays in Legal History, Bobbs Merrill, 1965; University of Florida Law Review, contributor, 1950. *Memberships:* Chairman Rules Committees, District Court; Member of numerous Bar Groups; Vice-president, Tallahassee World Future Society, 1986-88; Board of Directors, 1965-80, Wentworth Foundation Historical Society, Pensacola. *Honours:* Phi Beta Kappa, 1948, Alpha Chapter of Florida State University; National Humanities Endowment award for justice seminar, American University, Washington DC, 1976. *Hobbies:* Music; Gardening; Writing; Child development; Women's Network Groups. *Address:* Florida First District Court of Appeal, 300 Martin Luther King Blvd, Tallahassee, Florida 32301, USA.

WENZEL Donna R, b. 12 Feb. 1953, Lafayette, Indiana, USA. Office Manager; Safety Officer. m. Dennis J Wenzel, 6 May 1979. 1 son. *Education:* Graduate, Rochester Business Institute, 1972-73. *Appointments:* Accountant/Computer Operator, Faculty of Pharmacy and Pharmaceutical Sciences, University of Alberta, Edmonton, 1984-87; Office Manager, SynPhar Laboratories Inc, Edmonton, 1987-. *Memberships:* Women's Inter-Church Council of Canada, Member of Council and Executive; Sec, Alberta North Synodical-Evangelical Lutheran Women; Peace w/Justice Enabler for Lutheran Church Women. *Honour:* Educational

Exchange to Zimbabwe, 1985. *Hobbies:* Music; Human Rights Issues (particularly for women); Travel; Safety; Girl Guides; Drama. *Address:* 630 Lee Ridge Road, Edmonton, Alberta, Canada T6K 0N8.

WERA Anne R., b. 1 June 1936, Winona, Minnesota, USA. Administration Researcher; Music Teacher. *Education:* BA, Music Education, Piano & Organ, Viterbo College, Wisconsin, 1958; MM, Applied Piano, University of Minnesota, 1960; MA, Administration, Loras College, Iowa, 1978. *Appointments include:* LaCrosse Public Schools, 1958-64; University of Iowa, 1964-65; Head, Music Education, University of Nevada, 1965-66; Assistant Professor, Music, Universities of Whitewater & River Falls, Wisconsin, 1966- 67; Music Specialist, 4-12, Dubuque Community Schools, 1967-86; Substitute Instructor, various public schools, 1987-. Also: Various consultantships, research, choir conductor. *Memberships include:* National Association of Secondary School Principals; American Association of School Administrators; Association for Supervision & Curriculum Development; National Band Association; American Symphony Orchestra League; National Organists Guild; Music Teachers National Association; Life member, Music Educators National Conference, American Association of University Women. *Honours include:* Various committees & responsibilities, professional associations; Boards, American Youth Symphony & Chorus, Dubuque Symphony, Dubuque Girls Club; Award, instrumental music for the blind & deaf, & trainable retarded children, 1960- 64, 1970-79; Numerous biographical recognitions. *Hobbies:* Travel; Research; Performing; Reading; Walking. *Address:* 1008 LaCrosse Street, Onalaska, Wisconsin 54650, USA.

WERBIL Jennifer Lee (Vinson), b. 8 Jan. 1952, Madison County, Anderson, Indiana, USA. Publications Director and Adviser; Teacher. m. David Olin Werbil, 22 May 1974. *Education:* BS, Teaching, Journalism, Radio/TV, 1974, MA, Journalism, Public Relations, Advertising, 1976, Ball State University; English Certification, Indiana University, 1988. *Appointments:* Clerk/PR, Hoyt Wright Company, 1974-76; Teacher, Publications Director, Senior Class Sponsor, Quill and Scroll Sponsor, Indianapolis Public Schools, Indiana, 1977-. *Publications:* Short stories and how to's in magazines. *Memberships:* Indianapolis Education Association; Indiana State Teachers Association; National Education; English Teachers Council of Indianapolis; Indiana High School Press Association; Quill and Scroll; Women in Communications; Kappa Alpha Theta; Sigma Delta Chi; Republication Party. *Hobbies:* Writing; Reading; Swimming; Water- skiing; Plants and garden work; Running; Walking; Animals; Children: Environmental concerns. *Address:* 7137 McIntosh Lane, Apartment 2A, Indianapolis, IN 46226, USA.

WERSTIUK Eva Susanne Gabrielle, (neé Törzs)b. 25 Feb. 1939, Budapest, Hungary. Associate Professor; Researcher; Lecturer. m. Nick Henry Werstiuk, 20 Sept. 1965, divorced 1976. 1 son, 1 daughter. *Education:* BSc, First Class Honours, Chemistry, Physiology, 1961; PhD Organic Chemistry, 1964, University of London, England. *Appointments:* Research Fellow, Department of Chemistry, The John's Hopkins University, Baltimore, USA, 1964-66; Research Fellow, Department of Chemistry, Imperial College of Science and Technology, London, England, 1966-67; Research Associate, Department of Biochemistry, 1967-80, Member of Faculty, Department of Neurosciences, 1980-, McMaster University, Hamilton, Ontario. *Publications:* Recent Advance in Pyrazine Chemistry, with G W H Cheeseman, 1972; Quinoxaline Chemistry: Developments 1963-75, with G W H Cheeseman, 1978; Antipsychotics: II Butyrophenoses, with M Steiner, 1987. *Memberships:* New York Academy of Science, 1987; American Association for Advancement of Science, 1978; Society for Neuroscience, 1978; Canadian College of Neuropsychopharmacology, 1985. *Honours:* University of London Postgraduate Scholarship, 1961-64; Research Fellowship, Ontario

Mental Health Foundation, Toronto, Canada, 1978- 81; Long-term Research Fellowship, 1981-90. *Hobbies:* Classical music; Playing the piano; Theatre; Swimming; Tennis; Philosophy and History of Science; Archaeology. *Address:* Department of Biomedical Sciences, McMaster University, 1200 Main Street West, Hamilton, Ontario, Canada L8S 3Z5.

WESCHLER Anita, b. New York City, USA. Sculptor; Painter. *Creative Works:* Solo Shows in New York City & Nationwide; Group Shows in Metropolitan Museum of Art; Museum of Modern Art; works in Metropolitan Museum of Art, Whitney Museum; public and private collections. *Memberships:* Fellow, MacDowell Colony; Yaddo; Architectural League; Art Students League; Delegate, Fine Arts Federation of New York; Pennsylvania Academy of Fine Art, University of Pennsylvania. *Address:* 136 Waverly Place, New York, NY 10014, USA.

WEST Benita Louise, b. 27 Mar. 1956, Cleveland, Ohio, USA. Learning Disabilities Teacher. *Education:* BSc, The Defiance College, 1978; Certificate, The Institute of Children's Literature, 1985; MEd, Cleveland State University, 1986. *Appointments:* Clerk Typist, Coyahoga County Welfare Department, 1973-74; DH Teacher, Virgin Islands Dept of Education, 1979-85; SBH Teacher, Mental Development Center, 1985-87; Learning Disabilities Teacher, Cleveland City Schools, 1987-. *Memberships:* American Federation of Teachers; Order of Eastern Star, Prince Hall Affiliation; East View United Church of Christ (past Sunday school Assistant Superintendent). *Hobbies:* Sewing crafts; Bowling; Writing children's stories. *Address:* 3455 Milverton Road, Shaker Heights, Ohio 44120, USA.

WEST Stacy Ellen, b. USA. Public Relations Executive; Lawyer. *Education:* AB, Government, Cornell University, 1980; JD, Washington University School of Law, St Louis, Missouri, 1983; Admitted, Pennsylvania Bar, 1983. *Appointments include:* Associate, Attorney, Government Regulation Section 1983-86, Director, Client Relations 1986-, Morgan, Lewis & Bockius law firm, Philadelphia. *Publications:* Articles: Washington University Law Quarterly, Congressional Quarterly. *Memberships:* Vice Chair, Marketing Administrators Committee, Economics of Law Practice Section, American Bar Association; National Association of Law Firm Markting Administrators; Philadelphia Bar Association; Various community organisations. *Hobbies:* Skiing; Tennis; Squash; Travel; Walking; Jazzercise. *Address:* Morgan, Lewis & Bockws, 2000 One Logan Square, Pennsylvania 19333, USA.

WESTINGHOUSE Anna Marie, b. 21 Mar. 1931, Cincinnati, Ohio, USA. Administrator. Divorced, 1 son, 1 daughter. *Appointments:* Talk Show Host, WYCA Radio, WLNR Radio, 1968-85; Director, Programme Development, Greater Hammond county Services, 1981-82; Executive, Marketing & Public Relations, Home Nursing Service Association, 1982-86; Dorchester Retirement Home Business Centre, 1986-88. *Publications:* Author, Women's Networking Director; Author, Producer, Host, Women's Issues, Minority & Drug and Alcohol, Radio Shows; Writer/Lecturer, Women's Issues. *Memberships:* Purdue University Advisory Board Member; Seton Academy Advisory Board; Lake County Women's Business Executive Board; Red Cross Nursing Committee Board, etc. *Hobbies:* Toastmasters; Writing; Research - Gerontology; Self Help Groups. *Address:* 511 Conkey Street, Hammond, IN 46324, USA.

WESTLANDER Gunnela A M, b. 4 Oct. 1930, Stockholm, Sweden. Director, Division of Social Psychology. m. 29 Mar 1953, div. 1972. 3 sons, 1 daughter. *Education:* BA 1953, MA 1969, PhD 1976; Associate Professor, University of Stockholm, Department of Psychology; Full Professor, Institute of Occupational Health, 1987; Authorised Psychologist, 1969. *Appointments:* Institute of Psychotechniques, 1962-65; Swedish Council of Personnel Administration,

1966-78; National Board of Occupational Safety & Health, 1978- 87; Institute of Occupational Health, 1987-; Department of Psychology, University of Stockholm, 1975-87. *Publications:* 60 books and articles including: Equality between the sexes in an organizational per. spec., 1984; Office automation as a driving force, 1986; Government Policy and Swedish Health Care: The Swedish Alternative, 1988. *Memberships:* Swedish Association of Psychologists. *Honours:* Editor, Board Memberships: The Journal of Women and Health, USA; Nordish Psyhologi/ Scandinavia. *Hobbies:* Music, piano; Politics; Literature; Creative homework. *Address:* National Institute of Occupational Health, S-171 84 Solna, Sweden.

WESTMORELAND Barbara F, b. 22 July 1940, New York City, USA. Physician. *Education:* BS, Chemistry, Mary Washington College, 1961; MD, University of Virginia Medical School, 1965; Internship, Vanderbilt Med Ctr, 1965-66; Neurology Residency, University of Virginia, 1966-70; Fellowship in EEG, Mayo Clinic, 1970-71. *Appointments:* Mayo Clinic, 1971-; Asst Prof of Neurology 1973-75, Assoc Prof of Neurology 1975-78, Prof of Neurology 1978-, Mayo Medical School. *Publications:* Co-author of book: Medical Neurosciences; Author and co-author of various articles and chapters on EEG, Evoked Potentials and Epilepsy. *Memberships:* President 1987-88, Treasurer 1978-80, American Epilepsy Soc; Secretary, American EEG Society, 1985-87; President 1979-80, Sec-Treasurer 1976-78, Central Asst of EEG; Pres, Sigma Xi Mayo Chapter, 1987-88; Board Member, American Board of Qualifications in EEG, Alpha Omega Alpha. *Honours:* Colgate Darden Award (Highest Honours) Mary Washington College, 1961; Teacher of the Year Award for Neurology, Mayo Medical School, 1976. *Hobbies:* Bicycling; Skiing; Music. *Address:* 200 First St SW, Rochester, MN 55905, USA.

WESTON Dawn Thompson, b. 15 Apr. 1919, Joliet, Illinois, USA. Artist; Researcher. m. Arthur Walter Weston, 10 Sept. 1940. 2 sons, 1 daughter. *Education:* BS, Northwestern University, 1942; Postgraduate research, 1960-62; MA, Educational administration, 1970; Postgraduate studies at University of Illinois, Art Institute of Chicago and Philadelphia Institute for the Achievement of Human Potential. *Appointments:* Art Therapist, USN Hospital, Gt Lakes, Illinois, 1940-45; Teacher, Holy Child and Waukegan and Lake Forest High Schools, Illinois, 1946-76; Elementary and Jr High Art Director, Lake Bluff, Illinois, 1954-58; Educational Director, Grove School for brain-injured, 1958-66. *Creative works:* One woman shows, Evanston Woman's Club, Northwestern University, Illinois; Represented in permanent collections: ARC, Victory Memorial Hospital Waukegan, Etchings for Country Gentleman Mag, 1956. *Memberships:* Chairman, Board of Grove School for Brain-injured children, 1982-87; Delegate to Methodist Convention/Northern Illinois District, 1982-89. *Honours:* Highest Rank for the artwork from Columbia University, New York as Art Editor of Evanston Township HS Year Book, 1937; President of Penn Hall Alumni Association for Chicago Area, 1938-40; Selected to dance in the prized Waamu shows of Northwestern University, trained by Martha Graham, 1938-42; Elected to Pi Lambda Theta, Honorary Educational Society, 1970. *Hobbies:* Reading; Creative writing; Children of the world; Research on uneven growth and shifting visual imagery due to trauma; Travel. *Address:* 349 E Hilldale Place, Lake Forest, IL 60045, USA.

WESTON Margaret Kate, (Dame) b. 7 Mar. 1926, Carmarthen, Wales. Former Director, Science Museum. *Education:* BSc., Engineering, London University; CEng. *Appointments:* Engineering Apprenticeship then post with General Electric Company Limited, 1944-55; Assistant Keeper, 1955, Department of Electrical Engineering & Communications, Keeper, Museum Services, 1967, Director 1973-86, The Science Museum; The National Railway Museum York; The National Museum of Photography, Film and Television, Bradford, The Wellcome Museum of the History of Medicine, all set up as part of the Science Museum in period of Directorship. *Memberships Include:*

President, Association of Railway Preservation Societies; Governor, Member, Management Council, Ditchley Foundation; Governor, Imperial College of Science & Technology; Trustee, Queen's Gate Trust; member: Museums and Galleries Commission; 1851 Commission; RSA Council; etc. *Honours:* Honorary Doctorate of Science, University of Aston, 1974; Honorary Fellowship, Imperial College, 1975; Fellowship, Museum's Association, 1976; President, 1977; Elected Companion, BIM, 1977; DBE, 1979; Honorary DSc., University of Salford, 1984; etc. *Hobbies:* Music; Travel; Gardening. *Address:* 7 Shawley Way, Epsom, Surrey KT18 5NZ, England.

WESTON Theodora White, b. 31 Dec. 1955, Chicago, USA. Attorney; Judge. Divorced, 1 son, 1 daughter. *Education:* BS. Education, Illinois State University, 1976; JD, St Louis University, 1981. *Appointments:* Solo Law Practice, 1982-; Provisional Municipal Judge, 1988-; Municipal Port Attorney, 1988-. *Publications:* St Louis Court Handbook, 1986; Co- Editor; BALSA Reports, 1980-81. *Memberships:* Mound City, Chicago, National, American Illinois, Bar Associations; American Arbitration Association; Bar Association of Metro St Louis. *Honours:* Outstanding Young Woman of America, 1987. *Hobbies:* World History; Music; Writing. *Address:* 1221 Locust, Suite 1000, St Louis, MO 63103, USA.

WESTWOOD Pamela S, b. 25 July 1945, Kenton, Ohio, USA. Nurse. m. Michael D. Westwood, 13 May 1978, 1 stepson, 1 stepdaughter. *Education:* Diploma of Nursing, Miami Valley Hospital School of Nursing, Dayton, 1966; Primary Care Nurse Practitioner, School of Health Care Sciences, Sheppard Air Force Base, 1976; BA, Social Psychology, Park College, 1978; MA Psychology, University of Northern Colorado, 1982; Air War College, 1987. *Appointments:* Miami Valley Hospital, 1966-67; Air Force 1967-, Assignments and Rank: 2nd Lieutenant, General Duty Nurse, Offutt Air Force Base, Nebraska, 1967-69; 1st Lieutenant, General Duty Nurse, Clark Air Force Base, Philippines, 1969-70; Captain, General Duty Nurse, Wurtsmith Air Force Base, Michigan 1970-73; Captain, Charge Nurse, Zaroagoza, Spain, 1973-75; School of Health Care Science, Primary Care Nurse Practitioner School, 1975-76; Major, Primary Care Nurse Practitioner, Nellis Air Force Base, Nevada, 1976-79; Major, Primary Care Nurse Practitioner, Seymour Johnson Air Force Base, North Carolina, 1979-81; Lieutenant Colonel, Primary Care Nurse Practitioner, Wright Patterson Air Force Base, Ohio 1981-84; Lietenant- Colonel, Primary Care Nurse Practitioner, Quality Assurance Co-ordinator, Hickam Air Force Base, Hawaii, 1984-86; Wilford Hall Medical Center, Lackland Air Force Base, Texas, 1986-. *Memberships:* American Nurses Association; Air Force Association; Uniformed Nurse Practitioners Association. *Honours:* Air Force Tactical Air Command Scholastic Achievement Award, 1977; Air Force Chief Nurse Badge, 1980; Air Force Accomodation Medal 1979, 1981; Air Force Meritorious Service Medal 1984 and 1986. *Hobbies:* Golf; Jogging; Tennis. *Address:* 6027 Watertown Drive, San Antonio, TX 78249, USA.

WETSTONE Janet Meyerson, b. Spartanburg, South Carolina, USA. Designer; Journalist; Realtor. m. 1947, divorced 1973, 2 sons, 1 daughter. *Education:* University of Missouri, 1945-47; Georgia State University, 1970, 1980. *Appointments:* President, Jan's Interiors, Atlanta, 1965-67, Wetstone Craft Co., Atlanta, 1967-80; Consultant, Enterprise Paint Co., 1967-79; Plaid Enterprises, 1979-87; Realtor Associate, Strathmore Realty Co., Sarasota, 1985-. *Publications:* Rags to Riches with Mod Podge; Specially Yours; Decorating with Sheets and Mod-Podge; The Creative Frame Maker; inventor of Modge Podge patnted in US; various other inventions patented. *Memberships:* First President, Education Guild John & Mabel Ringling Museum of Art, Sarasota, 1963-65; Chairman, First Childrens Art Carnival Ringling Museum, 1963-64; League of Women Voters; Democratic Women of Georgia; Vice President, Women in Film, Atlanta, 1982-83; United Inventors and Scientists of America; Sarasota Board of Realtors. Nominee, Florida State Legislature, 1988; Million Dollar

Club Real Estate. *Hobbies:* Riding; Golf; Photography; Painting; Sailing; Art; Music; Politics. *Address:* 3969 Glen Oaks, Manor Drive, Sarasota, FL 34232, USA.

WHALEY Peggy Elaine Ellis, b. 30 Nov. 1939, Cleveland, Tennessee, USA. Advertising Executive. m. Leo J Whaley, 29 Mar. 1957. 3 daughters. *Education:* Attended: Cleveland Community College, 1964-65; Dalton College, 1970-72; Numerous professional seminars and workshops. *Appointments:* Office Manager/Corp Offr, Southern Gen Products, 1967- 73; Office Manager, Joe Goodson, CPOA, 1974-78; Comptroller, Professional C & C, 1980-83; Publisher, Peggy Whaley News Report, 1982-85; Editor, Southeast Floor Covering Magazine, 1975-76; Owner, Whaley & Associates, 1983-. *Publications:* Co-author, Today and Tomorrow Become Yesterday; numerous articles for magazines and newspapers. *Memberships:* Small Business Administration; Dalton Regional Library; Dalton Library Foundation Board; National Association for Female Executives; National Association of Accountants; National Association for Floor Covering Women; Toastmasters International; NY Business Press Editors, Inc; World Trade Council; Chamber of Commerce; Pilot Club; League of Women Voters. *Honour:* Feature in 1985 Daily Citizens News, Professional Woman Profile. *Hobbies:* Swimming; Writing; Reading. *Address:* P O Box 205, Dalton, GA 30722, USA.

WHARE Wanda Snyder, b. 5 Nov. 1959, Columbia, Pennsylvania, USA. Attorney. m. James Robert Snyder, 14 Nov 1987, 1 son. *Education:* BA, Franklin & Marshall College, 1981; JD, Dickinson School of Law, 1984. *Appointments:* Bureau of Workers' Compensation, Department of Labour & Industry, 1984-87; Gibbel, Kraybill & Hess, 1987-89; Irex Corporation, 1990-. *Publications:* Editor-in-chief, high school literary magazine 1977, Franklin & Marshall Yearbook 1981, Dickinson School of Law Yearbook 1984. *Memberships:* Co-Chairperson of Class of 1981; Class Agents, Franklin & Marshall College; Staff-Parish Relations Committee, & Commission on Status & Role of Women, 1st United Methodist Church, Lancaster, Pennsylvania. *Honours:* Semi-finalist, National Merit Scholarship, 1977; Quill & Scroll, 1977; Dean's List, Franklin & Marshall College, 1978-81. *Hobbies:* Cross-stitch; Hiking; Reading. *Address:* 17 Lark Street, Pine Manor, Middletown, Pennsylvania 17057, USA.

WHARTON Cynthia Lee, b. 3 June 1947, Greensboro, North Carolina, USA. Financial Executive. *Education:* BA, University of North Carolina, Chapel Hill & Greensboro, 1969; MPA, Woodrow Wilson School of Public & International Affairs, Princeton University, 1975. *Appointments:* Research assistant: International Council for Educational Development 1969-72, International Bank for Reconstruction & Development (World Bank) 1972-73; Consultant, Brazil, US Agency for International Development , 1974; Assistant Vice President, Wells Fargo Bank, NA, 1975-78; Programme Administrator, Charles H. Revson Foundation Inc, 1978-79; Vice President, Bank of America NT & SA, 1979-83; Vice President, Merrill Lynch Capital Markets, 1983-90. *Memberships:* Women's Economic Round Table; Board, UNCG Excellence Foundation; Board, One Pierrepont Street Corporation; Sustainer, Junior League, Brooklyn. *Honours:* Phi Beta Kappa, UNC, 1969; Scholastic financial scholarship, UNC, 1965-69; Karl H. Prickett Fellowship, Woodrow Wilson School, 1973-75. *Address:* One Pierrepont Street, Brooklyn Heights, New York 11201, USA.

WHEATLY Michele Gaye, b. 4 June 1956, London, England. University Professor. m. Stanley Keck Smith, 30 May 1987. *Education:* BSc., Honours, 1977, PhD, Zoology, 1980, University of Birmingham, England. *Appointments:* Postdoctoral Research Fellow, University of Calgary, Canada, 1980-83; Assistant/Associate Professor, Zoology, University of Florida, USA, 1984-. *Publications:* 31 refereed primary publications; 34 published abstracts. *Memberships:* Society for Experimental Biology; Canadian, American Societies of Zoologists; American Physiological Society; Crustacean Society; Sigma Xi; International Association of Astacology. *Honour:* Society for Experimental Biology - Presidential Medal, 1988. *Address:* Zoology Dept., University of Florida, 223 Bartram Hall, Gainesville, Fl 32611, USA.

WHEATON Elaine Esther, b. 11 June 1952, Biggar, Saskatchewan, Canada. Climatologist; Research Scientist. 2 sons. *Education:* BSc, 1973; MSc, Climatology, 1979. *Appointments:* Lab Instructor 1973-77, Lecturer 1977-79, University of Saskatchewan; Res Ass, Saskatchewan Inst of Pedology, 1979; Research Scientist, Climatologist, Saskatchewan Research Council, 1980-. *Publications:* Co-authored the Canadian portion, The Impact of Climatic Variations on Agriculture, ML Parry, TR Carter and NT Konijn (Eds), 1987; Vol 1 Assessments in Cool Temperature and Cold Regions. *Memberships:* Canadian Meteorological and Oceanographic Society Chairperson, Saskatchewan Local Centre; Canadian Association of Geographers Member of Organizing committee, EIA, 1986; Water Studies Institute, former Chair; Assoc Editor, Climatological Bulletin. *Honours:* Griffith Taylor Medal and Prize, Geography, 1974; Hantelman Humanities Scholarship; University Prize in Science, 1973. *Honours:* Horseback riding (dressage); Crosscountry skiing; Reading. *Address:* PO Box 4061, Saskatoon, Saskatchewan, Canada S7N 4E3.

WHEELER Catherine deVeer Werneke, b. 27 Dec. 1907, Washington, DC, USA. Artist. m. Judson Broughton Wheeler, 26 Dec. 1936. 1 son, 1 daughter. *Education:* Private Art lessons from Matilda Leisinring, 1919-25; Art School, Washington, 1927-29; British Academy, Rome, Italy, 1931; Famous Artist School, Bridgport, Connecticut, 1957. *Appointments:* Commercial artist, Tri-Utility Comp, New York, 1929-31; Mural Artist, WPA project 1933; Commercial artist, Rochon Hoover Studio, Washington, 1935-41; Freelance, Harwood Martin Adv. Agency, 1944-50. *Creative Works:* Illustrated Childrens Book, Sounds the Letters Make, 1940; Numerous portraits for private individuals; Painting of Horses, 1979-; Exhibited with AAEA since 1980 in Middleburg Virginia, Massachusetts, California, South Carolina, Kentucky. *Memberships:* Charter Member, National Museum of Women in the Arts, Washington DC; American Academy of Equine Art, Middleburg; Former Member, Washington Arts Club. *Honours:* Special Awards, Paper book cover, Famous Artists School Magazine Competition, 1957; Two popular vote awards from AAEA Exhibitions; Selected entry for inclusion in Anniversary issue of Polo Magazine, 1985. *Hobbies and Interests:* Sewing; Literature; Music; Medicine; Politics; World conditions. *Address:* 8360 Greensboro Drive, No 726, McLean, VA 22102, USA.

WHEELER Gloria Eileen, b. 6 June 1943, Twin Falls, Idaho, USA. University Professor. *Education:* BS, Montana Stat University, 1965; MA, MS, PhD, Univeity of Michigan. *Appointments:* Rensis Likert Associates, 1971-78; Faculty Member, 1978-, Assistant Professor, 1978-82, Associate Professor, 1982-, Brigham Young University. *Publications:* various journal articles. *Membership:* Decision Sciences Institute. *Honours:* NASPAA Federal Faculty Fellowship, 1980-81. *Hobbies:* Camping; Hiking; Travel; Reading; Church & Community Service. *Address:* Institute of Public Management, Box 108 TNRB, Brigham Young University, Provo, UT 84602, USA.

WHEELER Helen Rippier, b. USA. Educator; Consultant. *Education:* BA, Barnard College; MS, Columbia University; MA, Social Science, University of Chicago; Ed.D., Education, Columbia University. *Appointments:* Proprietor, Womanhood Media, 1973-; Faculty member: University of California, Louisiana State University, etc. *Publications:* Getting Published: An International Interdisciplinary Professional Development Guide Mainly for Women Scholars, 1989; Bibliographic Instruction Course Handbook, 1988; Womanhood Media, 1972, 1975; Basic Collection for the Community College, 1968; Community College Library, 1965; In Press: Aging Womanhood; chapters in various books; articles in professional journals. *Memberships:* Council, American Library Association; Board, Special Libraries Association; Founding Member, Aging and Ageism Caucus, National Womens Studies Association, etc. *Honours:* Phi Lambda Theta, Merritt Humanitarian Fund, Women's Institute for Freedom of the Press Course Proposal Awards; Visiting Scholar in Women's Studies, Japan; etc. *Address:* Womanhood Media, 2701 Durant Avenue, Box 14, Berkeley, California, USA 94704.

WHEREAT Suzanne Joy, b. 10 Jan. 1943, Australia. Medical Practitioner. m. Rodney George Whereat, 9 Sept. 1968, 2 daughters. *Education:* MBBS, University of New South Wales, 1967; D(Obst), RCOG, 1977. *Appointments:* Resident Medical Officer, Prince Henry Prince of Wales Hospital, 1967; Registrar, Royal Brisbane Childrens Hospital, 1968-69; Registrar, Grey's Hospital, 1969-70; Registrar, Obstetrics & Gynaecology, Grey's Hospital, 1971; General Practice, 1971-. *Memberships:* Australia Medical Association; Royal Australian College of General Practitioners. *Hobbies:* Reading; Theatre; Bush Walking. *Address:* 36 Raglan St., Mosman, NSW 2089, Australia.

WHITBECK Caroline Ann, b. 8 Jan. 1940, New York, USA. Educator; Research Scholar. 1 daughter. *Education:* BA, Mathematics, 1962; MA, Philosophy of Science, Boston University, 1965; PhD, Philosophy, MIT, 1970. *Appointments:* Lecturer, 1968-70, Assistant Professor, 1970-71, Philosophy, Yale Univerity; Research Associate, Psychiatry, Yale University School of Medicine, 1971-73; Assistant Professor, Philosophy, SUNY, Albany, 1973-78; Post-doctoral Fellow, 1977-78; Associate Professor, University of Texas Medical School, 1978-82; Research fellow, 1982-83, Visiting Associate Professor, 1983-86, Lecturer, 1986-, Senior Lecturer, 1988-, MIT. *Publications:* Articles in professional journals. *Memberships:* American Association for the Advancement of Science, Fellow; American Association of University Professors; American Philosophical Association; Association of MIT Alunmnae. *Honours:* Recipient, various honours and awards. *Address:* Center for Technology & Policy, MIT E40-223, Cambridge, MA 02139, USA.

WHITBY Julie Louise, b. 16 Nov. 1948, London, England. Poet; Author; Actress. *Education:* Bedales Trained for stage, Central School of Speech and Drama; Drama Centre, London; Trinity College, Oxford, 1 year. *Appointments:* Actress, Repertory companies and Theatre-in- Education; Poetry recitals nationally; Receptionist, Berlitz School of Languages. *Publications:* Poetry published in national magazines, newspapers and literary journals; Arts Council Anthology; Included in The Big Little Poem Card Series; Poems have also been broadcast. *Memberships:* Writers Guild of Great Britain; National Poetry Secretariat. *Honours:* Marjorie Kendal Scholarship, Central School of Speech & Drama; Described as The Best Woman Poet Now Writing, Under Forty, Books and Bookmen. *Address:* c/o Bernard Stone, Turret Bookshop, 42 Lamb's Conduit Street, London WC1 N3LJ, England.

WHITCOMB Kay (Also known as Kathryn N Keith), b. 20 May 1921, Arlington, Massachusetts, USA. Artist; Craftsman; Enameller. m. Dr Michael John Keith, 12 July 1952, divorced 1956. 1 son, 1 daughter. *Education:* RI School of Design, 1939-40 and 1941-42; Cambridge School of Art, 1940- 41; Apprenticeship in enamelling, Doris Hall, Cleveland, 1946-47. *Creative Works:* Architectural enamel on steel, 20 years; Enamel on copper, 40 years; Champleve enamel on copper; Cloisonne enamel beads techniques of enamelling, 1979-; Numerous exhibitions including: Society of Arts and Crafts, Boston, 1988; 2nd International Email (3), Coburg, West Germany, 1987; Masterworks 87, Taft Museum, Cincinnati, Ohio, 1987; Ubiquitous Bead Invitational, Bellevue Museum of Art, Washington, 1987. *Memberships:* San Diego Art Guild, Chairman, 1968-69; Enamel Guild: West, founder, 1st president

1976-78; Cloisonne Collectors Club, 1989-; American Pen Women; La Jolla Visual Art Program, Chairman 1989-90. *Honours include:* Young Americans, ACC, 1950; Decorative Arts, Wichita, Kansas, 1962; Internl Biennale, Art of Email, Limages France, 1978; Internl Exhibition, Tokyo, 1981, 1985; Quilt Design, San Diego, 1976. *Address:* 1631 Mimulus Way, La Jolla, California 92037, USA.

WHITE Cynthia Carol, b. 16 Oct. 1943, Fort Worth, Texas, USA. Sales Co-ordinator. m. (1)Franklin E. Owen, 20. Oct. 1961, divorced 1987, 1 son, 3 daughters, (2)John Edward White, 1 Jan. 1988. *Education:* BBA, Management, University of Texas, Arlington. *Appointments:* Keypunch Operator, Can-Tex Ind., Mineral Wells, 1966-67; Secretary, Midland Corp., Mineral Wells, 1967-68; Executive Secretary to Vice President, Sales, Panbburn Company, 1972-78; Bookkeeper Secretary, CB Sevice, 1978-82; Sales Co-ordinator, Square D Company, 1982-. *Memberships:* National Association of Female Executives. *Hobby:* Miniature Golf. *Address:* 125 Plaza Blvd., No 1031, Hurst, Texas 76053, USA.

WHITE Eunice Francesca Brandt (Sue), b. 6 Sept. 1929, Hartford, Connecticut, USA. Travel Consultant. m. Donald James White, 10 Aug. 1960, 1 son, 1 daughter. *Education:* Wilson College, 1952; Hartford Art School, 1954; Fugacy Travel School, 1970; Personal Placement, Harvard Seminars, 1983, 1984. *Appointment:* Travel Consultant. *Publications:* Poetry; Art. *Memberships:* CLIA; President, Admiral Gaspard de Caligny Huguenots Society; President, Tampa Bay Colony; etc. *Hobbies:* Travel; Photography of Flowers. *Address:* 30 Woodland St., Hartford, CT 06105, USA.

WHITE Frances Victoria, b. 1 Nov. 1936, Adel, Yorkshire, England. Actress. m. Anthony Marlowe Hone, 13 Nov. 1965, divorced 1974, 1 daughter. *Education:* Central School of Drama, London, 3 years. *Appointments:* Season at Dundee Repertory Theatre, 1960-61; The Victorian Chaise Longue, BBC TV, 1962; Fit to Print, Duke of Yorks Theatre, 1962; Blue and White, ATV, 1963; A Severed Head, Criterian Theatre, 1969; The Pumpkin Eater, film, 1964; The World of Coppard, BBC TV, 1967; Mary Queen of Scots, film, 1971; A Raging Calm, Granada TV, 1974; The Secret Agent, BBC TV, 1975; I Claudius, BBC TV, 1976; Prince Regent, BBC TV, 1979; Appearances, Mayfair Theatre, 1980; I Woke Up One Morning, BBC TV, 1st series, 1985, 2nd series, 1986; A Very Peculiar Practice, BBC TV, 1986; Paradise Postponed, Euston films, 1986. *Honours:* Associated Rediffusion Scholarship, 1959; Elsie Fogerty Prize for Best All Round Performance by a Woman, 1960; Dundee Repertory Contract Prize, 1960. *Address:* c/o Bryan Drew, Mezzanine Quadrant House, 80/82 Regent Street, London W1, England.

WHITE Gillian Mary, b. 13 Jan. 1936, Woodford, Essex, England. Professor. m. Colin Arthur Fraser, 1 Apr. 1978. *Education:* LL.B., 1957; PhD, London, 1960; Barrister, Gray's Inn, 1960. *Appointments:* Executive Officer, Estate Duty Office, 1954-57; Research Assistant to E. Lauterpacht, QC, Cambridge, 1961-67; Lecturer, Law, 1967-71; Senior Lecturer, 1971-73; Reader, 1973-75, Professor, 1975-, University of Manchester. *Publications:* Nationalization of Foreign Property, 1961; The Use of Experts by International Tribunals, 1965; Articles in legal periodicals; book reviews; chapters in collections of essays on International Law; Editor, Melland Schill Monographs in International Law, 1983. *Memberships:* American Society of International Law; British Institute of International & Comparative Law; International Law Association, British Branch, Council Member. *Hobbies:* Classical Music; Walking; Travel; Cricket; Cooking; Political & International Affairs. *Address:* Faculty of Law, University of Manchester, Manchester M13 9PL, England.

WHITE Jan, b. 11 May 1943, Bridgeport, Connecticut, USA. Executive. m. (1)David Dustin Tuttle 10 July 1972, divorced 1988. (2)Benjamin W. White. *Education:* MS

Mathematics, Bates College, 1965; MBA Marketing, Columbia University Graduate School of Business, 1967. *Appointments:* Corporate Staff, Systems Engineer, Marketing Representative, Harvard University Account Manager, IBM Corporation, 1966-72; Assistant to the Director of Information Processing Services, Massachusetts Institute of Technology, 1972-75; Managing Director, Tuttle Family Trust, 1975-81; VAX Prodcut Marketing Manager, Senior Product Management Manager, VAX Systems Marketing Programs Manager, Artificial Intelligence Market Conditioning Manager, Financial Systems Group Market Conditioning Manager, Digital Equipment Corporation, 1981-. *Creative works:* Guest speaker, Massachusetts Institute of Technology/Sloan School Marketing Club; 55 Minute composite video segments for Decworld TV; 15 Minute video: Robots and Beyond: The Age of Intelligent Machines; National film debut in Disney Channel special film, Silver Men. *Memberships include:* American Association for Artificial Intelligence; Founding Director, Columbia Club of New England; Columbia Club of New York; Founding Director, Columbia Business Club of Boston; First woman Board Member, Columbia University Graduate School of Business Alumni Association; Chairman, Concord Council, Boston Symphony Orchestra; Guild Board, Opera Company of Boston; Ladies Association Board, Concord Antiquarian Museum; Chairman, Emerson Hospital Auxiliary; Museum of Science, Boston; Board and Life Member, Hannah Duston Garrison House Association; Charter Life Member, Harwich Historical Association, etc. *Honours:* Nominated to White House Fellows Program; VAX Tenth Anniversary Celebration Certificate of Appreciation, 1988. *Hobbies:* Music; Dance; Floral and other fine and performing arts; Sailing (Instructor); Swimming (Instructor); Skiing; Tennis; Golf; Riding; Hiking; Biking; Horticulture; Preservation of natural spaces and species worldwide. *Address:* 77 Francis Avenue, Cambridge, Massachusetts 02138, USA.

WHITE Janet Lynn, b. 14 July 1949, Yonkers, New York, USA. Company President; Business Consultant; Author; Lecturer. m. Frank White, 7 Aug. 1967, divorced 1986, 1 son. *Education:* BA, Accounting, Columbia Pacific University, 1984. *Appointments Include:* Assistant General Manager, Greyhound Food Management Corp; Assistant Chief Cost Accountant, United Bank, Denver; Accounting Supervisor, Payless Stores Corp, Oakland; Controller, Cost Accounting Manager, I T Corp; President, J W Business Solutions. *Publications:* Cost Accounting Principles & Applications for Layman Use; articles in professional journals. *Memberships Include:* National Association of Accountants, Bay Area Society of Information Centres; Entrepreneur Association of Diablo Valley; Contra Costa Council; InT'L Trade Association; Pleasanton and Walnut Creek Chambers of Commerce (Ambassador for Each). *Honours Include:* Arbitrator, American Arbitration Association; Certificates of Merit, National Association of Accountants. *Hobbies:* Cross Country Skiing; Equestrian Sports; Walking in Woods. *Address:* 2121 N. California Blvd., Suite 1010, Walnut Creek, CA 94596, USA.

WHITE Katherine Patricia, b. 1 Feb. 1948, New York City, USA. Attorney. *Education:* BA English, Molloy College, 1969; JD, St John's University School of Law, 1971. *Appointments:* Attorney, Western Electric Co., Inc, New York City, 1971-79; Attorney, AT & T, New York City, 1979-83; Attorney, AT & T Communications, Inc, New York City, 1984-; Adj. Professor of Law, New York Law School, 1987-88; Adj. Professor of Law, Fordham University, New York City, 1988-. *Memberships:* Board of Governors, Women's National Republican Club; President, 1986-88, St John's University Law School Alumni Association, LI Chapter; President, 1980-81, Catholic Lawyers' Guild for Diocese of Rockville Center; New York State Bar Association; Association of the Bar of the City of New York; Wharton Business School Club of New York; Metropolitan Club. *Honours:* Lambda Iota Tau, International Literature Honour Society, 1969. *Hobbies:* Racing sailboats, Figure

skating, Golf, Tennis. *Address:* 5 Starlight Court, Babylon, NY 11704, USA.

WHITE Katherine Ann Inman, b. 15 Dec. 1951, Arlington, Virginia, USA. Foreign Language Teacher. m. Michael Henry White, 25 May 1974. *Education:* BA magna cum laude 1973, MEd 1978, University of North Carolina, Greensboro (UNC-G). *Appointments:* Mendenhall Junior High School, 1973-84; Grimsley High School, 1984-. *Creative work includes:* Frequent speaker, local, regional & national foreign language conferences. Topics: Games & warm-up/wind-up activities in the language classroom. *Memberships include:* North Carolina Association of Educators; National Education Association; Past NC Secretary, American Association of Teachers of Spanish; American Association of Teachers of French; American Council of Teachers of Foreign Languages; Offices, Foreign Language Association of North Carolina; Former Coordinator, Guilford County Foreign Language Association; Past Office, Delta Kappa Gamma; Various community associations. *Honours:* Alumni scholarship, UNC-G, 1969-73; Phi Beta Kappa, 1973; Pi Delta Phi (honorary French), Sigma Delta Pi (honorary Spanish), 1972. *Hobbies:* Bridge; Travel; Reading; Cooking. *Address:* 5204 Bennington Drive, Greensboro, North Carolina 27410, USA.

WHITE Lori Ann, b. 23 May 1962, Grangeville, Idaho, USA. Fiction Writer. *Education:* BA, English/Creative Writing, University of Idaho, 1980-85; Science Fiction Writer's Workshop, Michigan State University, Clarion, 1983. *Appointments:* Argonaut, University of Idaho, 1981-82; Freelance Fiction writer, 1981-. *Publications:* Short stories: Separate Rhythms; Old Mickey Flip had a Marvellous Ship; Knives; The Reason for the Rhyme; Gracious Hostess; All I Want for Christmas is My Two Front Teeth; Strange Attractions. *Memberships:* National Honour Society; Phi Beta Kappa; Phi Kappa Phi; Science Fiction Writers of America. *Honours:* National Scholastic Writing Awards, 3rd place, 1979; National Merit Finalist, 1979; Honorable Mention, World of Poetry, 1981; 3rd place, Writers of the Future, 1985. *Hobbies:* Skiing; Running; Weight-lifting; Dance; Theatre; Music; Technological advances of all types. *Address:* 1235 Wildwood Ave No 294, Sunnyvale, CA 94089, USA.

WHITE Mary Jane, b. 14 June 1953, Charlotte, North Carolina, USA. Poet; Translator; Attorney. *Education:* BA, Reed College, 1973; MFA, Writer's Workshop, 1978, JD, College of Law, 1979, University of Iowa; HS, North Carolina School of Arts, 1971. *Appointments:* Assistant, Winneshiek County Attorney, 1979-81; Solo Practitioner, Law, 1979-85; Poet; Translator, 1985-. *Publications:* The Work of The Icon Painter, chapbook, 1979; Russian Poetry the Modern Period, contributing translator, 1979; Starry Sky To Starry Sky, Holy Cowl, poetry and translations, 1988. *Memberships:* PEN; AWP; Iowa Arts Council; Artists in the Schools. *Honours:* Hallmark Undergraduate Poetry Award, 1973; NEA Poetry Fellowship, 1979; Breadloaf Waitress Scholarship, 1979; NEA Translation Fellowship, 1985; Kenneth Rexroth Memorial Translation Fellowship, 1988. *Address:* Box 159-A, RR No 2, Deconah, IA 52101, USA

WHITE Patricia Rosalie Smith, b. 13 Dec. 1928, Greenville, USA. Community Resource Development Educator; Nutritionist; Realtor. m. Winfield Horace White, 21 June 1949, divorced 1969, 1 son, 2 daughters (1 deceased). *Education:* BS, University of Rhode Island, 1950; MS, 1972, PhD, 1981, University of Maryland. *Appointments:* Stat. Quality Control Technologist, Oscar Mayer, 1954; Textile Research, 1965-67; Ext. Agent, Home Economics Co-op.Ext. Serv., University of Maryland, 1967-77; Supervisory Agent, EFNEP, Pr.Geo.Co., 1969-77; Area Agent, Community Resource Development, 1978-. *Publications:* Articles in professional journals. *Memberships Include:* Community Development Society; Community Resource Development Association; League of Women Voters; American Home Economics Association. *Honours:*

Recipient, many honour & awards. *Hobbies:* Reading; Bicycling; Hiking; Camping. *Address:* Rt. 2 Box 82-1, Leonardtown, MD 20650, USA.

WHITE Ruth S., b. USA. Composer; Author; Publisher. *Education:* BFA (Piano) 1948, BFA (Music Composition) 1948, MFA (Music Composition) 1949, Carnegie Mellon University. *Appointments:* Supervisor, Demo School, University of California Los Angeles, 1951-59; President, Rhythms Productions 1955-, Cheviot Corporation 1961-. *Creative work includes:* Classical compositions, recorded USA, Canada, Europe; Approx. 75 children's musical albums; Multi-media Productions; Music for films, commercials. *Memberships include:* Board, & National Trustee 1972-76, Recording Academy; Music Educators National Society; Audio Engineering Society; Musicians Union; International Association of Women Composers; Classical Music Society. *Honours:* 1st prize, music composition, National Society for Arts & Letters, 1951; Fellowship, Huntingdon Hartford Foundation, 1966; Notable Recording, American Library Association, 1983; Parents Choice, recording, 1983; Award, computer film score, Atlanta Film Festival, 1971. *Hobbies:* Camping; Running; Rafting. *Address:* Box 34485, Los Angeles, California 90034, USA.

WHITE Sally Blanche Fox, b. 25 Nov. 1924, Waxahachie, Texas, USA. Director, Public Relations & Fashion. m. Joseph A. White, 25 Dec. 1947, 1 son. *Education:* University of Mexico, 1945; BJ Honours, University of Texas, 1946; Scheil School of Art, 1954; Dallas School of Commercial Art, 1956; Virginia Commonwealth University, 1967-68. *Appointments include:* Publicity Chair, United Fund, Richmond, Virginia; Admissions Counsellor, William Woods College, Fulton, Missouri; Feature writer, advertising manager, Daily Texas; Copywriter, layout artist, Joske's, San Antonio; Commentator, continuity writer, San Angelo Radio; Advertising manager, Meacham's, Fort Worth; Freelance fashion commentator, publicist, sales trainer, Chicago, Dallas & New Orleans. Current: Director of Public Relations, Neiman Marcus, Atlanta, Georgia, 1972-. *Memberships include:* Fashion Group Inc; Womens Chamber of Commerce; Charter member, Atlanta Press Club; Atlanta Botanical Gardens Associates; Womens Commerce Club; High Museum of Art; Atlanta Historical Society; School Support Group, Rabun-Gap-Nacoochee Club. *Honours include:* Elected, Leadership Atlanta; Womens Chamber of Commerce, 1980; Governor's Art Award, Embroiders Guild of America, 1987; Biographical recognition. *Address:* c/o Neiman Marcus, 3393 Peachtree Road NE, Atlanta, Georgia 30326, USA.

WHITE Vicki Lee, b. 18 Feb. 1960, Steubenville, USA. Banker. m. John Robert White, 12 Apr. 1980. *Education:* Applied Diploma: General Banking, 1986, Retail Banking, 1987. *Appointments:* Teller, New Accounts, 1979-84, Computer Operations, 1985-, Miners & Mechanics Bank. *Publications:* Songs: David, Magic & Love, 1977; Illustrator, Rainbow (poetry book), A Poem for You, 1978. *Memberships:* American Institute of Banking; Ancient Mystical Order of Rosae Crucis; Steubenville Art Association. *Hobbies:* Acrylic-Oil Painting; Stamp & Coin Collecting; Photography; Non-fiction Reading. *Address:* Sugar Street, Richmond, OH 43944, USA.

WHITEHEAD Geraldine Boyd, b. 28 Feb. 1953, Syracuse, New York, USA. Social Services. m. William 29 Sept. 1979, divorced 3 May 1988. 2 sons. *Education:* BA, Hamilton College, 1975; MSW, Syracuse University, 1979; Education Administration-Certificate in Advance Studies, Sacred Heart University, completion 1989. *Appointments:* Facility Counselor, Onondaga County Juvenile Detention Facility, Hillbrook Detention Home, 1976- 79; Family Counselor II, Family Services, Woodfield, Bridgeport, 1979-845; Senior Probation Officer, State of Connecticut/Judicial Department/Office of Adult Probation, 1984-86; School Social Worker, City of Bridgeport, Board of Education/Pupil Personnel Department of Special Educational Services,

1986-; Program Coordinator, City of Bridgeport/Board of Education/Youth Services Summer Program, 1988. *Memberships:* National Board of Advisors, Outstanding Young Women of America Program, 1988; Charter Member, Outstanding Young Americans, 1988; National Association of School Social Workers, 1986-; Connecticut Association of School Social Workers, 1986-; National Association of Negro Business and Professional Womens Clubs (Corresponding Secretary, Bridgeport Chapter 1987), 1985-. *Honours:* One of 10 Outstanding Young Women in America Program Finalists' for 1987 Award Recipient, 1988; Professional Accomplishment Award, National Association of Negro Business and Professional Womens Clubs, 1988; Connecticut Outstanding Citizen Award, Connecticut Jaycees and WVIT Channel 30, 1988. *Hobbies:* City of Bridgeport Mayor's Drug Abuse Prevention Council; Boy Scouts of America; Youth Community Activities. *Address:* 106 B Smoke Valley Road, Stratford, Connecticut 06497, USA.

WHITEHEAD Helen May, b. 1 Sept. 1951, Harrisburg, Pennsylvania, USA. Small Business Entrepreneur/Marketing Consultant. m. Gregory James Whitehead. 1 son. *Education:* AA, Liberal Arts, University of Maryland, European Division, Germany, 1978; Certificado de Suficencia, University of Zaragoza, Spain, 1978; BS, Marketing, Northeastern University, Boston, 1982; BS, Business administration Hons, Auburn University, Montgomery, Alabama, 1983; MBA, Simmons College, Graduate School of Management, Boston, Massachusetts, 1987. *Appointments:* Staff Sergeant, US Air Force, Scott AFB, Illinois, 1971-75; USAF Europe, Ramstein, Federal Republic of Germany, 1975-78; Manager, Sales Representative, M&S Indian Jewelry, Griesheim, Germany, 1978-79; Training Department Coordinator, Aviation Simulation Technology Inc, Bedford, Massachusetts, 1982-84; Regional Sales Manager, Huang's Trading Co, Skokie, Illinois, 1984-86; President, Uniques, Bedford, Massachusetts, 1983-87; Staff Engineer, CTA Inc., Burlington, Massachusetts, 1989-. *Memberships:* Scholarship Chairperson, Hanscom AFB Officers' Wives Club; Substitute Teacher, Hanscom AFB Education Systems; Substitute Teacher, Quincy School System; National Association of Female Executives; Alpha Sigma Lambda. *Honour:* US Air Force Commendation Medal, 1974. *Hobby:* Speaker on entrepreneurship. *Address:* 107 Dundee Road, N Quincy, MA 02171-1305, USA.

WHITEHORN Katharine Elizabeth, b. London, England. Journalist. m. Gavin Lyall, 2 sons. *Education:* MA, Honours, Newnham College, Cambridge; Postgraduate Study, Cornell University, USA. *Appointments:* Picture Post, 1956-57; Womans Own, 1958; Spectator, 1959-61; Observer. *Publications:* Cooking in a Bedsitter, 1960; Roundabout, 1961; Only on Sundays, 1966; Social Survival, 1968; Observations, 1970; How to Survive in Hospital, 1972; How to Survive Children, 1975; Sunday Best, 1976; How to Survive in The Kitchen, 1979; How to Survive Your Money Problems, 1983. *Membership:* National Union of Journalists. *Honour:* LLB, St Andrews, 1985. *Hobby:* River Boat. *Address:* The Observer, Chelsea Bridge House, Queenstown Road, London SW8 4NN, England.

WHITEHOUSE Constance Mary, b. 13 June 1910, Nuneaton, England. m. Ernest Raymond Whitehuse, 23 Mar. 1940, 3 sons. *Education:* Cheshire County Training College, 1930-32; Special Art Course, Art College, Wolverhampton (part-time). *Appointments:* Art Mistress, Brewood Grammar School, 1943-45; Senior Mistress, Head, Art, Madeley Modern School, Shropshire, 1959-64; Co-Founder, Clean Up Tv Campaign, 1964; President, National Viewers and Listeners Association, 1965-. *Publications:* Cleaning Up TV; Who Does She Think She Is?; Whatever Happened to Sex?; A Most Dangerous Woman; Mightier Than the Sword, 1985. *Honours:* CBE, 1980. *Hobbies:* Photography; Gardening. *Address:* Blachernae, Dead Lane, Ardleigh, Colchester, Essex, CO7 7RH, England.

WHITELEY Angela Mary, Lady, b. 28 May 1931,

Kent, England. Lighting Consultant. m. Peter John Henry, 18 July 1955, 2 sons, 1 daughter. *Education:* Beneden School. *Appointments:* Extra Lady in Waiting to Her Royal Highness Princess Alexandra, 1985-. *Memberships:* Vice Patron, Riding for the Disabled Association; Past Member, Council of Riding for the Disabled Association. *Hobbies:* Art; Opera; Ballet; Travel; Cooking; Gardening. *Address:* Harsfold Farmhouse, Wisborough Green, Billingshurst, Sussex RH14 0BD, England.

WHITESIDE Elizabeth Ayres, b. 24 Feb. 1960, Columbus, Ohio, USA. Attorney. *Education:* Indiana University, 1978-80; BFA, University of Wisconsin, Milwaukee, 1982; JD, Ohio State University, 1985. *Appointments:* Franklin County (Ohio) Municipal Court Clerk's Office, 1981; Chester, Hoffman & Willcox, 1983-84; Porter, Wright, Morris & Arthur, Columbus, Ohio, 1984; Squire, Sanders & Dempsey, Columbus, Ohio, 1985-87; Shearman & Sterling, New York, 1987-. *Publication:* Administrative Adjudications: An Overview of the Existing Models and Their Failure to Achieve Uniformity and a Proposal for a Uniform Adjudicatory Framework, 1985, reprinted in part, 1986. *Memberships:* American Bar Association; District of Columbia Bar; Ohio State Bar Association; American Judicature Society; Phi Delta Phi Legal Fraternity, Swan Inn, Magister; Columbus Bar Association; Cap City Young Republican Club; Alpha Lambda Delta and Phi Eta Sigma Honorary fraternities; Ohio State Law Journal; United Methodist Women; Bar Admissions: Ohio 1985, District of Columbia 1986; United State Tax Court, 1986; United States Court of Appeals, District of Columbia and Sixth Circuits, 1986; United states District Court, Northern and Southern Districts of Ohio, 1986. *Hobby:* Playing the violin. *Address:* 260 West 52 Street, No 5K, New York, NY 10019, USA.

WHITESITT Linda Marie, b. 13 Jan. 1951, Great Falls, Montana, USA. Musicologist; Violinist. m. Bennett Lentczner, 16 Jan. 1982. *Education:* BM, Violin, Peabody Conservatory, 1973; MM, Music History, 1975; PhD, Musicology, University of Maryland, 1981. *Appointments:* Instructor, Gettysburg College, 1975; Assistant Professor, Radford University, 1978-84; Violinist, South Carolina Philharmonic Orchestra, 1988-; Violinist, Roanoke Symphony, 1978-84, 1986-87; Violinist, New River Valley Symphony, 1980-88, West Virginia Symphony, 1984-88; Adjunct Professor, Roanoke College 1986-88; Sales Coordinator, ICS-Texicon, Charlotte, NC. *Publications:* The Life and Music of George Antheil, 1900-1959, 1983; articles and reviews in various journals. *Memberships:* American Musicological Society, Secretary/Treasurer, Southeast Chapter; College Music Society; Sonneck Society; American Association of University Women. *Honours:* NEA, 1982; Virginia Commission for the Arts, 1983; NEH Summer Fellowship, 1984; AAUW Educational Foundation Individual Research Project Grant, 1986-87; Music for Women Fund Grant, 1986-87. *Hobbies:* Hiking; Drawing. *Address:* 2067 Malvern Road, Rock hill, SC 29730, USA.

WHITFIELD Vallie Jo Fox, b. 18 Mar. 1922, Nashville, Tennessee, USA. Writer; Publisher. m. Robert Edward Whitfield, 26 Mar. 1943, 2 sons, 2 daughters. *Appointments:* Shell Development Company, 1943-45; Writer- Publisher, Whitfield Farm, 1962-68; Real Estate Agent, Realities, Pleasant Hill & Walnut Creek, 1968-85; Publisher, Whitfield Books, 1978-. *Publications include:* Whitfield History & Genealogy of Tennessee, 1964; Whitfield, McKeel, Fox, Schiefer Families, 1965; Virginia History & Whitfield Biographies, 1976; History of Pleasant Hill, California, 1981; Heritage History, 1988. Also articles in: Historical & Genealogical Magazine; Concord Life Magazine; Trades. *Memberships:* Contra Costa Board of Realtors, 1968-85; Past Regional Vice President, Conference of California Historical Societies; International Toastmistress Clubs. *Honours:* Numerous awards, biographical recognitions. *Hobbies:* Reading; Establishing library archives, Pleasant Hill Historical Society; Cataloguing records, Contra Costa Historical Society; Civic & research interests; Community work.

Address: 1841 Pleasant Hill Road, Pleasant Hill, California 94523, USA.

WHITLEY Alice, b. 6 Feb. 1913, Sydney, Australia. Educator. *Education:* BSc., Sydney University; PhD, London University, England, 1954. *Appointments:* Mathematics Teacher, Brighton College, Manly, New South Wales, 1935-37; Sydney Church of England Girls' Grammar School, 1938-40; Teacher, Mathematics & Science, 1941-52, Head of Science, Deputy Headmistress, 1955-59, Headmistress, 1960-72, Methodist Ladies College, Burwood, New South Wales; Demonstrator, Chemistry, University of New South Wales, 1955-65; Member (foundation), Commonwealth Science Advisory Committee, 1965-73; Consultant to Australian Schools Commission, 1973-. *Publications:* A New Approach to Chemistry, co-author; Design of Science Rooms, co-author; Schools in Australia, co-author; articles in professional journals. *Memberships Include:* Fellow, Australian College of Education; Associate, Royal Australian Chemical Institute; Australian Federation of University Women, New South Wales, President 1979-81; Teacher's Guild of New South Wales; Royal Society of New South Wales; etc. *Honour:* MBE, 1966. *Hobbies:* Reading; Needlework. *Address:* 1/39 Belmore St., Barwood, NSW 2134, Australia.

WHITMAN Ruth, b. 28 May 1922, New York City, New York, USA. Poet; Translator; Teacher. m. Morton Sacks, 6 Oct. 1966, 1 son, 2 daughters. *Education:* BA magna cum laude, Radcliffe College, 1944; MA, Classics, Harvard University, 1947. *Appointments:* Director in Poetry, Cambridge Center for Adult Education, 1964-68; Director, Poetry in the Schools, Massachusetts Council on the Arts, 1970-73; Poet-in-Residence: Hamden-Sydney College, Virginia, 1974, Harvard Alumni College, 1974, 1975, Holy Cross College, 1978, Centre College, Kentucky, 1980, 1987; Visiting Professor: Trinity College, Hartford, 1975, University of Denver, 1976, Massachusetts Institute of Technology, 1979, 1989-; University of Massachusetts, Boston, 1980: Lecturer, Poetry: Radcliffe Seminars, Radcliffe College, 1969-, Harvard Writing Program, 1979-84; Writer-in-Residence, Kentucky Arts Commission, 1981, Hebrew University, Jerusalem, Israel, 1984-85; Reviewer, Choice, 1980-; Poetry Editor, Radcliffe Quarterly, 1980-; Readings/recordings, USA, England, Israel, Egypt. *Publications:* Blood & Milk Poems, 1963; An Anthology of Modern Yiddish Poetry, 1966, 2nd Edition, 1979; The Marriage Wig & other poems, 1968; The Selected Poems of Jacob Glatstein, 1972, The Passion of Lizzie Borden: New & Selected Poems, 1973; Poemmaking: Poets in Classrooms, 1975; Tamsen Donner: A Woman's Journey, 1977; Permanent Address: New Poems 1973-1980, 1980; Becoming a Poet: Source, Process, and Practice, 1982; The Testing of Hanna Senesh, 1986; The Fiddle Rose: Poems 1970-1972 by Abraham Sutzkever, 1990; Laughing Gas: Poems New and Selected 1963-1990, 1991; Essays & translations; Author, Narrator, Sachuest Point (TV documentary), 1977. *Memberships:* Phi Beta Kappa; Modern Languages Association; Signet Club, Harvard; Poetry Society of America (Regional Vice-President, New England, 1968-87), PEN; Authors Guild. *Honours:* Senior Fulbright Writer-in-Residence Fellowship, 1984-85; Numerous other awards & honours. *Hobby:* Listening to chamber music. *Address:* 1559 Beacon Street, Brookline, MA 02146, USA.

WHITMIRE Kathryn J, b. Houston, Texas, USA. Mayor. m. Jim Whitmire, deceased. *Education:* Honours Graduate, Business Administration, 1968, MSc., Accountancy, 1970, University of Houston. *Appointments:* Associate, CPA, National CPA firm, Houston, 8 years; Faculty Member, Business Management, University of Houston; Partner, with late husband, Public Accounting Practice; Elected City Controller, 1977, re-elected 1979; Inaugurated 48th Mayor of the City of Houston, 1982, re-elected for 3rd term, 1986-. *Memberships:* Vice President, President-elect, US Conference of Mayors, 1982-86; US 4th Conference of Mayors Literacy Task Force and Task

Force on Drug Control; President, Texas Municipal League, 1989; etc *Honours:* 1st Woman in City of Houston to be elected to any city office; Awarded Distinguished Alumnus Award, College of Business Administraitorn, University of Houston, 1979, and Distinguished Alumnus Award, 1982; Recipient, Public Service Award, CPA's 1982; Named Woman of the Year, Texas Women's Political Caucus, 1984; City and State Outstanding Mayor, 1988; etc. *Address:* PO Box 1562, Houston, TX 77251, USA.

WHITMORE Beatrice Eileen Ott, b. 15 Mar. 1935, Harrisonburg, Virginia, USA. Staff Representative, International Association of Fire Fighters. m. Dale W Whitmore, 3 May 1967. 2 sons, 1 daughter. *Appointments:* US Air Force, 1953-55; Clerk Typist, USAF Civil, Eglin AFB, Florida, 1956-58; Clark AFB, Philippines, 1958-60; Secretary, Wright-Patterson AFB, Ohio, 1960-75; Fire Inspector, Wright-Patterson AFB, Ohio, 1975-85; Federal Staff Representative, International Association of Fire Fighters, 1985-89; Secretary, National Coffee Service Association, 1989-90; Secretary, National Association Rehabilitation Facilities, 1990-. *Memberships:* National Association Female Executives; IWC; Staff Representatives Union; Lodge: Job's Daughters; IAFF Local F88- Wright-Patterson AFB, Ohio, Sec Treasurer 1977-83, President 1983-85, President Emeritus 1985-; Leader, Organizer Little Sparkies, Wright-Patterson AFB, 1976-79; Den Mother, Boy Scouts of America. *Honour:* National Fire Protection Association Award for Fire Prevention, 1977. *Hobbies:* Sewing; Crocheting; Gardening; Reading; Playing organ; Birds; Cats. *Address:* 2311 Glade Bank Way, Reston, VA 22091, USA.

WHITMORE Menandra Sabina, b. 27 Oct. 1936, Huaraz, Ancash, Peru. Librarian. m. Jacob L. Whitmore, 7 Jan. 1965. 2 daughters. *Education:* BA Social Work, Universidad Catolica, Lima, 1967; MLS (Library Science), Universidad de Puerto Rico, 1974; MLS, Catholic University of America, Washington DC, USA, 1984. *Appointments:* Social Worker: Cornell Univ. Project, Vicos, Peru, 1960-62; American Friends Service Committee, Mexico & Peru, 1963-65; Librarian: American College of Puerto Rico, as Director of Libraries, 1977-80; Cataloger, Government Printing Office, Washington DC, 1981-83; In charge of Acquisitions Section, Pentagon Library, 1984-. *Publications:* Bibliographies published on mangroves, insects and forest history. *Memberships:* American Library Association; Seminar on the Acquisition of Latin American Library Materials; REFORMA (National Association to promote Library Services to the Spanish-Speaking: Treasurer, 1988-). *Honours:* Fellowship, Cornell University, 1960; American College of Puerto Rico, 1980: Commencement Ceremony dedicated to Menandra Whitmore; Awards for Exceptional Performance, Department of the Army, 1985 and 1988. *Hobbies:* Design and fabrication of women's clothing; Gardening; Comparison of the English and Quechua languages. *Address:* Chief, Acquisitions Section, Pentagon Library, Department of Defense, Washington, DC 20310, USA

WHITNEY Barbara T., b. 27 Aug. 1942, Chicago, Illinois, USA. Executive Director, Lincoln Park Zoological Society. m. John Alden Whitney, 27 June 1964, 1 son, 2 daughters. *Education:* BA, Writing, Denison University, Granville, Ohio, 1964. *Appointments:* Researcher, Book Division, Time Inc, 1964-66; Freelance Writer, 1966-75; Executive Director, Lincoln Park Zoological Society, Chicago, Illinois, 1975-. *Publications:* Articles in Animal Kingdom, 1981, 1984. *Memberships:* Fellow, Professional Member, American Association of Zoological Parks and Aquariums (various committees, Representative 1981); Economic Club of Chicago (Membership Committee 1979-82, Chairman of Membership Subcommittee 1982); American Association of Fund Raising Executives; Publicity Club of Chicago. *Honours:* Servian Award, University of Chicago Cancer Research Fund, 1971; Leadership Award, Direct Mail Marketing Association, 1978; Golden Pyramid Award, International Specialty

Advertising Association, 1980; Chicago Industry Colleagues Award, Women's Advertising Club, Chicago, 1980. *Address:* The Lincoln Park Zoological Society, 2200 N Cannon Drive, Chicago, IL 60614, USA.

WHITTEMORE Margot, b. 15 July 1959, New York City, USA. Financial Consultant. *Education:* BS, Marketing 1981, Boston University School of Public Communication; MBA, Graduate School of Business Administration, New York University, 1984; International Management Exchange Program, Universita Bocconi, Milan, Italy, 1984; London Polytechnic, 1980. *Appointments:* Assistant Account Executive, Barrett Card Limited, London, England, 1980; Management Director, Business Connections, Boston, MA, USA, 1980-82; Assistant Accountant, Conrac Corp, Stamford, 1983; An International Entrepreneurial Study, Spencer & Rubinow, New York, 1984; Financial Consultant, Fith Avenue Financial Center, Merrill Lynch, New York, 1985-. *Membership:* Vice President, Graduate Finance Association, 1984. *Honours:* Placed 13th of 11,000 Consultants, 1987; Place 12th of 11,000 Consultants, 1988; Dean's List, Boston University School of Public Communication. *Hobbies:* Dance; Water sports; Entrepreneurial ventures; Travel. *Address:* 15 East 11th Street, No. 4G, New York, NY 10022, USA.

WHITTEMORE Nena Louise Thames, b. 17 Apr. 1939, New Orleans, Louisiana, USA. College administrator. m. Robert Aalbu Fliegel, 2 Apr. 1983. 1 son. *Education:* BA, Carleton College, 1961; MA, Hunter College, 1963; PhD, City University of New York, 1968. *Appointments:* Lecturer & Teaching Fellow, Hunter, 1961-68; Instructor, Rutgers University, 1969-70; Asst Prof, John Jay College, 1970-75; Dir of Alumni 1976-82, Sr Devel Officer 1981-84, Carleton College; Exec Dir Dev & College Rel, Hollins, 1984-87; VP Institutional Adv, Bryant College, 1988-89. *Publications:* Less is More, Handbook for Alumni Administration, 1989; Mainstreaming Young Alumni, 1983; Roman Generals on the March, 1980; The Palm Tree Impresa in the New Arcadia, 1975; Educated Woman, 1971. *Memberships:* Council for the Advancement & Support of Education, Board Member District 5, Chair, Fund Raising Track, District III; National Association of Fund-Raising Executives, Board of Directors, Roanoke Chapter, 1985-88; Board of Directors, National Conference of Christians and Jews, Roanoke Chapter, 1985-88. *Honours:* Graduate Dissertation Fellowship, 1965-66; City University of New York Teaching Fellowship, 1961-63; Hunter College Distinction in English; Honours in English, Cum Laude, Carleton College, 1961. *Hobby:* Poetry. *Address:* 4867 Hunting Hills Dr., Roanoke, Virginia 24014, USA.

WHITTLESEY Faith Amy Ryan, b. 21 Feb. 1939, Jersey City, USA. United States Ambassador to Switzerland/Federal Official. m. Roger Whittlesey, deceased 1974, 2 sons, 1 daughter. *Education:* BA, Wells College, 1960; Ford Foundation Grant, Academy of International Law, The Hague, Netherlands, 1962; JD, University of Pennsylvania Law School, 1963. *Appointments Include:* Law Clerk, 1965; Special Assistant Attorney General, Pennsylvania Department of Justice, 1967-70; Assistant United States Attorney, Eastern District of Pennsylvania, 1970-72; Member, Pennsylvania House of Representatives, 1972, re-elected 1974; Affiliated with Philadelphia Law Firm, Wolf, Block, Schorr and Solis-Cohen, 1980-81; US Ambassador to Switzerland, 1981-83, 1985-; Assistant to President for Public Liaison, Senior White House Staff, The White House, Washington DC, 1983-85. *Memberships Include:* Pennsylvania, and International Bar Associations; etc. *Honours:* Outstanding Legislator Award, Delaware county School Boards Legislative Council, 1976; Certificate of Achievement, Pennsylvania Federation of Professional Womens Clubs, 1977; Certificate of Award, Pennsylvania State Society, Daughters of the American Revolution, 1977; etc. *Address:* United States Embassy, 93 Jubilaumstrasse, 3005 Bern, Switzerland.

WICKER Veronica DiCarlo, b. Monessen, USA. US

District Judge. m. Thomas C. Wicker, 1 son, 1 daughter. *Education:* BFA, Syracuse University, 1952; JD, Loyola University, 1966. *Appointments:* US Magistrate US Courts, Eastern District of Louisiana, 1977-79; US District Judge, US Courts, Eastern District of Louisiana, 1979-. *Memberships:* Louisiana, American, Fedral, New Orleans Bar Associations; Maritime Law Association; Federal Judges Association; Association of Women Judges; Association of Women Attorneys; American Justinian Society of Jurists. *Address:* US Courthouse, Room 406, 500 Camp St., New Orleans, LA 70130, USA.

WICKES Mary, b. St Louis, Missouri, USA. Actress. *Education:* BA, Honorary Doctor of Arts, 1969, Washington University, St Louis. *Appointments:* Stage Appearances include: Oklahoma, Palace Theatre, New York City; Park Avenue, Shubert Theatre; The Man Who Came to Dinner, Music Box Theatre; Stage Door; Blithe Spirit; Show Boat; Films Include: New Voyager; The Trouble with Angels; White Christmas; TV: Title Role, Mary Poppins; Alice, Halls of Ivy; The Canterville Ghost; The Lucy Show; MASH; Co-Star Father Dowling Mysteries, NBC, 1989. Seminars taught at Washington University. *Memberships:* Academy of Motion Picture Arts & Sciences; Academy of Television Arts & Sciences; Actors Equity association; Screen Actors Guild; American Federation of Television and Radio Artists; Phi Mu; etc. *Honours:* Nominated for TV Academy Emmy; Best Actress Award, Variety Clubs Outstanding Achievement Award in Entertainment Industry, by York Rite Masons of California, et. *Hobbies:* Friends; Volunteer Work in Hospital & Church. *Address:* c/o Artists Agency, 10000 Santa Monica Boulevard, Los Angeles, CA 90067, USA.

WICKSTEIN Zena Winifred, b. 9 Dec. 1940, Cleve, South Australia. Farmer & Grazier; Teacher. m. Richard Neil Wickstein, 10 Jan. 1962, 1 son, 1 daughter. *Education:* Teacher's Certificate, 1965. *Appointments:* Junior Primary Teacher, Cleve, 1960-65; Teacher-Librarian, 1971-76; Relief Teacher, 1977-88; Bureau of Census & Statistics, Census Collector, 1986. *Publications:* Co-Editor, Editorial Writer, A Century of Education in the Cleve District, 1886-1986; Amateur Painter in Oils; Tapestry Kneelers. *Memberships:* Cleve Area School Council Secretary, 12 years; Sims Farm Operations Association, Secretary; State Executive, SA Association State Schools Organisation; Anglican Church Cleve, Treasurer; etc. *Honours:* Centenary Year Award, Century of Education in Cleve District 1886-1986, 1986. *Hobbies:* Church Organist; Reading; Tapestry; Knitting; Crosswords; Swimming; Music; Golf; Painting; many others. *Address:* Box 177, Cleve, SA 5640, Australia.

WICKSTEN Mary Katherine, b. 17 Mar. 1948, San Francisco, USA. Associate Professor. *Education:* BA, 1970; MA 1972; PhD, 1977. *Appointments:* Lecturer, (Los Angeles), 1978-79, (Northridge), 1979, California State University; Associate Professor, Biology, Texas A&M University, 1980-. *Publications:* Articles in professional journals. *Memberships:* American Society of Zoologists; Biology Society of Washington; Southern California Academy of Sciences; Sigma Xi; Pacific Science Association; Western Society of Naturalists. *Hobbies:* Underwater Photography; Aquarium Keeping; Equitation. *Address:* Dept. of Biology, Texas A&M University, College Station, Texas 77843, USA.

WICKWIRE Patricia JoAnne Nellor, b. Sioux City, Iowa, USA. Consultant; Trainer; Lecturer. m. Robert James Wickwire, 7 Sept. 1957, 1 son. *Education:* BA cum laude, University of Northern Iowa, 1951; MA, University of Iowa, 1959; PhD, University of Texas, Austin, 1971; Postgraduate work, several universities/academies. *Appointments:* Teacher, various independent schools, Iowa; Reading Consultant, Dormitory Head, University of Iowa; Teacher, School Psychologist, Psychological Services Coordinator, Administrator, District Guidance, Student Services & Special Education, South Bay Union High School District, California; Director, Multi-District Consortium for Special Education, California; Lecturer, Loyola-Marymount University; Consultant, State Department of Education, California; Independent Contractor, Consultant, Trainer, Lecturer; President, Wickwire & Associates, California. *Publications:* The Academic Achievement and Language Development of American Children of Latin Heritage; Contributor, professional & popular journals, magazines, newspapers. *Memberships:* Chair, International Career Association Network; Executive Board: American Association for Career Education; Association for Measurement & Evaluation in Counseling & Development; Committee on Women, American Association for Counseling & Development; Network Director, National Association of Female Executives; President's Committee on Employment of the Handicapped; American Association of School Administrators; World Future Society; California Executive Board, American Association of University Women; Executive Board or President, many state & area bodies. *Honours:* Special Citation for Achievement in Education in California; South Bay Woman of the Year; Numerous achievement awards. *Hobbies:* Reading; Writing; Walking; Gardening; Photography; Career & leadership development; Professional ethics; Equal opportunity. *Address:* 2900 Amby Place, Hermosa Beach, CA 90254, USA.

WIDENER-BURROWS Dawne Delane, b. 7 July 1955, Hampton, Virginia, USA. Marketing Research Company President. m. Lawrence B. Burrows, 1 Jan. 1980. *Education:* BS, Journalism, Spanish, University of Florida, 1976. *Appointments:* Research Analyst, Rife Market Research, Miami, Florida, 1976-78; Research Manager, Earle Palmer Brown Advertising, Washington DC, 1978-79; Vice-President, Director of Research, Needham Harper & Steers Advertising, Washington DC, 1979-85; Vice-President, Director of Strategic Planning, Rosenthal Greene & Campbell, Bethesda, Maryland, 1985-86; Partner, Migliara Kaplan & Widener, Baltimore, Maryland, 1986-87; President, Widener-Burrows & Associates, Annapolis, Maryland, 1987-. *Memberships:* Marketing Research Association, Mid-Atlantic Chapter President 1985; American Marketing Association; Advertising Association of Baltimore; Women in Advertising and Marketing. *Hobbies:* Cycling; Travel; Teaching; Speaking on subjects of advertising and advertising research. *Address:* 31 Old Solomon 1st Road, Suite 200 B, Annapolis, MD 21401, USA.

WIDETZKY Judi, b. 22 May 1941, Minneapolis, USA. Acting Chairman, World Labour Zionist Movement, 1982-; President of Council of Women's Organizations in Israel Education. BA, Political Science, Hebrew University, Jerusalem, 1964; Teachers Certificate, oranim Teachers Seminary, 1959. *Appointments:* Assistant Editor, English Language Science Journals, Weizman Science Press, Jerusalem, 1965-67; Assistant to Mr David Ben Gurion, 1st Prime Minister of Israel in Keren Hanegev, fundraising arm of Sde Boker College, 1967-70; elected Secretary General, World Movement of Young Labour Zionists, 1970-75, Director, Young Leadership, Department of Moetzet Hapoalot Pioneer Women, 1975; Representative, Dor Hemshech Young Leadership Department of World Zionist Organisation in USA and Canada, 1975-78, Executive Director, Moshe-Sharett Institute of Socialist Zionist Education, 1978-82. *Publications:* Echoes of the Past, 1982; Refugees, Their Aclimitization into the Mainstream Culture - the Israeli Experience, 1985. *Memberships:* Permanent Budget & Finance Committe of WZO and Jewish Agency; etc. *Hobbies:* Painting; Music. *Address:* 28 Remban Street, Jerusalem, Israel.

WIEDER Marcia Ellen, b. 5 Oct. 1956. President and Chief Executive Officer. *Education:* BA, TV & Film Production, University of Maryland, 1978; Certified Instructor, Technologies for Creating Results Seminars. *Appointments:* Writer/Producer, Westinghouse; Executive Producer, Global PR & Communications Projects, Wieder Enterprises; President and Chief Executive Officer, TVI Creative Specialists. *Publications:* Making It In The Media; Venture Into Video. *Memberships:* Vice President, Managing Director,

National Association of Women Business Owners; Advisory Board, Maryland Film Commission; Advisory Board, University of Maryland, School of Business. *Honours:* National Communications Award, 1988; Chivas Regal Young Entrepreneur of the Year, 1988; Small Business Admin, Women in Business Advocate, 1988. *Hobbies:* Public speaking; Teaching or mentoring start-ups. *Address:* 1325 Eighteenth St NW, No 908, Washington, DC 20036, USA.

WIEGERSMA Nancy Ann, b. 16 July 1942, Worcester, Massachusetts, USA. Professor of Economics. 1 daughter. *Education:* BS, Northeastern University & University of Maryland, 1966; MS 1969, PhD 1976, University of Maryland. *Appointments:* Economist, US Department of Agriculture, 1969- 73; Lecturer, Women's Studies, San Diego State University, 1973-74; Associate Professor of Economics, Northern Virginia Community College, 1974-79; Professor of Economics, Fitchburg State College, 1979-. *Publications:* Books: Agriculture in Vietnam's Economy, 1973; Vietnam: Peasant Land, Peasant Revolution, 1988. Article, Asiatic Mode of Production in Vietnam, Journal of Contemporary Asia, 1982; Adviser, Annual Editions in Economics, 1976-77; Advisory Board, Vietnam Generation, 1988-. *Memberships:* Offices, past/present, Massachusetts State College Faculty Association; Coordinator, Women's Work Project, 1974-79; Northeast Feminist Scholars; American Economic Association; Union for Radical Political Economics. *Honours:* Distinguished Service Award, USDA, 1972; Achievement grant 1980, 5 professional development grants 1984-, Fitchburg State College; Grant, study of war & social consequences, William Joiner Centre, 1987; Various honour societies. *Hobbies:* Hiking; Cross-country skiing; Photography; Stained glass work; Town of Montague Arts Cuncil, 1985-88. *Address:* 80 Leverett Road, Montague, Massachusetts 01351, USA.

WIELAND Joyce June, b. 30 June 1931, Toronto, Canada. Artist; Film Maker. *Education:* Central Technical School, Toronto. *Appointments include:* Animator, with George Dunning, 1957-59; Currently artist & film maker. *Creative works include:* Book, True Patriot Love, 1971; Book, Joyce Wieland, 1987; 20 films including 1 feature- length, The Far Shore; Paintings; Quilts; Collages; Sculpture. *Memberships:* Royal Canadian Academy; Arts & Letters Club, Toronto. *Honours:* 2 awards, 3rd International Filmmaker Festival, New York, 1969; Victor M. Lynch-Staunton Award, Canada Council, 1972; 3 Canadian film awards, 1977; Officer, Order of Canada, 1983; Award, Ann Arbor Film Festival, 1986. Winner, Toronto Arts Award, 1987; Mayoral reception in honour, Toronto, 1987. *Address:* 497 Queen Street East, Toronto, Ontario, Canada M5A 1V1.

WIENER Hermine Beate (Lauber), b. 27 Jan. 1934, Nurnberg, Germany. Businesswoman; Local Government Councillor. m. (1) Otto Stern, 24 Dec. 1954, div. 1976, 2 sons, (2) Morton Wiener, 24 Oct. 1976. *Education:* Studies, City College of New York, USA. *Appointments:* Chief Executive Officer, Nurnberger Wach-und Schliessgesellscaft mbH, & Sicherheitsgesellschaft am Flughafen Nurnberg mbH, Germany, 1975-; Councillor, Town of Palm Beach, Florida, USA, 1987-. *Memberships:* Offices: Greater Palm Beach Symphony; Graham Eckes Palm Beach Academy; Norton Gallery of Art; Anti-Defamation League. Member: Chaine des Rotisseures; Rotary International. *Honour:* Donor, David & Lisa Lauber Prize, promising artists, Nurnberg, Germany; Recepient: City of Hope Hospital, Humanitarian of the Year Award, 1990; Recepient: Haym Solomon Award of the Anti-Defamation League of B'Nai Brith, 1990. *Hobbies:* Travel; Photography; Classical music; Interior design. *Address:* 215 Nightingale Trail, Palm Beach, Florida 33480, USA.

WIER Dara, b. 30 Dec 1949, New Orleans, Louisiana, USA. Poet; Professor of English. m. Michael Pettit, l Sept 1983, 1 son, 1 daughter. *Education:* BS, Longwood College, 1971; MFA, Bowling Green University, 1974. *Appointments:* Hollins College, 1975-80; University of Utah 1980; University of Texas 1983; University of Alabama 1980-85; University of Massachusetts, 1985- . *Publications:* Books of poems: The Book of Knowledge 1988; All You Have In Common 1984; The 8-Step Grapevine 1980; Blood, Hook and Eye, 1977. *Memberships:* Associated Writing Programs, Board member 1975-80; lst Woman President, 1979-80; PEN; MLA. *Honour:* National Endowment for the Arts Poetry Fellowship, 1980-81. *Address:* 504 Montague Road, Amherst, MA 01002, USA.

WIER-CRITZ Nancy, b. 13 Feb. 1954, Cincinnati, Ohio, USA. Director, Social Services Clermont Nursing Center. 1 daughter. *Education:* Associate in Science, Social Work, 1974, BSc, Social Work, 1978, University of Cincinnati. *Appointments:* Director of Social Services, Our Lady of Mercy Hospitals, Cincinnati, Ohio 1976-86; Director of Social Services, Clermont Nursing Center, 1986-. *Memberships:* NASW, Hospital Nursing Home Communication Council; Sigma Delta Tau Alumni Association. *Hobbies:* Biking; Sailing; Photography. *Address:* 3966 Piccadilly Circle, Cincinnati, Ohio 45230, USA.

WIEST Elizabeth H, b. 3 July 1936, Lancaster, USA. Nurse Educator; Administrator. m. Donald K Wiest, 8 Mar. 1980. *Education:* BSN, 1966, MS, 1968, University of Maryland; Ed.D., University of Wyoming, 1980. *Appointments:* Staff Nurse, Lancaster General Hospital, 1957-63; Staff Nurse, University Hospital, Baltimore, 1965-66; Clinical Instructor, Lancaster General Hospital School of Nursing, 1966; Assistant Professor, University of Maryland, 1967-74; Assistant to Associate Professor, Universiy of Wyoming, 1974-83; Director, Off Campus Nursing Programmes, Universiy of Wyoming, 1983-. *Memberships Include:* American, Wyoming, District Nurses Associations; National League for Nursing; Wyoming League for Nursing; Wyoming commission for Nursing and Nursing Education, Vice Chairman; numerous other professional organisations. *Honours:* USPHS Traineeship for Graduate Study, 1966-67; Kemper Scholarship to Rutgers Summer School of Alcohol Studies, 1969; Sigma Theta Tau, 1969. *Hobbies:* Reading; Quilting; Needlepoint; Walking. *Address:* 1930 Sheridan, Laramie, WY 82070, USA.

WIESTER Linda Marie Chisholm, b. 5 July 1946, Boston, Massachusetts, USA. President, Cleany Boppers Inc. m. Thomas C Wiester, 23 June 1972. 1 son, 1 daughter. *Education:* Catonsville Community College, 1980; Arlington Bible Institute, 1974-76. *Appointments:* Bookkeeper, Endicott & Johnson's, 1965-67; Waitress, Flower Drum Inn, 1976-86; President, Cleany Boppers, Inc, 1986-. *Memberships:* Business Partners Inc; National Association of Women Business Owners, Program Chair; Better Business Bureau; Liberty Road Community Council; Building Service Contractors Association International, Professional Member. *Hobbies:* Reading; Needlework; Tennis. *Address:* 9319 Samoset Road, Randallstown, MD 21133, USA.

WIGGINS Sue Ann, b. 4 Apr. 1948, El Paso, Texas, USA. Management, Oil Refinery Turnarounds. divorced. 2 sons. *Education:* BS, Management, Park College, 1983; Graduate work, University of Maryland, 1988. *Appointments:* Training Specialist, IVD Courseware Developer, Contracting Officer's Rep, US Army, 1980-88; Management, Oil Refinery Turnarounds, 1989-. *Publications:* Articles for Army Air Defense periodicals; Paper on IVD Courseware Development, Society of Applied Learning Technology. *Memberships:* Assn of US Army; Society of Applied Learning Technology; Federal Women's Programme. *Honour:* Commander's Award for Civilian Service, 1984. *Hobbies:* Music; Travelling; Walking for exercise & sport (Volksmarch). *Address:* 4716 Blossom, El Paso, TX 79924, USA.

WIGGS Sheila Naismith, b. 7 Dec. 1946, Irvine, Ayrshire, Scotland. Musician; Musicologist; Teacher. *Education:* GRSM, ARCM, LRAM, Royal College of Music, London, 1965-68; M.Mus., Research, Oxford

University, 1970. *Appointments:* Teacher, 1968-76, Curator of Instruments, 1970-76, Royal College of Music; Westminster Abbey Choir School, 1970-78; Mander Portman Woodward Tutorials, 1970-78; Epsom College, 1980-87; Glendower School, London, 1988-. *Publications:* Contributor to many musical journals including: Classical Music; Music Quarterly. *Memberships:* Royal College of Music Union; Incorporated Society of Musicians; National Trust. *Honours:* Internal Prizes, Royal College of Music. *Hobbies:* Languages; Tennis; Golf; Crosswords; Cooking. *Address:* Tudor Croft, Blundel Lane, Cobham, Surrey KT11 2SP, England.

WILBORN Letta Grace Smith, b. 12 May 1936, Arkansas, USA. Teacher. m. Leonard B. Wilborn, 7 June 1959, 1 son, 1 daughter. *Education:* BA, University of Arkansas, 1958; MA, California State College, 1969. *Appointments:* Teacher, Simmons High School, 1958-59; Teacher, Rowland Unified School Disrict, 1964-. *Memberships:* Summit Climbers International; Pan Hellenic Council; Sigma Gamma Rho. *Honours:* Service Award, Our Authors Study Club, 1986; Quality of Life Award, Sigma Sigma Chaper, Sigma Gamma Rho, 1986; 25 Year Service Award, Rowland Unified School District, 1989. *Hobbies:* Travel; Bowling; Reading. *Address:* 5934 Blair Stone Drive, Culver City, CA 90232, USA.

WILCHER Shirley J., b. 28 July 1951, Erie, Pennsylvania, USA. Attorney. *Education:* Certificat Pratique de Langue francaise, with honours, University of Paris, France, 1972; AB cum laude, Philosophy, French, Mount Holyoke College, 1973; MA, Urban Affairs, Policy Analysis, New School for Social Research, 1976; New York State Assembly Fellow, Albany, 1976; JD, Harvard Law School, 1979; Admitted to Bar of State of New York, 1980. *Appointments:* Auditing Examiner, Prudential Insurance Company, Boston, Massachusetts, 1973-74; Research Associate, New School for Social Research, New York City, 1975; Summer Law Clerk, NAACP Legal Defense & Education Fund Inc, New York City, 1977, 1978; Associate Attorney, Proskauer Rose Goetz & Mendelsohn, New York City, 1979-1980; Staff Attorney, National Women's Law Center, Washington DC, 1980-85; Associate Civil Rights Counsel, Committee on Education and Labor, US House of Representatives, Washington DC, 1985-. *Publications:* The Implications of the Feminization of Poverty for Black American Women, 1984; Co-author: Home Health Care Needs in New York City, 1975; The Special District Zoning Concept in New York City, 1975; Sex Discrimination in Education: Legal Rights and Remedies (with N.Campbell, M.Greenberger, M.Kohn), 1983; Sex-Based Employment Quotas in Sweden (with C.Brown), 1907, Report to US Department of Labor Congress, 1986, 1987, US Department of Education Congress, 1988. *Memberships:* National Conference of Black Lawyers (Co-Chair, Section on Women's Rights, 1983-87, National Board of Directors, 1985-87, Former Board Member, Chair, Women's Issues Committee, Vice-Chair, Washington DC); Board of Directors, Recording Secretary, National Political Congress of Black Women, 1985-87; Coalition on Women's Appointments, National Women's Political Caucus, 1988-89; Other bodies concerned with women's & black issues. *Honours:* Recipient of various scholarships, fellowships & prizes. *Hobbies:* Collecting Oriental art & antiques; Music; *Address:* 9039 Sligo Creek Parkway 1014, Silver Spring, MD 20901, USA.

WILCOX Paula, b. 13 Dec. 1949, Manchester, England. Actress. m. Derek Seaton, 18 Apr. 1970, deceased 1979. *Appointments:* Stage Appearances include: Anya, The Cherry Orchard; Juliet, Romeo & Juliet, Bristol Old Vic; Ellie Dunn, Heartbreak House, Shaw, Harrogate Festival; Kay, Time & the Conways; Peter Pan, Sheffield Crucible Theatre; Starred in Pantomime, Lincoln, Bristol, Birmingham, Australia, Middle & Far East; TV Work includes: many plays and drama series: Play for Today; Remember the Lambeth Walk, musical documentary for BBC; Most Well Know for Hit Situation Comedy Series, The Lovers, Man About the House, Miss Jones & Son; New Series, Channel 4, The Bright Side, many radio plays; 2 films based on TV shows, The Lovers and Man About the House. *Hobbies:* Swimming; Watching Football & Cricket. *Address:* Marment Management, Langham House, Regent Street, London W1, England.

WILDE Dawn Lee, b. 26 Oct. 1959, Pittsburgh, USA. Computer Systems Analyst. m. Nicholas Paul Wilde, 2 June 1984. *Education:* BA, 1981, M.Eng., 1982, Operations Research, Cornell University. *Appointments:* Computer Systems Analyst, Air Force Budget, Pentagon, Washington, 1982-84; Computer System Analyst, Cruise Missile Simulations Office, 1984-88, Offuh AFB, NE; Associate Programmer, IBM, Boulder, CO, 1985-. *Membership:* Association for Computing Machinery. *Honour:* CDP, 1987. *Hobbies:* Downhill Skiing; Swimming; Bicycling; Knitting; Crochet; Cooking. *Address:* 2134 S. Walnut St 19, Boulder, CO 80302, USA.

WILDERMUTH Jo Ann Voisard, b. 17 Oct. 1951, Oxfordshire, England US citizen. Publishing Company Executive; Teacher. m. Rickey Lynn Wildermuth, 16 Aug. 1974, 1 son, 2 daughters. *Education:* Edison State College, Ohio, USA, 1982. *Appointments:* Machinist, Copeland Corporation, Sidney, Ohio, 1974-78; Timekeeper, Baumfolder Corporation, 1978-80; Engineering Clerk, Piqua, 1980-84; Cost Accountant, Broadway Companies Inc, Dayton, 1984-86; Projects Director, Antioch Pubishing Company, Yellow Springs, 1986-; Instructor, Edison State College, 1987-; Consultant, Glasco Inc, Springfield, 1988. *Memberships:* Past President, American Business Women's Association; Offices, American Production & Inventory Control Society; National Association of Female Executives. *Honour:* Woman of Year, 1988-89. *Hobby:* Freelance photographer. *Address:* 2400 Co Road, 25A, PO Box 661, Sidney, Ohio 43565, USA.

WILDES Linda Kathleen Ellis, b. 2 June 1949, Quincy, Illinois, USA. Senior Computer Analyst. m. Bradley Eugene Wildes, 22 Aug. 1980. 1 son. *Education:* BS, University of Illinois, 1970; MS, Engineering Management, Milwaukee School of Engineering, 1978. *Appointments:* Internal Auditor 1970-72, Methods Analyst 1972-74, Supervisor Material Control 1974-79, Senior Computer Analyst 1979-, Wisconsin Electric Power Co, Milwaukee, Wisconsin. *Memberships:* Vice President, Cedarburg, WI Community Scholarship Fund, 1977; Cedarburg Jaycettes, 1972-79 (Treasurer 1973, State director 1975). *Honour:* Outstanding Young Woman, YWCA, Milwaukee, 1970. *Hobbies:* Bridge; Crocheting. *Address:* N99 W6564 Lexington St, Cedarburg, WI 53012, USA.

WILHELM Gloria Jean, b. 6 Aug. 1947, Brighton, Sussex, England. Headmistress; Teacher. m. Isaac Olufemi Wilhelm, 24 Jan. 1970, divorced 1988, 1 son, 2 daughters. *Education:* Sheffield College of Education, 1969-72. *Appointments:* Herries Comprehensive School, Sheffield, 1972-74; Head, Biology, Head, Boarding House, Edgerley Memorial Girls Secondary School; Head, Grange School, Lagos, 1983-. *Memberships:* Lioness Movement, Secretary 1987-88; Founder Member, Private Schools Sports Administrators Association, 1987-. *Honours:* Secretary of the Year, Lioness District 1987-88. *Hobbies:* Reading; Classical Music; Singing; Watercolour Painting; Theatre. *Address:* PO Box 22, Ikeja, Lagos State, Nigeria.

WILKEN Claudia Ann, b. 17 Aug. 1949, Minneapolis, Minnesota, USA. Magistrate. m. John M. True, 14 Dec. 1984, 1 son. *Education:* BA, Stanford University, 1971; JD, University of California, Berkeley, 1975. *Appointments:* Assistant Public Defender, US District Court, 1975- 78; Lecturer, 1978-84, University of California; Law Partner, Wilken & Leverett, 1978-84; U S Magistrate, 1983-; Professor, New College, 1980-85. *Memberships:* California State, American, Alameda County Bar Associations; California Women Lawyers; National Association of Women Judges; Women Lawyers of Alameda County; Board, Berkeley

Community Law Centre. *Honours:* Order of the Coif; Phi Beta Kappa, 1971 *Address:* 450 Golden Gate Ave, Room 19426, PO Box 36002, San Francisco, CA 94102, USA.

WILKERSON Marjorie Joann Madar, b. 2 Dec. 1930, Spokane, Washington, USA. m. Billy E Wilkerson, 9 Jan. 1953. 1 son. *Education:* Student, University of Puget Sound, 1948; BA, UCLA, 1949; Postgraduate, So Methodist University, 1958. *Appointments:* Personnel Management to Agent, Travellers Ins Cos, Houston & Dallas Texas, 1952-63; Senior Acct. Agent, Allstate Ins Cos, Tacoma Washington, 1966-; Author, Lecturer, Consultant on Insurance, Teacher. *Publications:* Author, Sex and Society, 1976; Editor, Chiropractic Education Newsletter; Newsletter Editor, Women's Political Caucus, Washington; Grantee activist to study Women's Issues for Washington Comm. for Humanities, 1974-75. *Memberships:* Board of Directors, Washington State Women's Political Caucus; Lobbyist, Women's ERA & Rights; Worker Right to Know, Olympia; Spokesperson Community effort to protect zoning, Dallas, Texas & Tacoma, Washington; Secretary & Board of Directors, Beaumont Texas Art Museum, 1954-57; President, Walnut Hill League, Dallas, Texas; Lobbyist, Toxic Agent Exposures, Olympia, Washington, 1981-; Established First Girl Scout Troop in Beaumont Texas, 1955. *Honours:* Numerous Sales Awards, Allstate Ins. Co, including Divisional Agent of the Year, 1984; Top Commercial Producer, Washington, Idaho, Oregon, 1975; Medallion of Honor, 15 years of winning Honor Ring, various top producer in all lines of insurance. *Hobbies:* Furthering and advancing the Youth of America; Lobbying safer, cleaner, healthier environment. *Address:* 15 Oregon, Suite 304, Tacoma, WA 98409, USA.

WILLIAMS Melva Jean, b. 11 June 1935, Burke, South Dakota, USA. Oil and Gas Company Executive. m. J B Williams, 29 Apr. 1977. 1 son, 3 daughters. *Education:* Graduate, Roberta's Finishing School, Miami, Florida, 1950; Charron-Williams Commercial College, 1954. *Appointments:* President, 1979-83, Vice Chairman Board, 1983-, Southeastern Resources Corp., Ft Worth and Rising Star, Texas, 1968-; Director, SERPCO, Inc., Fort Worth, 1977-87; Vice president, 1980-84, President, 1984-88; Secretary, Treasurer, J J & L Drilling Co, Inc, Ft Worth and Cisco Texas, 1979-82; General Partner, B & W Real Estate Investments, Nashville, 1980-; F & W Real Estate Investments, Fort Worth, 1981-; Director, Rising Star Processing Corporation, Fort Worth, Secretary/Treasurer, 1981-; Director, Brownwood Pipeline Corporation, Fort Worth 1983-; Secretary/Treasurer 1983; Director Glenwil Energy Corporation, Fort Worth and Houston, Texas, 1983-; Secretary/Treasurer 1983-; Westward Properties, Ft Worth; Director, Aero Modifications Internat. Inc, Ft Worth and Waco Texas. *Hobbies:* Golf; Travel; Reading; Music. *Address:* 6150 Indigo Ct, Fort Worth, TX 76112, USA.

WILKINS Caroline, b. 12 May 1937, Texas, USA. Consultant. m. Billy Hughel Wilkins, 31 Aug. 1957, 1 son. *Education:* BA, University of Texas, 1961; MA, University of the Americas, Mexico City, 1964. *Appointments:* Instructor, History, 1966-68; Administrator, Consumer Services, Oregon, 1977-81; Consultant, 1980-. *Publications:* Credit & Financial Issues, co-author, 1981; Consumer Handbook, 1980; Consumer Pocketbook, 1978; Consumer and the State Agency, 1978; Implications of the US-Mexican Water Treaty for Inter-regional Water Transfer, 1968. *Memberships:* National Trust for Preservation; Zonta International, past President; etc. *Honours:* Corvallis OSU Woman of Achievement, 1973; Corvallis First Citizen Nominee, 1985; etc. *Hobbies:* Photography; Cooking; Breeding Pembroke Welsh Corgies. *Address:* 3311 NW Roosevelt Dr., Corvallis, OR 97330, USA.

WILKINSON Doris, b. 13 June 1936, Lexington, Kentucky, USA. Professor. *Education:* BA, University of

Kentucky, 1958; MA, 1960, PhD, 1968, CWRU; MPH, Johns Hopkins University, 1985. *Appointments:* Associate Full Professor, Macalaster, 1970-77; Executive Associate, American Sociological Association, 1977-80; Professor, Howard University, 1980-84; Visiting Professor, University of Virginia, 1984-85; Professor, University of Kentucky, 1985. *Publications:* Articles in professional journals. *Memberships:* Society for the Study of Social Problems, President 1987-88; Eastern Sociological Society, Chair Publications Committee, 1987-88; American Sociological Association. *Honours:* Valedictorian, 1954; Dean's List, 1955-58; Woodrow Wilson Fellow, 1959-61; AWS Outstanding Teacher, 1969; Phi Beta Kappa, 1978. *Hobbies:* Piano; Creative Writing. *Address:* Dept. of Sociology, University of Kentucky, Lexington, KY 40506, USA.

WILLADSEN Jytte, b. 30 Nov. 1928, Copenhagen, Denmark. Psychiatrist. m. Leif Klinken, 27 Sept. 1962. *Education:* MD, University of Copenhagen, 1955; Psychiatrist, 1964; Internships: Psychiatric Hospitals, Arhus, Vordingborg and Copenhagen. *Appointments:* Psychiatrist in Chief, Copenhagen County Psychiatric Hospital, Nordvang, Glostrup, 1969-. *Publications:* Depression, dit navn er kvinde, 1983; Din og min psykiatri, 1988; Many articles and essays on women's health and psychiatry. *Memberships:* Danish Medical Association; Danish Psychiatric Association. *Honours:* WHO Fellowship for studies in USA on depression in women, 1980; Rosenkjaer Prize for Scientific Communication in the Media, Danish Broadcasting Corporation, 1987. *Hobby:* Hiking. *Address:* Copenhagen County, Psychiatric Hospital, Nordvang, DK-2600 Glostrup, Denmark.

WILLIAMS Ann Houston, b. 18 Dec. 1943, Red Bank, New Jersey, USA. Associate Professor. m. Delbert E. Williams, 31 July 1976. *Education:* BS, Biology, University of South Carolina, 1965; MAT, Biology, Duke University, 1972; PhD, Zoology, University of North Carolina, 1977. *Appointments:* Biology Teacher, A C Flora High School, 1966-73; Teaching Assistant, University of North Carolina, 1973-77; Post Doctoral Research Associate, Duke University, 1977-78; Assistant Professor, Biology, Southwestern University, 1978-80; Assistant Professor, 1980-85, Associate Professor 1985-, Auburn University. *Publications:* Papers in various journals. *Memberships:* American Society Zoology; AAAS; Ecological Society of America; Alabama Academy of Science, Secretary 1985-; Gamma Sigma Delta; Sigma Xi; Board of Directors, Organisation for Tropical Studies; Board of Directors, Auburn University Fed. Credit Union. *Honours:* Recipient various honours & awards including: Teaching Fellow, University of North Carolina, Zoology, 1977; Certificate of Merit, ZTA Alumni, 1984; Outstanding Paper published in Journal Alabama Academy of Science, 1986. *Hobbies:* Gardening; Scuba Diving; Stained Glass Work. *Address:* Dept. of Zoology & Wildlife Science, 101 Cary Hall, Auburn University, AL 36849, USA.

WILLIAMS Camilla, University Professor; Opera Singer. *Appointments:* Created role of Madame Butterfly as first black contract singer, New York City Center, 1946; Created first Aida, New York City Center, 1948; Tours of Alaska, Europe, Israel, Formosa, Australia, New Zealand, Korea, Japan, Philippines, Laos, South Vietnam, Poland; Appeared with: Royal Philharmonic; Vienna Symphony; Berlin Philharmonic; New York Philharmonic; Chicago Symphony; BBC Orchestra; Stuttgart Orchestra, etc; Professor of Voice: Brooklyn College, 1970-73, Bronx College, 1970, Queen's College, 1974; First Black Professor of Voice, Indiana University, Bloomington, 1977-. *Honours:* Recipient, numerous honours and awards including: Harlem Opera & World Fellowship Society Award, 1963; Camilla Williams Park designated in danville, Virginia, 1974; Sigma Alpha Iota; Honoured Guest, New York Philharmonic 10,000th Concert Celebration, 1982; First Black Professor, Voice, Central Conservatory of Music, Beijing, China, 1983; Honorary Doctorate, Virginia State

University, etc. *Address:* School of Music, Indiana Univerity, Bloomington, IN 47405, USA.

WILLIAMS Carol J, b. 12 Aug. 1944, New Brunswick, New Jersey, USA. Associate Professor. m. 4 July 1980. *Education:* BA, 1966; MSW, 1979; MS, Computer Science, 1987; PhD, 1981. *Appointments:* Associate Professor, Social Work Program, Kean College, 1979- ; Research Consultant, New Jersey Division of Youth and Family Services, 1979-; Research Consultant, Association for Children of New Jersey, 1985-88. *Publications:* Reports: Out of Balance: New Jersey's Juvenile Family Crisis Intervention System; Passate County DYFS Evaluation; Assessment of the Kean College Social Work Program, Interim Report. *Memberships:* Council on Social Work Education; National Association of Social Workers; Association for the Advancement of Higher Education, Assessment Forum; Association for Computing Machinery; National Organization for Women; Academy of certified Social Workers. *Honours:* Academic Council, Thomas A Edison College, 1985-; Assessment Advisory Committee, Thomas A Edison College, 1988-; NIMH Fellowship for Dissertation Research, 1978-79; Award for Involvement in Alternative Education, 1979; Alpha Delta Mu, Social Work Honor Society, Honorary Member, 1983-. *Hobbies:* Travel; Camping. *Address:* 32 Halstead Road, New Brunswick, NJ 08907, USA.

WILLIAMS Carolyn Ruth Armstrong, Dr., b. 17 Feb. 1944, Birmingham, USA. Dean; Educator. m. James Alvin Williams, Jr., 16 Mar. 1968. *Education:* BS, Tennessee State University, 1966; MA,, Northwestern University, 1972; MA, 1978, PhD, Postdoctorate Studies, Harvard University, 1978, Cornell University. *Appointments:* Assistant Dean/Associate Professor, Engineering, Vanderbilt University, 1987-. *Publications:* several papers; books in progress. *Memberships:* Phi Delta Kappa; Phi Alpha Theta; Delta Sigma Theta; National Association of Minority Engineer Programme Administrators; Association Women in Science; Society of Women Engineers; National Association of Women Deans Administrators and Counselors; Board Member of Women in Science; Society of Women Engineers; National Technical Paper Coordination; Chair of Women in Academia. *Honours:* Phi Delta Kappa; Woodrow Wilson Administrative Fellow; Women of Achievement Recognition Award. *Hobbies Include:* Bowling; Tennis; Cross Country Skiing; Playing Harp. *Address:* 36 Morningside Drive, Cortland, NY 13045, USA.

WILLIAMS Christina, b. 9 Apr. 1952, Tallahassee, USA. Director. m. John D. Williams, 15 June 1974, 1 daughter. *Education:* DA, Theatre, 1974. *Appointments:* Founder, Director, Young Actors Theatre, 1975-. *Memberships:* Vice President, Childrens Theatre Association of FIA; America Theatre Associatiron; Youth Theatre Directors of America. *Honours:* Certificate, Very Special Arts Festival; several other awards. *Hobbies:* Travel; Films; Theatre; Swimming. *Address:* 916 Brookwood Drive, Tallahassee, FL 32308, USA.

WILLIAMS Debra Sue McCulloch, b. 19 May 1957, Lebanon, Tennessee, USA. Energy Consultant. m. Scott Williams, 5 Nov. 1983, 2 sons. *Education:* BS, Vocational Home Economics, Middle Tennessee State Univesity, 1979. *Appointments:* Energy Adviser, Tennessee Valley Authority, 1979-88; Residential Energy Consultant, Murfreeesboro Electric Department, 1988-. *Membership:* Electrical Women's Roundtable. *Hobbies:* Decorating; Sewing; Travel. *Address:* 602 Irongate Boulevard, Murfreesboro, Tennessee 37129, USA.

WILLIAMS Dolores Louise, b. 20 Apr. 1931, Rockford, USA. Telecommunications Executive. m. Hence Williams, 10 June 1960, deceased 1979, 1 daughter. *Education:* BA, 1959; Kansas & Tennessee Teaching Certificates. *Appointments:* Teacher, US Dept. Int., 1959-62, Navajo Reservation; Assistant Director, Health & Welfare, 1971; Director, US H.E.W. Headstart, 1971-73; Unit Supervisor, Bell System, 1974-81; Assisant Manager AT & T Bell South, 1981-.

Memberships: South Central Bell's Speech Masters; NAACP; American Management Association; Nashville Urban League. *Honours:* O.M. Council of Excellence, 1986, 1987, 1988; Achieveer's Sales Award, 1987; Sales Excellence Round Table, 1987; many other honours & awards. *Hobbies:* Piano & Organ Playing; Classical Music; Hiking; Dancing; Singing; Reading. *Address:* 500 Michele Drive, Antioch, TN 37013, USA.

WILLIAMS Elynor Alberta, b. 27 Oct. 1946, Baton Rouge, USA. Director, Public Affairs. *Education:* BSc., 1966. *Appointments:* Publicist, General Food Co; Communicaitrons Specialist, NC Agricultural Extension Service; Director, Corporate Affairs, Hanes Group; Director Public Affairs, Sara Lee Corp. *Memberships:* International Association of Business Communicators; Public Relations Society of America; National Association for Female Executives; National Womens Political Caucus; NAACP; AKA. *Honours:* Honorary Doctorate, Clinton Junior College, 1984; Boss of the Year, Winston Salem Chapter, Professional Secretaries International, 1984-85; Outstanding Congribution in Business Award, Winston Salem Chapter, National Council of Negro Women, 1985; Black Womens Hall of Fame Foundation's Kizzy Image, 1988; YMCA's Black & Hispanic Achievers Industry Award, 1988; Selected One of 10 Black Women in Corporate America, Essence Magazine, 1989; *Hobbies:* Piano; Reading. *Address:* 2335 North Commnwealth 3, Chicago, IL 60614, USA.

WILLIAMS Jewel Carmichael, b. 11 Feb. 1937, Canton, Mississippi, USA. Board of Alderman, City of Canton; Insurance Salesman. m. Frank Williams, 22 Mar. 3 sons, 2 daughters. *Education:* AA, Business Admin, Mary Holmes College, 1967; Soc, Jackson St University, 1969-71; Tougaloo College, 1987. *Appointments:* Staff 1966-68, Secretary 1968-73, Director 1973- 85, Child Development Group of Mississippi; Social Worker, Canton Public School, 1985- ; Insurance Salesman. *Memberships:* Board of Alderman, City of Canton; National Council Negro Women; Lucy C Jefferson Federated Club; Marnette Social & Civic Club; Chairman, Tougaloo College Scholarship Fund; NAACP; Fried of Library, Canton. *Honours:* Outstanding Community Work, Project Unity, 1979, 1981, 982; Community Work, NAACP, 1986; Civil Rights, 1986, 1987; Women for Progress, 1983, 1984. *Hobbies:* Community affairs; Travelling; Sewing; Needlepoint; Reading. *Address:* 513 Cauthen St, Canton, MS 39046, USA.

WILLIAMS Margaret Lu Wertha Hiett, b. 30 Aug. 1938, Midland, Texas, USA. Registered Nurse. m. (1)James Troy Lary, 16 Nov. 1960, divorced 1963, son, (2)Tuck Williams, 11 Aug. 1985. *Education:* BS, Texas Woman's University, 1960; MA, 1964, MEd., 1974, Teachers College, Columbia University; Certified Psychiatric Mental Health Nurse (R.N.C.). *Appointments:* Nurse Aid, 1955-56, Staff Nurse, Head Nurse, 1960- 63, Midland Memorial Hospital; Instructor, Odessa College, 1964-66; Director, Laredo Junior College, 1966-70; Assistant Professor, Pan American University, 1970-72; Nursing Practitioner, St Lukes Hospital, 1972- 79; Field Supervisor, We Care Home Health, 1983-87; Senior Staff Psychiatric Nurse, Glenwood A Healthcare International Inc., Psychiatric Hospital, 1987-89; Nurse IV Supervisor Region 3 Pasarr Program Texas Department of Health. *Memberships:* American Nurses Association; Texas Nurses Association. *Honours Include:* Outstanding Young Woman of America, 1965. *Hobbies Include:* Public Speaking. *Address:* 505 N. Gray, PO Box 1218, Stanton, TX 79782, USA.

WILLIAMS Meta Talbot, b. 7 July 1918, Brisbane, Australia. Voluntary Community Worker. m. Roderick Guildford Williams, 11 Dec. 1943, 1 daughter. *Appointments:* Adult Guide Leader, 1936-44; Division Commissioner, 1961-65; State Guide Adviser, 1965- 70; Region Commissioner, 1972-73; HQ Commisisoner, 1973-76; Chairman, State Executive, 1976-81; Member, Australian Executive Committee, 1976-81. *Publications:* The Continuing Challenge, 1984. *Memberships Include:* Assistant State Archivist, Girl

Guides Association, Queensland; Former State Treasurer, YWCA; Former State Treasurer, Victoria League; Former Member, Save the Children Fund. *Honours:* Red Kangaroo, 1969; Queen Elizabeth II Silver Jubilee Medal, 1977; Queensland Mother of the Year, 1981; OBE, 1985. *Hobbies:* Porcelain Art; Gardening; Reading. *Address:* Brisbane, Queensland, Australia.

WILLIAMS Mollie Ann, b. 12 Nov. 1946, Deport, Texas, USA. News Editor. m. Michael N Williams, 28 Nov. 1964. 3 daughters. *Education:* Michael's School of Cosmotology, 1963; Instructor's Training, Paris Beauty School, 1969. *Appointments:* Owner/operator, Beauty Fashion, Bogata, Texas; Operator, Carol's Beauty Shop, Odessa, Texas; Instructor, Paris Beauty School, Texas; Operator, Red River Haven Beauty Shop, Texas; Editor, Reporter, Photographer, Bogata News. *Publications:* Feature stories and articles in: Talco Times; Bogata News; Blossom News; Deport Times. *Memberships:* President, Bogata PTO; Red River Valley Girl Scouts, Leader; Pub Ch Assembly of God Church; Pub Ch PTO Bogata; Vol program, Red River Haven Nursing Home, Bogata. *Hobbies:* Writing; Reading; Sewing. *Address:* Box 526, Bogata, TX 75417, USA.

WILLIAMS Sheila Elizabeth, b. 27 Sept. 1956, Springfield, Massachusetts, USA. Managing Editor. m. David W Bruce, 15 Aug. 1987. *Education:* BA, Elmire College, Elmira, New York, 1978; Studied at London School of Economics, London, England, 1976-77; MA Philosophy, Washington University in St Louis, 1982. *Appointments:* Editorial Assistant, Assistant and Associate Editor, 1982-85, Managing Editor, 1985-, Isaac Asimov's Science Fiction Magazine (Davis Publications, Inc). *Publication:* Editor with Cynthia Manson, Tales from Isaac Asimov's Science Fiction Magazine, 1986. *Memberships:* Science Fiction Writers of America; New York Women in Science Fiction. *Address:* Davis Publications, 380 Lexington Avenue, New York, NY 10017, USA.

WILLIAMS Shirley, Rt. Hon., b. 27 July 1930, London, England. Politician. m. Bernard Williams, 1955, divorced 1974, 1 daughter. *Education:* Opus Scholar, Sommerville College; MA, Oxford University; Fulbright Scholar, Columbia University, USA. *Appointments:* General Secretary, Fabian Society, 1960-64; Labour MP, Hitchen, 1964-74, for Hertford & Stevenage, 1974-79; Social Democratic Party Member of Parliament for Crosby, 1981-83; Parliamentary Private Secretary, Minister of Health, 1964-66; Parliamentary Secretary, Minister of Labour, 1966-67; Minister of State, Education & Science, 1967-69; Minister of State, Home Office, 1969-70; Opposition Spokesman, Health & Social Security, 1970-71, Home Affairs, 1971- 73, Prices & Consumer Affairs, 1973-74; Secretary of State for Prices & Consumer Protection, 1974-76. *Publications:* Politics is For People, 1981; A Job to Live, 1985; Contributor of pamphlets on European Community and economics for Central Africa. *Memberships:* Faculty Member, IMI Geneva, Switzerland; Director, Turing Institute. *Honours:* Visiting Fellow, Nuffield College, Oxford, 1967-75; Trustee, Twentieth Century Fund, USA; Honoray DEd, CNAA; Honorary Dr Pol. Econom, University of Leuven, Belgium; Honorary LLD, Leeds University, 1979; Southampton University, 1981. *Hobbies:* Riding; Rough Walking; Music. *Address:* c/o SDP, 4 Cowley Street, London SW1P 3NB, England.

WILLIAMS Susan Eva, b. 17 Aug. 1915. Lord-Lieutenant of South Glamorgan. m. Charles Crofts Llewellyn Williams, 1950. *Appointments:* JP, 1961; High Sheriff, 1968; DL 1973, Glamorgan; Lieutenant, South Glamorgan, 1981-85; Lord Lieutenant of South Glamorgan, 1975-. *Hobby:* National Hunt Racing. *Address:* Caercady, Welsh St Donats Cowbridge, S Glamorgan CF7 7ST, Wales.

WILLIAMS Ulysses Jean, b. 15 Sept. 1947, Memphis, Tennessee, USA. Teacher. m. Foster Williams, Snr, 5 Dec. 1966. 3 sons, 1 daughter.

Education: Philander Smith College, 1964-67; BSE 1967-69, MSE 1970-73, University of Central Arkansas; Certification, Emotional Disturbances 1978-79, Certification, Elementary Admin (Night School) 1987-88, Arkansas State University. *Appointments:* Secretary, Cotton Plant School, 1969-70; Teacher, Helena, West Helena, 1970-78; Educational Specialist, Adolescent Department, East Ar Regional Mental Health Center, 1978-80; Teacher, Elaine Public School District, 1981-. *Creative works:* Developed programmes of use to Learning Disabled, Graduate and Undergratudate Chapters of Zeta Phi Beta Sorority Inc and Therapeutic Foster Homes. *Memberships:* National Education Association; Arkansas Education Association; Classroom Teachers' Association, Building Representative; Elaine Teachers' Association; NAACP; Chamber of Commerce and many others. *Honours:* Outstanding Elementary Teacher of the Year, 1970; Outstanding Community Leader, 1973; Zeta of the Year, Local Chapter, 1982; Arkansas Zeta of the Year, 1985; Outstanding Regional Coordinator, Voter Education, Voter Registration, 1987; Kappa E Ta, Educational Honor Society. *Hobbies:* Speaking; Crocheting; Knitting; Bowling; Reading; Working with the community and people. *Address:* 239 Desota Street, West Helena, Arkansas 72390, USA.

WILLIAMS Ursula Moray, b. 19 Apr. 1911, Petersfield, Hampshire, England. Housewife. m. Peter Southey John, 28 Sept. 1935. 4 sons. *Education:* Private; 1 year in France; 1 year at Winchester College of Art. *Appointments:* Justice of the Peace, Evesham, 1959-81; Vice Chairman, 4 years, Chairman of Juvenile Bench. *Publications:* Author of 70 books; Contributions to American and British magazines; including Lady. *Memberships:* PEN Club; West of England Writers Association; National Book Club. *Hobbies:* Writing; Gardening; Reading; Music; Village Life; Grandchildren. *Address:* Court Farm House, Beckford, Tewkesbury, Glos, GL20 7AA, England.

WILLIAMS-GRAVES Patricia L. Faciane, b. 10 Dec. 1941, Louisiana, USA. Consultant. m. John T Graves, 28 June 1986, 1 daughter. *Education:* AA, Political Science, Los Angeles City College, 1970; various courses at: UCLA. *Appointments:* Labour Relations Specialist, UAW, 1968-; Founder, Faciane and Associates; Commissioner: Los Angeles County Highway Safety Commission, 1983-, State of California Employment Training Panel, 1983-; LA County Highway Safety Commission (Commissioner); Employment Training Panel (Commissioner); Los Angeles Private Industry Council; State of California Public Procurement Advisory Council (Commissioner); Ex. Vice President(UAW-Labor Employment and Training CORR). *Memberships;* National Women of Achievement; Women Aware, Vice President; Jack and Jill of America; Lullaby Guild of the children's Home Society; etc. *Honours:* Notre Dame Academy Mother of the Year, 1987; various other honours and awards. *Hobbies:* Writing; Antique Collection. *Address:* 6605 Bedford Avenue, Los Angeles, CA 90056, USA.

WILLIAMSON Alicia Ann, b. 7 June 1938, Bournemouth, England. Headmistress. m. John Williamson, 11 Aug. 1961, 1 daughter. *Education:* DipEd, Whitelands Training College, Putney, 1958; BSc(Hons), London University, 1968; New Hall Cambridge, 1971-72, BA (Part I), 1972. *Appointments:* South Croydon Secondary Modern, 1958-61; Bexley Grammar School, 1961-66, 1967-70; Bromley Technical School for Girls, 1966-67; Head of 3rd Year, Highfield Comprehensive, 1972-74; Headmistress, Stratford House School, Bromley, Kent, 1974-. *Memberships:* Secondary Heads Association, Member of Council, Executive, Chair of Public and Parliamentary, Committee, Vice-Chair of Sports Committee; GSA; National Association of Head Teachers; ISAI; Mathematics Association; British Federation of University Women; Vice-Chair, Bromley Young Enterprise Board; Magistrate; AFA. *Honour:* Fencing Blue, Cambridge, 1971. *Hobbies include:* Young enterprise; Bromley Operatic Society; Drama; Fencing;

Rugby; Bridge; Travel; Reading; Sleeping. *Address:* Stratford House School, 8-10 Southborough Road, Bickley, Bromley, Kent BR1 2DZ, England.

WILLIAMSON Jean Esther, b. 19 Nov. 1934, Long Beach, California, USA. Psychologist. m. Robert Wayne Williamson, 23 July 1955. 1 daughter. *Education:* AA, Fullerton College, 1954; BA 1955, MA 1961, California State University, Long Beach; Licensed Marriage, Family, Child Counselor, 1968-. *Appointments:* Teacher, Fullerton, California, 1955-59; Graduate Assistant, California State University, Long Beach, 1962; Remedial Tutor, Fullerton, 1959-62; Psychologist, El Rancho Unified School District, 1963-; Instructor, Pepperdine University, 1968-69; Instructor, Chapman College, 1980- 81. *Memberships:* Treasurer, Pi Lambda Theta, 1963; Psi Chi, 1961; American Mensa Selection Agency; Chairperson, El Camino Mental Health Advisory Board, 1983-87; Whittier YMCA Board of Managers, 1979-88; Vice President, Rio Hondo Catholic Charities Board, 1984-88; Ordained Deacon, United Presbyterian Church in the USA, 1959; Chairman, Rio Hondo Association of School Psychologists, 1967-68. *Honours:* Life Member, California Scholarship Federation, 1952; Life Member, Alpha Gamma Sigma, 1954; Honorary Life Service Award, Calif. Congress of Parents & Teachers, 1980; Honorary Service Award, PTA,(Obregon School), 1983. *Hobbies:* Photography; Reading; Gardening; Volunteer work with Mental Health and charitable agencies. *Address:* 638 Nenno Avenue, Placentia, California 92670, USA.

WILLIAMSON Susan Mary (Sue), b. 21 Jan. 1941, Lichfield, England. Artist. m. Anthony Gerald Williamson, 30 May 1962 (div. 1983), 1 son, 2 daughters. *Education:* BA studies, University of Natal, South Africa, 1959-61; Art Students League, New York, USA, 1964-69; Advanced Diploma, Fine Art (Distinction), University of Cape Town, SA; Scholarship: Edita Norris Foundation for Peace and Culture, Paris, 1990. *Creative works include:* Art: Modderdam Postcards (demolished squatter camp), 1978; Last Supper an installation, demolished Coloured people's homes, Cape Town, 1981; A Few South Africans portraits, courageous men & women, Helen Joseph, portfolio of prints, 1983-88. 5 Solo exhibitions, South Africa, 1975-, exhibition toured USA, 1986-88; Group exhibitions, '87 Artists Against Apartheid, USA, Italy, UK, Sweden, Norway, W. Germany, 1968-. Book, Resistance Art in South Africa protest art in SA, 1989. *Memberships:* Chair 1978-80, Women's Movement for Peace; Committee 1982-83, Artists Guild. *Hobbies:* Wilderness Trips; Indigenous Art. *Address:* 8 Blake Street, Observatory 7925, Cape Town, South Africa.

WILLIS Barbara, b. Jersey City, New Jersey, USA. Area Director of Public Relations. *Education:* BA, English Education, Rutgers University, 1973; MA, Media, Montclair State College, 1976. *Appointments:* Editor of Corporate Publications, Chief Copywriter, Vornado Inc, Garfield, New Jersey, 1975-76; National Publicity Representative, The Salvation Army, New York City and Verona, New Jersey, 1977-82; Director of Public Relations, Bloomfield College, Bloomfield, New Jersey, 1982-84; Independent Public Relations Consultant/ Writer, 1984-; Director of Public Relations, Jersey City Medical Center, New Jersey, 1986-87; Area Public Relations Director, Melvin Simon & Associates, Jersey City, 1987-. *Memberships:* Public Relations Society of America; Board Member, The Salvation Army Advisory Organization; Board Member, The Education Arts Team, Jersey City; Past Vice-President, Rutgers Newark College of Arts and Sciences Alumni Association; Former Member, National Association for Female Executives. *Honours:* Phi Beta Kappa, Rutgers University, 1973; Outstanding Senior Award, Rutgers University, 1973; Greater New York Blood Programme Recognition Award, 1987. *Hobbies:* Film and theatre history; Photography; Writing. *Address:* Melvin Simon & Associates, 30-228 Mall Drive West, Jersey City, NJ 07310, USA.

WILLIS Connie E, b. 31 Dec. 1945, Denver, Colorado,

USA. Science Fiction Writer. m. 23 Aug. 1967. 1 son, 1 daughter. *Education:* BA, University of Northern Colorado, 1967. *Appointments:* Elementary School Teacher; Nursery School Teacher. *Publications include:* Water Witch, 1982; Fire Watch, 1985; Lincoln's Dreams, 1987; Light Raid, being published shortly. Numerous articles to magazines and journals. *Memberships:* Science Fiction Writers of America; United Church of Christ. *Honours:* National Endowment for the Arts Creative Writing Grant; Nebula Award for A Letter From the Clearys; Nebula Award for Fire Watch; Hugo Award; John W Campbell Award. *Hobbies:* Reading; Counted cross-stitch; History. *Address:* 1716 13th Avenue, Greeley, CO 80631, USA.

WILLIS Olive Christine (Lady), b. 20 Nov. 1895, Hampstead, England. m. 1916, 2 daughters. *Education:* Oxford Higher, 1st Class Honours; Newnham College, Cambridge University, Mathematical Tripos. *Appointments:* Part-time Mathematics Teacher, St Margaret's Girl's School, Bushey, Herts; Voluntary Welfare Worker, Naval Wives, Malta, 1946-48, Portsmouth 1948-50. *Memberships:* 1950-80: English Speaking Union; British Legion; President, Portsmouth Hospital Management; Chairman, Girl Guides; Save the Children; Petersfield Drama & Musical Festival. *Honours:* CBE. *Address:* c/o Lady MacDonald, Spinners Ash, Tilmore, Petersfield, Hants GU32 2JH, England.

WILLIS Wincey (Winsome), b. 8 Aug. 1954, Gateshead, England. Television Presenter. m. Malcolm Willis, 7 Dec. 1977. *Education:* University in Strasbourg, France. *Career:* Travel Courier; Radio Presenter and Promotions Manager; Record Industry Promotion (Artists and Records); Television Presenter; Actress; Author. *Creative works:* Articles on Animal Husbandry and Bird Breeding; Short Stories for children (used on television); It's Raining Cats and Dogs. *Memberships:* Life Member, Jersey Wildlife Preservation Trust; International Herpetological Society; Association for the Study of Repitilia and Amphibia; Royal Society for the Protection of Birds; The British Chelonia Group; Muffin The Mule Club; Sooty's Friendship Circle; Winston PA Club; World Wildlife Fund; Patron of the Lemur Lifeline, Marwell Zoo. *Hobbies:* Parrot Breeder; Running Injured Bird Hospital; Music; Painting; Aerobic Exercise; Animal Keeper; Food; Travel; Wishing on Falling Stars; Roller Skating; Playing Poo Sticks; Dancing.

WILLY Margaret Elizabeth, b. 25 Oct. 1919, London, England. Lecturer; Author. *Education:* Honours Diploma, Humanities, Goldsmiths' College, University of London, 1940. *Appointments:* Lecturer. British Council, 1950-, City Literary Institute, London, 1956-85; Goldsmiths' College, 1959-75; Morley College, London, 1975-85; Centre for Continuing Education, University of Sussex, 1985-. *Publications include:* Author: Invisible Sun, poems, 1946; Every Star a Tongue, poems, 1951; Life Was Their Cry, 1950; South Hams, 1955; Three Metaphysical Poets, 1961; English Diarists, 1963; Three Women Diarists, 1964; Wuthering Heights: Critical Commentary, 1960; Browning's Men & Women: Critical Commentary, 1968. Editor: English (journal), 1954-75; Numerous anthologies. *Memberships:* Elected Fellow, Royal Society of Literature, 1960. *Honours:* W. H. Hudson Memorial Prize 1938, Gilchrist Medal 1940 (Literature), University of London; Atlantic Award, Literature (young British writers, careers interrupted by war), Rockefeller Institute, 1946. *Hobbies:* Reading; Travel; Painting; Music; Walking. *Address:* 19 Hillview Road, Findon Valley, Worthing, West Sussex BN14 0BU, England.

WILMS Dorothee, b. 11 Oct. 1929, Grevenbroich, Germany. Politician. *Education:* Diploma Degree Economic Science, PhD, University of Cologne. *Appointments:* Employee 1956-73, Head, Research Department for Educational & Social Development 1977-82, Institut der Deutschen Wirtschaft; Deputy Executive Director, Federal Christian Democratic Union (CDU), 1974-76; Head, Central Division Politik, CDU Federal Office, 1974-75; Member, German Federal Parliament, 1976-; Minister, Education & Science,

1982-87; Minister, Intra-German Relations, 1987-. *Memberships:* Christian Democratic Union; Central Committee, German Roman Catholics. *Hobbies:* Walking; Classical Music; Historical books. *Address:* Ministry for Intra-German Relations, Godesbergerallee 140, D-5300 Bonn 2, Federal Republic of Germany.

WILPON Bonnie Vivian, b. 31 July 1952, Coral Gables, Florida, USA. Market Research Manager. *Education:* BS, Management, Florida State University, 1973; MS, Management, University of South Florida, 1977. *Appointments:* Co-ordinator, Project Community School, Waltham, 1973-75; Programme Director, Gulf Coast Epilepsy Foundation, Tampa, 1976-77; Manager, Walker Data Source Tampa, 1977-. *Publications:* Annotated Bibliography of Books about Disabilities for Young People, co-author, 1975; Come and Get to Know Me, co-presentor, 1975. *Memberships:* Eastlake Square Mall Merchant's Association, Vice President, Treasurer, President; Business & Professional Women; National Association of Female Executives; WEDU; Tampa Bay Mensa; Vice-President, Special Events West Coast Chapter, American Marketing Association; Board of Trustees, SERVE; Publicity and Finance Committees, Tampa Bay Camera Club. *Honours:* Rotary International Group Study Exchanges to Japan, 1986; various other honours & awards. *Hobbies:* Postcard Collecting; Travel; Photography; Circus Sideshow History & Biographies; Games. *Address:* 8310 Coors Place, Tampa, FL 33615, USA.

WILSON Ann, b. 29 July 1947, Yokohama, Japan. Correctional Supervisor. *Education:* BA, William Penn College, 1966-70; MA, Bridgewater State College, 1975. *Appointments:* Recreational Director 1971-74, Correctional Officer 1976-82, Massachusetts Correctional Institute, Framingham; Correctional Officer, Iowa State Penitentiary, Ft Madison, 1982- 84; Correctional Supervisor, Iowa Correctional Institution for Women, Mitchellville, 1984-. *Memberships:* Alpha Chi Honour Society, 1968-70; National Association for Female Executives; American Correctional Association; Iowa Correctional Association. *Honour:* Outstanding Young Women of America, 1972. *Hobbies:* Reading; Sports, volleyball, softball, racquetball, tennis, jogging, swimming and fishing; Belong to health club. *Address:* 3007 57th Street, Des Moines, IA 50310, USA.

WILSON Elizabeth Hornabrook, Lady b. 25 Jan. 1907, Adelaide, South Australia. Community Voluntary Service. m. Sir Keith Cameron Wilson, 24 May 1930, 2 sons, 1 daughter. *Appointments:* Founding President, Milpara Nursing Home Auxiliary; President, Volunteer Association of the Child & Family Health Services, 1981-83. *Memberships Include:* Executive Member, 1930-, Chairman, 1951-54, Vice President, 1961-, Victoria League (SA); Royal Commonwealth Society; Commandent, Red Cross Aids SA Division, 1939-51; President, Tusmore Red Cross Branch, 1939-69, 1973-, Chairman of the Australian Red Cross Society (SA Division) 1968-71, Member of Divisional Council 1947-; Chairman, National Committee, Victoria League, 1952-58, 1967-70; Member of the Burnside War Memorial Hospital Board, Governor since 1950; Patron Civilian Widows Association since 1960; Patron of the Cornish Association in South Australia since 1975; etc. *Honours:* MBE, 1946; CBE, 1959. *Hobbies:* Gardening; Creating Floral Displays; Family; Community Activities. *Address:* 79 Tusmore Avenue, Tusmore, SA 5065, Australia.

WILSON Elizabeth Anne Martin (Lady), b. 7 Sept. 1911, Melrose, Scotland. Lexicographer. m. Sir Archibald Duncan Wilson, GCMG, 17 July 1937. 1 son (deceased), 2 daughters. *Education:* 1st class Hon Mods, 2nd class Greats, Lady Margaret Hall, Oxford, 1930-34. *Appointments:* Teacher, Sherborne (Girls), 1934-36; Worked in Russia, Jan to May 1937; Taught at intervals; Lexicographer, 1974-. *Publication:* Compiled The Modern Russian Dictionary for English Speakers, 1982. *Memberships:* Foreign Office Wives, Chairman, 1962-64; Assocation of Teachers of Russian; British Association of University Slavists. *Hobbies:* Walking;

Music; Amateur botany. *Address:* Cala Na Ruadh, Port Charlotte, Islay, Argyll PA48 7TS, Scotland.

WILSON Evelyn Gail, b. 9 Aug. 1945, Anniston, USA. Retial Chain Official. m. (1)Jimmy Ray Rust, 28 June 1960, deceased 1970, 1 son, deceased 1986, (2)William O. Wilson Junior, 26 June 1971, 1 stepson, 1 stepdaughter. *Education:* Business College, 1965; University of Alabama, 1975-76; Certified Professional Secretary, Billing Clerk. *Appointments:* Secretary, Church of St Michael & All Angels, Anniston, 1963-66; District Secretary, Aalbama, Vocatonal Rehabilitation Service, 1966-76; Personnel Administrator, Super Valu Stores Inc., Anniston, 1976-; Instructor, Secretarial Procedures, Anniston Junior Achivement; Instructor, Written Communication, American Institute of Banking, 1981-82. *Memberships:* American Society of Personnel Administrators, Vice President, 1981-82; International Management Association, President 1987-88; many civic organisations. *Address:* 4212 Brian Dr., Anniston, AL 36201, USA.

WILSON Irene K, b. Boston, Massachusetts, USA. Freelance Writer; Advisor. m. Edward O Wilson, 30 Oct. 1955. 1 daughter. *Appointment:* Consultant/Advisor, 1988-. *Publications:* Wildflowers of the Mind, Poetry book, 1981; Poetry published widely in numerous literary magazines and anthologies. Short Stories: Reflect Magazine, 1984; Mystery Time Anthology, 1986-87; Haiku, Japan; Haiku Society of America Magazine; Wind Chimes; Dragonfly. Recent Publications: Redbook Magazine, Callapalco-lO; Perspectives, Biology and Medicine; Byline; Poets for Peace, Harvest Books Inc; Odessa Poetry Review; Amelia Maga Magazine; The Cathartic; Poet; Dan River Anthology; Parnassus Literary Review; Piedmont Literary Review. *Memberships:* International Platform Association; Poetry Society of America; Associate, Academy of American Poets; Massachusetts State Poetry Society; Poets and Writers; Affiliate, Mystery Writers of America. *Honours:* Hall of Fame Author Award, 1985-86; Golden Poet, 1988; Book Publication Grant, American Poets Fellowship Society, 1981; Haiku Award, Bardic Echoes Magazine, 1984; Cicada Magazine, 1986: Honorable Mention, Story Time Magazine, 1984; Midwest Poetry Review; Various others. *Hobbies:* Watercolour painting; Exhibiting in juried shows; Photography; Birdwatching. *Address:* 9 Foster Road, Lexington, MA 02173, USA.

WILSON Jacqueline, b. 17 Dec. 1945, Bath, Somerset, England. Writer. m. William Millar Wilson, 28 Aug. 1965, 1 daughter. *Publications:* Adult crime novels: Hide and Seek, 1972; Truth or Dare, 1972; Snap, 1973; Let's Pretend, 1975; Making Hate, 1976; Books for children and young adults: Nobody's Perfect, 1982; Waiting for the Sky To Fall, 1983; The Other Side, 1984; The School Trip, 1984; The Killer Tadpole, 1984; How To Survive Summer Camp, 1985; Amber, 1986; The Monster in the Cupboard, 1986; Glubbslyme, 1987; The Power of the Shade, 1987; This Girl, 1988; Stevie Day series: Supersleuth, 1987; Lonelyhearts, 1987; Ratrace, 1988; Vampire, 1988; Radio plays: Are You Listening?; It's Disgusting At Your Age; Ask A Silly Question. *Hobbies:* Browsing in second-hand bookshops; Collecting toy animals; Going to art galleries; Swimming; Cross-stitch samplers. *Address:* c/o Gina and Murray Pollinger, 222 Old Brompton Road, London SW5 0BZ, England.

WILSON Joyce Muriel (Stranger), b. Forest Gate, London, England. Writer; Dog Behviour Consultant. m. K.B. Wilson, 28 Feb. 1944, 2 sons, 1 daughter. *Education:* BSc., Zoology, London University, 1942. *Appointments:* Research Chemist, 1942-46. *Publications:* 55 books, best known include: Running Foxes; Flash; A Walk in the Dark; Kym, A Dog in a Million; Three's a Pack; Double or Quit; forthcoming: Spy - The No Good Pup; articles in: Dog & Country; Kennel Gazette; Off Lead (USA); Western Mail; Cat World. *Memberships:* Institute of Journalists; Society of Authors; President, Anglesey Cat Club; Vice President, Findon Downs Dog Training Club. *Hobbies:*

Competing with German Shepherd Dogs in Working Trials; Training Dogs & Training Owners to Train Dogs. *Address:* c/o Aitken & Sone, 29 Fernshow Road, London SW10 0TG, England.

WILSON Lynette Ann, b. 29 Dec. 1932, Campbell Town, Tasmania. m. Rex Croydon Wilson, 15 May 1954, 3 sons, 1 daughter. *Education:* Teachers Diploma, Art, University of Tasmania, 1953. *Appointments:* Art Teacher, Education Dept. of Tasmania, 1954-. *Creative Works:* Paintings represented in public collections, Tasmania, & private collections throughout Australia, England, Canada & America. *Memberships:* Life Member, Former Secretary & President, Art Society of Tasmania; President, Tasmanian Art Group. *Honour:* Life Member, Art Society of Tasmania, 1986. *Hobby:* Choral Singing. *Address:* 60 Bellevue Parade, Newtown, Tasmania 7008, Australia.

WILSON Margaret Dauler, b. 29 Jan. 1939, Pittsburgh, USA. Professor. m. Emmett Wilson, 12 June 1962. *Education:* AB, Vassar College, 1960; AM, Harvard University, 1963; PhD, Harvard University, 1965. *Appointments:* Teaching Fellow, Harvard, 1962-63, 1964-65; Assistant Professor, Columbia Univerity, 1965-67; Assistant Professor, Rockefeller University, 1967-70; Associate Professor, 1970-75, Professor, 1975-, Princeton University; Visitor, Institute for Advanced Study, 1983. *Publication:* Descartes, 1978. *Memberships:* American Philosophical Association; Leibniz Society of North America, President, 1986-90; International Berkeley Society. *Honours:* Woodrow Wilson Fellowship, 1960-61; Knox Fellowship, 1963-64; Guggenheim Fellowship, 1977-78; Immanuel Kant Lecturer, Stanford University, 1982; ACLS Fellowship, 1982-83. *Hobbies:* Environmental Issues; Animal Welfare. *Address:* Box 262 RD 1 Canal Rd, Princeton, NJ 08540, USA.

WILSON Marie Frances, b. 27 Dec. 1940, Butte, Montana, USA. Writer; Publisher. div. *Education:* AA, Social Sciences, 1985. *Appointments:* NATO HQ, Oslo, Norway; American Embassy, Oslo, 1970-75; California Optometric Association, USA, 1979-83. *Publications:* Over 250 articles and photographs in magazines across USA and overseas; 4 major publications; Buying the Best, all self-published. *Memberships:* California Writers Club; COSMEP Publishing. *Hobbies:* Scuba diving; Skiing; Reading; Travel worldwide (lived in 5 countries). *Address:* Mission Btn 12th-13th Avenue, Carmel-by-the-Sea, CA 93921, USA.

WILSON Rubie Stein, b. 2 July 1932, Memphis, Tennessee, USA. Chief Executive Officer; Company Owner. m. Fred Wilson, 16 Nov. 1960, 2 sons, 2 daughters, 3 stepchildren. *Education:* AA, Business Administration, Owens-Henderson, Memphis; Los Angeles City College. *Career:* Over 10 years in Radio from age 14; Announcer and Disc Jockey Show, A Date with Rubie, 1949-55, 1960-65; 1st female to interview Elvis Pressley, WHHM Memphis, early 50s; Worked for WDIA, WCBR, KTYM, KBLA Los Angeles; Woman's Programme Director, Continuity Director and Traffic Manager, 3yrs in radio; Clerical Supervisor, State Department of Social Welfare, Los Angeles, California, 1959- 71; Owner, Vice-President, Chief Executive Officer, Wilson Enterprises, Mail Order Company, nationwide services, DBA Ms Rubie's Secrets, Cosmetics, Owner, Chief Executive Officer, Ms Rubie's Creative Designs jewellery company, 1971-. *Memberships:* Alpha Gamma Chi; National Association of Female Executives; Chamber of Commerce; Bank of America Small Business Alliance; Listed in Dun & Bradstreet. *Honours:* 3rd Class Operator's License FCC for Radio; 2 State of California Merit Awards for teaching Seminars and Classes in Organisation and Administration; On VIP List, Caesars Palace, Las Vegas. *Hobbies:* Music including piano and organ playing; Public speaking; Travel; Sports. *Address:* 2424 Gramercy Park, Los Angeles, CA 90018, USA.

WILSON Sandra Jean, b. 31 Aug. 1946, Kansas City, Missouri, USA. Psychologist. m. Virgil Ray Wilson, 11 June 1982, 1 son, 1 daughter. *Education:* BS, University of Central Arkansas, 1968; MA, University of Arkansas, 1973. *Appointments* Director, Evalution Team, Psychiatric Department, Arkansas Children's Colony, 1968-74; Coordinator, Cons & Education, Human Services Inc, West Central Arkansas, 1974-76; Coordinator, County Clinic, Delta Counselling & Guidance Centre, 1976-79; Director, County Centre, SW Arkansas Counselling & Mental Health Centre, 1979-; Private practice, consultant (management, administration, medical records), 1987-. *Publications:* Various papers, pamphlets, professional presentations, *Memberships include:* President, Arkansas School Psychology Association; American Psychological Association; Fellow, offices, Arkansas Psychological Association; Offices Spasmodic Dysphonia Association of Arkansas; National Association of School Psychologists; County Mental Health Task Force. *Honours:* 5-year appointment, Arkansas Board of Examiners in Psychology; Governor's Commendation, public sevice; Recognition, community service, Optimist Club; High school honour graduate. *Hobbies:* Porcelain & antiques; Designing clothes & jewellery; Flower gardening; Reading; Writing; Painting. Main interests: Child abuse & neglect, adolescent rebellion, developmental stages of marriage, effect of religious beliefs on coping skills, stress management. *Address:* Route 1, Box 332-0A, DeQueen, Arkansas 71832, USA.

WILSON Suzanne Fischer (Sue), b. 16 July 1946, Pittsburgh, Pennsylvania, USA. Owner, Sue Wilson Express Services. Divorced. 2 sons. *Education:* BA, Southern Methodist University, 1969. *Appointments:* Teacher, Dallas Independent Schools, 1969-71; Model/Sales, Dallas Apparel Market, 1972-77; Employment Industry 1978-; Owner, Sue Wilson Express Services, Permanent/Temporary Employment Services, 1980-. *Creative Works:* Publications: How to improve your Typing Speed in Five Days; How to Write a Resume. Guest Speaker for numerous seminars on topics including Changing Trends of Personnel Practices; Female Entrepreneurs; The Changing Trends of Medical Careers; How to Prepare for the Job Market, etc. *Memberships:* Governor's Business Advisory Council, Committee to review the States Economic Development Efforts, Education Review Committee; Greater Albuquerque Chamber of Commerce, Board of Directors, 1986-; Honorary Base Commander to Kirtland Air Force Base 1550th Helicopter Training Unit; Better Business Bureau, 1985-, Board of Directors; Great Southwest Council of Boyscouts, Executive Board, 1986-; Lovelace Clinic, Advisory Board, 1986-; United Way, of Propecting Committee, 1987-; New Mexico Association of Personnel Consultants, President 1984, Treasurer 1988; Governmental Liaison, New Mexico State Job Training and Co-ordinating Committee, Executive Committee, Chairman and Marketing Co-ordination. *Honours:* National Certification, Certified Personnel Consultant, 1984; Certificate of Appreciation, Office Education Administration, 1986; Award from Express Services, National Headquarters, 1988. *Hobbies:* Tennis; Oil Painting; Home Decorating. *Address:* Sue Wilson Express Services, 4600 Montgomery NE, Suite One, Albuquerque, New Mexico 87109, USA.

WILSON OF RADCLIFFE Freda, Lady, b. 23 Jan. 1930, Bolton, England. m. Alfred, Lord Wilson of Radcliffe, 10 June 1976, died 1983. *Appointments:* Personal Assistant to Scientific Director of International Isocyanate Inst. *Hobbies:* Gardening; Walking; Travel. *Address:* The Bungalow, 4 Hey House Mews, Holcombe, Bury BL8 4NS, England.

WILSON-NESBITT Judy Lynn, b. 13 Mar. 1952, Pittsburgh, USA. Vice President. m. Robert H. Nesbitt, 23 Aug. 1986. *Education:* BSN, 1974, MN, 1976, University of Pittsburgh; MPA, New York University, 1983. *Appointments:* Clinical Specialist, Children's Hospital of Pittsburgh; Cardiac Counselor, Cleveland Clinic; Assistant Director, University Hospital of Cleveland; Associate Director, Columbia Presbyterian; Senior Manager, Ernst & Whinney; Vice President, HBO

& Company. *Publications:* Articles in journals. *Memberships:* HFMA; ACHE; Board American Heart Association. *Honours:* Sigma Theta Tau. *Hobbies:* Golf. *Address:* 69 West Shore Drive, Pennington, NJ 08534, USA.

WILSON-NEWBY Bonita Wesley, b. 21 Mar. 1951, Pittsburgh, Pennsylvania, USA. Physician. m. James M Newby, 24 Oct. 1987. 1 son, 1 daughter. *Education:* BS 1971, MD 1976, Howard University; Pediatric Internship & Residency, Boston City Hospital, 1976-79; Chief Resident Pediatrics, 1981, Allergy Fellowship, 1982-84, Howard University. *Appointments:* Assistant Professor, Pediatrics and Allergy, Howard University, 1984; Allergist, Group Health Association, Washington, 1985-; Private Practice, 1986-. *Memberships:* Alpha Omega Alpha; Fellow American Academy Pediatrics; American Academy Allergy and Immunology; American Association Certified Allergists; Board of Directors of National Capital Health Ministries; DC Medical Society; National Medical Association; American Medical Association. *Hobbies:* Bike riding; Reading; Crochet. *Address:* 6323 Georgia Ave NW, Suite 208, Washington, DC 20011, USA.

WINCH Jean Rosemary Vera, The Hon. b. 30 Oct. 1928, London, England. m. 14 Dec. 1950. *Publications:* Oil Paintings, Watercolours, Bronzes. *Hobbies:* Flat Racing and Breeding. *Address:* Castle Barn, Penhyndeud Raeth, Gwynedd, Wales.

WINDSOR Patricia, b. 21 Sept. 1938, New York City, USA. Author; Lecturer; Educator. m. (1) Laurence C Windsor, 3 Apr. 1959, 1 son, 1 daughter, divorced 1978, (2) Stephen E. Altman, 21 Sept. 1986, separated 1987. *Education:* Bennington College and New York University. *Appointments:* Assistant Editor, Mademoiselle Magazine, New York City; Information Manager, Family Planning Association, London; Faculty, University of Maryland, Institute of Childrens Literature; Editor in Chief, Easterner, Washington DC; Director, Wordspring Literary Agency, New York. *Publications:* Novels: The Summer Before, 1973; Something's Waiting for You, 1974; Mad Martin, 1976; Divina for Roses, 1976; Killing Time, 1980; The Sandman's Eyes, 1985; The Hero, 1988; 10 novels, and numerous articles in professional journals. *Membership:* Childrens Book Guild. *Honours:* Best Book, ALA, 1973; New York Times Outstanding Book for Young Adults, 1976; Austrian State Award, 1980; Edgar Allan Poe Award, 1985; Best News Story, IABC, 1979; etc. *Hobbies:* Skiing; Painting; Writing as Therapy Tool for Disturbed Teens; Meditation. *Address:* c/o Writers House, 21 West 26th St., New York, NY 10010, USA.

WINDSOR-MORGAN Gillian, b. Bodmin, Cornwall, England. Art Historian & Antiquities Conservator; Writer; Educator. m. George Michael Hind, divorced, 1 daughter, (2) Terry Lane Mason, divorced. *Education:* PhD, Fine Arts/Conservation Restoration. *Appointments:* Computer Systems Conservator 1983-84; Director, CEO: California Institute for The Restoration & Conservation Arts, 1984-86; Director, Windsor Morgan Institute, 1988; Founder, Chairman, European Decorative Arts Forum, USA. *Contributor To:* Various journals & magazines. *Memberships:* American Institute for the Conservation of Historical Works; Art Deco Society. *Address:* 3556 Sacramento Street, San Francisco, CA 94118, USA.

WING Adrien Katherine, b. 7 Aug. 1956, Oceanside, California, USA. Lawyer. m. Enrico A Melson, 28 Apr. 1983, 2 sons. *Education:* BA, Magna cum Laude, Princeton University, 1978; MA, University of California, 1979; JD, Stanford Law School, 1982. *Appointments:* Curtis Mallet Prevost Colt and Mosle, 1982-86; Rabinawitz Boudin Standard Krinsky & Lieberman, 1986-87; Professor, University of Iowa Law School, 1987-. *Creative Works:* Annotated Bibliography: Proof and Pleading of Foreign Law in Domestic Jurisdictions, in Stanford Journal of International Law, 1985; Amendments to the Foreign Sovereign Immunities Act:

The Act of State Doctrine, 1986. *Memberships:* Council on Foreign Relations; National Conference of Black Lawyers; Young Lawyers, American Bar Association; Director, Association of Black Princeton Alumni; Trustee, Princeton Class of 1978 Foundation; American Society of International Law, Executive Council. *Honours:* Frederick Douglas Award, 1978; Afro-American Studies Thesis Prize, Honorable Mention, 1978; Academic Fellow Award, University of California, Los Angeles, 1979; Stanford African Student Award, 1982. *Hobbies:* Writing; Poetry; African Dance & Music; Jogging. *Address:* University of Iowa Law School, Iowa City, IA 52242, USA.

WINKEL Nina, b. 21 May 1905, Borken, West Germany. Sculptor. m. George Winkel, 10 Dec. 1934. *Education:* Academy of Fine Arts, Duesseldorf, 1922. *Appointments:* Freelance Sculptor, 1944-. *Creative Works:* Solo Exhibitions, 1944, 1947, 1968; various group exhibitions. *Memberships:* National Academy of Design, Fellow; National Sculpture Society, Secretary, 1965-68; Sculptors Guild; Sculpture Centre, President 1970-73, President Emeritus. *Honours:* Numerous including, Benhett Prize, 1976; Liskin Purchase Prize, 1981; Citation, State of New York, 1983. *Address:* Dunham Road, Keene Valley, NY 12943, USA.

WINNER Anne Moore Windle, b. 4 Sept. 1921, West Chester, Pennsylvania, USA. School Psychologist. m. 14 Apr. 1944. 1 son, 3 daughters. *Education:* BA, Swarthmore College, 1942; MA, Bucknell University, 1961; CASE, Johns Hopkins University, 1974; DEd, Pennsylvania State University, 1988. *Appointments:* Social & CW work, 1944-61; Clinical Psychology, 1961-63; School Psychology, Baltimore City and Public Schools, 1963-; Private practice. *Creative Works:* Research: The Bundu-? and Draw A Person with black elementary school children, 1971; Academic performance of children treated for lead poisoning, 1988. *Memberships include:* Maryland Delegate, International School Psychologists; American Psych. Association; Maryland Psych. Association; Charter Member, National Association of School Psychologists; Maryland Association of School Psych.; Founder, President and other offices, Balto City Association of School Psychologists; Founder and Officer, N Central Pennsylvania Chapter, NASW; Founder, Society of Friends, Lewisburg, Pennsylvania, etc. *Honours:* Scholar, Bucknell University, 1960-61; Scholar, University of Pennsylvania School of Social Work, 1945-46. *Hobbies:* Music; Art; Reading; Gardening; Breeder Golden Retriever dogs, 1973-83. *Address:* 102E Chestnut Hill Lane, Reisterstown, MD 21136, USA.

WINOGRAD Audrey Lesser, b. 6 Oct. 1933, New York City, USA. Advertising Executive. m. Melvin H Winograd, 29 Apr. 1956. 1 daughter. *Education:* BA, University of Conn, 1953. *Appointments:* Assistant Advertising Manager, T Baumritter Co Inc, New York City, 1953- 54; Assistant Director, Creative Merchandising & Public Relations, Kirby Block & Co Inc, New York City, 1954-56; Division Merchandise Manager, Director of Advertising & Sales Promotion, Wingorad's Department Store Inc, Pt Pleasant, New Jersey, 1956-73; Vice President 1960-73, Executive Vice President 1973-86, President 1976-, AMW Associates, Ocean Twp, New Jersey. *Publications:* Editor: Shop Talk and The Communicator; Business Newsletters. *Memberships:* National Retail Merchants Association; New Jersey Public Relations & Advertising Association; Monmouth County Business Association; New Jersey Women Business Owners; Monmouth & Ocean Development Council; Ocean Chamber of Commerce; American Society of Advertising & Promotion; ASPCA; Humane Society of USA; Animal Protection Institute, and many more. *Honours:* Jasper, Norma Advertising Awards, 1976-88. *Hobbies:* Animal & wildlife protection; Gourmet cooking; Skiing; Collecting animal paintings and figurines. *Address:* AMW Associates Advertising & Public Relations, 10 Pine Lane, Ocean, New Jersey 07712, USA.

WINSBERG Gwynne Sandra Roeseler, b. 28 Nov.

1930, Chicago, USA. Management Consultant; Health Care Executive. m. David Melvin Winsberg, 1 Dec. 1950, divorced 1984, 1 son, 1 daughter. *Education:* MS, 1962, PhD, 1967, University of Chicago. *Appointments:* Instructor, University of Chicago, 1965-67; Assistant Professor, Northwestern University Medical School, 1967-75; Associate Dean, Loyola University, 1975-81; President, GRW Associates Inc. Chicago, 1981-; Vice President, Efficient Health Systems Inc., 1987. *Publications:* Articles in professional journals; Record Album. *Memberships:* President, New Music Chicago, 1986; Board Member, Organic Theater, 1988; American Public Health Association; National Academy of recording Arts and Sciences; American Association of Preferred Provider Organizations. *Honours:* USPHS Predoctoral Research Fellow, 1965-67; USPHS Awards, 1973, 1974; NEH Award, 1974. *Hobbies:* Backpacking; Bicycling; Avant Garde Music; Theatre. *Address:* 5533 N. Glenwood, Chicago, IL 60640, USA.

WINSLOW Helen Caudle, b. 24 Mar. 1916, New Salem, North Carolina, USA. Artist; Teacher. m. Randolph Winslow, 30 Nov. 1940, 1 daughter. *Education:* BA, Florida Southern College, 1936; Art Students League, New York City, 1936-41; Otis Art Institute, 1954-57. *Appointments:* Art Teacher, Exhibiting Artist, 1956-88. *Creative Works:* Paintings: Roberts Gallery, LA, 1966-; Brentwood Gallery, 1967-68; Vallis & Sensen, Sna Francisco, 1967; Gallery Fair, Mendocino, California, 1968-80; Austin Gallery, Scottsdale, 1974, 1977, 1984. *Membeships:* Royal Society of Arts, Art Associate; Art Students League, Life Member; Society of Western Artists. *Honours:* Recipient, various honours and awards. *Address:* 9934 Westwanda Dr., Beverly Hills, CA 90210, USA.

WINSOR Eleanor Margaret Webster, b. 1 Dec. 1941, Champaign, Illinois, USA. Businesswoman; Educator. m. Curtin Winsor, 6 May 1972, 1 daughter. *Education:* AB, Hollins College, Virginia, 1963; MA, University of Pennsylvania, 1966. *Appointments:* Adjunct Professor, Earth & Environmental Sciences, Wilkes College, Wilkes Barre; President, Winsor Associates, 1986-. Also numerous business & civic activities including: Chairperson, Lower Merion Township Planning Commission, 1974-; Advisory Committee to the Maurice K. Goddard Chair, Pennsylvania State University College of Agriculture, 1980-; Trustee, Agnes Irwin School, Rosemont, PA, 1985-; Environmental Affairs Committee, PA Chamber of Business & Industry, 1987-; Government Affairs Committee, Water Pollution Control Federation, 1987-; Chairperson, Steering Committee, PA Council of Mediators, 1988-; Board, Community Dispute Settlement Programme, Delaware County, 1988 . *Publications include:* Numerous papers, articles, lectures, environmental protection & allied subjects. *Memberships:* Numerous civic & governmental bodies. *Honours:* Awards, American Society of Public Administration 1981, Anglers Club of Philadelphia 1985, PA Environmental Council 1986; Conservationist of Year, North Area Environmental Council, 1984; Honorary DSc, Wilkes College, 1986. *Hobbies:* Fly fishing; Cycling; Community work. *Address:* 101 Cherry Lane, Ardmore, Pennsylvania 19003, USA.

WINSTON Sarah, b. 15 Dec. 1912, New York City, USA. Writer. m. Keith Winston, 11 June 1932, 2 sons. *Publications:* V-Mail, Letters of a World War II Combat Medic, 1985; Not Yet Spring, 1976; Everything Happens for the Best, 1969, 1970; Our Son Ken, 1969; And Always Tomorrow, 1963; Everything Happens for the Best, And Always Tomorrow and V-Mail have been recorded by The Library of Congress as Talking Books for the Blind and Handicapped, Our Son, Ken recorded by Recording for the Blind, Inc. *Memberships:* League of Women Voters; National League of American Penwomen; Common Cause. *Honours:* 1st Prize, National League of American Penwomen Biennial Contest, 1970; NLAPW Biennial Contest, 1st Prize, 1972; Nominee (twice), Gimbel Achievement Award, 1970, 1972; etc. *Hobbies:* Oil Painting; Sculpture; Piano; . *Address:* 1838 Rose Tree Lane, Havertown, PA 19083, USA.

WINTER Patricia Lue, b. 6 Feb. 1924, Wadsworth, Ohio, USA. Technical Consultant. m. Frederic W. Hammesfahr, 19 Feb. 1949, 3 sons. *Education:* Louisiana State University, 1941-42; University of Akron, Ohio, 1942-44; BS, University of Illinois, 1945; JD, Rutgers University, 1981. *Appointments:* Systems Engineer, International Business Machines Inc, 1945-49; Computer Systems Engineer, Firestone Tire & Rubber Company, 1949-50; Vice President 1976-85, President 1985-, Hammesfahr, Winter & Associates Inc. *Publications:* Technical Articles, Energy Progress journal. *Memberships:* Advisory Board, Pittsburgh Coal Conference; State Board of New Jersey Women Business Owners; Rutgers Law School Alumni; American Society of Professional & Executive Women; Women in Energy; Association of Energy Engineers. *Honours:* Alpha Lambda Delta, 1942; Pi Mu Epsilon, 1942. *Hobbies:* International Travel; Hiking; Genealogy. *Address:* PO Box 536, Bernardsville, New Jersey 07924, USA.

WINTERS Anne, b. 13 Oct. 1939, St Paul, Minnesota, USA. Poet; College Instructor. *Education:* BA, New York University, 1961; MA, Columbia University, 1963. *Appointments:* Instructor in English Literature: Boston State College, Massachusetts, 1966-69; Massachusetts Institute of Technology, 1981; University of California, Davis, 1983-85; St Mary's College, California, 1985-87. *Publications:* Salamander: Selected Poems of Robert Morteau (translated and with introduction), 1979; The Key to the City, poems, 1986; Poems in Poetry, Kenyon Review, The New Republic, and in anthologies. *Hobby:* Modern Language Association. *Honours:* Jacob Glatstein Memorial Prize for translations from the French of Robert Marteau, Poetry magazine, 1979; Phi Beta Kappa, 1981; Woodrow Wilson Fellow, 1981; Nominated for National Book Critics Circle Prize for The Key to the City, 1987; Individual Artist's Grant, National Endowment for the Arts, 1987-88. *Hobbies:* Gardening; Madrigals. *Address:* c/o English Department, University of California at Berkeley, Berkeley, CA 94720, USA.

WINTERS Wendy Anne (Wendi), b. 25 May 1953, San Diego, California, USA. Public Relations Executive. m. Lt Tod A. J. Geimer, 22 Aug. 1987. *Education:* Associate, Occupational Studies, Tobe-Coburn School; BAF, Virginia Commonwealth University; Student, School of Visual Arts, Fashion Institute of Technology. *Appointments:* Intern, Area Manager, Time Inc, New York City, 1972-78; Assistant Buyer, Abraham & Strauss, Brooklyn, New York, 1976-78; Regional Director, Merchandise Manager, Lady Madonna Management Corporation, New York City, 1978-81; With Eleanor Lambert Division, Creamer Inc, New York City, 1981-82; President, Owner, Wendi Winters Public Relations, New York City, 1982-88; Syndicated Fashion Writer, Copley News Service, San Diego, California, 1985-86; Partner, President, The Fashion Vanguard Inc, New York City, 1986-; Fashion Columnist, The West Side Spirit, New York City, 1987-; Executive, The Rowland Company Inc, New York City, 1988-. *Memberships:* Tobe-Coburn Alumni Association, New York City, Chairman 1982-86; Tobe-Coburn Alumni Association Inc, Vice-President, Current Activities, 1986-87; Alumni Board, Virginia Commonwealth University School of Arts, Richmond; The Fashion Group, Publications Committee; AWARE, Co-Chair, Programme Committee; Tobe-Coburn Alumni Association, Chairman 1983-86. *Honour:* T Award for Outstanding Young Alumna, Tobe-Coburn Alumni Association, 1980. *Hobbies:* Writing; Drawing; Designing costume jewellery and clothing; Roller skating; Computers. *Address:* 102 East 22nd Street 4H, New York, NY 10010, USA.

WINTERS-MARLIN Deborah Ann, b. 23 Aug. 1951, Garden City, Kansas, USA. Medical Doctor. m. Clyde E. Marlin Jr, 21 Dec. 1975, 1 son, 2 daughters. *Education:* BA cum laude, German, Southern Missionary College, 1973; Volunteer State Community College, 1973-74; Middle Tennessee State University, 1974; MD, Loma Linda University, Medical School, 1978, Internship and Residency (Diagnostic Radiology),

Medical Center, 1979-82, Loma Linda University. *Appointments:* Kern Radiology, Bakersfield, California, 1983-84; River Park Hospital, McMinnville, Tennessee, 1984-; Warren Regional Hospital, McMinnville, 1984-; Coffee Medical Center, Manchester, Tennessee, 1986-. *Publication:* Cholecystojejunostomy Complicated by Massive Hemocholecyst, 1982. *Memberships:* American College of Radiology; Radiological Society of North America; American Association of Women Radiologists; Tennessee Medical Association; Warren County Medical Society, Vice-President 1986, President 1987; Tennessee Radiological Society; River Park Hospital Medical Staff, Secretary-Treasurer, 1988, Vice-Chief of Staff, 1989. *Honours:* Betty Crocker Homemaker of Tomorrow Award, 1969; High School Valedictorian, 1969; Standard Secondary Certificate for Teaching, Certified, 1973; Alpha Mu Gamma. *Hobbies:* Tole and decorative painting; Creative cooking and baking; Interior decorating; Crafts; Cave exploring; Travel; People; Collecting cookie cutters; Collecting recipes; Collecting Bible story colouring books; Promoting interest in women's health. *Address:* River Park Hospital, Sparta Highway, McMinnville, TN 37110, USA.

WINTERSON Jeanette, b. 27 Aug. 1959, Manchester, England. Writer. *Education:* St Catherine's College, Oxford, 1978-81; MA Hons, English. *Publications:* Oranges Are Not The Only Fruit, 1985; The Passion, 1987, Penguin Edition 1988. *Honours:* Whitbread First Novel Award, 1985; Publishing for People Award, 1985; John Llewelyn Rhys Prize, 1987; Commonwealth Writers Award (with Bruce Chatwin), 1988. *Hobbies:* Philosophy; Gardening; Classic cars; Cats. *Address:* c/o Pat Kavanagh, Ad Peters Ltd, 5 The Chambers, Chelsea Harbour Lots Road, London SW10, England.

WINTHROP Leslie, b. 11 Aug. 1949, Queens, New York, USA. Company President. m. Robert Siegel, 21 Mar. 979, 2 step-sons, 1 step- daughter. *Education:* BBA, 1970, MBA, 1972, Bernard M. Baruch College. *Appointments:* Merchandise Manager: Hoescht & Fibers, New York City, 1972-74, W. Coast, Los Angeles, 1974-76; Director, Advertising, Alex Colman, Borden (LA), 1976-77; President, Gilda Miros Ltd., 1977-80; President, Advertising Agency Register, 1980-; Instructor, Parsons School/New School, New York, 1985-. *Memberships:* Advertising Club; Board of Directors, Advertising Club, New York, 1985-87; Advertising Women of New York; Ad-Net; American Advertising Federation. *Honours:* Crystal Prism award, Americcan Advertising Federation, 1985; Andy Award, Advertising Club, New York, 1986. *Hobby:* Tennis. *Address:* 425 East 58 Street, New York, NY 10022, USA.

WIRTSCHAFTER Irene Rose, b. 5 Aug, Elgin, Illinois, USA. Tax Consultant. m. Burton S Wirtschafter, deceased. *Education:* BCS, Columbus University; Real Estate Appraiser, Philadelphia Board of Realtors. *Appointments:* Military service, commissioned Ensign, US Navy 1944, retired with rank of Captain, 1976; Internal Revenue Agent, US Treasury Office of International Operations, International banking specialist; Real Estate Associate; Real Estate Appraiser; Insurance Broker; Statistician; Accountant; Elected to House of Representatives, Silver Haired Legislature, District 32, Florida, 1985-. *Memberships:* Numerous including: Director, Florida Spacecoast Philharmonic; Director, Cocoa Beach Citizens League; President, Friends of Cocoa Beach Library; Cocoa Beach Constitution Bicentennial Committee; Special Events Comm and Military Affairs Com of Cocoa Beach Area Chamber of Commerce, etc; Veterans Administration Advisory Committee on Women Veterans; National Trustee of Association of Naval Aviation; Director, Silver Wings Fraternity, etc.; Member of Code Enforcement Board of Cocoa Beach. *Honours:* Woman of the Year Award, Silver Wings Fraternity, 1985; Honorary Citizen: Winnipeg, Canada, Atchison, Kansas and New Orleans, Louisiana; Honorary Commissioner of Agriculture, Louisiana; Key to the City of Atchison, Kansas, 1989, Name inscribed in Memory Lane, International Forest of Friendship, Atchison; Kentucky Colonel; Louisiana

Colonel; Honorary Deputy Fire Marshal, State of Florida; 99 Achievement Award; Certificate of Appreciation, Florida Silver-Haired Legislature, 1987. *Address:* 1825 Minutemen Causeway Apt 301, Cocoa Beach, Florida 32931, USA.

WISDOM Guyrena Julia Knight, b. 27 July 1923, St Louis, USA. m. 3 July 1976. *Education:* BA, Education, Harris-Stowe State College; MA, Educaitonal Psychology, University of Illinois. *Appointments:* Elementary School Teacher, 1945-63; School Psychologist, 1963-74, 1984-85; Private Psychologist, 1985-88; Assessment Specialist, St Louis Regional Centre for Developmentally Disabled, 1988-. *Publications:* Booklets, Self Esteem, and Learning Disabilities; Co-author, BKKS Apperception Survey. *Memberships:* National Association of School Psychologists; National Association of Children with Learning Disabilities; Council for Exception Children; Association for Supervision and Curriculum Development. *Honours:* Kappa Delta Pi; Pi Lambda Theta. *Hobbies:* Attending Ballet Performances; Musical Comedy; Concerts. *Address:* 5046 Wabada Ave., St Louis, MO 63143, USA.

WISEMAN Shirley Mcvay, b. 17 June 1937, Arkansas, USA. Homebuilder. m. 5 Dec. 1977, 1 son, 1 daughter. *Education:* University of Kentucky; American University. *Appointments:* Pesident, Wiseman Construction & Development Company Inc., 1965-84. *Memberships Include:* Vice President, Treasurer, 1987, First Vice President, 1988, President, 1989, National Association of Home Builders; Home Builders Association of Kentucky, various offices including, Board of Directors, 1974, 1975; Home Builders Association of Lexington, Board Member, 1972-78; Home Owners Warranty Corporation of Lexington, President, 1976; Board of Directors, 1977-78. *Honours:* Recipient, various honours and awards. *Address:* 153 Patchen Dr., Suite 1, Lexington, KY 40502, USA.

WISHART Betty R., b. 22 Sep. 1947, Lumberton, North Carolina, USA. Composer. *Education:* BMus, Queens College; MMus, University of North Carolina, Chapel Hill; Studied with Wolfgang Rose, Michael Zenge, Richard Bunger. *Appointments:* Teacher of Piano and Composition, Kohinoor Music; Vice-President, Final Copy, 1981-; Owner, Teacher, Wishart Studio, 1984-. *Creative works:* Hymn for the Children, commission for third, Scots and Mariners Presbyterian Church; Illusion, suite for piano; Kohinoor Sonata, piano; Sounds, organ; Memories of Things Unseen, Chi'en, Experience, instrumental ensemble; Oriental Excursions, piano; Salute, 2 pianos. *Memberships:* American Society of Composers, Authors and Publishers; International League of Women Composers; Various offices, Delta Omicron; Broward County Music Teachers Association (President 1987-89, Recording Secretary 1985-87); District VI Executive Board, Florida State Music Teachers Association. *Honours:* Star of Delta Omicron, 1969; Honours Concert (performer and composer), University of North Carolina, 1971; Outstanding Young Women of American, 1973, 1975; Area Chairman of the Year, Delta Omicron, 1973. *Address:* 11051 NW 33rd Street, Coral Springs, FL 33065, USA.

WITHROW Mary Ellen, b. 2 Oct. 1930, Marion, Ohio, USA. Treasurer of the State of Ohio. m. Norman David Withrow, 4 Sept. 1948, 4 daughters. *Education:* Graduated, Marion Harding High School, 1948. *Appointments:* President, Elgin Board of Education, 1972; Deputy Registrar, State of Ohio, 1972-75; Deputy County Auditor, Marion County, Ohio, 1975-77; County Treasurer, Marion County, Ohio, 1977-83; Treasurer, State of Ohio, 1983-. *Memberships Include:* 1st Vice-President, National Association of State Auditors, Comptrollers and Treasurers; Vice President, 10 State Midwestern Region of National Association of State Treasurers; Fairness Commission Member, Democratic National Committee; Co-Chairperson, Midwest Farm Crisis Task Force, Democratic National Committee; Women Executives in State Government; Member, Business and Professional Women; Member, Executive

Committee adn Governing Board for the Council of State Governments. *Honours:* Inductee, Ohio Women's Hall of Fame, 1986; Recognized for Professional Achievement by Investment Dealers of Ohio Inc., 1986; Intelligent Investor of the Year, Ryan Financial Strategy Group, 1986; Outstanding Elected Democratic Woman Holding Public Office award, 1987, by the 300, 000 member National Federation of Democratic Women; Fellowship Award to attend the John F.Kennedy School of Government at Harvard University, 1987, by th eWomen Executives in State Government; Advocate of the Year Award by the US Small Business Administration, 1988; Honorary Member, Ohio Chapter, Delta Kappa Gamma; Honorary Member, Delta Sigma Pi; . *Hobby:* Painting. *Address:* 1991 Newmans-Cardington Road, Waldo, OH 43356, USA.

WITTE Jeanne Marie, b. 5 June 1938, Elgin, Illinois, USA. Registered Nurse. m. Raymond Witte 19 Nov. 1960, divorced 1986. 3 sons, 2 daughters. *Education:* St Francis College, 1959; St Charles Hospital School of Nursing, 1959. *Appointments:* Medical/Surgical Nursing, Pediatric Nursing, St Charles Hospital, 1960-65; Obstetrics, Copley Hospital, 1970-75; Director of Nursing, North Aurora Center, 1975-76; Asst Director of Nursing, Fox Valley Nursing Home and Director of Rehabilitation and Education, St Charles Medical Center, 1976-77; Rehabilitation Consultant, Chubb Insurance, 1977-80; Regional Rehabilitation Supervisor, CNA Insurance, 1980- 81; Catastrophic Case Management Specialist, Crawford & Co, 1981-86; Regional Manager, American International Health and Rehabilitation Services, 1986-89. *Creative works:* Lectured as guest speaker at Rehabilitation Institute of Chicago. *Memberships:* Board of Directors, Playmakers Inc; RING (Rehabilitation Insurance Nurses Group; Illinois Nursing Associa6tion; Association Rehabilitation Nurses; National Female Executive Assoc; National Association Rehabilitation Providers in the Private Sector. *Honours:* Awarded, Certified Insurance Rehabilitation Specialist, 1985; Named in Charter Edition, National Distinguished Service Registry, Library of Congress, Medial & Vocational Rehabilitation. *Hobbies:* Music, soloist; Theatre; Sports; Gardening; Reading; Decorating; Crafts. *Address:* 901 Warrenville Road Suite 300, Lisle, Illinois 60532, USA.

WITTELS Beatrice, b. 5 Jan. 1910, Philadelphia, USA. Nutritionist; Author; Artist; Publisher; Advertising Executive. m. David G. Wittels, 18 Jan. 1934, 3 sons, 1 daughter. *Education:* University of the Arts, 1926; The Barnes Foundation, 1928; Pennsylvania Academy of Fine Arts, 1938. *Appointments:* Fashion Artist, 1928-38; Fine Arts Painter, 1940-; Advertising Manager, Nan Duskin, 1944-46; Sales Promotion Director, Nan Duskin, 1958-60; Founder, Beatrice Wittels Advertising Agency, 1961-. *Publications:* Editor, Publisher, CSC Reports, 1977-: The Grainarian Gourmet, Sprouts, Dim sum & Soups, Beatrice Wittels I Choose to Be Well Diet Cookbook. *Memberships:* President, Founder, Cooking for Survival Consciousness, 1977; The Fashion Group of Philadelphia, Regional Director, 1959-61; World Food Day National Committee, 1981-. *Honours:* Neographics Award, 1972; Philadelphia Art Directors Award, 1976; DaVinci Art Alliance Award, 1948. *Hobbies:* Music; Piano; Dancing; Physical Fitness; Cooking. *Address:* Box 26762, Elkins Park, PA 19117, USA.

WITTER Geraldina Porto, b. 31 Jan. 1934, Mogi das Cruzes, Brazil. Psychologist; University Teacher. m. Jose Sebastiao Witter, 3 July 1954, 1 son, 2 daughters. *Education:* BA, School of Education, 1961; Educational Specialist, 1964, PhD, 1969, Livre docencia in School of Psychology, 1977, Universidade de Sao Paulo, Brazil. *Appointments:* Teacher, School Psychology, Universidade de Filosofia Ciencias e Letras de Rio Claro, 1962-65; Teacher, Philosophy, Science & Letters, 1965-69, Adviser, Institute of Psychology, 1970-87, University of Sao Paulo; Adviser, School of Educatiron, Universidade Federal de Paraiba Joao Pessoa, 1977-82; Teacher, Pontificia Universidade Catolica de Campinas, 1985-87. *Publications:* Privacao Cultural, 1971, 1976; Avalia cao de Instrucao Programada, 1972;

Condicionamento Verbal, 1975; Ciencia Ensino e Aprendizagem, 1975; pesquisas Educationais, 1979; preescolar : Enfoque Conportamental, 1980; Educaao de Adultos, 1983; Psicologia da Aprendizagem, 1984. *Memberships Include:* Secretary, Academia Paulista de Psicologia; Conselho Federal de Psicologia; Conselho Estadual de Psicologia; Sociedade de Psicologia de Sao Paulo; Interamerican Society of Psychology; International Psychology Association. *Honours:* Luiz Horta Lisboa Prize for History, 1949; Honour by Works, Conselho Federal de Psicologia, 1974-78, Conselho Estadual de Psicologia, 1979; Centenario de Psicologia Cientifica Prize, 1979; Honour, Reseacher, Instituto Nacional de Pesquisas da Amazonia and Conselho Nacional de Pesquisa, 1979. *Hobbies:* Av. Pedroso de Morais 144, apt 302 Pinheiros, O5420, USA.

WOHLFAHRT Barbara Robbins, b. 30 Oct. 1947, Chicago, Illinois, USA. Executive Vice President. m. Timothy H Wohlfahrt, 23 Aug. 1969. 2 sons, 2 daughters. *Education:* BSc, Mechanical Engineering, University of Wisconsin, 1969. *Appointments:* Technical Writer, Gilman Engineering, Janesville, 1969-70; Sales, Wausau Metals Corp, Wausau, 1970-71; Executive Vice President, Modu-Line Windows, Inc, Wausau, 1972-85; Executive Vice President, Major Industries, Inc, Wausau, 1983-; Executive Vice President, Prime Consultants, Inc, Wausau, 1983-; Executive Vice President, Republic Industries, Inc, Wausau, 1988-. *Publication:* The Art of Tipping: Customs and Controversies, 1984. *Memberships:* Director, Lutheran Social Services, 1975-78; Director, Tippers International Ltd, 1983-. *Honour:* Pi Tau Sigma, Engineering Honor Society, 1969. *Hobbies:* Reading; Cooking; Nutrition. *Address:* 3012 Hubbill Avenue, Wausau, WI 54401, USA.

WOLF Charlotte Elizabeth, b. 14 Sept. 1926, Boulder, Colorado, USA. Sociologist; University Professor. m. Rene A Wolf, 3 Sept. 1952. 1 son, 1 daughter. *Education:* BA, MA, University of Colorado; PhD, University of Minnesota. *Appointments:* Lecturer, Sociology, University of Maryland, Ankara, Turkey, 1965-67; Assistant Professor, Colorado State University, 1968-69; Assistant Professor, Colorado Women's College, 1969-74; Chair/Professor, Ohio Wesleyan University, 1974-83; Chair/Professor, Sociology, Memphis State University, 1983-. *Publications:* Garrison community: A study of an Overseas Military Colony, 1969; Articles in numerous professional journals; Ankara: A Social-Historical Study, 1968; Chapters in books; Monograph: People in New Situations. *Memberships:* Offices, American Sociological Association; Vioe President, North Central Sociological Association; Treasurer Offices, Society for Study of Social Problems; Executive Board, Western Social Science Association; President, Denver Chapter/ National Board Member, National Organisation for Women. *Honours:* Woman of the Year, Denver National Organisation for Women, 1972; Delta Tau Delta; Award, scholarly production, Ohio Wesleyan University, 1982; Research grant, faculty, Memphis State University, 1986. *Hobbies:* Reading; Swimming; Hiking; Music; Ballet. *Address:* Department of Sociology, Memphis State University, Memphis, TN 38152, USA.

WOLF Gertrude O, b. 27 Sept. 1923, Williamsburg, Brooklyn, New York, USA. Freelance Journalist; Poet. m. Dr Milton Wolf, 3 Aug. 1947, divorced 1969. 1 son, 3 daughters. *Education:* BA, English Education, Brooklyn College, 1944. *Appointments:* Director, Production Department, Interscience Publishers, New York, 1944; Associate Editor, Cosmetic and Drug Preview, New York, 1946; Reporter and Assistant to the Editor, The Somerset Messenger-Gazette, Somerville, 1944-46; Reporter, feature writer, assistant theatre editor and drama critic, The Columbus Citizen, 1947-51; Advertising copywriter, Eaton Paper Corporation, Pittsfield, 1951-52; Suburban newspaper correspondent, The Evening and Sunday Bulletin, Philadelphia; The Main Line Times, Ardmore; West Chester (Pa) Daily Local News, 1966-70; Appointment Desk, Receptionist, Medical Records Assistant, Founder, Editor, Chief Writer of Newsletter, LaGuardia Medical

Group, 1971-80; Queensborough Public Library, 1981-87. *Publications:* Autobiographical essays and book: Gertrude W: Memoirs; Poetry: Golden Tinsel and the Stars; Seashells at Mantoloking; Lonely Landscape; Movie Sheet Scene; Surrealistic; Castle of Dreams; First Snow of Winter. *Memberships:* Parents Without Partners, Queens Chapter, No 16; Union, District Concil 37, AFSCME. *Honours:* New York State Regents Scholarship, Morris High School; Senior High School Graduation Medals for: Highest Ranking Graduate, French, Journalis; Junior High School Commencement Medals for: Highest Ranking Graduate, Journalism and All-round Scholarship, Service and Achievement; Bible recitation at graduation exercises; Voted, Girl Most Likely to Succeed, Morris High School Senior Class.Dean's Honours List, Brooklyn College. *Hobbies:* Photography; Essays; Travel. *Address:* 65-10 Parsons Boulevard, Apartment 1D, Fresh Meadows, New York, NY 11365, USA.

WOLF-DEVINE Celia, b. 14 Sept. 1942, Philadelphia, Pennsylvania, USA. Professor; Freelance Writer. m. Philip Devine, 28 June 1986. *Education:* BA, Smith College, 1964; MA 1971, PhD 1984, University of Wisconsin. *Appointments:* Various universities & colleges including: Simmons College; Tufts University; College of St Benedict, St John's University, 1985-86; St Cloud State University, 1986-87; Stonehill College, 1987-. *Publications:* Abortion & the Feminine Voice; More Abortion and Feminine Voice, Public Affairs Quarterly July 1989; An Inequity in Affirmative Action (in Journal of Applied Philosophy), 1988; From New Age Christianity to the Catholic Church (in New Catholics, ed. O'Neil); Various contributions, Review of Metaphysics, New Oxford Review, National Catholic Register, including series of articles on need for community in the Catholic Church. *Honours:* Merit scholarship, 1959-60; Research grants, Stonehill College, 1988, 1989. Monograph, Descartes' Theory of Vision. Music. *Address:* Philosophy Department, Stonehill College, North Easton, Massachusetts 02401, USA.

WOLFE Terri Linn, b. 13 June 1954, Flint, Michigan, USA. Marketing Engineer; Mass Spectrometry; Forensic Scientist. m. Thomas J Richards, PhD, 21 May 1989. *Education:* BSc, Human Medicine, Michigan State University, 1979; MBA, University of Notre Dame, 1990. *Appointments:* Michigan State Police, 1980-83; Gamma Biologicals, 1983-86; Amtec Diagnostics International, 1985-86; Genetic Systems (Bristol-Myers), 1986-88; Finnigan Corporation, 1988-. *Creative works:* Lectures given in the areas of Blood transfusion and Immunohematology; Forensic Serology, Toxicology and Expert Witness Testimony. *Memberships:* American Academy of Forensic Sciences; American Association of Blood Banks; American Chemical Society; American Society for Clinical Pathologists; Illinois Association of Blood Banks; Chicagoland Blood Bank Society. *Honour:* ASCP (MT and SBB) Specialist, Blood Banking, 1985. *Hobbies:* Gourmet cooking; Personal computing; Jazz bands, symphonies; Clarinet, woodwinds; Landscape, architecture; Gardening; Clothing design and sewing. *Address:* 1011 West Stratford Drive, Peoria, Illinois 61614, USA.

WOLHUTER Rowena Victoria, b. Johannesburg, South Africa. Managing Director. m. (1) 1 son, 2 daughters. (2) 1 Nov. 1983. *Appointments:* Senior Executive, RV Food Enterprises cc; Director, Rowena & Brian Cosmetics (Pty) Ltd, 1983; Partner, B & R Properties, 1987; Director, IPM, 1972-82. *Memberships:* Wanderers Club; SA CCL for the Aged; Johannesburg Chamber of Commerce. *Honours:* Small Business Woman of the Year, Sarie/Old Mutal, 1987; Lifegro Top 10 Business women of the Year, Lifegro/Volkskas, 1986; Finalist in the Hill Samuel R100 000 Award, 1986; Invited to be one of the first Lady Menmbers, Fellowship of Excellence, Fedics Organisation, 1988. *Hobbies:* Game farming; Reading; Interior decorating. *Address:* P O Box 2441, Randburg 2125, South Africa.

WOLPE Claire Fox, b. 24 June 1909, New York, USA. Therapist. m. Arthur Wolpe, 25 Dec. 1932, deceased, 2 daughters. *Education:* BA, Mills College, 1930; MA, 1936, MSW, 1965, University of Southern California; PhD, Marquette University, 1970. *Appointments:* University Religious Conference, 1932; Los Angeles County Hospital, 1934-38; Gateways Mental Health Center, 1962-63; Executive Director, Bay Cities Hospital, 1965-68; Marriage Guidance Institute, 1968-70; Private Practice, 1970-88. *Publications:* articles in professional journals. *Memberships:* National association of Social Workers, Boad; LA Jewish FederationCouncil, Board; many other professional organisations. *Honours:* Los Angeles Times Woman of the Year, 1950; Conference Jewish Women's Organisation Award, 1950. *Hobbies:* Painting; Travel; Walking. *Address:* 234 So Orange Drive, Los Angeles, CA 90036, USA.

WOLRIGE GORDON Anne Marie, b. 16 Oct. 1936, London, England. Writer; Gardener; Magistrate. m. Patrick Wolrige Gordon, 2 June 1962, 1 son, 2 daughters. *Education:* Ancaster Gate, 1946-49; Ancaster House, 1949-54. *Publications:* Peter Howard Life & Letters; Dame Flora; Play, Blindsight. *Honour:* JP, 1986. *Hobbies:* Gardening; Music; Walking; Cooking; Law; Education; Faith. *Address:* Ythan Lodge, Newburgh, Ellon, Aberdeenshire AB4 0AD, Scotland.

WOMACK Barbara Jean, b. 14 Jan. 1944, Birmingham, Alabama, USA. Associate Real Estate Broker; Homemaker. m. Henry O Womack, 5 Jan. 1974. 2 sons, 1 daughter. *Education:* Diploma, Southern Business University, 1962; Certificate, Fortune Sales Seminar, 1973; Real Estate Sales, Clayton Junior College, 1973; Real Estate Brokerage, Real Estate Academy, 1976; Certificate, Lotus 1-2-3, Clayton State College, 1988. *Appointments:* Typist, J R Wilson Company, 1961-64; Secretary, American Moistening Corporation, 1965-66; Executive Secretary/Office Manager, Republic National Life Insurance, 1966-70; Sales Associate, Washburn Realty, 1972-75; Sales Associate, Griswold Realty, 1975-76; Corporate Secretary/Treasurer: Capitol City Realty Inc, 1976-; Womack Contractors Inc, 1983-; Womack Builders Inc, 1983-; Corporate President/Owner, Simply Beautiful Inc, 1985-89; Corporate Secretary/Treasurer, Womack Development Inc, 1980-. *Creative work:* Secretarial Handbook for Republic National Life Insurance Field Offices, 1970. *Memberships:* American Society of Professional and Executive Women; Arts Clayton Inc; National Association of Women in Construction; Chamber of Commerce. *Honours:* Received Cap and Chevron 1971, Chevron 1972, 1973, 1974, Clayton General Hospital Auxiliary; Outstanding Young Women of Clayton County, 1972. *Hobbies:* Oil painting; Flower arrangements; Interior designs; Walking and travelling abroad. *Address:* 7715 Ciboney Drive, Jonesboro, Georgia 30236, USA.

WONG Lisa Sueng, b. 13 Oct. 1950, Los Angeles, California, USA. Designer; Architect. *Education:* AB Architecture 1973, MArch 1980, University of California, Berkeley; Licensed Architect, California, 1987. *Creative work includes:* Designer & Architect for: Wong House & Studio, Stockton, CA, 1980-89; Eaton Medical Centre, Tracy, CA, 1988; Tracy Store, 1988; Santos Avenue Elementary School, Ripon, CA, 1989; Interiors, Stockton Radiology, 1989; Wok Express & Sherwood Mall, Stockton, CA, 1990-. Competition entries: Class of 1954 Pedestrian Gate, UCB, 1987; Stephen Hannah Corporation Architectural Competition, Dream House, 1989. *Memberships:* American Institute of Architects; Sierra Valley Chapter, AIA. *Hobbies include:* Art; Music; Ballet; Film; Theatre; Travel, lived & worked in London (UK) 3 years 1974-77, also visited Europe & Japan. *Address:* 704 North Stockton Street, Stockton, California 95203, USA.

WOOD Harriett Faith, b. 27 Dec. 1927, Linden, New Jersey, USA. Poet; Teacher; Lecturer; Writer. m. William Wood, 14 Feb. 1961, div. 1970, 1 daughter. *Education:* AA, Applied Art, Fashion Institute, 1955; BA, English Literature, Sierra University, 1987. *Appointments:*

Poetry Writing Workshops, 1980-; Instructor in Prose and Poetry, Santa Monica College, Santa Monica, California, 1984-; Founder, The World Mother Press, 1988. *Publications:* Poetry: The Mermaid's Farewell; The Return; The Lion Cub (sonnet); Poems in anthologies: Letter to Colette; Letter to Masako; Talk of Masako; After Masako; Stories: Bring Your Heart Next Thursday; In a Cave of Trees; Critical essays on poetry, Beverly Hills Times; Article on poetry, The Movement Newspaper; Poets in Profile, interview/poetry reading, KCET Los Angeles Public Broadcasting service; Poetry of Walt Whitman, guest lecture, University of California. *Memberships:* Los Angeles Arts Council; Associated Writing Programs; California Poets in the Schools. *Honour:* Fellowship, MacDowell Colony, Peterborough, New Hampshire, 1959-60. *Hobbies:* Dancing; Hiking. *Address:* 1038 Lake Street, Venice, CA 90291, USA.

WOOD Joanna Harriet, b. 3 July 1954, Henley-on-Thames, England. Interior Design Consultant. m. Edward Orlando Charles Wood (Honourable), 19 Dec. 1977, 1 daughter. *Appointments:* Founder, Joanna Trading interior design consultancy, 1979-; Retail shops, Joanna Wood Ltd, 1985-. *Memberships:* International Society of Interior Designers; Interior Decorators and Designers Association. *Hobbies:* Art; Literature; Hunting; Skiing. *Address:* 33 Eaton Terrace, London SW1, England.

WOOD Jodine Janish, b. 12 Dec. 1929, Southbend, Indiana, USA. Clinical Director, Broderick & Wood; Clinical Psychologist. m. Don C Wood, 14 Feb. 1952. 2 sons, 1 daughter. *Education:* BS, Mills College, 1951; MA, California Study Center, 1982; MFCC License No 18139, 1982; PhD, Clinical Psychology, Cambridge Graduate School, 1987. *Appointments:* Office Manager Dental office, 1959-83; USC Dental School Clinician, 1974; Lecturer/Dental Practice Management, Israel, Germany, Peru, New Zealand, Egypt; Director for Women's Colleges in Southern California, 1968-82; Therapist, Guidance Center, 1980-82; Family Service of Long Beach, 1981-; Family Center, 1981-; Director, Broderick, Wood and Associates, 1983-. *Creative Works:* Presenter Professional Workshop, California Family Study Center, 1982; Presenter, Professional paper, AMCAP, 1982; Presenter, International Conference in Russia, 1985. *Memberships:* AAMFT; SCAMFT; Association of Mormon Counselors & Psychoterapists (AMCAP). *Honours:* Approved Supervisor certification Status, AAMFT, 1987. *Address:* 5252 Orange Avenue, Suite 110, Cypress, California 90630, USA.

WOOD Judith Louise Barlow, b. 2 June 1940, Wilkes County, North Carolina, USA. Librarian; Assistant Professor. m. Robert Emerson Wood, 2 June 1964. *Education:* BS, Wake Forest College, 1962; MSLS 1975, PhD 1983, Case Western Reserve University (CWRU). *Appointments:* Medical Bibliographer 1975-78, Research Assistant 1979-81, CWRU; Associate Researcher, Tantalus Library Management Consultants, 1981-83; Assistant Professor, School of Information & Library Science, University of North Carolina (UNC), 1983-. *Publications:* Co-author, Consolidation of Information: Handbook on Evaluation, Restructuring & Repackaging Scientific & Technical Information; Articles, Professional Journals, Growth of Scholarship 1987, Correspondence of Document File Structure to Discipline Structure 1988. *Memberships:* Director, North Carolina Special Libraries Association; President, Secretary, Chapel Hill Toastmasters; American Association of University Professors; American Library Association; American Society for Information Science; Association for Library & Information Science Education; Medical Library Association. *Honours:* Co-investigator, National Science Foundation Grant, 1987-89; University Research Council Grant, 1986-87; Junior Faculty Development Award, 1986; 4.0 grade average, CWRU, 1976-83; Medical Technology Scholarship, 1961-62; Hankins Scholarship, Tri-Beta, 1958-61. *Hobbies:* Cycling; Gardening; Recycling & Conservation of Natural Resources; Reading; Public Speaking. *Address:* School of Information & Library Science, CB

3360, 100 Manning Hall, University of North Carolina, Chapel Hill, NC 27599, USA.

WOOD Kathleen Oliver, b. 17 Sept. 1921, New York, USA. Writer; Editor; Teacher; Radio Show Hostess. m. John Thornton Wood, 1941, divorced 1947, (2) Clifford Emanuel Huff, 1948, divorced 1955, 1 son, 2 daughters. *Education:* Swarthmore College, 1938-39; Antioch College, 1940-41; University of New Mexico, 1949; Cleveland College, 1960-61. *Appointments:* Announcer, DJ, WCLV 1968-69; Show Hostess, WERE, 1971-72; Writer, Editor, Highlights, University Circle, 1971-81; Weekly Radio Show, CRRS, 1979-; Tutor, Vocational Information Programme; Freelance Writer, Editor, 1980-; Publicity Specialist, AARP Tax-Aide Program, NE Ohio, 1987-88; Exec. Secretary Cleveland Cultural Garden Federation, 1988-. *Publications:* Writer, Jefferson Encyclopedia; Author, Greenwood, 1967; Editor-Publisher, Frog in the Milk Pan, 1963; Editor, Office Gal Magazine, 1962-63, Graffiti Magazine, 1967, Smorgasbrain Magazine, 1968-. *Memberships:* Zonta International, Past Director; Mensa; IABC; PRSA; AMMPE; VP for US; Cultural Garden Federation; Advertising Women of Cleveland, etc. *Hobbies:* Theatre; Esperanto; etc. *Address:* PO Box 5612, Cleveland, OH 44101, USA.

WOOD Kathleen Ringwood Doran, b. 27 June 1946, Morristown, New Jersey, USA. Actress; Lecturer; Talkshow Host; DJ. m. 25 Jan. 1969, divorced 1977, 1 son. *Education:* BS, West Chester University, 1975; MA, Speech Communication, Universiy of Houston, 1982. *Appointments:* Lecturer, Speech & Communications, University of Houston, 1986-; Lecturer, Alvin Community College, 1986-87. *Publications:* Creator, Editor, Vocare, 1987-; Creator, Producer, Host, Access, Cable TV, 1983-85. *Memberships Include:* Women in Cable, Founding Member, Publicity Chair, Newsletter Editor, Treasurer; Theatre Network of Houston, Founding Member; Pasadena Little Theatre; etc. *Honours:* Honorary Deputy Sheriff, Harris County, Texas, 1981; Certificates of Recognition: American Cancer Association, American Heart Association, US Marine Corps, Boy Scouts of America, etc, 1982-85. *Hobbies:* Announcing; MC; Performing.

WOOD Larry (Mary Laird), b. Sandpoint, Idaho, USA. Journalist; University Educator; Environmental Consultant; Author. 1 son, 2 daughters. *Education:* BA magna cum laude, University of Washington, Seattle, 1938; MA 1940; Postgraduate Stanford University, 1941-42; University of California, Berkeley, 1943-44; Certificate in Photography, 1971; postgraduate Journalism, University of Wisconsim, 1971-72; University of Minnesota, 1971- 72, University of Georgia, 1972-73; Postgraduate Art, Architecture and Marine Biology, University of California, Santa Cruz, 1974-76, 1977-80, Stanford University, 1979-80. *Appointments include:* By-line columnist Oakland (Calif) Tribune, San Francisco Chronicle, 1946-62; Feature writer, Western region Christian Science Monitor, CSM Radio Syndicate and Internat. News, 1973-; Register and Tribune Syndicate, Des Moines, 1975-; also Times' Mirror Syndicate, CHEVRON USA, Calif. Todaty Magazine; Contributing editor: Travelday magazine, 1976-; No. Calif. Fashion Showcase, Dallas; Bus. Ins. Crain Communications, Los Angeles; Spokane magazine; Photographer/feature writer Scholastic Publications, 1974-; Feature writer: Donnelley Publs., Oak Brook, Illinois; Meridian Publs., Ogden, Utah; Fawcett Boating Books, 1976-; Dir. public relations No Calif. Assn. Phi Beta Kappa, 1969-; Cons., feature writer Met. Transp. Commn. No Calif. 1970-; Contributing editor, Fodor Travel Guides, 1981-, Principles of Science, 1982, etc. *Publications include:* Co- author: Fodor's San Francisco, Fodor's California; California (State publ), 1986; syndicated photographer, feature writer Linguapress, English lang. mags. Guest numerous spl. sci press trips, also others. Numerous articles to magazines; Author, Natural Resources, USA (Crown Books, N.Y.), 1988; Award winning Author of Social Issues Resures, Earth Sciences, 1988. *Memberships* *include:* Sec. Jr Center of Arts, Oakland, 1952- ; Trustee, Calif. State Parks Found., 1976-; Advisory Board, KRON-TV, National NBC on Programming, 1986-; Lifetime membership, University of Washington Alumni Association; University of California, Berkeley Alumni Association; Stanford University Alumni Association; Charter member, Ocean Sciences Alumni Association; Communications Alumni Assoc. University of Washington, etc.; Author for Wolters-Noordhoff-Longman English Language Texts, (Great Britain, The Netherlands, 1988-.) *Honours include:* Recipient numerous honours and awards including: Citations: US Forest Service, 1975, Nat. Park Service, 1976, Oakland Mus. Assn. 1978-79, 1981, Port Dirs. Assn. 1979; Named Calif. Woman of Achievement, 1979, 1980, 1981; Citation BC Totem Pole series, 1982-; Calif. Underwater Parks features, 1982; honoured by Oakland C of C, San Francisco C of C, Chevron USA for work on Oakland..The Other City on the Bay, 1983; Plaque for hydrofoil coverage from missile ship squadron, Key West, 1983; Named to University Wash/Broadway High Hall of Fame, Seattle, 1984; Collected works selected for Bell & Howell microfilm libraries worldwide, also special collection in Oakland Public Library, U. Waseback; Columbia: Alaska's Receding Glacier - rated one of USA's top science articles for 1988. *Hobbies:* Riding; Skiing; Architecture especially historic buildings of American West. *Address:* 6161 Castle Drive, Oakland, California 94611, USA.

WOOD Laura Lee, b. 24 May 1951, Lexington, Kentucky, USA. Nursing Manager; Freelance Writer. *Education:* Diploma, Kentucky Baptist Hospital School of Nursing, 1972; BA Nursing course, Bellarmine College, Louisville, current. *Appointments:* Transitional Care Manager 1978-81, Coronary Care Manager 1981-, Clinical Coordinator, Total Artificial Heart Project 1984-87, Highland Baptist Hospital, Louisville. *Publications include:* Numerous booklets & abstracts; Articles, Nursing Care of the Artificial Heart Patient 1987, Heart to Heart 1988; Book chapter, Post-Op Care of the Patient with an Artificial Heart. *Memberships:* International Affairs Committee, American Association of Critical Care Nurses (AACCN); Kentucky & Greater Louisville Heart Associations. *Honour:* Speaker, AACCN National Teaching Institute. *Hobbies:* Flying; Sky diving; Scuba diving; Golf; Reading; Cats (3). *Address:* c/o Humana Hospital, 1 Audubon Plaza, Louisville, Kentucky 40201, USA.

WOOD Lynette Eva, b. 11 Jan. 1951, Sydney, Australia. Marketing. m. Maxwell John Berghouse, 8 Sept. 1979, 1 son, 1 daughter. *Education:* MA, University of Sydney, 1975; MBA, University of New South Wales, 1984; AGSM. *Appointments:* Director, Sales & Marketing, American Express Int. Inc., 1975-81; Marketing Division Head, Myers Ltd., 1981-83; Marketing Director, Citibank Ltd., 1983-85; Associate Director, Schroders Aust. Ltd., 1985-; Director, Schroders Aust. Property Management Limited. *Memberships:* Director, Unit Trust Association of Australia; Director, AGSM Alumni Association. *Hobbies:* Reading; Victorian House Restoration; Tennis; Photography. *Address:* Schroders Aust. Ltd., 31st Floor, Grosvenor Place, 225 George Street, Sydney 2000, Australia.

WOOD Marguerite Noreen, b. 27 Sept. 1923, Ipswich, Suffolk, England. Writer. m. Douglas James Wood, 12 Apr. 1947. 1 son, 1 daughter. *Education:* Chartered Physiotherapist, MCSP, 1944; BA Hons Open University, 1982. *Appointments:* NHS Hospitals, 1944-58; Justice of the Peace, 1968-; Freelance poet. *Publications:* Stone of Vision, 1964; Windows Are Not Enough, 1971; Crack Me The Shell, 1975; A Line Drawn In Water, 1980; Jeanne La Pucelle, a song cycle, 1987. *Memberships:* The Poetry Society, UK; The Suffolk Poetry Society; The Magistrates' Association. *Honours:* Various poetry prizes. *Hobbies:* Painting; History. Address: Smallgains House, Castle Road, Hadleigh, Ipswich, Suffolk IP7 6JH, England.

WOODARD Susan Marie Zeits, b. 22 Jan. 1952,

Detroit, Michigan, USA. Registered Nurse; Businesswoman. m. Johnzelle Woodard, 7 Dec. 1973, 1 son. *Education:* Manatee Junior College, 2 years; LPN, Ben Hill Technical Vocational School, Eastman, Georgia, 1978; ADN, Middle Georgia College, 1980; BSN in progress. *Appointments include:* Dodge County Hospital, 1980-83; Bleckly County Hospital, 1983-84; Co-owner, manager, now president, S&J Woodard & Son Inc (store, mobile home repairs removals & rentals, radio parts), 1984-; CCU/ICU Charge nurse, 3 Rivers Hospital, 1987- ; Independent Nursing Registry, 1987-. *Creative work includes:* Complete restructure & editing, Policy & Procedure Manual (labour & delivery, postpartum, & nurseries), Obstetrics Department, Dodge County Hospital, 1982; Various quality assurance studies, Dodge County Hospital, 1980-83. *Honours:* White M Club, scholastic achievement, 1968; Several 1st & 2nd place awards, art work, Georgia State Fair, 1974-80; Graduated 1st in class, nursing, Middle Georgia College, 1980. *Hobbies:* Oil painting, landscapes; Craft work; Swimming. *Address:* Route 6, Box 525, Eastman, Georgia 31023, USA.

WOODFORD Cecile, b. 5 Feb. 1913, Eastbourne, Sussex, England. Author; Journalist. m. David Woodford, 19 Nov. 1938, deceased 1970, 1 son, 1 daughter. *Appointments:* Founder, Crown Quality Books, 1964-. *Publications:* A Sip from any Goblet; Sussex Ways & Byways; Jane Anne's Story Book; Yuletide Festival; Portrait of Sussex, 4 editions, 1972; Stir the Witches Cauldron; By the Crown Divided; In the High Woods; Caroline's Kingdom; The Art of Inning; A Devil in Paradise; History Notebook, etc. *Memberships:* Society of Authors; Civic Society of Eastbourne, Secretary 1967-72; Member, Mass-Observation Team, Sussex University. *Honours:* Art Awards, 1924- 30. *Hobbies Include:* Archaeological Digs; Research into History of Sussex. *Address:* 19 Carmen Court, Willingdon, Eastbourne, Sussex BN20 9NP, England.

WOODFORD Peggy Elizabeth Lainé, b. 19 Sep. 1937, Shillong, Assam, India. Writer. m. Walter Stafford Aylen, 1 Apr. 1968, 3 daughters. *Education:* St Anne's College, Oxford, England, 1956-59; MA(Hons) Oxon, English. *Appointments:* Research Assistant, BBC TV, London, England, 1962-63; Senior Tutor, Padworth College, Reading, Berkshire, 1965-68. *Publications:* Abraham's Legacy, 1963; Mozart, Illustrated Biography, 1977, 1984; Schubert, Illustrated Biography, 1978, 1984; Rise of the Raj, Illustrated history of the growth of trade in British India, 1600-1859, 1978; Teenage novels: Please Don't Go, 1972, Paperback Edition, 1987; Backwater War, 1975; See You Tomorrow, 1979; The Girl With A Voice, 1981; Love Me, Love Rome, 1984; Monster in Our Midst, 1988; Collections of short stories: The Real Thing, 1977; You Can't Keep Out The Darkness, 1980; Misfits, 1984; In the Beginning, verse libretto of Jazz Oratorio (music Annette Batam), 1st performance 1976; Hyenas in Petticoats, dramatic dialogue, performed 1981. *Honours:* Italian Government Research Scholarship, Rome, 1959-60. *Address:* c/o Murray Pollinger, 222 Old Brompton Road, London SW5 0BZ, England.

WOODRUFF Marian, m. 1952, separated 1977, 3 sons, 1 daughter. *Education:* Apprenticed, Leather Craft Shop, Florence, Italy; Rhode Island School of Design; Smith College. *Appointments:* Guide, Metropolitan Museum of Art, 1945-46; Lecturer, Childrens Programme, Museum of Art, Rhode Island School of Design, 1946-51; Programme Dirctor, Nashua Arts & Science Centre, 1968-69; Adjunct Instructor, Fine Arts White Pines College, 1979-81, 1986; Director, Education, Currier Gallery of Art, 1970-. *Memberships Include:* Nashua Public Library; Grants Reviewer, Institute of Museum Services, Washington, 1985, 1987; League of New Hampshire Craftsmen. *Address:* 587 Maple Street, Manchester, NH 03104, USA.

WOODS Dorothy Mae, b. 29 Mar. 1942, Hermanville, Mississippi, USA. Owner of boutique. divorced. 5 sons, 5 daughters. *Education:* AA, Human Behaviour, University of Laverne, 1985; Diploma,

Rhema Bible Institute, 1986; BA, Sociology, Cal State, LA, 1989; Diploma, State of Calif Word Processing; Diploma, State of Calif Child Development. *Appointments:* President, From Prison to Peace Inc, 1986; Manager, Da'thy Discount Boutique, 1987-. *Membership:* NAACP. *Hobby:* Tennis. 2990 N Glenrose Ave, Altadena, CA 91001, USA.

WOODS Joan Shirley LeSueur, b. 5 Sept. 1932, Phoenix, Arizona, USA. Piano Consultant; Writer; Clinician. m. Dr Kenneth Ray Woods, 21 Mar. 1952. 1 son, 3 daughters. *Education:* Brigham Young Univ; Arizona State Univ; Columbia Univ Graduate School, NYC, 1970-73; York Univ, York, England, 1971; Mozarteum, Salzburg, Austria, 1971; Vienna Cultural Center, Vienna, 1973; Texas Christian University, Ft Worth, Texas, USA, 1974-76; Dale Carnegie Course, 1973; PhD, 1973. *Appointments:* Piano Faculty, Northern Arizona Univ, Flagstaff; Piano Pedagogy Consultant, Instructor, Tempe, Phx AZ Public Schools; National Piano Foundation Clinician, Arizona; Instructed Broadway Show Classes, NYC, 1960-67; Conductor, Piano Ensembkes, 1970-89; Teacher of Advanced Piano, Theory and Composition, NYC and AZ, 1952-89; Teacher of Writing Seminars; Employed by film star Michael Landon, 1986-88; Adjudicator for contests and student performances, 1960-89; Performer and teacher of radio, TV artists, 1948-89. *Creative works:* Children's Book, 1964; Jazz Study Program for 12 Levels, 1985-88; Consultant, The Song Shoppe Books, 1986; Script & Music Consultant, The Celebrity Series, teleplay, 1986; Songs, NYC productions, 1964-88; TV Teleplays, 1988; Contributor to numerous magazines; Numerous recordings. *Memberships include:* Phx Piano Teachers Association, 1968-86; Pres, AZ State Music Teachers Association, Central District, 1985-87. *Honours include:* TV, Radio & Composition Contest Awards. *Hobbies:* Reading; Theatre; Travel. *Address:* 1401 West Pepper Place, Mesa, AZ 85201, USA.

WOODS Sandra K, b. 11 Oct. 1944, Loveland, USA. Company Vice President. m. Gary A Woods, 11 June 1967, 1 son, 1 daughter. *Education:* BA, 1966, MA, 967, University of Colorado. *Appointments:* US Civil Service Commission, 1967; Department of Health Education & Welfare, 1968-69; Dept. Housing & Urban Development, 1970-80; Director, Programme Analysis, Regional Director, Community Planning & Development; Vice President, Corporate Real Estate, Adolph Coors Co. *Memberships Include:* Various professional organisations. *Honours:* Phi Beta Kappa; Leadership Denver, 1976; Outstanding Young Women in America, 1978; White House President's Exchange Programme, 1980; Phi Alpha, 1987. *Hobbies:* Skiing; Tennis; Travel. *Address:* Corporate Real Estate Dept. RR856, Adolph Coors Company, Golden, CO 80401, USA.

WOODS Willie G., b. 3 Nov. 1943, Yazoo City, Mississippi, USA. University Educator/Administrator. *Education:* BA, Education, Shaw University, 1965; MEd, Duke University, 1968; PhD work, Indiana University of Pennsylvania. *Appointments include:* Instructor to Associate Professor, 1969-82, Coordinator, Basic Studies, 1978-83, Professor, English & Education, 1982-, Director, Academic Foundations Program, 1983-87, Assistant Dean, 1987-, Harrisburg Area Community College, Harrisburg, Pennsylvania. *Publications:* Handbook for Tutors, 1977. *Memberships include:* Board, Charter Member, Past President, other past offices, Pennsylvania Association of Developmental Educators; PA Act 101 Western Region Directors Council (Past Chair/Vice-Chair); Representative Council, Harrisburg Coordinator, Past Secretary/ Associate Editor, PA Black Conference on Higher Education; Council on Black American Affairs, American Association of Community & Junior Colleges; National Council of Teachers of English; PA Department of Education Act 101 Planning Council, 1986-88; Secretary, Education Committee Chair, Board of Advisors, Youth Urban Services, Harrisburg YMCA; Board, Alternative Rehabilitation Communities Inc; Past Treasurer, National Political Congress of Black Women, Greater Harrisburg Area; National Association for the Advancement of Colored People; Past Executive Committee, Epsilon Sigma Omega, Alpha Kappa Alpha. *Honours include:* Member, Alpha Kappa Mu; PA Black Conference on Higher Education Service Awards, 1980, 1982; Outstanding Community Service Award, Epsilon Sigma Omega, Alpha Kappa Alpha, 1983; Volunteer of the Year Award, Greater Harrisburg Area YMCA, 1983; Member, Pennsylvania Invitational Forum, American Council on Education's National Identification Program for Women in Higher Education Administration, 1983; Award for Exemplary Support & Dedication to Educational Development of Minority Students, 1984, Certificate of Recognition, 1986, HACC Black Student Union; Tribute, HACC Minority Caucus, 1989; *Hobbies:* Travel; Bowling; Listening to Music; Reading; Sewing. *Address:* Harrisburg Area Community College, 3300 Cameron Street Road, Harrisburg, PA 17110, USA.

WOODWARD Deborah Boros, b. 13 May 1950, Cleveland, Ohio, USA. Writer; Editor. m. Arthur Quincy Woodward, 6 May 1973, 1 son. *Education:* BA, English, University of Michigan, 1972. *Appointments:* Editor, Richmond Magazine, 1978-79; Freelance Writer Editor, 1979-85; Rudisill Inc., Film Production Co., 1985-86; Freelance Writer, Editor, 1986-. *Publications:* The Commonwealth of Women (finalist, American Film Festival), 1984; articles in: Boston Globe; Pittsburgh Press; Miami Herald; Virginia Business; Style Weekly; Commonwealth. *Hobbies:* Dancing; Embroidery; Renovating Victorian Homes. *Address:* 2039 West Grace Street, Richmond, VA 23220, USA.

WOOLDRIDGE Patrice Marie, b. 6 Mar. 1954, Chicago, Illinois, USA. Marketing professional. m. Patrick J Wooldridge, 27 June 1981. *Education:* AS, Moraine Valley College, 1974; BA 1976, MA 1977, Govs State University; MBA, Loyola University, Chicago, 1983. *Appointments:* Community Prof, Govs State University, Illinois, 1977-78; Counselor, Social Worker, Bloom Twp High School, Illinois, 1977-78; Market Analyst, Dr Scholl Footcare, Chicago, 1978-79; Supr Consumer Research Unocal Schaumburg, Illinois, 1979-84; Group research dir, Tatham-Laird & Kudner, Chicago, 1984-87; Vice President, Associate Director, Strategic Planning & Research, Bayer Bess Vanderwarker, Chicago, 1987-; Instr dancing, 1969-; T'ai Chi the Sch of T'ai Chi Chuan, New York City, 1986-; Arica the Arica Inst, New York City, 1978-; Performer the Anawim Players, Chicago, 1985-; Treasurer, Karma Thegsum Choling, Chicago, 1987; Board of Directors, Illustrated Theatre Co, Chicago, 1987; Adv Bd, N W Suburban Boy Scouts, Schaumburg, 1984. *Membership:* American Marketing Association. *Address:* 2 East Oak, Apt No 1110, Chicago, IL 60611, USA.

WOOLF Nancy Jean, b. 27 July 1954, Fort Sill, Oklahoma, USA. Research Psychologist. m. Larry L Butcher, 24 Dec. 1983. 1 son, 1 daughter. *Education:* BS Psychobiology 1978, PhD Neuroscience 1983, UCLA, Los Angeles. *Appointment:* Assistant Research Psychologist, UCLA, Los Angeles, 1984- *Publications:* Author of numerous articles to professional journals. *Memberships:* Society for Neuroscience; New York Academy of Science; Association of Academic Women. *Honours:* Women of Distinction, College of the Desert, Palm Desert, California, 1976; Graduate Women of the Year, Association of Academic Women, UCLA, 1983; ARCS Scholar, 1980-82; Mental Health Training Program Trainee, 1982-83; Travel Grant, Graduate Division, UCLA, 1979; Research Grant, Chancellor's Patent Fund, UCLA, 1983. *Address:* Dept of Psychology, University of California, Los Angeles, CA 90024, USA.

WOOLNOUGH Hilda Mary, b. 11 Feb. 1934, Northampton, England. Artist. m. Reshard Gool (dec. 1989), 2 sons, 1 daughter. *Education:* NDD, Painting, Chelsea School of Art, London, 1955; MFA, Experimental Etching, University of Guanajuato, Mexico, 1966. Postgraduate: Metal techniques, Central School of Art, London 1966-67, Nova Scotia College of Art, Canada 1971. *Appointments:* Instructor, etching, San Miguel de Allende Institute, 1965-66; Established

Etching & Lithography Department, Jamaica School of Art, Kingston, West Indies, 1966-69; Design Consultant, RDC, 1970- 71; Sessional Lecturer, Fine Arts, University of Prince Edward Island, Canada, 1970-78; Visiting artist, Canterbury College of Art, UK, 1987. *Creative works:* Work in collections of: Canada Council Art Bank; Art Galleries, Ontario, New Brunswick, Nova Scotia; University Art Galleries, McMaster, Carleton, St Mary's; Canadian Broadcasting Company; Air Canada; Shell & Esso Corporations; Jutland Museum, Visby, Sweden; Jamaica Art Gallery. *Honours:* Graphics scholarship, University of Guanajuato, 1965; Awards, Canada Council, Arts Council; Joint recipient with R. Gool, PEI Arts Council Award for Distinguished Services, 1989; Featured, various films. *Hobbies:* Gardening; Cooking; Music; Swimming. *Address:* RR 4, Breadalbane, Prince Edward Island, Canada C0A 1E0.

WOOLSEY Suzanne Haley,. b. 27 Dec. 1941, San Francisco, California, USA. Management Consultant; Psychologist. m. R James Woolsey, 15 Aug. 1965. 3 sons. *Education:* BA, with distinction, Phi Beta Kappa, Stanford University, 1963; MA 1965, PhD 1970, Harvard University. *Appointments:* Associate Professor Psychology, Federal City College, 1968-70; Planning & Evaluation, office of Secretary of HEW, 1970-75; The Urban Institute, 1975-76; Associate Director, Office of Management and Budget, 1976- 80; Partner, Coopers & Lybrand, 1980-. *Publications:* Numerous editorial and op-ed pieces to The Washington Post; Pied Piper Politics and the Child-Care Debate, 1975-76. *Memberships:* Humanities & Sciences Council, Stanford University; Visiting Committee, Duke University Institute for Policy Science; Chair, TIAA-CREF Nominating Committee for Boards of Trustees; National Advisory Board, Private Sector Council; Principal, Center for Ezxcellence to Government. *Honour:* Tribute to Women in International Industry, National YWCA. *Hobbies:* Sailing; Skiing; Snorkeling; Scuba diving. *Address:* 1800 M Street NW, Washington, DC 20036, USA.

WOOLSTON-CATLIN Marian, b. 20 Jan. 1931, Seattle, Washington, USA. Physician. m. Randolph Catlin, 5 July 1959, 1 son, 2 daughters. *Education:* BA cum laude, Vassar College, 1951; MD, Harvard Medical School, 1955; Intern, residents' training, Boston, 1956-59. *Appointments:* Teaching fellow, psychiatry, Harvard & Tufts Universities, 1957-59; Fellow, 1975-78, instructor 1978-82, child psychiatry, Harvard (at Massachusetts Mental Health Centre (MMHC), & Gaebler Children's Unit, Waltham); Private practice. *Creative works include:* Co-founder, Harry C. Solomon Award (MMHC), 1959-. *Memberships include:* American Psychiatric Association; American Academy of Child & Adolescent Psychiatry; Membership chairman, New England Council for Child Psychiatry; American Medical Association; Massachusetts Medical Society; Boards, various community organisations & services. *Honours:* Speaker, Rhodes House Conference, Women in the Professions, 1961; Ames Cup, Hunnewell Memorial Garden, Womens Exhibition Committee, Massachusetts Horticultural Society, 1975; Commonwealth fellow, child psychiatry, Gaebler Children's Unit, 1975-78. *Hobbies:* Landscape design; Sculpture. *Address:* 314 North Street, Medfield, Massachusetts 02052, USA.

WOOTTON OF ABINGER Baroness (Barbara Frances), b. 1897, Cambridge, England. m. (1) John Wesley Wootton, 1917, deceased 1917. (2) George Percival Wright, 1935, deceased 1964. *Education:* Girton College, Cambridge (MA Cantab). *Appointments:* Director of Studies and Lecturer in Economics, Girton College, 1920-22; Research Officer, Trades Union Congress and Labour Party Joint Research Department, 1922-26; Principal, Morley College for Working Men and Women, 1926-27; Director of Studies for Tutorial Classes, University of London, 1927-44; Professor of Social Studies, University of London, 1948-52; Nuffield Research Fellow, Bedford College, University of London, 1952-57; Governor of the BBC, 1950-56; Deputy-Speaker, House of Lords, 1967-. *Publications:* (As Barbara Wootton): Twos and Threes, 1933; Plan or No

Plan, 1934; London's Burning, 1936; Lament for Economics, 1938; End Social Inequality, 1941; Freedom Under Planning, 1945; Testament for Social Science, 1950; The Social Foundations of Wage Policy, 1955; Social Science and Social Pathology, 1959; Crime and the Criminal Law, 1964; In a World I Never Made, 1967; Contemporary Britain, 1971; Incomes Policy: an inquest and a propoal, 1974; Crime and Penal Policy, 1978; Frequent contributor to New Society and other sociological journals. *Memberships:* Departmental Committee, National Debt and Taxation, 1924-27; Royal Commission on Workmen's Compensation, 1938; Interdepartmental Committee on Shop Hours, 1946-49; Royal Commission on the Press, 1947; UGC, 1948-50; Royal Commission on the Civil Service, 1954; Interdepartmental Committee on the Business of the Criminal Courts, 1958-61; Council on Tribunals, 1961-64; Interdepartmental Committee on the Criminal Statistics, 1963-67; Royal Commission on the Penal System, 1964- 66; Penal Advisory Council, 1966-79; Advisory Concil on Misuse of Drugs, 1971- 74; Chairman, Countryside Commission, 1968-70 (National Parks Commission, 1966-68); JP in the Metropolitan Courts, 1926-70 (on the Panel of Chairmen in the Metropolitan Juvenile Courts, 1946-62). *Honours:* Created Life Peer of Abinger Common, 1958; CH 1977; Honorary Doctorates from: Columbia, New York; Nottingham; Essex; Liverpool; Aberdeen; York; Hull; Aston in Birmingham; Bath; Southampton; Warwick; Cambridge and London Universities. Honorary Fellow: Girton College, Cambridge, 1965-; Bedford College, London, 1964-; Royal College of Psychiatrists, 1979. *Hobby:* Country Life. *Address:* House of Lords, Westminster, London SW1, England.

WORBOYS Annette Isobel, Novelist. m. 20 Sept. 1946. 2 daughters. *Publications:* As Annette Eyre: Three Strings to a Fortune, 1962; Visit to Rata Creek, 1964; Valley of Yesterday, 1965; A Net to Catch the Wind, 1966; Return to Bellbird Country, 1966; House of Five Pines, 1967; A River and Wilderness, 1967; A Wind from the Hill, 1968; Thorn-apple, 1968; Tread Softly in the Sun, 1969; The Little Millstones, 1970; Dolphin Bay, 1970; Rainbow Child, 1971; The Magnolia Room, 1972; Venetian Inheritance, 1973; Chosen Child, 1973. As Vicky Maxwell (pseudonym): The Other Side of Summer, 1977; Way of the Tamarisk, 1974; High Hostage, 1976; Flight to the Villa Mistra, 1973. As Anne Worboys: The Lion of Delos, 1974; Every Man a King, 1976; The Barrancourt Destiny, 1977; The Bhunda Jewels, 1980; Run, Sara, Run, 1981; A Kingdom for the Bold, 1986. *Memberships:* Crimewriters Association; Romantic Novelists Association; Society of Women Writers & Journalists; Tonbridge Wells and District Writers Circle; Society of Authors. *Honour:* Romantic Novelists Association award for best of year, 1977 for Every Man a King. *Hobbies:* Theatre; Gardening. *Address:* The White House, Leigh, Tonbridge, Kent TN11 8RH, England.

WORLEY Jo-Anne, b. 6 Sept. 1939, Lowell, Indiana, USA. Freelance Actress. m. Roger Lee Perry, 11 May 1975. *Education:* Midwestern University; Pasadena Playhouse. *Appointments:* Appearances include: Hello Dolly, Pittsburgh Civic Light Opera; Heaven Sent, Palm Beach, Florida; Beautiful Lady, Mark Taper Forum, Los Angeles, California; Die Fliedermaus, Fort Worth, Texas Opera Association; Playing Our Song, Hawaii, etc; Appearances in TV Films; TV Talk Shows; Theatre Musicals; Game Shows; Musicals and Non-Musicals; Night Clubs; Opera; Concerts; Kid Shows; Theatre on Broadway and Off-Broadway; Commercials; national touring companies. *Publication:* Jo Anne Worley's Chicken Joke Book. *Memberships:* Board of Directors of Actors and Others for Animals. *Honours:* 2 Drama Logue Awards; Best Actress in a Musical. *Address:* 315 S. Beverley Drive, Beverly Hills, CA 90212, USA.

WORNY Christine May, b. 3 May 1941, Chicago, Illinois, USA. Psychotherapist; Administrative Director. m. (1) 4 daughters, (2) Marvin R. Cohen, 27 Oct. 1984. *Education:* BA, Psychology, Mundelein College, Chicago, 1972; MA, Clinical Psychology, Roosevelt University,

Chicago, 1974. *Appointments:* Psychologist, 1974-77, Psychologist, Team Leader, 1977-83, Madden Mental Health Center; Psychotherapist, Director of Community Education, 1974-87, Psychotherapist, Administrative Director, 1988- Centrum Counseling and Phobia Clinic, Oak Park, Illinois. *Memberships:* Phobia Society of America; Association to Advance Ethical Hypnosis; Anxiety Treatment Specialists Society; Association of Mental Health Private Practitioners; National Academy of Certified Clinical Mental Health Counselors; American Association for Counseling & Development; American Mental Health Counselors Association. *Hobbies:* Travel; Reading; Hiking; films and theatre. *Address:* Centrum Counseling and Phobia Clinic, 1100 Lake Street, Suite 250, Oak Park, IL 60301, USA.

WORTH Helen (Mrs Arthur M Gladstone), b. July 1913, Cleveland, Ohio, USA. Author; Poet; Educator. *Education:* BA, University of Michigan; Graduate Work, New School for Social Research. *Appointments:* Lecturer, Food & Wine Appreciation Course, various Universities; National Magazine and Newspaper Food Editor; Helen Worth syndicated Food/Wine Feature, 1980. *Publications:* Performer and Writer of Verses to accompany husband's macrophotography for slideshow, The Down on the Farm Cook Book, 1943, reissued 1983; Shrimp Cookery, 1952; Cooking Without Recipes, 1965, reissued 1984; Hostess Without Help, 1971; Damnyankee in a Southern Kitchen, 1973; Small Secrets: A Creature Garden of Verses, 1984. Contributions to: Talk; House Beautiful; Brides; Wine West. *Honours:* Outstanding Cookbook Award, 1972; Runner-up, Cookbook Award, 1974; Federated Women's Clubs of America, Outstanding Journalism Award, 1977. *Memberships include:* Authors League; American Society of Journalists and Authors; National Book Critics Circle; National and Virginia Federations of Press Women. *Address:* 1701 Owensville Road, Charlottesville, VA 22901, USA.

WREN Jill Robinson, b. 30 Apr. 1954, Summit, New Jersey, USA. Lawyer; Author. m. Christopher G. Wren, 12 June 1976. *Education:* University of Delaware, 1972-74; BA, George Washington University, 1976; JD, Boston University School of Law, 1980. *Appointments:* Law Clerk, Wisconsin Department of Justice, 1979; Judicial Law Clerk, Dane County Circuit Court, Madison, WI, 1981-83; Author, law books, 1982-; Editor, Continuing Legal Education, Wisconsin State Bar, 1984-86; Legal Affairs Editor, Adams & Ambrose Publishing, 1986-. *Publications:* Co-author, Legal Research Manual: Game Plan for Legal Research & Analysis, 1983, 1986; Co-author, Teaching of Legal Research, article (Law Library Journal), 1988. *Memberships:* American Bar Association; Wisconsin State Bar; Authors Guild; Society of Professional Journalists; American Association of Law Libraries; American & Wisconsin Civil Liberties Unions; Wisconsin Democratic Party. *Honours:* Invited speaker, legal research, numerous groups, USA & Canada; Legal Research Manual named one of 50 Most Useful Reference Works, Legal Information Alert, 1987. *Address:* c/o Adams & Ambrose Publishing, PO Box 9684, Madison, Wisconsin 53715, USA.

WRIGHT Belinda (Brenda), b. 18 Jan. 1929, Southport, England. Prima Ballerina; Ballet Teacher. m. Jelko Yuresha, 4 Nov. 1961, 1 son, 1 daughter. *Education:* Diploma, Elementary, Intermediate (Honours), Advanced, Solo Seal, Royal Academy of Dancing, London, 1945. *Appointments:* Ballet Rambert, 1945-58; Ballet de Paris, 1959-51; London Festival Ballet, 1951-62; Grand Ballet Marquis de Cuevas, 1954-55; Royal Ballet, London (Guest Artist), 1963; Principal Ballerina, Royal Ballet, 1964-65; National Ballet of Cuba, 1967; TV appearances include: Music for YOu, Music in Camera, All Kinds of Music, Gala Performance, What's My Line, TV Panel Game; French TV in Harald in Italy. *Creative Works:* Created Vision of Marguerite, 1952; Alice in Wonderland, 1953; Copelia, 1956; Snow Maiden, 1961; Pheadre, 1964; Armida, 1971; Pas de Sylphes, 1967; La Camelia; Co-Producing Giselle, Central Ballet of China, with Kelko Yuresha, 1984.

Memberships: London Studio Centre; Dance Works; Dance Centre; Ballet Panel, SWET. *Honours:* ARAD, Solo Seal, 1945; Anna Pavlova Trophy, 1937; The Dancing Times Cup, 1939; Errol Addison Cup. *Hobbies:* Painting: Reading. *Address:* 8 Deanery Street, London W1, England.

WRIGHT Bobbie Jean, b. 3 Apr. 1933, Oklahoma City, USA. Professor. m. Donald K. Wright, 23 Nov. 1955, divorced, 3 daughters. *Education:* BA, Oklahoma State University, 1954; MRE, Southern Baptist Theological Seminary, 1957; Ed.D., Nova University, 1976. *Appointments:* Director, Student Nurses, Highland Hospital, 1955-56; Assistant Executive Director, YWCA, Allentown, 1961-64; Assistant National Teenage Consultant, National Board, YWCA, New York City, 1964-65; Professor, Sociology, Thomas Nelson Community College, 1968-; Co-Owner, Manhattan Janitorial Service, 1969- 77; Co-owner, VIP Yard Signs, 1988-89. *Publications:* Articles in professional journals. *Memberships:* Virginia Sociological Association, President, 1980; Delta Kappa Gamma, 1986; Tidemill Civic Association. *Honours:* 1st Place, Oklahoma's High School State Tournament, Tennis, Table Tennis and Badminton, 1949-50. *Hobbies:* Tennis; Racketball; Table Tennis; Swimming; Collecting Clowns. *Address:* 213 Deerfield Blvd., Hampton, VA 23666, USA.

WRIGHT Celeste Turner, b. 17 Mar. 1906, St John, New Brunswick, Canada. Poet (Retired Professor of English). m. Vedder Allen Wright, 26 June 1933. 1 son. *Education:* AB, University of California, Los Angeles, 1925; MA 1926, PhD 1928, University of California, Berkeley. *Appointments:* Instructor, Asst Prof, Assoc Prof, Full Professor 1928-48, Full Professor 1948-73, Professor Emeritus 1973-, University of California, Davis; Chair, Dept of English, University of California, Davis, 1928-55. *Publications:* Anthony Mundy: An Elizabethan Man of Letters, 1928; Collections of Poems: Etruscan Princess, 1964; A Sense of Place, 1973; Seasoned Timber, 1977. Memoir: University Women, 1981; Poems and research in numerous journals. *Memberships:* Academy of American Poets; Poetry Society of America; Modern Language Assoc of America; Phi Beta Kappa. *Honours:* Annual Medal, Faculty Research Lecturer, University of California, DAvis Senate, 1963; Reynolds Lyric Prize, Poetry Soc America, 1963; Silver Medal for A Sense of Place, Commonwealth Club of California, 1973; Grand Prize, California Statewide Competitions, Ina Coolbrith Society, 1961, 1965, 1970. *Hobbies:* Aerobics class; Sponsor and judge, University of California Davis, Annual contest for student poets, 1979-. *Address:* 1001 D Street, Davio, California 95616, USA.

WRIGHT Erma Naomi, b. 18 Oct. 1930, Detroit, Michigan, USA. Teacher; Dance Therapist. m. Aug. 1949, 3 sons, 2 daughters. *Education:* AA, Wayne County Community College, 1977; BA 1979, MEd 1980, University of Michigan; Chauffeurs' Training School, 1988. *Appointments:* Detroit Councils, Arts 1980, Olympiad 1984; Los Angeles County Host Committee, XXIII Olympiad; Los Angeles County Children's Services, 1984-85; Detroit Department of Parks & Recreation, 1988-89; Detroit Board of Education. *Publications:* Meaning & Purpose of Dance, Black Dance, & Dance Therapy; Dances of African Origin & Their Therapeutic Value & Effect on the Mental Health of the Community; Dances of African Origin & Their Therapeutic Values. *Memberships include:* Detroit Federations, Musicians, Teachers; American Guild of Variety Artists; American Dance Therapy Association; American Forum for International Study; Los Angeles Dance Alliance. *Honours include:* Service award, Detroit Public Schools, 1987; Cool Cat Award, Los Angeles County Children's Services Department; Performing Arts Award, University of Michigan, 1978; 1st New World Festival, African Diaspora, Brazil, 1978. *Hobbies:* Dance; Music; Ethnic foods; Theatre; Shopping; Health & nutrition; Interior decorating. *Address:* 246 Madison Avenue no. 431, Harmonie Park, Detroit, Michigan 48226, USA.

WRIGHT Helen L Kimbro, b. 17 July 1932, Nashville,

Tennessee, USA. Author; Lecturer. *Education:* BS, Journalism, University of Tennessee, 1977. *Appointments:* President, Helen L Wright, Inc (Yacht Sales and Leasing, Incorporated in 1981). *Publications:* Metropolitan Opera House; Unlimited Powers; The Art, Power and Technique of Writing; Panic in New York; News for Opera Lovers: The Met is Still There. *Memberships:* National Association for Female Executives, New York; Marble Collegiate Church, New York. *Hobbies:* Reading; Music. *Address:* P O Box 2451, Westport, CT 06880, USA.

WRIGHT Lorna Lenore, b. 6 Feb. 1949, Sioux Lookout, Canada. Consultant; Assistant Professor. m. Prasetyo Sumantri, 28 Dec. 1983. *Education:* BA, Wilfred Laurier University, 1969; MA, University of Essex, 1974; PGCE, University of London Institute of Education, 1975; MIM, American Graduate School of International Management, 1982; PhD, University of Western Ontario, 1989. *Appointments:* Educator, CUSO, Thailand, 1969-73; Advisor, CIOA, Indonesia, 1975-78; Educator, Nagoya University, Japan, 1979-82; Consultant, Salasan Associates Inc., & Kanchar International Inc., Canada, 1984-; Assistant Professor, Queen's University, School of Business, Canada, 1986- . *Publications:* Articles on international management in various journals. *Memberships:* Chairman, Canadian-Indonesian Business Council; Academy of International Business; Academy of Management; Administrative Sciences Association of Canada; Society for Intercultural Education Training and Research; Canadian Council for SE Asian Studies. *Honours:* Barton Kyle Yount Award, 1982. *Hobbies Include:* Tae Kwon Do; Flying; Hiking; Crochet; Reading; Ikebana. *Address:* School of Business, Queen's University, Kingston, Ontario, Canada K7L 3N6.

WRIGHT Margaret Taylor, b. 8 Nov. 1949, Wilmington, USA. Global Marketing Consultant. *Education:* BA, University of North Carolina, 1972; MBA, Wake Forest University, 1978. *Appointments:* Marketing, American Home Products, 1978-80; Ted Bates Advertising, 1981; Marketing, Foremost McKesson, 1981-83; Marketing, Sara Lee Corp, 1983-86; President, Wright Marketing Blueprint, 1986-. *Publication:* Developed & introduced oreo Cookies n Cream Ice Cream, 1984. *Memberships:* American Marketing Association; Restaurant Association; Snack Food Association; Princeton Club; *Honours:* Youth Chairman, Gubernatural Campaign for Governor Holshouser NC, 1972. *Hobbies:* Travel; Tennis; Golf; Sailing. *Address:* Wright Marketing Blueprint Inc., 59 East 54th Street, Suite 72, New York, NY 10022, USA.

WRIGHT Mary Patricia, b. 10 May 1932, Warlingham, Surrey, England. Author. m. Richard M. Wright, 25 Apr. 1959, 2 daughters. *Education:* Associate, Royal Institute of Chartered Surveyors, 1955; Associate, Land Agents' Society, 1956; 1st Class degree (External), London University, 1964. *Career:* Chartered surveyor, agricultural land agent, Sussex, Devon & London, 1951-59; Teacher, 1965-79; County Councillor, 1981-. *Publications:* Woman's Estate, 1959; Conflict on the Nile, 1950; Ilena, 1974; Journey Into Fire, 1977; Shadow of the Rock, 1978; Storm Harvest, 1980; This My City, 1981; While Paris Danced, 1982; I Am England (award), 1987; That Near & Distant Place, 1988. As Mary Napier: Blind Chance, 1980; Forbidden Places, 1982; State of Fear, 1984; Heartsearch, 1988; Powers of Darkness, 1990. *Honour:* Georgette Heyer Historical Novel Prize, 1987. *Hobbies:* Local history & archaeology; Gardening; Prairie- busting in local churchyrd. *Address:* Whitehill House, Frant, East Sussex, England.

WRIGHT Patricia Chapple, b. 10 Sept. 1944, Doylestown, Pennsylvania, USA. Assistant Professor of Biological Anthropology. m. James Alfred Wright, 11 June 1967. 1 daughter. *Education:* BA, Biology, Hood College, 1966; PhD, Anthropology, City Univ of New York, 1985. *Appointments:* Adjunct Lecturer, Dept of Anthropology 1983-84, Research Assoc, Primate Ctr 1983-, Visiting Asst Prof 1985-87, Assistant Professor 1988-, Duke University; Visiting Research assoc, Calif Inst Tech, 1986-88. *Publications:* Authored a number of articles for scientific journals and magazines. *Memberships:* AAS; International Primatologist Society; American Society of Primatologists; Assoc for Tropical Biology; Animal Behavior Society; American Assoc Physical Anthropology; American Assoc of Anthropologists. *Honours:* John D. and Catherine T. MacArthur Fellow, 1989-; International Director, Ranomafana National Park Project, Madagascar, 1987- ; S L Washburn Prize for Outstanding Student paper, American Assoc of Physical Anthropologists, 1982; Consultant for Aotus breeding project, Yemassie Monkey Ctr, Yemassie, S Carolina, 1987-; Member, International Advisory Committee, Duke Primate Center, 1987-. *Hobbies:* Conservation; Wildlife; Rain forests; Monkeys; Lemurs. *Address:* Biological Anthropology and Anatomy, Wheeler Bldg, 3705-B Erwin Road, Duke University, Durham, NC 27705, USA.

WRIGHT Rosemarie, b. Chorley, Lancashire, England. Concert Pianist. m. Michel Brandt, 2 sons. *Education:* Diploma, Vienna State Academy; Royal Academy of Music, with Harold Craxon; Licentiate & Associate, Royal Academy of Music; Studied piano with Edwin Fischer, Chamber Music with Pablo Casals. *Appointments:* Debut: Vienna, 1960; Concerts with orchestras, recitals and braodcasts in France, Germany, Austria, Italy, Switzerland, Portugal, Greece, Turkey, Holland, Belgium, Norway, Denmark, USA, Australia, UK; Performances at numerous festivals; Pianist in Residence, Southampton University, 1972-80; Examiner, Associated Board, Royal Schools of Music, 1972-; Adjudicator, British Federation of Music Festivals, 1983-; Professor, Piano, RNCM, 1973-78; Professor, Piano, Royal Academy of Music, 1978-; Records, Piano music by Edward MacDowell. *Honours:* Albanesi Prize; Chappell Silver Medal; Kate Steel Prize; Matthay Fellowship; Haydn Prize, Vienna, 1959; Bosendorfer Prize, 1960. *Hobbies:* Art; Education. *Address:* 84 Filsham Road, Hastings, East Sussex, England.

WRIGHT Sara Elizabeth, b. 4 May 1950, Aiken, South Carolina, USA. Family Psychologist. m. Paul Conrad Rosenblatt, 9 June 1983, 1 daughter. *Education:* BS, 1972, MEd., 1975, University of Texas; PhD, University of Minnesota, 1985. *Appointments:* Co-Ordinator, Middle Earth Drug Crisis Centre, 1971-72; Director, Emergency Services, Trinity Valley Mental Health-Mental Retardation, 1975-78; Programme Dirctor, Andrew, Inc., 1978-79; Family Psychologist, Dakota Centre, 1979-. *Publications:* Articles in: Journal Marriage & Family Therapy; American Journal Family Therapy; Family Relations; Medical Aspects Human Sexuality; Family Therapy Networker. *Memberships:* American Association Marriage & Family Therapy, Board, Newsletter Editor; Minnesota Women Psychologists, Steering Committee; Phi Kappa Phi; Kappa Delta Pi. *Hobbies:* Writing; Gardening; Parenting. *Address:* 1712 W. Eldridge Ave., Roseville, MN 55113, USA.

WRIGHT Wendy, b. 9 Aug. 1947, London, England. Landscape & Garden Designer; Consultant; Lecturer. m. John Charles Wright, 2 June 1978, 1 son, 1 daughter. *Education:* Dip. ISGD, Inchbald School of Design. *Appointments:* Lecturer, Inchbald School of Garden Design, 1986-; Lecturer, English Gardening School, Chelsea Physic Garden, 1988-; Principal, The Garden School In The North. *Memberships:* Advisory Council, Inchbald School of Design; Fellow, Society of Landscape & Garden Designers, 1987. *Hobbies:* Gardening; Horses; Bridge. *Address:* c/o Bursar's House, 5 Travelyan College, Elvet Hill Road, Durham, DH1 3LN, England.

WRIGHT (Geraldine) Jere Hathaway, b. 25 Aug. 1926, Salem, Oregon, USA. Public Relations Consultant. m. John Grant Wright Jr, divorced. 2 sons, 1 daughter. *Education:* BA, University of Maryland; YWCA Professional School. *Appointments:* YWCA Youth Director, Wash DC Metro Arca, 1950- 53; Composer, Lyracist, Performer & Homemaker, 1956-70; Consult to Mrs Jouett Shouse, Fndr Wolftrap Farm Park/ Performing Aerts, 1970-79; Cons, United Cable TV,

1981-; Cons Fairfax Symphony, 1979-81; Consul, Barter Theatre, Geo Mason Univ, 1982; Consul, Clewes Communications, 1986, 1987; Cons, Straight Drug Treatment. *Creative works:* Children's LP: Smokey Bear & Ranger Hal; Producer, Tribute to Freedom, featuring Senator Everett Edw Dirksen, USA. *Memberships:* Co-Chair, Intl Children's Festival, Wolf Trap; Past VP Fairfax Symphony; Co-Chair, Women of the Year, 1985; Natl Cap Area YWCAS; V Chair, American Festival Mime, 1980; Member Board Dirs, No Virginia Community Foundation and Fairfax County Council Arts; Pres, Director, Board of Trustees, Scholarship Fund, Am Soc Civil Engrs; Natl Capital Area. *Honours:* Natl Public Serv Award; Natl Public Relations Soc/America; Thoth Award, PRSA, Wash DC; Communications Award, Fairfax Co Chamber Commerce; Fairfax County Council/ Arts Service Award. *Hobbies:* Piano, organ music; Tap dancing; Wildlife; Politics; Capital Speakers Club. *Address:* 11060 Thrush Ridge Road, Reston, Virginia 22091, USA.

WRIGHT-HECKER Eleanore Reidell, b. 17 June 1915, Mattoon, Illinois, USA. Retired. m.(1)Curtis Wright, 21 Mar. 1941. (2)Arthur O Hecker, 14 Feb. 1956, 1 son, 1 daughter. *Education:* BS, BM, MD, University of Illinois; University of Michigan; FACN. *Appointments:* Intern, Augustana Hospital, Chicago; private Practitioner; Resident, Psychiatry; Guest Lecturer, University of Illinois Law School; Guest Lecturer, University of Michigan Law School; Director, Out-Patient Department, Friends Hospital, Philadelphia; Faculty Womens Medical School, Philadelphia; Clinical Director, Embreeville State Hospital, Embreeville, Pennsylvania; Regional Director, Mental Health Programme for Eastern Pennsylvania; Superintendent, Embreeville State Hospital, retired 1971. *Publications:* Family Physician After Care-Mental Hospitals, 1960; Forced Motivation, 1962; The Employment of Patients as Full Time, 1962; Comparative Clinical Experience with Five Antidepressants, 1960; Clinical Evaluation of Fluphenazine-Diseases of Nervous System, 1961; Preliminary Results with Fluphenazine, 1960; Open Doors (totally unlocked hospital), 1959, 1960; A Study of PerDiem Cost for Three Catagories; Alcoholism: A Need for Diagnostic Classification, 1966; Reassessing Hospital Treatment Practices, 1968. *Memberships:* Illinois Medical Society; American Medical Society; Champaign County Medical Society; Michigan Medical Society; American Psychiatric Association; Pennsylvania Medical Society; Chester County Medical Society. *Honours:* Honorary Award of FACN, 1965; National Register of Prominant Americans, 1967. *Hobbies:* Crafts; Bridge; Politics. *Address:* 1657 Elk Forest, Elkton, MD 21921, USA.

WRIGHTSON Denelle Cole, b. 20 Sept. 1956, Fort Wayne, Indiana, USA. Architect. m. John Mowll Wrightson, 15 Aug. 1981, 1 son. *Education:* BA, Kalamazoo College, 1978; MArch, University of Wisconsin, 1981. *Appointments:* Cole Mattot Architects, 1978-80; City of Milwaukee, 1980-81; Hidell Architects, 1982-. *Memberships:* American Institute of Architects; Texas Society of Architects; Dallas Museum of Art. *Honour:* Women in Architecture Exhibition, 1988. *Hobbies:* Sports; Art; Travel. *Address:* 7135 Dalewood Avenue, Dallas, Texas 75214, USA.

WROTTESLEY Mary Ada Van Echten, Lady, b. 5 Mar. 1929, Cape Town, South Africa. Housewife. m. Major R. Wrottesley, 5 Mar. 1955, 2 sons. *Education:* BA, University of Capetown. *Hobbies:* Swimming; Reading; Social. *Address:* 18 Sonnehoogte, Thomas Road, Kenilworth, Cape 770, South Africa.

WU Daisy Yen, b. 12 June 1902, Shanghai, China, Retired. m. Hsien Wu, 20 Dec. 1924. 2 sons, 3 daughters. *Education:* BA, Gin Ling College, Nanking, China, 1917-21; Graduate student, Smith College, Northampton, MA, USA,. 1921-22; Graduate Student, Chicago University, Chicago, IL, Summer, 1922; MA 1923, Graduate Study 1925, Columbia University, New York; Diploma in French Language, L'Academie Sino-Francaise, Peking, 1944; Diploma in French Language,

UN Language Training Course, NYC, 1963. *Appointments:* Assistant, Biochemistry, Peking Union Medical College, 1923-24; Research Associate, Biochemistry, Med College of Alabama, 1950-53; Technical Associate, Nutrition, Food Conservation Div, UNICEF, NYC, 1960-64; Associate in Nutrition 1964-70, Special Lecturer in Nutrition 1970-71, Institute of Human Nutrition, Columbia University; Consultant, Nutrition & Metabolic Res, St Luke's Hosp Ctr, NYC, 1971-86. *Publications:* Papers of original research in professional journals in USA, China and Japan; Hsien Wu in Loving Memory, as editor and compiler; A Guide to Scientific Living by Hsien Wu, editor; Author, Supplement to Hsien Wu's Principles of Nutrition. *Memberships include:* American Institute of Nutrition; Society of the Sigma XI; American Public Health Association (Fellow); Royal Society of Health, London (Fellow); New York Academy of Sciences. *Honour:* Trustees' Scholarship, Ginling College, Nanking, China, 1918; Founder of the Ming Ming School, Peking, China, 1934. *Hobbies:* Reading; Writing; Investigating; Research. *Address:* 449 E14 Street, New York, NY 10009, USA.

WU Felicia Ying-Hsiueh, b. 27 Feb. 1939, Taipei, Taiwan, Republic of China. Professor; Biochemist. m. Cheng-Wen Wu, 10 Nov. 1963, 2 sons, 1 daughter. *Education:* BS, Chemistry, National Taiwan University, 1961; MS, Organic Chemistry, University of Minnesota, USA, 1963; PhD, Organic Chemistry, Case Western Reserve University, 1969. *Appointments:* Research Associate: Cornell University, 1969-71, Yale University, 1971-72; Associate, 1972-73, Instructor, 1973-78, Assistant Professor, 1978-79, Albert Einstein College of Medicine; Visiting Professor, Institut Pasteur and Insitut Gustave-Roussy, Paris, France, 1979-80; Associate Professor, Pharmacological Sciences, State University of New York, 1981-; Professor, National Taiwan University; Researcher, Insitiute of biomedical Sciences, Academia Sinica, Taipei, Taiwan, 1988-. *Publications:* Articles in numerous journals including: Tetrahedron Letters; Biochemistry; Journal of the American Chemical Society; Journal of Biological Chemistry; etc. *Memberships:* American Society of Biochemistry and Molecular Biologist; Biophysical Society; American Chemical Society. *Honours:* Recipient, various honours and awards. *Hobbies:* Piano; Coin & Stamp Collecitons; Sports. *Address:* 7 West Meadow Road, Setauket, NY 11733, USA.

WU Margaret Anne, b. 11 Apr. 1935, Chicago, Illinois, USA. Computer Scientist; Educator. m. 24 June 1907, 1 son, 1 daughter. *Education:* BS, Mathematics, Illinois Institute of Technology, 1956; MS, Mathematics, Northwestern University, 1958; PhD, Computer Science, University of Iowa, 1980. *Appointments:* Research Computer Scientist, Illinois Institute of Technology Research Institute, Chicago, Illinois, 1958-67; Research Associate, 1967-71, Visiting Assistant Professor, Management Science, 1979-, University of Iowa, Iowa City. *Publications:* Computers and Programming: an Introduction, 1973; Introduction to Computer Data Processing, 1975, 2nd Edition, 1979; Introduction to Computer Data Processing with Basic, 1980. *Memberships:* Association for Computing Machinery; Institute of Electrical and Electronics Engineers Computer Society. *Hobbies:* Music; Drama; Literature. *Address:* Phillips Hall, University of Iowa, Iowa City, IA 52242, USA.

WU Nancy, b. 1 Oct. 1919, Kiukiang, Kiangsi, China. Physician. m. Tse-Tsung Chow, 28 May 1959, 2 daughters. *Education:* MD, West China Union University Medical College, 1945; Residency in Anesthesiology, Boston City Hospital and Memorial Hospital, New York, USA, 1951-53; Postdoctoral Research Fellow, Cardiopulmonary Laboratory, Department of Internal Medicine, University of Texas Southwestern Medical School, Dallas, 1953-56; Certified, American Board of Anesthesiology, 1959. *Appointments:* Staff Anesthesiologist, Massachusetts Memorial Hospital, Boston, 1956-59; Chief, Anesthesiology, Lemuel Shattuck Hospital, Boston, 1959-65; Assistant

Professor, Anesthesiology, 1965-73, Clinical Associate Professor, Anesthesiology, 1973-75, University of Wisconsin; Consultant Anesthesiologist, Stoughton Community Hospital, Stoughton, Wisconsin, 1975-76; Associate Professor, Anesthesiology, University of Texas Southwestern Medical School, Dallas, 1976-; Staff Anesthesiologist, Chief of Pain Clinic, Assistant Chief of Anesthesiology Section, Veterans Administration Medical Center, Dallas; Senior Attending Staff, Parkland Memorial Hospital, Dallas. *Memberships:* American Medical Association; Texas Medical Association; Dallas County Medical Society; American Society of Anesthesiologists; Texas Society of Anesthesiologists; Dallas County Anesthesiology Society; International Anesthesia Research Society; International Association for the Study of Pain; American Pain Society; Chinese American Medical Society; American Society of Regional Anesthesia; American Society of Pain Medicine. *Hobbies:* Antique collection; Travel; Reading. *Address:* VA Medical Center, Department of Anesthesiology, 4500 South Lancaster, Dallas, TX 75216, USA.

WU Yongtang, b. 28 Oct. 1938, Guangdon, People's Republic of China. Associate Professor. m. Law Wingyim, 27 Jan. 1962. 2 daughters. *Education:* Zhongshau University, 1956-60. *Appointments:* Teaching Assistant and Lecturer 1960-85, Associate Professor 1985-, Mathematics Department, Zhongshau University. *Publications:* The Learning and Application of Relational Database System; CM Automatic Programming System for numerical Control Tools; The Petri Net Theory and It's Application in Communication System. *Memberships:* Member of Council, Applied Mathematics Society of Guangdong; Member of Council, Management Software Society of Guangdon; Automatics Society of China; Mathematics Society of China. *Honour:* Prize for Outstanding Achievement in Science and Technology, 1981, 1984. *Hobbies:* Novels; Classical music. *Address:* Department of Mathematics, Zhongshau University, Guangzhou, Guangdong, People's Republic of China.

WURTS Janny, b. 10 Dec. 1953, Bryn Mawr, Pennsylvania, USA. Author; Illustrator. *Education:* BA, Hampshire College, 1975. *Appointment:* Freelance Author and Illustrator, 1975-. *Publications:* Novels: Sorcerer's Legacy; Stormwarden; Keeper of the Keys; Shadowane; Master of Whitestorm; Daughter of the Empire (in collaboration with Raymond E. Feist); Cover illustrator with artwork appearing on own novels. *Memberships:* Science Fiction Writers of America; Vice President, 1982 and 1983, Association of Science Fiction Artists. *Hobbies:* Horseback riding; Sailing; Music; Travel. *Address:* 50 Maple Street No 5, Plainville, Connecticut 06062, USA.

WURTZBURG Susan Jane, b. 29 Jan. 1960, Toronto, Canada. Archaeologist. m. 2 Jan. 1988. *Education:* BSc., Honours, 1984; MA, Anthropology, 1988. *Appointments:* Archaeological Projects in: Belize, 1982, England, 1984, Peru, 1983, Australia, 1985, 1986, Ontario, 1985, 1986, Mexico, 1987, 1988. *Publications:* Co-Author: Analyzing Residential Platforms at Sayil, Yucatan, Mexico, 1988, The Forgotten Beginning of Canadian Palaeo-Indian Studies, 1988. *Memberships:* American Anthropological Association; Council for British Archaeology; Society for American Archaeology; Ontario Archaeological Society. *Honours:* SUNY Benevolent Award, 1987, 1988. ssa 2OHobbies: Outdoors; Travel; Photography. *Address:* Dept. of Anthropology, State University of New York, Albany, NY 12222, USA.

WYANDT Loretta, b. 23 Jan. 1931, Seffner, Florida, USA. Real Estate Broker-Salesman; City Councilperson. m. James Howard, 4 Aug. 1951. 2 sons. *Education:* Political Science, Saint Pete Jr College, 1978. *Appointments:* City Councilperson, 1979-81 and 1988-90; Real Estate Salesman, 1986-89; Real Estate Broker, 1989-. *Creative work:* Composition on Real Life Politics, SP Jr College. *Memberships:* Home Owners Assoc; Oldsmar Rec Center; Founder, Oldsmar Top of the Bay;

Garden Club; Pinellas Ct EMS Adv Bd; Metropolitan Planning Orig Cac of Pinellas Ct. *Honours:* Appointed to Governors Crime Prev & Law Enforcement Comm, 1989; Oldsmar Chamber of Commerce (One in a Million), 1986; Emergency Medical Services of Pinellas Ct, Service to Community, 1988; Pinellas County Metropolitan Planning Orig, Service to Community; Blue Ribbon for Petticoat Fern, Fl State Fair, 1975. *Hobbies:* Collecting butterflies for home; Reading non-fiction & government articles; Growing plants for garden club and state fairs; Attending State legislative sessions and local meetings. *Address:* 601 Shore Drive East, Oldsmar, FL 34677, USA.

WYATT-CUMMINGS Thelma Laverne, b. 7 June 1945, Amarillo, Texas, USA. Judge. 1 son, 1 daughter. *Education:* BA, University of California, Los Angeles, 1965; JD, Distinction, Emory University School of Law, 1971. *Appointments Include:* Field Representative, Atlanta Urban League, 1965-67; Private Legal Practice, 1971-77; Visiting Professor, Law in Real Property, Emory University, 1974-75; Consultant, ABC Management Inc., 1975; Seminar Presenter, 1982-; Judge: State Court of Fulton County, 1985-. *Publications:* The Incompetence of a Husband and Wife to Testify so as to Illegitimae a Child, Georgia State Bar Journal, 1970; Justice or Just Us?, Cascade Chronicle, 1986. *Memberships Include:* Georgia State, American, National, GateCity, Atlanta Bar Associations; National Judicial Council, Past Chairman; American Judicature Society. *Honours Include:* Award of Excellence, National Association of Blacks in Criminal Justice, 1988; Distinguished Service Award, National Judicial Council, 1988; many others. *Hobbies:* Reading; Swimming; Horticulture; Scrabble; etc. *Address:* 160 Pryor Street, SW, Room 204, Atlanta, GA 30303, USA.

WYCICHOWSKA Ewa Aleksandra, b. 29 Nov. 1949, Poznan, Poland. Prima Ballerina; Dance Educator; Choreographer. m. Tomasz Gatebiowski, 4 Mar. 1971, divorced 1978, 1 daughter. *Education:* Ballet School, Poznan, 1968; Scholarship, Ministry of Culture, L'Academie Internationale de la Danse, Paris, France, 1974-75; MA, Academyof Music, Department of Dance Pedagogy, Warsaw, 1981; International Course for Professional Choreography and Composition with Robert Cohan, London, England, 1985. *Appointments:* Soloist of Ballet, 1968, Prima Ballerina, 1980, Choreographer Debut 1980, Grand Theatre, Lodz; Dance Educator, Academy of Music, Lodz, 1981-84. *Creative Works:* Numerous leading roles in traditional and modern ballets including: Romeo and Juliet; Snow White; La Fille; Green Table; Sylphides; Giselle; Coppelia; Compositions: The Voice of Woman; Concerto F- Minor; Chopin; Serenade; M. Katowicz; Rock Ballet; Republika. *Memberships:* Zaiks. *Honours:* 1st Prize, All-Polish Choreographic Competition, Category of Soloists, Lodz, 1973; City of Lodz Award, 1983; Gold Cross of Merit for Artistic Output, 1984; Prize for Young Artists in St Wyspianski (the 1st degree). *Hobbies:* Painting; Sculpture; Old Inkas Culture; Theatre; Collecting Buttons. *Address:* ul Tamka 6/73, Lodz 91-403, Poland.

WYETT Jo Ann Powers, b. 28 Aug. 1938, Custer City, Oklahoma, USA. Coordinator of Guidance and Counseling. m. Bobby G Wyett, 22 Apr. 1957. 3 sons, 1 daughter. *Education:* BS, Panhandle State University, 1961; MS 1965, Oklahoma State University; Counseling Cert 1973, Post graduate in Adm 1979, Texas Tech University. *Appointments:* Science/Math Teacher, Guymon, Oklahoma, 1965-69; Biology Teacher, Lubbock, Texas, 1969-74; Sophomore Counselor, Lubbock, 1974-82; Special Services Counselor, Lubbock, 1982-88; Coordinator of Guidance & Counseling, 1988-89. *Memberships:* Classroom Teachers Assn; Life member, NEA; Life member, TSTA; LEA; Member-at-Large, West Texas Assn of Counseling & Development; Alliance for the Nineties: Substance Abuse Task Force; Advisory Board, Lubbock Council of Alcoholism & Drug Abuse; Advisory Board, Child Advocacy Research and Education Center. *Honours:* Phi Kappa Phi, 1965; AYI, Natl Science Foundation, 1961; Teacher-of-the- Year, Coronado High School, 1972-73;

Counselor-of-the-Year, WTACO, 1989. *Hobbies:* Reading; Family activities; Church activites, Deacon, Second Baptist Church; Golfing; Snow skiing; People. *Address:* 1628 19th Street, Lubbock, Texas 79401, USA.

WYLIE Betty Jane, b. 21 Feb. 1931, Winnipeg, Canada. Writer. m. William Tennent Wylie, 1 June 1952, deceased. 2 sons, 2 daughters. *Education:* BA, double honours, 1951; MA 1952, University of Manitoba. *Publications include:* Plays: The Horsburgh Scandal; Mark; A Place on Earth; Kingsayer; The Old Woman and The Pedlar; Beowulf (musical-record album), 12 others produced. Books: The Clear Spirit, 1967; Beginnings: A Book for Widows, 1977, 3rd edition, 1988; Encore: The Leftovers Cookbook, 1979; No Two Alike, 1981; Betty Jane's Diary: Lessons Children Taught Me, 1982; Tecumseh, 1982; John of a Thousand Faces, 1983; The Book of Matthew, 1985; Everywoman's Money Book, 1984, 4th edition 1989; The Betty Jane Wylie Cheese Cookbook, 1984; The Best is Yet to Come, 1985, 2nd edition 1989; Successfully Single, 1986; All In the Family, 1988; Something Might Happen, 1989. *Memberships:* Playwrights' Union of Canada; The Writers' Union of Canada; CAPAC; Bereaved Families of Ontario; Dramatists' Guild; International Society of Dramatists; Board Member, Investors' Syndicate Mutual Funds. *Honours:* Education Award, Ontario Psychological Foundation, 1987; Media Award, Canadian Nurses' Association, 1988. *Hobbies:* Theatre; Swimming; Birds; Wine. *Address:* c/o The Writers' Union of Canada, 24 Ryerson Avenue, Toronto, Ontario, M5T 2P3, Canada.

WYNN Susan Rudd, b. 25 Dec. 1955, Louisville, Kentucky, USA. Physician; Author. m. Ralph T Wynn, MD, 29 May 1982. 2 sons. *Education:* BS 1979, MD 1981, Texas A & M University; Mayo Graduate School of Medicine, Fellowships in Pediatrics and Allergy, 1987. *Appointments:* Columnist, International Medical News, 1986-88; Staff Pediatrician, Mayo Clinic, 1987; Allergist in Private Practice, Fort Worth, 1988. *Memberships:* Chair, Medical Student Section; Chair, Women in Medicine Project, American Medical Association; American College of Allergists; American Academy of Pediatrics; American Academy of Allergy; Alpha Omega Alpha; Amer. Med. Women's Association. *Honours:* President's Scholar, Texas A & M, 1974; Leon Unger Award, American College of Allergists, 1985; Geigy Fellowship, American College of Allergists, 1987; Outstanding Young Women of America, 1979. *Hobbies:* Writing; Travel; Photography. *Address:* 5929 Lovell Avenue, Fort Worth, Texas 76107, USA.

WYNNE Martha V, b. 18 Nov. 1951, St Louis, Missouri, USA. Corporate Finance Officer. *Education:* BA, University of Texas, 1972; MBA, University of Houston, 1981. *Appointments:* Speechwriter, Lt Gov William P Hobby Jr, 1973; Department Manager, Tracy-Locke, 1973-77; Securities analyst, Fayez Sarofim & Co, 1977-81; Vice President, Corporate Finance, Rotan Mosle, 1981-85; Corporate Finance Manager for leaveraged buyouts, G E Capital Corporation, 1985-87; Principal, Corporate Finance Specialists, 1987-. *Creative works:* Currently writing book, Business Valuation for John Wiley & Sons, publishers. *Memberships:* Board, Association for Corporate Growth, Dallas; Board, Houston Society of Financial Analysts; Board, Houston Symphony League; Board, Treasurer, Houston Business Forum; President and Founder, Encorps. *Honours:* Gubernatorial Appointee to Texas Council on Disabilities, 1989-1991; Gold H Award, 1969; Houston AMSO Delegate, 1981; Commencement Speaker, University of Texas School of Humanities, 1973; Outstanding Women of Houston, 1985; Deacon, Highland Park Presbyterian Church, Dallas. *Hobbies:* Sailing; Squash; Tennis. *Address:* 6542 Northwood Road, Dallas, TX 75225, USA.

WYNTER Dana, b. 8 June 1931, England. Actress; Writer; Journalist; Documentary-Maker. m. Gregson Edward Bautzer, 10 June 1956, 1 son. *Education:* Rhodes University, Republic of South Africa. *Appointments:* Broadway Play, Black Eyed Susan, 1954;

Radio Series, Private Lives of Harry Lime, London, 1953; appeared on numerous TV programmes including: Wagon Train, 1961; Studio One, 1953; Playhouse, 90, 1955; Virginian, 1962; The Man Who Never Was, co-starring in TV Series, 1968; Gunsmoke, 1968; Medical Centre; Marcus Welby; Ironside; To Rome with Love; The FBI Story; It Takes a Thief, 1970; Ben Casey; The Invaders; The Wild Wild West; Cannon; Macmillan and Wife; Hawaii Five O; Alfred Hithcock Presents; appeared in numerous films including: Invasion of the Body Snatchers; The View from Pompey's head; D Day 6th June, 1955; Sink the Bismarck, 1960; On the Double, with Danny Kaye; Fraulein; Airport (No 1); Produced and appeared in 6 TV specials, Dana Wynter in Ireland, 1976, 1978; A Royal Romance, CBS TV, 1983; Radio interview with Dr Christiaan Barnard for RTE Ireland, 1983-84; latest film, Le Sauvage. *Publications:* Contributor of numerous articles in newspapers and magazines including The Guardian. *Address:* c/o Contemporary-Korman, 132 South Lasky Drive, Beverly Hills, CA 90212, USA.

WYNYARD Ann Lindsay, b. 7 Jan. 1929, Northampton, England. Farmer; Freelance Canine Journalist; Judge, Pedigree Dogs. m. 10 June 1950, 3 daughters. *Appointments:* Assistant Secretary to a Director of Elizabeth Arden, London; Private Secretary to Montague Skitt; Hon. Secretary, British Utility Breeds Association, 1972-81. *Publications:* The Dog Directory - Guide to The Tibetan Spaniel, 1974; The Dog Directory Guide to Owning a Tibetan Spaniel, 1980, 1986; Dogs of Tibet, 1982; The American Tibetan Spaniel Handbook, co-author, 1986. *Memberships:* English Kennel Club; Vice President, BUBA, & Tibetan Spaniel Association, King Charles Spaniel Association; Deputy Chairman, Japan Animal Welfare Society (UK) Ltd. *Honours:* Breeder, 72 Tibetan Spaniel Champions (Worldwide). *Hobbies:* Raising Money for Charities; Breeding, Exhibiting Tibetan Spaniels. *Address:* Sedgebrook Hall, Chapel Brampton, Nr. Northampton, NN6 8BD, England.

WYSE Lois, b. 30 Oct. 1926. Advertising Executive; Author. 1 son, 1 daughter. *Education:* Case Western University. *Appointments:* Co-Founder, Wyse Advertising, New York City. *Publications:* 48 books including: Novels: The Rosemary Touch; Kiss, Inc; Far from Innocence; The Granddaughter; Poetry: Love Poems for the Very Married; Are You Sure You Love Me?; I Love You Better Now; A Weeping Eye Can Never See; Essays: What Kind of Girl Are You, Anyway? Lovetalk; The Six Figure Woman; Company Manners; Funny You Don't Look Like a Grandmother. *Memberships:* Board of Directors, Consolidated Natural Gas; Trustee, Beth Israel Medical Center; Board of Directors, Catalyst. *Address:* Wyse Advertising, One Madison Avenue, New York, NY 10010, USA.

WYSOCKA Ewa Katarzyna Joanna, b. 25 Nov. 1961, Gdansk, Poland. Psychologist. *Education:* MA Pedagogy, 1987; MA Psychology, 1988. *Appointments:* Assistant Professor, Silesian University, 1987. *Publications:* Articles in professional journals. *Memberships:* Polish Psychological Society; Polish Pedagogical Society. *Hobbies Include:* Oriental & Classical Music; Literature; Sailing; Windsurfing. *Address:* ul. Ukanska 5/139, 40-887 Katowice, Poland.

WYSOCKI Sharon, b. 20 Feb. 1955, Detroit, Michigan, USA. Therapist; Writer; Visual Artist. *Education:* BSc, Eastern Michigan University, 1977; Warwich University, UK. Certified Addiction Counsellor, Licensed Social Worker, Michigan; Masters of Social Work, University of Michigan, 1989. *Appointments include:* Psychodrama Therapist, Woodway Grange Intermediate Treatment Centre, Coventry, England, 1975; Officer, Federal Correctional Institution, Milan, Michigan, 1977; Substance Abuse Counsellor, Self-Help Addiction Rehabilitations, Detroit, 1977-79; Drug & Alcohol Outpatient Therapist, WOMAN Centre, Detroit, 1979; Detoxification Therapist, Midwest Mental Health Clinic at Doctors' Hospital, 1979-88; Substance Abuse Therapist, Insight, Inc., 1979-; Founder, Women for Better Working Conditions in Corrections; Research

Consultant, The Mirrored Image (advises on topics of prisons chemical dependency and mental health issues for literary and film projects; currently employed as a Chemical Dependency Outpatient Therapist, Greenbrook Recovery Center, Saline, Michigan. *Publications:* Layperson's Exploratory Drama Manual; Exploratory Drama/Self Awareness; Everybody is a Star, Self-Awareness Through Drama; Ariadne's Thread; Article, Sobering Thoughts. Also: Numerous appearances, radio & television; Editor, Art of the Journal, Journal Art; Presenter, workshops in field; Art work exhibited, numerous group exhibitions, USA, Canada, Hungary, India. *Hobbies:* Advocate, women working in penal institutions & how their images are portrayed in media; Interested, Dada & Fluxus art movements. *Address:* Progressive Press, 7320 Colonial, Dearborn Heights, Michigan 48127, USA.

X

XIAO Zhangling, b. 20 Mar. 1930, Putian, Fujian, People's Republic of China. Associate Professor. m. 30 Sept. 1965. 1 son, 1 daughter. *Education:* Bachelor's degree, Chemistry, 1952, Postgraduate in Catalysis, Dept of Chemistry 1963, Xiamen University, People's Republic of China. *Appointments:* Assistant Teacher 1952-59, 1963-77, Assistant Professor 1978-82, Associate Professor 1983-, Dept of Chemistry, Xiamen University, China; Visiting Scholar, School of Medicine, Washington University, St Louis, USA, 1985-87; Visiting Scientist, Dept of Biochemistry St Jude Children's Research Hospital, Memphis, Tennessee, 1987-. *Publications:* Author of numerous articles in USA and China. *Memberships:* Chemical Learned Society, People's Republic of China; Chemical and Chemical Technological Learned Society, Fujian, Chuina; Council of Chemical and Chemical Technological Learned Society, Fujian, China; Editorial Board, Petro-chemical Technology Journal, China; Society of Chinese Bioscienties, America. *Honours:* Scientific and Technological Achievement Award, Fujian Province, China, 1981; Scientific and Technological Achievement Award, Higher Education Dept, Fujian Province, China, 1984; Scientific and Technological Achievement Award, National Division of Education, China, 1985 and 1987. *Hobby:* Work in laboratory. *Address:* Department of Chemistry, Xiamen University, Xiamen, Fujian, People's Republic of China.

Y

YABLON Babette, b. 21 Mar. 1931, New York City, New York, USA. Attorney. m. Lawrence H. Yablon, 23 Nov. 1952, 2 sons. *Education:* BA, Washington Square College, New York University, 1950; JD, Law Review, New York University School of Law, 1953. *Appointments:* Samuel B. Weingrad, 1953-56; Private Practice, 1956-73; Jessel Rothman PC, 1973-75; Managing House Counsel, Eagle Insurance Co, 1975-78; Shayne, Dachs, Stanisci & Corker, 1978-. *Publications:* Women Trial Lawyers, How They Succeed in Practice and in the Courtroom (contributor), 1986; Automobile Accident Deposition (co-author); Deposition, Interrogatories and Trial (co-author). *Memberships:* Nassau County Bar Association (Moot Court Competition-Judicial Panel). *Address:* 941 Glenwood Road, West Hempstead, NY 11552, USA.

YAGER Ellen Kahn, b. 3 May 1930, Brooklyn, USA. Consultant. m. 6 Jan. 1952, 1 son, 1 daughter. *Education:* BA, 1951, BS, 1954, MA, 1954, University of Minnesota; MLS, St John's University, 1974. *Appointments:* Executive Director, Minnesota UN Association, 1952-53; Librarian, New York Public Library, 1977-81; Freelance Editor, 1981-88; Adjunct Professor, Political Science, Palm Beach Community College, 1988-. *Publication:* Editor, Newsletter, Ripon Society. *Memberships:* Board of Directors, Ripon Society, 1982; Board of Directors, Minnesta University Alumni Association; Special Libraries Association; New York Library Club. *Honours:* Recipient, honours & awards; SPAN: Foregn Study. *Hobbies:* Music; Reading. *Address:* 1020 D Summit Trails Circle, West Palm Beach, FL 33415, USA.

YALOW Rosalyn Sussman, b. 19 July 1921, New York, USA. Medical Investigator. m. A Aaron Yalow, 6 June 1943. 1 son, 1 daughter. *Education:* AB, Hunter College, New York City, 1941; MS 1942, PhD 1945, University of Illinois, Urbana. *Appointments:* Assistant in Physics 1941-43, Instructor 1944-45, University of Illinois; Lecturer and Temp Assistant Professor in Physics, Hunter College, 1946-50; Consultant, Lenox Hill Hospital, 1952-62; Consultant, Radioisotope Unit 1947-50, Physicist and Asst Chief, Radioisotope Service 1968-70, Acting Chief 1968-70, Chief, Nuclear Medicine Service 1970-80, Director, Solomon A Berson Research Laboratory 1973- , VAH; Research Service Professor 1968-74, Distinguished Service Professor 1974-79, Solomon A Berson Distinguished Professor-at-Large 1986-, Mt Sinai School of Med, CUNY; Chief, VA Radioimmunoassay Reference Laboratory, 1969-; Senior Medical Investigator, VA, 1972-; Distinguished Professor-at-Large 1979- 85, Professor Emeritus 1985-, Albert Einstein Col of Med, Yeshiva University; Chairman, Dept of Clinical Sciences, Montefiore Medical Center, 1980-85. *Publications:* About 500 publications. *Memberships:* Fellow, NY Acad of Science; Radiation Research Soc; American Assoc of Physicists in Med; Assoc Fellow in Physics, American College of Radiology; Biophysical Soc; American Diabetes Assoc; American Physiological Soc; Endocrine Soc; Soc of Nuclear Medicine. *Honours:* Recipient of 40 Honorary Degrees and numerous awards and prizes; Nobel Prize in Physiology or Medicine, 1977; Foreign Associate, French Academy of Medicine, 1981; Designation of Berson Laboratory as American Nuclear Society Nuclear Historic Landmark, 1986. *Address:* Senior Medical Investigator, Veterans Administration Medical Center, 130 West Kingsbridge Road, Bronx, NY 10468, USA.

YANCEY Laurel Guild, b. 12 Dec. 1953, Santa Rosa, California, USA. Broadcast Attorney. m. Arthur H. Yancey, 19 June 1988. *Education:* BA, Simmons College; JD, Boston College Law School. *Appointments:* Senior Attorney, Advisor, Low Power TV Branch, Mass Media Bureau, 1985-88; Attorney Advisor, TV Branch, Mass Media Bureau, Federal Communications Commission, 1988-. *Publications:* Associate Editor,

University of California Los Angeles Black Law Journal, 1978. *Memberships:* District of Columbia Bar Association; American Women in Radio and Television; Massachusetts & District of Columbia Bar. *Honours:* Outstanding Young Women of America, 1980; Community Service Award, FCC, 1980; Performance Award, 1988. *Hobbies:* Equestrian-Dressage; Downhill Skiing; Tennis; Cable Production. *Address:* 15544 Brandywine Road, Brandywine, MD 20613, USA.

YANKOWITZ Susan, b. 20 Feb. 1941, Newark, New Jersey, USA. Novelist; Playwright. m. Herbert Leibowitz, 3 May 1978. 1 son. *Education:* BA, Sarah Lawrence College, 1963; MFA, Yale School of Drama, 1968. *Creative works:* Major publications: Slaughterhouse Play, 1971; Boxes, a play, 1973; Portrait of a Scientist As A Dumb Broad, screenplay, 1974; Terminal, play, 1975; Silent Witness, novel, 1976; Short fiction, monologues, essays, 1977-87; Alarms, play, 1988. Major play productions: Terminal, 1971- 73; Qui Est Anna Mark? 1979; Baby, 1982; A Knife in the Heart, 1983; Alarms, 1987; Deronda, an opera, 1988. Television and film: The Prison Game, 1977; Silent Witness, 1980; The Amnesiac, 1982; Sylvia Plath, 1989. *Memberships:* PEN; WGA East; Dramatists Guild; New Dramatists; Authors League. *Honours:* US/Japan Fellowship Grant; NEA Creative Writing Fellowship; Guggenheim Fellowship; CAPS Award; Rockefeller Foundation Grant; Vernon Rice Drama Desk Award; Joseph E Levine Fellowship. *Address:* 205 W 89th Street, 8F, New York, NY 10024, USA.

YAO York-Bing Katherine, b. 24 Dec. 1941, Canton, China. Investment Firm Executive; Academic Professional. *Education:* MS, University of Michigan, USA, 1963; PhD, Columbia University, 1972. *Appointments:* Vice President & Director, Yao Shih-Chin Corporation 1965-, Chou Pei-Chuang Corporation 1976-, New York, USA. *Publication:* Book, Education in China, 1984. *Membership:* American Management Association. *Honours include:* College scholarships; University fellowships; Academic prizes; Professional awards. *Hobbies:* Writing; Reading; Music; Travel. *Address:* 485 Fifth Avenue, New York, NY 10017, USA.

YARBOROUGH Valerie Louise, b. 24 Aug. 1928, San Antonio, Texas, USA. Internal Auditor; Consultant. 3 daughters. *Education:* AA, Santa Clarita Junior College, 1972; BA, California State University, Northridge, 1973. *Appointments:* Manager, Adams & Associates, Seattle, Washington, 1973-76; Staff accountant, George Braby CA, 1977-78; Corporate accountant, Westin Hotel Company, 1978-79; Staff auditor 1979-85, Senior Auditor & Board of Directors 1979-, Christopher & Associates, Seattle, 1986-88; Board of Directors, Caprice Inc, 1988-. *Memberships:* Delta Tau Kappa; Past President, National Federation of Womens Clubs; American Society of Women Accountants; National Association of Management Accountants; League of Women Voters. *Address:* Westin Building, 2001 6th Avenue, Seattle, Washington 98121, USA.

YARIV Frances, b. 27 Aug. 1939, Bridgeport, Connecticut, USA. Writer. m. Amnon Yariv, 9 Apr. 1972, 1 daughter. *Education:* BA, MA, Syracuse University. *Appointments:* Teacher of English, Los Angeles Public Schools, California, 1965-76; Writer (Novelist, Screenwriter), 1975-. *Publications:* Novels: Elena; Leaving; Aegean Enchantment; Last Exit; The Hallowing; Safe Haven. *Memberships:* PEN; The Authors Guild; Women in Film. *Honour:* Winner, W G A East Foundation Fellowship in Screenwriting, 1987-88. *Hobbies:* Travel; Volunteer work; Reading. *Address:* 2257 Homet Road, San Marino, CA 91108, USA.

YARON Gilah, b. 10 Dec. 1941, Tel Aviv, Israel. Singer. m. Yehuda Yaron, 28 Mar. 1961. *Education:* Music Teachers Seminary, 1961-64; Singing lessons with Hede Tuerk-Boernstein, 1962-70; Futher studies, singing, Jennie Tourel, Guenter Reich, George London, Elisabeth Schwarzkopf; Scholarships, American-Israel

Cultural Foundation, Sharet Fund for Young Artists, 1963-70; Further scholarships, study abroad, Germany, Switzerland, Austria. *Appointments:* Music teaching for retarded children, 1961-76; Member, Rinat Chamber Choir (director, Gary Bertini), 1962-76; Instructor, Vocal Department, Rubin Academy of Music, Jerusalem, 1982-; Performances, soprano soloist, all major orchestras in Israel, conductors including Bertini, Weller, Maag, Paray, Markevitch; Metha Chamber Music Productions; International festivals, Berlin, Frankfurt, Salzburg, London, Brighton, Bergamo, Zurich, Turin, Lourdes. *Honour:* Prize for Young Artists, Israel Philharmonic Orchestra, 1970. *Hobbies:* Educational subjects; Languages; Gardening. *Address:* c/o Ruth Shahar Concert Management, 62 Ben-Gurion Boulevard, Tel Aviv 64589, Israel.

YATES Juanita, b. 14 Dec. 1924, Monroe County, Missouri, USA. Freelance Journalist. m. George A Yates, 25 Apr. 1945. 4 sons, 7 daughters. *Education:* Attended: Northeast Missouri State University, 1943-46; Varied classes at Missouri University. *Appointments:* Shelbina Bank, 1944-45; Monroe City News, 1964-84; Freelancing: 1984-88; Wrote for 20 newspapers and magazines; editor, Best Shots magazine. *Publications:* Lake Country Faces and Places; Freelancing; Fun and Profit; The Lighter Side; The Biggs Kids and the Accordion Summer. *Memberships:* Missouri Press Women, District Vice President; Missouri Mothers, Inc; American Mothers, Inc; MC Sheltered Workshop; Hannibal Community Concert Association. *Honours:* Missouri Press Woman Communicator of the Year, 1976; Missouri Press Woman of Achievement, 1981; Missouri Mother of the Year, 1982; Missouri Family Award, 1987; Scholarship, Northeast Missouri State University, 1940. *Hobbies:* Music; Reading; Writing; Speaking; Work with handicapped and abused children; Help start Cerebral Palsy School, Sheltered workshop; Amnesty International. *Address:* Rt 3, Box 46, Monroe City, Missouri 63456, USA.

YATES Marypaul, b. 24 Nov. 1957, Knoxville, Tennessee, USA. Textile Design Executive. m. Benjamin H. Weisgal, 5 June 1983. *Education:* University of Georgia, 1973-75; BFA magna cum laude, Syracuse University, 1977; AAS, Fashion Institute of Technology, 1979. *Appointments:* Adjunct Instructor: Hunter College 1978-82, Fashion Institute of Technology 1985, Parsons School of Design 1988-; Design assistant, Jeffrey Aronoff Inc, 1978-81; Independent design consultant, 1981-82; Stylist, Gerli & Company, 1982-83; Design Director, Maharam, 1983-87; Principal, Yates Weisgal Inc, 1987-. *Creative work includes:* Book: Textiles: Handbook for Designers, 1986. Group exhibitions: FIT at Forty, Fashion Institute of Technology, 1984, Textiles for the 80's, Rhode Island School of Design, 1985. *Memberships:* American Craft Council; Association for Contract Textiles; Interior Colours Forecasting Committee, Colour Association of US; Colour Marketing Group; Industry Advisory Board, Fashion Institute of Technology; Textile Study Group, New York. *Honours:* Designer, collections winning: IBD Bronze Award (healthcare fabrics) 1986, Roscoe Award 1982, Coty Award (men's accessories) 1980; Grant, Ford Foundation, 1976; Art Competitive Scholarship 1975-77, E. B. Furgatch Memorial Scholarship 1976, Syracuse University. *Hobbies:* Writing; Textile research; Travel. *Address:* 185 East 85th Street, 20F, New York, NY 10028, USA.

YATES Sandra Ann Rohn, b. Lincoln, Nebraska, USA. Administrative Vice President. m. Thomas A. Yates, 15 May 1975. *Appoinments:* Public Relations Assistant, Bankers Life, Nebraska, 1966-75; Administrative Vice President, Yates & Associates, 1982-. *Memberships:* Welcome Wagon, Vice President, 1984; Newcomers, Vice President, 1985; Theatre Arts for Children, Board of Directors, 1987-. *Honours:* NITA Distric Champion, 1982. *Hobbies:* Tennis; Golf; Bridge; Art; Music; Theatre. *Address:* 6447 Boxelder Drive, Lincoln, NE 68506, USA.

YEVICK Jean Evelyn, b. Pittsburgh, Pennsylvania,

USA. Mortgage Broker; Nurse. *Education:* Mercy School of Nursing; University of Pittsburgh. *Appointments:* Leo H. Criep, MD, 1958-60; Mayer A. Green, MD, 1960-64; Psychophysiological Laboratory 1965-70, Renal Research Divisions 1970-80, Pulmonary Medicine 1980-83; University of Pittsburgh School of Medicine; Allergy Supervisor, Brentwood Medical Group, 1969-; Managing Director & Corporation Treasurer, Overland Financial Network Inc, 1984-. *Creative work includes:* Text & tape sets: Recycling Cash, Getting Started, Financing; Tape sets: Money Savings Management Techniques, Save Big Dollars on Your Real Estate Offers; National speaker. *Memberships:* Secretary, Mount Washington Chamber of Commerce, Treasurer, Real Estate Leadership Association of America; President, American Congress of Real Estate, 1982-83, 1984-89; Vice President, Pennsylvania Residential Owner Association. *Hobbies:* Tennis; Speaking; Travel; Reading; Bridge. *Address:* PO Box 6068, Pittsburgh, Pennsylvania 15211, USA.

YOCHELSON Kathryn Mersey, b. 22 Oct. 1910, New York City, USA. Teacher; Author. m. Dr Samuel Yochelson, 21 June 1930. 1 son, 1 daughter. *Education:* BA, Art Education, New Haven Teachers College, 1926-30; Graduate work, Yale, Albright Art School, American University and University of Maryland. *Appointments:* Art Teacher, New Haven School Systems, 1930-39; Volunteer, Ed Dept, Albright-Knox Art Gallery, Buffalo, 1940-60; Chairman, Seven Painters of Israel Exhibition, 1953; Organized permanent art collection, Buffalo Jewish Center, 1952; Chairman, 20 Artists for Israel, 1968; Personal Vision: Yochelson Collection of Israeli Art, 1987. *Creative works:* Authored articles in Israeli art and artists; Reviewed newly published books on Israeli art for local press; Israeli Art: Golden Threads, memoir of encounters in documenting historic facts. *Memberships:* Sunday Scholar Series Committee; Life Member, Albright-Knox Art Gallery; Life Member, Brandeis Women's Committee; Secy, Washington Watercolor Society; National Am Pen Women, Capitol Branch. *Honour:* Honorary mention, New Haven School System. *Address:* Apartment 824 East, 4201 Cathedral Avenue, Washington, DC 20016, USA.

YOCHEM Barbara J. (Runyan), b. 22 Aug. 1945, Knox, Indiana, USA. Sales Representative. m. (2) Donald Heard, 12 Dec. 1988. 1 son, previous marriage. *Appointments:* Coach, trapshooting, 1975-; Publisher, By By Productions, 1980-; Employee 1980-86, Sales Manager 1983-85, Hunter Woodworks Inc; Sales Representative, Commercial Lumber & Pallet, 1986-. *Publication:* Barbara Yochem's Inner Shooting. *Honours include:* Trapshooting recognitions: World Bronze Medallist, 1980; USA Bronze Medallist, 1977; All American Trapshooting Team, 5 years; High National Allround Average Leader, 1976, 1977 Trap & Field; California State Trapshooting Team, 3 years; High National Doubles Leader, 2 years Trap & Field. Biographical listings. *Hobbies include:* Amway Business. *Address:* PO Box 1676, Glendora, California 91740, USA.

YONGE (Ida) Felicity Ann, b. 28 Feb. 1921, Edinburgh, Scotland. Political Secretary. *Education:* Convent of the Holy Child, St Leonards-on-Sea, Sussex, 1934-38. *Appointments:* Women's Royal Naval Service, 1940-46 (2nd Officer, 1943-46); Junior Assistant Purser, P & O Steam Navigation Company, 1947-50; Personal Assistant, Chairman of Conservative Party, 1951-64; Private Secretary, Leader of the Opposition, 1964-65; Opposition Chief Whip (Conservative), 1965-70 & 1974-79; Assistant Private Secretary, Leader of the House of Commons, 1970-74; Special Adviser, Government Chief Whip's Office, 1979-83. *Honours:* MBE, 1958; DBE, 1982. *Hobbies:* Bridge; Gardening. *Address:* 58 Leopold Road, Wimbledon, London SW19 7JK, England.

YORBURG Betty, b. 27 Aug. 1926. Professor; Author. m. Leon Yorburg, 23 June 1946, 1 son, 1 daughter. *Education:* PhB, 1945, MA, Sociology, 1948, University of Chicago; PhD, New School for Social

Reseach, 1968. *Appointments:* Instructor, College of New Rochelle, 1966-67; Professor, Sociology, City College, Ciy University of New York, 1967-; Lecturer, new School for Social Research, 1972-75. *Publications:* Utopia and Reality, 1969; The Changing Family, 1973; Sexual Identity, 1974; The New Women, 1976; Introduction to Sociology, 1982; Families & Societies, 1983. *Memberships:* American Sociological Association; American Association for the Advancement of Science; New York Academy of Sciences; National Council of Family Relations. *Honours:* Research Assistantship, Professor Clifford Shaw, Chicago Area Project, 1947-47; Fellowship Award, 1987; etc. *Hobbies:* Reseach on Family, Women, Politics, Aging. *Address:* 20 Earley Street, City Island, NY 10464, USA.

YORK Susannah, b. 9 Jan. 1942, England. Actress; Writer. m. Michael Wells, 1960, 1 son, 1 daughter. *Education:* Royal Academy of Dramatic Art. *Appointments:* Acting Debut in Repertory; TV Appearances include: Jane Eyre, TV special for NBC, 1971; TV Films: Slaughter on St Teresa's Day, Fallen Angels, Golden Gate Murders, 1979; Prince Regent, A Christmas Carol, Second Chance, We'll Meet Again; Films Include: Tunes of Glory; Freud; Tom Jones; They Shoot Horses, Don't They?; A Man for All Seasons; The Killing of Sister George; Oh What a Lovely War; The Battle of Britain; Brotherly Love; Zeb & Company; Happy Birthday Wanda June; Images; The Maids; Gold; Eliza Fraser; Conduct Unbecoming; Heaven Save us from Our Friends; Skyriders; The Silent Partner; Superman I; The Shout; Superman II; Falling in Love; Alice; The Awakening; Loophole; Bluebeard; The Falcons Malteser; Stage appearances include: Hedda Gabbler; Penthesilea; The Human Voice; Fatal Attraction; The Applecart; The Woman. *Publications:* Lark's Castle; In Search of Unicorns; articles in Redbook & other publications. *Honours:* Best Actress for Images, Cannes Film Festival; Best Supporting Actress, They Shoot Horses Don't They?, Academy Award Nominee. *Hobbies:* Reading; Writing; Travel; Languages; Houses; Gardening; Horse Riding. *Address:* c/o Jeremy Conway, 109 Jermyn St., London SW1, England.

YORK Tina, Artist. *Education:* School of the Museum of Fine Arts, Boston, 1967-69; George Dergalis, Apprenticeship, Wayland, 1967-75; BA with honours, Brandeis University, 1978; MD Programme, New York Medical College. *Appointments:* Violinist, child prodigy, 1955-66. *Creative Works:* One Man Shows: Copley Society, Boston, 1972, 1973; Cambridge Art Association, Massachusetts, 1975; The Creation, 7 painting series, 1975; Rose Art Gallery, Brandeis University, 1979; Group Shows, Boston Area, New York Area, Frankfurt & Munich in West Germany, 1968-86; The University within Us, a 54 painting series based on electro scans of the body; The Story of Cholestrol, a 14 painting series published as a calender in 90 countries, 1988; Work in private collections in USA, Germany, England, Spain, Italy, Switzerland, France, Austria, Canada, Argentina. *Honours:* Recipient of various prizes and awards. *Address:* Postfach 730146, 8500 Nürnberg 173, West Germany.

YORKE Margaret, b. 30 Jan. 1924, Surrey, England. Writer. *Publications:* Over 30 novels including No Medals for the Major; The Scent of Fear; Safely to the Grave. *Memberships:* Crimewriters Association (Chairman 1979-80); Society of Authors; PEN; Detection Club; Mystery Writers of America. *Honours:* Award for Best Translated Crime Novel, Swedish Academy of Detection, 1982. *Address:* c/o Curtis Brown, 162-168 Regent Street, London W1R 5TB, England.

YOUNATHAN Margaret J Tims, b. 25 Apr. 1926, Clinton, Mississippi, USA. Professor. m. Ezzat S Younathan, 11 Aug. 1958. 2 daughters. *Education:* BA, University of So Mississippi, 1946; BS 1950, MS 1951, University of Tennessee; PhD, Florida State University, 1958. *Appointments:* Instr food and nutrition, Oreg State University, 1951- 55; Postdoctoral research Assoc, Florida State University, 1958-59; Sr Nutritional Cons, Ark Dept Health, Little Rock, 1962-68; Instructor,

Pediatrics, University Ark School Medicine, Little Rock, 1962-65; Assistant Professor 1965-68, Associate Professor human nutrition and food 1971-79, Professor 1979-, Louisiana State University, Baton Rouge. *Publications:* Contributed articles on food and nutrition research to professional journals. *Memberships:* Inst Food Technologists; Am Inst Nutrition; LA Home Econs Assoc; Sigma Xi; Phi Kappa Phi; Gamma Sigma Delta; Omnicron Nu; Phi Upsilon Omnicron. *Honours:* LA State Univ Council on Research summer faculty grantee, 1980; LA Home Econs Assn, dist D, outstanding home economist, 1988; Lou Ana Food Inc, grantee, 1987; Chosen for: International nutrition work in Sierra Leone 1984 and Jamaica 1987. *Hobbies:* House plants; Bird watching. Address: 1048 Castle Kirk Dr, Baton Rouge, LA 70808, USA.

YOUNG Christine Brooks, b. 13 July 1944, Suffolk, Virginia, USA. Real Estate Investor. m. Hubert Howell Young, Jr, 31 Dec. 1964, 1 son. *Education:* Mary Washington College, 1962-64. *Appointment:* Owner, Young Properties, 1979-. *Creative works:* Business renovations featured, Old House Journal, Country Living, Olde Times, Suffolk Magazine. *Memberships:* Suffolk Team Advancing Revitalisation (STAR); Board, Riddick's Folly. *Honour:* Delegate, National Republican Convention, 1984. *Address:* 444 North Main Street, Suffolk, Virginia 23434, USA.

YOUNG Eddye Vivian Pierce, b. 2 May 1947, Fort Worth, Texas, USA. Concert artist; Opera singer; College professor. m. 26 May 1984. (divorced). 1 daughter. *Education:* Bachelor of Music, 1969; Master of Music, 1973. *Appointments:* San Jose State University, 1973-76; Miami University of Ohio, 1976-84; Pennsylvania State University, 1984-; Pennsylvania State University, 1984-89; Self employed (Professional singer, New York), 1986-; Sara Lawrence College, Bronxville, New York, 1989-. *Memberships:* American Guild of Mus Artists; National Association of Teachers of Singing. *Honours:* Metropolitan Opera National Auditions, 1970; San Francisco Opera Florence Bruce Award, 1976; Metropolitan Opera National Council Grant Recipient, 1980, 1984, 1989; Numerous regional opera and singing awards 1970-; Citation, City of Philadelphia for contribution to music and education, 1988; Outstanding Young Women of America (Ohio), 1978. *Hobbies:* Needlework; Collecting china and crystal; Antiques. *Address:* 425 Riverside Drive Apartment 15E, New York, NY 10025, USA.

YOUNG Fredda Florine, b. 11 Feb. 1937, USA. Supervisor. 2 sons. *Appointments:* Simpson Electric Co., 1955-57; American National Bank, 1957-60; Atlantic Liquour Co., 1960-70; General Time Corp, 1974-76; Republic Steel Corp, LTV Steel, Gulf State Steel, 1976-. *Honours:* Appointed 1st Female Production Supervisor, 1977. *Hobbies:* Needlework; Travel. *Address:* 115 Elsmore Blvd., Gadsden, AL 35901, USA.

YOUNG Genevieve, b. 25 Sept. 1930, Geneva, Switzerland. Publisher. *Education:* BA, Wellesley College, USA, 1952. *Appointments:* Harper & Row, 1952-70; Vice President, Executive Editor, J. B. Lippincott, 1970-77; Senior Editor, Little Brown & Company, 1977-85; Editor-in-Chief, Literary Guild, 1985-88; Editorial Director, Bantam Books, 1988-. *Memberships:* Trustee, Phillips Academy, Andover, Massachusetts, 1975-78; Executive Council 1975-78, 1985-, General Publishing Division, Association of American Publishers; President 1981-82, Women's Media Group; Director 1985-, Youth Counselling League, President 1989-. *Honours:* Alumnae achievement award, Wellesley College, 1982; Matrix award, Women in Communications, 1988. *Hobbies:* Tennis; Skiing; Cooking. *Address:* Bantam Books, 666 Fifth Avenue, New York, NY 10103, USA.

YOUNG Janet Mary, b. 23 Oct. 1926, Widnes, England. Minister of State, FCO. m. Dr G T Young, 15 July 1950, 3 daughters. *Education:* MA (PPE), Hon. Fellow, 1978, St Anne's College, Oxford. *Appointments:*

Baroness in Waiting, 1972-73; Party Under Secretary of State, DoE, 1973- 74; Minister of State, DES, 1979-81; Chancellor, Duch of Lancaster, 1981-82; Leader of House of Lords, 1981-83; Lord Privy Seal, 1982-83; Minister of State, FCO, 1983-. *Memberships:* Vice Chairman, Conservative Party Organisation, 1975-83, Deputy Chairman, 1977-79; Co-Chairman, Womens National Commission, 1979-83; Councillor, Oxford City Council, 1957; etc. *Honours:* Created Life Peer, 1971, Baroness Young of Farnworth in the County Palatine of Lancaster; PC, 1981. *Hobby:* Music. *Address:* House of Lords, London SW1A 0PW, England.

YOUNG Lesley Margaret, b. 3 Mar. 1954, Mossman, Australia. Concert Pianist. *Education:* BMus; ARCM (Performance); LMus.A; A.Mus.A. *Appointments:* Concert Pianist; Debut, Wigmore Hall, London, 1977; Concerto Performances with major Australian Symphony Orchestras, QCM Chamber Orchestra, RNCM Symphony Orchestra, Orchestra Da Camera, etc; Recitals for Australian Society for Keyboard Music, International Society for Contemporary Music, Incorporated Society of Musicians, Manchester Midday Concerts Society, various music clubs; Radio Broadcasts; TV appearances in Australia. *Honours:* 1st prize, Open Piano Championship, Australian National Eisteddfod, 1973; State Winner, Commonwealth Finalist, ABC Instrumental And Vocal Competition, 1973, 1974; 1st Prize, Commonwealth Finals, ABC Instrumental & Vocal Competition, 1975; 1st Prize, National Piano Concerto Competition, Dudley, 1976. *Hobbies:* Theatre; Art; Travel. *Address:* 23 Woodside Road, Tonbridge, Kent TN9 2PD, England.

YOUNG Lois Catherine Williams, b. 10 Mar. 1930, Ohio, USA. Public Administration/Consultant. m. William Walton Young, Sr, 14 Sept. 1952. 2 sons, 1 daughter. *Education:* BS, New York University, 1957; MS, Hofstra University, 1962; Prof Diploma 1967, EdD 1981; MPA, Florida International University, 1988. *Appointments:* Teacher, Copiague Schools, New York, 1957-59; Research Associate, Columbia & Hofstra University, New York, 1964-69; Teacher, Half Hollow Hills Schools, Dix Hills, New York, 1970-72; Instructor, Connecticut Col, 1972-73; Supervisor/Supt Rdg Specialist, Hempstead Schools, new York, 1975-85. *Publications:* Poetry; Contributing author: Proceedings, South African Project, Florida Memorial College, 1987; Multilateral Project, United Nations Association of USA, 1987, 1988. *Memberships:* Chapter Secretary, Jack & Jill of America, Inc, 1960-62; Board of Directors, New York University Alumni Federation, SEHNAP, 1983-89; Board of Directors, United Nations Association, USA, 1987-; American Society for Public Administration, 1987 . *Honours:* Honorary Life Member, National Parent Teacher Association, 1965; Laurel Wreath Award, Doctoral Association, New York Educators, 1982; Fellow, Florida and Outstanding Achievement Award, 1988, International University, Public Affairs & Services, 1987-88. *Interests:* Member Alpha Kappa Alpha Inc (global affairs); Member, Tuskegee Airmen, Inc (aviation). Hobbies: Writing; Travel; Radio reading for unsighted; Performing arts. *Address:* 14320 South West 105 Terrace, Miami, Florida 33186, USA.

YOUNG Louise Buchwalter, 20 July 1919, Springfield, Ohio, USA. Writer. m. Hobart P. Young, 3 June 1944, 1 son, 2 daughters. *Education:* AB cum laude, Vassar College, 1940; MSc, Geophysical Sciences, University of Chicago, 1980. *Appointments:* Research Associate, Massachusetts Institute of Technology, 1942-44; Science Editor, American Foundation for Continuing Education, 1960-73; Freelance writer, 1972-. *Publications:* Power Over People, 1973; Earth's Aura, 1977; Blue Planet, 1983; Unfinished Universe, 1986. *Memberships:* Boards: Open Lands Project 1962-, Lake Michigan Federation 1974-78, Citizens for Better Environment 1977-83; Environmental Advisory Committee, US Department of Energy, 1978-81. *Honours:* Awards & recognitions: Friends of American Authors, 1973; Friends of Chicago Library, 1983; Society of Midland Authors, 1983; Garden Club of America, 1988. *Hobbies:* Photography;

Sailing; Flying Gliders. *Address:* 1420 Sheridan Road, Apt. 3F, Wilmette, Illinois 60091, USA.

YOUNG Margaret Elisabeth Jane, b. 21 Dec. 1922, London, England. Retired Hospital Physicist. m. Lawrence Young, 5 Jan. 1951. *Education:* Royal Holloway College, University of London, 1940-43; BSc, 1943, MSc, 1949, London. *Appointments:* Lecturer in Physics, Royal Free Hospital School of Medicine, University of London, 1943-49; Physicist, Medical Research Council Radiobiological Unit, Harwell, 1949-51; Physicist, Ottawa Civic Hospital, 1951-52; Physicist, Charing Cross Hospital, London, 1953-55; Physicist, British Columbia Cancer Control Agency, Vancouver, Canada, 1956-85. *Publications:* Radiological Physics, 1957, 3rd Edition, 1983. *Memberships:* Hospital Physicists Association, UK; Canadian College of Physicists in Medicine; American Association of Physicists in Medicine. *Hobbies:* Walking; Gardening; Riding. *Address:* 3226 West 51st Avenue, Vancouver, British Columbia, Canada V6N 3V7.

YOUNG Margaret Labash, b. 17 Aug. 1926, Bridgeport, Connecticut, USA. Editor. m. Harold Chester Young, 7 June 1958. 1 son, 1 daughter. *Education:* BA, Cornell University, 1948; Summer course, Radcliffe College, 1953; Summer Travel Course, Lausanne University, Switzerland, 1955; MA Library Science, University of Michigan, 1959. *Appointments:* Marketing Course Asst, Harvard Business School, 1949-52; Science Teacher, Willard Day School, Troy, 1952-53; Arthur D Little, 1953-57; Library Assistant, Cambridge, Massachusetts Public Library, 1957-58; Librarian, Salzburg Austria, Seminar in American Studies, 1981-83; Gale Research Co, 1964-. *Publications:* Co-editor, Directory of Special Libraries, 1976- 81; Scientific & Technical organizations and Agencies Director, 2 editions, 1985-87; Life Sciences Organizations and Agencies Directory, 1st edition, 1988. *Memberships:* Special Libraries Assoc-Chair of Publishing Division, 1985-86; Editor, Bulletin, 1984-85; Beta Phi Mu, Honorary Society Library Science, 1959; Professional Editors Network, 1986-. *Honours:* National Honor Society, 1943-44; Prize essayist, 1944; Beta Phi Mu, 1959. *Hobbies:* Tennis; Swimming; Gardening; Collecting bookmarkers, paperweights and stamps; American Field Services (International student exchange); American business history; International travel. *Address:* 313 Farmdale Road West, Hopkins, Minnesota 55343, USA.

YOUNG Marjorie Ann Harris, b. 1 Sep. 1946, Bartow, Florida, USA. Director of Youth Services (Juvenile Corrections). m. Francis H. Young, 10 Jan. 1970, 1 daughter. *Education:* Graduated with honours, Union Academy High School, Bartow, Florida; BA cum laude, Psychology, Morris Brown College, 1969; MEd, Rehabilitation Counselling, 1972, MPA, 1979, Georgia State University, Atlanta. *Appointments:* Counsellor, 1972-76, Programme Coordinator, 1976-79, District Director, 1979-81, Rehabilitation Services, Atlanta, Georgia; Director, Human Development, Atlanta, 1981-83; Director, Division of Youth Services, Department of Human Resources (Juvenile Correction), Atlanta, 1983-. *Publications:* Perceived Authority and Alienation, 1980; How Can Women Overcome the Barriers to leadership Opportunities in Rehabilitation. *Memberships:* Vice-President, Chairperson of Administrators Council, National Association of Juvenile Correction Agencies; Board Member, Commission on Accreditation for Corrections; Secretary, Governor's Criminal Justice Coordinating Council; Steering Committee, Governor's Juvenile Justice Coordinating Council; Chairperson, State Advisory Board to Georgia Legislative Black Caucus; Coalition of 100 Black Women, Atlanta; Morris Brown College Alumni Association; Alpha Kappa Alpha Sorority Inc. *Honours:* Outstanding Dogwood Festival, 1983; Outstanding Young Woman of America, 1985; Status Achievement Award, National Alumni Association, Morris Brown College, 1987. *Hobbies:* Writing; Sewing; Cooking; Track; Dancing; Girl Scouts of America; Church activities. *Address:* 878

Peachtree Street NE, Room 817, Atlanta, GA 30309, USA.

YOUNG Patricia Janean, b. 30 Nov. 1953, San Diego, California, USA. Speech-Language Pathologist. *Education:* AA, Palomar Community College, 1971; BA, 1976, MA, 1981, California State University; Credential, Speech & Hearing Specialist, 1981; Certificate, Clinical Competence, American Speech-Language-Hearing Association, 1982; Licensed Speech-Language Pathologist, California, 1982. *Appointments:* Management Trainee, J.W.Robinson's Department Store, Los Angeles, California, 1977-78; Screening Coordinator, 1978-81, Speech Pathologist, 1981-1983, Riverview Hearing, Speech & Language Centers, Long Beach, California; Speech Pathologist/Director/Owner, Speech Pathology Services, Carlsbad, California, 1984-; Producer, Cable TV shows, Communication Disorders, 1983; Coordinator, Public Service Announcement, Disabilities Awareness Week, 1986, Coordinator/Interviewee, Inside San Diego, Disabilities Awareness Week, 1988, ABC TV. *Publications:* Poetry in Phi Delta Journal, 1984. *Memberships:* California Speech Pathologists & Audiologists in Private Practice; American and California (Division Representative 1985-88) Speech-Language-Hearing Associations; Vice-President, Past Secretary, Phi Delta Gamma; National Association for Hearing & Speech Action (Chair, Benefit, 1983); Life Member: Zeta Tau Alpha; California Scholastic Federation; Public Awareness Subcommittee, Senator Ellis/Assemblywoman Bentley's Advisory Committee for Developmentally Disabled; Association for Retarded Citizens. *Honours:* Presentation (with JoAnn Yates), West Orange County Consortium of Special Education, 1981; Certificate of Recognition, Senator Jim Ellis, for contribution to Disabled Awareness Week, 1986; Awards: Outstanding Service to Department, 1981, Outstanding Clinical Competence, 1982, California State University, Long Beach; Outstanding Young Women of America, 1983; Outstanding Achievement, California Speech-Language-Hearing Association, 1987. *Hobbies:* Writing; Horseback Riding; Fashion; Dancing; Theatre; Nature. *Address:* 2880 Andover Avenue, Carlsbad, CA 92008, USA.

YOUNG Rebecca Conrad, b. 28 Feb. 1934, Clairton, Pennsylvania, USA. State Legislator. m. Merwin Crawford Young, 17 Aug. 1957. 4 daughters. *Education:* BA, University of Michigan, 1955; MA Teaching, Harvard University, 1963; JD, University of Wisconsin, 1983. *Appointments:* Commissioner, State Highway Commission, Madison, 1974-76; Deputy Secretary, Wisconsin Department of Admin, Madison, 1976-77; Associate, Wadsack, Julian & Lawton, Madison, 1983-84; Elected Representative Wisconsin State Assembly, Madison, 1984-. *Creative work:* Translator: Katanga Secession, 1966. *Memberships:* Chair, Dudgeon-Monroe Neighborhood Association, Transporation Comm 1980-81; Spokesperson, Coalition for Community Schools, 1978-79; Vice president, Wisconsin Coalition for Balanced Transp 1972-74; Vice president, Child Development Inc, 1972; Vice president, Dudgeon School PTA, 1969-70; Vice President/Board member, League of Women Voters of Dane Co, 1967-70; Volunteer, Headstart, classes for emotionally disturbed children, 1968-70; ACLU; Wisconsin Law Alumni Board of Visitors, 1988-. *Honours:* Public Interest Award, Center for Public Representation, 1980; YWCA Woman of Distinction, 1981; Congress for a Working America, for exemplary work on passage of Industrial Revenue Bond Reform Act, 1986; Clean 16 Environmental Award, 1985-86 and 1987-88; National Women's Political Caucus of Wisconsin Annual Toast & Roast, 1985; Wisconsin Pro-choice Community in Support of Reproductive Freedom, 1987; Wisconsin Coalition for Advocacy Community Building Award, 1988; Legislative Leadership Award, Maternal Child Health Coalition, 1988; Gaylord Nelson Human Service Award, Wisconsin Community Action Program Association, 1989. *Hobbies:* Charades; Scrabble. *Address:* Room 110 North, State Capitol, PO Box 8953, Madison, WI 53708, USA.

YOUNG LIVELY Sandra Lee, b. 31 Dec. 1943, Rockport, Indiana, USA. Charge Nurse. m. Kenneth L. Doom, 4 May 1962, divorced 1975, 3 daughters. *Education:* AS, Vincennes University, 1979. *Appointments:* Nursing Aide, Nurse, forest Del Nursing Home, Princeton, Indiana, 1975-80; Charge Nurse, Welborn Baptist Hospital, evansville, 1979-80, 1982-83; Staff Nurse, Longview Regional Hospital, Texas, 1980-82; Staff Nurse, Assistant Director, Leisure Lodge Home Health, Overotn, Texas, 1983-84; Staff Nurse, Director, Laird Hospital Home Health Services, 1984-86; Charge Nurse, Branchville Training Centre, Indian Department of Corrections, 1987-. *Memberships:* Vincennes University Alumni Association; Smithsonian Institute; National Association of Female Executives; Menninger Foundation. *Address:* 435 S Lincoln Ave, Rockport, IN 47635, USA.

YPERIFANOS Nell Arhos, b. 25 Feb. 1931, Texas, USA. Art Gallery Owner; Jewellery Designer. m. Nicolas S. Yperifanos, 14 Sept. 1958, 1 daughter. *Education:* BFA, University of Texas, 1952. *Appointments:* Partner, Zolotas Jewellery, USA, 1966-72; Partner,Yperifanos Jewellery Inc., 1976-82; Partner, Carminel Gallery, 1987; Nell Yperifanos Gallery Inc., 1988-. *Memberships:* National Arts Club, New York City; Doubles; many professional organizations. *Hobbies:* International Travel; Art & Antique Collector; Languages; Theatre; Metaphysical Studies. *Address:* 400 East 58th Street, New York, NY 10022, USA.

YU Priscilla Chang, b. 24 Oct. 1933, New York City, USA. Librarian. m. George Tzuchiao Yu, 11 Aug. 1957, 2 sons. *Education:* BA, University of California, 1955; MLS, Columbia University, 1957. *Appointments:* Head, Gifts & Exchange, 1976-78, Documents Bibliographer, 1980-84, Assistant History Librarian, 1984-, University of Illinois. *Publications:* Articles in professional journals. *Memberships:* ALA; Chinese-American Librarians Association; Illinois Library Association; International Association of Orientalist Librarians; American Historical Association. *Honours:* Recipient, various honours and awards. *Hobbies:* Piano; Singing; Reading; Travel. *Address:* History Library, 424 Library, University of Illinois Library, 1408 West Gregory Drive, Urbana, IL 61801, USA.

YUKL Trudy Ann, b. 5 Feb. 1947, Portsmouth, New Hampshire, USA. Psychologist. *Education:* BA, Psychology, University of Kentucky, 1969; MS, Counselling, Suffolk University, 1984; Advanced Graduate Study, Harvard University, 1984-85; EdD, Counselling Psychology, Boston University, 1989. *Appoinments:* Co-founder/Director, MGH Indian Clinic, 1973-86; MGH-Medical Social Worker, Emergency Ward, 1969-86, Clinical Fellow, Psychology, West End Group Practice, Massachusetts General Hospital, Boston, 1986-87; VA, Outpatient Clinic, Honolulu, Hawaii, 1987-88; Psychologist, Crisis Team, North Essex Mental Health Center, Haverhill, MA, USA, 1988-89. *Publications:* Author, 4 publications in profesional journals. *Memberships Include:* Board of Directors, Secretary, Hui Hoa Aloha, Honolulu; Mental Health Consultant, Kalaupapa, Molokai; Office of Hawaiian Affairs, Volunteer; American Psychological Association; Boston Indian Council, Health Consultant, Advisory Board. *Honours Include:* Outstanding Professional, Human Services, 1974-75; Phi Delta Kappa; Panel Member, Dana Farber Cancer Institute, 1983; *Hobbies:* Travel; Photography; Music; Piano; Guitar; Native American Culture. *Address:* North Essex Mental Health Center, 66 Winter Street, Haverhill, MA 01830, USA.

YUNGER Libby Marie, b. 20 Feb. 1944, East Cleveland, Ohio, USA. Technical Manager; Analytical Biochemist. m. Richard D. Cramer, 22 May 1979. *Education:* BA, Earlham College, 1966; MA 1971, PhD, 1974, Neuroscience, University of Iowa. *Appointments:* Research Biochemist, Lederle Labs, 1975-78; Associate Senior Investigator, Smith Kline & French Labs, 1978-83; Manager, Bioanalytical Research, Pitman Moore Inc., 1983-; Adjunct Associate Professor, Animal Science, University of Illinois, 1987-. *Publications:* Over

20 research articles in professional journals. *Memberships:* Society of Neuroscience; American Chemical Society; International Society Immunopharmacology; New York Academy of Science; Sigma Xi, Executive Committee, ISU Chapter, 1988-. *Honour:* Phi Beta Kappa, 1966. *Hobbies:* Historic Preservation; Travel; History; Photography. *Address:* IMC Pitman Moore Inc., PO Box 207, Terre Haute, IN 47808, USA.

YUTHASASTRKOSOL Charin, b. 30 Dec. 1930, Bangkok, Thailand. Real Estate Corporation Officer. m. 23 Feb. 1953. 2 sons, 1 daughter. *Education:* Associate Degree, Strayer College, Washington DC, 1959. *Appointments:* Bookstore Manager, International School of Bangkok, 1961-68; Owner & Operator, Anita Ballet School, Bangkok, 1961-70; Director Public Relations, 1979-89, Senior Vice President, 1989-, Twining Land Corporation, Baltimore, USA. *Memberships:* Life Member, Business & Prof Womens Association, under the Qeen of Thailand's patronage, 1961-; Philadelphia-Delaware Vall Restaurant Assoc, 1976-77; Faculty Member, Temple Uni Ass for Retired Professional, 1980- *Honours:* Recieved plaque in Ballet Dancing Award, Former Queen of Thailand, 1969; Received over 190 plaques and medals, Ballroom Dancing awards, 1978-; Award for dancing, Queen of Thailand, 1984; Plaque Award in Dancing, Foundation for the Blind of Thailand, 1989. *Hobbies:* Practising design arts; Teaching and playing piano; Performing ballet, jazz and tap dance. *Address:* Twining Corp, 4004 Greenway, Baltimore, MD 21218, USA.

Z

ZACHER Candace M. Naumowicz, b. 8 Mar. 1950, Milwaukee, Wisconsin, USA. Instructional Technology Consultant. m. James A. Zacher, 25 Oct. 1980, 1 daughter. *Education:* BA, Northwestern University, 1971; MS, Syracuse University, 1975; PhD, Purdue University, 1984. *Appointments:* Training Coordinator, Milwaukee Medical Complex 1978-80, Indiana Highways Department 1981-82, Purdue University 1985-87; Instructional developer consultant, 1982-85; Instructional technologist, AT&T Bell Laboratories, 1987-. *Creative works:* Articles: Developing Effective Documentation for Computer Software, 1987; Dynamic Viewing-Effective Computer Screens for CAI, 1987; Assessment of Micro-based Art Activities, 1984. Multimedia presentation, US, 1974. *Memberships:* Association of Educational Communications & Technology; National Society of Performance & Instruction (NSPI); Vice President, Indiana Chapter, NSPI; Chicago Chapter, NSPI. *Honours:* Outstanding Woman Leader of Tomorrow, Quota Club, 1967; Pi Lamba Theta, 1975; Phi Delta Kappa, 1978. *Hobbies:* Ballet; Watercolour painting; Outdoor photography; Travel. *Address:* Property Loss Research Bureau, 1501 Woodfield Road, Suite 400W, Schaumburg, IL 60173, USA.

ZACHERT Virginia, b. 1 Mar. 1928, Jacksonville, Alabama, USA. Research Professor Emerita. *Education:* AB, Georgia State Womans College, 1940; MA, Experimental Psychology, Emory University, 1947; PhD, Industrial Psychology, Purdue University, 1949. *Appointments Include:* Various positions, 1940-55; Research Associate, Auburn Research Foundation, Auburn University, 1955-58; Director, Sturm O'Brien Consulting Engineers, Auburn, 1958-59; Project Field Director, Keesler AFB, Biloxi, 1959- 62; Private Consultant, 1960-71; Associate Professor, Medical College of Geogia, 1963-70, Research Professor, 1970-84, Research Professor Emerita, 1984-. *Publications:* Articles in numerous professional journals. *Memberships:* Life Member, American Psychological Association; Sigma Xi; Fellow, Georgia Psychological Association; etc. *Honours:* Recipient, various honours & Awards. *Address:* Dept. of OB & Gyn MCG, Augusta, GA 30912, USA.

ZADORA Magdalena Joanna, b. 24 June 1949, Legnica, Polan. Psychologist. *Education:* Master's degree 1975, studies of psychology, sociotherapy 1986, 1988, Master of Psychology Diploma 1988, University of Wroclaw. *Appointments:* Gdansk Psychiatric Hospital, 1975-78; Psychologist, Gdansk School System, 1976-. *Membership:* Polish Society of Psychology. *Honours:* Awards: Inspector of Schools 1982, Schools Administrator 1986. *Hobbies:* Singing; Animals; Gardening; Sport; Languages; Resting in woods; Friendship; Writing verses & song lyrics. *Address:* 81-881 Sopot, Str. O. Kolberga 14B/20, Poland.

ZAFT Alice Emily, b. 10 Jan. 1947, Far Rockaway, New York, USA. Lawyer. m. Jon Ruston Weissman, 15 Dec. 1969, 1 son, 1 daughter. *Education:* BA, Smith College, 1979; JD magna cum laude, Western New England College, 1983. *Appointments:* Law Clerk to presiding Justices, Superior Court, Commonwealth of Massachusetts, 1982-83; Partner, Cooley, Shrair, Alpert, Labovitz & Dambrov PC. *Memberships:* Vice President, Women's Bar Association; Massachusetts Bar Association; Association of Trial Lawyers of America; Past office, Hampden County Bar Association; Massachusetts Association of Women Lawyers; Massachusetts Association of Trial Attorneys; Smith College Club. *Honours include:* American Jur Award, excellence in Trusts & Estates. *Hobbies:* Batik; Gardening; Cross-country skiing. *Address:* 227 Mountain Road, Wilbraham, Massachusetts 01095, USA.

ZAHRA-NEWMAN Margaret-Anne, b. 23 June 1958, Sydney, Australia. Computer Software Developer; Publisher. m. Anthony Edward Zahra-Newman, 1 son. *Education:* B.Com., University of New South Wales. *Appointments:* Company Director, MATZN Pty Ltd., 1980-; Medical Practice Manager, 1980-; Managing Director, JAM Software Pty Ltd; Computer Software Developer Publisher. *Publications:* Article, Fa'a Samoa - The Samoan Way of Life, 1981; Assertion and Social Skills, Co-autjor with George Sent; Josephine Zammit MBE, A Maltese Woman in Australia, 1989; Software Publications: Macintosh Computer Software; JAM Appointment Diaries; Smart Alarms; The Medical Electronic Desktop including MED Patient (aka MacMED); MED Billing; MED Search; MacList; Technofile; Other Customised computer databases. *Hobbies:* Art; Oil Painting; Pottery, *Address:* 27A Nowranie St., Summer Hill, NSW 2130, Australia.

ZAIDEL Dahlia W, b. 3 Oct. 1944. Professor; Scientist. m. Eran Zaidel, 23 Oct. 1965, 2 sons. *Education:* BA, Psychology, Queens College, 1966; PhD, Cognitive Psychology, UCLA, 1981. *Appointments:* Postdoctoral Fellow, Psychiatry, 1982-83, Assistant Professor, psychology, 1984-, UCLA. *Publications:* numerous articles in professional journals. *Memberships:* AAAS; APA; Sigma Xi; Neuroscience Society. *Honours:* NIMH Pre-doctoral Fellowships, 1979-81; NIH Grant, 1984-; Fulbright Fellowship, Oxford, England, 1988-89. *Hobbies:* Archaeology; Films; Hiking. *Address:* Dept. of Psychology, UCLA, Los Angeles, CA 90024, USA.

ZAIMONT Judith Lang, b. 8 Nov. 1945, Memphis, Tennessee, USA. Composer. m. Gary E. Zaimont, 18 June 1967, 1 son. *Education:* Juilliard School, Prep. Division, 1958-64; Master in Piano, Long Island Institute of Music, 1966; BA, Music, Queens College, City University of New York, 1962-66; MA, Music Composition, Columbia University, 1967. *Appointments:* Composer. *Publications:* Commissions from Connecticut Opera, Exxon Fund, Florilegium Chamber Choir, Baltimore Dance Theatre, Greenville Symphony (SC), Gregg Smith Singers, Baltimore Chamber Orchestra, Hopkins Symphony. Compositions: oratorios: Lamentation, 1982; Sacred Service, 1976; Cantatas: The Chase, 1972; Parable, 1986; Chamber Opera: Goldilocks and the Three Bears; Orchestral: Monarchs, 1988; Tarantelle, 1985; Chroma, 1986; Piano Concerto, 1972; Great Land, 1982; The Magic World, 1979; Sky Curtains, 1984; Dance/Inner Dance, 1985; Editor in Chief: Book Series, The Musical Woman: A International Perspective Vol. 1, 1983, Vol. II, 1985-86; Principal Editor, Contemporary Concert Music by Women, 1984; Author, Twentieth Century Piano Music: A Graded Annotated Selective List, 1980, Composition. *Honours Include:* Woodrow Wilson Fellowship, 1966-67; Gottschalk Competition 1st Prize Gold Medal, 1970; Debussy Fellowship, Alliance Française, 1972; NEA Grant, 1982; Guggenheim Fellowship, 1983; Presser Foundation Award, 1984. *Address:* 47 Lawrence Street, North New Hyde Park, New York 11040, USA.

ZAITZOW Barbara Hope, b. 6 Dec. 1955, San Diego, California, USA. Research Associate. m. Peter D Villanova, 21 July 1985. *Education:* BA, Sociology, San Diego State University, 1974-82; MS, Sociology 1982-85, PhD Candidate, Sociology 1985-, Virginia Polytechnic Institute and State University. *Appointments:* Undergraduate Teaching Assistant 1978-82, Graduate Teaching Assistant 1982-86, Editorial Assistant, Sociological Inquiry, 1984-86, Course Instructor, 1985-87, Research Associate 1987-, Public Opinion Laboratory Social Science Research Institute. *Publications:* Paper: What Price? No Pain, No Gain: Some Further Thoughts on Teaching Sex Roles, The Humanist Sociologist, with J K Skipper, 1984; Papers presented at Conferences; Technical Reports. *Memberships:* Alpha Kappa Delta, International Sociology Honor Society; American Correctional Association; American Sociological Assocation; John Howard Association; Western Society of Criminology. *Hobbies:* Travel; Music; Horseback riding; Reading; Prison reform. *Address:* Public Opinion Laboratory,

Social Science Research Institute, Third & Locust Streets, DeKalb, Illinois 60115, USA.

ZALOSCER Hilde, b. 15 June 1903, Tuzla, Bosnia. University Professor. *Education:* Doctor of Philosophy, Vienna University, 1927. *Appointments:* Editor, Art Magazine; Professor, Alexandria University, Egypt, 1947-67; Professor, Carleton University, Ottawa, Canada, 1969-72; Lecturer, Vienna University, Austria, 1972-74. *Publications include:* La Collection Abbas el Arabi; Porträts aus dem Wüstensand, 1947; Die Kunst im Christlichen Agypten, 1962; Vom Mumienbildnis zur Ikone, 1974; Der Schrei, Signum einer Epoche; Eine Heimkehr gibt es nicht Nicht, 1984; Das Bildzitat im Oeuvre von Thomas Mann, 1984. *Memberships include:* Archaeological Society, Alexandria; Society for Coptic Archaeology, Cairo; Thomas-Mann- Gesellschaft; AICA, Paris. *Honours:* Adolf Scharf Prize, Vienna, 1944; Theodor Korner Prize, Vienna, 1970; Golden Doctorate, Vienna, 1977. *Hobbies:* Golf; Music. *Address:* Franz Koci Strasse 6/15/12a, A-1100 Vienna, Austria.

ZANDER Janet Adele, b. 19 Feb. 1950, Miles City, Montana, USA. Psychiatrist. m. Mark Richard Ellenberger, 16 Sept. 1979. 1 son. *Education:* BA, St Olaf College, 1972; MD 1976, Residency in Psychiatry 1976-79, Fellowship in Psychiatry 1979-80, University of Minnesota Medical School. *Appointments:* Staff Psychiatrist, St Paul Ramsey Medical Center, 1980-; Assistant Professor in Psychiatry, University of Minnesota, 1981-; Director of Inpatient Psychiatry, St Paul Ramsey, 1986-. *Memberships:* American Psychiatric Association; Minnesota Psychiatric Association; Minnesota Medical Association; American Medical Women's Association; Ramsey County Medical Society. *Honours:* Phi Beta Kappa, 1971; National Merit Scholar, 1968; Chief Resident in Psychiatry, 1978-79. *Hobbies:* Choral singing; My child. *Address:* 640 Jackson Street, St Paul, MN 55101, USA.

ZAREMSKI Barbara Maria, b. 28 June 1937, Chicago, Illinois, USA. Psychotherapist (Family and Transpersonal); Author; Swim Coach. m. Sherman C. Zaremski, 14 May 1962, 2 sons. *Education:* BSc. Psychology, Sociology, University of Illinois, 1959; BSCU, Avila College, 1975; St Paul Methodist Seminary, Kansas City, 1980; MDiv, William Lyon University; PhD, Psychology, 1988. *Appointments:* Michael Reese School of Nursing, 1959-60; Caseworker, Department of Welfare, Cook County, 1960-62; Head Swim Coach, Oak Park YMCA, 1960-63; Swim Coach, Kansas City Jewish Community Center, 1969-70; Biofeedback & Optimal Performance Center, Leawood, Kansas, 1975-; Masters Swim Coach, 1982-; Sport psychology work with world record holders in swimming and masters weightlifting; Internationally ranked Masters competitive swimmer. *Publications:* Hurting, Winning and Preparing, 1981; Students Fine Gold Work - The Design and Creation of Jewelry; Robt von Newman, Physical Ecology and Athletic Endeavor, 1982; Excellence over the Years - Study of Top Ten Masters Swimmers, 1985. *Memberships:* NASW; American Swim Coaches Asociation; Masters Swim Coaches Association; American Association of Family Counselors and Mediators; Approved Supervisor, American Association of Marriage and Family Therapists; Professional Member, American Association of Pastoral Counselors; BNLP; North American Sector, Psychology of Sport and Physical Activity, International Society for Sport Psychology. *Honours:* General Robert E.Wood Scholarship, 1954-59; Awards, Burmese and Russian Blue cats, Tomahawk Cattery, 1969-73; National Champion, Masters Competitive Swimming Short and Long Courses, yearly, 1977-, World Champion, 1978, 1979, 1988; World Record Holder, 2 mile open water swim, 50-50 year age group, 1988. *Hobbies:* Jewellery creation; Meditation; Singing. *Address:* Biofeedback and Optimal Performance Center, 9931 Lee Court, Leawood, KS 66206, USA.

ZATLIN Phyllis, b. 31 Dec. 1938, Green Bay, Wisconsin, USA. Professor. m. George Boring Kelly, 20 Aug. 1962, 1 son, 1 daughter. *Education:* BA, Rollins College, 1960; MA, 1962, PhD, 1965, University of Florida. *Appointments:* Various positions, Rutgers University, New Brunswick, New Jersey, 1963-, including Associate Dean, 1974-80, Full Professor, 1979-, Departmental Chair, 1980-87. *Publications:* Lengue y lectura: un repaso y una continuacion, with teacher's manual and tapes, (with Matilde O. Castells), 1970; Elena Quiroga, 1977; Victor Ruiz, 1980; Jaime Salom, 1982; Editor: El rapto (Francisco Ayala), 1971; El lando de seis caballos (Victor Ruiz Iriarte), 1979; La piel del limon (Jaime Salom), 1980; Noviembre y un poco de verba. Petra Regalada (Antonio Gala), 1981; The Contemporary Spanish Theater. A Collection of Critical Essays (with Martha T. Halsey), 1988; Combate de Opalos y Tasia. Sombra y quimera de Larra. La magosta (Francisco Nieva), forthcoming; Numerous articles. *Memberships:* American Association of University Professors (National Council 1987-); Modern Language Association (Commission on the Status of Women 1978-81); Women's Equity League (National Board, 1973, 1976-77. *Honours:* Fulbright Fellow, 1960; Woodrow Wilson Fellow, 1961; Distinguished Alumnus, Rollins College, 1985. *Interests:* Research; Contemporary Hispanic theatre; Cross-cultural approaches to theatre; Narrative of contemporary Spanish women writers; Translation studies. *Address:* Department of Spanish and Portuguese, Rutgers University, New Brunswick, NJ 08903, USA.

ZAVADA Mary Roberta, b. 11 Jan. 1936, Passaic, New Jersey, USA. Vice-President, Publications; Writer. *Education:* AB magna cum laude, College of St Elizabeth, 1957; MA, Creative Writing, De Paul University, 1959; London University, England, 1962, 1963-64. *Appointments:* Managing Editor, Educational Testing Service, 1974-82; Director, Press Relations, 1982- 86, Vice-President, Publications, 1986-, Insurance Information Institute. *Publications:* Articles and stories in numerous publications including Vogue, The New York Times, The Washington Post, College Board Review. *Memberships:* New York Women in Communications; Kappa Gamma Pi, President, Boston Chapter, 1967-69, 2nd National Vice-President, 1969-71. *Honours:* 1st Prize, Vogue magazine Prix de Paris Writing Contest, 1957; All-expense award to London University, Washington DC Branch, English- Speaking Union, 1962; Designated 1 of 60 Outstanding Women in Communications, New York Women in Communications, 1983. *Hobbies:* Travel; Sewing. *Address:* Apt 6A, 6040 Boulevard East, West New York, NJ 07093, USA.

ZAWODNY LuRae Jean, b. 9 Feb. 1949, Chicago, USA. Artist. m. Janusz K. Zawodny, 18 Sept. 1971, 1 son. *Education:* BA, University of Nebraska, 1970; MFA, Claremont Graduate School, 1982. *Creative Works:* Solo Exhibitions: Libra Gallery, Claremont, 1982; Olympia Federal, 1983; University of Portland, 1984; Columbia Arts Centre, 1985; Group Shows: Chaffey College, 1977; Lang Gallery, 1978; KNBC TV, Los Angeles, 1981. *Memberships:* American Council for the Arts; Oregon Art Institute; Maryhill Museum. *Address:* 23703 NE Margaret Road, Brush Prairie, WA 98606, USA.

ZAYACHEK Mary Katherine, b. 18 Aug. 1943, Jersey City, USA. Hospital Administrator; RN. m. Jon Martin Zayachek, 24 Sept. 1966, 2 sons, 1 daughter. *Education:* BSN, 1965; MA, Southwestern University, 1985. *Appointments:* RN, St Barnabas Medical Centre, 1965-66; Nurse, Critical Care, Spohn Hospital, 1966-67, Overlook Hospital, 1968-74; Clinical Instructor, Passaic County Community College, 1975-76, Clara Mass School of Nursing, 1975; Utilization Supervisor, 1976-80, Quality assurance, 1980-85, Assistant Administrator, 1985-86, Assistant Vice President, 1986, The Mountainside Hospital. *Memberships:* NJ Association of Quality Assurance Professionals; National Association of Quality Assurance Professionals; NJ Association healthcare Risk Managers, Charter Member. *Honours:* Recipient, various honours & awards. *Hobbies:* Sailing; Aerobics. *Address:* The Mountainside Hospital, Bay & Highland Aves, Montclair, NJ 07042, USA.

ZEBROWSKI Rachel Katharine Williams, b. 25 July 1951, Cleveland, Ohio, USA. Architect. m. Joseph A. Zebrowski, 29 Sept. 1984, 2 daughters. *Education:* BA, Sarah Lawrence College, 1972; MArch, School of Architecture & Urban Planning, University of California, Los Angeles, 1975. *Appointments:* Paolo Soleri, 1972; Lyman, Gittleson, Walters Architects, 1973-76; Charles Kober Associates, 1976-78; Coy Howard & Company, 1978-81; Urban Design Group, 1982-84; Williams Resources, 1984-87; Page- Zebrowski Architects, 1987-. *Creative works include:* Project Architect: McCafferty residence, Gross residence; Architect, Williams residence. *Memberships:* American Institute of Architects; Advisory Board Chair, Board of Directors, Tulsa Centre for Contemporary Arts. *Honours:* Dean's Award, design excellence, graduate thesis, UCLA; Various design awards, Progressive Architecture, 1978, 1980. *Hobbies:* Horses; Photography; Gardening; Skiing; Music. *Address:* Page- Zebrowski Architects, 233 South Detroit, Suite 310, Tulsa, Oklahoma 74120, USA.

ZEDLER Beatrice Hope, b. 14 May 1916, Milwaukee, USA. Professor Emerita. *Education:* BA, 1937, MA, 1938, Marquette University; PhD, Fordham University, 1947. *Appointments:* Teacher, Philosophy, Marian College, 1939-40, College Misericordia, Dallas, 1941-43; Professor, 1946-86, Professor Emerita 1986-, Philosophy, Marquette University. *Publications:* How Philosophy Begins, 1983; Translator: G. Menage's, The History of Women Philosophers, 1984, Thomas Aquinas' On the Unity of the Intellect Against the Averroists, 1968; 23 articles, 40 book reviews. *Memberships:* American Catholic Philosophical Association; American Association of University Professors; Medieval Academy of America. *Honours:* Appointed to Marquette University Women's Chair of Humanistic Studies, 1967-69, Re- appointed 1969-71; Faculty Award for Teaching Excellence, 1981; Aquinas Lecturer, Marquette University, 1983. *Hobbies:* Reading; Listening to Music. *Address:* 5305 W. Wisconsin Ave., Milwaukee, WI 53208, USA.

ZEI Alki, b. 15 Dec. 1927, Athens, Greece. Author; Translator. m. Georges Sevasticoglou, 3 Nov. 1947, 1 son, 1 daughter. *Education:* Literature, University of Athens; Acting, Athens School of Drama, & Centro Sperimentale Cinematografia, Italy; Screenwriting, Institute Cinematografy, Moscow, USSR. *Publications:* Novels: Wildcat Under Glass, translated 14 languages; Petros War, translated 8 languages; Sound of the Dragon's Feet, translated English; Uncle Platon; A Sunday in April, translated French; Anniba's Football Shoes; Boots & Shoes; Achille's Fiancee. *Membership:* Greek Writers Association. *Honours:* Mildred Batchelder Awards (USA), novels, 1970, 1974, 1976. *Address:* Leoforos Alexandras 194, 115-21 Athens, Greece.

ZEITLIN Marianne Langner, b. 31 Mar. 1928, Toronto, Canada. Novelist; Playwright. m. Zvi Zeitlin, 5 May 1951, 1 son, 1 daughter. *Appointments:* Manager, Clarion Music Society, 1963-65; Public Relations Manager, Theatre Guild, 1965-67. *Publications:* Mira's Passage; Next of Kin (novel); Numerous articles and short stories in Helicon 9, Jerusalem Post, Gannett Press, Jewish Roots. *Memberships:* Trustee, Friends of Rochester Public Library. *Address:* 204 Warren Avenue, Rochester, NY 14618, USA.

ZELDIN Xenia Valerie, b. 6 June 1957, Roanoke, Virginia, USA. Professor of Philosophy. *Education:* AB, Bryn Mawr College, 1979; MA Philosophy 1983, PhD Philosophy 1988, The University of Texas at Austin. *Appointments:* Visiting Assistant Professor, Philosophy, Texas A&M University, 1987-88; Adjunct Assistant Professor, Philosophy, Iowa State University of Science and Technology, 1988-. *Publications:* Author of papers presented at Universities. *Memberships:* Society for the Advancement of American Philosophy; Iowa Philosophical Society; American Philosophical Association; Southern Conference on Slavic Studies; American Association for the Advancement of Slavic Studies. *Honour:* Maria Rosa Scholarship Award, American Institute for Italian Culture, Bryn Mawr

College, 1979. *Hobby:* Photography. *Address:* Department of Philosophy, Iowa State University, Ames, Iowa 50011, USA.

ZEMANS Joyce Lynn, b. 21 Apr. 1940, Toronto, Canada. Art Historian; University & Arts Administrator. m. Frederick H.S. Newton Mozah Zemens, 6 June 1960, 1 son, 2 daughters. *Education:* BA, University of Toronto, 1962; MA, 1966; University of London, 1960-61. *Appointments:* Director, Canada Council, 1989-. *Publications:* Jock Macdonald, 1986; Christopher Pratt, 1985; J.W.G. Macdonald: The Inner Landscape, 1981; Art, 1976. *Memberships:* Canadian Association of Fine Arts Deans; International Association of Fine Arts Deans; Universities Art Association of Canada; International Association of Art Critics. *Address:* 99 Metcalfe St., PO Box 1047, Ottawa, Ontario K1P 5V8, Canada.

ZEMO Nina Vera, b. 28 Sept. 1947, Stamford, Connecticut, USA. Marketing Executive; Writer. *Education:* BA, Anna Maria College, Paxton, Massachusetts, 1969; MA, California State University, San Francisco, 1973; Alliance Francaise; Graduate courses, University of California, Berkeley. *Appointments:* Assistant editor, Progressive Architecture Magazine, 1969; Assistant buyer, I. Magnin & Company, San Francisco, 1971-74; Research associate, Justice Department Grant, SF, 1974-75; Director of Marketing, Institute for Contemporary Studies, SF, 1975-79; Director, Public Relations, Bank of California, SF, 1979-80; Product Manager, Levi Strauss & Company, SF, 1980-84; Marketing Director, Technical Instrument Company, SF, 1984-87; Cahners Publishing Company (Reed International), Stamford, Connecticut, 1988-. *Honour:* Outstanding Young Women in America, 1979. *Hobbies:* Writing poetry, plays, novel in progress, articles; Calligraphy; Drawing; Aerobics; Wine; Opera. *Address:* One Strawberry Hill Court 3E, Stamford, Connecticut 06902, USA.

ZERBE Kathryn J, b. 17 Oct. 1951, Harrisburg, Pennsylvania, USA. Psychiatrist. *Education:* BS with BA equivalent, double major, Duke University, 1973; MD, Temple University School of Medicine, 1978. *Appointments:* Staff Psychiatrist 1982-, Section Chief 1987-, C F Menninger Memorial Hospital. *Publications:* Numerous articles, transactions, book reviews, presentations, and papers to professional journals, magazines and conferences. *Memberships:* American Medical Association; American Medical Women's Association; American Psychiatric Association; Affiliate Member, American Psychoanalytic Association; American Society of Psychopathology of Expression. *Honours:* Cum Laude, Duke University, 1973; Seeley Fellow 1979-80, 1980-81 and 1981-82, Menninger School of Psychiatry; Annual Laughlin Award for Merit, The National Psychiatric Endowment Fund, 1982. *Hobbies:* Reading; Hiking; Art history; Travel; Writing. Professional interests: Psychoanalysis; long-term psychotherapy and hospital treatment; teaching and supervision; eating disorders; psychobiographical studies of artists, professional development growth in women; applied psychoanalysis. *Address:* Menninger, Box 829, Topeka, KS 66601, USA.

ZERNOVA Ruth, b. 15 Feb 1919, Odessa, Russia. Writer. m. Ilya Serman, 15 Nov. 1943, 1 son, 1 daughters. *Education:* MA, Leningrad University, 1947. *Publications:* In Russian: Scorpio Berries, 1961; Light and Shadow, 1963; Bakalao, 1963; A Long Long Summer, 1967; Sunny Side, 1968; Stories About Anton, 1968; Mute Rings, 1974; Womens Stories, 1981; It Has been in Our Times, 1988. *Memberships:* Union of Soviet Writers, from 1965-76; Union of Writers of Israel. *Hobbies:* Songs & Their History. *Address:* POB 23118, Ramot, Jerusalem, Israel.

ZEVON Susan Jane, b. 23 July 1944, New York City, USA. Architecture Editor. *Education:* BA, Art History, Smith College; International studies (Smith College junior year), University of Geneva, Switzerland.

Appointments: Assistant Editor, Trends & Environments, House & Garden magazine, 1970-80; Senior Editor, Self magazine, 1980-81; Account Supervisor, Jessica Dee Communications, 1982-85; Architecture Editor, House Beautiful magazine, 1985- . *Publications include:* Co-author, book, Decorating on the Cheap; Contributing reporter, Home Style pages, New York Post; Contributor, Home section, NY Times. *Memberships:* Past President, past Vice President, Smith College Club, New York City; Architectural League, NYC. *Hobbies:* Art; Literature; Gymnastics; Films. *Address:* 400 East 55th Street, New York, NY 10022, USA.

ZHANG Hou-can, b. 10 Apr. 1927, Beijing, China. Professor of Psychology. m. Z. H. Wang, 1946, 2 sons, 2 daughters. *Education:* Department of Psychology, Fu-Ren University, 1945-48. *Appointments include:* Chair, Department of Psychology, Beijing Normal University, 1982- 87; Vice President, Chinese Psychological Society, 1984-; Deputy Chair, Psychological Measurement Committee, CPS, 1984-; Vice Director, Beijing Psychological Society. *Publications:* Books: Psychological & Educational Statistics; Experimental Psychology. Also: Deputy Chief Editor, Chinese Encyclopaedia of Psychology. *Memberships:* Assembly, International Union of Psychological Science; International Society for Study of Behaviour Development; President, Educational Statistics & Measurement Association, of Chinese Educational Society. *Honours:* Research award, National College Entrance Exams, 1987; Award, outstanding college text book, State Educational Commission, 1988; Outstanding Woman in Beijing, 1988; Biographical recognition, USA, 1987. *Hobbies:* Extensive. *Address:* Department of Psychology, Beijing Normal University, Beijing 100875, China.

ZHANG Kaiming, b. 22 Oct. 1933, Jaingsu, China. Professor. m. Shaolian Zheng, 19 Jan. 1958, 1 son, 1 daughter. *Education:* Graduate, Mathematics, Fudan University,, Shanghai, 1953; Graduate School, Leningrad University, USSR, 1958-60. *Appointments:* Assistant, Mathematics, 1953- 58, Lecturer, 1960-74, Lecturer, Computer Science, 1974-78, Associate Professor, Professor, Physics, 1978-, Fudan University, Shanghai. *Publications:* Computational Physics, 1987; scientific papers in professional journals. *Memberships:* Council Member, Computational Physics Society; Vice Chairman, Council, Shanghai Molecular Science Research Association; Editorial Board, Chinese Journal of Computational Physics; Journal of Molecular Science. *Honours:* 2nd Award, Sciences & Technology Progress, National Education Committee 1985. *Address:* Physics Dept., Fudan Unlvesity, Shanghai, Peoples Republic of China.

ZHOU Lingdi, b. 18 Feb. 1934, Nanjing, China. Professor. m. Youngkang Liu, 23 Jan. 1960, 2 daughters. *Education:* Graduate, Chongqing University, 1955; Nanjing University, 1957-59. *Appointments:* Assistant Tutor, Changchun Geologicla College, 1955-57, 1959-61; Assistant Researcher, Institute of Geology, Academia Sinica, 1961-66; Assistant Researcher, 1966-80, Associate Professor, 1980-86, Professor, Mineralogy & Geochemistry, 1986-, Institute of Geochemistry, Academia Sinica. *Publications:* A Handbook of Identification of Pt-group Minerals, co-author, 1981; Pt-group Minerals and Their Formation, in Geochemistry of Pt-group Elements and Pt-group Minerals in Pt-bearing Geological Bodies in China, 1981. *Memberships:* Chairperson, Academic Commission, Institute of Geochemistry, Academia Sinica; Commissioner, Mineralogical Commission, chinese Geologicla Society; Chinese Society of Mineralogy Petrology & Geochemistry. *Honour:* 2nd Award, Academia Sinica, 1980. *Address:* Institute of Geochemistry, Academia Sinica, Guiyang, Guizhou Province, Peoples Republic of China.

ZHOU Yu-liang, b. 10 Feb. 1923, Tianjin, China. Professor. m. Liang-cheng Cha, 23 Dec. 1949, died 1977, 2 sons, 2 daughters. *Education:* BS, Catholic University, Beijing, China, 1946; MS, 1949, PhD, 1952, University of Chicago, USA. *Appointments:* Associate Professor, 1953-79, Professor, 1979-, Biology, Nankai University. *Publications:* Mycology, 1986; Molecular Microbiology, by J.B.G. Kwapinski, edited & translated to Chinese, 1986. *Memberships:* Sigma Delta Epsilon; Sigma Xi; Chairman, Mycology Committee, Chinese Society for Microbiology; Board of Directors, Chinse Society for Microbiology. *Address:* Dept. of Biology, Nankai University, Tianjin, China.

ZICH Sue Schaab, b. 18 Oct. 1946, Buffalo, New York, USA. Nursing Administrator. m. Timothy J. Zich, 25 Nov. 1976, 2 sons. *Education:* BSN, Villa Maria College, Erie, Pennsylvania, 1968. *Appointments:* Staff Nurse, Team Leader, Charge Nurse, Buffalo Children's Hospital, 1968- 71; Staff Nurse, Plasmapheresis Unit, Roswell Park Memorial Institute, 1971- 72; Health & Safety Officer, Camp Nurse, Boy Scouts of America, summers 1971, 1973-75; Staff Development Coordinator, Episcopal Church Home, Buffalo, 1975- 77; Paediatric Charge Nurse, Loudoun Memorial Hospital, 1977; Nursing Instructor, Northern Virginia Mental Health Institute, 1977-78; Director, Nursing Service, Barcroft Institute, 1978-. *Memberships:* Offices, Northern Virginia Directors of Nursing Association; Past Chapter President, Villa Maria College Alumnae Association; Life member, Mount St Mary Alumnae Association; Numerous offices, Boy Scouts of America, & Metropolitan Soccer Referees Association. *Honours:* Scouting Awards: Key Leader 1981, District Award of Merit 1985, Prince William District; Den Leader Training Award 1982, Coach Training Award 1985; Scouter's Training Award, 1984. *Hobbies:* Sewing; Reading; Sports; Macrame; Craft activities; Wreath making; Cooking; Camping. *Address:* 9709 Evans Ford Road, Manassas, Virginia 22111, USA.

ZIEGLER Dhyana, b. 5 May 1949, New York City, USA. Professor. *Education:* BS, Baruch College, City University of New York, 1981; MA, 1983, PhD, 1985, Southern Illinois University. *Appointments:* Production Intern, CBS TV, 1980-81; Instructor, Southern Illinois University, 1981-84; Assistant Professor, Jackson State University, 1984-85; Professor, Broadcasting, University of Tennessee, 1985-. *Publications:* Documentaries: A Visit with Alex Haley, 1986; Single Parenting: A Woman's Perspective, 1987. *Memberships:* Society of Professional Journalists; Sigma Delta Chi; Kappa Tau Alpha; Broadcast Education Association; Phi Delta Kappa; Delta Sigma theta; Women in Communications. *Honours Include:* Outstanding Faoulty Member of the Year, 1988, Chancellor's Citation for Extraordinary Service, 1988, Kappa Tu Alpha, 1988, University of Tennessee. *Hobbies:* Music; Writing; TV; Arts; Collecting Leaves & Rocks. *Address:* University of Tennessee, Dept. of Broadcasting, 295 Communications Building, Knoxville, TN 37921, USA.

ZIFFRIN Marilyn Jane, b. 7 Aug. 1926, Moline, Illinois, USA. Composer. *Education:* BM, University of Wisconsin, Madison, 1948; MA, Columbia University, New York, 1949; Composition with Alexander Tcherepnin and Karl Ahrendt. *Appointments:* Head, Music Department, NW Mississippi Junior College, Senatobia, 1949-50; Assistant Head, Transcriptions, WGN Radio- TV, Chicago, Illinois, 1950-52; Office Manager, W M Simeral & Co, Chicago, 1952-56; Teacher, Chicago Public Schools, 1956-61; Assistant Professor, Northeastern Illinois University, Chicago, 1961-67; Associate Professor, New England College, Henniker, New Hampshire, 1967-82. *Compositions:* Letters, Symphony for Voice and Orchestra; Three Movements for Guitar; Sono, cello and piano; Fantasia, solo bassoon; Haiku, soprano and viola, keyboard; Conversations, double bass, harpsichord; Piano Trio; String Quartet; Rhapsody for guitar; Trio for soprano, xylophone, tuba; Songs; Suite for Piano. *Memberships:* American Women Composers Inc; American Society of Composers, Authors & Publishers; Sigma Alpha Iota Society of Composers Inc; League of Women Composers; Composers Forum Inc; American Music Center; The Sonneck Society; National Association of

Composers, USA; Music Teachers National Association; College Music Society; Music Educators National Conference. *Honours:* 2nd Prize, Suite for Piano, Chicago Chapter, International Society for Contemporary Music, 1955; 1st Prize, Haiku, Delius Composition Competition, 1972; Semi-finalist, Sono, Kennedy Center Freidheim Awards, 1983; 2nd Prize, Piano Trio, Bradley University Arts Festival, 1985; Fellow, MacDowell Colony, 1961, 1963, 1971, 1977, 1980, 1989; ASCAP Awards, 1981-89; NH Commission on the Arts, 1983; Resident, Virginia Center for the Creative Arts, 1987. *Hobbies:* Playing chamber music; Walking; Reading; Jazz; Completing biography of composer Carl Ruggles. *Address:* PO Box 179, Bradford, NH 03221, USA.

ZILVERSMIT Charlotte Perlman, b. 21 Feb. 1933, Syracuse, New York, USA. Clinical Social Worker. m. Arthur Zilversmit, 26 Dec. 1955. 1 son, 1 daughter. *Education:* BS, Cornell University, 1954; MSW, University of California, Berkeley, 1958. *Appointments:* The Virginia Frank Child Development Center of Jewish Family & Community Service, 1973-84, Supervisor, Family Therapy Training, 1983-84; Jewish Family & Community Service, Chicago, 1973-88; Private Practice, 1988-. *Publications:* Teaching Family Therapy, 1988; Use of Family Agency Resources in Response to one Family's needs in the Many Dimensions of Family Practice with H Frankle and L Wineberg. *Memberships:* Board Certified Diplomate, Clinical Social Work, NASW; ACSW; CSW; AGPA (American Group Psychotherapy); AAMF (American Association of Marriage and Family Therapy); Illinois Society of Clinical Social Workers; Societa Italiana di Terapia Familiare. *Honour:* Omicron Nu, Honor Society Cornell University, College of Human Ecology, 1954. *Hobbies:* Painting; Art; Travel. *Address:* 320 Spruce Avenue, Lake Forest, Illinois 60045, USA.

ZIMMER Maude Files, b. 29 Nov. 1905, Oak Ridge, Louisiana, USA. Writer. m. (1) 1 son, (2)Joseph E. Zimmer, 16 June 1945. *Education:* Diploma, Louisiana State Normal College, 1924; Colorado University, 1925; Mexico University, 1937. *Appointments:* Teacher, Oak Ridge High School, Oak Ridge, Louisiana, 1924-26, 1932-38; Assistant Editor, Lands of Romance magazine, 1937-38; Secretary, 1939-41; Supervisor, US Office of Censorship, 1942-45; Columnist, Hartford Times, Hartford, Connecticut, 1947-59. *Publications:* Books: A Time to Remember, 1963; A Village So Small, 1965; Door Without A Lock, 1972; Book reviews; Articles for numerous magazines and newspapers. *Memberships:* National League of American Pen Women (several offices in 2 branches); Pierian (Literary) Club, Oak Ridge; Fine Arts Club, Monroe, Louisiana; YWCA, Monroe; First United Methodist Church, Monroe. *Honours:* 4th Prize, Short Story Contest, Writers Digest, 1961; 1st Prize for Short Story, 2nd Prize for Inspirational Books, National League of American Pen Women, 1974; Maude Files Zimmer Day, statewide celebration held in Oak Ridge, sponsored by Oak Ridge Pierian Club and Caddoan Club. *Hobbies:* Lectures and book reviews; Various organisations; Travel, USA, West Indies, Mexico, Canada, South America. *Address:* Westchester Square, Apt 106, 2701 Sterlington Road, Monroe, LA 71203, USA.

ZIMMERMAN A. Jeannine, b. 29 Oct. 1930, St Joseph, Missouri, USA. Crime Laboratory Specialist. m. (1)James T. Vaughan, 2 Mar. 1950, 1 son, (2)Frank Zimmerman, 9 Jan. 1958, 3 sons, divorced. *Education:* BA, Colorado Womens College, 1975; MA, Criminal Justice, University of colorado, 1982. *Appointments:* Self-employed Questioned Document Examiner, 1970-77; Questioned Document Examiner, Aurora, Colorado Police Dept., 1977-. *Publications:* Articles in various journals including: Police Science Abstracts; Journal of Forensic Science; Comparison of the writing on historical papers in, In Search of Butch Cassidy, 1976, by Larry Pointer. *Memberships:* American Academy of Forensic Sciences, Fellow; Southwest Association of Forensic Document Examiners; International Association of Identification. *Honours:* Meritorious Service Commendation, Aurora Police Department,

1987; Excellence Bonus Award, Aurora Police Department, 1988. *Hobbies:* Tennis; Antique Glassware & Oriental Rugs; Art. *Address:* Aurora Police Dept., 15001 E. Alameda Drive, Aurora, CO 80012, USA.

ZIMMERMAN Frances, b. 10 Oct. 1924, Kansas City, Missouri, USA. m. Eugene R Zimmerman, 8 Dec. 1945. 2 sons, 2 daughters. *Education:* BA, Park College, Parkville, 1945; University of Michigan, 1976; University of Kansas, 1980; University of Missouri, 1975. *Appointments:* Instructor, Department of Labor Employment & Training Adm, 1975-82; Public Relations, Missouri Division of Employment Security, 1962-75; President, Zimmerman & Associates, Consulting firm, 1982-. *Creative works:* Paintings: Daughters; Portraits. Slide Programs: Communications; Images; Brandy. *Memberships:* Soroptimists International; International Association of Personnel; Lioness International Mid-American Association of Assoc Executives; Starlight Women's Committee. *Honours:* A NOW Speaker and Consultant to clubs, organizations, women's meetings, high schools and colleges throughout area. *Hobbies:* Oil paintings; Writing; Photography; Travelling. *Address:* Zimmerman and Associates, 10568 Century Lane, Overland Park, Kansas 66215, USA.

ZIMMERMAN Helene Loretta, b. 26 Feb. 1933, Rochester, New York, USA. University Professor. *Education:* Regent's Diploma, 1949; BS, Business Education, 1953; MS, Business Education, 1959; PhD, Business Education, 1969; Certified Records Manager, 1977. *Appointments:* Williamson Central School, Williamson, New York, 1953-69; University of Kentucky, 1969-70; Central Michigan University, 1970-. *Publications:* General Business, high school textbook (co-author), 1977; Application Projects, workbook in records management (co-author), 1987. *Memberships:* International Vice-President for English-speaking Countries, Past President, US Chapter, International Society for Business Education; Secretary, Board of Regents, Institute of Certified Records Managers; President, Michigan Business Education Association; National Business Education Association; Association of Records Managers and Administrators; State President of Michigan, Delta Kappa Gamma; Gamma Sigma Sponsor, Delta Pi Epsilon. *Honours:* Leadership Award, Michigan International Council, 1979; Leadership Award Phi Delta Kappa, 1988; Distinguished Service Award North-Central Business Education Association, 1989. *Hobbies:* Travel; Crafts; Sewing. *Address:* 1405 Lincoln Court, Mt Pleasant, MI 48858, USA.

ZIMMERMAN Jo Ann, b. 24 Dec. 1936, Keosauqua, Iowa, USA. Lieutenant Governor. m. Tom Zimmerman, 1956, 3 sons, 2 daughter. *Education:* Nursing Diploma, 1958; BA, Drake University, 1973. *Appointments Include:* Assistant Head Nurse, obstetrics House Nursing Supervisor, Obstetrics Nursing Supervisor, Broadlawns Medical Centre; Maternity Nursing Instructor, Broadlawns School of Nursing; Lieutenant Governor, State of Iowa. *Publications:* Various articles in professional journals. *Memberships:* numerous professional organisations including: League of Women Voters; Iowa Womens Political Caucus; National Organization of Women; Iowa Department of Education. *Address:* Office of Lieutenant Governor, State Capitol, Des Moines, IA 50319, USA.

ZIMMERMAN Naoma, b. 2 Aug. 1914. Psychiatric Social Worker; Family Therapist; Communication Specialist; Lecturer; Consultant; Author. *Education:* MA, University of Chicago, 1940. *Appointments:* Case Worker, Therapist, Family Service of S. Lake Co., Illinois, 1958; Consultant, Family Therapy to HS.s., Social Work Agencies, etc; Private Practice; Lecturer; Teacher, Family Therapy, Summer Faculty, University of Chicago, 1967-71. *Publications:* Sleepy Forest, 1943; Timothy Tic-Tock, 1943; Sleepy Village, 1944; The New Comer, 1944; Baby Animals, 1955; Little Deer, 1956; Farm Animals, 1966; Corky Meets a Spaceman, 1960; Corky in Orbit, 1962. *Memberships:* American Ortho.Psych.

Association; National Association of Social Workers. *Address:* 465 Drexel Ave., Glencoe, IL 60022, USA.

ZIMMERMAN Winona Estelle,b. Mankato, USA. Farming Writer. 1 son, 1 daughter. *Education:* The Redding Ridge Institute of Literature, (eight years). *Appointments:* Writer, short stories and articles; State Reporter/Columnist, Draft Horse Journal; Farming and Le Center Economic Development Corporation Promotion and Publicity Director; Minnesota Department of Agriculture State Farm Advocate. *Memberships:* Minnesota Farmers Union; Minnesota Pork Council Women; Minnesota Pork Producers; Minnesota Agri-Women Dist. and President, 1987-89; Belgian Draft Horse Corporation of America; Minnesota Horse Breeders Association; FGJ Marine Corps League Auxiliary President, 1989; VFW Ladies Auxiliary President, 1988-89; American Legion Auxiliary; Rural Family Life Center Advisory Board - University of MN; CARE Advisory Board Le Sueur County; Life Work Planning Center Adv. Board; Community Education Advisory Board; United Way Advisoryy Board/Executive Secretary; American Biographical Institute Advisory Board; numerous other organisations. *Hobbies:* Bridge; Chess; Gardening; Reading; Drawing; Decorating. *Address:* Route 2, Road 9, Box 70, Le Center, MN 56057, USA.

ZINDEL Bonnie, b. 3 May 1943, New York City, USA. Writer. m. Paul Zindel, 25 Oct. 1973, 1 son, 1 daughter. *Education:* BA, Psychology, Hofstra University, 1964. *Appointments:* Director, Public Relations, The Cleveland Play House, 1969-72; Producer, Show Intermission Feature, Boston Symphony, Station WCLV-FM, Cleveland, 1970-72. *Publications:* A Star for the Latecomer, 1980; Hollywood Dream Machine, 984; Playwright: I Am a Zoo- Jewish Repertory Theatre - The Troup Theatre, 1976; Lemons in the Morning, A.M Back Alley Theatre, 1983; Thee Latecomer, Actors Studio, 1985; Adriana Earthlight-Student Shrink, 1987. *Memberships:* Playwrights Unit, Actors Studio; Women in Film. *Address:* c/o Curtis Brown, Ten Astor Place, New York, NY 10003, USA.

ZINER Feenie, (Florence), b. 22 Mar. 1921, Brooklyn, New York, USA. Writer; Teacher. m. Zeke Ziner, 17 Sept. 1941, 4 sons, 1 daughter. *Education:* BA, Brooklyn College, 1941; MSS, Columbia University School of Social Work, 1944. *Appointments:* Institute for Juvenile Research, Chicago, 1947-48; Park Ridge School for Girls, Illinois, 1949-51; New School for Social Research, 1971-74; State Univesity of New York, Purchase, 1972-74; Associate Professor, University of Connecticut, 1974-. *Publications:* True Book of Time, 1953; Wnderful Wheels, 1955; Little Sailors Big Pet, 1958; Counting Carnival 1960; Pilgrims & Plymouth Colony, 1963; A Full House, 1967; Bluenose, Queen of Grand Banks, 1970; Duck of Billingsgate Market, 1975; Within this Wilderness, 1978; Cricket Boy, 1978; Sauanto, 1988; Book Reviewer, Montreal Star; New York Times etc. *Memberships:* American Association of University Professors; PEN, American Centre; Authors' Guild. *Address:* 182 Shore Drive, Branford, CT 06405, USA.

ZITCER Diane Susan, b. London, England. Television Presenter; Journalist. m. Cary Haskell Zitcer, 22 Sept. 1981. 2 daughters. *Education:* Stage Management Diploma, Central School of Speech & Drama, 1978-80. *Appointments:* On the Road, BBC2, 1987; Style on a Shoestring, Lifestyle Satellite Channel, 1988; Storytime, BBC1, 1989. *Membership:* National Union of Journalists. *Hobbies:* All sport, particularly Snow & Water skiing; Interior design and Do-it-Yourself; Embroidery and needlework; Theatre; Cinema. *Address:* 2 Sidmouth Road, London NW2 5JX, England.

ZOBEL Jan, b. 8 Feb. 1947, San Francisco, USA. Tax Consultant. *Education:* BA, Whittier College, 1968; MA, University of Chicago, 1970. *Appointments:* Teacher, Chicago Public Schools, 1969-70, San Francisco Public Schools, 1971-78; Private practice, Tax Consultant, 1978-; Teacher, University of California, San Francisco State University, San Mateo Community College District, San Francisco Community College District, 1986-. *Publications:* Editor: People's Yellow Pages, 1971-81; Where the Child Things Are, 1977-80. *Memberships:* Finance Committee, Bay Area Women's Building, 1974-88; National Association of Enrolled Agents; California Association of Enrolled Agents; National Association of Tax Preparers. *Honours:* Key to City of Buffalo, 1969; Certificate of Honour, San Francisco Board of Supervisors, 1974; Small Business Adminsitrations Accountant Advocate of the Year, 1987. *Address:* 56 Cumberland, San Francisco, CA 94110, USA.

ZOLDBROD Aline Penny, b. 11 Dec. 1947, Pittsburgh, Pennsylvania, USA. Psychologist; Stress Trainer. m. Lawrence Osterweil, 6 Nov. 1977, 1 son, 1 daughter. *Education:* BA magna cum laude, high honours in Sociology and Anthropology, Oberlin College, Oberlin, Ohio, 1969; Clinical Intern, Massachusetts Mental Health Center, Boston, 1971-72; PhD, Heller School, Brandeis University, 1978. *Appointments:* Staff Psychologist, Pequod- Cambridge, Massachusetts, 1970-83; Consultant, Greenery Nursing Home, Brighton, Massachusetts, 1973-78; Instructor, Social Work Theory and Methods, Suffolk University, Boston, Massachusetts, 1978-79; Private Practice in Psychotherapy, Lexington, Massachusetts, 1981-; Lecturing, teaching. *Publication:* The Emotional Distress of the Artificial Insemination Patient, 1988. *Memberships:* Board of Directors, Resolve Inc; American Orthopsychiatric Association; American and Massachusetts Psychological Associations; Boston Society for Gerontological Psychiatry; Fellow, American Board of Medical Psychotherapists. *Honours:* Phi Beta Kappa, 1969; HEW Grant for Research, 1975; Invited Lecturer, national and international groups, 10 years. *Hobbies:* Gardening; Reading; Swimming; Lecturing; Writing; Playing with her children. *Address:* 12 Rumford Road, Lexington, MA 02173, USA.

ZOPF Evelyn LaNoel Montgomery, b. 10 July 1932, Laurel, Mississippi, USA. Guidance Counsellor. m. Paul Edward Zopf Jr, 5 Aug. 1956, 1 son. *Education:* MusB, 1953, MA, 1954, Education, University of Southern Mississippi. *Appointments:* Private Music Teacher, Voice, Piano, Clarinet and Trumpet, 1953-61; Guidance Counsellor, University of Southern Mississippi, 1953-54; Guidance Counsellor, University of Florida, 1954-56; Teacher, New Orleans City Schools, Louisiana, 1956-57; Public School Music Teacher, Band Director, Choral Director, Putnam County Schools, Florida, 1957-59; Substitute Teacher, Guilford County Schools, 1959-; Advisor to foreign students, 1954-56, 1959-62; Speaker, various religious and art groups. *Memberships:* Arts Series Committee, Guilford College; New Garden Friends Meeting, Interim Choir Director 1961, Chairman of Music Committee 1974-76; First International Congress on Quaker Education Committee, 1987-88; Guilford College Sesquicentennial Committee 1985-87; Volunteer, American Red Cross; Volunteer, Boy Scouts of America; University of Florida Union Board, 1955-56; County Democratic Convention, Precinct Delegate 1977, 1979, Precinct and Campaign Worker 1980; Greensboro Friends of Music, Board of Directors 1970-71; Board of Directors, Greensboro Chapter, North Carolina Symphony Board; United Society of Friends Women, President 1979-81; International Fellwoship of Quaker Women; Guilford College Community Chorus; Phi Mu; Director, Women's Society; Guilford College Arts Appreciation, Vice-President 1980-81, President 1981-82; Guilford Gourmet. *Honours:* Voted Miss Mississippi Southern by student body, 1953; Voted Best Citizen by faculty, 1953; Hall of Fame, 1953; Awarded Life Membership, International Fellowship of Quaker Women, 1981. *Hobbies:* Music; Fitness; Cooking; Calligraphy; Art; Nature; Dance; Politics. *Address:* 815 George White Road, Greensboro, NC 27410, USA.

ZORIE Stephanie Marie, b. 18 Mar. 1951, Walla Walla, Washington, USA. Lawyer. m. Francis Benedict Buda, 18 Apr. 1981. *Education:* AA 1972; BA 1974; JD 1978. *Appointments:* Peace Group, Paraguay, 1974;

Attorney at Law, Richard Hardwick, Coral Gables, Florida, 1978-79; Attorney at Law, Brown, Terrell & Hogan, Jacksonville, 1979-80; Attorney at Law, Richard Nichols, Jacksonville, 1980; Private Practice, Jacksonville, 1981-84; Attorney at Law, Nolan Carter, Orlando, 1984-85; Attorney at Law, Blakeley & Zorie, PA, Orlando, 1985-86; Private Practice, Orlando, 1986- . *Publication:* Transexual Legal Rights. *Memberships:* Admitted to the following Courts: Supreme Court of Florida; US Court of Customs and Patent Appeals; US Court of Appeals for the Federal Circuit; US Court of International Trade; US Customs Court; US District Court for the Southern District of Florida; US District Court for the Middle District of Florida; US Court of Appeals, 11th Circuit; US Court of Appeals, 5th Circuit; US Court of Claims; US Tax Court; US Supreme Court. Phi Alpha Delta Law Fraternity; The Association of Trial Lawyers of America; Spanish American Law Society; University of Florida Honor Court; John Marshall Bar Association; American Bar Association; Orange County Bar Association; Executive Association of Greater Orlando; International Platform Association. *Honours:* Claude Pepper Award; Mortar Board Woman's Honourary. *Hobbies:* Windsurfing; Sailing; Cooking; Needlework; Currently writing a book on fish camps in Florida and out of the way Florida bars. *Address:* POBox 1468, Orlando, Florida 32802, USA.

ZOZOM Elizabeth, b. 12 June 1955, Bayonne, New Jersey, USA. Graphic Designer; Sculptor. *Education:* Associate in Specialised Technology, Art Institute of Philadelphia, 1975; Philadelphia Academy of Fine Arts, 1977-78. *Appointments:* Assistant Art Director, Philadelphia Magazine, 1975-76; Freelance Designer and Proofreader, 1976-83; Designer, 1981-82, Design Director, 1982-83, Director of Production and Design, 1983-, Running Press Book Publishers. *Creative works include:* Painting and sculpture in group shows: Pratt Institute, New York City, 1972; Provident Bank, Philadelphia, 1973; Women's Art League, Philadelphia, 1976; Gallery 3 1/2& 4, Philadelphia, 1976; Etage, Philadelphia, 1977; Art Institute of Philadelphia, 1977; Old City Art Spring Festival, Philadelphia, 1978; Race Gallery, Philadelphia. *Address:* USA.

ZUKIN Jane Shetzer, b. 20 Sept. 1948, Detroit, Michigan, USA. Director, Commercial Writing Service. m. Stanley Zukin, 6 Jan. 1969. 2 sons, 1 daughter. *Education:* BA, Mass Communications, Wayne State University, 1970. *Appointments:* Copywriter, WQRS FM, 1969; Program Content Editor, WDEE AM, 1970; Pub Rltns Jwish Welfare Federa, 1970-77; Owner, Starmakers Incorporated, 1977-84; Director, Commercial Writing Service, 1984-. *Publications:* Milk-Free Diet Cookbook, 1982; The Newsletter-For People with Lactose Intolerence, 1986-; *Mermberships:* American Medical Writers Assn; Professional Member, Natl Writers Club; Amercian Business Womens Assn. *Hobbies:* Fine Arts, art, music, theatre; Graphic design; City- School Affairs; Gardening. *Address:* Commercial Writing Service, 12 Arbury Drive, P O Box 3074, Iowa City, IA 52244, USA.

ZWILICH Ellen Taaffe, b. 30 Apr. 1939, Miami, Florida, USA. Composer. m. Joseph Zwilich, 22 June 1969, dec. June 1979. *Education:* BMus, 1960, MMus, 1962, Florida State University; DMusArts, Juilliard School of Music, 1975; Studies with Roger Sessions and Elliott Carter. *Career:* Violinist, American Symphony, New York City, 1965-73; Premiere Symposium for Orchestra, Pierre Boulez, New York City, 1975; Chamber Symphony and Passages, Boston Musica Viva, 1979, 1982; Symphony No 1, Gunther Schuller, American Composers Orchestra, 1982. *Creative works:* Einsame Nacht, 1971; Im Nebel, 1972; Sonata in Three Movements, 1973-74; String Quartet, 1974; Trompeten, 1974; Passages, for soprano and chamber ensemble, 1981; String Trio, 1982; Symphony No 1: 3 Movements for Orchestra, 1982; Passages for Soprano and Orchestra, 1982; Divertimento, 1983; Fantasy for Harpsichord, 1983; Intrade, 1983; Prologue and Variations, 1983; Double Quartet for Strings, 1984; Celebration for Orchestra, 1984; Symphony No 2 (Cello Symphony), 1985; Concerto Grosso, 1985; Concerto for Piano and Orchestra, 1986; Images for 2 Pianos and Orchestra, 1986; Tanzspiel (Ballet in 4 Scenes), 1987; Trio for Piano, Violin & Cello, 1987; Praeludium for Organ, 1987; Symbolon for Orchestra, 1988; Concerto for Trombone & Orchestra, 1988; Concerto for Bass Trombone, Strings, Timpani & Cymbals, 1989; Concerto for Flute & Orchestra, 1989. *Memberships:* Honorary Life Member, American Federation of Musicians; American Music Center, Board of Directors, Vice-President 1982-84; International League of Women Composers; Board of Directors, American Composers Orchestra. *Honours:* Elizabeth Sprague Coolidge Chamber Music Prize, 1974; G.B.Viotti Gold Medal, Vercelli, Italy, 1975; Grantee, Martha Baird Rockefeller Fund, 1977, 1979, 1982; Guggenheim Fellow, 1981; Citation, Ernst von Dohnani, 1981; Pulitzer Prize, 1983; National Institute of Arts and Letters Award, 1984; Grammy nomination, 1987; Honorary Doctorate, Oberlin College, 1987; Arturo Toscanini Music Critics Award, 1987; Composers Award, Lancaster Symphony Orchestra. *Address:* 600 West 246th Street, Riverdale, NY 10471, USA.

ZWINGER Ann Haymond, b. 12 Mar. 1925, Muncie, Indiana, USA. Freelance Writer & Illustrator (Natural History). m. Herman H. Zwinger, 18 June 1952, 3 daughters. *Education:* BA, Art History, Wellesley College, 1946; MA, Indiana University, 1950. *Career:* Instructor, art history, Smith College, 1950-51; Visiting Lecturer, Colorado College, 1985-. Also Director, American Electric Power, 1977-. *Publications:* Books: Beyond the Aspen Grove (award); Run, River, Run (awards); Wind in the Rock; A Desert Country Near the Sea; Colorado II (text only); Letters of John Xantus; John Xantus: Fort Tejon Letters; The Mysterious Lands; Land Above the Trees (with Beatrice Willard); Conscious Stillness (with Edwin W. Teale). Contributions, various journals including Audubon Magazine, Orion. *Memberships:* Authors Guild; Director, John Burroughs Association; Local Director, Nature Conservancy; Board President, Thoreau Society. *Honours:* Burroughs Medal, 1976; Award, Friends of American Writers, 1976; Honorary doctorates, Colorado College 1976, Carleton College 1984; Alumnae Award, Wellesley College, 1977; Award, nature & ecology, Indiana Authors' Day. *Address:* c/o Frances Collin, Rodell-Collin Literary Agency, 110 West 40th Street, Suite 20004, New York, NY 10018, USA.

Honours List

NAME:	Ms Dorothy Baker
ADDRESS:	90 Pakington Street Kew Victoria 3101 Australia
OCCUPATION:	Artist
YEAR OF ENTRY:	1986
CITATION:	An Outstanding Contribution to Art

NAME:	Isobel Bennett
ADDRESS:	30 Myola Road Newport Beach NSW 2106 Australia
OCCUPATION:	Marine Biologist
YEAR OF ENTRY:	1988
CITATION:	An Outstanding Contribution to Marine Biology

NAME:	Marlene K Blemel
ADDRESS:	6022 Constitution NE, Suite 3 Albuquerque NM 87110 USA
OCCUPATION:	Company Executive
YEAR OF ENTRY:	1986
CITATION:	An Outstanding Contribution to Commerce

NAME:	Henriette Hannah Bodenheimer
ADDRESS:	Sadja Gaon Street 8 Jerusalem Israel
OCCUPATION:	Writer (historian of political Zionismus)
YEAR OF ENTRY:	1988
CITATION:	An Outstanding Contribution to Education and to The State of Israel

NAME: Clarice A Bryan FIBA

ADDRESS: 245A Bourne Field
                    St Thomas
                    VI 00801
                    USA

OCCUPATION: Solicitor

YEAR OF ENTRY: 1987

CITATION: An Outstanding Contribution to The Law

NAME: Miss Billie Jeanette Burke OAM

ADDRESS: Department of Foreign Affairs
                    Canberra
                    ACT 2600
                    Australia

OCCUPATION: Personal Secretary

YEAR OF ENTRY: 1986

CITATION: An Outstanding Contribution to The Civil
                    Service and Australia

NAME: Phillita Toyia Carney

ADDRESS: 1200 N Nash Street No 1155
                    Arlington
                    VA 22209
                    USA

OCCUPATION: Business Executive

YEAR OF ENTRY: 1987

CITATION: An Outstanding Contribution to Business

NAME: Ms Antoinette Mary Clancy

ADDRESS: Cuan Aisling
                    The Cove
                    Tramore
                    Co Waterford
                    Republic of Ireland

OCCUPATION: President (and founder) of the Women's
                    Political Party (1982)

YEAR OF ENTRY: 1989

CITATION: An Outstanding Contribution to the cause
                    of Women

NAME:	Joyce Naomi Clark
ADDRESS:	1001 Carmel Parkway No 15 Corpus Christi TX 78411 USA
OCCUPATION:	Nurse
YEAR OF ENTRY:	1987
CITATION:	An Outstanding Contribution to Nursing

NAME:	Lady Gloria Florence Clayton
ADDRESS:	PO Box 164 Applecross WA 6153 Australia
OCCUPATION:	Public Relations Director
YEAR OF ENTRY:	1989
CITATION:	An Outstanding Contribution to the Community

NAME:	Irene Coates LFIBA
ADDRESS:	"Kalkadoon" 140 Station Street Blackheath NSW 2785 Australia
OCCUPATION:	Playwright and Artist
YEAR OF ENTRY:	1986
CITATION:	An Outstanding Contribution to Art

NAME:	Ms Jean Poindexter Colby
ADDRESS:	73 Eagles Nest Road Duxbury MA 02332 USA
OCCUPATION:	Author
YEAR OF ENTRY:	1989
CITATION:	An Outstanding Contribution to Children's Literature and to Sports Reporting

NAME: Jean Elizabeth Comeforo FIBA

ADDRESS: 616 North Lemon Street
                     Media
                     PA 19063
                     USA

OCCUPATION: Teacher of the Deaf

YEAR OF ENTRY: 1989

CITATION: An Outstanding Contribution to Teaching

NAME: Dr J Sue Cook

ADDRESS: 924 Dyer Lane
                     Modesto
                     CA 95350
                     USA

OCCUPATION: Professor of Nursing

YEAR OF ENTRY: 1986

CITATION: An Outstanding Contribution
                     to Education

NAME: Mrs Sara Mullin Graff Cooke

ADDRESS: Oak Hall
                     529 East Gravers Lane
                     Philadelphia
                     PA 19118
                     USA

OCCUPATION: Child Care, Fund Raiser, Marketing, Kin
                     dergarten Teacher

YEAR OF ENTRY: 1989

CITATION: An Outstanding Contribution to
                     the Community

NAME: Dr Joy Beaudette Cripps
                     LFIAP, LFWLA, Litt D

ADDRESS: 3 Mill Street
                     Aspendale
                     Victoria 3195
                     Australia

OCCUPATION: Publisher, Poet, Photographer, Regent for
                     CUAS & Regent for POET International

YEAR OF ENTRY: 1986

CITATION: An Outstanding Contribution
                     to Literature

NAME: Dr Margaret Corinne Devlin FIBA

ADDRESS: Health Science Centre 471
                       1200 Main Street West
                       Hamilton
                       Ontario
                       Canada L8N 3Z5

OCCUPATION: Graduate Nurse and Specialist in Obstet-
                       rics and Gynecology

YEAR OF ENTRY: 1989

CITATION: An Outstanding Contribution
                       to Medicine

NAME: Nancy Priscilla Dibley

ADDRESS: Flat 7, 23 Upper Berkeley Street
                       London W1H 7PF
                       England

OCCUPATION: Writer, Musician

YEAR OF ENTRY: 1987

CITATION: An Outstanding Contribution
                       to Writing and Music

NAME: Joanne Walton Dickinson
                       JD, FRSA, LFIBA

ADDRESS: 1111 City National Building
                       Wichita Falls
                       TX 76301
                       USA

OCCUPATION: Lawyer

YEAR OF ENTRY: 1987

CITATION: An Outstanding Contribution
                       to Law

NAME: Thelma Chapman Dixon

ADDRESS: PO Box 908
                       Andalusia
                       AL 36420
                       USA

OCCUPATION: Executive

YEAR OF ENTRY: 1987

CITATION: An Outstanding Contribution
                       to The Business

NAME: Ms Marjorie E T Ducote

ADDRESS: 2037 Bankhead Parkway
Huntsville
AL 35801
USA

OCCUPATION: Research Chemist

YEAR OF ENTRY: 1989

CITATION: An Outstanding Contribution
to Research

NAME: Mrs Estelle Cecilia D Dunlap
PhD, LPIBA

ADDRESS: 719 Shepherd Street NW
Washington
DC 20011
USA

OCCUPATION: Educator and Mathematician

YEAR OF ENTRY: 1986

CITATION: An Outstanding Contribution
to Education

NAME: Anne M Egry

ADDRESS: 108 Mattier Drive
Pittsburgh
PA 15238
USA

OCCUPATION: Teacher

YEAR OF ENTRY: 1987

CITATION: An Outstanding Contribution
to Education

NAME: Ms Elaine W Farrar

ADDRESS: 635 Copper Basin Road
Prescott
AZ 86301
USA

OCCUPATION: Painter, Sculptor, Graphic Artist
and Art Educator

YEAR OF ENTRY: 1987

CITATION: An Outstanding Contribution
to Art and Education of Critical Enquiry
through the Art

NAME: Dr Patricia Marquerita Fergus FWLA

ADDRESS: 510 Groveland Avenue
                     Minneapolis
                     MN 55403
                     USA

OCCUPATION: Writer, Consultant in Writing,
                     Professor Emeritus

YEAR OF ENTRY: 1986

CITATION: An Outstanding Contribution
                     to Higher Education

NAME: Arlene Mae Willging Frederick FIBA

ADDRESS: Rt 6 Box 338K3
                     Columbia
                     SC 29212
                     USA

OCCUPATION: Nurse

YEAR OF ENTRY: 1987

CITATION: An Outstanding Contribution
                     to Nursing

NAME: Ms Antoinette J Freitas-Krajcar MA CLU

ADDRESS: 2065 Spyglass Drive
                     San Bruno
                     CA 94066
                     USA

OCCUPATION: Manager

YEAR OF ENTRY: 1986

CITATION: An Outstanding Contribution
                     to The Insurance Industry

NAME: Joyce A Gandy LFIBA

ADDRESS: 42 Parsonage Road
                     Edison
                     NJ 08837
                     USA

OCCUPATION: Business Owner

YEAR OF ENTRY: 1987

CITATION: An Outstanding Contribution
                     to Business

NAME: Rose Helen Glennie LFIBA

ADDRESS: 1 Woodside Place
Dunlop
Kilmarnock
Ayrshire
Scotland KA3 4DB

OCCUPATION: Teacher, Educational Psychologist

YEAR OF ENTRY: 1987

CITATION: An Outstanding Contribution
to Education

NAME: Joan Estelle Godfrey
OBE, MEdAd, FCNA

ADDRESS: "Chandalay"
18/44 Brisbane Street
Toowong
Queensland 4066
Australia

OCCUPATION: Nursing

YEAR OF ENTRY: 1987

CITATION: An Outstanding Contribution
to Nursing Education

NAME: Ms Jean S Grey CPA

ADDRESS: 9 Spruce Lane
Stosset
New York
NY 11791
USA

OCCUPATION: Certified Public Accountant

YEAR OF ENTRY: 1986

CITATION: An Outstanding Contribution
to The Advancement of Women in the
Accounting Profession

NAME:	Louise Harris LPIBA, LFWLA, DDG
ADDRESS:	395 Angell Street No 111 Providence RI 02906 USA
OCCUPATION:	Researcher and Writer
YEAR OF ENTRY:	1986
CITATION:	An Outstanding Contribution to Research and Writing

NAME:	Noela J Hjorth
ADDRESS:	PO Box 6 (Luke Road) Clarendon 5157 South Australia
OCCUPATION:	Artist
YEAR OF ENTRY:	1987
CITATION:	An Outstanding Contribution to Art

NAME:	Ruth Ann Ross Jacobs
ADDRESS:	2000 S Ocean Blvd Penthouse K Boca Raton FL 33432 USA
OCCUPATION:	Retired
YEAR OF ENTRY:	1987
CITATION:	An Outstanding Contribution to Business

NAME:	Professor Sezin Karadede LFIBA
ADDRESS:	Faik Ail Sok Kilicci Apt Daire 9 Yenisehir Diyarbakir Turkey
OCCUPATION:	Ophthalmologist
YEAR OF ENTRY:	1986
CITATION:	An Outstanding Contribution to Ophthalmology

NAME:	Ms Marian J Karpen LFIBA
ADDRESS:	233 East 69th Street New York NY 10021 USA
OCCUPATION:	Financial Executive
YEAR OF ENTRY:	1986
CITATION:	An Outstanding Contribution to Finance

NAME:	Dr Vernette Landers LFIBA, LFWLA, LFABI
ADDRESS:	PO Box 3839 Landers CA 92285 USA
OCCUPATION:	Retired School Counsellor and Author
YEAR OF ENTRY:	1986
CITATION:	An Outstanding Contribution to Education and Writing

---

NAME:	Marge E Landsberg HE, FIBA, FWLA, AAABI, LFABI, DG, DDG
ADDRESS:	1 Shikmona Street Bat-Galim Haifa 35014 Israel
OCCUPATION:	Specialist, Linguist
YEAR OF ENTRY:	1987
CITATION:	An Outstanding Contribution to Linguistics

NAME:	Ms Ling-Ai Li
ADDRESS:	360 West 55th Street New York NY 10019 USA
OCCUPATION:	Lecturer and Writer
YEAR OF ENTRY:	1987
CITATION:	An Outstanding Contribution to Education and Writing

NAME:	Mrs Mia W Lord
ADDRESS:	174 Majestic Avenue San Francisco CA 94112 USA
OCCUPATION:	Director, Crusade to Abolish War and Armaments by World Law
YEAR OF ENTRY:	1988
CITATION:	An Outstanding Contribution to World Peace

NAME:	Dr Jean D'Arcy Maculaitis-Cooke
ADDRESS:	103 South Ward Ave Rumson NJ 07760 USA
OCCUPATION:	Business Owner, Author, Professor and Lecturer
YEAR OF ENTRY:	1988
CITATION:	An Outstanding Contribution to Education, Research and Business

---

NAME:	Ms Bridget Grace Marks
ADDRESS:	Green Gables Farm Bigelow Road Athol MA 01331 USA
OCCUPATION:	Graduate Student
YEAR OF ENTRY:	1986
CITATION:	An Outstanding Contribution to helping the developing Nations through the World Energy Foundation

NAME:	Ms Violet Sweet McFarland FIBA
ADDRESS:	PO Box 872
	Lake Elsinore
	CA 92330
	USA
OCCUPATION:	Author and Teacher
YEAR OF ENTRY:	1989
CITATION:	An Outstanding Contribution
	to Writing, Publishing and the field
	of Education

NAME:	Ms Johanna Mitchell
ADDRESS:	PO Box 850
	Saskatoon
	Sask
	Canada S7K 3V4
OCCUPATION:	Business Executive
YEAR OF ENTRY:	1987
CITATION:	An Outstanding Contribution
	to Business

NAME:	Ms Peggy Jean Mueller
ADDRESS:	1506 Hardouin Avenue
	Austin
	TX 78703
	USA
OCCUPATION:	Dance Teacher/Choreographer
YEAR OF ENTRY:	1990
CITATION:	An Outstanding Contribution
	to Dancing, Ranching and Trail Riding

NAME:	Mary Devon O'Brien LFIBA
ADDRESS:	594 Valley Street
	Maplewood
	NJ 07040
	USA
OCCUPATION:	Communications Executive
YEAR OF ENTRY:	1987
CITATION:	An Outstanding Contribution
	to Project Management

NAME: Eleanor Otto - Cultural Doctorate
                 World University

ADDRESS: Manhatten Plaza
                 400 W 43rd Street 27-T
                 New York
                 NY 10036
                 USA

OCCUPATION: Writer, Actress, Dancer and Singer

YEAR OF ENTRY: 1987

CITATION: An Outstanding Contribution
                 to Poetry

NAME: Lucie Pfaff PhD DBA

ADDRESS: 518 Morse Avenue
                 Ridgefield
                 NJ 07657
                 USA

OCCUPATION: Professor

YEAR OF ENTRY: 1987

CITATION: An Outstanding Contribution
                 to International Business Studies

NAME: Ms Lucile Brickner Brown Price

ADDRESS: 508 West Broadway
                 Decorah
                 IA 52101
                 USA

OCCUPATION: Retired College Administrator

YEAR OF ENTRY: 1989

CITATION: An Outstanding Contribution
                 to the expansion of consciousness, includ-
                 ing increased awareness of the human
                 potential

NAME:	Dr Marilyn Zwaig Rossner
ADDRESS:	PO Box 1455 Station H Montreal Quebec Canada H3G 2N3
OCCUPATION:	Professor of Special Educator Yoga, Behaviour Therapist, Therapist
YEAR OF ENTRY:	1987
CITATION:	An Outstanding Contribution to Special Education

NAME:	Barbara Hamilton Schaeffer
ADDRESS:	Monroe Heavy Equipment Inc Rentals DBA Magic Carpet Travel 2425 Enterprise Road Orange City FL 32763 USA
OCCUPATION:	Executive
YEAR OF ENTRY:	1987
CITATION:	An Outstanding Contribution to the Community

NAME:	Sylvia-Lou Shepherd Ed D
ADDRESS:	4657 Vista de la Tierra Del Mar CA 92014 USA
OCCUPATION:	Consultant, Music
YEAR OF ENTRY:	1988
CITATION:	An Outstanding Contribution to Music Education and Performance

NAME:	Dr Helen Chien-Fan Su
ADDRESS:	610 Highland Drive Savannah GA 31406 USA
OCCUPATION:	Research Chemist
YEAR OF ENTRY:	1988
CITATION:	An Outstanding Contribution to Chemistry

NAME:	Ms June Conran Sutherland LFIBA
ADDRESS:	29 Swinburne Avenue Hawthorn Vic 3122 Australia
OCCUPATION:	Midwife
YEAR OF ENTRY:	1989
CITATION:	An Outstanding Contribution to Midwifery

NAME:	Mrs Kathryn C Walden FIBA
ADDRESS:	PO Box 355 Headland AL 36345 USA
OCCUPATION:	Artist
YEAR OF ENTRY:	1986
CITATION:	An Outstanding Contribution to Art

NAME:	Ms Annita L C Walker
ADDRESS:	2920 Harwood Street Tallahassee FL 32301 USA
OCCUPATION:	(Retired Chemist) Asst Director of Information Services, Florida A & M University School of Journalism, Media and Graphic Arts, Tallahassee, FL, USA
YEAR OF ENTRY:	1989
CITATION:	An Outstanding Contribution to Chemical Research

NAME:	Mrs Eleanor P Weinbaum LPIBA LFWLA
ADDRESS:	Hotel Beaumont Apt 415 625 Orleans Street Beaumont TX 77701 USA
OCCUPATION:	Writer, Freelance Writer and Poet
YEAR OF ENTRY:	1986
CITATION:	An Outstanding Contribution to Writing

NAME: Angela Anderson Williams

ADDRESS: 4024 Apollo Drive
                     Anchorage
                     AK 99504
                     USA

OCCUPATION: Health Administrator

YEAR OF ENTRY: 1987

CITATION: An Outstanding Contribution
                     to Medicine

NAME: Ms Annie John Williams LPIBA

ADDRESS: 2021 Sprunt Avenue
                     Durham
                     NC 27705
                     USA

OCCUPATION: Retired Teacher

YEAR OF ENTRY: 1986

CITATION: An Outstanding Contribution
                     to Education

NAME: Lady Elizabeth H Wilson

ADDRESS: 79 Tusmore Avenue
                     Tusmore
                     SA 5065
                     Australia

OCCUPATION: Charity Worker

YEAR OF ENTRY: 1990

CITATION: An Outstanding Contribution
                     of Voluntary Service to the Community

NAME: Dr Sophie M Wolanin
                     LPIBA LFWLA

ADDRESS: 1608 Lafayette Road
                     Pittsburgh
                     PA 15221
                     USA

OCCUPATION: Business Administrator

YEAR OF ENTRY: 1986

CITATION: An Outstanding Contribution
                     to Commerce